Nations of the World

2012

Eleventh Edition

Nations of the World

A Political, Economic & Business Handbook

Grey House Publishing
4919 Route 22
Amenia, NY 12501

Grey House Publishing

PUBLISHER: Leslie Mackenzie
EDITOR: Richard Gottlieb
EDITORIAL DIRECTOR: Laura Mars
MARKETING DIRECTOR: Jessica Moody
PRODUCTION MANAGER: Kristen Thatcher

Grey House Publishing, Inc.
4919 Route 22
Amenia, NY 12501
518.789.8700
FAX 518.789.0556
www.greyhouse.com
e-mail: books@greyhouse.com

Central European Business Ltd

MANAGING DIRECTOR: Anthony Axon
PRODUCTION MANAGER: Elaine McCarthy
EDITORIAL: Anthony Griffin, Sue Hewitt, Patrick Ivory, Marianne Keating, Anthony Miller, Lena von Heimendahl, Sophie von Heimendahl

World of Information
11 Clarendon Street
Cambridge CB1 1JU, UK
Tel: +44 (0) 1223.351584

First edition published 2000
Eleventh Edition published 2012
Printed in Canada

Nations of the world: a political, economic & business handbook – 11th ed. (2012) – 2016p.

1. Almanacs, American. 2. Business travel – Handbooks, manuals, etc. 3. International trade – handbooks, manuals, etc.

HF1010.N37
658-dc21
ISBN: 978-1-59237-760-2

2001238305
softcover

Contents

INTRODUCTION

This eleventh edition of *Nations of the World: A Political, Economic & Business Handbook* profiles every nation and self-governing territory around the world. It offers political, economic and business information in an easy-to-access, single-volume format, supplemented by maps, charts and tables.

Praise for previous editions:

> *". . . this is the most current information available for the political and economic state of the world's nations. . . . helpful for business people interested in doing business overseas and for tourists interested in traveling to these countries."*
>
> American Reference Books Annual, 2011

> *". . . this sizable reference essentially offers an annual report on the welfare and status of every recognized nation-state. . . . prose overview relates political developments and subsequent pages detail . . . economic indicators, political machinery and social structure . . . Tourists will find the health precautions and business directory especially instructive."*
>
> CHOICE, May 2011

The year 2011 witnessed slow improvement to the US economy, and much unrest and instability in the rest of the world. Major events include the death of terrorist Osama bin Laden, the official end of the Iraq war, transitioning economies and governments in several developing countries, as well as tenuous finances in several others.

As the economies and leadership around the world continue to change, so do global markets, crucial to business worldwide. Tourism is often the lifeblood of otherwise impoverished nations. Education and technology are invaluable in controlling the most devastating diseases, and empowering rural villagers to learn how to support themselves and their families. *Nations of the World* provides the understanding necessary to advance on the world stage in business, education, and recreation.

The 2012 edition of *Nations of the World* offers tremendous insight into the living conditions, social standings and economic climates of 229 nations, from those in the news to those that seldom make headlines. New countries include South Sudan and Sint Maarten. Since the last edition, there have been 32 head of state elections, resulting in 17 new leaders, and 41 general elections, resulting in 10 changes in government.

Every country profile has been reviewed and updated. Contributors worldwide have written thoughtful, comprehensive country essays. These international correspondents, true experts in their fields, have contributed to some of the most influential books and periodicals in the world. See the Contributor list following this Introduction.

Nations of the World is a reliable, careful compilation of essential information that is presented in a useful, organized format. This reference is critical for anyone doing business or traveling overseas. It has also proved to be an important reference tool for students in secondary school through college, as well as for professionals in politics, the military, and reconstruction sectors.

Arrangement & Currency

Nations of the World is arranged alphabetically by nation or territory. Part one of each country chapter is a concise, independently written **Country Overview**. These overviews do not reflect the worldview of any particular government or intelligence agency. You will find current political and economic events, as well as an informed outlook toward the future. Most chapters include a **Map** with key places; some of the world's more obscure places are shown in relation to surrounding countries. All chapters include **Key Facts** – official country name(s), ruling parties, language, basic area, population, unemployment, and 2010 inflation figures, **Key Indicators** – charted over five years that end in 2010, include population, GNP, imports/exports, foreign debt, exchange rate, and **Risk Assessment** – rates politics, economy and general stability of the region.

Part two is a **Country Profile.** This section includes detailed historical information in easy-to-follow chronological order, political structure and parties, and a detailed look at the country's population, labor market, media, trade, industry, agriculture and energy. Business travelers will learn about that country's time zones, banking practices, entry requirements, dress codes, climate, health issues, hotels, working hours and the best way to travel to and from. *Noted are countries in political crises, with advice to visitors.*

The **Business Directory** – part three – has contact numbers and web sites for hotels, travel information and chambers of commerce, plus dozens of other useful numbers and addresses.

Following the country profiles are **Regional Worldwide Overviews:** Global Overview; Africa; the Americas; Asia and the Pacific; Europe; and the Middle East. Like individual country chapters, these overviews offer an expertly written narrative on the region's political and economic climate. They include **Key Indicators, Currencies**, and a **Map** of the region.

Plus, buyers of the print directory get Free Access to **Nations of the World Online**, where users can access individual Country Reports for download on http://gold.greyhouse.com. With online access, searching through this vast amount of text and finding specific country information has never been easier. Online access is available upon request to book buyers at no additional cost; use coupon at the back of the book.

With nearly 2,000 pages of critical political, economic and business information including narrative overviews, charts and maps, this newest edition of *Nations of the World: A Political, Economic & Business Handbook* – in both print and electronic format – is a timely and immensely valuable reference acquisition to all public, academic and special library collections.

Contributors

Guy Arnold is a freelance writer who specialises in north-south relations and African affairs. His most recent publications include *A Third World Handbook*, *Wars in the Third World Since 1945* and *The End of the Third World*.

Barry Baxter has spent most his working life in Africa. He has worked as a journalist for 45 years, reporting from Botswana, South Africa, Zambia (and northern Rhodesia), Zimbabwe (and Southern Rhodesia), Angola, Kenya, Tanzania and Uganda. Since 1994, he has operated *NewsWorld*, an Africa news agency serving Reuters, the South African Press Association, Agencia EFE and several magazines.

Daniel Brett is a freelance journalist contributing articles on agricultural economics, protest movements and trade-related issues in Africa and Latin America as well as the politics and economics of other developing countries.

Shanjukta Ghosh is a graduate of Delhi University and writes on socioeconomic themes of the Indian subcontinent, with emphasis on high-technology.

Anthony Griffin is a UK-based journalist specialising in emerging markets, with an emphasis on Spanish speaking countries. He regularly contributes articles to British and international publications, on Europe and South America.

Aileen Herlihy, based in Australia, writes on health and welfare issues, with an emphasis on developing countries as well as Australia.

Niki Johnson is a research fellow at the Political Science Institute, Universidad de la República, Montevideo, Uruguay.

Ali Khalil is a business journalist at the UK-based *Asharq Al-Awsat* Arabic newspaper and writes on the Middle East.

Asbed Kotchikian is a doctoral student and lecturer at Boston University, US, specialising in the Middle East and the Caucasus. He has lectured at universities in Armenia, Georgia and Latvia.

Marcela López Levy works as a researcher and editor at the UK-based Latin America Bureau, and writes on Latin America and the Caribbean.

Elaine McCarthy writes on agricultural and political trends within the European Union.

Ali Rafel al Mansour is an analyst based in the Middle East, who reports on the petroleum industry and OPEC.

Meldun Mawson is a Swedish writer who specialises in travel and tourism issues, and the social and cultural implications of political change in Latin America, as well as northern Europe.

Marianne Morse is a freelance political and economic country analyst. She edited the *Organization of American States – the next 50 years*.

Neamat Nojumi is a former Afghani mujahideen soldier. Since 1991, he has been living in the US and works as a commentator on Central Asian affairs. He is author of *The Rise of the Taliban in Afghanistan*.

Gergana Noutcheva is a researcher specialising in Eastern Europe at the Centre for European Studies, based in Belgium.

Anita Parameswaran is a business analyst for a leading insurance company working on corporate strategy. She writes on North Africa and the Mediterranean.

Craig Stenhouse is a researcher specialising in Africa and the Middle East.

Bernadeta Tendyra specialises in Eastern Europe and has worked as a BBC World Service journalist.

Marian White is a freelance writer specialising in the politics and economics of the Pacific Rim with a particular interest in emerging economies.

William R Thomson is a former director and vice president in charge of the Asia Development Bank's lending programmes in over 25 Asian and Pacific countries. He advises both international investment houses and governments on regional economic developments and investment opportunities.

José Luis Velasco lectures in Mexican politics and holds a doctorate in political science from Boston University. He is the author of *El Debate Actual Sobre el Federalismo Mexicano*, published by Instituto Mora.

Main sources

It should be noted that the methodology used by the International Monetary Fund (IMF), World Bank, Organisation for Economic Co-operation and Development (OECD) and other main gatherers of international data can vary not only from within itself, but also from each other and from individual central banks and government departments. In order to ensure consistency and to allow like to be compared with like, *World of Information* uses the same single source each year for the Key Indicator data. Readers should be aware, however, that occasionally a more up to date figure is used in the body of the text that might not have been calculated in the same way. The principal sources used are: the IMF, World Bank, Asian Development Bank (ADB), African Development Bank (AfDB), Eastern Caribbean Central Bank (ECCB), Economic Commission for Latin America and the Caribbean (ECLAC), individual central bank reports and national statistics. Statistics have also been gathered from UN agencies including FAO, UNHCR, Unicef and WHO.

Afghanistan

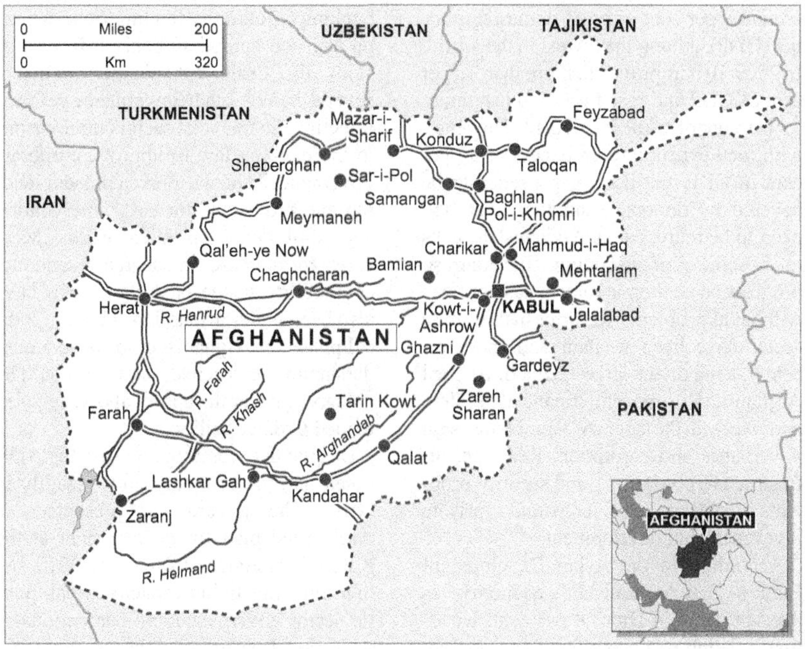

Western governments, for the most part anxious to disengage from Afghanistan, could be forgiven for failing to remember why their troops were in fact there. The original strategy, or plan, was disarmingly simple. The idea was to prevent Afghanistan continuing as a safe haven for the al Qaeda terrorist organisation whose declared objective was to murder the peaceful citizens of miscellaneous countries – apparently regardless of their religion. As is the case with so many apparently straightforward plans, things actually turned out to be less than straightforward. A large part of the problem was an inability to distinguish between those who were members of al Qaeda and those who were Afghanistan's peaceful citizens. Thus, the premise had to be that every Afghani was a terrorist unless proved otherwise. *Habeus corpus* became inverted.

The Afghanis could be forgiven for being fed up with foreign incursions into their rugged, mountainous country. Ten years of war with the USSR, five years of civil war waged by bloodthirsty warlords, five further years of barbarous Taliban rule followed by ten years of war with, or by, North Atlantic Treaty Organisation (NATO). By 2011, the strategists had reached the conclusion that there were in fact less than 100 card carrying members of al Qaeda operating in Afghanistan. Ranged against this perceived threat were thousands of troops from more than twenty countries, lead by the US. Western governments appeared to be speaking with forked tongues, telling the Afghanis that they were there for the long haul, to see the introduction of a fair and free functioning democracy. At the same time the folks back home were being fed a diet of 'firm dates' for the withdrawal of troops. Distinctions were now drawn between al Qaeda and the Taliban, the long standing military opponents. By 2011, it seemed, talks were taking place with the Taliban for a peaceful handover of power. Quite what was going to happen to the restoration of human rights, womens' rights, education, elections and so on was simply kicked into the long grass.

Poor? Us?

According to the International Monetary Fund (IMF) Afghanistan is still one of the

KEY FACTS

Official name: The Islamic Republic of Afghanistan

Head of State: President Hamid Karzai (since 2002; re-elected 20 Aug 2009)

Head of government: President Hamid Karzai

Ruling party: Members of the national assembly are elected as independent candidates

Area: 647,497 square km

Population: 29.12* million (2010) (some 1 million Afghanis are still in exile in Pakistan and Iran)

Capital: Kabul

Official language: Pashtu and Dari (named as official languages in the 2004 constitution)

Currency: Afghani (Af) = 100 puls

Exchange rate: Af43.00 per US$ (Oct 2011)

GDP per capita: US$515 (2010)*

GDP real growth: 8.20% (2010)*

GDP: US$15.50 billion (2010)*

Unemployment: 35.00% (2008)

Inflation: 7.70% (2010)*

Balance of trade: -US$-6.6 million (2009) (Aghanistan's highest export is opium, which is not included in the IMF export figure)

* estimated figure

poorest countries in the world, with annual per capita income estimated at about US$500. This places it well below its neighbours on most human development indicators. When the Taliban regime was replaced in 2001, Afghanistan's infrastructure and institutions were in disarray as a result of years of conflict and erratic policies. Half of the country's 1979 population was exiled, crippled, or dead and many of those who survived were living in abject poverty. The most pressing economic tasks involved restoring economic stability and rebuilding institutions. The challenge was even greater because of the inherently unstable security situation. In 2002 the IMF began to assist in rebuilding basic economic institutions and to provide advice to the government on economic policies and reforms. Afghanistan finally qualified for debt relief in January 2010, which lead to a 96 per cent reduction in its 2006 stock of external debt of nearly US$12 billion.

Some progress has been made in recent years toward the country's political, economic and social transformation. The initial IMF supported programme, which ended on 25 September 2010, aimed at continuing the process of rebuilding key economic institutions, putting public finances on a sustainable path and laying the foundation for economic stability, low inflation, growth and poverty reduction. During the programme's term, economic growth averaged a respectable 12 per cent per year. However, this growth has been volatile, ranging from 3 per cent in fiscal year 2008/09 to 21 per cent in 2009/10, thanks to a record harvest and a booming service sector fuelled by aid inflows. The authorities managed to control inflation after domestic prices surged in 2008 due to historically high world commodity prices. However, inflation picked up again after mid-2010, fuelled by rises in food and oil prices.

Balancing the books

Although revenue collection was initially disappointing, it improved in early 2009. For the three fiscal years prior to 2009, government revenues remained stagnant at around 8 per cent of gross domestic product (GDP), among the lowest in the world. In 2009/10 it improved to more than 10 per cent of GDP and rose further to just under 11 per cent of GDP in 2010/11. However, with total expenditure in excess of 20 per cent of GDP, the fiscal gap needed to be covered by donors, a situation that will need to be redressed as Afghanistan seeks to become self-sustaining. In contrast, progress on economic reform has not been without its problems. Reforms in the public sector have been hesitant and more recently, a run on the largest bank threatened Afghanistan's nascent financial system and exposed the country's problems with governance and corruption. Red tape, infrastructure bottlenecks and security problems continue to constrain private investment and development.

According to the Asian Development Bank (ADB) Afghanistan's economy has been growing at about 8 per cent. Headline inflation rose from 5 per cent in July 2010 to 18.4 per cent in January 2011, driven by higher international food prices and an accommodative monetary policy. Tax collection has been growing at an impressive 32 per cent per year. Economic policy has focussed on the need to keep monetary expansion under control with a view to lowering inflation and pressing ahead with revenue reforms to ensure continued increases in tax collection. As already noted, Afghanistan's financial sector was shaken by a run on the Kabul Bank in September 2010, forcing the authorities to adopt measures to reassure depositors, put the bank under the control of Da Afghanistan Bank (the central bank) and suspend shareholders' rights. As a result of the Kabul Bank scandal, the authorities strengthened the supervision of banks and were expected to enforce key banking regulations and impose sanctions on any non-compliant bank. IMF discussions also dealt with planned audits of several banks, other governance reforms affecting the financial sector and revisions to the banking law to improve corporate governance in banks, prevent insider lending and provisions for early intervention and resolution of problem banks. Measures to increase transparency and accountability in the banking system have also been under discussion. This is a critical phase for Afghanistan for once an understanding is reached, the IMF would be able to consider the approval of a new Extended Credit Facility.

Despite deteriorating security, the ADB noted that the economy grew steadily in 2010. The government presented an Afghan-led plan for development at the Kabul Conference of Donors in 2010, but low implementation capacity, weak public sector governance and perceptions of widespread corruption have inevitably raised concerns over implementation. Self evidently, sustainable, self-reliant growth requires significant improvements in security, progress in the Afghan-led reconciliation process and a better private sector environment.

Private consumption remains the economy's main driver, based on continued high external assistance inflows and security spending that fuels demand for production of goods and services, including construction. The wheat harvest was above average in FY2010/11, but agricultural growth was below FY2009's record. The size of the opium economy (not included in the official figures for economic activity) has been declining since 2007 because of enforced crop substitution policies, but in 2010 its farm gate price more than doubled, owing to plant disease-related lower production levels. This automatically boosted farmers' opium-sourced income, complicating the already slow pace of poppy eradication.

Afghanistan maintains a managed floating exchange rate regime. The currency, the Afghani, appreciated by around 10 per cent against the US dollar over the period January 2010–February 2011, on high inflows of foreign exchange in the form of

KEY INDICATORS **Afghanistan**

	Unit	2006	2007	2008	2009	2010
Population	m	*25.05	25.80	*28.14	*29.84	*29.12
Gross domestic product (GDP)	US$bn	7.05	9.89	10.20	13.30	*15.50
GDP per capita	US$	264	323	359	426	*515
GDP real growth	%	6.1	5.5	3.4	20.9	*8.2
Inflation	%	5.1	13.0	26.8	-12.2	*7.7
Exports (fob) (goods)	US$m	430.0	1,811.0	1.8	*2.2	–
Imports (fob) (goods)	US$m	2,960.0	6,744.0	7.8	*8.8	–
Balance of trade	US$m	-2,530.0	-4,933.0	-6.0	*-6.6	–
Current account	US$m	-145.0	-379.0	-192.0	-125.0	309.0
Exchange rate	per US$	49.32	49.53	50.25	45.18	46.45

* estimated figure

donor grants and remittances and on increased demand for domestic currency. This appreciation, alongside levels of inflation that had become higher than among trade partners, caused the real effective exchange rate to appreciate as well, potentially undermining exports.

To achieve stability both in domestic prices and the exchange rate, Da Afghanistan Bank targets reserve money (bank reserves and currency in circulation) as its key monetary tool, relying on the issue of its capital notes and foreign currency auctions to control the money supply. The absence of price pressures at the start of the fiscal year allowed it to adopt a relatively expansionary monetary stance for FY2010, in order to accommodate an increase in demand for money stemming from expected economic growth. It targeted reserve money growth in FY2010 at 18.9 per cent, 1.8 percentage points higher than in FY2009.

In view of these inflation pressures, however, the central bank was expected to increase its level of intervention in the market. Gross international reserves climbed to US$5.0 billion at end-March 2011 (a rise of 19 per cent from 12 months earlier), reflecting higher donor inflows. Reserves are sufficient to finance 14.3 months of imports and can facilitate market intervention to stabilise the economy and currency. As already noted, a run on deposits at Kabul Bank, the largest private bank, in the second half of 2010 raised concerns about financial stability, highlighting the need to strengthen central bank supervision. Although the government took steps to stabilise the crisis, the bank's losses (stemming from serious weaknesses in its corporate governance and management) could well constitute a heavy fiscal burden.

Following the surge in domestic revenue collection in FY2009, the government continued to improve in this area and collection was expected to reach 9.8 per cent of GDP in FY2010. This good performance was driven by improved tax administration, including a levying of business receipts tax at borders and other structural reforms. Still, the fiscal position (excluding grants) remained among the world's weakest.

Development expenditure is almost fully funded by external assistance while fiscal sustainability – domestic revenue as a share of recurrent spending – is expected to decline to around 65 per cent in FY2010 from 72 per cent a year earlier. This decline was due to upward pressures on recurrent spending, mainly from the higher wage bill caused by the expansion of the Afghan security forces and the rollout of pay and grading reforms for civil servants. Steps toward fiscal sustainability are particularly important given plans for Afghan-led security – since most International Security Assistance Force (ISAF) nations are already setting dates for withdrawing their troops.

At conferences in London and Kabul in January and July 2010, the government presented refinements to its Afghan-led medium-term plan for development and announced results-based national priority programmes to meet its objectives. It also set out public financial-management reforms. Only an estimated 20 per cent of donor funds are actually distributed, however, through the government budget, and to increase this share (as committed at the Kabul Conference), the government needs to improve its implementation capacity. It also needs to address broader issues of transparency and accountability in the public sector, including strengthening audits on the use of domestic funds.

The current account deficit (excluding grants) was estimated to have narrowed from 43.6 per cent to 37.6 per cent of GDP in FY2010. The narrowing trend reflects the fact that grant-related imports (and grant financing), though increasing in US dollars, are falling relative to nominal GDP. Including grants, the current account balance varies only slightly: it was expected to run a small surplus of 1.9 per cent of GDP in FY2010, a turnaround from the previous deficit of 1.4 per cent.

During the 2010 fiscal year imports increased by 3.7 per cent. The rise was attributed to continued high demand from donor-funded projects, particularly for fuel, capital equipment and food, which together make up almost 80 per cent of imports. Exports (much smaller than imports) rose by 6.9 per cent; the main items remained dried fruits, carpets and furs.

GDP growth rates for FY2011 and FY2012 are projected by the ADB at 8.0 per cent and 8.5 per cent respectively. These estimates assume that substantial development-partner funding continues; agriculture and services perform well; the resolution of the Kabul Bank crisis is not disruptive; and industry improves, aided by mining-related construction.

If managed effectively, mining has the potential to grow robustly, although its contribution to the budget over the next few years is likely to be modest. The World Bank estimates that even in a low-impact scenario the first significant investment, the Aynak copper mine, could generate budget revenue of around US$155 million a year in the construction phase (2011–15), increasing to US$365 million from royalties once the mine is operating. The Hajigak iron ore mine may also bring in revenues, of US$89 million a year after it starts construction in 2013. In the early years of development, combined receipts from these two mines could therefore be over one per cent of GDP, but that amount is contingent on strong management.

The government expects in the next few years to make further progress on revenue collection, particularly by the possible introduction of a value added tax and to increase its fiscal sustainability ratio to above 70 per cent. The tax take should also benefit from the increased mining activity, largely through indirect tax revenue in the construction phase. Meeting the 70 per cent target will, though, be challenging under continued pressure on recurrent expenditure. Although external assistance is set to gradually decline, it is likely to be needed to cover at least part of such spending for several years.

Foreign aid will inevitably continue to plug the balance of payments gap. The current account surplus is expected to fall slightly in FY2011, to 1.4 per cent of GDP, driven by increased imports as international commodity prices rise. Excluding official transfers, the balance should continue its gradual improvement to a deficit of 34.4 per cent of GDP as development assistance falls relative to the size of the economy (though nominally it expands). Inflation is projected to average 9.8 per cent and 9.1 per cent in FY2011 and FY2012, assuming that prudent monetary policy is adopted as planned and that it can mitigate the impact of rising international commodity prices.

The overall outlook is subject to several risks, notably worsening security conditions, political instability, weak governance, loss of export competitiveness and new barriers to trade with neighbouring countries.

The debt relief granted to Afghanistan under the extended heavily indebted poor countries initiative in 2010 has relieved the debt burden by US$1.6 billion, taking it to a sustainable level (around 8 per cent of GDP). Nevertheless Afghanistan will stay at high risk of debt distress, particularly if foreign grants (expected to decrease gradually in the medium term) fall heavily.

Risk assessment

Economy	Poor
Politics	Poor
National stability	Poor

COUNTRY PROFILE

Historical profile

1838–42 First Afghan War when Britain invaded Afghanistan to counter the threat to British India from expanding Russian influence in Afghanistan and was defeated by fierce resistance from Afghanistan's many ethnic tribes.
1878–80 Second Afghan War after Britain invaded Afghanistan again; parts of the country were absorbed into British India. Russia also seized parts of Afghani territory.
1907 Russia signed an agreement with Britain, promising no further interference in Afghanistan.
1919 Third Afghan War, after which Britain recognised Afghanistan's independence.
1926 Amanullah proclaimed himself King.
1929 Amanullah fled after civil unrest over his reforms; Mohammed Nadir Shah was proclaimed King. He reunited a fragmented Afghanistan and took steps to modernise the country, though less obtrusively than Amanullah.
1933 Nadir Shah was assassinated and his son, Zahir Shah, became King; his reign lasted 40 years.
1956 Afghanistan built a close relationship with the Soviet Union, gaining arms supplies and undertaking trade.
1964 A constitutional monarchy was introduced, which led to political polarisation and power struggles.
1965 The Communist People's Democratic Party of Afghanistan (PDPA) was formed.
1973 General Mohammed Daud deposed King Zahir Shah, who moved into exile in Italy; Afghanistan was declared a republic.
1978 General Daud was assassinated in the Saur (April) Revolution, a coup by the pro-Communists, led by the PDPA's leader, Noor Taraki, who was declared president.
1979 The Soviet Union invaded Afghanistan after the nationalist foreign minister, Hafizullah Amin, deposed Taraki. Amin was executed in December and replaced by the pro-Soviet Babrak Karmal. Numerous Afghan factions formed the Mujahidin and started a guerrilla war against the Soviet occupation forces. Backed by the US, Pakistan, China, Iran and Saudi Arabia, the Mujahidin inflicted heavy losses on Soviet troops.
1985 The Mujahidin gathered in Pakistan, forming an alliance against Soviet forces. Half of the Afghan population was displaced by the war.
1986 Babrak Karmal was replaced by Najibullah Ahmadzai, the head of the Afghani secret police, as head of the Soviet-backed regime.
1988 Afghanistan, USSR, the US and Pakistan signed peace accords.
1989 The Soviet Union withdrew its last troops from Afghanistan. Civil war continued as the Mujahidin refused to co-operate with the Najibullah regime.
1991 The US and Russia agreed to end military aid to both sides.
1992 Afghanistan was declared an Islamic republic after the capture of Kabul by Mujahidin factions and Najibullah was forced to seek the UN's protection in Kabul. Rival militias vied for power.
1993 Burhanuddin Rabbani, an ethnic Tajik, was proclaimed president, and Gulbuddin Hekmatyar, who was strongly backed by the US during the Soviet occupation, was appointed prime minister.
1994 The Pashtun-dominated Islamic fundamentalist Taliban, formed in Kandahar, south Afghanistan, emerged as the major challenge to the Rabbani government.
1995 The Taliban swept through southern Afghanistan.
1996 The Taliban captured Kabul and quickly imposed a strict version of *sharia* (Islamic law). President Rabbani fled to join the anti-Taliban alliance in the north.
1997 Only Pakistan and Saudi Arabia recognised the Taliban as legitimate rulers of Afghanistan. Hostilities increased in the north between the Taliban and the militias of the United National Islamic Front for the Salvation of Afghanistan (UNIFSA) (also known as the Northern Alliance).
1998 The Taliban captured Mazar i Sharif, the last major city that had been outside Taliban control; around 6,000 civilians were massacred following the city's capture. The US launched cruise missiles at suspected bases of Osama bin Laden, accused of bombing US embassies in Africa.
1999 The UN introduced economic sanctions against Afghanistan for harbouring bin Laden.
2001 The Afghan resistance leader, Commander Massoud, was assassinated. The giant statues of Buddha in Bamyan were destroyed by the Taliban. The US and Britain launched air strikes against the Taliban and al Qaeda, following the Taliban's refusal to hand over bin Laden, also blamed for masterminding the 11 September 2001 attacks on the twin towers in New York. Opposition forces seized Mazar i Sharif, then Kabul and other key cities. Afghan groups agreed an interim government in UN-sponsored talks in Bonn, Germany. The Taliban gave up Kandahar, its last stronghold, at the end of the year and Pashtun royalist, Hamid Karzai was sworn in as head of a 30-member interim power-sharing government.
2002 The first contingent of foreign peacekeepers arrived. Hamid Karzai was elected interim president by the *Loya Jirga* (a grand council of tribal leaders). Former monarch, Zahir Shah, returned to Kabul, but made no claim to the throne. He had been in exile for 29 years before his return. Karzai narrowly escaped an assassination attempt in his home town of Kandahar. After 23 years, the Asian Development Bank resumed lending to Afghanistan.
2003 The afghani was re-valued. Afghanistan introduced a law banning armed factions from politics. NATO forces took control of security in Kabul.
2004 Afghanistan ratified a new constitution including a presidential system. Presidential elections were won by Hamid Karzai with 55 per cent of the vote. President Karzai was sworn in as Afghanistan's first democratically elected leader. Afghanistan was guaranteed US$8.2bn in aid until 2007.
2005 Parliamentary elections were held where the turnout was 36 per cent in Kabul and 53 per cent across the country.
2006 There was a resurgence of Taliban activity and fighting with coalition forces in the south, culminating in the fiercely fought Operation Mountain Thrust. Responsibility for security in the south passed to NATO. The Paris Club of international creditors forgave the greater part of the country's external debt.
2007 Former King Zahir Shar died. A *jirga* began in Kabul to discuss means of combating the Taliban. Russia cut around US$10 billion from Afghanistan's outstanding debt, accrued during the Soviet Union's occupation 1979–89. The Asian Development Bank approved a loan of over US$170 million to complete the circular highway connecting Kabul and other major cities, in particular the section between Herat in the west and Mazar i Sharif in the north. The completed road will bypass the warring territory of the south, plus reduce travel times and transport costs. The highway will also facilitate trade with neighbouring countries in the north and west.
2008 The US reported that the government controlled only 30 per cent of the country, while the Taliban controlled about 10 per cent; the rest of the country was under the control of tribal chiefs. Government officials deny their control was so limited claiming the tribal chiefs supported central government and provided security in its stead.
2009 The US deployed a further 17,000 reinforcements, to 'meet urgent security needs', adding to the 36,000 military personnel already deployed. The UN reported that 2,118 civilians had been killed in 2008, an increase of 39 per cent

on the 2007 figure. Taliban insurgents were blamed for 55 per cent of the deaths while NATO and Afghan forces were held responsible for 39 per cent. In a UK-Afghan military operation on Taliban strongholds in Helmand province, US$71 million in heroin and drug manufacturing chemicals were seized, as well as factories making improvised bombs. A UK official estimated that 60 per cent of Helmand police were drug users in a province where police are poorly paid, where work is high risk and corruption is widespread. Japan announced it would pay the salary of around 80,000 police officers, as well as funding teacher training and the construction of schools and hospitals. The presidents of Afghanistan and Pakistan agreed to increase military co-operation against Islamic extremists operating from strongholds in their shared border areas. The first national park, Band e Amir, featuring deep blue lakes and natural dams of travertine, was established near Bamyan Valley, the site of the giant, 1,500-year old, Buddha statues destroyed by the Taliban in 2001. Following an election campaign that lacked credibility due to accusations of widespread fraudulent activities, presidential elections took place on 20 August. Hamid Karzai won 49.67 per cent of the vote and his closest rival Abdullah Abdullah 30.59 per cent. Post election challenges to the results continued until the Independent Election Commission (IEC) ruled that a run-off presidential election should take place between Karzai and Abdullah. However Abdullah withdrew from the election after his call for the head of the IEC to be sacked was rejected. The runoff election was cancelled and Karzai was declared winner be default. In his first speech after taking office he vowed to fight corruption. President Obama committed a further 30,000 US troops to be sent to Afghanistan, bringing US military strength to 100,000. Other foreign troops, around 32,000 at the end of 2009, were likely to be increased by 5,000.

2010 In February, Nato launched a major offensive against the Taliban in the southern province of Helmand. General Stanley McChrystal was sacked by President Obama on 23 June after he criticised US and Afghan leaders in an article in *Rolling Stone* magazine. General David Petraeus took command of the 130,000 strong international forces. A vital transit agreement was signed with Pakistan in July, allowing access to sea routes and the Indian market. President Karzai's timetable for transfer of control of security to domestic forces by 2014 was agreed at an international conference in July. Dutch troops withdrew on 1 August. In parliamentary elections, held on 18 September, 2,584 candidates stood for 249 seats in the Wolesi Jirga; all elected candidates were non-partisan.

2011 In January, the minister of education, Farooq Wardak, was reported in UK's *Times Educational Supplement* as saying that a 'cultural change' meant the Taliban were 'no more opposing girls' education'. On 18 June, in a move that was hoped to encourage the Taliban to join the political process, the UN announced it was splitting a sanctions blacklist for the Taliban and al Qaeda into two separate lists. On 19 June the (US) Defence Secretary confirmed that 'preliminary' talks between the US and the Taliban in Afghanistan had taken place. President Obama announced on 23 June that 10,000 US troops would leave Afghanistan in 2011 and a further 23,000 would leave by mid-2012. The remaining 70,000 are due to be withdrawn by 2014. In an unannounced visit on 11 July President Sarkozy of France announced that 1,000 troops would be withdrawn by the end of 2012. The half-brother of President Karzai was shot dead in his home on 12 July, in the southern city of Kandahar. The Taliban claimed responsibility for the murder although other reports said it was a member of his bodyguard. On 17 July Jan Mohammad Khan, an important tribal leader and aide to President Karzai, was killed in his home in Kabul. Bamiyan was the first province to be given responsibility for its own security on 18 July, when NATO handed over control to Afghan troops. 200 French troops that were part of a 4,000 military contingent stationed in the district of Surobi and the neighbouring Kapisa Province, were withdrawn from active service in the NATO mission in Afghanistan on 20 October. A further 200 were scheduled to be withdrawn by the end of December.

Political structure

Constitution

On 4 January 2004, Afghanistan ratified a new constitution, establishing an Islamic republic, in which the president rules with a national assembly; women are recognised as equal citizens and have one-fifth of the lower house seats.

Independence date

19 August 1919

Form of state

Islamic republic

The executive

The president is the Head of State, leading a cabinet, with two vice presidents and 29 ministers.

National legislature

The National Assembly has two chambers. The Wolesi Jirga (House of the People) (lower) has 249 directly elected members for five-year terms with the number proportional to the populations of the provinces. Under the constitution, the Kuchi (nomad) community is allocated 10 seats; female candidates are also guaranteed seats. According to the constitution, the chamber may set up commissions to inquire into government actions, endorse and enforce legislation not approved by the president (providing it has a two-thirds majority), question ministers, decide on government development programmes and the budget and approve or reject government sponsored appointments. The Wolesi Jirga ratifies laws and approves the actions of the president.

The Meshrano Jirga (House of Elders) (upper house) has 102 members who are either indirectly elected or appointed representatives. Members must be aged over 35 years. One member from each provincial council is elected to serve a four-year term in the upper chamber.

Legal system

The 2004 constitution guarantees an independent judiciary, consisting of a Stera Mahkama (supreme court), high courts and appeal courts.

The president appoints the members of the supreme court, with the approval of the Wolesi Jirga.

Last elections

20 August and 7 November 2010 (presidential and run-off (cancelled)); 18 September 2010 (parliamentary)

Results: Presidential: Hamid Karzai won 49.67 per cent of the vote and Abdullah Abdullah 30.59 per cent, Ramazan Bashardost 10.46 per cent, Ashraf Ghani Ahmadzai 2.94 per cent, Mirwais Yasini 1.03 per cent; 27 other candidates each won less than 1 per cent. Turnout was 38.7 per cent. Runoff: Abdullah withrew and Kazai was declared winner.

Parliamentary: all 249 elected candidates elected were non-partisan.

Next elections

2015 (presidential); 2015 (parliamentary)

Political parties

Ruling party

Members of the national assembly are elected as independent candidates

Main opposition party

Jami'at e Islami (Islamic Society of Afghanistan) leads a loose alliance.

Population

29.12* million (2010) (some 1 million Afghanis are still in exile in Pakistan and Iran)

Last census: June 1979: 13,051,358 (excluding nomad population)

Population density: 40 inhabitants per square km (2010) 2006

Annual growth rate: 1.7 per cent 2005 (ADB)

Ethnic make-up
Pashtun (Pathan) (38 per cent), Tajik (25 per cent), Hazara (19 per cent), Uzbek (6 per cent), minority groups include Aimaks, Turkmen, Baluch and others (12 per cent).
The Pashtuns largely reside in south-eastern Afghanistan. Tajiks, Hazaras and Uzbeks are the main communities in northern and central Afghanistan.
Religions
Almost the entire population is Muslim (84 per cent Sunni Muslim, 15 per cent Shi'ite); Hindu, Sikh and Jewish minorities.

Education
The UN Educational, Scientific and Cultural Organisation (Unesco) assists the Afghan government in the education sector's reconstruction by promoting universal primary education, especially for girls, and the expansion of primary schooling with access to secondary education.
Unesco has extended its support for a computer centre at Kabul University, including Internet access for the young. It also funds the printing of text-books for all levels of education.
In January 2011 the minister of education, Farooq Wardak, was reported in the UK's *Times Educational Supplement* that a 'cultural change' meant the Taliban were 'no more opposing girls' education'.
Literacy rate: 51.9 per cent and 21.9 per cent respectively for men and women; adult rates (Unesco 2000).
Enrolment rate: 15 per cent gross primary enrolment of relevant age group (including repeaters), rates for 2000–01 (Unesco 2002).

Health
WHO continues to support the IDPs by providing essential medical supplies to clinics within the camps. There is provision for night health services and nutrition centres for malnourished children. Harsh winters in the region cause acute respiratory infections, while hot dry summers lead to diarrhoeal diseases.
Despite on-going security problems, UN relief agencies and the WHO provide emergency medical supplies and assistance to local hospitals.
Polio is endemic. In 2006, a large outbreak of the disease, in the volatile southern regions, followed a drop in overall numbers of cases in previous years. The UN undertook immunisation against polio of around 1.3 million children in the southern provinces of Kandahar and Helmand in September 2007. The week-long campaign took place within the war zones while 10,000 health workers were given safe passage to undertake the operation.
Life expectancy: 42 years, 2004 (WHO 2006)
Fertility rate/Maternal mortality rate: 7.4 births per woman, 2004 (WHO 2006)
Child (under 5 years) mortality rate (per 1,000): 165 per 1,000 live births (2002), 49 per cent of children aged under five were malnourished (World Bank).
Head of population per physician: 0.19 physicians per 1,000 people, 2001 (WHO 2006)

Welfare
Many Afghans have fled the country due to war, drought and earthquakes. The UNHCR estimated that, at its peak, more than 3.7 million Afghans survive outside their homeland; between 1.1–1.5 million were internally displaced. Over 520,000 refugees returned in 2005, the largest group, of 453,000, came from camps in Pakistan. International agencies and the government have been working hard for their rehabilitation, as well as for the thousands who returned in previous years.
The WFP has been working with the Afghan government to rehabilitate irrigation systems and expand its activities to cover the reconstruction of schools, hospitals, roads and bridges.
In 2005, Japan donated US$29 million to *New Beginnings Programme* that offers ex-militia soldiers the opportunity of joining the official army or retraining in peacetime occupations such as farming or tailoring. Japan had already donated US$90 million to the project that required US$140 million to fund.

Main cities
Kabul (capital, estimated population 2.4 million in 2008), Kandahar (347,253), Mazar-i-Sharif (277,302), Herat (350,154), Jalalabad (143,525).

Languages spoken
The languages spoken by Afghanistan's two largest ethnic groups are Dari (Afghan Persian) (50 per cent) and Pashtu (35 per cent). Turkic languages (primarily Uzbek and Turkmen) (11 per cent), 30 minor languages (primarily Baluchi and Pashai) (4 per cent). Farsi (Persian) is spoken by the Tajiks. Some speak a second language, including English, Russian, French or German.
The use of English began to grow after the arrival of NATO forces in 2005, as many jobs in government and non-governmental organisations (NGOs) required a level of use. By 2009 there were several hundred private schools teaching English to thousands of Afghan students.
Official language/s
Pashtu and Dari (named as official languages in the 2004 constitution)

Media
All material is subject to *Sharia* (Islamic law) and regulatory bodies are controlled by the government. However, since 2001 there has been a strong growth in broadcasting and print media, with five TV stations and over 300 newspapers published nationwide; in a country with a low literacy rate the radio is the principal medium for news and information.
Press
Print journalism does not match broadcast journalism for professionalism and research with opinions offered instead of investigation and hard facts. Self-censorship is widely practiced by older writers and violence towards journalists has curbed the focus necessary for news gathering. The market for newspapers and advertising revenue is so small that private newspapers must rely on political factions and individuals for sponsorship.
Dailies: State-owned publications, in Dari and Pashtu, include *Daily Anis Eslah*, *Arman-e Melli* and *Eslah*. English dailies include *Kabul Times*. Private newspapers in Dari and Pashtu include *Hewad*, *Eradeh*, *Shari'at*, *Daily Afghanistan* (www.dailyafghanistan.com), *Tolafghan* (www.tolafghan.com) and *Payam e Mojahed* (www.payamemojahed.com). English private dailies include *Daily Outlook Afghanistan* (www.outlookafghanistan.net) and *Daily Cheragh* (www.cheraghdaily.af).
Weeklies: In Dari and Pashtu, *Aina-e-Zan* (Women's Mirror). In English, *Kabul Weekly* is an independent newspaper funded by the UN. *Omaid Weekly* is published in the US and is one of the most widely read Afghani publications in the world.
Broadcasting
National Radio and Television Afghanistan (NRTA) is under the ministry of information and culture.
Radio: There are many radio stations broadcasting regionally. The government-owned Radio Afghanistan is national; it has competition from several foreign radio broadcasting services. Commercial radio stations including the popular Arman FM (www.arman.fm) with programmes in local languages and English, Radio Killid (www.thekillidgroup.com) and Rana FM (www.ranafm.org).
Television: The popularity of television is growing and some stations are providing local programming. The National Television Afghanistan (NTA) is government run; other national, free-to-air private stations include Tolo TV (www.tolo.tv) which shows foreign and domestic programmes, Ariana TV (www.arianatelevision.com) with news in Pashtu, Dari and English and Ayna TV is based in the northern provinces and broadcasts in four local languages.
Television is also provided by foreign entities including the US-based satellite

networks Noor TV (www.noor-tv.com) and Payame Afghan TV (www.payameafghantv.com). Khorasan TV, is a local satellite network with Shamshad and Afghan TV (http://afghanistantv.org).

News agencies

National news agency: BNA (Bakhtar News Agency)
Pajhwok Afghan News: www.pajhwok.com
Afghan Islamic Press: www.afghanislamicpress.com

Economy

The economy has been in a state of renewal since 2001, after the fall of the authoritarian Taliban regime. Afghanistan has a strong agricultural sector, accounting for around 30 per cent of GDP, although its level of productivity has been blighted by civil conflict, exploitation and underinvestment since the 1980s, leaving a legacy of degraded natural resources (particularly in forests and pastures) and fragmented rural institutions. Consequently, the level of productivity is low with inefficient production systems and poor management so that Afghanistan relies on international food aid to feed its population. It is estimated that introducing modern technologies would increase capacity by 7.5 million hectares of cultivated land, and with proper irrigation 20 per cent could be double-cropped.
Natural resources include minerals and hydrocarbons. Industrial manufacturing, which accounts for around 25 per cent of GDP, is mostly small-scale production of locally required products such as soap, furniture, textiles and shoes. Exports are dominated by hand-woven carpets which provided revenue of over US$186 million in 2006/07.
The informal economy is dominated by the illegal production and trade in opium, which creates an obstruction to government efforts to raise legitimate revenue through taxation. Around 6,250 tonnes of (wet) opium was produced in 2009, which was a fall of 1,190 tonnes from the high of 7,440 tonnes in 2007/08. The 2009 drought may have had more of an adverse effect on harvests than counter-narcotic measures. Afghanistan accounts for around 90 per cent of the world's opium trade.
GDP growth had fallen in 2008 to 3.4 per cent, due to the high costs of imported food and petroleum products and the impact of the global economic crisis. However, by 2009 economic activity picked up and GDP growth climbed to 20.9 per cent as agriculture recovered from a drought and government and coalition forces increased their spending. In 2010, GDP growth fell to 8.2 per cent and domestic security deteriorated and world trade slowed. Inflation fell from a high of 26.8 per cent in 2008 (with a peak of 43 per cent in May 2008) to -12.2 per cent in 2009 as food prices fell and monetary policies introduced by government acted as deflationary pressures. It rose to an estimated 7.7 per cent in 2010. As the currency (Afghani) appreciated in value over 2008–09 the government managed the amount in circulation; money demand remained strong and the Afghani remained close to its five-year average in real terms.
Although per capita income is low, it has risen steadily, and in 2008 it was US$359, rising to US$426 in 2009 and estimated to have been US$515 in 2010. Corruption has been highlighted as one of Afghanistan's most insidious problems. The watchdog charity Integrity Watch Afghanistan (IWA) reported in July 2010 that a survey had shown corruption was rampant and becoming entrenched in all areas of Afghan life. At the same time international donors voiced their criticism that anti-corruption measures were not producing tangible results and that if economic support was to be channelled through the government's budget (from 33 per cent to 50 per cent as proposed by President Kazai), then measures for a strengthened financial system that cuts corruption and poor governance were required.

External trade

Much of the government's strategy for international trade is predicated on a future with secure, nationwide peace. It sees the future of Afghanistan as a hub for regional trade, with land links to surrounding countries.
The ministry of commerce and industry has undertaken negotiations in regional economic initiatives, which include the Economic Co-operation Organisation (ECO) and bilateral negotiations with neighbouring countries including Iran, India, Pakistan, Tajikistan and Uzbekistan. Plans include participation in the South Asia Free Trade Area (Safta) and the Central Asian Regional Economic Co-operation (Carec) programme. Afghanistan is also an observer member of the World Trade Organisation (WTO).
A suggested oil pipeline through Afghanistan to Pakistan would create an oil trade linking Central Asia with Pakistan.

Imports

Afghanistan mainly imports capital goods including construction items needed to repair its neglected infrastructure, foodstuffs, textiles and petroleum products.
Main sources: Pakistan (typically 36 per cent of total), US (9 per cent), Germany (8 per cent).

Exports

Opium, Afghanistan's largest, albeit illegal, export is primarily transported north through the Central Asian republics and on to Europe. Measures by foreign governments have been introduced in an attempt to eradicate the crop. Around 10 per cent of Afghan families rely on its production and as opium represents a large proportion of the country's exports this could lead to a serious drop in income if the campaign is successful.
Principal non-opium exports include hand-woven carpets, fruits and nuts, small scale industrial products, pelts and hides and semi-precious and precious stones. Afghanistan has been the world's largest exporter of raisins and a major producer of grapes, melons and other fruit.
Main destinations: India (typically 21 per cent of total), Pakistan (20 per cent), US (19 per cent).

Agriculture

Farming

The population is returning to the countryside and some rural areas have been transformed by the return of Afghan refugees from Pakistan and Iran. However, the level of productivity is low with inefficient production systems and poor management so that Afghanistan relies on international food aid to feed its population. A severe drought in 2009 not only reduced harvests but also increased soil erosion. It is estimated that introducing modern technologies increase capacity by 7.5 million hectares of cultivated land, and with proper irrigation 20 per cent could be double-cropped.
Twelve per cent of the total area is cultivated, another 10 per cent is pasture land and a further 5–6 per cent considered by some sources to have agricultural potential.
Most cultivated land is situated in river valleys or plains, which are often fertile; an estimated two-thirds of cultivated land is irrigated. Food output is frequently below what is required to feed the population. In total more than 12,000 out of 22,000 farming villages were abandoned or destroyed during the fighting of the 1990s.
Apart from the opium poppy, the main crops are wheat, fruit and vegetables, maize, rice, barley, cotton, sugar beet, sugar cane, oil seeds.
The livestock herd needs rebuilding. Livestock includes sheep, cattle, goats and poultry, with donkeys, horses, camels, mules and buffaloes kept as draught animals. Sheep provide a major source of protein and animal fat. Some 70 per cent of wool production, along with hides from karakul sheep, is exported.

After the fall of the Taliban, the farmers started to sow poppies again. In 2002, President Karzai banned opium poppy cultivation and trafficking, and offered farmers US$350 for each 0.2 hectare (ha) to be replanted with alternative crops. This was only a fraction of what the farmers could earn from the poppy crop. Around 6,250 tonnes of (wet) opium was produced in 2009, which was a fall of 1,190 tonnes from the high of 7,440 tonnes in 2007/08 – although the 2009 drought may have had more of an adverse effect on harvests than counter-narcotic measures. Afghanistan accounts for around 90 per cent of the world's opium trade. Until economic and social alternatives are developed, the local population remains dependent on the opium economy. The British army has been assisting the government in its efforts to irradicate poppy cultivation.

Forestry

Wooded land is limited to the eastern Hindu Kush region and along the Pakistani border. Many forests in these areas have been severely reduced due to trees being cut down and the wood smuggled out to surrounding countries.

Tourism

The continuing instability in the country hinders the development of a tourist sector in Afghanistan, although given the right conditions there is considerable potential. The country has a wealth of cultural, heritage and natural sites which have been out-of-bounds for much of the war. But, despite the on-going fighting with the Taleban and Al Qaeda, Afghans still welcomes visitors and there are escorted tours, for hardy travellers available either solely in Afghanistan or as part of a journey along the 'Silk Road'. Restrictions on travel in the south apply and such destinations should be avoided. A number of luxury hotels are available in Kabul that offer tight security, nevertheless terrorists target foreigners and all visitors should adhere to instructions given by their respective diplomatic representatives.

Environment

In April 2009, the first national park, Band e Amir, featuring deep blue lakes and natural dams of travertine, was established near Bamyan Valley, the site of the giant, 1500-year old, Buddha statues destroyed by the Taliban in 2001.

Mining

Natural resources include copper, chromite, lead, zinc, iron, salt, lapis lazuli, emeralds, talc and barium sulphate. Long-term mineral development projects include copper mining and smelting at Ainak and high-grade iron ore mining at Hajigak in northern Afghanistan.

A Chinese-owned mining company won a tender in November 2007 to develop one of the world's largest copper mines sited in Logar Province. It is estimated that the site has 13 million tonnes of copper. Australia, Canada, China and Russia all contested the tender, ultimately won by China Metallurgical Group with an investment of US$3 billion. The mine is expected to be operational in 2012 and offer employment to thousands of Afghan workers.

Hydrocarbons

Proven hydrocarbon reserves were in excess of 150 million barrels of oil and 12.7 billion cubic metres (cum) of natural gas, located in 29 fields in the north-western region of the country by Soviet Union in 1959. Since then very little of these resources have been exploited and further exploration, using modern technologies, had been curtailed due to the geopolitical situation and the series of conflicts in Afghanistan, although potentially oil producing sedimentary sections had been located in the south of the country. Limited seismic surveys of the northern oil and gas fields began in late 2004, conducted by the US Geological Survey and by 2006 it estimated that mean volumes were 1.6 billion barrels of oil and 444 billion cum of natural gas (although proven natural gas reserves, by this time, were 49.6 billion cum). Three oil and gas bearing blocks in the north, with proven reserves, were licensed for exploration and production, in 2009. In 2008 all Afghanistan's oil needs were imported, mainly from Pakistan and Turkmenistan.

Gas production from the Jowzjan province, amounted to 2.8 million cum per annum, used exclusively domestically.

There are small deposits of coal, estimated at 74 million tonnes located mainly in northern Afghanistan in the region between Herat and Badashkah. Production is typically just 1,000 tonnes per annum.

Energy

The energy sector was badly damaged during the years of upheaval. Afghanistan has installed capacity of 450MW, generated by hydropower, of which only 271MW are available. Some border areas receive supplies from neighbouring countries. Electricity supply is only available to around 6 per cent of the population and interruptions and blackouts are frequent.

Banking and insurance

Afghanistan has six banks (four of which have almost no assets) and two commercial banks – Pashtani and Milli – with assets. In 2003, two banking laws were passed: the Central Banking Law and the Commercial Banking Law. The first laid the groundwork for the Central Bank to focus on monetary policy, pricing stability and oversight of the commercial markets; the second allowed for private ownership of commercial banks. Standard Chartered (UK), Microfinance Bank of Afghanistan and National Bank of Pakistan opened in 2004.

An International Monetary Fund (IMF) report in February 2011 into the operations of Kabul Bank, Afghanistan's largest private bank, recommended that it be put into receivership, which would help the government in its plan to stabilise financial services in the country. The IMF identified problems of corruption, bad loans and mismanagement that had resulted in hundreds of million of US dollars being lost. The IMF also urged the government to announce plans to deal with the scandal that had become public in December 2010, to protect the rest of the banking system and that legal action should be taken against those responsible for the fraud. Abdul Qadeer Fitrat, central bank governor, resigned on 27 June saying he felt his life was in danger for investigating fraud at Kabul Bank. He said that he was being hindered in his investigations by the government, which in turn accused him of treason.

Central bank

Da Afghanistan Bank

Main financial centre

Kabul

Time

GMT plus 4.5 hours

Geography

Afghanistan is a landlocked country in south-western Asia. Its neighbours are Turkmenistan, Uzbekistan and Tajikistan to the north, Iran to the west, and Pakistan to the east and south. It also has a 76km border with the People's Republic of China to the north-east. The Hindu Kush mountains are in the north-east of the country.

There are three geographic areas: the central highlands (comprising over 60 per cent of the land), the arid southern region (25 per cent of the land) and the fertile northern plains.

Hemisphere

Northern

Climate

The climate is dry with large variations between day and night temperatures as well as swift seasonal changes. Maximum summer temperatures on the plains can reach 46 degrees Celsius (C), while the lowest winter temperatures, in the mountains, reach minus 26 degrees C; Kabul (at altitude 1,800 metres) has an average 16 to 33 degrees C in summer (July–August) and minus 8 to 2 degrees C in winter.

The rainy season is from October–April, although rainfall is very irregular; Kabul averages 335mm per annum.

Entry requirements

Passports
Required by all.
Visa
Required by all; application forms can be obtained via: www.embassyofafghanistan.org/main/consulate/visa.cfm or local embassies.
Business visas require a letter of introduction stating the purpose of visit and sponsorship information. A visa financial guarantee must be included with the application fee. For a multiply entry visa, a letter of introduction signed by the president of the organisation, must accompany the documentation.
Currency advice/regulations
Import and export of local currency is limited to Af500. Import of foreign currency is unlimited, although export of foreign currency is limited to the amount declared on arrival.
US dollars circulate widely. Travellers cheques are not readily accepted.
Customs
Alcohol is permitted for personal consumption.
All antiquities, carpets, furs and photography films require an export permit.
Prohibited imports
Illegal drugs, pornography; pork products in any form.
Cameras require an import permit.

Health (for visitors)

Mandatory precautions
Vaccination certificate for yellow fever if travelling from an infected areas.
Advisable precautions
Hepatitis A, anti-malarial precautions, polio, tetanus, typhoid. Diphtheria, hepatitis B, TB immunisations are recommended in some circumstances – seek further advice. Water precautions are necessary. There is a risk of rabies.
Emergency medical care is limited and visitors should ensure they have medical insurance that includes emergency evacuation. Hospitals and doctors require immediate cash payment before commencing treatment. The German Medical Diagnostic Center (www.medical-kabul.com), operates in Kabul, offering treatment that includes medical, radiological and pharmacy services. It does not offer emergency, obstetric or dental treatment.
Public hospitals are not up to Western standards and should be avoided. There are a limited number of private hospitals and some international aid groups operate medical facilities in cities and villages. Visitors should travel with all their necessary medications.

Hotels

Accommodation tends to be scarce and spartan. There are only a few international hotels in Kabul, including the Intercontinental Hotel, Bagh-I-Balla, Kabul and the Serena Hotel, Froshgah Street, Kabul.

Credit cards

Only Visa branded credit and debit cards are accepted at very limited outlets.

Public holidays (national)

Afghanistan uses the Persian calendar (although it used the Islamic calendar between 1999 and 2002). The Persian calendar has 12 months which differ from the Gregorian calendar: there are 31 days in each of the first six months of the Persian calendar, 30 days in each of the next five months and 29 days in the last month, except in leap years when it has 30 days.
Persian year 1389: 21 March 2010 to 20 March 2011 (year 1390: 21 March 2011 to 22 March 2012).
Dates of feasts vary according to the sighting of the new moon, so cannot be forecast exactly.
Fixed dates
21 Mar (Naw Roz/Persian New Year), 28 Apr (Islamic Revolution Day), 19 Aug (National Day).
Variable dates
Eid al Adha (three days), Ashura, Birth of the Prophet, First day of Ramadan, Eid al Fitr (three days).
Muslim holidays that occur on a Friday may be observed on Saturday.

Working hours

The weekend is Friday.
Banking
Sat–Wed: 0800–1200, 1300–1630; Thu: 0800–1330.
Business
Sat–Wed: 0800–1200, 1300–1630; Thu: 0800–1330.
Government
Sat–Thu: 0800–1600.
Shops
Commercial shops keep long but varying hours, usually Sat–Thu: 0700–2300.

Telecommunications

Mobile/cell phones
GSM 900/1800 services available in main cities only.

Electricity supply

220 volts AC, 60 cycle electrical system, using European round, two-prong plugs. Supplies may be seriously affected and power cuts frequent.

Weights and measures

Metric system (local units are also in use).

Social customs/useful tips

It is customary to shake hands on meeting and taking leave. Among men, embracing is a traditional form of greeting. Islamic conventions apply. When sitting cross-legged on sofas or cushions, soles of feet must not be shown.
Business meetings are usually conducted in English or Dari. Green or black tea, nuts and raisins are served. The form of greeting is *Salaam Aleykum* (peace be with you), followed by a firm handshake and placing the right hand over the heart. Several minutes are spent engaging in pleasantries about each other's countries. It is essential to build trust and to be patient.
Women should dress modestly in long skirts or trousers and avoid revealing tops and dresses.

Security

Foreign nationals are advised not to visit Afghanistan unless absolutely necessary. All visitors should register their presence with their diplomatic representative and keep up-to-date with local information on threat levels. Travel within the country should be kept to a minimum to lessen the risk of the threats posed by armed criminals and terrorists and between rival tribal armies.
Kidnapping, which is widespread, is the most serious threat to any visitor; seeking professional advice for security measures may be necessary.
Suicide-bombings have become more common and visitors must observe a high level of vigilance.
There is widespread danger from mines and unexploded ordinance throughout the country.
All street demonstrations and large gatherings should be avoided.

Getting there

The current security situation means that flights may be cancelled and roads closed at any time. It is advisable to check before travelling. The information that follows may also change.
Air
National airline: Ariana Afghan Airlines
International airport/s: Kabul airport (KBL), 16km from Kabul; facilites include a bank, bar and restaurant.
Airport tax: Departure tax: Af200
Surface
Road: There are links to Iran and Pakistan via the Asia Highway and to the CIS via road and rail. Hostilities have periodically closed the Pakistan route; check before travelling.
In 2007, a road bridge spanning the River Pyanj in northern Afghanistan opened, linking Tajikistan and Afghanistan. The bridge, costing US$37m, was paid for by the US.

The Regional Road Corridor Improvement Project, estimated at US$18 billion, to improve Central Asian roads, airports, railway lines and seaports and provide a vital transit route between Europe and Asia was agreed on 3 November 2007. Six new transit corridors, between Afghanistan, Azerbaijan, China, Kazakhstan, Kyrgyzstan, Mongolia, Tajikistan and Uzbekistan, of mainly roads and rail links, will be constructed, or existing resources upgraded, by 2013. Half the costs with be provided by the Asian Development Bank and other multilateral organisations and the other half by participating countries.
Rail: Links exist between Kabul and the CIS.

Getting about

The current security situation means that flights may be cancelled and roads closed at any time. It is advisable to check before travelling. The information that follows may also change.

National transport

Air: Ariana Afghan Airlines flies a limited service to Herat and Mazar-e-sharif.
Road: Main centres are linked by paved roads but secondary roads vary in condition and by season. There are approximately 22,000km of roads.
Buses: Bus service are unreliable and dangerous for internal travel.
Rail: On 25 May 2010 a 75-kilometer stretch of railway line connecting Mazar-e-Sharif to the northern border with Uzbekistan was inaugurated; it is scheduled for completion by the end of 2010 and will connect to Uzbekistan's rail network and allow the easier transport of exports to regional markets in Europe and Asia.
Water: There are 1,200km of navigable inland waterways, including the Amu Darya River.

City transport

Taxis: Taxis are available from Kabul airport to the city centre. Tipping is not usual. Fares are negotiable and can be high for foreigners.
Buses, trams & metro: A limited number of buses are operating.

Car hire

International driving licences are required for those hire cars available.

BUSINESS DIRECTORY

The addresses listed below are a selection only. While World of Information makes every endeavour to check these addresses, we cannot guarantee that changes have not been made, especially to telephone numbers and area codes. We would welcome any corrections.

Telephone area codes

The international dialling code (IDD) for Afghanistan is + 93, followed by the area code and subscriber's number. Landline telephones are still unreliable. Some of the numbers below are mobile/cell numbers.

Herat	40	Kandahar	30
Jalalabad	60	Marez-E-Sherif	50
Kabul	20	Mobil phones	70

Chambers of Commerce

Afghan Chamber of Commerce and Industry, Mohammed Jan Khan Wattt, Kabul (tel/fax: 290-196).

Banking

Afghanistan International Bank, House no 1608 Behind Amani High School, Wazir Akhbar Khan, Kabul (tel: 792 03158; fax: 202 103567).

Agricultural Development Bank, Jaddeh-Maiwand, Kabul.

Export Promotion Bank, Jaddah-Temorshahi, Kabul.

First Micro-finance Bank of Afghanistan, Street West of Park Shahr-i-Naw, Charahi Ansari, Kabul (tel: 0790 95705).

Industrial Promotion Bank, Shahr-i-naw, Kabul.

Mortgage and Construction Bank, Shahri-i-naw, Kabul.

National Bank of Pakistan, House No 2, Street No 10, Wazir Akbar Khan, Kabul (tel: 20-230 1660; fax: 20-230 1659).

Pashtany Tejaraty Bank, Mohmmad Jan Khan Watt, Kabul.

Standard Chartered Bank, P.O. Box 16019, House No. 10, Street No. 10 B, Wazir Akhbar Khan, Kabul (tel: 790 88888, 790 20833).

Central bank

Da Afghanistan Bank, Ibni Sina Watt, Kabul (tel: 240-7579).

Travel information

Ariana Afghan Airlines, PO Box 76; Street 10, Ansari Watt, Kabul (tel: 70-204-0913; fax: 870-600-142238; internet: flyariana.com).

Kabul Airport, PO Box 76, Anseri Watt, Kabul.

Ministries

Ministry of Communications (internet: www.af-com-ministry.org).

Ministry of Finance (internet: www.mof.gov.af).

Ministry of Foreign Affairs: Malak Azghar Road, Kabul (tel: 210 0366; e-mail: contact@mfa.gov.af).

Ministry of Information and Culture, Mohammad Jan Khan Watt, beside Spinzar Hotel, Kabul (internet: www.moic.gov.af)

Ministry of Rural Rehabilitation and Development (internet: www.mrrd.gov.af).

Ministry of Agriculture, Irrigation and Livestock, Darulman, Kabul (internet: www.agriculture.gov.af).

Other useful addresses

Afghan Islamic Press, House 208, Qafila Road, Tahkal Payan, Peshawar, Pakistan (tel: (+92- 91) 570-1100; fax: (+92- 91) 570-3355; e-mail: aip@pes.comsats.net.pk).

Afghanistan Embassy (USA), 2341 Wyoming Avenue, NW, Washington DC 20008 (tel: (+1-202) 234-3770; fax: (+1-202) 328-3516; e-mail: info@embassyofafghanistan.org; internet: www.embassyofafghanistan.org

Afghanistan Investment Support Agency, Opposite Ministry of Foreign Affairs, Kabul (tel/fax: 210-3404; internet: www.aisa.org.af).

Afghanistan Wireless Communication Corporation, Ministry of Communications Building, Mohammad Jan Khan Watt, Kabul (tel: 20-0000; fax: 20-0200; e-mail: info@afghan-wireless.com).

Arman FM (radio), PO Box 1045, Central Post Office, Kabul; House 3, St 12, Wazir Akbar Khan, Kabul (e-mail: info@arman.fm).

British Embassy, 15th Street, Roundabout Wazir Akbar, Khan, PO Box 334, Kabul (tel: 701-02000; fax: 701-02274; email: britishembassy.kabul@fco.gov.uk).

Fedex (Afghan Express), Karte 3, Khai Street, House 326, Kabul (tel: 25-00525; fax: 25-00524).

DHL Express, Street 10, Wazir Akbar Khan, House 310, Kabul (e-mail: kbl_hdesk@af.dhl.com).

TNT Express, Turabaz Khan Crossroads, Kabul.

National news agency: BNA (Bakhtar News Agency): www.bakhtarnews.com.af

Internet sites

Afghanistan Embassy (Australia): www.afghanembassy.net

Afghanistan Online: www.afghan-web.com

Afghanistan government website: www.af

Guide to Travellers to Kabul: www.afghanembassy.net/n_travel.html

UN Development programme: www.undp.org.af/projects/lofta_july.html

UN Development Business on-line subscription service: www.devbusiness.com

World Bank: www.worldbank.org/afghanistan

Albania

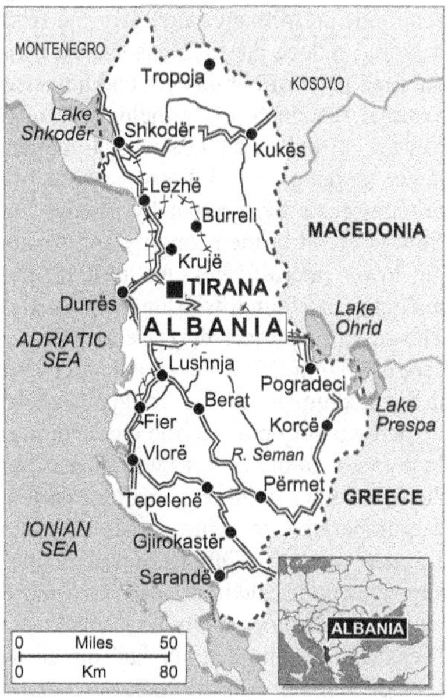

In the days of the Roman empire the emperors' legions, coming down the Appian Way to Brindisi to cross the Strait of Otranto would land on the coast of Albania to march east on what was the great military highway to Thessalonica and Constantinople. Albania was sporadically invaded by Goths and Normans, and subject to the rule of the Byzantine, Bulgarian, Serbian and Venetian empires. Then, for almost five centuries, the Ottoman Turks held sway, making Albania the only European Muslim state. Finally, the armies of Hitler and Mussolini made their presence felt. True Albanians are the descendants of the Illyrians, whose kingdom was conquered by Rome in 167BC. It was not until 1912 that Albania finally gained independence.

Internal conflict

Having thrown off the strictures of communism in 1990 by overthrowing its ruthless dictatorship under Enver Hoxh, Albania came close to imploding in 1997 when, after fraudulent pyramid investment schemes collapsed and many Albanians lost their life's savings, riots lead to a state of emergency and the resignation of President Berisha. In 2011 the situation seemed to be close to repeating itself through a crisis that could be traced back to the 1990s. In simple terms, none of the elections held in 'democratic' Albania have come close to what would be generally recognised as free and fair. The 2009 elections saw the leader of the opposition protest against the results by boycotting parliament. The boycott made the voicing of opposition complaints and views virtually impossible. It also enabled Albania's prime minister and veteran politician Sali Berisha (who has held top offices for more than half of Albania's post communist period) to do as he pleased. In the international rankings of political freedom Albania has slipped to the same levels as bastions of democracy such as Abkahzia, Nagorno-Karabakh and the Gambia.

Freedom and transparency are both victims of the widespread corruption that is rife in Albania. Albania came in at number 95 on the Transparency International Corruption Perceptions Index in 2009. The Berisha regime has cheerfully refused to dismiss cabinet ministers accused of dishonesty or incompetence. Albania's establishment institutions – even the judiciary – are tarred with the same brush.

The political conflict between Berisha and Edi Rama, leader of the opposition Partia Socialiste ë Shqipërisë (PSS) (Socialist Party of Albania), has deteriorated to the level of employing extra institutional measures to gain points over their opponents. Thus, Mr Berisha accuses Mr Rama of attempting to gain power through force, while Mr Rama returns the compliment by accusing Mr Berisha's government of being undemocratic, claiming instead that what Albania needs is a Tunisia style uprising. However, instead of an uprising, Albania in late January 2011 saw vicious street-fighting in which a three (some reports put the figure at four) people lost their lives. Things came to a head when the crowd tried to storm the office of Prime Minister Berisha. In a five-hour confrontation opposition supporters threw stones at the building as the police replied with tear gas and water cannon. The street battles were the vicious aspect of the feud between Messrs Berisha and Rama. In addition to being the leader

KEY FACTS

Official name: Republika ë Shqipërisë (Republic of Albania)

Head of State: President Bamir Topi (since 24 Jul 2007)

Head of government: Prime Minister Sali Berisha (elected 3 Jul 2005; re-elected 28 Jun 2009)

Ruling party: Coalition: Aleance per Ndryshim (AN) (Alliance for Change) led by the Partia Demokratike (ë Shqipërisë) (PD) (Democratic Party (of Albania)) with Partia Republikane (RP) (Republican Party), Partia Demokrate e Re (PDR) (New Democratic Party) and Partia për Drejtësi dhe Integrim (PDI) (Party for Justice and Integration); PD re-elected 28 Jun 2009; coalition took office 3 Sep 2009)

Area: 28,748 square km

Population: 3.20 million (2010)*

Capital: Tirana

Official language: Tosk Albanian; the Albanian language is divided into two dialects – Gheg, north of the river Shkumbinit, and Tosk in the south.

Currency: Lek (L) = 100 qindarka

Exchange rate: L104.80 per US$ (Oct 2011)

GDP per capita: US$3,716 (2010)

GDP real growth: 3.50% (2010)

GDP: US$11.80 billion (2010)

Labour force: 1.05 million (2010)

Unemployment: 13.70% (2010)

Inflation: 3.60% (2010)

Balance of trade: -US$2.76 billion (2010)

* estimated figure

of the opposition socialists, Mr Rama is also the mayor of Tirana.

After a rocky period in 1997, when riots followed the collapse of a pyramid 'investment' scheme, some sort of stability has been restored. However, the impasse between government and opposition and their respective leaders has resulted in public disillusion at a time when few European economies were performing satisfactorily. Albania had joined NATO in 2009 and had seen its European Union Schengen area visa requirements lifted. For most Albanians, however, what mattered more was the restoration of some form of 'normality' to their daily lives, starting at the top. For Albania's still impoverished electorate, the political feud seemed to have little to do with their interests, more to do with their leaders egos and the material interests of their respective circles.

The economy

Albania's gross domestic product (GDP) growth stood at 3.4 per cent in the first quarter of 2011, down from 5.4 per cent in the fourth quarter of 2010, according to the Albanian Institute of Statistics, INSTAT. Transport, industry and construction registered the biggest growth, while telecommunications and services all registered negative growth. The construction sector was helped by government investments in infrastructure that preceded the May 2011 local elections, while negative growth in the telecommunications sector was mainly a result of lower mobile phone rates.

INSTAT has published quarterly data on Albania's economic growth since the third quarter of 2008. Since then, the preliminary estimates have often been revised mainly downwards, prompting discussions about the credibility of preliminary government estimates, with some analysts complaining of political pressure to prompt positive forecasts. Albania's government has often been at odds with the International Monetary Fund (IMF), and with the opposition, over economic growth forecasts. The centre-right government of Prime Minister Sali Berisha estimates GDP growth at 3.5–4.0 per cent for 2011, a forecast that allowed for planned increases in expenditure. But the IMF more conservatively estimates 2.7 per cent growth for 2011. It has urged the ministry of finance to cut spending and increase taxes in order to keep the budget deficit and the ballooning public debt at bay.

In its June 2011 report on the Albanian economy, the IMF noted that the Albanian economy had shown some strength. According to the IMF, Albania weathered the 2009 global financial crisis well and, in contrast to most other European economies, avoided an output contraction and has again led growth in the region. The financial sector proved resilient and did not require public support. Throughout, inflation remained under control. Last, but not least, the rebalancing of the economy began as exports picked up and the high current account deficit began to narrow. Economic growth in 2010 was estimated by the IMF to be 3.5 per cent, projected to decelerate to 2.66 per cent in 2011, due to slack domestic demand and moderating exports. Over the medium term, growth might recover to some 4 per cent, with some improvements in external sustainability. These levels, although respectable, are well below the previous decade's average of 6 per cent, and also subject to downside risks, not least those stemming from the high level of public debt.

Fiscal policy is the priority for boosting economic performance and lowering risk. It would reduce the risks associated with the high level of public debt and advance external sustainability by helping to narrow the current account deficit. Moreover, lower deficits would boost sustainable private-sector led growth by raising the flow of credit to the economy and securing lower interest rates. As in 2010, the budget again found itself under pressure. The deficit is projected to rise to 4.66 per cent of GDP in 2011 and above 5 per cent in the medium term. This would push public debt up very close to the legal ceiling. In the view of the IMF, as was the case in 2010, another mid-year budget review was imperative to achieve cuts of some 1.5 per cent of GDP. Repeated budget slippages underlined the need for a more realistic macroeconomic framework. Weaker economic activity had put pressure on revenue collection, but the shortfall compared to the initial budget mainly reflected over-optimistic forecasts. The requisite fiscal consolidation will require credible measures and sustained effort. Already interest, wage, and entitlement spending claim more than two thirds of every lek the government collects in taxes and fees. Should the required spending cuts be seen as unrealistic, direct taxes or contributions will need to be raised. One measure could be to rescind the earlier cuts in social contributions, especially since they have not resulted in the hoped-for increase in compliance. Doing so would also help lower the pension deficit – which, at one per cent of GDP, is on the high side in the context of Albania's young and growing population. Albania's very low flat income tax rates could also be raised without imperiling Albania's competitive position.

The monetary policy framework of an inflation target and flexible exchange rate is, however, a fundamental strength of the Albanian economy. In spite of higher import prices and increases in administered prices and excises, inflation is projected to return within the Bank of Albania's target band. A better macroeconomic policy mix is nevertheless called for. Improved fiscal performance will be critical in ascertaining external sustainability as well as the

KEY INDICATORS — Albania

	Unit	2006	2007	2008	2009	2010
Population	m	3.15	3.15	*3.17	*3.19	*3.20
Gross domestic product (GDP)	US$bn	9.11	10.62	13.00	12.20	11.80
GDP per capita	US$	2,892	3,210	4,102	3,819	3,716
GDP real growth	%	5.0	6.0	7.8	3.3	3.5
Inflation	%	2.2	3.4	3.4	2.2	3.6
Unemployment	%	13.9	13.4	12.8	13.0	–
Exports (fob) (goods)	US$m	750.0	1,078.7	19,244.3	1,048.0	1,547.9
Imports (fob) (goods)	US$m	2,618.0	3,978.3	4,907.5	4,264.1	4,305.3
Balance of trade	US$m	-1,868.0	-2,899.6	-3,551.9	-3,216.1	-2,757.5
Current account	US$m	*-536.0	-625.0	-1,752.0	-1,874.9	-1,403.9
Total reserves minus gold	US$m	1,768.8	2,104.2	2,319.8	2,313.9	2,469.6
Foreign exchange	US$m	1,754.8	2,097.0	2,307.4	2,229.6	2,386.3
Exchange rate	per US$	96.73	90.43	83.89	94.98	103.94

* estimated figure

achievement of the inflation target at lower real interest rates. The limited fallout of the global financial crisis owes much to earlier proactive and forceful supervision and regulation. Still, balance sheet repairs have some way to go, financial innovation is progressing, and new international and domestic challenges are in the offing. Boosting productivity by attracting foreign investment is essential for higher sustainable growth. The last decade finally witnessed the arrival of relatively large-scale international investors in Albania, a critical factor in the transfer of technology and innovation, which in turn are essential for raising productivity and providing higher-wage employment in Albania. A favourable investment environment is a vital condition for success. Albania's EU perspective is one critical element in its attractiveness to investors. Other key requirements include the maintenance of a level playing field, the adoption of international best-practice regulations and their predictable enforcement by professional institutions. It will also be important to persevere with the remaining structural reform agenda.

Risk assessment

Economy	Good
Politics	Fair
Regional stability	Uncertain

COUNTRY PROFILE

Historical profile

1920s Italy withdrew from Albania and agreed to recognise its independence. Tirana was declared the capital city. Political instability followed. Prime Minister Ahmet Beg Zogu took the crown, proclaiming himself King Zog I.
1939 Italian troops under Benito Mussolini invaded Albania and King Zog fled.
1940 The Italians used Albania as their platform for the invasion of Greece.
1941 The Albanian Communist Party (ACP) was formed, with Enver Hoxha as its leader.
1943 German forces invaded and occupied Albania following surrender by the Italians.
1944 The Germans were forced out by Enver Hoxha's Communist resistance fighters. He proclaimed the constitution of the Democratic Government of Albania and became first secretary of the politburo. Albania became a Stalinist state and remained staunchly isolationist until the 1990s.
1945 The official language was based on Tosk Albanian.
1945–46 Tribunals were held which condemned thousands to death or imprisonment as 'war criminals' and 'enemies of the people'. Non-communists were purged from government positions.
1948 Albania broke its ties with Yugoslavia. The USSR began economic aid to Albania. The ACP was renamed the Partia e Punës (Party of Labour of Albania) (PLA).
1955 Albania became a founding member of the Warsaw Pact.
1961 Relations with the USSR soured when Albania supported China in the Sino-Soviet ideology dispute. Albania withdrew from the Council for Mutual Economic Assistance (Comecon).
1967 The Communist government outlawed religion, making Albania the world's only formal atheist state.
1968 Albania withdrew from the Warsaw Pact over the Soviet-led invasion of Czechoslovakia.
1976 A new constitution was adopted in which Albania declared itself the independent Peoples' Socialist Republic and reaffirmed its policy of self-reliance.
1985 Hoxha died and Ramiz Alia became first secretary of the politburo.
1989 Communist rule in Eastern Europe collapsed. Freedom of religion was restored.
1990 The PLA was renamed the Partia Socialiste ë Shqipërisë (PSS) (Socialist Party of Albania) and pursued a more liberal democratic ideology. Opposition parties were legalised. Thousands of people tried to flee the country when the right to travel abroad was granted.
1991 After an interim constitution was approved, multi-party elections were won by the PSS. Ramiz Alia was elected to the new post of executive president. Fatos Nano was forced to resign as head of government as the political and economic situation began to deteriorate. A caretaker government took power.
1992 The Partia Demokratike (ë Shqipërisë) (PD) (Democratic Party (of Albania)) won an overwhelming victory in parliamentary elections, ending five decades of communist rule. PD leader, Sali Berisha, was elected president. Aleksander Meksi was appointed prime minister. Ramiz Alia, Fatos Nano and several others from the old Communist regime were tried and jailed for corruption.
1994 A national referendum rejected a new constitution which would have given too much power to the president.
1995 Albania was admitted to the Council of Europe.
1996 The PD won a landslide victory in parliamentary elections, which were tainted by accusations of fraud.
1997 Leka, the son of King Zog, attempted to restore the monarchy but a referendum voted against it and he went abroad. Fraudulent pyramid investment schemes collapsed and many Albanians lost their life's savings, sparking weeks of rioting. President Berisha not only dismissed the prime minister and the head of the army but also closed down opposition newspapers and declared a state of emergency. The solution to the profound political crisis was fresh parliamentary elections in which the PSS were swept back into power and President Berisha resigned. The convictions of communist-era leaders were overturned; Fatos Nano was elected prime minister and Rexhep Majdani became president.
1998 Refugees from the war in Kosovo (Serbia) fled into Albania. Nano resigned due to protests over the economy, and was succeeded by Pandeli Majko. Voters approved Albania's first post-Communist constitution, which declared the country a parliamentary republic.
1999 There was a mass refugee exodus of Kosovans into Albania as thousands fled attacks by Serbian forces. Prime Minister Majko was succeeded by the Socialist, Ilir Meta.
2000 Albania joined the World Trade Organisation (WTO).
2001 Ilir Meta and the PSS won general elections.
2002 Prime Minister Ilir Meta resigned after failing to resolve an internal PSS feud with the president. Pandeli Majko became prime minister. Alfred Moisiu was elected president by parliament. Pandeli Majko resigned and Fatos Nano became prime minister again. The royal family returned from exile.
2003 Albania and the EU began Stabilisation and Association Agreement (SAA) talks.
2005 Albania signed a US$15 million deal with the US Occidental Petroleum Corporation for oil and natural gas drilling. The opposition PD won parliamentary elections and Sali Berisha became prime minister.
2006 The SAA with the EU was signed.
2007 Bamir Topi was elected president by parliament. Opposition parties had objected to his candidacy on the grounds that he was a representative of the ruling party.
2008. The electoral system was changed to the closed list proportional representation method.
2009 Albania joined Nato. Four coalition blocs contested parliamentary elections. The AN government coalition, including the PD and Partia Republikane (RP) (Republican Party), Partia Demokrate e Re (PDR) (New Democratic Party) and the Partia për Drejtësi dhe Integrim (PDI) (Party for Justice and Integration), was sworn into office; Sali Berisha remained in office as prime minister.
2010 The first Albanian sale of government bonds began in April; the US$398

million sale of five-year bonds, with a yield of 7 per sent was managed by the Deutsche Bank and J P Morgan Chase banks. Remittances were reported to represent 15 per cent of GDP, with most monies coming from Greece and Italy.
2011 On 21 January, over 21,000 anti-government protestors rallied in Tirana; three people were killed by security forces. On 14 May, violence broke out among political supporters following the announcement that the ruling PD's Lulzim Basha had beaten the incumbent PSS candidate Edi Rama in the 8 May mayoral election in Tirana.

Political structure

Constitution

Albania's communist constitution of 1976 was abrogated in 1991, when the democratic, Republic of Albania came into being under an interim constitution.
A new constitution was agreed by referendum and came into effect on 28 November 1998. It provides for multi-party elections and guarantees freedom of speech, religion, press, assembly and organisation.

Independence date

28 November 1912

Form of state

Unicameral parliamentary democratic republic

The executive

The president is head of state and shares control of the armed forces with the prime minister. The president is elected by parliament to a five-year term and is limited to two terms. The president appoints the prime minister nominated by the party or coalition of parties that has a majority of seats in the Assembly. If the Assembly fails to approve the president's appointee three times, the president dissolves parliament. The prime minister and Council of Ministers are in charge of the country's economic, social and cultural affairs. The president and prime minister are jointly responsible for foreign relations and security affairs.

National legislature

The unicameral parliament, Kuvendi ë Shqipërisë (Assembly of Albania) has 140 members, elected for four-year terms. In November 2008 the electoral system was changed to the closed list proportional representative method. There are now 12 multi-party constituencies corresponding to the12 national administrative regions, wherein parties must win at least 3 per cent of the vote (and pre-election coalitions 5 per cent) before they can be placed on the closed list to become deputies of the assembly. The new system tends to favour leading political parties.
The Assembly meets twice a year. In addition to passing legislation, the Assembly also elects the president and approves the president's appointment of the prime minister and the prime minister's choices for the Council of Ministers.

Legal system

The court system is headed by the Supreme Court. Its members are appointed by the president to nine-year terms with the consent of the Assembly. Judges in appeals and district courts are appointed by the president upon the recommendations of the Higher Judicial Council, which is headed by the president and includes the chair of the Supreme Court and the minister of justice. A separate constitutional court rules on constitutional matters and consists of nine members appointed by the president with the Assembly's consent.

Last elections

28 June 2009 (parliamentary); 20 July 2007 (presidential).
Results: Paliamentary: Aleance per Ndryshim (AN) (Alliance for Change) led by Partia Demokratike e Shqipërisë (PD) (Democratic Party (of Albania)) won 46.84 per cent of the vote and was allocated 70 seats (out of 140); Bashkimi për Ndryshim (BN) (Unification for Changes), led by Partia Socialiste e Shqipërisë (Socialist Party) 45.37 per cent (66); Aleanca Socialiste për Integrim (ASI) (Socialist Alliance for Integration), led by Partia Demokristiane e Shqipërisë (Democratic Party) 5.55 per cent (4); Poli i Lirisë (PL) (Pole of Freedom) 1.82 per cent (no seats).
Presidential: Bamir Topi won 85 votes of the presidential vote in parliament.

Next elections

July 2012 (presidential); 2013 (parliamentary)

Political parties

Ruling party

Coalition: Aleance per Ndryshim (AN) (Alliance for Change) led by the Partia Demokratike (ë Shqipërisë) (PD) (Democratic Party (of Albania)) with Partia Republikane (RP) (Republican Party), Partia Demokrate e Re (PDR) (New Democratic Party) and Partia për Drejtësi dhe Integrim (PDI) (Party for Justice and Integration); PD re-elected 28 Jun 2009; coalition took office 3 Sep 2009)

Main opposition party

Partia Socialiste ë Shqipërisë (PSS) (Socialist Party of Albania)

Population

3.20 million (2010)*
Last census: April 2001: 3,069,275 (provisional)
Population density: 120 inhabitants per square km. Urban population: 44 per cent (1996—2002).
Annual growth rate: 0.4 per cent (2005) (World Bank)
-0.2 per cent 1994–2004 (WHO 2006)

Ethnic make-up

Albanians make up 97 per cent of the population. The largest ethnic minority group is the Greeks, who account for around 2 per cent of the total. Other groups include Macedonian, Montenegrin, Vlach and Gypsy (Romany) groups.

Religions

Muslim (70 per cent), Christian Orthodox (20 per cent) and Roman Catholic (10 per cent).

Education

Despite its many failings, the communist regime virtually eliminated illiteracy. However, since 1991 the situation has deteriorated markedly, with equipment and buildings in a parlous state. Although high attendance rates in primary schools have been maintained, enrolment in pre-primary schooling and at the secondary or tertiary level has declined. In Albania, the government has closed down a third of public kindergartens and pre-school attendance has dropped dramatically. Unqualified teachers in elementary schools account for 10 per cent of teaching staff, and in the secondary schools, 8 per cent. The government has an ongoing programme to replace equipment and reconstruct buildings in urban areas and is also focussing on teacher training and enrolment rates. The current structure of the sector has resulted in a misalignment between the supply and demand of education. Consequently, the government is also engaged in a school construction programme to provide facilities for those areas where there are currently no school facilities.
The total expenditure on education is around 3 per cent of GDP.
Literacy rate: 99 per cent adult rate; 99 per cent youth rate (15–24) (Unesco 2005).
Enrolment rate: 100 per cent (primary); 71.5 per cent (secondary) (World Bank).
Pupils per teacher: 18 in primary schools.

Health

Although Albania's modest healthcare sector functioned adequately during the communist era, it suffered from substantial underfunding. The government recognises the problem and plans to strengthen managerial capacities and to decentralise health planning. It will take many years to create a system capable of providing even basic healthcare.

HIV/Aids

Albania had been screened from the initial impact of the Aids epidemic by the isolation imposed by the former communist state. However, the country opened its borders following the advent of

democratic government in 1991 and the first HIV case of HIV was detected in 1993. By 2003, 177 cases had been reported of which 37 had died of Aids. Between 2001–03 the percentage of HIV positive females increased and their numbers now match male infection rates.
Life expectancy: 72 years, 2004 (WHO 2006)
Fertility rate/Maternal mortality rate: 2.2 births per woman, 2004 (WHO 2006)
Birth rate/Death rate: 18.2 per 1,000 crude birth rate; 6.5 per 1,000 crude death rate (USAID 2003).
Child (under 5 years) mortality rate (per 1,000): 18 per 1,000 live births in 2003; 14 per cent of children aged under five are malnourished (World Bank).
Head of population per physician: 1.31 physicians per 1,000 people, 2002 (WHO 2006)

Welfare
Albania's social infrastructure is in a poor state. Never well developed, social disintegration in 1997 led to further deterioration of virtually all services as funds dried up.
The collapse of central government authority in 1997 has led to already poor tax collection rates falling further. Neither the funds nor the infrastructure exist to provide adequate welfare coverage. It has been estimated that more than one million people are living below the poverty line. The Albanian Institute of Statistics reported in late-1999 that over one-third of families have only one income source averaging US$64 per month.
The government is attempting to remedy this by introducing community-based social services for vulnerable groups and is in the process of reorganising the state pension system based on the actuarial model. The aim is to increase coverage in rural areas in order to reduce poverty.

Main cities
Tirana (capital, estimated population 399,999 in 2008), Durrës (Durrazzo) (130,269), Elbasan (105,852), Shkoder (Scutari) (90,620), Vlore (93,812), Korca (57,758), Fier (65,244), Berat (48,068).

Languages spoken
Greek, Romanian, Bulgarian, Serbian, Tosk and Gheg are also spoken.
English, Italian, German and French are also spoken in business circles.
Official language/s
Tosk Albanian; the Albanian language is divided into two dialects – Gheg, north of the river Shkumbinit, and Tosk in the south.

Media
Press freedom in Albania has been declared partly free by the US-based media watchdog, Freedom House, and the government has used criminal and tax laws to target and intimidate media sources it wishes to stifle.
Due to the country's poor infrastructure, mountainous terrain and low economic development, access to media can be poor.
Press
The print media is not sophisticated and tends towards sensationalism. Many newspapers are published by political parties and interest groups.
Dailies: In Albanian, policital party publications include *Rilindja Demokratike* (http://pages.albaniaonline.net/rd), and *Zeri i Popullit* (www.zeripopullit.com). Private newspapers include *Shekulli* (www.shekulli.com.al) the largest daily, *Gazeta Shqiptare* (www.balkanweb.com/gazetav4), *Koha Ditore* (www.koha.net), *Sot* (www.sot.com.al), *Korrieri* (www.korrieri.com) *Koha Jonë* (www.kohajone.com), are tabloids. In English, *Albanian Daily News* (www.albaniannews.com). And *Tirana Times* (www.tiranatimes.com).
Weeklies: In Albanian, general interest magazines include *Shqip* (www.shqip.al), and *Veriu Observer* (www.gazetaveriu.netfirms.com). *Sporti Shqiptar* (www.sportishqiptar.com.al) is a sports publication.
Business: In Albanian, *Biznesi* (www.biznesi.com.al) is a newspaper, *Monitor* (www.monitor.al) is a magazine. The Albanian Chamber of Commerce publishes *Probiznes News* (www.cci.gov.al) magazine.
Broadcasting
Radio Televizioni Shqiptar (RTSH) (www.rtsh.al) is the state broadcaster, operating from Tirana.
Radio: In Albanian, RTSH (http://rtsh.sil.at) operates three national stations, including an international service. There are two commercial national broadcasters, Plus 2 Radio (www.plus2radio.com.al) and Top Albania Radio (www.topalbaniaradio.com). Other local commercial radio stations include Radio Saranda (www.radiosaranda.com), Radio Planet (www.planet93fm.com) and Radio IMR (www.radio-ime.com), which has talk and information programmes.
There are foreign radio broadcasts received in foreign languages including, English, Italian, French and German.
Television: RTSH operates one national station; it also has a satellite service for expatriate communities in neighbouring countries. Funding is provided by government grants, subscription and commercial advertising. Programmes include news, current affairs and documentaries as well as popular shows. TV Arberia (www.telearberia.tv) is a private network.
Advertising
There is a total ban on cigarette advertising.
News agencies
National news agency: Albanian Telegraphic Agency (ATA)

Economy
Although the service sector accounts for almost 60 per cent of the economy, Albania is still a country where primary industries are important. Agriculture, including timber products, accounts for around 20 per cent of GDP and employs almost 60 per cent of the workforce. Other industries include mining of ores, cement, chemical and energy production. Manufacturing also accounts for around 20 per cent of GDP, with products geared to the export market.
GDP growth, which had been consistently high since 2000, was 7.8 per cent in 2008; but in 2009 as the global economic crisis cut world trade GDP growth fell to 3.3 per cent and remained almost constant at 3.5 per cent in 2010. While so many Western economies fell into recession Albania avoided an undermining of its economy. There had been a concerted effort made by the government to enhance the financial system and make progress towards a functioning market economy, according to a report by the European Union (EU), which in 2010 was assessing Albania's progress towards membership. The EU report commended the fiscal reforms already undertaken, then advised that Albania had to address weaknesses in infrastructure and human capital. Albania is one of the poorest countries in Europe, despite poverty levels having fallen from 25.4 per cent in 2002 to 12.4 per cent in 2008; GDP per capita had never been higher than US$4,102, but with the downturn in the economy this fell to US$3,819 in 2009 and further still to US$3,716 in 2010; per capita income is anticipated to rise to US$4,131 in 2011.
Remittances in 2009 amounted to 10.9 per cent of GDP, in 2010 remittances amounted to US$1.3 billion, which was only slightly more than the US$1.27 per cent in 2009.
EU membership is not expected before 2015; however the EU has signed a Stabilisation and Association Agreement and continues to fund infrastructure improvements. Other international financial institutions, such as the World Bank and IMF and the European Bank for Reconstruction and Development (EBRD) have all invested in projects of improvement. The rebuilding of the technical and physical infrastructure, from telecommunications to roads and railways, is a major priority.

While the government encourages foreign investment in agriculture, agri-processing, manufacturing and export-oriented activities, poor basic services, such as electricity, discourage investor interest. Efforts to develop a larger tourist industry are also hindered by poor infrastructure and under-investment. Efforts to counter the grey economy include a simplified tax system and structural reforms. The EU has warned that measures to kerb corruption and organised crime must be robust and continuous in order to improve foreign investment confidence.

External trade

Albania is a signatory of the Central European Free Trade Agreement (CEFTA), along with Bosnia and Hercegovina, Croatia, Macedonia, Moldova, Montenegro and Serbia and Kosovo.

Albania, Macedonia and Bulgaria have a trilateral agreement to build a new Balkan oil pipeline (AMBO), from Burgas, on the Black Sea, to the port of Vlore, in southern Albania. Its estimated cost was US$1.2 billion and had a supply target of 750,000 barrels per day, with the construction postponed until 2009; by late 2010 construction was still awaiting a start date.

Imports

Principal imports include machinery, capital goods, electrical and electronic goods, vehicles, minerals, fuels and oils.

Main sources: Italy (typically 26 per cent of total), Greece (16 per cent), China (7 per cent).

Exports

Principal exports are minerals, including hydrocarbons and hydroelectricity, chrome products, copper wire, ferro-nickel ore and bitumen, chemicals and iron and steel. Major manufacturing plants include cement, textiles and footwear and food processing, plus engineering products.

Main destinations: Italy (typically 63 per cent of total), Greece (7 per cent), Slovakia (6 per cent).

Agriculture

Farming

Agriculture, formerly the largest sector in the economy, has declined to less than 25 per cent of GDP, but remains an important social as well as economic factor in Albanian life. The sector is dominated by small-scale subsistence farming, which is underdeveloped and poorly financed.

There is minimal mechanisation and little use of fertilisers and pesticides. Despite government attempts to privatise farmland, outside financial assistance has been needed to develop farming.

Fishing

Albania's fish catch declined sharply following the collapse of Communism and has not recovered. The sector is in generally poor shape. The fishing fleet comprises ageing and poorly equipped vessels and there is a shortage of fishermen. Development of the marine fisheries, including rehabilitation and construction of ports and other infrastructure, is a government priority.

There is some freshwater fishing in rivers, lakes and reservoirs. Fish farming of marine and freshwater species is increasingly important. Internal consumption of fish has increased in recent years, leaving about half of the approximately 4,000 tonnes of production for export, mainly to Greece and Italy.

Forestry

Forests cover less than two-fifths of the land area, the equivalent of 991,000 hectares (ha).

The forest industry is small-scale and is based mainly on imported raw materials to meet domestic production needs.

Forestry is of little importance to GDP, with most timber production being used for domestic fuel. Timber processing and associated activities have been transferred to the private sector, but forest management remains in state hands.

Industry and manufacturing

The industrialisation policy of the Communist era was aimed at making Albania completely self-sufficient. Although this meant that Albania was one of the few countries in the world without any foreign debt, it also meant that the industrial sector relied on outdated and inefficient machinery which produced poor quality goods unable to compete in international markets.

A side-effect of the search for higher productivity was a complete absence of environmental concerns, with industrial wastelands, oil slicks and abandoned equipment littering the country. Combined with thousands of broken concrete bunkers and derelict factories, Albania faces major, long-term environmental problems.

The industrial sector has experienced a disastrous decline in output since 1990. The sector is focused mainly on engineering, chemicals, metals, construction materials, food processing and other agro-allied industries. The sector employs around 10 per cent of the workforce and accounts for around 19 per cent of GDP. There is virtually no light industry.

Foreign investment is the key to reviving industrial output, and consequently the government has been attempting to portray Albania as a low-wage manufacturing base with extensive natural resources on Western Europe's doorstep. Foreign companies have become involved in rehabilitating and modernising Albania's chrome industry by taking over a number of steel plants and mines.

Tourism

Albania's tourist and travel industry is modest, contributing just 7.6 per cent to GDP. The sector directly employs 67,000 workers (6.8 per cent of total employment) and indirectly employs 233,000 (23.9 per cent of total employment).

In 2011, direct foreign investment in the sector was estimated to be US$227 million (L22.8 billion), which was 4.6 per cent of total investment. International visitor numbers were predicted to be 2.58 million, with visitor spending expected to generate US$3.29 billion (L238 billion) in foreign earnings.

Attractions for visitors are typically Mediterranean beach resorts, unspoilt (undeveloped) countryside and historic sites. As the infrastructure grows and improves Albania as a destination for the less-seasoned European traveller will also develop.

Environment

Macedonia and Albania participate in the Lake Ohrid Conservation Project (LOCP) which is a bilateral project supported by the World Bank.

Mining

The mining sector contributes as much as 20 per cent to GDP and employs some 15 per cent of the workforce.

Albania used to be the world's third-largest producer and second-largest exporter of chromium. The industry is undergoing rehabilitation. As with all areas of the Albanian economy, the mining sector suffers from obsolete technology and techniques, the disruption of supply lines and lack of management skills.

There are extensive reserves of copper, iron, zinc and nickel. In addition, there are smaller reserves of uranium, titanium-magnetite, gold and silver. Most of these reserves are in remote and mountainous areas of northern Albania, which increases production costs.

Hydrocarbons

Proven oil reserves were 199 million barrels in 2008, with production at 6,000 barrels per day (bpd). However, consumption was 34,000bpd, all of which was imported, mainly from Russia. There are two small oil fields currently in production at Patos and Morinza, which account for most production.

The state-owned Albpetrol is responsible for policy, administration and exploitation of hydrocarbons in Albania, either solely or in partnership with foreign oil and gas companies.

Armo the former state-owned oil refiner, with two facilities at Ballsh and Fier with total capacity of 26,000bpd, was sold to

a US-Swiss investment group in 2008.
The Albanian Macedonian Bulgarian Oil (Ambo) pipeline, to carry Russian and Caspian oil through the Baltic from the Black Sea port of Burgas in Bulgaria to Vlore on the Albanian Adriatic, via Macedonia – and avoiding the congested Turkish straits – was proposed in 2004 and endorsed in 2007 but by 2011 construction has yet to start.
The Swiss-based Manas Petroleum Corporation announced oil and gas finds close to the border with Kosovo in north-western Albania in 2008. Estimates of oil were 2.98 billion barrels and 85.4 billion cubic metres (cum) of natural gas. If deposits are gas only the find could be as large as 792.9 billion cum. A call for tenders for the Albanian section of the Trans-Adriatic Pipeline (TAP) was issued in April 2011.
Proven natural gas reserves were 849.6 million cum in 2008, with production at 28.3 million cum, all of which is consumed domestically.
Albania has coal reserves estimated at around 700 billion tonnes, with production at 130,000 tonnes in 2008. Sufficient coal (of generally low quality) is produced for domestic consumption. Production is carried out at 21 mines in four basins run by various state-owned stock companies.

Energy
Total generating capacity was 1,684MW in 2007, producing around 5.5 billion kilowatt hours. The bulk of energy (around 90 per cent of total output) is produced from three hydropower plants in the north of Albania, although supplies are affected by drought conditions during summer.
There are small oil-fired power stations but imports have become prohibitively expensive, so that in April 2009 Albania announced plans to invest in three new hydroelectric schemes, based in the south and capable of producing an additional 40 per cent of hydropower. A new thermal power plant on the coast at Vlora, which will be fuelled by imported liquefied natural gas (LNG), has been planned since 2007 but is awaiting World Bank investment.
In 2008 the state-owned utility Kesh was in the process of being privatised, with the help of USAID. Kesh was under-funded and lacked commercial experience to provide a modern electricity service to all customers. The infrastructure was in poor condition; about a quarter of electricity generated was lost during distribution because of damaged network. Theft of electricity and non-payment of bills were common. Power cuts were frequent and to meet demands Albania imported energy mainly from Greece and Macedonia.
The discovery by Swiss-based Manas Petroleum Corporation of a huge and untouched natural gas and oil field in the north-west in 2008 could result in an overhaul of Albania's energy mix.

Financial markets
Stock exchange
The Tirana Stock Exchange opened in mid-1996. Since the collapse of the pyramid schemes in 1997, it has been faced with the daunting task of rebuilding the confidence of potential investors.

Banking and insurance
The European Bank of Reconstruction and Development (EBRD) is involved in the development and privatisation of the banking system. An attempt to privatise the Savings Bank of Albania, the last state-owned bank, failed in 2002 when two Italian banks pulled out of the tender.
Albania's central bank is the Banka e Shqipërisë (Bank of Albania). It has the power to authorise the creation of and supervise new banks, including those with foreign capital.
Central bank
Banka e Shqipërisë (Bank of Albania)
Main financial centre
Tirana

Time
GMT plus one hour (daylight saving, late March to late October, GMT plus two hours)

Geography
Albania's 28,748 square km are split into three main areas: a coastal plain, mountains and an inland plain. Albania shares a border with Montenegro and Serbia (Kosovo) to the north, the Former Yugoslav Republic of Macedonia (FYROM) to the north-west and Greece to the south. The Adriatic and Ionian Seas are to the west. The country's Albanian name, Shqipéria, which translates as 'land of the eagles', reflects its remote and mountainous nature; mountains cover over 70 per cent of the land area. The highest mountain entirely within Albania is Mt Jezerce (2,694 metres) in the north, although Mt Korab on the border with FYROM reaches 2,751 metres.
The longest river, the Drini (285km), drains into Lake Ohrid on the border with FYROM. To the north, the Drini joins the Buna river, the only navigable waterway in Albania. There are three natural freshwater lakes in Albania, all of which share borders with either Greece, Montenegro or the FYROM. Numerous artificial lakes have been created by hydroelectric power stations damming rivers, the largest of which are in the north around Kukes and Skhodra.
Hemisphere
Northern

Climate
Albania has a Mediterranean climate, with long, hot and dry summers and cool, cloudy and wet winters. Autumn has humid weather brought by the warm sirocco wind. The high inland mountains can become cold during the winter months. July is the hottest month; November, December and April are the wettest months. It is warmest in the south-west and coldest in the north-east.

Dress codes
During the summer, light clothing is recommended, with warmer clothes essential during the winter months, particularly in mountainous regions.

Entry requirements
Passports
Required by all.
Visa
Not required by most citizens of Europe, North America, Australasia and a few Asian countries for visits up to 90 days. A US$10 entry tax is levied. (For a full list of exemptions visit www.mfa.gov.al/english/info2.asp.) An entry-exit form is issued at the border: the entry portion is handed in at passport control and the exit portion should be kept until departure.
Currency advice/regulations
The import and export of local currency is not permitted.
The import of foreign currencies is allowed without limitation, although all amounts must be declared on arrival. Export of foreign currency is allowed within the limits of the declaration given, less the amounts exchanged or spent. Keep exchange receipts.
Travellers cheques are accepted by banks and large tourist hotels. ATMs are available in Tirana and other main towns.
Customs
Personal items may be taken into Albania without incurring duty.

Health (for visitors)
Medical facilities are limited and medicine is in short supply. Doctors and hospitals generally expect immediate cash payment for health services. Health care is free for citizens of countries with reciprocal health agreements. Full medical insurance is advisable.
Mandatory precautions
A vaccination certificate for yellow fever is required if travelling from an infected area.
Advisable precautions
It is advisable to have immunisations against hepatitis A and B, typhoid and tetanus. Polio immunisation is not recommended for adults who received childhood inoculations. There is a risk of rabies. Access to clean water in the

country is variable, and it is not usual to drink tap water.

Hotels
Hotel provision of all standards, including international hotels, is improving. Increasing numbers of hotels can be contacted directly by telephone. Bookings can be arranged online through Albania Holidays Ltd (www.albania-hotel.com).

Credit cards
Major international hotels in Tirana accept American Express, Mastercard and Diners Club (but not Visa). Cases of credit card fraud have been reported.

Public holidays (national)
Fixed dates
1 Jan (New Year's Day), 28 Nov (Independence and Liberation Day), 25 Dec (Christmas Day).
Variable dates
Orthodox Easter Monday, Labour Day (first Mon in May), Eid al Adha, Islamic New Year, Birth of the Prophet, Eid al Fitr.
Islamic year 1433 (26 Nov 2011–14 Nov 2012): The Islamic year contains 354 or 355 days, with the result that Muslim feasts advance by 10–12 days against the Gregorian calendar. Dates of feasts vary according to the sighting of the new moon (*hilal*), so cannot be forecast exactly.

Working hours
Banking
Mon–Fri: 0800–1600.
Business
Mon–Fri: 0800–1600.
Government
Mon–Fri: 0700–1500.
Shops
Mon–Sat: 0800–1200, 1500–1900.

Social customs/useful tips
It is customary to shake hands on meeting and taking leave. Business cards are exchanged. Albanian business meetings are reasonably relaxed. Delays to negotiations can be expected as bureaucratic tendencies still exist.
Albanians are a naturally friendly and curious people with a good sense of humour, and are keen to talk to and meet foreigners.
Small gifts are appreciated. Round up the bill slightly when in restaurants.
Local body language customs: nodding the head up and down indicates no, and side to side indicates yes.

Security
It is advisable to be extremely cautious in Albania. Security has improved in recent years, but crime is still a serious problem and armed criminal gangs operate in most areas. There are a large number of semi-automatic weapons in private hands. Travel to the north-eastern border areas between Albania and Kosovo is not recommended.
Avoid giving anything to women and children asking for money, as they target foreigners and will follow the compassionate whenever they see them again. Visitors should dress down and not display watches, cameras or other expensive items.

Getting there
Air
Albania is accessible by air from numerous European centres, including Athens, Bucharest, Budapest, Ioannina, Paris, Rome and Zurich.
National airline: Albanian Airlines.
International airport/s: Rinas Mother Teresa Airport (TIA), 25 km from Tirana.
Airport tax: US$10
Surface
Road: There are road links from all bordering countries, including Greece at Kakavia and Kristalopigi, and Kosovo (in Serbia) at Han-i-Hotit and Vrbnica, and Macedonia at Cafasan.
Rail: There are no passenger rail links between Albania and the rest of Europe and travel in some of the border regions is inadvisable.
Water: There are ferry services connecting Durrës and Vlora with Trieste, Ancona, Brindisi and Bari in Italy and Rijeka and Pula in Croatia. Others connect Durres to Kopa in Slovenia and Sarandra to Corfu.
Main port/s: Durrës, Vlora and Sarandra.

Getting about
National transport
Air: Ales Airlines (a private joint Italian-Albanian company licensed by the Albanian government) serves eight small airports across the country.
Road: Out of approximately 21,000km of roads, only 3,000km are paved. Road conditions can be unpredictable – narrow, unsurfaced and potholed, with the added risk of straying cattle or pedestrians. Mountain roads are often impassable. The roads are considered to be the worst in Europe.
Buses: Buses run frequently between Tirana and Durrës and other towns to the north and south. Tickets are sold on the bus.
Rail: The rail network is approximately 720km, single-track and unelectrified. Trains are diesel.
City transport
Taxis: The only city with a taxi service is Tirana. There are taxi transfers from Rinas airport to the city centre.
Buses, trams & metro: A flat-fare bus service operates in the main cities, including Tirana. Airport buses operate from the airport to the city centre every three hours. Journey duration is 30 minutes.

Car hire
Driving in Albania is only recommended for those with no other choice. An international driving permit or a national driving licence is required. It is advisable to hire a local car and driver through travel agencies. Traffic drives on the right.

BUSINESS DIRECTORY

The addresses listed below are a selection only. While World of Information makes every endeavour to check these addresses, we cannot guarantee that changes have not been made, especially to telephone numbers and area codes. We would welcome any corrections.

Telephone area codes
The international direct dialling code (IDD) for Albania is +355, followed by area code and subscriber's number:

Berat	32	Korca	82
Durrës	52	Shkoder	22
Elbasan	54	Tirana	4
Fier	34	Vlore	33

Useful telephone numbers

Police:	19
Fire:	18
Ambulance:	17

Chambers of Commerce
Albanian British Chamber of Commerce and Industry, PO Box 1547, Tirana (tel: 227-000; fax: 230-636; e-mail: info:abcci.com).

American Chamber of Commerce in Albania, Rruga Deshmoret e 4 Shkurtit, Tirana (tel: 259-779; fax: 235-350; e-mail: info@amcham.com.al).

Korça Chamber of Commerce and Industry, Bulevard Republika, Korça (tel/fax: 824-457; e-mail: albchamber1@albchamber.com).

Tirana Chamber of Commerce and Industry, Rruga e Kavajes 6, Tirana (tel: 230-284; fax: 227-997; e-mail: ccitr@abissnet.com.al).

Union of Chambers of Commerce and Industry of Albania, Rruga e Kavajes 6, Tirana (tel: 230-283; fax: 227-997; e-mail: root@ccitr.tirana.al).

Banking
Albanian State Agricultural Bank, Tirana (tel: 27-738).

Albanian State Bank for Foreign Relations, Tirana.

Alpha Credit Bank, Deshmoret e Kombit Blvd 47, Tirana (Internet site: www.alpha.gr).

Arab Albanian Islamic Bank, Deshmoret e Kombit, Tirana (tel: 23-873).

Bankandertregtare (Intercommercial Bank), Tirana Tower, Rruga e Kavajes 59,

Tirana (tel: 58-755/60; fax: 58-752; e-mail: icbs1@albaniaonline.net).

Banko Italo Albanese (Banka Italo Shqiptare) (Italian-Albanian Bank), Rruga e Barrikadave, Tirana (tel: 33-966; fax: 35-701).

Fefad Bank, Tirana (tel: 3-496, 37-958; fax: 33-481).

National Bank of Greece, Blvd. Deshmoret e Kombit, VEVE Business Centre, Tirana (tel: 33-621, 35-542).

National Commercial Bank of Albania, Tirana (tel: 50-955; fax: 50-960; e-mail: bkt@albmail.com).

Savings Bank of Albania, Rr Deshmoret e 4 Shkurti, 6 Tirana (tel: 24-540/051; fax: 23-587/695).

Tirana Bank, Blvd. Deshmoret e Kombit, NR55/1, Tirana (tel: 33-441).

Central bank

Banka e Shqiperise (Bank of Albania), Sheshi Skënderbej 1, Tirana (tel: 222-152; fax: 223-558; e-mail: public@bankofalbania.org).

Travel information

Lufthansa Tirana Rinas Airport Office (tel: 42-350/54/58; fax: 42-350/60).

Ministry of tourism

Ministry of Tourism, Blvd Deshmoret e Kombit, Tirana (tel: 28-123); fax: 27-922).

Ministries

Albanian Assembly, Kurvendi, Blvd Dëdhmotët e Kombit, nr 4, Tirana (tel: 42-37-418, 42-47-354; fax: 42-27-949; email: head-directory@parlament.al; internet: www.parlament.al).

Committee of Environmental Protection, Ministry of Health and Environmental Protection, Bulevari Bajran Curri, Tirana (tel: 42-682; 35-229; fax: 35-229).

Department of Economic Development and Foreign Aid Co-ordination, Tirana (tel: 28-467; fax: 28-363).

Industrialeksport – 4 Shkurti Street 6, Tirana (tel: 4550).

Institute of Statistics, Tirana (tel: 22-411; fax: 28-300).

Makinaimport (State Trade Organisation for the Import of Machinery), 4 Shkurti Street 6, Tirana (tel: 25-220, 25-221).

Mineralimpex (State Organisation for Export of Minerals), 4 Shkurti Street 6, Tirana (tel: 25-832, 23-848).

Ministry of Agriculture and Food, Blvd Dëdhmotët e Kombit Tirana (tel: 28-318, 32-675; fax: 23-806, 27-924).

Ministry of Energy and Mineral Resources (tel: 32-833; fax: 34-052).

Ministry of Finance and Economy, Dëdhmotët e Kombit, Tirana (tel: 28-405; fax: 28-494).

Ministry of Health and Environment, Ministria e Shendetesise, Tirana (tel and fax: 34-615).

Ministry of Industry, Transport and Trade, Sheshi Skenderbey, Tirana (tel: 25-353, 32-289; fax: 27-773, 616-835).

Ministry of Transport and Telecommunications, Sheshi Skenderbey, Tirana (tel: 25-353; tel/fax: 27-773/616/835).

National Agency for Privatisation (tel/fax: 27-937).

National Committee of Energy, Dëdhmotët e Kombit, Tirana (tel/fax: 28-475).

President's Office, Tirana (tel: 28-491; fax: 33-761).

Prime Minister's Office, Tirana (tel: 34-816; fax: 34-818).

Other useful addresses

Agroeksport – State Trade Organisation for the Export of Agricultural and Food Products, 4 Shkurti Street 6, Tirana (tel: 25-227, 25-229, 23-128).

Albanian Embassy (USA), 2100 S Street, NW, Washington DC (tel: (+1-202) 223-4942; fax: (+1-202) 628-7342).

Albanian Telecom, Myslim Shyri 42, Tirina (tel: 32-047; fax: 33-323).

Albkontrol (Organisation for Inspection of Exported and Imported Goods), Rruga Skënderbeu 15, Durrës (tel: 22-354; fax: 22-791).

Artimpex (State Organisation for Export), 4 Shkurti Street 6, Tirana.

British Embassy, Ruga Vaso Pasha 7/1, Tirana (tel: 34-973; fax: 34-975).

Bureau for the Registration of Patents & Trade Marks, Konferenca e Pezes Street 6, Tirana.

Business Economic Development Department, c/o Ministry of Industry and Trade, 3 Rruga Andon Zamo Cajupi, Tirana (tel: 34-673; fax: 34-658).

Foreign Investment Promotion Centre, Ekspozita Shqiperia Sot (Protokolli), Blvd Jeanne d'Arc, Tirana (tel: 27-626; fax: 28-439, 42-133).

Insig, Insurance Institute, Rruga e Dibres 91, Tirana (tel: 341-84, 341-69, 341-70; fax: 341-80, 238-38).

Small and Medium-Sized Enterprises (SME) Foundation, c/o Ministry of Industry and Trade, 3 Rruga Andon Zako Cajupi, Tirana (fax: 34-892); EU Expert (fax: 42-413, 34-609).

Transshqip (State Organisation for the Transport of Goods in Foreign Trade), 4 Shkurti Street 6, Tirana (tel: 23-076, 24-659).

US Embassy, 103 Rruga Elbasanit, Tirana (tel: 424-7285; fax: 423-2222; e-mail: wm_tirana@pd.state.gov).

National news agency: Albanian Telegraphic Agency (ATA) Bulevard Zhan D'Arc, 23, Tirane (tel: 251-152; fax: 234-230; internet: www.ata-al.net).

Internet sites

Albanian Daily News: www.albaniannews.com

Albanian parliament: parlament.al

Albanian Economic Development Agency: aeda.gov.al

Albanian Ministry of Foreign Affairs: www.mfa.gov.al

Albanian Telegraphic Agency: www.ata-al.net

Bank of Albania: www.bankofalbania.org

Algeria

KEY FACTS

Official name: Al Jumhuriya al Jazairiya ad Dimucratiya ash Shabiya (Democratic and Popular Republic of Algeria)

Head of State: President Abdelaziz Bouteflika (since 1999; re-elected Apr 2009)

Head of government: Prime Minister Ahmed Ouyahya (since 24 June 2008)

Ruling party: Coalition: Front de Libération Nationale (FLN) (National Liberation Front), Rassemblement National pour la Démocratie (RND) (National Rally for Democracy) and Mouvement de la Société pour la Paix (MSP) (Movement of the Society for Peace) (since 2002; re-elected 17 May 2007)

Area: 2,381,741 square km

Population: 35.70 million (2010)*

Capital: Algiers

Official language: Arabic

Currency: Algerian dinar (AD) = 100 centimes

Exchange rate: AD74.68 per US$ (Oct 2011)

GDP per capita: US$4,366 (2010)

GDP real growth: 3.30% (2010)

GDP: US$160.30 billion (2010)

Labour force: 10.81 million (2010)

Unemployment: 10.00% (2010)

Inflation: 4.30% (2010)

Oil production: 1.81 million bpd (2010)

Balance of trade: US$7.78 billion (2009)

Foreign debt: US$4.00 billion (2008)

* estimated figure

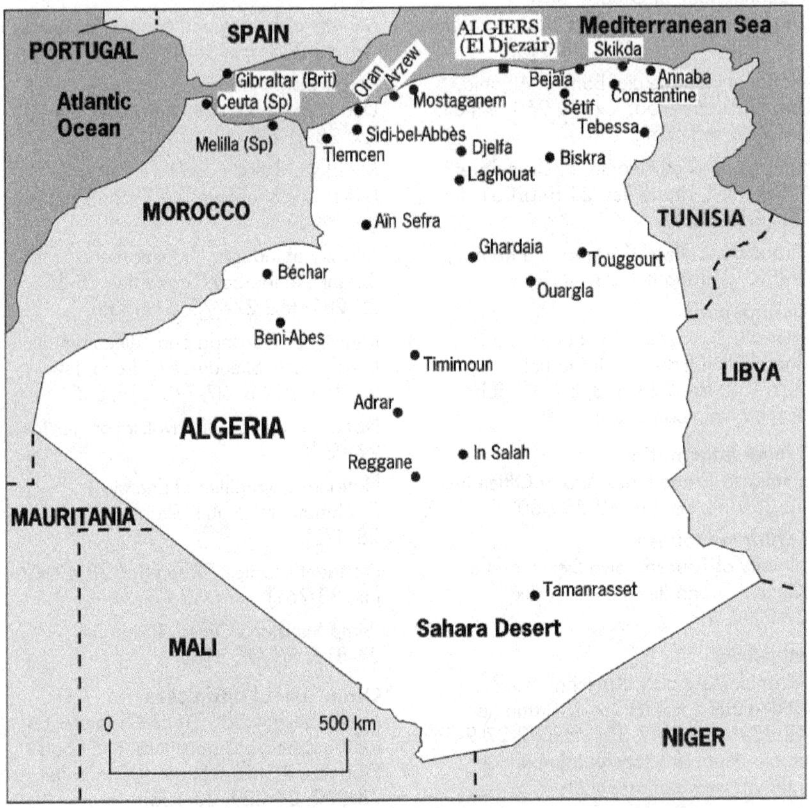

In their excellent book, *Algeria: Anger of the Dispossessed*, the authors Martin Evans and John Phillips point out that the post-independence history of Algeria is largely the story of 'rival groups claiming the mantle of revolution'. They go on to note that following the surprising appropriation of the revolution by the Islamist movement, there followed the 'most wretched period of Algeria's post war history, the 1990's, which saw them cheated at the polls and embark on a bloody terrorist war against the rest of the population.

Successive governments, nominally civilian, but in fact controlled by the military from behind the curtain, responded with indiscriminate violence, torture and political chicanery.' Civil wars all too easily produce innocent victims. In the case of Algeria its educated, Westernised minority became an obvious, if innocent, target.

Protests

Change was certainly in the Algerian air in the first half of 2011. In February a protest march was held in Algiers, seen by many as a predictable development of the simmering unrest that had existed in the capital's poorer quarters for some time. Algeria's violent twentieth century history has created a greater degree of sensitivity to unrest than was the case in neighbouring Tunisia. The February protests were centred on a coalition of political groupings labelled the National Co-ordination for Change and Democracy. The street protests passed off peacefully enough probably due to a massive police presence.

In fact the street protests were probably calmer than the atmosphere at the heart of Algerian politics, where Algeria's ageing president, Abdel Aziz Bouteflika faced the rivalry of the ambitious General

Muhammed Tewfiq Mediene, the army's *de facto* leader. President Bouteflika's political strategy had as much to do with outwitting the General as quashing the street protests. As the Arab Spring uprisings of 2011 claimed its third victory with the fall of Libya's Muammar Qadafi, Algeria began to feel itself increasingly isolated. The isolation was underlined by the protests that resulted from Algeria's ill-advised decision to grant refuge to various members of the Qadafi clan.

Lost in Libya

By September 2011 Algeria's attitude towards the Libyan uprising was beginning to look less than felicitous. Algeria had voted against the Arab League resolution in March 2011 that had approved the NATO military actions against the Qadafi regime. By the end of September, Algeria still had not recognised the Transitional National Council as Libya's legitimate government. This reluctance to sever links with the Qadafi régime and the asylum granted to members of the ruling family inevitably generated rumours of Algerian military and material support for Qadafi himself. These went as far as to suggest that Algeria had actually kept the maverick Libyan leader supplied with fuel, arms and transport. It was therefore hardly surprising that in Tripoli there developed a certain antipathy towards their neighbour to the west. This sentiment was shared by Algeria's opposition parties. The London *Economist* reported that there existed 'widespread disdain for the *pouvoir*, as the military-backed regime of President Bouteflika is commonly known. It also reported that 'one writer noted that it was hardly surprising that Algeria had not recognised Libya's council, 'since the *pouvoir* does not even recognise its own people.'

The economy

The International Monetary Fund (IMF) in its annual report on the Algerian economy reported that 'Prudent fiscal and monetary policies contributed to maintaining inflation low and, combined with a period of increasing oil prices, allowed Algeria to build a solid financial position, with large external reserves, sizeable budgetary savings in an oil stabilisation fund and low public and external debts.' However, despite efforts to diversify the Algerian economy, hydrocarbon revenues still represent 98 per cent of exports and two-thirds of budgetary revenues. The non-hydrocarbon sector is inward-oriented and largely sustained by public spending. On the back of solid non-hydrocarbon growth (about 6 per cent over the past decade), unemployment has fallen continuously, reaching 10.2 per cent by the end of 2009, but remains stubbornly high among younger Algerians.

The strong growth in non-hydrocarbon gross domestic product (NHGDP) was partially offset by the decline in hydrocarbon production. NHGDP growth reached 9.3 per cent in 2009, driven by an excellent cereal harvest and good performance in the Public Investment Programme (PIP)-led service and construction sectors. However, the substantial drop in hydrocarbon output (estimated at -6.0 per cent) lowered overall growth to about 2.5 per cent, a little lower than in 2008. The stabilisation of the hydrocarbon sector and the dynamic performance of the PIP-related sectors should lead to overall growth of 3–3.5 per cent in 2010.

Average total inflation rose to 5.7 per cent in 2009, the highest level of the past decade, due to substantial fresh food price inflation. Non-fresh food inflation remained low in 2009 at 2.3 per cent on average. In 2010, the increase in fresh food prices slowed down considerably but the rate of non-fresh food inflation appeared to be increasing. Overall, inflation was 4.3er cent in 2010.

Banking

The IMF notes that Algerian banks do not rely on external financing and have continued to benefit from a healthy growth in deposits, although these have slowed down since the end of 2009 (by 8.3 per cent in August 2009. The Banque d'Algérie (central bank) has continued its policy of absorbing excess liquidity generated by the PIP expenditure and the hydrocarbon sector. Overall, credit to the economy has increased by 12.5 per cent (August 2010, year-on-year). The growth in credit to the public sector has remained at a high level (excluding debt re-purchase by the Treasury) while growth in credit to the private sector (enterprises and households) slowed slightly as a result of a reduction in credit to households following the ban on consumer lending since August 2009.

The budget will remain in deficit despite the rise in hydrocarbon revenues in 2010 Algeria was expected to post its second consecutive budget deficit of the decade, which could reach 4 per cent of GDP following a deficit of about 7 per cent in 2009. The increase in hydrocarbon revenues will be more than offset by a 17 per cent increase in total expenditures. Reflecting the substantial increase in expenditures in recent years, the breakeven oil price that would correspond to a balanced budget increased from US$34 per barrel in 2005 to US$88per barrel in 2010. A reform of civil service wages and salaries, to rationalise their structure, led to a 34 per cent rise in the wage bill from 2008. As a

KEY INDICATORS — Algeria

	Unit	2006	2007	2008	2009	2010
Population	m	33.80	34.00	34.37	35.10	*35.70
Gross domestic product (GDP)	US$bn	114.83	131.57	158.97	140.80	160.30
GDP per capita	US$	3,397	3,825	4,940	3,926	4,366
GDP real growth	%	2.0	4.6	3.0	2.0	3.3
Inflation	%	2.5	4.6	4.5	5.7	4.3
Unemployment	%	12.3	13.8	11.3	10.2	–
Industrial output	% change	–	1.5	1.4	2.0	–
Agricultural output	% change	–	5.0	-5.3	2.6	–
Oil output	'000 bpd	2,005.0	2,000.0	1,990.0	1,811.0	1,809.0
Natural gas output	bn cum	84.5	83.0	86.5	81.4	80.4
Exports (fob) (goods)	US$m	59,839.0	59,870.0	78,590.0	45,186.0	–
Imports (fob) (goods)	US$m	25,312.0	25,160.0	38,070.0	37,402.0	–
Balance of trade	US$m	34,527.0	34,710.0	40,520.0	7,784.0	–
Current account	US$m	25,211.0	23,242.0	34,231.0	160.0	15,104.0
Total reserves minus gold	US$m	77,914.0	110,318.0	143,243.0	149.041	162,614.0
Foreign exchange	US$m	77,810.0	110,180.0	143,102.0	147.221	160,568.0
Exchange rate	per US$	69.83	67.21	61.66	72.65	74.39

* estimated figure

result, current expenditure is projected to grow by 31 per cent (including salary back payments for 2008–09 in the education sector).

Capital expenditure in 2010 was expected to have stabilised at its 2008–09 level with the continued implementation of the 2005–09 PIP. Non-hydrocarbon revenues recorded a further 19 per cent increase but yet covered only half of current expenditure. In total, the primary non-hydrocarbon deficit in 2010 was estimated to have remained broadly unchanged from 2009 at about 45 per cent of NHGDP, indicating a continued support of fiscal policy to non-hydrocarbon growth, which had decelerated from 2009. The overall deficit should be fully covered by non-bank financing, while the level of resources in the FRR could grow by about US$1.5 billion, roughly equivalent to 38 per cent of GDP.

Algeria's external balance was negatively affected during 2009 by the fall in the price of hydrocarbons, with the current account surplus falling to 0.3 per cent of GDP from 20 per cent in 2008. Nevertheless, official reserves increased by US$4 billion to US$149 billion at end-2009 (almost 3 years of imports of goods and services). During the first nine months of 2010, hydrocarbon export revenues increased by about 32 per cent, due to the steady rise in oil prices, while export volumes (in particular of gas) fell by 1.4 per cent. Imports decreased slightly from last year, contributing also to the improvement in the current account balance. Algeria's official reserves rose by about US$8 billion from-2009 to US$157 billion by end-September 2010.

Neighbours?

In 1994 Algeria closed the open frontier that had existed with Morocco for hundreds of years. The closure followed a guerrilla attack on a Marrakesh hotel. The response to the attack saw Algeria introduce an entry visa requirement which Morocco objected to. A major policy difference between Algeria and Morocco has been their opposing stances to the future of Wesern Sahara (Sahrawi Arab Republic). Since the departure of the Spanish, the barren territory has been claimed by both Morocco and the Polisario independence movement. Morocco has offered the territory some form of autonomy while Algeria has supported the claims of the Polisario. Regional tensions were relaxed when Morocco unilaterally lifted the visa requirement for Algerians in 2004. In 2005 Algeria reciprocated, also lifting the visa requirement, but – perversely – not actually opening the frontier. Algeria insists that a referendum on the future of the territory should be held as provided for in an international agreement signed by both countries in 2003.

Hydrocarbons

On the global energy map, Algeria can hardly be ignored, if only because it is the world's sixth largest natural gas producer and Africa's fourth largest crude oil producer. As a member of the Organisation of Petroleum Exporting Countries (OPEC) Algeria needs to observe production quotas, but its substantial production of condensate (450,000 barrels per day (bpd) in 2008) and natural gas liquids (357,000bpd) are not subject to such constraints. The US government's Energy Information Administration (EIA) estimated Algeria's total oil liquids production at 2.23 million bpd, of which domestic consumption only accounted for 13 per cent. Domestic consumption also accounted for some 30 per cent of natural gas production, the balance being exported.

According to the *BP Statistical Review of World Energy 2011* (BP 2011) Algeria's proven oil reserves at the end of 2010 were12.2 thousand million barrels, the fourth largest in Africa (behind Libya, Nigeria and Angola). The oil produced, the Saharan Blend, is considered to be among the highest quality in the world. This critical factor enables Algerian oil to comply with European Union (EU) criteria on the sulphur content of gasoline and diesel fuel.

In 2011 state-owned Sonatrach continued to dominate oil and gas production, although in recent years there has been an easing of regulations permitting foreign oil-producers to enter into a number of production agreements with Sonatrach. Sonatrach continues to operate the largest oil-field in Algeria, Hassi Messaoud, which alone produced some 400,000bpd of crude in 2008. Alongside Sonatrach foreign oil companies have steadily increased their share of Algeria's oil production; the largest of these is Anadarko of Texas with a total oil production capacity of over 500,000bpd from the Hassi Berkine South and Ourhound fields. Anadarko's gross oil production in late 2008 was put at 422,000bpd. The company is also developing seven new oil and natural gas fields in the Berkine Basin. Other foreign operators and investors include BG Group (UK), BP (UK), Cepsa (Spain) Conoco-Phillips (US), ENI (Italy) Gazprom (Russia), Repsol (Spain), Ruhrgaz (Germany), Shell (UK/Netherlands), Statoil (Norway) and Total (France). The 2008 bidding round, the first under the more relaxed regulations had met with a poor response. Eleven of the zones open to bids attracted no interest at all. The four winning bidders were ENI, Ruhrgas, Gazprom and the BG Group.

The US is the largest importer of Algerian oil; average imports of 547,000bpd represented around 4 per cent of total US oil imports in 2008 and corresponded to 28 per cent of total Algerian oil exports. Algeria has a total refining capacity of 450,000bpd; the refineries are all operated by Naftec, itself a subsidiary of state-owned Sonatrach. The principal hydrocarbon export port is Arzew, which handles about 40 per cent of all Algeria's hydrocarbon exports.

According to the BP11, Algeria's natural gas reserves at the end of 2010 totalled 159 trillion cubic feet (tcf), the eighth largest reserves in the world. Algeria is the sixth largest natural gas producer in the world and the second largest among member of Opec after Iran. Natural gas exports in 2007 were 3.03tcf, 0.93tcf were consumed domestically. Natural gas accounts for some 60 per cent of Algeria's total energy consumption. As in the case of oil production, Sonatrach controls natural gas production and wholesale production; Sonelgaz (also state-owned) controls retail distribution. Two thirds of Algeria's natural gas exports are carried by two natural gas pipelines to Europe. The Transmed pipeline runs from Algeria to Italy via Tunisia and Sicily. The MEG pipeline connects Algeria with Spain via Morocco. Three new pipelines are under construction linking Algeria to Spain, Italy and Nigeria.

Risk assessment

Economy	Good
Politics	Poor
Regional stability	Good

COUNTRY PROFILE

Historical profile

1830 Algeria was conquered by the French.

1831 The Légion Étrangère (French Foreign Legion) was established and based in Algeria to protect French colonial interests.

1848 Algeria became a *département* of France.

1954 The Front de Libération Nationale (FLN) (National Liberation Front) led the struggle for independence.

1962 Algeria gained independence and Ahmed ben Bella of the FLN was designated Algeria's first president.
1965 Ahmed ben Bella was ousted by Colonel Houari Boumédienne.
1976 Boumédienne won the presidential elections. He introduced a new constitution, which confirmed commitment to socialism, the FLN as the sole political party and Islam as the state religion. The constitution was approved by referendum. A programme of industrialisation began.
1973–76 Algeria supported the formation of the Frente Popular para la Liberación de Saguia el Hamra y Río de Oro (Polisario) (Popular Front for the Liberation of Saguia el Hamra y Río de Oro) in Spanish Sahara. The group wanted self-determination for Spanish Sahara (later known as Western Sahara). Spain handed the territory over to Morocco and Mauritania, Polisario announced the formation of the Saharawi Arab Democratic Republic (SADR) and formed a government-in-exile.
1977–85 Fighting continued between Moroccan military and Polisario forces. Morocco left the Organisation for African Unity (OAU) in protest at the SADR's admission to the body.
1988 Full diplomatic relations with Morocco were resumed.
1978 President Boumédienne died and the FLN candidate, Colonel Chadli Benjedid, was elected president; he was re-elected in 1984 and 1989.
1986–91 Rising inflation and unemployment, exacerbated by the collapse of oil and gas prices, led to strikes and violent demonstrations. A UN-monitored cease-fire began in Western Sahara.
1989 The National People's Assembly revoked the ban on new political parties and the Front Islamique du Salut (FIS) (Islamic Salvation Front) was founded.
1991 The FIS won the first round of the parliamentary elections and the second round was cancelled when it seemed certain the FIS would gain an absolute majority.
1992 Violent outbreaks followed the cancellation of the elections. The National People's Assembly was dissolved by presidential decree. President Chadli resigned and a five-member Haut Conseil d'Etat (HCE) (High Council of State) was instituted. The FIS was banned. A state of emergency was declared following clashes between FIS supporters and security forces. Mohammed Boudiaf, chairman of the HCE, was assassinated. The Armée Islamique du Salut (AIS) (Islamic Salvation Army), the military arm of the FIS, launched a campaign of guerrilla warfare.
1994 Liamine Zeroual became chairman of the HCE.
1995 Zeroual was elected president in the first multi-party democratic elections.
1997–98 The newly created Rassemblement Nationale Démocratique (RND) (National Democratic Rally) won the parliamentary elections.
1999 President Zeroual stood down (one year early) and Abdelaziz Bouteflika was elected president. A referendum approved Bouteflika's law on civil concord and thousands of members of the AIS and other armed groups were pardoned.
2000 Attacks continued by small groups of dissidents opposed to the civil accord. Ali Benflis became prime minister.
2001 The Berber community were granted greater cultural and political recognition following months of unrest in the Kabylie region.
2002 The Berber language, Tamazight, was officially recognised as a national language. Berber activists in Kabylie and several opposition parties elsewhere boycotted the parliamentary elections, which were won by the FLN.
2003 A major earthquake hit northern Algeria, the worst since 1980. The leader of the banned FIS and his deputy were freed from prison after serving 12-year sentences. President Bouteflika dismissed Ali Benflis as prime minister and appointed Ahmed Ouyahia in his place.
2004 President Bouteflika was re-elected and re-appointed Prime Minister Ouyahia.
2005 Nourredine Boudiafi, the head of the AIS, was arrested and his deputy killed. The government promised Berber leaders more investment in the Kabylie region and greater recognition for the Tamazight language. An official inquiry concluded that security forces abducted and killed over 6,000 citizens during civil unrest in the 1990s; the guerrilla campaign of the FIS was estimated to have killed 150,000 people. In a 'reconciliation' referendum there was overwhelming support for the government's granting of amnesty to many who were involved in the post-1992 killings.
2006 Ahmed Ouyahia resigned and Abdelaziz Belkhadem became prime minister. Measures to increase the state owned oil giant Sonatrach's role in oil and gas exploration and refining were introduced.
2007 The FLN won parliamentary elections, with a reduced majority, losing seats to its coalition partners in a low turnout. Prime Minister Belkhadem resigned and was re-appointed by the president.
2008 President Bouteflika appointed Ahmed Ouyahia as prime minister; he had previously served as prime minister 1996–98 and 2003–06. A referendum confirmed a change to the constitution allowing a president to run for a third-term in office.
2009 President Bouteflika won a third term in office, with 90.2 per cent of the vote. His closest rival was Louisa Hanoune with 4.22 per cent. Algeria, Nigeria and Niger agreed to build a US$13 billion pipeline across the Sahara, taking Nigerian natural gas to the Mediterranean gas network.
2010 In March, the Russian energy giant Gazprom, in partnership with the state-owned Sonatrach, began prospecting for natural gas in the Berkine basin, 500km south of Algiers. A report published in March warned that the Berber language (Tamazight) was in danger of dying out due to discrimination and neglect. The twentieth century was one of the driest periods, with multiple droughts in the Maghreb region, according to research published in May. In June parliament approved a US$1.48 billion fund for scientific research, in hopes of reversing the country's 'brain-drain'. Research programmes to benefit from further funding include agriculture, health and energy, with an emphasis on applied research and technology.
2011 Riots across the country on 8–9 January following steep rises in food prices were quelled by police at a cost of five dead, 800 injured (including 763 police officers) and thousands arrested. The government cut import duties and taxes on 10 January to curb prices that had risen by 30 per cent since 1 January. On 3 February President Bouteflika announced that the 19-year state of emergency would be lifted. The decision had been forced on the regime, following widespread protests not only in Algeria but also in a number of other Arab countries.

Political structure

Constitution

The 1976 constitution has been amended three times.

In 1997, the government banned religion-based parties and imposed a law restricting the formation of political parties. All political parties must hold a founding conference attended by 400–500 delegates elected by 25,000 supporters from 25 of the country's 48 provinces. This policy is intended to limit the number of political parties and place at severe disadvantage all parties that lack funding – particularly those, such as the Front Islamique du Salut (FIS) (Islamic Salvation Front), without access to state funds.

Independence date

1962

Form of state

Republic

The executive
The head of state is the president, elected by universal suffrage for five years. He appoints a prime minister, who in turn appoints a government.
The president has the power to dissolve the government and request elections.
National legislature
The bicameral parliament consists of the 380-member Al Majlis al Sha'abi al Watani (Assemblée Populaire Nationale) (National People's Assembly) and the 144-member Al Majlis al Umma (Conseil de la Nation) (National Council). Members of the Majlis al Sha'abi al Watani are elected in multi-seat constituencies by proportional representation for five-year terms and include eight seats reserved for Algerian voters abroad; it holds legislative power. In the Majlis al Umma 96 members are elected by local councils and 48 are appointed by the president.
Legal system
The legal system is based on French and Islamic law.
The judicial system consists of 183 courts and 31 appeal courts organised on a regional basis.
There are three special criminal courts in Oran, Constantine and Algiers, which deal with economic crimes against the state (against which there is no appeal) – the Court of State Security which is composed of judges and army officers, the court of audit and the Supreme Court in Algiers, which is the ultimate judicial authority.
Algeria has not accepted International Court of Justice (ICJ) jurisdiction.
Last elections
17 May 2007 (parliamentary); 9 April 2009 (presidential)
Results: Presidential: Abdelaziz Bouteflika won 90.2% of the vote, no other candidate won over 5 per cent; turnout was 74.54 per cent.
Parliamentary: FLN won 136 seats out of 389; RND 61; MSP 52; Parti du Travail (PT) (Workers' Party) 26; Rassemblement pour la Culture et la Démocratie (RCD) (Rally for Culture and Democracy) 19 seats; and independents and minor parties 68. Turnout was 35.65 per cent. The ruling three-party coalition of FLN, RND and MSP retained their majority with 249 seats.
Next elections
2014 (presidential); 2012 (parliamentary)

Political parties
Ruling party
Coalition: Front de Libération Nationale (FLN) (National Liberation Front), Rassemblement National pour la Démocratie (RND) (National Rally for Democracy) and Mouvement de la Société pour la Paix (MSP) (Movement of the Society for Peace) (since 2002; re-elected 17 May 2007)
Main opposition party
Parti du Travail (PT) (Workers' Party).

Population
35.70 million (2010)*
Last census: 16 April 2008: 34,745,000 (provision figure) (including 230,000 nomads)
Population density: 12 inhabitants per square km. Urban population: 58 per cent (1995–2001).
Annual growth rate: 2.8 per cent (2005) (World Bank)
1.6 per cent 1994–2004 (WHO 2006)
Ethnic make-up
The majority of Algerians are of Berber descent. The other significant ethnic group is Arab, although as a result of centuries of integration the two ethnic groups have become increasingly indistinguishable. The distinct Berber culture and language is best preserved in the north and eastern regions of Algeria.
The European population, most of whom are French, has declined from over one million before independence in 1962 to less than 50,000 in 2001.
Religions
Islam is the official religion. Approximately 99 per cent of the population is Sunni Muslim, while Christians make up about one per cent.

Education
Primary education lasts for six years. Secondary education, which begins at age 11, is divided into two courses of four years and three years. Approximately 13 per cent of students remain at tertiary level. Teaching is carried out in Arabic, although at higher levels French is widely used.
The government has encouraged girls to attend school to reduce the difference in literacy rates. A total of 86 per cent of girls are now educated to primary level, and 53 per cent to secondary level.
Total expenditure on education is 4–5 per cent of GDP.
Literacy rate: 69 per cent adult rate; 90 per cent youth rate (15–24) (Unesco 2005).
Compulsory years: 6 to 15.
Enrolment rate: 98 per cent gross primary enrolment of relevant age group (including repeaters); 63 per cent gross secondary enrolment (World Bank).
Pupils per teacher: 27 in primary schools.

Health
All Algerians are entitled to free medical care. Medicines are sold through the state monopoly at subsidised prices, and are provided free to children and the elderly, though there have been some cutbacks.
Health indicators point to a deterioration in public health, with infant mortality ratios and infectious diseases increasing.
Health care infrastructure and personnel show considerable urban-rural disparities.
Life expectancy: 71 years, 2004 (WHO 2006)
Fertility rate/Maternal mortality rate: 2.5 births per woman, 2004 (WHO 2006)
Child (under 5 years) mortality rate (per 1,000): 35 per 1,000 live births; 6 per cent of children aged under five are malnourished (World Bank).
Head of population per physician: 1.13 physicians per 1,000 people, 2002 (WHO 2006)

Welfare
During the 1990s, unemployment rates increased dramatically, poverty doubled and the purchasing power of the middle class experienced a huge drop.
Government expenditure on social protection is relatively high, but the welfare system is criticised as unsustainable and inefficient. The most serious challenge to the government is tackling unemployment.
The government continues to play a major role in providing housing and basic health services, particularly to urban populations.
Substantial housing shortages have proven persistent, despite the deregulation efforts the government undertook to promote private sector construction.

Main cities
Algiers (capital, estimated population 1.5 million in 2008), Oran (609,823), Constantine (462,187), Annaba (383,504), Batna (292,943).

Media
Despite laws guaranteeing freedom of access to information and freedom of expression in accordance with the constitution journalists are regularly targeted by not only the authorities but also militant Islamists. There are libel laws with large fines and *Sharia* (Islamic law) that can curb the media's ability to question and investigate; self-censorship is prevalent.
The law allows the formation of privately owned newspapers, but any new non-Arabic publication must first be approved by the independent Information Council.
In September 2011 the government announced sweeping media reforms to allow private radio and television stations to exist for the first time since independence in 1962.
Press
Most newspapers are in private ownership.
Dailies: In Arabic, *Ech Chaab* (www.ech-chaab.com) is state-owned, *Ech*

Chourouk (www.echoroukonline.com) and *El Khabar* are privately owned, with English editions. In French, *El Moudjahid* (www.elmoudjahid-dz.com) is state-owned, *El Watan* (www.elwatan.com), *Liberte* (www.liberte-algerie.com), *La Tribune* (www.latribune-online.com), and *Le Soir d'Algeria* (www.lesoirdalgerie.com) an evening newspaper, are all privately owned. *Le jeune indépendant* (www.jeune-independant.com) is a publication for the young.
Weeklies: In French, a privately owned, current affairs magazine is *Algérie Actualité*, while *El Hakika* is an Arab tabloid.
Business: In French, there are three publications, *Le Maghreb* (www.lemaghrebdz.com), an influential daily along with *Liberte Economie* (www.liberte-economie.com), with wide ranging topics; *Le Journal d'Affaires* (www.lejournaldaffaires.com) is more informal.
Periodicals: In French and Arabic, *El Manchar* is a bi-monthly satirical magazine.

Broadcasting
All broadcasting is state controlled. National public broadcasting is provided by Radiodiffusion Télévision Algérienne (RTA).
Radio: Algerian Radio (www.algerian-radio.dz), operated by RTA, has 35 stations providing three radio networks with local and international services in Arabic, French and Tamazight. International services are also provided in Spanish and English.
Television: The state-run Enterprise Nationale de Télévision (ENTV) (www.entv.dz) provides services in Arabic and French with online programmes. Satellite programming is provided by ENTV through Canal Algérie and Thalitha. ENTV also has collaborative links with French-based Berbère TV (www.brtv.fr).

Advertising
Although advertising is allowed and adverting agencies operate in Algeria, over 50 per cent of all advertising is placed by government entities and is controlled by the National Publishing and Advertising Agency (ANEP). The market is underdeveloped and the foremost form of advertising is through the print media.

News agencies
National news agency: Algerian Press Service (APS)
Other news agencies: Agence Algérienne d'Information (AAI) (in French): www.aai-online.com

Economy

With large reserves of hydrocarbons, 12.2 billion barrels of oil and 4.5 trillion cubic metres of natural gas at the end of 2009, the economy has been buoyed by strong exports that have provided a trade surplus since 2008. However, there is little investment in other sectors and the economy and without hydrocarbons remains weak.
Algeria has benefited from the sharp rise in global oil prices since 2005, tripling its record foreign exchange reserves between 2000–06. Oil and gas accounts for almost 30 per cent of GDP, 60 per cent of budget revenues and 95 per cent of export earnings. It has been able to pay back around 50 per cent of its outstanding debts to its Paris Club creditors since the government introduced new hydrocarbon laws that opened up the market to redevelopment with deregulated oil and gas prices.
The IMF warned that high revenue from oil production discourages growth elsewhere in the economy and the money from higher oil prices should be used to diversify, and reinvested to expand the economy. The government embarked on a five-year US$55 billion spending programme in 2004 and the results have shown improvement in infrastructure and employment prospects. GDP growth fell to 2.0 per cent 2006, while unemployment fell from a high of 28.4 per cent (and as much as 50 per cent in the youth group) in 2003, to 11.8 per cent in 2007.
Algeria has huge potential, mainly due to its rich natural resources, but also its strategic position close to the fast growing and fuel-hungry EU, to which Algeria has gas pipelines.
The government's policy of turning Algeria's command economy into a market economy is an unpopular one. Industrial action in protest at the sale of public enterprises has continued and the IMF is cautious about the balance between deregulating the market and the sharp rise in job losses this would cause, against the long term good of the market.
Government policy includes improving the investment climate in the tourist sector and the production of non-oil related goods. In reality, obstacles remain for non-oil trade, primarily due to the repatriation of revenue in foreign currencies. A climate of unrest and violence has resulted in reluctance on the part of private investors to put money into Algeria. This may improve with the pending WTO membership and the EU trade association agreements, although the current ban on alcohol imports is undermining these trade agreements.
Algeria is taking tentative steps towards breaking the stranglehold oil and gas has on its economy, but it remains to be seen if it can diversify at a time when windfall revenue from high oil prices negates the value of any other industry or business.

External trade

The strict control of imports has begun to be relaxed, nevertheless the government still has a great influence in planning the economy, with hydrocarbon exports providing a huge trade surplus each year. Algeria has large gas and oil reserves and a ready market for its natural gas, with a major pipeline already connecting, through Spain, to the rest of Europe.
Algeria has moved closer to full membership of the WTO with changes to its foreign trade policy and the backing of the US, both of whom signed a free trade agreement in 2004. However, in a bid to become a member Algeria must revise legislation on the importation of alcohol that may prove unpopular.
Algeria has an Association Agreement, including free trade, with the EU, signed in 2005, which provides for the gradual removal of import duties on industrial products and the liberalisation of Algeria's agricultural export market by 2012.

Imports
Principal imports are capital goods electrical and electronic goods, semi-finished goods, food and tobacco, transport equipment and raw materials.
Main sources: France (typically 22 per cent of total), Italy (8.6 per cent), China (8.5 per cent).

Exports
Principal exports are hydrocarbons; chemical fertilisers, iron and steel, wine, tobacco and foodstuffs.
Main destinations: US (typically 26.7 per cent total goods exports), Italy (16.6 per cent), Spain (9.1 per cent).

Agriculture

Farming
The sector employs about 25 per cent of the labour force and contributes around 10.5 per cent of GDP. Just over 40,000,000 hectares (ha) are given over to agriculture, or around 16 per cent of total land available, of which over 8,250,000ha are under arable and permanent crops.
Climatic conditions and the availability of water for irrigation directly affect crop yields. Despite extensive irrigation programmes and the dividing of state holdings into smaller units, agricultural output has failed to keep pace with the rate of population growth. Imports typically represent around 25 per cent of import costs. Government policy had been to reduce reliance on imported food, now, however, an open market is developing as state owned agricultural land is returned to private hands.
Underlying constraints to growth include soil erosion, desert encroachment, inefficient management in the state sector, poor marketing, recurrent droughts and

the inability of farmers to secure loan finance due to problems with land security. Government plans to reduce dependence on imports by a series of measures, included investing in new technology, financial incentives for state and private sector farms to buy equipment, encouraging foreign investment, less interference in the private sector and tree planting to arrest desertification.
There has been a large increase in the number of vineyards now operating in Algeria, providing a boost in export revenue. Although wine consumption is banned under Islamic law, production has been increasing; since the end of the 1990s it has doubled to around 500,000 hectolitres by 2005. It has provided a healthy income for farmers, in semi-arid regions, when other food crops have failed.
Main cash crops are grapes, oranges, olives, dates, tobacco, sugar beet and tomatoes. Hard and soft wheat and barley are grown for the home market, as are vegetables, and pulses.

Fishing

The fisheries sector largely consists of small-scale private sector operators, virtually all of whom do their fishing in the Mediterranean. Main catches include sardines, anchovies, sprats, tuna and shellfish.
The government plans to boost fisheries by modernising the Mediterranean ports, where most of the catch is landed. It has also set up a partnership with West African states for fishing in the Atlantic Ocean.

Forestry

Less than 2 per cent of Algeria's total land area is covered with forest or wooded land and the country is one of the largest importers of wood in Africa.
Algeria's forest resources cover some 3.5 million hectares (ha), with the state monopoly processing some 272,000 cubic metres of wood annually. All of the forest and arable land is in a broad coastal strip, around 400km wide. As part of plans aimed at reducing desertification the government has established an extensive tract of plantation forests.
Algeria is among the world's largest producers of cork. Other forestry products include sawn timber, wood-based panels and paper based on non-wood fibres. Most domestic demand for forest products is met through imports.

Industry and manufacturing

Industry represents 50 per cent of GDP and employs 23 per cent of the labour force. Algeria's industrial sector is dominated by large, inefficient state-owned companies that have largely survived only due to the credit extended them by the country's state-owned banks. Government attempts to privatise these industries have been frustrated by a lack of investor interest and the fear that the possible mass redundancies which may result will cause further social instability.
The largest company in Algeria is the state-owned hydrocarbons concern, Société Nationale pour la Recherche, la Production, le Transport, la Transformation et la Commercialisation des Hydrocarbures (Sonatrach).
Production is dominated by heavy industries such as steel, petrochemicals, fertilisers and cement, but the focus of development is changing to light industry. In 2005 the first laptop computers produced in Algeria went on sale. The manufacturers, EEPAD, an Algerian Internet service provider, aim at producing one million units a year, enough to supply every home in Algeria, by 2010.
Traditional agri-allied industries are also important, particularly textiles, food processing and tobacco and cigarette production. However past lack of investment and inefficiencies in these industries resulted in generally low productivity. In an effort to modernise the government has allowed some entities to be expanded, charge competitive prices and invest profits. Industry is opening up to more foreign involvement, particularly in large-scale projects such as motor vehicle assembly. Main constraints to development are shortages of vital inputs and skilled labour, high production and transport costs and maintenance problems. Industrial development is centralised in the northern coastal strip, but plans exist to extend industry to the high plateaux in the south.

Tourism

The tourist industry is small compared to neighbouring countries, but the government has intentions to grow the business. The country has cultural, coastal resorts and adventure tourism on offer, appealing primarily to European visitors. There were 1.91 million visitors to Algeria in 2009, which increased to over 2 million in 2010, of which 71 per cent belonged to the Algerian diaspora, predominately from France. Business based visitor numbers rose steadily 2008–10, accounting for 32 per cent of total growth. Foreign revenue was US$330 million in 2010.
In 2009 the government signed contracts with foreign and domestic interests for 283 new hotels with a total of 17,000 beds and 36,000 new jobs. In 2010 total accommodation was 90,000 beds, while there is a target of 160,000 beds by 2015. There are a good supply of airports and ports that could be utilised quickly, although the countrywide infrastructure still has to be redeveloped to expand tourism into the unspoiled Sahara region and seldom visited tribal areas.
In April 2011, the World Tourism Organisation listed Algeria as the fourth most popular destination in Africa (after Morocco, Tunisia and South Africa). However, the upheavals in North Africa due to the 'Arab Spring' and a series of terrorist attack on tourists and resorts (2009–10), have had a detrimental effect on foreign exchange earnings as visitor numbers fell. In partnership with Tunisia, the tourism ministry has implemented a promotion campaign to attract wary holidaymakers to return.

Mining

The mining and hydrocarbons sector employs 4 per cent of the labour force and contributes 40 per cent to GDP.
Algeria is rich in minerals, including iron ore, uranium, zinc, phosphates, gold, antimony, bituminous coal, tungsten, manganese, lead, mercury and salt. The mining of iron ore and phosphate for feedstocks (for local steel and fertiliser production, respectively) and for export are the most important.
Also located near the Moroccan border are iron-ore reserves estimated at two billion tonnes. The remote location and the Western Sahara/Morocco conflict have so far prevented exploitation.

Hydrocarbons

At the end of 2010, oil reserves stood at 1223 billion barrels (1.5 billion tonnes); new oil discoveries, improved data on existing fields and a recent increase in exploration are likely to mean that Algeria's reserves will be revised upwards. Production was 1.8 million barrels per day (bpd), a slight decrease of 0.3 per cent on the 2009 figure, while domestic consumption was 327,000 bpd, also a decrease of -0.1 per cent. Approximately 90 per cent of Algeria's crude oil exports go to Western Europe, with Italy as the main market followed by Germany and France. The Netherlands, Spain and Britain are other important European markets. Algeria's Saharan blend oil, 45 degrees API with negligible (0.05 per cent) sulphur content, is considered among the highest quality in the world. Algeria had a refining capacity of 22 million tonnes (161.3 million bpd) in 2008 and is planning to increase production to 50 million tonnes (366.5 million bpd) by 2014.
The state-run Sonatrach has responsibility for the oil and gas sectors including exploration, transportation, processing and marketing of hydrocarbons. It provides technical regulation and control including investment and development. In 2009 it let a contract with Swiss and Japanese engineering companies to construct new, and renovate existing, oil plants. The

contracts, totalling over US$1.7 billion, will provide large gas processing facilities at the Gassi Touil oil field as well as supply gas gathering plants and product pipelines. The project is scheduled to be completed by 2013.

Natural gas reserves were 4.52 trillion cubic metres (cum) at the end of 2010, with production of 80.4 billion cum. They are Africa's second largest deposits of natural gas (after Nigeria). Sonelgaz (Socièté Nationale de l'Electricité et du Gaz) (National Society for Electricity and Gas) is the state-owned company that has responsibility for the domestic distribution of electricity and natural gas. It has a quasi-monopoly over Algeria's international market in natural gas, as well as distribution and domestic sales of natural gas.

Exports of natural gas are destined to only five countries, with 27.56 billion cum exported to Italy alone, Spain received 12.05 billion cum, Portugal and Tunisia both imported around 1.3 billion cum and Slovenia 380,000 cum in 2010. The Medgaz (Algeria-Spain) sub-Mediterranean gas pipeline was completed in January 2009. The gas stream goes online in mid-2010, supplying 8 billion cum per annum. Another, the Galsi gas pipeline, is under construction between Algeria and northern Italy, which will also supply 8 billion cum per annum when completed in 2012–13. Existing gas pipelines include Pedro Duran Farell (Algeria-Spain) supplying 12 billion cum annually and the Trans-Mediterranean (Algeria-Tunisia-Italy-Slovenia) supplying 33.5 billion cum per year.

Algeria also exports liquefied natural gas (LNG) to many more destinations in Europe and the Far East, although none imported more than France's 7.85 billion cum in 2007.

In July 2009, two major contracts were signed. The first between Algeria, Niger and Nigeria was to build a 2,580km trans-Sahara gas pipeline (TSGP) traversing all three countries, which is estimated will cost US$13 billion and transport up to 30 billion cum of natural gas, destined for Europe. Three foreign energy companies also expressed an interest in investing in the project – Russia's Gazprom, France's Total and the Anglo-Dutch Shell. Algeria also expressed an interest in Nigeria's upstream element of TSGP, which would utilise its existing gas pipeline network and storage facilities. The second was with Canada's SNC-Lavalin Group to build new gas handling facilities in eastern Algeria near Qartzites de Hamra that will process and treat around 10 billion cum of natural gas, generated from the four oil fields. The US$1.1 billion project is due to be complete in 2012; the natural gas produced will be pumped to Arzew where it will be processed into 4.7 million tonnes per day of LNG for export.

Coal represents approximately 1 per cent of total energy consumption. Algeria's total recoverable coal reserves are estimated at 40 million tonnes. Imports of coal in 2007 totalled 10.7 million tonnes.

Energy

Total installed generating capacity was 6,500MW in 2007, all of which was generated by oil and natural gas. Ongoing investment has included three new generating stations, a new power grid, incorporating high voltage power lines and, in 2008, the beginning of an 18-year contract with US General Electrics to improve efficiency, output and reliability of 51 gas turbines in 13 power stations; by 2010 generating capacity is projected to be 14,000MW. Sonelgaz (Socièté Nationale de l'Electricité et du Gaz) (National Society for Electricity and Gas) is the state-owned company that has responsibility for the distribution of electricity and natural gas.

Financial markets

Stock exchange

The Algiers stock exchange (Bourse d'Alger) was formally opened in 1999.

Banking and insurance

The Algerian banking sector is dominated by six state-owned banks. There is a total of 17 commercial banks and 10 financial institutions. The sector has been inefficient, with the large state banks acting mainly as depository institutions and financing loss-making public sector companies. In 2006 the government began financial sector reforms and by 2008 the 17 commercial banks had opened up to foreign investors and restructuring of the six public sector banks was underway. However, fallout from the subprime crisis in the United States led to the postponement in January 2008 of the sale of 51 per cent of Crédit Populaire d'Algérie. Algeria remains underbanked with some 26,000 people per branch and the government has confimed that it will continue with reforms.

Central bank

Banque d'Algérie.

Time

GMT plus one hour.

Geography

Algeria is the second largest country in Africa. With a total land area of 2.38 million square km, the country comprises three distinct regions: a narrow coastal plain, which has the most fertile soils and houses the majority of the country's population, agriculture and industry; the uplands of the Atlas mountain chain, which tend to be semi-arid steppe in the valleys; and the vast sandy desert to the south. Algeria has borders with Morocco to the west, Tunisia and Libya to the east and Niger, Mali and Mauritania to the south.

Hemisphere

Northern

Climate

The coastal region has a temperate Mediterranean climate, averaging 13 degrees Celsius (C) to 24 degrees C throughout the year and rising to a daytime high of 32 degrees C during the summer (June to September). The rainy season is October to May, with rains especially heavy from November to February. The desert is constantly inhospitable, with temperatures rising to 45 degrees C during the day, falling to 10 degrees C at night, and with very little rainfall.

Dress codes

Western-style dress is acceptable, with lightweight or safari suits recommended in summer. Women should not wear revealing clothes.

Entry requirements

Passports

Required by all

Visa

Visas are required by most nationals: visit http://algeria.embassyhomepage.com/ for details and application form or contact your local Algerian embassy. Visas are usually valid for 90 days.

Business visas must be accompanied by an invitation from an Algerian company (in duplicate).

Prohibited entry

Nationals of Israel

Currency advice/regulations

The import of foreign currency is unlimited, but must be declared on arrival; export of foreign currency is permitted up to the amount declared on arrival. Local currency may be imported and exported. Visitors are advised to change money through official sources only; it can sometimes be difficult to reconvert dinars to foreign currency. Declaration forms, issued on arrival, should be kept and used at each successive currency change to be surrendered on departure. Failure to comply with these regulations may mean visitors are liable to forfeit the currency. Travellers cheques can only be used in very limited outlets; US dollars and euros have most recognition.

Health (for visitors)

Mandatory precautions

A yellow fever and/or cholera vaccination certificate is required if arriving from infected or endemic areas.

Advisable precautions

Hepatitis A and B, diphtheria, TB, typhoid, tetanus and polio vaccinations are advisable. There is risk of malaria in some areas, therefore prophylaxis is recommended. There is also a rabies risk. Water precautions should be taken throughout the country. Bottled water is often hard to find, particularly in southern parts of the country.

Hotels
There is a limited range of hotels on offer; hotels are either high-luxury or modest one- two-star hotels. It is advisable to book well in advance as accommodation in Algiers is difficult to obtain.
The service charge is usually 15 per cent.

Credit cards
The use of credit cards are restricted to urban areas.

Public holidays (national)
The weekend in Algeria changed from the traditional Thursday-Friday Arab alignment to the Saturday-Sunday European align in August 2009.
Fixed dates
1 Jan (New Year's Day), 1 May (Labour Day), 19 Jun (Revolutionary Readjustment), 5 Jul (Independence Day), 1 Nov (Anniversary of the Revolution).
Variable dates
Eid al Adha (two days), Eid al Fitr (two days), Islamic New Year, Ashura, Prophet's Birthday.
Islamic year 1433 (26 Nov 2011–14 Nov 2012): The Islamic year contains 354 or 355 days, with the result that Muslim feasts advance by 10–12 days against the Gregorian calendar. Dates of feasts vary according to the sighting of the new moon, so cannot be forecast exactly.

Working hours
The weekend in Algeria changed from the traditional Thursday-Friday Arab alignment to the Saturday-Sunday European align in August 2009.
Banking
Sun–Thur: 0900–1530.
Business
Sat–Tue: 0800–1200 and 1300–1700; Wed 0800–1200 and 1300–1600.
Government
Sat–Wed: 0800–1200 and 1400–1730; Thur 0800–1200.
Shops
Sat–Wed 0800–1230 and 1430–1800; Thu: 0800–1300.

Telecommunications
Mobile/cell phones
GSM 900/1800 services are available mostly in inhabited areas in the north and isolated towns in central and southern Algeria.

Electricity supply
Electricity supply varies from 127–220V; a compensator for use with electronic/computer equipement is advisable. A variety of plug fittings are used.

Social customs/useful tips
Business appointments should be made in advance. Business cards are exchanged after introductions. French-style courtesy should be adopted by visitors. Hospitality is regarded as very important, and visitors are usually entertained in restaurants and hotels. Wives seldom accompany their husbands to social engagements outside the home.
Care should taken to respect local customs, especially during the fasting month of Ramadan (approximately 21 August–19 September 2009).

Security
Violence was endemic during the 1990s. Although there have been fewer violent incidents since 2000, visitors should still take precautions by avoiding travelling alone and avoid the provinces of Tamanrasset, Djanet and Illizi in the south-east, where tourists have been targetted for kidnapping. Incidents of assaults on foreigners have increased in some urban and rural areas and visitors should avoid carrying valuables and large sums of money.

Getting there
Air
National airline: Air Algérie
International airport/s: Algiers (Houari Boumédienne) (ALG), 20km from city. Facilities include duty-free shop, restaurant, bank, post office, shops, car hire.
Other airport/s: Annaba (Les Salines) (AAE), 12km from city; Constantine (Ain El-Bey) (CZL), 9km from city; Oran (Es Senia) (ORN), 10km from city.
Airport tax: None
Surface
Road: The border between Algeria and Morocco is closed and access is denied. Roads are good in the coastal and northern Sahara networks, while access to Mali, by the trans-Saharan highway, is unsealed and its use is subject to seasonal conditions.
Rail: A daily train service (the Trans-Maghreb) links Tunis with Algiers and Oran.
Water: Regular ferry services connect Algieria with France and Spain.
Main port/s: Algiers, Annaba, Arzew, Bejaia, Oran.

Getting about
National transport
Air: There are frequent services from Algiers to Annaba, Constantine and Oran provided by Air Algérie. Regular flights also link these towns with other principal centres. Fares are generally low for domestic flights but overbooking can occur, especially in summer.
Road: Main roads are in good condition generally, but desert routes are rarely maintained.
Buses: Long-distance coach services are operated by Société Nationale des Transports de Voyageurs (SNTV) and Altour. Bookings for long trips should be made well in advance.
Rail: The service is operated by Société Nationale des Transports Ferroviaires (SNTF). There are two classes; some services are air-conditioned and some have couchettes.
City transport
Taxis: Taxis are widely available in main centres; they are radio-controlled in Algiers. Taxis are identified by a local colour code. They are supposed to be metered, but owing to demand, usually operate without a meter and use a minimum fare system instead. A surcharge is imposed after dark. Tips are usually 10 per cent of fare.
Buses, trams & metro: State-owned service operates in Algiers. Can be overcrowded during rush hours. Daily and longer duration tickets are available.
A new metro in Algiers was due to begin public operations in November 2011. Line One is 8.5km long and has 10 stations from Grande Poste in the city centre to Hai al Badr in Kouba southwest of the city. Stations open 0500–2300.
Car hire
Car hire is available in most main towns and at airports. An international driving licence and third-party insurance are required. The maximum speed limit is 50kph in towns and 100kph on main roads.

BUSINESS DIRECTORY

The addresses listed below are a selection only. While World of Information makes every endeavour to check these addresses, we cannot guarantee that changes have not been made, especially to telephone numbers and area codes. We would welcome any corrections.

Telephone area codes
The international dialling code (IDD) for Algeria is + 213 followed by the area code and subscriber's number:

Algiers	21	Ghardaia	29
Annaba	38	Oran	41
Béchar	49	Sétif	36
Boumerdes	24	Tiemcen	43
Constantine	31	Tindouf	49

Useful telephone numbers
Directory enquiries: 19
Telegrams: 13
Police: 17

Chambers of Commerce
Algerian Chambre de Commerce et d' Industrie, Palais Consulaire, 6 Boulevard

Amilcar Cabral, Place des Martyrs, PO Box 100, 16003 Algiers (tel: 715-160; fax: 710-174; e-mail: caci@wissal.dz).

Constantine Chambre de Commerce et d' Industrie, 6 Rue de 24 Novembre 1954, PO Box 394, 25000 Constantine (tel: 935-923; fax: 937-807).

Dhara Chambre de Commerce et d' Industrie, 1 Avenue Benyahia Belcacem, PO Box 99, Mostaganem (tel: 216-709; fax: 216-578).

French Chambre de Commerce et Industrie en Algerie, Villa Clarac, 3 Rue des Cèdres, El Mouradia, Alger (tel: 606-496; fax: 609-509; e-mail: cfcia@cfcia.org).

Oran Chambre de Commerce et d' Industrie, 8 Boulevard de la Soummam, Oran (tel: 391-299; fax: 396-312).

Banking

Banque Al Baraka, Haï Bouteldja Houidif, Villa No 1 Rocade Sud, Ben Aknoun, Algiers (tel: 916-450; fax: 916-457; e-mail: info@albaraka-bank.com).

Banque de l'Agrulture et du Developpement Rural, 17 Boulevard Colonel Amirouche, Algiers (tel: 634-922; fax: 635-146).

Banque de Developpement Local, 5 Rue Gaci Amar, Staoueli, Algiers (tel: 393-755; fax: 393-757).

Banque Extérieure d'Algérie, 3 Rue du Docteur Lucien Reynaud, Algiers (tel: 239-330; fax: 239-099; e-mail: dircom@bea.dz).

Banque Nationale d'Algérie, 8 Boulevard Ernesto Che Guevara, Algiers (tel: 714-719; fax: 712-424; e-mail: nb@bna.com.dz).

Caisse d'Epargne et de Prevoyance, 42 Rue Khelifa Boukhalfa, Algiers (tel: 713-395; fax: 714-131).

Crédit Populaire d'Algérie, 2 Boulevard Colonel Amirouche, Algiers (tel: 740-528; fax: 642-383).

Central bank

Banque d'Algérie, Villa Jolie, 38 Avenue Franklin Roosevelt, 16000 Algiers (tel: 230-023; fax: 260-856; e-mail: ba@bank-of-algeria.dz).

Travel information

Air Algérie, 1 Place Maurice Audin, PO 483, 1600 Algiers (tel: 653-340; fax: 509-389; e-mail: contact@)airalgerie.dz).

Algiers-Houari Boumediene Airport, BP130 Dar El-Baida, 16100 Algiers (tel: 506-000; fax: 509-219; e-mail: hlamyl@hotmail.com).

Ministry of tourism

Ministry of Tourism and Handicraft, Rue des Frères Ziata, 16070 Algiers (tel: 792-301; fax: 792-632).

National tourist organisation offices

ONAT (Entreprise Nationale Algérienne du Tourisme), 126 bis Rue Didouche Mourad, Algiers (tel: 744-448; fax: 743-214; e-mail: onat@onat.dz.com).

Ministries

Prime Minister's Office, Rue Docteur Saadane, 16001 Algiers (tel: 732-300; fax: 717-927).

Ministry of Agriculture and Rural Development, 12 Boulevard Colonel Amirouche, 16001 Algiers (tel: 711-712; fax: 745-986).

Ministry of Commerce, Rue Docteur Saadane, 16001 Algiers (tel: 732-340; fax: 735-478).

Ministry of Communications and Culture, Palais de la Culture, El-Anassers, 16502 Algiers (tel: 679-420; fax: 684-459).

Ministry of Defence, Avenue Ali Khodja, Les Tagarins, 16030 Algiers (tel: 711-515).

Ministry of Education, 8 Avenue de Pékin, 16070 Algiers (tel: 605-560; fax: 606-757).

Ministry of Energy and Mines, 80 Avenue Ahmed Ghermoul, 16014 Algiers (tel: 673-300; fax: 650-997).

Ministry of Finance, Immeuble Mauretania, Place du Pérou, 16001 Algiers (tel: 711-366; fax: 736-450).

Ministry of Fisheries and Marine Resources, 4 Rue des Quatre Canons, 16001 Algiers (tel: 433-947; fax: 433-168).

Ministry of Foreign Affairs, Place Med Seddik Benyahia, 16070, Algiers (tel: 504-545; fax: 504-242).

Ministry of Health, Population and Hospital Reform, 125 Rue Abderrahmane Laala, 16075 Algiers (tel: 279-900; fax: 279-641).

Ministry of Higher Education and Scientific Research, 11 Rue Doudou Mokhtar, 16033 Algiers (tel: 912-323; fax: 912-113).

Ministry of Housing and Urbanism, 135 Rue Didouche Mourad, 16001 Algiers (tel: 740-722; fax: 747-664).

Ministry of Industry and Restructuring, Immeuble le Colisée, 4 Rue Ahmed Bey, 16030 Algiers (tel: 693-156; fax: 693-235; e-mail: info@mir-algeria.org).

Ministry of the Interior and Local Communities, Rue Docteur Saadane, 16001 Algiers (tel: 732-340; fax: 605-210).

Ministry of Justice, 8 Place Bir Hakem, 16030 Algiers (tel: 921-608; fax: 921-243).

Ministry of Labour and Social Protection, 44 Rue Med Belouizded, Belcourt, Algiers (tel: 683-366; fax: 745-306).

Ministry of Participation and Reforms Co-ordination (MPCR), Chemin Ibn Badis el Mouiz, 16030 Algiers (tel: 929-885; fax: 929-884).

Ministry of Post and Telecommunications, 4 Boulevard Krim Belkacem, 16027 Algiers (tel: 711-220; fax: 730-047).

Ministry of Public Works, 3 Rue du Caire, 16050 Algiers (tel: 689-500).

Ministry of Religious Affairs and Endowments, 4 Rue de Timgad, Algiers (tel: 608-555; fax: 600-936).

Ministry of Small and Medium Enterprises, Immeuble le Colisée, 4 Rue Ahmed Bey, 16030 Algiers (tel: 601-144; fax: 592-658).

Ministry of Transport, 119 rue Didouche Mourad, 16001 Algiers (tel: 740-699; fax: 646-637).

Ministry of Vocational Training and Professional Education, Route de Dély Ibrahim, 16033 Algiers (tel: 911-528; fax: 912-779).

Ministry of War Veterans, 9 Avenue Benarfa Mohamed, 16030 Algiers (tel: 922-355; fax: 922-739).

Ministry of Water Resources, 8 Place de Bir Hakem, 16030 Algiers (tel: 283-837; fax: 747-543).

Ministry of Youth and Sports, 3 Rue Mohamed Belouizdad, 16600 Algiers (tel: 683-350; fax: 657-778; e-mail: mjs@wissal.dz).

Other useful addresses

Algerian Embassy (USA), 2137 Wyoming Avenue, NW, Washington DC 20008 (tel: (+1-202) 265-2800; fax: (+1-202) 667-2174; e-mail: embalg.us@verizon.net).

APSI (investment promotion agency), Boulevard du 11 Décembre 1960, BP 336 El-Biar, 16030 Algiers (tel: 914-225; fax: 914-303; e-mail: apsi@wissal.dz).

British Embassy, 6 Avenue Souidani Boudiemaa, BP08 Alger-Gare, 16000, Algiers (tel: 230-068; fax: 230-067).

FINALEP (Algero-European Financial Participation Company), 11 Route Nationale, Staouéli, Algiers (tel: 393-494; fax: 392-020; e-mail: finalep@wissal.dz).

National Office of Statistics, 8/10 Rue des Moussebilines, BP 202 Ferhat Boussad, 16000 Algiers (tel: 744-100; fax: 743-839; e-mail: ons@onssiege.ons.dz).

SAFEX (Algerian fairs and exports company), Palais des Expositions, Pins Maritimes, BP 366 Alger Gare, Algiers (tel: 210-123; fax: 210-630; e-mail: safex@wissal.dz).

SNTF (national rail company), 21-23 Boulevard Mohamed V, Algiers (tel: 711-510; fax: 748-190).

Sonatrach (national oil and gas company), 10 Rue Djenane El-Malik, Hydra, 16035 Algiers (tel: 548-011; fax: 547-700; e-mail: sonatrach@sonatrach.dz).

US Embassy, 4 Chemin Cheikh Bachir El-Ibrahimi, BP 408 Alger-Gare, 16000, Algiers (tel: 691-255; fax: 693-979).

National news agency: Algerian Press Service (APS) Agence Algérienne d'Information (AAI) (in French): www.aai-online.com

Internet sites

Africa Business Network: www.ifc.org/abn

Africa news outlet: allafrica.com

African Development Bank: www.afdb.org

Algeria Interface: www.algeria-interface.com

Algeria News Agency: www.aps.dz

Algeria On-Line: www.djazaironline.net

Mbendi AfroPaedia: www.mbendi.co.za

American Samoa

COUNTRY PROFILE

Historical profile

1722 The Dutch navigator, Jacob Roggeveen, was the first European to sight the islands.
1831 The London Missionary Society arrived to convert native Samoans and established a British presence.
1872 The US gained exclusive use of the deep-water whaling port of Pago Pago.
1889 The Treaty of Berlin between Britain, the US and Germany promised an independent Samoan government.
1899 The Berlin Treaty was annulled by the Tripartite Treaty, which granted the US the right to all eastern islands of the Samoan group, giving Germany the remainder. In exchange, Britain gained control of Germany's rights in Tonga, Niue and the Solomon Islands (excluding Bougainville).
1900 American Samoa officially became a US territory. Traditional rights were protected in return for a military base and coaling station. Islanders became US nationals, but not citizens; they cannot vote in US elections.
1941 The US entered the Second World War and American Samoa became a strategic location, for the US Pacific Fleet.
1945 The US Marine Corps withdrew.
1951 The territory was transferred to the US Department of the Interior.
1956 The US appointed Peter Tali Coleman as the first Samoan governor; he went on to become the first popularly elected governor.
1960 The constitution was promulgated.
1967 A revised constitution was introduced, which guaranteed the rights of inhabitants on issues such as land ownership and civil rights.
2002 Following fears of overfishing in American Samoa's exclusive economic zone (EEZ), the Western Pacific Regional Fishery Management Council approved a decision to limit access of fleets to EEZ waters.
2003 Governor Tause Sunia died, his deputy Togiola Tulafono was appointed acting governor.
2004 Cyclone Heta caused devastation and President Bush declared the islands a federal disaster area. Incumbent, Acting Governor Tulafono won the gubernatorial elections.
2005 Cyclone Heta's damage to the Manu'a islands was estimated at US$2 million. The government-owned KVZK-TV re-launched Channel 5, which had been off-air since 1991. Travellers from American Samoa were required to obtain entry permits to enter Samoa. The governor introduced legislation to ban human trafficking and involuntary servitude.
2006 Eni Faleomavaega was re-elected for a tenth term as Territorial Delegate in elections to the US House of Representatives.
2007 Samoa agreed to waive the US$30 entry permit fee for all American Samoan nationals who could prove a Samoan ancestor.
2008 In the run-off gubernatorial elections incumbent Togiola Tulfono won 56.5 per cent and Afoa Moega Lutu 43.5 per cent.
2009 Togiola Tulfono became governor. An earthquake, of 8.3 magnitude, struck offshore in the Pacific Ocean and caused a devastating *tsunami* that swept over several Samoan islands, killing more than 140 people, including 25 in American Samoa. US federal aid was provided including emergency supplies. Later, a media report accused the administration of having previously squandered millions of dollars of funds, which had been allocated for a *tsunami* warning system. The system had only progressed to the planning stage, including for an island-wide siren warning system, before the US had halted funding in 2007, due to misspending by American Samoan officials.
2010 The resident population took part in the United States census in April, which, after personal details, included questions on race, housing and internet and mobile phone access. In September, President Obama signed legislation to delay the increase in the minimum wage, scheduled for 2010 and 2011, in American Samoa.
2011 Following agreements with the state and federal authorities on tax incentives and exemption plus a freeze on the increase in minimum wages, in April the Starkist cannery company announced that it would begin re-hiring 500 workers and gave a long-term commitment to stay in American Samoa and to increase production. Further discussions to improve the business environment for Starkist included state help to reduce energy costs and increased provision of cold-storage.

KEY FACTS

Official name: Territory of American Samoa

Head of State: President of the United States of America Barack Obama (from 20 Jan 2009)

Head of government: Governor Togiola (Tala) Tulafono (since 2003; re-elected Nov 2008)

Area: 196 square km (five islands); Tutuila: 135 square km

Population: 68,000 (2010)*

Capital: Fagatogo (on Tutuila), usually known as Pago Pago

Official language: English and Samoan

Currency: US dollar (US$) = 100 cents

GDP per capita: US$8,000 (2007)*

GDP real growth: 3.00%

Labour force: 17,630 (2005)

Unemployment: 29.80% (2005)

* estimated figure

Political structure

Constitution

The 1960 constitution was revised in 1967.

American Samoa is represented in the US by a senator and a non-voting representative.

American Samoans are not US citizens; they are classified as US nationals and have freedom of entry into the continental US, but no voting rights.

Form of state

American Samoa is an unincorporated and unorganized territory of the US, administered by the Office of Insular Affairs, US Department of the Interior.

The executive

Local executive power rests with a popularly elected governor and lieutenant governor, who serve four-year terms.

National legislature

The bicameral Fono (Legislative Assembly), consists of the House of Representatives (lower chamber), with 21 members elected for two-year terms, of which 20 members are elected in single seat constituencies and one, non-voting member for Swains Island, decided by public meeting, and the Senate (upper chamber) with 18 members, all *Matai* (local chiefs), elected for four-year terms, according to Samoan custom.

Legal system

High Court – the chief justice and associate justices are appointed by the US Secretary of the Interior.

Last elections

4 and 18 November 2008 (gubernatorial); 7 November 2006 (US House of Representatives)

Results: Gubernatorial (first round): Togiola Tulfono won 41.3 per cent, Utu Abe Malae 31.4 per cent, and Afoa Moega Lutu 26.8 per cent. Run-off: Tulafono won 56.5 per cent, Malae 43.5 per cent.

US House of Representatives: Eni Faleomavaega (Democrat) won 47.1 per cent of the vote; Aumua Amata Coleman (Republican) 40.7 per cent; and Muavaefaatasi Ae Ae (Independent) 12.2 per cent.

Next elections

November 2012 (gubernatorial)

Political situation

The relationship between American Samoa and the US has exercised the leadership of both countries. Under the constitution American Samoa is an unorganised territory, so the people of American Samoa are US nationals but not citizens and they cannot migrate for work to other US states and territories without visas. In 2007 the US imposed a minimum wage, under federal laws, that threatened the viability of the island's largest employers – two tuna canning factories – raising wages from the local norm of US$2.63–4.09 per hour, depending on the industry, to US$7.25 by 2009. The US Congress, at the request of the American Samoan Congress representative, required three questions to be included in the 2008 political ballots: whether American Samoans should become US citizens, whether territorial senators should be elected by American Samoans and whether American Samoa should have it own federal district court and limited jurisdiction. Newly introduced, and some considered pre-emptive, measures to tighten immigration laws were also seen as another contentious issue that ignored the interests of local people.

In March 2011, the Republican controlled US-Congress voted to rescind the voting rites of representations of American Samoa, effectively disenfranchising their electorate in policies that directly affect them.

Population

68,000 (2010)*

Last census: April 2000: 57,291

Population density: 320 inhabitants per square km.

Annual growth rate: 1.6 per cent (2003)

Ethnic make-up

Samoan (Polynesian) (89 per cent), Tongan (4 per cent), Caucasian (2 per cent), others (5 per cent).

Religions

Approximately half the population are Christian Congregational, but Roman Catholics, Latter Day Saints and Protestants are also represented.

Education

Extra federal funds were provided in 2006 for schools with students from deprived backgrounds, aimed at those at risk of dropping out of education. There were also schemes for early reading and English learning, and support for children with disabilities. Specific funding for American Samoa of US$29.5 million will be added to improve the island's education system.

Compulsory years: Six to 18

Health

Life expectancy: 75.8 years (2005 estimate)

Fertility rate/Maternal mortality rate: 3.25 births per woman (2005 estimate).

Birth rate/Death rate: 25.9 births and three deaths per 1,000 population (2005 estimate)

Child (under 5 years) mortality rate (per 1,000): 9.3 deaths per 1,000 live births (2005 estimate)

Main cities

Fagatogo, the capital, on Tutuila, is usually known as Pago Pago (estimated population 4,388 in 2008), Tafuna (13,552), Nu'uuli (5,828), Leone (4,289), Faleniu (4,556).

Languages spoken

English is used for business and commerce but Samoan, (closely related to Hawaiian), is in common use among the local population.

Official language/s

English and Samoan

Media

Press

There are only two national, locally based daily newspapers, the *Samoa News* (www.samoanews.com) and the *Samoa Observer* (www.samoaobserver.ws).

A new, locally printed, five day publication began in 2006, the *American Samoa Tribune* is bilingual and owned by the Samoa Observer Newspaper Group.

Broadcasting

Radio: There are two commercial radio stations operating, both using their call signs, KKHJ 93FM (www.khjradio.com) with music and general interest programming and KNWJ 104 FM (www.fm104.org) with religious programmes; both broadcast in English. Several radio station broadcasts can be picked up from Samoa.

Television: The government owned KVZK Television operates three channels, broadcasting for eight hours each day. KVZK is an affiliate of US broadcasters PBS, ABC and CBS. There are several privately owned cable TV stations including K34HI, a Fox affiliate, WVUV-LP an NBC affiliate, American Samoa Cablevision, a CNN affiliate and K11UU. K21GL broadcasts religious programmes.

TV signals, by SBC TV1, neighbouring Samoa's public, commercial broadcaster, can be received.

News agencies

ABC Pacific Beat:
www.radioaustralia.net.au/pacbeat
Pacific Magazine:
www.pacificmagazine.net

Economy

The economy is based on agriculture, fishing, fish processing and aid from the US. Since September 2009 when the Chicken of the Sea tuna cannery closed, with the loss of over 2,000 jobs (12 per cent of a workforce of over 17,000), the economy has become precarious. The remaining tuna cannery, StarKist, laid off 600–800 workers in May 2010 as minimum wages legislation, introduced by the US, increased costs to the canning industry. Between them, the canneries had provided around 80 per cent of GDP. Other components of the economy such as agriculture and services, which each comprise a third of GDP, have been unable to absorb the volume of unemployed workers and has resulted in rising costs and welfare payments.

An agreement was reached in October 2010 for Tri Marine International to take

over the closed Chicken of the Sea cannery, which will be renovated and automated. The level of employment when the cannery is re-opened is not known but will be considerably lower than the 2,000 people originally employed.
A dependence on primary sectors has also meant the economy is particularly vulnerable to adverse weather conditions and disease. A devastating *tsunami* struck in September 2009 and caused damage to property and crops on low lying lands. Reconstruction aided GDP growth through 2010, as US aid topped $22.5 million. Around half of the government's revenue is from US aid, making international support essential to the island's development. Government efforts to attract investment to the territory and diversify the economy have had limited success. The island's natural beauty is an obvious tourist attraction, making it a fast growing sector of the economy, not only for the sun-worshipers but also the more intrepid eco-tourists. There are 10-year tax incentives for new businesses in the area, attempting to attract light manufacturing and service based industries. In January 2011 the Fono considered three possible revenue measures designed to cover the shortfall of US$7.2 million in government funding. They included an increase in business licences, higher import duties and a wage tax. The governor stated that without the new income, cuts to both work hours and the jobs of government workers were inevitable. In June 2011, the US Department of Homeland Security backed calls for American Samoa to be designated as 'high risk' over its accounting of government funds. This would mean a greater degree of scrutiny of all spending of federal funds and payments made in arrears will take longer to be paid.
US Army recruitment, which is a considerable source of income and employment, has dropped in recent years, the decrease is believed due to the war in Iraq, which has had negative publicity, arising from the death of a number of American Samoan servicemen.

External trade

American Samoa benefits from duty free entry into the customs territory of the US. Only one cannery exists and its production is almost exclusively destined for the US domestic market.

Imports

Materials for the canneries, processed food, machinery and parts, timber and petroleum products.
Main sources: US, Australia and Samoa.

Exports

Canned tuna, small industrial products and handicrafts.
Main destinations: US, Indonesia and India.
Canned fish to the US is not counted as an export.

Agriculture

Farming

The soil is volcanic. About 10 per cent of the land area is cultivable, half of which is under permanent cultivation.

Fishing

Tuna and deep-sea fishing is important to the economy. American Samoa is the main processing site for the US tuna fishing fleet in the Pacific.
The Chicken of the Sea Samoa Packing plant was closed in September 2009 with the loss of around 2,000 jobs. In May 2010 600–800 workers were laid off from the last operational cannery, StarKist. The governor of American Samoa called on the US Congress to provide US$18 million in a rescue package to save one of the territory's largest employers, which together with allied industries makes up about 80 per cent of its economy. Following agreements with the state and federal authorities on tax incentives and exemption plus a freeze on the increase in minimum wages, the Starkist cannery company announced that it would begin re-hiring 500 workers and provide long-term commitment to stay in American Samoa and increase production. Further discussions to improve the business environment for Starkist included state help to reduce energy costs and increased provision of cold-storage.
The government announced in October 2010 that the Chicken of the Sea tuna canning operation was to be re-instated. In partnership with the US-based Tri Marine International, the plant will be heavily automated and may only require around 100 workers. The plant is scheduled to open in 2011–12.

Industry and manufacturing

The private sector is dominated by the fish processing industry, which employs one-third of the workforce. StarKist has the world's largest tuna cannery in American Samoa and has a 44 per cent US market share. The two other producers are BumbleBee and Chicken of the Sea (a Thai owned company). Between them they produce 80–90 per cent of American Samoa's principal export, the majority of which is directed to the US market. The tuna canneries export around US$470 million processed tuna annually. StarKist and Chicken of the Sea employ more than 5,150 people or 74 per cent of the private sector workforce. Sales from StarKist canneries are reported to have increased sharply in recent years. American Samoa is fighting to exclude tuna from the US/Thailand Free Trade Agreement in order to save around 3,000 jobs.
Ecuador and Columbia are a threat to the tuna canneries as they have the production capacity to supply the entire US market and wipe out the economy of American Samoa.
Other industries include textiles, meat canning, dairy produce, jewellery, handicrafts and tourism. There are also factories processing soap, liquor and perfume. The US government is trying to encourage joint ventures and other foreign investment for any product with a 30 per cent local content.
The tuna cannery, Chicken of the Sea, announced in May 2009 that the jobs of 2,000 workers were in jeopardy as it planned to move its operations to mainland US by the end of September.
In May 2011, the government moved to take over the bankrupt MYD Samoa shipyard, for US$250,000. The government plans to invest in the shipyard and turn it into the South Pacific's key marine repair facility.

Tourism

Despite its obvious charms – blue lagoons, clean Pacific waters lapping against white sandy beaches and tropical weather to tempt any jaded traveller – American Samoa does not have a large tourist industry due to its remoteness and limited access, which has resulted in a lack of tourist infrastructure. Cruise ship arrivals have increased, but as they are based on the itineraries of foreign cruise liners visits are sporadic and result in economic feast and famine.
Ecotourism is a growing attraction.

Mining

The only natural resources are pumice and pumicite.

Hydrocarbons

There are no known hydrocarbon reserves. Consumption of petroleum products, including refined oil, is typically over 4,000 barrels per day (bpd), all of which is imported.
American Samoa does not import nor produce natural gas or coal.

Energy

Total installed generating capacity was 60MW in 2008. The American Samoa Power Authority is responsible for electricity generation and supply. There are two oil-fired power stations supplied by imported petroleum products. Any generator using renewable sources of energy and privately run may sell surplus electricity back to the utility.

Banking and insurance

The Bank of Hawaii and the Amerika Samoa Bank provide 24-hour full banking services and correspond with banks in the US and the Pacific.

Time
GMT minus 11 hours

Geography
American Samoa comprises the seven islands of Tutuila, Ta'u, Olosega, Ofu, Aunu'u, Rose Atoll and Swains Island, lying in the southern central Pacific Ocean, about 3,700km (2,300 miles) south-west of Hawaii. Pago Pago has one of the best natural deepwater harbours in the region.
Hemisphere
Southern

Climate
Tropical with annual rainfall around three metres. There are two main seasons: rainy (November—April) and dry (May–October). Temperatures range from 20–32 degrees Celsius.

Entry requirements
Passports
Required by all except US citizens with proof of citizenship; (all US nationals require a passport for re-entry to the US from January 2007).
Passports must be valid for at least 60 days beyond the intended length of stay.
Visa
US entry requirements apply. Visas required by all, except US citizens with proof of identity and foreign nationals from countries covered by the 'Visa Waiver Program', who are in possession of machine readable passports. All other visitors and passport holders must apply for a visa. Visas are valid for up to 90 days. A return/onward ticket is also required.
Further information can be found at http://travel.state.gov. More detailed information can be found at http://uscis.gov/graphics/services.
All visitors must have proof of adequate funds for up to 30 days and onward/return tickets. Entry to American Samoa does not give automatic entry to the US and visitors must apply separately through a US consulate.

Health (for visitors)
Mandatory precautions
Vaccination certificates required for yellow fever if travelling from infected area.
Advisable precautions
Vaccination for diphtheria, tuberculosis, hepatitis A and B, polio, tetanus and typhoid are advisable. There is a risk of rabies and dengue fever.

Public holidays (national)
Fixed dates
1 Jan (New Year's Day), 17 Apr (Flag Day), 4 Jul (Independence Day), 11 Nov (Veterans' Day), 25 Dec (Christmas Day).
Variable dates
Martin Luther King's Birthday (third Mon in Jan), Washington's Birthday (third Mon in Feb), Memorial Day (last Mon in May), Labour Day (first Mon in Sep), Columbus Day (second Mon in Oct), Thanksgiving Day (fourth Thu in Nov).

Working hours
Banking
Mon–Fri: 0900–1500; Sat: 0800–1200.
Business
Mon–Fri: 0730/0830–1730/1800; Sat: 0830–1200.
Government
Mon–Fri: 0730/0830–1730/1800; Sat: 0830–1200.
Shops
Mon–Fri: 0800–1700; Sat: 0800–1300.

Weights and measures
Imperial

Social customs/useful tips
Visitors should be sensitive to local conventions and respect local customs and practices. Care should be taken when dressed casually; bikinis and shorts are acceptable in hotels, but they are not considered appropriate when visiting urban and rural areas.

Getting there
Air
National airline: Hawaiian Airlines and Polynesian Airlines connect American Samoa to international air routes.
International airport/s: Pago Pago International (PPG), 11km from town; duty-free shop, restaurant and shops.
Airport tax: US$3, usually included in ticket price.
Surface
Main port/s: Pago Pago is an international port. It is served by a number of passenger cruise and cargo lines.

Getting about
National transport
Air: Samoa Air and Inter Island Air (a charter airline) serve the islands.
Road: There are approximately 150km of paved roads and 200km of unpaved or secondary roads, the majority of which are on Tutuila.
Buses: There is a local service operating between the airport and Pago Pago town centre. The 'aiga' bus service provides cheap travel between Pago Pago and outlying villages.
Water: A weekly service operates between Pago Pago and the Manu'a islands.
Car hire
An international driving licence or valid national driving licence is required. Minimum age of 21. Traffic drives on the right.

BUSINESS DIRECTORY

Telephone area codes
The international direct dialling (IDD) code for American Samoa is +1 684, followed by subscriber's number.

Useful telephone numbers
Police, fire and ambulance911

Chambers of Commerce
American Samoa Chamber of Commerce, PO Box 2446, Pago Pago 96799 (tel: 699-6214; fax: 699-2219; e-mail: chamber@samoatelco.com).

Banking
Amerika Samoa Bank, PO Box 3790, Pago Pago 96799 (tel: 633-5053; fax: 633-5057).

Bank of Hawaii, PO Box 69, Pago Pago 96799 (tel: 633-4226; fax: 633-2918).
Central bank
Federal Reserve System, 20th Street and Constitution Avenue, NW, Washington DC 20551 (tel: (202) 452-3000; fax: (202) 452-3819).

Travel information
Flight information: (tel: 699-9101, 0800-2200).

Pago Pago International Airport, PO Box 1539, Pago Pago 96799 (tel: 699-9101/2/3; fax: 633-5281).
National tourist organisation offices
Office of Tourism, Convention Centre, Pago Pago, 96799 (tel: 633-1091/92/93; fax: 633-1094).

Ministries
Department of Commerce, Economic Development, American Samoa Government, Pago Page, American Samoa 96799 (tel: 84-633-5155; fax: 684-633-4195; email: Azodiacal@doc.asg.as

Other useful addresses
Office of Economic Development and Planning, Territorial Planning Commission, Pago Pago, 96799 (tel: 633-5156).

Office of the Governor, American Samoa Government, Pago Pago (tel: 633-4828; fax: 633-2269).

Internet sites
Government website: www.asg-gov.net

Office of Tourism: www.amsamoa.com

Samoa News on-line: www.samoanews.com

US Office of Insular Affairs: www.doi.gov/oia

Andorra

COUNTRY PROFILE

Historical profile

One of the world's smallest countries, Andorra is also one of the oldest nations in Europe, established by Charlemagne in 803 as a buffer state against a Muslim Spain.

803 Charlemagne captured the area from Spanish Muslims and his son, Louis the Pious, presented the area's inhabitants with a charter of liberties.

843 The Valls d'Andorra (Valleys of Andorra) were granted to Sunifred, Count of Urgell.

1278 Co-principality established between France (originally represented by a nominee of the king, then the emperor and latterly the president himself) and Spain (in the person of the Bishop of Seu d'Urgel).

1419 A parliament, the Consell de la Terra (Council of the Land), was established to represent the Andorran people.

1866 The Consell General de las Valls (Council of the Valleys) replaced the Council of the Land, during the year of the New Reform, which introduced democratisation to Andorra.

1933–34 The Council of the Valleys was temporarily dissolved by the courts. Elections were held and all men over 25 years were granted the right to vote.

1981 Constitutional reforms were enacted to move power away from the feudal co-princes and towards the parliament.

1983 Income tax was introduced following public spending needed for storm damage and a general recession.

1985 Universal suffrage was introduced.

1991 Andorra joined a customs union with the EU.

1993 Andorra introduced a new constitution, establishing the country as a sovereign parliamentary democracy, and a new 28-member parliament, the Consell General (General Council). The first elections were won by Agrupament Nacional Democratic (AND) (National Democratic Grouping).

1994 A coalition government was formed, led by Unió Liberal (UL). Marc Forné Molné of the Partit Liberal Andorra's (PLA) (Liberal Party of Andorra) was elected prime minister by the General Council.

2001 The PLA was re-elected.

2002 The Organisation for Economic Co-operation and Development (OECD) blacklisted Andorra as a tax haven with 'prejudicial' tax practices. The principality refused to agree to lift the secrecy surrounding its banking sector. Préfet Philippe Massoni was appointed representative of the President of France in Andorra.

2003 Joan Enric Vives Sicília succeeded Joan Martí Alanís as Bishop of Seu d'Urgel and *ex officio* co-prince of Andorra.

2004 An agreement on a Savings Tax Directive concerning tax withholding and savings between the EU and Andorra was reached.

2005 The ruling PLA won general elections and Albert Pintat Santolària was elected head of government.

2006 Measures to reform the economy and improve the country's reputation as a financial centre were adopted

2007 Nicolas Sarkozy, as president of the French Republic, became co-prince.

2009 Andorra agreed to lift its banking secrecy laws, allowing it to be removed from the OECD blacklist. In parliamentary elections, the opposition PSD won 45.03 per cent of the vote, (14 seats out of 28). The ruling party contested the election as part of the Coalició Reformista (CR) (Reformist Coalition) (with three other parties) and together won 32.34 per cent (11 seats). Turnout was 75.3 per cent. In the first round of elections for Cap de Govern (head of government) held in May, no candidate won an absolute majority. In June Jaume Bartumeu (PSD) won a majority vote of 14 to become Cap de Govern.

2011 Parliamentary elections were held on 3 April – they had been called early due to the failure by parliament to pass the budget and important legislation on value added tax (VAT). The opposition, Demòcrates per Andorra (Democrats for Andorra) (Democrats), a successor to the RF, won 71.4 per cent of the vote (20 seats out of 28), PSD 21.4 per cent (six), Lauredian Union 7.1 per cent (two); two other political parties failed to win any seats. Turnout was 74.1 per cent. Antoni Marti, leader of the Democrats was elected prime minister by parliament on 11 May, with 21 votes (out of 28).

Political structure

Constitution

The first written constitution was adopted 14 March 1993 after a referendum. The

KEY FACTS

Official name: Principat d'Andorra (Principality of Andorra)

Head of State: Co-Princes: Bishop of Seu d'Urgel (Spain), Joan Enric Vives i Sicília (from 2003) and President Nicolas Sarkozy (France) (from 2007)

Head of government: Cap de Govern Antoni Marti Petit (from 11 May 2010)

Ruling party: Demòcrates per Andorra (Democrats for Andorra) (Democrats) (from 3 Apr 2011)

Area: 468 square km

Population: 85,000 (2010)*

Capital: Andorra la Vella

Official language: Catalan

Currency: Euro (€) = 100 cents

Exchange rate: €0.75 per US$ (Oct 2011)

GDP per capita: US$44,900 (2008)*

GDP real growth: 2.60% (2008)*

Labour force: 42,220 (2008)

Unemployment: 7.00% (2008)

Inflation: 2.30% (2008)

* estimated figure

constitution allows Andorra to hold full sovereignty, to be able to form trade unions and political parties, and to have an independent judiciary. It can also decide its own foreign policy and join international organisations.

Form of state

Andorra is a co-principality under the joint sovereignty of the President of France and the Spanish Bishop of Seu d'Urgel, who are represented locally by officials called *verguers*.

The executive

The co-princes (the Bishop of Seu d'Urgel and President of France), are titular heads of state. The country is governed by an administration formed by the party or coalition with the largest number of seats in the legislature.

National legislature

The unicameral General Council (Consell General, Consell General de les Valls) has 28 members, who serve for four-year terms, of which, 14 elected by proportional representation in a single national constituency and 14 are elected by seven *parroquies*, or parishes from a national list. The General Council elects the Cap de Govern (head of government) (subject to the approval by the co-princes), who is leader of the largest party and who presides over the executive council.

Legal system

Independent judiciary

Last elections

3 April 2011 (parliamentary)

Results: Parliamentary: Demòcrates per Andorra (Democrats for Andorra) (Democrats) won 71.4 per cent of the vote (20 seats out of 28), Partit Socialdemòcrata (PSD) (Social Democratic Party) 21.4 per cent (six), Unió Laurediana (Lauredian Union), 7.1 per cent (two); two other political parties failed to win any seats. Turnout was 74.1 per cent.

Next elections

2015 (parliamentary)

Political parties

Ruling party

Demòcrates per Andorra (Democrats for Andorra) (Democrats) (from 3 Apr 2011)

Main opposition party

Partit Socialdemòcrata (PSD) (Social Democratic Party)

Population

86,000 (2009)*

Last census: July 2000: 66,089

Population density: 147 people per square km.

Annual growth rate: 0.7 per cent 1994–2004 (WHO 2006)

Ethnic make-up

Of Andorra's total population, only about 33 per cent are natives with the right to vote. The rest include Spaniards (43 per cent), Portuguese (11 per cent), French (7 per cent), English, Australians, Moroccans and others (6 per cent).

Religions

Roman Catholicism is predominant.

Education

A range of universal, free public French, Spanish and Andorran lay schools provide education up to secondary level. Although schools are built and maintained by Andorran authorities, teachers are paid for the most part by France or Spain. The government provides free nursery schools, although supply falls short of demand. About 50 per cent of Andorran children attend the French primary schools, and the rest attend Spanish or Andorran schools. In July 1997, the University of Andorra was established, which serves principally as a centre for virtual studies, connected to Spanish and French universities. The only two graduate schools in Andorra are the Nursing School and the School of Computer Science.

Compulsory years: Four to 16

Health

Life expectancy: 80 years, 2004 (WHO 2006)

Fertility rate/Maternal mortality rate: 1.3 births per woman, 2004 (WHO 2006)

Birth rate/Death rate: 5.4 deaths to 10.29 births per 1,000 population (World Bank).

Child (under 5 years) mortality rate (per 1,000): 6 per 1,000 live births (World Bank)

Welfare

Social security in Andorra is based on a points system with two distinct programmes covering health and old-age insurance.

Health insurance covers illness, pregnancy, accidents at work, disability and death. Social security payments cover nearly 75 per cent and 90 per cent of expenditure relating to illness and hospitalisation respectively. There is no discrimination against disabled persons in employment, education, or in the provision of other state services.

Unemployment benefit includes 50 per cent of the average salary calculated in the first month and 66 per cent calculated from the second month onwards.

Pensions

People pay contributions towards their old-age pension and on retirement receive a pension proportional to the number of points collected. All salaried workers pay contributions to the Andorran Social Security Fund (CASS). Old-age pension is paid to those covered from the age of 65.

Family support

Maternity care and childbirth are fully covered by social security, while disability benefits are calculated in each individual case.

Main cities

Andorra la Vella (capital, estimated population 25,204 in 2008), Les Escaldes (16,387), Encamp (14,861), Sant Julia de Loria (10,041).

Languages spoken

French and Castilian

Official language/s

Catalan

Media

The constitution guarantees the freedom of speech and of the press.

Press

In Catalan, there are several newspapers including the *Diari d'Andorra* (www.diariandorra.ad), *Bondia* (www.bondia.ad), and *El Periodic d'Andorra* (www.elperiodico.com).

Broadcasting

Radio Televisio d'Andorra (RTVA) (www.rtvasa.ad) is the national broadcaster; Spanish TV also broadcasts in Andorra (www.tvc.cat). All TV services are provided by digital technology.

Radio: Radio Nacional d'Andorra (RNA) is the only public station. Privately-owned commercial stations include Radio Valira, Andorra 1 (www.andorra1.ad) and Andorra 7 (www.andorra7radio.com).

Radio signals from Spain and France can be picked up with ease.

Economy

With more than 10 million visitors a year, Andorra is heavily reliant on the tourist sector, which accounts for around 80 per cent of GDP. Financial services are an important magnet for foreign investment.

Andorra is a tax haven with a banking system aimed at attracting foreign private funds.

Andorra was removed from the OECD's list of unco-operative tax havens in 2009, following Andorra's agreement to operate equivalent measures in transparency and information exchange regarding taxation of income from savings as other EU member states.

There is a very small-scale agriculture sector, given Andorra has only some 2 per cent of arable land; tobacco and sheep farming are the principal produce. Consequently, there is a heavy reliance on food imports. Light industry in Andorra consists almost entirely of tobacco products, handicrafts and furniture, which are the primary exports.

The most important activities of the service sector are commerce and the hotel trade, which employ almost 40 per cent of the workforce. There are insufficient modern

and dynamic services, such as specialised services for businesses, and a reliance on traditional sectors limits the economy's potential.
Andorra is a member of the EU customs union and is treated as an EU member with no tariffs on manufactured goods when trading with EU members.

External trade
As a member of the European Union Customs Union with favourable excise duties Andorra is a major entrepôt for numerous European goods. However, Andorra is treated as a non-EU member and its agricultural products are subject to tariffs.
Spain and France are Andorra's main export partners.
The nearly 3km long Envalira tunnel, between Andorra and France, runs under the highest mountain pass in Europe. It is one of the longest road tunnels in the world.

Imports
Three-quarters of Andorra's revenue is from import tariffs. Main imports are foodstuffs, electricity, raw materials, manufactures and consumer goods.
Main sources: Spain (typically over 50 per cent of total), France (over 20 per cent), US (1 per cent)

Exports
The volume of exports is typically under 5 per cent of GDP, a figure far below that of most OECD countries, indicating the unusual nature of the economy, based on retail sales to tourists. Main exports include tobacco products and furniture.
EU members take 99.5 per cent of total exports.
Main destinations: Spain (typically over 50 per cent of total), France (over 30 per cent).

Agriculture
The agricultural sector is a small part of the economy and typically employs less than 1 per cent of the working population. Agricultural production is limited by a scarcity of arable land, and most food has to be imported. Milk is sourced domestically. Principal crops are tobacco and potatoes, rye, wheat, barley, oats. Some other vegetables are also grown.
The principal livestock activity is sheep husbandry.
Land use: 2 per cent permanent crops, 56 per cent forest and woodland, 20 per cent irrigated land.
Andorra imports fish from Spain for domestic needs. Trout are plentiful in streams.
Logs are transported to Spain. Most reforestation is in pines.

Industry and manufacturing
The industrial sector has fallen to around 20 per cent of economic activity. The small manufacturing sector primarily services tourism, but also includes cigarettes, cigars and furniture.

Tourism
The Andorran economy is heavily dependent on tourism with 10.5 million visitors in 2009. It is very well known as a winter destination, with an established infrastructure catering for its many skiing tourists. During summer it caters for the active tourist and those favouring spa holidays. It also relies on day-trippers who visit the principality to shop for duty-free consumer and luxury items. The number of visitors not arriving from either Spain or France did not rise above 40,000 in 2009.
Despite the detrimental impact on tourism in Europe of the global economic crisis, Andorra did not experience either a drop in visitor numbers or weakness in business growth in the tourist industry during the late 2000s. This was probably due to the perception of Andorra as a destination as good value for money for most Europeans.

Environment
Current issues are deforestation and overgrazing of mountain meadows contributing to soil erosion. Natural hazards include snowslides and avalanches.

Mining
Forges in Andorra were once famed. There are small amounts of iron ore and lead but access is a problem.

Hydrocarbons
Even though Andorra has good hydroelectric facilities, around three-quarters of energy consumed is by imported oil from France and Spain. It does not import coal or natural gas.

Energy
Electricity demand is estimated at 500GWh, of which around 50 per cent is supplied by Endesa of Spain, and the remainder by Electricité de France (EDF) and the country's only hydroelectric plant.

Banking and insurance
The banking sector with its tax haven status contributes substantially to the economy. Seven commercial banks operate some 34 branches. Strict secrecy laws are maintained.
Andorra's financial service sector is benefiting from the eurozone which provides greater stability and enhanced opportunities. After being denounced as an unco-operative tax haven by the OECD in 2003, Andorra conceded to EU standards regarding taxation of income from savings. From 2005 Andorra has imposed a withholding tax, up to 35 per cent, which is passed to the tax department of an EU citizen's country. Instead of informing the relevant EU country about the amount of money in savings accounts, the anonymity of the saver is preserved. In an effort to avoid joining the global list of non-co-operative tax havens, held by the Organisation of Economic Co-operation and Development (OECD), Andorra eased its banking laws to allow the sharing of bank data that cracks down on offshore tax evasion.
Andorra has also agreed to supply information on tax fraud, for criminal or civil trials, and notify EU member states about additional malpractices.

Central bank
European Central Bank (ECB)

Time
GMT plus one hour (daylight saving, late March to late October, GMT plus two hours)

Geography
Andorra lies high in the eastern Pyrenees mountains in south-western Europe. The lowest elevation is 838 metres, reaching to nearly 3,000 metres at the peak of Coma Pedrosa. Andorra is landlocked, sharing borders with France and Spain.

Hemisphere
Northern

Climate
Warm summers and moderately cold winters; temperatures range from 0–30 degrees Celsius.

Entry requirements
Passports
Required by all except for nationals of France and Spain, who only require an identity card.

Visa
Not required, but the relevant regulations of Spain and France, depending on point of transit, should be followed. Stays of up to three months without a visa are allowed.

Currency advice/regulations
No currency restrictions.

Health (for visitors)
Mandatory precautions
None

Advisable precautions
Up-to-date tetanus, Measles-mumps-rubella, varicella and polio immunisations are recommended; also influenza if visiting Nov-Apr.

Hotels
Around 270 hotels, most with modern facilities.

Public holidays (national)
Fixed dates
1 Jan (New Year's Day), 6 Jan (Epiphany), 14 Mar (Constitution Day), 1 May (Labour Day), 24 Jun (St John's Day), 15 Aug (Assumption Day), 8 Sep (Mare de Déu de Meritxell, National Day), 1 Nov (All Saints

Day), 4 Nov (St Charles Day), 8 Dec (Immaculate Conception), 24 Dec (Christmas Eve), 25–26 Dec (Christmas Holiday), 31 Dec (New Year's Eve).

Variable dates

Good Friday, Easter Monday, Ascension Day, Whit Monday.

Working hours

Banking

Mon–Fri: 0900–1300, 1500–1700; Sat: 0900–1200.

Business

Considerable variation in times, depending on whether following French or Spanish working practices.

Shops

Mon–Fri: 0900–2000; Sat: 0900–2100; Sun: 0900–1900.

Getting there

Air

International airport/s: The closest international airports are located in France (Toulouse-Blagnac, 180km) and Spain (Barcelona, 200km), connecting to inter- and intra-continental destinations. Approximately three hours drive. Regular shuttle bus services connect both airports with Andorra.

Surface

Road: From Spain: Barcelona-Andorra via Cervera; Barcelona-Andorra via Calaf; Barcelona-Andorra via Solsonal. Madrid-Andorra via Zaragoza. Buses run regularly from Barcelona and Madrid. Other road connections to Lleida, Puigcerdà, Tarragona and Girona. Mountainous roads exist over the Envalira pass to Perpignan, Tarbes and Toulouse.
From France: Paris-Andorra via Aix-les-Thermes; Marseilles-Andorra via Perpignan; Biarritz via St Gaudens.
A road runs from the Spanish to the French frontiers through Saint Julia, Andorra la Vella, Escaldes-Engordonay, Encamp, Camnillo and Soldeu.

Rail: From Spain: Barcelona to Puigcerda, then by bus to La Seu d'Urgel and Andorra. Madrid to Lleida, then bus to La Seu d'Urgel and Andorra.
From France: Paris to Aix-les-Thermes or L'Hospitalet, then bus to Andorra; Perpignan to La Tour de Carol, then bus to Andorra .

Getting about

National transport

Road: There are 269km of roads, of which 198km are paved. Roads can be blocked by snow in winter and congestion in summer.

Buses: Constant minibus services link all the villages.

BUSINESS DIRECTORY

The addresses listed below are a selection only. While World of Information makes every endeavour to check these addresses, we cannot guarantee that changes have not been made, especially to telephone numbers and area codes. We would welcome any corrections.

Telephone area codes

The international direct dialling (IDD) code for Andorra is +376, followed by customer's number.

Useful telephone numbers

Mountain rescue: 112
Police: 110
Fire: 118
Ambulance: 118

Chambers of Commerce

Andorra Chamber of Commerce, Industry and Services, C/Prat de la Creu 8, Edifice le Mans 204, Andorra La Vella (tel: 809-292; fax: 809-293; e-mail: ccis@andorra.ad).

Banking

Banc Agricol i Comercial d'Andorra, Mossen Cinto 6, Andorra la Vella (tel: 821-333).

Banca Cassany SA, Avinguda Meritxell 39-41, Andorra la Vella.

Banc Internacional, Avinguda Meritxell 32, Andorra la Vella (tel: 820-037).

Banca Mora SA, Placa Coprinceps 2, Les Escaldes (tel: 820-607).

Banca Reig, Avinguda Meritxell, Andorra la Vella (tel: 822-618).

Credit Andorra, Avinguda Princep Benlloch 19, Andorra la Vella (tel: 820-326).

La Caixa, Pl Rebés, Andorra la Vella (tel: 820-015).

Central bank

European Central Bank (ECB), Kaiserstrasse 29, D-60311 Frankfurt am Main, Germany (tel: +49(69) 13-440; fax: +49(69) 1344-6000).

Travel information

Caseta d'Informació i Turisme (tourism kiosk opposite Restaurant Martí), Andorra la Vella (tel: 827-117).

Sindicat d'Iniciativa Oficina de Turisme (national tourist office at the top of Carrer Doctor Vilanova between Plaça del Poble and Plaça Rebés), Andorra la Vella (tel: 820-214).

Ministries

Government of Andorra, C/ Prat de la Creu 62, Andorra La Vella (tel: 829-345; internet: www.govern.ad).

Ministry of Finance, Andorra la Vella (tel: 829-245).

Ministry of Commerce, Industry and Agriculture, Andorra la Vella.

Ministry of Tourism and Environment, C/Prat de la Creu, Andorra la Vella (tel: 875-7 02; fax: 860-184; e-mail: turisme@andorra.ad)

Other useful addresses

French Embassy, C/ Les Canals 38-40, Andorra La Vella (tel: 820-809).

French Post Office, C/Bonaventura Armengol, Andorra la Vella (tel: 820-408).

General Syndic's Office (tel: 821-234).

Pas de la Casa Customs Post (Andorran frontier with France) (tel: 855-120).

Police, Andorra la Vella (tel: 821-222).

Sant Julia de Loria Customs Post (Andorran frontier with Spain) (tel: 841-090).

Servei de Telecomunicacions d'Andorra STA, Avinguda Meritxell 110, Andorra la Vella (tel: 821-021).

Sindicat d'Iniciativa de les Valls d'Andorra, c/Dr Vilanova, Andorra la Vella (tel: 820-214).

Spanish Embassy, C/ Prat de la Creu 34, Andorra La Vella (tel: 820-013).

Spanish Post Office, c/o Joan Maragall, Andorra la Vella (tel: 820-257).

Internet sites

Only Andorra yellow pages: www.onlyandorra.com

Andorra information: www.andorra.ad/

Angola

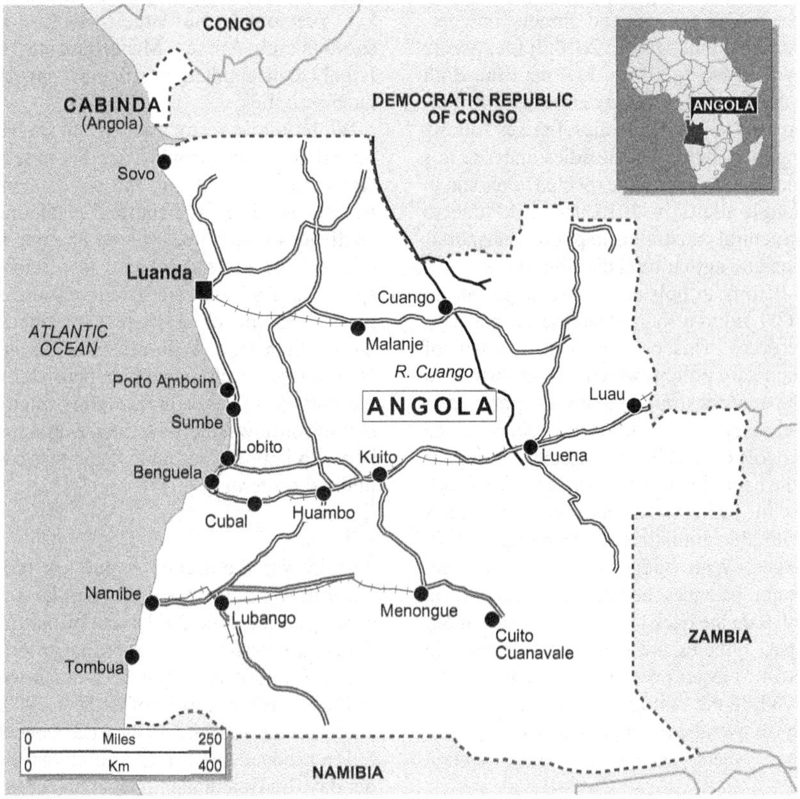

Angola, with its oil wealth, is one of the richest countries in Africa, yet the United Nations Development Programme estimates that some 54 per cent of the population lives on less than US$1.25 a day. The rural/urban divide is widening with official data putting the proportion of the rural population living below the national poverty line at. 58 per cent compared to 19 per cent in urban areas. On top of this Angola has slipped from 143rd to 146th on the United Nation's Human Development Index. In an attempt to rectify this the 2011 budget allocated a total of around 30 per cent for 'social expenditure'. Of this 8 per cent is for education, 3.8 per cent health, 12.8 per cent social protection, 1.3 per cent culture, 4.9 per cent housing and community development, and 0.8 per cent environmental protection.

After nearly 30 years or war, Angola is still struggling to improve its infrastructure. The administration and implementation of government planning is hampered by a lack of human resources, partly as a result of years of under-funding of education, partly because so many qualified Angolans have left the country, and partly because those that have stayed prefer to work in the urban centres, especially the capital, Luanda, rather than the country side.

The president rules

The Movimento Popular de Libertação de Angola (MPLA) (Popular Movement for the Liberation of Angola)'s landslide victory in the 2008 elections has led to a further concentration of power in the hands of President José Eduardo dos Santos, who has ruled since 1979. The constitution that was adopted in 2010 abolished presidential elections; in their stead the nominated leader of the ruling party becomes president and head of state. The vice president has replaced the prime

KEY FACTS

Official name: Republica de Angola (Republic of Angola)

Head of State: President José Eduardo dos Santos (since 1979; re-elected 1992)

Head of government: Vice President Fernando da Piedade Dias dos Santos (appointed 3 Feb 2010)

Ruling party: Movimento Popular de Libertação de Angola (MPLA) (Popular Movement for the Liberation of Angola) (from 30 Sep 2008)

Area: 1,246,700 square km

Population: 19,08 million (2010)*

Capital: Luanda

Official language: Portuguese

Currency: Kwanza (Kz) = 100 Lwei

Exchange rate: Kz94.69 per US$ (Oct 2011)

GDP per capita: US$4,329 (2010)

GDP real growth: 3.40% (2010)

GDP: US$82.50 billion (2010)

Labour force: 7.98 million (2010)

Inflation: 14.50% (2010)

Oil production: 1.85 million bpd (2010)

Balance of trade: US$18.17 billion (2009)

* estimated figure

minister as head of government in theory, but in fact is directly under the president's authority. Although the constitution sets a two term limit (of five years each) on presidents, the first elections under the new constitution will not be until 2012. If, as is expected, Mr Santos wins it is possible that he will be president until 2022, meaning he will have been in power for more than 40 years.The economy

Angola's economy is largely dependent on the oil sector, which accounts for 95 per cent of exports. The collapse in oil prices and demand in 2009 therefore had an adverse affect on the economy. For years one of the fastest growing economies in the world, Angola's gross domestic product (GDP) growth was just 3.4 per cent in 2010, after 2.4 per cent in 2009 (and down from 13.8 per cent in 2008). Despite the recovery in oil prices, growth was hampered by government arrears in construction and infrastructure payments. The outlook is good however and growth is expected to reach 7.5 per cent in 2011 buoyed by high oil prices and by the resumption of the government's Public Investment Programme (PIP).

According to the *African Economic Outlook 2010* (AEO), published jointly by the African Development Bank and the Organisation for Economic Co-operation and Development, the economy remains largely driven by public investment, which is blighted by political patronage and corruption. National planning programmes continue to highlight the need for better co-ordination of public policies, and there is a clear need for a national infrastructure development policy. Efforts are currently being taken to boost the private sector and decrease reliance on public investment.

Inflation remains a challenge for Angola. After years of sustained decreases, inflation rose by 6 per cent in 2008 to reach 13.7 per cent and climbed one percentage point again in 2010. It is expected to decrease in 2011 to 11.7 per cent. Both a deteriorating exchange rate and sharp increases in petrol and diesel prices following the removal of subsidies underlie this increase. Inflation is expected to remain in double digits in 2010 and 2011 due to structural constraints in public transportation and agricultural distribution.

Efforts to bolster the exchange rate in 2009 led to a sharp decrease in monetary reserves. This prompted an overhaul of monetary policy, which was enshrined in the new constitution that was approved in February 2010. The Banco Nacional de Angola (BNA) (National Bank of Angola) (the central bank) now shares responsibility for interest and exchange rate policies with the ministries of planning and finance. With budgetary and current account balances beginning to recover in 2010 on the back of rising oil prices, monetary policies are expected to loosen in 2011 to foster private sector activity.

While the non-oil sector has expanded by an average of 14 per cent over the past four years, economic diversification remains shallow. The construction and infrastructure sectors are heavily dependent on the PIP, while growth in agriculture more adequately reflects a catch up after the country's 27-year war that ended in 2002. Commerce, which developed informally during the war, was severely disrupted in 2010 by the government's displacement of the Roque Santeiro market, previously the largest market in sub-Saharan Africa. Manufacturing is largely concentrated in oil- and gas-related activities.

While public sector capacity to crowd out private investment in a number of sectors remains a concern, the government has managed great social and economic challenges since 2002 without any major outbreak of violence. There is a widespread lack of qualified human resources that acts as a major constraint to growth in the medium term. With an ambitious infrastructure development plan boosted by the country's first credit risk rating and by massive inflows of credit, the government hopes to improve access to basic services in the short term.

Oil

Angola was the second largest oil producer in Africa in 2010 after Nigeria. According to the June 2011 issue of the *BP Statistical Review of World Energy* Angola's oil reserves were 13.5 thousand million barrels at the end of 2010. In 2010, the oil sector was hard hit by a 1.2 per cent fall in production (to 1.78 million barrels per day (bpd)) although the partial recovery in world prices (from a 34.2 per cent drop in 2009, prices rebounded by 24.7 per cent in 2010) eased the effect. Production is expected to recover to 1.85 million bpd in 2011 (almost three times the production of 746,000bpd of a decade earlier) and 2.05 million bpd in 2012. Angola's production quota as set by the Organisation of the Petroleum Exporting Countries (Opec) is 1.65 million bpd.

Although uncertainty surrounds ultra deepwater extraction following the catastrophic Gulf of Mexico spill in 2010, several foreign companies are involved in prospecting off Angola's shores. The outlook remains good. In August 2010, French-owned Total announced works on the water fields north of Luanda that are estimated to contain about 500 million barrels of oil and production is scheduled to begin in 2014. The Italian company ENI also made two new discoveries in March 2010 in the waters off Soyo in the northern region of the country. The previous bidding round for offshore rights had

KEY INDICATORS — Angola

	Unit	2006	2007	2008	2009	2010
Population	m	*15.86	*16.33	*16.81	*17.31	*19.08
Gross domestic product (GDP)	US$bn	45.17	61.36	83.40	68.80	82.50
GDP per capita	US$	2,847	3,757	4,961	3,972	4,329
GDP real growth	%	18.6	22.6	13.8	2.4	3.4
Inflation	%	18.6	21.1	12.5	14.0	14.5
Industrial output	% change	20.0	19.6	9.8	0.4	–
Agricultural output	% change	8.9	21.0	1.8	29.0	–
Oil output	'000 bpd	1,409.0	1,723.0	1,880.0	1,784.0	1,851.0
Exports (fob) (goods)	US$m	31,862.0	44,396.2	63,913.9	40,827.9	–
Imports (fob) (goods)	US$m	9,586.0	13,661.5	20,982.2	22,659.9	–
Balance of trade	US$m	22,276.0	30,734.7	42,931.8	18,168.0	–
Current account	US$m	10,538.0	6,747.0	6,408.0	-7,571.7	-1,495.0
Total reserves minus gold	US$m	8,598.6	11,196.8	18,359.4	13,664.1	19,749.5
Foreign exchange	US$m	8,598.4	11,196.5	18,359.1	13,238.5	19,339.3
Exchange rate	per US$	80.28	75.10	75.01	79.33	91.91

* estimated figure

been suspended in 2008 following the first post-war legislative elections but the government is aiming to launch a new round in 2011.

Refining, storage, transportation and distribution of petroleum products are currently held under a monopoly by Sonangol, the state-owned oil company, but these activities are scheduled for liberalisation by 2012. Sonangol has increasing interests in foreign oil exploration and production, and in December 2010 it embarked on a joint venture with Venezuelan and Cuban state oil companies to develop oilfields in Venezuela. Sonangol has taken steps to increase transparency as it broadens its reach into new markets by hiring Ernst & Young to audit its accounts.

In terms of oil-related manufacturing, in 2010 Angoflex (a joint venture between Sonangol and French-owned Technip) became the first Angolan company to supply an oil industry project abroad, in Ghana. Angola is expecting to meet growing demand for pipes for gas and oil transportation in the West African market. Angoflex increased production from 80 to 200 pipes per day in the first quarter of 2010, and expects to grow further to 500 pipes daily.

The construction of Angola's long-awaited new oil refinery, Sonaref has begun and operations are expected to begin in 2014 with more than 1,000 jobs being created. The Sonangol-owned facility in Lobito will have an initial capacity to process 115,000bpd, 50 per cent of which will be exported. Despite being an oil-producing country, Angola imports energy and it is expected that Sonaref will enable the country to reduce its 2009 US$1.6 million bill on imported refined crude. Currently, the sole refinery in the country processes just 37,500bpd covering only 30 per cent of domestic needs.

Angola has substantial natural gas reserves estimated at 297 billion cubic meters (bcm), the second largest in Africa. In order the capitalise on this resource, the government has embarked on a project to build a natural gas plant (Angola LNG). Situated in Zaire province, Angola LNG represents the country's largest single investment ever and should process 5 million tonnes of liquefied petroleum gas (LPG) per year mostly bound for the US market. With the execution rate of construction running at 69 per cent in the second quarter of 2010, the first exports should be bound for Mississippi in the first quarter of 2012.

Diamonds, copper and iron ore

Mining is still concentrated on oil and diamonds although the resumption of pre-war exploitations of iron ore, gold and copper is underway. Although the diamond industry, Angola's second largest export commodity after oil, was hard hit by the steep drop in world prices and low demand in the wake of the global economic crisis, tariffs rose by 43.5 per cent in 2010 to US$114.2 per quilate. The state-run diamond company Empresa Nacional dos Diamantes de Angola (Endiama) contracted its production by 2.4 per cent in 2010, though this is expected to expand by 18.2 per cent in 2011 and 41.7 per cent in 2012. Endiama is resuming its pre-crisis investments and is reactivating the suspended fields.

The move to diversify Angola's mining base away from diamonds is underway. Copper mining, Angola's second production after diamonds prior to 1963, will soon resume in the Mavoio region in the northern province of Uíge. Monthly production of 20,000 tonnes of pure copper is expected. In September 2010, state-owned Empresa Nacional de Ferro de Angola (Ferrangol) (National Iron Ore Company of Angola) committed to investing US$1 billion over four years to develop the Cassinga project in the southern Huila province, an area rich in iron ore, manganese and gold deposits. Production in this region was interrupted by the civil war over 30 years ago.

Agriculture

Despite contributing only 10.6 per cent of GDP in 2009, agriculture is the fastest growing sector (up 11.5 per cent in 2010 and 25.9 per cent in 2009) although it has yet to recover from the losses of the civil war. With the help of international donors and a credit line from the China Development Bank, the government has been investing heavily in agriculture as part of a US$1.2 billion 2009–12 investment plan. It aims to tackle food insecurity which currently threatens 10–15 per cent of the population, to reduce costly food imports and to boost employment. With less than 30 per cent of arable land under cultivation, the potential for extensive agriculture is huge. Intensive farming is also needed to raise productivity. In 2010, a US$350 million credit line was set up for medium and small-scale producers and peasants' associations to enable them to finance the purchase of seeds, fertiliser and small-scale farming instruments, as well as to finance investments aimed at expanding farming areas and increasing production.

Refugees

The United Nations High Commission for Refugees (UNHCR) estimates that there are still over 100,000 Angolan refugees: 70,000 in the Democratic Republic of Congo (DRC), 25,000 in Zambia, 6,000 in Namibia and 2,000 in Congo (Brazzaville). At the end of 2011 these refugees will loose their war refugee status. Those that choose to return to Angola will give the government yet another challenge, in finding accommodation, education, health facilities and jobs.

HIV/AIDS prevalence remains low in Angola, a result of the isolation experienced during its long war. The official goal to keep HIV/AIDS prevalence below 3 per cent of the population is officially on track.

Unemployment is still very high and has been affected by the recent global economic crisis. It is estimated to be between 24.1 per cent and 26.3 per cent and the purchasing power loss to be 1.15 per cent for 2009 and 31 per cent for the 2003–09 period. The public administration remains the largest formal employer, revealing the limited extent to which growth has stimulated the creation of jobs in the private sector.

Risk assessment

Politics	Fair
Economy	Fair
Regional stability	Fair

COUNTRY PROFILE

Historical profile

1482 The Portuguese arrived in Angola, which became a staging post for trade with India and south-east Asia.

1575 The Portuguese founded Luanda. The country became a major source of slaves, who were transported to Brazil.

1836 The slave trade was abolished.

1885 The borders of Angola were set following the Berlin Conference of imperial powers who, with an eye on exploitable assets in Africa, agreed to formal boundaries. Angola provided Portugal with minerals and agricultural products.

1951 Angola's status changed from a colony to an overseas territory.

1956 The Movimento Popular de Libertação de Angola (MPLA) (Popular Movement for the Liberation of Angola) was founded as a guerrilla force fighting Portuguese rule.

1961 An uprising in which 50,000 Angolans were massacred led to increased repression by colonial security forces.

1962 The Frente Nacional para a Libertacao de Angola (FNLA) (National Front for the Liberation of Angola) was formed by refugees of the uprising, living mainly in what is now the Democratic Republic of Congo.
1966 The União Nacional de Independencia Total de Angola (Unita) (National Union for the Total Independence of Angola) was formed.
1972 The FNLA and MPLA assumed joint leadership of the liberation struggle.
1975 Angola gained independence from Portugal. Scheduled elections failed to take place when the MPLA took power. Unita and the FNLA formed an alliance aimed at defeating the MPLA government.
1979 José dos Santos (MPLA) became president, backed by the Soviet Union and Cuba. A civil war ensued, with Unita supported by the US and South Africa.
1988 An agreement between South Africa, Angola and Cuba was signed, all foreign troops to be withdrawn by mid-1991.
1990 A UN mission, to verify Cuban troop withdrawals, was initiated.
1991 The MPLA officially dropped its commitment to Marxism-Leninism in favour of social democracy. Talks with Unita began and Cuban troops withdrew. The Bicesse Accords, sponsored by the UN and signed by the MPLA and Unita, recognised fundamental rights and duties based on the principles of the major international treaties on human rights to which Angola is a signatory, and established multi-party politics.
1992 The first multi-party elections resulted in a coalition government formed by the MPLA and minor parties. The newly-legalised Unita lost and rejected the election results, ending the UN-brokered cease-fire.
1994 A cease-fire peace agreement, the *Lusaka Protocol*, was signed between the government and Unita.
1997 Unita joined the ruling MPLA in a power-sharing government of national unity, however, it did not disarm.
1998 Renewed hostilities between MPLA and Unita broke out.
2002 Jonas Savimbi, the leader of Unita, was killed by government forces. The Angolan government offered an amnesty for all Unita rebels who surrendered. A cease-fire was signed, ending the civil war. Fernando da Piedade Dias dos Santos became prime minister.
2003 The World Bank approved a US$125 million assistance programme.
2004 More than 3,000 people were arrested in a crackdown on illegal diamond mining and trafficking (around 11,000 illegal migrants were deported in four months).
2006 A cease-fire was signed between the government and the armed militia, Fórum Cabindês para o Diálogo (FCD) (Cabinda Forum for Dialogue), in Cabinda, the rebel Angolan enclave, followed by the formal signing of a *Memorandum for Peace and Reconciliation* in Cabinda. Angola joined the Organisation of Petroleum Exporting Countries (OPEC) as a full member.
2008 The first parliamentary elections since 1992 were finally held; the ruling MPLA won 81.64 per cent of votes and 191 seats (out of 220). International observers reported that the election had not been free and fair and that there had been faults with the voting systems, particularly in Luanda. The president appointed Paulo Kassoma (MPLA) as the new prime minister.
2009 TAAG, the national airline, posted a loss of US$70 million after it had been banned from EU airspace in 2007. Later, the EU allowed TAAG to operate out of Portugal only and only with certain aircraft and under very strict conditions. Russian President Dmitry Medvedev paid an official visit to Angola.
2010 A new constitution was approved by parliament in January. It abolished direct presidential elections; instead the leader of the largest party in parliament assumes the post of head of state and will not be limited to a fixed number of terms in office. The opposition called it 'a complete fraud' that would lead to 'excessive executive power'. Vice President Fernando da Piedade Dias dos Santos was appointed as head of government in February (in a new post that replaced the office of prime minister), along with a new government. In March the restrictions on TAAG operating in the EU were lifted. Between July–September compiling of a new voter registry began, with responsibility shared between the ministry of state and provincial governments.
2011 On 18 March Angola committed 10.6 per cent of the total US$241.6 million set aside for telecommunications within the public investment programme, for the construction and launch of a Russian-built Angolan satellite in 2012. On 22 June Angola and Russia signed a parliamentary protocol, aimed at sharing legislative and juridical experiences between their respective legislatures.

Political structure

Constitution

Parliament approved a new constitution on 21 January 2010, replacing the interim constitution formulated in 1975. The new constitution officially names the president as Head of State and government as well as commander-in-chief of the armed forces. Direct elections for the presidency were abolished with the majority party in parliament electing its leader as president. Presidential terms in office are limited to two five-year terms – although President Santos, if re-elected, could remain in office until 2022 as the two-term limit will not begin until the 2012 elections. The post of prime minister was abolished and all duties transferred to the office of vice president. The National Assembly can in future remove the president from office following approval by the Supreme Court. Land rights were rectified with the state assuming all land is owned by the state which can decide who may use it; only Angolan nationals and companies registered in Angola will have access to land rights.

Form of state

Unitary republic

The executive

The president is elected by the majority party in parliament and is Head of State and the executive, as well as commander-in-chief of the armed forces. Terms in office are limited to two five-year periods. Presidents appoint their own vice president.

National legislature

The unicameral Assembleia Nacional (National Assembly) has 220 members, of which 130 are elected by proportional representation and 90 elected by provincial councils. The assembly is presumed to sit for four-year terms, but only two general elections have taken place since 1992.

Legal system

The Head of State appoints judges to the Constitutional and Supreme Courts and Head of the Court of Audits. The Judicial Proctorate is appointed for a four-year term of office and may be re-appointed for another four-year term.

Last elections

29–30 September 1992 (presidential); 5–6 September 2008 (parliamentary).

Results: Parliamentary: Movimento Popular de Libertação de Angola (MPLA) (Popular Movement for the Liberation of Angola) won 81.64 per cent of the vote (191 seats out of 220), União Nacional para a Independência Total de Angola (Unita) (National Union for the Total Independence of Angola won 10.39 per cent (16), Partido Renovador Social (PRS) (Social Renewal Party) won 3.17 per cent (8), Nova Democracia União Eleitoral (NDUE) (New Democracy Electoral Union) won 1.20 per cent (2), Frente Nacional de Libertação de Angola (FNLA) (National Front for the Liberation of Angola) won 1.11 per cent (3). Turnout was 87.36 per cent.

Presidential: José Eduardo dos Santos received 49.6 per cent of the votes, making a run-off election necessary between him and second-place Jonas Savimbi; the run-off was not held and Savimbi's Unita disputed the results of the first election and led to a resumption of the civil war. Savimbi's death in 2002 resulted in a cease-fire and the end of the war.

Next elections

September 2012 (parliamentary); due by 2009 but postponed (presidential).

Political parties

Ruling party

Movimento Popular de Libertação de Angola (MPLA) (Popular Movement for the Liberation of Angola) (from 30 Sep 2008)

Main opposition party

União Nacional de Independencia Total de Angola (Unita) (National Union for the Total Independence of Angola)

Population

19.08 million (2010)*

Last census: December 1970: 5,646,166

Population density: 10 inhabitants per square km. Urban population: 34 per cent (1994–2000).

Annual growth rate: 2.6 per cent 1994–2004 (WHO 2006)

Internally Displaced Persons (IDP)

450,000 (UNHCR 2004)

Ethnic make-up

37 per cent Ovimbundu, 25 per cent Mbundu, 13 per cent Bakongo, 2 per cent Mestico (mixed European and indigenous descent), 1 per cent European.

Religions

Traditional beliefs (47 per cent), Christianity (38 per cent), mainly Roman Catholic.

Education

Primary school enrolment has increased slowly, although the increase in male enrolment has been higher than for females. Education expenditure amounts to round 6 per cent of the national budget.

The government allocated US$40 million to hire the graduates of a Unesco scheme, which is set to train around 29,000 school teachers as part of a development programme.

Total expenditure on education is around 3 per cent of GDP.

Literacy rate: 66.8 per cent total; 53.8 per cent female; adult rates.

Compulsory years: 6 to 9

Enrolment rate: 74 per cent gross primary enrolment of relevant age group (including repeater) (World Bank)

Pupils per teacher: 29 in primary schools

Health

Public health has become a priority as Angola's human development indicators are poor, it is recognised to having a high rate of infant mortality and has to repair the damage done by 27 years of civil war. One in four children under aged five are likely to die of malaria, the single largest cause of child mortality.

Until the country can exploit its vast natural resources and raise the living standards of the population as a whole, it has to contend with inadequate numbers of doctors and antiquated medical equipment. Preventative care has been described as almost non-existent and primary care, outside former provincial capitals, limited to infrequent and inadequate drug supplies.

Most doctors, who work within the private sector, live in the capital, Luanda. The government has prepared a large package of incentives to encourage health workers to work in the provinces, however most measures are awaiting the financial resources to implement them.

There were cases of polio reported to the World Health Organisation – Global Polio Eradication Initiative in 2006; the country had previously been free of the disease and its re-emergence was due to infected travellers.

The border between Angola and the Democratic Republic of Congo (DRC) was closed on 6 January 2009 due to an outbreak of Ebola in the Luande Norte province of DRC.

HIV/Aids

While the civil war wrought great destruction on the population, paradoxically it provided a buffer that stopped the disease from gaining a significant hold, as people were prevented from travelling. Now the citizens of Angola are free to travel and with a youthful population the government has taken measures to educate young people concerning the risks of HIV infection. A Unicef study presented in 2003 showed that almost 60 per cent of youths are sexually experienced by aged 15 years, and almost all by aged 18. A third of women had never heard of HIV/Aids and over half did not know that transmission could happen from mother to child. In October 2005 there had been 17,620 cases of HIV/Aids reported. While prevalence rates for countries in the region range between 25–40 per cent and the rate in Angola is only 3.9 per cent, UN agencies are still concerned the following years could determine whether Angola is engulfed by the pandemic, particularly if education and basic health provisions remain lacking.

HIV prevalence: 3.9 per cent aged 15–49 in 2003 (World Bank)

Life expectancy: 40 years, 2004 (WHO 2006)

Fertility rate/Maternal mortality rate: 6.7 births per woman, 2004 (WHO 2006); 1,700 maternal deaths per 100,000 live births (World Bank).

Child (under 5 years) mortality rate : 154 per 1,000 live births (2004); 42 per cent of all children are underweight for their age (World Bank).

Welfare

In 2005 plans to return 22,000 refugees living in Zambia got underway, however by November only 35,000 were able to make the return and the programme was extended into early 2006. The numbers of internally displaced persons (IDPs) total over 100,000 and are unable to return home due to poor access and mine infestation and lack of administrative capacity with basic services virtually non-existent. Mine clearance is ongoing as one in every 415 Angolans has been disabled by landmines, but it is estimated in 2005 that six million more remain to be destroyed.

Main cities

Luanda (capital, estimated population 2.5 million in 2008), Huambo (325,207), Lobito (142,105), Benguela (128,084), Lubango (245,196), Malanje (152,675).

Languages spoken

Local languages: principally Ovimbundu, Kimbundu (the language of the Mbundu), Bakongo and Chokwe.

Official language/s

Portuguese

Media

While the constitution ensures freedom of expression the UNHCR considers Angola does not have press freedom as the government harasses private media outlets and uses anti-defamation laws to protect officials from reports deemed 'offensive'. There is also a special committee that has censorship authority over the media.

Press

There is only one national daily newspaper, operated by the government, in Portuguese *Jornal de Angola* (), referred to as *JA*. Private, independent newspapers are all weekly, including *Angolense* (www.jornalangolense.com), *Semanário Angolense* (www.semanarioangolense.net), *Folha 8*, *A Capital*, *Actual*, *Cruzeiro do Sul* and *Agora*; *Diario de Luanda* is government-owned.

Broadcasting

National media is state-controlled. Independent media is largely based in major cities, particularly Luanda.

Radio: With high levels of illiteracy radio services are important sources of news and information; most households have radios. The state-run Radio Nacional de Angola (RNA) (www.rna.ao) is the only national radio service, which has a network of five stations broadcasting in Portuguese and local languages, as well as some foreign languages. Other private stations include Luanda Antena Comercial

(www.nexus.ao/lac) and Radio Ecclesia (www.recclesia.org), based in Luanda, run by the Roman Catholic Church. As a frequent critic of the government it was denied permission to extend its service into other areas of the country in 2005.
Television: There is a limited national service operated by Televisão Popular de Angola (TPA) (www.tpa.ao).
Pay-TV is available through JumpTV (www.jumptv.com) which carries Portuguese TV programmes from RTP Internacional (RTPi) (http://programas.rtp.pt). TV Cabo (http://www.tvcabo.pt) is a satellite TV network providing international programmes. These services are almost exclusively based in Luanda.

News agencies

National news agency: Angola Press (Angop): www.angolapress-angop.ao AngoNoticias (www.angonoticias.com).

Economy

Industry accounts for some 70 per cent of GDP, of which 5 per cent is manufacturing; oil extraction and refining accounted for around 85 per cent of GDP in 2008. As a result of high global oil prices in 2008, Angola's exports were a record US$61.66 billion, with production at an all-time high of 1,875,000 barrels per day (bpd); reserves were 13.5 billion barrels at the end of 2010. Diamond mining is the only other major industry, with exports increasing in value, so that by 2008 they were US$1.2 billion, and estimated to be US$1.3 billion in 2009. Services account for 26 per cent of GDP, and agriculture 7 per cent, of which subsistence farming for the majority of the population is still the norm; 40 per cent of the population live below the poverty line, according the UN's World Food Programme.
GDP growth dropped dramatically from a record high of 22.6 per cent in 2007 to 13.8 per cent in 2008, which then fell significantly to 2.4 per cent in 2009, as world trade almost ground to a halt and oil exports fell by about 5 per cent. The balance of trade was US$42.9 billion in 2008 and in 2009, although it remained positive, it fell to US$18.16 billion and in turn cut government revenue. GDP growth in 2010 began to rise but only to 3.4 per cent.
The government has undertaken to liberalise the economy but corruption is still seen as widespread and the government as inefficient, largely stemming from local patronage and the generally secretive nature of government.
In 2010, three international credit rating agencies put Angola's for risk rating as the same as Nigeria (B+ or equivalent). As Angola does not suffer the political instability and violence as seen in Nigeria's Niger Delta, the lower than expected ratings were seen as a reflection of international opinion of Angola's governance.

External trade

Angola signed a free trade agreement with the US in May 2009 and is in discussion with the World Trade Organisation (WTO) for membership. Angola is also a member of the Southern African Development Community (SADC).
Angola is the second largest exporter of petroleum in Africa (after Nigeria). Oil, combined with diamonds, accounts for 99.7 per cent of all exports. Angola has been criticised and warned that current accounting practices in the oil industry have led to widespread corruption with the loss of many millions of dollars each year. Oil revenue is mainly used to finance government spending. Tradable goods exports account for only 0.3 per cent. Angola is said to suffer from *Dutch Disease*, with all non-oil local industries being stifled by the otherwise mono-oil based economy.

Imports

Principal imports are refined petroleum products, electrical equipment, vehicles and spare parts, machinery, foodstuffs, medicines, textiles, consumer goods and military materials.
Main sources: Portugal (typically 20 per cent of total), China (15 per cent), US (12 per cent).

Exports

Principal exports are crude oil, gas and derivatives (typically 92 per cent of total), diamonds (8 per cent), marble, coffee, sisal, fish and fish products, timber and cotton.
Main destinations: China (typically 34 per cent of total), US (27 per cent), South Africa (10 per cent).

Agriculture

Farming

Agriculture's share of GDP has slowly begun to rise as production has increased, as more displaced persons and ex-combatants have returned to their farms. Production was still severely hampered by a list of problems in 2005, including lack of seed and animals, as well as fertilisers, equipment and vehicles, landmines, lack of infrastructure, reduced capabilities of institutions and little access to investment. International donors and financial institutions have provided relief funds and personnel to improve the situation.
Even so, food insecurity is widespread and around 50 per cent of the population is undernourished.
Of the major crops, only coffee is produced in exportable volumes, while the cultivation of sisal and cotton has virtually ceased. Several overseas companies are reportedly interested in rehabilitating sugar cane, cotton and sisal estates.
Livestock farming has been disrupted by insecurity, the neglect of veterinary services and recurrent droughts have affected much of the south and centre of Angola.

Fishing

The fishing sector represents less than 5 per cent of GDP. Government policy is aimed at increasing the amount of foreign fishing operations in territorial waters in order to increase foreign investment in the sector and increase licence revenue.
Angola's 1,600km coastline offers some of the richest fishing grounds in Africa, with the annual catch averaging 450,000 tonnes per year before independence. Production has shown a turnaround with an estimate of over 200,000 tonnes, largely due to increased government support for the sector.
In a meeting of African ministers in Namibia, held on 2 July, members discussed illegal and unregulated fishing, which is estimated to cost Africa US$1 billion per annum in lost revenue and the threat to stocks and local artisan fishing.

Forestry

Angola has around 18 per cent forest cover with an additional 43 per cent of other wooded land. Most forests are semi-deciduous and located in the north of the country. There are a large number of mangrove forests around Luanda, and in the south and west the forests give way to savannah forest. Around 6.6 per cent of the country's forests are protected, although Angola is the only African country which has not produced a forest law to bring forestry regulation up-to-date.
Angola has considerable timber resources. Valuable tree species, including rosewood, ebony, African sandalwood and mahogany, most of which can be found in the northern tropical forests that have not been commercially exploited since independence. Angola lost around 128,000 hectare of forest cover per year between 1990–2000, which is a modest 0.18 per cent per annum compared to the world average of 0.24 per cent and the African average of 0.78 per cent. In terms of wood products, Angola produces relatively small amounts of sawnwood, pulp and plywood panels. Most industrial roundwood is used for posts, poles and agricultural purposes. Averages annual charcoal production is under 240,000 tonnes and woodfuel just under 3.5 million cubic metres

Industry and manufacturing

Industrial production is centred on food processing, brewing, sugar, textiles and tobacco products. Also important are light manufactures, such as electrical goods

(eg radio production), construction materials, steel production, motor vehicles, detergents, bicycles and chemicals.
Manufacturing accounts for just 4 per cent of GDP.
Activity is concentrated in Luanda, Lobito and Huambo. Output is often sluggish due to shortages of foreign exchange, poor management and a low-paid labour force.
About 60 per cent of total production is accounted for by nationalised industries. The government has embarked upon a privatisation programme involving some 200 state-owned enterprises in a variety of industrial sectors. In early 2003, it passed laws to liberalise the sector and open it up to foreign investment.
The diamond industry has received a vital boom to the industry after De Beers agreed to a joint mining venture with Endiama. Angola is seeking to become one of the top three diamond producers in the world and increasing production to six million carrats.

Tourism
Much work still needs to be done to repair the war-damaged infrastructure, but visitor numbers continue to increase. The Ministry of Hotels and Tourism is attempting to attract foreign capital investment to rebuild the tourism sector. Hotels are in short supply and those that exist have a 99 per cent occupancy rate. The ministry estimates that 50 per cent of the hospitality sector's infrastructure needs renovating and coupled with the poor roads and internal air transport the sector has much to do but also much to gain.
Angola is in partnership with five of its southern African neighbours to establish a huge cross-border eco-tourism, game reserve and tourist resort. Angola has 13 national parks and reserves and has been underdeveloped since the 1960s so that once areas are designated free from landmines, tourism can expand into virtually untamed territories.

Mining
Before independence, Angola was a major producer of iron ore, gold and copper. However, the major disruptions to the country's infrastructure and economy throughout the war have meant that the country's considerable base metal and gold resources have been barely exploited.
Diamonds (mostly of gemstone quality) were the country's second-largest foreign exchange earner in 2004. Endiama is the state-owned diamond mining company dealing with all aspects of diamond exploitation.
Before the ban on Angolan 'conflict' diamonds in 2000, Angola was the fourth-largest diamond producer in the world, producing some US$600 million of rough diamonds per year. By 2003 US$1 billion rough diamonds were sold through the official trading company Sodiam, however the true figure can only be estimated as illegal mining and smuggling from the former Unita-held territories is still a major problem. Without punitive measures to deter this lucrative trade, the revenue from diamonds cannot be fully measured or used.
The government is introducing a register and to licence the many artisan prospectors and control the wholesale price of diamonds, and to establish an export certification scheme to identify legitimate production and sales.
Angola also has deposits of phosphates (Cabinda site, estimated 100 million tonnes; Kindonakasi, estimated 50 million tonnes), gold (at Cassinga and Lombige), copper, lead and zinc (in Tetelo and Alto Zambeze). There are deposits of marble and black granite in southern Angola. The production of ornamental stones was predominantly of black granite which was exported mainly to Spain and Portugal. Angostone Construction and Ornamental Rocks Ltd mines red granite from mines in Cunene province. With an initial investment of US$1.5 million, Angostone is producing 150 cubic metres of red granite per month.

Hydrocarbons
Proven oil reserves were 13.5 billion barrels at the end of 2010, with production at 1.8 million barrels per day (bpd), an increase of 3.8 per cent on the 2009 figure of 1.7 million bpd. Production increased at a time of maximum global price rises. Angola joined the Organisation of the Petroleum Exporting Countries (Opec) in 2007, and was allocated a quota of 1.9 million bpd in 2008. Most oil fields are located offshore near the city of Soyo and the Angolan enclave of Cabinda. Onshore exploration has been hampered by the destruction of so much infrastructure and unexploded ordinance from Angola's 21-year civil war.
Oil revenue contributed over 80 per cent of public revenue and over 50 per cent of GDP. It is mainly used to finance government spending, although it has been criticised and warned that its current accounting practices have led to widespread corruption with the loss of many millions of dollars each year. The Sociedade Nacional de Combustiveis de Angola (Sonangol) is the state-owned oil and gas company, which has a monopoly on exploration and production. There were nine oil projects planned to begin production from 2009 with the potential of providing 1.1 million bpd when all became operational.
There is one refinery, in Luanda, which provided 39,000bpd in 2007 with the needs of the modest domestic consumption of 62,000 bpd met by imports. The construction of a new refinery in Lobito will provide products for domestic and regional African markets and is expected to be operational by 2012.
Proven natural gas reserves were 269 billion cubic metres (cum) in 2008, which was a significant increase on the 56 billion cum in 2007. However, production remains low with only 11 per cent marketed, 14 per cent re-injected as part of oil recovery and 75 per cent vented or flared. The government is planning to increase the conversion of flared gas to liquefied natural gas (LNG) for export, with the construction of an LNG plant at Soyo, with an initial production capacity of five million tonnes (6.9 million cum).
Angola does not produce or import coal.

Energy
The state-owned monopoly Empresa Nacional de Electricidade (ENE) is responsible for all aspects of electricity production from generation and end-user supply. With the country's total electricity generating capacity estimated at 800MW, only 20 per cent of the population has access to electricity and blackouts are frequent. Around 30 per cent of this is provided by thermal generation and about 70 per cent through hydroelectric dams. Much of the country's electricity generation and transmission infrastructure was damaged during the civil war. There are three separate regional power grids operating in the north, south and middle of Angola. Two new turbines and power lines for the Capanda hydroelectric dam on the Kwanza River have been installed; with a further two planned Angola's electricity generating capacity will be doubled. A new hydroelectric dam, to be located at Baynes, on the Kunene River, was agreed by the governments of Angola and Namibia in 2007.
In 2009 the Italian-based energy company ENI and Sonangol, the state-owned oil and gas company, agreed to evaluate an onshore gas-fired power plant using associated gas from offshore oil fields.

Banking and insurance
The central bank is the Banco Nacional de Angola (BNA) (National Bank of Angola). It issues, and is responsible for, all foreign exchange transactions in conjunction with the ministries of planning, commerce and finance. The banking sector has long been undercapitalised and economically inept. However, the sector has seen some foreign interest, with Portuguese banks such as Banco Fomento Exterior and Banco Totta e Azores opening branches in Luanda.

In 2005 the Banco de Poupança e Crédito (Bank for Savings and Credit) and World Vision International, began a programme of micro-credit, by offering 1,900 families at least US$200 and 79 small farmers associations up to US$10,000 for agricultural purposes.

Central bank

Banco Nacional de Angola (BNA) started functioning in late-1996 as the central bank, ceasing its commercial activities, as part of the government's financial reforms.

Main financial centre

Luanda

Time

GMT plus one hour

Geography

Angola lies on the west coast of Africa, bordered by the Democratic Republic of Congo (DRC) to the north, Zambia to the east and Namibia to the south.The Cabinda district is separated from the rest of the country by the estuary of the River Congo and DRC, with the Republic of Congo lying to its north.

Hemisphere

Southern

Climate

In Luanda and northern regions, October–April is hot and humid with usual temperatures ranging from 28–32 degrees Celsius (C), with a maximum of 34 degrees C. April–September is hot but less humid with daytime temperatures ranging from 25–30 degrees C and cool evenings. Southern regions are more temperate and rainfall can be frequent and heavy, particularly in April.

Dress codes

Informal dress is suitable for most occasions. Lightweight suits are recommended for business meetings. Visitors to the central and southern plateaux will need warm clothes at night, as will visitors to the coastal region during May to September.

Entry requirements

Passport and visa requirements are liable to change at short notice. It is advisable to check with the local Angolan Embassy/consulate at the outset.

Passports

Required by all. Passport must be valid for at least six months and contain two blank pages for stamping. Return or onward ticket is also required.

Visa

Required by all (except transit passengers remaining within the airport). Must be obtained in advance of arrival. Valid for 90 days.

A business visitor must provide a letter of invitation from a local Angolan company or institution and an own company letter stating purpose of visit.

An exit permit, provided by the same office which issued the visa, is also required.

Currency advice/regulations

There are no restrictions on the amount of foreign currency that can be taken into Angola, but it must be declared on arrival. The export of foreign currency is limited to US$5,000; the export of Angolan currency is prohibited

Customs

Many goods may not be imported without government authorisation and licensing.

Health (for visitors)

Mandatory precautions

Yellow fever vaccination certificate is required on arrival and may be demanded by some airlines before departure.

Advisable precautions

Hepatitis A and B, typhoid, tetanus, meningococcus and polio vaccinations are recommended. Malaria prophylaxis is essential. There is a rabies and cholera risk.

Water precautions must be taken.

Travel insurance, including emergency medical evacuation, is essential. All medication, with prescriptions, should be carried by travellers.

Hotels

Hotel accommodation is in short supply, although much existing capacity has been upgraded. Bookings should be made at least one month in advance of travel. Bookings cannot be made by airline companies or at airports.

Credit cards

American Express accepted at Presidente and Tivoli hotels. Generally, credit cards are not accepted.

Public holidays (national)

Fixed dates

1 Jan (New Year's Day), 4 Jan (Martyrs of the Colonial Repression Day), 4 Feb (Anniversary of Start of Liberation War), 8 Mar (Women's Day), 4 Apr (Peace and Reconciliation Day), 1 May (Labour Day), 25 May (Africa Day), 1 Jun (International Children's Day), 1 Aug (Armed Forces Day), 17 Sep (Nation's Founder and National Heroes Day), 2 Nov (All Souls Day), 11 Nov (Independence Day), 25 Dec (Christmas Day).

Variable dates

Good Friday, Easter Monday.

Working hours

Banking

Mon–Fri: 0830–1130, 1400–1530.

Business

Mon–Fri: 0830–1230, 1430–1800; Sat 0830–1230.

Government

Mon–Fri: 0800–1200, 1400–1700.

Telecommunications

Telephone/fax

Telephone and mobile phone usage and infrastructure are expanding, but international connections are unreliable. Angola Telecom is the country's public telecommunications company.

Electricity supply

220V AC, 50 cycles.

Social customs/useful tips

Travel permits may be required for travel outside Luanda province. Visitors are advised to carry spare passport photographs. Visitors should not attempt to photograph any public building, infrastructure or security forces or use binoculars in the vicinity.

Security

Travel by car in many parts of Luanda is relatively safe by day, but doors should be locked, windows closed and packages stored out of sight. Walking in Luanda after dark should be avoided.

There is the possibility of banditry and danger from landmines laid during the civil war. Frequent checkpoints and poor infrastructure contribute to unsafe travel on roads outside Luanda. Police and military personnel are heavily armed and can be unpredictable; their authority should not be challenged. No travel should be undertaken on roads outside the city after nightfall.

Throughout Angola, taking photographs or using binoculars near anything that could be perceived as being of military or security interest, including government buildings, could lead to problems with authorities and should be avoided at all costs.

Getting there

Air

National airline: TAAG (Linhas Aéreas de Angola). *In July 2007 the European Union banned TAAG from EU air space, due to safety concerns.*

International airport/s: Luanda-4 de Fevereiro (Code: LAD), 4km from city, restaurant. No taxis, public telephones or banking services.

Airport tax: None

Surface

Road: Road travel is not generally practicable, though access is now possible across the Namibian frontier to the south.

Rail: Rail travel to Angola is difficult due to regional conflict and war damage which has destroyed railways and bridges. The Benguela railway, which ran from the Zambian copperbelt to the port of Lobito, is being repaired.

Water: Angola has several ports along its Atlantic seaboard with the possibility of passenger traffic from other coastal African countries.

Main port/s: Cabinda, Lobito, Luanda, Namibe. Lobito and Luanda are being repaired.

Getting about

National transport

Air: Most of the country is only accessible by air. TAAG operates domestic flights connecting to main centres but these can be unreliable. There are separate helicopter services to the Cabinda enclave and some commercial companies, connected to the oil and diamond industries, who operate jet aircraft, may carry passengers. All passengers must carry authorisation to travel (*guia de marcha*), and business travellers should alert their embassy or representative of their travel plans.

Road: Angola's roads and bridges are gradually being restored. Landmines are a continuing danger, but traffic is now free to travel along the main roads between provincial capitals. The condition of roads ranges widely from reasonable to dire. Night travel is to be strictly avoided.

Buses: There are buses throughout the country but the service is poor and the buses are generally very crowded.

Taxis: Difficult to find and expensive. Travellers arriving by air will need to be met by their sponsors or by their hotel transport service.

Rail: The railway system is under repair, following the damage caused during the civil war. There are irregular passenger services on three routes from Luanda-Malanje, and Lobito-Dilolo, and Namibe-Menongue. Refreshements are available but no sleeping accommodation or air-conditioning is provided.

City transport

Taxis: Unregulated taxis should be avoided. No taxi service from airport to Luanda.

Buses, trams & metro: There are local city buses.

BUSINESS DIRECTORY

The addresses listed below are a selection only. While World of Information makes every endeavour to check these addresses, we cannot guarantee that changes have not been made, especially to telephone numbers and area codes. We would welcome any corrections.

Telephone area codes

Telephone direct dialling code for Angola is +244 followed by area code and subscriber's number.

Luanda 2

Chambers of Commerce

Angolan Chamber of Commerce and Industry, 14 Largo do Kinaxixi, PO Box 92, Luanda (tel: 344-506; fax: 344-629; e-mail: ccira@ebonet.net).

Banking

Banco de Comercio e Industria, 86 Avenida 4 de Fevereiro, Luanda (tel: 333-684; fax: 333-823; e-mail: secretariado@bci.ebonet.net).

Banco Comercial Angolano, 83A Avenida Comandante Valódia, PO Box 6900, Luanda (tel: 449-517; fax: 449-516; e-mail: bca@snet.co.ao).

Banco Africano de Investimentos, 34 Rua Major Kanhangulo, Luanda (tel: 337-369; fax: 335-486).

Banco de Poupança e Crédito, PO Box 1343, Luanda (tel: 233-9158).

Central bank

Banco Nacional de Angola, 151 Avenida 4 de Fevereiro, PO Box 1243, Luanda (tel: 332-633; fax: 390-579; e-mail: sec.gvb@bna.ao).

Travel information

Direcção de Emigração e Fronteiras de Angola (visa queries), Defa, Luanda (tel: 330-314, 330-019).

TAAG-Angola Airlines (Linhas Aéreas de Angola), Rua da Missão 123, CP 179, Luanda (tel: 332-485; fax: 393-548).

Ministry of tourism

Ministerio do Comercio e Turismo (Ministry of Commerce and Tourism), Largo 4 de Fevereiro 3, Luanda (tel: 338-741).

Ministries

Ministry of Agriculture and Rural Development, 2 Avenida Comandante Gika, CP 527 Luanda (tel: 322-694; fax: 323-217).

Ministry of Defence, Rua 17 de Setembro, Luanda (tel: 337-530; fax: 392-635).

Ministry of Education and Culture, Avenida Comandante Gika, CP 1281 Luanda (tel: 322-797; fax: 321-592).

Ministry of Energy and Water, 105 Avenida 4 de Fevereiro, CP 2229 Luanda (tel: 393-681; fax: 393-687).

Ministry of Ex-Servicemen and War Veterans, 2 Avenida Comandante Gika, CP 5466 Luanda (tel: 321-117; fax: 323-561).

Ministry of Family and Women's Advancement, Edifício Palácio de Vidro, Largo 4 de Fevereiro, 1242 Luanda (tel: 338-745; fax: 330-028).

Ministry of Finance, 127 Avenida 4 de Fevereiro, CP 592 Luanda (tel: 332-122; fax: 332-069).

Ministry of Fisheries and Environment, Edifício Atlantico, Avenida 4 de Fevereiro, CP 83 Luanda (tel: 390-690; fax: 333-814).

Ministry of Foreign Affairs, 8 Avenida Comandante Gika, CP 1500 Luanda (tel: 323-250; fax: 393-246).

Ministry of Geology and Mines, Avenida Comandante Gika, CP 1260 Luanda (tel: 326-724; fax: 321-655).

Ministry of Health, Rua 17 de Setembro, CP 1201 Luanda (tel: 322-797; fax: 321-592).

Ministry of Hotels and Tourism, Edifício Palácio de Vidro, Largo 4 de Fevereiro, CP 1242 Luanda (tel: 331-323; fax: 338-211).

Ministry of Industry, 25 Rua Cerqueira Lukoki, CP 594 Luanda (tel: 397-070; fax: 334-700).

Ministry of Information, 1 Avenida Comandante Valódia, CP 2608 Luanda (tel: 342-818; fax: 343-495).

Ministry of the Interior, 204 Avenida 4 de Fevereiro, CP 2723 Luanda (tel: 391-049; fax: 395-133).

Ministry of Justice, Rua 17 de Setembro, CP 2250 Luanda (tel: 330-327).

Ministry of Petroleum, Avenida 4 de Fevereiro, CP 1279 Luanda (tel: 337-440; fax: 372-373).

Ministry of Planning, Largo 17 de Setembro, Luanda (tel: 390-722; fax: 339-586).

Ministry of Posts and Telecommunications, 42 Avenida 4 de Fevereiro, CP 1459 Luanda (tel: 337-799; fax: 330-776).

Ministry of Public Administration, Employment and Social Security, 32 Rua 17 de Setembro, CP 1986 Luanda (tel: 338-654).

Ministry of Public Works and Town Planning, Rua Ed Mutamba, CP 1061 Luanda (tel: 336-717; fax: 333-814).

Ministry of Science and Technology, 25 Rua Cerqueira Lukoki, CP 1288 Luanda (tel: 338-987).

Ministry of Social Assistance and Reintegration, 117 Avenida dos Massacres, CP 102 Luanda (tel: 340-370; fax: 342-988).

Ministry of Territorial Administration, 8 Avenida Comandante Gika, Luanda (tel: 320-638; fax: 323-238).

Ministry of Trade, Edifício Palácio de Vidro, Largo 4 de Fevereiro, CP 1242 Luanda (tel: 338-737; fax: 370-804).

Ministry of Transport, 42 Avenida 4 de Fevereiro, Luanda (tel: 337-744; fax: 337-687).

Ministry of Youth and Sports, Avenida Comandante Gika, CP 5466 Luanda (tel: 321-117; fax: 323-561).

Other useful addresses

Angolan Embassy (USA), 2100 16th Street, NW, Washington DC 20009 (Tel: (+1-202) 785-1156; fax: (+1-202) 785-1258; e-mail: angola@angola.org).

ANGOP (news agency), CP 2181, Luanda (tel: 334-945).

Associação Comercial de Luanda, CP 1275, Edificio Palácio de Comércio, le Andar, Luanda (tel: 322-453).

DHL International Ltd, Avenida Che Guevara 52–52a, CP 1545 (tel: 390-326, 390-376, 392-082).

Direcção dos Servicos de Comércio, CP 1337, Largo Diogo Cão, Luanda.

Direcção dos Servicos de Estatistica (statistical agency), CP 1215, Luanda.

Direcção da Aviacao Civil (National Civil Aviation Directorate), Rua Frederich Engels, 92-6 andar, CP 569, Luanda (tel: 339-412, 338-196, 338-596).

Direcção dos Caminhos de Ferro (National Railways Directorate), Rua Major Kanhangulo, CP 1250, Luanda (tel: 370-061).

Direcção Nacional de Correios e Telecomunicacoes (National Posts and Telecommunications Directorate), Rua Frederich Engels, CP 1459, Luanda (tel: 339-750).

Direcção Nacional da Marinha Mercante e Portos (National Merchant Navy and Ports Directorate), Rua Rainha Ginga, 74-4 andar, Luanda (tel: 332-032, 339-847, 339-848).

Direcção Nacional dos Transportes Rodoviarios (National Road Transport Directorate), Rua Rainha Ginga, 74-1 andar, Luanda (tel: 339-390).

Empresa Nacional de Construcão de Obrtas Industrials (National construction Company for Industrial Projects), Bairro do Cazenga, 5 Avenida Zona Industrial, CP 18612, Luanda (tel: 390-087, 391-478).

Empresa Nacional de Diamantes de Angola (Endiama), Rua Major Kanhangulo 100, CP 1247, Luanda (tel: 333 018; fax: 337 216; www.endiama.co.ao).

Empresa Nacional de Electricidada (ENE - National Electricity Company), Edeficio de Geologia e Minas 7, CP 772, Luanda (tel: 323-382, 337-498, 323-568, 321-498, 321-499).

Importang (state import agency), Calçada do Município 10, CP 1003, Luanda (tel: 392-787).

Institute Foreign Investment, Rue Serqueira Lukoki 25 (tel: 334-700).

Instituto Nacional do Cafe de Angola (INCA – National Coffee Institute of Angola), Rua Dr Alves Maciel 17-1D, Luanda (tel: 370-386).

Instituto Nacional de Estradas de Angola (National Roads Institute), Rua Amilcar Cabral 35-4, Caixa Postal 5667, Luanda (tel: 332-828, 391-536; fax: 335-754).

Radio Nacional de Angola, CP 1389, Luanda.

Sociedade Nacional de Combustiveis (SONANGOL-Angola National Fuels Company), Rua I Congresso do MPLA, Caixa Postal 1316, Luanda (tel: 334-143/9; fax: 333-542/6, 391-782).

Televisão Popular de Angola (TPA), CP 2002, Luanda.

US Embassy, 32 Rua Houari Boumedienne, Luanda (tel: 445-481; fax: 446-924).

National news agency: Angola Press (Angop): www.angolapress-angop.ao

Internet sites

AllAfrica.com: www.allafrica.com

African Development Bank: www.afdb.org

Africa Online: www.africaonline.com

Angola News: www.angolanews.com

Jornal de Angola: www.jornaldeangola.com

Anguilla

KEY FACTS

Official name: Anguilla

Head of State: Queen Elizabeth II; represented by Governor Alistair Harrison (from 21 Apr 2009)

Head of government: Chief Minister Herbert Hughes (AUM) (from 15 Feb 2010)

Ruling party: Anguilla United Movement (AUM) (from 15 Feb 2010)

Area: 96 square km (Anguilla 91 square km, Sombrero 5 square km)

Population: 15,000 (2010)*

Capital: The Valley

Official language: English

Currency: East Caribbean dollar (EC$) = 100 cents

Exchange rate: EC$2.70 per US$ (fixed rate)

GDP per capita: US$9,711 (2006)*

GDP real growth: -8.50% (2009)*

Unemployment: 7.80% (rates for under aged 25 typically 29 per cent) (last published rate 2002)

Inflation: 2.40% (2007)

Balance of trade: -US$125.92 million (2010)

Visitor numbers: 89,922 (2010)

* estimated figure

COUNTRY PROFILE

Historical profile

Anguilla was originally settled about 1,500BC by Arawak Indians, who called it Malliouhana, and later by Carib Indians.
1650 The British established a colony on Anguilla.
1745 and 1796 Anguilla repelled attacks by France.
1882 Anguilla became part of a larger colony governed from St Kitts.
1967 St Kitts-Nevis-Anguilla became a state, in association with the UK. (The status of an associated state allowed St Kitts-Nevis-Anguilla to become independent internally while the British government retained responsibility for external affairs and defence).
1969 Two brief Anguilla rebellions ended after British security forces were sent to install a British commissioner.
1971 The Anguilla Act was passed by the British parliament. A major provision of the Act stated that, should St Kitts-Nevis-Anguilla initiate legislative steps to terminate the status of association, Anguilla could be separated formally from the other islands.
1980 Anguilla separated from St Kitts-Nevis and became a British Dependent Territory.
1982 A new constitution gave Anguilla greater control over its internal affairs.
1994 The Anguilla United Party (AUP) was elected and its leader, Hubert Hughes, became chief minister.
1999 Hughes was re-elected, but lost his parliamentary majority when Victor Banks, leader of his coalition partner, the Anguilla Democratic Party (ADP), resigned.
2000 Hughes called a general election – four years early – in order to break the constitutional deadlock. Hughes and the ANP lost the election, which was won by the Anguilla United Front (AUF), coalition led by the Anguilla National Alliance (ANA) and the ADP; Osbourne Fleming (ANA) was appointed chief minister.
2002 Under UK legislation all British Dependent Territories became British Overseas Territories.
2005 The AUF coalition was re-elected. Andrew George was appointed governor.
2006 Wilhelm Bourne was appointed attorney general in succession to Ronald Scipio.
2007 A review of the constitution began.
2009 Anguilla Air Express, an executive air service to San Juan, Puerto Rico, began operations. Andrew George retired as governor and Alistair Harrison replaced him as governor.
2010 In parliamentary elections held in February, the opposition Anguilla United Movement (AUM) won more seats (four seats out of seven) in the national assembly, despite winning fewer votes than the outgoing AUF, due to the voting system of first-past-the-post. Herbert Hughes (AUM) became chief minister.
2011 In January the chief minister renewed his call for Anguilla to be given independence from the UK, following an announcement by Governor Harrison in December 2010 that he would not sign and pass the 2011 budget. On 4 April the governor approved the 2011 budget.

Political structure

Constitution

Anguilla Constitutional Order 1 April 1982 (amended 1990), gave greater control over its internal affairs.

Form of state

A self-governing, British Overseas Territory; residents have British citizenship (and by extension access to the European Union). Foreign affairs and defence are administered from the UK

The executive

Executive power rests with an appointed British governor, assisted by an executive council (chief minister, two *ex-officio* members and not more than three other ministers).

The governor, appointed from the UK, is responsible for defence and external affairs, but is required to consult the chief minister on matters relating to internal security, the police and civil service.

National legislature

The unicameral House of Assembly has seven members elected for five-year terms in single-seat constituencies, plus two nominated members and two *ex-officio* members.

Legal system

The legal system is based on English common law. Anguilla is a member of the Eastern Caribbean Supreme Court, which is responsible for the high court and court of appeals. Final appeal rests with the Privy Council in the UK.

Last elections
15 February 2010 (parliamentary)
Results: Parliamentary: Anguilla United Movement (AUM) won 32.68 per cent of the vote (four seats out of seven), Anguilla United Front (AUF) 39.37 per cent (two), Anguilla Progressive Party 14.71 per cent (one), independents 13.24 per cent (none).
Next elections
2015 (parliamentary)

Political parties
Ruling party
Anguilla United Movement (AUM) (from 15 Feb 2010)
Main opposition party
Anguilla United Front (AUF)
Political situation
The downturn in the global economy has had a severe negative effect on Anguilla, along with all of its neighbours. Not only has government revenue fallen, leading to spending cut backs, but the UK's Foreign and Commonwealth Overseas Territories office is demanding more commitment by the Anguillian government to good governance and public accountability. At the same time the US and EU want details of their citizens who may be possible tax evaders.
The AUF government's record was found wanting by the electorate when, in parliamentary elections held on 15 February, the opposition Anguilla United Movement (AUM) won more seats (four seats out of seven) in the national assembly, despite winning fewer votes than the outgoing AUF, due to the voting system of first-past-the-post. Herbert Hughes (AUM) became chief minister.

Population
15,000 (2010)*
Last census: October 2001: 11,430
Population density: 104.5 inhabitants per sq km.
Annual growth rate: 3.3 per cent (2003)
Ethnic make-up
Mainly of African descent; some of Irish descent.
Religions
Anglican (40 per cent), Methodist (33 per cent), Seventh-Day Adventist (7 per cent), Baptist (5 per cent), Roman Catholic (3 per cent).

Health
Life expectancy: 77 years (estimate 2003)
Fertility rate/Maternal mortality rate: Two births per woman (2003).
Birth rate/Death rate: 15 births per 1,000 population; five deaths per 1,000 population (2003).
Child (under 5 years) mortality rate (per 1,000): 23 per 1,000 live births (2003)

Main cities
The Valley (capital, estimated population 1,680 in 2008), Stoney Ground (1,395), North Side (1,976).

Languages spoken
Official language/s
English

Media
Press
The only local newspaper, *The Anguillan* (www.anguillian.com), is published weekly.
Dailies: *Chronicle* and *The Daily Herald* are published in St Martin and cover Anguillan news.
Periodicals: *What We Do in Anguilla* is an annual magazine with tourist information.
Broadcasting
Radio: The government-owned national radio station, Radio Anguilla, operates Radio Axa (www.radioaxa.com) with news, music and talk shows. There are several private radio stations including some with religious programming such as New Beginning Radio, The Caribbean Beacon and Voice of Creation. General interest stations include Klass FM (www.klass929.com), Heart Beat Radio (http://hbr1075.com) and Kool FM (www.koolfm103.com).
Television: The Caribbean Cable Communications operates Anguilla Television with two channels offering local and international programmes.
News agencies
Other news agencies: Caribbean Net News: www.caribbeannetnews.com

Economy
With so few natural resources Anguilla's economy is dominated by financial services, high-end tourism, export of lobsters and remittances, as well as grants-in-aid from the UK and EU. Anguilla is largely reliant on imported fuel and food.
GDP growth was 5.5–6.0 per cent in 2008 and was much the same in 2007, despite higher priced food imports pushing up inflation beyond headline inflation in the first half of 2008. Tourism accounted for 23.6 per cent of GDP over the period 2002–06. The financial sector was 18.3 per cent of GDP in 2008. By 2007 foreign direct investment (FDI), typically in tourist related projects, accounted for 29.5 per cent of GDP, rising from 26.4 per cent in 2006.
The global economic crisis drastically cut the number of visitors to Anguilla and resulted in a lower rating of its debt issue by the Caribbean Information and Credit Rating Services (CariCRIS), in October 2009. However by the winter or 2009–2010 visitor numbers had jumped, as they took advantage of special deals and packages and arrivals from the US were up by 15 per cent on the previous year.

External trade
Anguilla is an associate member of both the Caribbean Community (Caricom) and the Organisation of Eastern Caribbean States (OECS). However, as a British Overseas Territory (BOT), Anguilla is constrained in its full participation of trading agreements as negotiated by either organisation.
Anguilla's international trade is largely confined to financial services and small-scale production of mechanical and engineering parts and marine crafts and

KEY INDICATORS — Anguilla

	Unit	2006	2007	2008	2009	2010
Population	m	0.01	0.01	*0.01	*0.01	*0.01
Gross domestic product (GDP)	US$bn	0.20	–	–	*0.17	–
GDP per capita	US$	16,183	14,430	15,230	–	–
GDP real growth	%	0.1	12.0	0.0	*-8.5	–
IExports (fob) (goods)	US$m	12.3	9.2	11.5	26.2	12.7
Imports (fob) (goods)	US$m	197.1	218.2	239.2	153.4	137.6
Balance of trade	US$m	-184.8	-209.0	-227.7	-127.1	-125.9
Current account	US$m	-144.6	-184.0	-211.3	-102.4	-68.4
Total reserves minus gold	US$m	41.8	44.9	44.0	37.5	39.9
Foreign exchange	US$m	41.8	44.9	44.0	37.5	39.9
Tourist numbers	'000	116.8	114.6	89.3	76.5	89.9
Exchange rate	per US$	2.70	2.70	2.70	2.70	2.70

* estimated figure

agricultural products including seafood, livestock and foodstuffs.

Imports

Principal imports include petroleum, consumer goods, food products, chemicals, manufactures and textiles, vehicles.

Main sources: Typically US, Puerto Rico, UK

Exports

Principal exports include lobsters, fish and other seafood, livestock, salt, rum and concrete blocks.

Main destinations: Typically UK, US, Puerto Rico and other Caribbean islands.

Agriculture

The agriculture sector accounts for around 4 per cent of GDP. There is mainly small-scale farming of peas, corn, sweet potatoes, okra and tropical fruits. The average cultivated plot is less than 0.25ha. Traditional livestock raising (goats, sheep, poultry) is important, with some animals raised for export.

Fishing

Lobster fishing is a major employer and principal earner of foreign exchange; 70t are caught each year. The typical annual fish catch is 250t.

Industry and manufacturing

The manufacturing sector is based primarily on boatbuilding, construction and fish processing and contributes less than 1 per cent to GDP.

Tourism

Tourism is an important component of the economy, accounting for an estimated 23 per cent of GDP in 2011 with direct revenue of US$51 million (EC$137 million). Total revenue was forecast to be US$144 million (EC$389.3 million) in 2011. Tourism directly employs 23.9 per cent of the workforce, with 65.8 per cent of total employment having some involvement in the industry. The tourist and travel sector was forecast to attract 7.5 per cent of total foreign direct investment (US$8.6 million (EC$23.3 million)) in 2011.

The number of visitors peaked in 2007, with a total of 13,980, of which 3,303 arrived by air and 10,677 by sea. Numbers during the global economic crisis fell to 9,005 in 2009, but with a modest resurgence of 9,723 visitors in 2010. Visitors from North America account for around 60 per cent of total arrivals, with European and other Caribbean islands providing the remainder.

In November 2010 the government began work on its Sustainable Tourism Master Plan 2010–2020 (STMP), which includes public consultation on the industry's future and development. Initial discussions focussed on Anguilla's prime attractions – pristine beaches and a clean environment, high quality accommodation, fine dining, relaxed atmosphere with a distinctive Caribbean flavour, peace and tranquillity, safety, friendly people and various degrees of exclusivity.

Hydrocarbons

There are no known hydrocarbon reserves; all needs are met by imports.

Energy

Total installed generating capacity is over 28MW after a new 5.4MW generator was installed in mid-2009. Anglec (Electricity Company) is responsible for generation, transmission and sales.

Financial markets

Stock exchange

Eastern Caribbean Securities Exchange (ECSE)

Banking and insurance

The island's banking sector is well-regulated and internationally competitive. With a neutral tax jurisdiction and no foreign exchange restrictions, Anguilla's financial services sector has attracted a lot of foreign interest over the years. Around 5,000 companies are registered in Anguilla, with most of them classified as International Business Companies (IBCs).

The seven members of the Organisation of Eastern Caribbean States (OECS), Antigua and Barbuda, Dominica, Grenada, Montserrat, St Kitts and Nevis, St Lucia and St Vincent and the Grenadines, share a common currency and central bank. The British Virgin Islands and Anguilla are associate members.

As from 2005 Anguilla has chosen to adhere to an EU tax directive and inform EU citizens' tax departments about the amount of money in savings accounts and allow tax to be levied from the home country, rather than imposing a withholding tax while retaining a saver's anonimity. Anguilla has also agreed to supply information on tax fraud, for criminal or civil trials, and notify EU member states about additional malpractices.

Central bank

Eastern Caribbean Central Bank, St Kitts and Nevis.

Offshore facilities

The offshore financial services sector in Anguilla is the responsibility of the governor, with day-to-day regulation carried out by the government's financial services department. There are strict laws to combat money laundering and only banks with a previous good record can be licensed as offshore banks. Companies can be incorporated through the Anguilla Commercial Online Registration Network (ACORN).

Time

GMT minus four hours

Geography

Anguilla, a coralline island of 91 square km, is the most northerly of the Leeward Islands. It lies to the north-west of St Kitts and Nevis and 8km (5 miles) to the north of St Maarten, Netherlands Antilles. The island of Sombrero (48km north of Anguilla) is also included in the territory, as are several other uninhabited small islands.

Hemisphere

Northern

Climate

Subtropical with a mean annual temperature of 27 degrees Celsius. It is hottest from July–October, coolest from December–February. Cooling trade winds blow throughout the year. Rain mainly falls September–December.

Entry requirements

Passports

Required by all, except US nationals (all US nationals require a passport for re-entry to the US). Passports must be valid for at least six months after date of entry.

Visa

Required by all, except nationals of US, Canada, EU, Japan and a number of other countries visiting for no longer than six months. From May 2009 EU citizens may make a short-stay visit, for up to three months, without a visa. All visitors require onward or return tickets and sufficient funds for their stay.

Currency advice/regulations

There are no restrictions on the import of local and foreign currency, but it must be declared. The export of local and foreign currency is limited to the amount imported and declared. Travellers are advised to take travellers cheques in US dollars to avoid additional exchange rate charges.

Health (for visitors)

Mandatory precautions

Vaccination certificate for yellow fever required if arriving from an infected area.

Advisable precautions

Hepatitis A vaccination recommended. Water and food precautions advisable.

Hotels

Several high-quality hotels and a wide selection of villas and apartments.

10–15 per cent service charge is usually included in the bill, plus 10 per cent room tax.

Public holidays (national)

Fixed dates

1 Jan (New Year's Day), 1 May (Labour Day), 25 Dec (Christmas Day), 26 Dec (Boxing Day).

Variable dates

Good Friday, Easter Monday, Anguilla Day (May), Whit Monday, Queen's Official Birthday (Jun), August Monday (first

Mon in Aug), August Thursday (first Thu in Aug), Constitution Day (Aug), Separation Day (third Mon in Dec).

Working hours
Banking
Mon–Thu: 0800–1500; Fri: 0800–1700.
Business
Mon–Fri: 0800–1200, 1300–1600.
Government
Mon–Fri: 0800–1200, 1300–1600.

Telecommunications
Mobile/cell phones
GSM 850/1900 services are available throughout the country.

Electricity supply
110/220V AC, 50 cycles

Getting there
Air
National airline: Air Anguilla.
Anguilla Air Express, an executive air service between San Juan, Puerto Rico and Anguilla, began in February 2009.
International airport/s: Wallblake (AXA), 3km from The Valley. Daily air service with St Maarten (Netherlands Antilles) and St Thomas (US Virgin Islands) and regular air services from Antigua, St Kitts and San Juan (Puerto Rico). Air taxi and charter services are available from Air Anguilla and Tyden Air.
Airport tax: Departure tax US$20.
Surface
Water: Tropical Shipping and Bernuth Lines sail from Miami to Anguilla. Frequent ferry services operate between Blowing Point and Marigot Bay, St Martin (French Antilles).
Main port/s: Road Bay, Sandy Ground; Blowing Point is a smaller port.

Getting about
National transport
Road: There is no public transport. Use taxis or car hire to travel. Anguilla has about 105km of roads, of which 65km are surfaced, but not to good standard. Public roads cover all parts of the island.
City transport
Taxis: Most generally used form of transport; readily available and inexpensive.
Car hire
Readily available. National licence needed to obtain temporary local licence. Drive on left.

BUSINESS DIRECTORY

The addresses listed below are a selection only. While World of Information makes every endeavour to check these addresses, we cannot guarantee that changes have not been made, especially to telephone numbers and area codes. We would welcome any corrections.

Telephone area codes
The international direct dialling code (IDD) for Anguilla is +1 264, followed by subscriber's number.

Useful telephone numbers
Police, ambulance, fire: 911

Chambers of Commerce
Anguilla Chamber of Commerce and Industry, PO Box 321, The Valley (tel/fax: 479-2839; e-mail: acoci@anguillanet.com).

Banking
Bank of Nova Scotia, PO Box 250, George Hill, The Valley (tel: 497-3333; fax: 497-3344).

Barclays Bank Plc (UK), PO Box 140, The Valley (tel: 497-2301/2304; fax: 497-2980).

Caribbean Commercial Bank (Anguilla) Ltd, PO Box 23, The Valley (tel: 497-2571/3; fax: 497-3570; e-mail: ccbaxa@anguillanet.com).

Caribbean Development Bank, PO Box 408, Wildey, st Michael, Barbados (1246) 431-1600; fax: (1246) 426-7269).

National Bank of Anguilla, PO Box 44, The Valley (tel: 497-2101/2104; fax: 497-3310).

Central bank
Eastern Caribbean Central Bank, Agency Office, PO Box 1385, Fairplay Commercial Complex, The Valley (tel: 497-5050; fax: 497-5150).

Stock exchange
Eastern Caribbean Securities Exchange (ECSE): www.ecseonline.com

Travel information
Air Anguilla, PO Box 110, The Valley (tel: 497-2643; fax: 497-2982).

National tourist organisation offices
Anguilla Tourist Board, PO Box 1388, The Valley (tel: 497-2759; fax: 497-2710; e-mail: atbtour@anguillanet.com; internet: www.charmingescapescollection.com).

Ministries
Ministries: all located at The Secretariat, The Valley (tel: 497-2451).

Ministry of Finance, PO Box 60, The Secretariat, The Valley (tel: 497-5881/3881; fax: 497-5872; e-mail: anguillafsd@anguillanet.com).

Office of the Governor, Government House, PO Box 60, The Valley (tel: 497-2621/2, 497-3312/3; fax: 497-3314/3151; e-mail: govthouse@anguillanet.com).

Office of the Chief Minister, The Secretariat, The Valley (tel: 497-2518; fax: 497-3389).

Office of the Minister of Finance, Planning and Economic Development, The Secretariat, The Valley (tel: 497-2545/2451; fax: 497-3761).

Other useful addresses
Agriculture Department (tel: 497-2615).

All Island Cable TV, George Hill, PO Box 336 (tel: 497-3600; fax: 497-3602).

Anguilla Electricity Co Ltd, PO Box 400, The Valley (tel: 497-5200; fax: 497-5440).

Cable & Wireless (WI) Ltd, Telecoms House, PO Box 77, The Valley (tel: 497-3100; fax: 497-2501; internet site: http://www.anguillanet.com).

Caribbean Beacon Radio, PO Box 690, The Valley (tel: 497-4340).

Government of Anguilla Financial Services Department, The Secretariat, The Valley (tel: 497-5881; fax: 497-5872; e-mail: anguillafsd@anguillafsd.com; internet: www.anguillaoffshore.com).

Immigration Office (tel: 497-2451, Ext 129).

Radio Anguilla, The Secretariat, The Valley (tel: 497-2218; fax: 497-2751).

Internet sites
Anguilla Financial Services/ACORN: www.anguillafsc.com

Anguilla Guide: www.anguillaguide.com

The Anguillian newspaper: www.anguillian.com

Antigua and Barbuda

COUNTRY PROFILE

Historical profile

1493 Columbus sighted Antigua.
1632 Antigua and Barbuda was settled by the British.
1667 Control was passed to Great Britain after a brief period of French control.
1674 First sugar colony was set up in Antigua by Christopher Codrington.
1685 Codrington leased the island of Barbuda from the British crown and imported African slaves to help grow tobacco and sugar.
1834 The slaves of Antigua were freed.
1860 Barbuda reverted to the British crown.
1871–1956 Antigua and Barbuda were administered together as part of the Leeward Islands federation.
1946 Vere Bird formed the Antigua Labour Party (ALP).
1958–62 Antigua and Barbuda became a member of the short-lived Federation of the West Indies.
1967 The island of Antigua and its two dependencies, Barbuda and the uninhabited islet of Redonda, entered into a free association with other British dependencies in the Windward and Leeward Islands. Antigua became an associate member of the Commonwealth.
1969 A Barbuda separatist movement was formed
1972 The sugar industry was closed down.
1981 Antigua and Barbuda achieved full independence as a unitary state, but retained the monarchy. The ALP won the first post-independence elections with Bird becoming prime minister.
1990 Vere Bird Junior, son of the prime minister, was declared unfit for office by a judicial enquiry which uncovered links with money laundering.
1993 Prime Minister Vere Bird Senor resigned and was replaced by his son, Lester.
1994 The ALP, led by Lester Bird won the general elections.
1995 Riots erupted over the imposition of new taxes. Ivor Bird, brother of the prime minister was convicted of smuggling cocaine into the country. Hurricane Luis struck the islands and destroyed 75 per cent of all homes.
1998 Six Russian-owned banks were closed down by the government, which accused them of money laundering.
1999 The ALP won the elections. Hurricane José caused severe damage to the country's infrastructure.
2001 After an investigation by the UK and US into the islands' banking sector subsequent adoption of a series of recommendations resulted in the country being declared co-operative in the fight against international money laundering.
2002 The US$22 million Nevis Street pier was officially opened.
2004 The United Progressive Party (UPP) won parliamentary elections, ousting the ALP, which had dominated politics since the 1950s. Winston Baldwin Spencer was sworn in as prime minister.
2006 The dispute between Antigua and Barbuda and the US, involving the World Trade Organisation, over the US ban on internet gambling continued despite a WTO ruling in 2005 in favour of the islands. The newly constructed Parliament Building in St John's was dedicated.
2007 Louise Lake-Tack was sworn in as governor general. The WTO ordered the US to pay Antigua compensation for loss of earnings during the disputed online gambling.
2009 US financier Sir Allen Stanford was charged by US prosecutors for a US$8 billion investment fraud perpetrated through the Bank of Antigua. In parliamentary elections, the ruling UPP won nine out of 17 seats, the ALP seven, Barbuda People's Movement (BPM) one; the BPM voted with the government. Chief financial regulator, Leroy King, was sacked by the government for allegedly collaborating with Sir Allen Stanford .
2010 Diplomatic relations were established between Antigua and Barbuda and Egypt in July.
2011 On 4 January, Prime Minister Baldwin Spencer ratified the Revised Treaty of Basseterre, establishing the Organisation of Eastern Caribbean States (OECS) economic union. The trial of alleged swindler, Allen Stanford was postponed in January while he underwent a detoxification programme to rid him of heavy doses of anti-anxiety and anti-depressant drugs which rendered him incompetent to stand trial. On 1 August citizens of the Organisation of Eastern Caribbean States (OECS) – Antigua and Barbuda, Dominica, Grenada, St Kitts and Nevis, St Lucia and St Vincent and

KEY FACTS

Official name: Antigua and Barbuda

Head of State: Queen Elizabeth II, represented by Governor General Louise Lake-Tack (from 17 Jul 2007)

Head of government: Prime Minister Winston Baldwin Spencer (UPP) (sworn in 2004; re-elected 12 Mar 2009)

Ruling party: United Progressive Party (UPP) (elected 2004; re-elected 12 Mar 2009)

Area: 280 square km (Antigua), 160 square km (Barbuda)

Population: 86,000 (2010)*

Capital: St John's (Antigua); Codrington (Barbuda)

Official language: English

Currency: Eastern Caribbean dollar (EC$) = 100 cents

Exchange rate: EC$2.70 per US$ (fixed)

GDP per capita: US$12,849 (2010)

GDP real growth: -4.10% (2010)

GDP: US$1.11 billion (2010)

Inflation: 3.40% (2010)

Balance of trade: -US$404.81 million (2010)

* estimated figure

the Grenadines – were granted freedom of movement, allowing them to reside, work, establish businesses and provide services throughout the organisation.

Political structure

Form of state

Independent state; it is a member of the Commonwealth.

The executive

The British monarch is the head of state, represented by a governor general who acts on the advice of the prime minister and the cabinet.

National legislature

The bicameral parliament has a 19-member House of Representatives (lower house), of which 17 members (16 Antiguan seats and one Barbudan) are directly elected in single seat constituencies for five-year terms. The remaining two seats are occupied by the Speaker and *ex officio* Attorney General appointed by the governor general, mainly on the advice of the prime minister.

Universal suffrage is at age 18 years.

The prime minister and the cabinet can be held responsible by the parliament.

Legal system

The legal system embodies the principles of English statutory and common law. Antigua is responsible for its own magistrate's courts. The regional Eastern Caribbean Supreme Court is responsible for the high court and the court of appeals. The final court of appeal is to the Privy Council in the UK.

Last elections

12 March 2009 (parliamentary)

Results: Parliamentary: the United Progress Party (UPP) won 51.1 per cent of the vote (nine seats out of 17), the Antigua Labour Party (ALP) 47 per cent (seven), Barbuda People's Movement (BPM) 1.1 per cent (one).

Next elections

March 2014 (parliamentary)

Political parties

Ruling party

United Progressive Party (UPP) (elected 2004; re-elected 12 Mar 2009)

Main opposition party

Antigua Labour Party (ALP)

Political situation

The government, in June 2009, sacked the Antigua and Barbuda chief financial regulator, Leroy King, following his arrest and expected extradition to the US. King was alleged to have accepted US$100,000 in bribes, while aiding US financier Sir Allen Stanford (charged in February 2009 by US prosecutors for a US$8 billion investment fraud perpetrated through the Bank of Antigua), by conducting sham audits and diverting the financial authority from looking closely at Stanford's business dealings.

In December 2009, US senate members lobbied the IMF and World Bank to deny bailout monies to Antigua and Barbuda until the government of the islands took responsibility for compensating US victims of Stanford's frauds.

In parliamentary elections held in March, the ruling UPP won nine out of 17 seats, the Antigua Labour Party (ALP) seven, Barbuda People's Movement (BPM) one; the BPM votes with the government.

Population

86,000 (2010)*

Last census: October 2001: 77,426

Population density: 170 inhabitants per square km. Urban population: 37 per cent (2003).

Annual growth rate: 1.7 per cent 1994–2004 (WHO 2006)

Ethnic make-up

The majority of the population is of African descent; the remainder is of British, Portuguese, Lebanese and Syrian origin.

Religions

Anglican (90 per cent), Methodist, Moravian, Roman Catholic, Pentecostal, Baptist and Seventh Day Adventists.

Education

Literacy rate: 90 per cent (2003)

Enrolment rate: Primary education 6–11 years: 50 per cent; secondary education 33 per cent; tertiary education 20–24 years 6 per cent (2003).

Health

Life expectancy: 72 years, 2004 (WHO 2006)

Fertility rate/Maternal mortality rate: 2.3 births per woman, 2004 (WHO 2006)

Birth rate/Death rate: 18 births per 1,000 population; six deaths per 1,000 population (2003).

Child (under 5 years) mortality rate (per 1,000): 11 per 1,000 live births, 2003 (World Bank)

Main cities

St John's (capital of Antigua, estimated population 22,077 in 2008); Codrington (capital of Barbuda, 150).

Languages spoken

English patois is widely spoken. French also spoken by a small number of people.

Official language/s

English

Media

Press

Dailies: There are two local newspapers including *Antigua Sun* (www.antiguasun.com), which also produces a Sunday edition, and *The Daily Observer* (www.antiguaobserver.com).

Broadcasting

The Antigua and Barbuda Broadcasting Service (ABS) (www.cmatt.com), provides radio and TV services.

Radio: There are several radio stations, including ABS Radio and private, commercial stations, Observer Radio (www.antiguaobserver.com), ZDK Liberty Radio (www.radiozdk.com) and VIBZFM (www.vibzfm.com). Crusader Radio (www.crusaderradio.com) is owned by the United Progressive political party and the Caribbean Radio Lighthouse (www.mannelli.com/lighthouse) is a Christian station.

Television: The government-owned ABS TV operates two channels and a cable service.

KEY INDICATORS — Antigua and Barbuda

	Unit	2006	2007	2008	2009	2010
Population	m	*0.08	*0.08	*0.08	*0.09	*0.09
Gross domestic product (GDP)	US$bn	1.00	1.03	1.26	1.18	1.11
GDP per capita	US$	12,282	13,092	14,929	13,852	12,849
GDP real growth	%	12.2	6.9	4.2	-6.7	-4.1
Inflation	%	1.8	3.4	5.6	-0.6	3.4
Exports (fob) (goods)	US$m	72.0	75.6	78.2	71.5	34.8
Imports (fob) (goods)	US$m	615.0	648.9	671.0	589.4	439.6
Balance of trade	US$m	-543.0	-573.3	-592.8	-517.8	-404.8
Current account	US$m	-162.0	-379.9	-354.3	-261.6	-112.7
Total reserves minus gold	US$m	142.6	143.8	138.0	127.9	136.6
Foreign exchange	US$m	142.6	143.8	138.0	108.2	136.1
Exchange rate	per US$	2.70	2.70	2.70	2.70	2.70

* estimated figure

News agencies
Other news agencies: Caribbean Net News: www.caribbeannetnews.com

Economy
High-end tourism dominates the economy of Antigua and Barbuda, accounting for over half of GDP, which leaves the economy vulnerable to external shocks. The global economic crisis cut tourist numbers until 2010, when numbers returned as the tourist industry made special offers to stimulate its core business. Financial services are also an important component of the economy, offering offshore banking services.
The necessary diversification of the economy is a difficult challenge as labour is attracted to the higher wages of the service sectors and away from agriculture and manufacturing industries. One area into which the islands have successfully diversified is the growing industry of internet gambling sites.
Agriculture is centred on the domestic market, but the lack of fresh water limits production. Manufacturing is limited to a *maquila* sector, producing principally bedding and electronic components.

External trade
Antigua and Barbuda is a member of the Caribbean Community and Common Market (Caricom) which comprises a common market and customs union. It is also a member of the Eastern Caribbean Currency Union (ECCU) using the East Caribbean Dollar.
There is heavy dependence on imported food and energy. The large trading deficit is only partially offset by re-exports (mostly manufactured goods and fuel oil) and earnings from tourism and capital inflows.
Imports
Principal imports include chemicals, fuel and related materials, food and live animals, machinery and transport equipment, other manufactures.
Main sources: US (typically 58 per cent of total), UK (6 per cent), Japan (4 per cent).
Exports
Principal exports include petroleum products while small-scale manufacturing enterprises produce bedding and handicrafts, and mechanical and electronic components for export.
Main destinations: Netherlands Antilles (typically 31per cent total), US (24 per cent), Barbados (8 per cent).
Re-exports
Petroleum

Agriculture
Agriculture typically accounts for around 4 per cent of GDP. Farming is faced with several problems that could weaken its contribution to GDP still further. A limited water supply, soil depletion and drought cause hardship and workers are turning to more lucrative employment in tourism and construction.
The majority of food grown is consumed locally. Fruit and sea-island cotton are grown for export.
Government policy is to encourage self-sufficiency in food. To expand agricultural production capacity, the government, with assistance from the European Development Fund, is promoting livestock development.
An agreement with Cuba has seen Antigua and Barbuda provided with technical assistance in a range of agricultural sectors, including tobacco, fertilisers, pesticides and irrigation.
Fishing
Fishing is a growth area. There are shrimp and lobster farms in operation and the catch each year is over 300t. The typical annual fish catch is over 1,500t.

Industry and manufacturing
Activity is centred on food processing, galvanised sheet, paints and light industries (mainly assembly of household appliances, vehicles, garments, paper products). Industry contributes 19 per cent to GDP, of which the construction sector contributes about 13 per cent. Construction activity has been dominated by housing and infrastructure repair as a result of hurricanes.

Tourism
Tourism is the principal economic activity of Antigua and Barbuda, accounting for around 50 per cent of GDP, three-quarters of foreign exchange earnings and 35 per cent of the labour force. The sector was hurt by the depredations of several hurricanes in the 1990s, the global economic downturn and, to a lesser extent, the 11 September 2001 terrorist attacks in the US. The lucrative stay-over market is recovering, with most visitors coming from the US and the UK. Cruise tourism has been targetted for expansion by the government, including development of the St John's waterfront, which, in its first year of operation, resulted in an increase of 45 per cent of cruise-ship arrivals.

Mining
There are known deposits of high quality barytes, limestone and clay. Redonda island was once an important source of phosphates and guano.

Hydrocarbons
There are no known hydrocarbon reserves. Consumption of oil was 5,000 barrels per day (bpd) in 2008, all of which was imported.
In 2005, Antigua and Barbuda, plus a number of other Caribbean states, signed an agreement with Venezuela to establish PetroCaribe, a multi-national oil company to be owned by the participating states. PetroCaribe buys low-priced Venezuelan crude oil under long-term payment plans.

Energy
Total installed generating capacity was 27MW in 2007, producing over 100 million kilowatt hours. The state-owned Antigua Public Utilities Authority (APUA) is responsible for, among other utilities, overseeing electricity; it generates, manages the transmission lines and distributes electricity.

Financial markets
Stock exchange
Eastern Caribbean Securities Exchange (ECSE)

Banking and insurance
The seven members of the Organisation of Eastern Caribbean States (OECS), Antigua and Barbuda, Dominica, Grenada, Montserrat, St Kitts and Nevis, St Lucia and St Vincent and the Grenadines, share a common currency and central bank. The British Virgin Islands and Anguilla are associate members.
Central bank
Eastern Caribbean Central Bank, St Kitts and Nevis.
Main financial centre
St John's
Offshore facilities
There is an offshore financial sector offering full tax haven facilities to international business companies, trusts, banks and insurance companies. A corporate income tax was introduced in 1999. The International Financial Sector Regulatory Authority has full oversight of the offshore sector. Service providers are required to report suspicious transactions to the authority under the money laundering legislation.

Time
GMT minus four hours

Geography
The country comprises three islands – Antigua, Barbuda and the uninhabited rocky islet of Redonda. They are situated along the outer edge of the Leeward Islands chain in the West Indies. Barbuda is the most northerly, 40km north of Antigua; Redonda is 40km south-west of Antigua. Guadeloupe lies to the south of the country, Montserrat to the south-west and St Kitts Nevis to the west.
Hemisphere
Northern

Climate
Tropical with temperature range from 21–32 degrees Celsius. Little variation throughout year, although driest from January–March.

Entry requirements
Passports
Required by all.
Visa
Not required for most countries. For a full list of those who may visit for business or tourism without a visa visit www.antigua-barbuda.com. Visits must not exceed six months and visitors must have onward/return tickets, confirmation of accommodation.
Currency advice/regulations
No restrictions on import or export of local or foreign currency, as long as amount is declared on arrival and not exceeded on departure.

Health (for visitors)
Mandatory precautions
Yellow fever vaccination certificate if arriving from an infected area.
Advisable precautions
Hepatitis A vaccination recommended. Water and food precautions advisable. Take medical kit.

Hotels
An 8.5 per cent room tax and 10 per cent service charge are added to hotel bills.

Public holidays (national)
Fixed dates
1 Jan (New Year's Day), 7 Oct (Merchant Holiday), 1 Nov (Independence Day), 9 Dec (VC Bird Day), 25 Dec (Christmas Day), 26 Dec (Boxing Day).
Variable dates
Good Friday, Easter Monday, Labour Day (first Mon in May), Whit Monday, Queen's Official Birthday (Jun), Caricom Day (Jul), Summer Carnival (first Mon and Tue in Aug).

Working hours
Banking
Mon–Thur: 0800–1300, 1500–1700; Fri: 0800–1200, 1500–1700.
Government
Mon–Fri: 0800–1200, 1300–1630. Offices close at 1500 on Fridays.
Shops
Mon–Sat: 0830–1200, 1300–1700. Many shops close Thur 1200.

Telecommunications
Mobile/cell phones
GSM 850/1900 services are available throughout the country.

Electricity supply
220/110V AC, 60Hz. American-style two-pin plugs. Some hotels also have outlets for 240V AC; in this case European-style two-pin plugs are used.

Getting there
Air
National airline: Antigua is a shareholder in LIAT, the regional Caribbean airline.
International airport/s: VC Bird International (ANU), 8km north-east of St John's; duty-free shop, restaurant, post office, car hire.
Airport tax: Departure tax: US$20.
Surface
Main port/s: St John's Deepwater Harbour, Falmouth Harbour, English Harbour.

Getting about
National transport
Air: Scheduled daily services between Antigua and Barbuda.
Road: A network connects all main centres. Over 1,000km of roads, mainly all-weather.
Buses: Restricted service.
City transport
Taxis: Fixed rate system. Taxis are not metered and it is advisable to negotiate fares in advance.
Car hire
National or international licence required to obtain visitor's driving permit. Driving is on the left.

BUSINESS DIRECTORY

The addresses listed below are a selection only. While World of Information makes every endeavour to check these addresses, we cannot guarantee that changes have not been made, especially to telephone numbers and area codes. We would welcome any corrections.

Telephone area codes
The international direct dialling code (IDD) for Antigua and Barbuda is +1 268, followed by subscriber's number.

Chambers of Commerce
Antigua and Barbuda Chamber of Commerce and Industry, North and Popeshead Street, PO Box 774, St John's (tel: 462-0743; fax: 462-4575; email: chamcom@candw.org).

Banking
Antigua and Barbuda Development Bank, 27 St Mary's St, Box 1279, St John's (tel: 462-0838; fax: 462-0839).

Antigua and Barbuda Investment Bank Ltd, High St, Box 1679, St John's (tel: 462-0067/1653; fax: 462-0804).

Antigua Commercial Bank, St Mary's and Thames Sts, PO Box 95, St John's (tel: 462-1217/9/2085/1860/4; fax: 462-1220).

Bank of Antigua, 1000 Airport Blvd, Box 315, St John's (tel: 462-4283; fax: 462-0040).

Bank of Nova Scotia, High St, Box 342, St John's (tel: 480-1500; fax: 480-1554).

Barclays Bank plc, High Street, Box 225, St John's (tel: 485-5000; fax: 462-4910).

Caribbean Banking Corporation Ltd, High Street, Box 1324, St John's (tel: 462-4217; fax: 462-5040).

CIBC Caribbean Ltd, High St and Corn Alley, Box 28, St John's (tel: 462-0836/7/0998/1278).

Royal Bank of Canada, High and Market Sts, Box 252, St John's (tel: 462-0325/6; fax: 462-1304).

Swiss American National Bank of Antigua, High St, Box 1302, St John's (tel: 462-4460; fax: 462-0274).

Central bank
Eastern Caribbean Central Bank, Agency Office, PO Box 741, Factory Road, St John's (tel: 462—2489; fax: 462-2490).

Stock exchange
Eastern Caribbean Securities Exchange (ECSE): www.ecseonline.com

Travel information
Antigua Hotels and Tourist Association (AHTA), Lower Redcliffe St, PO Box 454, St John's (tel: 462-0374/3703; fax: 462-3702; e-mail: ahta@candw.ag).

LIAT (1974) Ltd, PO Box 819, VC Bird International Airport (tel: 462-0700; fax: 462-4765).

Ministry of tourism
Ministry of Tourism, Culture and the Environment, New Administration Building, Queen Elizabeth Highway, St John's (tel: 462-0787; fax: 462-2836).

National tourist organisation offices
Antigua and Barbuda Department of Tourism, PO Box 363, Long and Thames Streets, St John's (tel: 462-0480, 462-0029; fax: 462-2483).

Ministries
Minister of State in the Prime Minister's Office and Leader of Government Business in the Senate, Queen Elizabeth Highway, St John's (tel: 462-5933; fax: 462-3225).

Ministry of Agriculture, Lands, Fisheries, Planning and Co-operatives, Nevis and Temple Sts, St John's (tel: 462-1543/5571; fax: 462-6104).

Ministry of Education, Youth, Sports and Community Development, Church St, St John's (tel: 462-4959; fax: 462-4970).

Ministry of Finance and Social Security, High St, St John's (tel: 462-4301; fax: 462-1622/5093).

Ministry of Foreign Affairs, Queen Elizabeth Highway, St John's (tel: 462-4956; fax: 462-3225/9377).

Ministry of Health and Civil Service Affairs, Cross St, St John's (tel: 462-8783; fax: 462-9308/5003).

Ministry of Justice and Legal Affairs, Nevis St, St John's (tel: 462-8867; fax: 462-2465).

Ministry of Labour and Home Affairs, c/o State Insurance Building, Redcliffe St, St John's (tel: 462-0567; 462-1595).

Ministry of Public Utilities, Public Works and Energy, St John's St, St John's (tel: 462-3851/4772; fax: 462-4622).

Ministry of Trade, Industry and Commerce Affairs, Redcliffe Street, St John's (tel: 462-4951; fax: 462-5003).

Other useful addresses

Antigua and Barbuda Embassy (USA), 3216 New Mexico Avenue, NW, Washington DC 20016 (tel: (+1-202) 362-5122; fax: (+1-202) 362-5225).

Antigua Public Utility Authority (APUA), PO Box 416, St Mary's Street, St John's (tel: 462-4990; fax: 462-2516).

British High Commission, PO Box 483, 11 Old Parham Road, St John's (tel: 462-0008/9, 463-0010).

Cable and Wireless Telex Bureau, St Mary's Street, St John's (tel: 462-0840/2).

Directorate of Offshore Gaming, 2nd Floor, Mutual Finance Centre, 9 Factory Rd, Room 216, PO Box 588, St John's (tel: 481-3300; fax: 481-3305; e-mail: director@antiguagaming.com; internet site: http://antiguagaming.d2g.com).

Free Trade & Processing Zone, PO Box 817, St John's (tel: 460-5552; fax: 460-5553; e-mail: ftpzone@candw.ag; internet site: www.antiguafreezone.com).

Industrial Development Board, 34 Newgate Street, St John's (tel: 462-1038; fax: 462-2836).

Internet sites

Daily Observer: www.antiguaobserver.com

East Caribbean Central Bank: www.eccb-centralbank.org

Investment and general information: www.antigua-barbuda.com

Official travel guide: www.geographia.com/an

Argentina

KEY FACTS

Official name: República Argentina (Argentine Republic)

Head of State: President Cristina Fernández de Kirchner (FPV) (from 10 Dec 2007)

Head of government: President Cristina Fernández de Kirchner

Ruling party: Alianza Frente para la Victoria (FpV) (Front for Victory Alliance) (from 2005; re-elected Oct 2007)

Area: 2,766,889 square km

Population: 40.09 million (2010; census figure)

Capital: Buenos Aires

Official language: Spanish

Currency: Peso (P) = 100 centavos

Exchange rate: P4.20 per US$ (Oct 2011)

GDP per capita: US$9,138 (2010)

GDP real growth: 9.20% (2010)

GDP: US$370.30 billion (2010)

Labour force: 11.43 million (2010)

Unemployment: 7.80% (2010)

Inflation: 10.50% (2010)

Oil production: 651,000 bpd (2010)

Balance of trade: US$14.27 billion (2010)

Late October 2010 saw the sudden death of Argentina's former President – and husband of the current president – Néstor Kirchner. Mr Kirchner had been elected to the presidency in 2003. His political credentials were modest – he had been governor of the province of Santa Cruz in the 1990s. At the time Argentina was awash with problems – not least a sovereign default to the tune of US$80 billion and a dramatic devaluation. Mr Kirchner was elected by a political rather than an economic default. Few senior politicians wanted to take the reins at such a time of national crisis; when it came to the final run off between Mr Kirchner and former president Carlos Menem, the latter threw in the towel, allowing Mr Kirchner to make his mark. This he certainly did, soon sidelining Mr Duhalde (who been president briefly in 2002–03 before Kirchner was elected) and, in 2005, getting rid of the architect of Argentina's recovery from economic ashes, the respected economy minister Roberto Lavagna. Mr Kirchner's death left his widow without her principal ally, economic guru and political strategist. Mr Kirchner's replacement in his wife's kitchen cabinet appeared to be the trade union leader Hugo Moyano. Her most prominent rival is the governor of the Buenos Aires province, Daniel Scioli who was reported to be planning a bid for the presidency supported by Mr Duhalde and dissident Peronists.

Default

The tenth anniversary in 2011 of Argentina's default on what eventually amounted to US$100 billion of sovereign debt lead Nobel laureate Paul Krugman, writing in the *New York Times*, to observe that 'Surely the Argentine example suggests that default is a great idea.' Argentina chose to turn its back on the International Monetary Fund (IMF), blaming it for the collapse of the economy. As, in 2011, European economies shrank at the prospect of debt default, Argentina was probably the only country that could recount the experience of life after default. Much of the Argentine pre-default experience chimed closely with that of countries such as Greece as they struggled with ever increasing debt re-payments, political impasse and rampant social unrest. Argentina eventually chose – or was forced to – break the mould. Cold-shouldering the IMF certainly made it difficult, and expensive, to roll over existing debt. But by nationalising pension funds and creaming off cash held in the central bank, Argentina muddled through.

Ten years on

At first glance, the post default Argentine model looks attractive enough. Between default in 2001 and the global financial crisis in 2008, Argentina's economy grew by an impressive 65 per cent. Growth in the gross domestic product (GDP) for 2011 was forecast at an improved 8.2 per cent. A major bugbear of the default experience has been – still the case ten years on – the impossibility of securing loans from the world's capital markets. This means that Argentina's exchange rate has to answer to both fiscal and monetary demands. A balance of payments surplus is also a *sine qua non* of Argentine economic policy if both trade and fiscal surplus are to be maintained.

Attention to detail had been a key component of President Cristina Kirchner's predecessor (and husband) President Néstor Kirchner. Succeeded by his wife, it was assumed in Argentine political circles that, á la Putin, Mr Kirchner had remained the *éminence grise* behind the presidential throne. His unexpected death saw a slow relaxation in fiscal discipline, as the annual inflation rate edged up – to 9.7 per cent according to official circles, but to a far higher 25–30 per cent according to most independent analysts. Mrs Kirchner may appear to European politicians to be in the classic 'Evita' mould of Latin American politics. But under her leadership, the post default Argentina saw itself welcomed into the G20 group of the world's leading economies. And few international leaders are able to analyse so accurately the misguided advice handed out to Argentina by the IMF as well as the unhelpful role of the credit rating agencies.

Argentina watchers know only too well how the country has followed a pendulum pattern of progress from boom to bust over the post World War II years. Whether the post default boom can be maintained, or whether the ominous inflation figures will hold sway, remained uncertain in mid-2011. Argentina's terms of trade may have been favourable in 2010, but there were other negatives waiting in the wings. Productivity, by international standards, is depressingly low. Investment is also below par – private investors often preferring the safety of overseas investments and bank accounts. One report claimed that Argentina's educational standards were also falling behind. The boom-like growth figures were, for the most part, the result of primary product and raw materials prices and demand. Accepting that Argentina's inflation is somewhere between 10 and 30 per cent, the inevitable conclusion is that the Argentine currency will appreciate, eroding competitiveness. International investors, even those active in the hydrocarbons sector, are avoiding rather than rushing to Argentina. Recent boom-bust experiences are also instrumental in causing increased capital flight. Some estimates put the figure over 2008-2011 at a staggering US$60 billion, more than double estimates of the inward investment figure for the same period.

Quoted in the London *Financial Times* in mid-2011, former central bank director Martín Redrado (replaced in 2010) claimed that: 'The government has a pro-inflationary monetary and fiscal policy which is inconsistent with the exchange rate policy. Sooner or later they will collide. Argentina isn't going to explode as it did before, but it is heading into the path of a storm.' Perhaps surprisingly, according to the *Financial Times*, Argentina still has the region's highest per capita income on a purchasing parity basis, although its economy in 2010 was one sixth of the size of Brazil's and one third that of Mexico.

According to preliminary figures prepared by the United Nations Economic Commission for Latin America and the Caribbean (ECLAC), the Argentine economy recovered strongly in 2010, with GDP growth expected to be in the region of 8 per cent, with unemployment falling to about 7.5 per cent in the third quarter of the year. The factors holding back the economy already appeared to be reversing in the second half of 2009 as a result of both external and local developments.

KEY INDICATORS **Argentina**

	Unit	2006	2007	2008	2009	2010
Population	m	38.97	39.36	39.70	*40.13	40.09
Gross domestic product (GDP)	US$bn	212.71	260.00	326.50	310.10	370.30
GDP per capita	US$	5,458	6,606	8,214	7,726	9,138
GDP real growth	%	*8.5	7.5	6.8	0.9	9.2
Inflation	%	10.9	8.5	8.6	6.3	10.5
Unemployment	%	9.5	9.2	7.9	8.7	–
Industrial output	% change	–	7.5	4.0	-1.2	–
Agricultural output	% change	–	9.8	-2.5	-15.7	–
Oil output	'000 bpd	716.0	698.0	682.0	676.0	651.0
Natural gas output	bn cum	46.1	44.8	44.1	41.4	40.1
Exports (fob) (goods)	US$m	33,908.0	55,980.0	70,589.0	55,669.0	68,134.0
Imports (fob) (goods)	US$m	23,484.0	42,525.0	54,547.0	37,141.0	53,868.0
Balance of trade	US$m	10,424.0	13,456.0	16,041.0	18,528.0	14,266.0
Current account	US$m	5,156.0	7,355.0	6,857.0	8,794.0	3,082.0
Total reserves minus gold	US$m	30,903.0	44,682.0	44,855.0	46,093.0	49,734.0
Foreign exchange	US$m	30,421.0	44,175.0	44,360.0	42,922.0	46,619.0
Exchange rate	per US$	3.07	3.14	3.14	3.71	3.90

* estimated figure

Export demand recovered as a result of developments in agricultural product markets and the economic performance of major trading partners such as Brazil. The strong recovery in grain harvests, affected by a severe drought in the previous growing season, made a substantial contribution, (together with sales of manufactured goods), to a considerable upsurge in exports (which did not, however, attain the very high values of 2008). At the same time, domestic spending was stimulated by the behaviour of the private sector and by macroeconomic policies.

The absence of signs of fragility in the country's finances and currency, together with lower returns on external assets, held down demand for foreign exchange. Contrasting with the large outflow of private capital in the first half of 2009, there was a (small) net inflow in the same period of 2010, while the trade surplus remained substantial even though reduced by higher imports. In a context of low international interest rates, a gradual weakening of the nominal exchange rate against the dollar and expectations of rising domestic prices, there was a considerable increase in sales of durable goods, particularly automobiles, as activity recovered and worries about the possibility of falling incomes eased. In addition, demand resulting from transfers to poor families via the child allowance (a mechanism that began to be implemented in 2009) fed through to non-durable consumer goods markets.

Taken as a whole, public spending expanded strongly. ECLAC noted that investment more than kept pace with aggregate growth and the accumulation rate recovered as a result, although the capital stock probably grew less quickly than output. Discussions about the inflation trend influenced wage negotiations, which were held under conditions indicative of future growth in demand, which materialised over the course of the year. Besides macro-economic factors, changes in price aggregates were influenced by specific developments in the food sector, particularly a lower supply of beef resulting from a decline in the size of the cattle stock. At the same time, the rate of depreciation against the dollar slowed. The effect on the multilateral real exchange rate was moderated by the appreciation of other currencies that are important for trade.

Back to the IMF

In November, after eight years of near hostility, the government announced a request for technical assistance from the IMF to prepare a nationwide consumer price index (CPI). In general, economic policy was directed towards strengthening the growth of demand and activity. In the first 10 months of 2010, national tax revenues were more than 30 per cent up on the same period the previous year, with growth shared evenly across the main taxes. Public spending increased at a similar rate, with particularly large increases for transfers to the private sector (where the child allowance and assistance for the energy sector were major growth items) and social security benefits. The public sector had a significantly larger volume of funding than the year before, owing to the general growth in tax revenues and funds transferred by the Central Bank in the form of dividends on stated earnings, which were booked as current income. The primary balance of the national public sector is expected to come in at about 2 per cent of GDP for 2010.

Monetary policy focussed on the use of external and local asset operations to limit fluctuations in the exchange rate and financial variables. At the beginning of the year, a controversy arose about the use of international reserves for public debt servicing, the operations concerned having been executed following the removal of the Banco Central de la República Argentina (central bank) president from his post. The government put forward an offer to regularise debt whose bondholders had not taken part in the 2005 restructuring. The ensuing bond swap involved about three quarters of all liabilities in this category. At the same time, some negotiations were undertaken to regularise outstanding debts with the Paris Club of international debtors. The yield spreads implicit in the prices of public bonds came down appreciably, although they remained higher than those of other countries in the region.

Argentina's economic activity indicator rose by 9 per cent in the first nine months of the year by comparison with the same period in 2009, and year-on-year GDP increased by 9.4 per cent in the first half. Output in goods-producing sectors rose particularly strongly from the benchmark levels of the recession. Agricultural output growth was particularly vigorous at 44 per cent in the first half. The grain harvest, comprising cereals, oilseeds and other crops, recovered very strongly to come in at about 93 million tons, a figure more than 50 per cent higher than the previous period's total for a similar sown area and close to the record harvests of the 2006–08 period. Soybean production grew by some 70 per cent and accounted for over half the total harvest. Maize output also increased greatly to a record 23 million tons. Conversely, the harvest of wheat, exports of which were restricted, fell to less than 8 million tons, a low figure by historical standards.

Argentina's manufacturing index rose by 9.3 per cent in the first 10 months, with considerable diversity of performance according to industrial sectors. Automobile output exceeded the peaks of 2008 with an impressive year-on-year rise of over 40 per cent. There was also a considerable (27 per cent) increase in the output of the basic metals industries. Conversely, cold storage plant activity contracted owing to the decline in supplies of raw material, as did the output of paper industries. The reported year-on-year rise in the Greater Buenos Aires CPI was 11.1 per cent in October (although many independent analysts put the figure somewhere between 20 and 30 per cent). Wage negotiations certainly seem to have been based on perceptions of substantially higher inflation. In any event, the general wages index (covering public- and private-sector workers, both registered and informal) rose by 25.5 per cent in the year to September.

Energy

Argentina's hydrocarbon sector is of vital importance to the economy. However, this point seems to be lost on its government, which continues to impose heavy regulation, to such an extent that private investors have preferred to go elsewhere. Thus, although domestic demand continues to grow, production of both oil and gas have been in decline in recent years, creating a structural imbalance and forcing Argentina to depend on energy imports. Argentina is, in fact, self sufficient in crude oil, but has to import refined oil products. The unattractive investment climate has meant that oil exploration activity levels are low. This, combined with the decline in production from Argentina's maturing fields, has meant that oil production has steadily declined since peaking in 1998.

Argentina's energy sector is also distorted by continued subsidies from central government, designed to prevent the politically unacceptable prospect of increasing prices for residential customers. In July 2011 the government, robbing Peter to pay Paul, had to seek extra funding for the energy subsidies, having exhausted the budgeted amount by mid-year. A document signed by eight former energy secretaries in July 2011 estimated Argentina's energy trade deficit for 2011 to be around US$3 billion. In 2006 the energy surplus was US$5.6 billion. Energy subsidies were estimated at US$6.3 billion. To make matters worse, in 2010 and 2011, the sector has been beset by labour discord, causing production to fall by as much as 100,000 barrels per day (bpd). As the thirtieth anniversary of the Falklands (Las Malvinas) war with the United Kingdom (UK) approached, there was some speculation that important reserves were to be found, in fact no oil in any quantity was located. The Argentine government continued to raise objections to the Falkland exploration activities. In Argentine waters close to the Falklands, a consortium comprising Yacimientos Petrolíferos (YPF), Pan American Energy (PAE) and Brazil's Petrobras has been carrying out exploration activities.

According to the *Oil and Gas Journal* (OGJ) Argentina's reserves at the beginning of 2011 amounted to 2.5 thousand million barrels. One positive development in an otherwise depressed industry was the announcement by the Spanish-owned YPF of a discovery of 150 million barrels of shale oil in the southern province of Neuquén. YPF is owned by Repsol, but although the Spanish company appears to want to retain majority ownership, it has been reducing its shareholding. Argentina's second largest oil company is PAE owned (since 2010 when the UK's BP sold its shareholding) by Argentina's Bridas Corporation. Bridas Corporation is itself a joint venture between the China National Offshore Oil Corporation (CNOOC) and Brias Energy Holdings. Oil production in 2010 according to the June 2011 issue of the BP Statistical Review of World Energy (BP11) was in the order of 651,000bpd. Chubut is the largest producing province, followed by Neuquén, Santa Cruz and Mendoza. At the end of 2010 the Argentine oil interests of Occidental of the US were sold to China's Sinopec, reinforcing a trend of increased Chinese exploration activities throughout Latin America. Occidental had been among the five largest foreign oil companies present in Argentina.

Although the recent history of the Argentine energy industry has been patchy, one bright spot has been the development of bio-diesel production. Argentina is one of the world's largest producers, and is the largest exporter of bio-diesel. Soybean production reached 23,100bpd in 2009, most of which was exported to Europe. Domestic consumption of bio-diesel also grew rapidly in 2010 following legislation that obliged diesel producers to blend in a seven per cent bio-diesel component.

The recent narrative of Argentina's natural gas production echoes the travails of its oil industry. Although Argentina is the largest natural gas producer in mainland South America, production has fallen by an estimated ten per cent since 2008. In the same year, Argentina became a net gas importer, as supplies were needed to maintain electricity generation. Other major gas consumers are the domestic industrial and residential sectors, consuming 20 per cent each. The transport sector also accounts for a significant amount, as almost two million vehicles are run on compressed natural gas. Increased imports of natural gas will be needed if the summer (air conditioning) and winter (heating) shortages experienced in recent years are not to be repeated. To revitalise and generate interest in the sector, the Argentine government introduced a Gas Plus programme aimed at permitting Argentine companies to sell natural gas from new or unconventional (shale, for example) sources at a premium roughly double the existing tariff. About 230 million cubic feet of 'unconventional' gas was produced in 2010. The largest domestic producer is Total Austral, a subsidiary of France's Total. An analysis of Argentina's existing natural gas reserves presents a sorry story – 2011 reserves were estimated by the BP2011 at 12.2 trillion cubic feet (tcf), representing a dramatic decline of around 50 per cent from a decade earlier. All Argentina's energy hopes are pinned on its large reserves of recoverable shale gas. These are put at 774tcf, the third largest in the world after China and the USA. In a minor key, in 2010 YPF discovered reserves of shale and conventional gas estimated at 4.5tcf in its Loma la Lata field in Neuquén. Currently, roughly half of Argentina's natural gas comes from fields in Neuquén, with some ten per cent coming from offshore fields.

Argentina's principal solution to increasing gas shortages is its agreement with Bolivia to supply natural gas. In 2010 this provided some 5 billion cubic metres of gas per day, expected to rise to 7.7 million in 2011, and to 27.7 million by 2017. Imports of liquefied natural gas (LNG) come mainly from Trinidad and Tobago; LNG imports were expected to double in 2011.

Electricity supplies are bolstered by Argentina's nuclear generation programme. This is expected to be extended in 2012 by the commissioning of the Atucha II plant. Atucha 1 began generation in 1974 augmented later by the Embalse plant near Córdoba. Following the general pattern of infrastructure projects in Argentina, hydroelectric electricity generation has tended to decline recently. Wind-power generation is under review in Patagonia, the topography of this region lends itself to this type of plant.

Risk assessment

Economy	Fair
Politics	Fair
Regional stability	Fair

COUNTRY PROFILE

Historical profile

1916–22 and 1928–30 President Hipolito Yrigoyen was Argentina's first popularly elected president. He was ousted in his second term by the armed forces.

1939–1945 Argentina was neutral during the Second World War and initially refused to break diplomatic relations with Japan and Germany.

1943 A military government, with pro-fascist sympathies, assumed power.

1944 Argentina broke diplomatic relations with Japan and Germany and declared war on them.

1946 General Juan Domingo Perón, a leading figure in the military government, won a free presidential election. He and his wife, Evita, became increasingly popular as social services spending grew. However, foreign exchange reserves built up during the Second World War were squandered by nationalising the railways and other public utilities. President Perón became increasingly repressive towards his critics and the Catholic Church.

1949 A new constitution strengthened the power of the president and criticising the government became a criminal offence, leading to the jailing of Perón's opponents.

1951 Perón was re-elected with a large majority.

1952 Perón's populist wife, Evita, died of cancer and his grass roots support began to wane.

1955 An attempted coup by the navy was crushed by the army. However, the armed forces did seize power later and Perón was exiled. A series of unstable military and civilian governments in subsequent years saw the Perónists win the few elections held.

1973 Hector Campora was elected president, following a Perónist victory. He resigned following widespread civil disturbances and was succeeded by Juan Perón, who had returned from exile.

1974 Perón died and was succeeded by his third wife, Isabel María Estela Martínez Cartas de Perón (better known as Isabel Perón). The country sank into political and economic chaos.
1976 The armed forces overthrew the government and installed General Jorge Videla as president on 29 March.
1976–83 The military junta suppressed left-wing opposition groups and activists and up to an estimated 30,000 people 'disappeared' in the state-sponsored dirty war (Guerra Sucia), where violence and murder against citizens was undertaken by military and police forces, in extrajudicial activities.
1981 General Leopoldo Galtieri became president on 22 December.
1982 The military invaded the Falkland Islands/Islas Malvinas, which lead to a conflict with the UK lasting ten weeks. Following Argentina's surrender its dead numbered over 700 and cost the economy billions of US dollars which all but collapsed and ended the military's power in office. General Bignone replaced Galtieri and instigated civilian elections.
1983 Raul Alfonsín of the Unión Cívica Radical (UCR) (Radical Civic Union) won the presidential elections.
1989 Perónist, Carlos Ménem, became president and began a programme of economic austerity in an effort to stabilise and restructure the ailing economy.
1990 Full diplomatic relations with the UK were restored, although Argentina continued to claim the Falkland Islands.
1992 The peso was introduced as a new currency and was pegged to the US dollar at a one-to-one rate.
1995 Ménem was re-elected president.
1997 International pressure was applied when a judge in Spain called for the arrest of senior military officers involved in human rights violations during the 'dirty war'. However a blanket national amnesty protected them.
1998 Argentine judges ordered arrests in connection with the abduction of hundreds of children of women arrested during the 'dirty war'. A protracted recession began.
1999 Fernando de la Rúa won the presidency; his centre-left Alianza para el Trabajo, la Justicia y la Educación (Alianza) (Alliance for Work, Justice and Education) failed to secure an absolute majority in the lower house of Congress but still had to deal with the economy which was US$114 billion in debt.
2000 The IMF granted a loan of US$40 million. Private Argentine aircraft and boats were again allowed to visit the Falkland Islands.
2001 The amnesty laws allowing members of the armed forces to escape prosecution for human rights abuses were overturned. The economy, devastated by years of recession and near to collapse led to public protests and a general strike against government spending cuts. The Perónists won the mid-term parliamentary elections and both houses of Congress came under opposition control. President Fernando de la Rúa resigned; Ramon Puerta took over briefly before Adolfo Rodríguez Saa became president. Saa's presidency lasted only until mass demonstrations against his austerity measures caused his resignation. Eduardo Camaño became acting president.
2002 Perónist Eduardo Duhalde was elected president by the Legislative Assembly on 2 January. He become the fifth president in two weeks, initially for only a few months until elections were held. The peso was devalued breaking the link with the US dollar. The president was given the power to pass some laws without congressional approval for the next two years. The peso was floated.
2003 Carlos Saúl Menem withdrew from the presidential election leaving Néstor Kirchner to win by default.
2004 An international arrest warrant was issued for the former president, Carlos Menem, over allegations of fraud. Menem returned from exile in Chile, following the cancellation of two international warrants for his arrest. The IMF accepted that its handling of Argentina's financial crisis in 2001 had aggravated the deepening recession and that it had continued to lend Argentina money when its debt burden had become unsustainable.
2005 Argentina's US$100 billion debt restructuring offer was accepted. The country hosted a thirty-four nation Summit of the Americas; violent protests accompanied proceedings.
2006 Argentina cleared its debt to the IMF. Price controls were extended in a bid to counter inflationary tendencies.
2007 Cristina Fernández de Kirchner (FPV), the wife of the former president Néstor Kirchner (2003–07), became president.
2008 Former president Fernando de la Rúa was charged with 'aggravated bribery' by a federal court. He was accused of bribing senators during the 2001 Congress debate to vote in favour of labour reforms.
2009 Argentina laid claim to 1.7 million square kilometres of ocean around its coast, up to Antarctica and including island chains governed by the UK, including Las Malvinas/Falkland Islands. In elections for 50 per cent of seats in the Chamber of Deputies, the ruling Perónist coalition, led by Frente para la Victoria (FPV) (Front for Victory) won 47 seats and lost its overall majority. The newly formed Acuerdo Cívico y Social (ACyS) (Civil and Social Agreement) (coalition of three parties and others) won a majority 41 seats in both chambers. President Kitchner remained in office as head of government. Former military leader Raynaldo Bignone and five other retired generals went on trial on 3 November charged with kidnapping, torture, human rights violations and the disappearance and killing of hundreds of opponents of the regime in the late 1970s.
2010 In February the government was again thwarted in its attempt to tap US$6.5 billion of central bank funds to pay off debt when a court refused to allow the move. President Cristina Kitchner's original plan had been opposed by central bank governor, Martín Redrado, who was forced to resign. In February, Argentina called on the UN to facilitate a meeting with the UK government to discuss sovereignty of Las Malvinas/Falkland Islands, just as UK-licensed oil exploration companies began exploratory drilling offshore of the islands. General Bignone, the former *de facto* president of Argentina, was jailed for 25 years in April for his abuses while he was in charge of the country's second largest torture centre between 1978–79. By June, long-term creditors agreed to accept new government bonds for two-thirds of the outstanding debt in a deal worth US$12 billion. This meant that Argentina had settled 92 per cent of its outstanding debt (from 2001) and expected to be able to borrow on the international money market at a better interest rate than any since 2001. Former president Néstor Kirchner died suddenly of a heart attack on 27 October; he had been expected to run in the 2011 presidential election. A national census was conducted on 27 October. Former military ruler Jorge Videla was sentenced to life in prison on 22 December, for crimes against humanity.
2011 General Bignone, the last military leader of Argentina, was found guilty of human rights abuses during the 1976–83 junta rule and was sentenced to life in prison on 15 April; four other accused were also convicted. Tough anti-tobacco legislation, already passed by the Senate, was approved by the lower house of assembly in June. Advertising and sponsorship will be banned, as will smoking in bars, restaurants and the work place and sale of single cigarettes and all sales to under 18 year olds. On 15 June, the UK prime minister reaffirmed his government's determination not to negotiate over the sovereignty of Las Malvinas/Falkland Islands. On 21 June President Cristina Kirchner announced that she would stand for re-election in October. In July Iran was reported to have offered to help investigations into the

1994 bombing of a Jewish centre in Buenos Aires that killed 85 people.

Political structure

Constitution

Under the 1853 constitution which was reinstated by the military government in 1955, power is separated into executive, legislative and judicial branches at federal and state level. Each of the 22 states has its own subordinated constitution, elects its own executive and legislature and establishes its own judiciary.

Form of state

Federal presidential democratic republic

The executive

Executive power is vested in the president, who is elected by popular vote every four years, with a limit of two terms in office.

National legislature

The Congreso Nacional (National Congress) consists of two chambers. The Cámara de Diputados de la Nación (Chamber of the Deputies of the Nation) has 256 members, elected by proportional representation for four-year terms; every two years half the seats are up for election. The chamber has exclusive rights to raise taxes.

The Senado de la Nación (Senate of the Nation) has 72 members, elected for six-year terms. Elected members are chosen from three-seat constituencies (23 provincial and the federal capital), two seats go to the party or coalition winning most votes and one seat to the second largest party or coalition. Every two years one-third of the constituencies are elected.

Universal suffrage is from aged 18 years and voting is mandatory (with some exceptions).

Legal system

The judiciary is independent of the government and forms the third 'pillar' of the constitution. Since 1998, federal judges have been elected and dismissed by a body comprising lawyers and academics. The election of judges was intended to reduce the endemic political influence that had previously affected the Argentine legal system, especially at the local level, for many years. There is a Supreme Court system at national and provincial levels.

Last elections

28 June 2009 (parliamentary); 27 October 2007 (presidential).

Results: Presidential: Cristina Fernández de Kirchner (FPV) won 44.9 per cent of the vote, Elisa Carrio (Confederación Coalición Cívica (CCC) (Civic Coalition Confederation)) 22.9 per cent and Roberto Lavagna (UNA) 16.9 per cent; all other candidates won less than 10 per cent. Turnout was 74.14 per cent.

Chamber of Deputies (50 per cent of seats): Peronists, (coalition of three parties and others), 30.8 per cent (47 seats out of 150), Acuerdo Cívico y Social (ACyS) (Civil and Social Agreement) (coalition of three parties and others) 28.94 per cent (41), Propuesta Republicana (PRO) (Republican Proposal) 17.7 per cent (20), Total de Izquierda (TI) (Total Left-wing) 5.7 per cent (6), minor independent parties 16.77 per cent in total (13).

Senate (30 per cent of seats): Peronists eight seats out of 30, ACyS 14, minor parties two.

Next elections

2011 (presidential and parliamentary: 50 per cent of seats contested every two years)

Political parties

Ruling party

Alianza Frente para la Victoria (FPV) (Front for Victory Alliance) (from 2005; re-elected Oct 2007)

Main opposition party

Unión Cívica Radical (UCR) (Radical Civic Union)

Political situation

Population

40.09 million (2010; census figure)

Last census: November 2001: 36,260,130

Population density: 14 inhabitants per square km. Urban population: 88 per cent of total (1995–2001).

Annual growth rate: 1.1 per cent 1994–2004 (WHO 2006)

Ethnic make-up

White (97 per cent), principally descendants of Italian and Spanish immigrants. Minority groups include the Buenos Aires Jewish community and Anglo-Argentines throughout the country. The major indigenous nations are the Quechua of the north-west, the Mapuche of northern Patagonia and the Matacos, Tobas and others who inhabit the Chaco and north-eastern cities like Resistencia and Santa Fé.

Religions

Roman Catholic (92 per cent), Protestant (2 per cent), Jewish (2 per cent), others (4 per cent).

Education

Education is compulsory and free, so that Argentina has one of the highest literacy rates in Latin America. Secondary education consists of basic general education and polymodal education (multipurpose schools catering to ages between 15 and 18). In parallel to the polymodal cycle, there is a technical-,professional course, which leads after a further year's study to the title of *Técnico*. Higher education is provided by national and private universities, which are autonomous. There are 25 national universities. Technical institutes (Institutos de Formación Técnica) offer higher technical education, leading to the award of the *Título menor*. Professional courses are also available in a wide range of subjects.

Literacy rate: 97 per cent adult rate; 99 per cent youth rate (15–24) (Unesco 2005).

Compulsory years: 6 to 15

Enrolment rate: 120 per cent gross primary enrolment of relevant age group (including repeaters); 100 per cent gross secondary enrolment; 57 per cent in tertiary education (World Bank).

Pupils per teacher: 17 in primary schools

Health

Per capita total expenditure on health (2003) was US$1,067; of which per capita government spending was US$518, at the international dollar rate, (WHO 2006).

The healthcare sector was deregulated in 2001. In effect, this gives Argentinians the right to choose between the union-administered healthcare system, known as *obras sociales*, and private healthcare providers. The reorganisation meant that those who paid into, or were already members of, a private health scheme, would no longer have to pay 3 per cent of their salaries to the union-administered system.

Most children receive immunisations against childhood diseases.

HIV/Aids

HIV prevalence: 0.7 per cent aged 15–49 in 2003 (World Bank)

Life expectancy: 75 years, 2004 (WHO 2006)

Fertility rate/Maternal mortality rate: 2.3 births per woman, 2004 (WHO 2006); maternal deaths 38 per 100,000 live births (World Bank).

Child (under 5 years) mortality rate (per 1,000): 17 per 1,000 live births (2003); 5 per cent of children aged under five are malnourished (World Bank).

Welfare

The main portion of the Argentine social security system is borne by a pay-as-you-go system where employers' and employees' contributions fund payments. Workers must contribute 11 per cent of their pay regardless of whether workers participate in a private, or the public, social security system; employers must contribute the equivalent of 16 per cent of each workers' salary to the public system. Non-salaried workers must pay the full amount of 27 per cent of their income.

The whole social security system is adversely affected when employers fail to pay or withhold their social security contributions. However, the percentage of non-registered employees in Argentina is very high. According to non-official

records of the Argentine Ministry of Labour, 20 out of 100 employees are non-registered employees, thus depriving them of pensions. Measures have been taken by the Argentine Social Security Authority (SSA) to force employers to register employees and contribute to the social security fund.
Ten of the country's largest private pension funds were nationalised in October 2008 at a cost of US$30 billion. The decision was taken to save the funds from the global financial turmoil.

Pensions

Argentina reformed its pension system in 1994 to a mixture of the old government-administered system and an individual retirement account programme administered by the Retirement and Pension Fund Administrators (AFJPs).
Argentina has retained the pay-as-you-go system. This system provides basic, universal old-age coverage (known as PBU) for all workers who reach retirement age and who have contributed for at least 30 years including a portion of the wealthiest Argentines' pensions. Payment of retirement benefits begin at age 65 for men and age 60 for women.

Main cities

Buenos Aires (capital, estimated population 12.1 million (m) in 2008), Córdoba (1.5m), Rosario (1.2m), La Plata (731,458), Tucumán (818,672), Mar del Plata (584,702), Mendoza (919,824), Salta (540,478), Santa Fé (500,365), Tucumán (818,672).

Languages spoken

Italian, German and French are still maintained within their respective communities. English is generally spoken in business circles. There are 17 native Indian languages, the most widely spoken of which is Quechua.

Official language/s

Spanish

Media

Argentina has a sophisticated media industry with over 150 daily newspapers, based in cities or regionally, hundreds of private commercial radio stations and dozens of televisions stations.

Press

Dailies: In Spanish, *La Nación* (www.lanacion.com.ar) is a respected publication, *Página 12* (www.pagina12.com.ar) has left-wing views, *La Prensa* (www.laprensa.com.ar), *La Razón* (www.larazon.com.ar) is a popular national broadsheet and *Clarín* (www.clarin.com). Regional newspapers includes *La Mañana de Córdiba* (www.lmcordoba.com.ar), *La Capital* (www.lacapital.com.ar) and *El Tábano* (www.eltabano.com).
In English, *Buenos Aires Herald* (www.buenosairesherald.com), has a business supplement and *Buenos Aires Times* (www.buenosairestimes.com).
Weeklies: In Spanish, *168 Horas* (http://168horas.com.ar), *Noticias* (www.noticias.uolsinectis.com.ar) has features on business and current affairs, *Foco* (www.foco.uol.com.ar). In German, *Argentinisches Tageblatt* (www.tageblatt.com.ar).
Business: In Spanish, major newspapers include *El Cronista* (www.cronista.com), *Negocio Nea* (www.negocionea.com.ar), *El Economista* (www.eleconomista.com.ar) and *Ambito Financiero* (www.ambitoweb.com) with an online edition in English. Business magazines include *Alzas y Bajas* (www.alzasybajas.com.ar), *Apertura* (www.apertura.com), *Bolsafe Valores* (www.bolsafevalores.com), *Edicion i* (www.edicioni.com), *El Grafico* (www.elgrafico.uol.com.ar), *Estrategas* (www.revistaestrategas.com.ar), *Fortuna* (www.revista-fortuna.com.ar), *Gestion* (www.gestion.com.ar), *Merdado* (www.mercado.com.ar), *Prensa Economica* (www.prensaeconomica.com.ar) and *Realidad Economica* (www.iade.org.ar). Monthly magazines include *Tiempo Empresario* (www.tiempoempresario.com.ar) and *Negocios Magazine*.
Periodicals: There are numerous magazines available, covering all interests. *Viva Sophia* (www.vivisophia.com) is a monthly women's magazine.

Broadcasting

Radio: In Spanish, the national public radio is Radio Nacional (www.radionacional.gov.ar) with four channels. La Red (www.uol.com.ar) is a national, commercial network. Radio Intereconomía (www.intereconomia.com) has news and economic contents.
One of the most popular radio stations is based in Buenos Aires, Radio Rivadavia (www.rivadavia.com.ar) along with at least 40 other FM stations. All musical genres are broadcast, as well as news (Radio America, www.estoesamerica.com.ar), cultural (Radio Continental, www.continental.com.ar) and religious contents (Red Puerto Libre, www.redpuertolibre.com.ar).
Television: There are five national television networks operated through affiliates and many more local services. Canal 7 (www.canal7.com.ar) is the state-run national TV service specialising in cultural and educational programmes but with the lowest viewer numbers. Telefe (www.telefe.com) with the highest viewer figures produces local content programmes as well as showing internationally produced shows. Canal 13 (www.canaltrece.com.ar) is Telefe's rival, producing popular programmes as well as news and current affairs. America 2 (www.america2.com.ar) and Canal 9 (www.canal9.com.ar) are the remaining national networks.
Argentina has one of the world's highest take-up rate for cable television with over a dozen stations to choose from. Station contents can be specific to viewer interest such as sports, children's or lifestyle programming or general content.

Advertising

The Centro de Informaciones de Publicidad (www.cip.org.ar) has authority for advertising matters in Argentina.
Press advertising accounts for approximately 45 per cent of total advertising expenditure, with commercial television taking between 25 and 30 per cent. Outdoor sites for posters are usually controlled by a few major or local companies or local authorities.

News agencies

National news agency: Telam: www.telam.com.ar
Other news agencies: Agencia DIB (in Spanish): www.dib.com.ar
Agencia Nova (in Spanish): www.agencianova.com
Clave Noticias (in Spanish): www.clavenoticias.com.ar
Noticias Agrentinas (in Spanish): www.noticiasargentinas.com
Diarios y Noticias (DYN) (in Spanish): www.dyn.com.ar

Economy

Argentina has vast natural resources providing a good standard of living for the population. These include rich farmlands with yields destined for export, a diverse industrial base, an educated workforce and minerals such as petroleum and natural gas. Industry constitutes the single largest component of GDP at over 20 per cent. It uses the abundant agricultural produce (Argentina is a major global producer of soya beans, beef and wheat) in food processing and mineral resources in chemical and pharmaceutical manufacturing, for iron, steel and aluminium production and it has factories for motor vehicle and machinery assembly, plus shipbuilding. However, its financial services and tourism sectors jointly constitute the largest share of over 60 per cent of GDP.
GDP growth was 6.8 per cent in 2008, down from 8.76 per cent 2007, as the global economic crisis deepened. By 2009 GDP growth had almost collapsed with a rate of 0.9 per cent. However, in 2010 the economy bounced back and reached a growth rate of 9.2 per cent. An agreement (in March 2009) between

Argentina and China to swap US$10 billion worth of their currencies with each other will allow trade without recourse to the US dollar. Argentine business may buy Chinese imports directly in renminbi and the deal provides Argentina with hard cash. World prices of Argentina's commodities hit an all-time high in 2008 and boosted the trade surplus to US$13.2 billion, allowing Argentina to build up official reserves of US$44.9 billion (August 2009), which permitted it to repay US$12 billion to creditors on loans defaulted in 2001. This brought the total percentage of loans repaid, as of June 2010, to 92 per cent and should allow Argentina to borrow on global capital markets from which it has been barred since 2001. Argentina is the second largest economy in South America and the resumption of talks strengthened interest in government bonds in the international money market.

External trade

The EU and Mercosur have had a trading agreement since 2006. Argentina typically has a trade surplus with the EU, over 66 per cent of which is made up of food and live animals (Argentina is ranked third in the EU's total imports of agricultural products (including prepared foodstuffs) in 2008); there is also a surplus, in favour of Argentina, of foreign direct investment (FDI).

In 2004, twelve South American countries signed an agreement to launch the South American Community of Nations (CSN), modelled on the European Union. In 2007 the name was changed to Union of South American Nations (Unasur). Unasur seeks to integrate with the Andean Community of Nations and Mercosur in a single market by 2014, when tariffs on non-sensitive products are abolished with the remainder eliminated by 2019. However political tensions within the region have hampered the ongoing process.

Argentine plans to form a closer trading relationship with China have been in existence for some time due to the increasing trade in soya, coupled with Chinese investment in Argentina.

Imports

Principal imports include metal manufactures, machinery and equipment, vehicles, chemicals and plastics.

Main sources: Brazil (typically 31 per cent of total), China (12 per cent), US (12 per cent).

Exports

Mineral products, agricultural products, vehicles and parts, electrical machinery, live animals and related products, chemicals. Food processing particularly meat, flour and other canned items are the largest manufacturing activities. Argentina is the primary source of tannin and linseed oil worldwide.

Main destinations: Brazil (typically 20 per cent of total), China (9 per cent), US (8 per cent).

Agriculture

Farming

The agricultural sector as a whole contributes around 7 per cent to GDP and employs 11 per cent of the workforce, with the sector being composed predominantly of individual farmers and small companies. Arable land covers 12 per cent of Argentina's total land area. The country is an important producer of food, particularly soya beans, meat and wheat. Together, vegetable products and livestock account for nearly a quarter of total exports. Overall, the country is the fifth largest agricultural exporter in the world, with the sector accounting for 60 per cent of all Argentina's exports. It is the largest exporter of soy oil, soy flour oil and sunflower, the second largest exporter of corn after the United States, the third largest exporter of meat and the fifth largest flour producer.

Argentina's meat consumption is the highest in Latin America, at over 50kg per person per annum. Argentina is the world's third-largest organic meat producer, with 90 per cent of organic produce destined for export markets, particularly the EU. In previous years agricultural profitability has been hit by low international commodity prices, rising production costs, subsidiation of international competitors and an over-valued exchange rate which has diminished competitiveness.

The worst drought since the 1970s created an agricultural emergency by January 2009, particularly in the provinces of Buenos Aires, Cordoba, La Pampa and Entre Rios, where 90 per cent of the wheat crop was lost nationwide, and 800,000 head of cattle died. The cattle industry declined as herds fell in numbers from 57 million in 2005 to 48.6 million in 2010 (the lowest level since 1964). Years of drought and the quota on beef exports, in operation since 2006, resulted in exports falling by 57 per cent in 2010 to 166,265 tonnes.

Fishing

Argentina has recently increased its fishing production and exports of surplus stock are becoming a valuable export earner, especially when processed into oil and fish meal. Because of the Argentines' preference for beef, the domestic demand for fish is relatively weak. Principal fishing ports are Mar del Plata and Bahía Blanca. The typical annual fish catch is around 925,000 tonnes, including 550,000 tonnes marine fish and 350,000 tonnes shellfish.

For the first time, exports of fish and seafood at over 131,540 tonnes surpassed beef exports, (at around 70,000 tonnes) in the first quarter of 2011.

Forestry

About 12 per cent of Argentina's total land is covered by forest, equivalent to 34.6 million hectares, and a further 6 per cent of other wooded land.

Argentina is not self-sufficient in forestry goods, with most of the domestic harvest going towards lumber. Pine and cedar used for pulp are harvested in the north-west of the country. Significant quantities of sawn goods, wood-based panels and chemical pulps are produced from domestic hardwoods and softwoods. A large quantity of paper is imported, although Argentina's pulp and paper industry relies mainly on domestic pulp production.

Industry and manufacturing

Argentina's main industrial centres are Cordoba and to a lesser extent Buenos Aires. Industry as a whole contributes approximately 29 per cent to GDP and employs 24 per cent of the workforce.

Major sectors of production include food, textiles, machinery and transport equipment, consumer durables, industrial chemicals, metal working, engineering, paper, iron and steel and electrical equipment. The beef industry has given rise to a number of associated industries, including hides, leather, meat extracts and processed meats. Sectors that have gained in prominence in recent years include software and petrochemicals.

The automobile sector represents an important growth sector for the economy. In recent years the sector has suffered from poor consumer demand and an uncompetitive exchange rate. Many car assembly plants have been closed and operations have been transferred to Brazil, where labour costs are lower and there is a more lucrative domestic market. With the exception of the automobile industry however, the manufacturing sector has been boosted by the acceleration of economic integration within Mercusor.

Tourism

Tourism in Argentina has a wide variety of different activities, climates and terrains to offer visitors. Although the summer in the southern hemisphere (between December–February) offers the North American and European visitor a welcome break from a possible bleak winter, the majority of visitors to Argentina remain those from Brazil.

Tourist numbers for the summer season 2009–10 were the highest since the 1990s, reaching 9.5 million in January

(2010), representing year-on-year growth of 10.2 per cent from 2009 and all statistics indicated that the 2010 summer would be a record. Employment related to tourism also grew accordingly, with an estimated 669,000 jobs directly involved in tourism in 2011 (3.8 per cent of total employment). Tourism represented 6 per cent of GDP in 2009. Around two million tourists arrived in Argentina in 2009 (down by 14 per cent on 2008 numbers) with foreign earnings of US$2.7 billion; revenue was estimated to have risen by 9.3 per cent in 2011 (7.1 per cent of total exports). Since 2003, tourist numbers and their spending have doubled, while investment in tourist accommodation has risen by 1,000 per cent. The industry had been boosted by the favourable exchange rate between the peso and American dollar.
The government recognised the importance of tourism to the economy by creating a Ministry of Tourism in July 2010, with the remit to represent an alternative development sector, which 'boosts employment and modifies regional economies'. Investment in travel and tourism in 2011 was estimated to be P25 billion (US$6 billion).
In April 2010, China and Argentina agreed to promote bilateral tourism exchange programmes and increase the number of Chinese tourists visiting for cultural events.

Environment
Argentina's diverse environments have created a number of different ecological challenges from heavy pollution in Buenos Aires, deforestation in subtropical provinces to overgrazing in Patagonia.

Mining
The mining code was altered to create a more attractive investment environment in 1993, since when growth in the sector has picked up; mining exports in 2000 were estimated at US$1 billion and and had risen to US$2.3 billion by 2004. Altogether, there are over 70 companies with established projects in Argentina and some 40 companies actively seeking mining opportunities in the country.
Iron ore is the principal mineral extracted, mostly in Río Negro province, but output is only sufficient to supply about half of the requirements of the country's largest blast furnace complex, the remainder being made up from imports. Other minerals extracted include lead, zinc, tin, and uranium.
Argentina's largest mining project is the Alumbrera copper and gold mine in Catamarca province, thought to be the ninth largest copper mine in the world. Annual production of some 15 tonnes of gold is also expected until the end of its 20-year life in 2019. In addition, the Cerro Vanguardia silver and gold mine produces approximately five tonnes of gold per year. Now a significant gold producer Argentina – which occupies a top twenty world position – has recently seen considerable production activity in the north-west of the country, where the Veladero mine is situated. The Argentina-Chile border zone is particularly promising and output is predicted to rise in 2005 because of increased production in the area.

Hydrocarbons
Argentina had 2.5 billion barrels of proven oil reserves in 2010, with production of 651,000 barrels per day (bpd), although production has fallen recently due to the lack of new capacity to offset declines in mature fields. Nevertheless, Argentine is a net exporter of oil and the third-largest oil producer and exporter in Latin America. Domestic oil consumption was 557bpd in 2010, and any exports went mainly to Brazil and Chile.
Proven gas reserves amounted to 300 billion cum in 2010, with production at 40.1 billion cum (a fall of 3 per cent from 2009), gas has become the country's primary source of energy. Exports are principally to Chile, supplied solely from the Neuquén gas fields.
Argentina has total coal reserves of 130 million tonnes. It produces 340,000 tonnes per year and consumes around 1.54 million tonnes per year.
The oil and gas sectors are fully privatised and there are no restrictions on imports and exports. There are comprehensive pipeline links with surrounding countries.
As traditional inland sites of oil and gas fields have matured the government has licensed offshore exploration sites.

Energy
As the third largest power producer in Latin America, Argentina has a fully deregulated and diversified market. Most of its electricity generation comes from hydropower, followed by natural gas. Argentina has over 25 million KW of installed generation.
Hydroelectricity is of prime importance to the energy sector, particularly the Yacyreta hydroelectric dam, which helps power Argentina and neighbouring Paraguay. The Salto Grande dam is also co-owned by a bordering country, Uruguay, and as is the case with the Yacyreta, power generated from the project is shared equally between the two nations.
Argentina relies on the Atucha I and Embalse nuclear power projects, both of which are operated by Nucleoelctrica Argentina SA. Construction of a third nuclear power station, Atucha II, was halted in 1999, although the government announced plans 2005 that it would invest US$700 million to complete the construction. However, the primary problem with Atucha II is technological obsolescence and discussions with the Atomic Energy of Canada Limited (AECL) to upgrade the design are ongoing. A feasibility study for a fourth nuclear power station began in 2006. Argentina has inactive uranium mines and is able to enrich uranium to process fuel rods but does not have a solution for spent radioactive waste from power plants.
Contracts were agreed between Canada-based Dynamotive and the province of Corrientes in 2008 for two 15.7 MW electricity generating stations, fuelled by biofuel from wood waste and other biomass residue.

Financial markets
Stock exchange
Bolsa de Comercio de Buenos Aires (BCDA) (Buenos Aires Stock Exchange)
Commodity exchange
MATba (Mercado a Témino de Buenos Aires)

Banking and insurance
The country's economic crisis of 2001 severely undermined Argentina's banking system, when the freezing of deposit accounts and the conversion of deposits into pesos undermined liquidity in the financial system. The value of assets deteriorated throughout 2002 as the peso lost value and government bonds fell to a fraction of their purchase price. Banks were unable to meet claims on deposits, while savers filed law suits against institutions for failing to honour their deposits. As such, the entire banking system teetered on the edge of collapse in 2003. This led to the closure of many local subsidiaries of foreign banks. However, Argenina's recent economic recovery has enabled the sector to rehabilitate itself somewhat, with an increase in money supply demand and a significant recovery on bank deposits and loans. The acceptance of the national government's debt restructuring plan in early 2005 has led to a much needed increase in foreign capital inflow and greater stability in the sector. Despite this gradual upturn the banking sector remains very sensitive to macroeconomic conditions and though the level of credit is growing, it remains at a slow rate.
A new Bank of the South, with a headquarters in Venezuela, will be launched in 2008 to provide an alternative source of development funding for the participating countries. Assets of US$7 billion will underpin its operations.
The governor of the central bank, Martin Redrado was forced by the government to resign in January 2010 after he had refused to pay US$6.5 billion of the country's debts from central bank reserves.

Central bank
Banco Central de la República Argentina
Main financial centre
Buenos Aires

Time
GMT minus three hours

Geography
Argentina is situated in the south-east of South America, facing the Atlantic Ocean to the east. Argentina is bounded by Chile to the west, Bolivia and Paraguay to the north and Brazil and Uruguay to the north-east. There are four main geographic provinces: the Andes, the lowland north, the Pampas and Patagonia.
The Andes Mountains line Argentina's western edge, forming the boundary with Chile. The highest peak, Aconcagua, stands 6,960 metres (22,834 feet).
Gently rolling plains extend eastward from the base of the Andes and descend gradually to sea level. Open savannas alternate with almost impenetrable thorn forests in the western part of the region.
Vast, generally treeless plains of central Argentina gradually rise from the Atlantic coast to the Andes Mountains. These fertile plains are Argentina's breadbasket. They consist of the Humid Pampas along the coast and the Dry Pampas in the west and south.
Patagonia, south of the Pampas, is dry and desolate. The Patagonian steppes support flocks of sheep, the wool of which is exported to Europe.
The southernmost inhabited territory, Tierra del Fuego (Land of Fire), consists of various islands with the northern areas used for sheep farming, while the southern islands are mountainous and covered in glaciers and forests.
Hemisphere
Southern

Climate
Argentina's climate ranges from sub-tropical in the north to sub-antarctic in the south. The densely populated central zone (including Buenos Aires) is temperate. Summer, from December–March, is hot and humid with temperatures ranging from 26–35 degrees Celsius (C); autumn is April–May, with temperatures in the range 10–25 degrees C; winter is from June–August, with temperatures of 0–20 degrees C, when nights can be cold with temperatures below freezing; spring is from September–November, with temperatures of 12–25 degrees C.

Dress codes
Dress codes are fairly formal in Buenos Aires. Suits are worn for business appointments and, for men, jackets and ties are required for dining out and other social occasions. Casual clothing is often worn on the coast, but shorts and beachwear should be worn only at the beach or pool.

Entry requirements
Passports
Passports are required by all visitors except nationals of neighbouring countries with identity cards.
Visa
All business travellers are advised to contact an Argentine embassy for requirements, before departure.
Tourist visas are not required by most nationals of the Americas, Europe, Australasia and some Asian countries. Citizens of neighbouring countries of Argentina need only national identification cards.
In 2010 a presidential decree was passed requiring a 'reciprocity fee' to enter Argentina from citizens of the United States (US$131, multiple entries for 10 years), Canada (US$70, single entry) and Australia (US$100, multiple entry).
For further exemptions and details check with the appropriate embassy or consulate before departure.
Currency advice/regulations
There are no restrictions on the import and export of local or foreign currency.

Health (for visitors)
Mandatory precautions
None
Advisable precautions
Typhoid and hepatitis A vaccinations are recommended. Yellow fever vaccinations are advised for visitors to the north-eastern forest area. Malaria prophylaxis is advisable for visits to some lowland tropical areas. Water precautions should be taken outside main towns. There is some risk of dengue fever and anthrax outside urban areas.
Medical insurance is necessary and doctors often expect immediate cash payment before treatment. Take medical kit.

Hotels
Wide range available, graded from one to five stars. There is a 21 per cent tax, which may be included in hotel tariff.

Public holidays (national)
Fixed dates
1 Jan (New Year's Day), 1 May (Labour Day), 25 May (Anniversary of the 1810 Revolution), 19 Jun (Flag Day), 9 Jul (Independence Day), 8 Dec (Immaculate Conception), 25 Dec (Christmas Day), 31 Dec (New Year's Eve).
Variable dates
Maundy Thursday, Good Friday, Malvinas Day (first Mon in Apr), Death of General José San Martin (third Mon in Aug), Columbus Day (second Mon in Oct).

Working hours
Banking
Mon–Fri: 09/1000–1500.
Business
Mon–Fri: 0900–1300, 1500–1800.
Government
Mon–Fri: 0800–1700.
Shops
Mon–Fri: 0900–2200, Sat: 0900–1300.

Telecommunications
Mobile/cell phones
GSM 850/1900 services are available in highly populated areas only.

Electricity supply
220V AC, 50 cycles

Social customs/useful tips
The normal form of greeting is a handshake. In general, European practices are followed. Standards on punctuality differ though and visitors may be kept waiting. Commercial quotations should be made in US dollars.
In their public behaviour, Argentines are very conscious of civilities. It is considered polite to first extend a greeting like *buenos dias* (good day) or *buenas tardes* (good afternoon) if you are approaching a stranger to ask for information.
Tough anti-tobacco legislation was approved by the lower house of assembly in June 2011; the Senate had already passed the legislation. Advertising and sponsorship will be banned, as will smoking in bars, restaurants and the work place and sale of single cigarettes and all sales to under 18 year olds.

Security
Although street crime is increasing in Argentina, personal security is a minor problem compared to other Latin American countries. Violent crime is rare in Buenos Aires. Travellers should take precautions against petty theft such as bag snatching, especially on trains.

Getting there
Air
National airline: Aerolíneas Argentinas.
International airport/s: Ministro Pistarini Ezeiza (EZE), 35km south-west of Buenos Aires; duty-free shop, restaurants, bank, car hire. A bus service operates to the city, every 30 minutes between 0500–2300, taking 45 minutes. Taxis are also available. A coach service also connects to Aeroparque Jorge Newbery airport for domestic flight connections.
Other airport/s: Aeroparque Jorge Newbery (AEP), 8km north-east of Buenos Aires, domestic terminal; duty-free shop, restaurant, bank, car hire.
Airport tax: International departures US$18; regional and to Uruguay US$8. International arrivals US$10. These levies are subject to inflation.

Surface

Road: There are well-maintained roads between all the neighbouring countries. Branches of the Pan-American Highway run from Buenos Aires to the borders of Bolivia, Brazil, Chile and Paraguay. Entry from Uruguay is possible via bridges over the Uruguay River at Puerto Colón, Puerto Unzué and the Salto Grande Dam. The long distances involved can make car journeys time-consuming: for example, the distance from Santiago in Chile to Buenos Aires is over 1,400 km.

Rail: The major direct route is north from Buenos Aires to Asunción in Paraguay. There are also direct rail links with Bolivia, Brazil and Chile. Services are often disrupted and delays can be expected.

Water: Ferry and hydrofoil services on the Río de la Plata link Colonia and Montevideo (Uruguay) with Buenos Aires. Ferries also operate from Paraguay on the Paraná River.

Main port/s: Buenos Aires, Ensenada (La Plata), Rosario and Bahía Blanca. There are numerous smaller ports and some specialised terminals (for oil, cereals, raw materials, etc).

Getting about

National transport

Air: Given the great distances involved, air travel is the logical method for reaching domestic destinations. Internal flights for Buenos Aires land at Aeroparque Jorge Newbery, 10 minutes from city centre by taxi.

An extensive domestic service is offered to regional airports and demand for services is high, so it is advisable to book flights in advance.

Road: The network has been improved in recent years and links major centres. Tolls are collected on major roads, which are privately-owned.

Buses: Long-distance bus services are operated by a number of companies, mostly centred on Buenos Aires, and are extensive (e.g. routes to Mar del Plata, Córdoba, San Martín de Los Andes, Mendoza). The Buenos Aires bus terminal is next to *Retiro*, the central rail station.

Rail: Travelling by train is generally cheaper, but slower, than travelling by bus. A comprehensive rail system links main towns. Long-distance Pullman services, with air-conditioning, sleeping facilities and restaurants, are recommended. It is advisable to book well in advance.

Water: There are regular sailings to Rosario and Corrientes via the Paraná River. River transport company Flota Fluvial operates services on the Plate, Paraná, Paraguay and Uruguay Rivers. Patagonian ports are also served, but sailings are irregular.

City transport

Taxis: Taxis, of which there are some 32,000 in Buenos Aires, generally have yellow roofs. They can be hailed or found on ranks and are metered within cities. For trips in the Buenos Aires centre which are less than six blocks, it is usually faster to walk than to take a taxi. Tips are not necessary, though generally expected from tourists.

There is also a widely available and much-used system of cars called *remises*, which offer a safer and more comfortable service. *Remises* are also available for travel to and from the airports, where they can be booked at separate counters. Journey time from Ezeiza airport to city centre is 40 minutes and 10 minutes from Aeroparque Jorge Newbery.

Buses, trams & metro: All major towns have good local services. In Buenos Aires there is a comprehensive public transport system with 'pay as you board' bus services, operating round the clock.

The Buenos Aires metro, known as *Subte*, has five lines and 80 stations; it operates from early morning to late at night. Tokens can be purchased at booking offices.

Ferry: The principal ferry connection in Buenos Aires is to Colonia in Uruguay and is frequented by tourists heading for the Uruguayan resort town of Punta del Este. River buses in the suburb of Tigre serve communities in the river delta and are a popular tourist attraction on weekends.

Car hire

Car hire is available in Buenos Aires and most main urban centres. An international driving licence, in addition to home licence, is advisable

BUSINESS DIRECTORY

The addresses listed below are a selection only. While World of Information makes every endeavour to check these addresses, we cannot guarantee that changes have not been made, especially to telephone numbers and area codes. We would welcome any corrections.

Telephone area codes

The international direct dialling code (IDD) for Argentina is +54, followed by area code and subscriber's number:

Bahía Blanca	291	Resistencia	3722
Balcarce	2266	Rio Cuarto	358
Buenos Aires	11	Rio Grande	2964
Catamarca	3833	Rosario	341
Córdoba	351	Salta	387
Formosa	3717	San Juan	264
Las Calera	351	San Lorenzo	3476
La Plata	221	San Miguel de Tucumen	381
Mar Del Plata	223	San Pedro	3329
Mendoza	261	San Rafael	2627
Neuquén	299	Santa Fé	342
Paraná	343	Santa Rosa	2954

Useful telephone numbers

Fire: 107

Police: 101

Ambulance: 101

Chambers of Commerce

American Chamber of Commerce in Argentina, 1133 Viamonte, 1053 Buenos Aires (tel: 4371-4500; fax: 4371-8400; e-mail: amcham@amcham.com.ar).

Argentine Chamber of Commerce, 36 Avenida Leandro N Alem, 1003 Buenos Aires (tel: 5300-5000; fax: 5300-9058; e-mail: centroservices@cac.com.ar).

British-Argentine Chamber of Commerce, 457 Avenida Corrientes, 1043 Buenos Aires, CF (tel: 4394-2762; fax: 4394-3860; e-mail: info@ccab.com.ar).

Rosario Chamber of Commerce, 1868 Córdoba, 2000 Rosario (tel: 425-7147; fax: 425-7486; e-mail: ccer@commerce.com.ar).

Banking

Asociación de Bancos Argentinos (ADEBA), San Martín 1229, Piso 10, 1004 Buenos Aires, CF (tel: 4394-1430; fax: 4394-6340).

Banco Crédito-Op Cooperativo Ltdo, Reconquista 484, Zona postal 1003, Buenos Aires, CF (tel: 4394-0105/0122; fax: 4325-9104).

Banco de Crédito Argentino, Reconquista 2, Zona postal 1092, Buenos Aires, CF (tel: 4334-1181/89; fax: 4334-5618).

Banco de Galicia y Buenos Aires, Tte Gral Juan D Perón 407, Zona postal 1038, Buenos Aires, CF (tel: 4329-6000; fax: 4329-6100).

Banco de la Ciudad de Buenos Aires, Florida 302, Zona postal 1313, Buenos Aires, CF (tel: 4325-5881/89).

Banco de la Nación Argentina (BNA), Bartolomé Mitre 326, Zona postal 1036, Buenos Aires, CF (tel: 4347-6000; fax: 4347-8078); international banking division (tel: 4347-8092; fax: 4347-8078); foreign trade promotion (tel: 4347-8763; fax: 4347-8764).

Banco de la Pampa, Reconquista 319, Zona postal 1003, Buenos Aires, CF (tel: 4325-3410; fax: 4325-8750).

Banco de la Provincia de Buenos Aires, San Martín 137, Zona postal 1004, Buenos Aires, CF (tel: 4331-2561/3584; fax: 4331-5154).

Banco del Buen Ayre, Cerrito 740, Zona postal 1309, Buenos Aires, CF (tel: 4350-020/054; fax: 4837-890).

Banco del Sud, Maipú 277, Zona postal 1084, Buenos Aires, CF (tel: 4326-3313, 4326-2965; fax: 4325-3177).

Banco Francés del Rio de la Plata, Reconquista 165, Zona postal 1003, Buenos Aires, CF (tel: 4331-7071; fax: 4954-8009).

Banco General de Negocios, Esmeralda 120, Zona postal 1035, Buenos Aires, CF (tel: 4394-3003, 4394-2879; fax: 4394-2698).

Banco Hipotecario Nacional, Balcarce 167, Zona postal 1064, Buenos Aires, CF (tel: 4342-9732; fax: 4331-0620).

Banco Holandés Unido, Florida 361, Zona postal 1005, Buenos Aires, CF (tel: 4394-4553; fax: 4322-0839).

Banco Medefín UNB, 25 de Mayo 489, Zona postal 1339, Buenos Aires, CF (tel: 4313-4125; fax: 4312-9450).

Banco Quilmes, Tte Gral Juan D Perón 564, Zona postal 1038, Buenos Aires, CF (tel: 4331-8111/9; fax: 4334-5235).

Banco República, Sarmiento 336, Zona postal 1041, Buenos Aires, CF (tel: 4331-8385/87; fax: 4331-2130).

Banco Río de la Plata, Bartolomé Mitre 480, Zona postal 1036, Buenos Aires, CF (tel: 4331-7551, 4331-8361; fax: 4331-7551; internet site: http://www.bancorio.com.ar).

Banco Roberts, 25 de Mayo 258, Zona postal 1002, Buenos Aires, CF (tel: 4334-1723, 4334-6682; fax: 4334-6679).

Banco Sudameris, Tte Gral Juan D Perón 500, Zona postal 1038, Buenos Aires, F (tel: 4331-4061/9; fax: 4331-2793).

Banco Supervielle Société Générale, Reconquista 330, Zona postal 1003, Buenos Aires, CF (tel: 4394-4051/9).

Banco Tornquist, Bartolomé Mitre 531, Zona postal 1036, Buenos Aires, CF (tel: 4343-784/49; fax: 4342-6090).

Banco Velox, San Martín 298, Zona postal 1004, Buenos Aires, CF (tel: 394-0115/0665; fax: 4394-8255).

Banesto Banco Shaw, Sarmiento 355, Zona postal 1041, Buenos Aires, CF (tel: 4325-6500; fax: 4312-4743).

Caja Nacional de Ahorro y Seguro, Hipólito Yrigoyen 1750, Zona postal 1308, Buenos Aires, CF (tel: 4476-4216; fax: 4111-568).

Deutsche Bank, Bartolomé Mitre 401, Zona postal 1036, Buenos Aires, CF (tel: 4343-2511/9; fax: 4343-3536).

The First National Bank of Boston, Florida 99, Zona postal 1005, Buenos Aires, CF (tel: 4342-3051/61; fax: 4343-7303).

Lloyds Bank, Reconquista 101, Zona postal 1003, Buenos Aires, CF (tel: 4331-3551/9; fax: 4342-7487).

Central bank

Banco Central de la República Argentina, Reconquista 266, 1003 Buenos Aires (tel: 4348-3500; fax: 4334-6489).

Stock exchange

Bolsa de Comercio de Buenos Aires (BCDA) (Buenos Aires Stock Exchange) (www.bcba.sba.com.ar/BCBA)

Commodity exchange

MATba (Mercado a Témino de Buenos Aires; www.matba.com.ar)

Travel information

Aerolíneas Argentinas, Paseo Colón 185, Zona postal 1063, Buenos Aires, CF (tel: 4320-2000; fax: 44317-3585; internet: www.austral.com.ar).

Austral Líneas Aéreas (ALA), Avda Corrientes 485, Piso 9, Zona postal 1398, Buenos Aires, CF (tel: 4340-7800, 4317-3605; fax: 4317-3992).

Ministry of tourism

Secretaría del Turismo, Presidencia de la Nación, Suípacha 1111, Piso 21, Zona potal 1360, Buenos Aires, CF (tel: 4312-5624, 4311-2089; fax: 4313-6834; internet site: http://www.sectur.gov.ar/eng/menu.htm).

National tourist organisation offices

Asociación Argentina de Agencias de Viaje y Turismo (Travel Agents' Association), Viamonte 640, Piso 10, Zona postal 1053, Buenos Aires, CF (tel: 4322-2804).

Ministries

Ministry of Culture and Education, Pizzurno 935, Zona postal 1020, Buenos Aires, CF (tel: 424-1551/9, 445-666, 448-110).

Ministry of Defence, Av. Paseo Colón 255, Zona postal 1063, Buenos Aires, CF (tel: 343-1561).

Ministry of Economy, Public Works and Services, Hipólito Yrigoyen 250, Zona posal 1310, Buenos Aires, CF (tel: 342-6411, 342-6421/9, 349-8814, 349-8810/2; fax: 331-0292, 331-2619, 331-2090; internet site: http://www.mecon.ar/default.htm).

Ministry of Foreign Affairs and International Trade, Reconquista 1088, Zona postal 1003, Buenos Aires, CF (tel: 331-0071, 312-1775, 312-3434; fax: 312-3593, 312-3423).

Ministry of the Interior, Balcarce 50, Zona postal 1064, Buenos Aires, CF (tel: 342-6081, 343-0880).

Ministry of Justice, Av Gral Gelly y Obes 2289, Piso 7, Zona postal 1425, Buenos Aires, CF (tel: 803-1051/3, 803-5453; fax: 803-3955).

Ministry of Labour and Social Security, Av L N Alem 650, Zona postal 1001, Buenos Aires, CF (tel: 311-3303, 311-2945).

Ministry of Public Health and Social Action, Av 9 de Julio 1925, Zona postal 1332, Buenos Aires, CF (tel: 381-8911, 381-8919).

Office of the President, Balcarce 50, Zona postal 1064, Buenos Aires, CF (tel: 331-5041, 303-608, 331-3183).

Other useful addresses

Administration of Agriculture and Agroindustrial Markets, Paseo Colón 922, Piso 1, Of 131, 1063 Buenos Aires (tel: 4349-2272/4; fax: 4349-2272).

Administration of Fish and Marine Resources, San Martín 459, Piso 2, 1004 Buenos Aires (tel: 4394-1869, 4394-5961).

Administration of Forestry Production, Av Paseo Colón 982, Piso 1, 1063 Buenos Aires (tel: 4349-2101, 4349-2103; fax: 4349-2108).

Administration of Geological and Mining Resources, Julio A Roca 651, Piso 8, 1322 Buenos Aires (tel: 4349-3131).

Administration of Livestock Markets, Paseo Colón 922, 1063 Buenos Aires (tel: 4349-2287, 4349-2294; fax: 4362-5144).

Administration of Markets of Non-Traditional Products, Paseo Colón 922, Buenos Aires (tel: 4362-1738, 4349-2280/2; fax: 4349-2280).

Administration of Mining Development, Av Julio A Roca 561, Piso 8, 1322 Buenos Aires (tel: 4349-3133).

Administration of Native Forestry Resources, San Martin 459, Piso 2, 1004 Buenos Aires (tel: 4394-1869).

Argentine Embassy (USA), 1600 New Hampshire Avenue, NW, Washington DC 20009 (tel: (+1-202) 238-6400; fax: (+1-202) 332-3171; e-mail: info@embajadaargentinaeeuu.org).

Argentine Industry Association, Av L N 1067, Piso 10, 1001 Buenos Aires (tel: 4313-2012, 4313-2512, 4313-2561; fax: 4313-2413).

Argentine Institute of Plant Sanitation and Quality, Av Paseo Colón 982, 1063 Buenos Aires (tel: 4313-8311).

Argentine Petrochemical Institute, Av Santa Fe 1480, Piso 5, Buenos Aires (tel: 4813-3436; fax: 4813-3436).

Argentine Petroleum Institute, Maipú 645, Piso 3, Primer Cuerpo, Buenos Aires (tel: 4322-3233, 4322-3652, 4322-3244; fax: 4322-3233).

Association of Importers and Exporters, Av Belgrano 124, Piso 1, 1092 Buenos Aires (tel: 4342-0010/9; fax: 4342-1312).

British Embassy, Dr Luis Agote 2412/52, Casilla de Correo 2050, 1425 Buenos Aires (tel: 4803-7070/1; fax: 4803-1731).

Bolsa de Comercio de Buenos Aires (Stock Exchange), Sarmiento 299, 1st Floor, AR 1353 Buenos Aires (tel: 4311-1174, 4311-5231, 4311-5235; fax: 4312-9332, 4312-6636).

Bureau of Export Promotion, Av Julio A Roca 651, Piso 6, 1322 Buenos Aires (tel: 4334-2975; fax: 4331-2266).

Centre for Business Promotion, Buenos Aires Stock Exchange, Sarmlento 299, Piso 1, 1353 Buenos Aires (tel: 4311-5231/4, 4313-4812, 4313-4544; fax: 4312-9332).

Customs Authority, Hipólito Yrigoyen 250 Of 606, 1310 Buenos Aires (tel: 4331-7330; fax: 4331-9839).

Department of Public Works and Transport, 250 Hipólito Yrigoyen Street, 11th Floor, Office 1141, PC 1310, Buenos Aires (tel/fax: 4349-7728; e-mail: arco@meyosp.mecon.ar).

Federal Board of Investment, San Martín 871, 1004 Buenos Aires (tel: 4313-5557; fax: 4313-1486).

Junta Nacional de Carnes (National Meat Board), San Martin 459, 104 Buenos Aires (tel: 4394-5161; fax: 4322-9357).

National Administration of Customs, Azopardo 350, 1328 Buenos Aires (tel: 4343-0661/9, 4343-0101/9).

National Administration of Fishing and Aquaculture, Av Paseo Colón 982, Anexo Jardin, Piso 1, 1063 Buenos Aires (tel: 4349-2330/1; fax: 4349-2332).

National Administration of Fuels, Av Paseo Colón 171, Piso 6, Of. 620, 1063 Buenos Aires (tel: 4319-8030/1).

National Commission of Telecommunications, Sarmiento 151, Piso 4, Of 435, 1041 Buenos Aires (tel: 4331-1203).

National Institute of Industrial Technology, Av L N Alem 1067, Piso 7, 1001 Buenos Aires (tel: 4313-3013).

National Institute of Mining Technology, Parque Tecnológico Migueletes, Casilla de Correo 327, 1650 San Martín (tel: 4754-5151, 4754-4141; fax: 4754-4070, 4754-8307).

National Institute of Statistics and Census, Dirección de Difusión Estadistics, Centro de Servicios Estadísticos, Av Julio A Roca 615, 1067 Buenos Aires (tel: 4349-9651).

National Viticulture Institute, Av Julio A Roca 651, Piso 5, Of 22, 1067 Buenos Aires (tel/fax: 4343-3816).

Public Works and Transport Department, 250 Hipólito Yrigoyen Street, 11th Floor, Office 1141, PC 1310, Buenos Aires (tel/fax: 4349-7728; e-mail: arco@meyosp.mecon.ar).

Secretariat of Agriculture, Livestock and Fisheries, Av Paseo Colón 982, 1063 Buenos Aires (tel: 4362-2365, 4362-5091, 4362-5946; fax: 4349-2504).

Secretariat of Energy, Av Paseo Colón 171, Piso 8 Of 803, 1063 Buenos Aires (tel: 4349-8003/5; fax: 4343-6404).

Secretariat of Finance, Hipólito Yrigoyen 250, 1310 Buenos Aires (tel: 4331-0731, 4342-2937, 4341-8900; fax: 4331-0292).

Secretariat of Industry, Av Junio A Roca 651, 1322 Buenos Aires (tel: 4334-5065, 4342-7822; fax: 4331-3218).

Secretariat of International Economic Relations, Reconquista 1088, 1003 Buenos Aires (tel: 4331-7281, 4331-1073; fax: 4312-0965).

Secretariat of Mining, Av Junio A Roca 561, Sector 9, 1322 Buenos Aires (tel: 4349-3212, 4349-3232; fax: 4343-3525).

Secretariat of Public Works and Communications, Sarmiento 151, 1041 Buenos Aires (tel: 4499-481; fax: 4312-1283).

Secretariat of Transportation, Av. 9 de Julio 1925, 1332 Buenos Aires (tel: 4381-1435, 4381-4007).

Secretariat of Trade and Investment, Hipólito Yrigoyen 250, 1310 Buenos Aires (tel: 4331-2208).

Sociedad Rural Argentina (one of the main associations of big landowners), Florida 460, 1005 Buenos Aires (tel: 4392-2030, 4322-2111).

Subsecretariat of Economic Planning, Hipólito Yrigoyen 250, Of 843, 1310 Buenos Aires (tel: 4349-5079; fax: 4349-5730).

Superintendencia de Seguros de la Nación (Insurance Superintendency), Av Julio A Roca 721, 1067 Buenos Aires (tel: 4306-653).

Telecom Argentina Stet-France Telecom SA, Maipú 1210, 9th Floor, Buenos Aires (tel: 4968-3604, 4968-3606).

Trade Information and Opportunities, Reconquista 1098, 1003 Buenos Aires (tel: 4315-1125; fax: 4311-1331).

Undersecretariat of Air, River and Maritime Transport, Hipólito Yrigoyen 250, 1310 Buenos Aires (tel: 4349-7205; fax: 4342-6365).

Undersecretariat of Interior Security, Balearce 50 Post box 1064, Buenos Aires (tel: 4342-9440 Ext 579; fax: 4331-7051).

Undersecretariat of Investments, Hipólito Yrigoyen 250, Piso 10 Of 1010, 1310 Buenos Aires (tel: 4349-8515/6, 4349-5037; fax: 4349-8522).

Undersecretariat of Medical and Sanitary Inspection, 9 de Julio 1925, Piso 10, Of 1003, 1332 Buenos Aires (tel: 4383-1811; fax: 4381-8912).

Unión Industrial Argentina (main private sector industrial association), Avenida Leandro N Alem 1067, 11 Piso, 1001 Buenos Aires (tel: 4313-2762).

US Embassy, Avenida Colombia 4300, 1425 Buenos Aires (tel: 5777-4533; fax: 5777-4240).

World Trade Centre Buenos Aires, Moreno 584, Piso 6, 1091 Buenos Aires (tel: 4331-3432, 4331-2604; fax: 4343-4270).

National news agency: Telam: www.telam.com.ar

Internet sites

Argentina: www.surdelsur.com

Automóvil Club Argentino: www.aca.org.artigua-barbuda

Buenos Aires: www.buenosaires.com

Fundacion Invertir Argentina: www.invertir.com

Tourism Secretariat: www.turismo.gov.ar

Armenia

In June 2011 Russia's President Dimitry Medvedev, acting as mediator between Armenia and Azerbaijan over the disputed Nagorno-Karabakh region, met with the Armenian President Serge Sargisian and his Azerbaijani counterpart Ilham Aliyev in the Russian city of Kazan. This was the fifth time the two had met with Mr Medvedev, an indication of Russia's concern over the dispute between the two countries. Nagorno-Karabakh is a territory populated mainly by ethnic Armenians but surrounded by Azerbaijan. Following the collapse of the Soviet Union, the two countries went to war over the enclave, and an estimated 20,000 people died. Recovering the territory is a central feature of Azerbeijani foreign policy and the reason why Azerbaijan continues to allocate some US$3 billion a year to its military budget.

Russia and Turkey

Many regional analysts believe that Russia's interest boils down to increasing its regional influence in a potentially volatile part of what Russia considers to be its sphere of influence. Russia's fear is that if it fails to influence the dispute, Turkey the other regional power, will step into the gap. At the time of the Nagorno-Karabakh war Turkey had supported Azerbaijan; its relations with Armenia are historically flawed and increased Turkish influence in the region would be seen by Russia as the thin end of a NATO wedge. Attempts to restore relations have repeatedly failed. In 2009 Azerbaijan had prevented the re-opening of the border between the two countries. Tensions between the two countries are aggravated by the religious dimension – Armenia is a Christian country, Azerbaijan is Muslim.

KEY FACTS

Official name: Haikakan Hanrapetoutioun (Republic of Armenia)

Head of State: President Serge Sarkisian (since 1998; re-elected 9 Apr 2008)

Head of government: Prime Minister Tigran Sarkisian (no relation to the president) (appointed 9 Apr 2008)

Ruling party: Coalition led by Hayastani Hanrapetakan Kusaktsutyun (HHK) (Republican Party of Armenia) with Bargavadj Hayastani Kusaktsutyun (BHK) (Prosperous Armenia) Orinats Erkir (OE) (Rule of Law) (from May 2007). Hay Heghapokhakan Dashnaktsutiun (HHD) (Armenian Revolutionary Federation, member of coalition but withdrew 27 Apr 2009).

Area: 29,800 square km

Population: 3.30 million (2010)*

Capital: Yerevan

Official language: Armenian

Currency: Dram (D) = Luma 100

Exchange rate: D371.50 per US$ (Oct 2011)

GDP per capita: US$2,846 (2010)

GDP real growth: 2.00% (2010)

GDP: US$9.40 billion (2010)

Labour force: 1.12 million (2008)

Unemployment: 7.00% (2010)

Inflation: 8.20% (2010)

Balance of trade: -US$2.03 billion (2010)

* estimated figure

In April 2010 Armenia had announced that it was reneging on its agreement with Turkey to re-open the border between the two countries, claiming that Turkey had failed to drop preconditions attached to the agreement. The agreement had been signed in October 2009. President Sargisian's change of mind placed the US in something of a high profile dilemma. The Turkish delaying strategy was aimed at ensuring that US President Obama was unable to make any reference to the 1915 massacres on the 24 April anniversary of the massacres. In any event, the US had long been reluctant to make any reference to the massacres fearing that to do so would prejudice the October 2009 agreement. A US Congress Foreign Affairs Committee voted in March 2010 to recognise the Turkish genocide. The sensitivity of the issue is increased by the fact that both Armenia and Turkey have substantial, and vocal, diaspora within the US. Negotiations between Armenia and Turkey had been proceeding secretly in the two years leading up to the October 2009 agreement. The objective, which appeared to have been secured, was to open the Armenia-Turkey border, establish diplomatic relations and at least begin to discuss the emotional issue of the 1915 massacres within a stable framework, to be provided by a joint commission. Relations between Turkey and Armenia had worsened following the Armenian war with Azerbaijan over the ethnically Armenian enclave of Nagorno-Karabakh in Azerbaijan. After its military incursion, Armenia had controversially ended up in control of the enclave. The October 2009 agreement did not include any references to the Nagorno-Karabakh issue, but Turkey had introduced it as a delaying tactic on the agreement's ratification. Anticipating the problem, Armenia's parliament in early 2010 passed legislation permitting the President to withdraw his signature from ungratified treaties. However, Mr Sargisian decided not to apply the new legislation in the case of the agreement with Turkey, ostensibly out of respect for the countries that had helped the two countries reach agreement, the US, Russia and France.

New challenges

In its annual overview of the Armenian economy the International Monetary Fund (IMF) noted that Armenia was continuing to recover from the global financial crisis, although new challenges have emerged. In the second half of 2010, agricultural output collapsed, and overall economic growth fell below expectations to 2.1 per cent. Disruptions to local agricultural output compounded the effects of higher prices in international commodities markets, triggering a sharp increase in food and fuel prices. Overall inflation rose to 11.5 per cent in March 2010, but fell to 8.2 per cent for the year. At the same time, Armenia's external trade balance and remittances have rebounded. Against this background, the IMF noted that other sectors of the Armenian economy returned a solid performance, including industry and services. These trends to continued into 2011, and with improved conditions in agriculture, growth was expected to increase to 4.6 per cent.

With the potential of a knock-on from food inflation to other prices in Armenia, the inflationary environment will likely remain challenging. However, overall inflation should moderate and return to the target figure in the first half of 2012. The IMF also notes that Armenia's fiscal balance has improved significantly, with the overall deficit coming down to below 5 per cent in 2010 from around 8 per cent in 2009.

Armenia has, in the view of the IMF, continued to make progress improving its business environment. Recent initiatives to reduce the cost of complying with taxes and setting up businesses are likely to have a positive impact. Also, continuous efforts regarding financial sector development and the commitment to financial stability are achieving visible results.

Armenia had experienced one of the highest growth rates in the world prior to the global crisis. Growth of gross domestic product (GDP) averaged an impressive 12 per cent per year during 2000–07, leading to a sharp increase in per capita income and a fall in poverty. This growth largely depended on remittances, however, which were funnelled, in particular, to construction. The share of construction in GDP peaked at 26 per cent in 2008. The global crisis inevitably brought an end to this boom. The sharp contraction in exports, remittances, and foreign direct investment (FDI), and the postponement of an exchange rate devaluation led to a crisis of confidence in Armenia and an enormous drop in output. The strong response from the authorities, coupled with substantial support from the international community, helped to soften the impact of the crisis and to restore confidence, albeit at the cost of a substantial rise in public debt. The crisis underscored that a growth strategy predicated on private remittance inflows into 'non-tradeables' was not sustainable and exposed Armenia's vulnerability to external shocks.

Industry (excluding construction) was, in the view of the Asian Development Bank (ADB) the driving force of the recovery, expanding by 9.5 per cent in 2010, much of which was generated by export-oriented mining and metallurgy. Increased volumes of foodstuffs, drinks, and pharmaceuticals helped growth. Construction, which had propelled high growth in earlier years before its collapse took down the economy by 14.2 per cent in 2009, expanded by 3.7 per cent in 2010, mainly due to government anti-crisis spending.

Private expenditure and investment grew by an estimated 5 per cent, reflecting

KEY INDICATORS **Armenia**

	Unit	2006	2007	2008	2009	2010
Population	m	*3.39	*3.47	*3.55	*3.27	*3.30
Gross domestic product (GDP)	US$bn	6.41	7.97	11.90	8.70	9.40
GDP per capita	US$	1,982	7,974	3,361	2,668	2,846
GDP real growth	%	13.4	13.8	6.8	-14.4	2.0
Inflation	%	2.9	4.4	9.0	3.4	8.2
Unemployment	%	7.5	7.1	6.3	6.8	7.0
Industrial output	% change	18.5	11.7	7.2	-33.8	–
Agricultural output	% change	0.4	10.3	1.4	-1.0	–
Exports (fob) (goods)	US$m	985.0	1,196.7	1,124.0	748.9	1,175.4
Imports (fob) (goods)	US$m	2,192.0	2,796.9	3,763.4	2,830.1	3,204.9
Balance of trade	US$m	-1,207.0	-1,600.3	-2,639.4	-2,081.3	-2,032.5
Current account	US$m	-117.1	-589.6	-1,503.0	-1,369.5	-1,373.2
Total reserves minus gold	US$m	1,071.9	1,659.1	1,406.8	2,003.6	1,865.8
Foreign exchange	US$m	1,058.0	1,649.5	1,403.9	1,879.0	1,832.3
Exchange rate	per US$	367.25	301.12	305.97	362.28	373.66

* estimated figure

the gradual recovery in global activity and its impact on the domestic economy. Remittance inflows from workers abroad picked up by 15.4 per cent to US$1.1 billion after a weak performance in 2009, though they remained below their 2008 peak level of US$1.4 billion. FDI inflows amounted to around US$750 million in 2010, up by 3.5 per cent year on year, with communications, electricity, gas, and water the largest beneficiaries.

As inflation picked up, the central bank tightened monetary policy; despite this tightening and measures to de-dollarise the economy, the share of foreign currency loans in banks stayed high, increasing from 51.9 per cent at end-2009 to 57.4 per cent 12 months later, while the share of foreign currency deposits fell from 73.4 per cent to 69.0 per cent.

Fiscal policy aimed to continue supporting the recovery while addressing medium-term fiscal and debt vulnerabilities. A 14.5 per cent increase in tax revenue and restrained spending significantly eased the fiscal imbalance. Improvements in tax and customs administration, progress in introducing an electronic tax-filing system, and strengthened taxpayer services (such as taxpayer service centres) along with greater economic activity boosted tax receipts. But despite climbing slightly from 16.7 per cent in 2009 to 16.9 per cent in 2010, the tax-to-GDP ratio is still low internationally. The budget deficit of 4.9 per cent of GDP recorded in 2010 was well below the 6 per cent of GDP projected by the government in late 2009 and a sizable 7.6 per cent recorded in 2009. About 60 per cent of the deficit in 2010 was financed through domestic resources.

Exports surged by 46.9 per cent, much of which was generated by export-oriented mining and metallurgy, primarily due to soaring international prices of copper, molybdenum, and other nonferrous metals (but also due to a better global economic environment). After falling by 25.0 per cent in 2009, imports showed growth of 19.8 per cent in 2010, boosted by domestic demand that was lifted by improving investment and rebounding remittances. The trade deficit grew slightly to an estimated US$2.3 billion, but larger remittances and factor income helped narrow the current account deficit to 14.6 per cent of GDP in 2010 from 16.0 per cent.

Growth with inflation

Continued growth in Armenia will continue to depend heavily on that in the Russian Federation. A strong performance there will boost FDI inflows, migrants' remittances, and demand for exports. As a result of improved external conditions – along with a rebound in agriculture, which is expected to grow by 10 per cent this year – GDP is projected to expand by 4.0 per cent in 2011 and 4.5 per cent in 2012. Inflation pressures will persist in 2011, though inflation is expected to come down from its 2010 high.

The immediate to mid-term macroeconomic challenges include tightening the monetary and fiscal stances, ensuring debt sustainability through concessional financing, and reducing external imbalances. Fiscal consolidation will require action on both the revenue and expenditure sides. The authorities acknowledge the need for a faster pace of reforms in the areas of tax and customs administration.

Further efforts for better governance will also be important to improve social policy, improve the distribution of resources, and reduce poverty. The government is aware of oligopolies in key sectors of the economy that have strong links with entrenched elites. It therefore intends to continue its efforts to reduce corruption, enforce competition, modernise public expenditure management, and strengthen the civil service and judiciary.

Risk assessment

Economy	Fair
Politics	Fair
Regional stability	Poor

COUNTRY PROFILE

Historical profile

At its height, the Armenian empire stretched from the Caspian Sea to the Mediterranean, before being incorporated into the Roman Empire in AD301. In the eleventh century, Armenia was incorporated into the Turkish Seljuk Empire.

1915 The Ottoman Empire killed around 1.5 million Armenians in response to the independence movement.

1916 Armenia was conquered by Russia. It joined an alliance with Georgia and Azerbaijan.

1918–20 Armenia was an independent republic for two years.

1920 Turkey and Russia invaded Armenia. An agreement with Russia led to Armenia proclaiming itself a socialist republic.

1922 Armenia was incorporated into the Union of Soviet Socialist Republics (USSR).

1923 Stalin drew the current recognised borders that placed the mainly ethnic Armenian Nagorno-Karabakh in Azerbaijan.

1930s The country suffered under Stalin's purges, but also underwent a period of industrial development.

1988–93 An earthquake in northern Armenia in 1988 killed 25,000 people. Nagorno-Karabakh demanded unification with Armenia, and conflict between Azerbaijan and Armenia began. It lasted intermittently for five years.

1990 The Pan-Armenian National Movement (PNM) won the parliamentary elections. A declaration of independence was made, but ignored by Moscow.

1991 The republic boycotted the Soviet referendum on the preservation of the USSR. In a referendum held shortly after the failed anti-Gorbachev coup in Moscow, 94 per cent voted for secession from the USSR. Levon Ter-Petrossian was elected president. Independence was formally proclaimed by the President. Armenia joined the Commonwealth of Independent States (CIS). The US recognised Armenia's independence.

1992 Armenia joined the UN. Conflict over Nagorno-Karabakh turned into full-scale war between Armenia and Azerbaijan.

1994 The war with Azerbaijan over Nagorno-Karabakh settled into an uneasy stalemate, with local Armenians backed by Armenian forces in control of the disputed enclave. A Russian-brokered cease-fire between Azerbaijan and Armenia was generally honoured.

1995 The first post-independence parliamentary elections resulted in victory for the ruling party, PNM. A constitution was approved by referendum which gave the president substantial powers, including the right to pass decrees.

1996 Levon Ter-Petrosian was re-elected president. There were protests over alleged electoral fraud.

1998 President Levon Ter-Petrosian was forced out of office after stating his wish to open negotiations with Azerbaijan. Robert Kocharian was elected president. The domestic political scene experienced growing instability and politically motivated violence. Deputy minister of defence, Colonel Vagram Khorkhoruni, was murdered. Arkady Gukasian was elected president of Nagorno-Karabakh.

1999 Prime Minister Vazgen Sargissian and other politicians were assassinated in the National Assembly. Aram Sargissian, the former prime minister's younger brother, was appointed to succeed him. The gunmen accused the government of leading Armenia into political and economic ruin.

2000 Andranik Margarian became prime minister and admitted that those affected by the 1988 earthquake were still living in a disaster zone. President Arkady Gukasian of Nagorno-Karabakh was seriously wounded in an assassination attempt.

2001 Armenia became a full member of the Council of Europe. There was no result in the US-brokered talks on Nagorno-Karabakh between the presidents of Azerbaijan and Armenia.
2002 The first meeting between the foreign ministers of Armenia, Azerbaijan and Turkey was held in Iceland to try to find a settlement for the Nagorno-Karabakh conflict.
2003 Incumbent Robert Kocharian won the second round of the presidential elections and the ruling Hayastani Hanrapetakan Kusaktsutyun (HHK) (Republican Party of Armenia), loyal to President Kocharian, won the parliamentary elections. There were criticisms of both elections. A referendum rejected constitutional amendments giving more power to the National Assembly. The death penalty was abolished.
2005 A referendum endorsed constitutional changes to strengthen parliament and limit presidential power.
2006 The Orinats Erkir party withdrew from the coalition government. Armenia, together with Azerbaijan and Georgia, signed a European Neighbourhood Policy co-operation agreement with the EU.
2007 Prime Minister Andranik Margarian died of a heart attack. Serge Sarkisian was appointed in his stead.
2008 In presidential elections, former prime minister Serge Sarkisian was elected with almost 53 per cent of the vote in an election that 'mostly met international standards', viewed by the Organisation for Security and Co-operation in Europe (OSCE). However opposition members claimed the vote was rigged and street protests began. Civil protests led to rioting in Yerevan, which caused eight deaths and a declaration of a state of emergency with the deployment of the army on the streets of the capital. Police had started to clear a temporary encampment close to the parliamentary building, which had been passively protesting the result of the presidential elections, when protesters opposed the action and violence broke out. Another, three-week state of emergency was imposed. President Sarkisian was inaugurated and he appointed Tigran Sarkisian (no relation) as prime minister.
2009 The first Yerevan municipal elections in nearly 20 years were held in which the HHK swept to victory (47.4 per cent), in a poll which the Council of Europe described as largely democratic despite some 'serious deficiencies'. The two main opposition groups denounced the election as fraudulent. A rapprochement with Turkey included an official meeting in Switzerland to discuss normalising diplomatic relations and opening up border crossing points.
2010 Following the US resolution in March describing Turkey's killing of Armenians during the First World War as genocide, Turkey's attitude to its negotiations with Armenia hardened. The accord of normalisation was suspended in April, following Turkey's demand that Armenia resolves its dispute with Azerbaijan concerning the territory of Nagorno-Karabakh. In October, a deal was brokered by Russia, between Armenia and Azerbaijan for the return of prisoners captured during the Nagorno-Karabakh conflict.
2011 Prime Minister Tigran Sarkisian announced on 16 June that Armenia was ready to establish diplomatic relations with Turkey, without preconditions. At the same time he warned Azerbaijan that Armenia would defend its territory of Nagorno-Karabakh from foreign aggression. On 25 June, under the auspices of Russian President Medvedev, the presidents of Azerbaijan and Armenia discussed a settlement agreement for Nagorno-Karabakh. Despite encouragement from world leaders, they failed to sign it and risked future conflict.

Political structure

Constitution

Although the country has had a directly elected president since 1991, a constitution was only approved by referendum in July 1995. It gave the president substantial powers, including the right to pass decrees.

In 2005 a referendum endorsed a number of constitutionals amendments, including reducing the power of the presidency, strengthening parliament and the judiciary, and enshrining in the constitution human rights provisions.

Independence date

21 September 1991.

Form of state

Multi-party republic: divided into various *marz* (provincial divisions).

It is a member of the Commonwealth of Independent States (CIS).

The executive

The president has broad powers. He is elected by direct universal suffrage for a period of five years and has the right to pass decrees.

Under the 1995 constitution, the president is not the head of the executive power, but rather directs that power, by forming the government, appointing (and dismissing) the prime minister and on the proposal of the latter, the cabinet ministers.

The president is not a member of the government, but chairs the sittings and ratifies all government decisions. In consultation with the prime minister, the president has the power to dissolve the National Assembly. The president is commander of the armed forces, represents the country in international negotiations, signs agreements and treaties and appoints the chief prosecutor.

National legislature

The unicameral Azgayin Zhoghov (National Assembly) is the supreme legislative body and comprises 131 deputies, of which 56 are elected in single seat constituencies and 75 by proportional representation through party-lists, assigned among those parties that win at least 5 per cent of the total number of votes.

Legal system

The highest appellate court is the Court of Appeal, which ensures uniformity in how the country's laws are applied through its final review of cases. The Court of Appeal's members are nominated by the Council of Justice, an administrative body created to ensure independence of the courts, and then appointed by the president. Armenia also has a Constitutional Court, which is charged with ensuring that legislative decisions and presidential decrees are consistent with the constitution. Of the Constitutional Court's nine members, five are appointed by the president and four by the National Assembly. The president of Armenia heads the Council of Justice. The minister of justice and the prosecutor general serve as deputy heads of the council.

In January 1999, a new civil code came into effect which creates the legal framework for property rights and contract enforcement, as well as the legal and institutional framework necessary for commercial banking activities. Despite this, the enforcement of laws and contracts remains weak.

Last elections

12 May 2007 (parliamentary); 19 March 2008 (presidential).

Results: Presidential: Serge Sarkisian won 52.8 per cent of the vote, Levon Ter-Petrossian, 21.5 per cent and Artur Baghdasarian 17.7 per cent; all other candidates won less than 10 per cent.
Parliamentary: HHK won 32.82 per cent of the vote (64 seats out of 131); Bargavadj Hayastani Kusaktsutyun (BHK) (Prosperous Armenia) won 14.68 per cent (24 seats); Hay Heghapokhakan Dashnaktsutyun (HHD) (Armenian Revolutionary Federation) 12.72 per cent (16); Orinants Erkir (OE) (Rule of Law) 6.84 per cent (nine); and Zharangutyun (Heritage) 5.81 per cent (six). Turnout was 59.9 per cent.

Next elections

February 2013 (presidential); May 2011 (parliamentary)

Political parties

Ruling party

Coalition led by Hayastani Hanrapetakan Kusaktsutyun (HHK) (Republican Party of

Armenia) with Bargavadj Hayastani Kusaktsutyun (BHK) (Prosperous Armenia) Orinats Erkir (OE) (Rule of Law) (from May 2007). Hay Heghapokhakan Dashnaktsutiun (HHD) (Armenian Revolutionary Federation, member of coalition but withdrew 27 Apr 2009).

Main opposition party

Hay Heghapokhakan Dashnaktsutiun (HHD) (Armenian Revolutionary Federation) since it withdrew from the government on 27 April 2009.

Population

3.30 million (2010)*

Last census: October 2001: 3,002,594

Population density: 109 inhabitants per square km (2010)

Annual growth rate: -0.8 per cent 1994–2004 (WHO 2006)

Internally Displaced Persons (IDP)

50,000 (UNHCR)

Ethnic make-up

Armenians (93 per cent), Azerbaijanis (3 per cent), Russians (2 per cent); Kurdish and Yezidi minorities.

Religions

Armenian Apostolic Church (90 per cent), Armenian Catholic and Protestant (9 per cent), Russian and Greek Orthodox and Jewish.

Education

Primary education is followed by seven years of secondary school which is divided into a four-year first cycle (ages 12 to 16) and a three-year second cycle (ages 16 to 19). In the second cycle, students can opt between general or technical education. Higher education is provided by the Université Marien-Ngouabi, which is largely state subsidised. It has a yearly enrolment of about 12,000 students.

Literacy rate: 99 per cent, adult rates (Unesco 2005).

Compulsory years: 6 to 11

Enrolment rate: 96 per cent gross primary enrolment, 87 per cent gross secondary enrolment, of relevant age groups, (including repeaters) World Bank.

Pupils per teacher: 19 in primary schools.

Health

HIV/Aids

HIV prevalence: 0.1 per cent aged 15–49 in 2003 (World Bank)

Life expectancy: 68 years, 2004 (WHO 2006)

Fertility rate/Maternal mortality rate: 1.2 births per woman (2003); maternal deaths 35 per 100,000 live births (World Bank).

Birth rate/Death rate: 6 deaths to 12 births per 1,000 people (World Bank).

Child (under 5 years) mortality rate (per 1,000): 31 per 1,000 live births; 3 per cent of children aged under five are malnourished (World Bank).

Head of population per physician: 3.59 physicians per 1,000 people (2003) (WHO 2006)

Welfare

The poverty family allowance system is based on the principle of voluntary involvement and aims to target the most needy. Welfare issues concerning the elderly are crucial as almost 97 per cent of them need constant medication and 41 per cent need home care.

Pensions

In order to improve the state pension system, the government has increased the level of contributions for certain income groups. Under the state system, pensioners receive a uniform payment. There are no private pension funds.

Main cities

Yerevan (capital, estimated population 1.09 million in 2008), Vanadzor (116,929), Gyumri (168,918).

Languages spoken

Russian and Kurdish.

Official language/s

Armenian

Media

Despite censorship being prohibited in 2004 libel and defamation laws are often used to harass journalists, which has resulted in self-censorship particularly when reporting corruption and security matters particularly in Nagorno-Karabakh.

Press

The National Press Club (NPC) of Armenia formed is a self-governing, apolitical, non-profit, independent public organisation that aims to support free and democratic press in Armenia.

There are around 30 newspapers available but circulations are low with the largest being only 10,000. Productions costs have been traditionally high but following international aid a printing plant was opened and since 2005 has provided an alternative and competition for the semi-state-owned printing house. A number of publications have since increased their days of publishing and increased their circulations. Newspapers are generally owned by wealthy individuals or political parties.

Dailies: Most newspapers are published in Armenian, with Russian and English languages editions, including *Aravot* (http://new.aravot.am), a privately owned daily. Parliamentary publications include *Ayastani Anrapetutyun* (www.hhpress.am) and *Respublika Armenia* (www.ra.am). Political party publications include *Azg* (www.azg.am), *Yerkir* (http://yerkir.am), and *Aykakan Zhanamak* (www.hzh.am). In Russian, *Golos Armenii* (www.golos.am).

Weeklies: In Armenian, *Haykakan Zhamanak* is a popular weekly newspaper; with a Russian edition *Iravunk* (www.iravunk.com); with English editions *Eter* (www.eter.tv), *Lragir* (www.lragir.am), *Yerkir* (www.yerkir.am), and *168 Jam* (www.168.am). MFA Nagorno Karabakh (www.nkr.am) published in Stepanakert.

Broadcasting

Radio: The state-run Public Radio of Armenia (www.armradio.am) has two general interest stations, children's radio (http://lyunse.amradio.am) and (www.arevik.net) and an international service (http://int.armradio.am). There are a few private commercial radio stations including Hit FM (www.hit.am), Radio Van (www.radiovan.am) and City FM (www.cityfm.am).

Television: Television is the dominant media outlet. The state-run national service is provided by Public TV of Armenia (www.armtv.com) with local and imported shows most of which are translated into Armenian. Armenia TV (www.armeniatv.am) in the national commercial service. There are around 30 cable, digital and satellite TV stations broadcasting pay-to-view services.

Advertising

There is a complete ban on advertising of tobacco and alcohol. Advertising which targets children must only contain products suitable for them.

News agencies

National news agency: Armenpress

Economy

Industry dominates the Armenian economy, constituting around 45 per cent of GDP, of which manufacturing accounts for 15 per cent. Industries include mining of gold, silver, base ores and minerals (marble and granite). Manufacturing includes processing imported diamonds and jewellery manufacturing, metal cutting and forge-pressing, instrument making, food processing, viniculture and alcohol distilling, vehicle assembly, clothing manufacturing and microelectronics. The service sector constitutes over 35 per cent of GDP; the major component of this is transport and storage, followed by energy and financial and banking services. Agriculture constitutes over 15 per cent of GDP.

GDP growth, which had been running at over 13.0 per cent since 2005 dropped to 6.8 per cent in 2008 as the global economic crisis took hold and international trade and commodity prices fell sharply, particularly in non-ferrous metals. GDP growth in Armenia dropped to -14.4 per cent in 2009. However, in 2010 the economy recovered and the growth rate increased to 2.1 per cent. Remittances form an important part of the economy

and can be as much as 10 per cent of GDP. Armenia's trade deficit jumped from -US$589.6 million in 2007 to -US$1.5 billion in 2008, which has remained at such a high margin since; in 2010 the trade deficit was -US$1.37 billion.
Poverty reduction fell from 26.5 per cent in 2006 to 23.5 per cent in 2008; but it jumped to 24.6 per cent in 2009, as a reflection of the collapse in the economy. This prompted the government to introduce programmes on social welfare to ameliorate the effect of the economic downturn on the most vulnerable, including family benefit payments, unemployment insurance, paid public works and pensions.
In 2009 the output of cut diamonds and their export was cut by 70 per cent (down to 70,600 carats) and rough cut diamond imports were down by 30 per cent as demand fell. However, as demand picked up in 2010, rough cut diamond imports also grew, with 20,000 carats imported in January alone.
Armenia has had to adapt in a world where it has to compete not only with other regional countries with similar prospects but with other much larger economies. The government has made structural reform a priority with efforts to make the economy a free market and encourage new sectors, which now include processed precious stones and jewellery production, information and communication technology and a nascent tourism industry. Older industries such as chemicals, electronic components, machinery, processed food, textiles and synthetic rubber, all of which are highly dependent on outside resources, are only being supported if they are viable and necessary to modern Armenia.

External trade

Armenia has regional trade agreements (RTAs) with eight neighbouring countries. It is a member of the World Trade Organisation (WTO) and benefits from the Aid for Trade scheme (sponsored by WTO), which offers trade related skills and financial infrastructure to developing countries.
Armenia is a net exporter of electricity, supplying Georgia and the Nagorno-Karabakh region of Azerbaijan, although there has been external pressure applied to have its ageing nuclear power station closed down. Heavy industrial products have given way to light industrial products and agricultural produce for export. All imported rough cut diamonds are processed and exported. Precious metals, diamonds, pearls and other precious gems are worked into jewelry for export. In total, the European Union imports almost three times as much Armenian goods and services each year as Russia, although Russia is Armenia's single largest trading partner.

Imports

Imports of essential goods, including natural gas and petroleum, foodstuffs, tobacco products, capital machinery, tools and rough cut diamonds.
Main sources: Russia (typically 25 per cent of total), China (9 per cent), Ukraine (6 per cent).

Exports

Principal exports include electricity, diamonds, (other precious stones, pearls, lapis lazuli), precious metals and jewelry, base metals, mineral products, transport equipment, electrical equipment.
Main destinations: Germany (typically 17 per cent of total), Russia (16 per cent), US (10 per cent).

Agriculture

Armenia is a major producer of grapes, vegetables, dairy products and some cotton and sheep breeding. Agriculture contributes around 25 per cent to GDP and employs over 45 per cent of the work force. Armenia was the first former Soviet republic to privatise agricultural land.
There are around 335,000 family farms, which account for the bulk of agricultural output. Development has been inhibited by lack of private investment, an inadequate agricultural financing system and poor infrastructure.

Industry and manufacturing

The economy relies heavily on the industrial sector. Industry accounts for around 40 per cent of GDP and employs around 20 per cent of the workforce.
Industry is mainly based on the extraction and processing of natural resources, particularly ores and chemicals.
Other industries are mechanical engineering, electronic generators, textiles, synthetic rubber, wine and cognac, mineral water and food processing.

Tourism

The tourist industry is based on Armenia's historic and cultural heritage, attracting its visitors from its diaspora in Russia, the US and Iran. Armenia is also the site of Mount Ararat, the location traditionally thought to be where Noah's Ark landed.
Tourism has become increasingly important in the economy, so that by 2011 it was forecast to account for 1.8 per cent of GDP. Visitor arrivals in 2009 were 575,281, with an estimated growth of 5 per cent in 2010. Employment from travel and tourism was expected to be 70,000 (6.3 per cent of total employment) in 2011. Tourist venue was forecast at D138.7 billion (US$370 million) in 2011.
The Zvartnots International Airport, the closest to the capital, Yerevan, was upgraded in 2007 and handled 1.387 million passengers – increasing to 1.48 million in 2008. Further work, including a new terminal and other facilities are planned to be completed by the end of 2011.

Mining

Mining accounts for around 13 per cent of GDP and employs 3 per cent of the workforce.
There are large deposits of copper, zinc, aluminium and other metals, including gold. Copper accounts for 38 per cent of the reserve, iron and molybdenum 25 per cent each; gold 7.3 per cent, silver 1.6 per cent and lead and zinc 3.1 per cent.
Armenia is rich in varieties of building stone, such as marble, granite, tuffa, limestone and gypsum, and in semi-precious and ornamental stones, such as agates, jasper, amethyst and turquoise.
The major markets for Armenia's mining products are Belgium, Georgia, Iran, Liechtenstein, Switzerland and Germany.

Hydrocarbons

Armenia has no oil reserves and is completely dependent on imports of petroleum products, all of which are transported by rail or truck since there are currently no oil pipelines in Armenia. Oil imports were estimated at 410,000 barrels per day (bpd) in 2007. Plans for a hydroelectric power station on the Aras River were discussed at a ministrial meeting in a 2008 when Iran and Armenia agreed to build a pipeline from Tabriz (Iran) to Eraskh (Armenia).
Armenia has no natural gas reserves. A 20-year agreement with Iran began in 2007, whereby 3.6 billion cubic metres (cum) of Iranian natural gas will be exchanged for Armenian electricity. The initial amount of 1.8 billion cum per annum will be doubled by 2019, with Armenia providing three kilowatts per one cum. A 137km gas pipeline was part of the agreement. Armenia imports some 2 billion cum of gas per year from Russia, via a pipeline from Georgia.
Imports of coal typically amount to around one million tonnes.

Energy

Installed electricity capacity is 3.4GW, generated by thermal, hydro and nuclear power. The ministry of energy oversees infrastructure projects and commercial energy companies providing electricity to end-users. There are 32 hydroelectric plants, which account for 34 per cent of production. Thermal power plants supply the remaining 26 per cent. Armenia is linked to Iran's grid, permitting two-way exchange of electricity. In 2008 the energy minister announced the construction of a new nuclear power unit, at an

estimated cost of US$5 billion, to provide 1,000MW. The plant will replace the existing Metsamor nuclear station, which was reopened in 1995 after its closure following the 1988 earthquake. Armenia has been under international pressure to close the plant. With a shared history, participation in Armenia's energy production by Russian companies is ongoing, including Rosatom (nuclear electricity generating).
Armenia and Iran are co-operating on development of renewable energy sources, including a new wind power plant with a capacity of 10.4MW.

Financial markets

Non-banking financial institutions (such as leasing organisations, insurance companies and investment funds) are either non-existent or at an early stage of development.
A Securities and Exchange Commission was established in November 1998.

Stock exchange

Armenia Stock Exchange (Armex)

Banking and insurance

The banking system in Armenia is growing but still experiences difficulties in attracting deposits (representing less than 10 per cent of GDP). Most lending is available at short maturities only and at high interest rates. The range of facilities and services on offer to customers is increasing. HSBC Armenia was one of the most active banks.
There are over 30 commercial banks in the country.

Central bank

Central Bank of the Republic of Armenia

Time

GMT plus three hours

Geography

Armenia is a landlocked country of high mountains and fertile valleys situated in south-west Transcaucasia. Georgia lies to the north of Armenia, to the west is the border with Turkey. Azerbaijan is to the east of the country – the ethnic Armenian enclave, Nagorno-Karabakh, is wholly within Azerbaijan – and to the south Armenia has a short frontier with Iran. The autonomous republic of Nankhchivan, an Azerbaijani territory, is an enclave within southern Armenia. Lake Sevan is at an altitude of 1,924 metres and is surrounded by mountain ranges reaching 4,090 metres at Mount Aragats. Numerous rivers and streams flow from the mountains into the River Araks which marks the south-western border of the country, its basin forming a fertile lowland to the south of Yerevan – the Ararat Plain.

Hemisphere

Northern

Climate

Cool winters and hot summers characterise Armenia with the average January temperature in Yerevan at around 1 degree Celsius (C), while July averages 26 degrees C. Snow falls in early winter (November and December) and rain in April to June.
Annual rainfall in Yerevan averages 33cm but is much higher in mountain regions.

Entry requirements

Passports

Required by all. Must be valid at least four months after date of departure.

Visa

Required by all except nationals of CIS countries. An invitation is required for visits over 21 days.Visas can be obtained online: www.armeniaforeignministry.am/consular/visa.html.

Currency advice/regulations

There are no restrictions on import of local or foreign currency, but amounts over US$10,000 must be declared. Export of local or foreign currency unlimited, but cash restricted to US$10,000, amounts above which must be transferred through a bank.

Customs

Personal goods up to US$500 are duty-free. Advisable to declare valuables such as jewellery, cameras, computers and musical instruments.

Health (for visitors)

Mandatory precautions

None.

Advisable precautions

It is advisable to be in date for the following immunisations: tetanus (within 10 years), hepatitis A (moderate risk only); hepatitis B (if you need to spend more than six to eight weeks in the region); malaria precautions for western border areas only.
Any medicines required should be taken by the visitor. Take a medical kit including a disposable syringe. Food and water precautions should be observed.

Credit cards

Major credit cards and travellers cheques are accepted at the banks in Yerevan.

Public holidays (national)

Fixed dates

1–2 Jan (New Year), 6 Jan (Orthodox Christmas), 8 Mar (Women's Day), 7 Apr (Motherhood and Beauty Day), 24 Apr (Genocide Memorial Day), 9 May (Victory and Peace Day), 28 May (First Republic Day), 5 Jul (Constitution Day), 21 Sep (Independence Day), 7 Dec (Earthquake Memorial Day), 31 Dec (New Year's Eve).

Variable dates

Good Friday

Working hours

Banking

Mon–Fri: 0900–1800.

Business

Mon–Fri: 0900–1800.

Government

Mon–Fri: 0900–1730.

Shops

Mon–Fri: 0900–2000; Sat–Sun: 0900–1800.l

Electricity supply

220V AC 50Hz

Weights and measures

Metric system

Social customs/useful tips

The Armenians are very hospitable and will invite strangers into their homes. Being unable to speak their language will not be a problem. Dress in rural areas should be modest.
Do not photograph military installations or equipment and seek permission to photograph religious buildings.

Security

Visitors should not travel to Nagorno-Karabakh in the west or the military occupied area surrounding it.

Getting there

Air

Armenia is increasingly accessible by air with flights from Europe, the Middle East and especially Moscow.
National airline: Armavia.
International airport/s: Zvartnots (EVN), 10km south-west of Yerevan; facilities include business and VIP halls plus duty-free shops, post office and cafés.
Airport tax: A departure tax of US$20, excluding transit passengers.

Surface

Road: Access is from Georgia to the north and Iran to the south. Routes from Turkey and Azerbaijan are closed.
Rail: There is a service running from Batumi on the Black Sea, via Tbilisi and the Georgian border, to Yerevan. There are also connections fromTbilisi to Gyumri and to Vanadzor. The *gnatsk* is a through train, running on alternate days.
Pre-booking is advised.

Getting about

National transport

Road: There are 7,705km (4,788 miles) of roads. The main roads are in reasonable condition, but local roads can be very poor.
Buses: Coaches operate between towns and city centres.
Rail: The railway system is aged and the service is unreliable.

City transport

Taxis: Taxis in Yerevan are unmetered. Expect to negotiate a fare to destination beforehand.

Buses, trams & metro: Vans (*marshrutnis*), charging a cheap flat fare, are the best way of travel in Yerevan. There is a short, single-line metro in Yerevan, which is cheap and efficient.

Car hire

Car rental services are available in Yerevan, but it is usual and advisable to hire a car and driver. Traffic drives on the right.

BUSINESS DIRECTORY

The addresses listed below are a selection only. While World of Information makes every endeavour to check these addresses, we cannot guarantee that changes have not been made, especially to telephone numbers and area codes. We would welcome any corrections.

Telephone area codes

The international direct dialling (IDD) code for Armenia is +374, followed by area code and subscriber's number:

Abovyan	222	Vanadzor	322
Gyumri	312	Yerevan	10

Chambers of Commerce

American Chamber of Commerce in Armenia, Hotel Armenia, 1 Amiryan Street, Yerevan 375010 (tel: 599-187; fax: 599-151; e-mail: amcham@arminco.com).

European Union Chamber of Commerce in Armenia, 8/1 Khorenatsi Street, Yerevan 375010 (tel: 547-760; fax: 547-780; e-mail: info@eucca.am).

Chamber of Commerce and Industry of the Republic of Armenia, 11 Khanjyan Street, Yerevan 375010 (tel: 560-184; fax: 587-871; e-mail: armcci@arminco.com).

Kotayk Marz Chamber of Commerce and Industry, 11 Sevani Street, Abovyan 378510 (tel: 26-035; fax: 233-97; e-mail: ccikotayk@ccikotayk.am).

Yerevan Chamber of Commerce and Industry, 11 Khanjyan Street, Yerevan 375010 (tel: 560-184; fax: 587-871; e-mail: yercci@arminco.com).

Banking

Ardshinbank of the Republic of Armenia, 3 Deghatan Street, Yerevan (tel: 560-611; fax: 151-155, 584-761).

Arminpex Bank, 2 Nalbandian Street, 375010 Yerevan (tel: 589-927, 567-183, 565-873; fax: 151-786, 151-815).

HSBC Armenia Bank, 1 Vramshapouh Arka Street, Yerevan (tel: 151-717; fax: 151-886).

Armeconombank, 32 G.Nzdehi Street, Yerevan 375026 (tel: 562-705, 531-115; fax: 151-149).

Armagrobank, 7a Movses Khorenacu Street, Yerevan 375015 (tel: 534-342; fax: 390-712-6).

Mellat, 1 P.Byusandy, Yerevan (tel: 581-354; fax: 151-811).

Prometeus, 19 Kochari Street, Yerevan 375012 (tel: 273-000; fax: 274-818).

Haykap, 22 Sarian Street, Yerevan 375002 (tel: 532-080; fax: 390-703-3).

Erebuni, 13 Khagakh- Don Street, Yerevan 375087 (tel: 577-256).

Credit - Yerevan, 2/8 Vramshapouh Arkay Street, Yerevan 375010 (tel: 589-065; fax: 580-083).

Central bank

Central Bank of Armenia, Vazgen Sargsyan Street 6, 375010 Yerevan (tel: 583-841; fax: 523-852); e-mail: mcba@cba.am).

Stock exchange

Armenia Stock Exchange (Armex) www.nasdaqomx.am/en/index.htm

Travel information

Armavia Airline Co Ltd, 3 Amiryan Street, 50 Mashtotsi Avenue, 0010 Yerevan(tel: 593-316; fax: 582-604; e-mail: armavia@infocom.am).

Levon Travel Bureau, 10 Sayat Nova Avenue, 375001 Yerevan (tel: 525-210; fax: 561-483; e-mail: tourism@levontravel.am).

National tourist organisation offices

Armenia Tourism Development Agency, 3 Nalbandyan Street, 0010 Yerevan (tel: 542-303; fax: 544-792; e-mail: help@armeniainfo.am).

Ministries

Ministry of Agriculture and Food Supplies, 1 Government House, Republican Square, 375010 Yerevan (tel: 524-641; fax: 151-086, 151-583).

Ministry of Communications, 22 Sarian Street, 375002 Yerevan (tel: 526-632; fax: 151-446; 151-151); Union Bldg, Republic Square, Yerevan 375010.

Ministry of Culture, Youth and Sports, 5 Toumanian Street, 375010 Yerevan (tel: 528-869, 561-920; fax: 523-930, 523-922, 526-869).

Ministry of Defence, Proshian Settlement, 60 G. Shaush Road, Yerevan (tel: 357-822; fax: 526-560).

Ministry of Ecology and Natural Resources, 35 Moskovian Street, 375012 Yerevan (tel: 530-741; fax: 534-902).

Ministry of Economical Structural Reform, 1 Government House, Republic Square, Yerevan 375010 (tel: 151-069).

Ministry of Education and Science, 13 Movses Khorenatsi Street, 375010 Yerevan (tel: 526-602; fax: 151-150).

Ministry of Energy, 1 Government House, Republican Square, 375010 Yerevan (tel: 521-964; fax: 151-036).

Ministry of Finance and Economy, 1 Melik-Adamian Street, 375010 Yerevan (tel: 527-082; fax: 151-154).

Ministry of Foreign Affairs, 2 Government House, Republican Square, 375010 Yerevan (tel: 523-531; fax: 151-042).

Ministry of Health, 8 Tumanian Street, 375001 Yerevan (tel: 582-413; fax: 151-097).

Ministry of Industry and Trade, Division of Tourism, 5 Hanrapetutjan Street, 375010 Yerevan (tel: 560-274, 560-780, 589-472, 587-706; fax: 526-577).

Ministry of Internal Affairs and National Security, 2 Nalbandian, 375025 Yerevan (tel: 529-733).

Ministry of Justice, 8 Parliament Street, 375010 Yerevan (tel: 582-157; fax: 565-640).

Ministry of Local Government Affairs, 2 Government House, Yerevan (tel: 525-274).

Ministry of Operational Affairs, 1 Government House, Republican Square, Yerevan 375010 (tel: 151-036; fax: 520-321).

Ministry of Privatisation and Foreign Investment, 1 Government House, Republic Square, Yerevan 375010 (tel: 520-351; fax: 151-036).

Ministry of Social Security, 18 Issahakian Street, 375025 Yerevan (tel: 526-831; fax: 151-920).

Ministry of Statistics and Data, State Registrar, Republican Square, 375010 Yerevan (tel: 524-213).

Ministry of Transport, 10 Zakiyan Street, 375015 Yerevan (tel: 563-391; fax: 525-268).

Ministry of Urban Planning and Construction, 1 Government House, Republican Square, Yerevan (tel: 589-080; fax: 151-036).

Prime Minister's Office, 1 Government House, Republican Square, 375101 Yerevan (tel: 520-360; fax: 151-035).

Other useful addresses

Armenian Embassy (USA), 2225 R Street, NW, Washington DC 20008 (tel: (+1-202) 319-1976; fax: (+1-202) 319-2982).

Armenian Foreign Trade Organisation, V/O Armentorg, Dom Pravitelstva, Ploschad Lenina, 375010 Yerevan.

Armenian Foundation for SMEs, 19 Khandjian Street, 375010 Yerevan (tel: 578-231; fax: 151-690; e-mail: smeda@arminco.com).

Armenian State Foreign Economic and Trade Association, Str 25 Hr Kochar, 375012 Yerevan (tel: 224-310; fax: 220-034).

Azat Mamoul (Dashnak News Agency), Yerevan (tel: 563-493; fax: 565-728).

British Embassy, 28 Charents Street, Yerevan (tel: 151-842; fax: 151-807).

Business Communication Centres, 6 Baghramian Avenue 2, 375009 Yerevan (tel: 222-145; fax: 151-934; e-mail: ggv@bcc.arminco.com).

Committee of Privatisation and Management of State Property, Ul Budakhian 1, 375014 Yerevan (tel: 280-120).

Department of Emergency Situations, Government House, Republican Square, Yerevan 375010 (tel: 531-612; fax: 151-036).

EC Energy Centre, Institute of Energy, Amaranotsayeen 127, Yerevan (tel/fax: 151-730).

Enterprise Development and Foreign Investment Promotion Armenian Agency (EDIPA), 23/1 Vramshapuh Arkah, Yerevan 375002 (tel: 538-929; fax: 151-149).

Secretariat of the Council of Ministers (tel: 520-360, 522-482; fax: 151-035, 141-036).

State Commission for Tax Inspection, Movses Khorenatsi, Yerevan 375010 (tel: 538-101, 538-073).

State Department for Statistics, State Register and Analysis of the Republic of Armenia, 3 Government House, Republic Square, Yerevan (tel: 524-213; fax: 521-921).

State TV and Radio, 5 Alex Manoogian, 375025 Yerevan (tel: 555-033).

TACIS (Technical Assistance to Commonwealth of Independent States), Ministry of Economy, 1 Government Building, Republic Square, Yerevan 10 (tel: 528-803; fax: 151-164).

US Embassy, 18 Baghramyan Avenue, Yerevan 375019 (tel: 520-791; fax: 520-800; e-mail: usinfo@arminco.com).

National news agency: Armenpress, 4 Floor, 28 Isahakian Street, Yerevan 375009 (internet: www.armenpress.am).

Other news agencies: Arka: www.arka.am

Arminfo: www.arminfo.info

Noyan Tapan: www.nt.am

Mediamax: www.mediamax.am

Internet sites

Armenian Development Agency: www.businessarmenia.com

Armenian information: www.armgate.com

Armenian Stock Exchange: www.armex.am

Armenia Yellow Pages: www.armenian.com

Arminfo News Agency: www.arminfo.am

Aruba

KEY FACTS

Official name: Aruba

Head of State: Queen Beatrix of the Netherlands; Governor Fredis Refunjol (from 2004)

Head of government: Prime Minister Michiel (Mike) Godfried Eman (AVP) (from 31 Oct 2009)

Ruling party: Arubaanse Volks Partij (AVP) (Aruban People's Party) (from 25 Sep 2009)

Area: 193 square km

Population: 107,000 (2010)*

Capital: Oranjestad

Official language: Dutch

Currency: Aruban guilder (Af) = 100 cents (commonly called the florin)

Exchange rate: Af1.79 per US$ (Oct 2011)

GDP per capita: US$21,800 (2004)

GDP real growth: 2.50% (2005)

Unemployment: 6.90% (2005)*

Balance of trade: -US$1.08 billion (2010)

Visitor numbers: 112,700 (2010)

* estimated figure

COUNTRY PROFILE

Historical profile

1499 First European sighting of the islands of the Netherlands Antilles by Spanish mariners.
1636 Dutch took over; Spanish and Portuguese Jews escaping from persecution in Europe settled in the islands.
1800–02 British Protectorate.
1825 Gold discovered and mined until 1916.
1863 Slavery completely abolished.
1954 Internal autonomy was granted to Netherlands Antilles.
1986 Aruba seceded from Netherlands Antilles; both entities elected to remain part of the Kingdom of the Netherlands. Aruba has complete autonomy over its internal affairs; the Netherlands is constitutionally responsible for defence and external affairs.
2001 Movimiento Electoral di Pueblo (MEP) (People's Electoral Movement) won parliamentary elections and Nelson Oduber (MEP) became prime minister.
2003 A law was introduced in order to help fight money laundering more efficiently.
2004 Fredis Refunjol was sworn in as governor.
2005 MEP won parliamentary elections. The disappearance (and murder) of US-national, Natalee Holloway, caused an outcry in Alabama (her home state). A public protest began, calling for Aruba to be boycotted by all US tourists, for what was seen as an inept investigation and an accusation that Aruba's police service was incapable of protecting visitors. The risk to Aruba's tourist industry, with 930,000 US visitors spending US$2.3 million annually, prompted the US State Department to reassure its citizens and for the FBI to review the police case file.
2007 The chief prosecutor closed the official investigation into the case of Natalee Holloway (missing since 2005).
2009 In parliamentary elections held on 25 September, the opposition Arubaanse Volks Partij (AVP) (Aruban People's Party) won 48 per cent of the vote (12 seats of 21), the incumbent MEP won 35.9 per cent (turnout was around 85 per cent). Mike Eman (AVP) took office as prime minister.
2010 In January the sale of the Aruba refinery to the state-owned PetroChina was cleared, following an agreement by the US-based Valero Energy Corporation and the government resolving a long-standing dispute over business taxes. A Dutch citizen, Joran van der Sloot was arrested in Peru and confessed to the murder of a young Peruvian woman in May. He had also confessed to killing US tourist Natalee Holloway in Aruba in 2005, but had later recanted his confession and was released through lack of enough other evidence. In June Joran van der Sloot stood trial in Peru, charged with murder and pleaded guilty.
2011 Van der Sloot was still awaiting a trial verdict in Peru in July; if convicted he could serve up to 25 years.

Political structure

Form of state

Parliamentary democratic monarchy.
On 10 October 2010, the Caribbean islands of Curaçao and St Maarten joined Aruba (1986) as semi-autonomous countries within the Kingdom of the Netherlands; at the same time the Caribbean islands of Bonaire, St Eustatius and Saba became Bijzondere Gemeenten (special municipalities) of the Netherlands.

The executive

The Head of State is the monarch of The Netherlands, who is represented by a governor. The governor is appointed by the monarch, on the recommendation of the Aruban Council of Ministers.
Executive power is exercised by the governor and a prime minister who heads an eight-member council of ministers. The Council is accountable to the Staten (parliament).

National legislature

The unicameral parliament, Staten (Estates), has 21 members, elected for a four-year term by proportional representation.

Legal system

Aruba's judicial system, which has mainly been derived from the Dutch system, operates independently of the legislature and the executive. Jurisdiction, including appeal, lies with the Common Court of Justice of Aruba and the Supreme Court of Justice in The Netherlands.

Last elections

25 September 2009 (parliamentary)
Results: Arubaanse Volks Partij (AVP) (Aruban People's Party) won 48 per cent of the vote (12 seats out of 21),

Movimiento Electoral di Pueblo (MEP) (People's Electoral Movement) 35.9 per cent (8), and Partido Democracia Real (PDR) (Real Democracy Party) 5.7 per cent (1). Turnout was around 85 per cent.

Next elections

September 2013

Political parties

Ruling party

Arubaanse Volks Partij (AVP) (Aruban People's Party) (from 25 Sep 2009)

Main opposition party

Movimiento Electoral di Pueblo (MEP) (People's Electoral Movement)

Political situation

In 2009 Aruba and The Netherlands became embroiled in a governmental disagreement over who ultimately has power in Aruba. Under the auspices of the Kingdom Council of Minister, based in Willemstad (Holland), changes to the draft consensus of law establishing a joint court of justice and new constitutional relations were approved, after Aruba strongly objected then withdrew from talks. This provoked a series of complaints by Aruba that it had been sidelined as the only territory under consideration with direct concerns about the changes. By July, Aruba was threatening to take its complaint to the United Nation's Decolonisation Committee for adjudication, asserting the Netherlands would overrule its autonomy. In October 2010 the Kingdom of the Netherlands was reconfigured to consists of the European country (including Caribbean municipal entities) and the Caribbean territories of Aruba, Curaçao and St. Martin.

Population

107,000 (2010)*

Last census: October 2000: 90,508

Population density: 516 inhabitants per square km. Urban population: 51 per cent (1995—2001).

Annual growth rate: 0.2 per cent (2003)

Ethnic make-up

Carib and Arawak Indian, European and African heritage.

Religions

Roman Catholic (82 per cent), Protestant (8 per cent), Hindu, Muslim, Confucian, Jewish.

Education

Literacy rate: 97 per cent

Health

Life expectancy: 78.8 years (estimate 2003)

Fertility rate/Maternal mortality rate: Two births per woman (2003)

Birth rate/Death rate: 12 births per 1,000 population; six deaths per 1,000 population (2003).

Child (under 5 years) mortality rate (per 1,000): Six per 1,000 live births (2003)

Main cities

Oranjestad (capital, estimated population 32,748 in 2008), St Nicolas (18,126).

Languages spoken

Papiamento is the local language. Dutch, English and Spanish are widely spoken.

Official language/s

Dutch

Media

Press

In Papiamento, from Oranjestad, *Diario* (http://news.diario-aruba.com), *Bon Dia* (www.bondia.com), *AWE Mainta* (www.awemainta.com) and *Solo di Pueblo* (www.solodipueblo.com) published in Santa Cruz. In Dutch, with an English edition, *Amigoe* (www.amigoe.com). In English, *Aruba Today* (www.arubatoday.com).

Broadcasting

Radio: In Papiamento, Dutch and English, Radio Kelkboom (www.watapana-aruba.com) broadcasts news, talk and music. There are several other commercial music and religious programme stations including Hit FM (www.hit94fm.com), Magic 96.5 (www.magic965.com), Mega 88FM (www.mega88fm.com) and Cool FM (www.coolaruba.com).

Television: Tele-Aruba (www.telearuba.aw) provides a comprehensive service with locally produced news, current affairs, educational, cultural and sports as well as imported programmes. There are several cable and satellite TV stations, some of which are also US affiliates, including Cable TVAruba (CTA) (www.cta.aw), Venevisión, Flamingo TV, ATV and Caribbean Super Station.

Advertising

All newspapers accept advertising in English.

News agencies

Other news agencies: The Governor of Aruba: www.kabga.aw
Caribbean Net News: www.caribbeannetnews.com

Economy

The service sector is the major component of the economy, in particular tourism and financial services; the industrial sector is still important, as crude oil from regional sources is imported, refined and traded on. Construction, led by tourism, also provides employment and growth. Agriculture is largely composed of animal husbandry as the island's soil is arid and unproductive. Other, less obvious sources of economic growth include trade in fine art and collectables.

GDP growth averaged 3 per cent 2003–07, but as the global economic crisis took effect tourism from North America and Europe was particularly hard hit and coupled with the temporary closure of the oil refinery in 2009 growth fell from 1.4 per cent in 2007 to 0.7 per cent in 2008 and into recession of -7.7 per cent in 2009. Oil export revenues fell from US$1.3 billion in 2008/09 to US$200 million in 2009/10. The combined downturn in tourism and oil caused the biggest slump in any economy in the Caribbean in 2009. In response, the government loosened its fiscal policies, cut a business tax and increased social payments to mitigate the impact of the recession.

External trade

Aruba is an Overseas Country and Territory (OCT) of The Kingdom of the Netherlands and benefits from free trade with

KEY INDICATORS — Aruba

	Unit	2006	2007	2008	2009	2010
Population	m	0.11	0.12	0.12	0.11	*0.11
GDP per capita	US$	22,934	25,760	26,511	43,986	–
GDP real growth	%	2.4	1.4	0.7	*-7.7	–
Inflation	%	3.6	3.0	3.3	1.8	–
Unemployment	%	0.0	7.1	6.9	11.3	–
Exports (fob) (goods)	US$m	3,951.5	2,691.1	3,705.0	1,445.3	265.8
Imports (fob) (goods)	US$m	3,837.5	2,853.0	4,200.8	1,919.1	1,343.0
Balance of trade	US$m	113.9	-162.0	-495.8	-473.8	-1,077.3
Current account	US$m	213.4	-99.4	-151.5	157.1	-410.2
Total reserves minus gold	US$m	337.8	372.1	604.9	578.2	568.2
Foreign exchange	US$m	337.8	372.1	604.9	578.2	568.2
Tourist numbers	'000	94.8	105.4	112.9	110.9	112.7
Exchange rate	per US$	1.79	1.79	1.79	1.79	1.79

* estimated figure

any EU member. Aruba also has free trade agreements (FTA) with the US, Canada, Malaysia and India. Aruba has regional associations for trade with countries of the Economic Commission for Latin America and the Caribbean (Eclac), Caribbean Development Co-operation Committee (CDCC) and the Association of Caribbean States (ACS). Although not a member of the World Trade Organisation (WTO), Aruba uses developments within the WTO to determine its trading practices.
Trans-shipment brings in important foreign exchange and Aruba offers free trade zones (situated near the harbour of Oranjestad and Barcadera) and activities, to foreign interests. Oil refining is an important industry, taking crude oil from regional sources for trading on.

Imports
Crude oil is imported for refining. Other products include foodstuffs, machinery, electrical equipment and chemicals.
Main sources: US (typically 50 per cent of total), The Netherlands (16 per cent), UK (5 per cent).

Exports
Main exports include refined petroleum products, live animals, animal products, art and collectables, machinery and electronic equipment and vehicles.
Main destinations: Panama (typically 24 per cent of total), The Netherlands Antilles (21 per cent), Colombia (18 per cent).

Re-exports
Refined oil and petroleum products.

Industry and manufacturing
Oil processing is the dominant industry in Aruba, despite the expansion of the tourism sector.
The Lago refinery, originally owned by a subsidiary of Exxon, was closed in 1985, depriving the island of one-third of its revenue, and later sold to the Aruban government for a nominal amount. It was rehabilitated by Coastal Oil and Gas Corporation of Houston and reopened in 1990. US-based El Paso undertook typical production of around 170,000 barrels per day (bpd) of oil, around 50 per cent of the refinery's capacity. El Paso sold the refinery and related marine, bunkering and marketing affiliates for US$465 million to the US-Valero Energy Corporation The refinery has a throughput capacity of 315,000bpd.

Tourism
Aruba has many Caribbean attractions and offers diversions for holidaymakers including sports, natural history and leisure pastimes. Most visitors arrive from North America, plus Aruba has cultural ties to The Netherlands and northern South America.
Travel and tourism is expected to directly account for 23.2 per cent of GDP in 2011, with 26.2 per cent of direct employment in the sector (13,000 jobs) and 75.5 per cent of total employment indirectly related to the industry. Visitor numbers were up by 6.2 per cent year-on-year in January 2010, as arrivals from the US returned following the global economic crisis. Foreign exchange revenue was forecast to be Af2.55 billion (US$1.4 billion) in 2011.
Over 300 cruise ships visit Aruba each year and the ministry of tourism is active in attracting more vessels to visit and 'enhance the experience' of passengers when they arrive. The second annual Aruba International Film Festival (AIFF) was held in June 2011, with films from 13 countries. Construction of the new, 320-room Ritz-Carlton Hotel, sited in Palm Beach (considered one of the best Aruban locations for Caribbean beaches), is due to be completed in 2012.

Hydrocarbons
There are no known hydrocarbons reserves. Consumption of oil was 8,000 barrels per day (bpd) in 2008, all of which was imported. Crude oil makes up over 95 per cent of all oil imported and is re-exported as refined oil; refinery capacity is 271,000bpd. Oil exports are a major component of GDP and foreign exchange earnings.
Any use of natural gas or coal is commercially insignificant.

Energy
Total installed generating capacity was 150MW in 2007, producing over 80 million kilowatt hours. The state-owned, WEB Aruba NV is responsible for electricity generation, while NV Elmar is the sole provider of electricity on the island and responsible for transmission, distribution and sales.
The government is reviewing the installation of wind-powered generators.

Banking and insurance
The banking sector consists of six commercial banks, two of which are branches of banks established in The Netherlands and Curaçao, one is a subsidiary of a bank established in Curaçao and three have their head offices in Aruba.
Aruba is a signatory of a new EU tax agreement that was introduced in July 2005. It has agreed to pass on, to the tax department of an EU citizen's country, information concerning the amount of money in savings accounts, to allow tax to be levied from the account holder's home country.
Aruba has also agreed to supply information on tax fraud, for criminal or civil trials, and notify EU member states about additional malpractices.

Central bank
Centrale Bank van Aruba

Offshore facilities
The offshore banking sector has great potential. The Central Bank has been better equipped to regulate the banking sector since the enactment of the State Ordinance on the Supervision of the Credit System, 1998.

Time
GMT minus four hours

Geography
Located in the Caribbean Sea north of Venezuela, Aruba is a flat island with large white sandy beaches and sparse vegetation. The highest point is Mount Jamanota which is 188 metres above sea level.

Hemisphere
Northern

Climate
Aruba lies outside the Caribbean's hurricane zone. It has an almost constant temperature of 27 degrees Celsius with cooling trade winds and an absence of tropical storms and hurricanes. Low levels of humidity and rainfall.

Entry requirements
Passports
Required by all, except nationals of US and Canada, who only need proof of citizenship, and of EU countries with EU Travel Cards. (NB citizens of Canada and US require passports for re-entry to their countries).
Passports must be valid for at least three months after arrival. A return or onward ticket and adequate funds are required.

Visa
Not required, except by nationals of former Communist and some other countries. For details, visit http://www.visitaruba.com/travel/toaruba/customs.html or contact the nearest embassy.

Currency advice/regulations
Import/export of Aruban currency is forbidden. No restriction on import of foreign currencies, but a licence is required for export.

Customs
Besides articles for personal use, persons aged over 18 are allowed 2 litres of alcohol and 200 cigarettes, 50 cigars and 250 grammes of tobacco.

Health (for visitors)
Mandatory precautions
Yellow fever vaccination certificate required if arriving from an infected area.

Advisable precautions
hepatitis A and B and typhoid vaccinations.

Hotels
There are numerous tourist hotels. It is advisable to book in advance. There is a 17.66 per cent service and government tax on room prices and a 10–15 per cent charge on food and drinks.

Public holidays (national)
Fixed dates
1 Jan (New Year's Day), 25 Jan (G F Croe's Day),18 Mar (National Anthem and Flag Day), 30 Apr (Queen's Day), 1 May (Labour Day), 25 Dec (Christmas Day), 26 Dec (Boxing Day).
Variable dates
Good Friday, Easter Monday, Ascension Day.

Working hours
Banking
Mon–Fri: 0800–1600.
Business
Mon–Fri: 0800–1200, 1300–1700.
Government
Mon–Fri: 0800–1200, 1300–1700. Sat: 0800–1200.
Shops
Mon–Sat: 0800–1800. Some shops close 1200–1400 every working day. Malls and shopping centres open 9.30–1800.

Telecommunications
Mobile/cell phones
GSM 900/1800 services are available, with coverage throughout the island.

Electricity supply
110/120V 60 cycles

Getting there
Air
Regular flights from US, Venezuela, Colombia and The Netherlands.
International airport/s: Reina Beatrix (AUA), 2.5km from Oranjestad, duty-free shop, bar, restaurant, post office, car hire.
Airport tax: Except for transit passengers, US destinations US$36.75, all other international destinations US$33.50.
Surface
Main port/s: Oranjestad, Sint Nicolaas and Barcadera are deep-water harbours.

Getting about
National transport
Road: A well-developed road system connects all major towns.
Buses: Regular services in and around main centres. Also *jitney* services and sightseeing tours.
City transport
Taxis: Usually identified by 'TX' before the licence number. Taxis are not metered; fares are government-controlled according to destination.
Car hire
Prices are reasonable. An international licence is required. Driving is on the right.

BUSINESS DIRECTORY

The addresses listed below are a selection only. While World of Information makes every endeavour to check these addresses, we cannot guarantee that changes have not been made, especially to telephone numbers and area codes. We would welcome any corrections.

Telephone area codes
The international dialling code (IDD) for Aruba is +297, followed by subscriber's number.

Chambers of Commerce
Aruba Chamber of Commerce and Industry, 10 JE Irausquin Boulevard, PO Box 140, Oranjestad (tel: 582-1566; fax: 583-3962; businessinfo@arubachamber.com).

Banking
ABN-AMRO Bank NV, Caya GF Betico Croes 89, Oranjestad (tel: 821-515; fax: 821-856).

Aruba Bank NV, Caya GF Betico Croes 41, PO Box 192, Oranjestad (tel: 821-550; fax: 829-152).

Aruban Investment Bank NV, Middenweg 20, PO Box 1011, Oranjestad (tel: 827-327; fax: 827-461).

Banco di Caribe, Caya GF Croes 90, Oranjestad (tel: 832-168; fax: 832-422).

Caribbean Mercantile Bank NV, Caya GF Betico Croes 53, PO Box 28, Oranjestad (tel: 823-118; fax: 824-373).

First National Bank of Aruba NV, Caya GF Betico Croes 67, Oranjestad (tel: 833-221; fax: 821-756).

Interbank Aruba, Caya GF Betico Croes 38, Oranjestad (tel: 831-080; fax: 824-058).

Central bank
Centrale Bank van Aruba, JE Irausquin Boulevard 8, Oranjestad (tel: 525-2100; fax: 525-2101).

Travel information
Aruba Cruise Tourism, Royal Plaza Mall, Suite 230, LG Smith Blvd 94, Oranjestad (tel: 583-3648; email: info@ArubaByCruise.com; internet: www.arubabycruise.com).

National tourist organisation offices
Aruba Tourism Authority, L G Smith Boulevard 172, Eagle (tel: 821-019; fax: 834-702).

Aruba Tourism Authority P R, A Schutte Str 2, Oranjestad (tel: 823-778, 823-779, 837-254; fax: 830-075; internet site: www.arubatourism.com).

Ministries
Ministry of Economic Affairs and Tourism, Government of Aruba, L G Smith Boulevard 76, Oranjestad (tel: 826-977; fax: 835-084).

Ministry of Finance, Oranjestad (tel: 823-237; fax: 827-116).

Ministry of Foreign Affairs, J E Irausquinplein 2A, Oranjestad (tel: 583-4705; fax: 583-8108)

Ministry of Public Works and Public Health, L G Smith Boulevard, Oranjestad (tel: 824-900; fax: 826-826).

Ministry of Traffic, Communications and Utilities, Oranjestad (tel: 824-900; fax: 835-985).

Cabinet of the Minister Plenipotentiary of Aruba, R J Schimmelpenninckiaan 1, 2517 JN The Hague, The Netherlands (tel: (+3170) 356-6200; fax: (+3170) 356-6210).

Other useful addresses
Aruba Foreign Investment Agency, 85 Caya G F Betico Croes, Oranjestad (tel: 826-070; fax: 822-745).

Aruba Trade & Industry Association, Pedro Gallegostraat 6, PO Box 562, Oranjestad (tel: 827-593).

Department of Economic Affairs, Commerce and Industry, L G Smith Boulevard 160, Sun Plaza Building, Oranjestad (tel: 821-181, 821-482; fax: 834-494).

Internet sites
Aruba government: www.aruba.com

Aruba online: www.arubatourism.com

Visit Aruba: www.visitaruba.com

Ascension Island

KEY FACTS

Official name: Ascension Island

Head of State: Queen Elizabeth II, represented by Governor and Commander-in-Chief, Mark Andrew Capes (from 29 Oct 2011)

Head of government: Administrator of Ascension Island Ross Denny (from Sep 2008)

Area: 88 square km

Population: 880 (2010)*

Capital: Georgetown

Official language: English

Currency: Pound sterling (£) = 100 pence

Exchange rate: £0.64 per US$ (Oct 2011)

* estimated figure

COUNTRY PROFILE

Historical profile

1501 Ascension Island was sighted by the Portuguese mariner Juan da Nova.
1815 The UK took possession (on Napoleon's exile to St Helena) and established a garrison.
1823 Responsibility for the island was taken over by the Admiralty Board until 1922, when it became a dependency of St Helena.
1922–64 The Island was managed by the Eastern Telegraph Company (renamed Cable and Wireless in 1934).
1942 The US constructed a military airstrip by arrangement with the UK government and the island became an important transit point on the South African route between 1943–45.
1957 A US presence was re-established with the extension of the Eastern Test Range, and in 1967, a Nasa tracking station was built (since closed).
1964 In view of plans to establish BBC and Composite Signals Organisation (CSO) stations, an administrator was appointed.
1982 The island was re-garrisoned during the Falklands War and Ascension Island remains the intermediate stop for Royal Air Force (RAF) flights from the UK to the Falkland Islands.
1999 Geoffrey Fairhurst became the administrator.
2002 A referendum, in which 95 per cent of the islanders voted, agreed to the formation of an Island Council under the leadership of the administrator. Income tax and customs duties replaced the island's former tax-free status. Andrew Michael Kettlewell was appointed administrator. The first general election was held on 1 November.
2004 Michael Clancy became governor, resident in St Helena. Command of the renamed Ascension Island Base was transferred from Headquarters Strike Command (RAF High Wycombe), to the Permanent Joint Headquarters (PJHQ), Northwood, London.
2005 Michael Thomas Hill was appointed as the new administrator. Elections for the second Ascension Island Council were held.
2006 The Administrator's Office was renamed Administration Department.
2007 Six out of the seven island councillors resigned in protest at a decision by the UK Foreign and Commonwealth Office (FCO) not to grant UK Right of Abode, Land Tenure, Fiscal Development and Social Development as previously announced, when taxation and democratic representation was introduced. The FCO had said that it wanted to create a settled society but the projected costs for the plans proved prohibitive and were rejected by the UK government. The Ascension Island Council was dissolved and business suspended for twelve months, with interim power reverting to the governor.
2008 The governor published a consultation document setting out a framework for the new Island Council and offering a period of consultation. Ross Denny became the new Administrator. An election for the Island Council was held.
2009 The FCO minister announced a new constitution for Ascension Island, which included a bill of rights and limits to the power of the governor. The Island council later voted in favour of the proposed changes.
2010 A formal meeting of the Island council discussed the eur15.5 million (US$22.6 million) from the European Development Fund (EDF) (to be shared out between St Helena, Ascension Island and Tristan da Cunha) to provide finance for the road network. In June, the UN dismissed the claim of sovereignty rights, by the UK government, over 200,000 square kilometres of seabed around Ascension Island; the UK was interested particularly in the oil and mineral rights.
2011 Administrator Ross Denny announced in June that Colin Wells will be his replacement as the new Administrator of Ascension Island from September. On 23 September, Governor Gurr's term in office ended and Attorney General Ken Baddon was sworn in as acting governor on 24 September, until Mark Andrew Capes takes up the post in 29 October.

Political structure

Constitution

The Ascension Island is a dependency of St Helena, which is a British Overseas Territory. The governor of St Helena appoints an administrator, who is responsible for the daily management of Ascension Island.

The executive
The Ascension Island government (AIG) is headed by the administrator, under the jurisdiction of the governor of St Helena who has overall control of defence, external affairs, internal security and the public service. Local services are managed by the AIG; the UK government has overall responsibility for good governance and island security.
National legislature
A directly elected seven-seat Island Council, plus two *ex-officio* appointees, (a director of financial services and attorney general) advise the administrator on matters of law and policy.
Last elections
14 October 2008 (Island Council)
Results: The seven elected Councillors are independent members.
Next elections
February 2011 (Island Council)

Population
880 (2010)*
Last census: March 1998: 712
Population density: 14 inhabitants per sq km.
Ethnic make-up
St Helenians, UK and US citizens.
Religions
Anglican and Roman Catholic

Main cities
There are no cities. Georgetown is the administrative capital and port (estimated population 560 in 2003). Two Boats village is a residential area; Traveller's Hill is the RAF garrison; Cat Hill is the US base.

Languages spoken
Official language/s
English

Media
Press
The only newspaper is *The Islander* (www.the-islander.org.ac), which is published weekly.
Broadcasting
The Ascension Island acts as a relay station for the BBC World Service (www.bbc.co.uk/worldservice) that broadcasts to Africa and provides radio programmes to the island along with the British Forces Broadcasting Service (BFBS) and the US military's Volcano Radio and TV services, which are also available to residents.

Economy
Ascension Island's main importance to the United Kingdom (UK) is as a military base and communications centre. The cost of government net of revenue is about £1.85 million (US$3.0 million). Public services, public works, healthcare facilities and the pier head are funded by the military and commercial organisations on the island. They each contribute an agreed sum annually.
Tax and customs duties were introduced in 2002.
A building project is under way to construct new homes to be owned by residents, with a view to increasing the population to 1,500 over the next few years. The pier head facility was improved for both public and commercial use.
Cable and Wireless plc operates an international satellite telecommunications service and the Ariane Earth Station on behalf of the European Space Agency (ESA). The BBC operates its Atlantic relay station broadcasting to Africa and South America.
The prospect of oil and natural gas around the Ascension Island prompted the UK government to claim up to 200,000 square kilometres of the Atlantic Ocean for its mineral rights. But in June 2010, the United Nations Commission on the Limits of the Continental Shelf (CLCS) concluded that the volcanic shaft that is crowned by the Ascension Island was too slender to possess rights and the claim was dismissed. Under the UN convention of the sea, a state is allowed sovereignty across the ocean bed for up to 321km, if it can be demonstrated that there is continuity of the continental shelf.

Agriculture
Fishing
There is a species of marteralia or flying squid that inhabit the waters around Ascension.

Tourism
The prospects for the tourist industry are limited due to the isolated nature of the Ascension Island and the tourist infrastructure is minimal. However, for those that make the journey, diving is a popular pastime and the island is renowned for its wildlife. The only air access to the island is via Royal Air Force flights from the UK. By sea there are commercial ships; one is chartered to deliver supplies twice a year from Portland (UK) and another sails monthly from Cape Town (South Africa) and Walvis Bay (Namibia), via two other British South Atlantic territories (St Helena and Ascension Island). This ship is operated under contract by Passenger Services Department, Andrew Weir Shipping Ltd (see travel information addresses).

Environment
In 2002, the British government gave £500,000 to the Royal Society for the Protection of Birds (RSPB) to clear the Island of rats and feral cats that were destroying the seabird population. Ascension Island is also an important breeding colony for the green turtle.

Hydrocarbons
Ascension Island relies entirely on imports of hydrocarbons. It imports around 200 barrels per day of oil.

Energy
Energy is produced by a number of means, including diesel and six wind turbines providing a generating capacity of over 270MW.

Banking and insurance
International banking facilities are available through the Bank of St Helena, including exchanging travellers' cheques and credit card facilities; foreign currency exchange is not offered.

Time
GMT

Geography
Ascension Island lies in the South Atlantic, north-west of St Helena. It is a rocky peak of volcanic origin with 44 craters. The last eruption took place about 600 years ago. The highest point is Green Mountain.
Hemisphere
Southern

Climate
The climate is sub-tropical. Showers occur throughout the year with slightly heavier rain in January–April.

Entry requirements
There is an £11 entry permit fee.
Visa
All visitors must have the Administrator's written permission to land, before beginning their visit. An Ascension Island Entry Permit form can be downloaded from www.ascension-island.gov.ac/visitors.htm and faxed for submission on (+247) 6152. Entry is only granted with evidence a full medical insurance policy, including medical evacuation.
Customs
Customs duties exist on alcohol, tobacco and petrol/diesel. Small amounts of personal goods are duty-free (see website above).

Hotels
A new consortium operates all public accommodation, including the Georgetown Obsidian Hotel (www.obsidian.co.ac, tel/fax: 6246, e-mail: accommodation@atlantis.co.ac).

Working hours
Banking
Mon–Fri: 0830–1500, except Thur: 0830–1230
Government
Mon–Fri: 0830–1230, 1330–1630.

Telecommunications
Telephone/fax
Direct satellite telephones

Getting there

Air

There is a twice-weekly RAF Tristar flight (Mondays and Thursdays) that departs from RAF Brize Norton, Oxfordshire. Bookings can be made through Passenger Services Department, Andrew Weir Shipping Ltd (see travel information addresses).

Surface

Water: The RMS *St Helena* operates twice a year from the UK (Portland) and monthly from Cape Town to Walvis Bay (Namibia), St Helena and Ascension Island. The ship is operated under contract by Passenger Services Department, Andrew Weir Shipping Ltd (see travel information addresses).

Main port/s: Georgetown

Getting about

Car hire

Cars can be hired for £20 per day.

BUSINESS DIRECTORY

The addresses listed below are a selection only. While World of Information makes every endeavour to check these addresses, we cannot guarantee that changes have not been made, especially to telephone numbers and area codes. We would welcome any corrections.

Telephone area codes

The international dialling code (IDD) for Ascension Island is +247 followed by subscriber's number.

Travel information

Passenger Services Department, Andrew Weir Shipping Ltd, Dexter House, 2 Royal Mint Court, London EC N4XX, UK (tel: +44 (0)207-575-6480; fax: +44 (0)207-575-6200; internet: www.aws.co.uk; e-mail: reservations@aws.co.uk).

St Helena Line, Andrew Weir Shipping (SA) Pty Ltd, 3rd Floor, BP Centre, Thibault Square, Cape Town, South Africa (tel: +27-21-425-1165; fax: +27-21-421-7485; e-mail: sthelenaline@mweb.co.za).

Miss Kerry Yon, Solomon and Co Plc (agents for St Helena Line), Jamestown, St Helena, South Atlantic (tel: +290-2523; fax: +290-2423; e-mail: solco.shipping@helanta.sh).

Ministries

The AIG telephone number is 7000, which will take the caller to a pre-recorded menu, from which the caller can identify and dial the extension of the contact required.

Administrator's Office, Islander Building, Georgetown (tel: 6311; fax: 6152; e-mail: andrew.kettlewell@ascension.gov.ac; internet site: www.ascension-island.gov.ac).

Chief Executive Officer, Ascension Island Works and Services Agency (AIWSA), Jamestown, St Helena (tel: 6346; fax: 6139; e-mail: chiefexecutive.aiwsa@atlantis.co.ac).

Other useful addresses

St Helena Government Representative, Suite 5, 30b Wimpole St, London W1G 8YB, UK (tel: +44 (0)207-224-5025; fax: +44 (0)207-224-5035).

St Helena Desk Officer, Foreign and Commonwealth Office, Room, King Charles Street, London SW1A 2AH, UK (tel: +44 (0)207-270-2695).

Miles Apart (books, maps, videos on South Atlantic Islands), 5 Harraton House, Exning, Newmarket, Suffolk CB8 7HF, UK (tel: +44 (0)1638-577-627: fax: +44 (0)1638-577-874); 5929 Avon Drive, Bethesda, Maryland 20814, USA (tel/fax: +1301-571-8942; e-mail: familycarter@msn.com).

The Islander, Fort Hayes, Georgetown (tel/fax: 6327; e-mail: the-islander@org.ac; internet site: www.the-islander.org.ac).

Internet sites

Andrew Weir Shipping:
http://www.aws.co.uk

Ascension Island government:
http://www.ascension-island.gov.ac

St Helena Bank:
http://www.sainthelenabank.com/index.htm

St Helena web portal:
http://www.sthelenaonline.com

Australia

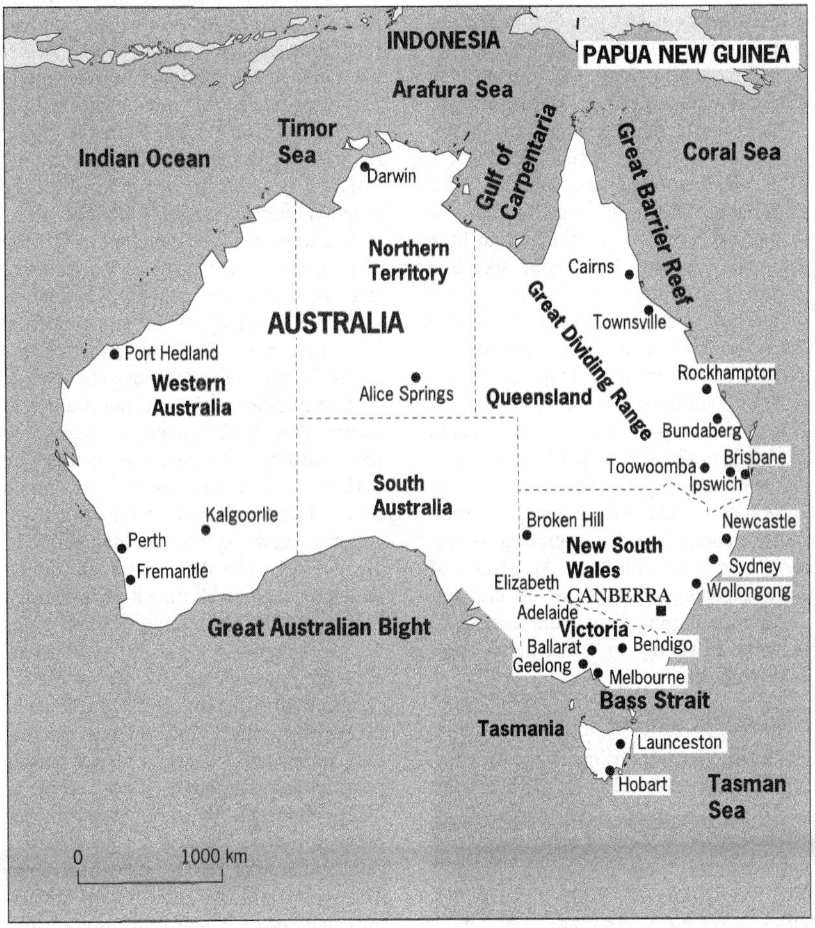

Australians are known for their direct, no-nonsense attitude to most things. The exception, it seemed in August 2010 was politics. After one of the most closely fought contests, neither the incumbent Prime Minister Julia Gillard nor her challenger, Tony Abbott, were able to claim a victory. Instead, each had to begin to seek coalition partners, something Australians had not seen for a long time – Australia had not experienced a hung parliament for years, and had not seen a coalition government since the end of the World War II in 1945.

The 5 per cent swing away from Julia Gillard, who had herself edged into the prime minister's office only two months earlier following a palace coup which saw her predecessor, Kevin Rudd accept the inevitability of an impending Labor Party ballot and step down from office. Mr Rudd had been in office for three years, elected in December 2007 with a seven per cent lead over the opposition Liberal Party. In 2010 the swing away from the Labor Party mirrored the swing in the opposite direction in 2007.

Bubbling down under

Unlike most of the economies in the Northern hemisphere, Australia went into the recessionary climate of 2008 in good shape. Demand for its natural resources, lead by China, risked outstripping production. Such were the inflationary pressures threatening the economy that in early 2008 the Reserve Bank had increased interest rates to their highest in 12 years, to

KEY FACTS

Official name: Commonwealth of Australia

Head of State: Queen Elizabeth II (since 1952), represented by Governor General Quentin Alice L Bryce (from 5 Sep 2008)

Head of government: Prime Minister Julia Gillard (ALP) (from 24 Jun 2010; elected 7 Sep 2010)

Ruling party: Australian Labor Party (ALP) (from 2007; re-elected 7 Sep 2010)

Area: 7,682,300 square km

Population: 22.27 million (2010)*

Capital: Canberra

Official language: English

Currency: Australian dollar (A$) = 100 cents

Exchange rate: A$1.03 per US$ (Oct 2011)

GDP per capita: US$55,160 (2010)

GDP real growth: 2.50% (2010)

GDP: US$1,236.00 billion (2010)

Labour force: 11.87 million (2010)

Unemployment: 5.23% (2010)

Inflation: 2.70% (2010)

Oil production: 562,000 bpd (2010)

Balance of trade: US$18.18 billion (2010)

* estimated figure

seven per cent. Although Chinese demand was in many respects reassuring, the economy's over-dependence on the world's largest manufacturer gave cause for concern. Australia's largest trading partner it may be, but the relationship does not seem to go much beyond that. Melbourne and Sydney's Chinatown districts do not add up to shared cultural or political values. One US journalist ascribed the relationship between the two countries to a shared passion for gambling.

None the less, Australia in 2011 found itself in the unnerving position of being a barometer for the Chinese economy. As international markets began to register concerns over the long term prospects of the Chinese economy, so Australia's 'lucky' run of 20 year's virtually uninterrupted economic expansion began to look a little risky. Australian government bond yields have long tended to track those of China. Around three-quarters of Australian government bonds are held overseas, giving them the role of instant economic indicators, to be sold or purchased according to market perceptions. According to Reuters, Australia's bond market is minuscule – corresponding to 5.5 per cent of GDP (compared to over 60 per cent in the US). So a little speculative selling can have an immediate, disproportionately large, effect.

Recovery

Australia's recovery is being driven by the mining boom, which has created a dilemma for the Reserve Bank of Australia, since, while unemployment is low, inflation has been on the high side. Mining companies may be booming, but the same is not the case for the retail and manufacturing sectors. Were the mining boom to falter, Australia risks finding itself dependent on a very weak traditional economy. Terms of trade are at historic highs, reflecting strong demand for commodities from China (Australia accounts for just over 70 per cent of China's iron ore imports) and other Asian economies. As a result, investment and job creation in mining and related sectors are also strong.

The real effective exchange rate has appreciated by 13.5 per cent since 2010, which has helped contain inflation pressures but presents a challenge for tradeable sectors that are not benefiting from high commodity prices. Household spending growth has slowed but higher saving should help strengthen household balance sheets. Australia's strong commodity demand is expected to be long lasting because of favourable prospects for sustained growth in emerging Asia, but there could be bumps along the road. Australia's macro-economic policy should continue to make room for the strengthening economy and not compound the emergence of capacity and price pressures. An additional policy challenge will be that the growing importance of mining raises the economy's exposure to swings in international commodity prices.

Favourable outlook

None the less, according to the International Monetary Fund (IMF), the economic outlook remains favourable. After a temporary setback in the first quarter of 2011 due to the extensive natural disasters, economic activity was expected to bounce back in the second quarter. The IMF projected GDP growth of 2 per cent for the calendar year 2011 and 3.5 per cent in 2012 on the back of strong demand for commodities and private investment in mining and liquefied natural gas. Employment was expected to grow at a slower pace than in recent years but the unemployment rate should remain below 5 per cent in 2011 and 2012. With the labour market approaching capacity, underlying inflation is likely to rise gradually. The external current account deficit is expected to narrow to 1 per cent of GDP in 2011 – due to the jump in the terms of trade – before progressively widening to about 6.5 per cent of GDP in the medium term, assuming the real effective exchange rate remains at its current level.

Most middle-aged Australians are well aware that their country's seemingly lucky history is distinguished as much by periods of recession as it is by boom times. The dominance of the natural resources sector has lead to a long period of appreciation for the Australian dollar, which reached an all time high in the first half of 2011. The mining sector shares with the energy sector an ability to generate large revenues for Australia while accounting for a disproportionate amount of investment capital and without creating very many jobs. There is also a serious geographic disparity: states such as Queensland and Western Australia may prosper, but the same is not the case for, say, Victoria or the Northern Territory. The sector is dominated by two companies, neither of which is wholly Australian. BHP-Billiton is an Anglo-Australian company whose 2011 half-yearly profits increased by 72 per cent on the previous year. The other major player is Rio Tinto, also Anglo-Australian, whose annual profits in 2010 increased by 162 per cent. Mining taxation has been something of a political hot potato in Australia. The former finance minister (head of the treasury) Ken Henry had come up with a proposal for a 'super profits tax' linked to a lower corporate tax rate, the idea being to spread the benefits through the business sector. However, when Labor prime minister Kevin Rudd adopted an amended version of the tax, he ran headlong into ferocious opposition from the mining companies. His successor Julia Gillard ditched the tax and negotiated a new arrangement with the mining companies; this was a less

KEY INDICATORS — Australia

	Unit	2006	2007	2008	2009	2010
Population	m	20.06	20.98	21.64	21.88	*22.34
Gross domestic product (GDP)	US$bn	755.95	908.83	1,010.50	982.10	1,236.00
GDP per capita	US$	36,442	43,312	46,907	44,895	55,160
GDP real growth	%	3.3	4.9	2.2	1.4	2.5
Inflation	%	3.5	2.3	3.7	2.1	2.7
Unemployment	%	4.8	4.3	4.2	5.6	5.2
Oil output	'000 bpd	544.0	561.0	556.0	559.0	562.0
Natural gas output	bn cum	38.9	40.0	38.3	42.3	50.4
Coal output	mtoe	203.1	53.1	219.9	228.0	235.4
Exports (fob) (goods)	US$m	124,913.0	142,133.0	189,919.0	154,788.0	212,850.0
Imports (fob) (goods)	US$m	134,509.0	160,047.0	194,205.0	159,003.0	194,670.0
Balance of trade	US$m	9,596.0	17,914.0	-4,286.0	-4,215.0	18,180.0
Current account	US$m	-41,690.0	-56,196.0	-42,940.0	-43,891.0	-31,990.0
Total reserves minus gold	US$m	53,448.0	24,768.0	30,691.0	38,950.0	38,659.0
Foreign exchange	US$m	52,821.0	24,237.0	29,867.0	33,002.0	32,793.0
Exchange rate	per US$	1.27	1.16	1.05	1.12	1.09

onerous 'resource tax' on iron ore and coal.

The overall state of Australia's finances in 2011 was more than satisfactory. The Gillard government's main priority was to get the budget back in the black by financial year 2012–13. The official forecast figure for 2010–11 was a deficit of 3.6 per cent of GDP. Australia's public finances are beefed up by its Future Fund which holds assets of over US$70 billion. In addition, Australia's superannuation funds add up to a reserve fund of US$1.3 trillion. Sadly, other surplus funds generated by the mining boon of 2006–07 were unwisely invested, with little to show for them, by the Howard administration.

Having peaked in 1999, productivity growth in Australia has since slowed, and the high level of the real exchange rate has generated pressure for efficiency improvements in the non-mining tradeable sector. Overall productivity growth ground to a halt at the turn of the century and began to actually move into negative figures in 2005. The severe drought played a part in this, but does not account for the total fall. During the financial crisis many companies put their staff on shortened hours rather than laying them off, which also lowered productivity. A May 2011 survey of Australia in the London *Economist* suggested that a major part of the problem was that Australia is still too highly, and often inefficiently, regulated. The same article suggested that Australians are more tolerant than most of regulation. This may also explain why Australia's banks were so surprisingly resilient to the global financial crisis, having already learned to live with sound regulation and supervision. Australia's rules, often tighter than the minimum international standards, such as higher loss-given-default assumptions, together with a pro-active approach to supervision, have helped maintain a relatively healthy and stable financial sector. Australia's level of household debt remains high, at around 150 per cent of disposable income and a rise in mortgage rates could lead to an increase in bad loans, although current arrears are modest. In addition, concentration in the banking sector has increased in the wake of the crisis with the assets of the four large banks now comprising about 75 per cent of total bank assets, although competition in lending has shown recent signs of recovery.

The view from Washington

The IMF considers the Australian dollar to be overvalued by some 10–20 per cent. Part of the overvaluation reflects higher interest rates in Australia than elsewhere and may dissipate over time with an eventual tightening by major central banks. The appreciation of the exchange rate has helped contain inflation pressures and has contributed to a structural shift of resources toward industries where Australia has a long-term comparative advantage.

Acccording to a study prepared for the IMF on the first ten years of the twenty-first century, GDP growth in emerging Asia was roughly twice as fast as average world growth. The study looked at the impact that this growth differential has had on Australia. The analysis suggested that roughly 25 per cent of Australia's growth over the last decade has been from emerging Asia's growth differential over that period. Looking ahead, the analysis suggests that should emerging Asia continue to grow in a similar fashion, Australia's growth dividend could almost double. On the other hand, if growth in emerging Asia remained strong, but became more balanced across the tradeable and non-tradeable goods sectors, then Australia's growth dividend would be slightly lower than the estimate for the last decade.

The likelihood of Australia's economic fortunes becoming increasingly tied to emerging Asia has several important policy implications. First, adjustment within Australia to the impact of emerging Asia implies significant resource reallocation. Second, Australia's longer-term growth potential will have a large externally determined component, the magnitude of which will likely be highly uncertain. Policies focused on long-term objectives will need to factor in this uncertainty. Finally, although the analysis assumes that emerging Asian growth occurs smoothly, in reality it is likely to be more variable. Australia will need to be well positioned to respond to the resulting volatility. For fiscal policy, this could imply allowing larger swings in the fiscal balance than would occur in economies less exposed to large exogenous shocks. Also financial sector regulation and supervision that erred on the safe side would also be prudent.

Energy

In addition to its reserves of iron ore, Australia has significant petroleum, natural gas and coal reserves and, according to the US-based Energy Information Administration (EIA) is one of the few countries belonging to the Organisation for Economic Co-operation and Development (OECD) that is a significant net hydrocarbon exporter, exporting about two-thirds of its total energy production. Australia is also the world's largest coal exporter and was the fifth largest exporter of liquefied natural gas (LNG) in 2007, after Qatar, Malaysia, Indonesia and Algeria. Australia's prospects for expanding these energy exports in the future are promising as Asian demand for both coal and LNG is rising. While Australia also exports crude oil and refined petroleum products, it is a net importer of oil.

Coal is Australia's largest hydrocarbon export earner, followed by crude oil and LNG. According to the June 2011 issue of the BP Statistical Review of World Energy (BP11) Australia had 4.1 thousand million barrels of proven oil reserves at the end of 2010. The majority of these reserves are located off the coasts of Western Australia, the Northern Territory and Victoria. The Carnarvon Basin accounts for 62 per cent of Australia's production of crude oil, condensate and liquefied petroleum gas (LPG).

Oil production in Australia peaked in 2000 at 828,000 barrels per day (bpd) and has since been declining. In 2010, oil production totalled 568,000bpd. Australia's onshore remains relatively unexplored ad exploration activity has concentrated on the offshore areas. Australia's main frontier for exploration has moved in recent years to the deepwater area of the Timor Sea, although the nearby Carnarvon Basin off the coast of Western Australia is still the busiest area in terms of overall drilling activity. After a rise in drilling activity in the late 1990s, several major discoveries are now in the process of being put into commercial operation. However, the new production that has come on-stream has not been able to compensate for the natural decline of the mature fields.

According to the BP11, Australia had 2.9 trillion cubic metres (tcm) of proven natural gas reserves at the end of 2010. Around 69 per cent of those natural gas reserves are located off the western coast in the Carnarvon Basin. Other important fields are the Cooper/Eromanga Basin (8 per cent) in central Australia and the Bass/Gippsland Basin (20 per cent) offshore southern Australia. The remainder comes from scattered small fields off the southern coast and in the central regions.

Natural gas production in Australia continues to increase steadily, reaching 50.4 billion cubic metres (bcm) in 2010. Although consumption is increasing as well, reaching 30.4bcm in 2010, production is growing twice as fast, according to the

Australian Department of Resources, Energy and Tourism. Exploration expenditure has increased significantly since 2007 and recent natural gas exploration in Australia has resulted in several important discoveries. Western Australia is the source of the greatest production increases and the largest producing basin in the country.

Risk assessment

Economy	Good
Politics	Good
Regional stability	Good

COUNTRY PROFILE

Historical profile

1778 Captain James Cook reached Australia and sailed the entire length of the East Coast. He claimed the land for Britain.
1788 British Naval captain, Arthur Phillip, founded a penal colony at Sydney. He had arrived with a fleet of 11 vessels and nearly 800 convicts.
1829 The Colony of Western Australia was established at Perth by Captain James Stirling.
1837 South Australia was established with Adelaide as its capital city.
1851 The discovery of gold in New South Wales sparked a wave of migration to Australia, known as the 'gold rush'. Within 10 years of the gold find, the population was estimated to have grown from 500,000 to 1.5 million. The Aborigines were treated badly.
1856 Australia became the first country to introduce the secret ballot for elections (known as the 'Australian ballot').
1877 The first Test cricket match between Australia and England was played in Melbourne.
1901 The Commonwealth of Australia was created. The former British colonies became the six states of Australia: New South Wales, Victoria, Queensland, Western Australia, South Australia and Tasmania. There are two self-governing states – the Northern Territory and the Australian Capital Territory.
1911 Canberra was founded as the capital city.
1914–1918 Australia fought alongside Britain during the First World War. Australian troops bore the brunt of the fighting in some theatres of war and suffered heavy casualties during the ill-fated beach landing at Gallipoli in Turkey in 1915.
1929–31 Following the Wall Street Crash, the Great Depression badly affected the Australian economy. Recovery was slow and uneven. The Labor government was defeated in the elections.
1939–45 Australia fought alongside Britain and the US during the Second World War. In 1942, Japanese aircraft bombed Darwin (Northern Territory), the only direct foreign attack on Australia since its creation.
1948 Australia began to promote immigration from Europe and between the 1940–70s more than a million people arrived, a third of which came from Britain.
1950 Australia participated in the Korean War.
1951 Australia, New Zealand and the US signed the Anzus Pact, a security pact for the South Pacific.
1963 The 'White Australia' policy of immigration restrictions was ended.
1965 Australia fought alongside the US in Vietnam. At the height of Australia's involvement, the task force numbered 8,500 troops.
1967 A national referendum approved changes to the constitution: the section which excluded Aboriginal people from the official census was removed and another change enabled the federal government to pass laws on Aboriginal issues.
1975 Australia restricted the immigration of non-skilled workers. The governor general, Sir John Kerr, dismissed Gough Whitlam's government following its repeated failure to pass the budget in the upper house of parliament. A caretaker government under Malcolm Fraser was installed.
1985 The issue of Aboriginal land rights was first addressed.
1986 Australia's legislative links with the UK were severed by the Australia Act, which abolished the UK parliament's residual legislative, executive and judicial controls over Australian state law.
1990 Bob Hawke and his Australian Labor Party (ALP) government narrowly won the federal election – the first ALP administration to win three consecutive elections.
1991 Paul Keating (ALP) succeeded Bob Hawke as prime minister.
1992 The Citizenship Act was amended to remove the obligation to swear an allegiance to the British Crown.
1993 The ALP won the general election with an increased majority. The Native Title Act granted the Aborigines compensation for the loss of land rights.
1996 The Liberal Party (LP)-National Party (NP) (referred to jointly as the Coalition) won a landslide victory in elections and John Howard, leader of the LP, took over as prime minister.
1998 The LP-NP coalition was re-elected at the general elections, but with a reduced majority.
1999 A national referendum opposed Australia becoming a republic by 55 per cent. After East Timor voted for independence from Indonesia, Australia led an intervention force to counter pro-Indonesia militia violence.
2001 Howard won a third term in the federal elections after gaining support for his 'Pacific Solution' – the policy of refusing entry to asylum seekers and directing them to other countries in Asia-Pacific.
2002 There were riots in the Woomera desert detention camp for asylum seekers. Eighty-eight Australian citizens were killed in a night club bombing in Bali, Indonesia.
2003 Australia sent 2,000 troops to the Iraq War. The Senate passed a no-confidence motion in Prime Minister Howard over his handling of troops in Iraq. Australia headed a peacekeeping Regional Assistance Mission to Solomon Islands (Ramsi) force to the Solomon Islands.
2004 The first passenger train service (the Ghan) to cross Australia from Adelaide in the south to Darwin in the north began services. A parliamentary committee cleared the government of lying about the threat posed by weapons of mass destruction in Iraq. With an increased majority, John Howard won a fourth term as prime minister.
2006 Australia experienced its worst drought on record. Troops were sent to aid the Timor-Leste government against mutineering soldiers.
2007 Heavy rain began to fall in south-east Australia, breaking a six-year drought, however it did not rain in the Murray-Darling river system, the principal crop-growing region. In parliamentary elections the opposition ALP won 44.0 per cent of the vote (86 seats out of 150); Kevin Rudd became prime minister. One of his first acts was to sign the Kyoto Agreement on greenhouse gas emissions targets.
2008 The prime minister made a formal apology to indigenous Aboriginal peoples for former government policies which included the forcible removal of Aboriginal children – 'the stolen generation' – from their families, in a policy of assimilation. Quentin Bryce, the first woman to hold the post, was sworn in as governor general of Australia.
2009 The worst forest fires ever recorded killed 173 people, injured around 500 and destroyed over 1,000 homes, with more badly damaged. Over 5,000 people were left homeless. The fires devastated 3,000 square km, including some towns in the state of Victoria. Arson was suspected to have caused a number of the fires. The Senate passed legislation setting a target of 20 per cent renewable sources of energy by 2020.
2010 In June, Kevin Rudd was replaced as leader of the ALP, just months before a general election and deputy leader of the ALP, Julia Gillard, was elected leader and

automatically became prime minister. There had been growing concerns that Rudd's policies on climate change and asylum seekers would lose the party support. Prime Minister Gillard called a snap general election for 21 August. The result was a hung parliament, as the ALP won 72 seats, the Coalition 73 seats, Greens one and independents four. Both major parties began coalition talks with non-aligned members of parliament. On 7 September, three independent members of parliament agreed to support Julia Gillard and her minority ALP government. Australia recorded 6,535 irregular maritime arrivals (IMAs) (asylum seekers and unauthorised migrants) during the year.
2011 At the beginning of January, after heavy rains had fallen since November 2010, major flooding in the State of Queensland caused widespread damage and mass evacuations. It was the worst recorded flooding since 1961 and steel and coal production were badly affected. By 12 January, floodwaters, which had inundated over 60 per cent of the state, were the worst in recorded history. Over 20 people were killed with over 70 missing in flash-floods. The capital, Brisbane, suffered flooding to its outer suburbs. Estimates were that the total damage would run to around US$13 billion in reconstruction. A bilateral agreement was signed on 7 May between the governments of Australia and Malaysia for IMAs attempting to land in Australia to be held in camps in Malaysia until their applications for settlement are processed. Annually, around 900 IMAs are expected to be held in Malaysia. Talks were also underway with Papua New Guinea and Nauru to provide more IMA camps. On 31 August, the High Court rejected government plans for a Malaysian IMA centre. The court said that Australia had signed treaties not to send asylum-seekers to another country that could not adequately protect them.

Political structure

Constitution

The Commonwealth of Australia is a constitutional monarchy with a parliamentary democracy. It consists of a federation of six states (New South Wales, Victoria, Queensland, South Australia, Western Australia and Tasmania) and two territories (Australian Capital Territory (ACT), Northern Territory). Each state has its own constitution, government, administration and judiciary. There are some 900 local government bodies at city, town, municipal and shire levels.
The federal government is located in Canberra, ACT. Federal responsibilities tend to be those with an international and national focus while state governments deal with regional issues. However, the overlap of power is considerable and companies must be prepared to deal with both levels of government.
Any amendment to the constitution must be passed by an absolute majority in each House of Parliament and must be approved in a referendum by the majority of electors in a majority of states and territories. In the past, three states (Tasmania, Queensland and Western Australia) have consistently blocked any changes to the constitution.
There is compulsory universal adult suffrage for Australian citizens, with a voting age of 18. An automatic fine of A$50 (US$35) is issued by post to those who fail to cast a vote, although this is rarely imposed through legal proceedings.

Form of state

Federal commonwealth, with the British monarch as Head of State.

The executive

The governor general represents and is appointed by the British sovereign. The role of governor general is largely ceremonial, but he has the power to dissolve parliament or the government and call new elections. He is also the commander-in-chief of the armed forces. If the governor general is ill, dies, resigns or is out of the country, an administrator is appointed to undertake the governor general's duties.
Day-to-day executive responsibility is held by the national government, which is composed of a cabinet of senior ministers formed by the party with a majority in the House of Representatives.

National legislature

The Parliament of Australia or Commonwealth Parliament has two chambers. The House of Representatives (lower house) has 150 members, elected by instant runoff voting (or alternative voting), whereby a candidate with a majority of preferential votes wins the seat. The number of seats is dependent on electoral distribution and may change at any given election. The Senate (upper house) has 76 members, 12 from each state and two for each territory, elected by proportional representation.
Under the constitution both Houses have equal standing and legislation must be passed by both chambers. Only the lower house can introduce legislation to raise taxes, therefore only the party or coalition in the majority in the lower house holds power.
Universal suffrage begins at age 18 years and voting is mandatory.

Legal system

The legal system is based on the constitution of 1901. The governor general and state governors appoint judges on the advice of the cabinets of federal and state governments. Each state has state courts, federal courts, family courts and a supreme court. The High Court of Australia, which has seven judges, is the ultimate court of appeal. The High Court has jurisdiction to hear and determine appeals and judgments, decrees, orders and the sentences of most lower courts, but since 1984 cases have only been referred to it if there is a difference of opinion at lower levels. The High Court's main task is to interpret the Australian Constitution.

Last elections

21 August 2010 (House of Representatives); 25 November 2007 (Senate)
Results: Parliamentary: Australian Labor Party (ALP) won 44.0 per cent of the vote (86 seats out of 150), the Liberal-National (LN) coalition won 41.8 per cent (62).
Senate: LN coalition won 18 seats (total 37 seats), ALP won 18 seats (total 32), The Greens won three (total five).

Next elections

1 July 2011 (Senate); 2013 (House of Representatives)

Political parties

Ruling party

Australian Labor Party (ALP) (from 2007; re-elected 7 Sep 2010)

Main opposition party

Liberal-National (LN) coalition

Population

22.27 million (2010)*
Last census: 8 August 2006: 20,061,646
Population density: Two inhabitants per square km (2000)
Annual growth rate: 1.2 per cent 1994–2004 (WHO 2006)

Ethnic make-up

The population is comprised mainly of immigrants and their descendants from over 120 countries, with Aboriginals and Torres Straits Islanders accounting for only 1.5 per cent of the population. The single largest immigrant group is from the British Isles, followed by Asians, New Zealanders, Italians, Croats, Serbs, Slovenes, Bosnians, Macedonians, Greeks, Germans, Vietnamese, Dutch, Poles and Lebanese. Over 20 per cent of the total population were born outside the country. More than half the Aboriginal population lives in urban areas.

Religions

Predominantly Christian (Anglican and Roman Catholic), although many are non-practising. There are significant Eastern Orthodox, Jewish, Muslim, Hindu and Buddhist communities in many cities.

Education

In most states, children start primary school at the age of five when they enrol in a preparatory or kindergarten year, after which primary education continues for either six or seven years followed by secondary education, available for either five or six years and may be completed by tertiary education of a student's level and choice.

State and Territory governments and the Federal government provide major financial support for primary and secondary education, delivered in public and fee-paying schools run by governments and non-government providers.

Links between the education and training sectors have been strengthened, through the introduction of the Australian National Training Authority (ANTA) national system of vocational education and training in co-operation with all levels of governments and industry. Two national communications campaigns began in late 2000 based on extensive market research into the vocational education and training needs of Australian individuals and enterprises.

Compulsory years: 6 to 15; Tasmania: 6 to 16.

Pupils per teacher: 18 in primary schools.

Health

While health care funds direct assistance to hospitals and rebates individuals under the Medicare national health insurance system, consideration of private medical insurance is central to federal health budget funding.

Primary healthcare is provided by independent and privately owned medical practices, offering general and specialist treatment including minor surgary. Hospitals may be state, or privately run institutions.

HIV/Aids

HIV prevalence: 0.1 per cent aged 15–49 in 2003 (World Bank)

Life expectancy: 81 years, 2004 (WHO 2006)

Fertility rate/Maternal mortality rate: 1.7 births per woman, 2004 (WHO 2006)

Birth rate/Death rate: Seven deaths per 1,000 people (World Bank).

Child (under 5 years) mortality rate (per 1,000): 4.6 per 1,000 live births (World Bank).

Head of population per physician: 2.47 physicians per 1,000 people, 2001 (WHO 2006)

Welfare

Social security payments are intended as a 'safety net' to help low income groups and anti-fraud measures are increasingly tough. In recent years, payments have been the subject of intense scrutiny to ensure that they are only distributed to those in genuine need, this has resulted in cuts in some benefits while other categories, especially disability and service pensions, have increased. Other priority groups have been defined as low-income: families with children; the long-term unemployed; and single parents.

Pensions

Australia has a forced savings 'superannuation' scheme for employees, the total value of which is approaching A$1 trillion (US$620 billion). The scheme involves compulsory contributions by employees of 9 per cent of their income. The scheme does not cover the self-employed or low-income workers. It is estimated that 94 per cent of pension schemes operate through trusts. Employees often have no choice in becoming a member and are ill-informed as to who heads the trust.

Main cities

Canberra, (national capital, 329,200 in 2008); state capitals – Sydney (estimated population 3.7 million (m)); Melbourne (3.6m); Brisbane (1.9m); Perth (1.3m); Adelaide (1.0m); Hobart (126,841; Darwin (61,769).

Languages spoken

Aboriginal dialects are becoming scarce. Italian is spoken by 2.6 per cent of the population and Greek by 1.8 per cent. A wide variety of other languages are spoken, particularly from Asia, reflecting the diverse origins of Australia's population.

Official language/s

English

Media

Press

In 2007 the government relaxed the laws on media cross-ownership of press and broadcasting and allowing greater levels of foreign ownership. Around 80 per cent of all print media is owned by four newspaper publishers, News Limited, Fairfax Media Publications, APN News and Media and West Australian Newspapers Holdings. All newspapers have a home market based on the major city and state in which they are published and very few are sold elsewhere.

Dailies: The only national daily is *The Australian* (www.theaustralian.news.com.au). Major regional publications include, in NSW *The Sydney Morning Herald* (www.smh.com.au), *Sun Herald* (www.sunherald.com.au) and *The Daily Telegraph* (www.news.com.au/dailytelegraph); in VIC *The Age* (www.theage.com.au) and *Herald Sun* (www.news.com.au/heraldsun) a tabloid with the biggest circulation; in *The Canberra Times* (http://canberra.yourguide.com.au); in QLD *Courier Mail* (www.news.com.au/couriermail), *The Brisbane News* (www.brisbanenews.net); in SA *The Advertiser* (www.news.com.au/adelaidenow); in WA *The Western Australian* (www.thewest.com.au); in NT *Northern Territory News* (www.ntnews.com.au); in Tasmania *Mercury* (www.news.com.au/mercury).

Weeklies: All major dailies produce weekend editions. The are a comprehensive range of magazine catering for all interests personal and professional. APC (www.acp.com.au) publishes many of the leading magazine titles including *The Australian Womens Weekly*, *TV Week* and *Cleo* (http://aww.ninemsn.com.au). *Beat Magazine* (www.beat.com.au) is an arts and entertainment magazine. *The Chaser* (www.chaser.com.au) and *Brainsnap* (http://brainsnap.com) are satirical publications.

Business: The only national daily is the *Australian Financial Review* (www.afr.com). All daily broadsheets have business sections. Weekly publications include *Western Australian Business News* (www.wabusinessnews.com.au), which has the largest circulation, *Business Review Weekly* (www.brw.com.au), with comprehensive articles on national matters, *Lloyds List DCN (Daily Commercial News)* (www.lloydslistdcn.com.au) dealing with transport matters and *Stock & Land* (http://sl.farmonline.com.au), reporting on agriculture. Monthly publications include *Sydney Business Review*,

There are numerous commercial and trade journals, including reports from the Australian Bureau of Agricultural and Resources Economics (Abare) (www.abareconomics.com).

Periodicals: For politics and culture *Monthly* (www.themonthly.com.au) and *Quarterly Essay* (www.quarterlyessay.com).

Broadcasting

The principal public broadcaster is the Australian Broadcasting Corporation (ABC), providing national, local and Pacific regional radio, TV and Internet services.

Radio: There are hundreds of commercial radio stations which in a combined number represent the largest audiences. They broadcast local interest shows and are affiliated to major, usually city stations, with personality presenters who command significant listenership numbers.

National radio services are provided by the public services ABC (www.abc.net.au) and SBS (www20.sbs.com.au) (with programmes broadcasts in many of the immigrant community languages), and commercial radio by Austereo (www.austereo.com.au), DMG Radio (www.dmgradio.com.au) and Southern Cross Broadcasting (www.southerncrossbroadcasting.com.au).

Radio Australia (www.abc.net.au/ra) is the ABC's external service.
Television: National, public TV is provided by the ABC (www.abc.net.au) and the Special Broadcasting Service (SBS), which provides multicultural programmes in over 50 languages. Both broadcast additional digital channels aimed children and world news programmes respectively. There are three, free-to-air, commercial channels, Seven (http://au.tv.yahoo.com), Nine (http://channelnine.ninemsn.com.au) and Ten (http://ten.com.au). Channels Seven and Nine regularly vie for top ratings, with domestically produced programmes and popular imports.
The conversion to digital services is expected to be completed by 2010. There are more than 250 privately owned regional TV stations that are affiliates to the metropolitan stations, the largest of which is WINTV (www.wintv.com.au).
Pay-to-view services have grown substantially since the 1990s, using terrestrial, cable and satellite platforms, including Foxtel (www.foxtel.com.au) and Optus (www.optus.com.au).

Advertising

Advertising is subject to the provisions of the Trade Practices Act, administered by the Australian Competition and Consumer Commission. Tobacco advertising is banned and alcohol has regulations for control. There is a voluntary code of conduct for advertising to children. The Advertising Standards Council interprets and applies all requirements and rules with punitive powers as necessary.
All forms of advertising are available, subject to privacy and consumer laws, including commercial press radio and TV, traditional outdoor advertising is available in many forms, along with direct mail facilities and house-to-house distribution of samples and literature. Modern advertising through personalised text-messaging and email adverts are all well established.

News agencies

AAP (Australian Associated Press): http://aap.com.au
ABC News: www.abc.net.au/news

Economy

Continent-sized Australia, with a modest sized population, has a range of productive industries, which not only provides for its own citizens but also allows for exports. By far the most profitable sector is mining, which is a world leader (in quantity) in brown coal, lead, uranium and zinc. Australia is ranked second for gold, copper, bauxite, silver and industrial grade diamonds; it is third ranked in producing manganese and fourth (by weight) in producing gem quality diamonds. Total exports of minerals in 2010-11 was around A$58.4 billion (US$59.58 billion), excluding oil and natural gas. At the end of 2010, petroleum production was 562,000 barrels per day; natural gas production was 50.4 billion cubic metres (an increase of 5.1 per cent on the 2009 figure) and coal production was 235.4 million tonnes of oil equivalent.
Australian agriculture, when not blighted by drought, exports grain and live animals, it has also become a world renowned wine producer with export sales reaching a record A$3 billion (US$3.9 billion) in 2006/07. However due to the global economic crisis exports in 2009 were only valued at A$2.27 billion (US$2.88 billion), despite an increase in volume sales.
GDP growth in 2008 was 2.2 per cent (down from 4.9 per cent in 2007) as both net exports and imports fell; the Reserve Bank of Australia (RBA) reduced its policy rate by 425 basis points to 3 per cent. In 2009 GDP growth fell further to 1.4 per cent and remained at the lowest level since the beginning of the economic crisis, as house prices fell leaving some with negative equity, and leading to a contraction in domestic demand and a decline in manufacturing output. Commodity exports, particularly to China, began to pick up in 2009-10. The Australian banking sector coped well and remained profitable while other countries were forced into recession. The RBA introduced wholesale funding and retail deposit guarantees to provide sufficient liquidity and helped maintain stability in the financial sector in 2009, staving off potential risk from sizable short-term wholesale funding. In 2010, as world trade picked up GDP growth was 2.5 per cent.
Australia was the first OECD and G20 country to lift its interest rates, with cash rates rising by 25 basis points to 3.25 per cent on 6 October 2009, as the Australian dollar reached a 14-month high of A$0.89 per US dollar. The rebound in the economy was the result first of China's continued purchases of Australian raw materials and secondly the strength of the banking sector which was less exposed to toxic debts than those in the US and Europe. Exports account for around 20 per cent of GDP; iron ore and coal are the highest exports by value. GDP growth had grown for five consecutive quarters by July 2010, although at a slower rate in the first three months (0.5 per cent) than in the same period in 2009 (1.1 per cent). Growth was due to exports to China and a stimulus package of increased public investment.

External trade

Australia is a member of the South Pacific Regional Trade and Economic Co-operation Agreement (Sparteca) along with 13 regional nations, which allows products duty free access by Pacific Island Forum members to Australian and New Zealand markets (subject to the country of origin restrictions).
Export marketing organisations established under government statutes supervise and promote the export of primary income-earning commodities, and the Export Market Development Grants scheme provides taxable cash grants for developing overseas markets. Australia has an industrial base that includes vehicle assembly, steel, aluminium and nickel smelting, textile and paper manufacturing and telecommunications and IT suppliers. There is a huge international trade in raw materials, minerals and agricultural produce supplying the Asia and Pacific region.
Australia has a free trade agreement (FTA) with the US (AUSFTA) and signed its biggest FTA with the Association of Southeast Asian Nations (Asean) and New Zealand in February 2009, under which tariffs will be reduced and trade in beef, dairy products and pharmaceuticals, as well as automotives and electrical machinery, are all expected to benefit.

Imports

Principal imports are finished products such as vehicles and parts, industrial machinery, computers and office equipment, electrical goods, textiles and crude oil and petroleum products.
Main sources: China (typically 18 per cent), US (11 per cent total, 2005), Japan (8 per cent).

Exports

Principal exports are minerals: coal, gold, diamonds, alumina, iron ore, uranium; agricultural products: wheat, meat, wool and live animals; manufactures include vehicles, processed food, computers and telecommunications equipment.
Main destinations: China (typically 22 per cent total), Japan (20 per cent), South Korea (8 per cent).

Agriculture

Farming

Agricultural output has doubled since the early 1960s, but the sector now only contributes 4 per cent of GDP, a reduction from 14 per cent, although agricultural production still accounts for 22 per cent of exports.
Larger, technologically-enhanced farms employing fewer workers are replacing many smaller operations; the number of farms has fallen by 25 per cent since the 1980s.
The long-running drought, which was only given a short-lived respite with rains in 2007, returned with greater force in 2008 with the driest June on record. Australia's principal food growing region, the

Murray-Darling basin, which produces 40 per cent of the country's fruit, vegetables and grain, was particularly hard hit. Nationwide wheat production in 2006–07 was down by 59 per cent and was at its lowest since 1982–83. Severe cuts in water allocations also cut rice and cotton production by 90 per cent and 42 per cent respectively, with some farmers abandoning parts of their crops in the field and using the reduced water to irrigate smaller areas and maximise their returns. In 2008, the government and land users agreed to water conservation plans with the commitment of A$3.7 billion (US$3.6 billion) in investment immediately and a further A$9.2 billion (US$9.5 billion) to restore the river system. It has been estimated that 10,000 farming families have been forced off the land since 2002 when the drought took hold, while those farmers that remain are adopting water efficient cropping methods.

Government involvement tends to be focussed on improving infrastructure as a means of facilitating investment.

Australia is the world's fourth-largest wheat producer, after the EU, the US and Canada. Since the 1980s, Australia has successfully diversified its wheat production, increasing the number of varieties grown and improving marketing. China's membership of the WTO has benefited Australian wheat growers, who have seen a rise in exports to Asia. As living standards improve in Asia, consumption of higher value commodities such as rice and noodles will increase.

A new variety of pineapple was launched in Queensland in September 2010, following 15 years of plant breeding. The Australian Jubilee has twice as much vitamin C of a typical pineapple. The pineapple industry is worth A$70 million (US$75 million) annually.

Fishing

Australia typically produces 220,000 tonnes of seafood and 13,000 tonnes of freshwater fish per annum. Around 80 per cent of annual fishing production is exported. Rock lobsters from Western Australia account for 30 per cent of exports by value. Other species include prawns, molluscs, carp and eels. The main destinations for fish exports are Japan, Hong Kong and Taiwan, while exports to the US and Europe have benefited from the weakness of the Australian dollar.

Following the annual meeting of the Commission for the Conservation of Southern Bluefin Tuna (CCSBT), held on Cheju Island, South Korea, all members agreed to a 20 per cut in the roughly 17,000 tonnes in 2009 bluefin tuna catches from 2010. Scientists had warned that without a cut fish stocks could crash as numbers had become dangerously low. For Australia, which had a larger proportion of the quota for the bluefin tuna catch, the overall cut was 30 per cent.

South Australia had the world's first tuna fish farm industry. However the last tuna cannery in operation, Port Lincoln Tuna Processors in South Australia, announced in February 2010 that it would close in May 2010 due to the lack of fish caused by the 2009 tuna quota cutbacks.

Forestry

There is a substantial forestry industry in tropical Queensland, producing approximately 22 million cubic metres (cum) of timber annually, worth over A$1 billion (US$694 million). Japan has traditionally been the sector's biggest customer, with New Zealand the second largest export market. The sector employs around 75,000 people. There are projects for new plantations to increase production by 300 per cent.

Industry and manufacturing

Australia embarked on a basic reorientation of its economy in the 1980s, and has transformed itself from an inward-looking, import-substitution economy to an internationally competitive, export-oriented economy. In the early 1990s, the sector suffered from poor investment, despite boosts to exports provided by the low exchange rate. However, having shed labour, gained more effective investment and a sharper export focus, Australian industry has become more competitive internationally with manufacturers of wood and paper products, food, beverages and tobacco becoming dominant.

The Liberal Party (LP)-National Party (NP) coalition government, first elected in 1995, quickly made clear its aim of transforming a traditional commodity-based economy by value-added processing of domestic raw materials into high-value consumer products for the global market. At the heart of industrial policy is a package to support innovation and improve access to venture capital for the commercial application of research and development. The government has also pledged to commit Australia to a free trade approach to the electronic market place – goods ordered and delivered electronically will remain duty free.

Tourism

Australia is a continental sized country with many of its major attractions thousands of mile apart. The tourist industry markets itself as three-centres, typically including the Great Barrier Reef (off the Queensland state coast), Uluru (Ayers Rock) in the centre of Australia and any one of its major cities. Likewise the distance Australia is from its potential markets shapes the way visitors view Australia as a place for an extended (and thus more expensive) visit. New Zealanders outnumbered all other visiting groups with 1.32 million visitors in 2009, followed by the UK (819,000), China (761,000) and the US (628,000).

The sector is managed with government backing, strong private investment and sophisticated sales and marketing, and has a network of tourist offices at federal, state and local levels to co-ordinate and target many niche markets.

The tourist industry suffered from a drop in the number of visitors during the global economic crisis of the late 2000s and suffered a resultant fall in revenue. International tourist expenditure fell by 2.9 per cent in 2009 over 2008 and overnight accommodation fell by 1.4 per cent; domestic tourist expenditure fell by 2.6 per cent and overnight accommodation fell by 3.6 per cent. Tourist revenue in 2011 was forecast to be A$41.8 billion (US$42.3 billion).

The forecast direct contribution of tourism to total GDP in 2011 was 3.3 per cent, A$47.6 billion (US$48.2 billion); the indirect contribution of travel and tourism to GDP was forecast to be A$187.1 billion (US$189.4 billion). Direct employment in the sector was expected to be 648,000 jobs (5.7 per cent of total employment) with 1.856 million indirect jobs related to travel and tourism. Investment in the industry was forecast to be A$21.7 billion (US$22 billion) in 2011, constituting 5.5 per cent of total investment in the economy.

The rising value of the Australian dollar in 2011 was identified as the sector's greatest threat to growth, while tourist promotions continue to highlight Australia's value for money.

Environment

Under the government's Eastern Australia Marine Bioregional profile, a new Coral Sea Conservation Zone, bounded by the Great Barrier Reef Marine Park, Solomon Islands, Papua New Guinea and Vanuatu was established in May 2009, offering environmental protection for one million square kilometres of ocean off Australia's north eastern coast. Existing users such as fishermen, scientific research and cruise ships will be allowed to continue work at current levels; expasion will be limited.

Australia, Philippines, Indonesia, Papua New Guinea and Solomon Islands are the countries with the most coral reef fish species.

In 2009 the Bureau of Meteorology in Melbourne announced that the gigantic hole in the ozone layer over Antarctica and Australasia had begun to shrink. News of an ozone hole in the 1980s and its significance to the welfare of the planet became the spark for awareness of the state of the planet and prompted the first worldwide action on the use of CFCs gases that were known to breakdown the ozone layer.

Mining

Mining contributed around 8.5 per cent of GDP in 2004 and employs 4 per cent of the workforce. Australia has major deposits of a variety of minerals, possessing the world's biggest economic reserves of lead, uranium, silver, zinc, tantalum, mineral sands and low-cost uranium. Australia is a significant producer of gold, iron ore, bauxite, nickel, diamonds, alumina, ilmenute, zircon and rutile. Australia is the largest exporter of gold and iron ore in the world.

In 2009 China won a bid to buy up to 17.5 per cent of the Australian mining company Fortescue Metals Group; the first in a series of bids. While cash-strapped Australian companies were looking for investment during a time of global economic downturn, China began hunting for all the vital raw materials it could secure.

Hydrocarbons

Australia is rich in natural resources and has considerable deposits of hydrocarbons. Proven oil reserves at the end of 2010 totalled 4.1 billion barrels, with production at 562,000 barrels per day (bpd), which was a 8.9 per cent increase on the 2009 production figure. The rate of production has been in decline since 2000, partly due to depleting reserves and the growing consumption of natural gas, nevertheless, oil consumption at 941,000bpd in 2010 means that imports are required to make up for its shortfall. Australia's main oil-fields are situated offshore in the Bass Strait and Carnarvon Basin; there are a number of smaller and younger fields becoming operational. There are also shale oil reserves in Queensland, estimated at around 30 billion barrels, but exploitation has been hampered by the cost of the technology necessary to utilise it, and environmental considerations.

There is a well-developed network of oil and gas pipelines that allow transport to domestic and export outlets. Refinery capacity was 740,000bpd in 2010, primarily producing petrol (gasoline) and diesel fuel. Refining production has fallen since 2002 due to overcapacity in refining in other Asian countries and the costs of shipping crude oil to Australia which made the end product uneconomic.

An oil rig in the Timor Sea, off the north-west coast of Australia, erupted in August 2009 spewing out around 400 barrels per day of oil and gas, making it Australia's worst drilling accident and causing serious environmental damage. An attempt to plug the leak on 14 October failed, and the oil platform was engulfed by fire. The leak was finally plugged on 3 November and the fire extinguished. Although the natural gas industry is wholly privately owned the government set up the Ministerial Council of Energy (MCE) in 2001, to provide a national oversight and co-ordination in the energy sector and provide national leadership in convergence issues across state and territories lines. On 25 May 2011, the Federal Government announced that a new national petroleum regulatory body for the offshore energy industry will be established to ensure best operating standards were applied. The new body is in response to the public inquiry into the 74-day oil and natural gas spill in the Timor Sea in 2009 that concluded the industry needed an independent, overarching body to implement and maintain world standards in production and safety.

The government funds seismic and geological data from Geoscience Australia for access free of charge by hydrocarbon companies to aid exploration of its on- and off-shore sites.

There were 2.9 trillion cubic metres (cum) of proven natural gas reserves at the end of 2010; production was 50.4 billion cum, an increase of 5.1 per cent on the 2009 rate and marks a steady trend of increase from the 29.8 billion cum in 1997. Projections have shown that Australia can maintain self-sufficiency in natural gas until at least 2016. There has been a steady growth in exports of liquefied natural gas (LNG) so that by 2010 Australia was the world's third largest exporter, with exports of over 25.36 billion cum, of which almost 17.66 billion cum went to Japan. The Gorgon Gas Project (GGP), when completed (scheduled for 2014), will be Australia's single largest resource project. It is due to convert natural gas from the offshore Carnarvon Basin gas field (Western Australia) into liquefied natural gas (LNG) on Chevron, the US-energy company's processing plant on Barrow Island. When the 15 million tonne per annum LNG plant is in full production it will be the one of the world's largest processing plants. On 20 May 2011, the Dutch energy company Shell announced that it would build the world's first floating LNG plant. Industry observers estimated the cost of the Prelude project could be between US$8–15 billion. The custom-built ship will be moored 200km off the Australian coast and process Australian natural gas to provide 3.6 million tonnes of gas per year delivered ready to go on-stream at any Asian importer's designated port.

Proven coal reserves were 76.4 billion tonnes at the end of 20109, representing 8.9 per cent of world reserves. However the majority of reserves (39.3 billion tonnes) are lower quality coking (brown) coal, which is used almost exclusively in power stations and produces a greater quantity of carbon dioxide emissions than other primary energy sources. Production in 2010 was 235.8 million tonnes of oil equivalent (mtoe) an increase of 2.9 per cent on the 2009 figure. Australia exports around 60 per cent of its production in both thermal and coking coal, of which 60 per cent is destined for Japan.

Total consumption of primary energy in 2009 was 118.2 mtoe.

Energy

Total generating capacity is over 4,900MW, with 240 billion kilowatt hours (KWh) produced in 2007. Around 75 per cent is produced by coal-fired power stations, most of the rest by gas and hydropower. In June 2009 a proposal to build Australia's biggest wind farm, near Broken Hill in New South Wales (NSW), was given permission to proceed. Around 600 wind turbines will generate enough electricity to provide NSW with almost 5 per cent of its energy needs. Plans for other wind farms are under consideration; the Senate passed legislation in August setting a target of 20 per cent renewable sources of energy by 2020.

Plans for a new hydroelectric power plant in Papua New Guinea (PNG) to supply electricity to northern Queensland were announced on 17 September 2010. The Australian power company Origin Energy and PNG's Energy Developments will build the power plant, with the first phase generating 1800MW to be supplied via an undersea cable to Weipa initially and then to Townsville, by about 2020.

The Australian Energy Regulator (AER) took control of the energy market from state entities in 2006 and is responsible for the economic regulation of energy markets. It promotes investment, ensures supply security and monitors prices faced by end users.

Although Australia has a nuclear power station in southern Sydney at Lucas Heights it does not generate electrical energy.

Financial markets

Stock exchange

Australian Securities Exchange (ASX)

Banking and insurance

In 2010 the government overhauled its taxation system to allow for growth in Islamic banking, finance and insurance products.

Central bank

Reserve Bank of Australia

Main financial centre

Sydney

Time
There are three time zones:
Queensland, New South Wales, ACT, Victoria, Tasmania (Eastern Standard Time (EST)) – GMT +10 hours.
South Australia and Northern Territory (Central Standard Time (CST)) – GMT + 9.30 hours.
Western Australia (Western Standard Time (WST)) – GMT + 8 hours
Daylight saving, plus one hour to GMT times in all states and territories except Western Australia and Queensland, (October to March).

Geography
Australia is an island continent with the Indian Ocean to the west, the Coral Sea to the east and the Tasman Sea and Pacific Ocean to the south. Australia is the flattest of the continents, the average elevation being less than 300 metres. It has three major landform features: the western plateau, the interior lowlands and the eastern uplands. Much of the land is desert.
Hemisphere
Southern

Climate
The climate ranges from tropical to temperate. About half of Queensland and Western Australia and 80 per cent of the Northern Territory are within the tropics. The remainder of the states and territories — New South Wales, Victoria, South Australia, Tasmania and the Australian Capital Territory — are in the temperate zone. Temperatures vary greatly from warm to very hot in summer (December—February) to cool and rainy in winter (June–August). In July, the temperature in Sydney averages 17 degrees Celsius (C) and in Melbourne 14 degrees C, but in the desert centre can reach 36 degrees. Average annual temperatures can vary from 25 degrees C in the far north to 13 degrees C in the far south. For most of Australia the hottest month is January.
Much of the country receives low rainfall, but some parts of Queensland, Tasmania, Victoria and New South Wales have annual rainfall of up to 4,200mm. Tropical cyclones develop over the seas to the north-west and the north-east in summer. An average of about three cyclones hit the Queensland coast every year. The Snowy Mountains in New South Wales, a famous ski resort, receives heavy snowfalls most years.
Some 70 per cent of the continent is arid, with extremes of daytime and night-time temperatures in the interior.

Dress codes
For business a suit and tie for men; suit, dress or skirt and blouse for women.

Entry requirements
Passports
Required by all.
Visa
Required by all and must be obtained in advance and from outside Australia.
Most citizens of EU and North America can apply for an Electronic Travel Authority (ETA) which can be issued by a travel agent or airline, or can be applied for online. See www.eta.immi.gov.au for details of those eligible, and follow links to the application site. ETA-eligible business visitors may stay for up to three months without additional documentation.
Those not eligible for an ETA must apply using form 456, through the nearest embassy or mission. Business visas will require a letter of invitation from a local company or organisation, a business letter from an employer stating purpose of trip and details of employee's function, proof of sufficient funds, and a full itinerary. Further details and application form can be obtained at www.immi.gov.au/business-services/index.htm.
Currency advice/regulations
This import and export of local and foreign currencies are unstricted but amounts over A$10,000 (or foreign equivalent) must be declared.
Travellers cheques are widely accepted.
Customs
Personal effects are exempt. Duty-free shops are open to international visitors on arrival in Australia.
Prohibited imports
Strict quarantine regulations make it inadvisable to carry food, fruit, vegetables, seeds, animals or plants without prior approval. Travellers are not permitted to carry fruit, vegetables or plants into the State of Victoria. Aircraft cabins are sprayed with insecticide before disembarkation.
Importation of certain items is prohibited, including narcotic and dangerous drugs, firearms and birds. Both import and export of protected wildlife or goods derived from (ie made from skins, feathers, shell, bone, etc) is strictly prohibited.

Health (for visitors)
Mandatory precautions
Vaccination certificates are required for yellow fever if travelling from an infected area.
Advisable precautions
UK nationals can obtain free hospital treatment through a reciprocal arrangement between the two governments, but they must pay for other medical treatment. Australia provides moderately expensive, good quality medical care.
Travellers should be wary of exposure to the sun and the use of sun screening creams is advised. Australia has a high incidence of skin cancer in peoples from northern Europe. The Northern Territory has occasional outbreaks of dengue fever; prevention measures include mosquito repellents, nets and clothing that fully cover the body at dawn and dusk.

Hotels
There is a full range of hotels in all cities, they should be booked well in advance, particularly during holiday seasons. A 10 per cent tip is optional.

Credit cards
Major international credit and debit cards are accepted by virtually everyone. Some taxis also accept credit card payments, check with the driver before the journey begins.

Public holidays (national)
In addition to official public holidays observed throughout Australia, extra statutory holidays are observed in individual states and the Australian Capital Territory (ACT).
Fixed dates
1 Jan (New Year's Day), 26 Jan (Australia Day), 25 Apr (Anzac Day), 27 Sep (Queen's Official Birthday, WA only), 25 Dec (Christmas Day), 26 Dec (Boxing Day).
If Christmas Day or New Year's Day falls on a Saturday, the next Monday is given as a holiday.
Variable dates
Good Friday, Easter Monday, Queen's Official Birthday (second Mon in Jun).

Working hours
Banking
Mon–Thu: 0930–1600; Fri: 0930–1700.
Business
Mon–Fri: 0900–1700.
Government
Mon–Fri: 0900–1700.
Shops
Mon–Fri: 0900–1700; Sat: 0900–1200.
Late night shopping (to 2100) in Sydney, Perth and Darwin on Thursday, and in Melbourne, Brisbane, Hobart and Canberra on Friday.

Telecommunications
In a move that will change the structure of Australia's broadband market major telecommunications companies Telstra and Optus agreed in June 2011 to join the government's A$36 billion (US$34 billion) plan to roll-out high-speed internet across the country. The two companies will close down their infrastructure and transfer customers to the National Broadband Network Company (NBNC). Government has plans to connect 90 per cent of households to a super-fast network and although both Telstra and Optus already have extensive broadband networks government considers it will be more

economical to bring the three parties together. Current broadband speeds in Australia are behind other industrialised countries.

Mobile/cell phones

GSM 3G service is available in major cities only, 900/1800 services are available in all most populated areas.

Electricity supply

220–250V AC, with 3-pin plug fittings (not UK style) and bayonet-type light sockets. Leading hotels also supply 110V outlets for razors and small appliances.

Weights and measures

Metric system

Social customs/useful tips

Australians tend to be informal, first names are quickly adopted. A handshake is normal for greetings. Business, with traditional blunt, straight-to-the-point talk, is often conducted over lunch or dinner accompanied by local wines and beers.

Australians love outdoor life and business tends to come to a standstill on weekends and public holidays, when there is a steady exodus to country areas, particularly beaches or ski-slopes depending on the season.

Visitors often complain about bureaucracy and patience is required in dealing with government departments and large corporations. There are no short-cuts and although sometimes an approach to the top official of a department might help speed up matters, this must be done with extreme caution as Australians do not tolerate queue-jumping.

Australia has strict drink-driving laws, police conduct random roadside breath tests and penalties can be severe.

Security

Australian cities are relatively safe though care should be taken, particularly at night. Each capital city has separate emergency numbers on the inside cover of phone books. Otherwise dial 000 and the operator will direct you to the appropriate service.

Getting there

Air

National airline: Qantas Airways.

International airport/s: All states have international airports (with the exceptions of the capital territory, (which is served by NSW), and Tasmania) with connecting inter- and intra-state flights.

NSW: Kingsford Smith (SYD), 8km south of Sydney; Victoria: Tullamarine (MEL), 21km from Melbourne; Western Australia: Perth (PER), 10km from Perth, all of which have duty-free shop, bar, restaurant, bank, post office, shops; Queensland: Brisbane International (BNE), 11km north-east of city, with duty-free shop, bar, restaurant; South Australia: West Beach (ADL), 8km from Adelaide, with bar, restaurant, post office, shops; Northern Terrritory: Darwin (DRW), 8km from city with bar, money exchange and duty-free shops.

Other airport/s: Tasmania: Hobart (HBA), 17km north of city, with restaurant and bar. Queensland: Cairns (CNS), 4km north-west of Cairns, with duty-free shop, hotel reservations; Townsville (TSV), 5km from city. (More information on local airports is provided on: www.airportsaustralia.com).

Airport tax: None

Surface

Water: There are regular sea links with New Zealand. Cruiseliners call at major ports in Australia. International shipping lines that maintain contacts with Australia may provide passenger services on cargo ships.

Main port/s: There are more than 30 ports. The main ports are at Sydney, Brisbane, Melbourne, Adelaide and Fremantle. Sea transport is extensively used for internal and international freight shipment. Containerised cargo facilities are available.

Getting about

National transport

Air: Air transport is widely used and well developed. Regular services linking main centres and nearly 440 airfields are operated by Australian Airlines, East-West Airlines, Air Queensland and over 25 other operators. Charter aircraft are also available. Travellers holding international air tickets can obtain concessionary air, rail and bus fares within Australia.

Road: All cities have good arterial roads. Despite the vast distances, there are good highways and bus services between all major centres, but conditions in the interior are rugged, with road transport more limited. Seek advice from the appropriate local automobile association before travelling in remote areas, as roads may be affected by weather conditions.

Buses: Air-conditioned express coach services link main centres, including Tasmania via ferries. Buses provide good services on main town routes, but convenient cross-town transport is not always available.

Rail: Railways, mainly government-owned and operated, provide express inter-urban passenger services, electrified suburban services and long-distance freight services, using a 38,563km network of tracks. Long-distance passenger trains are air-conditioned, with dining and sleeping facilities, they are generally a slower option of transport than road or air. Advance booking is recommended.

The Ghan passenger train runs directly from Adelaide to Darwin through the centre of Australia, via Alice Springs. The refurbished, 47-hour, 2,979km transcontinental journey, began its regular services in 2004. Alice Springs is the closest base for access to the region around Uluru/Ayers Rock national park and Kings Canyon.

There are rail extensions to the Ghan from other state capital cities of Melbourne, Sydney and Perth.

Water: There is a regular passenger/vehicle ferry link between Melbourne and Hobart, Tasmania.

City transport

Taxis: Metered taxis operate in all main cities and towns from major hotels, shopping areas and signposted taxi ranks. Radio-controlled taxis are listed in local telephone directories. Tipping is not expected, but a tip of the balance of the fare rounded up to the nearest dollar is sometimes given.

Buses, trams & metro: Sydney (NSW): the rail service AirportLink connects Sydney international airport with the city centre; trains depart at 10 minute intervals, journey time 13 minutes. State Transit run extensive services of buses, trains and ferries around the city and suburbs.

Melbourne (Vic): VicTrip operate trams, buses and trains around the cityand suburbs. See www.victrip.com.au for a journey planner. Skybus links the airport to city centre; services run 24 hours, everyday with daytime departures every 15 minutes, journey time 20 minutes.

Brisbane (Qld): Buses and trains link the airport to the city centre, journey time 20 minutes, as well as to all other parts of the city and suburbs.

Ferry: In Sydney, ferries are an easy, regular and enjoyable mode of transport to the city centre and harbour suburbs. The main ferry terminal is at Circular Quay. In Brisbane there are over a dozen passenger stops along the city's river.

Car hire

Hire cars are widely available. Current overseas licences are recognised, but International Drivers Permits are recommended. The required third-party insurance is normally included in car hire charge. Use of seat belts is compulsory and speed limit in towns is generally 60km per hour. Driving is on the left. Trams have the right of way. Drink driving rules are vigorously enforced, with sizeable fines.

BUSINESS DIRECTORY

The addresses listed below are a selection only. While World of Information makes every endeavour to check these addresses, we cannot guarantee that changes have not been made, especially to telephone numbers and area codes. We would welcome any corrections.

Telephone area codes
The international direct dialling (IDD) code for Australia is +61, followed by area code and subscriber's number:

Adelaide	8	Hobart	3
Brisbane	7	Launceston	3
Cairns	7	Melbourne	3
Canberra	2	Newcastle	2
Darwin	8	Perth	8
Gold Coast	7	Sydney	2
Wollongong	2	Townsville	7

Useful telephone numbers
Emergency Services: 000.

Chambers of Commerce
ACT and Region Chamber of Commerce and Industry, 12a Thesiger Court, PO Box 192, 2600 Deakin West (tel: 6283-5200; fax: 6260-3369; e-mail: chamber@actchamber.com.au).

Australian Business Chamber, 140 Arthur Street, Locked Bag 938, North Sydney, NSW 2059 (tel: 9458-7500; fax: 9923-1166; e-mail: moreld@abol.net).

Australian Chamber of Commerce and Industry, 50 Burwood Road, PO Box E14, Kingston, ACT 2604 (tel: 6273-2311; fax: 6273-3196; e-mail: acci@acci.asn.au).

Commerce Queensland, 375 Wickham Terrace, Brisbane, QLD 4000 (tel: 3842-2244; 3832-3195; fax: 3832-3195; e-mail: qcci@qcci.com.au).

New South Wales State Chamber of Commerce, Level 12, 83 Clarence Street, GPO Box 4280, Sydney NSW 2000 (tel: 9350-8100; fax: 9350-8199; e-mail: worldtradecentre@thechamber.com.au).

Northern Territory Chamber of Commerce and Industry, 5/2 Shepherd Street, GPO Box 1825, Darwin, NT 0800 (tel: 8936-3100; fax: 8981-1405; e-mail: darwin@ntcci.com.au).

South Australian Employers Chamber of Commerce, 136 Greenhill Road, Unley, SA 5061 (tel: 8300-0000; fax: 8300-0001; e-mail: enquiries@business-sa.com).

Tasmanian Chamber of Commerce and Industry, 30 Burnett Street, PO Box 793, 7001 Hobart (tel: 6234-5933; fax: 6231-1278; e-mail: admin@tcci.org.au).

Victoria Employers Chamber of Commerce asnd Industry, 196 Flinders Street, Melbourne, VIC 3000/ PO Box 4352QQ, Melbourne, VIC 3001 (tel: 8662-5333; fax: 8662-5462; e-mail: webmaster@vecci.org.au).

Western Australia Chamber of Commerce and Industry, 180 Hay Street, East Perth, WA 6004/ PO Box, East Perth, WA 6892 (tel: 9365-7555; fax: 9365-7550; e-mail: info@cciwa.com).

Banking
Australia and New Zealand Banking Group, 100 Queen Street, Melbourne, Vic 3000 (tel: 9273-5555).

Australia & New Zealand Savings Bank Ltd, Collins Place, 55 Collins Street, Melbourne, Vic 3000 (tel: 9275-5555).

Barclays Bank Australia Ltd, Barclays House, PO Box 3357, 25 Bligh Street, Sydney, NSW 2001 (tel: 9233-6622; fax: 9221-3060).

Colonial State Bank of New South Wales, PO Box 41, Sydney, NSW 2001 (tel: 9226-8000).

Commonwealth Bank of Australia, Pitt Street and Martin Place, Sydney, NSW 2000 (tel: 9378-2000; fax: 9312-9905).

Commonwealth Savings Bank of Australia, GPO Box 2719, Pitt Street & Martin Place, Sydney, NSW 2001 (9227-7111; fax: 9232-6573, 9235-1653).

National Australia Bank, 500 Bourke Street, PO Box 84A, Melbourne, Vic 3001 (tel: 9605-3500).

Natwest Australia Bank Ltd, 41st Level, Qantas International Centre, International Square, George Street, Sydney, NSW 2000 (tel: 9250-8500; fax: 9251-2763).

Rural & Industries Bank of Western Australia, PO Box E237, 54-58 Barrack Street, Perth, WA 6001 (tel: 9320-6206; fax: 9320-6444).

State Bank of Victoria, PO Box 267D, 385 Bourke Street, Melbourne, Vic 3001 (tel: 9604-7000; fax: 9602-2150).

State Bank of New South Wales, PO Box 41, Sydney, NSW 2001 (tel: 9226-8000).

State Bank of South Australia, 97 King William Street, PO Box 399, Adelaide, SA 5001 (tel: 9210-4411; fax: 9210-4758, 9212-3056).

Westpac Banking Corporation, 60 Martin Place, PO Box 1, Sydney, NSW 2001 (tel: 9226-3311).

Australian branches
Bank of New Zealand, 333 George Street, PO Box 507, Sydney, NSW 2001 (tel: 9290-6666).

Banque Nationale de Paris, 12 Castlereagh Street, PO Box 269, Sydney, NSW 2001 (tel: 9232-8733).

Central bank
Reserve Bank of Australia, 65 Martin Place, PO Box 3947, Sydney, NSW 2001 (tel: 9551-8111; fax: 9551-8000; e-mail: rbainfo@rba.gov.au).

Stock exchange
Australian Securities Exchange (ASX) (www.asx.com.au).

Australian Pacific Exchange (APX), Sydney (www.apx.com.au).

Travel information
Australian Capital Territory Tourist Bureau, Canberra Centre, Northbourne Avenue, Canberra City, ACT 2601 (tel: 6233-3666).

Automobile Association of the Northern Territory (AANT), 79-81 Smith Street, Darwin, NT 0800 (tel: 8981-3837).

Australian Tourist Commission, 80 William Street, PO Box 2721, Wooloomoloo, NSW 2011 (tel: 9360-1111; fax: 9361-1385; internet: www.atc.net.au).

Holiday WA Centre, 772 Hay Street, Perth, WA 6000 (tel: 9322-2999).

National Roads and Motorists Association (NRMA), 151 Clarence Street, Sydney, NSW 2000 (tel: 9260-9222).

NSW Government Travel Centre, 16 Spring Street, Sydney, NSW 2000 (tel: 9231-444).

Northern Territory Government Tourist Bureau, 31 Smith Street, Darwin NT 5750 (tel: 8981-6611/3).

Qantas Airways, Qantas Centre, QCA9, 203 Coward Street, Sydney, NSW 2020 (tel: 9691-3472; fax: 9691-4547; internet: www.qantas.com).

Queensland Government Tourist Bureau, Corner Adelaide and Edward Streets, Brisbane, QLD 4001 (tel: 3312-211; internet: www.tq.com.au).

Royal Automobile Club of Queensland (RACQ), 300 St Paul's Tce, Brisbane, QLD 4006 (tel: 3253-4444).

Royal Automobile Association of South Australia, 41 Hindmarsh Square, Adelaide, SA 5000 (tel: 8223-4555).

Royal Automobile Club of Tasmania (RACT), Corner Patrick & Murray Streets, Hobart, Tas 7001 (tel: 6382-200).

Royal Automobile Club of Victoria (RACV), 123 Queen Street, Melbourne, Vic 3174 (tel: 9790-2211).

Royal Automobile Club of Western Australia Inc (RACWA), 228 Adelaide Terrace, Perth, WA 6000 (tel: 9421-4444).

South Australian Government Travel Centre, 18 King William Street, Adelaide, SA 5000 (tel: 8212-1644).

Tasmanian Government Tourist Bureau, 80 Elizabeth Street, Hobart, Tas 7000 (tel: 6300-211).

Victoria Tourism Commission, 230 Collins Street, Melbourne, Vic 3000 (tel: 9619-9444).

VicRail Information: 619-1111 (Melbourne).

Ministry of tourism
Department of Tourism, Burns Memorial Building, 28 National Circuit, Forrest, ACT 2603 (tel: 6279-7111; fax: 6248-0734).

National tourist organisation offices
Tourism Australia, PO Box 2721, Sydney NSW 1006 (tel: 9360-1111; fax: 9331-6469; internet: www.tourism.australia.com)

Ministries
Department of Administrative Services, GPO Box 1920, Canberra, ACT 2601 (tel: 6275-3000; fax: 6275-3819).

Department of Communications and the Arts, GPO Box 2154, Canberra, ACT 2601 (tel: 6279-1000; fax: 6279-1901; internet site: http//www.dcita.gov.au).

Department of Defence, Treasury Building, Newland Street, Parkes, ACT 2600 (tel: 6265-9111; fax: 6273-3021; internet site: http://www.defence.gov.au).

Department of Employment, Education and Training, GPO Box 9880, Canberra, ACT 2601 (tel: 6240-8111).

Department of Finance, Treasury Building, Newlands Street, Parkes, ACT 2600 (tel: 6263-2222; fax: 6273-3021; internet site: http://www.dofa.gov.au).

Department of Foreign Affairs and Trade, Administrative Building, Parkes Place, Parkes, ACT 2600 (tel: 6261-9111; fax: 6261-3111; internet site: http://www://dfat/gov.au).

Department of Housing and Regional Development, GPO Box 9834, Canberra, ACT 2601 (tel: 6289-2222).

Department of Human Services and Health, GPO Box 9848, Canberra, ACT 2601.

Department of Immigration and Ethnic Affairs, PO Box 25, Belconnen, ACT 2616 (tel: 6264-1111; internet site: http://www.immi.gov.au).

Department of Industrial Relations, GPO Box 9879, Canberra, ACT 2601 (tel: 6243-7333).

Department of Industry, Science and Technology, GPO Box 9839, Canberra, ACT 2601 (tel: 6276-1000; fax: 6276-1111; internet: www.industry.gov.au).

Department of National Development and Industry, Tasman House, Hobart Place, PO Box 5, Canberra, ACT 2600.

Department of Primary Industries and Energy, GPO Box 858, Canberra, ACT 2601 (tel: 6272-3933; fax: 6272-5161).

Department of the Prime Minister and Cabinet, Locked Bag 14, Queen Victoria Terrace, Parkes, ACT 2600 (tel: 6271-5111; fax: 6271-5414; internet site: http://www.dpmc.gov.au).

Department of Social Security, Box 7788, Canberra Mail Centre, ACT 2610 (tel: 6244-7788).

Department of Transport, GPO Box 594, Canberra, ACT 2601 (tel: 6274-7111; fax: 6257-2505; internet site: http://www.dot.gov.au).

Department of the Treasury, The Treasury, Parkes Place, Parkes, ACT 2600 (tel: 6263-2111; fax: 6273-2614; internet site: http://www.treasury.gov.au).

Department of Veterans' Affairs, PO Box 21, Woden, ACT 2606 (tel: 6289-1111; fax: 6281-3822; internet site: http://www.dva.gov.au).

Foreign Investment Review Board, Department of the Treasury, Parkes Place, Parkes, ACT 2600 (tel: 6263-3795; fax: 6263-2940).

Other useful addresses
ACT Department of Business, Arts, Sport and Tourism, Level 8, FAI House, 197 London Circuit, Canberra, ACT 2601 (tel: 6207-5111; fax: 6205-0577).

Attorney-General, Suite MF 21, Parliament House, Canberra, ACT 2600 (tel: 6277-7300; fax: 6273-4102; internet site: www.law.gov.au).

Australian Bureau of Agriculture and Resource Economics, MacArthur House, Lyneham, ACT 2601 (tel: 6246-9111).

Australian Bureau of Statistics, Cameron Office, Chandler Street, Belconan, ACT 2617 (tel: 6252-7911).

Australian Dairy Corporation, Dairy Industry House, St Kilda Road, Melbourne, VIC 3004 (tel: 9819-4000).

Australian Embassy (USA), 1601 Massachusetts Avenue, NW, Washington DC 20036-2273 (tel: (+1-202) 797-3000; fax (+1-202) 797-3331; e-mail: library.washington@dfat.gov.au).

Australian Industrial Development Corporation (AIDC), 212 Northbourne Avenue; PO Box 3024, Canberra, ACT 2600 (tel: 6230-1300).

Australian Mining Industry Council, 216 Northbourne Avenue, Braddon, ACT 2601 (tel: 6249-8955).

Australian Securities Commission, Corporate Affairs Commission, National Mutual Centre, 15 London Court, Canberra City, ACT 2601 (tel: 6247-5011; internet site: www.asc.gov.au).

Australian Stock Exchange Ltd, Stock Exchange Center, 530 Collins Street, PO Box 1784 Q, AU Melbourne, VIC 3001 (tel: 9617-8611; fax: 9614-0303; internet site: www.asx.com.au).

Australia Trade Commission, Austrade Centre Cnr Bary Drive and Northbourne Ave, Canberra City, ACT 2601 (tel: 6276-5111; fax: 6276-5105).

Australian Trade Development Council, Department of Trade and Resources, Canberra, ACT 2600.

Australian Wheat Board, Ceres House, Lonsdale Street, Melbourne, VIC 3000 (tel: 9605-1555).

Australian Wool Corporation, Wool House, Royal Parade, Parkville, VIC 3000 (tel: 9341-9111).

British High Commission, Commonwealth Avenue, Yarralumia, Canberra City, ACT 2600 (tel: 6270-6666; fax: 6273-3236).

Business Council of Australia, Ethos House, 28 Ainslie Avenue, Canberra City, ACT 2601 (tel: 6247-8208).

Business Victoria, Level 13, 55 Collins Street, Melbourne, VIC 3000 (tel: 9651-9999; fax: 9651-9962).

BZW Australia Ltd, Level 22, 255 George Street, Sydney 2000 (tel: 9259-5913; fax: 9259-5477); Airports Team, GPO Box 4675, Sydney 1042 (fax: 9259-5477).

Confederation of Australian Industry, 12a The Siger Court, Deakin, ACT 2600 (tel: 282-2199); PO Box E14, Queen Victoria Terrace, Canberra, ACT 2600 (tel: 6732-311; fax: 6733-196).

International Trade Department Centre, Edgecliff Centre, 203 New South Head Road, Edgecliff, NSW 2027 (tel: 9329-297).

Major Projects Tasmania, 10/fl, 22 Elizabeth Street, Hobart, TAS 7000 (tel: 6233-5869; fax: 6233-5755).

New South Wales Department of State, Level 44, Grosvenor Place, 225 George Street, Sydney, NSW 2000 (tel: 9242-6963; fax: 9242-6970).

New South Wales Government Department of Industrial Development and Decentralisation, GPO Box 4169, Sydney, NSW 2001 (tel: 9927-2741).

Northern Department of Asian Relations, Trade and Industry, 1/fl Development House, 76 The Esplande, Darwin, NT 0800 (tel: 8999-5210; fax: 8999-5106).

Northern Territory Development Corporation, GPO Box 2245, Darwin, NT 5794 (tel: 8989-4211).

Queensland Department of Economic Development & Trade, Executive Building, 100 George Street, Brisbane QLD 4000 (tel: 3224-5970; fax: 3225-8914).

South Australia Department of Trade and Industry, Terrace towers, 178 North Towers, Adelaide SA 5000 (tel: 8303-2400; fax: 9303-2410).

Telecom Australia, 199 William Street, Melbourne, VIC 3000 (tel: 9606-5511).

US Embassy, Moonah Place, Yarralumla, ACT 2600 (tel: 6214-5600; fax: 6214-5970).

Western Australia Department of Industry and Trade, 170 St Georges Terrace, Perth, WA 6000 (tel: 9327-5666; fax: 9322-3361).

Western Australian Development Corporation, 28th Floor, City Mutual Tower, 197 St George's Terrace, Perth, WA 6000 (tel: 9322-7933).

World Trade Promotions (trade fairs and exhibitions), 291 Sussex Street, Sydney, NSW 2000 (tel: 9267-5122).

Internet sites

Austrade (information for overseas business people): www.austrade.gov.au/index.asp

Australian Broadcasting Corporation (ABC): www.abc.net.au

Australian Capital Territory government: www.act.gov.au

British Chamber of Commerce: www.whoswhere.com.au/abcc

Customs service: www.customs.gov.au

Department of Agriculture, Fisheries and Forestry: www.daff.gov.au

Department of the Environment and Heritage: www.environment.gov.au

Department of Health and Aged Care: www.health.gov.au

Foreign Affairs & Trade Dept: www.dfat.gov.au

Farmwide information on weather reports, commodity prices, etc: www.farmwide.com.au

Federal Government: www.fed.gov.au

Federal Parliament (Canberra): www.aph.gov.au/

General Information: www.about-australia.com

Immigration Department: www immi.gov.au

Invest Australia: www.investaustralia.gov.au

New South Wales state government: www.nsw.gov.au

Northern Territory state government: www.nt.gov.au/

Qantas: www.qantas.com.au

Queensland state government: www.qld.gov.au/

Reserve bank: www.rba.gov.au

South Australia: www.sa.gov.au

Stock Exchange: www.asx.com.au

Statistics: www.abs.gov.au

Tasmania state government: www.tas.gov.au

Taxation office: www.ato.gov.au

Tourism: www.australia.com

Tourism: www.tourism.australia.com

Victoria state government: www.vic.gov.au

Western Australia state government: www.wa.gov.au/

White pages: www.whitepages.com.au

Yellow pages: www.Yellowpages.com.au

Austria

Austrians tend to be gloomy rather than ebullient by nature. Thus, where the German observes that the situation is 'serious, but not hopeless', the Austrian will claim 'the situation is hopeless, but not serious'. In 1918, as the Austro-Hungarian empire was carved up, many Austrians shared the sentiments of Sigmund Freud: 'Austria-Hungary is no more' but 'I do not want to live anywhere else.' Things got worse; two decades later Austria disappeared completely, swept up into the German Reich. Modern Austria is a federation and the current federal government is a coalition of the two largest political parties. The coalition, in office since 2008, comprises the Sozialdemokratische Partei Österreichs (SPÖ) (Social Democratic Party of Austria) with the centre-right Österreichische Volkspartei (ÖVP) (Austrian People's Party). Also, in Austria's federal structure, considerable political power resides with the nine federal states. Thus, decision-making often requires building a consensus across different levels of government and political parties. The next federal elections are scheduled for 2013.

Corruption scandal

'Serious' was probably not how most Austrians would perceive their politicians' behaviour. 'Hopeless' was probably nearer the mark when former chancellor and leader of the ÖVP, Wolfgang Schüssel, announced in September 2011 that he was quitting parliament amid a widening corruption scandal centred on Telekom Austria. Schüssel himself had not been linked to the cases but his resignation took effect shortly afterwards following extensive Austrian media reports about supposed slush fund payments to politicians and lobbyists during Mr Schussel's period as chancellor. Mr Schüssel told a news conference he did not acknowledge any wrongdoing but that an independent investigation into corruption allegations had to be free of any political influence.

It had been reported that prosecutors had announced an investigation against former vice chancellor, Hubert Gorbach, of the far-right Freiheitliche Partei Österreichs (FPÖ) (Freedom Party of Austria). Gorbach allegedly took money from partly state-owned Austria Telekom in return for formulating a law biased in favour of the national telecoms provider. Telekom Austria, in which the state has a 28 per cent stake, commissioned an independent panel after the announcement to look into allegations of improper payments and compliance shortfalls. It is due to issue its report in 2012.

Mr Schüssel, 66, was chancellor from 2000 until 2007 under ÖVP coalitions with right-wing parties. He has been a regular member of parliament since 2008 and his name was mentioned among the candidates for the job of permanent European Council president which the European Commission leaders eventually gave to Herman Van Rompuy. Former ÖVP

KEY FACTS

Official name: Republik Österreich (Republic of Austria)

Head of State: Federal President Heinz Fischer (SPÖ) (from 2004; re-elected 25 Apr 2010)

Head of government: Chancellor Werner Faymann (SPÖ) (from 2 Dec 2008)

Ruling party: Coalition led by Sozialdemokratische Partei Österreichs (SPÖ) (Social Democratic Party of Austria) with Österreichische Volkspartei (ÖVP) (Austrian People's Party) (from 2 Dec 2008)

Area: 83,855 square km

Population: 8.39 million (2010)*

Capital: Vienna

Official language: German

Currency: Euro (€) = 100 cents (from 1 Jan 2002; previous currency schilling, locked at S13.76 per euro)

Exchange rate: €0.75 per US$ (Oct 2011)

GDP per capita: US$44,987 (2010)

GDP real growth: 2.00% (2010)

GDP: US$376.80 billion (2010)

Labour force: 3.61 million (2010)

Unemployment: 6.90% (2010)

Inflation: 1.70% (2010)

Balance of trade: -US$4.30 billion (2010)

* estimated figure

interior minister Ernst Strasser was also among the names mentioned by the local press as accused of receiving millions of euros from Telekom Austria decision-makers or lobbyists co-operating with the company. In March 2010, Mr Strasser resigned from his position of member of the European Parliament (EP), after being trapped by British journalists into accepting money in exchange for tabling amendments to legislation being passed in the EU assembly.

Habsburg revival?

Otto Habsburg, the oldest son of Karl I (Charles of Austria) and the last heir to the Habsburg throne, died in mid-2011. Otto was buried at the Imperial Crypt (Kapuzinergruft) in Vienna in July. Some 2,000 people – among them political leaders from all over Europe – attended a requiem in St Stephen's Cathedral. Following his death, the Schwarz-Gelbe Allianz (SGA) (Black-Yellow Association), a monarchy-endorsing movement formed in 2004, promised to compete in Austria's next general elections scheduled for 2013. Although not represented in any provincial parliament or town hall in Austria the SGA hopes to benefit from the nostalgia surrounding the Habsburg family which has been rekindled by the death of Otto.

The SGA had already tried to gain seats in the federal parliament in 2008, but was prevented from participating in the vote since it failed to garner the 2,600 statements of support that every political party has to present to election officials ahead of a federal ballot. It said it was certain many more Austrians would back its goals now than in 2008. The party told the magazine *Profil* that it wanted to create a commonwealth of the five countries that once formed the powerful Austrian-Hungarian Habsburg regime. The faction explained that it saw reasonable prospects of reaching this target by 2018. It explained that a member of the Habsburg family should head the confederation of states it had in mind. The SGA described its envisaged form of government as a 'democratic monarchy'.

Austrian political scientists concur that movements towards a monarchy will stand no chance in the foreseeable future in Austria regardless of political developments in and outside the country. Otto Habsburg's son Karl – who himself has refused to rule out a comeback in politics – represented the ÖVP in the EP for three years until 1999. He founded the Christlich-Soziale Allianz (CSA) (Christian-Social Alliance) after leaving the EP to enter the federal parliament in Vienna in the general vote of 1999 but failed. The party claimed only 1.5 per cent of the overall vote. Four per cent of votes are needed to win a seat in parliament. The Austrian public has been at odds over how to handle the Habsburg family in view of its legacy.

Serious about the economy

Luckily, a rebound in external demand had brought about a quick recovery in 2010. In contrast with other countries, in Austria private consumption and employment held up quite well during the recession. When external demand (especially from Germany) rebounded in the second half of 2010 the stage was set for a rapid recovery and GDP growth reached 2.1 per cent in 2010. The current account registered a surplus of 2.7 per cent of GDP, reflecting continued strong performance in services (mainly tourism and business services). Outward FDI recovered somewhat in 2010, but remained well below pre-crisis levels.

By mid-2011 the situation was anything but hopeless. GDP growth was expected to reach 3.3 per cent by the end of the year, buoyed up by external demand, re-stocking and equipment investment. This impressive level of growth was expected to moderate in 2012, as the cyclical recovery reached its end. In early 2011 Austria's inflation had already risen to well above the euro-zone average. The main risk factor facing Austria was possible turmoil in the euro area periphery, especially should it extend to core euro area countries or those of Central, Eastern and South-Eastern Europe (CESEE).

Austria's economic recovery and the current consolidation plan have succeeded in reducing the deficit, but not enough to put the debt firmly on a downward trajectory in the medium-term, a development needed to address fiscal risks. With a strong economy, low unemployment and supportive monetary policy, there is enough macro-economic space to tighten fiscal policy further, starting with the 2012 budget. Measures to strengthen incentives for older workers to retire later, improve efficiency in the provision of healthcare and rationalise subsidies would cut spending while at the same time making the government more efficient. A comprehensive fiscal federalism reform to better align spending and financing responsibilities would further underpin consolidation efforts.

Austrian banks have absorbed large credit costs on CESEE exposures and priorities for the banking sector are now those of strengthening private capital buffers, supervision and regulation. As profitability returns, priority will be given to building up high quality capital, as already required by forthcoming international standards, and exiting government support. Progress in enhancing bank supervision and macro-prudential regulation will continue, as well as co-ordination with continued international efforts.

Enhancing long-term growth prospects by increasing employment rates and human capital will gain importance. While overall unemployment is low, employment rates of low-skilled workers could be improved by reducing tax wedges. Productivity growth could also be boosted by

KEY INDICATORS — Austria

	Unit	2006	2007	2008	2009	2010
Population	m	8.26	8.28	8.29	8.30	8.39
Gross domestic product (GDP)	US$bn	323.83	373.94	415.30	381.90	376.80
GDP per capita	US$	39,190	45,181	50,098	45,989	44,987
GDP real growth	%	3.2	3.4	2.0	-3.6	2.1
Inflation	%	1.7	2.2	3.2	0.4	1.7
Unemployment	%	4.8	4.4	3.8	7.2	6.9
Exports (fob) (goods)	US$m	133,844.0	162,147.0	179,115.0	135,695.0	147,464.0
Imports (fob) (goods)	US$m	133,419.0	160,302.0	179,218.0	138,669.0	151,767.0
Balance of trade	US$m	425.0	1,845.0	-103.0	-2,974.0	-4,303.0
Current account	US$m	7,927.0	10,037.0	12,024.0	5,332.0	10,555.0
Total reserves minus gold	US$m	7,010.0	10,689.0	8,912.0	8,114.0	–
Foreign exchange	US$m	6,573.0	10,261.0	8,244.0	4,781.0	–
Exchange rate	per US$	0.75	0.69	0.68	0.78	0.76

educational reform, particularly to increase the number of university graduates in disciplines that complement research and development.

Public finances

While Austria's fiscal position compares favourably with other members of the euro area, the country's public finances had worsened sharply during the financial crisis and in the near future will face pressures from population ageing and health care costs, as well as risks from the large cross-border financial sector exposure. With increased market scrutiny of

sovereign debt risk in advanced countries, in the view of the International Monetary Fund (IMF) Austria needs to bring its public debt down more rapidly than envisaged under the current consolidation plan. However the Austrian authorities thought that current plans were adequate. In the financial sector, there was agreement that the challenges going forward are to increase the size and quality of private capital, improve liquidity management, take advantage of ongoing bank restructuring to address overcapacity in the Austrian market, and reduce risks from future foreign expansion through supervisory and regulatory reforms. Discussions also addressed structural reforms in labour markets and education.

Since 1990 increasing integration to the East has benefited the Austrian economy, but has also created vulnerabilities that came to a head with the global financial crisis. After the fall of the iron curtain, Austria's economic fulcrum moved eastward: trade with the CESEE became increasingly important, foreign direct investment (FDI) flows were directed to the region and Austrian banks entered the newly-opened markets. In many East European countries, rapid credit expansion fuelled not only economic growth but also a domestic demand boom and large current account deficits. In addition, credit was largely denominated in foreign currency, creating vulnerability to currency depreciation. After global money markets froze following the Lehman bankruptcy, the boom in the CESEE came to an abrupt halt and Austrian banks faced both a liquidity squeeze and deteriorating credit portfolios. Government intervention was necessary to support aggregate demand and stabilise the banking system, while a number of CESEE countries obtained support from international financial organisations and the Vienna Initiative, whereby foreign banks jointly committed to maintain exposures.

Outlook and risks

In the view of the IMF, supported by strong external demand, output growth was set to accelerate in 2011 and moderate thereafter, as the cyclical recovery will have run its course. Continuing the strong pace set at end-2010, in the first quarter of 2011 GDP grew by 0.9 over the previous quarter, surprising to the upside and triggering upward revisions by forecasters. Growth was led by exports, re-stocking and equipment investment, while construction activity remained weak and private consumption was subdued, reflecting declining real disposable incomes.

Confidence indicators point to a slowdown in the remainder of 2011. Both the IMF and the Austrian authorities agreed that 2011 GDP growth would be strong, with the IMF a bit more optimistic (3.3 per cent) than the central bank (3.2 per cent) and Austria's two leading research institutes (both 3 per cent). There was also agreement that growth will moderate to around 2 per cent in 2012. IMF staff viewed potential output as only marginally affected by the crisis, with the output gap all but closed next year.

The food and energy price shocks, higher excise taxes and the strong economy have pushed up consumer prices. In recent months, inflation in Austria has exceeded the euro area average: in June 2011, headline inflation was 3.7 per cent while core inflation was 2.8 per cent, about one per cent above the euro area indicators. The Austrian authorities assessed that indirect tax increases at the beginning of the year accounted for 0.4 percentage points of the differential and reckoned that it was too early to tell what might explain the rest. Demand pressures from the strong recovery may be an additional contributing factor. The reversal in commodity prices, the expected tightening of monetary conditions in the euro area and mildly constrained fiscal policy may help contain inflationary pressures in 2012 if wage settlements for the year remain moderate.

During 2007–10 the deficit had widened from 0.9 per cent to 4.6 per cent of GDP, while the public debt rose by almost 12 per cent of GDP. The government's multi-year fiscal consolidation plan would cut the deficit back to below 3 per cent by 2013 (in compliance with the EU excessive deficit procedure for Austria) and further to around 2 per cent in the medium term through a combination of tax increases and expenditure cuts. With growth so far in 2011 better than expected but with continued budgetary implementation risks in particular at the sub-national level, the IMF projected the deficit to decline to 3.4 per cent of GDP in 2011 and the structural deficit to stabilise at about 2 per cent of GDP in the medium term, with debt remaining above 70 per cent of GDP.

In Austria's banking system, profitability is improving despite growing non-performing loans (NPLs) and lessons from the crisis are being distilled. NPL ratios are high in CESEE subsidiaries, albeit with notable regional differences, while loans in Austria are performing relatively well. The large banks and most medium-sized banks were profitable in 2010 despite continuing significant provisioning costs. Interbank interest rates have normalised; and share prices for the large banks have recovered, but have not returned to pre-crisis levels.

Risk assessment

Politics	Fair
Economy	Fair
Regional stability	Good

COUNTRY PROFILE

Historical profile

For centuries the Austrian (later Austro-Hungarian) Empire covered most of central Europe.

1918 After the Austro-Hungarian Empire was defeated in the First World War, the first Austrian Republic was declared; three-quarters of the former Empire's territory was ceded to neighbouring states.

1933 Pro-fascist Engelbert Dollfuss (elected federal chancellor in 1932) gained dictatorial powers and banned all political opposition to his Vaterländische Front (VF) (Fatherland Front). Dollfuss forged a strong relationship with fascist Italy in an attempt to preserve Austria's independence.

1934 The government put down an uprising by Socialists in February. Dollfuss was assassinated in July by Austrian Nazis, who had been conspiring to oust the government and integrate Austria with Nazi Germany.

1938 The new chancellor, Kurt von Schuschnigg, met with Adolf Hitler in an attempt to preserve Austria's independence. After refusing to meet Hitler's demands for concessions for the banned Austrian Nazi Party, von Schuschnigg resigned as chancellor and was replaced by Arthur Seyss-Inquart (leader of the Austrian Nazi Party). Austria was integrated with Nazi Germany. Austria was renamed Ostmark.

1945 After Nazi Germany was defeated in the Second World War; Austria

re-emerged as an independent state but was divided into four zones of occupation by the US, UK, France and USSR. The conservative Österreichische Volkspartei (ÖVP) (Austrian People's Party) and the Sozialdemokratische Partei Österreichs (SPÖ) (Social Democratic Party of Austria) formed a coalition government.
1955 The 1955 State Treaty confirmed Austria's independence and banned re-integration with Germany. Austria joined the UN, declared its neutrality and the occupation forces withdrew.
1960 Austria joined the European Free Trade Area (EFTA).
1966 The ÖVP came to power after 20 years of a coalition.
1970-87 The SPÖ was in power until 1983, when it formed a coalition government with the Freiheitliche Partei Österreichs (FPÖ) (Freedom Party of Austria).
1986 The presidential election was won by Kurt Waldheim (independent but with ÖVP's backing). Controversy surrounded allegations of his implication in Nazi atrocities in the Balkans (1942–45), culminating in his listing as an undesirable alien by the US Department of Justice.
1987 Following an inconclusive election, the SPÖ and the ÖVP formed a coalition.
1992 Waldheim stepped down and was replaced by Thomas Klestil.
1995 Austria joined the EU. The one-year-old governing coalition collapsed over the 1996 budget.
1997 Franz Vranitsky led the government as chancellor from 1995 until his resignation in 1997, when he was replaced by Viktor Klima.
1998 Federal President Klestil was re-elected.
1999 After indecisive election results, the ÖVP-SPÖ coalition collapsed, leading to a coalition between the ÖVP and the far-right, FPÖ.
2000 The ÖVP's Wolfgang Schüssel became chancellor. The inclusion of the FPÖ in the government, with Susanne Riess-Passer (FPÖ) as vice chancellor led to EU diplomatic sanctions against Austria. Only after Joerg Haider stepped down as party leader of FPÖ were sanctions lifted.
2002 The euro replaced the Austrian schilling. After three FPÖ ministers resigned, Schüssel announced that ÖVP was withdrawing from the coalition government. The ÖVP won the snap election and Schüssel remained as Chancellor.
2003 ÖVP coalition government included the SPÖ and right-wing populist FPÖ.
2004 President Klestil died in office. Heinz Fischer (SPÖ) won the presidential elections.
2005 The FPÖ split; a breakaway faction, Bündis Zukunft Österreich (BZÖ) (Alliance for Austria's Future), was led by Joerg Haider. Austria began making payouts to those whose property had been looted during the Holocaust. Most of the victims are elderly and many resident in the US.
2006 In general elections, the SPÖ won 35.3 per cent of the vote, the ÖVP, won 34.3 per cent. Some states, led by far-right parties, introduced nationality laws for new citizens.
2007 After two months of negotiations, the SPÖ and ÖVP formed a coalition government and Alfred Gusenbauer became Chancellor. Former Austrian president and secretary general of the United Nations, Kurt Waldheim died.
2008 The ruling coalition government collapsed when the ÖVP withdrew, following disagreement over policy issues. In early elections, Chancellor Gusenbauer did not to stand for re-election. The SPÖ won 29.4 per cent of the vote the ÖVP 26 per cent and FPÖ 17.7 per cent; turnout was 76.6 per cent. Joerg Haider (BZÖ) was killed in a road accident. The SPÖ and ÖV formed a coalition in government, preventing the far-right BZÖ from forming a government. Werner Faymann (SPÖ) was sworn in as chancellor.
2009 German-based airline, Lufthansa took control of the state-owned Austrian Airlines in a privatisation deal by the government.
2010 In presidential elections held in April incumbent Heinz Fischer won a decisive 78.9 per cent of the vote.
2011 Plans by the state-owned estate company (Bundesimmobiliengesellshaft) dropped plans to sell two mountains for a total of €121,000 (US$70,000), in June, following a public outcry. Otto von Habsburg, the last heir to the throne of the long-defunct, Austro-Hungarian Empire, died on 4 July, aged 98 years.

Political structure

Constitution

The 1920 constitution was amended in 1929.

The state is a federal republic consisting of nine Länder (states), each with its own state Ländtag (legislature) and government. The nine states are Burgenland, Carinthia, Lower Austria, Upper Austria, Salzburg, Styria, Tyrol, Vorarlberg and Vienna. A considerable amount of political power is devolved to the state assemblies, although all matters of national interest are decided in Vienna. Each state parliament appoints its own state governor.

For some functions (for example, appointing the new president) the Nationalrat (National Council) and the Bundesrat (Federal Council) of the federal Bundesversammlung (parliament) meet in joint session, as the Nationalversammlung (National Assembly). Certain issues may be put to the popular vote in a national referendum and the people may also force a direct vote in the Nationalrat if any petition gathers more than 200,000 signatures.

Traditionally, the government has been required to work according to the principles of the *sozialpartner* (social contract). This informal organisation, comprising the Chamber of Economy, Chamber of Agriculture, Chamber of Labour and trade unions, is at the heart of the policy-making process. Such a system has served Austria well in the past as it both guarantees and feeds on national consensus and unity. However, it is becoming unworkable in a fully globalised world economy.

Form of state

Federal parliamentary democratic republic

The executive

Executive power rests with the head of the federal government, who is the chancellor appointed by the president, and usually the leader of the largest party in the Nationalrat.

The president is elected by popular vote every six years for a maximum of two terms. He has no executive powers in peace time. He has special emergency powers, as well as overseeing elections and swearing in new chancellors and governments, but in practice, he acts in accordance with the decisions of the government.

National legislature

The Nationalrat (lower house) has 183 members elected every four years by proportional representation. The seats are distributed first among 43 constituencies then among the nine states, and the remainder at federal level. The Bundesrat (upper house) has 62 members elected for between 4–6 years. Membership changes after every election of lower state assemblies. The Bundesrat may veto legislation passed by the lower chamber, although in practice such vetoes are suspensive and can be overridden by the lower chamber, except in cases of constitutional matters, rights of the Bundesrat and the jurisdiction of federal states. Although the two chambers are equal under the constitution, in practice the Nationalrat has more power. While in formal joint session both chambers constitute a third body, the Bundesversammlung (Federal Assembly).

Legal system

The legal system is divided between legislative, administrative and judicial power. There are three supreme courts Verfassungsgerichtshof (Constitutional Court), Verwaltungsgerichtshof (Administrative Court) and Oberster Gerichtshof (Judicial Court). There are around 200 local judicial courts (Bezirksgerichte), 17 provincial and district courts (Landes-und Kreisgerichte) and four higher provincial courts (Oberlandesgerichte) in Vienna, Graz, Innsbruck and Linz.

Last elections
25 April 2010 (presidential); 8 September 2008 (parliamentary).
Results: Presidential: Heinz Fischer (Sozialdemokratische Partei Österreichs (SPÖ) (Social Democratic Party)) won 78.9 per cent of the vote, Barbara Rosenkranz (FPÖ) 15.6 per cent, Rudolf Gehring (Christliche Partei Österreichs) (CPÖ) (Christian Party)) 5.4 per cent. Turnout was 49.2 per cent.
Parliamentary: the SPÖ won 29.3 per cent of the vote (57 seats out of 183) the ÖVP 25.9 per cent and Freiheitliche Partei Österreichs (FPÖ) (Freedom Party of Austria) 17.5 per cent (34), BZÖ-Liste Jörg Haider (BZÖ-Jörg Haider list) 10.7 per cent (21), Die Grünen-Die Grüne Alternative (The Greens-The Green Alternative) 10.4 per cent (20), no other party won enough votes to achieve gain a seat; turnout was 78.8 per cent.

Next elections
2016 (presidential); 2012 (parliamentary).

Political parties

Ruling party
Coalition led by Sozialdemokratische Partei Österreichs (SPÖ) (Social Democratic Party of Austria) with Österreichische Volkspartei (ÖVP) (Austrian People's Party) (from 2 Dec 2008)

Main opposition party
Freiheitliche Partei Österreichs (FPÖ) (Freedom Party of Austria)

Population

8.39 million (2010)*
Last census: May 2001: 8,032,926
Population density: Urban population: 65 per cent (1994–2000).
Annual growth rate: 0.2 per cent 1994–2004 (WHO 2006)

Ethnic make-up
Around 93 per cent are of German-Austrian origin. Minorities include Slovenes, Croats, Hungarians and Czechs and are mostly concentrated in the south-east. There are ethnic communities from Africa, the Middle East and Asia.

Religions
Roman Catholic (89 per cent); Protestant (6 per cent).

Education

Primary schooling lasts for four years. There are two main forms of secondary education; one academic and one geared more to technical and vocational education. The former, *Allgemeinbildende*, school may be attended for eight years or the latter, *Hauptschule*, attended for four years followed by a school offering specialised training of a technical or vocational nature. Tertiary education takes place in universities or specialist colleges including technology, music and art higher education institutions.
Compulsory years: 6 to 15
Enrolment rate: 103 per cent total primary enrolment, 99 per cent total secondary enrolment, 57 per cent tertiary enrolment; of relevant age groups (including repetition rates) World Bank.
Pupils per teacher: 12 in primary schools

Health

All Austrians have access to healthcare.

HIV/Aids
HIV prevalence: 0.3 per cent aged 15–49 in 2003 (World Bank)
Life expectancy: 79 years, 2004 (WHO 2006)
Fertility rate/Maternal mortality rate: 1.4 births per woman, 2004 (WHO 2006)
Child (under 5 years) mortality rate (per 1,000): 4.5 per 1,000 live births (World Bank)
Head of population per physician: 3.38 physicians per 1,000 people, 2003 (WHO 2006)

Welfare

Austrian social insurance is compulsory and covers health insurance, pension insurance, accident insurance and unemployment insurance. Contributions are shared by employers and employees.

Pensions
Reforms adopted in 2003, extended the years required for employee contributions from 40 to 45, before a worker can retire on a full pension with all benefits; the statutory retirement age was set at 65 for all; 10 disparate pension systems for various categories of workers were harmonised. This is expected to reverse the trend for early retirement. In 2003 the average age of retirement was 57.5, with less than 30 per cent of workers being in the 55–64 age range. With an ageing population the pension scheme will become progressively more expensive; it is expected that the new reforms wll limit spending by between 1.5–1.75 per cent of GDP a year. The government is proposing to stagger the rise in the official retirement age, while reducing state pensions by up to 30 per cent, in some cases.

Main cities

Vienna (capital, estimated population 1.6 million in 2005), Graz (223,297), Salzburg (143,259), Innsbruck (112,693), Klagenfurt (90,666), Linz (180,684), Villach (58,412), Wels (57,552), St Pölten (48,889), Dornbirn (43,005).

Languages spoken

About 94 per cent of Austrian nationals speak German, although a heavy dialect is in daily use. There are linguistic minorities of Slovenes, Croats, Hungarians, Slovaks and Czechs.

Official language/s
German

Media

Press
Almost all ownership of the print media is held by two Germany-based publishing houses, the Bertelsmann Media owns most magazine titles and Westdeutsche Allgemaine Zeitung (WAZ), through Mediaprint Group, controls most newspapers.
Dailies: In German, national newspapers include *Der Standard* (http://derstandard.at), *Die Presse* (http://diepresse.com), *Der Kurier* (www.kurier.at) a mass-circulation and *Neue Kronenzeitung* (www.krone.at), which has regional editions. Major regional newspapers include *Der Grazer* (www.grazer.at) from Graz, *Salzburger Fenster* (www.salzburger-fenster.at) from Salzburg and *Österreich* (www.oe24.at/zeitung), published in Vienna.
Weeklies: In German, *Profil* (www.news.at/profil), *Österreich Journal* (www.oe-journal.at), and *News Magazin* (www.news.at/magazin), for news and analysis, *Die Bezirksblätter* (www.noe-anzeiger.at), for regional and local news, *Wienerin* (www.wienerin.at), for women and *Wiener Zeitung* (www.wienerzeitung.at) a semi-official publication from Vienna.
Most daily newspapers have weekend editions, which tend to be bigger and contain a large amount of advertising.
Business: In German, *Wirtschafts Blatt* (www.wirtschaftsblatt.at) is a daily, *Industrie Magazin* (www.industriemagazin.at), and *Trend* (www.news.at/trend), are weekly magazines.

Broadcasting
Österreichischer Rundfunk (ÖRF) (Austrian Broadcasting Corporation) (www.orf.at) is the national, public broadcasting network.
Radio: ÖRF broadcasts four national radio networks (including Ö1 Hit Radio and FM4), 10 regional stations and two international channels (Radio Österreich 1 International and Radio 1476). Private, commercial radio stations includes Krone Hit (www.kronehit.at) a national network and local locally Energy 104.2 (http://energy.t-online.at) and Radio Anabella (www.radioarabella.at), from Vienna, Radio Osttirol (http://radio.osttirol.net) from Lienz, and Radio Fabrik (www.radiofabrik.at) from Saltburg.

Television: ÖRF (http://tv.orf.at) has two public channels ÖRF1 and ÖRF2, broadcasting domestically produced and imported programmes. Private networks include ATV (http://atv.at) and OKTO TV (http://okto.tv) is a non-profit community TV station. There are several cable and satellite TV networks including Pulse TV (www.puls4.com), Premiere Austria (www.premiere.at) and Austria 9 TV (www.austria9.tv). There are a number of German TV affiliates throughout Austria.

Advertising

The Österreichischer Werberat (ÖWR) (Austrian Advertising Council) (www.werberat.at) is the self-regulating body that applies the code and rules for the advertising industry.

Advertising and sponsorship on television is allowed in both public and private schedules; public programmes may only broadcast advertising between programmes. There are also three advert-free days each year including 24 December, Good Friday and 21 November. Adverts may only represent 5 per cent of the length of programmes and not more than 20 per cent of the day's schedule. Radio advertising is permitted on both private and public programmes.

Austria has an opt-in condition for commercial e-mails and telephony advertisements whereby customers must agree to their delivery.

Newspapers (especially weekend editions) and magazines are a popular location for adverts. Poster sites are available through municipal authorities. Advertising in cinemas and by direct mail is also widely used.

Economy

Austria is a small landlocked country of less than 84,000 square kilometres and a population of less than 10 million, but it is one of the richest countries in Europe with a per capita income that reached a record US$50,039 in 2008 and a ranking of 25 in the world for GDP. As with all post-industrial societies, the service sector is the largest component of the Austrian economy, with banking playing a major role, particularly as it is an important component of the rapidly growing Central, Eastern and South-eastern Europe (CESE) economies, into which Austrian-owned banks have expanded. Tourism is also an important sector of the economy; the country is in the top-15 countries visited worldwide, offering holiday destinations in both summer and winter.

GDP growth was 2.0 per cent in 2008 as the global economic crisis caused the economy to begin to contract. In response the government implemented a generous financial stimulus package of tax cuts of 0.3 per cent of GDP, including increases to pension payments and reduced unemployment insurance contributions. In 2009 the economy was in recession with an annual average growth rate of -3.9 per cent. Austria officially pulled out of recession in the third quarter of 2009 with GDP growth of 0.9 per cent, led by investment and exports, as global trade picked up. By 2010, growth had bounced back to 2.1 per cent and was forecast to rise to 3.3 per cent in 2011.

The banking sector was badly hit by the economic crisis, not only within Austria but also in the CESE where the added risk of lending in foreign currencies added to Austrian bank sectors' risks. The government had to provide special support amounting to €100 million (US$148.2 million). Lending in foreign currencies by Austrian subsidiaries in the CESE was halted (although remained active in euros) and there was little withdrawal of business from CESE countries.

External trade

As a member of the European Union, Austria operates within a community-wide free trade area, with tariffs set by a central body. Internationally, the EU has free trade agreements with a number of nations and trading blocs worldwide.

Foreign trade is a vital component of the Austrian economy and accounts for over 95 per cent of GDP of which 90 per cent is attributed to the motor vehicle sector, in particular engine and transmissions production. The EU accounts for around 65 per cent of both imports and exports while Germany is Austria's major trading partner accounting for 40 per cent of trade. Total trade with the US has grown, reaching US$8.9 billion in 2009, while Austria has invested heavily in Central, Eastern and South-eastern Europe (CESE) particularly in banking and industrial sectors.

Imports

Major imports are oil and oil products, chemicals, vehicles, machinery, foodstuffs and consumer durables.

Main sources: Germany (typically 40 per cent of total), Italy (7 per cent), Switzerland (6 per cent).

Exports

Major exports include machinery, vehicles and parts, paper and paperboard, chemicals (chiefly plastics and pharmaceuticals) and manufactured goods, electronic components, metal goods in ferrous and steel, textiles, foodstuffs.

Main destinations: Germany (typically 30 per cent of total), Italy (7 per cent), Switzerland (5 per cent).

Agriculture

Farming

The agricultural sector contributes 2.2 per cent to GDP and employs 6.9 per cent of the labour force. The sector is dominated by small scale farming (50 per cent of farms cover less than 10 hectares), although the trend is towards larger, more mechanised units leading to increased productivity.

About 18.2 per cent of land is crop land, 24.1 per cent permanent pasture land and 39 per cent forests and woodland. Farming is concentrated in Upper Austria, the northern part of Lower Austria, Burgenland and Styria.

Principal products are milk, beef, veal, pork, sugar beet, maize, barley, wheat and wine, but government is encouraging diversification to oilseeds, herbs, spices, hops and fast-growing timber. Quality wine, improved since a 1985 wine scandal, has become a major export product. Although output fluctuates, the country remains almost 90 per cent self-sufficient.

Fundamental reform to the Common Agricultural Policy (CAP) was introduced in 2005 in Austria. The subsidies paid on farm output, which tended to benefit large farms and encourage overproduction, were replaced by single farm payments not conditional on production. This is expected to reward farms that provide and maintain a healthy environment, food safety and animal welfare standards. The changes are also intended to encourage market conscious production and cut the cost of CAP to the EU taxpayer.

The growing of ornamental flowers and plants takes up much of Austria's horticultural land.

Fishing

The fisheries industry in Austria is based on professional lake fishing, which entails traditional breeding of trout, carp and other freshwater species. Austria promotes the EU's Common Fisheries Policy (CFP) as it benefits from the EU's structural funds for the development of aquaculture and the processing and marketing of products. Typically Austria's fishing haul is about 350 tonnes, amounting to 0.01 per cent of the EU total. Family firms run most businesses in both aquaculture and lake fishing. Despite its tradition of fish farming the sector suffers a lack of technical support.

Forestry

Forest and other wooded land occupy nearly a half of the total land area, with forest cover estimated at 3.8 million hectares (ha) in 2000. Forest cover increased an annual average of 0.20 per cent, the equivalent of 8,000ha between 1990–2000, as a result of afforestation in protected areas and natural extension onto agricultural land. Most of the forest is available for wood supply.

Forestry remains a major source of income within agriculture. Austria produces large quantities of paper and sawn wood, and is the fifth-largest exporter of sawnwood in the world with Germany, Italy and France the main export markets.

The wood processing industry places an emphasis on value-added production including skis and solid wood panel manufacturing. A large proportion of raw materials including roundwood, pulp and recovered paper are imported.

Industry and manufacturing

The industrial sector contributes 31 per cent to GDP and employs 34 per cent of the labour force.

Since 1985, the industrial workforce has fallen by more than 150,000 to just over 500,000, which can be partly explained by falling productivity growth and company restructuring during the late 1990s. Since then, the industrial sector has recovered. The steel industry in particular is flourishing. The sector's largest company, Voestalpine, has experienced record demand. Recent privatisation and deregulation of markets, along with tax and structural reform, have ensured that financially Austria is among the most successful of euro-zone nations.

Tourism

Austria has many cultural and historic attractions to offer its visitors, as well as a scenic terrain. As a mountainous country Austria also has two distinct holiday seasons offering either winter skiing or summer city or countryside and wildlife interests. Vienna, as the capital of the former Austro-Hungarian Empire, still boasts imperial institutions, including opera and chorale companies (Vienna Boys Choir), as well as the famous Spanish Riding School (of Lipizzaner stallions).

The gross value of tourism rose by 22.25 per cent between 1995–2009. Unlike many of its rival international markets, the global economic crisis did not affect Austrian tourism and visitor numbers remain consistent rising from 31.1 million in 2007 to 32.6 million in 2008, with a slight loss at 32.3 million in 2009. Travel and tourism was projected to directly contribute €12.8 billion (US$17.5 billion) to GDP in 2011 and indirectly €35.1 billion (US$49 billion).

Direct employment in the sector is around 5 per cent of total employment (196,000 jobs) and almost 13 per cent of indirect employment (523,000 jobs). Travel and tourism is Austria's biggest foreign exchange earner, with a forecast €17.3 billion (US$24.2 billion) going into the economy in 2011.

On 10 January 2011 the European Investment Bank (EIB) agreed to loan Austria €110 million (US$154 million), to support small tourist businesses. Investment in travel and tourism was estimated to be €2.8 billion (US$3.9 billion) of total investment scheduled for 2011.

Mining

The mining sector accounts for approximately 11 per cent of annual GDP and employs 1 per cent of the workforce.

There are deposits of various minerals, notably magnesite (of which Austria is the world's largest producer), iron, lead and zinc ores, salt, graphite, coal and gypsum. Commercial exploitation is restricted by the very small number of viable deposits and geological difficulties.

Hydrocarbons

Proven oil reserves are less than 70 million barrels, but with extraction relatively expensive reserves are under-exploited and are not expected to last beyond 2015. Consumption of oil amounted to 269,000 barrels per day (bpd), an increase of 0.2 per cent on 2009 figure. Natural gas reserves are modest at around 535 billion cubic metres (cum), whereas total imports of gas were 10.1 billion cum, of which 5.25 billion cum came from Russia. Although Austria has reserves of coal, it is low quality brown coal and production is not commercially viable. Imported coal amounted to two million tonnes oil equivaltent (mtoe) in 2010. Austria is poised to become an important European natural gas distribution hub with the completion of the Nabucco gas pipeline, between Turkey to Baumgarten (east Austria), in 2013, transporting gas from several central Asian producer countries.

The main oil and gas company, OMV Konzern (OMV), is the country's largest industrial conglomerate; the government is its largest shareholder with a 32 per cent stake.

Energy

Austria has 15 billion gigawatts installed capacity, of which hydropower is responsible for around 75 per cent of electricity generation. The Freudenau hydroelectric power plant on the Danube is one of the world's most advanced hydroelectric power generating facilities. Austria has committed itself to a green electricity production policy under its Eco-Power Act that requires the reduction in hydrocarbon energy production in favour of sustainable sources. Biomass, and in particular wood chip, which accounts for around 10 per cent of consumed energy, is being developed for domestic heating. Austria is also one of the leading European nations in terms of solar energy utilisation.

Financial markets

Stock exchange

Wiener Börse AG (WBAG) (Vienna Stock Exchange)

Commodity exchange

EXAA Abwicklungsstelle für Energieprodukte (EXAA) (EXAA Energy Exchange Austria)

Banking and insurance

Consolidation of the Austrian banking sector began in 1997 when Bank Austria, the largest bank, took over Creditanstalt and Erste Bank took over Giro Credit. In 1998, Bank Austria merged with Germany's HypoVereinsbank. Bank Austria officially merged with Creditanstalt in 2002. During the first half of 2005 Bank Austria Creditanstalt's (BA-CA) profits rose 59 per cent, up to €453 million.

There are around 1,000 national and local banks in Austria. Many are active in Central and Eastern Europe. Austria remains overbanked. In order to remain competitive in the new European market, significant consolidation is required.

In an effort to avoid joining the global list of non-co-operative tax havens, held by the Organisation of Economic Co-operation and Development (OECD), Austria eased its banking laws to allow the sharing of bank data that cracks down on offshore tax evasion.

Central bank

Österreichische Nationalbank (ÖeNB) (Austrian National Bank); European Central Bank (ECB).

Time

GMT plus one hour (daylight saving, late March to late October, GMT plus two hours)

Geography

Austria's land surface area is 83,855 square km. Austria is famous for its Alpine terrain, but the bulk of the country's economic activity and all of its major population centres are based on the low-lying areas around Vienna and Linz, in the north and east, and around Salzburg, on the German border.

Hemisphere

Northern

Climate

Climatic conditions vary widely across the country, with deep winter snows in the north and west, which are an essential element in the country's very important tourist economy. Seasonal variations are particularly marked: in Vienna, temperatures range from an average minus 1 degree Celsius (C) in January to 21 degrees C in July and August. Summers are often wet, with July and August recording averages of 84mm and 71mm of rainfall respectively.

Dress codes

Formality in dress is generally expected in business and for social events such as theatre and concerts. Warm clothing is essential for the winter months.

Entry requirements
Passports
Required by all, except nationals of countries which are signatories of the Schengen Accords, which includes most EU/EEA member states, who may visit on national IDs.
Visa
Visas are not required by nationals of EU and EEA countries; nationals of the US, Japan, Australia and a number of other countries do not need visas for visits of less than three months. For further exceptions contact the nearest embassy. A Schengen visa application (offered in several languages) can be downloaded from http://europa.eu/abc/travel/ see 'documents you will need'.
Currency advice/regulations
There are no restrictions on import or export of local or foreign currencies, although a permit is needed for export of over €7,000.
Customs
Personal items are duty-free. There are no duties levied on alcohol and tobacco between EU member states, providing amounts imported are for personal consumption.

Health (for visitors)
Nationals of the European Economic Area (EEA) countries and Switzerland can access reduced cost and sometimes free medical treatment using a European Health Insurance Card (EHIC) while visiting the EEA. Exceptions include nationals of the 10 countries which joined the EU in 2004 whose EHIC is not valid in Switzerland. Applications for the EHIC should be made before travelling.
Mandatory precautions
None
Advisable precautions
Vaccination for tick-borne encephalitis is recommended if visiting rural or forest regions.

Hotels
Generally of a high standard with a large selection available in most cities. Classified from five stars to one star. Rates vary according to category but are generally cheaper outside the capital.

Credit cards
Eurocard, Mastercard, Visa and, less widely, American Express and Diners Club are accepted.

Public holidays (national)
Fixed dates
1 Jan (New Year's Day), 6 Jan (Epiphany), 1 May (Labour Day), 15 Aug (Assumption Day), 26 Oct (National Day), 1 Nov (All Saints' Day), 8 Dec (Immaculate Conception), 25 Dec (Christmas Day), 26 Dec (St Stephen's Day).
Variable dates
Good Friday, Easter Monday, Ascension Day, Whit Monday, Corpus Christi.

Working hours
Banking
Mon–Wed and Fri: 0800–1500; Thu: 0800–1730.
Business
Mon–Fri: 0900–1800. Many offices do not work Friday afternoon.
Government
Mon–Fri: 0800–1230, 1300–1730. Many offices do not work Friday afternoon.
Shops
Mon–Fri: 0900–1800 (many shops close for two hours at midday); Sat: 0900–1300 or 1700. Longer opening hours exist in tourist areas.

Telecommunications
Mobile/cell phones
GSM G3 service operates in major cities only; 900 and 1800 services are available throughout the country

Electricity supply
220V AC

Social customs/useful tips
Appointments must be made in advance and punctuality is important; the usual form of address is *Herr* or *Frau*, followed by family or surname. People with an academic of professional title, eg *Doktor*, are addressed as *Herr* or *Frau Doktor*. Handshaking is universal in business and private meetings, both when arriving and leaving. Business is usually conducted in German. For restaurant meetings, dress formally, as for business meetings. Exchange pleasantries for a few minutes before getting down to business. When visiting private homes, it is usual to take flowers or confectionery for the host or hostess.

Security
There are no special problems and normal precautions apply. Vienna is possibly one of the safest cities in Europe.

Getting there
Air
National airline: Austrian Airlines
International airport/s: Vienna International (VIE), 18km south-east of city; facilities include duty-free shops, banks, bureaux de change, post office, restaurants, left luggage, conference facilities, medical facilities, tourist information, car hire.
Other airport/s: Graz (GRZ), 12km from city; Salzburg (SZG), 4km from city; Innsbruck (INN), 5km from city; Klagenfurt (KLU), 4km from city; Linz (LNZ), 15km from city.
Airport tax: None
Surface
Road: There are good road links with all surrounding countries. Motorists should check advisability of routes, especially in winter, with ÖAMTC or ARBÖ (Austrian automobile clubs).
Rail: Austria participates in European rail pass schemes.
Water: Ships provide regular passenger services and cruises on the Danube, starting at Passau or Regensburg in Germany, to Vienna. There are also links with the Rhine and Main rivers and the Black Sea.

Getting about
National transport
Air: Austrian Arrows operate regular flights between main cities.
Road: There is a good road network. A toll must be paid to travel on motorways and highways – stickers (*vignettes*) to display on windscreens can be purchased from petrol stations, tobacconists and offices of Austrian automobile associations. There are additional charges for certain major routes.
Buses: Services are provided by federal and local authorities, in addition to private companies. There are more than 1,800 services in operation.
Rail: State-owned network of almost 6,000km, most of which is electrified. Also about 20 private railways covering a total 660km. There are frequent intercity services from Vienna to Salzburg, Innsbruck, Graz and Klagenfurt.
Water: There is a passenger ferry service between Vienna and the Black Sea and on upper Danube in mid-May to mid-September. Austrian Federal Railways operate passenger services on all the larger lakes.
City transport
Taxis: Widely available from stands or via radio/telephone services. The taxi journey time to the city centre from the airport is 25–30 minutes. Fares are metered but expensive, and in some areas zone charges or set charges for standard trips apply; a 10 per cent tip is usual.
Buses, trams & metro: Vienna has a very efficient, integrated system which avoids the crowded city traffic. Public transport operates between 0500 and 2400 and tickets, for all services, can be bought for 24 hour/3 day and set periods. An airport bus operates 24 hours every 20 minutes, and takes approximately 30 minutes to get to the city centre.
Trains: The OBB train service S7 operates between 0511—2216 every hour, and takes 25 minutes from the airport to the city centre.
Car hire
Self-drive and chauffeur-driven services are available at railway stations, airports and in major cities. Rates per day vary with size of car, plus additional charge

per kilometre. A 'green card' (third party motor insurance) is compulsory. The speed limit is 100kph on most roads and 130kph on motorways, in built-up areas it is 50kph, unless otherwise stipulated.
EU issued driving licences are required, permitting the holders to drive in Austria for one year. Minimum driving age is 18.

BUSINESS DIRECTORY

Telephone area codes

The international direct dialling code (IDD) for Austria is +43, followed by area code and subscriber's number:

Baden bei Wein	2252	St Pölten	2742
Gmunden	7612	Salzburg	662
Graz	316	Steyr	7252
Innsbruck	512	Vienna	1
Kitzbühel	5356	Villach	4242
Klagenfurt	463	Wels	7242
Krems an der Donau	2732	Wien	2252
Linz	732	Wiener Neustadt	2622

Chambers of Commerce

American Chamber of Commerce in Austria, 35 Porzellangasse, A-1090 Vienna (tel: 319-5751; fax: 319-5151; e-mail: office@amcham.or.at).

Austrian Economic Chamber, 63 Wiedner Hauptstrasse, A-1045 Vienna (tel/fax: 059-0900; e-mail: wkoe@wko.at).

Burgenland Economic Chamber, 1 Robert-Graf-Platz, A-7000 Eisenstadt (tel/fax: 059-0907; e-mail: wkgbld@wkbgld.at).

Lower Austria Economic Chamber, 10 Herrengasse, A-1014 Vienna (tel/fax: 015-3466; e-mail: wknoe@wknoe.at).

Salzburg Economic Chamber, 1 Julius-Raab-Platz, A-5027 (tel/fax: 0662-8888; e-mail: wirtschaftskammer@sbg.wk.or.at).

Tirol Economic Chamber, 14 Meinhardstrasse, A-6020 Innsbruck (te/fax: 059-0905; e-mail: office@wktirol.at).

Upper Austria Economic Chamber, 3 Hessenplatz, A-4010 Linz (tel/fax: 059-0909; e-mail: wirtschaftskammer@wkooe.at).

Vienna Economic Chamber, 8 Stubenring, A-1010 Vienna (tel/fax: 514-50; e-mail: postbox@wkw.at).

Vorarlberg Economic Chamber, 9 Wichnergasse, A-6800 Feldkirch (te/fax: 0552-2305; e-mail: praesidium@wkv.at).

Banking

Bank Austria Creditanstalt AG, Am Hof 2, A-1010 Vienna (tel: 531-240; fax: 5312-4155).

Bank für Arbeit und Wirtshaft AG (BAWAG), Seitzergasse 2 - 4, A-1010 Vienna (tel: 534-530; fax: 5345-32930).

Erste Bank, Graben 21, A1010 Vienna (tel: 531-000; fax: 5310-0625); also at Schubertring 5-7, A-1010 Vienna (tel: 711-940; fax: 713-7032).

Österreichische Postsparkasse, Georg Coch-Platz 2, A1020 Vienna (tel: 514-000; fax: 5140-01700).

Österreichische Volksbanken AG, Peregringasse 3, A-1090 Vienna (tel: 313-400; fax: 3134-03683).

Raiffeisen Zentralbank Österreich AG, Am Stadtpark 9, A-1030 Vienna (tel: 717-070).

Central bank

Österreichische Nationalbank, Otto Wagner-Platz 3, PO Box 61, A-1011 Vienna (tel: 404-20-2398; fax: 404-20-666; e-mail: oenb.info@oenb.co.at).

European Central Bank (ECB), Kaiserstrasse 29, D-60311 Frankfurt am Main, Germany (tel: (+49-69) 13-440; fax: (+49-69) 1344-6000; e-mail: info@ecb.int).

Stock exchange

Wiener Börse AG (WBAG) (Vienna Stock Exchange) www.wienerborse.at

Commodity exchange

EXAA Abwicklungsstelle für Energieprodukte (EXAA) (EXAA Energy Exchange Austria) www.exaa.at

Travel information

ARBÖ (Auto-, Motor- und Radfahrerbund Österreichs), A-1150 Vienna, Mariahilfer Strasse 180 (tel: 891-217; fax: 891-236).

Austrian Airlines (Österreichische Luftverkehrs), PO Box 50, Fontanastrasse 1, Vienna A-1010 (tel: 683-5110; fax: 685-505).

ÖAMTC (Österreichischer Automobil-Motorrad und Touring Club), A-1010 Vienna, Schubertring 1-3 (tel: 711-990).

National tourist organisation offices

Österreich Werbung (Austrian National Tourist Office), 1 Margarethenstrasse, 1040 Vienna, (tel: 587-2000; fax: 588-6620; www.austria.info).

Ministries

Federal Chancellor's Office, Ballhausplatz 2, 1014 Vienna (tel: 531-150; fax: 535-0338).

Federal Ministry of Agriculture & Forestry, Environment and Water Resources, Stubenring 1, 1010 Vienna (tel: 711-000; fax: 715-9651).

Federal Ministry of Defence, Dampfschiffstr. 2, 1033 Vienna (tel: 515-950; fax: 515-9521).

Federal Ministry of Economic Affairs and Labour, Stubenring 1, 1010 Vienna (tel: 711-000; fax: 713-7995).

Federal Ministry of Education, Science and Culture, Minoritenplatz 5, 1014 Vienna (tel: 531-200; fax: 533-7797).

Federal Ministry of Finance, Himmelpfortgasse 8, 1015 Vienna (tel: 514-330; fax: 512-7869).

Federal Ministry of Foreign Affairs, Ballhausplatz 2, 1014 Vienna (tel: 531-150; fax: 533-2547).

Federal Ministry of the Interior, Herrengasse 7, 1010 Vienna (tel: 531-260; 531-263910).

Federal Ministry of Justice, Museumstrasse 7, 1070 Vienna (tel: 521-520; fax: 521-52727).

Federal Ministry of Public Affairs and Sport, Minoritenplatz 3, 1014 Vienna (tel: 531-150).

Federal Ministry of Social Security and Generations, Stubenring 1, 1010 Vienna (tel: 711-000; fax: 713-9311).

Federal Ministry of Transport, Innovation and Technology, Radetskystrasse 2, 1030 Vienna (tel: 711-620).

Other useful addresses

Austrian Business Agency, Opernring 3, A-1010 Vienna (tel: 202-588-5820; fax: 202-586-8659; e-mail: austrian.business@telecom.at; internet site: http://www.aba.qv.at).

Austria Presse-Agentur (APA) (Co-operative Agency of the Austrian Newspapers and Broadcasting Co), A-1199 Vienna, Gunoldstrasse 14 (tel: 36-050).

Austrian Telecommunications Regulatory Authority, Ministry of Science and Transport, Sektion IV, Kelsenstrasse 7, Vienna A-1030 (tel: 79731-4100; fax: 79731-4109; e-mail: Christian.Singer@bmv.gv.at).

Österreichisches Statistisches Zentralamt (Central Statistical Office), Hintere Zollamtstrasse 2b, A-1030 Vienna (tel: 711-280; fax: 7112-87728).

Post und Telekom Austria AG, Postgasse 8, 1010 Vienna (tel: 515-510; fax: 512-8414).

Vereinigung Österreichischer Industrieller (Association of Austrian Industrialists), A-1030 Vienna, Schwarzenbergplatz 4 (tel: 711-350).

News agencies:

APA (Austria Presse Agentur): www.apa.at

Presstext Austria (in German): www.pressetext.at

Internet sites

Statistics Austria: www.statistik.at/index_englisch.shtml

Azerbaijan

KEY FACTS

Official name: Azarbaijchan Respublikasy (Republic of Azerbaijan)

Head of State: President Ilham Aliyev (YAP) (from 2003; re-elected Oct 2008)

Head of government: Prime Minister Artur Rasizade (YAP) (from 2003; re-appointed Oct 2008)

Ruling party: Yeni Azerbaycan Partiyasi (YAP) (Yeni Azerbaijan Party) (from 2005; re-elected 7 Nov 2010)

Area: 86,600 square km

Population: 9.19 million (2010)*

Capital: Baku

Official language: Azeri (Turkic)

Currency: new manat (M) = 100 gopik (new currency introduced 1 Jan 2006)

Exchange rate: M0.79 per US$ (Oct 2011)

GDP per capita: US$4,807 (2009)

GDP real growth: 2.70% (2010)*

GDP: US$43.11 billion (2009)

Labour force: 5.87 million (2010)

Unemployment: 0.50% (official rate, 2009)

Inflation: 10.60% (2008)

Oil production: 1.04 million bpd (2010)

Balance of trade: US$19.73 billion (2010)

* estimated figure

March 2011 saw hundreds of pro-democracy demonstrators take to the streets of Baku, inspired by the 'Arab Spring' to give voice to their opposition to the rule of the Azerbaijani dictator Ilham Aliyev. As was the case with other totalitarian dictatorships, the Aliyev regime was quick to arrest protesters, meting out harsh penalties – one political activist was sentenced to two years in jail for trying to organise protests using Facebook.

Running scared?

Only two days before Azerbaijan had won the largely discredited Eurovision song contest with a song called, appropriately enough, *Running Scared.* Winning the contest was something of a public relations coup for Azerbaijanas victory meant that Baku would host the 2012 song contest. It was rumoured that the 2012 songfest would be hosted by the president's daughter, Leyla Aliyeva. In the manner of medieval oligarchs, the Aliyev clan has dominated Azeri politics since 1969. To all intents and purposes, the Aliyevs behave in the manner of a royal family. In 2005 the 'elections' were very much a stage managed affair, hardly worthy of the name. Both the Organisation for Security and Co-operation in Europe (OSCE) and the Council of Europe declared that the elections 'did not meet international standards despite some improvements' and opposition parties rejected the results out of hand. Although the ruling Yeni Azerbaycan Partiyasi (New Azerbaijan Party) lost its legislative majority, the result revealed that the main opposition parties had won only ten seats. The election of scores of pro-government independent MPs ensured that YAP would not be denied a majority on most issues. Illuminatingly, both President Aliyev's wife and uncle won seats in parliament, the thin end of a family wedge. The Aliyevs had, even under Soviet rule, managed to dominate Azeri politics. The election victories of sundry family members did little to dispel the notion that the Aliyev clan maintained their controlling interest in Azeri affairs; quite the contrary.

Macro-prosperity

Since winning independence from the USSR, Azerbaijan has conducted a geo-political balancing act, playing the US against Russia. Warned by Georgia's short war with Russia, the Baku government saw fit to recalibrate its international alignments. As the Putin regime has begun to flex its muscles, so Baku has needed to exercise more care in its relations with Russia. What is clear is that Azerbaijan will hold off seeking integration with NATO or the European Union. The Russian stance has been that the US and the EU in the shape of their oil giants have been happy to exploit Azerbaijani natural resources, but have given little in return – except, of course, money.

Oil dependent

Azerbaijan owes its macro-economic prosperity almost entirely to hydrocarbons. Although growth in oil output slowed in 2010, higher oil prices led to a large balance of payments surplus, while a revival in the non-oil economy, driven by public expenditure, led to solid but slower overall growth. Growth and the balance of payments were both predicted to remain strong in 2011 and 2012. Inflation was moderate but local and external factors will stoke price pressures in 2011. Supporting growth in the non-oil sector and reducing dependence on oil revenue represent a significant long-term challenge.

According to the Asian Development Bank (ADB), annual gross domestic product (GDP) growth at 5.0 per cent in 2010 was markedly lower than the very high rates of the previous few years when large investments rapidly expanded Azerbaijan's oil and gas resources. Growth in the hydrocarbon economy is estimated to have slowed to 1.8 per cent. The non-oil economy performed well, growing by 7.9 per cent, as it recovered from the headwinds of the global recession. With oil and gas production growth levelling off (oil production in 2010 was 377.4 million barrels), the outlook is for moderate overall growth based largely on non-oil activity. Robust growth in the non-oil economy in 2010 was driven largely by public investment, mainly in infrastructure projects that led to a 20.3 per cent expansion in construction activity. This was a marked recovery from the 8.3 per cent contraction in investment in 2009, when much lower oil prices and global crisis-related uncertainty reined in public and private investment. Non-oil manufacturing is estimated to have grown by about 6.8 per cent, after 2009's 12.6 per cent contraction. Several public and private industrial plants started operations and The State Oil Company of Azerbaijan Republic (SOCAR), the state-owned oil company, expanded into non-oil manufacturing.

Services growth was robust at 7.2 per cent, driven by the strong expansion in the non-oil economy as well as gains in gas transport services and new technologies in mobile communications and Internet access.

Agriculture performed poorly, contracting by 2.2 per cent in 2010 after 3.5 per cent growth in 2009. This reflected a 33 per cent drop in grain production that was caused by flooding, a decline in the area cultivated, and falling yields. Production of other agricultural products such as cotton and tobacco picked up.

The ADB noted that public investment, mainly in the non-oil sector, rose to 13 per cent of GDP, accounting for nearly three-quarters of overall domestic investment. Although private investment fell slightly as a share of total investment, it was well above its low of 2008. Foreign direct investment (FDI) in oil has been declining since 2006 with the completion of large investment projects as well as SOCAR's self-financing of new projects. Inflows into manufacturing, transport, and communications went up.

Inflation crept up steadily during the year, to 5.7 per cent in December 2010 year-on-year from 1.5 per cent in December 2009. The upturn was largely driven by rising prices of basic food items, including wheat, reflecting both higher import prices and the poor grain harvest. Non-food prices increased moderately over the year. Demand factors, such as a pay hike for public servants and a robust expansion in credit to the private sector, appear to have put some additional pressure on these supply-side factors. The State Oil Fund of Azerbaijan (SOFAZ), set up to save a part of the nation's hydrocarbon earnings, is channelling some of its revenue to the budget for financing public investment projects. Despite large transfers of this nature in 2010, SOFAZ assets surged by 52.8 per cent to US$22.8 billion at year-end, buoyed by higher oil prices.

Budget expenditure rose by 11.3 per cent in 2010, though as a share of GDP it moderated by about one percentage point to 28.3 per cent. Besides the salary hike, 2010 saw markedly higher social and defence outlays; public investment came in at 13 per cent of GDP. Tax collection increased by only 4.4 per cent in 2010, as customs revenue contracted because of lower imports of machinery and equipment. Total budget revenue declined by 2 percentage points to 27.4 per cent of GDP. The large gap between budget expenditure and revenue was again bridged by substantial SOFAZ transfers, keeping the overall budget deficit small, at 0.9 per cent of GDP.

Without the SOFAZ transfers the deficit would have been 15.1 per cent of GDP; these transfers have been rising in absolute terms and relative to GDP in recent years. They now make up over one-half of the government resources that finance budget expenditure. To arrest this trend,

KEY INDICATORS — Azerbaijan

	Unit	2006	2007	2008	2009	2010
Population	m	8.48	*8.55	*8.90	*8.97	*9.19
Gross domestic product (GDP)	US$bn	20.95	31.32	46.38	43.11	–
GDP per capita	US$	2,469	3,663	5,213	*4,807	–
GDP real growth	%	30.6	23.3	10.8	9.3	*2.7
Inflation	%	8.4	16.6	20.8	1.5	–
Industrial output	% change	–	32.8	10.0	2.5	–
Agricultural output	% change	–	4.0	6.1	6.0	–
Oil output	'000 bpd	654.0	868.0	914.0	1,033.0	1,037.0
Natural gas output	bn cum	6.3	10.3	14.7	14.8	15.1
Exports (fob) (goods)	US$m	7,649.0	21,269.3	30,586.3	21,096.8	26,476.0
Imports (fob) (goods)	US$m	5,269.3	6,045.0	7,574.7	6,513.9	6,745.6
Balance of trade	US$m	7,745.3	15,224.3	23,011.7	14,582.9	19,730.4
Current account	US$m	3,708.0	9,018.9	16,454.0	10,177.8	15,039.6
Total reserves minus gold	US$m	2,500.4	4,273.1	6,467.2	5,363.8	6,409.0
Foreign exchange	US$m	2,484.9	4,262.9	6,465.5	5,125.7	6,172.2
Exchange rate	per US$	87.00	0.85	0.82	0.80	0.80

* estimated figure

the government would need to increase revenue from taxes and other charges, though a substantial move would stymie policies that seek strong expansion in non-oil economic activity.

The Central Bank of Azerbaijan had adopted an expansionary monetary policy in 2009, aiming to counter the impact of the fall in growth from lower oil prices and an uncertain economic outlook. It set the refinancing rate at 2.0 per cent and the reserve requirement at 0.5 per cent. The Bank raised the refinancing rate to 3.0 per cent in November 2010 and again to 5 per cent in March 2011, responding to the strengthening in the non-oil economy and inflation pressures. It continues, however, to provide long-term loans and additional special financing support to private companies and banks at its discretion.

Evidence of recovery is seen in a 9.7 per cent rise in credit to the private sector and a 24 per cent expansion in the broad money supply, which in part reflected a rebound in net foreign assets as the overall balance returned to a large surplus. A sign of financial deepening and greater confidence in the banking system was that the ratio of broad money to GDP rose from 23.8 per cent in 2009 to 25.3 per cent in 2010.

On the external front, the marked global increase in oil prices led to an estimated 24 per cent gain in exports (oil and gas account for about 95 per cent of goods exports). Non-oil exports saw a small gain despite agriculture's contraction. Imports witnessed virtually no upturn despite the revival in non-oil growth. Similarly, net services and income payments were little changed from a year earlier while workers' remittances, a marginal item in the balance of payments but an important source of support for rural households, tumbled. Resting mainly on strength in oil pricing, the current account surplus was boosted to US$16.5 billion in 2010, about 31.9 per cent of GDP, from US$10.2 billion a year earlier. Gross international reserves jumped by nearly 20 per cent to US$6.4 billion at end-2010. With the surge in SOFAZ assets, total foreign assets amounted to about 56 per cent of GDP. Public external debt is relatively small at US$3.7 billion, about 9 per cent of GDP.

It all depends on oil

As oil prices rose in 2011 and are projected to remain high in 2012, the main challenge for the government will be to maintain macro-economic stability. Growth in oil revenue will allow a continued rise in social expenditure and investment in infrastructure that should spur private activity and improve the investment climate. The hydrocarbon economy is expected to grow steadily at about 3–4 per cent in the forecast period as oil and gas development sets the stage for faster expansion in later years. Robust growth of the non-oil economy is expected to stay driven by public sector investment. The government has planned investment spending of US$4.2 billion in 2011, which will drive a rapid expansion in construction with positive knock-on effects on the rest of the economy.

Higher oil export revenue should outweigh the import growth arising from strengthening investment and the rising income-related consumer spending. The current account surplus is expected to be 27.8 per cent of GDP in 2011 and 25.0 per cent in 2012, as import demand rises in response to growth of incomes and appreciation of the manat, and as growth in oil revenue slows.

The US-based Energy Information Administration (EIA) noted that while Azerbaijan's importance as a supplier of natural gas and oil is likely to increase, continued disputes with Armenia over the Nagorno-Karabakh region, as well as issues with Azerbaijan's access to the Nakhchivan enclave continue to provide a degree of political risk. Furthermore, the conflicting claims over the maritime and seabed boundaries of the Caspian Sea between Azerbaijan and Iran also provide continued uncertainty, with Iran insisting on an even one-fifth allocation between the five littoral countries (Turkmenistan, Uzbekistan, Iran, Azerbaijan and Russia) and challenging Azerbaijan's hydrocarbon exploration in disputed waters. Bilateral talks also continue with Turkmenistan on dividing the seabed and contested oilfields in the middle of the Caspian, while discussions with Georgia continue on the alignment of their boundary at certain crossing areas.

Azerbaijan's proven crude oil reserves were estimated at 7 billion barrels at the end of 2011, according to the June 2011 issue of the BP Statistical Review of World Energy (BP11). Azerbaijan's largest hydrocarbon basins are located offshore in the Caspian Sea, particularly the Azeri Chirag Guneshli (ACG) fields, which accounted for about 80 per cent of Azerbaijan's total oil output in 2009. SOCAR is Azerbaijan's state-owned oil and natural gas company and is responsible for producing oil and natural gas in Azerbaijan, operating the country's two refineries, running the country's pipeline system, and managing the country's oil and natural gas imports and exports. Although the Ministry of Industry and Energy handles exports as well as exploration and production agreements with foreign companies, SOCAR is party to all of the international consortia developing oil and gas projects in Azerbaijan. On its own, SOCAR produces less than 20 per cent of Azerbaijan's total output, with the rest (about 80 per cent) being produced by the Azerbaijan International Operating Company (AIOC).

AIOC is a consortium of 10 petroleum companies that have signed extraction contracts with Azerbaijan. It is led by British Petroleum (BP), but also includes Chevron, Statoil, Turkiye Petrolleri (TPAO), ExxonMobil, and SOCAR. AIOC has made significant direct investments in the development of the ACG fields, as well as the construction of the Baku-Tbilisi-Ceyhan (BTC) pipeline. BP is the largest foreign investor and has been involved in Azerbaijan since 1992.

Quadrupled production

Oil production in Azerbaijan increased from 283,000 barrels per day (bpd) in 1999 to more than one million bpd in 2010. Azerbaijan's production is expected to continue rising in 2011. The output likely was dampened in 2009 as a result of the prolonged partial shut-in at the offshore ACG project early in the year, which was necessitated by a gas leak.

The ACG fields are Azerbaijan's largest, located 62 miles east of Baku in the Caspian Sea. Total peak production was expected to reach 1.1 million bpd in 2010. The ACG fields have an estimated 9 billion barrels of reserves and are operated by BP on behalf of AIOC.

There were a number of projects in Azerbaijan's offshore that seemed promising, but were deemed disappointing after they turned out to either be dry holes or the oil discovered was deemed non-commercial, resulting in closure of several projects. In addition to the lack of new producing fields, political complications related to boundary disputes further dampened exploration. However, offshore exploration could receive renewed interest and additional foreign investment if the littoral states reach an agreement on legal status and borders in the Caspian Sea. Azerbaijan also has some onshore oil production, although it is modest compared to the offshore. There were nine onshore production sharing agreements in 2009 at various fields, accounting for only a fraction of total oil production.

Oil exports

Azerbaijan exported an estimated 876,000bpd in 2009, according to EIA, increasing more than 16 per cent compared with 2008 and nearly tripling since 2005. Most of Azerbaijan's oil is exported via pipeline, but small amounts are shipped by truck and railway. The majority of oil exports pass through the BTC pipeline system, which runs 1,110 miles from the ACG fields in the Caspian Sea, via Georgia, to the Mediterranean port of Ceyhan, in Turkey. From there the oil is shipped by tanker mainly to European markets. The BP-operated pipeline began exporting in July 2006 and has the capacity of 1.2 million bpd. The BTC pipeline is also used to export Kazakh oil, which travels by tanker across the Caspian to the Sangachal Terminal, near Baku.

The Baku-Novorossiysk pipeline is 830 miles long and has a capacity of 100,000bpd. The pipeline runs from the Sangachal Terminal to Novorossiysk, Russia on the Black Sea. SOCAR operates the Azeri section and Transneft operates the Russian section, which has at times complicated the operation of the pipeline as there is an ongoing dispute between SOCAR and Transneft concerning transportation tariffs on the pipeline. There are proposals to increase the capacity on the pipeline to between 180,000 and 300,000bpd, a key transportation addition as production grows in the ACG oil fields and throughput from Kazakhstan increases in the future.

The Baku-Supsa pipeline has an estimated capacity of 145,000bpd and runs 520 miles from Baku to Supsa, Georgia, on the Black Sea. It is operated by BP and owned by AIOC members. The pipeline is used by ExxonMobil Company to export its share of oil from the ACG fields because ExxonMobil, although it is a participant in AIOC, is not a participant in the BTC pipeline. In November 2010, Azerbaijan and Kazakhstan reached a preliminary agreement on maritime transport, which covers transport of Kazakh oil via the Caspian Sea and Azerbaijan through the BTC pipeline. With the continuing growth in Kazakh oil production and the expected boost in total Kazakh oil output with the commencement of the giant offshore Kashagan field (expected in 2012), the transportation issue between Azerbaijan and Kazakhstan will continue to gain importance. Azerbaijan has a crude oil refining capacity of 399,000bpd as of January 2010, according to the *Oil & Gas Journal* (OGJ). Azeri crude oil is refined domestically at two refineries: the Baku refinery, with a capacity of 239,000bpd, and the New Baku refinery, with a capacity of 160,000bpd. Domestic consumption of oil approximated 100,000bpd in 2009, falling by about 5,000bpd compared with a year earlier.

Natural gas

Also according to the BP2011, Azerbaijan had proven natural gas reserves of roughly 1.3 trillion cubic metres (tcm) as of the end of 2010. In 2010, Azerbaijan produced 15.1 billion cubic metres of natural gas and consumed 6.6 billion cubic metres. Almost all of Azerbaijan's natural gas is produced from offshore fields. The country's leading natural gas field is the Shah Deniz natural gas and condensate field, which started producing in 2006. The Guneshli field, part of the ACG oil and gas fields system, provides associated gas to the Azerigaz (a SOCAR subsidiary) system for domestic use via an undersea gas pipeline to Sangachal Terminal at Baku. The Sangachal Terminal, located south of Baku, is one of the world's largest integrated oil and gas processing terminals. It receives, stores, and processes both crude oil and natural gas from the ACG fields and from Shah Deniz, then ships these hydrocarbons through the BTC and the South Caucasus Pipeline (SCP) pipelines for export. Azerbaijan's natural gas production increases in the future are expected to come from the continuing development of the Shah Deniz field, which is the largest natural gas discovery since 1978. Shah Deniz is located offshore in the Caspian Sea, approximately 60 miles south-east of Baku.

A number of West European utilities are seeking to secure supplies for the Nabucco pipeline, which, if completed, will transport Caspian natural gas to Europe via Turkey. Azerbaijan's Phase 2 of the Shah Deniz project is a key supply source for the pipeline. In addition, the Italy-Turkey-Greece Pipeline (ITGI) as well as the Trans-Adriatic Pipeline (TAP) are expected to carry Shah Deniz gas to Europe.

Azerigaz is responsible for natural gas processing, transport, distribution and storage, mainly in the domestic market. Azneft, another SOCAR subsidiary, is responsible for exploration, development and production from the older onshore and offshore natural gas fields owned directly by SOCAR. AIOC is the largest foreign joint venture in association with SOCAR, and is involved in the development of the ACG oil and gas fields and the Shah Deniz gas field. Statoil and BP are the operators of the Shah Deniz gas field, and are the largest shareholders in the Shah Deniz consortium, each holding 25.5 per cent. Other shareholders include Total, LUKoil (Russia), SOCAR, Oil Industries' Engineering and Construction (OIEC) of Iran, each at 10 per cent, while Turkish Petroleum (TPAO) holds 9 per cent.

Natural gas exports

Azerbaijan became a net exporter of natural gas in 2007 with the start-up of the Shah Deniz natural gas field; in prior years it had been importing natural gas from Russia. In 2009, Azerbaijan exported an estimated 209bcf, mainly shipping it via the SCP. However, volumes of natural gas are also exported to Russia via the Gazi-Magomed-Mozdok pipeline and a small volume of natural gas is shipped to Iran via the Baku-Astara pipeline. Due to the tensions between Azerbaijan and Armenia, Azerbaijan had, in late 2006, began a swap deal with Iran that provides natural gas to Azerbaijan's geographically separate Nakhchivan enclave. Azerbaijan ships natural gas into Iran via the Baku-Astara Pipeline and Iran then delivers the gas via a new 30-mile pipeline into the enclave. Iran receives a 15 per cent commission on transit fees. In early 2010, Iran and Azerbaijan signed an additional gas supply deal for increased volumes of gas from Azerbaijan to be delivered to Iran for its own consumption, and volumes are likely to increase with the renovation of the pipeline and upgrades to the Astara gas compressor. In late November 2010, Azerbaijan and Iran signed a memorandum of co-operation on natural gas supplies and electricity swaps, which likely will expand energy trade between the two countries.

The main conduit for Azerbaijan's natural gas exports is the 555-mile SCP, also known as the Baku-Tbilisi-Erzurum pipeline (BTE), which runs parallel to the BTC oil pipeline for 429 miles, most of its route, before landing in Erzurum, Turkey. The pipeline began exporting in 2007, and has the capacity to transport about 770bcf of natural gas, according to IHS Global Insight. The Shah Deniz consortium owns and operates the pipeline.

Risk assessment

Economy	Good
Politics	Poor
Regional stability	Poor

COUNTRY PROFILE

Historical profile

Azerbaijan has at various times been part of the Persian, Muslim Arab, Turkish Seljuk, Mongol, Ottoman and Russian

empires. The modern Republic was formed from territory ceded to Russia by Iran following the second of the two Russian-Persian wars.
1848 The world's first oil well was drilled, just south of Baku.
1916 Azerbaijan joined an alliance with Armenia and Georgia.
1918–20 Azerbaijan existed as an independent republic until 1920, when it became part of the Soviet Union.
1936 The Azerbaijan Soviet Socialist Republic assumed the status of a full Soviet member.
1988–94 War broke out, and continued intermittently with Nagorno-Karabakh, an ethnic Armenian enclave that lies wholly inside Azerbaijan territory, when Armenians in the enclave voted to break away from Azerbaijan and join neighbouring Armenia. With the assistance of Armenian troops, separatists in Nagorno-Karabakh managed to expel Azeri forces by 1994 and have since maintained *de facto* independence from Azerbaijan. The self-proclaimed breakaway Nagorno-Karabakh Republic (Artsakh in Armenian) occupies approximately 4,400 square km, to which the separatists have added through military conquest some 7,700 square km of Azerbaijan proper. The six-year war threw Azerbaijan into political turmoil.
1989 Azerbaijan became the first Soviet Republic outside the Baltic to declare its national sovereignty.
1991 Formal independence was declared, with Ayaz Mutalibov, head of the Communist Party, as president.
1992 Violent demonstrations, over repeated failures in the Nagorno-Karabakh war, forced the Mutalibov to flee to Moscow. In presidential elections Abulfaz Elchibey leader of the Yeni Azerbaycan Partiyasi (YAP) (New Azerbaijan Party) came to power, declaring he would build a secular democratic system with close links to Turkey. Power was transferred from the Supreme Soviet council to a 50-person Milli Majlis.
1993 President Elchibey was forced to quit following an ultimatum issued by Colonel Suret Huseinov (Azeri commander in Nagorno-Karabakh). Elchibey invited his rival, Heidar Aliyev, a veteran politician, to become chairman of the parliament and then acting president. Suret Huseinov became prime minister. Aliyev won 98.8 per cent of the vote in presidential elections.
1994 A cease-fire agreement came into force between Azerbaijan and Armenia over Nagorno-Karabakh. The dispute had caused an estimated 35,000 deaths and created 850,000 internally displaced persons (IDPs), mainly Azeris, between 1988–94. In a guardian *coup d'état* President Aliyev removed Huseinov
1995 A new constitution was adopted.
1996 In National Assembly elections the Aliyev-backed YAP won a large majority. Artur Rasizade became prime minister.
1998 Opposition parties boycotted the presidential elections; Aliyev was returned to power.
2000 The ruling YAP won the general election, which was denounced as unfair by foreign observers, and leaders of five major opposition parties initiated a mass protest, calling for new elections.
2001 The government ordered that the local Azeri language should be written with a Latin, rather than Cyrillic, alphabet. Azerbaijan became a full member of the Council of Europe.
2002 US sanctions, imposed in 1992 following the outbreak of war with Armenia over the Nagorno-Karabakh enclave, were lifted after Azerbaijan agreed to participate in the US-led war on terrorism. Arkady Gukasyan was re-elected president of Nagorno-Karabakh. A referendum on amendments to the Azeri constitution was said to have received strong support from voters, but critics cited voting irregularities.
2003 President Aliyev collapsed and was taken to Turkey for hospital treatment. His son, Ilham Aliyev, was elected prime minister so that he could stand in presidential elections; he won a landslide victory. Artur Rasizade resumed his post as prime minister. Former president Heidar Aliyev died on 12 December.
2005 The Baku-Tbilisi-Ceyhan (BTC) oil pipeline was opened. The Artsakhi Demokratakan Kusaktsutyun (ADK) (Democratic Party of Artsakh) won parliamentary elections in Nagorno-Karabakh. In parliamentary elections in Azerbaijan, the ruling YAP and its allies won more than half the available 125 seats. Turnout was around 47 per cent. The Organisation for Security and Co-operation in Europe (OSCE) and Council of Europe observers declared that the election fell short of democratic norms. Around 15,000 people responded to opposition calls for election results to be annulled by marching in Baku. A new natural gas pipeline between Iran and Azerbaijan was inaugurated.
2006 A new manat was introduced, valued at one manat per 5,000 old manat. New parliamentary elections were held in ten constituencies, where ballots in the 2005 elections had been annulled. Azerbaijan, together with Armenia and Georgia, signed a European Neighbourhood Policy co-operation agreement with the EU.
2007 Bako Sahakian replaced Arkadiy Gukasian as president of Nagorno-Karabakh.
2008 Fierce fighting in Nagorno-Karabakh broke out; Azerbaijan accused Armenia of inciting the fighting. In presidential elections, incumbent Ilham Aliyev won a second term in office with about 89 per cent of the vote; turnout was around 76 per cent. The main opposition party, led by Isa Gambar, boycotted the election. International observers said the elections were neither free nor fair. Artur Rasizade remained in post as prime minister.
2009 A constitutional referendum to lift the two-term limit on the presidency was passed by 92 per cent of the vote.
2010 In parliamentary elections held on 23 May in Nagorno-Karabakh, Free Motherland won 46.6 per cent (14 seats out of 33), Democratic Party of Artsakh 28.6 per cent (six), Armenian Revolutionary Federation 20.3 per cent (six); turnout was 67.8 per cent. On 3 September Presidents Aliyev and Medvedev (Russia) signed a treaty to agree the demarcation of the border between the two countries. Approximately 2,500 candidates, in five political parties, registered to contest the parliamentary elections held on 7 November; however the electoral commission allowed only 690 candidates to stand. The ruling YAP won 74 seats (out of 125); 19 women in total were elected. Observers of the European Council and the US considered the elections as peaceful and participatory; however they also noted that limitations on the media and freedom of assembly weakened political discussion.
2011 On 17 April a number of protesters were arrested in Baku as they attempted to rally against President Aliyev's hard-line rule. On 25 June, under the auspices of Russian President Medvedev, the presidents of Azerbaijan and Armenia discussed a settlement agreement over the disputed territory of Nagorno-Karabakh. Despite encouragement from world leaders they failed to sign it, risking future conflict and leaving some 600,000 IDPs without hope of returning to their homes with security.

Political structure

Constitution

A constitution was adopted by national referendum in November 1995, and was amended following a referendum in 2002, which made changes to the parliamentary system. The changes included replacing proportional representation in the National Assembly with the majority system (first-past-the-post), and changing the election of the president from a two-thirds to a 50 per cent majority of the votes cast. On 18 March 2009, a constitutional referendum to lift the two-term limit on the presidency was passed by 92 per cent of the vote.
The Republic of Azerbaijan is officially a democratic, secular and unitary state, with

power separated among three branches: executive, legislative and judicial.
Administratively, the country is divided into 65 districts, the autonomous republic of Nakhichevan (which is separated from the main part of the country by southern Armenia), and the region of Nagorno-Karabakh (which has been occupied by Armenian forces since 1992).
Under the constitution, the autonomous republic of Nakhichevan is an autonomous state within the Republic of Azerbaijan. Executive power in Nakhichevan is implemented by the Cabinet of Ministers of Nakhichevan, which is appointed by the Nakhichevan prime minister on approval of the Milli Mejlis (National Assembly). However, presidential decrees have authority in Nakhichevan.

Independence date

18 October 1991

Form of state

Presidential republic, where despite democratic structures, there is no fair chance for the opposition.

The executive

The president is head of state. The president must be over 35-years-old and have been living permanently in the territory of Azerbaijan for over 10 years, having no previous convictions.
The president appoints a prime minister and Council of Ministers.
The president is also the supreme commander-in-chief of the armed forces and has powers to declare martial law and states of emergency.
Presidential elections are held every five years. The president is elected by a majority of half of all votes cast. If the presidential candidates fail to win a majority, a second round of elections is held between the two leading contestants. The candidate who wins the most votes in the second round is elected president.
According to the constitution, the president can only be removed from the post in cases of 'grave crimes'. In these cases the Supreme Court submits an application for removal to the Milli Mejlis (National Assembly), who must pass the application by a majority of 95 votes (over two-thirds majority).

National legislature

The unicameral Milli Mejlis (National Assembly) has 125 deputies, elected in single-seat constituencies for five-year terms. Legislative power of the Nakhichevan Autonomous Republic is held by a 45-member Ali Mejlis (Supreme Council), which independently settles questions of taxes, budget, economic development, social policy, environmental protection, tourism, health, science and culture as enacted by the Azerbaijan national assembly. It also has powers to appoint and dismiss the prime minister and Cabinet of Ministers of Nakhichevan. However, the Ali Mejlis lacks power to 'contradict' the constitution and laws of the Republic of Azerbaijan.

Legal system

The highest judicial body is the Supreme Court, which is divided into criminal and civil sections. There is also a Constitutional Court, Economic Court, ordinary and specialised courts.
Judges of the Supreme Court are appointed by the Milli Mejlis on the recommendation of the president. It is the highest judicial body in civil, criminal, administrative and other cases directed to general and specialised courts.
The Constitutional Court consists of nine judges appointed in the same way as in the Supreme Court. It is constitutionally bound to inquire into the activities of the president, Milli Mejlis, Cabinet of Ministers, Supreme Court and Milli Mejlis of the autonomous republic of Nakhichevan. In 2002, the constitutional changes included the remit of the Constitutional Court to hear cases brought by individuals. The Economic Court is the highest court on matters of economic dispute (as envisaged by legislation) and oversees activities in the relevant specialised courts.
Judicial power in the autonomous republic of Nakhichevan is exercised by the courts of Nakhichevan, although the Republic of Azerbaijan's laws apply in most cases.

Last elections

15 October 2003 (presidential); 7 November 2010 (parliamentary)
Results: Presidential: fomer president Heidar Aliyev's son, Prime Minister Ilham Aliyev (YAP), won a landslide victory with 79.5 per cent of the vote; his nearest rival, Musavat Party leader, Isa Gambar, had 12.1 per cent; turnout was 71.6 per cent. Opposition leaders alleged electoral fraud.
Parliamentary: Yeni Azerbaycan Partiyasi (YAP) (Yeni Azerbaijan Party) won 74 seats (out of 125), Vetendas Hemreyliyi Partiyasi (VHP) (Civic Solidarity Party) three seats, Ana Veten Partiyasi (AVP) (Motherland Party) two, independents and non-aligned 46; two other political parties did not win enough votes for any seats. Turnout 50.1 per cent.

Next elections

2013 (presidential); 2015 (parliamentary)

Political parties

Ruling party

Yeni Azerbaycan Partiyasi (YAP) (Yeni Azerbaijan Party) (from 2005; re-elected 7 Nov 2010)

Main opposition party

Azadliq (Freedom), an electoral alliance formed for the 2005 national assembly election and consisting of Müsavat Partiyasi (Equality Party), Azerbaycan Khalq Cabhasi Partiyasi (AXCP) (Popular Front of Azerbaijan), and the Azerbaycan Demokrat Partiyasi (ADP) (Azerbaijan Democratic Party) won 8 seats.

Population

9.19 million (2010)*
Last census: January 1999: 7,953,438
Population density: 104 inhabitants per square km (2010)
Annual growth rate: 0.8 per cent 1994–2004 (WHO 2006)

Internally Displaced Persons (IDP)

570,000 (UNHCR 2004)

Ethnic make-up

The majority are Azeri (90 per cent). Minority groups include Dagestani (3.2 per cent), Russians (2.5 per cent) and Armenian (2.3 per cent). Almost all Armenians live in the separatist Nagorno-Karabakh region.

Religions

The main religious affiliation is Shi'ite Muslim (93.4 per cent). Others include Russian Orthodox (2.5 per cent) and Armenian Orthodox (2.3 per cent).

Education

Compulsory schooling lasts for eight years, the last two of which can be undertaken in either general secondary schools, technical schools or vocational schools. Education is free, except for higher education for which there are student grants. There are approximately 4,500 schools, including 960 primary eight-year schools, more than 2,300 secondary schools, 20 higher schools, 74 colleges and 162 technical-vocational schools. In urban areas educational services are better than in rural areas.
Literacy rate: 97 per cent of the adult population
Compulsory years: Eight to 16
Enrolment rate: 85.5 per cent net primary enrolment; 84.7 per cent, male, 86.2 per cent, female (2009)
Pupils per teacher: 20 in primary schools

Health

In conjunction with the IMF, a new health policy was developed. The focus of government expenditure shifted away from input-based allocations (for example, based on the number of beds) to capital transfers based on the number and structure of local populations. Local autonomy was increased in healthcare and the elements of a basic package were developed, which the government provided free of charge in all public health facilities.
Healthcare is universal and virtually free of charge but there is a chronic shortage of basic medicines and despite pay increases doctors' morale remains low.
Over 60 per cent of health expenses goes to hospitals with acute care facilities and

staffed by specialised doctors rather than to preventive and basic health care. Fifty per cent of the population are severely iodine deficient.

HIV/Aids

HIV prevalence: 0.1 per cent aged 15–49 in 2003 (World Bank)

Life expectancy: 65 years, 2004 (WHO 2006)

Fertility rate/Maternal mortality rate: 1.8 births per woman, 2004 (WHO 2006); maternal deaths 43 deaths per 100,000 live births (World Bank).

Child (under 5 years) mortality rate (per 1,000): 75 per 1,000 live births; 10 per cent of children aged under five were malnourished (World Bank).

Head of population per physician: 3.55 physicians per 1,000 people, 2003 (WHO 2006)

Welfare

Although it has an abundance of natural resources, Azerbaijan is classified as the poorest country in Europe with 60 per cent of the population living in poverty. The former Soviet Union developed an extensive welfare system but price liberalisation and soaring inflation have rendered pensions, unemployment benefit and money paid to single parent families virtually worthless. The government intends to initiate a participatory poverty reduction strategy, as existing social safety nets are not enough to keep the unemployed out of poverty.

Main cities

Baku (capital, estimated population 2.1 million in 2005), Gyandzha (306,217, Sumgayit (268,522), Mingechaur (95,426), Ali Bayramli (70,626), Sheki (61,476).

Languages spoken

Azeri is spoken by 95 per cent of the population. Russian (3 per cent as first language) and Armenian (2 per cent) are also spoken. English language lessons are being introduced in schools and colleges. Some Azeris speak Russian as a second language although the use of Russian is being phased out.

Official language/s

Azeri (Turkic)

Media

Freedom of speech is guaranteed under the constitution however media outlets and journalist have been in subject to sporadic harassment by the government.

Press

The circulation of all newspapers is very small. Newspapers dropped Cyrillic script in favour of Latin in 2001.

Dailies: In Azerbaijani, national newspapers, some with online editions in Russian and English, include *525 Ci* (www.525ci.com), (Tues–Sat), *Yeni Azerbaycan* (www.yeniazerbaycan.com) a broadsheet, *Echo* (www.echo-az.com), *Azadliq* (www.azadliq.az), *Uc Noqta* (www.ucnoqta.com) and *Zerkalo* (www.zerkalo.az). In Russian, *Bakinskiy Rabockiy* (www.br.az), *Yeni Musavat* (www.musavat.com), *Nash Vek* (www.nashvek.com) and *Nedelya* (www.nedelya.az). In English, *The Azeri Times* (www.theazeritimes.com), *Baku Sun* (www.bakusun.az:8101), and *Azer News* (www.azernews.net).

Weeklies: In Azerbaijani, *Ayna-Zerkalo* (Azeri language) is a tabloid issued 156 days per year. In English *Our Century* (http://ourcentury.media-az.com),

Business: In Azerbaijani, *CBN Extra* (www.cbnextra.com) is a tabloid with a business section,

Broadcasting

Radio: Azerbaijan Radio (www.aztv.az), the national public radio is government-operated with two domestic stations (AzR 1 and 2) and one international channel. The independent, Public Television and Radio Broadcasting Company (www.itv.az) broadcasts in Azerbaijani, Russian and English. Private radio stations include Burc FM (www.burc.fm), Lider Jazz FM (www.lider.fm) and Antenn FM (www.antenn.az).

Television: AzTV () is the government-controlled, national public television service. The independent, Public Television and Radio Broadcasting Company (www.itv.az). Private TV stations include Space TV (www.spacetv.az), Lider TV (www.lidertv.com) and Azad TV.

Russian and Turkish TV channels are also available.

Advertising

There is a complete ban on tobacco advertising in all mediums. Advertising is allowed on national TV, radio, newspapers and bill posting.

News agencies

National news agency: Azar Tac www.azertag.com

Economy

The economy has seen huge increases in GDP growth since 2005, with a world record-breaking 34.5 per cent in 2006, as the benefits from the completion of the Baku-Tbilisi-Ceyhan (BTC) oil pipeline and the South Caucasus Pipeline (SCP) kicked in, allowing an expansion in exports of Azerbaijani hydrocarbons. The BTC transports oil from the Caspian Sea to the Mediterranean, while the SCP runs parallel with the BTC, transporting natural gas from the Caspian Sea to Turkey.

Large reserves of oil were seven billion barrels at the end of 2009, with production of one million barrels per day (bpd). Natural gas reserves were 1.30 trillion cubic metres at the end of 2010, with production of 1.1 billion cubic metres(a rise of 2.2 per cent on the 2009 figure).

The State Oil Company of the Republic of Azerbaijan (SOCAR) established a generation fund (State Oil Fund (Sofaz)) that will hold a proportion of the country's oil wealth in trust for future development.

The hydrocarbon industry accounts for over 90 per cent of the economy; the government, therefore, is keen to expand the non-hydrocarbon sector. Azerbaijan's ranking in the World Bank's *Doing Business 2010* report was 38 (out of 183) for ease of doing business and 17 for starting a business.

GDP growth in 2008 was 10.8 per cent, which fell to 9.3 per cent in 2009 as the effects of the global economic crisis caused a fall in the global price of oil thereby reducing fiscal oil revenues by 35 per cent; growth in 2010 was projected to have fallen to 2.7 per cent. Non-oil revenues remained on a par with 2008. The government used a transfer of resources from the Sofaz to limit the impact in the drop in revenue and repay foreign debt obligations and provide government-backed loans. Remittances in 2008 were US$1.55 billion, 3.4 per cent of GDP, and an estimated 1.24 billion in 2009. GDP growth was forecast to have been 2.7 per cent in 2010.

Oil companies represent most foreign direct investment (FDI); foreign interest has not extended to other areas of the Azeri economy. There are development projects underway, including a modern cement works, a thermal power plant and new infrastructure. Projects under consideration in 2011 include agribusiness, retail and financial services. The government has begun to privatise agricultural land and small- to medium-sized enterprises.

The conflict with Armenia over the Nagorno-Karabakh region has the potential to destabilise the country's economic progress. Although a cease-fire was signed in 1994, no final agreement has been reached.

External trade

Azerbaijan is a member of the CISFTA (free trade agreement of the CIS republics) along with Armenia, Belarus, Georgia, Moldova, Kazakhstan, Kyrgyzstan, Russia, Tajikistan, Ukraine and Uzbekistan.

International trade is vital to the economy; however hydrocarbons account for over 90 per cent of all exports and has a disproportionate influence on the economy. The second largest sector in the economy is shipbuilding; a memorandum of understanding was signed with South Korea's shipyard manufacturer STX Corporation and Azerbaijan investment interests to construct a modern port with new facilities at the new Baku Port; work began in 2009. Other export commodities include primary production and oil industry by-products.

Imports

Imports include machinery equipment, oil products, foodstuffs, metals and chemicals.

Main sources: Turkey (typically 19 per cent of total), Russia (17 per cent), Germany (8 per cent).

Exports

Exports are primarily oil and gas (over 90 per cent), with petroleum products including plastics and chemical fertilizers; other exports are ships and marine crafts, cotton fibre, machinery, foodstuffs.

Main destinations: Italy (typically 12 per cent of total), India (11 per cent), US (9 per cent).

Agriculture

Farming

Agriculture has declined by more than 50 per cent since independence, but it continues to employ 30 per cent of the labour force and contributes about 17 per cent to GDP. It is the second-largest export sector with large potential markets in the Middle East, Europe and the former Soviet Union.

Around 2 million hectares (ha) out of a total land area of 8.7 million ha is classified as arable. Some 70 per cent of the 77 per cent of land used for agricultural purposes is irrigated through an extensive canal system. Most farming takes place in the fertile lowlands surrounding the Kura and Araz rivers, in central Azerbaijan.

The whole country is well endowed with fertile land, although adversely affected by periodic drought. A wide range of crops is grown, notably cotton, tobacco, nuts, grapes, grain, tea, vegetables and citrus fruits. Cattle, sheep, pigs and poultry are reared.

Grain is the leading agricultural product, followed by raw cotton (the country's largest cash crop).

Livestock, dairy products and alcoholic beverages are also important products.

There is potential for agricultural development, greatly enhanced by the country's rich soils, wide agricultural plains and varied climatic conditions. There is scope for the cultivation of vegetables, fruits, cotton, tobacco, subtropical cultures, silkworm and sheep breeding.

However, agriculture comprises mainly smallholder farming, and is generally subsistence oriented. Despite the fact that 45 per cent of the country's population depend largely on agricultural income, the sector remains largely underdeveloped.

Fishing

Salyan on the Kura River is the main centre for processing and canning fish.

Azerbaijan once produced 10 per cent of the world's supply of caviar. The division of the Caspian Sea, which accounts for 90 per cent of world caviar production, has caused disputes between Azerbaijan and Russia. There is little effective policing of the Caspian, with smuggling and illegal fishing widespread. The Caspian is also being overfished, and combined with the threat of pollution, production levels are set to fall. International regulation of the trade in caviar was tightened in 2006 and is expected to further restrict, for the forseeable future, Azerbaijan's caviar industry.

Forestry

Forest and other wooded land, mostly concentrated in the mountainous north, account for little more than one-tenth of its total land area.

Forests in the flood plain areas remain in poor condition and are prone to overgrazing and pollution. There is no large-scale forest industry, with most wood products imported from the Russian Federation. Commercial exploitation is limited, and production is used mostly for domestic purposes. Most forest is classified as either 'protected' or 'preserved' and is public owned.

Industry and manufacturing

The oil industry dominates the Azeri economy, providing the driving force for all other sectors.

The emphasis on heavy industry, combined with substantial primary resources, enabled the development of a major oil equipment manufacturing sector in the Soviet era. However, the disintegration of the Soviet Union meant that supplies and markets dried up, leading to the virtual collapse of most industries.

It is hoped that the development of Azerbaijan's oil and gas industry will benefit all sectors of the economy, with widespread infrastructure improvements and developments essential. The construction industry has expanded particularly rapidly on the back of Azerbaijan's oil and gas boom (by 42 per cent in 2004).

In order to stimulate growth the government has developed a medium- and long-term strategy to restructure the economy in consultation with the IMF.

Tourism

Although the service sector only constituted 31.8 per cent of GDP in 2009, the Ministry of Culture and Tourism has had long-term plans to promote Azerbaijan as an elite destination, with tourism identified as potentially the country's top income source. At the beginning of 2011 there were 499 hotels in operation and 45 new hotels were under construction. A major investment, in the construction of the winter ski-ing and summer holiday resort of Shahdag, in the northeast of Azerbaijan, began in 2006 as a 10,000 guest per day, tourist centre with four- and five-star hotels as well as chalets and campsites and all necessary services to provide for visitor needs.

There are over six thousand historic sites and many more of natural beauty throughout the country, which are largely unspoiled by either the conflict in Nagorno-Karabakh or modern developments. However, Azerbaijan lacks an integrated tourist infrastructure to provide the sophisticated visitor with services to fully appreciate more than a packaged resort or the capital city, Baku.

The tourist industry grew by 6–7 per cent in 2010 and was forecast to contribute M704.4 million (US$893.7 million) (1.6 per cent) of total GDP in 2011 and M2.62 billion (US$3.32 billion) (9.4 per cent) indirectly to GDP. Investment in travel and tourism was estimated to be M157.5 million (US$199.7 million), constituting 2.1 per cent of total investment in the economy scheduled for 2011.

With the expectation of attracting over three million visitors in 2011, resulting in direct employment in the industry of 61,000 jobs (1.5 per cent of total employment); indirect employment in travel and tourism was predicted to be 230,000 (5.5 per cent of total employment) and to rise in coming years.

Having won the Eurovision Song Contest in May 2011, Azerbaijan will host the contest in 2012 and the government expects this will give a boost in tourism receipts of M60 million (US$75.5 million) as an additional 10,000–15,000 tourists visit for the competition.

Environment

Pollution comes from four main sources – agriculture, industrial plants, oil exploitation and domestic waste. It will take time and investment to clean up Azerbaijan's environment.

Mining

The mining sector accounts for 1 per cent of GDP and since independence has suffered from a lack of infrastructure investment.

The republic has abundant mineral resources, including iron, lead, zinc and copper ores, cobalt, bauxite, matrium sulphate, marl, limestone, marble, lake and rock salts, and some small amounts of gold and silver. The largest iron ore field in the Caucasus region lies within Azerbaijan.

Copper reserves are attracting foreign investors. Azerbaijan has several deposits of pure copper, the largest of which is the Karadag, in western Azerbaijan, with reserves of about 320,000 tonnes.

Hydrocarbons

Oil from the Caspian basin has dominated the economic history of Azerbaijan since the late 19th century. In 1891, half of the world's crude oil was extracted from Azerbaijan. The Caspian Sea is still the centre of oil exploration for Azerbaijan.

Proven oil reserves were 7.0 billion barrels in 2010, with production at 1.03 million barrels per day (bpd), almost all of which was derived from the Azeri-Chirag-Guneshli (ACG) oilfield. The majority is exported to Russia, Italy, Turkey and Germany via the Baku-Tblisi-Ceyhan (BTC) pipeline, running 1,673km from Baku to the Mediterranean port of Ceyhan in Turkey via Georgia.

The government places great store on the development of an oil-driven economic boom, which, while it may have negative implications for other industries, could generate huge earnings and inward investment for years. However, as the Azeri lack the necessary financial resources and expertise to develop their fields, foreign petrochemical corporations have been encouraged to invest. In order to keep control of the industry, the resulting exploration and production projects have usually been joint ventures between the State Oil Company of the Azerbaijan Republic (Socar) and foreign companies.

Proven natural gas reserves were 1.3 trillion cubic metres (cum) in 2010, with production at 15.1 billion cum. Around 50 per cent of the country's production comes from the offshore Bakhar oil and gas field, off the Absheron Peninsula. However, future development is likely to concentrate on the Nakhichevan, Gunashli and Shah Deniz fields, from where natural gas is being pumped through the South Caucasus Pipeline (SPC), which was financed in large part by the consortium behind the BTC. The 692km long pipeline from the Shah Deniz field to Erzurum in Turkey, via Georgia, had an initial capacity of 8.8 billion cum, which is scheduled to increase to 20 billion cum in 2012.

A deal was announced by the Russian gas company Gazrom in 2009 whereby it will import 500 million cum of gas from the Shah Deniz field once it begins production. Russia and the EU have rival plans to build pipelines to export gas — Russia across the Black Sea to Europe, and the EU across the Caucasus and Turkey into Europe. The EU is concerned that Russia may be trying to corner the market in gas exports to Europe.

Any coal produced or used is commercially insignificant.

Energy

Total installed generating capacity is 5,5000MW, of which eight state-owned thermal power plants produce 80 per cent of all electricity generated, consuming 7.4 million tonnes of oil equivalent (mtoe) produced by natural gas and 4.5mtoe by oil. Actual production is limited to around 4,300MW due to lack of public investment and ageing and dilapidated facilities. The energy needs of the international oil and natural gas pipelines have increased demand and Azerbaijan is an importer of electricity from surrounding countries, of around 10 per cent of its needs.

The state-owned Azerenerjy company has a monopoly on power generation and the national power grid, which is divided into five regional operations, which have been liberalised to accept foreign investment via open stock companies.

Financial markets

Stock exchange

Baki Fond Birjasi (BFB), (Baku Stock Exchange) (BSE)

Banking and insurance

Azerbaijan's banking sector is underdeveloped and dominated by four Soviet-era state-owned banks. The majority of Azerbaijani banks are undercapitalised and illiquid and during the course of 2005 several had their commercial licences revoked. In May 2005 there were 46 banks operating in Azerbaijan. Banking law states that foreign ownership of any bank in Azerbaijan cannot exceed 30 per cent.

Central bank

National Bank of Azerbaijan (NBA)

Main financial centre

Baku

Time

GMT plus four hours (daylight saving, late March to late October, GMT plus five hours)

Geography

Azerbaijan is situated in eastern Transcaucasia bordering Armenia, Georgia, the Russian Federation (Daghestan Autonomous Republic), Iran and the Caspian Sea. It is the largest of the three Transcaucasian republics, covering 87,000 square km. Azerbaijan is split in two, with the Nakhichevan Autonomous Republic separated from Azerbaijan proper by southern Armenia. Approximately 20 per cent of Azeri territory is occupied by Armenia. The ethnic Armenian enclave of Nagorno-Karabakh is an area of 4,000 square km situated in the south-west of the country.

The greater part of the republic includes the lowlands of the River Kura and the lower reaches of its tributary, the Araks. The oil-rich Apsheron Peninsula, on which the capital city, Baku, is located, juts out into the Caspian Sea.

The level of the Caspian Sea, the largest salt water lake in the world, is subject to continuous change. In 1929 its surface area was larger than the Black Sea at 422,000 square km, before it started to decline reaching a record low point in 1951. Since then it has risen to about 436,000 square km. Higher water levels are causing problems along the Azeri coast.

Hemisphere

Northern.

Climate

Azerbaijan is considered to contain nine of the world's 13 climatic zones, from Alpine meadows to the subtropics. In Baku the climate is dry and Mediterranean. Due to its diversity, there are extremes of temperature in many areas – harsh winters and hot summers. Baku and other places on the Caspian Sea have mild winters. Temperatures in Baku are 0–5 degrees Celsius (C) in winter and 25–35 degrees C in summer.

Dress codes

Business dress should include a jacket and tie for men, and smart 'business-like' clothes for women.

Entry requirements

Passports

Required by all. Must be valid for at least three months after departure date.

Visa

Required by all with the exception of CIS citizens other than Armenia and Turkestan.

Application must be accompanied by an invitation from an Azerbaijani body or citizen, submitted through the Consular Department of the Ministry of Foreign Affairs of Azerbaijan in Baku. Contact the local embassy for further explanation.

Currency advice/regulations

Import/export of local currency by non-residents is prohibited.

There are no restrictions on the import of foreign currency by non-residents, although declaration on arrival is required. There are no limitations on the export of foreign currency, up to the amount declared on arrival.

US dollars, pounds sterling and euros are the preferred currencies and can be exchanged at the airport, bureaux de change, hotels, some restaurants and major banks. Hotels, exchange bureaux and restaurants will not accept US dollar bills dated before 1992 or those which are torn or in any way disfigured. Travellers are advised to take banknotes in small denominations and change small amounts of money as required. Rates offered by banks and bureaux de change are unlikely to vary significantly.

Travellers'cheques are accepted only by the International Bank of Azerbaijan.

Customs

On arrival foreign currency and personal and valuable items must be declared.

Prohibited imports

Weapons, drugs, animals, anti-Azerbaijan literature and pictures, fruit and vegetables are prohibited.

Health (for visitors)

Only emergency medical treatment is available free to visitors, with small payments for medicines or hospital treatment. The level of care is limited. Private chemists in Baku stock a range of the more basic medicines. Travellers are advised to take out an insurance policy which includes emergency repatriation in case of serious illness or accident.

Mandatory precautions

None

Advisable precautions

It is advisable to be in date for the following immunisations: tetanus (within 10 years), typhoid, hepatitis A and B, tuberculosis. Anti-malarial prophylaxis are advisable. There may be some risk of meningitis, tick-borne encephalitis and leishmaniasis (cutaneous and visceral). Rabies is present.

It is advisable to take a supply of those medicines that are likely to be required (but check first that they may be legally imported). A travel kit including a disposable syringe is a reasonable precaution. Water precautions are recommended.

Hotels

Hotel space in Baku is very limited. Payment for the full stay is required in advance upon arrival at the hotel in cash (in US dollar bills which should be in good condition). VAT and service charges are included in all bills; tipping the waiters is appreciated but not compulsory.

Credit cards

Accepted in the major hotels, some restaurants and all banks in Baku. Credit cards can be used to purchase tickets at the airport.

Public holidays (national)

Fixed dates

1 Jan (New Year), 20 Jan (Day of the Martyrs), 8 Mar (Women's Day), 21 Mar (Novruz Bayramy), 9 May (Victory Day), 28 May (Republic Day), 15 Jun (Day of National Salvation), 26 June (Army and Navy Day), 18 Oct (Independence Day), 12 Nov (Constitution Day), 17 Nov (National Revival Day), 31 Dec (Solidarity Day).

Variable dates

Ramazam Bayram, Kurban Bayram.

Islamic year 1433 (26 Nov 2011–14 Nov 2012): The Islamic year contains 354 or 355 days, with the result that Muslim feasts advance by 10–12 days against the Gregorian calendar. Dates of feasts vary according to the sighting of the new moon, so cannot be forecast exactly.

Working hours

Banking

Mon–Fri: 0900–1700.

Business

Mon–Fri: 0900–1800.

Government

Mon–Fri: 0900–1300; 1400–1800.

Shops

Mon–Fri: 0900–1900.

Telecommunications

Mobile/cell phones

There are two GSM mobile phone companies, Azercell and Bakcell.

Electricity supply

Voltage is usually 220V, 50 Hz.

Weights and measures

Metric system

Social customs/useful tips

Azeri culture blends Soviet-style courtesy with Middle Eastern informality.

The approach to business is not very well developed by Western standards, although technical knowledge and education standards are high.

Although Azeris are Muslim, they are probably the most secular of all the Muslim people of the former Soviet Union, with many considering themselves Eastern European rather than Asian. Consequently, Azerbaijan bears little relation to the Middle East with the exception of its oil and gas reserves. Business and negotiation habits are more akin to those in the rest of the former Soviet Union than with Middle Eastern practices.

The business environment has been reported to suffer from a number of ills, including very low wages for civil servants which act as an encouragement to corruption, a lack of transparency in the legal system and the inability to make decisions at lower governmental levels.

Bribery and 'gifts' were part and parcel of everyday business life in the former Soviet Union, and little has changed since 1991. However, moderate gifts and souvenirs discreetly given are usually more suitable than offers of foreign trips and shopping sprees.

Security

Crimes against foreigners are in general rare, but since late 2005 there has been an increase in violent muggings at night in the city centre (sometimes with the collusion of taxi drivers). It is advisable to arrange in advance to be transported to and from your hotel and to be vigilant in moving around on foot. Travellers should carry their passports with them at all times and ensure they travel with photocopies of their passports in case of theft.

Avoid all travel to Nagorno-Karabakh.

Getting there

Air

National airline: Azerbaijan Hava Yollari (Azal) (Azerbaijan Airlines)

International airport/s: Heydar Aliyev International (GYD), is located 25km east of Baku. Facilities include car hire, bank/bureau de change and VIP lounge.

Airport tax: None

Surface

Road: Inter-city bus routes link Baku with Tbilisi (Georgia), Derben (Dagestan) and Istanbul (Turkey).

The Regional Road Corridor Improvement Project, estimated at US$18 billion, to improve Central Asian roads, airports, railway lines and seaports and provide a vital transit route between Europe and Asia was agreed, on 3 November 2007. Six new transit corridors, between Afghanistan, Azerbaijan, China, Kazakhstan, Kyrgyzstan, Mongolia, Tajikistan and Uzbekistan, of mainly roads and rail links, will be constructed, or existing resources upgraded, by 2013. Half the costs with be provided by the Asian Development Bank and other multilateral organisations and the other half by participating countries.

Rail: There are rail connections to Tbilisi (Georgia), Derben (Dagestan) and various cities in the Russian Federation, including Moscow.

Water: Passenger ferries on the Caspian Sea link Azerbaijan with the Russian Federation, Central Asia and Iran. Ferries sail regularly to Baku from Turkmenbashy in Turkmenistan and from Bandar Anzali and Bandar Nowshar in Iran. Winter storms may disrupt services.

Main port/s: Baku.

Getting about

Travel within some regions of the country is restricted and visitors must obtain special permission from the Ministry of Interior.

National transport

Road: Azerbaijan has more than 57,770km of roads, of which over 31,000km are paved. Roads are generally in poor condition. Buses connect Baku and the main cities. The main motorway runs from Baku to Russia via the Caspian Coast.

Rail: Azerbaijan has a rail network of approximately 2,100km (1,300km electrified). The rail network is the most important form of transport, handling an estimated 75 per cent of total traffic.

City transport

Taxis: Taxis can be distinguished by a sign on top. Agree a price beforehand. Taxis are cheap, but drivers are unlikely to speak English. As the cost of a trip can vary widely, it is better to use hotel taxis or pre-arrange a car with driver.

Buses, trams & metro: Buses tend to be overcrowded. More expensive but more comfortable are *marshruts* (privately–operated minibuses), which follow the same routes. There is a metro in Baku with a total length of 28km.

Car hire

Car hire is available in Baku. An international driving licence is needed. Traffic drives on the right.

BUSINESS DIRECTORY

The addresses listed below are a selection only. While World of Information makes every endeavour to check these addresses, we cannot guarantee that changes have not been made, especially to telephone numbers and area codes. We would welcome any corrections.

Telephone area codes

The international direct dialling code (IDD) for Azerbaijan is +994, followed by area code and subscriber's number:

Baku	12	Neftechala	153
Dashkasan	216	Sumgayit	164
Nakhichevan	136		

Useful telephone numbers

Fire: 01
Police: 02
Ambulance: 03

Chambers of Commerce

American Chamber of Commerce in Azerbaijan, ISR Plaza, 340 Nizami Street, Baku 370000 tel: 971-333; fax: 971-091; e-mail: info@amchamaz.org).

Azerbaijan Chamber of Commerce and Industry, 31/33 Istiglaliyyat Street, Baku 370001 (tel: 928-912; fax: 971-997; e-mail: expo@chamber.baku.az).

Banking

Azakbank (private), 25 Xagani Street, 370070 Baku (tel: 983-109, 932-491; fax: 932-085).

Azcombank, 1 Inshaatchilar Avenue, 370073 Baku (tel: 388-323, 387-206).

AzEkoBank (joint stock bank), 11/39 Mustafa Subhi Street, Baku 370001 (tel: 929-433; fax: 980-406; e-mail: ecob@ecob.crack.azerbaijan.su; internet site: http://www.azekobank.com).

Azerbaijan Agricultural Industrial Bank, 125 Qadirli Street, Baku 370006 (tel: 389-293; fax: 389-115).

Azerbaijan Commercial Savings Bank, 71 Fizuli Street, Baku 370010 (tel: 930-561; fax: 939-489).

Azerbaijan Industrial Investment Bank, 71 Fizuli Street, 370010 Baku (tel: 931-701; fax: 931-266).

Azerbaijan National Bank, 19 Bulbul Ave, Baku 370070 (tel: 935-058; fax: 937-374).

Azerdemiryolbank, 31 Qarabagh Street, Baku 370008 (tel: 972-380, 675-321; fax: 987-936).

Azerigazbank, 37 Tbilisi Avenue, 370065 Baku (tel: 385-021; fax: 390-243).

Azerturkbank, 5 Islam Safarli Street, 370005 Baku (tel: 948-090; fax: 983-702).

Bakobank (private), 35 Yusif Safarov Street, 370025 Baku (tel: 666-549; fax: 981-927).

British Bank of the Middle East, 1 Bakihanov Street, Baku (tel: 981-234; fax: 980-817).

International Bank of Azerbaijan (IBA), 67 Nizami Street, Baku 370005 (tel: 930-091; fax: 934-091; e-mail: ibar@bar.az; internet site: http://www.ibar.az).

Most-Bank, 70 Nizami Street, Baku (tel: 971-070; fax: 972-094).

Promtekhbank (joint stock commercial bank), 69 Fizuli Street, Baku 370014 (tel: 957-874; fax: 958-360; e-mail: bank@devi.baku.az).

Rabitabank, 1 Buniat Sardarov Street, Baku 370001 (tel: 926-099; fax: 926-157).

Tajbank (commercial investment bank), 185 Azadlyg Ave, Baku 370087 (tel: 691-464; fax: 691-474).

Central bank

National Bank of Azerbaijan, 32 R. Behbudov Street, Baku (tel: 931-122; fax: 935-541; e-mail: mail@nba.az).

Stock exchange

Baki Fond Birjasi (BFB), (Baku Stock Exchange) (BSE) (www.bse.az).

Travel information

Azal (Azerbaijan Hava Yollari) (Azerbaijan Airlines), Prospect Azadlig 11, Baku 370000 (tel: 934-434; fax: 985-237, 651-120).

Azerbaijani Railways, Dilara Aliyeva Str 230, 370010 Baku (tel: 984-467; fax: 984-280).

Azertur Travel Agency of the State Council for Foreign Tourism (tours, hotel reservations, translation and interpreting services), 1 Azadlyg Ave, Baku 370000 (tel: 933-481; fax: 933-481).

Eur Tourism, 82 Topchubashev Str, Baku (tel: 973-444; fax: 986-810; e-mail: eurotourbaku@azeri.com).

Improtex (travel tours and conferences), 115 Azi Aslanov Str, Baku 370000 (tel: 930-896, 933-941; fax: 651-238; e-mail: toor@impro.Azerbaijan.su).

Ministries

Ministry of Agriculture and Food, 4 Shihali Kurbanov Street, Baku 370079 (tel: 935-355; fax: 943-952).

Ministry of Communications, 33 Azerbaijan Ave, Baku 370139 (tel: 930-004; fax: 984-285).

Ministry of Culture, Government House, Azadlyg Square, Baku 370016 (tel: 934-398; fax: 935-605).

Ministry of Defence, 3 Azerbaijan Ave, Azizbekov Baku 370601 (tel: 394-362; fax: 382-296).

Ministry of Economics, Government House, Azadlyg Square, Baku 370016 (tel: 936-920; fax: 932-025).

Ministry of Education, Government House, 1 Azadlyg Square, Baku 370016 (tel: 937-266; fax: 984-207).

Ministry of Finance, Sameda Vurguna Ul 6, Baku 370000 (tel: 933-012; fax: 987-969).

Ministry of Foreign Affairs, Gandjlar Meydani 3, Baku 370004 (tel: 923-401; fax: 629-756).

Ministry of Foreign Economic Relations, Lermontov Street 69, Baku 370601 (tel: 929-492; fax: 980-011).

Ministry of Grain Products, 13 Yusifzade Street, Baku 370033 (tel: 667-451; fax: 939-023).

Ministry of Health, Malaya Morskaya Street 4, Baku 370014 (tel: 932-977; fax: 988-559).

Ministry of Information and Press, 12 Ahmad Javad Street, Baku 370001 (tel: 926-357; fax: 926-747).

Ministry of Internal Affairs, 7 Gusi Hajiyev Street, Baku 370005 (tel: 986-396; fax: 923-471).

Ministry of Justice, 13 Kirov Avenue, Baku 370601 (tel: 939-785; fax: 938-367).

Ministry of Labour and Social Protection, Azadlyg Square, Baku 370016 (tel: 930-542; fax: 939-472).

Ministry of Material Resources, 83-23 Alaskar Alakbarov Street, Baku 370141 (tel: 394-296; fax: 399-176).

Ministry of National Security, 1 Azadlyg Square 1, Baku 370016 (tel: 931-000; fax: 936-296).

Ministry of Trade, Government House, Azadlyg Square 1, Baku 370016 (tel: 985-074; fax: 987-431).

Ministry of Youth and Sports, 98a Fatali Han Khoyski Avenue, Baku 370072 (tel: 981-426; fax: 643-650).

Office of the President of the Azerbaijan Republic, 19 Istiglaliyyat Street, Baku 370066 (tel: 983-113).

Other useful addresses

Azerbaijan News Service, Block 504, 1128 Street, Baku 370073 (building of the Institute of Zoology) (tel: 929-221/3; fax: 989-498).

Azerbintorg Foreign Trade Association, 14 Boyuk Gala Str, 370004 Baku (tel: 920-481, 926-492, 924-545; fax: 983-292).

Azerigaz, 23 Yusif Safarov Street, Baku 370025 (tel: 677-447; fax: 674-255).

Azerkimia, 86 Samed Vurgun Street, Baku 373200 (tel: 937-620).

Azertaj State Information Agency, Bulbul Avenue 18, 370000 Baku (tel: 935-445; fax: 938-138).

Baku General Customs Board, 62 Neftchilar Ave, Baku 370601 (tel: 939-588).

Baku Statistics Office, 10 Tabriz Street, Baku 370008 (tel: 669-327, 672-265).

Baku Telegraph Office, 41 Azerbaijan Avenue, Baku 370000 (tel: 936-142).

Baku Television, M. Husein St 1, Baku.

Board of Azerbaijan Railways, 230 Dilara Aliyeva Street, Baku 370010 (tel: 984-467).

British Embassy, 2 Izmir Street, 370065 Baku (tel: 924-813; fax: 985-558).

Caspian Shipping Company, 5 Rasulzade Street, Baku 370005 (tel: 922-058; fax: 935-339).

Central Post Office, 36 Uzeyir Hajibeyov Street, Baku 370000 (tel: 985-251).

EU Co-ordinating Unit in Azerbaijan, Government House, 8th Floor, Room 851, Baku 370016 (tel: 936-018; fax: 937-638).

Radio Baku, M Husein St 1, 370011 Baku.

Scientific Research and Test Constructive Institute of Oil Machinery of Azerbaijan Republic (Azinmash), Aras Street 4, Baku 370029 (tel: 670-888; fax: 672-888).

SME Development Agency 83, Mr Vagif G. Alikperov, S Vurguna, Azneftiechimprom Bld. 5th Floor, PO Box 114, 37000 Baku (tel: 957832; fax: 957832; e-mail: quirin@smeda.baku.az).

State Committee for Statistics, 24 Inshaatchylar Ave, Baku-136 370136 (tel: 381-171; fax: 380-577).

State Customs Committee, 2 Inshaatchilar Ave, Baku 370073 (tel: 927-545).

State Oil Company of the Azerbaijan Republic (SOCAR), 73 Neftchilar Ave, Baku 370004 (tel: 924-480, 920-745, 920-685; fax: 936-492, 923-204).

Statoil Caspian Region, 96 Nizami Street, 370010 Baku (tel: 977-340; fax: 977-944).

US Embassy, 83 Azadliq Avenue, Baku 370007 (tel: 980-335; fax: 983-755; e-mail: webbaku@pd.state.gov).

National news agency

Azar Tac (www.azertag.com).

Other news agencies:

Turan (www.turaninfo.com).

Trend (http://news.trendaz.com)

Internet sites

Heydar Aliyev International Airport: www.airport–baku.com
President of Azerbaijan: www.president.az

Bahamas

KEY FACTS

Official name: Commonwealth of The Bahamas

Head of State: Queen Elizabeth II, represented by Governor General Sir Arthur Foulkes (from 13 Apr 2010)

Head of government: Prime Minister Hubert Ingraham (FNM) (elected 2 May 2007)

Ruling party: Free National Movement (FNM) (elected May 2007)

Area: 13,935 square km

Population: 353,658 (2010; census figure)

Capital: Nassau

Official language: English

Currency: Bahamian dollar (B$) = 100 cents

Exchange rate: B$1.00 per US$ (fixed)

GDP per capita: US$21,879 (2010)

GDP real growth: 0.50% (2010)

GDP: US$7.50 billion (2010)

Labour force: 184,000 (2009)

Inflation: 1.70% (2010)

Balance of trade: -US$1.89 billion (2010)

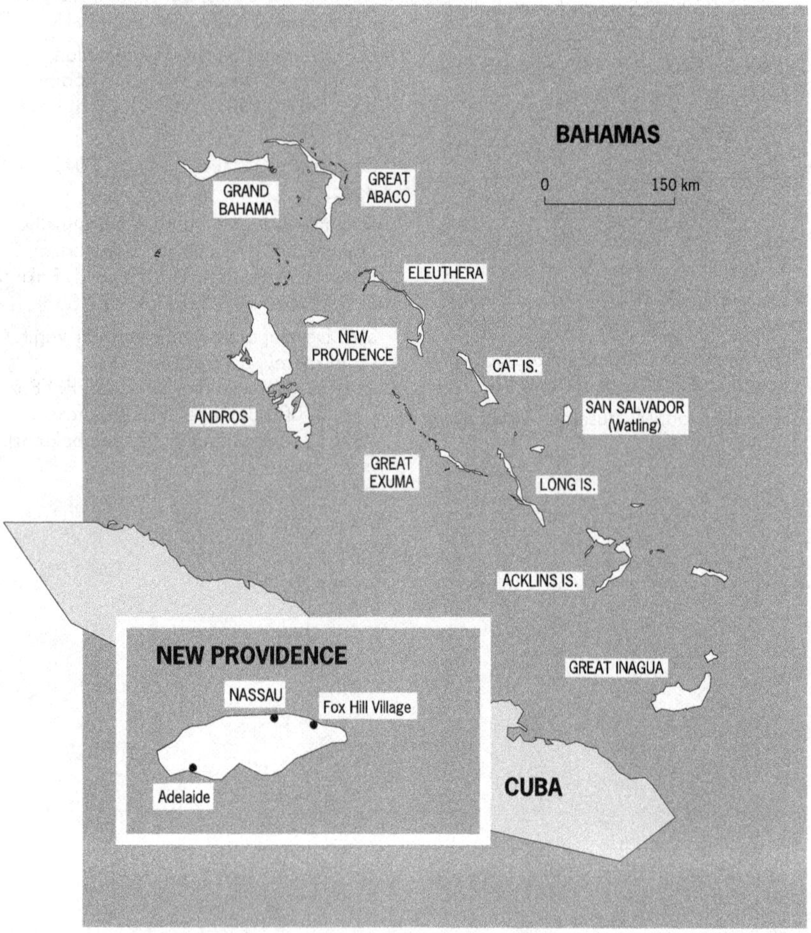

The economy of the Bahamas recovered slightly in 2010 with growth of 0.9 per cent, after a fall of 5.4 per cent in 2010. Tourism, the country's main foreign exchange earner, was the prime mover of the recovery, as visitors from the US, the biggest market, rebounded. The United Nations Economic Commission for Latin America and the Caribbean (ECLAC) reported that this rebound, together with buoyant activity in offshore financial services, helped to compensate for the weaker performance of the construction sector. Inflation declined as food and clothing prices fell. The fiscal situation deteriorated in fiscal year 2009/10 as revenues declined more sharply than expenditure, but there was an improvement in 2010/11. Meanwhile, the balance of payments current account deficit contracted moderately to 9.9 per cent of GDP, as higher tourism receipts outweighed the increase in the trade deficit.

Tourism recovers

Growth in the tourism sector has repercussions across the economy. Not only does the sector have a positive affect on the balance of payments, it is a major employer itself as well as generating employment through the construction industry. Work on the Baha Mar Resort Complex, the largest tourism project in the history of the Bahamas, started in February 2011. In the first year after completion, Baha Mar is expected to lead to US$1 billion of spending, create 6,500-7,000 permanent jobs and attract 430,000 stopover visitors (a 30 per cent increase).

According to ECLAC the economy is expected to continue recovering in 2011, with growth rising to 1.3 per cent, propelled by continued improvement in tourism and in construction linked to foreign direct investment (FDI). Inflation is expected to rise due to higher fuel prices. The fiscal deficit is projected to increase marginally and the balance of payments current account will widen as a result of higher oil prices and import payments relating to major projects.

Although domestic demand rallied and international fuel prices continued to strengthen, the rate of inflation rose slightly from 1.3 per cent in 2009 to 1.6 per cent in 2010. The main contributors to the decline in inflation were the heavily weighted food and beverage sub-sector, clothing and footwear, and miscellaneous goods and services. On the other hand, the cost of housing, water, electricity, gas and other fuels increased by 3.4 per cent and transport by 3.7 per cent, propelled in part by the hike in international fuel prices. Wage growth was contained in 2010 as salary increments for public officers were not paid and public employment was frozen in an effort to contain costs. Although there are no official figures, employment was expected to pick up in tourism and related segments of distribution as a result of the improvement in the tourism sector. Employment in construction and other sectors is expected to pick up in 2011, as work continues on the Baha Mar project.

British rule 1. Whose law?

On 22 June 2011 Prime Minister Ingraham told parliament that he intended to bring forward legislation to deal with 'the question of the imposition of the death penalty in The Bahamas'. This was after the UK-based Privy Council overturned the death penalty on a convicted killer (Maxo Tido) on 14 June sparking controversy concerning the sovereignty of the Bahamian justice system and the role of the Privy Council. The proposed legislation would prescribe specific categories for which the death penalty may be applied.

Rule 2. Her Majesty or His Majesty?

During the Commonwealth Heads of Government summit, on 28 October, the 16 countries in which the British monarch is Head of State unanimously agreed to change the royal line of succession from that of first born son to the first born child (regardless of its gender). The change will be enacted after the succession of Prince William

Risk assessment

Politics	Fair
Economy	Improving
Regional stability	Good

COUNTRY PROFILE

Historical profile

1647 The Bahamas (from the Spanish *Baja Mar* – meaning low tide), originally inhabited by Arawak Indians were occupied by British settlers in 1647.
1729 A parliamentary system of government was introduced.
1783 Recognised as a colony.
1834 Britain emancipated its slaves.
1964 Internal self-government was granted.
1967 In the first elections under full universal adult suffrage, the Progressive Liberal Party (PLP), led by Lynden (later Sir Lynden) Pindling won with the support of the United Bahamian Party (UBP).
1972 The PLP won a landslide victory and began independence talks with the UK.
1973 The Bahamas gained full independence on 10 July as a member of the Commonwealth.
1992 Sir Lynden Pindling and the PLP lost power to the Free National Movement (FNM).
1997 The FNM were re-elected.
2000 Sir Lynden Pindling died. The Bahamas was placed on the Organisation for Economic Co-operation and Development (OECD) Financial Action Task Force (FATF) list of Non-Co-operative Countries and Territories (NCCT) for having a financial system that did not comply with international banking regulation on money laundering and terrorist financing.
2001 The US awarded the Bahamas certification as being one of 20 countries fully co-operating with anti-drug efforts. Dame Ivy Dumont became the first female governor general.
2002 The PLP won the parliamentary elections. Perry Christie became prime minister.
2004 The FATF reported it remained concerned about the ability of the authorities to respond to foreign judicial and regulatory requests and would continue to monitor the situation. Hurricane Frances caused widespread damage.
2005 Dame Ivy Dumont retired; Paul Adderley, became acting governor general. The Bahamas banking system was removed from the FATF list of NCCT.
2006 Arthur Dion Hanna was inaugurated as governor general.
2007 In parliamentary elections the FNM won 23 out of 41 seats, defeating the incumbent PLP, which won 18 seats. The FNM leader, Hubert Ingraham, was sworn in as prime minister.
2009 Cuba and the Bahamas signed a bilateral co-operation agreement to promote trade and investment, as well as technical information exchange and joint programmes, particularly in the education and health sectors. The Bahamas Financial Services Board (BFSB), a regulatory body, was launched.
2010 Governor General Arthur Dion Hanna retired in April and Sir Arthur Foulkes was appointed and sworn into office as governor general on 13 April.
2011 The UK-based Privy Council overturned a death penalty on a convicted

KEY INDICATORS Bahamas

	Unit	2006	2007	2008	2009	2010
Population	m	0.33	0.33	0.34	0.34	0.35
Gross domestic product (GDP)	US$bn	6.24	6.59	7.50	7.30	7.50
GDP per capita	US$	19,917	19,895	22,156	21,529	21,879
GDP real growth	%	4.0	4.5	-1.3	-5.0	0.5
Inflation	%	1.9	1.9	4.5	2.1	1.7
Exports (fob) (goods)	US$m	692.1	801.9	997.2	710.7	702.4
Imports (fob) (goods)	US$m	2,626.0	2,956.9	3,131.0	2,536.7	2,590.6
Balance of trade	US$m	-1,933.9	-2,155.0	-2,133.9	-1,826.1	-1,888.2
Current account	US$m	-1,578.0	-1,315.1	-1,001.0	-863.6	-899.9
Total reserves minus gold	US$m	461.3	464.5	567.9	1,009.8	1,044.2
Foreign exchange	US$m	451.9	454.5	558.2	821.0	858.7
Tourist numbers	'000	93.5	90.9	86.8	91.9	103.8
Exchange rate	per US$	1.00	1.00	1.00	1.00	1.00

killer (Maxo Tido) on 14 June and sparked controversy concerning the sovereignty of Bahamian justice system and the role of the Privy Council. On 22 June Prime Minister Ingraham told parliament that he intended to bring forward legislation to deal with 'the question of the imposition of the death penalty in The Bahamas'. This legislation should prescribe specific categories for which the death penalty may be applied. On 27 June, the Bahamas Bar Association warned that abandoning the Privy Council could be 'treading in very dangerous water' and that a court of final appeal was essential to ensure justice for all. On 29 June legislation was introduced to amend the Parliamentary Elections Act, which included: re-registering for voters who have not moved home for over a year to cease; and limiting the circumstances for a recount following an election. A law banning shark fishing in Bahama's waters was signed on 5 July. It also prohibits the sale, import and export of shark products.

Political structure

Constitution

The 1973 constitution was enacted to validate independence. Rights of citizenship and freedom of the individual were guaranteed. The composition of parliament, with a senate and house of assembly, was mandated and the function and authority of the executive were set forth.

Voting eligibility is for citizens of the Bahamas who are 18 years or older.

Independence date

10 July 1973

Form of state

Constitutional multi-party parliamentary democracy; it is a member of the Commonwealth.

The executive

The British monarch is the nominal head of state, represented by the governor general. Executive power is exercised by the prime minister and cabinet, which advises the governor general on appointments and ratifies laws.

National legislature

The bicameral legislature consists of a House of Assembly (lower house) with 41 members elected for five-year terms in single-seat constituencies, and the Senate (upper house) with 16 members appointed by the governor general – nine members are appointed on the recommendation of the prime minister, four members are appointed on the recommendation of the leader of the opposition and three members are appointed on the recommendation of the prime minister and leader of the opposition together. The leader of the largest political party in the House of Assembly is made prime minister. The senate always reflects the political make-up of the House of Assembly.

The government may dissolve parliament at any time up to the parliament's five-year term.

Legal system

The Bahamian legal system is based on British common law with elements of former colonial legislation. Much of the business legislation enacted since independence is based on the US system. The Privy Council in London is the highest court of appeal.

Last elections

2 May 2007 (parliamentary)

Results: Parliamentary: the Free National Movement (FNM) won 56 per cent of the vote (23 of 41seats); the Progressive Liberal Party (PLP) won 44 per cent (18 seats). Turnout was 90 per cent.

Next elections

2012 (parliamentary)

Political parties

Ruling party

Free National Movement (FNM) (elected May 2007)

Main opposition party

Progressive Liberal Party (PLP)

Political situation

The establishment of a Financial Services Authority was announced in 2009, following the collapse in February of the insurance company CLICO Bahamas with liabilities in excess of US$9 million. This was the most tangible result of the downturn in the global economy in 2008–09. The Bahamas also had to contend with an unemployment rate of 12.1 per cent in New Providence and 14.6 per cent in Grand Bahama, with employment in the hotel and restaurant sector declining by 10 per cent and in the construction industry by 9 per cent. In May the five-star Four Seasons Resort, which had opened in 2003, closed due to insolvency.

Prime Minister, Hubert Ingraham, when he presented the 2009/10 budget, said that the economy had suffered but that the government would resume 'the path of social and economic progress temporarily interrupted by the global financial crisis' when the situation improved.

Population

353,658 (2010; census figure)

Last census: May 2000: 303,611

Population density: 30 inhabitants per square km. Urban population: 89 per cent (1995–2001).

Annual growth rate: 1.5 per cent 1994–2004 (WHO 2006)

Ethnic make-up

African (85 per cent), European and mixed race (12 per cent), other (3 per cent).

Religions

Baptist (32 per cent), Anglican (20 per cent), Roman Catholic (19 per cent), Evangelical Protestant (12 per cent), Methodist (6 per cent), Church of God (6 per cent).

Education

There is an extensive primary and secondary school system, and education is free. There are numerous options for tertiary education, including the College of the Bahamas, which is affiliated with the University of the West Indies (UWI). Local post-secondary vocational and technical training is available in mechanical, electrical and automotive engineering, television and radio, technology, computer science, electronics, construction, carpentry, secretarial services, bookkeeping, printing, photography, straw craft and dressmaking. A scholarship programme provides university training abroad in medicine, agriculture, engineering, science, education and other subjects considered necessary for national development but not available locally.

Literacy rate: 96 per cent of adults (2003)

Compulsory years: Five to 16

Enrolment rate: 98 per cent, gross primary enrolment (World Bank).

Health

There are three main hospitals in the Bahamas: Princess Margaret in Nassau and Rand Memorial in Freeport, both government owned, and the privately owned Doctors Hospital in Nassau. Lyford Cay Hospital is a smaller private establishment offering specialised treatment.

HIV/Aids

Deaths by Aids, once a leading cause, had by 2005 been halved due to the use of anti-retroviral (ARV) drugs – 1,600 patients received the treatment, up from 470 in 2002. Deaths from Aids dropped from 250 to 140 per annum between 2002–04.

Over 2,000 HIV positive patients are cared for by a speciality clinic in Nassau and it was reported that no new cases of infants born to HIV positive mothers were infected while patients. HIV-positive pregnant women's rate dropped from 2.7 per cent in 2001 to 1.6 per cent in 2004, nevertheless, child mortality was 25.21 per 1,000 live births in 2004.

HIV prevalence: 3.0 per cent aged 15–49 in 2003 (World Bank)

Life expectancy: 73 years, 2004 (WHO 2006)

Fertility rate/Maternal mortality rate: 2.3 births per woman, 2004 (WHO 2006)

Child (under 5 years) mortality rate (per 1,000): 11 per 1,000 live births (World Bank)

Welfare

Welfare conditions in the Bahamas are among the best in the Caribbean and the government is working towards ensuring that economic growth is accompanied by improvements in the social sector.
The National Insurance Act of 1972 set out the law governing social security. It provides for contributions from employers and employees to be paid to the National Insurance Fund. Anyone who is employed or self-employed is insured under the act, including non-Bahamians with work permits. Benefits include sickness and maternity payments, retirement and widows' pensions and social assistance payments.

Main cities

Nassau (capital and seat of government, on New Providence Island, estimated population 233,832 in 2005) and Freeport (on Grand Bahama Island, 27,270).

Languages spoken

English, Creole (among Haitian immigrants).

Official language/s

English

Media

Press

Dailies: Newspapers include the *Nassau Guardian* (www.thenassauguardian.com), *The Tribune* and the intellectual *Bahama Journal* (www.jonesbahamas.com);*Freeport News* (http://freeport.nassauguardian.net) is published on Grand Bahama.
Weeklies: Tabloid newspapers include *Punch* published twice weekly and has the largest circulation of all newspapers; *The Abaconian* is published once fortnightly, on Abaco.
Business: A quarterly magazine *The Bahamas Financial Digest* (www.bfsb-bahamas.com) is a government publication that reports on financial services and investments.

Broadcasting

The national public broadcaster is ZNS (www.znsbahamas.com), (the name is derived from its call sign: Zephyr Nassau Sunshine).
Radio: ZNS operates three commercial radio station; ZNS 1 and 2 from Nassau and ZNS3 from Freeport. There are around a dozen private stations include Splash FM (www.splash899fm.com), Radio Abaco (www.radioabaco.com) and 100 Jamz (www.100jamz.com).
Television: ZNS operates the only domestic TV station on the islands. Cable TV is available to around 96 per cent of the population offering a wide choice of imported TV programmes, sporting events and films.

News agencies

Other news agencies: Caribbean Net News: www.caribbeannetnews.com

Economy

Tourism and offshore financial banking are the mainstays of the economy. The tourist industry is the dominant sector, constituting over 60 per cent of GDP. GDP growth was -4.3 per cent in 2009, falling further from a negative growth of -1.7 per cent in 2008, caused by the global economic crisis that cut both tourist numbers and financial activity. There was also a cut of over 30 per cent in foreign direct investment. However, as tourism began to recover so did the economy, to a modest growth of 0.5 per cent in 2010, with a projected 1.5 per cent growth in 2011. During the worst of the recession, the annual unemployment rate was 14.6 per cent (almost double the typical annual rate as seen in years of growth), with workers in the tourist and construction sectors hit hardest.
Although the balance of payments in 2009 was in deficit, by around 12.5 per cent of GDP, external borrowing and a one-off Special Drawing Rights (SDR) from the International Monetary Fund (IMF) of US$179 million was more than adequate to cover the shortfall before the economy recovered in 2010. However, government debt by June 2010 was around 47 per cent of GDP, which affected Bahamas' sovereign rating, which was downgraded to BBB+/stable.
The high incidence of hurricanes in the Bahamas affects the economy, although due to the islands' general preparedness, the economic impact is kept to a minimum.
The World Travel and Tourism Council forecast tourism would contribute 47.4 per cent to GDP in 2011, while attracting investment constituting 16.5 per cent of total investment. Direct employment in the industry was forecast to be around 48,000 jobs (29.4 per cent of total employment) and a total of 91,000 jobs (55.1 per cent of total) through indirect employment. Foreign exchange from tourism was expected to be US$2.2 billion.
In May 2011, the state-owned Bahamas Petroleum Company (BPC) was seeking investors for rights to explore oil-sands deposits beneath the islands, with an offer of 25 per cent of well-head revenue returned in royalties to the government (less than the 33 per cent as contracted in the US).

External trade

Although the Bahamas was a founder member of the Caribbean Community (Caricom), it did not adopt the single market and economy (CSME), which was ratified by 12 other member states in 2006.

Imports

Principal imports include crude oil for refining, fuel oil, machinery and transport equipment, manufactured goods, livestock and foodstuffs, and chemicals.
Main sources: US (typically 91 per cent of total), Venezuela (2 per cent), Trinidad & Tobago (2 per cent).

Exports

Exports include chemicals, pharmaceuticals, rum, crawfish, agricultural products, salt, aragonite, sponges, cosmetics and perfume.
Main destinations: US (typically 72 per cent of total), The Netherlands (7 per cent), Canada (4 per cent).

Re-exports

Petroleum products

Agriculture

Farming

The agricultural and fisheries sector contributes approximately 3 per cent to annual GDP and employs about 5 per cent of the labour force.
Although only about 1 per cent of land area is cultivated, near self-sufficiency has been achieved in poultry, pork, eggs, fruit and vegetables. The expansion of export crops such as limes, pineapples, papayas, avocados, cucumbers and mangoes is being promoted.
The government has provided marketing facilities through the Product Exchange in Nassau for small-scale producers, and also supplies seed and fertilisers. There are special incentives to foreign investors in food production and processing.
The chicken industry accounts for 40 per cent of agricultural production.

Fishing

The sector employs around 9,000 Bahamians. The commercial harvesting of pearls and shells has seen a dramatic rise the annual harvest is typically 13,000 units. The harvest of sponges averages 70,000 per annum.

Forestry

Total forest cover is estimated at 842,000 hectares, equivalent of 15 per cent of the total land area. Most forests are concentrated on the four islands of the north-western Bahamas including Ahaco, Andros, Grand Bahamas and New Providence.

Industry and manufacturing

The industrial sector is small-scale, contributing around 10 per cent to annual GDP and employing 10 per cent of the labour force.
The largest contributor to the industrial sector is the crude oil transshipment terminal operated by Burmah Oil. Re-exports of crude and refined oil (mainly to the US) are estimated to account for around 16 per cent of GDP.

Other activity is centred on the production of rum, chemicals and pharmaceuticals for export. The companies manufacturing these products are largely foreign-owned and located in the Freeport trade area on Grand Bahama.

Other light industries include rum production, food processing, confectionery, garments, small boat building and furniture making.

The Bahamas Agricultural and Industrial Corporation (BAIC) is encouraging light manufacturing, furniture, toiletries, cosmetics, jewellery, linens, beachwear and the assembly of air conditioners and refrigerators.

The construction industry is also important, fuelled by the tourist trade and financial institutions requiring offices.

Tourism

The economy is dominated by the tourism industry, constituting over 60 per cent of GDP. Tourists from the US and Canada are the greatest in number, followed by Europeans and other Caribbean residents. Recording a rise of 15 per cent on the 2009 figures, over five million tourists visited the islands in 2010; cruise arrivals had grown by 18 per cent, with growth through the expanded docks at the newly enlarged cruise-liner port on Grand Bahama. The islands also offer luxury Caribbean holidays and conference locations

The Bahamas Ministry of Tourism and Aviation (BMOTA) co-ordinates and regulates the industry. The successful 2010 'Free Companion Airfare' promotion encouraged more US citizens to either return to the Bahamas or visit for the first time accounted for around 300,000 room occupancy. The reopening the Bimini Big Game Club resort for game-fishing, plus newly opened conference facilities and luxury resorts all added to a remarketing of the Bahamas after the global economic crisis had cut visitor numbers dramatically.

In 2011, total contribution of travel and tourism to GDP was forecast at 47.4 per cent with tourist related investment constituting 16.5 per cent of total investment. Total direct employment in the industry is put at 48,000 jobs (29.4 per cent of total employment) and indirect employment at 91,000 jobs (55.1 per cent). Foreign exchange in tourism was expected to be US$2.2 billion in 2011.

Mining

Mining contributes approximately 1 per cent to annual GDP and employs around 1 per cent of the labour force.

Crude salt is produced by solar evaporation in Great Inagua and Long Island and aragonite deposits are found near Bimini Island.

Hydrocarbons

There are no significant oil reserves; however, Bahamas is an important re-exporter of oil and transshipment earns the islands a significant amount of foreign exchange. Consumption of oil was 34,000 barrels per day (bpd) in 2008. The state-owned Bahamas Oil Refining Company (Borco) is the principal commercial entity in the petroleum market and has been involved in several joint ventures with larger international oil companies. In 2005, the Bahamas, plus a number of other Caribbean states, signed an agreement with Venezuela to establish PetroCaribe, a multi-national oil company, owned by the participating states. PetroCaribe buys low-priced Venezuelan crude oil under long-term payment plans.

Although the Bahamas was poised to increase its hydrocarbons re-export sector with the construction of two new liquefied natural gas (LNG) re-gasification terminals, one at Ocean Cay, processing LNG from Qatar.

Energy

Total installed generating capacity was 455MW in 2007, producing over 1.9 billion kilowatt hours. Conventional thermal power stations produce the Bahamas' domestic energy.

Financial markets

Stock exchange

Bahamas International Securities Exchange (BISX)

Banking and insurance

Central bank

Central Bank of the Bahamas

Main financial centre

Nassau

Offshore facilities

The Bahamas is one of the largest offshore financial centres in the world. It was taken off the OECD's blacklist of countries that did not meet international requirements on taxation and transparency after it enacted new legislation which eliminated banking operations that did not have a physical presence in the Bahamas, and allowed for the exchange of tax information and the establishment of a comprehensive anti-money laundering regime. It resulted in the number of banks and trust companies licenced in the offshore sector declining.

Time

GMT minus five hours (daylight saving, April–October, minus four hours)

Geography

The Bahamas archipelago, which consists of 700 islands and nearly 2,500 small islets or cays sprawled across roughly 259,000 square km, stretches south-east from the southern coast of Florida (US). Virtually all the islands are surrounded by coral reefs and sandbanks, and nearly all are low lying.

Hemisphere

Northern.

Climate

The Bahamas is said to have one of the finest climates in the world. There are two seasons: winter (November–April), which is cool and dry, and summer (May–October), which is warm and wet. The climate is semi-tropical with temperatures ranging from 20 degrees Celsius (C) in winter to 30 degrees C in summer. Hurricanes can occur between June–November.

Dress codes

Business dress is more formal in the Bahamas than elsewhere in the Caribbean or in Florida; a business suit and tie is recommended for men and conservative business dress for women.

Visitors should bring lightweight or tropical clothing and, during the wet season, rainwear.

If invited to a Bahamian's home for dinner, dress should be business attire for men and conservative evening wear for women. Formal attire is worn when attending church.

Entry requirements

Passports

Required by all, except nationals of the US and Canada with evidence of citizenship (all US and Canadian nationals require a passport for re-entry to their country). All passports must be valid for at least six months from the date of arrival and visitors must show proof of a return/onward ticket and sufficient funds to provide for maintenance during their stay.

Visa

Required, but nationals of various countries are exempt for periods ranging from two weeks to eight months. For details contact nearest consulate or embassy or consult www.bahamas.com.

From May 2009 EU citizens may make a short-stay visit, for up to three months, without a visa.

Currency advice/regulations

Permission is required from the Central Bank of the Bahamas to import local currency, which may be exported up to a maximum of B$70. The import and export of foreign currency is unlimited.

US dollars are accepted as legal tender.

To avoid additional exchange rate charges, travellers are advised to take travellers cheques in US dollars.

Prohibited imports

Illegal drugs, firearms and other offensive weapons, animals.

Health (for visitors)
Medical facilities are on a par with the US, but can be costly and therefore medical insurance is recommended.
Mandatory precautions
A yellow fever vaccination certificate is required if arriving from an infected area.
Advisable precautions
Recommended immunisations are typhoid, diphtheria, hepatitis A and B, and tetanus. Malaria prophylaxis is recommended for Great Exuma. Tap water is safe to drink, although it can often be salty in taste. Food precautions should be observed.

Hotels
Wide variety available. Bills usually include a service charge and a hotel room tax.

Public holidays (national)
Fixed dates
1 Jan (New Year's Day), 10 Jul (Independence Day), 25 Dec (Christmas Day), 26 Dec (Boxing Day).
Holidays which fall on a Saturday or Sunday are observed on the following Monday.
Variable dates
Good Friday, Easter Monday, Whit Monday, Labour Day (first Mon in Jun), Emancipation Day (first Mon in Aug), National Heroes Day (second Mon in Oct).

Working hours
Banking
Mon–Thu: 0930–1500; Friday: 0930–1700.
Business
Mon–Fri: 0900–1700.
Government
Mon–Fri: 0900–1730.
Shops
Mon–Sat: 0900–1700. Sunday closing laws are generally strictly observed, except for some grocers open for a few hours, as well as the tourist shops on Bay Street in Nassau if cruise ships are docked.

Telecommunications
Mobile/cell phones
A GSM 1900 service is available.

Electricity supply
120V AC, 60 cycles

Social customs/useful tips
Bahamians shake hands upon meeting and business cards may be exchanged. Address first-time business acquaintances by their last names – conversations generally move to a first-name basis more slowly than in most Western countries. Appointments for business meetings should be made in advance.
Business lunches are often held. If invited to dinner at home, it is customary to take a small gift for the hostess and send a thank-you card afterwards.

Security
Visits to the Bahamas are generally trouble-free. Crime exists in the main cities of Nassau and Freeport, including incidents of murder and armed robbery. Much of this is within the local community, but tourists are often perceived as wealthy and have been the victims of robbery, particularly when alone or in isolated locations. Passports are a particular target for theft.
Visitors should take sensible precautions and be vigilant at all times. It is advisable not to carry large amounts of cash or jewellery. Do not offer resistance in the event of an attempted robbery as the assailant may be armed.
The outlying Family Islands are relatively free of crime, but sensible precautions should still be taken.
Penalties for possession or trafficking of drugs are severe. Pack all luggage yourself and do not carry anything through customs for anyone else unless you are aware of the contents.

Getting there
Air
National airline: Bahamasair
International airport/s: Nassau International (NAS), 16km west of city, shop, restaurant, bank, post office, car hire; Grand Bahama International (FPO), 5km north of Freeport, shop, bar, restaurant, buffet, shops, car hire.
Other airport/s: Paradise Island (PID), 5km from Nassau; George Town (GGT), 6km from city.
Airport tax: Departure tax: US$18.
Surface
Water: All the major cruise lines operating out of Florida and liners from New York and Florida make calls in the Bahamas, either in Nassau or Freeport.
Main port/s: Freeport Container Port on Grand Bahama, Nassau on New Providence and Matthew Town on Inagua. There are modern berthing facilities for cruise ships at Potters Cay on New Providence, Governor's Harbour on Eleuthera, Morgan's Bluff on North Andros and George Town on Exuma.

Getting about
National transport
Air: An extensive air charter network covers the islands, serving over 50 landing sites. Local enquiries should be made for particular requirements.
Road: The main centres are well served by 1,535km of surfaced roads.
Buses: There are few conventional buses, which serve only in the main towns. Mini-buses (*jitneys*) operate in the Nassau and Freeport areas.
Rail: There is no passenger rail service.
Water: Ferry and mail-boat services are operated between the various islands in the archipelago, but for business travellers the length and frequency of journeys may prove a major drawback.
City transport
Taxis: Taxis are often metered and use a fixed-rate system, but the rate should be agreed before setting off. A 15 per cent tip is usual.
Car hire
A national or international licence valid for three months is required. Rates vary according to the season. Traffic drives on the left.

BUSINESS DIRECTORY
The addresses listed below are a selection only. While World of Information makes every endeavour to check these addresses, we cannot guarantee that changes have not been made, especially to telephone numbers and area codes. We would welcome any corrections.

Telephone area codes
The international direct dialling code (IDD) for Bahamas is +1 242, followed by subscriber's number

Chambers of Commerce
Bahamas Chamber of Commerce, Shirley Street and Collins Avenue, PO Box N-665, Nassau (tel: 322-2145; fax: 322-4649; e-mail: bahamaschamber@coralwave.com).

Grand Bahama Chamber of Commerce, The Mall and Pioneer Way, PO Box F-40808, Freeport (tel: 352-8329; fax: 352-3280; e-mail: info@thegrandbahamachamberofcommerce.com).

Banking
Bahamas Development Bank, West Bay Street, PO Box N-3034, Nassau (tel: 327-5780; fax: 322-6457).

Bank of the Bahamas Ltd, PO Box N-7118, Nassau (tel: 326-2560).

Bank of Nova Scotia, PO Box N-7518, Nassau (tel: 356-1400).

Banque Privée Edmond de Rothschild Ltd, 51 Frederick Street, PO Box N-1136, Nassau (tel: 328-8121; fax: 328-8115).

Barclays Bank, PO Box N-8350, Nassau (tel: 322-4921).

British-American Bank, PO Box N-7502, Nassau (tel: 327-5170).

Canadian Imperial Bank of Commerce (CIBC), PO Box N-7125, Nassau (tel: 322-8455).

Citibank, PO Box N-8158, Nassau (tel: 322-4240).

Commonwealth Bank, PO Box SS-6263, Nassau (tel: 328-1854).

Finance Corporation of Bahamas Ltd, PO Box N-3038, Nassau (tel: 322-4822).

Handelsfinanz-CCF Bank International ltd, Maritime House, Frederick Street, PO Box N-10441, Nassau (tel: 328-8644, 328-1737; fax: 328-8600).

Inter-American Development Bank, PO Box N-3743, Nassau (tel: 393-7159).

Lloyds Bank International (Americas), PO Box N-1262, Bolam House, King and George Streets, Nassau (tel: 322-8711; fax: 322-8719).

Royal Bank of Canada, PO Box N-7537, Nassau (tel: 322-8700).

Central bank

Central Bank of the Bahamas, Frederick Street, PO Box N-4868, Nassau (tel: 322-2193; fax: 356–4307; e-mail: queries@centralbankbahamas.com).

Stock exchange

Bahamas International Securities Exchange (BISX): www.bisxbahamas.com

Travel information

Bahamasair, Windsor Field, PO Box N-4881, Nassau (tel: 327-8451; fax: 327-7409).

Bahamas Hotel Association, Dele West Bay Street, sub Dean's Lane, PO Box N-7799, Nassau (tel: 322-8381; fax: 326-5346).

Nassau/Cable Beach/Paradise Island Promotion Board, Dean's Lane, Fort Charlotte, PO Box N-7799, Nassau (tel: 322-8381; fax: 326-5346).

Ministry of tourism

Ministry of Tourism, PO Box N-3701, Nassau (tel: 302–2000; fax: 302–2098; e-mail: tourism@bahamas.com).

Ministries

Ministry of Agriculture and Industry, Levy Building, East Bay Street, Nassau (tel: 325-7502; fax: 322-1767).

Ministry of Economic Development, Manx Building, West Bay Street, Nassau.

Ministry of Education, Youth and Sports, Shirley Street, Nassau (tel: 322-5495; fax: 322-3267).

Ministry of Financial Services and Investment, Sir Cecil V Wallace Whitfield Centre, Cable Beach, PO Bx N-10980, Nassau (tel: 327-5826; fax: 327-5006).

Ministry of Foreign Affairs, Post Office Building, East Hill Street, Nassau (tel: 322-7624; fax: 328-8212).

Ministry of Health, Ministry of Health Building, Royal Victoria Gardens, Nassau (tel: 322-7425; fax: 322-7788).

Ministry of Housing and Social Development, Frederick House, Frederick Street, Nassau (tel: 356-0765; fax: 323-3883).

Ministry of Justice, Post Office Building, East Hill Street, Nassau.

Ministry of Labour and Immigration, Post Office Building, East Hill Street, Nassau (tel: 323-7240; fax: 326-7344).

Ministry of Public Works, John F Kennedy Drive, Nassau (tel: 323-7814; fax: 325-2016).

Ministry of Tourism, PO Box N-3701, Bolam House, George Street, Nassau (tel: 302–2000; fax: 302–2098; e-mail: tourism@bahamas.com).

Ministry of Transport, Aviation and Local Government, Pilot House Complex, Nassau (tel: 394-0451; fax: 394-5023).

Office of the Deputy Prime Minister, Churchill Building, Bay Street, Nassau (tel: 356-6792; fax: 356-6087).

Office of the Prime Minister, Cecil V Wallace Whitfield Centre, West Bay Street, Nassau (tel: 322-2805; fax: 328-8294).

Other useful addresses

Bahamas Agricultural and Industrial Corporation, PO Box N-4940, Levy Building, East Bay Street, Nassau (tel: 322-3740; fax: 322-2133).

Bahamas Economic Development Corporation, Bahamas Development Bank, Adderley Building, Bay Street/Rawson Square, PO Box N-3034, Nassau (tel: 327-5780; fax: 327-5907).

Bahamas Electricity Corporation, Big Pond and Tucker Road, PO Box N-7509, Nassau (tel: 328-7700).

Bahamas Employers' Confederation, PO Box N-166, Nassau (tel: 328-1757, 326-6644; fax: 328-1346).

Bahamas Financial Services Board, PO Box N–1764, West Bay Street, Goodman's Bay Corporate Centre, Nassau (tel: 326-7001; fax: 326–7007; e-mail: info@bfsb-bahamas.com).

Bahamas Information Services, Nassau Court, PO Box N-8172 (tel: 325-6028).

Bahamas Investment Authority, Cecil Wallace Whitfield Centre, PO Box CB-10980, Nassau (tel: 327-5970/4; fax: 327-5907; e-mail: investbahama@batelnet.bs; internet site: http://www.opm.gov.bs).

Bahamas Telecommunications Corporation, J F Kennedy Drive, PO Box N-3048, Nassau (tel: 323-4911).

Bahamas Water and Sewerage Corporation, J F Kennedy Drive, PO Box N-3905, Nassau (tel: 323-3944).

British High Commission, Bitco Building, 3rd Floor, East Street, PO Box N-7516, Nassau (tel: 325-7471/2/3; fax: 323-3871).

Broadcasting Corporation of The Bahamas, PO Box N-1347, Nassau (tel: 32-4623, 322-4480).

Cabinet Office, Churchill Bldg, Rawson Square, PO Box N-7147, Nassau (tel: 322-2805; fax: 328-8294).

Central Post Office, Post Office Building, PO Box N-8302, Nassau (tel: 322-3344).

The Comptroller of Customs, Seaban Building, Oakes Field, PO Box N-155, Nassau (tel: 326-4401).

Gaming Board of the Bahamas, West Bay Street, PO Box N-4565, Nassau (tel: 327-7478).

Government Publications Office (import regulations), East Bay Street, PO Box N-7147, Nassau (tel: 322-2410).

Hotel Corporation of the Bahamas, PO Box N-9520, Nassau (tel: 327-8395; fax: 327-6978).

Port Department, East Hill Street, PO Box N-8173 Nassau (tel: 326-7354).

Securities Commission of the Bahamas, PO Box N-8347, Nassau (tel: 356-6271/2; fax: 356-7530; e-mail: secbd@batelnet.bs).

US Embassy, Mosmar Building, Queen Street, PO Box N-8197, Nassau (tel: 322-1181; fax: 328-3495; e-mail: embnas@state.gov).

Internet sites

Bahamas International Securities Exchange: www.bisxbahamas.com

Bahamas National Investment Policy: www.geographia.com/bahamas/investment

Ministry of Tourism: www.bahamas.com

The Bahamas Guide: www.thebahamasguide.com

Bahrain

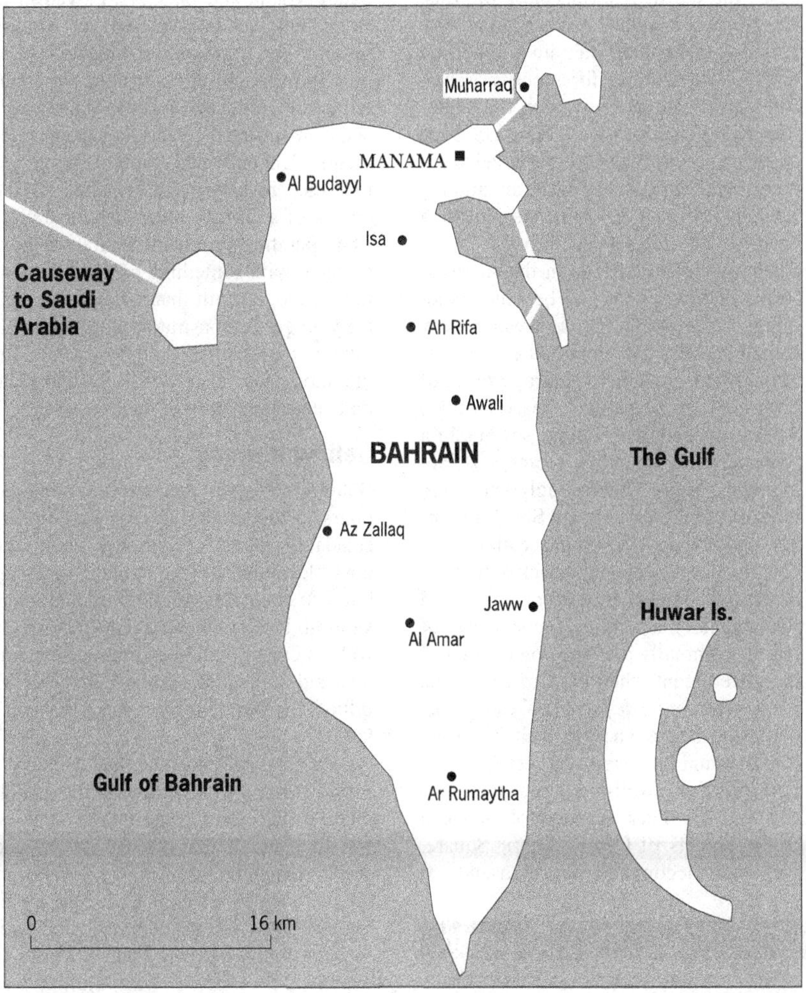

Bahrain is a small island (less than 50km long, and only 15km across), has a population of one million, (half of whom are not Bahrainis), little oil and, at least in comparison to its wealthy near neighbours, lacks a mouth-watering sovereign wealth fund. During World War II Bahrain served as an air-base for troops from both the US and the UK. In the period immediately after the war, it was the Gulf's staging post, where the aircraft of BOAC and Qantas refuelled on their flights half way round the world. In what at the time was the seminal work on the region, Richard H Sanger wrote that 'although its size and limited resources prevent Bahrain from becoming an important business and trading centre, wise expenditure and the investment of its oil revenues and wages have already brought the highest standard of living.' Mr Sanger also noted that the oil revenues had been 'quite fairly and usefully administered. Approximately one third has gone to the Sheikh to be spent by him and his family for their personal needs and charities. One third is invested so that Bahrain will have wealth to fall back on when oil production ends. And one-third is used for the operation and modernisation of the islands.' In 1953, it seemed, all was sweetness and light in the island state where a Sunni majority ruled over a Shi'a minority.

KEY FACTS

Official name: Al Mamlakah al Bahrayn (Kingdom of Bahrain)

Head of State: King Hamad bin Isa al Khalifa (ruler since Mar 1999; King since 14 Feb 2002)

Head of government: Prime Minister Sheikh Khalifah ibn Sulman al Khalifah (from 1999; re-appointed) Oct 2010)

Ruling party: There is no ruling party as such, but the Al Wifaq society are the largest single group in the Council of Deputies.

Area: 676 square km (35 islands)

Population: 1.26 million (2010)*

Capital: Manama

Official language: Arabic

Currency: Bahraini dinar (BD) = 1,000 fils

Exchange rate: BD0.38 per US$ (fixed)

GDP per capita: US$20,475 (2010)

GDP real growth: 4.10% (2010)

GDP: US$22.70 billion (2010)

Labour force: 578,000 (2008)

Inflation: 2.00% (2010)

Balance of trade: US$2.64 billion (2010)

* estimated figure

February – the cruellest month?

Bahrain continued as a relatively calm island, where Saudi Arabians could breach the island's fastness and drive over the 26km causeway, completed in 1986, linking the island to Saudi Arabia. But times change, immigration and birth rate differentials had seen to it that in the second half of the twentieth century, Bahrain's Sunni rulers held increasingly uncertain sway over a Shi'a majority. In the first ten years of the century, an estimated 65,000–100,000 Sunnis were added to the electoral roll, concentrated in large-scale government housing projects. Never-the-less, since the 2003 end of Saddam Hussein's rule in Iraq, Bahrain has found itself isolated as the only Shi'a majority country ruled by a Sunni elite. Many observers concur that Shi'a Iran has long sought to exacerbate tensions between the two communities. A desire to interfere in the internal affairs of Bahrain has long featured, albeit discreetly, in Iranian foreign policy. Iran has from time to time claimed Bahrain as its fourteenth Iranian province; the basis of this claim dates back to the eighteenth century when for a short period Bahrain recognised Iranian sovereignty. The periodic resurgence of the claim flies in the face of history; if anything it has probably lead to a modest level of Arab nationalism, evident in the rival nomenclature 'Persian' and 'Arabian' Gulf. Understandably, Bahrain's rulers are nervous of any Iranian interest in their country's affairs.

In the run up to Bahrain's 'elections' in October 2010 rumblings of dissent surfaced, anticipating similar undercurrents in Egypt, Libya, Syria, Tunisia and Yemen by several (largely unreported) months. As many as 150 protesters were detained in the October protests, principally targeting Shi'ite political and human-rights leaders, but including some who had done no more than join in the protests. Bahraini opposition leaders accused the US of ignoring these protests. The US Ambassador J Adam Ereli was reported as saying that 'Bahrain is important to the United States for security issues. But that doesn't mean we don't raise human rights issues as well.' The US State department, like many others, failed to appreciate the seriousness of the situation.

In late February 2011 matters came to a head, as Bahrainis lived through one of the most violent periods in the small island's history. What had become something of a peaceful backwater saw something of a bloodbath when nervous Sunni troops, unable to control crowds of protesters in Manama's Pearl ('Lulu') Square opened fire, killing seven Shi'a protesters and wounding scores, possibly hundreds, more. Interestingly, although most of the protesters were Shi'a, a number came from the Sunni community, equally incensed about the lack of true democracy, the prevalence of corruption and fundamental inequalities. Some degree of reason eventually prevailed on the part of the government when the Crown Prince, the government's *de facto* spokesman, ordered the troops back to their barracks. The Bahraini protesters had seen in Egypt how effective a well-organised street protest could be. Pearl Square took on some of the aspects of Cairo's Tahrir Square, with tents accommodating thousands of demonstrators, a Bahraini Speakers Corner and numerous, for the most part free of charge, food stands.

If things had looked grim in February 2011, by March they had taken a turn for the worse. Invoking the collective defence clauses of the Gulf Co-operation Council (GCC) on 14 March 2,000 troops from Saudi Arabia and the UAE moved in to shore up the beleaguered al Khalifa régime. The troop reinforcements lost no time in propping up their Bahraini counterparts, clearing public areas of protesters and dismantling the Pearl Square encampments. Unconfirmed reports suggested that the 'invasion' had resulted in the deaths of a further seven demonstrators. The operation provided the Iranian government with something of a public relations coup, a result that irritated many of the younger demonstrators who, again following the Egyptian example, seemed for the most part anxious to maintain the non-sectarian nature of their protest.

Getting it wrong

Bahrain's bigger, and wealthier, neighbours to the south and east were understandably nervous, not only about the possible outcome of the Bahraini uprising, but also about any possible Iranian intervention. It later emerged that Bahrain (as well as Oman) had been promised an annual aid stipend (from the US) of US$1 billion for the next ten years. Nervous? Us?

Bahrain is the base for the US Navy's Fifth Fleet; no small matter in the overall picture. The fleet comprises around 30 warships and 30,000 officers, sailors and staff. Immediately after the arrival of GCC troops in Bahrain US Secretary of State Hillary Clinton telephoned the Saudi foreign minister Prince Saud al Faisal to express her concern. Mrs Clinton was quoted as saying: 'the security challenges cannot be a substitute for a political resolution.' While in Tunisia she had earlier said of the invasion that 'We have said not only to the Bahrainis but to our Gulf partners that we do not think the security is the answer to what is going on.' The US was, predictably if improbably, joined by Iran in complaining about the Saudi presence in Bahrain. Iran sees Sunni Saudi Arabia as its sparring partner in the region.

Bahrain's royal family certainly appeared to have been wrong-footed by the Pearl Square demonstrations. After the shooting incident, King (Bahrain's rulers adopted the title of 'King' to replace the traditional 'Emir' in 1999) Hamad, the island's ruler, belatedly announced the

KEY INDICATORS **Bahrain**

	Unit	2006	2007	2008	2009	2010
Population	m	0.75	0.76	0.78	*1.04	*1.26
Gross domestic product (GDP)	US$bn	15.82	19.66	21.20	20.20	22.70
GDP per capita	US$	21,123	25,731	27,248	19,455	20,475
GDP real growth	%	6.5	8.1	6.1	2.9	4.1
Inflation	%	2.2	3.4	3.5	2.8	2.0
Natural gas output	bn cum	11.1	11.5	13.4	12.8	13.1
Exports (fob) (goods)	US$m	11,702.6	13,790.2	17,491.2	12,051.9	13,833.2
Imports (fob) (goods)	US$m	8,565.2	10,925.4	14,246.3	9,613.0	11,190.4
Balance of trade	US$m	3,137.4	2,846.8	3,244.9	2,438.8	2,642.8
Current account	US$m	2,112.0	2,906.5	2,256.9	560.0	770.1
Total reserves minus gold	US$m	2,910.0	3,000.0	–	–	–
Exchange rate	per US$	0.37	0.37	0.37	0.38	2.66

* estimated figure

release of 23 political prisoners. This gesture was not so much made willingly, but reluctantly in response to its imposition by Manama's protesters as a pre-condition to talks. Following the Saudi example, King Hamad also announced a one-off payment of 1,000 dinars to every Bahraini family. As has been the case in Egypt and in Libya, as well as Yemen, events in Bahrain added up to an uprising rather than a revolution, lacking as it did an obvious leader.

Tolerant no more?

The common perception of the Bahraini regime prior to the uprising was one of mild decency and tolerance. But the official response to the Pearl Square demonstrations was certainly not one of dialogue and discussion, nor of any degree of give and take. It was one of intolerance, harsh repression and summary punishment. The regime which, either by actually inviting or at least agreeing to the incursion of troops from Saudi Arabia and the UAE, had already shot itself in the foot, made matters even worse by detaining over 500 people. Human rights groups reported the deaths of four Bahrainis in detention; there were also reports of torture. The arrival of foreign troops in Bahrain was certainly a public relations disaster for the government. But there was worse: in April a military court sentenced four young Bahrainis to death for their alleged role in the death of two policemen. Three others received life sentences for their alleged role in the deaths. Amnesty International's Middle East director went on record as saying that 'Bahrain is in the grip of a deepening human rights crisis and the severity of the sentences… will do nothing to reverse that.' Significantly, a number of Bahraini politicians joined local human rights activists in acknowledging that the damage done to the country's reputation was beyond repair.

But the government's ham-fisted response continued to worsen. In mid-June 2011, a Bahraini military court tried 23 doctors and 24 nurses who had treated injured protesters. This was seen by virtually all neutral observers as a sad detachment of the regime from principled behaviour. The doctors and nurses' lawyers complained they had been tortured in custody. This was certainly not the behaviour expected of a once respected constitutional monarchy. The *London Times* went so far as to describe Bahrain as 'the world's newest pariah state'. The charges ranged from stealing medicine to stockpiling weapons to taking over a hospital. The defendants lawyers challenged the military court's jurisdiction, requesting also that their clients received independent medical examination.

Knowing it was on the ropes of international politics the Bahraini regime forlornly seized on the prospect of reinstating the Formula 1 Grand Prix that had been cancelled in March 2011 because of the protests. Crown Prince Salman had pounded Europe's political pavements in May, meeting with the UK's David Cameron and other leaders, optimistically endeavouring to restore his government's tattered image. It was reported that he had also been in touch with Formula 1 President Bernie Ecclestone. Local press reports alleged that in April a quarter of the staff employed at the Bahrain International Circuit (where the Grand Prix would have been held) had been sacked. Those who lost their jobs were all Sh'ia. The government's decision to end on 1 June the state of emergency that had been in place since March was thought to have more to do with reinstating the Grand Prix than any humanitarian concerns. The deadline for re-scheduling the Grand Prix was 3 June. At first it seemed as though the event would go-ahead. By mid-June, however, the decision to hold the Grand Prix seemed to have been reversed, not out of any moral or even political concerns, but because the risks to drivers and track officials were too high.

Oil gone

Bahrain is the oldest oil-producing state in the Gulf. The first strike was in 1932 and commercial production began in 1934 by the Standard Oil subsidiary, Bahrain Petroleum Company (Bapco), from the Awali field. Petroleum production and refining account for more than 60 per cent of Bahrain's export receipts, and 70 per cent of government revenues. Most of Bahrain's total energy consumption comes from natural gas, with the remainder supplied by oil. Hydrocarbons also provide the foundation for Bahrain's two major industries: petroleum refining and aluminium smelting. Bahrain's proven oil reserves stood at 125 million barrels in January 2011, according to the US-based *Oil and Gas Journal* (OGJ), all of which are located in the Awali field. In addition to the 46,000 barrels per day (bpd) produced in its territory, Bahrain and Saudi Arabia share the 300,000bpd of oil production from the offshore Abu Safah field. This figure is actually counted in Saudi oil production figures, but half of the output is allocated to Bahrain.

Unlike other Gulf states, Bahrain exports refined petroleum products rather than crude oil. Bahrain's domestic oil pipeline network is rather limited, focused primarily on delivering crude oil from the Awali field to the refinery at Sitra. Because domestic production is much lower than the country's refining capacity, Bahrain imports about 210,000bpd of Arab Light crude oil from Saudi Arabia via a sub-sea pipeline linking the two countries. Bapco (owned 60 per cent by the government and 40 per cent by Caltex since 1981) refines this crude oil and exports much of it via tanker. Most of Bahrain's exports go to India and other Asian markets. Crude oil production from the shared offshore Abu Safah field is sold from the Ras Tanura terminal in Saudi Arabia, the world's largest export terminal.

Bahrain's production remained relatively stable over the first decade of the twenty-first century. As domestic consumption has surged since 2005, exports have decreased, particularly since 2005. Perhaps surprisingly, the self contained nature and presence of Bahrain's hydrocarbons has meant that it has been to a degree cocooned from the uprising of the first few months of 2011. Exports were originally expected to continue to decrease in 2011, having already fallen from 27,000bpd in 2005 to 3,000bpd in 2009. However, diminished domestic demand resulting from the uprising may well make more production available for exports.

Risk assessment

Economy	Struggling
Politics	Poor
Regional stability	Precarious

COUNTRY PROFILE

Historical profile

1816 Bahrain's first treaty with Britain was signed

1861 The second treaty made it a British protectorate.

1869 Sheikh Isa bin Ali al Khalifa was named ruler.

1913 A treaty between Britain and Turkey recognised Bahrain as an independent state, but the country remained under British administration.

1923 After more than half a century of peace and stability, Sheikh Isa bin Ali al Khalifa abdicated in favour of his son, Sheikh Hamad.

1928 Iran claimed ownership of Bahrain; the dispute was not resolved until 1970 when Iran accepted a UN report stating that the vast majority of Bahrainis wanted their complete independence.

1932 Bahrain became the first country in the Gulf to strike oil.
1942–61 Sheikh Hamad died in 1942 and his son, Sheikh Sulman bin Hamad al Khalifa ruled Bahrain until his death in 1961, when he was succeeded by Sheikh Isa bin Sulman al Khalifa.
1968 Britain announced its intention to withdraw from the Gulf by 1971.
1971 Bahrain and Qatar became independent states.
1973–74 Bahrain's constitution was promulgated; it limited the Sheikh's powers and established an elected 30-member National Assembly.
1975 The National Assembly refused to ratify a bill to arrest and detain people for up to three years without trial, and was dissolved by the ruler, Sheikh Isa. The government subsequently ruled by decree.
1981 The political and economic union, Co-operation Council for the Arab States of the Gulf (CCASG) (known as Gulf Co-operation Council (GCC)) was formed by Bahrain, Kuwait, Oman, Qatar, Saudi Arabia and the United Arab Emirates (UAE).
1986 The opening of the 25km King Fahd Causeway between Bahrain and Saudi Arabia gave a boost to business and tourism.
1991 Bahrain actively supported the allied forces against Iraq in the Gulf military conflict.
1994 The majority Shi'ites staged demonstrations demanding better living conditions and the return of an elected parliament. The Sunnis, although once the majority but now in a minority, are dominant in both politics and business.
1999 Sheikh Isa bin Sulman al Khalifa, who had ruled since 1961, died and was succeeded by his son, Sheikh Hamad bin Isa al Khalifa.
2000 For the first time, non-Muslims and women were appointed to the 40 member Majlis al-Shura (Consultative Council).
2001 A referendum on political reform was approved, under which Bahrain would become a constitutional monarchy with an elected lower chamber of parliament and an independent judiciary.
2002 Hamad bin Isa al Khalifa was declared King, and the state became a constitutional monarchy. As part of the reform process, legislation was approved to allow women to vote in elections and run for national office. In legislative elections (the first since 1973), parliament became a mix of secular and Islamic candidates. The Shi'ite opposition boycotted the election resulting in a Sunni dominated parliament.
2004 The first woman to be appointed head of a government ministry, Nada Haffadh, was made health minister. A free trade agreement was signed with the US.
2005 King Hamad called for increased global co-operation to combat international terrorism. Thousands protested in favour of a fully elected parliament.
2006 Legislative elections were held in which Sunni representatives won 22 seats (out of 40) and Shi'ites won 18.
2007 There were several days of rioting in majority Shi'a areas with protesters demanding compensation for human rights violations between 1980–90.
2008 A common market was created between Bahrain, Kuwait, Oman, Qatar, Saudi Arabia and the UAE, the six wealthiest Gulf States. Citizens of these countries are allowed to travel between and live in any of the six states, where they may find employment, buy properties and businesses and use the educational and health facilities freely.
2009 Iraqi Airways began flights to Bahrain, after a gap of 20 years. The Nation Bank of Kuwait – Kingdom of Bahrain (NBK Bahrain), posted record profits of US$88.9 million for the first two quarters of the year (an increase of 55 per cent over the same period in 2008).
2010 In May the authorities suspended the news network Al Jazeera's operations in Bahrain and barred its workers, following the broadcast of documentaries on the treatment of Asian labourers and poverty in Bahrain. On 23 September, mainly Shi'a protesters were charged by the authorities with planning to overthrow the King. Parliamentary elections were held on 23 October in which 40 seats were contested. The Shia Al Wifaq National Islamic Society (Al Wifaq) won 18 seats (out of 40), but combined, the Sunni block won 22 seats, including 17 independent delegates. Sheikh Khalifah ibn Sulman al Khalifah resigned and was reappointed as prime minister on 23 October; he reappointed his previous cabinet members and made no changes to key ministerial posts.
2011 On March 6 protesters marched on the council of ministers building in Manama, calling on the prime minister to 'step down before Qadafi' (of Libya). On 15 March authorities asked Saudi Arabia to supply 1,500 troops to help their own forces restore order. A day later, security forces used tanks to oust protestors from Pearl Square, ending its two-week occupation. Ambulances were blocked from entering the square to provide aid. Later security militia carried out a sweep of hospitals, arresting any trauma patients being treated. It was reported by medical staff that they were also being intimidated and attacked by pro-government supporters. On 17 March the UN criticised Bahraini officials for commandeering all hospitals and the arrest by various security forces of protestors receiving medical treatment. On 7 April, the Turkish foreign minister, Ahmet Davutoglu, held talks in Bahrain with both the opposition group al Wifaq and King Hamad. Turkey was concerned that Bahrain could become the site of a proxy battle between Iran and the Arab Gulf states. On 26 May, Moody's downgraded Bahrain's sovereign credit rating to 'negative'. On 1 June, the King decreed that the state of emergency that had been imposed in March was to be lifted. On 6 June, trials began before the Court of National Safety of 47 medical personnel arrested for treating demonstrators during the civil unrest; 20 were charged with possessing unlicensed weapons, inciting others to overthrow the monarchy, unauthorised occupation of the hospital and stealing medical equipment; 28 others were accused of spreading false news and lying about the medical condition of some patients (one accused was tried *in absentia*). On 2 July, in a BBC interview, a doctor claimed that he had been subject to torture and coerced into making a false confession while under arrest; the family of other doctors made similar claims. National reconciliation talks between the Sunni-led government and Shi'a opposition, al Wifaq, began on 2 July, in which the King said that all the dialogue process would be inclusive. However, by 17 July al Wifaq had withdrawn from the talks, saying the national dialogue 'was not serious' and that they had been allocated too few seats. On ????? September 20 medical staff from the Salmaniya Medical Complex, who had treated injured persons during the February and March demonstrations, were convicted of by the National Safety Court. The security court gave long jail sentances to some 80 protesters. There was international condemnation of the harshness of the sentences and on 5 October the attorney general announced that after studying the court's judgement the 20 medical staff would be retried by the country's highest civilian court.

Political structure

Constitution

The 1973 constitution was suspended in 1975 and reinstated by royal decree, with significant amendments, in February 2002.

By a charter, agreed by referendum, Bahrain was declared a constitutional monarchy in 2002, with a bicameral parliament and independent judiciary. Women were given suffrage and although political parties remained illegal, eleven new political societies were licensed in 2001.

The King is the symbol of the country and is inviolate.

Independence date

15 August 1971

Form of state
Constitutional monarchy
The executive
Executive power rests with the King, who is Head of State, he appoints a prime minister and members of the Consultative Council, which is an advisory body that, since 2002, is empowered to make laws. The King may dissolve or extend the term of the Consultative Council. The King has the right to initiate, ratify and promulgate laws.
The King is the head of the armed forces and head of the Judiciary.
National legislature
A bicameral National Assembly consists of the Majlis an Nuwab (Chamber of Deputies (sometimes translated as 'Representatives')) (lower house) which has 40 popularly elected members and the Majlis al-Shura (Consultative Council) with 40 members appointed by the King. Membership of both houses is four years. The King may renew membership of the Council and dissolve the Chamber of Deputies by decree. Terms of both houses may be extended by the King for up to two extra years.
The King and prime minister present bills to the Chamber of Deputies for consideration before they are passed to the Consultative Council.
Legal system
The judiciary is a constitutionally independent body, whose function and organisation is regulated by law. It is a mixture, based on English common law and Sunni and Shi'a Sharia (Islamic law) traditions, where Sharia is the principal source of law.
The Supreme court is the final court of appeal for all civil, commercial and criminal matters.
Last elections
23 and 30 October 2010 (parliamentary, first and second round)
Results: Parliament (lower house, after two rounds): Al Wefaq National Islamic Society (Al Wefaq) won 18 seats (out of 40), Al Asalah Islamic Society (Al Asalah) three, Al Menbar National Islamic Society (Al Menbar) two, independents 17.
Next elections
2014 (parliamentary)

Political parties

Political parties in Bahrain are formally banned; MPs are members of political 'societies' of which the National Democratic Action Society (Wa'ad) represents an informal opposition.
Ruling party
There is no ruling party as such, but the Al Wifaq society are the largest single group in the Council of Deputies.

Population

1.26 million (2010)*
Last census: April 2001: 650,604
Population density: 966 inhabitants per square km, one of the highest in the world. Bahrain's population is highly urbanised (92 per cent).
Annual growth rate: 2.4 per cent 1994–2004 (WHO 2006)
Ethnic make-up
Bahrain's inhabitants are mostly Arab, with a sizeable minority of Iranian descent.
Approximately 38 per cent of the population are foreign residents, mostly from South Asia and other Arab countries,
Religions
According to the constitution, Islam is the state religion. Approximately 98 per cent of the indigenous population are Muslim – two-thirds Shi'as and the remainder belonging to the Sunni branch of Islam. There is no exact figure for the number of each; the Sunnis were in the majority up until the mid-1950s but are now in a minority, although remaining in power. The government have attempted to adjust the difference by a programme of naturalising Arab and non-Arab Sunnis for work in the police and military. The remaining 2 per cent are Jewish and Christian.
About half of the foreign population are non-Muslim, including Christians, Jews, Hindus, Baha'is, Buddhists and Sikhs.

Education

Primary schooling lasts for six years between the ages of six and 12. Secondary education lasts for three years and offers students a choice of three main branches: the general, the technical or the commercial.
The government is seeking to establish Bahrain as a regional centre for human resource development. In addition to several universities, there are a number of training centres, such as the Bahrain Training Institute (BTI) and the Bahrain Institute of Training and Finance (BITF) that are designed to prepare local graduates for the modern, technology driven workforce.
There are both government-owned and private schools.
Literacy rate: 91 per cent and 82.6 per cent for males and females respectively (World Bank).
Compulsory years: 6 to 15
Enrolment rate: 105 per cent boys, 106 per cent girls total primary school enrolment of the relevant age group (including repetition rates) (World Bank).

Health

Health services in Bahrain are of a high quality and all Bahrainis receive free health care from the state. There are a mixture of government and private hospitals, with additional government health centres and maternity hospitals.
HIV/Aids
HIV prevalence: 0.2 per cent aged 15–49 in 2003 (World Bank)
Life expectancy: 74 years, 2004 (WHO 2006)
Fertility rate/Maternal mortality rate: 2.4 births per woman, 2004 (WHO 2006)
Child (under 5 years) mortality rate (per 1,000): 12 per 1,000 live births (World Bank)
Head of population per physician: 1.9 physician per 1,000 people, 2004 (WHO 2006)

Welfare

The government provides direct financial assistance to those considered needy in addition to assistance provided by religious organisations and local charitable societies. There are seven social centres operated by the ministry of labour and social affairs (MoLSA) that provide training and assistance, especially to needy women. Public and private facilities for the elderly, handicapped and orphaned provide first class care, using the latest professional methods, approaches, and equipment. The number of needy families on government assistance lists has been growing for the past decade at double the rate of the population growth.
Family support
The social assistance programme provides approximately BD30 (US$80) per month to every family being assisted.

Main cities

Manama (capital, estimated population 140,616 in 2005), Rifa (97,194) Muharraq (58,254) Madinat Isa (40,665), Hammad (66,846), Jid Hafs (11,883).

Media

While press laws guarantee the independence of journalists, criminal penalties may be imposed for infringements, such as insulting the King; self-censorship is widespread.
Bahrain is striving to achieve a status as the primary media centre for the Middle East in competition with Dubai in United Arab Emirates.
Press
Dailies: In Arabic, *Akhbar al Khaleej* (www.akhbar-alkhaleej.com), *al Wasat* (www.alwasatnews.com), *al Ayam* (www.alayam.com), *al Meethaq* (www.almeethaq.net) and *al Waqt* (www.alwaqt.com). In English the *Bahrain Tribune* (www.bahraintribune.com) and *Gulf Daily News* (www.gulf-daily-news.com).
Weeklies: In Arabic, *Layalina* (www.layalinamag.com) and *Sada al-Usbu'*. In English, *Gulf Weekly*

(www.gulfweekly.com), has general news and information.
Business: In Arabic, *Akhbar al Khaleej* (www.akhbar-alkhaleej.com) has a business section. In English, the online website *Trade Arabia* (www.tradearabia.com), has a comprehensive range of business information topics and a hard copy *Gulf Industry* in English and Arabic, concerning the petroleum industry.
Periodicals: In Arabic, *Huna al Bahrain*, published by the Ministry of Information. In English, *Bahrain This Month* (www.bahrainthismonth.com).

Broadcasting

The state-owned Bahrain Radio and Television Corporation (BRTC) (www.bahraintv.com) operates the national public broadcasting networks.
Radio: BRTC operates Radio Bahrain (www.radiobahrain.fm) over three wave lengths, in the English language, offering news and current affairs, popular music and classical music. The Radio Bahrain Second Programme broadcasts general and cultural programmes including sports events and the Qur'an in Arabic. There are other private radio stations including Voice FM (www.voicefmbahrain.com), and, via satellite, Radio Sawa Gulf (www.radiosawa.com) and Monte Carlo Doualiya (www.rmc-mo.com) broadcasting in Arabic and French.
Television: BRTC operates five channels. The private and independent Orbit Satellite Television and Radio Network (www.orbit.net) operates 48 channels in Arabic and English by subscription. Residents also have access to hundreds of regional channels broadcasting via foreign satellite or cable TV companies.

News agencies

National news agency: Bahrain News Agency

Economy

Since Bahrain is the least wealthy of the six Gulf states and as its small hydrocarbon reserves is inexorably shrinking, it has had to adapt and diversify its economy to provide an income. The service, essentially banking and finance, sector now constitutes over 55 per cent of GDP. Industry and manufacturing constitutes over 40 per cent and agriculture less than 1 per cent of GDP. Alba, one of the world's largest alumina smelting plants is state-owned in partnership with the German company, BBS Kraftfahrzeugtechnik producing finished aluminium products for the automotive industry. There is also an automotive industry in performance car manufacturing using aluminium components. Bahrain is a major Middle Eastern banking centre and is a leading Islamic financial centre, with the largest concentration of Islamic commercial, investment and leasing banks, as well as Islamic insurance (*Takaful*) companies.
GDP growth was 6.1 per cent in 2008, having fallen from 8.1 per cent in 2007, when the global economic crisis cut trade, particularly in commodity sales. By 2009 GDP growth was 2.9 per cent and Bahrain just avoided going into recession. By 2010 the economy had picked up and had a growth rate of 4.1 per cent, although the forecast for 2011 was another slowdown to 1.5 per cent.
Large-scale tourist resorts and projects have become a significant source of revenue, with further development designed to attract greater regional tourism. Bahrain was the first Middle East country to build a Formula One racing circuit; Abu Dhabi was the second.
Infrastructure development has included a new port and expanded airport, strengthening Bahrain's position as a regional hub. The Economic Development Board (EDB) has been active in attracting foreign investment.
The Gulf Co-operation Council (GCC) was planning to issue a common currency in 2010, but the economic crisis and the experience of the fluctuating euro on the economies of the euro-zone gave the GCC pause for thought. If the currency is introduced it may have the effect of changing the medium of oil transactions from the US dollar to the new currency.
The anti-government riots in early 2011 set back the economy. Foreign Direct Investment (FDI) dropped over the year and the banking sector stagnated.

External trade

Bahrain is one of six members of the Gulf Co-operation Council (GCC) free trade agreement (FTA), a common market between Bahrain and the other five members of the GCC, which was launched in 2008. Citizens of these countries are now allowed to travel between and live in any of the six states, where they may find employment, buy properties and businesses and use the educational and health facilities freely. Bahrain is also a member of the Greater Arab free trade area, which co-ordinates shared standards and specification of Arab products, inter-custom fees and provides a platform for communication between members. A customs union was established whereby tariffs within GCC FTA are reduced by a percentage each year, until none remain.
The export of goods and services accounts for around 80 per cent of GDP. In the face of falling oil reserves the government has invested in processed aluminium which has become a major export commodity, while supporting many domestic downstream industries.

Imports

Main imports are crude oil, machinery, raw materials, chemicals and foodstuffs.
Main sources: Saudi Arabia (typically 26 per cent of total), Japan (9 per cent), US (8 per cent).

Exports

Main exports are petroleum and related goods, aluminium, vehicles and automotive parts, and textiles.
Main destinations: India (typically 4 per cent of total), Saudi Arabia (3 per cent), UAE (2 per cent).

Agriculture

Farming

The agricultural sector typically accounts for less than 1 per cent of GDP and employs 5 per cent of the workforce.
Apart from being a small island, development of agriculture is limited by labour shortages, lack of water and salinity of the soil. The major crop is alfalfa for animal fodder, although farmers produce modest amounts of crops including dates, watermelons, pomegranates, bananas, potatoes, eggplants and tomatoes for the local market.
Government agricultural plans emphasise drainage to reduce salinity, improvement of the soil and new irrigation and cultivation techniques; ther have also been experiments with hydroponics.
The land tenure system, under which over 60 per cent of cultivable land is held on three-year leases, discourages the stability needed for development.
The lack of grazing inhibits livestock production. One large dairy has annual milk production of 500,000 litres. Small dairy farmers, responsible for 15 per cent of production, have established a co-operative and constructed a milk pasteurising plant.

Fishing

The waters surrounding Bahrain have traditionally been rich fishing grounds, with more than 200 varieties of fish, many of which constitute a staple of the local diet.
The discovery of oil in 1935 led to a steady decline in the fishing industry, which has been unable to meet domestic demand, noticeably since the 1970s.
Moreover, pollution in the Gulf, since the 1980s, has increasingly threatened fish production and the shrimp industry.
Fish catches have dropped amid claims of illigal fishing, habitat destruction from land reclamation and environmental pollution that threatens overall fish stocks.
Pearl diving was once a major industry with 40 per cent of Gulf pearl exports coming from Bahrain. Diving has declined sharply since the 1930s, but Bahrain has been a leading pearl testing centre since 1990, and a new pearl and gem testing laboratory was opened in 2008.

Industry and manufacturing

The industrial sector contributed 39.6 per cent of GDP in 2004, of which manufacturing was 10.8 per cent. The sector typically employs 34 per cent of the labour force.

Bahrain's most prominent non-oil industry is the Aluminium Bahrain (Alba) plant, which supplies various downstream manufacturing plants as well as the Gulf Aluminium Rolling Mill Company (Garmco). Aluminium exports are one of Bahrain's biggest earners as a result of increased world prices. Alba dominates the manufacturing sector with a production capacity of 500,000 tonnes per year. More than 50 per cent of the aluminium produced at Alba is sold on the local and regional market, while the remainder goes mainly to the Far East.

Export-oriented small- and medium-sized industries have been attracted to free industrial zones established at Mina Sulman, Ma'amir, Abu Gazal and North Sitra, which enjoy tax and duty incentives. Industries located in these areas include plastics, paper, steel-wool and wire-mesh producers, marine service industries, aluminium, asphalt, cable manufacturing, prefabricated building and furniture.

Iron and steel production is increasing. The Bahrain Ispat Company, under the control of the Indian Ispat Group (based in London), operates a plant with a capacity of 1.2 million tpy of iron briquettes produced from iron pellets.

Tourism

Bahrain as a regional destination is the key strategy for its tourist industry. Government national plans include marketing Bahrain as a 'high-quality leisure and business tourism destination' for visitors primarily from the Middle East, but also Europe and Asia. Over seven million people visited the island in 2009, with visitor expenditure of over US$1.7 billion. Many visitors cross the causeway from Saudi Arabia for day-trips. The government is concerned that its traditional, historic towns are an asset that could easily be damaged by unfettered development.

The civil unrest and news reports of battles in the streets of Manama, together with the cancellation of the annual Grand Prix Formula One race resulted in tourism being adversely affected in 2011. Before the turbulence, the prospects for tourism had been good with travel and tourism directly providing 6.6 per cent of total GDP (16.5 per cent of indirect GDP), it had also been forecast to directly provide 33,000 jobs (7.1 per cent of total employment) and 79,000 jobs indirectly (16.9 per cent of total employment). Investment committed to tourism development in 2011 had been BD241.4 million (US$9.1 million). Bahrain will need a period of sustained peace and a serious promotional campaign to regain its reputation as a suitable destination.

Hydrocarbons

Proven oil reserves were negligible by 2010. Oil had accounted for around 65 per cent of government revenue and more than 60 per cent of exports, but the government has been diversifying the economy.

The Bahrain Petroleum Company has responsibility for all aspects of the hydrocarbon industry including exploration, production, refining and distribution in both domestic and international markets.

Bahrain had 200 billion cubic metres (cum) of natural gas at the end of 2010 and produced 13.1 billion cum, a 2.4 per cent increase on the 2009 figure. Unless further gas fields are found, current reserves are expected to be depleted by 2015. With the imminent loss, Qatar has signed an agreement to supply Bahrain with natural gas in the future.

Bahrain does not produce or import coal.

Energy

There was 2.3GW of installed electricity generating capacity in 2007 with peak domestic demand for electricity matching almost exactly total capacity of 2,230MW, with 9.2 billion kilowatt hours (kWh) generated. Consumption has grown steadily, and is projected to increase 7 per cent annually until 2020; independent power stations have been licensed, while state-owned facilities were privatised to meet the demand. A new, gas-fired power station, Al Ezzel, became operational in 2006 and was producing 950MW by 2007, and accounting for 30 per cent of all capacity available.

Construction of Bahrain's largest power plant, to provide around 30 per cent of Bahrain's total output, located at Al Dour, was begun in 2007. At a total cost of US$1 billion, it will provide an additional 1,250MW of electricity and 181,680 kilolitres of desalinated water. The US electrical engineers GE Energy are contracted to provide five gas turbines, equipped with advanced emission control technologies. Further plans to increase production in other existing plants should increase generation up to a projected need of 3,500MW by 2020.

A Gulf Co-operation Council (GCC) project to link the six member states (Saudi Arabia, Qatar, Bahrain, Kuwait, Oman and the United Arab Emirates) to an integrated power-grid began in 2005. The first phase of the GCC power grid was completed in July 2009 at a cost of US$1,095 million, linking Saudi Arabia, Bahrain, Kuwait and Qatar through 800km of transmission lines. Kuwait and Saudi Arabia will each receive an extra 1,200MW of power capacity and later, the UAE will receive 900MW, Qatar 750MW, Bahrain 600MW and Oman 400MW. In the first phase, a 400kV overhead line links Kuwait's Al Zour power station with Doha, and a 400kV submarine line to Saudi Arabia with Bahrain. The second phase will link the UAE with Oman. The resulting two mega-grids will be joined in the final phase.

Financial markets

Bahrain has a solid reputation as an international financial hub. It remains attractive as a result of a combination of factors, including its relative political stability, open and tax-free business climate, central geographical position, low costs, excellent communications and an accommodating government. The financial sector is one of the most diverse in the region and has the largest volume of transactions in the Middle East. The International Islamic Financial Market (IIFM) has attracted a number of major financial institutions to deal specifically in Sharia compliant deals.

Bahrain Islamic International Rating Agency (IIRA) is the sole credit ratings agency set up (in 2005) to provide a ratings system of capital instruments and Islamic financial products in predominantly Islamic countries. IIRA is sponsored by several multilateral development institutions, major banks, financial institutions and ratings agencies. It operates in 11 countries in which it also has shareholders as the *Sharia* complaint board of directors maintain an independence service

Stock exchange

Bahrain Stock Exchange (BSE)

Banking and insurance

In 2008 there were some 370 offshore banking units and representative offices in Bahrain, as well as 32 Islamic commercial, investment and leasing banks. Bahrain reportedly has the largest concentration of Islamic financial institutions, including *takaful* (insurance) companies, in the Middle East.

The Central Bank of Bahrain (CBB) has full regulations for its Islamic banking community.

An agreement was reached between Saudi Arabia, Kuwait, Bahrain and Qatar to establish the Gulf Co-operation Council (GCC) Monetary Council to be established (originally in 2009), marking plans to set up a regional central bank, to be based in Riyadh (Saudi Arabia). The GCC Monetary Council will oversee the introduction of a monetary union, due to be in operation by 2013.

Central bank

Central Bank of Bahrain (CBB) replaced the Bahrain Monetary Agency on 7

September 2006. It is responsible for maintaining monetary and financial stability.

Main financial centre

Manama

Time

GMT plus three hours

Geography

Bahrain is an archipelago of 33 islands. Only three of the islands are inhabited. The main island of Bahrain contains most of the population and is linked by a causeway to the island of Muharraq. Another causeway links Bahrain to Saudi Arabia.

Hemisphere

Northern

Climate

Summer temperatures are hot and humid, reaching 49 degrees Celsius (C) in the shade, while January, the coldest winter month, has temperatures ranging from 3 degrees C to 28 degrees C. Humidity, particularly on the coast, can be extreme. Between December and the end of March the climate is temperate, with temperatures ranging between 19–25 degrees C.

Dress codes

A lightweight suit or lightweight jacket and trousers are advised. A long-sleeved shirt with a tie should be worn at business and official meetings but a jacket need not be worn. Women should dress modestly. However, bikinis may be worn on certain beaches and at international hotel swimming pools. The dress code for women is less severe than in Saudi Arabia or some other Islamic countries.

Entry requirements

Passports

Passports are required by all.

Visa

Visas are required by all except nationals of Kuwait, Oman, Qatar, Saudi Arabia and the United Arab Emirates (UAE).
For details of requirements for business and tourist visas visit: www.bahrainembassy.org/visareq.html.
Tourist visas can be obtained on arrival at Bahrain airport, business visas must be applied for in advance. Journalists must make prior arrangements with the Ministry of Information.
Women arriving in Bahrain alone and without a visa could be refused entry. Lone female travellers are advised to obtain a visa before departure.

Prohibited entry

Israeli nationals or anyone holding a passport with an Israeli visa/stamp may be denied entry.

Currency advice/regulations

Any currency, including Bahraini, may be freely imported and exported.

Customs

Personal effects are duty free. The duty free allowance is 400 cigarettes or 50 cigars and two bottles of alcoholic beverages, for non-Muslim passengers only, and 227ml of perfume for personal use. Jewellery, drugs, firearms and ammunition are subject to import permits.

Prohibited imports

Pornographic and obscene literature and pictures, cultured or undrilled pearls, and goods of Israeli origin are prohibited.

Health (for visitors)

Medical services in Bahrain are of high quality with a good general hospital in Manama and modern health centres in smaller communities. Medical insurance is advised. Consultations are offered at the American Mission Hospital, 133 Isa Al-Kabeer Avenue, Manama (tel: 17-253-447; internet: www.amh.org.bh).

Mandatory precautions

Yellow fever certificate, for visitors arriving from infected areas.

Advisable precautions

Recommended immunisations are hepatitis A and B, polio, tetanus and typhoid. There is a risk of rabies.

Hotels

There are plenty of first class hotels. A 12 per cent service charge is usual. Major hotels and most restaurants are licensed.

Credit cards

All major credit cards are accepted.

Public holidays (national)

Fixed dates

1 Jan (New Year's Day), 16–17 Dec (National Day).

Variable dates

Eid al Adha (three days), Eid al Fitr (three days), Islamic New Year, Ashura, Prophet's Birthday.

Islamic year 1433 (26 Nov 2011–14 Nov 2012): The Islamic year has 354 or 355 days, with the result that Muslim feasts advance by 10–12 days against the Gregorian calendar each year. Dates of the Muslim feasts vary according to sightings of the new moon, so cannot be forecast exactly.

Working hours

Thursday and Friday are weekly holidays. Regular hours are subject to change during the month of Ramadan. Some banks and businesses close on Saturday.

Banking

Sat–Wed: 0730–1200; Thu: 0730–1100; some branches are open three days weekly in the afternoon; some offshore banking units close on Sunday; 1000–1330 during Ramadan.

Business

Sat–Thu: 0800–1530 or 0800–1300, 1500–1730.

Government

Sat–Tue: 0700–1415; Wed: 0700–1400. During Ramadan government offices open 0930–1430.

Shops

Sat–Thu: 0830–1230, 1530–1830; large superstores are open Sat–Thu: 0800–1900; late opening Wed and Thu: 0800–1200, 1530–2130; some are open for a few hours on Fri in the Souk.

Telecommunications

Mobile/cell phones

GSM 900/1800 services are available throughout the country.

Electricity supply

230V 50 cycles AC everywhere except Awali, which has 120V 60 cycles; various types of plug fitting, normally three-pin flat.

Weights and measures

Metric system (local measures are also used).

Social customs/useful tips

Traditionally much time is spent in exchanging small talk at business meetings; embarking on business matters before the atmosphere is favourable may cause offence. Decisions are often taken by consensus, according to the Arabian tradition, rather than exclusively on the advantages and disadvantages of the case submitted. In business, it is essential to create a mood of trust and to be persistent even when the case is apparently lost. Always shake hands on meeting and leaving. You may find the handshake lasts longer than in the West, but this is a sign of friendship. If you have made a good impression, the handshake on departure will be longer than that on arrival.
Muslims pray five times a day although shops and offices do not close during prayer. Although alcohol is not forbidden by law, like pork, it is forbidden by Islam and should be consumed with discretion. It is polite to avoid eating, drinking or smoking in the presence of Muslims during daylight hours in the month of Ramadan (it is illegal to do so in public). Unless addressing members of the royal family normal Western forms of address and greeting are usual.
Everyone, including the visitor, is subject to *sharia* (Islamic law) although it is less rigorously applied than in some other Islamic countries.

Security

Visitors to Bahrain should keep in touch with developments in the Middle East as any increase in regional tension might affect travel advice.
It is advisable to avoid village areas, especially after dark. Local security

precautions, religious and social sensitivities should be observed and respected.

Getting there

Air

National airline: Gulf Air (100 per cent owned by Bahrain since May 2007).

International airport/s: Bahrain International, Muharraq (BAH), 6.5km north-east of city, with bar, restaurant, buffet, bank, shops, hotel reservations.

Airport tax: International departures BD3; not applicable for transit passengers.

Surface

Road: The Saudi-Bahrain Causeway links Bahrain, Saudi Arabia and Qatar.

Water: There are passenger ferries running between Iran and Bahrain; the trip takes about 16 hours each way. There is a port tax of BD3.

Main port/s: Mina Sulman, Mina Manama and Mina Muharraq.

Getting about

National transport

Road: Bahrain's road network is fairly good. There are good tarmac roads between centres, and six-lane highways form a ring road by-pass system for Manama and Muharraq.

Buses: A national bus company provides public transport throughout the populated areas of the country.

Rail: There are no railways in Bahrain.

Water: Dhow trips are arranged most weekends to sand bars and nearby islands from the old wharf (Mina Manama) on King Faisal Road. Boat trips to neighbouring islands are frequently arranged on Friday and publicised in the local press.

City transport

It is easy to cover both Manama and Muharraq on foot, though renting a car will make it easier to get to farther-flung locations.

Taxis: Taxis (with orange side wings and black-on-yellow number plates) are plentiful and fares are regulated. Fares are by meter and only vary when coming from the airport or when travelling by night. Taxis are readily available for the 6.5km journey from Bahrain International airport to Manama, for which there is a charge in addition to the meter reading. Recommended fares from the airport are displayed outside the arrivals terminal. Shared taxis or 'pick-ups' can be hailed from any bus stop. They do not use meters. Fares vary depending on the destination, but are lower than standard taxi fares. However, they can be very cramped and uncomfortable. The 'pick-ups' have white and orange number plates, and a yellow circle with the licence number in black painted on the driver's door.

Car hire

Insurance is compulsory and international driving licences must be validated at the Ministry of Interior Traffic Headquarters before use in Bahrain. Car hire firms are listed in the local telephone directory, and it is generally recommended to compare prices. Driving is on the right. Seatbelts are compulsory for both the driver and front seat passenger, and young children must be seated in the back. Road signs are in English and Arabic. The maximum speed limit on highways is 100kph, and on inner city roads it is generally between 50–80kph. If an accident occurs, the vehicle must not be moved until traffic police get to the scene.

BUSINESS DIRECTORY

The addresses listed below are a selection only. While World of Information makes every endeavour to check these addresses, we cannot guarantee that changes have not been made, especially to telephone numbers and area codes. We would welcome any corrections.

Telephone area codes

The international direct dialling code (IDD) for Bahrain is +973 followed by subscriber's number.

Useful telephone numbers

Emergency service: 999
Directory enquiries: 181
International enquiries: 191
International bookings: 151
Operator: 100
Time in Arabic: 141
Time in English: 140
Telephone faults: 121

Chambers of Commerce

Bahrain Chamber of Commerce and Industry, Bld 122, Road 1605, Block 216, PO Box 248, Manama (tel: 17-229-555; fax 17-224-985; email: bastaki @ bahrainchamber.org.bh; internet: www.bahrainchamber.org.bh/english/index.htm)

Banking

Ahli United Bank Bahrain, 126 Government Avenue, PO Box 5941, Manama (tel: 17-221-700; fax: 17-224-322; e-mail: info@ahliunited.com).

Al Baraka Islamic Bank, PO Box 1882, Manama (tel: 17-535-300; fax: 17-533-993; e-mail: baraka@batelco.com.bh).

Arab Banking Corporation, ABC Tower, Diplomatic Area, PO Box 5698, Manama (tel: 17-543-000; fax: 17-533-163; e-mail: webmaster@arabbanking.com; internet: www.arabbanking.com).

Bahrain Development Bank, PO Box 20501, Manama (tel: 17-537-007; fax: 17-534-005).

Bahrain Islamic Bank, Al Salam Tower, Diplomatic Area, PO Box 5240, Manama (tel: 17-535-888; fax: 17-535-707; e-mail: bahisi@batelco.com.bh).

Bahraini Saudi Bank, PO Box 1159, Manama (tel: 17-211-010; fax: 17-210-989; e-mail: helpdesk@bahrainisaudibank.com).

Bank of Bahrain & Kuwait, 43 Government Avenue, PO Box 597, Manama (tel: 17-223-388; fax: 17-229-822; e-mail: bbkonline@batelco.com.bh).

First Islamic Investment Bank EC, PO Box 1406, Manama (tel: 17-218-333; fax: 17-217-555).

Gulf International Bank, PO Box 1017, Al-Dowali Building, 3 Palace Avenue, Manama (tel: 17-534-000; fax: 17-522-633; e-mail: info@gibbah.com; internet site: http://www.gibonline.com).

National Bank of Bahrain , PO Box 106, Manama (tel: 17-228-800; fax: 17-228-998; e-mail: nbb@nbbonline.com).

TAIB Bank, Sehl Centre, Diplomatic Area, PO Box 20485, Manama (tel: 17-533-334; fax: 17-533-174; e-mail: taib@taib.com).

Central bank

Central Bank of Bahrain (CBB), King Faisal Highway, Diplomatic Area, Block 317, Road 1702, Building 96, PO Box 27, Manama (tel: 17-535-535; fax: 17-533-342; web: www.cbb.gov.bh).

Stock exchange

Bahrain Stock Exchange (BSE) (www. bahrainstock.com).

Travel information

Bahrain International Airport, PO Box 586, Manama (tel: 17-321-151; fax: 17-324-096).

Bahrain Tourism Company, PO Box 5831, Manama (tel: 17-534-321; fax: 17-531-353; e-mail: btc@alseyaha.com).

Gulf Air, PO Box 138, Manama (tel: 17-228-820; fax: 17-224-452).

Ministry of tourism

Tourism Affairs, Ministry of Information, PO Box 26613, Manama (tel: 17-201-203; fax: 17-211-717; e-mail: btour@bahraintourism.com).

Ministries

Ministry of Cabinet Affairs, PO Box 26141, Manama (tel: 17-731-544; fax: 17-731-863).

Ministry of Commerce and Industry, PO Box 5479, Manana (tel: 17-531-531; fax: 17-530-455; email: drmansoor@ commerce.gov.bh; internet: www.commerce.gov.bh).

Ministry of Defence, PO Box 245, Manama (tel: 17-653-333; fax: 17-663-923).

Ministry of Education, PO Box 43, Manama (tel: 17-680-105; fax: 17-687-866).

Ministry of Electricity and Water, PO Box 2, Manama (tel: 17-546-666; fax: 17-533-035).

Ministry of Foreign Affairs, PO Box 547, Manama (tel: 17-227-555; fax: 17-212-603).

Ministry of Health, PO Box 12, Manama (tel: 17-255-555; fax: 17-252-569).

Ministry of Housing and Public Works, PO Box 5802, Manama (tel: 17-533-000; fax: 17-536-431).

Ministry of Information, PO Box 253, Manama (tel: 17-781-888; fax: 17-682-777).

Ministry of the Interior, PO Box 13, Manama (tel: 17-272-111; fax: 17-262-169).

Ministry of Justice and Islamic Affairs, PO Box 450, Manama (tel: 17-531-333; fax: 17-531-284).

Ministry of Labour and Social Affairs, PO Box 32333. Manama (tel: 17-687-800; fax: 17-686-954).

Ministry of Municipalities and Agriculture, PO Box 53, Manama (tel: 17-226-060; fax: 17-229-666).

Ministry of Oil, PO Box 1435, Manama (tel: 17-291-511; fax: 17-293-007).

Ministry of Transport, PO Box 10325, Manama (tel: 17-534-534; fax: 17-534-041).

Prime Minister's Office, PO Box 1000, Manama (tel: 17-200-000; fax: 17-532-839).

Other useful addresses

Aluminium Bahrain (Alba), PO Box 570, Manama (tel: 17-830-000; fax: 17-830-083; e-mail: alba@alba.com.bh).

Arabian Exhibition Management, PO Box 20200, Manama (tel: 17-550-033; fax: 17-553-288; aeminfo@batelco.com.bh).

Bahrain International Exhibition Centre, PO Box 11644, Manama (tel: 17-550-111; fax: 17-553-447; e-mail: biec@batelco.com.bh).

Bahrain National Gas Company (Banagas), PO Box 29099, Manama (tel: 17-756-222; fax: 17-756-991; e-mail: bng@banagas.com.bh).

Bahrain Petroleum Company (Bapco), PO Box 25555, Awali (tel: 17-704-040; fax: 17-704-070; e-mail: info@bapco.net).

Bahrain Stock Exchange, PO Box 3203, Manama (tel: 17-261-260; fax: 17-256-362; e-mail: info@bahrainstock.com).

Central Municipal Council, PO Box 53, Manama (tel: 17-276-060; fax: 17-263-666).

Consultative Council (Majlis al-Shura), PO Box 2991 Manama (tel: 17-714-422; fax: 17-715-715).

Customs Directorate, PO Box 15, Manama (tel: 17-725-333; fax: 17-725-534).

Ports Directorate, PO Box 453, Manama (tel: 17-725-555; fax: 17-725-534).

National news agency: Bahrain News Agency

Internet sites

Arab Net: www.arab.net

Arabia OnLine: www.arabia.com

Bahrain Economic Development Board: www.bahrainedb.com

Bahrain Financial Harbour: www.bfharbour.com/html.index.html

Bahrain Institute of Banking and Finance: www.bibf.com

Bahrain Islamic International Rating Agency (IIRA): www.iirating.com.

Bahrain Ministry of Finance and National Economy: www.mofne.gov.bh

Bahrain Promotions and Marketing Board: www.bpmb.com

Gulf business explorer: www.igulf.com/main.htm

Bangladesh

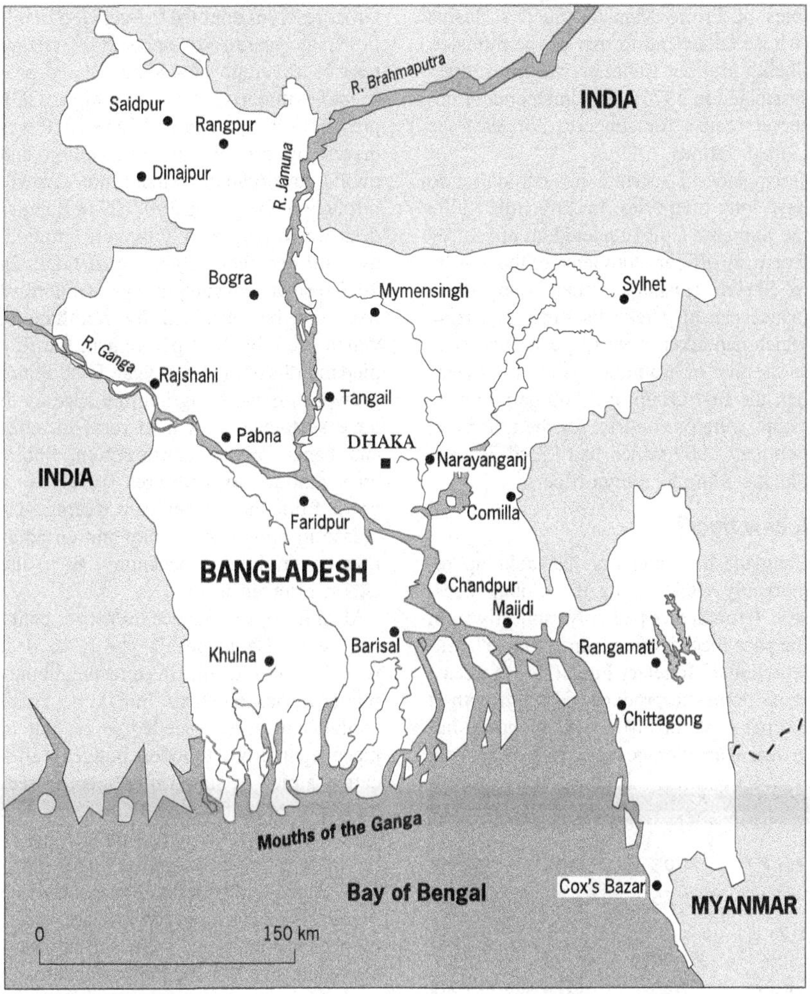

KEY FACTS

Official name: Gana Prajatantri Bangladesh (People's Republic of Bangladesh)

Head of State: President Hossain Zillur Rahman (from 11 Feb 2009)

Head of government: Prime minister Sheikh Hasina Wazed (Awami League) (from 6 Jan 2009)

Ruling party: The Mohajot (Grand Coalition) led by the Awami League (AL) (People's League) with the Jatiya Party (National Party) (since 29 Dec 2008)

Area: 143,998 square km

Population: 146.60 million (2010)*

Capital: Dhaka

Official language: Bengali (Bangla)

Currency: Taka (Tk) = 100 poisha

Exchange rate: Tk72.22 per US$ (Oct 2011)

GDP per capita: US$638 (2010)

GDP real growth: 6.00% (2010)

GDP: US$104.9 billion (2010)

Labour force: 73.87 million (2009) (does not include extensive expatriate numbers)

Unemployment: 4.80% (2010)* (does not include underemployment)

Inflation: 8.2% (2010)

Balance of trade: US$-5,4847.60 million (2010)

Annual FDI: US$9.50 billion (2009)

* estimated figure

If some fellow Asian countries have attracted the title 'lucky countries' for their combinations of natural and human resources, then Bangladesh probably deserves to be called the 'unlucky country'. Natural disasters are the main reason – the death toll from the 2007 cyclone was by Bangladeshi standards quite small, at an estimated 3,500. The previous cyclone, in 1991, killed over 140,000. As if cyclones and typhoons were not enough, inland areas also suffer from pollution, erosion and simple inundation from the 54 rivers which flow into Bangladesh from India. A lack of co-operation with India has resulted over the years in sedimentation of the river beds, changes in their direction, pollution and the increased salinity of ground waters. The gradually increasing level of the sea has also become a major preoccupation. All these factors place a heavy burden on the Bangladeshi economy, as they threaten agriculture, forestry, fisheries and livestock. But Bangladeshi party-leaders and politicians also have a lot to answer for:

not all of Bangladeshi bad luck can be attributed to natural causes. An unbelievable 3 million people are estimated to have died in the war of secession from India that ended in 1971.

Back to democracy?

After two years, Bangladesh's military-backed caretaker government had left office to be replaced by Sheikh Hasina's Awami League (AL)-led government in January 2009. In a high turnout election, the AL won more than the two-thirds parliamentary majority needed to pass constitutional amendments unchallenged. One of the League's main promises in the electoral campaign had been the establishment of a war crimes tribunal to mete out justice to those responsible for the violence in 1971. The government declared alleviating poverty and reducing consumer prices to be its top priorities. The prices of fertiliser and diesel were reduced, but the implementation of the ambitious election manifesto for economic reforms – needed to unlock Bangladesh's potential through private sector-led growth – has made slow progress.

War crimes

In seeking some sort of justice for the victims of the war of succession, almost 40 years ago, the AL needed to tread carefully. Not all Bangladeshi's had supported separation from what was then known as West Pakistan. A number of Islamist parties, including the majority supported Jamaat-e-Islami had been opposed. This opposition had its more violent expression in the activities of Jamaat-e-Islami's student wing under the banner of a para-military body called al Badr. On the incoming government's wish list was bringing to justice those Bangladeshis responsible for bloodshed at the time. The fact that those responsible for the bloodshed could so easily be matched with the political enemies of Prime Minister Sheikh Hasina (whose father and former prime minister, Sheikh Mujibur Rahman, was himself assassinated in 1975) gave independent observers cause for concern, not least the United Nations.

Bangladeshi politicians certainly do have long memories. In November 2009 the Supreme Court rejected an appeal by five army officers convicted of the murder of Sheikh Hasina's father. Bangladesh justice can also take its time. The trial, which had taken over 13 years, was seen as the first of a number. Also in November, the first group of 3,500 paramilitary troops were put on trial for the mutiny of February 2009 which had killed 74 people, including 57 army officers.

A new tiger?

Bangladesh's economy has held up remarkably well despite the global recession. Growth dropped only modestly from the pace recorded in recent years. The International Monetary Fund (IMF) forecast gross domestic product (GDP) growth at 5.4 per cent for 2010. The economy has grown at an average rate of 5 to 6 per cent per year since 1996. None the less, Bangladesh's growth rate remains well below the levels required to meet the millennium target of halving the number of people below the poverty line by 2015.

A mixture of strong foreign remittances, resilient exports and weak imports caused the current account of the balance of payments to record a surplus of almost three per cent of GDP in the year to June 2009. Gross reserves doubled to over US$10 billion in the year to November 2009, raising reserve coverage to 4.8 months of prospective imports, a 15-year high. GDP growth in the year to end June 2010 was driven by growth in consumption and public development expenditure. Growth throughout the period 2007–09 in Bangladesh was driven mainly by consumption, over 60 per cent of growth in GDP. In 2010, private consumption growth looked likely to be sustained by remittances, which grew by 17.4 per cent in the first nine months of the fiscal year. In addition, growth in non-rice agriculture appears to have sustained growth in rural incomes and hence private consumption. Public consumption expenditures received a boost from the 52 per cent average increase in public sector pay and an additional stimulus package for the export-oriented sectors.

Most European finance ministries could only envy Bangladesh's ability to deal with the crisis. Unlike in some neighbouring countries (such as India), no fiscal stimulus measures needed to be put in place, apart from a modest budget reallocation aimed at supporting specific sectors affected by the global downturn. The 2009/10 budget deficit remained below the budget target, despite revenue shortfalls. Faced with a possible rise in the rate of inflation and a rapid rise in share prices, monetary conditions were subsequently tightened, but insufficiently and through large high-cost government borrowing – with excess funds deposited in Bangladesh Bank (BB) (the central bank) – rather than sustained monetary policy operations.

For once, Bangladesh's fundamental economic weaknesses became its strengths. The limited impact of the global downturn on Bangladesh's growth reflected the low overall level of trade openness and the large share of basic textiles and garments as a proportion of total exports, which fared well. The resilience of Bangladesh's exports contrasts with the experience in both high and low income countries in Asia where exports remained well below the pre-crisis peak. Gross

KEY INDICATORS — Bangladesh

	Unit	2006	2007	2008	2009	2010
Population	m	155.96	158.84	*161.75	*164.71	*146.60
Gross domestic product (GDP)	US$bn	64.85	72.42	84.50	94.50	104.90
GDP per capita	US$	451	455	523	574	638
GDP real growth	%	6.4	5.6	6.0	5.4	6.0
Inflation	%	6.5	8.4	7.7	6.1	8.2
Industrial output	% change	9.7	8.4	6.8	6.5	–
Agricultural output	% change	4.9	4.6	3.2	4.1	–
Natural gas output	bn cum	15.2	16.3	17.3	19.7	20.0
Exports (fob) (goods)	US$m	11,553.7	12,449.1	15,501.8	15,067.1	19,238.7
Imports (fob) (goods)	US$m	14,443.4	16,665.3	21,505.9	19,759.8	24,723.4
Balance of trade	US$m	-2,889.7	-4,216.2	-6,004.1	-4,692.8	-5,484.6
Current account	US$m	762.0	334.0	926.2	3,344.6	2,502.4
Total reserves minus gold	US$m	3,805.6	5,183.4	5,689.3	10,218.9	10,564.3
Foreign exchange	US$m	3,803.9	5,182.2	5,686.7	9,499.9	9,904.1
Exchange rate	per US$	70.23	68.59	68.60	69.41	69.65

* estimated figure

international reserves exceeded US$10 billion in November 2009, almost double the level in November 2008. This is equivalent to 4.8 months of prospective imports, a 15-year high. The decline in international food and commodity prices contributed to a fall in inflation to 2.2 per cent in June. But with the accommodative monetary policy, upward pressure on real estate prices has become visible and the stock market rose by 40 per cent between March and October. However, as international food and commodity prices began to rise again, inflation rose to 6.7 per cent in October 2009. Bangladesh seems to be stuck in a low revenue-low capital spending balance as infrastructure bottlenecks continue to hold back growth. In the view of the IMF Bangladesh's financial soundness indicators are generally favourable although the weak condition of the state-owned commercial banks gives some concern.

Energy matters

Energy shortages, however, pose perhaps the biggest threat to Bangladesh's growth recovery. The World Bank considers that in the last two years, power generation has failed to keep pace with demand and Bangladesh is now in the midst of a serious power crisis. Studies show that poor quality power supply costs the country as much as 2 per cent in GDP growth each year. Manufacturers, surveyed in a World Bank investment climate assessment, estimated that power shortages cost them around 12 per cent in lost sales on an annual basis. The country's reliable base of generation capacity is about 4,300 Megawatts (MW). But peak demand is estimated to exceed 5,000MW on most days so many customers find themselves getting cut off when they most need power. Demand for electricity is expected to rise to 6,850MW within the next two years. Maximum generation currently available is between 3,800MW and 4,300MW. The estimated demand supply gap currently is 2,000MW in peak hours. Gas shortages account for at least half of this gap. Power and gas shortages have undermined external competitiveness. According to garment industry leaders, garment orders cannot be fulfilled because of energy constraints. Frequent power cuts and low gas pressure add to shipment time, forcing exporters to airfreight the merchandise at their own cost. Power cuts and gas shortages have reportedly rendered a significant part of the country's garment capacity idle. Progress in expanding power generation remains slow. The neglect of infrastructure may make itself most felt in the power sector, but it is part of a major and widespread problem. Bottlenecks of one sort or another delay lifting 40 per cent of the population – the some 60 million people that live on barely more than US$1 per day – out of poverty. In the view of the IMF Bangladesh needs to make the leap from an annual 6 to 6.5 per cent rise in GDP to over 8 per cent. The starting point in the equation would seem to be that of addressing power generation. To combat the acute power shortages, the government plans to increase power generation to around 7,000MW by 2013. However, power plants continue to suffer from gas shortages, despite some recent measures to increase gas supplies for power production. Short-term solutions being floated include diesel – and furnace oil-based rental power plants which can start generation within a short period of time – but these are higher cost routes and will reduce the competitiveness of firms. In 2009 and the first six months of 2010, 586MW of power were added to the national grid. However, no new plants have been built for some years and insufficient gas supplies limit the capacity of existing ones. An estimated US$9 billion of investment is needed to bring power to all Bangladeshis by 2020, an investment capacity that Bangladesh simply does not possess. Despite substantial supplies of high quality clean coal, little obvious attention seems to be given to coal-fired power generation.

The neighbours

Bangladesh is surrounded on three sides by India. The fourth frontier is the sea, or perhaps ironically given the close geographical relationship with India, the 710 kilometre coastline on the northern littoral of the Bay of Bengal, which constitutes what used to be known as 'the mouths of the Ganges' but in fact includes the mouths of two other important rivers, the Brahmaputra and the Meghna, this border too can be seen as 'Indian'. Since the war of secession and Bangladeshi independence, relations with India have been strangely distant. Things have begun to look as though they might change, however. The election victory of the Awami League in 2009 coincided with that of the Congress Party in India, setting the stage for renewed bilateral talks between the countries, in an atmosphere improved by counter-terrorism co-operation. In January 2010, Hasina travelled to New Delhi to meet with Indian Prime Minister Manmohan Singh, where they signed three agreements on mutual legal assistance in criminal matters, transfer of sentenced persons and countering terrorism, organised crime and illegal drug trafficking; and two memoranda of understanding on energy sharing and cultural exchange programmes.

Given Indian – and US – concerns about the stability of Pakistan, it is inevitable that wary glances should be directed at Bangladesh too. Given its size and location, a major crisis in Bangladesh could have important consequences for regional stability, particularly if significant refugee movements should ensue.

Visionary Vision

Under its 'Vision 2021' programme, the AL government has set out an ambitious year-by-year timetable to achieve a wide range of social and economic goals. These include 100 per cent net student enrolment at primary level by the end of 2010, the supply of pure drinking water for the entire population by the end of 2011, self-sufficiency in food by the end of 2012, universal hygienic sanitation by the end of 2013, a year in which the annual GDP growth rate is targeted to be 8 per cent (increasing to 10 per cent by 2017). In 2013 Bangladesh expects to generate 7,000 megawatt of electricity, increasing to 8,000 megawatt in 2015. The list – and it is a long list – goes on to forecast full literacy by 2014 and living accommodation for the entire population by 2015. There are a staggering 13 points on the check list to be achieved by 2021. Unless there are any more cyclones, of course. Or coups.

Risk assessment

Economy	Good
Politics	Fair
Regional stability	Fair

COUNTRY PROFILE

Historical profile

1200 The start of five-and-a-half centuries of Muslim rule over the region began with the Sultanate era.

1757 The region gradually came under the influence of British rule after the battle of Plassey.

1947 Named East Pakistan, Bangladesh became a province of Pakistan following the partition of India.

1949 The Awami League (AL) was established to campaign for East Pakistan's autonomy from West Pakistan.

1970 The AL, under Sheikh Mujibur Rahman, won the elections in East Pakistan, but West Pakistan refused to accept the result, resulting in civil unrest.

1971 The People's Republic of Bangladesh was unilaterally declared; a *de facto* secession from Pakistan followed the nine-month Indo-Pakistan war. Around 10 million Bangladeshis fled to India during the conflict.
1972 Sheikh Mujibur became prime minister and, in an attempt to improve living standards, began a programme of industrial nationalisation.
1974 Severe flooding destroyed much of the grain harvest. A state of emergency was declared as political unrest grew. A famine killed 100,000 people as wealthy farmers hoarded food that the poor could not afford to buy.
1975 Sheikh Mujibur became president, but was assassinated in a military coup. Martial law was imposed following the coup; Abu Sadat Mohammed Sayem became president on 6 November.
1976 Elections were postponed indefinitely. General Zia ur Rahman took over the post of Chief Martial Law Administrator previously held by President Sayem.
1977 General Zia assumed the presidency on 21 April, amending the constitution, making Islam, instead of secularism, its first basic principle.
1978 General Zia won the first direct presidential election.
1979 Parliamentary elections were won by Zia's Bangladesh Jatiyatabadi Dal (Bangladesh Nationalist Party) (BNP). Martial law was repealed and the state of emergency revoked.
1981 General Zia was assassinated.
1982 General Ershad seized power in a bloodless coup. The country was placed under martial law as the constitution and political parties were suspended.
1983–86 Bangladesh remained unstable, with opposition groups demanding the resignation of Ershad and his government. Ershad imposed Islam on the education system and forced teachers to teach in Arabic. This led to social unrest, particularly among the non-Muslim minority.
1986 Martial law ended and constitutional government was revived. Ershad was elected to a five-year term.
1987 A state of emergency was imposed during a wave of strikes and opposition demonstrations.
1988 Islam became the state religion. Floods covered around 75 per cent of the land and millions of people were made homeless.
1990 Ershad resigned following mass protests which made the country ungovernable.
1991 Elections resulted in a victory for the BNP, led by Begum Khaleda Zia, the widow of General Zia; she became prime minister. Ershad was jailed for corruption and the illegal possession of weapons. The position of president was made ceremonial and executive power was given to the office of prime minister.
1996 After two decades of military and authoritarian rule, the AL, led by Sheikh Hasina (Sheikh Mujibur's daughter), won the election.
1998 Floods covered two-thirds of the country, causing many deaths. Fifteen former army officers were sentenced to death for their involvement in the assassination of President Mujibur.
2000 Sheikh Hasina spoke out against military regimes and the government expelled a Pakistani diplomat for denying that three million Bangladeshis had been murdered by Pakistani forces in 1971. Diplomatic relations broke down between Bangladesh and Pakistan.
2001 There were violent clashes, strikes and a growth in Islamic fundamentalism in the build-up to parliamentary elections. The alliance led by Zia's BNP won a landslide victory. A Q M Badruddoza Chowdhury was sworn in as president.
2002 Chowdhury resigned and Iajuddin Ahmed was elected as president by parliament.
2004 The AL called 21 general strikes in a campaign to force early elections, accusing the government of being corrupt. The constitution was amended to reserve 45 parliamentary seats for women. Floods covered two-thirds of the country, killing over 800 people. Sheikh Hasina survived a grenade attack that killed 22 people at a party rally.
2005 A senior AL politician, Shah A M S Kibria, was killed in a grenade attack. There were hundreds of small bombings around the country; Islamic militants claimed responsibility.
2006 Bangladesh became a member of the South Asia Free Trade Agreement (Safta). The AL ended a yearlong boycott of parliament. General strikes, called by the AL, had disrupted the country for three months. Tension and violence continued in the lead-up to the end of the government's five-year term of office and the choice of a caretaker administration, until scheduled elections. President Ahmed assumed the role as chief adviser to break the impasse.
2007 President Ahmed resigned as chief adviser and Fazlul Haque became acting chief adviser after general elections were suspended; rioting broke out and a state of emergency was imposed. The suspended elections violated a constitutional requirement that elections be held within 90 days of the resignation of a government. The president announced that new voter lists were required to ensure elections were 'free, fair and credible'. Severe monsoon flooding caused death and destruction and left an estimated one million people in urgent need of international aid.
2008 The first passenger train since 1965 began operations between Dhaka and Kolkata (India). The Electoral Commission completed its registration of over 80 million voters; 13 million names were removed from the previous, discredited, list. In parliamentary elections the Mohajot (Grand Coalition) led by the AL won 262 seats (out of 299) and the BNP Alliance 32 (the alliance included the largest Islamist party, Jamaat e Islami, which failed to win any seats; turnout was 80 per cent.
2009 Sheikh Hasina (AL) became prime minister. Parliament elected Hossain Zillur Rahman as president. A two-day mutiny, over pay and conditions, at the Dhaka headquarters of the Bangladesh Rifles, the country's border guards, resulted in the deaths of 74 people, including scores of officers found in two mass graves the day after the mutineers surrendered. Around 1,700 border guards had been arrested in connection with the mutiny. Annual daylight saving time (DST) was introduced on 19 June, but was cancelled after confusion over how long the change might last. The Islamic organisation Hizb ut Tahrir, was banned.
2010 In August and September in the worst outbreak on record, anthrax killed over 325 people in the north of the country. After almost 40 years of living in the military owned house she had leased since a year after the assassination of her husband in 1981, former prime minister Khaleda Zia was evicted on 13 November. The eviction lead to violent protests as the BNP accused the government of cancelling the lease for political reasons. The Supreme Court rejected an appeal against the eviction on 29 November.
2011 Nobel laureate, Muhammad Yunus was sacked from the Grameen microfinance bank on 2 March. The Board of the Grameen Bank is dominated by the poor women who are the bank's main borrowers and shareholders; the board continued to support Yunus. The central bank, when dismissing him, said that he was over retirement age. Yunus began legal proceedings to challenge his sacking but lost his appeal on 8 March. In April the World Bank agreed a US$1.2 billion credit to build a 6km bridge across the Padma river, linking to the Dhaka-Chittagong Highway. The Bank estimated the road and rail connection would directly benefit 30 million people in the wider region. At present all traffic across the Padma relies on ferries, which are infrequent and often unsafe. Yunus finally stood down as leader of the Grameen Bank on 12 May following rejection of his final appeal. The Supreme

Court ruled on 12 May that Islamic clerics could issue fatwas (Islamic religious edicts) but that they could not be officially enforced. This ruling endorsed the same ruling made in 2001, which had followed an outcry due to a series of brutal punishments meted out by fatwas. Clerics had appealed against the earlier ruling saying fatwas were an integral part of Islamic religious practice. Bangladesh and India held a joint census in July, in an attempt to determine just how many Indians there are in the 51 enclaves in Bangladesh and how many Bangladeshis in the 100 Indian enclaves. There are possibly as many as tens of thousands of people on the wrong side of each border in enclaves which are historical anomalies of the partition of the subcontinent in 1947.

Political structure

Constitution

The constitution was enacted in 1972. It was suspended following the coup of 1982, restored in 1986, and has been amended several times.
In 1977, the constitution was amended making Islam, instead of secularism, its first basic principle.
The country has six political divisions: Dhaka, Chittagong, Rajshahi, Barisal, Sylhet and Khulna. These are further subdivided into districts, thanas (parish-level government) and villages.

Independence date

26 March 1971

Form of state

Parliamentary republic

The executive

The president, who is elected by the legislature for a five-year term, performs ceremonial functions. The president is also commander-in-chief of the armed forces. The cabinet is led by the prime minister, who is usually the leader of the ruling party. The elections are preceded by a 'caretaker' government which is supposed to have no political affiliation, in order to allow elections to be fought on an equal and fair basis.
Bangladesh's judiciary is separate from the executive – judges and magistrates are appointed by the Supreme Court.

National legislature

The unicameral Jatiya Sangsad (parliament) has 300 members elected by popular vote in single territorial constituencies every five years. In addition, 45 seats are reserved for women on a proportional representation basis, until 2014 when women will compete for parliamentary seats against male candidates.

Legal system

The judiciary is a civil court system based on the British model. The highest court of appeal is the appellate division of the Supreme Court.

Last elections

29 December 2008 (parliamentary); 11 February 2009 (presidential)
Results: Parliamentary: the Mohajot (Grand Coalition) including the Awami League (AL) (People's League) won 230 seats, with the Jatiya Party (National Party) 27 and others 5; the Bangladesh Jatiyatabadi Dal (BJD) (Bangladesh Nationalist Party) (BNP) won 29, others 3; turnout was 80 per cent. Five seats must be re-poled.
Presidential: Hossain Zillur Rahman was elected by parliament.

Next elections

2014 (presidential); December 2013 (parliamentary).

Political parties

Ruling party

The Mohajot (Grand Coalition) led by the Awami League (AL) (People's League) with the Jatiya Party (National Party) (since 29 Dec 2008)

Main opposition party

Bangladesh Jatiyatabadi Dal (Bangladesh Nationalist Party) (BNP)

Population

146.60 million (2010)*
Last census: January 2001: 123,151,246 (provisional)
Population density: 1,014 inhabitants per square km (2010)
Annual growth rate: 2.0 per cent 1994–2004 (WHO 2006)

Ethnic make-up

Bengalis (98 per cent) and Biharis. There are about one million tribal people, the majority of whom live in the Chittagong Hill Tracts in the east of the country. The tribes have distinct cultures of their own.

Religions

Islam (88 per cent), Hinduism (10 per cent), Buddhism and Christianity. Although Islam is the state religion, freedom of worship is guaranteed under the constitution.

Education

The investment in education amounts to 2.2 per cent of GDP.
In November 2003, the Asian Development Bank (ADB) announced it was leading the jointly financed Second Primary Education Development Program (PEDP-II), designed to reorganise primary education in Bangladesh, with a US$1.815 billion package, including US$654 million external financing, provided by, among others, 11 international donors. The programme will run over the six-year period 2004–09. The package includes a 32-year, US$100 million, loan. The objectives of PEDP-II are to raise standards in school governance, and teacher training, improve the quality of school buildings and enhance the accessibility of schooling for students, particularly those from poor families.
By 2004 nearly 18 million students were enrolled in over 78,000 primary level schools, in the world's largest primary education system. Bangladesh has gender parity and has strived to expand access to the very poor and disadvantaged, including those with special needs. Enrolment rates suggest that about four million primary school-aged children are absent from school and about one-third of children drop out before completing primary school; children in remote rural and tribal regions still have significantly less access to schooling. Despite Bangladesh's official policy of gender parity, gender differences in learning persist.
Micro level strategies for basic education in rural areas are being developed through concerted co-operation between local communities, NGOs, government, and international donors. The Bangladesh Rural Advancement Committee (Brac) has developed strategies for intense community participation, operating 35,000 schools, providing education to 1.2 million children with a strong emphasis on the recruitment of local female teachers. Schools operated by Brac have improved outcomes to state-run schools, with better life skills and higher transition to secondary schools. Satellite village schools linked with larger schools in the area bring education services to children living in remote parts of the country. International support in basic education helps combat the problem of child labour by giving incentives to educate children employed in industries. Government programmes include free education for girls up to class 10 and stipends for female students; food-for-education; and the total literacy movement.
Madrasas (schools offering an Islamic education to Muslim boys and girls) have increased in number from 1,500 in 1970 to 8,000 in 2004. Hindus and Buddhists also receive religious education at institutes called *Tol* and *Chatuspathi*.
Literacy rate: 41 per cent adult rate; 50 per cent youth rate (15–24) (Unesco 2005).
Compulsory years: Six to 10
Enrolment rate: 89.6 per cent net primary enrolment; 93.3 per cent, male, 86.0 per cent, female (2009). Bangladesh aims to achieve universal primary school enrolment by 2015.
Pupils per teacher: 55 overall, and 67 in state schools (ADB 2003)

Health

In the past decade, the infant mortality rate has been reduced by half – a faster reduction than any other country. With the highest incidence of malnutrition in the world, Bangladesh has made great efforts to improve the nutritional status of women and children.

Primary health care facilities have been expanded throughout the country and are provided though government sponsored Union and Thana Health Complexes; secondary health care facilities are provided by District level hospitals, and tertiary health-care facilities through Medical College Hospitals, Post-graduate Institutes and specialised hospitals at divisional and national levels.

It is estimated that at least 1.2 million people are exposed to poisoning by naturally occurring arsenic in groundwater, and about 40 million of Bangladesh's 144 million people are considered at risk. Since 1993, experts have found that tube wells in more than half of Bangladesh's 64 districts (mainly in the south-western, middle and north-eastern parts of the country) are likely to be contaminated with arsenic. The effects may take as long a 14 years to become visible but treatment can be successful before levels of poison reaches a certain level.

A cheap filter, costing around US$4, which can process 25–30 litres of drinking water a day, enough for a family of five is widely available.

HIV/Aids

The HIV prevalence rate among adults between is relatively low; the rates among high-risk groups are greater – sex workers 0.5 per cent and unregistered injecting drug uses 1.7 per cent (World Bank).

HIV prevalence: 0.03 per cent ages of 15-49

Life expectancy: 62 years, 2004 (WHO 2006)

Fertility rate/Maternal mortality rate: 3.2 births per woman, 2004 (WHO 2006); maternal deaths 440 per 100,000 live births (World Bank).

Birth rate/Death rate: 28 births and 8 deaths per 1,000 (World Bank)

Child (under 5 years) mortality rate (per 1,000): 46 per 1,000 live births (World Bank)

Head of population per physician: 0.26 physicians per 1,000 people, 2004 (WHO 2006)

Welfare

Over 67 million people live below the poverty line, and Bangladesh still has the highest incidence of poverty in South Asia; only India and China have higher numbers of poor. Added to which, Bangladesh has one of the highest density populations (roughly 800 people per square kilometre), however it has achieved near self sufficiency in food production and made good progress in improving natural disaster management and social safety nets. In the 2002/03 budget, an allowance of Tk125 each was given to 900,000 people, (up from a previous 600,000), deemed disadvantaged: orphans, retarded, very-old, widows, and deserted women.

The World Bank suggests that while economic development and lasting poverty reduction is being hampered by the absence of reliable power (an estimated 10 million rural households lack access to electricity), even poor households are eager to join community-based saving projects such as Safe Save, and the Social Investment Program Project designed to give the poor in remote areas access to decision-making processes through small-scale infrastructure and social assistance projects. Communities will be expected to provide participation by contributing at least 15 per cent of the expenditure needed and donors the remaining 85 per cent.

Main cities

Dhaka (capital, estimated population 11.7 million (m) 2005), Chittagong (3.7m), Khulna (872,087), Rajshahi (712,400), Mymensingh (447,974), Narayanganj (522,321), Comilla (297,352), Rajshahi (647,545), Rangpur (318,014), Bogra (211,969), Nawabganj (225,991).

Languages spoken

Bengali (Bangla) is spoken by 95 per cent of the population. The remaining 5 per cent speak various tribal dialects.

English is widely spoken and understood within the business community.

Official language/s

Bengali (Bangla)

Media

The constitution guarantees freedom of the press but pressure by politicians and the police is often exerted on journalists, who are also targeted but Islamist and Maoist groups. The government influences media outlets through awarding or withholding official advertising revenue.

Press

Dailies: Most newspapers are privately-owned, diverse and can be outspoken, with a strong tradition of owner-editorship. Newspapers that are published in English target the educated urban readership.

In Bengali *The Daily Ittefaq* (www.ittefaq.com), *Jugantor Daily News* (http://jugantor.com), *Prothom Alo* (www.prothom-alo.com), *Bhorer Kagoj* (http://bhorerkagoj.net) and *The Daily Inqilab* (www.dailyinqilab.com). In English, *The Bangladesh Today* (www.thebangladeshtoday.com), *The Daily Star* (www.thedailystar.net), *The Independent* (theindependent-bd.com), *Dhaka* (www.dhaka.com), *New Age* (www.newagebd.com), *New Nation* (www.nation-online.com), *The News Today* (www.newstoday-bd.com).

Weeklies: In Bengali, *Shaptahik2000* (www.shaptahik2000.com), *Anannya* (www.my-anannya.com), is a women's weekly, *Jai Jai Din* (www.jaijaidin.com), *Unmad* (www.homeviewbangladesh.com/unmad) is a satirical magazine and *Weekly Amod* (www.weeklyamod.com) comes from Chittagong. In English *Dhaka Courier* (www.dhakacourier.net) and *Holiday* (www.weeklyholiday.net) are news publications and *Blitz* (www.weeklyblitz.net) is a tabloid, *Weekly Evidence* (www.evidence-int.com) covers international news and comment.

Business: In English, *The Financial Express* (www.thefinancialexpress-bd.com), the *Independent Bangladesh* (www.independent-bangladesh.com) is in collaboration with *The Daily Commercial Times* from Chittagong.

Periodicals: In Bengali *At Tahreek* is an Islamic monthly publication. In English, *Business info Bangladesh* (www.bizbangladesh.com) is an annual trade and business directory.

Broadcasting

Radio: The state-owned broadcaster is Bangladesh Betar (www.betar.org.bd) with three national networks, A, B and C, as well as local stations, providing news, information, educational and cultural programmes as well as an external service in English, Hindi, Arabic, Urdu and Nepalese.

Private, commercial stations includes Radio Metrowave (www.metrowave-bd.com) Radio Foorti (www.proshikanet.com/radiofoorti), Radio Today (www.radiotodaybd.fm) and Capital FM (www.drivetimedhaka.com).

Television: The only terrestrial broadcaster is the national state-owned Bangladesh Television (BTV) (www.btv.com.bd). Other cable and satellite TV networks include Channel i (www.channel-i-tv.com), NTV (www.ntvbd.com), ATN Bangla (www.atnbangla.tv), RTV and Ekushey TV. ENB News (www.enbnewsbd.com) is a 24-hour news network.

Advertising

With illiteracy at around 50 per cent, radio, television and cinema advertising are primary sources of news and information. Newspapers accept advertising and some direct mail services are available. There are outdoor advertising sites in major towns.

News agencies

National news agency: Bangladesh Sangbad Sangstha (BSS)

BDNEWS24: www.bdnews24.com

Economy

The economy is largely based on agriculture, with the majority of the work force employed in the sector. Located at the Ganges-Brahmapurtra River Delta, Bangladesh has fertile land and plentiful water with an expanded irrigation network that provides three crops of rice per year in many regions. Other primary crops include jute, tea and maize. The service sector is the largest component in the economy, with larger employment groups in trade, hospitality, education, personal services and transport. Industries include mining, steel, chemicals paper and wood pulp.

Textile manufacturing was developed in the 1990s and exports of fabrics and clothes became the principal export in 2009. The industry employs mostly women for its assembly line production and has the world's lowest textile workers' payment. The Bangladesh textile industry is the world's third largest (after Turkey and China). Exports gained a fillip in 2008 when China's textile exports to both the US and EU were capped allowing Bangladesh to makeup the shortfall.

GDP growth was 6.0 per cent in 2008, a figure that has remained relatively constant since 2005, but which fell to 5.4 per cent in 2009. The economy was not unduly damaged by the global economic crisis, as its banking sector was not exposed to the losses experienced by high-income countries. Nevertheless, Bangladesh was hurt by falling world trade and the rising price of imports, particularly oil and food. Exports in 2008 were valued at US$14.2 billion; and in 2009 were estimated at US$15.6 billion. Imports in 2008 were US$19.5 billion and an estimated US$20.3 billion in 2009, so that Bangladesh typically carries a deficit in its balance of trade account -US$5.3 billion and an estimated -US$4.7 billion, in 2008 and 2009 respectively. Remittances are an important component of GDP, in 2008 at US$8.99 billion they accounted for 11.4 per cent of GDP; the estimate for 2009 was US$10.73 billion.

Bangladesh is a low income economy, as defined by the International Monetary Fund (IMF) in 2009, with a population of over 164 million. The high population density is a brake on development. Poverty rates, however, are in decline, with improvements in healthcare and education triggering social improvement. The infrastructure is vulnerable to typhoons and productive land is subject to recurring annual monsoon flooding. In 2010 the IMF concluded that Bangladesh could improve its growth rate if it implemented decisive tax reforms.

External trade

Bangladesh is a member of South Asia Association for Regional Co-operation, which operates a preferential trading arrangement that covers 6,000 products. In 2004 the South Asia Free Trade Area (Safta) was ratified, to be implemented between the seven member states (Bangladesh, Bhutan, India, Maldives, Nepal, Pakistan and Sri Lanka) by 2012.

In 2011, exports of the vegetable fibre jute were valued at over US$1 billion, a 30-year record since it fell out of favour in competition with man-made fibres. Its demand as a natural fibre with inherent bio-degradability has been growing steadily. Modern technology has also allowed it to be used in a greater variety of products, such as carpets, insulation material and bags. Bangladesh produces around 50 per cent of the world's supply of jute.

Imports

Main imports are manufactured goods, machinery and transport equipment, petroleum and petroleum products, chemicals and pharmaceuticals, cement, raw cotton, food, vegetable oil, fats and cereal crops.

Main sources: China (typically 15 per cent of total), India (15 per cent), Kuwait (8 per cent).

Exports

Main exports typically include jute manufactures and raw jute (over 20 per cent of total), cotton textiles, garments, frozen fish and seafood, leather, ceramics and tea. There is a ban on the export of natural gas.

Main destinations: US (typically 21 per cent of total), Germany (13 per cent), UK (9 per cent).

Agriculture

Farming

Agriculture dominates the economy and contributes around 20 per cent to GDP. It employs 66 per cent of the labour force and determines incomes and consumption for the vast majority of Bangladeshis. Bangladesh is largely self-sufficient in food grains, although a food deficit may occur when weather conditions are adverse.

Rice is the principal crop, accounting for about 70 per cent of cropped land. Improvements in rice production have been achieved through research, which has produced high-yielding rice varieties, improved farming methods, greater use of fertiliser and more widespread irrigation. Agricultural employment increased with the use of high-yield rice, which is between 20 and 50 per cent more labour-intensive than traditional varieties. In the 2009–10 sowing season, three new rice varieties were given their final testing. These stains of rice are designed to survive the annual monsoon flooding and are expected to improve the annual harvest. Over two million hectares are inundated by monsoon flash floods destroying millions of tonnes of rice each year. Another, high-yield rice strain, *Nerica*, was trial-grown in the Ganges delta in 2010–11. It was originally developed in Côte d'Ivoire, where it had been cultivated for Africa's dry lands, although seeds for this trial were imported from Uganda. It is fast-growing and drought-resistant and registered better than expected field results in 2010 so that 1,500 farmers nationwide grew it in 2011. Its short growing (90–100 days for *Nerica* verses 140–160 days for current rice strains) could overcome crop losses due to major natural disasters.

Other crops are pulses, wheat, jute, oil seeds, sugar cane, tea, spices, vegetables and fruit. The livestock sector contributes about 3 per cent to GDP.

The amount of cultivable land under irrigation has increased to about 35 per cent. Much of the land is broken into tiny plots. Farms of less than one acre account for about 40 per cent, while about 5 per cent of farm households own and operate more than 25 per cent of agricultural land. The government leases farm machinery to groups of farmers forming co-operatives and increasing farm sizes.

Bangladesh is the world's largest exporter of raw jute and jute goods, amounting to around half of the world shipments. The jute industry has been restructured and modernised with aid from the World Bank. In 2011, demand for the vegetable fibre jute reached a 30-year high since it fell out of favour in competition with synthetic fibres. Around five million farmers cultivate jute and its role in the rural economy is growing. Not only does the natural fibre have inherent bio-degradability but is also strong, versatile and long-lasting. Modern technology has also allowed it to be used in a greater variety of products, such as carpets, insulation material and bags. The government has given its backing by requiring all domestic food grains to be packaged by jute.

About 2 per cent of the world's tea is grown in Bangladesh on some 150 plantations in the north-east region of Sylhet. After meeting domestic demand, a significant amount is exported to other Asian countries and Europe.

Fishing

Fishing has been identified by the government as a rapidly growing sector with increased production, which could generate revenue and foreign earnings while improving local nutrition. The sector has grown by 8 per cent per year since 1996 and contributes 3.3 per cent to GDP and directly employs around 1.3 million people. The typical annual catch is over 1.7 million tonnes.

Development by government, NGOs and private initiatives include: new hatcheries, extensive marine fisheries in the Bay of Bengal, south of the country, supporting infrastructure and training programmes.

Forestry

Bangladesh's total forest cover is estimated at 1.3 million hectares. The forestry sector typically contributes about 2.5 per cent to GDP, providing raw materials for the construction industry.

Bangladesh is one of the world's most densely populated countries and, as a consequence, its forests are subject to heavy demand pressures, both in wood production and competing land uses. An estimated 80 per cent of wood production is used for fuel; most of the remainder is converted to sawnwood. Coastal forests comprise mangroves, which account for nearly half of total forest cover, and bamboo. Inland valley forests comprise *sal, gamari, chaplish, telsu, jarui, teak, garjan, chandon* and *sundari*.

Industry and manufacturing

The industrial sector accounts for around 26 per cent of GDP and employs 10 per cent of the workforce. Some 40 per cent of industrial capacity is publicly-owned, mostly in jute and textile milling, steel and chemical production. Around one-third of fixed assets in manufacturing enterprises are held by the public sector, but account for less than 10 per cent of output. The main activities are jute processing, contributing around 15 per cent to gross manufacturing output, and cotton spinning and weaving.

The garment industry, which is the principal exporter, grew rapidly during the 1990s, helped by economic liberalisation, fiscal incentives and a relatively disciplined workforce. It is the largest industrial employer, with about 1.5 million workers. Other industries include leather goods, newsprint, cement, refined sugar, beverages, pharmaceuticals, electronic components and fertilisers. The US$510 million fertiliser plant in Chittagong exports 500 tonnes of ammonia and 1,725 tonnes of urea a day, mainly to India and China; earnings are estimated at US$100 million a year.

Bangladesh has established export processing zones in Chittagong, Dhaka, and Gazipur. Improving the efficiency and flexibility of labour and the financial markets and public enterprise reform will be critical for the performance of the industrial sector.

Long-term financing is virtually impossible to obtain and few companies have access to overseas financing, resulting in only modest growth in the industrial sector, the garments industry aside. Low wage rates, labour and an entrepreneurial society make the country an ideal manufacturing base, although poor infrastructure, high tariffs, corruption and bad governance still need to be addressed. Power constraints are also cited as a reason for low investment, although the government has opened the energy sector to private and foreign investment.

Tourism

Tourism is undeveloped in Bangladesh. The government recognised the potential of the sector in the early 1990s, but promotion has been minimal. Bangladesh's proneness to natural disasters, especially flooding, is a disadvantage. Of around 200,000 visitors, only a fifth are holiday-makers.

Environment

A ban exists on the production and use of polythene bags which have caused serious problems blocking the drainage system.

Mining

The 550km of coastline hold large resources of beachsands with rare mineral deposits spread over 17 areas containing monazite, ilmenite, zircon, rutile and magnetite. There are large limestone deposits, which are used to produce cement. The Jaipurhat Limestone Mining and Cement Works extracts one million tonnes per year of limestone to operate the plant. Other mineral resources include peat, white clay and mineral-bearing sands.

The general trend of government incentives to foreign investors, including share holding and private investment in exploration activities, is likely to develop the mining sector.

Hydrocarbons

Proven oil reserves were negligible by 2010; the country is a net importer of oil of 101,000 barrels per day (bpd). Eastern Refinery, Bangladesh's only oil refinery, has benefited from a US$1 billion refurbishment, undertaken by a joint partnership by Saudi Arabia's Marasel Company and Beximco of Bangladesh, in 2010. The project will triple the output to almost 100,000 barrels per day (bpd) and increase the 40 per cent of demand it currently fulfils.

Petrobangla is the state-owned energy company which produces and markets oil and gas.

Bangladesh had proven natural gas reserves of 400 billion cubic metres (cum) at the end of 2010 and produced 20.0 billion cum, an increase of 1.3 per cent on the 2009 figure and over double the amount produced in 2000. A new gas field with an estimated 900 million cum in the Sunamganj-Netrakona districts of north-eastern Bangladesh was announced in September 2010.

The large gas reserves and the country's proximity to the potentially huge energy market in India could help Bangladesh to develop as a major natural gas transit corridor, linking India's easternmost states with West Bengal. However, there is strong opposition to natural gas reserves being used for earning foreign revenue through exports, with the view that domestic markets should be supplied first.

Around 80 per cent of gas consumption is used in power and fertiliser production and the remainder on industrial and household needs.

Bangladesh's coal reserves remained unexploited until recently. The Barapukuria coal mine in north-west Bangladesh, the first major coal mine was opened in 2003. The mine has a production capacity of one million tonnes per annum, which will be mainly used for electricity generation. Imports are typically around 500,000 tonnes.

Energy

Bangladesh has an electricity generation capacity of around 4,700MW, 95 per cent of which is generated by conventional thermal power, overwhelmingly natural gas, with 5 per cent hydropower. Production was 22.78 billion kilowatt hours (kWh) in 2007, while consumption was over 21.4 kWh.

The government has opened up the market to foreign involvement with joint projects to build new or refurbish existing power stations, plus support for small, local, generators up to 10MW in under-served areas, and rural electrification. Biomass plays a significant role in rural household energy supplies and is estimated to account for 50 per cent of all energy consumption. Nevertheless it remains a non-commercial element in Bangladesh's energy mix.

Financial markets

Stock exchange

Dhaka Stock Exchange (DSE)

Banking and insurance

The banking system dominates the financial sector, accounting for about 97 per cent of the market in terms of assets.

There are four nationalised commercial banks, six development banks, 27 private banks and 19 non-bank financial institutions. The four nationalised commercial banks have consistently accounted for over 60 per cent of assets since the mid-1990s, while private domestic banks account for about 32 per cent, and foreign banks for the remaining 6–7 per cent.

Successive Bangladeshi governments have failed to address the inefficiencies and mis-allocation of funds by the state-owned banks. The government's emphasis on private sector led growth, if implemented, requires the development of a more efficient, transparent financial sector. Development of a properly regulated banking system is one priority in this regard, the equity market is another.
Nobel laureate, Muhammad Yunus was sacked on 2 March 2011 from the Grameen microfinance bank, which he had founded. The BCB, when dismissing him, said that he was passed retirement age. Yunus began legal proceedings to challenge his sacking but lost his appeal on 8 March.

Central bank
Bangladesh Central Bank (BCB)

Main financial centre
Dhaka

Time
GMT plus six hours
Daylight saving time (DST), was introduced in 2009, beginning between 19/20 June and ending 31 December, allowing businesses to open an hour earlier during summer months. However, it was later cancelled and Bangladesh remains on GMT +6 hours.

Geography
Bangladesh is bordered mostly by India except for a short border with Myanmar to the south-east. The Bay of Bengal washes the southern edge of the country. The Ganges (Padma) and Brahmaputra (Jamuna) rivers flow from the Himalayas into the Bay of Bengal and each river has a massive and ever-changing delta system where they meet the sea. The silt deposits from these rivers have created a vast alluvial plain where the soils are among the most agriculturally rich in the world. Apart from some hills around Aylhet in the north-east and the Chittagong Hills in the south-east, the country is flat and low-lying, and is criss-crossed by numerous waterways.

Hemisphere
Northern

Climate
Bangladesh has a sub-tropical monsoon climate and is dominated by the seasonally-reversing monsoons. There are three main seasons: winter (November–February) with an average temperature of 19 degrees Celsius (C); summer (March–May) when the average temperature is 29 degrees C and the climate is remarkably equable; and monsoon (June–October) which is humid and warm and accounts for 80 per cent of the country's annual rainfall of 1,200–3,500mm. It is normal for monsoon floods to cover around one-third of the country each year.

Dress codes
Lightweight cottons and linens are suitable during all seasons except winter when warm clothing is required.
Most Bangladeshis wear traditional dress: *lungi* (sarong) and *kurta* (loose shirt) for men and *sari* for women. However, urban and professional men prefer Western clothes: trousers, suits and ties; very few women wear skirts.There is no recognised national dress, but at official functions, Bengali men are expected to wear a closed collar jacket and trousers; for less formal occasions, safari suits are popular. Visiting businessmen should wear a lightweight or tropical suit and tie, and women should dress modestly.

Entry requirements

Passports
Required for nationals of all countries. Passports must be valid three months beyond the intended length of stay. A return ticket is required.

Visa
Required by nationals of most countries, with the exception of a number of Commonwealth countries and several others (for a list of exemptions, see www.bangladeshhighcommission.org.uk). Applications for business and tourist visas must be accompanied by a letter of invitation or other specified documentation (see www.bangladeshhighcommission.org.uk).

Prohibited entry
Nationals of Israel

Currency advice/regulations
The import and export of local currency is limited to Tk500. The import of foreign currency is allowed but amounts greater than US$3,000 must be declared on arrival. The export of foreign currency is limited to US$3,000 or the amount declared on arrival.
All foreign currency exchanged must be entered on a currency declaration form. Travellers cheques can be exchanged on arrival at Dhaka Airport. To avoid additional exchange rate charges, it is advisable to take travellers cheques in US dollars or UK pounds sterling.

Customs
Personal effects duty-free provided they are declared on entry.

Prohibited imports
Firearms and some animals.

Health (for visitors)
Health regulations may change and it is advisable to make detailed enquiries before travelling.

Mandatory precautions
A vaccination certificate is required for yellow fever if travelling from an infected area.

Advisable precautions
Immunisations are recommended for tetanus, typhoid, polio and hepatitis A. In some circumstances, immunisations for hepatitis B and Japanese B encephalitis are advisable – seek medical advice. Malaria prophylaxis is recommended for areas outside Dhaka. There is a rabies risk. Water and food precautioons should be observed.

Hotels
Hotel bills must be paid in a major convertible currency or with travellers cheques.
Provincial towns have government rest-houses with fairly Spartan accommodation, for which booking well in advance is advisable.

Credit cards
Credit cards are accepted. There is limited acceptance of Mastercard, Diners Club and American Express outside Dhaka.

Public holidays (national)

Fixed dates
1 Jan (New Year's Day), 21 Feb (Shaheed Day), 26 Mar (National Day), 14 Apr (Bengali New Year), 1 May (Labour Day), 7 Nov (National Revolution Day), 16 Dec (Victory Day), 25 Dec (Christmas Day), 26 Dec (Boxing Day), 31 Dec (New Year's Eve).

Variable dates
Eid al Adha, Islamic New Year, Birth of the Prophet, July Bank Holiday (first Mon in Jul), Ascent of the Prophet, Shab e-Qadr, Eid al Fitr.
Islamic year 1433 (26 Nov 2011–14 Nov 2012): The Islamic year contains 354 or 355 days, with the result that Muslim feasts advance by 10–12 days against the Gregorian calendar. Dates of feasts vary according to the sighting of the new moon, so cannot be forecast exactly.

Working hours

Banking
Sun—Wed: 0900–1500; Thur: 0900–1300.

Business
Sunday–Thursday: 0900–1700.

Government
Sunday–Thursday: 0900–1700.

Shops
Saturday–Thursday: 0900–2000; Friday 0900–1230; 1400—2000.

Telecommunications

Mobile/cell phones
The use of mobile phones is limited to cities and urban areas.

Electricity supply
220V AC, 50 Hz with British-type 2 or 3 round pin plug fittings.

Weights and measures
Metric system

Social customs/useful tips
Normal Muslim customs predominate. Food and drink should be proffered with the right hand only. It is offensive to drink, eat or smoke in public or in the presence of Muslims during the month of Ramadan. Pork is considered unclean. However, alcohol is not prohibited and is available. Muslim women should not be photographed unless it is certain that no objection will be made. Females are expected to dress soberly and act discreetly. If travelling without a man, women sit together at the front of the bus.
People are usually warm and informal and do not hesitate to invite foreigners to their homes.
Gratuities in restaurants are around 10 per cent and 5 per cent for taxis.

Security
Thieving, armed robbery and kidnapping are a threat. Caution should be exercised when moving around, including in choice of transport. Ostentatious displays of wealth such as money, watches and cameras should be avoided.

Getting there
Air
National airline: Biman Bangladesh Airlines
International airport/s: Zia International (DAC), 20km north of Dhaka, with VIP lounge, duty-free shop, bank, post office, restaurant and car hire; Patenga (CGP), 22km from Chittagong.
Other airport/s: Sylhet (ZYL), in the north-east of the country catering for visitors to the highlands of Sylhet.
Airport tax: Tk300 for all passengers, excluding those under two-years-old and immediate transit passengers.
Surface
Road: It is possible to travel by road from a number of points in India, including West Bengal, Assam and Tripura. Travel may be difficult during monsoon seasons.
Main port/s: Chittagong, Chalna.

Getting about
National transport
Transport links in Bangladesh are often slow and prone to disruption by bad weather. Allow time for delays. In April 2011 the World Bank agreed a US$1.2 billion credit to build a 6k bridge across the Padma river, linking to the Dhaka-Chittagong Highway. The Bank estimates the road and rail connection will directly benefit some 30 million people in the region. At present all traffic across the Padma has to rely on ferries, which are infrequent and often unsafe.
Air: There are regular daily flights between main centres operated by Air Parabat. Biman Bangladesh also serves main centres.
There are regional airports at Barisal, Jessore, Saidpur, Sylhet, Cox's Bazar, Thakurgaon and Rajshahi. Local storms can disrupt schedules.
Road: Bangladesh has an extensive road system, but does not have the capacity to deal with the amount of traffic. An estimated 7 per cent of roads are paved, and around half are metalled. Travel on roads during the monsoon season is difficult. The 4.8km long road/rail bridge across the Jamuna River links the eastern and western parts of the country. Numerous ferry crossings sometimes make journey times unpredictable.
Buses: There are express buses and local ones which stop en route. The latter charge around 25 per cent less, but are slow. In remote areas local buses are often the only means of transport.
Rail: About one-third of Bangladesh is serviced by railways. Inter City (IC) trains are frequent, clean and reasonably punctual, especially in the eastern zone, although they may be relatively slow. Six classes of rail travel are available: 'first' and 'express' are recommended for air-conditioned coaches that also provide more room.
Water: The river is the traditional means of transport. There are 8,000km of navigable waterways, although flooding in the monsoon season, silting in the dry season, and fogs may make routes inaccessible. The main routes are covered by the Bangladesh Inland Waterway Transport Corporation (BIWTC), but there are many private companies operating on shorter routes. Passage should be booked well in advance.
City transport
Taxis: Taxis, generally identifiable by their black body and yellow top, are few and far between in Dhaka; they are available at main hotels and airports. Negotiate fares before travelling. A 10 per cent service charge is usual.
It is probably best to organise a car from the hotel for the 20km trip from Dhaka Zia International Airport; journey time is 30 minutes.
Rickshaws and autorickshaws are available, but are not recommended for use at night. Autorickshaws should be metered, but often are not. Negotiate fares in advance.
Buses, trams & metro: Buses are generally overcrowded and unreliable.
Car hire
There are a number of private car hire companies in Dhaka and other cities. The Bangladesh Parjatan Corporation (BPC), the government tourism organisation, has a fleet of air-conditioned and non air-conditioned cars, microbuses and jeeps for hire. The BPC also offers a transfer service for tourists between Dhaka airport and the city centre and main hotels.
Driving is on the left. A national licence or international driving permit is required.

BUSINESS DIRECTORY

The addresses listed below are a selection only. While World of Information makes every endeavour to check these addresses, we cannot guarantee that changes have not been made, especially to telephone numbers and area codes. We would welcome any corrections.

Telephone area codes
The international direct dialling code (IDD) for Bangladesh is + 880, followed by area code and subscriber's number:

Bagerhat	401	Khulna	41
Barisal	431	Kushtia	71
Bogra	51	Moulvi Bazar	861
Chittagong	31	Mymensingh	91
Comilla	81	Narayanganj	671
Dhaka	2	Patvakhali	441
Dinajpur	531	Rajshashi	721
Jamalpur	981	Sylhet	821

Useful telephone numbers
Police: 866-551/3
Fire: 9-555-5555
Ambulance: 112

Chambers of Commerce
American Chamber of Commerce in Bangladesh, Dhaka Sheraton Hotel, 1 Minto Road, Dhaka 1000 (tel: 861-3391; fax: 831-2915; e-mail: amcham@bangla.net).

Chittagong Chamber of Commerce and Industry, Agrabad Commercial Area, Chittagong (tel: 711-355; fax: 710-183; e-mail: ccci@globalctg.net).

Dhaka Chamber of Commerce and Industry, 65 Motijheel Commercial Area, Dhaka 1000 (tel: 955-2562; fax: 956-0830; e-mail: dcci@bangla.net).

Federation of Bangladesh Chambers of Commerce and Industry, 60 Motijheel Commercial Area, Dhaka 1000 (tel: 956-0102; fax: 861-3213; e-mail: fbcci@bol-online.com).

Foreign Investors Chamber of Commerce and Industry, 35-1 Purana Paltan Line, Inner Circular Road, Dhaka 1000 (tel: 831-9448; fax: 831-9449; e-mail: ficci@bangla.net).

Khulna Chamber of Commerce and Industry, 5 KDA Commercial Area, Khan-A-Sabur Road, Khulna (tel: 721-695; fax: 731-213).

Metropolitan Chamber of Commerce and Industry, 122 Motijheel Commercial Area, Dhaka 1000 (tel: 956-5208; fax: 956-5212; e-mail: sg@citechco.net).

Banking

Agrani Bank, Agrani Bank Building, 9D Motijheel Commercial Area, Dhaka 1000 (tel: 956-6160; fax: 956-2346).

Arab Bangladesh Bank, BCIC Bhaban, 30-31 Dilkusha Commercial Area, Dhaka 1000 (tel: 956-0312; fax 956-4122).

Bangladesh Krishi Bank (Agricultural Bank), 83-85 Motijheel Commercial Area, Dhaka 100 (tel: 956-0021; fax: 867-102).

Bangladesh Shilpa Bank (Industrial Bank), PO Box 975, 8 Rajuk Avenue, Dhaka (tel: 955-8326; fax: 956-2061).

Banque Indosuez, 47 Motijheel Commercial Area, Dhaka 1000 (tel: 956-6566; fax: 956-5707).

Citibank N A, Chamber Building, 122-124 Motijheel Commercial Area, Dhaka 1000 (tel: 955-0061; fax: 956-2236).

Dutch-Bangla Bank Limited, Sena Kalyan Bhaban, 195 Motijheel Commercial Area, Dhaka 1000 (tel: 956-8537, 956-8542-44; fax: 956-1889; e-mail: dbbl@bdmail.net).

Grameen Bank, Grameen Bank Bhaban, Mirpur, Section-2, Dhaka-1216, Bangladesh (tel: 900-5256; e-mail: grameen.bank@grameen.net).

Hongkong & Shanghai Banking Corporation, Anchor Tower, 1.1-B Sonargaon Road, Dhaka 1205 (tel: 966-0536; fax: 966-0554).

International Finance Investment and Commercial Bank, BSB Building, 8 Rajuk Avenue, Dhaka 1000.

Investment Corporation of Bangladesh, Dhaka.

Islam Bank Bangladesh, PO Box 233, Islami Bank Tower, 40 Dilkusha Commercial Area, Dhaka 1000 (tel: 956-3182; fax: 956-4532).

Janata Bank, Janata Bhadan, 110 Motijheel Commercial Area, PO Box 468, Dhaka 1000 (tel: 956-000; fax: 956-4644).

National Bank Limited, 18 Dilkusha Commercial Area, Dhaka 1000 (tel: 956-3081/5; fax: 956-3953; e-mail: nblho@citechco.net).

Pubali Bank Ltd, 26 Dikusha Commercial Area, Dhaka 1000 (tel: 956-9050; fax: 956-4009).

Rupali Bank Ltd, 34 Dilkusha Commercial Area, Dhaka 1000 (tel: 955-1624; fax: 956-4148).

Sonali Bank, Motijheel Commercial Area, PO Box 147, Dhaka 1000 (tel: 955-0426; fax: 956-1410).

Standard Chartered Bank, 18-20 Motijheel Commercial Area, Dhaka 1000 (tel: 956-1465; fax: 956-1758).

United Commercial Bank, 60 Motijheel Commercial Area, Dhaka 1000.

Uttara Bank, 90 Motijheel Commercial Area, Dhakar 1000 (tel: 955-1162; fax: 863-539).

Central bank

Bangladesh Central Bank, Motijheel Commercial Area, PO Box 325, Dhaka 1000 (tel: 956-6203; fax: 956-6212; e-mail: banglabank@bangla.net).

Stock exchange

Dhaka Stock Exchange (DSE): www.dsebd.org

Stock exchange 2

Chittagong Stock Exchange (CSE); www.csebd.com

Travel information

Automobile Association of Bangladesh, 3/B Outer Circular Road, Dhaka 17 (tel: 402-241).

Biman Bangladesh Airlines, Biman Bhaban, 100 Motijheel Commercial Area, Dhaka 1000 (tel: 240-151/90; fax: 863-005); airport (tel: 894-771/79); flight enquiries (tel: 894-350, 894-870).

Railway enquiries (tel: 409-686).

National tourist organisation offices

Bangladesh Parjatan Corporation, 233 Airport Road, Tejgaon, Dhaka 1215 (tel: 811–7855; fax: 812–6501; e-mail: bpcho@bangla.net).

Ministries

Ministry of Agriculture, Bangladesh Secretariat, Dhaka 1000 (tel: 869-277; fax: 867-040).

Ministry of Civil Aviation and Tourism, Bangladesh Secretariat, Dhaka 1000 (tel: 867-244; fax: 869-206).

Ministry of Commerce, Bangladesh Secretariat, Dhaka 1000 (tel: 869-679; fax: 865-741).

Ministry of Communications, Bangladesh Secretariat, Dhaka 1000 (tel: 864-977; fax: 866-636).

Ministry of Cultural Affairs, Bangladesh Secretariat, Dhaka 1000 (tel: 868-977; fax: 860-290).

Ministry of Defence, Ganabhaban Complex, Sher-e-Bangla Nagar, Dhaka 1207 (tel: 816-955; fax: 817-945).

Ministry of Disaster Management & Relief, Bangladesh Secretariat, Dhaka 1000 (tel: 868-744; fax: 869-623).

Ministry of Education, Bangladesh Secretariat, Dhaka 1000 (tel: 868-711; fax: 867-577).

Ministry of Energy and Mineral Resources, Bangladesh Secretariat, Dhaka 1000 (tel: 866-188; fax: 861-110).

Ministry of Environment & Forest, Bangladesh Secretariat, Dhaka 1000 (tel: 860-587; fax: 869-210).

Ministry of Finance, Finance Division, Bangladesh Secretariat, Dhaka 1000 (tel: 860-406; fax: 865-581).

Ministry of Fisheries and Livestock, Bangladesh Secretariat, Dhaka 1000 (tel: 864-700).

Ministry of Food, Bangladesh Secretariat, Dhaka 1000 (tel: 862-240; fax: 860-762).

Ministry of Foreign Affairs, Foreign Affairs Building, Segunbagicha, Dhaka 1000 (tel: 955-6020; fax: 956-2557).

Ministry of Health & Family Welfare, Bangladesh Secretariat, Dhaka 1000 (tel: 866-975; fax: 869-077).

Ministry of Home Affairs, Bangladesh Secretariat, Dhaka 1000 (tel: 864-611; fax: 869-667).

Ministry of Industries, Shilpa Bhaban, 91 Motijheel Commercial Area, Dhaka 1000 (tel: 956-3549; fax: 956-3553).

Ministry of Information, Bangladesh Secretariate, Dhaka 1000 (tel: 868-555; fax: 862-211).

Ministry of Jute, Bangladesh Secretariat, Dhaka 1000 (tel: 862-250; fax: 868-766).

Ministry of Labour and Manpower, Bangladesh Secretariat, Dhaka 1000 (tel: 862-141; fax: 868-660).

Ministry of Land, Bangladesh Secretariat, Dhaka 1000 (tel: 869-644; fax: 862-989).

Ministry of Law, Justice and Parliamentary Affairs, Bangladesh Secretariat, Dhaka 1000 (tel: 860-560; fax: 868-557).

Ministry of Local Government and Rural Development, Bangladesh Secretariat, Dhaka 1000 (tel: 869-176; fax: 864-374).

Ministry of Planning, Sher-e-Bangla Nagar, Dhaka 1207 (tel: 815-175; fax: 814-638).

Ministry of Post and Telecommunications, Bangladesh Secretariat, Dhaka 1000 (tel: 864-800; fax: 865-775).

Ministry of Primary and Mass Education, Bangladesh Secretariat, Dhaka 1000 (tel: 862-484; fax: 868-871).

Ministry of Religious Affairs, Bangladesh Secretariat, Dhaka 1000 (tel: 860-682; fax: 865-040).

Ministry of Science & Technology, Bangladesh Secretariat, Dhaka 1000 (tel: 866-144; fax: 869-606).

Ministry of Shipping, Bangladesh Secretariat, Dhaka 1000 (tel: 868-155; fax: 862-219).

Ministry of Social Welfare, Bangladesh Secretariat, Dhaka 1000 (tel: 860-452; fax: 868-969).

Ministry of Textiles, Bangladesh Secretariat, Dhaka 1000 (tel: 864-388; fax: 860-600).

Ministry of Water Resources, Bangladesh Secretariat, Dhaka 1000 (tel: 868-688; fax: 862-400).

Ministry of Women and Children Affairs, Bangladesh Secretariat, Dhaka 1000 (tel: 861-012; fax: 867-550).

Ministry of Youth and Sports, Bangladesh Secretariat, Dhaka 1000 (tel: 867-053; fax: 862-344).

President's Office, Bangabhaban, Dhaka 1000 (tel: 966-8041; fax: 946-6242).

Prime Minister's Office, Old Sangsad Bhaban, Tejgaon, Dhaka (tel: 888-160; fax: 813-244).

Other useful addresses

Asian Development Bank, Bangladesh Resident Mission, BSL Office Complex, Sheraton Hotel Annex, 1 Minto Road, Ramna, Dhaka 1000 (tel: 933-4017; fax: 933-4012; e-mail: abddrm@mail.asiandevbank.org).

Bangladesh Agricultural University, Mymensingh (tel: 4333, 4191/93).

Bangladesh Export Processing Zones Authority, 222 New Eskaton Road, Dhaka (tel: 832-553; fax: 834-963).

Bangladesh Jute Mills Corporation, Adanjee Court, Motijheel Commercial Area, Dhaka (tel: 238-182/6, 238-192/6; fax: 883-329, 883-985).

Bangladesh Small and Cottage Industries Corporation, 137-138 Motijheel Commercial Area, Dhaka (tel: 865-161).

Bangladesh Telegraph and Telephone Board, 36/1 Mymensingh Road, Dhaka (tel: 831-500; fax: 832-477).

Board of Investment, Shilpa Bhaban, 91 Motijheel Commercial Area, Dhaka (tel: 955-9378; fax: 956-2312).

Bangladesh University of Engineering & Technology, Ramna, Dhaka 2 (tel: 505-171-5).

British High Commission, United Nations Road, PO Box 6079, Baridhara, Dhaka 12 (tel: 882-705/9; fax: 883-437).

Chittagong Port Authority, Port Road, Chittagong (tel: 712-504; fax: 710-593).

Chittagong Stock Exchange, 1/F Kashfia Plaza, 923/A Sheikh Mujib Road, Chittagong (tel: 714-100; fax: 714-101).

Department of Environment, Poribesh Bhaban, Plot £16 Agargaon, Sher-e-Bangla Nagar, Dhaka (tel: 812-416).

Department of Fisheries, Matsa Bhaban Segunbagicha, Dhaka (tel: 956-9320).

Department of Immigration and Passports, 17 Segunbagicha, Dhaka (tel: 834-320; fax: 956-2787).

Department of Shipping, 8/F, 141-143, Motijheel Commercial Area, Dhaka (tel: 955-5128).

Department of Textiles, Bastra Bhaban, Kazi Nazrul Islam Avenue, Dhaka (911-6385).

Dhaka Electric Supply Authority, 1 Abdul Gani Road, Dhaka (tel: 956-3520).

Dhaka Stock Exchange, 9F Motijheel Commercial Area, Dhaka 1000 (tel: 955-1935; fax: 867-552).

Export Promotion Bureau, Chamber Building, 122-124 Motijheel Commercial Area, Dhaka 1000 (tel: 955-2245/9; fax: 956-8000; e-mail: epb.tic@pradeshta.net).

Infrastructure Development Co Ltd, c/o Economic Relations Division, Block 16, Room 3, Sher-e-Bangla Nagar, Dhaka (tel: 811-971; fax: 811-660).

Mongla Port Authority, Mongla, Bagerhat (tel: 416-2331; fax: 403-1224).

National Board of Revenue, Segunbagicha, Dhaka (tel: 838-120; fax: 836-143).

Planning Commission, G.O. Hostel, Sher-e-Bangla Nagar, Dhaka.

Power Development Board, WAPDA Building, Motijheel Commercial Area, Dhaka (tel: 956-2154; fax: 956-4765).

Privatisation Board, 14/F Joban Bima Tower, 10 Dilkusha Commercial Area, Dhaka (tel: 956-3763; fax: 956-3723).

Registrar of Joint Stock Companies and Firms, 24-25 Dilkusha Commercial Area, Dhaka (tel: 956-4005).

Securities and Exchange Commission, Jiban bima Tower, 10 Dilkusha Commercial Area, Dhaka (tel: 956-8101; fax: 956-3721).

US Embassy, Madani Avenue, Baridhara, Dhaka 1212 (tel: 882-4700; fax: 882-3744; e-mail: dhaka@pd.state.gov).

Water Sewerage Authority, 98 Kazi Nazrul Islam Avenue, Dhaka (tel: 816-792; fax: 812-109).

National news agency: Bangladesh Sangbad Sangstha (BSS), 68/2, Purana Paltan, Dhaka 1000 (tel: 955-5036; fax: 9557929; email: bssnews@bssnews.org; internet: www.bssnews.net).

Internet sites

Bangladesh Parjatan Corporation (National tourist organisation): www.bangladeshtourism.gov.bd

Bangladesh News: www.bangladeshnews.net

Virtual Bangladesh: www.virtualbangladesh.com

Barbados

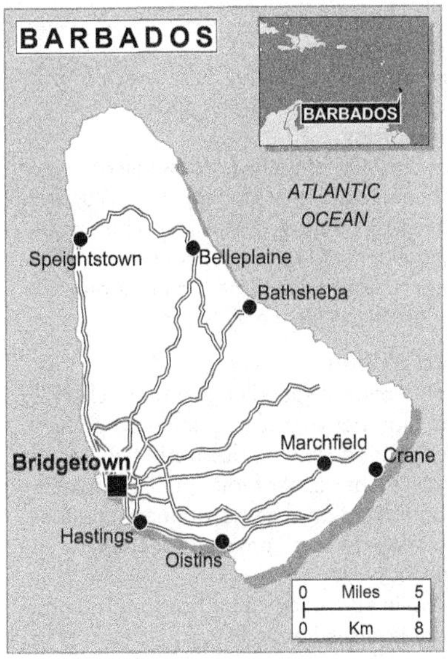

The economy grew by 2.8 per cent in the first quarter of 2011, continuing the recovery begun in 2010. This was largely on the back of tourism in general that had grown by 3 per cent in the January to September period in 2010, and an increase in stopover tourists from the United States and Canada as their economies recovered. On 25 June, the capital, Bridgetown, was added to the Unesco list of World Heritage Sites, as a well-preserved old town and nearby military garrison, and an outstanding example of British colonial architecture. It is hoped that this will attract more visitors.

On 29 June the government announced it would invest US$100 million in the sugar industry to promote its diversification into production of bagasse, ethanol, special sugars and molasses. Sugar had been the main agricultural crop in Barbados since the Dutch introduced it in 1642 but it slowly declined until the European Union was forced in 2009 to drop the preferential treatment given to former colonies. Prices fell by 40 per cent the sugar industry collapsed.

In July, a 16-member party from China, visiting to experience the Crop Over Festival (an annual carnival that used to celebrate the end of the sugar harvest), have said they will help promote the island on their return. At the same time, Barbados opened an embassy in China.

Risk assessment

Politics	Fair
Economy	Struggling
Regional stability	Good

COUNTRY PROFILE

Historical profile

Barbados was formerly a British colony and is now an independent sovereign state.
1951 Universal adult suffrage was introduced. The Barbados Labour Party (BLP) won the general election, and held office until 1961.
1955 The BLP split and a splinter group formed the Democratic Labour Party (DLP).
1961 Barbados achieved self-government. The DLP won the general elections, its leader Errol Barrow, became premier.
1966 Barbados gained independence; Errol Barrow became prime minister.
1967 Barbados joined the United Nations.
1973 Barbados, Guyana, Jamaica, and Trinidad and Tobago established the Caribbean Community and Common Market, later known just as Caribbean Community (Caricom).
1976–86 BLP retained power in elections.
1986 DLP won the general elections.
1994 The BLP won a landslide general election. Owen Arthur became prime minister.
2002 Barbados was removed from the Organisation for Economic Co-operation and Development's (OECD) blacklist of non-co-operative countries for its efforts to combat money laundering.
2003 The ruling BLP won the general elections.
2006 The opposition leader, Clyde Mascoll, resigned from the DLP and joined the ruling BLP.
2008 The opposition DLP won 52.5 per cent (20 seats out of 30) in parliamentary elections, the BLP 47.3 per cent, (10); turnout was 56.6 per cent. David Thompson (DLP) was sworn in as prime minister. The Barbados Defence Force received military aid of B$840,000 (US$1.68 million) from the Chinese Army. The

KEY FACTS

Official name: Barbados

Head of State: Queen Elizabeth II, represented by Governor General Sir Clifford Straughn Husbands (since 1996)

Head of government: Prime Minister David Thompson (DLP) (since 16 Jan 2008)

Ruling party: Democratic Labour Party (DLP) (since 15 Jan 2008)

Area: 430 square km

Population: 273,000 (2010)*

Capital: Bridgetown

Official language: English

Currency: Barbados dollar (BD$) = 100 cents

Exchange rate: BD$2.00 per US$ (Oct 2011)

GDP per capita: US$14,326 (2010)

GDP real growth: -0.50% (2010)

GDP: US$4.00 billion (2010)

Labour force: 142,000 (2010)

Unemployment: 10.80% (2010)

Inflation: 5.10% (2010)

Balance of trade: -US$912.80 million (2009)

* estimated figure

donation included computers, power generators and other equipment, and military training.
2009 An amnesty and new rules concerning Caricom nationals living and working in Barbados illegally were introduced. The mandatory death penalty for murder was abolished.
2010 In May Prime Minister David Thompson announced that he was unwell and in June that he would take a leave of absence while he recovered; Freundel Stuart became acting prime minister. In July, Barbados opened an embassy in China. On 23 October David Thompson died and Freundel Stuart was sworn in as prime minister.
2011 The economy grew by 2.8 per cent in the first quarter. On 25 June, the capital, Bridgetown, was added to the Unesco list of World Heritage Sites, as a well-preserved old town and nearby military garrison, and an outstanding example of British colonial architecture. On 29 June the government announced it would invest US$100 million in the sugar industry to promote its diversification into production of bagasse, ethanol, special sugars and molasses. In July, a 16-member party from China, visiting to experience the Crop Over Festival (an annual carnival), will help promote the island on their return. Sir Clifford Husbands retired and Elliot Belgrave took office as acting governor general on 1 November.

Political structure
Constitution
Promulgated on 30 November 1966.
Independence date
1966

Form of state
Parliamentary democracy, within a constitutional monarchy.
The executive
Executive power is vested in the British monarch, represented by a governor general, who is appointed by the monarch, and exercised by the prime minister and cabinet.
National legislature
Legislative power is exercised through the bicameral National Assembly, comprising a 30-member House of Assembly, popularly elected in single seat constituencies, for terms of five years and a 21-member Senate of appointed members for five-year terms.
Following National Assembly elections, the leader of the majority party or coalition assumes the post of prime minister, confirmed by the governor general. The cabinet is selected by the prime minister and confirmed by the governor general.
Legal system
The legal system is based on English common law. Judges are appointed by the service commissions for the judicial and legal service. There is no judicial review of legislative acts.
Last elections
15 January 2008 (parliamentary)
Results: Parliamentary: the DLP won 52.5 per cent, (20 seats out of 30), the BLP 47.3 per cent, (10); turnout was 56.6 per cent.
Next elections
2013 (parliamentary)

Political parties
Ruling party
Democratic Labour Party (DLP) (since 15 Jan 2008)

KEY INDICATORS Barbados

	Unit	2006	2007	2008	2009	2010
Population	m	0.27	0.28	*0.28	*0.28	*0.27
Gross domestic product (GDP)	US$bn	3.43	3.74	3.70	3.60	4.00
GDP per capita	US$	12,523	13,605	13,356	13,003	14,326
GDP real growth	%	3.9	4.2	0.6	-5.3	-0.5
Inflation	%	7.2	5.5	8.3	3.5	5.1
Unemployment	%	8.7	7.4	8.1	10.0	10.8
Exports (fob) (goods)	US$m	441.6	486.9	489.6	381.0	–
Imports (fob) (goods)	US$m	1,452.6	1,527.7	1,731.9	1,293.9	–
Balance of trade	US$m	-1,011.0	-1,037.8	-1,242.3	-912.8	–
Current account	US$m	-278.0	-311.2	-437.2	-312.0	-292.0
Total reserves minus gold	US$m	636.1	839.3	738.5	871.1	833.5
Foreign exchange	US$m	627.9	830.3	729.8	773.8	737.9
Exchange rate	per US$	2.00	2.00	2.00	2.00	2.00

* estimated figure

Main opposition party
Barbados Labour Party (BLP)

Population
273,000 (2010)*
Last census: May 2000: 250,010
Population density: 620 inhabitants per square km. Urban population: 51 per cent (1995–2001).
Annual growth rate: 0.3 per cent 1994–2004 (WHO 2006)
Ethnic make-up
African (90 per cent), mixed race (6 per cent), European (4 per cent).
Religions
Mainly Christian, with an Anglican majority and dozens of smaller sects, plus small Jewish, Hindu and Muslim communities. Anglican (40 per cent), Pentecostal (8 per cent), Methodist (7 per cent), Roman Catholic (4 per cent).

Education
Educational spending is around US$150 million per year. Expenditure on primary education typically fluctuates between 25–29 per cent of total public expenditure on education. The government provides assistance to all private secondary schools.
Public education at primary and secondary levels is free, although parents can opt to send their children to private schools. Primary education begins at aged five and lasts for six years.
The secondary school programme begins at aged 11 years and last until aged 16, when students choose between academic higher education or applied further education.
The Samuel Jackman Prescod Polytechnic (SJPP), the Barbados Community College (BCC), Erdiston College and the University of the West Indies cater for higher education. Eligible students also pursue their studies in North American colleges and universities.
Compulsory years: 5 to 16
Enrolment rate: 94.7 per cent to 100 per cent, primary school enrolment of the relevant age group.
Pupils per teacher: 18 in primary schools

Health
With 16 per cent of the population aged 60 years and over, Barbados has the highest percentage of elderly population in the English speaking Caribbean. Barbados provides high quality primary and secondary care with free treatment for young children. The Queen Elizabeth Hospital benefits from government aid. There is universal access to improved water and sanitation facilities.
HIV/Aids
HIV prevalence: 1.5 per cent aged 15–49 in 2003 (World Bank)

Life expectancy: 75 years, 2004 (WHO 2006)
Fertility rate/Maternal mortality rate: 1.5 births per woman, 2004 (WHO 2006)
Birth rate/Death rate: 13 births per 1,000 population; nine deaths per 1,000 population (2003).
Child (under 5 years) mortality rate (per 1,000): 13 per 1,000 live births (2003)

Welfare

The government provides an extensive welfare programme for the poor and the elderly. Assistance for the elderly comprises housing, transportation, home care and free utilities (water and utilities), assistance in kind, and food vouchers.
Financial assistance is provided to parents of underprivileged children as well as subsidies for school expenses.
Low rent housing is available to all residents; some housing is available to be purchased by low income earners.

Pensions

There is universal pension coverage from a non-contributory pension.

Main cities

Bridgetown (capital, estimated population 98,900 in 2003), Speightstown (3,600), Oistins, Holetown.

Languages spoken

A local Bajan dialect is spoken.

Official language/s

English

Media

Press

Dailies: There are two, *The Daily Nation* (www.nationnews.com) and the *Barbados Advocate* (www.barbadosadvocate.com).
Weeklies: Daily newspapers publish weekend editions. Others include *Eastern Caribbean News*, *Weekend Investigator* and *Caribbean Week* (published fortnightly).
Business: *The Broad Street Journal* (www.broadstreetnews.com) and *Business Monday* (www.barbadosadvocate.com), are business publications while most daily newspapers have business sections.
Periodicals: The Government Information Service (BGIS) (www.barbados.gov.bb) publishes data and research articles.

Broadcasting

The Caribbean Broadcast Corporation (CBC) (www.cbc.bb) is the nation public broadcaster.
Radio: CBC (www.cbc.bb) has three networks which cover news, cultural and sports events and all genre of music.
There are several private, commercial and religious radio stations operating including Voice of Barbados (VOB) (www.vob929.com), which competes with CBC for content, Hott FM (www.hott953.com), Mix 96.9 (www.mix969fm.com) and Gospel 97.5 (www.gospel975.com); the Barbados Broadcasting Service operates BBS 90.7 and Faith FM (www.barbadosadvocate.com).
Television: CBC (www.cbc.bb) is the only terrestrial TV network in operation, showing domestic news and current affairs, art and cultural programmes as well as imported shows. Programmes are also provided by Jump TV (www.jumptv.com), via the internet. It is the largest provider worldwide of internet programming.

News agencies

National news agency: Caribbean News Agency (Cana)
Other news agencies: Caribbean Net News: www.caribbeannetnews.com

Economy

The economy is characterised as having a strong service sector that caters for the tourist industry, with related construction and retail services. The financial sector, particularly offshore services, includes call centres in insurance targeted at the east coast of the US. Per capita income is one of the highest in the Caribbean. The global economic crisis hit hard in 2008 with the unemployment rate from within these sectors rising sharply. Government expenditure rose by over US$144 million to provide welfare and investment measures.
GDP growth was -0.2 per cent in 2008 and fell again to -5.5 per cent in 2009. GDP growth is estimated to show an improvement in 2010, but will still remain in recession. Growth in 2011 should be fully recovered and is forecast to rise to 3.0 per cent.
Overall, the economy in 2008–09 slumped as long-stay visitor numbers fell by 13.3 per cent and cruise passenger arrival numbers fell by 3.9 per cent. Barbados lost an estimated US$170 million in foreign exchange over the period and had to rely on the Special Drawing Rights (SDRs) provided to members of International Monetary Fund (IMF), to maintain foreign reserves.
As financial services began to pick up in 2009, the industry was overshadowed by the introduction, or extension, of regulatory actions by foreign governments on tax avoidance by their citizens. However, the IMF considered Barbados well placed and governed to adapt quickly to the changes.

External trade

As a member of the Caribbean Community and Common Market (Caricom), Barbados operates within the single market (Caribbean Single Market and Economy (CSME)), which became operational in 2006. It is also a member of the Organisation of American States (OAS). Barbados, as a member of the 15-country Caribbean Forum (Cariforum) has free trade agreements with the European Union (EU), Costa Rica, Dominican Republic, Colombia and Venezuela.
Barbados was the first single-crop agrarian economy to switch to the service sector provision of back office operations. Its financial sector, combined with the tourist sector, provides the greater percentage of GDP. The offshore financial centre utilises the well educated, English-speaking, workforce with its proximity to the US and Canada, as well as traditional links with the UK.

Imports

Principal imports are petroleum, consumer goods, food and beverages, construction materials, electrical components, vehicles, marine crafts and machinery.
Main sources: US (typically 40 per cent of total), Trinidad and Tobago (16 per cent), UK (5 per cent).

Exports

Principal commodity exports are sugar and molasses, rum and other foods and beverages, chemicals and electrical and electronic components.
Main destinations: US (typically 28 per cent of total), UK (10 per cent), Trinidad and Tobago (10 per cent).

Agriculture

Farming

The agricultural sector contributes around 7 per cent to GDP and employs around 5 per cent of the labour force.
Around 76 per cent of the total land area is under cultivation.
Emphasis has been placed on diversifying production away from sugar and towards the farming of sea island cotton, green vegetables and market garden produce.
The EU quota of just under 50,000 tonnes per year and its guaranteed price mechanism came to an end in 2007. The pressure is on Barbados to make the sugar sector profitable, although it seems unlikely that the island will be able to compete with low-cost producers and the heavily subsidised sugar beet farmers in North America and the EU. As well as trade liberalisation, the Barbados sugar sector has had to cope with environmental degradation and the rising price of land.

Fishing

There are complaints that the small fishing industry has not been supported by the government. The government issued fish importing licences permitting processors to import fish, when the domestic catch could have provided for domestic processing needs.

Industry and manufacturing

Manufacturing employs around 9 per cent of the workforce and construction and quarrying, 11 per cent.
Production is centred on light manufacturing and assembly of electrical and electronic

goods, food processing, clothing, sugar refining, petrochemicals and beverages.
Most new foreign-owned export-oriented industries are based on the island's nine purpose-built industrial estates, which are largely managed by the Barbados Industrial Development Corporation.
Emphasis is placed on expanding the number of value-added joint venture assembly industries.

Tourism

Barbados has a typical Caribbean experience for high-end visitors with unspoilt beaches and luxury accommodation. Sea sports (surfing and windsurfing) are very popular, along with diving and fishing.
The service sector typically constitutes 80 per cent of GDP. As the global economic crisis cut tourism the number of visitors to Barbados fell from a record 572,937 in 2007 to 567,667 in 2008, to 518,564 in 2009. The greatest reduction in visitors was those from the UK and the US, which, combined, had represented over 60 per cent of all arrivals in previous years. Visitor numbers from Canada improved by 11.2 per cent on the 2008 figures. Tourists arriving at the beginning of 2010 were showing an increase.
The only sector of the industry not to show a decrease in 2008–09 was Caribbean cruising. A cruise liner terminal in the capital, Bridgetown, has capacity for five ships at any one time. There were 460 visits by liners in 2009, disembarking a total of 635,746 passengers, an increase of 6.4 per cent up from 597,526 passengers in 2008. Private yachts are catered for at the Port Charles Marina and a villa complex in Speightstown.
The industry was forecast to directly employ around 20,000 workers in 2011, which constitutes 14.6 per cent of total employment. Indirect employment in the sector constitutes 46.6 per cent of total employment at around 65,000 jobs.
The forecast is for travel and tourism to directly contribute BD$1,155.8 million (US$557.9 million), or 14.2 per cent of GDP; indirect contribution is forecast at BD$3,824.9 million (US$1,912.5 million), or 47 per cent of GDP in 2011. Visitor exports were expected to be BD2,497.2 million (US$1,248.6 million), which constitutes 49.9 per cent of expected total foreign exchange. Investment in travel and tourism committed for 2011 was estimated at BD600.9 million (US$300.5 million), or 20.4 per cent of total estimated investment.

Hydrocarbons

Proven oil reserves were two million barrels in 2008, located offshore, producing 1,100 barrels per day (bpd), which is exported to Trinidad and Tobago for refining and re-importing. The state-owned Barbados National Oil Company (BNOC) is responsible for domestic production, its production accounted for 15 per cent of the island's annual consumption in 2008 (8,000bpd).
Natural gas reserves were 170 million cubic metres (cum) in 2008. In January 2009 Barbados awarded drilling rights to two blocks in its territorial waters in a bid to discover natural gas.
Any coal imports or use are commercially insignificant.

Energy

Total installed generating capacity was 210MW in 2007. Barbados relies on imported oil for most of its energy requirements. There are plans to expand solar and wind energy programmes.

Financial markets

Stock exchange
Barbados Stock Exchange (BSE)

Banking and insurance

The financial sector continues to expand.
Central bank
Central Bank of Barbados
Main financial centre
Bridgetown
Offshore facilities
Barbados is a major international business centre. It has several tax treaties in place with developed countries including Canada.

Time

GMT minus four hours

Geography

Barbados is the most easterly of the Caribbean islands, lying about 320km (200 miles) north-east of Trinidad. It is relatively flat and is one of the few coral-capped islands in the region.
Hemisphere
Northern

Climate

Generally warm but cooled by trade winds with temperature around 26–30 degrees Celsius (C) in the day and 15–18 degrees C at night. Rainy season, includes tropical storms: July–November. Humidity rises in the rainy season.

Dress codes

Business suits may be worn with jackets removed. Generally, smart casual wear is suitable in restaurants, although some restaurants may require suits and ties for men. Lightweight cottons are advised.

Entry requirements

Passports
Required by all.
Visa
Visas are not required by most European, American, Australasian and some Asian citizens. From May 2009 EU citizens may make a short-stay visit, for up to three months, without a visa. For a list of those that do, see www.barbados.org/docs.htm.
All visitors must have return/onward passage.
Currency advice/regulations
No restrictions on import of local currency, but it may not be exported. Unlimited foreign currency may be imported and exported, limited to the amount declared on arrival.

Health (for visitors)

Mandatory precautions
Yellow fever vaccination certificate if arriving from an infected area.
Advisable precautions
Typhoid/polio vaccination.

Hotels

There is wide range of first-class hotels available. A 5 per cent government tax and 10 per cent service charge are generally applied.

Public holidays (national)

Fixed dates
1 Jan (New Year's Day), 21 Jan (Errol Barrow Day), 28 Apr (National Heroes' Day), 1 May (Labour Day), 30 Nov (Independence Day), 25 Dec (Christmas Day), 26 Dec (Boxing Day).
Variable dates
Good Friday, Easter Monday, Whit Monday, Emancipation/Kadooment Day (first Mon in Aug).

Working hours

Banking
Mon–Thu: 0800–1500; Fri: 0800–1700.
Business
Mon–Fri: 0800–1600/1630; Sat: 0800–1200.
Government
Mon–Fri: 0800–1600/1630.

Telecommunications

Mobile/cell phones
GSM 900/1900, 900/1800 services are available throughout most of the island.

Electricity supply

110V AC, 50Hz. American-style two-pin plugs are in use.

Social customs/useful tips

Make and confirm appointments before travelling. Many hotels do not start check-in procedures until 1500 so advise the hotel if arriving earlier. Most hotels have a business centre, although facilities vary.

Getting there

Air
International airport/s: Grantley Adams International (BGI), 13km east of Bridgetown; duty-free shops, restaurant, bank, hotel reservations, car hire.
Airport tax: Departure tax BD$25; not applicable to transit passengers.

Surface
Water: Cruise-ship passengers may conclude their journey and depart by air, normal immigration and visa control standards would apply.
Main port/s: Bridgetown Harbour.

Getting about
National transport
Road: There are over 2,000km of surfaced road. Main roads radiate from Bridgetown.
Buses: Frequent and efficient standard fare services operate throughout the island.
City transport
Taxis: Taxis are easily available. They can be hailed, ordered by telephone or found on ranks. The Tourism Board publishes a list of standard fares.
Some hotels run pick-up services.
Car hire
A local driver's permit must be obtained; they are available at police stations and the licensing authority or through car rental agencies on presentation of a national driving licence or an international driving permit. A registration fee of B$10 will be due.
Traffic drives on the left and is often heavy during the rush hours. Strict speed limits of 20mph in Bridgetown and Speightstown and 30mph elsewhere.

BUSINESS DIRECTORY

Telephone area codes
The international direct dialling code (IDD) for Barbados is +1 246, followed by subscriber's number.

Chambers of Commerce
Barbados Chamber of Commerce and Industry, Nemwil House, Collymore Rock, St Michael (tel: 426-2056; fax: 429-2907; e-mail: bdscham@caribsurf.com).

Banking
Bank of Nova Scotia, PO Box 202, Broad St, Bridgetown (tel: 431-3000; fax: 426-0969).

Barbados Agency for Microenterprise Development Ltd (Fund Access), 30 Tudor Street, Bridgetown (tel: 228-1366; fax: 228-1343).

Barbados National Bank, PO Box 1002, Broad St, Bridgetown (tel: 431-5700; fax: 426-0969).

Barclays Bank PLC, PO Box 301, Broad St, Bridgetown (tel: 431-5151; fax: 436-7957).

Caldon Finance Merchant Bank Ltd, Hilton Hotel, 7 Shopping Arcade, St Michael (tel: 437-7550; fax: 436-4999).

Caribbean Commercial Bank, PO Box 1007C, Broad St, Bridgetown (tel: 431-2500; fax: 431-2530).

Caribbean Development Bank, PO Box 408 Wildey, St Michael, Barbados (tel: 431-1600; fax: 426-7269).

Intel Overseas Bank Inc, Suite No 7, Goding House, Spry St, Bridgetown (tel: 436-8826).

Mutual Bank of the Caribbean Inc, Triden House, Lower Broad St, Bridgetown (tel: 436-8335; fax: 429-5734).

Royal Bank of Canada, PO Box 68, Broad Street, Bridgetown (tel: 431-6700; fax: 427-8393).

Central bank
Central Bank of Barbados, Spry Street, PO Box 1016, Bridgetown (tel: 436-6870; fax: 427-3334; e-mail: cbb.libr@caribsurf.com).

Stock exchange
Barbados Stock Exchange (BSE): www.bse.com.bb

Travel information
Caribbean Airways, Terminal 1, Grantley Adams International Airport, Christ Church (tel: 428-1950; fax: 428-1652; e-mail: info@caribairways.com; internet site: www.caribairways.com).

Ministry of tourism
Ministry of Foreign Affairs, Tourism and International Transport, Tourism Division, Sherbourne Conference Centre, Two Mile Hill, St Michael (tel: 436-4830; fax: 436-4828).

National tourist organisation offices
Barbados Tourism Authority, Harbour Road, PO Box 242, Bridgetown (tel: 427-2623/4; fax: 426-4080; email: btainfo@barbados.org; internet: www.barbados.org).

Ministries
Ministry of Agriculture and Rural Development, Graeme Hall, Christ Church (tel: 428-4061; fax: 420-8444).

Ministry of Education, Youth Affairs and Culture, Jemmotts Ln, St Michael (tel: 426-5416; fax: 436-2411).

Ministry of Finance and Economic Affairs, Civil Service, Government Headquarters, Bay St, St Michael (tel: 426-3179; fax: 436-9280).

Ministry of Health and the Environment, Jemmotts Ln, St Michael (tel: 426-4669; fax: 426-5570).

Ministry of Home Affairs, Sir Frank Walcott Bldg, Culloden Rd, St Michael (tel: 431-7750; fax: 437-3794).

Ministry of Industry, Commerce and Business Development, Reef Rd, Fontabelle, St Michael (tel: 426-4452; fax: 431-0056).

Ministry of International Trade and Business, 1 Culloden Rd, St Michael (tel: 427-0427; fax: 429-6652).

Ministry of Labour, Community Development and Sports, National Insurance Bldg, Fairchild St, Bridgetown, St Michael (tel: 427-2326; fax: 426-8959).

Ministry of Public Works, Transport and Housing, The Pine, St Michael (tel: 429-3495; fax: 437-8133).

Ministry of Trade, Industry and Commerce, Savannah Lodge, Garrison, St Michael (tel: 427-270).

Prime Minister's Office, Government Headquarters, Bay St, St Michael (tel: 426-3179; fax: 436-9280).

Other useful addresses
Barbados External Telecommunications, Wildey, St Michael (tel: 427-5200; fax: 427-5808).

Barbados Investment and Development Corporation, Pelican House, Princess Alice Highway, St Michael (tel: 427-5350; fax: 426-7802; internet site: http://www.bidc.com/index.htm).

Barbados Manufacturers' Association, Prescod Blvd, Harbour Road, Bridgetown (tel: 426-4474, 427-9898; fax: 436-5182).

Barbados National Trust, 10th Avenue Relleville, St Michael (tel: 436-9033);

Barbados Tourism Investment Inc, 2nd Floor, Nemwil House, Collymore Rock, St. Michael (tel: 426-7085; fax: 426-7086; e-mail: btii@tourisminvest.com.bb; internet site: http://barbadostourisminvestment.com).

British High Commission, PO Box 676, Lower Collymore Rock, St Michael (tel: 436-6694; fax: 436-5398, 426-7916).

Caribbean Broadcasting Corporation, PO Box 900, Bridgetown (tel: 429-2041).

The Future Centre Trust, Edgehill Street, St Thomas (fax: 425-0075).

US Embassy, PO Box 302, Canadian Imperial Bank of Commerce Building, Broad Street, Bridgetown (tel: 436-4950; fax: 429-5246).

National news agency: Caribbean News Agency (Cana), Caribbean Media Corporation, Harbour Industrial Estate, Unit 1B, Building 6A, St Michael, BB11145 (tel: 467-1000; fax: 429-4355; email: admin@cmccaribbean.com; internet: www.cananews.net).

Internet sites
Barbados Cruise Tourism: www.cruisebarbados.com

Government information service: www.bgis.gov.bb

Barbados government portal: www.gov.bb

Travel and Tourism Encyclopedia: www.barbados.org

Belarus

KEY FACTS

Official name: Respublika Belarus (Republic of Belarus)

Head of State: President Aleksandr Lukashenko (from 1994; re-elected 19 Dec 2010)

Head of government: Prime Minister Sergei Sidorski (since 2003)

Ruling party: Coalition of Kommunisticheskaya Partuya Belarusi (KPB) (Communist Party of Belarus) and Agrarnaya Partiya Belarusi (APB) (Agrarian Party of Belarus) (since 1995; re-elected 28 Sep 2008)

Area: 208,000 square km

Population: 9.49 million (2010)*

Capital: Minsk

Official language: Belarusian since 1990 and Russian since 1995 referendum.

Currency: Rouble (R)

Exchange rate: R7,750.00 per US$ (Oct 2011)

GDP per capita: US$5,800 (2010)

GDP real growth: 7.6% (2010)

GDP: US$54.70 billion (2010)

Labour force: 4.61 million (2009)

Unemployment: 1.00% (official, 2009) (additional large number of underemployed)

Inflation: 7.70% (2010)

Balance of trade: -US$9,118.2 million (2010)

*Estimated figure

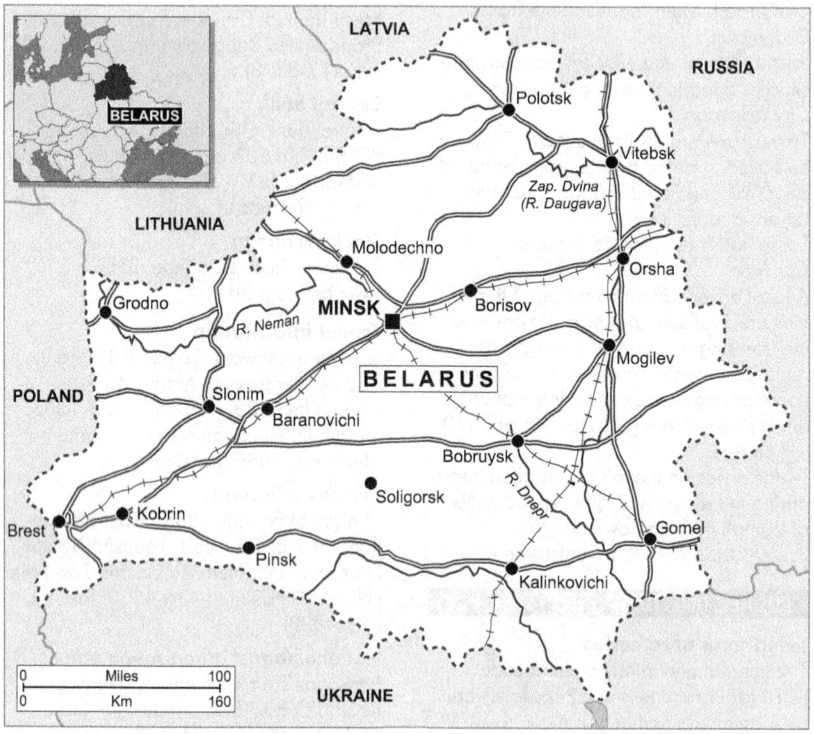

April 2011 saw Belarus' unpredictable dictator, Alexander Lukashenko, defy international criticism of his political repression by placing his main election challenger Andrei Sannikov, on trial. In December 2010 Mr Lukashenko had claimed his fourth term as President with 80 per cent of the votes in an election generally regarded as fraudulent. A former deputy foreign minister, Mr Sannikov came second in the election, with 2.5 per cent of the vote. Sannikov was also a founder of the human rights website Charter 97. His wife and well-known journalist Irina Khalip was also arrested but later released on bail.

Widespread arrests and EU Sanctions

Mr Sannikov, allegedly beaten up while in detention, was not the only activist to be arrested. Four of his co-defendants were charged with similar crimes. Among those arrested were 64-year old Vladimiir Neklyayev, Mikalai Statkevich, Ales Mikhaelevich and Vital Rymasheuski. All in all some two-dozen opposition politicians were arrested and faced jail sentences as long as 15 years.

In its response to these continued human rights abuses in Belarus, in August 2011 the US imposed further sanctions on the already isolated dictatorship. As relations between the US and Belarus steadily worsened, the US ambassador to Belarus, Kathy Stewart, was withdrawn. The US was not alone in so doing: the European Union (EU) had also imposed sanctions following widespread arrests. The sanctions imposed included a travel ban on recalcitrant President Aleksandr Lukashenko, two of his sons, the ministers of defence and the interior, as well as the director of Belarus' KGB. The Belarus government countered the steps with a hopeful statement: 'The imposition of new American economic sanctions goes contrary to the spirit of interaction and co-operation. As a result, Belarus has decided to freeze projects with the United States for exchanging highly enriched uranium fuel within the framework of initiatives for decreasing global threats.' The EU can exercise greater leverage over Belarus than the US. However, the attitude of the EU has tended to differ from that of the US, comprising efforts to improve relations and offers of greater credit and economic aid.

Bomb attack

Mr Lukashenko has long justified his dictatorial rule by claiming that he provides Belarus with stability. That claim was, quite literally, blown apart in April 2011 when a powerful bomb was detonated at the Oktyabrskaya metro station, some 100 metres from the President's office. Early reports gave the casualty figure from the bomb attack as 11 dead and dozens of seriously injured. Government sources hinted at the involvement of the anti-Lukashenko Belarus National Liberation Army, which had already claimed responsibility for similar bomb attacks in 2005 and 2008.

The economy

The World Bank considers that the unreformed and under-performing agricultural sector continues to be a burden on the state budget. The sector contributes 8 per cent to gross domestic product (GDP) while absorbing as much as 5 per cent of GDP in the form of state support. The sector is largely unprofitable, with enterprises registering soaring levels of debts that pose a significant fiscal risk. The reform agenda in agriculture requires a set of inter-related fiscal and structural reforms, including reduction of state support and agricultural subsidies. The energy market is profoundly affected by rising prices for energy imports from Russia. The fiscal cost of under-priced energy has risen to about 2 per cent of GDP. Energy subsidies are largely inequitable, discourage energy efficiency and deprive the energy sector of the financing needed for routine maintenance and investments. The analysis highlights the need to comprehensively reform the energy policy through tariff reforms and a strengthened regulatory environment to engender a climate conducive to private investments and competition.

Belarus operates one of the most extensive social assistance systems in the region, with total spending equal to 2.7 per cent of GDP and reaching about half of the population. Substantial social assistance benefits flow to households, including those with high incomes. In the view of the World Bank the system requires re-alignment of spending from untargeted to targeted programmes. Belarus' ageing population will put growing pressure on the pension system. As a consequence, the pension fund is expected to move from surplus into a structural deficit as early as 2014, while income replacement rates for future pensioners is expected to decline. The key challenge for the pension system in Belarus is to secure its long-term fiscal sustainability given the projected demographic changes, while allowing for a fiscally responsible reduction in contribution rates. Specific reform options include increases in the retirement age, indexation of benefits to inflation (as opposed to wages), reduction in contribution rates and introduction of notional accounts.

Market socialism

Belarus has seen limited structural reform since 1995, when President Lukashenko launched the country on a course of 'market socialism'. This saw the re-imposition of so-called 'administrative controls' over prices and currency exchange rates. The policy also increased the state's right to intervene in the management of private enterprises. Since 2005, the government has re-nationalised a number of private companies. In addition, businesses have been subjected to pressure by both central and local government, including arbitrary changes in regulations, numerous rigorous inspections, the retroactive application of new business regulations and arrests of businessmen and factory owners described as 'disruptive'. Continued state control over economic operations hampers market entry for businesses, both domestic and foreign. Government statistics, if they are to be believed, suggest that GDP growth has been strong, reaching 10 per cent in 2008, despite the apparent obstacle of a tough, centrally directed economy and a high rate of inflation. However, the global crisis pushed Belarus into recession in 2009. The drop in foreign demand for goods hit the industrial sector hard. The Minsk government has been forced into dependence on a standby-agreement with the International Monetary Fund (IMF) to compensate for balance of payments shortfalls. In line with IMF recommendations, in early 2009, Belarus devalued the rouble by approximately 20 per cent and tightened some fiscal and monetary policies. Nevertheless, Belarus was thought to have missed its 2009 budget targets with a deficit of about 2 per cent of GDP. On 1 January 2010, Russia, Kazakhstan and Belarus launched a customs union, with unified trade regulations and customs codes still under negotiation.

According to the National Statistical Committee, investment spending rose by 7.1 per cent in April 2010, only slightly down on the 7.5 per cent increase in March. With industrial production continuing to grow (by 6.4 per cent in April) and capacity utilisation increasing on the back of the upturn in economic activity, capital investment was expected to continue picking up. This was also to be further

KEY INDICATORS — Belarus

	Unit	2006	2007	2008	2009	2010
Population	m	9.71	9.69	9.67	9.48	*9.49
Gross domestic product (GDP)	US$bn	36.94	44.77	60.30	49.00	54.70
GDP per capita	US$	3,808	4,641	6,234	5,166	5,800
GDP real growth	%	9.9	8.2	10.0	0.2	7.6
Inflation	%	7.0	8.4	14.8	13.0	7.7
Unemployment	%	1.4	1.1	1.0	0.9	–
Industrial output	% change	*9.9	6.8	16.1	3.8	–
Agricultural output	% change	*9.9	4.7	8.5	1.3	–
Exports (fob) (goods)	US$m	19,739.0	24,380.4	33,043.3	21,360.7	25,347.8
Imports (fob) (goods)	US$m	22,323.0	28,346.8	39,154.5	28,317.7	34,466.0
Balance of trade	US$m	-2,584.0	-3,984.4	-6,111.2	-6,957.0	-9,118.2
Current account	US$m	-1,515.0	-2,944.0	-5,049.0	-6,388.7	-8,492.7
Total reserves minus gold	US$m	1,068.6	3,952.1	2,686.9	4,831.4	3,431.0
Foreign exchange	US$m	1,068.5	3,952.1	2,685.9	4,252.9	2,863.3
Exchange rate	per US$	2,142.00	2,156.50	2,136.40	2,789.50	2,978.50

* estimated figure

supported by increased foreign investment over the medium term.

Belarus' foreign exchange reserves fell to US$2.10 billion in June 2010, down from US$2.64 billion the previous month. This was their lowest level since November 2007, even despite the large influx of IMF and Russian emergency financial support. The IMF warned that this was a sign that both the Belarusian rouble peg and the broader financial system remain under considerable pressure, repeating its view that Belarus would need further inflows of multilateral aid to avert a more pronounced financial crisis.

Energy

A prolonged squabble over alleged unpaid gas debts has on numerous occasions resulted in Russia threatening to cut off natural gas supplies to Belarus, but Moscow is unlikely to let its dispute with Minsk jeopardise other energy relationships. In March 2010 Russia imposed a five-day deadline for Belarus to pay an outstanding debt of US$192 million or face a cut-off. While the Minsk government complained about a lack of ready cash to foot the bill, the Russian state-owned energy giant Gazprom was simultaneously making menacing noises about raising its charges as relations between the neighbouring countries faltered.

By threatening a gas shutdown the Kremlin has probably been seeking to pressure President Lukashenko in the run up to the presidential elections, according to analysts, some of whom suggested that the dispute had reached a critical point. Belarussian officials insisted that it was merely a contractual dispute and not a conflict over resources. Despite Belarus' claims that there wasn't enough money to pay the debt, Russian President Dmitry Medvedev continued to play hardball, responding that this was an 'insufficient explanation'. Gazprom, probably at the bidding of the Russian government, had suggested that gas supplies could be cut in proportion to the money owed, a 'solution' which would certainly exacerbate Belarus' cash flow problems. Belarus makes a profit from its gas transit role, buying Russian gas at discount rates and selling it on to Europe for a higher price.

The two countries are still struggling to complete a long-planned customs union, while there is lingering unhappiness in Russia that Belarus has still chosen not to recognise the independence of South Ossetia and Abkhazia, almost two years after Moscow supported the territories' bid to break away from Georgia.

Risk assessment

Economy	Poor
Politics	Poor
Regional stability	Fair

COUNTRY PROFILE

Historical profile

During the thirteenth and fourteenth centuries, Belarus was part of the Grand Duchy of Lithuania.

1500s The Grand Duchy was united with Poland.

1800s The dismemberment of Poland as it then was led to Belarus becoming a part of the Russian empire.

1918 Belarus became part of the Soviet Union, following the Russo-German treaty of Brest Litovsk.

1941–44 Belarus was occupied by Nazi Germany. After the war, Belarus was returned to its status as a Soviet republic, although, uniquely, it was granted membership of the UN in its own right.

1988 The Narodni Front Belarusi (NFB) (Belarusian Popular Front) was formed.

1991 Independence was declared. Following the disintegration of the Soviet Union, the Kommunisticheskaya Partuya Belarusi (KPB) (Communist Party of Belarus) quickly established itself as the main political force. Stanislau Shushkevich (NFB), a moderate reformer, was chosen as head of the Supreme Soviet, a body dominated by old-guard communists.

1994 Shushkevich was dismissed after a vote of no-confidence. The constitution was settled. Belarus was influential in the creation of the Commonwealth of Independent States (CIS). The first free presidential elections were won by Aleksandr Lukashenko.

1996 A constitutional referendum changed the structure of government and gave the president sweeping powers. It also extended President Lukashenko's term of office until 2001.

1997 Belarus and Russia ratified the treaty establishing a Union of Russia and Belarus.

1998 Belarus and Russia agreed to begin steps to merge their currencies and taxation systems.

2000 Parliamentary elections were boycotted by the opposition. The presidents of Belarus, Kazakhstan, Kyrgyzstan, Russia and Tajikistan (formerly the Customs Five) established the Eurasian Economic Community (EEC).

2001 President Lukashenko was returned to power and began a second five-year term amid controversy over the fairness of the election. The president appointed Henadz Navitski as prime minister.

2002 The IMF refused financial assistance, on the grounds that Belarus had not made sufficient economic reforms.

2003 President Lukashenko dismissed Prime Minister Navitski; he was succeeded by Sergei Sidorski. Russia, Ukraine, Kazakhstan and Belarus signed an economic union treaty.

2004 Parliamentary elections and a referendum were held on 17 October. Of the 110 seats in the House of Representatives, 107 were won by government supporters; the referendum approved a change to the constitution that enabled Lukashenko to stand for a third term as president.

2006 President Lukashenko was re-elected with 82.6 per cent of the vote. The EU and US considered the election seriously flawed.

2007 A second amendment to the constitution was adopted. Presidential terms in office are no longer limited to two.

2008 Belarus launched an international tender for the construction of a nuclear power plant. In parliamentary elections all 110 seats were won either by political parties or individuals loyal to the president. Protestors accused the administration of electoral fraud in anti-government demonstrations on the streets of the capital, Minsk. The Organisation for Security and Co-operation in Europe (OSCE) reported the elections as having fallen short of democratic principles of transparency and the count in 48 per cent of polling stations visited judged bad or very bad, with deliberate falsification of results observed.

2010 An ongoing dispute concerning Russian natural gas supplies and Belarusian payments for it resulted in a 'gas war', as Russian gas supplies to Europe, transiting Belarus, were shut down by Belarus in June. An agreement was reached and Belarus paid the outstanding debt and supplies resumed. On 6 June a customs union between Belarus, Russia and Kazakhstan became fully operational. International observers declared the presidential elections held on 19 December as 'deeply flawed'. Of the 10 candidates allowed to participate, incumbent Aleksandr Lukashenko won 79.7 per cent and his closest rival Andrey Sannikau won 2.6 per cent; turnout was 90 per cent. Following announcement of the results, thousands protested on the streets of Minsk, followed by violence and the arrest or abduction, by security forces, of seven presidential candidates and their supporters.

2011 The government closed the OSCE office in Minsk on 20 January after it had criticised the conduct of the December 2010 presidential election. Approval by the OSCE had been seen as crucial to Belarus's chances of receiving EU aid.

Alexander Lukashenko was sworn in for his fourth five-year term as president on 21 January. A number of political prisoners were released at the end of January, ahead of an EU foreign ministers' meeting to discuss re-imposing sanctions. On 31 January, both the EU and the US imposed tough sanctions and travel bans on President Lukashenko and his key political supporters, following a crackdown on the opposition after the flawed presidential elections. At least 14 people were killed and over 200 people injured by an explosion in the metro system in Minsk on 11 April. Andrei Sannikov, a former deputy foreign minister and co-founder of the Charter 97 group, went on trial on 27 April, accused of organising protests after the 2010 presidential election; he was one of seven presidential candidates arrested after Lukashenko won. Russia cut 50 per cent of the power it supplies in June; Belarus admitted it owed US$54 million. In the last week of May the Central Bank lifted exchange rate restrictions which resulted in a plunge in the value of the rouble that fell by 36 per cent against the US dollar. On 1 June, the government officially asked the IMF for a US$8 billion emergency loan to help it face its severe financial crisis. A team from IMF visited Belarus on 13 June to discuss a loan but declined to provide the funding until Belarus demonstrated a commitment to macroeconomic reforms. On 18 November, the presidents of Russia, Belarus and Kazakhstan signed an agreement to set targets for setting up an internal market, the Eurasian Union, by 2015. A Eurasian Commission will begin an overseeing role for integration on 1 January 2012.

Political structure

Constitution

The 1994 constitution vested legislative power in a 260-member Sejm (Supreme Council).

The first free presidential elections were held in 1994, after which differences emerged over the distribution of power between the president and the Supreme Council.

The constitutional referendum held in late 1996 and the subsequent introduction of a new constitution allowed an expansion of presidential powers and introduced a new two-chamber National Assembly, replacing the Sejm.

On 17 October 2007, the second amendment to the constitution was adopted. Presidential terms in office will no longer be limited to two.

Form of state

Authoritarian presidential republic, where political life is dominated by the president and no real opposition is allowed.

The executive

The president is directly elected for a maximum of two five-year terms and also serves as commander-in-chief of the armed forces, appoints the cabinet and prime minister and has the power to declare a state of emergency, but not to dissolve parliament.

National legislature

The Natsionalnoye Sobranie (National Assembly) is a bicameral parliament. In the Palata Pretsaviteley (Chamber of Representatives) (lower house), 110 deputies are elected by direct election in single-seat constituencies. The chamber has powers to call elections for the presidency, approve the nomination of the prime minister, draft laws and deliver a vote of no confidence in the government. The Soviet Respubliki (Council of the Republic) (upper house) has 64 members elected by regional governing councils and eight members appointed by the president. The council has the power to review proposed legislation, approve the nomination of top officials and consider decrees issued by the president.

All members of the national assembly serve four-year terms.

Legal system

Judicial power in the Republic of Belarus is vested in courts. The Constitutional Court adjudicates on whether law is constitutional. The prosecutor general is responsible for ensuring that all laws and presidential decrees are executed properly and uniformly across all state bodies and local Soviets.

Last elections

17 October 2004 (parliamentary); 19 December 2010 (presidential).

Results: Parliamentary: all 110 deputies elected were supporters of the president, with 12 of them representing political parties.

Presidential: Aleksandr Lukashenko won 79.67 per cent, Andrey Sannikau 2.56 per cent; eight other candidates each won less than 2 per cent. Turnout was 90 per cent.

Next elections

2012 (parliamentary); 2011 (presidential).

Political parties

Ruling party

Coalition of Kommunisticheskaya Partuya Belarusi (KPB) (Communist Party of Belarus) and Agrarnaya Partiya Belarusi (APB) (Agrarian Party of Belarus) (since 1995; re-elected 28 Sep 2008)

Main opposition party

No opposition political party or individual won any seats in the last election.

Population

9.49 million (2010)*

Last census: March 1999: 10,045,237

Population density: Approximately 48 per square km. Urban population: 71 per cent.

Annual growth rate: -0.5 per cent 1994–2004 (WHO 2006)

Ethnic make-up

Belorussian (78 per cent), Russian (13 per cent), Polish (4 per cent), Ukranian (3 per cent), other (2 per cent).

Religions

Eastern Orthodox (80 per cent), Roman Catholic, Protestant, Jewish and Islam (20 per cent).

Education

School education is divided into three stages: primary from aged four; basic from aged nine; then secondary schooling, from aged 11. Secondary schooling may be taught through gymnasiums, lyceums or colleges, as well as specialised or technical schools. Gymnasiums provide secondary education at a higher level, while lyceums provide vocational education. The certificate of lyceum education gives right of admission to any higher education institution.

Specialised secondary education lasts for two to four years. Colleges are a new type of institution in Belarus and provide advanced specialist training.

Public expenditure on education is estimated at some 6 per cent of annual gross national income.

Literacy rate: 100 per cent adult rate; 100 per cent youth rate (15–24) (Unesco 2005).

Compulsory years: 4 to 9.

Enrolment rate: 94.2 per cent net primary enrolment; 77.5 per cent net secondary enrolment, of the relevant age groups (including repetition rates), in 2002 (World Bank).

Pupils per teacher: 19 in primary schools.

Health

The population declined by 0.5 per cent per annum between 1994—2000 and is projected to decline at the same rate between 1999—2015. The Ministry of Statistics and Analysis reported that the cause of the decrease is due to the number of deaths exceeding the number of births. The dramatic fall in life expectancy since the early 1990s is caused by environmental degradation, economic distress and the ever-present radiation from Chernobyl fall-out which continues to affect health, particularly among children.

Medical care in Belarus is limited. There is a severe shortage of basic medical supplies, including anaesthetics, vaccines and antibiotics.

Life expectancy: 68 years, 2004 (WHO 2006)

Fertility rate/Maternal mortality rate: 1.2 births per woman, 2004 (WHO

2006); maternal deaths 28 per 100,000 live births (World Bank).
Birth rate/Death rate: 14 deaths to 9 births per 1,000 people (World Bank).
Child (under 5 years) mortality rate (per 1,000): 13 per 1,000 live births in 2003 (World Bank).
Head of population per physician: 4.55 physicians per 1,000 people, 2003 (WHO 2006)

Welfare

For some years now both economic and political standards have deteriorated under President Lukashenko. As long ago as 1998, a poll by the Ministry of Economy reported that almost 80 per cent of families believed their material well-being had worsened since the collapse of the Soviet Union. Although the state exercises control and mobilises funds for social care and protection, Belarus, along with other Eastern European countries, is planning to privatise its social security systems. Foreign citizens and people permanently living in Belarus have equal rights to social services.

Since independence, the number of local non-governmental organisations (NGOs) has increased dramatically in Belarus. To strengthen the NGO sector, USAID has created the Counterpart Alliance Program (CAP), which provides seed grants to social service organisations in Belarus.

There is a two tiered system of social security coverage: general employed workers and special employees (such as aviators, civil servants and certain medical personnel). Contributions are acquired from three sources: workers, 1 per cent of earnings; employer, 4.7–35 per cent of the payroll, dependent on industry or enterprise; government revenue covers the cost of social pensions and subsidies as needed.

Social security payments are made to the unemployed and those without pension rights through a general social insurance.

Pensions

Pensions are provided for old age (beginning for men at age 60 and women at age 55, with 25 or 20 years contributions, respectively), disabilities and survivors, including payments for sickness and maternity benefits.

Main cities

Minsk (capital, estimated population 1.9 million in 2005), Homel (Gomel) (548,770), Brèst (354,732), Hrodna (Grodno) (356,334), Mahileu (Mogilev) (401,261), Vitsebsk (Vitebsk) (378,186). Names in brackets are the Russian place-names.

Minsk is the headquarters for the Commonwealth of Independent States (CIS) organisation.

Languages spoken

Ukrainian, Polish and Yiddish.

Official language/s

Belarusian since 1990 and Russian since 1995 referendum.

Media

Press freedom is severely curtailed by presidential policy, with libel laws being both civil and criminal offences, resulting in either heavy fines or imprisonment. The government denies access by the opposition to the state-owned media and can close any independent publication house without judicial review. It appoints senior editors to state-run media outlets and decides on news content, even banning musicians performing pro-opposition music from radio airtime. The state-run press distribution monopoly has refused to deliver independent newspapers around the country and internet news websites are monitored by the State Centre on Information Security. In 2006, the US Media watchdog Freedom House ranked Belarus' freedom of the press as 185 out of 194 in the world and 'not free'.

A new media law was passed in parliament that independent journalists say will restrict online reporting and private media funding ahead of the 2008 parliamentary elections.

Press

All state-owned newspapers are heavily subsidised. Newspapers in the Russian language have the major share of the Belarusian market.

Dailies: In Russian, *Sovetskaya Belorussia* (www.sb.by), is the main government organ, *Respublika* (www.respublika.info), is a Council of Ministers newspaper, other government publications include *7 Dney* (http://7days.belta.by). Private newspapers include *Beloruskaya Gazeta* (http://www.belgazeta.by) and *Narodnaya Volya*. In Belarusion *Zvyazda* (www.zvyazda.minsk.by). In English *Belarus Today* (www.belarustoday.info).

Weeklies: In Russian, *Studenckaja Dumka* (http://studumka.iatp.by) is a youth magazine. In English *The Minsk Times* (www.sb.by/minsktimes), *Belarus* (www.belarus-magazine.by) are general news and interest magazines.

Business: In Russian, *BDG Delovaya Gazeta* (www.bdg.by), *Belorussky i Rynok* (www.br.minsk.by) and *Ekonomicheskaya Gazeta* (www.neg.by). *Delo (East+West)* (www.delobelarus.com) and *Entrepreneurship in Belarus* (www.nbrb.by/bv) are monthly magazines.

Broadcasting

The national, state-run broadcaster is Teleradiocompany (TVR) (www.tvr.by).

Radio: Belarus Radio operates a network of two national stations and three local, with internet broadcasting (www.tvr.by). Programming includes of news, music, cultural and sports events. External services are broadcast in English, German, Polish and Russian. Other radio stations include Radio Roks (www.roks.com), Unistar (http://unistar.by), Alfa Radio (http://alpha.by), and Pilot FM (in Russian).

Television: TVR operates TV-First (www.tvr.by), the only national public service, it also operates the satellite service Belarus TV. The majority state-owned Nationwide TV (ONT) (www.ont.by) is operated by Russia's Channel One.

Stolichnoye Televideniye (STV) (http://ctv.by) is a local Minsk broadcaster.

Advertising

The advertising market has been developing very slowly. Advertisers use radio, television, newspapers (rarely used by foreign advertisers) and posters.

News agencies

National news agency: Belta (Belarusian Telegraph Agency)

Economy

The economy is largely dominated by heavy industry, which accounted for 44.5 per cent of GDP in 2008, of which 32.9 per cent was manufacturing; services accounted for 45.8 per cent and agriculture 9.8 per cent. Belarus' manufacturing sector produces vehicles, particularly heavy, industrial units, motorcycles, household appliances, textiles, machine tools and fertilisers. There are mineral deposits and small reserves of oil and natural gas, all of which are exploited.

GDP growth had been strong since 2004 when it was a record 11 per cent; it remained high, reaching 10 per cent in 2008, but was severely disrupted by the global economic recession which cut the international trade on which Belarus relies. GDP growth in 2009 fell to 0.2 per cent.

Export of goods, which had grown by 1.5 per cent in 2008, fell dramatically by -12.7 per cent in 2009 (US$33 billion in 2008 down to a projected US$21.8 billion in 2009). Import of goods, which had grown by 14.3 per cent in 2008, fell by -15.8 per cent in 2009 (US$39 billion in 2008 down to a projected US$27.7 billion in 2009). Gross total external debt jumped from 25.2 per cent of GDP in 2008 to 42.8 per cent in 2009.

The World Bank, the European Commission and International Monetary Fund (IMF) have provided fiscal aid since 2007 (US$200 million, US$290 million and US$2.5 billion respectively), on condition the government reformed the economy and introduced measures to foster free-market practices, which had been weakened under the rule of President

Lukashenko, who had returned it to Soviet-style centralised planning, where less than 10 per cent of the economy was generated by the private sector. At the start of 2009 the exchange rate for the rouble against the US dollar was devalued by 20 per cent and its pegging to the US dollar replaced by a peg to a basket of currencies including the Russian rouble, US dollar and euro. This allowed a reduction in external vulnerabilities and offered the stability necessary to maintain confidence in the economy.
The economy began to pick up in 2010, buoyed by increased consumer spending and exports. GDP growth was 4 per cent and industrial output up by 5.9 per cent in the first quarter and a forecast annual growth of 11-13 per cent.
Russia is Belarus' principal trading partner and any change in their foreign relations that inhibit imports and exports has a direct influence on the Belarus economy.
On 1 June 2011, the government officially asked the IMF for a US$8 billion emergency loan to help it face a severe financial crisis. In the last week of May 2011 the Central Bank lifted exchange rate restrictions which resulted in a plunge in the value of the rouble of 36 per cent against the US dollar. The official exchange rate, a hangover from the soviet era and kept in place by President Lukashenko, had helped fend off intense economic fluctuations but the resulting pressure had swiftly diminished Belarus' foreign currency reserves. Imports that were held up waiting for banking transactions to be completed sparked a steady increase in inflation as goods in the market disappeared. On 1 July, the government froze the price of some staple foods and increased bank interest rates from 14 per cent to 16 per cent per annum.

External trade

Principal trading partners are Russia and CIS countries. Belarus concluded a custom union agreement with Russia and Kazakhstan in October 2010, which will improve exports to Russia. The customs union plans a single currency by 2020. Belarus is a major exporter of tractors worldwide.
On 19 October 2011, a free trade agreement (FTA) was signed by Russia with seven of its former Soviet republics: Armenia, Belarus, Kazakhstan, Kyrgyzstan, Moldova and Tajikistan. The FTA must be ratified by all relevant parliaments before its instigation in 2012.
On 18 November 2011, the presidents of Russia, Belarus and Kazakhstan signed an agreement to set targets for setting up an internal market, the Eurasian Union, by 2015. A Eurasian Commission will begin an overseeing role for integration on 1 January 2012.

Imports

Imports consist of petroleum and derivatives, rough diamonds, machinery and equipment, metal products, pharmaceuticals, foodstuffs, vehicles and products, chemicals and consumer goods.
Main sources: Russia (typically 59 per cent of total), Germany (8 per cent), Ukraine (5 per cent).

Exports

Principal exports include machinery, vehicles and parts, mineral products, chemicals, foodstuffs, iron, steel and energy.
Main destinations: Russia (typically 32 per cent of total), The Netherlands (17 per cent), Ukraine (8 per cent).

Agriculture

Farming

About 60 per cent of arable land is used for livestock (cattle and pigs), the rest being used for cultivation of potatoes, grain, sugar beet and flax. Although agricultural lands occupy 9.4 million hectares (45.2 per cent of the total area), more than 30 per cent of the land is still contaminated as a consequence of the Chernobyl nuclear plant explosion in Ukraine in 1986. Particularly badly hit was the area around Gomel, where high levels of contamination are still recorded.
The sector receives heavy state support in the form of tax reductions, consumer goods, fertilisers and fuels and remains collectivised, although there are huge unpaid wage arrears on collective farms.
The climate in Belarus means that production is concentrated on hardier crops, including grains, flax, sugar beet and potatoes, of which Belarus is a leading producer.
Belarus meets its own food needs except for feed grains, sugar and vegetable oils, which the government has targetted for increased production. Agriculture is oriented towards meeting domestic market demands for food products with a trend towards animal production.
There has been a steady growth in the amount of agricultural land under private ownership, although the process is slow and obstructed by political and bureaucratic problems.

Fishing

All fishing in Belarus is derived from rivers, lakes and reservoirs, mainly with drag nets by small teams moving from location to location. There is some fish farming, owned by the state or joint stock companies with government shareholdings.
Belarus has the capacity to process up to 20,000 tonnes per year of mainly smoked and salted fish, with a total of around 300 organisations involved in the fishery industry. The main traditional products include cold smoked fish, salted, preserved and canned fish. Government programmes include increasing the level of catches, the volume and efficiency of fish processing activity by introducing new technologies. Belarus has had an agreement with Russia since 2002, under which Belarus receives fish quotas in the Russian exclusive economic zone for 10 years, Russian-Belarussian joint ventures base their fleets in Russian ports and both countries co-ordinate their fisheries policies.

Forestry

Forest and other wooded land accounts for over two-fifths of the land area, with forest cover of 9.4 million hectares. About three-quarters of the forest is available for wood supply. Timber includes spruce and birch, which are generally of high quality. The state owns all forest and other wooded land. The Belavezhskaja Pusha Nature Reserve (north of Brest on the Polish border) is Europe's largest remaining area of primeval forest, totalling 1,300 square km in size.
In the period 1990–2000, afforestation increased forest cover at an annual average rate of 3.23 per cent, the equivalent of 256,000 hectares.
The forest sector in Belarus makes an important contribution to the economy. The government has attempted to turn back the sector's deterioration in recent years by increasing exports of wood, wood processing and pulp products. It has also investigated environmentally sustainable forestry and has launched a programme of information collation, using satellite technology, to assess the best use of forestry resources.
There is abundant roundwood production, which is mainly used for sawnwood in both large state-owned and small private enterprises. A significant proportion of roundwood and nearly half of pulpwood production is exported. There is very little domestic consumption of production of sawnwood and panels, but pulp and paper production do not meet domestic demand.

Industry and manufacturing

The industrial sector accounts for 25.5 per cent of GDP and employs 40 per cent of the workforce. It has benefited from Soviet-era industrialisation, which transformed Belarus from an agricultural economy into the region's industrial hub. The sector is diverse and comprises heavy machine production, micro-electronics, computers, chemical and mineral processing, synthetic fibre production, textiles, consumer durables and food processing. Raw materials have to be imported and manufacturing is reliant on energy imports, mainly from Russia.

One of the prime industrial sub-sectors is the automotive industry. Belarus is the world's third largest producer of tractors and also produces a large number of lorries, motorbikes and other vehicles, which are exported mainly to Europe. The Minsk Tractor Works (MTZ) produces up to 8 per cent of the world's tractors, which are exported to more than 100 countries.

Belarus' electronics sector is highly developed, due to its role in supplying the Soviet military machine. It manufactures radios, televisions and electronic devices used in engineering, as well as supplying consumer goods, including refrigerators and freezers, to countries inside and outside the former Soviet Union.

Production of chemicals is concentrated in Soligorsk, Gomel and Grodno. The chemical sector produces potassium and nitrate fertilisers, aminophosphate, medicines, polymers and plastics, chemical and synthetic fibres, pesticides, rubber goods and building materials.

Tourism

Tourist facilities are inadequate with poor quality hotels and bureaucratic obstacles hindering visitors; visas cost more than those charged by neighbouring states, border crossings are tedious and costly, while levies on hotel rooms for tourists put them out of the reach of most visitors. Investment in upgrading facilities and conserving historic tourist attractions is in short supply.

Environment

One-third of the nation's agricultural land has been unusable since it was contaminated by fall-out from the 1986 Chernobyl nuclear accident.

Mining

Belarus is not rich in natural resources, except for deposits of peat, used in power stations and for the manufacture of chemicals. There are significant deposits of potassium, which is a major export, and rock salt. Other resources include clay, sand, iron ore, cobalt, phosphate, silver and gold. Many known mineral deposits await development, while a full survey of the country's resources has yet to be carried out.

Hydrocarbons

Proven oil reserves were negligible by 2010. Consumption was 133,000 barrels per day (bpd) in 2010, the majority of which came from Russia. There are two refineries in the regions of Novopolotsk Vitebsk and Gomel with a total refining capacity of 493,000bpd.

Natural gas reserves were negligible by 2010. Consumption was 19.7 billion cubic metres (cum) in 2010 and is heavily reliant on Russian gas imports.

There are deposits of brown coal of little value. Coal is not produced; around six million tonnes are imported from Russia.

Energy

Belarus has a total electricity generating capacity of 7,850MW, but is dependent on imported Russian gas for production. The rising costs of fossil fuels encouraged the government to consider localising electricity generation and diversifying the fuel mix so that by 2012 25 per cent of electricity and heat will be generated by alternative energy sources. An agreement for importing electricity from Ukraine was signed in 2006, with supplies beginning with 1.5 billion kilowatt hours (kWh) in 2007, which is expected to steadily rise to 3.5 billion kWh.

Banking and insurance

The National Bank of the Republic of Belarus (NBRB) (central bank) and the Commercial Bank for Foreign Economic Activity (CBFEA) were established in 1991. All enterprises were instructed to transfer hard currency funds from the Russian Vnesheconombank to the CBFEA. The banking system has seen an increase in state participation since President Lukashenko was first elected in 1994. Priorbank is the largest private bank and holds 8 per cent of the total assets of the banking system, making it the fifth largest in Belarus. Foreign capital participation is present in 19 banks, including two which are wholly foreign owned. Credit to the private sector amounts to 9 per cent of GDP. In January 2003, Austria's Raiffeisen Bank bought a 50 per cent stake in Priorbank for US$30.5 million, injecting competition into the sector.

Central bank

The National Bank of the Republic of Belarus

Time

GMT plus two hours, (daylight saving, late March to late October, GMT plus three hours)

Geography

Belarus is situated in north-eastern Europe. It has frontiers with Poland, in the west, Lithuania in the north-west and Latvia in the north. It has long frontiers with Russia from the north to the east, and with the Ukraine from the east to the south. The land is a plain with numerous lakes, swamps and marshes. There is a region of low lying hills north of Minsk. The highest point, Mount Dzyarzhynskaya, is only 346 metres above sea-level. The southern part of the country is an extensive flat marshland. Forests cover some 30 per cent of the territory. The main rivers are the Dnepr which flows south to the Black Sea, and the Pripyat which flows eastwards to the Dnepr through the Pripyat Marshes.

Hemisphere

Northern

Climate

Temperature ranges from minus 6 degrees Celsius (C) in January, to a high of 18 degrees C in August. The average annual rainfall is 550mm to 700mm.

Dress codes

With grey, freezing winters and wet summers, fashion takes second place to practicality in Belarus. Smart dress is required for business.

Entry requirements

Passports

Valid passport required by all and must be valid for six months after departure.

All foreign nationals must register their passports at the local police station within three days of their arrival; if staying at a hotel, reception will do this automatically.

Visa

Visas are required by almost all and must be obtained by anyone travelling through Belarus by train, including international routes Warsaw-Moscow and St Petersburg-Kiev.

Some visa exceptions include nationals of the CIS, travelling as tourists. For further details of those exempt and full requirements for visas see www.mfa.gov.by/eng/consul/3.

Business visas allow stays for up to 90 days. Applications must include an invitation, (may be originally supplied as fax) on official letterhead and should have a signature of the head of a company as well as a corporate seal. It should also indicate the expected period of stay and a pledge by the host company to provide the invited person full support during their stay in Belarus including all possible medical expenses.

Visitors must register their stay with Belarus authorities for visits of over three days. Exit permits are required by foreigners intending to leave the country with expired visas.

Currency advice/regulations

Import and export of local currency is not permitted and all remaining money must be reconverted before departure. Import of foreign currency is unlimited; however, export of same is possible only to the amount declared on arrival. Currency exchange receipts should be retained and all transactions must be recorded on a currency declaration form, issued on arrival and surrendered on departure. The US dollar and euro currencies offer the best options for conversion. Many public services can only be paid for in hard currencies.

Traveller' cheques, in US dollars or euros, may be exchanged in large banks only, other currencies may be more problematic.

Customs

Small amounts of personal goods are duty-free. Valuable items such as jewellery, cameras, computers and musical instruments should be declared.

Health (for visitors)

Medical insurance is required by all foreign citizens visiting Belarus.

Mandatory precautions

None

Advisable precautions

Water precautions are recommended (water purification tablets may be useful). Dairy products, mushrooms and fruits of the forest (all of which may still be contaminated by radiation from the Chernobyl disaster) should be avoided. Some immunisations may be advantageous: polio, typhoid, diphtheria and tetanus, and hepatitis A for longer term visitors.

It is wise to carry adequate supplies of prescribed medicines, and have precautionary antibiotics if going outside major urban centres. A travel kit including a disposable syringe is a reasonable precaution.

Hotels

Minsk and Vitebsk boast two-, three- and four-star hotels; other cities have two and three-star hotels. There are no five-star Western-standard hotels in Belarus (as of 2006).

Credit cards

Large hotel, restaurants and at foreign currency shops accept major credit cards. There are a few ATMs in Minsk.

Public holidays (national)

Fixed dates

1 Jan (New Year), 7 Jan (Orthodox Christmas Day), 8 Mar (Women's Day), 15 Mar (Constitution Day), 1 May (Labour Day), 9 May (Victory Day), 3 Jul (Independence Day), 2 Nov (Dzyady/Remembrance Day), 7 Nov (Day of the October Revolution), 25 Dec (Christmas Day).

Variable dates

Good Friday, Orthodox Good Friday, Easter Monday, Orthodox Easter Monday.

Working hours

Banking

Mon–Fri: 0900–1700, including Priorbank, Minsk 2 airport.

Foreign exchange outlets are open all day until late, and some open 24 hours.

Business

Mon–Fri: 0900–1800 (appointments best between 0900–1000).

Government

Mon–Fri: 0900–1300, 1400–1800.

Shops

Most food stores are now open Mon–Sat: 0900–1400 and 1500–2000. Sat: 0900–1800.

General stores open Mon to Fri: 1000–1400 and 1500–1900. Sat: 1000–1800.

There are some 24-hour food stores.

Telecommunications

Mobile/cell phones

GSM 900/1800 services are available throughout most of the country.

Electricity supply

220V AC 50Hz. European-style round two-pin plugs are in use.

Social customs/useful tips

Business is conducted formally and appointments are essential. A firm handshake is important as is negotiating an agenda at the beginning of the meeting. Smoking in meetings is very common. Ask permission before lighting a cigarette and offer cigarettes generously.

Written communications are particularly important with large bureaucracies. Address the recipient formally and keep a copy of everything. It is customary to take a small gift on a business or social visit. Offering basic food is considered insulting; offer little luxuries. It is impolite to accompany guests who are not invited to a social function. Gratuities are not obligatory but are becoming more widespread. Vodka is the national drink.

Security

Crime is still negligible and visitors should avoid political demonstrations.

It is advisable to keep away from military establishments.

Getting there

Air

National airline: Belavia

International airport/s: Minsk 2 (MSQ), 43km east of the city, facilities include banks and bureaux de change, bars, car hire, duty-free shops, post office and restaurants.

Airport tax: None

Surface

Road: Good road connections exist with Ukraine, the Baltic States, Poland and Russia. Visitors arriving by car are advised to insure their vehicle with a Belarusian insurer (eg Belingosstrakh); offices can be found at crossing sites. Note that petrol is limited and only 4-star and diesel are available. Most petrol stations only accept cash.

A fee for drivers of foreign vehicles is collected at border checkpoints and varies according to the length of stay.

Rail: There are train connections with all neighbouring countries, with express trains from most European capitals.

Getting about

National transport

Road: There is road network of over 55,000km, the majority of which is hard surfaced. Petrol is limited; only 4-star and diesel are available; and most petrol stations only accept cash. Motorways connect many of the major cities.

Rail: Total railtrack is about 5,523km broad gauge, of which approximately 875km is electrified. Train tickets and reservations can be purchased at Francyska Skaryny Prospekt No 18, Minsk.

Water: Belarus is landlocked, but there is an extensive network of inland waterways (3,800km) which mainly convey cargo goods. The Mukhavets and Pripyat rivers in south Belarus are connected by the strategic Dnepr-Buh Canal, which in turn gives access to the Baltic and Black Seas.

City transport

Taxis: Taxis are plentiful; they can be found waiting in front of hotels, at the airport, railway station and bus station. Journey time from the airport to city centre is about 40 minutes.

Buses, trams & metro: The city of Minsk has a metro that covers the central district, with two lines and 23 stations. Trains run between 0600-0100; entry to the underground is by tokens which are obtainable from stations.

There are buses from the international airport to city centre, journey time about 60 minutes.

Urban buses, trams and trolleybuses run between 0535-0055; tickets for these can be purchased at news-stands or kiosks and must be punched when boarding.

Car hire

Cars can be rented, with or without a driver. An international driving licence with international permit is required. There are numerous restrictions that apply to driving. It is illegal to drive after consuming any amount of alcohol, no matter how little. Driving is on the right. International traffic signs and regulations are in use. Speed limits are 60kph (37mph) in towns and cities and 90kph (55mph) on country lanes and speed traps are widespread.

BUSINESS DIRECTORY

The addresses listed below are a selection only. While World of Information makes every endeavour to check these addresses, we cannot guarantee that changes have not been made, especially to telephone numbers and area codes. We would welcome any corrections.

Telephone area codes

The international direct dialling (IDD) code for Belarus is +375, followed by area code and subscriber's number:

Brest	16	Minsk	17
Gomel	23	Mogilev	22

Grodno	15	Vitebsk	21

Chambers of Commerce

Belarussian Chamber of Commerce and Industry, Communisticheskaya Street, 220029 Minsk (tel: 290–7249; fax: 290–7248; e-mail: mbox@cci.by).

Brest Chamber of Commerce and Industry, 14 Kubysheva Street, 224016 Brest (tel: 223-2400; fax: 223-4854; e-mail: bo@tppbrs.belpak.brest.by).

Grodno Chamber of Commerce and Indutry, Sovetskaya Street, 20023 Grodno (tel: 224-9070; e-mail: anat@grocci.belpark.grodno.by).

Minsk Chamber of Commerce and Industry, 65 Ya Kolas Street, 220113 Minsk (tel: 266-0473; fax: 266-2604; e-mail: secret@mdbcci.belpak.minsk.by).

Vitebsk Chamber of Commerce and Industry, Kosmonavtov Street, 210001 Vitebsk (tel: 236-3052; fax: 236-4674; e-mail: vitebsk@cci.by).

Banking

Belagroprom Bank, 44 Kropotkina Street, Minsk 220002 (tel: 503-958).

Bel Vnesh Econom Bank (Belarus Bank for Foreign Economic Affairs), 10 Zaslavskaya Street, Minsk 220004 (tel: 269-757, 267-022; fax: 269-759).

Commercial Bank for Reconstruction and Development (Belbusinessbank), 6a Partizansky Ave, 220033 Minsk (tel: 298-147, 768-942; fax: 298-147, 768-504).

Central bank

The National Bank of the Republic of Belarus, 20 F Skorina Avenue, 220008 Minsk (tel: 219-2303; fax: 227-4879; e-mail: email@nbrb.by).

Travel information

Belavia (Belarusian Airlines), 14 Nemiga Street, Minsk 220004 (tel: 210-4100; fax: 220-2383; email: info@belavia.by; internet: www.belavia.by/index_en.htm).

National tourist organisation offices

Belintourist, 19 Masherov Avenue, 220004 Minsk (tel: 226-9840; fax: 223-1143: email: office@belintourist.by; internet: www.belintourist.by).

Ministries

Department of Foreign Economic Co-operation (tel: 269-169).

Department of International Relations (tel: 269-187; fax: 269-936).

Ministry of Agriculture, Dom Pravitelstva, Minsk (tel: 271-377, 271-352, 205-492).

Ministry of Finance, Dom Pravitelstva, 220010 Minsk (tel: 296-949).

Ministry of Foreign Affairs, ul. K. Mark 16, 220050 Minsk (tel: 272-011; fax: 293-383).

Ministry of Information, Prospekt Mashirova 11, Minsk (tel: 237-574).

Ministry of Statistics and Analysis of the Republic of Belarus, 12 Partizan Avenue, Minsk 220658 (tel: 491-261, 495-200; fax: 492-204).

Ministry of Trade, Kirov St. Building, Minsk 220084 (tel: 276-121).

State Committee for Foreign Economic Relations, House of Government, Minsk 220010 (tel: 296-345).

State Committee for Economic Planning, Dom Pravitelstva, Minsk (tel: 296-944).

Other useful addresses

Belarusintorg, Foreign Trade Organisation, Ulitsa Kollektornaya 10, 220048 Minsk (tel: 207-812, 209-756, 208-188; fax: 209-470, 204-763).

British Embassy, 37 Karl Marx Street, Minsk 220016 (tel: 292-303/4/5, 172105920; fax: 292-306, 172292306); Visa and Consulate Section (tel: 292-310; fax: 292-311).

Minsk Expo Exhibition Company, pr. Masherova 14, Minsk 220035 (tel: 226-9193/9890; fax: 226-9192/9936; e-mail: minskexpo@brm.minsk.by; internet: www.minskexpo.com.by).

National Centre for Marketing and Price Study, 7-1117 Masherov Avenue, Minsk, PO 220004 (to reach the National Centre call for voice connection and/or fax: 266-758).

News Agency, Minsk (tel: 293-040).

Union of Enterpreneurs, 13 Internatsional'naya St, Minsk 220050 (tel: 172-587; fax: 271-596).

US Embassy, 46 Starovilenskaya Street, Minsk 220002 (tel: 210-1283; fax: 234-7853).

National news agency: Belta (Belarusian Telegraph Agency), 26 Kirov street, Minsk, 220030 (tel: 227-1991; fax: 227-1346; internet: www.belta.by).

Other news agencies: Belapan: http://en.belapan.com

Nashe Mneniye: www.nmnby.org

Internet sites

Belarus portal: http://www.e-belarus.org

Belarusian web links: http://www.belarusian.com/links

Belarusian web sites: http://www.ac.by/country/belwww.html

General information: http://www.belarus.net

Investment: http://www.ib.by

Chamber of Commerce: http://www.cci.by

Business information: http://www.delobelarus.com

General information: http://www.open.by

Belgium

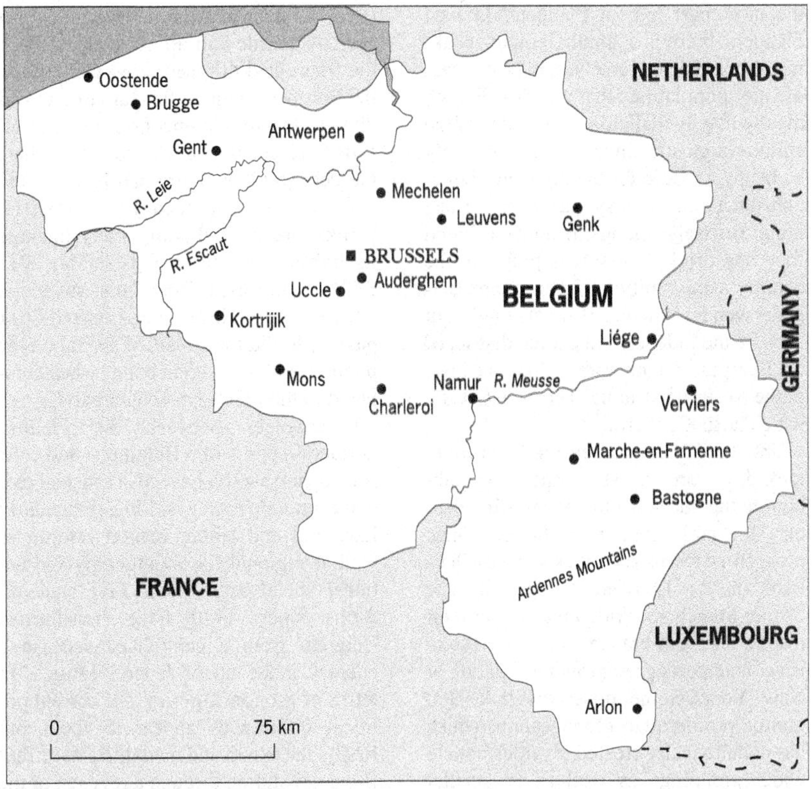

In February 2011 Belgium set a new world record for countries without an official government. Belgians accepted this embarrassing statistic with surprisingly good humour; the prevailing mood seemed to be one of ironic passivity rather than with protest. The atmosphere was almost one of jollity – in Ghent 249 people decided to strip in public – making one naked person for each day that the crisis had lasted. In Louvain-la-Neuve, citizens were promised free beer and chips. While North Africa was experiencing its Arab Spring, Belgium opted for a *Frites Revolution*. A well known Belgian actor undertook not to shave until his country had an administration; another joined forces with a prominent gynaecologist to call on Belgian women – á la Lysistrata – to go on a sex strike until political normality was restored.

The divided country

On a more serious note, in January 2011 tens of thousands of Belgians had responded to an internet proposal to take to the streets and simply demand a new government. Despairingly, Belgium's septuagenarian King Albert II appointed an *informateur* to see how the deadlock might be broken. He appointed a member of the Nieuw-Vlaamse Alliantie (N-VA), (New Flemish Alliance), one Bart De Wever, to look into the problem. Mr De Wever, a former history professor, turned out to be somewhat hamstrung by the rather obvious fact that the NVA advocated the dismantling of Belgium as a kingdom and the establishment of a Flemish-speaking republic. The NVA had won the largest share of the vote in the stalemated June 2010 elections. Not that this amounted to a substantial endorsement; the

KEY FACTS

Official name: Royaume de Belgique (French), Koninkrijk België (Dutch), Königreich Belgien (German) (Kingdom of Belgium)

Head of State: King Albert II (since 1993)

Head of government: Prime Minister Elio Di Rupo (PS) (from 6 Dec 2011)

Ruling party: Coalition of *Flemish parties*: Christen-Democratisch en Vlaams (CDV) (Christian Democratic and Flemish), Vlaamse Liberalen en Democraten (VLD) (Open Flemish Liberals and Democrats), Socialistische Partij-Anders (SP-A) (Socialist Party-Other); *francophone parties*: Parti Socialiste (PS) (Socialist Party), Mouvement Réformateur (MR) (Reform Movement), Centre Démocrate Humaniste (CDH) (Humanist Democratic Centre) (from 6 Dec 2011)

Area: 30,518 square km

Population: 10,88 million (2010)*

Capital: Brussels

Official language: Dutch (Flemish), French and German

Currency: Euro (€) = 100 cents (from 1 Jan 2002; previous currency Belgian franc, locked at Bf40.34 per euro)

Exchange rate: €0.75 per US$ (Oct 2011)

GDP per capita: US$42,630 (2010)

GDP real growth: 2.00% (2010)

GDP: US$465.70 billion (2010)

Labour force: 5.11 million (2010)

Unemployment: 8.30% (2010)

Inflation: 2.30% (2010)

Balance of trade: -US$2.33 billion (2010)

* estimated figure

NVA only garnered 38 per cent of the vote in Flanders, suggesting that not too many Flemish voters supported a split. To overcome the objections to Mr De Wever the King appointed a further battery of negotiators, two *édiateurs*, a *clarificateur*, a *conciliateur*, an additional *informateur* and, on top of then all, a *negotiateur*.

However, all that seemed to happen, was that the antipathy between the opposing groups worsened as prosperous Flanders sought to transfer the country's power base from the existing federal state to the three regions of Flanders (Flemish speaking), Wallonia (French) and Brussels (largely French). The very nature of the status of Brussels, known for its legally sanctioned use of two languages for official, administrative matters (*facilités*), was considered by many Flemish Belgians to be a step too far. The *facilités* allow the municipal authorities in the half dozen mainly French-speaking towns around Brussels, but technically on Flemish soil, to communicate in French with those citizens who wish to do so. There is some logic to the *facilités* since even in 2011 less than ten per cent of Brussels' inhabitants are Flemish speakers. In Flanders, citizens are already required to demonstrate that they have a reasonable command of Dutch.

Ratings slippage

In the absence of anything resembling a government, the so called 'caretaker' government lead by Yves Leterme, defeated in the June 2010 elections, was prevented from addressing the parlous state of Belgium's finances. The political vacuum resulted in the international credit agencies showing increased caution. Standard and Poor's (S&P's) revised Belgium's medium-term credit risk from stable to negative in December 2010.

The negativity hinges on the likelihood of the French-Flemish fault line developing into a fracture. About 60 per cent of the population speak Flemish (many resent the use of the term 'Dutch') and for the most part live in Flanders. In East Flanders, there is a small German-speaking minority. Conversely, the 40 per cent of the population that speaks French mostly live in Wallonia. Both sides of the culture-linguistic divide would probably be happy to settle for the division of their non-functional country was it not for one thing: Brussels. Alongside a love of good food and drink, Brussels is probably the country's only unifying factor. Some Belgians wonder whether Brussels might not become the independent capital district of the European Union, rather along the lines of the Australian Capital Territory (ACT), which hosts Canberra.

Until the 1960s, rustbelt Wallonia could look down on its less prosperous neighbour to the north. By the twenty-first century the tables had been turned. Once prosperous towns and cities such as Charleroi and La Louviére languished. The former French speaking elite sought their inspiration from France. Now their Flemish counterparts prefer to go to London or New York. Some observers link Belgium's problems to globalisation, which has paradoxically created loyalties both to wider groupings as well as to smaller ones. The prosperous Flemish community may have more in common with Spain's rebellious Catalans than with the Walloons. Not that governmental crises are exactly new to Belgium. In 2007, the London *Economist* had headlined its article on the problem *Time to call it a Day*.

Economic progress

In 1993 Belgium was the most heavily indebted nation in the European Union (EU). Its debt-to-GDP ratio was 134 per cent. A decade and a half later, in 2007, the figure had dropped to 84 per cent. In the European context this turnaround was thought to provide encouragement to efforts to rescue the Greek economy, where the debt to GDP figure had reached 160 per cent (and still rising) by mid-2011. Unlike Greece, Belgium largely finances itself from domestic savings; in May 2011 S&P's confirmed Belgium's sovereign ratings at A++. Nevertheless, as mid-2011 passed, so did the so-called spread on the interest paid on Belgian bonds when compared to their German counterparts.

Divergences between the Flemish northern part of Belgium and the francophone south have also affected federal economic policy making, particularly industrial and labour market reform, as well as regional fiscal autonomy and national social safety nets. Five state reforms since 1970 have transformed Belgium from a centralised state to a country made up of federal entities. In terms of economic policy, the current political differences appear to focus on: firstly, the extent and modalities of further fiscal devolution through a revision of the so-called Special Financing Act, which regulates the financial relations between the federal entities, and the transfer to the regions of part of personal income taxation as well as part of the responsibility for labour market policies, health care, child allowances, and the judiciary. And secondly, the financing of Brussels through higher compensation for public services provided to commuters and international civil servants in conjunction with streamlining its governing structures and improving the efficiency of its administration.

Growth held back

In its annual assessment of Belgium's economy, the International Monetary Fund (IMF) noted how the political deadlock inevitably hampered economic policymaking. None the less, in 2011, the Belgian economy was gradually recovering from the economic downturn but the protracted political negotiations and the

KEY INDICATORS — Belgium

	Unit	2006	2007	2008	2009	2010
Population	m	10.59	10.65	10.73	*10.81	*10.88
Gross domestic product (GDP)	US$bn	398.14	453.64	506.40	470.40	465.70
GDP per capita	US$	37,613	42,557	47,108	43,533	42,630
GDP real growth	%	3.0	2.7	1.1	-3.0	2.0
Inflation	%	2.3	1.8	4.5	-0.2	2.3
Unemployment	%	8.3	7.5	7.0	7.9	8.3
Exports (fob) (goods)	US$m	281,135.0	322,805.0	373,019.0	252,156.0	282,297.0
Imports (fob) (goods)	US$m	277,778.0	322,241.0	388,867.0	255,089.0	284,628.0
Balance of trade	US$m	3,357.0	564.0	-15,848.0	-2,933.0	-2,331.0
Current account	US$m	10,558.0	14,635.0	-12,891.0	1,298.0	4,481.0
Total reserves minus gold	US$m	8,783.0	10,384.0	9,318.0	15,907.0	16,499.0
Foreign exchange	US$m	7,619.0	9,298.0	7,767.0	7,801.0	7,880.0
Exchange rate	per US$	0.75	0.69	0.68	0.78	0.76

* estimated figure

absence of real government had certainly prevented important challenges being addressed. One particularly worrying factor was the, already mentioned, fact that the public debt-to-GDP ratio, having declined steadily during pre-crisis years, was on the rise again. A further factor was Belgium's ageing population. The related rising ageing costs were expected to put increased pressure on the public finances. Belgium's banking sector is in the midst of a restructuring but remained vulnerable to the knock-on effects of its sizeable foreign exposures, especially asset quality deterioration; and funding shocks.

Belgium's low employment rate and limited competition in both product and services markets has, in the view of the IMF, held back its economic growth, which is also crucial for fiscal consolidation. Belgium has also been adversely affected by the turbulence in the European sovereign debt markets. The political impasse has weakened market confidence in the country's resolve to bring its public debt under control. Despite high household savings and a strong external position, the 10-year sovereign bond spread (vis-à-vis the German Bund) increased from some 40 bps early in 2010 to around 100 bps in the latter part of the year and early 2011, the highest level among core euro area countries at the time. Preserving market confidence in Belgian sovereign debt is important to avoid adverse debt dynamics as well as to maintain sound bank balance sheets and funding conditions. In view of the inevitably large financing needs of Belgium's government and banks in 2011, it is urgent to address the above-mentioned economic policy challenges.

Modest recovery

Before accepting programmes to reduce the fiscal deficit in 2011–12, address the contagion problems in the financial sector and initiate reforms in the labour and services sector, the interim government considered that this would first require agreement on a new government and fiscal reform. The caretaker government prepared a draft 2011 budget law to ensure that the 2011 fiscal targets under Belgium's Stability Program will be reached while the financial authorities have intensified banking supervision.

Perhaps surprisingly, after being hit by a severe recession in 2008–09, the Belgian economy had staged a modest recovery, boosted by the rebound in world trade and by monetary and fiscal easing. GDP growth in 2010 was stronger than foreseen, estimated at 2 per cent, slightly above the euro area average of 1.7 per cent. As in other European countries, the expansion was driven by strong exports, notably to Germany and to the Asian emerging economies.

Industrial production in November 2010 had increased by about 7 per cent from the low point reached a year earlier. Both consumer and business confidence indicators had improved but despite employment expanding again, the unemployment rate increased further to almost 8.5 per cent in 2010, but remained below the euro area average of 10 per cent. Labour hoarding and use of reduced working time arrangements have mitigated the rise in unemployment. While core inflation remained subdued in 2010, headline inflation jumped up due to the energy price rise. Core inflation was weighed down by the sizeable output gap and remained low at 1.25 per cent in 2010. Headline inflation, however, picked up briskly to 2.3 per cent in 2010, well above the euro area average of 1.6 per cent. The inflation gap with the euro area was largely driven by rising oil prices and amplified by the sensitivity of the Belgian economy to energy price shocks.

Risk assessment

Economy	Fair
Politics	Poor
Regional stability	Fair

COUNTRY PROFILE

Historical profile

In the eighth and ninth centuries, the area which is now Belgium was part of the Charlemagne Empire. It achieved independence by the tenth century. Flemish towns, with their large textile industries, enjoyed great financial and political power.

1322 The area fell under French control again.

1419 The accession of Philip of Burgundy ended a period of instability.

1477 The Low Countries (Belgium and the Netherlands) passed to the Habsburgs of Spain on the death of Philip's son, Charles the Bold.

1500–55 Under the reign of Emperor Charles V, Antwerp was a leading commercial centre and financial centre.

1555–98 Reign of Philip II, King of Spain. The Belgians and the Dutch reacted against the tyranny of Philip II. There was turmoil between Protestant and Catholic communities.

1580s The northern Netherlands managed to secede. King Philip re-conquered the south, where Catholicism was imposed. The leading traders and intellectuals migrated to the north.

1598–1621 Under Archduke Albert and Archduchess Isabella (daughter of Philip II), the southern Netherlands (Belgium excluding Liège) became semi-autonomous.

1648 The Peace of Westphalia confirmed this position.

1700–13 The War of the Spanish Succession resulted in the southern Netherlands passing to the Austrian Habsburgs. Liège remained independent within the Holy Roman Empire.

1790 The United States of Belgium was established after a local revolution inspired by the French revolution.

1792 French troops conquered the southern Netherlands and Liège.

1793 The Austrians reoccupied the territory.

1794 The southern Netherlands and Liège were invaded by the French and the newly integrated territories were annexed to France. When Napoleon came to power, Belgium became part of the French empire.

1814–15 During the Congress of Vienna (after the defeat of Napoleon) it was agreed to unite the northern and southern Netherlands and the princedom of Liège under the rule of King William I. The Catholic Church refused to accept a protestant King, while William tried to impose Dutch rule in Flanders.

1828 The Catholics and young Liberals formed an association called Unionism and drew up a programme of demands.

1830 Revolution erupted in Brussels and the south broke away from the north. Belgium was declared independent of the Netherlands.

1831–65 Leopold I of Saxe-Coburg became the first King of Belgian.

1865–1909 King Leopold II, invested in expeditions to Africa and privately owned the Congo Free State, in which the treatment of Congolese natives by European officials was brutal. Belgian annexed the Congo Free State in 1908, shortly before the King's death.

1914 Following the outbreak of the First World War, Germany invaded Belgium and the country became a battlefield until the end of the war in 1918.

1918–39 Inter-war years saw rapid industrialisation, developing colonial wealth in Africa and the forging of regional links, leading to the Belgium-Luxembourg Economic Union (BLEU).

1940–45 Belgium was invaded and occupied by Nazi Germany.

1947 Belgium formed a customs union with Luxembourg and the Netherlands, known as Benelux.

1951 King Leopold III, who had been on the throne since 1934, abdicated in favour of his son, Baudouin (Boudewijn) I.

1958 Belgium was a founder member of the forerunner of the European Union (EU), the European Economic Community (EEC), with Brussels becoming the favoured location for the organisation.
1960 Belgium withdrew rapidly from the Belgian Congo.
1970s There was a succession of unstable coalition governments.
1979–92 Christian Democrat Wilfried Martens was appointed prime minister twice during this period, with Mark Eyskens serving for some months in 1981.
1992 Jean-Luc Dehaene was appointed prime minister.
1993 King Baudouin I died and was succeeded by his brother, Albert II. Belgium became a federal state.
1999 Belgium was one of the first 11 countries to adopt the euro.
2001 A government reform package approved more money for schools in the French-speaking communities of the south and more political influence for the Dutch-speaking Flemish around Brussels, even though they were in a minority.
2002 Euro currency replaced the Belgian franc.
2003 Parliamentary elections were won by the Vlaamse Liberalen en Demokraten (VLD) (Flemish Liberal and Democrats), a coalition was formed which included the Socialistische Partij Anders-Spirit (SPA-Spirit) (Socialist Party-Spirit), Parti Socialiste (PS) (Socialist Party) and Mouvement Réformateur (MR) (Reform Movement).
2004 Following conviction for racial incitement, the Vlaams Blok (VB) (Flemish Bloc) party reconstituted itself as Vlaams Belang (VB) (Flemish Interest)
2007 The VLD, SPA-Spirit, PS and MR formed a coalition government Prime Minister Guy Verhofstadt resigned; however he was re-appointed as a caretaker prime minister. His attempt at forming a coalition failed and to break the political impasse, the King asked Verhofstadt to form an interim government.
2008 After nine months of political stalemate, Yves Camille Désiré Leterme (CDV) was sworn in as prime minister leading a coalition government. The government initiated a US$2.8 billion stimulus package needed to avert a recession. Leterme resigned as prime minister following the collapse of the country's largest bank, Fortis, and a scandal over its rescue. Herman Van Rompuy took office as prime minister.
2009 Two predominantly Flemish-speaking towns of Halle and Affligem, were embroiled in controversy during EU elections, as Francophone political parties were denied advertising space on municipal billboards. The long-term result may be that the voting constituency of Brussels-Halle-Vilvoorde will be spilt along linguistic lines. Prime Minister Herman Van Rompuy resigned and Yves Leterme became prime minister again.
2010 Herman Van Rompuy became the EU's first permanent president on 1 January. The Leterme government resigned in April after a coalition partner withdrew over the voting future of Brussels-Halle-Vilvoorde. The lower house of parliament passed legislation banning the wearing of the *burka* (full Islamic face veil worn by women). In parliamentary elections held in June, the Flemish separatist party, Nieuw-Vlaamse Alliantie (NVA) (New Flemish Alliance) won 17.4 per cent of the vote (27 seats out of 150) and the right to form a coalition government.
2011 On 17 February, when there was still no government, Belgium achieved the dubious record of the longest time a democratic country had been without a government (249 days), as political parties from the Flemish-speaking north were unable to achieve unity with their French-speaking southern counterparts. On 16 May, Elio Di Rupo (PS) was asked to form a new government. However by 4 July he was still in coalition negotiations with others. On 14 September, caretaker prime minister, Yves Leterme, announced his resignation, to become deputy secretary-general of the OECD. On 21 November, Elio Di Rupo was unable to form a government and asked the King to relieve him of the responsibility. A new government was sworn into office, with Elio Di Rupo sworn in as prime minister, on 6 December, following a record-breaking 541 days since the general election caused a political deadlock. The six-party agreement to form a government was probably spurred on by the downgrading of Belgium's credit rating from AA+ to AA by Standard and Poor's on 25 November.

Political structure

Constitution

A new constitution was introduced in 1994, re-defining the federal structure and introducing devolution on both a regional and language-speaking level. In 2001, a constitutional amendment allowed greater autonomy in taxation, spending, agricultural and trade policy. The federal state is responsible for economic, domestic, foreign, defence, legal, welfare and health policy.
The are three Régions/Gewests (Regions) of Flemish, Wallonia and Brussels. Each has its own executive and assembly, responsible for regional policies (such as transport and housing).
Overlapping the Regions are three Communautés/Gemeenschaps (Communities), representing Belgium's Flemish, French and German-speakers. They are responsible for policy on language and cultural affairs. The French and German Communities operate separate parliaments. The Flemish Region and Community (which represent the same geographical area) operate a joint assembly. Language and cultural affairs in the Brussels Region are divided between the Flemish and French Communities.
In May 2003 electoral reforms allowed changes to electoral districts for the House of Representatives, which now match the borders of the provinces, a new system of distribution of seats, an electoral threshold and Belgians abroad allowed to vote.

Independence date

21 July 1831

Form of state

Federal parliamentary democratic monarchy

The executive

The monarch has a largely ceremonial role but, as Head of State, formally appoints the head of government, although this post is always the leader of the ruling coalition. The prime minister appoints a cabinet of ministers (limited to 15 and with an equal number of French and Flemish speakers); they do not sit in parliament but must present their policies and performance before parliament for review.

National legislature

The Federale Parlement – Parlement Fédérale – Föderales Parlament (federal parliament) has two chambers. The Kamer van Volksvertegenwoordigers – Chambre de Représentants – Abgeordneten Kammer (chamber of the people's representatives) has 150 members elected by proportional representation for four-year terms. The Senaat – Sénat – Senat (senate) has 71 members in total, of which 40 are directly elected for four-year terms by proportional representation, 21 members are appointed by the lower community parliaments and 10 members are appointed by other senators – sons and daughters of the monarch are customarily senate members. Both chambers can propose and veto legislation.
Universal suffrage is at age 18; voting is mandatory, although ballot papers allow an invalid or blank vote. Voting is almost entirely undertaken by electronic means, through the use of a computerised swipe card system. Although federal elections are scheduled every four years, early elections are possible when called for by the prime minister. The federal government is typically a coalition, with ministerial posts assigned to members of political parties within the ruling coalition.

Legal system

The *Code Napoléon*, became the basis of civil law in Belgium.

The constitution guarantees the independence of the judiciary from the executive and legislative branches. Court hearings are public and trials of a serious nature are heard before a jury of civilians.
The highest court is the Cour de Cassation (Supreme Court), composed of judges appointed by the Crown. A Cour d'Arbitration rules on conflicts of authority between the many layers of federal and national government and their legal instruments.
A Consultation Committee, made up of regional and national representatives including the prime minister, is the final recourse for conflicts of interest arising from devolution. Formed with equal numbers of French and Dutch/Flemish speakers, it makes its decisions by consensus.

Last elections
13 June 2010 (parliamentary)
Results: Parliamentary: (Chamber of Representatives) Nieuw-Vlaamse Alliantie (NVA) (New Flemish Alliance) won 17.4 per cent of the vote (27 seats out of 150), Parti Socialiste (PS) (Socialist Party) 13.71 per cent (26), Christen-Democratisch en Vlaams (CDV) (Christian Democratic and Flemish) 10.85 per cent (17), Mouvement Réformateur (MR) (Reform Movement) 9.28 per cent (18), Socialistische Partij-Anders (SP-A) (Socialist Party-Differently) 9.24 per cent (13), Vlaamse Liberalen en Democraten (VLD) (Open Flemish Liberals and Democrats) 8.64 per cent (13), Vlaams Belang (VB) (Flemish Interest) 7.76 per cent (12), Centre Démocrate Humaniste (CDH) (Humanist Democratic Centre) 5.53 per cent (nine); four other political parties won less than 5 per cent of the vote and shared the remaining 15 seats.
Senate: NVA won 19.61 per cent of the vote (nine seats out of 40), PS 13.62 per cent (seven), CDV 9.99 per cent (four), SP-A 9.48 per cent (four), MR 9.27 per cent (four), VLD 8.24 per cent (four), VB 7.6 per cent (three); three other political parties shared five other seats. Turnout was 89.2 per cent.

Next elections
2014 (parliament)

Political parties

Ruling party
Coalition of *Flemish parties*: Christen-Democratisch en Vlaams (CDV) (Christian Democratic and Flemish), Vlaamse Liberalen en Democraten (VLD) (Open Flemish Liberals and Democrats), Socialistische Partij-Anders (SP-A) (Socialist Party-Other); *francophone parties*: Parti Socialiste (PS) (Socialist Party), Mouvement Réformateur (MR) (Reform Movement), Centre Démocrate Humaniste (CDH) (Humanist Democratic Centre) (from 6 Dec 2011)

Population

10,88 (2010)*
Last census: October 2001: 10,296,350
Population density: Urban population: 97 per cent (1994–2000).
Annual growth rate: 0.3 per cent 1994–2004 (WHO 2006)

Ethnic make-up
Around 57 per cent of the population live in Dutch-speaking Flanders, 32 per cent in French-speaking Wallonia, 10 per cent in bilingual Brussels and 1 per cent in the German-speaking border region. There are also some 860,000 foreign expatriates and immigrants. The largest expatriate communities are Italian, French, Moroccan, Dutch, Turkish and Spanish. Foreigners comprise about 27 per cent of the population of Brussels.

Religions
Predominantly Roman Catholic (75 per cent). Also Protestant, Jewish and Muslim.

Education

Education budgets are set by the French, Dutch/Flemish and German language communities.
Most schools are state-run and free. Catholic and international schools are fee-paying. The Belgian education system is widely recognised as being of a very high standard. Government expenditure on education typically accounts for 3 per cent of GDP.
The teaching language is determined by the linguishic region in which a school is based: Dutch, French or German. Brussels is a bilingual region of its own, and here separate schools use the language appropriate to their pupils, drawn from the surrounding community. International schools (concentrated in Brussels and Antwerp), may teach in foreign languages and follow foreign curricula. Belgian French and Flemish schools follow the same school cycles. However exams are particular to each language. Primary schooling lasts from age six to 12 when students undertake exams to determine progression to one of four different schools and programmes: general, technical, artistic or vocational.
Universities and colleges offer a full range of subjects and qualifications.
Compulsory years: 6 to 18.
Enrolment rate: 103 per cent, gross primary enrolment; 146 per cent, gross secondary enrolment; of the relevant age group (including repeaters and training for the unemployed); 56 per cent teriary enrolment (World Bank).
Pupils per teacher: 12 in primary schools.

Health

Adequate healthcare is provided for all citizens. The patient pays for treatment, but the fee is reimbursed by his or her health insurance company. The reimbursement may cover almost all of the cost or very little, depending on the patient's choice of doctor. The *mutuelles* (health insurance companies) also have their own clinics where basic healthcare, optometry and dentistry can be obtained for a token fee.

HIV/Aids
HIV prevalence: 0.2 per cent aged 15–49 in 2003 (World Bank)
Life expectancy: 78 years, 2004 (WHO 2006)
Fertility rate/Maternal mortality rate: 1.7 births per woman, 2004 (WHO 2006); maternal deaths 8 per 100,000 (World Bank)
Child (under 5 years) mortality rate (per 1,000): 4 per 1,000 live births (World Bank)
Head of population per physician: 4.49 physicians per 1,000 people, 2002 (WHO 2006)

Welfare

A social insurance scheme covers welfare payments. Contributions are taken from all workers at 7.5 per cent of earnings and pensioners 0.5–2 per cent of pensions or pre-pensions; employers pay 8.86 per cent of the payroll and the government provides annual subsidies.
Old age pensions, disability, sickness, maternity benefits, survivors pensions are dependent on contributions to worker's insurance funds.
Workers' contributions cover around 70 per cent of social security costs. Unemployment benefits are administered by three regional offices, the Vlaamse Dienst Arbeidsbemiddeling Beroepsopleiding (VDBA) in Flanders, the Organisme de Formation et d'Emploi de la Wallonie (FOREM) in Wallonia and the Office Régional Bruxellois d'Emploi-Brusselse Gewestelijke Dienst voor Arbeidsbemiddeling (ORBEM-BGDA) in Brussels.

Pensions
The statutory age of retirement is 65 and 62 for men and women respectively; in 2009 it will be set at 65 for all.

Main cities

Brussels (Bruxelles, Brussel, Brüssel , Bruessel) (capital, estimated population 981,200 in 2003), Antwerp (Anvers, Antwerpen) (450,000), Gent (Ghent) (226,900), Charleroi (201,200), Liège (Luik, Lüttich, Liege, Luettich, Luttich) (185,700), Brugge (Bruges)(117,200), Namur (105,700), Mons (91,200).

Languages spoken

The northern part of Belgium, Flanders, is Dutch-speaking and the southern part, Wallonia, is French-speaking. Brussels is officially bilingual, but over 80 per cent of its population are French-speakers. There is also a small German-speaking area in eastern Wallonia, which became part of Belgium after the First World War. English, Luxembourgish, Italian, Spanish, Greek, Arabic and Turkish are also spoken.

Official language/s

Dutch (Flemish), French and German

Media

The linguistic division of Belgium society circumscribes its media.

Press

Dailies: Nation newspapers include, in Dutch, *The Nieuwsblad* (www.nieuwsblad.be),*Het Laatste Nieuws* (www.hln.be) is a tabloid and *De Morgen* (www.demorgen.be), *Belgisch Staatsblad* (www.ejustice.just.fgov.be) is a government gazette; in French, *La Libre Belgique* (www.lalibre.be) and *Le Soir* (www.lesoir.be); in German, *Grenz-Echo* (www.grenzecho.be).

Several regional newspapers are published by SudPress (www.lacapitale.be) including *La Capitale*, *La Meuse*, *La Gazette* and *Nord Eclair*; others include *Le Courrier Mouscron* (www.actu24.be), *Metro* (www.metrotime.be), and *Gazet van Antwerpen* (www.gva.be).

Weeklies: *Les Nouvelles du Dimanche Matin* is a Sunday newspaper. *Le 7e Soir* is a national weekly. Other weekly publications include *Knack* and *Le Vif/L'Express*.

Business: The principal daily financial newspaper is owned and published by Mediafin and in French called *L'Echo* (www.lecho.be) and in Dutch *De Tijd* (www.tijd.be). In French and Dutch, other weeklies include *Imediair* (www.imediair.be) and *Trends* (www.trends.be). *Forward* (www.vbo-feb.be) is the monthly publication of the Chamber of Commerce. In Dutch, *Impuls* (http://intersight.org/impuls) is an annual business directory.

Periodicals: Some daily newspapers publish weekend editions. In French and Dutch, *Flair* (www.flair.be), *Jet Magazine* (www.jetmagazine.be), and *Loving You* (www.lovingyou.be) are women's magazines. In English *New Europe* (www.neurope.eu), gives analysis of EU issues.In French and Dutch, monthly magazines include *Test Aankoop* (www.test-aankoop.be), a consumer magazine and *Meervoud* (www.meervoud.org) advocates Flemish sovereignty and *MM* (www.mm.be) is a magazine on marketing,

Broadcasting

National, public broadcasting is provided by Radio-Télévision Belge de la Communauté Française (RTBF) for the French-speaking community and Vlaamse Radio en Televisie (VRT) for the Dutch-speaking community.

Radio: There are two public and one commercial national networks, RTBF (www.rtbf.be/radio) has five stations and an international programme, VRT (www.vrt.be) has five stations and Belgischer Rundfunk (www.brf.be) transmitting programmes in German, has two stations. All broadcasters offer full internet access.

There are many independent, private, regional radio stations including C Dance Network (www.c-dance.be) and Topradio (www.topradio.be/); local stations include Crooze FM (www.crooze.fm) and Geel FM (www.geelfm.be) from Antwerp, Ciel Radio (www.cielradio.be) and Q Music (www.q-music.be) from Brussels and Zone 80 (www.zone80.be) from Liège.

Television: All terrestrial TV will be broadcast via digital technology by 2011. VRT is Belgium's leading broadcaster, which uses external production houses to provide domestic programmes. It has two TV channels, één (one) (www.een.be), which has a full range of programmes, Ketnet (www.ketnet.be) is for children and Canvas (www.canvas.be) is an in-depth news, alternative arts and entertainment channel. Ketnet shares its channel (0700–2000) with Canvas (2000–0100). RTBF (www.rtbf.be) operates two terrestrial, TV channels (La Une and La Deux) and a satellite network (www.rtbfsat.be). Vlaamse Televisie Maatschappij (VTM) (www.vtm.be) is the leading commercial TV network in the Dutch-speaking area, with three channels, VTM, Kanaal Twee (for children) and JIMtv.

There are many pay-to-view services provided via satellite or cable. TV Vlaanderen Digitaal (www.tvvlaanderen.be) and Liberty TV (www.libertytv.com) are satellite stations. Plug TV (www.plugtv.be) and AB3 (www.ab3.be) are cable TV services. Belgian TV viewers can also tune into a great number of channels from Germany, France, Luxembourg, The Netherlands, Spain, Italy and the UK.

Advertising

There are different authorities responsible for advertising in French and Flemish speaking communities.

There is a total ban on tobacco advertising and food adverts aimed at children are controlled by a self-regulatory code. Besides advertising carried by commercial television and radio channels (over 40 per cent of total advertising by expenditure), other popular forms of advertising include telemarketing, catalogues, direct mail, the internet and personalised mobile/cell phone texting.

Economy

Belgium has used its geographic situation to develop a sophisticated transport system of roads, rail, canals and ports that is important to trade in the European Union (EU). With this network in place, and although it has few natural resources and has to import almost all its raw materials, Belgium nevertheless has a diversified industrial sector, generally in the north (Flanders), based on a highly skilled, productive and multi-lingual work force. The service sector dominates at around 75 per cent of GDP, with industry constituting almost 25 per cent and agriculture, including fishing, 1 per cent. Antwerp is Europe's second largest port (after Rotterdam, The Netherlands); it processed 157.8 million tonnes of cargo in 2009, of which the single largest component was petroleum derivatives. Antwerp is also a world centre for diamond trading and processing, with imports of rough cut diamonds, cut and polished diamonds; most of the resulting production is exported. International trade in diamonds fell in 2009 as demand dropped in line with the global economic crisis.

GDP growth was 2.8 per cent in 2007, having been around that figure since 2005. In 2008, when the banking crisis struck and the country had to bail-out three of its largest banks that had over-extended their assets on non-performing loans (Fortis, Dexia and KBC Groep), GDP growth fell to 0.8 per cent. The crisis caused the downfall of the government as its attempts at selling Fortis left bank shareholders litigious and many bank-workers redundant. Belgium officially entered recession in the first quarter of 2009 with annual GDP growth of -3.0 per cent.

The effect of the global recession on Belgium was a drop in exports, a fall in domestic spending and a rise in unemployment. Per capita income that had been US$35,929 in 2005 jumped to US$47,185 in 2008 when the economy was buoyant, but within a year per capita income had fallen to US$43,533 in 2009.

When the economy is back to pre-crisis levels of growth, the government will have to tackle the imbalance of non-productive citizens and an aging population and the resultant public expenditure in their maintenance through social welfare and pensions.

External trade

As a member of the European Union, Belgium operates within a community-wide free trade area, with tariffs set as a whole. Internationally, the EU has free trade agreements with a number of nations and trading blocs worldwide.

It has a complex and open market economy; national and multinational companies have operations that import raw materials and semi-finished items that are readied and re-exported. While 75 per cent of all exports go to other EU states, international trade has been hampered by the high value of the euro.
Belgium's hand-made, quality chocolate confectioneries are some of the world's most sought after products. The raw chocolate is typically sourced from Africa, with the finished product consumed locally and exported.

Imports
Imports consist of petroleum and derivatives, rough diamonds, machinery and equipment, metal products, pharmaceuticals, foodstuffs, vehicles and products, chemicals and consumer goods.
Main sources: The Netherlands (typically 20 per cent of total), Germany (17 per cent), France (11 per cent).

Exports
Many companies export more than 80 per cent of their production. Principal exports include machinery and equipment, diamonds, steel, glass, pharmaceuticals and organic chemicals, motor vehicles, foodstuffs and carpets. A new biotechnology sector has developed.
Main destinations: Germany (typically 20 per cent of total), France (17 per cent), The Netherlands (12 per cent).

Agriculture

Farming
The agriculture sector accounts for around 1.4 per cent of GDP and employs 2.5 per cent of the workforce. Although small-scale, cultivation is intensive, especially in Flanders, which has better soils for arable farming. Here one quarter of the organically managed land is used for arable crops. Belgium is self-sufficient in sugar, eggs, butter and meat, and is an exporter of vegetables and horticultural produce. The amount of land under cultivation (approximately 25 per cent of total land area) is falling.
Reform to the EU Common Agricultural Policy (CAP) was introduced in 2005 in Belgium, whereby subsidies paid on farm output, which tended to benefit large farms and encourage overproduction, were replaced by single farm payments not conditional on production. This is expected to reward farms that provide and maintain a healthy environment, food safety and animal welfare standards. The changes are also intended to encourage market conscious production and cut the cost of CAP to the EU taxpayer.

Fishing
Fishing is a smaller and less important industry in Belgium than in neighbouring countries, largely because of its short coastline. The mussel- and oyster-bearing waters of the Scheldt estuary are bordered on both sides by the Netherlands. Belgium has a flotilla of small offshore trawlers, but no major deep sea fleet.

Forestry
Forest and other wooded land cover around 22 per cent of the land area – one of the lowest ratios in Europe. The majority of timber materials imported come from Germany and France.

Industry and manufacturing

The large-scale, export-based industrial sector accounts for 22 per cent of GDP and employs approximately 28 per cent of the labour force.
Belgium's industrial sector is strongly regional. Flanders, which accounts for some 60 per cent of GDP, has a modern industrial base. It is also more integrated into international markets than other regions, with around 85 per cent of its output going abroad and accounting for some 70 per cent of total Belgian exports. The region of Wallonia, on the other hand, accounts for 25 per cent of GDP and is burdened with declining heavy industry. The government has made considerable efforts to restructure the industrial base in Wallonia, with substantial investment incentives available.
The government's policy is aimed at facilitating the renewal and restructuring of industry so that it can adapt to new technologies and maintain its competitive position internationally. This includes encouraging domestic and foreign investment in industry with tax incentives, particularly in advanced technology fields.

Tourism

Belgium's historic towns and rich cultural heritage are particularly attractive to short-stay visitors, mainly from neighbouring countries. Around seven million tourist visit Belgium each year.

Mining

The mining sector accounts for approximately 0.3 per cent of GDP and employs 0.4 per cent of the workforce. There is no longer a mining industry. Only clay and sand are mined on any scale.

Hydrocarbons

There are no know oil or natural gas reserves. However it is a hub for the import and re-export of crude oil which it refines and liquefied natural gas (LNG) for which it is both a conduit and importer and blender of gas coming from The Netherlands, the UK, Norway, Germany and Russia. It imports 18 billion cubic metres of gas annually and 619,800 barrels per day (bpd) of oil. Belgian refineries had a total capacity of 791,000bpd.
Belgium's coal-mining industry has production of 122 million tonnes per annum largely produced by tip-washing; 214 million tonnes are imported to meet domestic demand.

Energy

Installed electricity capacity was 13.5GW. Nuclear power is the primary source of energy, accounting for around 60 per cent of electricity output; most of the rest comes from thermal sources, fired by gas, coal and oil. There are seven nuclear stations. Legislation provides for nuclear energy to be phased out by 2025, but Belgium's environmental obligations to the EU European Climate Change Programme are leading to revised considerations.

Financial markets

Stock exchange
NYSE Euronext NV

Commodity exchange
Liffe Connect

Banking and insurance

The banking sector is divided into three main groups – commercial banks, public credit institutions and private savings banks.
Belgium's efforts to meet the conditions for European Economic and Monetary Union (Emu) involved major restructuring of the financial sector.

Central bank
Banque Nationale de Belgique; European Central Bank (ECB)

Time

GMT plus one hour (daylight saving, late March to late October, GMT plus two hours)

Geography

Belgium is a small European state bordered to the north by the North Sea and The Netherlands, to the east by The Netherlands, Germany and Luxembourg, and to the south and west by France. It is flat near the coast, but hillier in the Ardennes region in the south-east.

Hemisphere
Northern

Climate

The country has a temperate climate; the proximity of the sea reduces the harshness of winter, but makes summers relatively cool.
Temperatures overall do not show great variations. The average for the hottest month, July, is 17 degrees Celsius (C) and for the coldest, January, 3 degrees C. Temperatures tend to be slightly higher along the coast and cooler in the Ardennes.
There is regular but moderate rainfall with average annual precipitation of 800mm.

Dress codes

Belgian dress codes are in general the same as those in other industrialised nations. Suit and tie for men are usual for business and formal occasions, but often a jacket and trousers are sufficient. For women, a suit, dress or skirt and blouse are suitable for most business and social occasions.

Entry requirements
Passports
Passport are required by all visitors, except EU citizens of Schengen Accord states, who require ID cards.
Visa
Required by all, except nationals of EU and Schengen area signatory countries, North America, Australasia and Japan. For further exceptions contact the nearest embassy. A Schengen visa application (offered in several languages) can be downloaded from http://europa.eu/abc/travel/ see 'documents you will need'.
Currency advice/regulations
No restrictions on foreign or local currency movements.
Customs
Personal items are duty-free. There are no duties levied on alcohol and tobacco between EU member states, providing amounts imported are for personal consumption.

Health (for visitors)
Nationals of the European Economic Area (EEA) countries and Switzerland can access reduced cost and sometimes free medical treatment using a European Health Insurance Card (EHIC) while visiting the EEA. Exceptions include nationals of the 10 countries which joined the EU in 2004 whose EHIC is not valid in Switzerland. Applications for the EHIC should be made before travelling.
Mandatory precautions
There are no mandatory health precautions.
Advisable precautions
No exceptional precautions are necessary; any necessary medication should be kept with its original packaging.

Hotels
It is advisable to book hotel or pension in advance either directly or through Belgium Tourist Reservations. By law, all tariffs must be displayed. Service charges are usually included. Tipping is roughly 10 per cent. Major credit cards are accepted.

Public holidays (national)
Fixed dates
1 Jan (New Year's Day), 1 May (Labour Day), 21 Jul (Independence Day), 15 Aug (Assumption Day), 1 Nov (All Saints' Day), 2 Nov (All Souls' Day), 11 Nov (Armistice Day), 15 Nov (Dynasty Day), 25 Dec (Christmas Day), 26 Dec (St Stephen's Day). Also community public holidays: 11 Jul (Flemish community); 27 Sep (French-speaking community).
Fixed-date holidays that fall on a Sunday are observed on the following day.
Variable dates
Easter Monday, Ascension Day, Whit Monday.

Working hours
Banking
Mon–Fri: 0900–1600. Banks are open most days, although a few small banks close at lunch-time.
Business
Mon–Fri: 0830–1730; Sat: 0900–1200.
Government
Mon–Fri: 0900–1700.
Shops
Mon–Sat: 0900/1000–1800/1900. In large cities, convenience stores *(magasins de nuit/avondwinkels)* stay open either all night or until around 2200 every day, including Sundays.

Telecommunications
Mobile/cell phones
There are G3 and 900/1800 GSM services available throughout the country.

Electricity supply
220V AC

Social customs/useful tips
It can be considered impolite to use French in Dutch-speaking Flanders or Dutch in Wallonia due to historical friction between the two language groups. English is quite widely understood and has made headway as a *lingua franca*, in Brussels in particular.
In Flanders, the names of Walloon cities are generally in Flemish and vice versa in Wallonia. There are also different names for German place names in both Belgium and Germany.
Business relations require some degree of formality and the use of the formal pronoun in French and Dutch (vous/U). It is customary to shake hands at the beginning and end of a meeting. Punctuality is valued.
Belgium has one of the highest ratios of police to population of any western European country and officers are permitted to undertake random identity checks. It is compulsory to have a passport or identity card with you at all times.
Alcohol is sold freely at any time of day or night. Smoking is banned in public places (including stations and airports).
Traffic coming from the right has priority in most situations (if the driver who has priority slows down or hesitates, he/she still has priority; a driver who has priority only loses this after having stopped and started moving again). Therefore, foreign drivers should be aware that vehicles could suddenly emerge from side-streets to their right.

Security
There is very little street crime or violence in Belgium, though the inner cities have isolated problem areas.

Getting there
Air
National airline: SN Brussels Airlines is an independent, Belgium airline.
International airport/s: Brussels Zaventem (BRU), 13km north-east of the city centre; amenities include, banks, restaurant, duty-free shops (arriving and departing), medical facilities and business centre. Antwerp International (ANR), 3km east of Antwerp; Brussels-South Charleroi (CRL), 55km south-east of Brussels; Ostend International (OST), 6km from city; Liège (LGG) 5km from the city centre.
Airport tax: Departure tax: Brussels Zaventem eur20.93; Brussels-South Charleroi: eur13.49; Antwerp and Ostend €10; Liège eur7.
Surface
Rail: Express trains (TEE) ensure rapid connection with all French, Dutch and German cities.
Water: There are daily crossings by ferry or jetfoil to Ostend or Zeebrugge from the UK and Norway.
Main port/s: Antwerp, Ghent, Zeebrugge, Ostend, Brussels, Liège.

Getting about
National transport
Road: There is an extensive road network. Toll-free motorways serve all main towns with the exception of those in the Ardennes.
Buses: Extensive coach services operate throughout the country, particularly to rural areas, run by Société Nationale des Chemins de Fer Belges (SNCB) and Société Nationale des Chemins de Fer Vicinaux (SNCV).
Rail: First- and second-class services run between all main towns. Combined tickets allowing stop-overs in main towns offer best value. Over half the railway network is electrified.
Water: There are over 1,500km of inland waterways. Services are operated by Administration des Voies Hydrauliques. Inland canals connect with major French, Dutch and German ports.
City transport
Taxis: Readily available throughout the country. The standardised, metered fare system includes a tip in the final price. Taxis booked to call for a pick-up include a surcharge in their fare. Chauffeur-driven cars are cheaper on long journeys.
Buses, trams & metro: Flat fares are charged on tram and bus service. There are metro services in Brussels and Antwerp.

Trains: Special airport shuttle service operates from Brussels Central Station and North Station, departing every hour.

Car hire

Available at aiports and in most main towns. The minimum age of a hire car driver is 23 years. A full driving licence, valid for at least one year remaining is required. All vehicles must carry a fire extinguisher and first aid kit

Speed limit: urban roads 60kph, main roads 90kph. Maximum speed on dual carrageways and motorways 120kph, minimum speed 70kph. Drive on the right. The wearing of seat belts throughout the vehicle is compulsory. Trams have right of way on any road.

BUSINESS DIRECTORY

The addresses listed below are a selection only. While World of Information makes every endeavour to check these addresses, we cannot guarantee that changes have not been made, especially to telephone numbers and area codes. We would welcome any corrections.

Telephone area codes

The international direct dialling code (IDD) for Belgium is +32, followed by area code and subscriber's number:

Antwerp	3	Ypres	57
Arlon	63	Liège	41
Bastogne	61	La Louvière	64
Brugge	50	Libramont	61
Brussels	2	Mechelen	15
Charleroi	71	Mons	65
Chimay	60	Ostende	59
Dendermonde	52	Verviers	87
Ghent	9	Zeebrugge	50

Chambers of Commerce

American Chamber of Commerce, 50 Avenue des Arts, 1000 Brussels (tel: 513-6770; fax: 513-3590; e-mail: gch@postl.amcham.be).

Antwerp Chamber of Commerce,12 Markgravestraat, 2000 Antwerp (tel: 232-2219; fax: 233-6442; e-mail: eic@kkna.be).

British Chamber of Commerce, Egmont House, 15 Rue d'Egmont, 1000 Brussels (tel: 540-9030; fax: 512-8363; e-mail: brit.cham@britcham.be).

Bruges Chamber of Commerce and Industry, 25 Ezelstraat, 8000 Bruges (tel: 333-696; fax: 342-297; e-mail: brugge@ccibkw.be).

Brussels Chamber of Commerce and Industry, 500 Avenue Louise, 1050 Brussels (tel: 648-5002; fax: 640-9328; e-mail: inscription@ccib.irisnet.be).

Charleroi Chamber of Commerce and Industry, 1a Avenue Général Michel, 6000 Charleroi (tel: 321-160; fax: 334-218; e-mail: info@ccic.be).

Federation of Chambers of Commerce and Industry of Belgium, 1-2 Avenue des Arts, 1210 Brussels (tel: 209-1550; fax: 209-0568; e-mail: fedcci@cci.be).

Ghent Chamber of Commerce and Industry, 41 Martelaarslaan, 9000 Ghent (tel: 266-1440; fax: 266-1441; e-mail: kkngent@cci.be).

Liège Chamber of Commerce and Industry, Palais des Congrès de Liège, 2 Esplanade de l'Europe, 4020 Liège (tel: 343-9292; fax: 343-9267; e-mail: info@ccilg.be).

Banking

AXA Bank Belgium, 214 Grotesteenweg, 2600 Antwerp (tel: 286-2211; fax: 286-2407; e-mail:contact@axa.be).

Dexia, Boulevard Pachéco 44, 1000 Brussels (tel: 222-1111; fax: 222-1122; e-mail: info@dexia.be).

Fortis Banque, 20 Rue Royale, 1000 Brussels (tel: 510-5211; fax: 510-5626 e-mail: info@fortis.com).

ING Belgium., 24 Avenue Marnix, 1000 Brussels (tel: 547-2111; fax: 547-3844; e-mail: info@ing.be).

KBC Bank and Insurance, Havenlaan 2, 1080 Brussels (tel: 429-1111; fax: 429-8123; e-mail: kbc.bank@kbc.be).

Central bank

Banque Nationale de Belgique, Boulevard de Berlaimont 14, BE-1000 Brussels (tel: 221-2111; fax: 221-3100; email: info@nbb.be).

European Central Bank (ECB), Kaiserstrasse 29, D-60311, Postfach 16 03 19, Frankfurt am Main, Germany (tel: (+49-69) 13-440; fax: (+49-69) 1344-6000; email: info@ecb.int; internet: www.ecb.int).

Stock exchange

NYSE Euronext NV: Palais de la Bourse, Place de la Bourse, 1000 Brussels (tel: 509.1211; fax: 509-1212; e-mail: info@euronext.be; www.euronext.com).

Stock exchange 2

Chi-X: www.chi-x.com

Commodity exchange

Liffe Connect: www.nyse.com/nyseeuronext

Travel information

Brussels International Airport Company (BIAC), Brussels Airport, B-1930 Zaventem, (tel: 2753-4200; email: info@biac.be).

Brussels International Tourism and Congress, Hôtel de Ville, Grand Place, 1000 Brussels (tel: 513-8940; fax: 513-8320; e-mail: info@brusselstourism.be).

SN Brussels Airlines, The Corporate Village, Da Vincilaan 9, 1935 Zaventem (customer service tel: 070 351-111; internet: www.flysn.be).

National tourist organisation offices

Belgian Tourist Office (Brussels and Ardennes), 61 Rue du Marché aux Herbes, 1000 Brussels (tel: 504-0390; fax: 504-0270; e-mail: info@opt.be).

Belgian Tourist Office (Tourism Flanders), 63 Rue du Marché aux Herbes, 1000 Brussels (tel: 504-0390; fax: 504-0270; e-mail: info@toerismevlaanderen.be).

Ministries

Ministry of Agriculture and Small and Medium-Sized Enterprises, 1 Rue Marie-Thérèse, 1000 Brussels (tel: 211-0611; fax: 219-6130).

Ministry of the Budget, 180 Rue Royale, 1000 Brussels (tel: 219-1911; fax: 217-3328).

Ministry for the Civil Service, Résidence Palace, 51 Rue de la Loi, 1040 Brussels (tel: 790-5800; fax: 790-5790).

Ministry of Consumer Affairs, Public Health and Environment, 7 Avenue des Arts, 1210 Brussels (tel: 220-2011; fax: 220-2067; e-mail: environment@health.fgov.be).

Ministry of Defence, 8 Rue Lambermont , 1000 Brussels (tel: 550-2811; fax: 550-2919).

Ministry of Economic Affairs and Scientific Research, 23 Square de Meeûs, 1000 Brussels (tel: 506-5111; fax: 514-4683).

Ministry of Employment, 51 Rue Belliard, 1040 Brussels (tel: 233-5111; fax: 230-1067; e-mail: info@cabmeta.fgov.be).

Ministry of Finance, 12 Rue de la Loi, 1000 Brussels (tel: 238-8111; fax: 233-8003; e-mail: contact@ckfin.minfin.be).

Ministry of Foreign Affairs, 15 Rue des Petits Carmes, 1000 Brussels (tel: 501-8211; fax: 511-6385; internet site: www.diplobel.fgov.be/default_em.htm).

Ministry of Interior Affairs, 60 Rue Royale, 1000 Brussels (tel: 504-8511; fax: 504-8500; e-mail: info@mibz.fgov.be).

Ministry of Justice, 115 Boulevard de Waterloo, 1000 Brussels (tel: 542-7911; fax: 538-0767; info@just.fgov.be).

Ministry of Mobility and Transport, 65 Rue de la Loi, 1040 Brussels (tel: 237-6711; fax: 230-1824).

Ministry of Social Affairs and Pensions, 62 Rue de la Loi, 1040 Brussels (tel: 238-2811; fax: 230-3895).

Ministry of Telecommunications, Public Enterprises and Participations, 7 Queteletplein, 1030 Brussels (tel: 250-0303; fax: 219-0914; e-mail: info@telcobel.be).

Prime Minister's Office, 16 Rue de la Loi, 1000 Brussels (tel: 501-0211; fax: 512-6953).

Other useful addresses

Belgian Association of International Trading Houses (ABNEI), 7 Israëlietenstraat, 2000 Antwerp (tel: 226-0712; fax: 231-9969; e-mail: tradechem@cmc.be).

Belgian Embassy (USA), 3330 Garfield Street, NW, Washington DC 20008 (tel: 202-333-6900; fax: 202-333-3079).

Belgian Foreign Trade Board, World Trade Centre, Tower 1, 30/36 Boulevard du Roi Albert II, 1000 Brussels (tel: 206-3511; fax: 203-1812; e-mail: info@obcebdbh.be).

Belgian Institute of Standardisation, 29 Avenue de la Brabançonne, 1000 Brussels (tel: 738-0111; fax: 733-4264; e-mail: info@ibn.be).

British Embassy, 85 Rue d'Arlon, 1040 Brussels (tel: 287-6211; fax: 287-6360; e-mail: info@britain.be).

Brussels Regional Development Agency, 6 Rue Gabrielle Petit, 1080 Brussels (tel: 422-5111; fax: 422-5112; info@sdrb.irisnet.be).

Ducroire/Delcredere (export credit agency), 40 Square de Meêus, 1000 Brussels (tel: 509-4211; fax: 513-5059; e-mail: ducroire@ondd.be).

Euler-Cobac (credit insurance), 15 Rue Montoyer, 1000 Brussels (tel: 289-311; fax: 289-329).

Federation of Belgian Companies (VBO-FEB), 4 Rue Ravenstein, 1000 Brussels (tel: 515-0811; fax: 515-0999; e-mail: info@vbo-feb.be).

Flemish Economic Alliance (VEV), 5 Brouwersvliet, 2000 Antwerp (tel: 202-4400; fax: 233-7660; e-mail: vev@vev.be).

Flemish Foreign Trade Board, 40 Boulevard du Régent, 1000 Brussels (tel: 504-8711; fax: 504-8899; e-mail: info@export.vlaanderen.be).

Investment Company for Flanders (GIMV), 37 Karel Oomsstraat, 2018 Antwerp (tel:290-2100; fax: 290-2105; e-mail: receptie@gimv.be).

National Institute of Statistics, 44/46 Rue de Louvain, 1000 Brussels (tel: 548-6365; fax: 548-6367; e-mail: info@statbel.mineco.fgov.be).

US Embassy, 27 Boulevard du Régent, 1000 Brussels (tel: 508-2111; fax: 511-2725; e-mail: ic@usinfo.be).

Walloon Business Union (UWE), 1-3 Chemin du Stockoy, 1300 Wavre (tel: 471-940; fax: 453-343; e-mail: info@uwe.be).

Walloon Export Agency (AWEX), 2 Place Sainctelette, 1080 Brussels (tel: 421-8211; fax: 421-8787; e-mail: mail@awex.wallonie.be).

Other news agencies: Belga News Agency: www.belga.be

Flandersnews (VRT news): www.deredactie.be

Internet sites

Belgium companies: www.belgium.com/business/tradecontact.php

Belgium Federal Information Service: www.belgium.fgov.be/

Belgium Foreign Trade Board: www.obcebdbh.be

Belgium White Pages: www.infobel.be

Europa (Gateway site): http://europa.eu.int

Export services: http://exportservices.be

Travel information: www.visitbelgium.com

Railway information: www.b-rail.be

Statistics: www.statbel.fgov.be

Le Soir (newspaper): www.lesoir.be

La Poste (newspaper) www.brusselspost.com

Government of Flanders: www.flanders.be

Government of Wallonia: www.wallonie.com

Hotels and restaurants: www.brussels-online.com

Belize

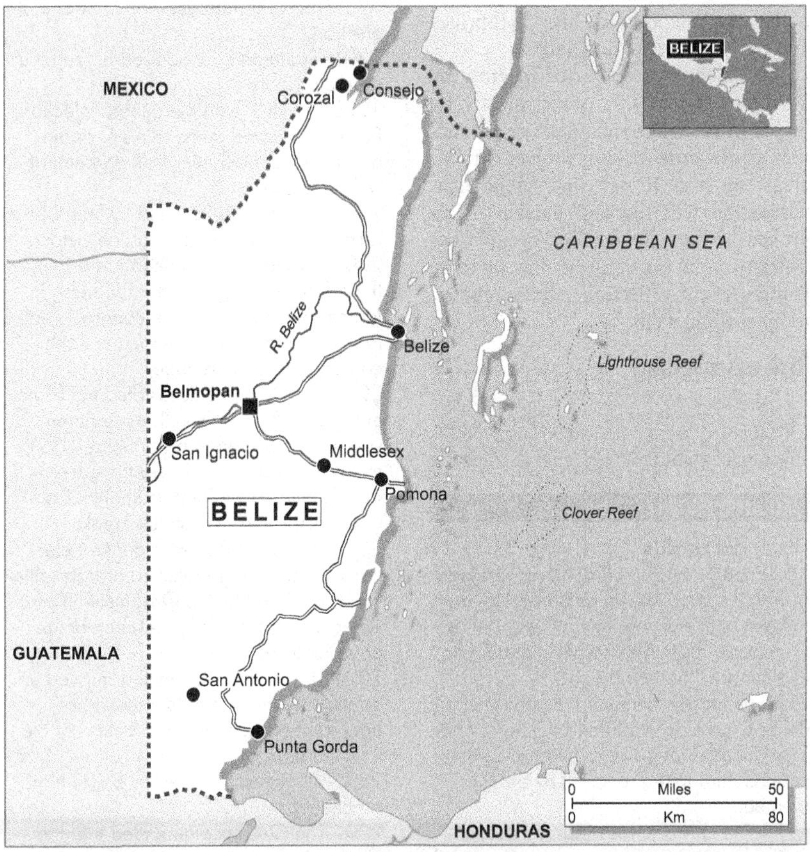

The Belizean economy did well in 2010, recovering to grow by 2.9 per cent, from zero growth in 2009. In the Caribbean Community (Caricom) only Suriname (4.4 per cent) and Guyana (3.6 per cent) did better. According to the United Nations Economic Commission for Latin America and the Caribbean (ECLAC) the economy was bolstered by a sharp rise in electricity generation and stronger growth in transport, communication and distributive trade. Tourism demand also improved owing to the recovery in major markets. Despite the upturn in activity, inflation remained flat (0 per cent) and higher employment was expected in recovering sectors. Notwithstanding the challenges presented by high debt levels and rising interest costs, the fiscal situation improved in 2010. Monetary policy sought to stimulate commercial bank lending to the private sector in order to facilitate the economic recovery. Meanwhile, robust growth in exports, combined with a modest rise in imports, led to a narrowing of the current account deficit by more than 50 per cent as a percentage of GDP.

The economy is expected to continue to expand in 2011 with growth of 2.5 per cent, driven by electricity, tourism and sugar production. Inflation is expected to rise to 2.0 per cent, led by higher fuel and other commodity prices, and employment is expected to show a modest improvement. The fiscal deficit is projected to contract marginally to 1.3 per cent of GDP, owing to flat growth in spending and a modest increase in revenue. A fall in service payments due to the downsizing of British military operations in Belize and reduced net exports of goods will contribute to a larger current account deficit.

KEY FACTS

Official name: Belize

Head of State: Queen Elizabeth II (since 1952); Governor General Sir Colville Norbert Young (since 1993)

Head of government: Prime Minister Dean Oliver Barrow (UDP) (from Feb 2008)

Ruling party: United Democratic Party (UDP) (from Feb 2008)

Area: 22,965 square km

Population: 312,000 (2010)*

Capital: Belmopan

Official language: English

Currency: Belize dollar (Bz$) = 100 cents

Exchange rate: Bz$1.99 per US$ (Oct 2011)

GDP per capita: US$4,159 (2010)

GDP real growth: 2.00% (2010)

GDP: US$1.40 billion (2010)

Labour force: 125,000 (2008)

Unemployment: 8.20% (2008)

Inflation: 0.50% (2010)

Balance of trade: -US$171.50 million (2010)

* estimated figure

Economic growth

ECLAC reports that growth has come from a substantial increase in electricity generation, owing to the full operation of the Vaca Dam and the bagasse plant belonging to Belize Cogeneration Energy Limited (Belcogen). Agriculture recovered marginally from the decline in 2009. Sugarcane deliveries expanded by 22.3 per cent to 1,122,765 long tons due partly to an extended crop season. Papaya output rose sharply thanks to higher yields, while output of most of the other major crops including citrus and bananas diminished.

After solid growth in 2009, manufacturing declined by 4.7 per cent in 2010. Despite the addition of a new well, low productivity from existing wells led to a 5.9 per cent decline in petroleum with annual production at 1.51 million barrels. Sugar production was also lower because the cane/sugar ratio worsened from 9.93 in 2009 to 12.73 in 2010, owing to the continuation of harvesting into the rainy season. Similarly, citrus juice output contracted due to lower deliveries and a lower yield of juice per box of fruit.

The services sector, including tourism and distribution, turned around from the decline of 2009 to grow by 3.7 per cent. Tourism recovered to grow by 5.5 per cent amid the growing recovery in major markets. The high-spending stay-over arrivals were up by 2.2 per cent to 222,632, while cruise passenger arrivals rose by 8.4 per cent. Net tourism receipts were up by 5.7 per cent to stand at US$228 million, reflecting an increase in visitor arrivals. Activity in wholesale and retail trade, transport and communications, and government services were up, buoyed by the recovery in tourism. Employment was expected to have picked up in the more dynamic sectors in 2010, including tourism and wholesale and retail trade. Inflation is expected to increase to 1.5 per cent in 2011, propelled by the continued high fuel prices and rising domestic demand.

The economy is projected to grow by 2.5 per cent in 2011, driven mostly by higher citrus, sugar and papaya production. Citrus production is projected to increase by over 10 per cent, while sugar production will rebound thanks to improved productivity. On the downside, petroleum output is forecast to drop by more than 3 per cent, reflecting reduced productivity at aging wells.

Risk assessment

Economy	Fair
Politics	Fair
Regional stability	Good

COUNTRY PROFILE

Historical profile

1802 Spain recognised British sovereignty of what became known as British Honduras, but after gaining their independence from Spain, both Mexico and Guatemala laid claim to the territory.

1970 Belmopan became the captial after Belize City was devastated by a hurricane.

1971 British Honduras joined the Caribbean Community (Caricom) as a full member.

1973 The territory was renamed Belize.

1981 Belize attained independence from the UK. However Guatemala refused to recognise Belize, citing its own territorial claims. British troops were stationed in Belize to protect it.

1984 After 30 years in power, the People's United Party (PUP) was defeated by the United Democratic Party (UDP). Manuel Esquivel became prime minister.

1989 The PUP narrowly won the general election.

1991 Guatemala recognised Belize as a sovereign state.

1993 The UDP won the general election; Esquivel became prime minister again and rejected the earlier PUP agreement with Guatemala.

1998 In elections, PUP, led by Said Musa, defeated the UDP in a landslide victory.

2000 The government began reforming the offshore banking sector following international criticism of the country's reputation as a tax haven. Hurricane Keith caused extensive damage.

2001 Hurricane Iris devastated the southern part of Belize. The UK government suspended its plan to grant Belize US$14 million of debt relief due to the government's failure to reform its financial services sector and abolish tax breaks.

2003 The ruling PUP won general elections. A referendum rejected a draft settlement, brokered by the Organisation of American States (OAS), between Belize and Guatemala

2004 The UK Privy Council dismissed an appeal by environmental protestors against the proposed construction of the Chalillo dam.

2005 Oil was discovered by Belize Natural Energy.

2007 The OAS recommended that the border dispute with Guatemala should be referred to the International Court of Justice.

2008 A new political party, the National Reform Party (NRP), was formed, led by Cornelius Dueck, a businessman from the Mennonite community. The number of deputies in the House of Representatives was increased to 31. In parliamentary elections, the UDP opposition won a landslide victory with 25 seats (out of 31), the ruling PUP won 6. Dean Barrow (UDP) became prime minister.

2009 Unesco added the Belize Barrier Reef Reserve System (the northern hemisphere's largest coral reef) to its list of endangered heritage sites. Unesco requested more action to limit human development and the loss of mangroves. Belize Telemedia Ltd was nationalised.

2010 Belize abolished the legal link with the UK's Review Committee of the Privy Council (RCPC) on 1 June. At the same time Belize endorsed the Caribbean Court of Justice as its supreme court. However

KEY INDICATORS — Belize

	Unit	2006	2007	2008	2009	2010
Population	m	0.30	0.31	0.32	*0.33	*0.31
Gross domestic product (GDP)	US$bn	1.21	1.27	1.38	1.34	1.40
GDP per capita	US$	4,028	4,098	4,310	4,045	4,159
GDP real growth	%	5.6	2.2	3.0	-1.1	2.0
Inflation	%	4.3	3.0	6.4	2.0	0.5
Unemployment	%	8.2	7.5	8.2	13.1	–
Exports (fob) (goods)	US$m	427.0	428.5	464.7	381.9	475.7
Imports (fob) (goods)	US$m	611.9	642.0	788.1	620.5	647.2
Balance of trade	US$m	-184.8	-213.5	-323.4	-238.7	-171.5
Current account	US$m	-27.0	-51.0	-158.0	-94.2	-45.7
Total reserves minus gold	US$m	113.7	108.5	166.2	213.7	218.0
Foreign exchange	US$m	104.4	98.4	156.1	175.4	180.5
Exchange rate	per US$	1.97	1.97	1.97	1.95	2.00

* estimated figure

the RCPC continued to adjudicate on legal matters referred to it the Belize courts. 2011 On 20 April the government signed two loan contracts with the American Development Bank (IDB), each for US$5 million, to finance the Integrated Water and Sanitation Programme and the Community Action for Public Safety (Caps), which will target youth involvement in major violent crimes in Belize City and violent behaviour in schools. On 24 June the Court of Appeal ruled that the nationalisation of Belize Telemedia was unconstitutional and the government moved to take it back into public ownership.

Political structure

Constitution

The governor general is advised by the cabinet (led by the prime minister) which holds executive power.

Form of state

Independent state with the British monarch as head of state, represented by the governor general.

The executive

The cabinet, led by the prime minister, holds executive power.

National legislature

The bicameral National Assembly consists of the House of Representatives (lower chamber), with 31 members elected by universal adult suffrage for a five-year term in single-seat constituencies. The Senate (upper chamber) currently has 11 members appointed by the governor general, of which seven were nominated by the prime minister, three by the opposition leader and one each from the Council of Churches, Chamber of Commerce and National Trade Union Congress; each to serve for a five-year term.

Last elections

7 February 2008 (parliamentary)

Results: Parliamentary: the PUP won 6 seats (out of 31), the UDP won 25 seats.

Next elections

March 2013 (parliamentary)

Political parties

Ruling party

United Democratic Party (UDP) (from Feb 2008)

Main opposition party

People's United Party (PUP)

Political situation

The government of Dean Barrow (UDP) has been trying to recover the loss of Bz$33.5 million (US$20 million) given in a promissory note by the previous administration of Said Musa (PUP) to the Belize Bank, in March 2007. The promissory note contravened laws that required any loan agreement over Bz$10 million to be sanctioned by parliament, which this note had not. In August 2008 the Central Bank required the Belize Bank to provide documentation for the authority to deposit US$10 million into the account of Universal Investment Holding (UIH) and to repay the two tranches of US$10 million, which had originally been donated to Belize by Venezuela and Taiwan for aid purposes. The Belize Bank complied and repaid US$10 million but the remaining amount was sequestered until the ruling of the High Court as to the validity of the transaction, which in May 2009 found in favour of the government, which awaits the return of the last tranche.

Population

312,000 (2010)*

Last census: May 2000: 240,204

Population density: 11 inhabitants per square km. Urban population: 48 per cent (1995–2001).

Annual growth rate: 2.4 per cent 1994–2004 (WHO 2006)

Ethnic make-up

Mestizos (44 per cent), Creoles (30 per cent), Mayans (15 per cent), Garifunas (7 per cent), Mennonites (3 per cent). Other races: Spanish, British, Lebanese, Chinese and Eastern Indian.

Religions

Roman Catholic (62 per cent), Anglican (12 per cent), Methodist (6 per cent), Mennonite (4 per cent), Seventh-Day Adventist (3 per cent).

Education

About 22.35 per cent of the budget expenditure in 2002/03 was allocated to the education sector, of which a total of Bz$61 million (US$31 million) and Bz$16 million (US$8.1 million) were budgeted for salaries and education grants respectively. Since 1998, dozens of new school buildings have been constructed, with more than 700 new classrooms catering for additional 3,000 students. The government contributes some Bz$20 million (US$10.1 million) towards higher education student loans for the University of Belize.

Literacy rate: 77 per cent adult rate; 84 per cent youth rate (15–24) (Unesco 2005).

Enrolment rate: 123 per cent for boys, 119 per cent for girls; total primary school enrolment of the relevant age group (including repetition rates) (World Bank).

Health

The ministry of health plans to implement the National Health Insurance as part of its overall health sector reform programme, with Bz$4 million (US$2 million) from the Social Security Fund.

HIV/Aids

HIV prevalence: 2.5 per cent aged 15–49 in 2003 (World Bank)

Life expectancy: 68 years, 2004 (WHO 2006)

Fertility rate/Maternal mortality rate: 3.1 births per woman, 2004 (WHO 2006)

Child (under 5 years) mortality rate (per 1,000): 33 per 1,000 live births (World Bank)

Welfare

As part of its poverty alleviation strategy, the Social Investment Fund (SIF) has sought assistance from the World Bank to spend some Bz$10.5 million (US$5.2 million) in water supply, sanitation, health, education and social services projects. Seven per cent of a worker's weekly earning is paid into the social security fund; a ratio is determined and divided between the employer and employee. Benefits include maternity, sickness, injury and dependant's grants.

Pensions

Old age pensions are paid to those aged between 60 and 65 who have made at least 130 contributions.

Main cities

Belmopan (capital, estimated population 10,277 in 2005), Belize City (51,535), Cayo (16,246), Orange Walk (14,964), San Ignacio (16,246), Dangriga (9,497).

Languages spoken

Spanish, Creole, Garifuna and Mayan dialects are widely spoken throughout the country.

Official language/s

English

Media

Press

Weeklies: There are no daily newspaper, the most widely read weeklies include *Amandala* (www.amandala.com.bz), and *The Reporter* (www.reporter.bz), *The San Pedro Sun* (www.sanpedrosun.net) is a community newspaper published on the island of Ambergris Caye. *The Belize Times* (www.belizetimes.bz) is the newspaper that speaks for the political party People's United Party and *The Guardian* (www.guardian.bz) for the United Democratic Party.

Broadcasting

Radio: There are around 10 radio stations, all of which are private and commercial. Most broadcast either music, religious or news contents, including People's Radio, (www.belizeweb.com), see news & entertainment, also includes Integrity Radio and Positive Vibes Radio. Others stations are Love FM, (www.lovefm.com) Krem FM (www.krembz.com) and Wave Radio (http://waveradiobelize.org).

Television: All TV stations are commercial. The privately-owned, Channel 5 (www.channel5belize.com) is the leading TV channel and, along with Channel 7 (www.7newsbelize.com) and Channel 9, is a terrestrial broadcaster. Centaur Cable Network, called CTV3 (www.ctv3belizenews.com) provides a subscriber cable services, with over 60 channels, to the region of Orange Walk in the north of the country.

News agencies

Other news agencies: Caribbean Net News: www.caribbeannetnews.com

Economy

The economy of Belize has more in common with the nearby Caribbean region than its Central American neighbours. A small enterprise economy, in the past it was dominated by the agricultural sector but by 2008 this contributed only 12 per cent of GDP. The service sector, which is dominated by tourism, accounts for 65 per cent of GDP, attributable to the rapidly expanding cruise sector and the growth in ecotourism. The industrial sector constitutes 23 per cent of GDP, despite the limitations of a small domestic market and relatively high labour costs (for the region). A number of US companies have out-sourced their operations to Belize, including petroleum, construction and garment manufacturing.

GDP growth was 3.8 per cent in 2008, which fell to 0.0 per cent in 2009 in the face the falling tourist numbers as the global economic crisis impacted on the countries of visitors. While revenues fell there was a corresponding increase in import commodity prices.

Belize's financial services attract foreign investors, along with onshore and offshore trust funds, Sharia compliant investment and company registration.

Damage from natural disasters has dogged the region. Belize was devastated by hurricanes in 2007 and heavy flooding in 2008, leaving the population to rebuild their lives and livelihoods. Remittances in 2009 were US$80 million (5.7 per cent of GDP), and was estimated to be US$88 million in 2010.

External trade

As a member of the Caribbean Community (Caricom) and Common Market, Belize operates within the Caricom Single Market and Economy (CSME), which became operational on 2006. Goods, services, businesses and money are free to move within CSME countries without barriers and tariffs.

Belize relies on imports of fuel and goods and services largely centred on tourism, clothing manufacture and food processing.

Imports

Main imports are machinery and transport equipment, food, beverages, tobacco, manufactured goods, fuels, chemicals and pharmaceuticals.

Main sources: US (typically 34 per cent of total), former-Netherlands Antilles (12 per cent), Mexico (9 per cent).

Exports

Principal exports are sugar, bananas, citrus, garments, fish and cultured shrimp, molasses and timber.

Main destinations: US (typically 45 per cent of total), UK (20 per cent), Costa Rica (17 per cent).

Agriculture

Farming

The agricultural sector forms the mainstay of the economy contributing approximately 20 per cent of total GDP and employing 25 per cent of the workforce. The sector accounts for about 65 per cent of foreign exchange earnings and the banana industry is the country's largest employer. Approximately 65 per cent of the country's land mass is considered to have arable potential but only 2 per cent is used for farming; 45 per cent of the total land mass is forest, much of which is commercially exploitable.

Sugar is the main cash crop though Belize has diversified into exporting other crops, particularly banana and citrus production (mainly oranges), and fisheries. Winter vegetables, papayas, mangoes and cocoa are also grown for export, while rice, maize, roots, beans and vegetables are produced for livestock consumption.

Hurricane Dean, which struck in 2007, destroyed the entire export crop of papaya, valued at over US$20 million and caused around US$1.2 million in damages to the sugar crop.

Fishing

Fishing, mainly for lobsters, conch and shrimp, contributes significantly to the economy.

Forestry

Forestry has played an integral role in the economy of Belize but the rise of the tourism industry has reduced its importance. Over half of the country's land mass is covered by forests, though the majority of this area has now been logged. Of the timber cut, the majority is sold in local markets including that of mahogany, soft pine, cedar, santa maria and yemeri. In recent years there have also been an increased harvesting of chicle (a latex gum of the sapodilla tree), throughout the country.

Industry and manufacturing

Centered on agricultural processing such as sugar-milling, citrus-processing and the processing of domestic foodstuffs, the industrial sector is small-scale. Garment manufacturing previously played a prominent role in the economy of Belize but has decreased in significance since the 1990s. In all, manufacturing contributes approximately one fifth of GDP (including a manufacturing contribution of 12.6 per cent). Manufacturing employs about 10 per cent of the workforce and construction employs 6 per cent.

Tourism

Belize is home to the largest coral reef in the northern hemisphere, designated as a Unesco world heritage site. Its atolls and lagoons are a popular destination for marine tourism. The mainland offers ancient Mayan temples and other archaeological sites, rainforests with diverse flora and fauna and a native culture to attract visitors.

The industry has been vital to the economy since the mid-1990s when, for the first time, tourism constituted over 20 per cent of GDP; since then it has steadily assumed a greater role, so that by 2010 it constituted 33.6 per cent of GDP. Nevertheless, this represents a fall from the record high of 37.5 per cent in 2007, before the global economic crisis cut the number of visitors. Employment in the industry was likewise cut from 34.1 per cent in 2007 to 30.9 per cent in 2010. However, in 2011 there was growth in both GDP growth and employment.

Around 250,000 tourists visit each year, either overland from other Central American countries, by air or via cruise liners, of which six major operators schedule some 19 liners to visit Belize City, mainly during the tourist season of November–June.

Environment

Scientists warned that the proposed Chalillo hydro project, which involves building a 50-metre high dam in the rainforest, would destroy rare habitat for jaguar, tapir and a sub-species of scarlet macaw. The Belize Supreme Court halted construction in 2002. However, in 2004, the Privy Council in London, ruled that work on the controversial Chalillo Dam could proceed.

Mining

Belize has insignificant mineral deposits. During the 1980s extensive drilling was undertaken in the country in a vain attempt to discover oil. Nowadays, mining mainly involves surface removal of gravel for use in the construction industry. Approximately 0.4 per cent of the workforce is employed in the mining and quarrying sector.

Hydrocarbons

Although there were oil reserves of 7 million barrels in 2008 they are not commercially viable. Consumption of oil was 7,000 barrels per day (bpd) in 2008, all of which was imported. In 2005, Belize, plus a number of other Caribbean states, signed an agreement with Venezuela to establish PetroCaribe, a multi-national oil company owned by the participating states. PetroCaribe buys low-priced Venezuelan crude oil under long-term payment plans.

Any use of natural gas or coal is commercially insignificant.

Energy

Total installed generating capacity was 81MW in 2007, producing over 210 million kilowatt hours. The privately owned Belize Electricity Limited (BEL) is the primary provider of electricity, distributing and selling electricity. It buys electricity from the Belize Electric Company Limited (Becol), which operates the Mollejon Hydroelectric facility in western Belize and the new 7MW Chalillo dam that became operational in 2006, and from Hydro Maya Limited in southern Belize. It also purchases electricity from Mexico.

The national power grid is connected to that of Mexico allowing transfer of energy during periods of maximum loads.

Banking and insurance

Belize's banking sector is small, but contains both an offshore and onshore sector. The offshore sector is undergoing continued expansion owing to generous tax schemes and there are now eight banks, one insurance house and more than 22,000 international business companies. The International Financial Services Commission acts as the regulator of the offshore sector.

The onshore sector is composed of five domestic commercial banks, seven international banks and three quasi-governmental institutions, with credit unions also being prominent. Belize Banking Ltd retains a dominant market position with 45 per cent of domestic banks' assets. The Central Bank of Belize supervises banking activity and the Register of Co-operatives is the Credit union regulator.

The country's insurance sector is also small with 17 firms competing in the market; six insurance houses, nine general companies and three composites. At present there are no reinsurance firms in Belize.

Central bank

Central Bank of Belize

Main financial centre

Belize City

Offshore facilities

Belize has an important offshore banking sector.

Time

GMT minus six hours

Geography

Belize lies on the Caribbean coast of Central America, with Mexico to the north-east and Guatemala to the south-west.

In the north the coastal area is low with fresh and sea water lagoons as well as swamps and mangroves. In the south, east and west the Maya mountain range, the Cockscomb range and the Mountain Pine Ridge, respectively, occupy around 40 per cent of the land and are dense rain forests. Close to the Guatemala border the land is relatively open. Belize possesses many small islands (Cayes) that straddle a coral reef which is the world's second largest, after the Great Barrier Reef in Australia.

Hemisphere

Northern

Climate

Sub-tropical with temperatures ranging from 10–30 degrees Celsius. Hottest months between March–September and rainy season June–October.

Entry requirements

Passports

Required by all and validity must be for at least six months longer than the intended period of stay.

Visa

Required by all, except north American, most European and Australasian citizens. For further exemptions contact the local embassy.

For a copy of the visa application visit www.un.int/belize/visappli.pdf.

All visitors should show that they have sufficient funds for the purpose and period of their stay and must be in possession of a valid return or onward ticket. Evidence in support of both funds and travel arrangements must be presented with applications for visas. Visitors are permitted to stay in Belize for up to 30 days.

Currency advice/regulations

A currency declaration form must be completed on arrival. Visitors are advised to keep a copy of the declaration form because travellers are not permitted to export more than this amount of currency.

Health (for visitors)

Mandatory precautions

Yellow fever vaccination certificate if travelling from infected area.

Advisable precautions

Typhoid, polio and rabies vaccinations. Malaria prophylaxis advisable. Water precautions should be taken.

Hotels

There are a good range of hotels. There are three charges likely to be levied locally: 8 per cent sales tax, 9 per cent hotel tax and a service charge of up to 10 per cent.

Public holidays (national)

Fixed dates

1 Jan (New Year's Day), 9 Mar (Baron Bliss Day), 1 May (Labour Day), 24 May (Commonwealth Day), 10 Sep (St George's Caye Day), 21 Sep (Independence Day), 12 Oct (Columbus Day), 19 Nov (Garifuna Settlement Day), 25–26 Dec (Christmas Holiday).

Variable dates

Good Friday, Easter Monday

Working hours

Banking

Mon–Thu: 0800–1300; Fri: 0800–1300 and 1500–1800.

Business

Mon–Fri: 0800–1200, 1300–1700. Some businesses are open on Saturday.

Government

Mon–Fri: 0800–1200, 1300–1700; closes 1630 on Fridays.

Telecommunications

Mobile/cell phones

A GSM 1900 service operates around the capital, and north and south along the coastline.

Electricity supply

110/220/V AC, 60Hz, with US style two-pin plugs.

Getting there

Air

Intercontinental flights usually arrive via the US, other international flights are regional.

International airport/s: PSW Goldson International (BZE), 16km west of Belize City; duty-free shops, bar. Taxis to the city

Airport tax: Departure tax US$36.25, payable in cash or travellers cheques only – credit cards are not accepted.

Surface

Road: Main routes are from Melchor de Mencos (Guatemala) and Chetumal (Mexico).

Main port/s: Belize City.

Getting about

National transport

Air: Maya Airways and Tropic Air operate domestic services to main centres. The charter flight company AeroBelize flies to minor airfields.

Road: Over 1,500km of surfaced road linking the eight major towns and cities, the network in the north is in better repair than south of Belize city. Occasionally during torrential downpours all-weather roads may be flooded, especially close to ferry crossings.

A new all-weather road to Charcoal, the largest and most important archaeological site in Belize, was completed in 2004 at a cost of around US$2.5 million.

Buses: Services operate within Belize City; long-distance coach services link major centres.

Water: Regular ferry services and small boats ply to offshore cayes.

City transport

Taxis: Taxis are available in towns and resort areas, and at the airport. They are easily recognised by their green licence plates.

Fixed rates apply within Belize City (higher at night). With no meters it is advisable to agree the fare beforehand. Tipping is discretionary.

Car hire

Foreign or international licences are acceptable for 30 days. Driver must be over 18 years old. Driving on the right.

BUSINESS DIRECTORY

The addresses listed below are a selection only. While World of Information makes every endeavour to check these addresses, we cannot guarantee that changes have not been made, especially to telephone numbers and area codes. We would welcome any corrections.

Telephone area codes

The international dialling code (IDD) for Belize is +501 followed by the area code and subscriber's number:

Belize City	2	Dangriga	5
Belmopan	8	Independence	6
Corozal	4	San Ignacio	92

Useful telephone numbers

Directory enquiries: 113.

Local and regional operator-assisted calls: 114.

International operator-assisted calls: 115.

Fire and ambulance: 90.

Police: 911.

Chambers of Commerce

Belize Chamber of Commerce and Industry, 63 Regent Street, PO Box 291, Belize City (tel: 227-3148; fax: 227-4984; e-mail: bcci@btl.net).

Banking

Alliance Bank of Belize Ltd, PO Box 1988, 18 Cnr New Road & Hydes Lane, Belize City (tel: 236-783, 236-784; fax: 236-785).

Atlantic Bank Ltd, PO Box 481, Cnr Cleghorn & Freetown Road, Belize City (tel: 234-123, 277-124; fax: 233-907, 234-150).

Atlantic International Bank Ltd, PO Box 481, Cnr Freetown Road & Cleghorn Streets, Belize City (tel: 230-681; fax: 230-677).

Banca Serfin of Mexico, PO Box 1636, Cnr Eyre & Hudson Streets, Belize City (tel: 027-8179, 027-8225; fax: 027-8970).

Bank of Nova Scotia, PO Box 708, Albert Street, Belize City (tel: 027-7027/030/415/416; fax: 027-7416).

Barclays Bank PLC, PO Box 363, Albert Street, Belize City (tel: 027-7211; fax: 027-8572).

Belize Bank Ltd, PO Box 364, 60 Market Square, Belize City (tel: 277-132, 272-390; fax: 272-712, 274-519).

Development Finance Corporation, PO Box 40, Bliss Parade, Belmopan, Cayo District (tel: 082-2360, 082-2350; fax: 082-3096).

National Development Foundation of Belize, PO Box 1210, 109 Cemetery Road, Belize City (tel: 027-2139, 027-2874; fax: 027-8437).

Provident Bank & Trust of Belize Limited, PO Box 1867, 1st Floor, 35 Barrack Road, Belize City (tel: 235-698; fax: 230-368).

Central bank

Central Bank of Belize, Gabourel Lane, PO Box 852, Belize City (tel: 223-6194; fax: 223-6226; e-mail: info@centralbank.org.bz).

Travel information

AeroBelize (air charter), PSW Goldson International Airport, Ladyville (tel: 252-535).

Belize Airport Authority, PSW Goldson International Airport, Ladyville (tel: 252-045; fax: 252-439).

Belize Port Authority, Caesar Ridge Road, Belize City (tel: 272-439; fax: 273-571).

Belize Tourism Industry Association (BTIA), 99 Albert Street, PO Box 62, Belize City (tel: 275-717; fax: 271-144; e-mail: btia@btl.net).

Maya Airways (administrative office), 6 Fort St, PO Box 458, Belize City (tel: 272-312; fax: 30-585); PSW Goldson International Airport, Ladyville (tel: 252-336).

Ministry of tourism

Ministry of Tourism, 14 Constitution Drive, Belmopan (tel: 223-394; fax: 222-862).

National tourist organisation offices

Belize Tourism Board, Lower Flat, New Horizon Investment Bld, 3 1–32 Miles Northern Highway, P.O. Box 325, Belize City (tel: 223-1913; fax: 223-1943; email: info@travelbelize.org; internet: www.travelbelize.org).

Ministries

Ministry of Agriculture and Fisheries, West Block, Belmopan (tel: 222-332, 222-241; fax: 222-409).

Ministry of Budget Management, Investment and Trade, Central Bank of Belize Building, Gaol Lane, Belize City (tel: 232-128, 236-194; fax: 235-097; e-mail: chalilio@bti.net).

Ministry of Economic Development, PO Box 42, Belmopan (tel: 222-526, 222-527, 222-023, 222-672; fax: 223-111, 223-673).

Ministry of Education and Public Service, West Block, Belmopan (tel: 222-329, 222-798, 222-067; fax: 223-389, 222-206).

Ministry of Energy, Science, Technology and Transportation, Belmopan (tel: 222-435; fax: 223-317).

Ministry of Finance, Belmopan (tel: 222-169; fax: 2222-886).

Ministry of Foreign Affairs, PO Box 174, Belmopan (tel: 222-322; fax: 222-854).

Ministry of Health and Sports, Belmopan (tel: 222-325; fax: 222-942).

Ministry of Home Affairs and Labour, Belmopan (tel: 222-281; fax: 222-016).

Ministry of Housing, Urban Development and Co-operatives, Belmopan (tel: 223-339; fax: 223-298).

Ministry of Human Resources, Community and Youth Development, Culture and Women's Affairs, Belmopan (tel: 222-161; fax: 223-175).

Ministry of National Security, Belmopan (tel: 222-225; fax: 222-615).

Ministry of Natural Resources, Belmopan (tel: 222-331, 222-249; fax: 222-333).

Ministry of Statistics, Central Statistical Office, Belmopan (tel: 222-207; fax: 223-206).

Ministry of Tourism and The Environment, Belmopan (tel: 223-394; fax: 222-862).

Ministry of Trade and Industry, Belmopan (tel: 222-199; fax: 222-329).

Ministry of Works, Belmopan (tel: 222-139; fax: 223-282).

Other useful addresses

Association of National Development Agencies (ANDA), Princess Margaret Drive, Belize City (tel: 35-115; fax: 32-362).

Attorney General's Ministry, Belmopan (tel: 222-504; fax: 223-390).

Belize Electricity Board, 115 Barrack Road, Belize City (tel: 277-141; fax: 231-905).

Belize Embassy (USA), 2535 Massachusetts Avenue, NW, Washington DC 20008 (tel: 202-332-9636; fax: 202-332-6888).

Belize Export and Investment Promotion Unit (BEIPU), PO Box 291, 63 Regent Street, Belize City (tel: 273-148, 274-394, 275-108/9; fax: 274-984).

Belize Information Service, P.O. Box 60, Belmopan (tel: 222-019; fax: 223-242).

Belize Marketing Board, 117 North Front Street, PO Box 479, Belize City (tel: 272-439; fax: 273-571).

Belize Port Authority (tel: 272-439; fax: 273-571; e-mail: portbze@btl.net).

Belize Offshore Centre (tel: 234-351; fax: 233-501; e-mail: cititrust@btl.net).

Belize Telemedia Ltd. St Thomas Street, PO Box 603, Belize City (tel: 232-868; fax: 277-600; internet site: www.btl.net).

Belize Trade and Investment Development Services (BELTRAIDE) (tel: 223-737; fax: 220-595; e-mail: beltraide@belize.gov.bz).

British High Commission, PO Box 91, Belmopan (tel: 222-146; fax: 222-717).

Central Statistical Office (CSO), Ministry of Finance, Belmopan (tel: 222-207; fax: 222-206).

Citrus Control Board, 87 Commerce Bight, Melinder Road, Dangriga Town (tel: 222-145, 222-447; fax: 222-686).

Customs & Excise, PO Box 146, Fort Street, Belize City (tel: 277-405; fax: 277-091).

Export Processing Zone, Ministry of Trade and Industry, Belmopan (tel: 222-199, 222-153; fax: 222-923).

Fisheries Department, Princess Margaret Drive, Belize City (tel: 244-552, 232-623; fax: 232-983; e-mail: species@btl.net).

Forest Department, Forestry Drive, Belmopan (tel: 223-629; fax: 222-083).

Geology and Petroleum Office, Unity Boulevard, Belmopan (tel: 222-178, 222-651; fax: 223-538).

National Development Foundation of Belize, 2882 Coney Drive Coral Grove, Belize City (tel: 231-207, 231-132; fax: 231-195).

Society for the Promotion of Education & Research (SPEAR), Corner Pickstock and New Road, PO Box 1766, Belize City (tel: 231-668; fax: 232-367).

Water and Sewerage Authority, Central American Boulevard, Belize City (tel: 224-757; fax: 224-759).

Internet sites

Belize hotels website: www.belizehotels.com/

Belize yellow pages: www.ipl.com.gt/cgi-bin/busca-beling

Inter-American Development Bank: www.iadb.org

Latin American Network Information Center: www.lanic.utexas.edu

Benin

KEY FACTS

Official name: République du Bénin (Republic of Benin)

Head of State: President Boni Yayi (from 2006: re-elcted 13 Mar 2011)

Head of government: Prime Minister Pascal Koupaki (from 28 May 2011)

Ruling party: Forces Cauri pour un Bénin Emergent (FCBE) (Cauri Forces for an Emerging Benin) (elected 2007; re-elected 30 Apr 2011)

Area: 112,622 square km

Population: 8.85 million (2010; census figure)

Capital: Cotonou (seat of government); Porto-Novo (administrative)

Official language: French

Currency: CFA franc (CFAf) = 100 centimes (Communauté Financière Africaine (African Financial Community) franc).

Exchange rate: CFAf488.90 per US$ (Oct 2011)

GDP per capita: US$711 (2009)*

GDP real growth: 2.70% (2009)*

GDP: US$6.67 billion (2009)

Labour force: 3.66 million (2007)*

Inflation: 1.90% (2007)*

Balance of trade: -US$607.50 million (2008)

* estimated figure

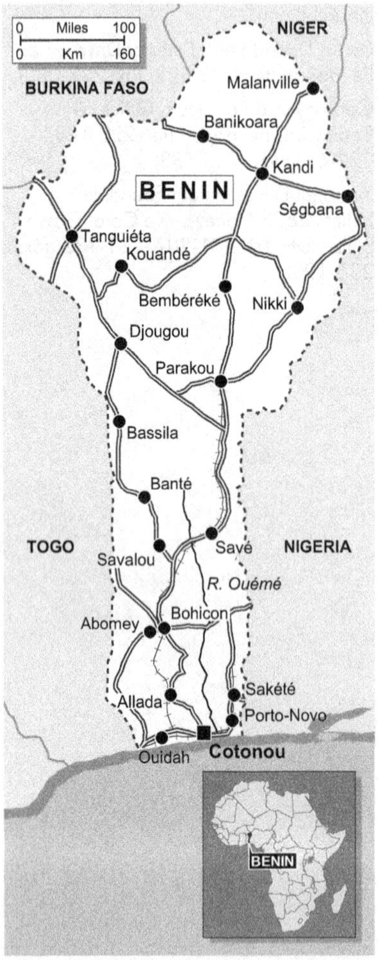

Benin has been in the vanguard of democracy in Africa since 1990 when it organised the first national conference that led to the emergence of a multi-party participatory democracy. Since then there have been five legislative elections, four presidential elections and two local consultations. At the head of the state, there have been three changes of regime. There have also been changeovers in parliament – although the April 2011 elections were won by the Forces Cauri pour un Bénin Emergent (FCBE) (Cauri Forces for an Emerging Benin), who increased their number of seats by six to a total of 41 (out of 83). Incumbent President Boni Yayi had earlier in the year won the presidential election. Freedom of the press is recognised and exercised and Benin's civil society has proven to be quite dynamic.

Since 2009, however, there has been a power struggle between the government and the parliament, which resulted in 2010 in the latter refusing to ratify international agreements. In December 2009, parliament had set the tone by rejecting the finance bill, judging it to be unrealistic, as was later confirmed by the drastic cuts that marked implementation of the budget. The government was forced to legislate by decree, as it had previously done to pass the supplementary budget in October 2008.

The economy

Benin's economy is characterised by a labour market dominated by the informal sector which involves about 95 per cent of the working population and plays a major role in income generation, reports the *African Economic Outlook 2010* (AEO), published jointly by the African Development Bank and the Organisation for Economic Co-operation and Development. In 2010, activity had been slowed down by low agricultural and cotton production, reduced public investment and floods. An estimated 8 per cent of the Beninese population, nearly one-third of which lives off agricultural activities, was directly affected. Growth in gross domestic product (GDP) in 2010, which was initially expected to be around 3 per cent, was in fact 2.1 per cent.

Macro-economic policy is implemented on the basis of agreements related to the Extended Credit Facility concluded with the International Monetary Fund (IMF) in June 2010, which is backed by other development partners in the form of financial and technical support for budget execution. Fiscal policy has been characterised since 2006 by a significant increase in public expenditure. The lethargy observed in the implementation of reforms, however, has prevented tax revenues from following the same upward trend. In the 2007–10 period, tax revenues increased on average by 12 per cent, whereas expenditure increased by nearly

20 per cent, with a peak between 2007 and 2008 due to rises in wages and investment expenditure.

In 2010, the balance of the state's financial operations showed a deficit down from 4.2 per cent in 2009 to 2.6 per cent. Budget execution has been projected to produce an overall deficit of 2.5 per cent in 2011. External accounts currently show a deficit (estimated at 7 per cent of GDP in 2010), due in particular to a low level of grants. The country's current account balance is projected to worsen in 2011 to 8 per cent of GDP, mainly as a result of a deteriorating trade balance and declining net services and public and private transfers, which will continue to suffer from the impact of the international economic crisis.

In 2011, real GDP is projected to grow by 2.5 per cent thanks to continuing major upgrading work, trade with Nigeria and the vigour of the cotton sub-sector. This modest recovery should be reinforced in 2012 as the major public works programme is boosted after the wait-and- see policy observed during the run up to the elections in 2010. Support for economic activity should materialise through completion of the installation and commissioning of the Maria Gleta gas turbine power station and continued modernisation of the Port of Cotonou (extension of the sand trap and construction of new quay berths).

The contribution to growth of the agricultural sector is projected at 0.7 points in 2011 copared to 0.6 points in 2010, supported by a reorganisation of the management of the cotton sub-sector, improvements in cotton-ginning factories and planned investment in 2011–12.

High under-employment

The official unemployment rate as defined by the International Labour Organisation (ILO) oscillates between 1 per cent and 3 per cent, with a significant fall in 2006–07 thanks in particular to the inception of major public works, significant hiring of teachers, and the enrolment of unemployed graduates in military service. Available rates for under-employment, however, show nubers swinging between 30 per cent and 50 per cent of the working population (rates in 2006 and 2007 were 53.2 per cent and 29 per cent, respectively). Growth projections are based on the assumption of a recovery in cotton production, a favourable trend in world cotton prices, a rise in international oil prices to no higher than US$90 per barrel and growth in trade with Nigeria.

Two developments could upset these projections in 2011–12. One is the international context and includes such threats as a higher than expected rise in oil prices, a fall in the price of cotton, poor results from trade with Nigeria as a result of circumstantial tariff-barrier-dismantling measures by the Nigerian government, a fall in used-vehicle re-exports to Nigeria and stricter measures to combat smuggling. The second is related to the domestic situation and national productivity – such as electricity supply problems and the possibility of fresh flooding.

Foreign trade and relations

These past few years, Benin has established new partnerships with emerging countries such as India, Saudi Arabia, Abu Dhabi, Kuwait and China. In all, these new partners contributed CFAf230 billion (US$0.47 billion) to its economy in 2005–10 and, in 2010 alone, 7 per cent of GDP. China is the most important in terms of volume and range of activities covered. It accounts for 76.5 per cent of this aid, followed by Kuwait (9.8 per cent) and Saudi Arabia (8.4 per cent). China assists Benin in infrastructure (roads, construction and health) and agriculture. Abu Dhabi and Saudi Arabia are active mainly in road infrastructure and construction. Kuwait is involved only in road infrastructure and India in the railway modernisation, fire-fighting equipment and agriculture.

The government maintains that Benin has set up a simple and non-binding operational framework for dealing with these partnerships. A request is generally submitted to the funds through which partner countries provide their support, then to their boards of directors. The emerging countries' practices differ from those of traditional partners in several points. They do not always take part in general discussions between the government and its partners. They prefer bilateral co-operation meetings. Their approach seems to be more pragmatic, and they seem eager to place their contribution within a true partnership. Accordingly, they address the investment needs expressed by the country itself, while traditional partners tend to direct their aid to country needs that they themselves have targeted.

Emerging countries have not, however, replaced the traditional partners. They supplement them in areas for which the latter rarely provide aid, such as road infrastructure and other major public works. Through their co-operation with African countries, emerging countries are seeking to increase their influence on the continent. In the sub-region, there is no alternative to their aid as each country has its specific needs. Benin is involved in trade only with China among its new emerging-country partners but it cannot be said that this trade has helped to make it more competitive.

Imports of goods increased by 6.1 per cent in 2010 compared with 9.7 per cent in 2009. This compares with 40 per cent and 10 per cent increases in 2007 and 2008, which reflected the high level of building materials and capital equipment imported as part of the preparations for the Community of Sahel-Saharan States (CEN-SAD) summit. The increase in imports in 2010 was mainly due to purchases of food products, intermediate products, energy products and capital goods. In terms of value, more than one-third of imports were

KEY INDICATORS — **Benin**

	Unit	2006	2007	2008	2009	2010
Population	m	8.63	8.88	*9.13	*9.38	8.85
Gross domestic product (GDP)	US$bn	4.76	5.43	6.72	*6.67	–
GDP per capita	US$	625	692	736	*711	–
GDP real growth	%	3.8	4.6	4.2	*2.7	–
Inflation	%	3.8	3.0	8.0	2.2	–
Exports (fob) (goods)	US$m	735.5	1,046.9	1,282.2	–	–
Imports (fob) (goods)	US$m	1,045.7	1,602.0	1,889.7	–	–
Balance of trade	US$m	-310.3	-555.1	-607.5	–	–
Current account	US$m	-327.3	-653.2	-618.6	*-467.0	–
Total reserves minus gold	US$m	912.2	1,209.2	1,263.4	1,229.8	1,200.1
Foreign exchange	US$m	908.9	1,205.6	1,259.9	1,148.5	1,120.1
Exchange rate	per US$	496.60	454.40	418.59	472.19	495.28

* estimated figure

consumer goods. The relative shares of food products and energy products have fallen from one year to the next but those of capital goods and intermediate products have tended to rise since 2006.

Exports stood at CFAf588.3 billion (US$1.2 billion) in 2010, up 4.6 per cent from 2009. They consisted mainly of agricultural products, principally lint cotton. The share of lint cotton in the total value of exports (including re-exports), which had reached an average of 50 per cent in the mid-2000s, has declined in the past five years due to difficulties in the sub-sector and declining production.

The other key characteristic of Benin's foreign trade is the high level of re-exportats, especially in the informal economy. Benin's primary trading zone for this kind of trade is the Economic Community of West African States (Ecowas), with Nigeria the principal destination. More than 40 per cent of Benin's export products go to Nigeria. The share of imports from Nigeria varies considerably from year to year but stood at 16 per cent in 2009. In informal trade, Nigeria is still the main source country for petroleum products, live animals and food products. Re-export goods are mostly meat and edible offal and vegetable oils. Developments in the import-export trade in goods, combined with a deficit trend in the balance of non-factor services resulting from high freight rate levels on imports, resulted in a deficit in the balance of goods and services estimated at 11.5 per cent of GDP in 2010. This represents a slight improvement over 2009.

Private sector

In 2010, implementation of the main reforms to the private sector continued with, as its ultimate goal, consolidation of the macro-economic framework and acceleration of growth. The government carried on with its reform of the cotton sub-sector by bringing into operation a new management structure and by transferring to a new mixed capital company, Société pour le Développement du Coton (SODECO), all the industrial assets of state-owned company, Société Nationale pour la Promotion Agricole (SONAPRA). Also, in an effort to improve the competitiveness of the Port of Cotonou and the Benin corridor, construction of two new container terminals has been started and a concession agreement signed for the port's main facilities. Work is also continuing to complete installation of a one-stop foreign trade counter at the Port of Cotonou as a means of improving competitiveness and combating fraud.

Similarly, work has started on concession of the former railway company, the Organisation Commune Bénin Niger des Chemins de Fer (OCBN). Reforms in the energy sector are also in progress. Ultimately, the national distribution utility Societe Beninoise d'Electricite et d'Eau (SBEE) is to be split into two distinct entities, a public asset-holding enterprise and a mixed-economy enterprise for the distribution of electricity. In telecommunications, the process of opening up the capital of public sector operator Bénin Télécoms is continuing.

Risk assessment

Economy	Fair
Politics	Fair
Regional stability	Fair

COUNTRY PROFILE

Historical profile

1960 Gained independence from France as the Republic of Dahomey. Hubert Maga, was elected president.

1963 Maga was overthrown by General Christophe Soglo leading a military *coup d'état*.

1965 Soglo declared himself head of state.

1967 A military coup deposed Soglo.

1969 Lieutenant Colonel Paul-Émile de Souza became president.

1970 Elections were scheduled but failed to take place due to irreconcilable differences between politicians of the north and south. Instead, a three-man presidential council was formed, with a two-year rotating presidency for each.

1972 Maga, the first president, was replaced, without incident, by Justin Ahomadegbé. Major Mathieu Kérékou led a *coup d'état;* he installed an 11-man government and declared Dahomey a Marxist-Leninist state.

1975 The Republic of Dahomey was renamed The People's Republic of Benin.

1990 With the country bankrupt and on the brink of social collapse, President Kérékou handed power to a national conference. The government abandoned Marxism-Leninism and committed itself to political and economic reform.

1991 Nicéphore Soglo became president and introduced sweeping austerity measures.

1995 Parties opposed to the president won a majority in the National Assembly in the legislative elections.

1996 Kérékou became president and Adrien Houngbédji, leader of the Parti du Renouveau Démocratique (PRD) (Party of Democratic Renewal), assumed the role of prime minister.

1998 Houngbédji resigned, a new government was formed without a post of prime minister.

1999 After National Assembly elections, the Parti de la Renaissance du Benin (PRB) (Benin Renaissance Party), led by former president Soglo's wife, Rosine, emerged as the largest single opposition party. Adrien Houngbédji (PRD) was elected president of the new Assembly.

2001 President Kérékou was re-elected for his last five-year term.

2002 The first municipal elections were held.

2003 A large coalition of parties backing President Kérékou won the National Assembly elections.

2004 An International Development Association (IDA) credit of US$45 million was approved to assist Benin in expanding electrification and restructuring its power sector. Benin and Nigeria agreed to redefine their mutual border.

2005 The International Court of Justice (ICJ) awarded Niger most of the river islands that had been disputed along the Niger/Benin border.

2006 Boni Yayi won presidential elections. Benin assumed control of nine islands in the Niger River in accordance with the 2005 ICJ ruling settling the border dispute; Niger received the large island of Lete and several others. President Boni's coalition, Forces Cauri pour un Bénin Emergent (FCBE) (Cauri Forces for an Emerging Benin), won parliamentary elections.

2008 Unreliable voter lists delayed local elections; four million registered voters had had their names omitted. At the Community of the Sahelian-Saharan States (CEN-SAD) Executive Council meeting in Cotonou, an investment guarantee agency was launched to provide funds for infrastructure projects.

2009 The European Union banned all air carriers from Benin from flying into its airspace, due to safety fears.

2010 In March, the World Bank agreed to fund the US$258 million refurbishment of the 998.8km West African coastal corridor road which runs through Benin from Abidjan (Côte d'Ivoire) to Lagos (Nigeria). Celebrations to mark 50 years of independence began on 1 August. Severe flooding in October killed 60 people and displaced around 120,000. Emergency relief was supplied for over 680,000 people affected by the devastation. A national census was held on 14 May.

2011 On 5 March, the date of the presidential elections was postponed by one week, following complaints that the electoral role was not yet ready, with over one million voters still to be registered. In the elections held on 13 March in which 14 candidates took part, incumbent Yayi Boni won 53.18 per cent and his closest rival Adrien Houngbédji 35.66 per cent. In parliamentary elections held on 30 April, the ruling FCBE won 41 seats (out of 83), increasing its number by six seats and cutting the opposition's combined total to 42; the Union Fait la Nation (UFN) (Unite the Nation) won 30 seats and six other political parties each won two seats. On 28 May Pascal Koupaki was named prime minister and a new government was appointed.

Political structure
Constitution
The 1990 constitution provides for multi-party politics and a president to be directly elected by popular vote. Presidential candidates cannot be aged over 70. No provision is made for a prime minister; the president is head of government.
Independence date
1 August 1960
Form of state
Republic
The executive
The president is directly elected by popular vote for a five-year term and has ultimate power and control.
National legislature
The directly elected Assemblée Nationale (National Assembly) has 83 members elected for a four-year term.
Legal system
The legal system is based on French civil law and customary law.
Last elections
30 April 2011 (parliamentary); 13 March 2011 (presidential)
Results: Parliamentary: Forces Cauri pour un Bénin Emergent (FCBE) (Cauri Forces for an Emerging Benin) won 41 seats (out of 83), Union Fait la Nation (UFN) (Unite the Nation) 30, Alliance Amana two, Alliance G13 Baobab two, Alliance Cauris 2 two, Force Espoir–Union pour la Relève (FE-UPR) (Hope Force-Union for Relief) two, Alliance Force dans l'Unité (AFU) (Strength in Unity Alliance) two, Union pour le Bénin (Union for Benin) two.
Presidential: Yayi Boni won 53.18 per cent of the vote, Adrien Houngbédji 35.66 per cent, Abdoulaye Bio-Tchané 6.29 per cent; 11 other candidates won less than 1 per cent each.
Next elections
2016 (presidential and parliamentary).

Political parties
There are over 100 registered parties in Benin, but only a handful are represented in parliament.
Ruling party
Forces Cauri pour un Bénin Emergent (FCBE) (Cauri Forces for an Emerging Benin) (elected 2007; re-elected 30 Apr 2011)
Main opposition party
Union Fait la Nation (UFN) (Unite the Nation)

Population
8.85 million (2010)*
Last census: February 2002: 6,769,914
Population density: 51 inhabitants per square km. Urban population: 43 per cent (1995–2001).
Annual growth rate: 3.2 per cent 1994–2004 (WHO 2006)
Ethnic make-up
African (99 per cent) (42 ethnic groups, most important being Fon, Adja, Yoruba, Bariba), European (1 per cent).
Religions
Animists (70 per cent), Christians (15 per cent) and Muslims (15 per cent).

Education
Annual expenditure on education is 3–3.5 per cent of GDP of which over 55 per cent is spent on primare education.
Literacy rate: 40 per cent adult rate; 56 per cent youth rate (15–24) (Unesco 2005).
Enrolment rate: 99 per cent gross primary enrolment, of relevant age group (including repeaters); 20 per cent net secondary enrolment (UN HDR)
Pupils per teacher: 52 in primary schools.

Health
HIV/Aids
70,000 people, 3,000 of whom are aged under 15 (World Bank). Half of sex workers have tested positive, so a pandemic could cause future problems if issues of contraceptive use are not addressed.
HIV prevalence: 1.9 per cent aged 15–49 in 2003 (World Bank)
Life expectancy: 53 years, 2004 (WHO 2006)
Fertility rate/Maternal mortality rate: 5.7 births per woman, 2004 (WHO 2006)
Child (under 5 years) mortality rate (per 1,000): 91 per 1,000 live births; 23 per cent of children aged under five were malnourished (World Bank).
Head of population per physician: 0.04 physician per 1,000 people, 2004 (WHO 2006)

Welfare
The National Social Security fund provides for general workers and farmers who have made contributions. The fund is supervised by the Ministry of Labour although its assets are autonomous and administered by trustees. Every employer must provide a contribution for each worker to cover disability and family allowances. Old age pension benefits are accrued by workers contributions to the fund.

Main cities
Cotonou (seat of government, estimated population 898,790 in 2003), Porto-Novo (administrative capital, 240,744), Parakou (175,792), Abomey (115,283), Natitingou (243,414).

Languages spoken
French; African languages (Yoruba, Bariba and Fon) are widely used in everyday life.
Official language/s
French

Media
Benin is considered one of the most liberal media markets in Africa.
Press
Dailies: In French, *Fraternite* (www.fraternite-info.com), *Le Matinal En Ligne* (www.actubenin.com) and *Le Nation* (www.gouv.bj/presse/lanation), is a government publication.
Weeklies: In French *La Gazette du Golfe* with political debate.
Business: The *Le Magazine de l'Entreprise* (www.creationdentreprise.org), is a magazine of regional business affairs.
Periodicals: In French, a fortnightly publication includes the government information bureau's *Journal Officiel de la République du Benin*.
Broadcasting
The state-owned Office des Radiodiffusion et Télévision du Bénin (ORTB) broadcasts radio and television services.
Radio: Radio is the prime medium for public news and information and phone-in programme are popular. The ORTB broadcasts Radio Benin (www.ortb.net, site under construction), in French, English and 18 local languages. Commercial stations include Golfe FM (www.eit.to), the pan-African Radio Africa No 1 (www.africa1.com) and Radio Planete (www.planetefm.com); Radio Maranatha (www.eit.to) and Radio Immaculee Conception (www.immacolata.com/fibenafr) are religious stations.
Television: Fewer residents watch TV than listen to radio. ORTB operated Television Nationale. Internet TV is provided Espace Informatique et Telecommunications (EIT) including Canal Sat Horizons (www.eit.to), LBC (www.lbcgroup.tv) and Future Television (www.future.com.lb). Television LC2 International (www.lc2international.tv) is a satellite station.
News agencies
National news agency: Agence Benin-Presse (ABP)

Economy
The principal component of the economy is the service sector, which constitutes over 45 per cent of GDP; trade is the major constituent (almost 20 per cent), followed by government services (11 per cent), education and healthcare. Agriculture represents 25 per cent of GDP, while forestry, livestock and fisheries constitutes a further

10 per cent. However, the single largest component of the economy is cotton, which at the height of its dominance accounted for around 40 per cent of GDP and around 80 per cent of export revenue in 2006. Although cotton exports have fallen as prices dropped on the world market it still remains, in 2010, a leading revenue earner. Other agricultural cash crops include palm oil, coffee and cocoa. Cultivation for domestic consumption includes among other produce, wheat, yams, legumes, groundnuts and pineapples. In July 2009 the UN Food and Agricultural Organisation (FAO) allocated US$500,000 to aid Benin in developing the cultivation of rice, which when under full production could bring in revenue of US$55 million. It was estimated the Benin imported 11 million tonnes of rice in 2010, a commodity that has risen sharply since 2008. Industry constitutes around 20 per cent of GDP (of which manufacturing is 8 per cent), with textile manufacturing is a leading industry.

GDP growth was 2.7 per cent in 2008, a fall from 5.0 per cent in 2007 as global trade fell and imports, particularly petroleum and foodstuffs, rose in price. However GDP growth in 2010 was projected to rise to 3.2 per cent and further still, to 4.4 per cent, in 2011.

With help from the International Monetary Fund (IMF), Benin addressed its serious problem of external debt which was cut by 58 per cent to 11.5 per cent of GDP in 2006 and since then has been kept relatively low, as macroeconomic reforms have been put in place to contribute to and enhance private sector growth.

Spending on poverty reduction has been focussed so that the poverty headcount fell from 37.4 per cent in 2006 to 34.4 per cent in 2009. GDP per capita was estimated at US$610 in 2008

Remittances in 2009 amounted to US$243 million (3.6 per cent of GDP), an amount that has fallen steadily since 2007, when it was US$282 million, and which probably reflects the lack of opportunity for workers overseas. Remittances in 2010 amounted to an estimated US$236 million.

Corruption and the informal sector also dog government control of the economy. Smuggling, including of people, between Benin and Nigeria, is rife and it has been estimated that the informal sector accounts for over 45 per cent of gross national income.

Benin is a member of Union Économique et Monétaire Ouest-Aficaine (UEMOA) (West African Economic and Monetary Union (WEAMU)), and its monetary policy is set by the Banque Centrale des États de l'Afrique de l'Ouest (BCEAO) (Central Bank of West African States) using the CFA franc (Communauté Financière Africaine franc).

External trade

Benin is a member of the World Trade Organisation (WTO); through its membership of Union Économique et Monétaire Ouest-Aficaine (UEMOA) (West African Economic and Monetary Union (WEAMU)) operates using the CFA franc (Communauté Financière Africaine franc). It has liberal trade agreements with other members, while the union has a trade agreement with the US.

Benin acts as a transit country for goods from Nigeria to Togo and its landlocked neighbours Niger, Burkina Faso and Mali.

Imports

Principal imports are refined oil and petroleum products, rice, foodstuffs, tobacco and capital goods.

Main sources: France (typically over 20 per cent of total), Ghana (less than 10 per cent), Côte d'Ivoire (less than 10 per cent).

Exports

Principal exports are cotton, palm oil, shea butter, coffee and cocoa.

Main destinations: China (typically over 30 of total), Indonesia (less than 10 per cent), India (less than 10 per cent).

Agriculture

Farming

The agricultural sector is the most important economic sector. It accounted for 36.9 per cent of GDP in 2004 and employs over 55 per cent of the workforce. Cotton is the principal cash crop and foreign exchange earner, farmed mainly on large industrial plantations. It is also important to the rural economy as it supports almost half of rural households.

Other cash crops include palm oil, coffee, sugar, cocoa, karité nuts and tobacco. Subsistence farming (mainly collectivised) shows low productivity but the country is virtually self-sufficient in food. Livestock farming is particularly important in the north. The principal food crops are yams, cassava, sorghum, beans, millet, maize and rice.

Fishing

Fishing is confined mainly to inland waters and augments local food supplies.

Industry and manufacturing

The industrial sector is small-scale, contributing 8.4 per cent to GDP and employing 6 per cent of the workforce.

Manufacturing activity is centred on processing primary products (palm oil, fats, sugar, beverages, cotton) for export, and the manufacture of consumer goods and construction materials for home consumption.

Cement production and oil refining are the main heavy industries.

The government has encouraged foreign investment in canning, paper processing, glass manufacturing, salt processing, agribusiness, pharmaceuticals, clothing, palm oil, building materials and chemicals.

In 2000, the cottonseed oil plant at Bohicon was extended and modernised, raising capacity to 12,000 tonnes of oil, and a sugar producing enterprise, which had been closed since 1990, was reopened.

Tourism

'Land of mystery' is the epithet given to Benin by its tourism ministry. As a country, it offers traditional African culture, ancient historic monuments and artefacts, plus a wealth of wildlife to entertain visitors. The government is investing in development to improve the tourist infrastructure and market beach, cultural and eco-tourism.

The tourism industry constitutes around 7 per cent of GDP, earning an average of US$673 million in 2008–09. The annual contribution jumped from US$540 million in 2007 to a record high of US$710 million in 2008, just before the global economic crisis cut visitor numbers. However, the contribution in 2011 is estimated at another record, of US$716 million.

Around 6 per cent of the working population is engaged in tourism; foreign exchange earnings are typically US$342–376 million per annum.

The Fishing Road project, sited along the coast between the capital Cotonou and the historic town of Ouidah, will be the largest tourist development ever undertaken in Benin, of 10-years duration. In 2008, the UAE-based Dubai World Africa began to invest not only in the Fishing Road project, helping with the purchase of 32km of seafront and ancillary land, but also by providing specialists in wildlife management to ecology experts to evaluate Benin's national parks.

Mining

The mining sector accounts for 5.5 per cent of GDP and employs 3 per cent of the workforce.

Activity is confined to extraction of limestone for the local cement industry, and marble. There is a limestone quarry at Onigbolo. There are known reserves of phosphate, chromite, uranium, low grade iron ore, marble and gold. The government has awarded a number of gold exploration licences to foreign investors.

Under Beninese law, all mineral resources belong to the state, which grants exclusive rights for exploration, development and mining activities.

Hydrocarbons

Proven oil reserves were eight million barrels in 2008, although there has been no production since 2003. All petroleum products are imported to meet domestic needs, which was 21,000 barrels per day (bpd) in 2008.

Proven gas reserves were 1.1 billion cubic metres in 2008; domestic consumption is negligible. Consumption of natural gas is expected to begin following the completion of the section of the West African Gas Pipeline (WAGP) from Nigeria's Escravos gas field to Benin. Although the pipeline supplies natural gas to Ghana, a spur line to Benin is still awaiting completion.

Energy

Total installed generating capacity was 59MW in 2007, producing over 120 million kilowatt hours.

Only 22 per cent of the population has access to electricity, the majority of these located in urban areas; rural populations rely on traditional fuels such as biomass and wood. Around 30 per cent of the energy mix is provided by hydropower. The joint Benin-Togo hydroelectric power project, producing 60MW, on the river Mono has been fully operational since the building of the Nangbeto Dam. Electricity is also imported from the hydroelectric Akosombo Dam in Ghana.

In 2008 the 32MW Takoradi, light fuel oil (LFO), power plant in Ghana was dismantled and transported to Benin, where it was broken down into three parts and distributed between three cities providing much-needed boosts to local power generation.

Communauté Electrique de Bénin (CEB) (Electricity Community of Benin) is a joint Benin-Togo entity responsible for developing electricity infrastructure within and between each country. In 2008 it began an upgrade of transmission lines to include fibre optics allowing residents access to telecommunications.

Financial markets

Stock exchange

Afribourse (Bourse Régionale des Valeurs Moblières) (BRVM)

Banking and insurance

Central bank

Banque Centrale des États de l'Afrique de l'Ouest

Main financial centre

Cotonou and Parakou

Time

GMT plus one hour

Geography

Benin is a narrow stretch of territory 700km long running north/south. The country has an Atlantic coastline of about 100km, flanked by Nigeria to the east and Togo to the west. In the north it is bordered by Burkina Faso and Niger.

Hemisphere

Northern

Climate

Equatorial in the south with average daytime temperatures reaching 30–38 degrees Celsius (C). Main dry season from January–March. Rainy seasons from May–July and from September–December. Very humid in coastal areas. The north is tropical with more extreme temperatures, and single dry and rainy seasons. Length of rainy seasons varies with location but it is generally very wet from July–October.

Entry requirements

Passports

Required by all except nationals of certain African countries who have identification documents.

Visa

Required by all, except for nationals of Economic Community of West African States (Ecowas) countries. For the latest requirements and to apply, contact the local embassy or representative.

Currency advice/regulations

There are no restrictions on import of local or foreign currency, but amounts of foreign currency must be declared on arrival.

Foreign currency exports are allowed up to the equivalent of CFAf500.

Health (for visitors)

Mandatory precautions

Yellow fever and cholera vaccination certificates required.

Advisable precautions

Inoculations and boosters should be current for cholera, tetanus, polio, hepatitis A, diphtheria, typhoid and yellow fever. There may be a need for vaccinations for tuberculosis, hepatitis B and meningitis. Malaria prophylaxis, which also provides protection for hepatitis B and yellow fever, include mosquito repellents, nets and clothing that cover the body after dark. There is a risk of rabies.

Other diseases that require preventative measures, such as condoms, are HIV/Aids and hepatitis B; to avoid bilharzia, avoid exposure to fresh water and use only well-maintained, chlorinated swimming pools.

Use only bottled or boiled water for drinks, washing teeth and making ice. Eat only well cooked meals, preferably served hot; vegetables should be cooked and fruit peeled. Dairy products are unpasteurised and should be avoided. There is a shortage of routine medications, including sun-screens, and visitors should take all necessary medicines with them. A first aid kit that includes disposable syringes, is a reasonable precaution. Healthcare is not to Western standards and medical insurance, including emergency evacuation, is necessary.

Hotels

Available in all main towns. Better class accommodation is found only in and around Cotonou. Advance booking is advisable. Service charge usually included in bill, otherwise 10 per cent tip.

Credit cards

Access, Mastercard, Visa accepted on limited basis. Some banks may advance cash on Visa cards, check with card company.

Public holidays (national)

Fixed dates

1 Jan (New Year's Day), 10 Jan (Traditional Day), 1 May (Labour Day), 1 Aug (Independence Day), 15 Aug (Assumption Day), 26 Oct (Armed Forces Day), 1 Nov (All Saints' Day), 30 Nov (National Day), 25 Dec (Christmas Day).

Variable dates

Good Friday, Easter Monday, Ascension Day, Whit Monday, Eid al Adha, Eid al Fitr, Birth of the Prophet.

Islamic year 1433 (26 Nov 2011–14 Nov 2012): The Islamic year contains 354 or 355 days, with the result that Muslim feasts advance by 10–12 days against the Gregorian calendar. Dates of feasts vary according to the sighting of the new moon, so cannot be forecast exactly.

Working hours

Banking

Mon–Fri: 0800–1100, 1500–1700.

Business

Mon–Fri: 0800–1230, 1530–1900. (Sat) 0900–1300.

Government

Mon–Fri: 0800–1230, 1500–1830.

Shops

Mon–Sat: 0830–1300, 1600–1930; (Sun) 0800–1200. Shops that open Sun mainly close Mon am.

Electricity supply

Electricity supply 220V AC 50 cycles.

Getting there

Air

International airport/s: Cotonou-Cadjehoun (COO), 6km west of city; taxi and limousine service (15–20 minutes to city centre), restaurant, business centre, 24 hours medical facility.

Airport tax: None

Surface

Road: There are routes from Burkina Faso, Togo, Nigeria and Niger.

Rail: A line linking Niger to Benin is under construction.

Water: Shipping lines from Marseille (France) and Lagos (Nigeria).

Main port/s: Porto Novo, Cotonou

Getting about

National transport

Air: Regular services between Cotonou, Parakou, Natitingou, Kandi and Djougou.

Road: Good main roads in south connecting towns to Cotonou and Porto Novo.
Mainly laterite, but the main coast road, which connects Lagos with Accra, is surfaced, and the road north from Cotonou is surfaced to Savalou.
In northern areas some roads are only passable in dry season.
Buses: Bus services link towns on these main routes.
Rail: There is only one operation railway line going north from Cotonou to Bohicon, Savé and Parakou. Facilities are limited.

City transport

Taxis: Fixed charge within towns, but advisable to negotiate fares in advance. Tipping is optional.

Car hire

Available in Cotonou. Chauffeur-driven services are recommended. Insurance/liability position should be checked. International driving licence required.

BUSINESS DIRECTORY

The addresses listed below are a selection only. While World of Information makes every endeavour to check these addresses, we cannot guarantee that changes have not been made, especially to telephone numbers and area codes. We would welcome any corrections.

Telephone area codes

The international direct dialling code (IDD) for Benin is +229, followed by subscriber's number.

Chambers of Commerce

Benin Chamber of Commerce and Industry, Avenue Général de Gaulle, PO Box 31, Cotonou (tel: 312-081; fax: 313-299; e-mail: ccib@bow.intnet.bj).

Banking

Bank of Africa Bénin (BOA), BP 08-0879, Ave Pape Jean Paul II, Cotonou (tel: 313-228; fax: 313-117).

Banque Centrale des Etats de l'Afrique de l'Ouest, BP 325, Ave Jean Paul II, Cotonou (tel: 312-466/7; fax: 312-465).

Banque Internationale du Bénin (BIBE) BP 03-2098, Carrefour des 3 Banques, Cotonou (tel: 315-549; fax: 312-365).

Continental Bank Bénin, 01 BP, Avenue Pope Jean Paul II, 2020 Cotonou (tel: 312-424, 313-393; fax: 315177).

Ecobank Bénin, BP 1280, Rue du Gouverneur Bayol, 01 Cotonou (tel: 314-023, 313-069; fax: 313-385, 313-718).

Financial Bank Bénin (FBB), BP 2700, Rue du Commandant Decoeur, Cotonou (tel: 313-100, 313-103, 313-104; fax: 313-102).

Central bank

Banque Centrale des États de l'Afrique de l'Ouest, PO Box 325, Avenue Jean Paul II, Cotonou (tel: 312-466; fax: 312-465; e-mail: webmaster@bceao.int).

Stock exchange

Afribourse (Bourse Régionale des Valeurs Moblières) (BRVM): www.brvm.org

Travel information

Transports Aériens du Bénin (tel: 314-797).

National tourist organisation offices

Office National du Tourisme et de l'Hôtellerie (ONATHO), BP 89, Contonou (tel: 315-402).

Ministries

Ministry of Public Service, Labour and Administrative Reform (tel: 313-112).

Ministry of Public Works and Transport, PO Box 16, Cotonou, Benin (tel: 313-380).

State Ministry of Government Co-ordination, Planning, Development and Employment Promotion (tel: 301-553).

Other useful addresses

Africa Rice Center (AfricaRice), 01 BP 2031, Cotonou (tel: 350 188; fax: 350 556; email: africarice@cgiar.org).

Agence Bénin-Presse, BP 120, Cotonou.

Benin Embassy (USA), 2737 Cathedral Avenue, NW, Washington DC 20008 (tel: 232-6656; fax: 265-1996).

Import/Export Alimentation de Bénin, BP 53, Cotonou.

Institut National de la Statistique et de L'Analyse Economique, BP 323, Cotonou (tel: 314-101/103).

Mission de Co-opération et d'Action Culturelle, BP 476, Cotonou (tel: 300-824).

Mission Permanente d'Aide et de Co-opération, BP 476, Cotonou (administers aid from France).

Organisation Commune Benin-Niger des Chemins de fer et des Transports (OCBN) (Benin Railways), PO Box 16, Cotonou, Benin (tel: 313-380).

Société Nationale d'Equipement, BP 2042, Cotonou (deals with capital goods).

Société Nationale de Commercialisation et d'Exportation du Bénin (Sonaceb), BP 933, Cotonou (tel: 312-822).

Société Nationale de Commercialisation des Produits Pétroliers (Sonacop), BP 245, Cotonou (tel: 312-290).

Société Nationale d'Importation du Bénin, BP 2042, Cotonou.

Syndicat National des Commerçants et Industriels Africains du Bénin, BP 367, Cotonou.

National news agency: Agence Benin-Presse (ABP), 01 BP 72 Cotonou (tel: 2131-2655; fax: 2131-1326; internet: www.gouv.bj/presse/abp).

Internet sites

Africa Business Network: http://www.ifc.org/abn

AllAfrica.com: http://www.allafrica.com

African Development Bank: http://www.afdb.org

Africa Online: http://www.africaonline.com

Benin: http://www.guide-benin.

Embassy in Paris: http://www.ambassade-benin.org

General tourist information: http://www.africaguide.com/

Mbendi AfroPaedia (information on companies, countries, industries and stock exchanges in Africa): http://mbendi.co.za

Mission to the UN: http://www.un.int/benin

Bermuda

Mark Twain said of Bermuda that 'You can go to heaven. I'd rather stay in Bermuda.' And indeed, tourism flourishes on these isolated island. The Bermudas or Somers Islands, consist of some 150 islands in the Atlantic Ocean about 917km (570 miles) off the coast of South Carolina. Ten of the islands are linked by bridges and causeways to form the principal mainland.

Although tourism is still important to the islanders, with, at the end of 2010, some 3,000 rooms providing 5,998 bed nights, the sector has been overtaken by international business as principal revenue-earner. Bermuda also operates a shipping register, allowing registration of unlimited ship type and tonnage within conditions agreed with the UK.

Employment

Tourism is the highest employer, with some 14 per cent, followed by the government with 10 per cent and business services, banking and other financial services, and international entities roughly equal on 8 per cent each. Gross domestic product (GDP) per capita is the highest in the world at around US$91,500, ahead of Qatar with US$87,600 and Luxembourg with US$79,400. This compares with the US at US$45,800.

COUNTRY PROFILE

Historical profile

1503 A Spaniard, Juan de Bermudez, sighted the islands.
1609 Settled by the British.
1612 A charter was given by James I to the Virginia Company to include Bermuda in the dominion. The first permanent settlers arrived shortly afterwards.
1684 The islands were sold to the City of London and became the property of the Crown.
1620 Bermuda was granted limited self-government when the House of Assembly was formed.
1700s Bermuda developed links with the American colonies of North America.
1815 Hamilton was named the capital city.
1834 Slavery was abolished.
1940 An agreement between the US and Britain granted about 10 per cent of Bermuda's land to the US for military use.
1963 The first political party was formed.
1968 Bermuda was granted internal self-government. The first elections held under universal adult suffrage were won by the United Bermuda Party (UBP).
1998 The UBP lost power for the first time since 1968 when the Progressive Labour Party (PLP) won the general election under Jennifer Smith. She was the first female party leader.
2001 Regulation to increase the transparency of the insurance sector was moved from the ministry of finance to the Monetary Authority.
2002 Implementation of Bermuda Companies Amendment Act simplifying the procedure for forming companies.
2003 PLP won parliamentary elections. Following an internal PLP revolt, Premier Jennifer Smith resigned and Alex Scott became premier. Hurricane Fabian, the most powerful storm since the 1950s, hit the islands and caused widespread destruction. A Constitutional amendment introduced 36 single seat constituencies within the islands (from the previous 20 dual seat constituencies).
2004 The PLP published plans for independence from the UK.
2005 Bermuda entered into a tax sharing agreement with Australia, only the second agreement signed after the US; it allows requests and information on specific tax matters under investigation or audit to be passed between states. The OECD welcomed the agreement as a measure to 'counter abuse of the financial system'.
2006 Ewart Brown was sworn in as premier, having replaced Alex Scott as leader of the PLP.
2007 Sir John Vereker retired and Sir Richard Hugh Turton Gozney became governor.
2008 The newly elected PLP government scrapped the public holiday on the Queen's official birthday, to be replaced by a National Heroes' Day (in October).
2009 The Organisation for Economic Co-operation and Development (OECD) added Bermuda to its 'white list' of countries and territories that had substantially implemented internationally agreed tax standards, after it had signed 12 tax information exchange agreements (TIEA) with various countries.
2010 Premier Brown gave his farewell speech in the last session of parliament in

KEY FACTS

Official name: Bermuda

Head of State: Queen Elizabeth II; represented by Governor Sir Richard Gozney (from 12 Dec 2007)

Head of government: Premier Paula Cox (PLP) (from 29 Oct 2010)

Ruling party: Progressive Labour Party (PLP) (since 1998; re-elected Dec 2007)

Area: 55 square km

Population: 65,000 (2010)*

Capital: Hamilton

Official language: English

Currency: Bermudan dollar (BD$) = 100 cents

Exchange rate: BD$1.00 per US$ (fixed)

GDP per capita: US$80,676 (2006)

GDP real growth: 2.50% (2005)

Labour force: 38,360 (2004)

Unemployment: 2.10% (2004)

Inflation: 3.10% (2005)

Balance of trade: US$487.00 million (2004)

Visitor numbers: 635,272 (2006)

* estimated figure

July, ahead of his retirement in October. Paula Cox (PLP) took office on 29 October as premier. Bermuda signed a TIEA with China on 4 December.
2011 Bermuda signed a TIEA with the Czech Republic on 4 February and with Indonesia on 27 June.

Political structure
Bermuda has had a broad measure of internal self-government since 1968. Queen Elizabeth II is represented by a UK-appointed governor who is responsible for defence, external affairs and internal security. The governor is guided on most internal matters by a cabinet appointed from the bicameral legislature.

Form of state
Representative democracy; crown colony of the UK.

The executive
The prime minister is chosen from the majority party and heads a cabinet of no more than 14 members of the legislature.

National legislature
The bicameral parliament comprises the House of Assembly (lower chamber), with 36-members, directly elected in single seat constituencies, for a maximum term of five years.
The Senate (upper chamber), has 11 senators, appointed by the governor, of which five are appointed on the advice of the premier, three on the advice of the leader of the opposition. The remaining three are appointed at the discretion of the governor, one of which becomes president of the senate, as voted on by the senate. The senate has the power to block constitutional changes, passed by the lower chamber, unless a two-thirds majority in senate votes in its favour.

Legal system
The legal system and Bermudian law are based on the British model. The ultimate court of appeal is the Judicial Committee of the Privy Council in the UK.

Last elections
12 December 2007 (parliamentary)
Results: Parliamentary: the ruling PLP won 52.5 per cent of the vote, 22 seats (out of 36) and the UBP 47.3 per cent, 14 seats.

Next elections
2012 (parliamentary)

Political parties

Ruling party
Progressive Labour Party (PLP) (since 1998; re-elected Dec 2007)

Main opposition party
United Bermuda Party (UBP)

Political situation
Despite its small size and negligible resource base, Bermuda has one of the highest per capita incomes in the world. The economy is based upon tourism and international business transactions, which take advantage of Bermuda's offshore banking status.
Inflation has been kept low through the policy of fixing the Bermudan dollar at parity with the US dollar. Bermuda has low levels of public debt and although borrowing has risen due to an increase in capital spending, debt remains well below the government's ceiling of 10 per cent of GDP.
The image of tax havens, such as Bermuda, suffered in 2008 as evidence of tax evasion schemes came to light. Coupled with the downturn in the global economy in 2008 and the collapse of some hedge funds, Bermuda has been forced to work harder for its share of the US$2 trillion worldwide hedge fund business, as well as offshore banking and insurance business. Some company headquarters have been moved to other less questionable destinations to bolster company images, prompting Bermuda to introduce new laws to provide greater transparency and good governance.
Following the enactment of a new regulatory framework in 2008, the Organisation for Economic Co-operation and Development (OECD) added Bermuda to its 'white list' of countries and territories that had substantially implemented internationally agreed tax standards. Bermuda had by then signed 12 tax information exchange agreements (TIEA) with various countries. The Bermuda Monetary Authority set up a supervisory regime to oversee Special Purpose Insurers (SPI) in 2009. In particular, SPIs include catastrophe or cat bonds that insure against extreme events where losses are particularly high.

Population
65,000 (2010)*
Last census: May 2000: 62,059
Population density: 1,280 inhabitants per square km. Urban population: 100 per cent.
Annual growth rate: 0.8 per cent (2003)

Ethnic make-up
African (58 per cent), European (36 per cent). Approximately 73 per cent of the population is Bermuda-born.

Religions
Non-Anglican Protestant (39 per cent), Anglican (27 per cent), Roman Catholic (15 per cent), African Methodist Episcopal (10 per cent), Methodist (6 per cent), Seventh-Day Adventist (3 per cent).

Health
Life expectancy: 77 years (estimate 2003)
Fertility rate/Maternal mortality rate: Two births per woman (2003)
Birth rate/Death rate: 12 births per 1,000 population; eight deaths per 1,000 population (2003).
Child (under 5 years) mortality rate (per 1,000): Nine per 1,000 live births (2003)

Welfare
An insurance scheme takes contributions from the employer and employee to benefit workers during sickness or disability, for maternity leave or survivors of deceased workers, funded by contributions of a set amount, paid by both the employer and employee, each paying 50 per cent of the sum per week.

Pensions
There is an old age pension scheme funded by contributions of a set amount, paid by both the employer and employee, each paying 50 per cent of the sum per week.

Main cities
Hamilton (capital city, estimated population 97,000 in 2003), St George's (St George's Island) (1,800).

Languages spoken
English and Portuguese.

Official language/s
English

Media

Press
Dailies: The only newspaper is *The Royal Gazette* (www.royalgazette.com).
Weeklies: Magazines include the *Bermuda Sun* (www.bermudasun.bm) and the *Mid-Ocean News* published by *The Royal Gazette*. *Worker's Voice* is published by the Industrial Union.
Periodicals: Monthly magazines include *Bermudian* and *Bermudian Business*. *Preview Bermuda* (www.previewbermuda.com) is a free publication for visitors. *Bottom Line* covers business matters and is published six times annually and issued free with *The Royal Gazette*.

Broadcasting
Radio: All stations are private and commercial. The Bermuda Broadcasting Company (BBC) operates four of the most listened to stations, providing a mix of programmes including news, music and local contents, however, the top ranking station is HOTT 107.5 (www.hott1075.com). VSB operates four channels including news, religious, music and tourist information. Radio Bermuda (www.marops.bm) gives shipping weather forecasts.
Television: There are two main networks, both commercial and free-to-air. The Bermuda Broadcasting Company (BBC) and DeFontes Broadcasting (Television) Ltd) (www.vsb-bm). There is ready access to satellite and cable TV services.

Advertising
Available in all forms of media from traditional newspaper ads to targeted mobile/cell texts and sponsorship.

News agencies
Other news agencies: Caribbean Net News: www.caribbeannetnews.com

Economy
Despite its small size and negligible resource base, Bermuda has one of the highest per capita incomes in the world. The economy is based on tourism and international business transactions, which take advantage of Bermuda's offshore banking status.
Inflation has been kept low through the policy of fixing the Bermudan dollar at parity with the US dollar. Bermuda has low levels of public debt and although borrowing has risen due to an increase in capital spending, debt remains well below the government's ceiling of 10 per cent of GDP.
Following the enactment of a new regulatory framework in 2008, the Bermuda Monetary Authority set up a supervisory regime to oversee Special Purpose Insurers (SPI) in 2009.

External trade
The large trade deficit is offset by net invisible earnings from tourism and international business, especially insurance and shipping registration. High import duties on all items are the government's main source of income.
Imports
Principal imports include foodstuffs, tobacco, clothing, fuels, chemicals, machinery, transport equipment, and live animals.
Main sources: US (typically 31 per cent), South Korea (27 per cent), Brazil (7 per cent).
Exports
Principal exports include foodstuffs, tobacco, clothing, fuels, chemicals, machinery, transport equipment, and live animals, pharmaceuticals and petroleum.
Main destinations: France (typically 66 per cent total), Spain (12 per cent), UK (5 per cent).
Re-exports
Pharmaceuticals and petroleum, machinery and transport equipment.

Agriculture
Agriculture contributes about 1 per cent to GDP annually. Less than 6 per cent of total area is cultivated arable land, most of which is used by tenant farmers for growing fruit, vegetables and flowers. Although self-sufficient in eggs and milk, around 80 per cent of food requirements need to be imported. There is a small fishing industry. The typical annual fish catch is over 350t, plus 25t per annum other seafood.

Industry and manufacturing
Manufacturing and construction combined contribute around 10 per cent to GDP and employ less than 5 per cent of the workforce. Major activities include ship repair, small boat building and manufacture of paints, perfumes, pharmaceuticals, mineral water extracts and handicraft souvenirs. The emphasis is on encouraging light industry in the Freeport area on Ireland Island North. Bermuda has large marine engineering interests, and operates one of the world's largest flag of convenience shipping fleets.

Tourism
Tourism, formerly the mainstay of the economy, is now second to the financial sector as a source of foreign exchange. Bermuda sits in the North Atlantic Ocean, over 1,000km from the east coast of the US. It is a British Overseas Territory and retains many characteristics of the old British colony. The capital, Jamestown, is a Unesco World Heritage Site, with many historic buildings
In 2010, 585,266 visitors spent time in Bermuda, of which most arrived by cruise liners or yachts. Visitors from the US are the largest single group, followed by Canadians, then UK and other Europeans. Tourism is second only in importance to the financial sector, with 18.3 per cent of GDP in 2010. Travel and tourism provides 23.4 per cent of all jobs and US$515 million in foreign exchange in 2010.
The Ministry of Business Development and Tourism was formed in 2010 to combine domestic and international business.

Hydrocarbons
There are no known hydrocarbon reserves. Bermuda consumed 5,000 barrels per day (bpd) in 2008, all of which was imported. The government maintains a fixed price for petrol (gasoline) and Esso and Shell are the only companies allowed to sell retail petroleum products in Bermuda.
Bermuda consumes more oil and gas annually than Antigua, Dominica, Grenada, St Lucia and St Vincent combined.
There is a liquefied natural gas (LNG) terminal supplying gas in cylinders; the French-owned Rubis Gaz distributes liquefied petroleum gas (LPG) to retailers as well as propane and butane to residential and commercial customers.

Energy
Total installed generating capacity was 175MW in 2007, producing over 67 million kilowatt hours. The Bermuda Electric Light Company is a subsidiary of the privately owned Belco Holdings Limited. Under Belco's proposals in 2009, five large-scale renewable energy projects are under consideration, a large catchment solar photovoltaic plant, commercial wind generation, wave energy, biomass and a sealed municipal waste burning plant. Another subsidiary, Purenergy Renewables, is offering several small-scale energy systems for private and commercial use, including micro-wind generation, solar photovoltaic and solar-thermal hot water.

Financial markets
Stock exchange
Bermuda Stock Exchange (BSX)

Banking and insurance
Central bank
Bermuda Monetary Authority
Main financial centre
Hamilton
Offshore facilities
The offshore banking sector plays a vital role in the economy.

Time
GMT minus four hours (GMT minus three hours from April to October).

Geography
The Bermudas or Somers Islands are an isolated archipelago, comprising about 150 islands in the Atlantic Ocean about 917km (570 miles) off the coast of South Carolina, USA. Ten of the islands are linked by bridges and causeways to form the principal mainland.
Hemisphere
Northern

Climate
Semi-tropical with temperatures usually ranging between 16—28 degrees Celsius, from winter (Nov–Mar) to summer (Apr–Oct), with no marked rainy season. Bermuda is located more than 1,600km north of the Caribbean and is subjected to occasional hurricane-force winds between June and September.

Dress codes
There is no occasion on the island when shorts cannot be worn. For the office, tailored shorts of one colour may be worn, with long socks to the knees with at least an inch to turn over.

Entry requirements
Passports
Required by all visitors except UK, US and Canadian nationals with other documentary proof of identification. All US and Canadian nationals have required a passport for re-entry to their country since 2007.
A return/onward ticket is required by all visitors.
Visa
Visas are not required by transit passengers and most citizens of the Americas, Europe, Australasia and some Asian countries, provided their stay does not exceed six months. For further details visit www.immigration.gov.bm, or contact a UK diplomatic or consular mission locally.
All visitors must have return/onward passage. Those wishing to travel to the US must have entry clearance for the country to be visited after leaving the US.

Currency advice/regulations
There is no limit to the import of local or foreign currency, provided it is declared on arrival. The export of local currency is limited to BD$250. The export of foreign currency is limited to the amount imported and declared.

Health (for visitors)
Mandatory precautions
Yellow fever vaccination certificate if travelling from an infected area.
Advisable precautions
Hepatitis, typhoid, tetanus and polio vaccinations.

Hotels
Generally expensive. Reduced rates are available in the November–March period. There is a 7.25 per cent occupancy tax payable at check-out in addition to room rates, and a 10–15 per cent tip is added unless a service charge has already been included in bill.

Credit cards
Credit cards are accepted at most hotels, restaurants and shops.

Public holidays (national)
Fixed dates
1 Jan (New Year's Day), 24 May (Bermuda Day), 11 Nov (Remembrance Day), 25–26 Dec (Christmas).
Variable dates
Good Friday, Cup Match and Somers' Day (first Thu and Fri of Aug), Labour Day (first Mon in Sep), Heroes' Day (Oct).

Working hours
Banking
Mon–Fri: 0900–1500; also 1630–1730 Fridays only.
Business
Mon–Fri: 0900–1700.
Government
Mon–Fri: 0900–1700.
Shops
Mon–Sat: 0900–1700. During summer many stores stay open until 2100.

Telecommunications
Mobile/cell phones
GSM 1900 coverage is available throughout the islands

Electricity supply
115–230V AC, 80 cycles

Getting there
Air
International airport/s: Bermuda International Airport (BDA), 16km from Hamilton; bar, restaurant, bank, shops, hotel reservations.
Airport tax: BD$25 is included in air tickets.
Surface
Main port/s: Hamilton, St George's. Weekly cruises link Bermuda with several east coast US ports during the summer months.

Getting about
National transport
Road: There are around 250km of well-surfaced roads.
Buses: Regularly scheduled buses operate at frequent intervals to most destinations throughout Bermuda. Passengers must have the exact fare, tokens or transport passes which provide unlimited travel by bus or ferry which can be purchased at the Central Terminal in Hamilton.
Water: Ferries to and from Hamilton, Paget, Warwick, Somerset and Dockyard.
City transport
Taxis: Metered taxis with 25 per cent surcharge between midnight and 0600; tariffs are fixed by law. Taxis displaying a small blue flag are approved by the Department of Tourism for sightseeing purposes.
Car hire
Foreign visitors are not permitted to drive cars. Motor-assisted cycles (mopeds and scooters) may be hired throughout the island and through hotel and guest-houses. Safety helmets must be worn and insurance is compulsory, although a driver's licence is not.

BUSINESS DIRECTORY

Telephone area codes
The international direct dialling (IDD) code for +1441, followed by subscriber's number.

Chambers of Commerce
Bermuda Chamber of Commerce, 1 Point Pleasant Road, PO Box HM 655, Hamilton HM CX (tel: 295-4201; fax: 292-5779; e-mail: info@bermudacommerce.com).

Banking
Bank of Bermuda, 6 Front Street, Hamilton HM DX (tel: 295-4000, 299-5005; fax: 299-6501, 295-1386).

The Bank of N T Butterfield & Son Ltd, PO Box HM 195, 65 Front Street, Hamilton HM AX (tel: 295-1111; fax: 295-0658).

Bermuda Commercial Bank Ltd, 44 Church Street, Hamilton HM 12 (tel: 295-5678; fax: 295-8091).

Central bank
Bermuda Monetary Authority, Burnaby House, 26 Burnaby Street, Hamilton HM 11 (tel: 295-5278; fax: 292-7471; e-mail: Info@bma.bm).

Stock exchange
Bermuda Stock Exchange (BSX), PO Box HM 1369, 3 F Washington Mall, Church Street, Hamilton HM FX (tel: 292-7212; fax: 292-7619; e-mail: info@bsx.com; internet: www.bsx.com).

Travel information
National tourist organisation offices
Department of Tourism, Global House, 43 Church Street, Hamilton HM 12 (tel: 292-0023; fax: 292-7537; internet site: www.bermudatourism.org).

Ministries
Ministry of Finance, Government Administration Building, 30 Parliament Street, Hamilton HM 12 (tel: 295-5151; fax: 295-5727).

Office of The Governor, Government House, 11 Langton Hill, Pembroke, Hamilton HM 13 (tel: 292-3600; fax: 292-6831; e-mail: governor@gov.bm).

Other useful addresses
Bermuda Broadcasting Company, PO Box HM 452, Hamilton HM BX (tel: 295-2828; fax: 295-4282).

Bermuda Hotel Association, 102 Reid Street, Hamilton HM 19 (tel: 295-2127; fax: 292-6671; internet site: http://www.bermudahotels.com).

Bermuda International Business Association (BIBA), Suite 203, 48 Par-la-Ville Road, Hamilton HM 11 (tel: 292-0632; fax: 292-1797).

Bermuda Insurance Management Association (BIMA), PO Box HM 1752, Hamilton HM GX (tel: 295-4864; fax: 292-7375).

Bermuda Small Business Development Corp, PO Box HM 637, Hamilton HM CX (tel: 292-5570; fax: 295-1600).

Department of Civil Aviation, Bermuda International Air Terminal, 2 Kindley Field Rd, St George's GE CX (tel: 293-1640; fax: 293-2417).

Government Information Services, Global House, 43 Church Street, Hamilton HM 12 (tel: 292-6384; fax: 292-5267).

Government Statistical Department, 43 Church Street, Hamilton HM 12 (PO Box HM 3015, Hamilton HM MX) (tel: 297-7761; fax: 295-8390).

Insurance Information Office, PO Box HM 2911, Hamilton HM LX (tel: 292-9829; fax: 295-3532).

The Registrar of Companies, Government Administration Building, 30 Parliament Street, Hamilton HM 12 (tel: 295-5151; fax: 292-6640; internet site: www.roc.bdagov.bm).

Internet sites
Bermuda Yellow Pages: www.bermudayp.com/

Bermuda online: www.bermuda-online.org

Bhutan

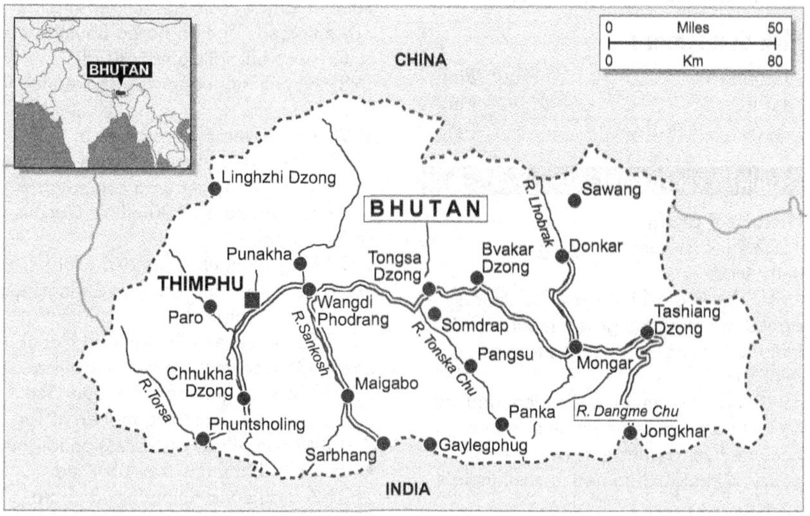

Possibly the most exciting event in Bhutan in 2011 was the marriage on 12 October in a monastery in the capital Thimpu of King Jigme. Like that other royal, in London, he too married a commoner, Jetsun Pema.

Hydro-powered economy

The economy of the Kingdom of Bhutan, population 726,000, is, quite literally, driven by its vast hydropower potential and the cycle of hydropower building and output. Two hydropower stations are being built and two other projects started pre-construction work in May 2010, ensuring strong growth for the medium term. The main challenges for the government are to try and diversify the economy and create job opportunities.

The *Asian Development Bank Outlook 2011* estimates growth to have accelerated to 7.0 per cent in financial year (FY) 2010 (ended 30 June 2010) from 5.7 per cent in FY2009. Construction revived with work on the Punatsangchhu I (1,200 megawatts (MW)) and Dagachhu (114MW) hydropower stations. Services, accounting for nearly two-fifths of GDP, contributed the bulk of the GDP gain, mainly construction related. Agriculture's growth was solid. Despite generating only about 16 per cent of GDP, it engages over 65 per cent of the labour force.

The electricity and water sector – nearly a quarter of GDP – did not contribute to the expansion, as no additional generation capacity has been added since Tala hydropower station came online in FY2007.

The global downturn had an adverse affect on tourism as visitor arrivals dropped by 9.3 per cent and foreign exchange earnings by 12.4 per cent.

As Bhutan is linked with India through trade (93.5 per cent of exports and 77.7 per cent of imports) and a currency peg, rising consumer prices in India tend to spill over. Year-on-year inflation rose to 6.1 per cent in the fourth quarter of FY2010 from 3.0 per cent a year earlier.

With the pickup in economic activity in 2010, growth in broad money accelerated to 30.1 per cent from 24.6 per cent, as domestic assets expanded. Domestic credit, primarily to the private sector, grew by 38.6 per cent in FY2010 from 31.1 per cent in the previous year, reflecting surging personal loans and credit to manufacturing.

The trade deficit is estimated to have worsened to 21.5 per cent of GDP in FY2010 from 7.5 per cent, as growth in merchandise imports accelerated markedly. Imports climbed by 39.0 per cent, mainly because of heavy needs for machinery, transport vehicles, and base

KEY FACTS

Official name: Druk-yul (The Kingdom of Bhutan)

Head of State: Druk Gyalpo (Dragon King) Jigme Kesar Namgyal Wangchuk (since 14 Dec 2006).

Head of government: Prime Minister Jigme Y Thinley (DPT) (from 9 Apr 2008)

Ruling party: Druk Phuensum Tshogpa (DPT) (Bhutan Peace and Prosperity Party) (from 23 Mar 2008)

Area: 47,000 square km

Population: 726,000 (2010)*

Capital: Thimphu

Official language: Dzongkha

Currency: Ngultrum (Nu) = 100 chetrums

Exchange rate: Nu48.98 per US$ (Oct 2011) (pegged to Indian rupee)

GDP per capita: US$1,978 (2010)

GDP real growth: 6.70% (2010)

GDP: US$1.41 billion (2010)

Inflation: 7.10% (2010)

Balance of trade: -US$144.70 million (2009)

Visitor numbers: 173,300 (2009)

* estimated figure

metals for the hydropower projects and housing.

Exports rose by only 5.5 per cent as sales of hydropower to India (about two-fifths of total exports) were pretty flat as capacity production has been reached. A jump in budgetary grants, mainly from India, held the current account deficit to 13.5 per cent of GDP in FY2010 from 1.6 per cent the previous year.

In addition to the construction of two hydropower stations, pre-construction works for Punatsangchhu II (990MW) and Mangdechhu (720MW) projects started in May 2010. Hydropower construction will therefore fuel GDP growth for the next 5 years, even as additional power production capacity and exports come online. Indeed, the government plans by 2020 to see new power stations increase generation capacity to 10,000MW, about seven times the present level. Accordingly, GDP is estimated to grow by 7.5 per cent in FY2011 and 8.0 per cent in FY2012.

High inflation in India, especially of food, is a concern. Projected higher global commodity price hikes will indirectly affect Bhutan, where inflation is expected to reach 8.0 per cent in FY2011 and moderate to 7.5 per cent in FY2012.

The current account deficit will deteriorate, mainly owing to imports of construction materials for power stations, as well as higher import prices of fuel. Export growth will likely be limited in the next couple of years. Expansion will need to come mainly from manufactured and commodity exports, as no additional power generation capacity will come online.

Although tourism revenue will grow, soaring imports are expected to push the current deficit out to around 20 per cent of GDP in both years. As with past projects, capital inflows from India to finance power plant construction, combined with development assistance, FDI, and some other borrowing, will likely suffice to finance the current account deficit.

Risk assessment

Economy	Fair
Politics	Fair
Regional stability	Fair

COUNTRY PROFILE

Historical profile

1907 The first hereditary king was enthroned.

1910 The Anglo-Bhutanese Treaty was signed, granting the government of British India full control of Bhutan's foreign relations.

1949 India became independent and the 1910 treaty was re-negotiated. Bhutan became free to pursue its own foreign policy, although it agreed to seek India's advice.

1952 King Jigme Dorji Wangchuk was enthroned and established the Tsogdu (National Assembly) in 1953.

1958 The Lhotshampa population of the southern districts of Bhutan was granted Bhutanese citizenship and tenure of lands.

1965 The Lodoi Tsokde (Royal Advisory Council) was established.

1972 King Jigme Singye Wangchuk was enthroned.

1979 Bhutan supported China in preference to India at the UN, beginning a gradual reorientation of foreign policy away from India.

1987 Bhutan's Sixth Five Year Plan included a policy of 'one nation, one people'. A code of traditional *Drukpa* dress and etiquette (*Driglam Namzhag*) was introduced.

1988 A census based on ethnicity branded many domiciled Nepalis as illegal immigrants, as a new citizenship law was enforced. Tibetan-based Bhutanese culture was officially emphasised.

1989 Nepali language was banned for use in schools.

1990 Anti-government protests in southern Bhutan led to ethnic violence as Bhutan People's Party began a campaign of violence; around 80,000 ethnic Nepalis fled to Nepal.

1998 King Wangchuk handed over full executive power to a Lhengye Zhungtshog (Council of Ministers).

1993 Talks between Bhutan and Nepal attempt to resolve the refugee problem.

1999 The King granted the Tsogdu the right to dismiss a reigning monarch. The WTO Working Party on Accession for the Kingdom of Bhutan was established.

2001 A draft constitution included proposals for a democratic system of government. Further talks took place concerning refugees between Bhutan and Nepal.

2002 The Ninth Five-Year Plan was drawn up to continue Bhutan's decentralisation process and promote 'Gross National Happiness'.

2003 A new government was installed with Jigme Yozer Thinley as prime minister.

2004 Indian insurgents entered Nepal and were reported to be working with Nepalese Maoists with a view to attacking Bhutan's royal palace.

2005 A draft constitution was unveiled that aimed to transform the country's absolute monarchy into a two-party democracy. Sangey Ngedup took office as prime minister. Crown Prince Jigme Khesar Namgyel Wangchuk undertook responsibilities held by the King, to gain experience before the King's abdication.

2006 The king appointed a chief elections commissioner and other officers to prepare for the first national elections. A mock election was held to train officials in the procedure. Khandu Wangchuk took office as prime minister. King Jigme Singye Wangchuk abdicated in favour of his son, Crown Prince Jigme Kesar Namgyal.

2007 Bhutan and India signed a treaty allowing Bhutan more control of foreign policy and military purchases. India was asked to provide increased security in border regions to prevent Assam Ulfa insurgents carrying out attacks in Bhutan. Lyonpo Khandu Wangchuk resigned as

KEY INDICATORS — Bhutan

	Unit	2006	2007	2008	2009	2010
Population	m	0.69	0.70	0.72	*0.74	*0.73
Gross domestic product (GDP)	US$bn	0.98	1.31	1.36	1.27	1.41
GDP per capita	US$	1,437	2,012	2,082	1,881	1,978
GDP real growth	%	11.0	22.4	6.6	6.3	6.7
Inflation	%	4.9	4.9	7.7	8.7	7.1
Unemployment	%	–	–	3.7	4.0	–
Exports (fob) (goods)	US$m	15,857.5	599.0	457.0	457.0	–
Imports (fob) (goods)	US$m	14,498.2	671.0	616.0	601.6	–
Balance of trade	US$m	1,359.3	-72.0	-159.0	-144.7	–
Current account	US$m	-29.0	116.0	160.0	-121.9	-73.0
Total reserves minus gold	US$m	545.3	699.0	764.8	890.9	1,002.1
Foreign exchange	US$m	543.3	696.8	762.6	879.2	990.7
Tourist numbers	'000	127.3	154.8	202.8	172.3	–
Exchange rate	per US$	44.43	41.35	43.50	48.40	45.73

* estimated figure

prime minister and Lyonpo Kinzang Dorji took office as the acting prime minister before the formation of the interim government and the first parliamentary general elections. Elections for the National Council of Bhutan (the upper house), were held for the first time since the King dissolved his absolute monarchy. Of the 25 members, 20 independent candidates were directly elected and five appointed by the King. Elections in five constituencies were postponed for one month as the minimum two candidates per district was not achieved.

2008 In the first parliamentary elections ever held in Bhutan, the Druk Phuensum Tshogpa (DPT) (Bhutan Peace and Prosperity Party) won 67.04 per cent of the vote (winning 45 seats out of 47), the People's Democratic Party (PDP) had 32.96 per cent (two seats); turnout was 79.4 per cent. Jigme Y Thinley (DPT) became prime minister. King Jigme Wangchuck was crowned. He became, at that time, the world's youngest monarch.

2009 Exiled Bhutanese in seven UNHCR-administered camps in Nepal launched a campaign for repatriation. An estimated 8,000 people were still awaiting a resolution of their plight; thousands more had already been offered access to third countries. An earthquake struck the eastern region, with a 6.1 magnitude.

2010 Two domestic airports at Bathbalathang and Yonphula were due to be opened with a domestic air service operated by the end of October, however completion was delayed.

2011 On 20 May, King Jigme announced to parliament his intentions of marrying commoner Jetsun Pema. They were married in a Buddhist ceremony on 12 October in a monastery in the capital Thimpu. Construction of a new domestic airport in Gelephu began on 2 July.

Political structure

Constitution

A draft constitution aiming to transform the country's absolute monarchy into a two-party democracy was drawn up in April 2005. It was approved by the people in a referendum during 2007.

Independence date

8 August 1949

Form of state

Hereditary monarchy

The executive

On 20 July 1998, King Jigme Singye Wangchuk handed over full executive power to the six-member Lhengye Zhungtshog (Council of Ministers).

The King is Head of State, assisted by the 10-member Lodoi Tsokde (Royal Advisory Council), the Tsogdu (National Assembly) and the monastic head of the kingdom's Buddhist priesthood.

National legislature

The bicameral parliament consists of the National Assembly (lower house) with between 47–55 directly elected members (dependent on the proportion of the population in each district) who serve five-year terms. The National Council (upper house) consists of 25 members (20 directly elected and five appointed by the monarch), all of which must be non-partisan; members serve five-year terms. The Druk Gyalpo (Dragon King) is also a member of the National Assembly.

Last elections

24 March 2008 (parliamentary)

Results: National Assembly: Druk Phuensum Tshogpa (DPT) Bhutan Peace and Prosperity Party won 67.04 per cent (45 seats out of 47), the People's Democratic Party (PDP) won 32.96 per cent (two seats); turnout was 79.4 per cent.

Political parties

Ruling party

Druk Phuensum Tshogpa (DPT) (Bhutan Peace and Prosperity Party) (from 23 Mar 2008)

Main opposition party

People's Democratic Party (PDP)

Population

726,000 (2010)*

Last census: May 2005: 634,982

In 2000 the United Nations (UN) *Statistical Yearbook* gave the population of Bhutan as 1,034,774, the CIA's *World Fact Book* had a figure of 2,005,222 and the World Bank's *World Development Report 2000/01* 782,000. Then in 2005 the Office of the Census Commission of the Royal Government of Bhutan conducted a census which gave a 2005 population count of 672,425. This figure does not include any Bhutanese refugees in camps outside Bhutan, which is put at over 100,000 by international aid agencies.

There are two possible reasons for the discrepancies in these figures. Firstly that in the early 1970s the government of Bhutan gave the UN an inflated figure so that Bhutan could become a member – at the time there was a cut-off point of one million. Thereafter a normal growth rate was added each year. A second possibility is that the western and central districts inflated their numbers to ensure their dominance over the southern and eastern districts. Again, once a figure had been established, each year an estimated figure was produced by using the population growth rate.

This publication has previously used the UN *Statistical Yearbook* figures. However, it now seems more realistic to start with the 2005 census figure. We have therefore taken the census figure of 672,425 and will increase the figure each year, until the next census, using the population growth rate, although even this figure (the World Health Organisation estimates 2.6 per cent 2000–15) is debatable. The *World Economic Outlook Database* of the International Monetary Fund, published in April 2009, has similar figures, although they start with a 2005 figure of 637,000 and increase by around 1 per cent per annum.

Population density: 18 inhabitants per square km (2010)

Annual growth rate: 2.2 per cent 1994–2004 (WHO 2006)

Ethnic make-up

There are many ethnic groups: the Sharchhop in the east (the largest group), the Ngalong in the west, the Lhotsampas, who speak Nepali, in the south and the Bumtaps, Khengpas, Layaps, Doyas and other nomadic groups.

Religions

Mahayana Buddhism is the state religion; Hinduism. Christianity is banned.

Education

The United Nations Children's Fund (Unicef) reported that in four decades, the government established 343 primary schools and a college that offers undergraduate degrees in arts and commerce. Since education remains a national priority in the country's development process, more than 150 community schools are available from which every school-age child may choose. However, classrooms are in short supply and most schools lack basic sanitation facilities. Each teacher may have an average of 37 students but in some schools, class sizes can reach 70 pupils.

Literacy rate: 61.1 per cent and 33.6 per cent for men and women respectively; adult rates (World Bank 2002).

Enrolment rate: 88.4 per cent net primary enrolment; 89.6 per cent, male, 87.2 per cent, female (2009).

Pupils per teacher: 37 in primary schools.

Health

Although improvement in the primary healthcare system has reduced the maternal mortality rate the figure is still one of the highest in south and east Asia. The United Nations Children's Fund (Unicef) reports that about four out of five women still deliver at home, without professional help.

Bhutan conducts national and regional immunisation days annually to achieve 90 per cent coverage. Unicef estimates that 22.2 per cent of households do not have safe drinking water.

Out-reach clinics spread across rural Bhutan provide low cost health care. A network of 145 basic health units supports the clinics, with each unit serving communities of 2,000 to 5,000 people. There

are 28 hospitals, which provide more advanced and referral treatment.
Unicef initiated model villages established in almost all the 202 sub-district blocks in the country have adopted a variety of health and education programmes. Its initial success has prompted Unicef to expand the model village experience into a more general community development programme.

Life expectancy: 63 years, 2004 (WHO 2006)

Fertility rate/Maternal mortality rate: 4.2 births per woman, 2004 (WHO 2006)

Child (under 5 years) mortality rate (per 1,000): 70 per 1,000 live births; around 19 per cent of children aged under five are malnourished (World Bank).

Head of population per physician: 0.05 physician per 1,000 people, 2004 (WHO 2006)

Welfare

In October 2001, the Bhutan government and the Asian Development Bank (ADB) signed a partnership agreement aimed at poverty reduction by 2012 through income and employment generation led by the private sector. Emphasis will be put on lifting monthly average rural incomes to about Nu3,000 (about US$65) per head. In March 2002, the ADB agreed to provide a US$700,000 grant to prepare a rural electrification and network expansion project.
There is a national pension plan and provident fund plan that currently provides for government employees and members of the armed forces. Between 16 per cent and 24 per cent of monthly earnings are paid into the funds, to provide for workers and their dependents. The amounts paid are split evenly between the employer and employee. These schemes are expected to be offered to other salaried workers over the next few years.

Pensions

Main cities

Thimphu (capital, estimated population 101,622 in 2003), Phuntsholing (113,262), Somdrup Jongkhar (15,091), Gaylegphug (15,091).

Languages spoken

There are 19 dialects and languages in Bhutan. Dzongkha bears similarities to Tibetan. English (the working language), Bumthangkha, Sharchop, Nepali and other dialects also spoken.

Official language/s

Dzongkha

Media

The government regulates the freedom of the media, excluding most private broadcasters.

Press

Weeklies: Weekly newspapers include, in Dzongkha *Kuensel* (www.kuenselonline.com); in English *Bhutan Observer* (www.bhutanobserver.com) and *Bhutan Times* (www.bhutantimes.bt) is published on Sunday.

Broadcasting

The government-operated Bhutan Broadcasting Service (BBS) (www.bbs.com.bt) is the only terrestrial television broadcaster.

Radio: The only independent radio station is Kuzoo FM (www.kuzoo.net), broadcasting in Dzongkha and English.

Television: The majority of programmes on the BBS are broadcast in Dzongkha (the national language and English (the working language).While the BBS is the only broadcaster, there is cable TV with many channels on offer.

Economy

This small landlocked country has achieved good economic growth and considerable improvement in its social indicators since the mid-1990s. According to the Bhutan Living Standard Survey (BLSS), the poverty headcount ratio was 23 per cent in 2007 and by 2010 Bhutan had either met or was on tract to meet its Millennium Development Goals. Government policy includes revitalising industry, expanding strategic infrastructure and investing in human capital (through healthcare and education). In 2008, agriculture, of which forestry was an important component, accounted for 19 per cent of GDP. Bhutan is almost entirely self-sufficient in the production of food and the agricultural sector employs over 80 per cent of the domestic labour force.
The service sector has remained static at around 35 per cent of GDP since the 1980s, which reflects a closed society that has only just moved to a democracy and openness. The economy is expected to develop with the expansion of entrepreneurial businesses catering for other new and established industries. Hydroelectricity generation and construction are the principal components of the industrial sector, which accounts for 46 per cent of GDP. The rugged terrain has required a greater than expected investment in roads and Bhutan has relied on foreign investment to gain its modernisation.
GDP growth was 5 per cent in 2008, a fall from the record high of 19.7 per cent in 2007. In 2009 growth returned to the 6.3 per cent, which had been typical before 2007 and is expected to remain at this level into 2010–11. GDP per capita has steadily increased from US$1,315 in 2006 to an estimated US$2,042 in 2010. Work has been carried out on tariff reform, liberalising foreign exchange and foreign direct investment (FDI) regulations, and deregulating interest rates.
Tourism has strong potential for growth, although travellers are restricted to pre-packaged holidays and arranged tours.

External trade

In 2010, Bhutan was in ongoing negotiations to join the World Trade Organisation. Trade, is limited to small-scale agricultural production and cottage industry manufacturing, as modern industrial production is limited. Bhutan's economy is closely linked to that of India, which provides financial and technical aid and manpower.

Imports

Principal imports are fuel and petroleum products, rice, machinery parts, vehicles and textiles.

Main sources: India (typically 78 per cent of total), Singapore (3 per cent), Japan (2 per cent).

Exports

Main exports include electricity (to India), cardamom, gypsum, timber, handicrafts, cement, fruit, precious stones and spices

Main destinations: India (typically 94 per cent of total), Bangladesh (3 per cent), Hong Kong (3 per cent).

Agriculture

Agriculture annually contributes around 26 per cent to GDP and employs 90 per cent of the workforce.
Approximately 15 per cent of the land area is fertile lowland arable and 72.5 per cent is forested. No trees can be cut down without a special permit.
Main crops are rice, maize, potatoes, citrus fruits, wheat, buckwheat, barley, millet, vegetables, mustard, apples and cardamom. Vegetable production is hindered by the cold climate.
Cattle, yaks, sheep, goats and pigs are raised.

Industry and manufacturing

The industrial sector contributes around 43 per cent to GDP annually. Manufacturing accounts for around 7.5 per cent of GDP, with cement as the principal product.
Small-scale local industries produce woodwork, fruit processing, weaving, textiles, soap, metals, handicrafts, carpets, matches and plywood manufacture. Most manufacturing industries are owned by the government.
Industrial growth has risen mainly because of increased value of electricity exports to India (from the Chukha hydroelectric plant). The Tala project alsdo enhanced growth when it came on stream in 2006–07. There has also been significant hydropower investment in industry.

Tourism
The tourist industry is comparatively young and the government has worked hard to maintain a balance between the needs of an emerging economy and Bhutan's historic (and unspoiled) culture that could so easily be damaged by unrestricted tourism. Bhutan prides itself on having a Gross National Happiness (GNH) indicator as part of its policy making process and its application to the development of the tourist industry (referred to locally as the 'tourism resource'), has at its centre the welfare of the people. In 2011 the government was at a stage of developing policies that respected the GNH index while balancing the pressures of growth and any free-market approach to tourism. The remoteness of Bhutan has helped regulate tourism, not only by the limited number of visitors that reach it within the Himalayas, but to travel overland or fly into the country all visitors must make arrangements through Bhutanese travel operators and obtain visas. The number of visitors in 2000 was 7,559 and the government has set a limit of 20,000 for 2012.

Mining
Mining contributes about 1 per cent to GDP and employs 1 per cent of the workforce.
Deposits of many minerals exist, but quarrying is restricted to limestone, dolomite, gypsum and slate due to difficulties of access. Talcum powder is the major mineral export.

Hydrocarbons
There are no known oil or gas reserves. Annual consumption is typically around 1,000 barrels per day of petroleum products.
Bhutan has coal reserves of 1.3 million tonnes and produces only 1,000 tonnes of coal per annum, which are used for domestic consumption. Some exploration is being carried out on the southern borders as the government encourages private sector investment in the sector.

Energy
Total installed generating capacity was 485MW in 2006, of which 97 per cent was provided by hydropower, which is Bhutan's most important economic asset. Domestic consumption is around 110MW and all surplus is exported to India, providing the largest component of Bhutan's total exports, which contributed 45 per cent of total revenues before the opening of the Tala Hydroelectric Project, which has increased energy export revenue to 60 per cent. The major hydroelectric facility, the Chukha plant, is connected to the Indian electricity grid. The India-backed Tala Hydroelectric Project, producing 1,020MW was completed in 2008, including six 170MW generators, with all of its production exported to India.
More than 90 per cent of Bhutan's domestic energy requirements are provided by biomass, such as firewood, due to low levels of rural electrification. Over 70 per cent of domestic energy consumption is accounted for by the household sector.

Banking and insurance
Central bank
Royal Monetary Authority (RMA)
Main financial centre
Phuntsholing

Time
GMT plus six hours

Geography
Bhutan is a landlocked country that lies in the Himalayan range of mountains, with Tibet (the People's Republic of China) to the north and India to the south.
Bhutan has three distinct regions. The high Himalayas is mountainous with little population. The tallest peak, at 7,554 metres is Kulha Gangri; there are 20 other peaks over 7,000m high.
The inner Himalayas is mostly rugged terrain, cut through with gorges and fast flowing snow-fed rivers. Mountain spurs that turn south divide the country and produce fertile, forest-lined valleys and terraced farming basins.
The southern foothills, including the Duar Plain, is only 20km wide; it is fertile flatland and home to some exotic wildlife: tigers, leopards, elephants and rhinoceros. Snow leopards, the world's rarest big cat, live at higher altitudes.
Hemisphere
Northern

Climate
There are three distinct climatic regions: the lowlands, along the border with India, are tropical with an annual monsoon, the middle band is temperate and the north is high frozen, glacial mountains. The capital Thimphu lies in the temperate zone with temperature variation ranging from: winter 12– minus 3 degrees Celsius (C) (day–night); summer 24–15 degrees C. The hottest region, in the south and Duar Plain, can range from: winter 20–11 degrees C (day–night); summer 31–23 degrees C. The monsoon usually arrives from mid-June to the end of August, with up to 4.5–5.0 metres of rain falling, although a high of 7.5 metres has been recorded.

Entry requirements
Passports
Required by all, except Indian nationals.
Visa
All visitors, except Indian nationals, require visas and these must be arranged prior to arrival.
Independent travel is not permitted, even for business purposes. Businessmen and tourists are admitted only in groups by pre-arrangement through registered tour operators in Bhutan. This can be done directly or through a travel agent abroad. A minimum daily tariff is regulated and fixed by the government. The rate includes all accommodation, meals, transport, and services.
Overseas Bhutanese embassies do not issue visas; they are issued from Thimphu. Visa applications should be made at least three months in advance. Add an extra three weeks for business visas, when a letter of introduction from a Bhutan company and an employer's guarantee, plus an itinerary should accompany applications.
The only airline servicing Bhutan is Druk-Air, which will only board travellers with visa clearance from the tourism authority. Entry is via India, Bangladesh, Nepal or Thailand.
At the point of entry, visas are stamped and a payment of US$20 is required, along with two passport photographs. The visa is required for exit from Bhutan.
If travelling overland from India a transit pass from the Indian authorities is required to permit passage through prohibited areas of the India-Bhutan border. For this, apply to the Indian Ministry of External Affairs in Delhi some months before travelling.
Enquiries can be made to the Bhutan Tourism Corporation (see travel information directory, below).
Although Bhutan has no formal diplomatic representation in Europe or the US, it has a Permanent Mission to the UN at 2 United Nations Plaza, 27th Floor, New York, NY 10017 (tel: (+1) (212) 826-1919), which has consular jurisdiction in the US. Informal contact is maintained between the Bhutanese and US Embassy in New Delhi (India).
Customs
All visitors will complete a customs declaration on arrival, when all videos, computer and personal electronic equipment must be declared,
Export of antiques and religious antiquities, plants and animal products is prohibited.

Health (for visitors)
Mandatory precautions
A vaccination certificate for yellow fever is required if arriving from an infected area.
Advisable precautions
Anti-malarial precautions are advisable. Bhutanese hospitals only provide basic care. Comprehensive medical insurance should therefore be obtained.

Hotels
All hotel bookings are made through the Bhutan Tourism Corporation. Private hotels are open only to Bhutan nationals, some Indian nationals and certain business contacts; state hotels are of adequate standard.

Credit cards
Of limited use, they may be accepted in a few shops; travellers cheques are accepted in many more places.

Public holidays (national)
Fixed dates
2 May (Third King's Birthday), 2 Jun (Coronation Day), 8 Aug (Independence Day), 11 Nov (three days, Birthday of HM Jigme Singye Wangchuck), 17 Dec (National Day).
Variable dates
Winter Solstice (Jan), Offerings Day (Jan), Losay (Lunar New Year) (two days Feb), Shabdrung Kuchoe (Apr/May), Buddha Parinirvana (May/Jun), Buddha's First Sermon (Jul/Aug), Third King's Death (Jul), Guru Rinpoche's Birthday (Jul), Blessed Rainy Day (Sep), Dashaim (Oct), Buddha Descension Day (Oct/Nov).
Bhutan uses a lunisolar calendar that follows, essentially, the Tibetan lunar calendar. There are 12 or 13 months in a year, each beginning and ending with a new moon (approximately 28 days), in a three year cycle. An extra month is added in the third year so that, on average, the calendar matches the solar year (365.25 days). Months do not have names and are referred to by their numbers. The new year begins in February and is called Losay. Buddhist festivals are declared according to local astronomical observations.

Working hours
Banking
Bank of Bhutan: 0630–0930 and 1200–1600. Other banks, Mon—Fri: 0900–1700; 0900–1300 (cash transactions); Sat: 0900–1100.
Business
Mon–Fri: 0900–1700.
Shops
Mon—Sun: 0900–2000. Closed Tuesday.

Telecommunications
Mobile/cell phones
GSM 900 service is available in major cities and towns.

Electricity supply
220 Volts, 50Hz.

Weights and measures
Metric system

Social customs/useful tips
Prior permission is required to visit some of the religious and administrative buildings (*Dzongs*) and special permits are required to visit certain areas.

Security
Most visits are trouble-free and the country is generally peaceful.

Getting there
Air
Air transport into Bhutan is by Druk-Air, which flies from India (New Delhi and Kolkata), Nepal (Kathmandu), Bangladesh and Thailand. Druk-Air bookings can only be arranged after a visa has been issued and must also be obtained from a Bhutanese tour operator.
National airline: Druk-Air (Royal Bhutan Airlines).
International airport/s: Paro (PBH), 8km south of Paro, 68km from Thimpu.
Airport tax: International departures Nu300
Surface
Road: There are two overland access routes, both from India. A new crossing between Assam and Samdrup Jongkhar in eastern Bhutan allows tours to travel on a single-lane road to the capital. The older crossing, from the Indian frontier (Jaigaon) to Phuntsholing, has the added problem for travellers of crossing the Indian state of West Bengal before reaching Bhutan. Whichever route is taken the journey is arduous.

Getting about
National transport
Air: No services exist.
Road: The road network comprises some 3,000km, largely surfaced. The mountain roads are hazardous and subject to landslides in the monsoon season. No roads exist in the northern high Himalaya regions.
Buses: Bus services are available between main centres, although local enquiries are recommended.
City transport
Taxis: The airport journey to Thimphu is 90 minutes.
Buses, trams & metro: There is a bus service to the airport from Thimphu, journey time 90 minutes.
Car hire
Certain services are available, and local enquiries are recommended. An international driving licence is needed.
Traffic drives on the left and 40kph is the average speed.

BUSINESS DIRECTORY

The addresses listed below are a selection only. While World of Information makes every endeavour to check these addresses, we cannot guarantee that changes have not been made, especially to telephone numbers and area codes. We would welcome any corrections.

Telephone area codes
The international dialling code (IDD) for Bhutan is +975, followed by area code and subscriber's number:

Jakar	3	Thimphu	2

Chambers of Commerce
Bhutan Chamber of Commerce and Industry, PO Box 147, Doybum Lam, Thimphu (tel: 322-742; fax: 323-936; e-mail: bsdbcci@druknet.net.bt).

Banking
Bank of Bhutan, (tel: 322-621, 322-266; fax: 323-433).

Bhutan National Bank, PO Box 439, Thimphu (tel: 322-767, 323-602; fax: 323-601; e-mail: mdbnb@druknet.net.bt).

Central bank
Royal Monetary Authority of Bhutan, PO Box 154, Thimphu (tel: 323-111; fax: 322-847; e-mail: rma@rma.org.bt).

Travel information
Association of Bhutanese Tour Operators (ABTO), PO Box 938, Thimphu (tel: 322-862, 327-715; fax: 325-286; email: abto@druknet.net.bt).

Bhutan Yodsel Tours and Treks, PO Box 574, Thimphu (tel: 323-912; fax: 323-589; e-mail: dawa@druknet.net.bt).

Department of Tourism PO Box 126, Thimphu, Bhutan (tel: 232-3251, 232-3252; fax: 232-3695; email: dot@tourism.gov.bt).

SITA Travels, SITA House, Presidential Business Park, C-9, Vasant Kunj, New Delhi 110070, India (tel: (+9111) 2612-1110; fax: (9111) 2612-1125; email: info@sitaindia.com and lokeshb@sitaindia.com; internet: www.sitaspecialtours.com).

Ministry of tourism
Bhutan Tourism Corporation Ltd (BTCL), PO Box 159, Thimphu (tel: 322-045, 322-854, 322-647; fax: 323-392, 322-479; e-mail: btcl@druknet.net.bt; ynorbu@druknet.net.bt; internet site: www.kingdomofbhutan.com).

National tourist organisation offices
Tourism Authority of Bhutan (supplies lists of operators and trekking agencies), PO Box 126, Thimphu (tel: 323-251/2, 325-121/2; fax: 323-695; e-mail: tab@druknet.net.bt).

Ministries
Ministry of Agriculture, PO Box: 252, Thimphu (tel: 232-3765; fax: 232-3153; internet: www.moa.gov.bt).

Ministry of Education PO Box 112, Thimphu (tel: 232-5325; fax: 232-5183; internet: www.education.gov.bt).

Ministry of Finance, PO Box: 117, Thimphu (tel: 232-2223; fax: 232-3154; internet: www.mof.gov.bt).

Ministry of Health, PO Box: 108, Kawangsa, Thimphu (tel: 232-2602, 232-2961; fax: 232-3113, 232-4649; internet: www.health.gov.bt).

Ministry of Home and Cultural Affairs Tashichodzong, Thimphu (tel: 232-6015; fax: 232-4320).

Ministry of Information and Communications, PO Box: 278, Thimphu (tel: 232-2144, 232-4439; fax: 232-1055; internet: www.moic.gov.bt).

Ministry of Labour and Human Resources, PO Box: 1036, Thongsel Lam, Lower Motithang, Thimphu (tel: 232-6732, 232-1482; fax: 232-6731; internet: www.employment.gov.bt).

Ministry of Trade and Industry, PO Box 126 Thimphu (tel: 23-251; fax: 23-695; internet: www.mti.gov.bt).

Ministry of Works and Human Settlement, PO Box: 791, Thimphu (tel: 232-7998, 232-2182; fax: 232-270; internet: www.mowhs.gov.bt).

Other useful addresses

Bhutanese Embassy, India, Chandragupta Marg, Chanakyapuri, New Delhi, 110 021 India (tel: (+91-11) 2688-9230/9806/7).

Bhutanese Permanent Mission to the UN, 2 United Nations Plaza, 27th Floor, New York, NY 10017 (tel: (+1-212) 826-1919; fax: (+1-212) 826-2998).

State Trading Corp of Bhutan, 52 Trivoli Court, Ballygange Circular Road, Calcutta, 700019, India.

United Nations Development Programme, United Nations Building, Dremton Lam, GPO Box 162, Thimphu (tel: 322 424; fax: 322-657; e-mail: fo.btn@undp.org).

Internet sites

Bhutan Experditions: www.bhutan-expeditions.com

Bhutan government portal: www.bhutan.gov.bt

Bhutan News Online: www.bhutannewsonline.com

Bolivia

KEY FACTS

Official name: Estado Plurinacional de Bolivia (Plurinational State of Bolivia)

Head of State: President Juan Evo Morales Ayma (since 22 Jan 2006)

Head of government: President Juan Evo Morales Ayma

Ruling party: Movimiento al Socialismo (MAS) (Movement towards Socialism) (from Dec 2005)

Area: 1,098,581 square km

Population: 10.23 million (2009)*

Capital: La Paz (administrative); Sucre (legislative and judicial)

Official language: Spanish

Currency: Boliviano (B) = 100 centavos

Exchange rate: B6.92 per US$ (Oct 2011)

GDP per capita: US$1,858 (2010)

GDP real growth: 4.20% (2010)

GDP: US$19.40 billion (2010)

Unemployment: 7.90% (2009) (additional widespread underemployment)

Inflation: 2.50% (2010)

Balance of trade: US$774.00 million (2009)

* estimated figure

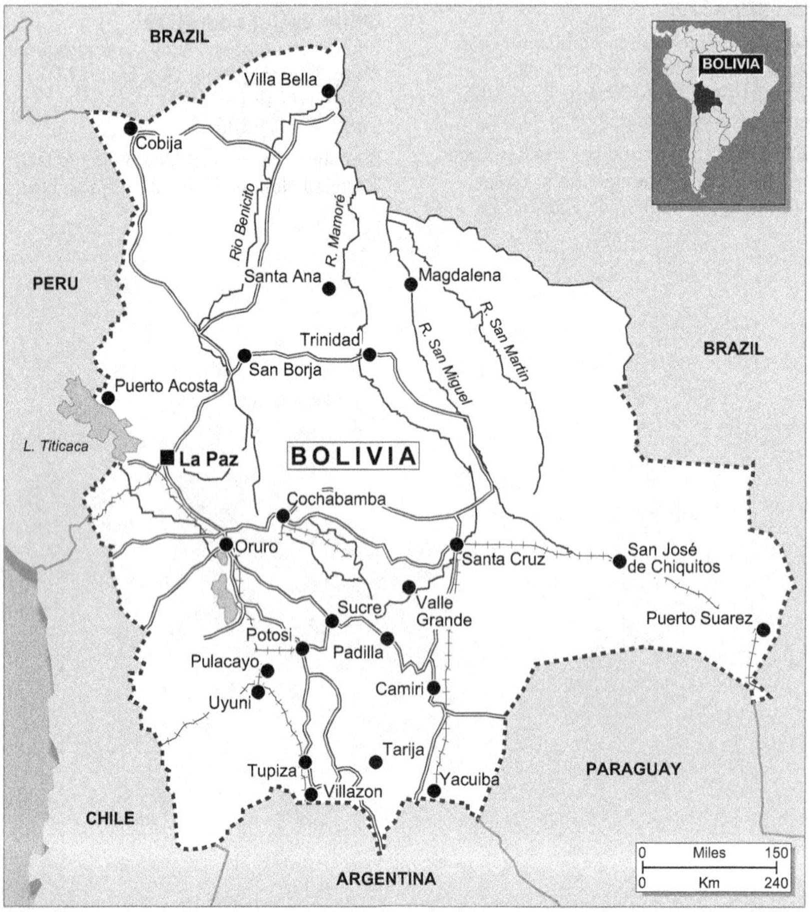

On the day after Christmas, 26 December 2010, the Bolivian government abruptly announced the removal of subsidies on diesel and gasoline – they cost the Bolivian exchequer an estimated US$666 million and were forecast to reach US$1 billion in 2011. In many countries this might have proved a manageable exercise. Not so in Bolivia, where the move represented a 73 per cent increase in pump prices. Subsidised petrol sold at an affordable US$0.50 a litre, less than half the price pertaining in Chile and Brazil. On the day of the announcement Bolivia's president Evo Morales, possibly foreseeing trouble, was visiting his ally, Hugo Chávez in Venezuela.

Setbacks

At the end of 2010 it had seemed that Sr Morales could do little wrong. But as 2011 progressed, his touch seemed to have deserted him, as he stumbled from one setback to another. The removal of fuel subsidies lasted only five days. Such was the intensity of the protests sweeping Bolivia, that President Morales had little option but to reverse the subsidy removal. Protestors had blocked Bolivia's roads, entered and burnt government offices. Bolivia's bus drivers had gone on strike. On top of paying a subsidy, which in effect encouraged the use of fuel, Bolivia's limited refining capacity means that it has to import refined petroleum and diesel.

Having backed down on the question of subsidies, Mr Morales' political vulnerability began to reveal itself. Graffiti displaying the slogan: 'Morales = Implosión' reflected the electorate's dissatisfaction, not only over the fuel subsidies, but also at increased food prices. In the twelve months to January 2011 inflation had risen to an annual rate of 8.4 per cent. Not only was food expensive, essentials such as sugar had become hard to find. Many of the price rises could be attributed to global increases, but government policies had also played their part. The imposition of price controls on certain crops had meant that farmers had simply avoided planting them.

Mr Morales' five years in government (he had comfortably won a second term with 64 per cent of the vote in 2009) had seen an unparalleled period of economic growth. There were two causes – high mineral prices on the world markets and largely cautious economic policies. But the removal of the fuel subsidies had seen that caution thrown to the wind. For the first time, Morales' popularity had seriously dipped; an Ipsos-Apoyo poll in Bolivia's urban areas showed an approval rating of only 32 per cent. Mr Morales' ruling coalition – Movimiento al Socialismo (MAS) (Movement towards Socialism) – is a tenuous grouping that risks disintegrating when faced with popular dissatisfaction. Its saving grace has been the absence of a cohesive opposition in Bolivia.

In October 2011, Mr Morales found himself on the back foot again, this time over heavyweight opposition to the construction of a road through the Isiboro-Sécure Indigenous Territory and National Park (TIPNIS). A 40 day march to the capital was organised which the police broke up; the heavy-handedness of the police was such that two members of Mr Morales' own cabinet, the defence and interior ministers, resigned in protest. In La Paz, where the march was due to end, a reported ten thousand or more attended a demonstration against the road.

Broadcasting control

In mid-2011 the Bolivian Congress passed a new telecommunications law that, *de facto*, gave the government greater control over broadcast media. Whereas before the law over 90 per cent of broadcasting was in the hands of private companies, the new law allocated one third of broadcasting licences to the state, the same proportion to the private sector and the remaining third to indigenous and social organisations. Associations of journalists and of broadcasters criticised the new law as a threat to constitutional rights. *Inter-alia* the new law would oblige radio and television stations to broadcast Morales' speeches at no cost to the government.

While most of the debate on the new law centred on broadcasting, the proposed legislation included a sinister clause that would allow the relevant governmental authorities to listen to telephone conversations. Telecommunications companies would be required to co-operate in providing information. The law would permit eavesdropping on politicians, ministers and journalists in cases affecting 'national security'.

The Loss of the Sea

Mr Morales is not the first Bolivian president to resort to the sensitive issue of the restoration of Bolivia's lost coastline. Nor, in all likelihood is he the first to do so when faced with a drop in popularity. On 23 March 2011, on Bolivia's Day of the Sea, he promised to sue the Chilean government in the international courts in a bid to force it to redress what he referred to as Bolivia's 'open wound', the loss of Bolivia's coastline to Chile after the War of the Pacific in 1879. Bolivia formerly possessed 400km of Pacific coastline, with a hinterland containing significant mineral resources in the region of the Atacama desert. The previous Chilean administration under President Michelle Bachelet had seen the two countries hold constructive discussions on the subject; under Chile's President Piñera, the discussions seemed to have been placed on the Chilean back burner, causing President Morales to impose a deadline of 23 March for Chile to come up with a serious proposal.

Bolivia has not had formal diplomatic relations with Chile since 1978, when negotiations over a sovereign corridor to the Pacific came to an inconclusive end. Peru, which also lost territory in the same war, has promised to back the Bolivian claims, going so far as to offer Bolivia the use of a Peruvian port to redress the 'unjust' situation.

Belt tightening

The diesel and gasoline subsidy reversal was emblematic of the problems confronting Mr Morales. According to the government Bolivia posted a fiscal surplus for the fifth year running in 2010. Not so, say some independent analysts, who claim that in fact a deficit was recorded. According to the United Nations Economic Commission for Latin America and the Caribbean (ECLAC) Bolivia's gross domestic product (GDP) was expected to show growth of 3.8 per cent in 2010 (in fact the figure was 4.2 per cent), while urban unemployment in the second quarter of the year registered 6.0 per cent (slightly lower than in the second quarter of 2009). The balance of payments current account was forecast to end the year with a larger surplus than in 2009, mainly due to a trade balance surplus and higher remittances from abroad. By contrast, the non-financial public sector accounts closed the year with a deficit for the first time since 2005.

During the first two quarters of 2010, the Central Bank of Bolivia relaxed its

KEY INDICATORS — Bolivia

	Unit	2006	2007	2008	2009	2010
Population	m	*9.63	*9.83	*10.03	*10.23	*10.52
Gross domestic product (GDP)	US$bn	11.23	13.19	17.40	17.60	19.40
GDP per capita	US$	1,125	1,342	1,737	1,724	1,858
GDP real growth	%	4.6	4.2	5.9	3.3	4.2
Inflation	%	4.3	8.7	14.0	3.5	2.5
Natural gas output	bn cum	11.2	13.5	13.9	12.3	14.4
Exports (fob) (goods)	US$m	3,863.0	4,490.4	6,447.8	4,917.5	–
Imports (fob) (goods)	US$m	2,809.0	3,249.2	4,641.0	4,143.6	–
Balance of trade	US$m	1,312.0	1,241.2	1,806.9	774.0	–
Current account	US$m	1,317.5	1,758.0	2,015.0	813.5	924.0
Total reserves minus gold	US$m	2,614.8	4,554.0	6,927.4	7,583.8	8,133.9
Foreign exchange	US$m	2,561.2	4,497.7	6,871.4	7,311.3	7,866.2
Exchange rate	per US$	7.99	7.64	7.28	7.02	7.02

* estimated figure

expansionary monetary policy stance through net bond issues in open market operations. This move was part of the central bank's monetary programme, which set targets for expanding total net domestic credit and net domestic credit to the non-financial public sector and for slightly reducing net foreign reserves. During the first half of the year, these targets were easily met.

The banking system's lending and deposit rates continued to drop in 2010. Between September 2009 and October 2010, the government's policy of boosting credit to the productive sector pushed average lending rates down from 7.6 per cent to 4.99 per cent and deposit rates from 0.5 per cent to 0.2 per cent. As lower interest rates stimulated borrowing, the gross loan portfolio increased by 24 per cent between December 2009 and October 2010, to reach a total of US$5.108 billion. The process known as 'bolivianisation' (or 'de-dollarisation') of the banking system continued in 2010, with over 50 per cent of loans and deposits held in bolivianos at year-end.

According to official information available to ECLAC in August 2010, the non-financial public sector was running a surplus of approximately 2.8 per cent of GDP. With respect to the same period in 2009, expenditure as a percentage of GDP was down by 0.3 percentage points and revenue by 2.1 percentage points. Although the results to September indicate a fall in both revenue and expenditure, Bolivia was expected to close 2010 with expenditure as a percentage of GDP at 1 percentage point higher than at year-end 2009 (from 32.4 per cent to 33.4 per cent), while revenue was projected to decrease from 31.3 per cent to 30 per cent of GDP.

Although tax revenue overall will likely inch up from 17.1 per cent to 17.3 per cent of GDP, receipts from the hydrocarbon tax are expected to fall from 9.8 per cent to 8.5 per cent of GDP. This fall is due mainly to the fact that it takes two to three quarters for a rise in oil prices to affect sales prices in the oil sector. The higher tax receipts will come principally from increased inflows of customs duties, which rose by an estimated 12.8 per cent in nominal terms in 2010 as a result of a 21.1 per cent increase in imports between September 2009 and September 2010. In the year to September 2010 current expenditure rose by 1 percentage point (from 12.7 per cent to 13.7 per cent of GDP), with a projected increase of 1.8 percentage points by the end of the year.

Construction, which grew by 10.2 per cent in 2010, was the most buoyant area of economic activity, thanks mainly to the boom in housing construction. Increased demand for gas in Brazil and Argentina spurred expansion of 6.4 per cent in the crude oil and natural gas sector. Mining, which – with growth of over 14 per cent – had been the most robust sector in 2009, expanded by only 0.72 per cent in 2010. In addition, during the second half of the year, strikes in the mining region of Potosí brought mining operations to a halt for almost an entire month. ECLAC forecasts economic growth at about 4.5 per cent for 2011.

Inflation in 2010 was 2.5 per cent, substantially higher than 0.3 per cent in 2009. Inflation was driven up by the rise in commodity prices, as some food items became costlier due to shortages caused by drought and flooding in various parts of the country. As a result, inflation rose by 1.2 per cent in October and by 1.1 per cent in November, which represented almost one half of the total cumulative inflation to that point. Between June 2009 and June 2010, the unemployment rate fell from 7.73 per cent to 6.03 per cent, owing mainly to a drop in female unemployment from 9.43 per cent to 6.89 per cent.

In 2010, Bolivia ran a current account surplus of about US$713 million, which was 12.34 per cent less than in 2009. Goods exports grew by US$788 million (16.02 per cent), owing in part to the surge in hydrocarbon exports (34 per cent) triggered by a recovery in demand from Brazil during the year. Imports rose by 22.32 per cent, leading to a goods balance of US$639.9 million, which was 17.71 per cent lower than in 2009. Workers' remittances were down by US$66 million (9.9 per cent) compared with the first half of 2009. The capital and financial accounts posted a surplus of US$76 million. Through October 2010, the net international reserves held by the central bank increased by US$609 million (7.1 per cent) to reach US$9.208 billion, which was equivalent to 21 months of import cover.

Oil

Although Bolivia exports natural gas to Brazil and Argentina, continued doubts about the size of its proved natural gas reserves have contributed to skepticism about its potential to be a significant fossil fuel producer and regional energy hub. Political risk has also characterised the energy sector and foreign involvement in it. Bolivia has asserted greater state control over the energy sector since Evo Morales and his MAS party assumed power in January 2006 and issued a nationalisation decree in May of that year.

Hydrocarbons, primarily natural gas, account for roughly 10 per cent of Bolivia's GDP, 30 per cent of government revenues and 40 per cent of export earnings. The state-owned oil company Yacimientos Petrolíferos Fiscales Bolivianos (YPFB) and private companies claimed to have invested around US$800 million in Bolivia's hydrocarbon sector in 2010, an increase of over 30 per cent from 2009.

Petroleum is responsible for roughly half of Bolivia's primary energy consumption, with most of the remainder natural gas. According to the International Energy Agency (IEA), combustible renewables and waste meet nearly 15 per cent of the country's energy needs. Traditional biomass is an important fuel for heating and cooking, especially for the 2.2 million Bolivians who still lack access to electricity. The electrification rate of 77.5 per cent masks enormous disparities for urban and rural populations: more than 98 per cent of city dwellers have access to electricity, compared to just 38 per cent of those in rural areas.

Historically, Bolivian oil consumption and production had been strongly correlated. Domestic production satisfied most of the country's demand, with a small surplus devoted to exports. Following the sector's reorganisation, oil production declined by nearly one-quarter between 2007 and 2009 and Bolivia became a net exporter to a net importer of petroleum. Bolivian oil production rebounded appreciably in 2010. Statistics from YPFB suggest that the increased production of natural gas liquids more than offset declines in crude oil production.

Bolivia has proven oil reserves of 465 million barrels, according to the US-based *Oil & Gas Journal* (OGJ). Estimates of Bolivia's proven reserves have been relatively consistent since the early 2000s, when they increased three-fold due to heightened exploration activity. Bolivia has only the sixth-largest oil reserves in South America and ranks among the smallest reserve-holders in the world. Bolivia claims another 391 million barrels of probable reserves and 255 million barrels of possible reserves.

Natural gas

Among mainland South American countries, Bolivia trails only Argentina and Venezuela in terms of natural gas production. Its production volumes have risen dramatically since 1999, when natural gas exports to Brazil began. The development and disposition of Bolivia's natural gas has been a source of considerable controversy. Violent unrest and government crackdowns in late 2003 became known as the Gas Wars because they were precipitated by opposition to a plan to export liquefied natural gas (LNG) via Chile, with which Bolivia has had troubled relations since it lost its sovereign access to the sea during the nineteenth-century War of the Pacific.

Roughly one-fifth of Bolivian natural gas production is used in the domestic market, which is dominated by electricity demand (over one-half of Bolivian natural gas consumption), industry (roughly one-quarter) and transport (just below one-fifth). Domestic natural gas prices are fixed at levels that range from US$.90 per thousand cubic feet (Mcf) to US$1.98 per Mcf, depending upon its end-use. Bolivia has proved natural gas reserves of over 26 trillion cubic feet (Tcf), according to the OGJ, which would rank as the second largest reserves in South America. However, some studies have suggested that the country's proved reserves are less than half that size. Most recently, YPFB accepted a Ryder Scott report that significantly downgrades the size of Bolivia's proved reserves to 9.9Tcf.

Bolivia produced an estimated 14.4 billion cubic metres (Bcm) of dry natural gas at the end of 2010, a substantial increase from 12.3Bcm the year before. Officially, the largest natural gas producer in the country is YPFB. However, as with the oil sector, Petrobras Bolivia is the operator of the Sabalo and San Alberto fields and is thus responsible for 60 per cent of the country's output. State-owned YPFB Chaco and YPFB Andina collectively produce 20 per cent of Bolivia's natural gas, with a number of privately held firms responsible for smaller stakes.

Brazil is the primary destination for Bolivian natural gas. Roughly 70 per cent of Bolivian natural gas output – or 85 per cent of exports – is directed to Brazil. Natural gas exports to Brazil began in 1999. The bilateral natural gas trade is governed by a 20 year contract between YPFB and Petrobras, under which Bolivia commits to supplying 1.1Bcf per day (30.08 million cubic meters per day (Mcm per day)). In October 2010, Bolivia agreed to supply Brazil with a further 78Mcf per day (2.2Mcm per day) of gas for a power plant in Cuiabá, which has been shuttered since Bolivian supplies were interrupted in 2007 due to unexpectedly low output and high domestic demand.

Bolivia began exporting natural gas to Argentina in 1972, which is now the destination for about 15 per cent of Bolivian natural gas exports. Official data suggest that Bolivian exports to Argentina averaged less than 173Mcf per day (4.9Mcm per day) in 2010, but Bolivia insists it is abiding by the terms of the agreement due to the relatively high heat content of its natural gas.

Risk assessment

Economy	Fair
Politics	Fair
Regional stability	Fair

COUNTRY PROFILE

Historical profile

Bolivia was inhabited by the ancient Aymará peoples, who were conquered by the Incas.

1538 The Incas were conquered by the Spanish.

1825 There were many revolts against Spanish rule; independence was finally gained under the leadership of Simón Bolívar.

1826 Bolivia's first constitution was established.

1879–83 War of the Pacific between Bolivia, Peru and Chile over disputed territory along the Pacific coast. Bolivia and Peru suffered a humiliating defeat by Chile's armed forces. A new elite, with mining interests, combined with the traditional ruling oligarchy, supported by external capitalist interests, gained power and polarised civil society into conservative and liberal factions.

1890s The exploitation of tin brought prosperity and peace after years of turbulent and unstable government. A new constitution established centralised political control and the separation of powers between the legislature, executive and judiciary. The indigenous population was disenfranchised when property and literacy were made a prerequisite.

1933–35 Defeat during the Chaco Wars with Paraguay led to a large part of the Chaco region, much of it arid and infertile, being annexed by Paraguay. The defeat discredited the ruling elite and formed the basis for a realignment of Bolivian politics with the middle-class joining the working-class and *campesinos* (peasant farmers) forming a broad revolutionary movement.

1941 Formation of the Movimiento Nacionalista Revolucionario (MNR) (Nationalist Revolutionary Movement), a broad multi-class coalition to resist the power of the traditional oligarchy and what was seen as US imperialism.

1951 A military *Junta* prevented the newly elected president, Victor Paz Estenssoro (MNR) from taking office. With the help of a militia, recruited from the national police, miners and peasants, a rebellion succeeded in installing a revolutionary council. It nationalised tin holdings and instigated land reform. Universal suffrage was extended to the indigenous population. A state-capitalist development programme was initiated, backed by the IMF and later by the US programme 'Alliance for Progress'.

1964 Vice President René Barrientos Ortuño led a *coup d'état*. The military continued to implement similar policies to the MNR's state-capitalist model.

1969 Barrientos died in a mysterious helicopter crash that many suspected was an assassination. A brief period of military populism was followed by the succession of the Bolivian left, the expulsion of the US Peace Corps and the creation of a Soviet-style People's Assembly.

1971 A violent coup led by Colonel Hugo Bánzer Suárez led to the repression of labour leaders and left-wing politicians in a period of a *Junta* known as the *Banzerato*.

1978 Strains within the ruling elite and pressure from US President Jimmy Carter forced Bánzer to call elections.

1978–1982 A period of political turbulence: seven military and two civilian governments held office for an average of six months each. Meanwhile, political parties split into different factions, resulting in 70 different parties – the MNR alone split into thirty parties – resulting in a weak civil society.

1979 The Acción Democrática Nacionalista (ADN) (Democratic Nationalist Action) was formed by Bánzer.

1982 Siles Zuazo was elected president; his rule was ineffective as he struggled to appease both the IMF and growing militant elements within the civilian population. Meanwhile, the Bolivian economy collapsed from hyperinflation and high levels of foreign debt.

1985 Siles resigned. President Paz Estenssoro (MNR) implemented austere fiscal policies and brought about economic liberalisation. He also signed a Pact for Democracy with the ADN to resolve the impasse between the executive and legislature.

1989 The new president, Paz Zamora (MIR), offered tax incentives for direct foreign investment in the mining industry.

1993 Gonzalo Sánchez de Lozada (MNR) won the presidential election.

1998 Hugo Bánzer was elected president following popular discontent with economic liberalisation measures initiated by the MNR. Bánzer's rule intensified efforts to restructure the economy prescribed by the IMF, while implementing a coca-eradication programme demanded by the US.

2001 Bánzer resigned due to ill health and was replaced by Vice President Jorge Quiroga.
2002 Hugo Bánzer died. Congress appointed Lozada (known universally by his nickname 'Goni') Gonzalo Sánchez de as president.
2003 Civil unrest throughout the year led to the resignation of President Lozada. Vice President Carlos Mesa was sworn in as president.
2004 President Mesa signed a natural gas export deal with Argentina. Opponents criticised the deal as a pre-emption of the following referendum on gas exports.
2005 President Mesa offered his resignation to Congress after 17 months in office, as a new wave of anti-government protests spread throughout Bolivia. He finally resigned in an effort to resolve the crisis over how to divide up the country's natural gas wealth. Eduardo Rodríguez was appointed president until the leftist candidate Evo Morales, leading the Movimiento al Socialismo (MAS) (Movement towards Socialism), won presidential and parliamentary elections.
2006 The oil and gas industry was nationalised. A constituent assembly was elected and opened proceedings to draft a new constitution, giving greater rights to the indigenous population.
2007 Bolivia, Brazil and Chile agreed to build a South American highway to link the Atlantic and Pacific coasts, running from Santos in Brazil, through Bolivia, to Arica and Iquique in Chile, at an estimated cost of US$600 million.
2008 Bolivia suspended operations with the US drug enforcement agency (DEA) in Bolivia.
2009 A constitutional referendum was held in which over 61 per cent of voters agreed to changes that included a separation of church and state, increased state control of the economy, (particularly natural resources) and tough laws preventing privatisation. More autonomy will be given to native peoples, including granting indigenous justice systems the same status as conventional courts (which are increasingly seen as inefficient and corrupt). The president began giving thousands of hectares of land, confiscated from large-scale owners, to indigenous farmers. A presidential agreement was signed between Bolivia and Paraguay, settling a border dispute which had led to the Chaco Wars in the 1930s. The accord leads the way to more development of oil and gas fields in the Chaco region. In national elections Evo Morales was re-elected president, and his political party, MAS, became the largest party in both chambers of parliament.
2010 In May, French, British and Bolivian-backed power companies were nationalised by the government as part of a move to control the electricity generating sector.
2011 In March, President Morales refused to restore the operations of the US DEA in Bolivia. On 24 March, Bolivia threatened that it would make a claim before the International Court of Justice (ICJ) to regain land lost during the 1879–83 war and ceded to Chile. If successful it will allow Bolivia access to the Pacific coast. President Morales signed a new law on 26 June that established state-owned companies set up to produce seeds and fertilisers, in a national effort to enhance food security. US$500 million will be invested in the project that will emphasise indigenous crops; the scheme will also include generous financial credits for small farmers.

Political structure

Constitution

The first constitution was promulgated in 1826. The 1947 constitution was revised in 1967, and again in 1994.

Bolivia is divided into nine departments, each of which elects three Senators. The prefect of each department is appointed by the president. There is obligatory universal adult suffrage.

A referendum to change the constitution was held on 25 January 2009. Over 61 per cent agreed to changes to include a separation of church and state, increased state control of the economy, particularly natural resources and tough penalties against privatisation. More autonomy will be given to native peoples, including granting indigenous justice systems the same status and conventional courts (which were increasingly seen as inefficient and corrupt).

Form of state

Presidential democratic republic

The executive

Executive power is vested in the president and his appointed cabinet.

The president is directly elected for a five-year term, but is chosen by Congress if no candidate gains a majority of the vote.

In the event of the president's death or failure to assume office, the next in line would be the vice president followed by the president of the Senate.

From 2009 presidential term limits were abandoned; all candidates that fail to win over 50 per cent of the vote and another candidate is within 10 per cent of the leader a runoff election will be held.

National legislature

The bicameral Congreso Nacional (National Congress), consists of the Cámara de Diputados (Chamber of Deputies) (lower house) with 130 deputies directly elected in single seat constituencies, plus 62 elected by proportional representation from party lists. Deputies must be aged over 25 years. The Cámara de Senadores (Chamber of Senators) has 27 senators, each of the nine departments return three representatives, of which two represent the winning political party and one from the second placed party. Senators must be aged over 35 years. Both Senators and Deputies hold office for five years.

From 2009 term limits were abandoned; all parliamentary candidates that fail to win over 50 per cent of the vote and when another candidate is within 10 per cent of the leader a runoff election will be held.

Legal system

There are five levels of jurisdiction headed by the Supreme Court.

From 1 June 2001, a criminal code was introduced which allows for public jury trials and a prosecution service independent of the police.

Last elections

6 December 2009 (presidential and parliamentary); 2 July 2006 (Constituent Assembly and constitutional referendum)

Results: Presidential: Evo Morales (MAS) won 62.51 per cent of the vote, Manfred Reyes Villa (PPB-CN) 28.2 per cent; six other candidates won less than 6 per cent of the vote each; turnout was 95 per cent.

Parliamentary: (Chamber of Deputies) Movimiento al Socialismo (MAS) (Movement towards Socialism) won 88 seats (out of 130), Plan Progreso para Bolivia-Concertación Nacional (PPB-CN) (Progressive Plan for Bolivia-National Convergence) 37, Frente de Unidad Nacional (FUN) (National Unity Front) 3, Nueva Alianza Social (NAS) (New Social Alliance) 2. Senate: MAS won 26 (out of 36 seats), PPB-CN 10.

Constitutional referendum: 57 per cent of the electorate voted against regional autonomy, although four out of the nine departments voted in favour.

Next elections

2014 (presidential and parliamentary)

Political parties

Ruling party

Movimiento al Socialismo (MAS) (Movement towards Socialism) (from Dec 2005)

Main opposition party

Plan Progreso para Bolivia-Concertación Nacional (PPB-CN) (Progressive Plan for Bolivia-National Convergence)

Population

10.23 million (2009)*

Last census: September 2001: 8,280,184

Population density: Seven inhabitants per square km. Urban population: 64 per cent (1995—2001).

Annual growth rate: 2.1 per cent 1994–2004 (WHO 2006)

Ethnic make-up

Official figures estimate that approximately 4.2 million Bolivians (50.6 per cent of the population) are indigenous, comprising 37 different indigenous and aboriginal peoples. Of these, most live in the Andean highlands.

Religions

In 1961, the church was separated from the state and there is complete freedom of worship. The majority of the population is Roman Catholic, although Protestant denominations are expanding. Many indigenous groups mix Christian symbolism with pre-Columbian worship.

Education

Education is free of charge. Nevertheless, the average schooling completed is less than seven years.

The need to integrate education policy into broader anti-poverty strategies is exemplified by a high rate of primary school drop out among poor children. In Bolivia the wealth gap contributes to more than 90 per cent of the shortfall in primary-school completion. Education deprivation and poverty intersects with gender disparities, particularly in the case of Bolivia's indigenous population. More than half of indigenous males and two-thirds of indigenous females do not complete primary education.

Public expenditure on education is equivalent to approximately 5 per cent of annual GDP and includes subsidies to private education at the primary, secondary and tertiary levels. Bolivia has one of the lowest levels of provision in the developing world.

Literacy rate: 87 per cent adult rate; 97 per cent youth rate (15–24) (Unesco 2005).

Compulsory years: Six to 14

Enrolment rate: 114 per cent gross primary enrolment of relevant age group (including repeaters); 84 per cent gross secondary enrolment; 39 per cent gross tertiary enrolment (World Bank).

Health

Infant mortality was halved by 2010 over the previous 20 years (142 down to 63 in under five year olds and 96 down to 50 in under one year olds), however, such mortality is still the highest in Latin America. Nevertheless, mortality rates have fallen quicker than in any other Latin American country since the government introduced the Universal Mother and Child Insurance scheme (SUMI) in 2002, which provides comprehensive healthcare for the age group and a cash transfer scheme for pregnant women.

Some companies provided private medical care for their employees.

International funding has been donated to provide increased family planning and community based healthcare.

Yellow fever continues to be an important public health problem in the Americas. In 2000, Bolivia introduced the yellow fever vaccine in their child vaccination schedule, as well as the vaccination of all age groups in enzootic areas.

HIV/Aids

HIV prevalence: 0.5 per cent aged 15–49 in 2003 (World Bank)

Life expectancy: 65 years, 2004 (WHO 2006)

Fertility rate/Maternal mortality rate: 3.8 births per woman, 2004 (WHO 2006)

Child (under 5 years) mortality rate (per 1,000): 53 per 1,000 live births (in 2003); 10 per cent of children aged under five tend to be malnourished (World Bank).

Head of population per physician: 1.3 physicians per 1,000 people 2001 (WHO 2006)

Welfare

Pensions

In December 2010 parliament endorse amendments to the system, with implementation in mid-2011.

The management of the private pension system was nationalised and a state entity, the Gestora Publica de la Seguridad Social de Largo Plazo (GSS) (Long Term Social Security Agency) was established to administer the pension fund. Workers continue to contribute 12.2 per cent of their earnings into individual accounts

A 'Solidarity Fund' was established, guaranteeing a minimum level of pension for all workers, using a semi-contributory system, based on the number of contributing years (minimum 10 years personal contributions) and is intended to provide pensions for the 60 per cent of Bolivians working in the informal sector in 2010.

The statutory retirement age for males was reduced from 65 to 58 (miners may retire at 56 and others working in unhealthy conditions at 51), for women the age was reduced to 55 (with an advance of one year for each live child born, for a maximum of three years.

The new pension fund will step up benefits for low-income households, with employers paying a higher contribution for their workers.

Main cities

La Paz (administrative capital, estimated population 812,986 in 2005), Sucre (legislative and judicial capital, 226,668), Santa Cruz (1.4 million), Cochabamba (592,594), El Alto (775,836), Oruro (214,058), Tarija (161,677), Potosi (143,281), Sacaba (136,746).

Languages spoken

Approximately half the population speak Spanish as their first language. The *campesinos* (peasant farmers) often speak only Aymará or Quechua, but these languages are seldom written and are of limited commercial importance. Aymará is mainly spoken in the departments of Oruro, La Paz and Potosí. Quechua (often mixed with Spanish) is spoken in the departments of Cochabamba, Potosí and Sucre.

Official language/s

Spanish

Media

Freedom of the press is generally expressed, although journalist do not have a reputation for reporting on sensitive topics such as corruption and drug trafficking.

Press

Dailies: In Spanish, *La Prenza* (www.laprensa.com.bo), *La Razon* (www.la-razon.com) and *El Diario* (www.eldiario.net) are published in La Paz; *El Deber* (www.eldeber.com.bo), *El Mundo* (www.elmundo.com.bo) are from Santa Cruz; *Los Tiempos* (www.lostiempos.com) from Cochabamba and *Correo del Sur* (http://correodelsur.com) is from Sucre.

Weeklies: In Spanish *Pulso* (www.pulsobolivia.com), reports on current affairs, as does *Samanario* (www.semanario.8m.net) based in Tarija.

Business: The weekly *Nueva Economía* (www.elmundo.es/nuevaeconomia) and *Periódico Jornada* (www.jornadanet.com) report on economics.

Broadcasting

The government-controlled broadcasting authority is the Dirección General de Telecomunicaciones.

Radio: Low literacy levels make radio listenership, particularly in rural areas, high and important for news and information broadcasting in not only Spanish but also the Aymará and Ouechua languages.

There are over 100 mostly private owned radio stations La Paz has around 40 radio stations alone. National networks include the government owned Radio Illimani (http://abi.bo) and the Catholic-run Radio Fides (www.radiofides.com), the independent Radio Panamericana (www.panamericana.bo), commercial stations include FM La Pas (www.fmlapaz.com), Melodia FM (www.melodiafm.com) and Radio WKM (www.wkmradio.com).

Television: There are several TV networks, all of which are commercial, including the government-run Television Boliviana (Canal 7) privates network include Bolivision (Canal 4) (www.redbolivision.tv), Unitel (Canal 9)

(www.unitel.tv) both from Santa Cruz and ATB Red Nacional (Canal 9) (www.atb.com.bo), Red Uno from (Canal 11) (www.reduno.com.bo) and Red PAT (Canal 13) (www.red-pat.com) from La Paz. The university television service, Televisión Universitaria (www.umsa.bo), provides educational programmes.

News agencies

National news agency: Agencia Boliviana de Informacion (ABI)

Other news agencies: Agencia de Noticias Fides (Catholic news agency): www.noticiasfides.com

Bolpress: www.bolpress.com

Economy

The economy is driven by Bolivia's primary industries, particularly natural gas extraction (it had proven reserves 300 billion cubic metres (cum) of natural gas at the end of 2010, with annual production of 14.4 billion cum) and tin mining and, more recently, lithium (reserves estimated at 4 million tonnes). Construction of a pilot, lithium production plant, at Salar de Uyuni, began in 2008 and completed in 2010, was expected to produce 30,000 tonnes of lithium carbonate, for export and use in batteries and high-tech equipment, by 2014. Agriculture is another key component of the economy, especially the growing of coffee, soybeans, wheat, rice and potatoes.

Bolivia is also the third largest coca cultivator in the world and while the leaf of the coca has been a traditional chewed stimulant by locals for generations, its refinement into the illegal narcotic cocaine and its subsequent smuggling abroad continues to be a source of tension between Latin America and the US and Europe (the main markets for the product). In a move that has angered international observers, particularly the United States, President Evo Morales has pledged to resist efforts to eradicate coca production, which he considers is part of his country's heritage.

GDP growth was 3.4 per cent in 2009, a fall from 6.1 per cent in 2008, when high global prices for natural gas boosted Bolivia's economy, and just at the time when the global economic crisis struck. In 2010 GDP growth was 4.2 per cent, reflecting the upturn in trade as the global economy recovered.

Under President Morales, there has been greater emphasis on state participation in the economy and public investment, which since 2007 has been consistently greater than private investment (averaging around 10 per cent and 6.5 per cent per annum respectively). The government has plans for further expansion and industrialisation in the hydrocarbon, energy and mining sectors, including improving the infrastructure. It favours partnerships with the private sector, so as to introduce modern management, financing and technological developments.

Remittances in 2009 were US$1.06 billion (6.1 per cent of GDP), and were forecast to have grown to US$1.064 billion in 2010.

In late-2010 parliament endorsed changes to the pension system. The plans were implemented in mid-2011 when the privately run pension system was nationalised, retirement ages were lowered and pensions were extended to include workers in the informal sector.

Of the 18 targets under the UN Millennium Development Goals that Bolivia committed itself to achieve by 2015, only five were showing improvement by 2009. These included a fall in the poverty rate (although the percentage of the population living in extreme poverty remains above the Latin American average), a fall in cases of malaria and an increase in the proportion of the population with access to drinking water and sanitation. Some targets remain constant such as skilled staff in attendance at births and some fell behind, such as the prevalence of HIV among 15–24 year olds grow and gender disparity in schools.

External trade

Bolivia is a full member of the World Trade Organisation (WTO) and is an associate member of Mercosur (the South American Common Market), which allows 80 per cent of trade to pass freely to other nations within Mercosur. The country is also a beneficiary of the US's Andean Trade Preference Act. Bolivia also has Generalised System of Preferences (GSP) status with the United States, the European Union and Japan.

Imports

Manufactured goods, petroleum products, plastics, paper, aircraft and aircraft parts, machinery and vehicles, chemical products and foodstuffs.

Main sources: Brazil (typically 18 per cent of total), Argentina (14 per cent), US (13 per cent).

Exports

Principal exports are natural gas, soya beans and soya products, zinc and tin.

Main destinations: Brazil (typically 32 per cent of total), South Korea (9 per cent), Argentina (8 per cent).

Agriculture

Farming

Although agricultural produce remains Bolivia's main export, agriculture's share of GDP has fallen from 30 per cent in the early 1960s to around 15 per cent by the end of the century. Yet it is still economically important, employing nearly half the country's labour force. Most agricultural activities in rural areas are performed in small family units with low levels of productivity and income.

The cultivation of commercial crops is central to the advancement of Bolivia's 'agricultural frontier' and an intrinsic element of Bolivia's export-oriented development programme. This development drive is backed by a major road-building programme and changes in land tenure laws.

Since the 1990s, the Bolivian government has fought a US-backed war against the production of coca leaves – the raw source of cocaine.The government has eliminated a total of 40,000 hectares of the crop, representing the eradication of 95 per cent of the country's coca fields since the programme began. Before the initiation of the eradication programme, coca production represented nearly 10 per cent of the country's GDP, so efforts are being made to replace coca production with alternative economic activities, such as commercial crops and textile manufacturing.

Unlike the Colombian drug fiefdoms, coca production in Bolivia was largely associated with indigenous peasants who have grown the crops as a traditional medicine since pre-Colombian times and, latterly, as a cash crop to alleviate their enduring poverty. Unsurprisingly, the government's efforts to destroy coca crops damaged the rural economy and inflamed social and racial tensions. Protests by coca farmers, who rely on the crop for their income, have culminated in mass unrest.

Significantly, President Evo Morales has underlined his opposition to the previous government's crackdown on coca production. In a hugely populist move he has pledged to reverse the policy.

Fishing

Bolivia produces approximately 6,000 tons of fresh water fish per year, almost entirely for the domestic market. Bolivia's lakes, among them Lake Titicaca the world's highest navigable lake, provide the basis for this yield. However, the fishing industry does suffer from limited access to external markets, which is exacerbated by poor road transport infrastructure owing to the extreme altitude of the lakes. In addition to the domestic catch, about 7,000 tons of marine fish are imported per year.

Forestry

With a total land mass of 1.1 million sq km (424,164 sq miles), 53 per cent of which is covered by forests and woodlands, Bolivia has the potential to be one of the world's most significant forestry nations.

Sawnwood accounts for more than 90 per cent of Bolivia's total export of forest products. Brazil nuts, palm hearts and rubber are also important sources of income and are mainly derived from the Amazon forests. The export of more value-added products, such as material for doors, window frames and furniture, has increased rapidly in recent years, surpassing the levels of sawn wood, Bolivia's traditional forest export. This diversification of forest products and improvement in production processes has increased the commercial viability of Bolivian forestry. There continue to be significant problems with the forestry sector however. Legal efforts to promote diversification and sustainability are limited and deforestation continues to out-pace forest regeneration. Forest cover decreased at an annual average rate of 0.30 per cent, the equivalent of 161,000 hectares in 1990–2000 and is still decreasing rapidly.

Though productivity has improved with the introduction of more sophisticated technology in the sawing and drying processes, there are still comparatively few sawmills for a country of Bolivia's forestry capacity and the industry suffers from poor transport infrastructure. The majority of the sawmills are located in the eastern region around Santa Cruz, where the standard of roads is particularly poor. Small- and medium-sized forestry companies that use old technology and outmoded production methods continue to operate with inefficient capacity and no method of producing value-added products. Valuable tree species such as mahogany, oak and cedar are dwindling in numbers. As well as contributing to the overall decline of biodiversity in the Amazon, these precious woods are now below commercial volumes. Efforts to control logging are limited as illegal colonisation of the forests and 'slash and burn' techniques continue.

Industry and manufacturing

Although it constitutes approximately 18 per cent to the total GDP of Bolivia, the industrial sector is considerably underdeveloped. Manufacturing in Bolivia is also capital intensive, employing just 14 per cent of the total work force.

Production is centred on the processing of minerals (mainly tin, lead and zinc smelting) and agricultural products. Oil refining and cement production are also important activities. There is a large workshop and artisan sector of small-scale domestic industries producing textiles, clothing and food. Bolivia is a producer of natural textile fibres: cotton, alpaca wool, llama wool, merino lambswool and rabbit fur. There is no heavy industry or electronics industry.

Bolivian industry is under pressure to become more competitive. Traditionally, unprocessed or semi-processed materials have dominated Bolivian exports. The government has created new and more decentralised industries, to stimulate the development of competitive industries, particularly agro-based industries.

Tourism

The Bolivian tourism industry is undergoing expansion. The country's wealth of diversity and cultural and natural attractions has made it a destination for eco-tourists and backpackers. Most of the country's hotels are located in the capital La Paz, but there has been an expansion of hotel accommodation in other cultural centres. The travel and tourism industry generated 9.2 per cent of total GDP in 2005 and visitor levels continued to rise. The continued expansion of the Bolivian tourism industry will depend significantly on the relative level of civil unrest in future years.

Mining

Mining has long been a mainstay of the Bolivian economy and its importance to the country continues today. The mining sector contributes up to one fifth of GDP and employs 10 per cent of the labour force. Mining accounts for approximately 45 per cent of the country's total export earnings and the country's unexploited mineral potential is significant.

The industry has continued to show an improved performance especially, the mining of tin, silver and gold. Total tin reserves are estimated at 1.6 million tonnes and are mainly composed of low quality ore and accounts for approximately 17 per cent of total mining production. Bolivia is the world's fifth-largest tin producer and one of the world's leading producers of antimony and tungsten. Other minerals extracted include zinc, silver, gold, lead, copper and limestone, while large reserves of iron ore, lithium and potassium are as yet unexploited. Zinc accounts for 27 per cent of total mining production. Gold production is significant, totalling some 14 tonnes per year.

Most mining operations are small and inefficient, with many of the more promising deposits occupied by co-operatives, with little exploration being carried out.

In 2010 construction of a pilot lithium production plant at Salar de Uyuni was completed at the site of a salt-lake that is estimated to contain 50–70 per cent of the world's reserves of lithium. When fully operational in 2014 it is expected to produce 30,000 tonnes of lithium carbonate per year, which accounts for around 30 per cent of the 2009-level of world supply.

Hydrocarbons

With 440 million barrels of proven oil reserves and meets all of its domestic oil needs. Production is over 60,000 barrels per day (bpd) and with consumption at over 50,000bpd Bolivia has a surplus to export into the South American oil market. Despite its significant reserves Bolivia lacks refining capacity and must import diesel. It also suffers from a poor transport infrastructure and a challenging topography which render the transportation of oil extremely difficult, as many of the country's oil fields are located in remote areas. Proven natural gas reserves were 300 billion cubic metres (cum) at the end of 2010 and production was 14.4 billion cum, an increase of 16.8 per cent on the 2009 figure and a doubling of output since 2001. Exports of natural gas in 2010 totalled 11.65 billion cum, of which 9.82 billion cum were delivered to Brazil and the remainder to Argentina. Brazil's Petrobras, Spain's Repsol and France's Total control almost 84 per cent of proven natural gas reserves while, since 2009 when it was newly re-nationalised, the state-owned Chaco is the fourth largest producer.

Due to the extensive exploration in recent years, there have been several large discoveries holding over 10 million cubic metres of natural gas. Estimates of Bolivia's total potential gas reserves are put at approximately 1.32 trillion cubic metres. There are discussion over supplying natural gas to Argentina, Bolivia, Brazil, Chile, Paraguay and Uruguay. Bolivia is also considering exporting to the large markets of the US and Mexico.

In 2006 the government nationalised 12 oil and gas companies in the south-eastern region that contains the country's richest hydrocarbon fields. The state-run Yacimientos Petroliferos Fiscales Bolivianos' had a 49 per cent stake in Chaco oil until January 2009 when the government seized control of 99 per cent of the BP-owned company, leaving 1 per cent in BP's hands. In 2008 the pipeline company Transredes was nationalised. Any coal production or use is commercially insignificantly.

Energy

Bolivia's capacity to generate electricity has improved markedly since the 1990s with an almost doubling of generation from a 0.8 GW to 1.4GW by 2005. Production in 2007 was an estimated 5.7 billion kilowatt hours (kWh) which was consumed domestically. The most is generated by conventional thermal plants fed by domestically supplied oil and gas. Some rural areas have unaffiliated power plants fuelled by biomass. Atypical of South America, Bolivia does not rely on hydropower, with only 460MW installed capacity, the largest being the Santa

Isabel plant in Cochabamba, producing 93MW.
The three, dominant, foreign owned energy companies, Brazil's Petrobras, Spain's Repsol and France's Total were forced to pay my taxes as the energy industry was progressively nationalised since 2006.

Financial markets

Stock exchange
Bolsa Boliviana de Valores

Banking and insurance

Bolivia's banking system has been undergoing extensive reform since the mid-1990s. The last decade has seen the full-scale privatisation of formerly state-owned banks and significant regulatory upheaval. A high level of dollarisation has meant that approximately 90 per cent of Bolivian deposits are denominated in US dollars and the holding of deposits is highly concentrated in the country's wealthy elite. This means that the banking system is highly dependent on the financial fortunes of a select number of wealthy Bolivians. Concern has been expressed in various quarters that President Evo Morales will seek to redistribute income to the poor. Thus the banking system may feel the effects of diminished holdings by wealthy clients in future years.
Bolivia's banking system has remained largely immune from the contagious effects of financial sector turmoil that inflicted the region in the early part of the decade. This fact owes to Bolivia's comparatively low exposure to international capital markets; the majority of Bolivia's debt is with foreign states and multilateral institutions, which have worked to change the structure of the country's debt portfolio and maintain vital foreign currency reserves.
A new Bank of the South, with a headquarters in Venezuela, will be launched in 2008 to provide an alternative source of development funding for the participating countries. Assets of US$7 billion will underpin its operations.
Central bank
Banco Central de Bolivia
Main financial centre
La Paz

Time

GMT minus four hours

Geography

Bolivia straddles the Andes and is made up of mountainous areas with cold desolate plateaux and semi-tropical and fertile lowlands. It is landlocked with Chile and Peru to the west, Brazil to the north and east and Argentina to the south. The Andean range is at its widest in Bolivia, some 650km.
The Western Cordillera separating Bolivia and Chile has peaks of between 6,000 metres and 6,500 metres above sea level and a number of volcanoes along its crest. Passes across the Cordillera are at 4,000 metres. To the east of the range lies the bleak treeless Altiplano also at around 4,000 metres. The Altiplano makes up about 10 per cent of the country and is divided into basins by spurs of mountains. Around 70 per cent of the population lives on the Altiplano, particularly the northern part where most of the larger cities are located. In the south, the parched desert landscape is mostly unpopulated.
Lake Titicaca, the highest navigable lake in the world, is situated at the northern end of the Altiplano. It is 171km in length, 64km in breadth and 280 metres at its deepest point. The immense depth of water keeps the lake at an even temperature of 10 degrees Celsius and modifies extremes of winter and night temperatures on the surrounding land, thereby making the basin favourable for farming.
The Eastern Cordillera rises sharply from the Altiplano in the east and four of its peaks rise to above 6,000 metres. These north-eastern slopes are heavily forested and are indented by fertile valleys in an area known as the Yungas.
In the north and east, the Oriente has dense tropical forest and in the centre there are plains covered with rough pasture, swamp and scrub.
Hemisphere
Southern

Climate

The climate varies with the area. It is tropical in the lowlands (eastern region) with an average temperature of 25 degrees Celsius (C); temperate in the highland valley regions (middle of the country), average temperature 15 degrees C, and cooler in the Altiplano (highland) areas (western region), average temperature 10 degrees C.
La Paz is in the Altiplano where temperatures vary between three degrees C in June and 25 degrees C in November and December. In the highlands the rainy season begins in December and ends in late March.

Dress codes

For business meetings men should wear a suit and tie, women a two-piece suit, or equivalent. Warm clothing is required in the high plateau region. Lightweight clothing is needed during the day and warmer clothing for the evenings in the valleys, and very lightweight clothing for both day and night in the tropical valleys.

Entry requirements

Travellers who arrive without the correct documentation will be fined.
Passports
Passports are required by all (valid for one year beyond departure date), except holders of Cedula de Identidad issued to nationals of Argentina, Paraguay, Peru and Uruguay.
Visa
A visa is not required for tourist visits up to 90 days, by nationals of most of the Americas, Western Europe, Australasia and some Asian countries. (For further details contact the local embassy or see www.embassyofbolivia.co.uk/visas.html#2.)
The 'specific purpose visa' for non-tourist visitors requires a letter of introduction, including an itinerary and letters of guarantee by employer and host company. (See www.embassyofbolivia.co.uk/visaformfiles/specificvisaform.html for application form.).
Currency advice/regulations
There are no restrictions on the import and export of local or foreign currency; currency must be declared.
US dollar travellers' cheques are the best form of currency to take. UK sterling cheques can sometimes be exchanged, but only with difficulty.
Customs
Visitors are not required to declare valuable personal effects such as cameras and radios. Business samples are duty-free as long as they are re-exported within 90 days.

Health (for visitors)

Mandatory precautions
A yellow fever vaccination certificate is required for visitors arriving from infected areas, and for those travelling to high risk areas such as the Departments of Beni, Cochabamba, Santa Cruz and the subtropical area of La Paz Department.
Advisable precautions
Typhoid, paratyphoid, hepatitis A, tetanus and polio vaccinations. Malaria risk exists in rural areas – prophylaxis recommended. Owing to the altitude of La Paz and other places in the Altiplano region, sufferers from heart or lung complaints should seek medical advice before leaving for Bolivia. Water precautions should be taken.

Hotels

There is a wide range available. Service charge and local tax are added to the bill. Tipping 5–10 per cent.

Credit cards

Mastercard, Diners Club, Visa and American Express have limited acceptance.

Public holidays (national)
Fixed dates
1 Jan (New Year's Day), 1 May (Labour Day), 6 Aug (Independence Day), 1 Nov (All Saints' Day), 25 Dec (Christmas Day). There are other additional holidays celebrated in individual provinces and towns.
Variable dates
Carnival (Feb, seven days), Good Friday, Easter Sunday, Corpus Christi (May/Jun).

Working hours
Banking
Mon–Fri: 0830–1200, 1430–1800; Sat: 0830–1200.
Business
Mon–Fri: 0830–1200, 1430–1830.
Government
Mon–Fri: 0800–1200, 1430–1830.
Shops
Mon–Fri: 0930–1230, 1500–1930; Sat: 1000–1500.

Telecommunications
Mobile/cell phones
GSM 1900 service available.

Electricity supply
110V and 200V in La Paz and 220V in Cochabamba and most other towns; US-type flat-prong plugs.

Weights and measures
The metric system is standard, although the Imperial is sometimes used.

Social customs/useful tips
In business circles, local customs are similar to those in Europe or North America. While English is widely used in commercial and business circles, a knowledge of Spanish is a valuable asset to the visitor. Correspondence in Spanish is almost essential. On business visits, cards are presented and it is normal to shake hands when arriving or leaving. It is advisable to arrange appointments before visiting. Bolivians are informal about observing prescribed times and will often arrive 30–45 minutes late.
It is customary to address persons by their professional title, eg, doctor, engineer and *licenciado* for social science graduates. Holders of law degrees are addressed as doctor.
It is offensive to refer to rural Indians as *indios*; they are referred to as *campesinos* (peasants).
It is customary to give gratuities in a hotel or restaurant of around 5–10 per cent even if a service charge has been added to the bill. The minimum drinking age is 21 years.

Security
Since the civil disruption in 2003, road blockades can happen on all main roads at any time. Visitors should not attempt to breach road blockades and should stay away from demonstrations.

Getting there
Air
National airline: Lloyd Aéreo Boliviano (LAB).
International airport/s: La Paz-El Alto (LPB), 14km from city, duty-free shop, bar, restaurant, bank, post office, hotel reservations.
Other airport/s: Cochabamba-J Wilstermann (CBB), 4km from city..
Airport tax: US$25 for all adults, excluding 12-hour transit passengers. An additional exit tax (US$25) is levied for all visitors staying over 90 days.
Surface
Road: Road access is possible from Peru, Argentina and Chile.
Travellers who use overland routes are generally advised to check border post opening hours.
Rail: Rail services connect La Paz with Chile (Arica and Calama) and Argentina (Buenos Aires). The Expreso del Sur is a special train service from La Paz to Buenos Aires.
Water: It is possible to take the steamer on Lake Titicaca from Puno (Peru) to Guaqui.
Main port/s: Although Bolivia is landlocked, access to the sea (and in certain cases free port facilities) has been granted by Paraguay (via River Paraguay), Brazil (Belem, Santos, Corumbá, Port Velho) and Argentina (Buenos Aires, Rosario).

Getting about
National transport
Air: Air transport is the best method of travelling around the country. Lloyd Aéreo Boliviano (LAB), Aerosur, TAM (army airline) and Aero Xpress (AX) operate domestic services to main centres.
Road: Around 50,000km of road exists, but only 5.5 per cent is paved and only 20 per cent can be classed as all-weather roads. The main centres are connected by highways of reasonable standard. A toll permit system is in operation; garage and petrol services are sparse outside main centres.
Buses: *Flotas* are long-distance buses, they mostly leave in the evening and travel overnight, except on the major routes where there are some daytime departures. It is advisable to book in advance and take warm clothing.
Rail: A north-south line runs from La Paz to Oruro and Uyuni, with spurs to Cochabamba, Uncia, Potosi, Sucre and Villazón at the Argentine border. The eastern system runs from Santa Cruz to Yacuiba and to Corumbá at the Brazilian border. Sleeper and first-class services are available; advance booking is essential.
Water: Half of Bolivia's territory lies in the Amazon Basin. Transport is by cargo boats, which carry passengers, vehicles and livestock. The tributaries of the Amazon are the Ichilo, Mamoré, Beni, Madre de Dios and Guaporé rivers.
City transport
Taxis: There are *remise* (yellow cabs) which have fixed rates applicable per passenger – the cabs are frequently shared. Within La Paz, *trufis* (cabs with green flags) ply along fixed routes. Tips are not expected.
Car hire
An international driving permit is required. This may be issued in Bolivia by the Federación Interamericana de Touring y Automovil Clubes (www.fitac.org) on presentation of a national licence, but it is advisable to procure one before travelling. At the frontier, drivers must also obtain a *hoja de ruta*, a form which notes the driver's itinerary.
Traffic drives on the right.

BUSINESS DIRECTORY
The addresses listed below are a selection only. While World of Information makes every endeavour to check these addresses, we cannot guarantee that changes have not been made, especially to telephone numbers and area codes. We would welcome any corrections.

Telephone area codes
The international direct dialling code (IDD) for Bolivia is + 591, followed by area code and subscriber's number:

Beni	3465	Potosi	262
Buena Vista	3932	Saavedra	3924
Cochabamba	441	Santa Cruz	33
La Belgica	3923	Sucre	4691
La Paz	22	Tarija	466
Montero	3922	Trinidad	346
Oruro	252	Villamontes	4672
Portachuelo	3924		

Useful telephone numbers
Police: 110
Fire: 119
Ambulance (La Paz): 118

Chambers of Commerce
American Chamber of Commerce of Bolivia, Avenida 6 de Agosto, Edificio Hilda, PO Box 8268, La Paz (tel: 244-3939; fax: 244-3972; e-mail: amgalin@caoba.entelnet.bo).

Cochabamba Chamber of Commerce, 336 Calle Sucre, Cochabamba (tel: 425-7715; fax: 425-7717; e-mail: sistema@cadeco.org).

Chuquisaca Chamber of Industry and Commerce, 64 Calle España, Sucre (tel: 645-1194; fax: 645-1850; e-mail: info@cicch.com).

National Chamber of Commerce, 1392 Avenida Mariscal Santa Cruz, La Paz (tel: 237-8606; fax: 239-1004; e-mail: cnc@boliviocomercio.org.bo).

Santa Cruz Chamber of Industry, Commerce and Services, 7 Avenida Las Américas esquina Saavedra, Santa Cruz (tel: 333-4555; fax: 334-2353; e-mail: cainco@cainco.org.bo).

Banking

Banco Bisa, Avenida 16 de Julio 1628, La Paz (tel: 359-471; fax: 316-597; e-mail: bancbisa@caoba.entelnet.bo).

Banco de Crédito de Bolivia, Calle Colón esquina Mercado 1308, La Paz (tel: 360-025; fax: 391-044).

Banco de la Nación Argentina, Avenida 16 de Julio 1486, La Paz (tel: 359-218; fax: 391-392; e-mail: bancnalp@caoba.entelnet.bo).

Banco Económico, Calle Ayacucho 166, Santa Cruz (tel: 361-177; fax: 361-184; e-mail: baneco@roble.scz.entelnet.bo).

Banco Ganadero, Calle 24 de Septiembre 110, Santa Cruz (tel: 361-616; fax: 361-617; e-mail: bangan@roble.scz.entelnet.bo).

Banco Mercantil, Calle Ayacucho esquina Mercado, La Paz (tel: 315-131; fax: 391-442; e-mail: bercant@caoba.entelnet.bo).

Banco Nacional de Bolivia, Avenida Camacho esquina Colón 1312, La Paz (tel: 318-732; fax: 359-146; e-mail: info@bnb.com.bo).

Banco Real, Avenida 16 de Julio 1642, La Paz (tel: 334-477; fax: 335-588; e-mail: real@caob.entelnet.bo).

Banco Santa Cruz, Calle Junín 154, Santa Cruz (tel: 369-911; fax: 350-114; e-mail: bancruz@mail.bsc.com.bo).

Banco Sollidario, Calle Nicolás Acosta 289, La Paz (tel: 484-242; fax: 486-468; e-mail: info@bancosol.com.bo).

Banco Unión, CalleLibertad 165, Santa Cruz (tel: 366-869; fax: 340-684; e-mail: info@bancounion.com.bo).

Interbanco, Calle Mercado No 1046, PO Box 14758, La Paz (tel: 317-707; fax: 316-787).

Central bank

Banco Central de Bolivia, PO Box 3118, Calle Mercado esquina Ayacucho, La Paz (tel: 409-090; fax: 406-598; e-mail: bancocentraldebolivia@bcb.gov.bo).

Stock exchange

Bolsa Boliviana de Valores: www.bolsa-valores-bolivia.com

Travel information

Automovil Club Boliviano, Avenida 6 de Agusto 2993, La Paz (tel: 431-132; fax: 431-139; e-mail: acblapaz@acelerate.com).

AeroSur, Calle Colón esquina Avenida Irala, Santa Cruz (tel: 364-446; fax: 365-246; e-mail: mail@aerosur.com).

Lloyd Aéreo Boliviano, Aeropuerto Jorge Wilstermann, Cochabamba (tel: 25-903; fax: 50-744; email: gergen@labairlines.com).

Ministry of tourism

Viceministerio de Turismo, Avenida Mariscal Santa Cruz, Edificio Palacio de Comunicacióónes, Piso 16, La Paz (tel: 236 7463/4; fax: 237 4630; e-mail: vturismo@mcei.gov.bo; internet:www.mcei.gov.bo).

National tourist organisation offices

Secretaría Nacional de Turismo, Calle Mercado 1328, Edificio Ballivián, La Paz (tel: 367-441; fax: 374-630).

Ministries

Ministry of Agriculture and Rural Development, Avenida Camacho 1471, La Paz (tel: 367-968; fax: 313-601).

Ministry of Defence, Avenida 20 de Octubre esquina Pedro Salazar, La Paz (tel: 431-364; fax: 433-159).

Ministry of Economic Development, Palacio de Comunicaciones, Avenida Mariscal Santa Cruz, La Paz (tel: 375-000, fax: 360-534; e-mail: contactos@desarrollo.gov.bo).

Ministry of Education, Culture and Sport, Avenida Arce 2147, La Paz (tel: 440-160; fax: 440-376).

Ministry of Finance, Palacio de Comunicaciones, Avenida Mariscal Santa Cruz, La Paz (tel: 392-220; fax: 359-955).

Ministry of Foreign Affairs, Calle Ingavi esquina Junín, La Paz (tel: 336-200; fax: 333-521; email: mreuno@rree.gov.bo).

Ministry of Foreign Trade and Investment, Palacio de Comunicaciones, Avenida Mariscal Santa Cruz, La Paz (tel: 343-519; fax: 377-451; internet site: http://www.mcei-bolivia.com).

Ministry of Government, Avenida Arce 2409 esquina Belisario Salinas, La Paz (tel: 440-114; fax: 442-589).

Ministry of Health and Social Security, Plaza del Estudiante, La Paz (tel: 371-373; fax: 391-590; e-mail: minsalud@ceibo.entelnet.bo).

Ministry of Housing, Avenida 20 de Octubre 2230, La Paz (tel: 372-241; fax: 371-335; e-mail: minviv@ceibo.entelnet.bo).

Ministry of Information, Edificio La Urbana, Avenida Camacho 1485, La Paz (339-027; fax: 391-607).

Ministry of Justice and Human Rights, Avenida 16 de Julio 1769, La Paz (tel: 361-083; fax: 392-982).

Ministry of Labour and Micro-enterprises, Yanacocha esquina Mercado, La Paz (tel: 407-740; fax: 406-867).

Ministry of Presidency, Palacio de Gobierno, Plaza Murillo, La Paz (tel: 371-082; fax: 371-388).

Ministry of Sustainable Development and Planning, Avenida Mariscal Santa Cruz 1092, La Paz (tel: 330-074; fax: 330-540).

Other useful addresses

Bolivian Embassy (USA), 3014 Massachusetts Avenue, NW, Washington DC 20008 (tel: 202-483-4410; fax: 202-3712; e-mail: embassy@bolivia-usa.org).

Bolsa Boliviana de Valores, Calle Montevideo 142, La Paz (tel: 443-232; fax: 442-308; e-mail: info@bolsa-valores-bolivia.com).

British Embassy, Avenida Arce 2732, La Paz (tel: 357-424; fax: 431-073).

Confederación de Empresarios Privados de Boliva, Avenida Mariscal Santa Cruz 1392, Edificio Camara Nacional de Comercio, La Paz (tel: 315-562: fax: 379-970; e-mail: cepbol@ceibo.entelnet.bo).

Empresa Nacional de Electricidad (ENDE), Calle Colombia 655, Cochabamba (tel: 59-500; fax: 59-509).

Eurocentro de Cooperación Empresarial de Bolivia, Calle Suárez de Figueroa 127, Santa Cruz (tel: 334-555; fax: 365-108; e-mail: eurocentro@cainco.org.bo).

US Embassy, Avenida Arce 2780 esquina Cordero, La Paz (tel: 430-120; fax: 432-051).

National news agency: Agencia Boliviana de Informacion (ABI). Dirección Av, Camacho 1485 Casilla, 6500 La Paz (tel: 200-373; fax: 200-246; internet: www.abi.bo).

Internet sites

Bolsa Boliviana de Valores SA (Bolivian Chamber of Commerce): www.bolsa-valores-bolivia.com

Bolivia Business Online: www.boliviabiz.com

Bolivia Government website: boliviaweb.com/gov.htm

Bolivian Times: www.boliviantimes.com

Bosnia and Hercegovina Republic

After several years of strong growth, increasingly accompanied by external and internal imbalances, the economy of Bosnia and Herzegovina Republic (BiH) fell into recession in 2009. Like elsewhere in the region, Bosnia and Herzegovina's pre-crisis growth relied on booming domestic demand financed from abroad. Sharp increases in government spending on wages and social transfers have added to demand pressures, which manifested in widening current account deficits and a spike in inflation. The global economic and financial crisis had triggered a collapse in the demand for BIH's exports and severely curtailed cross-border financial inflows. Private investment and spending on consumer durables collapsed, while private consumption softened to a lesser extent, on the back of moderate growth of wages and social benefits. The pre-crisis credit boom came to a sudden stop.

Faced with increasing financing pressures in 2009, the authorities put together a comprehensive programme supported by an International Monetary Fund (IMF) Stand-By Arrangement. The programme was designed to safeguard the currency board and cushion the effects of the deteriorating external environment, while adopting policies to redress fiscal imbalances and strengthen the financial sector. The authorities' approach included: gradual fiscal consolidation accompanied by structural fiscal reforms to bring public finances on a sustainable path; steps to strengthen the resilience of the financial sector alongside commitments from foreign parent banks to maintain their exposures to BiH and keep their subsidiaries capitalised; and substantial financing from the IMF

KEY FACTS

Official name: Republika Bosne i Hercegovine (BiH) (Republic of Bosnia and Hercegovina). BiH consists of two distinct entities: Federacija Bosne i Hercegovine (FBiH) (Federation of Bosnia and Hercegovina) and Republika Srpska (RS) (Serb Republic)

Head of State: Three-member rotating collective presidency (began with) Nebojsa Radmanovic (SNSD (Serb)) (from 2006; re-elected Oct 2010), Zeljko Komsic (SDP BiH (Croat)) (from 2006; re-elected Oct 2010), Bakir Izatbegovic (SDA (Bosniak/Muslim)) (elected Oct 2010)

Head of government: Prime Minister Nikola Spiric (SNSD) (from Jan 2007; re-elected 28 Dec 2007) remains (June 2011) as Chairman until a new chairman is agreed post the Oct 2010 elections; UN High Representative and EU Special Representative: Valentin Inzko (25 Mar 2009)

Ruling party: Seven-party coalition government (formed 9 Jan 2007)

Area: 51,129 square km

Population: 3.84 million (2010)*

Capital: Sarajevo (BiH)

Official language: Bosanski (Bosnian)

Currency: Konvertibilna marka (KM) = 100 fennings

Exchange rate: KM1.46 per US$ (Oct 2011)

GDP per capita: US$4,319 (2010)

GDP real growth: 0.80% (2010)

GDP: US$16.80 billion (2010)

Labour force: 1.21 million (2010)

Unemployment: 42.90% (2010)

Inflation: 2.10% (2010)

Balance of trade: -US$4.29 billion (2010)

* estimated figure

KEY FACTS

Official name: Republika Srpska (RS) (Serb Republic)

Head of State: President Milorad Dodik (from 15 Nov 2010)

Head of government: Prime Minister Aleksandar Dzombic (from 3 Feb 2011)

Ruling party: Stranka Nezavisnih Socijaldemokrata (SNSD) (Alliance of Independent Social Democrats) (re-elected 1 Oct 2006)

Area: 25,053 square km

Population: 1.49 million (2009)*

Capital: Sarajevo (*de jure*); Banja Luka (*de facto*)

Currency: Konvertibilna marka (KM) pegged to the euro at KM1 per €0.51 (since 2001); the KM is the only legal tender

* estimated figure

along with funds from the World Bank and the European Union (EU).

Bosnia and Herzegovina's stabilisation programme helped mitigate the impact of the global financial crisis on the economy. The IMF's financial support package also helped minimise the impact of revenue shortfalls on government spending, thus limiting output losses. It also helped stem the loss of foreign reserves by the central bank and shored up investor confidence. Confidence building steps, including BiH's participation in the European Bank Co-ordination Initiative and the increase of the scope and limit of deposit insurance coverage helped restore depositors' confidence in the banking system. Performance under the programme has been encouraging: fiscal restraint is addressing large imbalances of recent years and structural fiscal reforms have advanced, albeit at a slower pace than initially envisaged.

The economy appears to have bottomed out and is projected to have shown a modest recovery in 2010, paving the way for a rebound in 2011. Domestic demand will remain subdued, held in check by stagnant real wages and ongoing fiscal consolidation. This will contribute to a further narrowing of the current account deficit. Underlying inflation is projected to remain low. Private sector credit will pick-up slowly, as banks have yet to absorb the full losses due to non-performing loans in their portfolios. The programme targets a general government deficit of 4.5 per cent of gross domestic product (GDP) in 2010.

The importance of being European

Reported in the web edition of Agence France Presse, *EUBusiness* in May 2010, the Austrian EU Special Representative for Bosnia and Herzegovina, Valentin Inzko, had described Bosnia as a 'crisis-stricken country', which needed to 'get back on track to EU membership'. May 2010 saw an international summit meeting bring together EU representatives and officials from all the other Balkan states seeking EU membership. Bosnia may want to join the EU but the political impasse has blocked the vital reforms demanded by Brussels. Mr Inzko said that 'In the last four years overall the country has found itself in a political impasse. The political climate has deteriorated and political leaders now have their eyes set on general elections to be held in October (2010).' Mr Inzko lamented that 'negative rhetoric' was also on the rise in the run-up to the October voting. 'Suggestions that the dissolution of the country is possible (by Bosnian Serbs) have led to strong reactions from other political quarters' he added.

Since the end of the 1992–95 war Bosnia has been split into two entities, the Muslim-Croat Federacija Bosne i Hercegovine (FBiH) (Federation of Bosnia-Hercegovina) and the Serbs' Republika Srpska (RS) (Serb Republic). The two are linked by weak central institutions while each has its own government.

For some time the EU has been pushing for a change to the constitution to strengthen BiH's central government, which it says is necessary if the country is to become an EU member. However, Bosnian Serbs strongly oppose any strengthening of joint institutions at the expense of their entity's autonomy. In this they echo the views of hard-liners in Serbia itself, more favourably inclined towards Russia than Western Europe.

October 2011 elections

The BiH Republic has one of Europe's most complicated elections. First there is the three person rotating presidency, which means three different elections within the presidential election – one for the Croats, one for the Bosniaks and the third for the Serbs. In October 2010 these were won by Zeljko Komsic (of the Socijaldemokratska Partija BiH (Socijaldemokrati) (Social Democratic Party of BiH) (SDP BiH)), Bakir Izatbegovic (of the Stranka Demokratski Akije (SDA) (Democratic Action Party)), and Nebojsa Radmanovic (of the Savez Nezavisnih Socijaldemokrata (SNSD) (Alliance of Independent Social Democrats)), respectively. Nebojsa Radmanovic was the first to take on the presidency, on 20 October 2010. Each rotation lasts eight months, and each term in office is four years so that each of the three presidents serves twice.

Then there are elections to the Zastupnicki dom (House of Representatives) (lower house) whose 42 members in turn appoint the 15 members (five Bosniaks, five Croats and five Serbs) of the Dom Naroda (House of the Peoples) (upper house). The October 2011 election results were dominated by the Socijaldemokratska Partija BiH (Socijaldemokrati) (Social Democratic Party of BiH) (SDP BiH) who won eight seats (out of 42), Savez Nezavisnih Socijaldemokrata (SNSD) (Alliance of Independent Social Democrats) eight seats and Stranka Demokratski Akije (SDA) (Democratic Action Party), seven seats.

While these federal elections are going on, so too are presidential and parliamentary elections for Republika Srpska (RS) (Serb Republic) and Federacija Bosne i Hercegovine (FBiH) (Federation of Bosnia-Hercegovina).

By June 2011 there was still no Chairman of the Council of Ministers (prime minister) as the person proposed by the presidency, Slavo Kukic, was rejected by the Serbs. Nor was there an official ruling party. In both cases the previous incumbents – Prime Minister Nikola Spiric and the seven party coalition formed back in 2007 – remained in office.

Mr Inzko stressed that Bosnia's politicians would have to get back on the path to EU membership for the sake of their citizens, with polls showing that an overwhelming 85 per cent of Bosnians are in favour of EU membership. Not that Bosnia has failed to make any sort of headway towards EU membership. It signed a Stabilisation and Association Agreement (SAA), seen as the first step towards EU membership, back in 2008, but the process subsequently stalled as reforms could not be agreed upon. Agence France Presse cited political analyst Jacques Rupnik from the Paris-based Centre for International Research and Innovation (CERI) as saying that 'Bosnia will need to establish 'integrated, simplified and effective' government institutions. The perspective of entry into the EU needs not only a state but a state that functions, a government that functions. Bosnia's government is the most complicated, most absurd system I know as a political science professor. With this system you could never join the EU.' To complicate matters, in Bosnia itself there has been criticism, mainly from the Bosnian Serb side, that Mr Inzko's Office of the High Representative is actually contributing to the non-functioning of the Bosnian government. The eventual plan has always been to transform the High Representative's office into an office of the European Union special envoy to Bosnia. But this has been postponed several times, due to the continuing political instability.

'The perception of this country is still so bad that serious investors don't want to risk anything,' according to former foreign minister Mladen Ivanic quoted by Reuters. 'The main problem is the political system, not the economic system.' Bosnia's home market of an estimated 4.0 million citizens with around US$4,600 in GDP per capita is too poor to attract significant investment. Access to the larger neighbouring markets of Croatia and Serbia is vital, but there are many non-tariff barriers. The main potential for investment in the mountainous country, much of which is still patrolled by European peacekeepers, lies in energy and infrastructure; but political feuding and self-enrichment continue to thwart big projects. Energy investments are held up because Bosnia still lacks a functioning national electricity grid, despite repeated promises to remove political obstacles.

According to Reuters, a further brake on economic growth is land ownership. While other former Yugoslav republics have reformed their laws, Bosnia still labours under a system whereby the government owns the land and companies buy only the right to build on or use it. This divided system gives politicians a huge source of patronage, often requiring several layers of bribery to complete the construction of a building or run a business. Additionally, the lack of freehold ownership limits the amount companies can borrow and stifles growth.

There are some 400 state enterprises in the Muslim-Croat federation alone, whose board members and top management are all political appointees, not holding their jobs on commercial or professional criteria. Many informed Bosnians are understandably unhappy at this state of affairs.

Risk assessment

Economy	Poor
Politics	Poor
Regional stability	Fair

COUNTRY PROFILE

Historical profile

1463 Bosnia and Hercegovina (BiH) became a province of the Ottoman Empire. Many of BiH's Christian Slavic population (principally Serb and Croat) were converted to Islam.

1877–78 The Congress of Berlin assigned BiH to the Austro-Hungarian Empire following the end of the Russo-Turkish War.

1914 Gavrilo Princip, a Serbian nationalist, assassinated Austrian Archduke Ferdinand in Sarajevo (capital of BiH), precipitating the First World War.

1918 The defeat of the Austro-Hungarian empire during the First World War saw the creation of the Kingdom of the Serbs, Croats and Slovenes, encompassing BiH, Croatia, parts of Dalmatia and Macedonia, Montenegro, Serbia, Slavonia and Slovenia.

1929 The Kingdom was renamed Yugoslavia.

1941 Parts of Yugoslavia were occupied by the Germans, Italians, Hungarians and Bulgarians. Most of BiH was incorporated

KEY FACTS

Official name: Federacija Bosne i Hercegovine (FBiH) (Federation of Bosnia-Hercegovina)

Head of State: President Zivko Budimir (HDZ) (Hrvatska Stranka Prava (HSP) Croatian Party of Rights)) (from 17 Mar 2011)

Head of government: Prime Minister Nermin Nikšic (Hrvatska Demokratska Zajednica (HDZ) (Democratic People's Union)) (from 17 Mar 2011)

Ruling party: Coalition government with 16 members chosen from the quota of nationalies. There are eight Bosniak, five Croat and three Serb cabinet ministers.

Capital: Sarajevo

Currency: Konvertibilna marka (KM) (The Croatian kuna also circulate widely)

Exchange rate: KM1.51 per US$ (Jul 2004) (pegged at KM1.96 per euro)

GDP per capita: US$2,129*

Labour force: 722,000 (2007)

Unemployment: 42.00% (2009)

* estimated figure

into Croatia, which was granted independence by the Axis powers (Germany, Italy and Japan) and ruled by the country's fascist Ustasha movement. Two opposition movements, the communist Partisans led by Josip Broz Tito and the royalist Chetniks led by Draza Mihailovic and backed by the Allied powers, formed to resist Nazi rule.

1944–45 After hostilities broke out between the Chetniks and Partisans, the Allies withdrew support for the Chetniks and backed the Partisans. The Partisans then defeated the occupying forces, the Ustasha, and the Chetniks.

1945 BiH became a constituent republic of a new Yugoslav federation. Tito assumed power and adopted a Soviet-style constitution. The rest of the Yugoslav federation comprised Croatia, Macedonia, Slovenia, Montenegro, Serbia and the two autonomous regions of Vojvodina and Kosovo. In an attempt to create a Yugoslav unity, Tito imposed restrictions on religious worship, while socialism was encouraged as the country's national ideology.

1953 Constitutions adopted in 1953, 1963 and 1974 increased the autonomy of the constituent republics.

1989 Following the death of Tito in 1980 and the fall of communism elsewhere in eastern Europe, friction between the wealthier republics, Slovenia and Croatia, and the different ethnic groupings intensified.

1990 Multi-party elections in BiH brought to power a government which supported outright independence.

1992 After independence from Yugoslavia, civil war engulfed the whole of BiH.

1993 The Yugoslav dinar was replaced by the new dinar as the national currency.

1995 Hostilities were brought to an end by the Dayton Peace Agreement in late 1995. BiH was divided almost equally into two distinct entities, based along ethnic lines: the Federacija Bosne i Hercegovine (FBiH) (Federation of Bosnia and Hercegovina) (comprising the Croat and Muslim population, 51 per cent of BiH) and the RS (comprising the Serb population, 49 per cent of BiH). The disputed region of Brcko in the north-west of the country became a self-governing district within BiH. A multi-national Nato military force was deployed in BiH to enforce the military aspects of Dayton.

1996 A democratic government was elected comprising the main nationalist parties of the three ethnic communities: the Muslim Stranka Demokratski Akije (SDA) (Democratic Action Party), Hrvatska Demokratska Zajednica Bosne i Hercegovine (HDZ BiH) (Croatian Democratic Union of Bosnia and Hercegovina) and the Srpska Demokratska Stranka (SDS) (Serb Democratic Party). Alija Izetbegovic, Ante Jelavic and Zivko Radisic were elected to the three-member collective presidency.

1999 The new dinar was replaced by the Konvertibilna marka as the national currency.

2000 Nationalists did well in the general election and international hopes of multi-ethnic political co-operation declined. The Organisation for Security and Co-operation in Europe (OSCE) reported that several political parties abused the regulations during the elections.

2001 Ante Jelavic threatened to form his own government in Croat-dominated parts of the FBiH and was dismissed from the BiH presidency by UN High Representative Wolfgang Petritsch. Jozo Krizanovic became BiH president. Bozidar Matic resigned and the BiH parliament elected Zlatko Lagumdzija to replace him.

2002 Dragan Covic (Croat), Mirko Sarovic (Serb) and Sulejman Tihic (Muslim) were elected to the BiH presidency in the presidential elections. The SDA won the BiH parliamentary elections.

2003 Mirko Sarovic resigned from the BiH presidency after accusations of being involved with illegal arms sales to Iraq; he was replaced by Borislav Paravac.

2004 Sulejman Tihic became chairman of the presidency. UN High Representative, Paddy Ashdown, dismissed 60 top officials in the RS for failing to implement measures to catch Radovan Karadzic and General Ratko Mladic, both of whom were indicted on war-crimes charges. EU force (EUFOR) took over NATO's peacekeeping mission in Bosnia. Dragan Mikerevic, prime minister of the RS, resigned.

2005 RS parliament elected Pero Bukejlovic as prime minister. Dragan Covic was dismissed by the High Representative; Ivo Miro Jovic was appointed as the Croat member of the presidency. The EU agreed to stabilisation and association agreement talks as pre-entry measures for BiH to join the EU.

2006 The BiH rotating presidential elections were won by Haris Silajdzic, Nebojsa Radmanovic and Zeljko Komsic. In Zastupnicki dom (House of Representatives) elections the SDA won nine seats (out of 42); Stranka za Bosnu i Hercegovinu (SBiH) (Party of Bosnia and Hercegovina) won eight; Savez Nezavisnih Socijaldemokrata (SNSD) (Alliance of Independent Social Democrats) won seven; Socijaldemokratska Partija BiH (Socijaldemokrati) (Social Democratic Party of BiH) (Social Democrats) won five; HDZ BiH and SDS each won three seats and six political parties shared the remaining seven seats.

2007 Nikola Spiric became prime minister of BiH. Igor Radojicic (SNSD) was appointed acting-President of RS, following the death of President Milan Jelic. Spiric resigned as prime minister in protest at measures introduced by the UN High Representative to speed up decision making in the central parliament. BiH began reforms (seen as moves towards EU pre-membership) which are designed to strengthen central government and deny regional legislatures a veto on legislation. In RS presidential elections Rajko Kuzmanovic (SNSD) won with 41.8 per cent of the vote; his closest rival, Ognjen Tadic (SDP), had 35.2 per cent. Nikola Spiric was re-appointed prime minister of BiH.

KEY INDICATORS — Bosnia and Hercegovina Republic

	Unit	2006	2007	2008	2009	2010
Population	m	3.95	3.98	3.99	*4.00	*3.84
Gross domestic product (GDP)	US$bn	12.23	14.78	18.50	17.10	16.80
GDP per capita	US$	3,105	3,712	4,625	4,279	4,319
GDP real growth	%	6.2	5.8	5.5	-3.4	0.8
Inflation	%	7.5	1.3	7.4	-0.4	2.1
Unemployment	%	–	29.0	40.1	41.5	42.9
Exports (fob) (goods)	US$m	3,539.0	4,243.3	5,194.0	4,079.9	4,937.0
Imports (fob) (goods)	US$m	8,587.0	9,947.2	12,286.4	8,829.1	9,230.2
Balance of trade	US$m	-5,048.0	-5,703.9	-7,092.3	-4,749.2	-4,293.2
Current account	US$m	-1,025.0	-1,920.0	-2,766.0	-1,174.6	-916.0
Total reserves minus gold	US$m	3,372.0	4,525.0	3,516.0	3,245.0	4,383.0
Foreign exchange	US$m	3,371.0	4,525.0	3,515.0	3,241.0	4,383.0
Exchange rate	per US$	1.51	1.35	1.34	1.41	1.48

* estimated figure

2008 Haris Silajdzic became president of the BiH. BiH signed the Stabilisation and Association Agreement with the European Union. Full membership may not be achieved until 2018. The agreement was seen as a measure to bolster democratic values and counter ethnic tensions. Former Bosnian Serb leader Radovan Karadzic was arrested in Belgrade. Seven Bosnian Serbs were convicted of genocide in aiding the systematic killing of over 8,000 Bosnian Muslim men and boys during the siege of Srebrenica in 1995. All defendants had been members of either the police or army and were each given jail terms of 38–42 years. Local elections were won by nationalist political parties, which still divide communities along ethnic lines.
2009 Austrian diplomat, Valentin Inzko was appointed UN High Representative and EU Special Representative. Nedzad Brankovic resigned as prime minister of the FBiH. Former president Karadzic was charged with war crimes, genocide and crimes against humanity. The rail link between Belgrade (Serbia) and Sarajevo, closed since the conflict in the 1990s, was reopened.
2010 Haris Silajdzic became chairman of the rotating presidency in March. The Serbian parliament offered an apology for the 1995 Srebrenica massacre. In presidential and parliamentary elections held on 3 October, Zeljko Komsic (SDP BiH) won 60.6 per cent of the Croat vote, for the rotating federal presidency, along with Bakir Izatbegovic (SDA) with 34.9 per cent of the Bosniaks vote and Nebojsa Radmanovic (SNSD) with 48.9 per cent of the Serb vote. Milorad Dodik was appointed president of RS on 15 November. On 20 October Nebojsa Radmanovic (Serb) took office as the first in the rotating BiH presidency.
2011 President Dodik (of the RS) appointed Aleksandar Dzombic (SNSD) as prime minister of RS; he took office on 3 February. On 17 March, Zivko Budimir (Hrvatska Stranka Prava (HSP) (Croatian Party of Rights)) was elected president and Nermin Nikšic (Hrvatska Demokratska Zajednica (HDZ) (Democratic People's Union)) as prime minister of the Federation of BiH. The presidency proposed Slavo Kukic as federal (BiH Republic) prime minister on 14 June, but Serb representatives rejected his candidature on 17 June and the post remained unfilled.

Political structure

Constitution

The effective founding constitution of modern Republika Bosne i Hercegovine (BiH) (Republic of Bosnia and Hercegovina) is the 1995 Dayton Peace Agreement. This set out the federal state, divided between the Federacija Bosne i Hercegovine (FBiH) (Federation of Bosnia and Hercegovina) and the Republika Srpska (RS) (Serb Republic). The two republics are then subdivided into cantons based on the Swiss model. A European Union pre-membership agreement in December 2007 produced parliamentary reforms to strengthen the BiH central government, whereby FBiH and RS legislatures will no long be able to block and boycott a BiH vote.
The disputed region of Brcko in the north-west of the country was placed under international arbitration in 1995. In March 1998, the Brcko Tribunal declared the Brcko municipality a separate self-governing neutral district under the sovereignty of BiH.
In 2002, the FBiH and RS governments signed an agreement to make constitutional amendments designed to give equal status to all ethnic Muslims, Croats and Serbs in BiH.
Under the terms of the Dayton Agreement, the BiH is responsible for foreign affairs, foreign trade, monetary policy and law enforcement. The FBiH and RS are primarily responsible for fiscal policy, defence and law.
Constitutional government is not yet in full operation. The UN's Office of the High Representative (OHR) is responsible for overseeing and implementing the civilian aspects of the Dayton Agreement.
Universal suffrage at 18 years of age (16 years if employed). The 2001 election law only allows voters to cast ballots for members of their own ethnic group in elections for the collective three-member presidency. Voters may only vote in constituencies where they lived prior to the 1992–95 civil war.

Form of state

Confederated parliamentary democratic republic, separated into two constituent states – Bosnia-Hercegovina Federation and Bosnia Serb Republic (RS).

The executive

BiH has a three-member collective presidency, one representative from each of the three main ethnic groups. Although this is nominally the executive for the whole country, in practice, the RS appointed its own president and has frequently disregarded the authority of the three-man presidency. In 2002, the collective presidency was elected for a four-year mandate.
The government is formed from a Council of Ministers drawn from the Zastupnicki dom, which are nominated by the president and confirmed by the Zastupnicki dom. The council appoints a chairman (prime minister) as head of government; in 2005, the post of prime minister was enhanced, with the power to appoint and dismiss ministers.
The UN High Representative holds *de facto* power, delegated to local politicians.

National legislature

The central legislature is the bicameral Parlementarna Skupstina BiH (National Parliament of BiH), with representatives from both of the state parliaments as members. The Zastupnicki dom (House of Representatives) (lower house) has 42 members elected by party-list proportional representation, for a four-year term – 28 members from the FBiH (14 Bosniaks and 14 Croatians) and 14 from the RS. The Dom Naroda (House of the Peoples) (upper house) has 15 members appointed from the lower house and elected by the Zastupnicki dom, with equal representation of the three ethnic groups, five Bosniaks, five Croats and five Serbs.
BiH has two state parliaments (FBiH and NSRS – see below) and one central legislature.
The Federacija Bosne i Hercegovina (FBiH) (Bosniak/Croat Federation of Bosnia and Hercegovina) has a bicameral parliament with a House of Representatives (98 seats – members elected by popular vote for four-year terms); and a House of Peoples (30 Bosniak and 30 Croat seats).
The Narodna Skuptstina Republika Srpska (NSRS) (Serb Republic National Parliament) is unicameral, with 83 members elected for a four-year term by proportional representation.
The Brcko Distrikt (Brcko district), in north-east BiH, is under internationally administered supervision.

Legal system

Civil law system of former Yugoslavia. Legal infrastructure has been in disarray since the war.

Last elections

3 October 2010 (BiH presidency and parliament; state presidential and state parliaments)
Results: BiH Republic. Presidential (three-member rotating presidency): (Croats) Zeljko Komsic (SDP BiH) won 60.6 per cent of the vote, Borjana Kristo (HDZ BiH) 19.7 per cent, Martin Raguz (coalition) 10.8 per cent; four other Croat candidates each won less that 9 per cent. Bosniaks: Bakir Izatbegovic (SDA) won 34.9 per cent of the vote, Fahrudin Radoncic (SBB BiH) won 30.5 per cent, Haris Silajdzic (SBiH) 25.1 per cent; six other Bosniak candidates each won less than 3 per cent. Serbs: Nebojsa Radmanovic (SNSD) won 48.9 per cent of the vote, Mladen Ivanic (coalition) 47.3 per cent; one other candidate won less than 4 per cent.

Parlementarna Skupstina BiH (National Parliament of BiH), Zastupnicki dom (House of Representatives) (lower house): Socijaldemokratska Partija BiH (Socijaldemokrati) (Social Democratic Party of BiH) (SDP BiH) won eight seats (out of 42), Savez Nezavisnih Socijaldemokrata (SNSD) (Alliance of Independent Social Democrats) eight seats, (Muslim) Stranka Demokratski Akije (SDA) (Democratic Action Party), seven seats, Srpska Demokratska Stranka (SDS) (Serb Democratic Party) four seats, Savez za Bolju Buducnost BiH (SBB BIH) (Union for a better BiH) four seats, Hrvatska Demokratska Zajednica Bosne i Hercegovine (HDZ BiH) (Croatian Democratic Union of BiH) three seats; five other political parties and one coalition of three parties shared the remaining eight seats.
Republika Srpska presidency: Milorad Dodik (SNSD) won 50.52 per of the vote, Ognjen Tadic 35.92 per cent; eight other candidates each won less than 3 per cent.

Next elections
October 2014 (presidential and parliamentary)

Political parties

Ruling party
Seven-party coalition government (formed 9 Jan 2007)

Main opposition party
Socijaldemokratska Partija (SPD) (Social Democratic Party)

Population

4.00 million (2009)*
Last census: March 1991: 4,377,033
Population density: 76 inhabitants per square km. Urban population: 43 per cent (1994–2000).
Annual growth rate: 1.0 per cent 1994–2004 (WHO 2006)

Internally Displaced Persons (IDP)
330,000 (UNHCR 2004)

Ethnic make-up
Muslims (44 per cent), Serbs (31 per cent) and Croats (17 per cent). The RS is a mostly Serb enclave, while Muslims (also known as 'Bosniaks') and Croats control and inhabit the FBiH.

Religions
Islam (Muslims), Serbian Eastern Orthodoxy (Serbs), Roman Catholicism (Croats).

Education

The education system in BiH was largely destroyed by the civil war and is now influenced by politics. International aid and tax revenues are being used by the entity governments to re-build and fund the education system. In the FBiH, each canton has responsibility for education. The RS has responsibility for its own education system.
Despite the FBiH and RS signing the Declaration and Agreement on Education in BiH in 2000 to introduce much-needed reforms to the post-war education system, educational curriculums in each of the entities follow ethnic and religious lines. Segregation of students along ethnic lines is not uncommon.
BiH has universities at Banja Luka, Mostar, Sarajevo and Tuzla. Higher education is also poorly financed and most international aid has come from non-governmental organisations (NGOs).
Literacy rate: 95 per cent adult rate; 100 per cent youth rate (15–24) (Unesco 2005).

Health

The health system in BiH is poor and receives little funding from the central government, having handed down the funding responsibilities to cantonal and local government. The health system is largely dependent on aid but is also financed through employee insurance schemes.

HIV/Aids
HIV prevalence: 0.5 per cent aged 15–49 in 2003 (World Bank)
Life expectancy: 73 years, 2004 (WHO 2006)
Fertility rate/Maternal mortality rate: 1.3 births per woman, 2004 (WHO 2006)
Child (under 5 years) mortality rate (per 1,000): 14 per 1,000 live births (World Bank)
Head of population per physician: 1.34 physicians per 1,000 people, 2003 (WHO 2006)

Welfare

Higher spending on specific areas of the welfare system compared to other areas of the economy has become a major impediment to achieving economic growth in BiH. The welfare system is highly geared to supporting military veterans, war widows and their families, thus only benefiting around 230,000 people – about six per cent of the population.
According to the IMF, benefits and spending for military invalids and war widows in the FBiH and the RS account for 10–12 per cent of the country's government revenues. These payments also accounted for over 80 per cent of the annual pension fund.
The unemployment benefit system in BiH is of limited assistance to the claimant. Unemployment benefits – 30 per cent of the state average wage – in the FBiH are only available for six months – although these are available longer for those who had been in continuous employment for more than five years. Claimants need to have paid through an insurance scheme to gain unemployment benefits, while military invalids and war widows are funded by the state. As a result of the system, few register as unemployed, confusing official statistics of the unemployed in BiH. About 5 per cent of those registered as unemployed actually receive state benefits.

Main cities

Sarajevo (capital, estimated population 383,604 in 2005), Banja Luka (capital of RS) (173,748), Zenica (85,649), Tuzla (88,521), Prijedor (29,876), Mostar (the main town in Hercegovina province) (64,301), Bihac (39,195).

Languages spoken

Bosanski (Bosnian) is one of the southern Slavonic languages and is most closely related to Serbian, Croatian and Slovene. Croatian and Serbian are also spoken. Bosnian is written in Latin script but can also be seen written in the Cyrillic alphabet.
German is a useful language for the business traveller.
English is not widely spoken, but is becoming more common as a language for business.

Official language/s
Bosanski (Bosnian)

Media

The civil war of the 1990s resulted in a highly polarised media, which the Dayton Agreement addressed by developing a media to bridge inter-communal groupings. The media is partially free although state bodies and political parties have endeavoured to bring pressure on journalists and media outlets.

Press
Dailies: From Sarajevo in Bosnian, *Dnevni Avaz* (www.avaz.ba), and the independent *Oslobodjenje* (www.oslobodjenje.ba). From Banja Luka, in Serbian, *Nezavisne Novine* (www.nezavisne.com) and the Bosnian Serb government *Glas Srpske* (www.glassrpske.com). From Mostar, in Croatian, *Dnevni List* (www.dnevni-list.ba).
Weeklies: From Sarajevo in Bosnian, *Dani* (www.bhdani.com), *Slobodna Bosna* (www.slobodna-bosna.ba), and from Banja Luka *Reporter* an independent bi-weekly.

Broadcasting
National, public broadcasting is provided by Radio Televizija Bosne i Hercegovine (BHRT) (www.bhrt.ba), by Radio Televizija BiH in the Bosniak-Croat region (RTBiH) (www.rtvfbih.ba) and in the Serb region by Radio Televizija Republik Srpske (RTRS) (www.rtrs.tv).
Radio: Public radio has the highest listening figures. There are over 200 commercial radio stations; however the number has been restricted due to the inadequate advertising market.
The BHRT (www4.bhrt.ba) broadcasts two national networks and one international.

Popular commercial stations include Bosanska Radio Mreza (Boram) (www.boram.ba), BM Radio (www.bmradio.com), Radio Stari Grad (http://rsg.software.ba), Radio M (www.radiom.net), Radio Tuzla (www.radiotuzla.com) and Big Radio 2 (www.bigradiobl.com).
Television: BHRT, RTVBiH and RTRS provide public services in all local languages. There are over 40 channels to choose from, the majority are provided by foreign cable or satellite networks. Domestic commercial channels include Balkanmedia 7 (www.balkanmedia.com), BN TV Bijelina (www.rtvbn.com) and Mreza Plus (www.mrezaplus.ba).
News agencies
National news agency: FENA (Federal News Agency)

Economy

The economy is in need of revitalisation through structural reforms and private sector-led growth. BiH has natural resources in hydropower, coal, ore and minerals, good agricultural prospects, producing wheat, fruits and livestock, timber and forest products and an industrial manufacturing base in steel, aluminium, vehicle assembly and parts, textiles, furniture, munitions, domestic appliances, aircraft repair and oil refining. However it still has to deal with the after-effects of an internecine civil war, which has left deep divisions within civil society. Although the three rival federal regions have come together and agreed to strengthen central government the divergence complicates policymaking as conflicting views on the future of BiH impedes planning and investment. Growth in tourism, particularly along the Adriatic coast, is likely to boost the economy as it draws in ancillary sectors and provides employment
GDP growth in 2007 was 6.5 per cent, underpinned by growing exports, as exported goods were shifted towards higher-value added manufactured goods. This in turn increased the capital-intensive sector – in aluminium production and metals – and a growth in output and wages. However, employment fell as labour-intensive employment declined. GDP growth in 2008 was 5.4 per cent as the global economic crisis cut world trade. Per capita income that had been US$3,824 in 2007 jumped to US$4,636 in 2008 before falling back to US$4,279 in 2009, when the economy fell into recession and GDP growth was -3.4 per cent.
Unemployment in BiH is high at over 40 per cent, although unofficial statistics that include the grey economy estimates a rate of 18–22 per cent. Job creation is of primary importance and the lack of jobs accounts for a high level of migration for employment. Remittances in 2008 were US$2.73 billion (14.8 per cent of GDP), which fell to US$2.21 billion in 2009, as the value of the US dollar weakened and employment opportunities abroad were cut.
BiH entered a Stabilisation and Association Agreement (SAA) and Interim Agreement (IA) with the EU in 2008, which created a nascent free trade area to progressively open markets in BiH and foster economic and social developments. The agreement is expected to run until 2013 with a functioning free trade area to be fully operational before membership of the EU is confirmed. However in 2010, the EU called on BiH to limit its inconsistent implementation of reforms, to strengthen the fiscal system and foster a dynamic and competitive private sector and at the same time for BiH politicians to make compromises and foster unity.

External trade

As of September 2010, BiH was still working towards WTO membership. It is a member of the Central European Free Trade Agreement (Cefta), along with seven other countries in the region. Cefta has an association agreement with the EU, which is its primary trading partner. A Stabilisation and Association Agreement (SAA) with the EU was signed in December 2009, with the prospect of enhanced trading links.
The EU as a whole is BiH's largest trading partner, trading in miscellaneous manufactured articles, textiles, machinery and vehicle parts and raw materials (excluding hydrocarbons).
Industrial production includes heavy industries such as steel, aluminium and mining, with vehicle and aircraft assembly and oil refining. Lighter industries include furniture and domestic appliances manufacture.
Imports
Imports consist of fuels, foodstuffs, chemicals, machinery and equipment.
Main sources: Croatia (typically 15 per cent of total), Germany (11 per cent), Serbia (10 per cent).
Exports
Exports consist of mainly steel, minerals, clothing and textiles, aluminium and timber products.
Main destinations: Croatia (typically 17 per cent total), Germany (15 per cent), Serbia (13 per cent).

Agriculture

Farming
The legacy of war in the region has implications for BiH's agricultural policy. There is considerable uncertainty over land rights, with fragmented and small-sized farm units hindering any large-scale investment opportunities.
The varying climatic conditions in BiH offer wide possibilities both in terms of crop choice and cultivation of land farming, fruit-growing, vine-growing, vegetable-growing, forage crops and livestock production.
Agricultural activities in the RS extend over different farming systems including mixed farming enterprises (crops and cattle) on lower flat lands that alternate with more extensive sheep grazing systems in mountainous areas.
Most of the FBiH is mountainous, with farms in the south and south-east growing vegetables, fruits and rearing livestock. The issue of land mines in rural areas complicates policies related to post-war agricultural development.
Fishing
Fishing is of little importance to BiH's agricultural sector as a whole with the fish catch totalling some 2,500 tonnes per year.
Forestry
Over half of BiH's land area is forested, covering over 2.2 million hectares (ha). Three-fifths of woodland are used for wood supply, mostly for export. Most of the woodland is state-owned. The country has a small forest sector, which produces mainly sawnwood and wood-based panels from domestic resources.

Industry and manufacturing

Since the end of the civil war, the construction industry has been the main engine of industrial growth, and since the Zenica steelworks was sold to LNM Group in 2004 steel production has boosted state industrial production based on the resurgent metals sector, as well as the civil engineering projects and Balkan regeneration.
State-owned telecommunication entities are due to be one of the first organisations offered up for privatisation.

Tourism

There was little tourist infrastructure before 2004 and its market is centred on adventure holidays to its unspoilt mountains and lakes. Direct flights from the UK to Sarajevo have helped to provide access, with the re-opening of the bridge at Mostar, the national symbol of reconciliation, being used as a tourist attraction.

Mining

BiH has deposits of iron ores and good reserves of bauxite, as it used to be a major source of minerals for former Yugoslavia.

Hydrocarbons

There are no oil reserves. Consumption in 2008 was 29,000 barrels per day, all of which was imported, mainly from Russia.

Domestic downstream activities are limited to the Bosanski Brod oil refinery in Republika Srpska (RS), which had been closed from 2005–08 due to war damage. Following some refurbishment it now processes around 1,800 tonnes of crude oil per day. As part of the BiH government's privatisation programme majority shares in the oil refinery were sold to the Russian oil company Neftegazinkor, which promised strong investment in the plant, in 2007. However, scrutiny of the deal by BiH Transparency International highlighted what it saw as a flawed deal whereby Neftegazinkor paid for its shares with an advantageous loan from the RS government, using a below market estimation of the business and extended liabilities remaining the responsibility of the RS government.

Natural gas imports are supplied by Russia via the Bratsvo gas pipeline through Hungary and Serbia.

The EU and World Bank have backed plans for the Ionia-Adriatic Pipeline (IAP) to supply natural gas from the Middle East to BiH via Albania and Montenegro. Following IAP's detailed engineering phase, construction should begin in 2010–11.

BiH has deposits of coal and produces enough for its own consumption. The government has included the coal industry in the programme of its Agency for Privatisation. The Visca mines, near Tuzla in the north, produce 1,000 tonnes of coal a day, used in the domestic steel industry and power generation.

Energy

Total installed generating capacity was 4,300MW in 2007, generating 12.8 billion kilowatt hours (kWh); this figure is still only 90 per cent of pre-war output. As BiH consumption is lower than its capacity it is a net exporter of electricity. The state-owned Elektroprivreda Republika Srpska, operates one of the largest coal-fired power plants in BiH at Ugljevik. Plans for an additional 2,000MW are under consideration, in particular the Gacko II coal-fired power plant.

The energy market was opened up for competition for sales to commercial customers in 2008 and will be opened up for domestic customers in 2015. The transmission system has been unified into a single grid. Two joint stock companies have been created to undertake the operations of assets (Transco) and authorities (ISO).

Financial markets

Stock exchange

SASE (Sarajevska Berza) (Sarajevo Stock Exchange)

Banking and insurance

BiH's banking system has undergone reform since 1995. Although heavily indebted and close to bankruptcy, a number of banks underwent privatisation in the late 1990s. Foreign companies that have already invested in BiH banking have streamlined and modernised major banks. Croatia's Zagrebacka Banka has taken a major share in the banking sector, acquiring stakes in four banks. Three RS banks were granted licences from the Federation Banking Agency (FBA) and opened branches in the FBiH, assisted by the introduction of a harmonised banking code between the entities.

The central bank has responsibility as the monetary authority and currency board.

Central bank

The Centralna Banka Bosne i Hercegovine (CBBH) (Central Bank of Bosnia and Hercegovina)

Time

GMT plus one hour (daylight saving, late March to late October, GMT plus two hours)

Geography

BiH is a mountainous territory with only about 20km of coastline. Croatia forms its western border (running from north-west to south-east, along the Dinaric Alps) and its northern border. Serbia lies to the east and Montenegro to the south-east.

The ancient province of BiH lies between the Sava, Drina and Una rivers. There are fertile lowlands along the River Sava which forms the northern border.

Hemisphere

Northern

Climate

The climate in BiH is continental with warm summers and cold winters. The temperature averages one degree Celsius (C) in January and 21 degrees C in July. As the country is dominated by mountainous and hilly terrain, with central and southern BiH dominated by the Dinaric Alps, the weather can be unpredictable in valley areas in the spring and winter months.

Dress codes

During the summer, light clothing is recommended, with warmer clothes essential during the winter months.

Entry requirements

Passports

Required by all except nationals of Austria, Belgium, Finland, France, Germany, Greece, Italy, Luxembourg, The Netherlands, Norway, Portugal, Spain and Sweden, who only need a national identity card.

Visa

Not required by citizens of Europe, North America, Australasia, Kuwait, Qatar, South Korea, Malaysia and Brunei.

Currency advice/regulations

BiH has a cash economy. The Konvertibilna marka (KM) is the local currency. The dollar and euro, but not sterling, are the most acceptable foreign currencies, but it is likely that change will be supplied in KM. Credit card facilities are limited, although hotels, restaurants and shops in the major centres are beginning to accept them. Travellers cheques can be changed at only a few banks in major cities and are not recommended.

Import and export of local currency are permitted to a limit of KM200,000. There are no restrictions on import and export of foreign currencies.

Customs

A unified customs territory has been established in BiH. 200 cigarettes, 20 cigars or 200g of tobacco; one litre of wine or spirits; one bottle of perfume; and gifts up to eur76.70 are admitted duty-free.

Health (for visitors)

Medical services are not comprehensive. Visitors should carry a sufficient supply of medicines or prescription drugs.

Ensure that personal travel and health insurance covers all eventualities, including accident and evacuation.

Mandatory precautions

None.

Advisable precautions

Typhoid, tetanus and hepatitis A and B vaccinations are recommended.

Water and food precautions advisable.

Credit cards

Credit cards can be used in some shops, hotels and travel agencies (Croatia Airlines, Air Bosna) in Sarajevo and is accepted by the Privredna Banka Sarajevo for cash withdrawals.

Public holidays (national)

Fixed dates

1 Jan (New Year's Day), 7 Jan (Orthodox Christmas Day), 14 Jan (Orthodox New Year), 1 Mar (Independence Day), 1 May (Labour Day), 15 Aug (Assumption Day), 28 Aug (Orthodox Assumption Day), 8 Sep (Nativity of the Virgin Mary), 21 Sep (Orthodox Nativity of the Virgin Mary), 1 Nov (All Saints' Day), 2 Nov (All Souls' Day), 25 Nov (National Statehood Day), 25 Dec (Christmas Day).

Variable dates

Easter, Orthodox Easter, Eid al Adha, Birth of the Prophet, Eid al Fitr.

Islamic year 1433 (26 Nov 2011–14 Nov 2012): The Islamic year contains 354 or 355 days, with the result that Muslim feasts advance by 10–12 days against the Gregorian calendar. Dates of feasts vary according to the sighting of the new moon, so cannot be forecast exactly.

Working hours

Banking

Mon–Fri: 0800–1900.

Business

Mon–Fri: 0800–1700.

Government

Mon–Fri: 0730–1530, except Wed, 0730–1730.

Shops

Mon–Fri: 0800–1200 and 1700–2000, Sat: 0800–1500, but many shops open throughout day.

Telecommunications

Mobile/cell phones

GSM 900 facilities are available throughout most of the country.

Electricity supply

220V AC

Social customs/useful tips

Punctuality depends on the region: it is important in some, more casual in others. It is customary to shake hands on meeting and taking leave.

Security

Unexploded mines are still a danger away from main centres and routes and travellers should keep to roads or paved areas. There is a threat from terrorism. Visitors are advised to keep clear of demonstrations or crowds. Beware of pickpockets in Sarajevo and tourist areas.

Getting there

Air

National airline: B&H Airlines

International airport/s: Sarajevo International Airport (SJJ), 12km south of the city centre.

Other airport/s: Mostar (OMO) and Banja Luka(BNX).

Airport tax: US$12. Transit passengers remaining in airport transport area are exempt.

Surface

BiH is included in the Pan-European Corridor 5 scheme. The project has some 3,270km of railways, linking Kiev in the Ukraine with western Europe via Italy, and 2,850 of new and upgraded roads.

Road: From Zagreb (Croatia) the border can be crossed at Zupanja/Orasje, Stara Gradiska/Bosanska Gradiska, Maljevac/Velika Kladusa and Licko Petrovo Selo/Izacic.

From Split (Croatia): Kamensko/Livno and Metkovic/Capljina.

Rail: The newly reopened Belgrade (Serbia) and Sarajevo line takes six hours by train.

Water: Bosnia has 20km of coastline on the Adriatic, but no ports.

Getting about

National transport

Air: The BiH national airline is B&H Airlines. Air Srpska operates from the RS.

Road: Night travel by road is not advised and travellers on back roads risk landmines left over from the war. Drivers should also be aware of the local population's disregard for the country's traffic laws. Speeding, particularly on dangerous valley roadways, is commonplace. Horse transport is used by substantial numbers of the local population.

Buses: Buses run between Split and Zagreb to Sarajevo. Journey times from Split vary between five hours during the summer to six in the winter. Journey times from Zagreb take eight hours in the summer and 11 in the winter.

Rail: The country's two railway services are BiH's Zeljeznice Bosne i Hercegovina (ZBH) and RS's Zeljeznice Republike Srpska (ZRS).

City transport

Taxis: Inexpensive taxi services operate in all the main cities. All taxis are metered, but there is no basic charge. A 10 per cent tip is usual.

Buses, trams & metro: Most city centres are served by trams, while buses serve the suburbs. The service is generally cheap and regular. Bus transfers operate out of Sarajevo airport.

Car hire

Avis and Hertz and other international car hire companies operate in neighbouring Croatia. Although the majority of hire cars have Croatian licence plates and are normally insured for travelling within BiH, it is advisable to check before booking.

Car rental firms mainly operate from Sarajevo airport.

Because the international Green Card is not applicable in BiH, car insurance is restricted to Third Party only. Travellers are likely to be asked for either a large deposit or to leave an open credit card voucher with the hire company.

Should travellers have an accident in BiH which is reported to the police, the hire company will impose an automatic charge fine, over and above any other hire costs; check all agreements carefully.

Drivers should be 21 years with a minimum of two years' driving experience.

It is recommended that visitors who rent a car also hire a driver, especially if they intend to travel outside Sarajevo.

BUSINESS DIRECTORY

The addresses listed below are a selection only. While World of Information makes every endeavour to check these addresses, we cannot guarantee that changes have not been made, especially to telephone numbers and area codes. We would welcome any corrections.

Telephone area codes

The international direct dialling (IDD) code for BiH is +387 followed by area code and subscriber's number.

Banja Luka	51	Sarajevo	33
Mostar	36	Tuzla	35
Pale	57	Zenica	72

Useful telephone numbers

Vehicle assistance: 1282

Fire and rescue: 123/124

Police: 122

Ambulance: 124

Emergency hospital, Koldovorska Street, Sarajevo (English spoken): 611-111

Chambers of Commerce

American Chamber of Commerce in Bosnia and Hercegovina, 4 Zmaja Od Bosne, 71000 Sarajevo (tel: 269-230; fax: 269-232; e-mail: amcham@lsinter.net).

Bosnia-Hercegovina Chamber of Foreign Trade, 10 Branislava Durdeva, 71000 Sarajevo (tel: 663-631; fax: 663-632; e-mail: cis@komorabih.com).

Federation of Bosnia-Hercegovina Chamber of Economy, 10 Branislava Durdeva, 71000 Sarajevo (tel: 217-782; fax: 217-783; e-mail: info@kfbih.com).

Sarajevo Canton Chamber of Economy, 8 La Benevolencije, 71000 Sarajevo (tel: 250-100; fax: 250-137).

Banking

Aurobanka, Mostar (tel: 444-444, 444-445, 444-456; fax: 444-400; internet site: www.aurobanka.com; e-mail: aurobanka.com).

Gospodarska Banka, International Division, Ferhadija 11/III, 71000 Sarajevo (tel: 208-907, 667-688; fax: 444-605).

Hercegovacka banka, Kneza Domagoja Street, Sarajevo (tel: 320-555; fax: 324-771; internet site: www.hercegovacka-banka.com; e-mail: herbank@hercegovacka-banka.com).

Hrvatska Banka, Kardinala Stepinca bb, 88000 Mostar (tel: 312-112; fax: 312-121).

Hrvatska Postanska Banka, Kneza Domagoja, Mostar (tel/fax: 316-020; e-mail: hpb-hb@int.tel.hr).

Investment Bank of the Federation of Bosnia and Hercegovina, Igmanska 1, 71000 Sarajevo (tel: 277-900; fax: 668-952; e-mail: info@ibf-bih.com).

Komercijalna Banka, Dzafer mahala 65/67, 75000 Tuzla (tel/fax: 259-000, 252-630; internet site: www.kombanka.com.ba; e-mail: kombanka@kombanka.com.ba).

Privredna Banka Sarajevo, Obala Vojvode Stepe 19, 71000 Sarajevo (tel: 213-144).

Universal Banka, Branilaca sarajeva 20/V, 71000 Sarajevo (tel: 664-139; fax: 668-239; internet site: www.universalbanka.ba; e-mail: uniba@bih.net.ba).

Central bank

Central Bank of Bosnia and Hercegovina, Maršala Tita 25, 71000 Sarajevo (tel: 278-100; fax: 278-299; e-mail: contact@cbbh.ba).

Stock exchange

SASE (Sarajevska Berza) (Sarajevo Stock Exchange): www.sase.ba

Stock exchange 2

Banjalucka berza (Banja Luka Stock Exchange): www.blberza.com

Travel information

B&H Airlines, Kurta Schorka 36, Sarajevo(tel: 767-725; fax: 767-726; e-mail: opc@airbosna.ba).

Air Commerce, Sarajevo (tel: 663-396; fax: 663-395).

Avio Express, Sarajevo (tel/fax: 653-179).

Air Srpska, Veselina Maslese 28, 78000 Banja Luka (tel: 212-806; fax: 211-348).

Ministries

Ministry of External Trade and International Communication, 9 Musala, 71000 Sarajevo (tel: 664-831; fax: 655-060).

Ministry of Foreign Affairs of BiH, Musala 2, Sarajevo (tel: 281-100; internet site: http://www.mvp.gov.ba/Index_eng.htm).

RS Ministry of Foreign Economic Affairs, Vuka Karadzica 4, 51000 Banja Luka (tel: 331-430; fax: 331-436).

RS Ministry of Trade and Tourism, Vuka Karadzica 4, 51000 Banja Luka (tel: 331-523; fax: (331-499).

Other useful addresses

Agency for Privatisation in Federation of Bosnia and Hercegovina, Alipasina 41, Sarajevo (tel: 218-550; fax: 218-552; e-mail: apftbiro@bih.net.ba).

US Embassy of Bosnia and Hercegovina, 2109 E Street, NW, Washington DC 20037 (tel: 337-1500; fax: 337-1502; e-mail: info@bosnianembassy.org).

British Embassy, BFPO 543, 8 Tina Ujevica, Sarajevo (tel: 444-429; fax: 666-131; e-mail: britemba@bih.net.ba).

British Embassy Commercial Department, Petrakijina 22, Sarajevo (tel: 204-781, 204-782, 679-635; fax: 204-780).

Communications and Regulatory agency (CRA), Vilsonovo Setaliste 10, 71000 Sarajevo.

Directorate for Reconstruction and Development, Saravejo (tel: 650-563).

RS Directorate for Privatisation, Mladena Stojanovica 4, Banja Luka (tel: 308-311; fax: 311-245; e-mail: dip@inecco.net).

Elektrodistribucija (Power Distribution Company), Sarajevo (tel: 472-462).

Elektroprivreda BiH, Vilsonovo setaliste 20, 71000 Sarajevo (tel: 651-722; fax: 653-004).

Gras (Public Transport Company), Sarajevo (tel: 664-624).

Institute for City Development Planning, Saravejo (tel: 664-638).

Institute for City Construction, Saravejo (tel: 663-901).

Institute for Information and Statistics, Saravejo (tel: 664-450).

Office of the High Representative, Emerika Bluma 1, 71 000 Sarajevo (tel: 283-500; fax: 283-501).

Public Information Office HQ SFOR, Butmir Camp, 71 000 Sarajevo (tel: 495-149).

PTT (Post/Telegraph/Telephone), Sarajevo (tel: 664-813).

Sarajevo City Council, Reisa Dz Causevica Street No 3, Sarajevo (tel: 664-773; fax: 648-016).

Sarajevogas (Gas Company), Sarajevo (tel: 467-713).

Sarajevostan (Housing Company), Saravejo (tel: 663-522).

Sarajevski Sajam (trade fairs), Terezije bb, 71 000 Sarajevo (tel: 664-163, 201-208, 445-156; fax: 201-178, 201-208).

Telekom Srpske (e-mail: tskabinet@telekom-rs.com).

World Bank Resident Mission, Bosnia and Hercegovina, Hamdije Kresevljakovica 19, 71000 Sarajevo (tel: 440-293; fax: 440-108).

National news agency: FENA (Federal News Agency), (email: fena@fena.ba; internet: www.fena.ba).

Other news agencies: SRNA (Bosnian Serb): www.srna.co.yu

Onasa (independent): www.onasa.com.ba

Internet sites

RS Directorate for Privatisation: www.rsprivatizacija.com

Republika Srpska Government: www.vladars.net

United States BiH Embassy: www.bosnianembassy.org

World Bank Resident Mission: www.worldbank.org.ba

UN Office of the High Representative: www.ohr.int

Botswana

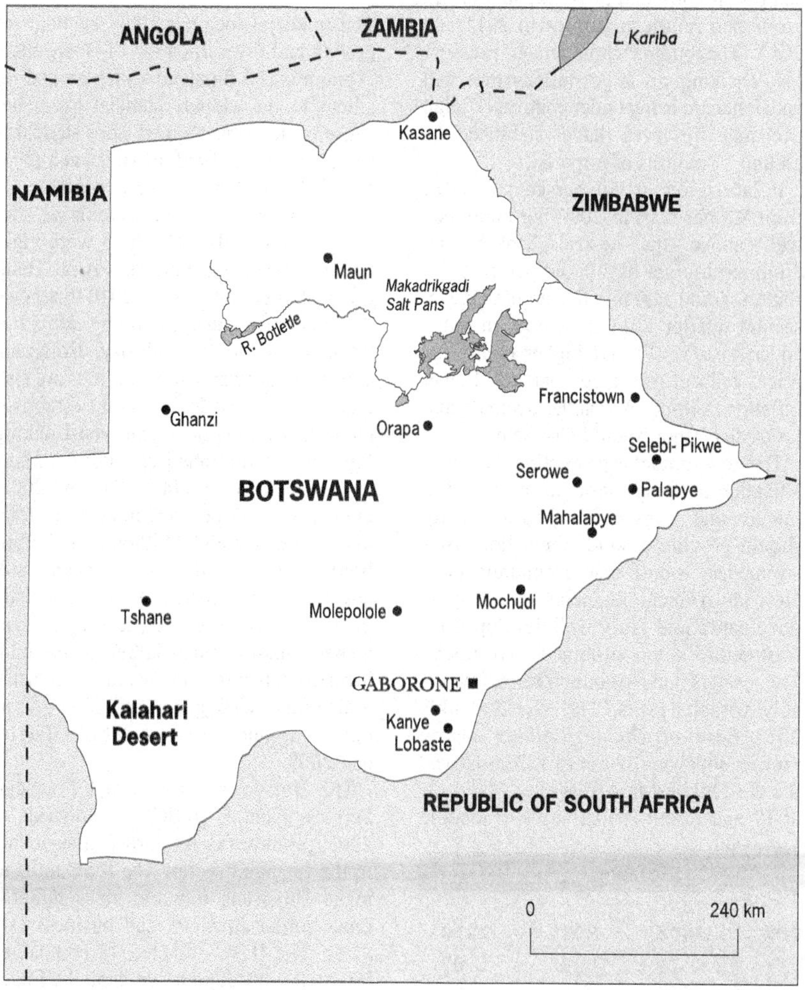

KEY FACTS

Official name: Republic of Botswana

Head of State: President Seretse Ian Khama (since 2008; elected 16 Oct 2009)

Head of government: President Seretse Ian Khama (since 2008; elected 16 Oct 2009)

Ruling party: Botswana Democratic Party (BDP) (since 1965; re-elected 16 Oct 2009)

Area: 582,000 square km

Population: 1.82 million (2010)*

Capital: Gaborone

Official language: English (official); Setswana (national).

Currency: Pula (P) = 100 thebe

Exchange rate: P7.25 per US$ (Oct 2011)

GDP per capita: US$7,627 (2010)

GDP real growth: 8.60% (2010)

GDP: US$14.00 billion (2010)

Inflation: 7.00% (2010)

Balance of trade: US$753.70 million (2009)

* estimated figure

Botswana, an article in the *Economist* reported in June 2011, 'has built an enviable reputation for good governance and political stability. It has a decent record on civil liberties and a relatively free press. Once one of the world's poorest countries, it now ranks among the richer middle-income ones.'

Diamonds are Botswana's best friend

All this success has been built on diamonds, of which Botswana is the largest producer. Diamonds account for some 50 per cent of government revenue, over half all exports and one third of gross domestic product (GDP). However, it is estimated that production has peaked and unless there are new discoveries, the diamonds will be gone by 2030. This makes it all the more important for the government to encourage and promote alternative industries.

The 2008–09 global economic crisis hit demand for diamonds, with production down by some 50 per cent to 17.73 million carats in 2009. That year, the GDP share of mining dropped to 28.3 per cent from 36.5 per cent in 2008. However in 2010, diamond exports recovered and were worth US$3.01 billion, compared with US$3.14 billion in 2008.

In September 2011 De Beers, which operates the world's two most valuable diamond mines in Botswana, announced that it would be moving many of its London-based staff to Gaborone. The move is part of a deal between the government and De Beers whereby Botswana has agreed to extend the sales agreement it has with the company by a further 10 years, double the length of the previous 5-year contracts. In return, Botswana will be allowed to independently market diamonds outside of De Beers sales channels. De Beers will move around 100 jobs, which handle the sorting, valuation and distribution of diamonds, by the end of 2013.

The rest of the economy

Botswana has developed from Least Developed Country (LDC) status at the time of independence in 1966 to Middle Income Country (MIC) status within three decades, largely owing to the effective use of revenues from mineral resources following the discovery of large diamond reserves. GDP per capita more than doubled, at current prices, from US$3,180 in 2000 to US$6,760 in 2008 but slipped to US$6,215 in 2009, reflecting the impact of the global slump on demand for diamonds and other minerals. Despite the impressive progress in per capita income, rates of poverty and inequality remain high.

The *African Economic Outlook 2010* (AEO), published jointly by the African Development Bank and the Organisation for Economic Co-operation and Development, agrees that Botswana's reliance on diamond exports is a challenge for sustainable economic growth. The global economic and financial crisis of 2008 saw the economy shrink 3.7 per cent in 2009, primarily because of a substantial fall in diamond demand, but it bounced back to growth of 6.4 per cent in 2010. The AEO forecasts that the economy will grow by 6.9 per cent in 2011 and 7.0 per cent in 2012. The current account deteriorated sharply in 2009 and 2010 but should improve and return to surplus in 2011 and 2012. The budget came under pressure too, chalking up large deficits that will take longer to bring under control. Foreign exchange reserves have stabilised at around 17 months of imports.

Inflation fell to 7.0 per cent in 2010 from 8.2 per cent in 2009 but continued well above the central bank's medium-term target of 3.0–6.0 per cent. Inflation should ease into the target range by second quarter 2011 as a hike in value added tax (VAT) and higher controlled prices fall out of the comparison. Lower inflation in South Africa, Botswana's major trade partner, should also help.

The government is promoting the diversification of the economy away from diamonds and Botswana's private sector should provide a solid foundation. Botswana has robust macroeconomic policies, an efficient financial sector, good governance and fairly well developed infrastructure after sustained investment. The result is that the country ranks favourably with its peers. The World Bank's 2011 *Ease of Doing Business* survey ranked Botswana 52 out of 183 countries, the third highest in Africa after Mauritius at 17 and South Africa at 34. Botswana could rank much higher had it not been for the costs of being a land-locked country. On the Corruption Perception Index compiled by Transparency International, Botswana was ranked 33 out of 178 countries in 2010, ahead of all its sub-Saharan African peers.

Financial sector

The financial sector is a key element for growth and diversification of Botswana's economy. The financial sector proved resilient to the global financial crisis because of the robust supervisory standards set down by the Bank of Botswana (central bank). No bailouts were required.

The Botswana banking sector is well developed. By end 2010, there were eight commercial banks, with ABN Amro Bank establishing a presence in 2010 to service the diamond industry, building on its traditional role in the industry. Botswana non-banking financial institutions are also making headway, following the establishment of a regulator – The Non-Banking Financial Institutions Regulatory Authority (NBFIRA) in 2008. By end-2009, there were 103 pension funds with total assets valued at P32.4 billion (US$4.5 billion). Pension funds in Botswana are, however, constrained by limited domestic investment opportunities, leading to over 60 per cent of its financial resources being invested offshore. The insurance industry is also significant, generating gross premiums of around 3.15 per cent of GDP by end-2009.

The Botswana International Financial Service Centre (IFSC) established in 2003, promotes cross-border investments in the financial sector. The IFSC aims to make Botswana a world class hub for cross-border financial and business services. The IFSC attracted 45 companies by 2010 with cumulative capital of over P6 billion (US$0.8 billion) and employing around 600 workers in specialised professions. Besides existing preferential treatment in processing of employment permits for its foreign employees, further changes in 2010 made it quicker to process residence permits for the IFSC's accredited companies.

The Botswana Stock Exchange (BSE), formally established in 1989, is an important part of the country's financial services sector. The BSE is one of the best performing stock exchanges in southern Africa with average aggregate returns of 24 per cent in the past 10 years and is the third largest in terms of market capitalisation. In 2010, the BSE introduced trading of an Exchange Trade Fund

KEY INDICATORS — Botswana

	Unit	2006	2007	2008	2009	2010
Population	m	1.75	1.77	*1.79	*1.81	*1.82
Gross domestic product (GDP)	US$bn	11.05	12.31	13.50	11.60	14.00
GDP per capita	US$	7,021	7,888	7,554	6,407	7,627
GDP real growth	%	3.4	5.7	2.9	-6.0	8.6
Inflation	%	11.3	7.1	12.6	8.1	7.0
Industrial output	% change	0.6	-1.0	3.2	-15.1	–
Agricultural output	% change	-0.7	6.8	1.8	30.4	–
Exports (fob) (goods)	US$m	4,567.0	5,051.9	4,706.9	3,337.3	–
Imports (fob) (goods)	US$m	2,603.0	3,445.4	4,488.4	4,091.1	–
Balance of trade	US$m	1,964.0	1,606.5	218.5	-753.7	–
Current account	US$m	1,947.0	2,074.0	502.2	-525.9	*-728.0
Total reserves minus gold	US$m	7,992.4	9,789.7	9,118.6	8,704.0	7,885.2
Foreign exchange	US$m	7,927.5	9,722.0	9,044.7	8,540.6	7,721.2
Exchange rate	per US$	6.18	6.50	6.82	7.16	6.79

* estimated figure

– a basket of shares that trade as a single security. It is hoped this initiative will boost liquidity on the BSE, which is currently very low. Market gains reflect the performance of the banking sector, which accounts for more than 60 per cent of BSE listed shares.

Public sector strike

A strike, the first by public sector workers, was called in April 2011 after a new law allowed public sector workers to join a trade union. The government held out against the Botswana Federation of Public Service Union's (BOFEPUSU) demand for a 16 per cent pay rise, offering a 5 per cent rise, conditional on future growth. The union claimed an 80 per cent turn out although the government maintained it was around 50 per cent. After two months the union accepted an unconditional 3 per cent, and the reinstating of all sacked workers. With the unemployment rate at 17 per cent, the government had felt it held a strong hand.

Tourism

Tourism has significant potential for foreign earnings in Botswana as over 17 per cent of the land is reserved as parks characterised by unique attractions. Among these are the Okavango Delta – the largest inland delta in the world – and Chobe National Park, home to a large elephant population. Although the contribution of the tourism sector to the overall economy is low, at around 4.2 per cent of GDP, the sector generates about 11,000 jobs. Initiatives underway to promote tourism include building up air services into the capital Gaberone and the upgrading of other airports around the country. A major challenge facing the tourism sector is lack of local experts.

Botswana is progressing well with the implementation of reforms required to meet the Millennium Development Goals (MDGs) by 2015. Significant progress has been made in education and in health although HIV/Aids remains a significant challenge despite proactive measures by the government. Botswana has one of the best Prevention of Mother to Child Transmission (PMCT) programmes in Africa where 96 per cent of babies born under the programme are HIV negative.

Botswana's central policy objective, as identified by National Development Plan 10 (2009–16), is to diversify the economy away from mining, a move seen as even more important following the global financial crisis and economic slump. To this end, the government has identified six areas for special attention – diamonds, transport and logistics, innovation, agriculture, education and health. The financial services and tourism sectors, led by the IFSC and Tourism Commission, aim to transform Botswana into a global financial centre and a South African tourist destination.

Risk assessment

Economy	Good
Politics	Fair
Regional stability	Fair

COUNTRY PROFILE

Historical profile

1885 Britain declared the country a protectorate and called it Bechuanaland, defining its modern borders.
1966 Independence for Botswana came a year after the territory's first election, which was won by Seretse Khama and his Botswana Democratic Party (BDP).
1980 On his death, Khama was succeeded by his vice president, Quett Ketumile Masire.
1984 and 1989 The ruling BDP easily won elections but was tainted by allegations of corruption.
1994 In the elections, the opposition party, Botswana National Front (BNF), took 13 seats and unseated three ministers.
1998 President Sir Quett Ketumile Masire retired from the presidency.
1999 The legislative elections were won by the BDP. The National Assembly chose Festus Mogae as president.
2001–02 The government's policy towards the San people (formerly called the Bushmen or Basarwa) in the Central Kalahari Game Reserve has been criticised internationally for its refusal to recognise the ownership rights of the Bushmen over the land they have lived on for at least 20,000 years. The Reserve was originally created in 1961 to constitute a refuge for the marginalised San people. However, the potential for tourism and diamonds increased the value of these marginal lands, leading the government to relocate the original inhabitants.
2003 A partnership between the government, a pharmaceutical giant and the Bill and Melinda Gates Foundation began providing free anti-retroviral drugs to the country's HIV-infected population.
2004 Festus Mogae won a landslide victory when he was elected for a second (and final) five-year term.
2006 The San people won a judicial ruling that the rights to their ancestral lands in the Kalahari Desert were enduring and their eviction by the government in 2005 was illegal.
2008 Seretse Ian Khama became president, following Mogae's retirement. Khama is the son of the independence leader and former president, Sir Seretse Khama, and paramount chief of the Bamangwato tribe of Botswana. Former president Mogae won the first Mo Ibrahim prize of US$5 million for good governance in office, given as an example for other African heads of states to follow.
2009 Botswana criticised Muammar al Qadafi (of Libya) for not allowing discussion at the African Union summit, of which he was chairman, concerning the warrant issued for the arrest of Sudan's president Omar al Bashir by the International Criminal Court (ICC). Only Botswana and Chad openly stated that President Bashir should go to the ICC and clear his name.
2010 In June, the African Development Bank granted Botswana's largest ever assistance package of US$1.5 billion, to help offset falling global diamond prices and 'fill part of the gap of the government's 2009–10 budget deficit...' In parliamentary elections held on 16 October the BDP won with 53.3 per cent of the vote (45 seats out of 57); the BDP re-elected Seretse Ian Khama as president.
2011 The high court ruled on 27 January that the Basarwa Bushmen had a right to drill for water in their traditional land within the Kalahari Game Reserve. On 13 June an eight-week strike by public workers, that closed hospitals, schools and government offices, was suspended as unions resumed talks with the government for a 16 per cent salary increase. In the end the workers settled for three per cent after the government insisted it could not afford a larger increase as the global economic crisis sapped demands for diamonds, the mainstay of the economy.

Political structure

Constitution
The constitution came into effect on 30 September 1966. It enshrines a code of human rights.
The approval of a 15-member House of Chiefs is needed for some measures, but it cannot veto legislation.
Form of state
Multi-party democratic republic
The executive
The National Assembly elects a president who has executive power for a maximumu of two five-year terms. He appoints a vice president and the cabinet, over which he presides. The president is an ex-officio member of the Assembly.
National legislature
The unicameral National Assembly has 57 directly elected members in single-seat constituencies for five-year terms. Four

members are co-opted and the president and attorney general are *ex-offico*. A growth in population, confirmed by census, will result in an expansion of directly elected members. The assembly is responsible for passing, amending and repealing laws.
Any law relating to tribal matters of property, organisation and traditional law, plus any change to the constitution, must be referred for their opinion to the House of Chiefs, a 15-member advisory council of hereditary chiefs. While the House of Chiefs has the power to summon any member of government to explain any policy or action it has no power of veto or legislation.

Legal system

Roman-Dutch law. Rural areas have customary courts.

Last elections

16 October 2009 (presidential and parliamentary)

Results: Parliamentary: the ruling Botswana Democratic Party (BDP) won with 53.3 per cent of the vote (45 seats out of 57), Botswana National Front (BNF) 21.9 per cent (6) and Botswana Congress Party (BCP) 19.2 per cent (four), Botswana Alliance Movement 2.27 per cent (one), independents 1.9 per cent (one); three other political parties failed to win any seats. Turnout was 76.7 per cent.
Presidential: The BDP voted Seretse Khama Ian Khama into office.

Next elections

October 2015 (presidential and parliamentary)

Political parties

Ruling party

Botswana Democratic Party (BDP) (since 1965; re-elected 16 Oct 2009)

Main opposition party

Coalition of Botswana National Front (BNF), Botswana Congress Party (BCP) and Botswana Alliance Movement (BAM).

Population

1.82 million (2010)*

Last census: September 2001: 1,680,863 (provisional)

Population density: Three inhabitants per square km. Urban population: 49 per cent (1995–2001).

Annual growth rate: 1.1 per cent 1994–2004 (WHO 2006)

Ethnic make-up

The Batswana, of which the largest group is the Bamangwato, comprise 79 per cent of the total population. The Kalanga 11 per cent, Basarwa (the Bushmen) 3 per cent, Kgalagadi and the rest 7 per cent.

Religions

Most of the population are Christians (about 49 per cent); other religions include various traditional beliefs, including animism, mostly in rural areas (50 per cent), and a small Muslim population.

Education

Primary education is free but with a high drop-out rate. In 2001, the gender gap in primary enrolment was 25 per cent, with net enrolment among girls remaining at only 50 per cent.
Secondary schooling starts from the age of 12 and lasts till the age of 18.
The National Policy on Education (1977) and the Revised National Policy on Education (1994) have provided the policy framework for the education system in Botswana.
The United Nations International Children's Emergency Fund's (Unicef) Girls' Education Programme has focussed on the prevention of HIV/Aids, particularly among children aged 6–15. Unicef in association with the government has been formulating primary school curricula and developing four 'model' community-based pre-schools.

Literacy rate: 79 per cent adult rate; 89 per cent youth rate (15–24) (Unesco 2005).

Compulsory years: 6 to 11 years.

Enrolment rate: 84 per cent, primary school enrolment; 10 per cent for girls and 24 per cent for boys gross enrolment for secondary schools.

Pupils per teacher: 28 in primary schools.

Health

An outbreak of a polio related disease in 2006 prompted an international alert and increased vigilance in Botswana's northern border region with Namibia, Zimbabwe and Angola. Acute Flaccid Paralysis (AFP) is classed as a symptom which may lead to polio and can attack adults as well as children.

HIV/Aids

Projections by UNAids show that the impact of HIV on firms could equal 4.9 per cent of their total wage bill between 1996–2004. It also reported that Botswana was the first country to begin providing antiretroviral drugs through its public health system, courtesy of a bigger health budget and drug price reductions negotiated with pharmaceutical companies.
UNAids said in September 2003 'rampant epidemics are under way in southern Africa' including Botswana, with a national adult HIV prevalence rising higher than thought possible.
Testing for HIV has been considered by most NGOs as best done voluntarily. In Botswana the testing has been changed to routine, any test that requires a blood sample will be checked for HIV/Aids, unless the donor expressly forbids it. This change in policy was initiated in January 2004 to overcome the reluctance of people to know their status regarding the disease. The head of the Botswana Aids Treatment Programme, Dr Darkoh, points out that without knowing their status patients cannot be treated in time or effectively. He also changed the method of testing with patients attending open, rather than separate, clinics. Testing for HIV/Aids has increased from 20 per cent to 95 per cent.
The change from voluntary to regular testing has not been welcomed by all, some rights activists fear the discrimination of patients if their results become public.

HIV prevalence: 37.3 per cent aged 15–49 in 2003 (World Bank). One of the highest in the world.

Life expectancy: 40 years, 2004 (WHO 2006)

Fertility rate/Maternal mortality rate: 3.1 births per woman, 2004 (WHO 2006)

Child (under 5 years) mortality rate (per 1,000): 82 per 1,000 live births; 17 per cent of children under aged five are malnourished (World Bank).

Head of population per physician: 0.4 physician per 1,000 people, 2004 (WHO 2006)

Welfare

Botswana provides a non-contributory social pension for about 80,000 elderly citizens of 65 years and older, a flat-rate 151 Pula each month. This income has become an important source of revenue for families and communities and has had a significant impact on poverty reduction, as it alleviates the needs of more than just the elderly. Studies have shown that multi-generational households derive a 'safety-net' against economic hardship and these pensions support families where grandparents are fostering children of HIV/Aids parents. Pensioners are economically independent and valuable family members, this contradicts any perception that they may be a financial burden on their offspring.

Pensions

Main cities

Gaborone (capital, estimated population 225,656 in 2005), Francistown (98,104), Molepolole (64,327), Selebi-Phikwe (54,472), Maun (52,488), Mogoditshane (48,936), Serowe (46,839), Mahalapye (44,330)

Languages spoken

Official language/s

English (official); Setswana (national).

Media

The constitution guarantees the freedom of the press. However, since 2006 the government has been moving to enact the Mass Media Communications (MMC) bill, which journalists claim with inhibit reporting as the government-appointed press council will adjudicate complaints and recommend disciplinary sanctions where necessary.

Press

Low circulations limit newspapers to mainly urban areas.

Dailies: There are few daily newspaper, including *Daily News* (www.mcst.gov.bw/dailynews) is government-owned and the private *Mmegi* (www.mmegi.bw).

Weeklies: Most newspapers are published weekly, including the *Botswana Guardian*, *Botswana Gazette* (www.gazette.bw), *The Midweek Sun*, *Sunday Standard* (www.sundaystandard.info) and *The Voice* (www.thevoicebw.com), for news and entertainment.

Business: The government-owned *Daily Business* is an imprint of the *Daily News*.

Broadcasting

Radio: Radio is the primary medium for public news and information. In English and Setswana, the national, state-run station is Radio Botswana (www.dib.gov.bw), which also operates the commercial Botswana 2 (RB2). Commercial stations include Yarona FM (www.yaronafm.co.bw), Gabz FM (www.gabzfm.com) and Duma FM.

Television: The government-owned national, public broadcaster is Botswana TV (www.btv.gov.bw). The pay-to-view, Kenyan satellite station, Prime (www.gtv.tv) provides around a dozen channels.

News agencies

National news agency: Bopa (Botswana Press Agency)

Economy

Botswana continues to live off its large diamond reserves, which is the world's largest by value. Trade was hit by the global economic crisis and production fell from 33.6 million carats in 2007 to 32.3 million in 2008 and dropped further to 17.7 million in 2009, resulting in a decline in diamond revenue of 50 per cent. This caused Botswana's worst trade deficit in its history, -US$659 million in 2009 (the trade balance had been US$1.6 billion in 2007). In June 2010, the African Development Bank (ADB) granted Botswana its largest ever assistance package of US$1.5 billion, to help offset falling global diamond prices. The International Monetary Fund (IMF) has predicted that unless global trade strengthens markedly, the trade deficit is likely to continue until 2013/14. The government introduced a number of fiscal measures including increasing value added tax from 10 per cent to 12 per cent, lowering public spending and raising non-mineral taxes.

Despite attempts to increase foreign involvement in non-mining sectors, through privatisation and other measures, diamonds are still the driving force of the economy, typically attracting the major share of foreign direct investment (FDI).

Botswana is a major tourist destination with the industry accounting for over 10 per cent of GDP. Agriculture accounted for 2 per cent of GDP in 2008, but has fallen in importance due in large part to natural conditions (floods and droughts) and animal diseases and a lack of basic infrastructure that limits access for farmers to markets. Government backed programmes have improved and increased the productivity of commercial crops, cattle husbandry, dairy production and poultry rearing. In recent years, the government has invested heavily in communications and water technology.

A high level of poverty (30.3 per cent in 2008) and unemployment, at an average 20 per cent, remain stubborn problems, exacerbated by the rise in the number of orphans of HIV/Aids victims. However by 2010 the efforts by the government to address the problems of HIV/Aids, with the introduction of antiretroviral drugs, have seen a decline in infection rates (17.6 per cent in 2008) and longer (and more productive) lives for those in treatment. Financial aid has also been given to orphans.

External trade

As a member of the Southern African Customs Union (SACU) Botswana trades freely with the other members (Lesotho, Namibia, South Africa and Swaziland) and operates a common customs border with them; SACU presents a united negotiating entity to foreign traders and importers.

In 2009 international donors pledged US$1 billion to upgrade transport links across eastern and southern Africa, in an initiative to carry goods to market cheaper and faster. Not only will roads and rail links be improved, but also time-consuming official procedures will be streamlined for efficiency.

Imports

Principal imports are electricity (80 per cent of the country's requirements), vehicles and machinery, electrical and transport equipment, food products and consumer goods, chemical and rubber products, textiles and tobacco.

Main sources: South Africa (typically 76 per cent of total), UK (6 per cent), China (3 per cent).

Exports

Principal exports are diamonds (typically 70–80 per cent of total) and copper-nickel ore, soda-ash, textiles, meat and meat products

Main destinations: UK (typically 53 per cent of total), South Africa (15 per cent), Norway (10 per cent).

Agriculture

Farming

The agricultural sector contributes around 3.5 per cent to GDP and employs 60 per cent of the workforce.

Production is divided between small, traditional farms and around 360 large-scale commercial units (including Barolong Farms, Pandamantenga and Tuli Block).

The climate and poor soil are suitable for extensive ranching, with the result that livestock produce accounts for about 80 per cent of marketed output. In the past, rearing of livestock has been hampered by frequent outbreaks of foot-and-mouth disease – now largely controlled – and more recently by drought. However, the livestock sector has predominated due to a lack of cultivatable land – only 5 per cent of the land is suitable for arable production – in a country which is mostly arid and contributes around 80 per cent of agriculture's share of GDP. Beef is one of the country's main exports and the Botswana Meat Commission (BMC) operates three abattoirs with a combined capacity of up to 2,000 head of cattle and smaller stock every day.

Government aims for self-sufficiency in basic foodstuffs, such as maize, millet, beans and sorghum, are far from being realised. There is potential for investment in adding value to primary products through increasing processing capacity. There is also a growing market in farm machinery, irrigation and water pumps.

Fishing

Botswana has a small freshwater fishing industry with annual average catches amounting to 2,000 tonnes.

Forestry

About 25 per cent of the total land area has forest cover. Another 20 per cent of its terrain is classified as wooded land. There are several large game reserves in the west, including the Central Kalahari Game Reserve, the largest protected area in Africa. There are no large-scale forest industries in the country. Some varieties of woods are used for fuel consumption and for the manufacture of wooden handicrafts.

Industry and manufacturing

The industrial sector as a whole contributes around 5 per cent to GDP and employs 10 per cent of the workforce.

The manufacturing sector is underdeveloped. There is a wide range of consumer products manufactured by a relatively small number of enterprises. There is also a large number of village industries, mainly producing handicrafts. The main

industrial base depends on the livestock sector. Beverages, chemicals, paper, plastics and electrical goods are also produced.
The small domestic market has hampered attempts to stimulate production. Emphasis is on expansion of the export market for traditional products, such as textiles, leather goods, processed meat and import substitution.
The government is pushing for increased value-added on the country's primary goods production. The soda ash industry has helped develop the local manufacture of detergents, potash and fertilisers. The country also produces electrical components, which utilise copper and nickel production.
The government has set up the Botswana Development Corporation (BDC) in an effort to promote industrial development, particularly in sugar refining, furniture, clothing, milling, brewing, packaging and handicrafts.

Tourism

Botswana's tourism sector is being actively developed as part of a strategy to diversify the economy away from dependence on diamond mining. The sector accounts for around 5 per cent of GDP. The main attractions are the country's rich variety of wildlife and its wilderness areas. Around 40 per cent of the land is dedicated to national parks, game reserves and wildlife management areas. Long-term sustainability is a key element of development policy. Botswana has tended to cater to up-market tourists, but in order to expand the market and the variety of the attractions, eco-tourism, in which private investors collaborate with local communities, is being fostered.

Mining

Exploitation of rich mineral reserves, notably diamonds, provided the key to Botswana's rapid economic growth, with the mining sector accounting for up to 50 per cent of GDP and employing 7 per cent of the workforce. Botswana's diamond reserves are expected to last until 2030 at current production rates.
Diamonds, together with copper and nickel production, are the main focus of prospecting activities and account for most of the country's export revenue. Botswana is the largest producer of diamonds, and second-largest producer of gem diamonds, in the world, after Russia. All diamond mining is carried out by De Beers Botswana Mining Company (Debswana), a company jointly owned by the government and UK-based De Beers of South Africa. De Beers produces 60 per cent of the world's diamond output, a significant proportion of which comes from Botswana.
As global sales of diamonds fell two mines – Damtshaa and Orapa No 2 – operated by Debswana, a company jointly owned by the government and De Beers, were closed for 2009, to be re-opened when demand picks up.

Hydrocarbons

There are no known domestic oil or natural gas reserves; all refined petroleum products are from South Africa.
Botswana has the largest known coal reserves in Africa – proven reserves are 17 billion tonnes, total reserves are estimated at about 50 billion tonnes, although of low quality. Coal output from the Morupule coal mine, which is mainly used in domestic power stations, is typically around one million tonnes per annum.

Energy

Total installed electricity generating capacity (all thermal) produces 979 million kilowatt-hours (kWh), while consumption is estimated at 2.57 billion kWh. Botswana relies on imported electricity of 1.95 billion kWh, chiefly from South Africa.
There is potential for hydroelectric generation and solar power. Half of total primary energy requirements are met by biomass, mainly fuelwood and charcoal.

Financial markets

In 2006 the African-owned, Pan African commodities and derivatives exchange (PACDEX Africa) was given the go-ahead by the African Union, the UN Conference on Trade and Development, the Pan African Commodities Platform and Botswana's finance ministry and services.
Stock exchange
Botswana Stock Exchange

Banking and insurance

Of the established commercial banks, the largest is Barclays Bank of Botswana, which was launched in 1950 and has approximately 42 branches and agencies. It has 19.6 per cent local equity with the rest held by the UK's Barclays Bank. Standard Chartered Bank of Botswana has been operating in the country since 1897 and has 14 branches and four agences.
Central bank
Bank of Botswana
Main financial centre
Gaborone

Time

GMT plus two hours

Geography

Botswana is a landlocked country in southern Africa, with South Africa to the south and east, Zimbabwe to the north-east and Namibia to the west and north. A short section of the northern frontier adjoins Zambia.
Botswana is a flat, arid country, 84 per cent of which is occupied by the Kalahari *sandveld*. The desert occupies most of the northern, central and western regions. There are some shallow valleys and low hills, notably the Tsodilo Hills, rising to 410m, located in the north-west. Other parts of the landscape, mainly along the south-eastern borders and the far north-west, are dotted with outcrops of rock and low hills.
There is little surface water outside the Okavango delta and the Chobe river areas in the north. The Okavango river rises in Angola and forms a 15,000km system of water channels, swamps, lagoons and islands, the largest inland delta in the world.
The majority of the population live in the south-eastern *hardveld*, which has a slightly higher elevation than the rest of the country. The rainfall is more reliable, but the agricultural potential remains low. The highest point in Botswana, Otse Mountain, which reaches 1,491m, is near Lobatse. 38 per cent of the country is given over to wildlife areas and national parks, including two-thirds of the Okavango delta.
Hemisphere
Southern

Climate

Sub-tropical, with hot summers and dry winters. Temperatures range from about 5–23 degrees Celsius (C) in July to 18–31 degrees C in January.

Entry requirements

Passports
Required by all. Passports should be valid for at least 12 months.
Visa
Required by all except citizens of North America, Western Europe, Australasia and Japan, plus transit passengers. All other visitors should confirm requirements from consular sections of local embassy before travelling.
Business visas should be accompanied by letters of invitation.
Currency advice/regulations
Import and export of foreign currency is unlimited, provided it is declared on arrival.
Import of local currency is unlimited but export is restricted to P50.
Customs
Member of Southern African Customs Union, therefore virtually no restrictions on movement of goods from South Africa, Namibia, Lesotho and Swaziland.

Health (for visitors)

Mandatory precautions
Yellow fever vaccination certificate required for visitors arriving from infected areas.

Advisable precautions
hepatitis A and B, tetanus, polio and typhoid immunisations are advisable.
Anti-malarial prophylaxis is recommended for visitors to northern regions. Insect repellant is a necessary precaution. A medical examination is advisable within 10 days if bitten by insects while visiting game reserves, in case of sleeping sickness.
AIDS infection rates are high throughout the country but particularly in Francistown and Gaborone.
Food, water, swimming and bathing precautions should be observed.
Medical insurance is essential.

Hotels
First-class hotels available in all main towns. Generally advisable to book in advance – essential at weekends and during public holidays.

Credit cards
American Express, Access/MasterCard, Barclaycard/Visa, Diners.

Public holidays (national)
Fixed dates
1–3 Jan (New Year), 1 Jul (Sir Seretse Khama Day), 18–19 Jul (President's Day), 30 Sep–1 Oct (Botswana Day), 25–27 Dec (Christmas Holiday).
Variable dates
Good Friday, Easter Monday, Ascension Day, President's Day (third Tue and Wed in Jul).

Working hours
Banking
Mon–Fri: 0900–1530; Sat: 0815–1045.
Business
Mon–Fri, Apr–Oct: 0800–1300, 1400–1700; Mon–Fri, Oct–Apr: 0730–1630.
Government
Mon–Fri: 0730–1230, 1345–1630.
Shops
Mon–Fri: 0830–1300, 1400–1700; Sat: 0830–1300.

Telecommunications
Mobile/cell phones
Mascom and Vista Cellular provide CSM 900 network, though coverage is limited to main towns.

Social customs/useful tips
A lightweight or tropical suit should be worn for meetings, casual clothes are acceptable at other times.
Most people rise early in the morning and nightlife is limited.
The noun for the people of Botswana is: singular, Motswana; plural, Batswana.

Getting there
Air
National airline: Air Botswana
International airport/s: The Sir Seretse Khama international airport (GBE) is 15km from Gabarone. Facilities include left luggage, bank, bar, restaurant, post office, shops and car hire.
There are no regular bus services to and from the airport but several hotels run minibuses
Taxis are available to the city centre.
Other airport/s: Francistown (FRW), 6km from city; Maun (MUB), Kasane (BBK) and Selebi-Phikwe (PKW).
Airport tax: US$20.
Surface
Road: Bitumised roads link Botswana with South Africa in the south, and Zambia and Zimbabwe in the north.
The Trans-Kalahari highway provides a shorter all-tarred road link between Namibia and South Africa's Gauteng province, crossing south-west Botswana, via Kanye and Ghanzi.
Botswanan border posts are at Ngoma Bridge and Shakawe. The road from Namibia, via Shakawe border post, is paved all the way to Maun.
Rail: There are good connections between South Africa and Zimbabwe with Botswana. Passengers are advised to take their own refreshments as the alternatives are limited. There are three classes, and sleeping compartments are available. First-class cars have comfortable reclining seats.
Plans to extend the network include the extension of the line into Namibia, following the construction of the Limpopo line from Zimbabwe to Mozambique.
Water: A car ferry operates across the Zambezi River to Zambia.

Getting about
National transport
Air: Air travel is the best way to get around Botswana.
Regular flights operated by Air Botswana connect Gaborone, Francistown, Maun and Kasane. Air Botswana and other operators provide direct charter flights to airstrips throughout the country.
Road: There are around 20,000km of well-developed roads, of which some 5,000km are tarred, the rest being gravelled or sand tracks.
Most major towns are connected by good roads. Travellers to Okavango should note that the road to Maun is tarred, but it is impossible to travel further without use of an overland vehicle.
Buses: Bus services remain underdeveloped. Services run between Gaborone and Francistown, going on to Nata and Maun.
Rail: Botswana's railway system consists of 641km of main line plus three branch lines – between Morupule and Palapye, Selebi-Pikwe and Serule, and between Sua Pan and Francistown.
The main Cape Town (South Africa)-Bulawayo (Zimbabwe) railway runs for over 700km through Botswana, linking several towns. This section is operated by Botswana Railways, along with freight-only lines to Selebi-Pikwe and Sua Pan.
Botswana Railways has lost a great deal of freight business to road transporters. It has established the Gaborone Container Terminal (Gabcon), a dry port facility acting as a container terminal, specifically for locally based importers and exporters.
City transport
Taxis: Taxis are available in the capital. Tips are not common; if offered, 10 per cent would be acceptable.
Car hire
National driving licence (in English) or international driving licence, valid for six months, is required. Speed limits: 120kph on main roads, 60kph in built-up areas. Seat-belts must be worn. Facilities are available to hire Avis car in South Africa and deposit it in Botswana, or vice versa. Hire cars are only available for driving from Botswana to Zimbabwe or Zambia by special prior arrangement.

BUSINESS DIRECTORY

The addresses listed below are a selection only. While World of Information makes every endeavour to check these addresses, we cannot guarantee that changes have not been made, especially to telephone numbers and area codes. We would welcome any corrections.

Telephone area codes
The international direct dialling (IDD) code for Botswana is +267, followed by subscriber's number:

Francistown	24
Gaborone	31,35,36,39
Jwaneng	58
Kasane	62
Lobatse	53
Maun	68
Selebe-Pikwe	26

Chambers of Commerce
Botswana Chamber of Commerce and Industry, PO Box 00290, Gaborone (tel: 359-292; fax: 372-467).

Botswana Confederation of Commerce, Industry and Manpower, Boccim House, Old Lobatse Road , PO Box 432, Gaborone (tel: 353-459; fax: 373-142; e-mail: boccim@info.bw).

Francistown Chamber of Commerce and Industry, PO Box 196, Francistown (tel: 241-2149; fax: 241-2175; e-mail: boccim@info.bw).

Banking
Barclays Bank of Botswana, PO Box 478, Barclays House, Plot 8842 Khama Crescent, Gaborone (tel: 352-041; fax: 313-672).

National Development Bank, PO Box 225, Development House, Plot 1123, The Mall, Gaborone (tel: 352-801; fax: 374-446).

Standard Chartered Bank Botswana Ltd, PO Box 496, 5th Floor, Standard House, The Mall, Gaborone (tel: 360-1500, 353-111; fax: 372-933, 353-446).

Central bank

Bank of Botswana, Private Bag 154, Khama Crescent, Gaborone (tel: 360-6000; fax: 391-6000; e-mail: webmaster@bob.bw).

Stock exchange 1

Botswana Stock Exchange: www.bse.co.bw

Travel information

Air Botswana, Sir Seretse Khama Airport, PO Box 92, Gaborone (tel: 395-2812; fax: 397-4802; commercial@airbotswana.co.bw).

Ministry of tourism

Department of Tourism, Ministry of Environment, Wildlife and Tourism, Private Bag 0047, Gaborone (tel: 395-3024; fax: 390-8675; e-mail: botswanatourism@gov.bw).

Ministries

Ministry of Agriculture, Private Bag 003, Gaborone (tel: 350-500; fax: 356-027).

Ministry of Commerce and Industry, Private Bag 004, Gaborone (tel: 360-1200; fax: 371-539).

Ministry of External Affairs, Private Bag 00368, Gaborone (tel: 360-0700; fax: 313-366).

Ministry of Finance and Development Planning, Private Bag 008, Gaborone (tel: 350-100, 355-272; fax: 356-086).

Ministry of Mineral Resources and Water Affairs, Private Bag 0018, Gaborone (tel; 352-452; fax: 372-733).

Ministry of Works, Transport and Communications, Private Bag 007, Gaborone (tel: 358-500, 355-563, 355-303; fax: 358-500, 313-303).

Office of the President, Private Bag 001, Gaborone (tel: 350-800).

Other useful addresses

Botswana Development Corporation Ltd, Private Bag 160, Gaborone (tel: 351-790; fax: 305-375).

Botswana Diamond Company (Pty) Ltd, Debswana House, The Mall, Gaborone (tel: 351-131; fax; 356-110).

Botswana Enterprise Development Unit (promotes industrial & rural development), PO Box 0014, Gaborone.

Botswana Meat Commission, Private Bag 4, Lobatse (tel: 330-321; fax: 330-530).

Botswana Power Corporation, Motlakase House, Macheng Way, PO Box 48, Gaborone (tel: 360-300; fax: 373-563).

Botswana Telecommunications Corporation, PO Box 700, Gaborone (tel: 358-000).

Botswanan Embassy (USA), Suite 7M, 3400 International Drive, NW, Washington DC 20008 (tel: 202-244-4990; fax: 202-244-4164)

Debswana Diamond Company, Gaborone (tel: 351-131; fax: 356-110).

Department of Geological Survey, Private Bag 14, Lobatse (tel: 330-0327; fax: 332-013).

Department of Information and Broadcasting, Private Bag 0060, Gaborone (tel: 365-8000, 365-3081; fax: 357-138, 301-675; e-mail: ib.publicity@info.bw).

Department of Mines, Private Bag 0049, Gaborone (tel: 352-641; fax: 352-141).

Department of Trade and Investment Promotion (TIPA), Private Bag 004, Gaborone (tel: 351-790; fax: 305-375).

Stockbrokers Botswana Ltd, Ground Floor, Barclays House, Khama Crescent, Post Bag 00417, Gaborone (tel: 357-900; fax: 357-901).

Water Utilities Corporation, Private Bag 00276, Gaborone (tel: 352-521).

National news agency: Bopa (Botswana Press Agency), (email: dailynews@gov.bw; internet: www.gov.bw/cgi-bin/news).

Internet sites

Africa Business Network: www.ifc.org/abn

AllAfrica.com: www.allafrica.com

African Development Bank: www.afdb.org

Africa Online: www.africaonline.com

Mbendi AfroPaedia (information on companies, countries, industries and stock exchanges in Africa): mbendi.co.za

Brazil

In early 2011 Brazil was not only poised to become the world's fifth largest economy; in 2014 it would be hosting the world football cup, and as if that was not enough, in 2016 the Olympic Games. In late 2010 the most popular president to have held the position stepped down; Luiz Inacio da Silva - Lula to every Brazilian - had distinguished himself in the trades' union movement, rising from being a factory floor employee to the nation's Presidency. He did more than simply cope with being President, he made the role his own, presiding over the most dizzying period of growth Brazil has ever seen, coinciding with a significant drop in poverty as increasing numbers of Brazilians aspired to become members of its fast-growing middle class. A July 2010 report in the London *Economist* quoted a report by the Fundação Getulio Vargas, noting that 'the number of people living in poverty has fallen by 20 million under Lula, from 49.5 million (or 28.5 per cent of the total) in 2003 to 29 million (16 per cent) in 2008.'

Being Dilma

Lula's successor, 62 year old Dilma Roussef is of Bulgarian ancestry. In Brazil's period of military government in the 1960s, Dilma was a student activist. Her radical opposition ended her up in jail for three years at a time when the Brazilian government considered torture to be an acceptable means of keeping things in check. Standing for president was her first stab at any electoral office, having garnered her political savvy as Lula's chief of staff. The electorate seemed uncertain whether her reputation for having a bad temper was a presidential asset or liability. Despite spending much of 2009

KEY FACTS

Official name: Republica Federativa do Brasil (Federative Republic of Brazil)

Head of State: President Dilma Rousseff (PT) (from 1 Jan 2011)

Head of government: President Dilma Rousseff (PT) (from 1 Jan 2011)

Ruling party: Coalition Lulista, led by Partido dos Trabalhadores (PT) (Workers' Party) with nine other political parties (from 2002; re-elected 2010)

Area: 8,511,965 square km

Population: 190.76 million (2010; census figure)

Capital: Brasília

Official language: Portuguese

Currency: Real (R$) (plural reais)

Exchange rate: R$1.77 per US$ (Aug 2010)

GDP per capita: US$10,816 (2010)

GDP real growth: 7.50% (2010)

GDP: US$2,090.30 billion (2010)

Labour force: 23.61 million (2010)

Unemployment: 6.70% (2010)

Inflation: 5.00% (2010)

Oil production: 2.14 million bpd (2010)

Balance of trade: US$20.22 billion (2010)

recovering from lymphatic cancer, Dilma steadily rose through the ranks, groomed as his successor by the astute Lula. Dilma's accession to the ruling Partido de los Trabahladores (PT) (Workers' Party) candidacy, was helped by a purge of many senior party members following a corruption scandal in Lula's first term as President.

Once elected, her first signs of a shift in foreign policy had a feminist touch. In sharp contrast to the cosy relationship between Lula and Iran's maverick President Mahmoud Ahmadinejad, she distanced herself from Iran's medieval attitude to women accused of adultery by condemning the stoning of a woman found guilty. Then a state visit to Argentina illuminated the differences in stature, stance and style between the two countries' presidents. Cristina Kirchner's 'bling' sits uncomfortably with Dilma's public diligence, demonstrated by the inclusion of a meeting with the Mothers of the Plaza de Mayo whose weekly demonstrations over the disappearances of their sons and grandsons have become an Argentine institution.

Brazil's foreign stature was boosted in March 2011 by a short state visit by US President Obama. While the Obama visit certainly trumped that of Ahmadinejad, implicitly welcoming Brazil into the fold of the world's major economic powers, it hardly added up to a comprehensive readjustment of relations between Brazil and the US. Gideon Rachman of the *Financial Times* was probably not the first visitor to Brazil to qualify Lula's affirmation that Obama 'looked like a Brazilian'. Mr Rachman observed that President Obama may resemble a Brazilian footballer, but looked nothing like the country's strikingly white élite. This, in a country where over half the population is either black or of mixed race.

The big loser in the election run-off was the candidate of the opposition Partido da Social Democracia Brasileira (PSDB) (Party of Brazilian Social Democracy), José Serra. Like many Brazilians, Mr Serra (who had been ahead in the polls for most of the pre-election period) had considered Dilma to lack the charisma and charm required of any successful Brazilian politician. If Dilma seemed to lack charisma, Mr Serra, the governor of the state of São Paulo was hardly George Clooney. His recipe for continued success echoed the policies his state government had implemented. Thatcherite in inspiration, these advocated a reduction in the size of Brazil's public sector alongside cuts in government spending.

Half-way house?

Lula's legacy was characterised by high growth, lower poverty and the apparent taming of the hyper-inflation that had once bedevilled Latin America's largest economy. Brazilian governments had long addressed the symptoms rather than the cause, happily crossing off a nought or two, finding it easier to issue new banknotes than to adopt unpopular economic measures. Cruzeiros became 'new' cruzeiros, which in turn, and just as confusingly, became 'cruzados' and later became 'reais' ('real' in the singular). Worryingly for Ms Roussef, as 2010 came to an end and her inauguration as president loomed near, inflation looked to be in danger of breaking through the government's target, already hovering around an annual rate of six per cent in December 2010. The worry was particularly acute for Ms Roussef, who had campaigned on a platform of increased poverty reduction and the maintenance of key welfare provisions such as the Bolsa Familia, a welfare provision handed out to around 12 million cash strapped families. Ms Roussef had also promised not to cut back the much needed infrastructure expansion programme. In the first test of wills between Dilma and an opposition that united not only members of the opposition PSDB but also trades' unions and even some renegade members of Dilma's own Partido dos Trabalhadores (PT) (Workers' Party) she came under opposition pressure for an inflationary increase in the minimum wage. Ms Roussef won the day, holding the increase to 545 reais per month, from the existing 510 (US$305).

While campaigning, Dilma Roussef had been happy to promise a lowering of Brazil's cripplingly high interest rates, at a time when Banco Central do Brasil (central bank) was already drawing up plans to do quite the opposite. At the end of 2010 Brazil's interest rate had already reached an annual 10.75 per cent, with some banks forecasting a rate of 13 per cent or more by the end of 2011. The inflationary trend could be traced back to the government's response to the global financial crisis of 2008. The downturn in demand for key Brazilian products - from raw materials such as hydrocarbons, timber and minerals to manufactures such as motor vehicles and aircraft, risked hitting the economy hard. The government's response - the acquisition of debt to boost government spending, worked well. Probably too well, as Brazilian economic growth soared away, reaching around 7 per cent. However, inflation was the price that had to be paid. In 2010 real estate prices in the smarter parts of Rio de Janeiro were estimated to have quadrupled,

KEY INDICATORS — Brazil

	Unit	2006	2007	2008	2009	2010
Population	m	*186.77	*187.64	*189.61	*191.61	*190.76
Gross domestic product (GDP)	US$bn	1,072.36	1,313.59	1,572.80	1,574.00	2,090.30
GDP per capita	US$	5,742	6,938	8,197	8,220	10,816
GDP real growth	%	3.7	5.4	5.1	-0.2	7.5
Inflation	%	4.2	3.6	5.7	4.9	5.0
Unemployment	%	8.4	9.3	7.9	8.1	6.7
Industrial output	% change	2.7	4.8	4.3	-6.7	–
Agricultural output	% change	4.1	5.9	5.8	-4.6	–
Oil output	'000 bpd	1,809.0	1,833.0	1,899.0	2,029.0	2,137.0
Natural gas output	bn cum	11.5	11.3	13.9	11.9	14.4
Coal output	mtoe	2.4	2.2	2.4	1.9	2.1
Exports (fob) (goods)	US$m	127,305.0	160,649.0	197,942.0	152,995.0	201,915.0
Imports (fob) (goods)	US$m	96,835.0	120,621.0	173,106.0	127,705.0	181,694.0
Balance of trade	US$m	30,470.0	40,028.0	24,837.0	25,290.0	20,221.0
Current account	US$m	13,621.0	3,555.0	-28,192.0	-24,302.0	-47,365.0
Total reserves minus gold	US$m	85,156.0	179,433.0	192,844.0	237,364.0	287,056.0
Foreign exchange	US$m	85,148.0	179,431.0	192,843.0	231,888.0	280,570.0
Exchange rate	per US$	2.15	1.78	1.83	1.99	1.76

* estimated figure

and some estimates anticipated a similar level of growth in 2011, fuelled by the coming World Cup and Olympics. If property prices had risen sharply, so too had senior executive salaries. Such was the growth in executive pay that according to a report in the London *Economist*, São Paulo salaries in 2010 had outpaced those of New York and London . To some extent this was no more than a reflection of the scarcity of qualified personnel in Brazil; the *Economist* reported that Brazil's universities only produce around 35,000 engineers each year, less than ten per cent of the number turned out in China, and insignificant to India's 250,000.

The continuity of economic policy was to some extent assured by the fact that finance minister Guido Mantega who had held the position under Lula stayed in place in the new Dilma government. But in an early sign of potential discord, at the end of 2011 Mr Mantega announced a number of anti-inflationary measures to be introduced under the new administration. These were to include reductions in the number of state-subsidised loans, cuts in the numbers of civil servants and, controversially, delays in the introduction of a number of the much vaunted infrastructure programmes. The jewel in the infrastructure crown is to be the US$22 billion showcase express train link between Rio and São Paulo. The *Wall Street Journal* quoted a Goldman Sachs banker as observing that 'A little fiscal restraint could solve a lot of problems, but the question is how much political will is there to do it.' There certainly is an international will to invest in Brazil; not in itself a particularly new phenomenon but one that has certainly accelerated since 2005, averaging an annual growth rate of over 25 per cent. Foreign direct investment (FDI) was just over US$48 billion in 2010. One report in the *International Herald Tribunel* put Chinese investment alone at a staggering US$37.1 billion since 2003. Much of this has been in the hydrocarbon and minerals sectors, which while benefiting the macro-economy do not generally create too many long-term jobs.

The IMF - same procedure as last year

In the generally unimaginative manner that has tended to characterise its largely predictable analyses of Latin American economies, the International Monetary Fund (IMF) in its mid-2011 report on the Brazilian economy noted that Brazil had recovered from the global financial crisis faster than most other comparable economies, already registering a full year of strong growth in 2009. After contracting by a cumulative 4.8 per cent in the fourth quarter of 2008 and the first quarter of 2009, Brazil's economy grew at a healthy annual rate of 8.9 per cent over the four quarters to March 2010, largely on the strength of domestic demand.

Brazil's strong macroeconomic framework and the government's prompt response helped contain the negative effects of the global crisis and laid the groundwork for the recovery. In the view of the IMF, much was due to the strength of Brazil's financial system and the combination of successful fiscal policies, exchange rate flexibility and inflation targeting.

As the crisis unwound, the supply of new credit from private banks to the economy fell significantly; however, a sizeable expansion of credit by public banks played a critical role in preventing a potentially large output loss. Responding to the significant capital inflows, in October 2009, the government imposed a 2 per cent tax on purchases of domestic bonds and equities by foreigners, which appeared to have some effect in slowing the rate of capital inflows. From early 2009, the stock market index rose by two-thirds and the Brazilian real appreciated by an impressive 25 per cent against a weak US dollar.

Responding to Brazil's inflationary pressures, the central bank raised interest rates in the first half of 2010 by a total of 200 basis points, to 10.75 per cent. By early 2011 the rate had reached 11.25 per cent. The central bank also reversed most of the cuts in reserve requirements, as well as the steps to support capital adequacy, implemented at the time of the crisis. In the fiscal area, the budget surplus was projected to rise from 2.1 per cent of GDP in 2009 to 3.3 per cent in 2010. The temporary tax incentives adopted to support domestic demand during the financial crisis were for the most part phased out.

The IMF attributed Brazil's stellar economic performance to a sharp growth in domestic investment, strong domestic consumption, and stronger-than-expected commodity exports. However, the IMF warned that, as Brazil's output neared its potential and as the unemployment rate declined to its lowest level in a decade, pressure on resources had inevitably built up and monetary policy rendered more complex by capital inflows.

In what amounted to an astonishing glimpse of the obvious, the IMF agreed that Brazil's monetary policy should remain focussed on keeping inflation expectations in check. The IMF also noted that Brazil's financial system has helped the country's economic expansion. However, the acceleration in lending to the household sector and its impact on overall demand growth required special attention.

ECLAC approval

An encouraging appraisal of Brazil's economic performance was also put forward by the United Nations Economic Commission for Latin America and the Caribbean (ECLAC) in its annual assessment of Latin American economies. In the view of ECLAC, Brazil's economic recovery took firm hold in 2010, with annual growth at 7.7 per cent, booming employment (more than 2.4 million jobs created between January and October) and a low unemployment rate averaging 6.3 per cent between August and October. On average, wages rose by 6.5 per cent in real terms. Personal loans were up 7.7 per cent, also in real terms, supporting a steady expansion of family consumption. Inflation, at 5.2 per cent for the 12 months to October, remained above the 4.5 per cent target. In the external sector, imports rebounded and income from FDI and portfolio investment was up sharply. ECLAC agreed this macroeconomic performance was due mainly to rising domestic demand spurred above all by public policies aimed at increased spending and financing, especially for investment.

In 2010 the Brazilian authorities withdrew most of the measures that had been put in place to deal with the effects of the global financial crisis in late 2008. The tax reductions targeting specific sectors (such as the automobile industry) were terminated. Compulsory bank deposits with the central bank returned to pre-crisis levels, and special credit lines to support Brazilian companies with external debts were also eliminated. However some investment supports were kept, such as the tax breaks on civil construction and more readily available credit for sectors producing capital goods. The Banco Nacional de Desenvolvimento Economico e Social (BNDES) (Brazilian Development Bank) received another capital injection to boost its financing capacity.

In the view of ECLAC Brazil's fiscal policy remained expansionary although some counter-cyclical measures were dropped. Non-recurrent revenue such as the dividends from state-owned companies (0.6 per cent of GDP), net revenue from the capitalisation of the Petrobras group (1.1 per cent of GDP) and rising tax revenues as activity picked up should make it possible to meet fiscal targets with a primary surplus of 3.1 per cent of GDP for 2010. For the 12 months to September 2010, this indicator stood at 2.9 per cent of GDP. Tax revenue, including that from payroll taxes, rose by 13 per cent in real terms during the period from January to September 2010 compared with the same period in 2009. Federal government spending increased by 12 per cent in real terms. Monetary policy in 2010 held the same expansionary course as in 2009. Public banks continued to perform well and became firmly established as the main sources of market financing, at 19.6 per cent of total credit. Improved economic performance, revenue and employment kept past-due credit below the 2009 level, at some 3.4 per cent of total credit. Credit reached 46.7 per cent of GDP in October 2010 compared to nearly 25 per cent of GDP in 2003.

With an estimated 7.7 per cent increase in GDP, output rose significantly in several sectors. Agriculture posted a gain of 11 per cent over 2009 and 1.9 per cent over the record set in 2008. Mining output continued to rise substantially, driven by iron mining (production at the largest company rose by 30.4 per cent during the first three quarters of 2010 compared with the same period in 2009). Manufacturing gained 13 per cent during the period, led by the rising production of capital goods (26.5 per cent). Nevertheless, output was still below the levels recorded before the September 2008 crisis, particularly for capital goods and consumer durables. Industrial output during the third quarter of 2010 showed virtually no change over the second quarter of 2010, declining by 0.5 per cent. This slowdown is associated with the impact of counter-cyclical policies, increased competition from imports and falling idle capacity in some sectors. Family and government consumption rose considerably, as did investment, which increased by 25.6 per cent in the same period of 2010. The national

indicator of civil construction compiled by the Brazilian Institute of Geography and Statistics (IBGE) rose by 6.3 per cent between January and October 2010, well above the 4.9 per cent increase during the same period in 2009. The investment rate for 2010 was expected to recover from the 16.7 per cent of GDP posted in 2009 and to return to the levels seen in 2008 when it reached 19.1 per cent of GDP. The upturn in production also led to a significant expansion of formal employment. The 2.4 million jobs created between January and October 2010 represent a 107 per cent gain over the same period in 2009. Unemployment was 6.1 per cent in October 2010; the national wage bill increased by 11.1 per cent between December 2009 and September 2010. Among the sectors adding the most jobs during the period was manufacturing (nearly 9 per cent). Strong domestic demand and rising commodity prices in the international market looked likely to affect inflation levels.

Most of the variations in Brazil's consumer prices have been due to fluctuating food prices, which rose 7.47 per cent in the 12 months to October 2010 compared to the 5.2 per cent overall variation in the extended national consumer price index (IPCA) during the same period a year earlier. Growing domestic demand fuelled the recovery of productive domestic activities that was reflected in the marked increase in value terms of goods imports (which rose by 43.8 per cent between January and October 2010 compared with the same period in 2009) in an environment of currency appreciation. Although exports increased by 27 per cent, the trade balance fell to US$14.63 billion in October and was not enough to finance the higher balance of services and income deficit that, at US$55.75 billion, was 38 per cent more than for the same period in 2009. The current account deficit worsened towards October 2010 and reached US$38.76 billion or nearly 2.37 per cent of GDP. Ample liquidity in the global economy enabled Brazil to finance this deficit mainly with US$21.78 billion in net foreign direct investment (FDI) income and US$61.27 billion in portfolio investments. The foreign currency surplus was absorbed by a US$43.31 billion increase in international reserves, which rose to US$284.90 billion at end October 2010. This is more than Brazil's total external debt, which was US$254.10 billion at the time.

Export commodity sales rose by 38.7 per cent and those of semi-manufactured goods by 37 per cent between January and October 2010 compared with 2009. Exports of manufactured goods increased by 19.3 per cent during the same period. Commodities accounted for the largest share of Brazil's exports (something that had not happened since the 1970s), amounting to 44.7 per cent of total exports during the first ten months. According to ECLAC, of Brazil's top ten exports between January and October 2010, nine were related to mineral and agricultural products. The number one export is iron ore; at US$22.00 billion, or 13.9 per cent of total exports, it surpasses second-ranked crude oil by 89 per cent and is one of the country's main sources of foreign exchange. The only manufactured products

among the top ten exports were passenger automobiles, at US$3.61 billion. A significant portion of export growth was due to rising prices during the period from January to October 2010. Virtually the opposite happened in terms of volume: manufactured goods were up by 9.2 per cent, commodities rose by 8.4 per cent and semi-manufactured goods saw a 4.2 per cent gain. Among export destinations, China - with a 15.85 per cent share - has become the principal buying country. Brazilian sales to Latin America were the fastest growing, expanding by 40.6 per cent (to nearly 21 per cent of total exports) between January and October.

Energy

According to the US-based *Oil and Gas Journal* (OGJ), Brazil had 12.9 billion barrels of proven oil reserves at the beginning of 2011, the second-largest in South America after Venezuela. The offshore Campos and Santos Basins, located off of the country's south-east coast, hold the vast majority of Brazil's proven reserves. In 2010, Brazil produced 2.7 million barrels per day (bpd) of liquids, of which 75 per cent was crude oil. Brazil's oil production has risen steadily in recent years, with oil production in 2010 about 150,000bpd, 6 per cent higher than in 2009. The US government Energy Information Administration (EIA), based on its January 2011 *Short-Term Energy Outlook*, forecast Brazilian oil production to reach 2.9 million bpd in 2011 and 3.0 million bpd in 2012. Brazil's domestic oil consumption averaged 2.52 million bpd in 2009. As a result Brazil became a net oil exporter in 2009.

Most Brazilian oil is produced in the south-eastern region of the country in Rio de Janeiro and Espírito Santo states. More than 90 per cent of Brazil's oil production is offshore in very deep water and consists of mostly heavy grades. Five fields in the Campos Basin (Marlim, Marlim Sul, Marlim Leste, Roncador, and Barracuda) account for more than half of Brazil's crude oil production. These Petrobras-operated fields each produce between 100,000 and 400,000bpd. International oil companies also play a role in Brazilian production. The Shell-operated Parque de Conchas project and the Chevron-operated Frade project are expected to achieve production levels of 100,000bpd and 68,000bpd, respectively. Recent offshore exploration efforts have yielded massive discoveries of pre-salt oil fields.

In its Short-Term Energy Outlook, the EIA projected that Brazil will continue to be a net exporter until the end of 2012. As pre-salt discoveries boost Brazilian production in the medium and long term, crude oil exports should steadily increase. However, this export growth could be moderated by increases in domestic consumption driven by rapid economic growth. Brazil still imports some light crude oil to meet the needs of its refinery fleet. According to the OGJ, Brazil has 1.9 million bpd of crude oil refining capacity spread among 13 refineries. Petrobras operates 11 facilities, the largest being the 360,000bpd Paulinia refinery in São Paulo. Petrobras plans to increase its Brazilian refining capacity to more than 3.0 million bpd by 2020. Under the company's 2010-14 business plan, Petrobras will build five additional refineries to meet this goal. Brazil is the second largest producer of ethanol in the world behind the United States. In 2009, Brazil produced 450,000bpd of ethanol, down from 467,000 in 2008. Despite this decline, the Brazilian Sugarcane Industry Association (UNICA) expected production to rise again following a successful 2010-11 harvest season. Although Brazil is the world's leading ethanol exporter, most of this added production will go to meet increasing domestic demand. All gasoline in Brazil contains ethanol, with blending levels varying from 20-25 per cent. Additionally, over half of all cars in the country are of the flex-fuel variety, meaning that they can run on 100 per cent ethanol or an ethanol-gasoline mixture.

Risk assessment

Economy	Good
Politics	Fair
Regional stability	Good

COUNTRY PROFILE

Historical profile

1500 First sighted by Portuguese mariner, Pedro Alvares Cabral. The area was claimed by the Portuguese crown.
Sugar cane plantations were started by the Portuguese, with Indian slave labour. The Indians were decimated by disease and the survivors fled to the interior. The Portuguese turned to Africa as another source of slaves.
1807 Portuguese imperial court moved to Brazil after the invasion of Portugal by Napoleon's armies and Brazil became a kingdom within the Portuguese empire. Following Napoleon's retreat, Prince Pedro, the son of João VI, became regent of Brazil.
1822 Brazil gained independence from Portugal and Emperor Pedro became Brazil's first monarch. The immediate post-independence period was marked by minor civil wars, slave rebellions and attempts at secession, with many in the south favouring a republican form of government.
1831 Pedro I abdicated following a period of political turmoil. Under a regency, his five-year-old son, Pedro II, succeeded him.
1840 At the age of 14, Emperor Pedro II was granted full powers as monarch. Although his reign was characterised by stability and a move towards political liberalism, wealth was concentrated in the hands of a small feudal elite while the rest of the population remained illiterate and poor.
1850 Pedro II abolished the slave trade.
1864-70 Brazil, Argentina and Uruguay were at war with Paraguay, ending with Paraguay's defeat and ruination.
1888 Pedro II abolished slavery, leading to a revolt by the country's landed gentry.
1889 The monarchy was overthrown by a revolution led by Manuel Deodoro da Fonseca and the king was sent into exile. A federal republic was established, although ruled in the interest of coffee plantation owners.
1929 Turmoil caused by the Wall Street crash led to a military coup which installed a civilian politician, Gertulio Vargas, as president in 1930.
1937 Vargas assumed dictatorial powers and began a revolution in welfare provision and reformed laws governing industry.
1939-45 Brazil remained neutral in the Second World War, but received a large number of exiled Nazis after the defeat of Germany.
1945 Vargas was ousted in a military coup. Elections were held under a new caretaker government and a new constitution was promulgated.
1951 Vargas was narrowly elected president.
1954 Vargas committed suicide after the military gave him the option of resigning or being overthrown.
1956 Juscelino Kubitschek, a strong democrat, came to power after fresh elections. Construction of the new capital, Brasília, began.
1960 Brasília was declared the country's new capital city.
1964 João Goulart was elected president, but after months of hyperinflation leading to the country's virtual bankruptcy he was overthrown by the military. General Humberto Castello Branco was installed as president, overseeing a period of political repression and economic growth based on state-owned industries.
Repressive military treatment of opposition led to human rights abuses and the disappearance of arrested suspects.
1974 General Ernesto Geisel became president and introduced reforms which allowed limited political activity and elections.
1982 Brazil defaulted on its foreign debt repayments, which were among the world's biggest.
1985 Tancredo Neves was elected president, but died before his inauguration. His vice-president, José Sarney, was declared president, taking over a country wracked by hyperinflation.
1986 Sarney introduced the Cruzado Plan which froze prices and wages in an effort to control inflation. However, growing public opposition led to the abandonment of the controls thereby maintaining hyperinflation.
1988 A new constitution was promulgated, reducing presidential powers.
1989 Fernando Collor de Mello was elected president. He introduced a radical economic reform, which involved trade liberalisation, privatisation and a controversial freeze on savings and bank accounts. However, this failed to meet expectations, inflation remained high and the country defaulted on its debt repayments.
1992 An Earth Summit was held in Rio. Collor resigned after being accused of corruption; he was later exonerated. Itamar Franco became president.
1994 Fernando Henrique Cardoso won the presidential election. A constitutional amendment limited presidential terms to four years.
1997 A constitutional amendment allowed presidents to run for a second term in office.
1998 President Cardoso was re-elected.
2000 Brazil's 500th anniversary celebrations were disrupted by protests by indigenous peoples on the issue of land reform and against the legacy of European colonialism, including genocide and the destruction of their cultures.
2001 Corruption scandals rocked the political establishment and a number of senior figures in government and Congress resigned.
2002 Luiz Inácio da Silva (known as Lula), leader of the Partido dos Trabalhadores (PT) (Workers' Party), was elected president.
2003 Lula was sworn in as president, heading a broad coalition government, led by the PT. The centrist Partido do Movimento Democratico Brasileiro (PMDB) (Democratic Movement Party) joined the coalition, ensuring a congressional majority to pass social security and tax reforms.

2004 The Moviemento dos Trabalhadores Rurais Sem Terra (MST) (Landless Workers' Movement) launched its biggest campaign, known as Red April, with a wave of farm occupations to force speedier expropriation and redistribution of unused farmland. Brazil applied for a permanent seat on the UN Security Council. The country launched its first rocket into space.
2005 Allegations of corruption were made against the ruling PT. President Lula apologised to the nation, while denying any personal responsibility for illegal actions.
2006 Elections took place for federal president, vice president and legislators (deputies and one-third of the senate) and state governors, lieutenant governors and members of state unicameral legislatures. In presidential elections Lula da Silva won a second term in office with over 60 per cent of the vote.
2007 Over 1,000 people were freed from sugar cane plantations in the Amazon by Brazil's ministry of labour's anti-slavery teams. The world's largest iron ore mine in the Carajas region, operated by Compañhía Vale do Rio Doce (CVRD), reached a record 972 million tonnes of ore processed.
2008 A previously unknown aboriginal tribe was found in the border region of Brazil and Peru. Brazil declined the offer to join the Organisation of Petroleum Exporting Countries (Opec).
2009 By May, severe floods, which struck in eight states across the north and north-east, had killed 42 people and forced 274,000 people to flee their homes.
2010 A controversial new hydroelectric dam, the world's third largest and to be built in the Amazon rainforest on the Xingu River, was given its environmental licence in January. When completed 500 square kilometres will be inundated and any indigenous communities within 100sq km living along the river will be displaced. In August, the Brazilian airline TAM Linhas Aereas and the Chilean airline LAN agreed to merge to form the region's largest carrier, with 115 destinations in 23 countries. The new company will be called the Latam Airlines Group, although the individual airline brand names will remain in use.

Political structure

Constitution

The 1988 constitution is the country's seventh charter since independence from Portugal in 1822. The federal republic consists of 26 states and one federal district (Brasília). Congress passed a constitutional amendment in 1997 allowing Fernando Henrique Cardoso to become the first president to stand for re-election.

Form of state

Federal presidential democratic republic

The executive

Executive power is exercised by the president, aided by ministers of state who are appointed by the president. The president is elected for a four-year term.
The president is also assisted by the Council of the Republic, an advisory body consisting of the vice president of the republic, the presidents of the Chamber of Deputies and the Senate, the leaders of the majority and minority in each house, the minister of justice, and six other members (two appointed by the president of the republic, two elected by the Chamber of Deputies and two elected by the Senate). These six members have a three-year term of office. The national defence council is the president's advisory body on defence matters. It consists of the vice president of the republic, the presidents of the Chamber of Deputies and the Senate, the minister of justice, ministers of the army, navy and air force, and the ministers of foreign affairs and planning.

National legislature

The bicameral, Congresso Nacional (National Congress) consists of the Senado Federal, (federal senate) (upper house) and Câmara dos Deputados (chamber of deputies) (lower house).
The federal senate has 81 members, of which two-thirds are directly elected and one-third indirectly elected. Members are elected in rotation for eight years. The chamber of deputies has 513 members elected by proportional representation to serve for four years.
All legislation proposed by the executive must be submitted to congress. As well as fiscal and budgetary control, congress must be consulted on matters concerning payments of external debt. Congressional committees have powers of oversight on nominations to important posts proposed by the executive. The senate must approve issues of treasury bills. Constitutional amendments must be approved by a three-fifths majority of both the chambers of the national congress.

Legal system

An 11-member Supreme Federal Tribunal is Brazil's highest judicial body. Judges are appointed by the president of the republic and approved by the Senate. It gives decisions in cases involving the president, vice president, ministers of state, members of Congress, its own members and judges of other courts. It interprets the constitution, judges disputes between the federal and state authorities, between different state authorities, between federal and state authorities and foreign governments, between different levels of the judicial system, and cases involving extradition, *habeas corpus* and *habeas data*.
The Higher Tribunal of Justice is composed of at least 33 members and gives decisions in cases involving state governors. Its members are appointed by the president and approved by the Senate. Regional federal tribunals have at least seven members, who are appointed by the president. The Higher Labour Tribunal is composed of 27 members appointed by the president and approved by the Senate. The Higher Electoral Tribunal includes at least seven judges, three from the Supreme Federal Tribunal, two elected by secret ballot from the Higher Tribunal of Justice and two appointed by the president. The labour and electoral tribunals each have regional counterparts. The Higher Military Tribunal is composed of 15 judges appointed by the president and approved by the Senate for life. Four of its judges are selected from the army, three from the navy and three from the air force. The remaining five are civilians. There is a federal court of appeal. The Federal Audit Court provides for the administrative review of national and state accounts.

Last elections

1 October 2006 (parliamentary); 1/29 October 2006 (presidential, first and second round).
Results: Presidential: (first round) Luis Inácio (Lula) da Silva won 48.61 per cent of vote, Geraldo Alckmin won 41.64, Heloísa Helena won 6.85 per cent. Second round da Silva won 60.83 per cent, Alckmin won 39.17 per cent; turnout was 83.2 per cent.
National congress (Chamber of Deputies): the PT won 15 per cent of votes (83 seats out of 513), the PSDB won 14.6 per cent (89), the PMDB won 13.6 per cent (65), the Partido da Frente Liberal (PFL) (Liberal Front Party) won 10.9 per cent (65), the Partido Progressista (PP) won 7.1 per cent (27); all other parties won less than 7 per cent of the vote.
Federal Senate (one-third (27 seats) up for re-election): The PT won 19.2 per cent, won six seats (giving 11 seats in total, out of 81), the PSDB won 12 per cent (15), the PMDB won 12.5 (5), the PFL won 25.7 (18); all other parties won less than 6 per cent of the vote. Turnout was 83.3 per cent.

Next elections

3 October 2010 (presidential, first round and parliamentary) and 31 October 2010 (presidential second round).

Political parties

Ruling party

Coalition government led by the Partido dos Trabalhadores (PT) (Workers' Party) (since 2002; re-elected 2006)

Main opposition party
Partido da Social Democracia Brasileira (PSDB) (Party of Brazilian Social Democracy)

Population
191.61 million (2009)*
Last census: August 2000: 169,799,170
Population density: 20 per square km.
Urban population: 82 per cent of the total population.
Annual growth rate: 1.5 per cent 1994–2004 (WHO 2006)
Ethnic make-up
European (54 per cent), mixed race (39 per cent), black (6 per cent) and Japanese (1 per cent). The major cities in the centre-south area of the country contain substantial communities of Portuguese, Italian, Lebanese and German immigrants. There are an estimated 210 indigenous groups in Amazonia, making up only 0.2 per cent of the total population of Brazil.
Religions
Catholic (90 per cent); Protestant (5 per cent). Brazil is the largest Catholic country in the world. There is freedom of worship and many other religions are represented.

Education
The investment in education amounts to 4.2 per cent of GDP.
State education is free from pre-primary level. Primary education begins at the age of seven and lasts for eight years. Secondary education, which is not compulsory, begins at the age of 15 and lasts for four years.
Primary and secondary education suffer from scarce resources. Although the initial enrolment rate is similar between the rich and the poor, the inequality is evident at later stages. Only 15 per cent of poor children compared to 80 per cent of children from the richest households complete primary school. Inequalities in budget affect enrolment patterns between those prosperous regions and the north-east where over half of rural children receive less than four years of schooling, and one-quarter of the population has had no schooling at all.
Brazil has doubled the number of students reaching their final year in secondary school but has only places for 11 per cent of them. If the country is to compete internationally it will have to increase this amount to at least 40 per cent, to match even its neighbour Argentina.
To combat the problem of lack of opportunity for poorer students in higher education, the president introduced tax concessions, in July 2004, for private universities who reserve at least 20 per cent of their places to black or native Indian students. It is expected that these tax breaks will provided places for up to 100,000 underprivileged students.
Literacy rate: 86 per cent adult rate; 94 per cent youth rate (15–24) (Unesco 2005).
Compulsory years: 7 to 14.
Pupils per teacher: 24 in primary schools.

Health
In theory, medical, pharmaceutical and dental treatment is free. However, in practice the social health system is underfunded and cannot meet the growing needs of the population. Private health insurance and healthcare facilities are widely available for those who can afford them. The National Social Security and Assistance Institute for Medical Care (INAMPS) is responsible for healthcare.
HIV/Aids
The UNAID/WHO reported that an estimated 105,000 Brazilians were receiving antiretroviral drugs, through the public health system.
HIV prevalence: 0.7 per cent aged 15–49 in 2003 (World Bank)
Life expectancy: 70 years, 2004 (WHO 2006)
Fertility rate/Maternal mortality rate: 2.3 births per woman, 2004 (WHO 2006); maternal mortality 160 per 100,000 live births (World Bank).
Birth rate/Death rate: 7 deaths to 20 births per 1,000 people respectively.
Child (under 5 years) mortality rate (per 1,000): 33.0 per 1,000 live births; 6 per cent of children aged under five are malnourished (World Bank).

Welfare
Employers pay 20 per cent of the payroll into the Social Insurance Scheme to cover payments for social benefits: pensions, invalidity pensions, sickness pay, family allowances, funeral grants, maternity grants, prisoners' family pensions, widows' pensions and special pensions for workers in dangerous jobs. The state sets aside taxes to cover the costs of collection and administration. Brazil shows a highly unequal distribution of income among households and individuals in both rural and urban economies. Pensions can vary from matching the minimum wage of R$130 to the maximum of R$1,200, dependant of contributions.
The Instituto Nacional de Providencia Social (INPS) (National Social Security Institute), administers the scheme for all workers except military personnel, civil servants and agricultural workers, who are covered by a separate system.
Pensions
The retirement ages for those in urban areas are 70 and 65 for men and women respectively, with 35 years contributions; in rural areas 60 and 55 for men and women respectively, with 30 years contributions.

Main cities
Brasília, (capital, estimated population 2.1 million (m) in 2005), São Paulo (10.1m), Rio de Janeiro (6.0m), Salvador (2.6m), Belo Horizonte (2.3m), Fortaleza (2.3m), Curitiba (1.7m), Manaus (1.6m), Recife (1.5m), Belém (1.4m), Porto Alegre (1.4m), Goiânia (1.1m), Guarulhos (1.2m), Campinas (1.0m), Nova Iguaçu (1.0m).

Languages spoken
Many business people and officials speak English. Spanish, Italian, French and German are also widely spoken, especially in tourist areas. There are nearly 200 indigenous languages.
Official language/s
Portuguese

Media
The constitution guarantees freedom of the press.
Brazil is the largest media market in South America and its media is dominated by a few domestically owned conglomerates of broadcasters and publishers.
Press
There are many publications for most interest groups.
Dailies: There are around 280 daily newspapers but the difficulty of distribution has limited readership to regional centres. Nevertheless, major media conglomerates supplies news and views through privately owned news agencies to local outlets.
In Portuguese, major city newspapers include *Correio Braziliense* (www.correioweb.com.br/cbonline) and *Tribuna do Brasil* (www.tribunadobrasil.com.br) from Brazíllia, *O Dia* (http://odia.terra.com.br) and *O Globo* (http://oglobo.globo.com) from Rio de Janeiro, *Folha de Sao Paulo* (www.folha.uol.com.br) and *O Estado de Sao Paulo* (www.estado.com.br) from Sao Paulo, *Correio da Bahai* (www.correiodabahia.com.br) from Salvador, *Super Notícia* (www.supernoticia.com.br) from Belo Horizonte and *O Povo* (www.opovo.com.br) from Fortaleza.
Weeklies: In Portuguese, *Istoé* (www.terra.com.br/istoe), *Veja* (http://veja.abril.uol.com.br) and *Época (http://revistaepoca.globo.com), are general news magazines.*
In English, *Brazzil Magazine* (www.brazzil.com) covers general news.
Business: In Portuguese, *Panorama Brazil* (www.panoramabrasil.com), *Prima Pagina* (www.primapagina.com.br), *Valor Economico* (www.valoronline.com.br) and *Gazeta Mercantil*

(www.gazetamercantil.com.br) offer a wide range of news and information. Magazines include the weekly *Carta Capital* (www.cartacapital.com.br) and the monthly *Amanhã* (www.amanha.com.br) and *Banco Hoje* (www.bancohoje.com.br) for banking news.

Periodicals: In Portuguese, monthly magazine include *Claudia* (http://claudia.abril.com.br) for women *Continente Multicultural* (www.continentemulticultural.com.br) for the Latin culture and (),

Popular magazines published in Portuguese include *Epoca*, *Isto E* and *Veja*. *Brazzil* is an English-language magazine covering the Brazilian economy, politics and culture.

Broadcasting

The responsiblity for radio and television broadcasting is overseen by the state body Empresa Brasileira de Radiodifusão (Radiobrás) (www.radiobras.gov.br).

Radio: There are over 2,000 radio stations, with an estimated 80 per cent of homes with access to a radio receiver.

The state-run public radio network Radiobrás (www.radiobras.gov.br) operates four radio stations over AM/FM. The largest commercial network is Globo Radio (http://globoradio.globo.com), others include Radio Eldorado (www.radioeldorado.com.br), Radio Bandeirantes (http://band.com.br), Radio Cultura (www.radiocultura.com.br) is a public cultural station.

Television: The conversion to digital TV began in São Paulo in 2007 and should be completed nationwide by 2016.

The state-run public TV network Radiobrás (www.radiobras.gov.br) operates four channels including news, documentaries and indigenous and cultural programmes. Large commercial TV networks include Rede Globo (http://redeglobo.globo.com), Sistema Brasileiro de Televisao (SBT) (www.sbt.com.br), TV Record (www.rederecord.com.br) and TV Band (http://band.com.br).

There are many cable TV providers, although most are foreign-owned, domestic networks include Televisão Abril (www.tva.com.br) and Rede TV (www.redetv.com.br).

News agencies

National news agency: Agencia Brazil (in Portuguese): www.agenciabrasil.gov.br

Other news agencies: Agencia Estado: www.ae.com.br/institucional

Agencia Globo: www.agenciaoglobo.com.br

Folha Press (business news): www.folhapress.com.br

PR Newswire (business news): www.prnewswire.com.br

Safras e Mercado (business news): www.safras.com.br

Economy

Brazil, the 'B' in BRIC, the acronym reputedly coined in a Goldman Sachs report of 2003, arguing that that by 2050 Brazil, Russia, India and China would be wealthier than most current major economic powers, has performed well recently.

Brazil has a large industrial base producing manufactured aircraft, motor vehicles, armaments and refined oil products, while the agricultural sector produces a significant quantity of exports, notably coffee and soya. It has vast natural reserves, which in 2009 included 12.9 billion barrels of petroleum with production of 2 million barrels per day (further reserves were found in 2010), natural gas (360 billion cubic metres (cum) with production of 11.9 billion cum), coal (9 billion tonnes, with production of 1.9 million tonnes of oil equivalent (mtoe)) and hydroelectricity (producing 88.5 mtoe).

GDP growth in 2007 was 6.1 per cent as global commodity prices were at an all-time high. GDP began to fall in 2008, to 5.1 per cent as exports declined, and by 2009 the economy fell into recession of -0.2 per cent as the commodity markets shrank. Nevertheless, Brazil is the eighth largest economy in the world and is expected to grow by 7 to 8 per cent in 2010.

Poverty remains a serious problem with large income inequalities and almost a third of the country living below the poverty line. The government provides limited welfare for over 12.5 million families through a *Bolsa Familia* programme of R$50 per what month (around US$50), with payments tied to school attendance.

External trade

In 2008, the União das Nações Sul-Americanas (Unasul) (Union of South American Nations) (known as Unasur from the Spanish Unión de Naciones Suramericanas), modelled on the European Union (EU) was ratified by three member states (out of 10 founding members plus two associate members). Unasur seeks to integrate with the Andean Community of Nations and Mercosur in a single market by 2014, when tariffs on non-sensitive products are abolished with the remainder eliminated by 2019. However political tensions within the region have hampered the ongoing process.

Brazil is the world's largest producer of coffee, sugarcane and oranges and has the largest commercial cattle herd. The majority of the Amazon rain forest is located in Brazil, covering 50 per cent of the land. The government called a halt to 70 per cent of all forest clearing in 2008, which will limit to amount of new land available for cattle pastures. Many international car manufactures have assembly plants in Brazil.

Imports

Principal imports include mineral fuels and oil products, machinery and electrical equipment.

Main sources: US (typically 16 per cent of total), China (13 per cent), Argentina (9 per cent).

Exports

Principal exports include vehicles and machinery, iron and steel, coffee, beef and other agricultural products, footwear and textiles.

Main destinations: China (typically 13 per cent of total), US (10 per cent), Argentina (8 per cent).

Agriculture

Farming

Brazil's agricultural sector accounts for 8.8 per cent of total GDP. This figure is no higher than that in comparable countries, but the significance of Brazil's agriculture sector lies in the fact that it has not declined as a percentage of GDP as development has gathered pace. Approximately 60 million hectares of the total land mass is used for agricultural purposes with another 90 million hectares available for cultivation. Large-scale farming is concentrated in the south and south-east of Brazil.

Brazil has shown remarkable progress in agribusiness development, which includes not just farming production but also increased investment in the sale of farm machinery and processing activities.

Brazil's agribusiness offers a diversified range of products from several regions and supplies cost-effective high quality food products. It accounts for over 40 per cent of the country's total exports.

Irrigated fruit growing in the São Francisco River and the Açu River Valleys, both located in north-eastern part of Brazil has contributed to its prosperous agribusiness sector.

Major agricultural exports include coffee (the world's largest producer and exporter), sugar cane (world's largest producer) and soya beans (world's second-largest producer after US). Orange juice (supplies 85 per cent of world market for orange juice concentrates), tobacco, cocoa, cotton, butter, maize and cattle (around 10 per cent of total world trade) are also significant.

Though agriculture has performed well in recent years, the sector's growth potential continues to be held back by poor transport infrastructure. Only 10 per cent of Brazil's roads are paved.

Fishing

Brazil has a coastline of 8,500km, 12 per cent of the world's freshwater reserves and two million hectares of flooded land.

The country is yet to fulfill its vast potential for marine and freshwater fishing despite efforts by the national government to promote fish as an export commodity. Brazil's annual catch is typically in the range of 980,000 metric tonnes (mt) including 505,957mt marine fish and 117,863mt shellfish.

Forestry

Brazil has vast forest areas; some 543.9 million hectares with the humid tropical areas of the Amazon forests in the north-west of the country accounting for 95 per cent of the total forested area. There are approximately five million hectares of forest plantations, the majority of which are pine and eucalyptus. However, vast areas of protected woodland land exist; 30 million hectares inclusive of state parks and national reserves.

In November 2009, the government reported that the annual rate of deforestation of the Amazon had fallen by 45 per cent and was the lowest level since 1988. The environmentalist campaign group, Greenpeace, claims government targets to reduce deforestation are too low, while others believe the downturn matches the global recession and will pick up when growth returns; the government plans to limit deforestation by 80 per cent by 2020.

Industry and manufacturing

Brazil's industrial sector is one of the most well developed in Latin America. Manufacturing contributes over 23 per cent to annual GDP and industrial goods account for up to 60 per cent of exports. Industry as a whole accounts for approximately 29 per cent of GDP and employs 20 per cent of the labour force.

Industry has relied primarily on imports of capital and intermediary goods, which are either higher quality or cheaper than domestically produced goods. This has caused balance of payments problems and depressed some sectors of industry, such as machine tools. In a drive to replace imports with domestically produced goods, the government has encouraged multinational investment in key sectors of industry. Problems arose in the pharmaceutical, biotechnology and computer industries when the government's desire for self-sufficiency caused it to ignore foreign patent rights and the payment of royalties.

Tourism

The Brazilian travel and tourism industry has developed massively in recent years. The tourism industry accounts for 7 per cent of total employment and 7.2 per cent of the country's total GDP.

The government began a shake-up of the sector's administration in 2003. The tourism authority, Embratur, was redefined as an agency to market Brazil abroad and the Ministry of Tourism was established. The Brazilian airline industry underwent upheaval in 2004, with the Department of Civil Aviation (DAC) introducing a new policy of fare control, whereby the government banned the sale of airfares it considered to be too low.

Investment in infrastructure and services, particularly in the north-eastern coastal area, is being pursued through the government's Tourism Development Programme (PRODETUR). Cultural and eco-tourism are being developed. Brazil has long been a destination for the world's backpackers and continues to be immensely popular at the budget end of the market.

Environment

Around 20 per cent of the Amazon rain forest was felled between mid-1960s and 2007. The land cleared was given over to cattle and soya bean production. Illegal logging accounted for a proportion of this deforestation and in January 2008 a presidential decree made it unlawful to trade in beef and soya produced on deforested properties.

In August 2010, the US agreed to convert US$21 million of Brazilian debt into a fund to halt deforestation and conserve the Atlantic coastal rainforest and the Cerrado and Caatinga ecosystems in Brazil. Around 90 per cent of the Atlantic coastal rainforest has been lost since Western explorers began to exploit the wealth of the region.

Mining

Brazil is a major mining nation, ranking twelve in the world gold production league (second in Latin America) with an annual output of 55 million tonnes. Forty tonnes is accounted for by formal mines and the remainder is generated by alluvial operations which are worked by prospectors.

The mineral potential of Brazil has not been fully assessed. Less than one-third of the country has been thoroughly prospected. The authorities are keen to exploit the country's raw material wealth and a comprehensive aerial survey has been completed by the government's National Mineral Resources Company (CPRM).

The centre of the mining industry is the state of Minas Gerais, named after the large number of gold and precious stone mines discovered in colonial times. Minas Gerais is also Brazil's main producer of mica, beryl, talc, marble, dolomite, graphite, zirconium, bauxite and nickel. There are also large known reserves of minerals scattered throughout the country with concentrations in the state of Rio Grande do Sul (copper, lead, zinc and wolfram), Bahia (lead, barite, quartz crystal and magnesite), Amapa (manganese) and São Paulo (lead, wolfram and zinc).

Brazil ranks as the world leader in production and reserves of niobium/colombium and as the world's top producer of tantalite (28 per cent of total world output). It is the second largest producer of iron ore, third largest producer of bauxite and fourth largest producer of tin. The Carajas mineral deposit contains most of these reserves.

Brazil has vast iron ore reserves, reportedly the world's sixth largest in volume, and is one of the world's leading iron ore exporters. Iron ore is produced from the Quadrilateral area of Minas Gerais in the south-east and the Carajas region in Southern Para. The privatised Companhia Vale do Rio Doce (CVRD), which operates the Carajas deposit with 67 per cent iron metal content, is one of the world's top iron ore exporters.

Brazil is also an important gold producer. Gold production has been decentralised and the market has become more accessible. Minas Gerais is Brazil's main gold producing area, accounting for 45 per cent of the sector's total exports.

Copper has been mined from two sources, the state-owned Caraiba Metals in Bahia and a small mine in Rio Grande do Sul. Production at these two sites is uneconomic. CVRD expects to initiate production from Salobo in the Carajas complex.

Hydrocarbons

Proven oil reserves were 12.6 billion barrels at the end of 2007, with production at 1.8 million barrels per day (bpd) (90.4 million tonnes), which is double the amount produced in 1997. Consumption was 2.1 million bpd in 2007, a rise from 1.9 million since 1997. Energy production is focussed on oil, with 48 per cent of domestic energy consumption coming from oil (including ethanol). Brazil's refining capacity is 1.9 million bpd; work began on a joint Brazil-Venezuela oil refinery in 2007, whereby Brazil expects to increase oil refining by 1.3 million bpd by 2015–20.

Oil exploration has intensified led by the state-owned entity Petrobrás, which announced in November 2007, that a new offshore oil field, Tupi, could hold between 5–8 billion barrels of recoverable light oil with reserves of natural gas. Tupi alone could represent 40 per cent of the oil reserves that Brazil has ever discovered, although drilling for and extracting the gas will be challenging and costly.

There are large reserves of oil shale concentrated in the south of the country, which have been exploited since 1880s.

Brazil is one of the world's largest ethanol producers, based on its sugar cane industry. It produced 390,000 bpd of ethanol in 2007 and is forecast to produce 530,000 bpd in 2009. All domestic automobile petrol uses 20–25 per cent ethanol blending.

Despite its large gas fields, with proven gas reserves totalling 360 billion cubic metres (cum) in 2007, production was only 11.3 billion cum, of which 9.88 billion cum was exported to Bolivia. Production has not increased significantly since 2003 and consumption of natural gas is only 7 per cent of total domestic energy production. Major gas fields are located in the Campos and Santos basins.

A new, 179km, natural gas pipeline was launched in February 2010, capable of carrying 40 million cum per day, from the Campos and Espírito Santo basins to intersect with Brazil's principal gas terminal, Cabinúnas, in Duque de Caxias.

Proven reserves of coal were 17 billion tonnes in 2007, although it was sub-bituminous and lignite, used primarily in power stations; recoverable reserves only amount to 7 million tonnes. Production was 2.2 million tonnes oil equivalent (toe), a figure that has remained stable since 2004. Consumption of coal was 23.4 million tonnes in 2006; imports bridged the shortfall.

Eight areas around Brazil have been found to contain uranium, although production is little more that 5,000 tonnes per annum.

Energy

Brazil became a net exporter of energy, from sugar cane ethanol and hydroelectricity, in 2006. It has the largest hydroelectric resources in the Americas, with installed electric capacity of over 1,000MW of which hydropower provides over 80 per cent of all generation. Brazil and Paraguay jointly run one of the world's largest hydroelectric complexes, Itaipú on the Paraná River, which has a capacity of 13.3GW. Brazil financed its building, using Paraguay's resources; all excess electricity produced by Itaipú is sold to Brazil. In May 2009 a review of the contractual agreement was discussed at ministerial level as Paraguay considered the price paid by Brazil for its electricity had not increased since Itaipú became operational in 1973; Brazil considered Paraguay must consider the investment Brazil originally made. Future developments include the construction of more plants including a 4.1GW extension to Tucuruí and 37GW in other locations.

Other electricity generation comes from coal and natural gas. Conventional thermal plants generate only 7.4 per cent of Brazil's total electricity. President Lula has expressed his administration's desire to expand hydroelectric power plants, leaving the future of conventional thermal generation unclear.

A controversial new hydroelectric dam, to be built in the Amazon rainforest on the Xingu River, was given its environmental licence in January 2010. When completed, at a cost of US$11 billion, the facility will produce 1.1GW of electricity. However 500 square kilometres will be inundated to provide the water catchment area and any indigenous communities within 100sq km living along the river will be displaced.

Nine out of 27 states, including the cities of Rio de Janeiro and São Paulo, experienced a major powercuts, on 10 November 2009. The damage was caused by a storm that brought down two power lines from the Itaipú hydroelectric power station, which automatically closed down, losing its entire output for several hours.

Brazil has two nuclear power plants, both of which are operated by a subsidiary of Electrobras, Electronuclear, producing 2.5 per cent of electrical generation in 2005. The construction of the country's third nuclear facility, Angra-3 has been slowed by political disagreements and a shortfall in funds.

Financial markets

Stock exchange

Bolsa de Valores de São Paulo (Bovespa) (São Paulo Stock Exchange)

Commodity exchange

Maringá Mercantile and Futures Exchange, São Paulo

Banking and insurance

The government of President Lula da Silva, signalled its more cautious approach to bank privatisation, with the cancellation of the sale of a 17.8 per cent stake in Banco do Brasil, Latin America's largest retail bank. Less than a quarter of the banking industry in Brazil is owed by foreign institutions. The major market operators are domestic finance houses.

A new Bank of the South, with a headquarters in Venezuela, will be launched in 2008 to provide an alternative source of development funding for the participating countries. Assets of US$7 billion will underpin its operations.

Central bank

Banco Central do Brasil

Main financial centre

Rio de Janeiro and São Paulo

Time

GMT minus three hours (daylight saving GMT minus two hours): most eastern cities, São Paulo, Rio de Janeiro and Brasília

GMT minus two hours (no daylight saving): Fernando de Noronha Archipelago

GMT minus four hours (no daylight saving): Amazonas State

GMT minus five hours (no daylight saving): Acre State

Daylight saving time is determined and set locally.

Geography

Brazil borders all South American countries except Chile and Ecuador. The distance from north to south is 5,320km, and from east to west 4,328km. Brazil has a land frontier of 15,719km and an Atlantic coastline of 7,408km.

Although Brazil's topography varies greatly, it can be divided roughly into five zones: the Amazon basin, the River Plate basin, the Guiana highlands, the Brazilian highlands and the coastal strip.

The densely forested Amazon basin covers some 40 per cent of Brazil's territory but has only one inhabitant per square km. It receives heavy rainfall and floods annually.

The River Plate basin in southern Brazil is less heavily forested. The land is higher and the climate cooler. The Guiana highlands, north of the Amazon, are part forest and part scrubland. The Brazilian highlands, lying between the Amazon and the River Plate basin, form a tableland from 300 metres to 900 metres high. There are a few mountain ranges, mostly in south-eastern Brazil.

Hemisphere

Southern

Climate

The average annual temperature increases from south to north. On the equator in the Amazon basin, average temperatures are 27 degrees Celsius (C) with no seasonal variation. From the latitude of the port of Recife to the border with Uruguay, the average temperature range is 17–19 degrees C. The two winter months in the south are June and July. Humidity is relatively high in Brazil, particularly in the Amazon basin and on the coast. The rainy seasons are January–April in the north, April–July in the north-east and November–March in the southern coastal area.

Dress codes

Suits are normally worn to business meetings, particularly in Brasília. They are also worn for formal social events and in exclusive restaurants and clubs. For other occasions smart casual clothes are suitable.

Lightweight clothing is advisable for all seasons in the north and for all but the two winter months in the south, when warmer clothing is necessary. Rainproof clothing or umbrellas are necessary during the rainy seasons.

Entry requirements

Passports

Required by all, except nationals of Argentina, Chile, Paraguay and Uruguay. Must be valid for at least six months from date of entry.

Visa

Required by all, except nationals of most EU member states, South America, Israel and some other countries. It is advisable to check online or with the nearest embassy or consulate for latest details.

Currency advice/regulations

There is no restriction on the import and export of local currency. Foreign currency import is unlimited but amounts must be declared; export of foreign currency is allowed up to US$4,000. Regulations may change at short notice. International credit cards are widely used, though cash advances are only paid in local currency.

Health (for visitors)

Mandatory precautions

A yellow fever certificate is required from travellers arriving from an infected country and any of the following countries: Angola, Bolivia, Cameroon, Colombia, Democratic Republic of Congo, Ecuador, Gabon, Gambia, Ghana, Guinea Republic, Liberia, Mali, Nigeria, Peru, Sierra Leone and Sudan.

Advisable precautions

Yellow fever vaccinations are essential for visits to infected areas within Brazil; these include Mato Grosso, Rondônia and states surrounding the Amazon.

Typhoid, tetanus and hepatitis A and B vaccinations are recommended. Malaria prophylaxis is advisable for visits to Amazon regions. There is a high risk of catching dengue fever. Rabies is also a risk. Water precautions should be taken.

Hotels

Graded from one- to five-stars. Wide range available in main towns but sometimes heavily booked (especially during Carnival) and advance booking advisable. Listings available from local tourist offices. Only five-star hotels are not price controlled.

A service charge is usually included in bill; if not, a 10 per cent tip is usual.

Credit cards

Amex, Diners, Mastercard and Visa widely accepted for purchases other than fuel.

Public holidays (national)

Fixed dates

1 Jan (New Year's Day), 21 Apr (Tiradentes Day), 1 May (Labour Day), 7 Sep (Independence Day), 12 Oct (Our Lady Aparecida, Patroness of Brazil), 2 Nov (All Souls' Day), 15 Nov (Proclamation of the Republic), 25 Dec (Christmas Day).

Variable dates

Carnival (five days, Feb), Good Friday, Easter Sunday, Corpus Christi (May/Jun).

Working hours

In Rio de Janeiro and São Paulo there is no siesta break; in Brasília there is a three-hour siesta from 1200–1500.

Banking

Mon–Fri: 1000–1600.

Business

Mon–Fri: 0900–1200; 1400–1800.

Government

Mon–Fri: 0930–1800.

Shops

Mon–Fri: 0900–1830/1900, Sat: 0900–1300. Shopping centres Mon–Sat: 0900–2200.

Telecommunications

Mobile/cell phones

GSM 900 and 1800 services available in most regions of the country.

Electricity supply

127V AC (Bahia (Salvador) and Manaus); 220V AC, 60Hz (Brasília and Recife); 110/220V AC, 60Hz (Rio de Janeiro and São Paulo).

Most hotels provide 100V and 220V outlets, transformers and adaptors.

Social customs/useful tips

There is generally a relaxed attitude towards timekeeping in Rio de Janeiro and the north-east, but people are much more punctual in São Paulo and Brasília. It is the usual practice to shake hands in greeting and on departure. When invited to someone's home for a meal, a gift of flowers for the hostess is customary.

Security

The Brazilian authorities insist on extensive personal documentation. This should be carried at all times.

Brazil's big coastal cities, particularly Rio de Janeiro and those situated in the north-east, have serious crime problems. Street robberies are common and press estimates put the number of armed assaults on bus passengers in Rio alone at about 20 per day.

First-time visitors to Rio are advised to be extremely cautious in allowing strangers to engage them in conversation, especially in areas such as the Avenida Atlantica (the Copacabana sea-front) and the western suburbs. It is inadvisable to visit the Baixada Fluminense, where a murder rate of 20 deaths per day makes the district one of the most violent areas in the world.

Getting there

Air

National airline: Varig (Viação Aérea Rio Grandense, privatised in July 2006).

International airport/s: Brasilia-International (BSB), 11km from city, with duty-free shop, bar, restaurant, buffet, bank, post office, shops, hotel reservations, car hire; Rio de Janeiro Galeão-International (GIG), 15km north of city, bank, hotel, taxi, duty-free shop, restaurant; Sâo Paulo-Cumbica (GRU) 25km north-east of city; Recife (REC).

Other airport/s: Fortaleza (FOR), Salvador-Dois de Julho (SSA), Belem-Val de Cans (BEL), Belo Horizonte-Pampulha (BHZ).

Airport tax: US$36, but should be included in ticket price.

Surface

Road: It is possible to reach Brazil by road from Argentina, Bolivia, Paraguay and Uruguay.

Rail: There are rail connections to Argentina and Uruguay.

Water: There are boats sailing along the Rio Paraguay between Asunción in Paraguay and Corumba. There are also boat services to Peru along the Amazon.

Getting about

When travelling between cities on public transport, visitors must carry passports as proof of identity is required.

National transport

Air: Regular domestic and charter flights to all main cities. Air is the main form of long-distance travel. Air taxis are available at most domestic airports. Advance booking is not necessary for shuttle flights between Rio de Janeiro and São Paulo (about one hour). Domestic flights are expensive, although safety and quality of service are good.

Road: All main centres are connected by surfaced highways, with particularly good roads in the north. Many of the local roads are in need of urgent repair. In total, around 1.6 million km of roads are supervised by the Departmento Nacional de Estradas de Rodagem (DNER).

Buses: Buses are the most popular means of transport with frequent inter-city bus services between main centres. Standards are variable although many routes are now served by modern high quality coaches. Sleeping berths (*leito*) are available on some routes.

Rail: State- and privately-owned railways operate limited services to most main centres throughout the country. Service is generally slower than bus and long distance travelling can be uncomfortable. Good sleeper services with restaurant cars operate between São Paulo, Rio de Janeiro and Belo Horizonte.

Water: Services on São Francisco River between Juazeiro and Pirapora and up the Amazon to Manaus. Hydrofoil service between Rio de Janeiro and Niteroi.

City transport

Taxis: Metered taxis, identified by their roof lights, are available almost everywhere in urban areas. They are inexpensive and often rudimentary. The fare is regularly adjusted according to a table posted on the inside of a rear window. In Rio de Janeiro, there are several types; these include so-called 'common' taxis (yellow with checkered stripe) and the more expensive radio taxi (white, with a red and yellow stripe). A 40 per cent surcharge operates between 2300–0600, on Sundays and public holidays. Tipping is optional.

Travellers arriving by plane are advised to use the main taxi companies which operate desks at major airports and run on a fixed-charge basis. Their cars are big and air-conditioned and although rates are more expensive than those officially charged by standard taxis, it is advisable to use them to avoid frequent exploitation of unwary travellers by individual operators.

Buses, trams & metro: Extensive services operate in all main centres. Efficient though crowded. Two types – regular and special (*fresces*).

Metro: Two-line service in Rio de Janeiro. Line one goes from Botafogo Station to Saenz Peña Station (Tijuca): Mon–Sat: 0600–2300. Line two cuts across the city's centre, from Estácio Station to the Maria de Graca Station: Mon–Sat: 0600–2000.

There is also a two-line network in São Paulo.

Integrated bus/metro tickets available.

Car hire

Car hire is expensive.

An international driving licence is advisable. Traffic is often congested in main cities. Petrol is of poor quality and expensive.

Service stations are rare on some roads and often close on Sundays.

BUSINESS DIRECTORY

The addresses listed below are a selection only. While World of Information makes every endeavour to check these addresses, we cannot guarantee that changes have not been made, especially to telephone numbers and area codes. We would welcome any corrections.

Telephone area codes

The international dialling code (IDD) for Brazil is +55 followed by the area code:

Belem	91	Porto Alegre	51
Belo Horizonte	31	Recife	81
Brasilia	61	Rio de Janeiro	21
Campinas	19	Salvador	71
Curitiba	41	Santos	132
Fortaleza	81	São Paulo	11
Manaus	92		

Chambers of Commerce

American Chamber of Commerce in Brazil (Rio de Janeiro), Praça Pio X 15, 20040-020 Rio de Janeiro (tel: 2203-2477; fax: 2223-0438; e-mail: achambr@amchamrio.com.br).

American Chamber of Commerce in Brazil (São Paulo), Rua da Paz 1431, Chácara Santo Antônio, 04713-001 São Paulo (tel: 5180-3804; fax: 5180-3777; e-mail: amhost@amcham.com.br).

Brazilian International Chamber of Commerce, 1.200 Rua Timbiras, 30140-060 Belo Horizonte (tel/fax: 3273-7021; e-mail: camint@camint.com.br).

British Chamber of Commerce in Brazil (Rio de Janeiro), Avenida Graça Aranha 1, Centro, 20030-002, Rio de Janeiro (tel: 2262-5926; fax: 2240-1058; e-mail: rio@britcham.com.br).

British Chamber of Commerce in Brazil (São Paulo), Rua Ferreira de Araújo 741, Pinheiros, 05428-002 São Paulo (tel: 3819-0265; fax: 3819-7908; e-mail: britcham@britcham.com.br).

Rio de Janeiro Chamber of Commerce and Industry, Rua da Assembléia 93, Centro, 20011-001 Rio de Janeiro (tel: 2532-0089; fax: 2532-1918; e-mail: chamber@ccirj.com).

São Paulo Associaçâo Comercial, 51 Rua Boa Vista, Centro, 01014-911 São Paulo (tel: 3244-3322; fax: 3244-3355; e-mail: infocem@acsp.com.br).

Banking

Banco America do Sul, Alameda Ribeirão Preto 87, 7 andar, Zona postal 01331, PO Box 8075, São Paulo (tel: 287-7955; fax: 287-2762).

Banco Bandeirantes, Rua Boa Vista 162, 7 andar, Zona postal 01014-902, São Paulo (tel: 823-1122; fax: 239-5959).

Banco Boavista, Familia Paula Machado, Zona postal 20091-040, PO Box 1560, Rio de Janeiro (tel: 211-1711; fax: 253-9036).

Banco Bozano Simonsen, Av Rio Branco 138, Zona postal 20057, PO Box 3074, Rio de Janeiro (tel: 271-8232; fax: 271-8160).

Banco Brasileiro Iraquiano, Praça Pio X 54 Centro, Zona postal 20091, Rio de Janeiro (tel: 253-2020/ 2255; fax: 253-3498).

Banco Chase Manhattan, Rua Alvares Penteado 131, Zona postal 01012, São Paulo (tel: 345-751; fax: 239-0594).

Banco de Credito Nacional, Rua Boa Vista 208, Zona postal 01014-030, PO Box 4222, São Paulo (tel: 235-1079, 235-1118; fax: 356-892).

Banco de la Nación Argentina, Av Paulista 2319, Sobreloja, Zona postal 01311, PO Box 22-25, São Paulo (tel: 280-2674; fax: 881-4630).

Banco de la Provincia de Buenos Aires, Rua L Badaró 425, 26 andar, Zona postal 01009, São Paulo (tel: 258-8798; fax: 257-4557).

Banco de la República Oriental del Uruguay, Av Paulista 1776, 9 andar, Zona postal 01310, São Paulo (tel: 251-2699/ 2454; fax: 289-8245).

Banco de Montreal, Trav do Ouvidor 4, Zona postal 20149, Rio de Janeiro (tel: 270-209/ 0210; fax: 221-2706).

Banco do Estado de São Paulo, Praça Antonio Prado 06, 6 andar, Zona postal 01062-900, PO Box 35565, São Paulo (tel: 259-6622, 259-7722; fax: 348-523).

Banco Exterior de España, Av Paulista 1963, 1 andar, Zona postal 01311, PO Box 51623, São Paulo (tel: 251-4344; fax: 288-8015).

Banco Francés e Brasileiro, Av Paulista 1294, 12 andar, zona postal 01310-915, PO Box 8017, São Paulo (tel: 252-7163/64; fax: 283-0794).

Banco Geral do Comercio, Rua Funchai 160, 5 andar, Zona postal 04551-060, São Paulo (tel: 828-7322; fax: 828-7208).

Banco Mercantil de São Paulo, Av Paulista 1450, 9 andar, Zona postal 01310-917, PO Box 4077, São Paulo (tel: 252-2121/2228; fax: 284-3312).

Banco Mitsubishi Brasileiro, Rua Libero Badaró 6633/641, Zona postal 01009-904, PO Box 8449, São Paulo (tel: 239-5244; fax: 362-128, 362-060).

Banco Noroeste, Rua Alvares Penteado 216, 3 andar, Zona postal 010102, PO Box 8119, São Paulo (tel: 239-0844, 378-401; fax: 354-858).

Banco Real, Av Paulista 1347, 3 andar, Zona postal 01310-916, PO Box 5766, São Paulo (tel: 285-5645, 251-9796; fax: 251-9222).

Banco Region de Desenvolvimento do Extremo Sul, Rua Uruguai 155, Porto Alegre (tel: 228-9200; fax: 228-8283).

Banco Safra, Av Paulista 2100, Bela Vista, Zona postal 01310, PO Box 9139, São Paulo (tel: 251-7575; fax: 251-7211).

Banco Sogeral, Av Paulista 1355, 12 andar, Zona postal 01311-924, São Paulo (tel: 251-5533; fax: 283-1449).

Banco Sudameris Brasil, Av Paulista 1000, 14 andar, Zona postal 01310-100, PO Box 3481, São Paulo (tel: 283-9251/9260; fax: 283-9269).

Unibanco-União de Bancos Brasileiros, Av Euzébio Matoso 891, 4 andar, Zona postal 05423-901, PO Box 8185, São Paulo (tel: 817-4322; fax: 815-5084).

Central bank
Banco Central do Brasil, Setor Bancário Sul, Quadra 03, Bloco B, Edificio Sede, PO Box 08670, 70074-900 Brasília DF (tel: 3414-2401; fax: 3321-9453; e-mail: cap.secre@bcb.gov.br).

Stock exchange
Bolsa de Valores de São Paulo (Bovespa) (São Paulo Stock Exchange), La Bolsa 64, Santiago (Tel: 698-2001; fax: 697-2236

Alvares Peuteado 151, São Paulo (tel: 233-2147; fax: 233-2226; www. bovespa.com.br).

Bolsa de Valores do Rio de Janeiro (BVRJ), (Rio de Janeiro Stock Exchange)

Praça 15 de Novembro 20, 2010 Rio de Janeiro (tel: 271-1001; fax: 221-2151; www.bvrj.com.br).

Commodity exchange
Maringá Mercantile and Futures Exchange, São Paulo

Brazilian Mercantile Futures Exchange (BM&F Bovespa), www.bmfbovespa. com.br

Travel information
Car Club do Brasil, Rúa Mexico 11, Rio de Janeiro 20006-900 (tel: 2533-1129; fax: 2220-2400; e-mail: viasat@carclubdobrasil.com.br).

EMBRATUR (Empresa Brasileira de Turismo), Rua Mariz e Barros 13, Rio de Janeiro 20270 (tel: 273-2212).

VARIG SA, Edif Varig, Avenida Almirante Silvio Noronha 365, 20021 Rio de Janeiro (tel: 272-5000; fax: 272-5700).

Ministry of tourism
Conselho Nacional de Turismo (CNTUR), Ministry of Infrastructure, Rua Mariz e Barros 13, 5 andar, 20270 Rio de Janeiro (tel: 273-0691).

National tourist organisation offices
Centro Brasileiro de Informação Turística (CEBITUR) (Brazilian Tourist Office), Rua Mariz e Barros 13, 6 andar, Praça da Bandeira, 20270-000 Rio de Janeiro (tel: 293-1313; fax: 273-9290).

Ministries
Ministry of Administration, Esplanada dos Ministérios, Bloco C, CEP 70046-900 Brasília-DF (tel: 224-2682; fax: 225-8927).

Ministry of Agrarian Policy, SBN Ed Palácio do Desenvolvimento, CEP 70057-900 Brasilia-DF (tel: 223-8852; fax: 226-8727).

Ministry of Agriculture, Esplanada dos Ministerios, Bloco D, 8 andar, CEO 70043-900 Brasília DF (tel: 226-5161, 226-5380; fax: 225-9046).

Ministry of the Air Force, Esplanada dos Ministérios, Bloco M, CEP 70045-900 Brasília-DF (tel: 321-5303; fax: 223-2592).

Ministry of the Armed Forces, Esplanada dos Ministérios, Bloco Q, CEP 70049-900 Brasília-DF (tel: 223-5356; fax: 321-2477).

Ministry of the Army, QG/EX, Bloco A, SMU, CEP 70630-900 Brasília-DF (tel: 315-5200, 224-2844; fax: 223-1145).

Ministry of Communications, Esplanada dos Ministerios, Bloco R, 80 andar, CEP 70040-900 Brasília DF (tel: 225-9381, 224-9723; fax: 226-3980).

Ministry of Culture, Esplanada dos Ministérios, Bloco B, CEP 70068-900 Brasília-DF (tel: 224-6064; fax: 225-9162).

Ministry of Education, Esplanada dos Ministérios, Bloco L, CEP 70047-900 Brasília-DF (tel: 321-1076; fax: 224-3618).

Ministry of Environment, Water Resources and Amazonia, Esplanada dos Ministérios, Bloco B, CEP 70068-900 Brasília-DF (tel: 322-7819; fax: 226-7101).

Ministry of External Relations, Esplanada dos Ministérios, Palácio do Itamaraty, CEP 70170-900 Brasília-DF (tel: 211-6100; fax: 223-7362).

Ministry of Finance, Esplanada dos Ministérios, Bloco P, CEP 70048-900 Brasília-DF (tel: 314-4805; fax: 322-5009).

Ministry of Health, Esplanada dos Ministérios, Bloco G, CEP 70058-900 Brasília-DF (tel: 224-5269).

Ministry of Industry, Trade and Tourism, Esplanad dos Ministerios, Bloco J, CEP 70056-900 Brasília DF (tel: 325-2001; fax: 325-2209).

Ministry of Institutional Reform, Palácio do Planalto, Praca dos Tres Poderes, CEP 70150-900 Brasília-DF (tel: 322-9619; fax: 211-1192).

Ministry of Justice, Esplanada dos Ministérios, Bloco T, Ed Sede, CEP 70064-900 Brasília-DF (tel: 226-2296; fax: 322-6817).

Ministry of Labour, Esplanada dos Ministérios, Bloco F, CEP 70056-900 Brasília-DF (tel: 226-6137; fax: 226-3577).

Ministry of Mines and Energy, Esplanada dos Ministerios, Bloco U, 70 andar, CEP 70065-900 Brasília DF (tel: 218-5447, 223-9059; fax: 225-5407).

Ministry of the Navy, Esplanada dos Ministerios, Bloco N, 20 andar, CEP 70055-900 Brasília DF (tel: 223-6858, 312-1000; fax: 312-1202).

Ministry of Planning and Budget, Esplanada dos Ministérios, Bloco K, CEP 70048-900 Brasília-DF (tel: 224-0679; fax: 225-4032).

Ministry of Science and Technology, Esplanada dos Ministérios, Bloco E, CEP 70067-900 Brasília-DF (tel: 224-4364; fax: 225-1141).

Ministry of Social Security, Esplanada dos Ministérios, Bloco F, CEP 70059-900 Brasília DF (tel: 224-5914; fax: 223-2293).

Ministry of Sport, Esplanada dos Ministérios, Bloco A, CEP 70054-900 Brasília-DF (tel: 224-5285; fax: 224-3618).

Ministry of Transport, Esplanada dos Ministerios, Bloco R, CEP 70040-900 Brasília DF (tel: 224-0185, 224-0995; fax: 226-4864).

President's Office, Palácio do Planalto, 40 andar, CEP 70150-900 Brasília-DF (tel: 211-1303, 211-1034; fax: 226-2078, 321-5804).

Other useful addresses
Associação do Comercio Exterior do Brasil (Exporters' Association), Avenida General Justo 335, Rio de Janeiro (tel: 240-5048).

British Consulate-General, Praia do Flamengo 284, 22210-030 Rio de Janeiro (tel: 553-3223; fax: 553-6850).

British Embassy, Setor de Embaixadas Sul, Quadra 801, Loto 8, Conjunto K, 70408-900 Brasília DF (tel: 225-2710, 223-5357; fax: 225-1777).

Companhia Vale do Rio Doce (CVRD – State Mining Company), Avenida Graca Aranha 26, Bairro Castelo, 20005 Rio de Janeiro (tel: 272-4477).

Confederação Nacional de Agricultura (CNA – National Agriculture Federation), Brasília DF (tel: 225-3150).

Confederação Nacional da Industria (CNI – National Confederation of Industry, comprising the 21 state industry federations), Edificio Roberto Simonsen, 16 andar, 70040 Brasília DF (tel: 224-1328).

Council of the State's Reform Programme, Av Borges de Medeiros, No 1501, 7 Andar, CEP 90119-900, Porte Alegre, Rio Grande do Sul (tel: 228-2708, 334-5275; fax: 226-5893, 382-4607).

Departamento Nacional de Telecomunicaes (Dentel), Via N2, Anexo do Ministerio das Comunicações, Esplanada dos Ministerios, Bloco R, 70044 Brasília DC (tel: 223-3229).

Divisão de Feiras e Turismo-Departamento de Promocão Comercial (Organisers of Trade Fairs and

Tourism), Ministerio das Relacões Exteriores, Esplanada dos Ministerios, 2 andar, 70170 Brasília (tel: 211-6644).

Fundacão Instituto Brasileiro de Geografia e Estatistica (IBGE – Brazil Institute of Geography and Statistics), Avenida Franklin Roosevelt 166, Castelo, 20021 Rio de Janeiro (tel: 220-6671).

National Department of Foreign Trade, Avenida Presidente Vargas 328, 11 andar, 20091 Rio de Janeiro (tel: 271-7504).

Petrolo Brasileiro-Petrobras Segen/Gasbol (State Oil Company), Rua General Canabarro 500, CEP 20271-201, Maracana, Rio de Janeiro (tel: 566-3733; fax: 566-5723/5299).

Rede Ferroviaria Federal (SA – Federal Railway Corporation), Praça Procopio Ferreira 86, 2221 Rio de Janeiro (tel: 223-5795).

Secretaria Especial de Desenvolvimento Industrial (Industrial Development Council), Ministerio de Desenvolvimento da Industria e Comercio, Lotes 2/5-2/8, Bloco G, 8 andar, 70070 Brasília DF (tel: 225-7556).

Superintendencia da Zona Franca de Manaus (Manaus Free Zone Authority), Rua Ministro João Gonçalves de Souza, Cidade Universitaria, Distrito Industrial, 69000 Manaus (tel: 237-3288).

US Embassy, Avenida das Naçoes, Lote 3, 70403-900 Brasília DF (tel: 321-7272; fax: 225-9136).

World Trade Centre (WTC), Av das Naçoes Unidas, 12-551, Sao Paulo (tel: 893-7113; fax: 893-7101).

National news agency: Agencia Brazil (in Portuguese): www.agenciabrasil.gov.br

Internet sites

Banco do Brasil: www.bancobrasil.com.br

Banco Itaú: www.itau.com.br

Brazilian Embassy in London: www.brazil.org.uk

Brazilinfo: www.brazilinfo.net

Brazil American Chamber of Commerce: www.amcham.com.br/

Brazil Statistics: www.ibge.gov.br

Brazzil (English-language magazine): www.brazzil.com

National Industry Confederation (markets and industry information): www.cni.org.br

British Virgin Islands

KEY FACTS

Official name: British Virgin Islands

Head of State: Queen Elizabeth II; represented by Governor Boyd McCleary (from 20 Aug 2010)

Head of government: Premier Ralph O'Neal (sworn in 23 Aug 2007)

Ruling party: Virgin Islands Party (VIP) (elected 20 Aug 2007)

Area: 153 square km

Population: 23,000 (2010)*

Capital: Road Town

Official language: English

Currency: US dollar (US$) = 100 cents

Exchange rate: US$1.00 per US$ (Oct 2011)

GDP per capita: US$16,000 (2004) (US$15,600 (2007) (BVI stats))

GDP real growth: -0.60% (2008)*

Inflation: 1.90% (2005)

Visitor numbers: 784,000 (2005)

* estimated figure

COUNTRY PROFILE

Historical profile

1493 The islands were sighted by Columbus.
1595 Sir Francis Drake visited the channel which runs through the islands and which now bears his name.
1648 The islands were settled by the Dutch.
1666 English settlers arrived.
1672 Tortola was taken over by the English.
1872 The islands became part of the UK colony of the Leeward Islands. The British Virgin Islands (BVI) continued to come under the authority of the governor of the Leeward Islands until 1960.
1960 An appointed administrator (renamed governor in 1971) assumed responsibility for the islands.
1967 Lavity Stoutt of the Virgin Islands Party (VIP) became the first chief minister as the islands were granted internal self-government.
1995 The VIP won the elections.
1997 The National Democratic Party (NDP) was formed.
1999 The VIP was re-elected.
2002 Islanders became British citizens under the British Overseas Territories Act.
2003 The NDP won parliamentary elections and Orlando Smith became chief minister.
2004 A review of the constitution, by the BVI Constitutional Review Commission, began.
2005 The BVI began imposing a withholding tax on EU citizens' savings. The tax is passed to the relevant EU country, although without the savers' names. The BVI government purchased the Virgin Gorda Airport for US$2.9 million, to maintain the tourist interests of the territory's second most populated island.
2006 David Pearey was sworn in as governor.
2007 A new constitution was promulgated. In parliamentary elections, the opposition Virgin Islands Party (VIP) won 10 seats out of 13, defeating the National Democratic Party (NDP) with two, and one independent; turnout was 62.3 per cent. Premier Ralph O'Neal was sworn into office.
2008 Premier O'Neal became the first locally elected leader to chair a meeting of the Executive Council.
2009 The government signed an agreement with the Organisation for Economic Co-operation and Development (OECD), removing the BVI from the list of countries that do not implement international standards for tax disclosure.
2010 Governor David Pearey retired and V Inez Archibald became acting governor until Boyd McCleary took office on 20 August. The Securities, Investment Business (and Mutual Fund) Advisory (SIBA) Committee was established on 15 December, tol review regulations and recommend changes that govern BVI financial services.
2011 In March, the office of the Governor of US Virgin Islands official requested that BVI stopped practices that produce pollution for its neighbour, including open air rubbish burning at the BVI incineration plant on Tortola.

Political structure

Constitution

BVI is a British Overseas Territory with a large degree of internal self-government, based on a new constitution which was promulgated in 2007. A ministerial system of government is enshrined. It increases the authority of the BVI government, particularly with new powers for international affairs and internal security and direct local control of police matters. Fundamental human rights for individuals were included. The prime minister has greater influence for setting cabinet agenda and a new role of cabinet secretary has been created.
The post of premier replaced the former role of chief minister.
The British monarch appoints a governor as a representative.

Form of state

British Caribbean dependency

The executive

Executive power is exercised by the governor, appointed by the British monarch, the premier and four other ministers elected by members of the house of assembly.

National legislature

The unicameral, House of Assembly, comprises 13 members, plus an *ex-officio* attorney general and a speaker of parliament. Nine members are elected to represent each district, with the remaining four representing a territory-wide vote.

The premier nominates an executive council, which is appointed by the governor.

Legal system

The legal system is based on the English common law system with local variations. Justice is administered by the Eastern Caribbean Supreme Court. A resident puisne judge presides over the High Court, Admiralty and associated courts. There is a Court of Appeal. Final appeals go to the Privy Council in the UK.

Last elections

20 August 2007 (parliamentary)

Results: Parliamentary: Virgin Islands Party (VIP) won 10 seats (out of 13), the National Democratic Party (NDP) won two, and one independent; turnout was 62.3 per cent.

Next elections

2011 (parliamentary)

Political parties

Ruling party

Virgin Islands Party (VIP) (elected 20 Aug 2007)

Main opposition party

National Democratic Party (NDP)

Population

24,300 (2009)*

Last census: May 2001: 20,647 (provisional)

Population density: 121 inhabitants per square km.

Annual growth rate: 3.2 per cent (2003)

Ethnic make-up

African (83 per cent), white, Indian, Asian and mixed race.

Religions

Methodist (45 per cent), Anglican (21 per cent), Church of God (7 per cent), Seventh-Day Adventist (5 per cent), Baptist (4 per cent).

Education

The education sector will receive US$46.7 million from the 2004 Budget.

Health

Life expectancy: 76 years (estimate 2003)

Fertility rate/Maternal mortality rate: Two births per woman (2003)

Birth rate/Death rate: 15 births per 1,000 population; five deaths per 1,000 population (2003).

Child (under 5 years) mortality rate (per 1,000): 19 per 1,000 live births (2003)

Welfare

A social security scheme exists for workers between the ages of 16 and 65. The scheme covers old age pensions, disability and a survivors fund. Contributions are shared between the employer and employee, each providing 3.25 per cent of salary. Self-employed workers pay the full 6.5 per cent.

Main cities

Road Town, on Tortola island (capital, estimated population 9,100 in 2003), East End-Long Look (5,200).

Languages spoken

Official language/s

English

Media

Press

There are three local weekly newspapers including *Island Sun* (http://islandsun.com), *BVI Beacon* (www.bvibeacon.com) and the *BVI Stand Point* (www.vistandpoint.com).

Broadcasting

All broadcasting is private and commercial and listeners benefit from easy access to US Virgin Island media outlets.

Radio: There are four stations located on the islands and named after their call signs. Radio ZBVI (www.zbviradio.com), Isle 95, WJKC (www.isle95.com), and ZVCR (www.zvcr1069fm.com) playing island music; Zking Radio (www.zkingradio.com) is a religious broadcaster.

Television: The Virgin Islands Television Network (VITV) is privately-owned. Orbit Satellite TV (www.orbit.net) and Innovative (www.iccvi.com) cable TV, provide many channels.

News agencies

Other news agencies: Caribbean Net News: www.caribbeannetnews.com

Economy

The economy is driven by financial services and tourism. The islands have one of the highest per capita incomes of not only the Caribbean but the world, at over US$50,000 in 2008. BVI's large offshore banking business is particularly successful in trust management, mutual funds and captive insurance. Of the 456,000 active companies, incorporated in BVI, 630 were limited partnerships in 2010. The financial services are fully open and connect to the North American and European banking and financial systems. The sector contributed 63 per cent to GDP in 2009. BVI caters for wealthy tourists in high-end hotels and holiday lets and as a port of call for Caribbean cruise-liners; it is also an established charter yacht centre. Over 30 per cent of GDP is generated by the tourist sector. Apart from livestock, the agricultural sector is unable to provide sufficient for domestic consumption and most food has to be imported. Construction and light industry comprises 10 per cent of GDP, providing employment for around 40 per of the workforce.

Both dominant sectors of the market were affected by the global economic crisis so that in 2008 GDP growth was -0.6 per cent and inflation rose to 7.1 per cent. This prompted the government to cut spending on capital projects such as telecommunications and transport.

External trade

The trade deficit is offset by tourist spending, capital inflows and by workers' remittances. BVI is an associate member of Caricom and the Organisation of Eastern Caribbean States (OECS).

Imports

Principal imports are petroleum, foodstuffs, consumer goods, machinery and equipment, building materials and vehicles.

Main sources: US Virgin Islands, Puerto Rico, US

Exports

Principal exports are fruit, vegetables, live animals, fish, rum, gravel and sand.

Main destinations: US Virgin Islands, Puerto Rico, US

Agriculture

Farming

The agricultural sector contributes approximately 15 per cent to annual GDP.

About 60 per cent of the total land area is agricultural.

Production is centred on livestock farming, fishing (langoustine, prawns), food crops (mainly fruit and vegetables) and sugar cane for rum production.

Main areas of activity are Tortola, Virgin Gorda and Jost Van Dyke.

The expansion of the tourist industry has increased the dependence on imported foodstuffs, mainly from the US.

Industry and manufacturing

The industrial sector typically contributes around 10 per cent to annual GDP. Industries include construction, concrete and rum production.

Tourism

Tourism is primarily based on marine activities and water sports for visitors who enjoy tropical sunshine, white beaches and the company of other tourists. With a local population of around 25,000 and annual tourist numbers of around 800,000 the industry is the principal generator of business, employment and capital investment and is vital to the economy. The tourism sector constituted 57.2 per cent of GDP in 2010, a slight improvement on comparable rates in 2006–07 (56.4–56.5 per cent), but a marked improvement on a decade low of 52.9 per cent in 2009 when visitor numbers fell by 10.7 per cent, mostly during the height of the tourist season (January–April) when 16.3 per cent fewer tourists visited. There were 41,400 fewer cruise liner passengers, despite an increase in the number of visiting ships – 408 cruise liners in 2008

and 421 liners in 2009. Tourism exports also fell by -14.6 per cent in 2009 as well as employment. In 2003, tourism employed over 87 per cent of the workforce but by 2009 this had fallen to 61.1 per cent. However, in the 2010/11 season all indices recorded growth in the sector.
In July 2011 the BVI national culinary team won the gold medal in the annual Taste of the Caribbean culinary completion, held in New York. In August 2011, the US-based Marriott International announced its new luxury spa and marina, Scuba Island Resort, development to be built east on Tortola; it is expected to be operational by 2013.

Hydrocarbons
There are no known hydrocarbon reserves. All domestic energy needs are met by imported petroleum products.
Any coal or natural gas products used are commercially insignificant.

Energy
Total installed generating capacity was 39MW in 2008, from 11 power stations. The state-owned BVI Electricity Corporation has a monopoly on electricity generation, transmission and distribution.

Banking and insurance
The business and financial services sector is the largest contributor to government income, accounting for around 60 per cent of the total. There are over 500,000 International Business Corporations (IBC) incorporated in the British Virgin Islands, regulated by the Financial Services Commission (FSC). The FSC operates as an independent regulator and is responsible for domestic and offshore finance.
The seven members of the Organisation of Eastern Caribbean States (OECS), Antigua and Barbuda, Dominica, Grenada, Montserrat, St Kitts and Nevis, St Lucia and St Vincent and the Grenadines, share a common currency and central bank. The British Virgin Islands and Anguilla are associate members.
Under a new EU tax directive, introduced in July 2005 in a number of associate and dependent EU countries, the BVI imposed a withholding tax for EU citizens. The tax will be passed to the relevant EU tax department while retaining the anonymity of the saver. Withholding taxes began at 15 per cent and will rise to 35 per cent by 2011.
BVI has also agreed to supply information on tax fraud, for criminal or civil trials, and notify EU member states about additional malpractices.
Central bank
There is no central bank.
Main financial centre
Tortola
Offshore facilities
The British Virgin Islands Financial Services Commission licenses and regulates all service providers operating within the offshore sector.

Time
GMT minus four hours

Geography
At the northern end of the Leeward Islands, in the eastern Caribbean, the British Virgin Islands consist of more than 60 islands and cays, of which only 16 are inhabited. Most of the islands are mountainous and of volcanic origin; the coralline island of Anegada is the only exception of any size. They lie about 100km to the east of Puerto Rico and adjoin the US Virgin Islands.
Hemisphere
Northern

Climate
The climate is sub-tropical, with no marked seasonal variation in temperature – generally 24–30 degrees Celsius (C) during the day and 10 degrees C cooler at night. Rainfall is generally low, although the hurricane season, occuring between July–November, can produce violent, torrential downpours.

Entry requirements
Passports
Required by all
Visa
Not required by most tourists for visits up to one month, with return/onwards tickets, pre-arranged accommodation and sufficient funds for stay. Longer stays require premission from the immigration department.
Some visitors will, and business visitors may, require a visa; see www.bvitourism.com/immigration for more details.
Currency advice/regulations
No restriction on import of foreign currency but amounts should be declared. Exports limited to the amounts declared on arrival.

Health (for visitors)
Mandatory precautions
None.
Advisable precautions
Typhoid vaccinations. Dengue fever is a viral disease transmitted by mosquitoes, which are most likely to bite two hours after sunrise and two hours before sunset. Use an effective insect repellent on all exposed skin. Take water precautions.

Hotels
Expensive, but wide range available. There is a 7 per cent government tax and hotels may impose a 10 per cent service charge usually added to the bill.

Public holidays (national)
Fixed dates
1 Jan (New Year's Day), 1 Jul (Territory Day), 21 Oct (St Ursula's Day), 25–26 Dec (Christmas).
If a holiday falls at the weekend the following Monday is taken in *lieu*.
Variable dates
H Lavity Stoutt's birthday (first Mon in Mar), Commonwealth Day (second Mon in Mar), Good Friday, Easter Monday, Whit Monday, Queen's Official Birthday (Jun), August Festival Day (first Wed in Aug).

Working hours
Banking
Mon–Fri: 0900–1500; also Fri: 1600–1700.
Business
Mon–Fri: 0800/0900–1600/1700. Sat 0800–1200
Government
Mon–Fri: 1230–2030.
Shops
Open for longer than offices and bank and are open all day Saturday.

Telecommunications
Mobile/cell phones
GSM 900/1900 coverage throughout the islands.

Electricity supply
110 volts AC, 60Hz, using US two-pin plugs.

Getting there
Air
There are no direct North American or intercontinental flights to the islands, all major air-carriers arrive via regional hubs. There are around six air charter-hire companies operating in BVI that fly to surrounding Caribbean islands.
National airline: There is no national airline.
International airport/s: Terrance B Lettsome International Airport (EIS) on Beef Island, 15km from Road Town on Tortola. Only inter-island and intra-Caribbean flights arrive at this airport, including regular flights from Puerto Rico, US Virgin Islands and Antigua.
Airport tax: Departures tax US$20, not applicable to transit passengers.
Surface
Water: There are regular, daylignt running, ferries to and from St Thomas and St John on the US Virgin Islands.
There is a US$5 departure tax when leaving by boat and US$7 for cruise passenger leaving the islands.
Main port/s: Tortola: West End, Beef Island, Road Town; Virgin Gorda: Spanish Town, Yacht Harbour.

Getting about

National transport

Air: There are around 10 domestic air charter companies that fly between the islands.

Road: The main highway from Beef Island through Road Town to West End is surfaced. There is a bridge connecting Beef Island with Tortola. There is also a surfaced road on the northern ridge from east to west. Roads on Virgin Gorda are in variable condition.

Taxis: On Tortola taxis may be chartered by agreement.

Water: Various types of boats ply between islands. Regular ferry services operate between Road Town and West End (Tortola).

City transport

Taxis: Widely available with published fixed fares. The taxi rank in Road Town is opposite the central post office, and the Taxi Association on Wickhams Cay. Tipping is optional. Taxis can be hired on an hourly or daily basis.

Car hire

Vehicles can be hired on Tortola and Virgin Gorda. Drivers must be aged at least 25 years and hold their own valid, national driving licence. A BVI driving permit must be obtained, for a fee – the rental company can issue this.

Driving is on the left and roads can be steep and unpaved.

BUSINESS DIRECTORY

The addresses listed below are a selection only. While World of Information makes every endeavour to check these addresses, we cannot guarantee that changes have not been made, especially to telephone numbers and area codes. We would welcome any corrections.

Telephone area codes

The international direct dialling (IDD) code for the British Virgin Islands is +1284, followed by subscriber's number.

Chambers of Commerce

BVI Chamber of Commerce and Hotel Association, James Frett Building, PO Box 376, Road Town, Tortola (tel: 494-3514; fax 494-6179; e-mail: bviccha@surfbvi.com).

Banking

Banco Popular de Puerto Rico, PO Box 67, Road Town, Tortola (tel: 494-2117; fax: 494-5294).

Bank of Nova Scotia, PO Box 434, Road Town, Tortola (tel: 494-2526; fax: 494-4657).

Barclays Bank International, PO Box 70, Road Town, Tortola (tel: 494-2171; fax: 494-4315).

Chase Manhattan Bank, PO Box 435, Road Town, Tortola (tel: 494-2662; fax: 494-3863).

CITCO Ban (BVI) Ltd, PO Box 662, Road Town, Tortola (tel: 494-2217; fax: 494-3917).

Crorebridge Bank, PO Box 71, Road Town, Tortola (tel: 494-2233; fax: 494-3547).

Disa Bank BVI, PO Box 985, Road Town, Tortola (tel: 494-4977; fax: 494-4980).

Guyerzeller Bank, PO Box 3162, Road Town, Tortola (tel: 494-5414; fax: 494-5417).

London International Bank and Trust Company, PO Box 3151, Road Town, Tortola (tel: 494-3045; fax: 494-3050).

Rathbone Bank, PO Box 986, Road Town, Tortola (tel: 494-6544; fax: 494-6532).

The Bank of East Asia, PO Box 901, Road Town, Tortola (tel: 495-5588; fax: 494-4513).

United Chinese Bank, PO Box 901, Road Town, Tortola (tel: 494-6775; fax: 494-8180).

VP Bank, PO Box 3463, Road Town, Tortola (tel: 494-1100; fax: 494-1199).

Travel information

Air Sunshine Inc (tel: 495-8900; email: EMail@AirSunshine.com).

Caribbean Wings (tel: 495-6000; email: carwings@yahoo.com).

Fly BVI Ltd, PO Box 3347, Roadtown (tel: 495-1747; fax: 495-1973; email: info@fly-bvi.com).

Island Birds, PO Box 993 Road Town, Tortola; Beef Island Airport (tel: 495-2002; email: info@islandbirds.com).

Island Helicopters International Ltd, PO Box 2900, East End; Beef Island Airport, Tortola (tel: 495-2538; (emergency medical transfers, tel: 499-2663); internet: info@helicoptersbvi.com; internet: www.helicoptersbvi.com).

National tourist organisation offices

BVI Tourist Board, Joshua Smith Building, PO Box 134, Road Town, Tortola (tel: 43-134; fax: 43-866; internet: www.bvitourism.com).

Ministries

Governor's Office, Government House, PO Box 702, Road Town, Tortola (tel: 494-2345, 494-2370, 494-3520; fax: 468-4490).

Other useful addresses

BVI Hotel and Commerce Association, PO Box 376, Wickhams Cay, Road Town, Tortola (tel: 43-514, 42-947; fax: 46-179).

BVI Financial Services Commission, Pasea Estate, Road Town, Tortola (tel: 494-4190; fax: 494-9399; e-mail: commissioner@bvifsc.vg; internet site: http://www.bvi.org).

BVI Offshore Financial Centre, Financial Services Department, Ministry of Finance, Pasea Estate, Road Town, Tortola (tel: 494-6430; fax: 494-5016; internet site: http://www.bvi.org).

Cable and Wireless (West Indies), PO Box 440, Road Town, Tortola (tel: 44-444; fax: 42-506).

Immigration Department, Road Town, Tortola (tel: 494-3701, 494-3471; fax: 494-4399).

Trade and Investment Promotion, Trade Department, Central Administration Complex, Road Town, Tortola (tel: 494-3701; fax: 494-5676).

VITV (Virgin Islands Television) Network, Butu Mountain, PO Box 118, Road Town, Tortola (tel: 494-8488/2257; fax: 494-5323).

ZBVI Radio, PO Box 78, Road Town, Tortola (tel: 494-2250; fax: 494-1139).

ZRODFM (radio station), PO Box 992, Road Town, Tortola (tel: 494-1037/5832; fax: 494-4564).

Internet sites

BVI homepage: www.britishvirginislands.com

Caribbean Wings - BVI Airlines: www.bvi-airlines.com

Islands on-line: www.islandsonline.com

The Island Sun: www.islandsun.com

Brunei

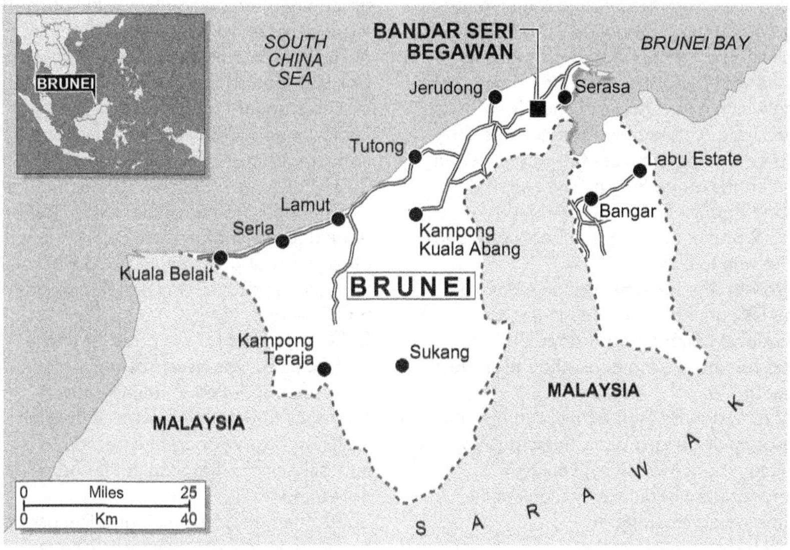

Brunei's oil reserves at the end of 2010 stood at 1.1 thousand million barrels, a lot of oil for a country with a population of less than 500,000. Yet this in itself could be a problem. The country's long-term challenge has to be to make the economy less dependent on oil and gas for when this finite resource runs out.

The *Asian Development Bank Economic Outlook 2011* reports that the increase in global price of oil in 2010 and 2011 will likely lead to moderately higher levels of production, but could also quicken the depletion of hydrocarbon reserves (unless offset by new discoveries).

A gradual transition to more diversified sources of growth will require progress in fostering a more conducive business environment for the private sector, improvements in the institutional capacity of the government, including service delivery, and finance sector development.

The authorities seem to have made a start: according to the *World Bank's Doing Business 2011* report, Brunei was in the top 10 countries to have improved its business environment over the previous year.

The country climbed 19 places in ease of starting a business (to 133 out of 183 countries) – though this is still a poor ranking – and ranks relatively well in ease of paying taxes (22) and trading across borders (52). However, the ranking remains low in investor protection (120), ease of obtaining credit (116), and ease of doing business (112).

As part of finance sector development, the government set up a Brunei Monetary Authority in January 2011 to improve regulation and supervision of the financial system.

According to the Asian Development Bank the economy recovered by an estimated 2 per cent in 2010 driven by higher production of oil and natural gas, stronger energy demand from traditional export markets such as Japan and South Korea, expansion of liquefied natural gas (LNG) production, and the opening of a new methanol plant in May 2010. Production of hydrocarbons, including LNG, accounts for nearly half of gross domestic product (GDP). Non-energy related private sector activity picked up moderately.

As the effect from the rebound in 2010 dissipates, economic growth is projected at the slightly higher than trend rates of 1.7 per cent in 2011 and 1.8 per cent in 2012, reflecting buoyant global energy markets and an increase in domestic demand. Oil and gas production is expected to rise moderately and the new methanol plant will contribute a full year's

KEY FACTS

Official name: Negara Brunei Darussalam (The Sultanate of Brunei)

Head of State: Sultan Haji Hassanal Bolkiah Mu'izzaddin Waddaulah, the Sultan and Yang Di-Pertuan of Brunei Darussalam (crowned Aug 1967)

Head of government: Sultan Haji Hassanal Bolkiah Mu'izzaddin Waddaulah, the Sultan and Yang Di-Pertuan of Brunei Darussalam

Ruling party: There is no ruling party.

Area: 5,765 square km

Population: 399,000 (2010)*

Capital: Bandar Seri Begawan

Official language: Behasa Melayu

Currency: Brunei dollar (B$) = 100 cents

Exchange rate: B$1.30 per US$ (Oct 2011) (the Brunei dollar is set at parity with the Singapore dollar.)

GDP per capita: US$31,239 (2010)

GDP real growth: 4.10% (2010)

GDP: US$13.00 billion (2010)

Labour force: 198,800 (2010)

Unemployment: 2.70% (2010)

Inflation: 0.50% (2010

Oil production: 172,000 bpd (2010)

Balance of trade: US$4.89 billion (2010)

* estimated figure

production to GDP. In the medium-term, the outlook for Brunei remains positive.

Risk assessment

Politics	Fair
Economy	Good
Regional stability	Good

COUNTRY PROFILE

Historical profile

1839 When an English explorer, James Brooke, arrived on the island of Borneo, he helped the Sultan to suppress an uprising against the rule of the Brunei Sultanate. As a reward for the role he played in quelling the rebellion, in 1841, the Pengiran Mahkota of Brunei made Brooke the Rajah of Sarawak on the north-west coast of Borneo (Sarawak is now the largest state in Malaysia). The British North Borneo Company began expanding its influence on the island.
1888 Brunei became a British protectorate, keeping the Sultanate out of the Malaysian confederacy. Brunei's monarch retained control over internal matters while the British took charge of external affairs.
1906 A treaty with Britain assured Brunei's status as a protectorate and the succession of the ruling dynasty. Executive power, including the right to advise the Sultan on all affairs except religion, was transferred to the British.
1929 Oil was discovered in the Seria field, ensuring the country's future prosperity.
1941–45 Brunei was occupied by the Japanese.
1959 An agreement was drawn up to allow Brunei internal self-government.
1962 In the run-up to Brunei's proposed amalgamation with Malaysia, the British pressured Sultan Omar Saifuddin into holding elections. The opposition Partai Rakyat Brunei (PRB) (Brunei People's Party) won a convincing victory, campaigning against unification, for complete independence from the UK and the creation of a constitutional monarchy. The Sultan's rejection of the result and his plans to unite with Malaysia led to an armed uprising which was quickly crushed (with British backing). A state of emergency was declared and political control was vested in the hands of the Sultan. The Sultan decided against union with Malaysia.
1979 Brunei concluded a treaty of friendship with the UK.
1984 Brunei became independent from the UK, under Sultan Haji Hassanal Bolkiah Mu'izzaddin Waddaulah, who had ruled since the abdication of his father in 1967.
1990 Sultan Bolkiah introduced his philosophy of Melaya Islam Berjaya (MIB) (Malay Islam Monarchy) which emphasises obedience and deters the questioning of authority.
1991 The sale of alcohol was forbidden. Nationals were required to wear Muslim garments.
1998 Prince al Muhtadee Billah, the Sultan's eldest son, was inaugurated as crown prince.
2000 Legal action was initiated against Prince Jefri Bolkiah, younger brother of the Sultan, for misusing US$15 billion while head of the state investment agency.
2002 Licences were awarded to two foreign consortiums, Royal Dutch/Shell and TotalFinaElf, to explore for oil deposits in Brunei's 200-mile Exclusive Economic Zone (EEZ) in the South China Sea.
2004 Parliament was reconvened for first time since 1984, with 21 appointed members.
2005 The Sultan sacked four members of his cabinet, replacing them with younger, more progressive candidates, and introduced reform measures. The constitution was changed so that the Sultan became infallible under the law. Parti Pembanguan (PP) (National Development Party) registered as a political party.
2007 Prince Jefri Bolkiah, former finance minister and brother of the Sultan, lost an appeal to the supreme court over the embezzlement of an estimated US$6 billion in public funds and was required to pay back the sum.
2008 A warrant for the arrest of Prince Jefri Bolkiah, was issued by a UK high court after he failed to attend a court summons to determine ownership of his exclusive luxury London home and to return billions of US dollars to the Brunei government.
2009 The new Sarawak legislative assembly building in Petra Jaya, was opened.
2010 In December, a border dispute that impeded oil exploration, was resolved when Brunei and Malaysia agreed to joint development of two exploration sites.
2011 On 7 July, the US trade representative warned Brunei that it risked being placed on a US Priority Watch List of intellectual property rights violators, due to continued infringements. The statement came at the start of Brunei's first legal copyright prosecution case.

KEY INDICATORS — Brunei

	Unit	2006	2007	2008	2009	2010
Population	m	0.38	0.39	0.39	*0.40	*0.40
Gross domestic product (GDP)	US$bn	11.56	12.39	14.60	10.50	13.00
GDP per capita	US$	30,626	32,167	37,053	26,325	31,239
GDP real growth	%	5.1	0.4	-1.5	-0.5	4.1
Inflation	%	0.2	0.4	2.7	1.8	0.5
Oil output	'000 bpd	221.0	194.0	175.0	168.0	172.0
Natural gas output	bn cum	12.3	12.3	12.1	11.4	12.2
Exports (fob) (goods)	US$m	7,627.0	7,691.6	10,697.7	7,171.9	–
Imports (fob) (goods)	US$m	1,585.9	1,991.8	2,857.7	2,282.4	–
Balance of trade	US$m	6,041.1	5,699.8	7,840.0	4,889.5	–
Current account	US$m	6,462.0	4,828.4	6,938.9	3,997.4	–
Total reserves minus gold	US$m	523.3	683.5	751.2	1,357.3	1,563.2
Foreign exchange	US$m	469.5	461.4	710.5	996.7	1,208.9
Exchange rate	per US$	1.54	1.45	1.42	1.45	1.36

* estimated figure

Political structure

Constitution

The Sultanate of Brunei (Negara Brunei Darussalam) became a fully independent sovereign state on 1 January 1984, when a ministerial system of government was established. Previously it had been a protectorate of Britain.

The Sultan rules partly by decree, and a state of emergency has been in force since a large-scale revolt in December 1962 which resulted in the suspension of sections of the constitution.

In lieu of democracy and to act as conduits of two-way communication between government and populace, there is a system of village and rural-district consultative councils.

In addition to the cabinet or council of ministers, three other councils advise the Sultan on the running of the country. These are:

- the Religious Council, which advises on all Islamic matters. The council also gives advice on legal matters; the Islamic court falls under its jurisdiction.

- the Privy Council, which is concerned with constitutional matters such as the exercising of royal prerogative and the awarding of honorary titles.
- the Council of Succession, which is empowered to determine the succession to the throne should the need arise.

In 2004 the Sultan signed a new constitution that will allow limited elections of up to 15 members to an expanded 45-seat legislative council; 30 council members will be appointed by the Sultan. No timetable for the elections was announced although a new parliament building was completed in 2009.

Independence date
1 January 1984

Form of state
Autocratic sultanate

The executive
The Sultan and Yang Di-Pertuan (paramount ruler) is the sovereign head of state and prime minister, retaining supreme executive authority. He is also head of the Islamic faith in Brunei and minister for defence.
A ministerial system of government was introduced following independence in 1984. The cabinet, presided over by the Sultan in his position as prime minister, consists mostly of members of the Sultan's family. Ministers are appointed to hold office at the Sultan's pleasure.

National legislature
The Legislative Council of 20 appointees was abolished at independence in 1984, ending a purely consultative role.
A General Assembly of 1,000 village chiefs from 150 villages and 35 *mukim* (village groups) took place in 1996, described as an expression of a 'grassroots political system' by the Sultanate. Chiefs were chosen by secret ballot of villagers but the Sultanate appointed the Assembly's advisers.

Legal system
Syariah (Islamic) courts were established in 1996 to handle family and criminal law. Their emphasis on publicly shaming offenders is designed to prevent anti-social and anti-Islamic activities.
Brunei has an independent legal system. It is a distinctive, separate branch of government, based on the English common law system. Apart from the *Syariah* courts, the legal system includes:
- the High Court, which hears appeals in criminal and civil matters from subordinate courts. It is presided over by the chief justice and various commissioners.
- the Court of Appeal, which hears appeals against High Court decisions. It consists of a president and two commissioners.
- subordinate courts, which have limited jurisdiction in civil and criminal cases, and are presided over by a chief magistrate.
- the Courts of Kathis, which deal with certain religious (Islamic) matters. These are marriage, divorce, inheritance and sexual crimes. The Courts of Kathis have jurisdiction over Muslims and supercede the civil law only in these matters.

Last elections
There have been no elections since 1962.

Political parties
There are three legally registered parties: Parti Perpaduan Kebangsaan Brunei (PPKB) (Brunei National Solidarity Party), Parti Kesedaran Rakyat Brunei (PAKAR) (Brunei People's Awareness Party) and Parti Pembangunan Bangsap (NDP) (National Development Party). As members of parliament, which was re-opened in 2004, are appointed, the parties have no representation at present. The constitution has been amended to allow election of a proportion of the parliament

Ruling party
There is no ruling party.

Main opposition party
No political parties are represented in the Legislative Council.

Population
399,000 (2010)*
Last census: August 2001: 332,844 (provisional)
Population density: 72 inhabitants per square km (2010)
Annual growth rate: 2.4 per cent 1994–2004 (WHO 2006)

Ethnic make-up
Indigenous (predominantly Malay) (69 per cent), Chinese (18 per cent), Indian (3 per cent), other (10 per cent). There are severe obstacles to further Chinese naturalisation and their emigration to China has been encouraged. The 50,000 Chinese living in Brunei play a negligible role in the country's political life, although they are vital to its economic success. Around a third of the Chinese population is naturalised. The same is true of the non-Malay indigenous population, which remains on the fringe of society but forms a crucial part of the workforce.

Religions
Sunni Islam (official faith and religion of all Malays). Members of the Chinese community are either Buddhist, Confucianist, Taoist or Christian. There are also ancient native religions.

Education
Primary schooling includes one year of compulsory pre-school education. Secondary education is divided into junior schools, lasting for three years between the ages of 12 and 15, and upper secondary schools, for another two years. Pre-university further education lasts for up to two years.
In 1985, the government established the University of Brunei Darussalam. In addition, there are two state-run teacher training colleges and six technical schools. If a university course is not available in Brunei, the government will pay for its students to study at a foreign university.
Education for expatriate children is provided by missionary schools, the International School and Chinese schools. All are fee paying and education at the International School follows a UK curriculum, but only caters for children up to the age of 12.
Literacy rate: 91 per cent, adult rates (World Bank)
Compulsory years: Five to 12

Health
The government has used its revenues from oil to provide one of the best healthcare systems in Asia. Health services are free for Brunei citizens, although there is a nominal fee for hospital and dentist treatment.
The healthcare system is based on health clinics, which provide primary care and include mobile clinics to reach the most isolated regions, health centres and district hospitals. The central hospital in Bandar Seri Begawan (Raja Isteri Pengiran Anak Saleha) has 550 beds and provides diagnostic and therapeutic facilities for the whole country. There are also government-operated hospitals in Tutong, Temburong and Kuala Belait. A Flying Medical Service reaches areas inaccessible by road. British Shell Petroleum (BSP) has its own private facilities in Seria.
The government is committed to increase its expenditure towards health care and building more clinics. Brunei continues to rely on expatriate doctors to run its health system. Government health surveys have shown that local doctors have made up only 10 per cent, and local dentists 32 per cent, of the medical workforce in the country.

HIV/Aids
HIV prevalence: 0.1 per cent aged 15–49 in 2003 (World Bank)
Life expectancy: 77 years, 2004 (WHO 2006)
Fertility rate/Maternal mortality rate: 2.4 births per woman, 2004 (WHO 2006)
Child (under 5 years) mortality rate (per 1,000): 5.0 per 1,000 live births (World Bank)

Welfare
The Employees Trust Fund or Tabung Amanah Pekerja (Tap) provides membership to a providence fund that is open to all government workers and private sector employees. The scheme requires

compulsory contributions from both the employer and the employee at a contribution rate of 5 per cent each. Universal old age pensions are granted those who have been residents for 30 years.
The ministry of culture, youth and sport oversees the distribution of pensions to citizens not holding contributory pensions and also provides welfare provisions for needy families and the handicapped. The government subsidises housing and food. Under the National Housing Scheme (NHS), the state grants housing to those who have lived under Temporary Occupation Licences (TOL). The Housing Scheme for Landless Citizens also gives land title deeds to those who have been occupying land under TOL.

Main cities

Bandar Seri Begawan (capital, estimated population 78,000 in 2003), Kuala Belait (27,800), Seria (oil field) (23,400).

Languages spoken

The national education system is formally bilingual for all, in Malay and English. Chinese is spoken; English is the principal commercial language.

Official language/s

Behasa Melayu

Media

With media ownership in the hands of, or controlled by, the royal family or if privately owned where self-censorship for political or religious reasons is widespread press freedom is severely curtailed. Legal sanctions against journalist can be up to three years imprisonment for 'false' reporting. The US-based media watchdog, Freedom House, rated Brunei as not free, with virtual no criticism of the government allowed.

Press

Publications that provide a variety of views and information beyond anything the newspapers controlled by the Sultan's family are able to achieve are either *The Straits Times* or Chinese publications produced in Sarawak and Singapore.
Dailies: In Malay, *Media Permata* (www.brunei-online.com/mp), in English, *Borneo Bulletin* (www.brunei-online.com/bb), and the independent *The Brunei Times* (www.bt.com.bn), which reports on international news.
Weeklies: In Malay, the official government newspaper *Pelita Brunei* is published every Wednesday, and in English, the *Brunei Darussalam Newsletter* (www.information.gov.bn/bdnewsletter) is a fortnightly publication and is also produced by the government.

Broadcasting

The only broadcasting organisation is Radio Televisyen Brunei (RTB) (www.rtb.gov.bn), which is government operated, under the control of the Department of Broadcasting and Information.
Radio: RTB (www.rtb.gov.bn) operates five radio stations, including an international service. There are several private stations broadcasting in Brunei but only Kristal FM (www.dst-group.com) is a domestic station; all others originate in Malaysia.
Television: RTB (www.rtb.gov.bn) operates channels 5 and 8 as well as an RBT International, broadcast via a satellite service. Foreign cable and satellite networks provide the only alternatives to the state-run broadcaster. Viewers with access to the internet may access foreign TV.

Advertising

Apart from traditional forms of advertising, new media has opened up opportunities for personalised advertising through emails and mobile/cell SMS texts.

News agencies

BruDirect (in English): www.brudirect.com
Brunei News (in English): www.bruneinews.net

Economy

The Brunei economy is dominated by the hydrocarbon extraction sector, which provided 70.1 per cent of GDP in 2008, when global prices for oil were at an all-time high and exports accounted for US$10.3 billion (out of US$10.7 billion total exports). The non-hydrocarbon sector is led by government services, construction and financial services. A manufacturing sector is deficient with over 70 per cent of all imports being manufactured goods, vehicles and parts and machinery; over 10 per cent of imports were food and live animals in 2008. Brunei is one of richest countries by GDP per capita of the Asean community but its non-hydrocarbon economy did not expand significantly in 2008 at the same time as hydrocarbon production was falling; although natural gas production had increased in 2007–08, it fell in 2009. GDP growth was 0.2 per cent in 2007, which fell into recession in 2008 at -1.9 per cent. The economy picked up in 2009 although it still remained in negative growth of -0.5 per cent. Brunei's highest GPD per capita was at a record high of US$36,707 in 2008, but it fell to US$26,325 in 2009.
The Brunei Investment Agency (BIA) invests around 50 per cent of the hydrocarbon income in an international portfolio; the exact value of these assets is secret.
Key to Brunei's policy of transforming Brunei into an offshore financial centre and tourist destination is economic diversification and an increase in foreign investment to maintain growth and long-term viability. Brunei's ambition is to become a service hub for trade and tourism (SHuTT) to take advantage of regional economic integration. Economic development has concentrated on infrastructure, roads, schools and numerous government buildings. In addition to promoting tourism, Brunei intends to increase the financial sector and energy-intensive industries, especially petrochemicals.
Major obstacles to growth include labour shortages, as many local unemployed workers are unwilling to do manual work. Complex bureaucracy and high wages are seen as deterrents to foreign investment. Brunei is a net receiver of migrant workers, although measures limit the length of their stay.

External trade

As the Association of Southeast Asian Nations (Asean) moves towards the creation of a comprehensive free trade area, it has already signed FTAs with China, Australia and New Zealand, India, Japan and South Korea. Brunei also belongs to the Asia Pacific Economic Co-operation (Apec) organisation
Most items can be imported under an open general licence. There are some restricted goods which require special licences, including used vehicles, certain listed drugs, livestock, some foodstuffs and gambling equipment (eg fruit machines). The government is encouraging exports from the non-hydrocarbons sector, which includes small-scale manufacturing in textiles, furniture and food processing. Primary production includes timber, marine and agricultural produce. Some items are heavily subsidised by the government and their export is consequently restricted. Such goods include rice, petrol, kerosene and diesel fuels as well as cigarettes.

Imports

Brunei's limited industrial and agricultural base requires a range of principal imports including machinery, transport equipment, manufactured goods, food and chemicals.
Main sources: Singapore (typically 34 per cent of total), Malaysia (19 per cent), Japan (8 per cent).

Exports

Crude oil (typically 50 per cent of the total exports) and liquefied natural gas (around 40 per cent) and refined products dominate the export schedule.
Main destinations: Japan (typically 44 per cent of exports), Indonesia (23 per cent), Australia (12 per cent).

Agriculture

Farming

The agricultural sector plays only a minor role in Brunei's economy, typically accounting for less than 3 per cent of GDP and employing 2 per cent of the workforce. Brunei has to import 80 per cent of its food needs. Only around 15

per cent of the total land area is cultivated or under grazing.
Brunei's agricultural base consists mainly of small farms growing rice and vegetables. Farming is primarily a part-time occupation. The main crops are rice, vegetables, arable crops and fruits. A wide range of tropical fruit varieties are produced, but in low volumes. Vegetable production is intensive and concentrated in the fertile alluvial plain close to the urban centres. With smallholding rice production declining, the government has initiated a pilot large-scale rice mechanisation project aimed at increasing output; it is hoped that once fully mechanised, 30 per cent of Brunei's rice needs will be met by domestic production.
Government attempts to increase the importance of the sector and moves towards self-sufficiency are hampered by the population's lack of interest in outdoor, manual work. Another disincentive is that farming is perceived as less lucrative than other areas of the economy, so reducing further the likelihood of significant small-scale development. High wage costs mean that the expansion of larger-scale production depends very much on increased mechanisation rather than labour-intensive techniques, unless large scale immigrant labour can be guaranteed.

Fishing

Since 1990, the government has attempted to expand the fishing industry. The ministry of industry and primary resources granted more fishing licences to match the extension of the country's fishing boundary to 200 miles offshore. Several other sites were located for aquaculture projects. The government also improved the distribution system to ensure that the local catch reaches more remote areas of the country. The trawling industry has also been developed. The important trawling areas are Pulau Tambisan and north of Sandakan (Marchesa and Labuk Bay).
Typical annual fish production is over 1,600 tonnes and other seafood over 400 tonnes.

Forestry

About 70 per cent of Brunei is covered by primary and secondary rain forest; 37 per cent of the country is designated as a national Forest Reserve. There is growing concern locally about the conservation of the forests and the environment, and exports of timber and logs are now strictly limited. Consequently timber production of logs and sawnwood is for domestic consumption only. Some natural rubber is produced. The government hopes to develop the forestry sector as part of its diversification strategy, but investment opportunities are limited by legal restrictions. Private companies wishing to become involved in the sector must have local business participation of 51 per cent.

Industry and manufacturing

The industrial sector, including hydrocarbons, accounts for approximately 44 per cent of GDP and employs almost a quarter of the workforce. The industrial structure, long dependent on export of oil and gas, consists mainly of small-scale enterprises. Apart from the energy and construction sectors, Brunei's industrial base is limited. The small domestic market, high wage costs, bureaucracy and poor co-ordination between government departments has deterred both local and foreign investment.
Despite the government's emphasis on diversification, the industrial sector remains underdeveloped. The manufacturing sector is small and consists mainly of the production of materials for the construction sector, petroleum refining, food-processing and garment manufacture. There are also factories producing canned food, mineral water and dairy products.
Areas the government wants to develop include the manufacture of furniture, pottery, tiles, cement, chemicals, plywood and glass. As part of the industrial development programme a number of industrial estates have been established. These include a 40 hectare site near Bandar Seri Begawan and the Beribi Light Industrial Complex, which consists of four blocks including textiles, food and electrical manufacturers.
The government is eager to promote the development of a financial centre and of export-oriented, value-added industries. Investment policy is open and flexible and welcomes investors, both local and foreign, in any productive industrial activity which furthers diversification.

Tourism

Tourism is relatively undeveloped, although the government is actively trying to promote the sector. Efforts have been made to attract visitors to such attractions as the 20ha Sungai Basong National Park at Bukit Bendera and the Jerudong Park Playground.
Brunei is marketing itself as a service hub for trade and tourism (ShuTT), using the country as a stop-off point for international travellers.
Despite areas of extensive natural beauty that could be visited by tourists, expansion of the sector is hampered by strict rules affecting clothing and alcohol and the difficulties associated with travelling caused by the relative scarcity of taxi drivers.

Environment

Brunei is prone to occasional typhoons, earthquakes and flooding. Environmental management is overseen by the ministry of development, ministry of health and the ministry of industry and primary resources. Brunei is party to major international environmental agreements that include endangered species, ozone layer protection, ship pollution and whaling.

Mining

Brunei possesses only limited raw materials. Its principal resources are clay and silica in the form of 20 million tonnes of high quality beach sands at Tutong.

Hydrocarbons

Total oil reserves were 1.1 billion barrels in 2010, with a production rate of 172,000 barrels per day (bpd), the majority of which is exported. Revenues from hydrocarbons make up over 50 per cent of GDP and 90 per cent of Brunei's exports and gives the country its international status.
Brunei has seven offshore fields of which the largest, Champion, contains about 40 per cent of total reserves. There are believed to be significant undeveloped oil reserves in the existing fields and these will be tapped by advanced technology and modern drilling methods. Brunei, along with China, Taiwan, Malaysia, The Philippines and Vietnam, claims the potentially oil-rich Spratly Islands. In June 2010, an agreement was reached between the governments of Brunei and Malaysia to share the revenue of two disputed oil blocks in territorial waters. The dispute had led to international oil companies declining to invest in exploration within the offshore waters while the countries haggled over its sovereign ownership.
Proven natural gas reserves were 300 billion cubic metres in 2010 with production at 12.2 billion cubic metres (cum). Brunei is south-east Asia's fourth-largest liquefied natural gas (LNG) producer with 8.83 billion cum in 2010, the majority of which is exported to Japan and the remainder to South Korea.

Energy

Total installed generating capacity was 759MW in 2006. All Brunei's electricity is produced in gas-fired power stations. Electricity demand is expanding by 7–10 per cent annually, making long-term electricity development a priority. A programme of electricity expansion has included the construction of a 110MW power plant in Tutong, opened in 2008, featuring new, more efficient combine cycle turbines.
Over 99 per cent of the population has access to electricity. The government agency Department of Electrical Services

(DES), is responsible for generation, transmission and distribution and sets the standards for usage in public buildings and installation maintenance. The private, independent power utility Berakas Power Company (BPC) also supplies electricity to the grid, although the grid is not integrated and is divided into three networks. Metering and cable supply has been privatised in order to introduce competition and efficiencies.

Banking and insurance

The regulatory system is based on the 1906 British Banking Act, although various modifications have been made to bring it up-to-date with modern banking requirements.

The fourth pillar of the Brunei International Financial Centre (BIFC), the International Insurance and Takaful Order, was set up, designed to provide for foreign investors in the banking scene. This will enable Brunei to have a fully operational foreign offshore banking sector.

The Royal Bank of Canada (RBC) became the first foreign bank to operate in the BIFC. RBC is focussing its activities on private bank services for the rich and assisting the management of Islamic funds.

Three local banks dominate the domestic banking sector – the Islamic Bank of Brunei (IBB), Baiduri Bank (BB) and the Development Bank of Brunei. Thw IBB conducts its savings and loans operations in accordance with Islamic law. The Sultan and his family own 80 per cent of IBB's paid up capital, Japan's Daiichi Kangyo Bank holds the other 20 per cent.

The three largest foreign banks in Brunei are Citibank, the Hong Kong and Shanghai Banking Corporation (HSBC) and Standard Chartered Bank. Other foreign banks include the Overseas Union Bank, Malayan Banking and the United Malayan Banking Corporation.

Central bank

Brunei has no central bank; the main duties are carried out by the ministry of finance.

Main financial centre

Bandar Seri Begawan

Time

GMT plus eight hours

Geography

Brunei lies 442km north of the equator on the northern coast of the island of Borneo. It consists of two wedges of land, within the Malaysian province of Sarawak and with the South China sea in the north. The country is divided into separate administrative districts: Brunei/Muara, Tutong and Seria/Belait in the western section, and Temburong, which makes up the entire eastern section of the country. Although there is a mountainous region in the eastern half of the country, Brunei mostly consists of a low-lying coastal plain. The highest peak is Bukit Pagon (1,841 metres). Brunei has four main rivers – the Belait, Tutong, Brunei and Temburong. Approximately 75 per cent of the total land area is covered by tropical rain forest.

Hemisphere

Northern

Climate

The climate is typically equatorial. Humidity averages 82 per cent, and daily temperatures range between 24 and 31 degrees Celsius (C). The rainy season lasts from September to January, although rainfall can be expected throughout the year. It can reach up to 7,500mm in the interior, but on the coast it tends to average around 2,500mm. The driest months are from January to April.

Dress codes

Lightweight clothing is suitable. In deference to the Islamic culture, Western business women should dress modestly at all times.

Entry requirements

Passports

Required by all. Must be valid for six months.

Visa

Required by all. Exceptions are granted for short stays of up to 14 or 30 days to nationals of certain countries and 90 days for US citizens (see www.mfa.gov.bn for details). Business visas require a sponsorship letter from a local company or government entity (for details see www.immigration.gov.bn/visiting.htm).

Prohibited entry

Holders of Israeli passports.

Currency advice/regulations

There are no restritions on the import of foreign and local currency, with the exception of the Singapore dollar, which is limited to B$1,000 equivalent, and Indian and Indonesian banknotes, which are prohibited. Export of local currency is restricted to B$1,000, while the export of foreign currency is limited to the amount imported. The Brunei dollar is at par with the Singapore dollar and the currencies are interchangeable in both countries.

Customs

Two litres of alcohol and 12 cans of beer; 200 cigarettes and 250g tobacco; 60ml perfume and 250ml eau de toilette allopwed duty free.

Prohibited imports

Trafficking and illegal importation of controlled drugs are very serious offences carrying the death penalty.

Health (for visitors)

Health services are not free for visitors, as it is for Brunei citizens, but there is only a very nominal charge for permanent residents and expatriate government officials and their dependants. Malaria has been eradicated in Brunei. Certificates of vaccination for both cholera and yellow fever are advisable. Normal precautions should be taken for food and drink. The authorities are becoming concerned over the growing amount of drug abuse.

Mandatory precautions

Vaccination certificates for yellow fever are required for travellers over one year of age travelling from an infected area.

Advisable precautions

Chest X-ray and blood film examination for malaria are required for the issue and renewal of labour permits as Brunei is malaria-free. Immunisations are recommended for hepatitis A, polio, tetanus, typhoid, and also advice should be sought regarding diphtheria, hepatitis A, Japanese encephalitis and TB. There is a risk of rabies.

Hotels

Rooms in major hotels have air-conditioning, telephones, TV, bathrooms and showers. A 10 per cent service charge is usual.

Credit cards

Major credit cards are accepted at some hotels and at some shops.

Public holidays (national)

Friday and Sunday are non-working days, if a holiday falls on these, then Saturday or Monday are substituted. Banks close on 30 June and 30 December.

Fixed dates

1 Jan (New Year's Day), 23 Feb (National Day), 31 May (Armed Forces Day), 15 Jul (Sultan's Birthday), 25 Dec (Christmas Day).

Variable dates

Chinese New Year (Jan–Feb), Hari Raya Aidiladha, Hari Raya Aidilfitra, Islamic New Year, Birth of the Prophet, Ascension of the Prophet, First day of Ramadan, Revelation of the Quran Anniversary.

Islamic year 1433 (26 Nov 2011–14 Nov 2012): The Islamic year contains 354 or 355 days, with the result that Muslim feasts advance by 10–12 days against the Gregorian calendar. Dates of feasts vary according to the sighting of the new moon, so cannot be forecast exactly.

Working hours

Banking

Mon–Fri: 0900–1500; Sat: 0900–1100. Many banks close during lunch hour.

Business

Mon–Thur: 0745–1215, 1330–1630; Sat: 0800–1200.

Government

Mon–Thu, Sat: 0745–1215, 1330–1630. Fasting month (Ramadan) 0800–1400.

Shops
Mon–Sat: 0800–1900/2100, 1000–2200 (most shopping centres). Post offices: Mon–Thu, Sat: 0730–1600; Fri: 0830–0930.

Telecommunications
Mobile/cell phones
There is a 900 GSM service available along with a G3 (2100) service.

Electricity supply
230V AC, with 3-pin round or 3-pin square plug fittings.

Weights and measures
Metric system.

Social customs/useful tips
The public sale and consumption of alcohol is prohibited by law. Muslims do not eat pork or drink alcohol. The right hand should be used for offering or receiving anything, from food to money. Refusal of offered refreshment is discourteous.
To point with the index finger is also considered discourteous; the thumb of the right hand should be used instead with the four fingers folded beneath it. To call a taxi or attract someone's attention, wave the whole hand with the palm facing downwards. Do not smack the fist of your right hand into your left palm; it has a different meaning in Brunei to that of Western countries. It is not customary to shake hands with members of the opposite sex. When visiting a mosque, shoes should first be removed. Do not pass in front of a person at prayer, or touch the Qur'an. Women should cover their heads, and not have their knees or arms exposed.

Security
There is no major problem with petty crime in Brunei.

Getting there
Air
National airline: Royal Brunei Airlines (RBA)
International airport/s: Brunei International Airport (BWN), 10km north of Bandar Seri Begawan, with car hire and taxi service.
Airport tax: Departures to Singapore and Malaysia B$5. All other international departures B$12.
Surface
Road: Road connections between Brunei and Sarawak (Malaysia) are good. There is a bitumen road between Miri and Kuala Belait.
Water: Most sea traffic is handled by the deep-water port at Muara, while the smaller port at Kuala Belait handles shallow-draught vessels.
Main port/s: Muara (27km from Bandar Seri Begawan), Kuala Belait, Lumut.

Getting about
National transport
Road: The total road network is around 2,500km. Brunei has 1,500km of main roads, 500km of district roads and 500km of unpaved road surface. There is no road connecting the Temburong district but a water taxi service is available. A main highway links Bandar Seri Begawan with Kuala Belait and Seria, with a road linking Muara and Tutong providing access to western districts.
Buses: There are six bus lines in Bandar Seri Begawan. Services operate betwen Bandar Seri Begawan and Kuala Belait and Seria, and also serve rural areas. Buses run from 0630–1800.
Water: The Brunei, Belait and Tutong rivers are the main inland waterways and are principally used for passenger traffic. River-going vessels use the old port at Bandar Seri Begawan. Large river taxis operate to the Temburong district; service starts at 0745 and ends at 1600.
River taxi and boat services are also available to Limbang in Sarawak and Labuan in Sabah.
City transport
The City Transport Service (CTS) is the easiest way to travel in the city. Fixed fare within the CTS zone.
Taxis: From the airport to the city centre, metered taxis are in operation 0700–0030. Metered taxis are also available from hotels and shopping centres near the capital to all parts of Brunei, but are otherwise scarce. Tipping is not usual.
Buses, trams & metro: From the airport to the city centre, buses operate 0630—1800, every 15—20 minutes.
Car hire
Self-drive and chauffeur-driven cars are available from major hotels and the airport. An international driving licence is required.

BUSINESS DIRECTORY

The addresses listed below are a selection only. While World of Information makes every endeavour to check these addresses, we cannot guarantee that changes have not been made, especially to telephone numbers and area codes. We would welcome any corrections.

Telephone area codes
The international direct dialling (IDD) code for Brunei is +673, followed by subscriber's number.

Useful telephone numbers
Police: 993
Fire: 995
Ambulance: 991
Flight information: 331-747
Directory enquiries: 0213
International calls: 000

Chambers of Commerce
Brunei Darussalam International Chamber of Commerce and Industry, PO Box 2246, Bandar Seri Bagawan 1922 (tel: 2 228382; fax: 2 228389).

Brunei Malay Chamber of Commerce, PO Box 1099, Bandar Seri Begawan 8672 (tel: 2 422752; fax: 2 422753).

Chinese Chamber of Commerce, 72 Jalan Roberts, PO Box 281, Bandar Seri Begawan 8670 (tel: 2 235494; fax: 2 235492).

National Chamber of Commerce and Industry, 144 2nd Floor Jalan Pemancha, Bandar Seri Begawan BS8711 (tel: 2 243321; fax: 2 228737).

Banking
Baiduri Bank Berhad (BB), 145 Jalan Pemancha, PO Box 2220, Bandar Seri Begawan 1922 (tel: 233-233; fax: 235-722).

Citibank, 12-15 Bangunan Darussalam, Bandar Seri Begawan (tel: 243-983; fax: 225-704).

Development Bank of Brunei Bhd, 1st Floor RBA Plaza, Jalan Sultan Bandar Seri Begawan 2085 (tel: 233-430; fax: 233-429).

HSBC, cnr Jalan Sultan and Jalan Pemancha, PO Box 59, Jalan Sultan, Bandar Seri Begawan (tel: 242-305/10, 242-204; fax: 241-316).

Islamic Bank of Brunei Berhad (IBB), lot 159, Jalan Pemancha, Bandar Seri Begawan (tel: 235-686/7; fax: 235-722).

Malayan Banking Berhad, 148 Jalan Pemancha, Bandar Seri Begawan 2085 (tel: 242-494).

Overseas Union Bank (OUB), Unit G5, RBA Plaza, Jalan Sultan, Bandar Seri Begawan 2089 (tel: 225-477; fax: 240-792).

Sime Bank Berhad, Unit G 02, Kompleks Yayasan Sultan Haji Hassanal Bolkiah , Bandar Seri Begawan (tel: 222-516; fax: 237-487).

Standard Chartered Bank, 51-55 Jalan Sultan, Bandar Seri Begawan (tel: 242-386; fax: 242-390).

Central bank
Brunei Currency and Monetray Board, Simpang 295, Jalan Kebangsaan, PO Box 660, Bandar Seri Begawan BS 8670 (tel: 238-3999; fax: 238-2232; e-mail: bcb@brunet.bn).

Travel information
Brunei Travel Service, Sdn Bhd, Bandar Seri Begawan (tel: 225-664).

Department of Civil Aviation, Ministry of Communications, Brunei International Airport, 2015 (tel: 330-483, 330-142/3; fax: 331-7066).

Royal Brunei Airlines, PO Box 737, Bandar Seri Begawan 1907 (tel: 240-500, 242-222; fax: 244-737).

Tourist information (on arrival level at airport) (tel: 331-747).

Ministries

Ministry of Communications, Old Airport, Berakas, Bandar Seri Begawan 1150 (tel: 383-838; fax: 380-127).

Ministry of Culture, Youth and Sports, Jalan Residency, Bandar Seri Begawan 1200 (tel: 240-585; fax: 241-620).

Ministry of Defence, Bolkiah Garrison, Bandar Seri Begawan 1110 (tel: 230-130; fax: 230-110).

Ministry of Development, Old Airport, Berakas, Bandar Seri Begawan 1190 (tel: 241-911; fax: 240-271).

Ministry of Education, Old Airport, Berakas, Bandar Seri Begawan 1170 (tel: 244-233; fax: 240-250).

Ministry of Finance, Bandar Seri Begawan 1130 (tel: 242-405; fax: 241-829).

Ministry of Foreign Affairs, Jalan Subok, Bandar Seri Begawan 1120 (tel: 241-177; fax: 224-709).

Ministry of Health, Old Airport, Berakas, Bandar Seri Begawan 1210 (tel: 226-640; fax: 240-980).

Ministry of Home Affairs, Bandar Seri Begawan 1140 (tel: 223-225).

Ministry of Industry and Primary Resources, Old Airport, Berakas, Bandar Seri Begawan 1220 (tel: 224-822; fax: 244-811).

Ministry of Law, Jalan Tutong, Bandar Seri Begawan 1160 (tel: 244-872; fax: 223-100).

Ministry of Religious Affairs, Bandar Seri Begawan 1180 (tel: 242-565).

Other useful addresses

Asean Investment Promotion Agency, Ministry of Industry and Primary Resources, Bandar Seri Begawan 1220 (tel: 238-119; fax: 238-811).

British High Commission, 2.01, 2nd Floor, Block D, Kompleks Bangunan Yayasan Sultan Haji Hassanal Bolkiah, Jalan Pretty, PO Box 2197, Bandar Seri Begawan 8711 (tel: 222-2231; fax: 223-4315).

Brunei Darussalam Embassy (USA), 3520 International Court, NW, Washington DC 20008 (tel: (+1-202) 237-1838; fax: (+1-202) 885-0560; e-mail: info@bruneiembassy.org).

Brunei Industrial Development Authority (BINA), Km 8, Jalan Gadong, BE 1118 (tel: 444100; fax: 423300; e-mail: bruneibina@brunet.bn).

Controller of Customs and Excise, Jabatan Customs and Excise Di-Raja, Bandar Seri Begawan (tel: 222-342).

Economic Development Board, Ministry of Finance, 2nd Floor, RBA Plaza, Jalan Sultan, Bandar Seri Begawan 2085 (postal address: Locked Bag 15, Bandar Seri Begawan 1999) (tel: 229-269; fax: 241-417).

University of Brunei Darussalam, Gadong, Bandar Seri Begawan (tel: 227-001).

US Embassy, 3rd Floor, Teck Guan Plaza, cnr Jalan Sultan and Jalan MacArthur, Bandar Seri Begawan (tel: 229-670; fax: 225-293).

Internet sites

Brunei Darussalam homepage: www.brunet.bn

Government of Brunei: www.brunei.gov.bn

Bulgaria

Bulgaria has certainly come a long way from the turbulent political and economic transition of the 1990s to a modern market economy. Today, Bulgaria (with just over 7.5 million people) is an upper middle-income economy – in 2009, its GDP per capita was US$6,423. But it hasn't been easy. A decade of reforms – some of them tough – preceded its 2007 accession to the European Union (EU). Drawing on World Bank policy advice, Bulgaria established prudent macro-economic policies and fiscal stability and it increased revenue collection. Up to 2007, Bulgaria had enjoyed a decade of sustained economic growth, but the global financial crisis of 2008–09 had a serious impact. In 2011 the Bulgarian economy has begun to recover well, with positive prospects for achieving smart, sustainable and inclusive growth

The economy

Bulgaria's recovery from crisis has been marked by remarkable adjustment. After contracting 5.5 per cent in 2009, the economy stabilised in 2010 growing 0.2 per cent on the back of strong export growth. Bulgaria's exports, which benefited from revived global demand and high international commodity prices, recovered to pre-crisis levels. Imports, however, remained subdued in line with depressed domestic demand stemming from high unemployment and economic uncertainty. The accompanying adjustment in external imbalances reduced the current account deficit from 23 per cent to 1 per cent of gross domestic product (GDP) between 2008 and 2010. With considerable slack in the economy, core inflation averaged one per cent in 2010, but rising energy and food prices drove average headline inflation to 3 per cent.

Strong policy action and large fiscal and financial sector buffers also helped Bulgaria weather the crisis well. Past fiscal surpluses saved in the fiscal reserve account boosted international reserves, underpinned confidence in the currency board arrangement and financed recent deficits (3.9 per cent in 2010, cash-basis). This combined with the prompt action to adjust government spending to the decline in revenues contained the fiscal deficit and debt and created the conditions for a

KEY FACTS

Official name: Republika Bulgaria (Republic of Bulgaria)

Head of State: President-elect Rosen Plavneliev (Gerb) (from 30 Oct 2011; due to take office on 23 Jan 2012)

Head of government: Prime Minister Boyko Metodiev Borisov (Gerb) (from 27 Jul 2009)

Ruling party: Grazhdani za Evropeysko Razvitie na Balgariya (Gerb) (Citizens for European Development of Bulgaria) (from 5 Jul 2009)

Area: 110,994 square km

Population: 7.60 million (2009)

Capital: Sofia

Official language: Bulgarian

Currency: Lev (Lev) = 100 stotinki

Exchange rate: Lev1.46 per US$ (Oct 2011)

GDP per capita: US$6,334 (2010)

GDP real growth: 0.20% (2010)

GDP: US$47.70 billion (2010)

Labour force: 3.40 million (2010)

Unemployment: 10.20% (2010)

Inflation: 3.00% (2010)

Balance of trade: -US$3.22 billion (2010)

NOTA

23 and 30 October 2011 following the first round and runoff presidential election Rosen Plavneliev (Gerb) won with 40.11 per cent and 52.58 per cent of the vote respectively, beating Ivaylo Kaflin (BSP) with 28.96 per cent and 47.42 per cent respectively.

quick exit from EU excessive deficit procedure. In the financial sector, non-performing loans had risen to 12.9 per cent by end-March 2011. However, the capital adequacy ratio remained high at 17.7 per cent and the banking system was profitable. Bulgaria's high level of capital and conservative regulatory regime going into the crisis enabled the Bulgarian National Bank (the central bank) to ease its regulatory requirements allowing banks to utilise some of their capital and provisioning buffers to absorb losses.

The recovery is expected to broaden to domestic demand. In 2011, real GDP is projected to rise to 3 per cent as continued strong export growth stimulates investment. As unemployment gradually declines, consumption will also gain momentum allowing real GDP to recover its pre-crisis levels in 2012. Over the medium term, growth is expected to recover to about 4 per cent reflecting the rebalancing between domestic and external demand. Against this backdrop, the current account deficit is expected to be contained to moderate levels. In the longer run, absent reforms, structural bottlenecks and population aging could constrain growth potential.

The recovery in consumption, however, is held back by increases in inflation and precautionary savings amid heightened regional uncertainty. As a result, imports remain subdued and the current account deficit is expected to move closer to balance. Higher food and fuel prices are projected to increase headline inflation to 4.25 per cent in 2011, before easing to 3 per cent in 2012. Given the moderate speed of recovery and ongoing shift away from non-tradeables to tradeable sectors, a quick reduction in unemployment is unlikely.

While there is scope for better-than-expected outcomes, risks are tilted to the downside. Growth would be higher if exports surprise, confidence improves to allow consumption to revive strongly, or if the absorption of EU funds exceeds expectations. Such a strengthening in demand, if accompanied by a return of large scale capital inflows, could test the correction in the current account. However, at this juncture, downside risks – largely related to the external environment – dominate and have a greater potential impact. Growth would be lower and the recovery more protracted if world oil prices were to rise further or if growth in Western Europe were to falter and reduce export demand. Tensions in the financial and sovereign debt markets of the euro area periphery could also impact on Bulgaria, but its international and fiscal reserves constitute critical buffers to counter such a tail risk.

Organised crime

Not far behind Greece and Romania, according to Transparency International, Bulgaria can claim to be the most corrupt member state of the EU, ranking 57th out of the 183 countries surveyed in 2011. Since his assumption of power in 2009, Bulgaria's maverick Prime Minister Boyko Borisov can at least say he has begun to make inroads into Bulgaria's organised crime. The colourful Mr Borisov can claim to be a man of the people, if only because of his interesting background; he worked, inter alia, as a fire-fighter and judo coach before becoming the mayor of Bulgaria's capital city Sofia and later rising through the political ranks to the leadership of the centre right party Grazhdani za Evropeysko Razvitie na Balgariya (Gerb) (Citizens for European Development of Bulgaria) and finally gaining the post of prime minister in the 2009 elections.

Mr Borisov's time in office has coincided with a wave of arrests of some of those suspected of involvement in organised crime. Styling himself 'Batman', the prime minister has overseen the arrest of colourfully named gangs such as The Killers (reported to be available for contract killings), The Impudent (kidnappings) and The Crocodiles (highway robberies). Mr Borisov named his anti-gang campaign Operation Octopus. A report published by the ministry of the interior in 2010 claimed that the leaders of 50 gangs (out of an estimated total of 223) had been arrested. According to the ministry, this still left some 1,200 gangsters still plying their trade. A high profile illegal activity is the smuggling of cigarettes (estimated to be worth some US$307 million annually), followed by drugs (US$123 million) and the sex trade (US$84 million). If Mr Borisov is Batman, his arch enemy is one Alexei Petrov, rumoured to be the brains behind a web of illegal activities. Nicknamed 'The Tractor' Mr Petrov also harbours political, even presidential ambitions. Mr Petrov was arrested in early 2011 on charges that included attempted murder, racketeering and extortion. Whether the charges against Mr Petrov can hold, however, is a different matter. Key witnesses appeared reluctant to come forward.

KEY INDICATORS — Bulgaria

	Unit	2006	2007	2008	2009	2010
Population	m	7.68	7.65	7.61	7.60	*7.53
Gross domestic product (GDP)	US$bn	31.69	39.61	52.00	47.10	47.70
GDP per capita	US$	4,120	5,186	6,857	6,223	6,334
GDP real growth	%	6.2	6.2	6.0	-5.0	0.2
Inflation	%	7.4	7.5	12.0	2.5	3.0
Unemployment	%	9.0	6.9	5.6	6.8	10.2
Industrial output	% change	8.3	14.0	3.0	30.3	–
Agricultural output	% change	-1.9	-29.7	24.6	5.6	–
Coal output	mtoe	4.6	8.1	4.8	4.5	4.8
Exports (fob) (goods)	US$m	15,101.0	18,523.5	22,585.5	16,502.7	20,608.2
Imports (fob) (goods)	US$m	23,179.0	28,664.9	35,450.3	22,176.2	23,825.6
Balance of trade	US$m	-8,078.0	-10,141.4	-12,864.8	-5,673.5	-3,217.4
Current account	US$m	-4,940.0	-8,464.0	-12,073.0	-4,339.6	-578.0
Total reserves minus gold	US$m	10,943.0	16,477.9	16,815.5	17,127.3	15,420.5
Foreign exchange	US$m	10,892.1	16,424.2	16,757.4	16,116.8	14,427.5
Exchange rate	per US$	1.48	1.35	1.33	1.41	1.48

* estimated figure

Risk assessment

Economy	Fair
Politics	Poor
Regional stability	Good

COUNTRY PROFILE

Historical profile

The Bulgars were a Finno-Ugrian people, whose ancestors crossed the River Danube in the seventh century and merged

with the Slavonic population. Bulgaria is the oldest surviving state in Europe to have retained its original name.
681 The state of Bulgaria was founded.
811–927 After defeating the Byzantine armies at the Battle of Pliska, Bulgaria expanded into the Balkans.
1014–18 The Byzantines regained control of lost territory and much of Bulgaria was again part of the Byzantine Empire.
1185–97 The Bulgarians revolted against Byzantine rule. Bulgaria re-emerged as a state and major Balkan empire.
1396 Bulgaria was conquered by Ottoman Turkey and became its European stronghold for the next 500 years.
1800s The Ottoman Empire began to fall apart as many Balkan states launched uprisings.
1878 Russia defeated Turkey and Bulgaria came into existence again as a sovereign state.
1908 German Ferdinand Saxe-Coburg-Gotha proclaimed himself King of Bulgaria.
1912 The Balkan powers of Bulgaria, Greece and Montenegro defeated the remnants of the Ottoman Empire.
1913 In the Second Balkan War, Bulgaria tried to take Macedonia from Serbia, but was defeated. Balkan states ended the war by signing the Treaty of Bucharest, which also reduced the territorial size of Bulgaria.
1915 Bulgaria invaded Serbia and Macedonia, after joining on the side of the Central Powers (Germany and Austro-Hungary).
1918 The Entente powers (Great Britain, France and Russia) defeated Bulgaria and an armistice was signed in September. The Bulgarian defeat led to the abdication of King Ferdinand I and his son, Boris, was crowned.
1923 As internal divisions intensified between the peasants, ethnic Macedonians and communists, the army overthrew the government, which was dominated by agrarian parties. Prime Minister Alexander Stambolisky was assassinated. Alexander Tsankov formed a new pro-democracy government.
1924–25 Violence from communist militants and Macedonian nationalists prevented the Tsankov government from bringing political stability to Bulgaria.
1926 An ethnic Macedonian, Andrei Liapchev, replaced Tsankov as prime minister.
1929–31 The Great Depression devastated the Bulgarian economy. Thousands of jobs were lost and a wave of strikes hit the country. In the 1931 parliamentary election, the Liapchev government was defeated by the centre-left Naroden Blok (NB) (People's Bloc), led by Alexander Malinov.
1934 A coalition of political parties, led by the Zveno Group's Kimon Georgiev and Colonel Damyan Velchev of the Voenni Sayuz (VZ) (Military Union), overthrew Malinov's government. The new government introduced one-party rule and turned Bulgaria into an authoritarian state.
1935 Disillusioned by the government's authoritarianism, King Boris III began a personal dictatorship of Bulgaria.
1939–1941 Bulgaria was neutral at the start of the Second World War, but joined the Axis powers (Germany, Italy and Japan) in 1941. Bulgaria ruled German-captured Macedonia and Western Thrace in Greece.
1943 Boris III died of a heart attack. The heir to the Bulgarian throne, Simeon II, was too young to rule. A three-man regency was established to rule on King Simeon II's behalf and Prime Minister Bogdan Filov became the *de facto* head of state.
1944 The Soviet Union invaded Bulgaria. The Fatherland Front, a left-wing alliance dominated by the Soviet-backed Bulgarska Komunistieska Partija (BKP) (Bulgarian Communist Party), gained power.
1946 A referendum abolished the monarchy, which had ruled Bulgaria periodically since the ninth century.
1947 All opposition parties were abolished. Political trials and executions on the Stalinist model were carried out under Vulko Chervenkov until 1953 when Todor Zhivkov became the general secretary of the BKP.
1962–88 Zhivkov cemented his position as leader of Bulgaria and the country moved politically and economically closer to the Soviet Union.
1989 Petur Mladenov was appointed Zhivkov's successor.
1990 The BCK changed its name to the Bulgarska Socialistièska Partija (BSP) (Bulgarian Socialist Party). The BSP won the first multi-party elections in Bulgaria since the inter-war period. However, growing political infighting and nationwide strikes led to its fall. An interim government was confirmed, under the leadership of Dimitur Popov.
1991 The BSP lost power in the parliamentary elections. The Sajuz na Demokratienite Sili (SDS) (Union of Democratic Forces) formed a government.
1992 The SDS's Zhelyu Zhelev became Bulgaria's first directly elected president.
1994 The BSP returned to government in the parliamentary elections.
1996 Simeon (Borisov) Sakskoburggotski (son of Boris III) returned to Bulgaria. Amid a severe economic and political crisis, Petar Stoyanov won the presidential elections.
1997 An early general election was held, resulting in a win for the SDS-led centre-right coalition, the Obedineni Demokratièni Sili (ODS) (United Democratic Forces).
2001 The Nacionale Dvisenie Simeon Tvori (NDST) (National Movement for Simeon II) won the general election. The NDST's leader (former king Simeon II (1943–44)), became prime minister and formed a coalition government. The BSP's Georgi Parvanov won the run-off presidential elections.
2003 The IMF approved of Bulgaria's efforts to improve its macroeconomic situation with a loan of US$36 million.
2004 Bulgaria joined NATO.
2005 The Koalicija za Balgarija (KzB) (Coalition for Bulgaria) (led by the BSP) won parliamentary elections, defeating the ruling NDST. Sergey Stanishev became prime minister.
2006 The European Union (EU) officially agreed to Bulgaria's membership but curbs on organised crime and corruption and the use of EU funds were among the conditions imposed that were stronger than those placed on previous accession countries. In presidential elections Georgi Parvanov won a landslide victory with 77.3 per cent of the vote. However, turnout was low at 41.2 per cent, in what was seen as voter apathy towards long-term political ineffectiveness at fighting organised crime and implementing social justice and other reforms.
2007 Bulgaria joined the EU. After eight years in prison and two death sentences, commuted to life, six hospital workers (five Bulgarian nurses and a Palestinian born doctor) were released by Libya. They had been held responsible for the deliberate infection of Libyan children with HIV/Aids. The NDST became the Nacionalno Dvizenie za Stabilnost i Vazhod (NDSV) (National Movement for Stability and Progress).
2008 The EU judged that Bulgaria had not sufficiently tackled corruption and organised crime, as required by its entry agreement, and suspended millions of euros in aid to upgrade roads and agriculture. Bulgaria risked further loss, of not only US$1 billion in EU funds, but also of joining the Schengen area of passport-free travel in 2011.
2009 Weeks of energy shortages were endured by Bulgarians after Ukraine, in dispute with Russia, cut Russian natural gas supplies to Bulgaria. The EU requested the return of €33 million (US$46.3 million) in farming subsidies that it claimed had been fraudulently misappropriated. Parliamentary elections were won by Grazhdani za Evropeysko Razvitie na Balgariya (GERB) (Citizens for European Development of Bulgaria) with

116 seats; BSP won 40 seats. Boyko Borisov (GERB) became prime minister.
2010 In April parliament approved measures to raise revenue and to further tackle the budget deficit, including by the sale of minority government holdings in companies and increased taxes on gambling and insurance premiums. In August, French authorities repatriated to Bulgaria foreign-born Roma people living without permits in camps around France, sparking condemnation from the European Commission and human rights groups.
2011 On 9 June, The Netherlands announced that it would veto the EU decision to admit Bulgaria and Romania into the Schengen area for passport-free travel of citizens and goods, and impose a one-year delay, in view of the turmoil in the Middle East and the potential for Middle Eastern migration to the EU in 2011–12. Nevertheless the EU approved Bulgaria's inclusion in the Schengen area agreement on 8 June. Bulgaria officially recognised the Transitional National Council (TNC) in Libya on 28 June. Eighteen candidates took part in presidential elections held on 23 October. Rosen Plavneliev (Gerb) won 40.11 per cent of the vote in the first round and Ivaylo Kaflin (BSP) 28.96 per cent, as none of the candidates won over 50 per cent of the votes a runoff was held on 30 October; Plavneliev won 52.58 per cent and Kaflin 47.42 per cent; turnout was 48.06 per cent.

Political structure

Constitution

A democratic constitution was passed in July 1991, defining Bulgaria as a republic with a parliamentary form of government.

Independence date

22 September 1908.

Form of state

Parliamentary democratic republic

The executive

The Council of Ministers is the supreme executive body of the government and usually consists of elected members of the National Assembly. The right to initiate new legislation is vested in the deputies and the Council of Ministers.
The head of state is the president of the Republic, elected by a direct popular vote every five years, and assisted by a vice president. The president is not allowed to initiate or veto new laws, but can bring a law back to parliament for further consideration.

National legislature

The unicameral Narodno Sabranie (National Assembly) has 240 deputies elected for four-year terms by proportional representation in multi-seat constituencies.

Legal system

The legal system is based on the 1991 constitution.
The judiciary is the third component within the political system. It is an autonomous power with an independent budget. The Supreme Legal Council has 45 members. The Constitutional Court is the supreme arbiter.

Last elections

5 July 2009 (parliamentary); 23 and 30 October 2011 (presidential, first round and runoff)

Results: Parliamentary: Grazhdani za Evropeysko Razvitie na Balgariya (GERB) (Citizens for European Development of Bulgaria) won 39.72 per cent of the vote (116 seats out of 240), Koalicija za Balgarija (Coalition for Bulgaria) 17.7 per cent (40), Dvizhenie za Prava i Sobodi (DPS) (in Turkish, Hak ve Özgürlükler Hareketi) (Movement for Rights and Freedoms) 14.45 per cent (38), Natsionalen Sayuz Ataka (NSA) (National Union Attack) 9.36 per cent (21), Sinyata Koalitsia (Blue Coalition) 6.76 per cent (15), Red, Zakonnost i Spravedlivost (RZS) (Order, Lawfulness, Justice) 4.13 per cent (10); 12 other political parties failed to win enough votes to win seats. Turnout was 60.2 per cent.
Presidential (first round): Rosen Plavneliev (Gerb) won 40.11 per cent of the vote, Ivaylo Kaflin (BSP) 28.96 per cent, Meglena Kuneva (independent) 14 per cent; 15 other candidates each won less than 4 per cent of the vote. Turnout was 52.11 per cent. Runoff: Plavneliev won 52.58 per cent, Kaflin 47.42 per cent; turnout was 48.06 per cent.

Next elections

2013 (parliamentary); 2016 (presidential)

Political parties

Ruling party

Grazhdani za Evropeysko Razvitie na Balgariya (Gerb) (Citizens for European Development of Bulgaria) (from 5 Jul 2009)

Main opposition party

Bulgarska Socialistièska Partija (BSP) (Bulgarian Socialist Party)

Population

7.60 million (2009)

Last census: March 2001: 7,928,901

Population density: 74 inhabitants per square km. Urban population: 70 per cent (1994–2000).

Annual growth rate: -0.7 per cent 1994–2004 (WHO 2006)

Ethnic make-up

Turks, Gypsies (around one million in 2002), Russians, Armenians, Jews and Greeks.

Religions

Eastern Orthodoxy is the main religion, but Catholic, Protestant, Jewish and Muslim communities also exist.

Education

Primary education comprises basic education and pre-secondary education. Secondary school education lasts for four or five years and is provided in three types of schools – comprehensive (general secondary) schools, profile-oriented schools and vocational (technical and vocational-technical) schools. Universities, institutes and academies provide higher education. Some universities are private. Public expenditure on education is typically equivalent to 3.2 per cent of annual gross national income.

Literacy rate: 99 per cent adult rate; 100 per cent youth rate (15–24) (Unesco 2005).

Compulsory years: 7 to 18.

Enrolment rate: 100 per cent boys and 98 per cent girls, total primary school enrolment of the relevant age group, (World Bank).

Pupils per teacher: 17 in primary schools.

Health

Health care reform was initiated in 2000 with the introduction of outpatient care reform, with future plans for transforming the hospitals into commercial enterprises. The IMF and the World Bank agreed to extend a loan of over US$60 million towards the health fund reform.
The National Health Insurance Fund (NHIF) is responsible for the development of the compulsory health insurance scheme in Bulgaria. Health insurance financing by the NHIF will replace funding through taxes for nearly 90 per cent of hospitals.

HIV/Aids

HIV prevalence: 0.1 per cent aged 15–49 in 2003 (World Bank)

Life expectancy: 72 years, 2004 (WHO 2006)

Fertility rate/Maternal mortality rate: 1.2 births per woman, 2004 (WHO 2006); maternal mortality 1.5 per 1,000 live births (World Bank).

Child (under 5 years) mortality rate (per 1,000): 12.3 per 1,000 live births (World Bank)

Head of population per physician: 3.56 physicians per 1,000 people, 2003 (WHO 2006)

Welfare

The Bulgarian social security system consists of a public pay-as-you-go system, a mandatory state-funded system of privately managed savings accounts and an additional voluntary private contribution. The National Social Security Institute

(NSSI) administers mandatory insurance programmes for maternity, sickness, disability and old age benefits including those related to work injuries and occupational diseases. It is also responsible for the collection, control and information services for all obligatory contributions. The current system of funding benefits was instigated in 2002. A mandatory social insurance scheme provides universal coverage for all members; contributions by individuals to a private insurance fund provide for old age pensions. These schemes are open to all employees, farmers, and artists who pay 21.75 per cent of earning for the social insurance and 0.5 per cent for the private insurance. Employers pay 8.25 per cent of payroll as a whole into these funds. The self-employed pay 31 per cent in total to the funds. The retirement is at aged 61.5 years (men) and 56.5 years (women), however the age is being increased every year until 2009 when retirement will be at age 63 (men) and 60 (women).

Main cities

Sofia (capital, estimated population 1.0 million in 2005), Plovdiv (340,050), Varna (317,570), Burgas (196,378), Ruse (156,564), Stara Zagora (142,337).

Languages spoken

Turkish (permitted since 1992), Macedonian, Romani, Gagauz, Tartar and Albanian.

Official language/s

Bulgarian

Media

The constitution guarantees freedom of the press.

Press

There are no laws regulating the print media, with publishing entirely liberated since the end of Communist control in 1989. Hybrid tabloids, which integrates elements of good journalism from the quality press with sensational stories, dominate the market.

In 2006 there were over 900 print media outlets, of which 15 were national and 10 regional, daily newspapers. All dailies have suffered from a steady drop is circulation figures and a sustainable market is dissipating.

Dailies: In Bulgarian, but with English online editions, include *Dnevnik* (http://news.dnevnik.bg), the leading quality newspaper and *Standart* (http://standartnews.com); others include *24 Chasa* (www.24chasa.bg), *Trud* (www.trud.bg), *Novinar* (www.novinar.org), and the *Monitor* (www.monitor.bg). The only English-language newspaper is *The Sofia Echo* (www.sofiaecho.com).

Weeklies: There are a variety of magazines for all interest groups. In Bulgarian, *Tema* (www.temanews.com) is a leading magazine for politics and current affairs, others include *7 din Sport* (www.7sport.net), *Novo Vreme* (www.novovreme.com) and *Kultura* (www.online.bg/kultura), which is published by the government.

Business: In Bulgarian, *Pari* (www.pari.bg) is a daily, with an English online edition; *Capital* (www.capital.bg) and the *Banker* (www.banker.bg), are both weeklies.

Broadcasting

Radio: The Bulgarian National Radio (BNR) (www.bnr.bg) has the largest market share with two national, public stations and regional services as well as an international service. There are over 100 private commercial stations, with over 30 in Sophia alone. Darik Radio (http://dariknews.bg), is a private national network. Regional stations include Radio Info (www.inforadio.bg), with news and information, from Sophia, Jazz FM (www.jazzfmbg.com) from Blagoevgrad and Radio Mixx (www.radiomixx.net), from Burgas.

Television: There are three national, commercial networks broadcasting for 24 hours. They include the public, Bulgarian National Television (www.bnt.bg) operates Kanal 1 and a satellite channel, the private bTV (www.btv.bg) with the largest audience and Nova Televisia (www.ntv.bg). There are over 180 registered cable TV operates throughout the country with digital TV services due to be fully implemented by 2015.

News agencies

National news agency: Bulgarian News Agency (BTA)

Economy

Bulgaria has a mixed economy based on mature industries such as mining, iron and steel, construction material manufacturing, oil refining and light engineering. It has also increased its manufacturing sector in electronics, clothing, food-processing and automotive components. Tourism has grown slightly quicker than the European Union (EU), average, and far higher than other non-EU Eastern European destinations. Almost nine million people visited in 2008 the majority of which travelled from other EU countries; the figures did not drop significantly in 2009, suggesting that other visitors switched to Bulgaria to benefit from a strong euro at a time of global weak currencies, including the lev. Bulgaria is a net exporter of energy, which accounted for 22 per cent of total exports in 2008.

Since 1994 the government has implemented conservative fiscal policies and tax reforms that have allowed the economy to grow at a steady rate. By 2008 Bulgarian direct personal taxation was one of the lowest in the EU while taxes on production and imports were some of the highest in the EU. Unemployment, which had been in long-term double digits had by 2006 fallen to 9.0 and 5.6 in 2008. Investment as a share of GDP has grown steadily from a total of 13 per cent in 1998 to 33.4 per cent in 2008, of which business investment, including foreign direct investment (FDI) (at 18.2 per cent), was 27.8 per cent. FDI fell to 9.8 per cent of GDP in 2009 as global trade weakened and investors became less inclined to part with their money.

GDP growth was 6.0 per cent in 2008, having remained at around this since 2005. However, when the global economic crisis struck Bulgaria, in the fourth quarter of 2008 the economy went into recession. GDP growth was -5.0 per cent in 2009, which increased household debt and unemployment which rose to 9.3 per cent. The annual inflation rate, which had been below 8 per cent (2001–07) jumped to 12 per cent in 2008.

An 'anti-crisis' plan was introduced by the government, in co-ordination with a worldwide programme to keep the global economy moving and avoid a damaging depression. In April 2010, parliament approved measures to raise revenue and decrease the budget deficit that included sale of minority government holdings in companies and increased taxes on gambling and insurance premiums. A new flat rate value added tax (VAT) of 9 per cent on the tourism sector will be introduced in April 2011, to bring the industry into line with EU standards.

When Bulgaria joined the EU in 2007 one specific stipulation for membership was that the government must tackled corruption and organised crime. In 2008 the European Commission declared that this had not been sufficiently robust and suspended financial aid and in July 2009 requested the return of €33 million (US$46.3 million) in farming subsidies that it claimed had been fraudulently misappropriated. In 2010, the newly elected government committed itself to fighting corruption (including cronyism and nepotism).

External trade

As a member of the European Union, Bulgaria operates within a community-wide free trade area, with tariffs set as a whole. Internationally, the EU has free trade agreements with a number of nations and trading blocs worldwide.

Energy accounts for over 20 per cent of all exports.

Imports
Principal imports include crude oil and natural gas, mining, metallurgical and petroleum equipment, raw materials, perfumes and cosmetics, vehicles, chemicals and plastics.
Main sources: Russia (typically 16 per cent total), Germany (11 per cent), Italy (8 per cent).
Exports
Significant exports include energy, footwear and clothing, iron and steel, copper, machinery and equipment and fuels.
Main destinations: Germany (typically 11 per cent of total), Greece (9 per cent), Italy (9 per cent).

Agriculture
Farming
Agriculture accounts for around 11 per cent of GDP. About 16 per cent of Bulgaria's workforce is employed in farming. Land for agricultural use covers 6.16 million hectares (ha). Principal crops are wheat, maize, barley, sugar beet; other crops include sunflowers, grapes and tobacco.
Official policy towards land reform has mainly focused on restoring property rights, which included over 99.58 per cent of agricultural land and 90 per cent for wooded areas.
With the exception of cereals, farm prices and trade have been liberalised. The outlook for wheat producers has brightened since the reduction of a 15 per cent tax on wheat export earnings to 10 per cent.
There is a sizeable wine industry, which accounts for around a third of agricultural exports. Bulgaria exports 80 per cent of its wine output, amounting to about 220,000 litres, of which 25 prer cent are exported to the UK, still the biggest market for Bulgarian wine.
Long-term development of agriculture is based on further concentration and specialisation, mechanisation, improved irrigation, increased grain production and expansion of the dairy sector. The government offers subsidised credits to farmers owning more than 10 cows.
Fishing
Bulgaria's implementation of EU fisheries legislation is yet to be completed. Since progress in the compilation of standardised market data has been slow, privatisation of the processing and marketing sectors has been largely affected. Bulgaria is collaborating on a draft convention on fishing and conservation of resources in the Black Sea, which provides an abundance of fish for domestic and external markets, although it is under-utilised. The main species caught include sprats, mussels and turbot.
Forestry
Forest and other wooded land accounts for over a third of the total land area, with 3.6 million hectares of forest cover. The proportion of forest cover has been increasing as a result of afforestation intended chiefly for soil protection, rather than wood production. Plantations account for more than a quarter of the forest area.
Most of the forest and wooded land is available for wood supply with the main species being beech and oak. Coniferous species include Norwegian spruce and Austrian pine. Up until 1999, all of the forests were state-owned, but by 2002 some 33 per cent were state-owned, 50 per cent municipal and 17 per cent privately owned.
Local demand for sawn wood, panels, pulp and paper is generally met by using domestic wood. Large amounts of sawlogs are also exported.

Industry and manufacturing
The industrial sector accounts for around 30 per cent of GDP and employs 38 per cent of the workforce.
Economic growth in the 1990s was led by the manufacturing sector, which contributes around 18 per cent to GDP. The industrial sector is well-developed, and the metal processing, machine building, chemicals, pharmaceuticals, electronics, textiles and food-processing sectors are particularly strong.
The machine building sector includes over 400 enterprises specialising in various areas including casting, machine tools, wood processing machines, machines for the mining industry, machines for the textile industry, machines for the food processing industry, agricultural machines, shipbuilding, vehicle manufacture, fine mechanics, metal constructions and household instruments.
The Great Wall Motor Company (TGWMC) of China was scheduled to begin car production in Bulgaria in February 2011. Investment by TGWMC of US$400 million, with an initial US$114 million, will provide an annual output capacity of 1,000 units of a sport utility vehicle, with a planned sale price of less than US$15,000. The plant will be managed and operated by the Bulgarian company Litex Motors. At maximum capacity, the plant is expected to produce 50,000 mixed units with the principal market in Eastern Europe before expanding into southern Europe.
The key markets are the EU (particularly Germany and the Netherlands), Russia and North America.

Tourism
Bulgaria has become a major tourist destination, despite limited infrastructure. Winter ski-ing and Black Sea summer resorts are the main attractions for an increasing flow of tourists. Investment is urgently needed in the existing, increasingly inadequate infrastructure, which is in danger of being overwhelmed, and in new development. The sector is short of up-market facilities. The authorities are seeking to diversify away from package tourism and to spread the benefits of tourism throughout the country, by encouraging cultural, rural and eco-tourism. A Ministry of Culture and Tourism was created in 2005.
The majority of visitors come from south-eastern Europe, especially Greece, followed by Germany, the UK and Russia.

Mining
The mining sector accounts for 2 per cent of GDP and employs 2 per cent of the workforce.
Bulgaria has some deposits of iron, manganese and chromium, and large reserves of zinc, lead and copper.
Apart from zinc, lead and copper, the non-ferrous ores contain some gold, silver and other precious metals. The Chala gold deposit in the area of Haskovski Mineralni Bani is one of Bulgaria's richest. The average gold content is higher than that in Madjarovo where it exceeds three grams per tonne.
Large deposits of copper ore have been discovered in the Sredna Gora mountains.
There are deposits of marl, limestone, granite, sandstone and clay, and plenty of stone which can be used in the building industry.

Hydrocarbons
Proven oil reserves were negligible in 2010 and consumption was 93,000 barrels per day (bpd) leaving Bulgaria a net importer of oil, with most of its supply coming from Russia. Known oil and natural gas deposits are of small amounts and at considerable depth. Exploration for oil and gas is concentrated in the north of the country and in the Black Sea.
The Balkans are a major transit region for oil and gas. In 2008 Bulgaria ratified the US$1.2 billion pipeline deal previously agreed between Russia, Bulgaria and Greece in 2007. The pipeline will run inland from Burgas to the northern Greek town of Alexandroupolis on the Aegean Sea and carry 750,000 barrels per day. Russian oil will be transported via the 285km pipeline to the huge EU market, avoiding the busy Bosphorus exit to the Mediterranean, where oil tankers can wait for days. A Russian consortium will hold a 51 per cent stake in the deal to build and operate the pipeline and a joint Greek/Bulgarian consortium 24.5 per cent each.

Natural gas reserves and production were negligible in 2010 and Bulgaria is dependent on Russia for the 2.6 billion cubic metres it consumes annually. They have an agreement in place, lasting up to 2018, guaranteeing Russian gas supplies. Bulgaria also transits Russian gas to other countries in Europe.
Proven reserves of coal were 2.36 billion tonnes at the end of 2010, of which the majority is the lesser quality brown coal, with low calorific value, which is used in power stations. Production was 4.8 million tonnes in 2010.

Energy
The most recent published figures for 2006 show total generating power at 43.15 billion kWh, which was an increase of 1.4 billion kWh on the 2005 figure. Bulgaria's installed electricity capacity is approximately 1,250MW, composed of 580MW of coal-powered thermal power, 380MW of nuclear power and 290MW of hydroelectric power.
The coal-fired Maritsa Iztok complex accounts for 60 per cent of all power generated. A new thermal plant, agreed in December 2005, is to be constructed at Maritsa Iztok to replace capacity lost by the closure of two nuclear reactors at the Kozloduy power plant after the EU had raised safety concerns. The government has plans to build a new nuclear power plant on the river Danube, to take over when the remaining plants go off-line. Annual production was 3.3 million tonnes oil equivalent (mtoe). The new plant is expected to keep Bulgaria as the leading exporter of electricity in the Balkans.

Financial markets
Stock exchange
Balgarska fondova borsa (Bulgarian Stock Exchange) (BSE)
Commodity exchange
Sofia Commodity Exchange

Banking and insurance
There is a two-tier system in which an independent central bank supervises and regulates commercial banks and has exclusive rights over the issue of currency. There are approximately 33 commercial banks, with total bank credit to the private sector accounting for 14 per cent of GDP, one of the lowest rates of former Soviet countries.
Central bank
Bulgarska Narodna Banka (BNB) (Bulgarian National Bank)

Time
GMT plus two hours (daylight saving, late March to late October, GMT plus three hours)

Geography
Bulgaria lies in south-eastern Europe, on the east of the Balkan Peninsula. It is situated on the western shores of the Black Sea and shares borders with Romania to the north, Turkey to the south-east, Greece to the south, Macedonia (FYROM) to the south-west and Serbia to the north-west. The lower River Danube forms most of the border with Romania. The Balkan Mountains dominate central Bulgaria, running from west to east and separating the Danubian plains in the north from the Thracian plains of Eastern Rumelia in the south-east. The Rhodope Mountains occupy south-west Bulgaria and separate it from Greece and Macedonia.
The Sofia depression in the west of the country is hill country which separates the Balkan Mountains from the southern mountains. It is the main centre of population and communications.
The fertile Bulgarian plateau, between the Danubian border and the Balkan Mountains, averages some 100km in width and contains several tributaries of the Danube, the major one being the Iskur. The main rivers south of the Balkan watershed are the Struma and the Maritza which run into the Aegean Sea. The broad Maritza Valley, which leads on to the Thracian plains, is one of the principal agricultural areas.
Hemisphere
Northern

Climate
Summer is hot and dry, April–September average temperature 23 degrees Celsius (C). Cold winters, average temperature minus 1 degree C, with heavy snow.

Dress codes
Dress for business is usually quite conservative but not overly formal.

Entry requirements
Passports
Passports are required by all visitors.
As from 1 January 2006, all visitors staying for longer than 24 hours must be registered with the authorities; hotels will automatically undertake this task.
Visa
Not required by citizens of Europe, North America, Australasia and some Asian countries for either 90 or 30 days. Full details and information can be found at www.bulgariatravel.org and see 'getting to Bulgaria'.
Businessmen from visa-free states may visit without a visa for up to 30 days. All other businessmen must apply for visas and include a letter of invitation from a company registered in Bulgaria endorsed by the Bulgarian Chamber of Commerce.
All visitors, tourist and business, must have travel and medical insurance to cover emergency medical expenses, repatriation, transport of mortal remains, funeral and hospitalisation. A copy of the policy, with legible policy number, company name, duration of validity and sum of coverage or a letter from the insurance company including such data, should be submitted with the application.
Currency advice/regulations
The import and export of local currency up to Lev5,000 is allowed without restrictions. Between Lev5,000–20,000 import and export is permitted if the amount was declared on arrival. The import and export of over Lev20,000 is allowed only with written permission from the central bank.
Foreign currency may be import in unlimited amounts, but must be declared on arrival; export of foreign cannot exceed the amount imported and declared.
A *bordereaux* is issued to all visitors on arrival, to record all money exchanges and must be returned to the authorities when departing. Local currency can only be exchanged on departure with the *bordereaux*. Visitors are advised to exchange money in banks and hotels.
ATMs are widespread; check with the card provider concerning terms and conditions.
Travellers cheques are accepted in major hotels and establishments; US dollars and pound sterling attract less additional rate charges.
Customs
Small quantities of spirits, wines and beverages are allowed in duty-free. Valuable personal effects should be declared verbally to Customs on entry. There are no restrictions on goods bought for foreign exchange in duty free shops at ports of entry.

Health (for visitors)
Foreign travellers must present valid evidence of health insurance to the Bulgarian border authorities in order to be admitted into the country.
Mandatory precautions
None
Advisable precautions
Recommended immunisations: hepatitis A, polio, tetanus and typhoid.

Hotels
Deluxe, first- and second-class ratings system. Hotels have been upgraded to attract business people. Radisson, Sheraton and Hilton groups have hotels in Sofia.

Credit cards
Main international credit cards are accepted in larger hotels and stores in larger cities, and in some restaurants in Sofia.

Public holidays (national)
Fixed dates
1 Jan (New Year's Day), 3 Mar (National Day), 1 May (Labour Day), 6 May (St

George's Day), 24 May (St Cyril and Methodius Day/Culture Day), 6 Sep (Unification Day), 22 Sep (Independence Day), 24–26 Dec (Christmas).

Variable dates
Orthodox Good Friday, Orthodox Easter Monday.

Working hours
Banking
Mon–Fri: 0800–1230, 1330–1530; Sat: 0830–1130.
Business
Mon–Fri: 0800 (0900)–1730 (1800).
Government
Mon–Fri: 0800 (0900)–1730 (1800).
Shops
Mon–Fri: 1000–2000; Sat: 0800–1400.

Telecommunications
Mobile/cell phones
There is good GSM coverage of 3G, with nationwide coverage of GSM 900 and 1800.

Electricity supply
220–240V AC/50 HZ

Social customs/useful tips
A nod of the head means 'No', a shake of the head means 'Yes'. Shaking hands is the traditional form of greeting. It is usual to invite your host to a good restaurant.

Security
By Western standards, the streets of Sofia and other towns and cities are generally safe. Street crime is slowly rising and the usual precautions should be taken.

Getting there
Air
National airline: Bulgaria Air
Hemus Air connects Sofia to some European and Middle Eastern destinations.
International airport/s: Sofia (SOF) airport, 10km east of the city centre. Facilities include banks, post office, duty-free shops, restaurant and car hire.
By day, buses run every 10 minutes to the city, at night they run every 20 minutes between 2100–0030. Taxis are available, if the metre is not in use, a fare may have to be negotiated before travelling.
Other airport/s: Varna (VAR), 9km from city; Burgas (BOJ), 13km from city.
Airport tax: None, except US nationals who are charged US$20.
Surface
Road: The pan-European corridor, which is being built or existing roads upgraded, links Bulgaria to the European motorway network. Border crossings exist from all surrounding countries; new roads and border controls are planned with Turkey, Greece and Serbia. The Trans-European Motorway (TEM), includes routes connecting Budapest with Athens via Sofia and with Istanbul via eastern Bulgaria. In July 2006 the proposal for a north-south road tunnel under Shipka Mountain estimated at US$120 million, was still under consideration.
Rail: There are no direct rail services between Bulgaria and Western Europe. Links exist to Serbia, Turkey, Romania and Greece.
Water: Ships provide regular passenger service and cruises on the Danube, starting at Passau in Germany, to Vienna, passing through Slovakia, Hungary and Serbia. There are also links with the Rhine, Black Sea and Main.
Main port/s: Burgas, Varna.

Getting about
National transport
Air: Bulgaria Air operates a domestic flight from Sofia to Varna. Hemus Air connects Sofia to the Black Sea cities of Varna and Bourgas.
Road: The overall quality of the 13,000km of roads linking the major cities is good but some roads are in poor repair and full of potholes. International road signs are used and traffic drives on the right.
Rail: Approximately 6,500km of track connect all main towns. First-class travel is recommended. It is necessary to make reservations.
City transport
Taxis: Taxis are plentiful and cheap. Official taxis have meters, although some privately operated ones may not. A 5–10 per cent tip in local currency is usual.
Taxis to Sofia airport have a journey time of 15 minutes. Fares should be agreed before departure.
Buses, trams & metro: Efficient and cheap tram and bus services operate in Sofia. Flat rate fares are charged.
Trolleybus services are available in Plovdiv and Varna.
Buses to the city centre from the airport run every 10 minutes during the day and every 20 minutes between 2100–0030, and take 25 minutes.
Car hire
An international driving permit is required. A green card (international car insurance) is compulsory. Most car hire accounts are transacted in hard currency. Drivers are normally given special petrol coupons, which can be used throughout the country. Speed limits: out of town 90kph and 120kph on motorways, in town 50kph. Drinking and driving is strictly prohibited. There are tolls on motorways and other major roads.

BUSINESS DIRECTORY

The addresses listed below are a selection only. While World of Information makes every endeavour to check these addresses, we cannot guarantee that changes have not been made, especially to telephone numbers and area codes. We would welcome any corrections.

Telephone area codes
The international direct dialling (IDD) code for Bulgaria is +359, followed by area code and subscriber's number:

Blagoevgrad	73	Rousse	82
Burgas	56	Smoliyan	301
Dobritch	58	Sofia	2
Gabrovo	66	Stara Zagora	42
Lovech	68	Varna	52
Plovdiv	32	Veliko Tûrnovo	62

Useful telephone numbers
Ambulance: 150
Fire brigade: 160
Police: 166
Operator: 121 (domestic);
123 (international)
Directory enquiries: 144 (business);
145 (domestic lines)
Traffic police: 165
Road service: 91-146

Chambers of Commerce
American Chamber of Commerce in Bulgaria, Building 2, Mladost 4 Area, Business Park Sofia, 1715 Sofia (tel: 976-9565; fax: 976-9569; e-mail: amcham@amcham.bg).

British Bulgarian Chamber of Commerce, 8 Charles Darwin Street, 1113 Sofia (tel: 971-4756; fax: 738-331; e-mail: info@bbcc.bg).

Bulgarian Chamber of Commerce and Industry, 42 Parchevich Street, 1058 Sofia (tel: 987-2631; fax: 987-3209; e-mail: bcci@bcci.bg).

Burgas Chamber of Commerce and Industry, 12B L Karavelov Street, PO Box 644, 8000 Sofia (tel: 812-007; fax: 810-130; e-mail: bscci@bcci.bg).

Dobritch Chamber of Commerce and Industry, 14 Nezavisimost Street, PO Box 182, 9300 Dobritch (tel: 601-433; fax:601-434; e-mail: dbcci@bcci.bg).

Gabrovo Chamber of Commerce and Industry, 1Vazrazhdane Square, PO Box 217, 5300 Gabrovo (tel: 288-39; fax: 341-83; e-mail: gbcci@mbox.eda.bg).

Plovdiv Chamber of Commerce and Industry, 7 Samara Street, 4003 Plovdiv (tel: 652-645; fax: 652-647; e-mail: pcci@plovdiv-chamber.org).

Sousse Chamber of Commerce and Industry, 3 A Ferdinand Boulevard, PO Box 484, 7000 Rousse (tel: 825-884; fax: 825-873; e-mail: info@ chamber.rousse.bg).

Stara Zagora Chamber of Commerce and Industry, 66 GS Rakovski Street, 6000 Stara Zagora (tel: 461-94; fax: 260-33; e-mail: office@chambersz.com).

Varna Chamber of Commerce and Industry, 135 Primorsky Boulevard, 9000 Varna (tel: 615-140; fax: 612-146; e-mail: office@vcci.bg).

Banking

Biochim Bank, 1 Ivan Vazov Street, 1040 Sofia (tel: 926-9210; fax: 981-9151; e-mail: info@biochim.com).

BulBank Ltd, 7 Sveta Nedelya Square, 1000 Sofia (tel: 984-1111; fax: 988-4636, 988-5370; e-mail: infor@sof.bulbank.bg).

Bulgarian Post Bank, 1 Bulgaria Square, 1414 Sofia (tel: 963-2104/5; e-mail: iap@postbank.bg).

DSK Bank, 19 Moskovska Street, 1040 Sofia (tel: 939-1220; fax: 980-6477).

Central bank

Bulgarska Narodna Banka, 1 Alexander Battenberg Square, 1000 Sofia (tel: 91-459 fax: 980-2425).

Stock exchange

Balgarska fondova borsa (Bulgarian Stock Exchange) (BSE): www.bse-sofia.bg

Commodity exchange

Sofia Commodity Exchange, Sofia (tel: 952 6212, 952 6225, 952 6203; fax: 952 6232; e-mail: sce@sce-bg.com; www.sce-bg.com).

Travel information

Bulgaria Air, 1 Brussels blvd, Sofia Airport Sofia 1540 (tel: 402-0306; fax: 937-3254; email: office@air.bg; internet: www.air.bg/en/).

Balkantourist, 2 Enos Street, 1408 Sofia (tel: 981-9806; fax: 988-4177; email: sofia.agency@balkantourist.bg; internet: www.balkantourist.bg).

Central Railway Station, Maria Luisa Boulevard, Sofia (tel: 31-111; internet: www.sofia.com/transport).

Hemos Air, Airport Sofia, 1 Brussels Blvd, Sofia 1540 (tel: 942-0202; fax: 945-9147; email: office@hemusair.bg; internet: www.hemusair.bg).

Sofia Airport (email: public@sofia-airport.bg; internet: www.sofia-airport.bg/En).

National tourist organisation offices

Bulgarian Tourism Authority, 1 Sveta Nedelia Square, 1000 Sofia (tel: 987-9778; fax: 989-6939; email: webmaster@bulgariatravel.org; internet: www.bulgariatravel.org).

Ministries

Ministry of Agriculture and Forests, 55 Hristo Botev Boulevard, 1000 Sofia (tel: 981-1546; fax: 885-557).

Ministry of Culture, 17 Alexander Stamboliiski Boulevard., 1000 Sofia (tel: 980-5384; fax: 981-8145).

Ministry of Defence, 3 Vassil Levsky Street, 1000 Sofia (tel: 862-4135; fax: 873-626).

Ministry of Economy, 12 Kniaz Alexander Batenberg Street, 1000 Sofia (tel: 981-9965, 987-9778; fax: 981-2515, 981-5039).

Ministry of Education and Science, 2a Doundukov Boulevard, 1000 Sofia (tel: 84-81; fax: 987-1289).

Ministry of Environment and Waters, 67 Gladstone Street, 1000 Sofia (tel: 814-269; fax: 521-634).

Ministry of Finance, 102 Georgi Rakovski Street, 1000 Sofia (tel: 869-1870; fax: 980-6863); external department (tel: 869-223; fax: 876-008).

Ministry of Foreign Affairs, 2 Alexander Jendov Street, 1000 Sofia (tel: 714-3507; fax: 736-069).

Ministry of Health, 5 Sveta Nedelya Square, 1000 Sofia (tel: 86-31; fax: 875-040).

Ministry of the Interior, 23 Gurko Street, 1000 Sofia (tel: 877-511; fax: 824-047).

Ministry of Justice, 1 Slavianska Street, 1000 Sofia (tel: 86-01; fax: 876-3226).

Ministry of Labour and Social Policy, 2 Triaditza Street, 1000 Sofia (tel: 981-1717; fax: 800-609).

Ministry of Regional and Urban Development, 17 Kiril & Methodius Street, 1000 Sofia (tel: 83-841; fax: 872-517).

Ministry of Transport, 9 Levski Street, 1000 Sofia (tel: 872-862; fax: 885-094).

Council of Ministers, 1 Dondoukov Blvd., 1000 Sofia (tel: 8501; fax: 884-252).

Other useful addresses

Agency for Economic Co-ordination and Development, 1 Vassil Levsky Street, 1000 Sofia (tel: 543-386; fax: 833-323).

Agency for Privatisation, 29 Aksakov St, 1000 Sofia (tel: 873-188; fax: 882-938, 885-395).

Amex Representative Office, BICD, Rila Hotel, 6 Kalojan Street, Sofia 1000 (tel: 871-516).

Board of Customs Houses at the Ministry of Finance, 1 Aksakov Street, Sofia 1000 (tel: 869-528; fax: 884-909).

British Embassy, 38 Boulevard Vassil, Levski, Sofia 1000 (tel: 980-1220; fax: 988-5367).

Bulgarian Academy of Sciences, 1 7-mi Noemvri Street, 1000 Sofia (tel: 841-41; fax: 803-023).

Bulgarian Embassy (USA), 1621 22nd Street, NW, Washington DC 20008 (tel: (+1-202) 387-0174; fax: (+1-202) 234-7973; e-mail: office@bulgaria-embassy.org).

Bulgarian Foreign Investment Agency, 3 Sveta Sofia Street, 1000 Sofia (tel: 980-0918; fax: 980-1320; e-mail: fia@geobiz.com; internet site: www.bfia.org).

Bulgarian Industrial Association (BISA), 14 Alabin Street, 1000 Sofia (tel: 879-611, 872-960; fax: 872-604).

Bulgarian National Television, 29 San Stefano Str, 1504 Sofia (tel: 446-329; fax: 662-388).

Bulgarian News Agency (BTA), 49 Tzarigradsko Chaussee Blvd, 1024 Sofia (tel: 877-363, 877-739; fax: 802-488).

Bulgarian Telecommunication Company (BTC), 8 Totleben Blvd (tel: 870-143; fax: 875-885).

Bulgarian Telegraph Agency, Trakija Boulevard 49, Sofia (tel: 8461).

Bulgarian Translators' Union, 16 Graf Ignatiev Street, 1000 Sofia (tel: 661-602, 662-564; fax: 510-845, 661-233).

Bulgarreklama (trade show agency), 147 Tsarigradsko Chaussee Blvd, 1784 Sofia 1784 (tel: 965-5220; fax: 965-5230; email: bul-reklama@bulgarreklama.com; internet: www.bulgarreklama.com).

Central Co-operative Union, 99 Rakovski Street, 1000 Sofia (tel: 84-41; fax: 878-157).

Central Post Office, 4 Gurko Street, Sofia.

Committee for Energy, 8 Triaditsa Street, 1000 Sofia (tel: 861-91; fax: 876-279).

Committee for Forests, 17 Antim I Street, 1000 Sofia (tel: 861-71; fax: 873-235).

Committee for Geology and Mineral Resources, 22 Maria Louisa Blvd, 1000 Sofia (tel: 832-767; fax: 833-976).

Committee for Posts and Telecommunications, 6 Gourko Street, 1000 Sofia (tel: 889-646, 871-837; fax: 814-512, 800-044).

Committee for Television, 29 San Stefano Street, 1504 Sofia (tel: 43-481).

Committee for Standardisation and Metrology, 21 6-ti Septemvri Street, 1000 Sofia (tel: 85-91; fax: 801-402).

EU Energy Centre (Thermie), 51 James Boucher Blvd, 1407 Sofia (tel: 681-461, 683-542; fax: 681-461).

Euro Information Centre, Network/Correspondence Centre, 54 Dr GM Dimitrov Blv, 1125 Sofia (tel: 738-448; fax: 730-435).

First Bulgarian Stock Exchange, 1 Macedonia Square, 1040 Sofia (tel: 815-711; fax: 875-566; internet: www.bse-sofia.bg).

Foreign Aid Agency, 1 Vrabcha Street, 1000 Sofia (tel: 881-951; fax: 885-039).

Intercommerce (import, export, re-export and transit operations, compensation deals and foreign trade transactions), 21 Aksakov Str, 1000 Sofia (tel: 879-364; fax: 873-753).

International Fair – Plovdiv, G. Dimitrov Boulevard 37 (tel: 553-191, 553-146, 26-129, 26-139).

International Road Transport (SO MAT), Gorublyane, 1738 Sofia (tel: 712-121, 758-015; fax: 758-015).

Interpred World Trade Centre (representation of foreign companies), 36 Dragan Tzankov Boulevard, 1040 Sofia (tel: 7146-4646; fax: 700-006, 706-401).

Law Offices for Foreign Legal Matters (tel: 877-782).

Medical Industry Association, Bademova Gora Street 20-a, Sofia 1404 (tel: 592-111).

Scientific Institute for International Co-operation and Foreign Economic Activities, 3A 165 Street, Zh K Izgreva, 1113 Sofia (tel: 708-336; fax: 705-154, 700-131).

Small and Medium-Sized Enterprises (SME) Development Programme, Agency for Privatisation, 29 Aksakov Str, 1046 Sofia (tel: 871-913; fax: 871-912).

Sofia Press Agency, 113 Tsarigradsko Shosse Blvd. (tel: 878-428; fax: 883-455).

Sofia Customs Office, 1 Aksakov Street, 1000 Sofia (tel: 800-402; fax: 884-909).

State Insurance Institute, 3 Benkovski Street, 1000 Sofia (tel: 879-341; fax: 871-429).

Union for Private Economic Enterprise, 2a Suborna Street, 1000 Sofia (tel: 659-371; fax: 659-411).

National news agency: Bulgarian News Agency (BTA), 49 Tsarigradsko Chaussee Blvd, 1124 Sofia, (tel: 9262-279, 9262-205; email: dnews@bta.bg; internet: www.bta.bg).

Other news agencies: BGnes: www.bgnes.com

Focus: www.focus.bg

Mediapool: www.mediapool.bg

Novinite (in English): www.novinite.com

SEEnews (in English): www.seenews.com

Internet sites

Background information on the government and useful links: www.vii.org/afgrbulg.htm

Bulgaria business catalogue and useful links: www.bulgaria.com

Bulgarian Economic Forum: www.biforum.org

Bulgaria financial and business newspaper: www.pari.bg

Bulgarian International Business Association: www.biba.bg

Bulgarian News Agency: www.bta.bg/site/en/indexe.shtml

SG Expressbank AD: www.sgexpressbank.bg

Full list of air carriers at Sofia airport: www.sofia-airport.bg/flights/image/airlines_en.htm

Burkina Faso

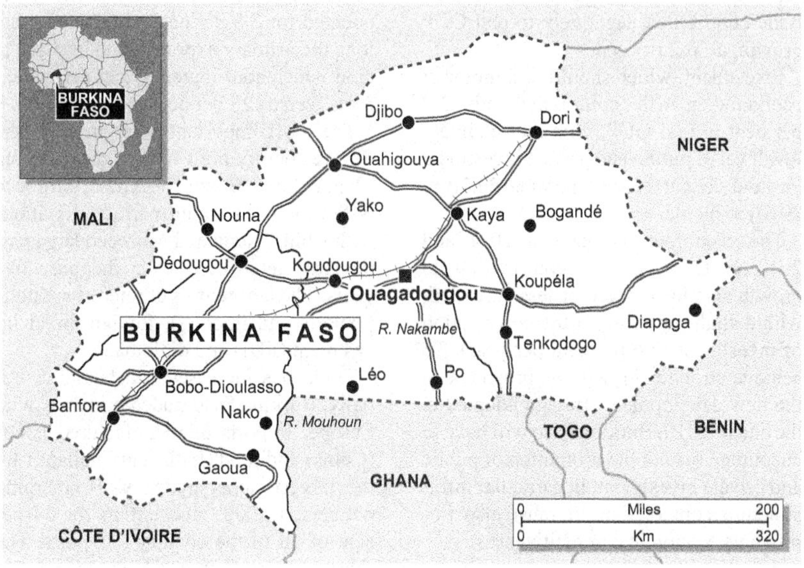

Seven candidates had taken part in presidential elections held on 21 November 2010. As expected incumbent President Blaise Compaoré won, with 81 per cent of the vote, his nearest rival, Hama Arba Diallo, won 8 per cent. Turnout was reported to be so low that the president turned to the media to encourage people to vote. The official declaration was a turnout of 53 per cent.

After the relatively trouble free presidential elections in 2010, 2011 turned into a bit of a nightmare for Burkina Faso. First, Prime Minister Tertius Zongo and his government resigned on 12 January. He was reappointed immediately and chose a new (but almost unchanged) cabinet on 16 January. Then on 14 April gunfire was heard in Ouagadougou, at an elite barracks of the presidential guard, as members rampaged through the city protesting at unpaid housing allowances. The mutiny lasted until a curfew was finally imposed on 16 April. A day later the government of Prime Minister Zongo was dissolved and on 18 April Luc-Adolphe Tiao (also of the Congrès pour la Démocratie et le Progrès (CDP) (Congress for Democracy and Progress)) was appointed prime minister. The unrest spread to the north as people demonstrated against the high cost of food. The mutiny spread to a fourth city by 19 April. On 21 April Compaoré appointed himself minister of defence in a cabinet reshuffle.

The economy

In 2010, economic growth, primarily driven by the secondary and tertiary sectors, with respective contributions of 2.3 points and 1.9 points, accelerated over 2009, with real GDP growth increasing from 3.2 per cent to 5.7 per cent. The *African Economic Outlook 2011* (AEO), published jointly by the African Development Bank and the Organisation for Economic Co-operation and Development reports the outlook for the economy in 2011 and 2012 to be for higher growth, with respective rates of 6.5 per cent and 6.2 per cent.

Agriculture (including cotton, livestock, forestry and fishing) represents 35.4 per cent of GDP, followed by trade and commerce, transport and communication at 18.1 per cent. These two sectors dominate the economy. The extractive industries are also highly dynamic, accounting for 5.1 per cent of GDP in 2010 versus 0.5 per cent in 2009.

Agriculture grew strongly (4.6 per cent) in 2010 compared with the previous year. This growth was due to the good

KEY FACTS

Official name: République Démocratique Populaire de Burkina Faso (Popular Democratic Republic of Burkina Faso)

Head of State: President Blaise Compaoré (from 1987; re-elected 21 Nov 2010)

Head of government: Prime Minister Luc-Adolphe Tiao (from 18 Apr 2011)

Ruling party: Congrès pour la Démocratie et le Progrès (CDP) (Congress for Democracy and Progress) (since 1997; re-elected May 2007)

Area: 274,000 square km

Population: 16.43 million (2010)*

Capital: Ouagadougou

Official language: French

Currency: CFA franc (CFAf) = 100 centimes (Communauté Financière Africaine (African Financial Community) franc).

Exchange rate: CFAf488.90 per US$ (Oct 2011) CFAf655.95 per euro (pegged from Jan 1999)

GDP per capita: US$564 (2009)

GDP real growth: 3.30% (2009)*

GDP: US$8.11 billion (2009)

Labour force: 6.67 million (2007) (excludes seasonal, expatriate numbers)

Inflation: -2.60% (2009)

Balance of trade: -US$513.00 million (2009)*

* estimated figure

distribution of rainfall during the 2010/11 agricultural season. To boost cereal production, the authorities have introduced several initiatives to support farmers: providing inputs (organic manure, improved seeds, fertilisers etc), organising training by agents from technical support units, and support of the sorghum, corn, cowpea, soya and groundnut sectors. These measures, combined with good rainfall, enabled a strong rise of 14.2 per cent in cereal production in 2010.

The cotton sector also performed well, with a 15 per cent rise in production over 2009, bringing the harvest from 414,500 tonnes to 476,700 tonnes in 2010. This strong increase was facilitated by incentive measures taken by the government to revive the sector including an increase in the advance purchase price of cotton from CFAf160 (US$0.33) per kilogram to CFAf182 (US$0.37), and the maintenance of price subsidies on fertilisers.

The modernisation of agriculture is key to the country's development policy. In 2010, the authorities adopted a series of eight application texts implementing land law in rural areas. The Millennium Challenge Corporation's programme drew on these measures to conduct work on the ground, notably in issuing deeds to rural property. In terms of promoting agriculture, the authorities continued discussions as part of the process of harmonisation and intervention co-ordination with a view to developing a national rural sector programme.

With strong food production and the rebound of cotton production, forecasts for the primary sector in 2011 and 2012 are improved, with food production expected to increase by 2.9 per cent and cotton by 4 per cent during the coming two years.

In terms of demand, the growth of real GDP in 2010 was primarily led by final consumption, with a contribution of 3.7 per cent. Private consumption was highly dynamic, with a 2.5 per cent share of GDP, while public consumption contributed at a rate of 1.2 per cent. External trade contributed negatively to real GDP growth, at -0.2 per cent.

Investment, which should be a motor of economic growth, contributed only 2.2 per cent to real GDP, with the relatively low level of public and private investment (around 23 per cent of nominal GDP in 2010) to blame.

The economic outlook for 2011 and 2012 in terms of the contribution to growth should be more or less sustained, with a slight upswing of the contribution of investment (2.6 per cent per year). To achieve stronger growth, as projected in the new development strategy adopted at the end of 2010, Burkina Faso will have to encourage further the promotion of public and private investment, in particular infrastructure construction. It must also improve its economic competitiveness.

International trade

In 2010, external trade was marked by good international prices for cotton and gold. In addition, gold production increased with the start of operations at the country's largest mine, Essakane. The positive effects of these two factors were dampened by the slight rise in international oil prices in the second quarter of 2010, by imports linked to the intensification of agriculture and mining activity, and by the investment needs for reconstruction and modernisation of socio-economic infrastructure following the floods of 2009 and 2010.

In 2010, the deficit on the trade account was 2.8 per cent of GDP. With the strong rise in gold exports (more than 40 per cent), the trade deficit was mostly absorbed compared to 2009, when it accounted for 5.8 per cent of GDP. Cotton, long the primary export, ceded its place to gold which contributed 57 per cent to exports, versus 23 per cent for cotton.

The most important emerging partners for the country are China, India, Taiwan, Thailand and Brazil. In Africa, Morocco is the main emerging partner. Relations with China, India and Morocco have particularly intensified over the past five years. The key centres of interest are trade (exports and imports), foreign direct investment (FDI) and diplomacy.

Trade has increased substantially; initially, Burkina Faso traded primarily with Europe. Imports of manufactured goods (China) and food (India and Thailand) are the largest items traded with emerging partners, in 2009 accounting for 34 per cent of all of the country's imports. The share of imports from China alone represented 16 per cent of total imports throughout the year. Exports of Burkinabé products to emerging countries in contrast remain low (6.5 per cent of total exports). China is the largest market for Burkina Faso goods (5 per cent of total exports).

This revival in trade was driven mainly by the private sector. Imports gave a large section of the population, particularly the poorest, access to a diverse range of low-cost products (two-wheeled vehicles, clothing, electrical products, etc). However, it is generally perceived that the quality of these products is very poor. Burkina Faso does not have good infrastructure for monitoring quality standards and in the view of the AEO should establish regulations.

The current account balance also improved in 2010. Its deficit was 2.7 per cent of nominal GDP, against 4.6 per cent the previous year. This trend should continue in 2011 and 2012, with respective deficits of 1.3 per cent and 0.4 per cent.

Three-quarters of the country's public debt is comprised of foreign debt. As a result, the public policy on debt consists of limiting new loans to concessional financing, with 'grant' elements above 35 per cent. In 2010, foreign debt accounted for 25 per cent of nominal GDP. The outlook for 2011 and 2012 indicates that this

KEY INDICATORS — Burkina Faso

	Unit	2006	2007	2008	2009	2010
Population	m	13.22	13.31	14.04	14.37	*16.43
Gross domestic product (GDP)	US$bn	6.12	6.98	8.29	8.11	–
GDP per capita	US$	456	508	591	564	–
GDP real growth	%	5.5	3.6	4.2	*3.3	–
Inflation	%	2.4	-0.2	10.7	2.6	–
Exports (fob) (goods)	US$m	563.0	575.4	624.0	–	–
Imports (fob) (goods)	US$m	897.0	1,730.1	2,278.0	–	–
Balance of trade	US$m	-334.0	-1,154.7	-1,654.0	*-513.0	–
Current account	US$m	-585.0	-1,361.4	-1,993.7	–	–
Total reserves minus gold	US$m	554.9	1,029.2	926.3	1,295.8	1,068.2
Foreign exchange	US$m	543.7	1,017.4	914.8	1,208.8	982.5
Exchange rate	per US$	496.60	454.40	418.59	472.19	495.28

* estimated figure

should increase to reach 26.2 per cent of GDP in 2011 and 28 per cent in 2012.

In terms of debt viability, Burkina Faso falls into the category of countries with a risk of high indebtedness in the medium term. Indeed, the ratio of net present value of debt to exports, which was 109.6 per cent in 2010, could reach 97.1 per cent in 2011 and 103.7 per cent in 2012.

Doing business and the private sector

Burkina Faso is attempting to improve its business environment. In the World Bank's *Doing Business* report for 2010, the country was ranked 151st out of 183 countries, a three-place improvement over 2009. The government's efforts have led to improvements in three of the ten indicators used in the *Doing Business*ranking. In terms of obtaining construction permits, the introduction of a construction permit facilitation centre (CEFAC) made it possible to reduce the number of procedures to obtain permits from 32 to 15, and to bring the time required down from 226 days to 15 days. The cost of executing contracts fell, while the number of documents required in international trade for both exporters and importers has begun to fall. However, the measures to protect property rights and enforce contract arrangements remain generally inefficient, among other reasons because of delays in obtaining judgements. According to the *Doing Business* report, debt recovery costs remain high in Burkina Faso, representing 81.7 per cent of the debt, versus 50 per cent on average in sub-Saharan African countries.

In 2010, privatisation focused primarily on the large cotton-ginning company Société Burkinabè des Fibres Textiles (Sofitex), which had been hard hit by the crisis in the sector following a sharp drop in world prices. After a recapitalisation in 2009, the state-owned 65 per cent of the company's capital. The importance of the cotton sector in the economy prompted the authorities to continue reforming the company in order to improve the sector's financial viability. Thus in 2010, the Sofitex board of directors undertook a new recapitalisation. In addition, the company committed to reforms with the aim of reducing operating costs. Notably, the company was restructured with a new internal audit department and the creation of a procedures manual and an information system for management.

In terms of the fight against corruption, the state monitoring authority – Autorité supérieure de contrôle de l'État (ASCE) – published its 2010 audit report, the contents of which were largely reported in the national press. This report clearly underlines responsibility for mismanagement. Still, the country fell in the 2010 report of Transparency International to 98th out of 178 countries assessed, down from 79th place in 2009. This fall was due to the fact that the majority of cases of financial malpractice brought to light by the monitoring authority went unpunished.

Poverty is endemic in Burkina Faso, despite good economic performances and the improving trend of social indicators. According to the results of the integrated survey of household living conditions (EICVM), poverty still affected 43.9 per cent of the population in 2009 (50.7 per cent in rural areas and 19.9 per cent in urban areas). The conflict in Côte d'Ivoire, which was resolved in 2011, had disrupted supplies to land-locked Burkina Faso and also pushed up prices for processed foods such as dried milk, sugar and vegetable oil.

Risk assessment

Economy	Poor
Politics	Poor
Regional stability	Fair

COUNTRY PROFILE

Historical profile

1958 The country was given self-government.
1960 Granted full independence from France as Upper Volta. Maurice Yameogo became first president.
1966 Yameogo was ousted in a military coup by Colonel Sangoule Lamizama.
1970 A new constitution was agreed by a referendum, it detailed the introduction of an elected president and civilian administration by 1975.
1974 Lamizama suspended the constitution and assumed the presidency.
1978 Multiparty elections for president and the National Assembly were held. Lamizama and his followers won and he retained the presidency.
1980 Yameogo, was overthrown in a coup by Colonel Saye Zerbo.
1982 Major Jean-Baptiste Ouédraogo overthrew Zerbo.
1983 Captain Thomas Sankara led a coup and took over as president.
1984 Upper Volta's name was changed to the Popular Democratic Republic of Burkina Faso.
1987 Sankara was assassinated. Captain Blaise Compaoré seized power backed by the Organisation pour la Démocratie Populaire-Mouvement du Travail (ODP-MT) (Organization for People's Democracy-Workers' Movement).
1991 A new constitution established a semi-presidential government. Compaoré was elected president, following the withdrawal of opposition candidates.
1992 The ODP-MT won a convincing victory in the national legislature elections.
1996 The ODP-MT merged with the Parti pour la Démocratie et le Progrès (Party for Democracy and Progress) to become the Congrès pour la Démocratie et le Progrès (CDP) (Congress for Democracy and Progress).
1998 Compaoré won the presidential election, which was boycotted by opposition parties.
1999 Prime Minister Ouédraogo and his cabinet resigned, but he and his cabinet were reinstated by presidential decree.
2000 The constitution was amended so that presidential terms were limited to two and a limit of five years per term was imposed. A UN report accused the president of not only allowing Burkina Faso to be involved in sanctions busting of UN embargoes on Angola but also of being in personal receipt of payments for diamond smuggling activities undertaken through his country by Unita rebels.
2001 International donors agreed to fund a US$85 million programme to combat Burkina Faso's HIV/Aids epidemic.
2002 The Chambre des Représentants (House of Representatives) was abolished. The CDP retained its majority in National Assembly elections.
2005 Opposition parties objected to President Compaoré's third time running for office saying it defied the constitution. The Constitutional Court ruled that since the constitution was changed after his first term in office his candidacy was acceptable. Blaise Compaoré was re-elected president with 80.3 per cent of the votes, while Bénéwendé Stanislas Sankara won 4.9 per cent. Turnout was 57.5 per cent.
2007 In the general elections the ruling CDP won 73 seats (out of 111). Tertius Zongo became prime minister following Paramanga Ernest Yonli's resignation.
2009 A national 'free birth certificate' programme began, which started the process of enfranchising all citizens. Other documentation and services such as passports and access to education will flow from the scheme and should cut, not only the ease with which trafficked children are exploited, but also deter child marriages. The ruins of Loropéni were added to Unesco's prestigious list of world heritage sites. Situated close to the border of Côte d'Ivoire, the stone enclosure is an historic site that is a tangible link with the past trans-Saharan gold trade.
2010 Heavy rains in July caused two dams in the east to brake and over 20,000 people were made homeless. Seven candidates took part in presidential

elections held on 21 November. As expected incumbent President Blaise Compaoré won, with 81 per cent of the vote, his nearest rival, Hama Arba Diallo, won 8 per cent. Turnout was reported to be so low that the president turned to the media to encourage people to vote. The official declaration was a turnout of 53 per cent.

2011 Prime Minister Zongo and his government resigned on 12 January. He was reappointed immediately and chose a new (but almost unchanged) cabinet on 16 January. The conflict in Côte d'Ivoire disrupted supplies to land-locked Burkina Faso and also pushed up prices for processed foods such as dried milk, sugar and vegetable oil. On 14 April gunfire was heard in Ouagadougou, at an elite barracks of the presidential guard, as members rampaged through the city protesting at unpaid housing allowances. The mutiny lasted until a curfew was finally imposed on 16 April. A day later the government of Prime Minister Tertius Zongo was dissolved. On 18 April Luc-Adolphe Tiao was appointed prime minister; the unrest had spread to the north as people demonstrated against the high cost of food. The mutiny spread to a fourth city by 19 April. On 21 April Compaoré appointed himself minister of defence in a cabinet reshuffle. On 1 July the World Bank announced a grant of US$23 million to enhance the information communication technology infrastructure in Burkina Faso.

Political structure

Constitution

Constitutional changes were adopted in January 1997. These included the abolition of the limit of two seven-year terms for the president, and an increase in the number of seats in the legislature from 107 to 111.

Form of state

Unitary and secular state

The executive

Executive power is vested in the head of state (the president), who is elected by universal suffrage for a seven-year term. The president may serve unlimited terms. The Council of Ministers is appointed by the president on the recommendation of the prime minister who is also appointed by the president, with the consent of the legislature.

National legislature

The unicameral Assemblée des Députés Populaires (ADP) (National Assembly) has 111 members, elected by proportional representation from party lists, to serve five-year terms.

The Chambre des Représentants (House of Representatives) (upper chamber) was abolished in 2002.

Last elections

6 May 2007 (parliamentary); 21 November 2010 (presidential)

Results: Presidential: Blaise Compaoré won 81 per cent of the vote, Hama Arba Diallo 8 per cent, Bénéwendé Stanislas Sankara 5.5 per cent; turnout was 53 per cent.

Parliamentary: Congrès pour la Démocratie et le Progrès (CDP) (Congress for Democracy and Progress) won 58.9 per cent (73 seats out of 111), Alliance pour la Démocratie et la Fédération–Rassemblement Démocratique Africain (ADF-RDA) (Alliance for Democracy and Federation–African Democratic Rally) 10.7 per cent (14), Union pour la République (UR) (Union for the Republic) 4.3 per cent (5), Union pour la Renaissance-Mouvement Sankariste (UpR-MR) (Union for Rebirth-Sankarist Movement 3.9 per cent, Convention des Forces Démocratiques de Burkina (CFDB) (Convention of the Democratic Forces of Burkina) 2.3 per cent (3), Union des Partis Sankarist (Union of Sankarist Parties) 1.7 per cent (2); a union of seven political parties together had 18.1 per cent (10). Turnout was 56.4 per cent.

Next elections

May 2012 (parliamentary); 2015 (presidential)

Political parties

Ruling party

Congrès pour la Démocratie et le Progrès (CDP) (Congress for Democracy and Progress) (since 1997; re-elected May 2007)

Main opposition party

Alliance pour la Démocratie et la Fédération-Rassemblement Démocratique Africain (ADF-RDA) (Alliance for Democracy and Federation-African Democratic Rally) is the largest opposition party.

Population

16.43 million (2010)*

Last census: 9 December 2006: 14,017,262

Population density: 39 inhabitants per square km. Urban population: 17 per cent (1995–2001).

Annual growth rate: 2.95 per cent according to 2007 government census.

Ethnic make-up

There are a number of ethnic groups, the most numerous of whom are the Mossi in the north (49 per cent), the Gourma in the east and the Bobo in the south-west. Other sizeable groups include the Fulani, the Hausa, the nomadic Tuareg with their Bella domestic serfs in the north-west and the Lobi in the south.

Religions

Animist (55 per cent), Muslim (40 per cent), Catholic (5 per cent).

Education

Only two in five children are able to attend school, due to the chronic lack of places.

Burkina Faso secured financial aid from the international donor community in 2002, in the form of a three-year package aimed at building capacity in education. The agreement encompassed the Education For All Fast Track Initiative (EFA-FTI) with the goal of providing every child with primary school education by 2015. The first phase of financing is aimed at the 1.2 million children currently unable to attend primary school. The initial financing will also be used to train new teachers, pay teachers' salaries, build new schools, help education systems, respond to HIV/Aids, and put in place other steps to ensure a quality primary education for all children.

French is the language used in schools, although most children will not have heard any spoken at home. School fees are charged although payment can be deferred until after harvest. About 10 per cent of schools are run outside the state system.

Literacy rate: 13 per cent adult rate; 19 per cent youth rate (15–24) (Unesco 2005).

Pupils per teacher: 47 in primary schools.

Health

A CFA6 billion, 10 year (2006–15) plan to make contraceptives available throughout the country is supported by the USAID and the UN Population Fund. The government believes that increasing the use of contraception will help reduce the maternal mortality rate, which at 484 per 100,000 births is one of the highest in West Africa.

HIV/Aids

Burkina Faso has the second highest infection rate in West Africa, next to Côte d'Ivoire. In February 2003, the UN Development Programme (UNDP) announced the provision of US$9.5 million in funding for the fight against HIV/Aids, poverty reduction and other activities in Burkina Faso. It is expected that half of the funding will be concentrated on the HIV/Aids programme, including prevention of HIV transmission, improved co-ordination and monitoring, and care for infected and affected persons.

A programme to provide anti-retroviral drugs was scaled down through lack of political commitment, poor infrastructure – with a lack of medical personnel – and a centralised distribution network, which are sited as major contributing factors in the programme's shortcomings.

HIV prevalence: 4.2 per cent aged 15–49 in 2003 (World Bank)

Life expectancy: 48 years, 2004 (WHO 2006)
Fertility rate/Maternal mortality rate: 6.6 births per woman, 2004 (WHO 2006)
Child (under 5 years) mortality rate (per 1,000): 107 per 1,000 live births; 34 per cent of children aged under five are malnourished (World Bank).
Head of population per physician: 0.06 physician per 1,000 people, 2004 (WHO 2006)

Welfare

The Social Insurance Scheme provides benefits for old age pensions, disability and a survivior's fund. The fund is open to workers who contribute 4.5 per cent of the wages and this is matched by their employer.

The government announced a national 'free birth certificate' programme in May 2009, which will begin the process of enfranchisement for all. Other documentation and services such as passports and access to education will flow from the scheme. It should also cut not only the ease with which trafficked children are exploited but also deter child marriages.

Main cities

Ouagadougou (capital, estimated population 1.0 million in 2005), Bobo Dioulasso (386,678), Koudougou (87,841).

Languages spoken

African languages include More, Dioula, Gourmantche and Peul. French is the universal medium for documentation.

Official language/s
French

Media

The government regulates the media through the Ministry of Communications and Culture.

Press

Dailies: In French, *Sidwaya* (www.sidwaya.bf), is the official government newspaper, other private publications include *Le Pays* (www.lepays.bf) and *L'Observateur Paalga* (www.lobservateur.bf).

Weeklies: In French, magazines or weekend editions of daily newspapers include *L'Observateur Dimanche* (www.lobservateur.bf), *Bendré* (www.journalbendre.net), *Indépendent* (www.independant.bf), *L'Opinion* (www.zedcom.bf), *Journal du Jeudi* (www.journaldujeudi.com), is a satirical magazine. *L'Evénement* (www.evenement-bf.net), is published fortnightly.

Broadcasting

The national, public broadcaster is Radio Télévision du Burkina (RTB) (www.tnb.bf).

Radio: For most of the population radio is the primary means of accessing news and information. There are many private and community stations in operation.

Radio Burkina (RTB) (www.radio.bf) has a national network with regional services, broadcasting in French and 13 local languages. Private stations include Savane FM (www.savanefm.bf), Africa No 1 (www.africa1.com), Radios Gambidi, Pulsar and Horizon FM and Radio Maria Burkina Faso (www.radiomaria.org) run by the Catholic Church.

Television: The public TV service is La Télévision du Burkina (RTB) (www.tnb.bf), which transmits programmes in French and local languages. Alternatively Canal 3 (www.tvcanal3.com), is a private, commercial TV station. There is satellite TV, primarily from French sources but with other international services available.

News agencies

National news agency: Agence d'Information du Burkina

Economy

Burkina Faso is one of the poorest countries in the world, with a per capita income of US$580 in 2009. The majority of the population work in agriculture, typically in subsistence farming, which constitutes 20 per cent of GDP and livestock (goats and cattle) a further 10 per cent. Cotton was the principle export revenue earner until 2010 when exports of gold provided the major source of foreign exchange. Industry, particularly gold mining, and manufacturing constitutes 15–20 per cent of GDP, while the service sector, including transport and communications, construction and government services constitutes around 50 per cent of GDP. However, unemployment is very high, estimated at around 77 per cent in 2004, which encourages migration.

GDP growth was an estimated 3.2 per cent in 2009, down from the estimated 5.2 per cent in 2008, due to the increased price of world commodities, a fall in remittances and a weakening of private sector activity. Recovery in the economy in 2010 is estimated to have reached GDP growth of 4.4 per cent.

The economy, despite positive developments, remains fragile and vulnerable to weather conditions and world commodity prices. The growing strength of the economy is encouraging foreign support for poverty reduction and reform; foreign donors provided US$63 per capita in 2008, up from US$30 in 2000. In 2008, the population living in poverty was 46.4 per cent. In January 2010 the government implemented a poverty reduction social expenditure programme, which focuses on education and health, committing 25.4 per cent of all government expenditure (6.4 per cent of GDP) to this programme.

Remittances have steadily fallen since 2007, when US$50 million was transferred into Burkina Faso; by 2009 remittances were US$49 million (0.6 per cent of GDP) and an estimated US$43 million in 2010. However, this may reflect a weakening economic situation and loss of opportunity in host countries rather than a fall in the numbers of migrants.

The civil unrest and ensuing instability in neighbouring Côte d'Ivoire has added to Burkina Faso's problems. Resources have had to be diverted for humanitarian assistance; over one million refugees have sought shelter and extra security measures have been implemented. The export of cotton via rail through Côte d'Ivoire to the coast has been curtailed.

External trade

As a member of the Economic Community of West African States (Ecowas), Burkina Faso is also a member of the West African Economic and Monetary Union (WAEMU) using the common currency, the CFA franc. Remittances from seasonal workers add to the balance of trade.

Industries include gold mining, processed food and cotton, brewing and bottling.

Imports

Main imports are machinery, foodstuffs, fuel and energy, and capital goods.

Main sources: Côte d'Ivoire (typically 24 per cent of total), France (20 per cent), Togo (6 per cent).

Exports

Main exports include gold, cotton, live animals, hides and skins.

Main destinations: Singapore (typically 17 per cent of total), Belgium (13 per cent), China (8 per cent).

Agriculture

Farming

The agricultural sector accounts for around a third of GDP and employs three-quarters of the workforce. It accounts for around 65 per cent of export earnings. Over 80 per cent of the population is engaged in subsistence farming and nomadic stock raising.

Burkina Faso is prone to drought and has poor soil. Only 10 per cent of the total land area is cultivated. There are plans to mechanise farming and open up new areas for development. Government figures released in June 2011 warned that deforestation was occurring by 110,550 hectares (he) every year (4 per cent of wooded area). The chief cause is agricultural encroachment. The eastern region of Kompienga was the worst hit with the loss of over 100,000he each year. Other factors in the loss of forests include the demand for firewood, decreased rainfall and bush fires. An increase in the population

has also placed an added burden on food production.
Principal food crops are sorghum, millet, yams, maize, rice and beans.
Cotton is the main cash crop and is the country's principal foreign exchange earner; others are sheanuts, sesame and sugar cane.
Livestock production is concentrated in the north, mainly for export to Côte d'Ivoire (which has severely restricted its Burkinabè beef imports in recent years) and Ghana.

Industry and manufacturing
The industrial sector as a whole contributes around 20 per cent to GDP and employs 10 per cent of the workforce; manufacturing contributes 13.5 per cent.
Production is centred on the processing of agricultural commodities (flour milling, sugar refining, manufacture of cotton yarn and textiles) and production of consumer goods, including moped/bicycle assembly, footwear and soap manufacture.
Foreign investment is minimal and development remains handicapped by the chronic shortages of raw materials and spares.

Tourism
Tourism is at an early stage of development. While hotel accommodation is expanding, most of it is confined to Ouagadougou and Bobo Diaoulasso, and access to some tourist sites is difficult. Europe is the main source of visitors, especially France, followed by Africa. The country comprises four tourist regions. Ouagadougou is an artistic and business centre, while the west specialises in indigenous culture, the Sahel in adventure holidays, and the east, which is home to two national parks, in safaris and hunting. The economic importance of the sector is recognised, with rural and eco-tourism being the focus of further development.

Environment
In June 2010 the African Union backed a proposal to build the 'Great Green Wall' project, of a 15km wide, 7,775km long, continuous belt of trees from Senegal in the west to Djibouti in the east (traversing 11 countries) in an effort to halt the advance of the Sahara Desert. The trees to be used would be drought-adapted, preferably native to the area from a list of 37 possible species, and should help to slow soil erosion and filter rain water.

Mining
The sector contributes around 7 per cent to GDP and employs 2 per cent of the workforce.
Activity is confined to extraction of gold-bearing quartz at Poura (reserves estimated at 30 tonnes), marble and antimony.
There are viable deposits of zinc and silver at Perkoa, and some 15 million tonnes of manganese deposits at Tambao, as well as known reserves of limestone, bauxite, nickel, phosphates and lead.
Exploitation of resources is hindered by weak infrastructure.
Burkina Faso has a geological structure similar to that of the world's richest gold producing areas.

Hydrocarbons
There are no known reserves of hydrocarbons and Burkina Faso relies entirely on imports of refined oil (9,000 barrels per day in 2008, mainly gasoline and distillate). Nigeria has used trade deals of oil with Burkina Faso as a way of improving relations.

Energy
Total installed generating capacity was 236MW in 2007, of which 85 per cent is supplied by thermal power. Electricity distribution is overseen by the Société Nationale Burkinabe d'Electricité (Sonabel). Only 14 per cent of the country, mainly the urban areas, has access to electricity and there is no national electricity grid. There are several dams producing hydropower, all publicly owned and accounting for 32MW, with an additional 75MW planned. Private energy generation is only used for private purposes. Some electricity is imported from Côte d'Ivoire. Electricity is regarded as crucial to the country's development and the government is keen to extend transmission lines and improve supply to meet growing demand. The rural population relies on biomass, typically wood fuel, for cooking, lighting and power, which is leading to deforestation and desertification in some areas.
In May 2009, the Canadian company Semafo announced its partnership with the government to undertake a feasibility study to construct a 20MW solar power system to provide low cost electricity.

Financial markets
Burkina Faso has no stock exchange.
Stock exchange
Afribourse (Bourse Régionale des Valeurs Moblières) (BRVM)

Banking and insurance
The banking sector has undergone liberalisation in recent years, with the government restricting its involvement to around a quarter of the sector.
Central bank
Banque Centrale des Etats de l'Afrique de l'Ouest (central banking authority for the members of the West African Monetary Union)
Main financial centre
Ouagadougou

Time
GMT

Geography
Burkina Faso is a landlocked country in West Africa, bordered by Mali to the west and north, by Niger to the east, and by Benin, Togo, Ghana and Côte d'Ivoire to the south.
Burkina Faso is a generally flat country. The north lies in the Sahel region, the semi-arid fringes of the Sahara desert. To the south-west there are hills. The highest point in the country, Ténakourou, which rises to 749m, is in this region. Rainfall is negligible in the Sahel area, but is heavier to south, supporting areas of wooded savannah, rice-growing and large plantations.
The main rivers, which flow southwards into Lake Volta in Ghana, are the Mahoun, Nakambé and Nazinon (formerly known as the Black, White and Red Volta rivers respectively). Other rivers include tributaries of the Niger. Only the Mahoun flows throughout the year, the rest being seasonal. There are many lakes.
Hemisphere
Northern

Climate
The climate is tropical. The dry season runs from November–March, when the Harmattan wind blows, keeping the humidity low. Temperatures in Ouagadougou range from 14 degrees Celsius (C) at night to over 35 degrees C during the day. The main rainy season is from June–October. The highest rainfall is in the south, lowest in the far north where an arid desert climate prevails.

Entry requirements
Passports
Required by all, except holders of national identity cards issued to nationals of Ecowas countries.
Passports must have at least six months validity.
Visa
Required by all, except nationals of Ecowas countries and transit travellers. Applications for tourist and business visas should include itineraries and vaccination certificates against yellow fever. Business visas require a company letter of introduction.
An onward or return ticket is also required.
Currency advice/regulations
There are no restrictions on the import/export of foreign currency or local currency.

Health (for visitors)
Mandatory precautions
Yellow fever vaccination certificate.

Advisable precautions
Typhoid, tetanus, hepatitis A and polio vaccinations are recommended. Malaria prophylaxis should be taken as risk exists throughout the country. Water precautions are also advisable. There is a risk of rabies. Visitors should seek advice with regard to vaccinations for diphtheria, hepatitis B, meningitis and tuberculosis.

Hotels
Hotels are available in Ouagadougou and Bobo Dioulasso with limited availability elsewhere. It is advisable to book in advance. Service is included in bills and gratuities are customary for taxis and porters.

Public holidays (national)
Fixed dates
1 Jan (New Year's Day), 3 Jan (Anniversary of the 1966 Coup d'État), 8 Mar (Women's Day), 1 May (Labour Day), 4 Aug (Revolution Day), 5 Aug (Independence Day), 15 Aug (Assumption Day), 15 Oct (Anniversary of the 1987 Coup d'État), 1 Nov (All Saints' Day), 11 Dec (Proclamation of the Republic), 25 Dec (Christmas Day).
Variable dates
Easter Monday, Ascension Day, Eid al Adha, Eid al Fitr, Islamic New Year, Birth of the Prophet.
Islamic year 1433 (26 Nov 2011–14 Nov 2012): The Islamic year contains 354 or 355 days, with the result that Muslim feasts advance by 10–12 days against the Gregorian calendar. Dates of feasts vary according to the sighting of the new moon, so cannot be forecast accurately.

Working hours
Banking
Mon–Thur: 0730–1130 and 1500–1600; Fri: open to 1700.
Business
Mon–Fri: 0730–1230 and 1500–1730.
Government
Mon–Fri: 0730–1230 and 1500–1730.
Shops
(Mon–Sat) 0800–1300 and 1500–1900; (Sun) 0800–1200.

Electricity supply
220/380 V AC, 50 cycles.

Getting there
Air
National airline: Air Burkina
International airport/s: Ouagadougou (OUA), 8km from city, banks, shops, post office, restaurants, car hire.
Other airport/s: Bobo Dioulasso (BOY), 16km from city.
Surface
Road: Most practical during dry seasons – from Mali (Bamako), Côte d'Ivoire (Abidjan) and Niger (Niamey), when buses operate on these routes. Land journeys are also possible from Ghana, Benin and Togo. Skirmishing between rival political factions makes it advisable to check conditions locally before departure.
Rail: Ouagadougou is linked to Abidjan (Côte d'Ivoire) by an express service, which operates up to three times a week. Sleeping and dining cars.

Getting about
National transport
Air: Air Burkina serves Ouagadougou, Bobo Dioulasso and other main centres. Bobo Dioulasso is the main domestic airport.
Road: Conditions vary; some roads are only passable in dry season, although international roads are all-weather.
Buses: Services between Ouagadougou and main towns. Advance booking advisable.
Rail: Daily service runs Ouagadougou-Bobo Dioulasso and on to Côte d'Ivoire; two classes; some trains have restaurant cars, sleeping accommodation and air-conditioning. Service can become overcrowded.
City transport
Taxis: Unmetered and available in main centres. A 10 per cent tip is usually given.
Buses, trams & metro: Frequent in Ouagadougou and Bobo Dioulasso.
Car hire
National licence plus permit or international driving licence required. Use of chauffeur-driven cars advised.

BUSINESS DIRECTORY

The addresses listed below are a selection only. While World of Information makes every endeavour to check these addresses, we cannot guarantee that changes have not been made, especially to telephone numbers and area codes. We would welcome any corrections.

Telephone area codes
The international direct dialling code (IDD) for Burkina Faso is +226, followed by subscriber's number.

Useful telephone numbers
Police: 17
Fire: 18
Ambulance: 3066-43/44/45

Chambers of Commerce
Burkina Faso Chamber of Commerce, Industry and Handicrafts , 118/220 Rue 3.119, 01 PO Box 502, Ouagadougou (tel: 306-114; fax: 306-116; e-mail: ccia-bf@ccia.bf).

Banking
Banque Internationale du Burkina, BP 1336, Av Nelson Mandela 800, Ouagadougou 01 (tel: 307-888, 307-878; fax: 310628).

Banque Internationale du Burkina SA, BP 362, Rue de la Chance, Ouagadougou 01 (tel: 306-170, 306-171; fax: 300-171, 310-094).

Banque Internationale pour le Commerce, l'Industrie et l'Agriculture du Burkina SA, BP 8, Avenue Dr Kwamé N'Krumah 479, Ouagadougou 01 (tel: 306-226/8, 306-227; fax: 311-955).

Caisse Nationale de Crédit Agricole du Burkina (CNCAB), BP 1644, Avenue Gamal Abdel Naser 2, Ouagadougou 01 (tel: 333-333).

Ecobank-Burkina, BP 145, Rue Maurice Bishop 633, Espace Fadima, Ouagadougou 01 (tel: 318-975, 318-980; fax: 318-981, 318-982).

Société Générale de Banque au Burkina (SGBB), BP 585, Rue du Marché 4, Ouagadougou 01 (tel: 323-232; fax: 310-561).

Central bank
Banque Centrale des Etats de l'Afrique de l'Ouest, Avenue Gamal Abdel Nasser, PO Box 356, Ouagadougou (tel: 306-015; fax: 310-122).

Stock exchange
Afribourse (Bourse Régionale des Valeurs Moblières) (BRVM): www.brvm.org

Travel information
Air Burkina, Avenue de la Nation, BP 1459, Ouagadougou 016 (tel: 5030-7676; fax: 5031-4517).

Direction du Tourisme et de l'Hôtellerie, BP 624, Ouagadougou 01(tel: 306-399; fax: 311-904).

Ministry of tourism
Ministry of Culture, Arts and Tourism, 03 BP 7007, Ouagadougou 03 (tel: 5033-0963; fax: 5033-0964; e-mail:webmestre–mcat@mcc.gov.bp).

National tourist organisation offices
Office Nationale du Tourisme Burkinabè, BP 1311, Avenue Frobénius, Ouagadougou 01 (tel: 311-959; fax: 314-434).

Ministries
Ministry of Agriculture, 03 BP 7005, Ouagadougou 03 (tel: 324-114).

Ministry of Administration, 03 BP 7034, Ouagadougou 03 (tel: 324-833).

Ministry of Commerce and Industry, 01 BP 365 Ouagadougou 01 (tel: 324-786).

Ministry of Communications, 03 BP 7045, Ouagadougou 03 (tel: 324-833).

Ministry of Defence, 01 BP 496, Ouagadougou 01 (tel: 307-214).

Ministry of Education, 03 BP 7032, Ouagadougou 03 (tel: 324-870).

Ministry of Employment and Social Security, 03 BP 7016, Ouga 03 (tel: 310-960).

Ministry of Energy and Mines, 01 BP 3922 Ouagadougou 01 (tel: 324-786).

Ministry of the Environment and Water, 03 BP 7044 Ouagadougou 01 (tel: 324-074).

Ministry of the Family, 01 BP 515, Ouagadougou 01 (tel: 310-960).

Ministry of Finance and Economy, 03 BP 7012, Ouagadougou 03 (tel: 306-995).

Ministry of Foreign Affairs, 03 BP 7038, Ouagadougou 03 (tel: 324-733; fax: 308-792; internet: www.mae.gov.bf/).

Ministry of Health, 03 P 7009 Ouagadougou (tel: 324-158).

Ministry of Higher Education and Scientific Research, 03 BP 7047, Ouagadougou 03 (tel: 324-567).

Ministry of Integration and African Affairs, 01 BP 6943, Ouagadougou 01 (tel: 324-833).

Ministry of the Interior, 03 BP 7011, Ouagadougou 03 (tel: 324-905).

Ministry of Justice, 01 BP 526, Ouagadougou 01 (tel: 324-833).

Ministry of Public Relations and Modernisation of Administration, 03 BP 7006, Ouagadougou 03 (tel: 306-995).

Ministry of Youth and Sports, 03 BP 7035, Ouagadougou 03 (tel: 324-786).

Other useful addresses

Burkina Faso Embassy (USA), 2340 Massachusetts Avenue, NW, Washington DC 20008 (tel: 202-332-5577; fax: 202-667-1882; e-mail: ambawdc@rcn.com).

Groupement des Petits Commerçants, BP 952, Ouagadougou.

Institut de la Statistique et de la Démographie, BP 374, Ouagadougou (tel: 335-537).

Office National de Commerce Extérieur, BP 389, Ouagadougou (tel: 336-225).

Société de Commercialisation, BP 531, Ouagadougou (tel: 333-007); BP 375, Bobo-Dioulasso (tel: 390-423).

Syndicat des Entrepreneurs et Industriels, BP 446, Ouagadougou.

Télévision Nationale du Burkina, BP 7029, Ouagadougou (tel: 336-801).

West African Economic Community, BP 643, Ouagadougou.

National news agency: Agence d'Information du Burkina, 01 BP 2507 Ouagadougou 01 (tel: 50 324-640; fax: 50 337-316; email: infos@aib.bf; internet: www.aib.bf).

Internet sites

Africa Business Network: www.ifc.org/abn

Air Burnina : www.air-burkina.com

AllAfrica.com: www.allafrica.com

African Development Bank: www.afdb.org

Africa Online: www.africaonline.com

Mbendi AfroPaedia (information on companies, countries, industries and stock exchanges in Africa): mbendi.co.za

Burundi

The local, presidential and legislative elections held in 2010 had been expected to cement the democratic gains achieved since the 2005 elections, which ended a decade-long civil war and brought to power the current ruling party, Conseil National pour la Défense de la Démocratie/Forces pour la Défense de la Démocratie (CNDD/FDD). The local elections in May were won by CNDD/ FDD, but the results were contested by most of the opposition, whose leaders withdrew from the remaining electoral process. As the opposition continued to complain openly about the results and press for fresh local elections, the government cracked down on its leaders. Most of those targeted, including Agathon Rwasa, Leonard Nyangoma and Alexis Sinduhije, three prominent opposition leaders, went into hiding and fled the country fearing for their lives. A large number of opposition members, particularly those from Rwasa's Forces Nationales de Libération (FNL) (National Liberation Forces), were killed in circumstances that official reports referred to as cases of banditry. The presidential election was held in June and legislative elections (for both the National Assembly and the Senate) in July, amid political tensions that undermined economic activity.

From a fairly good security situation before and during the electoral process, the country thus entered a period of insecurity characterised by killings and other crimes such as widespread theft. It is unlikely that Burundi will reach high and sustained levels of growth unless it can stabilise its political environment, strengthen its embryonic private sector and develop its human resources. The insecurity that followed the 2010 elections will have to be addressed in order to achieve the higher levels of investment and aid flows that are needed to raise growth rates.

Uncertainty returns

The elections affected the economy in three major ways. First, the uncertainty surrounding the electoral process, particularly after the withdrawal of the opposition, hampered economic activity as many investors decided to hold off on their investments until the political environment became clearer. One indication of this was the decline in banking activities: as of 30 September, the average amount of credit disbursed by the banking sector was 40 per cent lower than at the same date in 2009. Tax collection was also lower than usual. The swearing-in of a new government in late August clarified the situation, and economic activity picked up. Second, the elections were held in a politically fractionalised environment, diverting the attention of many people from productive activities to political activism. This was particularly the case in public institutions, and it is not surprising that the output of the public administration fell by 60 per cent in 2010. Third, the elections were partly financed by domestic revenue, taking away important resources that could have been used in the productive sectors.

The economy

In its 2010 issue on Burundi the *African Economic Outlook* (AEO), published jointly by the African Development Bank and the Organisation for Economic Co-operation and Development reported that the growth rate in the primary sector more than doubled from 1.8 per cent in 2009 to 4.6 per cent in 2010. This relatively high rate had an important effect on the overall rate of economic growth, since the primary sector is the backbone of the economy, accounting for 44 per cent of

KEY FACTS

Official name: Republika y'Uburundi (Republic of Burundi)

Head of State: President Pierre Nkurunziza (Hutu) (from 2005: re-elected 28 Jun 2010)

Head of government: President Pierre Nkurunziza

Ruling party: the Forces Nationales de Libération (FNL) (National Liberation Forces) (from Jul 2010)

Area: 27,834 square km

Population: 8.50 million (2010)*

Capital: Bujumbura (plans to build a new capital nearer to the centre of the country were announced in March 2007).

Official language: Kirundi and French

Currency: Burundi franc (Buf) = 100 centimes

Exchange rate: Buf1,270.80 per US$ (Oct 2011)

GDP per capita: US$180 (2010)

GDP real growth: 3.90% (2010)

GDP: US$1.49 billion (2010)

Inflation: 6.40% (2010)

Balance of trade: -US$343.00 million (2009)

* Estimated figure

GDP. Most of this performance was due to growth in the cash crop sector, which is dominated by coffee. The volume of coffee exported increased from 16,000 to 23,000 tonnes as a result of good weather and far-ranging reforms of the coffee sector, particularly improvements in quality. Exports of tea, the second main export crop, stabilised at about 6,000 tonnes.

Adverse climatic conditions during the first farming season had detracted from food production, particularly in the northern part of the country. Food output increased in the second farming season, however, as illustrated by the decline of food prices between May and July 2010. Overall, growth in the food sector was 1.5 per cent. The low technological level of the agricultural sector has kept Burundi's economy highly dependent on the vagaries of natural forces, particularly rainfall.

Although the direct effects of the food, economic and international financial crises were limited by Burundi's weak integration into the international economy, these crises affected the Burundian economy through indirect channels in 2010. Delays in aid disbursements due to the crisis in donor countries prevented the government from carrying out its expenditure and investment projects as planned. Moreover, the collapse of interest rates in Europe had a devastating effect on Banque de la République du Burundi's (central bank) resources. The amount of interest earned on central bank deposits dwindled from Buf23 billion (US$18 million) in 2009 to only Buf13 billion (US$10 million) in 2010, affecting the central bank's overall balance sheet and reducing its transfers to the central government.

The growth rate forecasts for 2011 and 2012 stand at 4.5 per cent and 5.2 per cent of GDP respectively. These forecasts, made before the elections, by the ministry of planning and reconstruction and the ministry of finance in the context of the preparation of the 2011–13 the Medium-Term Expenditure Framework (MTEF). They were based on: a) the elections in 2010 being transparent and peaceful and their results accepted by all, allowing the pursuit of economic reforms and creating an environment conducive to higher private investment; b) that the economy would take advantage of the recovery in world demand to increase its exports; c) that the increase in consumer prices would be slow owing to the reduction in international inflationary pressure; d) that rigorous implementation of economic and financial reforms would lead to a rise in coffee exports, while better management of water resources would increase irrigated agriculture, reorientation of budgetary allocations would increase the size and efficiency of public investment, and fiscal efficiency would improve; e) that there would be a gradual increase in imports to help the reconstruction effort; and f) that development partners would continue to assist the country's development efforts by providing external financial resources, in the form of grants and concessional loans.

The main risks to the forecasts for 2011 and 2012 are political, weather-related and external. The level of political risk will depend on whether the post-electoral tension abates, leading to a more peaceful political environment that will encourage domestic and foreign investment. Weather-related risks will continue to weigh on the country's economic performance, given Burundi's over-dependence on rain-fed agriculture. One important external risk is the possible reduction of aid disbursements to the country, particularly if there is no strong recovery in Western economies.

KEY INDICATORS — Burundi

	Unit	2006	2007	2008	2009	2010
Population	m	7.64	7.79	*8.94	*8.94	*8.50
Gross domestic product (GDP)	US$bn	0.91	1.00	1.17	1,321.00	1.49
GDP per capita	US$	120	128	147	*163	*180
GDP real growth	%	5.1	3.6	4.5	*3.5	*3.9
Inflation	%	2.8	8.4	24.4	11.3	6.4
Exports (fob) (goods)	US$m	58.7	52.9	69.6	66.0	–
Imports (fob) (goods)	US$m	249.4	257.6	338.1	343.0	–
Balance of trade	US$m	-190.7	-204.7	-268.4	-277.0	–
Current account	US$m	-132.0	-124.0	-305.4	-160.0	-163.6
Total reserves minus gold	US$m	130.5	176.3	265.7	322.0	330.7
Foreign exchange	US$m	129.7	175.4	265.0	217.0	217.4
Exchange rate	per US$	1,000.15	1,139.23	1,186.10	1,230.20	1,203.70

* estimated figure

Coffee and exports

Burundi has been characterised by a chronic trade deficit over the years. The dependence of the export sector on a single commodity, coffee, has made the economy vulnerable to upswings in coffee prices on the international market. Even when prices are high, however, Burundi does not benefit much because it exports such small quantities. In 2009, for example, only 16,000 tonnes were exported. In 2010, which was considered a good year in terms of coffee production, 23,000 tonnes were exported. The trade balance has therefore been dominated by imports. In 2010, imports and exports represented 24.1 per cent and 4.7 per cent of GDP respectively. The exports/GDP ratio has remained consistently low over the years, indicating that unlike many African countries, Burundi has not been able to generate export-led growth.

In 2011 and 2012, exports and imports are expected to remain at much the same levels as in 2010, which implies that the trade balance will not change substantially. Even if the volume of coffee exports increases as a result of the reforms under way in the coffee sector – the doubling of producer prices in just two years and the privatisation of coffee processing are expected to boost both output and better quality – international prices are not expected to remain at their 2010 level. As a result, the country will need to sell more coffee to maintain the same level of export revenue, which is unlikely given that coffee plants take three to four years to mature.

Burundi has a small and weak private sector, mainly because of a difficult business climate that discourages investment. According to the World Bank's 2011 *Ease of Doing Business* survey Burundi was ranked 180th out of 183 countries surveyed in 2010 – a clear indication of the challenges facing the development of the private sector.

Risk assessment

Economy	Poor
Politics	Poor
Regional stability	Fair

COUNTRY PROFILE

Historical profile

1899 Burundi and its neighbour, Rwanda, were incorporated into German East Africa.

1916 Belgium occupied the area.
1923 Re-named Ruanda-Urundi, Belgium continued its administration.
1959 Many Tutsi refugees from Rwanda sought shelter from ethnic violence.
1962 On 1 July the Kingdom of Burundi became independent from Belgium under a Tutsi King, Mwambutsa IV.
1963 Many Hutus fled into Rwanda due to ethnic violence.
1965 Hutu candidates won a majority in parliamentary elections. However, Mwambutsa refused to appoint a Hutu prime minister. A Hutu coup led by Michel Micombero failed and the Hutu elite were massacred in retaliation.
1966 Mwambutsa was deposed by his son Ntare V. Micombero led a successful *coup d'état* overthrowing the monarchy.
1972 Ntare was killed, supposedly by Hutus, sparking violence that led to the killing of 150,000 Hutus.
1976–87 Micombero was deposed by Tutsi Colonel Jean-Baptiste Bagaza. Bagaza's dictatorship was notorious for its violations of human rights.
1987 Bagaza was overthrown by Tutsi Major Pierre Buyoya.
1988 Thousands of Hutu were killed and many more fled into Rwanda
1992 A new constitution endorsed multi-party elections.
1993 Melchior Ndadaye, who was committed to reforming the Tutsi-dominated army, won the elections and became the first Hutu president. Ndadaye was assassinated by pro-Bagazza paratroopers. More massacres followed.
1994 Cyprien Ntaryamira, a Hutu, was appointed president by the National Assembly. He and the Hutu president of Rwanda were killed in a plane crash. Sylvestre Ntibantuganya, a Hutu, became president.
1995 A coalition government was formed under Antoine Nduwayu, a Tutsi. Ethnic violence continued.
1996 Major Pierre Buyoya seized power and suspended the constitution.
1998 Buyoya came to an agreement with parliament under a transitional constitution and was formally sworn in as president.
1999 Tutsi and Hutu factions agreed to talks brokered by former Tanzanian president Julius Nyerere.
2000 President Buyoya and 13 political parties signed the Arusha peace accord but two important Hutu groups refused to sign.
2001 In talks chaired by former South Africa president Nelson Mandela, it was agreed that Buyoya, a Tutsi, should remain president for 18 months of a new three-year transitional government, when a Hutu vice president would become president.
2002 The Burundi franc was devalued by 20 per cent to the US dollar. Violence between government forces and Hutu rebel groups continued.
2003 Vice President Domitien Ndayizeye was sworn in as president in accordance with the power-sharing agreement. The president and Pierre Nkurunziza, the leader of the main opposition group the Conseil National de Défense de la Démocratie-Forces de Défense de la Démocratie (CNDD-FDD) (Forces for Defence of Democracy), signed an agreement to end the civil war.
2004 A South African-style truth and reconciliation commission was set up. A new constitution was deferred until the transitional government was replaced with a fully elected Assembly.
2005 A referendum approved a new power-sharing constitution. The main former rebel Hutu group, CNDD-FDD, won the parliamentary elections. Pierre Nkurunziza was sworn in as president. Martin Nduwimana (Tutsi) and Alice Nzomukunda (Hutu) were appointed vice presidents.
2006 The 34-year old midnight-to-dawn curfew was lifted. A cease-fire between the government and the longest-established Hutu rebel group, the Forces Nationales de Libération (FNL) (National Liberation Forces), the armed wing of the Parti Pour la Liberation du Peuple Hutu (Palipe Hutu), was agreed. Burundi was admitted to membership of the East African Community (EAC).
2007 The Communaute Economique des Pays des Grands Lacs (CEPGL) (Great Lakes Countries Economic Community) was re-launched by Burundi, Democratic Republic of Congo and Rwanda. CEPGL is intended to promote regional economic co-operation and integration. Fighting between rival FNL factions resulted in 100 deaths; 40,000 civilians fled the fighting. Burundi joined the African Union (AU) peacekeeping force in Somalia.
2008 The UN assessment mission to implement the peace agreement was postponed due to fighting between government forces and the FNL.
2009 Agathon Rwasa, the leader of the FNL formally surrendered to AU troops in a ceremonial end to hostilities. They were the last rebel group to lay down their arms. The FNL became a political party – FNL under the leadership of Alain Mugabarabona Icanzo.
2010 By the beginning of June five candidates, including Agathon Rwasa, had withdrawn from the presidential election following criticism by the opposition of the electoral commission. When the presidential election took place on 28 June, incumbent Pierre Nkurunziza was the only candidate; he won 91 per cent of the vote (turnout was 76.9 per cent). All opposition parties boycotted the parliamentary elections, held on 23 July; the Forces Nationales de Libération (FNL) (National Liberation Forces) won 81 seats (out of 106) and Uprona 17, with turnout at 67 per cent. In July, the global anti-corruption watchdog organisation, Transparency International, stated that Burundi was considered the most corrupt state in Eastern Africa and that its neighbour, Rwandan was by far the least corrupt.
2011 On 30 June, the African Development Bank (AfDB) approved a US$67.23 million grant from the AfDB's Fragile States Facility (FSF) to fund phase two of the Gitega-Nyangungu-Ngozi road project. An attack on 19 September on a bar near Bujumbura by unidentified gunmen killed at least 36 people. Although the government blamed 'bandits' there were reports that the attackers wore army uniforms and had come from the DRC; there were also fears that a new rebel group had formed.

Political structure

Constitution

The constitution endorses multi-party elections by universal suffrage.
The 2005 referendum approved a new power-sharing constitution, under which Burundi's president has a deputy from each of the ethnic groups while 60 per cent of the cabinet is Hutu and 40 per cent Tutsi.
Representation in the National Assembly is apportioned on a 60/40 basis between the Hutu and Tutsi with three seats reserved for the Twa ethnic group. In the Senate (upper house) two members are elected from each of Burundi's 17 provinces (one Hutu and one Tutsi), plus three from the Twa ethnic group. Women must account for at least 30 per cent. Four former presidents were also co-opted as senators in July 2005.
The army and the police service are staffed equally along ethnic lines.

Independence date

l July 1962

Form of state

Republic

The executive

Executive power is vested directly in the elected president, with one each Hutu and Tutsi vice presidents.

National legislature

The bicameral parliament consists of the Assemblée Nationale (National Assembly) and Senate. The National Assembly has 100 deputies which are elected by proportional representation from party lists in 17 multi-seat constituencies. In addition, there are 18–21 co-opted members. The Senate has no fewer than 37 and no more that 54 members. Electoral colleges of communal councillors chose one Hutu and one Tutsi in each of the 17 constituencies. All members of parliament serve for five-year terms.

Legal system

Burundi law is based on Belgian and German law. The legal system is composed of a Supreme Court, Constitutional Court and a Courts of Appeal.

Last elections

23 July 2010 (parliamentary); 28 June 2010 (presidential)

Results: Parliamentary: the Forces Nationales de Libération (FNL) (National Liberation Forces) won 81 seats (out of 106), the Union pour le Progrès national (Uprona) (Union for National Progress) 17; turnout was 67 per cent.

Presidential: Pierre Nkurunziza won (unopposed) 91.62 per cent of the vote; turnout was 76.98 per

Next elections

2015 (parliamentary); 2015 (presidential).

Political parties

Ruling party

the Forces Nationales de Libération (FNL) (National Liberation Forces) (from Jul 2010)

Main opposition party

Front pour la Démocratie au Burundi (Frodebu) (Front for Democracy in Burundi)

Population

8.94 million (2009)

Last census: September 1990: 5,139,073

Population density: 250 inhabitants per square km. Urban population: 9 per cent (1995–2001).

Annual growth rate: 1.8 per cent 1994–2004 (WHO 2006)

Internally Displaced Persons (IDP)

381,000 (UNHCR 2004)

Ethnic make-up

The Hutu people are believed to comprise 85 per cent of the population, the Tutsi 14 per cent and the Twa 1 per cent, but there have never been any census statistics on ethnic groups.

Religions

Christianity (over 60 per cent), 32 per cent traditional beliefs.

Education

Burundi typically spends around 3 per cent of its public expenditure on education, however this will increase following an announcement by the president that primary education will be free. Primary education will be boosted by a US$4 million Unicef grant aimed at doubling enrolment by 2006. Classrooms are due to be refurbished and upgraded and 3,000 qualified teachers will be recruited, as well as training for less skilled teachers.

Secondary education is divided into two: academic and technical. Academic secondary education is available for four years between ages 12 and 16, then a national test determines access to higher education. Technical secondary education lasts from ages 12–19.

Kirundi is the language of instruction in primary schools and French in secondary schools.

Higher education is mainly provided by the Université du Burundi, which is largely financed by the government.

Literacy rate: 50 per cent adult rate; 66 per cent youth rate (15–24) (Unesco 2005).

Compulsory years: Six to 12.

Enrolment rate: 55 per cent boys and 46 per cent girls, total primary school enrolment for the relevant age groups (including repetition rates)
(World Bank).

Pupils per teacher: 42 in primary schools.

Health

Burundi's infant mortality rate is relatively high compared to the other African countries. Although women have a higher life expectancy, it is still less than the other East African countries. Immunisation campaigns have resulted in high levels of vaccinations against measles, TB, polio and other childhood deseases.

HIV/Aids

There were 220,000 adults living with HIV/Aids, of which 130,000 were women, as well as another 27,000 children diagnosed as HIV positive in 2003. The number of HIV/Aids cases has risen dramatically, particularly in rural areas. It is estimated that 20 per cent of the urban population, and six per cent of the rural population, are HIV positive. Infection rates in girls aged 15–19 are four times greater than boys of the same age and there are over 200,000 children orphaned by Aids.

HIV prevalence: 6.0 per cent aged 15–49 in 2003 (World Bank)

Life expectancy: 45 years, 2004 (WHO 2006)

Fertility rate/Maternal mortality rate: 6.8 births per woman, 2004 (WHO 2006)

Child (under 5 years) mortality rate (per 1,000): 114 per 1,000 live births (World Bank)

Head of population per physician: 0.03 physicians per 1,000 people, 2004 (WHO 2006)

Welfare

Burundi has 800,000 internally displaced people, while another 250,000 refugees fled to Tanzania.

The National Social Security Institute administers the old age, disability and survivor's pension insurance fund. It is a scheme funded by workers who contribute 2.6 per cent of their wages (3.8 per cent if working an arduous job), and employers contribute 3.9 per cent of the payroll (5.7 for arduous occupations). Old age pensions are paid at aged 60 (45 for arduous work).

Main cities

Bujumbura (capital, estimated population 384,461 in 2005), Gitega (25,412).

Languages spoken

French is the administrative language; KiSwahili is used commercially. English is a compulsory subject in secondary academic education.

Official language/s

Kirundi and French

Media

Press

There is a low readership for newspapers.

Dailies: In French, *Le Renouveau du Burundi* is a government-run newspaper that has had Unesco investment to allow it to publish every day and increase readership.

Weeklies: In French, *Arc-en-Ciel* and in Kirundi (local language) *Ubumwe* is government-run and the fortnightly *Ndongosi* is a Catholic publication and *Intahe* published by the Tutsi dominated political party, Union pour le Progrès national (Uprona) (National Progress Union).

Broadcasting

The government-controlled, Radiodiffusion et Télévision Nationale du Burundi is the national public broadcaster.

Radio: With low levels of literacy radio is the primary source of news and information. Radio Burundi (RTNB) broadcasts in Kirundi and Swahili as well as French and English. It also broadcasts an educational network. Radio Culture is funded partly by the health ministry. Private radio stations include Radio Isanganiro (www.isanganiro.org) and Radio CCIB+ is operated by the Chamber of Commerce. Bonesha FM (www.boneshafm.org) and Studio Ijambo (www.studioijambo.org) are funded by international organisations.

Television: The only TV station operating is the state-owned RTNB.

News agencies

National news agency: Agence Burundaise de Presse: www.cbinf.com

Burundi Information (in French): www.burundi-info.com

Burundi Quotidien (in French): www.burundi-quotidien.com

Iteka (in French and English): www.ligue-iteka.africa-web.org

Net press (L'Agence Burundaise d'Information): www.netpress.bi

Economy

Burundi is one of the poorest countries in the world. Sporadic fighting between ethnic groups has continued since the civil war ended in 2003, disrupting the social and economic fabric. The per capita income during the period of the civil war fell by 33 per cent (by 2009 it had only climbed to US$164). The IMF reported in 2009 that the latest estimates indicated 66.86 per cent of the population 'lives below the level of consumption that ensures the minimum vital to the individual'.
Agriculture, typically subsistence farming, is still the principal industry, constituting 45 per cent of GDP in 2009. Its regeneration is driving the economy, through revitalisation of food and export (cash) crops, development of livestock production (by rebuilding the national herd and improving cattle, pig and goat breeds), development of bee-keeping and fisheries and the revival of fish farming. Nevertheless, traditional crops of tea and coffee account for around 90 per cent of all foreign earnings.
GDP growth was 4.5 per cent in 2008. However it fell back to 3.5 per cent in 2009 due to lower private transfers and less foreign direct investment (FDI); it is expected to reach 3.9 per cent in 2010. As prices for imported oil and foods fell, headline inflation fell from 26 per cent to 4.5 per cent between 2008–10.
To assist agricultural development the government, with the help of international aid and financal institutions, is investing in infrastructure projects, such as inter-province link roads. A feasibility study has been undertaken to determine the possibility of linking such roads to the Tanzanian railway system. Deregulations of the coffee, tea and cotton industries were initiated by 2009 and have improved the prospects of coffee and cotton farmers whose industries had been in decline.
Despite the improving outlook for Burundi it still has much to do to make a significant impact on poverty and development. The mining industry is underdeveloped although there are, among other minerals, deposits of petroleum, nickel, gold, copper, uranium, platinum and rare earth oxides. Its manufacturing sector is small and caters for local needs.
In July 2010, the global anti-corruption watchdog organisation, Transparency International, rated Burundi to be the most corrupt state in eastern Africa.

External trade

As a founding member of the Common Market of Eastern and Southern Africa (Comesa), and the Economic Community of Central African States (ECCAS). Burundi operates a free trade zone to 13 of the 19 Comesa member states.
Burundi is a member of the East African Community (EAC) (with Kenya, Rwanda, Tanzania and Uganda). The East African Community Common Market Protocol (EACMP) was launched on 1 July 2010, which will lead to the free movement of labour, capital, goods and services between member states as well as employment opportunities and easier flow of investment capital. The signed protocol now requires that legislation in all states must be harmonised to conform to its jurisdiction.

Imports

Saudi Arabia (typically 18.9 per cent of total), Uganda (9 per cent), Belgium (8 per cent).
Main sources: Kenya (18.9 per cent total, 2006), Italy (15.1 per cent), Tanzania (11.1 per cent).

Exports

Principal exports are coffee (normally 75 per cent of total), manufactures, tea, sugar, cotton and hides.
Main destinations: UAE (typically 31 per cent of total), Switzerland (22 per cent), Germany (9 per cent).

Agriculture

Farming

The agriculture sector is the mainstay of the economy, although there was a sharp drop in agricultural output due to disruptions caused by the civil war. The sector has to contend with a damaged infrastructure, broken market networks and poor productivity. Internally displaced persons (IDP) caught up in the civil war were made to over-exploit land causing ecological damage. Although Burundi is potentially self-sufficient in food, large numbers of IDP rely on humanitarian assistance. Food products account for around 13 per cent of all imports.
The main cash crop is coffee, which accounts for up to three-quarters of the country's exports. More than 90 per cent of coffee production is arabica, which is being encouraged for its higher producer prices. The Burundian brand of coffee has won international best quality prizes.
Other cash crops include tea, cotton, palm oil and tobacco.
Agriculture traditionally employs around 90 per cent of the population and contributes around 50 per cent of GDP. Most land under cultivation is devoted to subsistence crops – mainly cassava, bananas, sweet potatoes, pulses, maize and sorghum
Cattle rearing is also an important source of food, as is fishing on Lake Tanganyika. Lake Tanganyika is a rich source of fish.

Forestry

Almost 4 per cent of the land area, around 95,000 hectares, is forest. Around 8.7 million cubic metres of wood is felled each year, of which 8 million cubic metres is used for firewood.

Industry and manufacturing

The industrial sector, which is centred almost entirely in Bujumbura, is based on import substitution and typically accounts for around 20 per cent of GDP. Production includes beer, soft drinks, cigarettes, glass, textiles, insecticides, cement, oxygen and coffee processing.
The civil war discouraged foreign investment and high import costs hampered development of industrial capital, with strengthening peace these trends are reversing.

Tourism

The sector has only had a few years since the civil conflict precluded tourists from visiting Burundi. Eco-tourism and the interest in the Eastern Lowland Gorillas, found in the border region with Rwanda and Uganda, have the potential of bringing in significant foreign exchange.

Mining

Gold and tungsten are mined.
Substantial nickel reserves (up to 5 per cent of world total) have been found, but low world prices and an inadequate infrastructure mean extraction is not economically viable. Deposits of vanadium and uranium are being surveyed.
Phosphates and limestone are used for cement production.

Hydrocarbons

There are no known deposits of hydrocarbons, making Burundi reliant on imported petroleum products, which represent 10 per cent of the country's energy needs, 15 per cent of all imports and cost up to 30 per cent of all foreign exchange earnings.
In 2009 the East African Community discussed oil and gas exploration and future exploitation including petroleum exploration in Burundi in the Ruzizi and Tanganyika basins, which have, as yet, yielded no commercial discoveries.
A feasibility study on the extension of an oil pipeline from Uganda to Bujumbura, was announced in 2009. The proposed pipeline will connect with one under construction between Kenya and Uganda.

Energy

Total installed generating capacity was 33MW in 2007, producing 9 million kilowatt hours; virtually all electricity is generated by hydropower. Burundi is considered to be one of the world's poorest countries; only Bujumbura and Gitega have a municipal electricity service. The majority of the population relies on non-commercial biomass, mostly fuel wood and peat for cooking, lighting and power; only around 1 per cent of the population has access to electricity.

There are two private companies in operation, the Régie de Production et Distribution d'Eau et d'Electricité (Régideso), which operates all thermal power stations and is responsible for urban distribution as well as some small hydro units in rural areas; and the Société Internationale des Pays des Grand Lacs (Sinelac) (a joint Burundi, Rwanda and Democratic Republic of Congo entity) which develops and maintains international power projects, including the major Ruzizi hydroelectric power plant, which is under consideration for an upgrade and extension.

Banking and insurance

Central bank

Banque de la République du Burundi

Main financial centre

Bujumbura

Time

GMT plus two hours

Geography

Burundi is a landlocked country lying on the eastern shore of Lake Tanganyika, in central Africa, just south of the Equator. It borders Rwanda to the north, Tanzania to the south and east, and the Democratic Republic of Congo to the west.

Plains rise from Lake Tanganyika in the west to a central sloping plateau; hills and valleys have cultivated fields and pastures. In the east the region in mostly savanna. The southern tributary of the Nile begins its 6,650km journey to the Mediterranean in the south. The highest peak is Karonje at 2,760 metre.

Hemisphere

Southern

Climate

Around Lake Tanganyika (including Bujumbura), equatorial with hot, humid temperatures 23–33 degrees Celsius (C), and frequent winds. Elsewhere is temperate with average temperatures of 20 degrees C. The rainy season is from October– May (except brief dry period December–January); the long dry season is from June–September.

Entry requirements

Passports

Required by all, with at least six months validity remaining at time of departure.

Visa

Required by all. Applications for tourist and business visas should include itineraries and vaccination certificates against yellow fever and cholera. Business visas require a company letter of introduction from the employer and a local host company.

Currency advice/regulations

Import and export of the local currency is limited to Buf2,000.

Import and export of foreign currency is unlimited but subject to declaration on entry. All currency exchanges must be made through the main banks in Bujumbura or Gitega.

Travellers cheques have a limited market and commissions can be high; to avoid extra exchange rate charges cheques are best in US dollars or euros.

Health (for visitors)

Mandatory precautions

Cholera vaccination certificates are required by all visitors. Visitors arriving from countries where yellow fever is endemic are required to have meningitis and yellow fever vaccination certificates.

Advisable precautions

Yellow fever and cholera vaccinations are considered essential. Occasionally a certificate for meningococcal meningitis is required when arriving. Vaccinations for hepatitis A, polio, tetanus and typhoid are recommended. Malaria prophylaxis should be taken as risk exists throughout the country. Hepatitis B is endemic; visitors should seek advice on diphtheria, dysentery and tuberculosis vaccinations. There is a rabies risk.

To avoid the risk of Bilharzia use only well-maintained swimming pools. Drinking water precautions are essential and water must first be boiled or otherwise sterilised for drinking, brushing teeth or making ice. Eat only well-cooked meat and fish, preferably served hot; vegetables should be cooked and fruit peeled. Pork, salad and mayonnaise and most dairy products, made from unboiled milk, may carry an inherent risk. Avoid food from street vendors.

HIV/Aids is widespread, with 15 per cent HIV positive among adults in Bujumbura. A travel kit including a disposable syringe is a reasonable precaution; all personal medications should be carried, along with their original packaging. Medical insurance, including repatriation is essential.

Hotels

Advisable to book in advance. Very little accommodation available outside Bujumbura. A 10 per cent tip is usual.

Public holidays (national)

Fixed dates

1 Jan (New Year's Day), 5 Feb (Unity Day), 12 Mar (Labour Day), 1 Jul (Independence Day), 15 Aug (Assumption), 13 Oct (Anniversary of Rwagasore's Assassination), 21 Oct (Anniversary President Ndadaye's Assassination), 1 Nov (All Saints' Day), 25 Dec (Christmas Day).

Variable dates

Easter (Mar/Apr), Ascension (May), Eid al Fitr.

Working hours

Banking

Mon–Fri: 0800–1130; 1500–1600.

Business

Mon–Fri: 0730–1200, 1400–1730.

Government

Mon–Fri: 0730–1200, 1400–1730.

Shops

Mon–Fri: 0830–1200, 1500–1800. Sat: 0830–1230.

Telecommunications

Mobile/cell phones

Several GSM 900 services operate in major areas of population in the north, west and south of the country.

Electricity supply

220V AC

Security

It is not recommended driving to and from Rwanda, unless travelling as part of a UN convoy; militia from rival political factions are likely to ambushed lone travellers.

Getting there

Air

The only direct intercontinental flights are from Europe.

National airline: Air Burundi (not approved by IATA)

International airport/s: Bujumbura (code: BJM), 11km north of city; café, currency exchange and post office.

Airport tax: Departure tax: US$20.

Surface

Road: All border crossings can be closed at very short notice depending on prevailing political conditions. There are reasonably passable roads from the Democratic Republic of Congo, either north or south, however the roads from Tanzania are generally in poor condition. The road from Kigali in Rwanda may be passable.

Water: There are connections across Lake Tanganyika, with ferries operating from Kigoma, (Tanzania), Kalenjie (DCR) and Mpulungu (Zambia).

Dar es Salam (Tanzania) is the closest sea port.

Main port/s: Bujumbura, Nyanza-Lac

Getting about

National transport

Air: There are no scheduled internal flights operating.

Road: Most of the roads leading to provincial towns are surfaced. Unsurfaced roads elsewhere can be difficult in the rainy season. Surfaced routes are being extended and local advice should be sought. Major roads are often closed after 1600 for security reasons. Driving outside the cities can be dangerous, particularly in border areas.

Buses: Very little public transport is available and buses are not recommended.

Water: Local boats are available on Lake Tanganyika, they can be slow depending on their cargo.

City transport
Taxis: Available in Bujumbura.
Car hire
Local firms only. International driving licence is required.

BUSINESS DIRECTORY

The addresses listed below are a selection only. While World of Information makes every endeavour to check these addresses, we cannot guarantee that changes have not been made, especially to telephone numbers and area codes. We would welcome any corrections.

Telephone area codes
The international direct dialling (IDD) code for Burundi is +257, followed by area code and subscriber's number:

Bubanza	42	Gitega	40
Bujumbura	2	Muramvya	43
Bururi	50	Ngozi	30
Cibitoke	41		

Useful telephone numbers
Police: 18, 19.

Chambers of Commerce
Burundi Chamber of Commerce, Industry, Agriculture and Handicrafts, Avenue du 18 Septembre, PO Box 313, Bujumbura (tel: 222-280; fax: 227-895; e-mail: ccib@cbinf.com).

Banking
Banque Commerciale du Burundi, PO Box 990, Libere Ndabakwaje; 84 Chaussee Prince Louise Rwagasore, Bujumbura (tel: 222-317; fax: 221-018).

Banque de Crédit de Bujumbura, PO Box 300, Avenue Patrice Emery Lumumba, Bujumbura (tel: 222-091; fax: 223-007; email: bcb@bi-network.com).

Interbank Burundi SA, PO Box 2970; 15 Rue de l'Industrie, Bujumbura (tel: 220-629; fax: 220-461; email: interb@cbinf.com).

Central bank
Banque de la République du Burundi, PO Box 705, Avenue du Gouvernement, Bujumbura, Burundi (tel: 225-142 fax: 223-128).

Travel information
Air Burundi, BP 2460, Avenue du Commerce, Bujumbura (tel: 223-460; fax: 223-452).

Bujumbura International Airport, PO Box 694, Bujumbura (tel: 223-707; 223-797; fax: 223-428).

Tourist office (for accommodation) 7 place de L'Indépendence, Bujumbura, BP 1402, (tel: 222-321, 220-704; email: nitra@cbinf.com).

National tourist organisation offices
Office National du Tourisme, 2 Avenue des Euphorbes, BP 902, Bujumbura (tel: 222-202/023; fax: 222-390; email: ontbur@cbinf.com); internet (in French): www.burundi.gov.bi).

Ministries
Ministry of Agriculture, Bujumbura (tel: 210-342; fax: 222-873).

Ministry of Commerce, Industry and Tourism, Bujumbura (tel: 217-775; fax: 225-595).

Ministry of Communication with the Government, Bujumbura (tel: 212-601; fax: 216-318).

Ministry of Community Development, Bujumbura (tel: 213-098; fax: 224-678).

Ministry of Defence, Bujumbura (tel: 219-994; fax: 225-686).

Ministry of Education, Bujumbura (tel: 217-776; fax: 226-839).

Ministry of Energy and Mines, Bujumbura (tel: 218-586; fax: 223-337).

Ministry of the Environment, Bujumbura (tel: 221-649; fax: 228-902).

Ministry of Finance, Bujumbura (tel: 217-918; fax: 223-827).

Ministry of Foreign Affairs and Co-operation, Bujumbura (tel: 217-595; fax: 226-313).

Ministry of Health, Bujumbura (tel: 218-200; fax: 229-916).

Ministry of Human Rights, Law Reforms and Relations with the National Assembly, Bujumbura (tel: 217-365; fax: 213-847).

Ministry of the Interior, Bujumbura (tel: 212-480; fax: 223-904).

Ministry of Justice, Bujumbura (tel: 210-595; fax: 222-148).

Ministry of Labour, Public Office and Professional Education, Bujumbura (tel: 217-928; fax: 224-079).

Ministry of Peace Process, Bujumbura (tel: 219-457; fax: 219-459).

Ministry of Planning, Development and Reconstruction, Bujumbura (tel: 219-079; fax: 224-193).

Ministry of Public Works and Equipment, Bujumbura (tel: 219-646; fax: 226-840).

Ministry of Repatriation of Displaced Persons, Bujumbura (tel: 218-184; fax: 218-201).

Ministry of Social Action and Promotion of Women, Bujumbura (tel: 210-376; fax: 216-102).

Ministry of Transport, Post and Telecommunications, Bujumbura (tel: 210-462; fax: 226-900).

Ministry of Youth Sport and Culture, Bujumbura (tel: 216-729; fax: 226-231).

Office of the President, Bujumbura (tel: 217-806; fax: 226-424).

Other useful addresses
APEE (export promotion) BP 3535, Bujumbura (tel: 225-997; fax: 222-767).

BCC (Burundi Coffee Co) BP 780, Bujumbura.

Burundi Embassy (USA), Suite 212, 2233 Wisconsin Avenue, NW, Washington DC 20007 (tel: (+1-202) 342-2574; fax: (+1-202) 342-2578).

Burundi Mining Co. BP468 Bujumbura (tel: 223-229).

CIGERCO (Cotton growers), BP 2571, Bujumbura (tel: 222-208).

National news agency: Agence Burundaise de Presse: www.cbinf.com

Internet sites
Africa Business Network: http://www.ifc.org/abn

AllAfrica.com: http://www.allafrica.com

African Development Bank: http://www.afdb.org

Africa Online: http://www.africaonline.com

Mbendi AfroPaedia (information on companies, countries, industries and stock exchanges in Africa): http://mbendi.co.za

Cambodia

KEY FACTS

Official name: Preah Réachéanachâkr Kâmpuchéa (The Kingdom of Cambodia)

Head of State: King Norodom Sihamoni (crowned 2004)

Head of government: Prime Minister Hun Sen (KPK) (since 1985; re-elected Sep 2008)

Ruling party: Coalition government: Kanakpak Pracheachon Kâmpuchéa (KPK) (Cambodian People's Party) and United National Front for an Independent, Neutral, Peaceful and Co-operative Cambodia (Funcinpec) (from 2004; re-elected 27 Jul 2008)

Area: 181,035 square km

Population: 14.30 million (2010)*

Capital: Phnom Penh

Official language: Khmer

Currency: Riel (R) = 100 sen

Exchange rate: R4,083.00 per US$ (Oct 2011)

GDP per capita: US$814 (2010)

GDP real growth: 6.00% (2010)

GDP: US$11.60 billion (2010)

Labour force: 8.80 million (2010)

Inflation: 4.00% (2010)

Balance of trade: -US$1.57 billion (2009)

* estimated figure

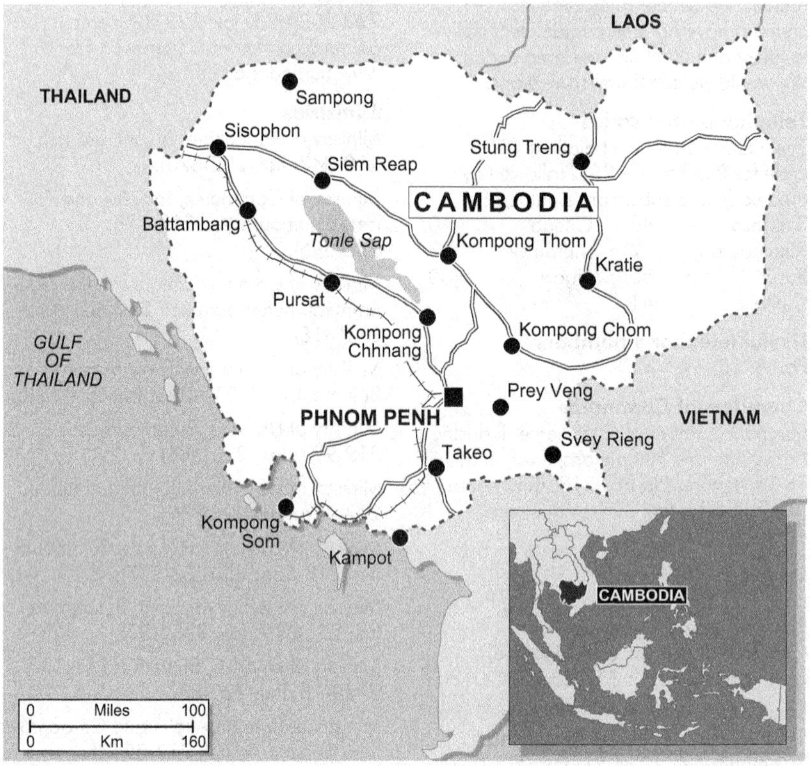

After the conviction in 2010 of Kaing Guek Eav (known as Duch) for the murder and torture of at least 15,000 inmates while in command of the notorious S-21 prison, in November 2011 three of the last remaining leaders of the Khmer Rouge were put on trial for genocide, war crimes and crimes against humanity. They are blamed for the deaths of up to 2.2 million people between 1975–79 and their trial will be the last of the high ranking Khmer Rouge to go on trial.

The scramble for Cambodia

Unlike the original scramble for Africa, Cambodia does not have the wealth of resources that attracted rivals to the dark continent. So why are China and Vietnam investing so much in this small country of no more than 14 million people? China, it seems, wants an ally in the Association of Southeast Asian Nations (Asean), organisation while Vietnam wants to counter the Chinese presence, especially since both are involved in the South China Sea where it is hoped oil will be discovered. Cambodia itself is keen to play one off against another. Whatever the reason, Cambodia is benefiting from strategic investments from both.

China is constructing a container terminal on the Mekong river, which, while other countries are exploiting for power generation, Cambodia is developing as a commercial highway. Quoted in an article in the London *Economist* in June 2011 the deputy director of the container terminal argues that the 'project is tailored to the war-ravaged country's needs: transport by water is cheaper than by road and requires less maintenance'. And there are few good roads anyway. China has already built the Prek Tamak bridge across the Mekong, started work in 2011 on a US$46 million road linking Phnom Penh to the province of Kampot on the coast, has built a hydro-electric power station that when fully operational by 2012 will supply as much as 50 per cent of Cambodia's power needs and plans to build three more.

Vietnam meanwhile has invested some US$2 billion in projects as diverse as telecommunications (through a subsidiary of the state telecommunication company Viettel), agriculture and retailing. Trade with Vietnam has grown from US$950 million in 2006 to US$1.8 billion in 2010. Others scrambling for influence in Cambodia include South Korea, Thailand and even Taiwan.

The economy

The *Asian Development Bank Economic Outlook 2011* reports that the recovery in tourism and clothing exports, together with a good paddy rice harvest meant a gross domestic product (GDP) recovery of 6.3 per cent in 2010, sharply up on the -2.5 per cent in 2009. Industry was the main contributor to GDP growth, expanding by an estimated 11.6 per cent after contracting in 2009. Demand for Cambodian garments, principally from the US and European Union (EU), rebounded in 2010. Data from the US department of commerce showed that US garment imports from Cambodia rose by 19 per cent in dollar terms. Construction activity remained sluggish, however, as foreign direct investment (FDI) in property was slow to recover from the global crisis. FDI in agriculture and garments, on the other hand, rose by 50 per cent to around US$801 million. Special economic zones attracted investments in light industry, especially in the capital, Phnom Penh, Sihanoukville and Svay Rieng.

Rice

The government adopted an ambitious plan in 2010 to increase paddy rice production and add value by promoting the milling of rice for export; some 70 per cent of the population earns a living from rice. The target is for one million tons of milled rice exports by 2015 (the government reckons that in 2009 the figure was just 13,000 tons). The plan includes expanding irrigation facilities; improving the use of water, seed, fertiliser and equipment; providing credit to farmers; encouraging the private sector to become involved in rice processing and export; and reducing transport costs.

Longer-term measures in the plan will focus on improving farm yields and export competitiveness, for example by building roads, railways and ports, and by improving land management. Chinese aid is going to be instrumental in the constructing of transport routes.

The ADB projects that GDP growth in 2011 will be 6.5 per cent and 6.8 per cent in 2012, posited largely on industrial growth of 10.8 per cent in 2012 as demand from the US and EU for garments holds up – US imports in January 2011 jumped by 41 per cent. In 2010 the recovery in global travel had seen tourist arrivals increase by 16 per cent to 2.5 million, with receipts up by 14.5 per cent to US$1.78 billion. The ADB expects this growth to continue into 2011 and 2012, with the biggest gains in arrivals from Asia.

Cambodia is still one of Asia's poorest countries with some 30 per cent of the population living in poverty in 2007, mostly in the rural areas. Higher food prices in 2008 increased the number of people reckoned to be under the poverty level. The government launched a social protection strategy in 2011, with immediate priorities to expand health care programmes and the pilot testing of programmes including conditional cash transfers and labour intensive public works.

The other blot on Cambodia's horizon is the unresolved border issue with Thailand. There has been sporadic fighting in recent years over parts of the border that have never been properly demarcated. As a result tensions have risen and in 2011 there were a number of incursions with thousands of villagers displaced by the fighting. The latest incident was in April 2011 when Cambodian soldiers opened fire on what the Thais called a 'normal patrol by the air force' that was flying along the border. The dispute goes back to the colonial era and in recent years has been aggravated by nationalists on both sides.

Risk assessment

Politics	Fair
Economy	Fair
Regional stability	Fair

COUNTRY PROFILE

Historical profile

1863 Cambodia was made a French Protectorate.
1941 Prince Norodom Sihanouk became King. Cambodia was occupied by the Japanese during the Second World War.
1945 Japanese occupation ended.
1946 France re-imposed its protectorate. A new constitution permitted Cambodians to form political parties. Communist guerrillas began an insurgency against French rule.
1953 Cambodia became independent with King Sihanouk as head of state.
1955 Sihanouk abdicated to pursue a political career as prime minister. His father, Norodom Suramarit, became King.
1960 King Suramarit died and Sihanouk became head of state.
1965 Sihanouk cut off relations with the US and gave support to North Vietnamese guerrillas fighting the US-backed regime in South Vietnam.
1969 The US began bombing Cambodia.
1970 Sihanouk was overthrown in a US-backed coup. General Lon Nol became president, proclaimed the Khmer Republic and began fighting the North

KEY INDICATORS — Cambodia

	Unit	2006	2007	2008	2009	2010
Population	m	14.16	14.58	13.39	*13.94	*14.30
Gross domestic product (GDP)	US$bn	7.26	8.60	11.30	10.80	11.60
GDP per capita	US$	512	600	825	775	814
GDP real growth	%	10.7	9.6	6.7	-2.5	6.0
Inflation	%	4.8	5.9	25.0	-0.7	4.0
Industrial output	% change	18.5	8.4	4.1	-2.5	–
Agricultural output	% change	5.5	5.0	5.7	5.6	–
Exports (fob) (goods)	US$m	3,693.0	4,089.0	4,708.0	4,301.8	–
Imports (fob) (goods)	US$m	4,749.0	5,423.6	6,533.6	5,875.8	–
Balance of trade	US$m	-1,056.0	-1,334.6	-1,825.8	-1,573.9	–
Current account	US$m	-146.0	-77.0	-1,216.0	-865.6	*-503.0
Total reserves minus gold	US$m	1,157.3	1,806.9	2,291.6	2,851.1	3,255.1
Foreign exchange	US$m	1,157.1	1,806.7	2,291.4	2,743.7	3,149.7
Exchange rate	per US$	4,025.00	3,950.00	4,054.00	4,139.00	4,184.90

* estimated figure

Vietnamese in Cambodia. Sihanouk formed a guerrilla movement, known as the Khmer Rouge, while in exile in China.
1970–75 Civil war and intensive American bombing caused widespread destruction.
1975 Lon Nol was overthrown by the Khmer Rouge, led by Pol Pot. Sihanouk briefly served as head of state.
1975–79 Under the Khmer Rouge regime, around 1.7 million people were killed and towns and industry destroyed. The cities were emptied and people were forced into the countryside to become agricultural workers.
1976 Sihanouk was replaced by Khieu Samphan as head of state and Pol Pot as prime minister.
1979 The Khmer Rouge was ejected by a Vietnamese invasion and the regime's policies were reversed.
1981 The pro-Vietnamese Kampuchean People's Revolutionary Party (KPRP) won the elections to the National Assembly, but the international community, led by the US, refused to recognise the new government. Instead, Cambodia was represented in the UN by the Khmer Rouge.
1985 Hun Sen became prime minister.
1989 Vietnam claimed to have withdrawn its remaining troops from the country. Hun Sen abandoned his socialist programme in an effort to appease the US and gain international recognition.
1991 The signing of a peace agreement brought to an end 13 years of civil war. A UN transitional authority was established to share power between the country's various factions. Sihanouk returned and became head of state.
1993 The UN organised elections. The Cambodian National Unity Party (Khmer Rouge) guerrilla group boycotted the poll. The two main parties, United National Front for an Independent, Neutral, Peaceful and Co-operative Cambodia (Funcinpec) and Kanakpak Pracheachon Kâmpuchéa (KPK) (Cambodian People's Party), agreed on a joint government under which they would share power. A constitutional monarchy was established and, in May, the country was renamed the Kingdom of Cambodia. The government-in-exile lost its seat in the UN.
1994 Thousands of Khmer Rouge fighters surrendered after the government called an amnesty.
1997 Second Prime Minister Hun Sen (KPK) seized power, removing First Prime Minister Prince Norodom Ranariddh (Funcinpec) from office, in a move condemned by the international community.
1998 The Khmer Rouge founder, Pol Pot, died. The KPK won the elections, but the opposition parties objected saying the election was fraudulent. A coalition government was formed with Funcinpec. Hun Sen became prime minister and Ranariddh became president of the National Assembly.
1999 Two Khmer Rouge leaders were arrested and charged with genocide.
2001 Parliament approved a law to create a special tribunal to bring genocide charges against Khmer Rouge leaders.
2002 The KPK scored an overwhelming victory in the country's first multi-party local elections, giving it control of over 98 per cent of the country's communes.
2003 Anti-Thai riots were set off by Thai claims that Angkor Wat belonged to Thailand and not to Cambodia. The KPK was re-elected in parliamentary elections, but failed to secure the two-thirds majority required under the constitution to govern alone.
2004 In July the two main political parties, KPK and Funcinpec, agreed to form a coalition government with Hun Sen remaining as prime minister, ending a government crisis that had crippled the kingdom for almost a year. Cambodia became a member of the WTO. Sihanouk went into self-imposed exile in January, first in Pyongyang, North Korea, and later to Beijing. He abdicated on 7 October. The Council of the Throne chose Prince Norodom Sihamoni as the new King.
2005 The UN agreed to the funding of a tribunal to try the leaders of the Khmer Rouge for genocide. Cambodia concluded a border agreement with Vietnam. The opposition leader, Sam Rainsy, was convicted *in absentia* for defaming prime minister Hun Sen.
2006 In the first senate elections, the ruling KPK won a majority. Sam Rainsy was given a royal pardon and returned from exile. The royalist political party, Funcinpec, dismissed Prince Norodom Ranariddh as leader.
2007 Prince Ranariddh was sentenced *in absentia* to 18 months in prison, for selling the headquarters of Funcinpec, for an alleged US$3.6 million. The most senior surviving member of the Khmer Rouge, Nuon Chea (Brother Number Two) was arrested and charged with crimes against humanity. The Khmer Rouge genocide tribunal began its first public hearings.
2008 The ruling KPK won a landslide victory and became the sole party in power. Hun Sen was re-elected prime minister unanimously (the opposition had boycotted the September parliamentary session.
2009 Opposition parties Pak Sam Rainsy (Sam Rainsy Party) (SRP) and Human Rights Party (HRP) created an alliance (Democratic Movement for Change) and agreed not to field candidates in competition with one another. Former Khmer Rouge leader, Kaing Guek Eav (known as Duch), was tried for murder and the torture of at least 15,000 inmates while in command of the notorious S-21 prison. Twenty ethnic Uighur asylum seekers were repatriated to China, just days before deals worth some US$1.2 billion were signed with the Chinese government.
2010 In July Kaing Guek Eav was found guilty and sentenced to 35 years in prison (reduced to 16 years, due to time served). He was the first Khmer Rouge official to be convicted of the 1975–79 genocide. A major stretch of the Pan-Asean railway project between Phnom Penh and Touk Meas near the Vietnam border was opened for freight transport in October. Further construction should connect Phnom Penh with the port city of Sihanoukville and the borders of Thailand and Vietnam by 2013. US$141.6 million in funding was provided by the central government, the ADB, the Opec Fund for International Development and the Australian and Malaysian governments. On 22 November, celebrants of the Water Festival, crossing the overcrowded Diamond Island Bridge in Phnom Penh, suddenly stampeded which resulted in the deaths of 351 people and injury of more than 700.
2011 A decision by the four-country Mekong River Commission to implement plans to build the controversial Mekong Xayaburi dam in Laos was due to be taken on 19 April, but following ecologically and socially adverse reports the decision was postponed. The Mekong River is a food source for millions of people along its length; the dam would reduce food production in favour of electricity generation. Construction of a new bridge across the Tonle Bassac River, close to Phnom Penh began on 6 July. Funded by China, the bridge will connect national highways one and two. The World Bank halted lending in August after villages were destroyed and thousands forcably evicted from an area in the centre of Phnom Penh which had been given over to a property developer to build luxury flats. Cambodia has become a major recipient of investment from China and may not be too concerned by the suspension of loans from the World Bank. On 21 November, three of the last remaining leaders of the Khmer Rouge were put on trial for genocide, war crimes and crimes against humanity. They are blamed for the deaths of up to 2.2 million people killed between 1975–79.

Political structure

Constitution

The 1993 constitution provides for a pluralistic, liberal democratic political system and for a limited monarchy.

To govern alone, a political party is required to have a two-thirds majority.

Independence date

9 November 1953

Form of state
Multiparty liberal democracy under a constitutional monarchy established in 1993.
The executive
Executive power is vested in the Council of Ministers led by the prime minister. The King appoints the prime minister from the representatives of the largest party in parliament on the recommendation of the president of the National Assembly.
National legislature
The bicameral parliament consists of the Radhsphea ney Preah Recheanachakr Kampuchea (National Assembly of Cambodia) with 123 members, elected by proportional representation for five-year terms, and the Sénat (Senate).
In 2006 the first elections for the Senate took place, whereby National Assembly members and councillors of subordinate assemblies voted for 54 members to represent their constituents and serve as Senators for six-year terms. In addition, two were appointed by the monarch and two were appointed by the National Assembly. The Senate, led by a 12-person cabinet, advises on all matters determined by law and the constitution.
Legal system
The judiciary is granted independence under the constitution. The Supreme Council of the Magistracy, chaired by the King, has the right to discipline any judge who breaks the law, but judges cannot be dismissed. The King has sole authority to appoint judges on the advice of the Supreme Council of the Magistracy.
Last elections
27 July 2008 (National Assembly); 22 January 2006 (Senate)
Results: Parliamentary: The Kanakpak Pracheachon Kâmpuchéa (KPK) (Cambodian People's Party) won 59.11 per cent of the vote (90 seats out of 123), Sam Rainsy Party (SRP) 21.91 per cent (26), Parti des droits de l'homme (Human Rights Party) (HRP) 6.62 per cent (3), Norodom Ranariddh Party (NRP) 5.62 per cent (2), United National Front for an Independent, Neutral, Peaceful and Co-operative Cambodia (Funcinpec) 5.02 per cent (2), League for Democracy 1.15 per cent (1); five other political parties failed to win any seats. Turnout was 81.5 per cent.
Senate: The KPK won 43 seats (out of the 54), Funcinpec nine, SRP two; two Senators were chosen by the King and two by the National Assembly.
Next elections
July 2013 (National Assembly); 2012 (Senate)

Political parties
Ruling party
Coalition government: Kanakpak Pracheachon Kâmpuchéa (KPK) (Cambodian People's Party) and United National Front for an Independent, Neutral, Peaceful and Co-operative Cambodia (Funcinpec) (from 2004; re-elected 27 Jul 2008)
Main opposition party
Pak Sam Rainsy (Sam Rainsy Party) (SRP)

Population
14.30 million (2010)*
Last census: 3 March 2008: 13,388,910 (provisional)
Population density: 79 inhabitants per square km (2010)
Annual growth rate: 2.2 per cent 1994–2004 (WHO 2006)
Religions
Theravada Buddhism, Christianity (Roman Catholicism).

Education
Primary school lasts between the ages of six and 12.
Secondary education is divided into lower secondary and upper secondary lasting for three years each. All students follow the same curriculum through the six years. Nearly 40 per cent of total expenditure in primary schools is paid through household contributions. Public expenditure on education typically amounts to around 3 per cent of annual gross national income.
Literacy rate: 69 per cent adult rate; 80 per cent youth rate (15–24) (Unesco 2005).
Enrolment rate: 123 per cent and 104 per cent for boys and girls respectively, total primary school enrolment of the relevant age group (including repetition rates) (World Bank).
Pupils per teacher: 44 in primary schools.

Health
In 2009 international research showed that there was an emergence of drug-resistant malaria in western Cambodia. The disease kills millions of people worldwide each year and with so few effective drugs the appearance of this new strain represents a global health catastrophe.
In 2010 the ministry of rural development said it aimed to provide one-third of two million rural households with access to proper sanitation facilities by 2015. The lack of facilities has led to one of the highest rates of under-five mortality rates in Asia. The NGO, International Development Enterprises (IDE) will provide assistance and work with rural communities to educate and provide facilities for sanitation and safe drinking water. Rural households will contribute to the construction of a latrine.
HIV/Aids
HIV prevalence: 2.6 per cent aged 15–49 in 2003 (World Bank)
Life expectancy: 54 years, 2004 (WHO 2006)
Fertility rate/Maternal mortality rate: 4.0 births per woman, 2004 (WHO 2006); maternal mortality ratio 470 deaths per 100,000 live births (World Bank).
Child (under 5 years) mortality rate (per 1,000): 97 per 1,000 live births; 47 per cent of children under aged five are malnourished (World Bank).

Welfare
Five Cambodian government ministries and their departments directly or indirectly offer social welfare support for the general population, including people with disabilities. There is provision for pensions of disabled veterans. There are no universal social security benefit entitlements in Cambodia.

Main cities
Phnom Penh (capital, estimated population 1.2 million in 2004), Bat Dâmbâng (158,124), Kâmpóng Saôm (175,891), Siem Réab (158,884), Sisophon (111,673).

Languages spoken
French is spoken. English is becoming the most commonly used business language, superseding French.
Official language/s
Khmer

Media
Press freedom, while not guaranteed, is practiced with the support of Prime Minister Hun Sen.
Press
Dailies: In Khmer, *Kaoh Santepheap* (www.kohsantepheapdaily.com.kh), *Reaksmei Kampuchea* and *Rasmei Angkor*. In Chinese, *Jian Hua Daily Cambodic and Con Rhuong Pao*. In English, *Cambodian Daily* (www.cambodiadaily.com).
Weeklies: In Khmer, the pro-communist *Trung Lap* and *Pracheachon* (Communist Party) published twice weekly. In English, *The Cambodian Magazine* (www.cambodianscene.com) and *Phnom Penh Post* (www.phnompenhpost.com) is published every Friday.
Business: In Chinese *The Commercial News* (www.thecommercialnews.com), has various news and economy articles.
Broadcasting
The unregulated ownership of satellite dishes allows full access to domestic and foreign broadcasts.
Radio: The National Radio of Cambodia (NRC) operates three stations, relayed nationwide and NRC International in English, French, Thai, Lao and Vietnamese. There are several other private commercial stations, including Radio 103 FM, Radio 97 FM, Radio 95 FM, Beehive 105 FM (www.sbk.com.kh), Bayon Radio is part of the Bayon TV network.

Television: The National Television of Cambodia (TVK) (www.tvk.gov.kh) is the state broadcaster. Other, private and commercial stations include TV3 (based in Phnom Penh), TV5 (www.ch5cambodia.com), CTN (www.ctncambodia.com), CTV9 (www.tv9.com.kh), Bayon TV (www.bayontv.com.kh) and Apsara TV. All TV stations provide satellite coverage, to which three other foreign channels are available.

News agencies

National news agency: AKP (Agence Kampuchea Presse)

Economy

Cambodia is, for the most part a rural, developing country which, despite extensive reforms and massive donor support, has an economic basis that remains weak. It is one of the least developed countries in the world, per capita income was US$825 in 2008, but in 2009 it fell to US$775 due to the cut in international trade and high prices of food during the global economic crisis.

Over 30 per cent of the population live below the poverty line, 80 per cent of whom live in rural areas. Agriculture accounts for around 30 per cent of GDP and is mostly subsistence farming. The service sector accounts for 40 per cent of GDP, concentrated in trading activities, and industry 30 per cent.

GDP growth was 10.2 per cent in 2007, which was mainly generated by increases in the tourism sector and clothing manufacturing, but GDP growth fell to 6.7 per cent in 2008 and finally fell into recession with GDP growth of -2.5 per cent in 2009. The US dollar has become integrated into the economy and is interchangeable with the domestic currency (riel).

Sustainable development is not possible without greater private sector commitment coupled with social programmes. The government is in the process of applying power to its trade policy machinery in expectation of improving the prospects of its nascent market economy. Economic growth has been driven by increases in clothing production (around 80 per cent of which is exported to the US), tourism with over two million visitors annually (over one million people visit Angkor Wat, Cambodia's main tourist attraction), and agriculture and construction activity. The infrastructure is weak and cannot provide the base for sustained growth in all sectors.

Despite the weakness of the economy, the International Monetary Fund (IMF) has advised that further investment should be applied to infrastructure development and high-impact social programmes. In 2009 the government indicated that it was planning to introduce a value added tax (VAT) on electricity imports. Cambodia is still a beneficiary of foreign assistance – US$600 million in 2008, in grants and concessional loans.

The major economic challenge for Cambodia over the medium term will be to encourage private sector growth that can create enough jobs for its young population, while improving the living standards of the population as a whole.

External trade

Cambodia is one of the world's least developed countries, its export market is dominated by the textile industry and the cut in global trade in 2008–09 cut exports to the US.

Cambodia is a member of Asean and is negotiating free trade arrangements with the other regional members.

Imports

Main imports are petroleum products, vehicles and machinery, construction materials, energy, pharmaceutical products, cigarettes, gold, artificial textiles and cotton yarns and textiles.

Main sources: Thailand (typically 27 per cent of total), China (16 per cent), Vietnam (13.9 per cent).

Exports

Major exports are clothing and footwear, timber and rubber, precious gems, rice, fish and tobacco.

Main destinations: US (typically 54 per cent of exports), Germany (8 per cent), Canada (6 per cent).

Agriculture

Agriculture accounts for 33 per cent of GDP and employs around 75 per cent of the workforce. Agriculture is hampered by poor soil fertility and irrigation and unclear land-ownership rights.

The principal crop is rice (both hill and lowland types), which is grown on 70 per cent of the cultivated land. Rice output accounts for around 17 per cent of GDP. Only 16 per cent of rice lands are irrigated and there have been no large-scale projects since the 1960s.

Other crops include rubber (a major export), maize, cassava and fruit and vegetables. The smuggling of rubber to neighbouring countries, to get a better price, is a problem. Cambodia also produces jute and sawn timber products.

Cattle stocks are improving, but fish represents the only animal protein for most people.

Tonle Sap (Great Lake), floods during the monsoon and is the breeding ground for many fish. It is one of the world's most productive inland fisheries; it provides around 75 per cent of the annual inland fish catch and 60 per cent of Cambodia's protein intake.

Industry and manufacturing

The industrial sector accounts for 29 per cent of GDP and employs around 20 per cent of the workforce.

Most of what little industry Cambodia possessed was wrecked during the 1970s under the Khmer Rouge, particularly by the virtual closure of the towns in the drive to force people back to the land. Development has been hampered by the absence of adequate transport and other infrastructure. The manufacturing sector is beset by shortages of power and raw materials and by poor quality products. A number of state factories have been leased to the private sector since 1990 and joint ventures established in enterprises such as hotels, rattan, mineral water, wood processing, a tannery, plywood, tyres and textiles.

Industrial expansion has been led by the growth in the garment-manufacturing sector, but the level of growth might be affected by the ending of garment quotas by the WTO in 2005. In order to offset this, the government will need to create a more investor-friendly environment.

In 2009 the US removed Cambodia from its economic black list and opened up opportunities for bilateral trade.

Tourism

The government has a target of three million tourists per annum by 2010. Particular focus is geared towards the cultural attractions such as the ancient city of Angkor Wat. Tourism, which has had to overcome the effects of years of upheaval, has led growth in the services sector. The main market is South Korea, followed by Japan, USA and the UK. Tourism is an important contributor to GDP. A new state airline, in partnership with Vietnam Airlines, Cambodia Angkor Airline, was launched in July 2009. The first route was from Preah Sihanouk Port to Angkor Wat.

A project begun in the 1960s to reconstruct the Baphuon monument was finally completed and re-opened in July 2011. The 11th-Century, intricately-carved three-tier tower, part of the Angkor temple complex, had been on the brink of collapse by the 1950s. A French team of archaeologists dismantled the tower, numbering each of the 300,000 sandstone blocks as they went. Work was interrupted by the civil war and the master plan to re-build the tower was destroyed. With the ending of the civil war in the mid-1990s, work began to solve the puzzle of putting the blocks back together. Angkor attracts some two million tourists each year.

Environment

The UN designated Tonle Sap (Great Lake) as an ecological hotspot and designated it a Unesco biosphere in 1997.

Between 2000–2005 it is estimated that logging of forests amounted to 140,500 hectares (ha) per year or 1.9 per cent annual deforestation. Primary forest cover has fallen from 766,000ha in 1999 to 322,000ha in 2005. Cambodia has 775 species of wildlife, of with 60 are under threat; it has 862 native tree species with 13 endangered and 10 critically endangered. Illegal logging, within the country and along Cambodia's borders, threatens not only the forests but also the communities that depend on these local resources.

Mining

The mining sector typically contributes 9 per cent to GDP and employs 1 per cent of the workforce.

There are deposits of iron ore, copper, manganese, gold and bauxite, but exploitation is hindered by the absence of transport facilities. Phosphates are the only economically viable mineral and are mined for use in the local fertiliser industries. Gemstones are also mined.

Hydrocarbons

There are no known oil or natural gas reserves. Cambodia is dependent on imports, which were over 4,000 barrels per day (bpd) in 2008, mainly from Thailand. Exploration is being undertaken particularly in offshore areas, where indications of oil and gas have been detected.

There are indications of small coal reserves.

Energy

Total installed generating capacity was around 190MW in 2006, producing 1.16 billion kilowatt hours (kWh); consumption was 1.18 billion kWh and imports of 250MW came from Vietnam and Thailand. Electricity imports of 500MW are expected in 2009.

About 15 per cent of the population have access to electricity, but only in Phnom Penh and provincial towns; consumption is growing. Current generation is small-scale and inefficient, mostly from oil-fired power stations with some hydropower. There is no national power grid and rural consumers as well as industries frequently use costly generators to ensure an uninterrupted supply.

There are major hydroelectric schemes planned for the north and east, along the Mekong River, the Srae Pok River and the Sesan River, providing a total of 2,000MW by 2020. Smaller hydro schemes, due to be operational by 2014, include the Attai River, Russey Chum and Ta Tai River dams being built by Chinese and South Korean companies.

The Asian Development Bank (ADB) has been involved in promoting the Greater Mekong Sub-region (GMS) electricity market to form a regional electricity grid which incorporates the uneven load demands and different resource bases. By 2008 a regional energy trading and sustainable development scheme was in place and bilateral arrangements included electricity imports and exports.

Financial markets

Stock exchange

Cambodian Securities Exchange

Banking and insurance

The banking system is underdeveloped. The economy is highly dollarised, with foreign currency making up 70 per cent of the total money supply. This hinders the central bank's ability to implement an effective monetary policy.

Since 2000, Cambodia has been reforming the banking sector, introducing a minimum capitalisation requirement of US$11 million. This led to the closure of 11 banks by 2002.

Central bank

National Bank of Cambodia

Time

GMT plus seven hours

Geography

Cambodia occupies part of the Indochinese peninsula in south-east Asia. It is bordered by Thailand and Laos to the north, by Vietnam to the east and by the Gulf of Thailand to the south.

Around 60 per cent of Cambodia is rain forest, of which 3 per cent is primary forest with extensive bio-diversity. The Tonle Sap (Great Lake) is the largest freshwater lake in south-east Asia, at 2,700 square km but only about one metre deep for most of the year. During the monsoon the lake grows by another 16,000 square km and its depth increases by nine metres. The lake flows out into the Mekong River. The highlands are located in the north-east and there are numerous islands along the south-west coast.

Hemisphere

Northern

Climate

Generally hot and very humid, with a rainy season from June to October/November. Likely temperatures in Phnom Penh are 22–30 degrees Celsius (C) from November–December and 24–34 degrees C in April.

Entry requirements

Passports

Required by all. Must be valid for six months from departure date.

Visa

Visas are required by all, with a few exceptions; to find a list and download a tourist one-month e-visa, see http://evisa.mfaic.gov.kh. An e-visa can only be used at Pochentong (Phnom Penh) and Siem Reap airports. Tourists can also get a visa on arrival at the Pochentong and Siem Reap airports, as well as the Poi Pet international checkpoint, overland from Thailand. If planning to arrive by boat from Vietnam, or overland at checkpoints other than Poi Pet, a visa must be obtained prior to arrival; the place of entry must be specified.

A business visa should be applied for before departure, contact the closest Cambodian consulate for further details.

Currency advice/regulations

Import and export of local currency is prohibited. Import of foreign currency must be declared on arrival; export of foreign currency can only be up to amount declared.

Health (for visitors)

Mandatory precautions

Vaccination certificates for yellow fever if travelling from an infected area.

Advisable precautions

Vaccinations recommended for diphtheria, tuberculosis, hepatitis A and B, Japanese B encephalitis. Anti-malarial precautions should be taken. There is risk of rabies.

Credit cards

Credit cards are only accepted in large hotels and shops.

Public holidays (national)

Fixed dates

1 Jan (New Year's Day), 7 Jan (Victory Day), 8 Mar (Women's Day), 14–16 Apr (Traditional Cambodia New Year), 1 May (Labour Day), 13–15 May (King's Birthday), 16 May (Royal Ploughing day), 18 Jun (Queen's Birthday), 24 Sep (Constitution Day), 29 Oct (Coronation Day), 31 Oct (last King's Birthday), 9 Nov (Independence Day), 10 Dec (International Human Rights Day).

Variable dates

Birth of Buddha Day (Visaka Buja Day) (May); Royal Ploughing Ceremony (Visakha Bochea Day) (May); three-day spirit festival (Pchum Ben festival) (Sep/Oct); three day Water Festival (Bonn Om Touk) (Nov).

The religious festivals are determined by the Buddhist lunar calendar.

Any public holiday that falls at the weekend is carried over to the next working day.

Working hours

Banking

Mon–Fri: 0800–1500.

Business

Mon–Fri: 0800–1200 and 1400–1700.

Government

Mon–Fri: 0800–1200 and 1400–1700.

Shops

0700–1800.

Telecommunications

Mobile/cell phones

There are 900 and 1800 GSM services available around main towns and cities only.

Social customs/useful tips

Business cards are essential and are usually exchanged during introductions; offering and receiving business cards with both hands is considered particularly polite.

Punctuality is important and visitors should allow plenty of time for travelling. It is acceptable to shake hands with both men and women.

In conversation speak clearly using a moderate pace and complete sentences. Always give time for your host to answer and maintain courtesies.

Even during difficult negotiations remain calm as anger will give a poor impression.

Criticism of the Royal Family and Buddhism should be avoided.

Learning some Cambodian greetings will both surprise and impress your host.

Photography is permitted although it is polite to ask permission before photographing Cambodian people, particularly monks.

Gratuities are welcome in restaurants and hotels.

The minimum drinking age is 18 years.

Security

The government has taken action to reduce crime but visitors are still advised not to walk alone at night in many areas of the city. Most hotels can arrange cars with drivers. When visiting the temples at Angkor Wat, travel by air to Siem Reap airport, remain within the main temple complex and do not attempt to travel to Banteay Srei or to other outlying temples.

Getting there

Air

National airline: Mostly foreign carriers provide international services and usually only from neighbouring countries. A new state airline, in partnership with Vietnam Airlines, Cambodia Angkor Airline, was launched in July 2009, initially flying domestic routes only.

International airport/s: Pochentong International (PNH), 8km from Phnom Penh.

Airport tax: International departures from Pochentong and Siem Reap airports US$25; from all other airports US$20.

Surface

Not all crossings are open to foreign visitors, check with local authorities before travelling. Some crossings will issue visas, but to avoid disappointment organise all visas before arriving at a crossing.

Road: Overland access is via Thailand, Vietnam and Laos.

Rail: The government is rehabilitating the railways to build links to Thailand by the Phnom Penh–Poipet line, and constructing a new line linking Phnom Penh and Ho Chi Minh City. These projects are part of the Asian Development Bank's (ADB) Greater Mekong sub-regional co-operation scheme. The Phnom Penh–Ho Chi Minh City link is part of the Trans-Asia railway aimed at linking Singapore to Kunming in Yunnan province of China.

Water: There are ferry services, via the Mekong River, from Vietnam and Laos. A sea-ferry runs from Thailand.

Main port/s: The Mekong river port of Phnom Penh, the seaport of Sihanoukville.

Getting about

National transport

Air: Domestic flights connect all major cities.

Road: There are 13,500km of roads. Only 12 per cent of national highways are paved, meaning that many communities are cut off during the rainy season.

The Phnom Penh–Ho Chi Minh City (HCMC) Highway refurbishment project is expected to be completed by 2012.

Buses: Some bus or passenger truck services are available.

Rail: There are 612km of track. Rail services operate between Phnom Penh–Aranyaprathet, and Phnom Penh–Kompong Som. There is a critical need to improve infrastructure over the medium-term.

Water: Ferries operate along the Mekong River.

City transport

The most convenient way to travel around the capital is by *cyclo* (tricycle) or *motodops* (motorcycles).

Taxis: There are ranks of cars with taxi signs at the airport and can be hired in all the main cities, but cruising taxis are not the norm.

Buses, trams & metro: Buses link all of Phnom Penh's suburbs.

Car hire

It is advisable to hire a car with driver as local conditions can overwhelm foreign visitors; most hotels can arrange the services of a car and driver.

BUSINESS DIRECTORY

The addresses listed below are a selection only. While World of Information makes every endeavour to check these addresses, we cannot guarantee that changes have not been made, especially to telephone numbers and area codes. We would welcome any corrections.

Telephone area codes

The international direct dialling (IDD) code for Cambodia is +855, followed by area code and subscriber's number.

Battambang	53	Pusat	52
Kampong Som	62	Stung Treng	74
Phnom Penh	23	Siem Riep	63

Useful telephone numbers

Police: 722-353

Fire: 723-555

Ambulance: 723-173

Local directory assistance: 1213

Chambers of Commerce

Phnom Penh Chamber of Commerce, 7B Street 81 corner Street 109, Sangkat Beung Raing, Daun Penh District, Phnom Penh (tel: 212-265; fax: 212-270; e-mail: ppcc@camnet.com.kh).

Banking

Acleda Bank Plc, P O Box 1149, #61, Preah Monivong Blvd., Sangkat Srah Chork, Khan Daun Penh, Phnom Penh (tel: 998-777; fax: 23 998-666).

Cambodia Mekong Bank Public Ltd, 1 Kramuon Sar Street, Khan Daun Penh, Phnom Penh (tel: 217-112; fax: 217-122).

Cambodian Commercial Bank Limited, 26 Monivong Road, Sangkat Phsar Thmei 2, Khan Daun Penh, Phnom Penh (tel: 426-145, 426-639, 213-601, 213-602, 426-638; fax: 426-116).

Cambodian Public Bank Ltd, Villa No. 23, Street 114, Vithei Kramounsar, Phnom Penh (tel: 426-067; fax:426-068).

Canada Bank Ltd, 265-269 Prash Ang Doung Street, Sangkath Wattphnom, Khan Daun Penh, Phnom Penh (tel:-266-046, 725-548).

Crédit Agricole Indosuez, 70 Blvd Norodom, Phnom Penh (tel: 427-233).

First Commercial Bank, 263 Ang Duong St, Phnom Penh (tel: 210-026; fax: 210-029).

Foreign Trade Bank of Cambodia, 24/26 Preah Norodom Boulevard, Phnom Penh (tel: 724-466, 723-866, 722-466, 723-466).

National Bank of Cambodia, PO Box 25, 22-24 Preah Norodom Blvd, Phnom Penh (tel: 428-105, 722-563; fax: 426-117).

Singapore Banking Corporation Ltd, 68 Samdech Pan Street (St. 214), Sangkat Beung Raing, Khan Daun Penh, Phnom Penh (tel: 217-771).

Singapore Commercial Bank Ltd, 316 Preah Monivong Boulevard, Sangkat Chak To Mok, Khan Daun Penh, Phnom Penh (tel: 427-471).

Union Commercial Bank Plc, UCB Bldg, No. 61, 130 Road, Psa Chas Quater, Khan Daun Penh, Phnom Penh (tel: 724-831, fax: 427-997).

Central bank

National Bank of Cambodia, 22-24 Preah Boulevard Norodom, Phnom Penh (tel/fax: 426-117).

Stock exchange
Cambodian Securities Exchange

Travel information
Canby Publications, PO Box 2349, Phnom Penh 3; House #23A, Street 55, Sangkat Chaktomuk, Khan Duan Penh, Phnom Penh (tel: 16-779-900; fax: 23-216-754; email: cambodia@canbypublications.com; internet: www.canbypublications.com).

Ministry of tourism
Ministry of Tourism, 3 Monivong Bld, Phnom Penh 12258 (tel: 211-593, 222-409; internet: www.mot.gov.kh).

National tourist organisation offices
Tourism of Cambodia, 262 Monivong Blvd, Khan Daun Penh, Phnom Penh (tel: 216-666; fax: 213-331; e-mail: info@tourismcambodia.com; internet: http://www.tourismcambodia.com).

Ministries
Ministry of Agriculture, 200 Norodom Blvd, Phnom Penh (tel: 723-689, 722-127).

Ministry of Commerce, Norodom Blvd, Phnom Penh (tel: 723-263; fax: 426-396).

Ministry of Culture, Monivong Blvd, Red Cross Street, Phnom Penh (tel: 724-769).

Ministry of Defence, Pochentong Blvd, Phnom Penh (tel: 725-697).

Ministry of Education, Youth and Sport, 80 Blvd Norodom, Phnom Penh (tel: 362-338; fax: 426-791).

Ministry of Finance, 60 St 92, Phnom Penh (tel: 426-841).

Ministry of Foreign Affairs and International Co-operation, Sisowath Quay, St 240, Phnom Penh (tel: 426-146, 724-441; fax: 26-144).

Ministry of Health, 153-153 Blvd Kampuchea Krom, Phnom Penh (tel: 725-833, 724-573).

Ministry of Industry, 45 Norodom Bld, St 45, Phnom Penh (tel: 723-477; fax: 427-840).

Ministry of Information, 62 Monivong Bld, Phnom Penh (tel: 723-369, 722-869).

Ministry of the Interior, 275 Norodom Blvd, Phnom Penh (tel: 426-494).

Ministry of Justice, Sothearos Blvd, Phnom Penh (tel: 724-543, 360-329).

Ministry of Planning, 386 Monivong Blvd, Phnom Penh (tel: 725-143, 724-543).

Ministry of Posts and Telecommunications, Street 13, Street 102, Phnom Penh (tel: 723-911, 426-817; fax: 426-786).

Ministry of Public Works and Transport, Norodom Blvd, Mahaksatriyani St, Phnom Penh (tel: 427-862; fax: 427-862).

Ministry of Religious Affairs, Sothearos Blvd, St 240, Phnom Penh (tel: 725-699).

Ministry of Rural Development, Pochentong Blvd, Phnom Penh (tel: 426-814).

Ministry of Social Welfare, 68 Norodom Blvd, Phnom Penh (tel: 725-191, 427-322).

Prime Minister's Office, 22 Street 214, Phnom Penh (tel:426-053 and 426-025).

Other useful addresses
ASEAN Investment Promotion Agency, Cambodian Investment Board, Government Palace, Sisowath Quay, Wat Phnom, Phnom Penh (tel: 50-428; fax: 61-616, 60-606).

ASEAN Secretariat, 70 A J1 Sisingamangaraja, Jakarta 12110, Indonesia (tel: 62(21)726-2991, 724-3372; fax: 724-3504, 739-8234).

Asian Development Bank, Cambodia Resident Mission, 93 Preah Norodom Boulevard, Phnom Penh (tel: 725-805; fax: 725-807).

British Embassy, 27-29 Street 75, Phnom Penh (tel: 427-124; fax: 427-124/5).

Cambodian Development Council (CDC), Phnom Penh.

Cambodian Embassy (USA), 4530 16th Street, NW, Washington DC 20011 (tel: (+1-202)- 726-7742; fax: (+1-202)-726-8381; e-mail: cambodia@embassy.org).

Cambodia Mine Action Centre, 22 Street 122, Phnom Penh (tel: 913-506).

Chemins de Fer du Cambodge, Moha Vithei Pracheathippatay, Phnom Penh (tel: 25-156).

Department of Civil Aviation, 62 Boulevard Norodom, Phnom Penh (tel: 427-141; fax: 26-169).

Global, Business Centre, 378 EO Sivutha Street, Group 1, Sangkat Olympic, Khan Chamcarmon, Phnom Penh (tel: 27-124; fax: 27-125).

Phnom Penh Port Authority (tel: 23-369).

National news agency: AKP (Agence Kampuchea Presse), 62 Monivong Blvd, Phnom Penh (tel: 430-564; fax: 427-945; email: akp@camnet.com.kh; internet: www.camnet.com.kh).

Internet sites
Asian Development Bank: http://www.adb.org/carm

Cambodia web sites: http://mekong.net/cambodia/links.htm

Cambodian web directory: http://www.kampuchea.com/

UN Food and Aid administration: http://www.fao.org/waicent/search/default.asp

Cameroon

KEY FACTS

Official name: République du Cameroun (Republic of Cameroon)

Head of State: President Paul Biya (from 1982; re-elected 9 Oct 2011)

Head of government: Prime Minister Philémon Yang (appointed 30 Jun 2009)

Ruling party: Coalition led by Rassemblement Démocratique du Peuple Camerounais (RDPC) (Cameroon People's Democratic Rally) with Union Nationale pour la Démocratie et le Progrès (UNDP) (National Union for Democracy and Progress) and Union des Populations du Cameroun (UPC) (Union of the Peoples of Cameroon) (since 1992; re-elected July 2007)

Area: 475,442 square km

Population: 19.41 million (2010)*

Capital: Yaoundé

Official language: French, English

Currency: CFA franc (CFAf) = 100 centimes (Communauté Financière Africaine (African Financial Community) franc)

Exchange rate: CFAf488.90 per US$ (Oct 2011); CFAf655.95 per euro (pegged from Jan 1999)

GDP per capita: US$1,101 (2010)

GDP real growth: 3.00% (2010)

GDP: US$22.50 billion (2010)

Labour force: 7.84 million (2010)*

Inflation: 1.30% (2010)

Oil production: 73,000 bpd (2009)

Balance of trade: -US$17.74 million (2010)

* estimated figure

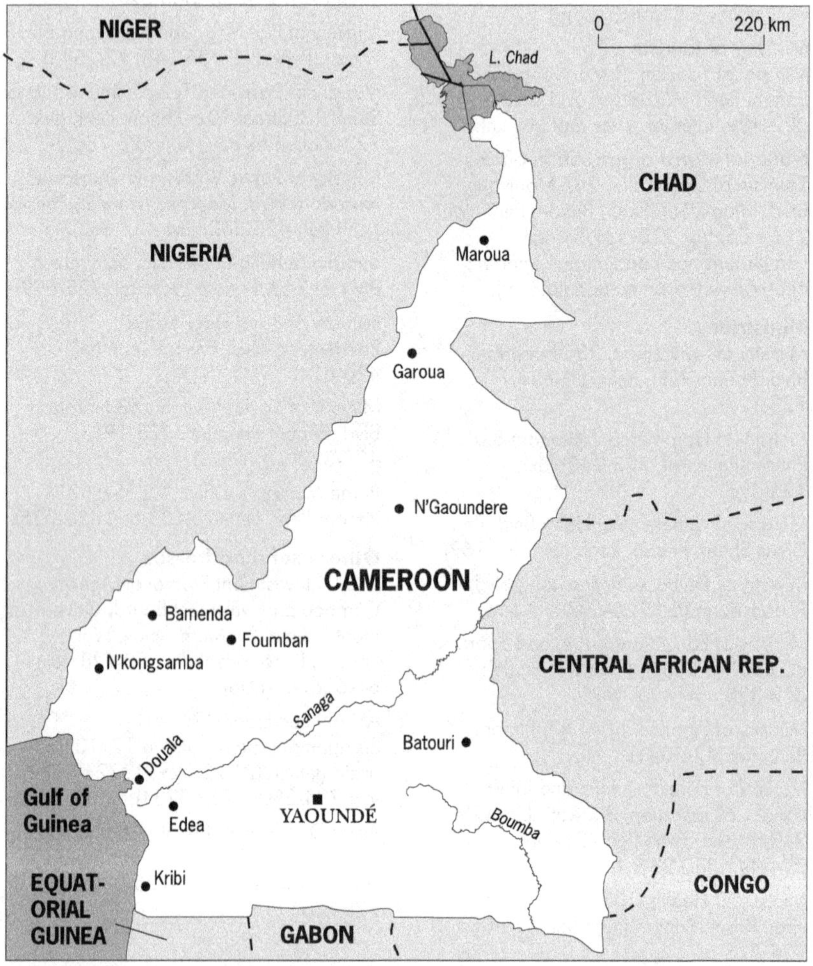

Following the 2006 elections President Paul Biya set up Elections Cameroon (Elecam) and put it in charge of organising, managing and supervising the whole electoral and referendum process. President Biya appointed several key figures from the Rassemblement Démocratique du Peuple Camerounais (RDPC) (Cameroon People's Democratic Rally), the governing party, prompting a challenge by the opposition. Since then, Elecam has recruited and posted its staff across the whole country. The domestic political event of 2010 was the series of meetings between Paul Biya and Ni John Fru Ndi, the chairman of the main opposition party, Front Social-Démocratique (SDF) (Social Democratic Front). These meetings, the first since the beginning of the 1990s, should help calm political life in Cameroon. The two key figures tackled the improvements to be made to Elecam in order to ensure the smooth conduct of elections. The October 2011 presidential elections were won Paul Biya with 77.99 per cent, John Fru Ndi came second with 10.71 per cent. The supreme court endorsed the result on 21 October, but France and the US denounced the election process as having 'many failures' and 'irregularities at all levels'. President Biya took office, for his sixth term, on 3 November.

The economy

In 2010, Cameroon's economic growth was driven by the global recovery with an upturn in certain non-oil exports, notably timber, coffee and cotton, which benefited from the price and volume effect as some developed countries rebuilt their stocks. The cocoa and aluminium markets, on the other hand, performed poorly, with falling prices. In addition to these falling prices, there was more than usual unplanned spending, mostly linked to the participation of the national football team in both the African Cup of Nations and the World Cup. Together with preparations to celebrate the 50th anniversary of independence, a large part of which was not included in the budget, the government had been forced to prepare a mini-budget half way through the year. The economy was also affected by the difficulties observed in some heavily indebted EU countries.

The *African Economic Outlook 2010* (AEO), published jointly by the African Development Bank and the Organisation for Economic Co-operation and Development, reported that the real rate of gross domestic product (GDP) growth, while positive between 2009 and 2010, stayed below the 7 per cent rate necessary to reduce poverty by half by 2015. The forecasts for 2011 and 2012 are dependent on the scale of the world economic recovery, the dynamics of domestic demand and the growth in public investment planned as part of the Growth and Employment Strategy Paper (GESP). The AEO expects that the rate of investment will rise from 18.5 per cent to at least 25 per cent of GDP, the minimum rate to guarantee sustainable economic growth and job creation.

Private sector growth

Cameroon's private sector is one of the most developed in Central Africa, with some 94,000 active businesses in 2009. The cities of Douala and Yaoundé have almost two-thirds of all businesses, which generate nearly three-quarters of total turnover. Two-thirds of businesses employ no more than five people and operate essentially in the tertiary sector. Nine out of ten are sole traders. Use of new information and communication technology is still modest, with barely one business in two connected to the Internet, and an even smaller proportion (one in four) with an intranet. Very few businesses invest significantly in new technology.

Traders complain a business climate unfavourable to the development of their activities at the administrative, judicial and financial levels. The most frequently cited obstacles in order of importance are: tax, corruption, access to credit, administrative systems, unfair competition, infrastructure and the cost of financing. The other big obstacles mentioned are insufficient dialogue between the public and private sectors, power cuts, transport and justice.

Confronted by these problems, the authorities have committed to a programme of structural and institutional reforms aimed at improving the business environment and the overall competitiveness of the economy. These measures include restructuring and privatisation of public enterprises; promotion of transparency and improvements in governance; reform of the financial sector and the civil service and consolidation of public finances. A new penal code of procedure had been introduced in 2007 and the Agence Nationale d' Investigation Financière (ANIF) (National Financial Investigation Agency) and the National Commission for the Fight against Corruption in Cameroon (CONAC) are now up and running. Despite these efforts, Cameroon has fallen 16 places in the World Bank's 2011 *Ease of Doing Business* survey – from 152nd in 2009 to 171st out of 183 countries evaluated.

Financial system

Cameroon's banking system is generally healthy and benefits from the trust of its depositors. It is composed of commercial banks, financial institutions, insurance companies, microfinance organisations and a stock market, the Douala Stock Exchange. After restructuring, employment in banking has risen, reaching about 3,000 employees. However the rate of banking is still very low, at 2–3 per cent of the active population.

The private sector

The privatisation of Société Nationale des Eaux du Cameroun (SNEC) (National Water Company of Cameroon) has been completed. This has enabled the creation of a publicly owned company, Camwater, and a service company, Camerounaise des Eaux (CDE), which is majority owned by the Moroccan Office National de l'Eau Potable (ONEP) (National Office for Drinking Water Supply).

Cameroon Airlines operations were suspended in February 2008. The creation and privatisation of the new airline company, the Cameroon Airlines Corporation, (Camair-Co) was finally completed in 2011 and the first flight from Doula to Paris took place in March. Cameroon Telecommunications (Camtel), Société de Développement du Coton du Cameroun (Sodecoton) (Cotton Development Company of Cameroon), Cameroon Development Corporation, Societé Camerounaise des Depots Petroliers (SCDP) (Cameroon Oil Distribution Company) and Camtainer (the state national transport and transit company) remain on the list of companies eligible for privatisation. Renovation and resizing works have been carried out at the Societe Nationale de Raffinage (Sonara) oil refinery, enabling the evaluation of the overall costs of the refinery. As a result, in 2011 Sonara, the only crude processor in Cameroon, will

KEY INDICATORS **Cameroon**

	Unit	2006	2007	2008	2009	2010
Population	m	*18.34	*18.86	*19.38	*19.93	*19.41
Gross domestic product (GDP)	US$bn	17.96	20.40	23.20	22.20	22.50
GDP per capita	US$	979	1,084	1,199	1,115	1,101
GDP real growth	%	3.5	3.3	3.4	2.0	3.0
Inflation	%	5.3	0.9	5.3	3.0	1.3
Oil output	'000 bpd	63.0	82.0	82.0	73.0	–
Exports (fob) (goods)	US$m	3,490.0	4,956.0	5,890.0	4,078.6	4,485.2
Imports (fob) (goods)	US$m	2,910.0	4,221.3	5,431.0	4,404.5	4,662.6
Balance of trade	US$m	580.0	734.8	459.0	-325.8	-177.4
Current account	US$m	118.0	285.7	-449.7	-1,136.5	-856.3
Total reserves minus gold	US$m	1,716.2	2,906.8	3,086.4	3,675.5	3,642.6
Foreign exchange	US$m	1,710.5	2,900.7	3,080.6	3,430.5	3,614.2
Exchange rate	per US$	496.60	454.40	418.59	472.19	495.28

* estimated figure

receive US$164 million from eight banks to fund its expansion. The refinery, based in Limbe, about 350km (217 miles) south-west of Yaoundé, will increase capacity to 4 million metric tons by 2015 from the current 2.1 million tons. The lender banks include UK-based Standard Chartered Plc, Societe Generale SA's unit in Cameroon, Lome-based Banque Atlantique and Commercial Bank Cameroon. The refinery, which is currently only able to process light crude, will be able to refine heavy crude after the refurbishment, the type pumped in Cameroon. The deal will guarantee the financial viability of the business, with knock-on effects on the pump price of oil products and less dependence on fluctuations in international crude oil prices.

Infrastructure

Infrastructure development is a constant concern, because it is part of the fight against poverty. Since the turn of the century, the authorities have committed to large projects in the transport, health, education and other sectors. These efforts can be seen in the construction sector. Raising the production capacity of cement as well as increasing import quotas have enabled improved availability of inputs. Ongoing construction works on the Lom Pangar dam and the port of Kribi offer prospects of positive growth. Even though road transport represents close to 70 per cent of overall transport activity, road maintenance is inadequate despite the privatisation process, as much for asphalted and non-asphalted roads (10.2 per cent of surfaced roads are in good condition, 31.9 per cent in normal condition, and 37.9 per cent in mediocre or poor condition). This is a more painful state of affairs given that the funding allocated to maintaining the national road network has grown over the same period. Other modes of transport are experiencing variable growth. Maritime transport rose in 2009 with a growth of 12.3 per cent in the tonnage of imported goods. In 2010, activity in this sector remained stable. In 2009, air transport suffered from the international economic situation but recovered in 2010. At the regional level, the Consensual Transport Master Plan for Central Africa (PDCT-AC), which aims to link all the capital cities by surfaced roads, is at the fundraising phase.

Natural resources management

The forestry sector accounted for 11.5 per cent of export revenues in 2008, second only to oil. In 2009, it was relegated to third place mainly because of cancelled orders and the withdrawal of several operators during the global economic slowdown. Export revenues thus dropped by 38.4 per cent in 2009. The authorities have adopted several measures, including widening the range of species to export in log form; lightening the tax burden through factory gate tax exemptions for 2nd and 3rd transformations; and simplifying the procedures of allocation and management of community forests. These reforms, continued in 2010, have enabled the supply chain network to take advantage of the upturn in world demand. In the area of replanting and regeneration, 2,225,167 trees were planted in 2009. In 2010, control of 70 per cent of forestry production was achieved under the forestry and environment sector programme. The policies applied take into account the constraints related to achieving the Millennium Development Goals (MDGs).

Agricultural reform

The agricultural sector remains strategic in Cameroon's development. The budget allocated to this sector is constantly rising. The directives of a major agricultural policy were reaffirmed by the head of state at the opening of the Comice Agropastoral agricultural show in January 2011. The directives include establishing a fertiliser production unit; setting up an assembly plant for agricultural machinery at Ebolowa; improving seed farms; preparing land reform to adapt to the needs of second-generation agriculture; strengthening the system of rural finance by opening the Agricultural Bank and a bank for small and medium-sized enterprises and industries.

Unemployment

While the unemployment rate in the strict sense as defined by the International Labour Organisation (ILO) remains low (4.4 per cent), youth unemployment remains of concern (13.7 per cent in 2007). Most of their participation (92 per cent) is in the informal economy, in jobs that are insecure and low-skilled. Under-employment remains very high (76 per cent), and many of those are young people who state that they are only doing their current job to survive until they find something better. In 2010, the government launched a huge recruitment drive to deal with the shortfall of civil servants in the administration. This was undertaken through direct competition or contractualisation. In this way, 7,261 teachers were put under contract and 1,304 graduates were recruited in different sectors. In 2008, in conjunction with the ILO, Cameroon had published a national report on child labour. This showed that of around 6 million children aged between 5 and 17, almost four out of ten children are economically active. This percentage is broadly the same for girls as for boys. But large disparities can be seen depending on the type of residence, the region surveyed and the age of the child. Many more children are economically active in rural areas (51.1 per cent) than in urban areas (17.9 per cent), unpaid in most cases.

Risk assessment

Economy	Poor
Politics	Fair
Regional stability	Fair

COUNTRY PROFILE

Historical profile

1470s Portuguese mariners arrived and gave Cameroon its name. Having found what they thought to be shrimps (*camaroes*) in the main river, they named it *Rio dos Camaroes*.

1884 Germany established the protectorate of Kamerun.

1916 The German administration was ousted by Allied forces in the First World War.

1919 A post-war League of Nations mandate gave some four-fifths of the territory to France, and the remainder, bordering Nigeria, to Britain.

1960 French East Cameroon gained its independence.

1961 British West Cameroon gained its independence.

1972 A unified state was formed, with the Union Nationale Camerounaise (UNC) (Cameroonian National Union) dominating both the executive and legislative branches.

1982 Prime Minister Paul Biya became president after the resignation of President Ahidjo.

1985 Biya renamed the ruling party the Rassemblement Démocratique du Peuple Camerounais (RDPC) (Cameroon People's Democratic Rally), and introduced a number of political reforms which were largely viewed as cosmetic.

1990 A multi-party political system was legalised. Although this change marked the gradual opening of the Cameroonian political system, subsequent elections were marred by irregularities and accusations of electoral fraud.

1996 In response to pressure from the Anglophone regional groups the constitution was amended to include a federal system with the addition of a senate in the

National Assembly. Presidential terms in office will in future last seven years.
1997 President Paul Biya was re-elected. The elections were boycotted by the three main opposition parties after their complaints about the handling of voter registration were ignored.
1999 English-speaking secessionists, led by the Southern Cameroon National Council (SCNC), announced a breakaway Federal Republic of Southern Cameroon.
2001 Demonstrations calling for decentralisation of power were banned and several southern Cameroon separatists were killed.
2002 The ruling RDPC increased its number of seats in the legislative elections. The International Court of Justice gave Cameroon sovereignty of the potentially oil-rich Bakassi Peninsula, claimed by Cameroon and Nigeria.
2003 The communications minister ordered the closure of an English-speaking private radio station, Magic FM, for running programmes critical of the government.
2004 Presidential Biya was re-elected. Ephraïm Inoni was appointed prime minister. Nigeria failed to withdraw troops from the Bakassi Peninsula.
2005 Presidents Obasanjo and Biya and UN Secretary General Kofi Annan failed to resolve the dispute concerning Bakassi Peninsula, thought to hold about 10 per cent of the world's oil and gas reserves.
2006 Nigeria ceded the Bakassi peninsula to Cameroon, in accordance with a 2002 International Court of Justice ruling.
2007 In the general elections, the ruling RDPC won 152 seats (out of 180) and the opposition SDF won 21.
2008 Parliament overwhelmingly voted to amend the constitution. The amendments included presidential immunity from prosecution for acts undertaken as president and an unlimited number of presidential terms in office. Nigeria finally surrendered sovereignty of the oil-rich Bakassi Peninsula.
2009 President Biya dismissed Ephraim Inoni as prime minister and appointed Philémon Yang as his replacement.
2010 In April, the parliamentary opposition claimed the figure of 19,406,100 million inhabitants as presented in the 2005 census was inaccurate and had been manipulated. Researchers agreed there could be inaccuracies as all figures presented were projections. Critics claim the projections for the English-speaking coastal region were 'exceptionally low', given overall growth rates. On 28 July national voter registration began, prior to the October 2011 presidential elections.
2011 On 7 July, the government presented a proposal to a parliament committee to give Cameroon's diaspora the right to vote in the upcoming presidential election. In presidential elections, held on 9 October, 23 candidates took part, but only two candidates won over 10 per cent of the vote. Incumbent Paul Biya won 77.99 per cent and John Fru Ndi 10.71 per cent; turnout was 65.8 per cent. The supreme court endorsed the result on 21 October, however both France and the US denounced the election process as having 'many failures' and 'irregularities at all levels'. President Biya took office, for his sixth term, on 3 November.

Political structure

Constitution

The constitution was promulgated in 1972 and revised in 1975 and 1996, when pressure from Anglophone regional groups resulted in constitution amendments, whereby a federal system of government would be introduced and a senate in the National Assembly instigated; neither of these provisions were implemented. However an increase in the presidential term in office extension to seven years was applied.
In April 2008 parliament overwhelmingly voted to amend the constitution, to include presidential immunity from prosecution for acts undertaken as president and an unlimited number of presidential terms in office.

Form of state

Unitary republic

The executive

Executive power is vested in the president, who appoints a cabinet. The president serves a seven-year term. A prime minister, who acts as head of government, is appointed by the president. The president names and dismisses cabinet members and judges, ratifies treaties, heads the armed forces, controls legislation and can rule by decree.

National legislature

The unicameral Assemblée Nationale (National Assembly) has 180 members, directly elected in single and multi-seat constituencies, to serve for five-year terms.

Legal system

Cameroon's legal system is based on French civil law with common law influences. The country has a Supreme Court, the judges of which are appointed by the president. Provisions in the 1996 constitution for judicial independence have not been put into force. Cameroon does not accept the compulsory jurisdiction of the International Court of Justice, but does belong to the International Court of Arbitration of the International Chamber of Commerce.

Last elections

22 July 2007 (parliamentary); 9 October 2011 (presidential)

Results: Parliamentary: The ruling RDPC won 152 seats (out of 180); SDF 15; Union Démocratique du Cameroun (UDC) (Democratic Union of Cameroon) 4; Union Nationale pour la Démocratie et le Progrès (UNDP) (National Union for Democracy and Progress) 4; Mouvement Progressiste (MP) (Progressive Movement) 1; undecided 4. Turnout was over 60 per cent.
Presidential: Paul Biya (RDPC) won 77.99 per cent, John Fru Ndi (SFD) 10.71 per cent, Garga Haman Adji (ADD) 3.21 per cent, Adamou Ndam Njoya (UDC) 1.73 per cent, Paul Abine Ayah (PAP) 1.26 per cent; 18 other candidates each won less than 1 per cent. Turnout is 65.8 per cent.

Next elections

2012 (parliamentary); 2018 (presidential)

Political parties

Ruling party

Coalition led by Rassemblement Démocratique du Peuple Camerounais (RDPC) (Cameroon People's Democratic Rally) with Union Nationale pour la Démocratie et le Progrès (UNDP) (National Union for Democracy and Progress) and Union des Populations du Cameroun (UPC) (Union of the Peoples of Cameroon) (since 1992; re-elected July 2007)

Main opposition party

Front Social-Démocratique (SDF) (Social Democratic Front)

Population

19.93 million (2009)*
Last census: April 1987: 10,493,655
Population density: 29 inhabitants per square km. Urban population: 50 per cent (1995–2001).
Annual growth rate: 2.1 per cent 1994–2004 (WHO 2006)

Ethnic make-up

Cameroon has a highly diversified population comprising some 200 ethnic groups, including Cameroon Highlanders (31 per cent), Equatorial Bantu (19 per cent) and Kirdi (11 per cent). There are about 200,000 Europeans in the country, mainly French speakers.

Religions

Indigenous beliefs are practiced by 40 per cent of the population, another 40 per cent are Christian, and 20 per cent are Muslim.

Education

Literacy rate: 68 per cent adult rate (Unesco 2005)
Enrolment rate: 107 per cent gross primary enrolment, 33 per cent gross secondary enrolment; of relevant age groups (including repeaters) (World Bank).
Pupils per teacher: 44 in primary schools.

Health

HIV/Aids

HIV prevalence: 5.5 per cent aged 15–49 in 2004 (World Bank)
Life expectancy: 50 years, 2004 (WHO 2006)
Fertility rate/Maternal mortality rate: 4.5 births per woman, 2004 (WHO 2006)
Birth rate/Death rate: 34.7 births and 15.4 deaths per 1,000 population (2005)
Child (under 5 years) mortality rate (per 1,000): 95 per 1,000 live births; 22 per cent of children aged under five are malnourished (World Bank).
Head of population per physician: 0.19 physician per 1,000 people, 2004 (WHO 2006)

Welfare

Cameroon's social insurance system provides cover for old-age pension, disability pension, sickness and maternity benefits, work injuries and family allowances.

Main cities

Douala (commercial centre, estimated population 1.9 million in 2004), Yaoundé (capital, 1.9 million), Garoua (287,586), Kousséri (176,241), Bamenda (229,109), Maroua (205,635), Bafoussam (185,635).

Languages spoken

24 major African language groups including Bamileke, Ewondo, Bassa and Bamoun are spoken. Around 80 per cent of the population speak French as a second language (francophone Cameroon) and 20 per cent speak English as a second language (anglophone – formerly British West Cameroon).

Official language/s

French, English

Media

The government maintains a tight control of media outlets with official restrictions and stringent libel laws that have regularly imprisoned journalists and led to self-censorship.

Press

Dailies: In French, the *Cameroon Tribune* is the official state-owned newspaper, with an English edition, published twice weekly, *La Nouvelle Expression* (www.lanouvelleexpression.net), is published three-times weekly. In English, *The Post* (www.postnewsline.com).
Weeklies: In French, private publications include *Le Messager* (www.lemessager.net), and in English *Postwatch* (www.postwatchmagazine.com).
Business: In French, *La Dépeche économique* is a bi-weekly publication.
Periodicals: In French, monthly publications include *La Voix du paysan* a farmer's magazine, *Dikalo* (http://www.dikalo.biz) and *Le Météo* an independent magazine.

Broadcasting

The national broadcaster is Cameroon Radio and Television (CRTV).
Radio: CRTV (www.crtv.cm) operates one national and several provincial services in French, English and local languages.
Other commercial stations include Nostalgie (www.cameroun-plus.com), Sky One (www.skyonecameroun.com) and the pan-African Radio Africa No 1 (www.africa1.com).
English-speaking separatists in the south of the country have used pirate-radio for propaganda.
Television: CRTV (www.crtv.cm) is the national public TV station. There are two private stations Canal 2 and STV (www.stvgroup.com) with two channels, which broadcast via satellite.

News agencies

Africa News Agency: www.africanewsagency.co.uk
APA: www.apanews.net
Panapress: www.panapress.com

Economy

Cameroon has a wealth of natural resources that underpin the economy, including mining, agriculture, forestry and oil and natural gas. Although the service sector constitutes around 50.4 per cent of GDP, industry 29.70 per cent of GDP (of which manufacturing was around 16 per cent) and agriculture 19.8 per cent in 2009, oil exports provide the largest export revenue. Other industries include aluminium smelting (from imported bauxite), hydroelectric generation, rubber production and timber felling. Manufacturing includes use of these raw materials for finished items. Agricultural produce includes cotton, coffee, cocoa and palm oil.
GDP growth was 2.0 per cent in 2009, a fall from 2.9 per cent in 2008 and 3.3 per cent in 2007. The fall in commodity prices following the global economic crisis had a detrimental effect on the economy, which also saw a rise in imported food prices, which in turn cut per capita income from US$2,224 in 2008 to US$1,114 in 2009. Estimates for 2010 show a rise in GDP growth to 2.6 per cent, but a further fall of per capita income to US$1,071.
Cameroon has a reputation for widespread corruption and has consistently ranked low in the World Bank's poll of ease of doing business, which in 2010 was 173 out of 183 countries, with enforcing a contract as the single most difficult element of the poll (142 out of 183).
The benefits gained through its natural resources, industry and commodity trading have not spread through its society and poverty is still widespread and public investment remains low. Remittances have steadily fallen since 2007 when US$167 million was transferred to Cameroon. By 2009 remittances were US$148 million (0.7 per cent of GDP), the estimate for 2010 was that remittances remained at US$148 million.
The government implemented its Growth and Employment Strategy Paper (GESP) in late 2009, which was designed to boost growth and create employment in the formal sector to reduce poverty over 2010–20. Unemployment, currently estimated at around 76 per cent, is being targeted as an ongoing programme to be reduced to less than 50 per cent. A reduction of the poverty rate from 39.9 per cent in 2007 to 28.7 per cent by 2020 is also a priority. The government will also increase its efforts in expanding the non-oil sectors to reduce the economy's vulnerability to external shocks.

External trade

As a member of the Communauté Économique des États d'Afrique Centrale (Economic Community of Central African States (ECCAS) Cameroon uses the CFA franc (Communauté Financière Africaine franc), issued by the Banque des États de l'Afrique Centrale (BEAC) (Bank of Central African States). ECCAS operates a customs and economic union with a common external tariff between its six members, with free movement of capital, people and goods and services.

Imports

Imports consist principally of crude oil, pharmaceuticals, vehicles, machines and electrical equipment, grain and foodstuffs.
Main sources: Nigeria (23.3 cent total, 2006), France (17.2 per cent), China (6.3 per cent).

Exports

Principal exports include crude oil and petroleum products, timber and finish wood items, rubber, coffee, cotton, cocoa and tobacco.
Main destinations: The Netherlands (typically 14 per cent of total), Spain (12 per cent), Italy (12 per cent).

Re-exports

Light crude oil for refining.

Agriculture

Farming

In order to broaden the country's economic base and increase the value added to domestic production, the government is encouraging development of its full agricultural potential. Some 70 per cent of Cameroon's labour force is employed in the agricultural sector, although only 2 per cent of Cameroon's land area is used for permanent crops. Principal crops include cocoa, coffee, bananas, cotton and oil palms. Virtually all food requirements are met by local production. Most agricultural production is in the hands of smallholders, with the exception of rubber and palm, which are run under the plantation system.

Mayuka, located in the northern region of Cameroon, is the centre of the cocoa industry, where business made sweeping profits as prices soared following the political crisis in Côte d'Ivoire. As demand for cocoa rises, so the government aims to double the amount of production.

Fishing

As a consequence of its short coastline and the intrusion on its territorial waters of Bioko Island, which belongs to Equatorial Guinea, Cameroon's fishing industry is underdeveloped. Offshore waters are not well stocked, as the currents which provide richer fishing grounds off Nigeria and other parts of West Africa do not flow close to Cameroon's coastline. Nevertheless, catches of both freshwater and marine fish have been steadily increasing in recent years.

Fisheries legislation in Cameroon contains specific clauses dealing with the aquaculture sector, covering issues related to registration and licensing, and the export/import of fish species. It aims to improve artisanal fishing methods, preservation and processing of fishery products.

Forestry

While the country is well-forested, with more than 40 per cent forest cover and an additional 30 per cent of other wooded land, unsustainable deforestation led to the loss of 222,000 hectares between 1990–2000. Nevertheless Cameroon is the second-largest area of tropical rainforest in Africa after the Democratic Republic of Congo (DRC). It is one of Africa's leading producers and exporters of tropical logs and sawn timber; smaller quantities of veneer and plywood are also exported. Important non-wood forest products include medicinal plants, nuts, wild fruits, rattan and bushmeat.

Three-quarters of Cameroon's forestry exports consist of industrial roundwood, with sawnwood accounting for another 18 per cent. Forestry imports to Cameroon are composed almost exclusively of paper and paperboard, totalling 96.5 per cent of forestry imports.

Industry and manufacturing

The industrial sector has been contracting, while services accounted for 40.5 per cent. However, the agri-industrial sub-sector has been growing, gradually substituting imports with domestically produced goods. The sector employs around 10 per cent of the workforce. Industrial output accounts for 25 per cent of Cameroon's exports.

The government has been a major participant in the industrial sector, mainly through the Société Nationale d'Investissement (SNI) (National Investment Agency), however economic imperatives have required that public entities become market driven and private enterprise has yet to become competitive. The Technical Commission for the Rehabilitation of Public Enterprises oversees privatisation and restructuring of all state-owned companies.

Tourism

There is considerable potential for tourism in Cameroon although development has been slow due to expensive air fares, the high cost of tourist visas, limited tourist infrastructure and the relatively high prices of hotels. A Tourist Development Plan is being undertaken in co-operation with the World Tourism Organisation (WTO). The government has devised a special investment code to encourage private investors. The deregulation of air traffic should help reduce air fares.

Environment

Cameroon's tropical forest is the largest in-tact rainforest in the world but it is being exploited at a faster rate than is sustainable threatening the habitat of numerous species and the long-term existence of elephants and gorillas.

As the forests have become more accessible, poachers are shooting antelope, chimpanzees and gorillas, for commercial purposes. In June 2006, as part of its commitment to debt relief, the French government agreed to invest in the conservation of Cameroon's natural resources, to include better management of protected areas, wildlife and forest production.

In 2005 a UN inspection team warned that a natural dam in the north-west province was in imminent danger of collapsing and flooding the Nyos Valley. The cost to repair the dam is estimated at US$15 million.

Mining

The mining sector accounts for around 10 per cent of GDP and employs 2 per cent of the workforce. Bauxite deposits of some 1,100 million tonnes at Adamaoua Province have been identified but remain unexploited, although an upturn in world aluminium prices encouraged Société des Bauxitese de Cameroun (SBC) to begin mining operations. There are deposits of iron ore at Kribi (reserves estimated at 197 million tonnes), and potential reserves of gold, diamonds, uranium, rutile, industrial clays and low-grade nickel and cobalt. Tin is mined on a very small scale. Investment by large mining companies is needed to exploit underground riches.

Hydrocarbons

Proven oil reserves were 200 million barrels in 2008, located offshore in the Niger Delta in Rio del Rey Basin. With production at 81,330 barrels per day (bpd) and consumption at 26,000bpd, Cameroon is a net exporter of oil. Stocks have been declining since the 1980s and without finding further oil fields it could become a net importer by 2020.

The state-owned Société Nationale des Hydrocarbures (SNH) is responsible for exploration and production of Cameroon's oil assets and has undertaken joint exploration projects with international oil companies.

Cameroon and Chad jointly operate the 1,080km Chad-Cameroon pipeline project (CCPP), with a capacity of 225,000bpd, transporting Chadian oil to the Cameroon Kribi port terminal. There is one refinery in Limbe with a capacity of 42,000bpd with plans to upgrade the facility and refine crude oil from regional oil producers. A contract, to revamp much of the Limbe refinery and upgrade to include a power generator and related facilities, was let in June 2010.

Proven natural gas reserves were 110 billion cubic metres (cum) in 2008, with production at 28 million cum which is entirely consumed domestically. Construction of the Logbaba gas and condensate facilities near Douala are almost complete and the UK-based Victoria Oil and Gas company expects commercial production to begin by January 2012. Initial production is set for 226.4 million cubic metres (cum) of gas per day, rising to 1.24 billion cum by 2014; at full capacity the plant will produce 1.69 billion cum.

The industry is still in its early stage of development and should take off dramatically since the territorial dispute with Nigeria over the Bakassi Peninsula was resolved in Cameroon's favour in 2007. The Bakassi Peninsula is estimated by some analysts to hold some 10 per cent of world oil and gas reserves. The government also believes there is considerable potential in two largely unexplored areas – the Logone Birni and Douala basins – and is also hoping for the discovery of big offshore finds. However, the coastline is limited and the country's maritime area is small.

Commercial quantities of coal are neither produced nor imported.

Energy

Total generation capacity was 875MW in 2007, nearly 90 per cent of which is hydroelectric. Although Cameroon has the second largest hydroelectric power potential in Africa (after the Democratic Republic of Congo), its hydro plants are old, having been built mainly in the 1950s, and operate well below capacity. Therefore, gas may have a more immediate influence on power generation as an alternative source of power, especially in the dry season. Cameroon expects its demand for power to double in the course of the next decade. There are four operational hydroelectric power stations including Edéa, Lagdo, Song-Loulou and Memve'ele.

The utility Société Nationale d'Electricité du Cameroun (AES-Sonel) is 51 per cent owned by the US's AES Corporation. AES-Sonel managed generation and distribution to over 500,000 customers, which is around 2 per cent of the population, who have access to electricity supplies; only 9 per cent of the capital's potential consumers use electricity. The remainder of the population relies on wood fuel as their primary source of energy.

To comply with a World Bank loan to develop the electricity sector emphasis on sustainable energy has increased. The Export-Import Bank of India agreed to lend Cameroon US$251.5 million, which resulted in a contract whereby the Indian engineering firm Angelique International will build two hydropower stations and drinking water and sanitation projects.

Financial markets

Stock exchange

Doula Stock Exchange (DSX)

Banking and insurance

Cameroon's banking sector has become significantly stronger as the result of IMF-led restructuring, but is still poorly developed. The last state-owned bank in Cameroon was bought by a French banking company in 1999. Cameroon's largest bank is the Société Générale de Banques au Cameroun (SGBC). The commercial banking sector is made up of nine commercial banks with 60 branches, but suffers from a lack of available capital, an unwillingness to take risks and outdated products.

Central bank

Banque des Etats de l'Afrique Centrale

Main financial centre

Douala

Time

GMT plus one hour

Geography

Cameroon lies on the Gulf of Guinea. Nigeria is to the west, Chad and the Central African Republic to the north-east and east, and the Republic of Congo, Gabon and Equatorial Guinea to the south.

The country can be divided into four main regions. The coastal plain is tropical but tempered by the effects of the sea. The tropical plateau in the south is heavily forested and cut through by a number of rivers flowing west into the Bight of Biafra or south-east to join the River Congo. The Adamawa and Bamenda highlands rise to 2,500 metres and are drier and cooler than the forest areas. The highlands are volcanic in origin, and include Mount Cameroon (4,070 metres). The savannah grasslands to the north lie between Nigeria and Chad, and stretch northwards to Lake Chad.

Hemisphere

Northern

Climate

In the north the single wet season is between April and September, and there is a dry season during the rest of the year.

It is tropical in the south with fairly constant average temperatures throughout the year, ranging between 18 degrees Celsius (C) at night and 30–32 degrees C during the day. In the south rainfall is distributed throughout the year with two wet seasons and two dry seasons.

Dress codes

Tropical clothes are advised, with warmer clothes required for the higher altitudes. Lightweight raincoats are recommended for the rainy season.

Entry requirements

Passports

Passports are required by all and should be valid for at least six months from date of arrival.

Visa

Required by all, except nationals of Central African Republic, Chad, Mali and Nigeria. Nationals of countries without Cameroonian diplomatic representation may be issued with a visa on arrival. A business visa requires a letter from applicant's company outlining purpose of visit and a letter from business partners in Cameroon (endorsed by the local police), plus a full itinerary.

An onward/return ticket and proof of sufficient funds are required.

Currency advice/regulations

There are no restrictions on the import or export of foreign currency.

Local currency import is limited to CFAf20,000 (approximately US$35) and export is limited to CFAf20,000 for tourists and CFAf45,000 (approximately US$80) for business purposes. Travellers cheques are accepted, but cash is advised.

Prohibited imports

Pornographic materials, illegal drugs, weapons and ammunitions may not be brought into Cameroon. Alcohol and other spirits (maximum 30 bottles) should be sent separately.

An invoice must accompany all furniture and electrical appliances to prove that they are more than six months old. Newer items are subject to customs duties and taxes. Home computers do not qualify as personal effects, and are subject to customs duties and taxes.

Health (for visitors)

Mandatory precautions

An international certificate of vaccination against yellow fever.

Advisable precautions

The principal health hazards are cholera, malaria and HIV. Vaccination against tetanus, typhoid, polio, meningitis, and hepatitis A and B are all advisable. Rabies and bilharzia also occur, and necessary precautions should be taken. Avoid swimming in fresh water; well-chlorinated swimming pools should be safe. Bottled water is readily available. Milk is unpasteurised and should be boiled; meat and vegetables should be cooked and fruit peeled.

Medical care is adequate, but can be expensive.

Hotels

Good hotel accommodation is available in main centres. Service charges usually added to bill.

Credit cards

There is limited acceptance of the major credit cards only.

Public holidays (national)

Fixed dates

1 Jan (New Year's Day), 11 Feb (Youth Day), 1 May (Labour Day), 20 May (National Day), 21 May (Sheep Festival), 15 Aug (Assumption Day), 1 Oct (Unification Day), 25 Dec (Christmas Day).

Variable dates

Good Friday, Easter Monday, Ascension Day, Eid al Adha, Eid al Fitr, Birth of the Prophet.

Islamic year 1433 (26 Nov 2011–14 Nov 2012): The Islamic year contains 354 or 355 days, with the result that Muslim feasts advance by 10–12 days against the Gregorian calendar. Dates of feasts vary according to the sighting of the new moon, so cannot be forecast exactly.

Working hours

Different hours are kept in the French-speaking (including Yaoundé and Douala) and English-speaking areas (south-west and north-west frontier areas) of Cameroon.

Banking

French-speaking areas: Mon—Fri: 0800—1200 and 1515—1630.

English-speaking areas: Mon—Fri: 0800—1330.

Business

French-speaking areas: Mon—Fri: 0730—1200 and 1430—1800.

English-speaking areas: Mon—Fri: 0730—1500; Sat: 0730—1200.

Government
French-speaking areas: Mon—Fri: 0730—1200 and 1430—1800.
English-speaking areas: Mon—Fri: 0730—1500; Sat: 0730—1200.
Shops
French-speaking areas: Mon—Sat: 0700/0800—1230 and 1430/1500—1830/1900.
English-speaking areas: Mon—Sat: 0700/0800—1200 and 1430/1530—1830—1900.
Post offices:
French-speaking areas: Mon—Fri: 0800—1200 and 1400—1700; Sat: 0800—1200
English-speaking areas: Mon—Fri: 0800—1200 and 1430—1700.

Telecommunications
Mobile/cell phones
Cellular telephones services are available.

Electricity supply
220V AC, 50 cycles; plugs are of the two-pin round type.

Social customs/useful tips
Handshaking is the customary form of greeting. Business is conducted primarily in English or French.
Care should be taken to respect Islamic and other local religious practices and conventions, and visitors should be aware of restrictions on food and drink in Muslim areas, particularly during the Islamic fasting period of Ramadan.
Visitors should take care when photographing. It is considered polite to ask permission to photograph traditional dances, and it is advisable not to take pictures of official buildings or military installations.
If there is no service charge included in a bill, gratuities in hotels and restaurants are up to 10 per cent.

Security
Muggings and petty crime have increased in recent years, mainly in the large cities. It is unwise to carry valuables or large amounts of cash in the street and thieves should not be resisted. Armed bandit attacks are a serious problem throughout the country. Journeys should be carefully planned and travelling in convoy is recommended. At the international airports, to avoid luggage being stolen, care should be taken to employ only the official porters.

Getting there
Air
National airline: Cameroon Airlines
International airport/s: Douala International (DLA), 10km from the city; duty-free shop, bars, restaurants, bank, post office and shops.
Other airport/s: Yaoundé-Nsimalen (YAO), 20km from the city; Garoua International (GOU), 6km from the city, also accept international flights.
Airport tax: Approximately US$18.
Surface
Road: Road access is possible from Nigeria, Chad, Gabon, Equatorial Guinea and the Central African Republic. These routes are rough and may become impassable during rainy seasons. Bush taxis and minibuses are available. Armed banditry is a problem in the area bordering the Central African Republic and in other parts of Cameroon.
Rail: Rail access is available from N'Gaoundal and Belabo in the Central African Republic.
Water: There are two boats a day from Calabar (Nigeria) across the Cross River to Oron, and from Ikang (Nigeria) there are speedboats to Ekondo Titi.
Douala offers more freight links with Europe than other Central African ports. Cameroon Shipping Lines (Camshiplines) maintains an office in Paris.
Main port/s: Douala. Other ports are at Limbe, Kribi and Garoua (on the River Bénoué), which handle river trade during the dry season.

Getting about
National transport
Air: Cameroon Airlines operates domestic services between the main cities, including several daily flights between Yaoundé and Douala. Early arrival at the airport terminal is advisable, as overbookings are common. However, air services are generally efficient and certainly the fastest means of travelling within Cameroon.
Road: Cameroon's road network totals 31,800km of roads. Surfaced roads run between main centres although there are no tarmac road links between Yaoundé and Ngaoundéré. Major routes are from Douala to Limbé, Buea, Bafoussam, Sangmelima, Bamenda and Yaoundé (all-weather road). Most other roads are unsurfaced and are often impassable during rainy season.
Buses: There are coach services between the main centres. Connections to rural areas are unreliable, dangerous and subject to suspension in the rainy season.
Rail: The track network extends 1,168km. Cameroon Railways (Camrail) links Kumba, Douala, Yaoundé and Ngaoundéré. An overnight service runs from Yaoundé to Ngaoundéré (12 hours). Second-class travel is cheap but uncomfortable. Sleeping facilities are available on some trains. There is an express three-hour service between Yaoundé and Douala with good facilities.

City transport
Taxis: Taxis are not metered but have a minimum fare and fixed prices. Long journeys and daily hire should be negotiated. A 10 per cent tip is optional. There are taxis from the airport to Douala city centre.
Car hire
Chauffeur- or self-driven cars are available in Yaoundé and Douala, but can be expensive. An international driving licence is required.

BUSINESS DIRECTORY

The addresses listed below are a selection only. While World of Information makes every endeavour to check these addresses, we cannot guarantee that changes have not been made, especially to telephone numbers and area codes. We would welcome any corrections.

Telephone area codes
The international direct dialling code (IDD) for Cameroon is +237 followed by the subscriber's number.

Useful telephone numbers

Police:	17
Fire:	18
Ambulance:	23-40-20

Chambers of Commerce
Cameroon Chamber of Commerce, Industry and Mines, Rue de Chambre de Commerce, PO Box 4011, Douala (tel:342-6855; fax: 342-5596; e-mail: cride-g77@camnet.cm).

Banking
Amity Bank Cameroon, PO Box 2705, Douala (tel: 432-055; fax: 432-046).

Banque Internationale pour le Commerce et l'Industrie du Cameroun (BICIC), PO Box 1925, Avenue du Général-de-Gaulle, Douala (tel: 428-431, 420-001; fax: 424-184, 424-116).

Commercial Bank of Cameroon, PO Box 4004, Douala (tel: 420-202; fax: 433-802).

First Investment Bank; PO Box 13276, Douala (tel: 431-304; fax: 428-423).

International Bank of Africa-Cameroon, PO Box 3300, Douala (tel: 428-422; fax: 428-423).

Société Générale de Banques au Cameroun, PO Box 4042, 78 Rue Joss, Douala (tel: 427-010, 427-004; fax: 430-353) .

Standard Chartered Bank Cameroon, PO Box 1784, Boulevard de la Liberté, Douala (tel: 424-191; fax: 422-789).

Central bank
Banque des États de l'Afrique Centrale, Direction Nationale, PO Box 83,

Yaoundé (tel: 223-0511; fax: 223-3380; e-mail: beacyde@beac.int).

Stock exchange 1

Doula Stock Exchange (DSX): www.douala-stock-exchange.com

Travel information

Cameroon Airlines, Littoral BP 4092, 3 Avenue General de Gaulle, Douala (tel: 422-525, 424-949; fax: 422-487, 423-459).

Douala International Airport, BP 3131, Douala (tel: 423-630, 423-577; fax: 423-758).

Ministry of tourism

Ministry of Tourism, Yaoundé (tel: 223-353, 235-258; fax: 221-295).

National tourist organisation offices

Société Camerounaise de Tourisme (Socatour), BP 7138, Yaoundé (tel: 233-219).

Ministries

Ministry of Agriculture, Yaoundé (tel: 234-085, 225-166, 231-190).

Ministry of Communications, Yaoundé (tel: 234-075; 223-155, 233-974).

Ministry of External relations, Yaoundé (tel: 220-133).

Ministry of Economy and Finance, BP 18, Yaoundé (tel: 234-000, 232-299).

Ministry of Environment and Forestry, BP 14276, Yaoundé (tel: 229-483, 221-225).

Ministry of Industrial and Commercial Development, Yaoundé (tel: 234-040, 225-085).

Ministry of Culture, Yaoundé (tel: 223-155, 233-974).

Ministry of Livestock, Fisheries and Animal Industries, Yaoundé (tel: 223-311, 220-443).

Ministry of Mines, Water and Energy, Yaoundé (tel: 233-404).

Ministry of Post and Telecommunications, Yaoundé (tel: 234-016; fax: 223-497).

Ministry of Public Works and Transport, Yaoundé (tel: 232-236).

Other useful addresses

British Embassy, Avenue Winston Churchill, BP 547, Yaoundé (tel: 220-545, 220-796; fax: 220-148).

Cameroon Development Corporation (CDC), BP 28, Bota, Limbe (tel: 332-251).

Cameroon Embassy (USA), 2349 Massachusetts Avenue, NW, Washington DC 20008 (tel: 202-265-8790; fax: 202-387-3826; e-mail: info@ambacam-usa.org).

Cameroon Press and Publishing Co, BP 1218, Yaoundé (tel: 234-012).

Cameroon Telecommunications, BP 1571, Yaoundé (tel: 234-065; fax: 230-303).

Commission Technique de la Mission de Réhabilitation des Entreprises due Secteur Public et Parapublic, SNI Building, 9th Floor, Yaoundé (tel: 239-750; fax: 235-108).

Centre National d'Assistance aux Petites et Moyennes Entreprises, BP 1377, Douala (tel: 425-858).

Centre National du Commerce Exterieur (CNCE), BP 2461, Douala (tel: 421-685).

Department of Statistics, BP 25, Yaoundé (tel: 220-788).

EU Delegate, BP 847, Yaoundé (tel: 221-387, 222-149).

FEICOM (Special Equipment and Intercommunity Intervention Fund), BP 718 Yaoundé (tel/fax: 231-759).

National Tenders Board, Mballa II, 4th Floor, PO Box 6604, Yaoundé (tel: 201-803; fax: 206-042; e-mail: DGTC@GCNET.CM).

Office National du Café et du Cacao (ONCC), – sole marketing agency for cocoa, coffee, cotton, groundnuts, palm kernels. BP 378, Douala (tel: 426-776, 425-088).

Office de Radiodiffusion-Télévision Camerounaise (CRTV), BP 1634, Yaoundé (tel: 234-088).

Regifercam, BP 304, Douala (tel: 407-159; fax: 423-205).

Société Camerounaise des Depots Petroliers, Siège Social BP 2271, Douala (tel: 405-445; fax: 404-796).

Société de Développement du Cacao SODECAO), BP 1651, Yaoundé (tel: 220-991).

Société de Développement du Coton, Headquarters, BP 302, Garoua (tel: 271-556; fax: 272-068).

Société Nationale des Eaux du Cameroun, BP 157 Douala (tel: 433-066, 430-067; fax: 422-945).

Société Nationale de Raffinage, Cape Limboh, PO Box 365, Limbe (tel: 423-815, 423-817; fax: 423-444, 424-199).

Société Nationale d'Investissement, BP 423, Place de la Poste, Yaoundé (tel: 224-499, 224-422).

Société de Recouvrement des Créances du Cameroun, BP 11991, Yaoundé (tel: 223-739, 220-911, 230-067; fax: 233-833).

Sydicate of Wood Producers and Exporters (SPEBC), BP 2064, Douala (tel/fax: 428-617).

Syndicat des Commerçants, Importateurs et Exportateurs du Cameroun (SCIEC), BP 562, Douala (tel: 420-304).

Syndicat des Industriels du Cameroun, BP 1516, Yaoundé (tel: 222-468; BP 673, Douala (tel: 423-058).

Technical Committee for Privatisation and Liquidations, SNI Building, 9th Floor, Yaoundé (tel: 239-750; fax: 235-108).

US Embassy, rue Nachtigal, BP 817, Yaoundé (tel: 234-014).

Internet sites

Africa Business Network: www.ifc.org/abn

AllAfrica.com: allafrica.com

African Development Bank: www.afdb.org

Africa Online: www.africaonline.com

Mbendi AfroPaedia (information on companies, countries, industries and stock exchanges in Africa): mbendi.co.za

Canada

Canada's economy has proved to be one of the industrialised world's most resilient since the global financial crisis. In July 2011 the Bank of Canada made a modest adjustment to its forecast for the whole year, dropping its growth projection from 2.9 per cent to 2.8 per cent. Hardly the stuff of crises. The same set of figures projected Canada's 2012 growth at 2.6 per cent.

Conservatives win majority

The May 2011 election saw the Conservative Party of Canada (CPC) win – for the first time – a clear majority. The Conservative victory appeared to polarise Canadian politics, but was seen by many Canadians as strengthening the Conservative's divisive policies. Their victory was seen as pushing Canadian politics further to the right. They ended up with 167 of the 308 seats in Canada's House of Commons, with forty per cent of the vote. Prior to the election the Conservatives had held 143 seats, not enough to give them a majority in the House. The Conservative leader and national prime minister, Stephen Harper, had won the previous two elections, but never held a majority government. The New Democratic Party/Nouveau Parti Démocratique (NDP) won 102 seats. The big loser was Liberal Party of Canada (LPC) (Party Libéral du Canada) with only 34 seats, their lowest ever number. For many post-war years the Liberals had been the 'natural' party of government; now their leader, Michael Ignatieff, lost his seat in the election and resigned as leader. In Québec, the governing LPC were tainted with allegations of corruption that had caused the party's poll ratings to slip through the floor. Given the buoyant state of Quebec's economy, this was something of a surprise, especially as Quebec's Liberal leader, Jean Charest, had managed to counter the separatist drift that had prevailed in the province. Another loser was the separatist Bloc Québecois (the Bloc), also long seen as a natural provincial leader. The Bloc were left with only four seats, having previously retained 47 seats. The surprise

KEY FACTS

Official name: Canada

Head of State: Queen Elizabeth II (since 1952), represented by Governor General David Johnston (from 1 Oc 2010)

Head of government: Prime Minister Stephen Harper (from 2006; re-elected 2 May 2011)

Ruling party: Conservative Party of Canada (CPC) (from 2006; re-elected 2 May 2011)

Area: 9,976,139 square km

Population: 34.10 million (2010)*

Capital: Ottawa

Official language: English, French

Currency: Canadian dollar (C$) = 100 cents

Exchange rate: C$1.04 per US$ (Oct 2011)

GDP per capita: US$46,215 (2010)

GDP real growth: 3.20% (2010)

GDP: US$1,574.40 billion (2010)

Labour force: 18.52 million (2010)

Unemployment: 8.00% (2010)

Inflation: 1.80% (2010)

Oil production: 3.34 million bpd (2010)

Balance of trade: -US$8.68 billion (2010)

* Estimated figure

victor in Québec was the NDP, which won 59 of the 75 seats.

Mr Harper's clear majority should enable him to proceed with a number of projects for which he had been unable to gain approval from his coalition partners. These included a tougher crime bill, a plan to lower corporate taxes from 21 per cent to 15 per cent over a five year period and the purchase of US manufactured F-35 fighter aircraft. Of particular interest internationally was Mr Harper's stated intention to give Canada greater clout in the Arctic. Mr Harper is not generally seen as a warm, or even friendly, politician. One headline in the *Toronto Globe and Mail* described him as 'nasty, brutish – and competent'.

The election outcome was something of a surprise for the majority of the political pundits. Canadians had been to the polls three times in seven years and Mr Harper called this one more correctly than most of his rivals. Like the Conservatives, the Liberals had also thought that a successful election campaign would enable them to break the country's political deadlock. The electoral polls had deceived, however. But one overwhelming statistic probably prevailed in the result: a staggering 85 per cent of Canadians do not pay any attention to politics.

Royalism OK?

In May 2011 the visit of the Duke and Duchess of Cambridge to Canada was generally thought to have been a huge success as crowds gathered to greet the recently married couple. The only fly in the royal ointment were the moments when, in Québec, the royal couple were faced with dissenting separatists. Not long after the royal visit, defence minister Peter MacKay announced that Canada's navy and air force, officially known since 1968 as the Maritime Command and the Air Command, would revert to their original names, the Royal Canadian Navy and the Royal Canadian Air Force. Similarly, the army – known as the Land Force Command – would be called the Canadian Army. The police force, the famous Mountie,' never lost its full title of the Royal Canadian Mounted Police. The restoration of some Royalist symbols was thought to be a carefully a calculated move by Mr Harper's ruling CPC. The latest edition of Canada's citizenship guide includes references to Queen Elizabeth and the Queen's portrait is now seen in many more public buildings.

Québec

The future of Québec and its sovereignty has traditionally dominated Québec's politics. Since the 1960s the paramilitary Front de la Libération du Québec conducted a series of attacks against government and establishment buildings, as well as kidnapping high profile political figures. This was against a legislative backdrop that made French the official language. Surprisingly, until 1968 Quebec did not have a political party that espoused independence. In that year the Parti Québécois (Québec Party) was founded in 1968, to promote Québec's independence, working alongside the federal Bloc Québécois which was only established in 1991, also to promote Québec's independence.

Québec's voters appear to be split on the issue of independence. Perhaps understandably, the province's English speakers are less than enthusiastic about the idea, as also is the case with Québec's older voters. In a 1980 referendum, just under 60 per cent rejected independence, A similar referendum in 1985 had returned a narrower victory, with just.50.6 per cent.

Plan Nord

In May 2011 Quebec launched its ambitious US$2.2 billion development plan which has the dual objectives of opening up the province's Northern region as well as strengthening environmental protection. Québec's northern region, the so-called Boreal Zone, covers an area twice the size of France – the Plan Nord envisages the region being opened up for mining, energy projects and forestry. Industrial activity would be banned in the northern half of the province and 12 per cent of the area would become a nature reserve. In this, Quebec was following the lead set by other provinces. Environmental protection has often been balanced by development projects. In Ontario an estimated 30,000 mining claims have been registered for the area to the west of James Bay and the province has passed a law protecting its northern area from development. Manitoba has approved legislation protecting 4 million hectares of forest. In Alberta the balance appears to have tilted in favour of development; energy enterprises took exception to plans to protect 20 per cent of the province. Alberta lags behind other provinces in environmental protection with virtually no limits on oil exploration. Paradoxically, the indigenous communities tend to favour the approval of exploration projects which create much needed jobs in otherwise underdeveloped regions. Their feelings were echoed at federal level where opposition plans to introduce a carbon tax were greeted with a statement by Mr Harper that they would 'screw everybody'. But in British Columbia the provincial legislature had gone ahead and introduced a carbon tax, which turned out to be surprisingly popular. Quoted in the London *Economist* one eminent academic from the University of Ottawa declared

KEY INDICATORS — **Canada**

	Unit	2006	2007	2008	2009	2010
Population	m	31.61	32.93	33.28	33.69	*34.10
Gross domestic product (GDP)	US$bn	1,269.10	1,432.14	1,511.00	1,336.40	1,574.10
GDP per capita	US$	39,115	43,485	45,428	39,669	46,215
GDP real growth	%	2.7	2.6	0.4	-2.5	3.2
Inflation	%	2.0	2.1	2.4	0.3	1.8
Unemployment	%	6.3	6.0	6.1	8.3	8.0
Oil output	'000 bpd	3,147.0	3,309.0	3,238.0	3,212.0	3,336.0
Natural gas output	bn cum	187.0	183.7	175.2	161.4	159.8
Coal output	mtoe	32.3	30.4	36.0	32.8	34.9
Exports (fob) (goods)	US$m	401,786	434,049	462,682	324,682	393,183
Imports (fob) (goods)	US$m	356,641	388,211	398,982	328,928	401,865
Balance of trade	US$m	45,146	45,838	63,700	-4,246	-8,682
Current account	US$m	20,792.0	13,263.0	9,652.0	-38,380.0	-49,682.0
Total reserves minus gold	US$m	34,994.0	40,991.0	43,778.0	54,238.0	59,998.0
Foreign exchange	US$m	33,198.0	39,314.0	41,537.0	42,602.0	44,888.0
Exchange rate	per US$	1.15	1.02	1.07	1.14	1.03

* estimated figure

that 'The carbon tax has been good for the environment, good for taxpayers and it hasn't hurt the economy.' British Columbia had demonstrated that a carbon tax could be acceptable, producing significant benefits at low cost. The left leaning NDP that had originally opposed the tax later said that it should have supported it, leaving the CPC alone in opposing the province's carbon tax.

Plan China

Like other mineral rich countries, Canada's relations with China are important. It was therefore surprising that after first being elected in 2006, Prime Minister Stephen Harper took over three years before arranging an official visit to China. At the beginning of his period in office, Mr Harper felt it appropriate to talk tough on China, promising that Canada 'would not sell out' in addressing the human rights issue with China. But by the time of his visit, in 2009, *realpolitik* had become the order of the day. Concerned about the lack of demand from the US, Canada needed to devote more time to increasing its exports to China, which in mid-2011 were estimated to account for an almost negligible 3.3 per cent of Canada's total exports. This figure was twice that of 2006, suggesting that for the time being, discussions on the sensitive issue of human rights would be firmly placed on Canada's back burner. In Canada's case, sales of minerals have been one of the economy's bright spots since 2008. The Canadian electorate seemed to have mixed feelings about foreign investment in the country's mineral resources. This concern was not limited to concern about Chinese takeovers; attempts by the Australian mining giant BHP-Billiton to take over Canada's PotashCorp for US$39 billion were rebuffed. The rejection was as much dictated by strategic as commercial considerations. Notably, the Canadian government saw fit to intervene, while at the same time re-asserting the importance the Canadian government attached to free trade. The prime minister of the province of Saskatchewan (where PotashCorp is located), Brad Wall observed that the province was 'welcoming foreign investment, but also balancing the strategic interests of this nation'. The (then) leader of the opposition Liberal Party noted that 'There's a difference between foreign investment and foreign control.'

Plan Israel

Canada's unequivocal support for Israel can be put down to Mr Harper. On becoming prime minister, he immediately brought an end to Canadian aid to the Palestinian Authority following the victory of Hamas in the Palestinian elections. Mr Harper refrained from criticising Israel's Gaza intervention and later stopped Canadian support for the United Nations' Relief and Works Agency (UNWRA). One Canadian minister went so far as to say that any attack on Israel would be regarded by the Canadian government as an attack on Canada. Government grants to pro-Arab charity groups have also been cut. The government has been at pains to defend its pro-Israeli stance; civil servants prefer to see it as a reflection of their prime minister's 'conviction politics'.

Energy abundance

According to the US government's Energy Information Administration (EIA), in 2008, Canada ranked fifth globally in total energy produced, generating a quadrillion British Thermal Units (Btu) of primary energy. The *Oil and Gas Journal* (OGJ) revised Canada's proven reserves of crude oil downward by over 1.5 per cent in 2010, which remained constant for January 2011. Despite the decrease from a previous estimate of 178.1 billion barrels, Canada's 175.2 billion barrels of proven reserves of crude oil places Canada third globally, behind Saudi Arabia and Venezuela. Canada is the only non-OPEC member among the top five reserve holders. Approximately 170 billion barrels (97 per cent) of Canada's reserves are unconventional, mainly from bitumen deposits. These unconventional deposits place Canada as one of the central sources of non-OPEC production growth in the coming decades.

Canada has a sophisticated, privatised oil sector that has seen increased consolidation and specialisation following the global economic downturn. International participation has risen rapidly in Canada's oil sector, although this has been for non-controlling stakes in projects. A recent regulation of foreign investment in Canada titled the Invest Canada Act outlines that any large investment in Canada must be of 'net benefit' to Canada, indicating a limit on foreign control of strategic commodities. Numerous Canadian oil firms have undergone significant corporate restructuring in the past two years. In August 2009, Suncor completed its acquisition of Petro-Canada, the former state oil firm, creating Canada's largest oil and gas firm. In December 2009, Encana completed its plans to spin-off its oil and traditional gas assets into a new, wholly independent firm, Cenovus. Other Canadian firms, such as Talisman Energy and Petrobank, have sought increased specialisation by creating separate entities to focus on specific areas, such as shale gas in British Columbia or shale oil in Saskatchewan and Manitoba. Asian firms have also been buying up Canadian assets through corporate acquisition.

Canada's regulatory framework is one in which federal and provincial bodies co-ordinate policy and regulation. Provincial authorities handle most of the oversight in the sector. The national regulatory body is the National Energy Board (NEB). The largest and most influential of the provincial regulators is the Alberta Energy Resources Conservation Board (ERCB).

Oil production in Canada comes principally from three sources: the oil sands of Alberta, the Western Canada Sedimentary Basin (WCSB), and the offshore oil fields in the Atlantic. Additional reserves are known to be under the Beaufort Sea in the Arctic, off the Pacific coast and in the Gulf of St Lawrence. Alberta provides the bulk of oil production and encompasses the major share of Canada's hydrocarbon resources. Moreover, production from the conventional offshore reserves off the eastern provinces comes from mature oil-fields, with few opportunities to replenish depletion rates. As such, western provinces will comprise an increasing proportion of overall Canadian oil production in the future. Total oil production in Canada amounted to 3.46 million barrels per day (bpd) in 2010, of which 2.65 million bpd was crude oil. Canada consumes around 2.3 million bpd, with consumption rates for petroleum relatively flat over the long-term, with a 0.1 per cent expected average growth rate through 2035, according to the EIA. This trend allows for any increase in production to be exported; Canada thus comprises a major source of non-OPEC oil production growth.

Of the 2.7 million bpd of crude produced in Canada in 2009, 1.35 million bpd of that was derived from the oil sands of Alberta. These volumes and growth from the oil sands will make them the largest single source of US crude imports, the additional conventional Canadian exports notwithstanding. Oil sands consist of a mineral called bitumen, an unconventional petroleum which is naturally found blended with sand, clay, and water. Once extracted, bitumen is a heavy, viscous type of crude oil. The bitumen must be 'upgraded' through a complex process which yields a light, sweet 'synthetic' crude. The technically sophisticated process by which bitumen is processed requires a separate facility known as an 'upgrader' and utilises significant amounts of water and diluents.

Chinese firms have begun to represent a significant presence in the oil sands. In January 2010, PetroChina finalised the acquisition of a 60 per cent stake in the MacKay River and Dover projects from Athabasca Oil Sands Company (AOSC). Sinopec acquired ConocoPhillip's stake in Syncrude Canada. Syncrude Canada Project produces 350,000 bpd and is one of the largest open-pit mines in the Athabasca Oil Sand region. China National Offshore Oil Company (CNOOC) also purchased a stake in the Christina Lake and Surmont oil sands projects from MEG Energy. The premier of Alberta, Ed Stelmach, even made an official state visit to Beijing in May 2010 to expand ties between the two countries and regions.

Gas

The OGJ estimates that Canada's proved natural gas reserves amounted to 61.95 trillion cubic feet (tcf) as of January 2011, a 7 per cent increase from the previous year. Despite its relatively small amount of reserves of natural gas, Canada is third in dry natural gas production, as well as the third largest net exporter of natural gas globally. Vast deposits of unconventional natural gas reside in the WCSB in the form of coal bed methane (CBM), tight gas and gas found in formations of shale. Although development of these resources is not as advanced as in the United States, they nevertheless make up a significant source of growth potential in natural gas production.

Although annual natural gas production over the last decade held steady with historical highs (averaging 182.33 billion cubic metres (cum)) it fell to 159.8 billion cum in 2010 (the lowest since the 1990s). In 2010 Canadian gas exports to the United States was 92.4 billion cum and typically accounts for over 90 per cent of the US's total pipeline imports.

Most of Canada's natural gas deposits reside in the WCSB, interconnected with the vast oil deposits in the same region. Although production of conventional natural gas is in decline in the WCSB, technological advances have spurred rapid investment in the region, especially in shale and tight gas plays in British Columbia and Alberta. Otherwise, reserves of natural gas are concentrated off the eastern shore of Canada, principally around Newfoundland and Nova Scotia, from the Arctic region, and off the Pacific coast.

As Canada develops its newly accessible reserves of natural gas, it will also have to expand exports to markets outside the United States. The extraction of shale gas in the US has led to an increase in domestic production that will require less imported gas in the future. Additionally, these smaller import volumes will increasingly be met by imports of liquefied natural gas (LNG), rather than from pipelines, the traditional mode of export from Canada to US markets. This has prompted firms to look to Asia for the necessary markets to sell the increasing amounts of gas, as well as attracting Asian investment.

Risk assessment

Politics	Good
Economy	Good
Regional stability	Good

COUNTRY PROFILE

Historical profile

1497 John Cabot claimed Newfoundland for Henry VII of England.

1534 Jacques Cartier explored Newfoundland and charted the Gulf of St Lawrence as far as what is now Québec city and Montréal. He claimed this land for France.

1600 King Henry IV of France granted fur trading rights in the Gulf of St Lawrence to a group of French merchants. The French settled in Acadia – the Canadian maritime provinces of what are now New Brunswick, Nova Scotia and Prince Edward Island.

1608 Founding of Québec as France's first colony by Samuel Champlain.

1629 Québec city was captured by the English fleet.

1632 Québec was returned to France by the treaty of St Germain-en-Laye.

1642 Founding of Ville Marie, which later became Montréal.

1660 The English Navigation Act prohibited foreigners from trading with English colonies.

1663 Louis XIV assumed personal control of the French settlements that included Québec, Montréal, Nova Scotia, New Brunswick and the area around the Gulf of St Lawrence and called this *Nouvelle France* (New France). Québec became a royal province.

1665 Jean Talon came from France to administer colonial affairs and brought about a significant expansion of the colony, encouraging agriculture, arts and business, stimulating immigration. By this time, the English, fighting for territorial dominance, controlled 10 colonies on the Atlantic coast and exceeded New France in terms of population and self-sufficiency.

1670 In competition with the French, the English established the Hudson Bay Company, giving themselves a monopoly on the fur trade in the Hudson Bay area.

1702 Queen Anne's War broke out between the English and the French. This led to the capture of Port Royal (capital of Acadia) by the English.

1713 Peace was established under the Treaty of Utrecht. This required France to surrender the Hudson Bay Area, Newfoundland and Acadia to Britain. France was permitted to keep Cape Breton Island and her inland colonies.

1754 The French and Indian War began in North America; it became the Seven Years War when fighting spread to Europe.

1755–56 The British attacked Québec, the nerve-centre of the French empire. Québec came under British rule.

1759 Montréal, cut off from reinforcements and supplies from France, fell to the British.

1774 Britain passed the Québec Act, which officially recognised French civil law and granted religious freedom to Roman Catholics. Britain assumed full control of the North Atlantic provinces of Canada, Nova Scotia, New Brunswick, Prince Edward Island and Newfoundland.

1858 British Columbia became a Crown Colony.

1862 The British withdrew troops from Canada.

1867 Ontario, Québec, Nova Scotia and New Brunswick joined together under the terms of the British North America Act to become the Dominion of Canada. These four territories became provinces with their own governments, law making bodies and lieutenant governors.

1870 Manitoba joined the Dominion, followed by British Columbia and Prince Edward Island. Hudson Bay became part of Canada and was renamed the Northwest Territories.

1898 The territory of Yukon was carved out of the Northwest Territories and entered the Dominion. The Territories, unlike the provinces that existed within their own right, were subject to federal legislative power. The federal government had the right to intrude in administrative and social affairs.

1905 Alberta and Saskatchewan became provinces of Canada.

1914–18 Canada joined the allies in the First World War.

1931 The Statute of Westminster was passed by the British parliament, granting dominion parliaments the right to reject the laws of the British parliament and allowing British dominions, including Canada, complete autonomy. Canada became a free associate of the British

Commonwealth of Nations, but had to swear allegiance to the British Crown.
1939–45 Canada joined the allies against Nazi Germany, Italy and Japan in the Second World War.
1949 Newfoundland became Canada's tenth province.
1969 Canada recognised English and French as its two official languages.
1977 Following an amendment to the Citizenship Act, Canadians ceased to be British subjects.
1980 A referendum to make Québec a separate country was rejected by the people of Québec.
1982 The Constitution Act stated that Canada no longer required British approval for new laws.
1995 The Canadian parliament passed a resolution recognising Québec as a distinct society within Canada. A referendum in Québec produced another 'no' vote for independence.
1999 Nunavut, created out of part of the Northwest Territories, became Canada's third territory.
2000 Jean Chrétien called snap elections, in which the Liberal Party of Canada (LPC) took 40.8 per cent of the vote, winning 172 seats.
2001 Québec's premier, Lucien Bouchard, resigned. Bernard Landry took over the post. Canada became the first country to legalise cannabis for people suffering from chronic medical conditions and terminal illnesses.
2002 Jean Chrétien announced he would resign in 2004.
2003 Toronto was seriously hit by an outbreak of the flu-like Sars virus. A power blackout – the biggest in North American history – hit Toronto, Ottawa and other parts of Ontario, as well as cities in the north-eastern US. Paul Martin took over as prime minister after Jean Chrétien's retirement.
2004 The ruling LPC won the parliamentary elections, but lost its majority.
2005 Haitian-born Michaëlle Jean was appointed as Governor General (GG).
2006 The Conservative Party of Canada (CPC) won elections but without an overall majority. Parliament approved the recognition of Quebec as a nation within a united Canada.
2007 Increased melting ice in Arctic waters opened the Northwest Passage between the Pacific and Atlantic Oceans, which become navigable during summer months. Canada asserted its territorial rights to manage the waterway ahead of any international recognition of its control.
2008 Prime Minister Harper dissolved parliament and called early parliamentary elections. The ruling CPC increased its share of the vote and its number of seats with 37.63 per cent and 143 seats (out of 308). However the total was less than the 155 seats necessary to achieve a majority. Stephen Harper remained in post as prime minister of a minority government.
2009 Canada imposed visa controls on visitors from Czech Republic and Mexico; there had been a disproportionate rise in asylum requests from the two countries. Parliament was prorogued for two months, conveniently while the winter Olympic Games took place in Vancouver. This was the second time Prime Minister Harper had employed this device to avoid critical parliamentary motions; this closure stalled attempts by parliament to force the government to release uncensored documents concerning torture of Afghan detainees.
2010 Parliament reopened in March. In April, a ruling by the Speaker of the House of Commons declared that the documents concerning Afghan detainees must be released or the government risked contempt of parliament. A parliamentary committee was formed in May and having taken an oath of confidentiality was allowed to review uncensored documents, to determine which, without threatening national security, would go forward for possible public release. David Johnston took up the appointment as the governor general 1 October.
2011 On 19 March, Canada joined in a five-country coalition (France, Italy, the UK and the US) to impose a no-fly zone over Libya. Three opposition parties rejected the budget on 23 March. The minority government of Steven Harper fell on 25 March following a parliamentary vote of no confidence. New, early elections took place on 2 May. The Conservatives won a decisive majority with 39.62 per cent of the vote (167 seats out of 308) giving Prime Minister Harper a clear majority. The New Democratic Party (Nouveau Parti Démocratique) (NDP) boosted their standing by winning 102 seats (up from 36 seats in 2008). The leaders of the Liberal Party, Michael Ignatieff and Bloc Québécois, Gilles Duceppe, quit their chairmanships following their defeat in the polls. Canada began to withdraw its combat troops from Afghanistan on 5 July. On 25 July the leader of the NDP, Jack Layton, announced he was stepping down 'temporarity' to fight cancer.

Political structure

Constitution

Although Canada is formally a constitutional monarchy with the British monarch as the nominal head of state, for all practical purposes the country is a sovereign state. The governor general is the Queen's representative in Canada.
The Canadian government has a federal structure, with 10 provincial governments plus the three northern territories of the Northwest Territories, Yukon and Nunavut on the lower tier and a national government on the upper tier.
The constitution is contained in the Constitution Act of 1982, although the province of Québec did not agree to this legislation. The division of power between the national and provincial governments is set out in the constitution which also contains a Charter of Rights and Freedoms. The federal government has authority over areas of national interest, while provincial governments have specific authority over local matters, including education, hospitals and public lands (including natural resources). The provinces exercise considerable autonomy over their affairs. Each province has an elected legislature together with an executive led by a provincial premier.
All Canadian citizens aged 18 years and over have the right to vote.

Form of state

Constitutional monarchy

The executive

The executive comprises the prime minister, appointed by the governor general, and his cabinet. The prime minister is the leader of the majority party in the House of Commons; the cabinet is also drawn from the ruling party's ranks.

National legislature

The House of Commons (lower legislature) does not have a fixed number of members, seats are apportioned based on the constitution. Seats are distributed among the provinces and reflect their population, however the provinces are also entitled to as many lower house seats as they have in the Senate and are entitle to as many seats as they had in 1976 or 1985, thus the current house has 308 sitting members. Members of the House of Commons sit for a maximum of five years and may be re-elected any number of times.
The Senate is a chamber of appointed members representing different political parties. The Governor General appoints members for a life-term, based on the recommendation of the prime minister. Seats are allocated to provide each province with equal representation. Over 50 per cent of membership is allocated to less-populated parts of the country to provide a balance of views. Senate tenure is guaranteed until aged 75. The Senate is a chamber of review whereby all legislatures must be passed before it for enactment. Legislature may be proposed by the Senate as long as it does not incur revenue collection.

Legal system

Based on English common law, except in Québec, where a French civil law system prevails.

The prime minister, through the governor general, appoints all judges to the federal courts, but not those to the provincial courts. Apart from this, the judiciary is independent of the executive. The Supreme Court of Canada is the highest court of appeal in both civil and criminal cases. Each province has its own court structure, headed by a provincial Supreme Court.

Last elections

2 May 2011 (parliamentary)

Results: Parliamentary: Conservative Party (Conservatives) won 39.62 per cent of the vote (167 seats out of 308), New Democratic Party (NDP) 30.63 per cent (102), Liberal Party 18.91 per cent (34), Bloc Québécois 6.04 per cent (four), Green Party 3.91 per cent (one); 13 political parties and two independent candidates each won less than 1 per cent and failed to win any seats. Turnout was estimated at 61.4 per cent.

Next elections

2015 (parliamentary)

Political parties

Ruling party

Conservative Party of Canada (CPC) (from 2006; re-elected 2 May 2011)

Main opposition party

New Democratic Party (Nouveau Parti Démocratique) (NDP)

Population

34.10 million (2010)*

Last census: 16 May 2006: 31,612,897

Population density: Three inhabitants per square km. Urban population: 77 per cent.

Annual growth rate: 1.0 per cent 1994–2004 (WHO 2006)

Ethnic make-up

British and Irish origin (28 per cent), French origin (23 per cent), other European origin (15 per cent), indigenous (2 per cent), other (including Asian, African, Arab) (6 per cent), mixed background (26 per cent).

In 2002, about 52 per cent of immigrants settled in Toronto, 15 per cent in Vancouver and 11 per cent in Montréal; the populations of many rural areas are declining.

Religions

Christianity is the prevailing religion in Canada. Approximately 45 per cent of the population belong to the Roman Catholic Church. The leading Protestant churches are the Anglican Church of Canada and the United Church of Canada. Orthodox Churches are also represented. Jews make up 1.2 per cent of the population and Muslims just under 1 per cent.

Education

Public investment in education amounts to 5.5 per cent of GDP. Universal primary education and gender parity, at this level and in secondary schools, have been achieved. Although methods of funding higher education vary from province to province, the federal and provincial governments fund approximately 85 per cent of the expenditure. Total government spending on education in 2002/03 amounted to C$25 billion (US$39 billion). Canada has strong initiatives to monitor and detect inequities in schooling across the provinces. There is stiff entrance exams for teaching courses and extensive in-service training for qualified teachers, which affords them high status in the community.

Each province is responsible for its own education system. In general, education is provided free of charge to the end of the secondary level. The number of private schools is small, except in the province of Québec. Levels of educational attainment continue to rise, with record numbers attending university. However, enrolments at elementary and secondary schools have steadily declined since the late 1960s, reflecting the decline in both the birth rate and the number of new immigrants.

The proportion of young people attending full-time university and college courses continues to expand, while part-time higher education courses for mature students are becoming increasingly popular. Canada has over 80 universities and 160 community and technical colleges, as well as 35 colleges of religious study.

Education services for indigenous students are an area of responsibility that is not clearly defined between provincial, territorial and federal government, who along with various local authorities have come up with different plans. There has been a rapid development of non-formal educational programmes, provided by non-governmental organisations. Citizenship education is a subject of renewed interest in the education curriculum.

Enrolment rate: 100 per cent total gross primary enrolment; 107 per cent boys, 106 per cent girls, gross secondary enrolment of relevant age groups (including repeaters) (Unesco).

Pupils per teacher: 16 in primary schools.

Health

Private expenditure averages 29 per cent of GDP, 39 per cent of which is funded by prepaid health plans and 52 per cent in out-of-pockets expenses.

Nationwide state-sponsored health insurance is achieved through a series of interlocking provincial plans, with the federal government providing substantial financial support through national Hospital Insurance and Medical Care Programmes. The insurance programmes are designed to ensure that all residents have access to medical services as needed. Most hospitals are run by non-profit, non-governmental, corporations.

HIV/Aids

HIV prevalence: 0.3 per cent aged 15–49 in 2003 (World Bank)

Life expectancy: 80 years, 2004 (WHO 2006)

Fertility rate/Maternal mortality rate: 1.5 births per woman, 2004 (WHO 2006)

Child (under 5 years) mortality rate (per 1,000): 5 per 1,000 live births (World Bank)

Head of population per physician: 2.14 physicians per 1,000 people, 2003 (WHO 2006)

Welfare

Canada has a comprehensive welfare system, which is administered at both federal and provincial levels of government. The system provides for social assistance, old age pensions, family allowances and unemployment insurance. Family allowances are credited for dependent children up to the age of 18.

Social assistance or welfare is the income programme of last resort in Canada. It helps people in need who are not eligible for other benefits. Benefit payments help pay for food, shelter and other health services.

The federal government provides monthly payments to parents or guardians on behalf of children under the age of 18, through a programme called the Child Tax Benefit. The amount is different according to family income, number of children and their ages. Successive federal governments have moved to target their financial support to families at the lower end of the income spectrum.

Pensions

Old age pensions become payable at the age of 65 and are indexed to inflation. There are essentially two social security programmes aimed at providing income for the elderly in Canada.

The Old Age Security (OAS) pension is given to people aged 65 and over, who meet residence requirements. Those who have little or no other income are eligible for the Guaranteed Income Supplement (GIS). People who have lived in Canada for less than 40 years receive a reduced pension.

The Canada and Québec Pension Plans are a form of insurance into which people must contribute during their working years to receive monthly payments starting at age 65. These plans also include survivor's pensions for the spouses of deceased pensioners, disability pensions and children's and death benefits.

Main cities
Ottawa (capital, estimated population 1.1 million (m) in 2005), Toronto (5.0m), Montréal (3.3m), Vancouver (2.1m), Calgary (1.0m), Edmonton (975,723), Québec City (696,886), Winnipeg (675,187), Hamilton (686,926).

Languages spoken
English is spoken by 61 per cent of the population, French by 26 per cent and both languages by 13 per cent. French predominates in the province of Québec (Montréal is the second largest French-speaking city in the world). A wide variety of other languages are spoken, reflecting the diverse origins of Canada's population.

Official language/s

English, French

Media
Press

Nearly all cities have at least one daily newspaper, and there is likely to be a tabloid if there is more than one on offer. The bilingual cities of Montreal and Ottawa offer newspapers in both English and French.

Dailies: The only national newspapers are the *National Post* (www.nationalpost.com) and *Globe and Mail* (www.theglobeandmail.com). The newspapers with the highest circulation include *Toronto Star* (www.thestar.com), *The Toronto Sun* (www.torontosun.com) a tabloid, *Vancouver Sun* (www.canada.com) and *The Gazette* (www.canada.com) from Montreal, and in French *Le Journal de Montréal* (www.canoe.com), and *La Presse* (www.cyberpresse.ca).

Weeklies: There are numerous local and community newspapers with dailies publishing weekend editions.

Business: National publications include *Canadian Business* (www.canadianbusiness.com), *The Northern Miner* (www.northernminer.com), Black Press has over 100 publications. Regional publications include *Business in Calgary* (www.businessincalgary.com) and *Business Edge* (www.businessedge.ca), from Alberta, *Business Examiner* (from Black Press), *Toronto Business Times* (www.torontobusinesstimes.com) and *Ottawa Business Journal* (www.ottawabusinessjournal.com) from Ontario and, in French, *Businest* (www.hebdosquebecor.com) and *Regard Économique* (http://www.linfonet.com) from Quebec.

Periodicals: There are a range of magazines published by central and regional government, including *Government Executive* (www.networkedgovernment.ca), *Municipal World* (www.municipalworld.com), and *The Hill Times* (www.thehilltimes.ca). News and current affairs are covered by *Inroads* (www.inroadsjournal.ca) published in November and May, *L'Actualité* (www.lactualite.com), published 20-times a year and *This Magazine* (www.thismagazine.ca) a bi-monthly with alternative political views. Monthly magazines include women's titles *Chatelaine* (http://en.chatelaine.com) in English and French and *Flare* (www.flare.com), others include *Our Times* (www.ourtimes.ca), and *Yourthink Magazine* (www.youthink.ca) for the young.

Broadcasting

The Canadian Broadcasting Corporation (CBC) is the national, public broadcaster with programmes in English and French that can be accessed by internet.

Radio: There are over 2,000 private, commercial radio stations providing entertainment, news and information for most tastes. CBC (www.cbc.ca/radio) operates four networks, including Radio One, Two, Radio Canada International and a radio station for indigenous communities with broadcasting news, cultural and speech-based programmes. Newcap (www.ncc.ca) has a network of 76 radio stations, and Rogers Broadcasting Limited (www.rogers.com) operates a pay-to-listen network, throughout the country. Local radio stations are found in all urban and many rural areas.

Television: Analogue TV is due to be replaced by digital TV by 31 August 2011. Until then all pay-to-view cable TV companies must supply a proportion of their output in analogue form until it has a digital subscription rate of 85 per cent.

CBC Television has three channels, CBCtelevision, CBCnews and CountryCanada with some domestic programmes broadcast in English and French.

CTV (www.ctv.ca) is the largest, English-language, privately-owned network, broadcasting mainly high rating US shows, as well as its own productions. The Global Television Network (Global TV) (www.globaltv.com) is the second English-language, privately-owned network, which relies on foreign programmes for its contents.

There are several French-language TV stations mainly based in Province of Quebec, including Télé-Québec (www.telequebec.tv) and CJNT-TV (www.cjntmontreal.ca) from Montreal.

The national, Aboriginal People's Television Network (www.aptn.ca) is based in Winnepeg.

There are many cable and satellite channels in English and French, available throughout the country offering all varieties of entertainments, news and educational programmes.

Advertising

Advertising Standards Canada is an independent, industry led agency created to ensure the integrity and viability of advertising. It regulates the Canadian Code of Advertising Standards through an Advertising Clearance Division, which preview adverts in five industries, specifically alcohol, children's advertising, cosmetics, consumer medications and food and soft drinks.

There is a full range of traditional and modern advertising media. Television accounts for the greatest part of net revenue, followed by magazines and newspapers.

Although the majority of Canadians speak English as their first language, the Francophone market, which is concentrated in Québec, is served extensively by its own French-language press, radio and television.

News agencies

Other news agencies: CBCNews: www.cbc.ca/news

CNW Group (in English and French): www.newswire.ca

The Canadian Press: www.thecanadianpress.com

Economy
Canada has vast natural resources of natural gas, timber, minerals and abundant fresh water and agricultural land that is used to produce beef, wheat, dairy products and fish, most of which is used in export trade. Its manufacturing sector is dominated by vehicle and aircraft construction, plus processing its natural resources.

GDP growth in 2007 was 2.5 per cent, but fell to 0.4 per cent in 2008 as the global economic crisis weakened the economy which slipped into recession in 2008, due to lower commodities prices and exports in general. By 2009 GDP growth was -2.6 per cent, but with the expectation that the economy will bounce back to growth of 3.1 per cent in 2010.

The Canadian banking system did not suffer the disastrous losses encountered elsewhere during the global economic crisis. This was due to the conservative nature of the sector, coupled with sound financial regulations and an economy that was already underpinned by high global commodity prices, historically low unemployment and low corporate and bank leverage rates that allowed the sector to ride out the downturn. Nevertheless, the impact on not only the volume of commodities exported but also the profits from the exports did reduce government revenue from US$242 billion in 2007/08 to US$234 billion in 2008/09 and a projected US$220 billion for 2009/10. As a result the country's current account balance, which fell from US$14.5 billion in 2007 to US$7.6 billion in 2008 fell further in 2009 to -US$36 billion and an expected -US$40 billion in 2010.

The federal government instigated measures, along with other countries, to stimulate the economy back into growth, including injections of public funds into money markets and guarantees for financial institutions.

As global trade picks up Canada's prospects will improve. But it is the health of the US economy that will have the greatest influence, as the two countries are comprehensively linked by trade with millions of jobs on both sides of their border relying on how well the other fares. Each is the other's largest export market; around 75 per cent of Canada's exports and 50 per cent of imports are with the US. China, which is buying up a large proportion of Canada's natural resources each year, has become Canada's second largest export market.

External trade

Canada's largest trading partner by far is the US and the country is now the leading export market for 35 separate US states. The North American Free Trade Agreement (Nafta), under which Canada has tri-lateral trade agreements with Mexico and the US, has been in operation since 1994. Canada's other top trading partners are China and Japan.

In the first six months of 2009 export commodities by rank were, crude oil, natural gas, motor vehicles, gold, pharmaceuticals, larger aircraft and wheat and rye. However, of the top 25 commodities exported only pharmaceuticals and larger aircraft registered a year-on-year increase in sales, with natural gas and crude oil losing a greater percentage than any other in the top 10, at 56 per cent and 51.8 per cent respectively.

Canada is the world's largest source of nickel, zinc and uranium and has large reserves of hydrocarbons, exported mainly to the US.

Imports

Main imports are machinery and equipment, vehicles and parts, industrial materials, crude oil, consumer goods, foodstuffs, durable consumer goods and construction materials.

Main sources: US (typically 50 per cent of total), China (11 per cent), Mexico (5 per cent).

Exports

Major exports include primary industry products such as wheat and agricultural products, fish, timber and minerals including gold and silver, as well as processed and manufactured goods such as vehicles and parts, industrial machinery, aircraft, telecommunications equipment; chemicals, plastics, fertilisers; wood pulp and aluminium.

Main destinations: US (typically 75 per cent of total), UK (3 per cent), China (3 per cent).

Agriculture

Farming

The agricultural industry is of considerable importance to the country's economy. Canada has somewhere in the region of 280,000 farms and is the world's second-largest wheat exporter, with its high-quality spring wheat commanding a premium price on world markets. The country is also a sizeable producer of other grains, notably barley, rapeseed (canola) and oats. Livestock rearing is as important a source of income as field crops.

Despite the relative importance of agriculture in the Canadian economy compared with other industrialised nations, the federal government tends to argue that it cannot afford to match the plentiful subsidies and other aid offered to farmers in the EU and US. However, delays in co-ordinated elimination of the world's farm subsidies through the WTO are focussing the government's attention on support programmes for Canadian farmers.

During the embargo of live cattle, plans were advanced to expand slaughtering facilities and increase the amount of Canadian processed beef, and open new export markets. The latest ban increased the enthusiasm for the plans, and has had added impetus since a US Senate decision in 2005 not to designate Canada as an area of 'minimal risk' from BSE, and a US cattle association won a temporary injunction blocking any US government move to reopen the border to live cattle imports.

Fishing

Canada remains the largest exporter of fish in the world. Approximately half of the country's sizeable annual fish catch is processed for export. Aggressive fishing depleted Canada's stocks causing the closure of Canada's Atlantic fisheries in 1992, which led to a bitter salmon war with the US when wild salmon stocks dipped to perilously low levels. Such were the tensions, annually renewed during the salmon spawning season, that Canada encouraged the capture of fish bound for rivers in Washington and Oregon, in retaliation for rising US catches of Canadian-origin salmon. A deal agreed in 1999 will be effective for 10 years along the coast and for 12 years along the Fraser River run, which should enable flexible reductions in catches through a managed scheme, replacing the more rigid quota system formerly in effect. Despite past tension between the national governments on this issue the US remains the largest market for Canadian fish exports.

Criticism has been raised that Canada has not protected its wild salmon population of fish. Three of the world's largest salmon farming companies operate in British Columbia and overall there are 17 companies managing 105 salmon farms. The fear is that Canada is raising non-native species of salmon and feeding them fish protein that creates risks for other species of wild fish. The resulting intermingling of populations risks the spread of disease, a competition for habitat and the alteration of the wild salmon gene pool. A salmon enhancement programme has been set up to enable the annual catch to reach 150,000 tonnes instead of the current average 70,000 tonnes.

Canada has imposed a moratorium on commercial cod fishing and has a 320km exclusion zone off its eastern coast, patrolled by an increased number of coast guard vessels.

Limited cod fishing in the northern and southern Gulf of St Lawrence resumed in the 2004–05 season, with maximum removals of up to 3,500 tonnes in the northern, and 3,000 tonnes in the southern, gulf.

Forestry

Over 70 per cent of Canada's total landmass is covered with forests and woodland. The country accounts for approximately 10 per cent of the world's forests and the forestry industry accounts for more than US$24 billion annually.

Canada is the largest exporter of newsprint, softwood timber and wood pulp worldwide. There is enormous variation in forest types across this vast country, including temperate softwood rainforests in coastal British Columbia, mixed boreal shield forests in central Canada, the maritime forests of New Brunswick and Nova Scotia on the Atlantic seaboard, and the sparse and slow-growing forests found at the Arctic tree line.

Québec, Ontario and British Columbia have the largest forest resources. Most forest and other wooded land is publicly owned, with 71 per cent under provincial jurisdiction and a further 23 per cent under the wing of the federal and territorial governments. Just 6 per cent is privately owned, and is generally located in the more productive regions. Large areas of forest land are under legislative protection, including the almost 8 per cent protected from harvesting.

Canada is the world's largest exporter of market pulp (almost 30 per cent of world total) and newsprint (near 40 per cent), with most production located in British Columbia, Ontario and Québec.

Non-wood forest products in Canada include maple syrup, berries, mushrooms, medicinal plants and game.

Industry and manufacturing

In a typical year for the Canadian economy the industrial sector contributes approximately 27 per cent to total GDP. The sector also accounts for around 18 per cent of the country's workforce.

Canada's traditional manufacturing sectors include petroleum refining, pulp and paper mills, motor vehicles, steel, sawmills and planing mills, the dairy products industry, motor vehicle spare parts and accessories, metal stamping and pressing, smelting and refining, industrial chemicals, food processing, commercial printing, communications equipment, feed industries, plastics fabricating industries and aircraft and aircraft parts. Notable new sectors are in advanced telecommunications and network technology.

Production of primary metals and transport equipment has grown in recent years, reflecting exceptional growth in the automotive industry. The vast majority of automobile production is exported to the US.

Tourism

Canada has huge wilderness areas situated within or close to the Arctic Circle; it also has impressive mountain ranges, wide prairies and many rivers and lakes, enough to keep even the most avid activity-tourist fully occupied. Those less keen on the great outdoors can visit Canada's major cities for cultural and historic interests. The Winter Olympics were held in Vancouver in December 2009, boosting what had been a slump caused by the global economic crisis in 2008.

In 2009 US citizens made over 11.6 visits to Canada, outnumbering visits by all other nationalities by around 3:1; however Canada's domestic tourist trade out-performs all international business by spending, domestically, 50 per cent more than all other visitors. Citizens from the UK and France were the next largest group of visitors. The majority of trips by US citizens were for the purpose of leisure, while for those travelling from UK and France it was evenly split between leisure and visiting family and friends.

In official figures for the third quarter of 2010, tourism was showing growth, particularly of visitors from Asia and other emerging markets which registered 20 and 32 per cent respectively, while UK visitors were showing a drop of 1.5 per cent on the 2009 year-on-year figure.

Travel and tourism 2011 was forecast to contribute C$23.5 billion (US$22.9 billion) of direct revenue in 2011, 1.4 per cent of total GDP, and indirectly C$84.8 billion (US$82.8 billion), or 4.3 per cent of total GDP. The industry was also forecast to directly employ 550,000 workers (3.2 per cent of total employment), the majority of which are employed in small to medium sized enterprises (SMEs), often family owned; employment including related jobs was expected to be 7 per cent of the total workforce (1.21 million jobs).

Foreign exchange earnings from tourism in 2011 are forecast at C$20.7 billion (US20.2 billion), which constitute 4.2 per cent of total foreign exchange. The industry was estimated to have had C$10.9 billion (US$10.6 billion) investment committed for 2011, or 2.8 per cent of total investment in the economy.

Environment

The Northwest Passage between the Pacific and Atlantic Oceans opened up in 2007 as a result of record ice melting in the Arctic. The ice shelf had retreated further than at any time in recorded history.

Mining

Canada remains a significant producer of gold and the country's reserves of the yellow metal more than trebled over the 1983–2003 period, to an estimated 1,500 tonnes. Other base metal and metal stocks have declined, but Canada remains a major producer of nickel, copper, zinc, lead, iron ore and diamonds.

Most of Canada's exploration is focused on diamonds, mainly in Northwest Territories, Alberta, Québec and Saskatchewan. The country's first diamond mine opened in 1998.

Hydrocarbons

Canada had considerable natural resources and in 2010 was the world's third largest producer of natural gas, after the Russian Federation and the US, and eighth largest of crude oil. Proven oil reserves were 32.1 billion barrels in 2010, second only to Saudi Arabia. However, over 95 per cent of deposits are oil sands and are comparatively difficult and expensive to extract and process compared to conventional crude oil. Production in 2010 was 3.3 million barrels per day (bpd), with consumption at 2.3 million bpd, allowing one million bpd to be exported, mainly to the US. Canada's refinery capacity is 1.9 million bpd; throughput in 2010 was 1.9 million bpd.

There are three main sources of oil production, the Western Canada Sedimentary Basin (WCSB), offshore oil fields in the Atlantic Ocean and the Athabasca oil sands deposits in northern Alberta. This is one of largest oil sands deposits in the world and provides Canada with its largest share of oil production. There are other oil sands deposits on Melville Island in the Canadian Arctic, and two smaller deposits in northern Alberta near Cold Lake and Peace River. Investment from Asian oil companies has grown in the 2000s as rising global oil prices have made oil sands production more profitable.

Canada's oil sector is wholly private, although its regulatory framework is one in which federal and provincial bodies co-ordinate policy and regulation. Provincial authorities handle most of the oversight in the sector. The national regulatory body is the National Energy Board (NEB). The largest and most influential of the provincial regulators is the Alberta Energy Resources Conservation Board (ERCB).

There are several oil companies in operation, the largest of which is Imperial Oil (majority owned by US-ExxonMobil); EnCana is the largest upstream operator and other significant companies include Talisman Energy, Suncor and EOG Resources,

Proven reserves of natural gas in 2010 were 1.7 trillion cubic metres (cum), with around 98 per cent of all natural gas production based in WCSB. Gas production in has been falling since the peak of 188 billion cum in 2006, when a severe winter had increased demand, to 159.8 billion cum in 2010. Domestic gas consumption is rising due to an increase in demand from the electricity-generating sector, driven by the economy and population growth.

Canada and the US operate an integrated gas market which means that any change in one country affects the other, including transport costs, weather and infrastructure constraints. Natural gas exports are exclusively destined for the US and totalled 92.4 billion cum in 2010. However, Canada also imports natural gas from the US when spot prices are cheaper than domestically produced gas, and which amounted to 20.91 million cum in 2010.

The Enbridge Pipelines cover 14,000km, delivering oil from Edmonton, Alberta, to Montréal, Québec, eastern Canada and refineries in the US Great Lakes region. The Trans-Mountain Pipeline (TMPL) delivers oil from Alberta to Vancouver and British Columbia as well as the US state of Washington. Gas production is steady throughout the year with spare capacity pumped into underground storage for winter peak use.

Canada's coal reserves were around 6.58 billion tonnes in 2010, with estimated coal production 34.9 million tonnes oil equivalent (mtoe). Coal consumption was around 23.4 mtoe and is primarily used for electricity generation with the remainder used in steel production.

Energy

Canada currently has one of the world's most diversified electricity generation bases. The country has hydroelectricity, natural gas, oil, coal and nuclear power

sources, which combined produce enough electricity to meet all domestic demand. The energy industry accounted for 5.6 per cent of national GDP in 2007 and employed 2.2 per cent of the labour force. At around 20 per cent of all export value, energy exports totalled C$90 billion (US$97 billion) almost all of which was sent to the US. Domestic energy demand grew by 2.8 per cent in 2007 due to population growth and economic expansion.
In 2007 total installed electric generating capacity was around 124 million kilowatts. Electricity generation and pricing are determined and controlled by each province with federal control exercised only for international and inter-provincial movement of energy. Environmental assessments of energy projects and the development of policies and regulations are also under federal control.
Hydroelectric power plants provide over 60 per cent of electricity generation; there are plans to increase this total through further expansion of power plants. Natural gas provides half the electricity of hydropower, and nuclear production half as much again. Natural gas alone provides 25 per cent of all domestic energy needs, supplied either directly to homes or in the production of electricity. There are 20 nuclear power reactors located in five sites, of which two are destined to be closed in 2011 and another in 2012 and 2013. However despite the decline in short-term energy production there has been a resurgence of interest in nuclear power generation. Sustainable energy production has increased with the growth in the use of wind turbines and in 2007 the government committed C$230 million (US$248 million) in investment in research for new technologies.

Financial markets

Stock exchange
Toronto Stock Exchange (TSX)
Commodity exchange
Bourse de Montréal (Montreal Exchange)

Banking and insurance

Toronto Dominion Bank is Canada's largest banking and financial services institution, in terms of both its retail network and overall personal deposits and lending, having merged with Canada Trust in 2000.
Financial legislation, (Bill C–8) allows foreign and local banks to increase stakes in Canadian banks and to encourage global competitiveness and economic growth. The legislation allows a single shareholder to hold up to 20 per cent of the voting shares of a big Canadian bank, and opened the way to strategic alliances with foreign banks.

Central bank
Bank of Canada
Main financial centre
Toronto

Time

Canada has six time zones:
Newfoundland – GMT minus 3.5 hours;
Atlantic standard time (Maritimes and Labrador) – GMT minus four hours;
Eastern zone (Québec and most of Ontario) – GMT minus five hours;
Central zone (Manitoba, north-west Ontario and eastern Saskatchewan) – GMT minus six hours;
Mountain zone (west Saskatchewan, Alberta and north-east Columbia) – GMT minus seven hours;
Pacific zone (Yukon and the bulk of British Columbia) – GMT minus eight hours;
Daylight saving operates, in all states except Saskatchewan, from early March to late October – local time plus one hour.

Geography

Canada is the second-largest country in the world (Russia is the largest) and it stretches from the Atlantic Ocean to the Pacific. Apart from the border with Alaska in the north-west, Canada's frontier with the US follows the upper St Lawrence Seaway and the Great Lakes, extending westwards along latitude 49 degrees N.
There are six principal geographical regions. The south-east corner is the most densely populated part of the country and comprises the Atlantic Provinces and the lowland area to the north of the Great Lakes and the St Lawrence Seaway. To the north and west of this region lies the Canadian Shield, which is covered by forests, bare rock and lakes. Further to the west are the Interior Plains which are largely prairies, while the coastal area along the Pacific is dominated by the Rocky Mountains. The Northwest Territories extend into the Arctic with a barren landscape and sparse population density.
Hemisphere
Northern

Climate

The climate is extreme, especially inland. Winter temperatures drop well below freezing, but summers are usually warm. There are often heavy snowfalls in winter, making travel difficult.

Dress codes

Canadians are generally casual about dress. It is best to ask about dress codes if you are unsure.

Entry requirements

Passports
Required by all, except permanently resident US citizens with photo-ID; (all US nationals require a passport for re-entry to the US from January 2007).
Visa
Are required by all, except citizens of EU, the Commonwealth and US. For further information see www.cic.gc.ca/english/index.html and choose 'to visit'.
Business travellers should seek further information from a Canadian consulate or see http://canadainternational.gc.ca/dbc/Business-travel-entering-canada-en.aspx.
Business visitors from exempted countries do not need to fulfil extra entry criteria, as long as their permanent employment is typically outside Canada, however work may not be undertaken beyond that allowed.
Currency advice/regulations
There are no restrictions on the import and export of currency.
Customs
Personal effects are allowed duty-free. Certain items, such as plants, meat, cereals, dairy products and live animals are subject to import licensing.
Prohibited imports
Include illegal drugs, marijuana, firearms, mace, pepper spray, switchblades (flick-knives) and fireworks. Vegetable matter including, apples, pears, stoned fruit, potatoes, fresh corn and firewood.

Health (for visitors)

Advisable precautions
No vaccinations or certificates are required. Comprehensive travel and medical insurance is essential though, as medical treatment can be very expensive.

Hotels

Many international hotel chains operate in most cities. However, it is advisable to book rooms in advance.
A goods and services tax of 7 per cent applies to all hotel bills, although visitors may be able to apply for a refund (for details and procedure see: www.nationaltaxrefund.com/eng/demarch.htm). Some states and provinces apply their own taxes.
Most large hotels have facilities for small displays or exhibitions, and smaller rooms may be rented as sample rooms. Most hotels impose a substantial surcharge on telephone calls.
For visitors travelling by car, good quality motels are available around all major towns and cities where rates are considerably less than those charged by city-centre hotels.

Credit cards

Credit cards are widely used.

Public holidays (national)

Fixed dates
1 Jan (New Year's Day), 1 Jul (Canada Day), 11 Nov (Remembrance Day), 25–26 Dec (Christmas).

When Canada Day falls on a Sunday, the next day is considered a holiday.
When Christmas Day or Boxing Day fall at a weekend, an extra day is given in lieu.
Additional holidays are observed by individual provinces and territories.

Variable dates
Good Friday, Easter Monday, Victoria Day (Mon preceding 24 May), Labour Day (first Mon in Sep), Thanksgiving Day (second Mon in Oct).

Working hours
Working hours vary throughout the country and government departments may work variable or flexible hours, especially during the summer months.

Banking
Mon–Wed: 1000–1500; Thu: 1000–2000; Fri: 1000–1600. Opening hours depend on the region and institution.

Business
Mon–Fri: 0830–1700.

Government
Mon–Fri: 0830–1700. Post offices Mon–Fri 0800–1745.

Shops
There is a five-day working week, but most retail stores in cities open on Saturday and a few on Sunday as well. Late shopping (to 2100) on Thursday or Friday is common in large cities; in suburban shopping centres, supermarkets often stay open until 2100 or 2200 Mon–Fri. Some convenience stores and supermarkets remain open 24 hours, especially in heavily populated areas.

Telecommunications
Mobile/cell phones
GSM 850/1900 services available in highly populated areas.

Electricity supply
120–240V (mostly 120V) 60 cycles AC, with two-pin flat-prong plug fittings (or three-pin with one round and two flat prongs) and screw-type lamp sockets. Adapters and transformers are available for appliances using other voltages.

Weights and measures
Metric system (Imperial and US systems also still in use).

Social customs/useful tips
When making introductions, the hand shake is considered rather formal unless you are meeting someone for the first time. To Canadians, eye contact is very important in conversation as it shows that you are paying attention.
It is best to avoid touching people unless you know someone fairly well. Touching someone of the opposite sex may well be considered harassment but touching the arm of your conversation partner is acceptable.
Tipping is expected and tends to be more generous in Canada than in other countries. 10 or 12 per cent would be considered frugal.

Getting there
Air
National airline: Air Canada
International airport/s: Ottawa (YOW) (www.ottawa-airport.ca), 13km south of the capital city. All major airports have full banking and catering facilities, duty-free shops and car hire. Airport-to-city bus and taxi services and, in some cases, rail links, are available.
Toronto Pearson International (YYZ) (www.gtaa.com), 27km north-west of Toronto, is Canada's busiest airport. It has three terminals catering for domestic and international flights; the latest was opened in 2004 and handles Air Canada's domestic and international passengers.
Other airport/s: Calgary (YYC) (www.calgaryairport.com), 8km north of city. Edmonton (YEG) (www.edmontonairports.com), 28km south of city. Montréal Dorval (YUL) (www.admtl.com), 25km west of Montréal. Vancouver (YVR) (www.yvr.ca), 15km south-west of city. Winnipeg (YWG), 10km north-west of city.
Airport tax: There are two taxes that may or may not be included in the price of the ticket.
Both levies vary depending on destination, the Airport Improvement Fee (AIF) is C$5 for intrastate, C$10 interstate and US, and C$15 for all other international flights; the Air Travellers Security Charge is C$12 for intrastate and C$24 for interstate and all international flights. Travel agents and airport information can provide last minute details.

Surface
Road: Numerous border crossings from the US link directly with the Canadian highway system. Avoid crossings during peak times at weekends during the summer months when there are long delays.
Rail: Via Rail Canada Inc provides links with the US. Routes include:
Montréal-New York; Toronto-New York; Toronto-Chicago; Toronto-Cleveland/Detroit.
Water: Ferries connect the east coast of the US with Canada across the great lakes. Hudson Bay ports are subject to closure during winter months.
Main port/s: On the Atlantic Ocean: Halifax (Nova Scotia), St John (New Brunswick) and St John's (Newfoundland). Montréal and Québec have ports on the St Lawrence Seaway (linking the Atlantic with the Great Lakes). Toronto's port is on the north-western shore of Lake Ontario. Montréal is the only port for passenger liners from Europe.
On the Pacific Ocean: Vancouver (British Columbia).

Getting about
National transport
Air: There are frequent and extensive air services connecting all towns and cities of importance with 68 major airports and over 700 smaller ones lacking control tower facilities. Privatised Air Canada serves the main routes, and several regional carriers operate as well. Air travel is the most widely recommended form of travel between major cities, except between Toronto, Montréal and Ottawa, where train service is comfortable, reasonably priced and usually punctual.
Road: There are about 392,000km of roads, about 84 per cent surfaced. Motorways connect some large industrial centres and most large cities have a motorway network. The trans-Canada highway at 7,821km is the longest national highway worldwide. It runs from Victoria in British Colombia in the west to St Johns in Newfoundland in the east. The speed limit on motorways is 100kmph, 80kmph on rural highways and 50kmph on urban roads. Seatbelts are compulsory for all passengers.
Buses: Long-distance coach services link all major centres. They are very well air-conditioned, and it is often recommended that travellers keep a sweater handy.
Rail: There is an extensive rail network that comprises around 100,000km of track. The Canadian National Railway (CN) and Canadian Pacific Rail are the two main railway services, but passenger services are operated by Via Rail Canada (Canrail), a government agency. Air-conditioning, refreshment facilities and sleeping accommodation are available on long-distance passenger services. The Transcontinental, runs a northern route through Saskatoon, Edmonton and Jasper, three times a week. It is advisable to book seats/sleepers as early as possible. Canrail passes give unlimited travel for certain areas and routes.
The southern route through Regina, Calgary and Banff was cut when government subsidies were stopped.
Water: The St Lawrence Seaway provides deep-water passage from the Atlantic to the Great Lakes; there are 3,017km of canals, mainly used for leisure.

City transport
Taxis: Good taxi services operate in all major cities; rates vary between cities.
Buses, trams & metro: Toronto, Montréal, Vancouver and Edmonton have efficient, safe and clean underground systems. Most cities have reliable and extensive bus services.

Car hire

Car hire is widely available. Overseas driving licences may be used for the first three months of a visitor's stay (six months in British Columbia). Driving is on the right-hand side of the road.

BUSINESS DIRECTORY

The addresses listed below are a selection only. While World of Information makes every endeavour to check these addresses, we cannot guarantee that changes have not been made, especially to telephone numbers and area codes. We would welcome any corrections.

Telephone area codes

The international direct dialling (IDD) code for Canada is +1, followed by area code and subscriber's number:

Calgary	403	Québec	514
Edmonton	780	Saskatoon	306
Fredericton	506	St John	506
Halifax	902	St John's	709
Kingston	613	Toronto	416
London	519	Vancouver	604
Montréal	514	Windsor	519
Niagara Falls	905	Winnipeg	204
Ottawa	613		

Chambers of Commerce

American Chamber of Commerce in Canada, 260 Adelaide Street, PO Box 160, Toronto, Ontario, M5A 1N1 (tel: 777-8512; fax: 738-7714; e-mail: info@amchamcanada.ca).

British Canadian Chamber of Trade and Commerce, PO Box 1358, Station 'K', Toronto, Ontario, M4P 3J4 (tel: 502-0847; fax: 502-9319; e-mail: central@bcctc.ca).

Canadian Chamber of Commerce, Delta Office Towers, 350 Sparks Street, Ottawa, Ontario, K1R 7S8 (tel: 238-4000; fax: 238-7643; e-mail: info@chamber.ca).

British Columbia Chamber of Commerce, 750 West Pender Street, Vancouver, British Columbia, V6C 2T8 (tel: 683-0700; fax: 683-0416; e-mail: bccc@bcchamber.org).

Halifax Chamber of Commerce, 7 Spectacle Lake Drive, Dartmouth, Nova Scotia (tel: 468-7111; fax: 468-7333;e-mail: info@halifaxchamber.com).

Kingston Chamber of Commerce, 67 Brock Street, Kingston, Ontario, K7K 1R7 (tel: 5448-4453; fax: 548-4743; e-mail: info@kingstonchamber.on.ca).

Manitoba Chamber of Commerce, 227 Portage Avenue, Winnipeg, Manitoba, R3B 2A6 (tel: 948-0100; fax: 948-0110; e-mail: mbchamber@mbchamber.mb.ca).

Montréal Board of Trade, 380 St Antoine Street West, Montréal, Québec, H2Y 3X7 (tel: 871-4000; fax: 871-1255; e-mail: info@ccmm.qc.ca).

North Vancouver Chamber of Commerce, 124 West 1st Street, North Vancouver, British Columbia, V7M 3N3 (tel: 987-4488; fax: 987-8272; e-mail: info@nvchamber.bc.ca).

Ontario Chamber of Commerce, 180 Dundas Street West, Toronto, Ontario M5G 1Z8 (tel: 482-5222; fax: 482-5879; e-mail: info@occ.on.ca).

Ottowa Chamber of Commerce, 1701 Woodward Drive, Ottowa, Ontario, K2C 0R4 (tel: 236-3630; fax: 236-7498; info@greaterottowachamber.com).

Québec Federation of Chambers of Commerce, 500 Place d'Armes, Montréal, Québec, H2Y 2W2 (tel: 844-9571; fax: 844-0226; e-mail: info@ccq.ca).

Toronto Board of Trade, 1 First Canadian Place, PO Box 60, Toronto, Ontario, M5X 1C1 (tel: 366-6811; fax: 366-8406; e-mail: info@bot.com).

Vancouver Board of Trade, World Trade Centre, 999 Canada Place, Vancouver, British Columbia, V6C 3E1 (tel: 681-2111; fax: 681-0437; e-mail: contactus@boardoftrade.com).

Winnipeg Chamber of Commerce, 259 Portage Avenue, Winnipeg, Manitoba, R3B 2A9 (tel: 944-8484; fax: 944-8492; e-mail: info@winnipeg-chamber.com).

Banking

Bank of Montréal, First Canadian Place, Concourse Level, PO Box 3, Toronto, Ontario M5X 1A1 (tel: 867-7662).

Bank of Nova Scotia, 44 King Street West, Toronto, Ontario M5H 1H1 (tel: 866-6161).

Business Development Bank of Canada, 3rd Floor, 5 Place Ville Marie, Montréal, Québec H4Z 1L4 (tel: 283-5904; fax: 496-8036).

Canadian Imperial Bank of Commerce (CIBC), Commerce Court, Toronto, Ontario M5L 1G9 (tel: 980-2211).

National Bank of Canada, 50 O'Connor Street, Suite 1224, Ottawa, Ontario K1P 6C2 (tel: 238-8383).

Royal Bank of Canada, 200 Bay Street, Royal Bank Plaza, Toronto, Ontario M5J 2J5 (tel: 974-5151; internet site: www.royalbank.com).

Toronto Dominion Bank, PO Box 1, Toronto Dominion Centre, 55 King Street, Toronto, Ontario M5K 1A2 (tel: 982-7730).

Central bank

Bank of Canada, 234 Wellington Street, Ottawa, Ontario, K1A 0G9 (tel: 782-8111; fax: 782-7713; e-mail: paffairs@bankofcanada.ca).

Stock exchange

Toronto Stock Exchange (TSX): www.tsx.com

CNQ (Canadian National Stock Exchange), Toronto: www.cnq.ca

Commodity exchange

Bourse de Montréal (Montreal Exchange): www.m-x.ca

Commodity exchange 2

ICE Futures Canada (Winnipeg Commodity Exchange): www.theice.com

Travel information

Tourism Industry Association of Canada, 130 Albert Street, Suite 1016, Ottawa K1P 5G4 (tel: 238-3883).

Air Transport Association of Canada, 99 Bank St, Suite 747, Ottawa, ON, K1P 6B9 (tel: 233-7727; fax: 230-8648).

Ministry of tourism

Tourism Canada, Federal Department of Industry, Science and Technology, 235 Queen Street, 4th Floor East, Ottawa K1A 0H6 (tel: 954-3851).

Ministries

Ministry of Agriculture and Agri-Food, Sir John Carling Building, 930 Carling Avenue, Ottawa, Ontario, K1A OC5 (tel: 995-8963).

Ministry of Foreign Affairs and International Trade, Lester B Pearson Building, 125 Sussex Drive, Ottawa, Ontario, K1A OG2 (tel: 996-9134; fax: 952-3904).

Ministry of Industry, CD Howe Building, 235 Queen Street, Ottawa, Ontario, K1A OH5 (tel: 952-4782).

Ministry of Natural Resources, 580 Booth Street, Ottawa, Ontario, K1A OE4 (tel: 995-0947; fax: 992-6424/5230).

Ministry of Public Works and Government Services, Sir Charles Tupper Building, Confederation Heights, Ottawa, Ontario, K1A OM2 (tel: 736-2027; fax: 736-23440).

Other useful addresses

Advertising Standards Canada, 350 Bloor Street, Suite 402, Toronto ON M4W 1H5 (tel: 961-6311; fax: 961-7904; email: info@adstandards.com; internet: www.adstandards.com).

Alberta Stock Exchange, 10th Floor, 300 Fifth Avenue SW, Calgary T2P 3C4 (tel: 974-7400; fax: 237-0450).

Bourse de Montréal (Stock Exchange), Tour de la Bourse, CP 61, 800 Square Victoria, Montréal H4Z 1A9 (tel: 871-2424; fax: 871-3553; e-mail: info@me.org).

British High Commission, 80 Elgin Street, Ottawa, Ontario, K1P 5K7 (tel: 237-1530; fax: 237-7980).

Canadian Broadcasting Corporation, 1500 Bronson Avenue, PO Box 8478, Ottawa, Ontario K1G 3J5 (tel: 724-1200; fax: 738-6843).

Canadian Embassy (USA), 501 Pennsylvania Avenue, NW, Washington DC 20001 (tel: 202-682-1740; fax: 202-682-7701; e-mail: webmaster@canadianembassy.org).

Canadian Importers' Association, 210 Dundas St West, Suite 700, Toronto, Ontario, M5G 2E8 (tel: 595-5333; fax: 595-8226).

Canadian Manufacturers' Association, One Yonge St, Toronto, Ontario, M5E 1J9 (tel: 363-7261; fax: 363-3779).

CTV Television Network, 42 Charles St East, Toronto, Ontario, M4Y 1T5 (tel: 928-6000; fax: 928-0907).

Department of Energy, Mines and Resources, 580 Booth St, Ottawa, Ontario, K1A 0E4 (tel: 995-3065; fax: 996-9094).

Department of Finance, 140 O'Connor St, Ottawa, Ontario, K1A 0G5 (tel: 992-1575; fax: 996-2690).

Department of Labour, Labour Canada, Ottawa, Ontario, K1A 0J2 (tel: 997-2617; fax: 953-0176).

Department of Regional Industrial Expansion, 235 Queen St, Ottawa, Ontario, K1A 0H5 (tel: 995-9001).

Economic Council of Canada, PO Box 527, Ottawa, Ontario, K1P 5V6 (tel: 993-1253; fax: 991-4904).

Investment Canada, PO Box 2800, Station 'D', Ottawa, Ontario, K1P 6A5 (tel: 996-2515; fax: 995-0465).

Ontario International Trade Corporation, 5th Floor, Hearst Block, 900 Bay Street, Toronto, Ontario, M7A 2E1 (tel: 325-6514; fax: 325-6509).

Retail Council of Canada, 210 Dundas St West, Suite 600, Toronto, Ontario, M5G 2E8 (tel: 598-4684; fax: 598-3707).

Statistics Canada, Statistical Reference Centre, Ottawa, Ontario, K1A OT6 (tel: 951-8116; internet site: www.statcan.ca/start.html).

Toronto Stock Exchange, The Exchange Tower, 2 First Canadian Place, Toronto, Ontario, M5X 1J2 (tel: 947-4700, 947-9301; fax: 947-4662).

Vancouver Stock Exchange, Stock Exchange Tower, 609 Granville Street, PO Box 10333, Vancouver, BC V7Y 1H1 (tel: 689-3334; fax: 688-6051).

Winnipeg Stock Exchange, 620 One Lombard Place, Winnipeg, Manitoba R3B 0X3 (tel: 987-7070; fax: 987-7079).

Internet sites

Asia-Pacific Economic Co-operation (APEC): www.apecsec.org.sg

Air Canada: www.aircanada.ca

Canada Online: strategis.ic.gc.ca

Canada Yellow Pages: www.canadayellowpages.com

Canadian Airlines: www.cdnair.ca

Canadian Automobile Association: www.caa.ca

Canadian Energy: www.centreforenergy.com

Canadian International Development Agency (CIDA): www.acdi-cida.gc.ca

Canadian Parliament: www.parl.gc.ca

Canadian Statistics: www.statcan.ca

Government of Canada (all dept): www.canada.gc.ca

Government of Alberta: www.gov.ab.ca

Government of Ontario: www.gov.on.ca

Government of Québec: www.gouv.qc.ca

Inuit and Artic news: www.nunatsiaq.com

North American Free Trade Agreement: www.nafta-sec-alena.org

Strategis (business and consumer site): strategis.ic.ca

Thomas Register: www2.thomasregister.com

Trans-Canadian highway: www.transcanadahighway.com

KEY FACTS

Official name: República de Cabo Verde (Republic of Cape Verde)

Head of State: President Jorge Carlos Fonseca (MPD) (9 Sept 2011)

Head of government: Prime Minister José María Neves (PAICV) (since 2001; re-elected 6 Feb 2011)

Ruling party: Partido Africano da Independência de Cabo Verde (PAICV) (African Party of Independence of Cape Verde) (since 2001; re-elected 6 Feb 2011)

Area: 4,033 square km (nine islands and 10 islets)

Population: 491,575 (2010; census figure)

Capital: Praia

Official language: Portuguese and Creole (national language)

Currency: Cape Verde escudo (CVE) = 100 centavos

Exchange rate: CVE79.48 per US$ (Oct 2011); (pegged CVEsc110.27 per euro)

GDP per capita: US$3,445 (2009)*

GDP real growth: 1.80% (2009)*

GDP: US$1.77 billion (2009)

Inflation: 1.20% (2009)

Balance of trade: -US$676.83 million (2009)

* estimated figure

Cape Verde

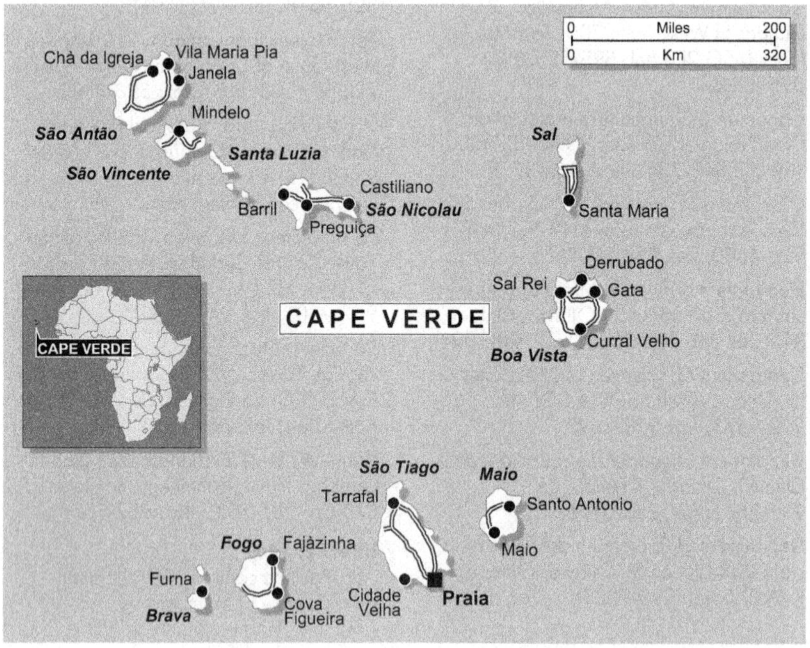

Cape Verde's economy showed signs of recovery from the impact of the global financial crisis with 2010 gross domestic product (GDP) growth estimated to reach 5.3 per cent compared to 3.6 per cent in 2009. In 2010 there were signs of recovery in tourism and air transport and strong support from the Public Investment Programme (PIP).

However, in 2010 foreign direct investment (FDI) and associated construction inflows continued to shrink. The *African Economic Outlook 2011* (AEO), published jointly by the African Development Bank and the Organisation for Economic Co-operation and Development reported that the outlook remains uncertain for 2011 as investment largely originates from the European Union (EU), which is growing only slowly. Remittances remained fairly constant in 2010 after a slight decrease of 2.2 per cent in 2009. The inflation rate was 2.1 per cent in 2010, down from 6.7 per cent in 2008, mainly as a result of the euro peg and the large import component of goods and labour of the PIP. Inflation is expected to rise slightly in 2011 because of increases in commodity and fuel prices and the weak resumption in private economic activity.

The government has put in place an ambitious strategy that addresses, on the one hand, the large PIP in infrastructure and, on the other, an improvement of the business environment through the creation of marketing and certification strategies. The extent to which these strategies generate direct benefits for the population and foster high value-added tourism will affect the resilience of the economy in the face of external shocks in the medium term, the trend in poverty rates and ultimately, the success of the government's PIP. In addition, the resumption in FDI flows will be key once the PIP is over as the country depends on external financing for large investment programmes.

To counter the impact of the crisis and to restructure the economy in view of Cape Verde's graduation to Middle Income Country (MIC) status, the government reinforced the 2010–12 PIP to address binding constraints: transport (particularly ports and roads), energy and water. In line with the PIP, the fiscal balance deteriorated considerably from -6.3 per cent in

2009 to -13.7 per cent in 2010 and is expected to remain large in 2011. International reserves are expected to remain at prudential levels in 2010–12, since the deficit is financed by external borrowing. Donor budget support increased considerably in 2010 to counter the crisis.

To reduce its strong dependence on fuel imports, Cape Verde has a US$300 million plan to cover 25 per cent of its needs with renewable energy by 2011 and 50 per cent by 2020. The country is developing 28 megawatt (MW) onshore wind farms expected to come into operation in June 2011 in Sal, Boavista, São Tiago and São Vicente islands. This is the first large-scale wind project in Africa and the first renewable energy Private Public Parnership (PPP) in sub-Saharan Africa.

Cape Verde is one of the few African countries that may meet the Millennium Development Goals (MDGs) by 2015. Four of the eight goals – achieving universal primary education, promoting gender equality, reducing child mortality and improving maternal health – were attained by the end of 2010. The sustainability of these outcomes largely depends on donor support. Some donors, however, phased out aid in 2010 from certain social sectors. With its graduation to MIC, Cape Verde faces reduced access to concessional loans and has requested an extension from 2012 to 2015 in order to access the Low Income Country (LIC) instruments under the assumption that this will prove sufficient to address key structural bottlenecks.

The PIP aims at crowding in private investment in 2011–12 by fostering growth clusters in line with the 2003 Economic Transformation Strategy (ETS): tourism, fisheries (export and processing), creating a transport hub, financial services and information technology. In spite of attempts to use its geopolitical situation and economic stability to find new partners, the country's trade and investment partners remain largely European. Diversification has been slower than expected under government plans.

Cape Verde has asked the EU to extend its LIC status until 2011 while negotiating new commercial agreements including services, favourable rules of origin and quotas for fish exports. Co-operation with Brazil is primarily in the fields of education and capacity building. Exchanges with China are linked to the construction of infrastructure. Cape Verde is reinforcing its relationship with the Economic Community of West African States (Ecowas). Since 2010 it has been hosting the West African Institute (WEA) and the Ecowas Centre for Renewable Energy and Energy Efficiency (ECREEE).

On the political front, 2011 was the year of the fourth democratic legislative and presidential elections in Cape Verde. Parliamentary elections took place on 6 February. After a tight race, the ruling Partido Africano da Independência de Cabo Verde (PAICV) (African Party of Independence of Cape Verde) won 37 out of 72 parliamentary seats. The main opposition party Movimento para a Democracia (MpD) (Movement for Democracy) picked up 33 seats. Presidential elections took place six months later. The run-off on 21 August was won by Jorge Carlos Fonseca of the MpD with 54 per cent; Manuel Inocêncio Sousa (PAICV) was the runner-up with 46 per cent.

Risk assessment

Economy	Fair
Politics	Good
Regional stability	Good

COUNTRY PROFILE

Historical profile

1462 The previously uninhabited islands were colonised by the Portuguese and became one of the most important slaving stations in West Africa.
1961 The movement for independence gathered strength, adopting guerrilla tactics against the Portuguese.
1975 Cape Verde gained independence after the fall of the dictatorship in Portugal.
1975–80 Moves to unite Cape Verde and Guinea-Bissau were made, but came to nothing following the overthrow of President Luiz Cabral in Guinea-Bissau.
1980 The constitution was adopted.
1981 A revision to the constitution was passed.
1990 A multi-party system was introduced.
1991 Cape Verde's first free multi-party elections were won by the Movimento para a Democracia (MpD) (Movement for Democracy) and a government under Carlos Veiga was formed.
1992 A new constitution was adopted.
1995 The MpD secured an absolute majority in the elections to the National Assembly.
1996 President Antonio Mascarenhas Monteiro (MpD) was re-elected; no other parties put up candidates.
1999 The constitution was amended.
2001 Pedro Pires was elected president.
2003 The IMF approved a three-year programme for US$11.5 million under the Poverty Reduction and Growth Facility (PRGF).
2004 Poor rainfall and locust damage resulted in reduced harvests and a larger than usual food deficit.
2006 PAICV won the general elections. Pedro Pires was re-elected president.
2007 Cape Verde withdrew its support for Polisario, the separatist movement in Western Sahara, and allied itself to Morocco. The WTO approved Cape Verde's membership.
2008 The Netherlands granted a three-year aid programme of US$14.2 million for education and vocational training. Cape Verde announced its backing of the Moroccan Sahara autonomy plan which allows Morocco and the Polisario to discuss the future of Western Sahara without pre-conditions.
2009 Cape Verde's first nomination to Unesco, Cidada Velha, located west of the capital Praia, was added the prestigious list of world heritage sites.

KEY INDICATORS — Cape Verde

	Unit	2006	2007	2008	2009	2010
Population	m	0.48	0.49	*0.50	*0.51	0.49
Gross domestic product (GDP)	US$bn	1.19	1.51	1.75	*1.77	–
GDP per capita	US$	2,457	3,080	3,469	*3,445	–
GDP real growth	%	10.8	6.9	6.2	*3.6	–
Inflation	%	4.8	4.4	6.8	1.2	–
Exports (fob) (goods)	US$m	111.0	76.5	115.7	94.0	–
Imports (fob) (goods)	US$m	498.0	743.6	830.7	770.8	–
Balance of trade	US$m	-387.0	-667.1	-715.0	-676.8	–
Current account	US$m	-0.6	-132.0	-205.5	-239.3	–
Total reserves minus gold	US$m	254.5	364.5	361.5	366.2	382.2
Foreign exchange	US$m	254.4	364.3	261.2	353.3	371.8
Exchange rate	per US$	85.50	75.50	75.29	79.37	83.26

* estimated figure

2010 An Economic Partnership Agreement with the EU was finalised in April, to provide new funding for Cape Verde and favourable export conditions. A memorandum of understanding (MOU) was signed in April to set up a joint Cape Verde and São Tomé company to run a high-speed ferry service between the two countries; however by July 2011 the service was still not operating. Tourist numbers increased due to the reduction in prices offered by the Cape Verdean tourist industry encouraging more visitors during the European winter so that by November several tour operators had booked more flights and hotel rooms.
2011 The ruling PAICV won parliamentary elections held on 6 February, with 50.9 per cent of the vote (37 seats out of 72); the MPD remained as the second party in the national legislature with 41.9 per cent (33 seats). The new PAICV government took office on 21 March; José Maria Neves remained in office as prime minister. Four candidates took part in the first round of presidential elections; but only Jorge Carlos Fonseca (MpD) who won 37.3 per cent of the vote and Manuel Inocêncio Sousa (PAICV) with 32 per cent, went forward to the runoff election on 21 August, in which Fonseca won 54.1 per cent, Sousa 45.9 per cent; turnout was 59.7 per cent. President Jorge Carlos Fonseca took office on 9 September. Former president, Pedro Verona Pires was awarded the US$5 million Mo Ibrahim prize for good governance (and who have voluntarily left office) in Africa, on 10 October.

Political structure

Cape Verde has a mixed presidential/parliamentary form of government.

Constitution

A new constitution was adopted in 1992 and amended in 1999. There are 17 municipios (administrative districts).

Form of state

Unitary republic

The executive

Executive power rests with the prime minister and the Council of Ministers, proposed by the prime minister and appointed by the president. The prime minister is appointed by the president, in consultation with the National Assembly. The president is elected by universal suffrage by electors registered in the electoral census in the national territory and abroad, for a five-year term. The presidential candidate must be a Capeverdean citizen by origin, thirty-five or more years of age on the date of his candidature, and, in the three years immediately preceding that date, have had permanent residence in the national territory.

National legislature

The unicameral Assembléia Nacional (National Assembly) has 72 members, of which 66 are elected by proportional representation, and six deputies are elected by Cape Verdeans living abroad (two each for Africa, the Americas and the rest of the world). All serve for five-year terms.

Legal system

The legal system is derived from that of Portugal.

Last elections

6 February 2011 (parliamentary); 7 and 21 August 2011 (presidential)

Results: Parliamentary: the Partido Africano da Independência de Cabo Verde (PAICV) (African Party of Independence of Cape Verde) won 50.9 per cent of the vote (37 seats out of 72), Movimento para a Democracia (MpD) (Movement for Democracy) 41.9 per cent (33), União Caboverdiana Independente e Democrática) (UCID) (Democratic and Independent Cape Verdean Union) 4.9 per cent; two other political parties each won less than 1 per cent of the vote and failed to win any seats. Turnout was 75.5 per cent.

Presidential (first round): Jorge Carlos Fonseca (MpD) won 37.3 per cent of the vote, Manuel Inocêncio Sousa (PAICV) 32.0 per cent, Aristides Lima (independent) 27.4 per cent and Joaquim Jaime Monteiro (independent) 2.0 per cent. Runoff: Fonseca 54.2 per cent, Sousa 45.8 per cent.

Next elections

2016 (presidential and parliamentary)

Political parties

There are six registered political parties.

Ruling party

Partido Africano da Independência de Cabo Verde (PAICV) (African Party of Independence of Cape Verde) (since 2001; re-elected 6 Feb 2011)

Main opposition party

Movimento para a Democracia (MPD) (Movement for Democracy)

Population

491,575 (2010; census figure)

Last census: June 2000: 436,863

Population density: 237 inhabitants per square km. Urban population: 63 per cent 1995—2001).

Annual growth rate: 2.4 per cent 1994–2004 (WHO 2006)

Ethnic make-up

Creole (71 per cent), African (28 per cent), European (1 per cent).

Religions

Constitutional separation of church and state allows for freedom of religion. Christian (97 per cent Roman Catholic).

Education

The National Development Plan of 2002–06 aims to increase vocational training and job creation and reduce illiteracy in an effort to generate foreign investment and therefore increase employment.

Literacy rate: 74 per cent adult population.

Enrolment rate: 100 per cent of children age six to 11 will enrol for school in 2015, Oxfam estimate.

Health

HIV/Aids

The government had a National Aids programme in place for the period 2001–04, financed by the World Bank.

Life expectancy: 70 years, 2004 (WHO 2006)

Fertility rate/Maternal mortality rate: 3.6 births per woman, 2004 (WHO 2006)

Child (under 5 years) mortality rate (per 1,000): 26 per 1,000 births (World Bank).

Head of population per physician: 0.49 physicians per 1,000 people, 2004 (WHO 2006)

Welfare

Around a third of the population live under the poverty line with around 14 per cent living in absolute poverty. Unemployment is estimated at 25 per cent, while underemployment is far higher. Poverty is worse in rural areas where employment opportunities are poor and incomes are declining. As a result, there is a steady migration to urban areas, creating pockets of extreme poverty within cities and towns.

Main cities

Praia, on Santiago Island (capital, estimated population 125,464 in 2005); Mindelo, on São Vicente (commercial centre, 67,452).

Languages spoken

Official language/s

Portuguese and Creole (national language)

Media

Press

The only daily is the government-run *Jornal Horizonte*, the only other local publications are *Expresso das Ilhas* (www.expressodasilhas.cv) and *A Semana* (www.asemana.cv). *Terra Nova* is a weekly based on São Vicente. Government publications include *Novo Jornal Cabo Verde* published twice a week and the periodical *Boletim Informativo*.

Broadcasting

The state-run broadcaster is Radio e televisão de Cabo Verde (RTC).

Radio: The state-run radio RTC (www.rtc.cv) has one station that has programmes relayed throughout the islands on a variety of frequencies. Private commercial stations include Praia FM (www.praiafm.biz), Mosteiros FM (www.mosteiros.com), Rádio Nova (www.radionovaonline.com) and Crioula FM (www.crioulafm.cv). Several foreign broadcasts, from Portugal and France, are readily available.

Television: RTC (www.rtc.cv) operates the country's only television station.

News agencies

National news agency: Inforpress (Agência de Notícias de Cabo Verde)
Voz di Povo: www.vozdipovo-online.com
APA: www.apanews.net
Panapress: www.panapress.com

Economy

Cape Verde has limited natural resources and much of the economy is dominated by the service sector, which constitutes 70 per cent of GDP, of which trade, transport and government services account for 55 per cent. Agriculture of any significant level is only possible on four of the 10 main islands as the rugged volcanic nature of the landscape is subject to erosion and persistent periods of severe drought; around 90 per cent of all food is imported.

GDP growth was 8.6 per cent in 2007, but it fell steadily, to 6.2 per cent in 2008 and further to 3.6 per cent in 2009. A three-year Policy Support Instrument (PSI), under the auspices of the International Monetary Fund (IMF), was completed in 2006, which grew international reserves and a programme of fiscal prudence so that when the global economic crisis struck in 2008–09 the economy was not plunged into recession and was able to weather the storm. Cape Verde reduced its poverty rate and graduated from UN least developed country (LDC) status.

GDP growth was projected to be 5.5 per cent in 2010, with inflation growing as the price of imported food increased.

Tourism is of growing importance to the economy, which typically attracts over 50 per cent of total foreign direct investment (FDI). However, the industry was hit by external shocks in 2008–09 with the record price of fuel and the weakness of foreign economies cutting tourist numbers so that the industry declined by -16.2 per cent, down from a record high of 23 per cent in 2007. As the global economy recovered so did the tourist numbers in 2010, with an industry growth of 3.9 per cent.

Remittances in 2008 were a record US$155 million, but this fell to US$145 million in 2009 (9.1 per cent of GDP) and was estimated to have fallen to US$144 million in 2010. There is a high level of unskilled workers (30–40 per cent of the population) and foreign investors are able take advantage of low wage rates. In May 2009, Prime Minister Neves called on the Cape Verdean student diaspora in the US to return home and take up business opportunities.

External trade

Cape Verde is a member of the Economic Community of West African States (Ecowas) and has indicated that it is interested in joining the West African Monetary Zone (WAMZ). Cape Verde became a member of the World Trade Organisation (WTO) in 2008.

There are free-trade zones (known as Foreign Trade Zones) which specialise in duty-free goods storage and raw materials for either re-export or manufacturing into goods for overseas markets.

Imports

Principal imports are foodstuffs such as foodstuffs: rice, wheat and maize, cooking oil and milk; and consumer goods, industrial products, transport equipment, fuels, machinery and textiles.

Main sources: Portugal (typically 45 per cent of total), The Netherlands (16 per cent), Spain (6 per cent).

Exports

Principal exports are fuel, fish, hides, salt and *entrepôt* trade.

Main destinations: Spain (typically 54 per cent total of total), Portugal (22 per cent), Morocco (7 per cent).

Re-exports

Petroleum, fish and crustaceans, clothing and shoes.

Agriculture

The agricultural sector forms the backbone of the economy, even though only 20 per cent of total area is cultivable, with 48 per cent of the population engaged in subsistence farming. Agriculture accounts for around 13 per cent of GDP. Most arable land is on the island of Sâo Tiago.

Recurrent drought, interrupted by torrential rains and floods, soil erosion, disease and a weak infrastructure have reduced agricultural production considerably, but there are schemes for water conservation and irrigation.

Beans and maize are the staple foodstuffs. Maize covers 25–80 per cent of cultivated land according to rainfall. Only 10 per cent of food is produced locally.

Other crops include bananas, sweet potatoes, yams, manioc, pumpkins, sugar cane, coffee and groundnuts. About 90 per cent of food requirements are met by imports, largely in the form of food aid.

Fishing

Although fishing (lobster and tuna) has been of growing importance, supporting some 20,000 people and accounting for over 60 per cent of export revenues and 4 per cent of GDP, it is under-exploited. A fishing port in Mindelo on São Vicente was completed in 2001.

Industry and manufacturing

The industrial sector accounts for around 19 per cent of GDP and employs 15 per cent of the workforce.

Industries include ship repair and fuelling, construction, fish processing and canning, flour milling, soft drinks, cigar manufacture and garment making. Construction and civil engineering contribute about 10 per cent of GDP and are primarily related to the development of the tourism sector. Two zones have been set up with industrial parks: Lazareto on São Vicente and Achada Grande Tras in Praia.

Tourism

Tourism is a primary contributor to the economy and is being vigorously developed as an engine of economic growth. Most tourist activity is centred on Sal, whose airport has been the only one catering to charter flights from Europe. Most visitors come from Portugal and Italy. In 2005, a new international airport was inaugurated on Santiago near the capital, Praia, which will open up Santiago and other islands to tourism. Other infrastructure works are in progress, including the Santiago Golf Club, a huge resort near Praia.

Environment

Cape Verde faces serious environmental problems, particularly concerning water management. Serious drought caused by global warming and the country's geographical location has undermined agriculture as well as plant cover. The government has drawn upon the Global Environment Facility (GEF) to help protect biodiversity and is supported by the UN's Food and Agriculture Organisation (FAO) in a forestry action plan.

Mining

The mining sector employs about 1 per cent of the workforce.

Activity is largely confined to exploitation of pozzolana (volcanic derivative) at São Antão, gypsum at Maio and production of salt on Sal and in Mindelo by evaporation method.

Hydrocarbons

There are no known oil or natural gas reserves. Consumption of oil was 2,000 barrels per day (bpd) in 2008, all of which was imported, mainly from Portugal and West African countries. The downstream industry is regulated by Direcão Geral da Energia and distribution is by Shell Capo Verde and Enacol.

Any use of natural gas or coal is commercially insignificant.

Energy
Total installed generating capacity was 77MW in 2007, producing over 50 million kilowatt hours. Although the majority of power is generated by conventional thermal power stations, there are six 300kW wind turbines in operation.
The state-owned Empresa Pública de Electricidade e Água (Electra) is responsible for generation, transmission, distribution and sales of electricity.

Financial markets
Stock exchange
Bolsa de Valores de Cabo Verde (BVC) (Cape Verde Stock Exchange)

Banking and insurance
Central bank
Banco de Cabo Verde
Main financial centre
Praia

Time
GMT minus one hour

Geography
Cape Verde is an archipelago of 10 islands and five islets in the North Atlantic Ocean, about 500km (300 miles) west of Dakar, Senegal.
Hemisphere
Northern

Climate
Hot with very little rainfall. Temperatures range from around 20 degrees Celsius (C) at night to 32 degrees C during the day. Hottest months are July, August and September and rain most likely from August–September.

Entry requirements
Passports
Required by all. Passport must be valid for six months.
Visa
Required by all, except nationals of Ecowas countries, former Cape Verde nationals (with proof of origin) and transit passengers.
Currency advice/regulations
Import and export of local currency prohibited. No restriction on import of foreign currency, but amounts must be declared on arrival. Export of foreign currency is limited to equivalent of CVEsc1,000,000 or the amount declared on arrival if higher.

Health (for visitors)
Mandatory precautions
Yellow fever certificates if arriving from countries having notified cases in the last six years.
Advisable precautions
Typhoid, tetanus, hepatitis A and polio vaccinations. Malaria limited risk exists September to November in Sâo Tiago Island. Water precautions should be taken. There is a rabies risk. There is a slight risk of cholera. Milk is unpasteurised and should be boiled. Dairy products should be avoided.

Hotels
Accommodation is available in all islands but the best establishments are situated in Fogo, Sal, Santiago, São Vicente.

Credit cards
Credit cards are only accepted in the bigger hotels.

Public holidays (national)
Fixed dates
1 Jan (New Year's Day), 20 Jan (Heroes' Day), 1 May (Labour Day), 5 Jul (Independence Day), 15 Aug (Assumption Day), 12 Sep (National Day), 1 Nov (All Saints' Day), 25 Dec (Christmas).
Variable dates
Carnival (Feb), Ash Wednesday, Good Friday.

Working hours
Banking
Mon–Fri: 0800–1400.
Business
Mon–Fri: 0800–1230, 1430–1800.
Shops
Mon–Fri: 0800–2000; Sat: 0900–1700.

Electricity supply
220V AC, 50Hz

Weights and measures
Metric system

Getting there
Air
TAAG of Angola flies weekly from São Tomé and Príncipe. South African Airlines, TAP Air Portugal and Tower Airlines also service Cape Verde.
National airline: Transportes Aéreos de Cabo Verde (TACV) guarantees daily inter-island flights and weekly flights.
International airport/s: Amilcar Cabral International (SID), 2km south of Espargos on Sal island; Praia International (RAI) on Santiago island.
Airport tax: None.
Surface
Water: A high-speed ferry service between Cape Verde and São Tomé is planned by the ferry company Expresso LDA with a one-way journey taking five days. The ferry will have 400 berths and a capacity of 800 passengers. The service was still not operational in July 2011.

Getting about
National transport
Air: Transportes Aéreos de Cabo Verde (TACV) flies daily to all islands except Brava and Santo Antâo. Discounted trips among the islands are available with the Cape Verde Airpass, which can be purchased when booking international flights with TACV. A charter service is provided by Cape Verde Express.
Buses: Buses available on main islands.
Water: Boats ply between the islands.
City transport
Taxis: Available on main islands. Taxis are available from Amilcar Cabral International Airport to city centre.

BUSINESS DIRECTORY

The addresses listed below are a selection only. While World of Information makes every endeavour to check these addresses, we cannot guarantee that changes have not been made, especially to telephone numbers and area codes. We would welcome any corrections.

Telephone area codes
The international dialling code (IDD) for Cape Verde is +238 followed by subscriber's number.
NB Standard and cellular numbers have seven digits: add '2' to the beginning of the existing standard number; add '9' to the beginning of the existing cellular number.

Useful telephone numbers
Praia, Santiago
Airport docks: 2615-821, 2615-646
Electricity Board: 2611-909
Fire brigade: 2612-727
Ambulance: 2612-462
Police: 2613-637

Chambers of Commerce
Barlavento Cámara de Comércio, Indústria, Agricultura e Serviços, Rua de Luz 31, PO Box 728, Mindelo, Saõ Vicente (tel: 2328-495; fax: 2328-496; e-mail: camera.com @mail.cvtelecom.cv).

Sotavento Cámara de Comércio, Indústria e Serviços, Rua Andrade Corvo, PO Box 105, Praia, Santiago (tel: 2617-234; fax: 2617-235; e-mail: cciss@mail,cvtelecom.cv).

Banking
Banco Insular (IFI), PO Box 556, Conjunto Residencial Comunidades, Lote Oito- Bloco D Fracção Oitava, Achada Santo Antonio-Praia (e-mail: bancoinsular@mail.cvtelecom.cv).

Banco Comercial do Atlantico, PO Box 474, Avenida Amílcar Cabral, Praia (tel: 2614-953; fax: 2613-235).

Banco Interatlântico, Avenida Cidade de Lisboa 131-A, Praia (tel: 2614-008, 2613-829, 2614-425; fax: 2614-712, 2614-752).

Caixa Económica de Cabo Verde SARL, PO Box 199, Avenida Cidade de Lisboa, Praia (tel: 2615-561; fax: 2615-560).

Central bank
Banco de Cabo Verde, Avenida Amilcar Cabral, PO Box 101, Praia (tel: 2615-526; fax: 2611-914; e-mail: drs@bcv.cv).

Stock exchange
Bolsa de Valores de Cabo Verde (BVC) (Cape Verde Stock Exchange): www.bvc.cv

Travel information
Agencia Cabetur, Viagens e Turismo, Rua Guerra Mendes 4, Praia (tel: 2615-551; fax: 2615-553).

Intertur SARL, Av Cidade de Lisboa, 2 Esq Fazenda, Praia (tel: 614-643; fax: 614-644); Rua 5 de Julho Espargos, Sal (tel: 2411-580/590).

Orbitur, Rua Roberto Duarte Silva, CP 161, Praia (tel: 2615-737; fax: 2613-888).

Praiatur, 100 Av Amilcar Cabral, CP 470, Praia (tel: 2615-746/7; fax: 2614-500).

Sal Amilcar Cabral International Airport, ASA-Empresa Nacional de Aeroportos E Seguranca Aerea-EP, PB 50, Ilha do Sal (tel: 2411-135, 2411-394, 2411-468; fax: 2411-570, 2411-323; e-mail: asacv@milton.cvtelecom.cv).

Transportes Aéreos de Cabo Verde (TACV), Av Amilcar Cabral, CP 1, Praia (tel: 2615-813; fax: 2615-905).

Ministries
Ministry of Agriculture, Alimentation and Environment, Praia (tel: 2615-716; fax: 2614-717).

Ministry of Defence, Praia (tel: 2610-372; fax: 2611-286).

Ministry of Economic Co-ordination, Avenue Amilcar Cabral, Praia (tel: 2613-210; fax: 2611-922).

Ministry of Education, Science and Culture, Praia (tel: 2610-507; fax: 2612-764).

Ministry of Foreign Affairs, Praia (tel: 2614-773; fax: 2611-960).

Ministry of Health and Social Promotion, Praia (tel: 2615-721; fax: 2613-991).

Ministry of Justice and Internal Administration, Praia (tel: 2615-687; fax: 2611-396).

Ministry of Sea, Praia (tel: 2616-662; fax: 2611-770).

Ministry of Transport and Infrastructure, Praia (tel: 2615-709; fax: 2614-822).

Prime Minister's Office, Palacio do Governo, Praia (tel: 2610-513; fax: 2612-288).

Other useful addresses
Associação Commercial e Agricola de Sotavento de Cabo Verde, CP 78, Praia (tel: 2612-991).

Associação Comercial Barlavento, CP 62, Mindelo, S Vicente (tel: 2313-281).

Cabo Verde Motors, CP 51-B, Praia (tel: 2612-345; fax: 2612-612).

Ceris, Sociedade Caboverdiana de Cerveja e Refrigerantes (beer and refrigeration), CP 320, Praia (tel: 2615-575; fax: 2614-488).

Direcção-Geral das Alfandegas (customs body), CP 98, Praia (tel: 2613-835, 2613-026).

Direcção-Geral do Comércio (trade body), CP 105, Praia (tel: 2614-159).

Direcção-Geral de Estatistica (Statistics Department of the Ministry of Economic Co-ordination), Avenida Amilcar Cabral, Praia (fax: 2611-922).

Direcção-Geral das Pescas (national fisheries authority), Praia (tel: 2612-976).

Direcção-Geral do Plano (Planning Department of the Ministry of Economic Co-ordination), Avenida Amilcar Cabral, Praia (fax: 2611-922).

Embassy of Portugal, Achada de S António, Praia (tel: 2615-602).

Empresa Nacional de Aeroportos e Segurança Aérea, Aeroporto Amilcar Cabral, Ilha do Sal (tel: 2411-394).

Empresa Nacional de Combustivels (national combustibles corporation), CP 1, Mindelo, S Vicente (tel: 2313-659).

Garantia (insurance company) (tel: 2615-661, 2615-662; fax: 2313-221, 2313-470).

Promex (Centro de Promoção Turística, do Investimento e das Exportações), CP89c, Praia (tel: 2622-736; fax: 2622-657; e-mail: promex@cvtelecom.cv).

Radio Nacional de Cabo Verde, CP 26, Praia (tel: 2613-729).

Shell Cabo Verde, CP 4, S Vicente (tel: 2314-470; fax: 2314-755).

US Embassy, R Abilio Macedo, Praia (tel: 2615-616).

National news agency: Inforpress (Agência de Notícias de Cabo Verde)

A Largo de Marconi, Achada de Santo António, Cabo Verde CP 40 (tel/fax: 262-2554; email: inforpress@mail.cvtelecom.cv; internet: www.inforpress.cv).

Internet sites
Africa Business Network: http://www.ifc.org/abn

African Development Bank: http://www.afdb.org

Africa Online: http://www.africaonline.com

Allafrica.com: http://allafrica.com

Mbendi AfroPaedia (information on companies, countries, industries and stock exchanges in Africa): http://mbendi.co.za

Cayman Islands

KEY FACTS

Official name: Cayman Islands

Head of State: Queen Elizabeth II; represented by Governor Duncan Taylor (from 15 Jan 2010)

Head of government: Premier (William) McKeeva Bush (from 20 May 2009)

Ruling party: United Democratic Party (UDP) (from 20 May 2009)

Area: 259 square km

Population: 54,397 (2010; census figure)

Capital: George Town (Grand Cayman)

Official language: English

Currency: Cayman Islands dollar (CI$) = 100 cents

Exchange rate: CI$0.82 per US$ (Oct 2011)

GDP per capita: US$46,500 (2006)*

GDP real growth: 1.10% (2008)*

GDP: US$2.25 billion (2008)

Labour force: 39,000 (2007; around 50 per cent are foreign workers)

Unemployment: 4.00% (2008)

Inflation: 7.00% (2005)

Visitor numbers: 1.97 million (2005)

* estimated figure

COUNTRY PROFILE

Historical profile

1503 Little Cayman and Cayman Brac were sighted by Christopher Columbus during his fourth and final voyage to the New World. The islands were first named Las Tortugas (turtles); the name was later changed to Lagartos (alligator or large lizard).

1540 The name Caymanas was given to the islands, derived from the Carib word for marine crocodile.

1585–86 Sir Frances Drake visited the islands.

During the sixteenth, seventeenth and eighteenth centuries, Dutch, English, Spanish and French ships used the islands for watering and provisioning.

1655 The islands came under British control when Jamaica was captured from the Spanish.

1670 In the Treaty of Madrid, Spain recognised UK sovereignty over Jamaica and the Cayman Islands. The early settlers were ex-soldiers from Oliver Cromwell's army, with other settlers from Jamaica, together with shipwrecked or marooned sailors.

1773 Grand Cayman's population reached 400.

1831 It was agreed that representatives should be appointed for the five different districts of Grand Cayman for the purpose of forming local laws for better government. After elections in the five districts, the legislative assembly met in George Town.

1833 Cayman Brac and Little Cayman were settled permanently.

1835 The proclamation declaring the emancipation of all slaves throughout the colonies was read.

1962 When Jamaica became independent, Caymanians retained direct links with the Crown and the Cayman Islands became a separate British Crown Colony.

1971 The first governor was appointed.

1972 A new constitution was adopted giving greater autonomy and making the islands a British Overseas Territory.

1994 A constitutional amendment introduced a ministerial form of government.

2000 Only independent candidates were elected to parliament.

2001 The United Democratic Party (UDP) was formed. Its leader, W McKeeva Bush, became the leader of government business.

2002 The People's Progressive Movement (PPM) was formed.

2003 The previously informal title for the government's chief minister, the Leader of Government Business, was formally recognised by the UK government.

2004 The worst hurricane since 1918, Hurricane Ivan, struck the islands, causing severe flooding and infrastructure damage.

2005 The PPM won the parliamentary elections; Kurt Tibbetts became Leader of Government Business.

2007 Public discussion in the Phase one of the Constitutional Modernisation Initiative began.

2009 Governor Stuart Jack stepped down. The opposition UDP won parliamentary elections. A referendum agreed, by 63 per cent of votes, to overhaul the constitution. W McKeeva Bush (UDP) became Leader of Government Business. The Cayman Islands agreed to adopt measures to allow the Organisation for Economic Co-operation and Development (OECD) to remove it from the OECD list of countries that do not implement international standards for tax disclosure. The new constitution was inaugurated; changes included the head of government becoming a premier, with a limit of two terms in office, and a bill of rights to be introduced in November 2012. Donovan Ebanks became acting governor.

2010 Duncan Taylor took office as governor in January. Legislation was introduced in February establishing bilateral agreements for exchanging tax information. A census took place over 10 October–24 November. Government financial statistics recorded a decline in GDP of -4 per cent, which was still an improvement on the 2009 fall of -9 per cent per; GDP per capita fell as a consequence from US$43,363 in 2009 to US$42,363.

2011 Preliminary results from the census, published in March, indicated that the population was fewer at 54,878, instead of the 2008 forecast of 57,000. Full results of the census are due in the fourth quarter of 2011. On 1 June a National Energy Policy Committee (NEPC) was convened for the first time to plan

Cayman Islands' response to rising fossil fuel prices and future energy needs.

Political structure

Constitution

The constitution of 1972, revised in 1994, created ministers and ministries and provided for a system of government headed by a governor, an Executive Council (ExCo) and Legislative Assembly. Unlike other Caribbean Overseas Territories, there is no chief minister, but a leader of government business. The appointed governor retains responsibility for the civil service, defence, external affairs and internal security.

On 6 November 2009, a new constitution was inaugurated; the head of government became a premier, with a limit of two terms in office. A bill of rights will be introduced in November 2012.

Form of state

Self-governing British Crown Colony

The executive

The British monarch is Head of State and is represented by the governor. Government is exercised by the Executive Council (ExCo) presided over by the governor, consisting of three official members appointed by the governor and five members drawn from the elected members of the Legislative Assembly. As ministers, the five elected members of the ExCo have direct responsibility for government portfolios.

National legislature

The Legislative Assembly has 18 members, 15 elected members (MLAs) for a four-year term in two-seat constituencies, and three *ex-officio* members.

Legal system

The legal system is based on English common law with local changes. Courts: Juvenile Court, Summary Court Grand Court and the Cayman Islands Court of Appeal. Final appeals go to the Privy Council in the UK.

Last elections

20 May 2009 (parliamentary)

Results: Parliamentary: United Democratic Party (UDP) won 44.21 per cent of the vote, (9 seats out of 15), the People's Progressive Movement (PPM) 29.78 per cent (5), independents 26.04 per cent (1); turnout was 73.4 per cent

Next elections

2013 (parliamentary)

Political parties

Ruling party

United Democratic Party (UDP) (from 20 May 2009)

Main opposition party

People's Progressive Movement (PPM)

Political situation

With a weird statistic that shows there are more companies register on the Cayman Islands than there are people living on them, business leaders were pleased when the Cayman Islands maintained its international ranking of sixth, in 2007, in total banking assets. Nevertheless, the Cayman Islands have come in for a battering from several sources. Bermuda set out to take a major share of the US$2 trillion hedge funds business from both the Cayman Islands and the British Virgin Islands and the 2007–08 crisis in US banking, has taken its toll on the Cayman Islands' reputation, as hedge funds have failed and tax evasion schemes have come to light. Officials from the UK and US treasury have begun investigations into offshore tax havens, with accusations of tax dodges and money laundering. Almost as soon as scrutiny began the Basis Capital Funds Management was declared bankrupt and in January 2008 Bear Stearns had two hedge funds falter.

The Cayman Islands has the highest standard of living of any other Caribbean country and it relies heavily on its offshore banking to maintain this and must judge the balance between offering a discrete, and no-questions-asked, banking service against the potential retaliatory action of foreign governments keen to stem the flow of revenue from their coffers.

Population

56,000 (2009)*

Last census: October 1999: 39,410

Population density: 150 inhabitants per square km.

Annual growth rate: 4.4 per cent (2003)

Ethnic make-up

Mixed race (40 per cent), white (20 per cent), black (20 per cent). Thirty-four per cent of the population are foreign residents, of whom 10 per cent are British or American.

Religions

Mainly Presbyterian with Anglican, Roman Catholic, Seventh-Day Adventists, Pilgrims, Pilgrim Holiness Church of God, Jehovah's Witnesses and Baha'i minorities on Grand Cayman. Baptists on Cayman Brac.

Health

The Cayman Islands have a variety of modern medical facilities. There are government-operated hospitals on Grand Cayman and Cayman Brac. The George Town Hospital on Grand Cayman is affiliated with the Baptist Hospital of Miami, USA, for patient referrals involving advanced care or treatment.

Life expectancy: 80 years (estimate 2003)

Fertility rate/Maternal mortality rate: Two births per woman (2003)

Birth rate/Death rate: 13 births per 1,000 population; five deaths per 1,000 population (2003).

Child (under 5 years) mortality rate (per 1,000): Nine per 1,000 live births (2003)

Main cities

George Town, on Grand Cayman (capital, estimated population 26,798 in 2005); West Bay (10,006), Bodden Town (8,084).

Languages spoken

Spoken English has a distinctive 'brogue'. The Jamaican patois and a stronger accent is also common. Spanish, particularly regional dialects of Central America and Cuba, is also spoken.

Official language/s

English

Media

Press

The private publisher Cayman Free Press (CFP) (www.caymanfreepress.com) has a variety of publications.

Dailies: There are two newspapers, *The Caymanian Compass* (www.caycompass.com) published by CFP and *Cayman Net News* (www.caymannetnews.com).

Weeklies: The *New Caymanian* newspaper is published on Friday. There are two TV guide publications.

Business: The *Cayman Observer* (www.caymanobserver.com) is a weekly publication. The *Cayman Islands Yearbook and Business Directory* is published yearly.

Periodicals: A free-issue tourist magazine *Key to Cayman* is a quarterly, *Inside Out* is a bi-annual home and lifestyle magazine, *The Journal* is a monthly general interest broadsheet; these are published by CFP. *Newstar* is a tourist publication.

Broadcasting

Radio: The public broadcaster is Radio Cayman (www.radiocayman.gov.ky), which has two networks, One (for news, information and music) and Two (for popular music). Private, commercial radio stations include Vibe FM (www.vibefm-cayman.com), Z99FM (www.z99.ky), Hot 106.1 (www.hot1041fm.ky), Kiss FM (www.kiss1061fm.ky) and X107.1 (www.x1071.ky).

Television: There are four commercial, free-to-air TV stations, Cayman International Television Network (CITN), called Channel 27 (www.cayman27.com.ky), transmits local, Caribbean and International news and entertainment, Cayman Television Service (CTS) with Island 24, which has evolved into a tourism information channel. There are two religious channels, CCTV and CATN.

There are four pay-to-view platforms. Digital cable providers include WestTel (www.weststartv.com) with 120 channels and CITN with 35-channels showing imported programmes. Satellite stations include Dish Direct TV with over 200 channels and Island TV.

News agencies

Other news agencies: Caribbean Net News: www.caribbeannetnews.com

Economy

In 2010 the service sector accounted for 94.6 per cent of GDP and dominates the economy, especially in offshore financial services and tourism, which provides virtually the sole sources of export earnings.

The land is not productive enough to feed the population and the islands are dependent on imports for the bulk of its consumption and investment requirements.

The economy is vulnerable to external shocks, such as the global economic crisis, which caused a downturn in trade and investment. As with other Caribbean countries, the Cayman Islands are susceptible to devastating hurricanes that injure people and damage property.

The first Islamic compliant bond (*Sukuk*) issuance programme to be listed on the London Stock Exchange in 2007 was issued by the Cayman Islands, valued at US$5 billion. The Cayman Islands have a growing reputation as a leader in Islamic finance

GDP growth in 2008 was 1.1 per cent. In the government budget for 2009, the fiscal year growth rate was -2.3 per cent, but the calendar growth rate forecast to be -5.7 per cent. The current account deficit was 15.9 per cent of GDP, which was forecast to increase to 19.7 per cent of GDP in 2009/10. The government has implemented measures to retain and enhance international business as well as identifying assets to be sold. The premier announced in February 2010 that residency may be purchased by financial workers for a one-off payment of US$1 million.

The Annual Economic Report published in July 2011 recorded a fall in GDP in 2010 of -4 per cent, which was still an improvement on the 2009 fall of -9 per cent; GDP in 2009 was forecast to be 0.9 per cent. GDP per capita fell as a consequence from US$43,363 in 2009 to US$42,363 in 2010. The construction, real estate and financial services sectors were hardest hit by the recession.

Over 50 per cent of the workforce are expatriates with most working in the financial industry. The Cayman Islands keep abreast of international compliance measures for money laundering.

In 2009 the Cayman Islands government was in need of a US$61 million loan to cover the shortfall in domestic spending; the UK, which is responsible for Cayman Islands' external affairs, provided security for the loan so long as fiscal reforms were implemented. In particular the UK wanted a commitment to cutting expenditure and an independent assessment of direct taxation to broaden the tax base.

External trade

The economy is heavily dependant on the financial services sector and tourism. A substantial deficit is traditionally run on the merchandise trade account, which is usually covered by invisible earnings and capital inflows from tourism and financial services .Trade is limited to small scale agricultural and marine production and manufactured consumer goods.

Imports

Principal imports are foodstuffs, petroleum and derivatives, consumer goods, machinery and transport equipment, tourist-related goods.

Main sources: US, UK, The Netherlands Antilles, Japan

Exports

Principal exports are aquaculture products including turtles and crustacean livestock and manufactured consumer goods.

Main destinations: US, Canada and other Caribbean islands.

Agriculture

Farming

Poor soil conditions and scarcity of land make agriculture uneconomic. Only about 8 per cent of the total land area is farmed. The Cayman Islands do not produce enough food to meet local demand and are reliant on imports. A National Tree Crop Husbandry Programme has increased the output of mangoes, citrus fruit and bananas. Government policies focus on sustainable development and using new technologies.

Fishing

The typical annual fish catch is 125t. All spawning areas for groupers were closed for fishing for a period of eight years from 2003, in a move aimed at preserving stocks for future generations. Groupers take eight years to mature.

Industry and manufacturing

The industrial sector makes only a very small contribution to the economy; diversification is hampered by factors such as high labour costs and a shortage of labour. Activity is centred on building materials (concrete blocks and tiles) and tourist-related industries such as jewellery, printing and food processing.

Tourism

The Cayman Islands offer typical Caribbean holidays based around its beaches. In 2011 the US-based TripAdvisor ranked the Cayman Islands as the world's top location for aquatic tours for the adventurous visitor, including scuba diving and yachting. The *Brides Magazine* also ranked the Cayman Islands as among the top 20 honeymoon destinations. Industry planning identified *niche* marketing based on 'sun, sand and surf' as the future of tourism in the Cayman Islands.

The industry has contributed over US$180 million per annum to GDP since 2007, although greatly below its peak of US$288 million in 2002. Tourism's share of GDP fell to 6.7 per cent in 2008–09; there was a slight improvement to 6.8 per cent in 2010. Real growth in tourism has been recovering since 2004 when a devastating hurricane inflicted so much damage on the islands that in 2005 tourism was in negative growth of -37.8 per cent. It recovered with growth of 18.2 per cent, helped by 1.93 million cruise-liner passengers visiting in 2006. The decline returned in 2007 with -3.4 per cent, which fell steadily until 2009 at -6.7 per cent, a time of maximum downturn in the global economic crisis. Since then tourism has picked up and grew by 2.7 per cent in 2010.

The tourist industry provided 8.3 per cent in direct employment in 2010 and 25.1 per cent of indirect employment; both of which have remained relatively static since 2006.

Hydrocarbons

There are no known hydrocarbons reserves and all domestic needs are met by imports, which were 3,000 barrels per day (bpd) in 2008.

Any use of natural gas or coal is commercially insignificant.

Energy

Total installed generating capacity was 115MW in 2007, producing over 490 million kilowatt hours. The Caribbean Utilities Company (CUC) is responsible for generation, distribution and supply of electricity; it has 18 generating units, including 16 diesel turbines.

Solar-photovoltaic panels have been installed in community centres such as hospitals but the uptake by households was, in 2009, low. According to CUC this was due to a lack of clear sell-back regulations which made it difficult for individuals to upload excess power to CUC, thus making the proposition of investing in the technology less attractive.

Financial markets

Stock exchange

Cayman Islands Stock Exchange (CSX)

Banking and insurance

Under an EU tax directive introduced in July 2005 in dependent EU countries, the Cayman Islands now informs all EU citizens' tax departments about the amount of money in savings accounts to allow tax to be levied from the home country while retaining a saver's anonyimity.

The Cayman Islands has also agreed to supply information on tax fraud, for criminal or civil trials, and notify EU member states about additional malpractices.

Central bank

The Cayman Islands Monetary Authority (CIMA) was established in January 1997.

Main financial centre

George Town, Grand Cayman

Time

GMT minus five hours

Geography

The Cayman Islands are located in the western Caribbean, south of Cuba and north-west of Jamaica.

The three islands of Grand Cayman, Cayman Brac and Little Cayman are limestone outcroppings, the tops of a submarine mountain range called the Cayman Ridge, which extends west-south-west from the Sierra Maestra range of the south-east part of Cuba to the Misteriosa Bank near Belize. There are no rivers or streams because of the porous nature of the limestone rock. All three islands are surrounded by healthy coral reefs.

Hemisphere

Northern

Climate

Prevailing north-east trade winds; moderate, otherwise hot climate. Average temperatures 24–29 degrees Celsius. The rainy season is May–Oct, but annual rainfall is low.

Dress codes

Neat, casual, tropical attire is appropriate. Public nudity and topless bathing are strictly prohibited by law.

Entry requirements

Passports

Required by all except citizens of the UK, US and Canada with proof of citizenship (authenticated birth certificate and photographic identity document) and a return ticket (all US and Canadian nationals require a passport for re-entry to their country from January 2007).

The pink immigration slip given upon arrival should be kept with travel documents and presented when departing.

Visa

Not required by transit passengers or nationals of the EU, North America, Australasia or Japan, provided their stay does not exceed 30 days. For further exceptions see http://cayman.com.ky/visiting/reqs.htm.

Salespeople planning to solicit business and take orders require a temporary work permit, applications should be obtained in advance from the Department of Immigration.

Currency advice/regulations

There is no restriction on import of foreign or local currency, apart from import of Jamaican dollars, which are restricted to J$20.

Customs

It is advised not to export products made from wild green sea turtles as they are illegal in most countries; farmed sea turtles may be allowed by a visitor's home country, however, the US prohibits its transshipment and will confiscate any such material.

Prohibited imports

Illegal drugs, including marijuana. Permits are necessary for firearms of any kind, including spearguns (or pole spears or Hawaiian slings), live plants and plant cuttings, raw meat and raw fruits and vegetables.

Health (for visitors)

Modern medical facilities are available, particularly on Grand Cayman and Cayman Brac. The George Town Hospital is well equipped for any diving accidents.

Mandatory precautions

None

Advisable precautions

Immunisation against typhoid, and less so TB, diphtheria and hepatitis B and C. Outbreaks of dengue fever and dengue haemorrhagic fever can occur. Hepatitis A has been reported in the northern Caribbean generally.

Tap water is safe to drink.

Hotels

There is a wide choice of hotels throughout the islands, mainly on the beach. There is a government room tax of 10 per cent and an automatic gratuity of 10 per cent of the room rate. Restaurants often add a 15 per cent gratuity to their bills.

Credit cards

Major credit cards are widely accepted.

Public holidays (national)

Fixed dates

1–2 Jan (New Year's holiday), 23 Jan (Heroes' Day), 15 May (Discovery Day), 12 Jun (Queen's Birthday), 3 Jul (Constitution Day), 31 Nov (Remembrance Day), 25–26 Dec (Christmas).

Some bank, legal and public holidays that fall on days other than Monday are moved to the following Monday. The above dates take this into account.

Variable dates

Feb/Mar (Ash Wednesday), Mar/Apr (Easter, three days).

Working hours

Banking

Mon–Thu: 0900–1600; Fri: 0900–1630.

Business

Mon–Fri: 0830–1700.

Government

Mon–Fri: 0800–1700

Post offices: Mon–Fri 0830–1530; Sat 0830–1200.

Shops

Mon–Sat: 0900–1700.

Telecommunications

Mobile/cell phones

There are 850/1900 and 900/1800 GSM services available throughout the islands.

Electricity supply

110V AC, 60Hz. American-style (flat) two-pin plugs are standard.

Getting there

Air

National airline: Cayman Airways.

International airport/s: Owen Roberts International (GCM), 3km from the centre of George Town, duty-free shop, bar, restaurant, buffet, money exchange, shops.

Other airport/s: Gerrard Smith (CYB) on Cayman Brac. Little Cayman is served by inter-island flights arriving at the Edward Bodden Airstrip.

Airport tax: Departure tax US$25

Getting about

National transport

Air: Cayman Airways operates a service from Grand Cayman to Cayman Brac. Island Air offers a four-times-a-day service between Grand Cayman and both Cayman Brac and Little Cayman.

Road: There are over 175km of road, mostly surfaced. Speed limits of 50, 40, 30, 25mph are strictly enforced. Most hotels have bicycles available for complimentary guest use.

Buses: Daily bus services start at 0600. There are regular bus services between West Bay and George Town, and between the latter and Bodden Town and East End. Mini-buses are operated by licensed operators.

City transport

Taxis: Taxis are readily available at hotels and airport. Fares are based on a fixed place-to-place tariff. Tipping optional.

Car hire

An international licence is recommended. A local permit is obtainable on production of a national licence. Traffic drives on the left. Wearing seat belts is mandatory.

BUSINESS DIRECTORY

The addresses listed below are a selection only. While World of Information makes every endeavour to check these addresses, we cannot guarantee that changes have not been made, especially to telephone numbers and area codes. We would welcome any corrections.

Telephone area codes
The international direct dialling code (IDD) for the Cayman Islands is + 1 345, followed by subscriber's number.

Useful telephone numbers
Emergency service (island-wide): 911.

Chambers of Commerce
Cayman Islands Chamber of Commerce, Harbour Centre, PO Box 1000, George Town, Grand Cayman (tel: 949-8090; fax: 949-0220; e-mail: info@caymanchamber.ky).

Banking
The Bank of Nova Scotia, PO Box 689, Grand Cayman (tel: 949-7666; fax: 949-0020).

Bank of Butterfield International (Cayman) Ltd, PO Box 705 G, Grand Cayman (tel: 949-7055; fax: 949-7761).

Barclays Bank International, PO Box 68 G, Grand Cayman (tel: 949-7300; fax: 949-7179).

Canadian Imperial Bank of Commerce and Trust Co (Cayman), PO Box 694 G, Grand Cayman (tel: 949-8666; fax: 949-7904).

The Cayman Islands Bankers' Association, PO Box 1321, Grand Cayman (tel: 949-0330).

Cayman National Bank and Trust Co, PO Box 1097, Grand Cayman (tel: 949-4655; fax: 949-7506); Galleria Branch, PO Box 1097, Grand Cayman (tel: 949-7137; fax: 949-7506).

First Home Banking, PO Box 914, Grand Cayman (tel: 949-7822; fax: 949-6064).

The Royal Bank of Canada, PO Box 245 G, Grand Cayman (tel: 949-4600; fax: 949-7396).

Swiss Bank and Trust Corporation Ltd, PO Box 852 G, Grand Cayman (tel: 949-7344; fax: 949-7308).

Central bank
Cayman Islands Monetary Authority, PO Box 10052 APO, Elizabethan Square, 80e Shedden Road, Grand Cayman (tel: 949-7089; fax: 949-2532; e-mail: cima@cimoney.com.ky).

Stock exchange
Cayman Islands Stock Exchange (CSX): www.csx.com.ky

Travel information
Cayman Airways, PO Box 1101, George Town, Grand Cayman (tel: 949-2311/8272; fax: 949-7607).

Ministry of tourism
Ministry of Tourism, Aviation and Commerce, Government Administration Building, Grand Cayman (tel: 949-7900; fax: 949-1746).

National tourist organisation offices
Cayman Islands Department of Tourism, PO Box 67, The Pavilion, Cricket Square, George Town, Grand Cayman (tel: 949-0623; fax: 949-4053; fax: 949-4053; internet sites: www.caymanislands.ky; www.divecayman.ky).

Ministries
Governor's Office, 4th Floor, Government Administration Building, Elgin Avenue, George Town, Grand Cayman (tel: 949-7900; fax: 945-4131).

Ministry of Agriculture, Environment, Communications and Works, Government Administration Building, Grand Cayman (tel: 949-7900; fax: 949-2922).

Ministry of Community Development, Sports, Women's and Youth Affairs, Government Administration Building, Grand Cayman (tel: 949-7900; fax: 949-0726).

Ministry of Education and Planning, Government Administration Building, Grand Cayman (tel: 949-7900; fax: 949-9343).

Ministry of Health, Drug Abuse, Prevention and Rehabilitation, Government Administration Building, Grand Cayman (tel: 949-7900; fax: 949-7544).

Ministry of Internal and External Affairs, Government Administration Building, Grand Cayman (tel: 949-7900; fax: 949-7544).

Ministry of Finance and Development, Government Administration Building, Grand Cayman (tel: 949-7900; fax: 949-9838).

Ministry of Legal Affairs, Government Administration Building, Grand Cayman (tel: 949-7900; fax: 949-1746).

Sports Office, Ministry of Community Development, Sports, Women's and Youth Affairs, Third Floor, Tower Building, Grand Cayman (tel: 914-3480; fax: 949-8487).

Other useful addresses
Cable and Wireless (West Indies) Ltd, PO Box 293, George Town (tel: 949-7800; fax: 949-5472).

Cayman Islands Port Authority, PO Box 1358, Georgetown, Grand Cayman (tel: 949-2055; fax: 949-5820; e-mail: info@caymanport.com).

Cayman Islands Stock Exchange, Fourth Floor, Elizabethan Square, P.O Box 2408GT, Grand Cayman (tel: 945-6060; fax: 945-6061; e-mail: csx@csx.com.ky; internet site: www.csx.com.ky).

Civil Aviation Authority, PO Box 278, George Town, Grand Cayman (tel: 949-7811).

Customs Department, PO Box 898GT, Grand Cayman (tel: 949-2473; fax: 945-1573).

Government Information Services, Broadcasting House, Grand Cayman (tel: 949-8092; fax: 949-5936).

Immigration Department (tel: 949-8344; fax: 949-8486).

Radio Cayman, PO Box 1110, George Town, Grand Cayman (tel: 949-7799).

Registrar of Companies, Ground Floor, Tower Building, Grand Cayman (tel: 949-7999; fax: 949-0969).

Internet sites
Cayman Islands information: www.cayman.com.ky/cayman.htm

Cayman Net News: www.caymannetnews.com

Central African Republic

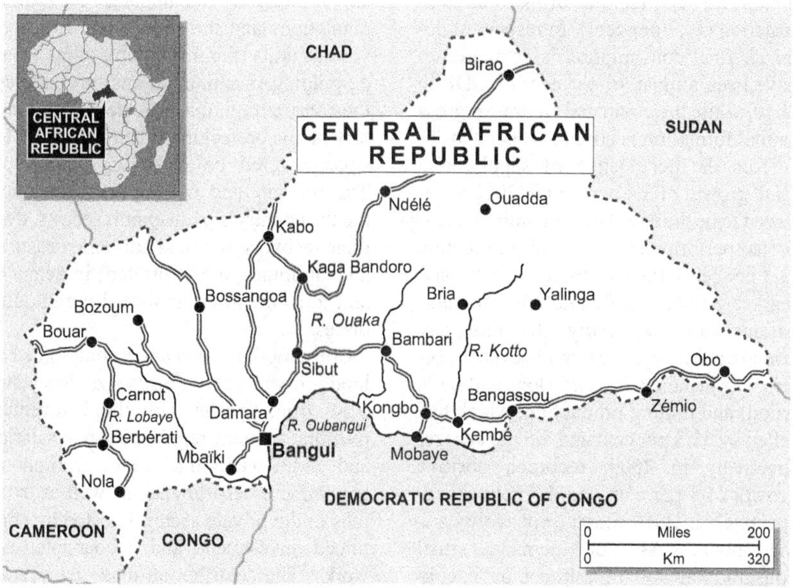

Presidential elections, originally scheduled for April 2010 were eventually held on 23 January 2011. Incumbent François Bozizé (of the Kwa Na Kwa party) won 66.08 per cent of the vote, his closest rival Ange-Félix Patassé (independent) won 20.1 per cent; three other candidates each won less than 7 per cent. The electoral commission confirmed President Bozizé's re-election on 26 January. After the second round of parliamentary elections held on 27 March, Kwa Na Kwa won a majority of 61 seats. All opposition parties, including 18 independent candidates, alleged electoral fraud.

The government signed a ceasefire agreement with the last active rebel group (Convention des Patriotes pour la Justice et la Paix (Convention of Patriotes for Justice and Peace (CPJP)), on 13 June 2011.

The recurring social, political and military crises of the past two decades have made the Central African Republic (CAR) a fragile, post-conflict state. These crises have damaged the economic fabric and destroyed the basic socio-economic infrastructure. However, the CAR has abundant natural resources, and is seeing an increase in economic stability and the implementation of financial and structural reforms, as well as the rehabilitation of basic social services.

Whether these economic and social improvements will be consolidated will depend largely on the country's capacity to complete the political stabilisation process and respect the peace agreements, notably through the Disarmament, Demobilisation and Reintegration (DDR) programme adopted during the Inclusive Political Dialogue (DPI) conference held in December 2008. The DPI conference brought together the presidential majority, the opposition, politico-military movements, civil society and public bodies. The success of the transition from a period of prolonged instability towards growth and development will also depend on the country's capacity to mobilise more resources than is currently the case. This concern led the government, in agreement with its main development partners, to organise a roundtable meeting for donors in 2011.

Somebody has to be last

The CAR has developed the knack or being near, or even at, the bottom of several international development lists and indexes. The World Bank's annual *Doing Business Index* in 2010 once again had the CAR in 183rd place out of 183. The UN Human Development Index had the CAR

KEY FACTS

Official name: République Centrafricaine (Central African Republic)

Head of State: President François Bozizé (Kwa Na Kwa) (since 2003; re-elected 23 Jan 2011)

Head of government: Prime Minister Faustin-Archange Touadéra (from 2008; re-appointed 19 Jan 2009)

Ruling party: Convergence Nationale 'Kwa Na Kwa' (KNK) (National Convergence) (from 2005; re-elected 27 Mar 2011)

Area: 622,984 square km

Population: 4.80 million (2010)*

Capital: Bangui

Official language: French

Currency: CFA franc (CFAf) = 100 centimes (Communauté Financière Africaine (African Financial Community) franc)

Exchange rate: CFAf488.90 per US$ (Oct 2011); CFAf655.95 per euro (pegged from Jan 1999)

GDP per capita: US$447 (2009)*

GDP real growth: 2.40% (2009)*

Inflation: 3.50% (2009)*

* estimated figure

down at 179 (out of 182 countries), it is ranked 153rd out of 177 countries in terms of gender equality and is far from completing most of the Millennium Development Goals. Some 86 per cent of the population have no access to basic social services, life expectancy is 45.1 years, access to safe drinking water stands at 30.2 per cent, well below the African average of 60 per cent, and access to sewerage stands at only 5.3 per cent, also below the African average, which is 31 per cent.

The economy

The economic recovery in the Central African Republic was confirmed in 2010, with real gross domestic product (GDP) growth estimated at 3.4 per cent. This positive growth came a year after the economy had suffered the full effects of the global economic and financial crisis that broke out in 2008. In 2010, the CAR also achieved the objectives set out in the 2008–10 poverty reduction strategy paper (PRSP) and the year saw its economic and financial programme negotiated with the International Monetary Fund (IMF), supported through the Extended Fund Facility (EFF) agreed upon with the IMF in December 2006. The sixth and final review of the EFF was approved by the IMF board on 25 August 2010, thus rewarding the efforts made in terms of economic and financial reform. The CAR also reached the completion point of the Heavily Indebted Poor Countries (HIPC) Initiative and the Multilateral Debt Relief Initiative (MDRI).

In 2010 sectoral distribution of the country's GDP was pretty much the same as in 2009, with a slight rise (0.3 per cent) in the share of agriculture to 54.9 per cent of GDP. Food crops (28.7 per cent of GDP) and agriculture (12.6 per cent) continue to dominate the primary sector, while trade (12.1 per cent) accounts for most of the tertiary sector, which overall has stabilised at 31.5 per cent of GDP. The secondary sector (13.5 per cent of GDP) is dominated by manufacturing and construction (10.3 per cent). In respect of demand, final consumption is estimated to have been almost 96 per cent of GDP in 2010, while the estimated figure for gross capital formation is around 13 per cent.

From the perspective of supply, real GDP growth of 3.4 per cent in 2010 is believed to be the result of the continued vigorous performance of food production (3.3 per cent), the construction sector and market services (trade and telecommunications) and especially the relatively strong recovery of the main export sectors. For instance, forestry (logs and sawn wood) and mining production, which had fallen by 31.8 per cent and 8.5 per cent respectively in 2009, recorded positive growth of 8 per cent and 4.5 per cent respectively in 2010, albeit from a low starting point. As for demand, final consumption and investment have contributed to the economic recovery.

The performance of food crops was essentially the result of continued aid to producers, especially through the distribution of insecticides and fertilisers, the re-establishment of security in cultivated areas, the opening of the CAR-Sudan corridor, and good rainfall. Livestock farming has benefited from the re-establishment of public security, as well as from livestock vaccination campaigns, training in the rational management of pasture areas, the replacement of small livestock in the areas concerned, and the introduction of credits to communities with the aim of increasing animal production.

Export crops, especially cotton and coffee, have also benefited from the good rainfall and the recovery in prices, as well as the ongoing maintenance of coffee plantations and the supply and fitting of various units (the installation of six small de pulping machines in two prefectures, the construction of a large de pulping factory in one prefecture, the installation of a solar-powered coffee-drying unit, etc). The forestry and mining sectors, which are the country's main export sectors, owe their recovery to fiscal support measures and an upturn (albeit limited) in demand, and to a rise in international commodity prices.

Consumption, the main driving force behind growth because of its size, has benefited from greater household revenues resulting from the regularisation of salaries and additional public sector workers in government departments, as well as extra jobs in the private sector, boosted by continued investment and labour-intensive works. The contribution made by overall investment to growth was limited to 0.7 percentage points in 2010, despite the public sector increasing its share by around 7 per cent. The effect of net external demand on growth was negligible. Increases in exports and imports largely cancelled each other out in terms of growth.

The *African Economic Outlook 2011* (AEO), published jointly by the African Development Bank and the Organisation for Economic Co-operation and Development, considers that economic recovery in 2010 should continue over the next two years. GDP growth is forecast to reach 4.3 per cent in 2011 and 4.5 per cent in 2012. This accelerated growth depends on the consolidation of the peace process and the improved political climate after the presidential and parliamentary elections. Major investment from mining companies and continued public and private investment alongside a recovery in food and cash crops will also contribute to the overall recovery. However, if the social climate and security situation get worse, this could discourage donors and affect investor confidence. Exogenous shocks, particularly the continued effects of the economic crisis on exports, could also hold back growth. Furthermore, the insufficient investment in infrastructure and the slowness of the improvement in the business climate could also delay the

KEY INDICATORS — Central African Republic

	Unit	2006	2007	2008	2009	2010
Population	m	*4.19	*4.27	*4.36	*4.44	*4.80
Gross domestic product (GDP)	US$bn	1.48	*1.71	*1.99	*1.99	–
GDP per capita	US$	*355	*402	*458	*447	–
GDP real growth	%	*4.0	*4.2	2.2	2.4	–
Inflation	%	6.6	*0.9	9.3	*3.5	–
Exports (fob) (goods)	US$m	166.1	187.9	147.2	135.3	–
Imports (fob) (goods)	US$m	213.0	264.1	308.6	257.1	–
Balance of trade	US$m	-47.3	-76.1	-161.5	-153.3	–
Current account	US$m	*-49.0	*-77.0	*-206.0	*-154.0	–
Total reserves minus gold	US$m	125.3	82.6	121.8	210.6	181.2
Foreign exchange	US$m	124.4	81.6	121.5	205.9	176.5
Exchange rate	per US$	496.60	454.40	447.81	472.19	495.28

* estimated figure

private investment that the CAR so badly needs to revive its economy.

Transport limitations

The low level of transport infrastructure is one of the CAR's main drawbacks to development. It remains among the lowest in Africa, even though the country's geographical position (a landlocked country with no direct access to the sea) makes such infrastructure essential for its economic development. The sector's main obstacles are: the absence of a permanent link for the development of imports and exports by sea; the inadequacy and poor maintenance of existing infrastructure; the lack of density of the network; and unbalanced land use. Despite this, transport infrastructure absorbs a large proportion of public investment. The country's landlocked position is exacerbated by the plethora of administrative checks that make transport expensive.

The main form of transport for travel, freight and supplies is by road. The country has 24,000km of roads, of which about 1,000 are asphalted. The network consists of 5,400km of national roads, 4,000km of regional roads and 15,000km of tracks. Like most countries in Central Africa, the CAR has abundant water and is crossed by tributaries of the Congo river, providing many potentially navigable waterways within its borders. There is only one international airport in the country, through which almost 90 per cent of traffic passes. The other three airports have paved runways in a poor state of repair.

Energy

There is a lack of energy, even though the country has a fairly dense river system with various sites that have a high potential for hydroelectricity, with outputs of between several hundred kilowatts (KW) and several dozen megawatts (MW). Firewood accounts for 90 per cent of energy consumption, the rest coming from imported oil products and hydroelectric resources, the latter providing barely 4 per cent. Development of the energy sector is in particular held back by a legislative and regulatory framework that is not adapted; the lack of an energy information system; deficiencies in the way the sector is run, especially in Enerca, the company that holds a monopoly on the production and commercialisation of electricity; and limited human and financial resources.

International partners

The CAR still relies upon aid from both traditional and emerging partners. This situation, brought about by two decades of armed conflict and political instability, has not significantly changed since the peace consolidation process began and the DPI took place in 2008. Nevertheless, China, and more recently in 2010 India, are increasing the number of initiatives to develop economic partnerships. Chinese co-operation is present in construction and the renovation of public and administrative buildings. China is also financing the construction of the 100 bed regional hospital in Bimbo, at a cost of CFAf4.5 billion (US$920 million). As of the end of 2010, the work was at a very advanced stage. The contract for the regional transport facilitation project for the Bangui–N'Djamena corridor was awarded to the China Communications Construction Company (CCCC).

Overall, the presence of traditional and emerging partners in the CAR remains very limited. But this situation is bound to change quickly because of the country's significant natural resources. Nevertheless, the CAR will have to improve its security and political situation and create the necessary conditions to attract direct investment. The authorities will also have to do more to produce a viable strategy to optimise future emerging partnerships.

The Central African Republic remains a fragile, post-conflict state, despite the efforts made. The implementation of the DDR programme, which was initiated following the DPI in 2008, was plagued by delays in 2010. The DDR, which aims to demobilise more than 8,000 former combatants, still encounters many political disputes, especially on the value of food subsidies to the rebels. In any case, the attacks on 17 July and 23 November 2010, including the taking of Birao, the main town in the north of the country, were a reminder of the need to be vigilant, even if, a few days later, the government regained control of Birao.

Among the efforts made, in accordance with the PRSP objectives, expenditure on reducing poverty, improving security and keeping the peace increased in 2009 and 2010. Education, health and targeted poverty-reduction programmes are being increasingly prioritised in the 2010–12 medium-term expenditure framework (MTEF).

Risk assessment

Economy	Poor
Politics	Fair
Regional stability	Fair

COUNTRY PROFILE

Historical profile

1889 The French established themselves at Bangui.
1907 The colony of Oubangi-Shari (named after two main rivers) was founded.
1958 The country was proclaimed a republic.
1960 David Dacko became the president of the independent and newly named country
1966 Dacko's cousin, Jean-Bedel Bokassa, an army commander, seized power, declaring himself life-president in 1972.
1977 Bokassa crowned himself emperor – the coronation consumed about one quarter of the country's annual income.
1979 Bokassa's repressive regime ended when French troops reinstated David Dacko.
1981 Dacko was ousted by the army chief of staff, General André Kolingba.
1986 Kolingba established a one-party state.
1990 Opposition groups united and forced the government to adopt a multi-party system.
1992 Elections were held but the results were nullified after several groups boycotted the poll.
1993 Ange-Félix Patassé became president in the first multi-party elections.
1995 A democratic constitution was adopted.
1996 Army mutinies erupted, the last of which degenerated into ethnic violence and was suppressed by French troops in January 1997.
1997 Patassé appointed Michel Gbezera-Bira at the head of an 11-party coalition government.
1998 Parliamentary elections were indecisive.
1999 A number of deputies defected to Patassé's Mouvement de Libération du Peuple Centrafricain (MLPC) (Movement for the Liberation of the Central African People), giving it a slight majority. Presidential elections confirmed support for Patassé. France withdrew its troops.
2001 Libya sent troops to protect Patassé.
2002 Rebels seized part of Bangui; they were fought off by the army, aided by Libyan warplanes.
2003 General François Bozizé led a military coup that captured Bangui while President Patassé was abroad. Bozizé proclaimed himself president, suspended the constitution and dissolved the National Assembly.
2004 The National Transitional Council created an independent commission to oversee elections. A new constitution was approved.
2005 The Convergence Nationale-Kwa Na Kwa (CN-KNK) (National Convergence-Kwa Na Kwa) coalition won parliamentary elections and incumbent François Bozizé

was elected president. Elie Doté was named as prime minister.
2006 President Bozizé ruled by decree for three months. Rebel activity continued throughout the year, causing the president to seek French military assistance.
2007 An agreement was signed between Sudan, Chad and the Central African Republic whereby no shelter would be given to rebel movements between these countries.
2008 Élie Doté resigned and the president appointed Faustin-Archange Touadéra as prime minister. Jean-Pierre Bemba was arrested (in Belgium) on charges that his troops allegedly committed atrocities in the Central African Republic in 2002. He faced charges at the International Criminal Court (ICC). Peace agreements with three rebel groups were signed allowing disarmament and the demobilisation of rebel fighters.
2009 Prime Minister Touadéra and his cabinet were dismissed; the president re-appointed him as head of a national unity cabinet, which included two senior members of two rebel groups and two opposition parliamentary members. The International Monetary Fund (IMF) approved the immediate payment of US$18.46 million for poverty reduction programmes, following CAR's successful economic performance under the Poverty Reduction and Growth Facility (PRGF),
2010 In February, the president decreed that presidential and parliamentary elections would take place in April; they were later postponed until 2011. In March, troops of the Lord's Resistance Army (LRA), a brutal and indiscriminate rebel force from Uganda, began attacking villagers in CAR. In November former president Jean-Bedel Bokassa was formally rehabilitated by presidential decree. Although he was accused of great cruelty during his reign, President Bozizé said that Bokassa had 'built the country but we have destroyed what he built'. His widow was awarded a state medal of honour.
2011 On 23 January, in presidential elections, postponed from 2010, incumbent François Bozizé (Kwa Na Kwa) won 66.08 per cent of the vote, his closest rival Ange-Félix Patassé (independent) won 20.1 per cent; three other candidates each won less than 7 per cent. After the second round of parliamentary elections held on 27 March, Kwa Na Kwa won a majority of 61 seats. All opposition parties, including 18 independent candidates, alleged election fraud. However, the electoral commission confirmed President Bozizé's re-election on 26 January. The government signed a ceasefire agreement with the last active rebel group (Convention des Patriotes pour la Justice et la Paix (Convention of Patriotes for Justice and Peace (CPJP)), on 13 June.

Political structure

Constitution
A new constitution was approved in December 2004.

Form of state
Republic

The executive
Under the new constitution, approved in December 2004, the presidential term has been reduced from six to five years. Presidents can only serve a maximum of two terms in office.

National legislature
The unicameral, National Assembly has 105 members elected in single-seat constituencies using a two-round voting method. All members serve for five-year terms.

Last elections
23 January 2011 (presidential and first round parliamentary); 27 March 2011 (second round parliamentary).

Results: Presidential: François Bozizé (Kwa Na Kwa) won 66.08 per cent of the vote, Ange-Félix Patassé (independent) 20.1 per cent, Martin Ziguélé (MLPC) 6.46 per cent, Emile Gros Raymond Nakombo (RDC) 4.64 per cent, Jean-Jacques Démafouth (APRD) 2.72 per cent; turnout was 54.01 per cent.
Parliamentary: Convergence Nationale 'Kwa Na Kwa' (KNK) (National Convergence) won a total of 61 seats (out of 105), independent candidates 26, Majorité Présidentielle (MP) (Parliamentary Majority) 11, Mouvement de Libération du Peuple Centrafricain (MLPC) (Movement for the Liberation of the Central African People) one, Rassemblement Démocratique Centrafricain (RDC) one. Five other seats were unaccounted for.

Next elections
2016 (presidential and parliamentary)

Political parties

Ruling party
Convergence Nationale 'Kwa Na Kwa' (KNK) (National Convergence) (from 2005; re-elected 27 Mar 2011)

Main opposition party
Collectif des Forces du Changement (CFC) (Combined Forces for Change)

Population
4.80 million (2010)*

Last census: 8 December 2003: 3,151,072

Population density: Five inhabitants per square km. Urban population: 42 per cent (1995–2001).

Annual growth rate: 1.8 per cent 1994–2004 (WHO 2006)

Ethnic make-up
Bayas (34 per cent), Bandas (27 per cent), Manzas (21 per cent), Saras (10 per cent), Mbums (4 per cent), Mbakas (4 per cent)

Religions
About 24 per cent of the population hold traditional beliefs; 25 per cent Protestants; 25 per cent Catholics; 15 per cent Muslims.

Education
Only 60 per cent of eligible children receive education. Basic education lasts for 10 years divided into six years' basic first stage and four years' basic second stage. General secondary school lasts for three years, which gives access to higher education. Only 10 per cent of secondary school-aged children are enrolled due to limited resources. Technical education at the secondary level is offered at two levels. School instruction is primarily in French, but the government has sought to promote Sango literacy and encourages its use in schools.
Higher education is offered at the Université de Bangui, which also has a teacher training college.

Literacy rate: 49 per cent adult rate; 59 per cent youth rate (15–24) (Unesco 2005).

Compulsory years: Six to 14

Health
Modern healthcare facilities exist only in Bangui (with one major hospital) and a few other towns.
In 2004, CAR launched a 10-year programme to reduce maternal deaths and infant mortality rates.

HIV/Aids
HIV prevalence: 13.5 per cent aged 15–49 in 2003 (World Bank)

Life expectancy: 45.1 years, 2010 (UN 2011)

Fertility rate/Maternal mortality rate: 4.9 births per woman, 2004 (WHO 2006); maternal mortality 1,100 per 100,000 live births (World Bank).

Child (under 5 years) mortality rate (per 1,000): 115 per 1,000 live births; 23 per cent of children under aged five are malnourished (World Bank).

Head of population per physician: 0.08 physicians per 1,000 people, 2004 (WHO 2006)

Welfare
The country is in deep poverty, with two out of three people earning less than US$1 a day. All social security programmes are administered by the Central African Social Security Office.

Main cities
Bangui (capital, estimated population 731,548 in 2005), Berbérati (62,319), Bouar (52,300), Carnot (66,346), Bambari (47,207).

Languages spoken
Sango, Banda, Baye and Zanda are widely spoken.
Official language/s
French

Media
Despite the repeal of press laws the resulted in criminal prosecution, journalist are still subject to harassment and imprisonment by government ministers.
Press
The press does not have a great influence due to the relatively costliness of newspapers and high levels of illiteracy.
Dailies: In the Sango-language *E Le Songo* is state-owned. In French, *Le Confident* (www.leconfident.net), is a private publication as are *Le Citoyen, L'Hirondelle Le Démocrate* and *L'Evenementiel*.
Weeklies: In French, *Centrafrique Presse* (www.centrafrique-presse.com) is a published newsletter, twice a week. There are several private newspapers including, *Les Collines de l'Oubangui, Temps Nouveaux*, and *Le Centrafricain*,
Periodicals: In French, *Journal Officiel de la République Centrafricaine* is a government publication.
Broadcasting
Radio: The state-owned Radio Centrafrique (www.radiocentrafrique.org) does not provide independent news, alternatively, Radio Ndeke Luka (www.radiondekeluka.org), a UN-sponsored station provides a balanced output and international rebroadcasts from France, UK and US.
Other radio stations and signals are provided by international organisations, including the pan-African, Radio Africa No 1 (www.africa1.com), the French Radio Nostalgie and the Roman Catholic Radio Notre Dame.
Television: Television Centrafricaine is state-run and the private, Tropic RTV, is the only other broadcaster.
News agencies
National news agency: Centrafrique Presse
Other news agency: Africa News Agency: www.africanewsagency.co.uk
APA: www.apanews.net
Panapress: www.panapress.com

Economy
The Central African Republic (CAR) is one of the poorest and least developed countries in the world. Its economy is dominated by subsistence agriculture, which constitutes around 50 per cent of GDP. Forestry is a major export revenue earner and is the single largest employer in the CAR, drawing on over 27 million hectares of exploitable forests. Major crops include, cotton, food crops (such as maize, cassava and yams), coffee and tobacco, however the sector is vulnerable to drought and regional political strife. The service sector, led by government services and transport, comprises around 35 per cent of GDP and industry the remaining amount. Mining is largely underdeveloped, but there are deposits of gold, uranium and other minerals. Diamond mining is the second largest export earner, but it has been estimated that 30 per cent of all diamond production is illegally smuggled abroad.
GDP growth was projected to reach 3.3 per cent in 2010, an increase from the estimated 1.7 per cent in 2009 as the export of commodities finally picked up with growth of 23.3 per cent in 2010. However it is not expected to surpass the 2007 or 2008 growth rates of 3.8 per cent and 3.7 per cent respectively, until 2011. Exports of commodities in 2007 grew by 13.2 per cent, but as the global economic crisis struck in 2008 exports fell by -17.1 per cent, and by -24.5 per cent in 2009.
In 2010 the UN Human Development Report ranked CAR at 159 out of 169, with a Human Development Index (HDI) value of 0.315, a value that deteriorated by 1 per cent 2005–10. The headcount poverty rate 2000–08 was 86.4 per cent of the population. Poverty is hindering development, as the workforce is largely unskilled with only half of the population over 15 years of age literate.
Serious reform is necessary to attract foreign investment. The economy would be enhanced by improved transport facilities and domestic reforms by the government. Under pressure from the World Bank and the IMF, CAR has privatised state-owned enterprises and introduced other measures to encourage investment and combat corruption.

External trade
The Central African Republic is a member of the Communauté Économique et Monétaire de l'Afrique Centrale (Cemac) (Economic and Monetary Community of Central Africa), which operates a customs union with import taxes and capital flowing freely among member states; import duties, levied on third parties, are pooled and shared between members.
International trade is largely based on the export of timber, (around 50 per cent of export earnings) and diamonds, although it is estimated that 30 per cent of all production is illegally smuggled abroad. There is a potential for a great deal more in mineral exports but a poor investment record and weak infrastructure hampers progress.
Imports
Principal imports are food, textiles, chemicals and pharmaceuticals, petroleum products, machinery, vehicles and electrical equipment.
Main sources: South Korea (typically 19 per cent of total), France (12 per cent), Cameroon (7 per cent).
Exports
Principal exports are timber, diamonds, gold, coffee, and natural rubber, tobacco, cotton and leather.
Main destinations: Belgium (typically 33 per cent of total), China (10 per cent), Indonesia (10 per cent).

Agriculture
Agriculture and forestry are the mainstays of the economy. Agriculture accounts for around 55 per cent of GDP and employs 66 per cent of the workforce. Around 12 per cent of the total land is arable; much of the rest is savannah.
The sector consists mainly of subsistence farming and animal husbandry. The main crops are maize, cassava, sorghum, groundnuts, sesame and rice. Cotton and tobacco are also cultivated. The main export crop is coffee.
Production is hampered by soil erosion, widespread drought and underdeveloped marketing and infrastructure, as well as poor internal security and mass migration.
Forestry
Forest covers 50 per cent of the country. There is significant forestry potential, including over 60 species of commercially viable trees, but it is under-exploited because of poor transport infrastructure.

Industry and manufacturing
The industrial sector typically accounts for around 18 per cent of GDP and employs 9 per cent of the workforce. Manufacturing accounts for around 9 per cent of GDP.
Manufacturing is relatively small-scale and is concentrated in the brewing, tanning, food processing, soap manufacture and textile sectors. There are also import substitution industries such as motor cycle and bicycle assembly.
The main industrial centre is the Bangui district.

Tourism
The tourist sector is under-developed, although with a wealth of natural resources, the potential, especially for eco-tourism, is considerable. Tourism is expected to contribute around 3.0 per cent to the economy per year and provide employment to 2.4 per cent of the workforce.

Mining
The mining sector officially accounts for around 4 per cent of GDP, employs 3 per cent of the workforce and generates 40 per cent of the country's export earnings. Smuggling is endemic and production and trade is likely to be far higher than official estimates.

Around 80,000 autonomous artisanal miners are engaged in mining production, mostly of diamonds and gold. Diamond output is around 500,000 carats per year, over half of which are gem quality. Other mineral deposits include uranium, limestone, iron ore, copper and manganese. The Bozizé government withdrew mining licences and seized mines belonging to foreigners and figures associated with the government of former president Patassé. The measures were taken as part of an anti-corruption campaign which targetted divested interests associated with vital revenue-generating sectors.

Hydrocarbons

There are no known exploitable oil or gas reserves, but exploration is being undertaken in regions where the geology gives rise to high expectations of deposits, typically crossing international borders.
Domestic consumption was 2,000 barrels per day in 2008, all of which was imported. The Central African Republic does not have any oil refining capacity.
There are no known reserves of natural gas; coal reserves are negligible and any amounts being imported or consumed are not recorded.

Energy

Total installed generating capacity was 40MW in 2007, producing 110 million kilowatt hours (kWh), little of which is provided to the general population. The state-owned Energie Centrafricaine (Enerca) is responsible for electricity generation and operates the Boali, M'Bali and Gamboula hydroelectric dams, which between them provide 19MW; an additional 137MW is planned through a mixture of upgrading and expansion or existing plants, and by new ones. There are small-scale, isolated diesel generators providing the majority of the country's community needs. The majority of the population relies on non-commercial biomass, mostly fuel wood for cooking, lighting and power.
Power lines cross the border into the Democratic Republic of Congo (DRC) from where power is accessed.
In February 2009 the World Bank approved a grant of US$8 million to help rehabilitate the power infrastructure, including hydropower facilities, such as the Boali hydroelectric dam, to ensure more reliable supplies.

Financial markets

Stock exchange
Afribourse (Bourse Régionale des Valeurs Moblières) (BRVM)

Banking and insurance

Central bank
Banque des Etats de l'Afrique Centrale

Main financial centre
Bangui

Time

GMT plus one hour

Geography

The Central African Republic is a landlocked country in the heart of equatorial Africa. It is bounded by Chad to the north, and Sudan to the east, by the Republic of Congo and the Democratic Republic of Congo to the south and Cameroon to the west.
Most of the land is rolling or flat plateau, apart from the rising land in the west. Around 36 per cent of the country is covered in tropical forest particularly in the south-west. Desertification in the north-east has resulted in scrubland. The Chari River runs through the centre from the east.
Hemisphere
Northern

Climate

Hot all year with temperatures up to 36 degrees Celsius. The dry season runs from November–February with cooler nights. The rainy season runs from May–October.

Entry requirements

Passports
Required by all
Visa
Visas are required by all except citizens of surrounding countries, Israel and Switzerland. Visas can be issued in neighbouring countries, generally within 24 hours but are expensive. Visas can be obtained in advance from the Central African Republic Embassy in Paris, 30 rue des Perchamps, 75116 Paris.
A business letter and itinerary must accompany the application for a business visa.
Proof of onward/return passage is required.
Currency advice/regulations
No restrictions on import of foreign currency, but amounts must be declared; export up to declared amount allowed. Unlimited import of local currency; export limited to CFAf75,000.

Health (for visitors)

Mandatory precautions
Yellow fever vaccination certificate required by all.
Advisable precautions
Typhoid, tetanus, hepatitis A and polio vaccinations are recommended. Malaria prophylaxis should be taken as risk exists throughout country. There is a rabies risk. Water precautions are necessary – bilharzia risk in some areas. AIDS risk.

Hotels

Good standard hotels are available in Bangui – limited accommodation elsewhere. Where service charge is not included in bill a 10 per cent tip is usual.

Public holidays (national)

Fixed dates
1 Jan (New Year's Day), 29 Mar (President Boganda's Remembrance Day), 1 May (Labour Day), 30 Jun (Prayer Day), 13 Aug (Independence Day), 15 Aug (Assumption Day), 1 Nov (All Saints' Day), 1 Dec (National Day), 25 Dec (Christmas Day).
Variable dates
Easter Monday

Working hours

Banking
Mon–Fri: 0730–1230.
Business
Mon–Fri: 0730–1530.
Government
Mon–Fri: 0700–1200, 1430–1700; Sat: 0700–1200.
Shops
(Mon–Sat) 0800–1200; 1600–1900.

Telecommunications

Mobile/cell phones
A GSM 900 service is available in limited areas.

Electricity supply

220/380V AC, 50 cycles

Weights and measures

Metric system

Security

Full civil control following the 2003 coup has yet to be restored. Visitors are recommended not to travel to the Central African Republic unless it is absolutely necessary. When travelling outside the capital extra precautions should be taken and advice sort from local authorities and diplomatic missions.

Getting there

Air
National airline: Air France and Sudan Airways serve CAR.
International airport/s: Bangui-M'Poko (Code: BGF), 4km from city, restaurant, post office, shops, car hire.

Getting about

National transport
Air: Small light aircraft can be chartered.
Road: Eight main roads run from Bangui to the main towns and those that are surfaced are toll roads. The Trans-African Lagos-Mombasa highway passes through the Central African Republic. Most other roads can become impassable during rainy season. NB Spare parts and petrol stations tend to be rare outside Bangui.
Buses: Limited coach service operates between Bangui and Bangassou.
Water: Large volume of freight is carried on rivers. The principal trading route is on the Oubangui River south of the capital

Bangui which runs into the River Congo, connecting Bangui to the Democratic Republic of Congo and the Congo Republic (including Brazzaville, from where railway runs to Pointe-Noire). Also services from Salo on the Sangha River.

City transport

Taxis: Available in Bangui; fares by negotiation.

Car hire

Self- or chauffeur-driven cars available. International driving licence required.

BUSINESS DIRECTORY

The addresses listed below are a selection only. While World of Information makes every endeavour to check these addresses, we cannot guarantee that changes have not been made, especially to telephone numbers and area codes. We would welcome any corrections.

Telephone area codes

Dialling code for Central African Republic: IDD access code +236 followed by subscriber's number.

Chambers of Commerce

Chambre de Commerce, d'Industrie, des Mines et d'Artisinat de Centrafrique, PO Box 252/ 813, Bangui (tel: 611.668; fax: 613-561; e-mail: ccima@intnet.cf).

Chambre de d'Agriculture, d'Elevage, des Eaux, Forêts, Chasses, Pêches et du Tourisme, PO Box 850, Bangui (tel:/fax: 619-052; e-mail: denissio@intnet.cf).

Banking

Banque de Crédit Agricole et de Développement, BP 801, Place de la République, Bangui (tel: 613-200).

Banque Internationale pour le Centrafrique, BP 910, Place de la République, Bangui (tel: 610-042; fax: 616-136, 613-438).

Banque Populaire Maroco-Centrafricaine, BP 844, Rue Guerlliot, Bangui (tel: 613-190, 611-290; fax: 616-230).

Caisse Nationale d'Epargne, BP 839, Siège social, Bangui (tel: 612-296).

Commercial Bank Centrafrique SA, BP 839, Rue de Brazza, Bangui (tel: 612-990; fax: 613-454).

Central bank

Banque des États de l'Afrique Centrale, Direction Nationale, PO Box 851, Bangui (tel: 612-405; fax: 611-995; e-mail: beacbgf@beac.int).

Stock exchange

Afribourse (Bourse Régionale des Valeurs Moblières) (BRVM): www.brvm.org

Travel information

Inter-RCA, BP 1413, Bangui.

Ministry of Water, Forests, Wildlife, Fisheries and Tourism, Bangui.

Office Centrafricain de Tourisme (OCATOUR), BP 655, Bangui (tel: 614-566).

Ministries

Ministry of Economy and Finance, Planning and International Co-operation, Bangui (tel: 610-811).

Ministry of Energy, Mines, Geology and Water Resources, Bangui.

Ministry of Posts and Telecommunications, Bangui (tel: 612-946).

Ministry of Rural Development, Bangui (tel: 612-800).

Ministry of Trade, Industry and Small- and Medium-scale Enterprises, Bangui (tel: 614-488).

Ministry of Transport and Civil Aviation, Bangui (tel: 612-307).

Other useful addresses

Central African Republic Embassy (USA), 1618 22nd Street, NW, Washington DC 20008 (tel: 202-483-7800; fax: 202-332-9893).

European Development Fund, BP 1298, Bangui (tel: 613-053, 610-113).

Office of the President, Palais de la Renaissance, Bangui (tel: 610-323).

Société Centrafricaine de Développement Agricole (SOCADA), ave David Dacko, BP 997, Bangui (tel: 613-033).

National news agency: Centrafrique Presse, (email: info@centrafrique-presse.com; internet: www.centrafrique-presse.com).

Internet sites

Africa Business Network: http://www.ifc.org/abn

AllAfrica.com: http://allafrica.com

African Development Bank: http://www.afdb.org

Africa Online: http://www.africaonline.com

Mbendi AfroPaedia (information on companies, countries, industries and stock exchanges in Africa): http://mbendi.co.za

Chad

KEY FACTS

Official name: République du Tchad (Republic of Chad)

Head of State: President Colonel Idriss Déby Itno (MPS) (from 1996; re-elected 25 Apr 2011)

Head of government: Prime Minister Emmanuel Nadingar (from 5 Mar 2010)

Ruling party: Mouvement Patriotique du Salut (MPS) (Patriotic Movement for Salvation) (since 1997; re-elected 20 Feb 2011)

Area: 1,284,000 square km

Population: 11.50 million (2010)*

Capital: N'Djamena

Official language: French and Arabic

Currency: CFA franc (CFAf) = 100 centimes (Communauté Financière Africaine (African Financial Community) franc)

Exchange rate: CFAf488.90 per US$ (Oct 2011); CFAf655.95 per euro (pegged from Jan 1999)

GDP per capita: US$687 (2009)

GDP real growth: -0.90% (2009)

GDP: US$6.85 billion (2009)

Inflation: 10.10% (2009)

Oil production: 122,000 bpd (2010)

Balance of trade: -US$2.23 billion (2009)

* estimated figure

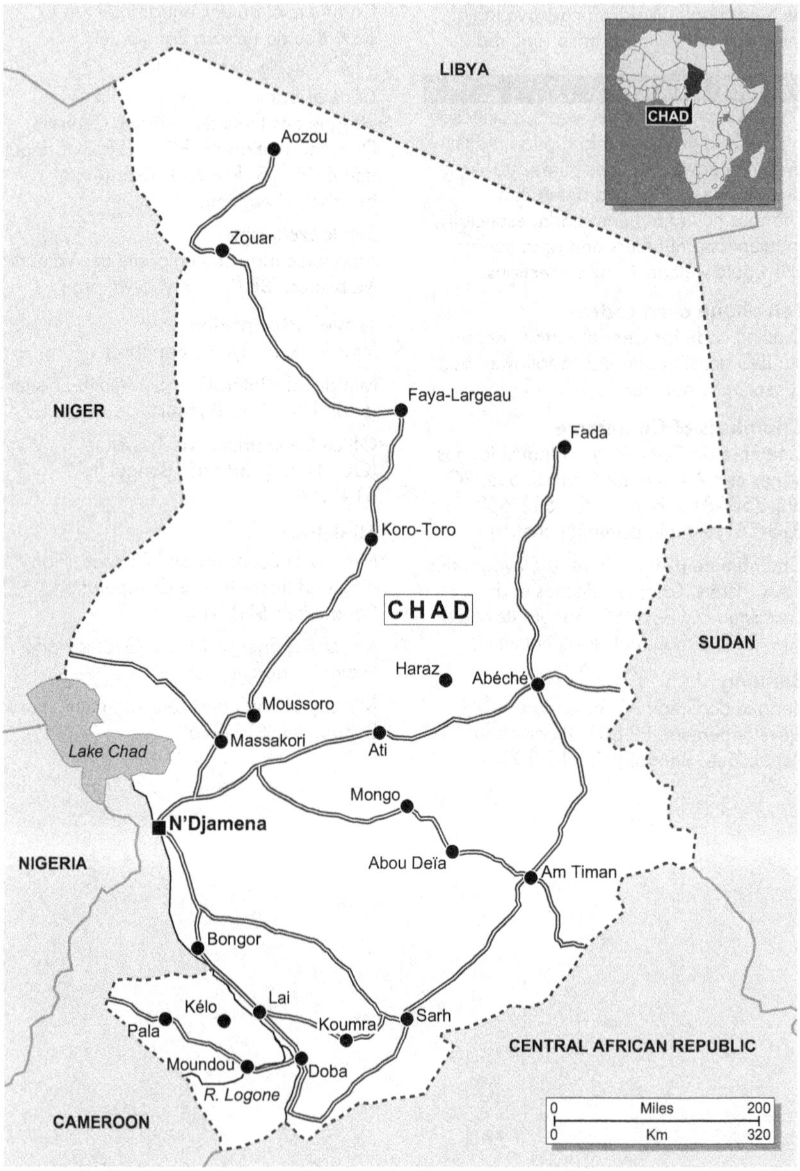

After decades of war, the lead up to Chad's latest elections was relatively calm. Even so, parliamentary elections that had been scheduled to take place on 28 November 2010 were postponed until 13 and 20 February 2011. The presidential election, which was due to be held on 3 April 2011 was finally held on 25 April, contested by three candidates, with a further three boycotting the vote claiming it would be an 'historic fraud' and that electoral reforms and issuance of new voter identification cards had failed. The general election was won by the ruling Mouvement Patriotique du Salut (MPS) (Patriotic Movement for Salvation) with 83 seats (out of 188) and, with the support of allies in parliament, retained power.

The presidential election was again won by Colonel Idriss Déby Itno of the MPS.

According to the *African Economic Outlook 2010* (AEO), published jointly by the African Development Bank and the Organisation for Economic Co-operation and Development, the economy did well in 2010, growing an estimated 5.9 per cent (up from 1.7 per cent in 2009), with the better security situation a key. For once there was no armed conflict in the country and the government tried to make up for lost time in several areas, including basic infrastructure, which significantly boosted growth (also spurred by higher world oil prices). Sparse rainfall and a bad 2009/10 harvest, which caused a food crisis, was offset by 7.2 per cent growth in the non-oil sector (up from 3.3 per cent in 2009). New investment produced modest oil sector growth of 0.6 per cent (after a 5.8 per cent contraction in 2009). As world demand picks up and construction, agriculture and oil sector investment continues, overall growth is expected to be 5.7 per cent in 2011 and 6.9 per cent in 2012, driven mostly by the non-oil sector, with growth rates of 6.8 per cent in 2011 and 7.4 per cent in 2012.

The primary sector was 58.1 per cent of GDP in 2010, with the economy's centrepiece, oil, 37.4 per cent of the sector, agriculture 9.7 per cent and livestock 8.7 per cent. The sector grew 3.6 per cent in the year (after contracting 3.8 per cent in 2009), helped by recovery from the previous bad harvest and investment to increase agricultural production. Oil output was practically the same as 2009, with 0.0 per cent growth (better than the 5.8 per cent drop in 2009) due to persistent water in deposits and lower pressure in oilfields. Despite a new refinery starting up soon, oil production will fall 1.1 per cent in 2011 and 3.6 per cent in 2012. With oil so dominant, the primary sector is expected in turn to shrink 3.3 per cent in 2011 and 2.6 per cent in 2012.

Oil and trade

Higher oil prices in 2010 greatly boosted the country's external position, with 33.8 per cent growth in goods exports and a strong 36.8 per cent increase in oil sector foreign direct investment (FDI). This reduced the overall balance of payments deficit to 2.4 per cent of GDP (from 10.8 per cent in 2009).

Goods exports were 44.4 per cent of GDP in 2010, 90 per cent of them oil, which increased 50.6 per cent mainly because of a rise in price of Chadian crude to US$72 a barrel (from US$52.8 in 2009), even though actual output fell slightly to 42.7 million barrels (from 43.1 million barrels in 2009) because of geological problems. All export items did well apart from cotton fibre, which was down 18 per cent (despite a 45 per cent world price increase) mainly owing to management problems at the state firm Société cotonnière du Tchad (CotonTchad) which holds the monopoly on all export sales.

Chad's economy is still heavily dependent on oil, which was 65.4 per cent of government revenue in 2010 and 90 per cent of export earnings. The country is in the process of joining the Extractive Industries Transparency Initiative (EITI), whose board approved its application in April 2010. On 9 June 2011 the EITI International Board extended Chad's Validation deadline by 6 months (until 15 October 2012), to allow Chad to bring its EITI reporting in line with the 2011 edition of the EITI Rules.

With oil dominant, no significant reform has been made in agriculture, which got only 2.8 per cent of primary sector current spending in 2010, with plans to raise it to 3.8 per cent in 2011, though this is far less than the 10 per cent set in 2003.

Goods imports were 27.7 per cent of GDP (up 0.4 per cent on 2009). Purchases of most items declined sharply because of the fall of the euro (to which the CFA franc is pegged) against the US dollar despite strong demand for equipment. But services imports rose 28.7 per cent, mainly due to robust government demand tied to major construction projects begun during the year, and increased demand (12.4 per cent) in oil sector construction and maintenance.

The current account deficit narrowed to 12.8 per cent of GDP in 2010 (from 16.9 per cent in 2009). The overall deficit of CfAO97.3 billion (US$200 million) (2.4 per cent of GDP) was funded mostly by the country's external reserves, which by the end of 2010 were sharply down to only 1.1 months of goods and services imports (from 1.7 months at the end of 2009). The current account deficit was expected to shrink further (to 9 per cent of GDP) in 2011–12 and the overall deficit was forecast to turn into a 2 per cent of GDP surplus. The steady decline in oil output may be amply compensated for by higher oil prices and the revival of cotton production. With the opening of an oil refinery and a cement factory, finished goods imports are expected to drop significantly, thus improving the external account.

The country's better external position, thanks to higher oil prices in 2010, also improved the debt situation and despite a 7.9 per cent nominal increase to US$2.1 billion at the end of 2010 (26.2 per cent of GDP, against 27.9 per cent in 2009), the ratio of debt to goods and services exports was much better, improving to 2.0 (from 3.1 in 2009).

The business climate did not improve in 2010 and Chad was still ranked 182nd out of 183 countries by the World Bank's 2011 *Doing Business* report on Ease of

KEY INDICATORS — Chad

	Unit	2006	2007	2008	2009	2010
Population	m	9.26	*9.49	*9.73	*9.97	*11.50
Gross domestic product (GDP)	US$bn	6.31	7.02	8.39	*6.85	–
GDP per capita	US$	680	*739	*862	*687	–
GDP real growth	%	0.1	*0.6	*0.3	*-0.9	–
Inflation	%	7.9	-7.4	8.3	10.1	–
Industrial output	% change	-3.7	2.5	5.5	–	–
Agricultural output	% change	3.2	-4.3	-4.6	–	–
Oil output	'000 bpd	153.0	144.0	127.0	118.0	122.0
Exports (fob) (goods)	US$m	3,479.0	3,875.0	4,526.9	*2,708.9	–
Imports (fob) (goods)	US$m	721.0	1,631.6	2,114.0	*2,539.0	–
Balance of trade	US$m	2,759.0	2,243.4	2,412.9	*171.3	–
Current account	US$m	485.0	*-745.0	*-1,511.0	*-2,230.0	–
Total reserves minus gold	US$m	625.1	955.1	1,345.5	616.7	632.4
Foreign exchange	US$m	624.6	954.5	1,344.9	612.0	627.8
Exchange rate	per US$	496.60	454.40	418.59	472.19	495.28

* estimated figure

starting a business. The time needed to set one up was 75 days, compared with an average 45.2 in the rest of sub-Saharan Africa and the number of procedures required was 13, above the regional average of 8.9. Annual tax on a firm's profits was 31.3 per cent (regional average 23.1 per cent) and the cost of importing and exporting goods about three times higher than the rest of the region. Property rights and business law are entrenched in the Organisation for the Harmonisation of Business Law in Africa (Ohada) rules that Chad ratified in 1996. Enforcement of them is hard, however, in the country's dysfunctional legal system. The private sector is also up against weak basic infrastructure and public services. Decades of war have seriously undermined the road network and energy supply, which is aggravated by landlocked Chad's capital being more than 1,000 kilometres from the nearest port, Douala (Cameroon).

The government stepped up efforts begun in 2009 to remedy the situation by investing much more (40.6 per cent of all public spending) in 2010, adopting a charter to improve the business climate and opening a one-stop shop to handle all formalities for setting up a business (involving taxes, customs, the justice and trade ministries and the social security department). The government also plans in 2011–12 to amend the investment and tax laws. It is already committed to such reforms under its 2008–11 poverty-reduction programme Stratégie Nationale de Réduction de la Pauvreté, deuxième génération (SNRP II) (National Strategy for the Reduction of the Poor II), but a May 2010 IMF report said political will to reform was still insufficient.

China and India

Since breaking with Chinese Taipei in 2006, Chad has been actively supported by Beijing, which has donated vehicles and constructed public buildings. Trade partnership, although important for motorcycle imports, is limited by the dynamism of neighbouring Nigeria, which supplies many manufactured goods.

China is, however, helping to fund an oil refinery being built at Djarmaya (45 kilometres from N'Djamena) and the laying of a 311km pipeline to carry crude from the Rônier and Mimosa oilfields at the rate of 20,000 barrels a day (with a maximum of 60,000 barrels a day). Work began in July 2009 with the aim of refining 1 million tonnes of crude a year from June 2011. China has a 60 per cent stake in the project through the China National Petroleum Corporation (CNPC) and the government has 40 per cent, which it paid for with a loan from Libya. Since Chad is landlocked, the refined oil will be sold on the local market and to neighbouring countries, starting with Niger and the Central African Republic (CAR). The refinery will also supply N'Djamena with about 20 megawatts (MW) of electricity.

China CAMC Engineering (a subsidiary of China National Machinery Industry Corporation), is building a CfAO37 billion (US$81.3 million) cement factory in the south-western town of Baoaré by mid-2011, the first time since independence that the country will be producing cement. Annual output will be 200,000 tonnes, partly meeting the country's needs of between 800,000 and 1,000,000 tonnes.

Another Chinese company, Soluxe International, a subsidiary of the Huayou Group, is building a US$150 million, 25 square-kilometre industrial park in Djarmaya, which will include hotels, factories making polypropylene fabrics, pressure vessels and plastic and a liquefied petroleum gas (LPG) bottling plant. China will pay for the whole project.

India is focusing on production facilities under its pan-African programme TEAM-9 (Techno Economic Approach for Africa-India Movement), which has loaned Chad US$50 million over 20 years at 2.5 per cent interest with five years grace. The Chadian government will contribute factory shells. The credit line, through the EXIM Bank, has already funded construction of a tractor assembly plant in N'Djamena, opened in November 2009 and turning out nine tractors a day (an annual production of 2,853 units), and renovation and reopening in December 2009 of a cotton mill at Sarh with an annual output of 8.5 tonnes of thread, 80 per cent of it for export. Also planned are a fruit-juice factory in the southern town of Doba, a plant producing rebar and a bicycle factory. The government fully owns all the factories built under the TEAM-9 programme but equipment and inputs are all imported from India or from Indian-owned firms. India plans to extend its aid soon to the pharmaceutical sector.

China and India take very different approaches to emerging-country partnerships. China reveals few details, with costs only estimated or sometimes unknown, and the partnership is run from the top, by the president or at ministry level. Senior officials say little about it. India, however, makes bilateral or multilateral agreements that are more open and initiatives often come from the emerging country.

China and India's activities have significant impact on the economy. The cotton mill has revived the industry in the countryside around Sarh and boosted exports of semi-finished textiles while encouraging local production. The tractor plant will help farming mechanisation and food self-sufficiency. The Djarmaya refinery will help Chad end the contradiction of producing oil but still importing it. By selling refined oil products to its neighbours, the country will improve its current account and also help regional integration. The cement factory will greatly boost construction as the country rebuilds. However, the activity of the emerging partners, especially China, has not created many jobs or increased transfer of skills, as most of the labour for the projects comes directly from the investing countries.

With peace being consolidated internally and externally, the biggest social challenge over the next few years is environmental. Chad is one of the world's most climatically vulnerable countries and in 2010 was hit by food shortages, severe flooding and a cholera epidemic that all seriously undermined social progress. The advancing desert and the drying-up of Lake Chad are already harming the nation's health and its agriculture, increasing poverty and threatening the peaceful cohabitation of farmers and the nomadic population. Preliminary results of the second population and housing census, RGPH2, which began in July 2008 and continued throughout 2009, showed a population of 11.2 million (50.7 per cent women, 49.3 per cent men), with a density of 8.7 per square kilometre in 2009 (up from 4.9 in 1993).

Risk assessment

Economy	Fair
Politics	Fair
Regional stability	Poor

COUNTRY PROFILE

Historical profile

1900s France defeated the local ruler, Rabeh Zubeit, at a battle in Kousseri in 1916, and the territory of Chad was formed.

1929 A northern, Saharan, segment was added.

1946 Chad was granted status as a French overseas territory with its own regional assembly.

1960 Chad was granted independence. A one-party regime was imposed under President Francois Tombalbaye. A series of rebellions against Tombalbaye's rule were repressed.

1975 Tombalbaye was killed in a coup and replaced by Colonel Félix Malloum. Malloum agreed to share power with rebel leader, Hissène Habré.
1979 Habré forced Malloum out of N'Djamena after a violent power struggle.
1980 A new alliance was formed between Habré and Goukouni Oueddei, which lasted until 1980 when Libya sided with Goukouni and Habré fled. Libyan troops and Chadian factions defeated Habré, at which point France intervened and the invading force was driven back from N'Djamena, leaving Habré in nominal control of the country.
1987 After several years of stalemate, President Mitterand of France and Colonel al Qadafi of Libya attempted to resolve the conflict, with both agreeing to withdraw their forces from Chad. The French troops withdrew but those of Libya did not. The French returned and pushed Libya back across the Chad-Libya border.
1989–90 A rebellion was launched by Idriss Déby, an army commander. Habré fled to Senegal and Déby proclaimed himself president.
1996 A new constitution was introduced, based on the French model. In Chad's first multi-party presidential elections, Idriss Déby was elected president.
1997 Legislative elections were won by the Mouvement Patriotique du Salut (MPS) (Patriotic Movement for Salvation).
2001 President Déby was re-elected. A peace agreement was signed in Libya between the Chadian government and the northern rebel movement, Mouvement pour la Démocratie et la Justice au Tchad (MDJT) (Movement for Democracy and Justice in Chad).
2002 The ruling MPS won the parliamentary elections. Haroun Kabadi was appointed prime minister by the president after the resignation of Nagoum Yamassoum.
2003 In January, Chad and the Central African Republic began peace talks. Moussa Faki became prime minister. Chad became an oil exporter, with the opening of a pipeline from its oil fields to Cameroon.
2004 Thousands of Sudanese refugees fleeing the unrest in the Darfur region of western Sudan arrived. Fighting between Chadian troops and pro-Sudanese government militias (Janjaweed) spilled across the border.
2005 Prime Minister Moussa Faki resigned and was replaced by Pascal Yoadimnadji. A referendum amended the constitutional with a 65.75 per cent approval vote, which removed the limit of terms in office for presidents; the senate to be replaced by a Cultural, Economic and Social Council.
2006 The World Bank suspended all loans to Chad as the government announced its intentions of steering oil revenue, originally destined for healthcare and education, to the military. Chad broke-off diplomatic relations with Sudan, following attacks on Chadian towns by Chad rebels based in the Darfur region of Sudan. An agreement was reached with the World Bank to resume loans and release oil revenue from an escrow account in return for an portion of petroleum profits being set aside for programmes for the poor. The presidential election, which was boycotted by the main opposition parties, was won by the incumbent Idriss Déby, giving him his third five-year term in office.
2007 An agreement was signed between Sudan, Chad and the Central African Republic, whereby no shelter would be given to rebel movements from each others countries. Prime Minister Pascal Yoadimnadji died; Adoum Younousmi became interim prime minister. Germany-based Transparency International declared Chad to be one of the most corrupt regimes in the world.
2008 A state of emergency was declared after a coup attempt. The rebels were defeated after two days and driven back towards the border with Sudan. The president dismissed Koumakoye and appointed Youssouf Saleh Abbas as prime minister. Former president, Hissène Habré, living in exile in neighbouring Senegal, was convicted of planning to overthrow the government and sentenced to death *in absentia*.
2009 A new rebel alliance, Union des Forces de Résistance (UFR) (Union of Resistance Forces) was established by eight local dissident groups. A UN peace-keeping force (Minurcat) took over from EU troops in eastern Chad.
2010 Chad and Sudan signed a peace agreement on 15 January. Youssouf Saleh Abbas resigned as prime minister in March and was replaced by Emmanuel Nadingar. At the request of Chad the UN agreed to withdraw its troops by the end of the year. According to the UNHCR in April, two million people were in need of food aid due to poor harvests in 2009–10. In August, the worst rains since the 1970s caused flooding that left thousands homeless as it destroyed entire villages and cultivated land.
2011 Parliamentary elections that had been scheduled to take place on 28 November 2010 took place on 13 and 20 February. The ruling MPS won 83 seats (out of 188) and, with the support of allies in parliament, retained power. The presidential election, which was due to be held on 3 April was finally held on 25 April, contested by three candidates, with a further three boycotting the vote claiming it would be an 'historic fraud' and that electoral reforms and issuance of new voter identification cards had failed. In presidential elections incumbent Idriss Déby (MPS) won 88.66 per cent of the vote; turnout was 64.22 per cent. By the end of April around 54,200 refugees had crossed the Sahara Desert to escape the conflict in Libya and were given refuge in camps in Chad. Senegal's foreign minister Madicke Niang announced on 10 July that Senegal was suspending the repatriation of Hissène Habré on the grounds that he might be tortured. Habré had been sentenced in 2008. President Déby took office again on 8 August; he immediately reappointed Emmanuel Nadingar as prime minister.

Political structure

Constitution

A new constitution was introduced in 1996, based on the French model with a strong executive branch and a legal system based on French civil law and Chadian customary law. However it has little *de facto* authority to provide civil liberties. Amendments agreed by referendum in 2005 removed the limit on terms in office for presidents; the justice system was subordinated to the executive branch; the senate was replaced by a Cultural, Economic and Social Council and the constitutional amendment process was moved to the president (rule by prerogative).

Form of state

Republic

The executive

The executive branch consists of the president who is head of state, and the prime minister and cabinet. The president is elected by popular vote to serve a five-year term; the prime minister is appointed by the president.

National legislature

The legislature consists of a National Assembly has 155 members elected by popular vote to serve four-year terms. However the president has not called for elections since 2002.

Legal system

Based on the French civil law system and customary law.

Last elections

13 and 20 February 2011 (parliamentary); 25 April 2011 (presidential)

Results: Parliamentary: Mouvement Patriotique du Salut (MPS) (Patriotic Movement for Salvation) won 83 seats (out of 188), Union Nationale pour la Démocratie et le Rénouveau (UNDR) (National Union for Democracy and Renewal) 10, Union pour le Rénouveau et la Démocratie (URD) (Union for Renewal and Democracy) eight, Rassemblement National pour la Démocratie au Tchad

(RNDT) (National Rally for Democracy in Chad) six; 21 other political parties shared the remaining 81 seats but none won more than four seats.
Presidential: Idriss Déby (MPS) won 88.66 per cent of the vote, Albert Pahimi Padacké (RNDT-le Réveil) 6.03 per cent, Nadji Madou (ASRI) 5.32 per cent; turnout was 64.22 per cent.
Next elections
2015 (parliamentary and presidential)

Political parties
Ruling party
Mouvement Patriotique du Salut (MPS) (Patriotic Movement for Salvation) (since 1997; re-elected 20 Feb 2011)
Main opposition party
Rassemblement pour la Démocratie et le Progrès (RDP) (Party for Democracy and Progress) and Front des Forces d'Action pour la République (FAR) (Action Forces for the Republic Front) have equal numbers of national assembly members.

Population
11.50 million (2010)*
Last census: April 1993: 6,279,931
Population density: Six inhabitants per square km. Urban population: 24 per cent (1995–2001).
Annual growth rate: 3.3 per cent 1994–2004 (WHO 2006)
Ethnic make-up
There are 200 distinct groups of Chadeans. In the north and centre: Arabs, Gorane (Toubou, Daza, Kreda), Zaghawa, Kanembou, Ouaddai, Baguirmi, Hadjerai, Fulbe, Kotoko, Hausa, Boulala, and Maba, most of whom are Muslim; in the south: Sara (Ngambaye, Mbaye, Goulaye), Moundang, Moussei, Massa, most of whom are Christian or animist. About 1,000 French citizens live in Chad. Of the population, 48 per cent of over 15s can read and write.
Religions
Muslim (44 per cent), traditional beliefs, Christians (33 per cent).

Education
As reform in the education sector has been slow following from the period of disturbances, local communities continue to play a greater role in financing and operating their schools. To rebuild the education system, the government of Chad developed an Education-Training-Employment strategy for 1990—2000 with the help of the International Labour Organisation, and other UN development agencies.
Five national programmes were developed including basic, secondary, higher education and research, vocational training and literacy. Estimates show that the programme has trained some 2,400 teachers and 1,000 classrooms have been built.
French is the primary language of instruction in most higher education institutions. The University of N'Djamena is the country's main university, with three faculties.
Literacy rate: 46 per cent adult rate; 70 per cent youth rate (15–24) (Unesco 2005).
Enrolment rate: 73 per cent gross primary enrolment, 12 per cent gross secondary enrolments; of relevant age groups, inlcuding repeaters (World Bank).
Pupils per teacher: 67 in primary schools.

Health
As one of the poorest countries in the world, Chad has the largest proportion of external resources committed to health at 62.9 per cent of all spending on healthcare.
Unicef and the Public Health Ministry began a campaign to inoculate nearly 90,000 children – half of them Sudanese refugees – against measles in the most remote areas, in 2004; their target was children aged between six months and 15 years. As well as the inoculations, staff distributed Vitamin A to children to reinforce their immune systems and protect them from blindness.
HIV/Aids
HIV prevalence: 4.8 per cent aged 15–49 in 2003 (World Bank)
Life expectancy: 46 years, 2004 (WHO 2006)
Fertility rate/Maternal mortality rate: 6.7 births per woman, 2004 (WHO 2006)
Child (under 5 years) mortality rate (per 1,000): 117 per 1,000 live births (World Bank)
Head of population per physician: 0.04 physicians per 1,000 people, 2004 (WHO 2006)

Welfare
An old age pension is paid at age 55 to workers with full contributions who pay 2 per cent of their wages. An employer pays 10 per cent of a worker's wage overall, for old age, disability and survivors' pensions. The government does not pay social security benefits. Roughly half the workforce has no jobs.
While Chad remains a traditional society, the role of women is expected to remain unchanged. Female Genital Mutilation (FGM) is practiced on 60 per cent of females, prior to puberty; and girls as young as 11 may be forced into an arranged marriage. Wives are subservient to their husbands and domestic violence is not uncommon. In 2003 a law was passed prohibiting FGM.

Main cities
N'Djamena (capital – formerly Fort Lamy – estimated population 751,288 in 2005), Moundou (140,830), Sarh (106,823), Abéché (77,296), Koumra (37,782).

Languages spoken
The language group in Chad is Afro-Asiatic; Arabic is spoken by most of the population and there are more than 50 African dialects.
Official language/s
French and Arabic

Media
Press
Newspapers are generally considered to be independent; however they have small circulations and are not distributed much beyond urban areas.
In French, daily newspapers include *Le Progres* and *Tchadien* (www.tchadien.com), other, weekly, private newspapers includes *N'Djamena Hebdo* (http://www.chez.com/ndjamenahebdo), and *Le Temps*, *Le Contact* is a bi-weekly.
Broadcasting
Radio: With high levels of illiteracy, radio services are the main medium of mass communication and sources of news and information.
The government-owned, Radiodiffusion Nationale Tchadienne, operates a national and three regional stations. Private radio stations include FM Liberté, owned by international human rights groups, Dja FM and Al Nassr are privately owned and La Voix du Paysan and Radio Arc-en-ciel are Roman Catholic stations.
Television: In Arabic and French, the only television station is the state-owned Téléchad, which favours the government.
News agencies
Afrik (French based): www.afrik.com/tchad
Africa News Agency: www.africanewsagency.co.uk
APA: www.apanews.net
Panapress: www.panapress.com

Economy
Chad is one of the poorest countries in the world, with a Human Development Index (HDI) ranking of 163 (out of 169) in 2010. Its economy is dependent on subsistence farming and foreign aid. The formal sector of GDP is officially made up of around 50 per cent industry, services at less than 40 per cent and the remainder by agriculture; a larger, more vibrant informal sector also operates. Exports include, cotton, cattle and gum Arabic, as well as some minerals including petroleum, gold, bauxite, natron and iron ore. Manufacturing production includes meat

packing, beer brewing and soft drinks bottling and construction materials.
GDP growth was -0.4 per cent in 2008, and fell further to an estimated -1.6 per cent in 2009, due to poor rainfall that cut agricultural production, and a fall in oil production (down from 127,000 barrels per day (bpd) in 2009 to 118,000bpd), at the same time as government expenditure grew. However, according to the International Monetary Fund (IMF) in a 2010 report GDP growth in 2010 was projected to have grown by 4.3 per cent as petroleum exports rose in value as world prices grew.
Development investment, in one of Africa's smallest oil fields, began in 2001 and oil production began in 2003, with the completion of the Doba oil pipeline (allowing Chad to export its oil via Cameroon). Despite production forecast to peak at 225,000 barrels per day (bpd), the country will remain dependent on imports of refined petroleum products as there are no refineries. Investment by the government in the project was only possible through support by the World Bank, which agreed to loans on the proviso that a proportion of dividend payments from the oil production should be invested in socio-economic growth to enhance the living standards of the population. However, the World Bank judged that Chad had failed to undertake the necessary measures and withdrew from the agreement, demanding repayment of its loans; Chad complied in 2009.
The economy has been undergoing a programme of liberalisation under the auspices of the IMF's Poverty Reduction and Growth Facility (PRGF). This has been coupled with debt service relief under an enhanced Heavily Indebted Poor Countries (HIPC) initiative. The government has privatised public enterprises, aimed at securing macroeconomic stability and strengthening its fiscal position.

External trade

Chad is a member of the Communauté Économique et Monétaire de l'Afrique Centrale (Cemac) (Economic and Monetary Community of Central Africa), which operates a customs union with import taxes and capital flowing freely among member states; import duties, levied on third parties, are pooled and shared between members.

Imports

Principal imports are machinery and transport equipment, industrial goods, petroleum products, foodstuffs and textiles.
Main sources: France (typically 18 per cent of total), Cameroon (13 per cent), China (11 per cent).

Exports

Principal exports are petroleum, raw cotton, fish, meat and cattle, hides, sodium carbonate (natron), ground nuts, gum Arabic and resins.
Main destinations: US (typically 90 per cent of total), France (5 per cent), China (2 per cent).

Agriculture

Farming

The agricultural sector forms the mainstay of the economy, accounting for around 40 per cent of GDP and 60 per cent of employment. Around 20 per cent of land is arable and most of this is the southern flood plains of the Logone and Chari rivers.
Rice is produced on the irrigated land along the banks of the Oubangi river north of Lake Chad. Subsistence farming and livestock predominate in the north.
The country's main food crops are sorghum, millet, dry beans, sesame, potatoes, rice and maize. Cash crops include oil seeds (groundnuts and sesame), sugar cane and tobacco. Cotton is the most important agricultural product.
Cattle farming involves nearly 40 per cent of the population. It contributes 39 per cent to total agricultural production and 20 per cent to Chad's GDP. About 90 per cent of beef production is exported to Nigeria.

Industry and manufacturing

The industrial sector contributes around 15 per cent of GDP and employs 10 per cent of the workforce.
The sector is small-scale and underdeveloped. Activity is centred in N'Djamena, Moundou and Sarh and is based on agriculture, particularly food processing, textiles, brewing, tobacco processing, leather and construction materials.

Environment

In June 2010 the African Union backed a proposal to build the 'Great Green Wall' project, of a 15km wide, 7,775km long, continuous belt of trees from Senegal in the west to Djibouti in the east (traversing 11 countries) in an effort to halt the advance of the Sahara Desert. The trees to be used would be drought-adapted, preferably native to the area from a list of 37 possible species, and should help to slow soil erosion and filter rain water.

Mining

Mining contributes less than 3 per cent to GDP. The only minerals extracted in any quantities are soda and rock salt (which are exported mainly to Nigeria) and natron from Lake Chad (used in preservation of meat and in tanning).
Known deposits of chromium, tungsten, titanium, iron, wolfram, gold, uranium and tin remain unexploited.
Other mineral deposits are thought to lie in the disputed Aouzou Strip along the Libyan border.

Hydrocarbons

At the end of 2007, Chad had proven oil reserves of 1.5 billion barrels, most of which is located in the Doba basin; production was 144,000 barrels per day (bpd). As a landlocked country oil is exported via the Chad-Cameroon oil pipeline, opened in 2003. There are no downstream facilities for refining and all exports are crude oil. Nigeria and Cameroon provide refined oil to Chad, which imports around 143,000bpd. There are plans to build a small refinery in N'Djamena to process the oil from Sedigi in the Lake Chad Basin. Industry experts consider Chad to have more undiscovered oil reserves; West Africa is one of the world's fastest growing oil regions.
The upstream oil industry is regulated by the Ministère des Mines, de l'Energie et du Pétrole (MMEP) (ministry of mines, energy and oil). The China National Petroleum Corporation (CNPC) and the government signed a memorandum of understanding in August 2009 to operate an oil refinery north of N'Djamena. Construction of the refinery began in 2008; it is 60 per cent owned by CNPC and 40 per cent by the government. CNPC also began construction of a 300 km oil pipeline from the Koudalwa oil field to the refinery in October 2009; it is scheduled to be completed by 2013.
Chad is not known to have either natural gas or coal reserves and nor does it import either in commercial quantities.

Energy

Chad had an installed electricity generation capacity of 30MW in 2007, which generated 90 million kilowatt hours. Only 2 per cent of the population have access to electricity with the rest relying on biofuel for domestic use. The electricity supply is provided by two power stations in N'Djamena and plants in Moundou, Sarh and Abéché. Imports from Nigeria and Cameroon provide most of Chad's power requirements. The World Bank has identified the necessity for an even distribution of regional energy, including electricity and gas, and in 2008 was prepared to find funding for a detailed assessment of the feasibility of such a programme of provision of infrastructure.
The Société Tchadienne d'Eau et d'Électricité (STEE) is the company responsible for electricity generation and supply in Chad.

Banking and insurance

The banking sector was fully privatised in 1999. The two main banks in Chad are the Banque Internationale de l'Afrique au

Tchad (BIAT) and the Société Générale de Banque Tchadienne (SGBT).

Central bank

Banque des Etats de l'Afrique Centrale.

Main financial centre

N'Djamena

Time

GMT plus one hour

Geography

Chad is a landlocked country in north and central Africa, bordered in the north by Libya, the east by Sudan, the south by the Central African Republic, the south-west by Cameroon, to the west by Nigeria and the north-west by Niger.

Lake Chad is a large body of freshwater that forms part of the border in the south-west and is fed largely by the Chari River.

There are tropical forests in the south and the Sahara desert stretches across the north, which includes Ennedi and Tibesti volcanic mountain ranges.

Hemisphere

Northern

Climate

Hot and arid in northern desert regions, and wet and tropical in the south. Southern rainy season from May to October, central rainy season from June to September with temperatures ranging from 20 degrees Celsius (C) at night to as high as 40 degrees C during the day. Dry season throughout the rest of the year, lower evening temperatures.

Entry requirements

Passports

Required by all except nationals of certain African countries. Passports must be valid for six months after date of visit.

Visa

Required by all, except a number of nationals of West and Central Africa.

Ordinary visas are issued for both business and tourist purposes, valid for one month. Apply at either a Chadian consulate or a French consulate.

All visitors must register with authorities on arrival. Exit permits must also be obtained if leaving via Niger or Sudan.

Currency advice/regulations

The import and export of CFA francs from outside the African Financial Community is limited to CFAf10,000; import of CFA francs from inside the community is unlimited. There is unlimited import of foreign currency but it must be declared on arrival; export of foreign currency is limited to declared amount.

To avoid extra exchange fees US dollars or euros are preferred.

Health (for visitors)

Mandatory precautions

Yellow fever vaccination certificate required if arriving from an infected area.

Advisable precautions

Hepatitis A, tetanus, typhoid and polio vaccinations. Malaria prophylaxis recommended as risk exists throughout the country. There is a rabies risk. Water precautions necessary outside the capital.

Hotels

Reservations should be made well in advance of visit. If service charge is not included in bill a 10 per cent tip is usual. Limited availability outside of N'Djamena.

Public holidays (national)

Fixed dates

1 Jan (New Year's Day), 13 Apr (National Day), 1 May (Labour Day), 25 May (Africa Day), 11 Aug (Independence Day), 1 Nov (All Saints' Day), 28 Nov (Proclamation of the Republic), 1 Dec (Day of Liberty and Democracy), 25 Dec (Christmas Day).

Variable dates

Easter Monday, Eid al Adha, Eid al Fitr.

Islamic year 1433 (26 Nov 2011–14 Nov 2012): The Islamic year contains 354 or 355 days, with the result that Muslim feasts advance by 10–12 days against the Gregorian calendar. Dates of feasts vary according to the sighting of the new moon, so cannot be forecast exactly.

Working hours

Banking

Mon–Thu and Sat: 0700–1300; Fri: 0700–1030.

Business

Mon–Sat: 0900–1230, 1600–1930.

Government

Mon–Thu and Sat: 0700–1400; Fri: 0700–1200. Specific times vary within this period.

Shops

Tue–Sat: 0900–1200; 1600–1930.

Telecommunications

Mobile/cell phones

GSM 900 services are available in populated areas only.

Electricity supply

220V AC, 50 cycles

Getting there

Air

National airline: Government owned Air Tchad provides only domestic flights. International flights are best provided by Air France.

International airport/s: N'Djamena (NDJ), 4km from city. Facilities include a post office, refreshments, bar, duty-free and car hire.

Airport tax: CFAf5,000 (tourist tax) and CFAf3,000 (security tax), except transit passengers continuing their journey within 24 hours.

Surface

Road: Access is possible via Sarh (Central African Republic), Bongor and Maroua (Cameroon). There is a paved road through the province of Kanem to Ngiugmi in Niger – the road runs to the Nigerian border.

Road conditions are variable and access can be very difficult, especially in the rainy season; driving is best undertaken between November and May.

It is dangerous to drive in the border region of Chad and Sudan, due to the situation in Darfur, Sudan.

Water: The main overland points of entry by ferry are via the Logone River (Cameroon) and Lake Chad (Nigeria).

Getting about

National transport

Air: Restricted domestic service operated by Air Tchad. Scheduled services occasionally commandeered by armed forces.

Road: Permits and four-wheel drive vehicles are required for all travel outside N'Djamena. Conditions are arduous, there are no emergency services; rest houses and petrol stations are not widely available. The government restricts travel in the central and northern territories. It is advisable to travel in convoy.

There are surfaced roads around N'Djamena; most other roads are not in good condition and are often impassable during rainy season (Jun–Oct).

City transport

Taxis: Available in N'Djamena and the principal towns – Sarh and Moundou; set-fare system in operation; 10 per cent tip is usual; can be hired on a time basis or by the day.

Car hire

Availablity is limited to N'Djaména only. French or international driving licence is required as well as a *autorisation de circuler*.

BUSINESS DIRECTORY

The addresses listed below are a selection only. While World of Information makes every endeavour to check these addresses, we cannot guarantee that changes have not been made, especially to telephone numbers and area codes. We would welcome any corrections.

Telephone area codes

The international dialling code (IDD) for Chad is + 235 followed by subscriber's number.

Chambers of Commerce

Chad Chamber of Commerce, Industry, Agriculture, Mines and Handicrafts, PO Box 458, N'Djamena (tel: 525-264; fax: 521-452; e-mail: cciamat@hotmail.com).

Banking

Banque Agricole du Soudan au Tchad, BP 1727, 1727 N'Djamena (tel: 519-041, 519-042; fax: 519-040).

Banque Commerciale du Chari Tchad, BP 757, N'Djamena (tel: 515-958, 515-231; fax: 516-249).

Banque de Développement du Tchad, BP 19, N'Djamena (tel: 522-829, 523-284; fax: 523-318).

Banque Internationale pour l'Afrique au Tchad, BP 87, Ave Charles de Gaulle, N'Djamena (tel: 525-684, 524-321; fax: 523-053, 522-345).

Banque Tchadienne de Crédit et de Dépôts, BP 461, N'Djamena (tel: 524-203, 522-801, 524-195; fax: 523-713).

Financial Bank, BP 804, N'Djamena (tel: 523-389, 522-660; fax: 522-905).

Central bank

Banque des États de l'Afrique Centrale, Direction Nationale, PO Box 50, N'Djamena (tel: 525-014; fax: 524-487; e-mail: beacndj@beac.int).

Banque des États de l'Afrique Centrale, (headquarters), 736 Ave Monseigneur Vogt, 1917 Yaoundé, Cameroon (tel: +237 223-4030/4060; fax: (+237) 223-3329/3350; email: beac@beac.int

Travel information

Air Tchad, 27 Avenue du Président Tombalbaye, BP 168, N'Djamena (tel: 515-090, 513-581, 514-564).

Direction du Tourisme, BP 86, N'Djamena (tel: 515-032, 512-303, 512-305).

Ethiopian Airlines, BP 989, N'Djamena (tel: 513-027, 513-143).

Sudan Airways, BP 167, N'Djamena (tel: 515-148).

National tourist organisation offices

Direction du Tourisme, BP 86, N'Dajmena (tel: 524-416; fax: 524 419).

Other useful addresses

Chad Embassy (USA), 2002 R Street, NW, Washington DC 20009 (tel: 202-462-4009; fax: 202-265-1937; e-mail: info@chadembassy.org; internet: www.chadembassy.org).

Chambre Consulaire du Tchad, BP 458, N'Djamena (tel: 515-264).

Commission for Trade and Industry, BP 453, N'Djamena (tel: 515-656).

European Development Fund, BP 532, N'Djamena (tel: 515-977, 512-276).

Office National des Céréales (ONC), BP 21, N'Djamena (tel: 513-731, 574-014).

Internet sites

Africa Business Network: http://www.ifc.org/abn

AllAfrica.com: http://allafrica.com

African Development Bank: http://www.afdb.org

Africa Online: http://www.africaonline.com

Chad: http://www.tchadrepertoire.com

Mbendi AfroPaedia (information on companies, countries, industries and stock exchanges in Africa): http://mbendi.co.za

Chile

KEY FACTS

Official name: República de Chile (Republic of Chile)

Head of State: President Sebastián Piñera Echenique (from 11 Mar 2010)

Head of government: President Sebastián Piñera (from 11 Mar 2010)

Ruling party: Coalition led by Coalición por el Cambio (CC) (Coalition for Change) (alliance of five parties) (from 2010)

Area: 756,626 square km

Population: 16.98 million (2009)*

Capital: Santiago

Official language: Spanish

Currency: Chilean peso (CH$) = 100 centavos

Exchange rate: CH$523.48 per US$ (Oct 2011)

GDP per capita: US$11,828 (2010)

GDP real growth: 5.30% (2010)

GDP: US$203.30 billion (2010)

Labour force: 7.10 million (2010)

Unemployment: 8.30% (2010)

Inflation: 1.50% (2010)

Balance of trade: US$15.86 billion (2010)

* estimated figure

By Latin American standards the Chilean population is politically relatively mature. They coped well with the limitations of the transition to democracy, not least the lingering popular support for the dictatorship's political parties. Chile has not seen any massive demand for change and confrontation and Chileans know that time takes care of many problems. Thus the same stoicism that enabled many Chileans to cope with the excesses of the dictatorship has also enabled them to understand and accept the limitations of democracy.

Growth

Chile's economy has been recovering from the global financial crisis since 2009, as well as the after-effects of a major earthquake in February 2010. Uncertainty over the knock-on effects of the European sovereign debt crisis initially caused gross domestic product (GDP) growth estimates for 2010 to be revised downwards to around 4.5 per cent; annualised output growth was 1.6 per cent in the first quarter. Thanks to a rebound in consumption, especially of durable goods and in machinery and equipment investment, GDP grew by 6.6 per cent in the second quarter and 7 per cent in the third. GDP growth for the year overall was expected to be around 5.5 per cent. A substantial upturn in investment during 2010 was estimated to have boosted potential GDP in 2011 by 5 per cent. GDP growth projections were put at between 6 per cent and 6.5 per cent for 2011.

A deficit of 1 per cent of GDP was estimated for 2010, corresponding to a structural deficit of 2.3 per cent. The trend towards lower deficits was to be maintained in 2011, given the slower spending growth stipulated in the budget bill presented by the new government. Consolidated central government spending was expected to expand by 5.5 per cent in real terms in 2011 which, in conjunction with the projected recovery in tax revenues and continuing high copper prices, was expected to give a structural deficit of 1.8 per cent.

Monetary policy continued to be guided by an annual inflation target of 3 per cent with a range of 1 per cent on either side. By October 2010 the monetary policy rate stood at an annualised rate of 2.75 per cent. Although the outlook for inflation was not expected to change substantially, it was thought that the Banco Central de Chile(BCC) (central bank) would continue to raise the reference rate as part of the gradual withdrawal of monetary stimulus.

Chile's exchange-rate policy continued to be based on a floating regime. As the dollar weakened against other currencies, terms of trade improved in 2010 and some foreign currency holdings were sold to cover the fiscal deficit. The peso posted an average nominal appreciation of 8 per cent over the first 11 months of the year relative to its average level in 2009. This is equivalent to an appreciation of some 6 per cent in the real exchange rate over that period.

In April 2010, on a seasonally adjusted basis, the economy had regained its output level of June 2008, the peak prior to the global financial crisis. The fastest-growing sectors were those that are linked to domestic demand, driven by the strength of spending. The highest growth rates were registered by the electricity, gas and water sectors.

In the fisheries sector, the effects of the salmon virus and the scarcity of deep-sea resources resulted in a negative performance. The agriculture and forestry sector has suffered the consequences of earthquake damage to export infrastructure, combined with slacker demand for forestry products. Mining has sustained a slow upturn since mid-2009 and manufacturing began to recover gradually in the second quarter following two years of continuous decline. According to the Instituto Nacional de Estadística de Chile (INE) (National Statistical Institute), industrial production peaked in March 2008, bottomed out in February 2009 and has followed an irregular pattern thereafter.

Chile's inflation has risen steadily from the negative values observed during the crisis, but has remained low and within its target range. As of October, the 12-month variation was 2 per cent and cumulative inflation over the year was 2.8 per cent. A pick-up in inflation during the whole of 2011 cannot be ruled out, however, given the rate at which idle capacity has been brought back into production in response to domestic demand well in excess of output growth.

In 2010 Chile's exports were sluggish, with little growth in most of the main categories. Mining exports were at a level similar to that of 2009, while exports of agricultural, forestry and fisheries products edged up thanks to the buoyancy of fruit exports. Indices for industrial exports, meanwhile, remained below their pre-crisis peaks and drifted downwards. By contrast, consumer and capital goods imports were strongly up in volume terms.

Copper prices began to climb in the second quarter of 2010 in a context of fairly low global copper inventories combined with dollar weakness and by October were just short of the high posted shortly before the global crisis. Conversely, with the exception of oil, most imported products did not rise significantly in price relative to 2009.

Against this background, the 2009 current account surplus of 2.6 per cent of GDP recorded was expected to be followed by a small deficit in 2010 partly caused by strong import growth resulting from vigorous domestic demand. This situation is expected to carry over into 2011, with a projected deficit of 2.5 per cent. Chile's balance of payments financial account was notable for the rapid growth of foreign direct investment (FDI) flows into Chile. This was accompanied by frequent capital outflows in the form of portfolio investment abroad and, on occasions, by outflows of other investments.

Unrest

In March 2010 President Piñera had been the nation's hero. His government was able to bask in the reflected glory surrounding the rescue, alive, of 33 trapped miners who had been underground for two months. By the middle of 2011, however, all that seemed to have been forgotten as Chile went from protest to protest and the president's popularity rating fell to a lowly 31 per cent, the lowest figure ever recorded.

The first serious protests that the government had to deal with were those triggered by the government's decision to approve the large HidroAysén hydroelectric project involving two rivers, the

KEY INDICATORS — Chile

	Unit	2006	2007	2008	2009	2010
Population	m	16.38	16.58	16.80	*16.98	*17.09
Gross domestic product (GDP)	US$bn	145.21	163.79	169.60	161.80	203.30
GDP per capita	US$	8,903	9,901	10,124	9,525	11,828
GDP real growth	%	4.0	5.0	3.2	-1.5	5.3
Inflation	%	3.4	4.4	8.7	1.7	1.5
Unemployment	%	6.0	7.2	7.8	9.8	8.3
Industrial output	% change	2.7	1.0	0.7	-4.1	–
Agricultural output	% change	3.5	1.7	2.1	0.5	–
Exports (fob) (goods)	US$m	58,485.0	67,644.0	66,455.0	53,735.0	71,028.0
Imports (fob) (goods)	US$m	35,899.0	43,991.0	57,610.0	39,754.0	55,174.0
Balance of trade	US$m	22,587.0	23,653.0	8,846.0	13,982.0	15,855.0
Current account	US$m	5,256.0	6,050.0	-3,439.0	4,217.0	3,802.0
Total reserves minus gold	US$m	19,392.0	16,386.8	23,072.4	25,283.5	27,816.3
Foreign exchange	US$m	19,224.9	16,695.3	22,848.6	23,849.3	26,317.8
Exchange rate	per US$	527.68	498.75	522.46	560.86	510.25

* estimated figure

Baker and the Pascua. Costing an estimated US$7 billion, the whole project will include five hydroelectric plants and a transmission network. The power generated will total 2,750MW, an increase of 35 per cent to Chile's current generating capacity. The approval of the project by local authorities sent the shares of the two designated engineering companies – Colbun and Spanish-owned Endesa – climbing. The decision also saw protests in the local town of Coyhaique as well as in downtown Santiago. Initially, the determination of the protesters took the authorities by surprise, but following the deployment of mounted police, water cannon and tear gas, the protests were brought under control and over 100 protesters arrested. The anticipated environmental damage to the area stemmed from the planned flooding of almost 6,000 hectares. Environmental protection group Conservación Patagónica claimed that the project not only risked ruining the landscape, but also decimating the population of South Andean deer and endangering fish stocks.

As the year wore on, the 'limitations of democracy' began to become increasingly apparent as national protests took hold. By August 2011, the demonstrations had merged with a two day general strike and hunger strikes that had entered their sixth week. That most of the protesters were students also gave the government cause for concern. Education has certainly been the Achilles heel of the Chilean social system. High growth rates may have brought prosperity; but not for all. Nowhere is this more apparent than in education, where the offspring of the country's wealthiest quartile are sent to well-equipped private schools and the remainder languish in schools that are manifestly inadequate in every respect. According to the Organisation for Economic Co-operation and Development (OECD) (which Chile joined in 2010) Chile spends less on education than any other member nation.

It was hardly surprising therefore, that union leaders saw education inequality as an excellent opportunity to attack Mr Piñera's government. In August 2011 union leaders launched a two day strike as the President's approval rating continued to drop, reaching 26 per cent. Endeavouring to take the high ground in the dispute, Mr Piñera acknowledged that Chile was facing a number of problems. On the eve of the strike he said that 'We are aware that our country has many overdue debts, many problems that have not yet been solved.' The contrast with the beginning of Mr Piñera's presidential term was marked. Immediately upon assuming power, he had seemed to deal competently with the chaos and after effects of Chile's earthquake. Then, against all the odds, the 33 miners had been rescued, allowing Mr Piñera's popularity rating to reach 63 per cent. In macro-economic terms, Chileans had little to complain about. But the striking workers felt, with some justification, that widespread reforms were needed. The slogan of the Confederación Unida de Trabajadores (CUT) labour confederation was that 'Chile can and must be different'.

As the unrest continued, Mr Piñera was forced on to the back foot, recognising that 'the Chilean model is not broken, but it does need some adjustment.' Others doubted whether their billionaire President and his cabinet of wealthy businessmen were really aware of their country's deficiencies. Mr Piñera's early successes, combined with Chile's macro-economic successes (growth in the second quarter of 2011 was 6.8 per cent) appeared to blind the President and his ministers to the need for reform. This included the educational reforms – in Chile's free market, students can end up on graduation with debts in excess of US$40,000. Mr Piñera has announced plans to provide an extra US$1 billion funding for Chile's poorer students. Other reforms sought by the protesters included tax, healthcare, labour and pensions, as well as a new constitution. Many saw the clashes as reflecting a rift in Chilean society that dated back to the divisions of the Pinochet era.

Peso weapon

The beginning of 2011 saw Chile girding its loins to participate in what had become known, rather melodramatically, as the 'global currency wars'. In early January the Banco Central de Chile (BCC) (central bank) announced that it would spend as much as US$12 billion in 2012 to restrain the national currency's strength. The objective was to rein in the peso's strength and give Chile's exporters a more competitive edge. The announcement coincided with the news that the peso had risen to a three year high against the dollar. The following day, it appeared that the policy was working, as the peso's value against the dollar fell by around four per cent. The BCC planned to spend US$50 million a day selling pesos. This corresponded to around six per cent of Chile's GDP.

Although the bank's intervention was essentially seen and defined by the BCC as an export promotion move, it later changed its tack, claiming that the move was aimed at creating a cushion of foreign currency reserves equivalent to 17 per cent of GDP to protect Chile from the possible effect of the eurozone debt crisis. The increased reserves, it was expected, would also protect Chile from the continued effects of low interest rates and the depreciation of the US dollar.

Chile was one of many Latin American economies where some sort of currency intervention had been adopted to weaken the effect of currency appreciation. By intervening early in the year, the BCC and the Chilean government, hoped to adhere to a forecast growth rate for 2011 of six per cent. The price of copper had continued to rise, reaching a record high of US$9,754 per tonne at the beginning of 2011. Interest rates in Chile stood at 3.25 per cent at the beginning of 2011, with inflation forecast at 3.3 per cent.

Easter Island

President Piñera's appointment of Pedro Edmunds Paoa as governor of the Pacific island in March 2010 did not go down well with the islanders. Before long there were murmurings that Mr Paoa was involved in land speculation. Mr Paoa tendered his resignation, but President Piñera sent a team of investigators to calm the colonial waters. These had been made choppier following the submission of a letter from the island's 'parliament' seeking secession from Chile. The islanders alternative would be some sort of link with the Pacific Polynesian states. The letter was addressed to President Piñera and also sent to the Pacific Island Forum. The parliament is in fact a pressure group representing the islands' indigenous people. The parliament represents about half the islands' population (of under 5,000). Mr Paoa was replaced by Carmen Cardinali in August.

Easter Island, a Unesco world heritage site, was annexed by Chile in 1888. The claimed links with Chile are at best tenuous – the islands are over 3,200km from the province of Valparaíso of which (technically) it forms a part. The islanders grievances centred on what they described as an 'uncontrolled' influx of tourists and government appropriation of ancestral land for state offices. Indigenous protesters have on occasion occupied state offices. Not all the island's indigenous community were in favour of secession. Alberto Hotus, the octogenarian head of the island's elders council went so far as to say that the territory could not survive without mainland support. Mr Hotus added that 'Chile is part of the American continent and we are part of Chile'.

Risk assessment

Economy	Good
Politics	Fair
Regional stability	Good

COUNTRY PROFILE

Historical profile

Inca rule barely touched Chile, with Aymara and Atacameno farmers and herders pre-dating the Incas. Chango Indians fished along the coastal areas while Diaguitas farmed the interior of Coquimbo. Beyond the central valley, Araucanian or Mapuche Indians resisted Inca aggression.

1535 Indigenous Araucaria people successfully resisted the first Spanish invasion of Chile.

1540 Santiago was founded by Pedro de Valdivia, who began the Spanish conquest of Chile.

1553 Araucarias captured and executed Valdivia.

1553–58 Indigenous people staged an uprising against Spanish colonialism; however most of the country was eventually subdued, although the Mapuche managed to hold onto their remaining territory for almost three centuries.

1578 Sir Francis Drake, an English adventurer, led a raid on the port of Valparaíso, which was repulsed by the Spanish armies.

1700 For most of the eighteenth century it was ruled by a small oligarchy of landowners.

1759 Chile began reforms under the auspices of the Bourbon monarchs, who succeeded the Habsburg dynasty in Spain.

1788 Irish-born Ambrosio O'Higgins y Ballenary began his tenure as governor of Chile. He outlawed slavery and forced labour, strengthened production and administration and bolstered the power of the military. Chile was granted more autonomy than most other Latin American colonies.

1807 Napoleon Bonaparte's invasion of Spain fuelled the independence movement in Chile.

1810 Independence leader Bernardo O'Higgins Riquelme, son of Ambrosio O'Higgins, led a revolt against José Miguel Carrera Verdugo, the Chilean leader who had brought more autonomy to the country.

1814 Spanish troops re-conquered Chile.

1818 Bernado O'Higgins joined forces with José de San Martín in Argentina and led successful battles against the Spanish that resulted in Chile's independence from Spain. Bernado O'Higgins became Chile's first post-independence leader.

1823 O'Higgins was forced to resign. Civil war between liberal federalists and conservative centralists ensued, lasting for seven years.

1830 The Conservatives won the civil war.

1851–61 President Manuel Montt liberalised the constitution, reducing the power of landowners and the Roman Catholic Church.

1879–84 Chile's victory in the War of the Pacific against Peru and Bolivia increased its territory by one-third.

1880s–90s The pacification of the Araucarias led to increased European immigration. Mining of nitrates and copper began.

1891 A civil war over a constitutional dispute between the president and congress led to a congressional victory, with the role of the president reduced to a figurehead.

1925 A new constitution saw the disestablishment of the church.

1927 General Carlos Ibañez del Campo seized power in a military coup and established a dictatorship.

1938–46 A Popular Front coalition was formed by communists, socialists and radicals.

1948–58 The Communist Party was banned.

1952 Carlos Ibañez was elected president, promising to strengthen law and order.

1964 Eduardo Frei Montalva was elected president, pledging to introduce limited social reform.

1970 Salvador Allende Gossens was elected president and imposed an extensive programme of nationalisation.

1973 The government failed to win a congressional majority in the elections as opposition to its policies mounted and the country faced ever-increasing economic problems. Food shortages followed high inflation and fighting broke out between pro- and anti-government activists. Backed by the CIA, the armed forces intervened. President Allende died during the military takeover. (In July 2011 an autopsy confirmed that he had in fact committed suicide and not been shot by the military.)

1974 General Augusto Pinochet Ugarte became president, remaining in power for 16 years.

1988 Chilean voters rejected Pinochet's bid to extend his power until 1997.

1989 The Concertación de Partidos por la Democracia (*Concertación*) (Coalition of Pro-Democracy Parties) was formed to contest the general elections. Patricio Aylwin (*Concertación*) defeated both Pinochet's protégé and a right-wing independent candidate in the presidential election.

1990 The *Concertación* won the general elections with 49.3 per cent of the vote in the Chamber of Deputies and 50.5 per cent in the Senate.

1993 Eduardo Frei Ruíz-Tagle won the presidential election. He began reducing the military's influence in government.

1998 Pinochet retired from the army and was made senator-for-life. He was arrested in the UK on a warrant issued by a Spanish magistrate on murder charges related to his 'caravan of death' in the 1970s.

2000 Ricardo Lagos Escobar (*Concertación*) won the elections and became Chile's first socialist president since 1973. The UK government declared Pinochet unfit for extradition to Spain and the former dictator was returned to Chile. A Chilean judge subsequently charged Pinochet with kidnap.

2001 Chile's appeal court ruled that Pinochet was mentally unfit to stand trial on human rights violation charges. The ruling centre-left *Concertación* held on to its majority in Congress.

2002 All charges against Pinochet were dropped after the Supreme Court upheld a verdict finding him mentally unfit to stand trial for human rights crimes. Pinochet resigned from his post as a lifelong senator.

2004 The right to divorce became law. Chile's court lifted Pinochet's immunity from prosecution, opening the way to possible trials of the octogenarian general on charges of human rights abuses during his 17-year rule.

2006 Michelle Bachelet (Partido Socialista de Chile (PS) (Socialist Party of Chile)) took office as Chile's first female president, after she won 53.5 per cent in the presidential election runoff; Sebastián Piñera, a moderate conservative won 46.5 per cent of the votes. Augusto Pinochet, former Head of State (1973–90), died. The controversy surrounding his rule denied him a state funeral. All senate membership became by direct election, replacing the system of appointments.

2007 Bolivia, Brazil and Chile agreed to build a South American highway to link the Atlantic and Pacific coasts, running from Santos in Brazil, through Bolivia, to Arica and Iquique in Chile, at an estimated cost of US$600 million.

2008 Chile recalled its ambassador from Peru, after Peru had asked the International Court of Justice (ICJ) to make a ruling over the disputed maritime border between them. The sea is a rich fishing ground. The Chaiten volcano in Patagonia erupted.

2009 Chile agreed with the Organisation for Economic Co-operation and Development (OECD) to implement international tax information exchange standards. In elections for the Chamber of Deputies, the Coalición por el Cambio (CC) (Coalition for Change) (alliance of five parties) won 43.44 per cent of the vote (58 seats out of 120), the ruling *Concertación*-Juntos Podemos won 44.36 per cent (57). In the Senate, where 18 seats were up for election (out of a total of 38), CC won nine seats, *Concertación*-Juntos Podemos nine, while Chile Limpio lost its only seat.

2010 Following two rounds of presidential elections, Miguel Juan Sebastián Piñera Echenique (Sebastián Piñera) (CC) won the run-off, held in January, with 51.6 per cent of the vote. A massive earthquake of 8.8 magnitude struck offshore near Chile's second city, Concepción, in February. Over 800 people were killed and many buildings were destroyed. Piñera was sworn in as president in March. In August, the Brazilian airline TAM Linhas Aereas and the Chilean airline LAN agreed to merge to form the region's largest carrier, with 115 destinations in 23 countries. The company became the Latam Airlines Group, although individual airline brand names remain in use.

2011 On 18 March the new 3,400km, US$1.3 billion, Carretera Interoceánica (Interoceanic Highway), was opened from Brazil's Atlantic coast to Peru's Pacific seaboard, bisecting the Amazon forest and crossing the Andes Mountains into Chile. On 23 March, Bolivia threatened to lodge a complaint against Chile in the ICJ for return of land won during the 1879–83 War of the Pacific. Since Chile annexed land from Peru and Bolivia following the war, Bolivia has been landlocked. Despite several attempts to resolve the issue, including the offer of free access to ports designated specifically for Bolivian trade, a peace deal has remained out of reach. Miners working for the world's largest copper mining company, Codelco, began a strike on 12 July, protesting plans to restructure the industry. In July an autopsy confirmed that Salvador Allende had in fact committed suicide in 1973 and not been shot by the military as they stormed the presidential palace during the coup led by General Augusto Pinochet. President Piñera reshuffled his cabinet on 20 July, in an effort to boost his popularity rating which had fallen to 30 per cent. He also reassured miners that there were no plans to nationalise Codelco.

Political structure

Constitution

The constitution dates from 1980, when it was accepted by two-thirds of voters in a plebiscite organised by the military government. Following a further plebiscite in 1989, 54 reforms passed into law. They included increasing the number of directly elected members in the Senate, abolishing Article 8 (which outlawed Marxist groups) and balancing the number of civilian and military representatives on the powerful Council of National Security. Further changes to the constitution require a two-thirds majority in both houses of the Congreso Nacional (National Congress).

Form of state

Presidential democratic republic

The executive

Executive power is held by the president and cabinet. The president is head of state and commander-in-chief of the armed forces. Elected for a fixed term of six years, the president cannot be re-elected for the following period.

The relationship between the executive and the armed forces is enshrined in the constitution. The president should take note of discussions within the Council of National Security. This consists of eight members, four military and four civilian. The four military members are the heads of the army, navy, air force and police. The four civilian members are the president of the republic, president of the Senate, president of the Supreme Court and the comptroller general of the republic. According to the constitution, the Council of National Security provides a forum within which it is possible to present, at the highest level, the military's opinion. The armed forces see the council as having the function of letting civilian governments know of potential conflicts between military and civilian interests, thereby acting to prevent future military intervention in government.

National legislature

The bicameral Congreso Nacional (National Congress), is composed of the Cámara de Diputados (Chamber of Deputies) (lower house) with 120 deputies directly elected in 60 two-member electoral districts, serving for four-year terms. The Senado de la República (senate) (upper house) has 38 directly elected members, serving for eight-year terms; around one-third of the membership is elected every four years.

Laws can originate in either of the chambers or be proposed by the president.

Legal system

The main tribunals of the independent judiciary system are the Supreme Court, 16 regional courts of appeal and the lower courts. The Supreme Court consists of 16 members appointed for life by the president from a list of five names proposed by the Supreme Court as vacancies arise. Members of the courts of appeal are appointed in the same way as those of the Supreme Court. Judges in lower courts are appointed in a similar manner, but from lists submitted by the court of appeal of the district in which the vacancies arise.

Last elections

13 December 2009 (parliamentary and presidential); 17 January 2010 (presidential run-off)

Results: Parliamentary: (Chamber of Deputies) Coalición por el Cambio (CC) (Coalition for Change) (alliance of five parties) 43.44 per cent (58 seats out of 120), Concertación de Partidos por la Democracia (*Concertación*) (Coalition of Pro-Democracy Parties)-Juntos Podemos (alliance of eight political parties) 44.36 per cent (57), Por un Chile Limpio (Chile Limpio) (For a Fair Chile) 5.4 per cent (three) independents 2.2 per cent (two); turnout was 87.7 per cent. Senate (18 seats elected, out of 38 total): Concertación-Juntos Podemos 43.3 per cent (nine seats), CC 45.1 per cent (nine) (Chile Limpio lost its only seat).

Presidential (first round): Sebastián Piñera Echenique (Coalición por el Cambio (CC)) (Coalition for Change) led by Renovación Nacional (RN) (National Renewal) won 44.03 per cent of the vote, Eduardo Frei Ruiz-Tagle (Concertación-PDC) 29.62 per cent, Marco Enríquez-Ominami Gumucio (independent) 20.12 per cent, Jorge Arrate Mac-Niven (Partido Comunista-Poder Democrático Social (PC- Podemos)) (Communist Party-Social Democratic Power) 6.21 per cent; turnout was 88 per cent. Run-off: Piñera won 51.6 per cent of the vote, Frei won 48.39 per cent.

Next elections

2013 (presidential, national congress and senate (half the membership)

Political parties

Ruling party

Coalition led by Coalición por el Cambio (CC) (Coalition for Change) (alliance of five parties) (from 2010)

Main opposition party

Concertación de Partidos por la Democracia (*Concertación*) (Coalition of Pro-Democracy Parties)

Population

16.98 million (2009)*

Last census: April 2002: 15,116,435

Population density: 20 inhabitants per square km. Urban population: 86 per cent.

Annual growth rate: 1.3 per cent 1994–2004 (WHO 2006)

Ethnic make-up

Mixed European and indigenous peoples (mestizos) account for approximately 75 per cent of the population, with a further 23 per cent of European descent and 2 per cent Indians, mainly Mapuches, in the south.

Religions
Approximately 85 per cent Roman Catholic, 10 per cent Protestant, with small minorities of Jews, Muslims and other religions.

Education
The investment in education amounts to 4.0 per cent of GDP. This figure has doubled since the early 1990s. Chile has achieved gender parity in both primary and secondary education and has extended the school year by around 15 per cent.
Education is free and compulsory for the first eight years, beginning at the age of five or six.
All other education institutions charge fees, either partly or in full. The subsidies system applies equally to municipal and private education but has been directed mostly to basic education. The role of the ministry of education is now limited to licensing private education and carrying out school inspections.
Over 80 per cent of children complete secondary education, which begins at the age of 13 or 14 years and is divided into a humanities/science programme or a technical/vocational programme. Higher education consists of universities, professional and technical institutes.
Literacy rate: 96 per cent adult rate; 99 per cent youth rate (15–24) (Unesco 2005).
Compulsory years: Five or six to 13 or 14 (eight years in total)
Enrolment rate: 103 per cent boys, 100 per cent girls, total primary school enrolment of the relevant age group (including repetition rates), (World Bank).
Pupils per teacher: 30 in primary schools

Health
Healthcare is distributed between the ministry of health and social security institutions as well as private funds and the public sector. Health and social security have increasingly come into the hands of pension fund administration companies (AFPs). Since 1999, over a quarter of Chileans had taken out private health insurance. The state is responsible for the financing of health promotion, protection and prevention through the National Health Fund. The decentralised national health service is able to provide healthcare at different levels. The most basic care is in the hands of regional health authorities, responsible for preventive medical services which are part of the health promotion and protection programmes.
Care for pregnant women, children under six and members of indigent and low income families is free. More specialised medical consultation and care is given at hospitals and maternity units. For patients who voluntarily choose the state system, a contribution of 25 to 30 per cent of the cost is required (depending on income). People under any social security scheme are entitled to preventive medical services (periodical health examinations) and in the case of illness, are granted full-paid sick leave. Occupational accidents or disease are covered by a special fund.
Life expectancy: 77 years, 2004 (WHO 2006)
Fertility rate/Maternal mortality rate: 2.0 births per woman, 2004 (WHO 2006)
Child (under 5 years) mortality rate (per 1,000): 8.0 deaths per 1,000 live births; 1 per cent of children aged under five are malnourished (World Bank).
Head of population per physician: 1.09 physicians per 1,000 people, 2003 (WHO 2006)

Welfare
The statutory age of retirement is 65 years for men and 60 years for women. The system requires 13 per cent of a worker's wage to be deducted and accumulated in one of seven independently managed mutual-fund companies selected by the worker, with a small part of the contribution going towards disability insurance. Neither employers nor the government contribute to the individual accounts. The contributions remain under the workers' control, if they change jobs, and are deferred from any tax.
However, critics of the Chilean pension model argue that given the country's poverty rate, some workers would never be able to save enough toward retirement. Besides, 42 per cent of the workforce, in the informal economy, are not covered by any pension system, according to government statistics. Although they can make voluntary contributions to the system, most workers' incomes are very low. Hence, the government guarantees a minimum pension to anyone who has worked as a regular employee for 20 years.
Monetary subsidies apply to those outside any social security scheme include a special family allowance for both pregnant women and children under 15, in extreme poverty, and a special pension allowance for people over 65, or the handicapped without economic resources.
The system allows up to 20 per cent foreign investment in pension funds and it is likely to push that limit to 35 per cent with new legislation.

Main cities
Santiago (capital, estimated population 4.8 million in 2005), Puente Alto (602,586), Viña del Mar (326,790), Antofagasta (313,054), Valparaíso (267,367), Talcahuano (252,800), San Bernardo (261,454), Temuco (285,766), Iquique (224,970), Concepción (390,639).

Languages spoken
English is the main second language.
Official language/s
Spanish

Media
Press
Dailies: In Spanish, national newspapers include the state-owned *La Nación* (www.lanacion.cl) and privately owned *El Mercurio* (http://diario.elmercurio.com) a long established publication *La Tercera* (www.latercera.cl) is it rival. Tabloids include *Las Ultimas Noticias* (www.lun.com) and *La Cuarta* (www.lacuarta.cl), which is written in Chilean vernacular. *La Segunda* (www.lasegunda.com) is an evening newspaper.
In Spanish, regional newspapers include from Santiago *La Hora* (www.lahora.cl) and *Publimetro* (www.publimetro.cl), which are free newspapers. From Los Angeles *La Tribuna* (www.diariolatribuna.cl), from Punta Arenas *La Prensa Austral* (www.laprensaaustral.cl), and from Antofagasta *La Estrella del Norte* (www.estrellanorte.cl). *Prensa Al Día* (www.prensaaldia.cl) carries a compilation of daily reported news. In English, the *Santiago Times* (www.tcgnews.com/santiagotimes) provides news and general information about Chile and Santiago.
Weeklies: Some daily newspapers have weekend edition and there are many magazines for all tastes and ages. Fortnightly publications include, in Spanish, *La Firme* (www.lafirme.cl), a analytical political magazine, *The Clinic* (www.theclinic.cl), a satirical magazine and *Ercilla* (www.ercilla.cl) for general information. Women's magazines include *Cosas* (http://www.cosas.cl) and *Vanidades* (www.vanidades.cl); *Conozca Más* (www.conozcamas.cl) for men and *Condorito* (www.condorito.com) is a humourus publication.
In German *Condor* (http://www.condor.cl), is a general news weekly.
Business: In Spanish, dailies include *Estrategia* (www.estrategia.cl) and *Diario Financiero* (www.diariofinanciero.cl), is an influential newspaper. Monthlies include *América Economia* (www.americaeconomia.com), was the first business magazine published, *Datos Sue* (www.datossur.cl) and *Estrategia* (www.capital.cl). *Punto Final* (www.puntofinal.cl) for fortnightly general business news. For Latin American news, *Business News Americas* (www.bnamericas.com) with an English daily on-line digest.

Broadcasting

The Ministerio de Transportes y Telecommunicaciones (www.mtt.cl) has overall authority for broadcasting.

The geography of Chile has resulted in more nationwide coverage of radio than TV signals.

Radio: There are over 300 radio stations, most of which are private, local and commercial. Several national networks include the private, Radio Cooperativa (www.cooperativa.cl) with news based programmes, Radio Agricultura (www.radioagricultura.cl), Bío Bío La Radio (www.radiobiobio.cl) and Radio Infinita (www.infinita.cl). Local stations in Santiago include Radio Tiempo (http://fmtiempo.cl), Radio Oasis (www.radiooasis.cl) and Radio Integral (www.radiointegral.cl).

Television: The national public, commercial broadcaster is Televisión Nacional de Chile (TVN) (www.tvn.cl). There are several other private TV networks, including Chilevision (www.chilevision.cl), Megavision (www.megavision.cl), Red TV (www.redtv.cl) and Canal 13 (www.canal13.cl).

There are many foreign and domestic channels available via satellite or cable.

Advertising

Advertising spending is dominated by TV (over 50 per cent), newspapers (over 10 per cent) and magazines (around 5 per cent).

News agencies

National news agency: Agencia Chile Noticias

Economy

Chile is the world's leading supplier of copper at around 30 per cent of global production. Copper provides over 14 per cent of national GDP, while combined mining represents over 16 per cent. Industry and manufacturing in 2009 constituted 13 per cent of GDP and the service sector over 60 per cent, of which financial services represented almost 16 per cent of GDP.

GDP growth in 2007 was 4.6 per cent, which began to fall in 2008 to 3.7 per cent as the global economic crisis weakened exports, particularly commodities. In 2009, the International Monetary Fund (IMF) deemed the banking system as 'well-capitalised' and the supervisory framework as strong, with a well-developed domestic capital market. International trade was at an all time high in 2007 with a trade balance of US$23.6 billion. It fell sharply to US$8.8 billion in 2008 as the economy fell progressively towards recession in 2009 with GDP growth of -1.5 per cent, in tandem with negative global growth. Inflation, which had remained fairly stable between 4.4–4.9 per cent (2006–07), jumped to 8.7 per cent in 2008, before falling back to 1.7 per cent in 2009 as domestic spending slumped.

A severe earthquake struck the central region, near the city of Concepción, in February 2010, killing 708 people, causing US$30 billion in damage to vital infrastructure and housing and disrupting energy production and copper mining. The necessary reconstruction led to an economic surge in GDP growth of 4.6 per cent in April and encouraged economists to predict annual growth for Chile of 4.5 per cent for 2010.

In July 2010 the government attempted to increase the mining royalties from 4–5 per cent to 4–9 per cent until 2013, which could have provided an extra US$1 billion to help reconstruction after the earthquake. However parliament rejected the proposal and the government will be forced to find other means to cover the public deficit of 2 per cent of GDP.

Chile's reputation for sound economic management has created a level of international confidence envied by much of Latin America. At the heart of these policies lies the government's concentration on sound monetary, fiscal and exchange rate policies. In June 2010 the central bank tightened its annual monetary policy rate (MPR), raising it 50 base points to 1 per cent and reigning in its monetary stimulus measures.

High unemployment has been a persistent trend at around 7 per cent for much of the 2000s. As the economic crisis deepened year-on-year unemployment reached 9.9 per cent in May 2009; employment growth became negative, at around -1.0 per cent.

External trade

Chile is an associate member of Mercusur, a member of the Organisation of American States (OAS) and has a free trade agreement with the European Union (EU) as well as other individual countries in Asia. It is also an associate member of the Unión de Naciones Suramericanas (Unasur) (Union of South American Nations), modelled on the European Union (EU), which seeks to integrate with the Andean Community of Nations and Mercosur in a single market by 2014, when tariffs on non-sensitive products are to be abolished with the remainder eliminated by 2019. However political tensions within the region have hampered the ongoing process.

Chile is the world's largest source of copper.

Imports

Main imports include petroleum and petroleum products, natural gas, chemicals, electrical and telecommunications equipment, industrial machinery and vehicles.

Main sources: US (typically 19 per cent of total), China (13 per cent), Argentina (12 per cent).

Exports

Major exports include copper, fruit and processed foods including wine and fish products, timber, paper and pulp.

Main destinations: China (typically 23 per cent of total), US (11 per cent), Japan (9 per cent).

Agriculture

Farming

The contribution of the agricultural sector to the Chilean economy is significant, employing 15 per cent of the total workforce and generating 6 per cent of GDP. Approximately 8 per cent of the total land mass is cultivated. The country's soil is fertile and well irrigated, particularly in the central area and main river valleys.

Dependence on imported foodstuffs has been reduced by improved wheat, sugar and vegetable oil production. Other important crops are oats, barley, rice, beans, lentils, maize and chickpeas. Important cash/export crops are maize, beans, asparagus, onions and garlic.

The production and export of a variety of fruit have all recorded impressive figures, given Chile's favourable growing conditions and good soil, relatively cost-effective labour and protection from disease. Table grapes, citrus fruits, avocados, pears, nectarines, peaches, kiwis, plums and nuts have done well. Chilean wine is growing in importance as a value-added agricultural product and a highly important export.

Livestock farming is concentrated in the south of the country.

Fishing

The Fishing industry in Chile is one of the economy's most important export industries. Chile is second only to Norway as a producer of fresh, frozen and prepared salmon, with annual exports totalling more than US$800 million. The productivity of the fishing industry is largely attributable to the large number of salmon farms in the south of the country.

Fishing and fish processing have become a diversified industry. Pilchards have traditionally been the main species of fish landed (75 per cent), with jack mackerel second. Abalone is exported to Japan, algae to Taiwan, hake to Spain, fresh salmon to the US and canned pilchards to the UK. Such diversification has been fuelled by substantial and continued increases in investment.

The typical annual fish catch is 4.3million tonnes, including 3.6 million tonnes marine fish and 164,477 tonnes shellfish.

Forestry

Chile has a significant amount of forested land, approximately 15.5 million hectares (ha), equating to 23 per cent of the total land area. In the period 1990–2000, deforestation accounted for a decrease of forest cover by an average of 0.13 per cent per annum or 20,000ha. Forestry is an important sector suitable for commercial exploitation.

Chile has abundant softwood plantations used for the manufacture of forest products. The forestry industry is primarily located in the south, stretching from the Seventh to the Tenth region, with the main concentration in the Eighth Region around Concepción. The three ports of the area (San Vicente, Lirquén and Talcahuano) handle up to 95 per cent of all forestry exports.

The sawn wood sector is characterised by a wide variety of producers, ranging from small portable sawmills to large highly automated mills. The larger sawmills tend to specialise in *pinus radiata*. Sawnwood production is largely a seasonal industry, with the highest activity occurring between spring and autumn (September to April). In the global market, Chile is the third-largest exporter of woodchips while nearly 50 per cent of its sawn timber, panels and softwood pulp production are exported.

Japan is the single most important purchaser of Chilean wood cellulose. Paper production has a large domestic market. The government has promoted private sector investment in forestry with land tax exemptions, rebates and subsidies.

Industry and manufacturing

Chile's manufacturing sector employs approximately one quarter of the country's total workforce. The sector also contributes around a third of Chilean GDP. Financial conglomerates control a substantial section of denationalised industries, although small firms with less than 10 employees still dominate.

Export-based industries include petrochemicals, pulp and paper, base metals, plastics, rubber and food processing (particularly fish and malted barley). Domestic market industries include textiles, footwear, cement, food processing, beverages and machinery.

Tourism

Chile's tourism industry continues to grow, with the country's variety of natural environments and climates attracting an increasing number of visitors. In line with the expansion of the industry Chile's infrastructure is being expanded to cater for the growth of the sector. The largest market is Argentina, but many tourists come from further afield, including a considerable number from the US and Europe.

Environment

Santiago suffers from a serious smog problem, which is at its worst May–September and is aggravated when the winter weather is interrupted by spells of milder temperatures.

Mining

The mining sector is of great importance to the Chilean economy, contributing 9 per cent to GDP and providing employment for 6 per cent of the workforce. It is the main export earner and a major focus of foreign investment in the country.

Activity is concentrated in copper, of which Chile is the world's leading producer and holds around 30 per cent of the world's proven reserves. The state-owned copper enterprise, Corporación Nacional del Cobre de Chile (Codelco), holds 70 per cent of national reserves and administers the four largest mines: Chuquicamata, El Teniente, Andina and El Salvador. Copper is also extracted from the Escondida mine, the biggest proven deposit in the world.

The sector was hit by falling copper prices until 2003 when demand for copper was fuelled by Chinese expansion in particular and prices rose. Copper continued to rise at a rapid rate in 2005, in line with increased demand in the international market.

Mining of silver, gold (the El Indio mine ranks among the highest grade mines in the world), iron ore, manganese and lead is also undertaken. Other mining sub-sectors include natural nitrates, mercury, marble, coal, sulphur and limestone

Proven and probable reserves at the Fachinal mine in southern Chile (Coeur d'Alene Mines Corporation) are estimated at 317,915 ounces of gold and 14.6 million ounces of silver.

Hydrocarbons

The country is a net importer of energy, with less than 10 per cent of its needs fulfilled by domestic hydrocarbon production. Domestic oil production, mainly from offshore fields at the Straits of Magellan and onshore at Tierra del Fuego and the southern mainland, provides less than 6 per cent of domestic consumption. Chile's oil reserves fell below 150 million barrels in 2008 and are no longer significant to its energy mix. Oil consumption was 314,000 barrels per day in 2010 which was imported either as refined products or crude oil to be process in the three oil refineries opertated by the state-owned Empresa Nacional del Petróleo (ENAP), which controls the energy sector.

Chile has less than 97 billion cubic metres of proven natural gas reserves, with production limited to the urban markets of central Chile, particularly Santiago.

However nationally, gas consumption has risen from 3.1 billion cubic metres (cum) in 2009 to 4.7 billion cum in 2010, despite a government push for conservation since consumption in 2004 was a record 8.7 billion cum.

Imported liquid natural gas (LNG) has increased, to become Chile primary source of energy. In 2010 LNG accounted for 3.07 billion cum, while piped natural gas from Argentina only amounted to 340 million cum.

There are two LNG terminals, one in Quintero on the central coast, the other in Mejillones in the north, centred on Chile's copperbelt.

Chile's coal resources come mainly from Lota/Coronel and the extreme south of Tierra del Fuego. All domestic coal production goes to power generation. Chile has total recoverable coal reserves of 1.3 million tonnes; production has fallen to around 40,000 tonnes a year.

Energy

Generation, transmission and distribution are entirely privately run entities. The sector is regulated by the Ministerio de Economía y Energía (MEE) (ministry of economy and energy) as a function of Comisión Nacional de Energía (CNE) (national energy commission).

Chile generated a total of 48.16 billion GWh of electricity in 2007, of which 60 per cent was generated by thermal and 40 per cent by hydroelectric power stations. Whenever possible hydropower is used as the lead source of energy but climatic conditions, particularly the lack of rainfall, have an impact on the need to use and ability to generate power. Demand for energy has almost doubled in the decade up to 2007, with a predicted year-on-year growth of 4.96 per cent for total electricity demand in 2008. Argentina withdrew its guaranteed supply of gas to Chile in 2004. In 2005 and 2007 supplies during August and May (winter months) were cut back by 60 per cent and 64 per cent respectively, with further restrictions in January 2008. The result was that more generation was forced on oil/coal fired power stations and Chile was forced to pay considerably higher energy costs. Renewable energy sources are only minor contributors to the remainder.

Financial markets

Stock exchange

Bolsa de Comercio de Santiago (Santiago Stock Exchange) (SSE)

Banking and insurance

Chile's banking and insurance sector was once an exclusive enclave of the economy where only the rich were able to access financial services. However, the 1990s saw an expansion of the banking sector throughout the country. Today Chile has one of Latin America's most developed and sophisticated banking sectors and Chilean banks have shown relative strength in a weak economic environment. The authorities do not allow new banks to enter the Chilean market, except via the purchase of an existing bank. Restrictions remain on the range of activities a bank can undertake, with pension fund management reserved for private pension fund companies.

Competitive pressures have increased with domestic banks facing increased competition from Spanish banks. Following Banco Santander Central Hispano's (BSCH) takeover of Banco Santiago and Santander Chile – two of Chile's largest banks – BSCH has a market share of just under 30 per cent.

Central bank

Banco Central de Chile

Main financial centre

Santiago

Time

GMT minus four hours (daylight saving, mid-October to mid-March, GMT minus three hours)

Geography

Chile occupies a thin strip of land, rarely more than 200km wide, which stretches 4,640km down the west coast of Latin America from north of the tropic of Capricorn to Cape Horn. Geography and climate range from hot deserts in the north to icy Andean peaks at almost 7,000 metres high in the east and thousands of rainswept islets in the south. Chile is bordered by the Pacific to the west, by Argentina to the east, by Bolivia in the north-east and Peru to the north. Several Pacific islands, including the Juan Fernandez archipelago and Easter Island, are Chilean.

There are three main geographical belts running from north to south – the Andes, the central valley, and the narrow coastal range. The Andes are characterised not only by their great height but also by being a broad mass, generally over 80km wide, and making a superb natural border with Argentina. West of the Andes, the central valley has a varied form. In the north, it is a high desert basin, characterised by inward drainage and near complete aridity. Further south it disappears, until re-emerging near Santiago. From Santiago to Puerto Montt, it constitutes the agricultural heart of Chile, until it disappears under the sea at Puerto Montt. The coastal range, significantly lower than the Andes and generally under 3,000 metres, forms a barrier between the populated central valley and the coast, except for certain gaps made by powerful rivers, as at Concepción in the south. Of the mainland area, 2.2 per cent is suitable for crops, 17.1 per cent for livestock and 10.8 per cent for forestry. The remaining 69.9 per cent is considered unproductive and is mostly covered by deserts or mountains.

Hemisphere

Southern

Climate

Generally hot and dry in north, Mediterranean in central region (cool nights) and wet and cold in the south. Temperatures in Santiago range from 10–33 degrees Celsius (C) in summer (December–March) and 2–20 degrees C in winter (June–September). The rainy season in the Santiago area is from May to September.

Dress codes

Relatively formal. A suit or a jacket and tie for men and skirts for women are usual for business.

Entry requirements

Passports

Required by all, with the exception of tourists travelling direct to Chile from Argentina, Brazil, Colombia, Paraguay and Uruguay, for whom national identity cards are sufficient. Entry will be permitted only with proof of return/onward passage and sufficient funds for stay.

Visa

Visas are not required by citizens of neighbouring countries or most EU states. For further details contact the local embassy. Business visas are not required by those citizens who do not need a tourist visa, all others, including those who do not normally require them but who are visiting on short-term contracts or receive fees from a local company, do need a visa.

On arrival a 'tourist card' is issued and must be returned when leaving.

Currency advice/regulations

No restrictions on import and export of foreign or domestic currency. International credit cards are widely accepted. Receipts for money changed on entry should be retained. Travellers cheques are readily acceptable in cities only.

Health (for visitors)

Mandatory precautions

None

Advisable precautions

Typhoid, polio, hepatitis A and tetanus vaccinations are useful.

Water precautions should be taken (avoid tap water) and eating unpeeled fruit or uncooked vegetables is not advised. Foreigners may get free primary health care from the state-run health service's hospitals, but for more serious cases they are required to pay the costs. Travel health insurance is advised if not already covered by one's own national health insurance.

Hotels

Numerous luxury and first-class hotels as well as good hotels in lower price range. The Stars Classification System is used. Bookings may be made at the Sernatur information office at Pudahuel Airport. An 19 per cent hotel tax is added to bill, unless paid for with foreign currency. Service charge is usually included, but an extra 5–10 per cent tip is usual.

Public holidays (national)

Fixed dates

1 Jan (New Year's Day), 1 May (Labour Day), 21 May (Navy Day), 26 Jun (St Peter and St Paul Day), 15 Aug (Assumption Day), 18 Sep (Independence Day), 19 Sep (Army Day), 12 Oct (Columbus Day), 1 Nov (All Saints' Day), 8 Dec (Immaculate Conception), 25–26 Dec (Christmas).

Variable dates

Mar/Apr (Good Friday, Holy Saturday), May/Jun (Corpus Christi), first Mon in Sep (Reconciliation Day).

Working hours

Banking

Mon–Fri: 0900–1400.

Business

Mon–Fri: 0900–1800.

Business visits are best made outside the summer month of February when the great majority of people are on holiday.

Government

Mon–Fri: 0830–1730.

Shops

Mon–Sat: 0900–2000. Supermarkets and many shopping centres are open continuously until 2100, including Sundays and public holidays.

Telecommunications

Mobile/cell phones

GSM 1900 services exist throughout most of the country.

Electricity supply

220V AC, with two-pin plugs.

Social customs/useful tips

People are expected to be punctual for business appointments. However, for social appointments, being 30 or 40 minutes late is quite usual. Chileans are very hospitable and do not necessarily expect reciprocity. Entertaining at home is common practice and a small gift of thanks is acceptable.

In Latin American Spanish it is acceptable to address others in a familiar form *tu*, or in a polite form *usted*. The latter is more appropriate for business although the familiar form is often rapidly adopted. Chileans are quite easy about smoking habits, but it is banned in cinemas, theatres, churches and public transport.

It is necessary to carry car documents when driving.

Security

Santiago is generally regarded as a safe city with low incidences of assault and mugging compared with other Latin American capitals. However, pickpocketing is common in the city centre and on buses.

Getting there

Air

National airline: LAN-Chile (Línea Aérea Nacional de Chile).

International airport/s: Santiago-Comodoro Arturo Merino Benítez (often known as 'Pudahuel') (SCL), 21km west of city; bar, restaurant, bank, post office, shops, tourist office, car hire. A bus service to the city runs 24 hours.

Other airport/s: Arica-Chacalluta (ARI), 18km from city; bar, restaurant, buffet, shops, car hire.

Airport tax: Departure tax: US$18

Surface

Road: The road system is dominated by the 3,455km Pan-American Highway, which links the Peruvian frontier to Puerto Montt in the south. Between Santiago and Puerto Montt, the Pan-American follows the course of the central valley. A trans-Andean highway links Valparaíso with the Argentine city of Mendoza. This is frequently closed during winter due to snow, when more southerly and lower passes have to be used.

Rail: Five lines to neighbouring Argentina, Bolivia and Peru are operated by the government-owned Ferrocarriles del Estado.

Water: Empremar (Valparaíso) is the principal port with developed passenger routes mainly to Argentina. Chile has around 60 ports.

Getting about

National transport

Air: Línea Aérea del Cobre (Ladeco) provides most domestic services. Lanexpress operates frequent flights to major centres only. Air taxi services also operate. The south of the country relies heavily on air links and seats must be booked well in advance.

Road: There are 80,000km of good roads including the Pan-American Highway running north-south and qualified as first-class. It is only possible to reach Punta Arenas by land from Rio Gallengos (Argentina).

Buses: Express coaches link main centres and are generally recommended (eg Santiago-Arica, typically one departure daily; Santiago-Valparaíso, approx hourly service).

Rail: A fast diesel-electric train service is available. The main line runs from Santiago to Puerto Montt (includes sleeper service, restaurant cars, air-conditioning, typical total journey time around 18 hours); Japanese-built train links between Santiago and Concepción (first-class service and a journey time around nine hours including bus service from Chillián to Concepción).

City transport

Taxis: From Santiago's Arturo Merino Benitez airport, there are metered taxis into town.

Taxis are cheap and widely available in main towns. An initial charge (*Bajada de Bandera*) is displayed on front windscreen. Large blue taxis do not have meters. Tipping is not customary. Radio taxis charge higher fares.

Within Santiago and Chile's main towns black and yellow taxis can be hailed but are scarce at rush hour. These taxis are mostly metered but for long journeys fares should be negotiated in advance. There are extra charges at night and on holidays.

Taxis operating from the airport require a special permit, and it is advised that visitors check a taxi's authenticity before boarding. The journey to central Santiago takes about 30 minutes. However, any taxi can go to the airport and the fare is often cheaper than from the airport.

Buses, trams & metro: Frequent inner city bus service. Shuttle service – mini-buses for several passengers – from airport to city centre.

Fast, frequent, clean and safe metro system in Santiago consisting of two main lines: line 1 San Pablo-Escuela Militar line; line 2 Lo Ovalle-Cal y Canto line which has 13 stations. Trains run 0700–2245.

Car hire

A national or international licence is accepted. Car hire can be arranged at the airport and in most major towns. A large deposit may be required. All car drivers require a 'Carnet de Passages et Douanes' issued by the Automobile Club. Traffic drives on the right.

BUSINESS DIRECTORY

The addresses listed below are a selection only. While World of Information makes every endeavour to check these addresses, we cannot guarantee that changes have not been made, especially to telephone numbers and area codes. We would welcome any corrections.

Telephone area codes

The international dialling code (IDD) for Chile is +56, followed by area code and subscriber's number:

Antofagasta	55	Linares	73
Arica	58	Punta Arenas	61
Chillán	42	Santiago	2
Concepción	41	Temuco	45
Coquimbo	51	Valparaíso	32
Iquique	57	Vina del Mar	32
La Serena	51		

Chambers of Commerce

American Chamber of Commerce in Chile, Avenida Kennedy 5735, Las Condes, Santiago (tel: 290-9700; fax: 212-0515; e-mail: amcham@amchamchile.cl).

British-Chilean Chamber of Commerce, Avenida Suecia 155-C, Providencia, Santiago (tel: 231-4366; fax: 231-8211; e-mail: cambrit@entelchile.net).

Antofagasta Cámara de Comercio, Servicios y Turismo, Latorre 2580, Antofagasta (tel: 225-175; fax: 55-222-053; e-mail: info@comercioantofagusta.cl).

Arica Cámara de Comercio, Industria, Servicios y Turismo, Rafael Sotomayor 252, Arica (tel: 224-643; fax: 253-718; e-mail: comercio@camaracomercioarica.cl).

Iquique Cámara de Comercio, Industria, Servicios y Turismo, San Martín 225, Iquique (tel: 412-942; fax: 414-090; e-mail: info@iquiquenegocios.cl).

Talca Cámara de Comercio, Servicios y Turismo, 2 Sur 1061, Talca (tel/fax: 233-569; e-mail: contact@camaradecomerciotalca.cl).

Temuco Cámara de Comercio, Servicios y Turismo, Vicuña Mackenna 396, Temuco (tel: 210-556; fax: 237-047; e-mail: camcotem@entelchile.cl).

Valparaiso Cámara Regional del Comercio y la Produccion, Pasaje Ross 149, Valparaiso (tel: 253-065; fax: 212-770).

Banking

Banco de A Edwards, Huérfanos 740, Santiago (tel: 388-3000; fax: 388-4100; e-mail: marketing@baenet.cl).

Banco de Chile, Ahumada 251, Santiago (tel: 637-1111; fax: 637-3434)

Banco de Crédito e Inversiones, Huérfanos 1134, Santiago (tel: 692-7000; fax: 699-0729; e-mail: consulta@bcl.cl).

Banco del Estado de Chile, Avenida Libertador Bernardo O'Higgins 1111, Santiago (tel: 670-7000; fax: 670-5478; e-mail: msoto9@bech.cl).

Central bank

Banco Central de Chile, PO Box 967, 1180 Agustinas, Santiago 8340454 (Tel: 670-2000; fax: 670-2099; e-mail: bcch@bcentral.cl).

Stock exchange

Bolsa de Comercio de Santiago (Santiago Stock Exchange) (SSE): www.bolsadesantiago.com

Bovalpo (Valparaíso Stock Exchange): www.bovalpo.com

Travel information

LADECO (Línea Aérea del Cobre), Avenida Américo Vespucio 901, Santiago (tel: 661-3131; fax: 639-5757; e-mail: josecotd@cmbchile.cl).

LAN-Chile (Línea Aérea Nacional de Chile), Avenida Américo Vespucio 901, Santiago (tel: 687-2525; fax: 687-2483; e-mail:sdelpino@lanchile.cl; internet: www.lan.com).

National tourist organisation offices

Servicio Nacional de Turismo (SERNATUR), (National Tourist Service) Avenida Providencia 1550, Santiago (tel: 236-1416; fax: 251-8469; internet: www.visit-chile.org; e-mail: sernatur@ctc-mundo.net or info@sernatur.cl).

Ministries

Ministry of Agriculture, Teatinos 40, Santiago (tel: 393-5000; fax:672-5654; e-mail: xbarrera@minagri.gob.cl).

Ministry of Defence, Edificio Diego Portales, Villavicencio 364, Santiago (tel: 222-1202; fax: 634-5339; e-mail: dn@defensa.cl).

Ministry of Economy, Mining and Energy, Teatinos 120, Santiago (tel: 672-5522; fax: 672-6040; e-mail: conomia@minecon.cl).

Ministry of Education, Avenida Libertado Bernardo O'Higgins 1371, Santiago (tel: 390-4000; fax: 380-0317; e-mail: ineduc@chilnet.cl).

Ministry of the Government, Palacio de la Moneda, Santiago (tel: 671-4103; fax: 699-1657).

Ministry of Housing, Avenida Libertado Bernardo O'Higgins 924, Santiago (tel: 638-0801; fax: 633-3892; e-mail: martinez@minvu.cl).

Ministry of the Interior, Palacio de la Moneda, Santiago (tel: 690-4000; fax: 699-2165; e-mail: alopez@interior.gov.cl).

Ministry of Justice, Morandé 107, Santiago (tel: 696-8151; fax: 696-6952).

Ministry of Labour and Social Security, Huérfanos 1273, Santiago (tel: 695-5133; fax: 671-6539).

Ministry of Mining, Teatinos 120, Santiago (tel: 671-4373; fax: 698-9262; e-mail: chileminero@mixmail.com).

Ministry of National Properties, Pdte. Juan Antonio Rios 6, Santiago (tel: 633-9305; fax: 633-6521; e-mail: aleonp@mbienes).

Ministry of Planning and Co-operation, Ahumada 48, Santiago (tel: 675-1400; fax: 672-1879; e-mail: misoto@mideplan.cl).

Ministry of the Presidency, Palacio de la Moneda, Santiago (tel: 690-4000; fax: 698-4656).

Ministry of Public Health, Enrique Mac-Iver 541, Santiago (tel: 639-4001; fax: 633-5875; e-mail: info@minsal.cl).

Ministry of Public Works, Morandé 59, Santiago (tel/fax: 361-2700; e-mail: mop.doh@chilnet.cl).

Ministry of Transport and Telecommunications, Amunategui 139 Santiago (tel: 672-6503; fax: 699-5138).

Ministry of Women's Affairs, Teatinos 950, Santiago (tel: 549-6100; fax: 549-6247; e-mail:sernam@entelchile.net).

Other useful addresses

Asociación de Exportadores de Manufacturas (ASEXMA Chile), Nueva Tajamar, Santiago (tel: 203-6699; fax: 203-6730; e-mail: asexma@asexmachile.cl).

Bolsa de Comercio de Santiago, La Bolsa 64, Santiago (Tel: 698-2001; fax: 697-2236; e-mail: fledermann@comercio.bolsantiago.cl).

British Embassy, Avenida el Bosque Norte 125, Piso 3, Las Condes, Santiago (tel: 231-3737; fax: 231-9771; e-mail: embsan@portal.cl).

Chilean Embassy (USA), 1732 Massachusetts Avenue, NW, Washington DC 20036 (tel: 202-785-1746; fax: 202-887-557; e-mail: embassy@embassyofchile.org).

Comisión Chilena del Cobre (Cochilco), Agustinas 1161, Santiago (tel: 382-8100; fax: 382-8300; e-mail: cochilco@cochilco.cl).

Comisión Económica para America Latina y el Caribe (CEPAL) (Economic Commission for Latin America – ECLAC), United Nations Building, Avenida Dag Hammarskjold s/n, Santiago (tel: 210-2000; fax: 208-0252).

Comité de Inversiones Extranjeras, Teatinos 120, Santiago (tel: 698-4254; fax: 698-9476; e-mail: investment@cinver.cl).

Corporación de Fomento de la Producción (CORFO) (Development Corporation), Moneda 921, Santiago (tel: 631-8692; fax: 631-8686; e-mail: drmetro@corfo.cl).

Corporación Nacional de Cobre (CODELCO), Huérfanos 1270, Santiago (tel: 690-3000; fax: 690-3059; e-mail: comunica@stgo.codelco.cl).

Empresa Nacional de Minería (ENAMI), MacIver 459, Santiago (tel: 664-7244; fax: 637-5436;e-mail: ghormaza@enami.cl).

Empresa Nacional de Petróleo (ENAP), Vitacura 2736, Santiago (tel: 280-3000; fax: 280-3199).

Instituto de Promoción de Exportaciones (ProChile), Avenida Libertador Bernardo O'Higgins 1315, Santiago (tel: 565-9000; fax: 696-0639; e-mail: info@prochile.cl).

Instituto Nacional de Estadísticas (INE), Avenida Presidente Bulnes 418, Santiago (tel: 366-7777; fax: 671-2169; e-mail: inecedoc@terra.cl).

Sociedad de Formento Fabril (SOFOFA)(Chilean Federation of Industry), Avenida Andrés Bello 2777, Santiago (tel: 391-3100; fax: 391-3200; e-mail: sofofa@sofofa.cl).

US Embassy, Avenida Andrés Bello 2800, Santiago (tel: 232-2600; fax: 330-3710).

National news agency: Agencia Chile Noticias, Carlos Antúnez 1884, Office 104, Comuna de Providencia, Santiago (tel/fax: 223-0205; email: prensa@chilenoticias.cl; internet: www.chilenoticias.cl).

Internet sites

Chile Business Directory: http://www.chilnet.cl/

Chile Trade Commission: http://www.prochile.cl

Government of Chile: http://www.gobiernodechile.cl

Latin Trade Online: http://www.latintrade.com

Latin World: http://www.latinworld.com

Organisation of American States: http://www.oas.org

China

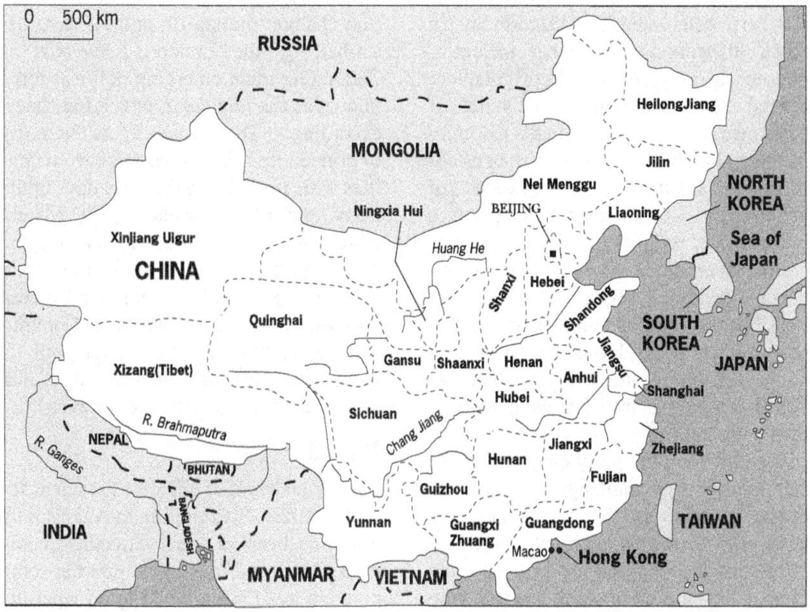

For the most part, China's international presence is superficially benign and beneficial. It is now the largest investor in Africa and in parts of Latin America. Most of its investment schemes in the developing world follow a formula involving the interchange of raw materials in payment of infrastructure and intermediate technology projects. China is also the world's largest holder of US debt. In 2011, however, there were parts of the world – notably in Africa – where Chinese benevolence was beginning to be mistrusted. The employment created by Chinese investment schemes was often for Chinese workers and the profits of so-called 'joint' enterprises were repatriated to China rather than paid as dividends in Africa or Latin America. The concept of 'ethical investment' has not yet bothered the Chinese government which prefers to turn a blind eye to human rights' infringements, seeking the same indifference from those Western companies investing in China.

Since 2001 China has progressed from being 'simply' the world's manufacturer, to becoming its banker. Representatives of cash strapped European countries, not to mention the European Union (EU), have made their way to Beijing, cap in hand. Not a global crisis summit goes by without the presence, if not always the participation, of Chinese official representatives. The development has happened to coincide with the arrival of a new kind of 'frontier-free' terrorism. The anti-terrorist campaign, following the attack on the Twin Towers in New York in September 2001, has been lead by the US. Apart from the possibly doubious prestige gained by China to be seen in such prestigious company as the President of the US and numerous European and Asian heads of state, the anti-terrorist counter campaign has provided China with a heaven-sent, if specious, excuse to clamp down harshly on its Tibetan, Uigur and Mongolian minorities.

The economy opens up – and the WTO

In this decade the Chinese economy has also opened up to private enterprise with a vengeance. The government's sub-plot here was the essential modernisation of the economy, which was seen as catalysed by the development of the private sector. The crowning glories were the successful

KEY FACTS

Official name: Zhonghua Renmin Gongheguo (Zhongguo) (People's Republic of China)

Head of State: President Hu Jintao (from 2003; re-elected 2008)

Head of government: Premier of the State Council Wen Jiabao (from 2003; re-elected 2008)

Ruling party: Zhongguo Gongchangdang (Chinese Communist Party) (CCP)

Area: 9,596,961 square km

Population: 1.34 billion (2010 census)

Capital: Beijing (Peking)

Official language: Putonghua (Mandarin Chinese – Beijing dialect).

Currency: Yuan (Renminbi) (Rmb) = 100 fen

Exchange rate: Rmb6.39 per US$ (Oct 2011)

GDP per capita: US$4,382 (2010)

GDP real growth: 10.30% (2010)

GDP: US$5,878.30 billion (2010)

Labour force: 779.95 million (2009)

Unemployment: 4.30% (2009)

Inflation: 3.30% (2010); 4.9% (month of Jan 2011)

Oil production: 4.07 million bpd (2010)

Balance of trade: US$254.18 billion (2010)

hosting of the Olympic games in 2008 and, in governmental circles almost as important, China's entry into the Word Trade Organisation in 2001. China's economic, political – and military weight – has been a world force. China's military expenditure may look small alongside that of the US (one sixth of annual US military expenditure) but it increases at around 10 per cent annually, enough to cause its neighbours – particularly Taiwan – a few concerns.

A distorted society?

By 2011, however, China's headlong rush into consumerism and material goods was beginning to create problems. The irony that Chinese society, under the banner of the Chinese Communist Party (CPC), should begin to show far greater degrees of inequality than the capitalist West had not been foreseen. And as inequality takes a grip on Chinese society so, to a much greater degree, does corruption and social injustice. Transparency International's 2011 index of corruption lists China in 74th place out of 183 countries. In a speech (in 2011) marking the 90th anniversary of the founding of the CPC, President Hu Jintao attacked the advance of corruption, warning that it could cost the party the trust and support of the people. While this may worry the government, its public face is certainly not one of humility. China's prime minister, Wen Jiabao, in March 2010 had claimed that uniquely, China's authoritarian state could 'make decisions efficiently, organise effectively and concentrate resources to accomplish large undertakings.'

90 years

At the end of June 2011, China's Communist Party celebrated its 90th birthday. In those 90 years the party has metamorphosed, shedding many of its original tenets and its strict adherence to the beliefs of Chairman Mao. In 2011 China's Communist party had become, as well as an establishment institution, a system of government. Communism in China is a bureaucracy, with its lounge suited mandarins, its entrance examinations, its limits on periods of office and of service. Possibly the biggest concern of China's party leaders in 2011 was the elimination of the corruption and cronyism that had risked bringing it into disrepute with its own body politic.

Just how long the party can continue to call the shots unchallenged is an open question. But as it approaches the hand-over to a new team of leaders in 2013, anxious looks will be directed at the fate of the one-party Arab leaders who failed to address the aspirations of their electorates. In 2011 the Chinese succession looked to be something of a *fait accompli*. Hu Jintao's posts of President, party chief and supreme military commander looked more than likely to go to Xi Jingping, the vice president. Prime Minister Wen Jiabao's position looked likely to be taken by Li Keqiang. Bo Xilai was the front runner for the position of internal security chief. These appointments would represent something of a generation change: messrs Bo and Xi were described by the London *Economist* as 'belonging to an emerging political force known as the *taisidang*, which translates, according to The *Economist*, as the 'party of princelings'. Both men come from families with close ties to the early days of the party and of the iconic Long March, which made them likely to endorse the party's traditions and to seek to maintain its grip on power. However much Chinese politics, in the framework of the Communist Party, have evolved, there will be those who already acknowledge that things can't stay as they are for ever.

The US

The official visit of US Vice President Joseph R Biden Jr to Beijing in August may not have been of great strategic importance, but it did manage to provide some pointers to Chinese thinking on what the rest of the world increasingly perceived to be a US economic crisis. The Chinese leaders, Vice President Xi Jingping and Prime Minister Wen Jiabao laboured to present the weaknesses of the US economy as a passing phase. They did not really have a great deal of room for manoeuvre; their country's economy is in many ways tied to that of the US. The Chinese government holds vast investments in US Treasury notes; its concern is that the value of its investments will be eroded by US inflationary trends, or – conversely – by the appreciation of the renminbi against the US dollar. Although the Chinese government might be able to control, to a degree, the macro-economic situation, the same was not the case with popular perceptions. And these certainly looked to be beyond the government's control if press reports were anything to judge by. These suggested that popular sentiment was increasingly critical as educated Chinese began to lose faith in the resilience of both the US economy and the US government.

Banking concerns

According to Reuters reports, the five biggest Chinese banks increased their combined earnings by 37 per cent in the first half of 2011. Fee income and improved

KEY INDICATORS — China

	Unit	2006	2007	2008	2009	2010
Population	m	1,314.10	1,321.29	1,328.02	*1,337.40	*1,334.74
Gross domestic product (GDP)	US$bn	2,644.64	3,250.83	4,401.60	4,909.00	5,878.30
GDP per capita	US$	2,011	2,461	3,315	3,678	4,382
GDP real growth	%	10.7	11.4	9.0	9.1	10.3
Inflation	%	1.5	4.7	2.9	-0.7	3.3
Unemployment	%	4.1	4.0	4.2	4.3	–
Industrial output	% change	12.5	8.1	9.3	9.9	–
Agricultural output	% change	5.0	3.9	5.5	4.2	–
Oil output	'000 bpd	3,684.0	3,743.0	3,795.0	3,790.0	4,071.0
Natural gas output	bn cum	58.6	69.3	76.1	85.2	96.8
Coal output	mtoe	1,212.3	1,311.4	1,414.5	1,552.9	1,800.4
Exports (fob) (goods)	US$bn	969.1	1,220.0	1,434.6	1,203.8	1,581.4
Imports (fob) (goods)	US$bn	791.6	904.6	1,073.9	954.3	13,272.2
Balance of trade	US$bn	177.5	315.4	360.7	249.5	2541.2
Current account	US$m	249,866.0	371,833.0	426,107.0	297,142.0	305,374.0
Total reserves minus gold	US$bn	1,068,5	1,530.3	1,949.3	2,416.0	2,866.1
Foreign exchange	US$bn	1,066.3	1,528.2	1,946.0	2,399.2	2,847.3
Exchange rate	per US$	7.82	7.37	6.94	6.80	6.77

* estimated figure

margins on lending generated increased profits, while bad debt levels subsided. None the less, by mid-2011 bank shares had fallen by some 25 per cent from their peak earlier in the year. This drop was considered to be attributable to a number of factors. First, although bad debt levels had fallen in the first half of the year, they looked set to rise. Loans overdue by less than three months rose by 36 per cent at the Bank of China. At the Industrial and Commercial Bank of China loans three to six months overdue also grew – in this case by 35 per cent. At the Minsheng Bank overdue loans more than doubled.

A second concern was attributed to what might be described as 'creative accounting' on the part of Chinese banks. Loans were bundled into 'wealth management' products enabling their clients to circumvent the one year deposit rate cap of an annual 3.5 per cent. Uncertainty surrounded the eventuality of bad debts in the case of these loans. Although Chinese banks were not technically liable for these bad debts, they risked having to account for them. The size of the funds classified in this way was staggering. Between them, the Agricultural Bank of China, Bank of Communications, China Construction Bank and Minsheng sold a total of seven trillion renminbi (US$1.1 trillion) of wealth management products in the first half of 2011.

Even if China's larger banks were soundly capitalised and enjoyed substantial liquidity, smaller banks were a different proposition. In the event of smaller banks defaulting, it would inevitably fall to the larger banks to bail them out. While this would probably be possible, the very possibility was enough to create some market uncertainty. Quoted in a far-reaching World Bank report published in November 2011, Tunc Tahsin Uyanik, Director of East Asia and the Pacific in the Financial and Private Sector Development Vice Presidency at the Bank was reported as saying that 'China has made considerable progress in developing a financial system that is more commercially-based and financially sound. He went on to say that: 'Reforms have accelerated since 2003, with the Chinese government adopting a series of policies to enhance the resilience of the financial sector and, on the structural side, strengthening a large number of domestic financial institutions and improving market confidence. However, China is confronted with some near term risks, reform challenges and development opportunities as it continues to modernise its financial sector that will require a strategic and holistic approach to reforms.

The World Bank report considered near term domestic risks for China's banks to be four-fold: first, the impact of the recent sharp credit expansion on banks' asset quality; second, the rise of off-balance sheet exposures and lending outside the formal banking sector; third, the relatively high level of real estate and commodity prices; and finally the increase of imbalances due to the current economic growth pattern. The report suggested that macro-economic and financial policies needed to be better aligned to create incentives for a durable transformation to a more commercially-oriented and effective financial system. In particular, the government was advised to reorient its role in the financial system, in order to improve credit allocation processes, promote financial markets and services that reduce the need for high levels of precautionary savings and strengthen institutional structures.

China also needed to continue its efforts to strengthen the financial sector's regulatory and supervisory regime. The People's Bank of China (PBC) (central bank) and the primary supervisory commissions needed to be empowered with focused mandates, operational autonomy and flexibility, increased resources and skilled personnel. Broader and more diversified financial products and services would also deepen and strengthen China's financial system. Fixed income markets needed to be further developed, alongside continued interest rate reforms. The continued development of the insurance sector, which has grown rapidly but has scope for further deepening, needed to be supported by more effective regulation and supervision. Finally, the report recommends that financial inclusion be improved through reforms that provide the right incentives for the provision of financial services to under-served sectors, foster market competition, improve legal and regulatory frameworks and financial infrastructure for financial inclusion and remove policies not properly aligned with the overall objective of improving access to finance.

Local government debt

The head of China's National Audit Office saw fit, in 2011, to warn that debts incurred by local governments and by investment companies established by provinces and municipalities were running out of control. Liu Jiayi estimated that this debt had risen to a staggering US$1.7 trillion, around 27 per cent of China's gross domestic product (GDP). The Chinese central bank had also expressed concerns, putting the debt figure even higher, at US$2.2 trillion, over 30 per cent of GDP. Analysts described these funds as 'loose' credit, often uncontrolled and unsecured. Often the collateral put forward did not exist, or its value was overstated. Much of this kind of lending was not subject to regulatory control; many local governments had even attempted to keep the scope of the lending secret.

Consumption and services

Taking a wider view of the Chinese economy, the Asian Development Bank (ADB) forecast that GDP would moderate in 2011 and 2012. Inflation was expected to rise in 2011, then decelerate in 2012. The new 5-year plan (2011–15) puts more emphasis on consumption and services as drivers of growth and on reducing both income inequality and pollution.

Better than expected economic growth in the second half of 2010 lifted the full-year rate of expansion to 10.3 per cent in a return to the pre-global recession double-digit pace. All sectors recorded solid growth, led by industry with a 12.2 per cent increase that contributed about two-thirds of total GDP growth. Services expanded by 9.5 per cent and agriculture by 4.3 per cent (helped by a good grain harvest). Investment and consumption accounted for 92 per cent of total growth, investment being the main contributor. The ADB considered that the easing of the aggressive fiscal stimulus put through during the global recession slowed the growth of fixed asset investment from the very high 31.0 per cent seen in 2009 to 24.4 per cent in 2010. Private consumption grew by 11.0 per cent in nominal terms (9.3 per cent in real terms), supported by higher incomes. Sales of household appliances and furnishings benefited from heavy investment in housing, while sales of automobiles continued to surge. Despite several years of solid growth in private consumption, however, it remains low as a share of expenditure based GDP at 34 per cent.

Net exports contributed positively to GDP growth in 2010 (by 0.8 percentage points), in contrast to 2009 when net exports fell as global trade slumped. Monetary policy supported growth, even as the authorities reined in the highly expansionary stance taken during the global recession. Growth in bank credit at Rmb8 trillion (US$1.25 trillion) also exceeded its target, by Rmb0.5 trillion (US$781 billion), although it was well below 2009's figure. This measure of credit is likely to understate the total as it excludes loans channelled through trust companies. Several estimates suggest that these off-balance-sheet loans amounted to about Rmb3.8 trillion (US$0.59 trillion) in 2010.

Abundant liquidity, rising food prices and higher costs of imported oil and commodities pushed up consumer prices during 2010, when inflation averaged 3.3 per cent. The government changed some of the weights in the consumer price index basket in early 2011, lowering that for food and raising the one for housing. Yet despite this, the index is still seen as understating inflation because its composition and weights have not been significantly adjusted to reflect the major changes in consumption patterns in the last decade.

Anxious to control inflation, the central bank raised the reserve requirement for banks six times in 2010 and three times in the first quarter of 2011 (to 20.0 per cent for large banks). It also lifted the benchmark interest rate twice in 2010 and once in the first quarter of 2011. The government also imposed price controls on some food items and increased subsidies for low-income earners.

Prices of residential property in cities rose strongly, propelled by rising incomes, investment demand and abundant liquidity. Overall property prices climbed by an average of 10.0 per cent in 70 major cities. Real estate investment surged by 33.5 per cent in nominal terms, outpacing overall investment growth. Government actions to curb house prices included raising both mortgage interest rates and down payments as well as directing banks not to lend for purchases of third (or more) homes. These changes damped the rate of increase during the year. Fiscal policy was supportive of growth in 2010, although less so than in 2009. Fiscal revenue and expenditure rose by 21.3 per cent and 17.4 per cent, respectively, well above the government's traditionally conservative targets. The strong revenue performance was a consequence of the robust economic growth and higher prices. The budget deficit narrowed to the equivalent of 2.1 per cent of GDP from 2.9 per cent in 2009.

International trade expands

Global recovery in trade in 2010 saw the country's trade flows soar by nearly 35 per cent to about US$3 trillion. Merchandise exports in nominal US dollar terms rebounded by 31 per cent. Imports rose even faster reflecting strong demand and higher prices for oil, other commodities and capital goods. The trade surplus at US$254 billion was little changed from 2009. However, China is diversifying its export markets in view of the slowdown in major industrial economies. It became Brazil's top trade partner in 2009 with bilateral trade showing a more than 12-fold increase in value since 2001. Some 85 per cent of its exports to Brazil are manufactured products, while soybeans and minerals account for two-thirds of its imports.

According to the ADB, foreign direct investment (FDI) reached US$105.7 billion in 2010, up by 12.4 per cent from the previous year. Manufacturing, real estate and services attracted the most FDI. The leading sources of FDI were (in order) Hong Kong, Taiwan, Singapore, Japan, the United States, the Republic of Korea and the United Kingdom. China's direct investment abroad increased by 23.4 per cent to US$59 billion in 2010. It targeted energy, mining and agriculture. Asia remained the top regional destination, although flows to South America and Africa picked up. Large investments in energy-related projects in some Central Asian countries have turned China into the second-largest investor there, after the Russian Federation.

Interestingly, China is also gaining prominence as a lender to developing countries: its lending in the past 2 years exceeded that from the World Bank (excluding the International Development Association, which makes grants and low-interest loans). These operations included loan-for-oil deals with Brazil, the Russian Federation and Venezuela; power-related projects in India; and infrastructure investments in Argentina and Ghana.

In 2010 China's current account surplus increased to US$305.2 billion, but as a ratio to GDP it declined to 5.2 per cent. The yuan appreciated against the US dollar by 3 per cent in nominal terms during the year, after the authorities indicated in June 2010 that they would gradually allow greater flexibility in the exchange rate. In real terms the yuan appreciated by 4.2 per cent in 2010. Efforts to 'internationalise' the currency resulted in much higher levels of yuan-denominated trade, estimated at Rmb70 billion in 2010 compared with just Rmb0.5 billion in 2009.

About 11.7 million new jobs were generated in urban areas in 2010, above the official target but still fewer than the average 24 million new job seekers who enter the labour market each year. Average minimum provincial wages rose by 24 per cent, illustrating government efforts to raise living standards and foster consumption.

12th Five year Plan 2011–15

The Plan, approved in March 2011, seeks to rebalance the pattern of growth. Its targets indicate that the authorities are willing to forgo some speed of GDP growth to enhance its sustainability. The ADB expected that fixed asset investment would remain the main driver of growth in 2011 and 2012, decelerating to 22 per cent in 2011 and to 20 per cent in 2012. Fiscal policy will be broadly expansionary, with a higher priority on education, health care, low-cost housing and research and development. The overall budget deficit is projected to be little changed at about 2 per cent of GDP.

Inflation pressures were prompting the authorities to tighten monetary policy, but their stance is expected to remain supportive of growth. They have trimmed the target for growth in M2 money supply to 16 per cent for 2011; a similar rate is assumed for next year. For new lending, the central bank has opted not to provide an annual target ceiling on new bank loans for 2011.

Energy

According to the US government's Energy Information Administration (EIA) China was a net oil exporter until the early 1990s but became the world's second largest net importer of oil in 2009. China's oil consumption growth accounted for over a third of the world's oil consumption growth in 2010. Natural gas usage in China has also increased rapidly in recent years and China has looked to raise natural gas imports via pipeline and liquefied natural gas (LNG). China is also the world's largest producer and consumer of coal, accounting for almost half of the world's coal consumption, an important factor in world energy-related CO_2 emissions.

Coal supplied the vast majority (71 per cent) of China's total energy consumption of 85 quadrillion British thermal units (Btu) in 2008. Oil is the second-largest source, accounting for 19 per cent of the country's total energy consumption. While China has made an effort to diversify its energy supplies, hydroelectric sources (6 per cent), natural gas (3 per cent), nuclear power (1 per cent) and other renewables (0.2 per cent) account for relatively small shares of China's energy consumption mix. The EIA projects coal's share of the total energy mix to fall to 62 per cent by 2035 due to anticipated increased efficiencies and China's goal to reduce its carbon intensity (carbon emissions per unit of GDP). However, absolute coal consumption is expected to double over this period, reflecting the large growth in total energy consumption.

Oil

According to the June 2011 issue of the BP Statistical Review of World Energy (BP Statistics) China had 14.8 billion barrels of proven oil reserves as of December 2010. China's largest and oldest oil fields are located in the north-east region of the country. China produced an estimated 4.07 million barrels per day (bpd) of total oil liquids in 2010, of which 96 per cent was crude oil. According to the *Oil & Gas Journal* (OGJ), China's oil production is forecast to rise by about 290,000bpd to over 4.5 million bpd in 2012. China consumed an estimated 9.2 million bpd of oil in 2010, up nearly 900 thousand bpd, or over 10 per cent from year-earlier levels. China's net oil imports reached about 4.8 million bpd in 2010 and it became the second-largest net oil importer in the world behind the United States in 2009. The EIA forecasts that China's oil consumption will continue to grow during 2011 and 2012 and the anticipated growth of 1.1 million bpd between 2010 and 2012 would represent almost 40 per cent of projected world oil demand growth during this 2-year period.

The Chinese government's energy policies are dominated by the country's growing demand for oil and its reliance on oil imports. The National Development and Reform Commission (NDRC) is the primary policy-making and regulatory authority in the energy sector, while four other ministries oversee various components of the country's oil policy. The government launched the National Energy Administration (NEA) in July 2008 in order to act as the key energy regulator for the country. The NEA, linked with the NDRC, is charged with approving new energy projects in China, setting domestic wholesale energy prices and implementing the central government's energy policies, among other duties. The NDRC is a department of China's State Council, the highest organ of executive power in the country. In January 2010, the government formed a National Energy Commission with the purpose of consolidating energy policy among the various agencies under the State Council.

China's total oil production was primarily due to new offshore production growth. China National Petroleum Corporation's (CNPC) Daqing field, in the north-east, produced about 797,000bpd of crude oil in 2010, according to FACTS Global Energy's most recent estimate. China Petroleum & Chemical Corporation's (Sinopec) Shengli oil field in the Bohai Bay produced about 547,000bpd of crude oil during 2010, making it China's second-largest oil field. However, Daqing, Shengli and other ageing fields have been heavily tapped since the 1960s and output is expected to decline significantly in the coming years. Recent exploration and production (E&P) activity has focused on the offshore areas of Bohai Bay and the South China Sea (SCS), as well as onshore oil and natural gas fields in western interior provinces such as Xinjiang, Sichuan, Gansu and Inner Mongolia.

Roughly 85 per cent of Chinese oil production capacity is located onshore, primarily in mature fields. Although offshore E&P activities have increased substantially in recent years, China's interior provinces, particularly in the north-west's Xinjiang Province, have also received significant attention. Recently, China announced its plan to make Xinjiang into the country's largest oil and gas production and storage base.

About 15 per cent of overall Chinese oil production is from offshore reserves and most of China's oil production growth will likely come from offshore fields. Offshore E&P activities have focused on the Bohai Bay region, the South China Sea (particularly the Pearl River Basin) and, to a lesser extent, the East China Sea. The Bohai Bay Basin, located in north-eastern China offshore Beijing, is the oldest oil-producing offshore zone and holds the bulk of proven offshore reserves in China. PetroChina initiated its phase one development of the Nanpu field in June 2007 and hopes to bring 200,000bpd of crude oil production on-stream by 2012. China National Offshore Oil Corporation (CNOOC) intends to double oil production in the offshore Bohai Bay, where over half of China's national oil company's (NOC) production is expected to originate by 2015. The NOCs made eight new discoveries in the Bohai Bay in 2009 and brought several fields online including Jinhzhou and Bonzhong. CNOOC's production in the Bohai Bay, including volumes from the East China Sea, was 317,000bpd in 2009.

In 2009, CNOOC's total oil production in the SCS was 191,000bpd. According to PFC Energy, CNOOC's proven hydrocarbon (oil and gas) reserves in 2009 in the SCS were 957 million barrels of oil equivalent, up 28 per cent from a decade ago. CNOOC and ConocoPhillips are developing the Panyu oilfields with output peaking at 60,000bpd. In 2010, CNOOC made another significant discovery of the Enping Trough in the shallow waters of the SCS, which could generate up to 30,000bpd. CNOOC tendered 13 blocks in May 2010 in the South China Sea.

But who owns what?

Territorial disputes in the East China Sea have so far limited large-scale development of fields in the region, including China and Japan's Exclusive Economic Zones (EEZs). The two countries have held negotiations to resolve the disputes. In June 2008, they reached an agreement to jointly develop the Chunxiao/Shirakaba and Longjing/Asurao fields. However, in early 2009, the agreement fell apart when China asserted sovereignty over the fields. Tensions in the second half of 2010 again surfaced between the two countries over the gas fields.

China also claims ownership of the potentially hydrocarbon rich Spratly Islands in the South China Sea, as do the Philippines, Malaysia, Taiwan and Vietnam. In June 2007, the UK's BP abandoned plans to conduct exploration activities near the Spratly Islands, citing ongoing uncertainty over competing ownership claims between China and Vietnam. The Paracel Islands, which China first occupied in 1974, are also claimed by Vietnam.

Natural gas

According to OGJ, China had 107 trillion cubic feet (tcf) of proven natural gas reserves as of January 2011, 27tcf higher than reserves estimated in 2009. China's production and demand for natural gas has risen substantially. In 2009, China produced 2.93tcf of natural gas, up around 8 per cent from 2008, while the country consumed 3.08tcf. China became a net natural gas importer for the first time in almost two decades in 2007.

The Chinese government anticipates boosting the share of natural gas as part of total energy consumption to 10 per cent by 2020 to alleviate high pollution from the country's heavy coal use. Consumption for 2009 rose from 2008 levels by over 12 per cent and the country imported over 140bcf of LNG to fill the gap. Although a majority of the gas consumption is dominated by industrial users (45 per cent in 2007 according to the National Bureau of Statistics), the growth of gas consumption in the past few years stems from the power, utilities and residential sectors. EIA projects gas demand to more than triple by 2035, growing about 5 per cent per year. To meet this anticipated shortfall, China is expected to continue importing natural gas via LNG and a number of potential import pipelines from neighbouring countries.

China's primary natural gas-producing regions are Sichuan Province in the south-west (Sichuan Basin); the Xinjiang Uygur Autonomous Region and Qinghai in the north-west (Tarim, Junggar and Qaidam Basins); and Shanxi Province in the north (Ordos Basin), producing about 65 per cent of China's total gas output. Several offshore natural gas fields are located in the Bohai Basin and the Panyu complex in the South China Sea.

Risk assessment

Economy	Good
Politics	Fair
Regional stability	Fair

COUNTRY PROFILE

Historical profile

From the nineteenth century onwards, the ruling Qing Dynasty (1644–1911) came under pressure from an increasing population and economic imbalances internally, and incursions from Western powers externally. Following defeat at the hands of the Japanese (1895) and escalating concessions to Western powers after the Boxer Uprising (1901), the centuries-old system of promotion to the civil service via examinations ended in 1905 and dynastic rule collapsed in 1911. Yuan Shikai failed to become emperor and a chaotic period of rule by 'warlords', regional power-brokers with military resources ensued.

1920s The Zhongguo Gongchangdang (Chinese Communist Party) (CCP) was formed and declared the southern province of Jiangxi an autonomous 'soviet' in 1927. The Communists were brutally suppressed by the rival Kuomintang (Nationalist Party).

1935 Mao Zedong took control of the CCP during the 'Long March', begun in October 1934, in which thousands of Communist fighters fled Jiangxi for the northern Shanxi province.

1937–45 The Japanese occupied increasingly large areas of China. The government of Chiang Kai-shek and the Kuomintang retreated to Sichuan province in the west of China.

1949 The People's Republic of China was established in October following the victory of Communist guerrilla forces led by Mao Zedong over the Kuomintang government, which fled to the island province of Formosa (now Taiwan).

1950 Tibet (Xizang), an independent region of western China, was occupied by the Chinese People's Liberation Army (PLA).

1958–60 In Mao's Great Leap Forward to collectivise agriculture and a socialist economic system, some 40 million people died from hunger.

1965 Tibet became an autonomous region of China, but has not enjoyed any real political or cultural autonomy.

1966 Chairman Mao launched the Great Proletarian Cultural Revolution in May. Some 800,000 died in the cities, but the wider effects of enforced rural re-education were widespread psychological trauma and the breakdown of industry and educational institutions.

1980–97 During this period, the CCP, with over 40 million members and political control, was dominated by China's elder statesman, Deng Xiaoping, who initiated gradualist economic reform designed to create a socialist market economy.

1986 The CCP Central Committee adopted a resolution redefining the general ideology of the CCP to provide a theoretical basis for the programme of modernisation and the open door policy of economic reform. An anti-corruption campaign was launched and there was significant liberalisation in the field of culture and the arts. However, student demonstrations in major cities were regarded by China's leaders as excessive 'bourgeois liberalisation'.

1987 In the ensuing clampdown of the 1986 demonstrations Hu Yaobang unexpectedly resigned as CCP general secretary, accused of 'mistakes on major issues of political principles'. The 'reformist' faction within the Chinese leadership emphasised the need for further reform and the extension of an open door policy. Li Peng became premier of the state council.

1989 The death of Hu Yaobang served as a catalyst for the most serious student demonstrations ever seen in China. The protests were against alleged corruption and nepotism within the government and sought a limited degree of Soviet-style *glasnost* in public life. A state of martial law was declared in Beijing. With the government fearing for its security, the army attacked protesters in and around Tiananmen Square, causing an unknown number of deaths. All over China, similar demonstrations were put down using force. The reformist Zhao Ziyang, CCP general secretary, was confined under house arrest. Deng brought in Jiang Zemin as general secretary to replace him. Jiang was also made chairman of the Central Military Commission (CMC) (head of the PLA).

1990 Martial law was lifted.

1992 The World Bank ranked China's economy third in the world after the US and Japan .

1993 Deng retired from his civilian offices, but continued to exert influence over the 'third generation' of leaders, including Jiang, who was elected state president.

1997 China regained sovereignty over Hong Kong, which had been in British control since a treaty signed in 1842.

1998 The NPC re-elected Jiang Zemin as president and approved major changes in the leadership, bringing in a new cabinet of younger technocrats.

2000 China signed bilateral trade deals with the EU and the US in preparation for its eventual accession to the World Trade Organisation (WTO) and consequent deeper integration within the global trading system.

2001 Tajikistan, China, Russia, Kazakhstan, Kyrgyzstan and Uzbekistan formed the Shanghai Co-operation Organisation (SCO). President Jiang Zemin offered China's support to the US for military action against terrorist activities following the 11 September attacks in the US. China was formally admitted to the WTO.

2003 The NPC elected Hu as state president and Zeng Qinghong as vice president; Wen Jiabao was appointed premier. China became the third country to put a man in space.

2004 Jiang Zemin resigned early as chairman of the CMC and President Hu Jintao assumed supreme authority. A landmark free-trade agreement was signed with the 10-member Association of Southeast Asian Nations (Asean).

2005 China threatened Taiwan with military force in the event of Taiwan's formal independence. Lien Chan was the first Taiwanese leader to visit China since 1949. China led the opposition to the proposal that Japan should become a permanent member of the UN Security Council citing Japan's failure to acknowledge its aggression during the 1930–40s. China scrapped its decade-old currency peg with the US dollar and sanctioned a 2.1 per cent revaluation of the renminbi against the dollar. Yao Wenyuan, last of the 'Gang of Four', died.

2006 China's Africa Policy, setting out its objectives for its relations with Africa, which promised investment and technical aid in return for African natural resources, was published. The Three Gorges Dam, the world's largest hydroelectric project, was completed. The 1,142km, railway line for passenger and freight between Quinghai and Tibet was completed. A China-Africa summit attracted 41 African heads of state and 48 heads of government to Beijing to meet hundreds of Chinese trade negotiators and business

people. The global annual trade surplus reached a record US$177 billion, an increase of 74 per cent.
2007 Vice Premier Huang Ju died. The Dalai Lama (Tibetan spiritual leader), announced that he was considering breaking a long tradition by naming his own successor, in an attempt to reduce the influence of CCP on his succession. China had taken into custody the chosen Panchen Lama, the second-highest spiritual leader in Tibetan Buddhism, Gedhun Choekyi Nyima, in 1995 and replaced him with its own, Gyancain Norbu, considered loyal to the communist party. The Panchen Lama chooses the succeeding Dalai Lama. Tibetan Buddhists fear that China will subvert their religion and culture by appointing its own Dalai Lama after the death of the reigning Dalai Lama.
2007 China's first high-speed train service began between Beijing and Shanghai.
2008 Hu Jintao and Wen Jiabao were re-elected president and prime minister respectively. A devastating earthquake of 7.9 magnitude struck the south-west province of Sichuan. A recorded 55,239 people died, 24,949 people were missing and 281,006 were injured by the earthquake. Over 5.46 million buildings collapsed and the authorities asked for 3.3 million tents from international aid to help house the 5.47 million people who were left homeless. The first regular, direct flights between China and Taiwan since 1949 began. China was given permission by the Convention on International Trade in Endangered Species (CITES) to import ivory. The government spent US$586 billion in a stimulus package to counter the effects of the worst of the global economic crisis.
2009 China and Russia signed a US$25 billion agreement, guaranteeing Russian oil to China until 2029. Ethnic violence in Xinjiang region erupted as young Uighurs demonstrated against discrimination. There were riots and attacks on the Han community; scores of people were killed and hundreds injured. Shanghai relaxed the one-child policy to encourage a second child to counter the social and economic effects of its aging population. The PRC celebrated 60 years in power with a huge parade involving 200,000 people along Beijing's Avenue of Eternal Peace. The populace had been told to view the spectacle on television and only the ruling elite were able to watch in person. Construction of a new six-lane bridge linking Hong Kong and Macao to China's mainland province of Guangdong began; when completed in 2016 it will be the longest sea-crossing bridge in the world (almost 50kms).
2010 China and Nepal agreed the height of Mount Everest to be 8,848m, the snow height, rather than the rock height as proposed by China. The economy grew by 11.9 per cent in the first quarter and overtook Germany as the world's second largest economy.
2011 A decision, by the four-country Mekong River Commission, to implement plans to build the controversial Mekong Xayaburi dam in Laos was due to be taken on 19 April, but following ecologically and socially adverse reports the decision was postponed. The Mekong River is a food source for millions of people along its length; the dam would reduce food production in favour of electricity generation. A smoking ban in public places came into force on 1 May, although smoking will still be permissible in workplaces. China had its first quarterly trade deficit (US$1.02 billion) in seven years in the first quarter of 2011. There was a trade surplus of US$140 million in March. The government increased the cost of electricity for industrial, agricultural and commercial users in a number of provinces from 1 June. The first ever audit of China's local government showed that at the end of 2010 there was a total debt of US$1.6 trillion. China's foreign exchange in the first quarter reached US$197 billion and in the second quarter US$153 billion. At 42.4km, the world's longest road bridge, spanning the coastal waters between the city of Qingdao and the suburb of Huangdao, in Jiaozhou Bay, was opened on 7 July. On 14 March, the Tibetan Dalai Lama announced that he was devolving power to his parliament-in-exile (in Dharamsala, India). Amendments to the Tibetan constitution (for the nation in exile), included an elected leader. The Dalai Lama retired from politics (aged 75), on 18 March. It was announced on 27 April that Lobsang Sangay would take over from the Dalai Lama as Kalon Tripa (prime minister) of the Tibetan government-in-exile. Sangay had won 55 per cent of the vote, beating two other candidates. Dr Sangay, a US university professor, was born in exile in India and has never visited Tibet. He was sworn in as the Tibetan premier on 8 August. On 24 July, 39 people were killed and almost 200 people injured when a high-speed train collided with another and derailed. There were accusations of design flaws in the signalling system and official corruption during construction. Tibet: On 7 November, the Dalai Lama answered Chinese criticism about a wave of self-immolation among monks and nuns (protesting about Chinese occupation of Tibet) saying that it was caused by Chinese 'cultural genocide' and that uncompromising officials had created a 'desperate' situation for Tibetans. In 2011, nine monks and two nuns committed public suicide in protest at what they saw as Chinese repression.

Political structure

Constitution

The current constitution came into effect in 1982 and mandates complete CCP rule of the country. China's constitution emphasises strict ideological homogeneity and forbids acts that endanger the state security. It states that the Chinese people must adhere to Marxism-Leninism and Mao Zedong Thought.
The People's Republic of China, a unitary state consisting of 22 provinces, four special municipalities under central government control and five autonomous regions, was established in October 1949. The provinces, special municipalities and autonomous regions elect local people's congresses and are administered by people's governments.

Form of state

People's republic

The executive

The executive is the 15-member State Council which is elected by the National People's Congress (NPC). State Council members, including the premier of the State Council, who is appointed by the president, may not serve more than two consecutive five-year terms. The NPC also elects the 155 members of the Standing Committee which convenes annually when the NPC is not in session.
Effective political control is in the hands of the CCP which has over 40 million members. All ministers are party members. The party's central committee of 175 full members meets irregularly for plenary sessions. A National Congress is usually held every five years when a new central committee is elected.
The political bureau (politburo) of the CCP sets policy and controls all administrative, legal and executive appointments; the nine-man politburo standing committee is the focus of power.
CCP committees are the key decision-making bodies in the provinces, cities and regions into which China is divided.
The president, who plays no formal role in administration, and vice president, are elected for a maximum of two consecutive five-year terms by the NPC.

National legislature

The unicameral Quanguo Renmin Daibiao Dahui (National People's Congress) (NCP) can have up to 3,500 members (currently 2,987), elected for five-year terms. Candidates are directly elected by voters of a local people's congress (village council) and raised to successive levels through a multi-tiered electoral system from provinces, municipalities, autonomous regions (including Hong Kong, Macao and Taiwan) and the armed forces to reach, eventually, the NCP.

The People's Political Consultative Conference (PPCC), with members drawn from a broader background coupled with the NCP make up the Lianghui (Two Meetings) to agree national political decisions.

Legal system

The Chinese legal system is an opaque mix of custom and statute. The judiciary and the government are closely connected. Much of the legal system remains at a partial stage of development.

The hierarchy of people's courts, ranging from Local People's Courts through Intermediate and then Higher People's Courts to the Supreme People's Court, is headed by the Ministry of Justice. The ministry was re-established in 1979 (it had been abolished in 1959 during Mao's 'Great Leap Forward'). Before 1979, arrests and sentences had to be approved by Communist Party committees. Although this practice was abolished in 1979, criminal law is still largely applied by the government as a form of public education, with periodic campaigns of mass arrests and executions used to frighten law-breakers.

People's courts, at all levels, deal with criminal, civic and economic matters in separate tribunals. Local people's mediation committees supplement the work of the courts by dealing with minor criminal offences and civil disputes, as well as helping implement government policy (such as the one-child per couple policy) at street level.

There is a similar hierarchy of people's procurates, re-established in 1978 after their abolition in the cultural revolution, extending from the localities to the Supreme People's Procurate. These monitor the work of state officials in the courts and the public security organs to ensure that they are observing the constitution and the law.

Supreme People's Court judges are appointed by the National People's Congress (NPC).

Last elections

October 2007 until February 2008 (NCP and PPCC); 15 March 2008 (presidential, indirect)

Results: Parliamentary: the CCP and the eight 'democratic' parties – all members of the China People's Political Consultative Conference – are allowed to stand in elections. The CCP forms the government.

Next elections

2012–13 (NCP and PPCC); 2013 (presidential, indirect)

Political parties

Ruling party

Zhongguo Gongchangdang (Chinese Communist Party) (CCP)

Main opposition party

Opposition parties are strictly controlled and do not offer alternative policies.

Population

1.34 billion (2010 census)

Last census: November 2000: 1,242,612,226

Population density: 140 inhabitants per square km (2010)

Annual growth rate: 0.8 per cent 1994–2004 (WHO 2006)

Ethnic make-up

The largest ethnic group is the Han, constituting 93.3 per cent of the population, which is largely concentrated around the basins of the main rivers (the Yellow River, the Yangtse and the Pearl River) and along the coast. Of the 55 other ethnic groups, 15 number over a million people each, including the Zhuang (Guangxi province), Hui (Muslims), Uygurs (in Xinjiang), Manchus, Tibetans, Mongolians and Koreans. The rest vary in size from several hundred thousand down to a few hundred.

Religions

China is officially atheist, but religion is tolerated to the extent that it does not challenge the state. Buddhism, Taoism, Islam, Catholicism and Protestantism all have followings. The formerly dominant belief system, Confucianism, continues to influence habits throughout society. Old temples, mosques and churches are being reopened and new ones built, but numbers are still far short of pre-revolutionary days. The Falun Gong religious movement is one of the religions considered to be subversive and its members have been arrested and imprisoned.

Education

The Ministry of Education in China estimates that 99 per cent of school-age children enter primary education, the length of which is six years. The retention rate in primary education for the whole country is 93 per cent.

Secondary education extends over six years, divided into general secondary education and vocational/technical secondary education. Both include two stages, junior secondary and senior secondary, of three years each. There are specialised schools and skilled workers' schools which cater for vocational training. The Ministry of Education estimated that 94 per cent of pupils finishing primary education enter secondary schools. It also says that half of pupils finishing junior secondary schools enter senior high education.

The Ministry of Education has encouraged the establishment of community colleges in major cities across China. Public expenditure on education was equivalent to less than 3 per cent of annual GDP in 2001 and included subsidies to private education at the primary, secondary and tertiary levels.

Literacy rate: 91 per cent adult rate; 99 per cent youth rate (15–24) (Unesco 2005).

Compulsory years: 7 to 16.

Pupils per teacher: 24 in primary schools.

Health

Employers pay for the medical care of most Chinese city-dwellers, while the rural population is in theory covered by local insurance schemes, village collectives or rural factories. The state and collective entities, such as factories or villages, run all large hospitals. There are a large number of private practitioners and privately run clinics.

It is estimated that more than one in five Chinese will be 60 years or older by 2030, which is likely to increase state expenses towards old age health care.

World Bank estimates show that 68 per cent and 24 per cent respectively in urban and rural areas have access to improved sanitation. Safe water facilities are available to 94 per cent of the urban population and 66 per cent of the rural population. Around 90 per cent of women use contraceptives, mainly due to the government's drive to keep down the birth rate.

Chinese consumption of tobacco products is popular and estimates say two-thirds of men smoke by the age of 25, with the vast majority maintaining the habit for many years. It is estimated that one third of Chinese men will die from smoking-related diseases, with the annual death toll reaching three million by 2050.

Hospitals rely on drug sales for 70 per cent of their budgets; in 2004 the Chinese government ordered price cuts for antibiotics, which account for 35 per cent of the Rmb49.6 billion (US$6 billion) pharmaceutical market. This measure is expected to have repercussions as it decreases hospital sales. Analysts say antibiotics are prescribed unnecessarily and the government is concerned about incentives, legal and illegal, that have resulted in hospital doctors prescribing them to about 80 per cent of in-patients.

In 2008, it was announced that a basic healthcare programme would be introduced for every citizen of China. Healthy China 2020 will provide universal health services to replace the patchy service that disadvantaged poorer patients, particularly the rural poor. The service will also monitor disease control and evaluate public health hazards.

The government announced that it was planning to invest an initial US$120 billion in healthcare reforms over the period 2009–11. Improving health insurance to include more people with basic cover and raising standards in public hospitals are priorities. The old state system was dismantled in the 1990s, during economic reforms, and since then there has been a growing disaffection among China's population, as around 50 per cent of all costs are met by the patient. Rural healthcare collapsed with secondary healthcare services provided only in towns and cities. With changes to the diet and a more Western lifestyle, which have led to Western afflictions such as heart disease and strokes, plus an ageing population, the health system is facing long-term challenges and a demand for more medical services, including screening and preventative measures.

Research in 2009 revealed that under the one-child policy selective abortion has left a marked imbalance between the sexes in China, with 32 million more males than females. Any measures, which may be introduced to re-dress the gender balance, will take many years to accomplish.

HIV/Aids

In 2003 there were over 840,000 people reported as living with Aids and there were 44,000 reported deaths due to Aids. The virus is now present in 31 regions and has exploited distinct risk groups. The prevalence of HIV infection among injecting drug users ranges from 35–80 per cent in Xinjiang, and 20 per cent of the population in Guangdong. Some rural communities in Anhui, Henan and Shandong have been hit by infection levels of 10–20 per cent, and as much as 60 per cent in the worst hit areas, where locals sold their blood plasma to supplement their poor incomes. Death rates in these areas are high, although not yet significant enough to affect national statistics.

In February 2009 government officials said that HIV/Aids was the leading cause of infectious death, at almost 7,000 by September 2008; tuberculosis and rabies fell to second and third causes of infectious deaths. Official statistics have become more reliable recently and there is a willingness by health officials to recognise HIV as a public health crisis; there had been reports of concerns of under-reporting by provincial and local officials. The disease has moved from high-risk groups into the mainstream population and officials are concerned that with growing industrialisation and with millions of migrant workers moving away from home the possibility of containing the disease has already been lost. Education programmes have been initiated.

HIV prevalence: 0.1 per cent aged 15–49 in 2003 (World Bank).
Life expectancy: 72 years, 2004 (WHO 2006)
Fertility rate/Maternal mortality rate: 1.7 births per woman, 2004 (WHO 2006); maternal mortality 55 per 100,000 live births (World Bank).
Birth rate/Death rate: 7 deaths and 16 births per 1,000 people
Child (under 5 years) mortality rate (per 1,000): 30 deaths per 1,000 live births (World Bank)
Head of population per physician: 1.6 physicians per 1,000 people, 2001 (WHO 2006)

Welfare

China's economic development is uneven, with a wide gap between cities and the countryside and between regions. China's social security expenses are typically equivalent to around 10 per cent of GDP.

The social insurance system includes provision for old age pensions, unemployment, medical care and industrial injury. Social insurance is implemented in accordance with state laws. The current focus of reform is on old age pension and unemployment insurance systems for urban enterprises. Social security entitlements have been allocated on a geographical footing with the working population being divided into urban and rural residents with the latter receiving far less in terms of benefits. Moreover, the urban population has been further split up into various layers depending on the size and importance of the employing enterprise or work unit. Therefore, a key state-owned enterprise (SOE) would offer better pension rights, wages and medical benefits than a smaller SOE or a township collective enterprise (COE).

The government increased the availability of the social security fund to more beneficiaries in 2003. The pension system is available to 150 million people, up from 130 million; the unemployment insurance system benefits approximately 110 million up from 100 million; and the medicare insurance system treats 100 million, an increase of 10 million people.

Another safety net beneath these systems is the minimum livelihood guarantee (MLG), which is administered by the Ministry of Civil Affairs (MCA). There are unemployment insurance schemes and some regions have started reforms of the basic medical insurance system.

Pensions

There is a partially funded pension scheme, which was launched in 1997, with two mandatory elements, a pay-as-you-go state pension administered by provinces, and individual pension accounts. There are also voluntary company pensions and for those most disadvantaged a social security fund. The pay-as-you-go system is based on contributions from employers and employees with the funds being pooled into a general account. In case of any shortfall, it is the responsibility of the local government to ensure funds are available to pay basic pension allowances. Government statistics indicate that SOEs contribute the majority of cash to pension funds.

In general, the contribution of the employer does not exceed 20 per cent of the overall wage bill of an enterprise. Employee contributions are between 4 and 8 per cent with employees in more developed areas paying the higher rate. The lower tier pension, known as the basic pension, is calculated at 20 per cent of the average wage of employees in the town or city.

As yet, China does not have a national policy for pension provision. Nevertheless the government is aware that with an ageing population and falling fertility rate China's dependency ratio – the numbers in work supporting the numbers in retirement – is projected to drop from 9:1 to 2.6:1 by 2045.

In August 2005 the government awarded operating licenses to 15 investment managers to operate China's new corporate pension scheme. Of the 15, four are foreign financial services ING, Fortis, Deutsche Bank and Bank of Montreal which are required to be in joint Chinese partnership. The new scheme will hold pension contributions in a legally distinct fund governed by trust law.

Main cities

Beijing (capital, estimated population 7.7 million (m) in 2004), Shanghai (10.8m), Tianjin (5.0m), Wuhan (5.1m), Shenyang (4.1m), Guangzhou (Canton, 5.0m), Nanjing (3.3m) Harbin (2.7m), Chongqing (2.4m), Jinan (2.1m), Changchun (2.4m), Chendu (2.5m), Taiyuan (2.0m), Jinan (2.1m), Dalian (1.7m), Qingdao (2.0m), Fushun (1.5m), Lanzhou (1.6m), Xi'an (2.9m), Zhengzhou (1.9m), Hangzhou (2.6m).

Languages spoken

There are seven main Chinese dialects, but the written language is the same for all dialects. Other languages include Tibetan, Uygur (a Turkic language) and Mongolian.

English is not widely spoken, especially outside the main cities, although there will usually be someone who can speak a little in hotels, restaurants and taxi stations.

Official language/s

Putonghua (Mandarin Chinese – Beijing dialect).

Media
All forms of media are tightly controlled by the authorities and recent labialisation has only been extended to distributions and advertising and not to editorial content.
The growth of the internet has resulted in 'the most extensive and effective legal and technological systems for internet censorship and surveillance in the world' according to an academic (industry?) report of 2005. China regularly blocks websites for groups it considers dissenting. Internet service providers and news organisations have agreed to Chinese censorship as part of their business contracts with China, which then allows access to its vast market.

Press
Dailies: The primary government-owned, Communist party, national newspaper, published in seven languages is *Renmin Ri Bao (People's Daily)* (www.people.com.cn), which has ten other separate newspapers. All cities have their own newspaper, typically published by the Communist party and therefore lacking much criticism of it. Corruption and inefficiency is reported but only after approval by Communist party officials. News outlets that have flouted this convention are subject to censure or swift closure.
In Chinese, *Zhongguo Qingnian Bao (China Youth Daily)* (www.cyol.net) aimed at Communist Young League, *Jie Fang Ri Bao (JF Daily)* (www.jfdaily.com) from Shanghai, *Dongnan Kuai Bao (Southeast Express)* (www.dnkb.com.cn), from Fujian, and *Guangzhou Metro Daily* (http://ycdtb.dayoo.com).
From Shanghai, in English, *Shanghai Daily* (www.shanghaidaily.com), *East Day* (http://english.eastday.com), includes business news, *The Shanghai News* (www.theshanghainews.net), *Shanghalist* (http://shanghaiist.com).
From Lassa, in Tibetan, *Bod Kyi Dus Bob (Tibet Times)* (www.tibettimes.net), in Chinese *Lasa Wan Bao* and online *China Tibet News* (www.chinatibetnews.com).
Weeklies: In Chinese, *Sanlian Shenghuo Zhoukan (Life Week)* (www.lifeweek.com.cn) a weekly of general interest, *Feng Hua Yuan (Chinese News & Culture Magazine)* (www.fhy.net), *Hau Xia Wen Zhai* (www.cnd.org) are bi-weeklies news magazines. *Trends* (www.trendsmag.com.cn) for women. In English, *Beijing Review* (www.bjreview.com.cn), is a national weekly news magazine and *Beijing Scene* (www.beijingscene.com), is a popular lifestyle magazine.
Business: There are several daily business newspapers, printed in Chinese, and some with English online editions, including *Jingii Ri Bao (Economic Daily)* (http://paper.ce.cn), *Jingii Guancha Bao (The Economic Observer)* (www.eeo.com.cn), *Guo Ji Shang Bao* (http://ibdaily.mofcom.gov.cn), *Qihuo Ri Bao* (www.qhrb.com.cn), *Zhongguo Gongshang Bao (China Industry & Commerce News)* (www.cicn.com.cn), *Zhongguo Jingji Shibao (China Economic Times)* (www.jjxww.com) and *Zhongguo Jinggii Bao (China Business)*, which specifically focusses on steel (www.chinaccm.com/0n). Other, major, regional cities have their own editions of the *Economic Daily*.
Magazines include a bi-weekly *Caijing (Business and Financial Review)* (www.caijing.com.cn).
Periodicals: In English, *Beijing This Month* is a semi-tourist magazine.

Broadcasting
All broadcasting is overseen by the Ministry of Radio, Film and Television.
Broadcast media, for most people, is limited to government-run organs, as foreign short wave radio signals are regularly jammed and the use of satellite receivers restricted. There are more than one billion television views and TV is a popular source of news and information.
Pay-to-view TV is a growing market and is expected to have around 130 million customers by 2010.
Radio: The government-run China National Radio has four national networks, plus China Radio International (CRI) (www.cri.cn) with services in 45 languages and a service devoted to Taiwan. Domestic radio services broadcast in the country's major languages and dialects. There are over 500 government-owned local radios stations, including the Beijing People's Broadcasting Station (BPBS), which has several services including a Special Educational Service, and Economic, Traffic and Literary stations.
The first foreign language radio station, in Beijing, Radio 774 (http://am774.bjradio.com.cn), was set up in 2004 by the Chinese government, specifically for foreign residents.
Television: The national state-run, China Central Television (CCTV) (http://english.cctv.com), has over 2,000 channels available for its viewers through a network of regional and municipal stations.
Non-domestic programmes are limited, with a few foreign TV companies providing services via either cable or satellite dishes.

Advertising
The Advertising Law of 1995 regulates all aspects of advertising under the auspices of the State Administration for Industry and Commerce. Certain products require additional approval before advertising such as tobacco, alcohol, pharmaceuticals and medical products and services.
As China's middle class has grown so has its consumerism, so that the advertising market in Asia is second only to Japan. It is worth over US$20 billion annually and has had a growth rate of over 10 per cent since 2004. Multinational corporations dominate the advertising industry with either products or techniques, but domestic enterprises are growing in importance and provision of services. Multinationals are as intent on protecting their brands as they are in promoting them throughout the country.

News agencies
National news agency: Xinhua (New China News Agency)

Economy
China has natural resources that provide many of the necessary basics for an advanced economy, including almost above all else a huge labour force (an estimated 813 million in 2010). However, around 40 per cent of this workforce is a peasant class engaged in agriculture, using technology to maintain intensive cultivation techniques, so that although China's arable land is only 75 per cent that of the US total, it produces around 30 per cent more than the US. China is the world's largest producer of rice and a significant producer of wheat, tea, pork and fish. Agriculture provides China with a high level of self-sufficiency in food; nevertheless agriculture's share of GDP fell from 28 per cent in 1978 to 11 per cent in 2008 as the industrial-manufacturing sector expanded. China's primary industries include coal mining, with reserves of 114 trillion tonnes and production of 1,553 million tonnes of oil equivalent (mtoe) in 2009. What it doesn't grow or produce it imports to power its manufacturing base which has turned China into the world's factory.
China, the 'C' in Bric, the acronym reputedly coined in a Goldman Sachs report of 2003, arguing that by 2050 Brazil, Russia, India and China would be wealthier than most current major economic powers.
Unlike the other Bric countries, China has an authoritarian government that has been able to plan and follow a strategy with a centralised economy based on set objectives, so that imports of natural materials were purchased on a national basis to be distributed and supplied at wholesale prices. Single item factory towns were built providing cheap labour for factories geared up for mass production, wholly for export sales. Before the global economic crisis took hold, the industry and manufacturing sector constituted 48 per cent of GDP and exports produced a trade

balance of US$261.9 billion and US$297 billion in 2007 and 2008 respectively. As global trade weakened, exports in 2009 fell, resulting in a trade balance of US$198.2 billion.
GDP growth in 2007 was 13.0 per cent, which fell markedly to 9.6 per cent in 2008 as global oil prices rose, due in large part to demand by China reaching around 10 per cent of total world use (only the US at around 20 per cent was higher). As the global economic crisis weakened the economies of trading partners, so exports fell. GDP growth in 2009 was 9.1 per cent and was predicted to rise to 10.5 per cent as global trade picked up. The State Council issued a new industrial plan in October 2009 to reduce overcapacity in seven heavy industries including cement, steel and aluminium smelting, following a boom in investment in infrastructure, paid for by public spending and lending by state-owned banks. This plan coincided with the publication of manufacturing statistics that recorded a straight seven-month expansion rate. Since becoming a member of the WTO, trade has grown so much that by 2010 China had overtaken Germany and Japan to become the world's second leading trading nation after the US.
Although China didn't slip into recession in 2008–09 it was worried that rising unemployment could trigger social unrest and social security was improved. Around 10 million (rural) migrant workers had lost their jobs by February 2009. In June 2010 migrant workers not only went on strike to demand better wages and working condition but also formed an independent and effective trade union. Inflation rose to a 28-month high of 28 per cent in November 2010.
Despite being a regime that espoused Communist principals China has been subject to the worst excesses of the West's malpractice, from petty provincial officials misappropriating land and government funds to capitalists manipulating China's only stock exchange through insider trading. However, when the authorities move to punish such felons, it is swift and harsh, typically ending in capital punishment.
The central bank de-linked the renminbi from the US dollar in 2005, and kept it within a 3 per cent margin of the US dollar. However it was re-linked in 2008 as the economic crisis cut Chinese exports but this left the renminbi undervalued and drew criticism from the US and India. In June 2010 the central bank announced an incremental revaluation of the currency, of 0.43 per cent, which raised the value of the yuan while not threatening export sales. The IMF noted that the yuan was still 'undervalued', although this was an improvement on the 'substantially undervalued' earlier comment.
Officials became concerned about the growth in property prices and a possible 'bubble' based on price speculation, so that from February 2011 permanent residents were restricted to the purchase of two apartments, while others were restricted to one only.
Inflation in July 2011 was 6.5 per cent and the government instigated measures to promote an economic slowdown and reduce inflation. Industrial production in August 2011 rose by 13.5 per cent on strong domestic demand when they reached a record high of US$155.6 billion, up 30.2 per cent on August 2010. However, in September 2011, the average minimum wage had risen by over 21.7 per cent, which increased production costs and may threaten China's pre-eminence as one of the world's cheapest manufacturing centres.
Imports in August 2011 showed strong domestic demand when they reached a record high of US$155.6 billion, up 30.2 per cent on August 2010. Exports rose by 24.5 per cent, resulting in a trade surplus of US$17.8 billion, down from US$31.5 billion in July.

External trade

Since becoming a member of the WTO trade has grown so much that by 2010 China had overtaken Germany to become the world's second highest trading nation after the US.
Its agricultural, manufacturing and industrial sectors export a huge range of items from seeds to hi-tech electronic equipment, from mass-produced garments to custom-built oil tankers; its service sector is not as well developed.
In November 2009 China pledged US$10 billion in concessionary loans (2010–13) to Africa, this was in addition to 50 previous co-operation agreements and US$5 billion to encourage Chinese firms to invest in Africa.
China and Taiwan signed a direct trade agreement ib 2008, enhancing trade links by increasing the number of flights between the countries, allowing many more passengers to visit. Tax free, direct cargo shipments are allowed between designated ports. Direct postal services have been improved and expanded.
Imports in August 2011 showed strong domestic demand when they reached a record high of US$155.6 billion, up 30.2 per cent on August 2010. Exports rose by 24.5 per cent, resulting in a trade surplus of US$17.8 billion, down from US$31.5 billion in July.

Imports

Main categories are petroleum, energy, light industrial and metal products, machinery and equipment, plastics, optical and medical equipment, organic chemicals, timber, iron and steel.
Main sources: Japan (typically 13 per cent of total), South Korea (10 per cent), Taiwan (9 per cent).

Exports

Principal exports include machinery and equipment, plastics, clothing, optical and medical equipment, finished goods, vehicles and parts, iron and steel.
Main destinations: US (typically 18 per cent of total), Hong Kong (14 per cent), Japan (8 per cent).

Agriculture

Farming

China's economy was traditionally based on agriculture, but since collectivisation and the Mao-era requirement for self-sufficiency in food was replaced with co-operatives in 1976, farming have experienced the progressively hard realities of the market place with large unprofitable state farms closing down and workers made redundant. Around 40 per cent of this workforce is employed in agriculture, using technology to maintain intensive cultivation techniques, so that by 2010 China became the world's largest consumer of fertilisers. China's arable land is only 75 per cent that of the US total, it produces around 30 per cent more than the US. China is the world's largest producer of rice and a significant producer of wheat, tea, pork and fish. Agriculture provides China with a high level of self-sufficiency in food; nevertheless agriculture's share of GDP fell from 28 per cent in 1978 to 11 per cent in 2008 as the industrial-manufacturing sector expanded.
With a burgeoning industrial base, China is experiencing rapid urbanisation and rural workers, looking for better wages and a share of China's increasing standard of living, have joined the factory line. A land reform law enabled farm collectives and members to sell their land; the government's ultimate aim is land privatisation. About 5 per cent of farmland, or 6.7 million hectares (ha), have been lost to mainly industrial development since 1997 and pressure on resources, such as water, is, in some areas, becoming critical. Land use and erosion have resulted in pollution and flooding, which prompted the government to modify the new reforms, including delisting 70 per cent of development zones, thus saving over 24,000 square kilometres of farmland.
Although all land is officially owned by the state, land ownership comes in the form of 'land use rights', which give the title-owner rights for between 30–70 years. Forty million farmers have lost the rights to their land since 1984 and rural

communities are protesting at the manner of the purchase and sale of farmland. Re-designated land use has also been initiated by the government with 5.4 million ha of arable land given over to forestry, while cotton growing has dropped by over 7 per cent. Both of these measures, and the reinforced embankment of the middle and lower reaches of the Yangtze and Yellow rivers, are measures designed to stem the disastrous flooding seen increasingly since the early 1990s.

Government policy, incorporating the changes that entry to the WTO has imposed, is mostly concerned with food security. The government's traditional agricultural policy has been to encourage farmers to increase production to meet the needs of the cities, while keeping prices low. This has involved guaranteeing farmers a price for a proportion of their crop and offering it at a subsidised price in the towns.

The government is attempting to increase farm incomes – which are markedly below those in the cities – in the hope that the sector can provide the impetus for growth of consumer products. The government is considering changing agricultural policy to focus more on grain quality rather than quantity in order to cope with external competition. There is likely to be increased rural poverty and unemployment in the medium-term as cheaper imports bite. The conundrum remains of how to increase rural incomes and provide food for a huge population without significant state intervention and, by extension, state distortion of the market.

From 2005, a policy that limits foreign producers of genetically modified (GM) seed crops from accessing the Chinese market runs concurrently with the country's own research and development to produce its GM crops in cotton and rice (US$121 million in 2004). The government's problematic position is hampered by its appreciation of the sales potential for unmodified crops in overseas markets that are reluctant to take GM crops, against the need for higher domestic yields and the possibility for sales of Chinese patented GM seed crops abroad.

According to the Centre for Chinese Agricultural Policy, China will need to produce more than 1.5 times the 1999 level of grain output to feed a population of 1.6 billion by 2030. The demand for livestock and aquatic products is forecast to double in the same period.

An agricultural reform and development plan was approved by the central committee in 2008. The plan aims to double the income of farmers in two decades.

Fishing

With its extensive river network and long coastline, China produces a substantial quantity of fish and exports much of it to its regional neighbours. The total marine fishing ground area is about 818,000 square nautical miles and China has a total of 150 commercially exploitable marine species in its waters. The main species are silver carp, bighead carp, grass carp and tilapia.

China's marine fishing production is made up of small-scale fisheries and the state-owned enterprises (SOEs). The small scale fisheries produce an estimated 90 per cent of the total seafood supply. The reform of SOEs has improved productivity in large-scale fishing operations. In common with other fishing grounds, stocks in the South and East China Seas are becoming depleted. Inland fishing is showing an increase, following a period of decline caused by the depletion of inland freshwater habitats due to dam-building, industrial pollution and land reclamation for agriculture.

Forestry

China has around 14 per cent forest cover, almost evenly divided between coniferous and broadleaved forests. Southern forests are mainly lowland rain forests and monsoon forests. In the north, the majority of forests are mixed coniferous.

The government has embarked on a policy of reforestation. Deforestation was partially blamed for the disastrous extent of the 1998–99 floods which killed thousands and swamped cities, agricultural land and industrial enterprises. Huge coniferous forests have been planted and it is hoped that slower-growing deciduous trees will augment them in the reforested areas.

The State Forestry Administration, has set ambitious targets for China to raise afforestation by 26 per cent by 2050.

China is one of the world's five largest wood-producing countries, although the majority of production is burned as fuel. It is a net exporter of wood products and also produces a large amount of non-wood forest products such as resins, tung oil, essential oils, bamboo poles and bamboo shoots, nuts, mushrooms, honey and medicinal plants.

Industry and manufacturing

China's industrial base is highly diversified and ranges from the production of metals and oil refining to light industry such as textiles and computer hardware. The manufacturing sector accounts for around 37 per cent of GDP. The major industries are mechanics, electronics, metallurgy, chemicals, building materials, furniture, woodwork, textiles, clothing, food, petroleum and coal processing. The government has been focussing on restructuring the industrial sector and introducing advanced technology. The government hopes to phase out small scale production and encourage foreign participation, particularly in the chemicals industry. The development of effective, low-cost chemicals for agricultural use is a top priority.

China has become a production centre for a multitude of labour-intensive assembly industries. China produces around 75 per cent of the global supply of textiles. There is considerable foreign investment coming from Hong Kong (which accounts for most of new funding in the Shenzhen Special Economic Zone), Japan and the US. China has the ability to exploit vertical economic linkages from its impressive natural resources to heavy industy and the manufacturing of white goods, which has shown impressive growth since the early 1990s.

China is a net exporter of aluminium and stands to become one of the world's largest aluminium producers. It is also a major exporter of magnesium, although competitors have complained that China has driven down global magnesium prices through price dumping on commodity markets. China is the world's largest steel producer.

Vehicle production is an important growth sector. On the basis of growth levels sustained since the late 1990s, China stands to become one of the world's largest car exporters by 2010.

China's attraction as a foreign investment destination has increased since it became a WTO member, since low production costs and cheap labour have encouraged many foreign businesses to transfer their operations to the mainland. The main concern is that increased competition will have a devastating effect on state-owned industries. More joint-venture companies are likely to evolve over time, leading to mixed-ownership control in the industrial sector.

Chinese industry is faced with an increasing domestic oversupply problem. At the same time, domestic demand has fallen as state-owned enterprises lay off workers as part of the government's restructuring programme. This has increased competition within Chinese industry, causing deflation and putting pressure on factory gate prices. The problems facing the industrial sector have led to concerns that Chinese companies, stimulated by the government's fiscal pump-priming of the economy, have been investing too much in increasing capacity.

Problems facing China's industrial sector are the lack of workable bankruptcy laws and the corruption of local officials, who are keeping failing industries afloat.

State-owned banks are forced to carry the burden of the industrial sector's debt, a burden that is unsustainable. An eventual clamp-down on non-performing loans

within the banking sector will affect the industrial sector. The government is encouraging investment in privately-owned industrial firms, with the possibility of opening up the sector to further foreign investment.
In June 2011 workers rioted for several days in the industrial city of Zengcheng after a market stall-holder was allegedly assaulted by security personnel. Although the stall-holder's refusal to move triggered the protests, there is long-held resentment among migrant workers (many from Sichuan province) of official corruption and abuse of power in Zengcheng. In August 2011, industrial output rose by 13.5 per cent on the same period in 2010. However, as inflation in July 2011 was a three-year high of 6.5 per cent, by September the average minimum wage had risen by over 21.7 per cent, which increased production costs as a time when China had instigated measures to promote an economic slowdown and reduce inflation. The rising production costs could weaken China's pre-eminence as one of the world's cheapest manufacturing centres.

Tourism
China is one of the world's most visited destinations and the tourism sector is being vigorously developed and promoted. Infrastructure was expanded and received extra impetus for the 2008 Olympic Games in Beijing. However, typical visa rules and restricting can pose an obsticle to potential visitors.
Visitor numbers to Tibet have increased to over four million per year. The increase has been put down to better marketing and the new high-speed rail service to China.
In 2008 an agreement was signed with Taiwan to allow 3,000 tourists per day into each country.

Environment
China is a land of contrast. While a project of land reclamation has been in operation since 2001 in the north- western Ningxia Hui autonomous region, where willows and grass are helping to beat back the desert, for many regions around China the prospects are not so good. The Yellow River typically runs dry before it reaches the sea due to the overuse of water for irrigation. Desertification is accelerating and threatens one-third of the country and 400 million people. The national policy of self-sufficiency in food in the past resulted in the cultivation of unsuitable grain crops in desert areas and, coupled with logging and over-exploitation exacerbated by a natural lack of water and rainfall, has led to rapid soil erosion. The beginnings of a forest have been planted in Yanchi in an effort to avert the spring sandstorms that sweep through Beijing each spring.
In contrast, the central and southern regions are hit every summer by severe floods. The worst affected areas are the middle and upper reaches of the Yangtze River, where the Three Gorges Dam is expected to bring some relief when it is completed. As it neared its completion, the risk to the environmental and ecology, wich included landslides and loss of drinking water, prompted officials to plan to relocate over four million people to the city of Chongqing from the immediate vicinity of the Three Gorges Dam between 2007–22.
In 2005 an explosion in a state-run chemical plant caused an 80km toxic benzene slick that flowed down the Songhua River endangering over nine million inhabitants who depend on the river for their supply. Many residents of the city of Harbin joined an exodus to avoid the danger when authorities halted river-water supplies and handed out thousands of bottles of water while the slick passed.
In 2008, China was reported to be the biggest carbon polluter in the world. The figures in the report came from provincial-level data from China's own Environmental Protection Agency. Nevertheless, the US per capita emission is still 5–6 times higher than China and any pressure to cap emissions in either country will require overcoming their no-harm-to-economic-growth stance.
The government declared a drought emergency in February 2009 in eight northern and central provinces. Around four million people lacked drinking water and half of the country's winter crops of wheat and rapeseed were threatened. Irrigation in the effected areas traditionally relies on rainwater; the drought is the worst since 1951.

Mining
China's mining industry ranks as one of the largest in the world, although production statistics are sketchy. Most of China's mineral production is consumed locally by state-owned enterprises (SOEs). There are around 80,000 SOEs and 200,000 collectively-owned mines. China is an important producer of copper, tungsten, antimony, lithium and molybdenum, and also produces significant quantities of zinc, lead, manganese, tin, mercury and rare earths. China ranks among the top five countries for its reserves of antimony, barite, graphite, magnesite, fluorite, molybdenum, tin and tungsten. China imports alumina, chromite, cobalt, copper, iron ore, manganese and other platinum-group metals. China is an extremely important market for the global minerals industry and is one of the largest mineral exporters, importers and producers in the world.
China is becoming increasingly important in the molybdenum market and has substantially more deposits of rare earth elements than the rest of the world, 97 per cent of them in the Bayan Obo iron ore mined in Inner Mongolia.
A Chinese-owned mining company won a tender to develop one of the world's largest copper mines sited in Logar Province in Afghanistan. It is estimated that the site has 13 million tonnes of copper. Australia, Canada, China and Russia all contested the tender, ultimately won by Metallurgical Group with an investment of US$3 billion.

Hydrocarbons
Proven oil reserves were 14.8 billion barrels at the end of 2010, with production at 4.0 million barrels per day (bpd), an increase of 7.1 per cent on the 2009 figure. However with consumption at 9.0 million bpd in 2009 China relies on imported oil to meet its needs and since the early 1990s has rapidly moved from being a net exporter of oil to the world's third largest net importer (after the US and Japan). It also has the second largest refining capacity in the world after the US, at 10.1 million bpd.
Around 85 per cent of Chinese oil production is located onshore, in the aging Daqing and Shengli fields in north-eastern and east China respectively. Exploration is concentrated in new offshore sites in the north-eastern Bohai Sea and the southern Pearl River Delta. Oil production is currently controlled by two state-owned oil firms, the China National Petroleum Corporations (CNPC) and the China Petroleum and Chemical Corporations (Sinopec), which combined dominate the upstream and downstream oil markets. CNPC, with a publicly listed subsidiary, PetroChina, concentrates on exploration and output, while Sinopec focuses on refining and distribution. In 2010, PetroChina was ranked as the second largest energy company (after the US-based ExxonMobil), based on capital value, in the world.
A US$25 billion deal was signed in 2009, whereby China is supplied with Siberian oil in exchange for Chinese loans to Russian companies. The Chinese Development Bank loaned Rosneft and Transneft, the Russian state oil company and pipeline company, US$15 billion and US$10 billion respectively. Some 300,000 barrels a day of oil annually began flowing through the pipeline in January 2011.
China considers the agreement to be strategically vital as it diversifies its hydrocarbon supplies away from the Middle East.

The inauguration of a new oil refinery in Guangxi Province took place on 9 September 2010. PetroChina, the owner/operator invested US$2.2 billion for the 200,000 barrels of oil capacity plant, located near the border with Vietnam, in the city port of Qinzhou.
China, along with Vietnam, Taiwan, Brunei, Malaysia and The Philippines, claims the potentially oil-rich Spratly Islands.
Proven natural gas reserves were of 2.8 trillion cubic metres (cum) in 2010, the majority of which are located in the south-western Sichuan Province, and the north-western region Xinjiang Uyghur Autonomous region. The latest discovery, the Puguang field in Sichuan Province, has proven reserves of 356 billion cum that could reach a total of 500–550 billion cum. Production in 2010 was 96.8 billion cum, which was an increase of 13.5 per cent on its 2009 levels. In 2007 China imported 3.3 billion cum of liquefied natural gas, which by 2010 had risen to 12.8 billion cum and total imports of natural gas were 16.35 billion cum. Indonesia and Australia are the source of the greatest proportion of natural gas imports. On 26 May 2011, PetroChina received its first LNG train of 145,000cum from Qatar at its new terminal at Rudong in Jiangsu Province.
China plans to replace coal with natural gas as the main source of power generation in homes in its major cities and the 4,000km west-east pipeline extending across the country to the urban coastal areas could eventually be extended to tap the large gas reserves of Central Asia.
The Sichuan-Shanghai natural gas pipeline became operational in September 2010. The US$9.2 billion pipeline is designed to transport 12 billion cubic metres of natural gas per year. China's consumption of natural gas was 3.4 per cent of total world gas consumption in 2010.
Coal is China's primary source of energy; there were proven reserves of 114.5 billion tonnes at the end of 2010, of which around 62 billion is thermal anthracite and 52 billion the lesser coking (brown) coal used in power stations. Production was 1,800.4 million tonnes of oil equivalent (mtoe), an increase of 9 per cent on the 2009 levels of 1,652.1mtoe. The main export destinations for Chinese coal are South Korea and Japan. China is becoming more open to foreign investment in its coal industry, in a bid to modernise the industry.

Energy

China's total installed generating capacity exceeded 700 million kW by 2007, of which around 70 per cent is produced by low quality and polluting coking coal, so there are plans to increase the number of natural gas electricity power stations. The giant Three Gorges dam was completed in 2006, with 26 generators capable of producing 847 million kilowatt hours (kWh) through hydropower. Another large hydroelectric project will involve a series of dams on the Yellow River, with 25 generating stations with a combined installed capacity of 158 million kW. The government is also expanding nuclear power generating capacity, with the construction of eight new nuclear power plants in joint ventures with Russian, French and Canadian firms.
The government hopes eventually to unify electricity distribution into one national power grid with power generators selling their electricity at rates determined by a free market. In the meantime there is a power shortage and the government increased the cost of electricity for industrial, agricultural and commercial users in a number of provinces from 1 June.

Financial markets

In 1986, the stock market in Shanghai, the largest in East Asia before 1949, reopened to trade shares and bonds. China has since opened securities exchanges in 44 cities, including the capital Beijing, but trading so far has been thin. Shanghai and the Shenzhen Stock Exchange (formally opened in 1991) remain the two major markets for both domestic and foreign investors. Both markets list 'A' shares (for domestic investors) and 'B' shares (for foreign investors) as well as bonds and warrants. As a result of further planned privatisation, Shanghai's total market capitalisation is expected to increase from US$600 billion in 2002 to US$2 trillion by 2010, although there are uncertainties surrounding the government's commitment to the privatisation programme. The market, driven by millions of retail investors, is thought to be overvalued and subject to illegal manipulations.
An equity market for small- and medium-sized companies (similar to the Alternative Investment Market in London) was established on the Shenzhen stock market in 2009. Called the Growth Enterprise Board it was expected to start operations in October.

Stock exchange

Shanghai Stock Exchange (SSE)

Commodity exchange

Dalian Commodity Exchange (DCE)

Banking and insurance

China's accession to the WTO in late 2001 means that reform in the country's banking sector became essential for China's domestic banks to compete with foreign-owned banks in the future. This meant eliminating corruption at the highest levels of management. Under the WTO agreement, foreign banks were allowed to offer renminbi banking services to Chinese corporations from 2004, and will be allowed to offer services to Chinese individuals from 2007.
In 2003, the country was dominated by four large banks, the Bank of China, the Agricultural Bank of China, China Construction Bank and Industrial and Commercial Bank of China, which between them controlled 80 per cent of banking services. WTO membership gives foreign banks the right to compete with domestic ones and all restrictions on the setting up, operation and licensing of foreign banks were eliminated by 2005. In addition, state-owned banks are to provide foreign currency services. In December 2001, HSBC became the first foreign bank to obtain equity in mainland China when it acquired 8 per cent in the Bank of Shanghai.

Central bank

People's Bank of China. The central bank became an autonomous financial institution in 1995.

Time

GMT plus eight hours
Despite its size, China works to one time zone only.

Geography

China is the third-largest country in the world after Russia and Canada. Its 28,000km land boundary touches North Korea, Russia, Mongolia, Afghanistan, Pakistan, India, Nepal, Bhutan, Myanmar, Laos and Vietnam.
China is bounded by the Yellow and East China Seas to the east and by the South China Sea to the south.
Deserts and semi-arid grasslands make up much of the western and northern parts of the country. Central and eastern China are the most heavily populated parts of the country. The plains of north and north-east China are flat and fertile, but frequently suffer from prolonged drought.
Mountain ranges occupy 33 per cent of China's area. Most of China's main rivers run west to east. The longest is the Yangtze River, followed by the Yellow River. The Yangtze River is known as Chiangjiang (long river) in China.
Much of China was once covered by forest, but due to dense settlement and intensive agriculture, most forests have disappeared.
There are 23 provinces including Henan, Guangdong, Shandong, Sichuan, Jiangsu, Hebei, Hunan, Anhui, Hubei and Zhejiang; four municipalities – Beijing (Northern Capital), Chongqing (Double Celebration), Shanghai (Above the Sea) and Tianjin (Heaven's Crossing); five autonomous regions – Guangxi (Western

Expanse), Neimengu (Inner Mongolia), Ningxia (Peaceful China), Xinjiang Uygur (New Frontier) and Xizang (Tibet) (Western Buddhists) and two special administrative regions – Hong Kong and Macau.

Hemisphere

Northern

Climate

China, with its extensive land mass, has a diverse climate with five temperature zones: cold-temperate, mid-temperate and warm-temperate, subtropical and tropical zone, as well as a plateau climate zone in Tibet.

Weather patterns for most of China are influenced by the monsoon periods that strike in different parts from April to October. Not only is there a series of monsoons drawn from the Pacific Ocean that dominate in turn, the south-east, eastern then northern regions but also one that is drawn from the Indian Ocean that strikes southern mainland China.

The average temperature in summer in Beijing is 28 degrees Celsius (C); Shanghai 16 degrees C and Guangzhou 32 degrees C.

Dress codes

Foreign businessmen generally wear suits and ties to negotiating sessions with Chinese counterparts, who have abandoned the Mao suit for Western dress. Less formal attire is acceptable outside the main cities.

Fashion-consciousness is growing among younger urban Chinese.

Entry requirements

Passports

All visitors need to hold a passport with validity of a minimum of six months. Passports should have at least a few blank pages for visas and entry and exit stamps.

Visa

Required by all, except transit passengers. Business visits can only be made with an invitation fom a Chinese organisation such as a ministry or commercial institution. Foreign firms may request such invitations from a trading corporation. An invitation in the form of a fax is usually sufficient for the visa application which should also include a business letter and itinerary. For up-to-date information concerning visas contact the nearest consulate.

It is possible for individuals to organise their own itinerary and when this has been confirmed by the authorities, the visitor must finance the cost of accommodation and the tour by depositing the amount, through a home bank, with China International Travel Service.

If arriving from Mongolia, airlines in Ulaanbaatar require holders of foreign passports to have a Chinese visa in order to board the aircraft for flights to Beijing. This requirement applies regardless of the length of time in transit at Beijing.

Currency advice/regulations

Export and import of local currency is limited to Rmb20,000; all exports of renminbi must be accompanied by a foreign currency conversion receipt, issued by domestic banks. Renminbi may be converted overseas within six months from any Bank of China operation but only with a foreign currency conversion receipt.

Import and export of foreign currency is unlimited but any amount over the equivalent of US$5,000 being exported must be declared.

Travellers cheques, preferably in US dollars, are accepted in major cities, in banks and four and five star hotels.

Customs

Certain items produced in China before 1949, such as embroidery, silks, porcelain, scrolls and *objets d'art*, may be subject to export restrictions. When arriving, listing electonic equipment and camera gear etc is compulsory on customs forms; if these items are not with the traveller on departure, the traveller is liable to pay duty on them. Receipts for any major purchases, especially paintings and antiques, should be kept.

Prohibited imports

Printed material, films, tapes that are viewed to be adverse to China's politics, economy, culture and ethics.

Health (for visitors)

Mandatory precautions

Vaccination certificates are required for yellow fever if travelling from an infected area.

Advisable precautions

Take precautions against HIV/Aids and malaria (generally confined to the southern part of China near the border with Myanmar and Vietnam, although in the summer months the Yangtze River basin is also affected). Rabies is endemic and bilharzia is present in southern and eastern parts of the country. Vaccinations should be taken against hepatitis A and B, diphtheria, tuberculosis, Japanese A encephalitis, polio, tetanus and typhoid. Drink only bottled water, avoid unpeeled fruit and salads and try to ensure all food has been thoroughly cooked. It is advisable to have emergency medical insurance; in Beijing two companies – Asia Emergency Assistance (AEA) and International SOS Assistance – offer evacuation services.

Hotels

There is no shortage of accommodation in peak seasons. The main hotels in major cities are of a reasonable standard, but many hotels are frugal, often with fixed-time, fixed-menu meals and even cold water only during certain hours in the evening and morning. There are new hotels built, with foreign assistance, in Nanjing, Guangzhou, Beijing and Zhjanjiang and international-standard joint-venture hotels in Tianjin, Hainan, Xiamen, Fujian, Hangzhou and Shenzen. Charges for government guest houses, which are used to accommodate hotel overflows, are high.

Reservations for business visitors are made by their host organisations. Joint venture hotels are able to accept bookings from outside China. Hotel reservations for over 70 Chinese cities are being computerised.

Tipping is officially forbidden in China, although small tips are occasionally 'expected' by porters in larger hotels. The custom is uneven, and tips will often be refused.

Credit cards

Credit cards are accepted at tourist hotels and tourist shops in major cities. Use of cash or traveller's cheques is more usual. Cash withdrawals from banks are possible with major cards, but are not encouraged and frequently entail long delays.

Public holidays (national)

Fixed dates

1–2 Jan (New Year's Holiday), 1–3 May (May Day), 1–3 Oct (National Day).

Variable dates

Chinese New Year (Jan/Feb)

Working hours

Banking

Mon–Fri: 0900–1200, 1400–1700.

Business

Mon–Fri: 0800–1130, 1300–1700.

Government

Mon–Fri: 0800–1200, 1300–1700.

Shops

Mon–Sun: 0900–1900.

Telecommunications

Telephone/fax

Telephone directories may not be readily available, visitors should keep a note of important telephone numbers.

Mobile/cell phones

GSM 900 service available in eastern provinces.

Electricity supply

220/240V AC, 50Hz. Two-pin sockets and some three-pin sockets used. Mostly flat plug fittings, with two-pin round as well in some hotels, and generally, screw-type light bulb fittings.

Weights and measures

Metric system (with Chinese units in use).

Social customs/useful tips

A ban on smoking in public places came into force on 1 May 2011. The new rules prohibit smoking in restaurants, hotels, railway stations and theatres, but not at

the office. It is estimated that up to a third of all smokers in the world are Chinese, and that there are some million smoking-related diseases diagnosed every year. The new rules have been criticised because they do not include punishments for those who choose to ignore them.
Doing business needs patience; punctuality is vital, being especially valued on the part of the visitor. It is customary to present a business card. The full title of the People's Republic of China should be used for formal communications.
If working towards a major contract, ir is a good idea to read the government's five-year plan (currently the 12th, 2011–15) so that you can relate your company or project to the overall picture of China's development. It is always advisable to have a local partner or representative, although personal meetings are important.
Bureaucratic procedures are many and the frustrations of grappling with the Chinese bureaucracy are considerable. The visitor should assume that virtually all negotiations are going to take far longer than expected.
It is advisable to have a destination written in Chinese characters.
Eating can be a tricky business but there are a few important things to remember to save embarrassment on the part of the foreigner. When dining with the Chinese, and certainly with professionals, you should wait until your seat is 'allocated' by a nod or a subtle indication by the host. The Chinese have great respect for authority and title and this determines where a person will be seated at a table. One should not begin eating until indicated to do so. Take care not to 'upset' the presentation of the food as this is considered very offensive. When eating with chopsticks do not position them upright in your ricebowl. The gesture is symbolic of death and should be avoided.
The Chinese are highly 'face' conscious and try to avoid self-embarrassment at all costs. It is important that foreigners endeavour not to mock, satirise or embarrass their Chinese counterparts in any way as this will definitely ruin any developing relationship.
Unofficial contact between foreigners and local Chinese was effectively banned until reforms gathered momentum in the 1980s and 1990s. The borderline of what is permissible remains unclear, and contact by Chinese with some categories of foreigners such as journalists may still attract adverse attention.
Taiwan (Formosa) is considered a province of China, and should not be referred to as a country. It is quite acceptable now adays to discuss Taiwan.

Security
China's cities probably rate among the world's safest after dark, although some, such as Shenzhen and Wuhan have a worse reputation. Thefts are relatively rare, perhaps because the authorities investigate and punish crimes against foreigners with special vigour. The usual precautions should be taken with valuables.
Organised gangs, some of them Hong Kong-based, are reported to operate in the southern city of Guangzhou (formerly Canton). Their methods include drugging and robbing businessmen.
Chinese criminal law is much harsher than in most Western countries, and Chinese society is still very puritanical in sexual matters.

Getting there

Air
An agreement was signed with Taiwan on 13 June 2008 to allow 36 direct flights (18 each) a week to start on 4 July. A further agreement will allow 3,000 tourists per day into each country from 18 July.
National airline: Air China.
International airport/s: Capital, Beijing (PEK), 26km north of the city, with duty-free shop.
Hongqiao (SHA), 12km from Shanghai, with restaurant, shops; Pudong International, 30km from Shanghai, 60 minutes by car. There are special buses; services to and from the city run from 0600–1900. Facilities include internet cafés and short-stay hotel rooms for passengers.
Baiyun International (CAN) 12km north of Guangzhou.
All airports have duty-free shops, banks, restaurants, post offices and business facilities.
Other airport/s: Include: Chengdu; Guilin; Haikou; Kunming and Tianjin.
Airport tax: Departure tax: domestic Rmb50; international Rmb90, to be paid in local currency only, excluding 24-hour transit passengers.
Surface
Road: Motorways have been built between Guangzhou and Shenzhen and Guangzhou and Zhuhai. These roads link the cities of Dongguan, Zhongshan, Foshan, Jiangmen, Huizhou and Shunde to Hong Kong and Macau. Motorway links to major cities from neighbouring countries are few, partly reflecting the fact that most of China's neighbours, including Laos and North Korea, are poorer than China itself.
The Regional Road Corridor Improvement Project, estimated at US$18 billion, to improve Central Asian roads, airports, railway lines and seaports and provide a vital transit route between Europe and Asia was agreed, on 3 November 2007. Six new transit corridors, between Afghanistan, Azerbaijan, China, Kazakhstan, Kyrgyzstan, Mongolia, Tajikistan and Uzbekistan, of mainly roads and rail links, will be constructed, or existing resources upgraded, by 2013. Half the costs with be provided by the Asian Development Bank and other multilateral organisations and the other half by participating countries.
Rail: The Kowloon-Canton Railway Corporation (KCRC) has express trains serving Kowloon-Guangzhou and an indirect Kowloon-Lowu service.
The Trans-Siberian Express operates two weekly services between Beijing and Moscow, one via Ulaanbaatar in Mongolia and a second via Harbin in northern China.
Nanning, in Guangxi province, is linked by rail to Hanoi, Vietnam. A second cross-border track runs from Kunming, the capital of China's south-western province of Yunnan, via Lao Cai, to Hanoi.
Water: Ferry services operate between Weihai and Inchon in South Korea, and between Shanghai and Osaka in Japan.

Getting about

National transport
Air: Air travel is the quickest way of getting around the country. There are several airlines including China Eastern, China Northern, China Southern and Yunnan Airlines. These provide regular services between the major cities, with first-class service on some routes. Flights are frequently overbooked and seats should be confirmed as a matter of course. Independent regional airlines also operate. Tickets not booked through an official guide/travel service should be booked and collected well in advance. Allow plenty of time for inevitable and often prolonged delays in services. Airport announcements are not multilingual.
Road: There are over 1.18 million km of internal roads, around 250,000km are paved, but most are narrow and poorly surfaced making long-distance travel time-consuming. A superhighway links Beijing and Tianjin, and a 138km four-lane toll highway links Hangzhou and the port of Ningbo in Zhejiang Province. These are linked into a network of 12 major highways across the country.
Buses: Extensive, long distance services are available, it is advisable to book seats in advance.
Rail: The rail network in 2011 was around 91,000km of track. Although many lines are electrified, many locomotives are steam-powered. Beijing is the hub of the rail network with lines radiating throughout the country. There are two major railway stations, the Beijing Railway Station and Beijing West Railway Station, which between them run various services

to Guangdong, Shanghai, Heilongjiang, Shanxi, Hebei and Kowloon.

In April 2011 Sheng Guangzu, railway minister, confirmed that the government would be spending US$428.8 billion on railway construction over the period to 2015. This was less than previously announced, but will still mean an expansion to 120,000km by 2015.

Operating speeds on bullet train lines was reduced from 350km per hour to 300km in April 2011. The Beijing–Shanghai line, scheduled to open in 2011, will also be reduced to 300km, from the planned 380km.

On 1 July 2006 the 1,930km passenger service between Quighai and Tibet, at elevations of 4,000–4,800 metres, began operating.

Rail services operate between main cities. Deluxe rail services, with opulent German-made sleeping cars and private dining coaches, are available. Generally, rail travel is comfortable and safe, but time-consuming because of the long distances involved.

The 2007/08 budget has set aside US$175bn for railway investment. The China Railway Construction floated on the Shanghai Stock Exchange in February 2008, raising Rmb22.25bn (US$3.1bn). The China Railway Group had previously raised US$5.5bn in December 2007.

Water: Hydrofoil and ferry services operate between Hong Kong and Guangzhou, and also serve Shekou, Shenzhen and Zhuhai. Inland waterways and coastal shipping services are an important form of transport.

City transport

Taxis: Taxi service is available in all major cities, from railway stations, hotels and shopping districts. Not all taxis are metered, but a standard rate per kilometre is regulation check before starting a journey. Taxis may be hailed in the street. Destinations may need to be written down in Chinese characters, as not many drivers speak a foreign language. It may be best to retain a taxi until returning to the hotel and paying the driver a small waiting fee during appointments or meals. Tipping is not practised.

Buses, trams & metro: Beijing has a serious transport problem with heavy congestion during the day and the risk of grid-lock during rush-hours. It has a metro system, with over 60 stations, with an upgrade and new lines, including the Olympic branch line, under construction, most of which are expected to be completed for the 2008 Olympic Games. However for the size of the city and population it is a small operation. The *yikatong* transport card is the only ticket that allows travel on most lines; individual lines have their own, non-transferable tickets. There are also buses, trams and trolleybuses but these are unsuitable for visitors without a working knowledge of Chinese.

There are metro systems in Chongqing, Guangzhou, Nanjing, Shanghai, Shenzhen, Tianjin and Wuhan.

There are extensive local bus services in all main cities, generally inexpensive but crowded and without timetables.

Trains: There are six main, metropolitan railway station that handle traffic from surrounding suburbs and districts.

Car hire

Most rental companies require the driver's passport as deposit, making car rental impractical. Cars with a driver can be hired for a day or week.

Bicycle hire is available in some towns, but it is advisable to carry proof of identity when riding.

BUSINESS DIRECTORY

The addresses listed below are a selection only. While World of Information makes every endeavour to check these addresses, we cannot guarantee that changes have not been made, especially to telephone numbers and area codes. We would welcome any corrections.

Telephone area codes

The International direct dialling (IDD) code for China is +86, followed by the area code:

Beijing	10	Qingdao	532
Chengdu	28	Shanghai	21
Dalian	411	Shenyang	24
Fuzhou	591	Shenzen	755
Guangzhou	20	Tianjin	22
Harbin	451	Wenzhou	577
Jinan	531	Wuhan	27
Lhasa	891	Xi'an	29
Nanjing	25		

Useful telephone numbers

Beijing

Police: 110

International calls, English-language: 337-431, 553-536

Local, long-distance enquiries: 116

Cable and telex information: 664-900

Taxis: 557-671

Airport-flight enquiries: 552-515, 555-531, ext 382

Shanghai

Ambulance: 120

Police: 110

Fire: 119

Taxis for disabled: 6215-5555

Chambers of Commerce

American Chamber of Commerce PRC, 1903 China Resources Building, 8 Jianguomenbai Dajie, Beijing 100005 (tel: 8519-1920; fax: 8519-1910; e-mail: amcham@amcham-china.org.cn).

British Chamber of Commerce in China, China Life Tower, 16 Chaoyangmenwai Avenue, Beijing 100020 (tel: 8525-1111; fax: 8525-1100; email: director@pek.britcham.org).

Banking

China Banking Regulatory Commission, Jia No 15 Financial Street, Xicheng District, Beijing 100140 (tel: 6627-9113; web: www.cbrc.gov.cn)

Agricultural Bank of China, Jia 23 Fu Xing Road, Beijing 100036 (tel: 6847-5321; fax: 6829-7160).

Bank of China, 410 Fuchengmen Nei Dajie, Beijing 100818 (tel: 6601-6688; fax: 6601-6869).

Beijing City Commercial Bank Corp Ltd, 2nd Floor, Tower B Beijing International Financial Building, 156 Fuxingmennei Street, Beijing 100031 (tel: 6642-6928; fax: 6642-6691/9).

Bank of Communications, 18 Xianxia Lu, Shanghai 200335 (tel: 6275-1234; fax: 6275-6784).

China Construction Bank, No 25 Finance Street, Beijing 100032 (tel: 6759-8050; fax: 6759-7353).

China Minsheng Banking Corporation Ltd, 4 Zheng Yi Lu, Dong Cheng District, Beijing 100006 (tel: 6526-9578).

Hua Xia Bank, Xidan International Mansion, No. 111 Xidan North Avenue, Xicheng District, Beijing 100032 (tel: 6615-1199, 6612-9139; fax: 6618-8484).

Central bank

People's Bank of China, 32 Chengfang Street, Xi Cheng District, Beijing 100800 (tel: 6619-4114; fax: 6601-5346; e-mail: webbox@pbc.gov.cn; internet: www.pbc.gov.cn/english).

Stock exchange

Shanghai Stock Exchange (SSE): www.sse.com.cn

Stock exchange 2

Shenzhen Stock Exchange: www.szse.cn

Commodity exchange

Dalian Commodity Exchange (DCE): www.dce.com.cn

Commodity exchange 2

Zhengzhou Commodity Exchange (ZCE): http://english.czce.com.cn

Travel information

Air China, Beijing Capital Airport, Beijing 100621 (tel: 6456-3201; fax: 6456-3831; e-mail: webmaster@airchina.com.cn).

Beijing Capital Airport, Beijing 100621(tel: 6456-4247; fax: 6457-0487).

China Eastern Airlines, 2550 Hingqiaolu, Shanghai 200335 (tel: 6268-6268; fax: 6268-6116; e-mail: webmaster@ce-air.com).

China International Travel Service (CITS), 103 Fuxingmennei Dajie, Beijing 100800 (tel: 6601-1122; fax: 6601-2021; e-mail: webmaster@cits.net).

China Southern Airlines, Baiyun International Airport, Guangzhou 510405 (tel: 8612-4738; fax: 8665-9040; e-mail: webmaster@cs-air.com).

Shanghai Hongqiao Airport, Shanghai 200335 (tel: 6269-0029; fax: 6269-0027).

Ministry of tourism

National tourist organisation offices

National Tourism Administration of the People's Republic of China (CNTA), 9A Jianguomennei Avenue, Beijing 100740 (tel: 6520-1114; fax: 6512-2096; internet: www.cnta.gov.cn/lyen/index.asp).

Ministries

Ministry of Agriculture, 11 Nonzhanguan Nanli, Beijing 100026 (tel: 6419-1114; fax: 64192468).

Ministry of Civil Affairs, 147 Beiheyan Dajie, Beijing 100721 (tel: 6523-5511; fax: 6513-5332).

Ministry of Communications, 11 Jianguomennei Dajie, Beijing 100736 (tel: 6529-2114; fax: 6529-2345).

Ministry of Construction, Baiwanzhuang, Haidian District, Beijing 100835 (tel: 6839-3970; fax: 6839-3333).

Ministry of Culture, A83 Dong'anmen Beijie, Beijing 100722 (tel: 6401-2255; fax: 6403: 1266).

Ministry of Defence, 20 Jinshanquianjie, Beijing 100009 (tel: 6673-0000).

Ministry of Education, 37 Damucang Hutong, Xidian, Beijing 100820 (tel: 6609-6114; fax: 6601-1049).

Ministry of Foreign Affairs, 2 Chaonei Dajie, Dongcheng Districti, Beijing 100701 (tel: 8596-1114).

Ministry of Health, 44 Beiheyan, Xicheng District, Beijing 100725 (tel: 6403-4433; fax: 6401-2369).

Ministry of Information Industry, 13 Xichang'anjie, Beijing 10084 (tel: 6601-4249; fax: 6201-6362).

Ministry of Justice, 10 Chaoyangmen Nandajie, Beijing 100020 (tel: 6520-5254).

Ministry of Labour and Social Security, 12 Hepingli Zhongjie, Dongcheng District, Beijing 100716 (tel: 6421-3240).

Ministry of Land and Natural Resources, 64 Funeidajie, Xicheng District, Beijing 100812 (tel: 6616-5566; e-mail: master@mail.mlr.gov.cn).

Ministry of Personnel, 12 Hepingli Zongjie, Beijing 100716 (tel: 6421-3240).

Ministry of Public Security, 14 Dongchang'anjie, Beijing 100741 (tel: 6512-1967).

Ministry of Railways, 10 Fuxinglu, Haidian District, Beijing 100844 (tel: 6324-0114; fax: 6324-2150).

Ministry of Science and Technology, 15 Fuxinglu, Haidian District, Beijing 100038 (tel: 6851-5544; fax: 6851-5004).

Ministry of State Security, 14 Dongchang'anjie, Beijing 100741 (tel: 6524-4702).

Ministry of Supervision, 4 Zaojunmiao, Haidian District, Beijing 100081 (tel: 6225-4129).

Ministry of Water Resources, 2 Ertiao, Baiguanglu, Xuanwu District, Beijing 100053 (tel: 6320-2114; fax: 6320-2650).

Other useful addresses

China International Trust and Investment Corporation (Citic), Capital Mansion, 6 Xinuan Nanlu, Beijing (tel: 6466-0088; fax: 6466-1186; e-mail: g-office@citic.com.cn).

China National Chemicals Import & Export Corporation (Sinochem), A2 Fuxingmenwai Dajie, Beijing 100046 (tel: 6856-8888; fax: 6856-8890).

China National Instruments Import & Export Corporation, Erligou, Xijiao, Beijing 100044 (tel: 6831-7393; fax: 6831-59251).

China National Light Industrial Products Import & Export Corporation (Chinalight), 910 Jinsongjiu Qu, Beijing 100747 (tel: 6776-6688; fax: 6774-7245).

China National Machinery Import & Export Corporation, PO Box 49, Erligou, Xijiao, Beijing (tel: 6849-4851; fax: 6831-4143).

China National Metals & Minerals Import & Export Corporation, Building 15, Block 4, Anhui Li, Chaoyang District, Beijing 100101 (tel: 6491-6666; fax: 6491-7031).

China National Offshore Oil Corporation, PO Box 4705, 6 Dongzhimenwai Xioajie, Beijing 100027 (tel: 8452-1010; fax: 8452-1044; e-mail: webmaster@cnooc.com.cn).

China National Petroleum Corporation, 6 Liupukang Jie, Xicheng District, Beijing 100724 (tel: 6422-2946; fax: 6426-6302; e-mail: webmaster@hq.cnpc.com.cn).

China National Technical Import and Export Corporation (CNTIC), Jiuling Building, 21 Xisanhuan Bei Lu, Beijing 100081 (tel: 6840-4106; fax: 6841-4877).

China Ocean Shipping Agency (PENAVICO), Tower Crest Plaza, 3 Maizidian Road West, Chaoyang District, Beijing (tel: 6461-1188; fax: 6467-3118; e-mail: general@penavico.com.cn).

Chinese Embassy (US), 2300 Connecticut Avenue, NW, Washington DC 20008 (tel: (+1-202) 238-5000; fax: (+1-202) 588-0032; e-mail: chinaembassy_us@fmprc.gov.cn).

Chinese Export Commodities Fair, 117 Liuhua Road, Guangzhou (tel: 8666-1664; fax: 8333-5880; e-mail: info@cecf-info.com).

General Administration of Customs, 6 Jiannei Dajie, Beijing 100730 (tel: 6519-4114; fax: 6519-4004).

Shanghai Advertising Corporation, 117 Xianggang Road, Shanghai 200002 (tel: 6321-7599; 6329-0068).

State Administration for Industry and Commerce, 8 Sanlihe Donglu, Xicheng District, Beijing 100820 (tel: 6803-2233; fax: 6857-0848).

State Administration of Entry-Exit Inspection and Quarantine, A10 Chaowai Dajie, Chaoyang District, Beijing 100020 (tel: 6599-4600; fax: 6599-4306).

National news agency: Xinhua (New China News Agency), Head Office, 20F Dacheng Plaza, 127 Xhuanwumen St (W), Beijing 100031 (email: xxp69@xinhuanet.com; internet: www.xinhuanet.com).

Internet sites

Archive of Chinese news digest, also contains links to other Chinese sites: www.cnd.org.

China Business Pages: www.chinapages.com.

China Web (investment data, Shanghai city information, stock prices, travel arrangements and a searchable directory of key figures in commerce, industry and government): www.comnex.com

China Window information on country, government and business activities: http://china-window.com

Shanghai business: www.sh.com

Colombia

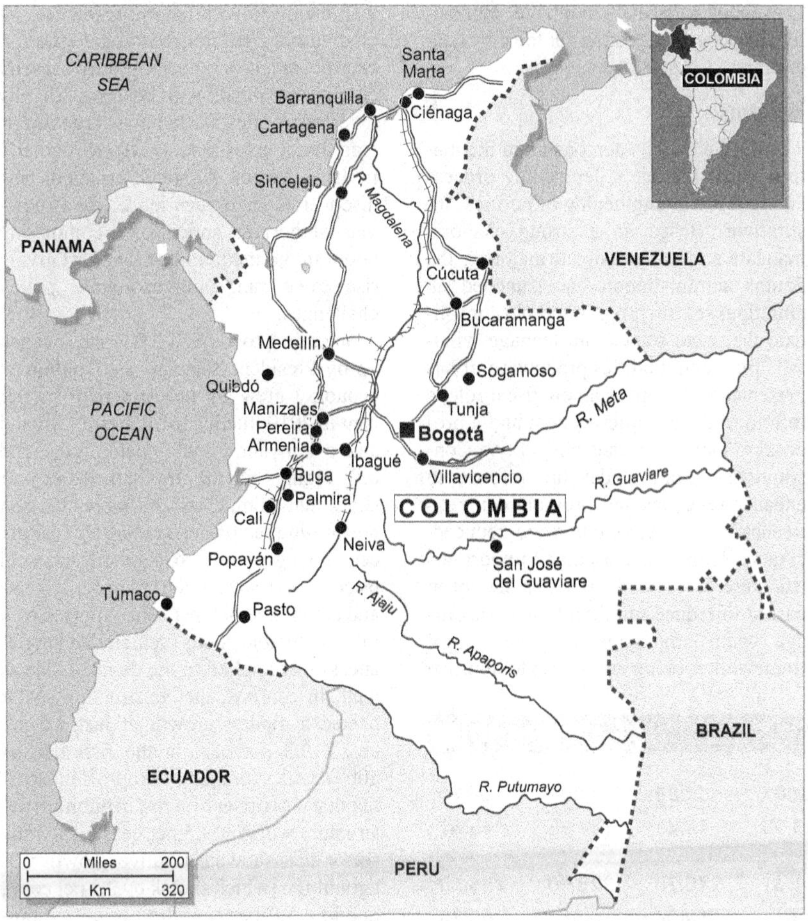

KEY FACTS

Official name: República de Colombia (Republic of Colombia)

Head of State: President Juan Manuel Santos (PSUN) (from 7 Aug 2010)

Head of government: President Juan Manuel Santos

Ruling party: Coalition led by Partido Social de Unidad Nacional (PSUN) (Social National Unity Party), with Parte de Integración Nacional (PIN) (National Integration Party) and Alas-Equipo (elected 2006; re-elected 14 Mar 2010)

Area: 1,138,914 square km

Population: 45.51 million (2010)*

Capital: Santa Fé de Bogotá

Official language: Spanish

Currency: Colombian peso (Col$) = 100 centavos

Exchange rate: Col$1,924.40 per US$ (Oct 2011)

GDP per capita: US$6,273 (2010)

GDP real growth: 4.30% (2010)

GDP: US$285.50 billion (2010)

Labour force: 20.93 million (2009)

Unemployment: 11.70% (2010)

Inflation: 2.30% (2010)

Oil production: 801,000 bpd (2010)

Balance of trade: US$2.15 billion (2010)

* estimated figure

President Juan Manuel Santos of the Partido Social de Unidad Nacional (PSUN) (Social National Unity Party) assumed office in August 2010 with a strong political mandate. Santos had won the second round of the presidential poll with more than 70 per cent of the vote, having campaigned on a continuation of former President Álvaro Uribe's democratic security and economic policies. The parliamentary elections held earlier in the year had already given his national unity coalition lead by the PSUN (together with Parte de Integración Nacional (PIN) (National Integration Party) and Alas-Equipo) a clear majority in Congress.

Sr Santos was certainly no stranger to Bogota's corridors of power. His great uncle Eduardo Santos had been Colombia's president from 1938 to 1942 and was the owner of Colombia's establishment newspaper, *El Tiempo*, where Juan Manuel had also worked as an editor.

Professional politician

Sr Santos' diplomatic and political career had seen him serve as head of his country's delegation to the London-based International Coffee Organisation as well as President of the United Nations Conference on Trade and Development (UNCTAD) and of the United Nations Economic Commission for Latin America and the Caribbean (ECLAC). His pet personal project has been Colombia's Good Government Foundation, aimed at improving the quality of government in Colombia. During his term as minister of defence he appeared to have risked sailing close to the political wind, to the extent that following the killing of FARC leader Raúl Reyes by Colombian commandos, an arrest warrant was issued for Sr Santos by the Ecuadorian government.

Less poverty, more jobs

On entering office, President Santos declared that his principal objectives had shifted away from that of security towards those of creating jobs and the fight against poverty. According to the World Bank, Colombia has one of highest levels of income inequality in Latin America and the Caribbean. Even the most casual observer cannot fail to be struck by the contrast between the affluence of Bogota's smarter suburbs and the poverty of *costena barrios*. Although the poverty level fell from 53.7 to 45.5 per cent over 2002–09, income inequality remained high. Encouragingly, however, there is evidence of an improvement in the equality of opportunities of children between 1997 and 2008, as measured by the World Bank's Human Opportunities Index, which captures coverage of key services necessary for children in life while adjusting for the fairness in its distribution among the population (coverage corrected for equity). Over the past decade, there have been significant improvements in terms of children's opportunities to receive health care, pre-school attendance, middle and high school completion and, access to electricity and telephones. While significant challenges remain (in terms of food security, nutrition, education quality, access to water and victimisation), improvements in the equality of opportunities are expected to eventually translate into better inequality and poverty outcomes for the next generation of Colombians.

Reforms

The 2010 elections demonstrated the maturity of Colombia's democratic process and reflect a strengthening of political institutions. Based on a strong electoral mandate and congressional majority, the Santos administration has launched an ambitious reform programme. To consolidate the fiscal stance and manage windfalls from commodities production, it has presented to Congress a new fiscal rule, a reform of the royalties system and a proposal to make fiscal sustainability a Constitutional right. Under the reform, to enhance revenues and promote competitiveness, tax exemptions were reduced, taxation loopholes closed and import tariffs were lowered. Legislation has been passed to reduce informality and encourage youth employment. A new legal framework is being introduced to improve the performance of the health system. Finally, to address social injustices arising during the country's civil conflict, a land titling reform and a law to compensate victims passed in Congress.

Economy accelerates

Colombia's economy is relatively diversified by regional standards. The country is well endowed with natural resources, including oil, coal and natural gas (see *Energy boom* below). The improved security climate, combined with business-friendly investment rules has led to a surge in foreign direct investment (FDI), particularly in the oil sector. Although no major new discoveries have been made, the Colombian authorities anticipate a commodity boom in the medium-term, in turn giving rise to a range of economic policy challenges.

According to the ECLAC – once headed up by President Santos – the Colombian economy grew by an estimated 4.0 per cent in 2010, fuelled by domestic demand and a buoyant mining sector (coal and oil). Figures for the first half of the year show that mining and oil were the best performing sectors, expanding by 14.3 per cent owing mainly to high oil and coal prices. Next were industry (6.5 per cent) and commerce (4.9 per cent), spurred by a rally in durable goods (vehicles and appliances) that applied to the demand side as well. In contrast, the construction sector posted a modest growth of just 2.5 per cent (10.3 per cent in the first half of 2009), with a temporary drop-off in building that was offset by a rise in public infrastructure works (19.5 per cent). The only sector that showed negative growth was agriculture (which shrank by 0.1 per cent), due to a 5.9 per cent drop in coffee production and the suspension of bilateral trade by Venezuela.

The acceleration in growth of the Colombian economy did not generate inflationary pressure thanks, among other factors, to currency appreciation and the marketing of surpluses that used to be exported. Inflation for the 12 months period to October 2010 was 2.3 per cent, with annual variations ranging from 2.7 per cent for core inflation to 1.7 per cent for food. Inflation expectations remained in the 2–4 per cent target range. For 2011, the Banco de la República (Bank of the Republic) (central bank) once again set target inflation in the same range.

The peso continued to appreciate, leading the government to adopt policies designed to control appreciation and mitigate its impact. In 2010 inflation

KEY INDICATORS — Colombia

	Unit	2006	2007	2008	2009	2010
Population	m	43.41	43.93	44.45	*44.98	*45.51
Gross domestic product (GDP)	US$bn	135.07	171.61	240.20	228.80	285.50
GDP per capita	US$	2,910	3,611	5,404	5,087	6,273
GDP real growth	%	6.8	7.0	2.5	0.1	4.3
Inflation	%	4.3	5.5	7.0	4.2	2.3
Unemployment	%	12.7	10.9	11.7	12.0	11.7
Industrial output	% change	4.3	–	–	2.4	–
Agricultural output	% change	2.4	–	–	-0.4	–
Oil output	'000 bpd	558.0	561.0	618.0	685.0	801.0
Natural gas output	bn cum	7.3	7.7	9.1	10.5	11.3
Coal output	mtoe	42.7	2.6	47.8	46.9	48,300.0
Exports (fob) (goods)	US$m	23,941.0	30,579.0	38,546.0	34,026.0	40,777.0
Imports (fob) (goods)	US$m	22,492.0	31,173.0	37,556.0	31,480.0	38,628.0
Balance of trade	US$m	1,449.0	-594.0	990.0	2,546.0	2,150.0
Current account	US$m	-2,909.0	-5,851.0	-6,765.0	-5,033.0	-9,032.0
Total reserves minus gold	US$m	15,296.0	20,767.0	23,479.0	24,748.0	27,766.0
Foreign exchange	US$m	14,673.0	20,096.0	22,810.0	23,158.0	26,349.0
Exchange rate	per US$	2,261.80	1,998.60	1,967.71	2,166.80	1,898.60

* estimated figure

remained under control; expectations were that the target of 2–4 per cent would be met. The new administration's economic proposals and the year-end indicators pointed to a 4.0 per cent growth of gross domestic product (GDP) in 2011.

Tax revenues at September 2010 indicated that the collection target of 12.4 per cent of GDP would be surpassed, mostly due to higher value added tax collections (up by 12 per cent compared to the same period in 2009) as the economy revived. Other factors were external taxes (15.1 per cent increase compared with the same period in 2009), which exceeded the target despite the global crisis and the suspension of trade with Venezuela. There was also a higher-than-expected income tax take thanks to larger payments by the state-owned petroleum company, Ecopetrol.

Public debt for 2010 was projected to be 35.1 per cent of GDP at year-end (similar to 2009) because the primary deficits are still negative. In June 2010 the central government debt balance was 34.5 per cent of GDP, 24 points of which corresponded to domestic debt. By the end of the year, this share remained virtually unchanged. The ministry of finance estimated that the consolidated public sector debt stood at 3.6 per cent of GDP and that central government debt was 4.4 per cent of GDP, 0.3 percentage points more than at year-end 2009.

With no major fluctuations in the inflation rate or prospects for higher inflation, the central bank held its monetary policy rate at 3.5 per cent until May 2010 and then lowered it to 3.0 per cent. Nominal loan interest rates had fallen more than the monetary policy rate since December 2008, except for mortgage loans. In real terms, all of the lending rates were at historical lows; Colombia's expansionary monetary policy had helped keep them stable. The commercial portfolio, which had been trending down on an annual basis, reversed the trend in July 2010 to post real annual growth of 8 per cent in September. Bank consumer and mortgage loan portfolios rose the most, by 10.6 per cent and 19.8 per cent, respectively, owing to the policy (in place since 2009) of subsidising new housing purchase interest rates.

Colombia saw substantial currency appreciation throughout the year. This trend, which began in 2009 and has adversely affected the export sector, is mainly due to external factors: monetary expansion in developed countries is weakening their currencies and sending capital flows streaming towards developing economies. To counteract the economic impact of appreciation, the administration eliminated the tax deduction for interest paid on external debt for certain activities, postponed planned monetisation projects amounting to US$1.5 billion and lowered tariffs on nearly 4,000 items (raw materials and capital goods), with the nominal tax going from 12.2 per cent to 8.3 per cent. In addition, the central bank has been intervening in the foreign exchange market since mid-September 2010. It had been buying US$20 million daily and planned to do so until March 2011. As of October 2010, the accumulated intervention amounted to US$2.24 billion. These interventions reversed the appreciation trend, which was a cumulative 8.6 per cent during the year to October and 8.4 per cent for the past 12 months.

Strong pressure on the labour market looked set to continue, with worker participation rates rising to 62.6 per cent at the national level and 65.5 per cent for urban areas – the highest in the previous six years. Despite job creation, the national unemployment rate remained at 11.9 per cent (annual average for the period from October 2009 to September 2010) and was unchanged from the previous period (12.0 per cent). The urban unemployment rate behaved in a similar fashion, going from 13.0 per cent to 12.7 per cent during the same period. Average real manufacturing wages increased slightly compared with 2009.

Colombia's trade balance for the first nine months of 2010 showed a surplus of US$1.32 billion fob, principally owing to the mining sector (along with oil and coal). The largest deficits were with Mexico (US$2.09 billion) and China (US$1.77 billion). Colombia has benefited from high oil and coal prices and rising production volumes, with tonnage growing by 29.3 per cent and 7.8 per cent, respectively, between January and September 2010 compared with the same period in 2009. The trade border with Venezuela remained virtually closed until October 2010, driving Colombia's exports to the latter down by an annual 69.2 per cent between January and September compared with the same period in 2009. Nevertheless, Colombia's total exports expanded by 21.2 per cent during the same period. Traditional exports (minerals, coffee and hydrocarbons) were up 45.5 per cent; non-traditional exports fell by 5.7 per cent. The destination countries whose share increased the most were the United States (from 37.8 per cent to 42.2 per cent, for oil) and Ecuador (from 3.7 per cent to 4.5 per cent, for fuel and vehicles).

Imports rose by 21.8 per cent between January–September 2010. However, there were, substantial jumps in imports of consumer goods (31.5 per cent), principally vehicles, as well as raw materials and intermediate products (31.9 per cent and 12.7 per cent, respectively, of the total variation in imports). Imports from China, which account for 12.9 per cent of all imports, were up by 43.3 per cent. The balance of payments still showed a current account deficit, but the healthy volume of FDI has yielded a financial account surplus. During the first half of the year, nearly 57 per cent of the FDI flowing into the country was for the oil and mining sector (including coal).

Energy boom

The higher levels of investment are one of the reasons for the dramatic increase in oil production in recent years following a period of steady decline. The Colombian government has enacted a series of regulatory reforms to make the sector more attractive to foreign investors. In addition, it has implemented a partial privatisation of the state oil company, Ecopetrol, in an attempt to revive its upstream oil industry. The security situation in the country has also improved over the last decade, with fewer attacks against oil and natural gas infrastructure. Expanded oil production will require further investment in both transport infrastructure and refining capacity.

According to the *Oil and Gas Journal* (OGJ), Colombia had 1.9 billion barrels of proven crude oil reserves in 2011, the fifth-largest in South America. These reserves are expected to increase with the exploration of several new blocks that were auctioned in 2010. Colombia produced an estimated 800,000 barrels per day (bpd) of oil in 2010, up from 686,000bpd in 2009. This trend has continued in 2011. The Agencia Nacional de Hidrocarburos (ANH) (National Hydrocarbons Agency) reported that Colombian production reached as much as 923,000bpd in May 2011. The US government's Energy Information Administration (EIA) reports that Colombia consumed 296,000bpd in 2010, allowing most of its oil production to be exported.

Before 2008, Colombia's oil production had flatlined for many years. This followed a period of steady decline that started in 1999, when Colombia's oil production peaked at 830,000bpd. The principle causes of the fall in oil production were natural declines at existing oil fields and a lack of sizeable new reserve discoveries. However, a combination of changes to the regulatory framework and the improved security situation has contributed to increasing levels of investment. The improvement in Colombia's security situation has also been a significant contributor to the renewed interest by international oil companies. Pipelines and other energy infrastructure are still the targets of attacks by guerrillas, but the number and severity of these attacks is much lower than in the past. According to the Colombian government, there were about 31 attacks against pipelines in 2010, compared with hundreds of such incidents that occurred per year in the early 2000s.

As a result of these improvements, Colombia has reversed the decline in its oil production and recently experienced rapid growth. The EIA forecasts that Colombia's oil production will increase in the next two years: the EIA projects that Colombian oil production will rise to 910,000bpd in 2011 and to surpass the one million barrel per day mark during the third quarter of 2012. The United States is the largest destination for Colombia's oil exports. In 2010, Colombia exported 365,000bpd of crude oil and refined products to the United States. China was Colombia's second-largest oil export destination in 2010, followed by Japan. China has recently expressed interest in financing new infrastructure projects in Colombia to facilitate the transport of oil to the Pacific coast for export.

According to the *BP Statistical Review 2011*, Colombia had proven natural gas reserves of 100 billion cubic metres (cum) in 2010 and produced 11.3 billion cum, while consuming 9.1 billion cum. A large portion of the country's gross natural gas production is re-injected to aid in enhanced oil recovery. The bulk of Colombia's natural gas reserves are located in the Llanos basin, although the Guajira basin accounts for the majority of current production.

As in the oil sector, natural gas production has risen substantially in the last few years, owing to greater investment at existing fields, rising domestic consumption and new export opportunities. Chevron is the largest natural gas producer in the country. The company also operates the offshore Chuchupa field in the Guajira basin, the largest non-associated natural gas field in the country. Chevron also operates the nearby onshore Ballena and Riohacha fields. The two biggest natural gas fields in the country, Cupiaga and Cusiana fields in the Llanos basin, were acquired from BP by Ecopetrol and Talisman Energy in 2010.

According to the World Energy Council, Colombia had 7,436 million short tons (MMst) of recoverable (mostly bituminous) coal reserves in 2008, the largest in South America. These deposits are concentrated in the Guajira peninsula in the north and the Andean foothills.

Colombia's coal is relatively clean-burning, with a sulphur content of less than 1 per cent. Production was 80.87MMst of coal in 2009, while consumption was only 6.69MMst. In 2009, Colombia was the fourth-largest coal exporter in the world.

Coal production, which is exclusively carried out by private companies, has nearly doubled since 2000. Preliminary estimates of 2010-production placed Colombia's coal output at 82.78 MMst – well short or the country's goal of 90MMst, but still a record for national production. Massive rains caused by the *el Niño* phenomenon in the latter part of 2010, which disrupted transportation networks and open-air mine operations, contributed to this shortfall. The Colombian government aspires to double production by 2019.

Risk assessment

Economy	Good
Politics	Good
Regional stability	Fair

COUNTRY PROFILE

Historical profile

1820 Colombia became independent from Spain.

1800s Outbreaks of fighting erupted sporadically throughout the nineteenth century, often between anti-clerical Liberals and pro-church Conservatives.

1899–1903 The (Civil) War of 1,000 Days in which some 100,000 people were killed. Panama separated from Colombia during the war and became an independent state.

1930 A Liberal president was elected, leading to social reform.

1948–57 The two major parties, the Partido Social Conservador (PSC) (Social Conservative Party) and the Partido Liberal (PL) (Liberal Party) became more extreme – the Conservatives veering towards fascism and the Liberals towards left-wing populism. Civil war broke out, resulting in up to 300,000 deaths.

1957 The civil war ended when the PSC and PL agreed on a power-sharing pact with the presidency going alternately to a PL then PSC member, with seats in cabinet and Congress to be split equally.

1965 The Ejército de Liberación Nacional (ELN) (National Liberation Army) and the Maoist People's Liberation Army were founded.

1966 Another and largest rebel group, the Fuerzas Armadas Revolucionarias de Colombia-Ejército del Pueblo (Farc) (Revolutionary Armed Forces of Colombia-Peoples' Army), was formed.

1971 After disputed elections, elements of the defeated Alianza Nacional Popular (Anapo) formed an armed movement (M-19) to fight the PSC government. They were joined by dissident members of the Farc.

1970s Guerrilla violence increased, at the same time as an increase in cocaine production.

1982 President Belisario Betancur granted guerrillas an amnesty and freed political prisoners.

1984 The assassination of the justice minister led to a step-up in the government war on drug traffickers.

1985 M-19 guerrillas stormed the Palace of Justice, killing 11 judges and 90 other people. The Andean volcano, Nevado del Ruiz, erupted and killed around 23,000 people in four surrounding towns.

1986 Virgolio Barco Vargas (PL) won an overwhelming victory in the presidential election. Violence became endemic as right-wing paramilitaries targeted PL politicians, left-wing groups carried out insurgency actions and death squads were controlled and sent out by drug cartels.

1989 A peace agreement between the government and M-19 allowed it to become a legal political party; other guerrilla groups remained active. PL and Unión Patriótica (UP) Patriotic Union (founded by Farc) presidential candidates were killed on the hustings, allegedly by drug cartels.

1991 A new constitution legalised divorce and gave indigenous people democratic rights.

1993 The infamous Medellin drugs lord, Pablo Escobar, was shot dead while trying to evade police arrest.

1994 Ernesto Samper won the presidential election.

1998 Andrés Pastrana Arango won the presidential election, bringing the Partido Conservador Colombiano (PCC) (Colombian Conservative Party) to power and ending 12 years of rule by the PL. In a move to allow peace talks to continue uninterrupted, the government agreed on a demilitarised area where military action against rebel groups would be suspended.

1999 President Pastrana began formal peace talks with the Farc in an attempt to end the region's longest-running civil war; after only two weeks the talks stalled. The two rebel movements, the Farc and the ELN, were estimated to control 40 per

cent of Colombia. The president's *Plan Colombia* won US$1 billion in US support through the anti-drug trafficking and insurgency plan. The peace talks broke down with recrimination on both sides.
2000 President Pastrana issued 11 emergency decrees to increase the armed forces from 10,000 to 42,000, with further increases to 52,000 by end-2001. The demilitarised area order was revoked.
2001 Pastrana agreed to extend the life of the demilitarised areas for a further eight months; Farc released 359 police and military in exchange for 14 rebel prisoners. An agreement to negotiate a cease-fire was signed.
2002 After three years of complex peace talks Pastrana broke off negotiations with Farc and ordered rebels out of the demilitarised area and stepped up a government crackdown. Threats from Farc and the Autodefensas Unidas de Colombia (AUC) (United Self-Defence Forces of Colombia) hindered electoral campaigning in rural areas, despite a security operation involving 150,000 troops and police; only 48 per cent of the population voted. Presidential candidate Ingrid Betancourt was kidnapped by Farc while campaigning. The PCC and the PL remained the largest groups in the legislature. Álvaro Uribe won the presidential election.
2003 Uribe's legislation raised tax revenues and boosted funding for the state pension system. Certain regional factions of the AUC disarmed.
2004 Farc guerrilla leader Ricardo Palmera was sentenced to 35 years imprisonment. The right-wing AUC movement and the government began peace talks.
2005 An international confrontation erupted when a leading Farc guerrilla commander was captured in Venezuela. The Presidents of both countries held a summit to resolve the matter. The national government passed new legislation, reducing jail terms for members of paramilitary groups who surrendered and disarmed. Tentative peace talks began, in Cuba, between the government and ELN, the second-largest rebel group.
2006 A disarmament agreement with right-wing paramilitaries led to a reported 20,000 fighters surrendering their weapons and being pardoned and retrained for civilian life. Colombia and the US signed a free-trade agreement. President Álvaro Uribe won re-election and the Partido Social de Unidad Nacional (PSUN) (Social National Unity Party) formed a coalition government in support of the president.
2008 Ecuador cut diplomatic relations with Colombia after Colombia took pre-emptive strikes against terrorists of Farc hiding out in Ecuador, killing senior Farc leader Raul Reyes. The founder and leader of Farc, Manuel Marulanda, died. Ingrid Betancourt, captured by Farc in 2002, was freed by government troops.
2009 Farc continued to release foreign and high profile hostages. The president offered a cease-fire with Farc in return for a cessation in criminal activities.
2010 In parliamentary elections held in March, over 2,500 candidates contested seats in both houses. The ruling PSUN coalition won 101 seats (out of 166) in the chamber of representatives and 58 seats (out of 102) in the senate. Following two rounds of presidential elections (in May and June) Juan Manuel Santos (PSUN) won with 69.1 per cent of the vote, Antanas Mockus (PV), his nearest rival, was runner-up with 27.5 per cent. President Chavez of Venezuela severed diplomatic ties with Colombia in July, objecting to claims by Colombia that Venezuela was harbouring Farc guerrillas.
2011 In the latest army tactic of combatting Farc by targetting high-ranking members, the Farc security chief was killed by the army on 4 June. In response Farc formed an elite unit (called Teófilo Forero) to engage in hit-and-run attacks on villages and military posts and kidnapping for extortion. On 23 June the UN reported that annual cultivation of coca fell by 15 per cent in 2010, a drop for the third year running, as acres of coca crops fell from 182,500 in 2009 to 155,000 acres in 2010. The on-going result was credited to *Plan Colombia*, in which billions of US dollars in aid funds efforts for countering drug trafficking. A trade agreement with the US was agreed by both houses of the US congress on 12 October.

Political structure

Constitution

The current constitution dates from 6 July 1991. Colombia has a representative democracy composed of an executive, legislative and a judicial branch.
Administratively, the country is divided into 32 departments ruled by governors, representing the executive branch, and a Departmental Assembly representing the legislative branch. Cities are governed by a mayor and a municipal council. All are elected by democratic vote.
Colombian citizens aged 18 and over are eligible to vote.

Form of state

Presidential democratic republic

The executive

Executive power is vested in the president, elected by universal adult suffrage for four years but not for consecutive terms. The president appoints a cabinet.

National legislature

The bicameral Congreso de la República (Congress of the Republic) (lower house) is composed of the Cámara de Representantes (Chamber of Representatives), with 166-members. The Chamber may examine the budget and treasury audit, review government actions and impeach senior national office holders. The Senado de la República (Senate of the Republic) (upper house) has 102 members. Among other things the Senate may approve or reject the resignation of the executive and military promotions and authorise the government to declare a war. All Congress members are elected for four-year terms by universal suffrage.

Legal system

The judicial system maintains formal independence but has experienced problems operating normally in circumstances that have extended to massed attacks using heavy firepower on major court institutions.

Last elections

14 March 2010 (parliamentary); 30 May and 20 June 2010 (presidential, first and second round)
Results: Chamber of Representatives: Partido Social de Unidad Nacional (PSUN) (Social National Unity Party) won 48 seats (out of 166), Partido Liberal Colombiano (PLC) (Colombian Liberal Party) 39, Partido Conservador Colombiano (PCC) (Colombian Conservative Party) 38, Partido Cambio Radical (PCR) (Radical Change Party) 14, Parte de Integración Nacional (PIN) (National Integration Party) 12, Polo Democrático Alternativo (PDA) (Alternative Democratic Pole) four, Partido Verde (PV) (Green Party) three; four other political parties won no more than two seats each. Turnout was 43.8 per cent.
Senate: PSUN won 25.8 per cent of the vote (28 seats out of 102), PCC 21.2 per cent (22), PLC 16.3 per cent (17), PIN 8.71 per cent (nine), PCR 8.34 per cent (eight), PDA 8.1 per cent (eight), Partido Verde Oxígeno (PV) 4.99 per cent (five), Movimiento Independiente de Renovación Absoluta (MIRA) 2.8 per cent (two), Compromiso Ciudadano por Colombia (CCC) (Citizen's Compromise for Colombia) 1.7 per cent (one); two seats are reserved for indigenous peoples. Turnout was 44.2 per cent.
Presidential first round: Juan Manuel Santos (PSUN) 47.3 per cent of the vote, Antanas Mockus (PV) 21.8 per cent, Germán Vargas Lleras (PCR) 10.3 per cent, Gustavo Petro (PDA) 9.3 per cent, Noemí Sanín (PCC) 6.2 per cent, Rafael Pardo (PLC) 4.5 per cent; turnout was around 49 per cent. Second round: Santos won 69.1 per cent of the vote, Mockus 27.5 per cent.

Next elections

2014 (presidential and parliamentary)

Political parties

Ruling party

Coalition led by Partido Social de Unidad Nacional (PSUN) (Social National Unity

Party), with Parte de Integración Nacional (PIN) (National Integration Party) and Alas-Equipo (elected 2006; re-elected 14 Mar 2010)

Population
45.51 million (2010)*
Last census: 22 May 2005: 41,468,384
Population density: 39 inhabitants per square km. Urban population: 79.1 per cent (2002).
Annual growth rate: 1.7 per cent 1994–2004 (WHO 2006)
Ethnic make-up
Mestizo 57 per cent, white 20 per cent, mulatto 14 per cent, Indian 1 per cent, and others 8 per cent.
Religions
Roman Catholicism is the official religion and the vast majority of Colombians consider themselves Catholic. There is freedom of worship.

Education
Financing for the education sector is decentralised and municipalities are required to use 30 per cent of the resources transferred to them from central government for education purposes.
Although the illiteracy rate averages 8 per cent among adults over 15 years of age, drop-out rates are increasing on an annual basis; Oxfam estimates that one in every four children drops out before completing primary education and girls' enrolment rates, estimated at 65 per cent, are at least 30 per cent lower than boys' enrolment rates. Primary education has also suffered due to cuts in government budget, while per capita spending is 12 times higher in the tertiary sector.
The New School Programme, known as the *Escuela Nueva*, was begun in the mid-1970s and governs the principles of the Colombian education system. It emphasises flexible school schedules and an appropriate curriculum catering to the needs of the poor rural areas.
Literacy rate: 92 per cent adult rate; 97 per cent youth rate (15–24) (Unesco 2005).
Compulsory years: Nine years in urban areas
Five years in rural areas
Enrolment rate: 113 per cent in primary; 67 per cent in secondary, of relevant age groups (including repitition rates) (World Bank).
Pupils per teacher: 25 in primary schools

Health
HIV/Aids
HIV prevalence: 0.7 per cent aged 15–49 in 2003 (World Bank)
Life expectancy: 73 years, 2004 (WHO 2006)
Fertility rate/Maternal mortality rate: 2.6 births per woman, 2004 (WHO 2006); maternal mortality 80 per 100,000 live births (World Bank).
Child (under 5 years) mortality rate (per 1,000): 18 per 1,000 live births; 7 per cent of children aged under five were malnourished (World Bank).
Head of population per physician: 1.35 physicians per 1,000 people, 2002 (WHO 2006)

Welfare
UN agency World Food Programme (WPF) stated that in 2003 there were two million internally displaced persons (IDP) who had fled their homes due to conflict and violence; 80 per cent of the two million lacked access to food production. Food aid is being provided for over 300,000 people, particularly in the northern states. International medical aid provides primary care, prenatal treatment and vaccinations for victims of the internal conflict, and the rural and urban disadvantaged.
Pensions
Colombia undertook major reforms in its pension system in the 1990s by shifting its priorities from government-run pay-as-you-go systems to multi-tier systems characterised by a privately run and fully-funded scheme. New workers have the choice of a pay-as-you-go defined-benefit as the primary system, if they prefer. An individual can only be a member of one scheme. In addition, there is a redistributive scheme for the elderly poor who are not entitled to a social insurance pension. Estimates show that only 30 per cent of individuals above the age of 60, or 2 per cent of the population, receive a pension. Consequently, compared to other industrial countries, the average pension remains very high and is estimated at about twice the GDP per capita.

Main cities
Bogotá (capital, estimated population 7.0 million in 2004, 2,640 metres above sea-level), Cali (2.3 million), Medellín (2.0 million), Barranquilla (1.4 million), Cartagena (853,900), Cucuta (657,100), Bucaramanga (542,400), Pereira (419,600), Ibagué (411,700), Santa Marta (404,800). More than 30 cities have populations of over 100,000.

Languages spoken
Some 200 Indian dialects are spoken. English is spoken in the business community.
Official language/s
Spanish

Media
Colombia is one of the most dangerous countries in the world for journalists to work in, with intimidation coming from drug runners, guerrillas, paramilitary groups and corrupt politicians.
Press
Dailies: There are many newspapers, in Spanish, including *El Espectador* (www.elespectador.com), *El Tiempo* (www.eltiempo.com) and *El Nuevo Siglo* (www.elnuevosiglo.com.co) are owned by political parties, *Vanguardia Liberal* (www.vanguardia.com) and *El Espacio* (www.elespacio.com.co) is an evening edition. Other provincial dailies include *El Colombiano* (www.elcolombiano.com) and *El Mundo* (www.elmundo.com) from Medellín, *Diario Occidente* (www.diariooccidente.com.co), from Cali and *El Heraldo* (www.elheraldo.com.co) from Barranquilla.
Weeklies: In Spanish, *Semana* (www.semana.com) is a news magazine with several specialist imprints. *Reviste Gatopardo* (www.gatopardo.com) and *Revista Diner* (www.revistadiners.com.co).
Business: In Spanish, dailies include *La Republica* (www.la-republica.com.co) is an authoritative newspaper, *Portafolio* (www.portafolio.com.co), *La Nota Económica* (www.lanota.com), also publishes special supplements. *Deporte y Negocios (Sports & Business)* (www.deporteynegocios.com) is a monthly magazine.
Broadcasting
The Comisión de Regulación de Telecommunicaciones is responsible for all broadcasting regulations. The national broadcaster is the Radio Televisíon Nacional de Colombia (RTVC) (www.rtvc.gov.co).
Broadcasting is closely controlled by the government although most programmes are produced by commercial companies.
Radio: RTCV operates Radio Nacional de Colombia (www.radionacionaldecolombia.gov.co) with music and cultural programmes for news. Radio Continental de Noticias (RCN) (www.rcn.com.co) operates a national network of 27 stations across the frequencies offering programmes of news, music and culture, for all audiences including the young and international listeners.
There are many local and regional commercial stations including La Z (www.laz92.com), Radio Activa (www.radioactiva.com.co) and Caracol Cadena Basica (www.caracol.com.co) with news programmes, from Bogota and Tropicana Estereo (www.tropicanafm.com) from Cartagena.
Television: There are over 30 TV stations broadcasting a wide variety of channels and programmes via cable and satellite facilities providing local, regional and national services. Most people gather their news from television.

RTCV operates Señal Colombia (www.senalcolombia.tv) with cultural and information programmes. Other national networks include Caracol TV (www.canalcaracol.com) and RCN Television (www.rcntv.com), showing domestically produced news, cultural, entertainment and sports programmes

Advertising

Advertising expenditure is equivalent to 2.1 per cent of GDP.

News agencies

Other news agencies: Prensa Latina: www.plenglish.com

Economy

The wealth of Colombia lies in its natural resources, which constitute the majority of its exports. At the end of 2009 oil reserves were 1.4 billion barrels (oil reserves 2009 increased, through new discoveries, by 32.5 per cent to almost 2 billion barrels); production was 685,000 barrels per day (bpd). At the same time natural gas reserves were 120 billion cubic metres (cum), with production of 10.5 billion cum; coal reserves were 6.8 billion tonnes with production at 46.9 million tonnes of oil equivalent (mtoe). Oil exports in 2009 topped US$10.27 billion and accounted for 3.2 per cent of GDP. Emerald exports in 2008 reached US$180 million, although the industry was considered under-developed and in need of foreign direct investment (FDI). Agricultural products for exports include coffee, bananas and cut flowers.

GDP growth in 2007 was 7.5 per cent, which fell sharply in 2008 to 2.4 per cent and 0.1 per cent in 2009 as the global economic crisis weakened foreign trade. However as international trade has begun to pickup, particularly with China which has an almost insatiable need for raw materials, GDP growth in 2010 is predicted to rise to 2.3 per cent.

In July 2010 the outgoing government of President Uribe announced proposals for setting up a new stabilisation fund to channel royalties from mining and petroleum profits, which the incoming administration of president-elect Santos confirmed it would consider. The plan is expected to generate 1.3 per cent of GDP, and help to avoid the 'Dutch disease' (ie when a currency appreciates too rapidly, due to sudden national wealth, thereby harming exports that become too expensive). The fund will siphon off windfall profits generated since the all-time high in global commodities and petroleum sales (in 2008).

Long-term unemployment is a problem, with a rate in double digits for all of the 2000s, with the national rate year-on-year of 12.1 per cent in May 2010. Some regional cities have fared worse than others with the highest unemployment rate of 21.3 per cent recorded in Pereira and 18.7 per cent in Armenia. Remittances were at a record high in 2008, at US$4.88 billion (2 per cent of GDP), but fell to an estimated US$4.1 billion as jobs were lost and salaries remained constant.

The illegal production and export of cocaine undermines the economy; in 2009 smuggled cocaine was estimated to be valued up to US$13 billion and with no of signs of reduction. Drug trafficking not only undermines the rule of law but denies the national treasury revenue that would otherwise come to it if the work undertaken was legitimate. It has promoted paramilitary organisations that have isolated regions of the country, which could otherwise be developed, and weakened the political system in general as they usurp legitimate government through violence, intimidation, bribery and political corruption.

External trade

Colombia belongs to the the Unión de Naciones Suramericanas (Unasur) (Union of South American Nations) – formerly known as the South American Community of Nations (CSN), modelled on the European Union (EU), which seeks to integrate with the Andean Community of Nations and Mercosur in a single market by 2014, when tariffs on non-sensitive products are to be abolished with the remainder eliminated by 2019. However political tensions within the region have hampered the ongoing process.

Coffee and petroleum, both commodities that react to world prices, are the main export products while Colombia is the world's second largest exporter of cut flowers (after The Netherlands).

Colombia is the world's largest exporter of illegal cocaine. A UN report in 2010 estimated that 400–600 tonnes of cocaine was produced and smuggled abroad, mainly to North America and Europe.

A US-Colombian free trade agreement was finally ratified by the US Congress on 13 October 2011 and was hailed by President Santos as historic.

Imports

Principal imports include industrial equipment, vehicles and equipment, consumer goods, chemicals, paper products, fuels and electricity, plastics and natural rubber products.

Main sources: US (typically 29 per cent in total), China (11 per cent), Mexico (7 per cent).

Exports

Principal exports are crude oil and derivatives, precious gems, coffee, coal, clothing, bananas and cut flowers.

Main destinations: US (typically 40 per cent of total), Venezuela (12 per cent), The Netherlands (4 per cent).

Agriculture

Farming

The agricultural sector has traditionally played a prominent role in the Colombian economy and it continues to contribute a sizable amount to total GDP. A wide variety of crops are grown throughout Colombia, depending on the altitude in a given region, but coffee is by far the most lucrative crop farmed.

Agricultural exports, primarily coffee, earn US$2 billion or more annually, and when prices have been high, have generated over half of the country's US dollar income. Colombia is the world's second largest producer of coffee after Brazil. Other important cash-export crops include bananas, exotic fruits, cut flowers, tobacco, cotton, sugar cane and cocoa. The illegal export of cocaine, and to a lesser extent marijuana, has been estimated to earn the country between US$500 million and US$1 billion per year.

The government has been successful in promoting the diversification of agricultural export crops and lessening the economy's dependence on coffee revenues. Projects included drainage and irrigation schemes to bring more land under cultivation, cheaper credit for farmers, the improvement of road networks and taking electricity to isolated areas. Basic food subsidies in favour of urban consumers were revised to increase incentives for farmers.

Colombia's flower industry began in 1970 and the country is now the world's second-largest exporter of cut flowers after The Netherlands. The US is the main destination for this product. Climatic conditions are ideal, with no special heating or cooling conditions required. Colombia produces over 3.5 billion flowers a year, mostly on the plains near Bogotá. Shipments of fresh and processed tropical fruit are also increasing.

Meat production was hit by guerrilla violence in ranching zones. The government has launched emergency development programmes in low-income farming districts as part of its plans to boost agricultural output and to passify politically turbulent regions.

Fishing

Despite a substantial coastline of 2,880km and recent modest successes in developing the shrimp and shellfish industries, the fishing industry as a whole remains underdeveloped. As a member state of the Andean Community Colombia has benefitted form special duty-free status and is increasing its shipments of

canned tuna to the EU. Exports of artificially reared shrimps are rising as the sector gathers strength.
The typical annual catch is 190,000mt, inclusive of 91,420mt marine fish and 20,580mt shellfish.

Forestry

Approximately half of Colombia's total landmass is forested. There are 49.6 million hectares (ha) of forests in the country. Most of the forests are located in the south-east of the country and form part of the Amazon jungle. Around 20 per cent of forested land is protected, with 40 national parks and reserves.
Despite its extensive forest resources, Colombia has a very modest production of industrial round timber. Sawn timber and panels have a large domestic market. Import of paper meets nearly one-third of the country's demand.

Industry and manufacturing

Manufacturing accounts for 14.3 per cent of Colombia's total GDP. Products include textiles and garments, chemicals, metal products, cement, cardboard containers, plastic resins and manufactures, beverages, wood products, pharmaceuticals, machinery and electrical equipment.
The industrial sector typically contributes a quarter of GDP, including the manufacturing sector which contributes 13 per cent, and employs 46 per cent of the workforce.
Food processing, beverages and textiles are the largest industries, followed by chemicals, leather goods, shoes and clothing, capital goods industries and motor vehicles. Metals, tobacco, cement, electrical engineering and paper are also important.

Tourism

Colombia's tourism industry is concentrated on the coastal region and the cities, especially Cartagena. Over the years Colombia's travel and tourism industry has suffered greatly from the ongoing civil conflict in the country. The industry has been severely damaged since its heyday in the 1990s, suffering from an image problem which was exacerbated by a reputation as the 'kidnap capital' of the world.
The travel and tourism industry is now beginning to make a moderate recovery. The industry now employs 5.9 per cent of the total workforce, a growth of 3.5 per cent year on year.

Mining

Mining in Colombia is concentrated on gold and other precious metals, iron ore, nickel and coal. In a typical year the mining industry contributes 4 per cent to the country's total GDP and employs 5 per cent of the total workforce. The industry is Colombia's main legal source of foreign exchange.
In recent years foreign investors have become fully aware of Colombia's potential for coal mining. With 20,000 tonnes of proven and inferred reserves the country's coal resource base is extensive and the quality of Colombian coal is high. Colombia is the second largest exporter of coal to Europe and the largest exporter to the US.
Colombia is one of the largest gold producers in the world, the fifth largest in Latin America after Peru, Brazil, Chile and Argentina. About 70 per cent of Colombian gold originates from the mines of Buritaca in Antioquia, using small-scale and primitive methods. Other precious minerals include silver and platinum (fourth largest producer of platinum), which are found in Choco Province along the Pacific coast.
Colombia is the world's top producer of high-grade emeralds, accounting for over 90 per cent of world output. The Muzo mine in the Eastern Andes near Bogotá is the world's largest emerald mine. Estimates put total emerald exports at US$250 million, of which a little more than 15 per cent is exported legally, for the most part (90 per cent) to Japan. Worker supervision in many of the emerald mines is minimal, fuelling the problems of smuggling.
Reserves of 100 million tonnes of iron ore assure Colombia of self-sufficiency until 2050. The known reserves are owned by Colombia's only steel company, Acerías Paz del Rio. The reserves are on the whole deep, expensive to extract and of low quality with a high sulphur content. A large part of the industry is located north-east of Bogotá, including the fully integrated steel works of Acerías Paz del Río.
Colombia has a high output of nickel supplying around 12 per cent of world demand. The country also mines copper, lime, sulphur, manganese, phosphates and salt.

Hydrocarbons

Colombia has one of the largest proven crude oil reserves in South America. At the end of 2007 proven oil reserves were 1.5 billion barrels, however, reserves have fallen from 2.6 billion barrels since 1997. Annual production of oil was 561,000 barrels per day (bpd), an increase of 0.4 per cent over the 2006 production. Nevertheless the trend is declining since production levels have fallen from a high of 838,000bpd in 1999. Colombia has managed to contain its consumption of oil, an average 237,000bpd since 1997, mainly by switching to other energy supplies.
Crude oil remains Colombia's largest export earner. It is a key source of foreign exchange earnings and is a major contributor to fiscal revenues. Expansion and exploration have therefore been at the forefront of the activities of the state owned entity, Ecopetrol, which announced plans to undertake US$6.2 billion in capital investment in new ventures over 2008–09. Geological features that match existing oil fields in Colombia suggest further hydrocarbon-rich territories.
With responsibility for all aspects of oil exploration, production, refining, transporting and trade in oil and gas, Ecopetrol is one of the world's top forty largest oil companies. In 2007 around 10 per cent of shares, worth US$2.8 billion, were sold to around 500,000 Colombian stockholders as a measure of privatisation. In 2008 Duff and Phelps (Colombia) rated Ecopetrol as triple A for corporate debt risk factors. A contract to increase the output of the Barrancabermeja refinery from 250,000bpd to 300,000bpd, which will also meet tougher clean fuel specifications, was let in November 2008.
There are five major oil pipelines, four of which link Colombia's largest oil field in the Cusiana/Cupiagua complex to ports in the Caribbean. But the ongoing civil conflict has resulted in attacks on its pipelines and sabotage of its installations by insurgent groups.
Colombia had 130 billion cubic metres (cum) of natural gas at the end of 2007, with production at 7.7 billion cum, which represents an increase of 5.6 per cent on the 2006 amount. Government policy through the *Plan de Masificación de Gas Natural* is to increase domestic consumption of natural gas.
There are plans to establish Columbia as an Andean regional gas hub with over 3,200km of gas pipelines providing national domestic supplies already. A new 230km pipeline for gas from Colombia to Venezuela was completed in October 2007, transporting 5.7 million cum per day; it may allow exports of Venezuelan gas at a later date.
Colombia had 6.9 billion tonnes of proven coal reserves at the end 2007. Production was 46.6 millions tonnes of oil equivalent (mtoe), which represented a 6.6 per cent increase on the 2006 production figure. The country has the second largest coal reserves in Latin America of high-quality and profitable bituminous coal most of which is exported. Sixty per cent of Colombia's coal reserves lie in the interior around Bogotá, where the giant El Cerrejón Norte mine is located. New development is centred on an open-cast mine in Guajira. Coal is Colombia's third

most important export after oil and coffee. With government investment in the promotion of the coal industry output doubled between 1997–2007.

Energy

Generating capacity in 2008 was over 50 billion-kilowatt hours (KWh); over 40 billion KWh (10.1mtoe) was consumed, which represented a 4.1 per cent increase on the 2006 figure. The surplus allows Colombia to be a net exporter of energy to neighbouring countries, particularly Ecuador. Around three-quarters of the energy produced came from hydropower, with conventional thermal and renewable sources constituting the remainder. Colombia has been self-sufficient in energy since 1984.

The energy sector has been deregulated since the 1990s and is composed of a mixture of private and publicly owned operators.

Financial markets

Stock exchange

Bolsa de Valores de Colombia (BVC), (Colombian Stock Exchange), Bogotá

Banking and insurance

Both Bancolombia and BBVA Colombia, two of the country's largest banking houses, have enjoyed significant profitability in recent years. Bancolombia, one of the oldest banks in Latin America, recorded pre tax profits of US$339 million in 2004, an increase of 53 per cent on the previous year's total. BBVA Colombia reported an earnings increase of 80 per cent in 2004. Both banks have indicated the likelihood of continued robust growth in 2005.

Following several years of a difficult economic and financial environment in the Colombia, the country's banking sector is now considered to be one of the leading markets in Latin America.

Central bank

Banco de la República

Main financial centre

Bogotá

Time

GMT minus five hours

Geography

Colombia, covering 1.14 million square km, is split between a coastal plain, high Andean peaks rising to more than 5,000 metres and a tropical Amazonian lowland. The only nation in South America with both Pacific and Caribbean coastlines, Colombia is bordered by Venezuela and Brazil to the east, Peru and Ecuador to the south and Panama to the north. Colombia owns the Isla de Malpelo in the Pacific and several Caribbean islands – including the San Andrés y Providencia islands. Its territorial waters border those of nations as distant as Honduras and Haiti.

Around 80 per cent of the population is concentrated in the Andean region, which covers around a quarter of the country's area. The Andes fan out northwards from the Ecuadorian border into three high *cordilleras* (parallel ranges) separated by deep valleys. Many of the peaks are volcanic. Colombia's highest mountain, the Pico Cristobal Colón, reaches 5,800 metres; it is 50km from the Caribbean coast in the Sierra de Santa Marta, which is isolated from the three main *cordilleras*. Just over half of the country lies east of the Andes. Known as Los Llanos, most of this region is virtually unexplored and sparsely populated jungle. A low plain fringes most of the coast in the west and the north. About a fifth of the population lives in this area, which is also about a fifth of the total land area.

Hemisphere

Northern

Climate

The equator runs across the south of Colombia. The low coastal plain and the jungle regions east of the Andes have a tropical climate, with frequent rains and temperatures between 24–28 degrees Celsius (C). Temperatures fall with the higher altitudes. In Bogotá, at 2,650 metres, temperatures average around 14 degrees C.

Dress codes

Dress codes in Colombia are partly determined by formality but mostly by climate. In the capital, Bogotá, at 2,650 metres, suits for men and skirts for women are usual for business. Residents recommend a light coat for the evenings. In low-lying cities such as Cali in the south or Cartagena on the Caribbean coast, informal lightweight clothing is common.

Entry requirements

Passports

Required by all with few exceptions (eg certain nationals of Ecuador and certain tourist visitors from Trinidad and Tobago).

Visa

Required for all business visits and must be obtained before arrival. A letter, issued by the traveller's company, giving name and position of applicant, a detailed summary of intended purpose of trip, an itinerary, and the acceptance of full responsibility for any expenses incurred during the term of stay must be submitted with the application, (an original and copy, to be translated into Spanish), which will be notarised by the Colombian embassy.

Tourist visas are not required by citizens of North America, most EU and West European and most South American countries for stays up to 90 days. For further details and confirmation, contact the nearest embassy.

Currency advice/regulations

There are no limitations on the import of foreign and local currency. The export of foreign currency is limited to US$25,000. Travellers' cheques are recommended. Banks are generally the only reliable location for changing travellers' cheques or cash.

Prohibited imports

Illegal drugs, food products, vegetables and plant material are prohibited. Permits are required for the import of firearms and ammunition.

Health (for visitors)

Mandatory precautions

None, although vaccination against yellow fever is essential for visitors travelling to certain parts of the country, notably the central valley of the Magdalena River, the inland border areas (with Ecuador, Peru, Brazil and Venezuela), Uraba district, the south-eastern part of the Sierra Nevada de Santa Marta and the forest area along the Guaviare River. A certificate of inoculation may be required by immigration officials.

Advisable precautions

Precautions should be taken against cholera, malaria, hepatitis; typhoid immunisation should be current. There are risks of dengue fever, TB, measles and rabies. Tap water is not considered safe to drink, boiled or bottled water should be used at all times. Milk is unpasteurised and should therefore be boiled or avoided. Meat and fish should be thoroughly cooked and preferably eaten hot. It is advised to avoid uncooked vegetables and dairy products made from local milk. Fruit should be peeled. Visitors to Bogotá should take it easy for a few days to get used to the altitude, which may induce drowsiness, dizziness or altitude sickness. Health insurance including medical evacuation is strongly recommended.

Hotels

Hotels are graded from one- to five-star by the Colombian Hotel Organisation. There are two seasonal tourist tariffs, low season is May–Nov and high season is Dec–Apr. A 5 per cent tax is imposed on all hotel bills. It is advisable to book well in advance. Service charge is normally added to bill, otherwise a 10 per cent tip is expected.

Credit cards

American Express, Diners, Visa and Master Card are widely used.

Public holidays (national)

Fixed dates

1 Jan (New Year's Day), ^6 Jan (Epiphany), ^19 Mar (St Joseph's Day), 1 May

(Labour Day), ^17 Jun (Corpus Christi/Thanksgiving Day), ^29 Jun (St Peter and St Paul Day), 20 Jul (Independence Day), 7 Aug (Battle of Boyacá), ^21 Aug (Assumption Day), ^16 Oct (Columbus Day), ^6 Nov (All Saints' Day), 8 Dec (Immaculate Conception), 25 Dec (Christmas Day).

Variable dates

Maundy Thursday, Good Friday, ^Ascension Day, ^Corpus Christi (May/Jun).
^ Holidays that do not fall on Monday are taken on the following Monday.

Working hours

Banking

In Bogotá: Mon–Fri: 0900–1500.
Other cities: 0800–1130 and 1400–1630.
On the last working day of the month, banks open up to 1200 only.

Business

Mon–Fri: 0800–1230, 1400–1800.

Shops

Mon–Fri: 0900–1900 or 2000.

Telecommunications

Mobile/cell phones

Some GSM 850 and 1900 services available in limited areas.

Electricity supply

110V AC 60 cycles; two-pin flat blade plugs.

Social customs/useful tips

It is customary to tip porters but not maids or clerks in hotels.

Security

With a virtual war being fought between the government, drug barons and Farc insurgents, realistic security measures must be carried out as kidnapping, armed robbery and bomb explosions are frequent hazards. Visitors should exert due care and vigilance at all times. It is advisable that embassy officials be informed of their national's presence in Colombia and itinerary, particularly if travelling to the north of the country.
Colombia has the highest murder rate in the Americas and one of the worst reputations, in South America, for street crime, which is common during daylight hours in main cities. Visitors are advised not to display jewellery and to carry as little cash and documentation as possible; watches and briefcases are prime targets. It is advisable to keep a copy of all documents in an hotel safe in case of mishap. Much crime is drug-related and visitors should be wary of any unwarranted attention from strangers.

Getting there

Air

National airline: Avianca (Aerovías Nacionales de Colombia).
International airport/s: Bogotá-El Dorado (BOG), 12km from city, duty-free shop, restaurant, post office, bank, shops, hotel reservations, car hire.
Other airport/s: Regional international flights also arrive at Barranquilla-Ernesto Cortissos (BAQ), 10km from city, car hire; Cali-Palmaseca (CLO), 19km from city, restaurant; Cartagena-Crespo (CTG), 2km north-east of city; Medellín-Rionegro (MDE), 15 minutes' flight by scheduled and frequent helicopter service to city, (36km south-east of Medellín).
Airport tax: International departures US$25–29 in cash, not applicable to transit passengers. An exit tax of US$19 is charged to travellers whose stay exceeds two months.

Surface

Road: Access is possible by road from Ecuador via Tulean to Ipiales and Venezuela from Christóbal to Cucuta.
Water: The rivers Meta, between Venezuela, Putumayo and a section of the upper Amazon in Peru, and the Orinoco between Brazil and Colombia, all act as borders. They are used by small boats.
Main port/s: Caribbean: Santa Marta, Barranquilla, and Cartagena. Pacific: Buenaventura and Tumaco. Upper Amazon: Leticia.

Getting about

National transport

Air: Domestic air travel is the most practical way of getting around the country. There are frequent and cheap air services between Bogotá and all main centres. Major international air carriers operate internal flights as well as smaller companies that operate domestic services.
Road: Travelling by road can be arduous and potenially dangerous. There are paramilitary groups in rural areas.
Fifty per cent of the main roads wind through steep *cordilleras*, with bridges and tunnels in constant need of repair. Only 4,600km of the country's 120,000km road network are considered to be in good condition and less than 13,000km are paved.
There are highway links for Bogotá-Cali; for other journeys local enquiries are advisable.
Buses: There are many bus companies providing services between coastal towns and cities. Bogotá-Medellín inter-city service is fairly reliable and comfortable.
Rail: There is no longer an intercity passenger rail service.
Water: Cargo boats that travel along the Magdalena, Guaviare, Caqueta, and Meta river systems offer passage to passengers; the is a slow means of travel. There are 10,000km of navigable rivers between the three main Andean ranges.

City transport

Taxis: Within Bogotá, taxis are usually metered with minimum charge and extra at night, holidays, Sundays and for out-of-town journeys. Tourist taxis (green and cream) are likely to have drivers able to speak English and can be hired by the hour/day from major hotels. Typical taxis can be hailed in the street and tipping is not usual. For unmetered, taxis fares should be agreed in advance of journey. Shared taxis, *colectivos*, operate within cities and suburbs.
Buses, trams & metro: Bogotá has a trolleybus system, buses and minibuses with flat rate fares.

Car hire

It is not recommended for foreign drivers as local conditions are so poor. Nevertheless, major car hire companies exist. Urban speed limits are 45–60kph while the rural speed limit is 80kph. An international driving licence (in Spanish) is required. Traffic drives on the right and during the working day is heavily congested in main towns.

BUSINESS DIRECTORY

The addresses listed below are a selection only. While World of Information makes every endeavour to check these addresses, we cannot guarantee that changes have not been made, especially to telephone numbers and area codes. We would welcome any corrections.

Telephone area codes

The international dialling code (IDD) for Colombia is +57 followed by the area code:

Armenia	67	Cartagena	5
Baranquilla	5	Cucuta	70
Bogotá	1	Manizales	69
Bucaramanga	73	Medellín	4
Cali	2		

Chambers of Commerce

American-Colombian Chamber of Commerce, 22-64 Calle 98, Bogotá (tel: 623-7088; fax: 621-6838; e-mail: info@amchamcolombia.com.co).

Barranquilla Chamber of Commerce, 36-135 Via 40, Barranquilla (tel: 330-3701; fax: 330-3750;e-mail: info@camarabaq.org.co).

Bogotá Chamber of Commerce, 16-21 Carrera 9, Bogotá (tel: 2381-0270; fax: 284-7735; e-mail: ccbcentro@ccb.org.co).

British-Colombian Chamber of Commerce, 77A-52 Carrera 12A, Bogotá (tel: 321-7077; fax: 321-7964; e-mail: britanica@cable.net.co).

Bucaramanga Chamber of Commerce, 36-20 Carrera 19, Bucaramanga (tel: 652-7000; fax: 633-4062).

Cali Chamber of Commerce, 3-14 Calle 8, Cali (tel: 886-1300; fax: 886-1399; e-mail: contacto@ccc.org.co).

Cartagena Chamber of Commerce, 32-41 Calle Santa Teresa, Cartagena (tel: 660-0795; fax: 660-0802; e-mail: camaradecomercio@ cccartagena.org.co).

Colombian Confederation of Chambers of Commerce, 27-47 Carrera 13, Oficina 502, Bogotá (tel: 346-7055; fax: 346-7026; e-mail: confecamaras@confecamaras.org.co).

Cucuta Chamber of Commerce, 4-38 Calle 10, Cucuta (tel: 571-5922; fax: 571-2502; e-mail: cccuc02@col1.telecom.com.co).

Manizales Chamber of Commerce, 26-60 Carrera 23, Manizales (tel: 884-1840; fax: 884-0919; e-mail: ccm@ccm.org.co).

Medellín Chamber of Commerce, 52-82 Avenida Oriental, Medellín (tel: 511-6111; fax: 513-7757; e-mail: subcontramed@camaramed.org.co).

Pereira Chamber of Commerce, 23-09 Carrera 8, Local 10, Risaralda, Pereira (tel: 252-587; fax: 250-957; e-mail: camarap@pereira.multi.net.co).

Banking

Banco Andino, Carrera 7a No 14-23, Piso 3, Apdo Postal 6826, Bogotá (tel: 284-8800; fax: 286-7919).

Banco Anglo Colombiano (associated to Lloyds Bank plc), Cra 8 No 15-46/60, Zonal postal 1, Bogotá (tel: 334-5088; fax: 286-1383).

Banco Cafetero, Calle 28 No 13 A-15, Apdo Postal 240332, Bogotá (tel: 282-7742; fax: 284-5430).

Banco Caldas, Calle 72 No 7-64, Apdo Postal 240332, Bogotá (tel: 282-7742; fax: 284-5430).

Banco Central Hipotecario, Carrera 6a No 15-32, Zona Postal 1, Bogotá (tel: 283-7100; fax: 283-2802).

Banco Colombo Americano, Carrera 7a No 16-36, Piso 10, Apdo Postal 12327, Bogotá (tel: 334-5530; fax: 283-2939).

Banco Colpatria, Calle 13, No 7-90, Piso 2, Apdo Postal 30241, Bogotá (tel: 283-1567; fax: 286-3914).

Banco Co-operativo de Colombia (Bancoop), Calle 98 No 14-41, Apdo Postal 12242, Bogotá (tel: 257-7411; fax: 218-1601).

Banco de Antioquia (Bancoquia), Calle 12 No 746, Bogotá (tel: 334-9040).

Banco de Bogotá, PO Box 3436, Calle 36 No 7-47, Bogotá (tel: 332-0032 fax: 338-3302).

Banco de Colombia, Calle 30A No 6-38, Zona Postal 1, Apdo Postal 6836, Bogotá (tel: 285-6767; fax: 287-0595).

Banco de Cio Exterior de Colombia (Bancoldex) (Foreign Trade Bank of Colombia), Calle 28 No 13A-15, Apdo Postal 240-092, Bogotá (tel: 341-0677; fax: 282-5071).

Banco de Crédito, Calle 27 No 6-48, Zona Postal 1, Bogotá (tel: 286-8400; fax: 282-7256).

Banco del Occidente, Carrera 5a No 12-42, Apdo Postal 7607, Cali, Valle (tel: 824-081; fax: 822-705).

Banco del Estado, Carrera 10 No 18-15, Apdo Postal 8711, Bogotá (tel: 282-8471; fax: 284-9775).

Banco Extebandes de Colombia, Calle 74 No 6-65, Zona postal 2, Bogotá (tel: 217-7200; fax: 212-5786).

Banco Ganadero, Carrera 9A No 72-21, Apdo Postal 53851/9, Bogotá (tel: 217-0100; fax: 255-2457).

Banco Industrial Colombiano, Carrera 52 No 50-20, Apdo Postal 768, Medellín, Antioquia (tel: 251-5216; fax: 251-4716).

Banco Latino de Colombia, Calle 72 No 10-07, Apdo Postal 056397, Bogotá (tel: 210-999; fax: 284-0056).

Banco Mercantil Colombia, Carrera 9A No 99-02, Zona Postal 8, Bogotá (tel: 618-2249; fax: 618-2111).

Banco Popular, Calle 17 No 7-35, Zona Postal 1, Bogotá (tel: 334-9640; fax: 282-4246).

Banco Real de Colombia, Carrera 7a No 33-80, Apdo Postal 034262, Bogotá (tel: 269-8523; fax: 287-0507).

Banco Sudameris Colombia, Carrera 8a No 15-42, Zona Postal 1, Bogotá (tel: 283-8700; fax: 281-6191).

Banco Superior, Carrera 10a No 64-28, Bogotá (tel: 217-3888; fax: 235-4352).

Banco Tequendama, Diagonal 27 No 6-70, Apdo Postal 29799, Bogotá (tel: 285-9900; fax: 287-7020).

Banco Uconal, Calle 72 No 8-56, Bogotá (tel: 310-5155; fax: 212-2094).

Banco Unión Colombiano, Piso 2, Carrera 7 N°71-52, Bogotá (tel: 3120411 fax: 3120843).

Caja de Crédito Agrario Industrial y Minero, Carrera 8a No 15-43, Zona Postal 1, Bogotá (tel: 334-9066; fax: 286-5824).

Caja Social, Calle 72 No 10-71, Apdo Postal 58175, Bogotá (tel: 310-0099; fax: 211-6036).

Citibank, Carrera 9a No 99-02, Bogotá (tel: 618-4455; fax: 618-2515).

Central bank

Banco de la República, Carrera 7, No 14-78, Bogotá (tel: 342-1111; fax: 286-1686; e-mail: wbanco@banrep.gov.co).

Stock exchange

Bolsa de Valores de Colombia (BVC), (Colombian Stock Exchange), Bogotá: www.bvc.com.co

Travel information

American Express, TMA, Cra.10 No 27-91, Offices 1-26, Bogotá (tel: 283-2955).

Avianca (Aerovías Nacionales de Colombia), Avenida, Eldorado 93-30, Piso 4, Bloque 1, Bogotá (tel: 413-9511; fax: 413-8325).

Colombian Hotel Organisation, Carrera 7, No 60–92 Bogotá (tel: 130-3640; internet: www.cotelco.org).

Fondo de Promoción Turistica de Colombia, Carrera 16A No 78-55 Of. 604, Bogotá (tel: 611-4330, 611-4185; fax: 236-3640; e-mail: turismocolombia@andinet.com; internet site: http://www.turismocolombia.com).

National tourist organisation offices

National Tourist Office, Calle 28 No. 13A-15 P 17 Y 18, Bogotá (tel: 283-9466; fax: 283-8945).

Ministries

Ministry of Agriculture and Rural Development, Avenida Jiménez No. 7-65, Santafé de Bogotá (tel: 334-1199; fax: 284-1775).

Ministry of Communications, Edificio Murillo Toro, Carrera 7 y 8 Calle 12 y 13, Santafé de Bogotá (tel: 286-6911; fax: 286-1185).

Ministry of Culture, Calle 8 No 6-67, Santafé de Bogotá (tel: 282-0854; fax: 282-0666).

Ministry of Economic Development, Carrera 13 No. 28-01, Apartado Aéreo 99412, Santafé de Bogotá (tel: 320-0077; fax: 287-6025).

Ministry of the Environment, Calle 38 No 8-61, Santafé de Bogotá (tel:288-6010; fax: 243-3004).

Ministry of Finance and Public Credit, Carrera 7a No. 6-45, Santafé de Bogotá (tel: 284-5400; fax: 284-5396).

Ministry for Foreign Affairs, Palacio de San Carlos, Calle 10 No. 5-51, Santafé de Bogotá (tel: 282-7811, 287-6800; fax: 341-6777).

Ministry of Foreign Trade, Calle 28 No. 13A-15 P 5,6,7,9, Santafé de Bogotá (tel: 286-9111; fax: 284-9537, 334-9908).

Ministry of Health, Carrera 13 No. 32-76, Santafé de Bogotá (tel: 336-5066; fax: 336-0116, 336-0296).

Ministry of the Interior, Palacio Echeverry, Carrera 8a No. 8-09, Santafé de Bogotá (tel: 283-0676, 283-6853; fax: 281-5884, 286-8025).

Ministry of Justice and Law, Avenida Jiménez No. 8-89, Santafé de Bogotá (tel: 286-0211, 286-5888, 286-9711; fax: 281-6384, 283-2761).

Ministry of Labour and Social Security, Carrera 7a No. 34-50, Santafé de Bogotá (tel: 287-3434/5045, 285-7092/7098, 285-8362/7361; fax: 285-7091, 287-3861/8342).

Ministry of Mines and Energy CAN, Santafé de Bogotá (tel: 222-4555, 2068, 222-0179; fax: 222-3651).

Ministry of National Defence, Avenida El Dorado Cra 52 CAN, Santafé de Bogatá (tel: 220-4999; fax: 222-1874).

Ministry of National Education, CAN, Santafé de Bogotá (tel: 222-2800; fax: 222-0324).

Ministry of Transport, CAN, Santafé de Bogotá (tel: 222-4411, 222-7577, 7966; fax: 222-1647, 222-1121).

Other useful addresses

Asociación Nacional de Industriales (ANDI), Carrera 13 No 26-45, Bogotá (tel: 334-6673, 281-0600).

Bolsa de Bogotá (Stock Exchange), Carrera 8a, No 13-82, Apartado Aéreo 3584, Bogotá (tel: 243-6501, 243-8471; fax: 281-3170).

Bolsa de Medellín S.A. (Stock Exchange), Carrera 50 No 50-48 Piso 2, Medellín (tel: 260-3000; fax: 251-1981).

British Embassy, Apartado Aéreo 4508, Torre Propaganda Sancho, Calle 98, No 9-03, Piso 4, Bogotá (tel: 218-5111; fax: 218-2330, 218-2460).

Caja de Crédito Agrario Industrial y Minero, Carrera 8 No 15-43, Bogotá (tel: 284-4600).

Carbones de Colombia (CARBOCOL), Carrera 7, No 31-10, Pisos 5-18, Bogotá (tel: 287-3100).

Colombian Embassy (USA), 2118 Leroy Place, NW, Washington DC 20008 (tel: 202-387-8338; fax: 202-232-8643; e-mail: emwash@colombiaemb.org).

Colombian Government Trade Bureau (Proexport Colombia) Calle 28 No. 13 A - 15 Piso 35, Santafé de Bogotá, (tel: 341-2066; fax: 282-8130, 282-8230).

Departamento Administrativo de Aeronáutica Civil (DAAC), Aeropuerto Internacional El Dorado, Bogotá (tel: 266-2237).

Departamento Administrativo Nacional de Estadísticas (DANE), Oficina 222, CAN-Avenida Eldorado, Bogotá.

Departamento Nacional de Planeación, Calle 26 No 13-19, Bogotá (tel: 282-4055; fax: 281-3348).

Empresa Colombiana de Mina (ECOMINAS), Calle 32, No 13-07, Apartado Aéreo 17878, Bogotá (tel: 287-7136; fax: 287-4606).

Empresa Colombiana de Petróleos (ECOPETROL), Carrera 13 No 36-24, Bogotá (tel: 285-6400).

Empresa Nacional de Telecomunicaciones (TELECOM), Calle 23 No 13-49, Bogotá (tel: 286-0077, 282-8280).

Federación Nacional de Cafeteros de Colombia, Calle 73 No 8-13, Apartado Aéreo 57534, Bogotá DE (tel: 217-0600).

Instituto Colombiana de Comercio Exterior (INCOMEX), Edifico Centro Comercio Internacional, Calle 28 No 13A-15, Bogotá (tel: 281-2200).

Instituto de Fomento Industrial (IFI), Calle 16, No 6-66, Pisos 7-15, Bogotá (tel: 282-2055).

Instituto Nacional de Investigaciones Geológico-Mineras (INGEOMINAS), Diagonal 53, No 34-53, Apartado Aéreo 4865, Bogotá (tel: 222-1811; fax: 222-3597).

Instituto Nacional de Radio y Televisión, Via del Aeropuerto Eldorado, Bogotá (tel: 222-0700; fax: 222-0080).

Invertir Corporation of Colombia (COINVERTIR), Cra 7 no 71-52 Torre A, Oficina 702, Bogotá (tel: 312-0312; fax: 312-0318).

US Embassy, Calle 38, No 8-61, Bogotá (tel: 285-1300; fax: 288-5687).

Internet sites

Business News, Latin Trade online: http://www.latintrade.com

Organisation of American States: http://www.oas.org

President of the Republic (in Spanish): http://www.presidencia.gov.co/webpresi/

Colombia Trade: http://www.coltrade.org/

Comoros

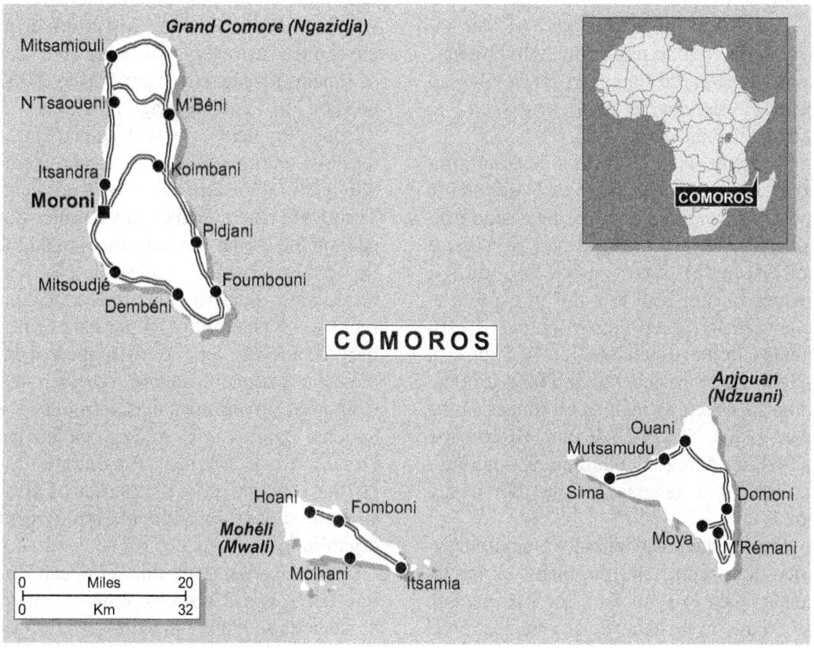

The Union of the Comoros is an archipelago of three islands (Grande Comore, Anjouan and Moheli). The economy is small and undiversified with few natural resources. On top of this, the country has suffered from chronic political instability for a number of years, with repeated coups and attempts at secession among the islands.

Constitutional reforms and the improvement of the political climate made the 2010 elections possible. In the first round of presidential elections, the Mohéli primary, held on 7 November, 10 candidates were in contention. Ikililou Dhoinine won 28.19 per cent of the vote, Mohamed Said Fazul 22.94 per cent, Abdou Djabir 9.88 per cent, Bianrifi Tarmidhi 9.31 per cent; six other candidates each won less than 9 per cent of the vote. In the second round, held nationally, Dhoinine won 61.12 per cent of the vote, Fazul 32.65 per cent, Djabir 6.23 per cent. Turnout was 67.1 per cent and 50.96 per cent respectively. The opposition's Mohamed Ali Said was re-elected as governor of Mohéli. The elections were considered by the international community to be generally free and fair

President Sambi's term of office expired in April 2011 and on 26 May Ikiliou Dhoinine, former vice president and Sambi supporter, took office as president of Comoros. Mouigni Baraka Said Soilihi had already, on 23 May, been sworn into office as governor of Grande Comore and Anissi Chamsidine had become governor of Anjouan. So ended, successfully for once, the latest round of political shinanigans.

Economy

While all that had been going on, the economy and social development had been neglected. However, in 2010 matters began to improve. In March the government of Qatar hosted a donor conference on development and investment in Comoros that drew pledges estimated at more than US$500 million, notably from the Gulf countries. Qatar itself also provided €20 million (US$26.8 million) of budget support that enabled Comoros to pay off wage and pension arrears. In June, the International Monetary Fund (IMF) considered Comoros had undertaken enough political and economic reforms to warrant debt relief under the Heavily Indebted

KEY FACTS

Official name: Udzima wa Komori (L'Union des Comores) (The Union of the Comoros) (from Jan 2002)

Head of State: President Ikiliou Dhoinine (from 26 May 2011)

Head of government: President Ikiliou Dhoinine (from 26 May 2011)

Ruling party: Únion-Presidential Movement (MP-Union) (Presidential Movement-Union) (from 24 Dec 2009)

Area: 2,171 square km

Population: 735,000 (2010)*

Capital: Moroni

Official language: Arabic and French

Currency: Comoros franc (Cf) = 100 centimes

Exchange rate: Cf366.68 per US$ (Oct 2011); (pegged Cf491.97 per euro)

GDP per capita: US$1,202 (2010)

GDP real growth: 2.10% (2010)

GDP: US$534.00 million (2010)

Inflation: 2.70% (2010)

Balance of trade: -US$156.36 million (2009)*

* estimated figure

Poor Countries (HIPC) initiative. The amount of debt to be cancelled was estimated at US$144.8 million. The interim debt reduction granted by creditors eased the pressure on Comoros' public finances.

Remittances from expatriates, which are a key source of finance and support for the Comorian economy, held up in 2010 despite the unfavourable international climate. These transfers were facilitated by the opening of branch offices of the Comorian post office in France.

Despite these improvements, the *African Economic Outlook 2011* (AEO), published jointly by the African Development Bank and the Organisation for Economic Co-operation and Development, considers that the Comorian economy has not fully recovered from the consequences of the country's period of instability, nor from the global recession of the last few years. However, in 2010, the real gross domestic product (GDP) growth rate was 2.1 per cent, up from 1.1 per cent in 2009.

The business climate remained much the same in 2010 as in 2009 – Comoros is still ranked 159th out of 183 countries in the World Bank's *Doing Business* report. Domestic lending rose moderately. This cautious monetary policy is conducted under the terms of the monetary co-operation agreement with France. In 2010, the mandatory reserve requirement of the Banque Centrale des Comores (BCC) (Central Bank of Comoros) was increased from 25 per cent to 30 per cent to offset the increase in money supply. This decision was taken to avert the possibility of an inflationary surge following the substantial grants provided to clear the government's wage arrears.

The agricultural sector had a lacklustre year in 2010. Vanilla production, still feeling the effects of the crisis that has affected this sector for a number of years, fell to 30 tonnes, compared to an average of 200 tonnes in the 1990s. Producer prices hit a historical low, leading many growers to abandon vanilla in favour of food crops.

Production of cloves showed an increase in 2010 to more than 3,000 tonnes, as against 1,700 tonnes in 2009. This increase was due to good prices and to strong demand from Asia.

Comoros is the world's leading producer of ylang-ylang, the essential oils of which are highly prized by the perfume industry. The global crisis had an adverse affect on the luxury products industry, which in turn lead to a fall in exports of ylang-ylang, even though output is estimated to have stabilised at 45 tonnes in 2010, the same level as in 2009; production had been as high as 60 tonnes in the late 1990s. The price decline observed in 2009 eased in 2010 but there was no indication of a reversal of the downward trend.

Despite the potential of the Comorian agricultural sector and the many initiatives undertaken to support it, food production continues to be hampered by the low level of mechanisation and difficulties in transporting and preserving food products.

Tourism is under-exploited and has yet to its full potential. In 2010, its performance was lower than forecast owing to the postponement of investments. The reconstruction of the Galawa Beach hotel complex has been transferred to Qatari industrialists, but this project, estimated at US$70 million, is not yet under way. The estimated €110 million (US$147 million) project of the Kuwaiti group, Comoro Gulf Holding, to develop the cliff overlooking Moroni has not started either. The delays in the implementation of these projects are due to the recent international financial crisis and the political uncertainty reigning in Comoros. The tourism sector, which is identified as a growth driver in the country's strategy, has set an objective of raising its capacity from 500 to 2,000 beds by 2014 and creating 2.500 jobs.

Unemployment is a widespread problem in Comoros, with an average unemployment rate estimated at 14.3 per cent. The global recession had only a minor impact on the labour market, since it had little effect on the trade, hotels and restaurants, construction and education sectors, which employ 54 per cent of tertiary sector workers. With support from the International Labour Office, the Comorian government has introduced a national employment strategy called the Decent Work Country Programme for 2010–11, combined with a series of measures to strengthen national employment organisations.

In the fisheries sector, the European Union (EU) and Comoros renewed their agreement on fishing in Comorian territorial waters. The fee paid by the EU is to be used to strengthen the sector's institutional framework and enhance its professionalism. In December 2010, Japan and Comoros signed a financial protocol of US$3 million to restart the national fisheries school on Anjouan, which had been closed when the island was shaken by separatist unrest.

KEY INDICATORS — Comoros

	Unit	2006	2007	2008	2009	2010
Population	m	0.63	*0.64	*0.64	*0.67	*0.73
Gross domestic product (GDP)	US$bn	0.40	0.44	0.53	0.53	0.53
GDP per capita	US$	645	680	817	799	1,202
GDP real growth	%	1.2	-0.5	1.0	1.1	2.1
Inflation	%	3.4	4.5	4.8	4.8	2.7
Exports (fob) (goods)	US$m	16.0	14.6	*6.5	*20.0	–
Imports (fob) (goods)	US$m	100.0	136.5	*175.9	*170.7	–
Balance of trade	US$m	-84.0	-121.9	*-169.4	*-156.4	–
Current account	US$m	-21.0	-32.9	*-58.6	*-42.3	*-36.0
Total reserves minus gold	US$m	93.5	117.2	112.2	150.3	145.3
Foreign exchange	US$m	92.7	116.3	111.3	139.0	131.8
Exchange rate	per US$	380.41	340.80	335.85	354.14	371.46

* estimated figure

International relations

China was one of the first developing countries to offer assistance to the new state. Co-operation between China and Comoros has steadily expanded and diversified ever since, and it now covers health, education and infrastructure.

Partnerships with Arab countries was a natural consequence of the admission of Comoros to the Organisation of the Islamic Conference and the Arab League. The 2006 election of Ahmed Sambi, the first Arabic-speaking president of Comoros, had been a turning point in the country's partnership with emerging countries and was instrumental in the holding of the donors' conference in Doha in 2010 and the appeal for investment in Comoros issued by the Arab League summit in Sirte.

The aftermath of the conference looks promising. The Arab League and the government of Comoros have undertaken to set up a specific follow-up mechanism. The IDB plans to establish a trust fund as an instrument for co-ordinating Arab countries' co-operation activities, with the aim of capacity building for the Comorian planning department and investment promotion by the IDB. The establishment of an Islamic bank in Comoros is also under consideration.

China is one of the first countries to have fulfilled the promises of the Doha conference, by signing two major contracts with the Comorian government. The first concerns the financing of the inter- and intra-island fibre-optic cable network; the second, the construction of the National Tourism Office, the cornerstone of which has already been laid.

These contributions should help to revive the Comorian economy. However, the political and social crisis that is shaking the Arab world may well prevent some countries in the region from living up to their commitments.

Risk assessment

Politics	Fair
Economy	Poor
Regional stability	Fair

COUNTRY PROFILE

Historical profile

1843 The Comoros was ceded to France by Portugal.
1886 The islands became a French protectorate.
1912 The islands became a French colony. The were administered from Madagascar.
1947 The Comoros became a separate French Overseas Territory and given representation in the French parliament.
1961 It achieved internal self-government.
1972 Elections produced a large majority for parties advocating independence and Ahmed Abdallah Abderrahman became president of the government council.
1973 Abderrahman was restyled president of the government.
1974 Mayotte voted to retain links with France while Grand Comore, Anjouan, Mohéli voted for independence.
1975 The Federal Islamic Republic of the Comoros claimed independence from France, Mayotte was the only island in the archipelago that voted to retain links with France.
1978 A constitution was approved by referendum.
1982 Constitutional amendments increased the president's power by reducing those of each island's governor.
1989 Abderrahman was assassinated.
1990 In Comoros' first democratic elections, Said Mohamed Djohar was elected president.
1992 A new constitution was approved that included the new post of prime minister.
1995 An abortive coup to topple Djohar was foiled by French troops.
1996 Mohammed Taki Abdoul-Karim won the presidential election. Constitutional changes adopted *sharia* as law.
1997 The islands of Anjouan (Ndzuani) and Mohéli (Mwali) declared their independence from the Comoros. Economic depression was given as the reason for their wish to reintegrate with France.
1998 President Taki Abdoul-Karim died. Tajidine ben Said Massonde became president.
1999 Colonel Azali Assoumani seized power in a bloodless coup and became president. In legislative elections on Anjouan, hardline secessionists won every seat.
2001 A military, unionist force on Anjouan took control in August. Attempts to wrest control from it failed and in December the Comoran government, by amending the constitution, implemented a change to unify the country in a loose federation as a decentralised Comoran Union of three autonomous islands: Anjouan, Mohéli and Grand Comoros.
2002 The country's name was changed to L'Union des Comores (The Union of the Comoros). In May, Assoumani was declared president of The Union. Mohamed Bacar was elected president of Anjouan. Mohamed Said Fazul was elected president in Mohéli, and Abdou Soule Elbak was elected president of Grande Comore.
2003 Power-sharing agreements were signed to allow national elections to take place and the presidency to rotate between the islands.
2004 Parliamentary elections took place for the Union. Opposition candidates to the Union president (Assoumani) formed an alliance: Camp des Îles Autonomes (CIA) (Autonomous Islands Party) and won 27 seats against six for the president's party. The first federal government was sworn in.
2005 Mount Karthala, a volcano on Grande Comore, erupted twice.
2006 Presidential elections for the Union took place. In the first round, held on Anjouan, 10 of the 13 candidates were eliminated. In the nation-wide second round, Ahmed Abdallah Mohamed Sambi won 58.02 per cent of the vote, Ibrahim Halidi Djaanffari 28.32 per cent and Mohamed Djaanfari 13.65 per cent. President Sambi took office.
2007 President Becar (of Anjouan) refused to give up his office, as according to the constitution he was required to do before scheduled elections. His forces clashed with the national army sent to enforce the constitution; the African Union (AU) also sent troops to support the constitution. Dhoihirou Halidi was appointed interim president of Anjouan. The constitutional court dismissed the president of Mohéli and Mohamed Ali Said was sworn in as its president.
2008 Forces of the AU overthrew the renegade president of Anjouan, Mohamed Bacar, and Moussa Toybou took office as president. Comoros was given full membership of the Islamic Development Bank (IDB).
2009 A referendum held in Mayotte (sponsored by the interior ministry of France), voted by 95 per cent to become an integral region of France. The government in Comoros claimed Mayotte as part of its territory and considered the referendum as provocative. The constitution was changed, extending the presidential term of office from four years to five. In parliamentary elections held in December the Únion-Presidential Movement (MP-Union) (Presidential Movement-Union) won 20 out of 24 seats.
2010 In June, the International Monetary Fund (IMF) considered Comoros had undertaken enough political and economic reforms to warrant debt relief under the Heavily Indebted Poor Countries (HIPC) initiative. The anticipated amount of debt to be cancelled was estimated at US$144.8 million. In presidential elections, held on 7 November, 10 candidates contested the first round (Mohéli primary), Ikililou Dhoinine won 28.19 per cent of the vote, Mohamed Said Fazul 22.94 per cent, Abdou Djabir 9.88 per cent, Bianrifi Tarmidhi 9.31 per cent; six other candidates each won less than 9 per cent of the vote. In the second round: Dhoinine won 61.12 per cent of the vote, Fazul 32.65 per cent, Djabir 6.23 per cent. Turnout was 67.1 per cent and 50.96 per cent respectively.
2011 On 21 January, the IMF agreed to the disbursement of US$2.42 million following the second review under its Extended Credit Facility (ECF) that registered the government's commitment to continued macroeconomic and structural reform, bringing the total amount disbursed to US$11.41 million. President Sambi's term of office expired in April. On 23 May, Mouigni Baraka Said Soilihi took office as governor of Grande Comore and Anissi Chamsidine became governor of Anjouan. On 26 May Ikiliou Dhoinine, former vice president and Sambi supporter, took office as president of Comoros.

Political structure

Constitution

The national constitution which was ratified by referendum in December 2001

created a federation – The Union of the Comoros – with each of the three islands having its own legislature, constitution and budget. Foreign relations, defence and currency were the responsibility of the Union. This inevitably caused some confusion with different election dates, different levels of authority on the islands and a mix of political parties holding power.
In an effort to sort out some these inconsistancies, constitutional changes were adopted on 17 May 2009 following a referendum in which 93.8 per cent of voters agreed to the changes; turnout was 52.7 per cent. Under these amendments, the island presidents were renamed governors, with the federal president assuming overall authority. President Ahmed Abdallah Mohamed Sambi's term of office was extended by one year so that the next presidential election (in 2011) coincides with that of the island governors.
More powers were transferred to the president, such as replacing the federal rotating presidency with a permanently elected office and allowing the president to declare a state religion.

Form of state
Federal republic

The executive
The presidency of the Union of the Comoros rotates between the islands of Grand Comore, Anjouan, and Moheli every four years according to the 2001 power-sharing constitution.
First round presidential elections are held on the island that will hold the next presidency; the top three candidates become the only candidates that the whole union votes on in the second round.

National legislature
The 33-member Assemblée de l'Union (federal parliament) has 15 members appointed by the three island legislatures (five each) and 18 elected through direct universal suffrage. Each island has its own assembly.

Legal system
French Nepolean Code and *Sharia* (Islamic) law in a new consolidated code.

Last elections
7 November and 26 December 2010 (presidential, first round on Mohéli and second round nationwide); 6/24 December 2009 (federal parliament); 17/ 21 March 2004 (autonomous islands' assemblies).
Results: Federal parliament: the Únion-Presidential Movement (MP-Union) (Presidential Movement-Union) and its allies won 20 seats (out of 33) the opposition won four; representatives of the Autonomous Islands' Assemblies (three from each) filled the remaining nine.
Autonomous Islands' Assemblies:
Grande Comore: supporters of the island president won 13 seats out of 20 and supporters of the Union president (Assoumani), seven.
Anjouan: supporters of the island president won 23 seats out of 25 and supporters of the Union president (Assoumani), two.
Mohéli: supporters of the island president won nine seats out of 10 and supporters of the Union president (Assoumani), one.
The opposition candidates to the Union president (Assoumani) formed an alliance: Camp des Îles Autonomes (CIA) (Autonomous Islands Party).
Presidential (first round (Mohéli primary)): Ikililou Dhoinine won 28.19 per cent of the vote, Mohamed Said Fazul 22.94 per cent, Abdou Djabir 9.88 per cent, Bianrifi Tarmidhi 9.31 per cent; six other candidates each won less than 9 per cent of the vote. Second round: Dhoinine won 61.12 per cent of the vote, Fazul 32.65 per cent, Djabir 6.23 per cent. Turnout was 67.1 per cent and 50.96 per cent respectively.

Next elections
2014 (federal parliament); 2014 (presidential)

Political parties
Comoros does not have a tradition of strong ideological political parties and political movements tend to support certain leaders. The only major issue of divergence is between those who favour a strong federal government and those who support autonomous island governments.

Ruling party
Únion-Presidential Movement (MP-Union) (Presidential Movement-Union) (from 24 Dec 2009)

Main opposition party
Convention pour le Renouveau des Comores (CRC) (Convention for the Renewal of Comoros)

Population
735,000 (2010)*
Last census: 1 September 2003: 575,660
Population density: 244 per square km. Urban population: 34 per cent (1995–2001).
Annual growth rate: 2.8 per cent 1994–2004 (WHO 2006)

Ethnic make-up
Antalote, Cafre, Makao, Oimatsaha, Sakalava.
The descendants of Arab traders, Malay immigrants and African peoples contribute to the islands' complex ethnic mix.

Religions
Sunni Muslim 86 per cent (official religion), Roman Catholic 14 per cent.

Education
Unicef concluded that school enrolment dropped due to insufficient classrooms and qualified teachers, among other infrastructural inadequacies. Education also suffers from poor performance and quality. A Unicef-sponsored humanitarian action plan in 2002 provided US$122,000 towards basic education.
Literacy rate: 59 per cent; adult rates (World Bank 2002).
Enrolment rate: 60 per cent (Unicef).

Health
The World Health Organisation (WHO), in 2003, funded health projects aimed at reducing mortality from common diseases and encouraging better use of existing health facilities, while improving the quality of healthcare overall. It also organised mosquito control activities to reduce the incidence of malaria.

HIV/Aids
Although prostitution is relatively rare, over 60 per cent of sex workers in Moroni tested HIV positive.
HIV prevalence: 0.12 per cent aged 15–49 in 2000
Life expectancy: 64 years, 2004 (WHO 2006)
Fertility rate/Maternal mortality rate: 4.7 births per woman, 2004 (WHO 2006); maternal mortality five per 1,000 live births (World Bank).
Child (under 5 years) mortality rate (per 1,000): 54 per 1,000 live births; 26 per cent of children aged under five years are malnourished (World Bank).
Head of population per physician: 0.15 physicians per 1,000 people, 2004 (WHO 2006)

Welfare
There is no minimum wage, there are no laws prohibiting bonded or forced labour and no protection for anti-union practices by employers. The labour code allows for one day off per week and one month of paid leave per year, although the government generally does not enforce the law due to a lack of provision.
The World Bank reported, in October 2003, that 47 per cent of households were living in poverty and 42 per cent of the population were malnourished. It stated that the government were poor in implementing, even in partnership, basic social infrastructure, and health and educational services tended to be of low quality and poorly utilised. Local communities were found to be keen to undertake projects in partnership with a World Bank poverty reduction plan, the 'Social Fund Project,' to creat small, income-generating activities. In future, proposed projects will rely mainly on village committees, community groups, NGOs and private firms.

Main cities
Moroni (on Grand Comore (Ngazidja) (capital, estimated population 60,200 in 2003), Mutsamudu (on Anjouan

(Ndzuani), (30,900), Mutsamudu (30,900), Mitsamiouli (21,400), Domoni (19,100), Fomboni (on Mohéli (Mwali) (13,300).

Languages spoken

Shikomor and numerous African languages are spoken. English is rarely spoken.

Official language/s

Arabic and French

Media

The government maintains tight control of the media, with newspapers and radio stations suspended and journalists risk arrest following items deemed disrespectful to its interests. Consequently self-censorship is prevalent.

Press

There are few commercial publications due to a small advertising market and a poor distribution network
In French, weeklies include *Al Watwan* (www.alwatwan.net) and *La Gazette de Comores* are official publications. Independent newspapers include *KashKazi* (www.kashkazi.com) (weekly), and *L'Archipel* (monthly).

Broadcasting

The national, state broadcaster is Office Radio et Télévision des Comores (ORTC) (www.radiocomores.km).
Radio: With high levels of illiteracy and poverty the radio is the principal medium for news and information.
ORTC operates Radio Comoros which broadcasts in Arabic, French, Comoran and Swahili. Two regional governments run their own stations, including Radio Television Anjouanaise (RTA) (www.rtanjouan.org) on Anjouan, and Radio Ngazidja on Grand Comore. Other stations include Radio Ocean Indien (www.radioceanindien.km) and Radio Dziyalandze (www.radiodziyalandze.com). Radio France International (RFI) (www.rfi.fr) has news programmes in French.
Television: ORTC operates the national, Television Nationale Comorienne (TNC). Other TV stations include RTA (www.rtanjouan.org) on Anjouan, TV Ulezi is a private provider while Mtsangani Television (MTV) broadcasts educational and cultural programmes. There are satellite services from Arabnet.
TV and radio services can be received from Mayotte.

News agencies

APA (African Press Agency): www.apanews.net
The Comoran Press: www.comores-online.com
Panapress: www.panapress.com

Economy

The islands of Comoros are largely formed from volcanic rock making it unsuitable for agriculture, what production is possible is subsistence farming. Nevertheless, according to a World Bank report in 2009, the economy in 2008 was dominated by agriculture, at 45.8 per cent, industry at 12 per cent, of which manufacturing was 4.2 per cent, and services went unreported. Around 80 per cent of the workforce is employed in agriculture, where meagre crops are supplemented by hunting, fishing and forest products. Food production in 2008–09 increased due to favourable weather.
GDP growth was 1.0 per cent in 2008, rising to 1.8 per cent in 2009 and is expected to have reached 2.1 per cent in 2010 due to donor aid, remittances and private sector construction. However the current account deficit is expected to widen to 10.2 per cent of GDP in 2010, up from 9 per cent in 2009, due to aid-funded imports.
A change in the political system in 2001 has resulted in centralised, national planning which has achieved a somewhat more effective economic policy. There is an increasing number of young people requiring education and social services before they will be productive members of the workforce. Comoros must rely on international aid, either through remittances which typically provides over US$12 million per annum paid directly into households and allowing private consumption, or disbursements from financial institutions. The Paris Club of creditors agreed to debt restructuring in November 2009, which was predicated on continued fiscal reforms. The World Bank and the International Monetary Fund (IMF) supports Comoros through a Heavily Indebted Poor Countries (HIPC) Initiative, which has resulted in enhanced growth, poverty reduction and debt sustainability. In September 2010, the IMF approved a US$21.5 million three-year loan.

External trade

Comoros is a member of the Common Market for Eastern and Southern Africa (Comesa), and operates within a free trade zone with 13 of the 19 member states. It is also a member of the Communauté Financière d'Afrique (CFA) (Financial Community of Africa), so that its currency is pegged to the French franc (pre-euro). Comoros runs annual deficits on its trade account, largely due to its limited export base.

Imports

Principal imports are rice and other foodstuffs, consumer goods; petroleum products, cement and transport equipment.
Main sources: France (typically 17 per cent of total), India (12 per cent), UAE (9 per cent).

Exports

Exports consist principally of agricultural plantation products, including cloves, essence of ylang-ylang (a major component of perfume) and vanilla, of which Comoros is a leading world producer.
Main destinations: Turkey (typically 25 per cent of total), France (20 per cent), Singapore (17 per cent).

Agriculture

Farming

The agriculture sector is the principal source of export earnings. It contributes around 40 per cent to GDP and employs 65 per cent of the workforce.
Although as much as 50 per cent of the total land area is cultivated, the agricultural sector remains underdeveloped (due to poor soil, adverse weather conditions and inadequate facilities) and over 50 per cent of the country's food requirements (notably rice) have to be imported.
Major food crops grown are cassava, sweet potatoes, rice and bananas; yams and coconuts are also produced, while main cash crops are cocoa, ylang-ylang (perfumes), vanilla and cloves.
Comoros produces around 1,700 tonnes of vanilla a year but its cultivation has suffered a drop in value due to overseas competition from new plantations and synthetic vanilla. Processed vanilla beans earned US$600 per kilo in 2003–04, while in 2006 the price had dropped to US$20–30.

Fishing

Fishing is underexploited, with tuna being the main catch. The fishing sector has received considerable aid from Japan and the EU.

Forestry

Deforestation, caused by clearing for the cultivation of the ylang-ylang crop, is an increasing ecological problem.

Industry and manufacturing

The industrial sector contributes around 13 per cent to GDP and employs 5 per cent of the workforce; manufacturing contributes 5.4 per cent. The sector is underdeveloped, with activity confined to distillation of essences and perfumes (particularly from ylang-ylang), vanilla processing, soft drinks, plastics and woodwork.

Tourism

The islands of Comoros offer pristine marine environments with tropical coral reefs, an active volcano and unique flora and fauna. However its low population has also resulted in a lack of tourism infrastructure and no direct flights from Europe (Comoros' primary market).

Tourism constituted over 11 per cent of GDP in 2000 but by 2009 had fallen to 4.5 per cent, due not only to the political instability in the islands but by the global economic crisis (2007–09), which cut visitor numbers. Likewise visitor spending was cut from 47.1 per cent of visitor exports in 2000 to 19.9 per cent in 2009. Total employment in travel and tourism was 9.8 per cent in 2000, which had fallen to 3.9 per cent by 2009.

In 2007 the government identified tourism as a key sector with potential growth for the economy. However, it has largely been foreign investment, particularly by the Gulf Co-operation Council (GCC), that has driven the market. Travel and tourism constituted 26.2 per cent of total capital investment in 2010, which was a dramatic reversal of the -12.7 per cent in 2009. By 2010 the tourism sector had grown by 1.7 per cent and was expected to have grown by 4 per cent in 2011.

Mining
There is no mining activity.

Hydrocarbons
There are no known hydrocarbon reserves. Consumption of oil was 1,000 barrels per day (bpd) in 2008, all of which was imported. The state-owned Société Comorienne des Hydrocarbures (SCH), was responsible for sourcing foreign oil through the French oil company, Total. However, since the global oil prices rose in 2007–08 the government has attempted to switch to alternative, and potentially cheaper, suppliers.

Any consumption of natural gas or coal is commercially insignificant.

Energy
Total installed generating capacity was 50MW in 2007, producing over 20 million kilowatt hours. Electricity is provided by the parastatal utility Electricite et Eaux des Comores (EEDC), which is operated by the French company and contracted to collect revenue.

The electricity infrastructure is poor and there are frequent blackouts, partly due to generator breakdowns and partly due to a lack of fuel. Solar-photovoltaic installations are used by small and rural communities.

Banking and insurance
The Banking sector is composed of the Banque Centrale des Comores (BCC), the central bank, the Banque de Développement des Comores (BDC), which focusses on development lending, and the Banque pour l'Industrie et le Commerce des Comores (BIC). The BDC stopped lending in 1997 due to liquidity problems, but still exists and is scheduled for restructuring some time in the future. The BIC is linked to France's BNP-Paribas and provides full international trade finance as well as local personal and business banking services.

Central bank
Banque Centrale des Comores (BCC)

Main financial centre
Moroni

Time
GMT plus three hours

Geography
The Comoros is an archipelago in the Mozambique Channel, between the island of Madagascar and the east coast of the African mainland. The group comprises four main islands (Grand Comore, Anjouan, Mohéli and Mayotte), and numerous islets and coral reefs. Mayotte, although geographically part of the Comoros group of islands, elected to remain as a French overseas territory, in 1975, and is politically separate from the Comoros.

Hemisphere
Southern

Climate
Tropical. Dry season May to October with average temperature 24 degrees Celsius (C). Rainy season from November to April with temperature 27–35 degrees C. Very hot and humid on coasts, cooler on inner highlands.

Entry requirements
Passports
Required by all.

Visa
Required by all.

Tourist visas obtained at the port of entry, are valid for 14 days. Visas valid for up to 90 days can be obtained in advance of travelling. Proof of return/onward passage is needed.

For business visas, information can be obtained from the Comoran Embassy 20 Rue Marbeau, 75116 Paris France (tel: (+33) 140-679-054; fax: (+33) 140-677-296).

Currency advice/regulations
There are no restrictions on the import of domestic or foreign currencies.

There are limited banking facilities for foreign travellers, credit cards are not universally accepted and travellers cheques can only be cashed in the Banque Internationale des Comores, in the capital. To avoid additional fees travellers cheques should be in euros. Foreign currency is exchanged in city and provincial banks.

Prohibited imports
Firearms, ammunition and radio transmission equipment, plants and soil.

Health (for visitors)
Mandatory precautions
Yellow fever vaccination certificates requested from visitors arriving from infected areas.

Advisable precautions
Typhoid, hepatitis A, tetanus and polio vaccinations recommended. Malaria prophylaxis advisable as risk exists throughout the country. Water precautions should be taken. There is a rabies risk. Seek further advice with regard to vaccinations for diphtheria, hepatitis B, meningitis and tuberculosis.

Hotels
Advisable to book in advance. Limited first-class accommodation available on Grande Comore, Anjouan and Mayotte (Maore), but several high-quality resort hotels have been built.

Public holidays (national)
Fixed dates
18 Mar (Death of Said Mohamed Cheikh Day), 25 May (Africa Day), 29 May (Death of President Ali Soilih Day), 6 Jul (Independence Day), 26 Nov (Death of President Ahmed Abdallah Day), 25 Dec (Christmas Day).

Variable dates
Eid al Adha, El am Hejir (Islamic New Year), Ashura, Eid al Fitr.

Islamic year 1433 (26 Nov 2011–14 Nov 2012): The Islamic year contains 354 or 355 days, with the result that Muslim feasts advance by 10–12 days against the Gregorian calendar. Dates of feasts vary according to the sighting of the new moon, so cannot be forecast exactly.

Working hours
Banking
Mon–Thu: 0730–1300; Fri: 0730–1100.

Business
Mon–Thu: 0730–1430; Fri: 0730–1130, Sat: 0730–1200.

Government
Mon–Thu: 0730–1200 and 1500–1730, Fri: 0730–1100, Sat: 0730–1200.

Shops
Closed daily between 1200–1500.

Telecommunications
Mobile/cell phones
A GSM 900 service is in operation.

Electricity supply
220V AC

Social customs/useful tips
Few people speak English, business is usually conducted in French or Arabic.

Getting there
Air
Regional flights from Africa are supplemented by scheduled flights from Paris, France and Dubai. Air Mohéli was set up in 2011 to fly the Moroni–Dubai route.

National airline: Air Comores International

International airport/s: Moroni International Prince Said Ibrahim (Code: HAH), 25km north of Moroni, on Ngazidja.

Facilities include refreshments and a post office. There are no money changing facilities. Taxis, with fixed prices are available.

Airport tax: None

Surface

Water: Cargo ships that carry passengers provide an irregular service from East Africa, Réunion, Madagascar and Mauritius.

Main port/s: Moroni (Grand Comore) and Fomboni (Anjouan): both have offshore anchorage for larger vessels.

Getting about

National transport

Air: Each island is served by Air Comores. There are regular flights between the islands.

Road: Surfaced roads on Grande Comore and Anjouan; other islands' roads can be difficult in rainy season. Mohéli has only very basic tracks.

Water: Small boats, which can be hired, ply between the islands.

City transport

Taxis: Service is provided by *taxi-brousse* (bush taxis) on each island. The journey from the International Airport to the city centre takes 30 minutes.

Car hire

International driving licence required.

BUSINESS DIRECTORY

The addresses listed below are a selection only. While World of Information makes every endeavour to check these addresses, we cannot guarantee that changes have not been made, especially to telephone numbers and area codes. We would welcome any corrections.

Telephone area codes

The international direct dialling code (IDD) for Comoros is +269, followed by the area code and subscriber's number:

Anjouan	71	Moroni	73
Mohali	72		

Useful telephone numbers

Emergency services: 744-890

Chambers of Commerce

Chambre de Commerce, d'Industries et d'Agriculture, PO Box 763, Moroni (tel: 730-958;fax: 731-983; e-mail: pride@snpt.km).

Banking

Banque de Development des Comores, Place de France, BP-298 Moroni (tel: 730-154, 730-818; fax: 730-397, e-mail: bdc@snpt.km).

Banque pour l'Industrie et le Commerce - Comores, BP 175, Place de France, Moroni (tel: 730-243, 730-225, 730-289; fax: 731-229).

Central bank

Banque Centrale des Comores, BP 405, Place de France, Moroni (tel: 73-1002/1814; fax: 73-0349).

Travel information

Comorian Association of Tourism (ACT) (tel: 732-847, 731-942; fax: 732-846).

Société Comorienne de Tourisme et d'Hotellerie (COMOTEL), Itsandra Hotel, Ngazidja (tel: 732-365).

International Prince Said Ibrahim Airport, BP 1003, Moroni (tel: 731-593, 732-452, 732-135; fax: 731-468).

Ministry of tourism

Ministry of Transport, Tourism, Post and Telecommunications, BP 97 Moroni (tel: 744-242; fax: 744-241).

Ministries

Ministry of Culture, Youth and Sports, Moroni (tel: 744-044).

Ministry of the Economy, Commerce, Handicrafts and Investment, BP 474 Moroni (tel: 744-232; fax: 730-144).

Ministry of Education, Professional Formation and Human Rights, BP 73 Moroni (tel: 744-185; 744-180).

Ministry of Equipment, Energy and Urbanism, Moroni (tel: 744-500).

Ministry of Finance, Budget and Privatisation, BP 324 Moroni (tel: 744-141; fax: 744-140).

Ministry of Foreign Affairs and Co-operation, BP 428 Moroni (tel: 744-100; fax: 744-111).

Ministry of Health, Population and Women's Affairs, Moroni (tel: 744-070).

Ministry of the Interior and Decentralisation, BP 686 Moroni (tel: 744-666; fax: 744-688).

Ministry of Justice and Islamic Affairs, Moroni (tel: 744-200).

Ministry of Production and the Environment, BP41 Moroni (tel: 744-630; fax: 744-632).

Ministry of Public Service, Employment and Labour, Moroni (tel: 744-540).

Other useful addresses

British Honorary Consulate, BP 986, Moroni (tel/fax: 733-182).

Comoros Embassy (France) 20 Rue Marbeau, 75016 Paris, France (tel: (+33) 1-4067-9054; fax: (+33) 1-4845-1365).

Comoros Mission to UN (US), 866 United Nations Plaza, Suite 418, New York, NY 10017 (tel: (+1-212) 750-1637; e-mail: comun@undp.org; internet: www.un.int/comoros).

Société Internationale des Comores, BP 175, Moroni (tel: 730-243).

Internet sites

Africa Business Network: www.ifc.org/abn

AllAfrica.com: http://allafrica.com

African Development Bank: www.afdb.org

Africa Online: www.africaonline.com

Mbendi AfroPaedia (information on companies, countries, industries and stock exchanges in Africa): http://mbendi.co.za

Congo

KEY FACTS

Official name: République du Congo (Republic of Congo)

Head of State: President Denis Sassou Nguesso (from 1997; re-elected 12 Jul 2009)

Head of government: Prime Minister Isidore Mvouba (appointed Jan 2005)

Ruling party: Coalition of Parti Congolais du Travail (PCT) (Congolese Labour Party), and its allies (since 2002; re-elected Aug 2007)

Area: 342,000 square km

Population: 3.90 million (2010)*

Capital: Brazzaville (political); Pointe-Noire (business)

Official language: French

Currency: CFA franc (CFAf) = 100 centimes (Communauté Financière Africaine (African Financial Community) franc)

Exchange rate: CFAf488.90 per US$ (Oct 2011); CFAf655.95 per euro (pegged from Jan 1999)

GDP per capita: US$2,538 (2009)*

GDP real growth: 8.80% (2010)

GDP: US$9.53 billion (2009)*

Inflation: 5.20% (2010)*

Oil production: 292,000 bpd (2010)

* estimated figure

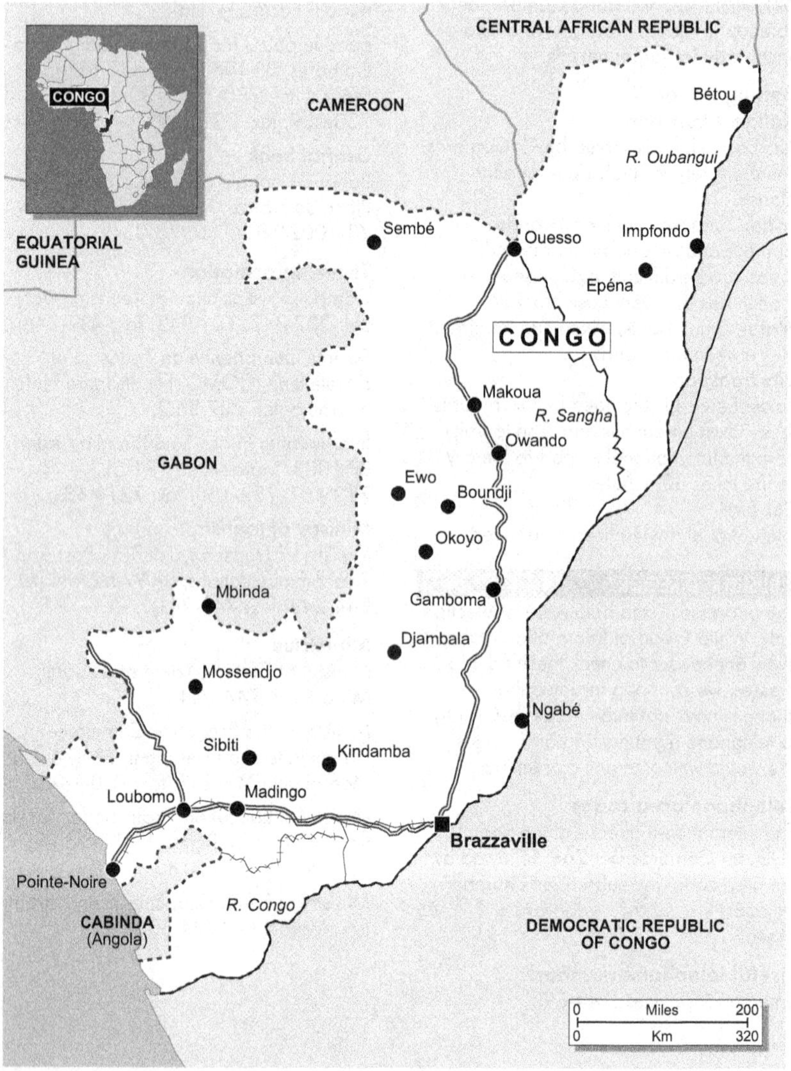

Congo's economic performance in 2010 owes a great deal to the increase in its oil production, reports the *African Economic Outlook 2011* (AEO), published jointly by the African Development Bank and the Organisation for Economic Co-operation and Development. Production reached a record level, estimated at 115 million barrels compared to 99 million in 2009. Fiscal reform and debt relief obtained under the Heavily Indebted Poor Countries (HIPC) Initiative also consolidated fundamental indicators and improved the budgetary balance. The result was a strong 10.2 per cent growth rate in 2010, with 8.4 per cent expected in 2011. These growth rates nevertheless remain fragile. They depend too heavily on the international oil market and maintenance of a high level of oil production. Medium-term forecasts show that oil production will gradually diminish unless new reserves are discovered. Diversification of the economy remains a crucial issue. Construction, public works and telecommunications continue to thrive.

The forestry sector seems to be recovering after having been penalised by the global crisis. Increased demand from Asian countries, particularly China, which is the leading buyer of Congolese timber, is ensuring the industry's survival.

The budgetary balance improved markedly in 2010 to reach 13.9 per cent of gross domestic product (GDP) and is forecast to reach 16.5 per cent in 2011. This is the result of a budgetary policy based on improving the quality of expenditure and implementation of the public contracts code and the public investment management system in line with the medium-term expenditure framework (MTEF). Revenue should increase 12 per cent in 2011, with oil revenue up 74.3 per cent and fiscal revenue up 17.8 per cent. The Republic of Congo should benefit from CFAf50 billion (US$0.12 billion) in 2011 in HIPC resources. Grants should reach CFAf45 billion (US$0.10 billion) and state borrowing CFAf115 billion (US$0.24 billion).

Congo's external position progressed in 2010 thanks to good oil price levels, improved productivity from certain reserves and a recovery in timber exports. The current account deficit fell to 2.6 per cent of GDP in 2010 thanks to the increase in exports. The inflation rate stood at 4.8 per cent in 2010 under the impact of strong domestic demand and an increase in international prices for food products.

International trade

Relations with emerging countries, notably India and China, go back to Congo's independence in 1960. More recently, relations have been forged with other Asian countries, such as Malaysia and Korea, Middle Eastern countries, such as Saudi Arabia and the United Arab Emirates, and Latin American countries, such as Brazil and Argentina.

Asia is Congo's biggest client. It accounted for 56 per cent of total exports in 2009, ahead of Latin America, where Mexico, Brazil and Argentina absorb 20 per cent of Congolese exports. China is the country's leading Asian partner, accounting for 40 per cent of Congo's export sales, principally in the form of oil and timber, compared with 10 per cent for Chinese Taipei. Imports from Asia nevertheless remain at a low level. They take the form mainly of food products and capital equipment but represent less than 8 per cent of the country's total foreign purchases.

Energy

Driven by the oil sector, which represents 66.3 per cent of GDP, the Congolese economy showed 10.2 per cent growth in 2010 in real terms after 6.8 per cent in 2009. According to the *BP Statistical Review of World Energy 2011* oil production reached a record 292,000 barrels per day (bpd) in 2010; proven reserves were 1.9 thousand million barrels at the end of 2010. The offshore oilfields, which produced more than 40 million barrels, kept their leading position.

France remains a major client. It and China are the biggest buyers of Djeno Blend quality oil and it and the United States are the main buyers of Nkossa Blend light oil.

Gas production increased by about 47 per cent, according to July 2010 data, rising from 75,405 tonnes in 2009 to 110,375 tonnes in 2010 thanks to good activity levels on the Nkossa field.

Oil is going to drive medium-term growth. In 2011, production should grow by 7.4 per cent before starting a period of decline unless new discoveries are made. The decline hypothesis seems unlikely to be realised, however, given the level of exploration work being carried out by numerous companies. In early 2011, the Italian national oil group Eni was due to start exploiting the tar sands in the Tchikatanga and Tchikatanga-Makola areas, 70km from Pointe-Noire. The tar or oil in nearly solid form produced will be processed in Italy at a rate of 40,000 barrels per day. Eni plans to build a tar processing plant on site in future, however.

On the domestic market, the activities of the Congolaise de Raffinage (Coraf) refinery which is owned by the state, produced contrasting results in 2010. Production fell 16.4 per cent to 276,500 tonnes, while sales increased 6.5 per cent. These results are explained by the low impact of world crude oil prices on prices at the pump and the fact that since November 2009 Coraf has been processing Nkossa Blend rather than Djéno Blend. Previous investment on the Nkossa oil field penalised Coraf's results in 2010. Prospects are promising nevertheless as the company continued to process Nkossa Blend in 2010, as well as carrying out a multi-year investment plan. Coraf can be expected to extend its coverage of the domestic market where it currently meets only 70 per cent of demand.

The economy

For three decades, Congo followed a centralised planning policy, marked by wide-ranging control of economic activity by the state, which granted monopolies, fixed prices and set up public-sector companies. Major distortions have resulted. Private initiative is not encouraged and support for the private sector has been neglected, penalising small and medium-sized enterprises. There is strong potential, however, in forest activities, agriculture, livestock rearing, fishing, mining and hydrocarbons. There are also numerous buoyant industrial sectors such as food processing, timber and construction materials.

According to the World Bank's *Doing Business* report for 2011, Congo lies in 177th position out of 183 countries in terms of the business climate. It has moved up a place since 2009 but its performance is still poor. A long list of

KEY INDICATORS **Congo**

	Unit	2006	2007	2008	2009	2010
Population	m	3.45	*3.55	*3.65	*3.76	*3.90
Gross domestic product (GDP)	US$bn	7.74	7.79	11.85	9.60	11.90
GDP per capita	US$	2,245	2,244	*3,245	*2,538	–
GDP real growth	%	6.4	-1.6	5.6	7.5	8.8
Inflation	%	4.7	2.5	6.0	*4.3	*5.2
Oil output	'000 bpd	262.0	222.0	249.0	274.0	292.0
Exports (fob) (goods)	US$m	6,387.0	*6,049.7	*8,041.4	*6,090.8	–
Imports (fob) (goods)	US$m	1,533.0	*2,781.7	*2,874.0	*2,490.5	–
Balance of trade	US$m	4,854.0	*3,270.2	*-5,167.4	*3,600.2	–
Current account	US$m	116.0	*-2,108.3	*-156.3	*1,198.7	–
Total reserves minus gold	US$m	1,840.9	2,174.3	3,871.8	3,806.3	4,446.9
Foreign exchange	US$m	1,839.9	2,173.2	3,870.7	3,695.5	4,388.1
Exchange rate	per US$	496.60	454.40	447.81	472.19	495.28

* estimated figure

handicaps continues to penalise the private sector. Poor infrastructure and poor legal, administrative and financial systems are compounded by bad governance and the lack of qualified labour.

The authorities plan to create a high council for public-private dialogue (HCDPP), which will be placed under the authority of the President and will bring together representatives of the private sector, the administration and public sector companies. This body will have the task of initiating the reforms necessary to improve the business climate.

Mining

The mining sector offers good prospects. In 2010, Soremi, a subsidiary of the American group Gerald Metals, continued to produce copper ore at Boko Songho and Yanga Koubanza. Production in 2010, which was estimated at 16,000 tonnes, represented more than double the 7,000 tonnes initially forecast. It was exported to China and Germany.

The Canadian company Mag Minerals Potasse du Congo, in which the Congolese government has a 10 per cent stake, is pursuing construction of a potassium plant. Carnallite is to be exploited to extract magnesium for production of a light alloy for use in the automobile industry and sodium chloride and potassium chloride for production of non-polluting fertilisers. The initial investment in this plant is estimated at US$1.6 billion. Annual production would be 600,000 tonnes, which would make Congo the biggest producer of potassium in Africa and the 13th biggest in the world. The Chinese company Complant has also expressed its interest in this sector.

Agriculture, forestry and fishing

Agriculture, livestock rearing and fishing contributed 3.4 per cent to GDP in 2010 compared to 5 per cent in 2009. Despite the fertile soil and heavy rainfall, the agricultural sector remains weak and turned mainly towards subsistence. It meets no more than 30 per cent of the country's food needs and makes use of less than 5 per cent of arable land. Imports represent 60 per cent of cereal and meat needs and 50 per cent of fish and seafood needs. Cassava production remained stable at 1.27 million tonnes in 2010, while plantain volumes increased 13.6 per cent to 96,800 tonnes. Groundnut production rose 4 per cent to 34,100 tonnes.

Some agro-industrial projects were launched in 2010, including one with South African partners for the production of alcohol from sugar cane. Malaysia-based companies also plan to produce biofuel from palm oil at a rate of up to 400,000 hectolitres per year, while Italy aims to produce up to 120,000 hectolitres per year.

The forestry sector continues to be penalised by the global economic crisis. Recovery is getting under way with difficulty. Its contribution to GDP is marginal at 0.3 per cent. Production of logs and sawn timber nevertheless continues to offer promising prospects. Still low prices for sawn timber on the international market resulted in a drop in production from 77,109 cubic metres in 2009 to 62,146 cubic metres in 2010. Nevertheless, increased demand from Asian countries should help the sector. China is the principal buyer of Congolese timber, ahead of Spain and Portugal. It takes 70 per cent of all timber exported.

In 2011, the authorities intend to maintain the measures they took to reduce the effect of the crisis in the sector. These allow the exportation of up to 30 per cent of logs and offer payment facilities for the felling tax. Wood processing remains an option for the future provided that an effort is made to train labour. The introduction of certification should enable the country to take full advantage of its potential in this sector. Congo and the European Union (EU) have signed a partnership to combat illegal forest exploitation. From July 2011, any cargo of wood entering the EU from Congo must have authorisation testifying that it only contains timber and wood products of legal origin. The agreement should open the way to sustainable development of the forestry sector and create new jobs.

Congo has about 12 million hectares of land exploitable for agriculture but its imports of foodstuffs in 2010 were estimated at CFAf130 billion (US$270 million). Exploitable areas are spread between Cuvette in the north and Sangha in the north-west. The development of plantations should create 20,000 jobs.

Despite a reduction in fishing resources in territorial waters, notably in the departments of Pointe-Noire and Kouilou, the volume of fish catches grew by 5 per cent to 4,500 tonnes in 2010. Fishing is handicapped by high production costs. Diesel fuel represents 35 per cent of costs in this activity. Other problems are the use of fishing gear that does not comply with EU regulations and non-compliance with designated fishing zones.

The dynamism of the construction sector, which represents 4 per cent of GDP, looks set to continue. It is one of the most promising non-oil sectors and is driven by a vast construction programme and upgrading work. The sector is nevertheless suffering from difficulties in getting supplies of building materials and a lack of qualified labour.

Telecommunications growth should speed up following the installation of optical fibre as part of a submarine cable project planned for 2011. This sector, which contributed 4.7 per cent to GDP in 2010, is continuing to progress rapidly.

Banking

The financial system was spared by the international crisis. The six Congolese banks have sufficient equity and reserves to meet all prudential norms. Despite the limited scale of the economic fabric, short-term prospects are good thanks to the launch of major infrastructure projects like the potassium plant, the gas power station and the modernisation of the port of Pointe-Noire.

The banking system counts six establishments: Crédit du Congo, which was taken over in 2009 by Morocco's Attijariwafa Bank; BGFI Bank Congo, a subsidiary of the private Gabonese BGFI Bank; Congolaise de Banque, a subsidiary of Morocco's BMCE Bank; Banque Commerciale Internationale, a subsidiary of France's Banque Populaire; Ecobank Congo; and the state-owned Banque Congolaise de l'Habitat. In 2010, banking activity progressed at a more moderate rate than in 2009. The balance sheet total increased 7.4 per cent compared to 35 per cent in 2008. The slowdown in the granting of gross credits to clients was significant.

Two new foreign banks were due to establish themselves in Congo in early 2011: the Indian group Besco, and Nigeria's United Bank of Africa. France's Société Générale is also interested in the Congolese market.

External trade

In an economy that is heavily dependent on oil, exports contributed 4.3 per cent to the formation of GDP in 2010. Buoyant oil production levels were supported by high prices and strong demand from Asian countries, especially China.

Congo's external position improved in 2010 thanks to exceptional oil revenue and the benefits accruing from attainment of the HIPC Initiative completion point. The trade surplus rose to 43.8 per cent of GDP in 2010 from 36.5 per cent in 2009. Export volumes increased thanks to good oil prices and higher productivity from certain oilfields, as well as a recovery in timber exports.

Exports represented 77.2 per cent of GDP in 2010 compared to 69.9 per cent in 2009. They mainly consist of oil, which represents 86 per cent of the total, minerals and timber. The total value of exports came to CFAf3.128 trillion (US$0.06 trillion) in 2010, up markedly in relation to 2009.

At the same time, imports of goods and service were kept under control in 2010 at a level close to the 33.4 per cent of GDP registered the previous year. This position is the result of a fall in imports of foodstuffs and energy products, countered by an increase in imports of capital goods.

The services deficit fell by 6 percentage points to 31.3 per cent of GDP in 2010 from 37.4 per cent in 2009. The current account balance was slightly in deficit in 2010 at 2.6 per cent of GDP but should be in surplus in 2011. This result cannot hide Congo's economic fragility, however. For this reason, a return to a current account deficit is possible from 2012 if measures are not taken before then to reduce dependence on oil.

Foreign direct investment (FDI) fell 18 per cent to CFAf 909 billion (US$2 billion) in 2009 from CFAf1.112 trillion (US$2.2 billion) in 2008. This fall was the result of the international financial crisis. At the same time, the recovery in Asian countries' demand for hydrocarbons should lead to a stronger flow of capital, notably in the oil and gas sector, but also in the mobile telephone sector.

Social indicators

Congo is lagging way behind on the Millennium Development Goals (MDGs). It will probably attain only two objectives by 2015 – universal education and sexual equality. Poverty has only slightly diminished, according to the latest study, carried out in 2009. The health situation remains worrying with high levels of infant and maternal mortality and still limited access to drinking water and sanitation. Unemployment remains high, especially among the young, and the average monthly salary level in the public sector does not exceed CFAf65,000 (US$134).

The government has committed to concrete action to revitalise the education system and ensure that all children get primary schooling. School fees have been abolished, school books are now free and teachers have been recruited.

On the employment front, the country continues to face a major problem with an unemployment rate of more than 17 per cent. Public-service salaries, which have been frozen for 15 years, will be raised in 2011. A new salary structure will be introduced, as will a simplified grading structure for public sector employees. This structure should take account of appointments, regradings and other administrative status changes. The minimum salary in the public sector, which currently stands at CFAf50,000 (about US$102), should be increased 25 per cent, according to official sources.

Risk assessment

Economy	Fair
Politics	Fair
Regional stability	Fair

COUNTRY PROFILE

Historical profile

From the fifteenth century, the Bakongo, Bateke and Sanga began settling in what is now the Republic of Congo.

1482 Portuguese explorer Diogo Cao mapped the coastline.

1880s The colonisation of what is now the Republic of Congo began in the late nineteenth century after the French explorer Pierre Savorgnan de Brazza signed a treaty with the Chief of the Batekes to establish a French protectorate over the north bank of the Congo river.

1910 Middle Congo, as the country was then known, became a colony of French Equatorial Africa.

1928 Africans revolted over forced labour which was used to build the Congo railway. More than 17,000 Africans died in the revolt.

1946 Congo was granted a territorial assembly by the French and representation in the French parliament.

1960 Congo became independent with a catholic priest, Abbé Fulbert Youlou, as president.

1963 Alfonse Massamba-Debat became president and Pascal Lissouba became prime minister. The country became a one-party socialist state.

1969 Captain Marien Ngouabi led a coup against Massamba-Debat and became president. The Parti Congolais du Travail (PCT) (Congolese Workers' Party) was declared the only legal political party.

1970 Ngouabi proclaimed Congo a Marxist state.

1977 Ngouabi was assassinated by forces loyal to Massamba-Debat, who in turn was executed for treason. Joachim Yhombi-Opango of the Comité Militaire du Parti (CMP) (Party of the Military Committee) became president.

1979 Colonel Denis Sassou-Nguesso took over the PCT, and remained in power under one-party PCT rule until 1992.

1990 The PCT abandoned Marxism.

1992 A new constitution was approved by a referendum. Multi-party legislative elections were won by the Union Panafricaine pour la Démocratie Sociale (UPADS) (Pan-African Union for Social Development), led by Pascal Lissouba. Lissouba was elected president, defeating Sassou-Nguesso.

1993 Political unrest forced new elections, which were won by UPADS.

1994 A peace agreement saw members of the opposition join the government. The currency was devalued.

1997 The government attempted to disarm rebel militia loyal to Sassou-Nguesso, resulting in a civil war. Thousands of people were killed and tens of thousands forced to flee their homes. After several months of fighting the Angolan Army invaded and sided with Sassou-Nguesso who succeeded in overthrowing the government of Pascal Lissouba.

Sassou-Nguesso assumed the presidency at the head of the Conseil National de Transition (CNT) (National Transitional Council).

1999 The warring factions signed a peace accord with the government. However, armed conflict continued.

2001 A peace conference proposed a new constitution and 15,000 militia were given financial incentives to demobilise. Lissouba was convicted *in absentia* of treason and corruption and sentenced to 30 years' hard labour. Congo signed a treaty establishing the Gulf of Guinea Commission.

2002 The new constitution, which strengthened the powers of the president, was endorsed by 80 per cent of the electorate. Sassou-Nguesso was elected president with almost 90 per cent of the vote after his rivals were either banned from running or withdrew. The legislative election for the new bicameral parliament led to the creation of a pro-Sessou-Nguesso coalition consisting of the PCT, the Forces Démocratiques Unies (FDU) (United Democratic Forces) and a number of independents. Electoral disputes between government forces and rebels in the south loyal to former prime minister Bernard Kolelas led to intense fighting, which reached Brazzaville. An agreement on power-sharing was reached between the government and two main rebel groups, but fighting continued in the east.

2003 All parties signed a peace agreement ending the civil war. A new constitution was adopted paving the way for elections.

2004 The Congo, which was held responsible for large-scale diamond smuggling from the Democratic Republic of Congo

(DRC), was expelled from the Kimberley Process Certification Scheme (for diamonds), when it was unable to explain why its exports outstripped its production. The move severely limited the Congo's exports of diamonds.
2005 The president appointed his close ally, Isidore Mvouba, as prime minister and caused a wave of criticism, as the constitution does not allow for presidential appointees. Bernard Kolelas was given an amnesty and allowed to return home after eight years in exile.
2006 Congo was chosen to hold the year's presidency of the African Union, after Sudan withdrew its candidacy amid diplomatic concern about its human rights record.
2007 Former Ninja rebels, who had been led by Pastor (Frederic) Ntoumi in support of Lissouba in the 1997–99 civil war, symbolically burned their weapons to demonstrate their commitment to peace. Around 40 political parties boycotted parliamentary elections. The ruling PCT won 88 seats (out of 137). The London Club (a group of private sector creditors) cancelled 80 per cent of Congo's debt.
2008 A government programme to demobilise, disarm and re-integrate ex-combatants of Paster Ntoumi, was launched.
2009 President Denis Sassou Nguesso was re-elected.
2010 In January, the World Bank and International Monetary Fund (IMF) announced a package of debt relief amounting to US$255.2 million, which will allow total debt savings of US$1.9 billion. In July, the president announced one of Africa's toughest child protection legal frameworks. Transparency International successfully appealed against a Paris court's ruling in 2009 that it could not act against foreign heads of state. On 9 November France's highest appeals court gave judges permission to proceed with investigations into assets held in France by President Denis Sassou-Nguesso, as well as by Teodoro Obiang Nguema of Equatorial Guinea and the late Omar Bongo, former president of Gabon.
2011 An ecology summit of heads of state, ministers and representatives of 35 rainforest countries was held in Brazzaville at the beginning of June. The meeting, to strengthen co-operation, issued a call for international funding for equatorial forest conservation (forests are deemed to provide an international service in carbon capture and provision of livelihood to an estimated 1.5 billion people worldwide). However, they failed to agree a formal structure of co-ordinated forestry policies. On 17 June the government announced that four economic zones would be established in 2012, in a move to diversify the economy from hydrocarbons to manufacturing and service industries. The zones will provide tax breaks and other incentives for participating companies. The Singapore Co-operation Enterprise signed a memorandum of understanding (MOU) for help to develop the zones. Several companies from various countries expressed an interest in the zones.

Political structure

Constitution
President Sassou Nguesso suspended the 2000 constitution in 2002 in favour of an older version in which presidential terms in office is seven years.

Form of state
Republic

The executive
Executive authority is vested in the directly elected president, who serves a seven-year term.

National legislature
The bicameral Parliament consists of the Assemblée Nationale (national assembly), with 153 members, elected in single seat constituencies for five-year terms. The Sénat (senate) has 72 members, elected by local, district and regional councils (six representatives for each of the 12 regions), to serve for six years.

Legal system
Based on the French civil, and traditional customary law

Last elections
12 July 2009 (presidential); 24 June/5 August 2007 (parliamentary (two rounds)).
Results: Presidential: Denis Sassou Nguesso won 78.6 per cent of the vote, Joseph Kignoumbi Kia Mboungou (independent) 7.46 per cent; turnout 66.42 per cent (official figure).
Parliamentary: (national assembly, first and second round) the PCT and its allies won a total 88 seats (out of 137), including the PCT with 46 and the Mouvement Congolais pour la Démocratie et la Développement Integral (MCDDI) (Congolese Movement for Democracy and Integral Development) 11. The opposition Union Panafricaine pour la Démocratie Sociale (UPDS) (Pan-African Union for Social Development) won 11 seats; Union pour la Démocratie et la République-Mwinda (UDR-Mwinda) (Union for Democracy and Republic-Mwinda) 1; Independents 37. Turnout was between 40–50 per cent.

Next elections
2016 (presidential); 2012 (parliamentary).

Political parties

Ruling party
Coalition of Parti Congolais du Travail (PCT) (Congolese Labour Party), and its allies (since 2002; re-elected Aug 2007)

Main opposition party
The Union Panafricaine pour la Démocratie Sociale (UPDS) (Pan-African Union for Social Development)

Population
3.90 million (2010)*
Last census: June 1996: 2,600,000 (provisional)
Population density: 7.6 inhabitants per square km. Urban population: 73 per cent (1995–2001) – the highest urbanisation rate in Africa.
Annual growth rate: 3.2 per cent 1994–2004 (WHO 2006)

Internally Displaced Persons (IDP)
100,000 (UNHCR 2004)

Ethnic make-up
Kongo (48 per cent), Sangha (17 per cent), Teke (17 per cent).

Religions
Traditional beliefs (over 50 per cent), Christianity (about 40 per cent, mainly Roman Catholic, some Protestant).

Education
Primary education is followed by seven years of secondary school which is divided into a four-year first cycle (ages 12 to 16) and a three-year second cycle (ages 16 to 19). In the second cycle, students can opt between general or technical education. Higher education is provided by the Université Marien-Ngouabi, which is largely state subsidised. It has a yearly enrolment of about 12,000 students.
Public expenditure on education typically amounts to 6 per cent of annual gross national income.
Literacy rate: 83 per cent adult rate; 98 per cent youth rate (15–24) (Unesco 2005).
Compulsory years: Six to 12
Enrolment rate: 120 per cent for boys, 109 per cent for girls, total primary school enrolment of the relevant age group (including repetition rates) (World Bank)
Pupils per teacher: 70 in primary schools.

Health
In 2004 a measles epidemics broke out in remote regions of northern Congo due to 'weak vaccination coverage' in earlier programmes and it was expected that, without a thorough immunisation campaign, measles would continue to return in two- to three-year cycles.
Pneumonic plague broke out in February 2005 in the north-east killing over 60 people and prompted control teams to be sent by international medical agencies to treat the victims. Many locals had fled the area and raised the fear of the infection spreading.

HIV/Aids
HIV prevalence: 4.9 per cent aged 15–49 in 2003 (World Bank)

Life expectancy: 54 years, 2004 (WHO 2006)
Fertility rate/Maternal mortality rate: 6.3 births per woman, 2004 (WHO 2006)
Child (under 5 years) mortality rate (per 1,000): 81 per 1,000 live births; 16 per cent of children aged under five were malnourished (World Bank).
Head of population per physician: 0.2 physicians per 1,000 people, 2004 (WHO 2006)

Welfare
In moves to encourage full cessation following the peace agreement of 2003, international donors have contributed over US$900,000 to projects set up to reintegrate demobilised soldiers into society. These projects were a second phase, the first built on credit offered by the World Bank of US$5 million.

Main cities
Brazzaville (political capital, estimated population 1.1 million in 2005), Pointe-Noire (economic capital, 630,883), Loubomo (114,869), Jacob (56,175).

Languages spoken
French is used for all business documentation. Other major languages are Lingala, Kikongo and Munukutuba. English is not much spoken.
Official language/s
French

Media
Despite the repeal of repressive press laws in 2000 the international human rights watchdog, Freedom House, described the Republic of Congo in 2006 as only partially free, as the government monopolised the broadcast media, which has a much larger share of the potential media audience.
Press
While there are many, small, independent newspapers published in Brazzaville few have a sustainable market outside the capital.
In French, the principal newspapers include the government-owned *Les Dépêches de Brazzaville* (www.brazzaville-adiac.com), the independent *Le Choc* (www.lechoc.info), and the Catholic publication *Semaine Africaine* (www.lasemaineafricaine.com).
Broadcasting
Radiodiffusion-Télévision Nationale Congolaise (RTN) is the state-run broadcaster.
Radio: RTN operates Radio Congo which broadcasts programmes in French, Lingala and Kikongo. The capital's own station, Radio Brazzaville, is also state-run and canal FM is a community station for the city. Radio Liberte is a private station. Foreign radio stations include Reveil FM, from Kinshasa (Democratic Republic Congo) and Radio France International (RFI) (www.rfi.fr) with news programmes in French.
Television: RTN operates the only locally broadcasting TV station, while satellite reception is available.
News agencies
National news agency: Les Dépêches de Brazzaville
APA (African Press Agency): www.apanews.net
Congopage (in French): www.congopage.com
Mwinda Press (in French): www.mwinda.org
Panapress: www.panapress.com

Economy
The economy is dominated by petroleum extraction, which accounts for most government spending. Foreign direct investment (FDI) is typically limited to petroleum extraction and forestry, the prime industry before oil was found; between them the two industries account for 75 per cent of GDP. However, these sectors are dependent on external markets and global commodity prices which fluctuate. Agriculture only accounts for 4 per cent of GDP, which is typically subsistence farming and is the country's largest employer. About half the area of forest is exploitable for commercial logging, while only 5 per cent remains protected from development. The service sector, both government and private are also largely supportive of the primary industries. Eco-tourism is a fledgling industry and in 2008 and 2009 measures were undertaken to preserve the environment of isolated regions and the Congo Basin for the indigenous pigmy (BaAka) tribes, gorillas, rainforests and bio-diversity in general.
GDP growth was 7.6 per cent in 2009, rising from 5.6 per cent in 2008. Before the international creditors, led by the Paris Club, agreed to reschedule the Republic of Congo's debts, the government had to demonstrate that it was implementing macroeconomic reforms. In 2008 US$643 million of debt was cancelled and in March 2010 a further US$2.4 billion was cancelled, which amounts to all bilateral debts. The debt-to-GDP ratio of 198.7 per cent of GDP at the end of 2004 was reduced to 55.6 per cent of GDP at the end of 2008. With the cancellation of its debts the International Monetary Fund (IMF) expects the ratio will move into surplus of 2.5 per cent in 2010.
World Bank donors pledged up to US$3.9 billion for sub-Saharan Africa in 2006, with around three-quarters of this sum being invested in the regional transportation system. Improvements to the roads and mass transit could further encourage foreign investment. For its own benefit the government will have to broaden the tax base and improve revenue collection.
The Congo's economic performance has improved steadily but the IMF advised that any windfalls from high oil prices should be spent on poverty-alleviation, such as providing basic health and education services. Remittances were US$14 million (0.2 per cent of GDP) in 2009, which fell in 2010 to an estimated US$13 million.
In 2010, the UN Human Development Index (HDI) ranked the Congo as 126 (out of 169 countries) for improvement in health, education and income and indicated that the Congo had had a consistently higher average improvement over other sub-Saharan African countries since 1990. The poverty rate was recorded as 54.1 per cent, and 55.9 per cent of households experienced at least three indicators of poverty.

External trade
As a member of the Communauté Économique des États d'Afrique Centrale (Economic Community of Central African States (ECCAS) Republic of Congo uses the CFA franc (Communauté Financière Africaine franc), issued by the Banque des États de l'Afrique Centrale (BEAC) (Bank of Central African States). ECCAS operates a customs and economic union with a common external tariff between its six members, with free movement of capital, people and goods and services.
There is a regular large trade surplus from oil export earnings, but invisibles and debt payments keep the current account in deficit.
Imports
Principal imports are manufacturing equipment, vehicles and machinery, construction materials and foodstuffs.
Main sources: France (typically over 25 per cent of total), China (over 15 per cent), US (around 10 per cent).
Exports
Principal exports are petroleum, timber, plywood, sugar, cocoa, coffee and diamonds.
Main destinations: US (typically 40 per cent of total), China (30 per cent), France (10 per cent).

Agriculture
The agricultural sector contributes around 25 per cent of GDP and employs a third of the workforce. Agriculture has been overshadowed by development of the petroleum industry.
Approximately a third of the total land area is given over to agriculture, of that almost all is pasture land. Only an estimated 2 per cent of the total land area is under cultivation (mainly in the alluvial

Niari Valley). Farming is small-scale with output concentrated on subsistence crops such as plantains, cassava, yams, groundnuts, manioc, potatoes, wheat, maize, beans and paddy rice. Despite some growth in food production, Congo relies heavily on food imports.

The main cash crops are coffee, cocoa, tobacco and sugar. Attempts to expand production of other cash crops include the rehabilitation of oil palm estates and a major new cocoa project.

Fishing

Fishing is underdeveloped but is practised commercially on a small scale.

Forestry

The main agricultural export is timber, mostly Okoumé logs (of which Congo is a major world supplier). About half the total timber output is used for wood processing. Approximately 60 per cent of the country is covered by woodlands and forests, much of it unsuitable for commercial exploitation. There are large eucalyptus (fast growing) plantations near Pointe-Noire.

Industry and manufacturing

The industrial sector contributes over 10 per cent to GDP and employs a fifth of the workforce. The manufacturing sector is largely underdeveloped, contributing less than 5 per cent to GDP. Construction contributes a further 5 per cent, although this figure could grow rapidly, particularly in the repair of the damaged infrastructure, if political stability remains calm and reconstruction efforts are sustained.

Most manufacturing enterprises operate in the Brazzaville and Pointe-Noire districts and in the Niari Valley. Activity is centred on agri-food and timber processing, textiles and oil refining.

There are also a few small-scale import substitution industries (footwear, soft drinks, metal working, chemicals) and a cement plant.

Structure and ownership of parastatals is being reformed and the privatisation programme is expected to be renewed after years of delay. Emphasis is on joint-venture enterprises, particularly in pulp/paper and light manufacturing.

Tourism

The tourist industry had great potential for eco-tourism, but until peace can by assured foreign governments continue to advise strongly that their citizens do not visit Congo unless absolutely necessary.

Mining

Congo has significant deposits of magnesium, gold, diamonds, cement, potash and salt. Commercial exploitation of these deposits was either damaged by the civil war or have yet to be developed.

In July 2004, Congo was expelled from the Kimberley Process, set up to curb the trade in 'conflict diamonds', when the Congo could not account for the discrepancy between reported production and its exports of rough diamonds. As these diamonds are mined mostly by artisans the government claimed it was unable to confirm production, or curb smuggling along its uncontrolled borders. The ban on Congo diamonds effectively suspended legal exports of diamonds.

Gold production from the Yangadou Mine experienced technical problems and production has only amounted to 4kg per month since it opened in 2003, instead of the 1,500kg as expected.

A major magnesium processing plant at Kouilou could have a significant role in the economy when it is up and running. The plan, by Canada's MagIndustries Corporation (MagMetals), is to construct a 72,000 tonnes per annum (tpa) smelter of the local magnesium salt deposits and produce 60,000tpa of magnesium alloy. However, by the beginning of 2005 the project was still awaiting financial backing.

As a by-product of the magnesium mining MagMetals also proposes to exploit the potash and salt deposits found in the locale, with a 300,000tpa potash fertiliser plant and 400,000tpa salt plant.

Hydrocarbons

Proven oil reserves were 1.9 billion barrels in 2007, with production at 222,000 barrels per day (bpd), which was a fall of 15.3 per cent on the 2006 figure of 262,000. French oil company Total E&F (Elf and Fino) announced in April 2008 that it was beginning production from the Moho Bilondo deep-water oil field, with an estimated 230 million barrels of recoverable oil.

Total E&F has the dominant role in Congo's oil sector although it has lost its monopoly status as other foreign companies, especially Italy's Agip, are also investing in the country's petroleum industry. Italy's Eni and Total E&F have said that they would invest in production of Congo's tar sands field. Total E&F has also invested in the only oil terminal in Congo, processing 250,000bpd from all domestic oil fields and able to handle one tanker every four days, loading from offshore buoys.

Oil refining capacity was 21,000bpd in 2007, which is more than adequate for domestic consumption of over 9,000bpd. Proven natural gas reserves were 90.6 billion cubic metres in 2007, most of which was oil-associated. A lack of infrastructure and investment means that most gas is vented or flared.

The French energy company Total announced, in early 2011, the discovery of two new hydrocarbon reserves, situated 70km offshore of Congo in deep waters. The 25MW gas plant in Djeno utilises gas for electricity production for supply to the Pointe Noire area.

Any use of imported coal is commercially negligible.

Energy

Total installed generating capacity was 121MW in 2006, although generating potential is estimated at 3,000MW, from unexploited hydropower. Around 25 per cent of the country's electricity requirements are imported from the Democratic Republic of Congo (DRC). The state-owned Société Nationale d'Électricité (SNE) is responsible for generating and distribution of energy but transmission is severely limited so that consumption is low and most rural inhabitants rely on wood fuel as a primary source of power.

Construction of a 300 megawatts gas-fired power plant began in 2008, at the coastal site of Mateve, 15km south of Pointe-Noire.

Banking and insurance

In 2004 the banking system was considered fragile by the IMF, with credit growth limited by the lack of viable projects and a reluctance by banks to make loans as loan recovery is problematic. Of the four domestic banks two have been classified as in good condition and two in either a fragile or critical condition and in need of restructuring.

Central bank

Banque des Etats de l'Afrique Centrale

Main financial centre

Brazzaville

Time

GMT plus one hour

Geography

The Republic of Congo is an equatorial country on the west coast of Africa. A flat, treeless plane stretches down from the highlands to the coast. The coastline stretches about 170km along the Atlantic Ocean. The rain-forested highlands extends northward to Cameroon and the Central African Republic. Congo is bordered by Gabon in the west, and with the Democratic Republic of Congo to the east. In the south there is a short frontier with the Cabinda enclave of Angola.

Hemisphere

Straddles the equator.

Climate

Equatorial or sub-equatorial. Main dry season from June–September with average temperatures ranging from 15 degrees Celsius (C) at night to 32 degrees C during the day. Rainy season from October–May with higher average temperatures and high humidity. Generally hotter and more humid in Congo Basin, drier and cooler in highlands.

Entry requirements

Passports

Required by all, valid for at least six months.

Visa

Required by all. Tourists must provide evidence of accommodation arrangements in Congo and of sufficient funds. If on business, a letter, issued by the traveller's company, giving a detailed summary of intended purpose of trip, a full itinerary including intended contacts with host company, and the acceptance of full responsibility for any expenses incurred during the term of stay, and repatriation expenses in case of emergency, must be submitted with the application to the local embassy.

Currency advice/regulations

There is no limit to the amount of foreign currency which can be imported, but amounts above US$335 must be declared; export of foreign currency is limited to the amount declared on arrival. The import and export of local currency is prohibited, except between countries in the CFAf zone.

Health (for visitors)

Medical and dental facilities are inadequate.

Mandatory precautions

A yellow fever vaccination certificate is required by all.

Advisable precautions

Typhoid, hepatitis A and B, polio and tetanus vaccinations are recommended. Malaria prophylaxis should be taken, as a risk exists throughout the country. Water precautions should be taken. Visitors should avoid uncooked fruit and vegetables. There is an Aids risk and a risk of rabies.

Hotels

Good hotels are available in Brazzaville, Pointe-Noire and Loubomo; there are few elsewhere. It is advisable to book well in advance. A 10 per cent tip is usual.

Credit cards

Two hotels in Brazzaville and several in Pointe Noire accept major credit cards.

Public holidays (national)

Fixed dates

1 Jan (New Year's Day), 5 Feb (President's Day), 8 Mar (Women's Day), 18 Mar (Marien Ngouabi Day), 1 May (Labour Day), 22 Jun (Army Day), 31 Jul (Revolution Day), 13–15 Aug (Independence celebrations), 25 Dec (Christmas Day), 31 Dec (Republic Day).

Variable dates

Easter Monday; Ascension Day.

Working hours

Banking

Mon–Fri: 0630–1300. Counters close at 1130.

Business

Mon–Fri: 0800–1200 and 1430–1730, Sat: 0800–1200.

Government

Mon–Fri: 0700–1400, Sat: 0700–1200.

Shops

Mon–Fri: 0800–1200 and 1530–1800. Sat: 0800–1200 and 1530–1800/1900. Some shops close on Mon afternoons; a few open Sun mornings.

Telecommunications

Mobile/cell phones

There there are two GSM 900 networks operating: CelTel Congo and Libertis Telecom; however, coverage is generally restricted to Brazzaville and Pointe Noire.

Electricity supply

220V AC 50 cycles; the voltage varies erratically.

Weights and measures

The metric system is used.

Getting there

Air

National airline: Lina Congo

International airport/s: Brazzaville-Maya Maya Airport (BZV), 4km from city; restaurant, car hire.

Other airport/s: Pointe-Noire Airport (PNR), 6km from city.

Airport tax: CFAf500.

Surface

Road: There is a road from Lambaréné, in Gabon, to Loubomo and Brazzaville; this is not surfaced all the way. Entry from Cameroon is only practicable in the dry season. There is a surfaced road from the Cabinda enclave of Angola.

Water: A ferry service across the River Congo is operational daily from 0800–1200 and 1400–1700 between Kinshasa (Democratic Republic of Congo) and Brazzaville. Cars can be carried. The ferry takes about half an hour. There is also a *vedette* service for passengers only, which takes 15 minutes. Both services are liable to short-notice cancellation or delay.

Main port/s: Pointe-Noire. Brazzaville is the inland river port.

Getting about

National transport

Air: Internal air service operated by Lina Congo from Brazzaville to Pointe-Noire and the main provincial towns.

Road: There are 1200km of tarred roads; other routes are mainly tracks which can be impassable in wet weather. There are very few metalled roads outside Brazzaville and Pointe-Noire, while the roads within the towns are generally poor. The main route from Pointe-Noire, through Brazzaville to Ouesso, is not uniform in quality; the section from Loubomo to Pointe-Noire is liable to become impassable in the rainy season.

Rail: The Congo-Océan railway runs from Pointe-Noire to Brazzaville, a distance of around 500km. The service has been improved, but the journey is slow. The only other line is the 280km Comilog railway from Mbinda on the Congo/Gabon border which links to the Congo-Océan railway and is used mainly for the carriage of manganese ore produced by Comilog. The railways suffer from lack of maintenance and general upkeep.

Water: The ferries on the rivers Congo and Oubangui are a principal form of transport.

City transport

Taxis: Freely available in Brazzaville and Pointe-Noire; tipping is not usual. Can be hired by the hour or day. Fares should be negotiated in advance of journey.

Car hire

Available from main hotels in Brazzaville and Pointe-Noire. International or national driving licence accepted. Traffic drives on the right.

BUSINESS DIRECTORY

The addresses listed below are a selection only. While World of Information makes every endeavour to check these addresses, we cannot guarantee that changes have not been made, especially to telephone numbers and area codes. We would welcome any corrections.

Telephone area codes

The international direct dialling code (IDD) for Congo is + 242, followed by subscriber's number.

Useful telephone numbers

Fire: 18.
Police: 17.
Ambulance: 822-365/368.

Chambers of Commerce

Congo National Chamber of Commerce, Industry and Agriculture, PO Box 1119, Brazzaville (tel: 832-956).

Brazzaville Chamber of Commerce, Industry, Agriculture and Crafts, Avenue Amilcar Cabral, PO Box 92, Brazzaville (tel/fax: 811-608; e-mail: cciam_brazza@hotmail.com).

Dolisie Regional Chamber of Commerce, Industry and Agriculture, PO Box 78, Dolisie (Tel: 910-017).

La Sangha Regional Chamber of Commerce, Industrie and Agriculture, PO Box 122, Ouessa (tel: 983-200).

Pointe-Noire Chamber of Commerce, Agriculture, Industry and Crafts, PO Box 665, Pointe-Noire (tel: 941-280; fax: 943-467; e-mail: cciampnr@cg.celtelplus.com).

Banking

Banque de Développement des Etats de l'Afrique Centrale, PO Box 1177, Brazzaville (tel: 811-885, 811-761; fax: 811-880).

Banque des États de l'Afrique Centrale, PO Box 126, Brazzaville (tel: 832-814/5, 833-626, 833-362; fax: 836-342).

Banque Internationale du Congo, PO Box 33, Avenue Amilcar Cabral, Brazzaville (tel: 830-308, 831-411; fax: 815-092, 835-382).

Crédit pour l'Agriculture, l'Industrie et le Commerce (CAIC), PO Box 2889, Brazzaville (tel: 810-978, 814-050; fax: 810-977, 835-352).

Mutuelle Congolaise d'Epargne et de Crédit, PO Box 13237, Brazzaville (tel: 837-001; fax: 837-930).

Union Congolaise de Banques; PO Box 147, Avenue Amilcar Cabral, Brazzaville (tel: 833-000; fax: 836-845).

Central bank

Banque des États de l'Afrique Centrale, Direction Nationale, PO Box 126, Brazzaville (tel: 813-684; fax: 811-094; e-mail: beacbzv@beac.int).

Travel information

Direction Générale du Tourisme et de Hotellerie, BP 2480, Brazzaville (tel: 814-030; fax: 815-549; e-mail:mcatcongo@yahoo.fr).

Ministries

Ministry of Construction and Urban Development, BP 1218, Brazzaville.

Ministry of Decentralisation and Regional Development, BP 630, Brazzaville.

Ministry of Defence, BP 1219, Brazzaville.

Ministry of the Economy, BP 2120, Brazzaville.

Ministry of Finance and the Budget, BP 64, Brazzaville (tel: 411-266; fax: 814-145).

Ministry of Foreign Affairs, BP 2070, Brazzaville.

Ministry of Industry, Fisheries and Crafts, Palais du Peuple, Brazzaville (tel: 835-130).

Ministry of the Interior and of Security, BP 64, Brazzaville.

Ministry of Trade and Small- and Medium-sized Enterprises, Brazzaville (tel: 831-827).

Ministry of Transport and Civil Aviation, BP 2146, Brazzaville.

Other useful addresses

Agence Congolaise d'Information (ACI), BP 2144, Brazzaville

Bureau pour le Développement de la Production Agricole, BP 2222, Brazzaville.

Direction de la Statistique, BP 2031, Brazzaville (tel: 834-324).

Institut de Développement Economique de la République Populaire du Congo, c/o The Presidency, Brazzaville.

Office du Café et du Cacao (OCC), BP 2488, Brazzaville (tel: 831-902).

Office Congolais des Bois (OCB), BP 1229, Pointe-Noire (tel: 948-248).

Office Congolais de l'Entretien Routier (OCER), BP 2073, Brazzaville.

Office National du Commerce (ONC), BP 2305, Brazzaville (tel: 834-399).

Republic of Congo Embassy (USA), 4891 Colorado Avenue, NW, Washington DC 20011 (tel: 726-5500; fax: 726-1860; e-mail: info@embassyofcongo.org).

Société Nationale de Recherche et d'Exploitation Pétrolières (Hydro Congo), BP 2008, Brazzaville (tel: 833-560).

Syndicat des Commerçants, Importateurs et Exportateurs de l'Afrique Equatoriale (Sycomimpex), BP 84, Brazzaville.

National news agency: Les Dépêches de Brazzaville

Les Manguiers, 76 Ave Paul Doumer, Brazzaville (tel: 532-0109; fax: 532-0110; email: belie@congonet.cg; internet: www.brazzaville-adiac.com).

Internet sites

Africa Business Network: http://www.ifc.org/abn

AllAfrica.com: http://allafrica.com

African Development Bank: http://www.afdb.org

Africa Online: http://www.africaonline.com

Congo-Brazzaville (French only, Actualité dossier): http://www.solcongolais.net/

Mbendi AfroPaedia (information on companies, countries, industries and stock exchanges in Africa): http://mbendi.co.za

Democratic Republic of Congo

Constitutional amendments were adopted on 21 January 2011, which, among other amendments, included electoral changes that will bring the presidential to a one- instead of two-round election; the opposition protested.

There were rumours of an attempted coup against the president on 27 February when 11 attackers and eight members of the security forces were killed – in March the government paraded 126 people accused of the coup attempt, many with untreated injuries.

Parliamentary and presidential elections took place on 28 November 2011. Results were scheduled for 6 December, but technical difficulties prevented the news for 48 hours. In the presidential elections, of the 11 candidates that took part Joseph Kabila won 48.95 per cent of the vote and Etienne Tshisekedi 32.33 per cent; the rest won less than 8 per cent each. Parliamentary results are not due for publication until 13 January 2012. International observers of the elections consider the results 'lack credibility' with numerous examples of problems with vote counting, as supporters of unsuccessful candidates took to the streets to voice their complaints. On 12 December, the Union pour la Nation Congolese (UNC) (Congolese National Party) announced it would challenge the result in the supreme court. President Joseph Kabila was sworn into office on 20 December.

The economy

The economy recovered well in 2010 after slowing in 2009 because of lower mining revenue and less foreign direct investment (FDI). Real GDP growth has been estimated to have reached 6.1 per cent, up from only 2.8 per cent in 2009. The *African Economic Outlook 2011* (AEO), published jointly by the African Development Bank and the Organisation for Economic Co-operation and Development reports

KEY FACTS

Official name: République Démocratique du Congo (Democratic Republic of Congo) (DRC)

Head of State: President Joseph Kabila (elected 2006; re-elected 28 Nov 2011)

Head of government: Prime Minister Adolphe Muzito (PLU) (appointed by the president 10 Oct 2010)

Ruling party: Caretaker-coalition led by Parti du Peuple pour la Reconstruction et la Démocratie (PPRD) (People's Party of Reconstruction and Democracy) with Parti Lumumbiste Unifié (PLU) (United Lumumbist Party) and Union des Démocrates Mobutistes (UDM) (Union of Mobutist Democrats) (elected 30 Jul 2006) *(Elections on 28 Nov 2011, results due to be published: 13 Jan 2012)*

Area: 2,345,409 square km

Population: 67.80 million (2010)*

Capital: Kinshasa

Official language: French

Currency: Congolese franc (Cf)

Exchange rate: Cf922.91 per US$ (Oct 2011)

GDP per capita: US$171 (2009)

GDP real growth: 2.80% (2009)

GDP: US$11.10 billion (2009)

Inflation: 46.20% (2009)

Balance of trade: -US$1.78 billion (2008)*

Foreign debt: US$10.00 billion (2006)

* estimated figure

that progress was mainly due to good performances in mining (up 11.8 per cent), construction (10.1 per cent) and wholesale and retail trade (6.3 per cent), while the building and repair of major roads increased movement of goods and people. But the water and energy sub-sector shrank 2.1 per cent in 2010 and continued to be a drag on the economy. Real GDP growth should be of the order of an annual 6 per cent in the next two years.

The revival of the mining sector, which grew 11.8 per cent in 2010 (from 7.1 per cent in 2009), was due to more exports and much higher world prices. The ban on mining in the east of the country that had been imposed in 2010 was lifted in March. Several mining firms that had shut down or reduced activity in 2009 resumed operations. In 2010, output of copper (467,000 tonnes) rose 54.3 per cent and cobalt (93,000 tonnes) 65.3 per cent from 2009. The sector contributes some 12.5 per cent of GDP.

Crude-oil production, however, fell to 7.9 million barrels on the year up to the end of November (from 8.6 million for the same period in 2009) because of delays in maintenance work by one of the sector's big enterprises, Perenco. On 17 March 2011 oil exploration in the old Virunga national park, which is also a Unesco World Heritage Site and important habitat for mountain gorillas, was suspended following outcries from environmental groups around the world.

Construction grew 10.1 per cent in 2010 (up from 5.3 per cent in 2009), because of more government road-repair projects, private housing projects and the reopening of the Cilu cement works in Lukala. Cement production rose 16.1 per cent in 2010 (up from 14.6 per cent in 2009).

Agriculture grew 18.6 per cent, thanks to higher production of logs (up by 89.8 per cent) and coffee (12.2 per cent) on the year up to the end of November, and because of better world prices. Agriculture is rather marginalised in government spending and gets only 0.64 per cent of the total budget, far below the 10 per cent spending target of African countries as a whole.

An agriculture law aimed at attracting investors will be debated soon by parliament and an agricultural-development strategy was drafted in April 2010, though it is not yet in operation. A national food-security programme was recently drawn up with the help of the UN Food and Agriculture Organisation (FAO) and adopted by the government.

The water and energy sector contracted 2.1 per cent (more than the 0.2 per cent fall in 2009) owing to supply shortages from the state-run electricity and water enterprises Société Nationale d'Electricité (Snel) and Régie de Distribution d'Eau (Regideso). Snel and Regideso have suffered from outdated equipment and maintenance failures, which hampered the manufacturing sector.

Growth in 2010 was boosted by increased private consumption, partly as a result of more household buying power after a significant drop in inflation. Private investment also rose with more government efforts to repair basic infrastructure and more private housing construction.

Public investment, especially in road and energy infrastructure, should also significantly help real GDP growth in the next few years.

Government projections are based on expectation of growing world demand for raw materials, thus higher prices and much more exports. Clouds on the horizon include social unrest, probable delays in structural reforms and persistent rebel activity in the east of the country. External uncertainties include erratic prices of raw-material exports and imported goods, on which the DRC is very dependent, and the country's ability to attract foreign funding.

The budget deficit improved in 2010 owing to more government revenue from the revival of the world economy and better prices of raw materials on which the country is very dependent, and also to use of a cash flow forecast and budget commitment plan in managing the deficit.

Special subsidies to supplement petroleum-product prices were suspended in November 2010, producing extra revenue of US$5 million a month.

Government outlay on health increased to 2.9 per cent of GDP (2.1 per cent in 2009). More money went to education than in 2009 but its GDP share fell slightly to 3.6 per cent (from 3.7 per cent).

Monetary Policy

Better monetary and budgetary policy co-ordination brought inflation down to 23.3 per cent in 2010, slightly less than the 23.6 per cent target in the government's economic programme, after reaching 46.2 per cent in 2009. After disruption mainly due to depreciation of the Congolese franc from January to mid-February and costlier petroleum products starting in mid-August, inflation was sharply reduced by lower prices for food and alcoholic beverages, transport, housing, water, electricity and fuel, and clothing and footwear. Core inflation fell from 30 per cent at the end of 2009 to 9.8 per cent at the end of 2010. Overall inflation is expected to decline to around 9 per cent in 2011 and 2012.

The Banque du Congo's (central bank) key interest rate was cut five times during the year and reached 22 per cent in November 2010. The real interest rate was 12.2 per cent in December. The volume of loans, however, due to lower real and nominal interest rates as well as lower prices, only rose 8.8 per cent, perhaps reflecting continued hesitation by investors because of the poor business climate.

KEY INDICATORS — Democratic Republic of Congo

	Unit	2006	2007	2008	2009	2010
Population	m	*59.27	*61.05	*62.88	*64.77	*67.80
Gross domestic product (GDP)	US$bn	8.54	10.14	11.60	11.10	13.10
GDP per capita	US$	146	166	175	171	186
GDP real growth	%	5.6	6.3	6.0	2.8	7.2
Inflation	%	13.2	16.7	18.0	46.2	23.5
Industrial output	% change	9.8	11.0	7.1	-4.2	–
Agricultural output	% change	2.5	3.0	3.0	3.0	–
Exports (fob) (goods)	US$m	2,044.0	*6,143.0	*6,836.0	*1,123.0	–
Imports (fob) (goods)	US$m	2,607.0	*5,257.0	*6,711.0	*4,949.0	–
Balance of trade	US$m	-563.0	*886.0	*125.0	*-3,826.0	–
Current account	US$m	-212.0	*-402.0	*-1,461.0	*-1,123.0	-898.0
Total reserves minus gold	US$m	154.5	182.9	77.7	1,615.4	1,840.9
Foreign exchange	US$m	154.2	179.6	71.8	1,002.8	1,297.0
Exchange rate	per US$	530.00	556.50	552.00	809.79	905.91

* estimated figure

A sharp rise in exports (60.4 per cent) and imports (52 per cent) was seen in 2010 after their slump in 2009, with exports responding to higher world prices for raw materials, especially minerals, and imports to demand for production machinery and manufactures.

These trends will continue to increase the current-account deficit, expected to widen to 15.7 per cent of GDP in 2010 (from 10.1 per cent in 2009) and 16.7 per cent in 2011, before improving in 2012.

Achieving Heavily Indebted Poor Countries (HIPC) Initiative completion point in June 2010 gives the country access to US$12.3 billion in debt relief (11.1 billion under the HIPC Initiative and 1.2 billion under the Multilateral Debt Relief Initiative (MDRI). Of this, US$491 million will come from the IMF and US$1,832 million from the International Development Association (IDA), with the rest from bilateral and commercial creditors. The DRC will no longer have a heavy debt-service burden undermining its revenue and exchange reserves. The government has already obtained relief of US$7.35 billion from the Paris Club, reducing debt servicing to 2.9 per cent of goods and services exports in 2010 (from 21.2 per cent in 2009) and to an expected 1 per cent in 2011. External debt is estimated at US$2.9 billion in nominal value and US$3.7 billion in current value.

Private sector

Doing business in the DRC is still not easy. The World Bank's *Doing Business* report has the DRC slightly improved at 175th place out of 183 countries in 2011 (from 182nd in 2010), mainly because of reforms involving setting up businesses, granting building permits and registering property. The DRC went up nine places (to 146th) for ease of starting a business after abolishing various formalities including presentation of the enterprise's seal, thus reducing the time for inscription in the trade register to five days, and two for obtaining a national identity number.

The country moved up 58 places to 81st for getting building permits, mainly thanks to cheaper permits (falling from 1 per cent to 0.6 per cent of the building's market value) and simpler procedures. Since the report, they have been obtainable within 30 days. Halving of proportional taxes and transfer fees for property (from 6 per cent to 3 per cent) earned the DRC a gain of seven places to 118th in the property registration ranking.

The main problems business people come up against are double taxation (at provincial and national level linked to decentralisation), access to bank loans for small and medium-sized enterprises, problematic application of administrative rules, and difficult supply of goods and services by major state enterprises dealing with transport , electricity, water and insurance.

Reforms under consideration include lifting the ban on foreigners running businesses, reducing fees for getting a national identity number, regulation of leasing, creating a property register, introducing a value-added tax in 2012 as the DRC ratifies its joining of Ohada (African business law harmonisation organisation) in February 2010, and implementing existing plans for better governance and transparency in managing natural resources (forests, mining and oil).

Despite government efforts at greater transparency in its operations, governance perception indicators, such as those compiled by the World Bank and the Mo Ibrahim Foundation, put the DRC well down on the list of African countries. Transparency International's 2010 Corruption Perceptions Index ranks the country at 164th position out of 178 countries.

Restructuring the central bank reached a milestone with the 2011 budget increase of its capital from Cf60 billion (US$65 million) to Cf213 billion (US$230 million). Dollarisation of the economy is still substantial, with foreign currency deposits in the country's banks (equivalent to Cf601.95 billion (US$0.65 billion)) making up 85.7 per cent of all deposits, and 84.7 per cent of those demand deposits.

Privatisation is going ahead despite resistance. A new legal framework for government divestment of commercial firms has been introduced and the statutes of such companies were changed at the end of December 2010. Financially compensated voluntary redundancies have been introduced at Regideso, the mining firm Gecamines and at the railway Société Nationale des Chemins de Fer du Congo (SNCC). The main obstacles are the companies' debts, insufficient capital and substantial wage-payment arrears.

Infrastructure

The DRC has about 152,500 kilometres of roads with nine main routes linking provincial capitals. The network is in very poor condition due to lack of maintenance and funding in recent decades. The electricity grid has a wide gap between supply and demand despite the country's huge generating potential of 100,000MW.

Hopes for improvement have risen with a new co-operation agreement with China and resumption of ties with funding sources as a direct result of announced higher government investment. Major projects include upgrading the Inga hydroelectric power stations and exporting more electricity to southern Africa through Zambia under the Domestic Electricity Markets for Consumption and Export Project (PMEDE) and the Southern African Power Market Project (SAPMP). The US$900 million scheme is being funded by the World Bank, the African Development Bank (AfDB) and the European Investment Bank. Another infrastructure project (costing some US$1.9 billion) will repair the tarred roads between Kinshasa and Lubumbashi (east-west) and Kisangani and Bunia (north-south).

The national electricity firm Snel is entering into more and more partnerships with the private sector, especially with mining enterprises, to rehabilitate power stations and provincial power lines in exchange for discounts on their electricity bills and arrangements for the resale of surplus power. Electricity production has been opened up to the private sector but distribution is still the monopoly of Snel.

Nationwide road projects have been estimated to amount to about 3.6 per cent of GDP for the period 2010–13. Government priorities are repairing tarred roads, reviving the national roads office and helping the population living along these routes. The government is still considering the plan to build a bridge over the Congo River to link Kinshasa and the Congo Republic capital of Brazzaville.

International relations

The DRC's most active emerging partners are led by China, followed by India and South Korea. Turkey is preparing to join them, while Brazil's presence is still small. These countries are very involved in mining, construction, information and communication, agriculture, technology transfer and social development.

China, which wants to expand its presence in the region, is involved in several economic sectors and projects as part of a long-term co-operation agreement with the government under which China builds infrastructure in exchange for mining concessions. China is also helping with major projects in education, health, water supply, electricity and rural development, funded in 2009–10 by grants amounting to Rmb140 million (US$21.9 million) interest-free loans of Rmb150 million (US$23.5 million) and soft loans. The latter included Rmb2.348 billion (US$0.37

billion), including Rmb490 million (US$76.7 million) to upgrade telecommunications and Rmb1.758 billion (US$0.28 billion) to build a national optic fibre network. A soft loan of Rmb376.5 million (US$58.9 million) will fund the 150MW Zongo-II hydroelectric project. China also plans to get more involved in the country's health system and agricultural training in the next few years.

The Indian government is providing low-interest credit lines over at least 25 years, along with capacity building and experience sharing. Indian credit lines since 2005 have included US$33.5 million in 2005 for urban transport in Kinshasa, for the mining enterprise Miba in Kasaï-Oriental and to build a cement factory in the Orientale province. Sixty tractors have also been supplied to revive agriculture. US$25 million in credit was provided in 2010 to buy water pumps, and US$263 million in 2009, including US$213 million for the Katende and Kakobola dams and the rest for rail transport. A project to refurbish DRC's railway network by 2015 was announced on 12 May 2011. The 3,000km, US$600 million programme of works is backed by the World Bank and Chinese investors. Railway tracks will be replaced and new rolling stock purchased, while personnel of the existing rail company, who have not been paid for over four years, will be either retired with a pension or re-employed.

India regularly provides professional training and university scholarships. It has also made grants for building ICT training centres and training women in farming and use of solar energy. Both governments have agreed on joint committees to discuss aid problems.

Korea and Brazil are currently focusing on technology transfer, and offer training, university scholarships and internships. Brazil is sending Congolese trainee technicians to more advanced countries as part of their training and also sending experts to the DRC. A similar scheme is being negotiated with South Korea, which is also involved in strengthening government institutions and negotiating to build a deep-water port in Banana (Bas-Congo). Talks are continuing with Brazil to extract oil from the central basin and in Ituri starting in 2012.

India's biggest telecommunication firm, Bharti Airtel, has bought the Congolese telecommunications company Zain and a new firm, Congo China Telecom (CCT), has been set up.

Emerging partners are different from 'traditional' ones because they attach no conditions to any aid, profitability comes first, implementation is efficient, they focus on neglected sectors and give the impression of wanting long-term involvement.

Co-operation with the DRC's emerging partners is defined by a formal agreement with China and a draft agreement with India. Agreements under mining and forestry laws give investors special facilities and tax and customs deductions. The Agence Nationale pour la Promotion des Investissements (Anapi) (National Office for the Promotion of Investments) is drafting a plan to create special economic zones.

Partnerships with emerging countries, which sub-contract to some Congolese firms, should produce significant benefits in the medium term, including more local jobs, cheaper consumer goods and technology transfer.

Risk assessment

Economy	Poor
Politics	Poor
Regional stability	Fair

COUNTRY PROFILE

Historical profile

During the sixteenth and seventeenth centuries, the British, Dutch, Portuguese and French bought slaves from the Kongo Empire.

1870 King Leopold II of Belgium set up a private venture to exploit the riches of the Kongo Empire.

1879–87 British explorer, Henry Stanley was commissioned to established Belgian authority over the Congo basin.

1884–85 European governments recognised Leopold's claim to the Congo basin.

1885 Leopold established the Congo Free State, which he headed.

1891–92 Belgium conquered Katanga.

1892–94 Belgium conquered eastern Congo, which was controlled by Arab and east African merchants.

1908 The Belgian state annexed Congo following atrocities carried out by Leopold's officials.

1959 A nationalist uprising based in Leopoldville (now Kinshasa) began the disintegration of Belgian colonial authority.

1960 Congo gained independence. Joseph Kasavuba became president. The Belgian community fled and too few professionals were left to run the government. Chaos ensued as the diamond and copper mining province of Katanga attempted to secede under the leadership of Joseph Tshombe.

1961 Prime Minister Patrice Lumumba was deposed and murdered, allegedly by Katangan separatists. Marshal Joseph Mobutu was appointed prime minister. UN soldiers began disarming the Katangese soldiers on behalf of the Kasavuba government.

1963 Tshombe agreed to end the Katangan separatist war.

1964 President Kasavuba dismissed Mobutu and appointed Tshombe as prime minister.

1965 Mobutu seized power after a coup.

1971 Congo was renamed Zaïre. Mobutu renamed himself Mobutu Sese Seko.

1973–74 Mobutu nationalised foreign firms and forced foreign investors out of the country.

1977 French, Belgian and Moroccan troops fought an attack on Katanga by Angolan-based rebels.

1989 Zaïre defaulted on its debt servicing to Belgium; the economy began to deteriorate as development programmes were suspended.

1990 Mobutu appointed a transitional government and lifted the ban on multi-party politics.

1991 A series of short-lived coalition governments were presided over by President Mobutu, who retained control of security and key ministries.

1993 Rival pro- and anti-Mobutu governments were formed

1996 Tutsi rebels, in eastern Zaire, captured much of the eastern border area

1997 Mobutu fled to Togo when the Alliance des Forces Démocratiques pour la Libération (AFDL) (Alliance of Democratic Forces for Liberation), led by Laurent-Désiré Kabila, seized Kinshasa, after a seven-month campaign. Kabila had been backed by Tutsi rebels and the Rwandan government. Zaïre was renamed the Democratic Republic of Congo (DRC). Kabila became president. All government institutions were dissolved and a new constitution drafted. Mobutu Sese Seko died in Morocco.

1998 The Rassemblement Congolais pour la Démocratie-Goma (RCD-Goma) (Congolese Democratic Coalition) was formed, supported by Rwanda, Burundi and Uganda, and aimed at overthrowing Kabila, who was backed by Zimbabwe, Namibia and Angola. A full-scale civil war broke out. Peace talks began in Zambia but were ultimately unsuccessful.

1999 A split developed between the Mouvement pour la Libération Congolaise (MLC) (Movement for Congolese Liberation) backed by Uganda and the RCD-Goma supported by Rwanda. The six countries involved in the war signed a cease-fire, and the RCD-Goma and MLC signed later.

2000 The UN authorised a 5,500-strong force to monitor the supposed cease-fire; fighting continued between government

and rebel forces and Rwandan and Ugandan forces.
2001 President Kabila was assassinated. His son, Major General Joseph Kabila became president. The currency was floated on 28 May. A peace agreement between DRC, Uganda and Rwanda allowed foreign troops to withdraw. An estimated 2.5 million people had died in the conflict; the UN reported that the warring parties had continued the fighting to mask plundering of DCR's rich mineral assets.
2002 Goma was devastated by the eruption of Mount Nyiragongo. Rwanda and the DRC signed a peace deal whereby Rwanda withdrew troops and DRC disarmed and arrested Rwandan Hutu militia held responsible for the genocide in Rwanda in 1994. The DRC government signed a peace deal with the two main rebel groups. UN sponsored power-sharing talks were undertaken in South Africa.
2003 A transitional constitution sanctioned an interim government pending democratic elections to be held within two years. Leaders of the principal former rebel groups were sworn in as vice presidents.
2004 The massacre of 160 mostly Tutsi DRC refugees in Burundi prompted renewed warnings of war, and the Tutsi-led RCD-Goma, the former main rebel group during the DRC's civil war, suspended its participation in the power-sharing government.
2005 Nine UN peacekeepers were killed in the north-east; UN troops retaliated, killing over 50 militia members. The national assembly adopted a draft constitution, which had been agreed by former rebel groups. A referendum on the new constitution was gave resounding approval for the changes, with 84.31 per cent voting 'yes'. The result paved the way for presidential and parliamentary elections.
2006 Etienne Tshisekedi, leader of the opposition Union pour la Démocratie et le Progrès Social (UDPS) (Union for Democracy and Social Progress) withdrew his call for a boycott of the general elections. In the first free democratic elections since the 1960s over 9,700 candidates contested 500 seats in the national assembly. In presidential elections, incumbent Joseph Kabila won 58.05 per cent of the vote and Vice President Jean-Pierre Bemba 41.95 per cent; turnout was over 70 per cent. Antoine Gizenga of the Parti Lumumbiste Unifié (Palu) (United Lumumbist Party) was appointed prime minister.
2007 In senate elections Kabila's Alliance pour la Majorité Présidentielle (AMP) (Alliance for a Presidential Majority) won 58 seats (out of 108). The Union pour la Nation Congolese (UNC) (Congolese National Party) coalition won 21 (including a seat for Jean Pierre Bemba, its leader). The Communaute Economique des Pays des Grands Lacs (CEPGL) (Great Lakes Countries Economic Community) was re-launched by Burundi, DRC and Rwanda. CEPGL is intended to promote regional economic co-operation and integration. Rebel leader, Laurent Nkunda, fighting in the eastern provinces of North and South Kivu, declared that the ceasefire with government forces had ended. Fighting displaced over 300,000 people from the area to UNHCR camps near the city of Goma, while many more fled into rebel held territory and out of reach of international aid. Renegade leader Kasereka Kabamba was forced to surrender to government forces in North Kivu province.
2008 Jean-Pierre Bemba was arrested (in Belgium) to face charges of war crimes at the International Criminal Court (ICC). Bemba had been in exile since being accused of high treason in DRC for refusing to disarm his militia, following his defeat in 2006 presidential elections. The president appointed Adolphe Muzito (Palu) as prime minister.
2009 Rwandan troops crossed into DRC in a joint military operation to eliminate Rwandan Hutu militia, exiled in DRC since 1994 and causing widespread mayhem in DRC's eastern province, destabilising the region. Former general and Tutsi rebel leader Laurent Nkunda (Conseil National pour la Défense du Peuple (CNDP) (National Council for the Defence of the People) was arrested in Rwanda, having fled from his stronghold in Bunagana. Another, Hema, militia leader, Thomas Lubanga, caught in 2005, went on trial before the ICC, charged with the use of child soldiers and the killing of rival militia of the Lendu tribe in Ituri Province. A Swiss court ruled that the assets of former president Mobutu Sese Seko, held in Swiss banks, must be returned to his family. It rejected the appeal that the money (over US$6 million) should be returned to DRC, because the legal claim to the money took too long to be brought before the court.
2010 The Paris Club of creditors agreed to forego almost half DRC debts in an agreement in February. Of the US$3 billion covered by the agreement, around US$1.3 will be cancelled and the remainder rescheduled and debt service payments deferred until 1 July 2012. The UN agreed to withdraw its peacekeeping troops from July, at the request of the government. A US$12 billion debt relief package was agreed by the International Monetary Fund (IMF) in July, the country will no longer have to carry its heavy debt service burden on its revenue and foreign exchange reserves. In October army commander Sadoke Kokunda Mayele was arrested on charges of encouraging the gang rape of more than 300 persons; he was handed over by his fellow rebels. On 22 November, the trial of former vice president, Jean-Pierre Bemba, at the ICC in The Hague (The Netherlands) began. He was charged with crimes against humanity and war crimes while leading his military forces in the Central African Republic in 2002–03; the abuses included murder, rape and pillage, which were alleged to have been 'widespread and systematic'.
2011 Constitutional amendments were adopted on 21 January, when among other amendments, electoral changes were introduced that stopped the presidential run-off process. There were rumours of an attempted coup against the president on 27 February when 11 attackers and eight members of the security forces were killed. On 7 March the government paraded 126 people accused of the coup attempt, many with untreated injuries. The ban on mining in the east of the country that had been imposed in 2010 was lifted in March. On 17 March oil exploration in DRC's old Virunga national park, which is also a Unesco World Heritage Site and important habitat for mountain gorillas, was suspended following outcries from environmental groups around the world. A project to refurbish DRC's railway network by 2015 was announced on 12 May. The 3,000km, US$600 million programme of works is backed by the World Bank and Chinese investors. Railway tracks will be replaced and new rolling stock purchased, while personnel of the existing rail company, who have not been paid for over four years, will be either retired with a pension or re-employed. Parliamentary and presidential elections took place on 28 November. Results were scheduled for 6 December, but technical difficulties prevented the news for 48 hours. In presidential elections, of the 11 candidates that took part Joseph Kabila won 48.95 per cent of the vote and Etienne Tshisekedi 32.33 per cent; the remainder won less than 8 per cent each. Parliamentary results are not due for publication until 13 January 2012. International observers of the elections consider the results 'lack credibility' with numerous examples of problems with vote counting, as supporters of unsuccessful candidates took to the streets to voice their complaints. On 12 December, the UNC announced it would challenge the result in the supreme court. Joseph Kabila was sworn into office on 20 December.

Political structure

Constitution

A draft of a new constitution was approved by the national assembly in May

2005, and by a majority (84.31 per cent) of the people in a referendum held in December. It was officially adopted on 18 February 2006. The new constitution increases the number of provinces from 10 to 26, allows greater autonomy for some of the mineral-rich regions and lowers the minimum age for presidents from 35 to 33, thereby allowing 33-year-old Joseph Kabila, who has been president since the death of Laurent Kabila (his father) in 2001, to stand for the presidency in the 2006 elections. The president, who is limited to two five-year terms, names the prime minister from the largest party.
The flag is blue, to symbolise peace, crossed by a red line (the blood of the four million people who died in the civil war) and hedged by two yellow lines (the vast mining deposits of the country).

Independence date
30 June 1960

Form of state
Presidential republic

The executive
Under an accord signed in 2002 by the government, rebel groups and the civilian opposition, President Joseph Kabila was expected to remain in office until election in 2004, however elections have been postponed to 2006. The president is assisted by four vice presidents, each representing the government, two armed rebel groups and the civilian opposition.

National legislature
The bicameral parliament consists of the Assemblée Nationale (national assembly; lower chamber) with 500 members, of which 61 are elected in single-seat constituencies and the remainder in multi-seat constituencies from an open list of candidates; the Senat (senate, upper chamber) has 120 members elected by representatives of subordinate assemblies.

Legal system
The civil code is based on the Belgian system, including the structure of the Supreme Court. Legal issues at the local level are usually dealt with according to tribal law.

Last elections
28 November 2011 (presidential and parliamentary); 19 January 2007 (senate)
Results: Presidential: Joseph Kabila won 48.95 per cent of the vote, Etienne Tshisekedi 32.33 per cent, Vital Kamerhe 7.74 per cent, Leon Kengo 4.95 per cent; seven other candidates each won less than 2 per cent. Turnout was 58.81 per cent.
Parliamentary: *interim results scheduled for publication on 13 January 2012*
Senate: the Alliance pour la Majorité Présidentielle (AMP) (Alliance for a presidential majority) won 58 seats (out of 108, of which PPRD won 22), the Union pour la Nation Congolese (UNC) (Congolese National Party) coalition won 21 (of which MLC won 14, including a seat for Jean Pierre Bemba, its leader).

Next elections
2016 (presidential and parliamentary); June 2012 (parliamentary, senate)

Political parties

Ruling party
Caretaker-coalition led by Parti du Peuple pour la Reconstruction et la Démocratie (PPRD) (People's Party of Reconstruction and Democracy) with Parti Lumumbiste Unifié (PLU) (United Lumumbist Party) and Union des Démocrates Mobutistes (UDM) (Union of Mobutist Democrats) (elected 30 Jul 2006) (*Elections on 28 Nov 2011, results due to be published: 13 Jan 2012*)

Main opposition party
Mouvement pour la Liberation du Congo (MLC) (Movement for the Liberation of Congo)

Population

67.80 million (2010)*
Last census: July 1984: 29,916,800
Population density: 20 inhabitants per square km. Urban population: 30 per cent.
Annual growth rate: 2.5 per cent 1994–2004 (WHO 2006)

Internally Displaced Persons (IDP)
3.4 million (UNHCR 2004)

Ethnic make-up
There are over 200 ethnic groups in DRC. The largest is the Kongo, which predominates in Bandundu province. The Mongo are mainly found in the heavily forested north and north-west. The Luba predominate in the two Kasai provinces and the Shabans and Bemba live mainly in Katanga (formerly Shaba) province. Other large ethnic groups include the Zande, the Bwaka, the Lulua and the Songe. There are a large number of people of Nilotic origin, mainly concentrated in the eastern North Kivu province.

Religions
Some 50 per cent of the population adhere to animist beliefs. The remainder are mostly Christian, of which a majority are Roman Catholic. Muslims make up some 10 per cent of the population, residing mainly in North Kivu province.

Education

Estimates by major non-government organisations show that at least four out of every 10 children of primary school age are denied the basic right to education in the DRC. Several obstacles towards accessing basic education include the inability of parents to pay school fees, massive displacement of population and destruction of school buildings during the civil war. Between 1997 and 2003, millions of children had no access to schools, leading to an increase in the dropout rate from 49 per cent to 75 per cent during the period.
The UN Children's Fund (UNICEF) has helped in the rehabilitation of seven schools and four health centres in Kisangani (damaged in 2000), which cater for 20,000 children. Unicef will also provide financial assistance towards training teachers and for various educational materials.
Literacy rate: 72 per cent men and 49 per cent women, adult rates (World Bank).
Compulsory years: Six to 12.
Pupils per teacher: 45 in primary schools.

Health

The Mobutu government had placed a low priority on standards of health and welfare, and continuing civil war inhibited improvement. From this low base, expenditure has slowly risen from the 1.5 per cent in 2000.
Only one-third of the population, mostly those in the larger cities, have access to local healthcare. There are more than 900 hospitals with a total capacity of over 75,000 beds, but many of these are not operating due to a lack of resources and loss of unpaid staff. There are an estimated 1,900 physicians working in the DRC, for a population of 58 million.
Tuberculosis incidence is about 260 per 100,000 population.
Unicef in association with the DRC government started a major measles immunisation campaign in October 2002, targetting some 15 million children initially.
Forty five per cent of the population have access to an improved water sources.
There were cases of polio reported to the World Health Organisation – Global Polio Eradication Initiative in 2006; the country had previously been free of the disease and its re-emergence was due to infected travellers.
The border between Angola and the Democratic Republic of Congo (DRC) was closed on 6 January 2009 due to an outbreak of Ebola in the Luande Norte province of DRC.

HIV/Aids
An HIV infection rate of 12 per cent has been characteristic for women who were caught up in civil war atrocities, or attacked by exiled Hutu Militia, and been raped. Such militia erroneously believe that raping a woman will be protection from HIV infection.
HIV prevalence: 4.2 per cent aged 15–49 in 2003 (World Bank)
Life expectancy: 44 years, 2004 (WHO 2006)
Fertility rate/Maternal mortality rate: 6.7 births per woman, 2004 (WHO

2006); maternal mortality 9.4 per 1,000 (World Bank)
Birth rate/Death rate: 15 deaths to 45 births per 1,000 people (World Bank 2001).
Child (under 5 years) mortality rate (per 1,000): 129 per 1,000 live births; 34 per cent of children aged under five were malnourished (World Bank 2004).
Head of population per physician: 0.11 physicians per 1,000 people, 2004 (WHO 2006)

Welfare
While several UN agencies and non-governmental organisations, through a diverse range of activities, manage the welfare situation in the DRC, there have been setbacks when humanitarian teams were withdrawn for safety reasons. The western provinces of the country have remained stable, but the eastern provinces, featuring unrivalled poverty and insecurity, are gripped by a humanitarian emergency. Over 3.3 million people are estimated to have been killed or died as a result of the war, to overthrow the DRC government, which started in 1998.
The UN estimates that there are 3.4 million internally displaced persons (IDPs), and the UN World Food Programme (WFP) estimates that 16 million people (including refugees from Angola), are in need of emergency food aid, or have been cut off from traditional means of subsistence. In early 2004, two million people benefited from WFP's programmes, at a total cost of US$196 million.
The UN reported that during 2002–03, there were 'unprecedented levels of violence by armed factions in eastern DRC, including cannibalism, systematic killings, rape and lootings,' despite some political stability following the installation of a government of transition in mid-2003. While there are no precise rape figures, records show over 40,000 cases were reported since the civil war of 1998 began, and exiled Hutu militia (from Rwanda) began attacking villagers in eastern DRC.

Main cities
Kinshasa (capital, estimated population 6.8 million in 2004), Lubumbashi (1.1 million), Mbuji-Mayi (938,000), Kolwezi (832,400), Kananga (557,800), Kinsangani (523,000).

Languages spoken
Among the many African languages spoken, Lingala, KiSwahili, Tshiluba and Kikongo are the most prominent in DRC.
Official language/s
French

Media
Press
Dailies: There are several dailies, all published in French, the majority of which are located in Kinshasa, including *La Potentiel* (www.lepotentiel.com), the independent, *La Référence Plus* (http://groupelareference.afrikart.net), *L'Avenir* (www.groupelavenir.net), *L'Observateur* (www.lobservateur.cd), *La Conscience* (www.laconscience.com), *La Phare* (www.lepharerdc.com), *La Prospérité* (www.laprosperiteonline.net), and *La République* (www.la-republique.com).
Weeklies: In French, *Le Soft* (www.lesoftonline.net), covers political matters.
Periodicals: In French, *Observatoire de l'Afrique Centrale* (www.obsac.com), a quarterly magazine with reviews of the news in Central Africa and the bi-monthly *C Retro Actuel* (http://c-retro-actuel.net), covering current affairs, politics, the economy and culture.
Broadcasting
The national, public broadcaster is Radio Télévision Nationale Congolaise (RTNC).
Radio: Radio services are the main medium of mass communication and sources of news and information.
RTNC operates La Voix du Congo (The Voice of Congo), which broadcasts programmes in French, Swahili, Lingala, Tshiluba and Kikongo. Private radio stations include the UN-backed Radio Okapi (www.radiookapi.net), Top Congo FM (www.topcongo.com) and Mangembo FM (www.mangembo-fm.com). There are also several stations broadcasting religious content. International transmissions from Radio France International (RFI) (www.rfi.fr) and the BBC World Service (www.bbc.co.uk/worldservice) (92.7 FM) are available through satellite and internet or relayed via local radio stations. There are many more private radio stations broadcasting in small localities throughout the country.
Television: Television coverage is almost nationwide, with four channels available including the government-owned RTNC. Commercial stations include RTGA (www.groupelavenir.net), Canal Tropical TV and Raga TV. There are many more private TV stations broadcasting in small localities throughout the country.
News agencies
National news agency: ACP (Agence Congolaise de Presse)

Economy
The Democratic Republic of Congo (DRC) has much potential, with huge mineral wealth of cobalt, copper, gold, diamonds and uranium, its rivers with abundant hydroelectric potential, fertile farmland and its virgin forests. It experienced exploitation during colonial times and civil war, and mismanagement during corrupt regimes following independence and is slowly beginning to develop its riches for itself, using foreign investment. There are still worrying risks of widespread violence in north-western and eastern provinces, coming from domestic insurgents, Rwandan Hutu militia, and more brutal attacks from the Ugandan Lord's Resistance Army. Such attacks cause deaths and maiming and displace communities and disrupt farming and commercial life.
The majority of the population is engaged in subsistence farming; a primary industry that remains the principal component of GDP, at 40.2 per cent in 2008; the service sector was 31.8 per cent and industry 28 per cent, of which manufacturing was 5.5 per cent. Although rich in so many ways, DRC is nevertheless one of the poorest countries in the world with per capita income of US$171 in 2009. In 2010, the UN Human Development Index (HDI) ranked the DRC as 168 (out of 169 countries) for improvement in health, education and income and indicated that DRC had had a consistently below average improvement rate compared to other sub-Saharan African countries since 1980. The poverty rate was recorded as 59.22 per cent, and 53.7 per cent of households experienced at least three indicators of poverty. The government signed a new Poverty Reduction and Growth Facility with the International Monetary Fund (IMF) in 2010, which provides loans at favourable rates for programmes to alleviate poverty.
GDP growth was 6.2 per cent in 2008, which fell to 2.8 per cent in 2009 as the global economic slowdown led to mine closures by multinational mining companies as they scaled back their operations. As a result almost overnight around 300,000 miners in Katanga Province lost their jobs. However, by late 2009 export sales of copper ore, in particular, began to pick up and GDP growth was forecast at 5.5 per cent for 2010. Inflation, which had been 18 per cent in 2008 jumped to 46.2 per cent in 2009, before falling back to an estimated 26.2 per cent in 2010 and forecast to fall further to 13.5 per cent in 2011.
External debt was estimated to be US$13.7 billion at the end of 2009. In February 2010, the Paris Club of international creditors agreed to reschedule debts of US$1.7 billion, while cancelling a further US$1.3 billion. In November 2010, international creditors agreed to cancel US$7.35 billion in foreign debt, much of it accrued under ex-president Mobutu, and deemed unsustainable.
Corruption is a major problem, especially in dealings in natural resources. The government has implemented reforms necessary to restore macroeconomic stability, cut corruption and apply measures of

good governance. However, with a country so large (the third largest in Africa, behind Sudan and Algeria) and a world market willing to accept dubious provenance, despite international sanctions, the authorities have a hard task securing the country's assets and borders. Diplomatic tension and militia fighting in the border region with Burundi has isolated the area from total government control and the smuggling of gold, diamonds and other minerals is rife.

The infrastructure is poor and in need of major investment, either foreign or domestic. DRC could become a powerhouse for Africa, supplying raw materials and surplus energy, if given time to develop a stable civil society.

External trade

The DRC is a member of the Common Market for Eastern and Southern Africa (Comesa), although in 2010 it was still not a member of the free trade area, as operated by 13 other member states, nor are there plans to join the customs union. It is also a member of the Economic Community of Central African States (ECCAS) and the Southern African Development Community (SADC).

DRC was a leading producer of industrial diamonds before its civil war and they remain dominant in the economy, accounting for around 50 per cent of exports.

The narrow export base is concentrated mainly on minerals, with some agricultural cash crops. The DRC's balance of trade is therefore susceptible to the vagaries of world commodity markets. Under-investment and regular strikes have further weakened the mining industry.

In April 2009 international donors pledged US$1 billion to upgrade transport links across eastern and southern Africa, in an initiative to carry goods to market cheaper and faster. Not only will roads and rail links be improved, but also time-consuming official procedures will be streamlined for efficiency.

Imports

Principal imports are foodstuffs, mining and other machinery, transport equipment and fuels.

Main sources: South Africa (typically 18 per cent of total), Belgium (10 per cent), China (10 per cent).

Exports

Principal exports are diamonds, copper, palm oil, cobalt, crude oil, rubber, cotton and coffee.

Main destinations: China (typically 49 per cent of total), US (15 per cent), Belgium (10 per cent).

Agriculture

Farming

Agriculture contributes around 50 per cent of GDP, around half of which is derived from subsistence farming, even though it provides the livelihood of 57 per cent of the population. There are almost 23 million hectares (ha) of agricultural land available, of which 7.8 million ha is given over to permanent arable and 15 million ha to pasture.

Despite enormous agricultural potential, the sector has been handicapped by transport problems, occasional drought, smuggling and inflexible pricing policies. Farmers in the eastern provinces have also had to contend with lethal Hutu militia, exiled from Rwanda, who target isolated farms and villages for supplies while often committing atrocities.

The government is developing the forestry sector with multilateral financial assistance.

Main food crops are cassava, maize, rice and plantain. Production is insufficient to meet demand, and poor transport restricts supplies to the urban areas. Main cash and export crops are plantation-grown coffee, cocoa, oil palm, rubber, tea, cotton, sugar and tobacco.

Fishing

Although the DRC has only a narrow coastline, the fisheries sector is evenly based between inland and coastal resources. Around 150,000 artisanal fisherman operate in the DRC, providing 90 per cent of the total national catch. Excluding subsistence production, inland fishing in the many rivers and lakes produces around 150,000 tonnes, comparable with the 160,000 for seafood production. The country is a substantial net importer of seafood and freshwater fish.

Forestry

DRC has 135.2 million hectares (ha) of tropical forest, roughly half the timber resources of the African continent. The first industrial exploitation started in 1930 at Mayumbe. The sector is vastly under-exploited and holds out much potential, particularly in terms of export revenue. From 1970 onwards, the focus of activity shifted from Mayumbe to the Cuvette region. The DRC produces large quantities of sawnwood, as well as plywood and veneer and tropical hardwood logs and sawnwood are the principal exports. However the principal use of timber is as domestic firewood.

An estimated US$12 million per annum is being lost through tax avoidance by international logging companies, according to Greenpeace in 2008. On 19 January 2009 almost 60 per cent of all timber contracts were cancelled, following a six-month review of 156 logging contracts, to clamp down on corruption and enforce environmental standards. The World Bank financed the review, which found that only 65 contracts for viable. New contracts, for logging 90,000 square kilometres of rainforest would be let at a later date.

Industry and manufacturing

The industrial sector contributes around 17 per cent to GDP and employs around 10 per cent of the workforce. Approximately three-quarters of production is centred around Kinshasa or in Katanga province, owing to the availability of electricity and adequate transport facilities in these areas.

In an environment of political instability, endemic corruption and poor regulation, few manufacturing industries have developed. The few that remain have also been hindered by a lack of technical and management expertise, the comparatively poor transport infrastructure and a chronic decline in domestic purchasing power eroded by inflation and lack of foreign exchange to purchase essential manufacturing inputs.

Output is geared towards the domestic market and is mainly concentrated on brewing, food processing, textiles, consumer goods, construction industry inputs and transport equipment.

Mismanagement and shortages of spare parts and materials have led to cut-backs in production with most firms operating at below half capacity. The government is attempting to increase production by encouraging foreign investment and offering substantial tax incentives.

Tourism

Tourism was never an important economic activity, but with its immense rainforests and rich bio-diversity, a peaceful DRC would provide a rich abundance of eco-tourist destinations for the adventurous traveller. The infrastructure deteriorated as a result of warfare and this will have to be improved if there is to be any major growth in the sector.

With the necessary investment and a return to civilian government the projected annualised growth in travel and tourism is 5.5 per cent (2006–15).

Environment

In 2008 the governments of DRC, Rwanda and Uganda agreed to joint measures to protect the mountain gorillas found within their shared border regions. Tourists visiting the area to view the endangered great apes raise a combined US$5 million for the countries concerned. However, poaching and civil strife have dropped the numbers of gorillas to critically endangered levels, so that a 10-year conservation project which focuses of security and encouraging local people to preserve the animals and habitat is seen as the only hope for the gorilla's survival.

Mining

The country is rich in mineral resources and is potentially one of Africa's richest countries. DRC's copper reserves are estimated at 75 million tonnes with iron at one billion tonnes, 240 million carats of diamonds and over 600 tonnes of gold.
In the past, mining contributed around a third of GDP and employed 5 per cent of the workforce. With around half of DRC's foreign exchange earnings gained from diamond exports, the industry watchdog called for stricter application of existing laws to reduce smuggling and exploitative practices that lead to less revenue for DRC than was possible.
Moves towards peace should lead to a resumption of investment in the mining sector, backed by planned new mining and investment codes. Mining is likely to be the driving force of the economy over the medium-term.
Diamonds are mined on a commercial scale by the Société Minière de Bakwanga (Miba) at Bakwanga in Kasai Oriental, but artisanal diggers account for almost three-quarters of total output.
There is tin mining and small-scale mining of cadmium, cassiterite and wolframite. Activity is concentrated in the copper-rich Katanga (formerly Shaba) province.
Twangiza gold deposits are estimated at 4.1 million tonnes of ore. With the exception of diamonds, these minerals have been hit by weak world demand.
Katanga Province is part of the Central African Copperbelt, which extends from Angola through the DRC into Zambia.
The state-run Gécamines has holdings containing the biggest concentrations of copper and cobalt in the world.
Gécamines' troubles are rooted in long-term problems of corruption and mismanagement. Its misfortune is exacerbated by the civil war, which has led to foreign partners scaling down or pulling out of joint ventures.
Australia's Anvil Mining has production of the Dikulushi copper and silver mine.
In 2006, the Canadian lawyer, Paul Fortin was appointed to run the state-owned mining company Gecamines, which had been plundered and left bankrupt by former president Mobutu Sese Seko, to restore the company to a viable entity and write draft national mining legislation. In October 2009 Mr Fortin resigned, in disappointment at what he saw AS widespread fraud preventing millionS of dollars of mining revenue from reaching state coffers, as reported in parliament.
An ambitious programme of development of DRC's minerals became defunct as the treasury lost US$450 million in 2008 alone through tax fraud, smuggling and illegal mining. Gold smuggling, in particular, had cost the state an estimated US$1 billion per year.
In March 2011, the ban on mining gold, tin and coltan was lifted in three provinces of eastern DRC. Following successful military action in the area to rout militia operations, the mining ministry dispatched officials to oversee legitimate shipments of ore from the region.

Hydrocarbons

Proven oil reserves totalled 180 million barrels in 2008, most of which are located off the Atlantic coastline and in the Congo River estuary. Oil production was 19,960 barrels per day (bpd) with consumption at around 11,000bpd. There is no domestic refinery and all crude oil must be exported, via the Moanda Oil Terminal.
Total natural gas reserves stood at one billion cubic metres in 2008, most of which is located beneath Lake Kivu, however the cost of exploiting this reserve has made production non-viable.
Coal reserves stood at 88 million tonnes, typical production is 10 million tonnes per annum. Mines are located at Luena and Kalemie.

Energy

Total installed generating capacity was 2,443MW in 2007; however the DRC has the potential to produce 419,210MW of economically feasible electricity, a figure which is greater than Africa's current total generating capacity, if it were able to harness the power of its rivers. The Inga Dam near the port of Matadi at the mouth of the Congo River produces 1,700MW supplying not only the capital but also the copper mines in Katanga. There are modest plans to invest in further plant which would boost capacity to 3,500MW. Inga provides DRC with its biggest foreign exchanger earner. Only 6 per cent of the population have access to the power grid; energy in rural areas is mainly derived from charcoal and wood.
DRC is a member of the Southern African Power Pool (Sapp); set up to provide reliable and economical energy supplies to all members in twelve countries. However, DRC is unable to receive electricity from Namibia due to a lack of high voltage lines in Angola.
In 2008 a forum, hosted by the World Energy Council, to discuss a new hydroelectric scheme at the Inga site, took place in London, between African leaders and international financiers. The plan under consideration was the building of the world's largest hydroelectric power station. The Grand Inga Project (GIP), estimated to cost some US$80 billion, producing output of 32,000MW, would have a 205-metre dam with a 15km reservoir and be operational by 2020–25. A new power grid would also be built extending north to Egypt and south to South Africa.
The parastatal utility company Société Nationale d'Electricité (SNEL) is responsible for production, transmission, distribution and sales of electricity, through subsidiary agencies.

Banking and insurance

The banking system is virtually non-existent as persistent hyperinflation has led to the collapse of all the country's banks.

Central bank
Banque du Congo

Main financial centre
Kinshasa

Time

Kinshasa and the western provinces – GMT plus one hour
Elsewhere – GMT plus two hours

Geography

The country is bordered by the Republic of Congo in the west, by the Central African Republic in the north, by Sudan in the north-east, by Uganda, Rwanda and Burundi in the northeast to east, by Tanzania in the east to south-east, Zambia in the south and Angola in the south to south-west. Lake Tanganiyka forms most of the border with Tanzania.
DRC is the second largest country in Africa (after Sudan), it is over two million square kilometres in area, encompassing a huge central basin of tropical rain forest, with mountains that rise in the east and the continent's second longest river (after the Nile) running through its northern and western regions. It has a tiny 37km coastline where the River Congo drains into the eastern South Atlantic seaboard. In its eastern range of mountains live the endangered mountain gorilla whose habitat is under threat from illegal logging and deforestation. Pic Marguerite on Mont Ngaliema (Mount Stanley) at 5,110 metres is the tallest peak. Close to the city of Goma are Africa's two most active volcanoes, Nyamuragira and Nyiragongo – which has the world's fastest flowing lava. The southern part of the country is savannah grassland.
Most of the population is concentrated in areas with the best communications, near Kinshasa in the far west, along the Congo River and other main rivers, and in the southern and eastern border regions.

Hemisphere
Straddles the equator, although most of the country is situated in the southern hemisphere.

Climate

The climate varies widely owing to the size of the country. The lowlands in the western region are hot and humid, including Kinshasa, where rain is concentrated in the period from November to March and temperatures reach 32 degrees Celsius (C) in the hottest month, January, with 26 degrees C in the coolest month, June. On the central plateau, the likely temperature range is 18–20 degrees C. In the south and the eastern province of Kivu the climate is a Mediterranean type and is slightly cooler, particularly in the winter months.

Dress codes
Business clothes may be casual and lightweight clothing is essential, especially if visiting during the rainy season.

Entry requirements
Visitors are advised to contact embassy representatives in advance to ascertain current entry requirements. Visitors are also advised to register their presence in DRC with their local embassy representative.

Passports
Required by all. All passports must be valid for six months from the date of departure. Proof of return/onward passage is also necessary.

Visa
Required by all.
Applications for a business visa requires a letter from a tour company stating the trip has been paid in full, or from an employer accepting responsibility for any expenses incurred; proof of status and a letter of finance giving proof of sufficient funds and a full itinerary. An official letter of invitation endorsed by the DRC authorities must also accompany the application. Travel regulations should be studied carefully before a visit as restrictions apply.

Prohibited entry
Those with visas/entry/exit stamps for Rwanda, Burundi or Uganda are likely to be refused entry.

Currency advice/regulations
The import or export of local currency is prohibited. Foreign currency import is limited to US$10,000 and must be declared. Currency declaration forms must be kept and all currency exchanges should be recorded.

Customs
Visitors are advised not to take in any equipment which may arouse suspicion, such as cameras, binoculars, maps or any kind of tools or military equipment.

Health (for visitors)
Mandatory precautions
Yellow fever vaccination certificate is required if arriving from an infected area.

Advisable precautions
Visitors should take precautions against all tropical diseases. Vaccinations for diphtheria, tetanus, hepatitis A, polio and typhoid are recommended. Other vaccinations that may be recommended are cholera, tuberculosis, hepatitis B and meningitis. There is a risk of rabies. Anti-malaria tablets are essential, and HIV/Aids is widespread among both men and women. Dysentery, typhoid and typhus are prevalent, especially outside Kinshasa. Bubonic plague exists in the Bunia region.
Tap water must be treated as unsafe unless boiled and filtered (bottled water is available in the main cities). Outside Kinshasa and Lubumbashi, eat only hot, cooked food and avoid raw salad, fruit, vegetables and ice cubes. Dairy products are unpasteurised and should be avoided. A first aid kit that includes disposable syringes, is a reasonable precaution. Medical insurance is essential, including emergency evacuation, and an adequate supply of personal medicines is necessary.

Hotels
Several major hotels in Kinshasa and other cities. Most tend to be expensive and are often heavily booked. A service charge is usually added to bill and further tipping is optional.

Public holidays (national)
Fixed dates
1 Jan (New Year's Day), 4 Jan (Commemoration of the Martyrs of Independence), 17 Jan (National Heroes' Day), 1 May (Labour Day), 17 May (National Liberation Day), 30 Jun (Independence Day), 1 Aug (Parents' Day), 17 Nov (Army Day), 25 Dec (Christmas Day).

Working hours
Banking
Mon–Fri: 0800–1130.

Business
Mon–Fri: 0730–1200, 1430–1700; Sat: 0730–1200.

Government
Mon–Fri: 0730–1500; Sat: 0730–1200.
It is normal practice for ministers and senior officials to work Mon–Fri: 0830–1300 and from 1600–2000.

Shops
Mon–Fri: 0800–1200, 1500–1700; Sat: 0800–1200.

Telecommunications
Mobile/cell phones
There are 900 and 1800 GSM services operating in highly populated areas.

Electricity supply
220V AC

Social customs/useful tips
With its vast range of ethnic groups and huge land area, there are many different traditions, according to the locality.
As in most French-speaking African countries, business etiquette when visiting government and (to a lesser degree) private commercial offices is more formal than in English-speaking Africa.
Do not openly criticise the government or attempt to photograph public buildings. Military installations are also best avoided if possible.

Security
The insecurity and lawlessness in eastern and northern DRC makes travelling to these areas dangerous. Visitors should consider whether their journey is vital before travelling in the rest of DRC.
Street crime is rife, especially in Kinshasa. Visitors are advised not to wear expensive jewellery or watches or to carry cameras conspicuously. To achieve anything expect to pay *katamulomo* tips, especially to soldiers (both genuine and fake), who are seldom paid and who man the roadblocks. Visitors should beware of unofficial 'porters' at N'djili airport. Those visiting for the first time should try to arrange for a local business associate or friend to meet them at the airport. Visitors are advised to stay in their hotels after dark. They should avoid public transport altogether and use hire cars rather than taxis whenever possible.
The DRC is undergoing profound political change which means that any official efforts which may be made to protect foreign visitors are unlikely to be effective outside Kinshasa. The best advice is to contact embassy representatives in advance in order to check the safety of the region to which you wish to travel.

Getting there
Air
National airline: Hewa Bora Airways
International airport/s: Kinshasa-N'djili International airport (FIH) is 25km from central Kinshasa. As N'djili is located a long way from the city, it is advisable to pre-arrange transport either with a hotel or local car hire firm such as Hertz (office within the shopping gallery at the Inter-Continental Hotel) or to arrange for a business or social contact to meet first-time visitors to the country at the airport.
Other airport/s: There are almost 60 airports and airfields around DRC.
Airport tax: Departure tax: Cf500

Surface
Road: There are 2,400km of poorly maintained asphalted roads leading to neighbouring countries. However, most borders are closed and the roads leading to them are considered very dangerous.
Rail: The three main lines into DRC are the Voie Nationale running from Matadi port to Kinshasa (366km); the eastern route entering from Tanzania at Kalemie and the northern route entering from the Sudan at Mungbere. There are also links to southern African states via Zambia.
An end to Angola's civil war would allow reconstruction of the Benguela line from

Shaba to Lobito port in Angola, but this could take several years.
Water: From Kinshasa there is a regular ferry service to Brazzaville, although it is subject to distruption.
Main port/s: The main port is Matadi, about 150km inland on the Congo River. Kinshasa is the main inland river port and the ferry crossing point from Brazzaville.

Getting about

National transport

Air: There are connections from Kinshasa-N'djili to over 40 local destinations. Charter facilities are available.
Road: There are indefinite restrictions on travel throughout the country. A permit from the interior ministry is required for travel outside Kinshasa.
The 240,000km road network is in poor condition outside main population centres and some parts have become impassable through lack of maintenance. Bridges should be checked before crossing and banditry is common.
Buses: Very irregular, crowded and infrequent service.
Rail: A network of over 5,000km is operated by Société Nationale des Chemins de Fer Zaïroise (SNCZ), but some parts are inoperable while others subject to disruption. Of the four classes – 'deluxe' and first-class are advisable.
A project to refurbish DRC's railway network by 2015 was announced on 12 May 2011. The 3,000km, US$600 million programme of works including railway tracks to be replaced and new rolling stock purchased, will be backed by the World Bank and Chinese investors.
Water: Inland navigation is important, particularly for freight on the Congo River between Kinshasa and Kisangani and the Kasai River from Ilebo to the Congo River north of Kinshasa. However, all routes around Kisangani have been disrupted by the civil war. When available, passenger services run on all major rivers and lakes. It is advisable to travel luxury or first class.

City transport

Shared taxis provide the best form of transport and are widely available. There is little or no public transport outside Kinshasa.
Taxis: Volatile inflation rates and political instability mean it is virtually impossible to keep track of taxi fares in local currency. If resorting to a local taxi, it is absolutely essential to negotiate a fixed fare before starting the journey.

Car hire

Self-drive cars are available in Kinshasa and at the airport. A deposit is required unless an acceptable credit card can be produced. International driving licence required. Traffic drives on the right.

BUSINESS DIRECTORY

The addresses listed below are a selection only. While World of Information makes every endeavour to check these addresses, we cannot guarantee that changes have not been made, especially to telephone numbers and area codes. We would welcome any corrections.

Telephone area codes

The international direct dialling (IDD) code for DRC is +243, followed by the area code and subscriber's number. In late 2006 the landline telephone system was not functioning. To call a mobile number (beginning with 8 or 9) dial +243 and then the number.

Kinshasa	12	Lubumbashi	2
Cellular network	8		

Chambers of Commerce

Fédération des Entreprises du Congo, 10 Avenue des Aviateurs, PO Box 7247, Kinshasa (tel: 880-7297; fax: 780-0660; e-mail: feccongo@hotmail.com).

Franco-Congolaise Chambre de Commerce et d'Industrie, 407 Avenue Roi Baudouin, PO Box 8.211, Kinshasa 1 (tel: 780-5871; fax: 880-7158).

Banking

Banque Commerciale du Congo SARL, BP 2798, Boulevard du 30 Juin, Kinshasa-Gombe (tel: 217-73, 217-76; fax: 221-770).

Banque Continentale Africaine (Zaire) SARL, 4 Avenue de la Justice, Kinshasa-Gombe (tel: 28-006, 28-537; fax: 25-243).

Banque Internationale de Credit SARL, 191 Ave de l'Equateur, Kinshasa-Gombe (tel: 882-0404, 884-1940/5631, 884-3159/3790, 880-1487; fax: 880-1125, 377-97900/34).

Citibank NA Congo, BP 9999, Citibank Building, Coin des Avenues Colonel Lukusa et Ngongo Lutete, Kinshasa-Gombe 1 (tel: 20555/57; fax: 40015).

Fransabank (Congo) SARL, BP 9497, Avenue du Port, 14/16 Immeuble Zaïre-Shell, Kin. 1, Kinshasa-Gombe (tel: 20121/2/3/4; fax: 12-27864).

Nouvelle Banque de Kinshasa, 1 Place du Marché, Kinshasa-Gombe 1 (tel: 12-20562-5, 12-0459-60, 12-3461-63; fax: 12-581-4961 80043).

Stanbic Bank Congo SARL, 12 Avenue de la Mongala, Kinshasa-Gombe (tel: 88-48445, 88-41984, 88-43453, 88-43419, 88- 04512; fax: 88-46216).

Union de Banques SARL, BP 197, Coin des Avenues de la Nation et des Aviateurs, Kinshasa-Gombe (tel: 88-4133, 88-43620, 88-44887; fax: 88-46628).

Central bank

Banque Centrale du Congo, 563 Boulevard Colonel Tshashi, PO Box 2697, Kinshasa-Gombe (tel: 20-704; fax: 880-5152; e-mail: cabgouv@bcc.cd).

Travel information

Air Zaïre, BP 10120, Airport de N'Djili, Kinshasa (tel: 20-939; fax: 20-940).

N'Djili International Airport, BP 10124, Kinshasa 24 (tel: 23-570).

SNCZ Railways, BP 597, Kinshasa.

Ministry of tourism

Ministry of Tourism, BP12.348, 15 Avenue Papa Ileo (ex des Cliniques), Kinshasa 1 (tel: 34-390, 88-02-394; fax: 88-44-987).

National tourist organisation offices

Office National du Tourisme de la République Démocratique du Congo, BP 9502, Kinshasa-Gombe 1 (tel: 89-32-2238, 815-091-627, 99-31-939; fax: 33-781; e-mail: ont-rdc@raga.net).

Ministries

Civil Service Ministry, Avenue des Ambassadeurs, BP 3, Kinshasa-Gombe.

Ministry of Agriculture, Boulevard du 30 Juin, Building Sozacom, 3e Etage, BP 8722 KIN I, Kinshasa-Gombe.

Ministry of Economy, Industry and Commerce, Boulevard du 30 Juin, Building Onatra, BP 8500 KIN I, Kinshasa-Gombe.

Ministry of Energy, 239 Avenue de la Justice, Building SNEL, BP 5137 KIN I, Kinshasa-Gombe.

Ministry of Environment and Tourism, 15 Avenue des Cliniques, BP 12348 KIN I, Kinshasa-Gombe.

Ministry of Finance, Boulevard du 30 Juin, BP 12998 KIN I, Kinshasa-Gombe.

Ministry of Foreign Affairs and International Co-operation, Place de l'Indépendance, BP 7100, Kinshasa-Gombe 14 (tel: 32-450, 30-248, 32-239, 30-996, 32-735, 33-325; fax: 88-02-368; internet site: www.minaffeci-rdcongo.net/).

Ministry of Health, Boulevard du 30 Juin, BP 3088 KIN I, Kinshasa-Gombe.

Ministry of Home Affairs, Kinshasa-Gombe.

Ministry of Information and Cultural Affairs, Avenue du 24 Novembre, BP 3171 KIN I, Kinshasa-Kabinda.

Ministry of International Co-Operation, Avenue de la Justice, Enceinte SNEL, Kinshasa-Gombe.

Ministry of Justice, 228 Avenue des 3 Z, Kinshasa-Gombe.

Ministry of Mines, 239 Avenue de la Justice, Building SNEL, BP 5137 KIN I, Kinshasa-Gombe.

Ministry of National Education, Enceinte de l'Institut de la Gombe, BP 3163, Kinshasa-Gombe.

Ministry of Planning and Development, 4155 Avenue des Coteaux, BP 9378 KIN I, Kinshasa-Gombe.

Ministry of Post and Telecommunications, 4484 Avenue des Huiles, Building Kilou, BP 800 KIN I, Kinshasa-Gombe.

Ministry of Public Works, Building Travaux Publics, Kinshasa-Gombe.

Ministry of Reconstruction, Boulevard Colonel Tshatshi, Building Travaux Publics, BP 26, Kinshasa-Gombe.

Ministry of Transport, Boulevard du 30 Juin, Building Onatra, BP 3304, Kinshasa-Gombe.

Ministry of Youth and Sports, 77 Avenue de la Justice, BP 8541 KIN I, Kinshasa-Gombe.

Other useful addresses

Democratic Republic of Congo Embassy (USA), 1800 New Hampshire Avenue, NW, Washington DC 20009 (tel: (+1-202) 234-7690; fax: (+1-202) 237-0748).

Democratic Republic of Congo Permanent mission the UN, 866 United Nations Plaza, Suite 511, New York (tel: (+1-212) 319-8061; fax: (+1-212) 319-8232; email: drcongo@un.int).

National news agency: ACP (Agence Congolaise de Presse), 44-48 Avenue Tombalbaye, BP 1595, Kinshasa (internet: www.un.int/drcongo).

Internet sites

Africa Business Network: www.ifc.org/abn

AllAfrica.com: http://allafrica.com

African Development Bank: www.afdb.org

Africa Online: www.africaonline.com

Congoplantet (gateway site): www.congoplantet.com

Democratic Republic of Congo (French only): www.congonline.com

Mbendi AfroPaedia (information on companies, countries, industries and stock exchanges in Africa): http://mbendi.co.za

Cook Islands

KEY FACTS

Official name: Cook Islands

Head of State: Head of State Queen Elizabeth II; represented Sir Frederick Goodwin (from 2001); High Commissioner Linda Te Puni (from 10 Mar 2010)

Head of government: Prime Minister Henry Puna (CIP) (from 18 Nov 2010)

Ruling party: Cook Islands Party (CIP) (from 18 Nov 2010)

Area: 234 square km (15 islands); Rarotonga (67 square km)

Population: 23,020 (2010)*

Capital: Avarua, on the island of Rarotonga

Official language: English and Cook Islands Mäori

Currency: New Zealand dollar (NZ$) = 100 cents; Cook Islands' own currency is defunct

Exchange rate: NZ$1.40 per US$ (Aug 2010)

GDP per capita: US$15,646 (2009)

GDP real growth: -0.10% (2009)

GDP: US$206.50 million (2009)

Inflation: 6.60% (2009)

Balance of trade: US$10.00 million (2008)*

Visitor numbers: 99,500 (2009–10)

* estimated figure

Tourism, together with the fishery sector, continue to be the main pillars of the Cook Island's economy. The first quarter of 2011 recorded an increase in the number of visitors from New Zealand, but a drop in arrivals from the US, Europe and Australia. The start on 5 July of direct flights from Sydney to Rarotonga International Airport is hoped to improve figures from the third quarter; as is a campaign to promote tourism. The Asian Development Bank forecasts growth of GDP for the financial year 2011/12 of 6.5 per cent. Inflation in 2010/11 was estimated at 3.5 per cent and is forecast to fall to 3.0 per cent in 2011/12.

COUNTRY PROFILE

Historical profile

1200 The islands were believed to have been settled by neighbouring Tahitians.
1596 The Spaniard, Alvaro de Mendana, was thought to be the first European to sight the islands.
1733 The islands were named in honour of Captain James Cook.
1789 Rarotonga, the main island, was sighted by the Bounty mutineers.
1888 The islands became a British protectorate.
1901 New Zealand became colonial administrators of the Cook Islands.
1965 The islands became self-governing, as a New Zealand dependency. Albert Henry of the Cook Islands Party (CIP) became prime minister.
1978 The Democratic Party (DP) won the election and Tom Davis became prime minister.
1994 The CIP won the general elections with 20 seats in the 25-seat parliament – the greatest margin of victory in 30 years. Geoffrey Henry became prime minister.
1997 The DP experienced internal conflict and a majority of party members broke away to become the Democratic Alliance Party (DAP). A faction of the DP became the New Alliance (NA) Party, led by Norman George.
1999 The CIP lost the general election and Terepai Maoate of the DAP formed a government with the NA.
2001 The Cook Islands was placed on the international money laundering blacklist of the Organisation for Economic Co-operation and Development (OECD).
2002 Maoate was ousted as prime minister in a vote of no-confidence. Robert Woonton (DAP) formed an all-party coalition.
2003 The DAP and the NA merged and reverted to their original name, Democratic Party (DP). Cook Islands Mäori became an official language.
2004 Jim Marurai, leader of DP was elected prime minister.
2005 After a dispute with his party, Marurai, remained prime minister with the support of the CIP. The Cook Islands was removed from the OECD international money laundering blacklist. Marurai's alliance with the CIP broke down and he returned to the DP for support, but not the party leadership.
2006 A by-election tipped the balance of power in parliament. The DP won snap elections, called by Prime Minister Marurai. A census was held in which 19,569 people were recorded, including tourists.
2008 Brian Donnelly became high commissioner but was forced to resign because of ill-health; he later died in New Zealand. Sophia Vickers became acting high commissioner until Tia Barrett was appointed acting high commissioner.
2009 The OECD published a list of countries that had not implemented international tax information exchange standards, of which Cook Islands was one, despite signing a co-operation agreement in 2002. High Commissioner Tia Barrett died suddenly in November.
2010 Linda Te Puni took up the post of acting high commissioner in March; she was later confirmed in the post in June. Sir Frederick Goodwin was re-appointed as the Queen's Representative, for the third time, on 10 August. Prime Minister Jim Marurai announced in October that candidates of the Democratic Party must sign a contract guaranteeing they will not change allegiance once elected, a move that had lead to political instability through shifting coalitions in the past. In a referendum, also held on 17 November, to reduce the number of parliamentary members, 76 per cent of the votes approved the motion; however as less than two-thirds of the voting population participated the proposed change was unsuccessful. In parliamentary elections held on 18 November, the opposition CIP won 16

seats (out of 24). Henry Puna became the new prime minister. Having lost the elections the guarantee demanded by Jim Marurai of his party colleagues became void.
2011 On 5 July the first direct flight from Sydney (Australia) landed at Rarotonga International Airport. On 6 July the government announced a proposal to tax savings and interest earned in all bank accounts by 15 per cent, which it said would be a temporary measure to overcome the government deficit. Opposition to the tax came from banks and their customers and the business community, which accused the government of failing to consult.

Political structure

Constitution

Under the 1965 constitution, New Zealand has responsibility for defence and foreign affairs and the Cook Islands is self-governing with full responsibility for internal affairs. Local affairs are handled by island councils and village committees in the outer islands.

Form of state

Self-governing state in free association with New Zealand.

The executive

Executive power is excised by the prime minister and cabinet, through the High Commissioner (Queen's Representative).

National legislature

The unicameral parliament comprises 25 members (10 representing the main island of Rarotonga, 14 representing constituencies on other islands, and one representing expatriate Cook Islanders), elected by universal suffrage for a five-year term. Parliament chooses a prime minister from among its members, who then appoints a cabinet.
The House of Ariki is a 15-member chamber of hereditary chiefs, which advises on matters of land and issues of tradition.

Last elections

17 November 2010 (parliamentary and referendum); 16 July 2008 (presidential).
Results: Parliamentary: Cook Islands Party (CIP) won 16 seats (out of 24), Democratic Party (DP) eight.
Referendum: 76 per cent of the votes approved the motion to reduce the number of members of parliament (MPs); however as a two-thirds majority of the voting population did not participate the referendum was unsuccessful.
Presidential: President Liverpool was re-elected unopposed.

Next elections

September 2015 (parliamentary)

Political parties

Ruling party

Cook Islands Party (CIP) (from 18 Nov 2010)

Main opposition party

Cook Islands Party

Population

23,020 (2010)*
Last census: 1 December 2006: 19,569
Population density: 97 inhabitants per square km (2010)
Annual growth rate: 8.6 per cent 2001–06 (2006 census)

Ethnic make-up

Polynesian (81 per cent), Polynesian and European mixed (8 per cent), Polynesian and non-European mixed (8 per cent), European 2 per cent.

Religions

The majority are Cook Islands Christian Church (70 per cent), although Roman Catholics, Latter Day Saints, Seventh-Day Adventists and Assembly of God are also represented.

Health

HIV/Aids

The first case of HIV infection by a resident of the Cook Islands was reported in December 2010.
Life expectancy: 72 years, 2004 (WHO 2006)
Fertility rate/Maternal mortality rate: 2.6 births per woman, 2004 (WHO 2006)
Child (under 5 years) mortality rate (per 1,000): 21 per 1,000 live births
Head of population per physician: 0.78 physicians per 1,000 people, 2001 (WHO 2006)

Main cities

Avarua, on the island of Rarotonga (capital, estimated population 10,500 in 2003).

Languages spoken

Rarotongan is spoken on Rarotonga; Pukapuka and Nassau both have their own quite different languages, while other islands have differing versions of Cook Islands Mäori. Most of the islanders also speak English.

Official language/s

English and Cook Islands Mäori

Media

Elijah Communications (EC) owns and operates radio and television stations and publishes a newspaper.

Press

Dailies: EC publishes the *Herald* (www.ciherald.co.ck), while the *News* (www.cookislandsnews.com) is another independent newspaper and both are weeklies.

Broadcasting

Radio: There are two radio stations with services that are broadcast in English and Mäori. The EC-owned Radio Cook Islands has a network that includes AM, FM and Internet streaming for coverage throughout the islands. It also operates HITZ 101.1 aimed at a young audience. Radio Ikurangi is also a private station.
Television: The EC-owned Cook Islands Television broadcasts for up to 18 hours per day. Services are provided via satellite and include not only domestic programmes but also some broadcast from New Zealand.

News agencies

ABC Pacific Beat:
www.radioaustralia.net.au/pacbeat
Pacific Magazine:
www.pacificmagazine.net
Pacific Islands New Association (Pina):
www.pina.com.fj

Economy

Tourism and some offshore financial services are the principal components of the economy. Subsistence agriculture and fishing, particularly of pearls, continue as important activities for the population. Remittances from migrant workers, aid from New Zealand and Australia, sales of postage stamps and export of agricultural produce also play a role. The pearl industry, based on the islands of Manihiki and Penrhyn, has become a significant export product and the government invests in the industry's future through quality control and marketing. There has been a shift to paid labour and small businesses on the southern atolls, although many still work their own plantations. A significant offshore banking business has developed; regulations have been revised and a Financial Supervisory Commission established, allowing for further improvements to be implemented. The sale of fishing licences to foreign fleets is a key revenue earner.
Major projects include expansion of the electricity system, installation of photovoltaic units in the Northern Group Islands, and improvements to telecommunications and the harbour and shipping services.
The government has problems in maintaining basic health and education services on the outer islands, due to continued migration of skilled workers to New Zealand.
The long term prospects for the Cook Islands economy is not particularly bright. The local population is not only aging but also in decline as migration takes the younger, productive workforce overseas. Although the subsequent remittances sustain elderly family members, who are no longer productive, the goods and services provided are increasingly based on their needs and are not necessarily used in capital investment.
Tourism remains steady; the industry catered for 99,500 visitors in 2009–10 and is expected to provide for over 101,000 in 2010–11.

External trade

The Cook Islands is a member of the South Pacific Regional Trade and Economic Co-operation Agreement (Sparteca) along with 12 other regional nations. This allows products duty free access by Pacific Island Forum (PIF) members (which includes the Cook Islands) to Australian and New Zealand markets (subject to the country of origin restrictions).

The Cook Islands suffer from an adverse balance of trade, particularly with New Zealand, with which it maintains a free trade agreement and free movement of workers.

Imports

Principal imports are manufactured goods, foodstuffs, textiles, fuels, timber, capital goods and live animals.

Main sources: New Zealand (typically 63 per cent of total), Fiji (18 per cent), Australia (7 per cent).

Exports

Principal exports are predominantly black pearls, copra, papayas, fresh and canned citrus fruit, fish, and pearl shells and clothing manufacture.

Main destinations: Japan (typically 49 per cent of total), New Zealand (7 per cent), Australia (3 per cent).

Agriculture

Farming

The rich volcanic soil on the southern islands helps subsistence farming cater for local consumption.

Fishing

Long-line fishing of tuna and billfish catches are most often exported to either American Samoa or Japan. The problems of the Cook Islands' huge fishery exclusive economic zone includes the continued attraction of illegal operators, too little data on migratory fish stock and the high cost of its operation. In order to develop the domestic fishing industry, the government introduced exemption on levies for fuel, bait and equipment, but labour shortages are a constant constraint. Since 2000 the number of licences issued for fishing has dropped from 60 to less than 20 boats and New Zealand has been approached for assistance.

Pearl farming used to be the second-largest income earner, after tourism. Commercial fishing generates three times as much export income as pearl production. The bases for pearl fishing are the northern group atolls Manihiki, Penrhyn and Rakahanga.

Industry and manufacturing

The Cook Islands economy earns around US$4.5 million per annum from its pearl industry. The other main secondary industries include agricultural exports, clothing manufacture, fruit canning/processing, electronic component assembly and handicrafts.

Tourism

Cook Islands' palm fringed, largely white beaches and azure seas fulfil most visitor's idea of a tropical paradise and the sector offers visitors as much of the local Polynesian culture as any could wish. The sector constituted around 60 per cent of GDP in 2010, which is higher than the regional average. There are direct, daily international flights from New Zealand and Australia, to the recently upgraded and expanded Rarotonga International Airport, opened in June 2010.

The government policy is to redirect the sector from a reliance on 'sea and surf' holidays to value-added geo-tourism, 'that sustains or enhances the geographical character of a place – its environment, culture, aesthetics, heritage, and well-being of its residents'.

The largest number of visitors are from New Zealand, with around 45 per cent share followed by Europe with 25 per cent and Australia with 14 per cent.

Mining

The Japanese government's Metal Mining Agency has discovered significant reserves of manganese in nodules on the seabed in Cook Islands territorial waters. New techniques are being developed to exploit this resource.

Hydrocarbons

There are no known hydrocarbon reserves. Consumption of oil was 1,000 barrels per day (bpd) in 2008, all of which was imported.

Energy

Total installed generating capacity was 8MW in 2007, producing 3 million kilowatt hours. The Rarotonga Electricity Authority is responsible for electricity supply to Rarotonga only.

Banking and insurance

Legislation to enable Cook Islands' development as an offshore financial centre and tax haven was enacted in 1981/82. There have been limited attempts to consolidate the banking sector, with 16 licensed banks in operation.

Main financial centre

Avarua (on Rarotonga).

Offshore facilities

The offshore financial industry provides 8 per cent of GDP.

Time

GMT minus ten hours.

Geography

The Cook Islands comprise 13 inhabited and two uninhabited islands located in the southern Pacific Ocean, between American Samoa to the west and French Polynesia to the east. The islands are spread over about two million square km (more than 750,000 square miles) of ocean, and form two groups – the Northern Group of the six atolls of Nassau, Pukapuka, Rakahanga, Penrhyn, Suwarrow and Manihiki, and the more populous Southern Group which includes Rarotonga, Aitutaki, Mangaia, Palmerston, and Takutea, all volcanic islands.

Rising sea levels as a result of global climate change are a potential threat to the low-lying islands.

Hemisphere

Southern

Climate

Damp and tropical, mild from Apr–Nov but Dec–Mar hot and humid, with likelihood of hurricanes. The mean temperature is 24 degrees Celsius, with average yearly rainfall over 2,000mm; heaviest on the forested volcanic slopes of the southern islands.

Entry requirements

Passports

Required by all, valid for six months beyond initial visa-free 31 days.

Proof of onward passage, adequate funds and suitable booked accommodation are also required.

Visa

For tourist purposes, visas are not required for stays of up to 31 days. Monthly extensions can be arranged up to a maximum of five months.

Currency advice/regulations

No restrictions on import of local and foreign currency. Export of local currency is limited to NZ$250 and of foreign currency to amount declared on arrival. .

Customs

Incoming passengers are permitted to bring in a maximum of 200 cigarettes, 1kg of tobacco or 50 cigars and two litres of wine or spirits or 4.5 litres of beer.

Health (for visitors)

Mandatory precautions

None.

Advisable precautions

Vaccinations for diphtheria, tuberculosis, hepatitis A and B, polio, tetanus and typhoid are recommended.

The World Health Organisation has warned of a high risk of catching dengue fever.

Hotels

A 10 per cent Government Turnover Tax applies. Tipping is not customary.

Credit cards

Visa and Mastercard are accepted.

Public holidays (national)
Fixed dates
1 Jan (New Year's Day), 25 Apr (Anzac Day), 25 Jul (Gospel Day, Rarotonga), 4 Aug (Constitution Day), 27 Oct (Gospel Day), 25 Dec (Christmas Day), 26 Dec (Boxing Day).
Variable dates
Good Friday, Easter Monday, Queen's Official Birthday (first Mon in Jun).

Working hours
Banking
Mon–Thur: 0900–1500; Fri: 0900–1100.
Business
Mon–Fri: 0800–1600.
Government
Mon–Fri: 0800–1600.
Shops
Mon–Fri: 0900–1600; Sat: 0900–1200.

Telecommunications
Telephone/fax
There are automatic telephone exchanges in Rarotonga and Aitutaki. International telecommunications are via Cable and Wireless and Peacesat satellite links.

Electricity supply
240V DC/50 cycle.

Social customs/useful tips
Bargaining is discouraged. Gratuities are not customary, as tradition requires that something is then given in return.
Dress: Brief attire (eg bikinis) should not be worn in towns or villages. Nude or topless sunbathing will cause offence.

Getting there
Air
There are direct, daily international flights from New Zealand and Australia.
International airport/s: Rarotonga (RAR), three kilometres west of Avarua. Restaraunts, duty-free shop, shops, car rental. Hotel coaches meet each flight and taxis and buses are also available.
Airport tax: Adults NZ$30; children three-12 years old NZ$15.
Surface
Water: Inter-island shipping services are provided by major passenger carrying cargo lines, operators include Express Cook Islands Line Shipping Ltd and Hawaii-Pacific Maritime Ltd.
Main port/s: Avatiu (on Rarotonga), and Aitutaki. Penrhyn Island (northern Cook Islands) is also a Port of Entry.

Getting about
National transport
Air: Air Rarotonga operates inter-island services. Airstrips for small planes on Aitutaki, Penryhn, Rakahanga, Mitiaro, Atiu, Mauke, Mangala and Manitiki. Services do not operate on Sunday.
Road: The Ara Tapu surfaced road runs 32km around Rarotonga coast. There is also an older inland road, which winds cross-country.
Buses: *The Island Bus* (yellow buses) – a round-the-island service in both directions (Mon–Fri 0700–1600; Sat 0800–1300).
Taxis: Taxi service is available on Rarotonga.
Water: There are harbours on Aitutaki, Atiu, Penrhyn and Suwarrow.
Car hire
Car, scooter and bicycle hire are available on Rarotonga and Aitutaki. Driving is on the left.
A local licence is required; they can be obtained from the police station on Avarua, on presentation of an international or Commonwealth national driving licence.

BUSINESS DIRECTORY

The addresses listed below are a selection only. While World of Information makes every endeavour to check these addresses, we cannot guarantee that changes have not been made, especially to telephone numbers and area codes. We would welcome any corrections.

Telephone area codes
The international direct dialling (IDD) for Cook Islands is +682 followed by subscriber's number.

Useful telephone numbers
Police: 999
Fire: 996
Ambulance: 998

Chambers of Commerce
Cook Islands Chamber of Commerce PO Box 242, Avarua, Rarotonga (tel: 20-925; fax: 20-969).

Banking
Bank of the Cook Islands, PO Box 113, Rarotonga (tel: 29-341; fax: 29-343).

Wall Street Banking Corporation Ltd, PO Box 3012, CITC House, Avarua (tel: 23-445; fax: 23-446; e-mail: info@wallbank.co.ck).

Westpac Banking Corporation, PO Box 42, Rarotonga (tel: 22-014; fax: 20-014).

Travel information
Air Rarotonga (tel: 22-888; e-mail: bookings@airraro.co.ck; internet site: http://www.airraro.com).

Flight information (24 hours) (tel: 25-890).

Government Information Office, PO Box 106 (tel: 29-304; fax: 20-856).

Principal Immigration Officer, Ministry of Foreign Affairs and Immigration, PO Box 105, Rarotonga (tel: 29-347; fax: 21-247).

Rarotonga International Airport, PO Box 90, Rarotonga (tel: 25-890; fax: 21-890; e-mail: aaci@airport.gov.ck).

National tourist organisation offices
Cook Islands Tourism Corporation, PO Box 14, Avarua, Rarotonga (tel: 29-435; fax: 21-435; e-mail: headoffice@cook-islands.com).

Other useful addresses
Asian Development Bank (ADB), South Pacific Regional Mission, La Casa di Andrea, Fr. Dr. W. H. Lini Highway; PO Box 127, Port Vila (tel: +678 2 23-300; fax: +678 2 23-183; email: adbsprm@adb.org; internet: www.adb.org/SPRM).

Cook Islands Development Investment Board, Rarotonga (tel: 24-296; fax: 24-298; e-mail: cidib@oyster.net.ck; internet: www.cookislands-invest.com).

Cook Islands Investment Corporation, Rarotonga (tel: 29-391; fax: 29-381; e-mail: ciic@oyster.net.ck).

Cook Islands News, PO Box 15, Rarotonga (tel: 22-999; fax: 25-303; e-mail: editor@cookislandsnews.com; internet site: www.cinews.co.ck).

Internet sites
Yellow pages: www.yellowpages.co.ck
Cook Islands government: www.cook-islands.gov.ck

Cook Islands News: www.cinews.co.ck

Cook Islands shipping movements: www.ck/shipping.htm

Cook Islands website: www.ck

Tourism Council of the South Pacific: www.tcsp.com

Costa Rica

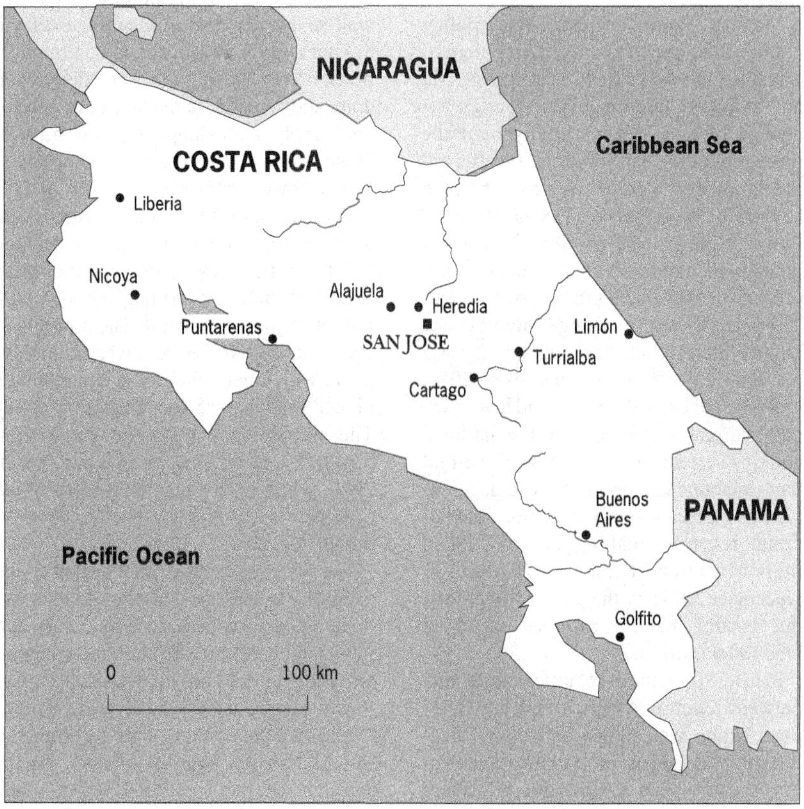

Google Earth (the internet atlas) nearly caused a war between Nicaragua and Costa Rica in late 2010 when in November Nicaraguan troops crossed into a disputed border area and planted a Nicaraguan flag on Costa Rica's Calero Island, claiming that Google Earth showed the island as Nicaraguan. Costa Rica immediately lodged a complaint with the International Court of Justice (ICJ).

On 8 March 2011, the ICJ ordered both sides to withdraw all personnel while judgement was pending. Both sides welcomed the ruling. On 8 April, Google Earth admitted that it had incorrectly marked the border between Costa Rica and Nicaragua. It blamed the US State Department for supplying incorrect data and began updating its map. In London and Paris they worry about whether they have been spotted on the golf course...

The economy

Having contracted by 1 per cent in 2009, the gross domestic product (GDP) of Costa Rica is expected to have shown growth of 4 per cent in 2010. This upturn is attributable to the strong performance by exports (8.1 per cent) and a moderate expansion in consumption (3.5 per cent) and gross fixed investment (3.4 per cent). The central government balance has continued to deteriorate and will likely close the year at 5.5 per cent of GDP (it was 3.4 per cent in 2009). Inflation is projected to stand at about 5.5 per cent, which is in line with the Banco Central de Costa Rica (BCCR) (central bank)'s target. The balance-of-payments current account deficit will end the year at 3.7 per cent (compared with 2 per cent in 2009), while the employment situation will show a modest improvement, as the unemployment rate

KEY FACTS

Official name: República de Costa Rica (Republic of Costa Rica)

Head of State: President Laura Chinchilla Miranda (PLN) (since 8 May 2010)

Head of government: President Laura Chinchilla Miranda (from 8 May 2010)

Ruling party: Partido Liberación Nacional (PLN) (National Liberation Party) (from May 2006)

Area: 51,060 square km

Population: 4.66 million (2010)*

Capital: San José

Official language: Spanish

Currency: Colón (CC) = 100 céntimos

Exchange rate: CC514.12 per US$ (Oct 2011)

GDP per capita: US$7,843 (2010)

GDP real growth: 4.20% (2010)

GDP: US$35.80 billion (2010)

Labour force: 2.12 million (2009)

Unemployment: 7.80% (2009)

Inflation: 5.70% (2010)

Balance of trade: -US$3.58 billion (2010)

* estimated figure

eases down from 7.8 per cent in 2009 to 7.3 per cent in 2010.

The United Nations Economic Commission for Latin America and the Caribbean (ECLAC) forecasts GDP growth of 3.5 per cent for Costa Rica in 2011. Sluggish activity among main trading partners and weaker trade flows will lead to a slowdown in the Costa Rican economy. Commitments related to transfers and compensation will continue to exert pressure on the fiscal balance, which will surpass the 5 per cent level in the absence of any significant improvement in fiscal revenues.

The BCCR predicts that inflation will once again be close to 5 per cent, as long as there are no external shocks.

Fiscal revenue is projected to have risen by 5.7 per cent in real terms in 2010, after falling by a marked 8.7 per cent in 2009. Because of the natural lag in the payment of taxes, income tax receipts will increase slightly, but most of the expansion will be in foreign trade and sales tax receipts. The tax burden will stand at 13.4 per cent of GDP.

Central government spending continued to climb rapidly in 2010, as commitments assumed in 2009 were paid out; the overall expected rise will be of 18.5 per cent in real terms. The wage bill will burgeon under a programme to gradually raise public-sector salaries, and transfers will increase following the creation of a special support fund for higher education.

The growing fiscal deficit was financed by issuing domestic debt, which thus increased from 40.9 per cent of GDP in September 2009 to 42.2 per cent of GDP in September 2010. External debt stood at 12.1 per cent of GDP in the same month, compared with 11.8 per cent in 2009. In September, Moody's Investors Service upgraded the country's government bond rating from Ba1 to investment grade of Baa3.

Monetary and exchange-rate policy continued to operate in an environment of transition towards a flexible exchange rate and inflation targeting. The foreign-exchange market was highly volatile throughout the year, trending towards appreciation of the colón. In November, the exchange rate averaged 513 colónes to the dollar (close to the 500 colón floor of the band), which represented a 10 per cent appreciation over the beginning of the year. The bilateral real exchange rate with the United States dollar appreciated by 8.5 per cent in the first nine months of 2010, as a result of capital inflows and lower foreign currency holdings in the national banking system. In September, the central bank announced a programme to accumulate, as a precautionary measure, international reserves totalling up to US$600 million between 2 September 2010 and 31 December 2011; by the end of November, the central bank's reserves stood at US$180.6 million.

In May 2010, the association agreement between Central America and the European Union was signed and the ratification process began. Free trade agreement negotiations with China and Singapore were concluded in April. With a view to further widening access to Asian markets, an agreement was reached with South Korea to begin discussions on a free trade agreement in 2011.

As the areas damaged by adverse weather events in 2009 return to production, annual growth of 5.7 per cent in 2010 is expected in the agricultural sector, as well as 5.1 per cent in manufactures and 5.7 per cent in transport and communications, driven by an upturn in external and domestic demand. In the face of continued oversupply and sluggish credit growth, however, the construction sector again shrank (by 6.4 per cent).

The consumer price index saw a slight upward movement of 1.5 percentage points, on the back of international price hikes for fuels and primary goods and a rally in domestic demand. The upswing in economic activity led to lower unemployment, which nevertheless remained much higher than before the economic crisis. The employment rate crept down from 55.4 per cent in 2009 to 54.8 per cent in 2010, while real wages increased by 3.8 per cent year-on-year in the first 10 months of 2010.

The wider current account deficit is due primarily to increased imports of intermediate goods (industrial components and inputs, including fuels) at a time when international prices are higher and the manufacturing industry is recovering. Goods exports are projected to grow by an annual rate of 10.1 per cent, particularly on the strength of the increased volume and value of agricultural products. Total exports from free zones slowed towards the end of the year, owing to a drop in sales of high technology products.

Services exports posted annual growth of 15.5 per cent, with particularly strong growth in business services. Foreign direct investment for the year as a whole is expected to total US$1.45 billion, which is US$100 million more than in 2009. Worthy of particular note were the entry of new competitors in the recently (2011) opened insurance sector and investment in business services exports.

KEY INDICATORS — Costa Rica

	Unit	2006	2007	2008	2009	2010
Population	m	4.35	4.44	4.53	*4.62	*4.66
Gross domestic product (GDP)	US$bn	22.52	26.24	29.80	29.30	35.80
GDP per capita	US$	5,173	5,905	6,580	6,345	7,843
GDP real growth	%	8.8	6.8	2.9	-1.1	4.2
Inflation	%	11.5	9.4	13.4	7.8	5.7
Unemployment	%	6.6	4.6	4.9	7.8	–
Industrial output	% change	11.0	8.0	-1.0	-5.0	–
Agricultural output	% change	10.8	7.1	-3.0	-4.7	–
Exports (fob) (goods)	US$m	8,238.0	9,267.8	9,554.4	8,846.8	9,375.4
Imports (fob) (goods)	US$m	11,547.0	12,255.4	14,568.5	10,874.2	12,951.2
Balance of trade	US$m	-3,309.0	-2,987.6	-5,014.2	-2,027.5	-3,575.8
Current account	US$m	-1,108.0	-1,519.0	-2,751.9	-537.0	-1,298.7
Total reserves minus gold	US$m	3,114.6	4,113.6	3,798.7	4,066.2	4,627.2
Foreign exchange	US$m	3,084.4	4,081.9	3,767.5	3,826.5	4,392.2
Exchange rate	per US$	517.94	498.86	526.24	573.29	525.83

* estimated figure

Risk assessment

Economy	Fair
Politics	Fair
Regional stability	Fair

COUNTRY PROFILE

Historical profile

1502 Christopher Columbus visited the region, naming it Costa Rica (Rich Coast).

1561 Colonisation of Costa Rica began. The country became a dependency of Nicaragua within the kingdom of Guatemala in the vice-royalty of Mexico, then known as Nuevo España (New Spain).
1808 Coffee was introduced into Costa Rica and became the country's main crop.
1821 The Central American provinces (Costa Rica, Guatemala, Honduras, Nicaragua and El Salvador) declared independence from Spain.
1822 Central American confederation annexed itself to the Mexican Empire, under General Agustín de Iturbde, later Emperor Agustín I.
1823 Agustín I was overthrown and Mexico became a republic. The Central American states formed the United Provinces of Central America.
1825 Costa Rica, Guatemala, Honduras, Nicaragua and El Salvador formed the Central American Federation (CAF).
1838 The CAF was dissolved and Costa Rica became a fully independent republic.
1849 Under the leadership of Juan Rafael Mora, Costa Rica helped organise Central American resistance against William Walker, the US bucaneer who took over Nicaragua.
1859 A *coup d'état* saw Mora lose power.
1870 Costa Rican leader, Tomás Guardía, began a process of development, encouraging foreign investment in the rail system.
1874 The United Fruit Company began operations in Costa Rica.
1889 The country embraced democracy and Bernardo Soto was elected as the country's first president.
1940 President Rafael Angel Calderón Guardía, founder of the Partido Unidad Social Christiana (PUSC) (Social Christian Unity Party), introduced social reforms, including labour rights and a minimum wage.
1948 The result of the presidential election was annulled after the government's candidate, Rafael Calderón, who came second, refused to accept defeat. An opposition leader, José Figueres Ferrer, led a revolt in favour of the winning candidate, Otilio Ulate. An interim regime was set up, the constitution was changed, the army was abolished and Otilio Ulate became president.
1953 José Figueres Ferrer, a democratic socialist and leader of the Partido Liberación Nacional (PLN) (National Liberation Party), won the election. He began social reforms with the help of the reformist bishop of San José and a communist union leader, remaining president until 1958.
1982 Luis Alberto Monge (PLN) was elected president. He introduced a programme of austerity measures designed to stabilise the deteriorating economy.
1986 Oscar Arías Sánchez (PLN) was elected president and began brokering a peace plan with the leaders of Nicaragua, El Salvador, Guatemala and Honduras to end regional political turbulence and civil war.
1987 Arías won the Nobel Peace Prize for securing a regional peace deal.
1990 Rafael Angel Calderón Fournier of the PUSC was elected president and enacted a series of austerity measures.
1994 José María Figueres (PLN) won the presidential election.
1998 Miguel Angel Rodríguez of the PUSC was elected president.
2000 Costa Rica and Nicaragua reached an agreement to end a dispute over navigation along the San Juan river, which serves as the border between the two countries.
2001 Privatisation of Costa Rica's Pacific ports began.
2002 The PUSC defeated the PLN in the parliamentary elections. Abel Pacheco de la Espriella (PUSC) won the run-off election and became president.
2003 Strikes were held by energy and telecommunications workers over President Pacheco's privatisation plans for the sector and by primary and secondary school teachers over problems in paying their salaries. The strikes led to the resignations of three ministers.
2004 Three former presidents – José María Figueres, Miguel Angel Rodríguez and Rafael Angel Calderón – were investigated over allegations of corruption.
2005 A national state of emergency was declared after days of heavy rainfall resulted in severe flooding along the Caribbean coast.
2006 Oscar Arías Sánchez and the PLN won presidential and parliamentary elections.
2007 Costa Rica cut diplomatic ties with Taiwan; President Arias said his country needed to attract more investment from China. The Central American Free Trade Agreement (Cafta) with the US was narrowly approved by referendum.
2009 President Arías renewed diplomatic ties with Cuba. At the G20 summit the leaders agreed to sanctions against Costa Rica, which the Organisation for Economic Co-Operation and Development (OECD) had labelled a secretive tax haven. Honduran President Manuel Zelaya was exiled to Costa Rica.
2010 In parliamentary elections held in February, incumbent PLN won 37.16 per cent of the votes (23 seats out of 57); in presidential elections, Laura Chinchilla (PLN) won 46.76 per cent of the vote; her closest rival Ottón Solís (PAC) won 25.17 per cent. Laura Chinchilla was sworn in as president on 8 May. In November Nicaraguan troops crossed into a disputed border area and planted a Nicaraguan flag on Costa Rica's Calero Island, claiming that Google Earth (the internet atlas) showed the island as Nicaraguan. Costa Rica lodged a complaint with the International Court of Justice (ICJ) immediately.
2011 On 8 March, the ICJ ordered both sides to withdraw all personnel while judgement was pending. Both sides welcomed the ruling. On 8 April, Google Earth admitted that it had incorrectly marked the border between Costa Rica and Nicaragua. It blamed the US State Department for supplying incorrect data and began updating its map. On 5 July, Costa Rica was removed from the OECD black-list of non-compliant tax havens, having introduced laws and practices, providing tax information to other OECD members.

Political structure

Constitution

Under the November 1949 constitution, government consists of three branches: legislative, executive and judicial.
In April 2003, the constitutional court annulled a constitutional reform enacted by the Legislative Assembly in 1969, barring presidents from running for re-election; the law reverts to the 1949 constitution, which states that presidents may run for re-election after being out of office for two presidential terms – eight years.
Voting: compulsory over 18 years.

Form of state

Presidential democratic republic

The executive

Executive power is held by the president, elected by popular vote for one four-year term — if a 40 per cent vote for any candidate is not obtained, a second ballot is held. The president is also head of government. The president appoints and is assisted by a 15-member cabinet.

National legislature

The unicameral Asamblea Legislativa (Legislative Assembly) has 57-members directly elected by proportional representation by provinces, for four-year terms. Although serving successive terms as a deputy is prohibited, a deputy may serve in a subsequent assembly after sitting out a term.

Legal system

The legal system is based on the Spanish civil law system. There are judicial reviews of legislative acts in the Supreme Court. Justices are elected for renewable eight-year terms by the Legislative Assembly. Costa Rica has not accepted compulsory International Court of Justice (ICJ) jurisdiction.

Last elections

7 February 2010 (presidential and parliamentary)

Results: Parliamentary: Partido Liberación Nacional (PLN) (National Liberation Party) won 37.16 per cent of the votes (23 seats out of 57); Partido Acción Ciudadana (PAC) 17.68 per cent (11); Partido Movimiento Libetario (PML) (Libertarian Movement Party) 14.48 per cent (10), Accesibilidad sin Exclusión (ASE) (Access without Exclusion) 9.17 per cent (four), Partido de Unidad Socialcristiana (PUS) (Social Christian Unity Party) 8.05 per cent (six), Partido Renovación Costariccense (PRC) (Costa Rican Renovation Party) 3.79 per cent (one); 12 other political parties won too few votes to gain any seats. Turnout was 69.08 per cent.

Presidential: Laura Chinchilla (PLN) won 46.76 per cent of the vote, Ottón Solís (PAC) 25.17 per cent, Otto Guevara (PML) 20.83 per cent; six other candidates won less than 4 per cent each. Turnout was 69.17 per cent.

Next elections

2014 (presidential and parliamentary)

Political parties

Ruling party

Partido Liberación Nacional (PLN) (National Liberation Party) (from May 2006)

Main opposition party

Partido Acción Ciudadana (PAC) (Citizens' Action Party)

Population

4.66 million (2010)*

Last census: June 2000: 3,810,179

Population density: 70 inhabitants per square km. Urban population: 60 per cent of total (1995—2001).

Annual growth rate: 2.3 per cent 1994–2004 (WHO 2006)

Ethnic make-up

The majority of the population, 98 per cent, is white or racially mixed, except in Limón province on the Caribbean coast, where an estimated 70,000 blacks and 5,000 Indians live. The Northern Guanacaste province also has a sizeable Indian population.

Religions

Roman Catholic (approximately 2.33 million followers); Methodist (estimated 6,000 followers); Baptist and Episcopalian.

Education

Education is compulsory at the elementary level, between the ages of six and 13, and is free at both elementary and secondary level. State-owned and private primary and secondary schools are of a high standard and the country has one of the highest literacy rates in Latin America. The adult illiteracy rate is estimated at 4.4 per cent and 4.3 per cent for men and women respectively. World Bank estimates show that the total primary school enrolment of the relevant age group typically stood at 104 per cent for boys and 103 per cent for girls (including repetition rates) between 1994 and 2000.

Costa Ricans are very proud of their education system, with about 12,000 university graduates joining the workforce each year. Costa Rica has 250,000 graduates from higher education per annum and 630,000 graduates from secondary academic schools and around 50,000 graduates of vocational schools.

Public expenditure on education typically amounts to 5–6 per cent of annual gross national income according to UN surveys.

Literacy rate: 96 per cent adult rate; 98 per cent youth rate (15–24) (Unesco 2005).

Pupils per teacher: 29 in primary schools.

Health

It is estimated that 10 per cent of all deaths are caused by prenatal or infectious diseases. Immunisation programmes against measles, diphtheria, polio and tetanus are very successful with between 85 and 95 per cent of all relevant ages being immunised.

Improved water sources and sanitation facilities are available to 98 per cent and 96 per cent of the population, respectively.

The Ministry of Health units operate a preventive health programme in all parts of the country. Most of Costa Rica's health services are supplied by the Caja Costarricense del Seguro Social (CCSS) (Costa Rican Social Security Agency), an independent state institution which operates a national insurance fund.

HIV/Aids

HIV prevalence: 0.6 per cent aged 15–49 in 2003 (World Bank)

Life expectancy: 77 years, 2004 (WHO 2006)

Fertility rate/Maternal mortality rate: 2.2 births per woman, 2004 (WHO 2006); maternal mortality 29 per 100,000 live births (World Bank).

Child (under 5 years) mortality rate (per 1,000): 8 per 1,000 live births; 5 per cent of children aged under five are malnourished (World Bank).

Welfare

The state-owned National Insurance Institute (INS) administers all social security insurance. Wage-earners and their dependants enjoy disability and retirement pensions, workers' compensation and family assistance. A pay-as-you-go system operates alongside voluntary individual accounts which provide second-tier benefits. The pay-as-you-go benefit, financed by employee, employer, and government contributions, is equal to a proportion of adjusted average monthly earnings.

Main cities

San José (capital, estimated population 1.5 million in 2004), Alajuela (791,900), Cartago (475,100), Puntarenas (397,700), Heredia (390,400), Limón (380,200).

Languages spoken

Business is conducted in Spanish, but many executives speak English. French, German and Italian are also spoken.

Official language/s

Spanish

Media

Press

Granma is the official publication of the central committee of the Communist Party of Cuba.

Dailies: In Spanish, major newspapers include *La Nación* (www.nacion.com), *La República* (www.larepublica.net), *Al Día* (www.aldia.co.cr), *Diario La Extra* (www.diarioextra.com) and *La Prensa Libre* (www.prensalibre.co.cr), which is an evening publication.

Weeklies: In English, *Tico Times* is an independent publication.

Business: In Spanish, *El Financiero* (www.elfinancierocr.com) is a daily, while *Actualidad Economica* (www.actualidad-e.com) and *EKA* (www.ekaenlinea.com), with an online version in English, are monthly magazines.

Broadcasting

Radio: There are over 100 commercial radio stations. Radio Nacional (www.sinart.go.cr) is the state broadcaster with cultural, news, information and music programmes. Other national networks include Radio Reloj (www.radioreloj.co.cr) and Radio Colombia (www.colombia.co.cr).

Television: Canal 13 (www.sinart.go.cr) is the national, public TV network. There are another seven national private TV stations offering a wide range of domestic and foreign programmes, including Repretel (www.repretel.com) with channels 4, 6 and 11 and Teletica (www.teletica.com) with channel 7. There has been a strong growth in cable and satellite TV with over a dozen companies offering international programming.

Economy

The economy of Puerto Rico is influenced and affected by the US economy, from which it derives much of its commercial investment and federal aid. Over 45 per cent of GDP is generated by the manufacturing sector, much of which is hi-tech industries, including capital-intensive industries and knowledge intensive industries, such as pharmaceuticals, electronics and biotechnology. The service sector, which generates over 50 per cent of GDP is dominated by financial services (15 per cent of GDP alone) and includes construction, transport, communications, utilities and public services. In 2007/08 tourism generated US$3.4 billion and provided employment for 60,000, from 5.06 million visitors. Agriculture accounts for less than 1 per cent of GDP.

Major improvements to Puerto Rico's business environment include the slashing of capital gains taxes and lowering operating costs for manufacturing plants. Puerto Ricans do not pay federal income taxes, and the local authorities have discretion to design tax incentives to attract foreign direct investment (FDI). The government has lobbied for permanent tax exemption status, saying this would be the best way to secure the Commonwealth's fiscal autonomy from the US federal government. With approximately 50 per cent of the economy supported by special exemptions for foreign firms, the repeal of tax incentives would severely undermine Puerto Rico's ability to compete with its Caribbean neighbours, prompting concern that the economy could collapse. Regional agreements such as the North American Free Trade Agreement (Nafta) have made countries such as Mexico attractive low wage, tariff free alternatives to Puerto Rico.

Always susceptible to external shocks due to the reliance on imports, particularly petroleum products, the economy has suffered with negative GDP growth since 2007 when it was -1.2 per cent, which fell further to -2.5 per cent and with a forecast of -5.5 per cent in 2009. Inflation fell from 13.5 per cent in 2007 to 8.0 per cent in 2008 to a forecast 4.5 per cent for 2009 as imports fall and domestic spending slows. High unemployment, which is categorised as a long-term problem, reached 16.5 per cent in 2009.

External trade

As an overseas commonwealth territory of the United States, the US has authority over interstate trade, commerce and customs administration. Puerto Rico is part of the North American Free Trade Agreement (Nafta).

Since Nafta was signed, the level of exported manufactured goods has fallen as Mexico, with its lower unit costs, has become a major supplier to the US and Canada. However, while low paid jobs were lost to Mexico there was an increase in pharmaceutical and hi-tech manufacturing in Puerto Rico.

The US accounts for over 75 per cent of imports and exports. Most trade is intra-company shipments, as parts from US companies are imported and finished goods are exported in return. This flow of materials and products creates profits for private companies and jobs for workers in Puerto Rico and the US.

Imports

Principal imports include petroleum and derivatives, chemicals, capital machinery and electronic components, textiles and yarns, raw and processed foodstuff, building materials and manufacturing raw materials.

Main sources: US (typically 50 per cent of total), Ireland (20 per cent), Nigeria (5 per cent).

Exports

Principal exports include chemicals, pharmaceuticals, medical products and equipment, finished goods, electronics, clothing, tuna and other fish products, beverages, tropical fruit, dairy and meat.

Main destinations: US (typically 76 per cent of total), Germany (5 per cent), The Netherlands (3 per cent).

Agriculture

Farming

Costa Rica's agricultural sector is an important contributor to the country's GDP. The sector represents approximately17 per cent of total GDP and employs a fifth of the workforce.

The most important cash crops are coffee, bananas and sugar. A considerable amount of meat, mostly beef, is also exported. The share of traditional agricultural exports declined from 95 per cent of total exports in 1990 to less than 30 per cent by 2004. Bananas account for just over a fifth of Costa Rica's exports. Costa Rica is the world's second-largest banana exporter, representing 12 per cent of the world's banana trade.

Around 10 per cent of the total land is cultivated arable land and 25 per cent is pasture.

Production of cash crops has risen in recent years, but increased exports have tended to be offset by falling prices.

Staple food crops including rice, maize and beans are grown, although Costa Rica is not self-sufficient in these.

Non-traditional products include tropical fruits, ornamental plants and cut flowers.

Fishing

industry has the potential for positive growth. However, the industry has suffered from a lack of organisation and infrastructure over the years.

The majority of the fishing industry is concentrated on the Pacific coastline. Shrimp fishing has decreased due to overfishing, but the potential for tuna, shark and sardine fishing has remained largely untapped due to a lack of investment in modern canning factories.

In a typical year the annual fish catch is 35,003mt, including 19,838mt marine fish and 6,341mt shellfish.

Forestry

Approximately 25 per cent of Costa Rica's total landmass is forested. Significant variations in elevation and topography have led to the development of a wide array of vegetative zones ranging from coastal mangroves to sub-alpine paramó. The predominant forests of Costa Rica can be broadly classified according to elevation and precipitation. The most extensive are lowland humid tropical forests in the south-east of the country and on the Peninsula de Osa. Common species are guacimo colorado (*Luehea seemanii*) and laurel (*Cordia alliodora*). Dry tropical forests are characteristic of the Guanacaste province in the north-west. The most extensive montane forests occur in the Cordillera de Talamanca mountain range in the south. Quercus are the most common trees at higher elevations. Costa Rica has an extensive network of protected areas with more than 25 per cent of the country's land area protected as forest reserves, national parks, and reservations for indigenous peoples.

Costa Rica produces a moderate amount of roundwood, three-quarters of which is used as fuel. The majority of industrial roundwood is used for sawn timber, but Costa Rica also has small wood-based panels and paper industries. Most pulp and paper is imported.

Industry and manufacturing

The Costa Rican industrial sector contributes approximately 23 per cent to the country's total GDP. The sector is also responsible for 24 per cent of Costa Rica's total level of employment.

The manufacturing sector alone contributes 18 per cent to GDP and is concentrated on export-oriented processing of agricultural products and electronic components. Costa Rica's manufacturing sector is divided into small- and medium-sized companies producing among other things shoes, packing materials, glass and leather goods, and larger companies involved in producing beer, cement, paper, textiles and palm oil.

There is also a growing number of companies involved in the processing of fish, fruit and meat. Other important industries are petroleum refining and pulp/paper processing.

There are industrial free zones (Zonas Francas), where incentives apply, at Puerto Limón, Puntarenas and Cartago.

The government's promotion of the manufacturing sector, with investment incentives and tax holidays, has largely been curtailed in the name of fiscal discipline.

Costa Rica has one of the lowest unit costs among developing countries for the creation of new jobs.

Tourism
Travel and tourism is one of Costa Rica's most significant economic sectors and now accounts for 13.7 per cent of total GDP.

Eco-tourism and resorts, coupled with the country's stability, are the main attractions. The sector doubled in size during the nineties, passing the million visitors mark by 1999. The US, together with Canada, is the main market, followed by Europe.

Environment
Since the 1960s and 1970s, the Costa Rican authorities have been increasingly anxious to protect the environment, so that by 2001, over a quarter of the total land area was protected. There has also been a great deal of success in protecting valuable natural resources in a sustainable way, while at the same time promoting a growing eco-tourism sector.

Mining
The mining sector in Costa Rica is not a substantial contributor to total GDP. However, Costa Rica does have substantial deposits of various precious metals and the industry is notable for the activity of Canadian firms in the country. In October 2005 two of the largest Canadian corporations operating in Costa Rica announced positive news. Glencairn announced that the Bellavista mine, which it operates, was nearing completion, while Vannessa Ventures Ltd announced the go-ahead of its Las Crucitas Project.

Gold and silver are mined in the western part of Costa Rica. Deposits of manganese, nickel, mercury and sulphur are largely unused. Petroleum deposits are found in the south, but not exploited. Salt is produced from seawater. Large gold deposits in Costa Rica are found near the border with Nicaragua, although estimates vary wildly on the level of reserves. The government is reluctant to explore other reserves found in national parks in the Peninsula de Osa region, due to the environmental impact.

Deposits of manganese, bauxite, aluminium, zinc, copper and sulphur exist in Costa Rica, although their quantity and potential for commercial mining is unknown. Discovery of a valuable bauxite deposit in Boruca area prompted large-scale investment in an aluminium smelting plant. Commercial deposits of iron ore may also be present.

Hydrocarbons
Although Costa Rica is thought to possess considerable oil reserves none has been proven. Consumption of oil was 45,000 barrels per day (bpd) in 2008, all of which was imported. Over 50 per cent of crude oil imports were refined domestically; refinery capacity is 24,000bpd.

The president re-iterated Costa Rica's 2002 ban of onshore and offshore oil exploration in March 2009.

Any use of natural gas is commercially insignificant.

Coal imports were over 70,000 tonnes in 2008, all used in power generation.

Energy
Total installed generating capacity was 1,962MW in 2007, producing 8.52 billion kilowatt hours. Hydroelectricity is responsible for 90 per cent of all power generated; the potential for more is considered very high. The government is backing investment in renewable energy sources including solar, wind, geothermal and biomass. The government plans to build 29 new hydroelectric power plants by 2020.

The state-owned Instituto Costarricense de Electricidad (ICE) (Light and Power Company) has exclusive rights to generate, distribute, transmit and sell electricity until 2040.

Financial markets
The main stock exchange in Costa Rica, the Bolsa Nacional de Valores (BNV), was established in 1976. Most transactions are in finance ministry debt and central bank monetary stabilisation bonds. The stock market index is the ALDESA and all shares are traded electronically. There is another exchange, the Bolsa Electrónica de Valores de Costa Rica (BEVCR), which trades in the same amount of paper and shares. The agricultural commodities exchange was set up in 1990 and trades in coffee, maize, potatoes and timber.

Stock exchange

Bolsa Nacional de Valores (Costa Rica Stock Exchange)

Banking and insurance
Costa Rica's financial services sector is composed of the Central Bank, three state-owned commercial banking houses, nineteen private commercial banks (including one jointly owned state bank), one workers' bank, one state-owned mortgage bank and four mutual house-building companies. There are also 15 private finance companies, 27 savings and loans co-operatives and 30 investment and retirement funds/trusts.

Both local and international companies have looked to raise capital abroad because of the poor service and high costs offered by the state banks in Costa Rica. Some of the larger private banks have capitalised on this by offering a wide range of international services and financing in dollars through offshore banks affiliated to them. However, reforms introduced under the administration of Manuel Angel Rodríguez (1998–2002) introduced regulations for the interbank market and for offshore banking operations and made the banking sector more flexible.

By opening up the financial sector to both domestic and foreign investors, Costa Rica is going down the same path as other Latin American countries which have secured economic stability by having a foreign presence in the financial sector.

The last few years have seen a number of joint ventures and takeovers by both domestic and foreign banking groups. The banks with the most presence in Costa Rica's banking system include Citibank, Banco de la Industria, Bancrecén, Banco de San José, Banco del Pacifíco, Banca Promérica and Scotiabank.

There is also a sizable offshore banking service with the financial services sector.

In recent years the Costa Rican authorities have co-operated with international agencies in order to guard against money laundering.

Central bank

Banco Central de Costa Rica

Main financial centre

San José

Time
GMT minus six hours

Geography
Costa Rica is the second smallest country in Central America after El Salvador. The country lies between Nicaragua and Panama and has coastlines on the Caribbean Sea and the Pacific Ocean. A low, thin line of hills between Lake Nicaragua and the Pacific extends into northern Costa Rica, broadening and rising into high and rugged mountains in the centre and south. The capital city, San José, lies in the Meseta central basin set in these highlands.

Both coasts have lowland areas. The sparsely inhabited east coast has a narrow swamp strip and tropical forests as the terrain rises inland. The Pacific coast has two peninsulas: the mountainous Nicoya peninsula in the north and the lowland Osa peninsula in the south. A rich lowland savannah patched by deciduous forests stretches along the Pacific coast between the two peninsulas.

Hemisphere

Northern

Climate
Costa Rica's weather is influenced by altitude. The Pacific coast is drier while the Caribbean coast has the most rainfall – about 300 days a year. It is hot and humid in lowland coastal areas; temperate and warm in central highlands. The dry season is December–May; the rainy

season runs from June–November. The temperature in San José ranges from a high of 24–27 degrees Celsius (C) to a low of 14–16 degrees C. The hottest months are March and April.

Dress codes

Formal dress is required for business engagements. Shorts, especially for women, are for the beach and should not be worn in restaurants or at parties. Women can wear trousers. Strapless dresses are only acceptable for evening events.

Entry requirements

Passports

Passports are required by all, and must be carried at all times. Passports must be valid for at least six months.

Visa

Required by all, except nationals of the Americas, Europe, Australasia and some Asian countries visiting either as tourists or for business purposes, for up to 30 or 90 days. For confirmation and further details contact the nearest consulate or email: miginfor@racsa.co.cr. Business visitors should carry a company letter stating that they represent a foreign company on legitimate business.

Those staying up to 90 days must obtain an exit visa from the Immigration Department in San José at least three days before leaving. Those whose stay is less than 30 days need only their disembarkation card (issued on arrival).

Prohibited entry

Entry is refused to persons of unkempt appearance or without sufficient funds (minimum US$200), who will be deported immediately.

Currency advice/regulations

No restrictions on import of foreign or local currency. Foreign currency should be changed only at banks and authorised bureaux. Street-corner foreign exchange transactions are illegal. Visitors may change excess local currency back to US dollars, but only at main offices of state commercial banks and on production of an onward airline ticket and passport.

Customs

It is prohibited to import arms and drugs. Import tariffs range from 1 to 20 per cent except for vehicles, textiles, shoes, clothing (which are higher). Food products and medicines require registration.

Health (for visitors)

Mandatory precautions

There are no compulsory vaccinations.

Advisable precautions

Typhoid, tetanus and hepatitis A vaccinations are advised.

There is a malaria risk in some low-lying areas – prophylaxis is advisable if visiting the provinces of Limón, Guanacaste, Alajuela and Heredia. Dengue fever mosquitoes are present throughout the country.

Water precautions should be taken outside of San José. There is a risk of rabies.

Hotels

It is advisable to book well in advance. A 3 per cent tourism tax, 10 per cent sales tax and 10 per cent service charge will be added to the bill. Gratuities of around 5–10 per cent are also expected.

Public holidays (national)

Fixed dates

1 Jan (New Year's Day), 19 Mar (Feast of San José (San José only)), 11 Apr (Anniversary of the Battle of Rivas), 1 May (Labour Day), 29 Jun (St Peter and St Paul Day), 25 Jul (Guanacaste Annexation), 2 Aug (Our Lady of the Angels), 15 Aug (Assumption/Mothers' Day), 15 Sep (Independence Day), 12 Oct (Columbus Day), 8 Dec (Immaculate Conception), 24 Dec (Christmas Eve), 25 Dec (Christmas Day), 31 Dec (New Year's Eve).

Most businesses close for Holy Week and between Christmas and New Year.

Variable dates

Maundy Thursday, Good Friday, Corpus Christi (Mon/Jun).

Working hours

Banking

Mon–Fri: 0900–1500.

Business

Mon–Fri: 0800–1200; 1400–1600.

Government

Mon–Fri: 0800–1600.

Shops

Mon–Sat: 0900–1800/1900.

Telecommunications

Mobile/cell phones

GSM 1800 service available.

Electricity supply

110/220V AC, 60Hz. Two-pin plugs are standard.

Social customs/useful tips

Appointments should be made in advance. It is customary to shake hands on meeting and taking leave. The usual form of address is Don for a man, and Doña for a woman, followed by the first name. Business cards to indicate academic/professional titles are exchanged after introduction.

Costa Ricans are not very punctual for social activities, except for football matches, the cinema and weddings, but are more formal with their business appointments.

Mothers are regarded as the leading family figures; grandparents and elders are highly respected.

The national pastimes are football and politics. The people have a strong sense of democracy.

Costa Ricans are called Ticos for short.

Although a service charge is added to restaurant and hotel bills, gratuities of 5–10 per cent are also expected.

Security

Petty crime is frequent. Thefts, especially in urban areas, and car break-ins are common. Thefts take place on the street and from cars. The loss or theft of a passport should be reported immediately to the local police and the relevant embassy. Some remote trails in national parks have been closed because of the low number of visitors and reported robberies of hikers in the area. Tourists should check with forest rangers for current park conditions. There are pickpockets in downtown San José. Beware of mugging in the national parks at night and of theft at beaches and ports.

Getting there

Air

National airline: Taca International Airlines

International airport/s: Juan Santamaría International (SJO), 22km from San José; duty-free shop, bar, restaurant, buffet, bank, post office, shops, car hire.

Airport tax: US$26; also payable in local currency or combination of both currencies.

Surface

Road: It is possible to travel overland from North or Central America. The nearest US town is Brownsville, Texas, on the Mexican border. From there it is about 4,000km by road on the Inter-American Highway to San José, crossing Mexico and going through Guatemala, Honduras, Nicaragua and into Costa Rica.

There is one major crossing point between Nicaragua and Costa Rica at Peñas Blancas, which is not a town, so there is nowhere to stay. There are two border crossings between Panama and Costa Rica.

Rail: There is no rail link with neighbouring countries.

Water: Cruise ships stop at Limón, Punterenas and Caldera. Freighters may accept a small number of passengers and private yachts cruise down the Pacific coast from North America.

Main port/s: Limón (Caribbean coast), Puntarenas and Caldera (Pacific coast).

Getting about

National transport

Air: SANSA is the main domestic carrier and operates cheap regular flights from San José to provincial towns. Travelair also provides domestic services. It is advisable to book in advance. A number of smaller airlines provide internal flights. There are over 200 small airfields throughout the country.

Road: Total network of some 30,000km of all-weather roads. Main routes are the Pan-American Highway; San José-Caldera; San José-Guapiles; and San José-Puerto Limón. Tolls are paid on all four-lane highways entering San José. Taxis are a form of public transport outside urban areas and can be hired by the hour, half-day or the day. Arrange the fare beforehand.

Buses: There are bus services around the country, but both the quality of services and prices vary considerably. Major tourist areas are better provided with short-distance bus services.

Rail: There is a short commuter train which links San José with Heredia and one which links Puerto Limón with the Río Estrella area. There is also a 'banana train' which travels on a section of track in the banana plantations around Guápiles.

Water: There are passenger and car ferries in operation.

City transport

Taxis: Taxis are red, except those serving Juan Santamaría International airport which are orange. Taxis are usually metered, but where there are no meters, it is advisable to agree a price before setting off. Taxis connecting to the airport or distant destinations charge a flat, official rate, but negotiation is possible.

Car hire

A temporary permit must be obtained from local traffic authorities on production of a national licence. Always carry a driving licence. There are tough drink-drive laws – the penalty includes having your driving licence impounded for a minimum of three years.

BUSINESS DIRECTORY

The addresses listed below are a selection only. While World of Information makes every endeavour to check these addresses, we cannot guarantee that changes have not been made, especially to telephone numbers and area codes. We would welcome any corrections.

Telephone area codes

The international direct dialling (IDD) code for Costa Rica is +506 followed by the subscriber's number.

Useful telephone numbers

Emergencies: 911
Ambulance: 128
Fire: 118
Police: 222-1365, 221-5337
Highway police: 222-9330, 222-8245

Chambers of Commerce

American-Costa Rican Chamber of Commerce, PO Box 4946-1000, San José (tel: 220-2200; fax: 220-2300; e-Mail: chamber@amcham.co.cr).

Costa Rican Cámara de Comercio, PO Box 1114-1000, San José (tel: 221-0005; fax: 233-7091; e-mail: servicos@camara-comercio.com).

Costa Rica Cámara de Industrias, PO Box 10003-1000, San José (tel: 281-0006; fax: 234-6163; e-mail: cicr@cicr.com).

Franco-Costa Rican Chambre de Commerce et d'Industrie, PO Box 912-1007 Centro Colon, San José (tel: 257-1138; fax: 257-1345; e-mail: cfcci@camarafranco-cr.org).

German-Costa Rican Cámara de Comercio, PO Box 2139-1000, San José (tel: 222-4789; fax: 221-1219; e-mail: cacoral@racsa.co.cr).

Unión Costarricense de Cámaras y Asociaciones de la Empresa Privada, PO Box 539-1002 Paseo de los Estudiantes, San José (tel: 290-5594; fax: 290-5596; e-mail: uccaep@uccaep.or.cr).

Banking

Banco Banex, Apdo 7983, 1000 San José (tel: 233-4855; fax: 223-7192).

Banco BCT, Apdo 7698, 1000 San José (tel: 233-6611; fax: 233-6833).

Banco Continental, Apdo 7969, 1000 San José (tel: 257-1155; fax: 255-3983).

Banco Co-operativo Costarricense, Apdo 8593, 1000 San José (tel: 233-5044; fax: 233-9661).

Banco Crédito Agrícola de Cartago, Apdo 5572, 1000 San José (tel: 251-3011; fax: 252-0364).

Banco de Costa Rica, Apdo 10035, 1000 San José (tel: 255-1100; fax: 255-0911).

Banco del Comercio SA, Apdo 1106, 1000 San José (tel: 233-6011; fax: 222-3706).

Banco de Fomento Agrícola, Apdo 6531, 1000 San José (tel: 231-4444; fax: 232-7476).

Banco de la Construcción, Apdo 5099, 1000 San José (tel: 221-5811; fax: 222-6567).

Banco de la Industria, Apdo 4254, 1000 San José (tel: 221-3355; fax: 233-8383).

Banco de San José, Apdo 5445, 1000 San José (tel: 221-9911; fax: 222-8208).

Banco Federado de Co-operativas de Ahorro y Crédito, Apdo 4748, 1000 San José (tel: 222-3323; fax: 257-1724).

Banco Fincomer, Apdo 57, Cartago (tel: 251-1351, 233-7822; fax: 222-0405).

Banco Germano Centroamericano, Apartado 2559, 1000 San José (tel: 233-8022; fax: 222-2648).

Banco Interfín, Apdo 6899, 1000 San José (tel: 221-8022; fax: 233-4823).

Banco Internacional de Costa Rica, Apdo 6116, 1000 San José (tel: 223-6522; fax: 233-6572).

Banco Lyon, Apdo 10184, 1000 San José (tel: 221-2611; fax: 221-6795).

Banco Mercantil de Costa Rica, Apdo 32101, 1000 San José (tel: 231-0724, 255-3636; fax: 255-3076).

Banco Metropolitano, Apdo 3932, 1000 San José (tel: 233-8111; fax: 222-8840).

Banco Nacional de Costa Rica, Apdo 10015, 1000 San José (tel: 223-2166; fax: 255-2436).

Corporación Costarricense de Financiamiento Industrial, Apdo 10507, 1000 San José (tel & fax: 221-2212).

Central bank

Banco Central de Costa Rica, Avenida Central y Primera, Calles 2 y 4, Apdo 10058, San José (tel: 243-3333; fax: 243-3011; internet: www.bccr.fi.cr).

Stock exchange

Bolsa Nacional de Valores (Costa Rica Stock Exchange) Central Street, 1st Avenue, PO Box 1736-1000, San José (tel: 221-8011; fax: 255-0131: www.bolsacr.com).

Travel information

American Airlines, Calle 26 & 28, Paseo Colón, San José (tel: 257-1266; fax: 222-5213).

British Airways, Calle 32, paseo Colón and Avenida 2, San José (tel: 223-5648; fax: 223-4863).

SANSA (Servicios Aéreos Nacionales), Apdo 999-1007, Centro Colón, San José (tel: 233-2714, 233-1673; fax: 255-2176).

Tourist Information Office, Plaza de la Cultura, Calle 5, Avenida 0-2, San José (tel: 223-1733 Ext 277; fax: 222-1090).

Ministry of tourism

National tourist organisation offices

Instituto Costarricense de Turismo (ICT), Edificio Genaro Valverde, Calles 5 y 7, Avenida 4, PO Box 777, 1000 San José (tel: 223-8423; fax: 223-5452).

Ministries

Ministry of Agriculture and Livestock, Science and Technology, Apdo 10094, 1000 San José (tel: 232-4496; fax: 232-2103).

Ministry of Culture, Apdo 10227, 1000 San José (tel: 223-1658; fax: 233-7066).

Ministry of Economy, Industry and Commerce, Foreign Commerce, Apdo 10216-1000, San José (tel: 222-1016; fax: 222-2305).

Ministry of Environment and Energy, Apdo 10104 1000 San José (tel: 257-1417; fax: 257-0697).

Ministry of Finance, Apdo 5016, San José (tel: 222-2481; fax: 255-4874).

Ministry of Foreign Affairs, Apdo 10027-1000, San José (tel: 223-7555; fax: 223-9328).

Ministry of Foreign Trade, Apdo 96-2050 Mtes de Oca, San José (tel: 222-5910; fax: 233-5090).

Ministry of Health, Apdo 10123, 1000 San José (tel: 233-0683; fax: 255-4997).

Ministry of Housing, Apdo 222-1002 Paseo de Los Estudiantes, San José (tel: 233-3665; fax: 255-1976).

Ministry of Information, PO Box 520-2010, Zapote (tel: 225-9936/9797; fax: 253-6984).

Ministry of the Interior, Police and Public Security, Apdo 10006, 1000 San José (tel: 223-8354; fax: 222-7726).

Ministry of Justice, Apdo 5685, 1000 San José (tel: 223-9739; fax: 223-3879).

Ministry of Labour and Social Security, Apdo 10133, 1000 San José (tel: 221-0238; fax: 222-8085).

Ministry of the Presidency and Planning, Apdo 520 Zapote, San José (tel: 224-4092; fax: 253-6984).

Ministry of Public Education, Apdo 10087, 1000 San José (tel: 222-0229; fax: 255-2868).

Ministry of Public Security, Apdo 55-4874, San José (tel: 226-0093; fax: 226-6581).

Ministry of Public Works and Transport, Apdo 10176, 1000 San José (tel: 226-7311; fax: 227-1434).

Ministry of Science And Technology, Apdo 5589-1000, San José (tel: 253-7446; fax: 224-8295).

Other useful addresses

British Embassy, Apdo 815, 11th Floor, Edificio Centro Colón, 1007 San José (tel: 221-5566, 255-2937; fax: 233-9938).

Centro de Promoción de Exportaciones e Inversiones (CENPRO) (Costa Rican Export & Investment Promotion Centre), PO Box 5418 San José (tel: 221-7166; fax: 223-5722).

Costa Rican Electricity Institute (ICE), PO Box 10032, 10 San José (tel: 220-7720; fax: 220-1555).

Costa Rican Embassy (USA), 2114 S Street, NW, Washington DC 20008 (tel: (+1-202)-234-2945; fax: (+1-202)-265-4795; e-mail: embassy@costarica-embassy.com).

Costa Rican Institute of Pacific Ports (INCOP), Calle 36, Avenida 3, San José (tel: 223-7111).

Costa Rican Investment and Development Corporation (CINDE), P.O. Box 7170-100 San José (tel: 220-0366, 220-4755; fax: 220-4750, 220-4754).

Costa Rican Investment Promotion Programme (CINDE-EUROPE), Eisenhowerlaan 128, 22517 KM Den Haag, The Netherlands (tel: (31-70)512-1212, 515-010).

Costa Rican Oil Refinery (RECOPE), Apdo 43351, 1000 San José (tel: 223-9611; fax: 255-2049).

Costa Rican Stock Exchange (BNVSA), Apartado 1736-1000, San José (tel: 222-8011; fax: 255-0131).

Ferias Internacionales SA (FERCORI), Apartado 1843, 1000 San Jose (tel: 233-6990; fax: 233-5791).

Free Zones Export Corporation, Apdo 96, 2020 Montes de Oca (tel: 222-5855).

Grupo Centro, PO Box 6133, 1000 San José (tel: 235-4509; fax: 240-7591).

National Association for Economic Development (ANFE), Apartado 3577-1000, San José (tel: 253-4497).

Red Nacional de Televisión, PO Box 7-1980, 1000 San José (tel: 231-333; fax: 231-6604).

Sistema Nacional de Radio y Televisión Cultural (SINART), PO Box 27941, Administración Central, 1000 San Jose (tel: 231-6474; fax: 231-6604).

Televisora de Costa Rica, PO Box 3786, 1000 San Jose (tel: 232-2222; fax: 231-7545).

TNT Correos de Costa Rica, Calle 34-36, Avenida 1RA, San Jose (tel: 233-4993; fax: 221-5046).

Union Pack de Costa Rica (UPS), Aveida 3, Calle 30 & 32, San Jose (tel: 257-7447; fax: 257-5343).

US Embassy, Pavas Frente Centre Comercial, Apdo 920-1200, San José (tel: 220-3939; fax: 220-2305).

Internet sites

Information about the country, investment and the Stock Exchange: http://incostarica.net

Côte d'Ivoire

KEY FACTS

Official name: République de Côte d'Ivoire (Republic of Côte d'Ivoire)

Head of State: President Alassane Ouattara (sworn into office 6 May 2011)

Head of government: Prime Minister Guillaume Soro (FN) (appointed 7 Dec 2010)

Ruling party: Coalition: Front Populaire Ivorienne (FPI) (Ivorian Popular Front); Forces Nouvelles (FN) (New Forces); Rassemblement des Républicains (RDR) (Rally of Republicans); Parti Démocratique de la Côte d'Ivoire (PDCI) (Democratic Party of Côte d'Ivoire) (formed 7 Apr 2007)

Area: 322,630 square km

Population: 21.40 million (2010)*

Capital: Yamoussoukro (administrative capital); Abidjan (economic and diplomatic centre)

Official language: French

Currency: CFA franc (CFAf) = 100 centimes (Communauté Financière Africaine (African Financial Community) franc). New notes have been issued; old notes cease to be legal tender from Jan 2005.

Exchange rate: CFAf488.93 per US$ (Oct 2011); CFAf655.96 per euro (pegged Jan 1999)

GDP per capita: US$1,036 (2010)

GDP real growth: 2.60% (2010)

GDP: US$22.80 billion (2010)

Inflation: 1.40% (2010)

Balance of trade: US$4.19 billion (2009)

* estimated figure

NOTA

11 December 2011, in parliamentary elections, the preliminary results were that the president's (Rassemblement des Républicains (RDR) (Republican Party) won 127 seats (out of 225), Parti Démocratique de la Côte d'Ivoire-Rassemblement Démocratique Africain (PDCI-RDA) (Democratic Party of Côte d'Ivoire–African Democracy Party) 77; other smaller parties won the remaining seats. Supporters of ex-president Gbagbo boycotted the elections.

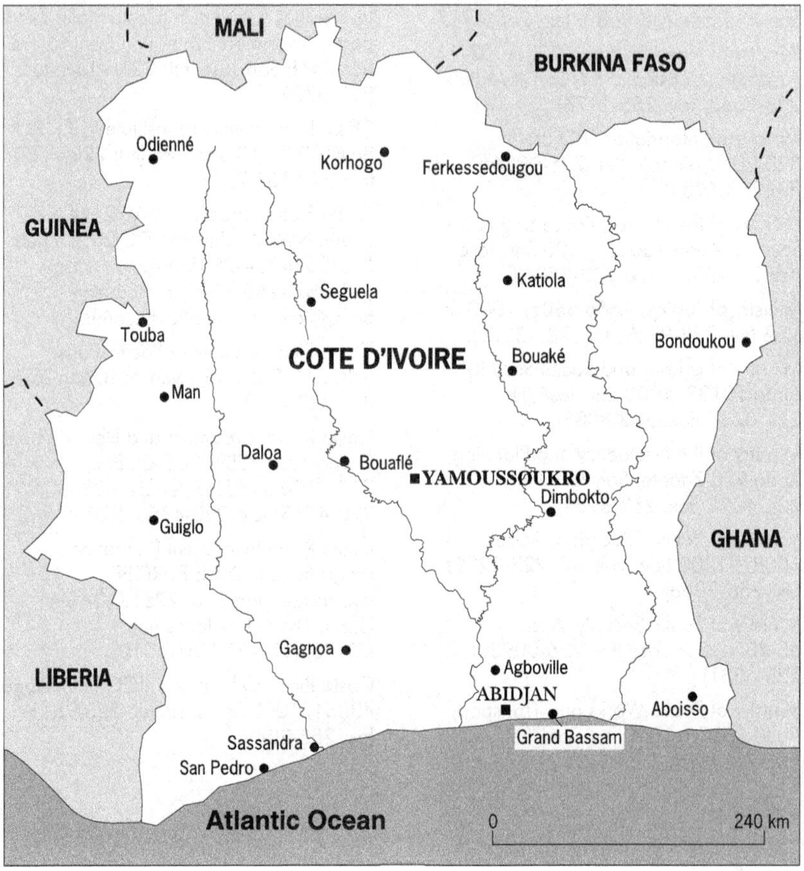

The political impasse in Côte d'Ivoire following the second round of the presidential elections on 28 November 2010 turned into an armed conflict between the defence and security forces led by the outgoing president Laurent Gbagbo and the republican forces loyal to Alassane Ouattara, the elected president recognised by the international community. After several days of heavy fighting, the pro-Ouattara forces arrested Gbagbo and several of his aides while they were in the bunker of the presidential palace. The escalation of the violence and the use of heavy weaponry increased the civilian death toll to more than 900 according to the United Nations (UN), with thousands more injured and massive numbers of Ivorian refugees, especially in neighbouring Liberia and Ghana.

This post-electoral crisis and the sanctions imposed by the international community had a strong impact on the economy, leaving the country cash-strapped. Nearly all the financial institutions and private firms had to cease operations due to the insecurity and the suspension of the clearing system by the Central Bank of West African States (BCEAO).

With this economic paralysis, the forecast for 2011 is for a strong fall of 7.3 per cent in real gross domestic product (GDP) growth. Nevertheless, a gradual recovery is expected in 2012 (around 5.9 per cent) based on the hypothesis of the security situation returning to normal in the second half of 2011, the sanctions being lifted and international co-operation being resumed. Also, the commitment of development partners to support the Ivorian authorities in their efforts for reconciliation and reconstruction will enable trust to be restored, thus fostering private-sector development.

The political crisis also made the already precarious humanitarian situation worse. By March 2011, around a million Ivorians had been forced out of their homes, while more than 79,000 more had fled, mainly to the Ghanaian border, but also to the Liberian border. There are enormous risks in terms of Côte d'Ivoire's progress in achieving the Millennium Development Goals (MDGs) by 2015. It is feared that many of the population will fall into poverty, with the level of poverty standing at 48.9 per cent of the population in 2008.

Côte d'Ivoire's medium-term economic and social outlook largely depends upon peace being restored and emergency reconstruction programmes being implemented. Despite the socio-political crisis of the last ten years, Côte d'Ivoire's economic partnerships with emerging countries have markedly increased, particularly those with Asian countries, including, notably, China, Korea, India, Singapore, Thailand, Brunei, Indonesia and Malaysia. Asia is Côte d'Ivoire's third largest trading partner (12.5 per cent), after Europe (44.0 per cent) and Africa (29.0 per cent). China, which is the country's leading Asian partner, still represents a modest share (3.2 per cent) of the economy compared with its wider performance in Africa.

The real rate of growth of the Ivorian economy was 2 per cent in 2010 after 3.7 per cent in 2009. This lower performance, reports the *African Economic Outlook 2011* (AEO), published jointly by the African Development Bank and the Organisation for Economic Co-operation and Development, can be explained principally by a dip in primary sector activity, which made a negative 0.1 per cent contribution to real GDP growth; electricity supply load-shedding; repeated strikes in several economic sectors and the unwillingness of the private sector to invest during an election period.

The poor performance of export agriculture is linked to the fall in the production of the main cash crops. Coffee production fell 35.2 per cent, from 144,700 tonnes in 2009 to 93,700 tonnes in 2010, after having risen 113.1 per cent in 2009 compared with 2008. Cocoa production dropped 6.1 per cent, from 1.30 million tonnes in 2009 to 1.23 million tonnes in 2010, after having increased 14.7 per cent in 2009. The reduction in the production of coffee and cocoa is partly the result of the ageing of plantations. Endemic cocoa diseases such as swollen shoot and brown rot, coupled with the abandonment of coffee plantations during periods when international prices were low, may also have contributed. An emergency programme has been set up to take charge of the phytosanitary treatment of the plantations most affected by parasites. Wider distribution of new varieties of coffee and cocoa and continued implementation of the plantation treatment programme should reduce disease. Efforts currently under way to restructure and modernise the coffee and cocoa sector and render its management more transparent should bring benefits some years hence. In early 2011 the 2010/11 cocoa season was starting to produce encouraging results. On 30 January 2011, total cocoa purchases had risen 19.1 per cent to a total 904,000 tonnes compared with 759,000 tonnes a year earlier. The volume declared to customs was up from 587,762 tonnes in the preceding year to 631,916 tonnes.

However, the political crisis and the temporary suspension of coffee and cocoa imports by the European Union (EU) had a negative effect on official production of these two crops and encouraged illegal trafficking with neighbouring countries. The Bourse du Café et du Cacao estimates that about 170,000 tonnes of cocoa leave Ivorian territory illegally every year for sale in neighbouring countries at a cost to the country of about CFAf17 billion (US$3.5 million).

The fall in export agriculture in 2010 has been tempered by positive results from cotton, cashew nuts, hevea and palm oil. After having fallen sharply in 2007 and 2008, cotton production improved markedly, rising by 31.8 per cent from 140,600 tonnes in 2009 to 185,300 tonnes in 2010. This vigorous recovery was attributable to the continued availability of public subsidies to producers for the acquisition of inputs. Coffee, cotton and cocoa, the main export products, provide livelihoods for around 9 million people, which is nearly half the Ivorian population. Cashew nut production has been showing remarkable, sustained growth since 2001. In 2010, Côte d'Ivoire produced 374,800 tonnes of cashew nuts compared with 340,300 tonnes in 2009, representing an increase of 10.1 per cent after a 9 per cent increase in 2009.

Oil and mining

Extractive production essentially concerns oil, gas and gold. The fall in the mining sector's growth rate, which stood at 15.9 per cent in 2010, is attributable to a reduction in oil and gold production. Oil production fell 19.1 per cent, from 18.54 million barrels in 2009 to 15 million barrels in 2010, under the combined effects of the temporary suspension of production on the Espoir field on block CI-26 and the natural depletion of the Lion-Panthère field on block CI-11. National gas production, on the other hand, recovered, increasing by 8.4 per cent, from 1.54 million cubic metres in 2009 to about 1.7 million cubic metres in 2010, after contracting 0.4 per cent in 2009. The increase in gas production is linked to the increase in gas production capacity from wells on the Espoir field and strong demand from local thermal electricity power stations.

KEY INDICATORS — Côte d'Ivoire

	Unit	2006	2007	2008	2009	2010
Population	m	17.38	20.16	*20.76	*21.39	*21.40
Gross domestic product (GDP)	US$bn	17.34	19.60	23.50	22.50	22.80
GDP per capita	US$	939	1,045	1,132	1,052	1,036
GDP real growth	%	-0.3	1.6	2.3	3.8	2.6
Inflation	%	4.9	2.1	6.3	1.0	1.4
Exports (fob) (goods)	US$m	8,144.0	8,475.9	10,390.1	10,503.3	–
Imports (fob) (goods)	US$m	6,067.0	5,931.6	7,068.6	6,318.1	–
Balance of trade	US$m	2,077.0	2,544.2	3,321.5	4,185.2	–
Current account	US$m	529.0	265.0	451.6	1,670.2	887.0
Total reserves minus gold	US$m	1,797.7	2,519.0	2,252.1	3,266.8	3,626.4
Foreign exchange	US$m	1,795.7	2,517.3	2,249.7	2,838.1	3,202.6
Exchange rate	per US$	496.60	454.40	418.59	472.19	495.28

* estimated figure

Despite this strong gas production performance, households and small and medium-sized enterprises (SMEs) have been facing shortages since the second quarter of 2010, the result of delays in the delivery of imported gas; maintenance stoppages at the Petroci oil company's gas canister filling plants; and increased demand for gas, which increased from 90,000 tonnes in 2006 to 120,000 in 2009.

The Espoir field represents about half the country's crude oil production, providing more than 25,000 barrels per day between 2006 and 2009. The field is operated by Canadian Natural Resources (CNR), which has 58.7 per cent of the rights. Its partners are Tullow Oil (21.3 per cent) and Petroci (20 per cent). Gas production from the Lion-Panthère field was 39 billion cubic feet (1.10 billion cubic metres) per day on average between 2006 and 2009. The field operator Afren has 48 per cent of the rights. Its partners are Petroci with 20.1 per cent, International Finance Corporation with 18.9 per cent and SK Energy with 13 per cent. Other fields are in operation. The Baobab field on block CI-40 had a production rate of more than 23,000 barrels per day on average between 2006 and 2009 and is the second largest field in terms of oil production.

Gold production contracted 28.0 per cent in 2010 after more than doubling between 2008 and 2009 with a remarkable 144.7 per cent increase. Uncertainty generated by the pre-election climate was one factor in this reduction. Among Côte d'Ivoire's solid ores, which are not yet heavily exploited, gold ore is the only one which has been mined on an industrial scale. Société des Mines d'Ity (SMI) has been active in the west of the country for more than 20 years, while Randgold is exploiting the seam near Tongon in the north. Gold reserves there are estimated at 90 tonnes. The start of production on these new reserves had been expected to produce an increase in output in 2011. Production had been expected to reach 5.33 tonnes in 2011 compared with 5.08 tonnes in 2010. The deterioration of the security situation made this forecast unrealistic.

In the 2011 edition of *Doing Business*, the World Bank's report on the business climate, Côte d'Ivoire is classed 169th out of 183 countries, dropping one place compared to its 2010 rank and six in relation to its 2009 rank. This unsatisfactory assessment indicates that considerable efforts are necessary to stimulate a recovery in economic activity based on the promotion of private investment and an improved business climate. In July 2010, a programme aimed at revitalising companies and improving their governance was officially launched. Its objective was to contribute to improving the performance of small and medium-sized enterprises and industries (SMEs/SMIs) and generally to improve the business climate. The government has taken other measures to improve the business climate, including providing training for legal executives specialising in trade as part of a project to support governance and capacity building in 2009. A reform plan that aims to improve the efficiency and equity of the judicial system and the publication of legal decisions has also been approved.

International trade

Economic partnerships between Côte d'Ivoire and emerging countries have shown marked progress. Several of these countries base their co-operation on the principles of sharing experience and knowledge, technology transfer and access to their markets. Côte d'Ivoire is particularly well placed in Africa for economic partnership with emerging countries by virtue of its agricultural, forest and mining resources and by its position in the WAEMU and ECOWAS economic zones. The country is all the more interested in co-operating with emerging countries because co-operation with its traditional partners, whether bilateral or multilateral, has become too narrow at a time when it needs to respond to numerous economic, scientific and technological challenges.

In Asia, China, South Korea, India, Singapore, Thailand, the Philippines, Brunei, Indonesia and Malaysia have all formed partnerships with Côte d'Ivoire. In the Middle East, Côte d'Ivoire has tried to diversify its range of partners by establishing relations with several countries in the region, including, notably, Saudi Arabia, Iran, Qatar and the United Arab Emirates, while at the same time preserving its traditional relations between Israel and Lebanon. Russia, Mexico and Brazil have also formed partnerships with Côte d'Ivoire.

Despite China's dominant position, trade with other emerging countries such as Brazil, India and Malaysia has also developed considerably in recent years, as has their investment in Côte d'Ivoire.

Consolidation of Côte d'Ivoire's links with emerging economies in the fields of development, international trade and direct investment is full of potential but can also create distortions. While it is true that the flow of exports and imports with China has increased strongly, Côte d'Ivoire still has a large trade deficit. The effect of these links on economic competitiveness can also have a negative impact on the Ivorian economy. Exportation of raw materials, for example, can result in loss of added value and failure to create jobs. The authorities therefore need to adopt measures to overhaul the structure of trade with emerging countries, while, at the same time, avoiding the pitfalls encountered in the course of co-operation with traditional partners. Furthermore, private investors in emerging countries have become increasingly wary since the start of the post-electoral crisis. Ivorian foreign policy towards emerging countries must take into account civil society associations and non-governmental organisations in order to forge closer partnerships and, above all, to facilitate the access of partner countries to the different social sectors. Furthermore, the real growth of the country depends on the training of personnel, low-cost technology transfer and innovation.

Elections

The first round of the presidential elections was successfully organised on 31 October 2010 after a campaign characterised by political pluralism as demonstrated by the presence of 14 candidates. The record 81 per cent rate of participation was seen as a sign of a real popular aspiration towards democracy. The second round resulted in a bipolarisation of the political field by setting the outgoing president Laurent Gbagbo and his La Majorité Presidentielle (LMP) against Alassane Ouattara of the Rassemblement des Houphouétistes pour la Démocratie et la Paix (RHDP). The RHDP is a coalition of the principal opposition parties: the Rassemblement des Républicains (RDR) (Rally of Republicans) and the Parti démocratique de la Côte d'Ivoire (PDCI) (Democratic Party of Côte d'Ivoire). The second round took place on 28 November 2010 and the participation rate was 71.28 per cent. Conflicting result announcements plunged the country into a political impasse, however. Alassane Ouattara was proclaimed the winner with 54.1 per cent of the vote by the chairman of the Independent Electoral Commission (CEI) but Laurent Gbagbo was declared the winner with 51.45 per cent of the vote by the Constitutional Council and refused to make way for his rival.

In its decision, the Constitutional Council took into account requests for results to be annulled in several départements under the control of the former rebel organisation the Forces Armées des Forces Nouvelles (FAFN), which was accused of massive fraud and human rights violations liable to distort the result of the vote.

According to the terms of the electoral legislation as laid down by the constitution and the electoral code, the material organisation of the vote is the responsibility of the Commission Electorale Indépendante (CEI) (Independent Electoral Commission) (Article 59 of the new electoral code), whose role it is to collect and announce the provisional results of the election. The same article provides that the commission should send a copy of the election report to the Constitutional Council, which, on the basis of Article 94 of the constitution, is responsible for announcing the final results.

The international community and the African Union recognised Alassane Ouattara as the victor. Confronted, however, with the political impasse created by Laurent Gbagbo's claim to retain the presidency, the international community applied economic, financial, diplomatic and political sanctions with the aim of isolating Gbagbo and forcing him to leave office. The conflict escalated in the first months of 2011 and in April Mr Gbagbo was arrested and Mr Ouattara resumed full power.

The post-electoral crisis and the sanctions imposed on Côte d'Ivoire are having a real impact on the economy. Security has broken down again and there has been an increase in the number of people displaced as a result of clashes between Laurent Gbagbo's Forces de Défense et de Sécurité (FDS) and Alassane Ouattara's FAFN. From an economic point of view, there has been a slowdown in activity, which has been aggravated by the closure one after the other of the majority of banks in the country. At the social level, poverty has been aggravated by numerous job losses and business closures. School closures in the Centre, North and West regions have resulted in the creation of substitute schools in the cities of Abidjan and Daloa for more than 3,000 pupils. According to humanitarian organisations, many Ivorians have taken refuge in neighbouring Liberia and Guinea. The former rebels, who have controlled several cities in the Centre, North and West regions for several years already, have made several incursions into the southern governmental half of the country. The capital, Abidjan, has been the scene of clashes between the FDS and the FAFN, with the loss of many human lives and large-scale material damage.

Risk assessment

Economy	Poor
Politics	Poor
Regional stability	Fair

COUNTRY PROFILE

Historical profile

1960 Côte d'Ivoire gained independence from France. Felix Houphouet-Boigny was selected to be the first president of Côte d'Ivoire by French colonial rulers as the most promising successor to their rule. Politicians, after independence, were drawn from oligarchs who had gained power through government positions or ran state-owned companies or gained positions in the ruling party, the Parti Démocratique de la Côte d'Ivoire (PDCI) (Democratic Party of Côte d'Ivoire).

1970s–1980s Economic decline increased pressure for political reform. Laurent Gbagbo, a lecturer and long-term dissident, emerged as the main opposition leader. He went into exile in 1982.

1988 Gbagbo returned from exile and founded the Front Populaire d'Ivoirie (FPI) (Ivorian Popular Front) to campaign for multi-party democracy.

1990 Houphouet-Boigny was forced to call elections, which were won by the PDCI. Houphouet-Boigny was re-elected president; Alassane Dramane Ouattara became prime minister.

1993 President Felix Houphouet-Boigny died after 30 years in power. Henri Konan-Bédié became president.

1995 Legislative and presidential elections were convincingly won by Konan-Bédié and the PDCI party.

1999 President Bédié was toppled in a military coup and General Robert Gueï seized the presidency. Tension between the Muslim north and Christian south was aggravated when Gueï banned Alassane Ouattara, the northern Muslim leader, from standing in the forthcoming presidential election.

2000 Laurent Gbagbo declared himself president following controversial elections. Gueï fled the country and supporters of Ouattara were killed after he called for new elections.

2002 An uprising split the country. The rebel Force Nouvelle (FN) (New Force) took control of the north and about 60 per cent of the country. Alassane Ouattara, leader of the Rassemblement des Républicains (RdR) (Republican Party) and head of FN, was granted citizenship, resolving his status for future elections. A cease-fire was negotiated and a French-manned buffer zone imposed between north and south. Former president Gueï was shot dead in Abidjan.

2004 UN peacekeepers were deployed, led by French troops. Rebels appointed ministers to join a coalition Government of National Reconciliation, but the PDCI pulled out amid ongoing violence. Abidjan was bombarded by rebel forces. When the Ivorian Air Force targeted Bouake, the northern stronghold of the FN, it killed nine French soldiers in the air raid. The French Air Force retaliated by destroying the Ivorian Air Force. Pro-government demonstrators rioted on the capital's streets, looting and threatening foreign, particularly French, targets.

2005 A UN report accused both rebel and government forces of atrocities including torture, systematic rape and mass execution. The government, FN and opposition leaders signed a deal to end the civil war. The Government of National Reconciliation was revived to take over until the next elections. Presidential elections were cancelled and President Gbagbo carried on as *de facto* president from his powerbase in the south. Presidents Obasanjo and Mbeki of Nigeria and South Africa respectively named Charles Konan Banny as interim prime minister. Banny was given powers to run an interim government (planned to end in 2006) and organise presidential elections; for this all militias had to be disarmed and voter registration undertaken.

2006 Banny faced his first test when international mediators called for the dissolution of parliament, which backed President Gbagbo. As a result, the ruling FPI briefly withdrew from the transitional government, accusing the mediators of a 'constitutional *coup d'etat*'. In the first meeting since 2000, the four main Ivorian leaders, Gbagbo (FPI), Bedie (PDCI), Ouattara (RdR) and Guillaume Soro (Mouvement Patriotique de Côte d'Ivoire (MPCI) (Patriotic Movement of Côte d'Ivoire)), attended a meeting with the prime minister to discuss plans for future elections and government. Militia loyal to Gbagbo failed to disarm as scheduled. Public identity hearings began to determine who could claim Ivorian citizenship and vote in the upcoming elections. The hearings were suspended following violent clashes between supporters of Gbagbo and Soro. Negotiators failed to agree terms for disarmament and voter registration. Presidential elections were postponed. The UN Security Council voted to extend President Gbagbo and Prime Minister Konan Banny's mandate for another year.

2007 A peace agreement was reached between President Gbagbo and Guillaume Soro (MPCI). A plan to integrate some members of the FN rebel militia with the regular army was mandated by presidential decree. Soro became prime minister. President Gbagbo visited the former rebel-held north and watched as weapons were destroyed at a peace party attended by five other African heads of state. The introduction of identity papers for all citizens sparked fears that large numbers would be fraudulently given to foreigners. A number of former northern rebels were absorbed into the regular army, the remainder were offered a three-month stipend to return to civilian life. Presidential and general elections were postponed.

2008 A public sector strike was settled when ministers cut their own wages by 50 per cent to help cover the cost of reintroducing subsidised fuel. Presidential and general elections were postponed.

2009 Presidential and general elections, delayed since 2005, were rescheduled; but were later postponed.

2010 Prime Minister Soro announced a new government in February, following the dismissal of his previous administration by the President, who had also dismissed the electoral commission. Voter registration was suspended after allegations of fraud as the lists were being drawn up. In March a newly appointed electoral commission set the presidential election for 31 October and tentatively set parliamentary elections for later in 2010. After six postponements, presidential elections were finally held on 31 October, in which Laurent Gbagbo won 38 per cent of the vote and Alassane Ouattara (Rassemblement des Républicains (RDR) (Republican Party) 32 per cent. However the opposition immediately lodged a formal challenge to the result in the constitution court, which failed on 7 November. International observers stated the elections were 'credible' despite some organisational deficiencies. As no candidate reached a necessary 50 per cent of the vote a run-off election was held on 21 November. The run-off lead to an immediate deadlock. On 1 December, supporters of Gbagbo accused the northern rebels of trying to steal the election on behalf of Ouattara and stopped an official of the electoral commission from reading out the results on national TV. Of the electoral regions nationwide, both candidates accepted the results from 13, but in the remaining seven under dispute, four were districts loyal to Ouattara, election commissioners loyal to Gbagbo prevented publication of the results. An attack on the offices of Ouattara, in which four supporters were killed by automatic gunfire, followed the failure of results being published within the 72-hour deadline. On 2 December, the chief electoral commissioner declared that Ouattara had won 54.1 per cent and Gbagbo 45.9 per cent. But Gbagbo's campaign team claimed because the results had not been announced in time they were therefore invalid and that Ouattara was in effect mounting a *coup détat*. On 3 December, the Constitutional Council annulled the electoral commission's results, and the votes from the seven disputed regions cancelled, stating that Gbagbo had won with 51.5 per cent of the vote, against 48.5 per cent for Ouattara. Foreign media were denied access and the country's borders were closed. Although the UN called on both sides to respect the outcome of the election Gbagbo was sworn into office on 4 December. On the same day Prime Minister Soro resigned, saying he recognised Ouattara as president-elect. President Gbagbo appointed Gilbert Marie N'gbo Aké as prime minister on 5 December. The AU suspended Côte d'Ivoire's membership on 10 December, until a 'democratically elected president effectively assumes state power'. Ouattara also took his official oath of office as president on 4 December and appointed Soro as his prime minister on 7 December. Parliamentary elections were postponed indefinitely. By 24 December the UN, US, EU, AU and Ecowas had all recognised Ouattara as the legitimate president of Côte d'Ivoire.

2011 On 3 January Laurent Gbagbo rejected the Ecowas and AU-sponsored talks which had offered him legal amnesty and residence in exile if he agreed to stand down as president. The AU, led by Nigeria, warned Gbagbo that he could be unseated militarily. Financial assets of Gbagbo were seized by Swiss banks on 19 January. Henri Dacoury-Tabley, governor of the central bank and a Gbagbo appointee, refused to accept Gbagbo's signature for funds and resigned on 22 January, following international pressure. On 26 January, Gbagbo ordered the assets of all local branches of the Central Bank of West African States (BCEAO) to be seized. By 14 February, major foreign banks, Paribas, Citibank and Standard Chartered, had suspended operations in Côte d'Ivoire due to 'security concerns'. Four domestic banks had also closed as depositors queued to withdraw their money. On 18 February, Gbagbo's administration took control of those foreign banks that had suspended operations. Ecowas asked the UN in March if it would adopt a mandate to use military intervention as a 'last resort'. By the end of March an estimated one million people had fled their homes due to the on-going political violence. At the request of the UN peacekeepers, French troops and tanks surrounded the presidential palace. Laurent Gbagbo was captured by French special forces, on 11 April; he was taken to the headquarters of Mr Ouattara. International sanctions began to be lifted after Gbagbo was deposed, but without a functioning banking system trade in cocoa was severely hampered. In mid-April the World Bank said it was ready to offer help, including reactivating programmes worth some US$100 million. The most notorious warlord, Ibrahim (IB) Coulibaly was killed by pro-Ouattara forces in Abidjan on 27 April. He had been a supporter of President Ouattara, but had refused to disarm after the capture of Gbagbo. The banks reopened on 28 April, leading to a rush to withdraw cash and receive delayed salaries. On 1 May President Quattara announced the setting up of a truth and reconciliation commission headed by former prime minister, Charles Konan Banny. On 5 May Switzerland moved to freeze assets (which had already been seized in January) of Gbagbo. The funds could to be blocked for up to three years, pending a request from Côte d'Ivoire for legal assistance to ensure the return of the funds. Alassane Ouattara took the oath of office on 6 May, with the inauguration ceremony held on 22 May, attended by French President Nicolas Sarkozy and the UN Secretary General Ban Ki-moon and several African heads of state. Amnesty International said in a report published in May that both sides in the recent conflict had committed war crimes. It also said that all those who had committed human rights violations should be prosecuted. On 12 July, the economic and finance minister reported that Côte d'Ivoire had been in default of its international debts since January and that it was unable to service its external debt in 2011, but would resume its payments to bondholders in 2012 following a deal agreed with the IMF. In July, officials from the National Museum of Abidjan reported to Interpol the loss of around 80 historic and culturally precious gold pieces stolen during the battle for Abidjan between the rival forces of Gbagbo and Ouattara. The stolen items included the best gold jewellery, masks and statues in the museum's collection, valued at an estimated US$6 million, which suggested insider knowledge and help given to the thieves. Michel Gbagbo (son of former president, Laurent Gbagbo) was arrested on 10 August and charged with post-election violence. On 16 August, Laurent Gbagbo himself was charged with economic crimes, including looting, embezzlement and armed robbery. A Truth, Reconciliation and Dialogue Commission was inaugurated on 28 September to consider the widespread violence following the presidential elections in 2010. Former prime minister Charles Konan Banny heads the Commission. Former president Gbagbo was flown to the ICC in

The Hague on 30 November, to stand trial for crimes against humanity committed between 16 December 2010–12 April 2011.

Political structure
Constitution
A multi-party system is enshrined in the constitution, but in practice no party other than Parti Démocratique de la Côte d'Ivoire (PDCI) (Democratic Party of Côte d'Ivoire) was allowed to operate until May 1990 when the government legalised party political activity.
A 1990 constitutional amendment allowed for the appointment of a prime minister, with the speaker of the National Assembly empowered to assume the office of president of the republic prior to a presidential election in the event of a sudden presidential vacancy.
The constitution was suspended following a military takeover in December 1999. In 2000, the constitution was revised, stipulating that presidential candidates must be of Ivorian origin, born of parents who are not naturalised Ivorians, should not have dual nationality and must have lived in Côte d'Ivoire for a minimum and uninterrupted period of five years. Those with at least 21 years of Ivorian citizenship are eligible to vote.
Form of state
Republic
The executive
Executive power rests with the president (elected by universal suffrage for a five-year term) who appoints the cabinet. The president can veto legislation, but his veto can in theory be overridden by a two-thirds vote of the National Assembly.
National legislature
The unicameral National Assembly has 225 members, elected for five-year terms. Internal political crisis and the civil war hampered parliamentary democracy. Elections in 2009 should restart the process.
Legal system
All civil, criminal, commercial and administrative cases come under the jurisdiction of the tribunaux de première instance (magistrates' courts), the assize courts and the court of appeal.
Last elections
31 October and 21 November 2010 (presidential); 10 December 2000 (parliamentary).
Results: Parliamentary: Parliamentary: Populaire Ivorienne (FPI) (Ivorian Popular Front) won 96 seats,); Parti Démocratique de la Côte d'Ivoire (PDCI) (Democratic Party of Côte d'Ivoire) 94. Presidential (first round): Laurent Gbagbo (FPI) won 38.3 per cent of the vote, Alassane Ouattara (Rassemblement des Républicains (RDR) (Republican Party) 32.1 per cent, Henri Konan Bédié 25.2 per cent; turnout was 85 per cent. Runoff: Ouattara won 54.1 per cent and Gbagbo 45.9 per cent. Turnout was 70–80 per cent.
Next elections
2011 (tentative parliamentary); 2015 (presidential)

Political parties
Ruling party
Coalition: Front Populaire Ivorienne (FPI) (Ivorian Popular Front); Forces Nouvelles (FN) (New Forces); Rassemblement des Républicains (RDR) (Rally of Republicans); Parti démocratique de la Côte d'Ivoire (PDCI) (Democratic Party of Côte d'Ivoire); Mouvement des Forces d'Avenir (MFA) (Movement of the Forces of the Future); Parti Ivoirien des Travailleurs (PIT) (Ivorian Workers Party); Union Démocratique et Citoyenne de Côte d'Ivoire (UDCY) (Citizens Democratic Union of Côte d'Ivoire) and Union pour la Démocratie et la Paix en Côte d'Ivoire (UDPCI) (Union for Democracy and Peace in Côte d'Ivoire) (formed 7 Apr 2007)

Population
21.40 million (2010)*
Last census: November 1998:15,366,672
Population density: 44 inhabitants per square km. Urban population: 43 per cent (1995–2001).
Annual growth rate: 2.2 per cent 1994–2004 (WHO 2006)
Ethnic make-up
Akan (the Baoule subgroup accounts for 23 per cent of the population), Kru (the Bete subgroup accounts for 18 per cent), Senoufo 15 per cent, Malinke 11 per cent, Agni, Mande. There are nearly 3 million foreign Africans (mainly from Burkina Faso and Mali) and an estimated 130,000–330,000 non-Africans (French 30,000 and Lebanese 100,000–300,000).
Religions
Islam (60 per cent), Christianity (mainly Roman Catholic) (22 per cent), traditional animist beliefs (18 per cent) (some of these are also numbered among the Christians and Muslims).

Education
Education is provided free of charge. Primary education lasts for six years from the age of six. Secondary education lasts for up to seven years from the age of 13. There are universities at Abidjan and Yamoussoukro, but many students attend French universities.
Only 50 per cent of girls attend primary school.
Literacy rate: 60 per cent, youth rate (15–24) (Unesco 2005)
Pupils per teacher: 41 in primary schools.

Health
HIV/Aids
Aids-related costs typically absorb 11 per cent of the total public health budget.
HIV prevalence: 7.0 per cent aged 15–49 in 2003 (World Bank)
Life expectancy: 44 years, 2004 (WHO 2006)
Fertility rate/Maternal mortality rate: 4.9 births per woman, 2004 (WHO 2006); maternal mortality six per 1,000 live births (World Bank).
Child (under 5 years) mortality rate (per 1,000): 117 per 1,000 live births; 24 per cent of children under aged five are malnourished (World Bank).
Head of population per physician: 0.12 physicians per 1,000 people, 2004 (WHO 2006)

Welfare
An employer must declare each worker employed to the Caisse National de Prevoyance Sociale (CNPS), the national social security fund, and is responsible for deducting social security contributions paid by the worker. Large firms are also expected to provide in-house medical care.
Social security is divided into three areas: family allowances, retirement pensions, medical care and compensation payments in case of accident at work. There are no payments for illness unconnected to work. Contributions are paid every quarter by firms employing fewer than 20, and each month for those employing over 20, people. The CNPS funds are ring-fenced from the government's main budget.
The social security system does not cover unemployment, which is paid monthly through labour exchanges and financed by a national solidarity contribution of 1 per cent of salary, which is levied on each employee's wages.
Child labour is used in domestic service, farming, mining and factory work as well as casual labour in street markets. Law restricting the age of employment is enforced in large enterprises but is more lax in small industries and the informal sector. Local opinion concerning child labour is equivocal; while rural children are needed for subsistence farming, and urban street children can avoid destitution through work, the need for change would seem to be moot.

Main cities
Abidjan (economic and diplomatic centre, estimated population 4.9 million in 2005), Yamoussoukro (political capital since 1983, 454,929), Bouaké (549,800), Daloa (309,363), Gagnoa

(215,664), Korhogo (349,953), San Pédro (202,714), Soubré (254,247).

Languages spoken

Approximately 60 local African languages are spoken, including Dioula, Baoule, Akan, Kru and Bete.

Official language/s

French

Media

According to the France-based media watchdog Reporters Without Borders, Côte d'Ivoire is one of the Africa's most dangerous places for journalists to carry out their work.

Press

Dailies: In French, national newspapers includes the government-owned, *Fraternité Matin* (www.fratmat.info) and *Notre Voie* (www.notrevoie.com) and *Le Partriote* (www.lepatriote.net), which are owned by the political parties PCT and UDR-Mwinda respectively. Other, national, private newspapers include *Le Nouveau Reveil,24 Heures* (www.24heuresci.com), *Le Front* and *Soir Info* (www.soirinfo.com). Newspapers with the same internet address (http://news.abidjan.net), include *L'Inter* and *Le Jour* and *Fraternité Matin*. Newspapers published in Abidjan include *Le Courrier d'Abidjan* (www.lecourrierdabidjan.info), *Le Matin d'Abidjan* (www.lematindabidjan.com) and *Nord-Sud* (www.nordsudmedia.info).

Broadcasting

For most of the population, radio is the principal medium for news and information. Radiodiffusion Télévision Ivoirienne (RTI) (www.rti.ci) is the national, public broadcaster funded through a license fee, advertising revenue and grants.

Radio: There are many private radio stations with a limited area of broadcasting around cities and other urban regions. RTI relays its two channels, RTI Frequence 2 (www.frequence2.ci) and La Nationale (www.lanationale.ci), with entertainment, news, education, information and cultural programmes, through a network of numerous, local stations. Other private stations include Nostalgie (www.nostalgie.ci) from Abidjan and Radio Jam (www.radiojam.ci), from Yamoussoukro. Religious stations include the Catholic Radio Paix Sanwi (www.radiopaixsanwi.net) and the Islamic Radio al Bayane (http://radio-albayane.com).

Television: The government controls the only terrestrial TV station although private, pay-to-view cable and satellite services are available through the French-owned Canal Satellite Horizons (www.canalhorizons.com).

RTI (www.rti.ci) operates La Premiere, a national channel and TV2, which for viewers of terrestrial TV can only be received within a radius of 150km of Abidjan. RTI also have dedicated sports and music channels. RTI services can be received throughout the country and also into some neighbouring countries via satellite services.

News agencies

National news agency: AIP (Agence Ivoirienne de Presse)

APA (African Press Agency): www.apanews.net

Panapress: www.panapress.com

Economy

The wealth of Côte d'Ivoire comes from its natural resources. It has small reserves of petroleum and natural gas and the country operates an oil refinery and hydroelectric power stations, which results in Côte d'Ivoire being a significant energy exporter in its region. Agriculture accounts for around 25 per cent of GDP, roughly the same as the industrial sector with the service sector constituting the remaining 50 per cent. Agricultural exports of cocoa (Côte d'Ivoire is the world's leading producer, providing around 40 per cent of total), coffee, bananas, rubber, palm oil and pineapples, along with tuna and timber and constitutes over 50 per cent of both export revenue and GDP. The 2010 cocoa harvest was a record crop and warehouses in the south of Côte d'Ivoire were stocked ready for export before a disputed presidential election in November 2010. However, the EU, Côte d'Ivoire's single largest market, rejected any purchases of cocoa from Côte d'Ivoire until the post-presidential election political crisis was resolved. On 8 March 2011, Laurent Gbagbo (who lost the election but was refusing to stand down as president) ordered his government to take control of all cocoa production and exports. His rival, Alassane Ouattara had called for a temporary ban on exports in an effort to deny Gbagbo the funds.

The country has a good and extensive infrastructure, including a large, modern port, which allows for rapid transport of goods and people.

GDP growth was 2.3 per cent in 2008 and rose to 3.8 in 2009, despite a reversal in GDP, down from US$23.5 billion in 2008 to US$22.5 billion in 2009; per capita income fell from US$1,132 in 2008 to US$1,052 in 2009. This was largely due to increases in global food prices as the global economic crisis cut raw material and commodity prices. Remittances were US$185 million in 2009 (0.8 per cent of GDP), but were estimated to have fallen to US$177 million in 2010.

In April 2009 the International Monetary Fund agreed to forgive US$3 billion of national debt under the Heavily Indebted Poor Countries Initiative (HIPCI) and agreed to lend Côte d'Ivoire US$565 million for poverty reduction and fiscal transparency, provided reform programmes were undertaken. Outstanding debt owed to the Paris Club of creditors was restructured and some payments deferred, in an agreement signed in May. Total repayments were reduced by 92 per cent from US$4.6 billion to US$391 million.

There was disruption to the economy caused by the disputed presidential elections in November 2010, when incumbent president Laurent Gbagbo refused to cede power in favour of the (internationally recognised) winner of the elections, Alassane Ouattara. US$163 million of the country's assets held in the central bank were seized by Gbagbo supporters and cocoa exports were slowed. By January 2011, it was predicted that GDP growth would contract by 5 per cent in the first quarter of 2011, as worry that an interest payment of US$29 million due to be paid in April 2011 by Gbagbo would be missed; the value of Côte d'Ivoire's US$2.3 billion Eurobonds fell to the lowest since they were issued in April 2010.

The economic future of Côte d'Ivoire is dependent on a resolution of the political crisis. The country has the potential for solid growth, with a history of foreign direct investment providing 40–45 per cent of total capital in domestic businesses, typically from French firms. However this record could be jeopardised if the instability continues and as international economic sanctions cut deeper into the regime of Gbagbo.

External trade

As a member of the Economic Community of West African States (Ecowas). Côte d'Ivoire is also a member of the West African Economic and Monetary Union (WAEMU) with a common external tariff and using the common currency, the CFA franc.

The northern region is the primary area for growing cocoa, the country's major export commodity, while the principal port for international trade is in the south. The country is a hub for international trade in West Africa and transhipment is an important element of the economy.

The UN banned the export of rough diamonds after it was found they were used in the purchase of weapons during the civil war. Since the peace accord was signed in 2007, calls for a relaxation in the ban have grown and the introduction of a state-run buying house to regulate and promote legitimate diamond sales.

Imports

Principal imports include fuel, capital equipment and foodstuffs.

Main sources: Nigeria (typically 21 per cent of total), France (14 per cent), China (7 per cent).

Exports

Principal exports include cocoa, coffee, timber, fuel, cotton, bananas, pineapples, palm oil, fish and diamonds (currently banned).

Main destinations: The Netherlands (typically 14 per cent total of total), France (11 per cent), US (8 per cent).

Agriculture

Farming

The agricultural sector is the mainstay of the economy. It accounts for around 30 per cent of GDP, earns over 60 per cent of export revenues and employs some 54 per cent of the workforce. The climate in some parts of the north is suitable for the production of wheat to support an estimated local consumption of about 200,000 tonnes a year.

The principal cash crops are cocoa and coffee. Côte d'Ivoire accounts for around 40 per cent of total world cocoa production. The cocoa and coffee sectors have undergone liberalisation and institutional reform since 1995. This has included transferring some responsibility for price stabilisation to the private sector, making operations more transparent, and reducing customs duties on cocoa and abolishing them for coffee. Price liberalisation was achieved for coffee in 1998 and cocoa in 1999, when Caistab, the price stabilisation fund, was disbanded and replaced by a private-sector operation. Privatisation of the coffee and cocoa sectors was highly controversial among farmer.

The Fonds de Regulation et de Controle (FRC), is the national cocoa and coffee marketing institution, which is owned by farmers (45 per cent), banks (20 per cent), insurance companies (20 per cent) and the government (15 per cent). The FRC determines minimum guaranteed farm-gate prices and bears the cost of implementing the price stabilisation mechanism, which cushions farmers' exposure to volatile international markets. Coffee and cocoa production is regulated by the Autorité de Regulation du Café et Cacao (ARCC), which determines export quotas. The 2010 cocoa harvest was a record crop and warehouses in the south of Côte d'Ivoire were stocked ready for export before a disputed presidential election in November 2010. However, the EU, Côte d'Ivoire's single largest market, rejected any purchases of cocoa from Côte d'Ivoire until the post-presidential election political crisis was resolved. On 8 March 2011, Laurent Gbagbo (who lost the election but was refusing to stand down as president) ordered his government to take control of all cocoa production and exports. His rival, Alassane Ouattara had called for a temporary ban on exports in an effort to deny Gbagbo the funds.

Fishing

Côte d'Ivoire is the second largest exporter of canned tuna in the world. The port of Abidjan handles more than 400,000 tonnes of fish a year. The government has launched a series of initiatives to modernise local fishing and assist local fishermen to benefit from the country's 150,000 hectares of lagoon and 350,000 hectares of lakes and rivers. The EU and Côte d'Ivoire run a fisheries agreement which provides EU fishermen with fishing rights in Côte d'Ivoire waters in return for the funding of research and training programmes.

Forestry

Côte d'Ivoire has 17 per cent forest cover and an additional 25 per cent of other wooded land. Ten per cent of forests are inside protected reserves, including the Parc National de Tai which has the largest tract of primary rainforest in West Africa. The southern half of the country, which was once covered by tropical forest, has suffered extensive deforestation for logging and agriculture. The northern half contains savannah woodland. Forestry is important and Côte d'Ivoire has been Africa's leading exporter of sawn timber. Wood is also an important source of domestic fuel.

Industry and manufacturing

The industrial and manufacturing sectors expanded rapidly following independence in 1960, but suffered some setbacks in the late 1980s as a result of increased foreign competition and a decline in consumer purchasing power. In addition, the industrial plant is ageing and has often not been renewed on account of the low level of private investment.

During the 1990s, privatisation reduced the state's role in industry and manufacturing. Policy has focussed upon encouraging private sector involvement in the hydrocarbons sector which it is hoped will encourage the expansion of the industrial and manufacturing sectors.

Environment

In July 2010 the Anglo-Dutch shipping company Trafigura was fined €1 million (US$1.3 million) by a court in The Netherlands after it had been found guilty of exporting and dumping toxic waste to Abidjan in 2006. In 2007 Trafigura had paid the government US$160 million without admitting liability and US$50 million shared among individuals harmed by the waste. Trafigura continues to deny responsibility for the spill.

Mining

The mining sector holds considerable potential and could become the second mainstay of the economy. It contributes around 3.7 per cent to GDP annually and employs 1 per cent of the workforce. A state company, Société pour le Développement Minier Ivorien (Sodemi) carries out exploration and production, in some cases in joint ventures with foreign companies. Gold is found in three main reserves: Issia, Lobo and Ity.

Diamonds have traditionally been mined by small independent prospectors, but the incidence of diamond smuggling and consequent loss of revenue prompted the Ministry of Mines to introduce licences for prospectors and diamond purchasing offices in 2000. Diamonds are produced at Séguéla and Tortiya. Reserves at Séguéla are estimated at 150,000 carats, and at Tortiya 450,000 carats.

Grand-Lehou produces 90,000 to 100,000 tonnes of manganese per year. A deposit, estimated at 1.2 million tonnes (47 per cent manganese), was discovered at Ziemougoula, near Odienne.

A large iron ore deposit at Monogaga-Victory has estimated reserves of 140 million tonnes. Further reserves, estimated at three billion tonnes, are located on the border with Guinea at Mount Nyumba and Mount Kalayo.

Hydrocarbons

Proven oil reserves were one billion barrels in 2008, with production at 70,000 barrels per day (bpd). The majority of oil reserves are located offshore in the shallow water Espoir field and the deep-water Baobab field. Domestic consumption is around 26,000bpd with the remainder exported, representing almost 30 per cent of foreign revenue, surpassing traditional export commodities of cocoa and coffee. The state-run Société Nationale d'Operations Pétrolières de la Côte d'Ivoire (Petroci) is responsible for the hydrocarbons industry through its four subsidiaries. Petroci Holding manages the oil sector; Petroci Exploration-Production is responsible for upstream hydrocarbon activities; Petroci-Gaz deals with the natural gas sector; Petroci Industries-Services manages all other related services.

In 2008 Côte d'Ivoire joined the Extractive Industries Transparency Initiative (EITI) and will have until 2010 to become compliant with EITI criteria. Further investment by foreign companies should be forthcoming through membership.

There is one operational oil refinery, with a capacity of 65,200bpd, sufficient to supply domestic requirements, as well as some export volumes for neighbouring countries. The refinery is connected to the Lion and Panther fields by pipelines and receives crude oil from Nigeria for processing. Construction of another refinery began in 2008, with a capacity of

60,000bpd. Both facilities are located in Abidjan.
Proven natural gas reserves were 28.3 billion cubic metres (cum) in 2008, with production over 1.3 billion cum, primarily consumed in domestic power stations.
Any coal produced or imported is commercially insignificant.

Energy
Installed electricity generating capacity was 1,086 MW in 2007. Around 70 per cent of annual production is generated by gas-powered plants, with a declining contribution from hydroelectric sources. Côte d'Ivoire is an exporter of electricity, supplying Ghana, Benin, Togo, Mali and Burkina Faso, through the West African Power Pool (Wapp). The state-owned Société d'Opération Ivoirienne d'Electricité (Sopie) is responsible for strategic planning and implementation of national standards in electricity provision.
The 288WM Azito power station provides around 30 per cent of the country's power and is located in Abidjan. A government sponsored rural electrification programme has extended access to electricity to the distribution system for around 50 per cent of the rural population. Investment in the programme is ongoing.

Financial markets
Stock exchange
Afribourse (Bourse Régionale des Valeurs Moblières) (BRVM)

Banking and insurance
Abidjan is traditionally a major regional banking centre. There is no clear distinction between commercial, merchant and development banks since they may all accept deposits and engage in long- and short-term financing. Local banks generally handle retail banking and export-crop financing as well as funding small- and medium-sized businesses and housing.
Some specialise in development of industry, agriculture and small businesses.
Côte d'Ivoire has a liberal policy towards foreign banks, but entry has become more difficult in recent years because of the large number of banks already present. A minimum capital is required for a new bank to start operating, but Ivorian participation is not obligatory.
Political instability has undermined the Ivorian banking sector, with the African Development Bank (AfDB) tranferring its head-quarters from Côte d'Ivoire to Tunisia in early 2003.
Central bank
Banque Centrale des Etats de l'Afrique de l'Ouest
Main financial centre
Abidjan

Time
GMT

Geography
Côte d'Ivoire is in West Africa on the Atlantic coast, bordered by Liberia and Guinea to the west, Mali and Burkina Faso to the north, and Ghana to the east.
To the south is a 470 kilometre coastline on the Gulf of Guinea, the eastern part of which is inset with lagoons.
The terrain rises from the coastal plains to a plateau, 300 metres high for most of its length, rising to 1,200 metres near the country's western border.
The three main geographical areas are the equatorial zone along the coast, the tropical rain forests of the south and the drier savannah belt in the north.
There are four main rivers, the Bandama, Comoe, Sassandra and Cavally, but they are not navigable for long distances due to rapids.
Hemisphere
Northern

Climate
There are four distinct seasons in the centre and south of the country. Here the climate is tropical, with a long dry season running from December–April, followed by the rainy season from May–July. From August–September a dry spell is followed in October–November by a short rainy spell.
Average temperatures on the southern coastal plains are 21–34 degrees Celsius (C). Humidity is 80–90 per cent. Annual rainfall can be as heavy as 2.5 metres spread over about 140 days. In the central region temperature ranges are 14–39 degrees C. Annual rainfall varies from 1–2.5 metres.
In the northern savannah the climate is more extreme, but less humid with temperatures between 21–40 degrees C. Rainfall averages 1.4 metres a year. There are two seasons, rains from July–November and the dry season from December–June.

Dress codes
When calling on senior personnel, businessmen should wear suits, even though this may be uncomfortable in Abidjan's hot and humid climate. The capital, Yamoussoukro, is less humid and at an altitude of 220 metres is cooler. In general loose-fitting, tropical lightweight clothing is advisable.
Women may wear sleeveless cotton dresses or lightweight skirts and blouses, and this mode of dress is adequate for business calls.

Entry requirements
Passports
Required by all except particular document holders of certain African countries.
Visa
Required by all except citizens of other Ecowas countries, and nationals of Andorra, Chad, Monaco, Morocco, Seychelles, Tunisia and Vatican City, for stays of up to three months. Applications for business visas require a letter from the visitor's company accepting responsibility for any expenses incurred, and a letter of invitation (can be faxed copy) from host company in Côte d'Ivoire.
Currency advice/regulations
The import of CFA francs is unlimited; export is limited to CFAf10,000. The import of euros is unlimited, all other currencies must be declared. Export of all foreign currencies is limited to CFAf25,000, or the amount declared on arrival.
Travellers cheques are accepted in banks and hotels.

Health (for visitors)
Mandatory precautions
Yellow fever vaccination certificate.
Advisable precautions
Cholera, hepatitis A and E and typhoid vaccinations are strongly recommended and polio immunisation is a benefit. Malaria prophylaxis should be taken as risk exists throughout the country all year.
Avoid tap water and drink only bottled beverages (including water) or beverages made with boiled water; cooked food is advisable and all fruit should be peeled.
Bilharzia is present, use only well chlorinated swimming pools. Rabies and sleeping sickness are a risk. It is advisable to pack a sterilised syringe kit.

Hotels
Abidjan and Yamoussoukro have several five-star hotels. There are a wide range of other hotels in the other main centres.
Tipping usually 10–15 per cent.

Credit cards
American Express and Mastercard are widely accepted; charge cards are of limited use.

Public holidays (national)
Fixed dates
1 Jan (New Year's Day), 1 May (Labour Day), 7 Aug (Independence Day), 15 Aug (Assumption Day), 1 Nov (All Saints' Day), 9 Nov (Day of Mourning), 15 Nov (Peace Day), 7 Dec (Félix Houphouët-Boigny Remembrance Day), 25 Dec (Christmas Day).
Variable dates
Easter Monday, Ascension Day, Whit Monday, Eid al Adha, Eid al Fitr, Birth of the Prophet, Ascent of the Prophet.
Some companies allow an informal one-day holiday before or after a Sunday holiday
Islamic year 1433 (26 Nov 2011–14 Nov 2012): The Islamic year contains 354 or 355 days, with the result that

Muslim feast advance by 10–12 dars against the Gregorain calendar. Dates of feasts vary according to the sighting of the new moon, so cannot be forecast exactly.

Working hours
Banking
Mon–Fri: 0800–1130 and 1430–1630.
Business
Mon–Fri: 0800–1200 and 1430–1700.
Government
Mon–Fri: 0730/0800–1200 and 1430–1730.
Shops
Mon–Fri: 0800–1200 and 1530–1830/1900, Sat: 0800–1200 and 1430–1730.

Telecommunications
Mobile/cell phones
There are several 900 and a 1800 GSM services operating in main urban areas.

Electricity supply
220V AC, 50 cycles

Social customs/useful tips
Ivorians like to shake hands and exchange greetings and other pleasantries before getting down to business.
It is considered polite to arrive punctually to social occasions when kissing on the cheek and hugging are reserved only for old friends.

Security
There are ongoing security problems in the country in general and increased trouble in the west – visitors are advised not to travel to the area. Foreign visitors should register their presence with their diplomatic missions on arrival, although many suspended their representation in 2005. Visitors must take added precaution for their own safety and take note of local warnings.

Getting there
Air
National airline: Air Ivoire: flies to France, South Africa and Dubai.
International airport/s: Abidjan-Félix Houphouet-Boigny (ABJ), is the country's airport hub accepting all intercontinental flights. It is 16km from city; duty-free shop, restaurant, bank, post office, pharmacy, car hire.
Yamoussoukro (ASK) accepts regional flights .
Airport tax: Departure tax: continental, CFAf3,000; intercontinental: CFAf5,000.
Surface
Road: There are good links from Ghana, Burkina Faso, Guinea and Liberia.
Rail: Travellers should check information concerning regular services from Burkina Faso, connecting Ouagadougou with Abidjan. Sleeping and restaurant facilities are available for these long journeys.

Getting about
National transport
Air: Air Ivoire no longer operates internal flights. Contact local airports for information on charter flights.
Departure tax: CFAf800.
Road: Extensive network of roads stretching from south to north with transverse roads interconnecting.
Buses: The once extensive service has been curtailed by the civil war. Contact local operators concerning services.
Taxis: Bush taxis run to all parts of the country.
Rail: A 1,145km network from Abidjan to Ouagadougou passes through Agboville, Dimbokra, Bouaké, Katiola and Ferkessedougou.
City transport
Taxis: In Abidjan, red taxis with meters can be hailed or ordered by telephone in main centres. Two tariffs operate: one from 0600–2400, the other 2400–0600. The early morning tariff is double that for the day and evening. Do not hesitate to haggle over the fare, especially if the meter is not running, or if arriving at the airport.
Buses, trams & metro: Buses usually run from 0600–2100 or 2200, operated in Abidjan by state-run Sotra.
Most hotels have their own airport buses. Check at hotel booths near the terminal exit.
Car hire
Self-drive and chauffeur-driven cars can be hired in Abidjan, Bouaké, Daloa, Gagnoa, Man and Sassandra.
An international driving licence is required (not less than 12 months old). Drivers must be at least 21-years-old. Seat-belts must be worn in front seats. Traffic drives on the right.

BUSINESS DIRECTORY

The addresses listed below are a selection only. While World of Information makes every endeavour to check these addresses, we cannot guarantee that changes have not been made, especially to telephone numbers and area codes. We would welcome any corrections.

Telephone area codes
The international direct dialling (IDD) code for Côte d'Ivoire is +225, followed by subscriber's number.

Useful telephone numbers
Ambulance (SAMU): 185, 2044-3445, 2044-5353.
Police (emergency): 111, 170.
International telephone enquiries: 160.
National telephone enquiries: 120.

Chambers of Commerce
American Chamber of Commerce, 01 PO Box 3394, Abidjan 01 (tel: 2021-4616; fax: 2022-2437; email: amcham@AfricaOnline.co.ci).

Côte d'Ivoire Chambre de Commerce et Industrie, 6 Avenue Joseph Anoma, PO Box 1399, Abidjan 01 (tel: 2033-1600; fax: 2032-3942; email: mail@ccici.org).

French Chambre de Commerce et d'Industrie, 141 Boulevard de Marseille, Immeuble Jean Lefebvre, 01 PO Box 189, Abidjan 18 (tel: 2025-8206; fax: 2024-1000; email: ccifci@ccif.ci).

Banking
Bank of Africa Côte d'Ivoire, BP 4132, 11 Ave Joseph Anoma, Abidjan 01 (tel: 2033-1536; fax: 2033-2398, 2032-8993).

Banque Atlantique (Côte d'Ivoire SA); BP 04, Immeuble Atlantique, Avenue Nogues, 1036 Abidjan 04 (tel: 2031-5950; fax: 2021-6852).

Banque de l'Habitat de Côte d'Ivoire, BP 2325, 22 Ave Joseph Anoma, Abidjan 01 (tel: 2022-6000; fax: 2022-5818).

Banque Internationale pour le Commerce et l'Industrie de la Côte d'Ivoire SA; Avenue Franchet d'Espérey, 01 BP 1298 Abidjan 01 (tel: 2020-1600, 2020-1700; fax: 2020-1700) .

Banque Paribas Côte d'Ivoire; BP 09, 17 Avenue Terrasson de Fougères, Abidjan 17 (tel: 2021-8686, 2021-3032; fax: 2021-8823).

BIAO-Côte d'Ivoire; BP 1274, 8/10 Avenue Joseph Anoma, Abidjan 01 (tel: 2020-0720, 2020-0722; fax: 2020-0700).

Caisse Autonome d'Amortissement Société d'Etat, BP 670, Immeuble SCIAM, Ave Marchant, Abidjan 01 (tel: 2021-0611, 2032-8575; fax: 2021-3578).

Cofipa Investment Bank Côte d'Ivoire, BP 411, Rue Botreau Roussel/ Ave Delafosse, Abidjan 04 (tel: 2021-8452; fax: 2021-8599).

Compagnie Bancaire de l'Atlantique en Côte d'Ivoire, 01 BP, Immeuble Atlantique, Avenue Nogues, 522 Abidjan 01 (tel: 2021-2804, 2030-1520; fax: 2021-0798).

Compagnie Financière de la Côte d'Ivoire; BP 1566, Tour BICICI 01, Rue Gourgas 15e étage, Abidjan 01 (tel: 2021-2732; fax: 2021-2643, 2020-1700).

Ecobank Côte d'Ivoire SA, BP 4107, Immeuble Alliance, 1 Av Terrasson de Fougères, Abidjan 01 (tel: 2031-9200, 2021-1041; fax: 2021-8816).

Société Générale de Banques en Côte d'Ivoire SA; BP 1355, 5 & 7 Avenue Joseph Anoma, Abidjan 01 (tel:

2020-1234, 2020-1111; fax: 2020-1482, 2020-1486).

Société Générale de Financement et de Participation en Côte d'Ivoire (SOGEFINANCE); BP 3904, 5-7 Avenue Joseph Anoma, Abidjan 01 (tel: 2022-5530, 2022-1234; fax: 2032-6760, 2020-1492).

Société Ivoirienne de Banque, BP 1300, Immeuble Alpha 2000, 34 Boulevard de la Republique, Abidjan 01 (tel: 2020-0000; fax: 2021-9741).

Central bank
Banque Centrale des Etats de l'Afrique de l'Ouest, Direction National, Angle Boulevard Botreau-Roussel et Avenue Delafosse, PO Box 1769, Abidjan (tel: 208-500; fax: 222-852).

Stock exchange
Afribourse (Bourse Régionale des Valeurs Moblières) (BRVM): www.brvm.org

Travel information
Air Ivoire, 2 Avenue du Général de Gaulle, PO Box 7782, Abidjan 01 (tel: 2021-3429; internt: www.airivoire.com).

Félix Houphouet-Boigny International Airport (tel: 2027-7322, 2023-4000).

Wagonlits (Railway Information), Boulevard de Marseille, Abidjan (tel: 2021-2066, 2021-3910).

Ministry of tourism
Ministry of Tourism, BP V184, Abidjan (tel: 2044-5500, 2044-5129, 2044-6474, 2044-6953; fax: 2044-5580).

National tourist organisation offices
Office Ivoirien du Tourisme et de l'Hôtellerie (OITH), Place de la République, BP 8538, Abidjan 01 (tel: 2020-2516; fax: 2020-3388; email: oith@tourismeci.org; internet: www.tourismeci.org).

Ministries
Ministry of Agriculture and Animal Resources, Immeuble de la Caisse de Stabilisation, BP V84, Abidjan (tel: 2021-3858; fax: 2021-4618; e-mail: minagra@cimail.net).

Ministry of Communication and Information Technology, Tour C, Tours Administratives, BP V138, Abidjan (tel: 2021-1116; fax: 2021-8495).

Ministry of Construction and Urbanism, Tour D, Tours Administratives, 20 BP 650, Abidjan (tel: 2021-8235; fax: 2021-3568).

Ministry of Defence and Civil Protection, Immeuble EECI, BP V 241, Abidjan (tel: 2021-2682; fax: 2022-4175).

Ministry of Economic Infrastructures, Immeuble Postel 2001, 18 BP 2203, Abidjan (tel: 2034-4273; fax: 2034-7322).

Ministry of Economy and Finance, Immeuble SCIAM, BP V163, Abidjan (tel: 2020-0842; fax: 2021-3208).

Ministry of Education, Tour D, Tours Administratives, BP V 120, Abidjan (tel: 2022-7406; fax: 2022-9322).

Ministry of Family, Women and Children, Tour E, Tours Administratives, BP 200, Abidjan (tel: 2021-7626; fax: 2021-4461).

Ministry of Foreign Affairs, Bloc Ministériel, Boulevard Angoulvand, BP V109, Abidjan (tel: 2022-7150; fax: 2033-2308).

Ministry of Health, Tour C, Tours Administratives, 01 BP V 04, Abidjan (tel: 2021-0871; fax: 2021-5240).

Ministry of Higher Education and Scientific Research, Tour C, Tours Administratives, BP V 151, Abidjan (tel: 2021-3316; fax: 2021-2225).

Ministry of the Interior and Decentralisation, Bloc Ministériel, Boulevard Angoulvand, BP V 121, Abidjan (tel: 2022-3816; fax: 2022-3648).

Ministry of Justice and Public Freedom, Bloc Ministériel, Boulevard Angoulvand, BP V 107, Abidjan (tel: 2021-1727; fax: 2033-1259).

Ministry of Labour, Civil Service and Administrative Reform, Immeuble Fonction Publique, Boulevard Angoulvand, BP V 93, Abidjan (tel: 2021-4290; fax: 2021-1286).

Ministry of Mines and Energy, Immeuble Postel 2001, BP V 40, Abidjan (tel: 2034-4851; fax: 2021-3730).

Ministry of Trade, Immeuble CCIA, Rue Jean-Paul II, BP V65, Abidjan (tel: 2021-6473; fax: 2021-6474).

Ministry of Transport, Immeuble Postel 2001, BP V 06, Abidjan (tel: 2034-7315; fax: 2021-3730).

Other useful addresses
Agence des Télécommunications de Côte d'Ivoire (ATCI), BP 2203, Immeuble Postel 2001, Rue le Coeur, Abidjan 18 (tel: 2034-4255; fax: 2034-4254).

Association of Businessmen and Industry of Côte d'Ivoire, Imm Lefébre, Bd de Marseille, 01 BP 464, Abidjan 01.

Association of Exporters of Coffee-Cocoa, Imm CCIA, 01 BP 1399, Abidjan 01 (tel: 2022-5446/5).

Association of Fishing Industry, Port de Pêche, 01 BP 14, Abidjan 01 (tel: 2025-7998; fax: 2025-2065).

Association of Import and Export Traders, Imm Résidence du Front Lagunaire 2 étage, 01 BP 3792, Abidjan 01 (tel: 2032-5427; fax: 2032-5652).

Association of West African Home Grown Product Dealers, Imm CCIA 7 étage, O & BP 5407, Abidjan 01 (tel: 2022-5795).

Bourse des Valeurs Abidjan, Ave Marchand 10, BP 1878, 01 Abidjan (tel: 2021-5783, 215742; fax: 2022-1657).

British Embassy, 3rd Floor, Immeuble Les Harmonies, Angle Boulevard Carde et Avenue Dr Jamot, BP 2581, Plateau, 01 Abidjan (tel: 2022-6850/2, 2032-8209; fax: 2022-3221).

Bureau National d'Etudes Techniques et de Dévéloppement (BNETD) (National Office for Technical and Development Studies), BP 945, 04 Abidjan (tel: 2044-2805, 2044-5877; fax: 2044-5666; email: nzoro@bnetd.sita.net; internet: www.bnetd.sita.net.).

Caisse de Stabilisation (CAISTAB), BP V132, Abidjan (tel: 2020-2700; fax: 2021-8994).

Centre de Commerce Internationale d'Abidjan (conference bookings), Abidjan (tel: 2022-4070).

Centre de Promotion des Investissements en Côte d'Ivoire (CEPICI), CCIA-WTR 5th Floor, BP V152, Abidjan 01 (tel: 2021-4070; fax: 2021-4071).

Committee of Insurers, Imm Les Arcades, 01 BP 3873, Abidjan 01 (tel: 2022-5437; fax: 2021-1835).

Committee of Privatisation, 6 Boulevard de l'Indénié, Abidjan-Plateau, BP 1141, Abidjan 01 (tel: 2022-2231/2232/2236; fax: 2022-2235).

Compagnie Ivoirienne pour le Développement des Textiles, BP 622, Bouaké (tel: 2063-3113, 2063-3013; fax: 2063-4167).

Conseil Economique et Social, 04 BP 301, Abidjan (tel: 2021-2060).

Côte d'Ivoire Embassy (USA), 3421 Massachusetts Avenue, NW, Washington DC 20007 (tel: (+1-202) 797-0300; fax: 20(+1-202) 265-2454).

The Customs Department, Boulevard de la République, BP V 25, Abidjan (tel: 2021-5223).

Direction et Controle des Grands Travaux, Département Industrie et Energie, Boulevard de la Corniche, Cocody, 04 BP 945, Abidjan 04 (tel: 2044-2118; fax: 2044-5866).

Energie Electrique de la Côte d'Ivoire, BP 1345, 1 place de la République, Abidjan (tel: 2020-6000; fax: 2032-7477).

French Embassy; BP 175, Rue Lecoueur 17, Abidjan 17 (tel: 2020-0404; fax: 2020-0447).

General Surveillance Co (Responsible for Import Controls), PO Box 795, Abidjan (tel: 2021-1290).

Ivorian Investment Promotion in Côte d'Ivoire (CEPECI), PO Box V 152, Abidjan 01 (tel: 2021-4070; fax: 2021-4071; internet site: http://www.cepici.go.ci).

National Enterprise Assistance and Promotion Centre (CAPEN), Immeuble La Pyramide, 9th floor, 08 BP 868, Abidjan 08 (tel: 2032-0145).

Organisation Centrale pour la Commercialisation de l'Ananas et la Banane (OCAB), Imm Corniche, 16 BP 1908, Abidjan 16 (tel: 2032-5882; fax: 2032-1060).

Port Autonome d'Abidjan, BP V85, Abidjan (tel: 2024-0866, 2024-2640; fax: 2024-2328).

Professional Association of the Oil Industry, 13 Impasse Paris Village, 01 BP 1777, Abidjan 01 (tel: 2021-7320; fax: 2022-2858).

Société des Mines d'Ity, BP 872, Abidjan 08 (tel: 2044-6363; fax: 2044-4100).

Société Ivoirienne de la Poste et de L'Epargne, BP 105, Abidjan 17 (tel: 2034-7004; fax: 2034-7107).

Société Ivoirienne de Raffinage (SIR), Boulevard de Petit-Bassam, BP 1269, Abidjan 01 (tel: 2027-0427, 2027-0160; fax: 2027-1798, 2027-3217).

Société Nationale d'Opérations Petroliéres de la Côte d'Ivoire, BP V194, Abidjan (tel: 2021-4058).

Société pour le Développement Minier de la Côte d'Ivoire, BP 2816, Abidjan (tel: 2021-2994).

SODEMI (State Company for Mineral Development), BP 2816, 31 Boulevard Latrille, Abidjan Cocody-Nord, Abidjan 01 (tel: 2044-0994; fax: 2044-0821).

US Embassy, 5 rue Jesse Owens, 01 BP 171, Abidjan 01 (tel: 2021-0979).

World Trade Centre, PO Box V 68, Abidjan (tel: 2021-6189, 2022-4072/3; fax: 2022-7112).

National news agency: AIP (Agence Ivoirienne de Presse), 04 Avenue Chardy, BP 312, Adidjan 04 (tel: 20-22-64-13; fax: 20-21-57-12; internet: www.aip.ci).

Internet sites

Africa Business Network: www.ifc.org/abn

AllAfrica.com: allafrica.com

African Development Bank: www.afdb.org

Africa Online: www.africaonline.com

Mbendi AfroPaedia (information on companies, countries, industries and stock exchanges in Africa): mbendi.co.za

Croatia

KEY FACTS

Official name: Republika Hrvatska (Republic of Croatia)

Head of State: President Ivo Josipovic (SPH) (from 18 Feb 2010)

Head of government: Prime Minister-elect Zoran Milanovic (SPH) (from 4 Dec 2011)

Ruling party: Kukuriku coalition, led by Socijaldemokratska Partija Hrvatske (SPH) (Social Democratic Party of Croatia), with Hrvatska Narodna Stranka-Liberalni Demokrati (HNS-LD) (Croatian People's Party- Liberal Democrats), Istarski Demokratski Sabor (IDS) (Istrian Democratic Assembly) and Hrvatska Stranka Umirovljenika (Croatian Pensioner's Party) (from 4 Dec 2011)

Area: 56,538 square km

Population: 4.43 million (2010)*

Capital: Zagreb

Official language: Croatian

Currency: Kuna (K) = 100 lipas

Exchange rate: K5.57 per US$ (Oct 2011)

GDP per capita: US$13,720 (2010)

GDP real growth: -1.40% (2010)

GDP: US$60.60 billion (2010)

Labour force: 1.75 million (2010)

Unemployment: 11.80% (2010)

Inflation: 1.00% (2010)

Balance of trade: -US$7.88 billion (2010)

* estimated figure

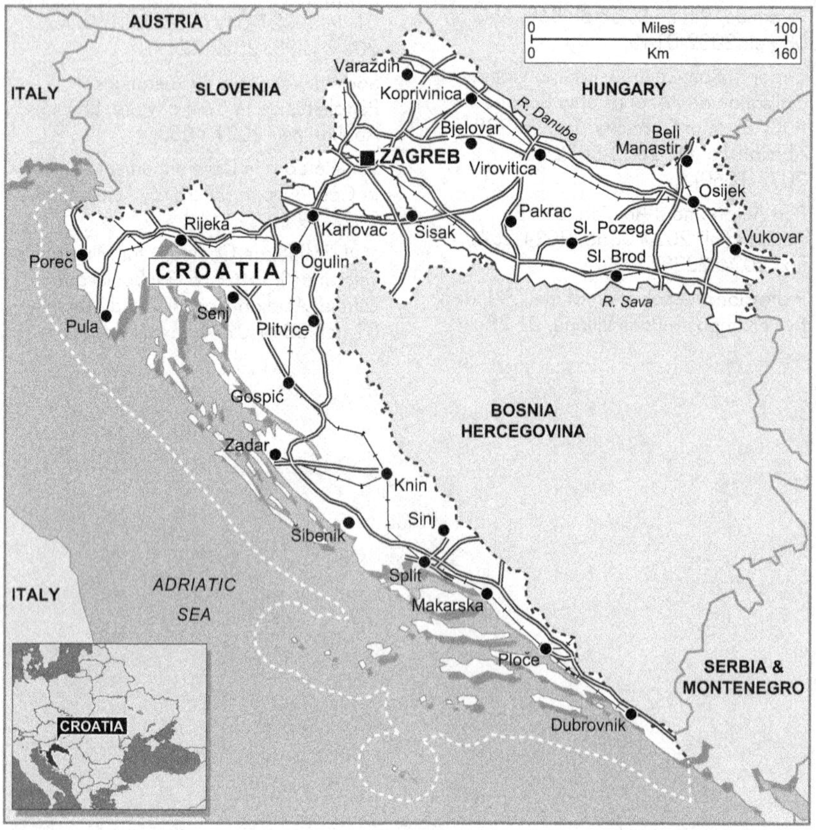

November 2011 saw Croatia's application to join the European Union (EU) finally approved, subject to a 'yes' vote in a referendum to be held in 2012. Assuming all goes well, Croatia will become the 28th member of the EU in mid-2013. Ironically, the political party that took the glory for the approval, the Hrvatska Demokratska Zajednica (HDZ) (Croatian Democratic Union), looked to be facing defeat at the hands of the improbably named opposition 'Kukuriku' (Croatian for cock-a-doodle-doo) in the 4 December 2011.

Work harder

The conservative HDZ has ruled for 16 of Croatia's 20 years as an independent state, but has been badly tarnished by a number of corruption scandals. The Kukuriku bloc, led by 45-year-old former diplomat Zoran Milanovic of the Socijaldemokratska Partija Hrvatske (SPH) (Social Democratic Party of Croatia), should it win the election as expected, will have as its first priority a reduction in state spending and dealing with a potential credit rating downgrade. Croats have been more concerned with the state of their economy than with the prospect of joining an EU that looks less than steady on its feet when facing the so called euro-zone crisis. Mr Milanovic has painted a dire picture of the economy, telling Croats they will have to work 'more, harder and longer' to turn the economy around before joining the EU in July 2013.

It's the economy

In the view of the World Bank, the Croatian authorities have so far managed the impact of the global crisis relatively well. Nonetheless, the crisis is having a significant impact on the economy and society. The challenge now is to implement further structural reforms needed for continued convergence with the EU member countries, with a special focus on reforms of the judiciary, public administration and fighting corruption, while striving for better living standards for its citizens. Despite Croatia's relatively high-income level, access to EU funds and the forthcoming EU membership, there is clearly a long way to go to reach even median EU status. Contagion from the market turmoil that has surged owing to renewed concerns about fiscal sustainability in Europe has increased risk aversion and uncertainty. Euro-zone events have pushed up the cost of borrowing and reduced capital flows to the region. The resultant plummeting of business and consumer confidence, coupled with fiscal austerity across the euro-zone combined with a slow down in the global economy, will almost certainly lead to a contraction in Europe in 2012. The Croatian economy remains reliant on economic cycles of the EU and, therefore, has a significant probability of another contraction after positive growth in 2011. Uncertainties emanating from the international banking system and financial markets remain major downside risks.

An expenditure-based fiscal adjustment is, in the view of the World Bank, a priority for Croatia to alleviate refinancing risks and protect its investment credit rating. The 2012 outlook for Croatia hinges on the implementation of a credible reform agenda. The country needs to enforce its fiscal responsibility act and reduce the fiscal spending and deficit. While all EU10 countries are tightening their fiscal positions in response to tightened financing and in order to re-build buffers, the general government fiscal deficit in Croatia will likely increase for the third consecutive year in 2011. In addition, Croatia needs to proceed with structural reforms to enhance productivity and thereby the competitiveness of the economy so that it is in a position to take advantage of an eventual global recovery. Structural reforms underpinning the expenditure adjustment will need to be implemented in early 2012 to have a full effect in 2013.

On the revenue side, introducing a modern property taxation system, rationalising quasi-fiscal fees and improving tax collection could help reduce pressures. In 2012, there will be no fiscal space for tax rate cuts. The acceleration of privatisation and the resolution of insolvent and illiquid companies would help reduce budget financing pressures. Unemployment in Croatia remains high: 60 per cent higher than before the 2008 crisis. Since 2008 the industry sector alone has lost around 38,000 jobs, while the construction and trade sectors have down-sized by another 65,000 jobs. About two thirds of the registered unemployed have been jobless for more than a year, which negatively affects their re-employment chances. The reform of labour regulation, retraining and horizontal business-sector support could reduce pressures on the labour market.

Croatia's economy has, according to the International Monetary Fund (IMF), yet to show signs of a sustained recovery from the effects of the economic crisis. Domestic demand continued to contract in 2010, as households reduced their debt levels and falling employment limited private consumption. Low confidence also hampered investment. Exports rebounded strongly, but given the narrow export base, were insufficient to pull Croatia out of the recession. Gross domestic product (GDP) thus fell by 1.25 per cent in 2010. The near-term outlook remained subdued and growth was only expected to reach 1 per cent in 2011, while medium-term growth is likely to be curtailed by weak competitiveness.

The government has made some progress in implementing the reforms outlined in its 2010 Economic Recovery Programme (ERP), aimed at addressing deep-rooted structural rigidities and competitiveness problems. The pension law was amended to gradually harmonise the retirement age between men and women at 65 years and discourage early retirement. The unemployment law was changed to reduce benefits and duration. Judicial reforms were instituted to strengthen bankruptcy procedures for companies and business registration procedures were streamlined. However, implementation of other reforms needed to improve competitiveness, such as increasing labour market flexibility and reducing the size of the public sector, have been hampered by strong social resistance.

The government's efforts did not, however, prevent fiscal deterioration in 2010. Despite the positive contributions from measures undertaken in 2009 and 2010, the general government's deficit widened to 5 per cent of GDP in 2010 on the back of falling revenues. This was caused by declining profit and income taxes and social contributions, as corporate profitability and employment plunged. Public debt stock rose to 41 per cent of GDP.

External vulnerabilities remain elevated despite substantial adjustment in the current account. The rising level of exports and the contraction in imports reduced the current account deficit to about 1.25 per cent of GDP in 2010 from just over 5 per cent of GDP in 2009. Capital inflows slowed down correspondingly due to excess capacity and weak economic prospects. Yet external debt amounts to 100 per cent of GDP and foreign currency debt of the public and non-financial private sector is even higher.

The largely foreign-owned banking sector has weathered the economic downturn relatively well. The banking system has ample liquidity and is sufficiently capitalised. Nevertheless, asset quality deteriorated, with the overall non-performing loan (NPL) ratio reaching 11 per cent at

KEY INDICATORS Croatia

	Unit	2006	2007	2008	2009	2010
Population	m	4.44	*4.44	*4.44	*4.44	*4.43
Gross domestic product (GDP)	US$bn	42.46	51.36	69.30	63.20	60.60
GDP per capita	US$	9,558	11,576	15,628	14,243	13,720
GDP real growth	%	4.6	5.8	2.4	-5.3	-1.4
Inflation	%	3.2	2.9	6.1	2.4	1.0
Unemployment	%	17.2	15.1	13.4	14.9	11.8
Exports (fob) (goods)	US$m	10,606.0	12,622.7	14,358.5	10,717.7	12,066.6
Imports (fob) (goods)	US$m	21,117.0	25,556.1	30,419.0	20,997.2	19,943.8
Balance of trade	US$m	-10,511.0	-12,933.4	-16,060.5	-10,279.4	-7,877.2
Current account	US$m	-3,377.0	-4,412.1	-6,519.0	-3,246.8	-900.7
Total reserves minus gold	US$m	11,487.8	13,674.5	12,957.3	14,894.5	14,132.5
Foreign exchange	US$m	11,487.4	13,674.0	12,956.8	14,419.0	13,665.4
Exchange rate	per US$	5.56	5.06	4.94	5.28	5.50

* estimated figure

end-2010. While aggregate profitability indicators have started to recover, several of Croatia's small banks reported losses. Credit growth to companies recovered somewhat, aided by official credit support schemes and accommodative monetary policy.

Risk assessment

Politics	Good
Economy	Fair
Regional stability	Fair

COUNTRY PROFILE

Historical profile

The Croats formed an independent kingdom during the tenth century.
1089 Inner Croatia came under the control of Hungary and then the Habsburg Empire, remaining that way for eight centuries.
1529 After Hungary's defeat by the Ottoman Turks, a militarised border was formed between Croatia and Bosnia-Hercegovina.
1918 The defeat of the Austro-Hungarian Empire during the First World War saw the creation of the Kingdom of the Serbs, Croats and Slovenes, encompassing Bosnia and Hercegovina (BiH), Croatia, parts of Dalmatia and Macedonia, Montenegro, Serbia, Slavonia and Slovenia.
1921 Prince Alexander, Regent of Serbia, became King.
1929 Following disputes between Serbs and Croats, King Alexander assumed dictatorial powers and the country was renamed Yugoslavia.
1934 King Alexander of Yugoslavia was assassinated in France by Croatian extremists. Power passed to Prince Paul, acting as Regent to 11-year-old King Peter II. He ruled with the support of the armed forces.
1939 Croatia was granted internal autonomy.
1941 A coup by air force officers replaced Prince Paul and the pro-Nazi Germany government with the 17-year-old King Peter II and established a pro-Allied government. In response, German and Italian forces invaded Yugoslavia, forcing the royal family and government into exile. The fascist Ustasha movement, led by Ante Pavelic, created the Nezavisna Drzava Hrvatska (NDH) (Independent State of Croatia).
1943 Civil war ensued between two rival groups, the communist partisans, led by General Josip Broz Tito, and the Royalist Chetniks. The partisans proclaimed their own government in liberated areas.
1944 King Peter II was deposed.
1945 The Federal People's Republic of Yugoslavia was proclaimed, with Tito as prime minister – a Croat opposed to expressions of Croat (or any other) nationalism. Croatia became a constituent republic of the federation. The other republics were: BiH, Macedonia, Slovenia, Montenegro, Serbia and the two autonomous regions of Vojvodina and Kosovo.
1953 Constitutions were adopted and Tito became president of Yugoslavia. Increased autonomy for the constituent republics was extended in 1963 and 1974.
1971 A mass movement in favour of Croatian nationalist revival was crushed by Tito.
1980 Tito died. A system of a collective (rotating) presidency was adopted.
1989 Differences and friction between the wealthier republics, Slovenia and Croatia, and the different ethnic groups intensified.

1990 Following Slovenia's secession from Yugoslavia, Croatia held its own free elections which were won by the nationalist Hrvatska Demokratska Zajednica (HDZ) (Croatian Democratic Community). Franjo Tudjman became the first president of the Republic of Croatia. In August, Croatian Serbs held their own referendum, which favoured maintaining their cultural autonomy. Rebel Serbs took control of the Krajina and two other regions in Croatia – Eastern and Western Slavonia. The secession of Croatia, Slovenia and BiH led to invasions of these republics by the Jugoslovenska Narodna Armija (JNA) (Yugoslav National Army).
1991 Independence from Yugoslavia was unilaterally declared.
1992–94 Croatia was recognised as an independent state by the then European Community (EC) on 15 January and became a member of the UN. Franjo Tudjman was re-elected president. The declaration of independence was followed by several months of war, first against the JNA and then against local rebel ethnic Serbs. JNA units had been incorporated into the ethnic Serb armies in the Krajina region. The Croatian government began to finance and support Bosnian Croat attempts to separate from BiH. This exacerbated the civil war in BiH between the Muslim and Bosnian Croats, until a cease-fire was achieved and the Muslim-Croat Federation was established in 1994.
1995 After nearly four years of Serb control, western Slavonia and Krajina were recaptured by the Croatian army. Tudjman's ruling nationalist HDZ won the parliamentary elections and Zlatko Matesa became prime minister. President Tudjman of Croatia, along with President Slobodan Milosevic of Yugoslavia and President Alija Izetbegovic of BiH, agreed to end the Bosnian civil war.
1996 Yugoslavia (by now consisting of Serbia and Montenegro and the two autonomous regions of Kosovo and Vojvodina) and Croatia signed an agreement on mutual recognition, formally ending five years of hostility.
1997 The HDZ won a majority in the upper house of the Sabor and President Franjo Tudjman was re-elected.
1998 Eastern Slavonia (some 5 per cent of Croatia's total territory) was handed back to Croatia by the UN Transition Authority for Eastern Slavonia (UNTAES).
1999 Franjo Tudjman died; Vlatko Pavletic became acting president.
2000 The Socialdemokratska Partija (SDP) (Social Democratic Party) won the general election. A centre-left coalition government was formed, led by the SDP, with Ivica Racan (SDP) as prime minister. Stjepan 'Stripe' Mesic of the Hrvatska Narodna Stranka (HNS) (Croatian People's Party) and regarded as an ally of the SDP, was sworn in as president.
2001 A constitutional amendment abolished of the upper house of parliament. Croatia agreed to extradite several suspected war criminals to the International Criminal Tribunal for former Yugoslavia (ICTY) at The Hague (The Netherlands). War veteran groups protested strongly at the government's co-operation.
2002 Ivica Racan resigned as prime minister, but was re-appointed and formed a new centre-left coalition government, comprising the SDP, HNS, Hrvatska Seljacka Stranka (HSS) (Croatian Peasant Party), Liberalna Stranka (LS) (Liberal Party) and Libra.
2003 Croatia submitted its formal application for EU membership. The nationalist HDZ, won parliamentary elections defeating pro-Western parties. Ivo Sanader (HDZ) became prime minister of a coalition government led by the HDZ with Hrvatska Socialna Liberalna Stranka, Demokratski Centar (HSLS, DC) (Croatian Social Liberal Party, Democratic Centre).
2004 Milan Babic, a Croatian Serb, was jailed for 13 years by the ICTY Tribunal in The Hague for war crimes during his leadership, in the early 1990s, of the self-proclaimed Krajina Serb republic.
2005 Stjepan 'Stripe' Mesic won the run-off presidential election. The EU began accession talks with Croatia; they had been stalled because Croatia was deemed unco-operative in handing over suspected war criminals. The fugitive, General Ante Gotovina was arrested in the Canary Islands and sent to the war crimes tribunal in The Hague.
2006 Croatia membership talks with the EU were caught up in internal discord about enlargement when the EU decided to wait until at least 2010 before offering Croatia membership. Talks with Croatia

continued with the EU, separately from Turkey, which had applied for membership at the same time.
2007 A coalition government between the HDZ and the Hrvatska Seljacka Stranka-Hrvatska Socijalno Liberalna Stranka (HSS-HSLS) (Croatian Peasant's Party-Croatian Social Liberal Party) was formed following parliamentary elections.
2008 An accession protocol with Croatia was signed by NATO ambassadors in Brussels.
2009 A border dispute with Slovenia that began in 1991 with the collapse of Yugoslavia impeded Croatia's efforts to join the EU. With such a short coastline (46km) Slovenia was intent on using the small Bay of Piran on the Adriatic Sea to give it access to international waters. Croatia wanted the border to be halfway through the bay and submitted maps and documents showing this to EU negotiators. Slovenia vetoed Croatia's first accession attempt and without an agreement by April Croatia was unable to join the EU in 2009. Croatia joined NATO in April. Ivo Sanader resigned and Jadranka Kosor became prime minister. Ivo Josipovic (Socijaldemokratska Partija Hrvatske (SPH) (Social Democratic Party of Croatia) won the first round of presidential elections.
2010 Josipovic won the run-off presidential elections held in January, with 60.3 per cent of the vote, Milan Bandic (independent) 39.7 per cent; turnout was 50.2 per cent. In a tit-for-tat move Serbia began legal action against Croatia at the ICJ for genocide committed in the early 1990s. The alleged genocide was said to have occurred during clashes between the two countries as Croatia fought for independence. The action was in retaliation for Croatia's refusal to drop a similar suit before the ICJ for atrocities by Yugoslav and Serbian forces against Croats in 1999. A referendum held in Slovenia on 6 June voted in favour of allowing international arbitrators to resolve the border dispute concerning the Bay of Piran. A five-person panel, including one Slovene and one Croat, will settle the matter. Sretko Kalinic, the assassin of Serbia's first democratically elected prime minister (Zoran Djindjic) in 2001, was extradited to Serbia on 25 August to serve a 30-year prison sentence; a Serbian court had found him guilty *in absentia*. Croatia signed a protocol in September to jointly found a new company, Cargo 10, with Macedonia, Serbia and Slovenia to incorporate their railway companies; later joined by Bosnia Herzegovina. Former prime minister, Ivo Sanader, left the country, just hours before parliament voted to lift his immunity from prosecution. An international arrest warrant was issued and he was arrested in Austria on 10 December on charges of bribery and corruption.
2011 A census, carried out on 31 March, recorded a population of 4,290,612 people residing in the country, of which 792,875 were in Zagreb. Extradition papers for Ivo Sanader's return to Croatia were signed in Austria on 12 July. Parliamentary elections took place on 4 December, in which the four-party Kukuriku coalition (led by SPH) won 40 per cent of the vote and replaced the incumbent coalition led by HDZ, which won 23.5 per cent (47). The HDZ coalition had been blamed for the poor state of the economy, rising unemployment and a number of corruption scandals, which marred the election campaign. The Kukuriku leader, Zoran Milanovic (SPH) had warned that he would introduce an austerity budget to avoid a credit agency downgrading and that he would approach the IMF for financial aid if necessary.

Political structure

Constitution

The written constitution was first adopted in December 1990, with amendments in 2000 and 2001 that cut back presidential powers and abolish the upper house of parliament.
Under the constitution there is a principle of the separation of power into legislative, executive and judicial branches, which are limited by the right to local and regional self-government.
The laws of Croatia must conform to the constitution
The electoral law gives the vote to all Croatians over the age of 18, including those living abroad. Ethnic minorities are equal with ethnic Croats according to the constitution. However, in recent years the international community has raised strong objections to laws that *de facto* discriminate against other groups – specifically returning Serb refugees. Until these problems are solved, Croatia is unlikely to be recognised as a fully democratic state.
The administration of Croatia is divided into 21 *zupanije* (counties). There are also two *kotari*, or special districts, at Glina and Knin, which are under direct Serb control.

Independence date

25 June 1991

Form of state

Unitary, democratic republic

The executive

Executive power is vested in the president who is Head of State and supreme commander of the armed forces and is directly elected for five years and a maximum of two terms.
The president appoints the prime minister and, by recommendation of the prime minister, other members of the government. These appointments are subject to confirmation by the House of Representatives.

National legislature

The unicameral Hrvatski Sabor (Parliament of Croatia) (known as Sabor) has between 100–160 members (exact numbers are determined by the Sabor), elected in multi-seat constituencies (up to a maximum of six), by proportional representation from party lists, to serve for four-year terms. Of the total number, eight seats are reserved for minority communities and five for expatriates.

Legal system

All civil and criminal cases are dealt with by basic and higher courts. The Supreme Court is the highest authority for civil and criminal law, charged with ensuring uniform application of laws and equality of citizens. All judges and other judicial officials are appointed by the Judicial Council, an elected body that is answerable to the parliament. The Judicial Council also acts as the Constitutional Court to determine the conformity of national legislation with the Constitution.
All prosecutions are the responsibility of the Office of the Public Prosecutor. There is also a Public Attorney. The Justice Ministry is the administrative authority of the Croatian judiciary. Its major instrument is the Croatian police, which falls under the jurisdiction of the interior minister.

Last elections

4 December 2011 (parliamentary): 27 December 2009/10 January 2010 (presidential first round and runoff)
Results: Parliamentary: Kukuriku coalition (of four political parties, led by Socijaldemokratska Partija Hrvatske (SPH) (Social Democratic Party of Croatia) won 40 per cent of the vote (80 seats, out of 151), the HDZ coalition (of three parties, led by Hrvatska Demokratska Zajednica (HDZ) (Croatian Democratic Union) 23.5 per cent (47), Hrvatski Laburisti-Stranka Rada (HL-SR) (Worker's Party-Labour Party) 5.1 per cent (six), Hrvatski Demokratski Sabor Slavonije i Baranje (HDSSB) (Croatian Democratic Assembly of Slovonija and Banranja) 2.9 per cent (six); four other political parties (two with seats reserved for ethnic minorities and other independent and community representatives) won the remaining 12 seats.
Presidential (first round): Ivo Josipovic (Socijaldemokratska Partija Hrvatske (SPH) (Social Democratic Party of Croatia) won 32.8 per cent of the vote, Milan Bandic (independent) 15 per cent, Andrija Hebrang (Hrvatska Demokratska Zajednica) (HDZ) (Croatian Democratic Union) 12.2 per cent, Nadan Vidosevic (independent) 11.5 per cent; all other candidates won less than 8 per cent each. Turnout was 44 per cent. Runoff:

Josipovic won 60.3 per cent of the vote, Bandic 39.7 per cent; turnout was 50.2 per cent.

Next elections

2011 (parliamentary); 2014 (presidential)

Political parties

Ruling party

Kukuriku coalition, led by Socijaldemokratska Partija Hrvatske (SPH) (Social Democratic Party of Croatia), with Hrvatska Narodna Stranka-Liberalni Demokrati (HNS-LD) (Croatian People's Party- Liberal Democrats), Istarski Demokratski Sabor (IDS) (Istrian Democratic Assembly) and Hrvatska Stranka Umirovljenika (Croatian Pensioner's Party) (from 4 Dec 2011)

Main opposition party

HDZ coalition (led by Hrvatska Demokratska Zajednica (HDZ) (Croatian Democratic Union), with Hrvatska Gradanska Stranka (HGS) (Croation Citizens Party) and Demokratski Centar (DC) (Democratic Centre)

Population

4.44 million (2009)*

Last census: March 2001: 4,437,460

Population density: 79.8 inhabitants per square km. Urban population: 58 per cent (1995–2001).

Annual growth rate: -0.3 per cent 1994–2004 (WHO 2006)

Internally Displaced Persons (IDP)

11,000 (UNHCR 2004)

Ethnic make-up

Croats (90 per cent of the population), plus Serbs, Hungarians and Gypsies. The April 2001 census, the first since the 1991—95 war, indicated that Serbs made up 4.5 per cent of the population (the figure was 12 per cent in the early 1990s).

Religions

Predominantly Roman Catholic, with Christian Orthodox, Muslim and Jewish minorities, living mostly in Zagreb.

Education

Primary education is compulsory and free of charge. Secondary education is between the ages of 14–18. Vocational schools offer courses lasting for three or four years, including a period of practical instruction. There are four universities offering courses in science, engineering and medicine that meet international standards.

Public expenditure on education typically amounts to 5 per cent of annual gross national income.

Literacy rate: 98 per cent adult rate; 100 per cent youth rate (15–24) (Unesco 2005).

Compulsory years: Six to 14

Enrolment rate: 99 per cent; gross primary enrolment, of the relevant age group (including repetition rates), (World Bank).

Pupils per teacher: 19 in primary schools

Health

The healthcare system has recovered since the internal conflict ended in 1995, but national coverage remains patchy, notably in the Krajina and Eastern Slavonia regions.

HIV/Aids

HIV prevalence: 0.1 per cent aged 15–49 in 2003 (World Bank)

Life expectancy: 75 years, 2004 (WHO 2006)

Fertility rate/Maternal mortality rate: 1.3 births per woman, 2004 (WHO 2006); maternal mortality 6 per 100,000 live births (World Bank).

Child (under 5 years) mortality rate (per 1,000): 6 per 1,000 live births; 1 per cent of children under five years are malnourished (World Bank).

Head of population per physician: 2.44 physicians per 1,000 people, 2003 (WHO 2006)

Welfare

The government faces a huge fiscal burden with an ageing population and a legacy of insufficient funds to pay retirees, particularly those who retired early following reforms of the late 90s. In 2002 the government introduced a dual social insurance and mandatory, privately managed, compulsory pension schemes, for all workers, with contributions that vary depending on the class of old age pension. Regular pensions require contributions of 10.75 per cent and 8.75 per cent (of payroll), from employee and employer respectively. Basic pensions require contributions of 8.75 per cent and 5.75 per cent (of payroll), from employee and employer respectively. Insurance contributions cover among other benefits, medical, disability and survivor's pensions. By 2020 projected pension fund assets should reach 25–30 per cent of GDP. In 2003 it was estimated there were over 50,000 Croatian refugees, of which 27,700 were internally displaced persons (IDP).

Main cities

Zagreb (capital, estimated population 699,164 in 2003), Split (192,589), Rijeka (141,063), Osijek (87,955), Zadar (71,457), Slavonski Brod (60,990), Pula (59,080), Sesvete (53,397), Sibenik (37,088), Sisak (35,664), Karlovac (48,057), Dubrovnik (29,916), Varazdin (41,801), Velika Gorica (35,238), Vinkovci (33,289), Vukovar (29,569).

Languages spoken

Croatian is written using the Latin alphabet. German and English are commonly used as second languages and business people are fluent in English. Bosnian and Serbian are also spoken and, near the Adriatic coast, Italian is spoken.

Official language/s

Croatian

Media

The constitution guarantees press freedom and bans censorship.

Press

Dailies: Most popular newspapers have a tabloid format with commercialised stories.

In Croatian, national newspapers include *Jutarnji List* (www.jutarnji.hr), *Vecernji List* (www.vecernji.hr), and *Vjesnik* (www.vjesnik.com). Regional newspapers include *Slobodna Dalmacija* (www.slobodnadalmacija.hr) from Split, *Novi List* (www.novilist.hr) from Rijeka, *24 Sata* (www.24sata.hr) from Zagreb and Glas Istre (www.glasistre.hr) from Pula.

Weeklies: In Croatian, the most influential news magazine *Globus* (www.globus.com.hr) has reported on corruption and organised crime that have been avoided by more mainstream publications. Another independent political magazine is *Nacional* (www.nacional.hr). *Gloria* (www.gloria.com.hr) is the most popular women's magazine and *Nogometni Magazin* (www.nogometni-magazin.com) is a sports publication.

Business: In Croatian, *Business.hr* (http://business.hr) and *Privredni Vjesnik* (www.privredni-vjesnik.hr with an English online edition) are both weekly newspapers.

Broadcasting

Television is the medium of choice for news and information for most people. Hrvatska Radiotelevizija (HRT) (www.hrt.hr) is the national, public broadcaster, which is funded through license fees and advertising revenue.

Radio: RTH operates three stations RTH1, 2 and 3, with a network provides by regional linking stations. There are numerous private stations centred on cities and regional centres, including Radio Samobor (www.radiosamobor.hr) with news and music, from Zagreb, Radio Mrežnica (www.radio-mreznica.hr) from the Central region, Radio Laus (www.radio-laus.hr) from Dubrovnik, Radio Istra (www.radioistra.hr) from Istria and Gradski Radio (www.eter.hr) from Slavonia.

Television: There are three national, commercial, networks including the government-owned HRT (www.hrt.hr) TV, which has two channels providing domestically produced news and entertainment programmes and foreign imports. The private TV channels include RTL Televizija

(www.rtl.hr) and Nova TV (http://dnevnik.hr). The Croatian media company OIV (www.oiv.hr) provides a comprehensive cable TV service, with 21 channels, to Croatia and neighbouring countries.
The conversion of terrestrial signals to digital is scheduled to be completed by 2010 and will provide the opportunity for transmission of many more channels.

Economy

Croatia has a free-market, service sector led, economy with its industrial sector, particularly shipbuilding, underpinning its international trade. Shipbuilding accounts for around 10 per cent of all exported goods and with manufacturing represents over 28 per cent of the structure of the economy. Farming includes crops for both a processed food industry and organic crops for export to other EU countries. The service sector represents over 65 per cent of GDP, with tourism as its principal sector and the country's major foreign exchange earner.
As Croatia is dependent on exports and tourism, GDP growth began to fall early in 2008 as the global economic crisis took hold and trade weakened and tourist numbers fell. Growth dropped from 5.8 per cent in 2007 to 2.4 per cent of 2008, before falling into recession in 2009 with GDP of -5.3 per cent. Recovery was slow and only managed -1.5 per cent in 2010, and only projected to return to a positive 2.0 per cent in 2011.
In 2009, the government introduced three supplementary budgets with measures that included expenditure cuts, freezing wages and pensions and raising value added tax (VAT). It also imposed a 'solidarity tax' on higher income earners. Although the measures helped improve financial market sentiment and the currency regained much of its strength, the overall fiscal deficit widened to just under 4 per cent of GDP.
Unemployment was typically high at 12.7–8.7 per cent (2005–08) but it rose sharply to 17 per cent in 2009. However in the first quarter in 2010, there was a pickup in industrial production and with growth in the construction sector unemployment was projected to fall to less than 10 per cent by the end of the year.
The International Monetary Fund (IMF) considered that Croatia had benefited from global growth before 2008 but had not used its gains to improve either its overall competitiveness through structural reforms or benefits in the tourist sector (which accounts for around 50 per cent of export goods and services) from large-scale foreign direct investment (FDI).
The World Bank ranked Croatia overall as 89 (out of 183) on its *Doing Business* list in 2010. Some aspects of business were considered harder, such as protecting investment at 131, while paying taxes and starting a business were considered easier, 42 and 56 respectively. The ranking placed Croatia as comparatively better than other Eastern European and Central Asian countries, but poorer than Organisation for Economic Co-operation and Development's (OECD) countries.

External trade

As a member of the European Union (EU), Croatia operates within a community-wide free trade area, with tariffs set as a whole. Internationally, the EU has free trade agreements with a number of nations and trading blocs worldwide.
International trade plays an important role in the economy. Shipbuilding is the major manufacturing industry, with ferrous steel and aluminium products also important. Electronics, including military applications, are part of the new technology industries, with pharmaceutical products and energy production. Traditional industries provide agricultural products such as timber, textiles, organic crops (prized in the EU) and processed food.

Imports

Principal imports are vehicles, machinery and electrical equipment, chemicals and foodstuffs, natural gas, electricity and petroleum products.
Main sources: Italy (typically 15 per cent of total), Germany (14 per cent), Russia (10 per cent).

Exports

Principal exports are ships, transport equipment, electronic equipment, textiles, chemicals, foodstuffs and energy.
Main destinations: Italy (typically 19 per cent of total), Bosnia and Hercegovina (13 per cent), Germany (11 per cent).

Agriculture

Farming

Almost half of the population lives in rural areas where agriculture continues to be the traditional source of income. The government has prepared a Rural Development Plan 2005–06 with four principal measures: farm investment, processing and marketing of agricultural and fish products, improved rural infrastructure and technical assistance. This programme is intended to align agriculture with conditions necessary for accession to the EU.
Of a total of 3.2 million hectares (ha) of arable land, 63 per cent is cultivated and the rest is pastureland. Only 68 per cent of agricultural land is privately owned.
Agriculture contributed 8.2 per cent to GDP, and recorded growth of 4.2 per cent in 2004; it employed 16.2 per cent of the workforce.
Family farms with an average holding of 2.8ha per farm, contribute to the overall animal and horticultural production. Crop production is especially well developed, covering the needs for cereals, while cattle breeding accounts for almost 50 per cent of agriculture-generated GDP. The warm weather and mild winters suit grape-growing.
The government is committed to initiating agricultural market reform and promoting private farming. Reform in the agrarian production sector is accompanied by rising food imports, mostly from the EU. Agriculture within the country meets the domestic demand for wine, wheat, corn, eggs and poultry. Croatia's oil and sugar processing facilities are big enough to provide exports. However, with high production costs and a series of free trade agreements farm products cannot compete internationally.

Fishing

There are rich marine resources concentrated on the Dalmatian Adriatic coast.

Forestry

Of a total of 1.7 million hectares (ha) of forest cover, nearly four-fifths of the forest is owned by the state, and the rest is in private hands. In 1990–2000, forest cover increased by an average of 0.11 per cent per annum, the equivalent of 2,000ha.
Croatia has a well-developed wood processing industry. Although a large amount of wood is reserved for domestic fuel consumption, the country manages to export industrial roundwood and sawnwood mainly to Slovenia and Italy respectively. Small volumes of wood pulp and panels are also exported, but paper is largely imported.

Industry and manufacturing

The industrial sector contributes around 30 per cent to GDP, it typically employs around 30 per cent of the workforce. Manufacturing accounts for around 20 per cent of GDP.
State owned enterprises (SOE) are due to be restructured, in preparation for the expected competition within the EU.
Privatisation of SOE has begun, although progress is slow. In 2005 government commitment to fiscal constraints, necessary for staff cuts, is still needed as SOE incur significant losses, particularly in the shipbuilding industry and the railway system.
Private enterprise in retail and wholesale businesses and manufacturing, as a whole, typically attracts 24 per cent of FDI.

Tourism

Tourism is one of the most important elements in Croatia's economy. It is the most important in foreign exchange earners, typically accounting for 20.6 per cent of GDP

The state still has a dominant position in tourism and the sector will have to be restructured in preparation for accession to the EU.
There are approximately 190,000 beds in hotels and apartments, with an equal number of beds in private accommodation. The majority of visitors come from Germany, Italy, Slovenia, Czech Republic and Austria.

Hydrocarbons
Proven oil reserves are modested, located in three regions: Slavonia, offshore in the Adriatic, near the Dalmatia coast and the Croatian region of the Pannonian Basin, where an estimated 1.2 million barrels per day (bpd) remains to be discovered. Consumption of oil is rising each year, with a forecast of 6 million barrels by 2012.
The Croatian state oil company INA is 51 per cent government-owned; in 2007 it began investing US$1.47 billion (spent by 2010) in upgrading two antiquated oil refineries so that production of imported Syrian and Egyptian oil could be increased. INA also invested US$500 million in exploration and drilling in the Middle East and Africa.
The 400,000bpd capacity Croatian Adriatic Oil (Adria) Pipeline, run by Jadranski Naftovod (JANAF) of Croatia, takes oil that arrives by tanker at the Croatian Adriatic port of Omisalj into the interior of Croatia. However there are plans to redirect the flow of oil, picking up Russian oil for delivery to the Adriatic for onward transportation. The negotiations, involving six countries, had not been concluded by 2011, but when agreement is reached an estimated 100 million barrels of crude oil, rising to 300 million barrels will be exported.
Natural gas reserves are modest. An estimate of undiscovered gas in the Pannonian Basin, to be shared with Hungary, is 210 billion cum but is likely to be from hard to reach sites. Imported gas comes primarily from Russia and Slovenia via pipeline.
Croatia has extensive coal reserves but production runs at less than 100,000 tonnes per annum, mostly for consumption by domestic power plants.

Energy
Croatia has 4,049MW of electricity generation capacity, of which almost 2,100MW is produced by hydropower, over 1,400MW by thermal power, 300MW by nuclear power plants and the remainder by alternative sources. Imports of electricity account for around 10 per cent of total energy consumption. Demand for electricity is increasing by around 5 per cent per year, creating an urgent need to increase generating capacity in Croatia. Hydroelectric plants are mainly located along the Adriatic coastline (Obrovac, Senj, Zakucac). Croatia does not operate a nuclear power plant but has joint ownership and responsibility for the plant in Krsko (Slovenia).
There is a geothermal resource in the north which could provide an estimated 839MW if harnessed, but which is currently used for heating spaces and swimming pools and balneology.

Financial markets
Stock exchange
Zagrebacka Burza (Zagreb Stock Exchange)

Banking and insurance
The central bank has general supervisory powers, endorsed by law, of the banking system. Legislation, since 2001, permits foreign investment in banks and since 2004 foreign banks may open branches in Croatia, although the EU is unimpressed about some of the restrictive stipulation necessary for this. Foreign exchange laws permit individuals opening foreign exchange accounts abroad and local banks offering foreign currency denominated loans.
There will be an amount of merging of supervisory authorities of the insurance, securities, investment funds and pensions into a financial services authority in line with EU requirements, before accession.
Central bank
Hrvatska Narodna Banka (HNB) (Croatian National Bank)
Main financial centre
Zagreb

Time
GMT plus one hour (daylight saving, late March to late October, GMT plus two hours)

Geography
Croatia is bounded by Slovenia to the north-west, Hungary to the north-east and the Serbian province of Vojvodina to the east. Bosnia and Hercegovina (BiH) takes a bite out of Croatia causing a rough horse shoe shape in the middle of the country from the east to the south-west. There is a very short border with Montenegro at the southern tip of the narrowing stretch of Croatia, near Dubrovnik. In the Adriatic Sea, Croatia also has maritime boundaries with Slovenia, Italy and Montenegro. There are 1,185 islands and islets along the 1,778km Croatian coast. At 56,538km square, the country consists of two principal parts: the Slavonian or Danubian plains of the north and east, through which the River Sava flows, and the extended Mediterranean coastal region of the Istrian peninsula and Dalmatia to the south-west and south-east. The hinterlands of this coastal region are the Dinaric Alps, which also extend into BiH.
To the south-west of Zagreb, a narrow neck of territory connects the two elongated parts of the country.
Hemisphere
Northern

Climate
In northern Croatia, the climate is continental, on the Adriatic it is Mediterranean, while in the mountainous regions, it is alpine. The coastal hinterlands have a colder climate with heavy snow in winter, but they can be very hot in summer. Temperatures inland average around 10 degrees Celsius (C), while average temperatures on the coastal areas are around 15 degrees C. During the summer months, temperatures along the coast are often in excess of 30 degrees C.
Precipitation is fairly constant country-wide throughout the year. The summer is the wettest season in the north, where the average annual rainfall in Zagreb is 890 millimetres. During the winter months, violent wind storms, known locally as the *Bora*, are common along the coast. A subsidiary sea of the Mediterranean, the Adriatic exercises a major influence on Croatia's climate, moderating the excesses of the continental climates of the north and east.

Dress codes
Business dress is formal, particularly in Zagreb.

Entry requirements
Passports
Required by all, except citizens of the EU, Switzerland, Norway and BiH who only need valid, official photographic identification.
Visa
Required by all, except nationals travelling as tourists from North America, Europe, Australasia, and some Asian countries, for stays of up to 90 days. Visitors are issued border passes on arrival, these must be kept until departure. For further details and exemptions see www.mfa.hr – visa requirements overview.
Nationals who do not require a tourist visa may visit for business purposes without a visa. All others business persons must apply for a business visa. Business visas require an official letter of invitation from a registered Croatian company or entity, on a formal declaration form that can be downloaded from www.hgk.hr. For further information contact the Croatian Chamber of Commerce e-mail: hgk@hgk.hr.
Currency advice/regulations
The import and export of local currency is limited to K15,000 in total, of which K500 is the maximum in banknotes. The import and export of foreign currency is unlimited. Amounts over K40,000

equivalent should be declared. Foreign currency can be exchanged in banks, by authorised dealers and post offices. Automated teller machines (ATMs) are common.
Travellers cheques in US dollars, pounds sterling or euros avoid extra exchange fees.

Customs
Goods for personal use up to the value of K300 can be imported free of duty.
Export of objects historic, cultural or scientific value must have a licence from the appropriate authorities.
A foreign national can be exempt from paying customs duties on equipment imported on the basis of a foreign investment contract. Appeals for exemption from duty should be submitted to the Ministry of Finance.

Prohibited imports
Illegal drugs. Firearms and ammunition must have the relevant Croatian permits.

Health (for visitors)
Nationals of the European Economic Area (EEA) countries and Switzerland can access reduced cost and sometimes free medical treatment using a European Health Insurance Card (EHIC) while visiting the EEA. Exceptions include nationals of the 10 countries which joined the EU in 2005 whose EHIC is not valid in Switzerland. Applications for the EHIC should be made before travelling.

Mandatory precautions
None

Credit cards
American Express, Diners' Club, Mastercard and Visa are accepted.

Public holidays (national)
Fixed dates
1 Jan (New Year's Day), 6 Jan (Epiphany), 1 May (Labour Day), 22 Jun (Anti-Fascism Day), ^25 Jun (National Day), 5 Aug (Thanksgiving Day), 15 Aug (Assumption Day), ^2 Oct (Independence Day), 1 Nov (All Saints' Day), 25–26 Dec (Christmas).
^ Some companies allow an informal one-day holiday before or after a Sunday holiday.

Variable dates
Mar/Apr Easter Monday, Jun Corpus Cristi

Working hours
Banking
Mon–Fri: 0700–1900; Sat: 0700–1300.
Business
Mon–Fri: 0800–1600.
Government
Mon–Fri: 0830–1630.
Shops
Food shops: Mon–Fri: 0700–2000, Sat: 0700–1500.
Non-food shops: Mon–Fri: 0800–1200, 1700–2000; Sat: 0800–1500.

Telecommunications
Mobile/cell phones
There are GSM roaming facilities available in the 900 band width, the 1800 is planned. Coverage is virtually throughout the country.

Electricity supply
220V AC, 50 Hz

Weights and measures
Metric system

Social customs/useful tips
Although Croats are a rather gregarious people, there is a growing tendency to reserved formality in business contexts. The formality extends to the exchange of business cards that state professional and acedemic status.
On balance, foreigners should avoid informality with their business and other hosts and should observe western business standards. Foreigners are advised to avoid discussions of a political nature in Croatia.
Trade fairs are part of the regular business life in Croatia and are a useful way to meet potential partners and gain entry to the market. The principal venue is Zagreb, although Rijeka, Split and Osijek also host fairs.

Security
There is some street crime in Zagreb and other major cities.

Getting there
Air
National airline: Croatia Airlines
International airport/s: Zagreb-Pleso International Airport (ZAG), 17km from the capital; business centre, bank, post office, restaurants, bars, duty-free shopping and car hire. Buses to the city run between 0700–2000. Taxis are available; travelling time 25 minutes.
Other airport/s: Dubrovnik International (DBV), 18km south-east of the city. Flights are inter-Euopean only. Facilites include money-changing offices, duty-free shopping, post office and car hire.
Airport tax: None

Surface
Croatia is included in the Pan-European Corridor 5 scheme. The project has some 3,270km of railways, linking Kiev in the Ukraine with western Europe via Italy, and 2,850 of new and upgraded roads.
Road: International buses connect Croatia with Austria, Italy, Hungary, France, Germany, Slovak Republic, Bosnia and Hercegovina.
Rail: There are international rail routes to Zagreb from Munich, Vienna, Venice, Budapest and Graz.
Water: Ferry services connect Rijeka and Pula with Durres and Vlora (Albania).

Getting about
National transport
Air: There are regular routes from Zagreb-Rijeka, Zagreb-Split and Zagreb-Ljubljana (Slovenia).
The main domestic airports are Rijeka (RJK), 25km from Rijeka and Split (SPU), 24km from Split.
Road: The government plans construction of 700km of new roads by 2011, making a total of 1,220km of highways and superhighways. The last 33km of the 380km Dalmatian Motorway, joining Zagreb and Split was opened on 26 June 2005.
Buses: Intercity bus services are available across the country.
Rail: Major rail links run from Zagreb to Rijeka and Varazdin.
Water: Split and Rijeka are connected by a daily sea-ferry service, but domestic sea connections with Dubrovnik are less frequent.

City transport
Taxis: Good taxi services operate in all main cities. All taxis are metered with a basic charge. A 10 per cent tip is usual.
Buses, trams & metro: Trams in Zagreb and Osijek only; buses in other cities and towns. Services are generally cheap and regular.

Car hire
A national driving licence is usually acceptable, although there have been instances where hire companies also requested an international driver's licence.
Traffic drives on the right. Speed limits are 130kph (81mph) on motorways, 100kph (62mph) on dual carriageways, 50kph (31mph) in built-up areas and 80kph (50mph) outside built-up areas. Right turns on red lights are strictly forbidden unless an additional green light (in the shape of an arrow) allows it. Right of way is always to the vehicle entering from the right.
Drink-driving is banned and subject to heavy penalties. The police also crack down on speeding and other road traffic offences. Croatia has a poor road safety record.

BUSINESS DIRECTORY
The addresses listed below are a selection only. While World of Information makes every endeavour to check these addresses, we cannot guarantee that changes have not been made, especially to telephone numbers and area codes. We would welcome any corrections.

Telephone area codes
The international direct dialling code (IDD) for Croatia is +385, followed by area code and subscriber's number:

Zagreb	1	Split	21
Dubrovnik	20	Rijeka	51

Useful telephone numbers

Emergency road help and information (Croatian Automobile Association (HAK), English speakers): 987
Police: 92
Ambulance: 94

Chambers of Commerce

American Chamber of Commerce in Croatia, 1 Krsnjavoga, 10000 Zagreb (tel: 483-6777; fax: 483-6776; e-mail: info@amcham.hr).

Croatian Chamber of Economy, 2 Rooseveltov trg, PO Box 630, 10000 Zagreb (tel: 456-1555; fax: 482-8380; e-mail: hgk@hgk.hr).

Dubrovnik County Chamber, 6 Pera Cingrije, 20000 Dubrovnik (tel: 411-376; fax: 412-044; e-mail: hgkdu@hgk.hr).

Rijeka County Chamber, 23 Bulevar Oslobodjenja, 51000 Rijeka (tel: 209-111; fax: 216-033; e-mail: hgkri@hgk.hr).

Split County Chamber, 4 Obala A Trumbica, 21000 Split (tel: 321-100; fax: 346-956; e-mail: hgkst@hgk.hr).

Zagreb County Chamber, 45 Draskoviceva, 10000 Zagreb (tel: 460-6777; fax: 460-6803; e-mail: hgkzg@hgk.hr).

Banking

Croatian Bank for Reconstruction and Development, Trg J J Strossmayera 9, 10 000 Zagreb (tel: 459-1620; fax: 459-1721).

Privredna Banka Zagreb, Corporate Finance Division, Capital Markets, Rackoga 6, Zagreb (tel: 472-3124; e-mail: capital.markets@pbz.hr; internet site: http://www.pbz.hr).

Central bank

Hrvatska Narodna Banka (Croatian National Bank), PO Box 603, Trg hrvatskih velikana 3, Zagreb 10002 (tel: 456-4555; fax: 461-0551; e-mail: info@hnb.hr).

Stock exchange

Zagrebacka Burza (Zagreb Stock Exchange): www.zse.hr

Travel information

Croatian Chamber of the Economy, Director of Tourism, Rosseveltov Trg 2, 10000 Zagreb (tel: 456-1570; fax: 448-618).

Croatia Airlines, Savska 4A, 41000 Zagreb (tel: 616-0066; fax: 530-475).

Croatian Railways (HZ-Hrvatske Zeljeznice), Mihanoviceva 12, Zagreb (fax: 457-7597).

Tourist Community of Zagreb, Kaptol 5, 41000 Zagreb (tel: 426-411; fax: 272-628).

Tourist Information Centre, Trg bana Jelacicá 11, 41000 Zagreb (tel: 278-855; fax: 274-083).

Ministry of tourism

Ministry of Tourism, International Relations Department, Ulica grada Vukovara 78, 10000 Zagreb (tel: 610-6300; fax: 610-9300).

National tourist organisation offices

Hrvatska Turisticka Zajednica (Croatian Tourist Board), Gunduliceva 3, 41000 Zagreb (tel: 424-637, 431-015; fax: 428-674).

Ministries

Government of the Republic of Croatia, Trg Svetog Marka 2, 10000 Zagreb (tel: 456—9222; fax: 630-3023).

Ministry of Administration, Republike Austrije 16, Zagreb 10000 (tel: 378-2111; fax: 378-2192).

Ministry of Agriculture and Forestry, Ulica grada Vukovara 78, 10000 Zagreb (tel: 610-6111; fax: 610-9200).

Ministry of Culture, Trg Burze 6, 1 000 Zagreb (tel: 461-0477, 456-9022; fax: 461-0489).

Ministry of Defence, Trg Kralja Petra Kresimira 4 br 1, 10000 Zagreb (tel: 456-7111; fax: 455-1105).

Ministry of Development and Reconstruction, Nazorova 61, 10000 Zagreb (tel: 378-4500; fax: 378-4551).

Ministry of Economic Affairs, Ulica grada Vukovara 78, 10000 Zagreb (tel: 610-6111; fax: 610-9120).

Ministry of Education and Sports, Trg Burze 6, 10000 Zagreb (tel: 456-9000; fax: 456-9087).

Ministry of Environmental Protection and Zoning, Ul Republike Austrije 20, 10000 Zagreb (tel: 378-2444; fax: 377-2822).

Ministry of European Integration, Ul grada Vukovara 62, 10000 Zagreb (tel: 456-9335, 456-9336; fax: 469-8310).

Ministry of Finance, Kataneiaeva 5, 10000 Zagreb (tel: 459-1333; fax: 492-2583).

Ministry of Foreign Affairs, Trg Nikole Subica Zrinskog 7–8, 10000 Zagreb (tel: 456-9964; fax: 456-9988, 455-1795; internet: www.mfa.hr).

Ministry of Health, Ulica baruna Trenka 6, 10000 Zagreb (tel: 459-1333, 460-7555; fax: 467-7076).

Ministry of Homeland War Veterans, Park Stara Tresnjevka 4, 10000 Zagreb (tel: 365-7888; fax: 365-7852).

Ministry of Immigration, Savska cesta 41/12, 10000 Zagreb (tel: 617-6011; fax: 617-6161).

Ministry of Internal Affairs, Savska 39, 10000 Zagreb (tel: 612-2111; fax: 612-2036, 612-2452).

Ministry of Justice, Administration and Local Self-Government, Ul Republike Austrije 14, 10000 Zagreb (tel: 371-0666; fax: 371-0772).

Ministry of Labour and Social Care, Prisavlje 14, 10000 Zagreb (tel: 616-9111; fax: 616-9200).

Ministry of Maritime Affairs, Transportation and Communication, Prisavlje 14, 10000 Zagreb (tel: 616-9111; fax: 615-6292, 619-6473).

Ministry of Physical Planning, Building Construction and Housing, Ulica Republike Austrije 20, Zagreb (tel: 378-2444; fax: 377-2555).

Ministry of Privatisation and Property Management, Gajeva 30a, 10 000 Zagreb (tel: 456-9103; fax: 456-9133).

Ministry of Public Works, Reconstruction and Construction, Ul Vladimira Nazora 61, 10000 Zagreb (tel: 378-4500; fax: 378-4598).

Ministry of Science and Technology, Trg J J Strossmayera 4, 10000 Zagreb (tel: 459-4444; fax: 459-4469; e-mail: office@science.hr; internet site: www.mzt.hr).

Ministry of Trades and Small and Medium Businesses, Ksaver 200, 10000 Zagreb (tel: 469-8300; fax: 469-8310).

Parliament of the Republic of Croatia, Trg Sv Marka 6 i 7, 10000 Zagreb (tel: 456-9222; fax: 492-0384).

Other useful addresses

Association of Croatian Hoteliers, Hotel Kvarner, Park 1 maja 4, 51410 Opatija (tel: 711-415; fax: 711-415).

British Embassy, Commercial Section, Vlaska 121 (3rd Floor), PO Box 454, 10000 Zagreb (tel: 455-5310; fax: 455-1685; email: commercial.section@zg.htnet.hr).

Croatian Parliament, Trg SV, Marka 6, 10000 Zagreb (tel: 456-9222, 630-3222; fax: 630-3018; email: sabor@sabor.hr).

Croatian Embassy (USA), 2343 Massachusetts Avenue, NW, Washington DC 20008 (tel: (+1-202) 588-5899; fax: (+1-202) 588-8936; e-mail: webmaster@croatiaemb.org).

Croatian Guarantee Agency, Ilica 49, 10000 Zagreb (tel: 484-6622; fax: 484-6612).

Croatian Investment Promotion agency, World Trade Centre Building, Avenija

Dubrovnik 15, 10000 Zagreb (tel: 655-4558; fax; 655-4563).

Croatian Privatisation Fund, Lueiaeeva 6, 10000 Zagreb (tel: 456-9119, 459-6377; fax: 456-9140, 611-5568; e-mail: croatia.eoi@hfp.hr; internet site: www.hfp.hr).

Croatian Securities Exchange Commission, Bogovieeva 3, 10000 Zagreb (tel: 481-1407; fax: 481-1507).

Croatian Shipbuilding Co Ltd (Hrvatska brodogradnja-Jadranbrod), Av V Holjevca 20, 10020 Zagreb (fax: 652-8420).

Economic Development Corporations – see Ministry of Development and Reconstruction.

Information Department, Ilica 1a, 10000 Zagreb (tel: 455-6455; fax: 455-7827; internet site: www.hic.hr/english/index.htm).

Luka Ploce (second largest Croatian Port), Trg Kralja Tomislava 21, 20340 Ploce (tel: 067-9601; fax: 067-9836; email: luka-ploce@du.tel.hr).

State Agency for Deposit Insurance and Bank Rehabilitation, Jurisiceva 1, 10000 Zagreb (fax: 481-3222: fax: 481-1907; e-mail: dragbank@zg.tel.hr).

State Bureau of Standards and Measures, Ul grada Vukovara 78, 10000 Zagreb (tel: 610-6111; 610-9324; e-mail: pisarnica@dznm.hr).

State Bureau of Statistics, Ilica 3, 10000 Zagreb (tel: 480-6111; fax: 481-7666; e-mail: ured@agram.dzs.hr).

Zagrebacki Velesajem (Zagreb fairs, exhibitions and conferences), Dubrovacka Avenija 2, Zagreb (fax: 520-6430).

Zagreb Stock Exchange, Ksaver 208, 41000 Zagreb (tel: 455-1866; fax: 455-1118; internet site: www.zse.hr).

Other news agencies: HIC (Croatian Information Centre): www.hic.hr

Hina (Croatian News Agency): http://websrv2.hina.hr

Internet sites

Croatia homepage: www.hr/english

Croatian Business Pages: www.hrvatska.com

Croatian Government: www.vlada.hr/english/contents.html

HINA, Croatian News Agency: www.hina.hr/nws-bin/ehot.cgi

Croatian Heritage Foundation: www.matis.hr/english/index.php

Hrvatska Radio Televizija: www.hrt.hr

Hrvatski Telekom: www.ht.hr

Cuba

KEY FACTS

Official name: República de Cuba (Republic of Cuba)

Head of State: President of the Council of State Raul Castro Ruz (since 24 Feb 2008)

Head of government: President of the Council of State Raul Castro (since 24 Feb 2008)

Ruling party: Partido Comunista de Cuba (PCC) (Cuban Communist Party)

Area: 110,860 square km

Population: 11.26 million (2010)*

Capital: Havana

Official language: Spanish

Currency: Cuban Convertible peso and Cuban peso (Cu$) (CUC) both = 100 centavos (NB From 2004, the US dollar was only to be used to convert to CUC)

Exchange rate: CUC0.82 per US$ (Oct 2011); (a government 10% surcharge is imposed on all US$ transactions converting to CUC, which was revalued by 8% in April 2005). Cu$ cannot be used for local payments, nor exchanged for any other currency.

GDP per capita: US$5,130 (2010)

GDP real growth: 2.10% (2010)

GDP: US$57.60 billion (2010)

Unemployment: 1.60% (2009)

Inflation: 2.90% (2010)

Balance of trade: -US$2.69 billion (2008)*

* estimated figure

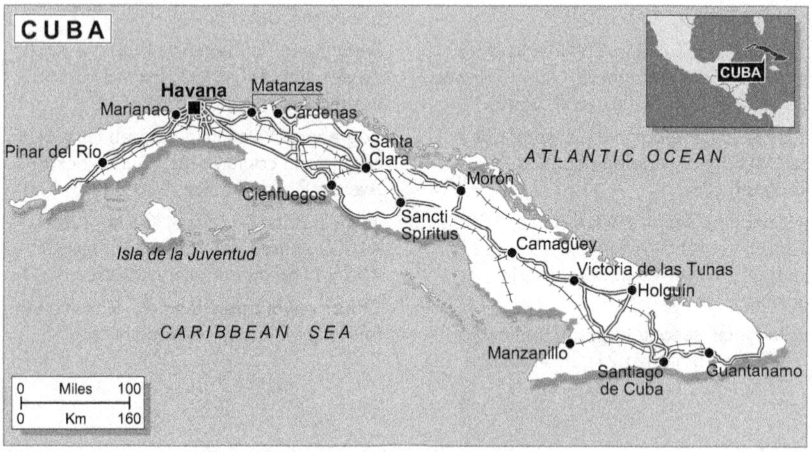

In 2011 Cuba things certainly 'ain't what they used to be' as the Castro dynasty totters to an uncertain end. For most Cubans, living in a confused blend of political anachronism and vacuum isn't a bundle of fun. Quite simply, everything has aged. Gone are the days of febrile four hour long political rallies, where the slogans of the leadership would be slavishly repeated over and over again. In 2011, the occasional *viva* is about as good as it gets. There simply isn't a great deal to celebrate: a scarcity of many basic food staples, a geriatric, dynastic government, over 50 years of one party rule. The Arab Spring may have gripped North Africa and parts of the Middle East, but Cuba was stuck with the wrong kind of Latin Autumn. Cuba's demographics differ from those of Tunisia or Egypt; it has an ageing, shrinking population that is unlikely to take to the barricades. The Cuban exile community – there are an estimated one million people of Cuban origin in the USA – seeks to clear its political decks, replacing the Castro administration with a Latin Tea Party.

Reading the runes

For political analysts, rallies do at least give some kind of insight into hierarchical shifts. Thus, on 26 July 2011 the faithful turned out for one such rally in the province of Ciego de Avila at which the keynote speaker was – predictably – expected to be Raúl Castro. But to everyone's surprise, Raúl, (the younger brother of Fidel), was not seated near the microphone. Instead, the keynote speech came from the dull voice of the Vice Chairman of the Council of State and Ministers, the octogenarian José Ramón Machado Ventura. Cuba watchers not only noted that Mr Machado Ventura lacked any charisma. He also lacked the historical credentials that the Castro brothers wore on their sleeve. Machado Ventura was not involved in the storming of the Montcada Barracks in 1953. Instead of inviting his listeners to stiffen their sinews, the boring Machado Ventura preferred to admonish his listeners for their failures.

Yoani Sánchez

In 2011, the most respected interpreter of Cuba's political runes was Yoania Sanchez, whose award winning blog *Generación Y* (Generation Y) provided the outside world with a daily interpretation of events. Thus Ms Sánchez observed that at the July rally, 'the triumphal harangues of yesteryear have given way to language that has all the urgency of a skipper in a foundering boat.' Ms Sánchez also speculated that 'perhaps what led Raúl Castro to delegate his speech was not just the absence of news and results suitable for announcement.' It was also the government's failure to stick to the promises made a year earlier. When Raúl Castro did take to the microphone, it was to criticise what he described as 'prejudice against the non-state sector' of the economy, shorthand for the once taboo 'private enterprise'. Promoting 'private economic activity' has become a critical economic reform in Cuba; in the short term the government envisages laying off as many as 1.8 million state employees, from a total workforce of 5.2 million. The only way in which these unemployed are likely to re-join the productive economy is by seeking employment in the private sector.

Alongside the development of the private sector, came the introduction of what Cuban media described as a 'tax culture'. This represented a sea change in official, and individual, behaviour. Government economists anticipated a 400 per cent increase in individual tax revenues. However, rendering unto Caesar has never sat comfortably in the Latin psyche, even in the region's more developed economies. In October 2010 the Cuban government published a tax code for those working in what were described as 'authorised occupations'. Although the introduction of the tax culture proved something of a challenge, Raúl Castro appeared determined to maintain the pace of reform. In 2011 it was planned to introduce legislation allowing Cubans to buy and sell their homes. Since the revolution, property rights have been non-existent in Cuba. Ironically, most Cubans do actually own their homes, but have not been allowed to sell them, only to exchange them for an equivalent property. In April 2011 the reform proposals were approved by the Communist Party Congress. During the period leading up to the April Party Congress, over 300,000 Cubans had applied for a business licence. The government expected that number to rise sharply as more public sector jobs were lost. Party veterans could only reflect on the replacement of the revolutionary spirit by an incipient business bureaucracy.

The *Y Generation*

Reliable information on Cuba of any sort – political, economic, even cultural – is hard to come by. Probably the most reliable source, started in 2007, is the website *Generación Y*. The name is an obscure reference to the number of Cubans of Yoania Sanchez' age whose names have Russian inspiration. The website is a daily blog on Cuban life written by Ms Sánchez and available in some 20 languages; it generates an estimated 14 million hits per month. The Cuban authorities have, unsuccessfully, sought to close down the website, as they have other media publishing honest accounts of life in Cuba.

Ms Sánchez' success – both in publishing her blog and avoiding closure or censorship – have made her an international media icon. She has met ex-President Jimmy Carter, published an interview with President Obama and has been included in its list of the 100 most influential people in the world by the US-based *Time* magazine. In contrast, former Cuban leader Fidel Castro has called her the leader of a group of 'special envoys of neo- colonialism, sent to undermine' his rule. One US academic noted that Ms Sánchez has probably replaced 'Che' and 'Fidel' among young progressive people interested in Cuba. Were this the case, the Cuban government's desire to close down Ms Sánchez's *Generación Y* would not be at all surprising. Nor would the closure of the blog represent a departure from the traditional stifling of accurate sources of information.

The US Obsession

It has long been a given that the Cuban Revolution had little to do with the rest of Latin America, and everything to do with US-Cuba relations. In 2011 the US economic embargo was still firmly in place. The embargo can only be lifted by a vote in Congress, and the mid-term Republican victories made anything like an ending of the embargo an impossibility. The Obama administration had at least reversed some of the tighter restrictions introduced by former President George Bush, who was beholden to the US Cuban lobby. In 2009 the Obama administration abolished the restrictions on travel and remittances by Cuban Americans introduced by Mr Bush. The effect of the loosening was significant and immediate: in 2010 over 400,000 US citizens visited Cuba, the highest number since before the revolution. At the end of 2010 the US ranked second (behind Canada) as the largest source of visitors to Cuba. Remittances from the US to Cuba are thought to be around the US$1 billion mark.

VeneCuba

Cubans could be forgiven for harbouring doubts about their future and the direction, or lack of direction, in which their leaders have steered the island country. No such doubts seemed to bother Venezuela's president, Hugo Chávez. During his period in office, billions of dollars in aid have been given to Cuba by Venezuela. In 2011 an estimated 50,000 Cubans were working in Venezuela, leading one Venezuelan commentator to describe their presence as Cuba's 'second invasion' of their country (the first being a failed incursion in 1967). Accumulated aid from Venezuela to Cuba in the period 1999–2009 was put at US$9.4 billion, roughly 70 per cent of Venezuela's total aid expenditure for the period. Two thirds of the Cubans working in Venezuela do so in the health sector.

The highest profile feature of the links between the two countries has been the visits to Cuba by Venezuelan President Chávez for cancer treatment. The relationship between the two countries is thought to be in the interest of both governments. In addition to untrammelled cash aid, Venezuela also provides Cuba with 115 million barrels of subsidised oil each day. The subsidy is calculated to cost Venezuela around US$3.5 billion per year (2010), although neither government has been prepared to ratify this figure.

Race

After 50 years of revolution, the elephant in the shabby room that is contemporary Cuban society is the question of race. Post-revolutionary society certainly moved towards racial equality, but not quickly enough. In 2011 a huge gulf existed between the white and Negro communities. The black and mulatto

KEY INDICATORS — Cuba

	Unit	2006	2007	2008	2009	2010
Population	m	11.37	*11.40	*11.20	*11.45	*11.26
Gross domestic product (GDP)	US$bn	–	*45.50	54.70	56.10	57.60
GDP per capita	US$	–	4,051	4,870	4,990	5,130
GDP real growth	%	–	6.5	4.3	1.4	2.1
Inflation	%	–	*2.8	0.9	1.5	2.9
Current account	US$m	–	–	-2,594.0	513.0	201.0
Exchange rate	per US$	0.82	0.82	0.82	0.82	0.82

* estimated figure

population was descended from slaves; like it or not, the prejudices from the era of slavery often remained in place. The coloured community for the most part supported the revolution and its aims. This suited the government, which saw itself *inter alia* as the defender of the rights of the less prosperous members of society. When the Soviet subsidies that had long sustained the Cuban economy began to dry up, it was the black and mulatto members of Cuban society who were hardest hit. No official figures are available on the make-up of Cuba's prison population, but evidence suggests that the black and mulatto component constitutes a majority.

According to the 2002 census, 66 per cent of the population are white, 10 per cent black and 24 per cent of mixed blood. One glaringly obvious area where no black faces are to be seen is that of the government itself. Paradoxically, and ironically, this contrasts sharply with the situation in the US, where black politicians regularly appear in ministerial positions.

Risk assessment

Economy	Poor
Politics	Poor
Regional stability	Good

COUNTRY PROFILE

Historical profile

1492 Christopher Columbus landed in Cuba and claimed the island for Spain.
1511 Diego Columbus, son of Christopher, settled the island. Spanish settlers established sugar plantations and exploited slaves from West Africa.
1514 The city of Havana was founded.
1607 Havana was named the capital of Cuba.
1762–64 Havana was captured by the British but was returned to Spain under the Treaty of Paris.
1868–78 The first war of independence ended in a truce after Spain promised reforms and greater autonomy – which were never fulfilled.
1886 Slavery was abolished.
1895–98 José Marti led a second war of independence; the US declared war on Spain.
1898 Spain was defeated and gave up all claims to Cuba, ceding it to the US.
1901 The constitution of the Republic of Cuba, modelled on the US constitution, was adopted.
1902 Cuba was officially granted independence from the US. Tomas Estrada Palma became its first president. However the US retained the right to intervene in Cuban domestic affairs.
1925 The Partido Comunista de Cuba (PCC) (Cuban Communist Party) was founded.
1933 Fulgencio Batista took power in a *coup d'état*.
1934 The US abandoned its right to intervene in Cuban internal affairs.
1940 A new constitution was promulgated.
1944 Batista retired from office.
1952 Batista seized power again, backed by the US government. His regime was oppressive and corrupt.
1956 Fidel Castro began a guerrilla war against Batista's dictatorship.
1958 US backing for Batista was withdrawn.
1959 The Cuban revolution concluded when Castro's revolutionaries defeated the Cuban army and assumed power, founding a socialist state.
1960 All US owned businesses in Cuba were nationalised without compensation; the US broke off diplomatic relations.
1961 The US sponsored an unsuccessful military invasion, by Cuban exiles, at the Bay of Pigs. Cuba was declared a Communist state and Castro allied it to the USSR.
1962 Castro's fear of US aggression resulted in the Cuban missile crisis when he agreed to deploy USSR nuclear missiles on Cuba. The US blockaded Cuba, published evidence of the missiles and US President Kennedy gave an ultimatum that they be removed or the US would bomb Cuba. The crisis was resolved when the USSR agreed and withdrew the missiles, and in return the US closed its missile sites in Turkey. The US imposed a full trade embargo on Cuba.
1976 A new constitution created a National Assembly, which held its first session and elected Fidel Castro as president.
1989 The USSR began to disintegrate and the trade in Cuban sugar for subsidised oil collapsed.
1991 Soviet troops left Cuba. The economy fell into depression.
1993 To ameliorate the economy some market reforms were adopted and the US dollar was made an official currency alongside the Cuban peso.
1998 US restrictions on remittances were eased.
2000 US approves the sale of food and medicines to Cuba.
2001 The first shipment in 40 years of US exported food arrived.
2002 The UN criticised Cuba for its poor civil rights. It was announced that at least 71 of Cuba's 156 sugar refineries were to be scrapped.
2003 A crackdown on dissidents resulted in international condemnation, as 75 people were imprisoned. The EU broke off diplomatic contacts.
2004 The official exchange rate of Cu$1 per US$ replaced the convertible rate of Cu$21 per US$. The US tightened restrictions on visits and money remittances to Cuba; the US dollar ceased to be legal tender and a 10 per cent commission for converting dollars to pesos was imposed.
2005 EU diplomatic relations with Cuba were re-established. President Hugo Chávez of Venezuela and Fidel Castro signed a co-operation agreement; Cuba supplied doctors and medical treatment to Venezuela in exchange for crude oil at a preferential price.
2006 The Non-Aligned Movement held its 14th meeting in Havana under Cuban chairmanship. Fidel Castro, amid rumours and speculation about his health, did not attend delayed celebrations of his 80th birthday or the 50th anniversary parade of his return to Cuba.
2007 In December a letter by Castro was read out on national television saying he would not hold on to power indefinitely.
2008 In parliamentary elections 614 candidates, including Fidel Castro, contested the 614 seats; turnout was 95 per cent. Fidel Castro announced he would not return to the presidency due to ill health. Raúl Castro was voted in unopposed as president. The Marxist ideologically driven system of equal pay for all was abandoned. The EU lifted sanctions imposed in 2003. Talks on mutual co-operation resumed between the European Commission and Cuba.
2009 Cuba offered to hold direct talks with the US, describing US President Obama as an 'honest man'. The US Congress voted to remove restrictions on family members travelling to Cuba, once a year, and sending remittances; trade in medicines and food was also eased. Costa Rica opened an embassy in Havana. The Organisation of American States (OAS) voted to lift Cuba's suspension of its membership.
2010 Political prisoner Orlando Zapata Tamayo died on 23 February after an 85-day hunger strike. Zapata was one of 75 dissidents jailed in 2003, and was serving a 25-year prison sentence for political activities against the régime. In March, El Salvador, the last Central American nation withholding diplomatic relations, opened an embassy in Havana. For the first time since 2006, Fidel Castro publicly addressed the National Assembly on 4 August, appearing fully recovered from his previous illness. Plans to lay-off up to a million state workers were announced on 14 September. It was hoped that the move would help revive the struggling economy. On 9 November President Raul Castro announced the first congress of the ruling communist party in 14 years would be held within months.

2011 On 14 January, the US further eased travel restrictions, allowing religious groups and students to visit Cuba. The payment of remittances of up to US$500 per quarter to non-family members for private economic activity, and greater amounts for religious institutions in Cuba, were allowed. The move is expected to improve civil life. US airports will be allowed to license chartered services to Cuba. Cuba suspended mail deliveries to the US on 22 January, due to new US security measures and the return of large quantities of mail. On 14 March, in an effort to stimulate the flagging economy by boosting exports and domestic production, the hard-currency convertible peso was devalued to match the US dollar, losing around 8 per cent in value. Not only will the devaluation increase the value of remittances from relatives in the US but will also increase the spending power of tourists. However, the convertible dollar will still be worth 24 domestic pesos, so the cost of imports will rise for most Cubans. On 17 April, during the first congress of the ruling PCC since 1997, President Raul Castro stated that top political jobs should be limited to two five-year terms in office and that the PCC leadership was in need of renewal and should be open to critical self-analysis. On 18 April the government announced that it will allow people to buy and sell their homes for the first time since the communist revolution in 1959. On 19 April, President Raúl Castro was elected first secretary of the PCC. Details to allow the buying and selling of private property and cars was published in *Granma* on 1 July. The proposed laws have still to be passed by parliament.

Political structure

Constitution

The 1979 constitution gives all legislative power to the Asamblea Nacional de Poder Popular (National Assembly of People's Power) which runs local and central government. An amendment in 2002 made the Partido Comunista de Cuba (PCC) (Cuban Communist Party) the permanent party of government.

Form of state

Socialist republic.

The executive

The president and the Consejo de Estado (Council of State) and council of ministers are appointed by the national assembly and drawn from the state (communist) party.

The council of state is the highest-ranking executive institution and is made up of a president, first vice president, and five vice presidents and 30 members. It has legislative powers when the national assembly is in recess. The council runs foreign trade and foreign relations, draws up the draft budget and is responsible for the general organisation of the revolutionary armed forces.

National legislature

The unicameral, Asamblea Nacional del Poder Popular (National Assembly of People's Power) has 609 members, elected for a five-year term from a closed list of PCC members. Its chief role is to approve laws put forward by the council of state. According to the constitution the national assembly is the 'supreme organ of state power and represents and expresses the sovereign will of all the working people'. Its role includes approving laws, discussing and approving the state budget and supervising other official bodies.

Legal system

While the constitution provides for independent courts it explicitly subordinates the courts to state control. The national assembly chooses all judges. The People's Supreme Court is the highest judicial body; it oversees a system of regional tribunals and is accountable to the national assembly.

Last elections

February 2008 (presidential election by National Assembly); 20 January 2008 (parliamentary).

Results: Parliamentary: 609 pro-government candidates stood for exactly the same number of seats in the National Assembly and were elected unopposed.

Next elections

January 2013 (parliamentary and presidential election by National Assembly).

Political parties

Ruling party

Partido Comunista de Cuba (PCC) (Cuban Communist Party)

Main opposition party

There is no opposition party.

Population

11.26 million (2010)*

Last census: September 2002: 11,177,743

Population density: Population density: 102 inhabitants per square km.

Annual growth rate: 0.4 per cent 1994–2004 (WHO 2006)

Ethnic make-up

The Cuban population is a product of the mix of four cultural groups: the indigenous people, Spaniards, Africans and Asians.

Mulatto (51 per cent), white (37 per cent), black (11 per cent), Chinese (1 per cent).

Religions

Many Cubans are agnostic or atheist, while unofficial estimates are of 75,000–100,000 practising Catholics. There is a smaller Protestant community. Practices based on African religions are reported to be increasing in popularity.

Education

Public expenditure on education amounts to 8.7 per cent of GDP. There is sustained investment in education with incentive rewards for excellence in pupils, teachers and schools. The education system promotes inclusively for learning outcomes and curriculum development between teachers and students.

Education is free at all levels. It is based on the Communist principle of combining learning with manual labour. Day nurseries and pre-school centres are available to all children after just six weeks. Primary schools are compulsory for six years until aged 12. Secondary schools are for 13- to 18-year-olds. State subsidies are available for workers returning to education to complete university courses.

Literacy rate: 97 per cent adult rate; 100 per cent youth rate (15–24) (Unesco 2005).

Compulsory years: 6 to 12.

Enrolment rate: 106 per cent gross primary enrolment, of the relevant age group (including re-enrolment); 81 per cent gross secondary enrolment, of the relevant age group (World Bank).

Pupils per teacher: 12 in primary schools.

Health

There are approximately 260 hospitals and over 400 clinics that provide full and free medical services in all regions of the country. However, current US economic embargoes limit access to internationally purchased branded medical supplies.

In 2005 US$100 million was allocated to invest in the pharmaceutical industry. Generic medicines have become a major export item.

HIV/Aids

HIV prevalence: 0.1 per cent aged 15–49 in 2003 (World Bank)

Life expectancy: 77.6 years, 2004 (MEDICC 2007)

Fertility rate/Maternal mortality rate: 1.4 births per woman; maternal mortality 52.2 per 100,000 live births (MEDICC 2007).

Birth rate/Death rate: 10.7 births per 1,000 population; seven deaths per 1,000 population (2003).

Child (under 5 years) mortality rate (per 1,000): 8 per 1,000 live births (World Bank)

Head of population per physician: 6.2 physicians per 1,000 people (MEDICC 2007)

Welfare

In a 2005 economist reported to Castro that the minimum monthly income to survive in Cuba was Cu$300 (US$14.4). The minimum monthly wage was increased to Cu$225 (US$10.8), and monthly pension payments to CU$150

(US$7.2) benefiting 54 per cent of state employees. Wages in other sectors grew in line with these increases. Pensions and social assistance were also increased by 50 pesos a month.
The 1976 constitution guarantees all Cubans the right and duty to have a job, while the state provides basic support for the aged, the disabled and others unable to work. Although the principle of full employment stands unchanged, the government has admitted that unemployment does indeed exist.

Main cities
Havana (estimated population 2.8 million in 2004), Santiago de Cuba (554,400), Camagüey (354,400), Holguín (319,300), Guantánamo (274,300), Santa Clara (251,800), Bayamo (191,100), Pinar del Río (180,400), Cienfuegos (171,500).

Languages spoken
The Spanish in use in Cuba is more Latin American than Castillian and many words are quite different from the Spanish used in Spain. Quite often the endings of words are dropped, shortened nouns are used and slang is prevalent. The further south in Cuba, the more pronounced the accent.
English is quite widely spoken, as it is the main foreign language taught in schools.

Official language/s
Spanish

Media
The constitution prohibits private ownership of electronic media and there are punitive laws which suppress journalists in a country where the media is tightly controlled and independent media and journalists are targeted for intimidation. The government strictly regulates Internet access.
Juventud Rebelde is Cuba's youth paper. The Cuban Communist party sees the media as an important tool for reinforcing socialist ideals within the scope of entertainment and education.
In December 2010 Cuba launched a Spanish language online encyclopaedia (www.ecured.cu) similar to Wikipedia. 'Its philosophy is the accumulation and development of knowledge, with a democratising, not profitable, objective, from a decoloniser point of view.'

Press
There are several news agencies publishing newspapers in six major languages.
Dailies: In Spanish, regional and local newspapers include *Cubahora* (www.cubahora.co.cu), *Periódic 26* (www.periodico26.cu) from Las Tunas, *Guerrillero* (www.guerrillero.co.co.cu) form Pinar del Rio, *Venceremos* (www.venceremos.co.cu) from Gauntanamo, with an English online edition, *Sierra Maestra* (www.sierramaestra.cu) from Santiago de Cuba, and *Vanguardia* (www.vanguardia.co.cu) from Villa Santa.
Weeklies: In Spanish, national publications include the government-run *Trabajadores* (www.trabajadores.cubaweb.cu), and Communist party-run *Granma* (www.granma.co.cu), *Cinco de Septiembre* (www.5septiembre.cu) from Cienfuegos, with an English online edition. Alternative magazines include *Bohemia* (www.bohemia.cubaweb.cu) an illustrated and *Dedete* (www.dedete.cubaweb.cu) is a humorous publication.
Business: In Spanish, *El Economista de Cuba* (www.eleconomista.cubaweb.cu), *Opiones* (www.opciones.cu), a weekly publication by the tourist industry and *Negocios en Cuba* (www.prensa-latina.cu) published by Prensa Latina.

Broadcasting
Services controlled by the Ministerio de la Informática y las Comunicaciones (Ministry of Information and Communications).
Radio: There are over 40 radio stations throughout Cuba, most local and catering for their captive audiences. National transmissions run parallel to international services provided via satellite and the Internet. Radio Cubana (www.radiocubana.cu) (with access to local radio streaming), Radio Havana Cuba (www.radiohc.cu) and Radio Rebelde (www.radiorebelde.com.cu) are the principal organs of state for news and propaganda.
Television: The national, state-run Cubavision (Sistema Informativo de la Televisión Cubana), (www.cubavision.cubaweb.cu) shows domestic programmes ranging from soap operas to university education and a wide range of imported material. There is also an international channel, Cubavision Internacional via satellite.
Cuba also joined Venezuela, Argentina and Uruguay – and later Bolivia, Ecuador and Nicaragua – to form a pan-American public news channel, Telsur (www.telesurtv.net) to broadcast programmes to offset what they saw as the overwhelming influence of popular, privately-run channels such as the US-run CNN en Español.
The only officially approved domestic satellite TV service is available to resident foreigners, tourist and approved Communist party officials. Illegal satellite provisions, using the US-based, anti-Castro TV Marti, have resulted in criminal convictions.

Advertising
Advertising facilities are limited and state-controlled and generally not available to foreign companies.

News agencies
National news agency: Agencia de Información Nacional (Cuban News Agency)
Other news agencies: Prensa Latina: www.plenglish.com.mx

Economy
Although 95 per cent of the economy is state-controlled, it is diverse and includes primary industries, such as agriculture and mining, secondary industries such as pharmaceuticals, and the famous cigar manufacturing and tertiary industries such as healthcare and tourism. The US embargo on the Cuban economy since the 1950s has been both a constraint, by limiting growth and innovation, and a spur to seek out alternative markets, technologies and inventiveness. Cuba has managed to survive with a make-do and mend regime during the economic siege.
However, the economic landscape has undergone a sharp change since 2008 when three hurricanes caused over US$10 billion in damage, tourist numbers fell due to the global economic crisis, which also resulted in a drop in nickel ore sales in much of 2009. These three shocks, falling within such a short period, caused a serious, progressive fall in GDP growth, down from 12.1 per cent in 2007 to 7.3 per cent in 2008, to 4.3 per cent in 2009, to an estimated 1.4 per cent in 2010.
While the economy did not fall into recession, Cuba is faced with harder requirements than experienced generally by other trading nations. The US is Cuba's biggest source of food and although food is not part of the long-standing embargo, the US requires that all imports have to be paid for before delivery. Cuba's cash-flow problems forced it to cut its imports in 2009 by 26 per cent, as it was faced with unpaid debts to foreign creditors. Cuba looked to other sources, such as Vietnam, for cheaper food and better terms of business.
During 2009, exports rose by 21 per cent, while imports only rose by 1 per cent, so that the trade deficit was cut by 7 per cent. Medical services from healthcare workers working overseas earned US$9.9 billion.
An embargo on remittances from Cuban exiles (mainly in Miami, US), which were estimated to bring the island over US$1 billion a year, was lifted in March 2009. The Cuban authorities require that any such remittances are used in special dollar stores where commodities are priced at a higher mark-up than elsewhere.
There are two currencies in Cuba: all local people use the Cuban peso (Cu$) while a convertible peso (CUC) is used for international trade and by foreign visitors.

The government maintains the price of certain basics for its citizens but all products outside this system must be paid for in CUC, which has led to a flourishing black market, estimated to be as much as 40 per cent of the economy.

The Marxist ideologically driven system of equal pay for all was abandoned in 2008 when the government announced that workers and managers would begin to earn performance bonuses. Workers earn a minimum 5 per cent bonus if targets are met and managers can earn up to 30 per cent when increased production can be demonstrated. Self-employment figures rose from 157,000 in 2010 to 295,000 in 2011.

In August 2010 President Raúl Castro announced that state control of the economy was going to be relaxed in a move to help revive the struggling economy. In September, the government announced that it was going to make redundant 500,000 state-workers, and encourage them to become self-employed or join new private enterprises, on which some restrictions were eased. However, some question how the funding for such businesses would be found and pointed to the wariness of foreign lenders who had experienced poor repayment and lack of foreign ownership rights, in the past.

In 2010 rationing of potatoes and tobacco was eliminated and subsidised worker's canteens were phased out in several ministries. There are plans to propose to the Communist Congress in April 2011 the removal of comprehensive food rationing. Rationing had been introduced in 1962 and allowed the government to counter the effect of the trade embargo, avoid absolute poverty and defuse possible social unrest. However, it also cost the country, as the loss of the profit motive flattened enterprise and initiative.

According to the World Bank, Cuba is an upper-middle income country, based on social criteria of life expectancy and education as well as water and sanitation infrastructure. However, without a fully functioning commercial economy, with entrepreneurial businesses and a free labour market Cuba is still a hybrid society with benefits of one system outweighing what could be the benefits of another.

On 14 March 2011, in an effort to stimulate the flagging economy by boosting exports and domestic production, the hard-currency convertible peso was devalued to match the US dollar, losing around 8 per cent in value. Not only will the devaluation increase the value of remittances from relatives in the US but will also give an increase in spending power for tourists. However the convertible dollar will still be worth 24 domestic pesos, so the cost of imports will rise for most Cubans.

External trade

The balance of payments is reliant on foreign currency earnings from tourism, remittances, nickel and cobalt. Sugar has fallen in importance as an export commodity and nickel and cobalt has expanded to take advantage of increasing world prices.

The US trade embargo continues to have a negative effect on trade, although Venezuela has been supporting Cuba with preferential oil imports in exchange for Cuban goods and services. China and Russia have both entered agreements for investment in Cuba.

Cuba has a trade co-operation protocol with the 15-member Caribbean Community and Common Market (Caricom).

Imports

Domestic companies require a licence to import certain goods, and the withdrawal of these licences a means for the government to control imports and its trade deficit, although the mechanism is regarded as heavy-handed.

Imports comprise petroleum, machinery and equipment, food, chemicals.

Main sources: Venezuela (typically 32 per cent of total), China (12 per cent), Spain (11 per cent).

Exports

Principal exports are included, nickel, cobalt, sugar tobacco, fish, bio-technical medical products, citrus and coffee.

Healthcare professionals are hired as a team to visit overseas countries (typically in South America and the Caribbean) to treat patients chosen by the host government.

Main destinations: China (typically 28 per cent of total), Canada (25 per cent), Spain (6 per cent).

Agriculture

Farming

Sugar is Cuba's most important export crop, however since its collapse as a top cash crop, there has been a concerted effort to diversify. The sugar industry has undergone restructuring to make the production more efficient and identify new markets. Over 70 of the 156 sugar refineries in Cuba have been decommissioned with some 100,000 workers laid off. Half of Cuba's 3.5 million hectares (ha) of sugar cane fields have been re-utilised to produce other crops, particularly foodstuffs for domestic consumption and reduce the need for imports.

Two new cocoa processing plants with a capacity of 45,000 tonnes are planned to provide exports of high quality cocoa butter.

Approximately 95 per cent of Cuba's coffee plantations are the highly prized arabica bean. Coffee exports should be enhanced by the refurbishment of seven processing mills. The international cost of coffee rose by 69 per cent 2010–11 and forced the authorities to reintroduce the practice of mixing roast peas with roast beans for sale and local consumption. In 2010 domestic consumption of coffee was 18,000 tonnes, whereas production was only 12,000 tonnes and imports costs rose to US$50 million. Investment in coffee production was US$9.5 million between 2005–10.

Cuba has begun developing organic farming, and there are over 100,000 small-to medium-sized organic farms reflecting the government's commitment to the 'greening of Cuba'.

In November 2011, the government relaxed its rules allowing farmers to sell their produce directly to hotels, restaurants and the public and to make a profit. The new rules are expected to cut out official middlemen, transportation costs and improve productivity.

Fishing

Catches have fallen since the mid-1980s. The contraction of fin fish catches by the deep sea fleet, partly as a result of changes in fishing agreements, has been largely responsible. Cuba is investing considerable resources in shrimp farming, but production has not been commercially significant.

Forestry

Forests cover around 2.3 million hectares (ha), around 15 per cent of the total land area. Since 1990 forest cover has increased by an average of 1.27 per cent per annum or 28,000ha.

Industry and manufacturing

The industrial sector contributes approximately 37 per cent to GDP.

Cuba's free trade zones, especially those of Wajay and Mariel have attracted a number of foreign companies. Mariel, located 48.2km west of Havana, is likely to play an important role in the future, especially if trade opens with the US.

The Hola processing plant in Havana toasts and grinds coffee beans for export to the UK, Ukraine, Bulgaria, the Bahamas and Spain.

The cigar industry is significant, with production increasing substantially in the late-1990s and generating annual revenues of an estimated US$150 million.

Tourism

The importance of tourism to Cuba has grown since it has had to deal with external and internal pressures that require not only hard currencies to buy commodities but also to maintain growth in its centralised economy. The US embargo on trade with Cuba has hindered development and all capital investment in the industry has been either government backed or in partnership with sympathetic foreign sources.

The sector has experienced a downturn as the share of direct contribution to GDP began to fall from 3.6 per cent in 2005 to 3.1 in 2006 to its lowest of 2.6 per cent in both 2009–10. Direct and indirect employment in the sector also fell during this time as visitor spending fell to its lowest US$2.106 billion in 2009, before a modest recovery in 2010. Although in 2009–10 government investment in the industry was cut, this had followed a period of higher outlay that matched investment in other sectors.

In May 2010, the government announced that it planned to allow foreign investment in golf courses, marinas and other tourist attractions, with the offer of medium- to long-term leases. Given the US ban on investment in Cuba, the prime candidates for investment are Canadians and Europeans.

In 2010, Cuba was a country unspoiled by mass tourism, but at the expense of a people held back from a potentially good living through tourism. Some of the current, quaint sights that enchant visitors, such as vintage cars left over from the days before the revolution, which have been lovingly conserved not for their good looks but because they were the only vehicles available, are likely to be lost (either snapped up by collectors or exchanged for a modern vehicle) in any headlong rush to modernise. It will require skilled management to move from an old Soviet style economy to a modern, open market where tourism provides a realistic living for workers and does not exploit them based on traditional poorer wages or overwhelm or monopolise local resources.

Environment

Incessant rain, following tropical storm Noel, falling from 11 October to 5 November 2007, caused the worst floods in forty years, destroying tens of thousands of homes, leaving roads impassable and damaging crops of sugar and coffee.

The drought that began in 2009 had by 2011 become the worst since the 1960s, as water levels in reservoirs fell to a fifth of normal amounts and tens of thousands of families became reliant on water lorries for their essential supplies. Even if the rainy season, in May–June, brings relief, normal rainfall will be insufficient to compensate for the deficit.

Mining

Mining contributes around 6 per cent to GDP. The island's extensive nickel and cobalt ore reserves, among the largest in the world, offer attractive large-scale mining opportunities. Cuba's rich mineral resources are open to foreign exploration and development.

Exploration for gold, silver and base metals is carried out by more than a dozen foreign firms in concession areas covering nearly a third of Cuba's national territory. Cuba has updated its mining legislation, bringing it into line with most other Latin American countries.

Nickel production has been boosted by the injection of Canadian capital and technology. Government figures for 2004–05 showed nickel production reached 35,000 tonnes and overtook sugar as Cuba's biggest merchandise export, earning US$545 million. Since 2000 Cuba has supplied over half the nickel China uses in the production of stainless steel, and to maintain supplies China agreed, in November 2004, to invest US$500 million in the nickel industry. Cuba intends to modernise its processing plants and continue exploration for other base and precious metals. More than half the production comes from the Comandante Pedro Sotto Alba processing plant at Moa Bay, jointly operated since 1994 by Sherritt (Canada) and a Cuban company, Compania General de Niquel (General Nickel Company). Cuba's two other operating nickel plants are being modernised with the help of export-linked revolving credits from Dutch, German and other foreign banks and trade houses.

Hydrocarbons

Proven oil reserves were 124 million barrels in 2008, with production at 52,000 barrels per day (bpd), however consumption was 176,000bpd which had to be met by imports. Four oil refineries have a capacity of 124,000bpd, since 2007, when the Cienfuegos refinery, a Soviet Russian era facility, was completed and upgraded by Cubapetroleo (Cupet) and the Venezuelan state-oil company. There are plans to increase production in this plant to 100,000bpd and national capacity to 161,000bpd.

The state-run Cupet is responsible for exploration, production and supply of all oil in Cuba, either solely or in partnership with international oil companies. Exploration has been located mainly onshore in the northern Matanzas Province. However, offshore exploration is expected to find larger deposits in the future; some analysts have predicted amounts up to 5.0 billion barrels, but most finds are likely to be in deep water which is difficult and expensive to exploit. Drilling offshore began in 2009. In May 2011, the Ministry of Basic Industry (Minbas) announced that plans for drilling five deepwater oil exploration wells were scheduled for August 2011. The Chinese engineering company Yantai Raffles has built a semi-submersible rig, completed by the Singapores's engineering company Saipem, to be delivered and fitted for oil production to begin and be completed by 2013.

In 2005, Cuba, plus a number of other Caribbean states, signed an agreement with Venezuela to establish PetroCaribe, a multi-national oil company, owned by the participating states. PetroCaribe buys low-priced Venezuelan crude oil under long-term payment plans. Since this agreement, up to 100,000bpd, have been sold to Cuba at a discounted rate (by anywhere up to 40 per cent of world prices) by Venezuela in exchange for thousands of its citizens travelling to Cuba for healthcare and Cuban doctors administering healthcare programmes for low-income patients in Venezuela.

Proven natural gas reserves were 70.8 billion cubic metres (cum) in 2008, with production at 396 million cum, all of which is consumed domestically in energy production.

Around 40,000 tonnes of coal are imported annually, for consumption in energy production. Any coal deposits are negligible and production insignificant.

Energy

Total installed generating capacity was 5,861MW in 2008, producing over 16,694 gigawatt hours (gWh) and the majority of which is produced by oil-fired power stations. Cuba has a system of distributed generation (DG), whereby small-scale plants are located around the country and closer to their end users. This has allowed Cuba to recover from Caribbean hurricanes, which strike annually, much more rapidly than countries which adopted more centralised power generation plants. Around 40 per cent of all electricity is provided by DG, most generators being powered by diesel but also by renewable sources such as photovoltaic panels and wind turbines. The government programme Energy Revolution, introduced in 2008 encourages energy awareness along with the installation of over 700 small generators (producing up to 1,700MW).

Hydropower was first introduced in the 1930s and produces around 500MW, with 10MW under construction. Other renewable energy sources include bagasse (residue of sugar cane, burned to produce energy) as an oil substitute and wave power.

Banking and insurance

The Cuban banking sector has been transformed from a closed and highly centralised Soviet-style model to a diversified two-tier banking system.

In a bilateral agreement signed in 2005 Cuba opened a subsidiary of the Foreign

Bank of Cuba in Caracas, Venezuela, while a subsidiary of the Industrial Bank of Venezuela has been approved to open in Cuba.

Central bank

Banco Central de Cuba (BCC)

Time

GMT minus four hours in summer, GMT minus five hours in winter (October – March).

Geography

Cuba is the largest island in the Caribbean, lying 150km south of Florida. Together with offshore islands and an archipelago of about 1,600 coral cays surrounding the main island, the country has an area of 110,860 square km. The largest offshore island is the Isla de la Juventud, formerly known as the Isla de Piños, which covers 2,200 square km. Most of the long, thin main island consists of plains and low ranges of hills. The highest mountains are in the Sierra Maestra in the extreme south-east, where the Pico Real de Turquino rises to 1,974 metres.

Hemisphere

Northern.

Climate

Subtropical, with an annual mean temperature of 26 degrees Celsius (C) the average summer shade temperatures can rise to 30 degrees C and higher. November–April is the cooler, dry season with maximum temperatures peaking at around 26 degrees C. Trade winds and sea breezes cool the air; there are sudden, short showers in summer. The months of June, September and October–November usually bring hurricanes. The north is wetter than the south and the south, in particularly Santiago Province, is much hotter than the north.

There is rainfall of up to 250mm a year in the mountains.

It can be humid between May and October with some heavy rain. Humidity averages 62 per cent. However, during September and October, humidity can reach 95 per cent.

Dress codes

Dress since the 1959 revolution has been casual. Cubans wear lightweight and loose-fitting clothes, and formal dress, such as a tie, is an extremely rare sight.

Entry requirements

Passports

Required by all. Passports of nationals of countries without diplomatic relations with Cuba must be valid for two months beyond date of arrival.

Visa

Required by all, except nationals of countries who have reciprocal visa-free agreements.

Business visas, valid for 90 days from issue, are only obtained through sponsorship by an appropriate Cuban government organisation. For sponsorship contact the relevant State Trading Organisation or the commercial office of a Cuban embassy. Without a sponsor a visa will not be issued and a tourist card does not provide local firms with the opportunity to trade with business visitors.

Tourist cards are provided by airlines and tour operators who are registered with Cubatur. Exit visas are required for visitors staying more than 90 days.

Currency advice/regulations

The import and export of local currency is forbidden. There are no restrictions on the import of foreign currency, subject to declaration of amounts over US$5,000. Currency can be exchanged at the airport or hotel for 'convertible pesos'. When departing, they can be converted back again.

Hard currency is generally required from visitors for most transactions, although the US dollar is no longer legal tender. Visitors arriving with US currency must change it into 'convertible pesos', for which a 10 per cent commission is charged.

Health (for visitors)

Mandatory precautions

A yellow fever vaccination certificate is required if arriving from an infected area.

Advisable precautions

Vaccinations are recommended for typhoid, hepatitis A, tetanus and polio, as well as malaria prophylaxis – mosquitoes are a problem outside Havana.

The water supply in most upmarket hotels is excellent but elsewhere water precautions should be taken. Bottled water is readily available.

Medical services are good and free to visitors in an emergency. Insurance is advisable in case repatriation is required. Resorts and major cities have international clinics for tourists but the US embargo often means branded medicines may not be available. An adequate supply of regularly administered medication should be carried.

A visitor admitted to hospital is likely to be tested for HIV/Aids and will be deported if found to be a carrier.

Hotels

The best hotels can be found in Havana and Varadero beach. Foreign currencies should be exchanged at official Cadeca outlets.

The practice of tipping is growing – restaurants 5–10 per cent.

Credit cards

Only credit cards which are not issued in the US (Visa, Eurocard, MasterCard, Access) are accepted, generally only at tourist sites.

Public holidays (national)

Fixed dates

1 Jan (Liberation Day), 1 May (Labour Day), 25 Jul (Rebellion anniversary, three days), 10 Oct (Anniversary of the War of Independence), 25 Dec (Christmas Day).

Variable dates

Carnival: Havana (Feb); Varadero (late Jan/Feb); Trinidad and Santiago de Cuba (Jun).

Working hours

Banking

Mon–Fri: 0830–1200, 1330–1500; Sat: 0830–1030.

Banks in resorts tend to stay open longer. Banks and post offices do not accept Eurocheques or American Express travellers cheques.

Business

Mon–Fri: 0830–1230 and 1330–1630; some offices open alternate Saturdays between 0800–1700.

Government

Mon–Fri: 0830–1230, 1330–1730.

Shops

Mon-Fri: 0900-1700; Sat: 0900-1200.

Shops are normally closed on Sunday, except those in tourist areas. Resort shops and supermarkets often open seven days a week and their hours vary according to demand.

Pharmacies are open daily 0800–2000; those with *turno permanente* signs are open 24 hours.

Telecommunications

Postal services

Cuba suspended mail deliveries to the US in January 2011. The move was thought to be in retaliation for the return of mail by the US as part of stricter security measures introduced after the attempt to mail explosives from the Yemen in 2010. President Obama had allowed the resumption of mail services, via third countries, in 2009; services had been suspended since 1969.

Cuba has very few official mail collection boxes, so visitors are advised to post mail in a hotel, or at the airport.

Mobile/cell phones

GSM 900 service available in main tourist areas and cities only.

In 2008 reforms were announced which gave Cubans unlimited access to mobile phones. However, payment has to be made in foreign currency.

Internet/e-mail

An under-sea fibre-optic cable from Venezuela improved internet down-load speed by some 3,000 times from early 2011. It also reduced international telephone costs. The 1,600km cable was paid for by the Bolivarian Alliance for the Peoples of

Our America (Alba) – a left-wing regional grouping founded by President Hugo Chavez of Venezuela.

Electricity supply
110V AC, 60 cycles
Most plugs in hotels are two-pin, flat-pin type, although some are the two-pin, round-pin variety.
Some electric shaver points can be 220/240V.
Lighting is usually of the screw in, rather than bayonet, type.

Social customs/useful tips
Foreign residents say there are few restrictions on foreign visitors, however, they advise against vociferous public criticism of the government.
Cuba has placed great emphasis on sports; baseball, originally imported from the US, is the national sport with boxing vying as the most popular spectator sport.
Cubans address each other, and often foreign visitors, as *compañero* or *compañera*, and the informal *tu* form is often used when speaking Spanish.
Photographing airports and sensitive sites is forbidden and permission should be sought before photographing public or religious buildings.

Security
Although Cuba is considered to be a generally safe country, the usual precautions should be followed.
Keep to the main busy areas in the cities. Keep valuables and money belt out of sight. Avoid going out alone if possible, especially at night.

Getting there
Air
National airline: Cubana de Aviación.
International airport/s: Havana-José Marti International (HAV), 25km from city, with duty-free shops, bank, tourist information, hotel reservation and car hire; Varadero-Juan Gómez International (VRA), 12km from Cuba's main beach resort.
Other airport/s: Santiago-Antonio Macea (SCU).
Airport tax: 25 convertible Cuban pesos, except transit passengers.
Surface
Water: There is no scheduled passenger traffic due to the US blockade. Some cruise vessels and private yachts visit Cuba.
Main port/s: Antilla, Cienfuegos, Guayabal, Havana, Mariel, Matanzas, Nuevitas, Santiago de Cuba.

Getting about
National transport
Air: Cubana operates limited domestic services to main centres. Internal flights by visitors are generally arranged through Cubatur.
Road: The Central Highway (Autopista Nacional) runs for over 1,100km, virtually from end to end of the island and gives access to a network of local roads. Total road system exceeds 30,000km, at least 40 per cent surfaced although some roads/tracks may not be passable in wet weather.
Buses: Cross-country buses are cheap and fairly reliable, but can be overcrowded. Coaches link main centres. An air-conditioned service operated by Viazul offers more comfortable travel around the island; payment in convertible pesos is required.
Rail: Cuba's rail capacity is not as extensive as it once was, due to natural disasters and lack of investment. There was 4,226km of public service track in 2003, an increase on the previous year. The main line connects Havana and Santiago de Cuba; some services on this route offer refreshments and air-conditioning. Other lines include between Havana-Cienfuegos and Cardenas-Jaguey. Railway stations in Cuba are immaculately clean, but timetables are often unreliable.
Water: Hydrofoils run twice daily from the southern port of Surgidero de Batananó to the Isla de la Juventud. There are also slower boats sailing three times a week, but a day trip is not possible using these.
City transport
Taxis: There are state and private taxi services, usually ordered through a hotel. Official taxis are metered and less expensive and more comfortable than private taxis, with which prior agreement on the fare is advisable. Turistaxis, the official taxi service for tourists, has stands at tourist centres and can also be flagged down in the street. Taxis can also be hired for the day; for travel outside Havana, taxis or cars with drivers are cheap but scarce.
Buses, trams & metro: Services in towns are generally considered erratic, inexpensive but invariably crowded. Cubanacan buses are available for tours of cities.
Car hire
Car hire is the most reliable form of transport for covering larger distances. Modern cars are available and can be booked in advance via the Internet through Cubatur (www.cubatur.cu). Hired locally, the price may rise sharply outside airport, city or tourist areas. Chauffeur-driven vehicles are also available.
A valid driver's licence is necessary. Traffic drives on the right; seat belts are not compulsory and the blood alcohol limit is 80mg/100ml.
Speed limits: autopista 100kph; paved roads 90kph; dirt roads 60kph; urban roads 50kph (40kph near schools).
Petrol is relatively easy to obtain and comes in two grades: *especial* and regular. Both are leaded and as a rule only the dearer *especial* is available to tourists. It is sold at 24-hour Servi-Cupet and Oro Negro petrol stations.

BUSINESS DIRECTORY

The addresses listed below are a selection only. While World of Information makes every endeavour to check these addresses, we cannot guarantee that changes have not been made, especially to telephone numbers and area codes. We would welcome any corrections.

Telephone area codes
The international direct dialling code (IDD) for Cuba is +53, followed by the area code and subscriber's number:

Camaguey	32	Manzanillo	23
Ciego de Avila	33	Matanzas	45
Cienfuegos	43	Pinar del Rio	82
Florencia	33	Santiago de Cuba	226
Havana	7	Villa Clara	42

Useful telephone numbers
There is an efficient, almost omnipresent, police service, but officers are unlikely to speak English.
Police: 116 can be dialled from any call box.
Havanautos (24-hour breakdown service): 338176 or 338177.

Chambers of Commerce
Cámara de Comercio de la República de Cuba, Calle 21, esq. A No 661, Vedado, Havana (tel: 551-321; fax: 333-042; e-mail: bic@camara.com.cu).

Banking
Banco de Inversiones SA, 5ta Ave No 6802 e/ 68 y 70, Miramar, Havana (tel: 243-374/5; fax: 243-373; e-mail: bdi@bdi.colombus.cu).

Banco Exterior de España, Línea esq a 2, El Vedado, Havana (tel: 334-560; fax: 334-559).

Banco Financiero Internacional SA, Línea No 1, Vedado, PO Box 4068, Havana 4 (tel: 333-003, 333-148; fax: 333-006).

Banco Internacional de Comercio SA, 20 de Mayo y Ayestarán, Apartado 6113, Plaza de la Revolución, Havana 6 (tel: 335-482/5484; fax: 335-112; e-mail: bicsa@bicsa.columbus.cu).

Banco Metropolitano SA, (successor of the international branch of the Banco Nacional de Cuba), Línea No 63 esq a M, Vedado, Plaza, Havana (tel: 553-116/7; fax: 334-241; e-mail: banmet@nbbm.columbus.cu).

Casas de Cambio SA (CADECA), Calle Aguiar No 411, e/ Obrapia y Lamparilla, Habana Vieja, Havana (tel: 335-673; fax:

335-673; e-mail: cadeca@cadeca.columbus.cu).

Grupo Nueva Banca SA (NB), Calle 1ra, No 1406 e/ 14 y 16, Miramar, Havana (tel: 247-564/67; fax: 245-674; e-mail: nbanca@nbanca.columbus.cu).

The Netherlands Caribbean Banking, 5ta Avenida No 6407 esq a 76, Miramar, Havana (tel: 240-419/21; fax: 240-472).

Central bank

Banco Central de Cuba, PO Box 746, Cuba 402, Habana Vieja, Havana (tel: 866-8003; fax: 866-6601; e-mail: webmaster@bc.gov.cu).

Travel information

Cubamar, Paseo 306 esq a 15, Vedado, Havana (tel: 662-523.4; fax: 333-111; e-mail: cubamar@cubamar.mit.cma.net).

Cubana, Calle 23, No 64 esq Infanta, Vedado, Havana (tel: 334-949/50; fax: 333-323; e-mail: eca@iacc.3.get.cma.net).

Havanatur/Infotur, Calle Obispo 358, (e/ Habana y Compostella), Old Havana (tel: 614-881); Plaza de Martí, Santiago de Cuba (tel: 23-302).

Ministry of tourism

Ministerio de Turismo Calle 19, No 710, Entre Paseo y A, Vedado, Havana (tel: 334 087; 334 318/9; fax: 334 086: Internet: www.cubatravel.cu; www.cubaweb.cu; www.ceniai.inf.cu).

National tourist organisation offices

Cubatur (Empresa de Turismo Nacional e Internacional), Calle F No 157 el Calzada y Novena, Vedado, Havana (tel: 835-4155; fax: 836-3170; e-mail: casamatriz@cubatur.cu).

Ministries

Ministry of Agriculture, Avenida Independencia, entre Cornill y Sta Ana, Havana (tel: 845-770; fax: 335-086).

Ministry of Basic Industries, Avenida Salvador Allende 666, Havana (tel: 707-711; fax: 333-845).

Ministry of Communications, Plaza De la Revolucion 'José Marti', CP 10600, Havana (tel: 817-654).

Ministry of Construction, Avenida Carlos M de Cespedes y Calle 35, Havana (tel: 818-385; fax: 335-585).

Ministry of Construction Materials Industry, Calle 17, esq 0, Vevado, Havana (tel: 322-541; fax: 333-176).

Ministry of Culture, Calle 2, No 258, entre 11y 13, Vedado, Havana (tel: 399-945).

Ministry of Economy and Planning, 20 de Mayo y Ayestaran, Plaza de la Revolucion, Havana (tel: 816-444).

Ministry of Education, Obispo 160, Havana (tel: 614-888).

Ministry of Finance and Prices, Obispo 211, esq Cuba, Havana (tel: 604-111; fax: 620-252).

Ministry of the Fishing Industry, Avenida 5 y 248 Jaimenitas, Santa Fé, Havana (tel: 297-034).

Ministry of the Food Industry, Calle 41, No 4455, Playa, Havana (tel: 726-801).

Ministry of Foreign Affairs, Calzada 360, Vedado, Havana (tel: 324-074).

Ministry of Foreign Investment and Economic Co-operation, Calle 1, No 201, Vedado, Havana (tel: 736-661).

Ministry of Foreign Trade, Infanta 16, Vedado, Havana (tel: 786-230; fax: 786-234).

Ministry of Health, Calle 23, No 301, Vedado, Havana (tel: 322-561).

Ministry of Higher Education, Calle 23, No 565, esq aF, Vedado, Havana (tel: 552-314).

Ministry of the Interior, Plaza de la Revolucion, Havana (fax: 733-5261).

Ministry of Internal Trade, Calle Habana 258, Havana (tel: 625-790).

Ministry of Iron and Steel, Metallurgical and Electronic Industries, Avenida Rancho Boyeros y Calle 100, Havana (tel: 204-861).

Ministry of Justice, Calle 0, No 216, entre 23 y Humboldt, Vedado, Havana (tel: 326-319).

Ministry of Labour and Social Security, Calle 23, esq Calle P, Vedado, Havana (tel: 704-571).

Ministry of Light Industry, Empedrado 302, Havana (tel: 624-041).

Ministry of the Revolutionary Armed Forces, Plaza de la Revolución, Havana.

Ministry of Sugar, Calle 23, No 117, Vedado, Havana (tel: 305-061).

Ministry of Transport, Avenida Independencia y Tulipán, Havana (tel: 812-076).

Other useful addresses

British Embassy, Calle 34, No 702/4, Miramar, Havana (tel: 24-1049; fax: 24-9214).

CariFin (financial services Cuba), 311 and 313 22nd Street, Between 3rd and 5th Avanues, Mirimar, Havana (tel: 244-468/70; fax: 244-140; e-mail: havana@cdc.com.cu).

Compañía Fiduciaria SA (investments), Calle 36A No 121 apto, 2 e/ 1ra y 3ra, Miramar Playa, Havana (tel: 247-434/5; fax: 249-745; e-mail: nbfid@nbfid.columbus.cu).

Cuban Investment Company, PO Box 30003, North Vancouver, B.C. Canada V7H 2Y8 (tel: 00(1-604)929-9694; fax: 00(1-604)929-3694; e-mail: cubaninvestments@idmail.com).

Etecsa (Empresa de Telecomunicaciones de Cuba SA), Havana (tel: 452-221, 451-221; fax: 578-036).

Financiera Nacional SA (FINSA) (non-banking activities), Calle G No 301, esq a 13, Vedado, Havana (tel: 553-177, 338-863; fax: 662-232; e-mail: finsa@finsa.columbus.cu).

TIPS (Technological and Commercial Information Promotion System), National Office, No 302, Calle 30, Miramar, Havana (tel: 331-797/798; fax: 331-799).

National news agency: Agencia de Información Nacional (Cuban News Agency)

Calle 23, 358 Vedado (tel: 662-049; fax: 325-541; internet: www.cubanews.ain.cu).

Internet sites

Cubana de Aviación airline: www.cubana.cu

Granma International (daily update in English, French, Spanish and Portuguese, with a summary in German): www.granma.cu

Viazul Bus Transportation: www.viazul.com

Curaçao

KEY FACTS

Official name: Curaçao (Kòrsou in *Papiamentu*)

Head of State: Queen Beatrix of The Netherlands, represented by Governor Frits Goedgedrag (from 10 Oct 2010)

Head of government: Prime Minister Gerrit Fransisco Schotte (MFK) (from 10 Oct 2010)

Ruling party: Coalition led by Movementu Futuro Korsou (MFK) (Movement for the Future of Curaçao), with Pueblo Soberano (Sovereign People) and Partido MAN (MAN Party) (from 10 Oct 2010)

Area: 444 square kilometres

Population: 142,180 (2010)

Capital: Willemstad

Official language: Dutch and Papiamentu (official)

Currency: Netherlands Antilles guilder (Naf) = 100 cents

Exchange rate: Naf1.79 per US$ (Oct 2011); (official rate pegged to US$ since Jan 2000)

GDP per capita: US$17,270 (2005 for The Netherlands Antilles)

GDP real growth: 3.50% (2008)*

GDP: US$5.08 billion (2008)*

Labour force: 63,000 (2008)*

Unemployment: 10.30% (2008)*

Inflation: 3.00% (2010)*

* estimated figure

COUNTRY PROFILE

Historical profile

The islands of the Netherlands Antilles were first inhabited by Carib and Arawak Indians.

1493 Christopher Columbus was the first European to sight the islands.

1499 The Spanish explorer, Alonso de Ojedo, visited Curaçao but left without establishing a settlement.

1527 The islands were settled, mainly by Spanish and Portuguese Jews escaping persecution.

1634 The Dutch East India Company took over the islands, 'persuading' the settlers to depart, first from St Maarten and later from Aruba.

1642–46 Peter Stuyvesant was governor.

1816 After a number of changes of possession, the islands – Curaçao, Aruba and Bonaire (known as the Leeward Islands), St Eustatius, Saba and Sint Maarten (half of which is the French territory of St Martin) (known as the Windward Islands) – were confirmed as Dutch territory.

1863 Slavery was abolished.

1916 The first oil refinery was opened in Curaçao.

1954 Internal autonomy was granted as associated states within a federacy.

1986 Aruba separated from the other islands and became a self-governing member of the Kingdom of The Netherlands. The remaining islands became the Antilles of Five.

1998 The general election resulted in a six-party coalition government under Prime Minister Suzanne Camelia-Römer.

1999 The Partido Laboral Krusado Popular (PLKP) (Labour Party People's Crusade) left the coalition, to be replaced by the Partido Antiá Restrukturá (PAR) (Party for the Restructured Antilles), with Miguel Pourier becoming prime minister.

2000 In a referendum, St Maarten voted in favour of separate status within the Kingdom of The Netherlands and relinquishing membership of The Netherlands Antilles government.

2002 The ruling coalition was returned to power in the elections.

2004 The coalition government avoided collapse, caused by a corruption crisis, when support was offered by the Democratische Partij (DP) (Democratic Party) of Bonaire. The government finally collapsed when the National People's Party (PNP) withdrew, citing its unwillingness to work with Justice Minster Ben Komproe. Prime Minister Louisa-Godett resigned and Etienne Ys became prime minister.

2005 The islanders of Curaçao voted to become an autonomous state within the Kingdom of The Netherlands and break with The Netherlands Antilles. The tiny neighbouring island, Sint Eustatius, decided to remain within the Antilles. The Movishon Antia Nobo (New Antilles Movement) was renamed Partido MAN.

2006 Emily de Jongh-Elhage became prime minister, following parliamentary elections. The islands of Curaçao and St Maarten signed an agreement of independence to become autonomous territories within the Kingdom of the Netherlands. At the same time Bonaire, Saba and St Eustatius agreed to become city-states of the Kingdom of the Netherlands. When these changes are enacted the Netherlands Antilles will cease to exist. A new terminal in the Curaçao International Airport was opened, designed to accommodate around 1.6 million passengers per year. The growth in tourism on the island and in the region is seen as a major industry and a phase two expansion is planned for when arrivals are expected to reach 2.5 million in 2031.

2007 Negotiations for a change in their status began between Bonaire, Saba and St Eustatius and The Netherlands.

2008 The Netherlands Antilles failed to have its name removed from the blacklist of tax havens by the Tax Directorate of the European Commission, despite being named a co-operative country by the Organisation for Economic Co-operation and Development (OECD) and the IMF.

2009 A national census was undertaken, which recorded 141,766 people.

2010 In January, in the last general election was held before The Netherlands Antilles ceased to exist as a country. Early general elections in Curaçao were automatically triggered when parliament failed to pass a new constitution. In August in the resulting parliamentary elections no single political party won outright power and a coalition was formed led by Movementu Futuro Korsou (MFK) (Movement for the Future of Curaçao), with Pueblo Soberano (Sovereign People) and Partido MAN (MAN Party). On 10

October the Netherlands Antilles ceased to exist and Curacao and St Maarten became semi-autonomous countries within the Kingdom of The Netherlands. Bonaire, St Eustatius and Saba became Bijzondere Gemeenten (special municipalities). Gerrit Schotte became prime minister on 10 October.
2011 A new airline InselAir, began a non-stop service between Caracas and Hato on 19 July.

Political structure

Constitution

A new constitution was adopted in September 2010.

Form of state

Parliamentary democratic monarchy.
On 10 October 2010, the Caribbean islands of Curaçao and St Maarten joined Aruba (1986) as semi-autonomous countries within the Kingdom of the Netherlands; at the same time the Caribbean islands of Bonaire, St Eustatius and Saba became Bijzondere Gemeenten (special municipalities) of the Netherlands.

National legislature

The staten (legislature) has 21 members, directly elected to serve four-year terms.

Legal system

The legal system is based on Dutch civil law, with some English common law. Judges are appointed by the monarch. Rights of appeal exist from The Netherlands Antilles Court of Appeals to the Supreme Court of The Netherlands, in The Hague.

Last elections

27 August 2010 (parliamentary)
Results: Parliamentary: Partido Antiá Restrukturá (PAR) (Party for the Restructured Antilles) won 30 per cent of the vote (8 seats out of 21), Movementu Futuro Korsou (MFK) (Movement for the Future of Curaçao) 21 per cent, (five), Pueblo Soberano (Sovereign People) 19 per cent, (four), Partido MAN (MAN Party) 9 per cent, (two), Partido Frente Obrero Liberashon 30 Di Mei (FOL Frente Obrero) (Party Workers' Liberation Front 30th of May) 7 per cent, (one), Partido Nashonal di Pueblo (PNP) (National People's Party) 6 per cent, (one); four other political parties failed to win any seats. Turnout was 65.81 per cent.

Next elections

2014 (parliament)

Political parties

Ruling party

Coalition led by Movementu Futuro Korsou (MFK) (Movement for the Future of Curaçao), with Pueblo Soberano (Sovereign People) and Partido MAN (MAN Party) (from 10 Oct 2010)

Political situation

Curaçao came into being on 10 October 2010, after the Netherlands Antilles ceased to exist and Curaçao and St Maarten became semi-autonomous countries within the Kingdom of The Netherlands. Bonaire, St Eustatius and Saba became Bijzondere Gemeenten (special municipalities) of the Netherlands.
An early general election in Curaçao had been automatically triggered when parliament failed to pass the new constitution in June 2010. On 27 August no single political party won outright power in parliamentary elections and a coalition was formed led by Movementu Futuro Korsou (MFK) (Movement for the Future of Curaçao), with Pueblo Soberano (Sovereign People) and Partido MAN (MAN Party). Gerrit Schotte became prime minister on 10 October.

Population

142,180 (2010)
Last census: July 2009: 141,766

Ethnic make-up

African and mixed race (85 per cent), Carib Amerindian, white, East Asian.

Religions

Baptist, Roman Catholic, Protestant, Jewish, Seventh-Day Adventist and others.

Education

Primary schooling lasts for six years (from age six to 12) and junior secondary school lasts four years (age 12 to 16). Following primary education, students have a choice of attending technical or vocational colleges in place of secondary school.
Higher education is provided by the Universiteit van de Nederlandse Antillen (University of the Netherlands Antilles). There is also a nursing school and a teacher training college in Curaçao.

Health

Curaçao has two general hospitals and one surgical hospital and receives patients from the other islands of The Netherlands Antilles. Most health professionals receive training in The Netherlands.
It is estimated that around 30 per cent of the population of the Netherlands Antilles suffer from hypertension; psychological problems are also highly prevalent among adults. The general standard of health among the Antilleans is poor, with poor nutrition and little or no exercise undertaken by the adult population. The Dutch government has assigned priority to encouraging the population to develop healthier lifestyles.

HIV/Aids

There is a national strategic action plan to halt the rapid spread of the disease. The drugs problem could prove to be a potent source of transmission.
Life expectancy: 76.3 years (estimate 2003)
Fertility rate/Maternal mortality rate: 2.1 births per woman (World Bank)
Birth rate/Death rate: 16 births per 1,000 population; 6.4 deaths per 1,000 population (2003).
Child (under 5 years) mortality rate (per 1,000): 11 per 1,000 live births (2003)

Welfare

A public insurance programme covers 100 per cent of health care costs for blue-collar workers. There is also an insurance fund for retired workers. Private companies also provide insurance plans for their employees. A social security fund covers employees of small private establishments.

Languages spoken

Papiamentu is a local patois mixture of Portuguese, Spanish, Dutch, English and French.
Spanish is widely understood and spoken.

Official language/s

Dutch and Papiamentu (official)

Media

Press

Dailies: The only regional daily newspaper is *Amigoe* (www.amigoe.com) with *Vigilante* (http://vigilante.nl) from Curacao as the local island publication
Business: Business publications include in English *Business Curaçao Directory* (www.businesscuracao.com) and the annual Trade Statistics by Central Bureau of Statistics (www.cbs.an).

Broadcasting

There are several radio stations with the three based in Curacao, Radio Hoyer (www.radiohoyer.com), Easy FM and Dolfijn FM (www.dolfijnfm.com). There are two commercial television channels operating and TeleCuracao is government owned.

Economy

The Netherlands Antilles economy, virtually devoid of natural resources, is heavily service-oriented, 84 per cent of GDP, and based largely on tourism with offshore financial services. Industry accounts for 15 per cent, primarily in oil-refining, transshipment, harbour and ship repair facilities. Agriculture only accounts for 1 per cent of GDP, producing aloes, sorghum, vegetables and tropical fruit. Dutch aid remains important to the economy.
The unemployment rate remains high at over 15 per cent. The islands have a higher per capita income and a well-developed infrastructure, compared with other countries in the region.

External trade

Trade is dominated by crude oil imports and the export of refined oil products.

Imports
Include crude petroleum, food and manufactures.
Main sources: Venezuela (typically 50 per cent of total), US (21 per cent), Italy (5 per cent).
Exports
Main exports include petroleum products.
Main destinations: US (typically 29 per cent of total), Panama (14 per cent), Mexico (9 per cent).

Agriculture
The agricultural sector contributes 1 per cent to GDP and employs 5 per cent of the workforce.
About 8 per cent of total area is cultivated arable land. Soil is generally poor and rainfall inadequate for most crops.
Small amounts of fruit and vegetables are grown for local consumption.

Industry and manufacturing
The industrial sector contributes about 19 per cent to GDP and employs 20 per cent of the workforce. It is dominated by petroleum refining and transshipment.
Manufacturing is concentrated on food processing and import substitution (paints, paper, soap, beer, chemicals).
The emphasis is on diversification into light export-based industries such as electronics and pharmaceuticals.

Tourism
The island of Curaçao offers a typical Caribbean experience of sun, sea and surf, it also has a historic capital town centre that is included in the list of Unesco World Heritage sites. It hosts an annual jazz festival in March, as well as other more sporting events, in particular diving among the coral reefs. The Curaçao-based airline InselAir has flights to a number of American destinations while Air Canada and Continental Airlines have expanded their services since independence in 2010 to include non-stop flights from Toronto-Pearson and Newark, respectively.
As a one-year old state in 2011, statistics for tourism in Curaçao are still presented within the statistics of the defunct Netherland Antilles until the Curaçao government can gather and present its own report. In general, travel and tourism was estimated to have contributed 34 per cent of GDP in the former Netherland Antilles, and provided a total of 36.9 per cent of all jobs.
Curaçao became a popular destination in 2010. Visitors from the Netherlands are the single largest group followed by Venezuelan visitors wishing to stay close to home; it is also a popular destination for the slightly older US traveller (rather than party-loving college students on package holidays) who can find pleasure in peaceful surroundings.

There are no known hydrocarbon resources. The 1914 discovery of oil in Venezuela was the impetus for the island of Curaçao's choice as the location of what was then the largest oil refinery in the world, which currently has a capacity of 320,000 barrels per day (bpd). Crude oil is imported mainly from Venezuela and Mexico under the San Jose Pact. Some of this is consumed domestically but the majority is refined and exported.
Any imported natural gas or coal used is commercially insignificant

Banking and insurance
Under an EU tax directive introduced in 2005 in a number of associate and dependent EU countries, impose a withholding tax to be passed to the relevant EU country but typically retains the anonymity of the saver. Withholding taxes began at 15 per cent and will rise to 35 per cent by 2011.
The Netherlands Antillies has also agreed to supply information on tax fraud, for criminal or civil trials, and notify EU member states about additional malpractice.
Main financial centre
Willemstad

Time
GMT minus five hours (minus six hours during summer daylignt saving).

Geography
Curaçao is located in the Caribbean Sea, 70km off the coast of northern South America, in the Netherlands Windward islands and consists of low hills.
Hemisphere
Northern

Climate
There are low levels of humidity and rainfall on Curaçao where temperatures average 29 degrees Celsus (C). Average annual rainfall is 550mm. There are higher levels of rainfall from May–December.

Entry requirements
Passports
Required by all and must be valid for at least three months from date of departure.
Visa
Not required by nationals of countries which are signatories of the Schengen Accords, which includes most EU/EEA member states; North America and Australasia for visits up to three months. Lists of nationals that do and do not require a visa can be found on the website of the Dutch Ministry of Foreign affairs: www.mfa.nl/lon-en/homepage under visas.
All visitors must provide evidence of sufficient funds for their stay and a return/onward ticket.

Currency advice/regulations
There are no restrictions regarding the import and export of local or foreign currencies.
Travellers cheques are widely accepted; US dollar cheques will avoid additional exchange charges.

Health (for visitors)
Mandatory precautions
Yellow fever vaccination certificate required if arriving from an infected area.
Advisable precautions
Inoculations and boosters should be current for tetanus and hepatitis A. There may be a need for vaccinations for diphtheria, typhoid, tuberculosis and hepatitis B.

Hotels
There are numerous tourist hotels. Government tax of 5 per cent and 10–15 per cent service charge is added to the bill.

Credit cards
All major credit and charge cards accepted. ATMs are available in major centres.

Public holidays (national)
Fixed dates
1 Jan (New Year's Day), 30 Apr (Queen's Birthday), 1 May (Labour Day), 2 Jul Curaçao Flag Day, 25–26 Dec (Christmas).
Variable dates
Carnival (Jan/Feb), Easter Monday (Mar/Apr) Ascension Day (Aug).

Working hours
Banking
Mon–Fri: 0830–1200, 1330–1630.
Business
Mon–Fri: 0800–1200, 1330–1630.
Government
Mon–Fri: 0800–1200, 1330–1630.
Shops
Mon–Sat: 0800–1200, 1400–1800. Gift shops open on Sundays and public holidays when cruise ships call.

Telecommunications
Mobile/cell phones
There are several 900, 900/1800 GSM services covering the island.

Electricity supply
Variable: 120/127/220V AC at 50 cycles or 60 cycles.

Getting there
Air
National airline: Windward Island Airways (Winair) (short haul flights only)
International airport/s: Curaçao (CUR), 12km north of Willemstad; with duty-free shops, bar, restaurant, hotel reservations and car hire. Taxis are available, fares are standard and should be agreed in advance.

Airport tax: Departure tax: Naf36 (international)

Surface

Water: There is a weekly ferry to Curaçao from Venezuela.

Getting about

National transport

Road: There is an all-weather network on the island.

City transport

Taxis: Taxis are usually identified by TX before the licence plate. Fares are standard and should be agreed before travelling. Tipping is discretionary.

Car hire

Car hire is widely available. An international licence is required.

BUSINESS DIRECTORY

Telephone area codes

The international dialling code (IDD) for Curaçao is + 599, followed by area code and subscriber's number:

Willemstad 9

Chambers of Commerce

Curaçao Chamber of Commerce and Industry, 1 Kaya Junior Salas, PO Box 10, Willemstad (tel: 9461-3918; fax: 9461-5652; e-mail: businessinfo@curacao-chamber.an).

Banking

Banco di Caribe, Schottegatweg Oost 205, PO Box 3785, Willemstad, Curaçao (tel: 9432-3410; internet: www.bancodicaribe.com).

Banco Industrial de Venezuela CA, Handelskade 12, PO Box 701, Willemstad, Curaçao (tel: 9461-1621; fax: 9461-6534).

Banco Mercantil Venezolano NV, A Mendez Chumaceiro Bvd; PO Box 565, Curaçao (tel: 9461-1566, 9461-2117; fax: 9461-1974; internet: www.bancomercantilcu.com).

Citco Bank Antilles NV, Schottegatweg Oost 44, Willemstad, Curaçao (tel: 9732-2322; fax: 9732-2330; email: curacao-bank@citco.com).

FirstCaribbean International Bank (Curacao) NV, De Ruyterkade 61, PO Box 3144, Willemstad (tel: 9433-8338; fax: 9433-8198; email: www.firstcaribbeanbank.an).

MCB Maduro & Curiel's Bank NV, Plaza Jojo Correa 2-4, PO Box 305, Willemstad, Curaçao (tel: 9466-1100; fax: 9466-1444; email: infor@mcb-bank.com).

MCB Maduro & Curiel's Bank, Schottegatweg Oost 130, Saliña, Curaçao (tel: 9466-1100; fax: 9466-1444; internet: mcb-bank.com).

Orco Bank N V, Dr H Fergusonweg 10, PO Box 3987, Curaçao (tel: 9737-2000; fax: 9737-6741).

Central bank

Bank van de Nederlandse Antillen, 1 Simon Bolivar Plein, Willemstad, Curaçao (tel: 9434-5500; fax: 9461-5004; e-mail: info@centralbank.an).

Travel information

National tourist organisation offices

Curaçao Tourist Board, PO Box 3266; Pietermaai 19, Curaçao (tel: 9434-8200; fax: 9461-5017: internet: www.curacao-tourism.com).

Ministries

Ministry of Finance, Pietermaai 4–4A, Willemstad, Curaçao (tel: 9461-2052).

Office of the Minister Plenipotentiary of the Netherlands Antilles, Badhuisweg 175, 2597 JP The Hague, The Netherlands (tel: (+31-70) 351-2811; fax: (+31-70) 351-2722).

Other useful addresses

British Consulate, PO Box 3803, Brombadiersweg z/n, Willemstad, Curaçao (tel: 9436-9366; fax: 9436-9533).

Curaçao Inc (for business information), International Trade Centre Bldg, Piscaderabay, PO Box 6112, Curaçao (tel: 9463-6250; fax: 9463-6485).

Curaçao Industry and International Trade Development Co (CURINDE), Emancipatie Boulevard 7, Curaçao (tel: 9437-6000; fax: 9437-1336).

Foreign Investment Agency Curaçao, Scharlooweg 174 Willemstad, Curaçao (tel: 9465-7044; fax: 9461-5788).

International Trade Centre, PO Box 6005, International Trade Centre Building, Piscadera Bay, Curaçao (tel: 9462-4433, 9463-6250; fax: 9462-4408, 9463-6485).

Island Government of Curaçao, Department of Economic Affairs, Hoogstraat 18, Curaçao (tel: 9462-4066; fax: 9462-6596).

Cyprus

KEY FACTS

Official name: Kypriaki Dimokratia-Kibris Cumhuriyeti (Republic of Cyprus)

Head of State: President Demetris Christofias (Akel party) (from 28 Feb 2008)

Head of government: President Demetris Christofias (from 28 Feb 2008)

Ruling party: Coaltion led by Dimokratikos Sinagermos (DS) (Democratic Rally), with Anorthotikon Komma Ergazomenou Laou (AKEL) (Progressive Party for Working People) (from Jun 2011)

Area: 9,251 square km (including the north)

Population: 1.10 million (2010)

Capital: Lefkosia (Nicosia); Greek spellings in use since 1995

Official language: Greek and Turkish

Currency: Euro (€) = 100 cents (from 1 Jan 2008; previous currency Cypriot pound, locked at C£0.58 per euro)

Exchange rate: €0.75 per US$ (Oct 2011)

GDP per capita: US$28,237 (2010)

GDP real growth: 1.00% (2010)

GDP: US$23.20 billion (2010)

Labour force: 404,000 (2010)

Unemployment: 5.40% (2010)

Inflation: 2.60% (2010)

Balance of trade: -US$6.38 billion (2010)

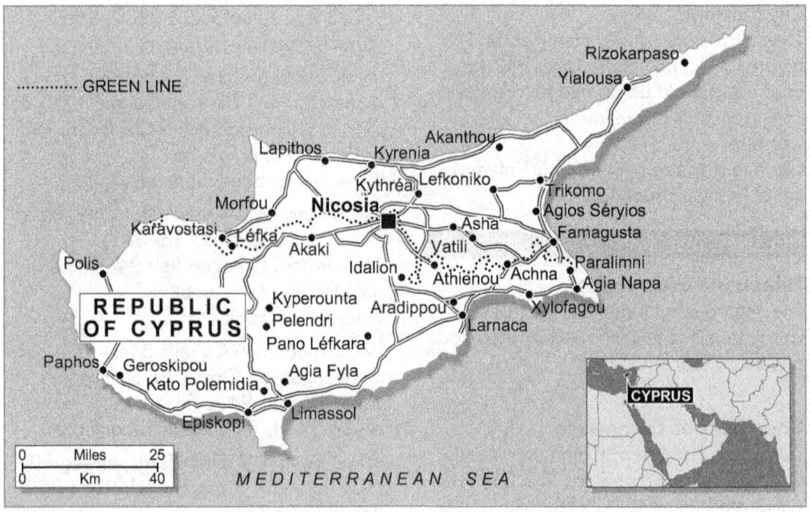

For some years Cyprus' economy, lead by its banking sector, has been punching above its weight. But 2011 is unlikely to go down as one of Cyprus' better years. In mid-2011 it had looked as though Cyprus, alongside Turkey, might even benefit from the Arab Spring, as tourists chose to avoid Egypt and Tunisia and hesitated about Greece as a holiday destination.

Split

Any visitor to Lefkosia (Nicosia) cannot fail to be perplexed by Europe's last remaining divided republic. The dividing frontier in Lefkosia is no Berlin Wall and its crossing points – manned by casual, cigarette smoking soldiers – lack the sinister aspect and deadly history once seen at Berlin's Check Point Charlie and other crossing points. Tourists cross from one side to the other quite casually and shops in the Turkish part of the capital accept euros as well as Turkish lira. Cyprus' division – now in its 38th year – looks quite likely to last longer than that of Germany. The patience of the United Nations (UN) is beginning to run thin and the prospect of a permanent partition starts to gain credibility.

The current round of talks, which got under way in 2008, have made little headway in ending the split, despite the fact that Messrs Demetris Christofias (the leader of the Greek Cypriot government) and Dervis Eroglu (the Turkish Cypriot leader) have met over 100 times. UN impatience became evident when, in November 2011, the UN Secretary General Ban Ki-moon summoned the two to meet with him in New York. Were the UN to give up the ghost on the talks, the parties would have to consider the possibility of a formal partition. Such an outcome would have disadvantages for both sides. But for the present Turkish Cypriot government under Mr Eroglu it would probably be their preferred solution. It would mean seeking international recognition of their state, their principal, if not overwhelming foreign policy objective, together with the consolidation of ties with Turkey. Although this ambition has yet to be achieved (only Turkey so far recognises northern Cyprus), representative trade offices have been set up in a number of countries, including the US, UK, Germany and as far afield as Australia. Officials have managed to gain observer status at the Organisation of the Islamic Conference and to send delegations to Assembly meetings of the Council of Europe. Northern Cyprus' economy is much smaller, more narrowly based and weaker than its southern counterpart. Per capita incomes in the north are a mere quarter of those in the south. As budget revenues only cover around two-thirds of administrative outlays, northern Cyprus is heavily dependent on Turkey for credits, grants and trade. Reliance on the Turkish lira also means there is no effective local control over monetary policy. The economy has therefore suffered for many years from high imported inflation (an average of 80 per cent between 1991–2000), weaknesses in the banking system (including the collapse of seven local banks in December 1999), constant annual trade deficits, limited foreign investment and a large public sector accounting for over 20 per cent of total employment and 20.3 per cent of gross domestic product (GDP).

For most of the 38 years since the Turkish invasion of Cyprus, international sympathy has tended to favour the Greek position. But by 2010 this, many observers suspected, was no longer the case. European Union members have become irritated by the disruption of EU business. The UK is bound by a condition of the 1960 (the year of Cyprus' independence) Treaty of Guarantee not to promote partition. Russia's new found political frindship with Turkey represents a significant regional shift and by 2011 Greece itself, laden with debt and in danger of default, was no longer the force it once was. Younger Greek Cypriots have only ever lived in a divided country and fail to see any obvious or immediate advantage in unification.

Ironically, Cyprus' first full year as an EU member state (2008), had seen it play a significant – and strangely paradoxical – role in one of the most contentious decisions to be made by the EU in decades: whether or not Turkey would be allowed to begin EU accession talks. At a March 2011 conference Mr Christofias said that 'progress had been zero since Mr Eroglu had been elected.' On their side, a spokesman for Mr Eroglu claimed that 'everyone wants peace, but not everyone wants a compromise.' At the same conference, the former Australian foreign minister and UN Special Envoy, Alexander Downer, said that more had been accomplished at the talks than was realised. According to Mr Downer agreement had been reached on the structure of a federated Cyprus, but not on issues such as property, territory and security.

However, the UN secretary general had not appeared to share Mr Downer's optimism following his earlier meetings, instead saying that 'The talks were losing momentum and needed a boost.'

July crises

If the Cyprus government had cause to be concerned over the future of the unification talks, it soon had other worries too. A decision by European governments to put pressure on Greek bond holders to accept a loss on their holdings (to 'take a haircut' in financial argot) had a disproportionate and adverse effect on Greek banks, two of which are Europe's largest holders of Greek bonds. The Bank of Cyprus was reported to hold ?2.4 billion (US$3.22 billion) in Greek debt and Marfin Popular Bank ?3.4 billion (US$11.36 billion). The latter bank held a total of ?12.5 billion (US$16.75 billion) in Greek loans, some 40 per cent ot its total lending. The yields on Cyprus 10 year bonds (maturing in 2014) reached 10.18 per cent, above the rates that had already forced Ireland and Portugal into accepting EU bail-outs. Moody's downgraded Cyprus bonds to two points above 'junk' status. Standard & Poor's lowered its rating on Greek sovereign debt from triple C to double C, the same level as Moody's. Coinciding with what looked like an incipient banking crisis, came a political deadlock as the government tried to force through its austerity programme, aimed at getting Cyprus' budget deficits under control. At the end of July, President Christofias, seeking to pre-empt talk of a possible EU bail-out, demanded the resignation of his entire cabinet. Analysts considered that Cyprus could be confronted by a financing gap of ?600 million (US$804 million) for the rest of 2011. Cyprus' banking sector had, simply, become too big for its small island. The billions that had gushed in meant that an artificial prosperity was created, disguising the reality of a small, precarious economy.

Explosion

That precariousness became clear when, on top of the parliamentary and banking crises, in late July 2011 came a third, altogether more unpredicable crisis. That a cache of Iranian weapons confiscated en route to Syria should explode, killing 13 people, was in itself serious enough. But that the weapons were being 'stored' in baking sun next to the country's largest power generation plant turned an accident into a catastrophe. The explosion destroyed the power station, plunging large parts of the island into darkness, leaving its industry unable to function and its offices unfit for purpose without any air conditioning.

A spokesman for the Association of Cyprus International Investment Firms painted a gloomy picture of the Cypriot economy after the power station ceased to function: 'If it wasn't for the explosion, Cyprus would probably get by.' But now, he continued, 'Cyprus has never found itself in a similar situation before – not since 1974.' The power station supplied more than half the island's electricity. The explosion was expected to push the economy into flat, or zero, growth for 2011 at a point when Cyprus was just beginning to emerge from recession. Before the explosion, government officials had forecast growth of 1.5 per cent for 2011. Credit rating agency Moody's forecast zero growth. Government economists calculated that the effects of the explosion were likely to add some ?200 million (US$268 million) to Cyprus' financing requirements for 2011.

KEY INDICATORS — Cyprus

	Unit	2006	2007	2008	2009	2010
Population	m	0.77	*0.78	*7.60	*0.80	*1.10
Gross domestic product (GDP)	US$bn	18.37	21.30	24.90	23.60	23.20
GDP per capita	US$	23,779	*27,326	32,772	29,620	28,237
GDP real growth	%	4.0	4.4	3.7	-1.7	1.0
Inflation	%	2.2	2.1	4.4	0.2	2.6
Unemployment	%	4.5	3.9	3.7	5.3	–
Exports (fob) (goods)	US$m	1,416.6	1,495.1	1,906.0	2,065.0	2,089.0
Imports (fob) (goods)	US$m	6,439.5	7,839.8	10,543.0	7,973.0	8,465.0
Balance of trade	US$m	-5,022.9	-6,344.7	-8,638.0	-5,907.0	-6,376.0
Current account	US$m	-1,090.6	-2,144.1	-4,566.0	-1,915.0	-1,807.0
Total reserves minus gold	US$m	5,646.8	6,118.6	616.8	796.2	514.9
Foreign exchange	US$m	5,621.5	6,100.1	585.5	562.9	276.2
Exchange rate	per US$	0.44	0.40	0.68	0.78	0.76

* estimated figure

The explosion very much looked like the last straw for the government of Mr Christofias. The President himself looked ill suited to deal with the crises that beset him. Any orderly re-shuffle of government ministers was knocked off course by the explosions, for which many Cypriots blamed their ministers. Allegations surfaced that civil servants and ministers had been warned of the dangers of storing the weapons close to the power station. Protest demonstrations outside the presidential palace called for Mr Christofias himself to resign. Instead Mr Christofias sought to weather the storm, delaying any reshuffle until the remaining ministers from the junior coalition partner, the Dimokratikos Sinagermos (Disi) (Democratic Coalition), had resigned. The government's crucial austerity programme was a casualty of the new crisis; first because there was no government in place with the authority to introduce a new crisis package of measures, second because the lower growth figures caused by the explosion would require the government to go back to the economic drawing board and recalculate its forecasts.

Risk assessment

Economy	Poor
Politics	Poor
Regional stability	Poor

COUNTRY PROFILE

Historical profile

1925 Cyprus became a British crown colony.
1955 The Greek Cypriots of the Ethniki Organosis Kipriakou Agonos (Eoka) (National Organisation of Cypriot Combatants) launched a guerrilla war against British authority. The Eoka wanted Cyprus to unify with mainland Greece.
1960 President Makarios oversaw Cyprus' independence, which followed a compromise agreement between Greek and Turkish Cypriots, with Britain retaining sovereignty over two military bases.
1961 Cyprus joined the IMF and World Bank.
1963 Makarios upset the Turkish Cypriots when he proposed constitutional change which would abrogate power-sharing arrangements. Inter-communal fighting erupted and the Turkish Cypriot community withdrew from the central government.
1964 A UN peace-keeping force was sent to the island.
1968–74 Talks on constitutional reform were inconclusive, as Turkish Cypriots sought separate municipalities in the five main towns.
1974 A brief Greek junta sponsored coup by supporters of a union with Greece toppled President Makarios who fled the island. Turkey invaded northern Cyprus and Greek Cypriots fled their homes in the north; 37 per cent of the island came under Turkish control, enforcing partition between north and south. The border between the two became known as the Green Line. The coup failed and Glafcos Clerides took over as the Greek Cypriot president, until Makarios returned at the end of the year.
1975 Northern Cyprus declared the formation of the 'Turkish Federated State of Cyprus' with Rauf Denktash as president and with the aim of eventually gaining independence.
1977 President Makarios died and was succeeded by Spyros Kyprianou.
1980 UN-sponsored peace talks resumed.
1983 Rauf Denktash suspended talks and northern Cyprus officially seceded as the Kuzey Kýbrýs Türk Cumhuriyeti (KKTC) (Turkish Republic of Northern Cyprus (TRNC)) introducing its own government and legal system. The international community rejected the secessionist move and only Turkey recognised it as a state.
1988 Georgios Vassiliou was elected Greek Cypriot president.
1992–93 Additional UN-sponsored talks with Rauf Denktash failed when the UN Security Council rejected Turkish demands for the recognition of separate sovereignty for the KKTC, including a right to secession.
1993 Glafcos Clerides defeated George Vassiliou in the presidential election.
1994 The European Court of Justice ruled that all direct trade between northern Cyprus and the EU was illegal.
1994–95 Talks continued between north and south with little progress. The Greek Cypriots and the UN pushed for a federal system, but this was rejected by the KKTC.
1996 Tension between the two sides increased and there was violence along the Green Line.
1997 UN-mediated talks between Clerides and Denktash failed.
1998 Clerides was narrowly re-elected for a second term. The EU listed Cyprus as a potential member.
1999 Further peace talks in the US failed to find a solution to Cyprus' division.
2000 Rauf Denktash was elected for a fourth five-year term as the KKTC president.
2001 The leaders of the two Cypriot communities held their first direct talks in four years and agreed to restart peace talks to pave the way for EU membership.
2002 A UN-sponsored plan for reunification as a federation with a rotating presidency was rejected by the KKTC, which insisted on international recognition. The EU invited Cyprus to join, however if the two estranged communities could not agree to reunification then only the Greek Cypriot part of the island would become a member.
2003 Tassos Papadopoulos of the Dimokratikon Komma (DIKO) (Democratic Party) won the presidency. A coalition led by the leftist, Anorthotikon Komma Ergazemenou Laou (Akel) (Progressive Party of the Working People) with Kinima Sosialdimokraton (Kisos) (Social Democrats Movement) won parliamentary elections. The UN deadline for agreement on reunification passed without agreement. Crossing points between the two zones were temporarily opened and the government lifted 20-year-old trade sanctions against the KKTC, thus allowing farmers in the north to sell produce in the south and export to the EU, and permitting Turkish Cypriots to work in the south.
2004 Twin referenda on the UN reunification plan and united EU entry saw Greek Cypriots voting against unification with the north by 76 per cent, while in the north, 65 per cent voted in favour of the proposal. The Republic of Cyprus joined the EU. Turkey agreed that it would recognise Cyprus as an EU member.
2005 Turkey agreed to extend a free trade accord with the EU, including Cyprus. Mehmet Ali Talat became president of KKTC. In Cyprus' worst ever air accident, 121 people on board a Helios Airways plane were killed in a crash as it approached Athens' airport.
2006 The ruling coalition won the parliamentary elections with a combined vote of 49 per cent.
2007 EU officials formally invited Cyprus to join the third stage of the European Monetary Union (EMU). The ruling coalition was dissolved as Akel nominated its own candidate for the 2008 presidential election. Ministerial posts were filled by technocrats. Cyprus became a member of the European Union Schengen area whereby all travellers may cross borders without a passport or visa.
2008 Cyprus adopted the euro as its official currency. Demetris Christofias became president. Ledra Street, which runs through the UN buffer zone in Lefkosia, was reopened; it had been closed since 1964. Five people were charged with manslaughter and causing death through negligence for the 2005 Helios Airways crash, two years after the airline became defunct.
2009 In KKTC elections the ruling CTP lost power to the Ulusal Birlik Partisi (UBP) (National Unity Party) and Dervis Eroglu (UBP), became prime minister; he is expected to adopt a more hard-line stance in talks with the government of the

Republic of Cyprus. Cyprus blocked progress of Turkey's accession (to the EU) talks when it refused to allow the start of talks in five policy areas unless Turkey changed its position on the Cyprus dispute.
2010 In KKTC presidential elections in April, Dervis Eroglu (UBP) won 50.4 per cent of the vote and incumbent Mehmet Ali Talat 42.9 per cent. The president of KKTC appointed Irsen Kucuk as prime minister of KKTC in May. Cyprus and Romania signed a Memorandum of Understanding (MoU) in May, covering technical and entrepreneurial development in renewable energy sources. UN-mediated talks on the future of northern Cyprus were held in November.
2011 In parliamentary elections held on 22 May, the opposition, centre-right, Dimokratikos Sinagermos (DS) (Democratic Rally) won 34.28 per cent of the vote (20 seats out of 56), while the ruling Anorthotikon Komma Ergazomenou Laou (AKEL) (Progressive Party for Working People) won 32.67 per cent (19 seats). Without enough seats for a majority in parliament, DS formed a coalition government with AKEL. An explosion on 11 July, in the arms depot of the Evangelos Florakis Naval Base on the south coast, killed 12 people and destroyed Cyprus' largest power plant. Total damage was estimated at US$2.8 billion; repairing just the power station, which had produced about half of the island's electricity, could cost US$1.4 billion. The governor of the central bank, Athanasios Orphanides, warned that as a result of the explosion the country faced a 'state of emergency' and that Cyprus could become the next southern eurozone member to look for a bail-out from the EU. He recommended a harsher programme of austerity measures. Cyprus began drilling for oil in the eastern Mediterranean in September; Turkey has said it will also start drilling, risking an escalation in tension between the two countries.

Political structure

The government of southern Cyprus is internationally recognised as the sole administration of the Republic of Cyprus. Occupied by Turkish troops since 1974, northern Cyprus has its own government and calls itself the Kuzey Kýbrýs Türk Cumhuriyeti (KKTC) (Turkish Republic of Northern Cyprus (TRNC)). It is only recognised by Turkey.

Constitution

The constitution was promulgated in 1960.
The voting age was extended to include all citizens above the age of 18 for the 1998 presidential election.
Northern Cyprus introduced its own consitution after declaring unilateral independence in 1983.

Independence date

1960

Form of state

Presidential republic

The executive

Executive power is held by the president who is directly elected for a five-year term by universal suffrage. A council of ministers is appointed by the president, who convenes and presides over its meetings. Ministers may not sit in the house of representatives, but may introduce bills.

National legislature

The unicameral Vouli Antiprosópon (House of Representatives) has 59 members elected for a five-year term, of which 56 members are elected by proportional representation; three members are observers representing the Maronite, Latin and Armenian communities and 24 seats are allocated to the Turkish Cypriot community but have not been filled since 1963.
In 1983, northern Cyprus introduced its own parliament, the 50-member Temsilciler Meclisi (House of Representatives).

Legal system

The Republic of Cyprus' legal system is embodied in the 1960 constitution and is based on British common law. The legal system in northern Cyprus is based on Turkish law.

Last elections

22 May 2011 (parliamentary); 17 and 24 February 2008 (presidential, first and second rounds); 19 April 2009 (KKTC parliamentary), 18 April 2010 (KKTC presidential).
Results: Parliamentary: Dimokratikos Sinagermos (DS) (Democratic Rally) won 34.28 per cent of the vote (20 seats out of 56), Anorthotikon Komma Ergazomenou Laou (AKEL) (Progressive Party for Working People) 32.67 per cent (19), Dimokratikon Komma (DK) (Democratic Party), 15.76 per cent (nine), Kinima Sosialdimokraton (KSD) (Movement for Social Democracy) 8.93 per cent (five), Evropaiko Komma (EK) (European Party) 3.88 per cent (two), Kinima Oikologon Perivallontiston (KOP) (Ecological and Environmental Movement) 2.21 per cent (one); four political parties and independents failed to win enough votes to win seats. Turnout was 78.7 per cent. Presidential: (first round), Ioannis Kasoulides 33.5 per cent, Dimitris Christofias 33.3 per cent and Tassos Papadopoulos 31.8 per cent; turnout was 89.6 per cent. Second round: Demetris Christofias 53.36 per cent of the vote, Ioannis Kasoulides 46.64 per cent.
KKTC parliamentary: Ulusal Birlik Partisi (UBP) (National Unity Party) won 44.07 per cent; 26 seats (out of 50), Cumhuriyetçi Türk Partisi (CTP) (Republican Turkish Party) 29.15 per cent (15), Demokrat Partisi (Democratic Party) (Democrats) 10.65 per cent (five), Toplumcu Demokrasi Partisi (TDP) (Communal Democracy Party) 6.87 per cent (two), Özgürlük ve Reform Partisi (ÖRP) (Freedom and Reform Party) 6.2 per cent (two); two other parties failed to win enough votes to reach the threshold for gaining a seat. Turnout was 81.42 per cent.
KKTC presidential: Dervis Eroglu (UBP) won 50.4 per cent of the vote, Mehmet Ali Talat (CTP) 42.9 per cent.
European parliament (June 2009): turn out was 59.4 per cent, compared to 72.5 per cent in 2004.

Next elections

February 2013 (presidential); 2016 (parliamentary).

Political parties

Ruling party

Coaltion led by Dimokratikos Sinagermos (DS) (Democratic Rally), with Anorthotikon Komma Ergazomenou Laou (AKEL) (Progressive Party for Working People) (from Jun 2011)

Main opposition party

Dimokratikos Sinagermos (Disi) (Democratic Coalition); KKTC parliament: Cumhuriyetçi Türk Partisi (CTP) (Republican Turkish Party)

Population

1.10 million (2010)
Last census: October 2001: 689,565 (excluding Northern Cyprus)
Population density: 82 inhabitants per square km. Urban population: 57 per cent (1994–2000).
Annual growth rate: 1.4 per cent 1994–2004 (WHO 2006)

Ethnic make-up

Greeks (84.1 per cent), Turks (11.8 per cent), Maronites (0.6 per cent), Armenians (0.3 per cent), Latins (0.1per cent), foreign residents (mainly British and Greek) (3.1 per cent).

Religions

Christian Orthodox (77 per cent), Muslim (18 per cent).

Education

Primary schooling lasts for six years between the ages of six and 12. Public general secondary education extends over six years. Almost 20,000 students, mostly from Turkey, Eastern Europe and the Middle East, attend six private universities in northern Cyprus.
Literacy rate: 97 per cent, adult rate (World Bank)
Compulsory years: Six to 15.

Enrolment rate: 100 per cent gross primary enrolment of the relevant age group (including repeaters) (World Bank)

Health

The government is looking for ways to persuade Greek-Cypriot medical specialists to return from overseas and offer high-quality healthcare services at a considerably lower cost than in Western Europe.

Life expectancy: 79 years, 2004 (WHO 2006)

Fertility rate/Maternal mortality rate: 1.6 births per woman, 2004 (WHO 2006)

Birth rate/Death rate: 8 deaths and 17 births per 1,000 people (World Bank)

Child (under 5 years) mortality rate (per 1,000): 4 per 1,000 live births (World Bank)

Head of population per physician: 2.34 physicians per 1,000 people, 2002 (WHO 2006)

Welfare

Cyprus offers a statutory social insurance scheme securing decent pensions and allows pensioners to continue working without affecting their pensions. The Social Insurance Scheme provides insurance for all employees who contribute 16.6 per cent on the insured income. The employer deducts 6.3 per cent of the employees' income and contributes 6.3 per cent, while the remaining 4 per cent is paid by the state. There is provision for a non-contributory social pension for elderly people who are not entitled to a pension from any other source. There is also a complementary public assistance scheme for people whose resources are not sufficient to meet their basic and special needs.

There is provision for unemployment and disability benefits. The National Social Security System allows women a paid 16-week maternity leave and a substantial birth allowance. Cyprus also offers crime victims a financial compensation programme.

Main cities

Nicosia municipal council voted to change the capital city's name to Lefkosia, Nicosia's Greek name, in 1995. The change was the result of a campaign to standardise place names according to their Greek pronunciation, although Nicosia is still the name in common use.

Lefkosia (capital, estimated population 197,600 in 2003), Lemesos (Limassol) (149,100), Larnaka (Larnaca) (48,200), Pafos (Paphos) (32,700).

In Turkish-occupied northern Cyprus, cities include Lefkosa (the part of Lefkosia under Turkish control – 45,800), Gazimagusa (35,700), Girne (19,000).

Languages spoken

English is widely spoken in tourist regions.

Official language/s

Greek and Turkish

Media

Media services have outlets in each zone operating under their own regulations.

Press

Dailies: In Greek, the most popular newspapers are all independents, including *Phileleftheros* (www.philenews.com), *Simerini (Today)* (www.simerini.com.cy), *Politis (Citizen)* (www.politis-news.com) and *Haravgi* (www.haravgi.com.cy). In Turkish important newspapers include *Kibris Gazetesi* (www.kibrisgazetesi.com) and *Halkin Sesi (Voice of the People)* (www.halkinsesi.org), both independents and *Yeni Kibris* (www.ykp.org.cy) published by the unification, YKP (New Cyprus Party), with Greek and English online versions. In English, *The Cyprus Mail*, (www.cyprus-mail.com).

Weeklies: In Greek, the SSP Media Group publishes several titles for women, men and lifestyle magazines (www.sppmedia.com). *To Periodiko* (www.toperiodiko.com) for current affairs, The Cyprus Government Gazette (www.cygazette.com) is a comprehensive weekly publication. In English, *The Cyprus Weekly* (www.cyprusweekly.com.cy) has the largest circulation, followed by the *Cyprus Observer* (www.observercyprus.com).

Business: Two publications that are closely linked are the *Financial Mirror* (www.financialmirror.com), published in English, with a Greek version *Xpress Economiki*.

In Greek, *Euro Kerdos (Euro Profit)* (www.eurokerdos.com) a financial and *Chrimatistiriaki* a stock exchange, monthly magazines.

Periodicals: Monthlies include, in Greek, *Flash* (www.flashcy.com) for young people, as is, in English, *Scoop* (www.scoop-magazine.com) and *Sports in the City* (www.sportsinthecitynews.com), *In Touch* (www.intouchcyprus.com) for lifestyle articles.

Broadcasting

Cyprus Broadcasting Corporation (CyBC) (www.cybc.com.cy) is state broadcaster for the Republic of Cyprus.

Bayrak Radio and Television Corporation (BRT) (www.brtk.cc) operates in Northern Cyprus.

Radio: CyBC operates three radio stations: the First Programme, International Programme, Third Programme and Fourth Programme, offering a range of news, talk, education, entertainment and music programmes, also in English, Armenian and Turkish.

BRT (www.brtk.cc) has five stations including Bayrak Radio, Bayrak FM, Baryrak International, Bayrak Classic FM and Bayrak Turkish Music, all broadcasting from Famagusta.

Private commercial radio stations include Radio Astra (www.astra.com.cy) Radio 91.4 FM (www.91.4coastfm.com) and Mix FM (www.mixfmradio.com).

Television: CyBC (www.cybc.com.cy) is the national public TV station, which operates two terrestrial channels, Pik 1, with news and factual programmes and Pik 2, with entertainment programmes and one satellite television channel (Pik TV).

BRT (www.brtk.cc) operates two TV channels Bayrak TV 1 and 2.

There are several other satellite and pay-to-view TV stations including Sigma (www.sigma.com.cy), Music Box TV (www.musicbox.com.cy) and Lumiere TV (www.lumieretv.com).

News agencies

National news agency: Cyprus News Agency (CNA)

Economy

The service sector, in particular tourism, but also financial services and real estate, constitutes almost 80 per cent of GDP, and employs over 70 per cent of the workforce. Over two million people visit the island each year. Manufacturing enterprises in ship repair and construction materials, pharmaceutical and clothing contributes less than 20 per cent of GDP, while agriculture comprises less than 3 per cent, providing potatoes, grapes, oranges, olives and wines for export.

Cyprus formally joined the Emu in 2008 and adopted the euro as its currency, not only to enhance its prospects of trading within the EU but also to gain a degree of safety from external shocks. However as tourist numbers fell during the global economic crisis so Cyprus' fortunes also weakened. GDP growth in 2007 was a strong 5.1 per cent, which fell to 3.6 per cent in 2008, before falling into recession in early 2009, with -1.7 per cent growth as tourism, the real estate market and local construction contracted sharply, as domestic demand fell and unemployment rose. The government introduced measures to ease the economy and aid its recovery, by allowing increased public debt. This increased its budget deficit to above 8 per cent of GDP, a figure that, in 2009, the EU Central Bank required to be lowered to 3 per cent by 2012. Measures to achieve this may include reducing the size of public employment.

Recovery began slowly, so that by the third quarter of 2010, GDP growth year-on-year was 1.7 per cent; the figure was not as high as expected due to a continued weakness in the construction industry.

Cyprus is highly dependent on imports of oil and commodities. International oil and

commodity prices are likely to push up inflation in the medium-term, which will increase the inflation differential with the euro area and erode Cyprus' competitiveness.
Northern Cyprus, which uses the Turkish lira, suffers from high inflation. Financial aid from Turkey and remittances from the more than 200,000 Turkish Cypriots living abroad are vital sources of revenue.

External trade

As a member of the European Union, Cyprus operates within a community-wide free trade area, with tariffs set as a whole. Internationally, the EU has free trade agreements with a number of nations and trading blocs worldwide.
In 2007 Cyprus licensed oil exploration in its territorial waters. This angered Turkish administered Northern Cyprus which argued that such exploration should be a joint venture and result in the benefit of both communities. In October 2010 Turkey announced plans to explore for oil off the coast of Northern Cyprus.

Imports

Cyprus has a large trade deficit as most goods must be imported, including cigarettes, crude oil, raw materials and machinery for manufacturing, and all transport vehicles.
Main sources: Greece (typically 20 per cent of total), Italy (11 per cent), UK (9 per cent).

Exports

Export of manufactured goods, including electric and electronic equipment, processed food, chemicals, paper, textiles and refined oil represent the largest portion of foreign earnings; important agricultural exports include potatoes, grapes, wine and citrus. Minerals exported include copper, pyrites, chrome, asbestos, and gypsum.
Main destinations: Greece (typically 22 per cent of total), Germany (9 per cent), UK (8 per cent).

Re-exports

Refined oil accounts for a significant share of total annual exports.

Agriculture

Farming

The agriculture sector contributes 5 per cent annually to GDP. Major crops are potatoes, grapes, citrus fruits and barley. Cattle, sheep and goats, swine and poultry are raised. Fresh pork, poultry meat and eggs satisfy local demand. Local production of beef, veal, mutton and lamb is supplemented by imports. Agriculture typically contributes 3.5 per cent to GDP and employs 7 per cent of the workforce.
The implentation of modern irrigation technologies has helped to address the sector's water shortage. A large-scale water development programme culminated in the Southern Conveyor Project that carries surplus water from the south-western part of the island to the central and eastern areas in an effort to broaden and boost agricultural production and alleviate water shortages.
Now a member of the EU, Cyprus is only eligible for full EU agricultural subsidies and rural development aid through the Common Agricultural Policy (CAP) from 2013.
During its transitional entry stage Cyprus has decided to implement the reform of the CAP on 1 January 2009. The reform was introduced throughout most of the EU in 2005, when subsidies on farm output, which tended to benefit large farms and encourage overproduction, were replaced by single farm payments not conditional on production. The change is expected to reward farms that provide and maintain a healthy environment, food safety and animal welfare standards. The changes are also intended to encourage market conscious production and cut the cost of CAP to the EU taxpayer.

Fishing

The fishing industry largely consists of inshore and trawl fishing, as well as aquaculture. Annual fish production typically totals 4,000 tonnes.

Forestry

Forest and other wooded land accounts for less than a third of the land area. Industrial wood and paper products are largely imported.

Industry and manufacturing

The industrial sector contributes around 12 per cent to GDP and accounts for 16 per cent of the workforce.
Major growth industries, which are mainly export-based, include cement, food and drink, footwear and clothing. Chemical and pharmaceutical products, plastics and publishing are also expanding areas. Foreign investment is encouraged. Industrial activity in northern Cyprus is limited to food and textiles.

Tourism

Cyprus markets itself as an island of ancient myth and culture. However, its political turmoil has cut the island in two and left relations fractious with not only its own Turkish community but also Turkey as its closest mainland neighbour. Tourists from the UK constitute the largest visitor group (1.242 million in 2008), followed by those from Russia (180,926).
In 2005 the tourist sector constituted 24.2 per cent of GDP, by 2009 this had fallen to 16.7 per cent, the lowest contribution since before 1989 (it peaked in 1994 at 34.4 per cent of GDP). Tourist arrivals peaked in 2005, with 2.470 million and the number slowly fell to 2.404 million in 2008 before dropping to 2.141 million in 2009 as the global economic crisis saw a drop in visitors from the UK, not only as their income was reduced, but as the pound sterling fell against the euro. In 2009 all indicators showed negative growth for the industry, as annual employment fell by -16 per cent, visitor spending fell by -19.2 per cent and capital investment dropped by -32.2 per cent. Government moved to reverse the decline by cutting value added tax (VAT) on tourist elements in the economy. Value for money package deals as well as special activity packages are promoted. In 2010 numbers picked up, with 2.172 million arrivals and increased spending.
An open sky policy for more budget airlines to land, plus a new terminal at Larnaca Airport, opened in 2009, and capable of processing 7.5 million passengers annually, should enhance the experience of travellers to Cyprus. There are marina projects being constructed around the south and west coasts to attract yachting enthusiasts and a cruise liner terminal, with facilities and berths for six ships, is planned.

Environment

The problems of water shortages, sewage disposal, industrial and agricultural pollution and waste disposal are acute. The government has introduced a programme of legislation incorporating the principle that the polluter pays. By July 2008, Cyprus had had no substantial winter rainfall since 2004 and water reservoirs were at their lowest since 1908 so that potable water had to be imported from the Greek mainland; contamination fears condemned a shipment of 40,000 cubic metres of water, which had to be discarded and pumped into the ground. Cyprus will import eight million cubic metres of water, costing US$70 million, by November 2008.
Northern Cyprus is particularly badly affected by water shortages, a problem accentuated by the Turkish soldiers stationed on the island. Shortages have caused many to stop cultivating the land as low rainfalls mean water reserves are used faster than they are replenished. The Turkish government has proposed building a water pipeline to northern Cyprus, capable of carrying 70–100 million cubic metres a year to the island. Since the 1990s, giant plastic 'sacks' of water have been pulled across the Mediterranean from Turkey to northern Cyprus; there is a concern about a long-term shortage of water.

Mining

Cyprus was once famous for its enormous copper reserves. It has a 3,000 year tradition of copper mining, which was the biggest source of the nation's revenue.

However after the 1974 Turkish invasion copper mining stopped.
Continued expansion in the construction industry has led to a boom in quarrying of construction materials and non-metallic minerals. Other quarried materials include marble, bentonite, umber, sienna, ochra and limonite.

Hydrocarbons
Although oil reserves are thought to be present in waters surrounding Cyprus and exploration has been undertaken, no commercial drilling is in operation. Oil exploration licences for the entire Cypriot territorial waters were issued to foreign oil companies from 2006 and evoked opposition from Northern Cyprus and Turkey which considered that any benefits from oil and gas finds would be garnered by the Republic of Cyprus. Cyprus began exploratory drilling for oil in the eastern Mediterranean in September 2011; Turkey has said it will also start drilling, risking an escalation in tension between the two countries.
Cyprus does not produce natural gas and any imports of liquefied natural gas (LNG) are negligible.
There are reserves of coal but production is not commercially recorded.

Energy
Total installed generating capacity was 1,124WM in 2007, producing 4.37 billion kilowatt hours.
The Electricity Authority of Cyprus (EAC) operates three power stations, two of which use heavy fuel oil. Valilikos Power Station, the third, and latest, plant, uses a combination of heavy fuel and gas. It will be extended to include additional turbines increasing the capacity by 480MW and powered by diesel, until a new natural gas terminal is built and they are converted to natural gas.
Cyprus is well suited to solar power with over 300 days of sunshine per annum. The government subsidises the installation of solar technology to a maximum 55 per cent of the cost, and has now started to subsidise wind power.
Cyprus began drilling for oil in the eastern Mediterranean in September; Turkey has said it will also start drilling, risking an escalation in tension between the two countries.

Financial markets
The Cyprus Stock Exchange (CSE) was transformed in 1996 from an over-the-counter market to an official stock exchange. The CSE became a fully computerised trading system in 1999. The overall supervision of the stock exchange is assigned to the minister of finance and is exercised by the minister through the Securities and Exchange Commission.

Stock exchange
Cyprus Stock Exchange (CSE)

Banking and insurance
The Bank of Cyprus, which was founded in 1899, leads the Cypriot banking sector. The Central Bank of Cyprus (CBC) oversees monetary policy. There are nine commercial banks. The abolition of the interest rate ceiling was part of a drive to reform banking practices in line with those of the EU.

Central bank
Central Bank of Cyprus

Time
GMT plus two hours (daylight saving, late March to late October, GMT plus three hours)

Geography
Cyprus is an island in the eastern Mediterranean Sea, about 100km south of Turkey. The landscape varies between rugged coastlines, sandy beaches, rocky hills and forest-covered mountains. The Troodos Mountains in the centre of the island rise to almost 1,950 metres.

Hemisphere
Northern

Climate
Mediterranean. Summers are long and dry. Winters are changeable with occasional rain. Temperatures range from 0–27 degrees Celsius (C) (in the mountains), 5–40 degrees C (inland) and 9–35 degrees C (on the coast). Hottest months are July and August; coldest are January and February. Average annual rainfall is 500mm.

Entry requirements
Passports
Required by all except citizens of EU, Switzerland, Iceland and Norway travelling with official national ID cards. Passports must have at least three months validity from the date of departure from Cyprus.

Visa
Required by all except citizens of most European countries, America and Japan. Contact the local embassy or High Commission for a full list of exceptions and application, see consular and protocol information in: www02.mfa.gov.cy. A Schengen visa application (offered in several languages) can be downloaded from http://europa.eu/abc/travel/ see 'documents you will need'.
For a business visa, applications should include an introductory letter from the employer, which gives details and the nature of business to be conducted.

Prohibited entry
Cypriot authorities do not recognise any ports of entry other than those in the Republic of Cyprus. Visitors with passports stamped in the Turkish Republic of Northern Cyprus must have their visa stamps cancelled by the Republic of Cyprus immigration authorities.

Currency advice/regulations
Local currency may be imported without restriction but must be declared; foreign currency over US$1,000 (or the equivalent) must be declared. The export of foreign and local currency is limited to the amount declared on arrival. Export of local currency withdrawn from Cypriot banks is permitted, provided a holding certificate is obtained.
To avoid extra exchange fees travellers cheques in UK pounds sterling or Cyprus pounds are advised.

Customs
Personal items are duty-free. There are no duties levied on alcohol and tobacco between EU member states, providing amounts imported are for personal consumption.
Unauthorised export of antiquities is prohibited; permission of the Cyprus Museum is required.

Health (for visitors)
Nationals of the European Economic Area (EEA) countries and Switzerland can access reduced cost and sometimes free medical treatment using a European Health Insurance Card (EHIC) while visiting the EEA. Exceptions include nationals of the 10 countries which joined the EU in 2004 whose EHIC is not valid in Switzerland. Applications for the EHIC should be made before travelling.

Mandatory precautions
None

Advisable precautions
Recommended immunisations include tetanus and polio, while long-term visitors are advised to consider a hepatitis A immunisation.
Tap water is safe to drink, but fruit, especially soft fruit, should be washed.

Hotels
There are over 500 hotels (from deluxe to one star). Visitors should book well in advance, especially during the peak holiday season (April–October). Cyprus Tourism Organisation (CTO) operates a rating system, both for hotels and any other licensed tourist accommodation. Tipping is not obligatory. A 15 per cent valued added tax (VAT) is charge on all bills.

Credit cards
Most leading cards are accepted in the main hotels, restaurants and shops.

Public holidays (national)
Fixed dates
1 Jan (New Year's Day), 6 Jan (Epiphany), 25 Mar (Greek National Day), 1 Apr (Greek Cypriot National Day), 1 May (Labour Day), 15 Aug (Assumption Day), 1 Oct (Cyprus Independence Day), 28 Oct

(Greek National Day/Ochi Day), 24–26 Dec (Christmas Holiday).

Variable dates

Green Monday (Feb/Mar), Greek Orthodox Easter (Mar/Apr, four days Thu–Mon); Pentecost (Festival of the Flood (Jun)).

Working hours

Banking

Mon–Fri: 0815–1230; Mon (only) 1515–1645, (year around).

In summer (Jun–Aug), in central districts, some banks have extended hours Tue–Fri: 1515–1645.

Business

Mon–Fri: 0800–1300 and 1500–1800 (winter), 0730–1300 and 1600–1830 (summer); Wed and Sat half-day (year round).

Government

Mon–Fri: 0730–1430; in winter Sept–June, Thu: 1500–1800.

Shops

Mon–Fri: 0800–1300 and 1430–1800 (winter), 0730–1300 and 1600–1830 (summer); Wed and Sat half-day 0800–1400.

Telecommunications

Mobile phones

GSM 900/1800 and G3 services are available in Greek Cypriot areas

Electricity supply

240V AC. Sockets are the UK flat three-pin style.

Weights and measures

The metric system is used.

Social customs/useful tips

It is considered impolite to refuse drinks offered at a first meeting. Cypriots customarily offer fruit preserves to guests. Between 1300–1600 hours is siesta time in the summer (May–September).

There are restrictions on photographing military installations in both south and north Cyprus.

Getting there

Air

International airport/s: Larnaka International (LCA), 8km from Larnaka (49km from Lefkosia); Pafos International (PFO), 10km east of Pafos (146km from Lefkosia).

Both airports offer tourist information, foreign exchange, hotel reservations and duty free shops.

Other airport/s: Northern Cyprus has an airport at Ercan with flights to and from Turkey. Flights are provided by a number of Turkish airlines and the northern Cypriot airline, Kibris Türk Hava Yollari (KYHY) (Cyprus Turkish Airlines). Visitors planning to arrive via Turkey are not allowed into southern Cyprus.

Airport tax: None

Surface

Water: Access by ship from Greece, Syria, Israel, Italy, Lebanon and Egypt.

Main port/s: Lemesos (Limassol)

Getting about

National transport

Buses: An efficient *intra-cud* (inter-town) bus service is available. All buses run from the central bus depots, connecting towns and villages. A rural bus operation is limited to once or twice a day, usually to the local market.

City transport

Taxis: An efficient service is operated throughout the island by metered taxis. The transurban service-taxis are shared taxis connecting all main towns. Prices are regulated. Between 2300–0600 an additional 15 per cent is charged. Tipping is standard practice.

Buses, trams & metro: Urban buses operate frequently during the day. In certain tourist areas during the summer, buses extend their operations until midnight.

Car hire

Car hire is available in all parts of the island, particularly from airports and commercial centres. Rates vary depending on the size of the car and are also subject to seasonal variations. For a higher price, a prestige service is also available. Cheap rates are available for hire periods of more than one week. Visitors should book cars well in advance during the period June–September. A national or international driving licence is required. Driving is on the left. Road signs are in both Greek and English.

BUSINESS DIRECTORY

The addresses listed below are a selection only. While World of Information makes every endeavour to check these addresses, we cannot guarantee that changes have not been made, especially to telephone numbers and area codes. We would welcome any corrections.

Telephone area codes

The international direct dialling codes (IDD) for Cyprus is +357, followed by area code and subscriber's number:

Larnaka	24	Lemasos	25
Lefkosia	22	Pafos	26

North Cyprus numbers are preceded by +90-392, in place of +357. Area code for Famagusta 366, Kyrenia 815.

Useful telephone numbers

Emergencies112

Chambers of Commerce

Cyprus Chamber of Commerce and Industry, Chamber Building, 38 Grivas Dighenis Ave and 3 Deligiorgis Street, PO Box 21455, 1509 Lefkosia (tel: 889-600; fax: 667-433).

Famagusta Chamber of Commerce and Industry, 339 Ayiou Andreou Street, Andrea Chamber Bldg, PO Box 3124, Limassol (tel: 370-165, 370-167; fax: 370-291).

Larnaka Chamber of Commerce and Industry, 12 12 Gregoriou Afxentiou Str, Skourou Bldg, 4th Floor, PO Box 287, Larnaka (tel: 655-051; fax: 628-281).

Lefkosia Chamber of Commerce and Industry, 38 Grivas Dighenis Ave and 3 Deligioris Str, Chamber Building, PO Box 1455, Lefkosia (tel: 449-500; fax: 367-433).

Limassol Chamber of Commerce and Industry, PO Box 347, 25 Spyrou Araouzou Street, Verengaria Building, PO Box 347, Limassol (tel: 362-556; fax: 371-655).

Pafos Chamber of Commerce and Industry, 32 Grivas Dighenis Avenue, Demetra Court, 2nd Floor, Flat 22, Pafos (tel:235-115; fax: 244-602).

Banking

Alpha Bank Ltd, Yiorkion Bldg, 1 Prodromou Street, 1095 Lefkosia (tel: 77-3799, 88-8888; fax: 77-3744).

Bank of Cyprus Ltd, Box 1472, 86-90 Phaneromeni Street, Lefkosia (tel: 46-4064; fax: 46-4340).

Cyprus Development Bank, PO Box 1415, Alpha House, 50 Archbishop Makarios III Avenue, Lefkosia (tel: 45-7575; fax: 46-4322).

Cyprus Investment and Securities Corporation, 60 Digenis Akritas Avenue, PO Box 597, Lefkosia (tel: 45-1535; fax: 44-5481).

Cyprus Popular Bank Ltd, PO Box 2032, 39 Archbishop Makarios III Avenue, Lefkosia (tel: 45-0000; fax: 44-9169).

Federal Bank of the Middle East Ltd, J & P Building, 90 Archbishop Makarios III Avenue, 1077 Lefkosia (tel: 88-8444; fax: 88-8555).

Hellenic Bank Ltd, Corner 92 Dhigenis Akritas Ave & Cretes Str, 1061 Lefkosia (tel: 86-0000; fax: 76-507).

Sociéte Générale Cyprus Ltd, PO Box 25400, 7-9 Grivas Dighenis Ave, 1309 Lefkosia (tel: 81-7777; fax: 76-4471).

Central bank

Central Bank of Cyprus, 80 Kennedy Avenue, PO Box 25529, 1395 Lefkosia (tel: 714-100; fax: 378-153; internet: www.centralbank.gov.cy).

Stock exchange

Cyprus Stock Exchange (CSE): www.cse.com.cy

Travel information

Cyprus Airways, PO Box 1903, 21 Alkeou Street, Lefkosia (tel: 44-3054, 2246-1800; fax: 44-3167, 2236-0075;

e-mail: marketing@cyprusair.com.cy; internet site: www.cyprusairways.com.cy).

Cyprus Hotel Association, PO Box 24772, Lefkosia (tel: 37-4251; fax: 36-5460).

Ministry of tourism

Ministry of Commerce, Industry and Tourism, 1421 Lefkosia (fax: 375-120).

National tourist organisation offices

Cyprus Tourism Organisation (main office, for postal enquiries only), 19 Limassol Ave, PO Box 4535, Lefkosia (tel: 315-715; fax: 313-022); (for personal and telephone enquiries only, open every morning except Sun, and on Mon and Thurs afternoons) Laiki Yitonia, East of Eleftheria Sq, Lefkosia (tel: 444-264); (24-hour service) Larnaka International Airport (tel: 654-389).

Ministries

Ministry of Agriculture, Natural Resources and Environment, Loukis Akritas Avenue, Lefkosia (tel: 30-0807; fax: 78-1156).

Ministry of Commerce, Industry and Tourism, 2 A Araouzos Street, Lefkosia (fax: 35-7120).

Ministry of Communication and Works, 28 Acheon Street, Lefkosia CY-1101 (tel: 30-2830; fax: 77-6272, 46-5462, 36-0578).

Ministry of Defence, 4 Emmanuel Roides Street, Lefkosia (tel: 80-7528; fax: 36-6225).

Ministry of Education and Culture, Gr Afxentiou Street, Lefkosia (tel: 30-5188; fax: 42-7559).

Ministry of Finance, Ex Secretariat Compound, Lefkosia (tel: 80-3530; fax: 36-6080).

Ministry of Foreign Affairs, Dem Severis Avenue, Government House No. 18-19, Lefkosia (tel: 30-0600; fax: 45-1881).

Ministry of Health, Ex Secretarial Offices, Lefkosia (tel: 30-9526; fax: 36-8883).

Ministry of Interior, Dem Severis Avenue, Ex Secretariat Offices, Lefkosia (tel: 51-0222; fax: 45-3465, 36-6709).

Ministry of Justice and Public Order, 12 Helioupoleos, Lefkosia (tel: 30-2355; fax: 76-1427).

Ministry of Labour and Social Insurance, Byron Avenue, Lefkosia (tel: 30-3481; fax: 45-0993).

Presidential Palace, Lefkosia (tel: 45-1333; fax: 44-5016).

Other useful addresses

British High Commission, Alexander Pallis St, PO Box 1978, Lefkosia (tel: 47-3131/7; fax: 36-7198).

Central Post Office, Eleftheria Square, Lefkosia (tel: 30-3219).

Cyprus Broadcasting Corporation, PO Box 4824, Lefkosia (tel: 42-2231; fax: 31-4050).

Cyprus Employers' and Industrialists' Federation, 30 Grivas Dhigenis Avenue, PO Box 1657, Lefkosia (tel: 44-5102; fax: 45-9459).

Cyprus News Agency, 7 Kastorias St, PO Box 3947, Lefkosia (tel: 31-9009; fax: 31-9006).

Cyprus Petroleum Refinery Ltd, PO Box 40275, 6302 Larnaka (fax: 2464-1401; e-mail: lambroug@cprl.com.cy).

Cyprus Telecommunications Authority, PO Box 4929, Lefkosia (tel: 31-3111).

Department of Customs & Excise, Customs Headquarters, 29 Katsonis Street, Ay Omoloyitae, Lefkosia (tel: 30-5404, 30-5737; fax: 35-5050).

Department of Statistics and Research, Ministry of Finance, 13 Andreas Araouzos Street, 1444 Lefkosia (tel: 30-9305, 30-3208; fax: 37-4830, 45-6712).

Embassy of the United States of America, Therissos St & Dositheos St, Lefkosia (fax: 45-9571).

Press and Information Office, Apellis Street, Ay Omoloyitae, 1456 Lefkosia (tel: 80-1155/1164/1177; fax: 36-6123; email: communications@pio.moi.gov.cy).

National news agency: Cyprus News Agency (CNA), 7 Kastorias Street, 2002 Strovolos, Lefkosia (tel: 556-009; fax: 556-103; email: news@cna.org.cy; internet: www.cna.org.cy).

Other news agencies: TAK (Arca Haber Ajansi) (in Turkish): www.arcaajans.com

Internet sites

Bridge to Greece and Cyprus: www.greekvillage.com/bridge/bridge.htm

Cyprus News: www.cyprusnews.com

Cyprus Telecommunications Authority: www.cytanet.com.cy

Cyprus Tourism Organisation: www.cyprustourism.org

Official Cyprus homepage: www.pio.gov.cy

Czech Republic

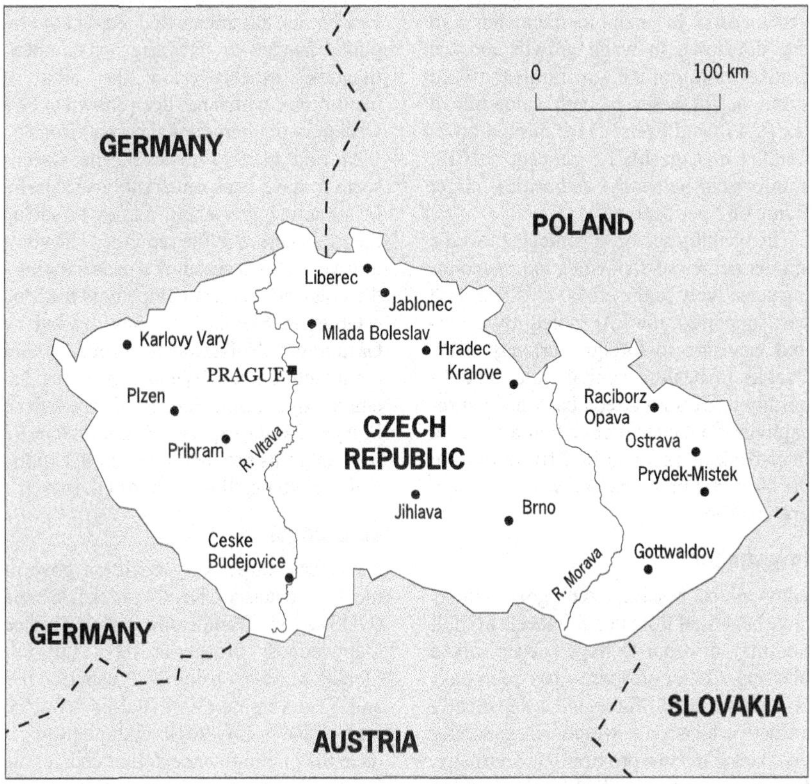

In 2011, the Czech Republic, once the leader of the pack of the ten ex-communist republics to have joined the European Union (EU), was grappling with the harsh realities of the post global financial crash rather than the post Soviet era. The Czech Republic's president, Vaclav Klaus, is a proud, even haughty man. Having been prime minister before becoming president, he can take some pride from the fact that, alongside Slovenia (when purchasing power is factored into the equation) the Czech Republic and Slovenia are the only two of the ten to be ahead of the poorest Western EU members, Malta and Portugal.

Growth resumes

In 2011 the Czech Republic returned to economic growth. In many respects the country resembles one of the smaller Western EU economies than its fellow ex-communist republics. A visitor to Prague in 2011 would find it hard to even imagine that only twenty years earlier the streets were devoid of attractive shops, clothes lacked colour and variety and for the most part the cars were either polluting Skodas or dated Soviet Ladas. By 2011, gross domestic product per capita (GDP) hovered around the US$25,000 mark, about 80 per cent of the EU average. By comparison, Germany's per capita is 116 per cent of the EU average, according to 2010 Eurostat figures. The GDP growth figure for 2010 was a more than respectable 2.3 per cent; however, this did not restore the economy to its pre-2008 levels – having shrunk by 4.1 per cent in 2009. Not only did growth fall, so did foreign direct investment (FDI) – a sector in which, through its respected promotion agency, CzechInvest (see *Investment* below) the republic had excelled. FDI did not dry up completely, but fell by some 50 per cent in 2009. Prior to 2009 the rule of thumb had

KEY FACTS

Official name: Ceská Republika (Czech Republic)

Head of State: President Václav Klaus (since 2003; re-elected 15 Feb 2008)

Head of government: Prime Minister Petr Necas (from 28 Jun 2010)

Ruling party: Coalition led by Obcanská Demokratická Strana (ODS) (Civic Democratic Party), with Tradice Odpovednost Prosperita 09 (TOP 09) (Tradition Responsibility Prosperity 09) and Veci verejné (VV) (Public Affairs) (from 30 Jun 2010)

Area: 78,864 square km

Population: 10.52 million (2010)*

Capital: Prague

Official language: Czech

Currency: Czech koruna (Kc) = 100 hellers

Exchange rate: Kc18.42 per US$ (Oct 2011)

GDP per capita: US$18,288 (2010)

GDP real growth: 2.30% (2010)

GDP: US$192.20 billion (2010)

Labour force: 5.42 million (2010)

Unemployment: 9.00% (2010)

Inflation: 1.50% (2010)

Balance of trade: US$2.81 billion (2010)

* estimated figure

been that FDI more than covered the budget deficit.

In its annual assessment of the Czech economy the International Monetary Fund (IMF) noted that 'market sentiment vis-á-vis the Czech republic remains relatively favourable, reflecting limited vulnerabilities.' Czech financial institutions had demonstrated a relatively sophisticated response to the crisis. Fiscal policy was described by the IMF as 'supportive' and the Czech National Bank (CNB) was the first central bank in Europe to start easing monetary policy, in August 2008.

Despite the financial authorities' largely positive reaction, the financial crisis, according to the IMF, impacted seriously on the fiscal position. During the years of healthy, rapid, growth the Czech authorities had not sought to secure any lasting fiscal consolidation. Thus, as the crisis made itself felt, the overall deficit widened sharply, accentuated by a rapid accumulation of debt and increased interest rate spreads. The consequences of this failure to protect the economy looked to last for some time, with the budget deficit unlikely to drop below 5 per cent of GDP in the medium term. Similarly, public debt looked more than likely to move in the wrong direction, probably doubling to an annual 60 per cent of GDP in less than a decade. The IMF estimated that a structural adjustment of around 0.7 per cent of GDP per year would be required to achieve the EU's notional deficit target of 3 per cent of GDP by 2013. To achieve this, the 2010 budget relied on permanent indirect tax increases and temporary expenditure cuts that were scheduled to expire in 2011.

In the view of the IMF, the economy's revival would be gradual and – given its international characteristics – closely linked to the pace of the global recovery. Worryingly for the government, consumer spending was expected to continue its decline, reflecting not only the continued increase in unemployment, but also the slowdown in wage growth and the gradual easing of the government's fiscal stimulus. Increases in both value added tax (VAT) and excise taxes pushed inflation to a manageable 1.5 per cent in 2010, comfortably below the authorities' target figure of 2 per cent.

The banking sector in general showed a similar degree of sophistication, responding sensitively to the crisis. This response was supported, the IMF noted, by a limited exposure to foreign currency risks. Thanks to healthy capital ratios and liquidity buffers no Czech bank needed recapitalisation, even though liquidity in the inter-bank market and in 2010 trading in the domestic bond market was still below pre-crisis levels.

Investment

Although successive Czech governments have benefited from healthy levels of FDI, this may turn out to have been a mixed blessing. Czech prosperity has been built on a cheap labour force and a logistically attractive location – which can generally be taken to mean a proximity to Germany. But as a report published by the London *Financial Times* (FT) in mid-2011 underlined, Czech economic development 'is going to have to come from productivity growth, research and development and entrepreneurship – things that have not been the country's strongest suit.' The FT went on to note the Czech Republic has one of the region's worst rankings in the World Bank's annual international survey of *Doing Business*. The prime minister, Petr Necas, has acknowledged that the republic needed to 'increase our competitiveness, especially in the area of institutions, which has been shown to be a weakness in international comparisons.'

At first glance, however, the Czechs seem to have been remarkably successful in attracting household names to set up their businesses in the republic. The automotive sector is certainly a case in point – the country's largest company is the long established Skoda Auto, now owned by Germany's Volkswagen Group. Other manufacturers are Hyundai of Korea, Japan's Toyota and Peugeot-Citroen from France. Skoda exports an impressive 92 per cent of its production; overall, exports make up some 70 per cent of GDP.

Euro angst

Mr Necas' three party coalition government (Obcanská Demokratická Strana (ODS) (Civic Democratic Party), Tradice Odpovednost Prosperita 09 (TOP 09) (Tradition Responsibility Prosperity 09) and Veci verejné (VV) (Public Affairs)) took office in July 2010, with plans to reduce the public finance deficit and get the country back on track for entry into the euro-zone (i e adoption of the euro as the national currency) by 2013. Previous governments had for some time been under pressure from Czech exporters to adopt the euro. Superficially, the arguments for joining the euro-zone seemed to make sense. However, as the crisis over the future of the euro staggered from bad to worse in the second half of 2011, the benefits of adhering to the koruna seemed to be gaining in acceptance. While the volatility of the koruna's exchange rate may give Czech exporters a headache, that pales into insignificance compared to the prospect (and the initial expense) of adopting an apparently doomed currency. Prime Minister Necas had wisely gone on record in early 2010 as saying that 'The government programme will not include any target date or promise to join the euro area. Exports are important, but this country is not only a country of exporters.' In July 2010 the koruna had gained 3.7 per cent against the euro, the highest appreciation rate of any of the 177 currencies

KEY INDICATORS — Czech Republic

	Unit	2006	2007	2008	2009	2010
Population	m	10.27	*10.27	*10.32	*10.48	*10.52
Gross domestic product (GDP)	US$bn	143.02	175.31	217.10	194.80	192.20
GDP per capita	US$	13,893	16,880	20,061	18,557	18,288
GDP real growth	%	6.4	6.5	3.2	-4.3	2.3
Inflation	%	2.5	2.8	6.3	1.0	1.5
Unemployment	%	7.2	5.3	5.4	8.1	9.0
Coal output	mtoe	23.7	18.9	22.8	22.8	19.4
Exports (fob) (goods)	US$m	95,119.0	122,791.0	145,697.0	112,606.0	126,414.0
Imports (fob) (goods)	US$m	92,139.0	116,878.0	139,328.0	103,088.0	123,600.0
Balance of trade	US$m	2,979.0	5,913.0	6,368.0	9,518.0	2,814.0
Current account	US$m	-4,462.0	-5,754.0	-6,669.0	-2,147.0	-7,188.0
Total reserves minus gold	US$m	31,182.0	34,550.0	36,642.0	41,157.0	41,909.0
Foreign exchange	US$m	31,054.0	34,445.0	36,459.0	39,670.0	40,335.0
Exchange rate	per US$	21.02	18.28	17.07	19.06	19.10

* estimated figure

tracked by the US financial information group Bloomberg. As an incipient euro crisis began to develop in mid-2010, a seemingly prescient Mr Necas was quoted: 'With the current state of the euro-zone, it wouldn't be politically wise to say that we will join on a certain date. After all, nobody knows what will happen in the euro-zone in two or three years, so a cautious approach is appropriate.'

Coalition blues

Mr Necas' coalition controls 115 of the 200 seats in the lower house of the Czech parliament. Since its election the coalition has staggered from one vote of confidence to another, seeing its poll ratings steadily fall. Much of the government's unpopularity is due to factors beyond its control as it endeavours to clear up the post financial crisis mess. In the midst of tending to the affairs of state, Mr Necas has also had to deal with the irritating unpredictability of the smallest member of the coalition, the populist Public Affairs party, whose demands for ministerial appointments have resulted in protracted squabbles. The coalition government's standing has also been eroded by allegations of corruption, which appear to touch a nerve with many Czechs. Public awareness of the corruption issue has been intensified at a time when cuts in public expenditure, high unemployment and lower salaries mean that more Czech families are finding it harder to make ends meet. As alarming for the government is the fact that the perception of corruption is widespread among the international business community. A survey by the German-Czech Chamber of Commerce in 2011 reported that one third of German companies established in the Czech Republic regretted the decision to invest. One western law firm established in Prague reported that the Czech republic had the highest number of law cases pending between the government and investors in Europe. However bad the perception may be, it does not seem to impact too harshly on the level of FDI, which in 2010 reached an impressive US$6.7 billion, substantially up on the US$2.9 billion registered in 2009.

Risk assessment

Economy	Good
Politics	Fair
Regional stability	Good

COUNTRY PROFILE

Historical profile

1918 Czechoslovakia's independence was established. Before this, Moravia and Bohemia had been ruled by Austria, while Slovakia had been governed by Hungary.
1938 Czechoslovakia ceded its German-speaking areas of Sudetenland to Germany.
1939–45 The country fell under German control until the end of the Second World War.
1946 The Czechoslovak Communist Party (CPCz) formed a power-sharing government following national elections.
1948 After mass protests and strikes orchestrated by the Communists, a government crisis left the CPCz with a majority in government. Czechoslovakia became a People's Republic, adopting a Soviet-style system.
1949–67 Stalinist-style rule, complete with party purges.
1968 Alexander Dubcek, the CPCz leader, introduced the policy of *socialism with a human face* – a period known as the 'Prague Spring' – which ended with the crushing of the reformist movement by the Soviet army.
1969–88 There were on-going protests at occupation by the Soviet troops. Václav Havel and a group of dissidents called for the restoration of civil and political rights. Mass demonstrations in 1988 marked the anniversary of the 1968 invasion.
1989 The new spirit of *glasnost* was met with scepticism as the government initially resisted political and economic change. However, large public demonstrations in the major cities, the 'Velvet Revolution', led to the resignation of the Communist Party leadership. Václav Havel was elected president and a pluralistic political system and market economy were introduced.
1990 The country was renamed the Czech and Slovak Federative Republic. The first free elections since 1946 resulted in a coalition government involving all major parties, with the exception of the CPCz, and Havel was re-elected president.
1991 The Soviet forces completed their withdrawal.
1992 In elections, the Czech voters backed the centre-right, while the Slovaks supported Slovak separatists and left-wing parties. Vladimir Meciar (a supporter of Slovak separatism) became Slovak prime minister. He opposed the rapid privatisation of the public sector proposed by the Czech prime minister, Václav Klaus. Neither was prepared to compromise and agreed to the separation of Slovakia, despite President Havel's objections.
1993 Czechoslovakia divided into two independent countries, the Czech Republic (comprising the regions of Bohemia, Moravia and Silesia) and the Slovak Republic (Slovakia). Václav Havel was elected president of the Czech Republic and Václav Klaus continued as prime minister.
1996 Klaus was reappointed prime minister in a minority coalition government, following the Czech Republic's first parliamentary election.
1997 The Klaus government resigned following the collapse of its coalition over disagreements on the economic reform programme and allegations of financial corruption.
1998 Milos Zeman, leader of the Ceská Strana Sociálne Demokratická (CSSD) (Czech Social Democratic Party), became prime minister and Václav Havel was re-elected president.
1999 The Czech Republic joined NATO.
2000 In elections, a coalition of four small liberal parties, the '4Koalice', became the strongest force in the upper house.
2002 Areas of Prague were flooded when the river Vltava rose to its highest level since 1890. The CSSD won parliamentary elections. President Václav Havel appointed Vladimír Spidla as prime minister.
2003 Parliament elected Václav Klaus as president. In a referendum to join the European Union (EU) 77.3 per cent voted in favour; turnout was 55 per cent.
2004 The Czech Republic became a member of the EU. The government resigned and Stanislav Gross formed a government.
2005 Gross resigned and Jirí Paroubek became prime minister; the new cabinet, unchanged in the key posts, was endorsed on the same day.
2006 Parliamentary (Chamber of Deputies) elections resulted in a stalemate, with both CSSD and Obcanská Demokratická Strana (ODS) (Civic Democratic Party) coalitions winning 100 seats in the lower house. After an initial rejection by parliament, the president appointed Mirek Topolánek as prime minister, who went on to form a government.
2007 The Czech Republic became a member of the European Union Schengen area whereby all travellers may cross borders within the area without a passport or visa.
2008 Incumbent Václav Klaus was re-elected president after two sets of three-rounds of voting. Visa-free visits by Czech nationals to the US was signed.
2009 The minority government lost a vote of no confidence, following an accusation that government advisors had attempted to stifle a critical television programme. Prime Minister Topolanek resigned. An interim government, with Jan Fischer as caretaker prime minister, was formed.
2010 Constitutional and legal wrangling set back the date of parliamentary elections several times (postponed from 2009)

until May. Three new political parties contested the Chamber of Deputies elections, but only two of them won enough votes to gain seats (Tradice Odpovednost Prosperita 09 (TOP 09) (Tradition Responsibility Prosperity 09) and Veci Verejné (VV) (Public Affairs)). The CSSD won 22.08 per cent of the vote (56 seats out of 200) and had the right to form a coalition government. However when the CSSD proved unable to form a government, Petr Necas (ODS) became prime minister on 28 June as the head of a three party coalition (ODS, TOP 09 and VV). In senate elections held in October, one-third of total seats (27) were in contention. The CSSD won 12 seats to take its senate number up to a total of 41, while the ODS lost 11 seats but retained eight for a total of 25 seats.

2011 In May, the Federated State of Micronesia (FSM) challenged Czech Republic government plans to expand Europe's second-largest coal-fired Prunerov Two power plant. Low-lying FSM is threatened by submersion as global warming adds to rising sea levels and if feels that expansion of this site, and the resulting increase in carbon dioxide output could exacerbate its problems. FSM will use a legal instrument of the UN Convention on Environmental Impact Assessment in a Transboundary Context (known as the EIA convention) in Czech Republic courts and if successful will challenge similar projects in other signatory countries where the EIA convention applies.

Political structure

Constitution

The constitution came into force on 1 January 1993. A majority of three-fifths of the members of parliament is required to change the constitution.

All citizens over the age of 18 are eligible to vote.

Independence date

1 January 1993

Form of state

Parliamentary democratic republic

The executive

The highest organ of executive power is the Council of Ministers, composed of the prime minister, the deputy prime ministers and ministers. It is answerable to the Chamber of Representatives.

The two legislative bodies together elect the president of the republic for not more than two five-year terms. The president's post is largely ceremonial but the president is the commander-in-chief of the armed forces. The president appoints the prime minister, and on the prime minister's recommendation, appoints the remaining members of the Council of Ministers.

National legislature

The bicameral Parlament (Parliament) comprises the Poslanecká Snìmovna (Chamber of Deputies) (lower house), with 200 members elected by proportional representation from party lists to serve for four-year terms and the Senát (Senate) (upper house), with 81 (possibly non-partisan) members. Every two years one third of the membership (27) is elected under a two-round majority system in single-member constituencies. Senators serve a six-year term.

Legal system

The civil law system is based on Austro-Hungarian codes. Judicial power is exercised by independent courts.

Last elections

28–29 May 2010 (parliamentary, first and second round); 15–16 and 22–23 October 2010 (senate, first and second round).

Results: Parliamentary (Chamber of Deputies): Ceská Strana Sociálne Demokratická (CSSD) (Czech Social Democratic Party) won 22.08 per cent of the vote (56 seats out of 200), Obcanská Demokratická Strana (ODS) (Civic Democratic Party) 20.22 per cent (53), Tradice Odpovednost Prosperita 09 (TOP 09) (Tradition Responsibility Prosperity 09) 16 .7 per cent (41), Komunistická Strana Cech a Morava (KSCM) (Communist Party of Bohemia and Moravia) 11.27 per cent (26), Veci Verejné (VV) (Public Affairs) 10.88 per cent (24); 21 other political parties won too few votes to win seats. Turnout was 62.6 per cent.

Senate (2008) (27 seats contested): ODS won three (resulting in 35 seats out 81), CSSD 23 (29), KSCM one (3); three minor political parties each lost one seat and seven other political parties did not win any seats. Turnout was 39.52 per cent (first round) and 29.85 per cent (second round).

Senate (2010) (27 seats contested) (first and second round): CSSD won 12 (total seats 41), ODS eight (total 25), Tradice Odpovednost Prosperita 09-Starostové a Nezávislí (Top 09-Stan) (Tradition Responsibility Prosperity 09-Mayors and Independents) two (total five), KDU-CSL, two (total five), Severočeši (North Bohemians) two (total two), independent one (total one).

Next elections

2013 (presidential); 2014 (Chamber of Deputies and Senate)

Political parties

Ruling party

Coalition led by Obcanská Demokratická Strana (ODS) (Civic Democratic Party), with Tradice Odpovednost Prosperita 09 (TOP 09) (Tradition Responsibility Prosperity 09) and Veci verejné (VV) (Public Affairs) (from 30 Jun 2010)

Main opposition party

Ceská Strana Sociálne Demokratická (CSSD) (Czech Social Democratic Party)

Population

10.52 million (2010)*

Last census: March 2001: 10,230,060

Population density: 133 inhabitants per sq km (2000). Urban population: 75 per cent (1995–2001).

Annual growth rate: -0.1 per cent 1994–2004 (WHO 2006)

Ethnic make-up

The chief minorities are Slovaks (3 per cent of the population), Poles (0.6 per cent), Germans (0.5 per cent) and Silesians, Roma, Hungarians and Ukrainians.

Religions

Christianity is the principal religion, although 40 per cent of the population define themselves as atheist. Roman Catholicism is the main denomination (39 per cent of the population), followed by Protestant (5 per cent), Orthodox (3 per cent). There is a very small Jewish community, mainly in Prague.

The state and the church are linked, but there is growing pressure for their separation and the state no longer exercises control over church affairs.

Education

Compulsory education is free. Basic schooling is divided into two cycles with primary lasting for five years from aged six to 11; the second cycle lasts for four years until aged 15. Secondary schooling is offered in one of three designated institutions, a secondary general, technical or vocational school. Technical school programmes last up to six years, vocational courses last between three and four years and general secondary education last for four years and leads to higher education.

There are three universities, Prague's Charles' University (the oldest in Central Europe, founded in 1348), Masarykova University in Brno and Palacky University in Olomouc.

Public expenditure on education typically amounts to 5.1 per cent of annual gross national income.

Literacy rate: Virtually universal.

Compulsory years: Six to 15

Enrolment rate: 104 per cent gross primary school enrolment; 95 per cent gross secondary enrolment, of the relevant age group (including repetition rates) (World Bank).

Pupils per teacher: 18 in primary schools.

Health
Since a market economy replaced the previously planned centralised economy healthcare has become more reative to local requirements, there are more clinics, many operated by foreign medical companies. Recently instituted heath insurance companies took in US$5.3 billion in 2004. The Czech constitution guarantees free health care for all citizens and sponsors health insurance through the General Health Insurance Company. Pure supplementary health care insurance is scarce and simply covers those items outside the mandatory state insurance. Some private companies cover four supplementary areas such as surgery, hospitalisation in the event of illness or accident, permanent disability and accidental death.

HIV/Aids

HIV prevalence: 0.1 per cent aged 15–49 in 2003 (World Bank)
Life expectancy: 76 years, 2004 (WHO 2006)
Fertility rate/Maternal mortality rate: 1.2 births per woman, 2004 (WHO 2006); maternal mortality 9 per 100,000 live births (World Bank).
Child (under 5 years) mortality rate (per 1,000): 3.9 per 1,000 live births (World Bank)
Head of population per physician: 3.51 physicians per 1,000 people, 2003 (WHO 2006)

Welfare
The social security scheme provides old age pension insurance, sickness insurance, state social support benefits, and social care. Those registered in contracted employment, as self-employed (including farming personnel), and informal employment (employed for household duties), pay insurance premiums.

Pensions

In 1999, the Czech government encouraged domestic savings through gradual reforms and development of a supplemental pension insurance programme. The amended law assured both employers and employees of significant tax relief. An employer who assists his employees to pay for supplementary pension insurance saves money both on tax payments for social and health insurance (to which supplementary pension insurance is not subject) and income taxes.
A contribution not exceeding 3 per cent of the gross pay is regarded as a tax-deductible expense. The pension scheme significantly altered the conditions for retirement savings. The minimum retirement age for both men and women gradually increases to 63 years by 2012 and the government is proposing stricter criteria for early retirement.
The Czech Republic has a challenge ahead. The current pay-as-you-go system, where employees pay the pensions of those already retired, is poorly suited to cope with a negative population growth. It has been estimated that the system, by 2020, will have debts amounting to Kc1.5 trillion (US$50 billion), with insufficient assets or income to fund pensions.
Proposals for private pension funds that rely on market equities to pay pensions also have their critics; market growth and volatility could fluctuate and disadvantage many. However, economic growth would be strengthened, and the government would only need to fund retirement for the poorest citizens.

Main cities
Prague (capital, estimated population 1.1 million in 2005); Brno (main city of Moravia) (365,182), Ostrava (Moravia) (310,652), Plzen (Pilsen) (161,910).

Languages spoken
The Czech and Slovak languages are mutually comprehensible. A large proportion of the population, particularly those engaged in industry and foreign trade, speak German. Hungarian, Romani and Polish are also spoken.

Official language/s

Czech

Media
Press

Dailies: In Czech, by popularity *Mladá fronta Dnes* (www.mfdnes.cz), (known as MF Dnes), *Právo* (http://pravo.novinky.cz) and *Lidové Noviny* (www.lidovky.cz).
Other national newspapers include the tabloid, *Blesk* (www.blesk.cz), *ZN Zemské Noviny*, *Hospodárské Noviny* and *Haló Noviny* (www.halonoviny.cz) which publishes political news.
Weeklies: Regional publications include weekly newsmagazine and special interest publications. One of the largest regional media groups, Vktava-Labe-Press (VLP) (www.vlp.cz) publishes daily newspapers in all major cities and regions under the *Deník* (daily) (www.denik.cz) suffix, such as *Brunenský Deník* (http://brnensky.denik.cz) from Brno.
In Czech, *Respekt* (www.respekt.cz), reports on political and economic issues, *Týden* (www.tyden.cz) is a newsmagazine *Mladý Svet*, takes a humorous view of the news. Some of the dailies publish weekend or supplementary weekly magazines. *Spy* (www.ispy.cz) is a tabloid
Business: In Czech, the daily *Hospodárske Noviny* (www.ihned.cz) is an authoritative newspaper. Magazines include *Ekonom* (http://ekonom.ihned.cz) and *Profit* (www.profit.cz). In English, *Czech Business Weekly* (www.cbw.cz) and the *The Prague Tribune* (www.prague-tribune.cz) have comprehensive coverage of news and the markets. The magazine *Finance New Europe* (www.financeneweurope.com) that began publication in 2006, was the first to focus on business matter within the new EU members; it is published every two months.
Periodicals: In Czech, *Sedmá Generace* (www.sedmagenerace.cz), is an environmentalist publication. The monthly *Awrot* (*The Return*) (www.zwrot.cz) is the largest Polish circulation.

Broadcasting

Radio: The national pubic radio station is Ceský Rozhlas (www.rozhlas.cz) operated several national services including Radio 1, Radiozurnal for news and information, Radio 2, Praha (www.radio.cz), for family audiences, Radio 3 Vltava, for culture, Radio 6 is a magazine style programme and Radio 7 (through Praha) is an international, multilingual service. There are also 12 regional stations.
There are numerous private stations broadcasting on FM and AM frequencies, including Evropa 2 (www.evropa2.cz) and Radio City (www.radiocity.cz), both from Prague, Kiss Hády (www.kisshady.cz) and Radio Petrov (www.radiopetrov.com) from Brno, and Radio Cas (www.casradio.cz) from Ostrava. Radio Blanik (www.radioblanik.cz) broadcasts in the western regions.
Television: All analogue TV is scheduled to be replaced by digital signals in 2012 as the TV services market share provided via satellite and cable grows.
Ceská Televize (CT) (www.ceskatelevize.cz), is the national, public broadcaster, operating channels CT1 and CT2, CT24 (www.ct24.cz), the 24-hour news channel and CTSport.
Other private TV stations include TV Nova (www.nova.cz) and Prima (www.iprima.cz).

Advertising

The advertising sector is well-developed with television typically gaining 50 per cent of the annual adspend. Magazines and newspapers each have around a 20 per cent market share. Most media expenditure is spent on advertising of food and drink. Tobacco is banned from advertising and alcohol and pharmaceuticals advertising are restricted.

News agencies

National news agency: CTK (Czech News Agency)

Economy
With an open market economy, based on manufacturing and engineering, the Czech Republic relies on its export trade (70 per cent of GDP) to provide its economic growth. Main industries include vehicle assembly, typically in partnership with foreign car manufactures, with output

destined for overseas markets (Škoda is the country's single largest employer and exporter), iron and steel production, metalworking, electronics, pharmaceuticals, textiles, brewing and traditional expertise in glass and crystal ware and ceramics. Cars and electrical appliances are manufactured by foreign-owned companies and specifically target export markets. Main agricultural produce includes sugar beets, potatoes, wheat and hops.
GDP growth in 2008 was 2.5 per cent, down from 6.1 per cent in 2007,. Growth had been at a steady 6.0–6.8 per cent rate since 2005. The economy had avoided damage during the first wave of the global economic crisis (2007/08) due to its sound banking system, but as global trade weakened and exports were cut GDP growth by 2009 had fallen into recession at -4.3 per cent. Since 2005 the trade balance has remained in credit, despite exports falling from US$145.7 billion in 2008 to US$108.9 billion in 2009. Domestic demand matched the trend with imports falling from US$139.3 billion in 2008 to US$103.1 billion in 2009. The economy was out of recession in the first quarter of 2010, with a forecast GDP growth of 1.7 per cent.
The Czech Republic decided in 2006 to postpone entry to the European Monetary Union (EMU) and adopting the euro as its currency. However in 2009 it became increasingly leery of joining the EMU, when the euro came under pressure and was stressed by the state of some weaker economies among its membership. In July 2010 Prime Minister Necas said that he would not commit his country to a target date for joining the EMU, as adopting the euro risked fuelling inflation and the economy would benefit from a flexible exchange rate and consumer prices converged with those in richer EU countries
Germany is the Czech Republic's single largest trading partner and, in the medium to long term, economic growth is as much dependent on the economic strength and growth of Germany as it is on the global recovery in trade.

External trade
As a member of the European Union (EU), the Czech Republic operates within a community-wide free trade area, with tariffs set as a whole. Internationally, the EU has free trade agreements with a number of nations and trading blocs worldwide.
The Czech Republic has several renowned exported products including beer (Pilsner beer is named after the Bohemian town in Czech Republic) and Bohemian crystal and porcelain. Vehicle manufacturing, led by Škoda, is typically in partnership with foreign car manufactures, with output destined for overseas markets.

Imports
The main classes of imports are machinery and transport equipment, typically around 45 per cent, raw materials and fuels, chemicals.
Main sources: Germany (typically 27 per cent of total), China (9 per cent), Russia (6 per cent).
Exports
Main exports are vehicles and machinery (over 50 per cent), chemicals, raw materials and fuel.
Main destinations: Germany (typically 30 per cent of total), Slovakia (9 per cent), Poland (3 per cent).

Agriculture
Farming
The agricultural sector accounts for around three per cent of GDP and 4.2 per cent of employment. Approximately 41 per cent of the country is arable land, 11 per cent permanent pasture and 2 per cent permanent crops. The most important crops are sugar beet, wheat, potatoes, maize, barley, rye and hops. The livestock industry is well developed with cattle, pigs, chickens and dairy products supplying the food processing industry.
Agriculture was collectivised during the communist period. Although production increased with the creation of large farms, soil erosion and the heavy use of machinery and chemicals have had a long-term detrimental effect on the landscape and environment. In 1991, parliament passed a law on land restitution, under which all land taken by the state after February 1948 was returned to its original owner or, if such a return was not possible, provided for the owner to be compensated.
Large-scale operations still dominate the sector, with many of the same problems experienced during the communist era. Agriculture remains labour intensive, relying on inefficient techniques, outdated technology and a poor distribution system. EU membership should eventually help the sector to modernise and redevelop.
Fishing
The Czech Republic has a long tradition in freshwater fishing and aquaculture, owing to the thousands of man-made fish ponds dating from the middle ages. The principal catch is the common carp. The Czech Republic produces around 25,000 tonnes of freshwater fish per annum, of which around 13,000 tonnes are exported. Being landlocked, the country also imports over 200,000 tonnes of seafood per year. There are 12 processing plants.
Forestry
Forests cover around 2.6 million hectares (ha), about one-third of the total land area, with the growing stock volume per hectare considered among the highest in Europe. Coniferous species make up more than four-fifths of the stock volume. There is no other wooded land.
Three-quarters of forest land is publicly-controlled, mainly at national level; the remainder is privately-owned. Forest output is moderate and the industry depends largely on processing of domestic raw materials. Austria and Germany are important export markets for roundwood and sawn wood respectively.
The domestic wood industry satisfies the majority of industrial needs for newsprint, plywood, furniture and traditional woodworking.

Industry and manufacturing
The industrial sector was among the most advanced in the world before the Second World War, with national GDP per capita the seventh highest in the world in 1938. The Communist takeover in 1948 led to the nationalisation of all enterprises and a concentration on heavy industry. Under communism there was insufficient capital investment, while a lack of management, marketing and financial skills handicapped the development of the sector. In common with its counterparts in other communist countries, Czech industry became characterised by outdated and inefficient technology, over-staffing and poor quality.
Since 1989, the Czech economy has diversified away from its heavy industrial base. Between 1986–98, industry's share of GDP fell from 60 per cent to 39 per cent as a flourishing services sector began to establish itself. In 2004, industry's share of GDP was 39.4 per cent, a drop from a high of around 40 per cent in 2001. The slowdown matched the global trend with manufacturing jobs increasingly being sourced in Asia.
Engineering is beginning to dominate the industrial sector. Automotive engineering accounted for 15.8 per cent of manufacturing exports in 2004.

Tourism
Tourism is a burgeonong sector, which has become a key contributor to the economy.The Czech Republic is one of the most popular tourist destinations in the world and Prague is one of Europe's favourite destinations.
A programme of renovation and moderisation has enhanced tourist facilities. Historic and cultural sites are the usual destinations for most visitors, but the health spas are increasingly popular.

Environment
One of the most lasting legacies of the communist era is pollution, with the Czech Republic one of the most despoiled corners of Europe. Not only is air pollution a major problem, water supplies have

become infected and raw sewage has reportedly been dumped in waterways by individuals as well as factories. Although environmental awareness has grown since 1989, the government and the majority of the population have focussed on economic transformation and improving living standards rather than on the environment.

Hydrocarbons
Proven oil reserves were 95 million cubic metres (cum) in 2008, with production at around 7,500 barrels per day (bpd). Consumption was 207.4 million bpd meaning the Czech Republic currently imports oil from both Russia and via Italy. International oil companies are still interested in the region and currently the Western Carpathians are being explored, although two wells have been found to be non-commercial. There are three oil refineries with a total capacity of 198,000bpd, with the Ceská Rafinérská being the largest.
Proven natural gas reserves were 3.96 billion cubic metres (cum) in 2008, while production was 141 million cum. However, consumption is typically around 9.3 billion cum per annum the balance of which is imported, mainly from Russia, Germany and Norway.
Reserves of coal were 4.5 billion tonnes at the end of 2007, with production at 23.6 million tonnes oil equivalent (mtoe), which has remained steady since 2003.

Energy
Electrical capacity is predominantly from thermal sources, with the remainder from hydroelectric and nuclear stations. The Czech Republic is a net exporter of electricity to Germany, Austria, Poland and Slovakia.
Ceské Energetické Závody (CEZ) is the dominant power company in the Czech Republic, supplying over 70 per cent of the Republic's power which was 82.9 billion kilowatt hours (kWh) in 2007. There was an 8 per cent increase in electricity from renewable sources. Consumption was over 60 billion kWh. CEZ operates two nuclear power station, at Dukovany and Temelin, as well as thermal and hydroelectric power plants. Electricity exports, particularly from the Temelín nuclear power station, are an important source of foreign earnings.
Construction of the controversial Temelin nuclear power station began in the 1980s. The first reactor became operational in 2000, but was shut down several times due to technical problems. A second reactor became operational in 2003, allowing Temelin to generate an extra 2,000MW of power. The power station must conform to EU safety standards by 2009.
In May 2011, the Federated State of Micronesia (FSM) challenged Czech Republic government plans to expand its coal-fired Prunerov Two power plant, Europe's second-largest. Low-lying FSM is threatened by submersion as global warming adds to rising sea levels. It feels this expansion, and its resulting increase in carbon dioxide output could exacerbate its problems. FSM will use a legal instrument of the UN Convention on Environmental Impact Assessment in a Transboundary Context (known as the EIA convention) in Czech Republic courts and if successful will challenge similar projects in other signatory countries where the EIA convention applies.

Financial markets
Stock exchange
Burza Cennych Papíru Praha (Prague Stock Exchange) (PSE)

Banking and insurance
The country is suffering from high levels of public debt, approximately 18.8 per cent of GDP. Most of this debt can be attributed to government bail-outs in the banking sector. The IMF has estimated that continued bank restructuring will take up a large percentage of the Czech Republic's GDP.
Much of the bank restructuring has been as a result of the government attempting to ensure that there is compatibility between Czech and EU laws, following EU membership in 2004. This also includes continued privatisation, not least in the banking sector, where state-owned stakes in banks will gradually be eliminated.
The Foreign Exchange Act introduced partial liberalisation for capital account and full convertibility for current account transactions in Czech koruna. It also cleared the way for Czech membership of the Organisation for Economic Co-operation and Development (OECD), enabled companies to accept credit from non-resident banks and eased restrictions on direct investment.
The accumulation of bad domestic and international debt and non-performing loans, particularly to Russia, has reduced the attraction of Czech banking corporations to foreign investors. However, with the introduction of more stringent financial regulations and an improvement in accounting standards, bank privatisation will likely gain momentum.
Central bank
Ceska Národnì Banka (CNB) (Czech National Bank).

Time
GMT plus one hour (daylight saving, late March to late October, GMT plus two hours)

Geography
The Czech Republic is a landlocked country in central Europe, bordering Germany to the west, Poland to the north, Slovakia to the east, and Austria to the south. The landscape varies greatly from lowlands to Alpine-type mountains. It has numerous rivers (the Elbe (Labe), and its largest tributary, the Vltava, provide important links to sea ports).
With a total area of 78,864km square the Czech Republic is slightly smaller than Austria and one-third the size of the UK. The country is split into two principal regions, Bohemia in the west and Moravia to the east. Surrounded by low mountains Bohemia is a plateau forming a basin drained by the Elbe and the Vltava – on which Prague is situated. The lowlands of Moravia are drained by the Morava River which flows into the Danube and by the Oder (Odra) eventually flows into the Baltic Sea.
Hemisphere
Northern

Climate
The climate is continental with warm, showery summers and cold, snowy winters. June is the hottest month and January the coldest. February and March are the driest months and June, July and August the wettest. The average temperature in winter is minus 5 degrees Celsius (C) and in the summer around 20 degrees C.

Dress codes
Most people wear standard casual clothes. They do, however, dress up when eating out or going to the theatre or a concert. Some more exclusive restaurants do not admit people in casual wear and it is useful to enquire beforehand. For business, a suit and tie is advisable for men and a suit or dress for women.

Entry requirements
Passports
Passport required by all, except nationals of EU/EEA and Switzerland, with valid national ID cards.
Visa
Required by all, except nationals of EU and Schengen area signatory countries, North America, Australasia and Japan. For further exceptions contact the nearest embassy. A Schengen visa application (offered in several languages) can be downloaded from http://europa.eu/abc/travel/ see 'documents you will need'.
See http://czech.embassyhomepage.com for a full list of exceptions to visa controls. Business visas for nationals requiring visas require evidence of invitation from a local company and business letter of intention from employer.

Currency advice/regulations
The import and export of local currency is limited to Kc200,000, while there are no restrictions on the import of export of foreign currency.
Travellers cheques are readily accepted but euros, US dollars, or UK pounds avoid extra exchange fees. ATMs are found in most banks.
Customs
Personal items are duty-free. There are no duties levied on alcohol and tobacco between EU member states, providing amounts imported are for personal consumption.

Health (for visitors)
Nationals of the European Economic Area (EEA) countries and Switzerland can access reduced cost and sometimes free medical treatment using a European Health Insurance Card (EHIC) while visiting the EEA. Exceptions include nationals of the 10 countries which joined the EU in 2004 whose EHIC is not valid in Switzerland. Applications for the EHIC should be made before travelling.
Mandatory precautions
None
Advisable precautions
Immunisation for hepatitis A and B may be useful.

Hotels
Prague has a wide range of hotels. Business travellers are advised to book rooms well in advance.

Credit cards
All major credit and charge cards are accepted.

Public holidays (national)
Fixed dates
1 Jan (New Year's Day), 1 May (Labour Day), 8 May (Liberation Day), 5 Jul (St Cyril and St Methodius Day), 6 Jul (Jan Hus Day), 28 Sep (Czech Statehood Day), 28 Oct (National Day), 17 Nov (Freedom and Democracy Day), 24–26 Dec (Christmas).
Variable dates
Easter Monday

Working hours
Banking
Mon–Fri: 0800–1800; some banks close early on Fri.
Bureau de Change in main city centres operate seven days a week until 1900.
Business
Mon–Fri: 0800–1700.
Government
Mon–Fri: usually 0800–1600, but may vary.
Shops
Mon–Fri: 0800–1800; Sat: 0900–1200; some shops remain open late on Thursday evening.

Telecommunications
Mobile/cell phones
GSM 900/1800 services are available throughout the country.

Electricity supply
Domestic: 220V, 50 cycles AC is almost universal, with two-pin continental plugs.

Weights and measures
The metric system is in use. In addition, the following measures are used: quintal or metric hundredweight = 100kg. Food is usually purchased by the decagram and kilogram.

Social customs/useful tips
A handshake is a traditional accompaniment to a greeting. Using a person's title is customary. Managing directors should be addressed as *reditel* and the chairman as *predseda*.
When visiting private homes it is customary to take flowers for the hosts. Visitors also generally leave their shoes in the hallway, partly as a mark of respect and partly because of pollution in the streets.
The difference between a Slovak and a Czech may be difficult to spot; however mistaking one for the other can cause offence.
Tipping is appreciated in any restaurant, usually 5 to 10 per cent.
Drinking and driving is strictly forbidden.
Illegally parked cars tend to be towed away by the police and it is advisable to park at attended car parks where the cost is relatively low.

Security
Street crime, especially in the centre of Prague, has increased since the 1989 revolution, as the police tend to keep a low profile. It is advisable to carry as little as possible in the way of valuables and cash.
Car vandalism and theft have also increased.
Report any robberies in central Prague to the Central Police Office, Jungmannova 9, Prague 1 (tel: 6145-1760), where interpreters are available.

Getting there
Air
National airline: CSA Czech Airlines
International airport/s: Prague-Ruzyne Airport (PRG), 20km north-west of the city. Facilities include duty free shopping, post office, money exhange, restaurants and car hire. An airport bus service runs every 30 minutes between 0600–2100, with a journey time of 30 minutes to the city centre. Taxis are available 24 hours.
Airport tax: Departure tax, from Prague only: Kc700
Surface
Road: Entry is possible from Germany, Poland, Slovak Republic and Austria.
Rail: As part of the European intercity network there are convenient routes to the Czech Republic from Western Europe including the cities of Berlin, Frankfurt, Munich, Zurich and Vienna. The most famous and fastest trains include the Kafka, Goethe and the Einstein, which are operated by the formerly state-owned Ceské Dráhy (CD) (Czech Railways).
The Vindobona Express operates daily from Vienna to Prague and on to Berlin.
For more rail information call (tel: 2422-4200).
Water: There are ferries along the Vltava River from Germany.

Getting about
National transport
Air: CSA Czech Airlines operates extensive low-cost domestic network.
There are regular daily flights from Prague to Brno, Ostrava, Presov, Holesov, Kosice, Piestany, Bystrica, Karlovy Vary and Poprad.
The approximate travel time from Prague to Brno is 45 minutes, one hour to Karlovy and 30 minutes to Karlovy Vary.
Road: There are several major highways linking Prague with the main towns (usually marked with an E). Motorways run from Prague to Plzen and Podebrady to Bratislava (Slovak Republic) via Brno. Users of the Czech motorways are required to purchase a *vignette* (season ticket) for each year.
Buses: The services of the national bus company, CAD, are faster and more comfortable than the train for many routes. Tickets can be bought in advance from larger stations.
Rail: The rail service is efficient and coverage is comprehensive, composed of approximately 9,365km of track. It is advisable to book seats in advance on the main routes. Fares are low, although supplements may be charged for travel on express trains.
Water: There are many navigable waterways in the Czech Republic. The main river ports are located at Prague, Usti nad Labem and Decin.
City transport
Taxis: Taxis travelling to and from the airport are allowed to charge higher rates. Within the city, it is advisable to either negotiate a price before travelling or agree the use of the meter. Higher charges are usually levied for night services.
Buses, trams & metro: The bus network is extensive, covering many areas not visited by rail. In addition to a flat-fare service, the buses are reliable and comfortable.
In Prague, tickets can be bought in advance from tabak shops and other shops displaying the sign *Predprodej Jizdenek*.

On boarding the buses, insert your ticket into the top of the machines attached to the poles, then pull the handle towards you. Passes do not need to be punched. City buses operate predominantly on the outskirts of towns. City bus 119 leaves daily every five to seven minutes (peak times) or every 15 minutes (off-peak) for round trips from Dejvicka metro station to the airport. From the metro, follow the exit signs for Ruzyne Airport. An ordinary city transport ticket or pass is required before boarding. The CSA Czech Airline bus service operates every 30 minutes from its terminal, off Revolucni near the river, to the airport. It also stops at Dejvicka metro station. Look for the sign that says Ruzyne. For more city transport information see: www.dp-praha.cz/en/index.htm

Trams cover all the major streets and intersect with metro lines. There are tram services in Prague, Brno, Ostrava, Plzen and several other towns. Services usually operate between 0430–2400. After midnight, night trams run approximately every 40 minutes. Blue badges on tram and bus stops denote an all night service. Tram 91, the 'historic tram', stops at most of the city's top sights, except for the castle. These trams run Saturdays, Sundays and during holidays, making hourly stops during the summer. Tickets should be punched in the appropriate machine on entering the tram. Note that a separate ticket is required when changing tram routes.

Car hire

Many of the international car hire companies, including Avis, Eurodollar and Hertz, operate in the Czech Republic. Speed limits are 60kph in towns and villages, 90kph on the main roads and 110kph on motorways. The speed limit is reduced to 80kph on motorways in built-up areas. It is advisable to avoid driving in the city centre as illegal parking will result in the use of car clamps.

Traffic drives on the right. Seat belts are compulsory and drink driving is strictly prohibited. An emergency road rescue service is available by calling 154. A valid national driving licence is required.

BUSINESS DIRECTORY

Telephone area codes

The international dialling code (IDD) for the Czech Republic is + 420, followed by area code and subscriber's number:

Breclav	51	Ostrava	59
Brno	54	Plzen	37
Havirov	6994	Prague	2

Useful telephone numbers

Emergency calls: 158
Ambulance service: 112/155
Police: 158, 2121-1111
Traffic accidents: 154, 2121-3747
Emergency Medical Aid: 298-341 (24-hours: doctors speak English and German):290-651
Fire: 150
Directory enquiries: (Prague only): 120
International enquiries: 0135
Breakdown assistance: 154, 123, 777-521
Car repair service (24-hours): 733-351/3
Lost property office: 235-8887
Car repair service (24-hours): 733-351/3
Lost property office: 235-8887

Chambers of Commerce

American Chamber of Commerce, 10 Dusni, 11000 Prague 1 (tel: 2232-9430; fax: 2232-9433; email: amcham@amcham.cz).

Breclav Chamber of Commerce, 10 namisti TG Masaryka, 69002 Breclav (tel: 932-6116; fax: 937-4126; email: ohk@breclav.net).

British Chamber of Commerce, 3 Pobrezni, 18600 Prague 8 (tel: 2483-5161; fax: 2483-5162; email: britcham@britcham.cz).

Czech Chamber of Commerce, Freyova 27, 19000 Prague 9, (tel: 9664-6111; email: office@komora; internet: www.komora.cz).

Ostrava Regional Economic Chamber, 2224/8 Vystavni, 70900 Ostrava-Marianske Hory (tel: 747-9328; fax: 747-9324; email: info@rhko.cz).

Banking

ABN AMRO Bank NV, Amsterdam, Revolucni 1, 110 15 Prague 1 (tel: 2481-5141; fax: 2481-5100, 22481-5139).

Agrobanka Praha A S (largest private bank), Hybernska 18, 110 00 Prague 1 (tel: 2444-1111; fax: 2444-6199, 22444-1500).

Bankovni Asociace (Banking Association), Vodickova ulice 30, 110 00 Prague 1 (tel: 2422-5926; fax: 2422-5957).

BNP - Dresdner Bank, Vitezna 1, 150 000 Prague 5 (tel: 5700-6111).

Ceska Sporitelna A S (Czech Savings Bank), Na Prikope 29, 113 98 Prague 1 (tel: 2422-9268; fax: 2421-3455).

Ceskomoravska Stavebni, Ruzova 15, 110 00 Prague 1 (tel: 2407-2024; fax: 2407-2225).

Ceskomoravska Zarucni a Rozvojova Banks A S, Jeruzalemska 4, 115 20 Prague 1 (tel: 2423-0734).

Ceskoslovenska Obchodni Banka A S (CSOB), Na Prikope 14, 115 20 Prague 1 (tel: 2411-1111; internet: www.csob.cz).

Creditanstalt A S Praha, Siroka 5, 110 01 Prague 1 (tel: 2110-2111; fax: 2481-2185).

Evropabanka A S, Strosmayerovo nam 1, 170 01 Prague 7 (tel: 6671-2134).

GiroCredit Banka Praha A S, Vaclavske nam 56, PO Box 749, 111 21 Prague 1 (tel: 2403-3333).

HVB Czech Republic, Prague (tel: 2111-2111; internet: www.hvb.cz).

Interbanka A S Praha, Vaclavske nam. 40, 110 00 Prague 1 (tel: 2440-6111).

Komercni Banka A S, Na Prikop 33, 114 07 Prague 1 (tel: 2402-1111; fax: 2424-3020).

Podnikatelska banka A S, Rohacova 79, 130 79 Prague 3 (tel: 6121-6089; fax: 6121-6085).

Raiffeisenbank A S Praha, Vodickova 38, 110 00 Prague 1 (tel: 2423-1270; fax: 2423-1278).

Realitbanka A S, Antala Staska 32, 146 20 Prague 4 (tel: 6104-5439).

Royal banka CS A S, Krocinova 1, 110 00 Prague 1 (tel: 2422-8582; fax: 2422-4833).

Wustenrot - Stavebni Sporitelna A S, Jugoslavska 29, 120 00 Prague 2 (tel: 2400-7200; fax: 2400-7204).

Zivnostenka Banka A S, Na Prikope 20, 113 80 Prague 1 (tel: 2412-1111; fax: 2412-5555).

Central bank

Czech National Bank, Na Prikope 28, 110 03 Prague 1 (tel: 2441-1111; fax: 2441-2404; e-mail: info@cnb.cz).

Stock exchange

Burza Cennych Papíru Praha (Prague Stock Exchange) (PSE)

www.pse.cz

Travel information

Cedok (travel and hotel corporation), Na Prikope 18, 111 35 Prague 1-Nove Mesto (tel: 2419-7642; internet www.cedok.com).

Ceske Drahy (CD), Nábrezi Ludvíka Svobody 1222/12 110 15 Praha 1 (tel: 97-224-1881 reservations for inter-city trains only; internet: www.cd.cz/static/eng/).

Cestovni Kancelar, (national rail travel agency), V Celnici 6 110 00 Praha 1 (tel: 2423-9464; email: CKPHApob692@dop.pha.cd.cz; internet: www.czech-travel-guide.com).

CSA Czech Airlines, Airport Praha, Ruzyne 16008 (tel: 2480-6111; fax: 2481-5183; internet: www.czechairlines.com/en/; City Service Centre, V Ceinici 5, 110 00 Prague 1 (underground line B, station Namesti Republiky) (tel: 2010-4111);

sales and ticket reservations (tel: 2010-4310).

National tourist organisation offices
Czech Tourism, PO Box 46, Vinohradska 12041 Praha 2 (tel: 2158-0111; fax: 2424-7516; internet: www.czechtourism.com); tourist information (tel: 2011-3229, between 0800 and 2000 hours; 2011-4512, 24 hours a day).

Ministries
Ministry of Agriculture, Tisnov 17, 117 05 Prague 1 (tel: 2181-2111; fax: 2481-0478).

Ministry of Culture, Milady Horakove 220, 160 41 Prague 6 (tel: 5708-5111; fax: 2431-8156; email: minkult@mkcr.cz).

Ministry of Defence, Tychonova 1, 160 01 Prague 6 (tel: 2021-0255; fax: 2021-0257; email: otevrenalinka@army.cz).

Ministry of Education, Youth and Sport, Karmelitska 8, 118 12 Prague 1 (tel: 5719-3111; fax: 5719-3790).

Ministry of the Environment, Vrsovicka 65, 100 10 Prague 10 (tel: 6712-1111; fax: 6731-0308: internet: www.env.cz).

Ministry of Foreign Affairs, Loretanske Namisti 5, 125 10 Prague 1 (tel: 2418-1111; fax: 2431-0017; email: info@mzv.cz; internet: www.czech.cz/).

Ministry of Health, Palackeho nam 4, 128 01 Prague 2 (tel: 2497-1111; fax: 2497 2111; email: mzcr@mzcr.cz).

Ministry of the Interior, Nad Stolou 3, 170 34 Prague 7 (tel: 6142-1115; email: dotazy@mvcr.cz; internet: www.mvcr.cz).

Ministry of Justice, Vysehradska 16, 128 10 Prague 2 (tel: 2199-7111; fax: 2491-9927; email: msp@msp.justice.cz: internet: www.justice.cz).

Ministry of Labour and Social Affairs, Na Poøienim Pravu 1, 128 01Prague 2 (tel: 2491-8391; fax: 2192-2664).

Ministry of Regional Development, Staromestske Namisti 6, 110 15 Prague 1 (tel: 2486-1111; fax: 2486-1333).

Ministry of Transport and Communications, Naboøei Ludvika Svobody 12, 110 15 Prague 1 (tel: 5143-1111; fax: 2481-0596; email: utv0001@mdcr.cz).

Office of the Prime Minister, Naboøei Eduarda Benese 4, 118 01 Prague 1 (tel: 2400-2111; fax: 2481-0231).

Office of the President, Prague Castle, 119 08 Prague 1 (tel: 2437-1111; fax: 2437-3300).

Other useful addresses
Asociace Investicnich Fondu (Association of Investment Companies and Funds), Tynska 21, 110 00 Prague 1 (tel: 2481-0063; fax: 2481-0063).

Asociace Obchodnich Spolecnosti a Podnikatelu CR (Association of Trading Companies and Businessmen), Skretova 6, 120 59 Prague 2 (tel: 2421-5371/81; fax: 2423-0570).

Association of Czech Entrepreneurs, Skretova 6, 12059 Prague 2 (tel and fax: 2423-0580).

BBC (Radio), Na Porící 12, Prague 1 CZ-110 00 (tel: 2487-2545; fax: 2487-2546).

Board of Legislation and Public Administration, Vladislavova 4, PO Box 596, 117 15 Prague 1 (tel: 2419-1111; fax: 2421-5060).

British Embassy, Commercial Section, Palac Myslbek Na Prikope 21, 11719 Prague 1 (tel: 2224-0021/22/33; fax: 2224-3625).

Centrum Vnejsich Ekonomickych Vztahu (Centre For Foreign Economic Relation), Politickych Veznu 20, PO Box 791, 111 21 Prague 1 (tel: 2422-1586,22406-2421; fax: 2422-1575).

Cesky Statisticky Urad (Czech Statistical Office), Sokolovska 142, 180 00 Prague 8 (tel: 6604-2414).

Confederation of Industry of the Czech Republic, Mikulandska 7, 11361 Prague 7 (tel: 2499-5679).

CzechInvest (Czech Agency for Foreign Investment), Stepanska 15, 120 00 Prague 2 (tel: 9634-2500; fax: 9634-2502; e-mail: marketing@czechinvest.org; internet site: http://www.czechinvest.org).

Czech Republic Embassy (USA), 3900 Spring of Freedom Street, NW, Washington DC 20008 (tel: (+1-202) 274-9100; fax: (+1-202) 966-8540; e-mail: amb_pol_washington@embassy.mzv.cz).

Czech Television (CTV) - Public Corporation, Kavcí Hory, Prague 4 CZ-140 70 (tel: 6113-1111).

Euro Information Centre, Network/Correspondence Centre, NIS Havelkova 22, 130 00 Prague 3 (fax: 2423-1114).

Fond Narodniho Majetku (National Property Fund), Rasinovo Nabrezi 42, 120 00 Prague 2 (tel: 2491-1111; fax: 206-618).

Nejvyssi Soud CR (Czech Supreme Court), Buresova 20, 657 37 Brno (tel: 4132-1237; fax: 4121-3493).

NIS (National Information Centre of the Czech Republic), Havelkova 22, 130 00 Prague 3 (tel: 2421-5808–15, 2422-2026–9; fax: 322-1484, 2422-3177).

Prazska Informacni Sluzba (Prague Information Service), Senovazne Namesti 23, 110 00 Prague 1 (tel: 544-444; fax: 421-1989).

Sdruzeni Soukromych Zemedelcu Cech, Moravy a Slezska (Association of Private Farmers of Bohemia, Moravia and Silesia), Tesnov 17, 117 05 Prague 1 (tel: 491-3606; fax: 491-0162).

Svaz Prumyslu a Dopravy CR (Confederation of Industry of the Czech Republic), Mikulandska 7, 113 61 Prague 1 (tel: 2491-5253).

UNIDO (Federation of Czech Industries), Mikulandska 7, 113 61 Prague 1 (tel: 2491-5679; fax: 2491-5253).

Ustavni Soud CR (Czech Constitutional Court), Jostova 8, 660 83 Brno 2 (tel: 4216-1111).

National news agency: CTK (Czech News Agency), 5/7 Opletalova, 111 14 Prague 1 (tel: 2209-8111; internet: www.ctk.cz).

Internet sites
Atlas (the national coach company) http://jizdnirady.atlas.cz/

Brno Trade Fairs and Exhibitions Co Ltd (press information): www.bvv.cz/bvv

Ceské Dráhy, (national rail information) www.cd.cz/static/eng/

Czech business directory: www.muselik.com/czech/cbd.html

Czech directory: www.inform.cz/def.asp

Czech Embassy in Washington DC: www.mzv.cz/washington

Czech Ministry of Finance: www.mfcr.cz

Czech Ministry of Industry and Trade: www.mpo.cz

Czech Office for Protection of Competition: http://compet.cz

Czech Republic (provides links to information about the country): www.muselik.com/czech/toc.html

Czech Telecommunications Office: www.ctu.cz

Czech Trade Promotion Agency: www.czechtrade.cz/

Czech Trade Promotion Agency (in English): www.czechtradeoffices.com/Global

Hotels and history: www.abaka.com/Czech/

IPB (Investicni A Postovni banka as): www.ipb.cz

Office of Czech Republic: http://vlada.cz

Prague city transport www.dp-praha.cz/en/index.htm

Denmark

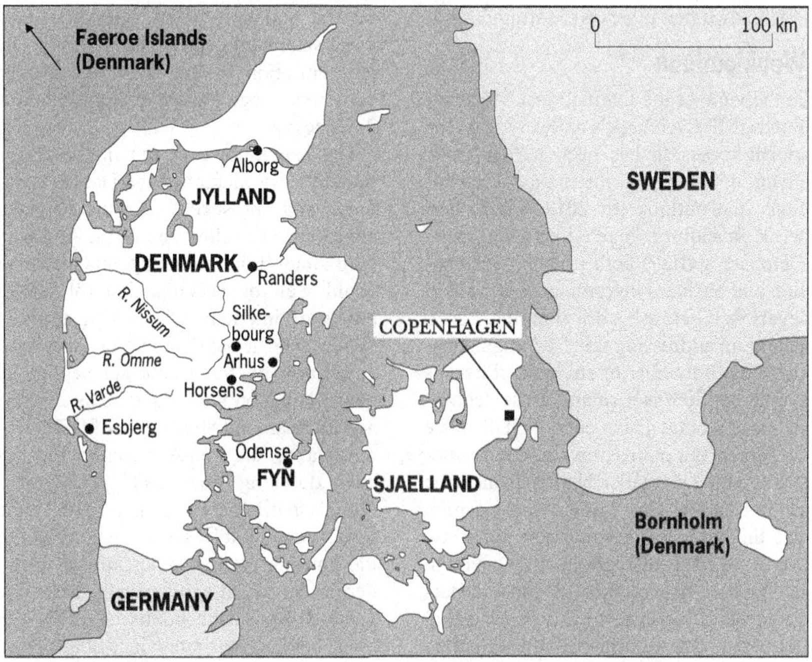

A decade of centre-right government ended in Denmark with the September 2011 election of the small Scandinavian country's first female prime minister. Helle Thorning Schmidt had entered the election with a manifesto that promised voters an end to austerity, offering in return a programme of increased spending.

Slim majority

On the morning after the election, Ms Thorning Schmidt's so called 'red block' looked to be on course to win 93 seats, seven more than the outgoing coalition government led by Prime Minister Lars Lokke Rasmussen. The result did not come as a surprise to Danish voters as the opinion polls had been indicating a narrow majority for the Socialdemokraterne (SD) (Social Democrats) for some time. The ousting of the coalition cut the minority Det Konservative Folkeparti (the Conservative People's Party) back to size. The price paid by the Liberal Alliance (founded in 2007 as the Ny Alliance (New Alliance)) for its coalition support had been the introduction of a number of jarring anti-immigration laws which sat uncomfortably with Denmark's tradition of consensus politics. In contrast to the adversarial politics of most European countries, in Denmark it has long been accepted that reforms to health, defence, education and welfare legislation require cross party agreement.

Prior to the election Mr Rasmussen's government had sought to save money by getting rid of Denmark's early retirement scheme and – in keeping with many other European countries – raising the pension age. It was the question of early retirement that had triggered the disagreement between the two main parties, prompting Helle Thorning Schmidt to make a Keynesian declaration that 'We would prefer to spend our way out of the crisis rather than save our way out.' The leader of the People's Party, Pia Kjaersgaard, preferred to leave early retirement as it was, but would have considered reform in return for even tighter immigration policies. Immigrants make up approximately 8 per cent of the country's population and of these nearly 50 per cent are Muslim The opinion tide had appeared to be on Ms

KEY FACTS

Official name: Kongeriget Danmark (The Kingdom of Denmark)

Head of State: Queen Margrethe II (since 1972)

Head of government: Prime Minister Helle Thorning-Schmidt (Socialdemokraterne) (from 4 Oct 2011)

Ruling party: Coalition Red Alliance, led by Socialdemokraterne (SD) (Social Democrats), with Det Radikale Venstre (DRV) (Social Liberal Party), Socialistisk Folkeparti (SF) (Socialist People's Party) and Enhedslisten (de-rød-grønne) (Enhedslisten) (Red-Green Alliance) (from 4 Oct 2011)

Area: 43,080 square km

Population: 5,55 million (2010)*

Capital: Copenhagen

Official language: Danish

Currency: Danish krone (Kr) = 100 ore

Exchange rate: Kr5.55 per US$ (Oct 2011); (pegged through the original European Exchange Rate Mechanism; trades around Kr7.43 per euro)

GDP per capita: US$56,147 (2010)

GDP real growth: 2.10% (2010)

GDP: US$310.80 billion (2010)

Labour force: 2.91 million (2010)

Unemployment: 5.90% (2010)

Inflation: 2.10% (2010)

Oil production: 249,000 bpd (2010)

Balance of trade: US$8.95 billion (2010)

Kjaersgaard's side earlier in the year when passport controls had been re-instated at Danish borders. This received a cool reception from the European Union (EU) in Brussels, where since 1995 open borders and the almost sacrosanct Schengen agreement were high profile symbols of the single market. The Danish government had insisted that the customs' checks were not in breach of the Schengen agreement. Denmark was not alone in expressing concerns about Schengen. For different reasons, largely due to north African immigration, othe EU countries had also considered revoking their Schengen commitment. Denmark's increased border controls were hardly far reaching, consisting of an extra 50 border agents and increased checks at Denmark's frontiers with Germany and Sweden. Surprisingly, however, immigration had not turned out to be the big election issue that many had feared. The Danish electorate turned out to be far more concerned with the future of their economy.

Growth?

Ms Thorning Schmidt had promised measures to restore economic growth that included increased expenditure on both health and education. This would be financed by increased taxes on banks and on Denmark's high earners. Central to the debate about the future of the economy was the size of Denmark's budget deficit, forecast to reach 4.6 per cent of gross domestic product (GDP) in 2012. The challenges of an ageing population and shrinking revenues from North Sea oil (although in Denmark's case these had never been particularly significant) meant that left to itself, the size of the deficit would inevitably increase. Predictably, Denmark's financial sector was nervous of the new government's plans to raise taxes on banks. In 2011 two small Danish banks had been taken into state control and it was known that others were struggling.

Weak outlook

In the view of the International Monetary Fund (IMF) Denmark's recovery from the global recession has been hesitant and, given deteriorating international conditions, the outlook for 2012 was at best weak. In addition, in relation to the size of Denmark's GDP) both private consumption and business investment continued at levels well below historical norms. Fortunately, in addressing this challenge, Denmark has a number of strengths. First, its public net debt is zero and gross debt remains at around 45 per cent of GDP, some 10 percentage points of which funds a deposit with Danmarks Nationalbank (the central bank). This strong fiscal position and the buffer of precautionary liquidity, guard against disruptions in sovereign and/or bank debt markets. Second, the targeted fiscal response to the recent global economic crisis cushioned the effect of the downturn while at the same time advancing Denmark's structural reform agenda. Third, the government's aim is to return gradually to fiscal balance over the medium run, which is considered appropriate by the IMF. And, as a result of the krone's peg to the euro, Denmark's monetary policy stance is one of stimulation. The current account surplus exceeds 5 per cent of GDP and the net international investment position is in modest credit. The narrow band peg to the euro is also strong. Even at the nadir of the global crisis, net outflows from Denmark were modest and only brief. Both price and wage setters take the peg as a fact of life, with inflation in line with the average euro-zone wage growth at slightly below 2 per cent.

This is not, however, to paint an exceptionally rosy picture of the Danish economy and prospects. Export demand appeared set to slow into 2012. And with euro-zone strains mounting, this softening could well be accompanied by further bursts of international banking turmoil. While Danish bank claims on distressed euro area sovereign debt are negligible, bank claims on the euro-zone as a whole add up to around 80 per cent of GDP. Domestically, the house price bubble has been deflating since 2007, with prices broadly flatlining since early 2010. While associated credit losses remain low so far, the housing market trends appear to underpin the recent extraordinary leap – by some 8 percentage points of GDP – in household savings rates since 2008. Thus, while household net wealth is strong, Denmark stands out with high levels of gross household debt averaging around 300 per cent of disposable income. Though this phenomenon is not new, partly reflecting the effects of mandatory private pension schemes, household borrowing on this scale represents a macro-economic and financial vulnerability.

One high priority is the urgent introduction of the proposed reforms to early retirement, as well as actions on planned reforms for student grants, disability benefits and the flexi-jobs system. In the view of the IMF, these reforms need to be supported by a cautious settlement in the forthcoming 2012 round of wage negotiations. Wage increases that are seen to be below those of Denmark's main trading partners will underpin confidence in Denmark's economic prospects in what continues to be an uncertain global environment and may begin to reverse the erosion of Denmark's competitiveness over the past decade.

Denmark has made some progress in the past two years in strengthening the banking sector, notably with the so-called 'bank packages'. These include new

KEY INDICATORS — Denmark

	Unit	2006	2007	2008	2009	2010
Population	m	5.43	5.45	5.48	5.51	*5.55
Gross domestic product (GDP)	US$bn	276.28	311.90	340.80	309.30	310.80
GDP per capita	US$	50,904	57,044	62,238	56,115	56,147
GDP real growth	%	3.9	1.8	-0.9	-5.1	2.1
Inflation	%	1.9	1.7	3.4	1.3	2.3
Unemployment	%	4.0	2.9	1.8	3.4	5.9
Oil output	'000 bpd	342.0	312.0	287.0	265.0	249.0
Natural gas output	bn cum	10.4	9.2	10.1	8.4	8.2
Exports (fob) (goods)	US$m	90,557.0	101,235.0	114,884.0	91,811.0	96,061.0
Imports (fob) (goods)	US$m	87,778.0	101,985.0	116,424.0	84,247.0	87,109.0
Balance of trade	US$m	2,779.0	-751.0	-1,541.0	7,564.0	8,952.0
Current account	US$m	8,118.0	4,279.0	1,845.0	12,942.0	16,641.0
Total reserves minus gold	US$m	29,724.0	32,534.0	40,466.0	74,291.0	73,503.0
Foreign exchange	US$m	29,160.0	32,029.0	39,823.0	71,259.0	70,334.0
Exchange rate	per US$	5.64	5.17	5.09	5.83	5.62

* estimated figure

resolution procedures applying 'haircuts' to senior bank debt and signaling intent to reduce the implicit government bank guarantees. None the less, stress in the system has recently increased markedly, in part reflecting European developments, and this requires a continued robust policy response. The relatively large size of the financial sector in Denmark requires faster and further progress than that required elsewhere. This ought to reduce the macro-economic and fiscal risks associated with the financial sector, at the same time lowering funding costs and stimulating economic activity.

Denmark's proposed establishment of a committee of enquiry into the optimum structural arrangements for large banks is also welcome. In the interim, however, given increased stress in the international financial system, the capital requirements for large banks should continue to be actively reviewed taking into account their exceptional importance. One obvious proposal would be that these banks could be required to retain a proportion of earnings to further strengthen their balance sheets.

Moves to strengthen banking liquidity should include the continued expansion of reporting requirements on foreign currency liquidity positions. In view of the increased challenges in the international banking system to which Denmark is exposed, an early review of the adequacy of funding of the Danish Financial Supervisory Authority would seem appropriate.

Given Denmark's openness and its householders' high propensity to save, the IMF does not consider that this is the time to pursue immediate structural consolidation, preferring an unchanged structural fiscal balance for 2012. The accommodation thereby created should primarily be used to fund non-recurring and labour-intensive investments, notably the repair and maintenance of infrastructure and public buildings at the local government level.

In the view if the IMF, the immediate challenge confronting Denmark is the pressing need to raise productivity growth. Structural reforms to secure this aim will also strengthen the growth of household income and strengthen the tax base. Government action to reduce the size of the public sector and by extension the burden of taxation, to encourage a rebalancing of highly skilled workers from the public to the private sector and to encourage greater competition between Danish enterprises, should also play a key role in securing these long term goals.

Risk assessment

Economy	Fair
Politics	Fair
Regional stability	Good

COUNTRY PROFILE

Historical profile

Denmark is an ancient kingdom situated on an archipelago, which has historically served as a bridge between continental Europe and the Scandinavian Peninsula. During the Napoleonic era, the Danes sided with the French and, as a result of their defeat, lost their dominance in Scandinavia.

1397 The Union of Kalmar united Denmark, Sweden and Norway under a single monarch with Denmark the leading power.

1523 Denmark recognised Swedish independence.

1729 Greenland became a Danish province.

1814 Denmark ceded Norway to Sweden.

1849 Denmark became a constitutional monarchy with a bicameral parliament.

1903 Iceland was granted home rule from Denmark.

1918 Iceland became a sovereign state in union with Denmark.

1914–18 Denmark was neutral during the First World War.

1918 Denmark's transition to parliamentary government with universal suffrage was fully established after the First World War and has been suspended only during the Nazi occupation of the Second World War.

1939 Denmark signed a non-aggression pact with Nazi Germany.

1940 Germany invaded Denmark.

1945 The German occupation ended. Denmark recognised the independence of Iceland.

1948 The Faroe Islands were granted self-government within the Kingdom.

1949 Denmark was one of the founder members of NATO.

1953 A revision of the constitution allowed for female succession to the throne, abolition of the upper house of parliament and the introduction of proportional representation. Greenland became an integral part of Denmark.

1959 Denmark joined the European Free Trade Association (EFTA).

1972 Queen Margrethe ascended the throne.

1973 Denmark joined the European Economic Community (EEC).

1979 Greenland was granted home rule; Denmark retained control over Greenland's foreign affairs and defence.

1985 Parliament passed legislation to ban the construction of nuclear power plants.

1992 In a referendum, voters rejected the Maastricht Treaty on further European integration.

1993 Poul Schlüter, prime minister since 1982, resigned after a judicial enquiry criticised him for misleading parliament in 1989 over the Tamil visa scandal. A four-party coalition government was formed by Poul Nyrup Rasmussen.

1994 Rasmussen was returned to power after a general election.

2000 In a referendum, Denmark voted against joining Europe's single currency.

2001 The Venstre (Liberal Party), led by Anders Fogh Rasmussen, formed a minority government, in coalition with the Konservative Folkeparti (Konservative) (Conservative People's Party), relying on support from the far right Dansk Folkeparti (DF) (Danish People's Party).

2004 Crown Prince Frederik married Australian-born Mary Donaldson, (their first son was born on 15 October 2005). Denmark and US agreed a deal to modernise the US Thule airbase in Greenland, over the objections of many local people.

2005 A dispute with Canada over the ownership of the Hans Islands, halfway between Greenland and Canada, erupted. The dispute was settled with a draft protocol to manage their dealings concerning the island.

2006 Cartoons of Mohammed which had appeared in *Jyllands Posten* newspaper provoked protests and boycotts of Danish exports in Middle Eastern countries.

2007 Crown Princess Mary gave birth to a daughter. Danish troops were withdrawn from Iraq. Prime Minister Rasmussen called a snap parliamentary election 15 months earlier than was necessary. The ruling Venstre won 26.3 per cent of the votes (46 seats out of 175) and with their coalition parties secured another term in office. Prime Minister Rasmussen remained in office.

2008 Ny Alliance (New Alliance) was renamed Liberal Alliance. Denmark approved more autonomy for Greenland in which Greenlanders are recognised as a separate people under international law and the local government has more control of resources, including a bigger share of oil revenues, and control of internal security.

2009 Anders Fogh Rasmussen resigned as prime minister, to become Secretary General of NATO; Lars Løkke Rasmussen (no relation) became prime minister. Denmark hosted the UN Climate Change Conference in Copenhagen. Delegates from around the world, including 115 heads of state and governments, discussed measures necessary to halt global warming. The outcome was thought to be less than successful as, although a temperature rise of no more than 2 degrees

centigrade was an agreed limit, no limit was agreed on the emission of greenhouse gases.
2010 Pre-tax profits for the toy company Lego increased by 63 per cent to US$870 million, due to demand for its figurines of *Harry Potter* and sales of its building blocks.
2011 On 8 January Crown Princess Mary gave birth to twins (boy and girl). On 3 February, a Somali refugee was convicted of attempting to kill Kurt Westergaard, the cartoonist whose cartoon of Mohammed in 2006 had sparked Islamic protests across the Middle East. Despite its participation in the visa-free Schengen agreement, on 5 July Denmark introduced border controls by instituting spot checks to prevent criminals and illegal immigrants entering the country (via Germany and Sweden). In parliamentary elections, held on 15 September, Venstre won 26.7 per cent of the mainland vote (47 of 175 mainland seats), and Socialdemokraterne 24.9 per cent (44). These two parties lead opposing coalitions (known as the Blue Alliance and the Red Alliance, respectively) and their total share of the vote was Red Alliance 50.2 per cent (89 seats), Blue Alliance 49.8 per cent (86). Greenland returned two, and Faroe Islands returned one, candidates supporting the Red Alliance, giving it a total of 92 seats. Faroe Islands also returned one supporting the Blue Alliance. Total turnout was 87.2 per cent. On 16 September Prime Minister Lars Løkke Rasmussen (Venstre) resigned. Helle Thorning-Schmidt (Socialdemokraterne) became prime minister on 4 October.

Political structure

Constitution

Denmark has a written constitution – *The Constitution Act* – a revised constitution was adopted on 5 June 1953. It set out the rights and requirements of the monarchy, state, church, government, judiciary and the individual. It legalised female succession to the throne, abolished the upper house of parliament and introduced proportional representation.
The monarchy is governed by the *Succession to the Throne Act*, adopted 27 March 1953, whereby royal power is inherited.
The Faroe Islands are a Danish external territory, electing two members to the Danish parliament, which maintains responsibility for constitutional, foreign and defence matters. A High Commissioner represents the Danish government and advises on joint affairs.
Greenland is a special cultural community in the Kingdom of Denmark. Only foreign policy, defence, police and monetary policy are Danish state affairs. Greenland elects two members to the Danish parliament.

Form of state

Constitutional monarchy

The executive

Executive power is vested in the monarch, and legislative power vested jointly in the monarch and parliament. The King appoints the prime minister and cabinet, who form the Council of State; they are responsible to the Folketing (parliament). All legislation is subject to the constitution.

National legislature

The unicameral Folketing has 179 members, of which 135 are elected by proportional representation in 17 districts, plus 40 seats that are allocated to balance the difference between the district and national vote. All members serve four-year terms unless early elections are called by the prime minister. Two representatives each from the Faroe Islands and Greenland are elected separately.

Legal system

Denmark's highest court is the Supreme Court in Copenhagen, made up of 15 judges. It hears appeals from two superior courts in Copenhagen and Viborg. These courts deal with appeals from the 84 tribunals, or lowest courts of justice, around the country. They can also deal initially with cases of greater consequence.

Last elections

15 September 2011 (parliamentary)
Results: Parliamentary (2011): Venstre (Liberal Party) won 26.7 per cent of the mainland vote (47 of 175 mainland seats), Socialdemokraterne (SD) (Social Democrats) 24.9 per cent (44), Dansk Folkeparti (Danish People's Party) 12.3 per cent (22), Det Radikale Venstre (DRV) (Social Liberal Party) 9.5 per cent (17), Socialistisk Folkeparti (SF) (Socialist People's Party) 9.2 per cent (16), Enhedslisten (de-rød-grønne) (Enhedslisten) (Red-Green Alliance) 6.7 per cent (12), Liberal Alliance 5 per cent (nine), Det Konservative Folkeparti (Conservative People's Party) 4.9 per cent (eight). Mainland turnout was 87.7 per cent. Faroe Islands returned two candidates, one for Sambandsflokkurin (Union Party) and one for Javnaðarflokkurin (Social Democratic Party). Greenland returned two candidates, one for Inuit Ataqatigiit (IA) (Inuit Community) and one for Siumut (Forward). Total turnout was 87.2 per cent.

Next elections

2015 (parliamentary)

Political parties

Ruling party

Coalition Red Alliance, led by Socialdemokraterne (SD) (Social Democrats), with Det Radikale Venstre (DRV) (Social Liberal Party), Socialistisk Folkeparti (SF) (Socialist People's Party) and Enhedslisten (de-rød-grønne) (Enhedslisten) (Red-Green Alliance) (from 4 Oct 2011)

Main opposition party

Blue Alliance, led by Venstre (Liberal Party)

Population

5.55 million (2010)
Last census: January 2001: 5,349,212
Population density: 120 inhabitants per square km. Urban population: 85 per cent (1995–2001).
Annual growth rate: 0.4 per cent 1994–2004 (WHO 2006)

Ethnic make-up

Danes make up the majority of the population, along with some 9,000 Greenlanders and around 12,000 Faroese. The largest immigrant groups from outside the kingdom are Turkish, British and Norwegian. There is a small German minority in southern Jutland.

Religions

The majority of the population (90 per cent) belong to the Lutheran Church although there are small groups of other Christian denominations.

Education

There are 10 years of compulsory schooling, although the average student attends school for 15 years.
The participation rate at primary and secondary levels is close to 100 per cent of the relevant age groups. Forty-six per cent of the relevant age group attend education at a tertiary level. The cost of university or post-high school further education is financed by a system of student grants supplemented by bank loans carrying a state guarantee.
Compulsory years: Seven to 16.
Pupils per teacher: 10 in primary schools.

Health

Hospitalisation and treatment by general practitioners is free of charge, but there are part-charges for medicine prescribed by GPs. Treatment by dentists and opticians is subsidised but not free. Since 1988, several small private hospitals have opened, the fees for which can be covered by insurance schemes.

HIV/Aids

HIV prevalence: 0.2 per cent aged 15–49 in 2003 (World Bank).
Life expectancy: 78 years, 2004 (WHO 2006)
Fertility rate/Maternal mortality rate: 1.8 births per woman, 2004 (WHO 2006); maternal mortality 0.1 per 1,000 live births: (World Bank)
Child (under 5 years) mortality rate (per 1,000): 4.4 per 1,000 live births (World Bank)

Head of population per physician: 2.93 physicians per 1,000 people, 2002 (WHO 2006)

Welfare
There is an extensive cradle-to-the-grave social security system, however the size of the welfare system has gradually been reduced since the 1990s. In 2005, the system came under close scrutiny and a government commissioned appraisal recommended that the pension aged should be raised and early retirement phased out, and charges set for some healthcare and educational services.
Currently welfare benefits include unemployment benefits, supplementary benefits and rent and heating grants.
Social security and welfare spending as a share of GDP is approximately 5.8 per cent.

Pensions
Denmark was the first country to introduce old age pensions in 1895, funded by two general taxes. To sustain the current pensions, there is a three pillar approach to provision. Pillar one is a basic, mandatory, publically administered scheme, maintained to provide for the poor in old age and may be supplemented by other allowances. Pillar two are mandatory, privately administered schemes and workplace pensions, which are devised to attract contributions as high as 16 per cent of wages. Pillar three are privately administered schemes with individual and voluntary contributions. Other schemes exist and fall within the rules of the three pillars.

Main cities
Copenhagen (capital, estimated population 1.1 million in 2004), Aarhus (220,700), Odense (144,600), Aalborg (120,600), Esbjerg (72,700).

Languages spoken
English and German are widely spoken in business and administration.

Official language/s
Danish

Media
Press freedom is guaranteed by law, as demonstrated in 2006 by the international furores following the publication of images of the Prophet Mohammad by a Danish newspaper, which was un-censured.

Press
Most publications are privately owned and tend to have fairly strong political leanings.
Dailies: There are around 50 daily newspapers, with Sunday readership particularly high. The leading newspapers are *Morgenavisen Jyllands Posten* (http://jp.dk) *Ekstra Bladet* (http://ekstrabladet.dk) a tabloid, BT (www.bt.dk), Politiken (http://politiken.dk) and *Berlingske Tidende* (www.berlingske.dk).
Weeklies: Most daily newspapers publish weekend editions. In Danish, a variety of political magazines include *LO* (www.lo.dk), *Solidaritet* (www.solidaritet.dk), and *Danske Regioner* (www.regioner.dk). For general news *Weekend Avisen* (www.weekendavisen.dk), and *Grønland* (www.groenlandselskab.dk) for news from Greenland. In English, *The Copenhagen Post* (www.cphpost.dk).
In Danish, women's magazines include *Ingelise* (www.ingelise.dk), and *Alt for Damerne* (www.altfordamerne.dk); *Euroman* (www.euroman.dk) is for men. *Udfordringen (Showtime)* (www.udfordringen.dk) covers music and performing arts.
Business: In Danish, national dailies include *Net Posten* (www.netposten.dk) and *Scandinavia Now* (www.scandinavianow.com), national magazines include *Berlingske Nyhedsmagasin* (www.business.dk) and *Pengte & Privatøkonomi* (www.penge.dk). Regional newspapers from Copenhagen include *Børsen* (http://borsen.dk), *Erhvervs Bladet* (www.erhvervsbladet.dk), and *Okonomisk Ugebrev* (www.ugebrev.dk). *Ase Nyt* is a commercial quarterly.
Periodicals: Periodicals on general interest, life-style, consumer and commercial interest include *Blender, En Skør Skør Verden* and *Social Demokraten*.

Broadcasting
The national public broadcaster is DR (www.dr.dk).
Radio: DR (www.dr.dk/drdkradio) operates two national stations (P1 and P2), plus a regional station (P3) and a DAB, digital radio (P4), providing a comprehensive mix of all music genre, talk radio and information. A DR station also broadcasts in Nyheder (an Indonesian and Malaysian language).
There are many privately operated commercial radio stations and most located within relatively small areas or population centres. Regional and national networks include The Voice (www.thevoice.dk), Radio Mojn (www.mojn.dk) and Hit FM (www.hitfm.nu).
Television: Analogue transmissions will begin to be closed down by late 2009, with High Definition TV transmissions begun in January 2008.
DR (www.dr.dk) operates two national channels DR1 and DR2.
Other commercial TV services are provided by either cable or satellite, of which TV 2 (http://tv2.dk) the government-owned network is a multi-channel service. Foreign-owned services, include the Swedish, MTG (www.mtg.se), SBS (www.sbsbroadcasting.com) and US Disney Channel, which provide a wide variety of programmes.

Advertising
Press and cinemas advertising is the most popular form of medium, while direct mail is limited to a customer requesting material. There is limited advertising on radio, and poster sites are heavily regulated.
On television and radio, there are advertising restrictions, with bans of tobacco and alcohol and a limit on pharmaceutical products and items for children. Only 12 minutes per hour is given over to advertising with a maximum of 15 per cent of total daily output.

Economy
Although the economy is balanced with a well-developed, export-based manufacturing sector and an important agricultural sector, like all post industrial societies services account for the largest share of GDP, at over 60 per cent. Agriculture and food industries combined are Denmark's largest industry employing around 150,000 people, with annual sales of over eur15 billion (over US$20 billion), it is also a net exporter of food. Even so agriculture accounts for only 5 per cent of GDP, while industry and manufacturing account for over 30 per cent. Denmark is a net exporter of energy and has oil reserves producing 265,000 barrels per day (in 2009).
GDP growth in 2007 was 1.7 per cent, a fall from 3.4 per cent in 2006 as imported raw materials were at record high prices, and exports suffered a downturn as the global economic crisis affected Denmark's chief trading partners. GDP growth fell further to -0.9 in 2008 as the economy entered recession, and there was a budget surplus of US$11.75 billion. By 2009 GDP growth had fallen further to -5.1 per cent and it was predicted there would be a budget deficit of Kr9 billion (around US$1.68 billion) or 0.5 per cent of GDP. Denmark provides revenue to the governments of Greenland and the Faroe Islands (59 per cent and 6 per cent of their GDP, respectively).
The banking system, which is fully integrated into the global system, was severely damaged by the crisis and in 2008 several banks required public funds to remain solvent, so that by 2009 around KR100 billion (US$18.75 billion) in government bailout money had been provided. The central bank interest rate was raised twice within one month at the end of 2008 as it scrambled to keep the krone pegged to the euro. The turbulent relationship between the krone and euro has put in doubt Denmark's membership of the eurozone in the foreseeable future.

When the Greek economic crisis in April–May 2010 weakened the euro the krone also fell, which meant that exports were more competitive. In measures to stimulate the economy the government announced that it would increase the deficit in 2010 to Kr86.3 billion (US$16.57 billion), through spending and public investment. However, observers have said that as Denmark's GDP is so dependent on exports until global trade has recovered fully expectations for growth are weak in the medium to long term.

External trade

As a member of the European Union (EU), Denmark operates within a community-wide free trade area, with tariffs sets as a whole. Internationally, the EU has free trade agreements with a number of nations and trading blocs worldwide.
Denmark's heavy industrial base is limited by a lack of natural resources. However it has sophisticated hi-tech, pharmaceutical and bio-technical industries, an aircraft manufacturing base and is a net exporter of food and energy. It is also the home of the world-famous Lego, toy building blocks, designed in the 1930s.
Denmark is a world leader in export of pork and manufactured wind turbines.

Imports

Principal imports are machinery and equipment, raw materials and semi-manufactures for industry, chemicals, grain and foodstuffs and consumer goods.
Main sources: Germany (typically 21 per cent of total), Sweden (13 per cent), The Netherlands (7 per cent).

Exports

Principal export commodities include machinery and instruments, pork and meat products, dairy products, fish, chemicals and pharmaceuticals, furniture, ships.
Main destinations: Germany (typically 17 per cent of total), Sweden (13 per cent), UK (9 per cent).

Agriculture

Farming

The agricultural sector typically contributes around 3 per cent of GDP and employs 4 per cent of the labour force. The sector is organised into local co-operatives which are united in national federations.
Agriculture benefits from the Common Agricultural Policy (CAP), which imposes import duties on products entering the EU from other countries in order to equalise the price of imported commodities with those produced within the union. Efforts to reform the CAP could have a significant impact on future production.
The government primarily acts as a regulator in the agricultural sector. It sets veterinary standards and lays down the rules for farm mergers and ownership. The government does not set production or export and import targets, and as a member of the EU, agriculture is subject to the EU agricultural production quota regime.
Intensive farming is concentrated on livestock production, mainly pig-meat, beef, veal, poultry and dairy produce.
Denmark has large world market shares in products such as pig-meat, dairy products, seeds, mink pelts and fish products.

Fishing

Typical seafood catches total around 1.7 million tonnes per annum (tpy), yielding over 140,000 tpy of fish oils.
Denmark ranks fourth among the world's leading seafood exporters. It continues to export significant quantities of processed seafood, fish oil and meal mainly processed from imported raw material. Decreased Danish cod catches are putting pressure on prices and import substitutes. Cod and other fish imports from other countries have considerably increased.

Forestry

Forest and other wooded land accounts for only one-eighth of the land area, with forest cover estimated at 455,000 hectares (ha). Plantations constitute about 75 per cent of the forest area, with the remainder classed as semi-natural. Less than 25 per cent of the forest is under public ownership, with the rest shared between individuals and private institutions. Demand for forest products is high and is mostly met by imports. Most of the softwood logs are processed locally while high quality hardwood logs are increasingly imported. The furniture industry depends on imported raw materials and exports most of its production.

Industry and manufacturing

Denmark has a highly developed and diversified industrial sector, which is almost wholly under private ownership. The industrial sector contributes around 25 per cent of GDP and employs a quarter of the labour force.
As a country with a market economy and free external trade, government industrial policy plays a relatively minor role, especially as there is no significant state ownership in the industrial sector. The World Bank ranked Denmark in its at 8 for ease of doing business, and 15 for starting a business, out of 155 in 2005.
Government support for industry is largely confined to export credit arrangements and funds for research and development.
The engineering, food processing and wood-paper industries are the economy's three biggest production areas.

Tourism

Tourism plays an important role in Denmark's economic life. It is a modern, highly developed country with extensive infrastructure and can cater for millions of tourist each year. As tourism is a combination of elements such as attractions, amenities, infrastructure and accompanying services, they are unlikely to be controlled by a single authority and the industry has an organic nature with growth dependent on local or individual stimulation. The industry is considering the impact of tourisim on the environment and society, with schemes proposed that will manage its influence, both beneficial and harmful.

Mining

The mining sector contributes under 1 per cent to Denmark's GDP. Denmark has no exploitable raw materials other than sand and gravel for construction.
In Greenland, there are substantial deposits of coal, iron ore, uranium, gold and diamonds, none of which are currently being exploited.

Hydrocarbons

Denmark had proven oil reserves of 1.57 billion barrels of oil with production of 312,000 barrels per day (bpd) in 2007. Proven reserves of natural gas were 120 billion cubic metres (cum) in 2007, with gas production of 9.2 billion cum. Oil and gas production comes from 19 fields in the North Sea, connected by pipelines to the port of Kaergard in Jutland. Mærsk Olie and Gas operates 15 of these fields, DONG E&P operates three and Amerada Hess A/S operates one.
Oil production is forecast to decline from 2007–2011 from 19 million cum to 16.6 million cum while gas is expected to fall from 9.1 billion cum to 7.8 billion cum. Current indications suggest that self-sufficiency in oil is expected to be exceeded by 2016, however with new technological development and further exploration oil reserves are predicted to last until around 2030.

Energy

Total electricity capacity amounts to around 12,969MW, in thermal power stations fuelled primarily by coal, followed by gas, wind, oil and biomass.
In 2007 Denmark had 5,212 wind turbines in operation, producing a total of 3,124 megawatts (MW), including the largest wind farm in the EU at Nysted, with a trend for fewer but larger turbine wind power plants. Wind power accounted for 19.7 per cent of domestic electricity supplies; the target is to reach 50 per cent of capacity by 2030.

Financial markets

Stock exchange

The Københavns Fondsbørs (Copenhagen Stock Exchange) (CSE)

Banking and insurance

Denmark has a healthy banking sector which is open to foreign competition. There are around 100 commercial banks in operation, although the two largest account for 60 per cent of total bank assets.

Central bank

Danmarks Nationalbank

Main financial centre

Copenhagen

Time

GMT plus one hour (daylight saving, late March to late October, GMT plus two hours)

Geography

Denmark is a low-lying country in northern Europe. Its only land frontier is with Germany and totals 67.7km, while the coastline exceeds 7,300km. Nowhere is more than 52km from the sea. Norway lies to the north of Denmark, across the Skagerrak – a gulf in the North Sea. Sweden lies to the north-east, its most southerly region being separated from Zealand by a narrow strait.

Outlying territories of Denmark are Greenland and the Faroe Islands in the North Atlantic Ocean.

The mainland consists of the peninsula of Jutland, the islands of Zealand, Funen, Lolland, Falster and Bornholm and 401 smaller islands. The average elevation of land above sea level is 30 metres and its highest point is only 173 metres above sea level. Denmark lies between the North Sea to the west and the Baltic Sea to the east.

Hemisphere

Northern

Climate

Predominantly western winds bring warm, moist air from the West Atlantic, tempering the climatic influences from the east. In winter these can take the form of long periods of frost with ice-bound waters and, in summer, occasional high temperatures and drought. The average temperature in Denmark is 7.5 degrees Celsius (C); the temperature varies from minus 0.1 degrees C in the coldest months to 16 degrees C in July. The average rainfall amounts to 664mm and is distributed fairly evenly over the year, with August normally being the wettest.

Dress codes

Danes are generally informal about clothing. Businessmen usually wear jackets and ties at meetings and only adopt a dinner jacket (or long dresses for women) on very formal occasions.

Entry requirements

Passports

Required by all, except EU visitors travelling on national ID cards.

Visa

Required by all except nationals of EU, North America, Australasia or Japan. For further exceptions contact the nearest consulate. Denmark is a member of the Schengen visa accord and all visitors that require a visa must apply to a Danish consulate; when a visa has been issued a visitor may travel to any other Schengen zone without further visas.

Business trips can be undertaken on a Schengen visa, nevertheless, an original invitation from a business contact in Denmark is necessary when applying. A Schengen visa application (offered in several languages) can be downloaded from http://europa.eu/abc/travel/ see 'documents you will need'.

Currency advice/regulations

There are no restrictions on import and export of local or foreign currency, however sums over eur15,000 should be declared on arrival. Some banks refuse to change large denomination foreign notes. ATMs are plentiful. Travellers cheques in US dollars, pound sterling and euros save additional exchange fees.

Customs

Personal items are duty-free. There are no duties levied on alcohol and tobacco between EU member states, providing amounts imported are for personal consumption.

Health (for visitors)

Nationals of the European Economic Area (EEA) countries and Switzerland can access reduced cost and sometimes free medical treatment using a European Health Insurance Card (EHIC) while visiting the EEA. Exceptions include nationals of the 10 countries which joined the EU in 2004 whose EHIC is not valid in Switzerland. Applications for the EHIC should be made before travelling.

Mandatory precautions

None.

Advisable precautions

Hotels

There is no official rating system. Tarrifs include 15 per cent service charge. It is advisable to book accommodation in Copenhagen in advance, especially during summer.

Credit cards

All the usual credit and charge cards are accepted.

Public holidays (national)

Fixed dates

1 Jan (New Year's Day), 5 Jun (Constitution Day), 24–26 Dec (Christmas).

Variable dates

Maundy Thursday, Good Friday and Easter Monday, Great Prayer Day, Ascension Day, Whit Monday.

Public holidays that fall on the weekend are not carried over to a weekday.

Working hours

Banking

Mon–Fri: 0930–1600; Thu: 0930–1800.

Business

Mon–Fri: 0800/0900–1600/1700; offices frequently close early before the weekend or on the eve of public holidays.

Government

Mon–Fri: generally 0900–1700.

Shops

Mon–Thu: 0900–1730; Fri: 0900–1900/2000; Sat: 0900–1300/1400. First Saturday in each month most shops open: 0900–1600/1700.

Telecommunications

Mobile/cell phones

The GSM 1800 and 900 networks operate throughout the country.

Electricity supply

220/380V AC.

Social customs/useful tips

Shaking hands is the acceptable way to greet and depart from both business contacts and friends. Punctuality is expected on all occasions.

Service is normally included on bills and further tipping is not necessary in hotels, restaurants or taxis.

Security

Apart from the occasional pickpocket, the streets of Copenhagen are generally safe.

Getting there

Air

National airline: Scandinavian Airline System (SAS) – jointly owned with Sweden and Norway.

International airport/s: Copenhagen (CPH) at Kastrup, 8km south-east of capital. Business/conference centre, Internet access, duty-free shops, bars, restaurants, bank, post office, transfer hotel (maximum stay 18hrs), shower and sauna facilities. Car hire available. A new rail link between the airport and main railway station in Copenhagen takes 12 minutes. There are also regular bus services from the airport departing every 10–20 minutes taking 20 minutes.

Other airport/s: Aalborg (AAL), 6km north-west of city; Aarhus (Tirstrup) (AAR), 44km north-east of city; Billund (BLL), 2km east of city, Esbjerg (EBJ), 8km from city.

Airport tax: None

Surface

Road: The 18km Great Belt bridge and tunnel, linking Copenhagen to the island of Funen (Fyn), provides the first seamless surface connection from mainland Europe to Copenhagen. It includes a 6.5km long suspension bridge, the world's second

longest. A second bridge and tunnel, the Øresund connection, links Copenhagen with Malmø in Sweden consisting of an 8km bridge and an 8km tunnel connected by an artificial island. Tolls are applicable on both bridges.
Rail: High-speed Intercity trains via Copenhagan airport connect to Funen (1 hour) and Jutland (2 hours) with additional connections to Malmø (Sweden) on a 30-minute journey via the Øresund link. Access from other European countries is via Germany.
Water: Regular ferry services from UK, Norway, Sweden, Poland, Iceland, the Faroe Islands and Germany.

Getting about

National transport

Air: The network of scheduled services radiates from Copenhagen. Domestic airports are generally situated between two or more cities which are within easy reach of each other. Domestic flights are usually of no more than 30 minutes duration.
Road: About 70,000km of roads including 593km of motorway. The road system in the Danish archipelago makes frequent use of ferries. Motorways are not subject to toll duty.
Buses: There are few private long-distance coaches.
Rail: Approximately 2,500km of railways are operated by Danish State Railway (DSB) and a few private companies, providing a very efficient service linked to the ferry services. Country bus network operates where there are no railways.
Water: Ferry services connect the islands of Zealand, Funen and Lolland and Jutland peninsula, operated by DSB.

City transport

Taxis: There is a good service in all major towns. Taxis can be hailed in the street when they display their green 'Fri' sign, or by telephone or at ranks. Fare includes a tip.
Buses, trams & metro: Good bus service in Copenhagen, including night buses until 0230. Frequent, efficient services in other main towns. Flat-rate fares are usual.

Car hire

Hire cars are available throughout the country at main DSB stations and all airports. They can be booked in advance through stations, international car hire firms and travel agents. A valid driving licence is required, which must be carried when driving. Most firms stipulate a minimum age between 20–25. The speed limits are 130kmph on motorways, 80kmph on highways, and 50kmph in urban areas; speed traps are commonplace. Even for minor speed limit offences, drivers are liable to pay heavy on-the-spot fines; if payment cannot be made, the car may be detained. Avoid drinking and driving, as the laws of misuse are tough. Seatbelts, throughout a vehicle, are compulsory.

BUSINESS DIRECTORY

The addresses listed below are a selection only. While World of Information makes every endeavour to check these addresses, we cannot guarantee that changes have not been made, especially to telephone numbers and area codes. We would welcome any corrections.

Telephone area codes

The international direct dialling code (IDD) for Denmark is +45, followed by subscriber's number.

Useful telephone numbers

Fire, police, ambulance	112
Emergency dental treatment	3138-0251
24-hour chemist	3314-8266

Chambers of Commerce

American Chamber of Commerce in Denmark, 28 Christians Brygge, 1559 Copenhagen V (tel: 3393-2932; fax: 3313-0507; e-mail: mail@amcham.dk).

Danish Chamber of Commerce, Børsen, 1217 Copenhagen K (tel: 7013-1200; fax: 7013-1201; e-mail: hts@hts.dk).

Banking

BG Bank, 68 Nørre Voldgard, 1390 Copenhagen K (tel: 7011-9999; fax: 3914-4899; internet: www.bgbank.dk).

Den Danske Bank AS (commercial bank), Holmens Kanal 2-12, DK-1092 Copenhagen K (tel: 3344-0000; fax: 3118-5873; internet: www.danskebank.com).

Finansrådet (bankers' association), Bankernes Hus, Amaliegade 7, DK-1256 Copenhagen (tel: 3312-0200; fax: 3393-0260; internet: www.finansraadet.dk).

Jyske Bank (Bank of Jutland, private bank), Vestergade 8-16, DK-8600 Silkeborg (tel: 8922-2222; fax: 8922-2499; internet: www.jbpb.com).

Spar Nord Bank AS, 15 Skelagervij, PO Box 162, 9100 Aalborg (tel: 9634-4000; email: ine@sparnord.dk; internet: www.sparnordbank.com).

Sydbank, PO Box 169, 4 Peberlyk, DK-6200 Aabenraa (tel: 7463-1111; fax: 7463-1320; email: info@sydbank.dk; internet: www.sydbank.dk).

Nordea Bank AS, PO Box 850, Christiansbro Strandgade 3, DK-0900 Copenhagen C (tel: 3333-3333; email: hotline@nordea.dk; internet: www.nordea.dk).

Central bank

Danmarks Nationalbank, Havnegade 5, DK-1093 Copenhagen (tel: 3363-6363; fax: 3363-7103; e-mail: info@nationalbanken.dk).

Stock exchange

The Københavns Fondsbørs (Copenhagen Stock Exchange) (CSE): www.omxnordicexchange.com

Travel information

Copenhagen Airport, PO Box 74, Lufthavnsboulevarden 6 DK-2770, Kastrup (tel: 3231-3231; fax: 3231-3132; email: cphweb@cph.dk; internet: www.cph.dk).

Copenhagen Airtaxi, Copenhagen Airport Roskilde, DK-4000 Roskilde (tel: 391-114).

DSB (Danish State Railways), 1349 Sølgade 40, 1349 Copenhagen (tel: 3314-0400).

Forenede Danske Motorejere (FDM) (the Danish motoring organisation), Blegdamsvej 124, DK-2100 Copenhagen Ø (tel: 7013-3040; fax: 4527-0993).

Scandinavian Airlines System (SAS), Frosundaviks Alle 1, Stockholm S-16187, Sweden (tel: (+46-8) 7970-000; fax: (+46-8) 858-741).

National tourist organisation offices

Danmarks Turistrad (tourist board), Vesterbrogade 6 D, 1620 Cogenhagen V (tel: 3311-1415; fax: 3393-1416).

Ministries

Ministry of Agriculture, Fisheries and Food, Holbergsgade 2, 1057 Copenhagen K (tel: 3392-3301; fax: 3314-5042; e-mail: fvm@fvm.dk).

Ministry of Business and Industry, Slotsholmsgade 10-12, 1216 Copenhagen K (tel: 3392-3350; fax: 3312-3778; e-mail: em@em.dk).

Ministry of Business and Industry, Invest in Denmark, Slotsholmsgade 10-12, Copenhagen K, DK-1216 (tel: 3392-3350; fax: 3312-3778; e-mail: Investdk@em.dk; internet site: www.investindk.com).

Ministry of Culture, Nybrogade 2, 1203 Copenhagen K (tel: 3392-3370; fax: 3391-3388; e-mail: kum@kum.dk).

Ministry of Defence, Holmens Kanal 42, 1060 Copenhagen K (tel: 3392-3320; fax: 3332-0655; e-mail: fmn@fmn.dk).

Ministry of Economic Affairs, Ved Stranden 8, 1061 Copenhagen K (tel: 3392-3222; fax: 3393-6020; e-mail: oem@oem.dk).

Ministry of Education, Fredriksholms Kanal 21-25, 1220 Copenhagen K (tel: 3392-5000; fax: 3392-5547; e-mail: uvm@uvm.dk).

Ministry of Employment, Holmens Kanal 20, 1060 Copenhagen K (tel: 3392-5900; fax: 3312-1378; e-mail: am@am.dk).

Ministry of the Environment and Energy, Hojbro Plads 4, 1200 Copenhagen K (tel: 3392-7600; fax: 3332-2227; e-mail: mem@mem.dk).

Ministry of Finance, Christiansborg Slotsplads 1, 1218 Copenhagen K (tel: 3392-3333; fax: 3332-8030; e-mail: fm@fm.dk).

Ministry of Foreign Affairs, 2 Asiatisk Plads, 1448 Copenhagen K (tel: 3392-0000; fax: 3254-0533; e-mail: um@um.dk; internet site: www.um.dk/english).

Ministry of Health, Holbergsgade 6, 1057 Copenhagen K (tel: 3392-3360; fax: 3393-1563; e-mail: sum@sum.dk).

Ministry of Housing and Urban Affairs, Slotsholmgade 1, 3, 1216 Copenhagen K (tel: 3392-6100; fax: 3392-6104; e-mail: bm@bm.dk).

Ministry of the Interior, Christiansborg Slotsplads 1, 1218 Copenhagen K (tel: 3392-3380; fax: 3311-1239; e-mail: inm@inm.dk).

Ministry of Justice, Slotsholmsgade 10, 1216 Copenhagen K (tel: 3392-3340; fax: 3393-3510; e-mail: jm@jm.dk).

Ministry of Research, Bredgade 43, 1260 Copenhagen K (tel: 3392-9700; fax: 3332-3501; e-mail: fsk@fsk.dk).

Ministry of Social Affairs, Holmens Kanal 22, 1060 Copenhagen K (tel: 3392-9300; fax: 3393-2518; e-mail: sm@sm.dk).

Ministry of Taxation, Slotsholmsgade 12, 1216 Copenhagen K (tel: 3392-3392; fax: 3314-9105; e-mail: skm@skm.dk).

Ministry of Transport, Fredriksholms Kanal 27, 1220 Copenhagen K (tel: 3392-3355; fax 3312-3893; e-mail: trm@trm.dk).

Parliament, Christiansborg, 1240 Copenhagen K (tel: 3337-5500; fax: 3332-8536).

Prime Minister's Office, Christiansborg, Prins Jorgens Gard 11, 1218 Copenhagen K (tel: 3392-3300; fax: 3311-1665; e-mail: stm@stm.dk).

Other useful addresses

American Embassy, Dag Hammarskjolds Alle 24, DK-2100 Copenhagen Ø (tel: 423-144; fax: 430-223).

British Embassy, Kastelsvej 36, DK-2100 Copenhagen Ø (tel: 264-600; fax: 381-012, 431-400).

Central Telegraph Office, Købmagergade 37, DK-1150 Copenhagen K (tel: 3312-0903).

Copenhagen Stock Exchange, Nikolaj Plads 6, DK-1067 Copenhagen K (tel: 3393-3366).

Danish Convention Bureau, 27 Skindergade, 1159 Copenhagen K (tel: 3332-8601; fax: 3332-8803).

Danmarks Agentforening (association of commercial agents of Denmark), Børsen, DK-1217 Copenhagen K (tel: 3314-4941).

Danmarks Statistik, Sejrøgade 11, DK-2100 Copenhagen Ø (tel: 3917-3917; fax: 3118-4801).

Dansk Arbejdsgiverforening (employers' confederation), Vester Voldgade 113, DK-1503 Copenhagen V (tel: 3393-4000; fax: 3312-2976).

Det Okonomiske Rad (economic council), Kampmannsgade, DK-1604 Copenhagen V (tel: 3313-5128).

Grosserer Societetet, Børsen (royal exchange), DK-1217 Copenhagen (tel: 3391-2323).

Industriraadet (Confederation of Danish Industries), H C Andersen's Boulevard 18, DK-1790 Copenhagen V (tel: 3377-3377; fax: 3377-3410).

IPC (International Press Centre), Snaregade 14, DK-1205 Copenhagen K (tel: 131-615; fax: 911-613).

Regional Development Organisation (Copenhagen Capacity), Kongens Nytorv 6, 4, sal DK-1050 Copenhagen K (tel: 3333-0300; fax: 3333-7333).

Ritzaus Bureau 1/S (news agency), Mikkel Bryggersgade 3, DK-1460 Copenhagen K.

Royal Danish Embassy (USA), 3200 Whitehaven Street, NW, Washington DC 20008 (tel: (+1-202) 234-4300; fax: (+1-202) 238-1470; e-mail: wasamb@um.dk).

Teknisk Forlag AS (technical press-publishing house), Skelbaekgade 4, DK-1717 Copenhagen V.

Thomson Communications (Scandinavia) AS, Hestemøllestrede 6, Postboks 2181, DK-1017 Copenhagen K.

Internet sites

Danish web index: www.web-index.dk

Interactive travel site: www.visitdenmark.com

Statistical Office: www.dst.dk

Trade directory for Denmark: http://uhk.dk

White pages: http://infobel.com/denmark/default.asp

Yellow pages: www.yellowpages.dk

KEY FACTS

Official name: République de Djibouti/Jumhouriyya Djibouti (Republic of Djibouti)

Head of State: President Ismail Omar Guelleh (from 1999; re-elected 8 Apr 2011)

Head of government: Prime Minister Dileita Mohamed Dileita (since 2001; re-appointed 2005)

Ruling party: Coalition called Union pour la Majorité Présidentielle (UMP) (Union for a Presidential Majority), (consists of five political parties, all supporters of President Ismail Omar Guelleh) (since 2005; re-elected 8 Feb 2008)

Area: 23,200 square km

Population: 890,000 (2010)*

Capital: Djibouti-ville

Official language: French/Arabic (Somali/Afar are the national languages)

Currency: Djibouti franc (Df) = 100 centimes

Exchange rate: Df175.00 per US$ (Oct 2011)

GDP per capita: US$1,383 (2010)

GDP real growth: 4.50% (2010)

GNP per capita: US$1.14 billion (2010)

Inflation: 4.00% (2010)

Balance of trade: -US$373.30 million (2009)

* estimated figure

Djibouti

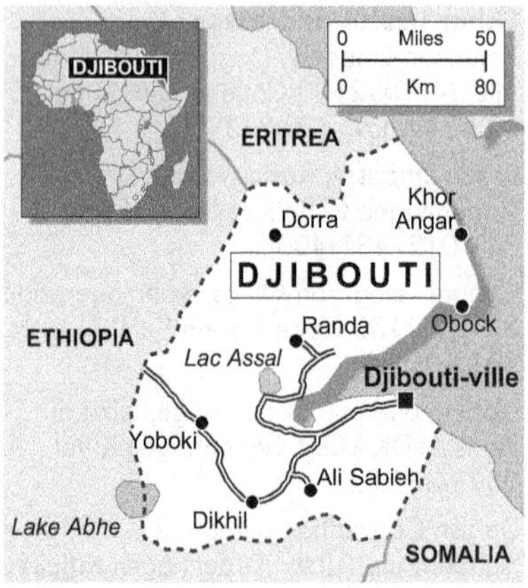

The run-up to the 8 April 2011 presidential election was rough. For starters, the largest anti-government demonstration since independence took place on 18 February in Djibouti-ville. Around 30,000 people called on President Ismail Omar Guelleh to quit office and the security forces used teargas and rubber bullets to disperse the crowds. Opposition groups, including the Union pour l'Alternance Démocratique (UAD) (Union for Democratic Change), decided to boycott the election and called on voters to do likewise. They warned that voting would not be free and fair and would most likely be rigged.

Security forces arrested four opposition political leaders on 11 March, as they planned to head another demonstration against Guelleh. On 15 March, international observers (funded by the US) quit Djibouti, after they were declared 'illegal' by the foreign minister, Mahmoud Ali Youssouf, and accused of failing to maintain neutrality. On 5 April, parliament voted to allow unlimited terms in office for a president (they had already been increased from two terms to three in 2010). The result of the election was another win for incumbent President Guelleh. He won 80.58 per cent of the vote, with Mohamed Warsama Ragueh attracting just 19.42 per cent; turnout was 69.68 per cent. Parliamentary elections had been due to take place at the same time as the presidential election but were postponed until 2013. The previous elections, in 2008, had also been boycotted by the opposition, leaving the Union pour la Majorité Présidentielle (UMP) (Union for a Presidential Majority) with all 65 seats in the Assemblée Nationale (National Assembly).

The economy

Djibouti benefits from a geographically strategic position by the Red Sea, allowing the country to position itself as a trade hub. It is located at the crossroads of Africa, Asia and Europe and next to a very busy shipping route. Over the years successive governments have thus endeavoured to take advantage of this great positioning and build modern, competitive port infrastructure, with a bulk port, a petroleum port, a container terminal, a free-trade zone and modern information and communication technologies.

According to the *African Economic Outlook 2011* (AEO), published jointly by the African Development Bank and the Organisation for Economic Co-operation and Development, at 4.4 per cent, real gross domestic product (GDP) growth slowed slightly in 2010, but remains steady. Concentrated in the tertiary sector, the drivers of growth are still port operations, including transit trade with Ethiopia, and FDI. Nevertheless these two sectors were less dynamic than in 2009 and 2008.

Private sector investment accelerated in 2010, while FDI, which has been the driving force of economic growth for several years, fell to US$74 million, down from US$93.5 million in 2009 and US$234 million in 2008.

Port operations include trade in oil and gas and dry freight transported in bulk or in containers to Ethiopia or for trans-shipment. During the first three quarters of 2010, the number of containers entering Djibouti fell by around 30 per cent compared with the same period in 2009. There was a particularly marked fall in trans-shipment activity (down 75 per cent). Trans-shipment used to account for between 50 per cent and 60 per cent of containers entering Djibouti. In the third quarter of 2010, that figure slumped to just 25 per cent. The number of incoming containers bound for Ethiopia, however, remained stable.

Dry bulk freight was less affected, falling by 17 per cent during the first three quarters of 2010, mainly in that bound for Ethiopia. Trade in oil and gas slowed slightly, shrinking by 10 per cent during the first three quarters of 2010 compared with the previous period.

Nevertheless, thanks to the recovery in Ethiopia, Djibouti's main trade partner in the region, and in FDI, economic growth is forecast to accelerate to 4.6 per cent and 5.1 per cent in 2011 and 2012 respectively. The FDI is mainly linked to the enlargement of the container terminal at Doraleh port, the construction of the trans-shipment port in the town of Tadjourah, the project to exploit the geothermal energy potential of Lake Assal and the construction of 1,600 housing units. There are also plans to extend the free-trade zone to accommodate processing activities, and possibly industrial activities. This will only be possible, however, once the energy constraints that weigh so heavily upon the country have been eased. FDI is forecast to reach US$161 million in 2011 and US$149 million in 2012.

The Djiboutian economy is not a particularly balanced one. It is heavily reliant on transport and communication activities, which contribute 28.4 per cent to GDP, trade and tourism (18.7 per cent), non-market services (13.9 per cent), and the banking and insurance sector (13.8 per cent).

There is limited agricultural production which provides only 10 per cent of the country's fruit and vegetable consumption. Djibouti has to import 90 per cent of its food products, resulting in structural food insecurity, which is made worse by chronic drought. In November 2010, the United Nations (UN) launched an appeal for US$39 million to provide humanitarian aid to 120,000 people affected by the prolonged drought in Djibouti. Low rainfall over the past four years has destroyed the harvests of small farmers, wiped out more than 70 per cent of livestock and caused widespread malnutrition. To reduce the country's vulnerability, a food security body, the Société Nationale de Sécurité Alimentaire (SNSA), was set up to oversee the farming of arable land in other countries. Djibouti reached agreements with Sudan and Ethiopia for the concession of 5,000 hectares in each country for growing food products for the national supply.

Furthermore, although Djibouti has 372km of coastline, with an estimated exploitable potential of 47,000 tonnes of fish resources per annum, the fisheries sector remains underdeveloped. Only around 4.2 per cent of the potential resources are exploited (approximately 2,000 tonnes a year). This under-exploitation is caused by the limited number of boats, the poor training of fishermen, and unsuitable fishing techniques.

Although the economy stood up fairly well to the financial crisis of 2008–10, it remains particularly vulnerable because of the country's strong dependence on foreign trade. New sectors of activity, such as telecommunications, the finance and insurance sector, and tourism and construction have emerged over the past few years.

Doing business

The World Bank's 2011 Doing Business report ranks Djibouti 158th out of 183 countries, one place below its 2010 ranking. Although Djibouti still has a respectable rating of 60th for paying taxes, it has fallen 22 places since 2010, when it was ranked 38th. The country also scores well for trading across borders (38th), but doing business is hindered in particular by the poor protection of investors (179th), the difficulty in getting credit (176th), and the problems in starting a business (175th). Entrepreneurs are also confronted with the high costs of input such as energy and telecommunications, in addition to the limited availability of electricity and the lack of qualified manpower. Financial intermediation plays a modest role because of the high cost of credit, in a context of low inflation and monetary stability.

The authorities have taken some measures to improve Djibouti's ranking. In 2010 there was an overhaul of the investment code with the revised text passed by the National Assembly. It provides tax and non-tax incentives to investors, such as tax exemptions, exemptions from domestic consumption tax and registration fees, and preferential tariffs for energy and land acquisition. Legislation governing companies and forms of bankruptcy was also passed, and the labour code was revised. The most notable changes related to the abolition of the minimum wage, which was compensated for by the introduction of industry-specific labour agreements.

A one-stop shop to facilitate business start-ups, the Agence Nationale pour la Promotion des Investissements (ANPI) (National Agency for the Promotion of Investments), was created to encourage investment and promote private-sector development. But to strengthen its position as a trade hub, Djibouti must overcome its energy, water and food constraints. The energy deficit is hindering the development of the economy and is an obstacle to the introduction of new industries and manufacturing activities.

Djibouti has natural resources that have not yet been exploited, particularly perlite and salt. Perlite reserves are estimated at 23 million tonnes. The potential salt resources in Lake Assal are estimated at 1.2 million tonnes per year. Despite the investment of an American company in the sector, the resources have not yet been exploited. Prospecting for gold and oil is in progress. The country also has tourism potential, which is not sufficiently exploited. A strategic plan to develop the tourism sector has been prepared. The main tourist sites are Lake Assal, Lake Abbé, Day Forest, Le Goubet, the Seven Brothers

KEY INDICATORS **Djibouti**

	Unit	2006	2007	2008	2009	2010
Population	m	*0.75	*0.77	*0.78	0.82	*0.89
Gross domestic product (GDP)	US$bn	0.77	0.85	0.98	1.05	1.14
GDP per capita	US$	1,030	1,099	1,253	1,305	1,383
GDP real growth	%	4.8	5.1	5.8	5.0	4.5
Inflation	%	3.5	5.0	12.0	1.7	4.0
Exports (fob) (goods)	US$m	55.2	58.1	68.8	77.4	–
Imports (fob) (goods)	US$m	335.7	473.2	574.1	450.7	–
Balance of trade	US$m	-280.5	-415.2	505.3	-373.3	–
Current account	US$m	-99.1	-171.4	-225.4	-71.1	-77.0
Total reserves minus gold	US$m	120.3	132.1	175.5	241.8	249.0
Foreign exchange	US$m	117.8	130.3	173.7	219.6	230.6
Exchange rate	per US$	174.70	175.47	176.01	175.80	177.72

* estimated figure

islands, Moucha Island and Maskali Island. Initiatives have been undertaken by the Djibouti tourism agency, which now has around a dozen local promoters.

International relations

The authorities are determined to participate actively in regional integration. The introduction of VAT in 2009 was a preparatory step for the common external tariff to be introduced by the Common Market for Eastern and Southern Africa (COMESA). Djibouti is negotiating trade agreements with Kuwait, Kenya, Turkey, Saudi Arabia, Tunisia and Ethiopia.

Ethiopia and Djibouti have an interest in maintaining good relations with each other, as the two countries are interdependent. Ethiopia depends on the port of Djibouti for the transit of its imports and exports. Djibouti, for its part, imports its food through Ethiopia. Eventually, Ethiopia hopes to reduce its dependence on the port of Djibouti by developing other trade routes, particularly via Port Sudan and the ports of Berbera in Somaliland and Mombasa in Kenya. Nevertheless, Djibouti remains the best in terms of security and distance.

The country is home to major foreign military bases thanks to its strategic geographical location in the Gulf of Aden. In 2002, an American military base was added to the already existing French base. German and Japanese military contingents are also present, as is the European anti-piracy Operation Atalanta.

Risk assessment

Economy	Fair
Politics	Poor
Regional stability	Fair

COUNTRY PROFILE

Historical profile

1862 France reached agreements with local leaders which gave the French the right to settle in Djibouti. They also acquired the port of Obock. The country was called French Somaliland.
1888 Construction of Djibouti-ville began on the southern shore of Tadjoura Bay. At the end of the century, France signed an agreement with the Emperor of Ethiopia designating French Somaliland as the 'official outlet of Ethiopian commerce'. The agreement led to the construction of the vital Addis Ababa-Djibouti railway.
1892 Djibouti-ville became the capital of French Somaliland.
1917 The Addis Ababa-Djibouti railway was completed.
1946 French Somaliland was made an overseas territory, with its own parliament and representation in the French parliament.
1967 A referendum favoured continued French rule. French Somaliland was renamed the French Territory of the Afars and the Issas.
1977 The re-named Republic of Djibouti was granted independence by France after several years of growing protests and demonstrations. Hassan Gouled Aptidon of the Rassemblement Populaire pour le Progrès (RPP) (Popular Rally for Progress) was elected president.
1981 Djibouti became a one-party state, with the RPP as the only legal political party.
1991 The Front pour la Restauration de l'Unité et de la Démocratie (FRUD) (Front for the Restoration of Unity and Democracy) launched a civil war in northern Djibouti. The ethnic Afar organisation called for multi-party elections.
1992 Following several months of fighting, Aptidon agreed to a referendum, which led to a limited, multi-party constitution. In the elections to the Chamber of Deputies only four parties are allowed to take part; the RPP won 72 per cent of the vote while a newly formed alliance led by the Parti du Renouveau Démocratique (PRD) (Party of Democratic Renewal) won the remainder.
1993 President Aptidon was re-elected for a fourth term.
1994 Despite the new constitution, FRUD did not end its armed struggle until December, when the government and FRUD signed a peace accord confirming the constitutional and electoral reforms of 1992.
1997 President Aptidon was re-elected for a fifth term. FRUD joined RPP in a coalition government.
1999 The 83-year-old president resigned after 22 consecutive years in power. Ismael Omar Guelleh was elected president.
2001 Dileita Mohamed Dileita replaced Barkat Gourad Hamadou as prime minister.
2002 The law limiting four parties to contest elections, passed in 1992, expired. US led coalition troops arrived, in preparation for military action in Afghanistan and against al Qaeda targets in the region.
2003 The first fully multi-party elections held since independence, were won by parties supporting President Guelleh. Large numbers of illegal immigrants – estimated at 15 per cent of the population – were deported.
2005 In presidential elections, Ismail Omar Guelleh, the only candidate, was re-elected with 100 per cent of the vote.
2008 The opposition boycotted the parliamentary elections, won by the UMP coalition (consisting of five political parties, all supporters of President Ismail Omar Guelleh). Border clashes in the Mount Gabla area – also known as Ras Doumeira – that killed nine Djibouti troops and injured many more – were blamed, by the US, on 'military aggression' by Eritrea. The US and France called for a cease-fire and troop withdrawals on both sides and for negotiations to begin.
2009 Eritrea denied it had troops in Djibouti, contrary to a UN Security Council announcement that Eritrea had failed to withdraw.
2010 Parliament amended the constitution in April; a president may now serve for more than two terms although the mandate was reduced to five years in office and an upper age limit of 75 years was set. The amendment meant that President Guelleh would be allowed to run for office in 2011.
2011 The largest anti-government demonstration since independence was held on 18 February in Djibouti-ville. Around 30,000 people called on President Guelleh to quit office. Security forces used teargas and rubber bullets to disperse the crowds. On 8 March opposition groups decided to boycott the upcoming presidential election and called on voters to do likewise. The opposition warned that voting would not be free and fair and would most likely be rigged. Security forces arrested four opposition political leaders on 11 March, as they planned to head a demonstration against Guelleh. On 15 March, international observers (funded by the US) quit Djibouti, after they were declared 'illegal' by the foreign minister, Mahmoud Ali Youssouf, and accused of failing to maintain neutrality. On 5 April, parliament voted to allow unlimited terms in office for a president. The presidential election took place on 8 April, incumbent President Guelleh won 80.58 per cent of the vote and Mohamed Warsama Ragueh 19.42 per cent; turnout was 69.68 per cent. Parliamentary elections that had been due to take place at the same time as the presidential election were postponed until 2013. On 8 July, the UN issued an emergency appeal for US$136.3 in funds to provide aid for thousands of malnourished people caught up in the drought in the Horn of Africa.

Political structure

Constitution

The constitution was amended in April 2010 so that a president may now serve for more than two terms, although the mandate was reduce to five years in office and an upper age limit of 75 years was set.

The executive
Executive power is vested in the president as Head of State, who is directly elected by absolute majority vote, is typically leader of the largest political party in parliament. The president appoints a prime minister as head of government and leader of the council of ministers, both of which are responsible to the president. There is no term limit on the presidency, although there is an upper age limit of 75 years. The term in office is five years.
National legislature
The unicameral Assemblée Nationale (National Assembly) has 65 members elected in multi-seat constituencies for five-year terms. Membership includes 30 representatives of Somali groups (of which 21 are Issa) and 32 Afar peoples.
Last elections
8 February 2008 (parliamentary); 8 April 2011 (presidential).
Results: Parliamentary: four-party coalition called Union pour la Majorité Présidentielle (UMP) (Union for a Presidential Majority) won 94.1 per cent of the votes (all 65 seats); the opposition boycotted the elections. Turnout was 72.6 per cent.
Presidential: Ismail Omar Guelleh won 80.58 per cent of the vote, Mohamed Warsama Ragueh 19.42 per cent; turnout was 69.68 per cent.
Next elections
2013 (parliamentary); 2016 (presidential).

Political parties
Ruling party
Four-party coalition called Union pour la Majorité Présidentielle (UMP) (Union for a Presidential Majority), led by the Rassemblement Populaire pour le Progrès (RPP) (Popular Rally for Progress) (since 2005; re-elected 8 Feb 2008)
Main opposition party
Union pour l'Alternance Démocratique (UAD) (Union for Democratic Change), has no seats in parliament having boycotted the 2008 elections.

Population
818,159 (2009, census)
Last census: (December 1960: 81,200). According to the 2009 census, 70.6 per cent of the population live in urban areas, with 58.1 per cent of the population resident in the city of Djibouti, especially in the Balbala and Boulaos neighbourhoods. The rest of the population is spread across the different regions: Dikhil (10.9 per cent), Ali Sabieh (10.6 per cent), Tadjourah (10.6 per cent), Arta (5.2 per cent) and Obock (4.6 per cent). There are 161,132 nomadic people, accounting for 19.7 per cent, while the sedentary rural population accounts for 9.7 per cent of the total. Of the total population 53.8 per cent are male and 46.2 per cent female and 60.7 per cent of the population are aged between 15 and 59 years old.
Population density: 28 inhabitants per square km. Urban population: 84 per cent (1995–2001).
Annual growth rate: 2.7 per cent 1994–2004 (WHO 2006)
Ethnic make-up
About 60 per cent of the national total are Issas, of Somali origin and about 35 per cent are Afars who have links with Ethiopia; there are about 5 per cent European residents.
The population also includes refugees from the Ogaden and Eritrean wars in Somalia and Ethiopia.
The nomadic population (principally Afars) totals around 100,000.
Religions
Islam (94 per cent), Christianity (6 per cent)

Education
Literacy rate: 75.6 per cent men, 54.4 per cent women; adult rates (World Bank).
Enrolment rate: 45 per cent boys, 33 per cent girls, total primary school enrolment of the relevant age group (including repetition rates) (World Bank).

Health
The results of this spending appear limited, due mainly to poor management and the high costs of foreign staff and medicines.
HIV/Aids
This percentage is high enough to pose a significant threat to the country's future prosperity. Under a funding agreement in June 2004, US$12 million from the Global Fund to fight Aids, tuberculosis (TB) and malaria, will be spent on antiretroviral drugs to be supplied to Aids suffers until 2007. From an initial 200 patients it is expected that 4,000 patients will be treated, however the estimate of HIV positive cases in Djibouti is 9,000, with only 1,000 people registered – gaining them access to free treatment – though there has been an improvement in the numbers of people being tested.
HIV prevalence: 2.9 per cent aged 15–49 in 2003 (World Bank)
Life expectancy: 56 years, 2004 (WHO 2006)
Fertility rate/Maternal mortality rate: 4.9 births per woman, 2004 (WHO 2006)
Child (under 5 years) mortality rate (per 1,000): 97 per 1,000 live births; 18 per cent of children aged under five are malnourished (World Bank).
Head of population per physician: 0.18 physicians per 1,000 people, 2004 (WHO 2006)

Welfare
The average unemployment rate in the country is about 45 per cent. Although poverty is more acute in the rural areas, 72 per cent of those defined as living in absolute poverty reside in urban areas. Djibouti has been severely affected by the large influx of refugees from Ethiopia, Somalia and Eritrea, putting great strain on its financial resources. In August 2003 thousands of refugees and illegal immigrants were given an ultimatum to leave the country. Most had fled the wars in Somalia and Ethiopia and their numbers were as high as 100,000, or 15 per cent of the Djibouti population. The reason given by the government for their expulsion was security. By February 2004, 3,361 had been repatriated to Somaliland, by the UN High Commission for Refugees (UNHCR), who provided food and other provisions for each person, to last for the first nine months. Other refugees ended up in camps in Ethiopia as internally displaced persons.

Main cities
Djibouti-ville (capital, estimated population 547,100 in 2003).

Languages spoken
English is understood by the larger trading houses. Cushitic languages, as well as Somali and Saho-Afar are widely spoken.
Official language/s
French/Arabic (Somali/Afar are the national languages)

Media
Although the constitution provides for a free press, in practice the government maintains tight control of media outlets and circulation of information is highly restricted. Journalists generally have to avoid sensitive issues covering human rights, the army, and the government, relations with Ethiopia and foreign financial aid. A law prohibits the dissemination of false information and regulates the publication of newspapers, which has led to journalists exercising self-censorship. Journalists are largely untrained and poorly paid.
Press
In French, the main locally published newspaper *La Nation* (www.lanation.dj) is government owned. Political parties, Parti National Démocratique publishes *La Republique*, and Union pour l'Alternance Démocratique publishes *Le Renouveau*.
Broadcasting
The government owns the only radio and television stations allowed within the country with news programmes uncritical of the government or government policy. External services are available.
Radio: Radio Télévision Djibouti (RTD) (www.rtd.dj) provides a national network

for news, information, religious and musical programmes. External services via AM and local FM relays provide foreign broadcasts.
Television: RTD (www.rtd.dj) has a monopoly in broadcasting, providing a few hours TV per day.
News agencies
National news agency: ADI (Agence Djiboutienne d'Information)
(internet: (in French): www.adi.dj).
Presidential Press Office: www.spp.dj

Economy
Djibouti's location on the Horn of Africa is the main economic asset of a country that is mostly barren. It is strategically located at the mouth of the Red Sea, close to the world's busiest shipping lanes and the Arabian oilfields; it is the terminus of rail traffic into Ethiopia.
Djibouti's economy is reliant on services, which constitute around 80 per cent of GDP. The agricultural sector is small and industry only constitutes less than 20 per cent of GDP, of which manufacturing is less than 5 per cent. Economic activity centres on the port and the adjacent free trade zone, which in 2009 sustained GDP growth at a time when the economy in general was sluggish. The trans-shipment of goods from the port to Ethiopia, in particular, and other hinterlands is the primary activity for the port. The authorities are planning to develop the port into a shipping hub; however the prevalence of Somali pirates in the region may harm this strategy.
The railway and other support services, along with the presence of foreign military, provides directly and indirectly around half the country's income. The French military presence has been joined by the US which uses Djibouti as a military base for activities in the region, while the port is used by foreign navies patrolling the busy, but vulnerable, shipping lanes leading to the Suez Canal.
GDP averages 5 per cent. Although an International Monetary Fund (IMF) report of 2009 said that while Djibouti had successfully attracted foreign direct investment (FDI), and enjoyed the benefits of the expansion in port facilities and increased military personnel, GDP per capita had remained fairly constant at US$1,253–US$1,382 from 2008–10, despite inflation reaching a high of 12 per cent in 2008. International food prices rose sharply in 2008 and the impact on low-income earners was disproportionately high. Around half the population live below the poverty line and the number is growing; rising unemployment is a significant problem with around 50 per cent of the population living without a job.
Remittances in 2009 were US$28 million (2.7 per cant of GDP), and in 2010 it was estimated to have remained at that figure. In 2010, the UN Human Development Index (HDI) ranked Djibouti as 147 (out of 169 countries) for improvement in health, education and income and indicated that the Djibouti had consistently trailed the average improvement in other Arab countries since it was included in the ranking in 2005. The poverty rate was unavailable, but 47.3 per cent of households experienced at least three indicators of poverty.

External trade
Djibouti is a member of the Common Market for Eastern and Southern Africa (Comesa), and operates within a free trade zone with 13 of the 19 member states. The country has few assets with an unskilled labour force, limited natural resources and little scope for agriculture with poor, unproductive soil. The majority of foreign earnings come from its strategic function as a trans-shipment corridor for goods transported to and from the Port of Djibouti and Ethiopia.
There is a free trade zone near the port of Djibouti.
Imports
Principal imports are fresh fruits and vegetables (from Ethiopia), foods, beverages, transport equipment, construction material, chemicals and petroleum products.
Main sources: France (typically 31 per cent of total), UAE (19 per cent), Saudi Arabia (6 per cent).
Exports
Principal exports transiting Djibouti are live animals, cotton, sugar, cereals, salt, skins, leather and coffee.
Main destinations: Ethiopia (typically 35 per cent of total), France (20 per cent), Somalia (12 per cent).

Agriculture
Farming
The underdeveloped agricultural sector contributes only 3 per cent to GDP.
Due to poor terrain (mostly desert), most agricultural producers are nomads engaged in herding goats, sheep and camels. Drought has severly affected the livelihoods of the herd owners. Around 95 per cent of food requirements are imported.
Projects under consideration include increasing the amount of arable land by irrigation schemes and rehabilitation of water dams and wells.

Industry and manufacturing
The industrial sector is limited to construction and small-scale concerns such as mineral water bottling, tanning, dairy and animal food plants. New industries set up in Djibouti include cement, tiles, paints and meat processing. Foreign investment is being encouraged and should be aided by renewed political stability in the region.

Tourism
The sector is small and underdeveloped and any visitor will need to be experienced in self-sufficiency to enjoy anything on offer outside the capital of Djiboutiville. There are sites of natural wonder, such as active volcanoes, the bay of black lava, turned dark green near the western end of the Gulf of Tadjoura and the rare trees being conserved in the Day Forest National Park on Mount Goda.

Environment
In June 2010 the African Union backed a proposal to build the 'Great Green Wall' project, of a 15km wide, 7,775km long, continuous belt of trees from Senegal in the west to Djibouti in the east (traversing 11 countries) in an effort to halt the advance of the Sahara Desert. The trees to be used would be drought-adapted, preferably native to the area from a list of 37 possible species, and should help to slow soil erosion and filter rain water.

Mining
Surveys have indicated the presence of minerals such as copper, gypsum and sulphur. No minerals are mined commercially. Salt is extracted and exported.

Hydrocarbons
There are no proved oil reserves; consumption of oil was 13,000 barrels per day in 2008, all of which were imported. Djibouti relies entirely on oil to generate electricity; it opened the Doraleh oil terminal, in 2006, which can manage and store up to 240,000 tonnes of oil.
Any import and use of either natural gas or coal is commercially insignificant.

Energy
Total installed generating capacity was 150MW in 2008, producing over 250 million kilowatt hours. Djibouti is constrained in its energy generation by having no natural resources to exploit, it is without oil, natural gas and hydroelectric potential.
The state-owned Electricité du Djibouti is responsible for generation, transmission and distribution of electricity, which is only available in cities and a few small towns, plus those villages that have financed their own diesel-powered generators. In urban areas that are supplied with electricity around 99 per cent of the population use it for lighting only, kerosene is commonly used for other domestic purposes such as cooking and heating.
Djibouti has been recognised as a country with high a potential for renewable power generation from solar, wind and geothermal sources.

The government signed an agreement with the Icelandic Reykjavik Energy Invest (REI) in 2008 to initially build a 50MW geothermal power plant in the Rift Valley, which, along with an additional seven other geothermal plants, will produce a total of 900MW.

Banking and insurance
Central bank
National Bank of Djibouti
Main financial centre
Djiboutiville

Time
GMT plus three hours

Geography
Djibouti is in the Horn of Africa, at the southern entrance to the Red Sea. It is bounded on the north, west and south-west by Ethiopia, and on the south-east by Somalia. The land is volcanic desert.
Hemisphere
Northern

Climate
Very hot and arid from April–August; average temperature 32 degrees Celsius (C) and can reach 45 degrees C. Slightly cooler from October–March, with occasional light rain.

Dress codes
Djibouti has a large Muslim population so visitors should dress modestly, especially in the city. However, it is far less strict than other Islamic countries.

Entry requirements
Passports
Required by all. Must be valid for six months beyond date of departure.
Visa
Required by all, except French nationals. For business visits, a letter of invitation from a company in Djibouti is necessary.
Currency advice/regulations
No restrictions on import/export of local or foreign currency.

Health (for visitors)
Mandatory precautions
Yellow fever vaccination certificate if arriving from an infected area.
Advisable precautions
Yellow fever, typhoid, tetanus, hepatitis A and polio vaccinations. Malaria prophylaxis recommended as risk exists throughout the country. There is a rabies risk. Water precautions should be taken. Eat only well cooked meals, preferably served hot. Pork, salad and mayonnaise may carry increased risk. Vegetables should be cooked and fruit peeled.

Hotels
Available in Djibouti-ville – limited elsewhere. Service charge is normally included. Tipping is not usual.

Credit cards
Generally not accepted, except by airlines and Sheraton Hotel.

Public holidays (national)
Fixed dates
1 Jan (New Year's Day), 1 May (Labour Day), 27 Jun (Independence Day), 25 Dec (Christmas Day).
Variable dates
Eid al Adha, Eid al Fitr, Islamic New Year, Birth of the Prophet.
Islamic year 1433 (26 Nov 2011–14 Nov 2012): The Islamic year contains 354 or 355 days, with the result that Muslim feasts advance by 10-12 days against the Gregorian calender. Dates of feasts vary according to the sighting of the new moon, so cannot be forecast exactly.

Working hours
Banking
Sat–Thu: 0715–1145.
Business
Sat–Thu: 0630–1300.
Government
Sat–Thu: 0630–1300.
Shops
0730–1200, 1600–1900; closed Fri.

Telecommunications
Telephone/fax
A 100 per cent automatic service; outside Djibouti-ville there are very few telephones.

Electricity supply
220V AC, 50 cycles.

Getting there
Air
International airport/s: Djibouti-Ambouli (JIB), 5km south of city; restaraunts, duty free shops, bureau de change, car hire.
Airport tax: US$20
Surface
Road: There is a surfaced road from Addis Ababa (Ethiopia). Local advice should be taken as to when to travel by road as it can be difficult, with problems caused by the political situation.
Rail: There is a rail link with Ethiopia with a daily service, but it is not reliable or safe.
Main port/s: Djibouti-ville.

Getting about
National transport
Air: Djibouti Airlines operates a daily domestic service to Obock and Tadjoura from Djibouti. Dikhil and Ali-Sabieh can be reached by chartered aircraft.
Road: There are surfaced roads to the Ethiopian border and to Arta, and from Djibouti-ville to Tadjoura; most roads are in need of repair. Take local advice when planning to travel by road.
Rail: Some towns are served on the Djibouti– Addis Ababa railway.
Water: Ferry service links Djibouti-ville with Tadjoura and Obock.
City transport
Taxis: They are available in main towns. Tipping is not usual as fares include gratuities; there is an official tariff, but it is usual for visitors to be charged 50 per cent more; there is a similar increase at night.
The journey from the airport to the centre of Djibouti-ville takes 10 minutes.
Car hire
Available in Djibouti-ville and at the airport. Valid international driving licence recommended. A temporary licence can be obtained on presentation of national licence. Traffic drives on right.

BUSINESS DIRECTORY

The addresses listed below are a selection only. While World of Information makes every endeavour to check these addresses, we cannot guarantee that changes have not been made, especially to telephone numbers and area codes. We would welcome any corrections.

Telephone area codes
The international dialling code (IDD) for Djibouti is + 253 followed by subscriber's number.

Useful telephone numbers
Police: 17
Fire: 18

Chambers of Commerce
Djibouti International Chamber of Commerce et Industry, Place de LaGuarde, PO Box 84, Djibouti (tel: 351-070; fax: 350-096; e-mail: cicid@intnet.dj).

Banking
Banque de Développement de Djibouti; PO Box 520, Angle Ave Georges Clémenceau et rue Pierre Curie, Djibouti-ville (tel: 353-391; fax: 355-022).

Banque Indosuez Mer Rouge; PO Box 88, 10 Place Lagarde, Djibouti-ville (tel: 353-016; fax: 351-638).

Banque pour le Commerce et l'Industrie-Mer Rouge; PO Box 2122, Place Lagarde, Djibouti-ville (tel: 350-857; fax: 354-260).

Central bank
Banque Centrale de Djibouti, Avenue Saint Laurent du Var, PO Box 2118, Djibouti-ville (tel: 352-751 fax: 356-288; e-mail: bndj@intnet.dj).

Travel information
Daallo Airlines (Airline of Horn of Africa), PO Box 1954, Djibouti-ville (tel: 353-401, 356-660; fax: 351-765).

Djibouti Airlines, Place Lagarde, PO Box 2240, Djibouti-ville (tel: 351-006; fax: 352-429).

Djibouti Airport, BP 204, Djibouti-ville (tel: 340-101 ext 300, 382-322; fax: 340-723).

Puntavia Airline de Djibouti, CP 2240, Djibouti-ville (tel: 351-036, 351-006; fax: 353-429, 356-660).

National tourist organisation offices

Office National du Tourisme de Djibouti, BP 1938, place du 27 Juin, Djibouti-ville (tel: 353-790; fax: 356-322; e-mail: onta@intnet.dj).

Ministries

Ministry of Agriculture and Rural Development, BP 453, Djibouti-ville (tel: 351-297).

Ministry of Commerce, Transport and Tourism, BP 121, Djibouti-ville (tel: 352-540).

Ministry of Foreign Affairs and Co-operation, BP 1863, Djibouti-ville (tel: 353-342).

Ministry of Industry and Industrial Development, BP 175, Djibouti-ville (tel: 350-340).

Other useful addresses

British Consulate, BP 81, Gellatly Hankey et Cie, Djibouti-ville (tel: 355-718; fax: 353-294); c/o Inchcape Shipping Office, Djibouti-ville (tel: 353-836/844).

Central Post Office, boulevard de la République, Djibouti-ville (tel: 350-669).

Compagnie du Chemin de Fer Djibouti-Ethiopien, BP 2116, Djibouti-ville (tel: 350-353).

Djibouti Embassy (USA), 1156 15th Street, NW, Washington DC 20005 (tel: (+1-202)-331-0270; fax (+1-202)-331-0302).

Office National d'Approvisionnement et de Commercialisation (ONAC), BP 75, Djibouti-ville (tel: 350-327).

Office of the Prime Minister, BP 2086, Djibouti-ville (tel: 351-494; fax: 355-049).

Radiodiffusion Télévision de Djibouti (RTD), BP 97, Djibouti-ville (tel: 352-294).

Service de Statistique et de Documentation, BP 1846, Djibouti-ville (tel: 353-331).

US Embassy, BP 185, Villa Plateau du Serpent, Boulevard Maréchal Joffré, Djibouti-ville (tel: 353-995).

National news agency: ADI (Agence Djiboutienne d'Information), (internet: (in French): www.adi.dj).

Internet sites

Africa Business Network: http://www.ifc.org/abn

AllAfrica.com: http://allafrica.com

African Development Bank: http://www.afdb.org

Africa Online: http://www.africaonline.com

Information on Horn of Africa: http://www.djibouti.com

Local online newspaper: http://www.djiboutipost.com

Mbendi AfroPaedia (information on companies, countries, industries and stock exchanges in Africa): http://www.mbendi.co.za

Dominica

COUNTRY PROFILE

Historical profile

1493 Chritopher Colombus visited the island and named it Dominica (Sunday Island).
1627 Despite attempts by the Earl of Carlisle, who was put in charge of Dominica by England, initial attempts at colonisation are fiercely resisted by the indigenous Carib community.
1635 France claimed Dominica. Resistance by the Carib Indians continued.
1763 Britain won possession of Dominica in accordance with the Treaty of Paris, which had ended the Seven Years' War between France and Britain. Britain established a legislative assembly, representing only the minority white population.
1831 Britain conferred political and social rights on free non-whites.
1834 Slavery was abolished.
1838 Dominica become the first British colony in the Caribbean to have a black-controlled legislature.
1865 Britain replaced the elected assembly with one consisting of one-half elected members and one-half appointed.
1896 Dominica became a crown colony again.
1940 The administration of Dominica was transferred to the Windward Islands.
1951 Universal adult suffrage was established.
1958 Dominica became part of the UK-sponsored West Indies Federation.
1960 Dominica was granted self-government by the UK.
1961 Edward leBlanc (Dominica Labour Party) (DLP) became chief minister.
1974 LeBlanc retired and was replaced by Patrick John (DLP).
1967 Full autonomy of its internal affairs was gained.
1978 Dominica became an independence republic and a member of the Commonwealth. Patrick John (DLP) became prime minister.
1980 The Dominica Freedom Party (DFP) won a convincing victory and Eugenia Charles become prime minister – the first female prime minister in the Caribbean.
1981 Two attempted coups failed and the Dominican Defence Force was disbanded.
1995 The United Workers' Party (UWP), led by Edison James, won the general election, defeating the ruling DFP.
2000 The UWP lost the election to a coalition composed of the Dominica Labour Party (DLP) and the DFP. Prime Minister Roosevelt Douglas died suddenly and Pierre Charles was appointed as his successor. Under legislation, the National Commercial Bank was permitted to engage in offshore financial services.
2002 Dominica ended the sale of passports under its economic citizenship programme.
2003 Dr Nicholas Liverpool became president, elected by parliament despite an opposition boycott of the sitting.
2004 Prime Minister Pierre Charles died; Roosevelt Skerrit was sworn in as his successor. Diplomatic relations with Taiwan was cut in favour of China, which agreed to provide aid of US$100 million over five years. An earthquake damaged buildings in the north of the island and cost millions of dollars in repairs.
2005 Roosevelt Skerrit's DLP won the parliamentary elections; the DFP, the junior partner in the former coalition government, lost both of its seats – the first time in 35 years that the DFP did not win a seat.
2006 A section of the fibre optic cable, which when completed will traverse the entire Eastern Caribbean (around 1900km in length), reached Dominica.
2007 Hurricane Dean ruined around 99 per cent of the banana crop, severely damaging the country's principal industry.

KEY FACTS

Official name: The Commonwealth of Dominica

Head of State: President Nicholas Liverpool (from 2003; re-elected Jul 2008)

Head of government: Prime Minister Roosevelt Skerrit (DLP) (from 2004; re-elected 18 Dec 2009)

Ruling party: Dominica Labour Party (DLP) (since 2000; re-elected 18 Dec 2009)

Area: 750 square km

Population: 68,000 (2010)*

Capital: Roseau

Official language: English

Currency: East Caribbean dollar (EC$) = 100 cents

Exchange rate: EC$2.70 per US$ (fixed)

GDP per capita: US$5,167 (2010)

GDP real growth: 1.00% (2010)

GDP: US$376.00 million (2010)

Inflation: 2.90% (2010)

Balance of trade: -US$159.31 million (2010)

* estimated figure

However, the tourist infrastructure remained largely untouched.
2008 President Liverpool agreed to serve another term in office.
2009 Dominica formally applied for US$5 million from the IMF Rapid-Access Component of the Exogenous Shock Facility (ESF). The ESF is intended to assist small islands respond to adverse external economic conditions, brought about by the global financial crisis. The ruling DLP won parliamentary elections; Roosevelt Skerrit remained in office as prime minister.
2010 Dominica celebrated 40 years of membership in *La Francophonie*, the international organisation of French speaking countries, in March.
2011 An agreement to jointly fund a project to drill exploratory geothermal wells was signed on 12 April between the government, Agence Francaise de Development (French Development Agency) and the EU, with work beginning at the end of July. The launch of a new ferry service was announced in June; a proposed service by the *L'Express Des Iles* will carry up to 350 passengers between Dominica, St Lucia and other neighbouring French-speaking islands. On 21 July, Former ambassador Irwin LaRacque was appointed as Secretary General of the Caribbean Community. On 1 August citizens of the Organisation of Eastern Caribbean States (OECS) – Antigua and Barbuda, Dominica, Grenada, St Kitts and Nevis, St Lucia and St Vincent and the Grenadines – were granted freedom of movement, allowing them to reside, work, establish businesses and provide services throughout the organisation.

Political structure

Independence date

1978

The executive

Executive power rests with the prime minister who acts on the advice of the cabinet.
The role of the president, as Head of State, is largely ceremonial. The president is nominated by the prime minister, in consultation with the leader of the opposition, and is then elected by the House of Assembly for five years, renewable once.

National legislature

The unicameral House of Assembly has 32 members, of which 21 (representatives) are directly elected in single seat constituencies for five-year terms. Senators are elected (by votes of Assembly representatives) or may be appointed (a maximum of five senators by the president on the advice of the prime minister and four on the advice of the leader of the opposition). There is also an *ex officio* member with the remaining seat is held by the speaker of the Assembly.
The assembly appoints the president, who is a ceremonial head of state. The prime minister is the leader of the majority in the House of Assembly and the leader of the opposition is appointed by the president as leader of the main grouping outside the government.

Legal system

The legal system is based on English common law. There are three local levels of judiciary courts. The Eastern Caribbean Supreme Court, located in St Lucia, hears appeals. The Privy Council in the UK is the highest court of appeal.

Last elections

18 December 2009 (parliamentary); July 2008 (presidential).
Results: Parliamentary: Dominica Labour Party won 61.21 per cent of the vote (17 seats out of 21), United Worker's Party 34.85 per cent (four); three other political parties won less than 2.5 per cent of the vote each and failed to win any seats. Turnout was 37.9 per cent.
Presidential: President Nicholas Liverpool was re-elected by parliament unapposed.

Next elections

2014 (parliamentary)

Political parties

Ruling party

Dominica Labour Party (DLP) (since 2000; re-elected 18 Dec 2009)

Main opposition party

United Workers' Party (UWP)

Political situation

Dominica has been struggling to replace the export revenue it used to earn from bananas. The end of the so called 'banana wars' was signalled in December 2009 when Europe, the world's biggest banana market, initialled the treaty to halt the preferential treatment it gave to Africa, Caribbean and Pacific (ACP) countries. The banana producing countries of the ACP, like Dominica, are mostly small islands which will struggle to meet the economies of scale of their competitors in central and south America. Agriculture still dominates the economy, employing some 30 per cent of the workforce. The government has encouraged the diversification of the agricultural sector into other high-value crops suitable for small-holders, such as coffee, patchouli, aloe vera, cut flowers, and exotic fruits.
Dominica does not have the typical white sandy beaches of other Caribbean islands and missed out on the first wave of tourist destinations. It has, however, managed to promote its landscape of mountains, hot-springs and fresh water lakes to a more adventurous holiday maker. Cruise ship stop-overs have also increased since the construction of a new dock with waterfront facilities in Roseau.
Dominica is still one of the poorest countries in the Caribbean and receives aid from both the IMF Rapid-Access Component of the Exogenous Shock Facility (ESF) and the joint Caricom and Caribbean Development bank, Caribbean Catastrophic Risk Insurance Facility (CCRIF) when necessary.
In the last elections, held in December 2009, the Dominica Labour Party was re-elected and Roosevelt Skerrit continued as prime minister. The president is elected by the prime minister in consultation with the leader of the opposition.

Population

68,000 (2010)*
Last census: May 2002: 69,625
Population density: 97 inhabitants per square km. Urban population: 73.9 per cent (2007).

KEY INDICATORS — Dominica

	Unit	2006	2007	2008	2009	2010
Population	m	0.07	0.07	*0.07	*0.07	*0.07
Gross domestic product (GDP)	US$bn	0.30	0.31	0.36	0.36	0.38
GDP per capita	US$	4,203	4,333	4,978	4,949	5,167
GDP real growth	%	4.0	0.9	3.2	-0.3	1.0
Inflation	%	2.6	2.7	6.4	0.0	2.9
Exports (fob) (goods)	US$m	44.3	39.0	43.9	37.8	34.4
Imports (fob) (goods)	US$m	146.9	172.3	217.4	205.4	193.7
Balance of trade	US$m	-102.6	-133.3	-173.5	-167.7	-159.3
Current account	US$m	-49.9	-87.0	-136.1	-123.2	-96.8
Total reserves minus gold	US$m	63.0	60.5	55.2	75.5	76.1
Foreign exchange	US$m	63.0	60.5	55.1	64.5	66.4
Exchange rate	per US$	2.70	2.70	2.70	2.70	2.70

* estimated figure

Annual growth rate: 0.5 per cent 1994–2004 (WHO 2006)

Ethnic make-up

Black, mixed black and European, European, Syrian, Carib.

Religions

Roman Catholic (77 per cent), Methodist (5 per cent), Pentecostal (3 per cent), Seventh-Day Adventist (3 per cent), Baptist (2 per cent).

Education

Literacy rate: 94 per cent, adult rate (2003)

Compulsory years: Five to 16

Health

The country has experienced notable improvements with a decline in infant and maternal mortality and communicable diseases and an increase in life expectancy; chronic and other non-communicable diseases are now the leading causes of death and ill-health, even as new problems such as HIV/Aids present themselves.

Life expectancy: 74 years, 2004 (WHO 2006)

Fertility rate/Maternal mortality rate: 2.0 births per woman, 2004 (WHO 2006)

Birth rate/Death rate: 17 births per 1,000 population; seven deaths per 1,000 population (2003).

Child (under 5 years) mortality rate (per 1,000): 12 per 1,000 live births (2003)

Welfare

Dominica has a national insurance system in which employee contributions are 3 per cent of salary and employer contributions are 7 per cent.

Main cities

Roseau (capital, estimated population 20,000 in 2003), Berekua (3,900), Portsmouth (3,600).

Languages spoken

English and French-Creole.

Official language/s

English

Media

Press

There are no daily newspapers. Weekly publications include *The Chronicle* (www.dachronicle.com) *The Times*, *The Sun* and *The Tropical Star*.

Online news is carried by Dominica News (www.dominicanewsonline.com), Dominican Weekly (www.dominica-weekly.com) News-Dominica (www.newsdominica.com) and Cakafete (www.sakafete.com).

Broadcasting

Radio: DBS (Dominica Broadcasting Services) (www.dbcradio.net) is the government-operated radio service. Commercial stations include Q95 FM (www.wiceqfm.com), Kairi FM (http://kairifmonline.com) and Voice of Life Radio (www.voiceoflife.com) plays religious programmes

Television: There is no national TV service although a Marpin Telecoms (www.marpin.dm) provides a cable service with 52 channels.

News agencies

Other news agencies: Caribbean Net News: www.caribbeannetnews.com

Economy

The economy is still largely dependent on primary industries, particularly agriculture, with around 30 per cent of the workforce employed in farming, fishing and forestry. Mining of minerals, such as pumice and gravel, for the construction industry is also important. Manufacturing is dependent on agriculture as it uses domestic produce to make foodstuffs, such as fruit juice and alcohol, and soap from coconuts. The service sector, in particular tourism, has grown to be the largest component of GDP. Over 88,000 visitors arrived in Dominica in 2008, just before the downturn in growth, but numbers, particularly those arriving by cruise liners, were expected to rise in 2010.

Dominica is subject to extreme weather conditions as hurricanes have caused widespread devastation. The island has one of the highest rainfalls in the Caribbean (averaging 150cm–370cm on the coast, 635cm in the highlands), and following the commercialisation of its water resource since 2009, has benefited from the export of fresh water.

GDP growth was 3.2 per cent in 2008, which fell to -0.3 per cent in 2009 as the global economic crisis cut trade and depressed the construction industry, as well as reduced the number of visitors to the island. However in 2010 Dominica came out of recession, with growth of 1.4 per cent and with a projected growth of 2.5 per cent in 2011.

Around 5.5 million expatriate workers sent US$23 million (6.7 per cent of GDP) in remittances in 2009, which were projected to increase to US$25 million in 2010, with money flowing directly into family budgets. Private enterprise is still considered to be the long term solution to high unemployment and poverty. GDP per capita fell from US$5,006 in 2008 to US$ 4,976 in 2009, before expecting to rise to US$5,148 in 2010. Although the rise mirrored the rise in GDP growth, the rate was less than the rate established in earlier years.

In July 2010 the European Investment Bank provided credit of US$10 million to support small and medium enterprises (SME) and projects for renewable energy in Dominica. The EU has also provided assistance in the development of the government's tourism development plan, which seeks to promote Dominica's ecotourism, as well as help to develop geothermal energy resources.

External trade

Dominica is a member of the Caribbean Community and Common Market (Caricom) and operates within the single market (Caribbean Single Market and Economy (CSME)), which became operational in 2006. As a member of the Eastern Caribbean Currency Union (ECCU) Dominica uses the common Eastern Caribbean Dollar.

Light manufacturing has become more important to Dominica's export trade as banana exports to the EU were cut in the mid-2000s.

Imports

Principal imports include manufactured goods, machinery and equipment, food and chemicals.

Main sources: US (typically 40 per cent of total), Trinidad and Tobago (21 per cent), UK (6 per cent).

Exports

The principal exports include, soap, bay oil, vegetables and citrus fruit, foodstuffs and fresh water. Bananas are still an export commodity, despite their fall in production and pre-eminence.

Main destinations: Jamaica (typically 16 per cent of total), Antigua and Barbuda (15 per cent), France (14 per cent).

Agriculture

The agriculture sector is the mainstay of the economy, accounting for around 18 per cent of GDP and employing 40 per cent of the labour force. About 25 per cent of the total land area is agricultural. Bananas are the main crop, with exports destined mainly for the UK. Banana exports are controlled through the Dominican Banana Marketing Board (DBMB), a government agency. Dominica's climate makes the banana crop highly vulnerable. Hurricanes occur periodically and in the past have wiped out as much as 95 per cent of the crop.

The government is trying to promote new crops as part of its diversification plan, for when the market is fully liberalised in 2006; these include coffee, mangos, and aloe vera.

Fishing

The typical annual fish catch is over 1,100t, plus 4t of other seafood.

Forestry potential is not exploited.

Industry and manufacturing

Industry accounts for 24 per cent of GDP. The manufacturing sector is small-scale and centred on soap production, construction, agricultural processing (mainly coconut oil and copra), canned fruit juices, cigarettes, cigars and rum. Water bottling for export is also important.

Tourism
Dominica is a small island with diverse terrain of high peaks, deep gorges, hot springs, a rich rain forest and the world's largest active boiling lake; it also has a wealth of marine life. It has adopted the slogan 'Nature Island of the Caribbean' for its tourism promotion.

The tourist industry constituted 24.9 per cent of GDP in 2010, which was a fall of -0.1 per cent on the 2009 contribution. This was the fourth consecutive year of loss as tourist numbers fell due to a series of hurricanes in 2005 that caused damage to travel and tourism infrastructure. The global economic situation from 2007 has also had an adverse affect. Employment associated with tourism was 22.8 per cent of the working population in 2010; the percentage had been steadily falling since a high of 27 per cent in 2006, but in 2011 it rose by 0.1 per cent. Around 30 per cent of all visitors arrive from North America and around 15 per cent from Europe; visitors from the Caribbean region account for around 50 per cent of all tourists. Of the 466,181 tourists in 2008, 386,414 arrived on 211 cruise-liners.

Hydrocarbons
There are no known hydrocarbon reserves. Import of oil was 1,000 barrels per day in 2008. In 2005, Dominica, plus a number of other Caribbean states, signed an agreement with Venezuela to establish PetroCaribe, a multi-national oil company, owned by the participating states. PetroCaribe buys low-priced Venezuelan crude oil under long-term payment plans.

Any use of natural gas or coal is commercially insignificant.

Energy
Total installed generating capacity was 24MW in 2006. The Dominica Electricity Services (Domlec) has exclusive rights, until 2025, to provide generation, distribution, transmission and sale of electricity. Power is generated by both hydro and conventional thermal plants.

Plans for the commercial development of a geothermal-fuelled power plant, developed by the Eastern Caribbean Geothermal Development Project (ECGDP) (or Geo-Caraïbes), which is estimated will provide 60–120MW overall, will be operated by the West Indies Power Limited (WIPL), and owned by ECGDP countries.

Financial markets
Stock exchange

Eastern Caribbean Securities Exchange (ECSE)

Banking and insurance
The seven members of the Organisation of Eastern Caribbean States (OECS), Antigua and Barbuda, Dominica, Grenada, Montserrat, St Kitts and Nevis, St Lucia and St Vincent and the Grenadines, share a common currency and central bank. The British Virgin Islands and Anguilla are associate members.

Central bank

Eastern Caribbean Central Bank, St Kitts and Nevis.

Offshore facilities

The offshore financial sector makes a significant contribution to Dominican GDP and it is an area that the government would like to see progress. The government introduced anti-money laundering legislation and in 2003 Dominica was removed from the OECD blacklist of non-compliant countries.

Time
GMT minus four hours

Geography
Dominica is situated in the Windward Islands group of the West Indies, lying between Guadeloupe to the north and Martinique to the south.

The island has a rugged mountainous interior. It has volcanic activity, with the second largest boiling lake in the world (after Rotorua, New Zealand), where a waterfall feeds water onto a crater that is thought to have a magma chamber below. Morne Diablatins is the highest peak at 1,447 metres.

Much of the island is virgin rain forest with steep rivers flowing down to the shore of either black volcanic or golden sands.

Hemisphere

Northern

Climate
Sub-tropical with year-round tradewinds moderating the heat. Daytime temperatures range from 24–32 degrees Celsius; coolest from December–March. It is driest from January–May. The hurricane season, when storms can be very violent, is from June–October; rainfall is much higher in mountain areas. Annual rainfall in Roseau is 125–200cm and much higher inland.

Dress codes
Formal business attire.

Entry requirements
Passports

Required by all except, Canadian citizens travelling with proof of citizenship with photo ID and French nationals using their national *Carte identite*. Proof of onward/return passage is also required. Canadian nationals require a passport for re-entry to their country from January 2007).

Visa

Tourist visas up to 21 days are valid for all visitors who can show proof of a return/onward ticket and sufficient funds for the duration of the stay. Longer visa-free stays are only granted to designated nationals of the Americas, Europe and Australasia. Business visas will be issued to visitors who represent foreign companies, who must present proof of employment.

Contact the nearest High Commission or embassy for further information and application form.

Currency advice/regulations

The import of local and foreign currency is unlimited but must be declared, export is limited to the amount imported.

Travellers cheques are accepted but to avoid extra exchange fees US dollar denominations are recommended. ATMs are available.

Health (for visitors)
Mandatory precautions

Yellow fever vaccination certificate required if arriving from infected area.

Advisable precautions

Immunisation for hepititis A is useful. Other lesser risks include typhoid, bacillary and amoebic dysentery and occasional outbreaks of dengue fever as well as haemorrhagic dengue fever. Water precautions should be taken in rural areas. As visitors are required to pay up-front for treatment, it is strongly recommended to take out full medical insurance.

Hotels
Most hotels are family-run and situated around the capital. Hotel bills include a 10 per cent service charge.

Credit cards
All major cards are accepted.

Public holidays (national)
Fixed dates

1 Jan (New Year's Day), 3 Nov (Independence Day), 4 Nov (Community Service Day), 25–26 Dec (Christmas).

Variable dates

Carnival (Feb), Good Friday, Easter Monday (Mar/April), May Day (first Mon in May), Whit Monday (last Mon in May), August Monday (first Mon in Aug).

Working hours
Banking

Mon–Thu: 0800–1500; Fri: 0800–1700.

Business

Mon–Fri: 0800–1600. Sat: 0800–1300.

Government

Mon: 0800–1300, 1400–1700; Tue–Fri: 0800–1300, 1400–1600.

Telecommunications
Mobile/cell phones
GSM 850 and 900/1900 services available throughout most of the islands.

Electricity supply
220/240V AC, 50 cycles, with European three pin plugs.

Social customs/useful tips
Dominica's national dish is made from a large land frog, the *crapaud* or mountain chicken. In 2004, a ban was placed on hunting the amphibians, which are facing extinction.

Getting there
Air
National airline: None
International airport/s: Melville Hall (DOM), 64km north-east of Roseau; Canefield (DCF), 5km north of Roseau. Both of these airports are too small for international jets; access by air is via Antigua, Barbados, Costa Rica, Martinique or Guadeloupe.
Airport tax: Departure tax: EC$55, for a stay of more than 24 hours.
Surface
Water: There are ferries to surrounding islands.
Main port/s: Roseau (Woodbridge Bay) and Portsmouth (Prince Rupert's Bay).

Getting about
National transport
Air: Regional airline Carib Express based in Barbados.
Road: The network is over 750km, most of which is classified as first class.
City transport
Taxis: Available at airports and through hotels. Fixed rate system.
Car hire
A temporary local driver's permit is required, priced EC$30, and can be obtained on production of an national driving licence. Drivers must be aged between 25–65 years with at least two years experience.
The speed limit is generally 20mph.

BUSINESS DIRECTORY

The addresses listed below are a selection only. While World of Information makes every endeavour to check these addresses, we cannot guarantee that changes have not been made, especially to telephone numbers and area codes. We would welcome any corrections.

Telephone area codes
The international direct dialling code (IDD) for Dominica is +1 767, followed by subscriber's number.

Chambers of Commerce
Dominica Association of Industry and Commerce, 6 Cross Street, PO Box 85, Roseau (tel:448-2874; fax: 448-6868; e-mail: daic@marpin.dm).

Banking
Agricultural, Industrial & Development Bank (AID Bank), Charles Avenue, Goodwill (tel: 448-2853).

Bank of Nova Scotia, 28 Hillsborough Street, PO Box 520, Roseau (tel: 448-8580).

Banque Française Commerciale Antilles Guiyane, Queen Mary Street, PO Box 166, Roseau (tel: 448-4040).

Barclays Bank, 2 Old Street, PO Box 4, Roseau (tel: 448-2571).

Dominica Co-operative Credit Union, Great Marlborough Street, Roseau (tel: 82-191).

National Commercial Bank of Dominica, 64 Hillsborough Street, PO Box 271, Roseau (tel: 448-4401).

Royal Bank of Canada, Bay Front, PO Box 19, Roseau (tel: 448-2771).

Central bank
Eastern Caribbean Central Bank, Agency Office, PO Box 23, Dorsett House, Corner Old Street and Hodges Lane, Roseau (tel: 448-8001; fax: 448-8002).

Stock exchange
Eastern Caribbean Securities Exchange (ECSE): www.ecseonline.com

Travel information
Cardinal Airlines, 26 King George V Street, PO Box 661, Roseau (tel: 449-8922; fax: 449-8923).

Ministry of tourism
Ministry of Tourism, Port and Employment, Government Headquarters, Kennedy Avenue, Roseau (tel: 82-401).

National tourist organisation offices
Dominica Tourist Board, National Development Corporation, PO Box 293, Roseau (tel: 82-045; fax: 85-840).

Division of Tourism (National Development Corporation), PO Box 73, Valley Road, Roseau (tel: 82-186, 82-351; fax: 85-840).

Ministries
Ministry of Agriculture and the Environment, Government Headquarters, Kennedy Avenue, Roseau (tel: 82-401; fax: 87-999).

Ministry of Communications, Works and Housing, Government Headquarters, Kennedy Avenue, Roseau (tel: 82-401; fax: 84-807).

Ministry of Community Development and Women's Affairs, Kennedy Avenue, Roseau (tel: 82-401; fax: 98-220).

Ministry of Education, Sports and Youth Affairs, Government Headquarters, Kennedy Avenue, Roseau (tel: 82-401; fax: 80-080).

Ministry of External Affairs, Legal Affairs and Labour, Government Headquarters, Kennedy Avenue, Roseau (tel: 82-401; fax: 85-200).

Ministry of Finance, Industry and Planning (The Economic Development Unit), Government Headquarters, Kennedy Avenue, Roseau (tel: 82-401; fax: 80-054).

Ministry of Health and Social Security, Government Headquarters, Kennedy Avenue, Roseau (tel: 82-401; fax: 86-086).

Ministry of Privatisation and Foreign Investment (National Development Corporation), PO Box 293, Valley Road, Roseau (tel: 82-045).

Ministry of Trade and Marketing, Government Headquarters, Kennedy Avenue, Roseau (tel: 82-401; fax: 86-103).

Office of the Prime Minister, Government Headquarters, Kennedy Ave, Roseau (tel: 82-406).

Other useful addresses
Co-operative Citrus Growers' Association, 21 Hanover St, Roseau (tel: 82-062).

Dominica Banana Marketing Corp (DBMC), Corner of Queen Mary St and Turkey Lane, Roseau (82-671).

Dominica Broadcasting Corporation, Victoria Street, Roseau (tel: 83-283; fax: 82-918).

Dominica Embassy in US, 3216 New Mexico Ave, NW Washington DC 20016 (tel: (+1-202) 364-6781).

Dominica Export-Import Agency (Dexia), PO Box 173, Roseau (tel: 82-780; fax: 86-308).

Dominica Hotel Association, PO Box 270, Roseau (tel: 84-436).

Dominica National Development Corporation (NDC), PO Box 293, Valley Road, Bath Estate, Roseau (tel: 82-045; fax: 85-840; internet site: http://ndcdominica.dm/index.htm).

International Business Unit, Ministry of Finance, Government Headquarters, Kennedy Avenue, Roseau (tel: 82-401; fax: 80-406; e-mail: ibu@cwdom.dm).

Internet sites
Tourist website:
www.avirtualdominica.com

Dominican Republic

KEY FACTS

Official name: República Dominicana (Dominican Republic)

Head of State: President Leonel Fernández Reyana (PLD) (since 2004; re-elected 16 May 2008)

Head of government: President Leonel Fernández Reyana

Ruling party: Partido de la Liberación Dominicana (PLD) (Dominican Liberation Party) (from 2010)

Area: 48,400 square km

Population: 9.38 million (2010; census figure)

Capital: Santo Domingo de Guzmán

Official language: Spanish

Currency: Dominican Republic peso (RD$) = 100 centavos

Exchange rate: RD$38.22 per US$ (Oct 2011)

GDP per capita: US$5,228 (2010)

GDP real growth: 7.80% (2010)

GDP: US$51.60 billion (2010)

Unemployment: 16.00% (2008)*

Inflation: 6.30% (2010)

Balance of trade: -US$6.74 billion (2009)

Visitor numbers: 4.12 million * (2010, excludes cruise passengers)

* estimated figure

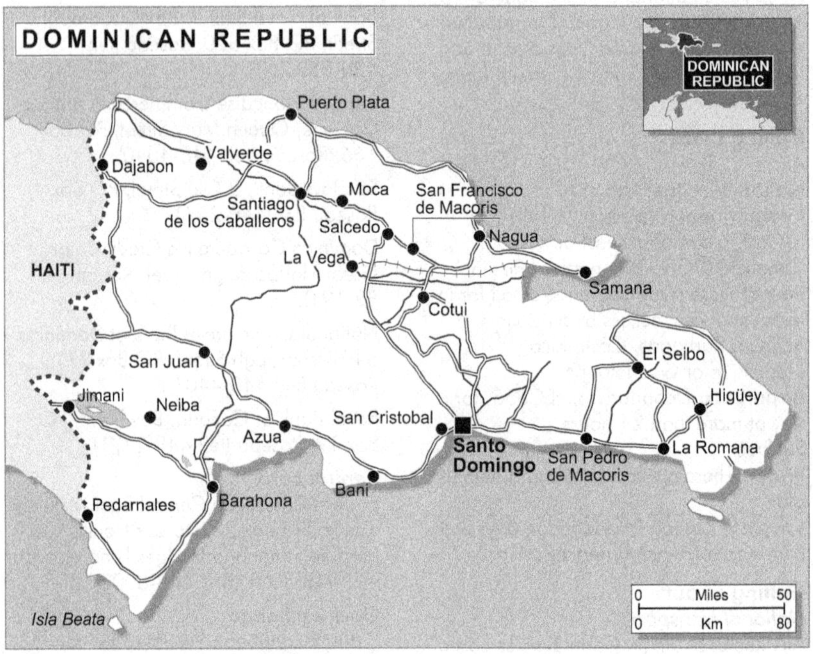

The Dominican Republic shares the island of Hispaniola with Haiti, so that 2010 was largely dominated by the aftermath of the devastating earthquake that struck close to Haiti's capital of Port au Prince in January. In the first months after the earthquake much of the traffic of aid, construction and personnel passed through the Dominican Republic and Santo Domingo de Guzmán became a focal point for summit meetings and conferences concerning relief efforts for its neighbour.

The legislative elections held in May passed without too many disruptions. An agreement was signed on 25 January 2011, whereby the Organisation of American States (OAS) will provide technical assistance in reforming Dominican Republic's electoral law to provide a more transparent system in time for the next presidential elections in 2012 and parliamentary in 2014.

The economy

Fuelled by stimulus measures, according to the United Nations Economic Commission for Latin America and the Caribbean (ECLAC), the economy of the Dominican Republic expanded by 7 per cent in 2010. However, the impact of growing domestic demand on imports and the rising oil bill have pushed the current account deficit up; it is expected to end the year in the area of 7 per cent. Thanks to ample productive capacity, this strong performance has not generated inflationary pressures. The economic slowdown of 2009 had a lagged impact on tax collections, and the planned scale-back of subsidies for the electricity sector was delayed. The authorities therefore cut spending in order to meet the central government's deficit target, equivalent to 2.6 per cent of GDP.

The economic upswing boosted property and consumption tax collections, but relatively slow growth during 2009 also had a delayed impact on direct collections and this led to poor current revenue performance. As a result, during the first half of the year the central government deficit neared the RD$30 billion mark (US$0.78 billion) (3.3 per cent of GDP for the period) agreed with the International Monetary Fund (IMF) for the entire year. To address the situation, the administration amended the budget to hold the central government deficit to no more than 2.6 per cent of GDP.

The deficit was financed virtually entirely with external resources, although monthly auctions of government bonds with maturities of up to 10 years were conducted during the year in order to foster the development of a national debt market. Total non-financial public sector debt ended the year at a level equivalent to 29 per cent of GDP. This is half of a GDP point above the 2009 level.

Projected tax revenues for 2011 were revised downward from the targets agreed with the IMF in late 2009. The tax pressure is expected to be 13.3 per cent instead of the original 15 per cent. The administration announced its intention to make current spending cuts a priority, highlighting cutbacks in transfers to the electricity sector. In view of the above, the 2011 budget provides for a central government deficit equivalent to 1.6 per cent of GDP.

After holding the benchmark rate at a historically low 4 per cent, the Banco Central de la República Dominican (central bank) raised the overnight interest rate by 100 basis points between October and November 2010 in an effort to check the growth of credit to the private sector, which as of October had expanded by more than 16 per cent in nominal terms (11 per cent in real terms).

GDP growth in 2010 was due to buoyant domestic demand. Improving labour conditions and easier access to credit supported consumption. Investment (which expanded by nearly 20 per cent after contracting 14.7 per cent in 2009) has benefited from credit to the private sector and from the flows of foreign direct investment (FDI) and public investment in infrastructure.

During the first nine months of 2010, growing domestic demand lifted the construction sector (15 per cent) and commerce (12.6 per cent). The communications sector also performed well (9.7 per cent). Local manufacturing rose in line with GDP for the first time since 2005, owing to rebounding consumption and to demand from Haiti for finished goods. After contracting for five years, manufacturing in free zones showed signs of recovery in the third quarter, with 3.4 per cent year-on-year growth as operations shifted from textiles to medical equipment manufacturing, jewellery and footwear.

The 5 per cent projected growth for 2011 reflects the impact of less expansionary public policies and falling demand from the United States.

With core inflation stable, the behaviour of fuel prices lessened the impact of indexing the gasoline and diesel fuel taxes. Inflation for 2010 was 6.3 per cent (5.8 per cent in 2009). The shift in monetary policy and the slowdown in activity are expected to keep inflation below 6 per cent for 2011.

Owing to the recovery, the labour participation rate was 54.9 per cent during the first half of 2010. But employment is still 1.4 percentage points below the level recorded in 2007. The broad unemployment rate (which includes persons who did not look for work but are willing to work) fell by half a percentage point to 14.4 per cent.

International trade

Goods exports expanded by 17.3 per cent to the third quarter of 2010 thanks to an upturn in demand from the United States and, to a lesser degree, to greater demand from Haiti for finished goods. Nevertheless, buoyant domestic demand and the increase of more than 40 per cent in the oil bill drove imports up by 27.7 per cent during the period. The result was a trade deficit of nearly 11 per cent of GDP. The surplus in the services trade balance shrank as the nearly 3 per cent increase in tourist arrivals did not offset the rise in freight costs.

Despite slackening external demand, exports in 2011 are expected to benefit from the resumption of nickel exports and the start-up of gold exports from the Pueblo Viejo mine. Along with slower growth and greater energy product price stability, the current account is projected to show a deficit equivalent to 6 per cent of GDP.

Risk assessment

Economy	Fair
Politics	Fair
Regional stability	Good

COUNTRY PROFILE

Historical profile

1492 The island was visited by Christopher Columbus. He named it Hispaniola (Little Spain).
1496 Colombus' brother, Bartolomeo, founded the city of Santo Domingo and his son, Diego was the first governor of the Spanish colony.
1697 Western part of island (Haiti) given to France under Treaty of Ryswick.
1795 Remainder of island (Santo Domingo) ceded to France.
1808 Santo Domingo regained by Spain, after revolt by Spanish creoles.
1821 Independence gained following uprising against Spanish rule.
1822 Annexed by Haiti under Jean-Pierre Boyer.
1844 Boyer was overthrown and the eastern part of the island became independent as the Dominican Republic.
1861–63 President Santana returns republic to Spanish rule.
1864 Spain annuls its annexation of the Dominican Republic after a popular revolt.
1965 Second Dominican Republic declared.
1906 US and Dominican Republic sign 50-year Treaty of Accord.
1916–24 US armed forces occupied the island, following internal disorder.
1930–1961 General Rafael Trujillo leads *coup d'état*, overthrowing President

KEY INDICATORS — Dominican Republic

	Unit	2006	2007	2008	2009	2010
Population	m	8.65	8.78	*8.90	*9.03	9.38
Gross domestic product (GDP)	US$bn	31.72	36.40	45.60	46.70	51.60
GDP per capita	US$	43,827	4,147	5,117	5,176	5,228
GDP real growth	%	10.7	8.5	5.3	3.5	7.8
Inflation	%	7.6	6.1	10.6	1.5	6.3
Industrial output	% change	13.1	2.8	1.7	-2.2	–
Agricultural output	% change	9.9	1.2	-3.4	12.5	–
Exports (fob) (goods)	US$m	6,441.0	7,237.2	6,747.5	5,519.0	–
Imports (fob) (goods)	US$m	11,190.0	13,817.1	15,992.9	12,259.8	–
Balance of trade	US$m	-4,749.0	-6,579.9	-9,245.4	-6,740.8	–
Current account	US$m	-1,122.0	2,230.2	-4,518.6	-2,158.5	-4,435.0
Total reserves minus gold	US$m	2,115.6	2,546.4	2,271.6	2,885.1	3,475.8
Foreign exchange	US$m	2,091.2	2,447.8	2,235.6	2,609.5	3,358.0
Exchange rate	per US$	33.75	33.37	35.45	36.03	36.88

* estimated figure

Horacio Vazquez and becoming a dictator.
1961 Trujillo was assassinated.
1962 Democratic election of Juan Bosch, in the first free elections in 38 years.
1963 Bosch deposed by military.
1965 Civil revolt resulted in another intervention by US armed troops.
1966 Joaquín Balaguer (protégé of Trujillo) won the presidential election, leading the Partido Reformista Social Cristiana (PRSC) (Social Christian Reform Party). He was re-elected in 1970 and 1974, and survived several coup attempts.
1978 Sivestre Antonio Guzmán, (Partido Revolucionario Dominicano (PRD) (Dominican Revolutionary Party)) defeated Balaguer in presidential elections.
1979 The economy deteriorated following two hurricanes that caused US$1 billion in damage and left 200,000 people homeless; fuel prices rose and sugar prices fell.
1994 The constitution was established, setting out the power of the executive.
1996 Leonel Fernández Rayana of the Partido de la Liberación Dominicana (PLD) (Dominican Liberation Party) narrowly won the presidency.
1998 PLD won a majority in both chambers of parliament.
2000 Rafael Hopólito Mejía Domínguez (PRD) won the presidential election.
2002 The PRD won legislative elections. Former president Joaquín Balaguer died.
2004 A two-day general strike was held in protest at the sharp devaluation of the peso. The Dominican Republic joined the Central American Parliament.
2007 The Central American Free Trade Agreement (Cafta) with the US was ratified.
2008 Incumbent Leonel Fernández Rayana (PLD) won the presidential elections.
2010 Following a severe earthquake in Haiti in January, the Dominican Republic became a focal point for summit meetings and conferences concerning relief efforts for its neighbour. A 49 per cent stake in the state-owned Refidomsa oil refinery (near Haina Occidental port) was sold to the Venezuelan PdVSA in May, for US$130 million. In legislative elections held in May, the ruling PLD won 54.61 per cent of the vote (105 deputies and 31 senators), the PRD 41.9 per cent (75 deputies); turnout was 54.15 per cent.
2011 An agreement was signed on 25 January, whereby the Organisation of American States (OAS) will provide technical assistance in reforming Dominican Republic's electoral law to provide a more transparent system. On 12 July the Inter-American Development Bank (IDB) announced that it will disburse US$324 million over the year, of which US$200 million will be used by the government for budgetary support, and in line with macroeconomic stability as stipulated by the IMF in February. This brings the total loans to the Dominican Republic by the IDB up to US$1.9 billion.

Political structure

In addition to their unicameral national parliaments, El Salvador, Guatemala, Honduras, Nicaragua, Panama and Dominican Republic also return directly-elected deputies to the supranational Central American Parliament.

Constitution

The 1994 Constitution prevents the re-election of an individual as president for consecutive periods.

The executive

Executive power rests with the president, who is also head of government and commander-in-chief of the armed forces. The president is directly elected for a one-off four-year term. The cabinet is appointed and presided over by the president. The president, by constitutional decree, names the provincial governors, who are his representatives in each province.

National legislature

The bicameral Congress of the Republic is comprised of a Chamber of Deputies, with 178 deputies, elected for four-year terms by preferential vote and block votes by provinces with one representative per 50,000 citizens, with a minimum of two per province. The 32-member Senate is elected for a four-year term, one member for each province plus one for the Distrito Nacional. The Senate elects the members of the judiciary.

Last elections

16 May 2008 (presidential); 16 May 2010 (parliamentary).

Results: Presidential: Leonel Fernández (DLP) won 53.8 per cent of the vote, Miguel Vargas (DRP) 40.5 per cent, and Amable Aristy (Social Christian Reformist Party) 4.6 per cent.

Parliamentary, Chamber of Deputies: Partido de la Liberación Dominicana (PLD) (Dominican Liberation Party) coalition won 54.6 per cent of the vote (105 seats out of 183), the Partido Revolucionario Dominicano (PRD) (Dominican Revolutionary Party) coalition 41.9 per cent (75), Partido Reformista Social Cristiana (PRSC) (Social Christian Reform Party) 1.46 per cent (3); eight other political parties did not win enough votes to gain any seats. Senate: the PLD won 31 seats out of 32, the PRSC 1. Turnout was around 54.1 per cent.

Next elections

2012 (presidential); 2014 (parliamentary)

Political parties

Ruling party

Partido de la Liberación Dominicana (PLD) (Dominican Liberation Party) (from 2010)

Main opposition party

Gran Alianza Nacional coalition led by Partido Revolucionario Dominicano (PRD) (Dominican Revolutionary Party)

Population

9.38 million (2010; census figure)

Last census: October 2002: 8,562,541

Population density: 168 inhabitants per square km. Urban population: 66 per cent (1995—2001).

Annual growth rate: 1.5 per cent 1994–2004 (WHO 2006)

Ethnic make-up

Mixed race (73 per cent), white (16 per cent), black (11 per cent).

Religions

Roman Catholic (95 per cent). There is also a small Protestant community.

Education

Primary education lasts for six years and is free of charge. There are two systems of secondary education in operation, the traditional has six years of study divided into two-year then four-year cycles. The reform system has two cycles of three years. The emphasis of the former is academic and the latter scientific/technical. Both systems allow for specialised studies.

Secondary schooling is subsidised in private schools.

Literacy rate: 84 per cent adult rate; 92 per cent youth rate (15–24) (Unesco 2005).

Compulsory years: Seven to 17

Pupils per teacher: 28 in primary schools.

Health

Seventy-nine per cent of the population have access to an improved water source.

HIV/Aids

The HIV/Aids infection rates is one of the largest in the Caribbean.

HIV prevalence: 1.7 per cent aged 15–49 in 2003 (World Bank)

Life expectancy: 67 years, 2004 (WHO 2006)

Fertility rate/Maternal mortality rate: 2.7 births per woman, 2004 (WHO 2006)

Birth rate/Death rate: 24 births per 1,000 population; seven deaths per 1,000 population (2003).

Child (under 5 years) mortality rate (per 1,000): 29 per 1,000 live births (World Bank)

Main cities

Santo Domingo de Guzmán (capital, estimated population 2.2 million in 2004), Santiago de los Caballeros (501,800), La Romana (198,0000), San Pedro de

Macoris (167,100), Puerto Plata (133,400), San Francisco de Macoris (131,300), San Cristobal (121,800).

Languages spoken

English is widely spoken.

Official language/s

Spanish

Media

Press freedom is guaranteed by law although some contentious matters are generally avoided, such as the army and Roman Catholic Church.

Press

Dailies: In Spanish, there are several national and regional newspapers including *El Caribe* (www.elcaribecdn.com), *Hoy* (www.hoy.com.do), *Listín Diario* (www.listin.com.do), *Diario Libre* (www3.diariolibre.com) *La Información* (www.lainformacionrd.net), *El Día* (www.eldia.com.do), *Nuevo elDiario* (www.elnuevodiario.com.do) and *El Observador Cibaeño* (www.observador.tk) from Santiago de los Caballeros. An evening newspaper is *El Nacional* (www.elnacional.com.do).

In English, from the northern coast, *Dominican Today* (www.dominicantoday.com), *Gringo News* (www.gringo-times.com) is a humours publication and *The Adscene* (www.theadscene.com) is also in Spanish and German.

Weeklies: In Spanish *(A)Hora* (www.ahora.com.do), covers general interest news.

Periodicals: In English the monthly *The Puerto Plata Report* (www.popreport.com), is a regional magazine from the northern coast.

Broadcasting

The national government-owned broadcaster is Corporación Estatal de Radio y Televisión (CERTV).

Commercial broadcasting companies are generally owned by a few either economically or politically powerful entities.

Radio: There are over 200 FM radio stations. CERTV (www.certvdominicana.com) operates three stations, Dominicana FM, Quisqueya FM and 620 AM. Commercial stations include LA91 FM (www.la91fm.com), Super Mix (CDN) (www.elcaribecdn.com.do), La Nueva 106.9 FM (www.lanueva106fm.com) and Radio Moca (http://cima100fm.com).

Television: The national public broadcaster is CERTV (www.certvdominicana.com), which operates Canal 4. There are many cable and satellite services including the government-run, commercial Antena Latina (http://antenalatina.antena-sin.com) Canal 7. Private stations include Hola Gente (www.holagente.com.do), Color Vision (www.colorvision.com.do), Telemicro (www.telemicro.com.do), Cadena de Noticias (CDN) (www.elcaribecdn.com) news TV, Aster TV (www.aster.com.do) for children, Telesistema (www.telesistema11.tv) and Teleantilles (www.tele-antillas.tv).

Advertising

All forms of media accept advertising, which is widely distributed.

News agencies

Other news agencies: Caribbean Net News: www.caribbeannetnews.com
Prensa Latina: www.prensalatina.com.mx

Economy

The Dominican Republic has become a middle income country, as ranked by the World Bank. The economy has moved from a typically agrarian to a service based, open market system, following the opening up of the economy to foreign investment and domestic macroeconomic reforms. The manufacturing sector is centred on foreign owned operations, based in a number of free-trade zones, and involved in assembly or light manufacturing. Other, service orientated companies, such customer service call centres, also operate from these zones. Tourism is the single, principal industry and leading employer, while mining of ferronickel, gold and silver are the major export commodities, along with agricultural products such as sugar, coffee, tobacco, cocoa, meats and consumer goods.

GDP growth was 5.3 per cent in 2008, falling to 3.5 per cent in 2009 as the impact of the global economic crisis cut trade as well as export commodities and tourism. However by 2010 GDP was estimated to have grown to 5.5 per cent and this is projected to remain stable in 2011. On 12 July 2011, the Inter-American Development Bank (IDB) announced that it will disburse US$324 million over the year, of which US$200 million will be used by the government for budgetary support, and in line with macroeconomic stability as stipulated by the IMF in February. This brings the total loans to the Dominican Republic by the IDB up to US$1.9 billion.

Remittances from expatriate workers make an essential contribution to the economy; 1.5 million live abroad, mostly in the US but increasingly in Europe and in 2009 US$3.5 billion (7.3 per cent of GDP) was injected into the economy, particularly into family economies. Remittances were estimated to have fallen to US$3.3 per cent in 2010 as the economies of host countries adjusted following the economic crisis.

External trade

The Dominican Republic is the only Caribbean member of the Central America Free Trade Agreement (DR-Cafta), which includes Costa Rica, El Salvador, Guatemala, Honduras and the US; it is also a member of the Caribbean Community Common Market (Caricom), along with 15 other members.

There are a number of free trade zones (FTZ) which manufacture clothes and footwear, leather goods and jewellery, electronic and medical products, pharmaceuticals and tobacco for export.

Imports

Foodstuffs, petroleum, industrial raw materials, cotton and fabrics, chemicals and pharmaceuticals, consumer goods and foodstuffs.

Main sources: US (typically 40 per cent of total), China (10 per cent), Venezuela (5 per cent).

Exports

Ferro-nickel, sugar, gold, silver, coffee, cocoa, tobacco, meats and consumer goods.

Main destinations: US (typically 62 per cent of total), Haiti (14 per cent), The Netherlands (2 per cent).

Agriculture

Farming

The principal commercial crop is sugar cane, production of which has fluctuated due to vagaries of weather, falling export demand and labour shortages.

The main agricultural exports – sugar, coffee, cocoa and tobacco – account for just under a half of the country's export earnings. Rice, vegetables and citrus fruits are grown for home consumption.

Cattle-raising has expanded considerably and commercial fishing is being developed.

Estimates of cultivated arable land vary between 18–25 per cent; pasture 17–30 per cent; woodland/forest 25–40 per cent. Soil is generally fertile and rainfall/water availability is adequate.

Agriculture is becoming more commercialised. The country benefits from agreements that provide it with duty free access to the US markets. These include the Generalised System of Preferences, the US Caribbean Basin Initiative.

Industry and manufacturing

The industrial sector contributes around a third of GDP and employs up to a quarter of the workforce.

Activity is centred on sugar refining (which is the dominant industry), cement production, the processing of foodstuffs, tobacco, beverages and textiles. The country is the largest exporter in the Caribbean region of apparel to the US. Some of the best known labels are manufactured in the Dominican Republic. The Caribbean Basin Initiative allows the country's textiles duty-free entry to the US market. However, with China now a member of the WTO this trade is threatened.

Other light industries include plastics, rubber, chemicals and paper.
The emphasis is on encouraging joint ventures that utilise a high percentage of local materials, expanding facilities at the main industrial free zones (La Ramona, San Pedro de Macoris, Santiago) and overcoming the serious supply/energy problems. The free trade zone programme is the country's leading earner of foreign exchange.

Tourism
Orbitz, a leading, US-based, travel company ranked the Dominican Republic fourth most popular Caribbean destination in 2008, with typical resort facilities and sports activities, plus Caribbean cultural events.
Tourism constituted 17.5 per cent of GDP and 16.1 per cent of all employment in 2010. Since 2005, the Dominican Republic has received an annual average of 4.3 million air passenger arrivals, of which 4 million were tourists. Overwhelmingly, the largest contingent of visitors over the period was from the US, with an average 1.1 million. Arrivals by sea have grown steadily since the new, exclusive Marina Royale in Samaná was opened in 2006, peaking in 2009 with 496,728 arrivals. The Haiti earthquake in January 2010 may have had a detrimental effect on visitors, as numbers were estimated at 352,539, for the year. Tourists may not have wished to be seen relaxing in close proximity (Haiti and the Dominican Republic share the island of Hispaniola) to so much devastation.
In January 2011, a new, award-winning website, 'My Paradise' www.godominicanrepublic.com), was launched to promote tourism.

Mining
The mining sector as a whole typically accounts for 2 per cent of GDP and employs 3 per cent of the workforce.
Gold, silver and ferro-nickel are all mined in significant quantities. Gypsum, limestone and marble are mined for the domestic market. Deposits of copper, iron, titanium and platinum also exist.
In March 2003, Canada-based Placer Dome was given ownership of the Pueblo Viejo gold mine for 25 years, following a vote in the Senate. The mine, which has reserves of 15–30 million troy ounces, is set to see around US$350 million of investment between 2003–08.
The country's largest mining facility is operated by Falconbridge, a Canadian company, which exports 33,000 tonnes of nickel per year.
Some industry analysts believe that large deposits of nickel, copper and gold have yet to be discovered.

Hydrocarbons
There are no known hydrocarbon reserves. Consumption was 119,000 barrels per day (bpd) in 2008, all of which was imported. In 2005, the Dominican Republic, plus a number of other Caribbean states, signed an agreement with Venezuela to establish PetroCaribe, a multi-national oil company, owned by the participating states. PetroCaribe buys low-priced Venezuelan crude oil under long-term payment plans. In June 2009 is was agreed that a 49 per cent stake in the state-owned refinery would be sold to Venezuela for US$130 million in exchange for oil supplied via Petrocaribe.
There are no known reserves of natural gas but imports were 254.8 million cubic metres of liquefied natural gas (LNG). There is a regasification terminal that feeds two gas-fired power plants with LNG imported from Trinidad and Tobago. Around 750,000 tonnes of coal is consumed in energy production.

Energy
Total installed generating capacity was 5,550MW in 2007, producing over 13 billion kilowatt hours. The energy market has been deregulated and the US-AES Corporation is the single largest private energy provider, owning seven power plants with a total capacity of 988MW, including a regasification terminal that feeds liquefied natural gas to two separate gas-fired power plants with a total capacity of 555MW and a coal-fired power station at Itabo with a capacity of 295MW. Hydropower accounts for over 400MW of all electricity produced and there are plans to double capacity.

Financial markets
Stock exchange
Bolsa de Valores de la República Dominicana (Dominican Republic Stock Exchange)

Banking and insurance
The foreign investment law of 1997 permits overseas banks to operate banks in the Dominican Republic.
The banking sector hit a crisis in 2003 when the Banco Intercontinental (Baninter) collapsed as a result of massive fraud.
The Women's Development bank (Banmujer) began operations in 2001, lending small loans of around US$1,000 to women for entrepreneurial ventures.
Central bank
Banco Central de la República Dominicana.
Main financial centre
Santo Domingo.

Time
GMT minus four hours

Geography
The Caribbean island of Hispaniola is divided north/south into the Dominican Republic in the east, occupying around 65 per cent of the land, and Haiti in the west. The closest other islands are Jamaica in the south-west, Cuba in the west, the Turks and Caicos in the north and Puerto Rico in the east.
In the centre of the island the *Cordillera Central* is the tallest mountain range with peaks over 3,000 metres. Lake Enriquillo, the largest lake and lowest spot, is located in the south-west.
Hemisphere
Northern

Climate
Tropical with temperatures ranging from 27 degrees Celsius (C) during the dry season (November–April) to 37 degrees C from June–October when humidity is highest.

Entry requirements
Passports
Required by all. The exception is nationals of US and Canada, who may travel with proof of citizenship including photo ID, birth certificate or driving licence and after purchasing a tourist card (US$10). All US and Canadian nationals require a passport for re-entry to their country from January 2007.
All passports must have twice as much time left of validity as the length of stay in the Dominican Republic.
Visa
Required by all. Some exceptions can be found at www.dr1.com/travel/prepare/documentation.shtml; a list of nationals that may enter with a tourist card is also given.
Business visitors and visitors from countries that may not use a tourist card should contact the nearest Dominican Republic consulate.
Currency advice/regulations
The import and export of local currency is prohibited. Only a limited number of foreign currencies may be exchanged in the Dominican Republic. While the accepted currencies include the euro, the Canadian dollar, and pound sterling, the US offers the maximum exchange rate. On departure up to 30 per cent of exchanged currency can be reconverted, in US dollars only, on presentation of official exchange reciepts.
Import of foreign currency must be declared and export cannot exceed the imported amount. Travellers cheques, in US dollars, are accepted in most locations. ATMs, dispensing the Dominican Republic peso only, are found in city and tourist centres.

Customs

Prohibited imports

Illegal drugs, weapons, plants and vegetables and pornographic material.

Health (for visitors)

Mandatory precautions

Yellow fever certificate if travelling from an infected area.

Advisable precautions

Vaccinations for meningitis, typhoid, diphtheria polio and TB; other lesser risks include hepatitis A and B and dengue fever. Bilharzia is endemic; use only well chlorinated and maintained swimming pools. Malaria precautions are recommended. Rabies is a risk.

Water precautions are essential; use only bottled or boiled water. Eat only well cooked meals, preferably served hot. Pork, salad and mayonnaise may carry increased risk. Vegetables should be cooked and fruit peeled.

Health insurance (to include emergency medical repatriation) is strongly recommended, as medical care is limited and variable in quality. All personal medication should be carried, with their prescription.

Hotels

Following intensive tourist development, there are a full range of hotels available. Tourist locations charge more than city hotels and in general hotels are considerably more expensive during the winter. Bills usually include 12 per cent government tax and 10 per cent service charge.

Public holidays (national)

Fixed dates

1 Jan (New Year's Day), 6 Jan (Epiphany), 21 Jan (Our Lady of Altagracia), 26 Jan (Duarte's Birthday), 27 Feb (Independence Day), 1 May (Labour Day), 16 Jul (Restoration Day), ^24 Sep (Our Lady of las Mercedes), 6 Nov (Constitution Day), 25 Dec (Christmas Day).

^ Businesses may take Mondays *in lieu*.

Variable dates

Good Friday (Mar/Apr), Corpus Christi (May/Jun).

Working hours

Banking

Mon–Fri: 0830–1700.

Business

Mon–Fri: 0800–1200, 1400–1800.

Government

Mon–Fri: 0800–1500.

Telecommunications

Mobile/cell phones

There are 1800/1900 GSM services available in most urban areas.

Electricity supply

110–120V AC, 60 cycles.

Weights and measures

The metric system has been adopted. However, certain other units are still in use, eg ounces and pounds are used in weighing solids, petrol and motor oils are measured in imperial gallons, cooking oil is retailed in pounds and fabrics are measured by the yard. Land surfaces in rural areas are generally measured by tarea – equal to 624 square metres.

Getting there

Air

International airport/s: Santo Domingo-Las Américas (SDQ), 30km east of city, duty-free shop, bar, restaurant, bank, post office, shops, hotel reservations, car hire; Gregorio Luperon International Puerto Plata (POP), 18km from city, bank, duty-free shop, restaurant, bar, car hire.

Airport tax: International departures US$10, excluding transit passengers.

Surface

Road: The main route runs from Haiti via Elias Pina.

Main port/s: There are 14 ports, including Santo Domingo (the largest) and Haina.

Getting about

National transport

Air: There are flights between Santo Domingo, Santiago, Samana, Punta Cana and Puerto Plata. These are provided by Bavaro Sun Flight, Aerolineas Santo Domingo and Dorado Air.

Road: There are about 17,120km of roads. Highways link Santo Domingo-Hinguey, Montecristo, Dajabon, San Juan, Elias Pina. There is a direct route from Santo Domingo to Port-au-Prince in Haiti.

Buses: There are bus stations in all towns. Fairly numerous services from Santo Domingo to Puerto Plata, La Romana – journey times vary. Also to Barahona and Samana.

Rail: There are a number of freight-only railways.

City transport

Taxis: In Santo Domingo taxis are freely available in the main business districts. These are not metered and it is advisable to agree the price with the driver before setting out. Taxis which travel off these routes may be difficult to find, especially at night. No tip is expected.

Buses, trams & metro: Buses in Santo Domingo are cheap, though crowded.

Car hire

National or international licence required. Chauffeur-driven cars can be negotiated with taxi drivers outside main hotels. Car hire facilities are good, but fairly expensive.

BUSINESS DIRECTORY

The addresses listed below are a selection only. While World of Information makes every endeavour to check these addresses, we cannot guarantee that changes have not been made, especially to telephone numbers and area codes. We would welcome any corrections.

Telephone area codes

This international direct dialling code (IDD) for the Dominican Republic is +1 809 followed by subscriber's number.

Useful telephone numbers

Santo Domingo

Emergency (Ambulance, Police): 911

Police:	682-3151
Police (radio patrol):	533-1074
Centro Médico Nacional (hospital):	682-0171
Fire Department:	682-2000
Red Cross:	682-4545

Chambers of Commerce

American Chamber of Commerce of the Dominican Republic, Avenida Sarasota 20, Torre Empresarial, PO Box 95-2, Santo Domingo (Tel: 381-0777; fax: 381-0286; e-mail: amcham@codetel.net.do).

British Chamber of Commerce of the Dominican Republic, Avenida San Martin 253, Edificio Santanita, PO Box 718-2, Santo Domingo (tel: 616-2335; fax: 616-2336; e-mail: britcham@tricom.net).

Santiago Cámara de Comercio y Producción, Avenida Las Carreras 7, Edificio Empresarial, Santiago (tel: 582-2856; fax: 241-4546; e-mail: csantiago@camarasantiago.com).

Santo Domingo Cámara de Comercio y Producción, Calle Arzobispo Nouel 206, PO Box 815, Santo Domingo (tel: 682-2688; fax: 685-2228; e-mail: camara.sto.dgo@codetel.net.do).

Banking

Banco BHD, Ave 27 de Febrero esq, Winston Churchill, Santo Domingo DN (tel: 243-3232; fax: 541-4949).

Banco del Exterior Dominicano, Ave Abraham Lincoln No. 756, Piantini, Santo Domingo (tel: 565-5540; fax: 565-5547).

Banco de los Trabajadores De La República Dominicana, Av México Esq Calle Altagracia, Santo Domingo (tel: 682-0171; fax: 685-6536).

Banco de Reservas de la República Dominica, Isabel La Catolica No. 72, Santo Domingo (tel: 688-2241; fax: 685-0602).

Banco Dominicano del Progreso, Ave John F Kennedy No. 3, Miraflores, Santo

Domingo (tel: 563-3233; fax: 563-2451).

Banco Gerencial y Fiduciario Dominicano, Ave 27 de Febrero No 50, El Vergel, Santo Domingo (tel: 541-9400; fax: 567-6747).

Banco Latinoamericano, Gustavo Mejía Ricart Esq Agustín Lara, Ens Piantini, Santo Domingo (tel: 562-2662; fax: 562-1915).

Banco Mercantil, Ave Bolivar No. 308 Esq Jose Joaquín Pérez Gazcue, Santo Domingo (tel: 221-7151; 688-0608).

Banco Metropolitano, Ave Lope de Vega Esq Gustavo Mejía Ricart, Edif. Goico Castro, Ens Naco, Santo Domingo (tel: 562-4242; fax: 540-1566).

Banco Nacional de Crédito, John F Kennedy Esq Tiradentes, Ens Naco, Santo Domingo (tel: 540-4441; fax: 567-4698).

Banco Popular Dominicano, Av. John F Kennedy No 20 Esq Máximo Gómez, Torre Popular, 11 Avo. Piso, Santo Domingo (tel: 544-5900; fax: 544-5999).

Bank of Nova Scotia, Ave. John F Kennedy Esq Lope de Vega, Ens Naco, Santo Domingo (tel: 544-1700; fax: 542-6302).

Citibank, Ave John F Kennedy No 1 Esq San Martín, Santo Domingo (tel: 566-5611; fax: 567-2255).

Central bank

Banco Central de la República Dominicana, PO Box: 1347, Calle Pedro Henríquez Ureña, Esq Leopoldo Navarro, Santo Domingo (tel: 221-9111; fax: 686-7488; e-mail: info@bancentral.gov.do).

Stock exchange

Bolsa de Valores de la República Dominicana (Dominican Republic Stock Exchange): www.bolsard.com

Travel information

Aerolíneas Argo, Avenida 27 de Febrero 409, Santo Domingo (tel: 566-1844).

Dominicana de Aviación, Leopoldo Navarre, Edificio San Rafael, PO Box 1415, Santo Domingo (tel: 687-7111).

Santo Domingo-Las Américas International Airport, Santo Domingo (tel: 549-0450/0480).

Ministry of tourism

Secretaría de Estado de Turismo, PO Apdo 497, Avenida México esp, 30 de Marzo, Ofiinas Gubernanentales Bloque B, Santo Domingo (tel: 221-4660; e-mail: dominicantourism@globalserve.net).

Other useful addresses

Asociación Dominicana de Empresas de Inversión Extranjera (ASIEX), Av Independencia Santo Domingo, RD (tel: 535-6165; fax: 535-1744).

Asociación Dominicana de Exportadores (ADOEXPO), Av W Churchill 5, Santo Domingo (tel: 532-6779; fax: 533-9734).

Asociación Dominicana de Zonas Francas (ADOZONA), Gustavo Mejía Ricart 72, Santo Domingo, RD (tel: 566-0230, 566-0437).

British Embassy, Floor 7, Edificio Corominas Pepín, Avenida 27 de Febrero No. 233, Santo Domingo (tel: 472-7111; fax: 427-7574).

Centro Dominicano de Promoción de Exportaciones (CEDOPEX), Av 27 de Febrero, Plaza de la Independencia, Santo Domingo, RD (tel: 530-5549; fax: 530-8208).

Consejo Nacional de Zonas Francas de Exportación, Leopoldo Navarro 61, Edif San Rafael 5ta Planta, Santo Domingo (tel: 686-8077; fax: 686-8079).

Corporación de Fomento Industrial, Av 27 de Febrero, Plaza de la Independencia, Santo Domingo, RD (tel: 530-1686; fax: 530-1303).

ITT-America Cables and Radio Inc, Julio Verne 21, Santo Domingo (tel: 682-3115).

Public Enterprise Reform Committee, Gustavo Mejía Ricart No 73, Santo Domingo (tel: 683-3591; fax: 683-3964).

RCA Global Communications Inc, Edificio Diez, Calle Conde 203, Santo Domingo (tel: 682-3722).

Secretariat of State for Finance, Avda México, Santo Domingo, DN.

Secretariat of State for Industry and Commerce, Edif. de Oficinas Gubernamentales 7, Avda México, Santo Domingo, DN (tel: 685-171).

Internet sites

Dominican Republic One: http://www.dr1.com/

Export promotion (in Spanish): http://www.cedopex.gov.do/

Easter Island

COUNTRY PROFILE

Historical profile

1680 Work on the *moai* (the large stone statues for which Easter Island is famous) ceased due to tribal wars induced by overpopulation and famine.
1722 The Dutch navigator, Jacob Roggeveen, came to the island on Easter Sunday, hence its name.
1770 Spaniards came from Peru and named the island San Carlos.
1774 Captain Cook visited the island.
1862–63 More than 1,000 islanders were kidnapped and despatched to Peru to work on the guano islands and plantations. Only 15 survived to be repatriated, but some were carrying infectious diseases which quickly decimated the population.
1866 Catholic missionaries converted the remaining population to Christianity.
1871 Conflict between the missionaries and a French settler, who had established a sheep farm, forced the missionaries to leave with around 100 followers. Around 110 natives remained on the island.
1888 The island was annexed by Chile.
1966 The international airport opened and Chile declared the island a province.
1986 The airport runway was extended for use as an emergency landing strip for the US Nasa space shuttle.
1996 Easter Island was declared a World Heritage Site by Unesco.
2002 The first outbreak of dengue fever in Chile occurred on Easter Island.
2003 Unesco awarded a German company a contract for US$11.5 million to restore the stone *moai*. Work was completed in 2005.
2006 Melania Carolina Hotu Hey was appointed as *Intendenta* (provincial governor).
2008 A Finnish visitor was arrested for damaging an ancient monument when he chipped off a piece of a *moai*, while wishing to find how hard the stone was. He was later forced to make a public apology, pay a fine of US$17,000 and was banned from the island until 2011.
2009 In a referendum, residents voted by up to 90 per cent in favour of legislation to curb the number of migrants from Chile allowed to live and work on the island. As tourism developed, hundreds of Chileans from the mainland migrated to work in bars, hotels and as taxi drivers. Luz Zasso Paoa became mayor.
2010 Pedro Edmunds Proa (a pro-independence politician) was appointed provincial governor of Easter Island in March. On 7 August, around 70 people, who had been squatting on public land in Hanga Roa were evicted; the squatters claimed the land was ancestral and therefore theirs. Pedro Edmunds resigned and Carmen Cardinali was appointed to the post of *Intendenta* on 13 August. Clashes between native islanders of the Rapu Nui group and Chilean police occurred on 4 December, after the group refused to leave buildings occupied earlier in 2010; they claimed the buildings had been 'illegally taken' from their ancestors. Security forces used pellet guns and rubber bullets, injuring around 19 demonstrators, one of whom was air-lifted to Chile for emergency medical treatment; arrests were made and reinforcements travelled to the island.
2011 Police evicted a group of native Rapa Nui from a luxury hotel on 6 February. The indigenous Hitorangi clan had occupied the Hangaroa Village and Spa since August 2010, protesting that their ancestors had been cheated out of ownership of the hotel land. They were also protesting at plans to develop Easter Island.

Political structure

Easter Island is administered as a province of Chile (part of the Valparaíso region), with a governor and locally elected council.
Elections are held every four years for six councillors, who then elect the mayor.
A Council of Elders was formed in 1983 to represent the interests of the native *Rapa Nuis* (Easter Islanders).

Form of state

Province of Chile

Political parties

Island politicians belong to a number of national political parties including Partido Demócrata Cristiano (PDC) (Christian Democratic Party), Partido Humanista (PH) (Humanist Party), Unión Demócrata Independiente (UDI) (Independent Democratic Union) and the Partido por la Democracia (PLD) (Democratic Party)

Political situation

The pro-independent movement in Isla de Pascua (Easter Island) (Rapa Nui) was given tacit support by the former governor Pedro Edmunds Proa when, in 2010 he

KEY FACTS

Official name: Isla de Pascua (Easter Island) (Rapa Nui)

Head of State: President of Chile: Verónica Michelle Bachelet Jeria; represented by *Intendenta* (provincial governor) Carmen Cardinali (from 13 Aug 2010)

Head of government: Mayor Luz Zasso Paoa (since 2009)

Area: 180 square km

Population: 4,781 (2009)*

Capital: Hanga Roa (only inhabited township)

Official language: Spanish

Currency: Chilean peso (CH$) = 100 centavos

Exchange rate: CH$523.48 per US$ (Oct 2011)

Visitor numbers: 40,000 (annually)*

* estimated figure

allowed islanders to squat on government land close to the centre of Hanga Roa. Despite claims that it was ancestral land and denials that they were trespassing the central government in Chile moved quickly to diffuse the situation by replacing Governor Pedro Edmunds Proa with another islander politician Carmen Cardinali, on 13 August. Governor Cardinali authorised the eviction of the protestors and demolition of their temporary structures.

Population
4,781 (2009)*
Last census: 2002: 3,791
Annual growth rate: 0.0 per cent (2003)
Religions
Christianity

Main cities
Hanga Roa is the only inhabited township.

Languages spoken
Rapa Nui, an Eastern Polynesian language, is spoken. English is not used.
Official language/s
Spanish

Media
Press
News publications are pamphlets and internet connections, such as *Te Rapa Nui* (www.rapanui.co.cl). Newspapers from the mainland have to be flown in and may be days old. The bi-annual (May and October) *Rapa Nui Journal* (www.islandheritage.org) is an academic publication.
Broadcasting
Radio: There are several radio stations, broadcasting in Spanish, including the (Chilean) government-run Radio Cooperativa (www.cooperativa.cl), the private Radio Activa (www.radioactiva.cl) from Santiago, ADN Radio (www.adnradio.cl) and Armada de Chile broadcasts to military personnel. Radio Manukena is a community radio station broadcasting in the local language.
Television: Satellite television is broadcast from Chile (TV Chile: www.tvchile.cl) with reception available on the island.

Economy
Tourism is the principal industry, which offers employment to a significant proportion of the population. There are a number of hotels and guesthouses catering for visitors interested in archaeological and activity pursuits. The Rapa Nui National Park and open museum encompasses almost the entire island and is run by the inhabitants. Flights link the island with Santiago, Chile, and French Polynesia.
Fishing and commerce also provide income.

External trade
As a province of Chile, all international trade agreements are negotiated by the government in Santiago.
Imports
Main imports are food, fuel, construction materials and machinery from Chile.
Exports
Main exports are tuna, avocados and pineapples to Chile.

Agriculture
Traditional subsistence farming is carried out.
Although the island is predominantly grassland, pine, eucalyptus and fruit trees have been planted.
The island's main crops are bananas, pineapples, sweet potatoes, yams, sugar cane, maize, potatoes, tomatoes, castor beans, melons, grapes and avocados. Sheep farming has declined rapidly since the mid-twentieth century due to soil erosion. There are wild horses in addition to those used as draught animals and for riding. Poultry bred on the island includes pigeons, quail and ducks.
Lobster, tuna and king fish are an important local source of protein.

Industry and manufacturing
There is a small manufacturing sector, based on the production of local handicrafts.

Tourism
Easter Island is famous for its giant stone heads, called *moai* (statues), of which nearly a thousand of these ancient sculptures are strewn along the coastline and extinct volcano. Easter Island was awarded Unesco status as a world heritage site in 1995 and in 2005, the *moai* were restored by Unesco. Easter Island is visited by around 40,000 tourists each year not only to see the *moai* but also, they are attracted in early-February by the Tapati Festival. Many visitors arrive either by airplane or cruise ships, which because the island lacks a deep-water harbour must land passengers and crew by tenders. There are over a dozen hotels and a number of hostels catering for visitors. There are also opportunities for hiking, horse-riding, cycling and swimming.

Hydrocarbons
There are no known oil reserves; all domestic needs are met by imports from Chile.

Energy
The former state-owned and now limited company, Sasipa (Sociedad Agricola y Servicios Isla de Pascua) manages the supply of electricity on the island. In 2007 a 15-year contract began to develop and plan the provision of a comprehensive electrical service, including the investment needed and projected growth.

Banking and insurance
Central bank
Banco del Estado de Chile

Time
GMT minus six hours

Geography
Easter Island is a small volcanic rock, measuring 166 sq km, in the southern Pacific Ocean. It lies about 3,500km off the coast of Chile, the closest land mass. The nearest inhabited island (Pitcairn) is about 1,600km to the west. The island is roughly triangular in shape, with a rugged coastline and few beaches. Inland are low rolling hills and grasslands. There is no flowing water; volcanic craters round the edge of the island hold standing water.
Hemisphere
Southern

Climate
Subtropical, cooled by constant winds. Average rainfall is 1,250mm falling mainly in June–July; average temperature ranges from 16–27 degrees Celsius.

Entry requirements
Passports
Required by all, with the exception of tourists travelling from Argentina, Brazil, Colombia, Paraguay and Uruguay, for whom national identity cards are sufficient. Entry will be permitted only with proof of return/onward passage and sufficient funds for stay.
Visa
As a province of Chile, the requirements are the same. Citizens of neighbouring countries or most EU states do not need visas. For further details contact the local embassy. Business visas are not required by those citizens who do not need a tourist visa; all others, including those who do not normally require them but who are visiting on short-term contracts or receive fees from a local company, do need a visa.
On arrival a 'tourist card' is issued and must be returned when leaving. Onward/return passage is necessary.

Health (for visitors)
Mandatory precautions
Vaccination certificates are required for yellow fever if travelling from an infected area.
Advisable precautions
Vaccinations for diphtheria, tuberculosis, hepatitis A and B, polio, tetanus and typhoid are recommended. There is a risk of rabies.

Telecommunications

Telephone/fax

There is a limited telephone service available. There is no direct international dialling, although satellite links enable calls to be made through the international operator in Chile.

Getting there

Air

National airline: Lan-Chile

International airport/s: Mataveri International (IPC), 1.6km south of Hanga Roa.

Surface

Main port/s: Hanga Roa.

Getting about

National transport

There are few surfaced roads. Four-wheel drive vehicles, motor cycles and horses are the main means of transportation. Minibuses are used by tourists.

Car hire

Make local enquiries regarding availability of car hire.

BUSINESS DIRECTORY

The addresses listed below are a selection only. While World of Information makes every endeavour to check these addresses, we cannot guarantee that changes have not been made, especially to telephone numbers and area codes. We would welcome any corrections.

Telephone area codes

The international direct dialling (IDD) code for Easter Island is +56 (Chile) followed area code 32 and Easter Island number 100 + subscriber's number.

Other useful addresses

Gobernación Provincial, Isla de Pascua (tel: 100-254)

Internet sites

Easter Island Foundation:
www.netaxs.com/~trance/rapanui.html

KEY FACTS

Official name: República del Ecuador (Republic of Ecuador)

Head of State: President Rafael Vicente Correa Delgado (from 2007; re-elected 26 Apr 2009)

Head of government: President Rafael Correa

Ruling party: Movimiento PAIS (Patria Altiva i Soberana) (Proud and Sovereign Fatherland Movement) (from 26 Apr 2009)

Area: 270,670 square km

Population: 14.31 million (2010; census figure)

Capital: Quito

Official language: Spanish

Currency: US dollar (US$) = 100 cents

Exchange rate: US$1.00 per US$ (Oct 2011)

GDP per capita: US$3,984 (2010)

GDP real growth: 3.20% (2010)

GDP: US$58.90 billion (2010)

Labour force: 4.48 million (2010)

Unemployment: 7.60% (2010)

Inflation: 3.60% (2010)

Oil production: 495,000 bpd (2010)

Balance of trade: US$78.00 million (2009)

Ecuador

Between 2001 and 2008, according to the World Bank, the Ecuadorian economy grew at an average annual rate of 5 per cent. In 2009, as a result of the global crisis, gross domestic product (GDP) growth dropped to 0.4 per cent, recovering in 2010 to 3.6 per cent. Inflation has remained relatively low since the 'dollarisation' of the economy in 2001. The government's current strategy has been to sustain economic growth by significantly increasing public spending by, mostly, investing in housing, transportation and energy projects. As a result of these policies, public spending has increased by 305 per cent between 2005 and 2010. To finance public spending, the government has used additional resources besides the traditional revenue services, which have included foreign bilateral loans, loans from social security funds held by the Instituto Ecuatoriano de Seguridad Social (IESS) (Ecuadorian Social Security Institute), extraordinary oil revenues, and tax reforms. Income poverty (according to the national poverty line) decreased form 37.6 per cent in 2006 to 32.8 per cent in 2010, likewise extreme poverty fell from 16.9 per cent in 2006 to 15.4 per cent in 2009. Poverty and inequality continue to be Ecuador's main challenges, this has been acknowledged by the government and has driven the large scale expansion of social programmes. The 2009–13 Development Plan has a strong emphasis on reducing poverty, as well as stressing social inclusion, equality and justice.

The economy

Following a sharp slowdown in 2009, according to the United Nations Economic Commission for Latin America and the Caribbean (ECLAC) Ecuador's economy was expected to have grown by 3.5 per cent in 2010, on the strength of higher oil prices and an upturn in private consumption and domestic credit. Nevertheless, public-sector accounts and the balance of payments current account are running a deficit. Against a backdrop of higher public investment, 3.5 per cent growth was projected to be maintained in 2011, subject to oil prices and the availability of financing for investment projects.

Tax receipts rose significantly in 2010 owing to a reduction in tax evasion and an increase in economic activity. Between January and September 2010, value added tax receipts shot up by 21.5 per cent over the same period in 2009. Other tax receipts were up sharply, too, with the exception of income tax, which was still feeling the effects of the 2009 downturn. Higher international oil prices pushed up petroleum revenues; central government revenues are therefore expected to climb from 22.3 per cent of GDP in 2009 to 25.5 per cent in 2010.

Current and capital expenditure grew at a moderate rate because of the difficulties in securing financing for investment projects, especially in the first half of the year. Therefore, although the central government had budgeted for a larger increase, estimates are that expenditure has only risen from 27.3 per cent of GDP in 2009 to 28.3 per cent of GDP in 2010. With higher revenues and lower-than-expected expenditures, the projected central government deficit of 2.9 per cent of GDP is lower than the budgeted 5.6 per cent. The problems caused by the limited availability of financing began to improve in April 2010, thanks to initial disbursements on a series of loans from the Andean Development Corporation for a total of US$755 million. In addition, the government received a US$1 billion loan from the China Development Bank in August. These loans took external public debt from US$7.39 billion at year-end 2009 (14.2 per cent of GDP) to US$8.59 billion in October 2010 (15.5 per cent of GDP). As a result, domestic public debt rose from US$2.84 billion at the end of 2009 (5.5 per cent of GDP) to US$4.52 billion in October 2010 (8.1 per cent of GDP).

During the first half of 2010, the real exchange rate appreciated moderately. However, the appreciation of the currencies of Ecuador's main trading partners and the general weakness of the dollar led to a period of real depreciation that began in June and continued for the rest of the year.

In the second quarter, the banking sector began to step up lending to the private sector. Demand for credit escalated as the economy improved. In October 2010, private bank lending to the private sector was up 18.3 per cent from October 2009. Although public banks account for less than 10 per cent of total credit to the private sector, their share of overall financing has been growing steadily..

Unlike 2009, private consumption and gross fixed capital formation looked set to be the most robust components of aggregate demand in 2010. However, public consumption slackened because of financing problems early in the year. The manufacturing, construction, trade and financial sectors all looked likely to post brisk growth in 2011. In contrast, the electricity and water sectors will contract because low water levels in late 2009 and early 2010 cut hydroelectric output. Oil refining was also down during 2010, as maintenance work at the Esmeraldas refinery reduced its production capacity.

Modest inflation

During 2010, prices grew at a moderate and steady rate and average inflation of 3.6 per cent was projected for the year. Labour indicators improved in 2010 in line with the economic recovery. Unemployment fell from 9.1 per cent in the first quarter to 7.4 per cent in the third quarter. Although under-employment also fell, it still hovered at about 50 per cent of the economically active population. Thanks to the increase in nominal wages and the low rate of inflation, real wages were up by 6.3 per cent compared with 2009.

Ecuadorian exports were expected to have surged by 22.9 per cent in 2010 compared with 2009, owing mainly to petroleum exports (although only because prices have risen) and to some traditional exports (coffee, shrimp and cacao) and non-traditional exports (flowers, wood, mineral products, vehicles and other metals manufactures). Nevertheless, imports rose by a larger margin and were up by 31.9 per cent. Although imports of all types of goods rose, imports of consumer durables, fuels and some intermediate goods stood out, driven by the increase in aggregate demand and the phase-out, in early 2010, of the balance of payments safeguards implemented the previous year. These factors together were expected to widen the merchandise trade deficit to 2.1 per cent of GDP.

KEY INDICATORS — Ecuador

	Unit	2006	2007	2008	2009	2010
Population	m	*13.54	13.34	13.92	14.12	14.31
Gross domestic product (GDP)	US$bn	41.45	44.18	54.70	57.30	58.90
GDP per capita	US$	3,080	3,218	3,928	4,059	3,984
GDP real growth	%	4.2	1.9	6.5	0.4	3.2
Inflation	%	3.3	2.2	8.4	5.1	3.6
Unemployment	%	7.8	7.4	6.9	8.5	7.6
Industrial output	% change	2.0	2.8	1.7	-4.1	–
Agricultural output	% change	4.1	1.2	-3.4	-16.1	–
Oil output	'000 bpd	545.0	520.0	514.0	495.0	495.0
Exports (fob) (goods)	US$m	12,728.0	13,852.4	19,147.0	14,347.0	–
Imports (fob) (goods)	US$m	12,114.0	12,591.4	17,776.0	14,269.0	–
Balance of trade	US$m	614.0	1,261.0	1,371.0	78.0	–
Current account	US$m	1,503.0	1,464.0	1,087.0	-268.0	-2,570.0
Total reserves minus gold	US$m	1,489.5	2,816.4	3,738.2	2,873.2	1,434.8
Foreign exchange	US$m	1,456.1	2,764.9	3,685.5	2,819.8	1,383.5
Exchange rate	per US$	1.00	1.00	1.00	1.00	1.00

* estimated figure

Compared with the same period in 2009, overseas remittances fell by 5.6 per cent in the first three quarters of 2011, owing in particular to the worsening employment situation in Spain and Italy, two of the main destinations of Ecuadorian migrants. This will have an impact on the current account deficit, which was expected to end the year at 2.9 per cent of GDP.

Energy

Ecuador is one of Latin America's largest oil exporters, with net oil exports estimated at 285,000 barrels per day (bpd) in 2010. The oil sector accounts for about 50 per cent of Ecuador's export earnings and about one-third of all tax revenues. Despite being an oil exporter, Ecuador must still import refined petroleum products due to the lack of sufficient domestic refining capacity to meet local demand. As a result, the country does not always enjoy the full benefits of high world oil prices: while these high prices bring Ecuador greater export revenues, they also increase the country's refined product import bill.

In 2007, Ecuador re-joined the Organisation of the Petroleum Exporting Countries (Opec), after leaving the organisation at the end of 1992. Ecuador is the smallest oil producer in Opec, with an assigned production quota of 434,000bpd. Despite an increasingly challenging investment environment, data available indicate that Ecuadorian production was increasing in 2011. A growing share of Ecuador's exports are going to China, which has secured a fixed supply in exchange for loans from the China Development Bank.

According to the *Oil and Gas Journal* (OGJ), Ecuador held proven oil reserves of 6.51 billion barrels in January 2011 – the third largest reserves in South America after Venezuela and Brazil. Ecuador is the fifth-largest producer of oil in South America, producing 486,000bpd of oil in 2010 (almost all of which was crude oil), down from a 2006 peak of 536,000bpd. Data from the first half of 2011 show a rebound in production, which averaged 501,000bpd in the period up to June 2011.

According to the US government's Energy Information Administration (EIA) in 2010, Ecuador exported 212,000bpd of oil to the United States, accounting for less than two per cent of total US oil imports. Other destinations for Ecuadorian crude in 2010 included Chile, Peru and China. Ecuador has begun to look towards the Asian market, namely China, as an alternative export market and source of investment. Since 2009, Ecuador has agreed to three separate loan agreements with China which were explicitly backed by oil deliveries. Under these agreements, Ecuador is required to invest a share of the loaned amount in infrastructure projects involving Chinese companies and repay the loans in crude oil shipments. In addition to these formal arrangements, China has made numerous other large-scale loans to Ecuador that have coincided with oil supply agreements.

Petroecuador, the state-run oil company, controls most of the crude oil production in the country. Major foreign-owned oil companies operating in Ecuador include Repsol-YPF (Spain), Eni (Italy) and Andes Petroleum, a consortium of Chinese companies. In November 2010 the government of Ecuador completed renegotiating its contracts with oil companies under a new hydrocarbons law. The new law mandates 'service agreements', in which oil companies will receive a fixed fee per barrel rather than shares of production, with the remainder of the revenue accruing to the government. This measure, designed to increase government revenue, led companies such as Petrobras (Brazil) and Noble Energy (US) to exit the country. Negotiations over fair compensation for their assets continue.

Ecuador's most productive oil fields are located in the north-east corner of the country. Crude oil production increased sizably in 2003 with the opening of the Oelducto de Crudos Pesados (OCP) pipeline, which removed a chokepoint on crude oil transportation in the country. However, production has leveled off in recent years, the result of natural decline, a lack of new project development and operating difficulties at existing oil fields. However, production levels are again set to surpass 500,000bpd in 2011 with the inauguration of the Panacocha field in the Ecuadorian Amazon – the first new production expansion since the current government took office in 2007

Natural gas

According to OGJ, Ecuador had 282 billion cubic feet (bcf) of natural gas reserves as of January 2011. In 2009, Ecuador produced a total of 49bcf of natural gas, almost all of which was associated gas from oil production. Ecuador's natural gas utilisation rates are due mainly to the lack of infrastructure to capture and market natural gas. According to the National Oceanic and Atmospheric Administration, Ecuador flares the second largest amount of natural gas in South America behind Venezuela.

The only large-scale natural gas project in Ecuador is the Amistad field, located in the Gulf of Guayaquil, which produces an estimated 23.5 million cubic feet (MMcf) per day. Petroecuador took over this project after US-based Noble Energy opted to exit the country rather than renegotiate its production contract. All of Amistad's natural gas production flows to the Machala facility, a 130 megawatt (MW), onshore, gas-fired power plant that supplies electricity to the Guayaquil region.

Risk assessment

Economy	Good
Politics	Fair
Regional stability	Fair

COUNTRY PROFILE

Historical profile

1530 Ecuador formed part of the Inca Empire until its conquest by Francisco Pizarro of Spain who landed on the Ecuadoran coast en route to Peru and defeat the Incas.

1822 Antonio José de Sucre Alcalá defeated the monarchist forces of Spain at the battle of Pichincha. Ecuador gained its independence as part of the federation of Gran Colombia.

1930 Ecuador seceded from Gran Colombia and became an independent republic.

1941 Peru invaded the mineral-rich province of El Oro.

1942 Ecuador lost about 200,000 square kilometres of the disputed land to Peru.

1960s and 1970s A series of elected and appointed presidents (usually by the armed forces) ruled Ecuador. Few saw out their full terms of office.

1967 A new constitution was came into law.

1968 Jose Maria Velasco was elected president for the fifth time. As support declined he had assumed dictatorial powers by 1970.

1972 Ecuador became a significant oil producer. General Guillermo Rodriguez Lara became president after overthrowing Jose Maria Velasco

1978 A new constitution was approved, providing for presidential elections.

1979 Jaime Roldós became president. Democratisation was encouraged and supported by US policy.

1981 Roldós was killed. Oswaldo Hurtado became president.

1984 President Febres Cordero introduced free-market economy measures. An earthquake destroyed a long section of Ecuador's only oil pipeline.

1992 Sixto Durán Ballén became president. Ecuador resigned its membership of the Organisation of Petroleum Exporting

Countries (Opec) in order to increase production.
1997 President Abdala Bucarem was removed from office; he was accused of corruption and mental incompetence. Fabian Alarcón, became interim president. Popular protests called for a national assembly and new constitution.
1998 A new constitution was inaugurated. Jamil Mahuad Witt became president.
2000 With the economy in recession and inflation running at almost 60 per cent, the US dollar was adopted, by presidential decree, as Ecuador's currency. The rate for changing the sucre was set at 25,000 sucre per US$1. Mahuad was ousted during widespread protests. Vice President Gustavo Noboa assumed the presidency.
2002 Colonel Lucio Gutiérrez became president. Indigenous peoples protested against the oil companies, bringing production to a halt and demanding that more revenue be spent on their communities.
2003 Former president Noboa escaped to Dominican Republic to avoid corruption charges.
2004 The Congress dismissed and replaced most members of the Supreme Court. Gutiérrez accused the former court of bias in favour of the opposition.
2005 Congress voted (60–2) to remove President Gutiérrez; Vice President Alfredo Palacio became interim president. Former president Gutiérrez was arrested on conspiracy charges following his return from exile in Colombia.
2006 The Partido Renovador Institucional de Acción Nacional (Prian) (Institutional Renewal Party of National Action) won parliamentary elections, but Rafael Correa (PAIS Alianza) won the presidency.
2007 The president called for a Constituent Assembly to reform Congress. Although most members boycotted the session the Congress agreed to a referendum on the proposal. Congress later withdrew its support, claiming the president had changed the agreed text. An electoral tribunal was empowered to conduct the referendum, despite members being threatened with impeachment by Congress. The supreme electoral court dismissed 57 Congress members for attempting to obstruct the referendum; 21 substitute Congress members were sworn in, achieving the 50-plus quorum. The referendum was passed when 81.72 per cent voted in favour of the proposition to re-write the constitution and form a Constituent Assembly (turnout 71 per cent). Elections to the new Constituent Assembly were won by the president's political party PAIS Alianza. Having dissolved Congress, the Constituent Assembly was given a mandate to draft a new constitution to replace the congress. All visitors were required to buy a permit to land on the Galápagos Islands. As a conservation measure, the Tarjeta de Control de Transito (TCT) (transit control card) limits the number of people who may visit the islands at any one time.
2008 Ecuador cut diplomatic relations with Colombia for three months, following pre-emptive strikes by Colombia against its domestic terrorists, Fuerzas Armadas Revolucionarias de Colombia-Ejército del Pueblo (Farc) (Revolutionary Armed Forces of Colombia-Peoples' Army) hiding out in Ecuador and Venezuela. Over a dozen Farc members including the senior Farc leader Raul Reyes were killed. The new draft constitution was agreed by a majority of the Constituent Assembly and put to a national referendum. The new constitution was approved by 64 per cent of the vote. President Correa declared that Ecuador would default on billions of US dollars of foreign debt, which he described as 'illegitimate'.
2009 In early presidential elections, incumbent Rafael Correa won 51.99 per cent of the vote, his closest rival, former president Lucio Gutiérrez, won 28.24 per cent. In parliamentary elections for the new National Congress, Movimiento PAIS (PAIS Movement) won 45.78 per cent of the vote (59 seats out of 124) and Partido Sociedad Patriótica 21 de Enero (PSP) (January 21 Patriotic Society Party) 14.9 per cent (19).
2010 The UN withdrew the Galápagos Islands from its list of endangered world heritage sites in July, after the government improved its protection of the natural environment and unique biodiversity. In August, the government signed a US$3.6 billion trust fund deal with the UN not to develop and exploit the Yasuni National Park, which contains an estimated one billion barrels of oil and thousands of species of trees, endangered mammals such as jaguars, monkeys and otters, as well as hundreds of bird species. The rich Amazon rainforest is also home to rarely seen indigenous aboriginal tribes. The UN Development Programme (UNDP) will administer the money raised from governments, organisations and individuals to pay for the trust fund. A 48-hour state of emergency was imposed as President Correa was held by protesting police for 10 hours in a hospital until rescued by the army. The Police had been protesting against civil service reforms that would have cut their benefits. President Correa described the attack as an attempted coup. A national census was held on 28 November.
2011 In March, scientists launched a campaign to catch and kill thousands of invasive rats that threaten indigenous animals on the Galápagos Islands. Year-on-year GDP growth for the first quarter was 8.6 per cent compared to the same period in 2010, according to the Central Bank of Ecuador and was the highest growth in ten-years. Preliminary results of the 2010 census, published on 11 July, recorded a population of 14.3 million inhabitants (to go in database) and an Ecuadorian annual population growth of 1.24 per cent.

Political structure

Constitution

28 September 2008, A new constitution was approved by 64 per cent of the vote. Among the 144 articles, the president may now hold office for two consecutive four-year terms; the president may dissolve congress within three years of its four-year term; control of strategic industries has been tightened and monopolies reduced; some foreign national loans were declared illegitimate; farm land that remains inactive may be expropriated and redistributed; free health care for elderly citizens will be provided by the state and civil marriage for single-sex partners is now allowed.
The 1979 constitution was amended in 1998 to strengthen the executive branch of government and abolish mid-term congressional elections and restrict the power of congress to dismiss cabinet ministers. Ecuador comprises 24 provinces, including the Galapagos Islands, each is administered by an appointed governor.

Form of state

Presidential democratic republic

The executive

Executive power rests with the president, elected by direct vote for a four-year term. The president appoints and presides over a cabinet.

National legislature

The unicameral Congreso Nacional (National Congress) consists of 100 members elected from party-lists by proportional representation, for four-year terms. Each of the country's 24 provinces returns a minimum of two deputies, plus an additional member for every 200,000 inhabitants. The 130-member Asamblea Constituyente (Constituent Assembly) dissolve the National Congress on 29 November 2008. The Constituent Assembly has a four-year term.

Legal system

The Supreme Court heads the judiciary. Its judges are appointed by Congress for four-year, renewable terms.

Last elections

26 April 2009 (presidential and parliamentary)
Results: Presidential: Rafael Correa won 51.99 per cent of the vote, Lucio Gutiérrez 28.24 per cent, Álvaro Noboa

11.41 per cent. Turnout was 75.29 per cent.
Parliamentary: Movimiento PAIS (PAIS Movement) won 45.78 per cent of the vote (59 seats out of 124), Partido Sociedad Patriótica 21 de Enero (PSP) (January 21 Patriotic Society Party) 14.9 per cent (19), Partido Social Cristiano (PSC) (Social Christian Party) 13.58 per cent (11), Partido Renovador Institucional de Acción Nacional (PRIAN) (Institutional Renewal Party of National Action) 5.79 per cent (seven); 14 other political parties each won less than 5 per cent of the vote and won no more than five seats of the remaining 28 seats available. Seven other political parties failed to win any seats.
Next elections
2013 (presidential)

Political parties
Ruling party
Movimiento PAIS (Patria Altiva i Soberana) (Proud and Sovereign Fatherland Movement) (from 26 Apr 2009)
Main opposition party
Partido Sociedad Patriótica 21 de Enero (PSP) (January 21 Patriotic Society Party)
Political situation
In the 15 October 2006 parliamentary elections the Partido Renovador Institucional de Acción Nacional (PRIAN) (Institutional Renewal Party of National Action) won 28 of the 100 seats in the national congress, the Partido Sociedad Patriótica 21 de Enero (PSP) (January 21 Patriotic Society Party) won 23, the Partido Social Cristiano (PSC) (Social Christian Party) won 13, and the Partido Roldosista Ecuatoriano (PRE) (Ecuadorian Roldosist Party) won six. No candidates stood for the Alianza Patria Altiva y Soberana (PAIS Alianza) (Proud and Sovereign Fatherland Alliance)). In the first round of the presidential election, Álvaro Noboa (PRIAN) won 26.8 per cent of the vote, Rafael Correa (PAIS Alianza) 22.8 per cent, Gilmar Gutiérrez 17.5 per cent, León Roldós Aguilera 14.8 per cent and Cynthia Viteri 9.6 per cent. The run-off took place on 26 November; Correa won 57 per cent of the vote against Noboa with 43 per cent. Noboa called for a recount, claiming vote rigging by his opponent; the electoral commission confirmed the result on 28 November.
In the 30 September 2007 Asamblea Constituyente (Constituent Assembly) the PAIS Alliance won 74 seats (out of 130).

Population
14.31 million (2010; census figure)
Last census: November 2001: 12,156,608
Population density: 42 inhabitants per square km. Urban population: 63 per cent (1995—2001).
Annual growth rate: 1.5 per cent 1994–2004 (WHO 2006)
Ethnic make-up
Mestizo (mixed Indian and white) (65 per cent), Indian (25 per cent), white and others (7 per cent), black (3 per cent). The indigenous Indian population is composed of eight main groups, five in the Oriente and three on the coast, each with their own language. One of the Oriente groups, the Quechua, also live in the highlands (sierra).
Religions
Over 95 per cent of the population is nominally Roman Catholic, although Protestant churches have made inroads in recent years. There is freedom of worship.

Education
The education sector in Ecuador needs increased funding and technology.
Enrolment in primary schools has been increasing at an annual rate of 4.4 per cent per year, although many children drop out before the age of 15.
Public universities have an open admissions policy. The number of people entering university, however, has increased and this is putting a strain on resources, contributing to a decline in academic standards.
Literacy rate: 91 per cent adult rate; 96 per cent youth rate (15–24) (Unesco 2005).
Compulsory years: Six to 15
Enrolment rate: 117 per cent gross primary enrolment (including repeaters); 59 per cent gross secondary enrolment (World Bank).
Pupils per teacher: 25 in primary schools

Health
Improved water sources and sanitation facilities are available to 71 per cent and 59 per cent of the population, respectively.
HIV/Aids
HIV prevalence: 0.3 per cent aged 15–49 in 2003 (World Bank)
Life expectancy: 72 years, 2004 (WHO 2006)
Fertility rate/Maternal mortality rate: 2.7 births per woman, 2004 (WHO 2006); maternal mortality 160 per 100,000 live births (World Bank).
Child (under 5 years) mortality rate (per 1,000): 24 per 1,000 live births; 14 per cent of children, aged under five, are malnourished (World Bank).

Welfare
The Ecuadorian Social Security Institute operates under the ministry of social welfare and offers old-age benefits, sickness and maternity coverage, work, injury and unemployment benefits. The system covers only around 30 per cent of the working population. Coverage is particularly poor in rural areas.

Main cities
Quito (capital, estimated population 1.5 million (m) in 2005), Guayaquil (2.2m), Cuenca (305,772), Santo Domingo (238,325), Alfaro (212,924), Machala (228,351), Manta (201,700), Portoviejo (187,369).

Languages spoken
Quechua and Jarvo are spoken. There is pressure from indigenous groups for Quechua to be made an official language.
English, taught to all schoolchildren, is also widely spoken.
Official language/s
Spanish

Media
Freedom of the press is guaranteed but foreign investment in the media is prohibited. Journalists operate a form of self-censorship particularly concerning perceived sensitive issues and defamation is a criminal offence and liable to up to three years in prison.
Press
Dailies: In Spanish, national newspapers include *El Comercio* (www2.elcomercio.com) and *El Universo* (www.eluniverso.com). Regional publications include *El Telégrafo* (www.telegrafo.com.ec) and *Expreso* (www.expreso.ec) from Guayaquil, *La Hora* (www.lahora.com.ec) and *Hoy* (www.hoy.com.ec) from Quito, *Correo* (www.diariocorreo.com.ec) from Machala and La Prensa (www.laprensa.com.ec) from Chimborazo.
Business: In Spanish, *El Financiero* (www.elfinanciero.com) is published weekly.
Broadcasting
The government seized TC Television in Quito and Guayaquil and Gamavision in Quito in July 2008, in a dispute lnked to the collapse of banks in the late 1990s. The Deposit Guarantee Agency (AGD) seeks to recover funds from banks that closed or went bankrupt in the financial crisis.
Radio: Radio is the most popular medium for entertainment, news and information and there are hundreds of stations, some in rural areas broadcasting in indigenous languages. Private, national commercial radio stations include Radio Sucre (www.radiosucre.com.ec), JC Radio (www.jcradio.com.ec) and Radio Caravana (http://radiocaravana.com); from Quito Radio Megaestacion (www.radiomegaestacion.com) and Radio i99 (www.i99.com.ec); from Guayaquil Radio America (www.americaestereo.com) and Radio

Latina (www.radiolatina.com.ec). There are several religious radio stations.
Television: There are several national, commercial broadcasters, programming mostly consists of Latin American soap opera shows and US imports, but domestic productions are growing. News, sports and music are also featured. Ecuavisa (www.ecuavisa.com), ETV Telerama (www.etvtelerama.com), Teleamazonas (www.teleamazonas.com), Telesistema (www.rts.com.ec) and Gamavision (www.gamavision.com).
The satellite TV station RTU (www.rtu.com.ec), which began transmitting in 2005, offers news and current affairs programmes.
News agencies
Other news agencies: Prensa Latina: www.prensalatina.com.mx

Economy
The economy is heavily dependent on the oil industry, manufacturing for the domestic market, commerce and agriculture. Exports are dominated by petroleum (51 per cent of total export earnings in 2009), although Ecuador is a leading exporter of bananas and plantains as well as a major exporter of shrimp (prawns) and, to a lesser extent, fresh flowers, canned fish and vehicles. The mining industry is in need of further development, but produces gold and copper. A wide range of cash and subsistence crops are produced, including coffee, cacao (cocoa beans), sugar, tropical fruits rice and livestock
GDP growth was 6.5 per cent in 2008, as oil, copper and gold prices reached record high prices, but the economy fell to 0.4 per cent in 2009 as the global economic crisis cut trade, particularly in commodities. Growth in 2010 recovered and was 2.9 per cent, with a projected 2.3 per cent in 2011. At the height of the 2008 boom inflation peaked at 8.4 per cent as a result of corresponding high prices of imports.
The political influence of President Correa has re-focussed the economy. He championed investment in public services, education and health, which resulted in increased income tax. Ecuador's poverty index decreased from 37.6 per cent in December 2006 to 33 per cent in June 2010. Remittances in 2009 were US$2.5 billion (4.5 per cent of GDP) and were estimated to have risen to US$2.54 billion in 2010, as funds were provided directly into family funds.
In December 2008 Ecuador officially defaulted on US$10 billion of its foreign debts, which it considered 'illegitimate'. Around 20 per cent of GDP was used in foreign debt and the president claimed that some of the debt was contracted illegally by previous administrations and that the debt will be restructured. According to the Alternate Governor of the Bank of Ecuador, Katiuska King Mantilla foreign debt was 13.8 per cent of GDP in August 2010 and the total service for this debt (public and private) was reduced to 9.6 per cent of GDP.
Chinese company Sinohydro pledged foreign direct investment of US$1.682 billion in 2010 for the future construction of Ecuador's largest hydroelectric project.

External trade
Ecuador belongs to the South American Community of Nations (SACN) (which combines the Andean Community of Nations and Southern Common Market (Mercosur)) in the creation of an economic and legislative union.
Imports
Principal imports are vehicles, pharmaceuticals and medical products, telecommunications equipment and electricity.
Main sources: US (typically 17 per cent of total), China (11 per cent), Colombia (10 per cent).
Exports
Principal exports are petroleum, bananas, fresh flowers, shrimp, canned fish and vehicles.
Main destinations: US (typically 33 per cent of total), Panama (14 per cent), Peru (7 per cent).

Agriculture
Farming
Prior to the rise in significance of the oil industry and other related economic activities, the agricultural sector was Ecuador's most prominent economic activity. In recent years output from the sector has fluctuated due to the adverse effects of the *El Niño* weather phenomena in the 1990s and shifts in world cocoa and banana prices.
Virtually the whole of the country is suitable for some form of agricultural exploitation. However, the sector has suffered from low levels of mechanisation and irrigation, and lack of financial incentives.
In coastal regions the main crops are bananas, cocoa, coffee, oil palms, sugar cane, cotton, rice and maize, while the sierra produces legumes, maize, wheat, potatoes, rye and barley. Ecuador is the world's largest producer of bananas.
Cattle are mainly reared in the highlands. There is small-scale poultry farming in Manabi province.
Rose growing and cut-flower production started in the early 1980s and the country has a number of rose growing enterprises. The potential for rose exports from Ecuador is enormous since all-year-round production is possible with no heating or cooling costs.
Temperate crops include blackberries, tamarillos (tree tomatoes), lemons, limes and avocados. In warmer regions, mangoes, pineapple, passion fruit, papaya, pepper, heart-of-palm and orito (kind of banana) thrive. In colder and temperate areas, broccoli, strawberry, asparagus, artichoke and peppers are grown. In addition, cucumbers, okra and melons are cultivated. The majority of the annual pineapple harvest is sold to the US and to Europe.
Fishing
Over recent years the fishing industry has increased in importance. Both sea and shrimp fishing have become more economically significant, with shrimp now being the second most important foreign exchange earner in the agricultural sector, after bananas.
Government policy has concentrated on the development of sea food, including tuna, fish oil and fishmeal for export.
The fisheries union in Ecuador has pressed for immediate reforms within the sector, asking for modernised management. The country's fishing legislation lacks organisation with poorly defined fishing rights.
In a typical year the annual fish catch is over 654,500mt, including 5,645mt freshwater fish and 64,200mt shellfish.
Forestry
Over 40 per cent of Ecuador's total land mass is forested; approximately 10.5 million hectares (ha).
Forests are mostly concentrated in the eastern Amazonian region characterised by lowland humid tropical rainforests. Forest plantations are mainly eucalyptus.
Large quantities of sawn timber and wood based panels are produced, although exports remain limited. Production of hardwoods and balsa wood is dependent on the Andean market. Most of the paper and pulp demand is met by imports.
According to some critics, there will be no forests left in Ecuador by 2030 and the government has been supporting a project which aimed to re-forest 500,000 hectares by the end of 2005, both for commercial and ecological reasons, with an emphasis on profitable exotic species.

Industry and manufacturing
Approximately 20 per cent of Ecuador's total GDP is generated by activity in the industrial sector, which is geographically concentrated in Quito and Guayaquil.
The sector accounts for 15 per cent of the entire labour force in a typical year.
A free trade zone (FTZ), offering incentives for the manufacture of export products, was established at Esmeraldas.

Tourism
The tourism sector is playing an increasingly important role in the economy of

Ecuador. The sector is the country's third most important economic activity, after petroleum and bananas. Travel and tourism employs around 8 per cent of Ecuador's total labour force and constitutes around 10 per cent of total GDP.
The mixture of environmental systems, including rain-forest and mountains, and especially the Galapagos Islands, favours eco-tourists as well as attracting trekkers, climbers, divers and backpackers. Ecuador converted to the US dollar in 2000, making it a more expensive country to visit than neighbouring countries. Visitor numbers have been rising steadily over recent years.

Environment
All visitors are required to buy a permit to land on the Galápagos Islands. As a conservation measure, a Tarjeta de Control de Transito (TCT) (transit control card) was instituted in 2007 to limit the number of people who may visit the islands at any one time.

Mining
Mining concessions can be found over approximately 5.6 million hectares of Ecuador's total land mass. Approximately 36,000 miners make their living in the informal sector, which represents about 1 per cent of the country's labour force.
Despite a growing foreign presence, Ecuador's mining industry is very much in its infancy, although it could become one of the economy's most dynamic sectors. The government is keen to make mining a high priority in view of its enormous production potential and the opportunity it offers to diversify the country's export base as an alternative to oil.
The most important mineral is gold, which is mined on a small-scale basis, although a number of foreign and local companies are negotiating with miners to take over their operations and introduce more technical expertise. Interest has been shown in gold, with a joint government and private mining venture in the Nambija region.
There are also major deposits of limestone, clay, plaster, barytine, feldspar, silica, phosphate, bentonite and pumice stone (Ecuador has one of the biggest reserves of pumice stone in the world). Kaolin, marble, puzzolan and gypsum are mined.

Hydrocarbons
Total oil reserves were 6.2 billion barrels in 2010, with production at 495,000 barrels per day (bpd). Consumption was 226,000bpd, which allowed the remainder to be exported. As Ecuador is one of South America's largest oil exporters the sector dominates the economy and provides around 50 per cent of total export earnings and 33 per cent of tax revenues.
However, Ecuador does not possess sufficient refining capacity, 176,000bpd from three refineries, so it relies on imported refined oil for domestic purposes. In 2008 a contract was signed with the South Korean KS Engineering to refurbish and upgrade the largest refinery, Esmeraldas.
Although the state-owned Petroecuador is responsible for exploration, production and transport of all hydrocarbons it typically works in partnership with foreign oil and gas companies and only produces around 50 per cent of crude oil. In 2007 the government began to transform contracts with foreign oil companies into service agreements, whereby oil companies act as government agents in producing oil and are given a fee in compensation for production. In 2009, the largest foreign oil producer, the Argentinean company, Repsol-YPF, agreed to the new contract structure.
Petroecuador utilises the older Sistema Oleducto Trans-Ecuatoriano (Sote), to transport oil to the Balao oil terminal on the Pacific coast, for export. The latest pipeline, which parallels Sote, the Oleducto de Crudos Pesados (OCP), has allowed private oil companies to double output.
Total natural gas reserves were 8.9 billion cubic metres (cum) in 2009, however domestic demand is negligible and the infrastructure to increase use is limited. All natural gas output is used in energy generation. The oil industry produces 3.3 billion cum, but all of it is lost due to the lack of infrastructure for its capture.
Although, there are small reserves of recoverable coal (lignite and sub-bituminous) estimated at 23.5 million tonnes, any consumption is commercially insignificant.

Energy
Total installed electricity capacity was 3,567MW in 2007, producing 14.8 billion kilowatt hours (kWh), which was more than sufficient to provide for consumption of 12.9 billion kWh. The majority of energy is provided by hydropower and the remainder by conventional thermal power stations. Although there is a net electricity surplus, supplies are often affected during the dry season of October-March when hydroelectric output declines. Ecuador imports electricity from Colombia during periods of shortfall.
The state regulator of energy is Consejo Nacional de Electricidad (Conelec) (National Electricity Council), under the mandate of the Ministerio de Energía y Minas (MEM) (Ministry of Energy and Mining). It has responsibilities for policy, planning and regulation of the independent utility companies.
Ecuador's largest power plant is the massive Paute River hydroelectric dam in Azuay Province, producing over 50 per cent of all domestic energy needs. In 2008 a new hydroelectric dam in San Francisco, Quito, which was inaugurated in 2007 and supplied 12 per cent of the country's electricity, became the focus of international disagreement between the government and its Brazilian backers and builders, Odebrecht. In June 2008 it was shut down by the government for claimed structural defects that had interrupted power supplies. Four contracts totalling US$800 million with Odebrecht were annulled by presidential decree, while Ecuador demanded repairs and recompense, while loans of US$243 million to the National Economic and Social Development Bank of Brazil (BNDES) were withheld. Other, smaller, hydropower projects are under construction.
The worst drought since the 1960s forced the government to introduce electricity rationing in November 2009, aimed at reducing consumption by 5–10 per cent. Water levels in the Paute River hydroelectric dam were at an historic low, with water flowing at 20–30 cubic metres (cum) per second instead of the average 70–80cum expected.

Financial markets
Stock exchange
Bolsa de Valores de Quito (BVQ) (Quito Stock Exchange)

Banking and insurance
A new Bank of the South, with a headquarters in Venezuela, will be launched in 2008 to provide an alternative source of development funding for the participating countries. Assets of US$7 billion will underpin its operations.
Central bank
Banco Central del Ecuador
Main financial centre
Guayaquil and Quito

Time
Mainland Ecuador: GMT minus five hours
Galapagos Islands: GMT minus six hours

Geography
Ecuador has three main regions – a low coastal strip, a high Andean *cordillera* with peaks rising to more than 6,000 metres, and a tropical lowland in the Amazon basin. The Andes, which here comprise two parallel ranges running north to south, form a barrier between 100 and 120km wide.
Chimborazo, an extinct volcano, is the highest mountain, at 6,310 metres, and there are several active volcanoes. Quito itself, which lies at 2,850 metres above sea level, is the second highest capital in South America, and visitors are advised to

take things easy for a few days after arrival to avoid altitude sickness.
To the north, Ecuador is bordered by Colombia and to the east and south by Peru. To the west lies the Pacific Ocean. Of the Spanish-speaking nations of South America, only Uruguay is smaller in area.
Hemisphere
Straddles the Equator

Climate
Although the equator crosses the north of the country (and gives it its name), only the eastern lowlands (the Oriente) and the northern coastal region have a typically tropical climate, with abundant rains, high humidity and little seasonal change in temperature, which averages around 25 degrees Celsius (C). The port city of Guayaquil is in the tropical zone and has most rain between January and April. In the Andes, the climate varies from the cold of the high glaciers to the temperate zone of the central valley around Quito, where the mean annual temperature is between 13 degrees C and 19 degrees C. Days are warm and nights are cool all year round. The rainy season in the valley lasts from November–May.

Dress codes
In government offices and private businesses in Quito, dress is relatively formal. Women usually wear skirts, while the men wear suits or jacket and tie. Dress is generally less formal in Guayaquil, the largest city and Ecuador's major port.

Entry requirements
Passports
Passports are required by all. Passports must be valid for six months.
Visa
Nationals of most countries do not need a visa for stays up to three months, but travellers should contact the local embassy for confirmation.
Currency advice/regulations
No restrictions on import or export of foreign or local currency.
International credit cards are generally accepted in Quito and Guayaquil. Travellers cheques can be difficult to exchange outside main towns. US dollar travellers cheques are the most easily negotiable.
Prohibited imports
Firearms, ammunition, illegal drugs, fresh or dry meat and meat products, plants and vegetables are prohibited/restricted unless prior permission is obtained.

Health (for visitors)
Mandatory precautions
A yellow fever certificate is required if arriving from infected areas and for those intending to visit Pastaza province in the east.
Advisable precautions
Typhoid, tetanus and hepatitis A and B vaccinations are recommended. Malaria prophylaxis is advisable; the malaria risk is high and widespread all the year. Yellow fever vaccinations are recommended for most areas east of the Andes. There is a rabies risk.
Tap water is not safe to drink. Bottled mineral water is widely available.

Hotels
Wide range available in Quito and Guayaquil. A government tax of 5 per cent and a service charge of 10 per cent payable on all rates.

Credit cards
Major credit cards are generally accepted.

Public holidays (national)
Fixed dates
1 Jan (New Year's Day), 1 May (Labour Day), 24 May (Battle of Pichincha Day), 10 Aug (Independence Day), 12 Oct (Columbus Day), 2 Nov (All Souls' Day), 25 Dec (Christmas Day), 31 Dec (New Year's Eve).
If New Year's Day falls on a Sunday, 2 Jan becomes a holiday instead. Holidays falling on a Tuesday are observed on the preceding Monday, while those falling on Wednesday and Thursday are moved to Friday. The exceptions to the latter rule are 1 Jan, 1 May, 2 Nov and 25 Dec.
Variable dates
Carnival (two days), Maundy Thursday, Good Friday.
Carnival is celebrated on Shrove Tuesday and Ash Wednesday (six weeks before Good Friday).

Working hours
Banking
Mon–Fri: 0900–1330, 1430—1030; Sat: 0900–1800.
Business
Mon–Fri: 0800–1630.
Government
Mon–Fri: 0830–1630.
Shops
Mon–Fri: 0900–1300, 1500–1900. Sat: 1000–2000. (Shopping centres, Mon–Sat: 1030–2030; Sun: 1030–1830.)

Telecommunications
Mobile/cell phones
GSM 850 service available in cities and large towns.

Electricity supply
110/120V AC, 60 cycles

Weights and measures
The metric system is in use.

Social customs/useful tips
Speak Spanish; if not, ensure that promotional material is in Spanish or has Spanish inserts.
Ecuadoreans prefer to deal with people they have spent time getting to know; lunches/business meetings can last from 1330 to 1800, dinners from 2000 onwards. Meetings often start late.
Ecuadoreans are polite and formal. Do not be discouraged by lack of enthusiasm; they like to be convinced. The use of the title Doctor, Engineer or Economist is common.

Security
Guayaquil has a serious street crime problem. Crime in Quito is on the increase, especially in the colonial centre of town, and police advise visitors to be wary of thieves and pickpockets and to watch luggage at all times.

Getting there
Air
National airline: TAME (Línea Aérea del Ecuador); Lan Ecuador.
International airport/s: Quito-Mariscal Sucre (UIO), 8km from city centre, duty-free shop, bar, restaurant, buffet, bank, post office, shops, car hire, tourist information. Guayaquil-Simón Bolivar (GYE), 5km north of city centre, duty-free shop, restaurant, buffet, currency exchange, post office, shops, car hire, tourist information;
Airport tax: US$25.
Surface
Access is possible from Colombia and Peru, although the quality of roads and railway services may vary.
Road: Buses run between Colombia and Ecuador via Tulcán, and between Peru and Ecuador via either Huaquillas or Macará.
Water: All visitors are required to buy a permit to land on the Galápagos Islands. As a conservation measure, a Tarjeta de Control de Transito (TCT) (transit control card) was instituted in 2007 to limit the number of people who may visit the islands at any one time.
Main port/s: Guayaquil, Manta and Esmeraldas.

Getting about
Passport checks are frequently made by the police, especially near the borders.
National transport
Air: Air transport is the usual mode of travel between cities. TAME, the commercial wing of the Ecuadorian Air Force, and several other airlines operate domestic services to main centres. Air-taxi and charter services are available from Guayaquil and Quito.
With the exception of flying to the Galápagos Islands, internal flights are

cheap. All visitors are required to buy a permit to land on the Galápagos Islands.
Road: Most parts of the country are accessible by surfaced or all-weather roads. Major routes run north-south in the coastal lowlands and the sierra. The Pan-American Highway runs from Tulcan via Ibarra, Quito, Riobamaba, Cuenca, Loja to Macara. Good roads link the sierra to the coastal ports.
Buses: Bus services link main towns, including Quito-Esmeraldas, Quito-Manta, Guayaquil-Manta and Quito-Guayaquil. Most towns have a *terminal terrestre* (central bus terminal). Reservations in advance should be made for long-distance services. Timetables are changed frequently and not always adhered to.
Rail: Routes include Quito-Riobamba, Guayaquil-Bucay, Alausi-Huigra, Sibambe-Cuenca and Ibarra-San Lorenzo. Rail travel is generally uncomfortable and unreliable.
Water: Boats are a frequent mode of travel, particularly in the Oriente region, and on the north-west coast.

City transport

Taxis: Taxis are cheap. They can be hailed or found on ranks. It is best to ask the fare beforehand. At weekends and at night, fares are 25–50 per cent higher. Journey time from airport to city centre 20–30 minutes. Tips are not expected.

Car hire

Major companies operate from Quito and Guayaquil. An international permit is required. Traffic drives on the right. Police checks are common.

BUSINESS DIRECTORY

The addresses listed below are a selection only. While World of Information makes every endeavour to check these addresses, we cannot guarantee that changes have not been made, especially to telephone numbers and area codes. We would welcome any corrections.

Telephone area codes

The international direct dialling code for Ecuador is +593, followed by area code:

Ambato	3	Machala	7
Cuenca	7	Manta	4
Esmeraldas	6	Portoviejo	4
Guayaquil	4	Quito	2

Useful telephone numbers

Police:	101
Fire:	102
Ambulance (Quito):	131

Chambers of Commerce

American-Ecuadorian Chamber of Commerce, Avenida 6 de Diciembre y La Niña, Edificio Multicentro, Quito (tel: 250-7450; fax: 250-4571; e-mail: info@ecamcham.com).

British-Ecuadorean Chamber of Industry and Commerce, Avenida El Tiempo 464 y El Telegrafo, Quito (tel: 244-9239; fax: 225-7433; e-mail: info@egbcc.org).

Guayaquil Cámara de Comercio, Avenida Francisco de Orellana y Miguel H Alcivar, Centro Empresarial Las Cámaras, Guayaquil (tel: 268-2771; fax: 268-2725; e-mail: info@lacamara.org).

Quito Cámara de Comercio, Avenida Amazonas y República, Edificio Las Cámaras, Quito (tel: 244-3787; fax: 243-5862; e-mail: ccq@ccq.org.ec).

Banking

Banco Bolivariano, Junín 200 y Panamá, Guayaquil (tel: 562-777; fax: 565-025).

Banco de Guayaquil, Pichincha 105 y P Icaza, Guayaquil (tel: 514-209; fax: 512-427; e-mail: glasso@bankguay.com).

Banco del Pacifico, P Icaza 200 y Pedro Carbo, Guayaquil (tel: 566-010; fax: 564-636; e-mail: webadmin@bp.fin.ec).

Banco del Pichincha, Avenida Amazonas 4560 y Pereira, Quito (tel: 980-980; fax: 981-280).

Banco la Previsora, Avenida 9 de Octubre 100, Guayaquil (tel: 561-656; fax: 566-665; e-mail: blp@bprevisora.fin.ec).

BancoUnion, Cordova 916 y VM Rendon, Guayaquil (tel: 566-555; fax: 313-295; e-mail: info@banunion.com).

Filanbanco, Avenida 9 de Octubre 203 y Pichincha, Guayaquil (tel: 322-780; fax: 326-916).

Superintendencia de Bancos (Banking Supervisory Agency), Avenida 12 de Octubre 24-185, Quito (tel: 554-422).

Central bank

Banco Central del Ecuador, Avenida 10 de Agosto y Briceño, Plaza Bolivar, Quito (tel: 519-384, 571-807).

Stock exchange

Bolsa de Valores de Quito (BVQ) (Quito Stock Exchange): www.ccbvq.com

Bolsa de Volores de Guayaquil (BVG) (Guayaquil Stock Exchange): www.mundobvg.com

Travel information

Ecuatoriana Airlines, Reina Victoria y Colón, Edificio Torres de Almagro, Quito (tel: 563-003; fax: 563-920).

SAETA Airlines, Avenida Carlos Julio Arosemena Km 2.5, Guayaquil (fax: 201-153; e-mail: ehbuzon@saeta.com.ec).

TAME Airlines, Avenida Amazonas 13-54 y Colón, Quito (tel: 509-392; fax: 509-594).

Ministry of tourism

Ministry of Tourism, Av Eloy Alfaro N32-300 y Carlos Tobar, Quito (tel: 228-303, 507-560; fax: 507-564, 229-330; e-mail: mtur1@ec_gov.net).

National tourist organisation offices

Asociación Ecuatoriana de Agencias de Viajes y Turismo (ASECUT), Avenida Amazonas 2468, Quito (tel: 552-617; fax: 552-916).

Corporación Ecuatoriana de Turismo (CETUR), Reina Victoria 514 y Roca, Quito (tel: 527-002; fax: 568-198).

Ministries

Ministry of Agriculture, Avenida Amazonas y Eloy Alfaro, Quito (tel: 504-433; fax: 504-922).

Ministry of Defence, Exposición 208, Quito (tel: 512-803; fax: 569-386).

Ministry of Education, San Gregorio y Juan Murillo, Quito (tel: 583-337; fax: 580-116).

Ministry of Energy and Mines, Santa Prisca 223, Quito (tel: 552-533; fax: 502-092).

Ministry of the Environment, Avenida Eloy Alfaro y Amazonas, Quito (tel: 540-920; fax: 255-172).

Ministry of Finance and Public Credit, Avenida 10 de Agosto 1661 y Jorge Washington, Quito (tel: 503-328; fax: 500-702).

Ministry of Foreign Affairs, Avenida 10 de Agosto y Carrión, Quito (tel: 503-093; fax: 227-025; e-mail: dgproeco@mmree.gov.ec).

Ministry of Foreign Trade, Avenida Amazonas y Eloy Alfaro, Quito (tel: 529-076; fax: 507-549).

Ministry of Government, Espejo y Benalcázar, Quito (tel: 584-919; fax: 580-067).

Ministry of Housing and Urban Development, Avenida 10 de Agosto 2270 y Cordero, Quito (tel: 238-060; fax: 566-785).

Ministry of Labour, Luis Felipe Borja y C Ponce, Quito (tel: 566-148; fax: 503-122).

Ministry of Public Health, Juan Larrea 445, Quito (tel: 529-163; fax: 569-092).

Ministry of Public Works, Avenida Orellana y Juan León Mera, Quito (tel: 222-749; fax: 223-077).

Ministry of Social Welfare, Robles 850 y Páez, Quito (tel: 227-975; fax: 563-469).

Other useful addresses

Bolsa de Valores de Quito (Stock Exchange), Avenida Amazonas 540 y Carrión, Quito (tel: 526-805; fax: 500-942; e-mail: informacion@ccbvq.com).

Bolsa de Valores de Guayaquil, 9 de Octubre 110 y Pichincha, Guayaquil (tel: 561-519; fax: 561-871; e-mail: earosemena@bvg.fin.ec).

British Embassy, Avenida Naciones Unidas y República de El Salvador, Quito (tel: 970-800/1; fax: 970-809).

Corporación Financiera Nacional, Juan León Mera 130 y Patria, Quito (tel: 564-900; fax: 223-823).

Ecuadorian Embassy (USA), 2535 15th Street, NW, Washington DC 20009 (tel: (202) 234-7200; fax: (202) 667-3482; e-mail: embassy@ecuador.org).

Empresa Estatel de Telecomunicaciones (EMETEL), Avenida 6 de Diciembre y Colón, Edificio Partenon, Quito (tel: 200-700; fax: 568-000).

Instituto Nacional de Estadística y Censos, Juan Larrea 534 y Riofrio, Quito (tel: 529-858; fax: 509-836).

National Bureau of Mines (DINAMI), Baquedano E7-13 y Reina Victoria, Edificio Araucaria, Quito (tel: 554-110; fax: 554-110; e-mail: dinami@accessinter.net).

National Council for the Modernisation of the State (CONAM), Edificio Corporación Financiera, Avenida Juan León Mera 130 y Patria, Quito (tel: 509-432; fax: 509-437).

Petroecuador, Avenida 6 de Diciembre y Paul Rivet, Edificio El Pinar, Quito (tel: 561-250; fax: 524-766).

Secretary General of the Administration, García Moreno 1043, Quito (tel: 580-750; fax: 580-751).

Superintendencia de Compañías del Ecuador (Companies Supervisory Authority), Roca 660 y Avenida Amazonas, Quito (tel: 529-960; fax: 565-685).

US Embassy, Avenida 12 de Octubre y Patria, Quito (tel: 562-890; fax: 502-052).

Internet sites

Economic Commission for Latin America (gateway site): http://www.eclac.cl/index1.html

Inter-American Development Bank: http://www.iadb.org

Latin Trade Online: http://www.latintrade.com

Latin World (directory of Internet resources): http://wwwlatinworld.com

Organisation of American States: http://www.oas.org

Egypt

KEY FACTS

Official name: Jumhuriyat Misr al Arabiya (Arab Republic of Egypt)

Head of State: *De facto* President Field Marshal Mohamed Hussein Tantawi (Chairman of Supreme Council of the Armed Forces (SCAF)) (from 11 Feb 2011)

Head of government: Prime Minister Essam Abdel-Aziz Sharaf (from 29 Jan 2011)

Ruling party: Awaiting announcement from SCAF

Area: 1,001,499 square km

Population: 81.12 million (2010)*

Capital: Cairo

Official language: Arabic

Currency: Egyptian pound (LE) = 100 piastres

Exchange rate: LE5.97 per US$ (Oct 2011)

GDP per capita: US$2,789 (2010)

GDP real growth: 5.10% (2010)

GDP: US$218.50 billion (2010)

Labour force: 26.18 million (2010)

Unemployment: 9.00% (2010)

Inflation: 11.70% (2010)

Oil production: 736,000 bpd (2010)

Balance of trade: -US$16.82 billion (2009)

Annual FDI: US$4.03 billion (2008/09)

* estimated figure

NOTA

13 January 2012, the final results of three rounds of parliamentary election were posted. The Democratic Alliance for Egypt (DAE) (a coalition of five political parties, led by the Freedom and Justice Party, plus independents) won 127 seats by proportional representation (PR) and 108 seats by first-past-the- post (FPTP) for a total of 235 seats. Although the DAE will have overall legislative powers the military council (SCAF) retains presidential powers until a new president is elected later in the year.

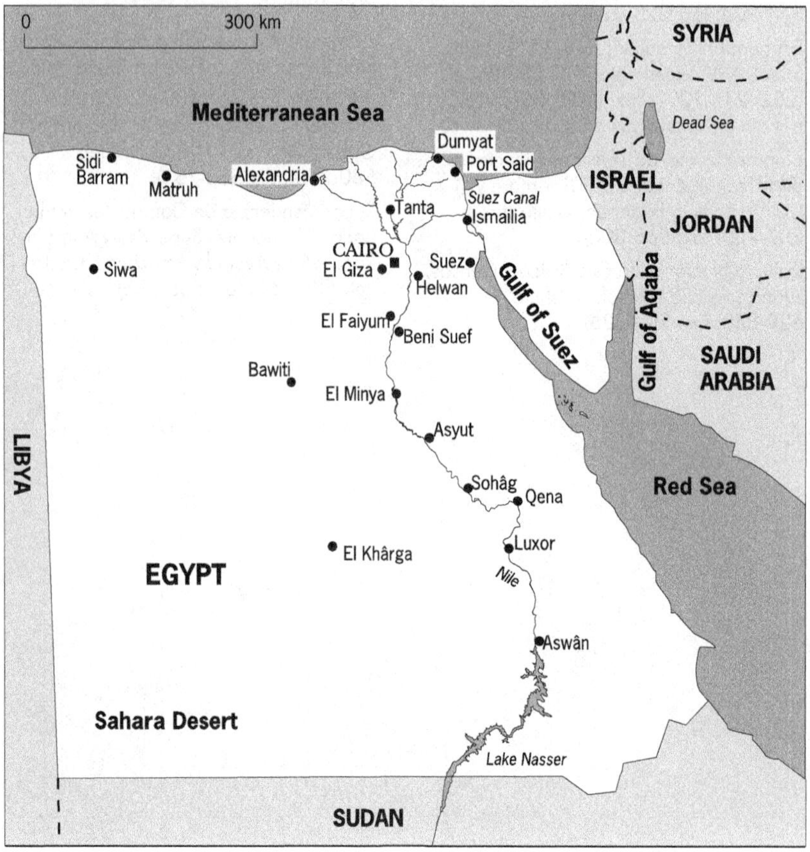

The nineteenth century witnessed what came to be known as the Arab Awakening, a revival of pride in Arab culture and a resentment of foreign domination. By the twenty-first century, the resentment had begun to be directed not so much at foreign powers, but against leaders who, for the most part were not democratically elected. These currents began to boil over in 2011, in what quickly became known as the Arab Spring.

Mubarak goes

If the Arab Spring had one pivotal moment, it was the removal from power, in February 2011, of Hosni Mubarak, Egypt's octogenarian president of 30 years. This may well turn out to have been a critical development, not only for Egypt, but also for the region as a whole. Mr Mubarak went, not at the sharp end of an Islamic uprising, but defeated by a new, younger, generation seeking not only better living conditions and jobs, but also increased freedom and, for want of a better word, dignity. This was a young generation that had had enough of corruption and coercion. The events centred on Cairo's Tahrir Square represented an uprising rather than a revolution. The democratic forces present were certainly strong; but they lacked any obvious leadership and were, inevitably, ill-organised. Once the uprising had achieved its first priority – the unceremonious ejection of Mubarak – progress to some form of democracy was probable, if not certain. Popular opinion had become mobilised, and a degree of dignity restored.

The importance of Egypt's position in the Arab equation cannot be underrated. Not only does Egypt have the region's largest population (81.12 million), its capital city Cairo is the biggest city in the Arab world with a population of over 11 million. The counterpoint to the burgeoning middle classes of Cairo and Alexandria is the depressing reality that virtually half Egypt's population earn less than US$2.00 per day.

Uprising or revolution?

Appropriately enough, the adoption of Tahrir Square held symbolic overtones. Named Midan Tahrir in 1952 to mark the Egyptian Revolution of that year, the name translates as Liberation Square. Initially, the groups that assembled in the square in early 2011 were for the most part students and Cairo's disaffected youth. Before long what had started as a student protest began to attract other social strata. Trades unionists and more radical left wing groups joined the protesters, as did Egypt's middle classes. There was one significant absentee from this somewhat anarchic coalition. The geriatric leaders of the Muslim Brotherhood were certainly among those who failed to grasp the importance of what was going on. The Brotherhood had initially favoured boycotting the protest completely, convinced that after a matter of days it would be routed by Egypt's security apparatus. The Brotherhood were wrong-footed by their belief that the burden of revolutionary protest rested with them rather than any other body. Their U-turn was catalysed by the realisation that most of the Brotherhood's younger members shared the protesters' beliefs.

The protest movement, as represented by the Tahrir Square demonstrations, brought together several strands of Egyptian discontent. These focussed on the restoration (perhaps more accurately defined as the introduction) of democracy, an end to the overwhelming security apparatus and its powers, the adoption of more equitable social and economic policies and a re-balancing of Egyptian foreign policy away from its close association with the perceived policy objectives of the US. To some extent, Egypt's middle classes differed in their priorities, seeking the establishment of democracy, but not necessarily advocating a break from the market economy or a de-coupling from the US.

In the post-uprising period, a degree of polarisation in Egyptian politics began to make itself evident. In April 2011 the Alliance of Socialist Forces was formed, comprising the Egyptian Socialist Party, the Popular Democratic Alliance (which incorporated the former Tagammu party), the Democratic Labour Party, the Socialist Revolutionary Party and the Egyptian Communist Party (itself formerly part of the Tagammu Party). Rather confusingly, alongside the Alliance was established a 150 member National Council incorporating most of Egypt's left-wing groupings, which include trades unionists (Egypt has some fifty independent trades unions), alongside agricultural labour groupings. Some of the more radical fringe political parties such as the Jamaat al Islamiya appeared to have abandoned their terrorist tactics in favour of pursuing more peaceful politics.

In mid-2011 the right-wing of Egypt's political spectrum appeared to be less well organised than their left-wing opponents. The Al Hizb al Watani al Dimuqrati (National Democratic Party) (NDP), which had long been the *de facto* single political party (and had been re-elected as recently as December 2010) was in the process of dissolution and no obvious replacement had emerged.

Encouragingly, in the referendum on Egypt's constitution held in mid-March 2011, the 41 per cent turnout of the 45 million on the electoral roll was the highest turnout ever recorded. Fourteen million voted in favour of the new constitution, only 4 million voted against. The general election that was originally mooted for June 2011 had, by September, slipped back to November 2011. The amendments approved by the referendum's majority limited future presidents to two terms each of four years (Mubarak had ruled for 30 years). Presidents would not be eligible if they held dual nationality or were married to a non-Egyptian. Future presidents were also obliged to appoint a vice president within 60 days of their election. The referendum was, in the view of many left wing and secular protesters, something of a stitch-up between the *ancien régime* and the Supreme Military Council. Rather than reflecting some form of conspiracy, the referendum's shortcomings probably reflected a lack of time for preparation.

The Brotherhood

For better or for worse, under the Mubarak regime and under that of Sadat before him, the Muslim Brotherhood had been the only opposition political party tolerated and even tacitly supported by the regime. None the less, in the general elections of November and December 2010 not a single Brotherhood candidate was elected. Technically banned from standing, the Brotherhood's candidates stood as independents. Mid-June 2011 saw the surprising announcement that the Muslim Brotherhood's Freedom and Justice Party was joining forces with the long-established Wafd party which had supported the Mubarak regime's opposition to radical Islam as represented by the Brotherhood. The Freedom and Justice party was reportedly based on the tenets of Turkey's ruling Adalet ve Kalkinma Partisi (AKP) (Justice and Development Party), which won a third election in June 2011.

KEY INDICATORS **Egypt**

	Unit	2006	2007	2008	2009	2010
Population	m	72.13	73.57	76.80	*76.70	*81.12
Gross domestic product (GDP)	US$bn	107.38	127.93	162.40	188.00	218.50
GDP per capita	US$	1,489	1,739	2,160	2,450	2,789
GDP real growth	%	6.8	7.1	7.2	4.7	5.1
Inflation	%	4.2	10.9	11.7	16.2	11.7
Unemployment	%	10.6	9.0	8.7	9.4	9.0
Oil output	'000 bpd	678.0	710.0	722.0	307.0	736.0
Natural gas output	bn cum	44.8	46.5	58.9	62.7	61.3
Exports (fob) (goods)	US$m	19,036.0	24,455.0	29,849.0	23,089.0	–
Imports (fob) (goods)	US$m	30,653.0	39,354.0	49,608.0	39,907.0	–
Balance of trade	US$m	-11,617.0	-14,900.0	-19,759.0	-16,818.0	–
Current account	US$m	2,635.0	412.0	-1,415.0	-3,349.0	-4,318.0
Total reserves minus gold	US$m	24,462.0	30,188.0	32,216.0	32,253.0	33,612.0
Foreign exchange	US$m	24,341.0	30,054.0	32,108.0	30,947.0	32,351.0
Exchange rate	per US$	5.71	5.54	5.31	5.69	5.79

* estimated figure

Originally opposed to political participation, in 2011 the Brotherhood had not only formed the Freedom and Justice Party, but dissident factions had also produced less conservative parties known as 'the Middle' (al-Wasat), and another named Renaissance (al-Nahda). Younger members of the Brotherhood found the new political climate refreshing, if more complex. The Brotherhood now had to cope with the realities of multi-party politics; it could no longer cast itself in the role of official opposition. The melting pot of Tahrir Square and the ability to express political views openly, meant that, often for the first time, rigid political positions and views were aired and challenged. Having been left behind at the beginning of the uprising, the Brotherhood appeared to be making up ground. It was rumoured by some secular parties that the Brotherhood had made some sort of deal with the army's ruling Supreme Council.

The Brotherhood's preparations for the planned elections were centred on its Council of Ulemas or Religious Constitutional Council, whose brief was to ensure that planned legislation conformed to Sharia (Islamic law). The Council was perceived by many Egyptians as an idea borrowed from the Iranian revolution where a similar council rules over the elected government. This ran counter to the apparent moderation of the Freedom and Justice Party. While the AKP has sought to reinforce Turkey's Islamic culture, it is seen outside Turkey as a 'mildly' Islamic political party. The Egyptian political and historical context made it unlikely that the Brotherhood could ever aspire to any form of political mildness. This probably accounted for the scepticism of Egypt's secular middle classes – notably in Cairo and Alexandria – towards the Brotherhood's affirmations of more liberal attitudes.

Implicit in the Brotherhood's approach to the elections as exemplified by the formation of the Religious Constitutional Council was that secular parties and non-Muslim parties would in fact become illegal. Significantly, this stricture would apply to Egypt's Christian Copts, representing some ten per cent of the population. Following the Tahrir Square uprising, Egypt's Copts found themselves increasingly attacked, their churches burned down. The attacks were attributed to the minority Salafists – Muslims embracing a Saudi-inspired form of Islamic extremism. The puritanical Salafists' violent behaviour was apparently caused by rumours of Muslim women converting to Christianity to extricate themselves from unhappy marriages. The Salafist interpretation of Islam does not allow Muslims to leave the faith. Other attacks on Christian churches were attributed to Muslim mobs responding to exaggerated rumours that Christians were in possession of arms or illegally building churches. Although the Brotherhood's Religious Constitutional Council appeared to favour the Salafist interpretation of Islam, the two branches of Islam have long been enemies, reflecting the rivalry of their two 'host' countries.

Elections begin

In November 2011, Cairo's iconic Tahrir Square again became the focal point of the shifting tectonic plates that had begun to characterise Egyptian politics. Egyptian soldiers and police fired tear gas and set fire to protest tents in the square in an effort to drive out thousands of protestors demanding a speedier transfer of power from increasingly discredited military rulers to a civilian government. Eleven protesters were reported killed just one week before Egypt's first free elections. The pro-democracy protesters had lost patience with Egypt's ruling (and for the most part seriously wealthy) generals, suspecting them of seeking to cling to power following the election of parliament and a new president.

Shortly after the violence in Tahrir Square, in the first round (of three) of voting the political groupings that sought a more general application of Sharia (Islamic law) won a clear majority of the votes. The Muslim Brotherhood's Freedom and Justice party emerged in front with 37 per cent of the 10 million or so valid votes. The Brotherhood managed to prevail even in more sophisticated political centres such as Cairo and Alexandria, where Egypt's more liberal parties had hoped to exhibit their greatest strength. The second placed Nour Party won 24 per cent of the vote. The Nour party is dominated by the more extremist Salafis, and did not even exist until mid-2011. It also seeks to impose strict Sharia.

The second and third rounds of voting were due to take place in January 2012. Of concern to the more liberal elements of the Egyptian population was the inevitability that the Islamists' parties grip on a future parliament looked invincible, especially since the remaining election rounds were due to take place in areas where the Islamist parties were strong. Perhaps ironically, Egypt's liberals might find themselves eventually grateful to the unpopular military.

One of the tasks for the new parliament will be to appoint a committee to draft a constitution that many Islamists envisage being based to a large degree on the principles set out in the Koran. But the ruling military council has indicated that it will choose 80 of the committee's 100 members. Troubles ahead?

Sharika al Geish

Just how much of the US$1.5 billion granted by the US to Egypt, or more accurately to the Egyptian Army, each year ended up being spent on defence apparatus is a matter of speculation. What is certain is that the aid money allowed the Egyptian army to become a significant economic and commercial force, known as Sharika al Geish – Army Incorporated. While other ranks in the army are conscripts the officer corps is exclusively made up of professional soldiers. The army's overweening presence in both Egyptian business and politics meant that it was an obvious target for criticism and opposition from the protest movement. Responding to this sensitivity, the Army seemed prepared to take a back seat, apparently uncertain about the nature of its role in Egypt's future government. The army seemed almost relieved that progress towards genuine democracy would allow it to adopt a lower profile.

The IMF – just how wrong can we be?

The events that shook Egypt in January 2011 caught many observers by surprise. Egypt's well funded intelligence services certainly seemed to have fallen asleep at the wheel, as did the US's CIA. Another agency that, perhaps less surprisingly, mis-read all the signs, was the International Monetary Fund (IMF). In what had become a long-established pattern of unimaginative economic strategies, in its April 2010 Article IV Consultation Statement, the IMF had gone so far as to praise the Mubarak regime for implementing 'neo-liberal' economic measures. Paradoxically, having complained about Egypt's slow progress in introducing key fiscal reforms (which included the introduction of a property tax, broadening VAT revenues and phasing out energy subsidies) all of which were likely to increase popular discontent, the IMF went on to endorse the overall policies of the Mubarak regime.

The IMF report, re-iterating its naïve belief in one-size fits all economic policies, encouraged the expansion of Public

Private Partnerships (PPPs) which would involve increased privatisation and outsourcing from the public to the private sector. This seemed to have scant political sensitivity for the concerns and aspirations of Egypt's middle and working-classes. The coffee shop test – that is to say half an hour spent in conversation with Egypt's articulate middle class – would perhaps have increased the IMF's awareness of the massive scale of corruption, at all levels of government. The traditional and accepted format of IMF 'staff visits' to most member countries remained one of hermetic meetings with government officials. Rumours of the Mubaraks' illicit wealth were rife in the streets of Cairo and Alexandria, rumours which were later borne out by declarations from banks in France, Spain, Switzerland and the UK of sizeable bank deposits held on behalf not only of the Mubarak family, but also other members of the regime. Failing to appreciate the size of the problem, the IMF did no more than make a passing reference to a Transparency International report that noted: 'accountability and transparency, and weaknesses in the legal/regulatory system were key reasons for Egypt remaining 111th out of the 180 countries on its Corruption Perception Index.' No recommendations, no criticism.

Having got this observation out of the way, the IMF continued: 'Decisive action to continue the earlier reform momentum should focus on addressing the remaining (sic) structural weaknesses.' In addition to sound economic macroeconomic policies, the IMF insisted, 'efforts should focus on: resuming privatisation and increasing the role of carefully structured and appropriately priced PPPs, should assist fiscal adjustment and mobilise private resources for infrastructure investment.'

The IMF's response to the Egyptian uprising consisted of a veritable flurry of briefings and reports. First came in an interview with the organisation's director for the Middle East Masood Ahmed, published in the *IMF Survey* E-magazine. Mr Ahmed said that the events in Egypt 'will clearly have a negative economic impact in the short run, but over the longer term they can position Egypt to better exploit its potential to achieve higher standards of living and employment for all sections of its population.' No doubt, growth will take a hit this year (2011), falling below the 5.5 per cent rate registered in the last two quarters or 2010, as tourism and foreign investment will decline. The budget deficit, already high, is likely to increase this year with lower economic activity, higher food prices, higher interest rates, and any new spending initiatives. Finally, unemployment has long been high – and especially so among the youth at 25 per cent – and it could worsen this year with lower economic activity.

In what amounted to something of a *volte-face* for the IMF, Mr Ahmed appeared to steel himself to acknowledge that the IMF in endorsing the Mubarak regime so wholeheartedly had simply got Egypt wrong. 'However, it is also important to recognise that greater transparency, competition and a broader ownership of the national economic reform agenda should enable Egypt to tackle some of the constraints that have held back an inclusive and sustainable improvement in living standards. This will then leverage the country's inherent strengths: a dynamic and young population, a large domestic market, access to key markets, a privileged geographic position, a strong financial sector, and a comfortable level of reserves.' There was no acceptance by the IMF that it's policy of supporting and endorsing the Mubarak regime had, if anything, worsened the position of the average Egyptian. Instead of contrition, there was a vague acceptance that the Egyptian people had made the critical move: 'The Egyptian government and the Egyptian people will define the economic policies that suit Egypt the best to emerge from this period of unrest. The IMF can help by providing the needed technical and policy advice to support the Egyptian authorities confront their short- and medium-term challenges and bring about more inclusive growth, based on its global experience. And this is something we are already doing. As with all other members, if the Egyptian authorities decide that financial support would also be useful, the Fund would be ready to help, based on an assessment of the financial needs.' A handy combination of waffle spiced with rather unacceptable self-satisfaction.

A team from the IMF visited Cairo again in early April 2011. Representatives of the interim Egyptian administration visited Washington later in April to take part in the Spring Meetings of the IMF and World Bank. Egypt had indicated that it anticipated a financing need of some US$10–12 billion for the period to June 2012 from the international community. Egypt had approached bilateral and multilateral partners, including the IMF, to provide the financial support for the programme.

In April Egypt reached agreement with the IMF on a draft 12-month US$3 billion financing package, to support the proposed economic reforms during the transition to democracy. It was left to Ratna Sahay, the IMF's deputy director for the Middle East to announce that: 'Following a revolution and during a challenging period of political transition, the Egyptian authorities have put in place a home-grown economic programme with the overarching objective of promoting social justice.' The proposed reforms, which were announced in Cairo on 5 June, contained measures aimed at supporting economic recovery, generating jobs, and assisting low-income households, while maintaining economic stability. Egypt was the first recipient of IMF financial assistance in the Middle East and North Africa since the events of the Arab Spring. Later, at the G8 Summit meeting in May 2011 in France, the IMF announced that it could make available as much as US$35 billion in financial assistance to the region.

Egypt's budget deficit inevitably widened in the months following the departure of Mubarak. This was largely due to extraordinary spending measures taken by the government as a result of the protests. The larger deficit will be financed in part through foreign grants and loans from bilateral and multilateral development partners, including the IMF. According to the IMF, expenditure in the new budget will focus on human capital and social investment, as well as labour-intensive public works to generate job-intensive growth.

The budget also included a number of tax reforms to generate resources for additional social spending as well as a moderate increase in the improvement of the tax system. These reforms coincided with possibly optimistic efforts to strengthen tax administration and improve compliance. The government's plan also envisaged a number of structural reforms, including the transition to a VAT-like consumption tax and reform of the highly inequitable and costly system of subsidies. Additionally the World Bank pledged US$4.5 billion in support to Egypt over a two-year period to address Egypt's budget and reserve shortfalls and to finance reforms that would strengthen its credit and investment prospects. Saudi Arabia, Qatar, the United States and other countries also promised substantial assistance.

The oil still flows

Egypt's importance in international oil markets is due to its position as a key transit route between the oilfields of the Arabian Gulf and Europe via both the Suez Canal and the Sumed pipeline. The spring 2011 uprising had no effect on oil supplies, even if it did contribute to increased oil-market nervousness. Total oil production, according to the *BP Statistical Review of World Energy 2011* (BP 2011), has declined since the country's 1996 peak of close to 935,000 barrels per day (bpd) to the current level of about 736,000bpd. Egypt's consumption (757,000bpd) is slightly higher than production and the country has begun to rely on a small volume of imports to meet domestic demand. Egypt also has the largest oil refining sector in Africa and since refining capacity now exceeds domestic demand, some non-Egyptian crude oil is currently imported for processing and re-export.

This drop in Egypt's oil production has been offset by the rapid development of the natural gas sector for both domestic consumption and export. Over the past decade, Egypt has become a significant natural gas producer and a strategic source for European natural gas imports. Egypt currently has a pipeline network for exports to Eastern Mediterranean countries in addition to liquefied natural gas (LNG) exports to Europe, Asia, and the Americas. However, increasing domestic demand for natural gas has led the government to stall natural gas export expansion plans. The government has been actively working to attract foreign investments in the sector to increase exploration, production and downstream activities.

Egypt's natural gas sector is expanding rapidly with production quadrupling between 1998 and 2009. According to BP2011, Egypt's estimated proven gas reserves were 78 trillion cubic feet (tcf) at the end of 2010, a slight increase from end 2009 reserves of 77.3tcf and the third highest in Africa after Nigeria (187tcf) and Algeria (159tcf). In 2009, Egypt produced roughly 61.3 billion cubic metres (bcm) and consumed 45.1bcm. With the expansion of the Arab Gas Pipeline, and LNG facilities, Egypt will continue to be an important supplier of natural gas to Europe and the Mediterranean region.

According to Cedigaz (an international association dedicated to natural gas information), in 2009 the electricity sector accounted for the largest share of natural gas consumption (54 per cent), followed by the industrial sector (29 per cent). While still a relatively small share, Egypt is beginning to incorporate natural gas into the transport sector through the use and development of compressed natural gas vehicles and fuelling stations.

The government is also encouraging households, businesses and the industrial sector to consider natural gas as a substitute for petroleum and coal. In January 2008, the World Bank approved loans for the Natural Gas Connections Project, which serves to switch consumption of liquefied petroleum gas (LPG) to natural gas through investment in new connections and to further expand natural gas use in densely populated, low income areas.

As is the case with the oil sector, the Egyptian General Petroleum Corporation (EGPC) is the state entity charged with managing upstream activities including infrastructure, licensing and production. The promotion of the sector along with the development strategy is managed by the Egyptian Natural Gas Holding Company (EGAS). Both EGPC and EGAS work with private companies in joint venture partnerships.

The Egyptian government has an established policy to allocate one third of proven natural gas reserves for domestic market requirements, one third for future generations and the remaining third for exports. Given increasing domestic demand, combined with popular pressures in recent years against LNG and gas export contracts (particularly with Israel), the then oil minister declared in mid-2008 that no new gas export contracts would be made. These policies delayed plans to expand the export infrastructure and have also deterred some investment in the more expensive offshore areas.

According to the US government's Energy Information Administration (EIA), exploration and production activities in Egypt's natural gas sector continue to grow. While there have been marked decreases in the production of natural gas associated with oil extraction, new finds of non-associated gas fields combined with growing domestic demand and export capacity, are increasing interest in the Egyptian natural gas sector. To promote exploration in the more expensive deepwater offshore, the Egyptian government revised pricing policies by agreeing to pay more for natural gas produced in these areas, assuring continued international interest in developing these potential resources. Over 80 per cent of Egypt's natural gas reserves and 70 per cent of production is in the Mediterranean and Nile Delta but exploration and production continue in all major hydrocarbon rich areas including the Western Desert.

Risk assessment

Politics	Uncertain
Economy	Poor
Regional stability	Uncertain

COUNTRY PROFILE

Historical profile

1571 Egypt became part of the Ottoman Empire. Mohammed Ali assumed the rule of Egypt. His descendants ruled until 1952.

1859–69 The Suez Canal was built.

1882 Britain occupied Egypt and although it remained under Ottoman suzerainty, it became *de facto* a British colony.

1914 Britain eliminated the Ottoman suzerainty and the country became a British protectorate – the Egyptian Sultanate.

1922 Following the revolution of Saad Zaghloul in 1919, Britain granted partial independence to Egypt, but retained the right to defend the Suez Canal and Egypt itself. Egypt was renamed Kingdom of Egypt.

1928 Muslim Brotherhood founded by Hasan al-Banna.

1936 Signing of the Anglo-Egyptian Treaty, which restricted British military presence to the Suez Canal Zone.

1947–49 Egypt contributed to a pan-Arab military force that failed to occupy the newly-created state of Israel.

1952 The 23 July Revolution, led by the army, ousted King Fu'ad, who had just succeeded his father, King Faruq.

1953–56 Egypt was declared a republic under President Mohammed Neguib in 1953. Neguib relinquished power in 1954 to Colonel Gamal Abdel Nasser, who was officially elected in 1956.

1956 Nasser nationalised the Suez Canal to fund the construction of the Aswan High Dam to regulate the annual flooding of the Nile River. Egypt blockaded the Israeli Red Sea port of Eilat; Israeli forces attacked and occupied the Sinai Peninsula, later being joined by Britain and France seeking to regain control of the Canal Zone. In the face of strong international opposition, particularly from the US, all three withdrew their forces.

1958 Egypt and Syria formed the United Arab Republic (UAR) in the first step towards their aim for Arab unity.

1961 Syria withdrew from the union with Egypt but Egypt remained known as the UAR.

1967 Egypt again blockaded Eilat; Israel launched and won the Six Day War against Egypt, Jordan and Syria, taking control of the Sinai Peninsula and the Gaza Strip, which had been Egyptian

territory. Crucially, they also took control of the Golan Heights, overlooking Syria. The Suez Canal was closed.
1968–70 The War of Attrition was a limited war fought between Egypt and Israel, initiated by Egypt as a way to recapture the Sinai Peninsula from Israel; the war ended without changes to the frontiers.
1970–73 Anwar al Sadat was elected president following the death of Nasser. He renamed the country the Arab Republic of Egypt and ruled it as a one-party state. The Aswan High Dam was inaugurated by the President. In the 6 October War (also known as the Yom Kippur War), Egypt and Syria invaded Israel to reclaim some of the land lost in the Six Day War, but despite early strategic gains for Egypt and Syria, Israel counter-attacked and repelled the invasion, re-conquering the Golan Heights from Syria.
1975 The Suez Canal reopened, having been closed since the 1967 war.
1977 Sadat visited Jerusalem, which led to the Camp David Peace Accords, the signing of the Egyptian-Israeli Peace Treaty in 1979 and the eventual Israeli withdrawal from the Sinai Peninsula in 1982.
1981 President Sadat was assassinated by Islamic extremists. A national referendum approved Hosni Mubarak as president and also allowed political opposition parties for the first time. A State of Emergency (known locally as emergency laws) was declared, extending police powers, suspending constitutional rights, legalising censorship, and curtailing political activity and street protests.
1979 Egypt was expelled from the Arab League.
1989 Egypt re-joined the Arab League.
1991–94 Egypt contributed to the US-led military campaign against Iraq. Egypt was a party to peace agreements between Israel and the Palestinians, which began negotiations on the status of the former Egyptian territory of Gaza.
1996–2000 The Al Hizb al Watani al Dimuqrati (National Democratic Party) (NDP) was re-elected in the 1996 and 2000 elections. Mubarak was re-elected president for a fourth term.
2003 Emergency powers established when Sadat was assassinated in 1981 were extended for another three years.
2004 Ahmed Nazif became prime minister. In November, the funeral of Palestinian leader, Yasser Arafat, was held in Cairo.
2005 Egypt hosted the Sharm El Sheik summit, at which Palestinian President Abbas and Israeli Prime Minister Sharon signed a truce; Israel was to withdraw from Gaza and the Palestinian authorities curb the violence of militant groups opposed to Israel. Egypt resumed diplomatic ties with Israel. A constitutional amendment allowed multiple candidates in the presidential elections, which was won by incumbent Mubarak, for a fifth consecutive term.
2006 Emergency laws, which gave broad powers of arrest and detention to the security forces, were extended by two years.
2007 A referendum amended 34 articles in the constitution, including items aimed at banning political activities and the establishment of political parties based on race, religion and ethnicity; it also increased the power of the president and adopted an anti-terrorism law to replace emergency laws.
2008 Hamas militants breached several sections of the Egypt-Gaza Rafah border crossing allowing thousands of Palestinians to cross into Egypt, many to stock up on food and other necessities. Israel demanded that the border be closed to prevent the restocking of Hamas armouries. While foreign-led negotiations failed to provide a permanent solution, Hamas and Egyptian officials reached their own agreement.
2009 Egyptian forces closed the last breach along the Gaza border. In a crackdown on Islamist militants 25 leading members of Hizb al Wasat (Muslim Brotherhood) were jailed. Liberal democrat and opposition politician Ayman Nour (El Ghad), was released from jail on health grounds. Egypt sponsored talks between Palestinian rivals, Fatah and Hamas, over a proposed unity government.
2010 In January Mohammed Badi was named as leader (*general guide*) of Egypt's outlawed opposition Islamist movement, the Muslim Brotherhood. Analysts consider him a conservative who would likely steer the Brotherhood away from political activism and focus on religious and social work. In February, the World Bank approved a US$280 million loan for a second terminal at Cairo's international airport. In March Sheikh Mohammed Sayed Tantawi, Grand Imam of the al Azhar mosque and head of the al Azhar University, died in Saudi Arabia, aged 81. In May President Mubarak issued a decree renewing the country's emergency laws for a further two years. On 14 May, Egypt signed an agreement with Ethiopia, Uganda, Tanzania and Rwanda to redistribute their relative share of Nile waters; negotiations had begun in 1997. In the June elections for the Majlis al Shura, the ruling NDP won 80 seats in total (out of 132), four other political parties won one seat each and four independents were elected; there are also 44 unelected members. On 1 December, all opposition parties withdrew from further involvement in the general elections, following results that showed the NDP had won 209 out of 221 seats. The ruling NDP won an overwhelming majority of 420 seats (out of 518). The opposition, which had quit the election after the first round, cited extensive electoral fraud.
2011 Following mass-protests in Cairo's Tahrir Square at the leadership of President Mubarak, which began on 24 January, Mubarak dismissed his government on 29 January and appointed Ahmed Shafiq as prime minister in an attempt to pacify the protestors. However, the protests continued and on 11 February, Mubarak resigned and control of Egypt was taken over by the of Supreme Council of the Armed Forces (SCAF)), led by Field Marshall Mohamed Hussein Tantawi (defence minister); Ahmed Shafiq remained as prime minister. The SCAF refused to lift the emergency laws. Mr Mubarak and his family retreated to their residence in Sharm el Sheikh, the Red Sea resort. By 11 February there had been 384 confirmed deaths related to the demonstrations; of which 232 deaths were in Cairo. On 20 February, all prisoners arrested since 25 January were released and an investigation into officials responsible for violence towards demonstrators was begun on 28 February. A constitutional referendum was held on 20 March, in which 77.27 per cent of voters agreed to constitutional changes that included limiting the presidential term to four years and a two-term limit. On 28 March the SCAF announced that Mubarak and his family had been placed under house arrest. Essam Abdel-Aziz Sharaf became prime minister on 3 March. The former ruling-NDP was dissolved on 16 April and its assets, including its headquarters and other buildings, were seized and handed over to the government treasury. The prosecutor general ordered the arrest of Mubarak and his sons, Ala and Gamal, on charges of corruption. In April the Muslim Brotherhood announced it was setting up a new political party, the Freedom and Justice Party (FJP). It said it would be a civil, not a theocratic, group and would contest up to half the seats in the upcoming September election. It was officially recognised as a political party on 7 June. On 1 June Nabil al Arabi became secretary general of the Arab League. From 28 May the Egyptian government relaxed restrictions at the Rafah border crossing into Gaza, allowing women, children and men over 40 to pass freely. Men aged between 18 and 40 will still require a permit, and trade is prohibited. Prime Minister Essam Sharaf reshuffled his cabinet in mid-July, after protesters complained about the slow rate of reform. Many of the ministers, especially foreign minister Mohamed el Orabi, were said to have been close to former President Mubarak. On 8 July, thousands of

protestors gathered in Tahrir Square, Suez and Alexandria, as part of the 'Friday of Determination' demanding immediate reforms and a quicker prosecution of former government officials. Al Orabi resigned on 16 July. On 26 July, the news agency Mena disclosed that Hosni Mubarak was 'depressed and refusing food' in hospital. On 3 August Mubarak was put on trial for corruption and complicity in the deaths of protestors, during the Arab Spring uprising. On 15 August the judge at Mubarak's trial announced that it would be merged with that of former interior minister, Habib al-Adly, who is also accused of ordering the killing of protesters. The judge adjourned the trial until 3 September and said the trial would nolonger be televisied live. A state of emergency was declared on 10 September after an attack on the Israeli embassy by demonstrators in Cairo. Changes to the issuance of visas were announced it September, including halting the facility whereby US and many European citizens could obtain a visa on arrival. The move is expected to have an adverse affect on tourism, although the government denied this. An amendment to the election law was granted by the Supreme Council of the Armed Forces, on 2 October to allow one-third of parliamentary seats that had been set aside for political parties to be contested by independent candidates. There were clashes between Copts and security forces on 9 October. The clashes led to the resignation of finance minister, Hazem el-Beblawi, who objected to the way the government handled the protest. On 3 November, a government-sponsored set of guidelines for drafting the constitution were published and caused controversy with plans to exempt the military and its budget from civilian scrutiny and by giving the military a veto over legislation dealing with its affairs, as well as limiting the power of parliament to select a panel to write the constitution. On 14 November, the Higher Administrative Court ruled that former members of the NDP (former-president Mobarak's political party) were allowed to stand for parliament as independent candidates. Prime Minister Sharaf and his government resigned on 21 November, following three days of violence as demonstrators again occupied Tahrir Square in Cairo, protesting at the military's entrenchment of its power in the political life of Egypt. By 22 November, 26 people had been killed and many more maimed and wounded; Field Marshal Tantawi declared that scheduled parliamentary elections would take place and presidential elections would be held in July 2012 (brought forward from late-2012 or 2013). However, protestors continued to call for the military rulers to step aside. There were protests and injuries in other cities as well. On 24 November, the ruling Supreme Council of the Armed Forces (SCAF) appointed Kamal Ganzouri as prime minister. Parliamentary elections for the lower chamber began on 28 November, and were held in three rounds (the second on 5/6 December and the third on 14/15 December) to allow judicial supervision of each round. Over 40 political parties fielded a combined total of around 6,000 candidates to contest the 498-seat lower house, of which two-thirds will be chosen by proportional representation using party lists; the remaining one-third are open to all who are nominated regardless of affiliations - of these half must be 'professional' and the other half 'workers' or 'farmers'.

2012 The final results of three rounds of elections were posted on 13 January. The Democratic Alliance for Egypt (DAE) (a coalition of five political parties, led by the Freedom and Justice Party; plus independents) (Islamic, Muslim Brotherhood) won 127 seats by proportional representation (PR) and 108 seats by first-past-the-post (FPTP) for a total of 235 seats. Although the DAE will have overall legislative powers the military council retains presidential powers until a new president is elected later in the year.

Political structure

Constitution

Under the 1971 constitution, amended in 1980, Egypt is an Arab Republic with a democratic socialist system. The constitution states that there should be no discrimination on the grounds of race or religion. The country is divided into 26 governorates, with governors appointed by the president. There is universal suffrage with a voting age of 18.

On 20 March 2011, in a constitutional referendum, 77.27 per cent of voters agreed to constitutional changes that included limiting the presidential term to four years and to a two-term limit. Other changes included the appointment, by the president, of a vice president within 60 days of taking office; the power of the president to declare a state of emergency to be circumscribed by a parliamentary majority; presidential candidates to be aged over 40 years and not of dual-nationality, nor married to a non-Egyptian; the judiciary to be responsible for monitoring the electoral process; the Supreme Court to have the power to adjudicate electoral challenges and disputes; civilians to no-longer be tried by military courts and the newly elected parliament must write a new constitution within 60 day of its election in 2011.

Independence date

1922 (Britain supervised until 1946)

Form of state

Democratic socialist republic

The executive

Executive power rests with the president, who is elected by universal suffrage for a six-year term (and may be re-elected), having been nominated by at least one-third of the People's Assembly and approved by at least two-thirds. The president may choose one or more vice presidents, and appoints, and may dismiss, the prime minister and cabinet.

The president may take emergency measures, but these must be approved by a referendum within 60 days; he may also dissolve the People's Assembly (the legislative body) prematurely, but a referendum and elections must be held within 60 days. The president is supreme commander of the armed forces and head of the police.

National legislature

The bicameral parliament consists of the Majlis al Shaab (People's Assembly, lower house), with 454 members directly elected by universal suffrage and 10 members appointed by the president. All members serve for a five-year term. The Majlis al Shura (Advisory Council, upper house) has 264 members of which 174 are directly elected and the remainder appointed by the president, to serve for six-year terms. Every three years elections for an alternate half the membership takes place. Legislative powers of the Advisory Council are limited; the People's Assembly has ultimate power.

Legal system

The legal system is based on the constitution of 1971. Officially, Egyptian law is based on *Sharia* (Islamic law), although in practice it is based on English common law and the French Napoleonic code. Christians and Jews are subject to their own jurisprudence in personal status affairs. The Court of Cassation, consisting of five judges, is the highest court of appeal. Courts of appeal (three judges) sit in Cairo and four other cities. Assize courts (three judges) deal with serious crimes. Central tribunals (three judges) handle ordinary civil and commercial cases. Summary tribunals (one judge) deal with both civil and criminal cases and have the power to impose fines and decree three-year prison terms.

Last elections

28–29 November, 5–6 and 14–15 December 2011 (parliamentary); 6 September 2005 (presidential); 1 and 8 June 2010 (parliamentary: Majlis al Shura (upper house))

Results: Parliamentary (combined total after three rounds): Democratic Alliance for Egypt (a coalition of five political parties, led by the Freedom and Justice Party, plus independents) (Islamic, Muslim Brotherhood) won 127 seats by proportional

representation (PR) and 108 seats by first-past-the-post (FPTP) for a total of 235 seats; the Islamic Bloc (a coalition of three political parties, led by the Al Nour Party) 69 PR, 27 FPTP, total 123 seats; New Wafd Party 36 PR, two FPTP, total 38 seats; Egyptian Bloc (a coalition of three political parties, led by the Social Democratic Party), 33 PR, one FPTP, total 34 seats; Al Wasat Party 10 PR, total 10 seats; Reform and Development Party eight PR, one FPTP, total nine seats; The Revolution Continues Alliance (a coalition of five political parties, led by the Socialist Popular Alliance Party) seven PR, two FPTP, total nine seats; eight other political parties and 21 independent candidates won the remaining 40 seats. Ten seats are reserved for presidential appointees.
Presidential: Hosni Mubarak (NDP), won 88.6 per cent of the vote; Ayman Nour (al Ghad) 7.3 per cent. On 11 February 2011, Mubarak resigned.
Parliamentary (Majlis al Shura): NDP won 80 seats in total (out of 132), four other political parties won one seat each and four independents were elected; unelected members 44.

Next elections

19 January –22 February 2012 (parliamentary, upper house); June-July 2012 (presidential)

Political parties

Ruling party

Awaiting announcement from the Supreme Council of the Armed Forces (SCAF)

Main opposition party

Awaiting announcement from the SCAF

Population

81.12 million (2010)*

Last census: 11 November 2006: 72,798,013

Population density: 63 inhabitants per square km. Urban population: 43 per cent of the total (1995–2001).

Annual growth rate: 1.9 per cent 1994–2004 (WHO 2006)

Ethnic make-up

Eastern Hamitic (99 per cent); the remaining 1 per cent comprises minorities including Armenian, Italian and Greek.

Religions

Muslim (mostly Sunni, but including between six and seven million Sufis) (92 per cent); Coptic Christian and others (8 per cent).

Education

Primary education is compulsory and free; followed by three years of intermediate school and two years of secondary school, which are also free, but not compulsory. University graduates have long been guaranteed employment by the state, and this has contributed to the growth of a bloated and overstaffed state bureaucracy. The desire by graduates for office-based professional employment has led to a shortage of skilled technical labour. The government is encouraging more students to go into technical education.

Literacy rate: 56 per cent adult rate; 73 per cent youth rate (15–24) (Unesco 2005).

Compulsory years: 6 to 12

Enrolment rate: 101 per cent, total primary school enrolment of the relevant age group (including repetition rates); 78 per cent, total enrolment of the relevant age group, in intermediate and secondary schools, (World Bank).

Pupils per teacher: 23 in primary schools

Health

Healthcare in the private sector has become increasingly popular in recent years, especially in Cairo, with the construction of a number of private hospitals that provide an alternative to the severely over-stretched public health service. However the general decline in living standards has placed many private sector healthcare institutions in financial difficulties.

Family planning is widely available and officially encouraged, although many religious leaders continue to preach that it is against Islam. The population continues to grow and the government expects it to double to 110 million over the next 30 years, even if the target of halving the average family size is achieved.

Improved water sources and sanitation facilities are available to 95 per cent and 94 per cent of the population, respectively.

HIV/Aids

HIV prevalence: 0.1 per cent aged 15–49 in 2003 (World Bank)

Life expectancy: 68 years, 2004 (WHO 2006)

Fertility rate/Maternal mortality rate: 3.2 births per woman, 2004 (WHO 2006); maternal mortality 170 per 100,000 live births (World Bank).

Child (under 5 years) mortality rate (per 1,000): 33 per 1,000 live births; 4 per cent of children aged under five were malnourished (World Bank).

Head of population per physician: 0.54 physicians per 1,000 people, 2003 (WHO 2006)

Welfare

Social security provisions include sickness benefits, pensions, health insurance, training and subsidies on basic goods, including pharmaceuticals. The government places particular stress on the improvement of rural living standards and has established rural social units to provide health, education and agricultural services. Social services include care for mothers and children, the aged, the handicapped and prisoners, family planning, cultural education and literacy courses. The government, employers and employees contribute to a national insurance scheme that covers pensions and sickness benefit. A social development fund provides retraining, unemployment insurance and assistance to people who lose their jobs as a result of reforms and the privatisation of public enterprises.

Main cities

Cairo (capital, estimated population 7.7 million in 2010); Greater Cairo, 10.6 million, is the largest city in Africa.
Other cities include Alexandria (4.0 million), Giza (2.7 million), Shubra al Khaymah (1.0 million), Port Said (548,900), Suez (488,200), Luxor (421,500), Asyut (401,600), El Faiyum (305,100), Ismailia (297,500), Aswan (256,100), El Minya (235,400).

Media

Egypt is the centre for pan-Arab electronic broadcasting having been the first with its own satellite (Nilesat 101) (www.nilesat.com.eg), it has the largest production facilities for Arabic films and TV shows and is the most influential news broadcasting and publishing centre in the Middle East.

While libelling the president, state institution and foreign heads of state may carry a penality of imprisonment, criticism of the regime in unexceptional.

Press

Dailies: In Arabic, *Al Ahram* (www.ahram.org.eg) the oldest Arabic newspaper anywhere and the government-owned *Al Jumhuriyah* (www.algomhuria.net.eg), and the semi-state owned *Al Akhbar* (www.elakhbar.org.eg). Party political newspapers include and *Al Messa* (www.almessa.net.eg), *Almasry Alyoum* (www.almasry-alyoum.com), and *Al Ahali* (www.al-ahaly.com). Other private newspapers include *Al Wafd* (www.alwafd.org), *El Akhbar* (www.elakhbar.org.eg) and *El Fagr* (www.elfagr.org).

In English, the state-owned *The Egyptian Gazette* (www.algomhuria.net.eg/gazette) and *Daily News Egypt* (www.dailystaregypt.com).

In French, in government-owned *Al-Ahram Hebdo* (http://hebdo.ahram.org.eg) and *Le Progrès Egyptien* (www.progres.net.eg).

Weeklies: Some daily newspapers have weekend editions. In Arabic, the political magazine *Al Watan al Arabi* (www.alwatanalarabi.alqanat.com) covers regional news, *Akidaty* for general interest and *Horreyati* (www.horreyati.net.eg) for entertainment. Women's magazines

include *Nisf el Dunia* with social and women's issues, *Hawwa* covers home and family issues and *Kolenas* is distributed internationally.
In English, the *Middle East Times* (www.metimes.com) provides general interest and commercial and financial news, *Watani* (www.wataninet.com), and *Al-Ahram* (http://weekly.ahram.org.eg).
Business: Most daily newspapers have sections on business matters. The only dedicated newspaper is the *Business Today Egypt* (www.businesstodayegypt.com), in English, which has a section called *In the Black* specifically covering commercial and corporate news.
In Arabic the weekly *Al Ahram Iktisadi* covers analysis of Egyptian business.
Periodicals: Monthly publications in Arabic includes the influential *Sabah el Kheir* (www.rosaonline.net/sabah) which covers general interest features. The quarterly *Al Siassa al Dawlya* covers domestin and international politics.
IBA Media is Egypt's leading English-language publisher with *Egypt Today* (www.egypttoday.com), published six times per year.

Broadcasting

The national, public broadcaster is the Egypt Radio Television Union (ERTU) (www.ertu.org).
Radio: ERTU provides cultural, news, entertainment, youth and sports programmes through a network of eight national radio stations with two external services. Private, commerical stations include El Gouna Radio (www.romolo.com) and Nile FM (http://nilefmonline.com), both playing western music.
Television: ERTU operates two national and local channels. There are numerous satellite TV stations available, led by the ERTU Nile Channel, (www.nilesat.com.eg), Dream TV and Al Mihwar (www.elmehwar.tv) are privately owned.
Egyptian broadcasters transmit over 80 channels throughout the Middle East and the Mediterranean region.

Advertising

There is a total ban on cigarette and tobacco advertising; cosmetics, medications, and food products require a permit from the relevant ministry.
Traditional print and broadcast advertising is becoming sophisticated with western style high-concept and teaser ads. Posters and billboards are popular in city locations. Electronic advertising is offered through websites and individual mobile/cell phone reception.

News agencies

National news agency: MENA (Middle East News Agency)

Economy

Despite natural resources of petroleum, natural gas, phosphates, gold and iron ore, plus agricultural produce of wheat and cotton, and a major tourist industry, manufacturing in pharmaceuticals, vehicles and parts, the economy could only provide a per capita income of just US$2,450 in 2009. Egypt is Africa's second most populous country (after Nigeria) and Cairo is the continent's largest city. Egypt's population is over 75 million, of which, according to the UN Human Development Indices (2009), 23.4 per cent are classified as poor and live below the poverty line.
GDP growth in 2007 was 7.1 per cent, which was maintained in 2008 at 7.2 per cent. The global economic crisis had little effect on the Egyptian economy, as its banking sector is not being greatly integrated into world financial markets, there being relatively low private credit. Banking regulation over 2004–07 increased bank asset requirements, a major buffer to the weakness suffered by foreign banks in Western markets. In fact at no time did the economy slip into recession and the 4.7 per cent growth in 2009 is expected to rise to 5.0 per cent in 2010. Nevertheless, inflation, which had been in single digits up to 2006, jumped to 11 per cent in 2007 as global food and fuel prices rose. The international credit agency Moody's upgraded Egypt's sovereign rating from negative to stable in October 2009, as inflation modified, falling from a headline inflation rate of 24 per cent in August 2008 to 11.4 per cent in April 2009.
Trade between Egypt and the US increased year-on-year by 22.2 per cent in the first quarter of 2010, reaching US$2.24 billion, up from US$1.82 billion in 2009, which was largely due to the overall competitiveness of Egyptian products and the fall in the Egyptian pound against the US dollar.
The economy is also sustained traditionally by Suez Canal tolls and remittances from expatriate workers. However, both recorded declines as global trade slowed and employment became scarce. Suez Canal tolls fell from a high of US$5.2 billion in 2007/08 to US$4.7 billion in 2008/09; short term projections do not indicate a return to profit of over US$5 billion before 20011/12. Remittances reached an all time high of US$7.4 billion in 2007/08 but have since fallen with a 26 per cent reduction in 2009. There was a decline of US$1.7 billion in the third quarter of the 2008/09 financial year, down from US$2.3 billion in the previous quarter.
The hydrocarbon sector is the mainstay of the economy. Oil exports in 2007/08 were US$11.2 billion due to a record high in world prices, but have since fallen to between US$7.9–8.8 billion. Natural gas exports have remained constant at between US$3–4 billion.
Agriculture accounted for 13 per cent to GDP in 2008 and although it has been deregulated and is largely in private hands, certain commodities deemed strategic to the economy such as cotton, sugar and rice, are still regulated by the government.
Textile and garment manufacturing is a major sector in the economy, not only as a large employer but also as an exporter. Around 25 per cent of non-hydrocarbon exports are made up of finished clothes and fabrics. Egypt has the continent's largest garment industry; the spinning industry was restructured in 2006 with the aid of European Union funding along with government investment.
The Islamic Development Bank (IDB) and the World Bank announced in October 2010, that they were setting up a regional initiative of up to US$1 billion to help close the infrastructure gap in the Middle East and North Africa (Mena) and help boost economic growth. The World Bank considers that the Mena region requires US$75–100 billion per year to sustain the growth of recent years and boost economic competitiveness. However private sector investment is limited and the new initiative should address the shortfall in investment, through Shari'a-compliant and conventional investment. The initiative should benefit Egypt, Morocco, Jordan and Tunisia in particular.
The crisis that toppled the regime of Hosni Mubarak was estimated to have cost the country over US$301 million per day. Economic growth was also affected as the tourist industry was immediately affected, followed by investment and trade.
On 12 May 2011, the Egyptian government officially requested a loan of US$2 billion from the IMF to underwrite its 2010/11budget deficit, which was expected to reach 9–10 per cent. It was predicted that Egypt would need an extra US$10 billion in 2011/12. Egypt had already agreed loans with the African Development Bank (ADB) and the World Bank.

External trade

Egypt, as a member of the Common Market for Eastern and Southern Africa (Comesa), operates within a free trade zone (FTZ) with 13 of the 19 member states. It also signed the Agadir Agreement which proposes to set up a FTZ between Egypt, Jordan, Tunisia and Morocco. In 2005 the Greater Arab Free Trade Area (Gafta) was ratified by 17 members, including Egypt, creating an

Arab economic bloc. A customs union was established whereby tariffs within Gafta are reduced by one per cent each year, until none remain. It is also a signatory of the Euro-Mediterranean Partnership agreement, which provides for the introduction of free trade between the EU and 10 Mediterranean countries by 2012.

Imports

Principal imports are machinery and equipment, foodstuffs, chemicals, wood products and fuels.

Main sources: US (typically 11 per cent of total), China (8 per cent), Saudi Arabia (6 per cent).

Exports

Principal exports are crude oil and petroleum products, cotton, textiles, metal products and chemicals. Other exports include refined sugar cane, raw cotton, potatoes, rice and oranges.

Main destinations: Italy (typically 11 per cent of total), India (7 per cent), The Netherlands (6 per cent).

Agriculture

Farming

Irrigation is supplied by the River Nile and the government is looking at ways to improve the efficiency of water use through the construction of lined canals and pipes. Problems surrounding the ecological effects of the Aswan High Dam persist. Fertile land is found in the Nile Valley and Delta – the cultivable area accounts for only 2.4 per cent of the total land area at around 3.1 million hectares.

The construction of the Aswan High Dam in the 1970s initially improved crop yields by providing a constant source of water for irrigation. However, the dam had a damaging long-term effect on agriculture. It has permanently raised the water table, causing serious drainage problems and high salinity as well as depriving the Nile valley of annual silt, a natural fertiliser, previously brought down by the river during the flood season. The silt has had to be replaced by costly chemical fertilisers.

Virtually all water in Egypt comes from the River Nile, from which Egypt is allowed to take 55.5 billion cubic metres of water a year, under its agreement with nine other Nile basin countries. This imposes strict limitations on the expansion of agriculture.

A number of major irrigation schemes are under way. These are along the coast north-west of Alexandria, the Nile border with Sudan, East Oweinat in the desert and the largest project of them all, the Southern Valley Scheme. The cost of the Southern Valley Scheme is projected to reach US$85 billion by 2017. Saudi investment will build the largest farm in the world (six times bigger than Singapore) which will reach full production in 2010 and will employ 25,000 people permanently, as well as additional seasonal labour.

Agricultural production in Egypt is highly labour-intensive. Output suffers from crop infestation, price controls, fragmented land tenure, increased soil salinity and consumer preference for imported foods. Major subsistence crops include maize, sorghum, rice, wheat, beans and vegetables. Egypt's wheat consumption far outstrips local production, with Egyptian wheat crops supplying just 40 per cent of annual domestic demand. Some 65 per cent of food requirements are imported, making Egypt's annual food import bill around US$5.5 billion.

Cotton is a major export crop; however, WTO agreements, which came into force in 2005, removed tariffs and trade and will put enormous pressure on the industry as it attempts to compete with Asia that has lower production costs and lower prices. Egypt produces high-quality long staple cotton that has been traditionally exported to Europe, the US and Japan, and it may have to lose many jobs as it carves out a niche market in quality cotton rather than competing for the mass market.

Fishing

There are active fishing industries in the Mediterranean and the Red Sea, as well as more limited freshwater fishing on the Nile and Lake Nasser. Egypt typically produces over 300,000 tonnes of seafood and 190,000 tonnes of freshwater fish per annum. Virtually all of this is used for domestic consumption. Eleven lakes used to provide an annual 173,000 tonnes of fish but this rate has declined in recent years due to overfishing, lack of investment and pollution.

Forestry

Forests covers less than 1 per cent of Egypt's land area.

Industry and manufacturing

Industrial production, with a growth rate estimated at 2.5 per cent in 2004, is an important component of the economy, providing 32.1 per cent of GDP, while manufacturing provides 18.2 per cent. However, individually they were both outperformed by the total services industry that provided 52.4 per cent of GDP in 2004, of which tourism represented the lion's share.

The government places emphasis on: industrial diversification and import substitution, the development of downstream chemicals, and of heavy industry such as the Helwan Iron and Steel Company, the Nag Hammadi aluminium plant and El Dikheila integrated steel works. Industry and manufacturing has been dominated by state-owned companies however there is a renewed interest by the government to sell off enterprises, including metallurgical, food, wood pulp, and chemical processing, and various smelting works.

A number of cotton concerns are also on the privatisation list, although these companies are at risk, not from the shift in economic rationalisation, by rather global trading dynamics. World Trade Organisation (WTO) rulings that came into practice on 1 January 2005 removed all global tariffs and subsidies on processed cotton. Egypt, as a major manufacture of cotton thread and cloths, could lose thousands of jobs and millions of dollars in export sales. However, a niche market is being formed, supplying cotton apparel to the US under the Qualified Industrial Zones (QIZ) protocol, whereby manufactured goods from nominated QIZ, which must contain 11.7 per cent Israeli input, will be given free access to US markets.

The petrochemical sector is a leading contributor to GDP and has a predicted 6 per cent annual growth.

Egypt has a growing automotive industry, supplying both vehicles and components. There are 18 vehicle manufacturers operating under joint trade agreements with foreign companies. BMW invested US$35 million in a new factory, providing jobs for 500 workers, which opened in 2004. There are plans to invest a further US$25 million in more facilities. Nissan will open a new assembly plant, geared to produce 3,800 cars a year, which is scheduled to be operational by 2007.

Tourism

Egypt has a wealth of archaeological and historic sites, coastal resorts and is the outlet for the longest river in Africa, the Nile, which is a major waterway, offering tourists cruise trips down to Aswan. It is close enough to its target market of Europe to be recognisable and exotic enough to provide interest for those looking for more stimulation than a beach holiday.

According to the World Travel and Tourism Council (WTTC), tourism has provided steady income for Egypt, with tourist numbers averaging 11 million visitors annually. Tourism's total contribution to the economy was US$37.8 44 billion in 2010. Despite a fall in 2009 when the global economic crisis cut the number of visitors travelling worldwide, the tourist industry has been growing steadily each year, providing around 15 per cent of all employment in Egypt. Capital investment in the sector fell in 2009 by -13.6 per cent, rather than the previous average of 20 per cent growth per annum.

The tourist industry was badly affected by the civil unrest of the Arab Spring at the beginning of 2011. Foreign governments

initially advised their citizens not to visit Egypt and both tour operators and individuals cancelled their bookings. However, as the political situation eased, the sector returned to normal, following a short burst of promotion.
Changes to the issuance of visas were announced it September, including halting the facility whereby US and many European citizens could obtain a visa on arrival. The move is expected to have an adverse affect on tourism, although the government denied this.

Mining

Government policy aims to encourage foreign and local companies to explore for and exploit raw materials. Agreements have been reached for exploration and production of sulphur, phosphate and gold. The government is keen to extend franchises for other minerals, especially titanium and silver. Among non-oil raw materials, only iron ore, phosphate rock and limestone is produced on a significant scale. Other minerals produced include baryte, clay, feldspar, fluorspar, gypsum, kaolin, quartz, salt, silica sand and talc. Manganese and chrome deposits have also been exploited, while commercial deposits of zinc, tin, lead and copper have been discovered in Sinai.
A contract to mine sulphur in Sinai is held by Freeport Egyptian Sulphur Company, a wholly owned subsidiary of US firm Freeport McMoran. The annual production capacity is thought to be around 250,000 tonnes per year (tpy). Egypt also has deposits of uranium.
Although Egypt has no bauxite, it has developed a significant aluminium industry based on electric power from the Aswan High Dam. Production was initially used for basic consumer goods but Egypt now exports a wide range of basic aluminium products.

Hydrocarbons

Proven oil reserves were 4.1 billion barrels in 2007, with production of 665,080 barrels per day (bpd). However consumption was 680,000bpd, the balance being imported. Mature oil fields are declining in production and considerable effort is being expended on enhanced oil recovery. The discovery of a new oil field, Ak Zahraa, in East Ras Qattara (ERQ), with an estimated flow rate of 2,615bpd, was announced in August 2009.
Egyptian General Petroleum Corporation (EGPC) is responsible for oil exploration. Its subsidiary Petrobel is a joint venture with the Italian Agip and is exploring for and operating wells in Badr el Din, near the Gulf of Suez.
Egypt has Africa's largest oil refinery sector with nine refineries; total annual production is 726,000bpd. EGPC operates the largest refinery of El Nasr at Suez. The government has plans to upgrade facilities to increase production of value-added petroleum products.
Proven natural gas reserves were 2.03 trillion cubic metres (cum) in 2007, with production at 46.5 billion cum, an increase of 4.2 per cent on the 2006 figure of 44.7 billion cum. Reserves are expected to last until the 2040s given current levels of production. Domestic consumption in 2007 was 32 billion cum while 2.35 billion cum was exported to Jordan via a pipeline (generating 80 per cent of Jordan's electricty). The remainder was exported worldwide as liquefied natural gas (LNG). Under a 20-year agreement signed in 2008 Egypt exports gas to Israel (constituting 40 per cent of Israel's requirements);
Natural gas began flowing to the Lebanese Beddawi gas-fired power plant in September 2009. In June 2011 the gas pipeline was hit by an explosion for the third time in six months.
Coal reserves total some 27 million tonnes, but there is no commercial production.

Energy

Total installed generating capacity was 20.47 gigawatts (GW) in 2006, producing over 110 billion kilowatt hours. The state-owned Egyptian Electricity Authority (EEA) plans to increase capacity to 32GW by 2011, through use of gas-fired turbines at 11 new power stations and by expansion of its existing stations.
The Aswan High Dam, in Upper Egypt, provides 12 per cent of the country's electricity. Renewable energy schemes include photovoltaic panels (solar energy) which accounts for 45MW and installed wind energy accounting for 230MW.
Egyptian natural gas was scheduled to begin flowing to the Lebanese Beddawi gas-fired power plant in September 2009. When at full capacity around 850,000cum of natural gas will operate two turbines.
In November 2010 the World Bank agreed to two new loans, totalling US$820 million, for the construction of a 1,500MW combined cycle gas turbine power plant north of Giza, and the development of a wind turbine power project to be located in the Gulf of Suez.

Financial markets

On 27 January 2010 the stock exchange was closed while political unrest was ongoing; it re-opened in March following consultations with the new prime minister. The Egyptian stock exchange (EGX) had, until its closure, been one of the most dynamic in the Middle East, but it had lost 16 per cent in value of the benchmark EGX 30 Index in the two days before closure. The stock exchange authorities set up new rules to avoid further slumps, including suspending trading for 30 minutes if stocks move by up to 5 per cent and cutting, by one hour, trading hours.

Stock exchange

Cairo and Alexandria Stock Exchange (EGX)

Banking and insurance

The banking sector is dominated by four public-sector commercial banks – Banque Misr, Bank of Alexandria, Banque du Caire and the National Bank of Egypt – which hold about 60 per cent of deposits, 70 per cent of assets and 65 per cent of loans, and are the main conduit for public-sector trade, savings and financing.
In 2004, Egypt was removed from the OECD list of non-co-operative countries on money laundering after reforms had been implemented.
The Central Bank of Egypt (CBE) strengthened the monetary policy framework over 2004 which should aid it as it manages and limits inflationary pressures while stimulating market driven interest rates. The IMF in a 2005 report stressed that the CBE independence from political interference should be maintained.
As part of the privatisation programme under way by the government two state banks are in the process of being sold off to the commercial sector. In 2006, bids for the Bank of Alexandria valued the bank at US$1.6 billion – a figure over five times greater than the government's own valuation. Proceeds of the sale will go to re-capitalising other state-owned banks and a reduction in Egypt's public debt.

Central bank

Central Bank of Egypt

Main financial centre

Cairo

Time

GMT plus two hours (GMT plus three hours from May to September).

Geography

Most of Egypt is located in the north-east corner of Africa between the Mediterranean Sea, the Red Sea, Sudan and Libya. The Sinai peninsula, separated from the African continent by the Suez Canal and the Red Sea, borders Israel. The peninsula also faces Jordan and Saudi Arabia across the Gulf of Aqaba.
The world's longest river, the Nile, flows through deep gorges from mountains in the south, before ending its journey in the Nile delta on Egypt's northern coast, with outlets into the Mediterranean Sea. Its influence on Egypt has been profound as over thousands of years the river has been the lifeblood of the country, its flood plains have provided fertile agricultural land and the necessary freshwater for life

in an arid landscape. About 95 per cent of Egypt is uninhabitable desert and over 90 per cent of the population lives within 20km of the Nile.
The Awan Dam, completed in 1970, created Lake Nasser, the world's third largest reservoir. Its hydroelectric power station produces about half of Egypt's electricity and maintains a steady flow of water downstream.

Hemisphere
Northern

Climate
The climate is dry with very little rainfall, hot in summer and cool in winter. Temperatures in Cairo in the north vary from 43 degrees Celsius (C) maximum in summer to 18 degrees C maximum in winter. Sandstorms (the *khamsin* or *simoon* winds) can disrupt air traffic between March and May.
Rainfall is largely confined to the Mediterranean coast, with around 200 millimetres a year in Alexandria. Egypt is dependent on the Nile for nearly all its water needs. The government is pressing ahead with desert reclamation schemes, but these are also dependent on limited Nile waters as reserves of water under the desert have so far proved relatively insignificant.

Dress codes
Lightweight clothing is necessary for the hot summer months (May to September). Business dress is formal – suits are worn for all occasions. Men should not wear shorts, except at the beach and women should wear modest clothing in public, covering their arms and legs.

Entry requirements
Passports
Required by all. Some exceptions are allowed for a few nationals of the Middle East. Contact the nearest Egyptian Consulate for more information.
Passports must be valid for six months beyond the intended length of stay.
Visa
Required by all, except citizens of some adjacent countries, for full list of exceptions contact the local embassy or visit http://egypt.embassyhomepage.com.
Business and tourist visas, valid for three months, available for most Europeans and North Americans, were obtainable at the point of entry until September 2011 when it was announced that visas would have to be required before arrival. There are a number of exceptions to this ruling (including tourist groups, family groups through travel agencts) and it is advisable to check with an Egyptian embassy before travelling.
All visitors, except those Europeans and US nationals on tourist visas, must register at the Office of Foreigners and Nationality within seven days of arrival. Hotels will normally undertake this on the visitor's behalf.
Currency advice/regulations
The Import of local currency is unlimited, however its export is prohibited. The import and export of foreign currency is unrestricted.
Customs
It is permitted to import one bottle of alcohol and 200 cigarettes. Camera, video equipment and computers should be declared at customs.
Prohibited imports
Illegal drugs, firearms and cotton.
Export of any antiquity older than 100 years must have a clearance from the Ministry of Cultural Affairs.

Health (for visitors)
Mandatory precautions
A vaccination certificate against yellow fever is required if travelling from an infected area.
Advisable precautions
Typhoid, hepatitis A, tetanus vaccinations are recommended. Malaria exists from June–October in the El Faiyum area. There is also a rabies risk. Polio was eradicated in 2005.
Avoid drinking tap water and use bottled water instead; water used for brushing teeth or making ice should be boiled first or otherwise sterilised. All fruit should be peeled and only well-cooked meat, vegetables and fish, served hot, should be eaten. Salad and mayonnaise may carry increased risk, except in top-class restaurants. Avoid food sold on the streets.

Hotels
There is a wide range available. Bills are quoted in US dollars and may be settled in Egyptian currency. A 20 per cent tax and service charge should be added to all prices.

Credit cards
Most credit cards are widely accepted. Excepting airline tickets, the free market exchange rate is used in calculating credit card transactions.

Public holidays (national)
Fixed dates
^7 Jan (Coptic Christmas Day), 25 Apr (Sinai Liberation Day), 1 May (Labour Day), 23 Jul (Revolution Day), 6 Oct (Armed Forces' Day), 24 Oct (Suez Victory Day).
Variable dates
^Coptic Easter Monday, Eid al Adha, Eid al Fitr, Islamic New Year, Birth of the Prophet.
^ Followers of the Coptic faith observe this holiday.
Islamic year 1433 (26 Nov 2011–14 Nov 2012): The Islamic year contains 354 or 355 days, with the result that Muslim feasts advance by 10–12 days against the Gregorian calendar. Dates of feasts vary according to the sightings of the new moon, so cannot be forecast exactly.

Working hours
As a Muslim country the official weekend begins on Friday. Embassies and the offices of some foreign companies also close on Saturday and Sunday. Some companies treat Thursday as a half day. Hours may also vary between winter and summer.
Banking
Sun–Thu: 0830–1400. Money exchanges in city centres also 1700–1900 or 1800–2000.
Business
Sat–Thu: 0900–1700.
Government
Sun–Thur: 0900–1500.
Shops
Sat–Thur: 0900—1300 and 1600—2000 (summer); 1000—1800 (winter). During Ramadan Sat–Thur: 0930—1530 and 2000—2200.
Department stores offer extended hours and local shops may vary their hours to suit.

Telecommunications
Mobile/cell phones
There are GSM 900 services operating in all popluated areas.

Electricity supply
220–440V AC in most areas; in some rural districts 110–380V AC is still found.

Weights and measures
Metric system (local units also in use).

Social customs/useful tips
Hospitality is considered a prime virtue and it would be rude for visitors not to accept a token drink or other invitation. Many hosts will not allow a guest to pay for anything during his or her stay. Guests should therefore not squabble over paying at a restaurant, for example. In address, use the first name with the appropriate title (for instance Mr, Madame, Doctor, Engineer). Business cards in Arabic are appreciated.
In June 2010 authorities in Alexandria began enforcing a smoking ban in government buildings. The ban will extend to cafes in 2012 with the plan to make Alexandria the first non-smoking city in Egypt. Egyptians smoke some 19 billion cigarettes annually, including the traditional shisha water pipes which are found in many coffee shops.

Security
Violent crime against foreigners is rare. However, thieves operate in busy tourist areas such as Giza and Luxor. In these

areas it is best to avoid wearing flashy or expensive jewellery.
Given its strategic position in the Middle East, Egypt is particularly sensitive regarding national security. Photographing bridges, railway stations and military installations is forbidden. Carrying a video camera can cause problems with the Egyptian authorities.

Getting there

Air
National airline: Egyptair
International airport/s: Cairo International (CAI), 24km from city, facilities include incoming/outgoing duty-free shops, banks, post office, restaurants and car hire. Borg el Arab-Alexandria International (HBE), 60km from city, including business centre, bank, post office, restaurant, shops, pharmacy and car hire. Luxor Airport (LXR) 5.5km from the city.
Taxis and bus services run to all.
Airport tax: None
Surface
Road: There are road links from Libya and Israel.
A new road from Aswan to Port Sudan was under construction in 2003 but has yet to be completed. Until then no roads to Sudan are recommended.
Water: There are ferry services to Port Said and Alexandria from many destinations across the Mediterranean, run by Menatours. There are ferries between Aqaba in Jordan and Nuweiba on the Sinai peninsular and to Suez from Jeddah in Saudi Arabia. There are steamer services across Lake Nasser from Sudan, although these are suspended during periods of instability in Sudan.
Main port/s: Alexandria, Al Ghardaqah, Aswan, Bur Safajah, Damietta, Marsa Matruh, Port Said and Suez.

Getting about

National transport
Air: Egyptair operates domestic services from Cairo to Luxor, Aswan, Hurghada, Abu Simbel and Alexandria. Air Sinai operates services to North and South Sinai. If planning to fly south, book well in advance. Travel to certain areas of the Nile Delta is restricted.
Road: There is a 31,000km surfaced network which includes good roads linking Cairo-Alexandria, Cairo-Port Said, Ismailia-Suez-Sinai, Cairo-El Faiyum-Luxor-Aswan.
Buses: There are four intercity bus companies: luxury service Superjet, West Delta Bus Company, East Delta Bus Company, and Upper Egypt Bus Company. There are fast and comfortable services between most towns and cities, although they tend to be crowded, and tickets should be booked in advance where possible.
Rail: There are train services to all main cities and towns in Egypt, including express and through trains from Cairo to Alexandria, Luxor and Aswan. Four classes available; certain routes have air-conditioned sleeping cars and buffet service. Tickets must be reserved, sometimes up to two days in advance.
Water: Traditional sailboats (*felucca*) offer rides along the Nile river.
City transport
Taxis: Metered and unmetered taxis are readily available, but meters where fitted are often not used. Fares should be agreed in advance.
Air-conditioned limousines are available at airports and main hotels. Chauffeured taxis from Cairo airport to the city centre are recommended. Hotels have their own shuttle services. Hotel taxis or chauffeured hire cars are more efficient and can be hired by the day, subject to negotiation. Fares are usually listed in the major hotels.
City centre taxis are cheap, although often uncomfortable and never have air-conditioning. If you are travelling beyond the city centre, it is a good idea to carry a map to guide the taxi driver. The journey time from Cairo International Airport to the city is about 40–60 minutes. Tipping is usually 10 per cent.
Buses, trams & metro: Local buses are numerous, cheap and crowded, as are the few trams still in existence. The Cairo metro is fast, inexpensive and not too crowded, it has 43 stations, five of which run through central Cairo.
Ferry: Several routes run north and south of the city plied by waterbuses.
Car hire
An international driving licence and third-party insurance are needed. Hire charges should be negotiated in advance. The maximum speed limit on main roads is 90kph, rising to 100kph on the Cairo-Alexandria desert road; fines for speeding are substantial. Traffic in Cairo is heavily congested.

BUSINESS DIRECTORY

The addresses listed below are a selection only. While World of Information makes every endeavour to check these addresses, we cannot guarantee that changes have not been made, especially to telephone numbers and area codes. We would welcome any corrections.

Telephone area codes

The international direct dialling code (IDD) for Egypt is +20, followed by area code and subscriber's number:

Alexandria	3	Ismailiya	64
Ashara Ramadan	15	Kafr El Sheik	47
Aswan	97	Luxor	95
Asyut	88	Maeria	3
Benha	13	Mahalla	43
Beni Suef	82	Mansoura	50
Cairo	2	Marsa Matruh	3
Damanhur	45	Port Said	66
Damietta	57	Pyramids	2
El Arish	68	Sacheia	16
El Minya	86	Sohag	93
Fayoum	84	Suez	62
Giza	2	Tanta	40
Heliopolis	2	Zagazig	55

Useful telephone numbers

Cairo
Police: 122
Fire: 125
Ambulance: 123
Aswan
Police: 22147
Alexandria
Police: 960-151-122
Suez
Police: 23-929

Chambers of Commerce

Alexandria Chamber of Commerce, 31 El-Ghorfa El-Togaria Street, Alexandria (tel: 809-339; fax: 808-993).

American Chamber of Commerce in Egypt, 33 Soliman Abaza Street, Doki-Giza, Cairo (tel: 338 1050; fax: 338-1060; e-mail: info@amcham.org.eg).

Aswan Chamber of Commerce, Abtal El-Tahreer Street, Aswan (tel: 323-084).

Cairo Chamber of Commerce, 4 Midan El-Falaki, Cairo (tel: 354-2943; fax: 355-7940).

Damietta Chamber of Commerce, Saad Zaghloul Street, Damietta (tel: 322-799; fax: 320-632).

Egyptian-British Chamber of Commerce, PO Box 4EG, 299 Oxford Street, London W1A 4EG (tel: 020-7499-3100; fax: 020-7499-1070; e-mail: info@theebcc.com).

Fayoum Chamber of Commerce, El-Nadi El-Reyadi Street, El Fayoum (tel: 322-148).

Federation of Egyptian Chambers of Commerce, 4 Midan El-Falaky, Cairo (tel: 795-1136; fax: 795-1164; e-mail: fedcoc@menanet.net).

Ismailia Chamber of Commerce, 163 Saad Zaghloul Street, Ismailia (tel: 221-663; fax: 322-515).

Port Said Chamber of Commerce, Benayet Souk El Goumla, Port Said (tel: 222-733; fax: 236-141).

Red Sea Chamber of Commerce, Old City Council Building, Hurghada (tel: 440-761).

Suez and South Sinai Chamber of Commerce, 47 Salah Eldin Elayoubi Street, Suez (tel: 227-783).

Banking

Alexandria Commercial and Maritime Bank, PO Box 2376, 85 El Horreya Avenue, 21519 Alexandria (tel: 392-1237, 392-1556, 392-9203; fax: 391-3706).

Arab African International Bank, 5 Midan Al-Saray Al Koubra, Garden City, Cairo (tel: 794-5094/5/6; fax: 795-8493).

Arab International Bank, 35 Abdel Khalek Sarwat Street, Cairo (tel: 391-8794, 391-6391; fax: 391-6233).

Bank of Alexandria, 49 Kasr El Nil Street, Cairo (tel: 393-6262, 391-1203; fax: 391-0481, 391-980).

Bank of Commerce & Development, 'Al Tegaryoon', PO Box 1373, 13 26th July Street, Sphinx Square, Mohandessin, Cairo (tel: 302-8156, 302-1623; fax: 302-3963).

Cairo Barclays Bank, PO Box 110, Maglis El Shaab, 12 Midan El Sheikh Youssef, Garden City, Cairo (tel: 366-2600; fax: 366-2810/11).

Cairo Far East Bank, PO Box 757, 104 El Nil Street, Dokki, Cairo (tel: 336-2516/18; fax: 348-3818).

Crédit International d'Egypte, 46 El Batal Ahmed Abdel Aziz Street, Mohandessin, Cairo (tel: 336-1897, 336-1898; fax: 360-8673).

Delta International Bank, PO Box 1159, 1113 Corniche El Nil Street, Cairo (tel: 575-3492; fax: 574-3403).

Egyptian American Bank, PO Box 1825, 4 & 6 Hassan Sabri Street, Zamalek, Cairo (tel: 738-0126, 738-0136, 738-2661; fax: 738-0609, 738-0450).

Misr Exterior Bank; Cairo Plaza Building, Cornish El Nil, Boulaque, Cairo (tel: 778-701, 778-619, 766-381, 766-360; fax: 762-806, 578-0238).

Misr International Bank, PO Box 218, Embaba, 54 El Batal Ahmed Abdel Aziz Street, Mohandessin, Cairo (tel: 749-4424, 749-7091; fax: 700-928).

National Bank for Development (NBD), PO Box 647, 5(A) El Borsa El Gedida Street, 11511 Cairo (tel: 392-3245; fax: 390-5681).

National Bank of Egypt, PO Box 11611, National Bank of Egypt Tower, 1187 Corniche El Nil, Cairo (tel: 574-9101; fax: 576-2672).

Nile Bank, PO Box 2741, 35 Ramses Street, Abdel Moneim Riyad Sq, Cairo (tel: 574-1417, 574-3502, 575-1105; fax: 575-6296, 575-3640).

Suez Canal Bank, PO Box 2620, 11 Mohamed Sabri Abu Alam St, Cairo (tel: 393-1066, 393-1048, 393-1215; fax: 391-3522).

Central bank

Central Bank of Egypt, 31 Kasr el Nil Street, Cairo (tel: 392-6211; fax: 391-7168; email: info@cbe.org.eg).

Stock exchange

Cairo and Alexandria Stock Exchange (EGX), www.egyptse.com

Travel information

Cairo Airport, Airport Road, Heliopolis, 11776 Cairo (tel: 265-4611; fax: 263-7132; internet: www.cairo-airport.com).

Egyptair, New Administrative Complex, Airport Road, Cairo (tel: 267-4700–4709; fax: 418-3715; internet: www.egyptair.com).

Ministry of tourism

Ministry of Tourism, Misr Tourist Tower, Abbassiya Square, Abbassiya (tel: 284-1707; fax: 285-9551; email: mot@idsc.gov.eg).

National tourist organisation offices

Egyptian Tourist Authority, Misr Travel Tower, Abbassia Square, Cairo (tel: 286-4509, 284-1970; fax: 285-4363; internet: www.touregypt.net).

Ministries

Ministry of Agriculture, Anal and Fish Wealth and Land Reclamation, Nadi El Seid Street, Dokki, Giza (tel: 702-677; fax: 703-889; email: capi@idsc.gov.eg)..

Ministry of Cabinet Affairs and Administrative Development, 1 Magles El Shaab Street, Cairo (tel: 354-1722; fax: 355-6306; email: cabinet1@idsc.gov.eg).

Ministry of Culture, 2 Shagaret El Dor St, Zamalek Cairo 03 (tel: 341-5568; fax: 340-6449; email: mculture@idsc.gov.eg).

Ministry of Defence and Military Production, 5 Ismail Abaza Street, Cairo (tel: 355-3063; fax: 354-8739; email: mod@idsc.gov.eg).

Ministry of Economy and International Co-operation, 8 Adly St, Cairo (tel: 390-6796; fax: 390-3029; email: mineco@idscl.gov.eg; internet site: www.sis.gov.eg).

Ministry of Education, 4 Ibrahim Naguib St, Garden City, Cairo (tel: 355-7952; fax: 356-2952; Email: moe@idsc.gov.eg).

Ministry of Electricity and Energy, Ramses Street, Abbassia, Nasr City Cairo (tel: 261-6514; fax: 261-6302; email: mee@idsc.gov.eg).

Ministry of Finance, Lazoughly Square, Justice and Finance Building, Cairo (tel: 354-1055; fax: 354-5433; email: mofinance@idsc1.gov.eg).

Ministry of Foreign Affairs, Maspero, Cairo (tel: 574-9820; fax: 574-9533).

Ministry of Information Maspero, Corniche El Nil, Cairo 02 (tel: 574-8986; fax: 574-8781; email: minexter@idsc1.gov.eg; internet: www.mfa.gov.eg).

Ministry of Health and Population, Magles El Shaab St, Cairo (tel: 354-1076; fax: 355-3966; email: moh@idsc.gov.eg).

Ministry of Higher Education, 4 Ibrahim Naguib Street, Garden City, Cairo (tel: 355-7952; fax: 356-2952; email: mheducat@idsc1.gov.eg, info@sti.sci.eg).

Ministry of Housing, Reconstruction and New Urban Communities, 1 Ismail Abaza St, Cairo (tel: 355-3320; fax: 355-7836; email: mhuuc@idsc1.gov.eg).

Ministry of Industry and Mineral Wealth, 2 Latin America Street, Garden City (tel: 355-7034; fax: 354-8362; email: moimw@idsc.gov.eg).

Ministry of Information, Maspero, Corniche El Nil, Cairo (tel: 747-193; fax: 757-144; email: rtu2@idsc.gov.eg).

Ministry of Insurance & Social Affairs, El Sheikh Rihan Street, Bab El-Louq, Cairo (tel: 337-0039; fax: 337-5390; email: msi@idsc.gov.eg).

Ministry of Interior, El Sheikh Rihan St, Cairo (tel: 355-7500; fax: 355-7792; email: moi1@idsc.gov.eg).

Ministry of Justice, Justice and Finance Building, Lazoughli Sq, Cairo 15 (tel: 355-1176; fax: 355-8103; email: mojeb@idsc1.gov.eg).

Ministry of Land Reclamation, Nadi El Seid St, Cairo 10 (tel: 703-011).

Ministry of Local Administration, Kasr El Aini St, Cairo 04 (tel: 355-3566).

Ministry of Manpower and Immmigration, 3 Youssef Abbas St, Nasr City, Cai (tel: 260-9363; fax: 260-9891; email: mwlabor@idsc1.gov.eg).

Ministry of Petroleum, 16 El Mokhayyam El Da'em Street, Nasr City (tel: 262-2268; fax: 263-6060; email: mopm@idsc1.gov.eg).

Ministry of Planning, Salah Salem Road, Nasr City (tel: 602-935; fax: 263-4747).

Ministry of Public Enterprises, Magles El Shaab Street, Cairo (tel: 355-8026; fax: 355-3606); PEO, 2 Latin America Street, Garden City, Cairo (tel: 794-3484; fax: 795-9233).

Ministry of Public Works and Water Resources, El Nil St, Embaba, Cairo 04 (tel: 354-5884; fax: 355-8008; email: mpwwr@idsc.gov.eg).

Ministry of Rural Development, 4 Shooting Club Street, Dokki, Cairo (tel: 349-7470; fax: 349-7785).

Ministry of Shipping, 7 Abdel Khalek Sarwat St, Cairo, 01 (tel: 764-343).

Ministry of Social Affairs and Insurance, El Sheikh Rihan St, Bab El Louk, Cairo 06 (tel: 354-2900; fax: 917-799).

Ministry of State for Administrative Development and Environment and Ministry of the Public Enterprise, 1 Magles El Shaab Street, Lazoughli Square, CAI 06 (tel: 355-8026; fax: 355-5882; email: mops3@idsc.gov.eg).

Ministry of State for the Affairs of the People's Assembly and the Shoura Council, Magles El Shaab St, Cairo 04 (tel: 355-7750; fax: 355-7681; email: parli@idsc.gov.eg).

Ministry of State for Environmental Affairs, Helwan Road, Cairo (tel: 375-7306; fax: 378-4285; email: eeaa@idsc.gov.eg).

Ministry of State for Military Production, 23 Kobri Al Kubba St, Cairo 36 (tel: 257-8697/2915).

Ministry of State for Planning and International Co-operation, Salah Salem Street, Nasr City (tel: 401-4615; fax: 401-4733; email: miceu@idsx.gov.eg).

Ministry of State for Scientific Research Affairs, 101 Kasr El Aini St, Cairo 04 (tel: 355-7952).

Ministry of Trade and Supply, 99 Kasr El Aini St, Cairo 04 (tel: 355-0360; fax: 354-4973; email: msit@idsx.gov.eg).

Ministry of Transport, Communications and Civil Aviation, 105 Kasr El Aini Street, Cairo (tel: 354-3623; fax: 355-5564; email: garb@idsc.gov.eg).

Ministry of Waqfs, 5 Sabry Abou Alam Street, Bab El-Louq, Cairo (tel: 392-6163; fax: 392-6305; email: mawkaf@idsc1.gov.eg)

Prime Minister's Office, 1 Magles El Shaab St, Lazoughli Square, Cairo 04 (tel: 354-7376; fax: 355-8048).

President's Office, Abdipalace, CAI 06 (tel: 391-0130).

Other useful addresses

Arab League, The Arab League Building, Corniche El Nil, Cairo (tel: 393-4499; fax: 775-626).

Arab Organisation for Industrialisation, 2D Abassiya Square, PO Box 770 (tel: 823-377; fax: 826-010).

Arab Republic of Egypt National Telecommunications Organisation (ARENTO), 26 Ramses Street (tel: 760-333; fax: 771-306).

British Embassy, 7 Ahmed Ragheb St, Garden City, Cairo (tel: 354-0852; fax: 354-0859).

Cabinet Office, 1 Maglis El Shaab Street, Lazoughli Square, CAI 04 (tel: 354-7376; fax: 355-8048).

Cairo Regional Center for International Commercial Arbitration, 3 Aboul Feda Street, Zamalek, Cairo (tel: 340-1330; fax: 340-1336).

Cairo Stock Exchange, 4 Sharia esh-Sherifein, Cairo (tel: 392-1402; fax: 392-8526).

Capital Market Authority, 20 Emad El Din Street, Sixth Floor, Downtown (tel: 777-774; fax: 755-339).

Central Agency for Public Mobilisation and Statistics (CAPMAS), Saleh Salem Street, Nasr City, Cairo (tel: 603-717; fax: 604-099).

Central Post Office, Ataba Square, Cairo.

Commercial International Investment Company (CIIC), 66-68 Mohie El-Din Abou El-Ezz St, Dokki, Cairo (tel: 335-8035, 335-7093, 337-6251; fax: 335-7095).

Commercial Representation Office, 96 Ahmed Orabi Street, Mohandiseen (tel: 347-1892; fax: 345-1840).

Commission of the European Communities Delegation in Egypt, 6 Ibn Zenki Street, Zamalek, Cairo (tel: 340-8388; fax: 340-0385).

Customs Information Centre, 4 El Tayaran Street, Nasr City (tel: 260-5711; fax: 261-2672).

Egyptian Electricity Authority, Abassia, Cairo (tel: 261-6537; fax: 261-6512, 401-1630).

Egyptian Embassy (USA), 3521 International Court, NW, Washington DC 20008 (tel: (+1-202) 895-5400; fax: (+1-202) 244-5131).

Egyptian General Petroleum Corporation (EGPCC), 4 Palestine Street, Fourth Sector, new Maadi (tel: 353-1438; fax: 353-1457).

Egyptian Radio and Television Corporation (ERTC), Radio and TV Building, Sharia Maspiro, Corniche el Nil, PO Box 504, Cairo (tel: 749-508; fax: 746-989).

Faud Nemah (Interpreter Service), 40 Kasr El Nil Street, Cairo (tel: 746-394).

General Authority for Control of Imports and Exports, Atlas Building El Sheikh Maarouf and Ramses Streets (tel: 574-2830; fax: 766-971).

General Authority for Investment and Free Zones, 8 Sharia Adly, PO Box 1007, Cairo (tel: 390-6804).

General Organisation for Industrialisation (GOFI) 6 Khali Agha Street, Garden City (tel: 355-7005; fax: 354-4984).

General Organisation for International Exhibitions and Fairs (GOIEF), Exhibition Ground, Nasr City, Cairo (tel: 260-7811; fax: 260-7845, 260-7848).

International Finance Corp (IFC), 5 El Fallah Street, Mohandessin, Cairo (tel: 347-8081; fax: 347-3738).

Internatinal Monetary Fund (IMF), 31 Kasr El Nil Street, Central Bank, Cairo (tel: 392-4257; fax: 351-7137).

Kamel Bros Ltd (interpreter service), 20 Hassan Sabri Street, Cairo (tel: 817-575).

Local Governorates, El-Islah El-Zerai Building, 10th Floor, 4 Nadi El-Seid Street, Dokki (tel: 349-4770; fax: 349-7788).

Sales Tax Authority, 4 El Tayaran Street, Nasr City (tel: 260-7500; fax: 260-7501).

Social Fund for Development (SFD), Hussein Hegazy and El Aini Streets, Cairo (tel: 354-8339; fax: 355-0628).

Taxation Authority, 5 Hussein Hegazi Street (tel: 355-7784; fax: 355-5438).

US Embassy, 5 Sharia Latin America, Garden City, Cairo (tel: 355-7371).

National news agency: MENA (Middle East News Agency)

Internet sites

Arab Bank: www.arabbank.com

Egypt Business Directory: www.telefax.com.eg/default.htm

Egypt corporate information: www.corporateinformation.com/egcorp.html

Egypt economic indicators: www.economic.idsc.gov.eg/

Egypt www index: http://ce.eng.usf.edu/pharos/

El Salvador

KEY FACTS

Official name: República de El Salvador (Republic of El Salvador)

Head of State: President Mauricio Funes (FMLN) (sworn in 2 Jun 2009)

Head of government: President Mauricio Funes

Ruling party: Frente Farabundo Martí para la Liberación Nacional (FMLN) (Farabundo Marti National Liberation Front) (sworn in 2 Jun 2009)

Area: 21,400 square km

Population: 6.82 million (2009)

Capital: San Salvador

Official language: Spanish

Currency: US dollar (US$) (from 1 Jan 2001; previous currency colón locked at C8.75 per US dollar)

Exchange rate: US$1.00 per US$ (fixed)

GDP per capita: US$3,701 (2010)

GDP real growth: 0.70% (2010)

GDP: US$21.70 billion (2010)

Labour force: 2.50 million (2008)

Unemployment: 5.90% (2008) (plus additional underemployment)

Inflation: 1.20% (2010)

Balance of trade: -US$3.61 billion (2010)

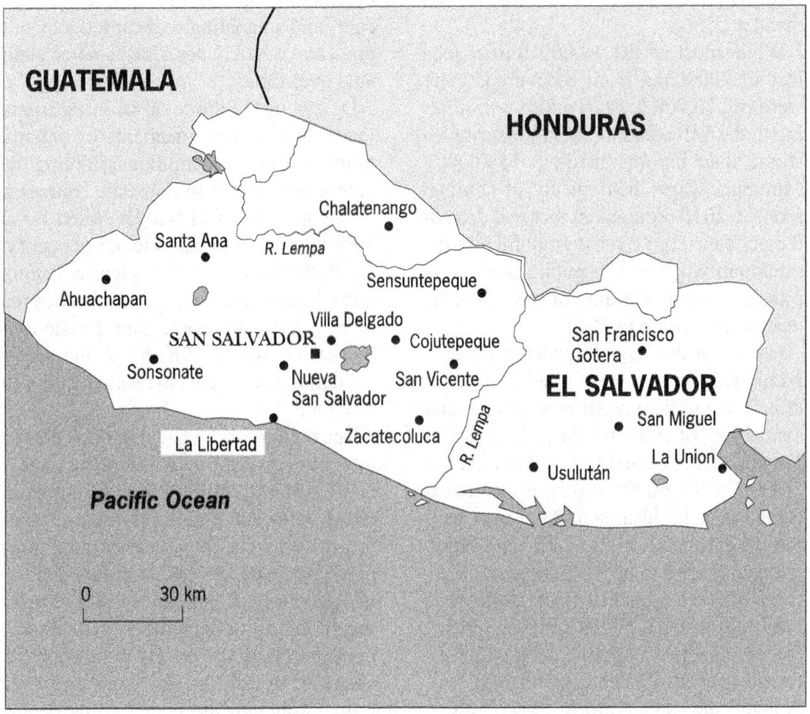

El Salvador emerged from a bitter civil war in the 1980s, during which an estimated 75,000 people died, following the signature of a peace agreement in 1992. Since the end of the conflict, El Salvador has made significant progress towards consolidating peace and democracy. The country's political transformation led to major structural reforms and stable macro-economic policies that resulted in strong economic performance (an average yearly growth of around 6 per cent) during the 1990s. The structural reforms embarked upon included trade liberalisation, financial sector privatisation, a comprehensive reform of the tax system and improvements in the investment climate. The adoption of the United States dollar as legal tender in 2001 helped in reducing inflation and consequently the uncertainty of business and interest rates. The 1992 peace accord implemented by the United Nations allowed former guerrillas of the Frente Farabundo Martí para la Liberación Nacional (FMLN) (Farabundo Marti National Liberation Front) to form a legitimate political party and participate in elections. In March 2009, Mauricio Funes was elected president of El Salvador, a first in history for an FMLN candidate. Mr Funes took office in June 2009 after 20 years of Alianza Republicana Nacionalista (Arena) (Nationalist Republican Alliance) as the ruling party. Although macro-economic stability and the promotion of pro-poor social development and inclusion were key elements of Funes' election platform, the global crisis has constrained the government's fiscal space and made evident the need to address structural vulnerabilities in order to implement a sustainable social programme.

The economy

In 2010, according to the United Nations Economic Commission for Latin America and the Caribbean (ECLAC) the economy of El Salvador did not perform as well as anticipated, with projected growth for the year only 1 per cent. Inflation was expected to have approached the 2 per cent mark, owing to food and energy price hikes late in the year. The current account deficit would be around 2.8 per cent of gross domestic product (GDP) because of a rise in the trade deficit and a slowdown in the flow of remittances. The relative improvement in economic activity, combined with the impact of the 2009 tax reform and the cutback in subsidies for the electricity sector, pushed the non-financial public sector (NFPS) deficit down to the equivalent of 4.8 per cent of GDP.

GDP grew by 0.6 per cent in the second quarter of 2010 after falling for five straight quarters. Growth had been spurred by an agricultural sector that, after severe losses in 2009, grew by more than three per cent in 2010. Because of weak domestic demand (which is expected to increase by 3.2 per cent after contracting by 12.8 per cent in 2009), the manufacturing and services sectors are expected to have shown growth of less than 1 per cent. Consumption, which is projected to grow by some 3 per cent, was affected by the labour situation in El Salvador and in the United States. Persistently high unemployment among the population of Latin American origin in the United States has slowed the growth of remittance flows.

The 0.7 per cent decline in the construction sector, combined with the contraction of credit for the private sector, was forecast to translate into a 0.3 per cent drop in gross fixed capital formation.

Thanks to the slow growth of domestic demand (due in part to the scarcity of credit for the private sector) and to a lag in some price pass-throughs, accumulated inflation to the third quarter of 2010 was just 1.1 per cent. However, it was estimated that year-on-year inflation will be in the area of 2 per cent because of the effect that rains had on some agricultural prices in October and because of energy price subsidies. Inflation is projected to be nearly 3 per cent in 2011 as domestic demand picks up.

While most of the 18,000 formal jobs lost in 2009 had been recovered, there were still 20,000 fewer workers contributing to the Salvadorean Social Security Institute than before the crisis (580,000). Minimum wages held steady in nominal terms in 2010 (equivalent to a real drop of 0.6 per cent), but a substantial hike in the minimum wage and in public sector employee pensions was announced late in the year to take effect in 2011.

In view of the lagged impact of the economic recovery in the United States, the effect of public investment and greater availability of credit for the private sector, growth was expected to top 2 per cent in 2011. The 12 month inflation rate is expected to be in the area of 3 per cent, as is the current account deficit. The NFPS deficit is projected to be 3.7 per cent.

For 2010, the goal of fiscal policy had been to lower the NFPS deficit to ensure the sustainability of public debt, which estimates put at 50 per cent of GDP. Although the tax reform has had a less-than-expected impact because the modest upturn in economic activity delayed implementation of some measures, total receipts for the first nine months of 2010 had been up by 8.7 per cent in real terms.

During the same period total expenditure rose by 1.2 per cent in real terms. Protecting social spending has been a priority, but the combination of real increases in personnel expenses and procurement of goods and services (1.7 per cent) and stagnating real capital expenditure (down by 0.3 per cent) is not sustainable over time.

Delays in the approval of international loans held up disbursements by international financial institutions, forcing the authorities to turn to domestic sources of financing. The 2011 budget called for an NFPS deficit equivalent to 3.5 per cent of GDP, thanks to more efficient collection and a freeze on current expenditure in real terms. With the wage and pension increases announced for the public sector, the deficit is expected to reach 3.7 per cent of GDP.

The medium-term fiscal outlook was for total public sector debt as a percentage of GDP to start to fall in 2011. Although interest rates have not returned to their pre-crisis levels, they were coming down gradually. Despite this decrease, deposits had grown by 2 per cent in real terms in the period up to September 2010. During the same period, lending to the private sector contracted by 4.4 per cent in real terms, although the pace of this decline later slowed. The private sector credit situation contrasted with ample levels of capitalisation and liquidity in the banking sector; banks have used the excess liquidity to improve their liabilities profile and become more profitable.

KEY INDICATORS — El Salvador

	Unit	2006	2007	2008	2009	2010
Population	m	7.01	7.13	5.78	5.82	*6.18
Gross domestic product (GDP)	US$bn	18.65	20.37	22.10	21.10	21.70
GDP per capita	US$	3,270	3,547	3,822	7,366	3,701
GDP real growth	%	4.2	4.6	2.4	-3.5	0.7
Inflation	%	4.0	3.8	7.3	0.5	1.2
Unemployment	%	6.0	6.2	5.9	–	–
Industrial output	% change	3.5	3.4	1.6	27.5	–
Agricultural output	% change	7.5	8.6	7.3	12.5	–
Exports (fob) (goods)	US$m	3,567.0	4,039.1	4,610.7	3,929.8	4,576.7
Imports (fob) (goods)	US$m	7,628.0	8,143.6	9,004.2	7,037.7	8,188.7
Balance of trade	US$m	-4,061.0	-4,104.6	-4,393.5	-3,107.9	-3,612.0
Current account	US$m	-854.9	-1,183.1	-1,595.9	-304.2	-488.3
Total reserves minus gold	US$m	1,814.9	2,110.0	2,443.1	2,868.8	2,569.6
Foreign exchange	US$m	1,777.3	2,070.5	2,404.6	2,612.0	2,317.4
Exchange rate	per US$	1.00	1.00	1.00	1.00	1.00

* estimated figure

International trad

Negotiations on the Association Agreement between the European Union (EU) and Central America that had been completed in May 2010 are expected to impact in 2011. The agreement seeks to foster Central American integration enabling El Salvador to diversify its exports and attract greater flows of foreign direct investment (FDI) from the EU.

The expansion of non-traditional exports (benefiting from rising demand in the United States) was not enough to offset the upturn in imports. This upturn was due in part to recovering consumption but was triggered above all by an oil bill increase of more than 40 per cent.

Under the integrated export promotion policy that is part of the 2010–14 Five-Year Development Plan, export credit guarantees have been available from the Multisectoral Investment Bank since October. Taking into account the 2.5 per cent growth in remittances (16 per cent of GDP), projections showed a current account deficit equivalent to 2.8 per cent of GDP. Because of the delay in disbursements from international financial institutions, approximately half of that deficit will be financed with international reserves.

These reserves ended 2010 at some US$2.70 billion (9.3 per cent less than in 2008), which is equivalent to four months' imports. The remainder of the deficit was financed equally from the capital and financial accounts. The approximately 16 per cent drop in FDI flows contrasts with the extraordinary levels posted in 2009, associated with the sale of assets in the financial sector. Nearly half of these assets had gone to the commerce and financial sectors.

By October 2010 the real effective exchange rate had depreciated by 1.6 per cent, owing to the appreciation of other Central American currencies and of the Mexican peso against the dollar. This should benefit the export sector in the short run. If the economy continues to recover in 2011, the current account deficit is expected to surpass 3 per cent.

Risk assessment

Economy	Fair
Politics	Fair
Regional stability	Fair

COUNTRY PROFILE

Historical profile

1821 The Central American provinces (Costa Rica, Guatemala, Honduras, Nicaragua and El Salvador) declared independence from Spain.
1825 Costa Rica, Guatemala, Honduras, Nicaragua and El Salvador formed the Central American Federation (CAF).
1838 The CAF was dissolved and El Salvador became an independent republic. By the twentieth century, the majority of the indigenous population had been reduced to poverty and discontent, having been pushed off their land, which had been turned over to crops for export. Most of El Salvador's income came from coffee exports.
1929 Coffee prices plummeted following the US stock market crash.
1932 During the uprising of peasants and Indians an estimated 30,000 people were killed by the military, referred to as *La Matanza* (the massacre).
1961 The right-wing Partido de Conciliación Nacional (PCN) (National Reconciliation Party) came to power following a military coup.
1969 Honduras and El Salvador fought what became known as the 'soccer war', which was prompted by land disputes and El Salvador's win in the World Cup play-offs between the two countries; over 3,000 people died.
1970s There were demonstrations, civil disobedience and strikes. The *esquadrones de muerte* (death squads) were formed. Thousands of Salvadorians were kidnapped, tortured and murdered.
1977 General Carlos Romero was elected president.
1979 Romero was ousted by reformist military officers, although this failed to stem the number of deaths at the hands of military-backed death squads.
1980 Napoleón Duarte became El Salvador's first civilian president since 1931.
1980s Civil war between the US-backed right-wing government and a leftist guerrilla group, Frente Farabundo Martí para la Liberación Nacional (FMLN) (Front for National Liberation), was based largely in the countryside. Right-wing groups carried out indiscriminate street killings of 'subversives'. Some rural communities were targeted by the security forces for eradication.
1982 The far-right Alianza Republicana Nacionalista (Arena) (Nationalist Republican Alliance) came to power following violent parliamentary elections.
1984 Duarte won the presidential election and began to negotiate a settlement with the FMLN.
1989 Arena's Alfredo Cristiani was elected president.
1992 A formal cease-fire, under UN auspices, came into effect. An estimated 75,000 people had been killed in the 12-year civil war.
1994 Political killings and threats continued right up to the elections. Arena's Armando Calderón Sol was elected president.
1997 Arena won the Assembly elections.
1999 Francisco Flores (Arena) won the presidential election.
2000 The FMLN become the largest party in the National Assembly. Arena formed a coalition government with the PCN, giving the right-wing block a majority in the Assembly.
2001 The US dollar was adopted as the official currency. Around 1,500 people were killed in the worst earthquakes for more than a decade and 1.5 million were made homeless.
2003 A free trade agreement (FTA) with Panama came into effect.
2004 Antonio Saca (Arena) won the presidential elections. El Salvador, along with the Dominican Republic, Costa Rica, Guatemala, Honduras and Nicaragua, agreed to a proposed Central American Free Trade Agreement (Cafta) with the US.
2005 The OAS human rights court voted to re-open an investigation into the El Mozote massacre in 1981. Thousands of people fled the area surrounding the Ilamatepec volcano after it erupted and a tropical storm caused many deaths and damaged the surrounding area.
2006 Arena won 34 seats in the national assembly elections; the FMLN won 32 seats. The newly defined border between Honduras and El Salvador was inaugurated.
2007 Three members of Arena were murdered in Guatemala. After eight years of conflict, the International Court of Justice (ICJ) ruled on a new maritime boundary between Honduras and Nicaragua. The result gives both countries equal access to the rich fishing grounds and oil and gas exploration waters in the area.
2009 In parliamentary elections, the opposition and former revolutionary guerrilla group, FMLN won 42.6 per cent, (35 seats out of 84), the ruling Arena 38.6 per cent (32). In the presidential election, opposition leader, Mauricio Funes (FMLN) won 51.3 per cent, Rodrigo Avila (Arena) 48.7 per cent. Mauricio Funes became president. Diplomatic ties with Cuba were restored after a break of 50 years.
2011 On 30 April the Supreme Court disbanded the Christian Democratic Party (CDP) and the National Conciliation Party (NCP), as neither conservative party had won the minimum level of votes (of 3 per cent) required in the 2004 presidential election. The parties will cease to exist once the terms of office of their mayors and legislators have ended. A draft bill set before parliament in July for a new wealth and estate tax came in for criticism. It was considered that a levy on investment and entrepreneurial achievement could lead to de-capitalisation in El Salvador.

Political structure

In addition to their unicameral national parliaments, El Salvador, Guatemala, Honduras, Nicaragua, Panama and Dominican Republic also return directly-elected deputies to the supranational Central American Parliament.

Constitution

The constitution came into effect in December 1983. It delineated the three arms of government – legislative, executive and judicial – granting them official autonomy. Executive power is held by the president who serves a non-renewable five-year term of office. Legislative power, formed of members elected on three-year terms is held by the unicameral National Assembly – which also holds the power to appoint a president if no candidate gains an absolute majority in the elections. In 1991 constitutional reforms strengthened the judicial and electoral systems. There are 14 *departamentos* (administrative divisions) which each have a governor and an elected local council headed by a mayor.

Form of state

Presidential democratic republic

The executive

Executive power is vested in the president (who is elected every five years in March), assisted by the vice president and council of ministers. A second round of elections must be held within 30 days of the declaration of the result of the first round if no candidate secures an absolute majority (51 per cent) at the first attempt.
The presidential term begins on 1 June. The president is both the head of state and head of government.

National legislature

The unicameral Asamblea Legislativa (Legislative Assembly), has 84 members directly elected for three years by proportional representation, of which 64 are elected in 14 multi-seat constituencies relating to the 14 departments (returning between 3–16 deputies each, depending on population sizes) and 20 deputies selected in a single national constituency. Deputies may serve successive terms.

Legal system

Since 1993, El Salvador has undergone a full-scale review of its judicial structure. In order to achieve a basic level of judicial independence, judicial appointments are the responsibility of the Legislative Assembly, and funding for the courts has been ensured. In 1998, the Legislative Assembly replaced the 1860 criminal code and code of criminal procedure with more efficient procedures. With a US$22.2 million loan from the Inter-American Development Bank (IDB), approved in 1996, El Salvador began a programme of judicial training, the renovation and expansion of efforts to educate juvenile offenders, and projects to strengthen administration and planning. The process of reform is continuing and is more autonomous and professional than at any time in El Salvador's history.

Last elections

15 March 2009 (presidential); 18 January 2009 (parliamentary).
Results: Presidential: Mauricio Funes (FMLN) won 51.3 per cent, Rodrigo Avila (Arena) 48.7 per cent.
Parliamentary: Frente Farabundo Martí para la Liberación Nacional (FMLN) (Farabundo Martí National Liberation Front) won 42.6 per cent, (35 seats out of 84), Alianza Republicana Nacionalista (Arena) (Nationalist Republican Alliance) 38.6 per cent (32), Partido de Conciliación Nacional (PCN) (National Conciliation Party) 8.8 per cent (11), Partido Demócrata Cristiano (PDC) (Christian Democratic Party) 6.6 per cent (5), Cambio Democrático (CD) (Democratic Change) 2.1 per cent (1).

Next elections

2014 (presidential); 2012 (parliamentary)

Political parties

Ruling party

Alianza Republicana Nacionalista (Arena) (Nationalist Republican Alliance); ((Frente Farabundo Martí para la Liberación Nacional (FMLN) (Farabundo Marti National Liberation Front) (from 1 May 2009)

Main opposition party

Alianza Republicana Nacionalista (Arena) (Nationalist Republican Alliance)

Population

6.82 million (2009)
Last census: 12 May 2007: 5,744,113
Population density: Is high, with around 280 inhabitants per square km.
Annual growth rate: 2.0 per cent 1994–2004 (WHO 2006)

Ethnic make-up

Approximately 94 per cent of the population are *mestizo*, 5 per cent Amerindian and 1 per cent white.

Religions

Predominantly Roman Catholic (75 per cent); most of the remaining 25 per cent belong to a number of Protestant churches.

Education

Low levels of literacy and educational skills are regarded by the government as a major impediment to foreign investment.
Literacy rate: 80 per cent adult rate; 89 per cent youth rate (15–24) (Unesco 2005).
Enrolment rate: 112 per cent gross primary enrolment of relevant age group, including repeaters; 56 per cent gross secondary enrolment; 17 per cent gross tertiary enrolment (World Bank).
Pupils per teacher: 33 in primary schools

Health

Approximately 55 per cent of the population has access to safe water.

HIV/Aids

HIV prevalence: 0.7 per cent aged 15–49 in 2003 (World Bank)
Life expectancy: 71 years, 2004 (WHO 2006)
Fertility rate/Maternal mortality rate: 2.8 births per woman, 2004 (WHO 2006): maternal mortality 1.2 per 1,000 live births (World Bank).
Child (under 5 years) mortality rate (per 1,000): 32 per 1,000 live births; 11 per cent of children aged under five are malnourished (World Bank).
Head of population per physician: 1.24 physicians per 1,000 people, 2002 (WHO 2006)

Welfare

El Salvador operates a mandatory private insurance system, introduced into law in 1996 and implemented in 1998 as part of the government's privatisation strategy. The law ensured state provision for those aged over 36-years in 1996 but was closed to new entrants. The new private system is funded through a mixture of contributions made by workers and employers.
The state also operates a welfare system for benefits covering sickness, maternity and work injury. These are based on contributions by the employer and worker and subsidised by the state, but exclude casual workers and those involved in domestic work. Agricultural workers are denied sickness and maternity pay and teachers are excluded from work injury benefits.

Pensions

Old-age pensions are available to men aged over 60 and women over 55 with 25 years of contributions. There is no minimum age requirement for those with more than 30 years' contributions. The 1996 pension reform created five private pensions funds, but in September 2000 three of these were merged into a new fund – AFP Crecer, run by Spanish bank BBVA – which in 2002 controlled around 60 per cent of the country's pensions market.

Main cities

San Salvador (capital, estimated population 521,366 in 2005), Soyapango (300,388), Santa Ana (181,131), Mejicanos (201,517), San Miguel (181,819).

Languages spoken

Nahua is spoken by some Amerindians. English is widely spoken in business circles.

Official language/s

Spanish

Media

Press freedom is guaranteed by constitution.

Press

Dailies: In Spanish, Most newspapers include sections on business and economic matters.
National newspapers include *El Diario de Hoy* (www.elsalvador.com) and *La Prensa Gráfica* (ultra-conservative) (www.laprensagrafica.com) and *El Mundo* (www.elmundo.com.sv), an evening newspaper. Local newspapers include *Diario Co Latino* (www.diariocolatino.com) from San Salvador and *El Pais* (www.elpais.com.sv) from Santa Ana. *El*

Faro (www.elfaro.com.sv) is a weekly publication.

Broadcasting

Radio: There are over 80 commercial radio stations. Radio El Salvador (www.radioelsalvador.com.sv) is the state-run network with local stations providing nationwide coverage. Most stations provide services for a localised area and the majority are located around San Salvador.

Television: There are 17 TV channels provided by around five networks. One of the largest private, commercial network is Telecorporacion Salvadorena (TCS), with ESMI TV (www.esmitv.com), which has five channels, covering news, sport, music and drama and entertainment. Agape TV (www.agapetv8.com) has both commercial and religious programmes. Iglesia del Camino (www.delcamino.org.sv) is run by the Catholic Church. The government runs a cultural and educational channel (canal 10).

There are many pay-to-view digital, cable and satellite services available.

Advertising

All advertising methods are available through the press, cinemas, commercial TV and radio, periodicals and posters. Modern venues such as website and individual mobile/cell phone advertising are available to a lesser extent.

News agencies

Other news agencies: Prensa Latina: www.prensalatina.com.mx

Economy

The service sector constitutes around 60 per cent of the economy and is estimated to employ about 49 per cent of the total labour force; the industry sector comprises a total of almost 30 per cent of GDP, of which manufacturing accounts for almost 20 per cent, and agriculture around 10 per cent. There are free trade zones to encourage export industries (*maquila*), beginning with textile and garment manufacturing but expanding into customer service industries such as offshore call centres, all of which employ around 70,000 workers. As to the general economy retail, financial services and ancillary service businesses have grown as the economy has expanded. Agriculture produce includes coffee, sugar, and livestock and are included in exports products, along with manufactured goods in iron and steel, paper, pharmaceuticals and foodstuffs.

GDP growth was 2.4 per cent in 2008 but the economy fell into recession in 2009 with growth of -3.5 per cent. However, by 2010 it had recovered and growth was 1.0 per cent with a projected increase to 2.5 per cent in 2011.

The economy is steadily strengthening, although it suffers risk from external shocks, such as natural disasters (a devastating earthquake struck in 2001 and hurricanes are an annual risk). It also felt the downturn in foreign economies during the global economic crisis in 2008. The government is committed to reducing the public debt-to-GDP ratio and an increase in tax revenue of up to 1.5 per cent of GDP is considered the likely step, to be undertaken by 2012. This action should also allow a sustainable base for social, security and infrastructure spending while the fiscal deficit declines.

High levels of unemployment and underemployment persist and remain a government priority. The ability to earn foreign exchange is hampered by El Salvador's comparative disadvantage in terms of productivity, due to low levels of capital investment. However, world prices for coffee, the main agricultural export, have risen steadily since 2004.

Worker remittances in 2009 were US$3.53 billion (15.7 per cent of GDP). This is projected to rise to US$3.65 billion in 2010, delivering funds directly into typically poorer family budgets.

External trade

l Salvador is a member of the Central American Free Trade Agreement (Cafta) along with the US, Costa Rica, Guatemala, Honduras and Dominica Republic. The *maquila* sector dominates trade with manufactured goods (in particular garments) exported, typically, to the US. Other such enterprises include light manufacturing and offshore call centres. Agricultural produce for export includes coffee, sugar and livestock. There has also been an increase in non-traditional exports such as shrimps, sesame seeds, nuts, fruits and honey.

Imports

Principal imports include raw materials, consumer goods, capital goods, fuels, foodstuffs, petroleum and electricity.

Main sources: US (typically 30.7 per cent of total), Guatemala (8.9 per cent), Mexico (7.1 per cent).

Exports

Principal exports include offshore assembly exports, coffee, sugar, shrimp, textiles, handcrafts, chemicals and electricity.

Main destinations: US (typically 49.6 per cent of total), Guatemala (14.4 per cent), Honduras (8.8 per cent).

Agriculture

Farming

The agricultural sector of El Salvador's economy employs approximately a third of the country's total workforce. The sector contributes about 12 per cent to total GDP. Approximately 34 per cent of total land is arable; 30 per cent permanent pastures.

Coffee is the most important crop. Other major crops are cotton, sugar cane, maize, beans and rice. There has been some diversification within the sector, with non-traditional exports such as sesame seeds, nuts, vegetables, fruits, honey and, above all, shrimps, taking an increasing share.

Fishing

The Gulf of Fonseca is regarded as one of Central America's greatest natural resources with rich fisheries and diverse marine life, which is shared by Honduras, Nicaragua and El Salvador. Typically, the annual catch is over 18,000mt per year.

Forestry

The forestry industry in El Salvador is relatively small.

Industry and manufacturing

Contributing approximately 28 per cent to total GDP and employing around a fifth of the total workforce, the industrial sector is a significant part of El Salvador's economy.

The national government has made efforts to shift the industrial sector towards manufacturing for export through the development of the *maquila* (in-bond manufacturing) sector and the creation of free zones. *Maquila* exports have accounted for the bulk of growth in the export sector since 1992. Investment incentives in the free zones include a 10-year income tax exemption, import duty exemptions or reduced exposure to taxes on equity or assets for 10 years.

Tourism

Tourism has traditionally played an insignificant role in El Salvador's economy. However, the travel and tourism sector is continuing to expand and now accounts for around 8 per cent of total GDP. The industry employs round 7 per cent of the total labour force.

Mining

Mining has been a stable sector of the El Salvadorian economy for several years. Gold, silver, sea salt and limestone are mined or quarried and there are deposits of copper, iron ore, sulphur, mercury, lead, zinc and perlite. There are two gold mines, one at San Cristobal and the other near San Salvador which also mines silver. However, the mining sector is small and underdeveloped, contributing only 0.1 per cent to GDP. There are two cement works, the 240,000 tonnes per year (tpy) Cemento Mayan at Canton Tecomapa and the 684,000tpy Cemento de El Salvador at El Ronco.

Hydrocarbons

There are no known hydrocarbon reserves, although oil exploration is ongoing. The country is totally reliant on imported products, of which oil imports were 46,000 barrels per day (bpd) in 2008, with consumption at 45,000bpd; refinery capacity is 22,000bpd, at the Acajutla Port site.

In 2006 an association of 20 municipal mayors signed an agreement with Venezuelan to buy oil on preferential terms. In 2009 a presidential scheme began, to take over the purchase of oil from Venezuela for national distribution and have El Salvador considered for membership of the Petrocaribe programme, through which Venezuela provides oil at below market prices to participating Caribbean countries.

The first ethanol producing plant was opened in 2006 at Acajutla Port, processing 227,000 kilolitres per year. In 2008 the US Southridge Enterprises arranged with major domestic sugar cane growers to use their crops for ethanol production of up to 75,700 kilolitres per year. All ethanol is exported to the US.

Any natural gas or coal imports are commercially insignificant.

Energy

Total installed generating capacity was 1,236MW in 2007, producing over 5.3 billion kilowatt hours. The energy market is open to competition but subject to the autonomous regulatory body of the Superintendencia General de Elécticidad y Telecomunicaciones (Siget) (Superintendent General of Electricity and Telecommuncations).

El Salvador is the largest producer of geothermal electricity in Central America. The privately owned LaGeo operates the Ahuachapán and Berlin geothermal power plants. Hydroelectric installations include Guajoyo, Cerrán Grande, 5 de Novembre and 15 de Septembre.

Financial markets

Stock exchange

Bolsa de Valores de El Salvador (BVES) (El Salvador Stock Exchange)

Banking and insurance

The banking system of El Salvador remained under state ownership until 1991. Thereafter the government implemented market reforms that handed control to private investors. Interest rates are determined by the market.

Central bank

Banco Central de Reserva de El Salvador

Time

GMT minus six hours

Geography

El Salvador lies on the Pacific coast of Central America. Guatemala is to the west and Honduras to the north and east. The basins in the centre of the country rise to little more than 600 metres at San Salvador. Across this upland and surmounting it, run two more or less parallel rows of volcanoes, 14 of which are over 900 metres. Lowlands lie to the north and south of the high backbone. The ash and lava from the volcanoes have produced an ideal soil in which to grow coffee.

Hemisphere

Northern.

Climate

The climate is semi-tropical. The dry season is from November–April; temperatures range from 15–23 degrees Celsius (C); the rainy season runs from May–October, when the average temperature is 28 degrees C. Generally, the temperature depends on the altitude; coastal areas are hotter and more humid than upland areas.

The driest month is February with just 5mm average rainfall. The wettest month is June with 328mm. The coldest month is December when the average daily temperature varies between 16 and 32 degrees C. In May, the hottest month, the variation is only slightly different, ranging between 19 and 33 degrees C.

Dress codes

Light cotton suits and ties are the generally accepted form of dress for businessmen, although some Salvadoreans will dress less formally in *guyaberas* (styled cotton shirts worn outside the trousers), particularly in the warmest months. Businesswomen should wear a light suit or equivalent. Dress as for business if invited to a social occasion unless suggested otherwise.

A sweater or light jacket will be required for evenings and for the highlands.

Entry requirements

Passports

Required by all. Passports must be valid for six months from date of departure.

Visa

Required by all, except citizens of most Central American, EU and some Asian countries (for a full list visit www.elsalvador.org or contact the local embassy). Business visas require, in Spanish, a letter of invitation from an El Salvadorian company and a letter from the foreign company being represented.

Currency advice/regulations

There are no restrictions on the import or export of local or foreign currencies. In the case of foreign currencies, the quantity being imported, especially if sizeable, should be declared, as there is a restriction on export of larger amounts to the level imported.

Prohibited imports

Fruit, vegetables, plants and animals.

Health (for visitors)

Mandatory precautions

A yellow fever vaccination certificate is required if arriving from an infected area.

Advisable precautions

Typhoid, polio, hepatitis A and tetanus vaccinations. Dengue fever cases have risen, visitors should avoid exposing their skin during early morning and evening when the risk of being bitten by mosquitoes is highest. Malaria is not a virulent strain but prophylaxis should be taken as there is some risk in the Santa Anna province and rural locations. There is a high rabies risk. Water precautions are essential and only well-cooked food should be eaten. Milk is unpasteurised and should be boiled.

Hotels

The best hotels can be found in the capital. A 10 per cent tip is usual.

Public holidays (national)

Fixed dates

1 Jan (New Year's Day), 1 May (Labour Day), 4 Aug (Transfiguration Bank Holiday), 15 Sep (Independence Day), 12 Oct (Columbus Day), 2 Nov (All Souls' Day), 24 Dec (Christmas Eve), 25 Dec (Christmas Day), 31 Dec (New Year's Eve).

Variable dates

Holy Wednesday, Maundy Thursday, Good Friday.

Working hours

Banking

Mon–Fri: 0900–1700. Sat: 0900–1300.

Business

Mon–Fri: 0900–1800.

Government

Mon–Fri: 0800–1730.

Shops

Mon–Sat: 0900–1200, 1400–1800. Supermarkets Mon–Sat: 0800–2200. The main shopping centres are open on Sunday.

Electricity supply

110V AC, 60Hz

Social customs/useful tips

Appointments should be made in advance. Salvadorans have a distinctly Latin sense of time and can be among the least punctual people in Central America, although many businessmen and bankers, particularly those with export experience, keep *horas inglesas* (punctual time). Business relationships and meetings tend to be formal in early stages. Use proper titles such as Licenciado (college graduate), Ingeniero (engineering graduate) and Doctor (physicians and lawyers), followed by the person's surname. Handshaking before and after meetings is important. First names should not be used until a business relationship has been consolidated. Upon introduction it is

important to exchange cards; a supply of Spanish-printed cards is advisable. Business is conducted in Spanish although some executives speak English. Some knowledge of spoken Spanish is much better than none.
Meetings over meals, including breakfast, are becoming common. Working lunches and dinners can be lengthy. Gratuities in restaurants and hotels are around 10 per cent.

Security

El Salvador has a poor personal security environment, with a homicide rate twice that of Los Angeles. Kidnappings, carjackings, and robbery are common and can occur anywhere. There is a risk of murder for those robbed, even if they do not resist. Downtown San Salvador should be avoided at all times, as should roads outside the city after dark. Reports indicate the border with Guatemala has been a site for attacks on vehicles. Jewellery or large amounts of cash should not be carried.
Business travellers should arrange to be met at the airport and be accompanied by a local representative, as this has been shown to reduce problems.

Getting there

Air

National airline: TACA Airlines.
International airport/s: El Salvador International (SAL), 35km south of San Salvador; bank, car hire, restaurants, shops. The airport and the highway that runs to it are the most modern and developed in the region. It is expanding its services in order to become an international cargo warehousing and distribution centre.
Airport tax: US$27.15.

Surface

Road: Roads run from Guatemala and Honduras. Duty is paid at the border when entering or leaving the country by land. It is advisable to carry small denomination notes to pay the border duties.
Rail: Lines run through El Salvador from Guatemala to Honduras.
Main port/s: Acajutla, La Unión/Cutuco, La Libertad (fishing only). Major ports on the Pacific are Puerto Barrios and Santo Tomás de Castilla.

Getting about

National transport

Air: Scheduled internal services from San Salvador to San Miguel, La Unión and Usulután. Charter flights are available.
Road: There is a network of 9,800km of paved roads. The Pan-American Highway (over 300km) runs through the country linking San Salvador with Santa Ana in the west and San Miguel in the east; Carretera Litoral runs south of the Pan-American Highway linking the capital with Sonsonate, Zacatecoluca and Usulatan. Many roads have fallen into considerable disrepair as a result of the war and cuts in government spending.
Buses: The bus system is excellent, with services between major towns. The buses are often crowded and run frequently.
Rail: There are 602km of railway, including 429km of line from Guatemala to Honduras. A narrow gauge line links the western town of Ahuachpan and the port of Acajutla with San Salvador, which is in turn connected to La Union in the east. The railway is used largely for freight traffic.

City transport

Taxis: Taxis are bright yellow. The regular taxi line is Taxi Acacya. Taxis can be hailed or ordered by telephone. The fixed rate system is not rigidly followed – check before proceeding. No taxis have meters. Tipping is unusual but 10 per cent of fare is appreciated. Taxi from airport to city centre journey time is 25 minutes.

Car hire

A national or international permit valid for 30 days is required. Traffic drives on the right.

BUSINESS DIRECTORY

The addresses listed below are a selection only. While World of Information makes every endeavour to check these addresses, we cannot guarantee that changes have not been made, especially to telephone numbers and area codes. We would welcome any corrections.

Telephone area codes

Dialling code for El Salvador: IDD access code +503 followed by subscriber's number.

Useful telephone numbers

Emergency:	121
Information:	114
International enquiries/ calls (operator):	119, 120
For collect calls (US only):	190
Migration Office:	222-7328
Foreign Office:	222-6611

Chambers of Commerce

American Chamber of Commerce of El Salvador, Paseo General Escalón 5432, San Salvador (tel: 264-7609; fax: 263-3237; e-mail: contact@amchamsal.com).

El Salvador Cámara de Comercio e Industria, 9a Avenida Norte y 5a Calle Poniente, PO Box 1640, 1118 San Salvador (tel: 244-2000; fax: 271-4461; e-mail: camara@camarasal.com).

Banking

Ahorromet Scotiabank, Avenida Olímpica 129, Edificio Torre Ahorromet Scotiabank, San Salvador (tel: 245-1211; fax: 245-2884).

BANCASA (Banco de Construcción y Ahorro), 75 Avenida Sur 709, Colonia Escalon, San Salvador (tel: 263-5508; fax: 263-5506).

Banco Agrícola Comercial, Paseo General Escalón 3635, Colonia Escalón, San Salvador (tel: 224-0283; fax: 224-3948).

Banco de Comercio de El Salvador, 25 Avenida Norte y 23 Calle Poniente, San Salvador (tel: 226-4577; fax: 225-7767; e-mail: webmaster@banco.com.sv).

Banco Creditomatic, 55 Avenida Sur y Alameda Roosevelt, Centro Roosevelt, San Salvador (tel: 298-1855; fax: 224-4138).

Banco Cuscatlan, Km 10 Carretera a Santa Tecla, Edificio Pirámide Cuscatlán La Libertad (tel: 228-7777; fax: 228-9999).

Banco Hipotecario, Pje. Senda Florida Sur, Paseo General Escalón, San Salvador (tel: 223-3753; fax: 298-0447).

Banco Salvadoreño, Alameda Dr Manuel Enrique Araujo 3550, San Salvador (tel: 298-4444; fax 298-0102).

Grupo Capital, Alameda Dr Manuel Enrique Araujo, Edificio Century Plaza, San Salvador (tel: 245-6000; fax: 224-3303).

Unibanco, Alameda Roosevelt 2511, San Salvador (tel: 245-0651; fax: 298-5261).

Central bank

Banco Central de Reserva, Alameda Juan Pablo, entre 15 y 17 Avenida Norte, PO Box 106, San Salvador (tel: 281-8000; fax: 281-8013; e-mail: comunicaciones@bcr.gob.sv).

Stock exchange

Bolsa de Valores de El Salvador (BVES) (El Salvador Stock Exchange): www.bves.com.sv

Travel information

Corporación Salvadoreña de Turismo (CORSATUR), Boulevard del Hipódromo 508, San Benito, San Salvador (tel: 243-7835; fax: 243-0427).

TACA International Airlines, Edificio Caribe, San Salvador (tel: 298-5055; fax:279-4345).

National tourist organisation offices

Instituto Salvadoreño de Turismo (ISTU) (El Salvador Tourist Board), Calle Rubén Darío 619, San Salvador (tel: 228-000, 222-8699, 222-8144, 222-9366; fax: 221-208).

Ministries

Ministry of Agriculture and Livestock, Final 1a Avenida Norte 13 Calle Oriente y Avenida Manuel Gallardo 704, San Salvador (tel: 279-1579; fax: 224-2944).

Ministry of Defence, Alameda Manuel Enrique Araujo, Carretera a Santa Tecla, San Salvador (tel: 223-0233; fax: 298-2005).

Ministry of Economy, Alameda Juan Pablo II Calle Guadalupe, Centro de Gobierno, San Salvador (tel: 281-7134; fax: 221-2797).

Ministry of Education, Alameda Juan Pablo II Calle Guadalupe, Centro de Gobierno, San Salvador (tel: 281-0256; fax: 281-0257).

Ministry of Environment, Alameda Roosevelt y 55 Avenida Norte, Torre El Salvador, San Salvador (tel: 260-8876; fax: 260-3092).

Ministry of Finance, Edificio Las Tres Torres, Avenida Alvarado, San Salvador (tel: 225-6500; fax: 225-7491).

Ministry of Foreign Affairs, Alameda Manuel Enrique Araujo 5500, San Salvador (tel: 243-3805; fax: 243-3710).

Ministry of Health, Calle Arce 827, San Salvador (tel: 271-0008; fax: 221-0985).

Ministry of Interior, Centro de Gobierno, San Salvador (tel: 221-8582; fax: 281-5959).

Ministry of Justice and Public Security, 6a Calle Oriente 42, Antiguo Local Policia Nacional, San Salvador (tel: 271-2655; fax: 245-2650).

Ministry of Labour, Paseo General Escalón 4122, San Salvador (tel: 263-5423; fax: 263-5272).

Ministry of Public Works, 1a Avenida Sur 603, San Salvador (tel: 293-6603; fax: 271-0163).

Other useful addresses

Asociación Nacional de la Empresa Privada (ANEP), 1a Calle Poniente y 71a Avenida Norte 204, Colonia Escalón, San Salvador (tel: 224-1236; fax: 223-8932; e-mail: anep@telesal.net).

Asociación Salvadoreña de Industriales (ASI), Calles Roma y Liverpool, Colonia Roma, San Salvador (tel: 279-2488; fax: 279-2070; e-mail: unatias@sv.cciglobal.net).

Bolsa de Valores de El Salvador, Alameda Roosevelt 3107, Edificio La Centroamericana, San Salvador (tel: 298-4244; fax: 223-2898; e-mail: webmaster@bves.com.sv).

British Embassy, Paseo General Escalón 4828, Edificio Inter-Inversiones, San Salvador (tel: 263-6527; fax: 263-6516; e-mail: britemb@sal.gbm.net).

Corporación de Exportadores de El Salvador (COEXPORT), Condominios del Mediterráneo A-23, Colonia Jardínes de Guadalupe, San Salvador (tel: 243-3110; fax: 243-3159; e-mail: service@coexport.com).

El Salvador Embassy (USA), 2308 California Street, NW, Washington DC 20008 (tel: (202) 2265-9671; fax: (202) 234-3834; e-mail: correo@elsalvador.org).

Fundación Salvadoreña para el Desarrollo Económica y Social (FUSADES), Urbanización y Boulevard Santa Elena, Edificio FUSADES, Antiguo Cuscatlán, La Libertad (tel: 278-3366; fax: 278-3369; e-mail: fusades@fusades.com.sv).

Superintendencia del Sistema Financiero, 7a Avenida Norte 240, San Salvador (tel: 281-24444).

Unión de Dirigentes de Empresas Salvadoreñas (UDES), Condominios del Mediterráneo C-22, Colonia Jardines de Guadalupe, San Salvador (tel: 243-2746; fax: 243-3145).

US Embassy, Boulevard Santa Elena Final, Antiguo Cuscatlán, La Libertad (tel: 278-4444; fax: 278-6011).

Internet sites

El Salvador trade and investment: http://www.elsalvadortrade.com.sv/

Fundación Salvadoreña para el Desarollo Económico e Social (Salvadorean Foundation for Social and Economic Development) (Spanish): http://www.fusades.com.sv/

Equatorial Guinea

KEY FACTS

Official name: República de Guinea Ecuatorial (Republic of Equatorial Guinea)

Head of State: President Teodoro Obiang Nguema Mbasogo (PDGE) (since 1979; re-elected 2002)

Head of government: Prime Minister Ignacio Milam Tang (from 8 Jul 2008)

Ruling party: Partido Democrático de Guinea Ecuatorial (PDGE) (Democratic Party of Equatorial Guinea) (from 1993; re-elected 4 May 2008)

Area: 28,051 square km

Population: 1.19 million (2010)*

Capital: Malabo

Official language: Spanish and French

Currency: CFA franc (CFAf) = 100 centimes (Communauté Financière Africaine (African Financial Community) franc)

Exchange rate: CFAf488.90 per US$ (Oct 2011); CFAf655.95 per euro (pegged from Jan 1999)

GDP per capita: US$9,579 (2009)

GDP real growth: 0.90% (2010)*

GDP: US$12.22 billion (2009)

Inflation: 12.70% (2010)

Oil production: 274,000 bpd (2010)

Balance of trade: US$5.94 billion (2010)*

* estimated figure

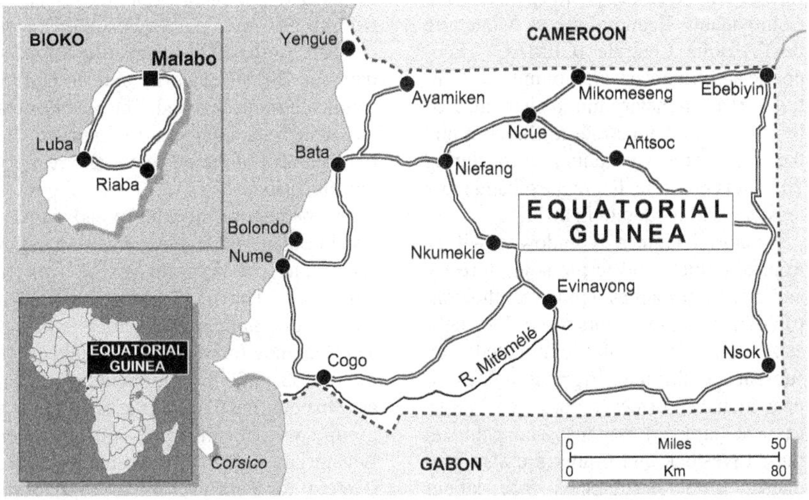

President Teodoro Obiang Nguema Mbasogo has been in power since 1979 and is now the longest serving African president (after the demise in October 2011 of Muammar al Qadafi of Libya). In the latest presidential elections in November 2009 he won 99 seats in the 100-seat parliament with 96.7 per cent of the votes. The ruling Partido Democrático de Guinea Ecuatorial (PDGE) (Democratic Party of Equatorial Guinea) also has an overwhelming majority in all 30 municipalities. The results were disputed by the opposition, which won the one remaining seat in parliament. The conditions imposed by the government on international observers were severely criticised for not permitting them to carry out an independent monitoring function.

In January 2010, President Obiang Nguema Mbasogo named his cabinet, fulfilling a constitutional requirement to form a new government after a presidential election. The new cabinet, comprising 26 ministers, was 50 per cent larger in size than the previous cabinet. Over the course of 2010 the government showed few signs of political easing or weakness. Tensions have nevertheless declined somewhat since the attack on the presidential palace in early 2009. In 2010, four top officials were sentenced to death for their role in these events while several Nigerians were sentenced to long prison sentences. The death sentences were carried out shortly after they were announced by the military tribunal.

In the absence of a truly participative democratic system, concerns are already being voiced about the future stability of the current regime. The president is now 68 years old and the rumours about his health are intensifying. He has made it known he favours his eldest son, Teodoro Nguema Obiang Mangue, as his successor. 'Little Teodoro', as he is known in Equatorial Guinea, is the current minister of agriculture and forestry. In July 2010, he was designated vice president of the ruling PDGE and in October 2010, he was promoted to the rank of lieutenant colonel in the armed forces.

The economy

According to the *African Economic Outlook 2011* (AEO), published jointly by the African Development Bank and the Organisation for Economic Co-operation and Development Equatorial Guinea's economy did not have a particularly good year in 2010. Having weathered the global downturn in 2008 and 2009, growth in 2010 was 1.2 per cent of gross domestic product (GDP), sharply down on the 12.4 per cent in 2009. The drop was mainly as a result of the fall of oil output and the main oil-producing fields reaching their maturity. The economy has been on a downward trend since 2004, when real GDP growth peaked at 38 per cent. 2010 experienced one of the lowest growth rates since the exploitation of hydrocarbons began in the mid-1990s. It is expected to recover and return to high growth rates of 5.0 per cent and 7.5 per cent in 2011 and 2012. Even though outputs from the oil industry will be lower, growth will be sustained by the international demand for hydrocarbons and the construction of major infrastructure projects, including those for the hydrocarbon industry.

The recovery of oil prices, despite the fall in production, has had a positive effect on the government budget with the deficit reaching 2.6 per cent of GDP in 2010, up from a deficit of 9.6 per cent of GDP in 2009. Driven by falling imports, the current account rose to a surplus of 2.7 per cent of GDP in 2010, compared to a 7.6 per cent deficit in 2009; it is projected to remain in surplus of 2.9 per cent in 2011 and 3.8 per cent in 2012. The inflation rate for 2010 was 4.7 per cent. As a result of continued high levels of capital expenditure, inflation is expected to remain in the region of 6.3 per cent in 2011. Equatorial Guinea faces no debt problems due to a budget surplus and external reserves. External debt at the end 2010 was close to 5 per cent of GDP, or CFAf307 billion (US$1.06 billion).

A persistent concern for authorities has been the possible 'Dutch disease' effects of the oil boom – the situation wherein a boom in the natural resource sector leads to an appreciation of the real exchange rate, hurting the export potential of other productive sectors. The rapid boom in the oil sector in Equatorial Guinea has led to a substantial appreciation of the real effective exchange rate over the past decade, which might have had a subsequent negative impact on all other productive sectors such as cocoa, the main export prior to the oil boom, or timber, now the main export commodity after oil and gas. Given that Equatorial Guinea belongs to the Communauté Economique et Monétaire de l'Afrique Centrale (CEMAC) (Economic and Monetary Community of Central Africa) monetary union characterised by a fixed exchange rate to the euro and the significant weakening euro during 2010, it is possible that real exchange rate tensions will moderate in 2011.

Equatorial Guinea is endowed with a tropical climate and fertile soils, forestry and marine resources. However, the contribution of these sectors to GDP is modest. Agriculture is dominated by subsistence farming. Agricultural products include coffee, cocoa, rice, yams, cassava (tapioca), bananas and palm oil nuts. Livestock and timber are also produced. Rural occupations face labour shortages as workers migrate to Bata on the mainland and Malabo on the island of Bioko. The country claims an exclusive maritime fishing zone of 300,000 square kilometres.

Corruption and mis-management

The AEO notes that sound management of Equatorial Guinea's vast oil and gas resources is crucial to reducing poverty and promoting human development. The perceived high level of corruption and lack of transparency in the management of the resources in the hydrocarbons sector has affected the country's attempts to join the Extractive Industries Transparency Initiative (EITI), initiated in September 2007. The EITI seeks to promote good governance in the management of natural resources by requiring resource extraction firms to publish what they pay to governments and the latter what they receive from firms. Compliant countries are those deemed by the EITI as meeting its standards. In 2010 Equatorial Guinea had its candidate status revoked. The government has stated its intention to improve the management of the oil sector and reapply for admission

The perception of widespread corruption in Equatorial Guinea remains a major issue. The country ranked 168 (jointly with Angola) out of 178 countries in 2010 on the *Corruption Perception Index* of Transparency International. It ranked 151 out of 163 in 2006. The main corruption case in court in 2010 was the one against a group of ex-employees of Guinea Ecuatorial de Telecomunicaciones (Getesa) for a crime of misappropriation.

The environment for private-sector activity also remains difficult. Equatorial Guinea still ranks among the bottom countries in the World Bank's *Doing Business Index*. It slipped three places in the ranking in 2011 to 164 from 161 in 2010. Key constraints include construction permits, import licences, the perceived high level of corruption, elaborate procedures and an unpredictable judicial environment.

Millennium Development Goals

Over 70 per cent of the population in Equatorial Guinea falls below the poverty line, raising questions about the extent to which the country's oil wealth has benefitted the majority of the population. Maternal and infant mortality rates are still very high. Measuring progress towards the Millennium Development Goals (MDGs) with precision is an extremely difficult task because of data deficits and an ongoing controversy about the population census (see below). The country is on track to achieve the MDGs of universal primary education, reducing child mortality, improving maternal health, and combating HIV/Aids, malaria and other diseases. However, it is not on track to achieve the MDGs of ensuring environmental sustainability and promoting gender equality and empowering women.

International relations

Oil wealth has attracted the attention of emerging economies in recent years.

KEY INDICATORS — **Equatorial Guinea**

	Unit	2006	2007	2008	2009	2010
Population	m	1.17	1.21	*1.24	*1.28	*1.19
Gross domestic product (GDP)	US$bn	8.56	12.57	18.42	12.22	–
GDP per capita	US$	7,315	8,702	14,859	9,579	–
GDP real growth	%	5.6	9.8	*5.8	12.4	1.2
Inflation	%	4.4	2.9	4.3	7.1	12.7
Oil output	'000 bpd	358.0	363.0	361.0	307.0	274.0
Exports (fob) (goods)	US$m	*8,290.0	*10,250.0	*14,846.0	*8,495.0	*9,781.0
Imports (fob) (goods)	US$m	*2,020.0	*2,365.0	*3,667.0	*5,258.0	*3,845.0
Balance of trade	US$m	*6,270.0	*7,885.0	*11,179.0	*3,237.0	*5,936.0
Current account	US$m	*679.0	*524.0	*2,225.0	-1,684.0	*-1,950.0
Total reserves minus gold	US$m	3,066.7	3,845.9	4,431.2	3,251.9	2,346.4
Foreign exchange	US$m	3,066.1	3,845.2	4,430.5	3,211.3	2,306.4
Exchange rate	per US$	496.60	454.40	418.59	514.03	495.28

* estimated figure

However, the country remains relatively closed. Equatorial Guinea's main emerging partner is China. There is a small presence of Chinese Taipei, Cuba, Argentina, Brazil and Russia. The country's hydrocarbons industry is still dominated by United States (US) companies but Chinese companies are increasingly active providing significant credit lines. Equatorial Guinea lacks the administrative capacity to engage strategically with the emerging partners.

Equatorial Guinea, and therefore its president, had the chair of the African Union in 2011, which entailed hosting the 2011 African Union Summit of Heads of State. As ever with these events, there were a number of important real estate developments including one a few kilometres south-west of Malabo at Sipopo. It is rumoured to have cost some ?580 million (US$777 million) and consists of 52 luxury villas for all heads of state and government attending the summit, a large conference hall, a four kilometre-long seafront promenade and a five-star hotel with 200 rooms. A 120-bed hospital and a motorway linking the site to Malabo were also completed in early 2011.

Equatorial Guinea has also been chosen to co-host the 2012 Africa Cup of Nations football tournament in partnership with Gabon. Two stadiums are being upgraded to Fédération Internationale de Football Association (FIFA) (International Federation of Association Football) standards for the event, one in Bata with a capacity of 45,000 and another in Malabo, with a capacity of 16,000.

President Teodoro Obiang Nguema Mbasogo maintains very close relations with some traditional partners, especially France (although there was a blip in November 2009 when France's highest appeals court gave permission to proceed with investigations into corruption and the assets held in France by the President). The French Group Bouygues, with close connections to the entourage of the president, remains the lead construction firm active in Equatorial Guinea. It was commissioned to build the luxury hotel and accompanying 18-hole golf course for the African Union Summit. The presence of Spanish firms is particularly evident in the food and distribution sectors; however, the inputs for these activities come from imports rather than local suppliers.

Data dispute

An enduring controversy regarding population data remains an issue in Equatorial Guinea; population data affect the reliability of many economic and social statistics. There is a major discrepancy between government population statistics and those of development partners. Estimates from the United Nations Population Division put the population at 693,000 in 2010, a figure adopted by most international institutions, including the World Bank and the International Monetary Fund (IMF). However, the government claims that a 2002 census recorded a population of a little over 1 million. The government explains the discrepancy as largely due to the influx of migrants, drawn to Equatorial Guinea principally from neighbouring countries by the oil boom and the expectation of better jobs and prospects. A difference of such a large magnitude has an enormous impact on variables expressed as a percentage of population. This affects the measurement of economic and social progress and complicates making informed policy decisions. The government has declared its commitment to resolve the controversy regarding the population data with a new census and a household expenditure survey.

Risk assessment

Politics	Poor
Economy	Fair
Regional stability	Fair

COUNTRY PROFILE

Historical profile

1470 The island of Anobon was first visited by the Portuguese, who subsequently settled it and the other islands in the Gulf of Guinea, including Bioko.
1477 Portugal ceded Bioko to Spain. Bioko became an important slave-trading base for several European nations up to the nineteenth century.
1844 Spanish began settling the mainland region of Río Muni.
1904 Río Muni and Bioko became the West African Territories, later named Spanish Guinea.
1968 Spanish Guinea was granted independence from Spain and renamed the Republic of Equatorial Guinea. Macias Nguema became president.
1972 Nguema became 'President for Life' and his presidency degenerated as democratic institutions and practices were dismissed. The regime used terror to maintain power and up to one third of the population fled the country as the economy collapsed.
1979 Teodoro Obiang Nguema Mbasogo (the president's nephew) seized power in a *coup d'état*. Macias Nguema was executed. Even though a ruling Supreme Military Council (SMC) was established Obiang retained all effective power.
1982 A new constitution was drafted with the help of the UN Commission on Human Rights. It came into effect on August 15 and the SMC was abolished
1984 and 1989 President Obiang was re-elected unopposed.
1992 The president dismissed the government as a prelude to the introduction of multi-partyism.
1993 The first multi-party elections were won by the president's Partido Democrático de Guinea Ecuatorial (PDGE) (Democratic Party of Equatorial Guinea); the main opposition parties boycotted the election.
1995 Zafiro, the country's largest oil field was discovered off Bioko Island.
1996 President Obiang won the presidential elections, which were described as 'a farce' by international observers.
1999 PDGE won 75 seats in the first fully contested parliamentary elections. Opposition parties alleged fraud and boycotted parliament.
2000 Equatorial Guinea and Nigeria signed a treaty agreeing to the demarcation of their maritime border.
2002 Opposition members accused the government of mass human rights abuse. President Obiang was re-elected.
2004 The ruling and allied parties won the 25 April parliamentary elections; foreign observers criticised both the poll and the results. Perpetrators of an alleged coup were arrested in Harare, Zimbabwe, when their plane landed for refuelling. Nineteen mercenaries accused of the planned overthrow were convicted, including opposition leader, Severo Moto, who was sentenced to 63 years in prison
2005 Sir Mark Thatcher, son of the former UK prime minister, Margaret Thatcher, was arrested in South Africa and pleaded guilty to financing the helicopter used in the 2004 attempted coup; he was fined US$500,000 and given a suspended gaol sentence. Spain overturned the asylum status of opposition leader, Severo Moto, after receiving evidence he had been involved in a number of coup attempts.
2006 The government resigned following accusations by the president of corruption and incompetence.
2008 President Obiang announced that presidential elections would take place in 2010. Opposition leader, Severo Moto, was arrested in Spain and charged with trafficking weapons into Equatorial Guinea. He had been given political asylum by Spain in 1986; political asylum had been revoked in 2005 after he was accused of attempting to promote a *coup d'etat* from Spain, but it was re-instated in

2008. In parliamentary elections, the ruling PDGE, allied to the Front of Democratic Opposition (FOD), won 99 seats out of 100, the Convergencia para la Democracia Social (CPDS) (Convergence for Social Democracy) won one seat. The government of Prime Minister Nfubea resigned; Ignacio Milam Tang was appointed in his stead. British national Simon Mann was sentenced to more than 34 years in jail over a 2004 coup plot in Equatorial Guinea but was later given a presidential pardon and deported.
2009 Gunmen attacked the presidential palace in the capital Malabo in February, but were repelled by security guards. The thirty-year anniversary of President Obiang's coup was celebrated. Obiang Nguema won the presidential elections with 95.8 per cent of the vote. Opposition and human rights organisations claim the voting was neither free nor fair.
2010 The parliament of Economic Community of Central African States (ECCAS), Communauté Économique des États d'Afrique Centrale (EEAC, French), Comunidade Económica dos Estados da África Central (CEEAC, Portuguese) was opened in Malabo on 15 April. An agreement to export two million barrels of oil a year (beginning in July) to Ghana was announced in May. Transparency International successfully appealed against a French court's ruling in 2009 that it could not act against foreign heads of state and on 9 November France's highest appeals court gave permission to proceed with investigations into corruption and the assets held in France by President Teodoro Obiang Nguema, as well as by Denis Sassou-Nguesso of Congo and the late Omar Bongo, former president of Gabon.
2011 On 30 January, President Mbasogo became the 2011 chairman of the African Union (AU). He described criticism of his chairmanship by human rights groups a 'un-African'. The AU lost direction as President Mbasogo offered AU support for the regime of Colonel Qadafi, while other African leaders supported the Libyan rebels. A referendum was held on 13 November to vote on limiting the number of presidential terms in office to two and to establish the post of vice president, with a provision for the serving president to choose a successor; the existing proviso on a president's age limit was also to be removed. Opposition leaders called the referendum a 'sham' and reported there was evidence of 'ballot stuffing'; human rights campaigners said the changes 'will strengthen the near-absolute powers of President Teodoro Obiang Nguema Mbasogo and further deprive citizens of their civil and political rights'. The post of vice president was considered an opportunity for Mbasogo's eldest son Teodoro to be groomed to succeed his father.

Political structure

Constitution

A new constitution designed to usher in multi-party politics was adopted on 16 November 1991. It provided for the separation of powers between the president and prime minister and gave the president protection from impeachment, prosecution and *subpoena* before, during and after his term of office.

Form of state

Republic

The executive

The president is elected for a seven-year term by universal suffrage. The prime minister is appointed by the president.

National legislature

The unicameral Cámara de Representantes del Pueblo (House of People's Representatives) has 100 members directly elected by proportional representation from party lists, who serve five-year terms.

Legal system

Judges are appointed, transferred and dismissed for political reasons, even though the constitution provides for judicial independence. The judicial system does not appear to operate independently, thus undermining basic rights.

Last elections

4 May 2008 (parliamentary); 29 November 2009 (presidential)

Results: Parliamentary: Partido Democrático de Guinea Ecuatorial (PDGE) (Democratic Party of Equatorial Guinea), allied to the Front of Democratic Opposition (FOD), won 99 seats out of 100, the Convergencia para la Democracia Social (CPDS) (Convergence for Social Democracy) won one.
Presidential: Teodoro Obiang Nguema Mbasogo (PDGE) won 95.8 per cent of the vote, Plácido Micó Abogo (CPDS) 3.6 per cent; turnout was 93.5 per cent.

Next elections

2016 (presidential); 2013 (parliamentary)

Political parties

Ruling party

Partido Democrático de Guinea Ecuatorial (PDGE) (Democratic Party of Equatorial Guinea) (from 1993; re-elected 4 May 2008)

Main opposition party

Convergencia para la Democracia Social (CPDS) (Convergence for Social Democracy).

Population

1.19 million (2010)*

Last census: 1 February 2002: 1,014,999

Population density: 16 inhabitants per square km. Urban population 49 per cent (1995–2001).

Annual growth rate: 2.4 per cent 1994–2004 (WHO 2006)

Ethnic make-up

The mainland region of Rio Muni is occupied by 75 per cent of the population, 90 per cent of whom belong to the Fang ethnic group. The island province of Bioko consists of Bubis, Fangs and Creoles.

Religions

Christianity (98 per cent, mostly Roman Catholic), traditional beliefs (2 per cent).

Education

Public expenditure on education typically amounted to 2.3 per cent of annual gross national income between 1994–1997 according to World Bank estimates.

Literacy rate: 83.2 per cent adult rate; 92.5 per cent male rate (Unesco).

Enrolment rate: 126 per cent gross primary enrolment of relevant age group (including repeaters); 115 per cent gross secondary enrolment.

Pupils per teacher: 41 in primary schools.

Health

Approximately 43 per cent of the total population is under 15 years. World Bank surveys show that 43 per cent of the population have access to improved water sources.

HIV/Aids

The government has failed in its commitments to eradicate the continuing epidemics of malaria and yellow fever, while allowing HIV prevalence to increase. There are an estimated 1,100 people living with HIV/Aids – most sufferers are over the age of 15.

Life expectancy: 43 years, 2004 (WHO 2006)

Fertility rate/Maternal mortality rate: 5.9 births per woman, 2004 (WHO 2006)

Child (under 5 years) mortality rate (per 1,000): 97 per 1,000 live births (World Bank)

Head of population per physician: 0.3 physicians per 1,000 people, 2004 (WHO 2006)

Welfare

Welfare conditions in the country are virtually non-existent, with limited access to primary healthcare, education and job opportunities.
In 2003 the Government introduced a two-tier system that created a separate wage system for private sector workers inside and outside of the oil sector. The minimum monthly wage for all private sector workers was set at CFAf77,000 (approximately US$154), and an

additional differential payment is made dependent on a worker's skills.
However the minimum wage law does not apply to public sector workers who are generally paid much less than their counterparts in the private sector.
Under-age youths perform both family farm work and street vending. The government does not enforce the legal minimum age for child employment.
Equatorial Guinea is also a destination and transit point for the trafficking in children (as unpaid workers) and women (for prostitution).
Human rights conditions in the country are considered, by Amnesty International, as 'alarming' as the security forces continue to harass civilians and political dissidents; imprisonment, torture and extrajudicial killings have been cited in all parts of the country.

Main cities
Malabo (capital, on island of Bioko, estimated population 100,677 in 2005), Bata (Rio Muni) (71,901).

Languages spoken
Fang, Bubi Ibo and Creole (pidgin English) are spoken.
Official language/s
Spanish and French

Media
In 2006 Equatorial Guinea was ranked 137 out of 168 for press freedom by the French-based, Reporters without Borders. Despite a constitutional guarantee of freedom of the press, rights to freedom of opinion, expression, the sharing and publication of information are severely restricted, with the government using military courts, repressive laws and arbitrary arrests and prosecutions to restrict political freedom and civil rights.
Press
There are few newspapers available. In Spanish, *Ebano* is state-owned and *La Nacion* and *La Opinion* (a weekly), are privately owned. *La Gaceta (de Guinea Ecuatorial)* (www.lagacetadeguinea.com) is published monthly.
Periodicals: In Spanish, *La Diaspora* (Spanish) is published overseas every other month.
Broadcasting
Radio: There are two radio stations broadcasting in Spanish and local African languages Radio Nacional de Guinea Ecuatorial is state-run and the commercial, Radio Asonga, is run by Teodorino Obiang Nguema (the president's son). The French-based RF1 and several foreign Christian radio stations broadcast into the country.
Television: There is a limited service provided by the state-run Television Nacional.
News agencies
AFP (Agence France-Presse): www.afp.com
AllAfrica: www.allafrica.com
APA (African Press Agency): www.apanews.net
Panapress: www.panapress.com

Economy
Oil is transforming the economy; however it has yet to achieve a fully developed, economically diverse, open-market. The country's GDP has increased forty-fold (1995–2010), which has allowed the government to embark on an ambitious infrastructure programme; investment between 2004–07 rose from US$13.7 million to US$455.2 million (2 per cent to 21.4 per cent of total capital expenditure), which in turn has enhanced related skills in construction. Nevertheless, the majority of the working population is engaged in subsistence farming and while the GDP per capita is estimated at over US$10,000, inequality within society is widespread, with capital expenditure on social programmes between 2004–07 remaining static at around 18 per cent. Equatorial Guinea was ranked 117 out of 169 countries in the 2010 UN Human Development Index (HDI) list. There was an improvement in Equatorial Guinea's HDI, compared to other sub-Saharan counties, since 2005, but the trend was less favourable compared to world trends.
GDP growth was 21.4 per cent in 2007 as energy prices reached an all-time high, but fell back to 10.7 per cent as global trade fell and exports of hydrocarbons fell; growth in 2009 was 5.3 per cent. The trade balance in 2008 was US$10.55 billion with total exports of US$14.46 billion, of which hydrocarbons were US$14.36 billion. In 2009 the trade balance had fallen to US$3.23 billion with total exports of US$8.49 billion, of which hydrocarbons were US$8.36 billion. The sharp drop in revenue caused the country's current account to plummet from US$1.67 billion in 2008, to -US$1.95 billion in 2009. Around 80 per cent of hydrocarbon revenue accounts for government revenue, with value added tax and trade taxes largely making up the remainder.
The government is attempting to reduce the predominance of hydrocarbons in the economy. However balancing an economy that is prone to distortion by one overarching sector is proving difficult. Much of the remainder of the economy is underdeveloped even though Equatorial Guinea is rich in timber, fishing and agricultural land. There are also undeveloped mineral resources of titanium, iron ore, manganese, uranium, and alluvial gold. The cocoa industry has suffered from falling world prices, a higher foreign exchange rate than competitor countries and stagnation due to a loss of immigrant farm labourers and farmers leaving the land to seek higher wages in the oil and related sectors.
High unemployment rates, of around 30 per cent, indicates a segmented employment pattern with the majority of the population dependent on primary industries and too few employed in value-added secondary or tertiary industries.

External trade
As a member of the Communauté Économique des États d'Afrique Centrale (Economic Community of Central African States (ECCAS) Equatorial Guinea uses the CFA franc (Communauté Financière Africaine franc), issued by the Banque des États de l'Afrique Centrale (BEAC) (Bank of Central African States). ECCAS operates a customs and economic union with a common external tariff between its six members, with free movement of capital, people and goods and services.
As a primary producer over 90 per cent of exports are unprocessed petroleum, timber, coffee and cocoa.
Imports
Principal imports are petroleum sector equipment, general equipment, vehicles and construction materials.
Main sources: China (typically 20 per cent of total), US (17 per cent), Spain (15 per cent).
Exports
Principal exports are petroleum, methanol, timber and cocoa.
Main destinations: US (typically 30 per cent of total), China (213 per cent), Japan (9 per cent).

Agriculture
Farming
Agriculture typically accounts for around 5 per cent of GDP, but employs 70 per cent of the workforce. The main cash crop, cocoa is grown on Bioko and Rio Muni, which also produces timber and coffee for export. Main food crops are cassava, sweet potatoes, bananas, palm oil and kernels.
Fishing
The fishing sector is a developing, and potentially lucrative, sector of the economy. The industry has been partially restored, since the 1970s when former President Nguema had banned fishing and destroyed the entire fishing fleet. Nevertheless, the industry is held back by low levels of investment and President Obiang's reluctance to permit a potential conduit that might allow access into the country by those opposed to his regime. The government is developing the 314,000 square kilometre exclusive maritime economic zone surrounding the

island of Anobon, off the mainland territory coastline, which is one of the Atlantic's richest fishing fields.

An EU-Equatorial Guinea fisheries agreement, gives EU trawlers the right to capture 5,500 tonnes of fish per year. Under the deal, the EU pays Equatorial Guinea eur412,500 (US$458,000) per year, much of which goes into expanding and improving local fishing production.

Forestry

Equatorial Guinea has 63 per cent forest cover and logging is an important economic sector.

Industry and manufacturing

The industrial sector used to contribute around 90 per cent of GDP but since the boom in oil exports industry and manufacturing have been reduced to minor elements in the economy. Most production is related to the oil sector although as of 2005 there is no refining capacity. The manufacturing sector is very small, contributing less than 2 per cent of GDP. The non-oil industrial sector is underdeveloped, with activity centred on very small-scale food and timber processing. The traditional industries of cocoa and coffee suffer from a lack of investment. Industrial production remains around 30 per cent.

Tourism

The political situation in Equatorial Guinea has an inhibiting effect on tourism and the industry is localised and underdeveloped. The country's natural beauty and rich bio-diversity is secondary to business travel, related to the oil industry. However, investment from the latter is being redistributed into the former, with infrastructure projects to provide roads and tourist resorts for future growth.

Mining

Industrial production in mining is underdeveloped, activity is limited to artisan exploitation of alluvial gold. There are reserves of copper, iron ore, uranium, tantalum and manganese.

Hydrocarbons

Proven oil reserves were 1.8 billion barrels in 2007, with production rising sharply from 5,000 barrels per day (bpd) in 1995, to 363,000bpd in 2007 from offshore in the Alba and Zafiro fields of the Gulf of Guinea. However domestic consumption has remained negligible at around 1,000bpd and the sale of the surplus has allowed Equatorial Guinea's GDP to grow in step with the new industry. As sub-Saharan Africa's third largest exporter of oil (after Nigeria and Angola) oil exports account for over 90 per cent of all foreign earnings.

The national oil company of Equatorial Guinea, GEPetrol, is responsible for safeguarding the interests of the government in all aspects of production sharing agrements (PSAs) and joint ventures with foreign oil companies, which undertake upstream activities in the country. Legislation ensures that GEPetrol has a minimum 35 per cent stake or share allotted to it, of all investment in the hydrocarbon sector, to guarantee local participation.

Downstream activities are limited as a monopoly exists on distribution. The country is without refining facilities and the infrastructure to deliver petroleum products beyond the cities is rudimentary.

Proven natural gas reserves were 36.8 billion cubic metres (cum) in 2007, most of which is associated natural gas from offshore Bioko Island, where there is a newly completed liquefied natural gas (LNG) facility. Production subsequently rose from 28 million cum in 2001 to 1.3 billion cum in 2006, with growth expected as the policy to end gas flaring is implemented.

A second LNG facility is planned, to process surplus natural gas from Nigeria and Cameroon, totalling around 30 million cum.

The state-owned Sociedad Nacional de Gas de Guinea Ecuatorial (Sonagas) manages all assets and the development of an industrial and residential natural gas market. It is also responsible for the exploration, production, distribution and marketing of natural gas reserves. Legislation ensures that Sonagas has a minimum 35 per cent stake or share allotted to it, of all investment in the hydrocarbon sector, to guarantee local participation.

Any coal production or imports are of insignificant amounts.

Energy

Total installed generating capacity was 131MW in 2006 produced by conventional thermal and hydroelectric plants. However capacity is well below the potential of 11,000MW that could be produced through hydro-power alone. The system is hampered by aging equipment and the transmission network, which alone limits output from the upgraded natural gas-fired power station on Bioko Island to 28MW. Increased capacity, of an expected 4–6MW, is due with the construction of an adjacent plant. There are plans to expand the network; in the meantime small diesel powered generators are widely used during the frequent power outages.

The government has been unsuccessful in its attempt to privatise the state-owned Sociedad de Electricidad de Guinea Ecuatorial (Segesa), due to lack of interest by foreign investors.

Banking and insurance

Central bank

Banque des Etats de l'Afrique Centrale

Main financial centre

Malabo

Time

GMT plus one hour

Geography

Equatorial Guinea is situated on the west coast of Africa. The country comprises the island of Bioko (formerly Fernando Po), 40km off the coast of Cameroon; the mainland territory of Río Muni, 250km south of Bioko; and the islands of Annobón, Corisco, Great Elobey and Small Elobey. The Río Muni enclave is bounded to the north by Cameroon and to the east and south by Gabon.

The islands, in the Gulf of Guinea, are volcanic and mountainous with beaches. Malabo, the capital, is located on Bioko, which covers 2,000 square km. Annobón (17 square km), together with the other smaller islands, are close to the mainland and are all part of Río Muni region.

The mainland is heavily forested with some mountains. There is a coastal plain, which supports plantations. The south of the region is fairly inaccessible.

Hemisphere

Northern

Climate

Equatorial with heavy rainfall for most of the year except for slightly drier period from December–February. The mainland Rio Muni is drier and cooler than Bioko. Average temperature is 26 degrees Celsius throughout the year, and generally very humid.

Entry requirements

Passports

Required by all, valid for six months beyond date of departure.

Visa

Required by all, except US nationals. Business visas require a letter of invitation from a local company and proof of visitor's status and a letter of finance giving proof of sufficient funds for length of stay and a full itinerary.

Currency advice/regulations

Import of local and foreign currencies is unrestricted, provided that amounts in excess of CFAf50,000 (approximately US$90) are declared on arrival. Export of currencies is limited to the amount declared. Failure to declare excess currency risks forfeiture of any amount over the CFAf50,000 limit when departing.

Equatorial Guinea is a cash economy and CFA francs is the only form of payment accepted. Foreign currency should be exchanged at banks, which are few in number.

Health (for visitors)

Mandatory precautions

A yellow fever vaccination certificate is required if arriving from an infected area.

Advisable precautions
Vaccinations against hepatitis A and B, tetanus, diphtheria, polio, typhoid and meningitis are strongly recommended. Malaria prophylaxis is advisable as risk exists throughout the country. There is a rabies risk. Water precautions should be taken.
Medical facilities are limited so it is advisable to pack any personal medications required.

Hotels
Accommodation is very limited but there are hotels in Malabo and Bata. It is essential to book a hotel before travelling, preferably through local business contacts. Food is rarely available at the Bata Hotel and, in Malabo, air-conditioning is available only in some rooms in the Apartotel Impala.
When there is no service charge, gratuities are around 10 to 15 per cent.

Public holidays (national)
Fixed dates
1 Jan (New Year), 8 Mar (Women's Day), 1 May (Labour Day), 25 May (Africa Day), 5 Jun (President's Day), 3 Aug (Armed Forces Day), 15 Aug (Constitution Day), 12 October (Independence Day), 10 Dec (Human Rights' Day), 25 Dec (Christmas Day).
Variable dates
Good Friday, Corpus Christi (May/Jun), Human Rights Day (Dec).

Working hours
Banking
Mon–Sat: 0800–1200.
Business
Mon–Fri: 0800–1500.
Government
Mon–Fri: 0830–1500; Sat: 0830–1200, (alternate Sat) 1000–1200.
Shops
(Mon–Sat) 0800–1300 and 1600–1900.

Electricity supply
220 V AC, 50 cycles

Social customs/useful tips
Corruption is endemic. Special permits from the Ministry of Information and Tourism are required for most photography, including the presidential palace and its environs, military installations, government buildings, airports, harbours and other areas.

Getting there
Air
Several European airlines link Malabo with Madrid, London, Paris, Amsterdam and Zurich.
International airport/s: Malabo Airport (SSG), 7km from the capital city on the island of Malabo.
Bata Airport (FGBT), 6km from city, on the mainland of Equatorial Guinea.
Surface
Road: There is access by semi-surfaced road from Gabon to Mbini and Bata, although this route is not generally recommended.
Main port/s: Malabo, Bata, Luba, Mbini and Kogo.

Getting about
National transport
Air: There are a number of small airlines serving domestic routes, especially Ecuato Guineana, which operates between Bata and Malabo. They do not meet international standards and most of them have been grounded.
Road: On Bioko a surfaced road links major towns in the north. On mainland Río Muni a surfaced road links Bata with Mbini and a partly surfaced road links Bata with Ebebiyin (near Gabon border). Other roads are unsurfaced and can be difficult.
Water: There is a boat service between Malabo and Bata.

BUSINESS DIRECTORY

The addresses listed below are a selection only. While World of Information makes every endeavour to check these addresses, we cannot guarantee that changes have not been made, especially to telephone numbers and area codes. We would welcome any corrections.

Telephone area codes
The international direct dialling code (IDD) for Equatorial Guinea is +240 followed by area code and subscriber's number:

Bata	8	Malabo	9

Chambers of Commerce
Camara Oficiel de Comercio, Agricola y Forestal, 43 Avenida de la Indepencia, PO Box 51, Malabo (tel: 923-43; fax: 932-66).

Banking
Banco de Crédito y Desarrollo (credit and development bank), 1 Avenida de la Libertad, PO Box 39, Malabo (tel: 2146).

Banco Exterior de Guinea Ecuatorial, Carretera de Aeropuerto, Malabo (tel: 2001).

Banque Internationale pour l'Afrique Occidentale, Calle de Argelia No 6, PO Box 686, Malabo (tel: 2367, 2887).

Caisse Commune d'Epargne et d'Investissement en Guinée Equatoriale (CCEI-GE); PO Box 428, Malabo (tel: 2003, 2910; fax: 3311).

Société Générale de Banque GE; PO Box 686, Calle Argelia, Malabo (tel: 3337; fax: 2743).

Central bank
Banque des Etats de l'Afrique Centrale, Direction Nationale, PO Box 501, Malabo (tel: 20-10; fax: 20-06; e-mail: beacmal@beac.int).

Other useful addresses
Comite Sindical de Cacao (cocoa growers' organisation), Bioko.

Dirección General de Correos y Telecomunicaciones, Malabo.

Empresa Estatal de Comercio Interior y Exterior, Malabo.

Empresa General de Industria y Comercio (EGISCA), Malabo.

Empresa Guineano-Española de Petróleos (Gepsa), Malabo.

Internet sites
Equatorial Guinea oil: http://www.equatorialoil.com/

Africa Business Network: http://www.ifc.org/abn

AllAfrica.com: http://allafrica.com

African Development Bank: http://www.afdb.org

Africa Online: http://www.africaonline.com

Mbendi AfroPaedia (information on companies, countries, industries and stock exchanges in Africa): http://mbendi.co.za

Official site (in Spanish): http://www.guineaecuatorial.net/ms/main.asp

KEY FACTS

Official name: Hagere Ertra (State of Eritrea)

Head of State: President Issaias Afewerki (since 1991; elected president 1993)

Head of government: President Issaias Afewerki

Ruling party: People's Front for Democracy and Justice (PFDJ) (formerly the Eritrean People's Liberation Front (EPLF))

Area: 125,000 square km

Population: 5.25 million (2010)*

Capital: Asmara

Official language: There is no official language but the working languages are Tigrinya, Arabic and English.

Currency: Nakfa (Nk) = 100 cents

Exchange rate: Nk15.00 per US$ fixed (pegged from 1 Jan 2005)

GDP per capita: US$398 (2010)

GDP real growth: 2.20% (2010)

GDP: US$2.12 billion (2010)

Labour force: 2.06 million (2008)

Inflation: 12.70% (2010)

Balance of trade: -US$40.00 million (2008)*

* estimated figure

Eritrea

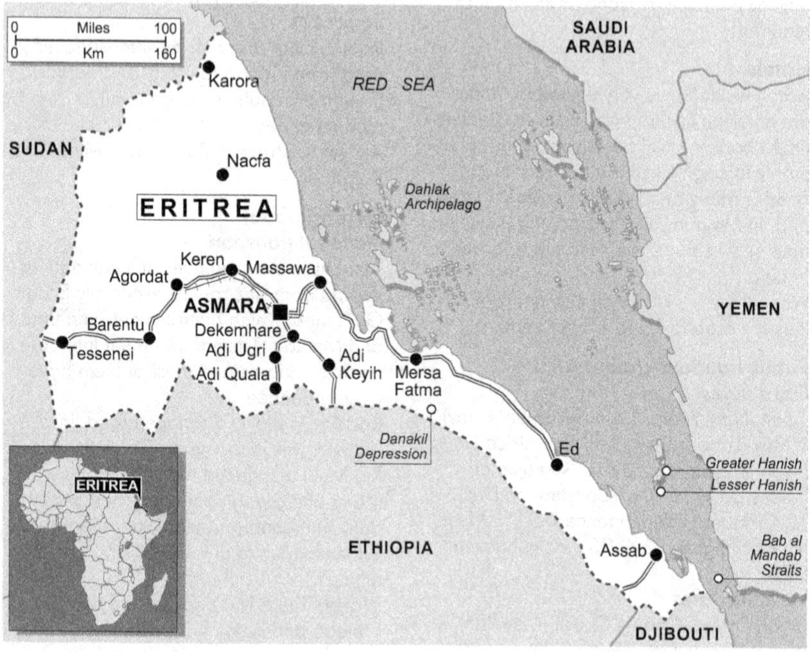

It took decades for Issaias Afewerki, co-founder of the Eritrean People's Liberation Front (EPLF) (renamed the People's Front for Democracy and Justice (PFDJ) in 1994) in 1970, to finally overthrow Ethiopian Colonel Mengistu's forces and liberate Eritrea in 1991. He became president in 1993 and it looks likely that he won't give it up easily. He stated in 2008 that democratic elections don't need to be held for 'three or four decades'.

Former US Ambassador to Eritrea, Ronald McMullen, was quoted in a leaked memo as saying that 'Isaias is an austere and narcissistic dictator whose political ballast derives from Maoist ideology fine-tuned during Eritrea's 30-year war for independence.' As a one-party state, with a leader trained as a political commissar in China under Mao Tse-Tung, the only way Eritrea can gain democracy is to either outlive the regime or replace it - and in this case, that won't come easily, and probably not without a fight.

The economy

Mining and remittances from the extensive Eritrean diaspora are the major sources of foreign earnings. Commodities for export include gold, copper, iron ore, potash and petroleum. Global prices for all these have risen significantly since 2007 (gold prices trebled over 2007-11) and in 2010 contributed US$2.12 billion to gross domestic product (GDP).

Gross domestic product (GDP) in 2010 was estimated to be US$2.11 billion, with growth of 2.2 per cent. There is a high level of subsistence farming (estimated at around 80 per cent of households), leaving the population vulnerable to the vagaries of the weather.

Lousy neighbour

Eritrea has been a poor neighbour to all in the Horn of Africa. A border dispute with Ethiopia has been unresolved since a bloody conflict erupted in 1998. The fighting was so acrimonious that the United Nations had to withdraw it's peace-keeping force (UNMEE) several times, although the final straw came in 2008, when Eritrea cut off fuel supplies to the troops and they left for good. Eritrea has also picked fights with Yemen and Djibouti and in 2010, the UN refused to lift sanctions against Eritrea because it said Afewerki's regime still supported armed opposition groups destabilising the region, and had still to comply with the agreement to withdraw troops from Djibouti.

On 6 December 2011, the UN Security Council imposed tougher sanctions against Eritrea for providing sanctuary for militant Islamist groups (particularly al Shabab), and for attaching neighbouring countries including Somalia. Foreign mining companies were required to impose tighter control over their funding of the industry.

Migration

People are demonstrating with their feet and leaving the country. Eritrea was among the top 10 emigration countries in 2010; the World Bank considers that some 34 per cent of emigrants are skilled workers, notably medical personnel. Around 2,000 refugees reach the Shagarab refugee camp in Sudan every month and most come from Eritrea, escaping compulsory military service. The head of the UN High Commission for Refugees (UNHCR) has warned that human traffickers begun targeting refugee camps in 2011, to kidnap refugees either for money or to kill them and to harvest human organs.

There is an adage in defence that says it only takes one missed attack to bring disaster, so you have to prepare for all attacks. Perhaps for Afewerki, like Qadafi in Libya and Ben Ali of Tunisia, it's the strike he doesn't see coming that will bring him down and give Eritrea a chance of change, to grow and prosper.

Risk assessment

Economy	Poor
Politics	Poor
Regional stability	Poor

COUNTRY PROFILE

Historical profile

1889–1941 Under Italian rule. Eritrea first emerged as a political entity following the Italian occupation of the Red Sea port of Massawa and other coastal enclaves in the 1880s. In 1889, Italy signed the Treaty of Ucciali with the Ethiopian Emperor, Menelik, and in 1890, named the country Eritrea.

1941 The UK defeated Italy during the Second World War and Eritrea became a British protectorate.

1952 UN-sanctioned federation with Ethiopia.

1962 Eritrea was annexed to Ethiopia as a province under Emperor Haile Selassie.

1991 The Eritrean People's Liberation Front (EPLF) overthrew Ethiopian Colonel Mengistu's forces and liberated the territory; Issaias Afewerki assumed power.

1993 A vote resulted in a virtually 100 per cent acceptance of independence.

1994 Eritrea achieved nationhood and Afewerki was elected president by the National Assembly.

1998 Eritrea and Ethiopia resumed border warfare. The Permanent Court of Arbitration in the Hague ruled that Yemen should have the Red Sea island of Greater Hanish, fought over in 1995 by Eritrea and Yemen, and it was announced that Eritrea would return it to Yemen. The nakfa was introduced as Eritrea's national currency, to be used alongside the Ethiopian birr.

2000 UN peacekeepers opened a 1,000km cease-fire land corridor between Ethiopia and Eritrea and the two countries signed a peace deal in Algiers, ending the two-year war.

2001 The UN established a buffer zone along the border between Ethiopia and Eritrea.

2002 Eritrea and Ethiopia accepted a ruling on the border dispute, made by the Boundary Commission at the Permanent Court of Arbitration of The Hague. A new 1,000km boundary was established between the two countries.

2003 The UN Mission in Ethiopia and Eritrea (UNMEE) mandate was extended.

2004 Eritrea suffered a harsh drought, resulting in severe drinking-water problems both for humans and animals. Implementation of the peace process that was to resolve the border conflict between Ethiopia and Eritrea remained stalled.

2005 New Bank of Eritrea regulations required all transactions to be conducted in the national currency, the nakfa. The new currency was pegged against the US dollar at Nk15 per US$. Eritrea restricted the movement of UNMEE peacekeepers along the Eritrea/Ethiopia border, leading to fears that the war would flare up again. The independent commission at the Permanent Court of Arbitration in The Hague, set up as part of the peace deal signed in Algiers in 2000 between Eritrea and Ethiopia, ruled that Eritrea had launched unlawful attacks against Ethiopia in 1998, thereby triggering the border war between the two countries.

2006 Tensions continued in the border dispute with Ethiopia. Eritrea rebuffed international attempts to mediate. Eritrea was accused of arming Islamist opponents of the Somali transitional government, which was supported by Ethiopia.

2007 Talks, set by the Ethiopia-Eritrea Border Commission, to confirm the demarcation between Ethiopia and Eritrea, failed to reach an agreement on time. The Commission considered the border it drew in 2006 to be binding in the face of the impasse. While Ethiopia and Eritrea accepted the ruling neither attempted to implement its recommendations and 1,700 UN peace-keeping troops remained in the area in a notionally demilitarised zone.

2008 United Nation's troops along the disputed border began what was described as a 'temporary relocation' out of Eritrea, after the government cut off fuel supplies. Border clashes in the Mount Gabla area – also known as Ras Doumeira – that killed nine Djibouti troops and injured many more was blamed by the US, on 'military aggression' by Eritrea. The US and France called for a cease-fire, troop withdrawals on both sides and for negotiations to begin. The Security Council terminated the UNMEE.

KEY INDICATORS — Eritrea

	Unit	2006	2007	2008	2009	2010
Population	m	4.54	4.85	*5.01	*5.16	*5.25
Gross domestic product (GDP)	US$bn	1.21	1.32	1.38	1.87	2.12
GDP per capita	US$	267	271	276	363	398
GDP real growth	%	-0.9	1.3	-9.8	3.6	2.2
Inflation	%	15.0	9.3	19.9	34.7	12.7
Exports (fob) (goods)	US$m	64.0	–	–	–	–
Imports (fob) (goods)	US$m	564.0	–	–	–	–
Balance of trade	US$m	-501.0	–	–	–	–
Current account	US$m	-43.0	-9.0	-75.0	-94.0	-122.0
Total reserves minus gold	US$m	25.4	34.3	57.9	90.0	114.1
Foreign exchange	US$m	25.3	34.3	57.9	84.3	108.6
Exchange rate	per US$	13.50	13.24	15.00	15.00	15.38

* estimated figure

2009 The Eritrean national football team refused to return to Eritrea after playing in the Senior Challenge Cup in Nairobi and applied for, and eventually found, asylum in Australia. Eritrea denied it had troops in Djibouti, contrary to UN Security Council announcement that it had failed to withdraw. The UN imposed arms and travel sanctions and froze assets on top politicians and military personnel from Eritrea due to their support of insurgents in Somalia.
2010 In April, President Afewerki invited foreign and domestic journalists to visit military installations in an attempt to influence the UN to lift sanctions against Eritrea. In June Eritrea and Djibouti signed a mediation agreement over their border dispute, with Qatar as a mediator. However despite Eritrea's step towards 'constructive engagement' with Djibouti, the UN refused to lift sanctions, saying that President Afewerki's regime still supported armed opposition groups destabilising the region as well as non-compliance with the agreement to withdraw troops from Djibouti.
2011 On 12 June the Nabro volcano erupted (for the first time in recorded history), and forced airline flights in East Africa to be curtailed. On 12 July, 13 top Eritrean football players refused to return to Eritrea after playing in an East African tournament and applied for asylum in Tanzania. On 6 December, the UN Security Council imposed tougher sanctions against Eritrea, due to its giving sanctuary to militant Islamist groups (particularly al Shabab) that have attacked neighbouring countries. Foreign mining companies will be required to maintain more control over their funding of the industry, including foreign investment; remittances are also likely to be affected by the sanctions.

Political structure

Constitution

A new constitution was adopted in May 1997.

A 150-member National Transitional Council was set up, with 75 seats allocated to the People's Front for Democracy and Justice (PFDJ), 60 to the Constitutional Assembly and 15 to overseas Eritreans.

The president governs with the help of his 24-member Consultative Council. The Consultative Council is composed of ministers and regional governors.

There are six administrative regions, each with regional, sub-regional (55) and village administrations (651). The regions enjoy a degree of autonomy.

Independence date

24 May 1993

National legislature

The unicameral Hagerawi Baito (National Assembly) has 150 members, of which 75 were appointed by the ruling PFDJ and 75 were elected. Eritrea is effectively a one-party state as no opposition parties are legally recognised.

The original intention, in 1991, was for 399 elected members to represent regional constituencies but in 2001 it was decided that no elections would take place until all of the territory claimed by Eritrea was under its control. Regional and local assemblies are in operation with attendant elections.

Last elections

24 May 1993 (presidential)

Results: Presidential: Issaias Afwerki was elected by the National Assembly with 95 per cent of the vote.

Next elections

No information available

Political parties

Ruling party

People's Front for Democracy and Justice (PFDJ) (formerly the Eritrean People's Liberation Front (EPLF))

Main opposition party

Opposition parties are not allowed.

Population

5.25 million (2010)*

Last census: May 1984: 2,748,304

Population density: 32 inhabitants per square km. Urban population: 19 per cent (1995–2001).

Annual growth rate: 3.3 per cent 1994–2004 (WHO 2006)

Internally Displaced Persons (IDP)

59,000 (UNHCR 2004)

Ethnic make-up

There are nine ethno-linguistic groups.

Religions

Tigrigna-speaking Christians (mainly Orthodox), are the traditional inhabitants of the highlands, with some Protestant and Roman Catholic communities (49 per cent); Muslim communities of the western lowlands, northern highlands and east coast are 49 per cent. A small number of the population adhere to traditional beliefs.

Education

There are approximately 260 primary schools and over 50 secondary schools. It has been estimated by Oxfam that 93 per cent of children age 6–11 will enrol for school in 2015.

Literacy rate: 67 per cent men, 36 per cent woman; adult rates (World Bank 2002).

Enrolment rate: 53 per cent gross enrolment, of relevant age group, in primary education (World Bank 2001).

Pupils per teacher: 44 in primary schools.

Health

Access to an improved water source is available to 46 per cent of the population.

HIV/Aids

A survey published in 2001 revealed that 4.6 per cent of soldiers were HIV-positive and 22.8 per cent of female bar workers were affected as well. By 2002, more than 13,000 people had been registered as infected with HIV/Aids. The main incidences are in Asmara, the capital, and Assab, the sea port, where prostitution is rife. Up to 30 per cent of prostitutes are HIV positive.

HIV prevalence: 2.7 per cent aged 15–49 in 2003 (World Bank)

Life expectancy: 60 years, 2004 (WHO 2006)

Fertility rate/Maternal mortality rate: 5.4 births per woman, 2004 (WHO 2006); maternal mortality 10 per 1,000 per live births (World Bank).

Child (under 5 years) mortality rate (per 1,000): 45 per 1,000 live births (2003); 44 per cent of children aged under five were malnourished (World Bank).

Head of population per physician: 0.05 physicians per 1,000 people, 2004 (WHO 2006)

Welfare

A post-war rehabilitation project, implemented by the UN Development Programme (UNDP), has put metal roofs, doors and windows back on houses that were deserted and ransacked during the border war with Ethiopia. An estimated 60,000 children were left crippled by the war, and another 45,000 orphaned. A large proportion of the population is dependent on food aid.

Main cities

Asmara (capital, estimated population 543,707 in 2005), Keren (86,483), Dek'emhare (30,180), Massawa (Mitsiwa) (24,419).

Languages spoken

The principal language group in Eritrea is Afro-Asiatic; Arabic, Afar, Bilen, Hedareb, Kunama, Nara, Saho, Tigray and Tigrinya are spoken. English is rapidly becoming the language of business and is the medium of instruction at secondary schools and at university.

Official language/s

There is no official language but the working languages are Tigrinya, Arabic and English.

Media

In 2006 Eritrea was ranked 166 out of 168 and one of the three worst press freedom violators (after North Korea and Turkmenistan) worldwide. Journalists have been imprisoned and media outlets were closed down in 2001, so that, in 2008, government organs have a monopoly, which led the Paris-based Reporters Without Borders to condemned Eritrea as isolating its population from the world and subjecting it to 'propaganda worthy of a bygone age'.

Press

There are no daily newspapers, all publications are government-owned, including in Tigrinya and Arabic *Hadas Eritrea* (*New Eritrea*), *Tirigta* (owned by the PFDJ political party) and *Geled* for a youth readership and in English *Eritrea Profile*.

Broadcasting

Radio: Two radio stations exist, Radio Zara and Dimtsi Hafash Radio (Voice of the Broad Masses of Eritrea) operates two networks that broadcast in Arabic and local languages. Services can also be received via Arabsat satellite.

Television: The government-owned ERI-TV broadcasts in Arabic, and local languages although transmissions are limited to Asmara and surrounding areas.

News agencies

Erina (Eritrean News Agency): www.dehai.org/erina

Economy

Subsistence farming is the mainstay of the economy, sustaining around 80 per cent of the population, despite only 10 per cent of arable land being cultivated. Agricultural products include grains and potatoes, cotton and flax, fruit and vegetables, dairy products and meat. In 2009, agriculture constituted 14.4 per cent of GDP, the service sector 63.4 per cent and industry 22.2 per cent, of which manufacturing was 5.6 per cent. Agriculture directly employed 17.3 per cent of the workforce in 2009, services 59.5 per cent and industry 23.2 per cent. Industrial production is centred around mining, of gold, copper, iron ore, potash and petroleum. Manufacturing production includes food processing (using local produce), drinks (including alcoholic beverages), leather goods and textiles, construction materials, chemicals and salt, paper and matches.
The service sector provides resources for most of agriculture and industry; however with a command economy in operation government services constitutes most paid employment in Eritrea.
Using an old-style, Communist, centrally planned economy, Eritrea has to deal with problems inherent in that system (lack of investment, suppressed entrepreneurial enterprise, limited diversity, lack of swift change due to changing circumstances). In addition there is an inadequate and still war-ravaged infrastructure, a lack of hard currency to pay for imports, a weak tax collection system and the predominance of unproductive subsistence agriculture, which is subject to harsh climate changes.
A severe drought in 2008 resulted in a 25 per cent loss in agricultural productivity for that year, forcing the government to import food, just at a time when world food prices had risen sharply. The drought was only one reason for low productivity – manpower shortages and unexploded ordnance (UXO) (landmines) continue to be problems. The global recession meant Eritrea was hit by a reduction in remittances from its diaspora. Private transfers from abroad and remittances typically account for over 30 per cent of GDP.
GDP growth was 1.4 per cent in 2007, falling to -9.8 per cent in 2008, but rising to 3.6 per cent in 2009, and forecast to remain positive, albeit at a low growth rate of 1.8 per cent, in 2010. Inflation fell to 9.3 per cent in 2007 but rose to 19.9 per cent in 2008 and higher still to 34.7 per cent in 2009, as food shortages and import prices impacted on the population; inflation eased back to 20.5 per cent in 2010.
The country's economic future depends on the government adopting an open market economy, which it has claimed it is committed to introduce, and its ability to eradicate the widespread illiteracy and unemployment. Eritrea was one of the countries that was not included in the 2010, UN Human Development Index, which gave a quantitative ranking of national development in health, education and income. The border between Ethiopia and Eritrea, implemented after the UN Boundary Commission ruling in 2002, ought to have encouraged stability and allowed Eritrea to focus on these problems, but relations between the two countries remain fractious and continuing tensions are likely to deter investment until a lasting accord is reached.
In the long term, Eritrea may benefit from the development of offshore oil, fishing and a tourism industry.

External trade

Eritrea is a member of the Common Market of Eastern and Southern Africa (Comesa), however due to its command economy and tightly controlled import/export policies it does not have plans to join the customs union and free trade area as agreed by other member states.

Imports

Principal non-petroleum imports include machinery, food and manufactured goods.

Main sources: Germany (typically over 20 per cent of total), Italy (20 per cent), France (15 per cent).

Exports

Principal exports include livestock, sorghum, textiles, food and small manufactures.

Main destinations: Italy (typically over 35 per cent of total), US (15 per cent), Belarus (5 per cent).

Agriculture

Fishing

Fishing for sardines, anchovies, tuna, shark and mackerel is practised in the Red Sea on a very small scale. There are over 1,000 different species of fish off Eritrea's shores, with the stocks virtually untouched since the 1950s. The government believes there is potential for exporting 80,000 tonnes of fish annually. The sector has been badly affected by the closure of its market in Yemen as a result of a territorial dispute.
The majority of timber harvested is used for domestic purposes.

Industry and manufacturing

The industrial sector contributes around 27 per cent of GDP and employs 10 per cent of the workforce.
The industrial base is traditionally centred on the production of glass, cement, footwear and canned goods, but most industrial enterprises have been badly damaged by war. All state-owned distribution and import/export enterprises established by the former government have been dissolved.
Major problems include outdated machinery and techniques, supply of energy, and the need for imports throughout the sector. With a lack of foreign currency and investment, industry is suffering from outdated machinery and intermediary goods which need to be imported.

Tourism

The government designated the entire coastline as an environmentally protected zone in 2006. Among other attractions, include active volcanoes and the Afar Triance or Danakil Depression where three tectonic plates, the Arabian and two African plates, are pulling away from each other. The resulting split can be seen in the East African Rift Zone. There are also traditional dwellings and a few remaining native wildlife areas.
Eritrea has been experiencing prolonged military action with neighbouring Ethiopia and tourists are advised to find alternative destinations.

Environment

In June 2010 the African Union backed a proposal to build the 'Great Green Wall' project, of a 15km wide, 7,775km long, continuous belt of trees from Senegal in the west to Djibouti in the east (traversing 11 countries) in an effort to halt the advance of the Sahara Desert. The trees to be used would be drought-adapted, preferably native to the area from a list of 37 possible species, and should help to slow soil erosion and filter rain water.

Mining

Fighting along the border regions disrupted mining activities, although exploration continued elsewhere in Eritrea. The Phelps Dodge Exploration Corporation conducted exploration on the Debarwa copper-zinc deposits and identified up to four million tonnes of reserves, including at least two million tonnes of mineable high-grade copper and a large amount of gold.

Gold-bearing seams exist in highland areas. There are over 15 gold mines and a large number of prospects close to Asmara. The potential for new discoveries in the area is good. Substantial gold reserves have also been identified at Adi Nefas by LaSource Development SAS. Artisanal mining production is estimated to produce around 550kg per year.

Despite Eritrea's mining potential, salt and marble remain the country's main exported minerals.

Hydrocarbons

Following several oil exploration projects it was determined that there are no exploitable oil and gas reserves in Eritrea; it is dependent on imports at around 5,000 barrels per day (bpd) of oil to supply its requirements.

In December 2008 Iran deployed military personnel in Eritrea in return for refurbishing the defunct refinery at the Red Sea port of Assab, which had a crude oil capacity of 18,000bpd before it was closed down in 1997.

Energy

Total installed electricity generating capacity is 154MW, powered mainly by diesel-fired generators. However until an upgrade in the dated power grid, to be completed in 2009, becomes operational the electricity supply will remain available only in mainly large urban areas, leaving the majority of the population without access.

Some villages provide themselves with electricity from community diesel generators for water pumps, while photovoltaic electricity generation of around 2KW are used to a limited extent in health centres and schools to power operating theatres, refrigerators and lighting.

Banking and insurance

Central bank

Bank of Eritrea

Time

GMT plus three hours

Geography

Eritrea extends inland from the Red Sea coast of eastern Africa. To the south, the country has a long frontier with Ethiopia, and a short frontier with Djibouti. Sudan lies to the north and west.

The coastal area is a desert plain, around 50km wide in the south, and one of the driest places in the world. Inland, the terrain becomes hillier, rising to 2,000m, in the north-west, while further south it turns to rolling plains.The highlands are cool and receive up to 60cm of rainfall annually; fertile valleys support agricultural activity.

Hemisphere

Northern

Climate

Coastal and lowland regions very hot and dry throughout the year. On the plateau, which includes Asmara, the dry season runs from October–May with temperatures ranging from as low as 6 degrees Celsius (C) in December to 26 degrees C in March (light rain from February–April). Temperatures can fall sharply at night during the dry season.

The rainy season runs from June–September with average temperature 21 degrees C. Rainfall is less than 500mm per year in lowland areas, increasing to 1,000mm in the highlands. The temperature gradient is similarly steep: average annual temperatures range from 17 degrees C in the highlands to 30 degrees C in Massawa. The Danakil depression in the south-east, which is more than 130 metres below sea-level in places, experiences some of the highest temperatures recorded, frequently exceeding 50 degrees C.

Entry requirements

Passports

Required by all, valid for three months beyond intended length of stay.

Visa

Required by all except nationals of Kenya and Uganda. Business visas are valid for one month, but can be extended on application to the Eritrean Foreign Ministry. A business letter giving proof of sufficient funds for length of stay, a full itinerary and copy of return/onward ticket, should accompany application.

Currency advice/regulations

There are no restrictions on import or export of local and foreign currency. From January 2005, all transactions have been conducted in the national currency, the nakfa.

Health (for visitors)

Mandatory precautions

A yellow fever vaccination certificate is required if travelling from or via an infected area.

Advisable precautions

Inoculations and booster should be current for diphtheria, polio, tetanus, hepatitis A, and typhoid. There may be a need for vaccinations for, tuberculosis, hepatitis B and meningitis. Use malaria prophylaxis if travelling in areas below 2000 metres.

Malaria and hepatitis B are caused by mosquitoes, precautions including mosquito repellents, nets and clothing covering the body after dark should be used. There is a risk of rabies in rural areas. There is a shortage of routine medications and visitors should take all necessary medicines with them. A first aid kit that includes disposable syringes, is a reasonable precaution. Use only bottled or boiled water for drinks, washing teeth and making ice. Eat only well cooked meals, preferably served hot; vegetables should be cooked and fruit peeled. Dairy products are unpasteurised and should be avoided, unless cooked.

Healthcare is not to Western standards and medical insurance, including emergency evacuation, is necessary.

Hotels

Both Asmara and Massawa suffer from a severe shortage of hotel space; booking is advisable. Standards are low but are being improved. Service charge of 10 per cent and a small tip is usual in addition to service charge. Visitors are expected to pay bills at government-run hotels in US dollars or denominated traveller's cheques.

Credit cards

Credit cards are only accepted at a few outlets in Asmara.

Public holidays (national)

Fixed dates

1 Jan (New Year's Day), 8 Mar (Women's Day), 24 May (Independence Day), 20 Jun (Martyrs' Day), 1 Sep (Start of the Armed Struggle), 25 Dec (Christmas Day).

Variable dates

Eid al-Fitr, Eid al-Adha, Prophet's Anniversary, Easter.

Islamic year 1433 (26 Nov 2011–14 Nov 2012): The Islamic year contains 354 or 355 days, with the result that Muslim feasts advance by 10–12 days against the Gregorian calendar. Dates of feasts vary according to the sighting of the new moon, so cannot be forecast exactly.

Working hours

Banking

(Mon–Fri) 0800–1200, 1400–1700; (Sat) 0800–1200.

Business

Mon–Thu: 0700–1200, 1400–1800; Fri: 0700–1130, 1400–1800.

Shops

Mon–Fri: 0830–1300, 1430–2030.

Electricity supply

220V AC, 50 cycles.

Weights and measures

The metric system is in force.

Security

Street crime such as theft and robbery is rare in most cities. However, it is advisable not to walk around alone late at night in any town, particularly Asmara and Massawa. Valuables, especially cameras and including passports, should be kept out of sight.

Getting there

Air

National airline: Eritrean Airlines
International airport/s: Asmara (ASM), 6km from city, restaurant, currency exchange, post office, duty-free.
Airport tax: International departures: US$20; domestic departures Nk15.

Surface

Road: There are no roads considered safe to enter the country. The 300km road from Kassala in Sudan, to Tessenai, is largely unsurfaced.
Main port/s: Massawa and Assab.
Assab's cargo levels are very low. The port had previously relied on Ethiopia for 90 per cent of its trade.

Getting about

National transport

Road: The extensive road network is undergoing major rehabilitation with US$27m allocated by the government to road reconstruction.
There are 622km of asphalt roads. The Massawa-Asmara main route (107km) is open. Other main routes (largely unsurfaced) are Asmara-Keren to Afabet-Nacfa in the north, and Asmara-Tessenai to the west. In many parts of the country, roads are difficult or impassable during the rainy season. There are extensive mine fields in Eritrea, especially near the border with Ethiopia. Travelling on main roads outside of the border areas is generally safe, but it is advisable not to drive off-road or travel after dark in rural areas.
Buses: Some bus services available, including one service to Addis Ababa.
Taxis: Taxis are available for trips outside the city, but the fares are higher.
Rail: The link from Asmara to the coast is functioning.

City transport

Taxis: The journey time by taxi from the Asmara International Airport to the city is 15 minutes. Taxi drivers do not expect a tip.

BUSINESS DIRECTORY

Telephone area codes

The international dialling code (IDD) for Eritrea is +291 followed by 1 and subscriber's number.

Chambers of Commerce

Eritrean National Chamber of Commerce, 46 Aboit Avenue, PO Box 856, Asmara (tel: 121-589; fax: 120-138; e-mail: encc@eol.com.er).

Banking

Commercial Bank of Eritrea; PO Box 291, 212 Liberty Avenue, Asmara (tel: 116-005, 121-844/48; fax: 124-887l, 121-849).

Eritrean Development & Investment Bank; PO Box 1266, 29 Atse Yohannes Street, Asmara (tel: 123-787, 114-520, 126-777).

Housing & Commerce Bank of Eritrea; PO Box 235, Bahti Meskerem Square, Asmara (tel: 120-350; fax: 120-401).

Central bank

National Bank of Eritrea, Zeraai Derres Square, PO Box 849, Asmara (tel: 123-033; fax: 122-091; e-mail: tekieb@eol.com.er).

Travel information

Ministry of tourism

Ministry of Tourism, PO Box 1010, Asmara (tel: 126-997).

Ministries

Ministry of Agriculture, PO Box 124, Asmara (tel: 181-499; fax: 181-415).

Ministry of Defence, PO Box 629, Asmara (tel: 113-349; fax: 114-920).

Ministry of Education, PO Box 5610, Asmara (tel: 113-044; fax: 113-866).

Ministry of Energy and Mines, PO Box 5285, Asmara (tel: 116-872; fax: 127-652); Department of Energy (fax: 112-339); Department of Mines (fax: 112-994).

Ministry of Finance and Development, PO Box 896, Asmara (tel: 113-633; fax: 117-947).

Ministry of Fisheries, PO Box 923, Asmara (tel: 114-271; fax: 112-185).

Ministry of Foreign Affairs, PO Box 190, Asmara (tel: 113-811; fax: 123-788).

Ministry of Health, PO Box 212, Asmara (tel: 112-877; fax: 112-899).

Ministry of Information, PO Box 242, Asmara (tel: 115-171; fax: 119-847).

Ministry of Justice, PO Box 241, Asmara (tel: 111-822).

Ministry of Local Government, PO Box 225, Asmara (tel: 113-006).

Ministry of Public Works, PO Box 841, Asmara (tel: 119-077).

Ministry of Trade and Industry, PO Box 1844, Asmara (tel: 118-386, 113-910; fax: 120-586).

Ministry of Transport and Communications, PO Box 204, Asmara (tel: 110-444; fax: 127-048).

Other useful addresses

African Minerals Inc (AMI), PO Box 3508, Asmara (tel: 120-280, 120-030; fax: 120-332).

British Consulate, 27 Lorenzo Tazaz Street, PO Box 997, Asmara (tel: 123-415; fax: 127-230).

Communications and Postal Authority, PO Box 234, Asmara (tel: 112-900; fax: 110-938).

Eritrean Association in London, UK (tel: (0)181-748-0547).

Eritrean Business Licence Office, PO Box 3045, Asmara (tel: 114-809, 114-752; fax: 126-694).

Eritrean Shipping Lines, PO Box 1110, Asmara (tel: 120-308/359/257; fax: 120-331).

Grain Board of Eritrea, PO Box 1234, Asmara (tel: 115-624; fax: 120-586).

Investment Promotion Centre, Asmara (tel: 118-822, 118-124; fax: 124-293).

Prima Eritrea Oil Company, Asmara (tel: 120-050; fax: 120-099).

Red Sea Trading Corporation (import/export services operated by the PFDJ), 29/31 Ras Alula Street, PO Box 332, Asmara (tel: 127-846; fax: 124-353).

US Embassy, PO Box 211, Asmara (tel: 120-004, 120-009; fax: 127-584).

Voice of the Broad Masses of Eritrea (Dimtsi Hafash), Ministry of Information, Radio Division, PO Box 872, Asmara.

Internet sites

Eritrean news: http://www.messelna.com

Africa Business Network: http://www.ifc.org/abn

AllAfrica.com: http://www.allafrica.com

African Development Bank: http://www.afdb.org

Africa Online: http://www.africaonline.com

Estonia

KEY FACTS

Official name: Eesti Vabariik (The Republic of Estonia)

Head of State: President Toomas Hendrik Ilves (since 2006; re-elected 29 Aug 2011)

Head of government: Prime Minister Andrus Ansip (RE) (elected 2005; re-elected 6 Mar 2011)

Ruling party: Reformierakond (RE) (Reform Party) (from 2005; re-elected 6 Mar 2011)

Area: 45,227 square km

Population: 1.34 million (2010)*

Capital: Tallinn

Official language: Estonian

Currency: Kroon (plural krooni) (EEK) = 100 senti

Exchange rate: EEK0.75 per US$ (Oct 2011)

GDP per capita: US$14,836 (2010)

GDP real growth: 3.10% (2010)

GDP: US$19.80 billion (2010)

Labour force: 687,000 (2010)

Unemployment: 16.90% (2010)

Inflation: 2.90% (2010)

Balance of trade: -US$330.70 million (2010)

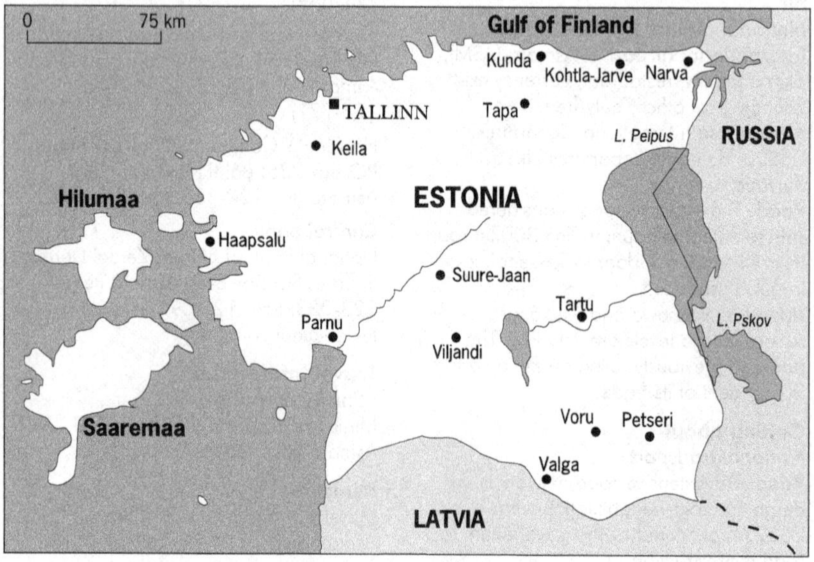

The Estonian authorities could be forgiven for feeling a certain smugness in 2011. Surrounded by economic turmoil, Estonia was one of the very few European countries that met the European Union's (EU). criterion of an annual budget deficit below 3 per cent of gross domestic product (GDP). Not only that, the forecast 2010 budget deficit, at 2.95 per cent, was surprisingly low; Estonia's government debt was minimal, and inflation was low. The government had responded swiftly to the global crisis: spending cuts were tough, infrastructure projects were accelerated, many financed by the EU. This 'normalcy' was also attributed by some observers to the fact that Estonia has managed its Russian community more successfully than have the other Balkan countries. Around a quarter of Estonians would describe themselves as 'Russian' compared to a third in Latvia. The relationship with what amounts to the former colonial power has been handled differently by each Baltic state. Ethnic Russian communities inevitably hankered after the 'good old' days of the Soviet Union, looking to Moscow rather than Brussels for guidance, even inspiration. Quoted in the *Baltic Times* the London *Economist's* Central and Eastern European correspondent Edward Lucas made the point that the Baltic states seemed to have missed a trick in not encouraging the formation of a 'Baltic Russian' identity as an alternative to the Kremlin's idea of what being Russian is all about. Interestingly Estonia's President Toomas Ilves has been quoted as saying that 'the Baltic states are the best place in the world to be a Russian'. The only trouble is that not many Baltic Russians would agree. However, Russian claims that the Russian minorities are a 'victimised' underclass seemed exaggerated. For some time, Estonia has effectively been a 'post-communist' republic. This is pretty understandable. Many, but no longer most, Estonians still recall that Stalin's defeat of Hitler also brought with it nearly fifty harsh years of annexation, deportation and Russification. Older Estonians still feel strongly about deprivations suffered during the Soviet era. The Estonian parliament only ratified its border treaty with Russia after inserting clauses referring to the Russian occupations of 1940–41 and 1945–91. Unsurprisingly, Russia responded by stating that the treaty was null and void.

The economy

Estonia's annual gross domestic product (GDP) growth rate in the first quarter of 2011 was a rip-roaring 8.5 per cent, the highest of the EU's 27 member countries. Breaking records is something of Estonia's forte. The Baltic country also boasts of the lowest public debt level in the EU, only 6.6 per cent of GDP and it can also claim to be among the continent's ten best sovereign risks. No pain, no gain has very much been the order of the day; locked in to the euro, Estonia could not resort to monetary policies to re-balance its economy. Instead, the government launched a far-reaching fiscal adjustment – amounting to a nine per cent austerity programme. Estonia's export growth has been, by any reckoning, exceptional. Exports grew by 53 per cent in the year up to May 2011, industrial production by 26 per cent. Swedish electronics manufacturer Ericsson is the country's largest exporter.

The International Monetary Fund (IMF) in its November 2011 report on the Estonian economy noted the vibrant recovery that marked Estonia's first year in the euro area, albeit amid nascent tensions. The economy's strong rebound has been grounded in a proven track record of prudent macro-economic policies, which also underpinned a successful euro adoption and a recent credit rating upgrade. But coming on the heels of one of the EU's deepest economic contractions, the recovery has exposed underlying difficulties. Price pressures continued and unemployment, while declining, remains high with long-term joblessness on the rise. Following the strong growth seen in 2011, the pace of economic activity and price increases looked set to moderate in 2012. In line with weakening export markets, growth is projected to slow to about 3 per cent. This is expected to be only partially offset by stronger final domestic demand. The output gap is expected nonetheless to continue to narrow in 2012. Inflation should also moderate as the impact of global food and fuel prices shocks dissipate. Core inflation's outlook remains uncertain given wage pressures largely stemming from labour shortages and mismatched skills. So far, wages increases have not exceeded productivity gains. As a result, economy-wide profitability and external competitiveness have improved. These trends are likely to continue but pressures could remain on core inflation.

With continued volatility in global financial markets, downside risks to the outlook have risen at end-2011. With two-thirds of Estonia's exports going to the EU, recent European and global developments have tilted risks to the downside. Besides the domestic risk that the unwinding of past real and financial sector imbalances will be more protracted and weigh on domestic demand, external risks associated with the euro area sovereign debt crisis prevail.

Summarising the situation, the IMF observed that Estonia faces an increasingly challenging environment as it looks to continue implementing policies preserving macro-economic policy credibility and safeguarding sustainable growth. Following a strong recovery in its first year in the euro area, Estonia's economic activity was likely to slow down in 2012. Inflation was poised to slow even though pressures on core inflation would probably remain. In addition to a possible slowdown in exports, the generalised confidence fallout from the euro area sovereign debt crisis could spill over to Estonia despite its strong fundamentals.

In the view of the IMF Estonia's fiscal position will remain strong but there will be a need to limit the impact of the 2012 budget. Looking beyond the current scenario, the authorities' medium-term target can safeguard Estonia's strong fiscal position. This will require continued expenditure restraint to counter spending pressures that are likely to emerge. The authorities' ongoing efforts to enhance central government productivity through centralisation of accounting and personnel management can help. Still, without raising taxes, achieving the fiscal target on a sustainable basis, implementing the authorities' plan to reduce labour taxation, and restore fiscal buffers will require reducing non-wage goods and services by at least two percentage points of GDP in the medium term. The pace of consolidation should be mindful of long-term investment needs and cyclical developments.

Banking

For the financial sector, the challenge entails safeguarding stability in the context of heightened global financial tension. Estonian banks have little direct or indirect exposure to euro area sovereign debt, while at the same time capital and liquidity buffers have increased substantially since 2007. However, the legacy of the previous crisis continues to burden balance sheets and dependence on financing from parent banks remains high, although both of these factors are declining. The latter has proven a stable source of financing, but parent banks in turn rely on short-term wholesale funding. Limiting potential contagion will thus require continued improvements in cross-border supervision. Developing regional crisis resolution tools – in close co-operation with relevant authorities – can provide critical backstop to Estonia's sizable fiscal and financial buffers. The scheduled December 2011 high-level meeting of Nordic regulators provides an opportunity to make progress in this critical area. In addition, an early and gradual institutional adoption of Basel III requirements can reduce funding risks, but its implementation should avoiding creating headwinds for credit conditions.

Financial resilience can also be supported by further enhancing the regional and domestic resolution frameworks for banks, and addressing weaknesses in Estonia's bankruptcy law. The recent

KEY INDICATORS **Estonia**

	Unit	2006	2007	2008	2009	2010
Population	m	1.35	1.34	1.34	1.34	*1.34
Gross domestic product (GDP)	US$bn	16.61	21.28	23.20	19.10	19.80
GDP per capita	US$	12,353	15,851	17,299	14,267	14,836
GDP real growth	%	11.1	7.1	-3.6	-14.1	3.1
Inflation	%	4.4	6.6	10.4	-0.1	2.9
Unemployment	%	5.9	4.7	5.5	13.8	16.9
Exports (fob) (goods)	US$m	9,635.1	11,087.1	12,630.1	9,125.2	11,641.3
Imports (fob) (goods)	US$m	12,373.6	14,697.8	15,350.2	9,903.2	11,972.0
Balance of trade	US$m	-2,738.5	-3,610.7	-2,720.1	-778.0	-330.7
Current account	US$m	-2,575.0	-3,684.0	-2,143.0	893.2	673.2
Total reserves minus gold	US$m	2,781.2	3,262.7	3,964.9	3,971.9	2,555.9
Foreign exchange	US$m	2,781.1	3,262.6	3,964.8	3,874.7	2,460.4
Exchange rate	per US$	12.10	10.83	10.69	11.27	11.81

* estimated figure

adoption of a domestic resolution law provides a welcome tool to minimise the cost of a bank failure. This could be supplemented by introducing a bank-asset separation authority as well as by developing cross-border bank resolution tools in co-ordination with the EU and regional partners. In addition, legal clarifications regarding the Reorganisation Act for corporations have improved its effectiveness, while the recent adoption of an analogous law for individuals ensures broader coverage. Reforms are still needed to shorten the lengthy and costly bankruptcy process.

More broadly, sustainable growth will entail enhancing Estonia's attractiveness for foreign direct investments (FDI), addressing skill mismatches, and increasing human capital. Estonia's 2020 Competitiveness Strategy highlights the need for further improvements in the business environment to continue to draw FDI. The urgency of boosting knowledge-based activities and remaining an attractive destination for FDI has been heightened by growing competition from emerging markets. Furthermore, fully drawing on Estonia's resources and developing their potential will also require addressing skill mismatches and continuing attention to foster human resources in technical fields as well as to attract highly-trained individuals to support sustainable income convergence to EU levels.

The ruling Reformierakond (RE) (Reform Party) has been in power since 2005, having been re-elected in March 2011. In many European countries the knee-jerk reaction to times of austerity has been to ditch the pilot. In Estonia the response has been more complex – flying in the face of received wisdom by taking the surprising step of joining the euro-zone's beleaguered currency from January 2011. The move came at a time when many countries were giving serious consideration to doing just the opposite.

Risk assessment

Economy	Fair
Politics	Good
Regional stability	Good

COUNTRY PROFILE

Historical profile

Around 3,000 BC the Finno-Ugric peoples began to migrate from Eastern Europe to the north-east coast of the Baltic Sea.
1219 Valdemar II of Denmark and the German Sword Brethren, a crusading order, conquered Estonia.
1346 The Danes sold their share of Estonian territory to the Livonian Order of Teutonic Knights (an alliance of the Sword Brethren and the German Order of Teutonic Knights).
1524–39 The State of Teutonic Knights, including Estonia, renounced religious allegiance to Rome and converted to Lutheranism.
1561 In the secularisation and partition of the State of Teutonic Knights, Estonia (now northern Estonia) became part of Sweden. Livonia (now Latvia and southern Estonia) was placed under Polish rule.
1721–1917 Estonia became a Baltic province of Russia.
1918–40 Estonia was an independent republic.
1940–88 Estonia was a constituent republic of the USSR.
1988 Estonia declared its sovereignty.
1989 Economic autonomy was granted.
1990 Independence from the USSR was declared. The break-up of the Soviet Union led to a sharp decline in industrial and commercial output.
1991 Independence was reaffirmed.
1992 Following the country's first free elections since independence, a coalition of various right-wing conservative parties, operating under the name Isamaa Pro Patria, was the heart of the government coalition, headed by Mart Laar as prime minister. Lennart Meri became president. A new constitution was adopted based on the 1938 model that provided the legal continuity to the Republic of Estonia prior to the Soviet occupation. Inflation soared to nearly 1,000 per cent as the Soviet energy and food supply system crumbled and hard currency was required for imports. A new currency, the kroon, was introduced and pegged to the Deutsche mark under a currency board system of a ratio of eight to one.
1994 GDP growth was registered for the first time since independence. Estonia joined the NATO Partnership for Peace programme (PfP). Laar lost a vote of no-confidence and Andres Tarand became caretaker prime minister until elections could be held.
1995 The governing coalition parties lost ground in the parliamentary elections. A centre-left government was formed under Tiit Vähi as prime minister. Estonia applied to join the EU. The government collapsed when the Eesti Keskerakond (EK) (Estonian Centre Party) left the government.
1996–97 The re-formed coalition collapsed when six ministers resigned and the resulting minority government also collapsed after Vähi's resignation. The ECP leader, Mart Siimann, became prime minister and formed a minority government with the Estonian Rural Union (EM) and independents.
1999 The EK became the largest party in parliament; Mart Laar remained in office as prime minister. Estonia joined the World Trade Organisation (WTO).
2000 The economy recovered from the 1998 Russian crisis and foreign investment picked up.
2001 Arnold Rüütel was elected president by the electoral college.
2003 Juhan Parts formed a coalition government comprising Uhendus Vabariigi Eest-Res Publica (ResP) (Union for the Republic-Res Publica), the Reformierakond (RE) (Reform Party) and Eestimaa Rahvaliit (ER) (Estonian People's Union). Estonians voted to join the EU.
2004 Estonia joined NATO and the EU.
2005 The failure to pursue a controversial tough anti-corruption plan led to the demise of the government. Andrus Ansip (RE) was appointed prime minister of a new, three-party coalition government of RE, Keskerakond and ER.
2006 Parliament voted for Toomas Hendrik Ilves, to replace the incumbent president, Arnold Rüütel.
2007 In parliamentary elections the ruling RE-ER-Keskerakond coalition won with an increased majority of 66 seats (out of 101). Estonia became a member of the European Union Schengen area whereby all travellers may cross borders without a passport or visa.
2008 An agreement allowing visa-free visits of citizens to the US was signed.
2009 The international ratings agency Standard and Poor's cut Estonia's long-term sovereign foreign currency credit rating from A to A-, due to Estonia's dependence on external financing.
2010 In May, the Organisation for Economic Co-operation and Development (OECD) voted unanimously to admit Estonia as a member. In July EU finance ministers agreed that Estonia should adopt the euro as its currency on 1 January 2011, at an exchange rate of 15.6466 kroon to the euro. The new threat of concerted cyber-attacks attracted almost 40 countries to a conference in Tallinn in June to discuss possible counter-measures. The Estonian government, banks and other institutions had collectively been one of the first to experience an all-out attack on their computers in 2007; the perpetrators were never caught, despite suspicion falling on Russia.
2011 Estonia adopted the euro as its currency on 1 January, at an exchange rate of 15.6466 kroon to the euro. In parliamentary elections held on 6 March, the ruling RE won 28.6 per cent of the vote and increased its seats to 33 (out of 101). On 24 March a coalition government was agreed between the RE and the Isamaa ja

Res Publica Liit (IRL) (Union of Pro Patria and Res Publica (Party of National Affairs)); Prime Minister Ansip (RE) remained as prime minister. Trade figures released on 13 July showed a year-on-year increase in exports of 53 per cent and a decrease in the deficit. On 29 August, parliament re-elected Toomas Hendrik Ilves as president. The eleventh population and housing census will be held in two parts, with the first undertaken on 31 December and the second on 31 March 2012.

Political structure

Constitution

The constitution was adopted on 28 June 1992. It is based on the 1938 model, that provides legal continuity to the Republic of Estonia prior to Soviet occupation.

The constitution defines the areas of responsibility of the government as: to implement domestic and foreign policies; to direct and co-ordinate the work of government institutions; to organise and implement legislation, the resolutions of the Riigikogu (parliament) and edicts of the president; to submit draft laws and foreign treaties to the parliament; to prepare drafts of the state budget and to implement and report on the budget and to organise relations with foreign states.

Only Estonian citizens are allowed to vote, leaving the 38 per cent non-Estonian population largely disenfranchised. The constitution can only be amended by referendum and two successful passages through the Riigikogu.

Estonia is divided into 15 counties and six towns (the other 27 towns form part of the counties). The counties are divided into 193 parishes.

There is universal suffrage – for Estonian citizens only – from age 18.

Form of state

Democratic republic

The executive

Executive power is vested in the president who is directly elected for a five-year term by an electoral college consisting of 101 parliamentary deputies and 266 local government representatives. The winning candidate has to secure a majority within two rounds of voting otherwise the election returns to parliament.

The president nominates the prime minister who then forms a government. In case of the failure of the president's candidate(s) to form a government (the constitution permits the president two nominations), the parliament will name a prime minister to form a government. The prime minister alone nominates the ministers of his cabinet, who are formally appointed by the president and swear an oath before the parliament. Members of the government need not have any political party affiliation nor be members of the parliament.

National legislature

The unicameral Riigikogu (parliament) has 101 representatives elected by proportional representation for four-year terms. Its prime constitutional function is legislation, but it also has constitutional duties to review the activities of the executive and directly represent voters.

Legal system

Estonia's legal system is similar to that of continental Europe. The Civil Code underwent large-scale reforms in 2002, the most notable being the implementation of the Law of Obligations Act, which overhauled old contract laws that dated back to the Soviet era.

The Supreme Court has seventeen justices, of which the chief justice is appointed by the parliament after nomination by the president; the rest are appointed by the parliament after nomination by the chief justice. Justices are appointed for life. The Supreme Court can hear appeals, either in full session, or by means of a special *ad hoc* panel.

There are town and county courts where cases are heard by a judge and assistant judges, elected by popular vote.

Last elections

6 March 2011 (parliamentary); 29 August 2011 (presidential, indirect)

Results: Parliamentary: the Reformierakond (RE) (Reform Party) won 28.6 per cent of the vote (33 seats out of 101), Eesti Keskerakond (Keskerakond) (Estonian Centre Party) 23.3 per cent (26), the Isamaa ja Res Publica Liit (IRL) (Union of Pro Patria and Res Publica) 20.5 per cent (23), Sotsiaaldemokraatlik Erakond (SDE) (Social Democratic Party) 17.1 per cent (19); five other political parties and all independent candidates each won less that 4 per cent and fail to gain any seats. Turnout was 63.51 per cent.

Presidential: Toomas Hendrik Ilves won 73 votes (out of 101).

Next elections

2016 (presidential, indirect); 2015 (parliamentary)

Political parties

Ruling party

Reformierakond (RE) (Reform Party) (from 2005; re-elected 6 Mar 2011)

Main opposition party

Eesti Keskerakond (Keskerakond) (Estonian Centre Party)

Population

1.34 million (2010)*

Last census: March 2000: 1,370,052

Population density: 33.2 inhabitants per square km. Urban population: 69 per cent (1995–2001).

Annual growth rate: -1.0 per cent 1994–2004 (WHO 2006)

Ethnic make-up

Estonians make up the majority of the population (62 per cent), followed by Russians (30 per cent), Ukrainians (3 per cent) and Belarussians (2 per cent). Russians are in the majority in many towns.

Religions

The main religious denominations are Lutheran, Russian Orthodox and Baptist, with Lutherans in the majority.

Education

Schools may be private, municipal or state run. The backbone of the education system is general comprehensive schooling, which caters for children of all ages and abilities. Pre-school attendance is high but is not a prerequisite for primary schooling. This is part of basic school education, lasting for nine years, starting from the age of seven.

On completion of basic education (aged around 16 – a student may choose to extend or abbreviate their study), a student may continue in an upper secondary or vocational school. The majority of schools offer a general curriculum. Some specialise in a branch of the humanities or sciences.

The oldest university is Tartu University, founded in 1632. Since 1999, some selected post-secondary vocational schools have been given the right to offer vocational higher education. There are six public universities, nine private universities and seven state vocational education institutions. The usual duration of studies is three to four years.

Literacy rate: 100 per cent adult rate; 100 per cent youth rate (15–24) (Unesco 2005).

Compulsory years: 7 to 17

Enrolment rate: 95 per cent boys, 93 per cent girls, total primary school enrolment of the relevant age group (including repetition rates) (World Bank).

Pupils per teacher: 17 in primary schools.

Health

Private healthcare provision is negligible. Overall indices show an improvement in health in the general population.

HIV/Aids

HIV prevalence: 1.1 per cent aged 15–49 in 2003 (World Bank)

Life expectancy: 72 years, 2004 (WHO 2006)

Fertility rate/Maternal mortality rate: 1.4 births per woman, 2004 (WHO 2006); maternal mortality 50 per 100,000 live births (World Bank).

Child (under 5 years) mortality rate (per 1,000): 8 per 1,000 live births (World Bank)

Welfare
The guiding principle behind the government's social welfare development policy is the complete dismantling of the state-centred Soviet system. Government priorities include the establishment of an adequate social security system, funded by contributions from employers and employees.
Estonia is moving away from the pay-as-you-go pension system to a three-tier partially state-funded pension scheme. The first tier is financed by a 33 per cent social tax, 20 per cent of which is kept for pensions. The fully funded second pillar came into effect in 2002. The scheme offers additional pension coverage and it is suggested it be mandatory only for people currently under the age of 18. The third tier consists of voluntary contributions administered by private pension funds and insurance companies.
In 2002, the retirement age was 63 years for men and 58 years for women, which is likely to increase gradually to 63 years by 2016.

Main cities
Tallinn (capital, estimated population 392,555 in 2005), Tartu (100,672), Narva (67,288), Kohtla-Järve (41,311), Pärnu (43,758).

Languages spoken
Estonian belongs to the Baltic-Finnic group of the Finno-Ugric languages, which also includes Hungarian and Finnish. The Latin alphabet is used. Various other languages spoken include Latvian, Lithuanian, Ukrainian, Belarusian, Russian, Finnish, Yiddish and German. English has replaced Russian as the primary business language.
By law, all transactions, contracts and company returns have to be in Estonian. Notarised transactions in English often accompany these.

Official language/s
Estonian

Media
Press
Dailies: There are 11 daily newspapers, of which six are distributed nationally. In Estonian the highest circulating newspapers are *Postimees* (www.postimees.ee), *Eesti Päevaleht* (www.epl.ee), *Maaleht* (www.maaleht.ee), *SL Õhtuleht* (www.sloleht.ee) is an evening tabloid. In Russian, *Vesti Dnya* (www.vesti.ee) *Sillamyaesky Vestnik* (www.vestnik.ee) and *Narva* (www.narvaleht.ee).
Weeklies: In Estonian *Kesknädal* (www.kesknadal.ee), for general interest, *Eesti Loodus* (www.eestinaine.ee) for cultural items, *Kroonika* (www.kroonika.ee) is a tabloid and *Sirp* (www.sirp.ee) another popular publication. In English, the *Baltic Independent* and *Baltic Times* (www.baltictimes.com).
Business: In Estonian, *Aripäev* (www.ap3.ee) is published daily, with on-line English and Russia editions.

Broadcasting
Eesti Rahvusringhääling (ERR) (Estonian Public Broadcasting) (www.err.ee) replaced Eesti Televisioon (Estonian Television) and incorporated Eesti Raadio (Radio Estonia), as the combined national, public broadcasting service, in June 2007.
Radio: Eesti Raadio (Radio Estonia) (www.er.ee) operates five stations catering for all domestic demographics and foreign listeners. The private, national, commercial radio network, U-Pop (www.u-pop.ee) has five stations including Radio Elmar (Estonia music), Radio Uuno and Radio Kuku. There are many local commercial radio stations broadcasting throughout Estonia.
Television: ERR has one TV channel. There are several private TV stations, some of which are foreign and broadcast through cable or satellite channels. Domestic TV includes Kanal 2 (www.kanal2.ee) and TV3 (www.tv3.ee), showing foreign imports, Seitse (www.seitse.tv) and Alo TV, based in Tartu.

Advertising
Adspend is typically over US$70 million, the majority of which is spend in newspapers (around 45 per cent) television (30 per cent) and magazines (10 per cent). Tobacco advertising is banned as well as any that promotes the consumption of alcohol. It is forbidden to use newscasters or political commentators in advertising.

Economy
Although the economy is structured around the service sector, which constitutes over 60 per cent of GDP, including telecommunications and information technology, business services, retail, construction and real estate, the industrial sector still contributes almost 20 per cent to GDP, in particular, engineering, electronic components, as well as more traditional manufacturing of textiles, foodstuffs and timber and paper products linked to Estonia's forestry wealth. Agriculture accounts for less than 5 per cent of GDP, providing dairy, cereals, potatoes and livestock. Export commodities include minerals, electricity, manufactured goods and agricultural products.
GDP growth was 6.7 per cent in 2007, but because Estonia had restructured and opened up its economy, adopting Western banking business practices, when the global economic crisis struck in 2008–09 it was caught-up quickly in the international recession, which exposed its underlying weaknesses. GDP growth was -5.1 per cent in 2008, which fell further to -13.9 per cent in 2009.
The International Monetary Fund (IMF) determined that Estonia's problems going into the recession were that its competitiveness was poor and that salaries had exceeded productivity, public expenditure was unsustainable as job losses cut tax revenue and private sector indebtedness had grown beyond assets and income. This resulted in a sudden halt in domestic demand as well as a severe fall in export demand; output declined by over 15 per cent in 2008–09, and wages fell by 6.5 per cent by the end of 2009. Inflation that had been rising in 2007 jumped from 6.6 per cent to 10.4 per cent in 2008, before crashing to -0.1 per cent in 2009. Many companies shed staff to remain in business and the unemployment rate, which had fallen to 5.9 per cent in 2006 (down from a high of 13.6 in 2000) rose swiftly to around 20 per cent by 2010.
Estonia had to undertake policies that maintained macroeconomic stability and at the same time support its currency so that it could go forward to become a member of the European Monetary Union (EMU) (in 2011), which required, as a member, a fiscal deficit limit of 3 per cent of GDP. Estonia managed this task by halting benefit and wage increases and increasing its competitiveness. As global trade picked up, the economy grew and in 2010 GDP growth was a modest 1.8 per cent, with 3.5 per cent projected for 2011.
In July 2010 EU finance ministers agreed that Estonia should adopt the euro as its currency on 1 January 2011, at an exchange rate of 15.6466 kroon to the euro.

External trade
As a member of the European Union, Estonia operates within a community-wide free trade union, with tariffs determined centrally and as a whole. Internationally, the EU has free trade agreements with a number of nations and trading blocs worldwide.

Imports
Principal imports are machinery and equipment, chemical products, textiles, foodstuffs and vehicle equipment.
Main sources: Russia (typically 11 per cent of total), Finland (10 per cent), Germany (9 per cent).

Exports
Main exports include electrical and electronic equipment, wood, charcoal and paper, textiles, food products, metals, chemical products and vehicle parts.
Main destinations: Russia (typically 17 per cent of total), Finland (16 per cent), Sweden (11 per cent).

Agriculture

Farming

The agricultural reform programme has produced mixed results. Most large state-run farms have been dismantled but some co-operatives and state-owned farms persist.

Government agricultural policy is designed to provide affordable food for Estonians while balancing farm income and guaranteeing farm workers equivalent earnings to industrial workers.

Estonia is eligible for EU subsidies and rural development funds through the Common Agricultural Policy (CAP). However, like the other new EU member countries, it will only get the full amount by 2013. The EU decided to introduce CAP support funds gradually over a 10-year period. During its transitional entry stage Estonia has decided to implement the reform of the CAP in 2009. The reform was introduced throughout most of the EU on 1 January 2005, when subsidies on farm output, which tended to benefit large farms and encourage overproduction, were replaced by single farm payments, not conditional on production. The change is expected to reward farms that provide and maintain a healthy environment, food safety and animal welfare standards. The changes are also intended to encourage market conscious production and cut the cost of CAP to the EU taxpayer.

Fishing

Some 130,000 tonnes of fish are caught per annum. The total catch has fallen dramatically as disputes with Latvia over territorial waters and falling investment have contributed to lower catches. Estonia has been a net fish importer since independence, although the value of exports has increased.

Forestry

Forest makes up 40 per cent of available land in Estonia. As with all sectors the forestry industry suffers from outdated machinery, equipment and a lack of finance and investment, yet despite this, total timber production has increased.

The government has established special credits for the forestry industry to develop technology. Traditionally most Estonian timber exports were of logs and for paper. A further increase in the overall value of timber exports is anticipated as paper related exports decline and the export of finished timber products increases.

The timber-processing industry has developed quickly, and the export potential for Estonian timber products is good, principally in Scandinavia, but also in Russia and Ukraine.

Estonia's only pulp mill at Kehra is owned by Horizon Pulp and Paper, part of the Singapore-based Tolaram group. In 2006, Estonian Cell, which is owned by Norway's Larvik Cell, will begin constructing a pulp mill at Kunda in northern Estonia. The mill, which will cost around US$184 million, will be partly financed by the European Bank for Reconstruction and Development (EBRD).

Industry and manufacturing

During the Soviet era, the Estonian industrial sector was characterised by a high degree of concentration (20 per cent of enterprises produced two-thirds of industrial output), dependence on imports from the Soviet Union (80 per cent of all imports) and a reliance on the markets of the Soviet Union (90 per cent of exports).

Since independence in 1990 industry has undergone much restructuring, with long-term investment following privatisation. Traditional industries such a furniture making are still thriving accounting for around 10 per cent of exports, to modern advanced biomedical research and production with an emphasis on gene research and technologies. Electronics factories provide high-tech components for international corporations such as Nokia and Philips.

Estonia's relatively cheap labour, energy and raw materials are the main reasons for the country's industrial competitiveness, coupled with tax incentives for businesses and a well-educated and motivated workforce.

Tourism

Tourism is an important sector of the economy that is expected to contribute US$574 million or 4.9 per cent of GDP. In line with the lack of direct foreign investment, travel and tourism is expected to attract US$706 million, however this represents 21.3 per cent of total capital investment. The sector should generate US$1.5 billion in total exports and employ 17.7 per cent of the workforce.

Travel links, especially by air, and infrastructure continue to improve. The visitor attractions are mainly heritage-related, with Tallinn being the main destination, but other sectors, including rural and adventure tourism, are being developed. Visitor numbers in 2004 were 1.7 million; Finland continues to be the principal market, accounting for over 50 per cent of visitors.

Mining

Estonia has a limited range of mineral resources, principally for use in the construction industry. Mining and quarrying activities contribute less than 1 per cent of GDP.

Hydrocarbons

There are no proven crude oil reserves; however there is a substantial amount of oil shale in the north-east, exploited by Eesti Põlevkivi (Estonian Oil Shale), run by Eesti Energia, the state-owned energy company. Since Estonia joined the EU oil shale production has been significantly cut back as the country has tried to meet EU environmental regulations. Oil consumption in 2007 was 28,000 barrels per day (bpd).

The Estonian port of Tallinn remains ice-free during winter and is an important transit point for Russian oil into the EU.

National gas consumption was 1.5 billion cubic metres (cum) in 2007, all of which was imported, primarily through a 250-mile pipeline from Russia. There are no coal reserves and Estonia relies entirely on imports.

Energy

Total installed generating capacity is over 2,380MW and Estonia is a net exporter of electricity, mainly to Latvia and north-west Russia. The Narva thermal power plants produce over 90 per cent of all the electricity generated. It is divided into two major, shale oil fired stations, the Balti power plant and the Eesti power plant. New technology, installed since 2003, has reduced some of the environmentally damaging emissions derived from burning shale oil. EU environmental regulations have challenged the country to find alternative, cleaner energy sources.

The Estlink project, connecting an underwater cable linking the Baltic States with the Scandinavian and Nordic power grids, is sponsored by Estonia and Finland and partly funded by the EU; it became operational in 2007.

Natural gas, petroleum and by-products are all imported, mainly from Russia. The Connectbaltic project is a plan to build a natural gas pipeline between Finland and Estonia, laid across the Baltic seabed, supplying 2 billion cubic metres of gas per annum. The environmental impact assessment was completed in 2008 and a decision on whether to continue will be made in 2009.

Financial markets

Stock exchange

Tallinn Stock Exchange (TSE)

Banking and insurance

The commercial banking sector is licensed by the central bank. Foreign-owned banks are permitted to operate and bank shares are freely traded.

Central bank

Eesti Pank (Bank of Estonia)

Main financial centre

Tallinn

Time

GMT plus two hours (daylight saving, late March to late October, GMT plus three hours)

Geography
Estonia is situated in north-east Europe, the northernmost of the three Baltic States, bordering the Russian Federation to the east and Latvia to the south. Its northern coastline is on the Gulf of Finland and its western coastline in the Gulf of Riga and the Baltic Sea. From north to south the country measures 240km, from east to west 360km. With a total land area of 45,227 square km, Estonia is the smallest of the Baltic states and about the same size as Denmark.
The terrain is flat and heavily wooded; there are numerous lakes, rivers and bogs. Offshore, there are around 1,500 islands.

Hemisphere
Northern

Climate
The mildest areas are along the Baltic coast. Summer is short, with sunshine lasting up to nine hours a day, and an average temperature of 15 degrees Celsius (C). Winters are cold, with slush, ice and repeated light coverings of snow (average minus 4 degrees C). Spring and autumn are very short.

Dress codes
Warm clothes are required during winter, with a raincoat and umbrella necessary during the summer. Business dress is conservative but relatively informal, with a jacket and tie expected for meetings.

Entry requirements
Passports
Required by all, except nationals of EU/EEA countries and Switzerland

Visa
Required by all, except nationals of EU and Schengen area signatory countries, North America, Australasia and Japan. For further exceptions contact the nearest embassy or see full list can be found at www.vm.ee. A Schengen visa application (offered in several languages) can be downloaded from http://europa.eu/abc/travel/ see 'documents you will need'.

Currency advice/regulations
There are no restrictions on the import and export of local or foreign currency.

Customs
Personal items are duty-free. There are no duties levied on alcohol and tobacco between EU member states, providing amounts imported are for personal consumption.

Health (for visitors)
Nationals of the European Economic Area (EEA) countries and Switzerland can access reduced cost and sometimes free medical treatment using a European Health Insurance Card (EHIC) while visiting the EEA. Exceptions include nationals of the 10 countries which joined the EU in 2004 whose EHIC is not valid in Switzerland. Applications for the EHIC should be made before travelling.

Mandatory precautions
No specific requirements.

Advisable precautions
Vaccinations may be advised for hepatitis A and diphtheria.
Take mosquito lotion if travelling outside the towns. There is a risk of rabies.

Hotels
There are numerous good quality western style hotels in Tallinn. It is advisable to book a hotel before travelling.
For the peak period of June and July, the Estonian Tourist Board suggests the traveller books in January.
Bills must be paid in Estonian kroons if credit cards are not accepted.

Credit cards
Most major hotels and restaurants and a few shops accept American Express, Visa, Eurocard and Diners' Club.

Public holidays (national)
Fixed dates
1 Jan (New Year's Day), 24 Feb (Independence Day), 1 May (Spring Day), 23 Jun (Victory Day), 25 Jun (St John's Day, Midsummer), 20 Aug (Restoration of Independence Day), 24 Dec (Christmas Eve), 25 Dec (Christmas Day), 26 Dec (St Stephen's Day).

Variable dates
Good Friday.

Working hours
Banking
Mon–Fri: 0900–1600.

Business
Mon–Fri: 0830–1830. Lunch around 1300. Some offices stop work at 1630.

Government
Mon–Fri: 0900–1700.

Shops
Mon–Fri: 0930–1900, Sat: 0930–1600.

Telecommunications
Mobile/cell phones
Estonia has three mobile service providers, operating on a GSM system.

Social customs/useful tips
Estonians can be quite reserved and are not particularly talkative. Shaking hands is the normal form of greeting. Flowers are generally acceptable as a gift.
There is a service charge of 10 to 15 per cent, but a small tip in addition is appreciated.
Saunas are popular in Estonia, usually followed by a substantial meal washed down with liberal quantities of beer and vodka.
Until you are sure of the ethnic background of your host avoid talking about Russians and the communist past. Many Estonians have relatives who were sent to Siberia, which has left strong feelings when it comes to Russia. Also avoid asking what your host did during the Soviet occupation – it may sound as if you are asking if they were a member of the Communist Party or even if they were sent to Siberia.
There is a strong sense of national pride and identity among Estonians and they do not appreciate being lumped together with Latvia and Lithuania as 'the Baltic states', or even being described as part of eastern Europe.

Security
Estonia is a safe place to visit compared to some of the other former Soviet republics, although muggings do occur in urban areas, especially at night. Car theft is also a problem.

Getting there
Air
National airline: Estonian Air
International airport/s: Tallinn (TLL) airport, 5km north-west of city. Includes a business centre, bank, post office, restaurant, bar, shops and car rental. Conference facilities also available. Bus no 2 runs between the city and the airport, taking 15 minutes. A shuttle bus to the main hotels and the city centre meets all flights.
Airport tax: There is no airport tax.

Surface
Road: Foreign cars are flagged down at borders to examine the documents in an attempt to block the flow of stolen foreign cars. Check insurance before travelling and do not buy cheap insurance at the frontier. There are direct routes along the Baltic coast connecting Latvia and Lithuania and also the Russian Federation.
Rail: International lines run from surrounding countries, although rail travel between Estonia, Latvia and Lithuania is time-consuming.
Water: Ferry services run between Stockholm and Tallinn, Helsinki and Tallinn and Rostock (Germany) and Tallinn via Helsinki.
Main port/s: Muuga is Tallinn's port and is the most modern in the country.

Getting about
National transport
Air: There is limited domestic air travel with Baltic Aeroservis, which serves the islands of Kuressaare and Kärdla. Charter flights to other destinations can also be booked.
Road: Estonia has a high density of roads although there are few major highways. Signs are not illuminated and fairly small, so driving at night is best avoided. In winter roads can be icy and ungritted.
The high level of car crime in the Baltic States means that border crossings can be

very lengthy processes and insurance can be difficult to find.

Buses: Estonia has a very extensive bus network linking every area of the country. Tickets should be booked in advance.

Rail: The majority of major cities are covered. Tallinn and Tartu are connected by an express service.

City transport

Taxis: Taxis in Tallinn are relatively cheap. There is a good taxi service from Tallinn International Airport to the city centre, with a journey time of 10 minutes. Private services should display the name of the company and its number on the roof. Fares should be agreed upon beforehand. There are also minibuses called *Marshrut-taxis*, which operate on set routes, stopping at fixed destinations and seating up to 10 people.

Buses, trams & metro: All parts of the city can also be reached by bus, trolley-bus and tram. Tickets can be bought from stalls in the main shopping areas.

Car hire

Car hire can be arranged at the airport. Never drink and drive – no level of alcohol is permitted. Speed limit is 50km per hour in built-up areas, 90km per hour in the country and 110km per hour on motorways. In towns there are parking permits, fines and wheel clamps. Driving is on the right. EU nationals should be in possession of a national driving licence. The international car hire firms Avis, Hertz and Europcar all have bureaux in Estonia. Roads, although deteriorating, are of a reasonably good standard but can be dangerous in winter due to ice.

BUSINESS DIRECTORY

The addresses listed below are a selection only. While World of Information makes every endeavour to check these addresses, we cannot guarantee that changes have not been made, especially to telephone numbers and area codes. We would welcome any corrections.

Telephone area codes

The international direct dialling code (IDD) for Estonia is +372, followed by area code and subscriber's number:

Haapsalu	47	Rapla	48
Jögeva	77	Tallinn	none
Narva	35	Valga	76
Pärnu	44	Viljandi	43
Polva	79	Voru	78

Useful telephone numbers

Fire brigade: 01

Police: 02

Ambulance: 03

Gas: 04

NB Numbers 01–04 cannot be dialled from mobile telephones; 112 should be dialled instead.

Chambers of Commerce

American Chamber of Commerce Estonia, Tallinn Business Centre, 6 Harju, 10130 Tallinn (tel: 631-0522; fax: 631-0521; e-mail: acce@acce.ee).

British-Estonian Chamber of Commerce, 21 Suur-Karja, 10148 Tallinn (tel: 640-5872; fax: 640-5873; e-mail: info@becc.ec).

Estonian Chamber of Commerce and Industry, 17 Toom-Kooli, 10130 Tallinn (tel: 646-0244; fax: 646-0245; e-mail: koda@koda.ee).

Banking

Eesti Forekspank (Estonian Forexbank), Narva mnt 9a, Tallinn (tel: 630-2100; fax: 630-2200; e-mail: bank@forex.ee); international settlements (tel: 640-6400).

Eesti Hoiupank (Estonian Savings Bank), Kinga 1, Tallinn (tel: 630-2600; fax: 630-2602; e-mail: mailbob@esb.ee).

Eesti Investeerimispank (Estonian Investment Bank), PO Box 26, Narva mnt 7, Tallinn (tel: 620-0800; fax: 620-0812/0801; e-mail: info@estib.ee); international settlements (tel: 620-0828).

Eesti Krediidipank (Estonian Credit Bank), Narva mnt 4, Tallinn (tel: 640-5000; fax: 631-3533; e-mail: krediidipank@ekp.ee).

Eesti Maapank (Land Bank of Estonia), Tallinna 12, Rakvere (tel: 43-821; fax: 43-617); in Tallinn (tel: 646-6295; fax: 646-6649/6313-720); international settlements (tel: 640-8321).

Eesti Pangaliit (Estonian Association of Banks), Pärnu mnt 19, Tallinn (tel: 245-5400; fax: 245-5401; e-mail: panagaliit@teleport.ee).

Eesti Uhispank (Union Bank of Estonia), Tartu mnt 13, Tallinn (tel: 610-4300, 631-2728; fax: 610-4302); international settlements (tel: 640-3516, 640-3519).

Hansapank, Liivalaia 8, EE0001 Tallinn (tel: 631-0311/310; fax: 631-0410; e-mail: webmaster@hansa.ee).

Merita Bank Ltd (foreign bank's branch), Harju 6, Tallinn (tel: 631-4040; fax: 631-4153; e-mail: merita@estpak.ee).

Tallinna Aripanga Aktsiaselts (Tallinn Business Bank), Estonia pst 3/5, Tallinn (tel: 245-5349; fax: 242-3322; e-mail: tbb@torn.ee).

Tallinna Pank, Parnu mnt 10, Tallinn (tel: 631-0100/0102, 640-5880; fax: 631-0111; e-mail: info@tp.ee); international settlements (tel: 640-5829).

Central bank

Eesti Pank (Bank of Estonia), Estonia Boulevard 13, Tallinn 15095 (tel: 668-0719; fax: 668-0836; e-mail: info@epbe.ee).

Stock exchange

Tallinn Stock Exchange (TSE): www.omxnordicexchange.com

Travel information

Baltic Tours, Vene 23B, Tallinn (tel: 244-6331; fax: 244-0760).

Estonian Air, Vabaduse, Valjak 10, Tallinn (tel: 244-6383, 244-0295; fax: 631-2740).

Estonian Association of Travel Agents, Pikk 71, Tallinn (tel: 260-1705; fax: 242-5594).

Estonian Railways, 36 Pikk Str, Tallinn (tel: 240-1610; fax: 240-1710).

Finest Hotel Group, Parnu mnt 22, Tallinn (tel: 245-1510; fax: 244-6029).

Lufthansa Airport Office (tel: 638-8077; fax: 638-8077); Lufthansa city centre, Pärnu mnt 10, Tallinn (tel: 631-4444).

National tourist organisation offices

Estonian Tourist Board, Liivalaia 13/15, Tallinn (tel: 627-9770; fax: 627-9777; e-mail: tourism@eas.ee).

Ministries

Ministry of Agriculture, Lai 39/41, Tallinn (tel: 244-1166; fax: 244-0601).

Ministry of Citizenship and Immigration, Ministry of the Interior, Pikk 61, Tallinn (tel: 244-5080; fax: 260-2785).

Ministry of Culture and Education, Suur Karja 23, Tallinn (tel: 244-5077; fax: 244-0963).

Ministry of Defence, Pikk 57, Tallinn (tel: 239-9160/50; fax: 239-9165).

Ministry of Economic Affairs, Harju 11, Tallinn (tel: 244-0577; fax: 244-6860).

Ministry of Energy, Ministry of Economy, Kiriku 6, Tallinn (tel: 244-3941; fax: 244-8091).

Ministry of Environment, Toompuiestee 24, Tallinn (tel: 245-2507; fax: 245-3310).

Ministry of Finance, Suur Ameerika 1, Tallinn (tel: 268-3445; fax: 268-2097).

Ministry of Finance (Foreign Affairs Dept), Kohtu 8, Tallinn (fax: 245-2992).

Ministry of Foreign Affairs, Ravala 9, Tallinn (tel: 231-7091; fax: 277-1677, 231-7099; internet site: http://www.vm.ee).

Ministry of Industry and Energy, Gonsiori Str 29, Tallinn (tel: 242-3550; fax: 242-1133); Foreign Relations Dept (fax: 242-5468).

Ministry of the Interior, Pikk 61, Tallinn (tel: 266-3611; fax: 260-2785, 244-1112).

Ministry of Justice, Suur Karja 19, Tallinn (tel: 244-5120; fax: 224-6235).

Ministry of Reform, State Chancellery, Lossi Plats 1a, Tallinn (tel: 231-6730; fax: 244-0372).

Ministry of Social Affairs, Gonsiori 29, Tallinn (tel: 242-3434; fax: 242-1862).

Ministry of Trade and Commerce, Kiriku Tn 6, Tallinn (tel: 244-3941, 244-5921); Foreign Relations Dept (fax: 244-8091).

Ministry of Transport and Communication, Viru 9, Tallinn (tel: 239-7613; fax: 239-7606); Foreign Relations Department (fax: 244-9206).

Prime Minister's Office, Losi Plats 1a, Tallinn (tel: 231-6701; fax: 244-0372).

Other useful addresses

A/S Seesam Insurance, Kreutzwali 2/Narva mnt 24, Tallinn (tel: 243-3518; fax: 242-4886).

A/S Central (shipping agents), Hospidali 6, Parnu (tel: 244-0707).

Asker (building advice), Roosikrantsi 12, Tallinn (tel: 244-2165, 277-1304/124; fax: 277-1189).

Association of Construction Materials Producers of Estonia, Jaama 1A, Tallinn (tel: 251-2230; fax: 650-6178).

Baltic Insurance Co, Olevimagi 12, Tallinn (tel: 260-1384; fax: 260-1790).

Baltic Trade Company (commercial service organising exhibitions, seminars, joint ventures), Ravala Str 27, Tallinn (tel: 245-5089; fax: 244-5768).

Baltlink, Tartu mnt 13, Tallinn (tel: 242-1003; fax: 245-0893).

British Embassy, Kentmanni 20, 20001 Tallinn (tel: 631-3461/2; fax: 631-3354); commercial section (fax: 631-3463).

Business Advisory Services Centre, Lei 9, Tallinn (tel: 260-9675; fax: 631-3523).

Confederation of Estonian Industry, Gonsiori 29, Tallinn (tel: 242-2235; fax: 242-4962).

Department for Foreign Economic Relations, Suur Ameerika 1, Tallinn (tel: 268-3559; fax: 268-3622).

Department of Statistics, Endla 15, Tallinn (tel: 245-3889; fax: 245-3923; internet site: http://stat.vil.ee/K.E.S-ENGL.htm).

Eesti-Estline, Sadama 29, Tallinn (tel: 244-9051; fax: 242-5352).

Estonian Association of Construction Entrepreneurs, Ravala 8, Tallinn (tel/fax: 243-3213).

Estonian Business Advisory Services, Tallinn BAS Centre, Lai 0, Tallinn (tel: 260-9795; fax: 631-3523).

Estonian Embassy (USA), 1730 M Street, NW, Washington DC 20036 (tel: 202-588-0101; fax: 202-588-0108; e-mail: info@estemb.org).

Estonian Export Council, Kiriku 2/4, Tallinn (tel: 244-4703; fax: 244-3615).

Estonian Foreign Trade Association, Uus 32/34, Tallinn (tel: 260-1462; fax: 260-2184).

Estonian Institute for Market Research, Vaike-Karja 1, Tallinn (tel: 244-8605; fax: 244-1378, 277-1675).

Estonian Institute (information service), PO Box 3469, Tonismagi 8, Tallinn (tel: 244-0513; fax: 268-2057; e-mail: einst@einst.ee; internet site: http://www.einst.ee).

Estonian Investment Agency (EIA), Ravala Str 6 (room 602B), Tallinn (tel: 641-0166; fax: 641-0312).

Estonian Maritime Industry, Sadama 17, Tallinn (tel: 260-1723; fax: 244-4808).

Estonian Shipping Co, 3/5 Estonian Blvd, Tallinn (tel: 244-3802; fax: 242-4958, 243-1228).

Estonian State Energy Department, 29 Gonsiori Str, Tallinn (tel: 242-1579; fax: 242-5468, 242-1908); external department (tel: 242-1480).

Estonian Trade Council, Kiriku Str 2/4, Tallinn (tel: 244-4703; fax: 244-4615).

Hanson Insurance, Narva mnt 24, Tallinn (tel: 261-2440; fax: 242-5977).

Loksa Shipyard, Tallinn (tel: 257-5241; fax: 263-91230).

Municipality of Tallinn, Vabaduse Valjak 7, Tallinn (tel: 266-6146; fax: 244-1230).

National Customs Board, Ravala pst 9, Tallinn (tel: 231-7722; fax: 231-7727).

Port of Tallinn Authority, Sadama 25, Tallinn (tel: 242-7009; fax: 242-2950).

Radio Estonia – Foreign Service, Gonsiori 21, Tallinn (tel: 243-4282; fax: 243-4139).

Reklaam/Television Ltd, Tonismagi 2, Tallinn (tel: 243-4606; fax: 231-1077).

Ookean State Stock Corporation (Estonian Fishing Company), Paljassaare Str 28, Tallinn (tel: 247-1421, 249-7212; fax: 249-8190).

State Department of Foreign Trade, Komsomoli 1, Tallinn (tel: 268-3559; fax: 268-3097).

State Chancellery, Lossi Plats 1a, Tallinn (tel: 231-6730; fax: 244-0372).

Swiss Baltic Re-Advisers, Lai 27, Tallinn (tel: 244-8949; fax: 274-6469).

Tallink, PO Box 3495, Tallinn (tel: 244-0770; fax: 244-5224).

Tallinn New Port, Maardu tee 57, Tallinn (tel: 223-6500, 223-4313; fax: 223-8805).

Tallinn Stock Exchange, Tallinn (tel: 244-1920; fax: 244-9382).

Other news agencies: BNS (Baltic News Service): www.bns.ee

Delfi (in Estonian): www.delfi.ee

Internet sites

Estonia Business: http://www.ee/www/Business/welcome.html

Estonia Country Guide: http://www.ciesin.ee/estcg/

Estonia Investment: http://www.investinestonia.com

Ethiopia

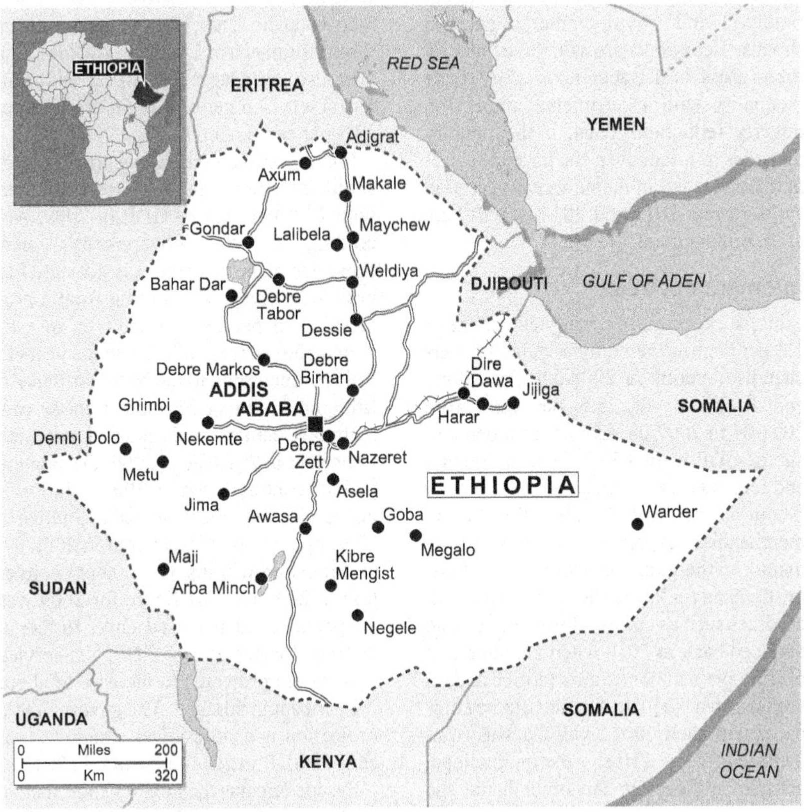

Ethiopia seems set to remain effectively a one-party state for the next five years, since none of the opposition parties managed to get a seat in parliament. The May 2010 elections had gone relatively smoothly, although political tensions had been expected to rise. However, inference may be drawn from the fact that the ruling Ethiopian People's Revolutionary Democratic Front (EPRDF) and its allies won all but two (independent) seats in parliament - thus controlling 99% of parliament. Many in the opposition have complained about the lack of political space and government intimidation. Although development partners largely remained silent about the election and its result, the European Union (EU) election observers noted that the election was not conducted in a free and fair environment and hence was below international standards. The African Union (AU) declared that the elections were 'free and fair' and had met all AU election standards.

The economy

Growth in Ethiopia has been strong over the last five years. Gross domestic product (GDP) grew by 8.8 per cent in 2010 compared with 9.9 per cent growth in 2009. The *African Economic Outlook 2010* (AEO), published jointly by the African Development Bank and the Organisation for Economic Co-operation and Development, predicts growth for 2011 and 2012 will continue, based on the government's recent forecasts.

Growth is mainly driven by the service sector (14.5 per cent), followed by industry (10.2 per cent) and agriculture (6 per cent). Within the agricultural sector, the fishing sub-sector rebounded in 2010 while the other sectors remained fundamentally unchanged. The service sector's leading role was primarily driven by high

KEY FACTS

Official name: Ityopia (Federal Democratic Republic of Ethiopia)

Head of State: President Girma Wolde Giorgise (elected by parliament 2001; re-elected 2007)

Head of government: Prime Minister Meles Zenawi (from 1995; re-elected 4 Oct 2010)

Ruling party: Coalition Ethiopian People's Revolutionary Democratic Front (EPRDF), an alliance of the Tigray People's Liberation Front (TPLF), the South Ethiopian Peoples' Democratic Front (SEPDF), the Amhara National Democratic Movement (ANDM), and Oromo People's Democratic Movement (OPDM) (from 1991, elected 1995, re-elected 2010)

Area: 1,251,282 square km

Population: 85.00 million (2010)*

Capital: Addis Ababa

Official language: Amharic

Currency: Birr (Birr) = 100 cents

Exchange rate: Birr17.17 per US$ (Oct 2011)

GDP per capita: US$350 (2010)

GDP real growth: 8.00% (2010)

GDP: US$29.70 billion (2010)

Inflation: 2.80% (2010)

Balance of trade: -US$5.28 billion (2009)

* estimated figure

growth in hotels and restaurants, public services and real estate.

In 2010 the government launched a new five-year plan – the Growth and Transformation Plan 2010/11–2014/15. This plan, beginning in fiscal year 2010/11, sees the agricultural sector to be the major source of economic growth. The plan calls for a shift to high-value crops, a focus on high-potential areas, the commercialisation of smallholder farming, and the development of large-scale, commercial agriculture Industrial growth is also a particular focus and the government plans to promote the sector using both export-oriented and import-substituting industrialisation policy. The industrial sector is thus expected to grow at a faster rate than other sectors.

Except for the last three years when inflation and foreign exchange became major problems, macro-economic performance has been good. However, growth projections for the agricultural sector are based on unprecedented expectations given the traditional dependence on rain-fed agriculture. The sustainability of this growth is questionable when the low level of domestic resources and the shortage of foreign exchange are taken into account.

There is a need to focus on bringing about major structural change in the economy to ensure the sustainability of economic growth. Although Ethiopia has experienced significant growth in the last five years, when judged in the context of the structural problems maintaining this level of growth will be difficult. Growth has not been accompanied by structural improvements, rather it has come about as a result of intensive use of resources, especially labour and land, with the outcome still depending on good weather. Productivity growth played little part. This should not come as a surprise, however, given an economy that is operating with low technology levels, rain-dependent agriculture, and is vulnerable to external shocks. Economic growth, especially in urban areas, is also accompanied by rising inequality with a detrimental impact on poverty reduction. Thus, if the country manages to attain even the base case scenario envisaged in the new five-year plan for the years 2011 and 2012, it will be a great achievement.

International trade

Ethiopia experienced a marginal decline of 1.2 per cent in the nominal value of merchandise exports in 2008/09 after hitting annual growth of 25.5 per cent from 2003/04 to 2007/08. Exports as a percentage of GDP were 4.5 per cent in 2008/09 and remained fairly unchanged in 2009/10 (about 4.6 per cent of GDP). The drop in merchandise exports in 2009 was due mainly to the global economic crisis hurting demand for key traditional export commodities such as coffee. However, demand bounced back in 2010 when although two of Ethiopia's major exports (coffee and oil seeds) saw a small decline in volume compared with their 2009 level, this was compensated for by a rise in the international price of coffee. On the other hand, the international price of oilseeds declined. Among the other two key exports, khat and pulses, pulses showed a rise in both volume and price while khat increased in volume, with a small drop in its price. The combined effect left the level of exports in 2010 fairly unchanged compared to its level in 2009. Foreign exchange earnings in 2010 were helped by the positive change in service balance. This improvement reflects the performance of Ethiopian Airlines. The year also saw a large level of current transfer (about 14.6 per cent of GDP), up from 13.3 per cent in 2009.

Imports remained strong in 2010 at about 27.2 per cent of GDP, compared with 24.0 per cent of GDP in 2009. According to the government's new five-year plan, this figure is projected to grow over five years starting from a projected 30.5 per cent in 2011 to an estimated 35.0 per cent of GDP in the years to follow. According to the National Bank of Ethiopia, imports of consumer goods, raw materials, capital goods and fuel remained important in 2010, as in 2009. Despite the global economic crisis in 2009, Ethiopia's net service exports expanded at a remarkably high rate of 145 per cent in 2008/09, as compared with its 31 per cent contraction in 2007/08. The figure for 2009 was 1.3 per cent and increased a little further in 2010 to 1.6 per cent of GDP. Net service exports are projected to increase to about 2.1 per cent in 2010/11. The government's projection is a little lower, about 1.5 per cent of GDP in 2011 and again in 2012.

Europe remains the largest export market for Ethiopia though its share declined from 47.6 per cent in 2006/07 to 42 per cent in 2007/08 and further to 41.7 per cent in 2009. Ethiopian exports to Asia, by contrast, went from 30.2 per cent in 2007 to 35.2 per cent in 2008, and to 35.6 per cent in 2009. China, Saudi Arabia and United Arab Emirates have become increasingly important partners in 2009 and 2010. Among European importers of Ethiopian goods, Germany, Italy and the Netherlands were the most important trading partners in 2010. About 65 per cent of Ethiopia's imports came from Asia, followed by Europe at 24.8 per cent.

The private sector

Ethiopia's private sector is predominantly small scale, informal and service-oriented. The public sector dominates most economic activities, except for smallholder agriculture in rural Ethiopia. Private investment as a percentage of GDP not only remains low but has actually declined since 2003/04. The country performed poorly in a number of the World

KEY INDICATORS **Ethiopia**

	Unit	2006	2007	2008	2009	2010
Population	m	76.63	*78.65	*80.71	*82.81	*85.00
Gross domestic product (GDP)	US$bn	15.17	19.43	26.40	32.30	29.70
GDP per capita	US$	202	253	333	390	350
GDP real growth	%	11.6	11.5	11.2	9.9	8.0
Inflation	%	12.3	15.8	25.3	36.4	2.8
Industrial output	% change	7.4	–	10.4	8.9	–
Agricultural output	% change	11.2	–	7.5	6.4	–
Exports (fob) (goods)	US$m	1,024.0	1,248.9	1,554.7	1,538.1	–
Imports (fob) (goods)	US$m	4,105.6	5,155.6	7,206.3	6,819.0	–
Balance of trade	US$m	-3,080.9	-3,870.8	-5,651.6	-5,280.9	–
Current account	US$m	-1,785.9	-828.0	-1,805.7	-2,190.7	*-1,277.0
Total reserves minus gold	US$m	832.7	1,289.9	870.5	1,780.9	–
Foreign exchange	US$m	821.6	1,278.1	859.0	1,741.7	–
Exchange rate	per US$	8.85	9.09	9.60	11.78	14.41

* estimated figure

Bank's 2011 *Ease of Doing Business* survey which ranked Ethiopia 104th in 2011, down on place on 2010.

Banking and finance

The financial sector in Ethiopia has been too weak to support the private sector. Stringent collateral requirements for access to credit from banks is usually the major impediment. The banking system performs poorly when it comes to using modern banking technology and innovative financial instruments. It is also characterised by weak customer service. The situation is complicated by weak regulatory capacity that could make the banking sector potentially vulnerable to financial crises. The Commercial Bank of Ethiopia (CBE) is the main bank; there has been fast growth of private banks, both in the mobilisation of deposits and disbursement of credit. The sector is still closed to foreign-owned banks so it performs in a sheltered and globally non-competitive environment.

The government has a vital role to play in engaging the private sector if the five-year plan is to be successful. This is not difficult from a policy perspective, but what is still missing is the political will and a detailed action plan to be put forward by the joint private-public partnership (PPP) forum, which the government established in 2010. It is hoped that the PPP will be active in promoting the private sector's needs and concerns to the government.

There are a number of outstanding issues that are important for private sector development. Among them are reforms of the legal institutions such as competition legislation and the legislation related to collaterals; an improvement in the business climate (including government-business partnerships); good governance and building institutions that are able to facilitate private sector development; access to land and finance; improvement in tax administration; and maintaining a stable macroeconomic environment.

In 2010/11, the government has been attempting to address some these issues. It has established the PPP forum; issued a competition law and begun implementing it; and attempted to provide a stable macro-economic environment despite the uncertainty surrounding exchange rate instability and inflation witnessed at the beginning of 2011. On the down side, the government has introduced price controls on 18 major commodities, thereby adding to the challenges and uncertainties the private sector already faces.

Chinese investment

The last decade has seen growth in new partnerships between Ethiopia and emerging economies, particularly those of China, India and Turkey. The partnership with China is the most significant one as shown by the level of trade and investment, which includes the financing and construction of infrastructure such as roads, power and communications. India and Turkey are far behind in this new and emerging set of partnerships

China is currently the leading export destination for Ethiopia, overtaking Germany. It is also the leading source of imports for Ethiopia, having overtaken Saudi Arabia. Total trade (both imports and exports) between the two grew from US$100.12 million in 2002 (of which Chinese exports to Ethiopia took up US$96.43 million with Ethiopia's exports to China being US$3.69 million) to over US$700 million (Ethiopia's exports growing to over US$120 million) in 2006 and over US$1 billion in 2009/10.

In the last five years the boom in Ethiopian-Chinese economic relations has been felt in areas like road construction, the supply of manufactured goods from China, telecommunications development, the installation of big electric power stations by Chinese companies and investments in the manufacturing sector.

Difficulties with Eritrea linger

Ethiopian foreign policy is still dominated by tense relations with Eritrea, as the long-standing border dispute has not yet been settled despite several attempts at diplomatic solutions. The independent Eritrea-Ethiopia Boundary commission (EEBC) closed its operation in November 2007 and the UN Security Council decided to withdraw its peacekeeping force – the UN Mission in Ethiopia and Eritrea (UNMEE) in July 2008. This has raised the risk of conflict between the two countries, a risk still unresolved in 2011. Moreover, tensions in the region remain high as a result of the insecurity in Somalia. There is also a new development in Sudan, following the referendum on the independence of South Sudan. It is still unclear what the implications will be for Ethiopia.

Risk assessment

Economy	Improving
Political	Fair
Regional stability	Fair

COUNTRY PROFILE

Historical profile

100 BC A kingdom including part of modern-day Ethiopia existed around Axum.

450 AD The kingdom converted to Christianity and the Ethiopian church became part of the Coptic community.

1896 Italy tried to seize Ethiopia but lost the Battle of Adwa. The Italians held on to Eritrea on the Red Sea coast.

1916 Ras Tafari, later known as Emperor Haile Selassie, gained power over local lords but his appeal to the League of Nations for help against the occupying Italians went unheeded.

1936 Benito Mussolini's Fascist Italian army invaded Ethiopia, which became part of Italian East Africa. Haile Selassie went into exile in Bath, England.

1941 British and Commonwealth troops along with the *Arbegnoch* (patriots), Ethiopian resistance fighters battled the Italian occupiers. Emperor Haile Selassie returned to Addis Ababa on 5 May 1941.

1962 Eritrea was annexed by Ethiopia.

1974 Haile Selassie was deposed in coup led by Teferi Benti.

1975 Haile Selassie died in custody.

1977 Benti was killed and replaced by Colonel Mengistu Haile Mariam, who led a brutal regime known as the Dergue. At least 100,000 opponents or critics were killed.

1977 Somalia tried to annex part of Ethiopia's Ogaden region, where most people are ethnic Somalis. Cuban and Soviet troops and tanks assisted Ethiopia in repelling the Somali invasion.

1984 Drought led to a famine in which as many as one million people may have died.

1987 A Soviet-style constitution was adopted and the People's Democratic Republic of Ethiopia was formed. The regime was supported by the Soviet Union.

1991 Rebellions in Eritrea, led by the leftist Eritrean People's Liberation Front (EPLF) and, in Tigray province, by the Tigray People's Liberation Front (TPLF) ensued. Mengistu fled to Zimbabwe as the EPLF took control of Eritrea and a TPLF-led coalition, the Ethiopian People's Revolutionary Democratic Front (EPRDF), marched into Addis Ababa.

1995 A general election was held and won by the EPRDF. The country was officially renamed the Federal Democratic Republic of Ethiopia. Negaso Gidada became president.

1998 Border disputes resulted in Eritrea and Ethiopia resuming full-scale fighting in mid-year and sporadic clashes thereafter.

1999 Eritrea refused to withdraw from the disputed Badme area.

2000 The EPRDF parties won the legislative elections. UN Mission in Ethiopia and Eritrea (UNMEE) peacekeepers opened a 1,000km cease-fire buffer zone between Ethiopia and Eritrea after the two countries signed a peace deal in Algiers, ending the two-year war.
2001 President Gidada quit the ruling coalition but finished his term in office. Girma Wolde Giorgise was elected, by parliament, to the largely ceremonial position of president.
2002 Eritrea and Ethiopia accepted a ruling by the international Boundary Commission in The Hague on their border dispute and a new 1,000km frontier was established. Ethiopia, ravaged by drought, requested food aid for nearly six million people.
2004 A resettlement programme started to move over two million people away from parched, over-worked highlands to the pastoral, but disease rife plains of south-west Ethiopia. Long-term drought in Afar region resulted in over 350,000 people needing food aid, when livestock deaths became widespread.
2005 The ruling EPRDF and its allies won parliamentary elections. The independent commission at the Permanent Court of Arbitration in The Hague, set up as part of the peace deal signed in Algiers in 2000 between Eritrea and Ethiopia, ruled that Eritrea had launched unlawful attacks against Ethiopia in 1998, thereby triggering the border war between the two countries. The Ethiopian government said that it would lodge a claim for compensation. Donors put on hold US$375 million of budget support because of a government crackdown on opposition supporters.
2006 A new Alliance for Freedom and Democracy was formed by several opposition parties and rebel groups. Ethiopian troops intervened in Somalia to support the transitional government against Islamist militia forces. Ethiopia, together with Eritrea, rejected international proposals to settle their continuing border dispute.
2007 A limited census was undertaken; it did not include populations in Afar and Somali which were due to be recorded separately at a later date. Ethiopia, which uses the Coptic calendar of 13 months and is seven years later than the Gregorian calendar, celebrated its millennium. Parliament re-elected President Giorgise. Talks on an Ethiopia and Eritrea border agreement reached an impasse. The Ethiopia-Eritrea Border Commission duly considered the border it drew in 2006 to be binding. While Ethiopia and Eritrea accepted the ruling neither attempted to implement its recommendation; the 1,700 United Nations Mission in Ethiopia and Eritrea (UNMEE) peace-keeping troops remained in the area in a notional demilitarised zone.
2008 Ethiopia severed diplomatic ties with Qatar because of 'its hostility to Ethiopia' and the *Al Jazeera* media coverage of Ethiopian affairs. The UN Security Council terminated the UNMEE mandate. A new national coffee exchange was established in Addis Ababa. Ethiopia is Africa's largest coffee producer. Ethiopia consolidated its coffee collection and sales to increase quality and pay farmers a better return on their crop.
2009 Ethiopia began withdrawing its troops from Somalia.
2010 Israel restarted the immigration scheme for Ethiopians of Jewish descent after halting it in August 2008. Members of the Falash Mura community, who had been pressurised into converting to Christianity in the nineteenth century and the last remaining Jewish community in Ethiopia, trace their roots back to King Solomon. Some 20,000 Ethiopians had been admitted in 2003. In parliamentary elections held on 23 May the EPRDF won 59.8 per cent of the vote (327 seats out of 547), which, coupled with seats won by its allies, gave the ruling party 499 seats out of 547; opposition parties won only two seats. The opposition rejected the results as 'completely fraudulent'. International observers claimed that government intimidation of voters for a period of months before the election had influenced the outcome, although voting on the day remained 'peaceful and calm' and the AU declared that the elections were 'free and fair' and had met all AU election standards. Opposition leader, Birtukan Mideksa, was released after serving five years of a life sentence.
2011 On 9 February the UN World Food Programme (WFP) appealed for US$226.5 million in relief funds as the worst drought for over 50 years, resulting in ruined crops and the death of herds, and threating 1.3 million southern Ethiopians with severe hunger. In May, the consumer price index (CPI) for food increased by over 40 per cent. On 28 June, the UN estimated that 10 million people in the Horn of Africa were affected by severe food insecurity. On 13 July the WFP increased its appeal for US$477 million to cope with the developing disaster as food aid was scaled up. Refugees for Somalia added to Ethiopia's food supply problems as thousands crossed the border to find relief from the famine.

Political structure

Constitution

A constitution was adopted 8 December 1994 which established a federal system of government. The constitution formally came into force in August 1995 when the Federal Democratic Republic of Ethiopia was proclaimed.
Ethiopia comprises 11 semi-autonomous administrative regions organised loosely along major ethnic lines.

Form of state

Federal democratic republic

The executive

The role of president is largely a figurehead position. The prime minister, who is elected by parliament for a five-year term, holds executive power.
The president is elected by parliament for a six-year term.

National legislature

The bicameral Federal Parliamentary Assembly consists of the Yehizbtewekayoch Mekir Bet (Council of People's Representatives) with 527 members, elected for a five-year term in single-seat constituencies, of which 22 are reserved for representatives of minority peoples, and the Yefedereshn Mekir Bet (Council of the Federation) with 117 members, elected by subordinate assemblies, of which 22 represent each of the designates minority nationalities and the remainder representatives of the professional sector and any other interests so designated.

Last elections

23 May 2010 (parliamentary); 9 October 2007 (presidential)
Results: Presidential: Girma Wolde Giorgise was elected by parliament with 430 votes in support, 88 against and 11 abstentions.
Parliamentary: the Ethiopian People's Revolutionary Democratic Front (EPRDF) (coalition of four political parties) won 59.8 per cent of the vote (327 seats out of 547), Coalition for Unity and Democracy (coalition of four political parties) 19.9 per cent (109), United Ethiopian Democratic Forces (coalition of five political parties) 9.5 per cent (52), Somali People's Democratic Party 4.3 per cent (24), Oromo Federalist Democratic Movement 2.0 per cent (11); six political parties and an independent candidate all won less than 2 per cent and shared the remaining 24 seats. Turnout was 90 per cent.

Next elections

2013 (presidential); 2015 (parliamentary)

Political parties

Ruling party

Coalition Ethiopian People's Revolutionary Democratic Front (EPRDF), an alliance of the Tigray People's Liberation Front (TPLF), the South Ethiopian Peoples' Democratic Front (SEPDF), the Amhara National Democratic Movement (ANDM), and Oromo People's Democratic Movement (OPDM) (from 1991, elected 1995, re-elected 2010)

Main opposition party
No effective opposition party exists in parliament.

Population
85.00 million (2010)*
Last census: 28 May 2007: 73,918,505. The country's third national census was taken over a nine-day period and cost US$45.7 million.
Population density: 49.9 inhabitants per square km. Urban population: 16 per cent (1995—2001).
Annual growth rate: 2.6 per cent 1994–2004 (WHO 2006)
Internally Displaced Persons (IDP)
132,000 (UNHCR 2004)
Ethnic make-up
Oromo (40 per cent), Amhara and Tigrayan (32 per cent), Sidamo (9 per cent), Shankella (6 per cent), Somali (6 per cent), Afar (4 per cent), Gurage (2 per cent).
Religions
The Ethiopian Coptic Church is influential, particularly in the north. There is a large Muslim community in the south, made up mainly of Arabs, Somalis and Oromos.
Ethiopian Orthodox (40 per cent), Muslim (40 per cent), animist and other (20 per cent).

Education
Ethiopia has one of the world's lowest school enrolment rates. The government aims to enrol 5.3 million children in primary schools by 2005. The pattern of enrolment shows large gender gaps with girls being more likely to drop out in the early stages. Oxfam estimates that fewer than one-third of boys and one-tenth of girls aged 6—11 start school and one quarter of these drop out during the first two grades. Female literacy rates are only 32 per cent and girls of primary school age work 14—16 hours a day on a variety of tasks, either helping out at home or earning an income. In regions where tuition fees have been abolished, school enrolment has increased by up to 20 per cent.
In secondary schools, English has replaced Amharic as the medium of instruction, although several local languages are also used.
Literacy rate: 42 per cent adult rate; 57 per cent youth rate (15–24) (Unesco 2005).
Pupils per teacher: 43 in primary schools.

Health
The government aimed at reorganising health services through a twenty-year health development strategy, with a series of five-year investment programmes; the second phase began in 2003. The system provides access to health services for only about half of the population, mainly in the urban areas. Estimates suggests that 24 per cent and 15 per cent of the population respectively had access to improved water and sanitation facilities.
In 2005 the World Health Organisation – Global Polio Eradication Initiative (WHO – Polio Eradication) launched an Africa-wide mass polio immunisation programme, this coincided with the first case of the desease reported in Ethiopia in four years; its re-emergence was due to infected travellers. In a synchronised campaign with Somalia and Kenya, inoculation began for under fives by WHO – Polio Eradication and the country's health authorities in 2006.
HIV/Aids
There were 1.4 million people HIV positive in 2003, of which 770,000 were women, plus 120,000 children were HIV positive and 720,000 children were made orphans. There were 120,000 deaths due to aids in 2003.
The loss in annual GDP growth per capita was projected to be 0.6 per cent between 2002–10 due to the impact of the disease.
In Addis Ababa the prevalence rate of HIV/Aids has been falling from a high of 24 per cent in 1995 to 11 per cent in 2004.
HIV prevalence: 4.4 per cent aged 15–49 in 2003 (World Bank)
Life expectancy: 50 years, 2004 (WHO 2006)
Fertility rate/Maternal mortality rate: 5.7 births per woman, 2004 (WHO 2006); maternal mortality 18 per 1,000 live births (World Bank).
Child (under 5 years) mortality rate (per 1,000): 112 deaths per 1,000 live births; 47 per cent of children aged under five were malnourished (World Bank).
Head of population per physician: 0.03 physicians per 1,000 people, 2003 (WHO 2006)

Welfare
Ethiopia is one of the poorest countries in the world, with annual income per capita below US$100. Following the end of the border conflict with Eritrea in 2000, the government of Ethiopia started to implement an ambitious adjustment and reform programme and renewed its commitment to poverty reduction.

Main cities
Addis Ababa (capital, estimated population 3.1 million in 2005), Dire Dawa (274,252), Nazret (212,062), Gondar (154,787) Debre Zeyit (104,537).

Languages spoken
Oromigna and Tigrigna are widely spoken. English is taught in schools; as well as Arabic, French and Italian, it is used in business circles and understood in most hotels and major towns. Over 80 local languages are also spoken.
Official language/s
Amharic

Media
Press
Newspaper circulation is limited to the urban literate. The government maintains a strict control over journalists and many are in exile.
Dailies: In Amharic, *Addis Zemen* (www.ethpress.gov.et) is a state-owned, *Addis Admass* (www.addisadmass.com) is privately owned. In English, the *Ethiopian Herald* (www.ethpress.gov.et) is a state-owned, *The Africa Monitor (with The Daily Monitor, as an imprint) (www.theafricamonitor.com) is privately owned.*
Weeklies: There are a few magazines published in Amharic and English, including *Ethiopian Weekly Press Digest* and *The Sun*. There are many more online publications.
Business: In English, weekly publications include *Capital* (www.capitalethiopia.com) and *Addis Fortune* (www.addisfortune.com), both provide business news and features.
Broadcasting
The national broadcaster is the Ethiopian Radio and Television Agency (ERTA) (www.erta.gov.et).
Radio: Radio services are the main medium of mass communication and sources of news and information.
The government-owned Radio Ethiopia (www.angelfire.com/biz/radioethiopia) operates nationally over several AM frequencies in 11 languages including Amharic, Arabic, English, French and local languages.
The are just a few private, independent radio stations, including Radio Fanaa (www.radiofanaa.com) and Radio Jigjiga (www.radiojigjiga.com). External services include Voice of America (VOA). Ethiopia admitted jamming the Amharic broadcasts of VOA in March 2010.
Television: The state-controlled Ethiopian Television (www.erta.gov.et) is a monopoly, which broadcasts to most of the country via a microwave link-up. Foreign satellite services are available from Jump TV (www.jumptv.com).
News agencies
National news agency: Ethiopain News Agency
AllAfrica: www.allafrica.com
The Reporter:
http://en.ethiopianreporter.com
Walta Information Centre (WIC):
www.waltainfo.com

Economy
The World Bank rates Ethiopia as a low income economy, with agriculture as the principal component of the economy, albeit it most often subsistence farming. Nevertheless, agriculture constitutes over 40 per cent of GDP and provides over 85 per cent of exports. Ethiopia is ranked first in Africa for livestock, with over 49 million cattle, 22 million goats, 17 million sheep and 38 million chickens in 2008–09. Its coffee and teas are considered some of the best in the world and it exports spices, fruit, vegetables and flowers to Europe and other African countries. Ethiopia, Africa's largest coffee producer, established a national coffee exchange in 2008, to consolidate its coffee collection and sales to increase quality and pay farmers a better return on the value of their crop. In 2007/08 coffee exports amounted to US$525 million. There are, among others, mineral reserves in iron ore, gold, platinum and copper that have yet to be fully exploited. The tourist sector is still dependent on intrepid, self-reliant travellers who can provide for themselves, visiting world-renowned archaeological sites (the cradle of Mankind) and wildlife and game reserves. The private sector is mostly small-scale, informal and service-orientated.

GDP growth was 11.2 per cent in 2008, which had remained the same since 2006, growth in 2009 dropped by a couple of percentage points to 9.9 per cent in 2009, and further still to 8.5 per cent in 2010. This was partly due to a drought in 2009 and the devaluation of the birr in September 2010, but offset by a bumper harvest and higher exports of gold. Inflation has been a long-term problem and although the consumer price index (CPI) inflation fell from a high of 36.4 per cent in 2009 to 2.8 per cent in 2010, non-food inflation in 2009/10 was 15.6 per cent.

Although Ethiopia is one of the poorest countries in the world, despite a wealth of resources, economic development has been retarded by various factors, including poor infrastructure, desertification, recurrent droughts, deterioration in the terms of trade and the effects of the war with Eritrea. The International Monetary Fund (IMF) has emphasised the importance of tax reforms for macroeconomic stability, which should raise government revenue from domestic sources to at least 11.3 per cent of GDP.

Through a series of reform programmes to alleviate poverty that included targeted spending on education, health and infrastructure, and with a reduction in the poverty rate to 36.5 per cent in 2005, Ethiopia is on target to reach a poverty rate of 22 per cent by 2015. However, with rising food prices and poor harvests in 2008–09 the rate of those just above the poverty line increased, as over 70 per cent of the population lived on less than US$2 dollars a day. Remittances in 2010 were estimated at US$387 million, a rise from the US$353 million (1.3 per cent of GDP) in 2009.

The Export and Import Bank of China agreed to fund parts of the US$336 million new, approximately 5,000km railway project, launched in October 2010 by the Ethiopian Railway Corporation (ERC). The new railway is part of a five-year infrastructure expansion plan, coupled with a new boost of 10,000MW of electricity to the current 2,000MW, to enhance Ethiopia's ability to gain growth from its productive potential.

External trade
Ethiopia is a member of the Common Market of Eastern and Southern Africa (Comesa), which in 2009 launched a customs union between all 19 member states. In 2009, Ethiopia became a member of the Comprehensive Africa Agriculture Development Programme (CAADP), which under the auspices of the African Union (AU) promotes economic growth through agricultural-led development, designed to eliminate hunger, reduce poverty and food insecurity and enable expansion of exports.

Ethiopia is the origin of the coffee plant, and coffee beans are still a major export product providing over 30 per cent of the country's foreign earnings (a fall from over 60 per cent in the mid-1990s due to a slump in world prices).

Imports
Principal imports are food and live animals, petroleum and petroleum products, chemicals, machinery, motor vehicles, cereals, textiles, semi-manufactured goods and fertilisers.

Main sources: China (typically 24 per cent of total), Saudi Arabia (12 per cent), India (8 per cent).

Exports
Principal exports are coffee, khat, gold, leather products, live animals, oilseeds, marble and other minerals.

Main destinations: China (typically 15 per cent of total), The Netherlands (9 per cent), Somalia (8 per cent).

Agriculture
Farming
The agricultural sector is the mainstay of the economy, accounting for around 45 per cent of GDP, 85 per cent of employment and 62 per cent of exports. Only about two-thirds of Ethiopia's 122 million hectares of land is suitable for agriculture, of which around 15 per cent is actually cultivated. Large parts are affected by soil erosion. Intensive subsistence agriculture has depleted the soil and Ethiopia can no longer feed its population, even when the weather is good. Very little of the cultivated area is irrigated.

Ethiopia, as Africa's largest coffee producer, has benefited from rising coffee prices and the establishment of a new national coffee exchange opened in 2008. It will consolidate coffee collection and sales to increase quality and pay farmers a better return on the value of their crop. In 2007/08 coffee exports amounted to US$525 million.

Many growers have responded by switching to the production of qat. While coffee fell from 60 per cent of total exports to 35 per cent, export of qat increased to 15 per cent from 6 per cent.

Other cash crops include cotton and sugar, as well as the mildly narcotic plant qat, which has a traditional market in the Middle East. The main food crops are maize, sorghum, wheat, barley, millet and teff.

Despite the insurity and harrassing from bandits, a booming trade in livestock has thrived for more than two decades along the borders between Somalia, Ethiopia and Kenya.

Forestry
Only 4 per cent of Ethiopia's land area is forested. Since the mid-1970s, there has been extensive deforestation with up to 75 per cent of forest cover cleared or degraded, according to the UN's Food and Agriculture Organisation (FAO). The overwhelming majority of timber production is used as domestic fuel.

Ethiopia is one of the world's largest exporters of natural gum and gum resin (gum Arabic). Between 1996–2002 it exported over 13,000 tonnes of natural gum, worth US$17 million. However, industry experts warned, in March 2006, that damage from forest fires, woodfuel harvesting and improper gum tapping was causing serious damage to the resources, added to which, resettlement programmes were also destroying woodland habitats.

Industry and manufacturing
The industrial sector contributes 12.4 per cent of GDP and employs about 7 per cent of the workforce. Manufacturing of small handicrafts and other small industry sub-sectors make up around 7 per cent of GDP.

Industry is primarily based on the processing of agricultural raw materials. Principal among these is food processing, but textiles, handicrafts, and leather production are also significant.

Growth is constrained by a lack of raw materials, outdated machinery and techniques and the need for imports throughout the sector.

Tourism
Although visitor numbers have risen consistently each year since 1991, tourism is under-developed. The economic importance of the sector and Ethiopia's potential as a destination are recognised and priority is being given to improving the infrastructure and the country's image, which has suffered from the conflict with Eritrea and natural disasters. Ethiopia was selected by the World Tourism Organisation as one of the first beneficiaries of the Sustainable Tourism and Elimination of Poverty initiative, which provided experise and attract funding for tourism proposals.

Environment
In June 2010 the African Union backed a proposal to build the 'Great Green Wall' project, of a 15km wide, 7,775km long, continuous belt of trees from Senegal in the west to Djibouti in the east (traversing 11 countries) in an effort to halt the advance of the Sahara Desert. The trees to be used would be drought-adapted, preferably native to the area from a list of 37 possible species, and should help to slow soil erosion and filter rain water.

Mining
The mining sector accounts for around 6 per cent of GDP.
The government says there are at least 500 tonnes of proven gold reserves in the country. Activity is limited to small-scale gold mining.
The country has substantial reserves of iron ore and untapped reserves of platinum, tantalum (used in the electronics industry), nickel, phosphate, diatomite, copper, zinc, soda ash and potash. Tantalum reserves are estimated at 25,000 tonnes at one site alone.
The output of non-metallic minerals such as limestone and marble has increased significantly.
A number of foreign mining companies have been awarded exploration concessions.

Hydrocarbons
Ethiopia does not produce oil, but there is considered to be commercial potential and foreign interest and investment in the sector is high. An exploration deal between the Ethiopian government and White Nile (UK) was signed in 2008, one of many inward investments into the oil industry. Ethiopia relies on imports of refined oil to meet energy requirements, which was 35,000 barrels per day (bpd) in 2007. Sudan became an important source of supplies from 2003, when shipment by tanker truck along a new road began.
Natural gas reserves were 24.9 billion cubic metres in 2007.
Coal is not imported and any produced or used is commercially insignificant.

Energy
Ethiopia has 813.82MW installed electricity-generating capacity, of which 85 per cent is produced by hydropower. Full hydroelectricity potential is estimated at 45,000MW but the Ethiopian Electric Power Corporation (EEPCO), which is responsible for generating, distributing and sales of electricity, has only eight hydropower stations. There are, nationally, 22 stations in total, mostly small diesel powered plants and one geothermal plant at Aluto Langano. Around 22 per cent of the population has access to electricity and EEPCO has electrified 1,658 towns and the programme is ongoing. The joint Ethiopian-UAE, Grand Millennium Dam hydroelectric project, designed to regulate the flow of the Nile River and produce 5,000MW for export to neighbours, will not reduce the flow of water to Egypt, according to the Minister of Industry Tadesse Haile, in July 2011. The US$4.5 billion project, under construction since April 2011, should have a strong influence on Ethiopia's future economic prospects.

Financial markets
Commodity exchange
Ethiopia Commodity Exchange (ECX)

Banking and insurance
Central bank
National Bank of Ethiopia
Main financial centre
Addis Ababa

Time
GMT plus three hours
The Ethiopian day officially begins at 0600 (midnight elsewhere).

Geography
Ethiopia extends inland from the Red Sea coast of eastern Africa. The country has a long frontier with Somalia near the Horn of Africa. Sudan lies to the west, Djibouti to the east, Eritrea to the north and Kenya to the south.
The country is a high central plateau, at 1,800–3,000 metres above sea level which is dissected by the Great Rift Valley that runs diagonally across the country. The tallest peak is Mount Ras Dashen, at 4,620 metres in the Simien Mountains, in the rugged north. In the north-west the Blue Nile rises in Lake Tana. The landscape in the south is flatter and more suited to agriculture.

Climate
Dependent on altitude. Lowland regions are very hot and dry throughout the year. On the plateau (including Addis Ababa) dry season from October–May with temperature range from as low as 6 degrees Celsius (C) in December to 26 degrees C in March (light rain from February–April). Temperatures can fall sharply at night during the dry season. Rainy season from June–September with average temperature 21 degrees C.

Entry requirements
Passports
Required by all. Must be valid for at least six months.
Visa
Required by all. For business visas, an application should be accompanied by a letter from a sponsoring organisation or company. For those self-employed, a letter from a solicitor, accountant or business registration authority should suffice. Visas are usually issued for a one month period; heavy penalties may be imposed for unauthorised extensions. If necessary, contact the Immigration Office for an Alien's Registration Card and an exit visa. Visa application forms can be downloaded from a number of Ethiopian embassy websites (www.mfa.gov.et/Consular_Affair_Diplomatic/Consular_Affair.php).
An international certificate of vaccination against yellow fever is required when applying.
Foreign nationals are advised to register their arrival with the consular representative of their embassy.
Currency advice/regulations
Up to Birr100 can be imported, if a visitor has a re-entry permit Birr100 may be exported, or else local currency export is prohibited.
Unlimited foreign currency may be imported but it must be declared on arrival. Export of foreign currency is allowed up to the amount declared.
Travellers cheque are accepted and are best taken as either US dollars or pound sterling.
Customs
Skins, hides and any antique articles require an export certificate. Laptop computers must be declared upon arrival and departure. Tape recorders require special customs permits.

Health (for visitors)
Health facilities are extremely limited in Addis Ababa and inadequate outside the city. Travellers should bring their own prescription drugs and a doctor's note describing the medication. If the quantity of drugs exceeds that expected for personal use, a permit from the ministry of health is required.
The altitude in Addis Ababa may cause health problems.
Mandatory precautions
A yellow fever inoculation certificate.

Advisable precautions
Visitors should be in date for the following vaccinations: yellow fever, polio, typhoid, tetanus, hepatitis A and B, meningitis. There is a rabies risk.
Malaria prophylaxis recommended before visiting the lowlands. There is no malaria risk in Addis Ababa.
Tap water must be treated as unsafe unless boiled and filtered (bottled water is available in the main cities). Eat only well cooked meals, preferably served hot; vegetables should be cooked and fruit peeled. Dairy products are unpasteurised and should be avoided
A first aid kit that includes disposable syringes, is a reasonable precaution. Medical insurance is essential, including emergency evacuation, and an adequate supply of personal medicines is necessary.

Hotels
Hotels are available in Addis Ababa and other main centres. A service charge of 10 per cent and a tax of 2 per cent are added to bills but a small tip is usual in addition to the service charge. Payment is generally required in foreign currency.

Credit cards
Credit cards are accepted by airlines and the larger hotels only.

Public holidays (national)
Fixed dates
^7 Jan (Genna/Ethiopian Christmas Day), ^19 Jan (Timket/Epiphany), 2 Mar (Victory of Adwa Day), 28 May (Downfall of the Dergue), ^11 Sep (Enkutatash/New Year's Day), ^26 Sep (Meskel/Finding of the True Cross).
Variable dates
^Ethiopian Good Friday, ^Ethiopian Easter Day, Eid al Adha, Birth of the Prophet, Eid al Fitr.
^ Coptic Christian feasts only.
Ethiopia follows the Julian calendar, instead of the Gregorian calendar, used in most other parts of the world. The Ethiopian calendar year is divided into 13 months: 12 months of 30 days each and one month of five days (six in a leap year). The Ethiopian year commences on 11 September and runs seven years and eight months behind the Gregorian calendar.
Islamic year 1433 (26 Nov 2011–14 Nov 2012): The Islamic year contains 354 or 355 days, with the result that Muslim feasts advance by 10–12 days against the Gregorian calendar. Dates of feasts vary according to the sighting of the new moon, so cannot be forecast exactly.

Working hours
Banking
Mon–Thu: 0800–1500; Fri: 0800–1100, 1330–1500; Sat: 0830–1100.
Business
Mon–Thu: 0830–1230, 1330–1730; Fri: 0830–1130, 1330–1730. Most private businesses also work on Saturdays.
Government
Mon–Thu: 0830–1230, 1330–1730. Fri: 0830–1130, 1330–1730.
Shops
Mon–Sat: 0800–1300, 1400–2000. Local variations.

Telecommunications
Mobile/cell phones
A GSM 900 service is available in large cities and towns only.

Electricity supply
220V, 50 cycles AC. Plugs are of the two-pin variety.

Social customs/useful tips
Handshaking is the usual mode of greeting. The first name is followed by that of the father – there are no family names. The words Ato, Woizero and Woizrity are the equivalents of Mr, Mrs and Miss respectively, and should be used when addressing people.
Smoking is not popular among traditional people, or in front of priests. Dress should be modest. Shoes are removed on entering churches/mosques. Private formal entertaining is common in Addis Ababa, and cocktail parties are not uncommon.
Ethiopian law strictly prohibits the photographing of military installations, police/military personnel, industrial facilities, government buildings and infrastructure.

Security
Crime is an increasing problem in Addis Ababa. Normal precautions should be taken.
Exercise caution if travelling to the northern Tigray and Afar regions (within 50km of the Ethiopian/Eritrean border) because of landmines and unsettled conditions in the border area. Travel to the Ogaden Region is considered very dangerous and should not be attempted. Limit road travel outside major towns to daylight hours only.

Getting there
Air
National airline: Ethiopian Airlines
International airport/s: Addis Ababa-Bole International (ADD), 8km from city, bar, restaurant, bank, post office, shops, car hire.
Airport tax: International departures US$20 in cash and exact amount, excluding transit passengers.
Surface
Road: Entry by land into Ethiopia is possible, if difficult, via Dewale and Galafi (Ethiopia-Djibouti), Moyale (Ethiopia-Kenya), Humera and Metema (Ethiopia-Sudan), Jijiga (Ethiopia-Somalia). The road linking Nairobi and Addis Ababa forms part of the Trans-East African Highway.
Rail: The rail route from Djibouti to Addis Ababa is subject to disruption.
Water: Ethiopia has been landlocked since Eritrea gained independence.
Main port/s: Until the outbreak of hostilities with Eritrea in 1998, Ethiopia relied heavily on the Eritrean ports of Assab and Massawa. Djibouti has subsequently become Ethiopia's principal trading gateway.

Getting about
National transport
Air: Ethiopian Airlines operates domestic service to main towns.
Road: An all-weather road network connects principal towns. The road system is undergoing expansion.
There are border posts at Moyale on the Kenyan border, Adwa and Adigrat near the border with Eritrea, and Dewelle for Djibouti.
Roads are impassable to Lalibela from June to September.
Drivers bringing their own vehicles to Ethiopia will require a *carnet de passage*.
Buses: Coach services (liable to suspension) Addis Ababa-Gondar.
Rail: A line runs from Addis Ababa to Dire Dawa (and on to Djibouti). However, visitors are advised not to use this line for security reasons.
City transport
Taxis: In Addis Ababa, the National Tour Operations (NTO) provides taxis at the main hotels and the airport, although independent and communal cabs are available. It is advisable to check the fare and the destination before entering the cab. The most reliable taxis are available from the office of the Hilton Hotel. The taxi journey from the airport to the city centre takes about 30 minutes. Tipping is not usual.
Buses, trams & metro: Journey time from airport to city centre 30 minutes.
Car hire
Car hire (with or without driver) is available in the main centres. A valid international driving licence is required. Traffic drives on the right.
Payment for car rental is generally required in foreign currency.

BUSINESS DIRECTORY

The addresses listed below are a selection only. While World of Information makes every endeavour to check these addresses, we cannot guarantee that changes have not been made, especially to telephone numbers and area codes. We would welcome any corrections.

Telephone area codes

The international dialling code (IDD) for Ethiopia is +251 followed by area code and subscriber's number.

Addis Ababa	11	Gondar	58
Awassa	46	Jimma	47
Bahir Dar	58	Mekelle	4
Dire Dawa	25	Nazareth	22

Chambers of Commerce

Addis Ababa Chamber of Commerce, PO Box 2458, Addis Ababa (tel: 515-055; fax: 511-479; e-mail: aachamber1@telecom.net.et).

Awassa Chamber of Commerce, PO Box 167, Awassa (tel: 200-375; fax: 205-197).

Bahir Dar Chamber of Commerce, PO Box 48, Bahir Dar (tel: 200-481; fax: 201-787).

Dire Dawa Chamber of Commerce, PO Box 198, Dire Dawa (tel: 113-082; fax 112-468; e-mail: luiji@telecom.net.et).

Ethiopian Chamber of Commerce, PO Box 517, Addis Ababa (tel: 518-240; fax: 517-699; e-mail: ethcham@telecom.net.et).

Gondar Chamber of Commerce, PO Box 50, Gondar (tel: 110-320; fax: 115-656).

Mekelle Chamber of Commerce, PO Box 503, Mekelle (tel: 402-529; fax: 408-914).

Nazareth Chamber of Commerce, PO Box 36, Nazareth (tel: 112-083; fax: 122-699).

Banking

Awash International Bank SC; PO Box 12638, Bole Road, Addis Ababa (tel: 614-482/83, 612-919; fax: 614-477).

Bank of Abyssinia SC; PO Box 12947, Addis Ababa (tel: 514-130, 514-752; fax: 511-575).

Commercial Bank of Ethiopia; PO Box 255, Unity Square, Addis Ababa (tel: 511-271, 515-004; fax: 514-522, 512-166).

Construction and Business Bank, PO Box 3480, Addis Ababa (tel: 512-300; fax: 515-103).

Dashen Bank SC; PO Box 12752, Garad Building, Debre Zeit Road, Addis Ababa (tel: 661-380, 655-525; fax: 661-640, 653-037).

Development Bank of Ethiopia, PO Box 1900, Josep Broz Tito, Addis Ababa (tel: 511-188; fax: 511-606).

Wegagen Bank SC; PO Box 1018, Addis Ababa (tel: 655-015; fax: 653-330).

Central bank

National Bank of Ethiopia, PO Box 5550, Addis Ababa, Ethiopia (tel: 517-430; fax: 514-588; email: nbe.excd@telecom.net.et; internet: www.nbe.gov.et).

Commodity exchange

Ethiopia Commodity Exchange (ECX): www.ecx.com.et

Travel information

Addis Ababa-Bole Airport, PO Box 978, Addis Ababa (tel: 180-455; fax: 612-533).

Antiquities Authority, National Museum of Ethiopia, PO Box 76, Addis Ababa (tel: 117-150; fax: 553-188).

Ethiopian Airlines, PO Box 1755, Bole International Airport, Addis Ababa (tel: 612-222; fax: 611-474); town office (tel: 517-000; fax: 611-474; internet: www.flyethiopian.com).

National Tour Operations (NTO), PO Box 5709, Addis Ababa (tel: 512-955; fax: 517-688).

National tourist organisation offices

Ethiopian Tourism Commission, PO Box 2183, Addis Ababa (tel: 517-470, 150-609, 513-962; fax: 513-899; internet: www.visitethiopia.com).

Other useful addresses

African Union, PO Box 3243, Addis Ababa (tel: 557-700; fax: 511-299).

British Embassy, Commercial Section, Fikre Mariam Abatechan Street, Addis Ababa (tel: 612-354; fax: 610-588).

Central Statistical Office, PO Box 1143, Addis Ababa (tel: 113-010).

Department of Immigration and Refugee Affairs, PO Box 5741, Addis Ababa (tel: 553-899).

Djibouti–Ethiopian Railway Corporation, PO Box 1051, Addis Ababa (tel: 517-250; fax: 513-533).

Ethiopian Customs Office, PO Box 3248, Addis Ababa (tel: 513-100; fax: 518-355).

Ethiopian Embassy (USA), 3506 International Drive, NW, Washington DC 20008 (tel: 202-364-1200; fax: 202-686-9551; e-mail: ethiopia@ethiopianembassy.org).

Ethiopian Investment Authority, PO Box 2313, Addis Ababa (tel: 510-033; 514-396).

Ethiopian Privatisation Agency, PO Box 11835, Ethiopian Investment Authority Building, Bole Road, Addis Ababa (tel: 521-833; fax: 513-955).

Ethiopian Private Industries' Association, PO Box 8739, Addis Ababa (tel: 512-384; fax: 552-633).

Ethiopian Television, PO Box 5554, Addis Ababa.

Ethiopian Tourist Trading Enterprise, PO Box 8640, Addis Ababa (tel: 612-277; fax: 610-500).

Maritime and Transit Services, PO Box 1186, Addis Ababa (tel: 510-666; fax: 514-097).

Ministry of Culture and Information, PO Box 1364, Addis Ababa (tel: 551-011; fax: 551-609).

Ministry of Economic Development & Co-operation, PO Box 2428, Addis Ababa (tel: 519-684; fax: 517-988).

Ministry of Foreign Affairs, PO Box 393, Addis Ababa (tel: 517-345; fax: 514-300).

Ministry of Trade and Industry, PO Box 2559, Addis Ababa (tel: 518-200; fax: 514-288).

Voice of Ethiopia, PO Box 1020, Addis Ababa.

Wildlife Conservation Department, PO Box 386, Addis Ababa (tel: 510-455; fax: 510-168).

National news agency: Ethiopain News Agency, PO Box 530 Addis Ababa (tel: 155-0011; fax: 155-1609; internet: www.ena.gov.et).

Internet sites

Africa Business Network: http://www.ifc.org/abn

AllAfrica.com: http://www.allafrica.com

African Development Bank: http://www.afdb.org

ENA - Ethiopian News Agency: http://www.telecom.net.et/~ena

Ethiopian Mission to the UN: http://www.undp.org/missions/ethiopia

Ethiopian Privatisation Agency: http://www.undp.org/missions/ethiopia

Mbendi AfroPaedia (information on companies, countries, industries and stock exchanges): http://mbendi.co.za

Falkland Islands/Islas Malvinas

KEY FACTS

Official name: Falkland Islands

Head of State: Queen Elizabeth II, represented by Governor Nigel Robert Haywood (from 16 Oct 2010)

Head of government: Chief Executive Dr Tim Thorogood (since 7 Jan 2008)

Area: 12,173 square km (including East and West Falkland and adjacent islands)

Population: 3,140 (2010)*

Capital: Stanley

Official language: English

Currency: Falkland pound (Fl£) = 100 pence

Exchange rate: Fl£0.64 per US$ (Oct 2011)

GDP per capita: US$25,000 (2003)

GDP real growth: 2.00% (2006)*

Inflation: 3.60% (2004)*

* estimated figure

COUNTRY PROFILE

Historical profile

1592 First sighted by English mariners (Captain John Davis in ship *Desire* – the motto of the islands became Desire the Right).
1690 The first landing was by British Captain John Strong in the ship, *Welfare*. The Falkland Islands were named after the then Treasurer of the Navy, Viscount Falkland.
1764 French settlement was recorded. The islands were named Les Malouines after the French town of St Malo, hence the Argentine name of Malvinas for the islands.
1765 Captain John Byron (British) took formal possession of the islands at Port Egmont.
1767 The French settlement was sold to Spain and named Puerto de la Soledad.
1770 The Spanish ousted the British from Port Egmont.
1771 The British garrison was re-established.
1774 The garrison was withdrawn, leaving a plaque 'as a mark of possession' and a flag 'left flying'.
1820 The flag of the United Provinces of La Plata (Spanish) was hoisted at Puerto de la Soledad.
1823 The governor of the islands was nominated by the United Provinces Government (but did not visit).
1824 A German merchant, Louis Vernet, was given land by grant of the Buenos Aires government and a settlement of mixed nationalities, over the next few years, was established at Puerto de la Soledad.
1828 Vernet was appointed governor by the United Provinces. He attempted to stop sealing operations by other nations.
1831 The US protested about these actions and sent *USS Lexington* to sack Puerto de la Soledad (with the US president's approval). The islands were again unpopulated.
1833 Port Louis (Puerto de la Soledad) was taken over by the British, asserting full rights under naval superintendents until 1842.
1842 The first British governor, Richard C Moody, took up residence.
1981 The Falkland Islands and its dependencies were designated as British Dependent Territories.
1982 Argentina invaded the Falkland Islands. The UK despatched a military force, composed of naval ships and troops. The UK recaptured the islands.
1983 The British Nationality (Falkland Islands) Act gave islanders full British citizenship.
1990s The UK and Argentina resumed diplomatic relations. Both sides agreed to a formula to protect their respective positions on sovereignty and maritime jurisdiction, while discussing other matters. The UN committee on decolonisation urged the UK and Argentina to negotiate an ending to the dispute. The UK remained adamant that the self-determination of Falkland Islanders was paramount. Argentina adopted a constitutional amendment asserting its sovereignty over the islands.
1999 In an effort to improve relations, Argentine nationals were allowed to visit the islands for the first time since 1982.
2001 The UK agreed to allow Argentinean private aircraft and shipping to visit the islands.
2002 The Falkland Islands and its dependencies were designated as a self-governing British Overseas Territories (BOT).
2003 The 33rd General Assembly of the Organisation of American States (OAS) passed a statement of support for Argentina's claim to the Falkland Islands. The OAS called on Britain and Argentina to resume negotiations over the South Atlantic archipelago as soon as possible.
2004 Relations between Argentina and the UK deteriorated as Argentina banned charter flights to and from the Falklands crossing its airspace, and an Argentinean ice breaker, the *Almirante Irizar*, began 'policing' a Falklands conservation zone by challenging fishing vessels, demanding details of their permits. Argentina also gave permission for Aerolineas Argentinas to begin direct flights to the Falkland Islands, without regard for any UK agreement.
2006 The BBC ceased its broadcasts to the Falklands Islands, after 62 years. Alan Huckle became governor.
2007 Argentina terminated a 1995 agreement with the UK on oil exploration in the vicinity of the Falkland Islands. An agreement with BHP Billiton for at least two exploration wells to be drilled by 2010 was signed.

2008 Dr Tim Thorogood became chief executive of the Falkland Islands. Following an Anglo-Argentine feasibility study, it was estimated that there were 20,000 unexploded ordinances (UXO) that had yet to be disarmed, and which 'would present significant technical challenges and risks'.
2009 Argentina laid claim to 1.7 million square kilometres of ocean, including the Falklands Islands and other island chains governed by the UK. Argentina passed the Falkland Islands, South Georgia and the South Sandwich Islands and the British law, which defined the southern-most Argentine province as Tierra del Fuego, Antarctica and the Southern Atlantic Islands, including the Falkland Islands and part of Antarctica. The law means Argentine local government could try and collect royalties from oil companies with offshore operations that had previously been levied by the Argentine federal government.
2010 In May Rockhopper Exploration announced that it had made a 'significant oil discovery'. In retaliation for the drilling, the Argentine government decreed that all vessels sailing to and from Argentina, the Falklands, South Georgia and South Sandwich Islands were first to request authorisation from the Argentine government. The UK responded with a note to Argentina's chargé d'affairs in London, pointing out that the UK considers that Argentine Presidential Decree 256/2010 and Disposition 14/2010 'are not complaint with International Law including the UN Convention on the Law of the Sea'. The note also reaffirmed British sovereignty over the Falklands and South Atlantic Islands, and stated it has 'no doubt that the surrounding maritime areas of the Falkland Islands, and South Georgia and the South Sandwich Islands are not Argentine jurisdictional waters'. The island government released its Economic Development Strategy for public consultation, in July. It aims for a sustainable financial future of the islands, ensuring employment, maximising income and facilitating growth, using private and public interests. In September Uruguay denied entry to *HMS Gloucester*, the frigate charged with guarding the Falklands. The frigate was en route to the Falklands and the captain had requested permission to take on fuel and provisions in Montevideo. Nigel Haywood was sworn in as governor on 16 October. In his annual Christmas message Prime Minister Cameron assured the Falkland Islanders that there were '... no doubts whatsoever about the United Kingdom's sovereignty over the Falkland Islands; and there can and will be no negotiations on the sovereignty of the Islands unless you, the Falkland Islanders, want them.'
2011 The points system in the immigration policy for a permanent resident's permit was deemed to be too difficult to achieve and members of the legislative assembly (MLA) agreed to review and discuss altering the criteria used.

Political structure

Constitution

The original constitution, which dated from 1985, with amendments in 1997 and 1998, was replaced by a new constitution in January 2009. The islander's rights to self-determination are prescribed. The operations of the Governor and Executive and Legislative Councils are mandated under the constitution. The first chapter enshrines the Falkland Islanders's right to self-determination in accordance with the United Nations Charter, although Argentina has never accepted the principle as applying to the Falkland Islands. Defence and foreign affairs are the responsibility of the UK government.

Form of state

Overseas territory of the United Kingdom

The executive

Supreme authority is vested in the British monarch and exercised by the governor with the advice and assistance of the Executive and Legislative Councils.
The governor presides over a five-member Executive Council (three elected and two *ex-officio* members). The governor is obliged to consult the Executive Council, except for defence and security issues (when the Commander of the British Forces in the islands advises and directs). If the governor opposes the Executive Council an immediate report must be presented to the UK government in explanation. The governor is responsible for external affairs and the public service.

National legislature

The Legislative Council is composed of eight members (three from Camp (countryside) constituency and five from the Stanley constituency) elected by universal adult suffrage and two *ex-officio* members – the chief executive and the financial secretary. The council has a substantial measure of responsibility for the island's affairs.

Legal system

English common law

Last elections

17 November 2005 (legislative council)
Results: Legislative council: eight out of the ten seats were filled by election of non-partisan candidates, the remaining places being filled by ex-officio members.

Next elections

Political situation

Along with all other British Overseas Territories, a new constitution, proposed by the UK government, was agreed by the Falkland Islanders in 2008. The UK government was keen to see all of its territories take more responsibility for themselves, while maintaining implacable support for Falkland Islands' self-determination in the face of Argentina's adamant refusal to give up any part of its claim on the Falkland Islands.
The islands are prospering with the growth in tourism, a low unemployment rate and the continued quartering of military staff. In 2010, oil and gas exploration was underway and in May Rockhopper Exploration announced that it had made a 'significant oil discovery' offshore. On 9 July, the island government released its *Economic Development Strategy, for public consultation. It set out the aims for the economic and sustainable financial future of the islands, ensuring employment, maximising income and facilitating growth, using private and public interests.*

Population

3,140 (2010)*
Last census: 8 October 2006: 2,955
Population density: 4.8 inhabitants per square km.
Annual growth rate: 1.1 per cent (2003)

Ethnic make-up

White, almost exclusively of British descent. Workers from St Helena make up about 10 per cent of the population.

Religions

Anglican, Roman Catholic, United Free Church, Evangelist Church, Jehovah's Witnesses, Lutheran, Seventh-Day Adventist.

Main cities

Stanley (capital, estimated population 2,181 in 2005)

Languages spoken

Official language/s

English

Media

Press

The two weekly newspapers are *Teaberry Express* (www.falklandnews.com) and *Penguin News* (www.penguin-news.com). Official announcements and government directives are published in periodic publications of *The Falkland Islands Gazette*. The Falkland Islands News Area Network (www.falklandnews.com) provides a news agency service covering local headlines and from other regional newspapers such as *SAFIN Magazine*, *St Helena News*, *The Islander Newspaper* and the *Antarctic Sentinel*.

Broadcasting

Radio: The Falkland Islands Broadcasting Service and British Forces Broadcasting Service operate a local radio station and provide 24 hours/day listening on FM and MW. Satellite radio services are also available.

Television: Apart from the BFBS which provides satellite and cable TV services primarily for the military personnel stationed on the islands, KTV (www.ktv.co.fk) also operates a satellite service which distributes nine channels including BBC, CNN, TNT and HBO. Falkland Islands Television Limited (FITV) was set up in 2010 to broadcast locally produced news programmes.

Economy

The Falkland Islands is self-financing with an economy largely dependent on tourism and agriculture, of which fisheries is the main sector, with the sale of fishing licences to foreign trawlers typically generating over £20 million (around US$32 million) annually. *Illex argentinus* (Argentine shortfin squid) catches in 2008 were down, but the on-shore fishery has expanded. The general failure of the fishing season led to a deficit of around US$11 million in 2008/09.

Almost 80 per cent of the total marine catch is exported to Spain. The Falkland Islands Development Corporation (FIDC) is keen to enhance the island's development prospects through a National Aquaculture Strategy. After fishing, wool is the largest component of farming income. High quality wool is exported to the UK while FIDC is attempting to increase value added features. Other developments include a new abattoir designed to meet EU standards in order to exploit the islands' certification as a country producing organic food. Exports go to Denmark, Sweden and Spain as well as the UK.

The other key element of the economy is tourism. Over 40,000 tourists typically visit each year, most arriving by cruise ships. Land based tourism generated over £3 million (around US$4.8 million), encouraged by the new inter-island ferry service. Improved hotel accommodation and access have been included in development plans. There are regular, scheduled flights from Chile and the UK, via the RAF military airbase at Brize Norton in Oxfordshire. Although the RAF and Falkland Islands Tourist Board are committed to providing a comprehensive service for travellers, the route and distance still places a limitation on the numbers visiting by air.

External trade

As a UK Overseas Territory the Falkland Islands is a part of the European Union's Association of Overseas Countries and Territories (OCT Association), and some EU laws apply, specifically animal slaughter and commercial food hygiene regulations.

There are several rural associations that market local meat, wool, hides and fish.

Imports

Principal imports include fuel, food and drink, building materials and clothing.

Main sources: UK (typically 70 per cent of total), US (15 per cent), The Netherlands (9 per cent).

Exports

Wool, sheepskins and hides were virtually the only exports until the arrival of the fishing industry, which has grown to dominate commodity exports. Finfish, including hake, and *Dissostichus eleginoides (Patagonian toothfish, also known as Chilean sea bass), plus Illex argentinus* (Argentine shortfin squid) are, together with wool, the main exports.

Main destinations: Spain (typically 80 per cent of total), US (6 per cent), UK (5 per cent).

Agriculture

Farming

Soil quality is generally poor – peat over clay (peat is used as fuel). Virtually all available land has been used for sheep farming although small areas of arable land are cultivated (eg potatoes, hay crops, vegetable crops grown by individual households).

A hydroponic garden facility constructed in Stanley yields good quality vegetable crops for local and shipping consumption.

There is an indigenous tussock (or tussac) grass (*Poa Flabellata*, which will grow to a height of 3–4 metres) but because of its palatability for livestock, it has been over-grazed in most places.

Constant strong winds affect the suitability of all flora, and only the hardiest will survive. Indigenous grass covering large areas is known locally as 'whitegrass' (*Cortaderia Pilosa*) and a heather-like plant 'diddle-dee' (*Empetrum Rubrum*) is common.

There are around 90 farms. The average size is 10,000ha, with an average of 6,400 sheep. Sheep stock are a Corriedale/Polwarth mixture with small admixture of other breeds, eg Romney. The average clip per sheep is over 3.55kg.

Certain sheep diseases found elsewhere (eg foot rot, skin complaints/parasites) are either absent or not considered a problem on the islands.

An abbattoir meeting EU standards was opened in 2001 and is an important part of the Islands' organic farming programme. Farmers are being encouraged to diversify. The Islands have accreditation as organic under the brand name, Falklands' Finest.

Mutton is the principal source of protein and is supplemented during winter by beef. A dairy farm on East Falkland provided an important proportion of the islands' milk was closed in July2009. The pasture is improved by nitrogen fertiliser in quantities that would be uneconomic over a larger area.

Fishing

The Interim Conservation and Management Zone inaurgurated by the British government in 1986, was substanially revised in 2005. The revised law regulates the new system of transferable fishing rights. The Falklands have managed and policed a fish reserve and generated significant revenues through the annual award of fishing licences. These go to support the islands' health, education and welfare system. They have dropped to around £15 million (US$30 million) in recent years as a result of drop in Illex (squid) catches. Squid accounts for 75 per cent of the fish taken.

The Fisheries Department monitors marine activity daily and restrictions have been imposed on seismic fleets, especially during the fishing season.

The Falkland Islands Fishing Companies Association (FIFCA) was formed in 2007 to represent the fishing industry.

Industry and manufacturing

Small industrial units serve both onshore and offshore commitments. Hand-knitted local garments are produced for sale to visitors.

The Falkland Islands' largest private company, Falkland Islands Holdings plc, is quoted on the London Stock Exchange where it began trading in 1998. Activities are mainly retail trading and provision of services to the Falkland Islands. It controls about 80 per cent of retail sales, is the agent for Land Rover, the most popular vehicle, owns the Darwin Shipping Line and operates the port in Stanley.

Tourism

Tourists to the islands typically have to display determination to visit the islands down in the South Atlantic, 500km from South America and 770km from South Africa. Arriving by air requires either a flight on an RAF aeroplane from the UK (Brize Norton), which involves an 18 hour flight with two refuelling stops or a once weekly LAN scheduled connecting flight from Punta Arenas, Chile, to Mount Pleasant International airport.

The islands have little in the way of tourist infrastructure, but the islanders are welcoming and can provide accommodation, typically on a bed-and-breakfast basis. Wildlife tourism is popular, as is visiting the battlegrounds of the 1982 military conflict.

Between October 2007–April 2008, 62,200 passengers from visiting cruise ships were given clearance to land. This shows an annual growth of 21 per cent for the 2007–08 season, with a growth in passenger numbers averaging 16 per cent per annum since the 2001–02 season. Of the 46 different vessels that visited in the 2007–08 season, 10 were maiden calls. The Falkland Islands Tourist Board (FITB) (www.falklandislands.com) provides current and vital information for all visitors.

Mining

There is speculation that the great blanket bogs which obscure much of the inland geology of the islands may hide some diamond-bearing kimberlites and exploration is under way. There has been some evidence of gold.

Hydrocarbons

Although there is potential in the oil sector in the Falkland Islands, currently no oil is being produced and the islands rely on the import of petroleum products. Coal and gas is neither produced nor imported. Oil consumption is 2,600 barrels per day. Exploration for oil began in 1996 and in 2002 Falkland Oil and Gas Ltd (FOGL) was formed to manage exploration and operations of any potential oil field finds. Geological mapping has included most offshore regions surrounding the islands and it is thought to contain a potential 200–250 million barrels of oil. The first drilling of an exploratory began in 2009. In May 2009 a previously designated oil well was redefined as a natural gas discovery, possible holding 96 billion cubic metres.

An announcement on 27 June 2011 by the UK-based, Rockhopper Exploration confirmed that commercially viable oil and natural gas deposits offshore, in the North Falkland Basin, in a field known as Sea Lion had been recorded. However, no production was intended in the near future.

Energy

The majority of households use oil for heating. Stanley has a power station that generates 9.0MW of electricity. Outside Stanley, settlements generate their own power on an individual basis. There is a plentiful supply of peat (turf), although few houses have peat stoves.

The Sand Bay Wind Farm has three turbines, installed in 2007, producing 300,000 units of electricity, and around 25 per cent of all electricity consumed in Stanley, saving the island 20–25 per cent of annual oil imports as the existing diesel generators are used less. Another three wind turbines are being installed, to be completed during 2009–10.

Time

GMT minus four hours (GMT minus three hours April–September)

Geography

The Falklands Islands, comprising two large islands and about 700 smaller ones, are in the south-western Atlantic Ocean, about 770km (480 miles) north-east of Cape Horn, South America. They are 500km (300 miles) from the South American mainland.

The coastlines are marked by rocky headlands and sandy beaches. Vegetation comprises low grasses, ferns and shrubs. There are many small lakes and peaty pools and three rivers: the San Carlos on East Falkland and the Warrah and Chartres on West Falkland. There are hill ranges on both main islands, the highest points being Mount Usborne on East Falkland (705m) and Mount Adam on West Falkland (700m).

Hemisphere

Southern

Climate

Temperatures range from minus 6–21 degrees Celsius (C) with occasional lows of minus 10 degrees C and highs of 25 degrees C. Rainfall is around 700mm per year. Strong to gale-force winds are frequent during spring and early summer.

Entry requirements

Passports

Valid passports required by all, valid for three months.

Visa

Not required by nationals of EU/EEA countries, North America, Australasia and other commonwealth countries, Argentina, Chile, Brazil, Uruguay, Japan, Hong Kong, South Korea, Israel, Andorra, Liechtenstein, San Marino and Vatican City. For further confirmation and exceptions contact the Travel Co-ordinator in London (+44-(0)207-222-2542). Booking forms for the flight from the UK include details and purpose of visit and are required to be completed before or on arrival. All visitors are required to have a return ticket, accommodation and sufficient funds.

Currency advice/regulations

There are no restrictions on the import and export of local or foreign currency. The Falkland Islands has its own currency which is equivalent to UK sterling. The notes and coins cannot easily be exchanged for sterling or other currencies outside the Islands. Sterling is freely used on the islands and dollars are accepted.

Customs

200 cigarettes, 50 cigars, 100 cigarillos or 250 grams of tobacco; one litre of alcohol, two litres of wine; and 10 litres of beer or cider.

Import licences are required for plants, foodstuffs and firearms.

Prohibited imports

Uncooked or cured meat and plants are only allowed in under licence. Livestock is allowed on any in-coming aircraft.

Health (for visitors)

Mandatory precautions

None

Advisable precautions

Yellow fever vaccination in case of any stopover in Africa en route.

Radiation alerts are issued with local weather forecasts when the ozone hole stretches over the islands. Precautions against skin cancer should be taken with high factor suncream and clothing protection.

Credit cards

Credit cards are generally accepted at hotels and retail outlets.

Public holidays (national)

Fixed dates

1 Jan (New Year's Day), 21 Apr (Queen's Birthday), 14 Jun (Liberation Day), 8 Aug (Battle Day), 25 Dec (Christmas Day), 26 Dec (Boxing Day), 28–29 Dec (Stanley Races).

Variable dates

Good Friday, Peat Cutting Day (first Mon in Oct).

Working hours

Business

Mon- Fri: 0800-1200. 1300-1700.

Government

Mon–Fri: 0800–1200, 1300-1630.

Shops

Mon-Fri: 0900-1200, 1300-2000.

Telecommunications

Telephone/fax

Direct satellite telephone and telefax links are in operation throughout the Islands.

Postal services

A new post code for the islands has been issued through the Universal Postal Union: FIQQ 1ZZ.

Electricity supply

Voltage and plugs for electrical appliances are the same as in the UK, 240V 50Hz.

Getting there

Air

Flights to the Falkland Islands depart from RAF Brize Norton, Oxfordshire, UK, six or seven times per month. For information, contact a travel agent or the Falklands Islands Government office in London (tel: +44 (0)207-222-2542). LanChile operate weekly flights from Santiago via Puerto Montt and Punta Arenas. Details from any travel agent or from International Tours and Travel in Stanley (tel +500-22041; fax +500-22042).

Air Seychelles are contracted by the brokers to run the Brize Norton flights from 24 January–30 September 2010.

International airport/s: Mount Pleasant International Airport (MPN); 56km from Stanley.

Other airport/s: Stanley Airport

Airport tax: Embarkation tax of £22 per passenger (applicable departure flights only).
Surface
Water: Cruise ships stop in at Stanley.
Main port/s: Stanley.

Getting about
National transport
Air: Depending on bookings and weather conditions, the Falkland Islands Government Air Service (FIGAS) operates daily services to the majority of settlements with a fleet of eight-passenger Britten-Norman Islander aircraft.
Road: There is a limited amount of surfaced road mainly around Stanley and Mount Pleasant. Gravel roads are a common feature.
Water: There is an inter-island ferry service between East and West Falkland.
City transport
Taxis: There is a limited taxi service in Stanley and at the airport, provided by Stanley and Lowes Taxis (tel: (+500) 21381) and Cindy Cars (tel: (+500) 22123).
Buses, trams & metro: There is a bus service from the airport to Stanley, operated by Falkland Islands Tours & Travel (+500-21775).
Car hire
4X4 vehicles can be rented from Falkland Islands Company Ltd, Crozier Place, Stanley (tel: (+500) 27678).

BUSINESS DIRECTORY

The addresses listed below are a selection only. While World of Information makes every endeavour to check these addresses, we cannot guarantee that changes have not been made, especially to telephone numbers and area codes. We would welcome any corrections.

Telephone area codes
The international dialling code (IDD) for the Falkland Islands is +500 followed by subscriber's number.

Chambers of Commerce
Falkland Islands Chamber of Commerce, PO Box 378, West Hillside, Stanley (tel: 22-264; fax: 22-265; e-mail: commerce@horizon.co.fk).

Banking
Standard Chartered Bank, Box 166, Ross Road, Stanley (tel: 27-220; fax: 27-219); UK contact (tel: +44(0) 20-7280-7500).

Travel information
Falkland Islands Company Travel Services, Stanley (tel: 27-633; fax: 27-603).

Falkland Islands Government Air Service (FIGAS), c/o Falkland Islands Government, Stanley Airport (tel: 27-219; fax: 27-309; e-mail: figas@horizon.co.fk).

Falkland Islands Tourist Board, London, UK (e-mail: manager@tourism.org.fk) issues an accommodation guide.

Falkland Islands Tours & Travel (tel: 21-775; e-mail: astewart@horizon.co.fk).

RAF Brize Norton, Oxfordshire, UK (tel: +44 (0)1993-897-366).

Travel Co-ordinator, Falkland Islands Government Office, Falkland House, 14 Broadway, Westminister, London SW1H 0BH, UK (tel: (+44 -20) 7222-2542; fax: (+44-20) 7222-2375; e-mail: travel@figo.u-net.com).

National tourist organisation offices
Falkland Islands Tourist Board (FITB), Shackleton House, Stanley (tel: 22-215; fax: 22-619; e-mail: jettycentre@horizon.co.fk; internet site: www.falklandislands.com).

Ministries
Chief Executive, Thatcher Drive, Stanley (tel: 27-110; fax: 27-109).

Department of Agriculture and Mineral Resources, Stanley (tel: 27-355; fax: 27-352).

Department of Civil Aviation, Stanley Airport (tel: 27-300; fax: 27-302).

Department of Education, 23 Ross Road, Stanley (tel/fax: 27-292).

Department of Fisheries, PO Box 598, Stanley (tel: 27-260; fax: 27-265).

Department of Oil, Ross Road, Stanley (tel: 27-322; fax: 27-321).

Department of Public Works, Stanley (tel: 27-193; fax: 27-191).

Governor's Office, Government House, Stanley (tel: 27-433; e-mail: gov.house@horizon.co.fk).

Treasury, Falkland Islands Government, Thatcher Drive, Stanley (tel: 27-143; fax: 27-144).

UK Government Office, Falkland House, 14 Broadway, Westminster, London SW1H 0BH, UK (tel: +44 (0)20-7222-2542; fax: +44 0)20-7222-2375; e-mail: rep@figo.u-net.com).

Other useful addresses
Attorney General, PO Box 143, Stanley (tel: 27-273/4; fax: 27-276).

British Geological Survey, Petroleum Geology Group, Murchison House, West Mains Rd, Edinburgh, EH9 3LA (tel: +44(0)131 667-1000; fax: +44 (0)131 668-4930).

Cable & Wireless, Stanley (tel: 20-800; fax 22-206).

Customs & Immigration, Stanley (tel: 27-340; fax: 27-342).

Falkland Islands Development Corporation, Stanley (tel: 27-211; fax: 27-210).

Falklands Islands Co Ltd (FIC), Crozier Place, Stanley (tel: 27-600; fax: 27-603).

Medical Services/King Edward VII Memorial Hospital, Stanley (tel: 27-415; fax: 27-416).

Meteorological Office, RAF Mount Pleasant (tel: 73-557).

Overseas Territories Department, Foreign & Commonwealth Office, King Charles St, London SW1A 2AH (tel: +44(0)20-7270-3000; fax: (0)20-7270-2086).

The United Kingdom Falkland Islands Trust (administers the Shackleton Scholarship fund), c/o 14 Broadway, Westminster, London SW1H 0BH, UK (tel: +44 (0)20-7222-2542; fax: +44 (0)20-7222-2375).

Internet sites
Falkland Islands Government: http://www.falklands.gov.fk

Falkland Islands information: http://www.falklands-malvinas.com/

Falkland Islands web portal: http:/www.falklandislands.com

Falkland Islands News Network: http://www.sartma.com

United Kingdom Falkland Islands Trust: www.ukfit.org.uk

Faroe Islands

KEY FACTS

Official name: Føroyar (Faroe Islands)

Head of State: Queen Margrethe II of Denmark, represented by the High Commissioner Dan M Knudsen (from 1 Jan 2008)

Head of government: Prime Minister Kaj Leo Johannesen (SF) (from 26 Sep 2008)

Ruling party: Coalition led by the Sambandsflokkurin (SF) (Union Party), with the Fólkaflokkurin (FF) (People's Party) and the Javnaðarflokkurin (JF) (Social Democrats) (from 19 Jan 2008)

Area: 1,399 square km (18 islands)

Population: 49,000 (2010)

Capital: Tórshavn

Official language: Faroese, Danish

Currency: Faroese krone (FKr) (same value as Danish krone)

Exchange rate: FKr5.55 per US$ (Oct 2011)

Labour force: 29,430 (2008)

COUNTRY PROFILE

Historical profile

The first Norse settlers arrived in the Faroes from neighbouring Denmark and the Orkneys in the ninth century.

1380 Early administration was undertaken by a parliamentary body known as the Alting. The end of parliamentary procedures saw the Alting renamed the Løgting and becoming a royal court.

1397 The Faroes become a Danish province, with the political merger of Norway and Denmark into the Kalmar Union.

1849 The first Danish constitution included the Faroe Islands, administered under the Danish county Roskilde.

1939–45 The Faroe Islands were occupied by the British during the Second World War, although they remained largely self-governing. With continuous war work the economy improved steadily and was sustained.

1946 The Faroe Islands returned to Danish control. In a referendum, a very small majority voted in favour of becoming an independent state. Negotiations and diplomacy led to a home rule arrangement instead.

1948 The Home Rule Act made the Faroes security, foreign and economic affairs the responsibility of Denmark.

1998 Anfinn Kallsberg replaced Edmund Joensen as prime minister. Offshore oil prospecting began.

2001 A referendum to be held for approval of legislative amendments to enable a gradual winding-down of Denmark's authority on the islands was shelved after Denmark's Prime Minister Poul Nyrup Rasmussen said that subsidies would stop after four years if the islanders voted for independence.

2004 Jóannes Eidesgaard (JF) became prime minister, leading a coalition of the SF, the Javnaðarflokkurin (JF) (Social Democrats) and the Fólkaflokkurin (FF) (People's Party).

2006 A trust fund agreement was signed with the World Bank, whereby the Faroe Islands provides development collaboration with the Pacific island of Palau. Iceland and the Faroe Islands signed a special economic treaty granting many free trade arrangements for goods, services, capital and workers.

2008 In parliamentary elections, the Tjóðveldisflokkurin (TF) (Republican Party) won 23.3 per cent of the vote (8 seats out of 33), the Sambandsflokkurin (SF) (Union Party) 21 per cent (seven), the FF 20.1 per cent (seven), the JF 19.4 per cent (six), the Mioflokkurin (MF) (Centre Party) 8.4 per cent (three), and the Sjálvstýrisflokkurin (Home Rule Party) 7.2 per cent (two). Turnout was 89.2 per cent. Jóannes Eidesgaard remained as prime minister until the coalition collapsed and Kaj Leo Johannesen (SF) took over.

2009 Plans for an Arctic military force were announced by Denmark, with a base in the Faroe Islands, to protect Danish activities as the ice cap melts and opens up access to the polar region.

2010 In July, an association of five interested parties (including Faroe Petroleum) began deep sea oil prospecting in the Atlantic margin offshore, in Faroe Islands' territorial waters.

2011 A new licensing open-door policy was introduced by the government that allows any prospector to search for oil and gas without a pre-arranged contract under license.

Political structure

Constitution

The Faroe Islands were administered as a Danish county until they achieved home rule in 1948. The Faroe Islands are a Danish external territory, electing two members to the Danish parliament, which maintains responsibility for constitutional, foreign and defence matters. A High Commissioner represents the Danish government and advises on joint affairs.

Form of state

Parliamentary democratic dependency

National legislature

Internal affairs are under the legislative control of the Løgting (parliament) which has 33 members. New elections laws were introduced in 2008 under which the Faroe Islands is comprised of one constituency with a fixed number of members, elected for up to four years. Universal suffrage is 18 years.

The Landsstyri (a government of nine members) is formed, based on the strength of the parties in the Løgting. The Løgmadur (prime minister) has to ratify all Løgting laws.

All Danish legislation must be submitted to the Landsstyri before becoming law.

Last elections

19 January 2008 (parliamentary)

Results: Parliamentary: the Tjóðveldisflokkurin (TF) (Republican Party) won 23.3 per cent of the vote (eight seats out of 33), the Sambandsflokkurin (SF) (Union Party) 21 per cent (seven), the Fólkaflokkurin (FF) (People's Party) 20.1 per cent (seven), the Javnaðarflokkurin (JF) (Social Democrats) 19.4 per cent (six), the Mioflokkurin (MF) (Centre Party) 8.4 per cent (three), and the Sjálvstýrisflokkurin (Home Rule Party) 7.2 per cent (two). Turnout was 89.2 per cent.

Next elections

January 2012 (parliamentary)

Political parties

Ruling party

Coalition led by the Sambandsflokkurin (SF) (Union Party), with the Fólkaflokkurin (FF) (People's Party) and the Javnaðarflokkurin (JF) (Social Democrats) (from 19 Jan 2008)

Main opposition party

Tjóðveldisflokkurin (TF) (Republican Party)

Political situation

The rise in importance of oil exploration has grown in the 2000s. The independent energy company, Faroe Petroleum, was awarded rights to explore for oil and gas in regions between Scotland and the Faroe Islands, and subsequently found oil. In 2010 it bought a significant stake in the North Sea oilfield, for over US$100 million, as well as exploration sites elsewhere. Oil was also discovered by Cairn Energy in Faroe waters in 2010.

In July 2009, the Danish government announced plans to set up a permanent military presence in the Arctic and establish a regional joint service command in the Faroe Islands. Untapped natural oil and gas reserves under the melting Arctic ice could spark a scramble by all countries with a claim to the region.

Population

49,000 (2010)

Last census: July 2002: 47,350

Population density: 33 inhabitants per sq km (2000).

Annual growth rate: 1.2 per cent (2003)

Ethnic make-up

Scandinavian

Religions

Evangelical Lutheran Church of Denmark (85 per cent). The Faroe Islands are a diocese under the Danish national church. Of the various smaller religious communities the largest is the Plymouth Brethren.

Health

Life expectancy: 79 years (estimate 2003)

Fertility rate/Maternal mortality rate: Two births per woman (2003)

Birth rate/Death rate: 14 births per 1,000 population; nine deaths per 1,000 population (2003).

Child (under 5 years) mortality rate (per 1,000): Seven per 1,000 live births (2003)

Main cities

Tórshavn (Thorshavn), on the island of Streymoy (capital, estimated population 18,573 in 2005), Klaksvík (4,722).

Languages spoken

Faroese (derived from Old Norse) and Danish. Icelandic, English, Norwegian and Swedish are also widely spoken and understood.

Official language/s

Faroese, Danish

Media

Press

In Faroese, the only newspapers are published daily, including *Sosialurin* (www.sosialurin.fo), *Dimmalætting* (www.dimma.fo) and *Vikublaðið* (www.vikublad.fo).

Broadcasting

The national, public broadcasting company is Kringvarp Føroya (www.uf.fo).

Radio: The public network Útvarp Føroya (ÚF) and three other stations broadcast on several frequencies to provide national radio coverage. Rás (www.ras2.fo), Linden Kristligt Kringvarp (www.lindin.fo) a Christian broadcast, and Sundfelli broadcast in Faroese.

Television: The public network Sjónvarp Føroya (Svf) (www.svf.fo) provides between eight hours (weekdays) up to 15 hours (weekend) with local news and information and imported, dubbed, foreign entertainment programmes.

Advertising

Print material, outdoor and television attract most advertising revenues. There is no advertising on radio, and poster sites are heavily regulated.

Economy

The economy is heavily dependent on fishing and processed fish and is sensitive to the international market in fish. As a result the economy can fluctuate significantly between years and this can affect the rest of the economy significantly. The central bank of the Faroe Islands stated in 2009 that fish products accounted for about 95 per cent of the total exports. The total fish catch in 2008 was 521,306 tonnes, down from 582,000 tonnes in 2007. The fall in catches was also reflected in an overall fall in value of the catches. Fish farming has, since the 1980s, grown into the second largest export industry. Employment in the fishing industry is less than 16 per cent; employment in public administration and services accounts for 35 per cent of the workforce, while other service sector employment accounts for another 33 per cent. Unemployment in mid-2008 was less than 1.5 per cent; however the rate had grown to 4.4 per cent by the third quarter of 2009, due in large part to a fall in global trading.

GDP growth was 0.0 per cent in 2008 and was forecast to fall to about -3.3 per cent in 2009, before reviving in 2010 to around 3 per cent. These results followed two years of high GDP growth, which were due to an increase in credit-finance, private consumption and investment growth; all of which were cut by the global economic crisis in 2008.

Oil business activities have also improved the economic situation. In July 2010, deep sea oil prospecting began in the Atlantic margin offshore the Faroe Islands' territorial waters, by an association of five parties (including Faroe Petroleum).

The tourism industry is small and not only dependent on external factors but subject to the domestic infrastructure schemes necessary to provide service-based tourism.

External trade

As an autonomous overseas territory of Denmark the Faroe Islands negotiates it own bilateral trade agreements. It has executive and legislative powers over marine resources and trade relations. It is also a separate customs territory from Denmark and the EU.

Foreign trade is mainly with other EU countries, which provides around 58 per cent of imports, mainly consumer goods and raw materials. However the single largest import product is petroleum and its derivatives. Around 95 per cent of exports are destined for the EU. Of total exports over 80 per cent are fish and their products, of which Atlantic salmon accounts for the bulk at around 23 per cent, followed by cod at around 17 per cent and saithe (coalfish) at around 14 per cent. Processed fish is typically frozen for export, but also includes traditional salted and smoked fish, destined specifically for Danish and other Scandinavian markets.

Imports

Petroleum, machinery and vehicles, consumer goods, raw materials and semi-manufactures, foodstuffs and agricultural products.

Main sources: Denmark (typically 32 per cent of total), Norway (21 per cent), Germany (8 per cent).

Exports

Fish and fish products (over 80 per cent), postage stamps and fishing vessels.

Main destinations: UK (typically 20 per cent of total), Norway (16 per cent), Denmark (12 per cent).

Agriculture

Farming

Sheep-rearing is an important activity on the Faroe Islands. There are 70,000 sheep ranging free on the islands, providing meat and wool for the use of the inhabitants. Cattle are also kept for milk and meat. The islands have to import meat and other agricultural products, but have become self-sufficient in milk. Increasing co-operation among agricultural organisations has been fostered to make the islands as self-sufficient as possble. Potatoes are grown and also hay for the cows reared for milk production.

Fishing

Fishing is the dominant economic activity, acounting for 97 per cent of exports. The main fish stocks are cod, haddock and coalfish. Annual fish catches in excess of 600,000 tonnes have been the basis of sustained growth. The rising global price of fish has also contributed to the industry's profits as well as the investment in salmon and trout sea farming. Nevertheless, the business is highly vulnerable to fluctuations in not only world prices but also in amounts caught.

Industry and manufacturing

Most industrial activities are connected to the fishing sector. They include processing plants and shipyards, as well as the making of nets, ropes, etc. Small industries include breweries, building components, fibreglass boats, computer software, food and milk products, tinned fish and spun and wollen goods.

Tourism

The isolation of the islands limits the potential for tourism. Even so tourism is the second largest industry in the economy, and has developed since the 1990s. Greenland, Iceland and Faroe Islands have combined in an initiative to promote new tourism activities, with short and long-term stays at selected destinations combined with conferences, cruises and themed holidays.

Hydrocarbons

There is a possibility of offshore oil between the Faroe and Shetland Islands but by 2008 any finds were deemed uneconomical to develop.

The Faroe Islands relies on imported petroleum products. It does not currently produce or import gas and coal.

Energy

Installed generating capacity was 836MW in 2005, of which imported oil and petrol accounts for 90 per cent of energy demand. The total energy production mix is 30–40 per cent hydro- and wind-power and the remainder through diesel generation.

SEV, the Faroese electricity company, joined in partnership with Voith Siemens to produce a new SeWave, 1MW electricity generator, fuelled by wave power, which began operation in 2007 in Nípan on Vágar; it supplies 1 million kilowatt hour per annum. The installation site of another SeWave has been identified at Søltuvík on Sandoy.

Banking and insurance

Monetary policy and administration is headed by the Danish central bank (Danmarks Nationalbank).

When the banking crisis began in 1992, there were two big banks, one small private bank and savings banks in the Faroe Islands. One of the big banks was owned by Den Danske Bank. By the end of the crisis, the small bank had gone into bankruptcy, the two big banks had merged and were taken over by the Home Rule authorities and the savings banks were still in business. The savings banks and the merged bank function as banks under the same law.

Central bank

Danmarks Nationalbank

Time

GMT (daylight saving, end-March to end-September, GMT plus one hour).

Geography

The Faroe Islands are a group of 18 islands (of which 17 are inhabited) in the North Atlantic Ocean, south-east of Iceland and north-west of the north coast of Scotland. The main island is Streymoy and nowhere on the archipelago is over 3km from the sea. The islands are rocky with little opportunity for growing crops or forestry, although grass is plentiful.

Hemisphere

Northern

Climate

Mild winters and cool summers; usually overcast; can be foggy and windy.

Entry requirements

Passports

Required by all.

Visa

Even though a Danish territory, visas for Denmark are not valid for the Faroe Islands unless specified on the permit. For a business visa, an original letter of invitation from a local company or organisation, giving details about purpose of visit and duration of stay must accompany an application, along with evidence of hotel reservations.

Health (for visitors)

As for Denmark.

Advisable precautions

Without appropriate clothing for the climate hypothermia is a hazard.

Public holidays (national)

Fixed dates

1 Jan (New Year's Day), Apr 25 (Flag Day, afternoon only), 5 Jun (Constitution Day), 28 Jul (St Olav's Eve, afternoon only), 29 Jul (St Olav's Day), 24–26 Dec (Christmas Holiday), 31 Dec (New Year's Eve).

Variable dates

Maundy Thursday, Good Friday, Easter Monday, Prayer Day (Apr/May), Ascension Day, Whit Monday.

Working hours

Banking

Mon–Fri: 0930–1600 (Thu 0930–1800).

Business

Mon–Fri: 0800–1600 or 0830–1630.

Government

Mon–Fri: generally 0900–1700.

Shops

Mon–Fri: 0800–1700 or 0900–1730, Sat: close at 1300 or 1400.

Telecommunications

Mobile/cell phones

GSM 900 services cover virtually the entire territories.

Getting there

Air

National airline: Atlantic Airways has regular flights to Denmark, Norway, Iceland, Scotland, England and Greenland.

International airport/s: Vágar Airport (FAE) on the island of Vágar, located near the town of Sørvágur, a ferry links the island to Streymoy. Facilities include bank, restaurant, bar and shops.

BUSINESS DIRECTORY

The addresses listed below are a selection only. While World of Information makes every endeavour to check these addresses, we cannot guarantee that changes have not been made, especially to telephone numbers and area codes. We would welcome any corrections.

Telephone area codes

The international direct dialling (IDD) for the Faroe Islands is +298. There are no area codes.

Useful telephone numbers

Emergency services 000

Chambers of Commerce

Faroe Islands Trade Council, 12 Bryggjubakki, PO Box 259, Tórshavn 110 (tel: 353-100; fax: 353-101; e-mail: trade@trade.fo).

Banking

Central bank

Landsbanki Føroya, Müllers hús, í Gongini, PO Box 229, Tórshavn 110 (tel: 318-305; fax: 318-537; e-mail: landsbank@landsbank.fo).

Danmarks Nationalbank, Havnegade 5, DK-1093 Copenhagen (tel: (+45) 3363-6363; fax: (+45) 3363-7103; e-mail: info@nationalbanken.dk).

Travel information

Atlantic Airways, Vagar Airport, FR-380 (tel: 333-700; fax: 333-380).

Maersk Air, Aarvegur 6, PO Box 3225, FO-110 Tórshavn (tel: 333-700; fax: 318-670; e-mail: ff@olivant.fo).

Smyril Line, Jonas Broncksgota 37, PO Box 370, FO-110 Tórshavn (tel: 315-900; fax: 315-707; e-mail: office@smyril-line.fo).

Air Iceland, Vagar Airport, FO-380 Sorvagur (tel: 332-755; fax: 332-280).

The Faroe Islands Tourist Board Copenhagen, Hovedvagtsgade 8, 2, DK-1103 Copenhagen K, Denmark (tel: (+45) 3314-8383; fax: (+45) 3393-8575).

Faroe Travel, PO Box 1199, FO-110 Tórshavn (tel: 312-600; fax: 319-200).

National tourist organisation offices

Faroe Islands Tourist Board, Undir Bryggjubakka 17, PO Box 118, FO-110 Torshaven, (tel: 355-800; fax: 355-801; email: tourist@tourist.fo; internet site; www.tourist.fo).

Other useful addresses

British Consulate, Yviri vid Strond 19, PO Box 19, FR-3800 Tórshavn (tel: 313-510).

The Faroese Government, PO Box 64, FR-110 Tórshavn (fax: 314-942).

Faroese Press Agency, P/f Salvará, Tjarnardeild 12, Tórshavn.

Sjónvarp Føroya (television broadcasting), PO Box 21, FR-3800 Tórshavn (tel: 317-780).

Útvarp Føroya (general broadcasting), PO Box 328, FR-3800 Tórshavn (tel: 316-566).

Internet sites

Danish embassy with useful information on the Faroes: www.denmarkemb.org

Faroe business news: www.news.fo

Faroe Islands general site: www.faroe.com

Faroe Islands tourist site: www.faroeislands.com

Fiji

In January 2011, the 92 year old, former president, Josefa Iloilovatu Uluivuda (commonly known as Ratu Josefa Iloilo) and ally of current Prime Minister Frank Bainimarama, died. While in office in 2007, President Iloilo had overseen the repeal of the constitution, excluded the four major political parties from the political discussions on the future of Fiji and suspended, then sacked, the entire judiciary.

I have a plan

Prime Minister Frank Bainimarama has stayed resolute in the face of international condemnation and censure. He claimed that, according to the *People's Charter for Change, Peace and Progress; the Roadmap for Democracy and Sustainable Socio-Economic Development 2009–14; and the Strategic Framework for Change*, parliamentary elections would be held in 2014. He has stayed true to this date, despite sanctions against Fiji, himself and other senior members of the ruling regime (as well as, on one occasion, following New Zealand's decision to deny him a student visa, Bainimarama's son). However, while he refers all-comers to the plan – devised without the input of all political parties, nor the Methodist Church (the largest religious group in Fiji) – the ex-Army Chief of Staff and son of former president Sir Kamisese Mara, Tevita Mara declared that Bainimarima has no intention of holding parliamentary elections in 2014 as promised.

Friends at your back

Lieutenant Colonel Tevita Mara was appointed as Army Chief of Staff, the fourth highest in the Fijian military hierarchy, on 3 February 2011, but by May he had been accused of mutiny following his call for regime change. From then on he was a hunted man and had to leave Fiji by devious means on 9 May, ending up in Tonga, with the help of the Tongan navy that claimed it had 'rescued' Mara at sea. From Tonga he travelled to Australia and New Zealand and despite Fiji's attempt to extradite him he remains in exile – a critical voice Fiji is unable to silence.

The economy

The three mainstays of the economy in 2011 were tourism, mining and fishing, while the service sector in general suffered along with agriculture, which had to deal with the aftermath of the cyclone that struck in March 2010, causing severe flooding in Fiji's northern islands. Ironically, this was followed by a drought, which lowered harvest yields even further.

Tourism

The economy has been kept alive by the growth in tourism, with visitor arrivals increasing by 16.5 per cent in 2010, to a record 633,000 tourists. The majority of visitor came from Australia, followed by China and India. However as the Fijian dollar was devalued in 2009, coupled with price discounting, the overall growth in tourism earnings only kept pace with tourist arrivals. In 2011, discounting of holidays continued.

Gold

Between 2007–11 the global price of gold trebled, and the production of the Vatukoula mine of 59,000 grams was a year-on-year (August 2009–2010) rise of almost 80 per cent. Production is expected to reach an annual rate of 100,000 grams in 2011.

Prospects

The Asia Development Bank stated in its 2011 report of Fiji that the economy was confined to a low-growth path due to its weakness in investment, with both public and private investment estimated to have fallen by 14 per cent of GDP in 2010 (down from an average of 18 per cent ovee 2000–05). Private investment was estimated to be as low as 3 per cent of GDP.

Without the promised elections being deemed free and fair, there will be no return of significant donor assistance for infrastructure and other projects. Without this Fiji's economic prospects will remain poor. Internally, investors are concerned about a raft of regulations that appear opaque and subject to change without consultation.

KEY FACTS

Official name: Republic of the Fiji Islands

Head of State: President Ratu Epeli Nailatikau (took office 5 Nov 2009)

Head of government: Head of government: Prime Minister (interim) Commodore Voreqe 'Frank' Bainimarama (from 2007; re-appointed 13 April 2009)

Ruling party: Interim military government (from 2007; re-appointed 13 April 2009)

Area: 18,333 square km (about 332 islands, 110 inhabited)

Population: 861,000 (2010)

Capital: Suva (on Viti Levu)

Official language: English, Fijian and Hindi

Currency: Fijian dollar (F$) = 100 cents

Exchange rate: F$1.84 per US$ (Oct 2011)

GDP per capita: US$3,518 (2010)

GDP real growth: 0.10% (2010)

GDP: US$3.10 billion (2010)

Inflation: 5.40% (2010)

Balance of trade: -US$674.90 million (2009)

Visitor numbers: 116 (2010)

On 7 January 2012, Prime Minister Frank Bainimarama lifted the public emergency regulations that had been in force since April 2009 and which restricted so much of civil society. However, this was the day after new public order decrees had been issued to replace the emergency power, limiting political opposition and with continued detention for up to 14 days as directed by the commissioner of police. The 6 January public order decrees had also includes the creation of a media council with powers to ensure the government's control over what was published. It seems that Bainimarama may be positioning the country for those promised elections, but only on his terms and critics and the economy will have to trail along behind him.

Risk assessment

Economic	Poor
Political	Poor
Regional stability	Good

COUNTRY PROFILE

Historical profile

1643 The islands were first sighted by a European.
1874 Fiji became a British crown colony.
1879–1916 Over 60,000 Indian indentured labourers were imported to work on sugar plantations. The government in India stopped the recruitment of labourers.
1920 All indenture labour agreements were ended.
1963 General elections were held with the first majority Indian-led political party standing. The great council of chiefs signed the *Wakaya Letter* that asserted Fijian paramountcy.
1966 The Fijian Alliance Party was formed.
1968 Ratu Sir Kamisese Mara, Fiji's first prime minister was given the first instruments of independence. The Fijian Alliance Party won elections by appealing to both Indians and Fijians.
1970 On 10 October Fiji became independent and introduced a British-style political system with a new constitution. The British monarch remained Head of State, a bicameral parliament was introduced and a separate electoral roll for each ethnic group was provided.
1972 The first independent general elections were won by Ratu Mara's Fijian Alliance Party.
1977 Internal dispute between the leaders of the (ethnic Indian) National Federation Party (NFP), which had won a majority in the lower house of parliament elections resulted in a failure to form a government and Ratu Mara was recalled to power. The Fijian Alliance Party had won a majority in the upper house of parliament.
1981 The ethnic Fijian Western United Front political party was formed.
1985 The Fijian Labour Party (FLP) was formed, led by Timoci Bavadra.
1987 The NFP-FLP won the general elections and formed the first Indian-dominated government, led by Timoci Bavadra. The Alliance Party became defunct. Lieutenant Colonel Sitiveni Rabuka led two coups that overthrew the government as a republic was declared and all ties to the British monarch severed. Fiji was expelled from the British Commonwealth and overseas aid was suspended.
1990 A new constitution was promulgated and considered by foreign observers as racist, as it enshrined the supremacy of ethnic Fijians by allocating 37 seats to Fijians, 27 seats to Indians and 6 to others in the lower house of parliament.
1992 The Soqosoqo Duavata ni Lewenivanua (SDL) (Fijian People's Party), led by Rabuka won general elections. Rabuka became prime minister.
1994 The great council of chiefs appoint Ratu Sir Kamisese Mara as president.
1995 The president appoints a team to review the 1990 constitution.
1997 After three years of discussion a new non-discriminatory constitution was enacted. Fiji was re-admitted to the Commonwealth.
1999 The FLP won general elections and formed a coalition government with the Christian Democratic Alliance, Party of National Unity and the Fijian Association Party. Mahendra Chaudhry, the first Fijian of Indian descent, became prime minister. President Ratu Sir Kamisese Mara was sworn in for a five-year term.
2000 In a coup, led by George Speight, Chaudhry and his cabinet were held captive by an armed group seeking more power for ethnic Fijians and forced to resign from office. The great council of chiefs ordered President Mara to sack the government. Supporters of Speight rioted in Suva while he called for the 1997 constitution to be scrapped. The Commonwealth suspended Fiji's membership. All the hostages were freed as Commodore Frank Bainimarama seized power and restored order. President Mara retired from office and the great council of chiefs appointed the father-in-law of Speight, Josefa Iloilovatu Uluivuda (commonly known as Ratu Josefa Iloilo) as president. Laisenia Qarase was appointed prime minister of an all-Fijian interim government. The High Court ruled that the deposed government of Mahendra Chaudhry should be reinstated.
2001 The Court of Appeal ruled that the interim government was illegal, and stated that the 1997 multi-racial constitution should remain in place. President Iloilo was re-appointed by the great council of chiefs for a five-year term; he re-appointed Laisenia Qarase as caretaker prime minister. In general election, observed by the Commonwealth, Qarase's SDL won, but since it failed to secure an outright majority, it joined with the Matanitu Vanua (MV) (Conservative Alliance Party) in a coalition government. Qarase was sworn in as prime minister; his cabinet barred all ethnic Indians.
2002 Samisoni Speight Tikonasau, the brother of George Speight, was elected to parliament, reflecting the extent of

KEY INDICATORS — Fiji

	Unit	2006	2007	2008	2009	2010
Population	m	0.86	0.87	0.87	0.88	*0.88
Gross domestic product (GDP)	US$bn	3.17	3.41	3.60	3.10	3.10
GDP per capita	US$	3,674	3,882	4,095	3,464	3,518
GDP real growth	%	3.6	-6.6	-0.1	-2.5	0.1
Inflation	%	2.5	4.8	7.8	3.7	5.4
Exports (fob) (goods)	US$m	711.0	1,210.1	871.7	625.9	–
Imports (fob) (goods)	US$m	1,802.0	2,890.4	2,055.8	1,300.9	–
Balance of trade	US$m	-1,091.0	-1,680.4	-1,184.1	-674.9	–
Current account	US$m	-552.0	-586.0	-638.0	-238.2	-222.0
Total reserves minus gold	US$m	312.8	527.6	321.5	569.1	719.4
Foreign exchange	US$m	492.7	492.7	286.6	438.9	615.7
Tourist numbers	'000	100.6	99.0	107.3	99.5	116.0
Exchange rate	per US$	1.66	1.55	1.59	1.95	1.92

* estimated figure

George Speight's support among the voting public.
2003 A cyclone destroyed homes and flooded wide areas of the north and east of the country. The High Court ruled that the FLP should be allowed its seats in the cabinet.
2004 Ratu Sir Kamisese Mara died. The FLP declined a government role in favour of official opposition duties.
2006 Prime Minister Qarase agreed to review the *Reconciliation, Tolerance and Unity Bill*. President Ratu Uluivuda was re-appointed. The MV agreed to dissolve as a party and its members to merge with the ruling SDL, after it changed its stance on working to free its party members convicted of coup related offences. The ruling SDL won 36 out of 71 seats in the general elections and the FLP won 31 seats. The FLP entered into coalition with the SDL. In a bloodless, military *coup d'état* led by Commodore 'Frank' Josaia Voreqe Bainimarama, the president and government were dismissed. Bainimarama assumed the presidency and Jona Senilagakali Baravilala was appointed as the interim prime minister. Fiji was suspended from the Commonwealth.
2007 Under pressure from the great council of chiefs, Bainimarama reinstated Ratu Josefa Iloilo Uluivuda (commonly referred to a Ratu Josefa Iloilo) as president and Bainimarama became interim prime minister. Bainimarama announced that parliamentary elections would be held in 2010. Bainimarama dismissed the great council of chiefs, which refused to endorse his government and proposed his own vice president. A six-month long state of emergency was finally lifted following two failed coup attempts; public gatherings and restrictions on the media were not lifted.
2008 Bainimarama convened a great council of chiefs with himself as chairman. Fiji withdrew its participation in the Pacific Islands Forum – Joint Working Group on Fiji, leading to fears that the parliamentary elections would not go ahead. A political row between New Zealand and Fiji resulted in each country expelling the other's diplomats, following New Zealand's decision to deny a student visa to the son of interim Prime Minister Bainimarama. Bainimarama delayed democratic elections until reforms to what he considered 'racist' election laws are undertaken.
2009 Growing opposition to the government of Bainimarama came from leaders of the Pacific Forum in January, who said that he must hold general elections as promised. The former prime minister, Laisenia Qarase, reported during a tour of Australia in February that his life was in danger from the Bainimarama administration. He had been told by the administration that in future he would be denied an exit visa. A former vice president, Ratu Joni Madraiwiwi, criticised the government in February for being complacent and failing to address the country's problems. The Samoa prime minister, Tuilaepa Sailele Malielegaoi, accused Bainimarama of lying to the Pacific Forum about Fiji's political future and its return to democracy and urged Fijians to reclaim their government. In reply Bainimarama said Sailele had 'acted unprofessionally and unbecomingly' by criticising another country's leader. The International Bar Association voiced concern in March about the influence the military backed interim government had on the judiciary, as the rule of law had steadily deteriorated since 2006. In March, Bainimarama rejected demands for general elections, which followed the Commonwealth's threat to suspend Fiji's membership from September if elections were not carried out. Leaders of two opposition parties were denied invitations to the crucial agenda-setting meeting, set for 13 March, to discuss the course back to parliamentary democracy. Details of the 2007 census were released in March, which showed the percentage of Indo-Fijians had fallen from 51 per cent in 1966 to 37.5 per cent and is expected to fall further due to a steady stream of emigration. On 9 April the Court of Appeal found the interim government of Commodore Frank Bainimarama, appointed after the military *coup d'état* in 2006, to be illegal. President Ratu Josefa Iloilo repealed the 1997 constitution, became Head of State and sacked the judiciary and postponed elections until 2014. The four major political parties were excluded from the political process. The former military government was re-installed on 13 April, with Bainimarama as prime minister. The UN Security Council condemned the repeal of the constitution and called for an early general election. Fiji was suspended from the Pacific Islands Forum on 2 May. Following an erroneous media report that omitted any criticism of Fiji and that the EU wanted to assist Fiji, the EU reaffirmed its opposition to Bainimarama's military government and its refusal to hold democratic elections before 2014. The EU also confirmed that all financial assistance to Fiji had been suspended. The high court was re-opened on 27 May after six weeks closure following the coup in April when the constitution was suspended and the entire judiciary summarily sacked. A presidential decree de-registered all legal practitioners who had to apply to the chief registrar, a former military lawyer, for a new licence. In a national address on 1 July, Prime Minister Bianimarama announced that before parliamentary elections can be held in 2014, political reforms must be undertaken. He also called on donor countries to be understanding and offer financial help over the period. In September the Commonwealth again suspended Fiji's membership. This will mean Fiji will no longer be eligible for technical assistance, and, perhaps more importantly for keen supporter Mr Bianimarama, Fiji's rugby-7 team will not be able to participate in the 2010 Commonwealth Games; they got the bronze medal in 2006. Acting President Ratu Epeli Nailatikau was appointed to the post on 29 October; he was confirmed in the office on 5 November.
2010 Tropical cyclone Tomas struck Fiji on 15 March and caused some US$38 million of damage to agricultural crops, homes, infrastructure and native flora. The government announced in March that any politician who had engaged in national politics since 1987 would be banned from contesting the proposed 2014 parliamentary elections, so that no current politician may stand for re-election. Eight men accused of attempting to kill Mr Bainimarama in 2007 were found guilty and jailed.
2011 Former president Ratu Josefa Iloilo died on 6 February, aged 92 years. On the 3 March, the government introduced to parliament a proposed new system of electoral campaigning, changing from targeted ethnic groups to open-list proportional representation. Of the 71 seats in the lower house of parliament, 45 will be open to any candidate of any ethnic group. On 7 March, Ratu Inoke Takiveikata was convicted of inciting a military mutiny at the Queen Elizabeth Barracks in 2000. The nobleman was sentenced to life in prison. Fiji joined the Non-Aligned Movement (NAM) in May. Lieutenant Colonel Ratu Tevita Mara left Fiji by devious means on 9 May, ending up in Tonga, with the help of the Tongan navy that claimed it had 'rescued' Mara at sea. On 14 May, Mara issued a condemnation of Bainimarima's regime and called for tougher sanctions to be applied. Mara was subsequently charged with mutiny by the Fijian government. Fiji also officially demanded that Tonga extradite Mara to stand trial in Fiji, but a decision was deferred. On 10 June Ratu Tevita Mara was granted permission to address the Fijian democratic movement in Canberra (Australia). He is expected to reiterate his belief that Bainimarima has no intention of holding parliamentary elections in 2014 as promised. On 15 June, Fiji called on Australia to extradite Tevita, but Australia also deferred its decision to comply with its bilateral extradition agreement. On the same day, Solomon Islands' Prime Minister Danny Philip said

he was reluctant to grant entry to Tevita and risk upsetting relations with Fiji.

Political structure

Constitution

The constitution was promulgated on 25 July 1990 and amended on 25 July 1997 to allow non-ethnic Fijians more say in government and to make multi-party government mandatory. Bars against non-Fijians becoming prime minister and president were removed.

The Court of Appeal upheld the 1997 constitution in 2001.

The constitution states any political party with more than 10 per cent of the seats in parliament must be offered a cabinet position.

Voting: universal suffrage, over 21 years.

Independence date

10 October 1970

The executive

Executive authority is vested in the president, who is elected by the Great Council of Chiefs for a maximum of two five-year terms. A presidential council advises the president on matters of national importance. The president is the commander-in-chief of the military forces.

National legislature

There is a bicameral parliament – the Senate (upper house) (34 seats – 24 appointed by the Great Council of Chiefs, nine appointed by the president, and one appointed by the council of Rotuma) and the House of Representatives (lower house) (71 seats – 23 reserved for ethnic Fijians, 19 reserved for ethnic Indians, three reserved for other ethnic groups, one reserved for the council of Rotuma constituency encompassing the whole of Fiji and 25 open seats). Members serve five-year terms.

The prime minister is usually the leader of the majority party or coalition in parliament and is appointed by the president for a five-year term. The 18-member cabinet is appointed by the prime minister from among the members of parliament and is responsible to parliament.

The government announced in March 2010 that any politician who had engaged in national politics since 1987 would be banned from contesting the proposed 2014 parliamentary elections, so that no current politician may stand for re-election.

The *Bose Levu Vakaturaga* (Great Council of Chiefs) (GCC) comprises the highest-ranking members of the traditional chief system. The composition of the GCC was changed from 24 August 2007, when the number of members was reduced from 55 to 52, made up of 42 members representing chiefs from the 14 provinces, six co-opted members, three representatives of the chiefs of Rotuma and the Fijian affairs minister. The president, vice president and prime minister are no longer members, and commoners are excluded.

Legal system

Based on the British legal system.

Last elections

6–13 May 2006 (parliamentary)

Results: Parliamentary: Soqosoqo Duavata ni Lewenivanua (SDL) (United Fiji Party) won 44.6 per cent (36 seats out of 71); Fiji Labour Party (FLP) won 39.2 per cent of the vote (31 seats); United People's Party (UPP) 0.84 per cent (two seats); and Independents 4.9 per cent (two seats). Turn-out was 87.7 per cent.

Next elections

2013 (parliamentary)

Political parties

Ruling party

Interim military government (from 2007; re-appointed 13 April 2009)

Main opposition party

Soqosoqo Duavata ni Lewenivanua (SDL) (United Fiji Party)

Political situation

Population

861,000 (2010)

Last census: September 2007: 837,271

Population density: 46 inhabitants per square km (2010)

Annual growth rate: 1.0 per cent 1994–2004 (WHO 2006)

Ethnic make-up

Ethnic Fijians represent about 51 per cent of the population. Indians comprise about 44 per cent. There are also some Europeans, other Pacific islanders and Chinese.

Religions

Methodist (37 per cent), Roman Catholic (9 per cent), Hindu (38 per cent), Muslim (8 per cent).

Education

Fiji showed remarkable progress in access to basic education in the years following 1996. Basic education was boosted with the introduction of tuition assistance for primary schools in 1994. Totalling about F$4.8 million (US$2.3 million) annually, this assistance enabled primary schools to meet their annual development costs.

Primary schooling lasts for eight years; secondary education lasts for a possible seven years, with intermediate stages of four-year junior secondary, two-year senior secondary and one-year seventh form schooling. Progression through all stages culminates in examinations. Lessons are taught mainly in English but may also be taught in Fijian and Hindi.

The University of the South Pacific, which serves 10 English-speaking territories in the South Pacific, is the main provider of higher education.

Government expenditure on education increased through the 1990s and typically amounts to 16.21 per cent of the national budget.

The EU funded a US$44 million programme aimed at improving the quality of education in Fiji, by assisting more than 70 per cent of primary schools and 50 per cent of secondary schools.

Literacy rate: 93 per cent adult rate; 99 per cent youth rate (15–24) (Unesco 2005).

Compulsory years: 6 to 14.

Enrolment rate: 110.45 per cent gross enrolment in primary education (including repitition rates).

Health

In October 2010, the health minister declared that Fiji was free of typhoid, a disease that had been a constant threat across the region. On 30 November 2011, the Asia Pacific Observatory on Health Systems and Policies (APOHSP) reported that life expectancy in Fiji had fallen from 72.9 years to 67.8 over from 2000–05. The drop in expectancy was attributed to several factors, in particular political and economic pressures and including social and cultural changes.

Health care facilities in Fiji are barely adequate for routine medical problems. Two major hospitals, the Lautoka Hospital and the Colonial War Memorial Hospital in Suva, provide emergency and outpatient services. Other hospitals and clinics provide only a limited range of health services.

Access to clean water is available to 47 per cent of the total population.

HIV/Aids

HIV prevalence: 0.1 per cent aged 15–49 in 2003 (World Bank)

Life expectancy: 67.8 years (APOHSP 2011)

Fertility rate/Maternal mortality rate: 2.9 births per woman, 2004 (WHO 2006); 31.1 deaths per 1,000 live births (Ministry of Health, 2008).

Birth rate/Death rate: 20.7 births per 1,000 population; 7.1 deaths per 1,000 population (2007).

Child (under 5 years) mortality rate (per 1,000): 22.4 per 1,000 live births (Fiji Ministry of Health, 2008)

Head of population per physician: 3.26 physicians per 100,000 people, 2007 (Fiji Statistics 2008)

Welfare

Analysis in 2010, by economist Professor Waden Narsey, of the Fiji Islands Bureau of Statistics *Household Income and Expenditure Survey for 2008–2009*, concluded that almost one-third of citizens will be living in poverty by 2011.

Main cities
Suva (capital, on Viti Levu, estimated population 177,300 in 2003), Lautoka (on Viti Levu, 45,700), Nadi (on Viti Levu, 32,600), Labasa (on Vanua Levu, 25,400), Nausori (on Viti Levu, 22,800).

Languages spoken
English is widely used in business circles. Fijian dialects are spoken by the indigenous Fijians (Bauan is the most spoken). The Indian community speaks Fiji-Hindi. Cantonese is also spoken.
Since 2003, compulsory classes teaching the Fijian and Hindi languages have been introduced in some primary and secondary schools in order to avert the threat of losing the ethnic languages of the country.
Official language/s
English, Fijian and Hindi

Media
In April 2010 the government introduced new media laws (a code of standards and ethics and practice) to control the content of news reports and provide punishments of prison terms and heavy fines for any illegality. Foreign media ownership was severely curtailed and all media outlets must pledge allegiance to Fiji. Officials of the Fiji based, Pacific Islands New Association (Pina) have called for the organisation to be moved to another member state to avoid the growing censorship in Fiji.
Press
Journalistic standards are generally regarded as vigorous.
Dailies: In English, newspapers include *Fiji Daily Post* (www.fijidailypost.com), with its Fijian *The Fiji Times* (www.fijitimes.com) has business news and *Fiji Sun* (www.sun.com.fj), which is a tabloid.
According to new media laws that came into effect on 28 June 2010, which required all directors and 90 per cent of all shareholders of media organisations to be either Fijian or permanent Fijian residents, the *Fiji Times* had until 28 September 2010 to find new owners or be closed down. The *Fiji Times* was owned by News Limited (owned by media tycoon Rupert Murdoch) and a strong critic of the military government. The Fiji-based Motibhai Group took over control of News Limited's *Fiji Times* just before the September deadline.
Weeklies: In Fijian *Nai Lalakai* takes stories from *The Fiji Times* (www.fijitimes.com/nailalakai.aspx) and *Na Volasiga*, covering current affairs. Two Hindi language publications include *Sartaj* and *Shanti Dut* which features national and international news. The Pacific University Journalism publishes *USP Bulletin* and online news (www.usp.ac.fj/journ/).
Business: In English *Fiji Islands Business* (www.islandsbusiness.com) and *Island Business* are twin publications with varing domestic or international markets.
Periodicals: In English, the monthly *Pacific* (www.pacificmagazine.net) has regional news articles.
Broadcasting
Radio: Radio is the most popular medium for entertainment, news and information, particularly on remote islands.
The Fiji Broadcasting Corporation (FBCL) (www.radiofiji.com.fj) network has five stations providing a range of programmes based on the Fijian-, English or Hindi-languages. The Communications Fiji Ltd (www.cfl.com.fj) has a commercial network of five stations broadcasting to difference audiences including Radio Navtarang, in Hindi and Viti FM, in Fijian and FM96 for the under 25 years age group. Another commercial station, in English, is Radio Fiji Gold (www.radiofiji.com.fj).
The UK-based BBC World Service, the French Radio Internationale and Radio Australia are broadcast through local FM relay stations.
Television: The national public TV station is Fiji TV (www.fijitv.com.fj), which also has a satellite, pay-to-view service, provided by Sky Fiji, with over 20 channels. Local programmes are provided in Fijian, Hindi and English. Services are also transmitted to other Pacific territories, for a fee.
Advertising
Local press, radio and cinema outlets, as well as a few outdoor poster and billboard sites, provide venues for advertising.
News agencies
ABC Pacific Beat:
www.radioaustralia.net.au/pacbeat
Pacific Magazine:
www.pacificmagazine.net
Pacific Islands New Association (Pina):
www.pina.com.fj

Economy
The service sector constitutes around 60 per cent of the economy with industry accounting for up to 25 per cent and agriculture around 15 per cent. Tourism is the principal sector of the economy – in 2009 there were over 400,000 tourists plus a further 150,000 on business and visiting family, which brought in a total of US$1.589 billion in foreign earnings. The industrial sector is dominated by mining of gold, silver and limestone, all contributing to Fijian exports. Remittances from expatriates are also an important source of foreign exchange, which in 2009 was US$113 million (3.4 per cent of GDP), rising to an estimated US$128 million in 2010.
GDP growth in 2006 was 1.9 per cent, but following the coup led by Commodore Bainimarama the economy has been in recession as two corresponding international pressures compounded Fiji's situation. In 2006, the World Trade Organisation required the US and the EU to stop preferential imports from Fiji of textiles and sugar respectively. Both of these industries went into decline. The EU had agreed to provide financial aid to allow reinvestment in agriculture, but since the 2006 coup it set a proviso of democratic reforms and an improvement in human rights in Fiji. In the face of concerted opposition by international bodies and governments the Fijian military government rejected all calls to evolve a democratically inclusive regime. As such, financial aid that might have been forthcoming has been restricted and has had a direct effect on the economy. In 2007 GDP growth was -0.5 per cent, which rose to -0.1 per cent in 2008, but was adversely affected not only by the global economic crisis that cut the number of tourists, but Fiji was also hit by floods that damaged crops and tourist infrastructure, so that GDP growth fell further to -2.2 per cent in 2009. In December 2009 the currency was devalued by 20 per cent, which improved Fiji's international credit rating and stimulated growth. However it also reduced the value of sugar exports by 15 per cent, while the cost of petroleum imports rose.
Tropical cyclone Tomas struck Fiji in March 2010 and caused some US$38 million worth of damage to agricultural crops, homes and infrastructure. GDP growth in 2010 was estimated at 1.8 per cent, spurred on by reconstruction and a return of tourist numbers. However the biggest risk to the economy was deemed to be the level of government debt and contingent liabilities (debts incurred by government owned and guaranteed enterprises), totalling 70 per cent of GDP. The balance of trade, which had peaked at -US$1,108 million in 2008, fell to a five-year low of -US$7.14 in 2009.
In January 2010, a licence for a new bauxite mine was issued to a Chinese company. If sugar production falls further, mining may become the second largest component of the economy by 2015.

External trade
Fiji is a member of the South Pacific Regional Trade and Economic Co-operation Agreement (Sparteca) along with 12 other regional nations, which allows products duty free access by Pacific Island Forum members to Australian and New Zealand markets (subject to the country of origin restrictions). It is also a member of the Melanesian Spearhead Group (with

Papua New Guinea, Solomon Islands and Vanuatu) as a sub-regional trade group, whereby customs tariffs have been harmonised under the Melanesian free trade agreement (MFTA).

Imports

Principal imports are manufactured goods, petroleum products, chemicals, machinery and transport equipment and food.

Main sources: Singapore (typically 28 per cent of total), Australia (22 per cent), New Zealand (16 per cent).

Exports

Principal exports are sugar, garments and shoes, gold, timber, fish, molasses and coconut oil.

Main destinations: Singapore (typically 16 per cent of total), Australia (16 per cent) UK (15 per cent).

Agriculture

Farming

The agricultural sector typically accounts for around 16 per cent of GDP and employs 40 per cent of the workforce.

Historically, 85 per cent of land is granted to Fijian clans *(Mataqali)* and by law cannot be sold. This has led to underutilisation of some land. The soil is generally fertile and easily worked.

Sugar normally accounts for half agricultural output, but has declined both in quality and quantity. The sugar industry supports about 25 per cent of the working population, consumes around 12 per cent of all goods and services and earns more than 40 per cent of export income. The Fiji Sugar Corporation aims to diversify into ethanol and to encourage other uses for spare land, especially rice (50 per cent of which is imported).

The European Union announced in May 2009 that it would no longer pay a subsidised price for Fiji's sugar crop, worth over US$30 million annually. This was the second year in a row where Fiji missed out on business with the EU due to its unwillingness to adhere to democratic principals, which breached the Cotonou Agreement and the EU's opposition to Bainimarama's military government and its refusal to hold democratic elections before 2014.

Fishing

Fishing for local consumption includes skipjack, yellowfin and commercial species. Prawns and oysters are raised in fish farms. Bêche-de-Mer, shark-fins, trochus, mother-of-pearl and turtle shells are collected and sold.

The typical annual fish catch is over 44,700t with over 14,000t of other seafood. One million pieces of coral are harvested annually as well as 160,000 units, pearls and shells.

The prawn industry was given an investment boost in July 2011, with the introduction of a species of giant freshwater prawn, which has a better survival rate than the local species. The new species, to be farmed, should boost employment and the economy.

Forestry

In addition to natural rain forest, large new plantations of pine and hardwood were established in the late 1970s. There are exports of pine chips to Japan and sawn pine to Australia. The clearing of forests has caused soil erosion.

Industry and manufacturing

The industrial sector as a whole accounts for 26 per cent of GDP and employs 15 per cent of the workforce. The manufacturing industry (excluding sugar milling) accounts for 13 per cent of GDP and sugar accounts for one-third of industrial output.

Sugar cane is crushed at local mills and exported as raw sugar and molasses. In 2003, two mills were closed as part of the government's restructuring of the sector.

Copra milling, which produces coconut oil and oil cake for export, is carried on at Suva and Savusavu. There are two breweries, a flour mill and a steel-rolling mill.

Tourism

Fiji can offer the quintessential tropical holiday, with white sandy beaches and azure lagoons with colourful coral gardens just offshore. Although Unesco has yet to award the status of World Heritage Site to any of the four sites proposed, they are nevertheless highlights of a trip to Fiji. The sites include a range of natural sights and the traditional township of Levuka, Ovalau. The tourist industry is geared up to cater for visitors arriving by air for packaged holidays and offers eco-tourist activities in its lush forests, water sports and traditional cultural encounters.

Australians are overwhelmingly the largest group of tourists, followed by tourists from China, India, New Zealand and the US.

Although the political turmoil has taken its toll on the economy and Fiji has had international sanctions imposed in 2000 and 2006, the tourism sector maintained its level of significance for the economy. In 2005, travel and tourism constituted a record high of 36.9 per cent of GDP; however since then it has steadily fallen as the world economic downturn lead to a cut in the number of visitors and by 2011 its share of GDP was 27.7 per cent, a figure similar to that of 2000. Likewise, 30 per cent of total employment was typically found in travel and tourism, but fell to 25 per cent in 2010. Tourism began to pick-up in 2011.

Mining

The mining sector accounts for around 3 per cent of GDP and employs 2 per cent of the workforce.

Gold is Fiji's second largest export. Production is centred on one large mine, Vatukoula, owned by Emperor Gold Mines, which produces 120,000–160,000 ounces per annum and has reserves of around 3.5 million ounces. Accessible ore is expected to be exhausted within 10 years. Another smaller mine at Mount Kasai is operated by Pacific Island Gold and was reopened in 1997 following a 50-year closure.

Hydrocarbons

Fiji has no proven hydrocarbons reserves and relies on imports, which amount to 10,000 barrels per day.

Oil exploration has been undertaken but the government curtailed all further development as the cost of extraction outweighs the return on investment, as well as environmental reasons.

No gas is produced or imported. Consumption of imported coal amounts to 14,000 tonnes per annum.

Energy

The Fiji Electricity Authority (FEA) is responsible for providing and maintaining national power, as well as regulating the market. The FEA is encouraging the use of renewable energy sources to reduce the country's dependence on imported diesel.

A mini-hydroelectric scheme in Vanua Levu supplies electricity to 40 villages and other processing industries. Annual electricity generation is around 1 billion kilowatt hours (kWh).

The ongoing rural electrification programme will include a larger proportion of solar energy systems from 2009. A new financing system will help domestic and community users to purchase photovoltaic (solar) panels. Community projects will be able to lease the solar panels which will be installed and maintained as part of the contract. The World Bank and the Australian-based ANZ bank have provided to initial investment to provide start the renewable energy project.

Savusavu was selected as the site of Fiji's first geothermal power plant in May 2011, with a second planned for Labasa, if a thermal source is proven. Energy will be taken from naturally occurring hot springs, with surface temperatures of 40 degrees C. Geothermal energy production will initially supplement rather than replace existing energy production.

Financial markets

Stock exchange

South Pacific Stock Exchange (SPSE)

Banking and insurance
Central bank
Reserve Bank of Fiji

Time
GMT plus 12 hours

Geography
Fiji comprises more than 800 islands, of which 100 are inhabited, situated about 3,100km north-east of Australia and 5,000km south-west of Hawaii, in the Pacific Ocean. The four main islands are Viti Levu, Vanua Levu, Tavenui and Kadavu. Plains and valleys, including flood plains, and low mountains provide agricultural land. High mountains are rugged and volcanic.
Hemisphere
Southern

Climate
Hot and damp, tempered by cool winds from May–October. Maximum temperature during summer (December–April) 32 degrees Celsius (C), when hurricanes and cyclonic storms sometimes occur; rarely falls below 18 degrees C during the rest of the year.

Entry requirements
Passports
Required by all. Passports must be valid for three months beyond the the date of departure and visitors must possess sufficient funds and return/onward passage.
Visa
Visitor's visa (for stays up to four months) are issued on arrival to many foreign nationals from the Americas, Europe, Australasia and some Asian countries. Business visas, by representatives of overseas companies, from countries that do not require a visa may visit without further documentation.
Contact the nearest Fiji Consulate for further information.
Currency advice/regulations
There is no restriction on the import of local or foreign currency although it must be declared. Export of all currencies can only be up to the amount declared on entry.
Travellers cheques are accepted and are recommended in Australian dollars or pound sterling, to avoid added exchange fees.
In a review of currency designs in 2005 it was decided to retain the image of the head of the British monarch on the currency, even though Fiji has been a republic since 1987.
Customs
Personal effects allowed duty-free. Strict animal and plant quarantine regulations; fruit or plant material should not be brought in. Many agricultural and manufactured items subject to import embargoes and licensing and the list is subject to alteration. Details available from the Ministry of Commerce and Industry in Suva.
Prohibited imports
Strict animal and plant quarantine regulations apply; fruit or plant material are prohibited. Many agricultural and manufactured items are subject to import embargoes and licensing; a list and details are available from the Ministry of Commerce and Industry in Suva.

Health (for visitors)
Mandatory precautions
Vaccination certificates are required for yellow fever if travelling from an infected area.
Advisable precautions
Vaccination for diphtheria, tuberculosis, hepatitis A and B, polio, tetanus, typhoid and dengue fever. There is a rabies risk. In rural areas water should be boiled before drinking.

Hotels
There are many tourist hotels of all standards and types, frequently in scenic locations around the islands.
Tipping is not encouraged but visitors may give a gratuity for excellent service.

Credit cards
Most major credit cards accepted at hotels, restaurants, shops and rental car agencies, tours, cruises and travel agencies. American Express, Diners Club, Visa, JCB and Master Card have representatives in Suva.

Public holidays (national)
Fixed dates
1 Jan (New Year's Day), 25–26 Dec (Christmas Holiday).
Variable dates
Good Friday, Easter Monday, National Youth Day (first Fri in May), Ratu Sir Lala Sukuna Day (last Mon in May), Queen's Official Birthday (Jun/Jul), Fiji Day (Oct), Diwali (Oct/Nov), Birth of the Prophet Mohammed.
Muslim and Hindu festivals are timed according to local sightings of various phases of the moon.

Working hours
Banking
Mon–Thu: 0930–1500; Fri: 0930–1600. Foreign exchanges Mon–Fri 0830–1700; Sat: 0830–1200.
Business
Mon–Fri: 0830–1630/1700 (some business close early on Fri).
Government
Mon–Thu: 0800–1300, 1400–1630; Fri: 1400–1600.
Shops
Mon–Fri: 0800–1700; Sat: 0800–1300.

Telecommunications
Mobile/cell phones
A GSM 900 service is available throughout most of the islands.

Electricity supply
240/415V AC, with flat three-pin plug fittings. Larger hotels have 110V conversion units for electric shavers.

Social customs/useful tips
Lightweight suit and tie for men and lightweight suit or equivalent for women. It is customary to shake hands on meeting and taking leave. On social occasions punctuality is appreciated, and dress should be formal.
An invitation to a traditional village is regarded as an important occation. When visiting a *bure* (a native thatched cottage) shoes must be removed and head lowered when entering. Hats must be removed and an invitation to drink kava should be accepted to avoid insult.
Clothing may be casual, but should be modest: swimsuits are not acceptable anywhere except on beaches and around hotel pools.

Getting there
Air
National airline: Air Pacific
International airport/s: Nadi International (NAN), 8km north of Nadi, 200km from Suva; duty-free shop, restaurant, bank, post office, car hire.
Other airport/s: Nausori (SUV), 21km from Suva.
Airport tax: Departure tax F$30; not applicable to 24 hour transit passengers.
Surface
Water: Regular ferries operate between Kiribati, Nauru, Samoa and Tuvalu.
Main port/s: Labasa, Lautoka, Levuka, Savusavu and Suva.

Getting about
National transport
Air: Air Fiji operates several daily flights between Nadi International and Nausori Airport and most other domestic services, however, it was grounded in April 2009 due to financial problems. Air Pacific operates the main route between Nadi and Suva. Sunflower Airlines and Turtle Island Airways operate on parts of Viti Levu and are available for charter. Helicopters can be chartered from Pacific Crown Aviation, Suva.
Road: There is a 3,300km road network, about one-third of which is metalled. On Viti Levu, a 500km coastal highway links main centres. A trans-insular road on Vanua Levu connects Labasa with Savusavu.
Buses: Air-conditioned buses operate daily between Suva, Nadi and Lautoka; fares are cheap. Air-conditioned coaches for longer distances.

Water: Small inter-island vessels operate from Suva and Lautoka. A regular ferry service connects Suva and Labasa, Ovalau and Koro Island. Ferries also connect the majority of the major coastal areas of Viti Levu and Vanua Levu with all the major islands. It is also possible to charter boats.

City transport

Taxis: Metered taxis are available in main centres. It is advisable to negotiate fares for long journeys, in advance. Journey time for a taxi from the airport to the city centre is around 10 minutes.

Buses, trams & metro: Journey time from airport to city centre 20 minutes; buses operate 0700–1830.

Car hire

Chauffeur-driven and self-drive car hire available. Current overseas or international licence acceptable for six months. Driving is on the left-hand side of the road, speed limits are 50kph in towns and villages, 80kph on highways.

BUSINESS DIRECTORY

The addresses listed below are a selection only. While World of Information makes every endeavour to check these addresses, we cannot guarantee that changes have not been made, especially to telephone numbers and area codes. We would welcome any corrections.

Telephone area codes

The international dialling code (IDD) for Fiji is +679 followed by the customer number.

Useful telephone numbers

Police, fire and ambulance: 000

Chambers of Commerce

Suva Chamber of Commerce, 7th Floor, Honson Building, Thomson Street, PO Box 337, Suva (tel: 331-3505).

Banking

Australia & New Zealand Banking Group Ltd, PO Box 179, ANZ House, 25 Victoria Parade, Suva (tel: 321-3000; fax: 330-0267).

National Bank of Fiji, 107 Victoria Parade, PO Box 1166, Suva (tel: 331-4400; fax: 330-2190, 330-2032).

Westpac Banking Corporation, 6th Floor, Civic House, Town Hall Road, Suva (tel: 330-0666; fax: 330-0718).

Central bank

Reserve Bank of Fiji, Private Mail Bag,Viti Levu Island, Suva (tel: 331-3611; fax: 330-1688; email: rbf@reservebank.gov.fj).

Stock exchange

South Pacific Stock Exchange (SPSE): www.spse.com.fj

Travel information

Air Fiji, 185 Victoria Parade, Suva (tel: 331-5055, 331-4495; fax: 330-0771, 337-0693).

Flight information (24 hours) (tel: 672-2599).

Hotel reservations (available 24 hours on arrival concourse) (tel: 672-2433).

Nadi International Airport, Civil Aviation Authority of Fiji, Private Mail Bag (tel: 672-2500, 672-1555; fax: 652-1500, 672-3795).

Tourist information (0800–1700 hours) (tel: 672-2433).

National tourist organisation offices

Fiji Visitors' Bureau, Thomson Street, PO Box 92, Suva (tel: 330-2433; fax: 330-0970, 330-2751; e-mail: infodesk@fijifvb.gov.fj; internet site: http://www.bulafiji.com).

Ministries

Ministry of Primary Industries and Co-operatives, PO Box 358, Rodwell Road, Suva (tel: 331-1233).

Prime Minister's Office (tel: 321-1201; fax: 330-6034).

Other useful addresses

Asian Development Bank (ADB), South Pacific Regional Mission, La Casa di Andrea, Fr. Dr. W. H. Lini Highway; PO Box 127, Port Vila (tel: +678 2 23-300; fax: +678 2 23-183; email: adbsprm@adb.org; internet: www.adb.org/SPRM).

Bureau of Statistics, PO Box 2221, Government Buildings, Suva (tel: 331-5144, 331-5822; fax: 330-3656).

Commonwealth Development Corporation, 371 Victoria Parade, Suva (tel: 330-2577).

Department of Information, PO Box 2225, Government Buildings, Suva (tel: 321-1250/1; fax: 330-0776).

Fiji Posts and Telecommunications Ltd, PO Box 40, Suva (tel: 321-0329; fax: 330-5591; internet site: www.TelecomFiji.com.fj).

Fiji Trade and Investment Board, PO Box 2303, Government Buildings, Suva (tel: 331-5988; fax: 331-5783).

Forum Secretariat, Ratu Sukuna Road, Suva (fax: 330-3069).

National Marketing Authority of Fiji, PO Box 5085, Raiwaqa, Suva (tel: 338-5888).

Pacific Islands News Association Secretariat (PINS), Private Mail Bag, Level II, Damodar Centre, 46 Gordon Street, Suva (tel: 330-3623; fax: 330-3943).

Internet sites

Fiji government: www.fiji.gov.fj

Fiji information: www.fijiatoz.com

Fiji Statistics: www.statsfiji.gov.fj

Tourism Council of the South Pacific: www.tcsp.com/destinations/fiji

Finland

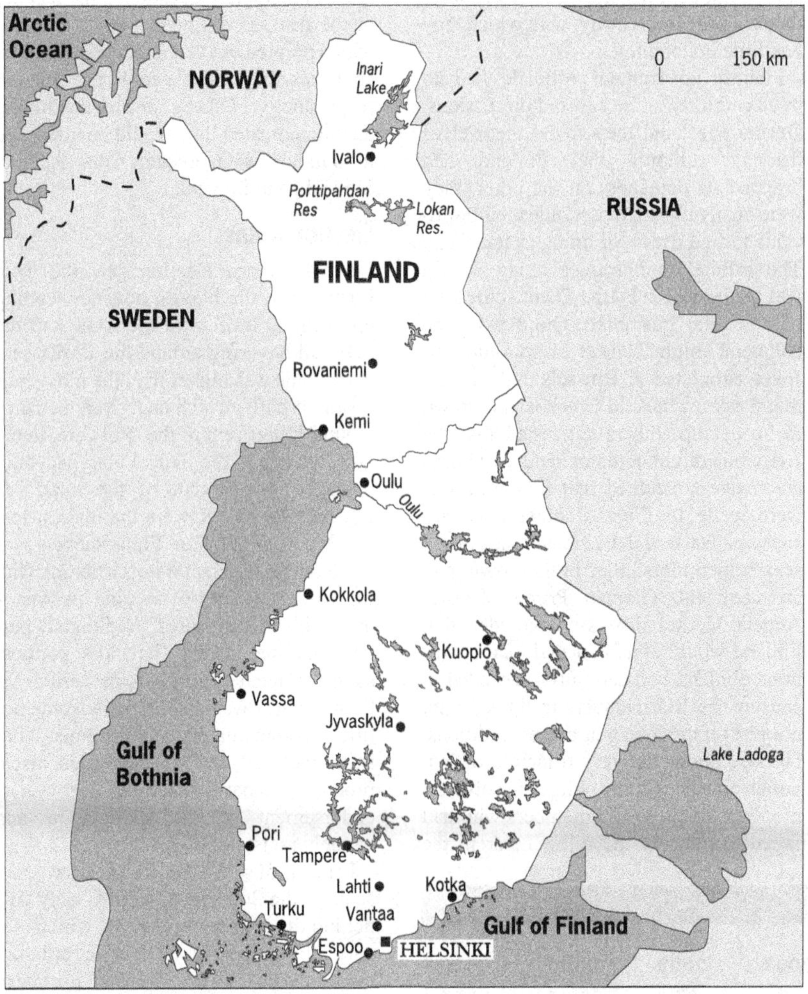

The first years of the 21st century went some way to explaining why it was that in the 20th century Finland's democracy survived virtually intact. This phenomenon became most apparent when, in 1939, Finland managed to resist Soviet aggression, upsetting the Kremlin's expectation that the Finnish proletariat would welcome its forces with open arms. Finland, unlike most of its neighbours, managed to navigate a course of self-interest through the Second World War that enabled its independence to remain intact; the most significant aspect of this was the avoidance of any formal alliance with Nazi Germany. In wrong-footing both the Soviet Union and Nazi Germany, the Finns showed that they could on occasions when push came to shove, be uncomfortably unpredictable.

Unpredictable?

That stubborn streak of unpredictability may have long lain dormant, but surfaced again in March 2011, when – after months of negotiations – the Finnish government looked likely to oppose the conditions of the European Union's (EU) €440 billion (US$590 billion) 'bail-out fund'. Behind the Finnish hesitation over endorsing the fund's creation lay the rapid rise of the Perussuomalaiset (PerusS) (True Finns)

KEY FACTS

Official name: Suomen Tasavalta: Republiken Finland (Republic of Finland)

Head of State: President Tarja Halonen (SDP) (since 2000; re-elected Jan 2006)

Head of government: Prime Minister Jyrki Katainen (NCP) (from 23 Jun 2011)

Ruling party: Coalition led by Kansallinen Kokoomuspuolue (KOK) (National Coalition Party) (NCP), with Suomen Sosialidemokraatinen Puolue (Social Democratic Party of Finland) (SDP), Vasemmistoliitto (VAS) (Left Alliance), Vihreä Liitto (VIHR) (Green League), Svenska Folkpartiet i Finland (SFP) (Swedish People's Party), Suomen Kristillisdemokraatit (KD) (Finnish Christian Democrats) (from 23 Jun 2011)

Area: 338,144 square km

Population: 5.36 million (2010)*

Capital: Helsinki

Official language: Finnish and Swedish

Currency: Euro (€) = 100 cents (from 1 Jan 2002; previous currency markka, locked at M5.95 per euro)

Exchange rate: €0.75 per US$ (Oct 2011)

GDP per capita: US$44,489 (2010)

GDP real growth: 3.10% (2010)

GDP: US$239.20 billion (2010)

Labour force: 2.67 million (2010)

Unemployment: 8.40% (2010)

Inflation: 1.70% (2010)

Balance of trade: US$4.40 billion (2010)

* estimate

party, lead by Timo Soini. At the heart of the bail-out project lay the requirement that all the EU's Triple A countries, which includes Finland, would agree to double their loan guarantees. Finland was alone in blocking the increase, prompting finance minister Jyrki Katainen (who also heads up the centre-right Kansallinen Kokoomuspuolue (KOK) (National Coalition Party) (NCP), to admit that 'We haven't had that many friends in the last round, that's true.'

Mr Katainen's KOK had, in the weeks preceding the Brussels summit, overtaken the then (before the April 2011 elections) ruling Suomen Keskusta (KESK) (Centre Party of Finland) lead by Mari Kiviniemi which, according to a TNS Gallup poll, found itself in third place behind both the KOK and the True Finns. Interviewed by the London *Financial Times*, Ms Kiviniemi acknowledged that Finland was playing the role of troublemaker in the bail-out negotiations. The circumstances, however, were hardly favourable. Finland's next general election was to take place on 17 April, which meant that the Finnish legislature was already dissolved. Within Parliament, the Europe Committee opposed the increase in Finland's loan guarantee. Ms Kiviniemi, whose KESK draws much of its support from rural Finland, told a press conference: 'I don't have the mandate from Parliament to increase them (the loan guarantees). It would be very, very difficult. I would say impossible, because this topic is a very hot one.'

It was not only the three leading political parties who noted that their supporters were opposed to any increase in the bail-out provisions. The opposition Suomen Sosialidemokraatinen Puolue (Social Democratic Party of Finland) (SDP), lead by Jutta Urpilainen had also given up their pro-EU stance, voting against the Greek and Irish bail -outs. The SDP's working class supporters failed to see why their tax revenues should be spent sorting out the financial mess of a country thousands of miles away, with which they had little in common.

Finnish government officials had to tread carefully in the bail-out discussions. On the one hand they found themselves denying rumours that Finland had dropped its demands, on the other, they were busily trying to persuade their politicians to find a way of doing exactly that. The official compromise being sought was the provision by the EU of some kind of collateral guarantee. Quite what the collateral might consist of was unclear. Jokes circulated in Brussels that Finland might ask for the odd Greek island or two to be put up; others suggested that the Acropolis might come in handy. EU officials were concerned that if concessions were made to Finland, other countries such as Austria and the Netherlands might seek something similar in their own loan arrangements. German Prime Minister Angela Merkel dismissed the idea that Finland would obtain special loan conditions. Finland had certainly succeeded in causing the EU members to think again, not just on the loan guarantee conditions, but also about the very principle of low deficit countries being obliged to solve the problems of those EU members who had failed to play by the rules. Later in the year, however, the possibility of a Finnish/Greek side agreement was to surface again. It was then reported that the two countries had agreed on arrangements whereby Athens would deposit million of euros into an escrow account to insure against any default by Greece on the Finnish quota of any loan. The Dutch government immediately questioned the legality of the deal, as did credit-rating agencies which pointed out that if extended to other countries similar deals could prove counter productive. Other countries that immediately indicated they would be interested in similar arrangements were Austria, Slovakia and Slovenia.

Election gains

Finland's April election saw the True Finns make the biggest advance, ending up virtually level with the KOK and the SDP, all hovering around the 19 per cent mark. This was higher than the most optimistic of polls, which had given the party around 15 per cent of the total vote. In the 2007 election, the True Finns had only managed 4 per cent of the total. Ms Kiviniemi's KESK were the biggest losers. Much of the True Finns success was attributed to the electorate's irritation with the so-called Euro-Crisis and its weariness with the so-called 'traditional' parties that had called Finland's political shots for much of the post-war period. Mr Soini's party was dismissed by some political commentators as 'extremist', despite the fact that it advocated fiscal probity. The party's Achilles heel was its endorsement of anti-immigration and vaguely racist policies.

In terms of seats, the True Finns won 39 seats in the 200 seat assembly, only five behind the conservative KOK which, despite the pressures of public opinion, continued to stand for greater European integration. The opposition SDP came in with 42 seats, only two behind the NCP. The KESK, which had previously headed the governing coalition, lost 16 seats, with only 35 seats. Finnish newspapers all featured photographs of a triumphant Mr Soini on their front pages. But it fell to the leader of the KOK party, Jyrki Katainen, to head up the new government. His appointment was greeted with some relief in Brussels; as Finland's finance minister he had established a reputation for moderate, pro-EU policies and a supportive stance towards the bail-outs. The True Finns' members of parliament had little experience of national politics, for the most part coming from municipal and local politics.

KEY INDICATORS — **Finland**

	Unit	2006	2007	2008	2009	2010
Population	m	5.27	5.26	5.29	5.35	*5.36
Gross domestic product (GDP)	US$bn	210.84	245.01	271.10	238.10	239.20
GDP per capita	US$	39,828	46,469	50,891	44,492	44,489
GDP real growth	%	4.8	4.4	1.2	-7.8	3.1
Inflation	%	1.3	1.6	3.9	1.6	1.7
Unemployment	%	7.7	6.8	6.4	8.2	8.4
Exports (fob) (goods)	US$m	77,552.0	89,905.0	96,918.0	62,688.0	69,401.0
Imports (fob) (goods)	US$m	66,046.0	78,045.0	86,709.0	57,679.0	64,998.0
Balance of trade	US$m	11,505.0	11,860.0	10,210.0	5,008.0	4,404.0
Current account	US$m	9,550.0	11,268.0	8,206.0	3,444.0	7,477.0
Total reserves minus gold	US$m	6,494.2	7,063.1	6,979.4	9,710.6	7,326.7
Foreign exchange	US$m	6,134.6	6,689.2	6,397.6	7,403.2	4,919.9
Exchange rate	per US$	0.75	0.69	0.68	0.78	0.76

* estimated figure

After weeks of negotiation, the True Finns did not join the governing coalition, having refused to soften the party's hard-line attitude towards the EU bail-outs. Mr Katainen's final coalition consisted of six parties – the SDP and four smaller parties.

Immigration

Before 1995, the year in which Finland joined the EU, immigration barely registered on the scale of Finnish political preoccupations. Even in 2011, by comparison with many other EU members, the total number of immigrants was small. Estimates put the total immigrant population at four per cent. For most Europeans this would not be of consequence. But for a section of the high profile True Finns party, it is important enough to have become their principal political platform. Finland's foreign minister Erkki Tuomioja sounds resolute enough: 'There's no question of putting a stop to immigration. For Finland's economic and cultural development, for our future, immigration remains essential.' Extremist websites are monitored by the Finnish Security and Intelligence Service, which considers Finland's extremists to lack a political agenda.

The economy – double-dip

Finland's economy was dealt a severe blow by the global crisis and, as is the case with many euro-zone countries, the recovery is worryingly slow. Due to the high dependence of its exports on both countries and commodities that have been adversely affected by the downturn, Finland experienced the worst recession in the euro-area in 2009, with gross domestic product (GDP) falling by a staggering 8 per cent. Economic growth had still been negative in both the final quarter of 2009 and the first quarter of 2010, technically putting Finland into a double-dip recession. There was a resumption of growth – to 3.1 per cent – in 2010, with the International Monetary Fund (IMF) projecting growth of around 2 per cent in 2011, although the outlook is unusually uncertain.

Fortunately the government's measures meant that the impact of the crisis on employment and inflation was partially contained. The unemployment rate rose relatively little from 6.5 to 8.25 per cent during 2008–09 reflecting the government-subsidised temporary employment-support programme. The labour market is anticipated to lag behind the pick-up in activity, with unemployment still at 8 per cent in 2010. Inflation turned down markedly in 2010, to 1.7 per cent. However, it has outpaced the EU average since late 2008, in part as the result of the generous multi-year collective wage agreements made in 2007 that were generally in excess of productivity gains. As a result, external competitiveness has deteriorated, although in the view of the IMF remains adequate.

Finland's banking system has weathered the global turmoil well thanks to healthy capital buffers and prudent management. Finnish banks have limited exposure to opaque structured products or vulnerable countries, including those within Europe. The country's rigorous regulatory and supervisory environment has helped shield the financial sector from the worst of the crisis.

Nokia falters, Finland falters

Finland's iconic manufacturer of mobile telephones, Nokia, has long been regarded as a mainstay of the country's economy. It is also a symbol of Finnish economic performance, to the extent that as long as Nokia is declaring profits and maintaining market share, Finns can sleep peacefully. But times change and 2011 showed signs that all was not well with the mobile telephone giant. Nokia may be getting more revenue from selling phones, but its profits are falling. Nokia's problems have been accentuated since the third quarter of 2008 – when Android began to become a factor in smartphone sales. It's with ancillary products and services, notably 'apps' that Nokia faces its toughest challenge. Apple has had it easy: there's essentially one product that developers write to – the iPhone. Nokia, with its much bigger and more diverse range of phones, has much more of a challenge. In the view of one industry expert, 'this great company has lost market share and bungled the most basic innovations since Apple launched iPhone in June 2007.'

Risk assessment

Economy	Fair
Politics	Fair
Regional stability	Good

COUNTRY PROFILE

Historical profile

Before independence in 1917, Finland was controlled by Sweden and later Russia. Prior to Sweden's conquest of Finland in the 1150s, the country had been a feudal and tribal society.

1150–1293 Sweden was in control of Finland.

1362 Finland was granted the full rights of a Swedish province.

1523 Treaty gave Russia part of Karelia (area between Finland and Russia).

1721 Russia took control of the whole of Karelia.

1809 Finland was conquered by Russia.

1905–06 Strikes were held by the population demanding rights and liberties. Parliamentary government and universal suffrage were established; in 1906, Finland became the first European country to give votes to women.

1917 Collapse of the Russian Empire. A Finnish declaration of independence was followed by a brief civil war.

1919 Establishment of a republic; Kaarlo Ståhlberg became Finland's first president. In the following 70 years, more than 60 governments, mainly minority coalitions, held power.

1939–41 The Soviet Union invaded Finland and after the bitter conflict of the 1939–40 'Winter War', Finland entered the Second World War on the side of Nazi Germany. In December 1940, German troops were invited by the Finnish government to occupy parts of the country and Finland joined Germany's invasion of the Soviet Union in 1941.

1944 Finland signed a peace treaty with the Soviet Union and its troops withdrew from Soviet territory. Finnish troops were then engaged in the 'Lapland War' in northern Finland against withdrawing German soldiers.

1945 Following the end of the Second World War, punitive reparations and the cession of Southern Karelia and its only Arctic port, Petsamo, were forced on Finland by the Soviet Union.

1948 The Treaty of Friendship, Co-operation and Mutual Assistance was signed by Finland and the Soviet Union. It lasted until 1992 after the Soviet Union's break-up.

1956–82 The powers of the strong executive presidency allowed for in the constitution were further enhanced by President Urho Kekkonen. He was succeeded by President Mauno Koivisto in 1982.

1987 The Suomen Keskusta (KESK) (Centre Party of Finland) was replaced after 50 years in government. Conservatives were in the coalition government for the first time in 21 years. Harri Holkeri was appointed Finland's first conservative prime minister since 1946.

1994 Martii Ahtisaari was elected as president. The Suomen Kristillinen Liitto (SKL) (Christian League of Finland), which opposed EU membership, withdrew from the coalition after Finland completed negotiations on joining the EU.

1995 Finland joined the EU. The Suomen Sosialidemokraatinen Puolue (SDP) (Social Democratic Party) won the parliamentary elections and formed a coalition government, with the SDP's Paavo Lipponen as prime minister.

1999 The SDP was again returned as the strongest party in the parliamentary elections; a five-party government coalition was formed. Lipponen was re-elected as prime minister.
2000 Tarja Halonen was elected as president – Finland's first female president. The powers of the president were reduced, following the introduction of a new constitution.
2001 Finland joined other EU states to support the US's military action in Afghanistan, following the 11 September terrorist attacks.
2002 The Vitireä Liitto (VIHR) (Green League) left the coalition government after parliament voted to proceed with plans to build Finland's fifth nuclear reactor.
2003 Anneli Jäätteenmäki became Finland's first female prime minister, heading a coalition of her own KESK, which won the March parliamentary elections, the SDP and the SFP/RKP. Jäätteenmäki was forced to resigned as prime minister; she was unable to form a working coalition as she was seen as untrustworthy following her revelations of secret international undertakings by the former prime minister, during the election campaign. Parliament elected the defence minister, Matti Vanhanen, as prime minister.
2004 Former prime minister Jäätteenmäki was acquitted of charges of illegally obtaining secret documents about the Iraq War while she was opposition leader.
2005 Former prime minister, Paavo Lipponen, stepped down as party leader of the SDP; Eero Heinäluoma replaced him. The popularity of the EU fell, in line with a number of other EU member states that had rejected the new EU constitution in referenda, as a poll conducted in showed that 49 per cent of Finns would vote 'no' to EU membership if given a choice at that time.
2006 The incumbent president, Tarja Halonen, won another term in office.
2007 In parliamentary elections the ruling KESK won 23.1 per cent of the vote (51 seats out of 200), only one seat more than its rival, the Kansallinen Kokoomuspuolue (KOK) (National Coalition Party). Prime Minister Matti Vanhanen (KESK) began talks with other parties immediately to form a coalition government.
2008 Former president Martii Ahtisaari was awarded the Nobel Peace Prize.
2009 GDP declined by 7.6 per cent in the first quarter. In May, the start-up date for the Olkiluoto nuclear power plant (OL3) was postponed until 2012.
2010 Prime Minister Vanhanen resigned on 18 June and Mari Kiviniemi became prime minister on 22 June. Permits for two new nuclear reactors were granted on 1 July, in a measure to cut Finland's dependency on Russian oil and natural gas. The decision sparked protests, including a 10-hour blockade of the Olkiluoto nuclear power plant, in August.
2011 Parliamentary elections were held on 17 April, amid controversy concerning Finland's contribution to the economic bailout of other, collapsing euro economies. The ruling SDP and NCP coalition approved the EMU's efforts, but called for modifications in the procedures. The nationalist, PerusS opposed any Finish economic help. The NCP won 20.4 per cent of the vote (44 seats out of 200) and the SDP 19.1 per cent (42). Notably, the share of votes for PerusS jumped from 4.1 per cent in 2007 to 19.1 per cent and its parliamentary seats increased from five to 39; it became the leading opposition party. A coalition government was formed with Jyrki Katainen (NCP) as prime minister; it took office on 23 June.

Political structure

Constitution

Finland's republican constitution, approved in 1919, was based on the principle of a unicameral parliament and a strong executive president.
In 2000, a new constitution reduced the president's powers, and increased the role of the government – consisting of a prime minister and cabinet – who exercise power in conjunction with the president.

Independence date

17 June 1919, Declaration of independence

Form of state

Constitutional republic

The executive

The president is Head of State and is directly elected, by universal vote, for a six-year term, and is allowed to stand for office for two further consecutive terms. The president and government exercise executive power over matters of foreign policy and national security. The president is expected to approve or reject all measures adopted by the Eduskunta (parliament) within a period of three months, and if no decision is reached, a bill lapses.

National legislature

The unicameral Eduskunta (Riksdag (Swedish)) (Parliament) has 200 members elected by proportional representation in 16 multi-seat constituencies, dependent on population sizes, except Åland which returns one member regardless. All serve for four-year terms.
The parliament appoints the prime minister and the 17–18 members of the Valtioneuvosto (Council of State/cabinet). Most of its members are drawn from within the parliament, but a few may come from outside. It is responsible to parliament for the general administration of the country. Because Finland has a loose, multi-party system, the cabinet always contains a coalition of parties and may be re-formed frequently. The president is empowered to order elections, but the parliament decides when, typically the third Sunday in March.

Legal system

The legal system is based on Swedish civil law and is codified. The judicial system is divided between ordinary civil and criminal jurisdiction and special courts of litigation.
The president appoints a chancellor of justice who is not a cabinet member. His function is to oversee the Council of State and to submit an annual report on its legal conduct.
The Court of the Realm is supreme constitutional court, six of whose 13 members are elected by parliament for a term of four years. The final court for civil and criminal cases is the Korkein Oikeus (supreme court), whose president and 21 members are appointed directly by the state president; the supreme administrative court is the Korkein Hallinto-Oikeus. Composed of 21 presidentially-appointed judges, it is the highest tribunal of administrative appeal.

Last elections

29 January 2006 (presidential); 17 April 2011 (parliamentary)
Results: Parliamentary: Kansallinen Kokoomuspuolue (KOK) (National Coalition Party) (NCP) won 20.4 per cent of the vote (44 seats out of 200), Suomen Sosialidemokraatinen Puolue (Social Democratic Party of Finland) (SDP) 19.1 per cent (42), Perussuomalaiset (PerusS) (True Finns) 19.1 per cent (39), Suomen Keskusta (KESK) (Centre Party of Finland) 15.8 per cent (35), Vasemmistoliitto (VAS) (Left Alliance) 8.1 per cent (14), Vihreä Liitto (VIHR) (Green League) 7.3 per cent (10), Svenska Folkpartiet i Finland (SFP) (Swedish People's Party) 4.3 per cent (nine), Suomen Kristillisdemokraatit (KD) (Finnish Christian Democrats) 4.0 per cent (six), Åland representative 0.3 per cent (one); turnout was 70.5 per cent.
Presidential: Tarja Halonen (SDP) won 46.3 per cent of the vote; Sauli Niinistö 48.2 per cent; six other candidates failed to win through to the runoff round.

Next elections

January 2012 (presidential); March 2015 (parliamentary).

Political parties

Ruling party

Coalition led by Kansallinen Kokoomuspuolue (KOK) (National Coalition Party) (NCP), with Suomen Sosialidemokraatinen Puolue (Social Democratic Party of Finland) (SDP), Vasemmistoliitto (VAS) (Left Alliance), Vihreä Liitto (VIHR) (Green League),

Svenska Folkpartiet i Finland (SFP) (Swedish People's Party), Suomen Kristillisdemokraatit (KD) (Finnish Christian Democrats) (from 23 Jun 2011)

Main opposition party

Perussuomalaiset (PerusS) (True Finns)

Population

5.35 million (2009)

Last census: December 2000: 5,181,115

Population density: 17 inhabitants per square km.

Annual growth rate: 0.3 per cent 1994–2004 (WHO 2006)

Ethnic make-up

Virtually all the population is of Finnish origin, apart from a small foreign population of around 20,000, a small number of Romany Gypsies, a Sámi (Lapp) minority in the north and a significant Swedish-speaking minority in the west.

The Estonians are close cultural relatives of the Finns. There are some small ethnic groups related to the Finns living in Russia.

Religions

Nearly 90 per cent of the Finnish population belongs to the Evangelical Lutheran Church. The Orthodox Church accounts for most of the remainder; there are Catholic, Jewish and Pentecostal minorities.

Education

Unesco reported, in 2004, that Finland achieved the highest overall scores in international tests for educational quality. Public expenditure on education amounts to 5.7 per cent of GDP. Universal primary education and gender parity, at this level and in secondary schools, have been achieved.

A sustained investment in education has resulted in high standards with the most rapid rise seen among those achieving a tertiary level qualification. The younger age groups are now more highly educated than their elders with about 83 per cent of people aged 25–34 having at least an upper secondary qualification in 1997, as against only 23 per cent of the population over the age of 65 achieving the same.

The education system consists of comprehensive secondary schools, post-comprehensive general and vocational education, higher education and adult education each lasting for three years. Vocational institutions provide initial apprenticeship training, in nearly all fields. A three-year vocational qualification gives access to all forms of higher education.

The Finnish higher education system comprises polytechnics and universities. The polytechnic system is founded on a nationwide network of 29 regional polytechnics. There are 20 universities, all of which are in the public sector. In addition to degree programmes, universities also provide adult education and various research and consultant services.

Compulsory years: 7 to 16

Enrolment rate: 99 per cent, for both boys and girls, total primary enrolment of the relevant age group. Enrolment in secondary and tertiary levels of the relevant age group was 118 per cent and 74 per cent respectively (World Bank).

Pupils per teacher: 18 in primary schools.

Health

The national healthcare system is excellent and few take out private health insurance. Employers pay towards national health insurance through social security contributions. Health services have traditionally been free, but the 1990s saw changes and nominal charges introduced on a range of basic services.

HIV/Aids

HIV prevalence: 0.1 per cent aged 15–49 in 2003 (World Bank)

Life expectancy: 79 years, 2004 (WHO 2006)

Fertility rate/Maternal mortality rate: 1.7 births per woman, 2004 (WHO 2006); maternal mortality 0.06 per 1,000 live births (World Bank).

Birth rate/Death rate: 10 deaths and 11 births per 1,000 people (World Bank).

Child (under 5 years) mortality rate (per 1,000): 3.1 per 1,000 live births (World bank)

Head of population per physician: 3.16 physicians per 1,000 people, 2002 (WHO 2006)

Welfare

Finland has a well-developed system of social welfare, and the high level of support has proved to be a stabilising factor in social terms. However, the government has been forced by a steadily rising budget deficit to seek ways of cutting its social spending. Welfare spending, despite cuts, typically totals over 50 per cent of GDP. Finland has an ageing population; those aged over 65 are expected to constitute over a quarter of the population by 2030, one of the highest proportions in the world. Pension regulations have permitted earlier retirement than in many other countries. These factors, combined with high life Most Finns receive health insurance, unemployment benefit, pension and family allowances.

Main cities

Helsinki (capital, estimated population 568,676 in 2005), Esbo (230,711), Tampere (204,580) Vantaa (186,238), Åbo (177,078),

Languages spoken

Finnish belongs to the Baltic-Finnic group of the Finno-Ugric languages, which also includes Estonian and Hungarian and is also related to Sámi, the language of the indeginous people of northern Scandinavia.

English is widely understood in business circles; German and Russian are also spoken.

Official language/s

Finnish and Swedish

Media

Press

The constitution guarantees the freedom of the press.

Dailies: There are over 50 newspapers published daily, of which 10 are national. In Finnish, morning newspapers include *Helsingin Sanomat* (www.hs.fi), which has the largest subscription circulation and *Aamulehti* (www.aamulehti.fi) with the second highest, *Borgåbladet* (www.bbl.fi), *Turun Sanomat* (www.turunsanomat.fi). The largest circulation newspaper in Swedish is *Hufvudstadsbladet* (www.hbl.fi). Evening newspapers are tabloid including *Ilta-Sanomat* (www.iltasanomat.fi) and *Ilalehti* (www.iltalehti.fi) which has the third largest circulation in Finland. There are also a number of newspapers sponsored by political parties.

Weeklies: Most daily newspapers publish a weekend edition. There are a full range of magazines for all interests, *Katso* (www.katso.fi) features popular entertainment, *Urheilulehti* (www.urheilulehti.fi) is a sports magazine and *Äpy* (www.apy.fi) is the country's oldest humorous magazine.

Business: Prominent publications include *Kauppalehti* (www.kauppalehti.fi), *Talous Sanomat* (www.taloussanomat.fi), and *Talouselämä* (www.talouselama.fi), which is a economic journal.

Periodicals: There are over 3,000 magazines on offer, most popular are of general interest.

Broadcasting

The national, public broadcaster is YLE (Yleisradio Oy) (www.yle.fi), which is funded by a licence fee. It typically attracts 44 per cent of TV viewers and over 50 per cent of radio listeners.

All analogue services were switched to digital in September 2007, allowing a mix of free-to-air and pay-TV services.

Radio: YLE operates seven radio stations through either digital or FM/MW/SW frequencies, which cater for all genres including cultural, music, talk, news, entertainment and education, in Finnish, Swedish and the Sámi-language. Radio Finland provides external services, including worldwide news in Latin.

There are many private national and local radio stations including Radio Nova (www.radionova.fi), Groove FM (www.groovefm.fi) from Helsinki, Radio 957 (www.radio957.fi) from Tampere and

Radio Iskelmä (www.iskelma.net) from Lahti.

Television: There are over 20 TV stations of which the public broadcaster YLE (www.yle.fi) has six channels showing a full range of programmes. MTV3 (www.mtv3.fi) is the most popular commercial station, Nelonen (www.nelonen.fi) has 50 per cent foreign and domestic programming, Sub TV (www.subtv.fi) is aimed at the young.

Advertising

The typical adspend is over US$1 billion per annum, with over 50 per cent spent in newspapers, followed by television (20 per cent) and magazines (15 per cent). There are restrictions on tobacco, alcohol, advertising to children and across-the-counter medicines.

Direct mail advertising and direct response advertising via printed, broadcast media and internet and mobile/cell phone are steadily increasing in market penetration.

News agencies

National news agency: STT (Finnish News Agency)

Economy

The economy is strong, open and export-led, with paper and card, telecommunications equipment and engineering foremost. Finland is a world leader in innovation, by investing heavily in research and development (3.5 per cent of GDP) and has a highly-educated workforce. Its industrial base is mineral extraction of gold, silver, copper, limestone, lead, zinc, chromium and iron ore. Around 70 per cent of the country is forested and the timber it produces is used in quality products such as furniture and veneer boards as well as general products such as paper and wood pulp. However, the service sector is the largest component of the economy, constituting over 65 per cent of GDP and employing the majority of the workforce in public services, financial and banking services and the private sector.

GDP growth was 5.3 per cent in 2007, which fell to 0.9 per cent in 2008 as the economy began to weaken as the global economic crisis cut trade and imports of petroleum in particular were at a record high. By 2009 Finland was in recession with GDP growth of -8.0 per cent, the worst fall of any country within the euro-area. In 2010 a modest growth was recorded, with GDP growth of 1.2 per cent. The unemployment rate, which had been at 6.5 per cent in 2008 rose to 8.2 per cent by 2009 as domestic and foreign demand slumped. The government backed programmes of temporary employment, however it is anticipated that unemployment will remain at around 8 per cent until the economy is fully restored.

Nokia is a leading world brand of mobile (cell) phones and had a global market share of 38 per cent in 2009. Exports have been falling as other, typically US, manufacturers have introduced more popular models, such as Apple iPhones. Year-on-year Nokia global sales in 2008–09 fell by 7 per cent and it made a net loss of US$1.4 billion in the third quarter of 2009.

The banking sector was not unduly damaged by the global turmoil as Finland's strong regulatory and supervisory environment helped shield the financial sector. Any weakness exposed in 2008 was fully recovered by 2009. However, the future growth of the economy is largely dependent on the wellbeing of the global economy and when exports pick up.

External trade

As a member of the European Union (EU), Finland operates within a community-wide free trade area, with tariffs determined centrally and as a whole. Internationally, the EU has free trade agreements with a number of nations and trading blocs worldwide. Its economy is export-oriented, with over 40 per cent of production being shipped abroad and export trade representing 70 per cent of GDP.

Timber, wood pulp and paper constitute Finland's core export base.

Imports

Main imports are foodstuffs, including grain, fuel and petroleum products, chemicals, transport equipment, machinery, textile yarn and fabrics, and industrial raw materials such as iron and steel.

Main sources: Russia (typically 16 per cent of total), Germany (15 per cent), Sweden (10 per cent).

Exports

Main exports are forestry products (Finland is the world's second largest forestry exporter, after Canada), mobile phones and wireless network technology, vehicles, machinery and equipment, bio-technology, chemicals.

Main destinations: Sweden (typically 10 per cent of total), Germany (10 per cent), Russia (9 per cent).

Agriculture

Farming

The opening up of Finland's agricultural sector was a major issue in the negotiations for EU membership.

Finnish agriculture is based on small family farms, with the average agricultural area of a farm about 25 hectares (ha). Forests are an integral part of the country's farms, and the average forest area of farms is 43ha. About 43 per cent of the farms produce food crops. Wheat and rye are cultivated on about 10 per cent of the arable land, and about 9 per cent is used for growing other crops including potatoes and sugar beets.

Agriculture typically contributes 1.1 per cent of GDP, although active farms employ 5 per cent of the workforce. On average, only about half of the income of farm families is obtained from agriculture, while farm forestry usually provides 10 to 15 per cent of the income.

Production is based on livestock, and about 80 per cent of the agricultural area is used as pasture or for arable fodder cropping. About 33 per cent of the farms are dairy farms. Finland is 85 per cent self-supporting in food grains, dairy products and root crops.

The EU's Fundamental reform to the Common Agricultural Policy (CAP) was introduced in Finland in 2005. The subsidies paid on farm output, which tended to benefit large farms and encourage overproduction, were replaced by single farm payments not conditional on production.

Fishing

Fishing, aquaculture and fish processing are a traditional part of Finnish industries. The food fishing industry is managed in accordance with the EU's Common Fisheries Policy (CFP), which covers resource, market and structural policies including inland waters and sea fishing as well as a monitoring system.

Fish farming is carried out both in the sea and in inland waters. The most important economic fish for sea fishing are Baltic herring and salmon. Although employment in the sector has dropped considerably, the catch remains stable due to the adoption of more efficient fishing techniques. The total catch is around 120,000 tonnes, of which less than a third is used for human consumption.

The annual production of farmed fish is around 17,500 tonnes consisting mainly of large rainbow trout.

Forestry

Nearly three-quarters of the country is covered by forest, estimated at 21.9 million hectares (ha). Forest resources have been increasing steadily, as annual growth exceeds felling and natural losses. About two-thirds of the forest area is privately-owned, mainly by small-scale farmers. Timber products account for nearly one third of export products and nearly one third of manufacturing output. There is a high level of product specialisation, aided by the fact that the transport and machinery sectors tend to cater for the forest industry. The most common species of tree growing are Scots pine, spruce and birch.

Industry and manufacturing

Industry in Finland is concentrated in three areas: paper and pulp production;

machinery and other metal products; and hi-tech electronics (particularly mobile phone production). The metals, engineering and electronics sector account for over 50 per cent of the country's work force and exports. Finnish exports have underpinned its strong economy and only a severe global downturn could leave the country vulnerable, not only to industry-specific shocks affecting its three principal sectors, but also performance in its key markets.
Research and development (R&D) investment in Finland is one of the highest in the world.

Mining

The sector accounts for only 0.3 per cent of GDP.
There are around a dozen ore mines, producing mainly chromium, mercury, zinc, silver, copper and nickel.
Deposits are small. Prospecting is being intensified to curb imports; refining technology is a major focus of development work. Outokumpu, the mining and metals group, has modernised the production facilities at its Harjavalta plant through an investment programme. The programme includes the copper smelter and nickel production line located at Harjavalta and the copper refinery located at Pori, both towns in western Finland.

Hydrocarbons

There are no known oil resources and there are no current exploration plans. All demand for oil is met by imports amounting to around 220,000 barrels per day (bpd). There are two refineries in Finland with a joint capacity of 252,000bpd; both are located on the southern coastline.
There are no gas resources although consumption is typically around 4.4 billion cubic metres (cum), with imports mainly from Russia. In February 2009 Finland was still considering joining the consortium responsible for building a natural gas pipeline between Russia's Siberian natural gas fields to the energy hungry German, French and Dutch markets, via the Baltic Sea.
There are no coal reserves and the country's needs are met by imports from Poland, Russia and the US amounting to 3.4mtoe in 2008.

Energy

Finland has a sophisticated energy mix, which include oil, natural gas, hydro, nuclear, geothermal, solar, wind and biomass, including wood, coal and peat-fired power stations. Total installed generating capacity is around 18.6GW, with consumption of over 80 billion kilowatt hours (kWh) per annum.
Owing to the high proportion of energy-intensive industry, long distances between population centres and geographic situation with a cold climate, Finland's per capita energy consumption is one of the highest among International Energy Agency (IEA) countries.
There are four nuclear reactors – two Russian and two Swedish-built. Expansion of nuclear power has reduced dependence on imported coal and oil. Around 33 per cent of the energy mix is met by nuclear energy. The fifth nuclear power plant, in Olkiluoto on the west coast, began construction in 2005, but construction problems have delayed completion and commercial electricity production of 1,600MW is not expected until 2012. The Finnish electricity company, Teollisuuden Voima Oy (TVO), oversees construction. Approval for two new nuclear reactors was given in July 2010; this should make Finland self-sufficient in electricity by 2020.
Natural gas fulfils around 11 per cent of Finland's energy needs and wood fuels around 10 per cent of electricity generation and 15 per cent of the total energy requirement, which is one of the highest rates among industrialised nations.

Financial markets

Stock exchange
Helsingin Pörssi (Helsinki Stock Exchange)

Banking and insurance

There are around 341 banks in Finland. Nordea, the largest bank in the Nordic region is Finnish. Other major banks in Finland include Oko Bank, Sampo Bank and Sweden's Svenska Handelsbanken AB.
Central bank
Suomen Pankki (Bank of Finland); European Central Bank (ECB).

Time

GMT plus two hours (daylight saving, late-March to late-September, GMT plus three hours).

Geography

Finland is the fifth-largest country in Europe, but is one of the most sparsely populated. The land frontier with Sweden to the north-west is 586km long, while the far northern border with Norway runs for 716km and the eastern border with Russia for 1,269km. Finland's western and southern shores are washed by the Baltic Sea.
The coastal regions consist of flat clay plains, where most agriculture is undertaken. The lake district, which is estimated to contain over 55,000 lakes and is densely wooded forests, occupies much of the south-east. Northern Finland is within the arctic circle and is mostly scrubland.
Hemisphere
Northern

Climate

Finland's climate varies widely across the country, with exceptionally strong differences between the summer and the winter norms. Temperatures average 5 degrees Celsius (C) in Helsinki and minus 0.4 degrees C in the north. January is the coldest of the long winter months, with an average minus 9 degrees C. Peak average temperatures in Helsinki are reached in July (18 degrees C).
Average annual rainfall in Helsinki is 675mm. Spring months are relatively dry, declining to 36mm in March, but higher rainfall starts in July, reaching a peak of around 70mm in the August–October period. Finland's snow season usually runs from November to April (although it runs up to May further north).

Dress codes

Formal dress, including dark-coloured suits for men, is normal for business purposes. In winter, heavy, warm clothing is essential for outdoor wear. A fur cap and winter boots or overshoes are also strongly recommended.

Entry requirements

Passports
Passports are required by all and must be valid for up to six months beyond the date of stay. Nationals of countries which are signatories of the Schengen Accord may visit on national IDs.
Visa
Visas are required by all except nationals of Schengen Accord countries, North America, Australasia and some Asian countries, for up to three months. All visas issued will adhere to Schengen Accord requirements. For business visas a letter of invitation from a local business contact, stating nature and duration of stay, plus proof of return/onward ticket and travel insurance, with a minimum coverage of US$25,000, or other medical insurance that covers Finland, must accompany the application.
For further information see http://formin.finland.fi/doc/eng/services/entry/main.html or contact the consular section of the nearest embassy. A Schengen visa application (offered in several languages) can be downloaded from http://europa.eu/abc/travel/ see 'documents you will need'.
Currency advice/regulations
There is unrestricted import of local and foreign currency.
Travellers cheques are widely accepted.
Customs
Personal items are duty-free. There are no duties levied on alcohol and tobacco between EU member states, providing amounts imported are for personal consumption. Visitors aged less than 22 years

may not import alcohol over 22 per cent proof.

Prohibited imports

Alcohol drinks over 60 per cent by volume are prohibited. Certain plant material and food, firearms and works of art are subject to restrictions and formalities. The Finnish tourist board can provide further advice.

Health (for visitors)

Nationals of the European Economic Area (EEA) countries and Switzerland can access reduced cost and sometimes free medical treatment using a European Health Insurance Card (EHIC) while visiting the EEA. Exceptions include nationals of the 10 countries which joined the EU in 2004 whose EHIC is not valid in Switzerland. Applications for the EHIC should be made before travelling.

Mandatory precautions

No special requirements are necessary.

Advisable precautions

All imported medication that are narcotics must be accompanied by a doctor's letter. Mosquito repellent is advised for visits to the north in summer.

Hotels

In Helsinki and the surrounding area, hotels are classified into five price categories. Generally of a high standard. Rates vary depending on location, facilities and season. Accommodation should be booked well in advance, especially during summer. If accommodation is unobtainable, a place may be found through *Hotellikeskus* (accommodation clearing-house) at the Central Railway Station in Helsinki. Gratuities are not expected, with the exception of porters. Service is included in restaurant bills, although a little extra can be added.

Credit cards

All major international credit cards are accepted.

Public holidays (national)

Fixed dates

1 Jan (New Year's Day), 6 Jan (Epiphany), 1 May (May Day), 6 Dec (Independence Day), 24–26 Dec (Christmas Holiday).

Variable dates

Good Friday, Easter Monday, Ascension Day, Midsummer's Eve, All Saints' Day.

Working hours

Finns tend to take fairly frequent holidays during the summer months. As a result, business visits between mid-June and mid-August should be undertaken only after making sure that the other party will be available. September to May is the favoured time for business visits. Some businesses and shops close from midday on the day before public holidays.

Banking

Mon–Fri: 0915–1615. Post offices may close later than commercial, savings and co-operative banks.

Business

Mon–Fri: 0800–1600; in summer businesses frequently close at 1530.

Government

Mon–Fri: 0800–1600.

Shops

Mon–Fri: 0900–1700; Sat: 0900–1300. Large department stores and supermarkets open Mon–Fri: 0900–2000; Sat: 0900–1800.

Telecommunications

Mobile/cell phones

There are extensive GSM 900/1800 and G3 services available.

Electricity supply

220V AC, 50Hz. Continental two-pin plugs are standard.

Social customs/useful tips

Finns appreciate punctuality. A gift of flowers is usual when visiting a business partner's home for the first time. Guests should not start drinking before their hosts have proposed their health.

Tips are small, except for unusually good service.

Think twice before refusing to go to a sauna with a host, since such an invitation is seen as a gesture of confidence and friendship by your host. Business meetings are sometimes conducted in saunas.

There are strict laws on drinking and driving.

Security

Street crime is a relative rarity in Finland; normal precautions apply.

Getting there

Air

National airline: Finnair

International airport/s: Helsinki-Vantaa (HEL), 19km north of capital; facilities include banks/bureaux de change, duty-free shops, car hire, hotel reservations, VIP lounge, conference rooms and restaurants.

Other airport/s: Jyväskylä (JYV), 21km from city; Kemi (KEM), 6km from city; Kokkola (KOK), 22km from city; Oulu (OUL), 15km south-west of city; Rovaniemi (RRVN), 10km from city; Tampere (TMP), 15km from city; Turku (TKU), 7km from city; Vaasa (VAA), 12km from city.

Airport tax: None

Surface

Road: The majority of road routes include sea ferry links from Sweden or Germany. There is a land link via Norway or Sweden to Finnish Lapland, involving travel through the Arctic Circle.

Rail: There are rail/sea links from Hamburg, Copenhagen and Stockholm to Helsinki or Turku. A rail connection to Stockholm is available from Haparanda/Tornio in the north. There are daily trains to Moscow and St Petersburg.

Water: Daily ferry services from Sweden, twice weekly from Germany and Poland. Reservations should be made in advance as these tend to be heavily booked, especially during summer and at weekends. Also regular services to Estonia and St Petersburg (Russia).

Main port/s: Helsinki, Kotka, Hamina, Mariehamn, Vaasa, Turku, Pori, Sköldvik, Rauma and Oulu.

Getting about

National transport

Air: Finland has one of the densest internal networks in Europe. Finnair provides connections between Helsinki and Ivalo, Joensuu, Jyväskylä, Kajaani, Kemi, Kittilä, Kokkola, Kuopio, Kuusamo, Lappeenranta, Mariehamn, Mikkeli, Oulu, Pietarsaari, Pori, Rovaniemi, Saonlinna, Tampere, Turku, Vaasa and Varkaus.

Road: Finland's 77,000km network of public roads include 12,000km of high-grade national highway and 30,000km of secondary routes, but there is only just over 600km of motorways. Traffic is light but distances are great, the roads remain passable at all times of the year, although weight restrictions are imposed during April and May in southern Finland and May to June in northern Finland.

Buses: Efficient coach services cover the entire country, and are the main form of transport in Lapland.

Rail: Network of around 6,000km (including 1,600km electrified), operated by state railway company, Valtionrautatiet (VR). Relatively inexpensive and there are several passes available allowing travel over a set period. Seat reservation is obligatory on special express trains. Tickets are valid for one month. Sleeper services are available on the main connections.

Water: Important method of transport, owing to large number of lakes (187,888), which cover 31,500 square km.

City transport

Taxis: Taxis have a yellow *taksi* sign, which is lit when the taxi is vacant. They can be hired at taxi ranks or signalled from the street. Fares are more expensive at night. Taxi drivers are not tipped.

Buses, trams & metro: An efficient and integrated bus, metro and tramway service, suburban rail lines and ferry services to Suomenlinna Islands, operates in Helsinki. A common fares system applies to

all the modes (including the ferries) with a zonal flat fare and free transfer between services. Multi-trip tickets are sold in advance, as are various passes.
Regular bus services, including Finnair City Bus, operate from the airport to the city, taking 35 minutes. Some Helsinki hotels run courtesy coaches.

Car hire

Available in most major towns. Rates include maintenance and insurance. The minimum age varies (usually 20–25) and at least one year's driving experience is a requirement for all drivers. The speed limits are 50kph in built-up areas, 80kph on normal roads and 120kph on motorways. The wearing of seat belts is compulsory. The use of headlights at all times is obligatory. Traffic drives on the right. A national driving licence or International Driving Permit is required. Driving around Helsinki is not recommended due to the lack of parking spaces. Any accident involving elk or raindeer must be report to the police.

BUSINESS DIRECTORY

The addresses listed below are a selection only. While World of Information makes every endeavour to check these addresses, we cannot guarantee that changes have not been made, especially to telephone numbers and area codes. We would welcome any corrections.

Telephone area codes

The international direct dialling (IDD) code for Finland is +358, followed by area code and subscriber's number:

Hämeenlinna	3	Mikkeli	15
Helsinki	9	Oulu	8
Imatra	5	Pori	2
Joensuu	13	Rovaniemi	16
Jyväskylä	14	Tampere	3
Kotka	5	Tornio	16
Kuopio	17	Turku	2
Lahti	3	Vaasa	6

Useful telephone numbers

Emergencies 114

Chambers of Commerce

Central Chamber of Commerce of Finland, 17 Aleksanterinkalu, PO Box 1000, Helsinki 00101 (tel: 696-969; fax:650-303; e-mail: keskuskauppakamari@wtc.fi).

Central Finland Chamber of Commerce, 4 Sepänkatu, Jyväskylä 40100 (tel: 652-400; fax: 652-411; e-mail: info@centralfinlandchamber,fi).

Helsinki Chamber of Commerce, 12 Kalevakatu, Helsinki 00100 (tel: 228-601; fax: 2286-0228; e-mail: kauppakamari@helsinki.chamber.fi).

Kuopio Chamber of Commerce, 2 Kasarmikatu, Kuopio 70110 (tel: 282-0291; fax: 282-3304; e-mail: kauppakamari@kuopiochamber.fi).

Lapland Chamber of Commerce, 29 Maakuntakatu, Rovaniemi 96200 (tel: 318-877; fax: 318-885; e-mail: kauppakamari@lapland.chamber.fi).

Turku Chamber of Commerce, 1 Puolankatu, Turku 20100 (tel: 274-3400; fax: 274-3440; e-mail: kauppakamari@turku.chamber.fi).

Banking

Nordea Bank Finland, Aleksanterinkatu 36 B, Helsinki, Fin-00020 Helsinki (tel: 1651; fax: 1654-2838).

Nordic Investment Bank, Fabianinkatu 34, PO Box 249, Fin-00171 Helsinki (tel: 18-001; fax: 180-0210).

Oko Bank, PO Box 308, Fin-00101 Helsinki (tel: 4041).

Sampo Plc, Unioninkatu 22, Fin-00075 Helsinki (tel: 105-1515).

Suomen Pankkiyhdistys r y (Finnish Bankers' Association), Museokatu 8 A, Box 1009, Fin-00101 Helsinki (tel: 405-6120; fax: 4056-1291).

Suomen Säästöpankkiliitto (Savings Bank Association), Pohjoisesplanadi 35A, 00101 Helsinki 10 (tel: 13-341).

Central bank

Suomen Pankki (Bank of Finland), Rauhankatu 16, PO Box 160, FI-00101 Helsinki (tel: 108-311; fax: 174-872; e-mail: info@bof.fi); European Central Bank (ECB), Kaiserstrasse 29, D-60311 Frankfurt am Main, Germany (tel: (+49-69) 13-440; fax: (+49-69) 1344-6000).

Stock exchange

Helsingin Pörssi (Helsinki Stock Exchange): www.omxnordicexchange.com

Travel information

Finland Travel Bureau Ltd, Mail Department, PB319, 00101 Helsinki 10 (poste restante service).

Finnair, Tietotie 11A, Helsinki-Vantaa Airport (tel: 81-881; fax: 818-4401; internet site: http://www.finnair.com).

Finnish State Railways (internet site: http://www.vr.fi/e-index.htm).

Helsinki-Vantaa Airport (tel: 82-771).

Helsinki Tourist Office, Pohjoiiesesplanadi 19, Helsinki.

National tourist organisation offices

Finnish Tourist Board (Matkailun Edistamiskeskus), Töölönkatu 11, PO Box 625, SF-00100 Helsinki (tel: 4030-1211; fax: 4030-1301/1333; e-mail: mek@mek.fi; internet site: http://www.mek.fi).

Ministries

FINNIDA (Finnish International Development Agency), c/o Ministry for Foreign Affairs, Merikasarmi, Laivastokatu 22, 00160 Helsinki (tel: 134-151; fax: 629-840).

Ministry of Agriculture and Forestry, Hallituskatu 3 A, PO Box 232, 00171 Helsinki (tel: 1601 (exchange); fax: 160-2190).

Ministry of Defence, Et. Makasiinikatu 8 A, PO Box 31, 00131 Helsinki (tel: 16-161; fax: 653-254).

Ministry of Education, Meritullinkatu 10, PO Box 293, 00171 Helsinki (tel: 134-171; fax: 135-9335).

Ministry of the Environment, Kasarmikatu 25, PO Box 380, 00131 Helsinki (tel: 19-911; fax: 1991-9545).

Ministry of Finance, Aleksanterinkatu 3, PO Box 286, 00171 Helsinki (tel: 1601 (exchange); fax: 160-3120).

Ministry for Foreign Affairs, Merikasarmi, Laivastokatu 22, PO Box 176, 00161 Helsinki (tel: 134-151; fax: 1341-5070).

Ministry of the Interior, Kirkkokatu 12, 001070 Helsinki (tel: 1601; fax: 160-2927).

Ministry of Justice, Eteläesplanadi 10, PO Box 1, 00131 Helsinki (tel: 18-251; fax: 1825-7730).

Ministry of Labour, Eteläesplanadi 4, PO Box 524, 00101 Helsinki (tel: 18-561; fax: 1856-7950).

Ministry of Social Affairs and Health, Snellmaninkatu 4-6, PO Box 267, 00171 Helsinki (tel: 1601 (exchange); fax: 160-4716).

Ministry of Trade and Industry, Aleksanterinkatu 4, PO Box 230, 00171 Helsinki (tel: 1601; fax: 160-3666).

Ministry of Transport and Communications, Eteläesplanadi 16, 00130 Helsinki (tel: 1601 (exchange); fax: 160-2596).

Prime Minister's Office, Snellmaninkatu 1 A, Fin-00170 Helsinki (tel: 3589-1601).

Other useful addresses

American Embassy, Itäinen Puistotie 14B, 00140 Helsinki (tel: 171-931; fax: 635-332).

British Embassy, Itäinen Puistotie 17, 00140 Helsinki (tel: 2286-5100; fax: 2286-5262).

Confederation of Finnish Industries, Eteläranta 10, SF 00130, Helsinki 13 (tel: 661-665).

Council of State, Aleksanterinkatu 3 D, 00170 Helsinki (tel: 1601 (exchange); fax: 160-2163).

Finnish Embassy (USA), 3301 Massachusetts Avenue, NW, Washington DC

20008 (tel: 202-298-5800; fax: 202-298-6030; e-mail: info@finland.org).

Finnish Foreign Trade Association, Arkadiankatu 2, PO Box 908, 001001 Helsinki (tel: 69-591; fax: 694-0028).

Helsinki Stock Exchange, Fabianinkatu 14, 00100 Helsinki 10 (tel: 624-161).

Invest in Finland Bureau, Aleksanterinkatu 17, 00100 Helsinki (tel: 696-9125; fax: 6969-2530; internet site: http://www.investinfinland.fi).

Liiketyönantajain (Confederation of Commerce Employers), Eteläranta 10, 00130 Helsinki 13 (tel: 19-281).

Main Post Office, Mannerheimintie 11, 00100 Helsinki 10.

Meilahti Hospital Haartmanink 3, Helsinki (tel: 4711).

Nesté (largest industrial corporation), Keilaniemi, 02150 Espoo, Helsinki (tel: 4501).

Oy Suomen Tietotoimisto (news agency), Lönnrotinkatu 5, 00120 Helsinki 12 (tel: 646-224).

Statistics Finland, Työpajankatu 13, PO Box FI-00022, Helsinki (tel: 17-341; fax: 1734-2279; internet site: http://tilastokeskus.fi/index_en.html).

Suomen Työnantajain Keskusliitto (Finish Employers' Confederation) Eleläranta 10, Helsinki 13 (tel: 17-281).

Tullihallitus (Board of Customs), Erottajankatu 2, 00120 Helsinki (tel: 6141).

Ulkomaankaupan Agenttiliitto (Finnish Foreign Trade Agents' Federation) Mannerheimintie 42A 00260 Helsinki 26 (tel: 446-768).

National news agency: STT (Finnish News Agency), Albertinkatu 33, 00180 Helsinki (tel: 695-811; fax: 695-81203 internet: www.stt.fi).

Internet sites

Virtual Finland: http://virtual.finland.fi

Finnish company information (top 100 Finnish companies): http://www.nedecon.fi

France

KEY FACTS

Official name: La République Française (The French Republic)

Head of State: President Nicolas Sarkozy (UMP) (from 16 May 2007)

Head of government: Prime Minister François Fillon (UMP) (appointed 17 May 2007)

Ruling party: Union pour un Mouvement Populaire (UMP) (Union for a People's Movement)

Area: 543,965 square km

Population: 62,96 million (2010)*

Capital: Paris

Official language: French

Currency: Euro (€) = 100 cents (from 1 Jan 2002; previous currency French franc, locked at Ff6.56 per euro)

Exchange rate: €0.75 per US$ (Oct 2011)

GDP per capita: US$41,019 (2010)

GDP real growth: 1.40% (2010)

GDP: US$2,582.50 billion (2010)

Labour force: 28.27 million (2009)

Unemployment: 9.40% (2010)

Inflation: 1.70% (2010)

Balance of trade: -US$71.21 billion (2010)

* Estimated figure

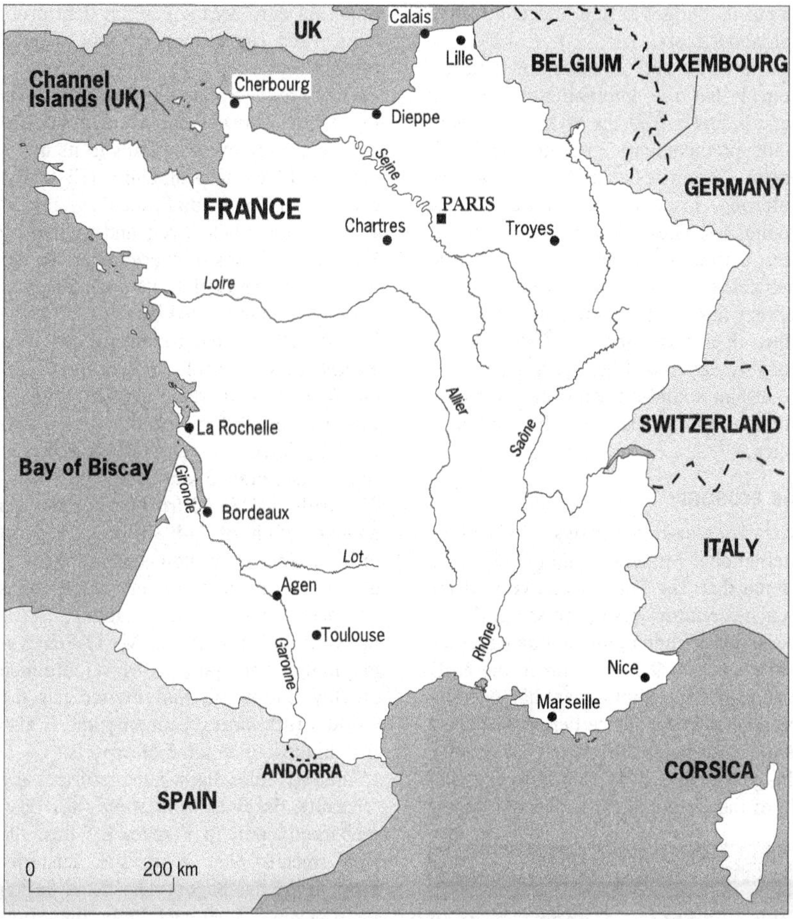

The latter stages of Mr Sarkozy's term as President began to be shaped by one overruling preoccupation. Mr Sarkozy's reputation, his 'standing' would be irreparably damaged were there to be a downgrading of French debt during his Presidency. To correct any image of weakness, Mr Sarkozy chose to stand alongside the German Chancellor, Angela Merkel, as a steward not only of European economic stability, but of the euro-zone currency itself. To a degree, in so doing, Mr Sarkozy was swimming against the tide, or at least against a number of local currents. Within the euro-zone, France certainly comes second to Germany in economic importance. But, France's debt as a percentage of gross domestic product (GDP) at 85.3 per cent, is higher than Germany's (80.1 per cent) and is the highest of any Triple A rating country in Europe. France's forecast budget deficit for 2011 is 5.7 per cent, more than three times higher than the 1.9 per cent deficit forecast for Germany. Many analysts consider that French promises to Brussels to cut its budget deficit to below 6 per cent in 2011 presupposed austerity measures that would inevitably restrict domestic consumption. To bring the deficit to below 3 per cent (as forecast for 2013), will require ?100 billion (US$134 billion) of cuts and new revenues.

Mr Sarkozy's positioning of France alongside Germany also meant that France, after Germany, was the largest contributor to the ?440 billion (US$590 billion) European Financial Stability Facility (EFSF), designed to prevent the European debt crisis spreading from manageable economies such as Greece to larger economies, notably Italy and Spain. The elephant in the Elysée corridors of power is that were this to happen, France might not be able to make further contributions to the EFSF. Once that became apparent, there was a clear risk that not only the future of the EFSF, but of the euro itself, would be called into question.

By mid-2011, it was apparent that the French economy was flatlining. Official growth forecasts – which had foreseen an annual GDP growth figure of 2 per cent for 2011 – were being revised downward. The French economy grew by 1.4 per cent in 2010, showing signs of sclerosis, particularly in the labour market, which is riddled by restrictions.

Reflecting aspects of concern to make the quick fix, in the second half of 2011 France rushed through belt-tightening measures, announcing ?65 billion (US$87 billion) of tax increases and budget cuts over five years. Most analysts thought this reflected Sarkozy's desire to protect the Triple A credit rating without irrevocably damaging his chances of re-election in 2012. Labour minister Xavier Bertrand was reported as saying 'Positive growth means tax revenue, but there isn't enough growth so we have to manage our budget like you do at home, or like a company chief,' after disappointing GDP data were released in November 2011. 'If there's not enough money coming in then there must be less money going out.'

A report by the respected Lisbon Council said France's inability to make rapid adjustments to its economy should be ringing alarm bells for the euro-zone. The Council ranked France 13th out of 17 economies for its overall health, including its growth potential, employment rate and consumption, and 15th for its progress on economic adjustments, particularly on reducing its budget deficit and controlling unit labour costs.

Towards the end of his term in office, it seemed that the international financial markets had wised up to France's economic predicament, ignoring the President's promises and aspirations, preferring instead their more prosaic prognostics. Thus, Mr Sarkozy's promises were discounted almost before he had been able to make them. As President, Mr Sarkozy has remained the politician he is, rather than becoming the statesman he probably never will be. He is known for the instant sound-bite and the short term initiative rather than for the measured policy.

The economy

In a rather rose-tinted analysis, in 2011 the International Monetary Fund (IMF) considered that 'the gradual recovery of the French economy was progressing.' However, France's unemployment rate seemed firmly stuck at 9.5 per cent; in the early months of 2011 employment had been increasing and confidence benefited from a period of stronger activity in core Europe. This growth in early 2011 had, by the middle of the year, rather fizzled out, as the crisis over the future of the euro continued to create uncertainty. The short-lived boost to growth had been led by strong private consumption and stock-building, bolstered by a recovery in investment. France's exports remained unimpressive; the IMF noted that 'an unsettled external environment continues to pose risks, especially related to possible spillovers from lingering euro area sovereign debt problems, and uncertainty about energy prices.'

The Front National (FN) (National Front)'s Marine le Pen attributed much of France's economic problems to its membership of the European Union (EU): 'Everything that made up France's grandeur' – a concept much loved and quoted by French politicians of every hue – 'its dynamism, its innovation, its openness, was completely annihilated by the EU' Ms le Pen told Philip Gourevitch of the *New Yorker* in late 2011. According to Mr Gourevitch in an article entitled *No Exit: Can Nicolas Sarkozy – and France – survive the European crisis?* Ms le Pen continued that France was 'ruined... It has ?1.6 trillion (US$2.1 trillion) in debts, an annual deficit of ?140 billion (US$188 billion) and 4 million unemployed. It doesn't export anything any more. It has no specific voice among nations.' As is the way with politicians Ms le Pen was playing to the gallery; Mr Gourevitch quickly points out that France has the world's fifth largest economy and is also fifth highest by volume of exports.

The IMF notes that what it describes as a 'sizeable fiscal consolidation' has been embarked upon in France. By this, the IMF means that a drastic austerity programme has begun. The fiscal deficit in 2010 was 7.1 per cent, better than foreseen, and a sizeable upfront adjustment is being made in 2011 to restore sustainable public finances. The overall budget deficit is to be reduced to 3 per cent of GDP by 2013 and 2 per cent of GDP by 2014. The adjustment is to be implemented through binding multi-year restrictions on more than three-quarters of central government expenditures and minimum yearly targets for the reduction in tax expenditures. Critically, the government's ability to achieve the targeted adjustment also depends on the pace of the global economic recovery, particularly in Europe. The 2012–13 targets might prove to be a bridge too far if actual growth falls short of the government's (probably ambitious) projections.

By 2011 the French banking sector had overcome most of the after effects of the global financial crisis and had returned to

KEY INDICATORS — **France**

	Unit	2006	2007	2008	2009	2010
Population	m	61.40	63.71	62.45	62.60	*62.97
Gross domestic product (GDP)	US$bn	2,252.11	2,560.26	2,866.80	2,675.90	2,582.50
GDP per capita	US$	36,706	41,940	46,035	42,747	41,019
GDP real growth	%	1.9	1.8	0.3	-2.5	1.4
Inflation	%	1.9	1.6	3.2	0.1	1.7
Unemployment	%	9.2	8.3	7.4	9.5	9.4
Coal output	mtoe	0.2	0.2	0.1	0.1	0.1
Exports (fob) (goods)	US$m	483,110.0	548,030.0	601,850.0	473,860.0	517,150.0
Imports (fob) (goods)	US$m	520,810.0	601,410.0	691,990.0	535,830.0	588,360.0
Balance of trade	US$m	-37,690.0	-53,390.0	-90,150.0	-61,960.0	-71,210.0
Current account	US$m	-28,192.0	-33,386.0	-64,776.0	-51,860.0	-44,500.0
Total reserves minus gold	US$m	42,652.0	45,710.0	33,617.0	46,633.0	55,800.0
Foreign exchange	US$m	40,287.0	43,587.0	30,382.0	27,729.0	36,211.0
Exchange rate	per US$	0.75	0.69	0.68	0.73	0.76

* estimated figure

profitability. Bank capital remains below some European peers, but is increasing, and the major French banks should be able to meet the Basel III capital requirements by 2013/14. At the same time, the large French banks remain highly reliant on wholesale funding and are exposed to peripheral euro countries; French banks are particularly exposed to Greek debt. Institutional reforms, including the unification of banking and insurance supervision and inclusion of consumer protection mandates, as well as the creation of a national systemic risk board have further strengthened supervisory arrangements in France, which will also benefit from proposed European reforms aimed at strengthening cross-border elements of supervision. House prices in France increased rapidly in the year to mid-2011, but in the view of the IMF financial stability risks linked to rapid house price increases seemed manageable.

France is challenged to lift potential growth and reduce unemployment, in particular the lack of jobs for young, unskilled, and senior workers. The reduction in unemployment is, in part, due to labour market reforms. A number of government programmes provide incentives for education and innovation. Efforts are also under way to improve competition in product and services markets where progress remains limited.

The opposition

The roll of a dice, fortune's dictates – or a possible criminal charge – can change not only the fortunes of individuals, but of whole countries. Such was the case in France where not only the fortunes of the opposition Parti Socialiste (PS) (Socialist Party), but possibly those of the nation, were opened up by the accusations of rape brought against Dominique Strauss-Kahn (DSK) by a hotel chambermaid in New York in mid-2011. The sudden decline and fall of DSK and his elimination from the Socialist leadership race was as surprising as it was significant. A large majority of French voters had seemed inclined to vote for DSK rather than for the unpopular incumbent, Nicolas Sarkozy.

Following the forced withdrawal of DSK, the likely success of the uncharismatic François Hollande in the leadership primary elections was attributed not only to chance, but also to intensive campaigning and Mr Hollande's ability to reflect and articulate the preoccupations of the French electorate. His electoral platform combined greater social equality with economic discipline. This chimed with the proposed social-democratic platform of DSK. Until the withdrawal of DSK, the 57 year old Hollande – nicknamed *Flanby* (cream caramel) by French media (and also *Monsieur Normal*), had been unable to establish any electoral lead, this despite having played a role in the PS's leadership for eleven years. Mr Hollande had been the partner of the former presidential candidate Ségolène Royal, with whom he had four children. His emergence as the party's leader appeared to coincide with the end of the relationship with Ms Royale, replaced in Mr Hollande's affections by the journalist Valérie Trierweiler.

There was, in fact, little to choose between Mr Hollande and the likely runner up, Martine Aubry, Hollande's successor as party leader and mayor of the northern city of Lille. Both candidates belonged to France's *Enarque* (graduate of the elite Ecole Nationale d'Administration (ENA) (National School of Administration)) meritocracy. Both endorsed the Sarkozy administration's (optimistic) plan to reduce the budget deficit to below 3 per cent by 2013. Both Aubry and Hollande have close links with the euro's original architect, Jacques Delors. Ms Aubry is his daughter; Mr Hollande was once a protégé of the veteran politician.

Family connections were also a feature of France's far-right, where the daughter of long-time party leader Jean-Marie Le Pen, Marine Le Pen, had taken over the leadership of the FN. Representing a new generation of rightists, Marine Le Pen had certainly given the party a new look and a new popularity. In an August 2011 interview with the *American Spectator* magazine, Ms Le Pen certainly didn't mince her words. On the future of the euro: 'Collapsing now, before our very eyes. And when it goes, the European Union in its present form will disappear along with it. Then the nations of Europe will regain their sovereignty.' Ms Le Pen's economics were, for the man on the Paris Métro easy enough to grasp: 'We would simply return to the franc. The parity would be one franc for one euro.' Just as easy to grasp, but more worrying for many French citizens, are Ms Le Pen's views on immigration and race relations. In her interview Ms Le Pen went on to say: 'Today there are entire neighbourhoods in France where our Republican laws are not applied. Often they are run by Islamists.' Once again, the Le Pen solution is disturbingly simple: 'We must actively discourage immigration. That means cutting social benefits to foreigners, no access to public housing and giving preference to French citizens for jobs.' Ms Le Pen is at pains to stress that the FN is not an extreme party: 'We are no more far right than Charles de Gaulle.' Ms Le Pen also argues that she is not against Islam, but against its incursions into France's secular state. Her arguments often seem rather odd and ill founded; 'Today in the Paris region, most meat sold in supermarkets is *halal* (lawful under Islamic law) and customers don't know it.' The Front's website makes the strange claim that eating *halal* meat may lead to conversion. From Mr Sarkozy's point of view, the preference would be to find himself running against Marine Le Pen in the second round. This would require him to group as many centre-right candidates alongside him. However, in October 2011 the polls suggested that Mr Sarkozy was more than likely to come third in the first round and simply be eliminated.

Immigration

There is no doubt that in focussing on immigration as one of its key issues, the FN is likely to gain rather than lose votes. As elsewhere in Europe, problems of race and religion have been the second elephant in the French political room. Everyone knows it is there, but no one really knows how to deal with it. France's Islamic community is probably the largest in Europe, estimated at six million. Ms Le Pen has fanned the flames by demanding that French Muslims (French women were banned from wearing the all-embracing *Burqua* in 2011) assimilate more and accept the modalities of modern French society.

Libya – Ecole Militaire?

In North Atlantic Treaty Organisation (NATO) circles France has long been seen as a junior partner. France's limited contribution to the NATO Afghanistan campaign, where France had 4,000 troops stationed (with 74 killed), did little to change the perception. In 2011, however, things improved for France following President Sarkozy's determined effort to secure a major role in moves to topple Libyan dictator Muammar Qadafi. Although the initial NATO air strikes were very much lead by the US, using Tomahawk missiles to destroy or impair air defence systems, the first manned air raid into Libyan territory was carried out by French aircraft. By late August the French contribution to the Libyan campaign was third, behind those of the US and the United Kingdom (UK). France also deployed the only aircraft-carrier in the campaign, the *Charles de Gaulle*. Some estimates put the cost of the French Libyan involvement at US$2 million per day, a total of some US$300 million by the end of August 2011. US expenditure to the end of July 2011 was estimated at US$896 million.

Le Printemps Arabe

In fact President Sarkozy and his advisors had been slow off the mark in understanding the importance of the Arab Spring. President Sarkozy's epiphany came about through a February telephone call from his friend Bernard-Henri Lévy who was in Benghazi. The wake-up call, and the opportunities it offered, was the answer to a maiden's prayer for Sarkozy. The President seized it rapidly, slipping into Action Man role, hoping as one observer put it, to 're-presidentialise'. Although the military intervention in Libya had been carried out under the aegis of the NATO, Sarkozy milked it to maximum electoral advantage.

Less charitable commentators saw the NATO Libyan intervention as an ill-conceived attempt by the President to reassert his authority and regain some of the international assurance France is perceived to have lost on Mr Sarkozy's watch. Many saw it as Sarkozy's last chance saloon, surprised and shocked by the characteristically impetuous decision to go to war and to recognise the Libyan rebels' provisional government in Benghazi. The Libyan scenario bore signs of Mr Sarkozy's sudden intervention in the 2008 stand-off between Georgia and Russia. Writing in the London *Financial Times* (FT), the newspaper's Paris correspondent Peggy Hollinger quoted one Sarkozy friend as saying that 'Bitterness is his *leitmotif.* He has a complex. He thinks he is not tall enough, not good looking enough, he wants to be loved. He thinks his ministers don't defend him enough.' Hollinger added that President Sarkozy would probably always be considered an outsider in France. The son of a Hungarian immigrant and a French mother of Greek-Jewish descent, Sarkozy reportedly chose in 1968 to march in favour of the de Gaulle regime. Unlike most French politicians and senior civil servants, he did not attend the élite ENA government academy. But above all else, the polls suggested that most French voters wanted their President to busy himself creating jobs for their children rather than going to war in North Africa.

Les Vacances des francais

The travails of the euro-zone, as well as the French involvement in Libya, will not have allowed new father Mr Sarkozy to take much of a holiday in 2011. As those of your correspondent's generation who learned about this French phenomenon from the classic film *Les Vacances de M Hulot* will remember, the annual departure for *les vacances* is almost sacrosanct. Not that the French are lacking in holidays for the rest of the year. The contrast with the US and many other European countries is impressive. An article *Vive les Vacances* by John Laughland in the London *Spectator* pointed out that there are school vacations every six weeks. In November there are two public holidays, followed by Christmas which generally adds up to a week or so off. These are followed in February by a mid-term skiing break when every train and flight from Paris to the ski-slopes is fully booked. Then comes the Easter break, followed by Whitsun.

The French summer vacation is almost a ritual in its own right; for many French middle class families the summer holiday is an annual *pélérinage* to their family's region of origin. A month's holiday is the norm, beginning either on 14 July, Bastille Day, or at the end of August when many large enterprises simply close down. This means that for at least a six-week period, from mid-July until the end of August, France is running at half (or less) speed.

France is the biggest country in Europe by area, but much of its territory is no more than extensive empty areas. These contrast dramatically with the over-populated capital city and its drab and deprived low cost suburbs. France, according to Mr Laughland, has the highest rate of second-home ownership in the world. But many second homes are in a poor state of repair, shared by extended families who only ever meet on these vocational opportunities. Mr Laughland's closing paragraph distils the whole phenomenon into one word: leisure. The tradition of leisure is still hard-wired into the French make-up. 'The French are not lazy: people work very hard when they have to. But since leisure is, in fact, the precondition for civilisation, they continue to understand that it constitutes the very point of life.'

This same 'understanding' governs the French approach to the working week. This is governed by legislation introduced in 2001 by the then socialist government, which set the working week at 35 hours. In France's private sector only lip service is paid to the 35 hour week – on average employees of French companies work 39.4 hours per week, still below the European average of 40.4. In the run-up to the 2012 elections, there was little the Sarkozy administration – lagging in the polls – dared do to amend the law. This despite the fact that since its introduction, French productivity has nose-dived in relation to that of Germany. Writing in the FT, Peggy Hollinger pointed out that France's hourly labour costs, once 10 per cent lower than Germany's, have risen to the same level. One depressing report suggested that within the euro-zone, French exports had fallen from a total share of 17 per cent in 1998 to 13.1 per cent in 2010. The same report put the cost of exemptions and benefits related to the 35-hour limit at US$29 billion.

Risk assessment

Economy	Fair
Politics	Good
Regional stability	Good

COUNTRY PROFILE

Historical profile

1337–1453 The Hundred Years' War took place between the English and the French. The English were defeated in 1453 and driven out of Aquitaine in southern France.

1789 The lack of representation for the increasingly powerful middle class, opposition to France's absolute monarchy and economic problems led to the French Revolution and the overthrow of Louis XVI.

1792 The First Republic was declared.

1804 Napoléon Bonaparte declared himself emperor and launched a military campaign in Europe.

1815 Napoléon's defeat at Waterloo by the British, Belgians, Dutch and Prussians saw the end of his reign. Louis XVIII became King of France.

1848 An uprising led by students and workers, although quickly crushed, again led to the overthrow of the monarchy. Louis Napoléon (nephew of the first Napoléon) was elected president.

1852 Louis Napoléon declared himself emperor.

1871 France's defeat in the Franco-Prussian War resulted in the annexation of Alsace-Lorraine by the Germans.

1914 France was invaded by Germany.

1918 Following the end of the First World War and Germany's defeat, France regained Alsace-Lorraine.

1939 After Germany's invasion of Poland, France and the UK entered the Second World War by declaring war on Germany.

1940 France signed an armistice after Germany had invaded the country. The Germans installed a puppet government, the Vichy, led by Henri-Philippe Pétain. A Free French resistance built up in the UK under the leadership of General Charles de Gaulle.
1944 Following the liberation of France by the Allied powers, a provisional government took office under General de Gaulle.
1945 After the war in Europe General de Gaulle retired from public office. The Fourth Republic was created with a constitution giving ultimate power to the Assemblé Nationale (National Assembly).
1946–1958 France had 26 different governments, many including large communist elements.
1958 The Fifth Republic was created after the introduction of a new constitution, which allowed for the creation of a powerful presidency. General de Gaulle was elected president. France became a founder member of the forerunner of the EU, the European Economic Community (EEC), along with Belgium, Italy, Luxembourg, The Netherlands and West Germany.
1962 Algeria, which had been a *département* of France since 1948, gained its independence, following a brutal insurgency.
1968 Discontent with low wages, lack of social reform and poor education policies led to a revolt by students and workers. The general strike was settled by the granting of generous wage rises and the student revolt collapsed, although De Gaulle's political position was fatally weakened.
1969 De Gaulle resigned from the presidency after losing a referendum on his programme for strengthening regional governments. He was succeeded by Georges Pompidou (1969–74) who was followed by Valéry Giscard d'Estaing (1974–81).
1970 Former president Charles de Gaulle died.
1981 François Mitterrand became the first socialist president since 1958 following Giscard d'Estaing's electoral defeat, governing with the first left-wing cabinet for 23 years.
1995 Jacques Chirac succeeded François Mitterrand as president. Pacific and Oceania countries condemned French nuclear testing in French Polynesia.
2002 The euro replaced the franc as France's currency. President Chirac defeated Jean-Marie Le Pen in elections. Prime Minister Lionel Jospin resigned and Chirac appointed Jean-Pierre Raffarin (UMP) in his place. After legislative elections, a coalition government was formed, led by the Union pour un Mouvement Populaire (UMP) (Popular Movement Party), with Union pour la Démocratie Française (UDF) (French Democracy Party), the Démocratie Libérale (DL) (Liberal Democracy) and allies.
2003 France was crippled by a series of public sector strikes over pension reform.
2004 Voting in regional elections showed national discontent with the government, as the left-wing opposition carried 21 out of the country's 22 mainland regions. Prime Minister Raffarin resigned, but was immediately re-instated.
2005 France held a referendum on the European Constitution in which almost 55 per cent voted No, with 45 per cent in favour; turnout was about 70 per cent. Prime Minister Raffarin resigned the next day; Dominique de Villepin was appointed prime minister. Rioting in disadvantaged and disaffected immigrant communities broke out, first in the Paris suburb of Clichy-sous-Bois, then elsewhere in the capital and in other towns and cities. Final figures reported by the French police were 8,973 vehicles burnt and 2,888 arrests forcing the government to declare a state of emergency for several weeks.
2006 France provided 1,700 troops for UN peace-keeping duties in the Lebanon. France and Germany combined to apply pressure on the EU demanding tougher conditions for Turkey's proposed membership.
2007 Nicolas Sarkozy (Rassemblement pour la République (RPR) (Party of the Republic)), won the presidential elections, defeating Ségolène Royal (Parti Socialiste (PS) Socialist Party)). François Fillon (UMP) was appointed prime minister.
2008 Société Générale, one of France's largest banks, lost US$7.1 billion through fraud by a rogue trader. President Sarkozy married Carla Bruni at the Elysée Palace. Parliament scraped the 35-hour working week, 10 years after it was introduced, so that companies could organise working patterns based on agreements with their workforces.
2009 An economic stimulus package of US$33.1 billion was launched. The Natixis corporate and investment bank declared it had 'toxic assets' of US$44 billion and losses of US$2.8 billion in the first quarter of the year.
2010 A national disaster was declared on 1 March following devastating storms that caused death and destruction, particularly along the Atlantic coast. Legislation banning the wearing of the burka (full Islamic face veil worn by women) in France was ratified in July. The penalties for wearing a burka and forcing a female to wear a burka include fines and imprisonment. The US, UK, Germany and France placed a ban on all cargo from Yemen in November, due to Al Qaeda activity in Yemen. Over three million French protestors took part in marches and widespread strikes in October, called to object to government plans to increase the age of retirement from 60 to 62 years by 2018; the legislation was finally enacted on 24 October.
2011 On 10 March, France became the first country to formally recognise the Libyan Transitional National Council (TNC) as the legitimate government of Libya. On 19 March, it joined a five-country coalition (with Canada, Italy, the UK and the US) to impose a no-fly zone over Libya. On 29 March a referendum was held in Mayotte to decide whether it should become a French Département d'Outre-Mer (DOM) (Overseas Department). The result was 95.24 per cent of votes in favour. On 3 March the island of Mayotte became France's fifth DOM. Comoros, which claimed the territory, protested the action of France. On 28 June, the French finance minister, Christine Lagarde was appointed as managing director of the International Monetary Fund (IMF), and took up her post on 5 July. On 29 June a supply of weapons (including assault rifles, machine guns and rocket launchers) was parachuted into rebel held territory of Libya by the French military. The AU condemned the move saying it puts the whole region at risk. The French stated that this was a one-off decision to re-arm a town cut off from supplies from its allies. In an unannounced visit to Afghanistan on 11 July President Sarkozy announced that 1,000 French troops would be withdrawn by the end of 2012. In indirect elections held on 25 September the left wing Socialist Party and its Communist and Green allies won enough seats to win control of the upper house. The conservatives had held power in the Senate since the formation of the Fifth Republic in 1958. 200 French troops that were part of a 4,000 military contingent stationed in the district of Surobi and the neighbouring Kapisa Province, were withdrawn from active service in the NATO mission in Afghanistan on 20 October. A further 200 were scheduled to be withdrawn by the end of December. On 24 November, France announced that it would no longer buy Iranian oil, typically amounting to 49,000 barrels per day, on a 'national basis',. The French ban was in response to Iran's continued nuclear programme. France also joined its EU partners in joint sanctions.

Political structure

Constitution

The 25 September 1958 constitution of the Fifth Republic maintained the original French republican ideals of liberty,

fraternity and equality. It was designed to end post-war political deadlock by granting greater powers to the president. It guarantees the unity and indivisibility of the French state.
Since 1982 much administrative and financial power, traditionally held by the state, has been devolved to the 22 *régions* (regions) and 96 *départements* (departments) of metropolitan France. In March 2003, parliament approved constitutional amendments which allow all of the regions and departments a greater amount of autonomy.
In mid-2000, legislation was passed granting semi-autonomy to the island of Corsica as a single administrative unit, replacing its previous status as two standard *départements*. France's overseas territories are either classed as Département d'Outre-Mer (DOM) (Overseas Department) or Térritoire d'Outre-Mer (TOM) (Overseas Territory), depending on the level of autonomy.

Independence date

14 July 1789.

Form of state

Semi-presidential democratic republic

The executive

Executive power is held by the president, elected by universal adult suffrage for a five-year term which can be renewed only once. A two-round voting system operates for presidential elections, with the second round a run-off between the two highest polling candidates from the first round.
The president appoints the prime minister and other members of the government, can dissolve the Assemblée Nationale and can also veto laws. In practice, the president traditionally accepts as prime minister the leader of the largest party in the National Assembly, and approves the prime minister's choice of government ministers.
The presidential term of office was reduced from seven years to five with effect from the 2002 presidential elections.

National legislature

The bicameral Parlement (Parliament) consists of the Assemblée Nationale (National Assembly) with 577 deputés (deputies) directly elected in single seat constituencies, for five-year terms. The Sénat (Senate) has 321 seats in total, of which 304 are elected for six-year terms by an electoral college of elected representatives from each department; the remainder are elected by overseas regions, departments, collectivities and territories.

Legal system

The country has no supreme court but this role is filled by a nine-member Conseil Constitutionel (Constitutional Council). Its task is to ensure that law treaties and regulations are in keeping with the constitution and that elections are conducted in a regular manner. The highest court of appeal is the Cour de Cassation, which can overrule decisions in all lower courts, but not government legislation. Since the signing of the Single European Act in 1986, the European Court of Justice (ECJ) has been the highest authority in certain areas of French law. France also accepts International Court of Justice (ICJ) jurisdiction.

Last elections

22 April/6 May 2007 (presidential); 10/17 June 2007 (parliamentary).
Results: Presidential: Nicolas Sarkozy (Union pour un Mouvement Populaire) (UMP) (Union for a Popular Movement) won 53.06 per cent of the vote; Ségolène Royal (Parti Socialiste (PS) (Socialist Party)) 46.94 per cent.
Parliamentary: Majorité présidentielle (Presidential Majority) coalition (led by UMP) 49.66 per cent (345 seats out of 577), L'Unité de la Gauche (United Left) coalition (led by PS) 49.08 per cent (277); all other parties won less than 1 per cent.

Next elections

22 April and 5 May 2012 (presidential); 10 and 17 June 2012 (parliamentary).

Political parties

Ruling party

Union pour un Mouvement Populaire (UMP) (Union for a People's Movement)

Main opposition party

Parti Socialiste (PS) (Socialist Party)

Population

62.60 million (2009)
Last census: 1 January 2006: 61,399,541
Population density: 107 inhabitants per square km. Urban population: 76 per cent (1995–2001).
Annual growth rate: 0.4 per cent 1994–2004 (WHO 2006)

Ethnic make-up

The population is predominantly Western European. North Africans form the principal ethnic minority, with smaller communities from former French colonies in Asia and sub-Saharan Africa.

Religions

There is no state religion, but Roman Catholicism predominates (90 per cent of population), with a significant Protestant minority concentrated in southern France (2 per cent) and Muslim and Jewish communities in major urban areas (1 per cent each).

Education

Compulsory education is provided for free. Primary schooling lasts to the age of 11, after which all pupils transfer to a four-year course in secondary school. At the age of 15 there are two options: either a three-year course leading to the *baccalauréate* examination or a two-year vocational course. An average of 80 per cent of schoolchildren are expected to achieve the *baccalauréate*, which is the minimum entry qualification to university. Educational expenditure is typically equivalent to 6 per cent of gross national income.
Compulsory years: Six to 16
Pupils per teacher: 19 in primary schools

Health

France's liberal state-subsidised medical system allows doctors and dentists to establish private practices. Patients, who are free to choose their own providers, are reimbursed by the state for up to 85 per cent of medical costs. The government makes full provision for people who are unable to make any contributions, by treating them as private patients covered by insurance.
Proposed reforms to reduce the cost of the health system have met with vociferous opposition from doctors, nurses and health professionals. Fraud is estimated to cost the system more than US$980 million per year, and ease of access to prescription drugs is thought to be the principal reason for the fact that French consumption of drugs and medicine is more than three times the European average.

HIV/Aids

HIV prevalence: 0.4 per cent aged 15–49 in 2003 (World Bank)
Life expectancy: 80 years, 2004 (WHO 2006)
Fertility rate/Maternal mortality rate: 1.9 births per woman, 2004 (WHO 2006); maternal mortality 0.1 per 1,000 live births (World Bank).
Child (under 5 years) mortality rate (per 1,000): 4.4 per 1,000 live births (World Bank)
Head of population per physician: 3.37 physicians per 1,000 people, 2004 (WHO 2006)

Welfare

France's extensive social security system, including health insurance, family allowances and retirement insurance, covers 99.2 per cent of the population. In common with other industrialised nations, France's ageing population is an increasing concern.

Pensions

In June 2010, pension reforms were introduced, to be implemented by 2012, including raising the retirement age from 60 to 62, with workers having worked for a minimum of 41.5 years. France's pension deficit for 2010 was estimated at US$39.5 billion and could treble by 2050 if measures to stem the costs are not employed.

Main cities
Paris (capital, estimated population 2.1 million in 2005), Marseille (771,153), Lyon (454,478), Toulouse (402,905), Nice (344,338), Nantes (278,056), Strasbourg (268,062), Bordeaux (216,683).

Languages spoken
Breton is spoken in Brittany and Euskera (Basque) is spoken in the south-west, while in Alsace and Lorraine, in the east, German is widely spoken.
English is spoken in the business community, but an understanding of French is considered essential for visitors.
Flemish, Catalán, Occitan, Corsu, Arabic, Kabyle and Antillean are also spoken.
Official language/s
French

Media
Press
French newspapers are editorially free from government control and censorship, and cover the full political spectrum.
There are 85 daily newspapers published, of which 24 are nationals. There are around 870 newspapers and 6,000 magazines published reaching over 45 per cent of adults. Regional newspapers have a larger readership than national titles.
Dailies: In French, major newspapers include *Le Monde* (www.lemonde.fr), *Le Figaro* (www.lefigaro.fr) is a conservative newspaper, *Libération* (www.liberation.fr) a left-wing newspaper, *Ouest France* (www.ouest-france.fr) has the largest circulation, *Le Parisien* (www.leparisien.fr) a centrist newspaper and *La Croix* (www.la-croix.com) a Catholic newspaper.
Weeklies: In French, the *Courrier Intenational* (www.courrierinternational.com), *L'Epress* (www.lexpress.fr) and *Le Point* (www.lepoint.fr) report on news and current affairs, *Le Journal du Dimanche* (www.lejdd.fr) is a popular Sunday newspaper. Special interest publications include *Maghreb Hebdo* concerning north African news and *La Marseillaise* a communist publication and two humourist magazines are *Le Canard Enchaîné* and *Le Herisson*. In English *The Riviera Times* (www.rivieratimes.com).
Business: In French, daily newspapers include *Les Echos* (www.lesechos.fr), *La Tribune* (www.latribune.fr) and *Investir* (www.investir.fr). Monthly publications include the popular economics magazine *Capital* (www.capital.fr), *L'Expansion* (www.lexpansion.com) and *Valeurs Actuelles* (www.valeursactuelles.com) a weekly and *Le Revenu* (www.lerevenu.com) a bi-weekly magazine. *Jeune Afrique Economie* is an Africa-oriented bi-weelkly.
Periodicals: In French, monthly publications include *Le Monde Dipomatique* (www.monde-diplomatique.fr) a left-wing magazine, *Entrevue* (www.entrevue.fr) a tabloid entertainment magazine, *Lire* (www.lire.fr) a cultural magazine and *Le Nouvel Afrique Asie* a left-wing third world-orientated monthly magazine. Influential women's magazines include *Vogue* (www.vogue.fr) and *Marie Claire* (www.marieclaire.fr).
Broadcasting
France is a world leader in broadcasting, providing international news and entertainment services to most continents, via radio, satellite, pay-to-view digital services and internet links.
Radio: The national public radio service is Radio France (www.radiofrance.fr) with seven stations offering a range of genre including classical, news, sport, information, culture and modern music. Radio France Internationale (RFI) (www.rfi.fr) is funded wholly by the French ministry of foreign affairs; it broadcasts worldwide in 19 languages, other than French.
Nationally, there are 17 commercial radio stations including Europe 1 (www.europe1.fr), Fun Radio (www.funradio.fr), RTL (www.rtl.fr) a major news and entertainment network, Sud Radio (www.sudradio.fr), NRJ (www.nrj.fr), a leading music network and Alouette (www.alouette.fr).
Apart from private local and regional radio stations, many are affiliates of national networks.
Television: The national public broadcaster is France Télévisions (www.francetelevisions.fr) with five networks. Some channels carry advertising. Channels are designated France 2, 3, 4, 5 and RFO (www.rfo.fr) for overseas territories. Combined, France Télévisions typically has 40 per cent of the audience share and 30 per cent of revenues.
TF1 (www.tf1.fr) is the leading commercial TV channel with typically 35 per cent audience share and almost 50 per cent of advertising revenues. Programmes include locally made and foreign imports. TFI operates a national 24-hour news channel, La Chaine Info (http://tf1.lci.fr), as well as a major digital and internet TV service, France 24 (www.france24.com), with a wide range of international news and current affairs in French, English and Arabic. All analogue services will be switched to digital services by 2011.
Advertising
The typical annual ad-spend is around €10 billion (US$7.2 billion), of which the greater part is spent by retail advertising at over €2 billion (US$1.4 billion). Television and magazine advertising typically carry around 30 per cent of the market each.
Numerous advertising agencies operate throughout the country. Television advertising is strictly controlled, by Régie Française de Publicité (RFP), and is expensive. There is limited advertising available on radio. All other media are widely used for advertising, although newspapers and magazines dominate. There are over 50,000 poster panels available. New advertising media is available through the internet and mobile/cell phones.
Tobacco and alcohol may be advertised but only under strict rules.
News agencies
National news agency: Agence France Presse

Economy
The French economy, following on after Germany and the UK, is Europe and the EU's most productive economy. It manufactures some of the biggest global brands of automobiles and luxury goods, space technology and heavy machinery, pharmaceuticals and construction materials, foodstuffs and cultural items. It is a major exporter of energy, particularly electricity from its network of nuclear power stations and it was reported in 2010 that it had three of the world's top-ten largest banks, operating worldwide.
GDP growth in 2007 was 2.3 per cent, which fell to 0.3 per cent in 2008 as the global economic crisis struck; the trade deficit was 37 per cent higher than in 2007, at US$71.4 billion, due to record high petroleum prices coupled with weakened export trade. The financial sector was caught up in the US mortgage-based toxic debt, which caused the economy to fall further to -2.2 per cent in 2009, so that France officially fell into recession in the first quarter of 2009. The government was forced to bail out six of the country's banks at the cost of US$14 billion to its taxpayers. At the same time as the global banking system was going into meltdown a trader working for Société Générale lost US$7.2 billion of the bank's money by speculating on the stock market through bogus transactions. It was the largest loss in France's corporate history and resulted in the bank being downgraded by two international credit ratings agencies.
Some much-needed reforms, notably in pensions, were begun in June 2010. They included raising the retirement age from 60 to 62, to be implemented by 2012; workers will also have to have worked for a minimum of 41.5 years. France's pension deficit for 2010 was estimated at US$39.5 billion and could treble by 2050 if measures to stem the costs are not employed. Another major priority for the government continues to be unemployment, which is around 10 per cent and, more

worryingly, with disproportionately high youth unemployment.

External trade

As a member of the European Union, France operates within a community-wide free trade area, with tariffs set as a whole. Internationally, the EU has free trade agreements with a number of nations and trading blocs worldwide. France has several overseas *départements* which are treated as *de jure* mainland France with fully implemented treaties with the EU.

France is a leading world trader; it is a major exporter of agricultural produce and processed food, its industrial base includes vehicles, aerospace and high-speed trains, telecommunications, weapons and consumer goods.

Imports

Principal imports are machinery and equipment, vehicles, crude oil, aircraft, plastics and chemicals.

Main sources: Germany (typically 15 per cent of total), Italy (9 per cent), Belgium (8 per cent).

Exports

Principal exports include machinery and vehicles, trains and other rail equipment, aircraft, plastics, chemicals and pharmaceuticals, iron and steel, food and beverages.

Main destinations: Germany (typically 16 per cent of total), Belgium (8 per cent), Italy (8 per cent).

Agriculture

Farming

France is a major European food producer with self-sufficiency in dairy produce and is a substantial exporter of livestock produce, wine, fruit and vegetables. Agriculture contributes around 3.1 per cent to GDP and employs 5 per cent of the labour force.

The EU's Fundamental reform to the Common Agricultural Policy (CAP) was introduced in France in 2005. The subsidies paid on farm output, which tended to benefit large farms and encourage overproduction, were replaced by single farm payments not conditional on production.

With the growing global demand for Champagne, which reached a record of almost 151 million bottles in 2007, the government extended the growing region, officially allowing vintners within the newly expanded area to designate their sparkling wine as Champagne. An area of 33,500 hectares in north-eastern France is the only place worldwide allowed to use the coveted Appellation d'Origine Controlee (AOC) and to label its wine Champagne. The last expansion of the Champagne region was in 1927; the latest enlargement will become operational in 2009, with the new AOC Champagne expected to be ready for sale by 2019.

Fishing

Although oyster farming remains highly vulnerable to the risk of disease, France is the top European producer of oysters and among the first three producers of mussels (from both fishing and aquaculture).

France is also the top European producer of fresh water trout and has remained competitive with European regions with more favourable environmental conditions. Sea bass and sea bream represent the majority of marine farm production with turbot farming expanding. Only part of the production is for domestic consumption, the remainder being exported.

Forestry

Forestry is France's richest natural resource with over a quarter (15 million hectares) of metropolitan France covered by forest, giving it the largest tree-covered area in the EU. The Office National des Forêts (ONF) (National Forestry Office) manages over a quarter of this area. Forestry is concentrated in the east, south and south-west of the country, with the largest area being the Landes, coastal forests south of Bordeaux. Deciduous forests account for 61 per cent of the total, while 38 per cent are coniferous or mixed.

About 8 per cent of the wooded area is brushwood.

Although it is a net importer of sawn softwoods and pulp for its paper industry, France remains the largest producer of sawn hardwood in Europe.

The forestry industry supplies raw materials to several industries. About 60 per cent of French wood production is used in the construction industry.

Industry and manufacturing

France has a broad industrial base incorporating a large capital-intensive state-owned sector, composed mainly of small- and medium-sized manufacturing enterprises, which together contribute around 25 per cent to GDP and employ 27 per cent of the labour force.

Industrial policy is generally aimed at developing the domestic market, promotion of 'new technology' sectors and internationalisation of state-owned companies.

Government protection of industry is an important economic issue and one which threatens both to retard the efficiency of domestic markets and alienate France's European partners.

Leading sectors include agri-foodstuffs, telecommunications, aerospace, motor industry, metallurgy, chemicals, parachemicals and pharmaceuticals, textiles and clothing.

Tourism

France has a reputation for haute cuisine, couture and culture, as offered in world class restaurants, cities and museums and galleries; it has historical sites that stretch back to the Roman Empire and others that have an importance to the modern world, it produces outstanding wine and cheeses. It was the birthplace of sun-worshipping holidays along its Mediterranean coast and any number of winter skiing resorts.

France is the number one tourist destination in the world, attracting over 79 million visitors in 2008, of which around 60 million arrived by road. The record number of tourists in 2008 was despite the beginning of a slump caused by the global economic crisis that cut tourism worldwide. By the first quarter of 2009 year-on-year international tourist arrivals to France had fallen 19.6 per cent and accommodation by 20.3 per cent. Despite Europe experiencing the greatest fall in growth in 2010 (exacerbated by the grounding of flights due to a volcanic ash cloud during the busy tourist season) France's premier position was not threatened, as tourists returned to pre-2009 numbers.

Travel and tourism in 2011 is forecast to directly contribute 3.9 per cent of GDP, and 9.1 per cent through total indirect contribution. Direct employment in the sector was predicted to be 4.5 per cent of total (1.15 million jobs) and 10.2 per cent of indirect employment (2.6 million jobs).

Tourism was expected to generate €43.5 billion (US$60.8 billion) in foreign exchange and the industry to have had direct investment of €12.3 billion (US$17.2 billion), 3 per cent of total investment committed for 2011.

Mining

The mining sector typically contributes 7 per cent to annual GDP and employs less than 1 per cent of the workforce. France is a significant producer of iron ore, bauxite and potash. In an effort to reduce dependence on imported minerals, exploration for lead, zinc, barium and tungsten has been intensified.

Hydrocarbons

Proven oil reserves were 1,220 million barrels in 2007. Crude oil production has declined since about 1990 from 67,000 barrels per day (bpd) to 19,840bpd in 2007 France is a heavy consumer of oil, amounting to two million bpd, most of which is imported from Norway, Russia and Saudi Arabia.

Although France has a lack of crude oil supplies the French oil company TotalFinaElf is one of the world's largest and most active international oil producers.

On 6 July 2011, parliament voted to ban hydraulic fracturing of shale oil and gas development. France is the first country to ban the technique (commonly referred to as fracking), that releases hydrocarbons from shale after being bombarded by high-pressure water, but has also been blamed for causing substrata instability. Proven natural gas reserves were 9.6 billion cubic metres (cum) in 2007, but consumption is typically over 45 billion cum and imports are required to make up the shortfall. Gaz de France (GdF), the majority government-owned utility, dominates gas activities and since energy markets inside the EU was opened to competition, around 30 per cent of GdF customers live outside France. The majority of gas pipelines are operated by GdF, including intra-European links.

Negotiations began in 2009 between the majority state-owned energy company EDF and Russia to invest in the South Stream gas pipeline between Russia and Bulgaria in exchange for a long-term contract. EDF aims to acquire 15 per cent of gas volume sales in France, Germany, Italy and the UK by 2015.

The coal-mining industry ended with the closure of the last mine in 2004, but some coal is imported for the remaining coal-fired power stations and the steel industry.

Energy

France is one of the world's largest nuclear power producers and is Europe's largest electricity net exporter. Total electricity generation capacity was 116 gigawatts (GW) in 2007, producing 542.4 billion kilowatt hours (kWh). Over 80 per cent of French electricity is generated by its 58 nuclear power stations, comprising 34 reactors of 900MW, 20 reactors of 1.3GW and 4 reactors of 1.45GW. In 2007 France consumed over 450 billion kWh or 100 million tonnes of oil equivalent. The government plans to expand the sector with the construction of a new generation of reactors as well as upgrading existing assets.

The leading electricity entity is EDF (Electricité de France), which is a limited-liability corporation, with 85/15 per cent government/private ownership, responsible for producing electricity, supplying around 95 per cent of all electricity in the country and delivering it nationally. Overseas, EDF has partnerships with electricity companies in North and South America, Africa, Asia and Europe.

Financial markets

Stock exchange

Euronext Paris

Commodity exchange

Liffe Connect

Banking and insurance

Central bank

Banque de France; European Central Bank (ECB)

Time

GMT plus one hour (daylight saving, late March to late October, GMT plus two hours)

Geography

France is bordered to the north by the English Channel (La Manche), and to the north-east, east and south-east by Belgium, Luxembourg, Germany, Switzerland and Italy, respectively. The Mediterranean Sea forms the southern boundary, and Spain the south-western, while the west coast faces the Atlantic Ocean.

France, the largest country in the west of Europe, has lush farming land, extensive forest and a large alluvial salt mash that makes up much of the province of the Camargue. The overall impression is of a rolling landscape from the south-west to north-east and mountainous regions for the rest of the country. There are four major river systems (the Seine, Loire, Rhone and Marne) that drain into either the Atlantic Ocean, English Channel or the Mediterranean Sea. The highest mountain, Mont Blanc (4,810 metres), is situated in the French Alps in the south-east.

Hemisphere

Northern

Climate

France has a moderate maritime climate in the north with a small temperature range and abundant rainfall. By contrast, southern France has a Mediterranean climate, with hot dry summers and mild, moist winters. Eastern France has a continental climate, with thunderstorms prevalent in summer. The average temperature in Paris in January is three degrees Celsius (C) and in July 18 degrees C. Annual rainfall in Paris is 573mm.

Dress codes

Western dress is the norm.

Entry requirements

Passports

Passports are required by all, expect nationals of EU countries with national ID cards. Passports must be valid for three months beyond the length of stay.

Visa

Required by all, except citizens of EU countries, North America, Australasia and Japan, for stays up to three months; this includes business trips by representatives of foreign entities with an invitation from a local company or organisation. Proof of adequate funds for stay, an itinerary, a guarantee of repatriation if necessary and return/onward ticket are also required. For further exceptions, full details and a copy of the application form visit www.diplomatie.gouv.fr/thema/dossier.gb.asp and follow the path (entering France) to the database. A Schengen visa application (offered in several languages) can be downloaded from http://europa.eu/abc/travel/ see 'documents you will need'.

Currency advice/regulations

There are no limits to the amount of local or foreign currency imported or exported, although amounts exceeding €7,600 must be declared.

Customs

Personal items are duty-free. There are no duties levied on alcohol and tobacco between EU member states, providing amounts imported are for personal consumption.

Plant material, meat products from Africa and valuable art or antique objects must be declared.

Health (for visitors)

Nationals of the European Economic Area (EEA) countries and Switzerland can access reduced cost and sometimes free medical treatment using a European Health Insurance Card (EHIC) while visiting the EEA. Exceptions include nationals of the 10 countries which joined the EU in 2004 whose EHIC is not valid in Switzerland. Applications for the EHIC should be made before travelling.

Mandatory precautions

None

Advisable precautions

There are no particular health hazards in France, although rabies is a problem in some rural areas.

Medical insurance is advisable for visitors of non-EEA countries as healthcare costs can be high. Only medication for personal use may be bought into France.

Hotels

Classified into deluxe and one- to four-star. Reservations (either direct or through centralised booking offices) should be made in advance during holiday seasons. Single rooms are rare and rates are usually quoted for double rooms. A tip of around 12–15 per cent of the bill is usual, provided no service charge has already been added.

Credit cards

All major credit cards are accepted.

Public holidays (national)

Fixed dates

1 Jan (New Year's Day), 1 May (Labour Day), 8 May (Victory Day), 14 Jul (Bastille Day), 15 Aug (Assumption Day), 1 Nov (All Saints' Day), 11 Nov (Armistice Day) and 25 Dec (Christmas Day).

The months of July and August are traditionally when the French take their holidays.

Variable dates

Easter Monday, Ascension Day, Whit Monday.

Working hours
Anyone intending to visit France for business purposes should avoid the traditional holiday month of August, when most businesses and government departments have only a skeleton staff at work.

Banking
Mon–Fri: 0900–1200 and 1400–1600. Some banks close on Mondays and all close early on the day before a Bank Holiday.

Business
Mon–Fri: 0900–1200 and 1400–1800.

Government
Mon–Fri: 0830–1800.

Shops
Mon–Fri: 0900–1830 (most shops are closed between 1200–1430). Some shops open on Sundays and some close on Mondays.

Telecommunications
Mobile/cell phones
There are 900/1800 and 3G GSM services available throughout all of the country.

Electricity supply
220V AC

Social customs/useful tips
In France, strangers and acquaintances shake hands at the beginning and end of a meeting.
Most offices traditionally have a long lunch hour, lasting from 1200 until at least 1400. Lunchtime remains a popular time for doing business, with a number of restaurants in big cities catering expressly for business clients.
French nationals must carry identification at all times. Visitors should carry their passports. Spot identity checks are not uncommon and it is illegal to be without identification.

Security
Serious crimes represent only a tiny percentage of the total number reported, while there has been a big rise in delinquency, vandalism and petty theft. Pickpockets operate particularly in train stations and subways.
France has one of the highest road accident rates in Europe.

Getting there
Air
France has a number of airports located in the various regions receiving international flights.
National airline: Air France
International airport/s: Paris-Charles de Gaulle Airport (CDG), 23km north-east of Paris. Facilities include a business centre, bank, post office, restaurants, bars, duty-free shopping, medical centre and pharmacy. Car hire is available.
Other airport/s: Orly (ORY), 14km south of Paris; Bordeaux (BOD), 12km from city; Lille (LIL), 15km from city; Lyon (LYS), 24km east of Lyon; Marseille (MRS), 24km north of city; Nice (NCE), 6km west of Nice; Toulouse (TLS), 10km from city; Biarritz (BIQ); Nantes (NTE); Perpignan (PGF) and Strasbourg (SXB).
Airport tax: None

Surface
France has good rail, road and sea connections with all surrounding countries.
Rail: The Eurostar service is provided by Belgium, UK and French railways, operating high speed rail connections between London, Paris and Brussels. Road vehicles are transported through the tunnel in Le Shuttle trains.
Water: There are regular cross channel ferries from the UK and Mediterrean ferries to Corsica, Spain (Balearic Islands) and North Africa.
Main port/s: Marseille (Europe's third-largest port), Boulogne, Nice, Calais, Dieppe, Dunkirk, Cherbourg, Le Havre, Rouen.

Getting about
National transport
Air: Paris is the most important business destination in France and is served by the two main airports, at Orly and Charles de Gaulle. Major cities are linked by Air France. Some services operate only during summer.
Road: France has the densest road network in the world. There are 806,000km of roads, including 7,100km of motorways, most of which are *autoroutes à péage* (toll roads).
Buses: There are good local bus services and some long-distance coach services.
Rail: French transport policy favours the railways. The Société Nationale des Chemins de Fer Français (SNCF) (French National Railroad Company) operates a nationwide network reaching to almost every part of the country. The most important rail lines radiate from Paris. Three high-speed train (TGV) lines link northern- and southern France. These trains are modern and comfortable; seats can be booked in advance.
Water: There are approximately 9,000km of inland navigable waterways. Major canal areas are situated in the north and north-east of Paris, where the majority of the navigable rivers, including the Seine, the Rhine, the Midi, Brittany and the Loire are connected with canals.

City transport
Paris has one of the best urban transport networks in the world. A *Carte Orange Hebdomadaire* allows unlimited travel for one week on most forms of public transport.
Taxis: From Charles de Gaulle and Orly airports to the city centre, limousines and taxis are available.
Taxis are only available from *stations de taxi* (taxi ranks). Day and night rates should be displayed inside the vehicle. Note that extra charges are usually levied for journeys to racecourses, stations and airports. Tipping is usually 10–15 per cent.
Buses, trams & metro: In Paris, the same tickets may be used on buses and the metro; a carnet of 10 tickets is cheaper. Buses operate between 0600–2100; some exceptional routes operate until 0030.

Car hire
All major international hire companies have offices in Paris and other main towns. Drivers must carry at all times: a passport or national ID card, a valid driving licence, car ownership papers and proof of insurance.
Traffic drives on the right. *Priorité à droite* applies, particularly in built-up areas – cars coming out of a side turning on the right have priority, unless suspended where a sign indicates. Speed limits: 130kph on toll motorways, 110kph on dual carriageways, 90kph on other roads and 60kph in towns. Note that these limits are reduced when wet. Speed limits for drivers who have held their licence for less than two years are 110kph on motorways, 100kph on dual carriageways and 80kph on other roads.
Wearing of seat belts is compulsory in front seats.

BUSINESS DIRECTORY

Telephone area codes
The International direct dialling (IDD) code for France is +33, followed by area code and subscriber's number:

Paris	1
North-west (Nantes, Rouen, etc)	2
North-east (Lille, Strasbourg etc)	3
South-east and Corsica (Lyon, Marseilles, etc)	4
South-west (Bordeaux, Toulouse, etc)	5

Useful telephone numbers
Police: 17
Fire: 18
Medical emergency and ambulance: 15

Chambers of Commerce
American Chamber of Commerce in France, 156 Boulevard Haussmann, 75008 Paris (tel: 5643-4567; fax: 5643-4560; e-mail: amchamfrance@amchamfrance.org)

Assemblée des Chambres Françaises de Commerce et d'Industrie, 45 Avenue d'Iéna, PO Box 3003, 75773 Paris Cedex 16 (tel: 4069-3700; fax: 4720-6128; e-mail: contactdie@acfci.cci.fr).

Boulogne-sur-Mer Chambre de Commerce et d'Industrie, 98 Quai Gambetta, 62204 Boulogne-sur-Mer (tel: 2199-6200; fax: 2199-6201; e-mail: ccibco@boulogne-sur-mer.cci.fr).

Bordeaux Chambre de Commerce et d'Industrie, 12 Place de la Bourse, 33076 Bordeaux (tel: 5679-5000; fax: 5569-5265; e-mail: bourse@bordeaux.cci.fr).

British-French Chamber of Commerce and Industry, 31 Rue Boissy d'Anglas, 75008 Paris (tel: 5330-8130; fax: 5330-8135; e-mail: information@francobritishchamber.com).

Calais Chambre de Commerce et d'Industrie, 24 Boulevard des Alliés, PO Box 199, 62104 Calais Cedex (tel: 2146-0000; fax: 2146-0099; e-mail: ccic@calais.cci.fr).

Grenoble Chambre de Commerce et d'Industrie, 1 Place André Malraux, PO Box 297, 38016 Grenoble Cedex 1 (tel: 7628-2828; fax: 7628-2747; e-mail: ccig@grenoble.cci.fr).

Loiret Chambre de Commerce et d'Industrie, 23 Place du Martroi, 45044 Orléans Cedex 1 (tel: 3877-7777; fax: 3853-0978; e-mail: direction@loiret.cci.fr).

Lorraine Chambre de Commerce et d'Industrie, 10 Viaduc J-F Kennedy, CS 4231, 54042 Nancy Cedex (tel: 8390-1313; fax: 8328-8833; e-mail: crci@lorraine.cci.fr).

Lyon Chambre de Commerce et d'Industrie, Palais du Commerce, Place de la Bourse, 69289 Lyon Cedex 2 (tel: 7240-5858; fax: 7837-5346; e-mail: info@lyon.cci.fr).

Nantes Chambre de Commerce et d'Industrie, 16 Quai Ernest Renaud, PO Box 90517, 44105 Nantes Cedex 4 (tel: 4044-6060; fax: 4044-6090; e-mail: administrator@nantes.cci.fr).

Nice Chambre de Commerce et d'Industrie, 20 Boulevard Carabaçel, PO Box 1259, 06005 Nice Cedex 1 (tel: 0820-422-222; fax: 9313-7399; e-mail: mde.nice.carabacel@cote-azur.cci.fr).

Rennes Chambre de Commerce et d'Industrie, 2 Avenue de la Préfecture, CS 64204, 35042 Rennes Cedex (tel: 9933-6666; fax: 9333-2428; e-mail: info@rennes.cci.fr).

Rouen Chambre de Commerce et d'Industrie, Palais des Consuls, Quai de la Bourse, PO Box 641, 76007 Rouen Cedex 1 (tel: 3414-3737; fax: 3514-3838; e-mail: ccir@rouen.cci.fr).

Strasbourg Chambre de Commerce et d'Industrie, 10 Place Gutenburg, 67081 Strasbourg Cedex (tel: 0388-752-525; fax: 0388-223-120; e-mail: direction@strasbourg.cci.fr).

Banking

Association Française de Banques, 18 Rue la Fayette, 75009 Paris (tel: 4246-9259).

Banque Nationale de Paris SA, 16 Boulevard des Italiens, 75009 Paris (tel: 4014-4546; fax: 4014-5599).

Banque Paribas, 3 Rue d'Antin, 75078 Paris Cedex 02 (tel: 4298-1234; fax: 4298-0433).

Caisse Centrale des Banques Populaires, 10-12 avenue Winston Churchill, 94677 Charenton Le Pont Cedex (tel: 4039-0000; fax: 4039-3940).

Caisse d'Epargne, 19 Rue du Louvre, 75001 Paris (tel: 4041-3031; fax: 4233-4518).

Compagnie Financière de Crédit Industriel et Commercial (CIC Group), Rue de la Victoire 66, 75009 Paris (tel: 4280-8080).

Crédit Agricole, Boulevard Pasteur 91-93, 75015 Paris (tel: 4323-5202).

Crédit Commercial de France (CCF), 103 Avenue des Champs-Elysées, 75008 Paris (tel: 4070-7040; fax: 4070-7353).

Crédit Foncier de France, SA, 19 Rue des Capucines, 75001 Paris (tel: 4244-8000; fax: 4244-7822).

Crédit Local de France, 7-11 Quai André Citroen, 75015 Paris (tel: 4392-7777; fax: 4592-7672).

Crédit Lyonnais SA, Boulevard des Italiens 19, 75002 Paris (tel: 4295-7000).

Crédit Mutuel, 88 Rue Cardinet, 75017 Paris (tel: 4401-1010; fax: 4401-1227).

Société Générale, Boulevard Haussmann 29, 75009 Paris (tel: 4298-2000).

Central bank

Banque de France, 31 Rue Croix des Petits Champs, 75001 Paris (tel: 4292-4292; fax: 4292-3940; e-mail: infos@banque-france.fr).

European Central Bank, Kaiserstrasse 29, D-60311 Frankfurt am Main, Germany (tel: (+49-69) 13-440; fax: (+49-69) 1344-6000; e-mail: info@ecb.int).

Stock exchange

Euronext Paris: www.euronext.com

Stock exchange 2

Chi-X: www.chi-x.com

Commodity exchange

Liffe Connect: www.nyse.com/nyseeuronext

Travel information

Air France (head office), 1 Place Max-Hymans, Paris 75757 Cedex 15 (tel: 4323-8181; internet site: http://www.airfrance.fr).

Airport office: 45 Rue de Paris, Roissy Charles de Gaulle, Paris 95747 (tel: 4156-7800).

Maison de la France (tourist office), 8 Avenue de l'Opéra, Paris 75001 (tel: 4296-1023; fax: 4286-8052).

Roissy Charles de Gaulle and Le Bourget airports, BP 20101, 95711 Roissy Charles de Gaulle Cedex (tel: 4862-1212, 4864-6807) (24 hours).

Ministries

Ministry of Agriculture, Fisheries and Food, 78 Rue de Varenne, 75700 Paris (tel: 4955-4955; fax: 4955-4039).

Ministry of Capital Works, Housing, and Transport, 246 Blvd Saint-Germain, 75007 Paris (tel: 4081-2122; fax: 4081-3099).

Ministry of the Civil Service, Administrative Reform and Decentralisation, 72 Rue de Varenne, 75700 Paris (tel: 4275-8000; fax: 4275-8970).

Ministry of Culture and Communication, 3 Rue de Valois, 75042 Paris (tel: 4015-8000; fax: 4261-3577).

Ministry of Defence, 14 Rue Saint-Dominique, 75700 Paris (tel: 4219-3011; fax: 4505-4091).

Ministry for the Economy, Finance and Industry, 139 Rue de Bercy, 75572 Paris Cedex 12 (tel: 5318-4000; fax: 5318-9701; internet site: www.minefi.gouv.fr).

Ministry of Employment, Rue de Grenelle, 75700 Paris (tel: 4438-3838; fax: 4438-2010).

Ministry of the Environment, 20 Avenue de Segur, 75302 Paris 07 SP (tel: 4219-2021; fax: 4219-1120).

Ministry of Foreign Affairs, 37 Quai d'Orsay, 75700 Paris (tel: 4317-5353; fax: 4551-6012).

Ministry of Industry, the Post Office and Telecommunications, 101 Rue de Grenelle, 75700 Paris 9 (tel: 4319-3636; fax: 4319-3052).

Ministry of the Interior, Place Beauvau, 75800 Paris (tel: 4927-4927; fax: 4266-1280).

Ministry of Justice, 13 Place Vendome, 75042 Paris (tel: 4477-6060; fax: 4477-6000).

Ministry of Labour and Social Affairs, 127 Rue de Grenelle, 75700 Paris (tel: 4438-3838; fax: 4056-6710).

Ministry of National Education, Higher Education and Research, 110 Rue de Grenelle, 75700 Paris (tel: 4955-1010; fax: 4955-1556).

Ministry for Relations with Parliament, 69 Rue de Varenne, 75700 Paris (tel: 4275-8000; fax: 4081-7300).

Ministry of Small- and Medium-Sized Enterprises, Trade and Artisan Activities, 80 Rue de Lille, 75700 Paris (tel: 4319-2424; fax: 4319-3767).

Ministry of Town and Country Planning, Urban Affairs and Integration, 35 Rue Saint-Dominique, 75700 Paris (tel: 4275-8000; fax: 4275-7755).

Ministry of Youth and Sport, Rue Olivier de Serres, 75015 Paris (tel: 5369-3000; fax: 5369-4370).

Prime Minister's Office, 57 Rue de Varenne, 75700 Paris (tel: 4275-8000; fax: 4544-1572).

Other useful addresses

ANIT (public information service), 8 Avenue de l'Opéra, 75001 Paris (tel: 4260-3738).

La Bourse de Paris (Stock Exchange), 39 Rue Cambon, 75001 Paris (tel: 4927-7000; fax: 4289-7868).

Bureau International des Expositions (International Exhibition Bureau), 56 Avenue Victor-Hugo, 75116 Paris (tel: 4500-3863; fax: 4500-9615).

Caisse Centrale de Co-opération Economique (CCCE), 233 Boulevard Saint-Germain, Paris (tel: 4550-3220).

Centre Française du Commerce Extérieur, 10 Avenue d'Iéna, 75116 Paris (tel: 4505-3000).

Direction Générale des Impôts, Centre des Non-Résidents, 9 Rue d'Uzés, 75094 Paris.

France Telecom, 6 Place d'Alleray, 75505 Paris Cedex 15.

French Embassy (USA), 4101 Reservoir Road, NW, Washington DC 20007 (tel: (+1-202)-944-6000; fax: (+1-202)-944-6166).

Institut National de la Statistique et des Etudes Economiques (INSEE), 18 Boulevard Adolphe Pinard, 75675 Paris Cedex 14 (tel: 4117-5050; fax: 4117-6666; internet site: http://www.insee.fr).

Invest in France Network/DATAR, 1 Avenue Charles Floquet, 75343 Paris Cedex 07 (tel: 4065-1006; fax: 4065-1240).

Service de la Répression des Fraudes et du Contrôle de la Qualité, 44 Boulevard de Grenelle, 75732 Paris.

Post Office, 52 rue du Louvre, Paris (tel: 4028-2000).

National news agency: Agence France Presse, 11–15 Place de la Bourse, 75002 Paris (tel: 4041-4646; fax: 4041-4632; www.afp.com).

Other news agencies: Reuters: http://fr.reuters.com

Focus: www.focusinfo.eu

Internet sites

Ferry information: http://seafrance.com/ferries_to_france.html

France Bottin (provides market information on France's main companies): www.bottin.fr

French electronic phonebook (searches can be conducted by name or by regions): www.epita.fr:5000/11/english.html

Tourist information: www.francetourism.com

French Guiana

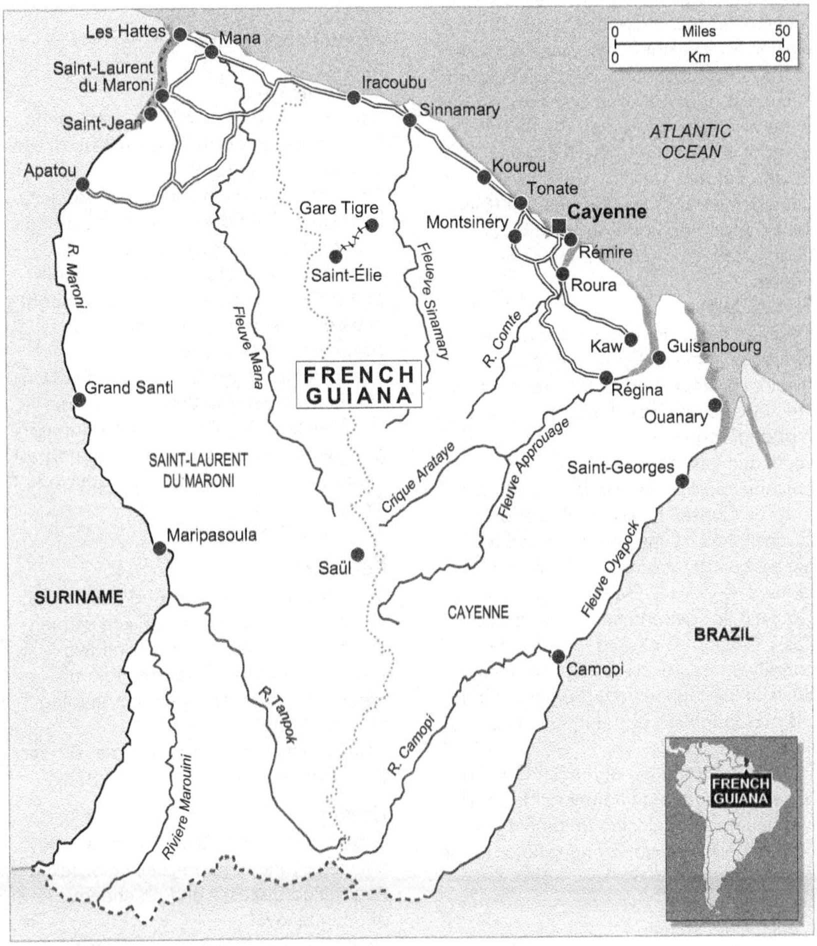

KEY FACTS

Official name: Guyane Française (French Guiana)

Head of State: President of France (Nicolas Sarkozy), represented by *Préfet* Daniel Ferey (from 8 Feb 2009)

Head of government: President of the Regional Council, Rodolphe Alexandre (from 26 Mar 2010); President of the General Council, Alain Tien-Liong (since Mar 2008)

Ruling party: Parti Socialiste Guyanais (PSG) (Socialist Party) (since 2000; re-elected 2004)

Area: 91,000 square km

Population: 231,000 (2010)*

Capital: Cayenne

Official language: French

Currency: Euro (€) = 100 cents (from 1 Jan 2002; previous currency French franc, locked at Ff6.56 per euro)

Exchange rate: €0.75 per US$ (Oct 2011)

GDP per capita: US$8,500 (2006)*

Labour force: 58,800 (2003)

Unemployment: 22.00% (2003)

Inflation: 1.50% (2003)

Balance of trade: -US$470.00 million (2003)

Foreign debt: US$1.20 billion (2003)

* estimated figure

COUNTRY PROFILE

Historical profile

Carib and Arawak Indians were the original inhabitants of French Guiana.

1496 First reported European sighting.

1604 The French established their first settlement on French Guiana.

1654–1915 There were numerous changes in control between the French, British, Dutch, Brazilian and Portuguese, as well as border disputes. During this period the economy of the region came close to collapse, particularly after the abolition of slavery in 1848. Black African slaves had previously worked on French Guiana's sugar plantations.

1946 French Guiana became a French Département d'Outre-Mer (DOM) (Overseas Department).

1953 Closure of penal colony on Devil's Island.

1964 The Kourou Space Centre was established.

1974 French Guiana was further incorporated into the French political system and granted the status of region of France.

1983 French Guiana was granted devolution. A Regional Council was established under the French decentralisation policy.

1998 The Parti Socialiste Guyanais (PSG) remained the single largest party in the Regional Council after the elections.

2000 There were pro-independence demonstrations and French Guiana sought to alter its relationship as a DOM.
2002 French Guiana adopted the euro as its official currency. Arianespace launched Intelsat 904 into orbit from Kourou. The satellite provides Internet, telecommunications and television services for Europe, Africa, Central Asia and Australia.
2003 A revision to the constitution began a process of change to the political and administrative organisation with the Regional Council assuming more influence.
2004 Early elections for the Regional Council were won by the PSG with 17 seats.
2005 Arianespace and the Russian Space Agency signed an agreement for construction of the Soyuz launch pad.
2007 Nicolas Sarkozy became head of state and president of the French Republic. Under a deal with the European Space Agency (ESA), the l'Ensemble de Lancement Soyouz (ELS) (Launch Pad for Soyouz) began construction
2009 Daniel Ferey became *Préfet*. The largest telecommunication satellite ever built, TerreStar-1, was launched from the Space Centre.
2010 The first flight of a medium-lift space launcher, which had been planned for 2009, took off from Kourou in January. Voters rejected the option of increased autonomy in a referendum in January. Rodolphe Alexandre was elected president of the Regional Council in March.
2011 On 27 April, Denis Labbé became *Préfet*. In July, the EU agreed to allow French Guiana to impose import tariffs from 1 July 2014 to protect 46 locally produced items, including food and manufactured goods. The target date for completion of the ELS for the Russian-built Soyuz-2 space rocket was postponed to 20 October. As planned, on 21 October, the ESA launched two satellites as part of Europe's development of its own global positioning system (GPS). To undertake this task not only was the completed ELS used for the first time, but the Russian giant Soyuz rocket was employed for the first time in French Guiana.

Political structure

Constitution

28 September 1958 (French Fifth Republic)

Under the 1946 constitution of the French Fourth Republic, French Guiana became a Départemente d'Outre-Mer (DOM) (Overseas Department) of France. In 1974, it was granted additional status as a region of France.

The president of France is represented by a préfet, appointed by the government in Paris. French Guiana is represented in the French National Assembly and in the French Senate by two deputies and one senator.

Since 1983, following the French government's policy of decentralisation, regional councils have been elected with powers similar to those of the regions.

The local government comprises a Conseil Régional (Regional Council) of 31-members and a 19-member Conseil Général (General Council), both directly elected for six-year terms. Since a revision to the constitution in March 2003 the political and administrative organisation has been in a state of change; the Regional Council is assuming more influence.

Form of state

Département d'Outre-Mer (DOM) (Overseas Department) of France, with additional status as a région (region) of France.

The executive

Executive power is vested in the president of France, represented by a Préfet (Commissioner), appointed by the president on the advice of the French Ministry of Interior.

National legislature

Local administration is provided by two unicameral councils with divergent powers. The Conseil Régional (Regional Council) has 31 members, elected in single seat constituencies, for four-year terms. The Conseil Général (General Council) (for department administration) has 19 members elected in single seat constituencies, for six-year terms. Presidents of the General and Regional Councils are appointed by the members of individual councils.

Three representatives of French Guiana are elected to the parliament of France: two deputies are elected to the French National Assembly and one senator to the French Senate.

Legal system

French legal system

Last elections

14 and 21 March 2010 (regional council); March 2006 (general council)

Results: Regional Council: Comité de Liaison de la Majorité Présidentielle (Liaison Committee for the Presidential Majority) (Presidential Majority) won 40.61 per cent of votes (21 seats), Parti Radical de Gauche (Radical Party of the Left) (Radical Left) 23.02 per cent 10; eight other parties each won less than 10 per cent of the vote and no seats. Turnout was 49 per cent.

Next elections

2014 (general council); 2012 (regional council)

Political parties

Ruling party

Parti Socialiste Guyanais (PSG) (Socialist Party) (since 2000; re-elected 2004)

Main opposition party

Union pour un Mouvement Populaire (UMP) (Union for the Popular Movement), Walwari Committee (aligned with the PRG in France)

Population

231,000 (2010)*

Last census: 1 January 2006: 205,954

Population density: Two inhabitants per square km.

Annual growth rate: 4.6 per cent (2003)

Ethnic make-up

Black or mixed race (66 per cent), white (12 per cent), East Indian, Chinese or Amerindian (12 per cent).

There are settlements of Hmong farmers from Laos. The troubles in neighbouring Suriname encouraged thousands of Surinamese to cross the border illegally and settle. The space centre has brought in thousands of scientists who live in a community of their own.

The minimum wage has attracted not only Surinamese but also Brazilians. These *clandestines* (illegal immigrants) are marginalised and forced to live in the poorest areas of the country, often without work.

Religions

Roman Catholic

Education

Schooling is compulsory and French Guiana has both public and private elementary schools, a high school, and two vocational schools. The condition of schools is, however, very poor, leading students to strike.

Literacy rate: 84 per cent, male; 82 per cent, female; adult rates (World Bank).

Health

Government health planning is seriously affected by the high prevalence of sexually transmitted diseases and an endemic level of dengue fever.

Health insurance is provided by the state-sponsored social security system, financed with compulsory contributions from salaries. People are usually reimbursed on the basis of rates negotiated between care providers and the social security.

Life expectancy: 77 years (estimate 2003)

Fertility rate/Maternal mortality rate: Three births per woman (2003)

Birth rate/Death rate: 21 births per 1,000 population; five deaths per 1,000 population (2003).

Child (under 5 years) mortality rate (per 1,000): 13 per 1,000 live births (2003)

Welfare

The official unemployment rate is 22 per cent with higher rates among young people. Jobs connected with satellite launching, combined with orderly French rule and an annual financial contribution amounting to US$500 million from Paris, have provided benefits such as good roads, decent health care, and a generous social security system.

Main cities

Cayenne (capital, estimated population 55,638 in 2005), St Laurent-du-Maroni (27,429), Kourou (main town around the space centre and rapidly growing, 27,132), Matoury (36,275), Rémire-Montjoly (20,823).

Languages spoken

French and French-Creole. Some business executives speak English, although business is generally conducted in French.

Official language/s

French

Media

Press

Daily papers are *Guyane-Matin*, *France-Guyane* and *La Presse de Guyane*. There are no English-language newspapers. US and metropolitan French papers are available. Several periodicals are in circulation but there are no trade publications.

Broadcasting

Radio-Télévision Française d'Outre-mer (RFO) broadcast in French. There are two independent radio stations: Cayenne FM and Radio Tout Mount.

Economy

The overall economy remains underdeveloped. The main activities are fishing, which accounts for 75 per cent of exports and forestry, which is under exploited due to poor infrastructure. An expanding sawmill industry has increased the exports of hardwood logs. Eco-tourism is beginning to grow in importance – although French Guiana has large tracts of unspoilt rain forests, it still has few facilities to cater for all but the hardiest.

The single major contributor to the economy, accounting for 25 per cent of GDP and half of tax revenues, is the Centre Spatial Guyanais (Guiana Space Centre) at Kourou, which launches commercial and government funded rockets, using either the European Ariane 5 or Russian Soyuz launchers. An estimated 24 per cent of the population work directly or indirectly in jobs connected with the space industry.

French Guiana is otherwise dependent on aid, technical assistance and imports from France. As a department of France, it receives the same benefits as mainland France: a minimum wage, free education and health care, and a large, well-paid civil service.

External trade

As a département d'outre-mer (DOM) of France, French Guiana is integrated as an outermost region of the European Union, which includes all EU trade agreements. There is heavy dependence on France for financial aid. The balance of trade deficit is mainly due to high imports of food and fuels, and undeveloped export potential.

Imports

Principal imports are food (grains, processed meat), machinery and transport equipment, fuels and chemicals.

Main sources: France (typically over 60 per cent), US, Trinidad and Tobago, Italy.

Exports

Principal exports are shrimp, timber and rosewood essence, gold, rum and clothing.

Main destinations: France (over 60 per cent total), Switzerland (7 per cent), US (2 per cent)

Agriculture

Cultivation is limited to the coastal area. Only 0.18 per cent of the total land area is cultivated and production is dominated by crops for domestic consumption such as rice, maize and bananas, while sugar cane is grown for rum production.

A small number of cattle farms have also been established.

Fishing

The typical total annual fish catch is over 5,000mt. Shellfish, molluscs and cephalopods account for another 2,700mt per annum.

The rainforest covers around 90 per cent of the land area. Poor infrastructure means the vast timber resources have not been fully exploited. Exports consisted of over 50,100 cubic metres of raw hardwood while imports were mostly processed sawnwood and wood panels used in construction.

Industry and manufacturing

The sector includes construction, shrimp processing, forestry products, rum and gold mining. Manufacturing is virtually non-existent, except for small factories processing agricultural or seafood products and a few sawmills. A tile and brick-making plant, based on important fields of red clay, operates in the Cayenne neighbourhood. Production of rum from sugar cane has declined. Industrial activity is limited to the area around the Kourou space centre.

Tourism

Tourism is an important area of the economy.

Mining

Bauxite deposits of 42 million tonnes and kaolin deposits of 40 million tonnes have been found, but extraction is not economically viable, although kaolin mining has begun in the Mana area. There are also reserves of silica, niobium and tantalite.

Gold is mined, both legally and illicitly, the latter activity on a large scale and causing serious environmental damage. Significant exploitation of the mineral resources will come about only with further improvements in infrastructure.

Hydrocarbons

French Guiana does not produce oil, gas or coal. It is heavily dependent on imports of petroleum products to meet its energy needs, importing around 11,000 barrels per day. Gas and coal are not imported.

Energy

Total installed generating capacity is around 300MW, produced by thermal power stations and French Guiana relies on petroleum imports from France to fuel them.

Banking and insurance

The Banque Nationale de Paris Guyane Sa (BNP Guyane) is a major commercial bank offering a wide range of services. There are branches in Cayenne, Kourou and Rémire-Montjoly.

Central bank

European Central Bank

Time

GMT minus three hours

Geography

French Guiana lies on the north coast of South America, with Suriname to the west and Brazil to the south and east. The country is largely low lying with hills no higher that 600 metres and covered in dense Amazonian rainforest that grows down to the mangrove fringed coastline.

Hemisphere

Northern

Climate

The climate is tropical. It is generally hot and humid with heavy rain. The dry season is August–December with an average temperature of 28 degrees Celsius (C). The rainy season is January–June with a temperature range of 22–32 degrees C.

Dress codes

For business meetings men should wear a lightweight or tropical suit and tie and women a lightweight suit or the equivalent.

Entry requirements

Passports

Passports are required by all except nationals of France and some francophone countries holding national identity cards. Passports should be valid for three months from the date of departure.

Visa

Required by all, except citizens of EU, North America, Australasia and Japan, for stays up to one month; this includes business trips by representatives of foreign entities with an invitation from a local company or organisation. Proof of adequate funds for stay, an itinerary, a guarantee of repatriation if necessary and return/onward ticket are also required. For further exceptions, full details and a copy of the application form visit www.diplomatie.gouv.fr/thema/dossier.gb.asp and follow the path (entering France) to the database.

Currency advice/regulations

There are no limits to the amount of local or foreign currency imported or exported, although amounts exceeding eur7,600 should be declared.

Travellers cheques are accepted; to avoid extra exchange fees, it is recommended that they be in euros, US dollars or pound sterling.

Health (for visitors)

Mandatory precautions

A yellow fever certificate.

Advisable precautions

Hepatitis A, B and D, typhoid and polio immunisations are recommended. Dengue fever is endemic. Malaria prophylaxis is advisable if travelling outside Cayenne. Water precautions should be taken, although tap water in Cayenne is safe. There is a rabies risk.

Hotels

There is a good standard of accommodation available in Cayenne, Kourou and St Laurent. Rates normally include service and taxes; if not, a 10 per cent tip is usual.

Public holidays (national)

Fixed dates

1 Jan (New Year's Day), 1 May (Labour Day), 8 May (Victory Day), 10 Jun (Abolition Day), 14 Jul (Bastille Day), 15 Aug (Assumption Day), 1 Nov (All Saints' Day), 11 Nov (Armistice Day), 25 Dec (Christmas Day).

Variable dates

Ash Wednesday (Carnival – Feb/Mar), Easter Monday (Mar/Apr), Ascension Day (Thur – May/June).

Working hours

Banking

Mon–Fri: 0730–1230, 1430–1730.

Business

Mon–Fri: 0800–1300, 1500–1800.

Government

Mon–Fri: 0730–1300, 1430–1830 (closed Wed and Fri afternoons).

Electricity supply

220V AC, 50 cycles

Social customs/useful tips

Appointments should be made in advance. It is customary to shake hands on meeting and taking leave. Business cards are exchanged after introduction.

Getting there

Air

International airport/s: Cayenne-Rochambeau (CAY), 15km from city; bar, post office, shops, hotel reservations, car hire.

Airport tax: None

Surface

Road: There is a coastal road to Suriname but there is no road access to Brazil.

Water: Ferries run regularly to Suriname, and from St George to Oiapoque (Brazil).

Getting about

National transport

Air: Air Guyane, Guyane Aero Service and Heli-Inter Service serve main centres and the interior of the country. (Bookings can be made through Air France.)

Road: There are 356km of national routes and 366km of departmental roads. Cayenne district is served by a good road system, but the streets of Cayenne itself are inferior. The only major road runs from Cayenne, via Kourou, to St Laurent on Suriname border.

Buses: Scheduled services on Cayenne to St Laurent route.

Water: Major form of travel. Motor boat serves some coastal towns. River boats and small planes link interior centres with coast. 400km rivers are navigable by small ocean-going vessels and river and coastal steamers but interior connections are made by local craft.

City transport

Taxis: Taxis are available in main towns. Fares include gratuities.

Car hire

Car hire is available in Cayenne and at the airport. An international licence required.

BUSINESS DIRECTORY

The addresses listed below are a selection only. While World of Information makes every endeavour to check these addresses, we cannot guarantee that changes have not been made, especially to telephone numbers and area codes. We would welcome any corrections.

Telephone area codes

The international direct dialling (IDD) code for French Guiana is +594 followed by another 594 and the subscriber's (six digit) number.

Useful telephone numbers

Talking clock: 3699

Times of tides: 378-300

Radio taxi: 307-305, 305-225

Bus service: 314-554

Fire: 18

Police: 17

Chambers of Commerce

Guyane Chambre de Commerce et d'Industrie, PO Box 49, Hôtel Consulaire, Place de l'Esplinade, 97321 Cayenne (tel: 299-600; fax: 299-634; e-mail: contact@guyane.cci.fr).

Banking

Banque Française Commerciale, 8 Place des Palmistes, 97300 Cayenne (tel: 291-111; fax: 301-312).

Banque de la Guyane, PO Box 35, 2 Place Victor-Schloelcher, Cayenne (tel: 310-515).

Banque Nationale de Paris Guyane, 2 Place Victor-Schoelcher, Cayenne (tel: 396-300; fax: 302-308).

Crédit Agricole, Angle av L Héder et rue Damas, 97300 Cayenne (tel: 318-000; fax: 317-524).

Crédit Martiniquais, 76 Av Gal de Gaulle, 97300 Cayenne (tel: 315-700; fax: 314-801).

Crédit Populairé Caisse Crédit Mutuel, 93 rue Lalouette, 97300 Cayenne (tel: 301-523; fax: 301-765).

Central bank

Banque de France, 31 Rue Croix des Petits Champs, 75001 Paris (tel: 4292-4292, 6480-2020; fax: 4292-3940; email: infos@banque-france.fr).

European Central Bank, Kaiserstrasse 29, D-60311 Frankfurt am Main, Germany (tel: (+49-69) 13-440; fax: (+49-69) 1344-6000; email: info@ecb.int).

Travel information

Air France, Cayenne (tel: 379-899).

Air Guyane, Aéroport de Rochambeau, 97351 Matoury (tel: 356-555; fax: 356-506).

AOM French Airlines (tel: 353-934).

Guyane Aero Services, Aéroport de Rochambeau, 97351 Matoury (tel: 356-162; fax: 358-450).

Héli-Inter Service Guyane, Aéroport de Rochambeau, 97351 Matoury (tel: 356-231; fax: 358-256).

Rochambeau International Airport, Cayenne (tel: 299-700).

Surinam Airways, c/o Atlas Voyages, 15 Rue Louis Blanc, 97300 Cayenne (tel: 317-298; fax: 305-786).

Syndicat Autonome des Hoteliers Restaurateurs et Cafétiers de Guyane, PK 9,2 Route de Rémire, 97354 Rémire Montjoly (tel: 354-100; fax: 354-405).

Syndicats d'Initiative Office du Tourisme, 7 Av du Président Monnerville, Cayenne 97300 (tel: 312-919).

TABA, PK 2,5 Route de Baduel, 97300 Cayenne (tel: 312-147; fax: 312-154).

National tourist organisation offices
French Guiana Tourist Board, 12, Rue Lallouette; BP 801; 97338 Cayenne (tel: 296-500; fax: 296-501; internet: www.tourisme-guyane.com/en).

Other useful addresses
Agence Régionale pour le Développement de l'Industrie Minière (Ardim), 111 rue Christophe Colomb, 973000 Cayenne (tel: 294-575).

British Consulate, 16 Ave G. Monnerville, B.P. 211, 97324 Cayenne (tel: 311-034; fax: 304-094).

Centre Spatial Guyanais, Korou (tel: 326-123).

Direction Régionale de l'Industrie, de la Recherche et de l'Environnement, pointe Buzaré, PO Box 7001, 97307 Cayenne (tel: 297-530; fax: 290-734).

Ligue pour la Protection des Oiseaux (LPO), Fonds Mondial pour la Nature (WWF), Cayenne (tel: 309-189).

Radio-Télévision Française d'Outre-mer (RFO), 43 bis Rue du Dr Devèze, BP 336, 97305 Cayenne (tel: 311-500).

Internet sites
Latin world, commercial directory: http://www.latinworld.com

Centre Français du commerce exterieur (site in French): http://www.cfce.fr

French Guiana Consular Information: http://travel.state.gov/french_guiana.html

French Polynesia

KEY FACTS

Official name: Territoire de la Polynésie Française (Territory of French Polynesia)

Head of State: President of France (Nicolas Sarkozy), represented by *Préfet* Richard Didier (from 24 Jan 2011)

Head of government: President of the Territorial Government President Oscar Temaru (from 1 Apr 2011)

Ruling party: Coalition of To Tatou Ai'a (Our Home), Union pour la Démocratie (UPLD) (Union for Democracy) and Tahoera'a Huiraatira (Popular Rally) (since Jan 2009)

Area: 3,600 square km (35 islands and 83 atolls)

Population: 271,000 (2010)*

Capital: Papeete (on Tahiti)

Official language: French and Reo Maohi (Tahitian)

Currency: Comptoirs Français du Pacifique franc (CFPf) = 100 centimes

Exchange rate: CFPf88.94 per US$ (Oct 2011); (pegged CFPf119.25 per euro)

GDP per capita: US$22,160 (2006)

GDP real growth: -2.10% (2008)*

GDP: US$5.50 billion (2005)*

Labour force: 87,843 (2004)

Unemployment: 10.90% (2004)*

Inflation: 3.40% (2008)

Balance of trade: -US$1.50 billion (2005)

Visitor numbers: 212,000 (2004)

* estimated figure

COUNTRY PROFILE

Historical profile

French Polynesia consists of 118 islands and was settled by Polynesians between 300 and 800 AD. From these islands, Hawaii, the Cook Islands and New Zealand were colonised.

1843 Tahiti, the largest island, and Moorea became French protectorates.

1880 Tahiti became a French colony. The other islands were annexed under the name Comptoirs Français de l'Océanie.

1957 The group of islands became the Territoire d'Outre-Mer (TOM, overseas territory) of French Polynesia, administered by a governor in Papeete on Tahiti.

1960 An international airport opened at Faa'a on Tahiti.

1963 French nuclear tests were conducted for the first time at Mururoa Atoll.

1977 Increased powers for the council of ministers were approved by the French government.

1984 New powers for the government, particularly in commerce, were approved by the French government.

1983 Despite strong local protests, French authorities insisted that nuclear tests would continue for 'as long as necessary'.

1984 Jurisdiction over certain local affairs (local budget, health services, primary education, culture, social welfare, public works, agriculture and sports) was conferred on the council of ministers. Gaston Flosse became president of the governing council.

1986 The Tahoeraa Huiraatira-Rassemblement pour la République (TH-RPR) (People's Servant-Rally for the Republic) won the Territorial Assembly elections.

1987 Following accusations of misappropriation of public funds, Flosse resigned as president.

1990 Amendments to the constitution augmented presidential and Territorial Assembly powers.

1996 Gaston Flosse was re-elected president. France ended nuclear testing. The French government relinquished control of all affairs except for defence, law enforcement, the judiciary and the local currency.

2002 An appeal court in Paris dismissed fraud accusations against President Flosse.

2004 France's President Chirac dissolved the Territorial Assembly and changed French Polynesia's status to Pays d'Outre-Mer (overseas country) (POM). Oscar Temaru (pro-independence, Tavini Huira'atira (People's Servant) (PS) was elected president of the new Assemblée de la Polynésie Française (APF) (Assembly of French Polynesia). Temaru was ousted by Gaston Flosse (TH-RPR).

2005 Oscar Temaru (PS), leader of the pro-independence movement and supported by the ADN, was elected president.

2006 President Temaru (PS) was ousted and Gaston Tong Sang (Tahoera'a Huiraatira (TH) (Popular Rally) was elected president, by the APF.

2007 In the first round of the postponed presidential elections for the APF, the incumbent, Gaston Tong Sang received the least votes and was eliminated. In the second round, Oscar Temaru (PS) won 27 votes and Édouard Fritch (TH) 17. A group of Tong Sang supporters broke away from the ruling TH and formed a new party, the O Porinetia To Tatou Ai'a (OPTTA). The French National Assembly approved a new parliamentary voting system of proportional representation and a minimum electoral threshold in a bid to bring a measure of stability to the islands' politics.

2008 The cabinet of President Oscar Temaru resigned. After two rounds in the general elections, the To Tatou Ai'a (Our Home) coalition (led by Temaru) won a total of 45.2 per cent of the vote (27 seats out of 57), the UPLD (led by Tong Sang) won 37.2 per cent (20) and the TH (led by Flosse) 17.2 per cent (10). Turnout was 76.9 per cent. A coalition of opposites, Our Home and TH, voted Flosse into the presidency, but he lost a vote of no confidence and was replaced by Tong Sang, with support from minor parties.

2009 President Tong Sang resigned. Oscar Temaru became president for the fourth time in 13 years. Former president, Gaston Flosse, was convicted of corruption and complicity to destroy evidence and abuse of public funds. He was stripped of all public offices and given a one-year suspended jail sentence, while further legal action was considered. President Temaru lost a vote of no confidence in parliament (29 votes to 24) and was replaced by Gaston Tong Sang.

2010 A general strike in June, called in protest at the cut in over 9,000 government jobs carried out by the government in an effort to limit its budget deficit, lasted for five days and resulted in grounded air flights and paralysed public services. In August, central government officials in Paris summoned political leaders from French Polynesia to discuss not only the instability of the government in the islands, following six years when the leadership changed nine times, but also the on-going financial crisis. Following an inconclusive end to the talks, Paris declared that without political reform economic support would be limited. The central government had sent a delegation in 2009 to audit the work of the French Polynesian government and recommended a reduced civil administration. However, this was rejected by President Tong Sang and the central government (in Paris) cut financial aid. Foreign borrowing by the French Polynesian government was found to be prohibitively expensive. The government in Paris said it would require a commitment to change, backed by a referendum on economic development and French Polynesia's status as a DOM, before it extended credit to the islands. In October the French minister for overseas territories, Marie Luce Penchard, on a visit to French Polynesia, proposed an electoral reform plan that would reduce the number of representatives in the APF and the proportion of seats set aside for remote island communities. In effect French Polynesia would be spilt into two parts for administrative purposes: the remote outer islands and the populated inner islands. Leaders of all political parties initially rejected the proposals; which were nevertheless enacted.

2011 Richard Didier took up his post of *Préfet* on 24 January. On 1 April, Gaston Tong Sang lost a vote of no-confidence in parliament (57:29) and his long-time opponent Oscar Temaru replaced him as president. This was the fifth time that Temaru had been voted into the presidential office. By the beginning of June electoral reform laws (introduced from Paris) were passed, whereby votes of no-confidence will be limited; in future, a ratio of three to five in favour of a parliamentary motion will be required before a call will be allowed. President Temaru announced severe cuts to public spending of up to 50 per cent. Gaston Flosse called for early elections to give voters an opportunity to decide on these policies. His critics opined that he wanted to return to parliament before a legal judgement banned him for up to five years. On 16 July President Sarkozy said he would veto any Polynesian plan to hold early parliamentary elections, saying that new laws of governance precluded elections at any interval except the prescribed time (due 2013). On 5 October, former president Gaston was sentenced by a criminal court to four years in jail for abuse of public funds.

Political structure

Constitution

In 1996, the French government relinquished control over all the territory's affairs except for defence, foreign affairs, law enforcement, the justice system and the local currency. France is represented by a high commissioner who has a supervisory role. The territory is represented in the French Parliament by two deputies and two senators.

The local government has control over the territory's more than three million square kilometres of sea, as well as shipping, civil aviation, work permits, mineral exploration, foreign investment and local economic affairs. Under the Statute of Autonomy, it has full control over its Exclusive Economic Zone.

French Polynesia became a Pays d'Outre-Mer (POM) (overseas country) of France in 2004 with the implementation of the Assemblée de la Polynésie française (Assembly of French Polynesia) statute. It has 57 members in the assembly representing six constituencies.

Under the autonomy law, the electoral list gaining the most votes in general elections wins a bonus of extra seats, amounting to a third of the seats in the local parliament.

Form of state

Autonomous Pays d'Outre-Mer (POM) (overseas country) of France

National legislature

The unicameral Assemblée de la Polynésie Française (Assembly of French Polynesia) has 57 members elected for a five-year term, either directly or by proportional representation, in six multi-seat constituencies. The assembly elects the president of the territorial government

In 2007, the French National Assembly approved an amendment to the parliamentary voting system in an attempt to streamline the chaotic nature of politics in French Polynesia. The new proportional representation system has two rounds of voting; to reach the second round any candidate must have at least 12.5 per cent of the vote from the first round and their party much achieve a minimum electoral threshold 5 per cent.

Last elections

27 January and 10 February 2008 (first and second rounds of national assembly)

Results: Parliamentary: the To Tatou Ai'a (Our Home alliance) won a total of 45.2 per cent of the vote (27 seats out of 57), the UPLD alliance won 37.2 per cent (20) and the Tahoera'a Huiraatira (Popular Rally) 17.2 per cent (10). Turnout was 76.9 per cent.

Next elections

2013 (national assembly)

Political parties

Ruling party

Coalition of To Tatou Ai'a (Our Home), Union pour la Démocratie (UPLD) (Union for Democracy) and Tahoera'a Huiraatira (Popular Rally) (since Jan 2009)

Main opposition party

None

Political situation

In August 2010, central government officials in Paris summoned political leaders from French Polynesia to discuss not only the instability of the government in the islands, following six years when the leadership changed nine times, but also the ongoing financial crisis. Following an inconclusive end to the talks, Paris declared that without political reform economic support would be limited. The central government had sent a delegation in 2009 to audit the work of the French Polynesian government and recommended a reduced civil administration. However, this was rejected by President Tong Sang and the central government (in Paris) cut financial aid. Foreign borrowing by the French Polynesian government was found to be prohibitively expensive. The government in Paris has said it will require a commitment to change, backed by a referendum on economic development and French Polynesia's status as a DOM, before it will extend credit to the islands. In October the French minister for the overseas territories, Marie Luce Penchard, on a visit to French Polynesia, proposed an electoral reform plan that would reduce the number of representatives in the assembly and the proportion of seats set aside for remote island communities. In effect French Polynesia would be spilt into two parts for administrative purposes: the remote outer islands and the populated inner islands. Leaders of all political parties initially rejected the proposals.

Population

271,000 (2010)*

Last census: 20 August 2007: 259,596

Population density: 63 inhabitants per sq km. Urban population: 53 per cent (1995–2001).

Annual growth rate: 2.5 per cent (2003)

Ethnic make-up

Polynesian (78 per cent), Chinese (12 per cent), local French (6 per cent), metropolitan French (4 per cent).

Religions

Protestant (54 per cent), Roman Catholic (30 per cent), other (16 per cent).

Education

Enrolment rate: 116 per cent gross primary enrolment, of relevant age groups, (including repeaters) (World Bank).

Health

Life expectancy: 73 years (men) 77 years (women), 2007

Fertility rate/Maternal mortality rate: 2.04 births per woman

Birth rate/Death rate: 16.93 births per 1,000 population; 4.63 deaths per 1,000 population.

Child (under 5 years) mortality rate (per 1,000): 8.44 deaths per 1,000 live births

Main cities

Papeete (capital, on Tahiti, estimated population 26,580 in 2005), Faa'a (on Tahiti, 29,076).

Languages spoken

English is spoken, especially in tourist and business circles.

In 2010, the French ministry for the overseas territories continued to reject the promotion of Tahitian as an official language of French Polynesia. Currently only French may be used in conducting government business; any decisions made in another language can and have been challenged. An appeal to the European Court of Human Rights in 2006 failed to get Tahitian recognised as an official language..

Official language/s

French and Reo Maohi (Tahitian)

Media

Press

Dailies: There are two newspapers available, in French, *La Dépêche de Tahiti* (Tahiti's largest newspaper) and *Les Nouvelles de Tahiti*.

Weeklies: In French *La Tribune Polynesienne* has general interest news. In English the *Tahiti Sun Press*, is a free-issue publication for tourists.

Periodicals: In French, monthly magazines include *L'Hebdo Maohi* (www.hebdo.pf) and the *Tahiti-Pacifique* (www.tahiti-pacifique.com) both covering current affairs.

Broadcasting

Radio: In addition to the government-operated RFO Polynésie (www.rfo.fr/polynesie.php) service, there are a number of private radio stations operating mostly on larger, inhabited islands, including Radio Bleue, Radio Tefana Te Reo, Radio Maohi and Radio Te Vevo, which all broadcast in Tahitian.

Television: The French overseas broadcaster RFO (http://polynesie.rfo.fr) provides all local produced news and imported French programmes, as well as internet TV services.

Advertising

Advertising is available in local newspapers and all such ads, correspondence and trade literature should be in French.

News agencies

National news agency: L'Agence Tahitienne de Presse (Tahitipress)

Economy

Around one million black pearls, valued at US$150 million are exported annually – French Polynesia is the Pacific region's second-largest source of loose pearls (after the Australian production of yellow pearls). Co-operatives and private producers farm quality cultured black pearls under strict guidelines introduced to maintain a healthy crop of oysters. The fisheries sector is growing with deep-sea resources (particularly tuna) fished, mainly by Asian fleets under licence. French Polynesia has the Pacific region's largest exclusive economic zone. Agriculture consists of smallholders growing fruit and vegetables, while plantations provide copra and coconut oil for export. However, the single largest component of the economy is the tourist sector. The global economic crisis in 2008–09 cut the number of tourists visiting French Polynesia by 6.2 per cent in 2009; the biggest drop was in visitors from North America and Europe. Also, the major tourist sailing-boat attraction, the Star Flyer, was withdrawn from service in 2010 and sent to the northern hemisphere, before its replacement was scheduled to by introduced in 2011, thus limiting tourist numbers further.

Another major source of revenue is financial transfers from France, which represent around 30 per cent of GDP; expatriate remittances, which amounted to US$690 million in 2009 and were estimated to have risen to US$771 million in 2010, are also an important source of revenue. There is a long-term and serious problem of unemployment, especially since France ceased its nuclear testing and withdrew most military personnel in 1996. France agreed to contribute funds as compensation for a limited period, but has since agreed that these payments be for an indefinite period.

Development of the remote archipelagos (Marquesas, Australs, Tuamotu and Gambiers) has begun with the construction of more airstrips and roads to improve port facilities and public services. Capital development throughout the territory has helped create new businesses, while strengthening social services.

External trade

Exports in 2010 were 6.4 per cent higher than in 2009, with pearls accounting for eur10.1 million (US$14.2 million) and fishing licences eur601,700 (US$841,941). Imports in 2010 totalled eur141.3 million (US$198 million).

Imports

Main imports are foodstuffs, consumer goods, capital goods, vehicles, fuels, machinery and equipment.

Main sources: France (typically 30 per cent of total), Singapore (11 per cent), US (10 per cent).

Exports

Typically, the main exports are black pearls (90 per cent of total exports), noni fruit and juice, coconut and its derivatives (flesh, oil and copra), beer, vanilla, fish and shark meat.

Main destinations: Hong Kong (typically 37 per cent of total), Japan (21 per cent), France (18 per cent).

Agriculture

Farming

Accounts for 4 per cent of GDP and employs 13 per cent of the workforce. Its development is a central plank of government policy. Primary products are copra, vanilla, mother-of-pearl shells, taro and cultured pearls.

Weather permitting, local production supplies over 60 per cent of overall demand for some vegetables.

Local production supplies about 28 per cent of demand for dairy products and 83–87 per cent of demand for pork. Fruit is produced for export, for fruit juice factories, and for the local market.

Fishing

Green mussel, prawn, live bait and freshwater shrimp aquaculture are under development. The fishing industry, in particular tuna, is growing. Typically, the annual catch is over 500,000mt including both fish and other seafood. The government aims to increase its commercial tuna-fishing fleet to around 150 vessels, which are to be built locally and overseas. Ship-building businesses in China and Fiji will probably be the main constructors.

Pearl farming is the second most important economic activity, after tourism, with over 800,000 harvested annually. Black pearls are the main merchandise export. They are mainly shipped to Japan and US.

Forestry

Although 70 per cent of the islands' land area is covered in forest, conditions limit exploitation to random felling, and almost all timber is imported. Plantations will yield productive forest of 11,250 hectares (ha) of Caribbean pine by 2025; 30ha of wood for local cabinet-making is planted per year.

Industry and manufacturing

The small manufacturing sector primarily processes agricultural products. It accounts for approximately 18 per cent of

GDP and employs 19 per cent of the workforce.
The oil mill, Huilerie de Tahiti, purchases all copra produced and processes it into coconut oil and meal (for animal feed), soap-making and monoi (scented coconut oil). Other industries include breweries, soft drinks and fruit juice factories and power station. Several small concerns produce textiles and handicrafts.

Tourism
Tourism is the most important economic activity, accounting for a quarter of GDP, and is the primary earner of foreign income.
An increase in cruise ship passengers has contributed to the improvement and the authorities are actively encouraging cruise visits.

Mining
Reserves of phosphate are present but not exploited.

Hydrocarbons
No oil, natural gas or coal is produced. Imported petroleum products amount to 6,300 barrels of oil per day.

Energy
The government-owned monopoly, Électricité de Tahiti, is responsible for power production, supply and sales in French Polynesia. On Tahiti, the largest island, peak demand was 97MW in 2007, producing 552 gigawatt hours (gWh), of which hydropower accounted for 30 per cent. Around 90 per cent of the population has access to mains electricity. On remote islands electricity is supplied by small hydro, solar and wind generated installations.

Banking and insurance
Although banking facilities in the principal urban centres are good, and include ATMs, financial service providers are scarce on some of the outlying islands.
Central bank
The Paris-based Institut d'Emission d'Outre-Mer (IEOM) provides all central banking services except foreign exchange reserves.

Time
GMT minus 10 hours

Geography
French Polynesia comprises several scattered groups of islands (120 islands in total) in the south Pacific Ocean, lying about halfway between South America and Australia.The Cook Islands are to the west and the Line Islands (part of Kiribati) to the north-west. The island groups in French Polynesia include the Iles du Vent (including the islands of Tahiti and Moorea) and the Iles Sous le Vent (about 160km north-west of Tahiti), which together constitute the Society Archipelago; the Tuamotu Archipelago which comprises 78 islands scattered east of the Society Archipelago in a line stretching north-west to south-east for about 1,500km; the Gambier Islands located 1,600km south-east of Tahiti; the Austral Islands lying 640km south of Tahiti; and the Marquesas Archipelago, 1,450km north-east of Tahiti.
Most islands are mountainous (volcanic) and ringed with coral reefs; the Tuamotu and Gambier groups are mainly low-lying atolls.
Hemisphere
Southern

Climate
French Polynesia is located in the tropical zone of the southern hemisphere. It has two seasons: warm and moist (Dec–Feb) average temperature 27 degrees Celsius (C); cool and dry (Mar–Nov), average temperature 21 degrees C. Rainfall varies, depending on relief of island and exposure to prevailing winds, but heaviest Nov–Mar.

Entry requirements
Passports
Required by all, valid for six months after date of departure.
Visa
Required by all, except nationals of EU, other European countries and Australia for stays up to three months and nationals of the US, Canada, New Zealand, Japan, South Korea and most Latin American countries for stays up to one month.
Customs
Visitors are allowed to bring 200 cigarettes, 100 cigarillos, 50 cigars or 200 grams of tobacco; one or two litres of spirits depending on strength; 50g perfume and 250ml eau de toilette; and goods to the value of CPFf5,000 duty free.
All baggage coming in from Fiji and Samoa, except hand luggage, is fumigated. Travellers should carry clothing and toilet articles for an overnight stay in their hand luggage and arrange for their hotel to collect other baggage from the airport after fumigation.
Prohibited imports
Import of foodstuffs, weapons and illegal drugs.

Health (for visitors)
Mandatory precautions
Vaccination certificate for yellow fever if travelling from an infected area.
Advisable precautions
Vaccination for diphtheria, tuberculosis, hepatitis A and B, polio, tetanus, typhoid are recommended. There is a rabies risk.

Hotels
Most of the major international hotel chains are represented. Hotels are expensive and tend to be clustered in resorts. Cheaper, but off the beaten track, are *pensions* (bed-and-breakfast type accommodation).

Credit cards
American Express, Diners' Club, Master Card and Visa accepted throughout Tahiti.

Public holidays (national)
Fixed dates
1 Jan (New Year's Day), 5 Mar (Missionary Day), 1 May (Labour Day), 8 May (Victory Day), 14 Jul (Bastille Day), 15 Aug (Assumption Day), 8 Sep (Autonomy Day), 1 Nov (All Saints' Day), 11 Nov (Armistice Day), 25 Dec (Christmas Day).
Variable dates
Good Friday, Easter Monday, Ascension Day, Whit Monday.

Working hours
Banking
Mon–Fri: 0800–1530.
Business
Mon–Fri: 0800–1200, 1330–1730; Sat: 0800–1200.
Government
Mon–Fri: 0800–1200, 1330–1730; Sat: 0800–1200.
Shops
Mon–Fri: 0730–1130, 1400–1700; Sat: 0730–1130.

Telecommunications
Tahiti has an automatic telephone network.

Electricity supply
220V AC, 60 cycles (check with hotel before using appliances).

Weights and measures
Metric system

Social customs/useful tips
Tipping is not customary, and is contrary to traditional Tahitian hospitality.

Getting there
Air
National airline: Air Tahiti Nui
International airport/s: Tahiti-Faa'a International Airport (PPT), 6km from Papeete; restaurant, bank and car hire.
Airport tax: None.
Surface
Main port/s: Papeete.

Getting about
National transport
Air: There are over 25 airfields in addition to Tahiti-Faa'a International Airport. Air Tahiti operates scheduled flights to Moorea, Huahine, Raiatea, Bora-Bora, Maupiti, Rangiroa, Manihi, Takapoto, Tubuai, Nuku-Hiva (Marquesas), Ua

Huka, Hiva Oa, Ua Pou, Anaa, Makemo, Hao, Rurutu and Mangareva (Gambiers) and several other atolls. Air Moorea operates daily services between Tahiti and Moorea. Both airlines also offer air taxi services, charters, circle island flights and transportation to other islands. Other air operators include Tahiti Conquest Airlines and Pacific Helicopter Tours.

Road: There are approximately 200km of road on Tahiti, including a circular 120km asphalt road around the main part of the island, and 100km of road on Moorea.

Buses: *Le truck* runs an unscheduled transport service between Papeete and outlying districts, leaving approximately every half hour for nearby areas and daily for distant points. The system also operates on Moorea, Bora Bora and some other islands.

Water: There is a scheduled boat service between Papeete and Moorea.

City transport

Taxis: Fares are controlled and should be displayed in each cab. In Tahiti, fares double between 2300 and 0500. Information on fares is available at GIE Tahiti Tourisme at the airport and in Papeete. The journey time from the airport to the city centre is 10 minutes.

Buses, trams & metro: Airport to city centre bus service operates 0400–2359 hours, every 15 minutes.

Car hire

There are numerous car hire establishments; rates include insurance. Drivers must hold a licence valid for at least one year and must be at least 21-years-old. Driving is on the right-hand side of the road.

BUSINESS DIRECTORY

The addresses listed below are a selection only. While World of Information makes every endeavour to check these addresses, we cannot guarantee that changes have not been made, especially to telephone numbers and area codes. We would welcome any corrections.

Telephone area codes

The international dialling code (IDD) for French Polynesia is + 689 followed by subscriber's number.

Useful telephone numbers

Police: 17

Fire: 18

Chambers of Commerce

French Polynesia Chamber of Commerce and Industry, PO Box 118, Rue Docteur Cassiau, 98713 Papeete (tel: 540-700; fax: 540-701).

Banking

Banque de Polynésie SA, PO Box 530, 355 Boulevard Pomare, Papeete (tel: 466-666; fax: 466-664).

Banque de Tahiti SA, PO Box 1602, Rue Cardella, Papeete (tel: 417-000; fax: 423-376).

Banque Socredo, PO Box 130, 115 rue Dumont d'Urville, Papeete (tel: 415-123; fax 433-661).

Central bank

Institut d'Emission d'Outre-Mer (IEOM), 5 rue Roland Barthes, 75012 Paris, France (tel : +33 1 5344-4141; fax : +33 1 4347-5134; e-mail: contact@ieom.fr).

Travel information

Air Moorea, BP 6019, Faa'a International Airport (tel: 864-141; fax: 864-299).

Air Tahiti Nui, Immeuble Dexter, Pont de l'Est, BP 1673, Papeete (tel: 460-303; fax: 460-222).

National tourist organisation offices

Tahiti Tourisme, Immeuble Paofai, Bvd Pomaré, BP 65 Papeete (tel: 505-700; fax: 436-619; e-mail: tahiti-tourisme@mail.pf; internet: www.tahiti-tourisme.com).

Other useful addresses

Institut Territorial de la Statistique, BP 395, Papeete, Tahiti (tel: 437-196; fax: 427-252).

Service des Affaires Economiques, BP 82, Papeete, Tahiti.

Syndicat des Importateurs et des Négociants, PO Box 1607, Papeete, Tahiti.

Syndicat d'Initiative de la Polynésie Française, BP 326, Papeete.

National news agency: L'Agence Tahitienne de Presse (Tahitipress)

Immeuble ICA/TNTV, Vallée de Putiaoro, Quartier de la Mission; BP 4635 Papeete RP, Tahiti (tel: 548-787; fax: 838-382; email: agence@tahitipresse.pf).

Internet sites

Tourism Council of the South Pacific: www.infocentre.com/spt.

Enterprise and development agency (in French): www.creation-entreprises.pf/

Gabon

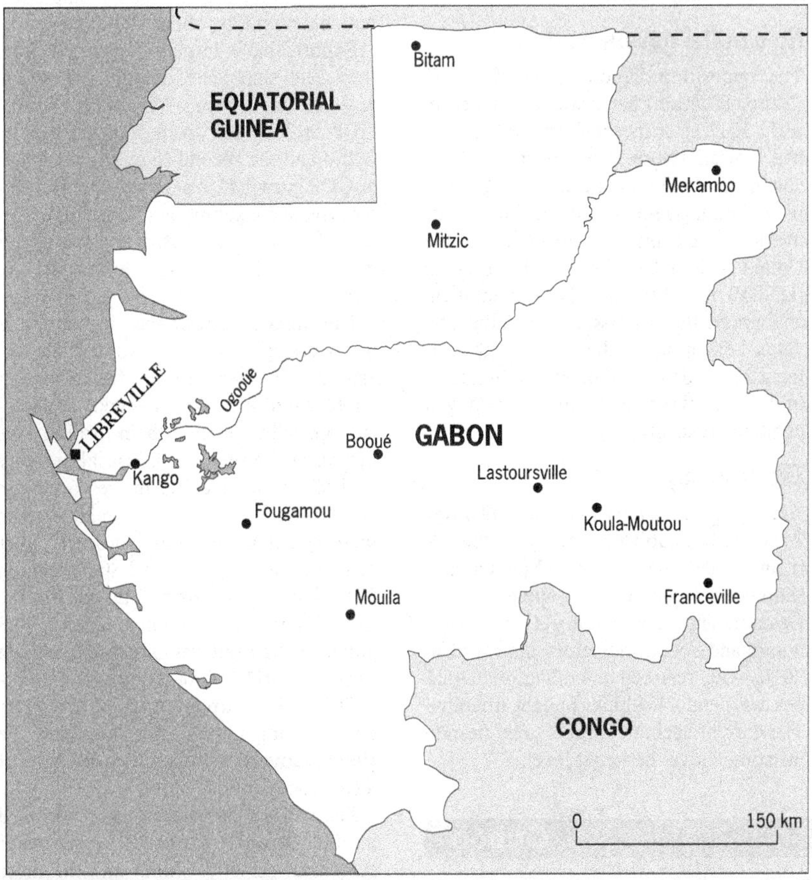

KEY FACTS

Official name: République Gabonaise (Gabonese Republic)

Head of State: Interim President Rose Francine Rogombé (sworn in 10 June 2009)

Head of government: Prime Minister Paul Biyoghé Mba (PDG) (from 18 Jul; re-appointed 16 Oct 2009)

Ruling party: Parti Démocratique Gabonais (PDG) (Gabonese Democratic Party) (since 1960; re-elected 17 Dec 2011)

Area: 267,667 square km

Population: 1.50 million (2010)*

Capital: Libreville

Official language: French

Currency: CFA franc (CFAf) = 100 centimes (Communauté Financière Africaine (African Financial Community) franc)

Exchange rate: CFAf488.90 per US$ (Oct 2011); CFAf655.96 per euro (pegged from Jan 1999)

GDP per capita: US$7,468 (2009)*

GDP real growth: -0.10% (2009)*

GDP: US$11.02 billion (2009)

Inflation: 2.10% (2009)*

Oil production: 245,000 bpd (2010)

* estimated figure

On 2 April, members of the oil workers union, the National Organisation of Oil Employees, went on strike for four days, shutting down Total and Royal Dutch Shell operations, in protest at the employment of foreign workers rather than local workers. The cost to the government and companies was estimated at US$131 million. Gabon's oil production has been steadily falling since the peak of 327,000 barrels per day (bpd) in 2001 – to 245,000bpd in 2010. Never-the-less, proved reserves at the end of 2010 were still a pretty healthy 3.7 thousand million barrels, the seventh highest in Africa.

Parliamentary elections were held on 17 December 2011; however, since the government rejected the suggestion of biometric voter registration to prevent fraud, the opposition and other community and civic groups called on voters to boycott the elections, declaring that they could not be free and fair and would be rigged in favour of the President's Parti Démocratique Gabonais (PDG) (Gabonese Democratic Party), which has been in power since 1968. The Union pour la Nouvelle République (UNR) (Union for a New Republic) (established in 2008) and Peuple Gabonais l'Union (PGU) (Union of the Gabonese People) chose to participate. Although voter turnout was low, the initial results were that PDG won 73 seats out of 120.

Constitutional amendments

The national constitution was amended by parliament on 28 December 2010 by 177–16, more than the required two-thirds majority. Parliament had moved that amendments were necessary after a disagreement about how to revise the electoral register for the 2009 presidential election had nearly resulted in a serious constitutional crisis. The president of the constitutional court also called for amendment to the electoral law and laws about the multi-party system, to bring the legislation into line with the constitution itself and improve the rule of law in Gabon.

The president of the parliamentary group of the majority PDG said the changes would correct 'weaknesses' in the constitution and settle the problem of challenges to election results, the length of political-transition periods and the eligibility of presidential candidates.

The main amendments were to extend the interim period to 45– 60 days were the presidency to be vacated; to specify the interim president's oath of office (not previously mentioned in the constitution); to alter clauses about freedom of association and of religion, which remain basic rights; to define the president's national defence powers; and to provide the president with extra powers when national independence and territory are seriously threatened.

Previously the time allowed between the presidency becoming vacant and elections to fill the presidency was 30 days. This was considered too short to allow for the drawing up of electoral lists, issuance of voting cards, declaring candidacies and establishing polling stations.

The amendments were criticised by the opposition who said that some of the changes gave the government a 'free hand' to rig the next elections and that the president would be allowed to decide when to hold an election, giving him an advantage. The PDG, which has been in power since 1968, were able to push the amendments through parliament, though one of its members opposed them and two others were disciplined for criticising the method of amendment.

No parallel governments

The opposition Union Nationale (UN) (National Union) party was disbanded in early 2011 after its secretary general had had himself sworn in as president of the country and appointed a parallel government. Fearing reprisals, on 25 January its members took refuge in the offices of the United Nations Development Programme (UNDP) in Libreville. The government announced the dismissal of all civil servants belonging to the parallel government and said the parliamentary immunity of the parallel president might be removed pending prosecution.

The economy

According to *African Economic Outlook 2011* (AEO), published jointly by the African Development Bank and the Organisation for Economic Co-operation and Development, the country's main economic and social indicators improved in 2010, with restored overall growth (5.5 per cent) and a healthier budget situation. The current account surplus grew despite inflation above the target level.

Recovery in 2010 was based on a 3.4 per cent increase in oil production with the opening of new oilfields, a 13.5 per cent rise in oil export prices and continuing efforts to extract marginal deposits. In the last quarter of 2010, the Anglo-Dutch company Shell brought into production an oilfield at Koula with estimated reserves of 64 million barrels, which should boost national output by about 10 per cent.

Exports have largely recovered from their 2009 slump and, though not yet back to 2008 level, were 59.7 per cent of real GDP in 2010 (up from 56.4 per cent in 2009) and the second-biggest contributor to GDP growth (2.2 percentage points) after private consumption (2.3 points). This contribution is projected to drop to 1.8 points in 2011 and rise again in 2012 to 2.5.

This mixed performance in exports is partly due to the reorganisation of the forestry sector where, a year after exports of unprocessed logs were banned, 11 factories opened to process them locally. This increased the sector's industrial capacity to 1.625 million cubic metres (cum) in 2010 (from 1.6 million cum in 2009). The industry will be required to process 75 per cent of all logs in 2011 and 80 per cent in 2012. Forestry's share of GDP growth fell from 1 percentage point in 2009 to 0.3 points in 2010 and was expected to remain steady in 2011 before rising to 0.4 points in 2012. The sharp fall was due to the ban on exporting unprocessed logs and the slight recovery will be due to the start of local processing.

The world manganese market slumped in 2009 because of stockpiling by major customers (mostly China) and the more than halving of the metal's price. With recovery of the world steel industry and China no longer drawing on its stocks, the GDP share of the mining sector grew to 3.0 per cent in 2010 (from 2.1 per cent in 2009). This share should more than double in 2011 to 6.5 per cent, before dipping slightly again (to 6.3 per cent) in 2012, thanks to investments since 2008 in new equipment, and the building of a plant to produce manganese metal (high manganese) to the tune of 20,000 tonnes a year and of another plant producing silicomanganese (65,000 tonnes). In addition, the Broken Hill Proprietary Company (BHP Billiton) has started operations in Franceville.

Efforts to encourage investment so as to further diversify the economy and expand industry continued in 2010. The government, aware that raw materials will not be the key to overall growth for ever,

KEY INDICATORS — Gabon

	Unit	2006	2007	2008	2009	2010
Population	m	1.40	*1.43	*1.45	*1.48	*1.50
Gross domestic product (GDP)	US$bn	9.55	*11.30	*14.54	*11.02	–
GDP per capita	US$	6,835	*7,887	*10,002	*7,468	–
GDP real growth	%	1.1	*5.5	*2.0	*3.5	–
Inflation	%	6.4	5.0	*5.3	*2.1	–
Industrial output	% change	-4.6	4.3	0.4	-2.5	–
Agricultural output	% change	2.1	5.3	-0.2	-1.1	–
Oil output	'000 bpd	232.0	230.0	235.0	229.0	245.0
Exports (fob) (goods)	US$m	6,054.0	*7,382.5	*7,602.5	*3,021.8	–
Imports (fob) (goods)	US$m	1,878.0	*1,873.2	*2,305.1	*1,764.7	–
Balance of trade	US$m	4,176.0	*5,509.3	5,297.3	*1,257.1	–
Current account	US$m	1,717.0	*1,892.6	*2,607.6	*1,283.0	–
Total reserves minus gold	US$m	1,113.4	1,227.2	1,923.5	1,993.2	1,735.9
Foreign exchange	US$m	1,112.2	1,226.0	1,922.3	1,784.2	1,530.5
Exchange rate	per US$	496.60	454.40	418.59	514.03	495.28

* estimated figure

recognises the need to boost small and medium-sized enterprises and industries (SMEs and SMIs). The private sector has been in steady decline for more than a decade for lack of clear, bold policy, and 80 per cent of the 10,000 firms set up every two years fail by the end of that time.

The business climate has remained sluggish owing to complex procedures, long delays and the cost of starting a firm in the country, aggravated by corruption, bad governance and the size of the informal sector, even though Gabon gained two places in the World Bank's annual *Doing Business report*, to 156th out of 183 countries, in 2010.

The government wants to help the private sector expand, attract FDI and produce strong and lasting growth that will generate jobs. To move in this direction, partnership agreements have been made with several emerging countries (China, Singapore and India) to boost the private sector with assistance and more financial services with easier access.

The Nkok special economic zone will focus on wood processing (and the sector's value chain in particular), which is one of the country's strategic sectors after oil, with Olam, owned by a Singapore sovereign fund, as the government's main partner. The zone is 27 kilometres east of Libreville and 40 per cent of its 1,146-hectare area will be occupied by industry, mainly wood processing with an annual capacity of 1 million cum, which should attract nearly US$1 billion in investments and create about 9,000 direct jobs.

Palm-oil plantations were inaugurated in October 2010 at Mouila (Ngounié province) and Tchibanga (Nyanga province), savannah areas in the south-west, with a first phase of 50,000 hectares for an investment of US$200 million and the creation of 7,000 direct and 21,000 indirect jobs. The second phase will be 150,000 hectares planted for US$600 million, and 4,000 direct and 8,000 indirect jobs. Output should reach 1 million tonnes and make Gabon one of Africa's leading palm-oil producers.

The partner will again be Olam, with 30 per cent of the plantations held by about 3,000 Gabonese farmers who will be given training in palm-oil plantation management. The new industry should eventually bring in annual export earnings of about US$800 million.

Gabon is jointly to hold, with Equatorial Guinea, the 2012 Africa Cup of Nations. Construction of facilities for the tournament has lead to an increase in investments for this and infrastructure projects associated with the 50th anniversary of independence celebrations.

Risk assessment

Economy	Fair
Politics	Fair
Regional stability	Fair

COUNTRY PROFILE

Historical profile

1472 Portuguese navigators arrived in the Ogooué estuary and Gabon soon became an important centre for slave trading for the Portuguese, Dutch, British and French.
1839 Having gained a dominant position in the area and despite Fang resistance, Gabon became part of the French Congo. The French began work to abolish the slave trade.
1910 Gabon became part of French Equatorial Africa.
1939–1945 Gabon was held by the Free French.
1946 Gabon became a province of French Equatorial Africa. In gratitude for the support of the local population for the Free French, President Charles de Gaulle of France granted French citizenship to all the territory's people.
1957 Gabon gained internal autonomy.
1958 It achieved self-government within the French community.
1960 Gained full independence from France, under President Léon M'Ba. The Parti Démocratique Gabonais (PDG) (Gabonese Democratic Party) assumed power.
1964 French forces restored M'Ba to the presidency after an abortive military *coup d'état*.
1967 President M'Ba died. Vice President Albert-Bernard Bongo became president.
1973 Bongo was re-elected and converted to Islam, adopting the forename Omar.
1981–89 Political unrest grew as people called for more democracy.
1990 After demonstrations by students and strikes by workers, President Bongo legalised opposition parties.
1991 A new constitution was introduced that formalised the multi-party system.
1993 Bongo narrowly won the presidential election, although the opposition claimed massive electoral fraud.
1996 Parliamentary elections gave the PDG an overwhelming majority.
1998 President Bongo won another seven years in power with more than two-thirds of the vote.
1999 The country was plunged into a deep recession due to the fall in the world price of oil.
2001 The PDG won the parliamentary elections.
2002 The PDG formed a coalition with the opposition to form the government.
2003 Constitutional changes made in July allow presidents to run for office for unlimited terms. The president modified his name to El Hadj Omar Bongo Ondimba.
2004 Gabon signed separate agreements to export around one billion tonnes of iron ore as well as oil to China.
2005 In presidential elections incumbent El Hadj Omar Bongo Ondimba won 79.2 per cent of the presidential vote; Pierre Mamboundou 13.6 per cent and Zacharie Myboto 6.6 per cent. Turnout was 63.3 per cent.
2006 Omar Bongo Ondimba was sworn in as president for a third seven-year term. Jean Eyeghe Ndong (PDG) was appointed prime minister. In parliamentary elections the ruling PDG won 82 out of the 120 seats, allied parties won 17, opposition 17 and independents four seats.
2008 Former foreign minister Jean Ping was elected chairman of the African Union Commission.
2009 The ruling PDG won senate elections. President Omar Bongo Ondimba had his assets in France frozen by the authorities and a French court ordered him to return a payment made to him for the release of a French businessman, jailed in Gabon. The president was thought to have around US$4 million held in French bank accounts; he claimed the money received was for the sale of a business and not for the release. In May, the president suspended his functions as head of state and was reported to be seriously ill. He died in Spain on 8 June and his body was flown back to Gabon for burial. Senate leader Rose Francine Rogombé became interim president on 9 June. In Ali Ben Bongo Ondimba (son of the late president Bongo) (PDG) won presidential elections. The Constitutional Court rejected opposition challenges to the official election results. Paul Biyoghé became prime minister.
2010 In August the government signed contracts, expected to generate up to US$4.5 billion in investment, with three Asian companies in a move designed to diversify the economy as oil reserves begin to dwindle. The contracts include the setting up of a special economic zone in Nkok (27km east of Libreville) with a capacity to process one million cubic metres of timber annually; improving the infrastructure, which would create around 50,000 jobs; developing a palm oil plantation of up to 300,000 hectares, and a palm oil refinery, with a possible new port for exports in the south east of Gabon. 5,000 low-cost homes are also included in the plans. Transparency International

successfully appealed against a Paris court's ruling in 2009 that it could not act against foreign heads of state. On 9 November France's highest appeal court gave judges permission to proceed with investigations into assets held in France by the late president, Omar Bongo and his family, as well as Teodoro Obiang Nguema of Equatorial Guinea and Denis Sassou-Nguesso of Congo. On 13 November, the Singaporea multinational, Olam International, agreed to invest US$1.7 billion in Gabon, including the construction of a fertiliser plant and palm oil plantations.
2011 On 2 April, members of the oil workers union, the National Organisation of Oil Employees, went on strike for four days, shutting down Total and Royal Dutch Shell operations, in protest at the employment of foreign workers rather than local workers. The cost to the government and companies was estimated at US$131 million. On 6 May, the opposition leader André Mba Obame was stripped of his parliamentary immunity as the government prepared to charge him with treason, following his TV broadcast in January, when he had declared himself the winner of the 2009 presidential election. Parliamentary elections were held on 17 December; however, since the government rejected the suggestion of biometric voter registration to prevent fraud, the opposition and other community and civic groups called on voters to boycott the elections, declaring that they could not be free and fair and would be rigged in favour of the President's PDG. The Union pour la Nouvelle République (UNR) (Union for a New Republic) (established in 2008) and Peuple Gabonais l'Union (PGU) (Union of the Gabonese People) chose to participate. Although voter turnout was low, the initial results were that PDG won 73 seats out of 120.

Political structure

Constitution

In 1991 a new constitution was introduced which restored multi-party elections and protected civil liberties. The constitution maintained a strong presidential role but allowed for a more influential prime minister.
In 2003, the constitution was changed to allow presidents to run for office for unlimited number of times, and the number of presidential election rounds was reduced from two to one.

Form of state

Presidential democracy

The executive

Executive power is divided between the president, elected by universal suffrage every seven years, and the prime minister and Council of Ministers (Cabinet) who are appointed by the president.
Government members must be more than 35 years of age and have at least seven years' professional experience.
The president is head of state, head of administration and chief of the armed forces.

National legislature

The bicameral parliament consists of the Assemblée Nationale (national assembly) with 120 members, of which 111 are elected in single seat constituencies and nine are appointed by the president, all to serve for five-year terms, and the Sénat (senate) with 91 members elected in single seat constituencies by representatives of subordinate assemblies, to serve for six-year terms.

Legal system

The legal system is based on the French civil law system and customary law. There is judicial review of legislative acts in the Constitutional Chamber of the Supreme Court.

Last elections

27 November 2005 (presidential); 17 December 2011 (parliamentary)
Results: Presidential: El Hadj Omar Bongo Ondimba won 79.2 per cent of the vote; Pierre Mamboundou 13.6 per cent and Zacharie Myboto 6.6 per cent. Turnout was 63.3 per cent.
Parliamentary: (initial results as of 20 December 2011) Parti Démocratique Gabonais (PDG) (Gabonese Democratic Party) won 73 seats out of 120.

Next elections

2016 (parliamentary); November 2012 (presidential)

Political parties

Ruling party

Parti Démocratique Gabonais (PDG) (Gabonese Democratic Party) (since 1960; re-elected 17 Dec 2011)

Main opposition party

Union du Peuple Gabonais (UPG) Union of the Gabonese People

Population

1.50 million (2010)*
Last census: 1 December 2003: 1,269,000 (provisional)
Population density: Five inhabitants per square km. Urban population: 82 per cent of total (1995–2001).
Annual growth rate: 2.3 per cent 1994–2004 (WHO 2006)

Ethnic make-up

There are some 40 different ethnic groups, of which the Fangs are the largest (40 per cent of the total); the Bapounous (20 per cent) are also highly significant. There are some 25,000 Europeans, mainly of French nationality.

Religions

Christianity (59 per cent), mostly Roman Catholic; indigenous animist beliefs (40 per cent). There is a small Muslim community (less than 1 per cent).

Education

School is compulsory and free for all children up to the age of 16 years. Secondary education covers seven years, divided into a lower cycle lasting four years and an upper cycle lasting three years. On completion of the upper cycle, pupils take the examinations for the *Baccalauréat* for advancement to university. On completion of the lower cycle, pupils may opt to take a 'short' or a 'long' course of technical secondary education. The former leads to the *Brevet de Technicien* and the latter to the *Baccalauréat technique*.
Two universities – Omar Bongo University and the University of Science and Technology of Masuku (USTM at Franceville) – as well as various independent institutions provide higher education. Universities enjoy a certain degree of autonomy, even though higher education is financed exclusively by public funds.
Public expenditure on education typically amounts to 2.5 per cent of annual GDP.
Literacy rate: 79.8 per cent, male; 62.2 per cent, female; adult rates (World Bank).
Enrolment rate: 62 per cent total primary school enrolment of the relevant age group (World Bank).
Pupils per teacher: 56 in primary schools.

Health

Gabon is plagued by poor health conditions, which are aggravated by the hot and humid climate and is the country worst affected by malaria in sub-Saharan Africa.
Gabon faces a growing crisis of male impotence affecting 25 per cent of all adult men, blamed on high levels of alcohol and tobacco use.

HIV/Aids

HIV/Aids is a rapidly growing crisis the World Health Organisation (WHO) estimates that 30,000 people in Gabon are being infected with HIV each year and Gabon is beginning to experience the serious effects of the African pandemic. Around 8,600 children have been orphaned by the disease. The main concentration of HIV/Aids cases is in the capital, Libreville. The government has launched a campaign to prevent the disease spreading further.
HIV prevalence: 8.1 per cent aged 15–49 in 2003 (World Bank)
Life expectancy: 57 years, 2004 (WHO 2006)
Fertility rate/Maternal mortality rate: 3.9 births per woman, 2004 (WHO

2006); maternal mortality 600 per 100,000 live births (World Bank).
Birth rate/Death rate: 16 deaths to 36 births per 1,000 population,
Child (under 5 years) mortality rate (per 1,000): 60 per 1,000 live births (World Bank)
Head of population per physician: 0.29 physicians per 1,000 people, 2004 (WHO 2006)

Welfare
Gabon's social welfare system, while deeply flawed, is one of the best in sub-Saharan Africa. It operates a social insurance system and healthcare system through separate funds administered by the National Social Security Fund (CNSS) and National Social Guarantee Fund (CNGS) for self-employed and state workers under contract through a pay-as-you-go system. As these funds have experienced financial difficulties and the government has undertaken to restructure them with a view to their long-term viability. Inadequate contributions have been blamed for the over-spending.
The social insurance system covers benefits including old age, disability, sickness, maternity and work injuries with provision for certain categories of self-employed workers. Old age pensions are available to men aged 55 with 20 years of insurance and 120 months of contribution during the last 10 years. It is set at a minimum of 40 per cent of average earnings during the last three or five years of pay. There is also provision for old-age settlement with a lump sum equal to 50 per cent of average monthly earnings for every six months of contribution, if the person is ineligible for pension.
Medical services are provided by hospitals and dispensaries operated by the CNSS, and by other establishments. Free maternity care is payable up to six weeks before, and eight weeks after, confinement.
A family allowance law also offers benefits to employees with one or more children under the age of 16 years. Family Allowance Benefits provide a month income for each child and a year school allowances for primary, secondary and technical school students.

Main cities
Libreville (capital, estimated population 673,995 in 2004), Port-Gentil (118,940).

Languages spoken
French is used for all documentation. The main native language is Fang, with a number of other Bantu dialects spoken.
It is essential that business visitors should be able to conduct business in French. Interpreters can be hired locally.
Official language/s
French

Media
The constitution guarantees freedom of speech and of the press, however, these are not always respected and this has led to self-censorship by local journalists.
Press
The national press is heavily influenced by government which owns the majority of newspapers used to discredit opposition political parties and independent media. While all newspapers may be critical of the government and political leaders, none are critical of the president. The government has shown itself to be quick to use libel laws, which can be both criminal and civil matters, and to suspend publications it deems unacceptable in their reporting.
Foreign newspapers and magazines are readily available in Libreville.
Dailies: The only newspaper is the government-owned *L'Union*, published in French.
Weeklies: In French, privately-owned newspapers include *Le Temps* which has a satirical tenor, *Le Temoin* covers general news and information, *La Lowe*, *La Relance* and the fortnightly *Le Journal*.
Business: In French, a monthly journal *Business Gabon* (www.gaboneco.com/busnessgabon/Business_Gabon.pdf) has business articles and information.
Periodicals: *L'Union* also publishes a monthly magazine, with a similar circulation. *M'Bolo* has three issues on holiday and travel.
Broadcasting
Gabon is developing as the centre of Francophone broadcasting for Central and West Africa, being the base of the radio service Africa No 1 and for the African operations of France's Canal Plus. The state has taken a financial interest in these broadcasting media, as well as in the main newspaper, directly and through parastatal groups. It therefore retains a high degree of control.
The government-owned, national, public broadcasting service, Radiodiffusion-Télévision Gabonaise (RTG), operates radio stations and a network of provincial stations.
Radio: RTG operates two national radio stations, based in Libreville, and a network of six regional stations broadcasting in French and local languages.
A major international station, Africa No 1, is 60 per cent government owned, with the rest owned by private Gabonese shareholders. It is in partnership with the French-owned Radio France Internationale (RFI), broadcasting throughout Africa.
Other, commercial stations include Black FM and Radio Emergence.
Television: RTG operates a network of provincial TV stations, which broadcast in French and local languages. RTG 1 is a national service, broadcast in Libreville and Franceville; while RTG 2 can be received only in the Libreville and the coastal area.
Téléafrica, is a private commercial channel that broadcasts 24 hours a day. Subscription TV is available through the French, Canal Horizons (Gabon), a channel designed to serve the whole of Francophone Central Africa.
News agencies
National news agency: Agence Gabonaise de Presse (AGP)
Gabonews: www.gabonews.ga
Internet Gabon: www.internetgabon.com

Economy
Gabon has sub-Saharan Africa's third-largest oil reserves – revenue from oil exports accounts for over 60 per cent of GDP. The dominance of oil in the economy has resulted in undue bias, not only in a weak non-oil sector but also a wide gap in pay levels. The 2005 criticism by the International Monetary Fund (IMF) of the Gabonese economy that it faced a 'lack of economic diversification and weak non-oil growth' remained true 2010. Although per capital income in 2009 was US$13,900 (by purchasing power parity), income is distributed extremely unevenly with 90 per cent of the wealth held by 5 per cent of the population. It has been estimated that over 50 per cent of the population lives below the poverty line and poverty is widespread particularly in rural areas.
Timber exports are an important source of foreign exchange, although coupled with farming, agriculture only accounts for 4 per cent of GDP. The service sector accounts for over 30 per cent of GDP, which typically provides support for the extractive industry.
GDP growth was a high of 5.6 per cent in 2007, as record global oil prices pushed up oil production and exports. As oil prices began to fall in 2008 the economy slowed to a growth figure of 2.3 per cent, then into recession in 2009 with GDP growth estimated at -1.4 per cent.
Public sector employment and wages are considered a drag on entrepreneurial enterprises, while domestic growth in non-oil activities has been modest and dominated by foreign companies.
Gabon has been criticised by the World Bank and the IMF for poor economic management. It also has a poor reputation with the Paris Club of creditor countries for the weak management of its debt and revenues. Nevertheless, a series of loans from the IMF and the Paris Club were approved by 2007; however,

following the death of former president Omar Bongo, and the financial and social upheaval this caused, Gabon was unable to meet its economic goals in 2009 leading to a strain in relationships with its lenders.

External trade

Gabon is a member of the Economic and Monetary Community of Central Africa (Cemac), the Economic Community of Central African States (ECCAS) and the Bank of Central African States, using the CFA franc. There is a common external tariff (CET) within Cemac.

Imports

Principal imports are foodstuffs, machinery and equipment, chemicals and construction materials.

Main sources: Russia (typically 31 per cent of total), US (17 per cent), China (16 per cent).

Exports

Principal exports are crude oil (over 70 per cent of total), timber, manganese and uranium

Main destinations: France (typically 32 per cent of total), US (8 per cent), China (7 per cent).

Agriculture

Farming

The agricultural sector in Gabon has been neglected, forcing the importation of a large percentage of the country's food needs. Only about 1 per cent of total land area is under cultivation and agriculture is further limited by the small size of the population. A shortage of cultivated lands has been the major problem facing the agricultural sector which, mostly through subsistence farming, supports a large portion of the population.

Principal cash crops are palm oil, cocoa and refined sugar, while subsistence crops are cassava, maize and plantains. Cocoa is grown mainly in Woleu Ntem province and coffee mainly in Ogooué-Ivindo, Ogooué-Lolo and Haut Ogooué provinces. Sugar cane is grown and refined by the Société Sucrérie du Haut-Ogooué (Sosuho). Annual sugar output is around 30,000 tonnes. Agrogabon set up three cattle ranches in the 1980s, importing tsetse fly-resistant cattle. They are located at Lekabi, Nyanga and N'Gounie. The only industrial-scale poultry farm is run by the Société Industrielle d'Agriculture et d'Elevage de Boumango (SIAEB).

Fishing

Gabon has well-stocked fishing grounds, which are only partially exploited. Domestic demand is estimated at around 36,000 tonnes. The typical annual catch is over 40,000 tonnes. Traditional fishing accounts for two-thirds of national fishing output. There are about a dozen fleets, most of which are foreign, engaged in industrial fishing in Gabonese waters.

Forestry

Exports of forest products amount to around US$320 million annually and timber is a source of employment for nearly a third of the working population outside the public sector. Forests cover almost 85 per cent of the land area, estimated at 21.8 million hectares (ha). Deforestation typically accounts for 0.05 per cent annually average decrease, or the equivalent of 10,000ha of forest cover.

The forestry industry is the second-largest industry in the country. Gabon commercially exploits and exports both soft and hard woods, but cultivation and processing of timber comprises the main portion of forestry activities. The country produces sawn timber, veneers and plywood. Tropical hardwood logs constitute the bulk of its roundwood exports. The potential commercial volume of live trees is estimated at 400 million cubic metres, 130 million of which is the much celebrated ebony gaboon wood.

Gabon is the fifth-largest world producer of timber, behind Finland, Canada, Sweden and New Zealand.

The forest is divided into three administrative zones. The coastal area is already fairly well exploited. The zone around Ngounie, Nyanga and Haut-Ogooué has the bulk of current activity. The Booue-Lastourville axis of the Transgabon railway is largely undeveloped. Seven large companies dominate okoume production. The largest is the majority state-owned Compagnie Forestière du Gabon (CFG).

Okoume, designated as the most important commercial timber, is selectively logged in a significant proportion of the country's forests. Exploitable forest potential is more than 300 million cubic metres. One-third of this is okoume, which is particularly suited to the production of plywood.

Industry and manufacturing

The main industrial activities are oil refining and timber processing, although these activities are treated separately from other industry in the national accounts. The other main manufacturing sectors are food processing, drinks and tobacco, metal transformation (primarily connected with shipyard activities and supplying the oil and wood industries) and building materials. Small sub sectors include textiles and chemicals (lubricants, paints, varnishes and detergents).

A fair proportion of the very modest industrial sector has been based on a policy of import substitution. This is now being abandoned as part of structural adjustment measures. The outlook for industry is therefore bleak even though there are plans to develop a regional export market within the Union Douanière des Etats de l'Afrique Centrale (UDEAC) (Central African Customs and Economic Union) countries. In theory, this larger potential market would allow industry to develop economies of scale that the small domestic market does not justify. In practice, however, high labour costs are likely to frustrate efforts to promote the regional market. Gabon's labour costs are high due to the well-established social security system, most of the cost of which is borne by employers, offering benefits that are not found in many other West and Central African countries.

Tourism

The tourist sector is still in its infancy, but since the global economic crisis cut trade in Gabon's principal export earners, timber and oil (a declining resource) the government has given tourism a higher profile in its long-term plans, not only to stimulate the economy but to encourage diversification. Gabon can offer tourists sights of spectacular natural wonder, traditional cultures, history and treasures. The number of arrivals in 2006 was 296,000, which by 2008 had grown to 358,000. Gabon's vast forests with their abundant flora and fauna, are becoming important centres for eco-tourism. Unesco designated the ecosystem and prehistoric landscape of Lopé-Okanda as a World Heritage site in 2007. A Gorilla sanctuary was established in 2001, on the island of Evangué-Ezango just north of the Loango National Park, to promote practical and sustainable tourism while curbing the trade in 'bush-meat' that threatens the survival of gorillas, which have been identified as a potentially lucrative source of foreign exchange.

Mining

Mining and hydrocarbons together contribute around 50 cent to GDP and employ 10 per cent of the workforce.

Gabon is one of the world's leading producers of manganese and uranium. Other areas of interest are gold and iron ore. Activity is concentrated on extraction and export of manganese ore (reserves of 200 million tonnes) and uranium (reserves of 35,000 tonnes). Both are crudely refined before export, the manganese as a 51 per cent concentrate and the uranium as 74 per cent pure yellow cake. Manganese goes mainly to Europe, but also to the US and the Far East. Uranium goes mainly to France (about 10 per cent of France's requirements), the rest to Belgium and Japan. Manganese and uranium account for 10 per cent of merchandise exports.

Manganese production is declining, while large deposits of iron ore, barytes (used in

paint-making) and niobium, discovered during construction of the Transgabon railway, have yet to be exploited.
There are 50 million tonnes of phosphate reserves.

Hydrocarbons
Gabon is sub-Saharan Africa's fourth-largest oil producer, after Nigeria, Angola and Equatorial Guinea. With income from oil exports representing around 40 per cent of GDP and 80 per cent of export revenue, Gabon's economy is highly dependent on this one commodity. The exports go primarily to Western Europe, although China also imports Gabonese crude oil.
Proven oil reserves were 3.7 billion barrels at the end of 2010, with production at 245,000 barrels per day (bpd), rising by 6.5 per cent on the 2009 figure. However, production has fallen from the high of 364,000bpd in 1997. The country's downstream industry consists of the Sogara refinery, which has a capacity of 17,000bpd.
The government has consistently maintained a market-oriented policy towards its sizeable oil reserves and has one of the most attractive hydrocarbons codes in Africa. Under this law, the state has a minimum 25 per cent holding in all oil-producing companies. Oil exploration permits are awarded under production-sharing agreements, which are individually negotiated.
Natural gas reserves totalled 34 billion cubic metres (cum) in 2007. All gas produced in Gabon is used for electricity or refinery fuel.
Any coal produced or import is commercially insignificant.

Energy
Gabon has a total electricity generating capacity of 400MW. In 2000 around 60 per cent of all energy was generated by conventional thermal power stations and the remainder by hydroelectricity. By 2007 the energy mix had changed as hydroelectric power stations provided 76 per cent of all energy and solar panels were being installed in remote villages. Around 90 per cent of urban households have access to electricity and 35 per cent of rural households.
The largest hydroelectric dams are Tchimbele (69MW) and Kinguele (58MW), on the M'Bei River. There is around 6,000MW of undeveloped hydroelectric potential and government plans to increase the role of hydropower while diminishing the role of thermal power, with commitments to upgrade and develop existing dams, power stations and the distribution network.
While the Société d'Energie et d'Eau du Gabon (SEEG) has a monopoly on electricity sales, production and distribution of electricity is open to commercial competition.

Banking and insurance
Central bank
Banque des Etats de l'Afrique Centrale
Main financial centre
Libreville

Time
GMT plus one hour

Geography
Gabon is an equatorial country on the west coast of Africa, with Equatorial Guinea and Cameroon to the north, and the Republic of Congo to the south and east.
The eastern boundary lies along the watershed of the Democratic Republic of Congo (DRC), so that all rivers flow broadly west through Gabon into the sea. The sandy coastal strip consists of palm-fringed bays, lagoons and estuaries. The uplands are heavily eroded by river action, and there is a wide coastal plain, which is largely alluvial in nature. The natural vegetation is dense rain forest.
Hemisphere
Straddles the equator; Liberville, the capital, is in the north.

Climate
The climate is equatorial with an annual mean temperature of 28 degrees Celsius and high levels of humidity. The rainy seasons are between October and mid-December, and between mid-January and May. The dry season is from June to September.

Dress codes
Lightweight or tropical clothing is suitable, with rainwear for the monsoon season. Businessmen should wear a lightweight or tropical suit and women a lightweight suit or equivalent.

Entry requirements
Passports
Required by all. Passports must be valid for more than six months after the date of departure.
Proof of return/onward passage is necessary.
Visa
Required by all and to be applied for before travelling. Applications for business visas require a letter from the representative's company accepting responsibility for any expenses incurred, a full itinerary and a letter of invitation from a host company in Gabon.
Currency advice/regulations
There are no limits on the import of foreign or domestic currency, although any sum should be declared on arrival. Export of local currency, to countries outside the CFA franc zone, is limited of CFAf200,000.
Visitors are advised to carry travellers cheques in euros to avoid extra exchange fees.

Health (for visitors)
Mandatory precautions
A yellow fever vaccination certificate is required.
Advisable precautions
Immunisations are advisable for yellow fever, hepatitis A, tetanus and typhoid. There is a rabies risk.
Malaria and HIV/Aids are prevalent and standard measures should be taken to avoid these diseases.
Water which is used for drinking, brushing teeth or making ice should first be boiled. Dysentery can be caught from contaminated raw fruit and vegetables and unboiled water. Dairy products made from local milk should be avoided. Meat and fish should be well cooked and eaten hot.

Hotels
Available in Libreville, Port Gentil, Lambaréné and other main centres. Service charge is usually included in bill, if not a tip of 10–15 per cent is usual.

Credit cards
Credit cards are not widely accepted.

Public holidays (national)
Fixed dates
1 Jan (New Year's Day), 1 May (Labour Day), 16 Aug (Assumption Day), 16–18 Aug (Independence Day celebrations), 1 Nov (All Saints' Day), 25 Dec (Christmas Day).
Variable dates
Easter Monday, Whit Monday, Eid al Adha, Eid al Fitr.
Islamic year 1433 (26 Nov 2011–14 Nov 2012): The Islamic year contains 354 or 355 days, with the result that Muslim feasts advance by 10–12 days against the Gregorian calendar. Dates of feasts vary according to the sighting of the new moon, so cannot be forecast exactly.

Working hours
Banking
Mon–Fri: 0730–1130, 1430–1630.
Business
Mon–Fri: 0730–1200, 1430–1800.
Government
Mon–Fri: 0730–1530 (30 minute lunch break); Sat: 0800–1300.
Shops
Mon–Sat: 0800–1200, 1500–1900.

Telecommunications
Mobile/cell phones
GSM 900 services are available in the most populated areas.

Electricity supply
220-30V AC, 50 cycles. Round two-pin plugs are standard.

Social customs/useful tips
Business is conducted in French. Appointments should be made in advance. It is customary to shake hands when meeting and taking leave. Business cards are exchanged after introduction.
Gratuities are between 10–15 per cent if no service charge is included.
The lifestyles of the middle classes in Libreville, Port-Gentil and Franceville have been heavily influenced by the French, and French etiquette has been largely adopted.
As elsewhere in Africa, it is extremely unwise to attempt to photograph any military installations or troop movements, security checkpoints, etc.

Security
Crime is increasingly a problem with incidents of robbery and armed attacks, particularly around Libreville and Port-Gentil. Avoid carrying valuables or wearing jewellery in public and walking alone at night.
Avoid travelling at night and always comply with the frequent police roadblocks.

Getting there
Air
National airline: Air Gabon (Compagnie Nationale Air Gabon).
International airport/s: Libreville-Léon M'Ba (LBV), 12km from city; restaurant, currency exchange; Port Gentil (POG), 4km from city.
Other airport/s: Franceville-Mvengue (MVB) has air charters. There are 65 other public and 50 private airfields linked mostly with the forestry and petroleum industries.
Airport tax: None
Surface
Road: The major routes are from the Republic of Congo, Cameroon or Equatorial Guinea. These are semi-surfaced but generally are in good condition and well maintained.
Water: There is a boat to and from São Tomé every five days.
Main port/s: The principal deep-water ports are Port Gentil, Owendo (Libreville). Mayumba and Nyanga are used for shipping timber. There is a fishing port in Libreville.

Getting about
National transport
Air: Air Gabon operates scheduled and charter flights to all main centres.
Road: There are an estimated 8,590km of roads, including 3,290km of main roads and 1,950km of secondary roads. Except for the routes Libreville-Ndende, Booué-Bitam, roads can be difficult in the rainy season. Travel by bush taxis and truck can be dangerous, especially in the rainy season.
Buses: Regular coach and minibus services link Libreville with Lambaréné, Oyem, Mouila and Bitam. Some services are subject to rainy season conditions.
Rail: Regular services operate on the Transgabon railway linking Libreville with Booué, Ndjolé and Franceville. There are two classes. The railcars are air-conditioned for some services but no refreshment or sleeping accommodation is scheduled. The rolling stock is generally new.
Water: The principal river is the Ogooué, navigable from Port-Gentil to Ndjole (310km), and serving the towns of Lambaréné, Ndjolé and Sindara.
A ferry service (taking two hours) operates between Libreville and Port-Gentil.
City transport
Taxis: Unmetered 'collective' and private taxis are available in main towns; tipping is not usual; rates vary according to the time of day. The journey from the airport to the Libreville city centre takes 10 minutes.
Car hire
Available in main towns, at airports and through hotels. International driving licence required. Charges are high.

BUSINESS DIRECTORY

The addresses listed below are a selection only. While World of Information makes every endeavour to check these addresses, we cannot guarantee that changes have not been made, especially to telephone numbers and area codes. We would welcome any corrections.

Telephone area codes
The international dialling code (IDD) for Gabon is + 241 followed by subscriber's number.

Useful telephone numbers

Police:	732-036	761-044
	760-950	720-951
Fire:	18	761-520
Ambulance:	732-771	762-344

Chambers of Commerce
Gabon Chamber of Commerce, Agriculture, Industry and Mines, PO Box 2234, Libreville (tel: 722-064; fax: 746-477).

Banking
Banque Gabonaise de Développement; PO Box 5, Rue Alfred Marche, Libreville (tel: 762-429, 762-489; fax: 742-699).

Banque Gabonaise et Francaise Internationale (BGFI), PO Box 2253, Blvd de l'Indépendance, Libreville (tel: 732-326, 764-035; fax: 740-894, 744-456).

Banque Internationale pour le Commerce et l'Industrie du Gabon SA, PO Box 2241, Avenue du Colonel Parant, Libreville (tel: 762-613, 763-811; fax: 746-410).

Banque Nationale du Crédit Rural, PO Box 1120, Avenue Bouët, Libreville (tel: 724-742, 766-144, 763-045; fax: 740-507).

Banque Populaire du Gabon, PO Box 6663, Blvd de l'Indépendance, Libreville (tel: 724-719; fax: 728-691).

Caisse Nationale d'Epargne, Siège Social, Libreville (tel: 766-509).

Centre de Chéques Postaux, Siége Social, Libreville (tel: 766-509).

Union Gabonaise de Banque SA, PO Box 315 & 2238, Avenue du Colonel Parant, Libreville (tel: 777-000; fax: 764-616).

Central bank
Banque des Etats de l'Afrique Centrale, Direction Nationale; PO Box 112, Libreville (tel: 761-352; fax: 744-563; e-mail: beaclbv@beac.int).

Travel information
ADL (Aeroport de Libreville), BP 363, Libreville (tel: 736-128).

Air Gabon (Compagnie Nationale Air Gabon), BP 2206, Aeroport International Léon M'ba, Libreville (tel: 730-027; fax: 731-156).

Eurafrique Voyages, BP 4026, Libreville (tel: 762-787; fax: 761-897).

Libreville Léon M'Ba International Airport, BP 363, Libreville (tel: 736-244/246/247; fax: 736-128).

Ministry of tourism
Ministry of Transport, Tourism and National Parks, BP 3974, Libreville (tel: 763-240).

Ministries
Ministry of Agriculture and Rural Development, BP 551, Libreville (tel: 721-579).

Ministry of the Arts, Culture and People Education, BP 1007, Libreville (tel: 724-028).

Ministry of Defence, Security and Immigration, BP 13493, Libreville (tel: 760-835).

Ministry of Economy, Finance, Budget and Privatisation, BP 9672, Libreville (tel: 721-571, 760-580; fax: 761-518).).

Ministry of Foreign Affairs and Co-operation, BP 2245, Libreville (tel: 762-251).

Ministry of Forestry and Environment, BP 199, Libreville (tel: 733-191).

Ministry of Higher Education, BP 3919, Libreville (tel: 763-252).

Ministry of Home (in charge of Local Collectivities and Mobile Security), BP 2110, Libreville (tel: 762-181).

Ministry of Housing, Land Registry and Town Planning, BP 512, Libreville (tel: 740-461).

Ministry of Justice, BP 547, Libreville (tel: 720-160).

Ministry of Labour and Human Resources, BP 2256, Libreville (tel: 732-739).

Ministry of Mining, Energy and Hydraulic Resources, BP 4041, Libreville (tel: 762-863).

Ministry of National Education and Professional Training, BP 6, Libreville (tel: 721-741).

Ministry of Public Health, BP 50, Libreville (tel: 762-522).

Ministry of Public Service and Administrative Reform, BP 496, Libreville (tel: 762-150).

Ministry of Shipping, BP 803, Libreville (tel: 733-210).

Ministry of Small and Medium Businesses, BP 4120, Libreville (tel: 720-636).

Ministry of Social Affairs, Family and Solidarity, BP 5684, Libreville (tel: 761-700).

Ministry of State Control, Decentralisation, Administration of Territory and Regional Integration, BP 178, Libreville (tel: 763-550).

Ministry of Trade Industry, BP 3906, Libreville (tel: 722-887).

Ministry of Youth and Sport, BP 3904, Libreville (tel: 763-576).

Other useful addresses

Compagnie Minière de l'Ogoué (Comilog), BP 578, Libreville (tel: 722-474).

Conseil Economique et Sociale de la République Gabonais, BP 1075, Libreville (tel: 762-668).

European Development Fund, BP 321, Libreville (tel: 732-250).

Gabonese Embassy (US), 2034 20th Street, NW, Washington DC 20009 (tel: (+1-202) 797-1000; fax: (+1-202) 332-0668).

Société de Développement de l'Agriculture au Gabon (Agrogabon), BP 2248, Libreville (tel: 764-082).

Société Equatoriale de Travaux Pétroliers Maritimes, BP 493, Libreville (tel: 753-509).

Société Gabonaise de Financement et d'Expansion, BP 2151, Libreville.

Société Gabonaise de Participation et de Développement, BP 1624, Libreville.

Société Gabonaise de Raffinage, BP 530, Libreville (tel: 752-365).

Société Nationale de Transports Maritimes (Sonatram), BP 3841, Libreville (tel: 740-632; fax: 745-967).

US Embassy, Boulevard de la Mer, BP 4000, Libreville (tel: 762-002).

National news agency: Agence Gabonaise de Presse (AGP), BP 168, Libreville (tel: 443507; fax: 443509; internet: www.agpgabon.ga).

Internet sites

Africa Business Network: http://www.ifc.org/abn

AllAfrica.com: http://allafrica.com

African Development Bank: http://www.afdb.org

Africa Online: http://www.africaonline.com

Mbendi AfroPaedia (information on companies, countries, industries and stock exchanges in Africa): http://www.mbendi.co.za

The Gambia

KEY FACTS

Official name: Republic of The Gambia

Head of State: President Yahya Abdul-Aziz Jamus Junkung Jammeh (APRC) (since 1994; re-elected 24 Nov 2011)

Head of government: President Yahya Jammeh

Ruling party: Alliance for Patriotic Reorientation and Construction (APRC) (since 1996; re-elected Jan 2007)

Area: 11,295 square km

Population: 1.73 million (2010)*

Capital: Banjul

Official language: English

Currency: Dalasi (D) = 100 butut

Exchange rate: D28.67 per US$ (Oct 2011)

GDP per capita: US$617 (2010)

GDP real growth: 5.70% (2010)

GDP: US$1.07 billion (2010)

Inflation: 5.00% (2010)

Balance of trade: -US$69.93 million (2010)

* estimated figure

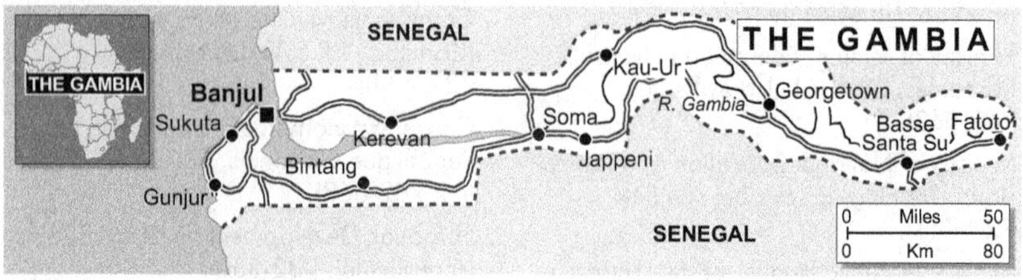

President Yahya Abdul-Aziz Jamus Junkung Jammeh came to power in 1994; he has remained stubbornly on-seat for the last 17 years, with no serious opposition. The election in November 2010 was no different, with President Jammeh winning 71.5 per cent of the vote. Ousainou Darboe (of the United Democratic Party (UDP)) was runner up with 17.4 per cent and the candidate for the National Alliance for Democracy and Development (NADD) (a five-party coalition)), Hamat Bah, third with 11.1 per cent; turnout was 83 per cent. Parliamentary elections are due in January 2012, but it would be very surprising if the Alliance for Patriotic Reorientation and Construction (APRC) did not return to power. Despite this apparent stability, there have been frequent cabinet reshuffles which have undermined government effectiveness.

Corruption remains a problem although improvements have been made since a government anti-corruption campaign started in 2003. Gambia was ranked 77 out of 178 countries in Transparency International's Corruption Perceptions Index for 2011, ninth of 48 sub-Saharan counties.

The economy

According to the *African Economic Outlook 2011* (AEO), published jointly by the African Development Bank and the Organisation for Economic Co-operation and Development, The Gambia has shown strong growth rates over the past three years. In 2010, growth slowed to 5.4 per cent from 6.7 per cent in 2009 as the global slump continued to affect re-exports, tourism and remittances. Growth should pick up to 5.6 per cent in 2011 and 2012. Good harvests – especially of rice – and gains in the construction and banking sectors drove economic growth.

The government managed to maintain macroeconomic stability in the face of external shocks such as a reduction in grant aid and trade revenues, as well as rising oil and food prices. Debt, both domestic and external, remains a problem and the burden is expected to increase further in the near future. Inflation picked up in the second half of 2010, partly reflecting the Central Bank of the Gambia's financing of the budget deficit. The central bank accordingly raised interest rates to 15 per cent and succeeded in keeping inflation below its 6 per cent target. Higher oil and food prices food prices drove up inflation in the first quarter of 2011.

The banking sector is developing, driven by foreign direct investment (FDI). Increased competition and capacity in the industry has increased deposits and credit supply. However, a large share of bank credit has been absorbed by the government and private sector demand for credit is limited.

Gambia has few natural mineral deposits so mining activity is minimal. Since 2006, however, mineral sands have been exported to China. The government recently awarded offshore and onshore oil exploration licences.

Industry, which accounted for 11.8 per cent of gross domestic product (GDP), grew 12.3 per cent in 2010. Bank lending to the construction sector, traditionally driven by remittances, helped sustain growth. There is little foreign interest in manufacturing, which is the preserve of mostly small companies engaged in processing groundnuts, fish and hides for export and bottling beverages for domestic markets. Manufacturing grew 5.7 per cent in 2010.

Growth in the service sector, accounting for 52.8 per cent of GDP, slowed to 2.3

per cent in 2010 from 7.2 per cent in 2009 as the distributive trade and hotels and restaurants slipped in the wake of the global recession. In particular tourism, accounting for about 12 per cent of GDP, contracted substantially, with revenues down 27.6 per cent during the first nine months of 2010 compared to the corresponding period in 2009. The government is looking to the World Bank and the United Nations World Tourism Organisation to help promote the industry.

Agriculture

Gambia is a low-income country with a structural food deficit. Never-the-less, agriculture is Gambia's most important economic sector with growth helping to offset declines in tourism and remittances. The sector is backward, however, in terms of technology and institutions to promote productivity, with weather the key variable. It is dominated by small-scale rain-fed crop production; semi-commercial groundnut and horticulture production, and artisanal fishery. Employing around 70 per cent of the working population, the sector accounted for some 26.9 per cent of GDP and 46.7 per cent of total food supply in 2010. Out of total cultivated land, 30 per cent was devoted to groundnuts, the principal export crop, and 18 per cent to rice. Most households have livestock. The years from 2008 to 2010 experienced good harvests, with agricultural production up 11.9 per cent annually. That performance suggests agriculture could potentially contribute more to the economy.

The government announced the Gambia National Agricultural Investment Plan (GNAIP 2011–15) in 2010, aimed at improving productivity through commercialisation and private sector participation. Spending on agriculture and land resources doubled to 6 per cent of the budget in 2011. Aligned with the New Partnership for Africa's Development (NEPAD)'s Comprehensive Africa Agricultural Development Programme (CAADP), the GNAIP aims to raise the budget allocation for agriculture to 10 per cent in the future. However, the plans do not address the key issue of reforming land ownership and tenure security. Land is traditionally held under communal ownership, making it difficult for individual farmers to reap the returns of investment. This undercuts effective land resource use and productivity, with knock-on effects all through the economy. Significantly, domestic food production has always fallen short of demand. According to the Food and Agriculture Organisation it is estimated that only 57 per cent of available arable land is being cultivated. Reform of land ownership and tenure is therefore a key first step to boost agriculture, on which the majority of the population depend for their livelihood.

International trade and relations

Re-exports continued to decline in 2010 as tariff harmonisation in the Economic Community of West African States (ECOWAS) and improving efficiency at other regional ports eroded Banjul's advantages as an entrepôt. The current account deficit widened to 12.2 per cent of GDP in 2010 from 10.1 per cent in 2009 and is projected at 11.9 per cent this year and 11 per cent in 2012.

Gambia has engaged with emerging country partners with mixed results. Chinese Taiwan remains Gambia's most important emerging country partner overall, but this has come at the expense of its relationship with the Peoples Republic of China. Cuba has provided doctors and medicines as well as scholarships while Venezuela has offered scholarships for engineers and university equipment. Gambia officials have said that while obtaining aid from traditional partners is a complicated process and takes a long time, the process with emerging country partners is simpler and carries few, if any, conditions.

Kuwait especially has become a more active partner, helping finance the University of the Gambia project.

Millennium Development Goals

Poverty remains high and is far more severe in rural than urban areas. Gambia has made significant progress towards achievement of the Millennium Development Goals (MDGs) on hunger, primary schooling, the share of women in non-agricultural sectors, child immunisation, the integration of sustainable development into country policies and developing global partnerships. However, much more needs to be done to halve extreme poverty, achieve full employment of the young and women, eliminate gender discrimination, reduce child and maternal mortality, and reverse the spread of HIV/Aids and malaria.

In keeping with high poverty rates, employment is a major problem. The most recent available data, the 2003 Population and Housing Census, show that only 38 per cent of the population was employed in 2003, up from 33 per cent in 1993. Most of the improvement took place in rural areas, where the ratio increased to 39 per cent from 33.1 per cent. In urban areas the ratio improved only slightly to 30.8 per cent from 29.4 per cent.

Risk assessment

Politics	Fair
Economy	Fair
Regional stability	Fair

COUNTRY PROFILE

Historical profile

When independence came to The Gambia in 1965, there were many who

KEY INDICATORS — The Gambia

	Unit	2006	2007	2008	2009	2010
Population	m	1.55	1.59	1.63	1.67	*1.73
Gross domestic product (GDP)	US$bn	0.51	0.65	0.82	0.74	1.07
GDP per capita	US$	325	411	503	440	617
GDP real growth	%	6.5	7.0	6.1	4.6	5.7
Inflation	%	2.0	5.0	4.5	4.6	5.0
Industrial output	% change	–	8.0	6.0	6.1	–
Agricultural output	% change	4.5	2.0	4.6	4.3	–
Exports (fob) (goods)	US$m	108.7	129.3	147.5	174.2	167.4
Imports (fob) (goods)	US$m	221.8	273.9	282.8	260.0	236.3
Balance of trade	US$m	-113.2	-144.6	-135.3	-68.9	-68.9
Current account	US$m	-58.0	-61.7	-51.5	29.2	-17.2
Total reserves minus gold	US$m	120.6	142.8	116.5	224.2	201.6
Foreign exchange	US$m	116.9	140.0	114.1	183.3	161.4
Exchange rate	per US$	28.25	24.87	22.19	28.50	28.01

* estimated figure

doubted that Africa's newest state would hold on to her status for any appreciable length of time. The oldest and most northerly of Britain's former West African possessions, The Gambia is surrounded, except on her Atlantic seaboard, by the bigger and more populous Senegal. It is said that but for the river the country would not have existed.
1455 The Portuguese established trading stations along the River Gambia.
1889 The boundaries of The Gambia were agreed by the British and French.
1894 The Gambia became a British protectorate.
1965 Following independence, Dawda Jawara, as the head of the People's Progressive Party (PPP), became prime minister, with the British monarch as head of state.
1970 Following a referendum, The Gambia became a republic. Dawda Jawara was elected president.
1981 Around 500 people were killed when Senegalese troops intervened in support of Jawara and suppressed a coup.
1982 Senegal and The Gambia formed a confederation called Senegambia intended to integrate military, economic and political institutions.
1989 The Gambia, the subordinate partner, withdrew from Senegambia and the confederation collapsed.
1991 The Gambia and Senegal signed a treaty of friendship.
1994 President Jawara was deposed by a military coup led by Lieutenant Yahya Jammeh. The 1970 constitution was suspended and all political parties banned.
1996 A new constitution was approved giving multi-party democracy. The Alliance for Patriotic Reorientation and Construction (APRC) were formed to support Yahya Jammeh in the presidential election. Three political parties were prohibited from taking part in the elections. Jammeh and the APRC were elected to the presidency and legislature, in what observers said were neither free nor fair elections.
2001 President Jammeh lifted the ban on opposition political parties. He was re-elected president.
2002 The centrist United Democratic Party (UDP) boycotted parliamentary elections, leaving the ruling APRC to win most seats unopposed in the parliamentary elections.
2005 Border tensions rose when Gambia doubled the price of ferry crossings across the river Gambia and Senegalese haulage firms, in protest, blockaded access routes. Senegal was effectively split in two as goods were hauled around Gambia on roads that were not all-weather and were unsuitable for heavy loads. Gambia experienced a shortage of goods in the marketplace due to the loss of revenue and blockaded imports. Nigeria, representing Economic Community of West African States (Ecowas), mediated between the protagonists.
2006 Thousands of refugees found sanctuary in The Gambia during fighting between the Senegalese army and Casamance separatists in southern Senegal. President Jammeh was re-elected.
2007 The APRC won 42 out of 48 seats in the national assembly. The UDP won four seats and the National Alliance for Democracy and Development (NADD) one seat and an independent one seat. The government expelled a senior UN official, Fadzai Gwaradzimba, after she criticised the president for his widely publicised herbal cure for HIV/Aids, which he claimed could cure the disease within days.
2009 Hundreds of villagers were rounded up and tested for activities in witchcraft, as ordered by President Jammeh.
2010 A trial began in June following the arrests in May of 12 foreign nationals in possession of two tons (1.8 tonnes) of cocaine bound for Europe, with a street value of US$1 billion. The Gambia has grown as a distribution point for Latin American drugs cartels that take advantage of the region's ties to Europe, the weak security and judicial systems and the poverty that provides a ready workforce. On 23 November the government ordered the withdrawal of all Iranian government representatives. No reasons were given but the move was thought to be related to an illegal shipment of arms, supposedly destined for Gambia, found by Nigerian customs officials in October. There was speculation that the arms were to be sent on to the Casamance region of Senegal. In November, in an interview with the Kenyan newspaper *The Nation* President Jammeh vowed not to seek another term in office.
2011 Presidential elections were postponed from early in the year but were finally held on 24 November, contested by three candidates. Incumbent Yahya Jammeh (APRC) won 71.5 per cent of the vote, Ousainou Darboe (UDP) 17.4 per cent and Hamat Bah (National Alliance for Democracy and Development (NADD) (five-party coalition)) 11.1 per cent; the turnout was 83 per cent. However, Ecowas condemned the elections an 'lacking legitimacy' having declared before the elections that they would not be free and fair because of high levels of ruling party intimidation.

Political structure

Constitution

The constitution was enacted in 1970, amended in 1982 and 1996.

Form of state
Democratic republic

The executive
Power rests with the president, who is elected by universal suffrage every five years. The president is both the head of state and head of government and appoints the cabinet.

National legislature
The unicameral National Assembly has 53 members, of which 40 belong to the rank of chieftain and each constitutes a constituency; three are elected to represent the capital and five to represent Kanifing Municipality. The remaining five are nominated by the president, to include the Assembly speaker and deputy. All serve for five-year terms.
The Assembly legislates, ratifies treaties and forms committees to review the work of the government.

Last elections
25 January 2007 (parliamentary); 24 November 2011 (presidential)
Results: Parliamentary: The ruling APRC won 42 seats out of 48 seats, the UDP won four seats and the National Alliance for Democracy and Development (NADD) one seat and an independent one seat. Five seats were filled by appointed members. Turnout was 41.7 per cent.
Presidential: Yahya Jammeh (APRC) won 71.5 per cent of the vote, Ousainou Darboe (UDP) 17.4 per cent and Hamat Bah (National Alliance for Democracy and Development (NADD) (five-party coalition)) 11.1 per cent; turnout was 83 per cent.

Next elections
2011 (presidential); January 2012 (parliamentary)

Political parties

Ruling party
Alliance for Patriotic Reorientation and Construction (APRC) (since 1996; re-elected Jan 2007)

Main opposition party
The United Democratic Party (UDP)

Population

1.73 million (2010)*
Last census: 15 April 2003: 1,364,507 (provisional)
Population density: 105 habitants per square km. Urban population: 33 per cent (1995–2001).
Annual growth rate: 3.2 per cent 1994–2004 (WHO 2006)

Ethnic make-up
Three major ethnic groups: Mandinka (42 per cent), Fula (18 per cent), Wolof (16 per cent). Other substantial ethnic groups: Jola, Serahule, Serere, Manjago, Bambara, Creole/Aku.

Religions
Muslim (90 per cent), Christian (9 per cent), animist beliefs (1 per cent).

Education
Primary schooling begins at aged seven and is free of charge and non-selective until aged 15. Secondary education is either vocational or academic. Basic vocational schools offer two-year courses and vocational secondary schools provide four-year courses. General secondary schools offer a three-year course leading to higher education provided by the University of The Gambia. The Gambia College offers vocational courses in agriculture, education, nursing, midwifery, and public health.
Literacy rate: Adult rates: 38.9 per cent, male; 31.9 per cent, female (World Bank).
Compulsory years: None
Enrolment rate: 77 per cent gross primary enrolment; 25 per cent gross secondary enrolment, of relevant age groups (including repeaters) (World Bank).
Pupils per teacher: 30 in primary schools.

Health
Improved water sources are available to 62 per cent of the population. Around 90 per cent of children are immunised against measles.
HIV/Aids
The Gambia has so far escaped much of the African pandemic. However, with 14 per cent of sex workers testing positive, there is a chance that the infection will spread.
HIV prevalence: 1.2 per cent aged 15–49 in 2003 (World Bank)
Life expectancy: 57 years, 2004 (WHO 2006)
Fertility rate/Maternal mortality rate: 4.6 births per woman, 2004 (WHO 2006); maternal mortality 1,100 per 100,000 live births (World Bank).
Child (under 5 years) mortality rate (per 1,000): 90 per 1,000 live births (World Bank)
Head of population per physician: 0.11 physicians per 1,000 people, 2003 (WHO 2006)

Welfare
The Gambia has two important funds, the social security fund and the housing finance fund, that receive contributions from employers and employees either directly or indirectly. The Department of Social Welfare in Banjul has been restructured with four major units covering child care, adult, elderly and disabled services. The Gambia government and the Social Security and Housing Finance Corporation (SSHFC) initiated mass housing projects including a rural electrification programme covering all major towns and villages.

Main cities
Banjul (capital, estimated population 46,700 in 2003), Serekunda (344,100), Bakau (82,300), Brikama (80,400).

Languages spoken
Mandinka, Wolof and Fula are local languages. French is taught in some secondary and high schools. German, Italian, Dutch and the Scandinavian languages are also spoken by tourism staff.
Official language/s
English

Media
Press
Dailies: In English. *Daily Observer* (www.observer.gm) and *The Gambia Daily News* (www.gambia.dk). Several online news outlets exist include Gambia News (www.gambianow.com), The Gambia Times (http://afrikanpath.com) which was launched on 5 July 2007 with local and regional news and Freedom Newspaper (www.freedomnewspaper.com).
Weeklies: The *Gambia News & Report* magazine, the Foroyaa (www.foroyaa.gm) is published bi-weekly and *The Point Newspaper* (www.thepoint.gm) thrice weekly; all are privately-owned.
Broadcasting
The state-owned Gambia Radio and Television Services (GRTS) provides a national network.
Radio: GRTS is non-commercial and broadcast in English and local languages. Other commercial stations, Radio 1 FM, West Coast Radio and City Limits Radio are privately owned.
Television: GRTS provides the only national service with a single channel which covers 60 per cent of the country. There are other private satellite, subscription channels, the most popular includes GAMTV and Premium TV Network which broadcasts throughout the coastal area.

Economy
The Gambia is one of the poorest countries in the world. The tourism industry is the highest single largest foreign earnings sector, while only providing paid employment for around 6 per cent of the workforce. Subsistence farming employs around 70 per cent of the workforce, which is reflected in per capita income at only US$606 in 2010. Groundnuts, in the form of peanuts, oil and cattle cake, account for 50 per cent of goods exported, while forestry and fisheries remain important sectors of agriculture. Major capital investment projects of infrastructure improvements, including a new terminal at the capital's international airport and improved port facilities, have aided exports. The port in Banjul brings in foreign earnings as well as trans-shipment costs for goods travelling between north and south Senegal. In 2009, exports were US$94.8 million, of which domestic exports were US$5.3 million.
GDP growth was 6.3 per cent in 2008, falling modestly to 5.6 per cent in 2009 and further still to 5 per cent in 2010. The strength of the economy was boosted by strong agricultural production. Nevertheless, at the end of 2009, external debt was 34 per cent of GDP and total public sector debt was 54 per cent of GDP. The country still faces a heavy debt burden, particularly interest on domestic debt, which consumes a large portion of government revenues, thereby reducing spending on social programmes. Remittances were US$60 million in 2009 (7.9 per cent of GDP) and estimated to have grown to US$61 million in 2010.
The UN Human Development Index (HDI) in 2010 recorded a headcount poverty rate of 60.4 per cent and a ranking of 151 out of 169 countries. With such deprivation The Gambia has grown as a distribution point for Latin American drugs cartels that take advantage of the region's ties to Europe, the weak security and judicial system and the poverty that provides a ready workforce. A trial began in June 2010 following the arrests in May of 12 foreign nationals in possession of two tons (1.8 tonnes) of cocaine from Latin America, bound for Europe, with a street value estimated at US$1 billion. The government has introduced capital punishment in an attempt to curb the growing problem.

External trade
The Gambia is a member of the Economic Community of West African States (Ecowas), which was set up to promote economic integration among members. It is also a member of the Anglophone West African Monetary Zone (WAMZ), which will introduce a common currency in due time. WAMZ will eventually be merged with the Francophone-members' currency (Communauté financière d'Afrique (CFA) (Financial Community of Africa), CFA franc) to produce a single currency (the eco) for the region. In the meantime The Gambia continues to use Dalasi as its currency.
With few natural resources, foreign exchange is dependent on remittances, tourism and the export of groundnuts (both raw and processed). Geographically, The Gambia is a long wedge separating the north and south of Senegal and as a result haulage firms must cross The Gambia to avoid the long and arduous route around it. Re-exports are estimated at over 30 per cent of total imports, which supply significant foreign exchange for the Gambian economy.
Imports
Principal imports are foodstuffs, manufactured items, fuel, machinery and transport equipment that support the transit trade.

Main sources: Côte d'Ivoire (typically 14 per cent of total), China (12 per cent), UK (9 per cent).

Exports

Principal exports are groundnuts (peanuts), fish, cotton lint, palm kernels and re-exports.

Main destinations: Senegal (typically 27 per cent total of total), Guinea (24 per cent), Guinea-Bissau (14 per cent).

Agriculture

Farming

Agriculture remains the main sector of the economy, typically contributing around 30 per cent to GDP and employing over 70 per cent of the workforce.

Approximately 17 per cent of the total land area is cultivated. Groundnuts are cultivated on about 60 per cent of the planted area, and provide 85 per cent of official export earnings. The Gambia is the second-largest producer of groundnuts in the world, after Senegal. Production of food crops (rice, maize, millet, sorghum, cassava) is insufficient to meet local needs, but receives a great deal of official encouragement. Small-scale fruit and cotton farming are also important while some livestock is exported to neighbouring countries for breeding.

The government, backed by international development agencies and donors, is attempting to increase agricultural production. The on-going US$2.5 million Lowlands Agricultural Development Project (LADEP) is aimed at developing 6,000 hectares for cultivation and the rehabilitation of 1,500 hectares in various lowland ecologies. US$2 million has been allocated to assist women's groups engaged in sheep, goat and poultry production while US$1.5 million is dedicated to an integrated rural development scheme.

Fishing

Fishing has also increased in importance with the annual catch rising to over 22,000 tonnes. The government, with assistance from the UN Development Programme (UNDP), is encouraging improved methods and modernisation of boats. Illegal fishing by foreign trawler fleets remains a problem.

Industry and manufacturing

The industrial sector contributes around 6 per cent to GDP and employs 4 per cent of the workforce.

The manufacturing sector is small-scale and underdeveloped.

The main activities (most of which are centred around Banjul, particularly in the Kanifing Industrial Estate) include groundnut and fish processing, brewing, footwear, perfume, cement and brick production.

Tourism

The Gambia is a popular destination for visitors from Western Europe who wish to avoid a cold winter season. It offers affordable resorts and activities focussed on its wildlife (bird-watching is of particular interest) sand and surf sports along its Atlantic coast, traditional culture and general sports, such a golfing and fishing.

In 2007, the travel and tourism sector accounted for of 21.8 per cent of GDP and 18.9 per of total employment but the global economic crisis interrupted the progress made in the sector's growth and the number of visitor arrivals fluctuated from 125,000 in 2006 to 143,000 in 2007, rising to 147,000 in 2008 before falling back to 142,000 in 2009. In 2007 the share of foreign exchange earnings attributed to tourism was 69 per cent, but in 2009 it had fallen to 49.9 per cent, before rising to 51.7 per cent in 2010.

Political uncertainty in 2009, caused when President Jammeh arrested hundreds of his citizens to be inspected for suspected witchcraft, ordered homosexuals to be flogged and announced that he had invented a miracle cure for HIV/Aids, caused not only donor countries to limit their involvement in The Gambia but left tourists disinclined to visit as well. Those that do visit are increasingly confronted by the negative influence of tourism on The Gambia with its high rate of youth unemployment, of prostitution, drugs peddling and begging.

The Gambia has two Unesco World Heritage sites, the James Island, with structures related to the North American slave trade, and ancient stone circles, tumuli and burial mounds at Senegambia.

Environment

Concerns are mounting over the ecological effects of tourism on the local environment, particularly shore erosion and the depletion of water resources.

Mining

Most mining activity is centred on the production of industrial minerals for local consumption. The Australian Carnegie Corporation is investigating the Brufut deposits located along the coast and around 11,000 tonnes of zircon has been found. There are known deposits of kaolin, tin, ilmenite and rutile, mostly unexploited.

Hydrocarbons

There are no proved hydrocarbon reserves and all domestic energy needs are met by imports. Consumption of petroleum products was 2,000 barrels per day in 2008.

Exploration for oil offshore in deepwater is underway. Legislation exists to harness any revenue if oil is discovered; downstream the market is unregulated.

Any use of natural gas or coal is commercially insignificant.

Energy

Total installed generating capacity was 30MW, producing 15 billion kilowatt hours in 2006. Power generation is typically from thermal power plants.

The Gambia is poorly resourced and has little potential for hydropower. However it is a partner in the West African Power Pool (Wapp), which is a regional integration project to improve power supply within the Economic Community of West African States (Ecowas) area, with affordable electricity as the goal for all. Four countries, Guinea, Senegal, Guinea Bissau and The Gambia, have agreed to build two hydroelectric power stations on the River Gambia at Kaleta in Guinea and Sambanglou in Senegal.

Banking and insurance

The banking sector is underdeveloped, but is growing as a result of increased economic activity and macroeconomic stability. The sector has seen consolidation, with two large mergers and privatisations.

It was announced in March 2005 that the introduction of the shared currency, the Eco, in The Gambia, Ghana, Guinea, Nigeria and Sierra Leone, which was due in July 2005, would be postponed. The currency was proposed to facilitate trade and growth with an ultimate plan to merge it with the CFA franc.

Central bank

Central Bank of The Gambia

Main financial centre

Banjul

Time

GMT

Geography

At its widest part The Gambia is only 48km wide as it straddles the River Gambia over its last 470km down to the Atlantic Ocean, where the country has a short coastline. The Gambia is the smallest country in Africa, and lies on both banks of the river, completely surrounded by Senegal. The land is low-lying, with mangroves towards the river mouth, and open savannah plains for most of the remaining land, with a maximum elevation of only 73 metres at the higher reaches of the river, in the east. During the dry season, when water levels drop, the river's width, at the capital Banjul, is only 5km across and tidal saltwater washes along its length for almost 250km turning the water brackish.

Hemisphere

Northern

Climate

Sub-tropical with distinct seasons. Dry season from November–May with temperatures around 21–27 degrees Celsius (C). The dry *harmattan* wind keeps the humidity low, but can obscure the sun and severely limit vision for days. Rainy season from June–October has high humidity and temperatures around 26–32 degrees C.

Entry requirements

Passports

Required by all. Passports must be valid for three months from date of departure.

Visa

Required by all, except citizens of countries with reciprocating visa-free entry for both tourism and business, (UK 30 days, others 90 days). See www.thegambia.net/visa.htm for initial details and contact the nearest embassy for confirmation All visitors must have onward/return tickets.

Currency advice/regulations

There is no restriction on the import or export of local currency – although exchanging local currency abroad may be difficult. The import of currency from Algeria, Ghana, Guinea, Mali, Morocco, Nigeria, Sierra Leone and Tunisia is prohibited. The import of all other currencies is unrestricted but must be declared; export is unlimited up to the amount declared.

Travellers cheques are accepted.

Health (for visitors)

Mandatory precautions

Yellow fever vaccination certificate required only if travelling from an infected area.

Advisable precautions

Inoculations and boosters should be current for cholera, tetanus, polio, hepatitis A, diphtheria, typhoid and yellow fever. There may be a need for vaccinations for tuberculosis, hepatitis B and meningitis. Use malaria prophylaxis (that also provide protection for hepatitis B and yellow fever) including mosquito repellents, nets and clothing that cover the body after dark. There is a risk of rabies.

HIV/Aids is prevalent. To avoid bilharzia, do not bath in fresh water lakes or rivers, use only well-maintained, chlorinated swimming pools.

Use only bottled or boiled water for drinks, washing teeth and making ice. Eat only well cooked meals, preferably served hot; vegetables should be cooked and fruit peeled. Dairy products are unpasteurised and should be avoided, unless cooked. There is a shortage of routine medications, including sun-screens, and visitors should take all necessary medicines with them. A first aid kit that includes disposable syringes, is a reasonable precaution.

Healthcare is not to Western standards and medical insurance, including emergency evacuation, is necessary.

Hotels

Book well in advance, especially if arriving during tourist season (Nov–May). Many Gambian hotels are geared to package holidays. 10 per cent tip is usual.

Credit cards

International credit cards are accepted; arrangements for hotel payment by credit cards should be arranged at the beginning of a stay. ATM exist in large towns but may be unreliable.

Public holidays (national)

Fixed dates

1 Jan (New Year's Day), 18 Feb (Independence Day), 1 May (Labour Day), 22 Jul (Revolution Day), 25 Dec (Christmas Day).

Variable dates

Eid al Adha, Good Friday and Easter Monday (Mar/April, Birth of the Prophet, Eid al Fitr.

Islamic year 1433 (26 Nov 2011–14 Nov 2012): The Islamic year contains 354 or 355 days, with the result that Muslim feasts advance by 10–12 days against the Gregorian calendar. Dates of feasts vary according to the sighting of the new moon, so cannot be forecast exactly.

Working hours

Banking

Mon–Thu: 0800–1330; Fri: 0800–1100 in Banjul; Mon–Fri: 0800–1200, 1600–1800 elsewhere.

Business

Mon–Thu: 0800–1600; Fri: 0800–1230.

Government

Mon–Thu: 0800–1600; Fri: 0800–1230.

Shops

Mon–Thu: 0800–1700; Fri–Sat: 0800–1300.

Electricity supply

220V AC, 50 cycles, with a mix of round and flat, three pin plugs.

Social customs/useful tips

In business, the personal approach is important; handshaking is widely used and the traditional greeting is *salam alaikum*. Jackets and ties should be worn at meetings; women may wear trousers.

Many Gambians are Muslim and their religious customs and beliefs should be respected. There are prohibitions concerning smoking and eating in public during Ramadan.

Getting there

Air

National airline: Gambia International Airlines (GIA)

International airport/s: Banjul International (BJL), 24km from city; bar, bank, restaurant, post office, shop and business lounge including internet connections. Taxis are available to the city.

Airport tax: Arrival tax at Banjul International (BJL) airport: either US$10, UK £5 or eur10.

Surface

Road: Road access to Banjul is possible from Dakar (Senegal), by the Trans-Gambia Highway which crosses the River Gambia by ferry between Farafenni and Mansa Konko. There is an alternative car ferry crossing between Barra and Banjul.

Water: Regular ferry services run between Banjul and Dakar (Senegal).

Getting about

National transport

Road: There are over 3,000km of roads, of which 450km are paved, particularly around Banjul; unsealed roads often become impassable in the rainy season. Highways run along each bank of the River Gambia; the Trans-Gambia highway runs north to south, crossing the river at Farafenni-Mansa Konko (car ferry).

Buses: The Gambia Public Transport Corporation (GPTC) operates cheap and reliable services linking Banjul with the coastal hotel area and other main centres.

There are several commercial bus services, such as Amdalaye and Transgambia services.

Water: There are around a dozen ferry crossing points where people, livestock and vehicles cross the river between the north and south shores. The Banjul-Barra ferry runs every 90 minutes (journey time 20—30 minutes) and there are small wooden ferries up-country which carry only three or four vehicles at a time.

A boat travels the length of the River Gambia, from Banjul to Basse, once a week. The journey takes about three days. It is possible to return overland by coach.

City transport

Taxis: Green (tourist) taxis have a diamond sign and a serial number on the side. They are licensed by the Gambia Tourism Authority and dedicated to serving tourists and other visitors. They are normally parked outside the hotels in the resort areas. The journey from the international airport to the city centre takes 30–40 minutes.

Yellow and Green taxis are mainly four-passenger saloon cars which run a shared taxi service between short distances or park by the roadside for individual hire.

The most common way of travelling is by collective *bush* taxis. These are mainly seven-passenger saloon cars, vans, minibuses and buses. They do not have a single colour and they operate a shared service between both short and long distances. It is advisable to agree the fare in advance when hiring collective taxis.

A 10 per cent tip is usual.

Car hire
International driving licence accepted for a period of three months. National licence can be used for a short visit. Traffic drives on the right.
Car hire facilities are somewhat limited and local enquiries through the tourist office are advised. Take care, there is a lack of adequate traffic signs.

BUSINESS DIRECTORY

The addresses listed below are a selection only. While World of Information makes every endeavour to check these addresses, we cannot guarantee that changes have not been made, especially to telephone numbers and area codes. We would welcome any corrections.

Telephone area codes

The international dialling code (IDD) for The Gambia is + 220 followed by subscriber's number.

Useful telephone numbers

Police	17
Fire	18
Ambulance (Banjul)	16

Chambers of Commerce

Gambia Chamber of Commerce & Industry, 1-3 Ecowas Avenue, PO Box 333, Banjul (tel: 4227-765; fax: 4229-671; email: gcci@qanet.gm).

Banking

Arab Gambian Islamic Bank Ltd, 7 Ecowas Avenue, Banjul (tel: 4223-773; fax: 4223-770).

First International Bank Ltd, PO Box 1997, 6 OAU Boulevard, Banjul (tel: 4202-000/5; fax: 4202-001, 4202-000).

International Bank for Commerce (Gambia) Ltd, PO Box 211, 11a Liberation Avenue, Banjul (tel: 4228-144, 4228-145; fax: 4229-312).

Standard Chartered Bank Gambia Ltd, PO Box 259, 8 Ecowas Avenue, Banjul (tel: 4228-681/4; fax: 4227-714).

Trust Bank Limited (TBL), PO Box 1018, 3-4 Ecowas Avenue, Banjul (tel: 4225-777, 4225-778/9; fax: 4225-781).

Central bank

Central Bank of The Gambia, 1-2 Ecowas Avenue, Banjul (tel: 4227-786; fax: 4226-969).

Travel information

Banjul (Yundum) International Airport, PO Box 285, Banjul (tel: 4473-000; fax: 4472-190).

Gambia International Airlines, Satellite House, PO Box 268, 68-69 Wellington Street, Banjul (tel: 4223-702, 4223-706; internet: www.gia.gm).

Gambia River Excursions, Lamin Lodge, Jangjangbureh Camp, PO Box 664 Banjul (tel: 4497-603; fax: 4495-526; internet: www.gambiariver.com).

West African Tours, PO Box 222, Serrekunda, (tel: 4495-258, 4495-532; fax: 4496-118; internet: www.westafricatours.gm).

Ministry of tourism

Department of State for Tourism and Culture, The Quadrangle, Banjul (tel: 4229-563, 4223-210).

National tourist organisation offices

Gambia Tourism Authority, Kololi, KMC, PO Box 4085, Bakau (tel: 4462-491–4; fax: 4462-487; email: info@gta.gm; internet: www.visitthegambia.gm).

Ministries

Ministry of Agriculture and Natural Resources (MANR), The Quadrangle, Banjul (tel: 4472-888; fax: 4237-034).

Ministry of Finance and Economic Affairs, The Quadrangle, Banjul (tel: 4227-221).

Other useful addresses

British High Commission, 48 Atlantic Road; PO Box 507, Fajara, Banjul, (tel: 4495-133–4; fax: 4496-134; email: bhcbanjul@gamtel.gm).

Central Statistics Office, Central Bank Building, Buckle Street, Banjul (tel: 4228-105).

Gambia Embassy (USA), Suite 905, 1156 15th Street, NW, Washington DC 20005 (tel: (+1-202) 785-1399; fax: (+1-202) 785-1425).

Gambia Hotel Association, c/o The Bungalow Beach Hotel, PO Box 2637, Serrekunda (tel: 4465-288; fax: 4466-180).

Gambia Investment Promotion and Free Zones Agency (GIPFZA), 5 Nelson Mandela Street, PO Box 757, Banjul (tel: 4222-4412, 4222-836; fax: 4222-829; e-mail: dipm.gipfza@qanet.gm; ceo.gipfza@qanet.gm).

National Investment Promotion Authority (NIPA), Independence Drive, Banjul (tel: 4228-332; fax: 4229-220).

US Embassy, 92 Kairaba Ave; PO Box 19, Fajara, Banjul (tel: 4392-856, 4392-858; fax: 4392-475; email: ambanjul@gamtel.gm).

Internet sites

Africa Business Network: www.ifc.org/abn

AllAfrica.com: allafrica.com

African Development Bank: www.afdb.org

Africa Online: www.africaonline.com

Gateway site: gambiagateway.tripod.com

Mbendi AfroPaedia (information on companies, countries, industries and stock exchanges in Africa): mbendi.co.za

The Gambia Tourism Authority: www.visitthegambia.gm

The Gambia website: www.gambia.net

Georgia

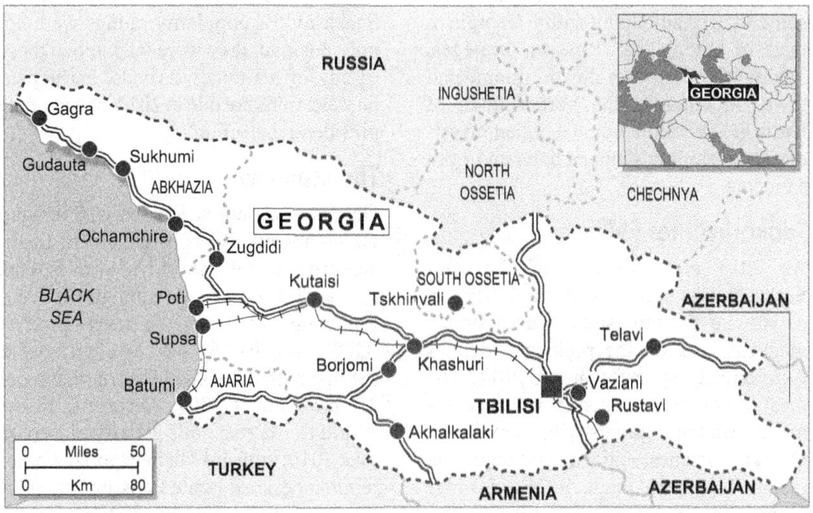

KEY FACTS

Official name: Sak'art'velos Respublika (Republic of Georgia)

Head of State: President Mikhail Saakashvili (from 2004; re-elected 6 Jan 2008)

Head of government: Prime Minister Nikoloz (Nika) Gilauri (from 6 Feb 2009)

Ruling party: Natshhionakhuri Modzraoba - Demokrathebi (NM-D) (National Movement - Democrats) (elected Mar 2004)

Area: 69,700 square km

Population: 4.41 million (2010)*

Capital: Tbilisi

Official language: Georgian

Currency: Lari (L) = 100 tetri

Exchange rate: L1.66 per US$ (Oct 2011)

GDP per capita: US$2,658 (2010)

GDP real growth: 6.40% (2010)

GDP: US$11.70 billion (2010)

Labour force: 1.92 million (2008)

Unemployment: 16.90% (2009)

Inflation: 7.10% (2010)

Balance of trade: -US$2.57 billion (2010)

* estimated figure

The latter part of 2009 and the first half of 2010 saw Georgia adopt a relatively low international profile. Not altogether surprisingly, a European Union (EU) enquiry, published on 30 September 2009, into the conflict between Georgia and Russia placed a large part of the blame on Georgia. Anticipating the EU-sponsored 'independent' report, Georgia had sought to pre-empt criticism by deploying the strange argument that it 'did not matter who fired the first shot'. The point at issue, ran Georgia's rationale, was Russia's continued 'occupation' of its sovereign territory and years of 'stoking tensions between Georgia and its rebel regions.'

Unwelcome report

Following the presentation of the report by the independent enquiry into the conflict, Georgia could only reflect that it was not entirely the conclusion it wanted to hear, even if it was half expected. Not mincing its words, the report concluded that Georgia's use of force on the night of 7 August 2008 was 'not justifiable in the context of international law.' The enquiry commission also said that it could not substantiate 'Georgian claims of a large-scale presence of Russian armed forces in South Ossetia prior to the Georgian offensive on 7/8 August.' The Georgian government's response, as expected, was to simply dismiss those comments, gaining little international credit by instructing state-owned television to announce in its news bulletins that the report pinned the blame on Russia.

Government ministers were quoted as saying that although most of the facts in the report were accurate, they disagreed with 'some elements of it'. Georgia was probably right in disagreeing with the report's conclusions that it used 'excessive force' in its opening attack on Tskhinvali (the capital of South Ossetia) pointing out that there was plenty of evidence of Russian troop deployment and going on to observe that these were not just peacekeepers'. 'One can hardly judge what is proportionate in this case' countered one minister.

Georgia had long insisted that Moscow was intent on subverting Georgia in an effort to 'divide and rule'. The EU report went a little way towards defending Georgia's position by saying that while 'the onus of having actually triggered off the war lies with the Georgian side, the Russian side, too, carries the blame for a substantial number of violations of international law.' A BBC report observed that the report's findings only emphasised the deep divide that exists between Georgia and Russia and that any hope of the two agreeing on the origins of the war was overly optimistic.

The Abkahzia question

In August 2011 Aleksandr Z Ankvab was elected president of Abkhazia, three years after the tiny enclave 'broke away' from Georgia following its recognition as a sovereign state by neighbouring Russia. By regional standards, as reported in the *International Herald Tribunel*, the Abkhazia elections were remarkable – if only because the outcome was not known in advance. The election was called following the death of President Sergei Bagapsh, the leader responsible for Abkhazia's breakaway from Georgia and for avoiding a complete annexation by Russia. Nevertheless, without Russian political and economic support Abkhazia could not survive as a notionally independent state. Its status owes everything to Russia's relationship – or the lack of it – with Georgia. After its victory over Georgia in the short-lived 2008 war, Abkhazia had joined South Ossetia in seeking independence from Georgia. Georgia continues to claim both states as integral parts of its territory.

Russia's relationship with Abkazia reveals some aspects of its objectives in the relationship. The presence of 5,000 'peacekeeping' troops in Abkhazia has given cause for concern not only to Georgia, but to many Abkhazia inhabitants. In the early 1990s Abkhazia had dislodged a Georgian military presence; the Russian presence at least provided some reassurance against a recurrence of Georgian incursions.

Georgia also offered the other breakaway region of South Ossetia something resembling an olive branch in the hope that it might think again. The Georgian authorities offered to hold talks with some hundred Ossetians, who had left at the same time as the Georgian troops, for destinations as far away as Israel and the Ukraine. Some Ossetians would prefer some form of autonomy within Georgia to that of living as Russian protégés. Tskhinvali is a run-down, dilapidated town. In contrast, the border town of Kurta has benefited from Georgian investment, developing shops, a hotel and even a cinema.

Saakashvili for PM?

As 2013 and the end of President Saakashvili's second and final term in power hove into sight, successionist manoeuvrings on the political sidelines were already apparent in late 2011. The most prominent protagonist was the enigmatic Bidzina Ivanishvili, reportedly Georgia's richest citizen (although the money had been made in Russia). Mr Ivanishvili's ambitions were not modest – his stated intention, if elected, was to make Georgia a model democracy. This would involve correcting the image that Mr Saakashvili's impetuosity had given the country. However, neutral observers had to acknowledge that Mr Saakashvili had given Georgia quite a lot more: not least a strong credit rating and a liberal economy.

Uncertainty also surrounded Mr Saakashvili's post-presidential ambitions. No clues had been given as to whether he wished to become prime minister, which the planned change from a presidential to a parliamentary system (approved by parliament in October 2010 and set to come into force from the 2013 presidential election) would allow. Wars and all, Mr Saakashvili's popularity ratings were not only positive, they were well above those of any of his putative rivals. Parliamentary elections are due in 2012, ahead of the presidential election.

The economy

Georgia's economic recovery, following the combined effects of the global financial crisis and the short war with Russia, appeared to be gaining strength in 2011, following the gross domestic product (GDP) growth of 6.6 per cent registered in the first half of 2010, after a contraction of 3.9 per cent of 2009. According to the World Bank, economic activity picked up over 2010, with growth in exports, worker remittances, real estate transactions, vehicle registrations and construction permits. Exports were up by 40 per cent (year-on-year) during the first half of 2010 and imports were up by a more modest 12 per cent (year-on-year). During the same period, value added tax (VAT) turnover increased by 27 per cent (year-on-year) after falling by 7 per cent during 2009. However, bank lending only showed signs of a modest pickup in 2010, while foreign direct investment (FDI) inflows remained well below pre-crisis levels and were well down, to US$273 million in the first half of 2010.

The economy was projected to grow by 4–5 per cent during the period 2011–13, although downside risks from global economic uncertainties are significant. Growth was expected to be generated by higher exports and private investment, supported by a pickup in bank lending. Exports, expected to play a key role in driving economic recovery, are projected to expand from 29.8 per cent of GDP in 2009 to 38 per cent during 2011–13. Export growth is expected to come primarily from metals and metal products, wines and other beverages, fruits and nuts and repaired and re-exported cars on the product side; and transport and tourism on the services side. Private investment is expected to benefit from the pickup in bank lending in 2010 and modest improvement in FDI inflows from 2011. There was, however, significant uncertainty regarding the pace of recovery and growth, as

KEY INDICATORS — Georgia

	Unit	2006	2007	2008	2009	2010
Population	m	4.40	4.37	*4.39	*4.38	*4.41
Gross domestic product (GDP)	US$bn	7.76	10.29	12.90	10.70	11.70
GDP per capita	US$	1,765	2,355	2,937	2,448	2,658
GDP real growth	%	9.3	12.4	2.3	-4.0	6.4
Inflation	%	9.1	9.2	10.0	1.7	7.1
Unemployment	%	13.6	13.3	16.5	16.9	–
Industrial output	% change	14.5	13.4	-5.5	–	–
Agricultural output	% change	-9.3	8.9	-2.1	–	–
Exports (fob) (goods)	US$m	633.0	2,104.1	2,428.0	1,893.2	2,462.2
Imports (fob) (goods)	US$m	1,463.0	4,976.5	6,261.2	4,292.6	5,034.5
Balance of trade	US$m	-830.0	-2,872.4	-3,833.2	-2,399.4	-2,572.3
Current account	US$m	-1,235.0	-2,028.0	-2,915.0	-1,364.3	-1,254.6
Total reserves minus gold	US$m	930.8	1,361.2	1,480.2	2,110.3	2,263.8
Foreign exchange	US$m	929.9	1,346.3	1,467.8	1,891.6	2,041.4
Exchange rate	per US$	1.78	1.67	1.49	1.67	1.78

* estimated figure

weakness in external markets undermins Georgian exports and tourism and raises refinancing costs for both the public and the private sector.

As FDI and other private inflows have fallen, official transfers have increasingly financed the current account. The external current account deficit adjusted significantly from 22.7 per cent of GDP in 2008 to 11.9 per cent in 2009, primarily due to a contraction in imports. With FDI and other private capital inflows falling sharply, the current account has increasingly been financed by higher public sector flows and International Monetary Fund (IMF) resources. The macro-economic framework is supported by an IMF Standby Arrangement. Since the economic downturn the Georgian authorities have allowed the exchange rate to adjust over time to facilitate external adjustment though they have periodically intervened to support the exchange rate in face of heavy foreign exchange pressure.

The inflation projection for 2011 has been revised up (to 8.5 per cent by end-year) on the back of rising food and fuel prices, but core inflation remains subdued. Balance of payment developments have been more favourable than anticipated in the first quarter owing to higher private inflows, including tourism. The current account deficit is still projected to widen moderately in 2011 (to 10.8 per cent of GDP) on account of higher import prices and to decline steadily thereafter. In April, the government issued a US$500 million Eurobond on very favourable terms. The proceeds were used to redeem, through a voluntary exchange, US$435 million of the US$500 million Eurobond maturing in 2013, reducing significantly the external debt rollover 'hump' of 2013.

The forecast 2011 fiscal deficit was lowered to 3.6 per cent of GDP (rather than 4.3 per cent), while allowing for an increase in social spending to alleviate the social impact of higher fuel and food prices.

Georgia's large current account deficit continues to be a source of vulnerability; additional fiscal adjustment is required to stabilise public debt, all the while meeting important social spending priorities. Strong first quarter economic activity indicators, including buoyant tax receipts, were consistent with GDP growth projections of 5.5 per cent in 2011. Year-on-year inflation peaked at 13.9 per cent in March before edging down to 13.5 per cent in April. Core inflation remained subdued, at a monthly 1.5 per cent in April 2011. High food and energy inflation reflected recent commodity price hikes and was expected to decline through the rest of the year. Balance of payment developments have been more favourable than anticipated. While higher import prices contributed to a sharp widening of the trade deficit in the first quarter, other inflows turned out stronger than projected, in particular tourism (40 per cent growth year-on-year in the first quarter) and net private capital inflows.

The favourable external developments contributed to an appreciation of the lari against the dollar, while allowing the central bank to make net purchases on the foreign exchange market. During the first four months of 2011, the lari appreciated by 7.6 per cent against the dollar and by 3.3 per cent in nominal effective terms. Depreciation pressures re-emerged in May, in connection to large-scale private foreign exchange purchases by one bank (to finance the Eurobond buy-back) and by non-financial companies. The central bank sold dollars at auction to avoid excessive volatility, but also allowed the rate to depreciate. Since the beginning of the year, the central bank has purchased US$20 million, on a net basis, on the foreign exchange market and net international reserves have now reached their pre-crisis level.

Risk assessment

Economy	Fair
Politics	Fair
Regional stability	Poor

COUNTRY PROFILE

Historical profile

1801–04 Most of what is now Georgia became part of the Russian Empire.

1917 Georgia joined an alliance with Armenia and Azerbaijan to become the Transcaucasian Federation.

1918 The Federation was dissolved and Georgia became an independent state.

1918–21 There was a brief spell of independence until the Russian Red Army invaded in 1921.

1922 Georgia was incorporated into the Soviet Union first as a Soviet Republic, and then as a member of the Transcaucasian Soviet Federative Republic (TSFR) along with Armenia and Azerbaijan.

1936 The TSFR was dissolved and the three states became republics of the Soviet Union.

1940–45 An estimated 10 per cent of the population perished in the Stalin purges.

1989 The killing of 20 people by Soviet troops during a national demonstration in Tbilisi triggered the final disillusionment with communism.

1990 Following a referendum which called for independence from the Soviet Union, Zviad Gamsakhurdia was elected the first president in July. Racist policies caused problems.

1991 Independence from Russia was declared. Prime Minister Teniz Sigua resigned.

1992 Gamsakhurdia was overthrown in a coup and Eduard Shevardnadze assumed power. Parliamentary elections were held, in which Shevardnadze was elected Chairman of the State Security Council. Shevardnadze re-appointed Teniz Sigua as prime minister. After Georgian independence the northern region of Abkhazia declared itself independent of the new state. The subsequent war killed an estimated 10,000 and created 300,000 internally displaced persons (IDP).

1994 A cease-fire was signed.

1995 After surviving a car bomb assassination attempt, Shevardnadze was elected by popular vote, and the Sak'art'velos Mokalaketa Kavshiri (SMK) (Union of Georgian Citizens) secured a majority vote in the parliamentary elections. A constitution was adopted. The Abkhaz parliament rejected the proposed status of autonomous republic within Georgia.

1996 In accordance with the constitution, a National Security Council was established.

1997 A Civil Code, second only to the constitution in importance, was adopted. Capital punishment was abolished.

1998 Shevardnadze survived a second assassination attempt.

1999 Georgia became a member of the Council of Europe.

2000 President Shevardnadze won the presidential elections. He said that he would not stand for a third term.

2001 Fighting erupted between Georgian security forces and Abkhazia separatists, despite the signing of a peace agreement. Mass demonstrations followed a raid by security forces on an independent television station, which had criticised the government for corruption.

2002 US special forces arrived to help train and equip Georgian forces for counter-terrorist operations. Russia accused Georgia of harbouring Chechen militants in South Ossetia and the Pankisi Gorge. Russian President Putin warned of military action if Georgia failed to deal with them.

2003 Work began laying the Georgian section of the 1,760km Baku-Tbilisi-Ceyhan (BTC) oil pipeline. Rigged elections resulted in mass protests and the storming of the parliament. President Shevardnadze was forced to resign; Nino Burdzhanadze became acting president. The Supreme Court later annulled the election results.

2004 Mikhail Saakashvili was sworn in as president and he nominated Zurab Zhvania for the re-introduced post of prime minister. A bloc led by the President's party won all the seats in the parliamentary elections.
2005 Prime Minister Zurab Zhvania died and Zurab Noghaideli became prime minister. The BTC oil pipeline, capable of carrying one million barrels per day of Caspian oil to Western markets, opened.
2006 Relations with Russia deteriorated as energy supplies to Georgia were interrupted and Georgia demanded withdrawal of Russian troops from South Ossetia and Abkhazia. Russia imposed embargoes on Georgian produce, transport and postal links, before and after Georgia arrested four Russians in Tbilisi on spying charges. In a referendum, over 90 per cent of South Ossetians voted for independence.
2007 A 15-day state of emergency was declared as opposition protesters accused the president of corruption and demanded new elections. Only state-television was allowed to report on the news, while Imedi TV, which had broadcast the views of opposition leaders, was suspended. The president acceded to protesters' demands and called for fresh elections. President Saakashvili replaced Zurab Noghaideli with Lado Gurgenidze as prime minister.
2008 Mikhail Saakashvili was re-elected president. The opposition challenged the result. International observers claimed the election had been democratic and that 'the outcome should be respected'. Within a month of his defeat in the presidential elections, Badri Patarkatsishvili died in exile in the UK, of natural causes. In parliamentary elections, the Natshhionakhuri Modzraoba (NM) (United National Movement) won a majority of seats. After days of fighting in South Ossetia (which wishes to cede from Georgia), the government sent in troops to restore order. Fierce fighting in the South Ossetia capital, Tskhinvali, resulted in the Georgian air force bombing surrounding areas. The Russian region of North Ossetia sent forces via the Roki tunnel in the Caucasus Mountains to aid South Ossetia. Georgia mobilised its army. Russia officially launched a 'peace enforcement' programme in support of South Ossetia. The Russian air force bombed the Georgian town of Gori as a convoy of Russian tanks and armoured vehicles arrived in the area. Russian troops engaged Georgian troops inside Georgia as thousands of refugees fled the area. Russia forced Georgian forces out of South Ossetia and adopted defensive positions within Georgia. Russia refused to withdraw completely and left a contingent to maintain a 'security buffer zone' of seven kilometres on either side of the South Ossetian border. The Russian government formally recognised the breakaway regions of South Ossetia and Abkhazia as independent states. President Saakashvili sacked Prime Minister Lado Gurgenidze and appointed Grigol Mgaloblishvili as prime minister. Aslanbek Bulatsev became prime minister of South Ossetia.
2009 Prime Minister Mgaloblishvili resigned and Nikoloz (Nika) Gilauri became prime minister. Parliamentary elections were held in Russian-backed South Ossetia, in which political parties committed to links with Russia won most votes. The elections were condemned by the EU and NATO as unauthorised by the sovereign state of Georgia. Georgia sent an initial 125 troops (later increased to 500) to join the NATO-led forces in Afghanistan, thereby strengthening its ties with NATO. Georgia will also allow NATO to use its territory as an alternative land bridge to Afghanistan. Russia vetoed the mandate of the UN Observer Mission in Georgia (Unomig) and obliged its withdrawal. Russian Prime Minister Putin announced that Russia would spend US$500 million in reinforcing its military base in Abkhazia. Russia claimed to have found evidence that Ukrainian troops and volunteers had fought alongside Georgians in the dispute over South Ossetia. Abkhazi President Bagapsh was re-elected for a second term in office.
2010 The Verkhny Lars-Kazbegi border checkpoint between Georgia and Russia, which had been closed in 2006, was reopened in March. In August, Russia deployed a S-300 missile system in Abkhazia; the system was already deployed in South Ossetia. Parliament approved, by 112 votes to 5, an amendment to the constitution on 16 October. The amendment moves primary political power from the president to the prime minister by introducing a number of checks and balances.
2011 A new Russian language TV news station, Kanal Pik, began broadcasting from Tbilisi on 25 January. It has a mandate to provide Georgian views on cross-border matters and to counter negative Russian reports concerning Georgia. President of Abkhazia, Sergey Bagapsh, died on 29 May; his deputy, Aleksandr Ankvab became acting president. In the presidential election held in Abkhazia on 26 August, Aleksandr Ankvab won 54.9 per cent of the vote, Sergey Shamba 21 per cent, Raul Khadjimba 19.8 per cent; turnout was 71.9 per cent. South Ossetia: President Eduard Kokoyty resigned on 10 December; Prime Minister Vadim Brovtsev became acting president. Elections will be held on 25 March 2012.

Political structure

Constitution
The 1995 constitution provides for a presidential republic with federal elements. The country is divided into nine districts and 64 regions.

Independence date
26 May 1918

Form of state
Presidential democratic republic

The executive
The president, who is head of state and head of government, is directly elected for five years and can serve no more than two terms. The head of state holds supreme executive power, together with the cabinet of ministers.

National legislature
The unicameral Sak'art'velos Parlamenti (Georgian Parliament) (also known as Umagheisi Sabcho (Supreme Council)) has 235 members elected by proportional representation, of which 150 are elected in multi-seat constituencies by party lists and 75 in single-seat constituencies; 10 members represent displaced citizens in the separatist region of Abkhazia.

Legal system
The legal system is based on the civil law system.

Last elections
21 May 2008 (parliamentary); 6 January 2008 (presidential).
Results: Parliamentary: the Natshhionakhuri Modzraoba (NM) (United National Movement) won 59.4 per cent of the vote (and around 120 seats out of 150), the Memarjvene Opozicia (MO) (Rightist Opposition) alliance won 17.6 per cent, all other parties won less than 10 per cent of the vote. Presidential: Mikhail Saakashvili won 53.5 per cent of the vote, Levan Gachechiladze won 25.7 per cent, and Badri Patarkatsishvili won 7.1 per cent; turnout is 56.2 per cent.

Next elections
2012 (parliamentary); 5 January 2013 (presidential).

Political parties

Ruling party
Natshhionakhuri Modzraoba - Demokrathebi (NM-D) (National Movement - Democrats) (elected Mar 2004)

Main opposition party
Memarjvene Opozicia (MO) (Rightist Opposition)

Population

4.41 million (2010)*
Last census: January 2002: 4,371,535
Population density: 64 inhabitants per square km (2010)
Annual growth rate: -1.3 per cent 1994–2004 (WHO 2006)

Internally Displaced Persons (IDP)
260,000 (UNHCR 2004)

Ethnic make-up
There are over 100 different ethnic groups in the country, including Georgian (70 per cent), Armenian (8 per cent), Russian (6 per cent) and Azeri (6 per cent). Other significant ethnic groups include Abkhazians and Ossetians.
Religions
Greek Orthodoxy is the main religion. There are also Shi'ite and Sunni Muslims, Jehovah Witnesses, Jews, Armenian Gregorians, Catholics and Baptists. There is inter-communal strife between the Christian Georgians and the Ossetian and Abkhazian ethnic Muslim minorities.

Education
Elementary schooling lasts for six years followed by two years of basic education. Secondary school education lasts for three years. Technical and vocational upper secondary education takes another two to four years.
There are 26 public higher education institutions in Georgia including eight universities and 14 technical and specialised institutes. In addition, 209 private higher education institutions have been established.
Public expenditure on education typically amounts to 5.2 per cent of annual gross national income (World Bank). Loans of US$60 million from the World Bank helped reform Georgia's secondary education.
Compulsory years: 6 to 14.
Enrolment rate: 89 per cent boys; 88 per cent girls, total primary school enrolment of the relevant age group (including repetition rates) (World Bank).
Pupils per teacher: 18 in primary schools.

Health
The population has 76 per cent and 99 per cent access to improved water and sanitation facilities, respectively.
HIV/Aids
HIV prevalence: 0.1 per cent aged 15–49 in 2003 (World Bank)
Life expectancy: 74 years, 2004 (WHO 2006)
Fertility rate/Maternal mortality rate: 1.4 births per woman, 2004 (WHO 2006); maternal mortality rate 70 per 100,000 live births (World Bank).
Child (under 5 years) mortality rate (per 1,000): 41 per 1,000 live births; 3 per cent of children aged under five are malnourished (World Bank).
Head of population per physician: 4.09 physicians per 1,000 people, 2003 (WHO 2006)

Welfare
Georgia has to cope not only with 58.5 per cent of its people living below the official poverty line but also an increased influx of refugees in the Pankisi Valley, 150km north of Tbilisi, inhabited largely by ethnic Chechens, known as Kists. The US Agency for International Development (USAID) has funded Georgia to implement community level activities, which benefit refugees, internally displaced people and others affected by ethnic violence and the deterioration of the social welfare system.
The benefits system includes pensions, unemployment benefits and family allowance, all paid at flat rates. The government provides 100 per cent electricity tariff discounts for war veterans and 50 per cent discounts for tax, customs, defence and security personnel.
Increased poverty in the urban areas leads to high incidence of wage and social transfer arrears. UN reports suggest that the average minimum wage is still insufficient to ensure an adequate standard of living for large parts of the Georgian population.

Main cities
Tbilisi (population 1.2 million in 2004), Kutaisi (268,800); Rustavi (181,400), Batumi (145.400).

Languages spoken
Russian and English are spoken and in the territory of Abkhazia, Abkhazian is sometimes spoken.
Official language/s
Georgian

Media
The constitution guarantees freedom of speech and of the press. However political turmoil during the 2008 presidential election saw intimidation of journalists by political leaders of on all sides of the debate.
Press
There are around 200 newspapers but most are small, local and without influence. Newspapers are typically subsidized by patrons, in business and politics, and editorial independence is correspondingly compromised.
Dailies: In Georgian *Sakartvelos Respublika* (*Republic of Georgia*) (www.opentext.org.ge/sakartvelos-respublika), was the official government newspaper. Other private publications include *24 Saati* (*24 Hours*) (www.24saati.ge), *Rezonansi* (*Resonance*). In Russian *Svobodnaya Gruzia* (*Free Georgia*) (www.svobodnaya-gruzia.com). In English *The Messenger* (www.messenger.com.ge).
Weeklies: In English, *The Georgian Times* (www.geotimes.ge) and *Georgia Today* (www.georgiatoday.ge).
Business: The EU-funded *Georgian Economic Trends* (www.geplac.org) is a quarterly with the best source of business news and information. It is published by the European Policy and Legal advice Center (Geplac) in English and Georgian.
Broadcasting
Georgian Public Broadcasting (GPB) (www.gpb.ge) provides national coverage.
Radio: The GPB (www.gpb.ge) has two radio stations, Public Radio offering a range of news, cultural and entertainment programmes and Radio Two offers Georgian music programmes, with part of the daytime schedule given over to educational, social and entertainment programmes. Private, commercial stations include, Radio Imedi (www.radio-imedi.ge) a national news and speech network and Fortuna FM (www.fortuna.ge) with local and international music of most genre.
Television: Most Georgians rely on TV to provide their news and information. The GPB (www.gpb.ge) has two TV stations, Public TV has a full range of programmes from news and current affairs to children's TV and sport and Channel Two has specialist programming but does not reach all regions of the country. There are a several commercial TV stations including Rustavi 2 (www.rustavi2.com.ge) is the most popular TV channel, Imedi TV (www.imedi.ge) and Mze TV (http://mze.ge), all providing locally produced and imported programmes.
A new Russian language TV news station, Kanal Pik (http://pik.tv/en), began broadcasting on 25 January 2011 from Tbilisi. It has a mandate to provide Georgian views on cross-border matters and to counter negative Russian reports concerning Georgia.

Economy
The economy is dominated by the service sector that constitutes almost 70 per cent of GDP, with industry contributing 21 per cent, of which manufacturing accounts for 12 per cent and agriculture 10 per cent. Agriculture employs over 50 per cent of the total work force. Major export commodities include wine and nuts, as well as ores and finished metals and electricity. However, Georgia remains reliant on imported fuel, food and pharmaceuticals to meet domestic demands.
GDP growth had been strong up to 2007 when it was 12.3 per cent, but as not only the global economic crisis struck in 2008 but also internal divisions resulted in a military confrontation with Russia, GDP growth fell to 2.3 per cent and then dropped further, into recession of -3.9 per cent in 2009 as the country was left to reconstruct its infrastructure and economy. Russia, which had been Georgia's largest trading partner, was suddenly an opponent.
The Baku-Tbilisi-Ceyhan oil pipeline, which commenced operations in 2005,

crosses 248km of Georgia; there are plans to either run a parallel gas pipeline or ship liquefied natural gas (LNG) to Europe via Georgia. In all of these programmes Georgia benefits, not only financially from transit fees for the supply of hydrocarbons from its neighbours to allies in Europe, but also by having a secure supply of fuel, which also avoids relying on Russian supplies for its domestic consumption.

External trade

Georgia had traditional ties with Russia which were, following the break-up of the Soviet Union, formalised through the Commonwealth of Independent States (CIS), however relations first became strained when Georgia moved towards the West and Russia imposed restrictions on Georgian imports and transport access. There was a military confrontation in 2008. The destination of exports to Russia has steadily switched to Turkey, Europe and the US.

Georgia is an important transit country for goods and hydrocarbons through Central Asia.

Imports

Imports typically include fuels, machinery and parts, transport equipment, grain and other foods and pharmaceuticals.

Main sources: Turkey (typically 15 per cent of total), Ukraine (11 per cent), Azerbaijan (9.4 per cent).

Exports

Merchandise exported includes metal and ore, machinery, nuts and wine and aircraft.

Main destinations: Turkey (typically 15 per cent of total), Azerbaijan (14 per cent), Ukraine (9 per cent).

Re-exports

Fuel, citrus fruits and wine.

Agriculture

Farming

The agricultural sector typically contributes over 30 per cent to GDP and employs about 50 per cent of the workforce. Georgia is a major agricultural producer and the warm climate favours the growing of a range of sub-tropical crops in the coastal region. Crops include tea, grapes, tobacco and fruit.

A great deal of Georgia's produce is exported to other former Soviet republics in return for much-needed supplies of manufactured goods.

Forestry

Over two-fifths of the land is covered by forests and woodland, of which only a fifth is available for wood production and another fifth is classified as primeval forest untouched by man. Around 60 per cent of Georgia's trees are broadleafed, including beech, oak, hornbeam and chestnut, and the rest are coniferous, mainly spruce and pine. Forests are important to protecting soil and water. The state owns all forests by law.

Georgia produces and exports roundwood (typically 65 per cent of forestry exports) and sawnwood (27 per cent) from hardwood species.

Industry and manufacturing

Industry accounts for a quarter of GDP and employs about 20 per cent of the workforce. Light industrial activities include food-processing and drinks production, metallurgy, shipbuilding, car production, consumer durables, garment manufacturing and oil-processing. Other industries include mining, chemicals, heavy engineering and steel-making. Levels of self-sufficiency in the manufacturing sector are low and export manufacturing potential is limited. The sector is troubled by a periodic lack of finance, the slow pace of rehabilitation of enterprises and low levels of management.

Tourism

The tourism sector has considerable potential to expand, but is hindered by government inactivity and political instability.

Mining

Georgia has major mineral deposits, notably manganese, copper and lead. Small quantities of iron ore are extracted.

There are reserves of about 200 million tonnes of manganese ore in Chiatura, of which 60 per cent is recoverable through underground mining and 40 per cent through open-pit mining. The Madneuli mining plant at Kazreti in southern Georgia is the country's only producer of copper concentrate. The Madneuli deposit contains the bulk of copper reserves, with reserves of around 460,000 tonnes of ore.

Hydrocarbons

Georgia has limited known oil reserves, estimated at 35 million barrels, but is believed to have greater potential. Exploration is underway both offshore in the Black Sea as well as onshore. Georgia, which consumes 14,000 barrels per day (bpd), produces around 1,000bpd and relies on imports from Russia and Azerbaijan.

Georgia has always been an obvious transport route for the oil from the Caspian Sea to the Black Sea and the Mediterranean. The 1,768km Baku-Tibilisi-Ceyhan (BTC) oil pipeline, was inaugurated in 2005 and carries 1 million bpd, 1 per cent of the world's oil requirements. It was targeted by Russian jets during the 2008 Georgia-Russian conflict, which emphasised the importance of this pipeline to European oil supplies as it diversifies supplies away from Russia.

Georgia had proven natural gas reserves of 84.9 billion cubic metres (cum) at the end of 2007. However, production is small and the country is dependent on imports of natural gas from Russia, although consumption has been falling since 2005 when consumption was 1.5 billion cum.

Coal reserves are estimated at 800 million tonnes, of which over a half are located at Tkibuli-Shaorskoye.

Energy

Total installed generating capacity is 4.4GW, of which 81 per cent is produced by 53 hydroelectric power stations, the remainder by three thermal power plants. Fuel shortages and a deteriorating infrastructure means the electricity sector operates below capacity and there are frequent power cuts. In order to meet demand, Georgia imports electricity from Armenia, Azerbaijan and Russia and has run up considerable debt on these imports, resulting in disputes with the suppliers. Poor electricity supply and high rates have prompted widespread non-payment among Georgian electricity customers.

The Russian state utility entity, Unified Energy Systems (UES), has bought 75 per cent of the electricity network and several generating facilities, effectively taking control of the energy market.

Financial markets

Stock exchange

Georgian Stock Exchange (GSE)

Banking and insurance

The banking sector has undergone reform since 1995 and the central bank, the National Bank of Georgia (NBG), has assumed a supervisory role. The NBG has concentrated on consolidating the banking sector to clamp down on poor management, corruption and non-performing loans. It has also progressively raised the minimum capital requirement, which has caused a dramatic fall in the number of banks operating in the country and forced many to seek foreign participation to survive.

Central bank

National Bank of Georgia (NBG)

Time

GMT plus three hours

Geography

Georgia is situated in west and central Transcaucasia on both sides of the Suram range. There are frontiers with Turkey and Armenia in the south, and with Azerbaijan in the south-east. The Black Sea coast is to the west. To the west of the Surams lies the more mountainous Kura basin. The Rion, which flows westwards into the Black Sea, and the Kura which flows eastwards through Azerbaijan into the Caspian Sea, are the country's two main rivers.

Hemisphere
Northern.

Climate
Hot and humid summers and mild winters. Georgia is protected against the cold air from the north by the Great Caucasus mountains. Temperatures range from 21 degrees Celsius (C) to 33C in July and from 0C to 10C in January. The west, including the Black Sea coast, lies in a sub-tropical zone with high humidity and heavy rainfall; temperatures average 5C in winter and 22C in summer. Eastern Georgia is more equable with lower humidity; temperatures average 2–4C in winter and 20–25C in summer. The mountain regions are dryer and cooler, while above 3,600m snow and ice prevail year-round.

Entry requirements
Passports
Required by all. Passports must be valid for six months after date of departure.
Visa
Required by all, except nationals of EU countries, CIS countries (other than Russia and Turkmenistan), Canada, Israel, Japan, Switzerland and US.
Business visas may in some cases require a letter of invitation from a local company or organisation and a letter of introduction from the employer.
Do not overstay the limit of the visa. The Georgian authorities can impose heavy penalties for non-compliance, including detention, fines and deportation, and all removals at the traveller's expense.
Currency advice/regulations
There are no restrictions on the import and export of local currency. The import of foreign currency is allowed, but export is limited to US$500.
Almost all payments are made in cash (US dollar notes are the most useful). Most foreign currency can be exchanged at special exchange shops in the streets of large towns.
Customs
Small amount of personal goods duty-free. On arrival declare all foreign currency and valuable items such as jewellery, cameras, computers and musical instruments.

Health (for visitors)
A reciprocal health agreement for urgent medical treatment exists with the United Kingdom. Some proof of UK residence will be required. Rabies is a health risk.
Mandatory precautions
A vaccination certificate is required for yellow fever if travelling from an infected area.
Advisable precautions
Water precautions are recommended (water purification tablets may be useful).
It is advisable to be in date for the following immunisations: tetanus (within 10 years), typhoid fever, hepatitis A (moderate risk only), hepatitis B, meningitis.
Any required medicines should be carried by the visitor, and it could be wise to have precautionary antibiotics if going outside major urban centres.
A travel kit including a disposable syringe is a reasonable precaution.

Credit cards
Only one or two outlets in Tbilisi can handle credit cards.

Public holidays (national)
Fixed dates
1 Jan (New Year's Day), 7 Jan (Orthodox Christmas Day), 19 Jan (Orthodox Epiphany), 3 Mar (Mothers' Day), 8 Mar (Women's Day), 9 Apr (Restoration Day), 9 May (Victory Day), 12 May (St Andrew's Day), 26 May (Independence Day), 28 Aug (Orthodox Assumption of the Virgin/Mariamoba), 14 Oct (Svetitskhovloba), 23 Nov (St George's Day/Giorgoba).
Variable dates
Orthodox Easter Monday

Working hours
Banking
Mon–Fri: 0930–1730.
Business
Mon–Fri: 0900–1800.
Shops
Mon–Sat: 0900–1700.

Electricity supply
220V AC 50Hz

Weights and measures
Metric system

Social customs/useful tips
Georgians are excellent hosts. Feasting is a central part of Georgian tradition. If you go to a dinner as the guest of honour, it is not unusual to be asked to sing a song or recite a romantic poem. When Georgians show friendship, it is sincere.

Security
There is a risk of terrorist activity, especially on the border with Chechnya.There has been an increase in the number of robberies, kidnappings and assaults involving foreigners, especially business people, in and around the capital, Tbilisi. Travellers should exercise caution in crowded places and markets, and when using public transportation. It is advisable not to walk alone at night and to avoid unofficial taxis.
Travellers should avoid unnecessary travel outside Tbilisi, especially at night. Train travel to Armenia, which is prone to incidents of theft and crime, should be avoided.

Getting there
Travellers intending to stay in Tbilisi for longer than three days must register with the Ministry of the Interior.
Air
National airline: Georgian Airways.
International airport/s: Tbilisi International Airport (TBS), 18km from city centre.
Airport tax: None
Surface
Road: Highways connect Georgia to the Russian Federation via the Caucasian Road Tunnel and the Georgian Military Highway to north Ossetia. The Verkhny Lars-Kazbegi border checkpoint between Georgia and Russia, which had been closed in July 2006, was reopened in March 2010.
Rail: Tbilisi has railway connections with Azerbaijan, Armenia and Iran. The conflict in Abkhazia has affected the rail link with the Russian Federation.
Water: International connections to main ports from the Black Sea ports of Odessa, Sochi, Trabzon and Istanbul. Connections are also available with the Mediterranean ports of Genoa and Piraeus.
Main port/s: The main ports are Batumi (deals mainly with oil exports), Poti and Sukhumi.

Getting about
National transport
The European Bank for Reconstruction and Development's (EBRD) plans for the transport sector include improving the maintenance of existing rail, road, port and airport systems; promoting the commercialisation and privatisation of the transport industries; developing Georgian links with the Euro-Asian corridor; encouraging better co-ordination between the Georgian transport systems and those of the other states in the region; and providing technical co-operation for policy development, structural reform, economic analysis, project specification and preparation, and economic and environmental assessment.
Road: Difficult terrain and weather conditions restrict road links. Note that reliable road maps and signposts do not exist. Independent drivers should note that fuel can be difficult to obtain without specialist local knowledge. An international driving permit is required.
Buses: Buses operate between major towns and cities. There is a small underground system in Tbilisi.
Rail: There is approximately 1,583km of track with a double-track railway between Marelisi and Sagandzile. There are regular services between Tbilisi, Azerbaijan and Russia. Reservations are required for all trains.

City transport
There are many forms of cheap public transport in Tbilisi. A knowledge of the local language with its own script could be very helpful.
Taxis: Both official and unofficial taxis are plentiful.
Fares should always be agreed in advance as fares for foreigners can be set extremely high. It is advisable to use only official taxis and not share with strangers.
Car hire
Although the roads are severely pot-holed, hiring a car and driver through your guide or business associate is the quickest form of transport. It is not recommended to drive yourself.

BUSINESS DIRECTORY

The addresses listed below are a selection only. While World of Information makes every endeavour to check these addresses, we cannot guarantee that changes have not been made, especially to telephone numbers and area codes. We would welcome any corrections.

Telephone area codes
The international direct dialling code (IDD) for Georgia is +995, followed by area code and subscriber's number:

Kutaisi	331	Tbilisi	32

Useful telephone numbers
Police: 02
Fire: 01
Ambulance: 03

Chambers of Commerce
American Chamber of Commerce in Georgia, 1 Nustubidze Street, 0177 Tbilisi (tel: 312-110; fax: 312-105; e-mail: amcham@amcham.ge).

Georgian Chamber of Commerce and Industry, 11 Chavchavadze Avenue, 0179 Tbilisi (tel: 230-045; fax: 235-760; e-mail: info@gcci.ge).

Banking
Bank of Georgia, 3 Aleksander Pushkin Street, 0105 Tbilisi (tel: 444-1729; fax: 444-182; e-mail: welcome@bog.ge).

People's Bank of Georgia, 74 Chavchavadze Avenue, Tbilisi 0162 (tel: 555-500; e-mail: info@peobge.com).

ProCredit Bank, 154 Agmashenebeli Avenue, Tbilisi 0112 (tel/fax: 202-222; e-mail: central@procreditbank.ge).

TBC Bank, 7 Marjanishvili Street, Tbilisi 0102 (tel: 777-000; fax: 772-774; e-mail: marjanishvili@tbcbank.com.ge).

United Georgian Bank, 37 Uznadze Street, Tbilisi 0102 (tel: 505-505; fax: 999-139; e-mail: admin@ugb.com.ge).

Central bank
National Bank of Georgia, 3/5 Leonidze Street, 0105 Tbilisi (tel: 996-505; fax: 999-346; e-mail: info@nbg.gov.ge).

Stock exchange
Georgian Stock Exchange (GSE): www.gse.ge

Travel information
Georgian Airways, 12 Rustaveli Prospect, Tbilisi (tel: 485-560; fax: 999-660; e-mail: info@georgian-airways.com).

National tourist organisation offices
Department of Tourism and Resorts, 12 Kasbegi Avenue, 0061 Tbilisi (tel: 525-301)

Ministries
Ministry of Agriculture and Food, Kostava 41, Tbilisi (tel: 996-261; fax: 933-300).

Ministry of Communications and Post, 2.9 April St, Tbilisi (tel: 999-528; fax: 934-419).

Ministry of Culture, 37 Rustaveli Ave, Tbilisi (tel: 937-433; fax: 999-037).

Ministry of Defence, 2 University St, Tbilisi (tel: 303-163; fax: 983-929).

Ministry of the Economy, 12 Czhanturia St, Tbilisi (tel: 230-925; fax: 982-743).

Ministry of Education, 52 Chkheixze St, Tbilisi (tel: 958-886; fax: 770-073).

Ministry of Environmental Protection and Natural Resources, 68a Kostava St, Tbilisi (tel: 230-664; fax: 983-425).

Ministry of Finance, 170 Barnovi, Tbilisi (tel: 226-805; fax: 292-368).

Ministry of Foreign Affairs, 4 Chitadze St, Tbilisi (tel: 989-377; fax: 997-249).

Ministry of Health, 30 Gamsakhurdia Ave, Tbilisi (tel: 387-071; fax: 389-802).

Ministry of Industry, 28 Gamsakhurdia Ave, Tbilisi (tel: 931-045, 386-558).

Ministry of the Interior, 10 D/Kheivnis St, Tbilisi (tel: 996-296; fax: 986-532).

Ministry of Justice, 19 Griboedov St, Tbilisi (tel: 989-252; fax: 990-225).

Ministry of Refugees and Accommodation, 30 Dadiani St, Tbilisi (tel: 663-302).

Ministry of Social Security, Labour and Employment, 7/2 Leonidze St, Tbilisi (tel: 938-989; fax: 936-150).

Ministry of State Property Management, 64 Czhavczhavadze Ave, Tbilisi (tel: 294-875; fax: 225-209).

Ministry of State Security, 4.9 April St, Tbilisi (tel: 982-383; fax: 932-791).

Ministry of Trade and Foreign Economic Relations, 42 Kazbegi Ave, Tbilisi (tel: 389-667; fax: 398-882).

Ministry of Urbanisation and Construction, 16 V Pshavela Ave, Tbilisi (tel: 374-276; fax: 220-541).

Other useful addresses
British Embassy, GMT Plaza, 4 Freedom Square, 0105 Tbilisi (tel: 274-747; fax: 274-792; e-mail: British.Embassy.Tbilisi@fco.gov.uk).

Business Communication Centre (BCC), 47 Kostava Street, Tbilisi (tel: 988-371; fax: 987-601).

Business Support Centre (BSC) Kutaisi, 124 Rustaveli Avenue, Kutaisi (tel: 310-1001; fax: 331-1001; e-mail: BSC@iberiapac.ge).

Committee for Socio-Economic Information of Georgia, 4 K Gamsakhurdia Avenue, Tbilisi (tel: 361-450, 938-936; fax: 995-892, 995-622).

Georgian Embassy (USA), Suite 300, 1615 New Hampshire Avenue NW, Washington DC 20009 (tel: (1+202)-387-2390; fax: (1+202)-393-4537; e-mail: georgiaemb@hotmail.com).

Georgian Stock Exchange, 74a Chavchavadze Avenue, Tbilisi 0162 (tel: 220=718; fax: 251-876; e-mail: info@gse.ge).

Independent Agency for the Development of Municipal Services, 89/24 D Agmashenebeli Ave, Tbilisi (tel: 951-003; fax: 986-950).

Sakenergo (state hydroelectricity company), 1 Vekua Street, Tbilisi (tel: 989-814; fax: 940-676).

Saknavtobi (state oil company), 65 M Kostava Street, Tbilisi 0175 (tel: 942-887; fax: 332-509).

Saktransgasmretsvi (state gas company), 22 Delisi III Lane, Tbilisi (tel: 932-981; fax: 227-746).

Telecom Georgia, Tbilisi (tel: 999-197; fax: 442-929; e-mail: info@telecom.ge).

Other news agencies: Prime-News: http://eng.primenewsonline.com

Civil Georgia: www.civil.ge

Internet sites
Information on government, elected officials and economic information: www.parliament.ge

Press office of the President of Georgia: www.presidpress.gov.ge/

Georgian Investment Centre: http://web.sanet.ge/gic/

Germany

In October 2011 Germany found itself at the centre of what Chancellor Angela Merkel described as the worst crisis to affect Europe since the Second World War. Mrs Merkel found herself between a rock and a number of hard places. She was confronted by French President Nicolas Sarkozy – desperate to avoid the collapse of the French banks that had lent to Greece; German MPs – many of whom saw no reason why the German electorate should have to hand over its savings to profligate European governments and financial institutions; and last but not least, she faced the anger of German voters themselves, many of whom had had quite enough of the euro and longed to return to the safety and security of the deutschmark. As each estimated figure for the bail-out funds seemed to grow, the more nervous the German public became. At stake was trust, trust between banks, between politicians and most important of all, trust between the German people and its government.

Rejection?

In the first of the seven state elections due to be held in 2011, Mrs Merkel's Christlich-Demokratische Union (CDU) (Christian Democrat Party), suffered an embarrassing defeat in Hamburg, where

KEY FACTS

Official name: Bundesrepublik Deutschland (Federal Republic of Germany)

Head of State: President Christian Wilhelm Walter Wulff (from 2 Jul 2010)

Head of government: Federal Chancellor Angela Merkel (CDU) (elected 2005; re-elected 27 Sep 2009)

Ruling party: Coalition: Christlich-Demokratische Union Deutschlands/Christlich-Soziale Union in Bayern (CDU/CSU) (Christian Democratic Union of Germany/Christian Social Union of Bavaria) and Freie Demokratische Partei (FDP) (Free Democratic Party) (CDU/CSU elected 2005; re-elected 27 Sep 2009; formed coalition 28 Sep 2009)

Area: 357,041 square km

Population: 81.78 million (2009)*

Capital: Berlin

Official language: German

Currency: Euro (€) = 100 cents (from 1 Jan 2002; previous currency Deutsche mark, locked at DM1.96 per euro)

Exchange rate: €0.75 per US$ (Oct 2011)

GDP per capita: US$40,631 (2010)

GDP real growth: 3.50% (2010)

GDP: US$3,315.60 billion (2010)

Labour force: 43.61 million (2010)

Unemployment: 7.70% (2010)

Inflation: 1.20% (2010)

Balance of trade: US$204.72 billion (2010)

its share of the vote was almost halved. The Sozialdemokratische Partei (SPD) (Social Democratic Party) on the other hand, saw a dramatic rise in its prospects, gaining an overall majority of seats. The SPD share of the Hamburg vote was 48 per cent, well above the national average of 26 per cent it was registering in the polls. On top of the Hamburg set-back in February, the defeat, in March, of the CDU in an area it had traditionally regarded as a part of its political heartland, Baden Wuttemberg, was a further setback for the Chancellor. Mrs Merkel's parliamentary majority remained intact – for the moment – but the two defeats looked likely to lead to more vociferous criticism of her leadership and its effects. Another by-product of her by-election defeat was the risk that her own party might decide to ditch her. Mrs Merkel had often appeared to be too hesitant and cautious. However, interpreting the Hamburg election results were was made complicated by the fact that it came close on the initial impact of the Japanese nuclear disaster, causing the economic debate to be intertwined with that of Germany's energy security.

Respite?

At least in the first 6 months of 2011, Germans felt confident as they left for their summer holidays that their country had avoided the economic crises that were bedevilling not only high profile Greece, but also Italy, Portugal, Spain and even (it was rumoured) France. The first weeks of 2011 saw the German economy, in true *donner und blitzen* style, galloping along at record growth. Worryingly, a number of leading German economists read the runes mistakenly. In May 2011 the chief economist at the Frankfurt-based Commerzbank, Jorg Kramer, was quoted 'Calling it a 'Wirtschaftwunder' is a bit aggressive, but I expect Germany to outperform for many years – so it may be a new paradigm.' At the time, Commerzbank raised its forecast for German growth from 3 per cent to 3.4 per cent. However, as the year progressed there were signs that the growth might be faltering – unemployment was still steadily falling and Germans could thank their unsteady neighbours to the south for weakening the euro sufficiently to stimulate German exports. The euro-zone crisis had, 'wihil-nihil' accelerated the emergence of Germany as – by a long chalk – the dominant partner in the European Union (EU). Thus while its euro-zone partners looked to it not only for guidance and workable solutions, they reacted quickly (and in the German view thanklessly) to German demands that its partners adhere to stricter budgetary disciplines and austerity measures.

Foreign trade booms

In March 2011, the Bundesverband Gross- und Aussenhandel eV (BGA) (German Foreign Trade Association) forecast that Germany's trade surplus, running at an annual surplus of €153 billion (US$205 billion), would begin to shrink. The BGA forecast that in 2011 German exports would reach the €1,000 billion (US$1,340 billion) mark in 2011. Germany's share in global exports would rise from 9 to 9.5 per cent, making Germany the world's second-placed exporting nation (behind China). Imports were expected to rise 12 per cent in 2011, reaching €903 billion (US$1,210 billion). The anticipated rise in purchases from other EU nations was 10 per cent, less than that from non-EU nations, which was expected to reach 15 per cent. Fears had been expressed that Germany was becoming too dependent upon China as an export market. These were dismissed by the BGA, which pointed out that only 7 per cent of German exports were destined for China in 2011, compared to the 60 per cent destined for other EU countries. Germany was the largest supplier of goods to the Middle East and North Africa, ahead of both France and Italy.

By mid-2011 the optimism that had characterised the first months of the year began to fade as analysts pointed out that although in 2010 the number of Germans employed, 40.5 million, had never been higher, the bulk of the new jobs – 300,000 – were in the services sector. The work-force in the manufacturing sector had actually shrunk by 140,000. Writing in *Die Welt*, analyst Olaf Gersemann said 'but no-one is saying out loud that this business model is not generating jobs, not even in a boom year like 2010'. A poll published at the beginning of the year by IW Consult showed that only 8 per cent of Germans felt that they had unambiguously benefited from German growth. Whistling in the wind, perhaps, Mrs Merkel had claimed in her New Year address that 'Together we have achieved an enormous amount.' One journalist described Mrs Merkel as 'divided from a German electorate that is seething about the botched handling of the euro-zone debt crisis.' Mrs Merkel had only herself to blame. In 2010 she had firmly announced that there was no possibility of extending rescue loans to Greece. Not much more than a year later, Mrs Merkel and her fellow European leaders had moved on to Greek bail-out number two. One poll showed 71 per cent of those polled having little or no faith in the single currency.

Entente?

The euro-zone crisis also meant that whether they liked it or not, Germany and France had become rather strange bedfellows. The relationship seemed to many to

KEY INDICATORS **Germany**

	Unit	2006	2007	2008	2009	2010
Population	m	82.29	82.20	82.12	82.03	*81.78
Gross domestic product (GDP)	US$bn	2,915.87	3,322.15	3,667.50	3,352.70	3,315.60
GDP per capita	US$	35,432	40,154	44,660	40,875	40,631
GDP real growth	%	2.8	2.5	1.3	-4.9	3.5
Inflation	%	1.8	2.2	2.8	0.1	1.2
Unemployment	%	9.8	8.4	7.8	7.5	7.7
Natural gas output	bn cum	15.6	14.3	13.0	12.2	10.6
Coal output	mtoe	50.3	86.0	47.7	44.4	43.7
Exports (fob) (goods)	US$m	1,135,730	1,354,120	1,498,190	1,144,870	1,303,330
Imports (fob) (goods)	US$m	934,860	1,075,430	1,232,430	956,650	1,098,610
Balance of trade	US$m	200,860	278,690	265,760	188,220	204,720.0
Current account	US$m	181,200	254,520	245,722	168,110	188,370
Total reserves minus gold	US$m	41,687	44,327	43,137	59,925	62,295
Foreign exchange	US$m	37,719	40,768	38,557	36,928	37,356
Exchange rate	per US$	0.75	0.69	0.68	0.78	0.76

* estimated figure

be flawed in a number of ways. First, the personal chemistry between Mrs Merkel and the French President had never been warm – Mrs Merkel was known to dislike Sarkozy's touchy-feely insistence on kissing her at international gatherings. Analysts who had labelled the relationship the 'Merkozy' duo missed the point that the relationship was not one of equals. While the German electorate quickly saw that, riding on Germany's coat tails, France's interest boiled down to one of avoiding an embarrassing bail-out for its own economy, the French government deeply resented having to play second fiddle to Berlin. If the German electorate objected to seeing their tax revenues used to save French bacon, the German government found its position as uncomfortable as it was unfamiliar. The situation provoked jokes a plenty, including the observation that in the Brussels headquarters of the European Commission, the first response to any new legislation was to ask what the German position on it would be.

Rather paradoxically, the beneficial effect of the weak euro on the German economy also enabled Angela Merkel to enter each more desperate round of the European bail-out discussions knowing that, in the final analysis, it would be in Germany's interest to give in to the demands of its neighbours, as well as those of the EU and the International Monetary Fund (IMF). Few Germans, however, would acknowledge the simple truth that the lion's share of German prosperity and wealth resulted from the rest of Europe buying German goods. The German government was well aware that Germany needed the euro-zone as much, or arguably more, than the euro-zone needed Germany. German manufacturers and German banks would suffer substantially if the euro-zone and its currency were to simply disintegrate.

The dilemma for Mrs Merkel was stark. To keep the euro-zone afloat, even in a reduced form, Germany would have to divert funds that otherwise might be used to provide the tax-cuts that German voters have long expected. But in mid-2011, there were moments – possibly brought about by a nagging French government – when Mrs Merkel's touch seemed to have deserted her. Were this to become the norm and Germany to lack firm leadership, an ailing Europe headed by a floundering France would be a less than attractive prospect for the international financial markets that seemed the likely arbiters of Europe's economic future.

The economy

Growth in German productivity continued to outpace the rest of Europe, making its exports more competitive. Thus, after some years in the political and even economic doldrums, Germany emerged in to the European sunlight at a time when most other European countries saw night approaching. But Germany's post-war history has made it a reluctant hero, anxious not to be seen as calling too many shots. Most Germans, the opinion polls suggested, did not want their country to be seen as the rescue option of last resort. The austerity their country has experienced had been overcome by hard work, not by hand-outs (or at least that was the mythology that chose to ignore benefits of the post-war Marshall Plan).

In the first quarter of 2011 German GDP surpassed its pre-crisis level following growth of 3.5 per cent in 2010, while employment was higher than before the crisis. The IMF projects the economy to expand by a healthy 3 per cent in 2011, but growth is expected to slow as the fiscal consolidation takes hold, the output gap closes and world trade growth decelerates. While Germany has so far escaped the crisis with little permanent damage, its long-term growth prospects remain low (about 1.25 per cent annually).

Rising commodity prices will temporarily lift German headline inflation from 1.2 per cent in 2010 to 2.5 per cent in 2011. Core inflation, however, is projected to rise only moderately. Germany's current account surplus, which rose to about 7.25 per cent of GDP just before the great recession, has since receded to about 5 per cent of GDP.

The authorities injected a sizeable fiscal stimulus in 2009–10 to counteract the economic downturn. With the economic recovery, they are moving towards a gradual consolidation. The pace of the recovery and the consolidation efforts imply that the objective of the European Union's Stability and Growth Pact (SGP), to bring the deficit below 3 per cent of GDP, can be achieved in 2011. The goal of the national fiscal rule, which targets a close-to-zero structural fiscal balance at the Federal level by 2016, is also within reach. The increased primary surplus will help bring down the debt-to-GDP ratio from its current level of over 83 per cent of GDP (having been boosted recently by banking sector support) to 73 per cent of GDP by 2016.

The banking system's return to broad stability reflects both the significant policy measures and the economic recovery. The German authorities injected significant capital into banks and provided the safety net of sovereign guarantees to access market financing during the crisis. In 2010 banks had raised their capital ratios and asset quality improved. However, pockets of vulnerabilities remained. Banks continue to be highly leveraged and the quality of their capital is low by international standards. Their profitability is also relatively low and expected to remain so.

The IMF welcomed Germany's impressive recovery buoyed by the strength of its export sector and the policies, including a fiscal stimulus and targeted measures to support the labour market and stabilise the financial sector. Directors underscored, however, the importance of structural measures targeting labour, capital and productivity to raise medium-term potential growth and domestic demand, particularly in the non-tradable sector, which would also support the role of Germany as an international locomotive and contribute to a reduction of global imbalances.

The multi-pronged agenda used to tackle Germany's long-standing structural issues could raise potential output growth. The implementation of such an approach, whose goal would be to boost labour participation, domestic investment and productivity, needed to include tax, education and innovation policies, complemented by an enhanced provision of risk capital and a more efficient insolvency process.

The measures adopted for German fiscal consolidation, while appropriate, also needed to allow room for fostering growth. Lowering the public debt-to-GDP ratio should enhance credibility. However, a reassessment of the speed of consolidation may be needed if Germany's growth turns out to be significantly weaker than expected. The use of fiscal instruments for stimulating growth should stay within the planned consolidation path.

In the view of the IMF, the German financial system has stabilised, although pockets of vulnerability remain. Improved capital ratios imply that the banks could absorb considerable stress. Nonetheless, German banks remain highly leveraged, achieve low profitability and the large banks remain highly dependent on market funding. While the overall level of direct exposure to spillover risks from elsewhere in Europe is limited, some banks are more exposed than others and indirect effects through banks outside of Germany could have cascading effects. A more timely publication of key financial data and enhanced transparency of the regulatory and supervisory regime, the operations of public sector banks and the deposit insurance schemes could only be beneficial to Germany's overall economic health.

Steps to limit systemic risk in the financial system are required in a number of areas. First, the legacy of the crisis still needs to be addressed, including establishing viable business models for the Landesbanken (regional commercial banks). Second, the regulatory and supervisory regime needs to be strengthened. Ensuring adequate and high-quality bank capitalisation is also important, especially where systemic risk considerations arise. Third, the harmonisation of the various deposit insurance schemes would allow for the possibility of the use of their resources for early intervention and help realise synergies with restructuring funds. Finally, the role of the Sparkassen (savings banks) would need to be considered in the context of an integrated and competitive European financial system.

Risk assessment

Economy	Good
Politics	Fair
Regional stability	Good

COUNTRY PROFILE

Historical profile

1871 Germany was unified under the Prussian royal house of the Hohenzollerns. Wilhelm I was appointed Germany's first Kaiser. After defeating France in the Franco-Prussian War, Alsace-Lorraine was annexed by Germany.
1880–1900 After Germany became Europe's leading industrial power, it attempted to expand territorially and become a world power, establishing colonies in Africa and trying to influence politics in the Balkans.
1914–18 Germany invaded Belgium and then France. The UK intervened, but the war in France became one of attrition until 1917, when US troops joined British and French forces. The First World War ended in 1918 with Germany's defeat. Kaiser Wilhelm II went into exile in the Netherlands. The Weimar Republic, a federation of 19 states, was declared in November 1918.
1919 Friedrich Ebert was appointed Germany's first president. Germany was called on to make massive financial reparations and to cede Alsace-Lorraine to France and parts of the Saarland to Poland, as part of the Treaty of Versailles. The Rhineland was de-militarised and occupied by the Western European powers.
1920s Germany was gripped by an economic depression, suffering from hyperinflation and high unemployment. As it could not afford to pay war reparations, France and Belgium occupied the industrialised Rhur as a protest.
1931 The instability of the economy and of democratic government led to the fascist National-Sozialistische Deutsche Arbeiterpartei (NSDAP) (Nationalist Socialist German Workers' Party) or Nazis, led by Austrian Adolf Hitler, becoming the largest party in the German parliament.
1933 Adolf Hitler was appointed chancellor of Germany.
1934 The Nazis consolidated their power. Hitler established himself as the führer (leader) of the Third Reich. The economy was rebuilt, all other political parties were banned and Hitler's opponents – Jews and other minorities – were placed in concentration camps.
1936 German troops re-took the Rhineland and provided military aid to Spanish nationalists fighting the Spanish Civil War. Germany, Italy and Japan formed an alliance.
1938 Austria became part of the German Third Reich after its pro-Nazi chancellor, Arthur von Seyss Inquart, invited German troops into the country. Annexation of Sudetanland, Czechoslovakia.
1939 Germany signed a non-aggression pact with the Soviet Union. Britain and France declared war on Germany after German troops invaded Poland.
1940 Germany captured most of Western Europe while most of Eastern Europe had pro-German puppet governments installed.
1941 Germany invaded the Soviet Union. Following Japan's attack on Pearl Harbor, the US declared a state of war with Japan; three days later, Japan's allies, Germany and Italy, declared war on the US.
1944–45 The US, Britain and the Soviet Union liberated Nazi-occupied Europe. Adolf Hitler committed suicide in Berlin. Following the end of the Second World War, Germany was occupied by the Allied powers.
1949 The Federal Republic of Germany (FRG) was established in the western zone by unifying the British, French and American zones of control, and the Deutsche Demokratische Republik (DDR) (German Democratic Republic (GDR)) was established in the east, under the Sozialistische Einheitspartei Deutschlands (SED) (Socialist Unity Party), following failure of negotiations to establish a unified administration. Konrad Adenauer became federal chancellor. Waltar Ulbricht became general secretary of the GDR's ruling communist party until 1971 when Erich Honeker replaced him.
1951 The FRG and France merged their coal and steel industries through the European Coal and Steel Community (ECSC).
1953 Severe food shortages and the policy of 'sovietisation' in GDR led to uprisings and strikes, suppressed by Soviet troops, causing large numbers of refugees to begin fleeing to the West.
1954 The FRG was admitted to NATO.
1955 The GDR became a member of the Soviet Union's Warsaw Pact.
1957 The FRG declared Berlin its capital. Bonn became the seat of government until reunification.
1958 The FRG became a founding member of the forerunner of the EU, the European Economic Community (EEC).
1961 The GDR constructed the Berlin Wall between eastern and western sectors to stem the flow of refugees to West Berlin.
1963–66 Ludwig Erhard succeeded Adenauer as federal chancellor.
1966–69 Federal Chancellor Kurt Georg Kiesinger's coalition comprised the two largest parties, Christlich-Demokratische Union (CDU) (Christian Democratic Union)/Christlich-Soziale Union (CSU) (Christian Social Union) and the Sozialdemokratische Partei Deutschland (SPD) (Social Democratic Party of Germany). He chose the mayor of Berlin, Willi Brandt, as his foreign minister.
1969 Willi Brandt (SPD) became chancellor. He implemented a policy of *ostpolitik*, orienting FRG foreign policy towards Eastern Europe and détente with the GDR.
1971 Erich Honecker became leader of the GDR, which became one of the most hardline members of the Warsaw Pact. In the late 1980s, Honecker resisted calls for democratisation on the Russian *glasnost* pattern.
1973 The FRG and GDR joined the UN.
1974 Helmut Schmidt became federal chancellor after the fall of Brandt in a security scandal. Disputes over the deteriorating economic situation, nuclear power and defence policy led to coalition instability and the withdrawal of the Freie Demokratische Partei (FDP) (Free Democratic Party)
1982 The CDU leader, Helmut Kohl, became federal chancellor.
1989–90 The Soviet Union withdrew support for the Honecker regime, prompting his resignation. With growing pressure for reunification, the Berlin wall was breached in a dramatic show of people-power as border guards declined to hold back protestors. After a further 11 months and a negotiated treaty the GDR acceded to the FDR and the two entities were reunified. Germany, France and the Benelux countries signed the Schengen Agreement abolishing passport controls between

them. Helmut Kohl won the first free German election since 1931.
1994 Federal elections resulted in a narrow victory for Chancellor Kohl and his CDU-led coalition.
1998 The SPD gained the largest share of the vote in the elections. Gerhard Schröder became chancellor and formed a coalition government with Bündis 90 (Alliance 90) and Die Grünen (Greens).
1999 Germany became a founding member of the European Economic and Monetary Union (Emu). Johannes Rau was elected as federal president.
2000 Helmut Kohl resigned as chairman of the CDU following revelations about illicit funding to the party during his time as chancellor. He was replaced by Angela Merkel.
2002 The euro replaced the Deutschemark. Gerhard Schröder was re-elected as chancellor by one of the narrowest margins in German election history.
2003 The Constitutional Court rejected a government request to ban the neo-Nazi National Democratic Party, after accusations that state agents had infiltrated the party's ranks, acting as *agents provocateurs* to discredit it.
2004 Horst Köhler took office as federal president.
2005 Chancellor Schröder called early elections which were deemed inconclusive with the CDU/CSU winning 35.2 per cent of the vote and the SPD 34.2 per cent. Angela Merkel became chancellor, leading a coalition government of CDU/CSU and SPD. She also became Germany's first woman chancellor and the first chancellor from the former communist eastern part of Germany.
2006 Parliament approved proposals to amend the constitution to reform the working of the federal structure. The government decided that German armed forces should engage actively in an international security role.
2007 China's economic growth overtook Germany's to become the world's third leading trading nation after the US.
2008 Chancellor Merkel addressed the Israeli parliament, the first given by a German head of government, during Israel's celebrations marking 60 years since its founding. The government came up with US$68 billion to save one of Germany's largest banks, Hypo Real Estate, from collapse. The German economy officially fell into recession.
2009 The government introduced a US$63 billion stimulus package to help shore up the economy. Horst Köhler was re-elected as Federal President. The German economy officially grew out of recession. In parliamentary elections the CDU/CSU won 38.4 per cent of the vote (239 seats of 622). Chancellor Merkel headed a CDU/CSU coalition government with FDP, to form a conservative, pro-business, liberal government.
2010 Chancellor Merkel persuaded parliament to commit €22.4 billion (US$30.68 billion) of German money to an EU fund providing a loan to Greece; there was popular discontent at the move. President Köhler resigned in May, following a political row sparked by his statement that Germany must sometimes deploy its military to protect its international interests 'for example free trade routes'. President of the Bundesrat, Jens Böhrnsen, became acting president, until the Federal Convention elected Christian Wulff; he took office on 2 July. The US, UK, Germany and France placed a ban on all cargo from Yemen in November, due to the Al Qaeda activity in Yemen.
2011 On 30 May, the government announced that all of Germany's nuclear reactors would be closed down by 2022. A virulent strain of E-coli killed 37 people and laid low over 3,228 people by 15 June; the outbreak was traced to a farm in Lower Saxony. German agricultural exports to Russia and Taiwan were suspended. On 19 June, Germany led Europe's second Greek bailout of US$126.5 billion (€90 billion), when the risk of Greece defaulting rocked European money markets and investors.

Political structure

Constitution

Federal republic; under the 1949 *Grundgesetz* (constitution), Germany has a high degree of devolution.
The federal structure is formed from 16 *Bundesländer* (regional states), including the city of Berlin. Each state has its own constitution, an elected legislature and a government with responsibilities including education and public order.

Form of state

Federal parliamentary democratic republic

The executive

Executive authority is held by the Bundesregierung (federal government). The chief executive and head of government is the Bundeskanzler (federal chancellor), chosen by the Bundestag (lower house of the federal assembly) and usually the leader of the ruling party, who then appoints his own ministers. The Bundespräsident (federal president) is elected for a five-year term by the members of the Bundesversammlung (federal assembly), but has largely ceremonial duties.

National legislature

The bicameral, Bundesversammlung (federal assembly), consists of the Bundestag (lower house) and Bundesrat (upper house). The Bundestag nominally has 598 members, of which 299 are elected in single seat constituencies and 299 allocated through party lists by proportional representation. Voters vote for both one candidate and one party per election. All members are elected for the term of the parliament, up to four-years.
The Bundesrat consists of 69 members chosen by the 16 Bundesländer (regional assemblies).

Legal system

The Federal Constitutional Court rules on constitutional issues, taking appeals from the lower courts. German law is largely code law that traces its roots to the Roman legal system. The court system below the Constitutional Court includes five branches: ordinary, labour, administrative, social and fiscal courts. Civil and criminal cases are normally in the jurisdiction of the ordinary court system, which is organised in local, regional and state tiers with a federal tribunal (Bundesgerichtshof), presiding over the system. Since the signing of the Single European Act in 1986, the European Court of Justice (ECJ) has been the highest court of appeal for rulings on matters affected by EU law.

Last elections

2 July 2010 (presidential, indirect); 27 September 2009 (parliamentary)
Results: Parliamentary: Christlich-Demokratische Union Deutschlands (Christian Democratic Union of Germany) (CDU) won 31.2 per cent of the vote (194 seats out of 622), Christlich-Soziale Union in Bayern (Christian Social Union of Bavaria) (CSU) 7.2 per cent (45), Sozialdemokratische Partei Deutschlands (SPD) (Social Democratic Party of Germany) 23 per cent (146), Freie Demokratische Partei (FDP) (Free Democratic Party) 14.6 per cent (93), Die Linkspartei (The Left Party) 11.9 per cent (76), Die Grünen (The Greens) 10.7 per cent (68). Turnout was 70.8 per cent.
Federal President: Christian Wulff was elected by the Federal Convention.

Next elections

September 2013 (parliamentary); 2015 (presidential)

Political parties

Ruling party

Coalition: Christlich-Demokratische Union Deutschlands/Christlich-Soziale Union in Bayern (CDU/CSU) (Christian Democratic Union of Germany/Christian Social Union of Bavaria) and Freie Demokratische Partei (FDP) (Free Democratic Party) (CDU/CSU elected 2005; re-elected 27 Sep 2009; formed coalition 28 Sep 2009)

Main opposition party

Sozialdemokratische Partei Deutschlands (SPD) (Social Democratic Party of Germany)

Population
81.78 million (2010)*
Last census: March 2004: 82,491,000
Population density: 235 inhabitants per square km. Urban population: 88 per cent.
Annual growth rate: 0.2 per cent 1994–2004 (WHO 2006)
Ethnic make-up
The majority of the population is Germanic. There is a small ethnic Slavonic (Sorbian) enclave in the south-east state of Saxony (approximately 60,000) and a Danish minority in the northern state of Schleswig-Holstein (approximately 50,000). There are an estimated 70,000 Sinti and Roma German nationals, mainly in the state's cities and towns . Some neighbourhoods in industrial cities are dominated by guest workers, mostly from Turkey, the Balkans and southern Europe.
Religions
The two principal religions are Roman Catholicism and Protestantism. The German Evangelical (Lutheran) church dominates in the overwhelmingly Protestant eastern, northern and central parts of the country. Members of the Catholic church form a majority in the south and west.

Education
Participation levels in primary and secondary education are almost 100 per cent, while 45 per cent attend some form of tertiary education. Approximately 4.8 per cent of GNP is spent on public education.
The public school system is administered by the individual states. Primary education is free and grants are made available for secondary education in institutions where fees are charged.
A year of kindergarten is followed by four years of primary school (*Grundschule*). Pupils are then screened for later admission into either advanced study or specialised and vocational training. Those in the advanced track continue at a *Gymnasium* to the age of 19, and then take the *Arbitur* comprehensive academic examination for admission to university. The majority of pupils attend vocational college after the age of 16.
Compulsory years: Six to 16
Pupils per teacher: 17 in primary schools

Health
There is no national health service, instead comprehensive healthcare is administered by the individual states. Health insurance provides 100 per cent of workers' salary for six weeks then drops to 80 per cent for 78 weeks. Health insurance also covers maternity and death benefits. Health insurance premiums, split by worker and employer in the case of those with high salaries, average 12.5 per cent of gross earnings.
HIV/Aids
HIV prevalence: 0.1 per cent aged 15–49 in 2003 (World Bank)
Life expectancy: 79 years, 2004 (WHO 2006)
Fertility rate/Maternal mortality rate: 1.3 births per woman, 2004 (WHO 2006)
Birth rate/Death rate: 8.6 births per 1,000 population; 10.3 deaths per 1,000 population (2003).
Child (under 5 years) mortality rate (per 1,000): 4.2 per 1,000 live births (World Bank)
Head of population per physician: 3.37 physicians per 1,000 people, 2003 (WHO 2006)

Welfare
Germany's health and social security systems are among the most generous in the world. Health, unemployment and retirement insurance are mandatory for most ordinary wage-earners under a wide-ranging social insurance system that has developed over more than a century. The system operates on a payroll withholding plan with contributions from workers, employers and government.
The welfare system provides assistance for all needy people who are unable to fend for themselves. There are funds for the support of widows, orphans and disabled people. The state makes available housing allowances for the poor in addition to its subsidies to low-income housing construction.
Changes introduced in 2005 affected the newly unemployed and those without work for more than a year, who received only a flat rate benefit and any additional sum was means tested, while measures to supervise and support those seeking work was stepped up. These measures were introduced to reduce the financial burden of the welfare system.
The Constitutional Court ruled that workers with children should pay a lower premium for the compulsory nursing insurance scheme than childless people.
Pensions
Of major concern is the rapidly changing demographic balance. As Germany's population continues to shrink, a smaller working population will have to bear the burden of an ever increasing number of pensioners. Pensions cost Germany the equivalent of 11–12 per cent of annual GDP and this is projected to rise to 18–19 per cent by 2040.
Contributions to the state pension scheme, which is mandatory except for workers with high salaries, range up to 18.7 per cent of gross income and are shared equally by worker and employer.
The normal retirement age is 63 for men and 60 for women.

Main cities
Berlin (capital, estimated population 3.4 million (m) in 2005), Hamburg (1.8m), Munich (1.2m, Bavaria), Cologne (965,300), Frankfurt am Main (648,000), Essen (588,800), Dortmund (587,600), Stuttgart (581,100), Düsseldorf (571,966), Bremen (527,900), Hanover (516,300), Duisburg (513,400), Nürnberg (486,700), Leipzig (486,100), Dresden (473,300), Bonn (307,500), Mannheim (306,100).

Languages spoken
English is widely spoken, especially in business circles; French is also spoken, particularly in the Saarland. In the north in Schleswig-Holstein, Danish is spoken by the Danish minority and taught in schools. Regional dialects often differ markedly from standard German. There is an ongoing debate on language reform in Germany. It is almost 100 years since language laws were last comprehensively reformed.
Sorbian, North and West Frisian, Romani, Turkish and Kurdish are also spoken.
Official language/s
German

Media
The constitution guaranteed freedom of the press. Germany has several international conglomerates that produce material for all media outlets, including Bertelsmann, ProSiebenSat.1 and Axel Springer.
Press
There are few national newspapers, most publications are regionally based and may be distributed nationally. Although newspaper circulations at over 21 million the figure has been falling since the 1990s. There are hundreds of newspaper titles, most of which are locally produced. Tabloid newspapers are referred to as 'boulevard press'. Most newspapers are subscribed to rather than purchased daily.
Dailies: Major national publications include, in German, *Bild* (www.bild.de) a tabloid with the highest circulation, *Süddeutsche Zeitung* (SZ) (www.sueddeutsche.de), *Frankfurter Allegemeine Zeitung* (FAZ) (www.faz.net), *Frankfurter Rundschau* (www.fr-online.de) and *Tageszeitung* (www.taz.de).
Foreign language newspapers are published in Berlin, in French and Spanish.
Weeklies: In German, an influential newspaper with more analysis and background information is *Die Zeit* (www.zeit.de); other news magazines include *Der Spiegel* (www.spiegel.de) with the largest circulation and has an English-language edition, *Stern*

(www.stern.de), *Focus* (www.focus.de) and the illustrated magazine *Superillu* (www.superillu.de). A few of the national dailies produce Sunday papers

Business: In German, *Börsen Zeitung* (www.boersen-zeitung.com) published Tuesday–Saturday is a financial newspaper, *Handelsblatt* (www.handelsblatt.com) and *Aktiv* (www.aktiv-online.info) for general business news; most national daily newspapers have sections on business and finance, including. Weekly publications include *WirtschaftsWoche* (www.wiwo.de) a economic magazine covering many aspects of business and *Kapital*, which looks at economic issues from a political standpoint; they are both published by the GWP Media Group (www.gwp.de).

There are numerous trade and business publications. The German Institute of Business Management publishes a range of periodical of specific interest, on company law and governance.

Periodicals: There are over 800 general magazines and 1,000 specialist periodicals of offer.

In German, the monthly, *NinetoFive* is an imprint of *WirtschaftsWoche* (www.wiwo.de) with lifestyle contents for the office worker. *Lieraturen* (www.literaturen-online.de) is a literary monthly magazine and *Brigitte* (www.brigitte.de) is a women's magazine published fortnightly.

In English, *Exberliner* (www.exberliner.com) is published bi-monthly.

Broadcasting

Public broadcasting is funded by licence fees.

Radio: ARD (www.ard.de) is a consortium of national, public broadcasters providing a nationwide service with regional based programmes; some collaborate to produce shows of common interest. Most produce their own programmes of news and genre music. Most operate on the FM bandwidth and some are available digitally (DAB). Another public network is DeutschlandRadio (www.dradio.de) operates two national networks, with news and cultural programmes and a music channel. Deutsche Welle (www.dwelle.de) provides an international service in seven foreign languages, with news in 23 other languages, broadcasting via radio, internet and mobile/cell phones.

There are an abundance of private, commercial regional radio stations. Large media conglomerates operate radio stations and well as private interests catering for all genres.

Television: Germany has the largest and most competitive television market in Europe. Two of the largest television channel, ZDF (www.zdf.de) and ARD (www.ard.de), are national public services. ARD is a network of regional channels while ZDF is a nationwide channel that also broadcasts in Austria, Luxembourg and Switzerland. Both produce their own contents in a full range of programmes. There are private, commercial channels including Europe's largest TV, radio and production company, RTL Television (www.rtl.de), Sat.1 (www.sat1.de) and pay-to-view channels, specialising in genres such as films (Premiere (www.premiere.de)), sport (Arena (www.arena.tv)), documentaries and music. All public and private, major networks deliver German satellite TV programmes to international subscribers.

Germany plans to begin halting analogue TV transmission from 2008, as regional digital services are made available, completing the switch by 2010.

Advertising

Typical annual spending on advertising is over US$11.8 billion, of which an equal share, of 30 per cent, is divided between television and magazines, with newspapers averaging 15 per cent of the total amount.

There are regulations governing the insertion of adverts on television and radio with a limit of 20 minutes and 90 minute per working day respectively. TV programme sponsorship is permitted. Advertising by new technologies requires that they are clearly recognisable. Cinema allows tobacco advertising as well as product placing and surreptitious advertising.

News agencies

National news agency: DPA (Deutsche Presse-Agentur)

Economy

In 2010, the German economy was the fourth largest in the world; it is certainly the largest economy in Europe and is a leading member of the EU's European Monetary Union (EMU).

Typical for advanced economies, the service sector, at over 69 per cent, is the largest component of GDP, agriculture has fallen progressively to around 3 per cent and the remainder is industry and manufacturing. Germany has many world-class products with global brands, including vehicles, pharmaceuticals, biotechnology and medical and genetic engineering, aerospace and precision machinery, electronics, building materials, beverages and foodstuffs and textiles. Primary industries include iron and steel, coal and natural gas production.

GDP growth in 2007 was 2.5 per cent and continued as positive in 2008, albeit at a reduced rate of 1.2 per cent, as the global economic crisis deepened. GDP growth in 2009 was -5.0 per cent; much of Germany's manufacturing is for export and trading partners were cutting back on spending as their economies weakened. However, by the second quarter of 2010 GDP growth was averaging 2.2 per cent, and was the fastest growth recorded since the 1980s, as a weaker euro helped to make German exports more competitive

The banking sector was caught up in the crisis from the beginning, when in 2007 the Sachsen Landsbank, a regional bank, was sold, as it neared collapse, to another larger banking entity, and had to rely on €17 billion (US$23.15 billion) of public funding. Other financial institutions hit by toxic debts due to the sub-prime mortgage failure in the US were, in February 2008, Germany's second largest bank, Commerzbank, which was forced to write-off US$1.1 billion; in April the Deutsche Bank warned of credit losses of US$3.9 billion and in October Hypo Real Estate was saved by a US$38.7 billion deal take-over deal with another private bank. Germany was the first advanced economy to fall into recession, but it was also one of first to come out, in the second quarter of 2009, with two consecutive months of growth as the government stimulus packages plus growing exports and increasing consumer spending contributed to growth.

Germany became the reluctant paymaster of the eurozone when the economic crisis in Greece, in April–May 2010, threatened to destabilise the euro unless it found help from other members of the EMU. Despite reluctance by the German public to underwrite a profligate economy, large amounts of Greek debt held in German banks were bought-up by the German government, as a US$146.2 billion (€110 billion) three-year loan was agreed, backed by the International Monetary Fund (IMF). In an effort to stabilise the euro the government in May 2010 banned temporarily its ten most important financial institutions from selling naked credit default swaps and the short-selling of government bonds, which it claimed was exacerbating the European debt crisis and resulted in the euro plummeting to a four-year low.

GDP growth in 2010 remained positive and was projected to reach 1.4 per cent, however growth to pre-crisis level is not expected before 2012.

External trade

As a member of the European Union, Germany operates within a community-wide free trade area, with tariffs set as a whole. Internationally, the EU has free trade agreements with a number of nations and trading blocs worldwide. It is Europe's leading export trader and the world's third largest vehicle exporter.

Exports account for over 70 per cent of GDP.

Imports

Include machinery, vehicles, chemicals, foodstuffs, textiles and metals raw materials.

Main sources: France (typically 8 per cent of total), The Netherlands (8 per cent), China (7 per cent).

Exports

Principal exports include machinery, vehicles and aerospace, chemicals and pharmaceuticals, electrical and electronic equipment and plastics.

Main destinations: France (typically 9 per cent of total), US (7 per cent), UK (7 per cent).

Agriculture

Farming

Germany has always provided incentives and subsidies for agriculture, which is generally regarded as a national resource.

Most of Germany's agriculture is now governed by the EU's Fundamental reform to the Common Agricultural Policy (CAP) was introduced in Germany in 2005. The subsidies paid on farm output, which tended to benefit large farms and encourage overproduction, were replaced by single farm payments not conditional on production.

Livestock production has long been the most important part of the sector, but is steadily declining.

Fishing

West German sea fishing has experienced a sharp decline in recent decades. The government makes some subsidies available, but policy is largely an EU matter. The total seafood catch declined rapidly to just over 300,000 tonnes per annum during the mid 1990s. Since then catches have fallen to around 250,000 tonnes per year. Freshwater catches have also seen a drop in quantity of about one-fifth over the same period.

The home ports of the east German deep-sea fishing fleets are Rostock-Marienehe and Sassnitz. The fleets work the waters off Iceland, Greenland, Labrador and Newfoundland and off the coast of West Africa. Inland fisheries account for only 4 per cent of the annual catch.

Forestry

Forest accounts for nearly a third of the land area estimated at 10.7 million hectares (ha) in 2000. These are located mainly in the south, centre and east of the country, with relatively little on the northern plain. Most of the forest area is available for wood supply. The growing stock per hectare is high and has been increasing. About 50 per cent of forests are publicly owned.

Germany has a strong forest industry and is one of the leading producers of wood-based panels and paper in the global market. The large-scale engineered wood product industry is dependent partially on sawnwood imports. Paper production is also partly based on imported wood pulp. It is one of the largest exporters and consumers of recycled paper.

Industry and manufacturing

The industrial sector accounts for 36.2 per cent of GDP and employs approximately 36 per cent of the workforce.

Germany is a leading European producer of motor vehicles and accessories, industrial plant, machine tools, electrical goods, scientific instruments, chemicals, pharmaceuticals and consumer goods.

Traditional industries (steel, shipbuilding) have contracted because of foreign competition and weaker demand. Some companies have moved into entirely new industries in order to take advantage of government deregulation and growth in service industries. The government has encouraged the modernisation of the industrial sector through the use of electronics and more flexible production techniques, having restructured industry in eastern Germany which had remained uncompetitive in terms quality.

High production costs in eastern Germany had prevented the region's companies from competing with their western counterparts but have shown a resurgence through a flexible approach to change, particularly in the electronics, food processing, printing, engineering and automotive sectors.

Tourism

Tourism accounts for 8 per cent of GDP and is a major employer, providing work for 2.8 million people. The main market is Europe, principally the Netherlands, followed by the UK and Switzerland. The US, which comes second after The Netherlands, is the most lucrative market. The sector is not a significant net foreign exchange earner, because so many Germans travel abroad.

Mining

Eastern Germany has huge deposits of lignite as well as significant deposits of the more valuable anthracite, potassium salts and uranium ore. However, there are relatively few feasibly accessible natural resources other than large supplies of black and brown coal, so Germany is largely dependent on imports. High extraction costs mean that exploitation of small deposits of iron ore, copper, lead, tin and zinc are limited.

Hydrocarbons

Total proven oil reserves stood at 367 million barrels in 2007, however with consumption at 2.5 million barrels per day (bpd) and crude oil production at 66,000bpd Germany has to import a major proportion of its needs. Germany is a major oil refining country with 14 sites and a total capacity of 2.4 million bpd. Germany is also the world's largest producer of bio-diesel, producing around 33,000bpd.

Proven natural gas reserves were 258 billion cubic metres (cum), located onshore in the north-western state of Niedersachsen. Offshore reserves, in the North Sea, provides 1.4 billion cum per annum but is subjected to tight environmental regulations that curtail further exploration, development and production. Germany is one of the world's largest consumers of natural gas, with supplies imported from Russia, Norway and The Netherlands. A new, direct 1,200km gas pipeline underneath the Baltic Sea, which would transport Russian gas between the Russian town of Vyborg to the German town of Greifswald was agreed in 2005.It will bypass existing pipelines that traverse the Ukraine, thereby minimising disruption caused by third-party, foreign disputes. The project is set to cost US$5billion, with German companies controlling a 49 per cent stake in the pipeline and the remainder in Russian hands. Work began amid complaints from Poland and the Ukraine that the project was designed to bypass its consumers.

Coal is Germany's main hydrocarbon resource. In 2007, coal reserves stood at 6.7 billion tonnes and production totalled 51.5 million tonnes oil equivalent (toe), an increase of 2.5 per cent on the 2006 figure. The majority of its coal is the less valuable sub-bituminous and lignite (brown coal), which is typically used in power stations, but is a heavy atmospheric pollutant.

Energy

There are over 2,800 power plants in Germany with an installed generating capacity of over 121 gigawatts (GW), producing over 592 billion-kilowatt hours (kWh) of electricity in 2007. The energy mix is divided between domestically produced brown coal (25.8 per cent), nuclear energy (20.7 per cent) and imported black coal (19.5 per cent); the remainder is produced from gas and renewable sources such as hydropower and wind, which accounted for 13 per cent of total electricity generating capacity in 2007. Germany has 17 nuclear reactors which provided 32 million tonnes oil equivalent (mtoe). In March 2011 four stations were closed following the earthquake and tsunami at the Fukushima plant in Japan. Then in May the government annouced that the seven oldest reactors, which were already subject to a moratorium, and the Kruemmel nuclear power plant, would not resume. Six other plants will be closed in 2021 and the last three in 2022.

Financial markets

There are eight German stock exchanges – located in Frankfurt, Dusseldorf, Munich, Berlin, Hamburg, Stuttgart, Hanover and Bremen. The Frankfurt Stock Exchange is the dominant trading floor with more than half the volume traded. Combined volume on the eight German exchanges exceeds that of all other European financial centres except London.

Stock exchange

Frankfurter Wertpapierbörse (FWB) Frankfurt Stock Exchange

Commodity exchange

Risk Management Exchange (RMX)

Banking and insurance

A sophisticated banking system underpins the country's economic strength.
There are three main categories: central bank; multi-purpose banks, including commercial, co-operative and (publicly owned) regional Landesbanks and savings banks; and specialist banks, including mortgage banks and instalment credit houses.
Many banks have important shareholdings in industrial companies and bankers sit on the supervisory boards of many companies.
In 2003, Josef Ackermann, the chief executive of Germany's main bank Deutsche Bundesbank, was put on trial for corruption. Although initially cleared, a retrial was ordered in December 2005 and Ackermann is facing increasing calls for his resignation.

Central bank

Deutsche Bundesbank; European Central Bank (ECB)

Time

GMT plus one hour (daylight saving, late March to late October, GMT plus two hours)

Geography

The Alps form the southern border with Switzerland and Austria. Germany's southern and eastern borders facing the Czech Republic are also demarcated by mountain ranges. The eastern border with Poland follows the Oder and Neisse rivers. The north is a low, wide coastal plain along the North and Baltic seas, which are separated by Denmark's Jutland peninsula. Germany's western borders join (in an anti-clockwise direction) the Netherlands, Belgium, Luxembourg, France and Switzerland.
Picturesque, forested highlands dominate the central and southern regions. The country is drained by the Danube, Rhine, Elbe, Weser and Oder river systems.
The highest mountain, with an elevation of 2,962 metres, is an alpine peak called Zugspitze, straddling the border with Austria. The main centres of population are concentrated in the west, along the middle and lower Rhine from Karlsruhe, near the French border, and from there northward through the highly industrialised Ruhr conurbation, to the Netherlands border. The German segment of the Rhine is 865km long, all of it navigable. On the south-east side of Europe's continental divide or watershed, the Danube flows eastward from its source in the Black Forest, through 647km of west Germany, to leave the country at the Austrian border at Passau on its way to the Black Sea. There is an important canal system allowing ships to sail from the Oder to the Elbe (to Prague).

Hemisphere

Northern

Climate

Moderate summers and rainy, bleak winters. Most of the country has a typical north-west coastal climate, heavily influenced by moist maritime air masses from the Atlantic. The eastern fringe of the country is sometimes influenced by the continental high pressure centre, making for somewhat colder winters and warmer summers. Prevailing winds are usually from the west.

Dress codes

It is customary to wear a suit and tie in banks, businesses and government offices.

Entry requirements

Passports

Required by all except citizens of Schengen agreement countries who may travel with national ID cards.

Visa

Required by all, except tourist and business visitors from EU, North America, Australasia and most of Europe for up to three months. For confirmation of exceptions and requirements see: www.auswaertiges-amt.de/ the website of the consular section of the German ministry of foreign affairs.
Germany is a member of the Schengen visa accord and all visitors that require a visa must apply to a Germany consulate; when a visa has been issued a visitor may travel to any other Schengen zone without further visas. A Schengen visa application (offered in several languages) can be downloaded from http://europa.eu/abc/travel/ see 'documents you will need'.

Currency advice/regulations

There are no restrictions on the import or export of local or foreign currency.

Customs

Personal items are duty-free. There are no duties levied on alcohol and tobacco between EU member states, providing amounts imported are for personal consumption.

Health (for visitors)

Nationals of the European Economic Area (EEA) countries and Switzerland can access reduced cost and sometimes free medical treatment using a European Health Insurance Card (EHIC) while visiting the EEA. Exceptions include nationals of the 10 countries which joined the EU in 2004 whose EHIC is not valid in Switzerland. Applications for the EHIC should be made before travelling.

Mandatory precautions

Vaccination certificates are not usually required, unless arriving from infected area.

Hotels

No official rating system. 10–15 per cent service charge. Advisable to book in advance, especially when trade fairs are being held. All major credit cards accepted.

Public holidays (national)

Fixed dates

1 Jan (New Year's Day), ^6 January (Epiphany), 1 May (Labour Day), ^15 Aug (Assumption Day), 3 Oct (German Unity Day), ^31 Oct (Day of Reformation), ^1 Nov (All Saints' Day), 25 Dec (Christmas Day), 26 Dec (Boxing Day).
Although not official holidays, many shops and businesses are also closed on Christmas Eve and New Year's Eve.

Variable dates

Good Friday, Easter Monday, ^Ascension Day, Whit Monday, ^Corpus Christi (May/Jun)
^ Holiday in certain areas only

Working hours

Banking

Mon–Fri: various hours between 0830–1300, 1400–1600; Thu: 0830–1300, 1400–1730. City centre branches do not close for lunch. Exchange bureaux: 0600–2200.

Business

Mon–Fri: usually 0800–1730.

Government

Mon–Fri: usually 0800–1700.

Shops

Mon–Fri: 0900–2000; Sat: 0900–2000. Sunday opening hours vary from state to state and can be limited.

Telecommunications

Mobile/cell phones

There are G3, 900 and 1800 services throughout the country.

Electricity supply
220V AC, 50 Hz. European-style round two-pin plugs are in use.

Social customs/useful tips
Handshaking is universal at the beginning and end of every social or business encounter. Germans acknowledge others, even strangers, with a standard greeting when entering or leaving a room, office, shop or railway compartment.
The focal point of German social life is frequently club membership. The thick web of traditional clubs, which are based on activities including pre-Lenten carnival and sports, card playing, animal husbandry and marksmanship, strongly contribute to social life. It is known as *Vereinsleben*, or club culture.
Germans are extremely aggressive drivers and politeness on the road is not rewarded. There is no speed limit on some parts of the *autobahn* (motorway network). Verbal public insults can result in lawsuits. There are also strict laws against racial slurs, especially anti-Semitism.
Do not try to pay bill if invited to a restaurant during business hours. If dining at a German's home, it is considered impolite to arrive late; a gift of flowers is a social 'must'; do not drink until the host has his or her glass. It is regarded as bad manners to keep your hands in your pockets when talking to someone.

Getting there
Air
National airline: Lufthansa
International airport/s: Berlin airports are small and do not receive intercontinental flights, arrivals are via continental or connecting flights. A redeveloped airport accepting intercontinental flights will not be ready before 2011. Frankfurt Airport (FRA), the principal German airport, is 13km south-west of the city, facilities include banks, post office, duty-free shops, restaurants and business suites. Extensive access to the city and other German connections are provided by trains (including international rail links), buses and taxis. Car hire and limousine services are available.
Other airport/s: Bremen (BRE) 4km south of city; Berlin-Tempelhof (THF), Berlin-Tegel (TXL) and Berlin-Schönefeld (SXF). Berlin-Schönefeld, in 2006, began redevelopment to replaced Berlin's three airports with the Berlin-Brandenburg International airport to be completed by 2011; Cologne/Bonn-Konrad Adenauer (CGN) 20km north of Bonn and 14km south-east of Cologne; Düsseldorf (DUS) 8km north of city; Hamburg (HAM) 13km north of city; Hanover (HAJ) 11km from city; Leipzig/Halle (LEJ); Munich (MUC) 11km north-east of city; Nuremberg (NUE) 8km north of city; Stuttgart Echterdingen (STR) 14km south of city.
Airport tax: None.
Surface
Road: There are good quality motorways and main roads linking all surrounding countries.
Water: Ships provide regular passenger services and cruises on the Danube between Regensburg, Vienna, Bratislava and Budapest and from Passau via Austria, Slovakia, Hungary, Serbia, Bulgaria to Romania and the Black Sea.
Main port/s: Bremen, Bremerhaven, Hamburg, Kiel, Rostock, Stralsund, Wilhelmshaven and Wismar.

Getting about
National transport
Air: Frequent services link Berlin, Hanover, Cologne/Bonn, Düsseldorf, Frankfurt, Hamburg, Bremen, Munich, Nuremberg and Stuttgart. Early morning flights provide direct links between many of these centres. Domestic flights are not cheap, but competition is bringing down prices.
Road: There are over 487,000km of roads with a modern network of motorways (*autobahnen*) linking all cities. Secondary roads in eastern Germany may not be of comparable standard with the west.
Buses: Good nationwide coach services are operated by Deutsche Bahn (DB) and other companies.
Rail: DB runs reliable Intercity Express and Sprinter services, with high-speed trains between major cities which include faster east–west links. First and second class travel is available and it is advisable to book in advance. For long-distance travel, trains can often be a quicker option than flying.
Water: Seaports on the Baltic and North Sea coasts are linked to inland waterways and railways. Navigable inland waterways are used extensively.
City transport
There are buses, trams, metro and electric railway services in many towns.
A Welcome Card entitles travellers to 48 hours of bus and rail travel. It can be bought at hotels or VBB (bus and train) offices. Otherwise, machines dispense tickets permitting three consecutive hours' travel on buses and trains.
Taxis: Good taxi services run in all main cities. In Berlin, the metered cabs are beige Mercedes with yellow taxi signs, available outside hotels or at well-signed ranks.
Car hire
Speed limits: built up areas 50kph, normal roads 100kph, *autobahns* 'recommended' top speed of 130kph.
Information is available from automobile clubs such as Allgemeiner Deutscher Automobil Club eV (ADAC), Automobil Club von Deutschland eV (AvD) and Deutscher Touring Automobil Club eV.
The wearing of seat belts is compulsory.

BUSINESS DIRECTORY

The addresses listed below are a selection only. While World of Information makes every endeavour to check these addresses, we cannot guarantee that changes have not been made, especially to telephone numbers and area codes. We would welcome any corrections.

Telephone area codes
The international direct dialling (IDD) code for Germany is +49 followed by the area code:

Berlin	30	Hamburg	40
Bonn	228	Hanover	511
Bremen	421	Leipzig	341
Cologne	221	Munich	89
Dortmund	231	Münster	251
Dresden	351	Nuremberg	911
Düsseldorf	211	Potsdam	331
Essen	201	Stuttgart	711
Frankfurt (Main)	69		

Useful telephone numbers
Police: 110
Fire: 112

Chambers of Commerce
American Chamber of Commerce in Germany, 12 Rossmarkt, 60311 Frankfurt am Main (tel: 929-1040; fax: 929-10411; e-mail: info@amcham.de).

Association of German Chambers of Industry and Commerce, 29 Breite Strasse, 10178 Berlin (tel: 203-080; fax: 203-081000; e-mail: dihk@berlin.dihk.de).

Berlin Chamber of Industry and Commerce, 85 Fasanenstrasse, 10623 Berlin (tel: 315-10666; fax: 315-10166; e-mail: service@berlin.ihk.de).

Bonn/Rhein-Sieg Chamber of Industry and Commerce, 17 Bonner Talweg, 53113 Bonn, (tel: 228-40; fax: 228-4170; e-mail: info@bonn.ihk.de).

British Chamber of Commerce in Germany, 60 Severinstrasse, 50678 Cologne (tel: 314-458; fax: 315-335; e-mail: info@bccg.de).

Cologne Chamber of Industry and Commerce, Unter Sachsenhausen 10-26, 50667 Cologne, (tel: 164-0551; fax:164-0129; e-mail: my@koeln.ihk.de).

Düsseldorf Chamber of Industry and Commerce, 1 Ernst-Schneider- Platz, 40212 Düsseldorf (tel: 355-70; fax: 355-7401; e-mail: ihkdus@duesseldorf.ihk.de).

Frankfurt am Main Chamber of Industry and Commerce, 4 Börsenplatz, 60313 Frankfurt am Main (tel: 219-70; fax:

219-71424; e-mail: info@frankfurt-main.ihk.de).

Hamburg Chamber of Industry and Commerce, 1 Adolphsplatz, 20457 Hamburg (tel: 361-38138; fax: 361-38401; e-mail: service@hk24.de).

Hanover Chamber of Industry and Commerce, 49 Schiffgraben, 30175 Hanover (tel: 31-070; fax: 310-7333; e-mail: schrage@hannover.ihk.de).

Munich Chamber of Industry and Commerce, 2 Max Joseph Strasse, 80333 Munich (tel: 511-6368; fax: 511-6290; e-mail: alberts@muenchen.ihk.de).

Münster Chamber of Industry and Commerce, 61 Sentmaringer Weg, 48151 Münster (tel: 707-0; fax: 707-325; e-mail: international@muenster.ihk.de).

Nuremberg Chamber of Industry and Commerce, 25–27 Am Hauptmarkt, 90403 Nuremberg (tel: 133-50; fax: 133-5200; e-mail: info@ihk-nuernberg.de).

Stuttgart Chamber of Industry and Commerce, 30 Jägerstrasse, 70174 Stuttgart (tel: 200-50; fax: 200-5354; e-mail: info@stuttgart.ihk.de).

Banking

Bayerische Landesbank, 18 Briennerstrasse, 80333 Munich (tel: 217-101; fax: 217-123579; e-mail: info@bayernlb.de).

Bremer Landesbank, 26 Domshof, 28195 Bremen (tel: 332-0; fax: 332-2322; e-mail: kontakt@bremerlandesbank.de).

Commerzbank, Kaiserplatz, 60261 Frankfurt am Main (tel: 136-20; fax: 285-389; e-mail: info@commerxbank.com).

Deutsche Bank, 12 Taunuslage, 60262 Frankfurt am Main (tel: 910-00; fax: 910-34225; e-mail: deutsche.bank@db.com).

Dresdner Bank, 1 Jürgen Ponto Platz, 60301 Frankfurt am Main (tel: 263-0; fax: 263-4831; e-mail: dresdner-bank@dresdner-bank.com).

DZ Bank, Platz der Republik, 60265 Frankfurt am Main (tel: 744-701; fax: 744-71685; e-mail: mail@dzbank.de).

Hamburgische Landesbank, 50 Gerhart Hauptmann Platz, 20095 Hamburg (tel: 333-30; fax: 333-32707; e-mail: info@hamburglb,de).

Hypovereinsbank, 16 Am Tucherpark, 80538 Munich (tel: 378-0; e-mail: info@hypovereinsbank.de).

Landesbank Baden-Württemberg, 2 Am Hauptbahnhof, 70173 Stuttgart (tel: 127-0; fax: 127-3278; e-mail: kontakt@lbbw.de).

Landesbank Berlin, 171 Bundesallee, 10889 Berlin (tel: 869-801; fax: 869-83074; e-mail: information@lbb.de).

Landesbank Hessen-Thuringen, 52-58 Neue Mainzer Strasse, 60311 Frankfurt am Main (tel: 913-201; fax: 291-517; e-mail: presse@helaba.de).

Landesbank Rheinland-Pfalz, 54-56 Grosse Bleiche, 55116 Mainz (tel: 113-01; fax: 113-2724; e-mail: lrp@lrp.de).

Landesbank Saar, 2 Ursulinenstrasse, 66111 Saarbrücken (tel: 383-01; fax: 383-1200; e-mail: service@saarlb.de).

Landesbank Schleswig-Holstein, 6 Martinsdamm, 24103 Kiel (tel: 900-01; fax: 900-2446; e-mail: info@lb-kiel.de).

Norddeutsche Landesbank, 10 Friedrichwall, 30159 Hannover (tel: 361-0; fax: 361-2502; e-mail: info@nordlb.de).

Westdeutsche Landesbank, 15 Herzogstrasse, 40217 Düsseldorf (tel: 826-2449; fax: 826-9683; e-mail: presse@westlb.de).

Central bank

Deutsche Bundesbank, Wilhelm Epstein Strasse 14, 60431 Frankfurt am Main (tel: 9566-3511; fax: 9566-4679; email: presse-information@bundesbank.de).

European Central Bank (ECB), Kaiserstrasse 29, 60311 Frankfurt am Main (tel: 13-440; fax: 1344-6000; email: info@ecb.int).

Stock exchange

Frankfurter Wertpapierbörse (FWB) Frankfurt Stock Exchange: http://deutsche-boerse.com

Stock exchange 2

Börse Stuttgart (Stuttgart Stock Exchange): www.boerse-stuttgart.de

Commodity exchange

Risk Management Exchange (RMX): www.rmx.eu/cnt

Travel information

Allgemeiner Deutscher Automobil Club (ADAC), 8 Am Westpark, 81373 Munich (tel: 767-60; fax: 767-62500; e-mail: adac@adac.de).

Automobil Club von Deutschland (AvD), 16 Lyoner Strasse 60528 Frankfurt am Main (tel: 660-60; fax: 660-6789; e-mail: avd@avd.de).

Deutsche Bahn (railway operator), 2 Potsdamer Platz, 10785 Berlin (tel: 297-0; fax: 297-1961; e-mail: info@bahn.de; internet site: http://www.bahn.de/index_e.html).

Lufthansa, 2-6 Von Gablenz Strasse, 50679 Cologne (tel: 696-0; fax: 696-3002; internet site: http://www.lufthansa.co.uk).

National tourist organisation offices

Deutsche Zentrale für Tourismus, Beethovenstrasse 69, 60325 Frankfurt am Main (tel: 757-20; fax: 751-903; e-mail: info@d-z-t.com).

Ministries

Office of the Federal Chancellor, 1 Schlossplatz, 10178 Berlin (tel: 400-0; fax: 400-01818; e-mail: internetpost@bundeskanzler.de).

Ministry of Consumer Protection, Food and Agriculture, Rochusstrasse 1, 53123 Bonn (tel: 529-05291; fax: 529-4262; e-mail: internet@bmvel.bund.de).

Ministry of Defence, 18 Stauffenbergstrasse, 10785 Berlin (tel: 200-400; fax: 200-48333; e-mail: poststelle@bmvg.bund.400.de).

Ministry of Economic Co-operation and Development, 40 Friedrich Ebert Allee, 53113 Bonn (tel: 535-0; fax: 535-3500; e-mail: poststelle@bmz.bund.de).

Ministry of Economy and Labour, 36 Scharnhorststrasse, 10115 Berlin (tel: 615-0; fax: 615-7010; e-mail: info@bmwa.bund.de).

Ministry of Education and Research, 2 Heinemannstrasse, 53175 Bonn-Bad Godesberg (tel: 57-0; fax: 573-601; e-mail:bmbf@bmbf.bund.de).

Ministry of the Environment, Nature Conservation and Nuclear Safety, 6 Alexanderplatz, 10178 Berlin (tel: 305-0; fax: 305-4375; e-mail: service@bmu.de).

Ministry of Families, Senior Citizens, Women and Youth, 42 Taubenstrasse, 10117 Berlin (tel: 206-550; fax: 206-551145; e-mail: poststelle@bmfsfj.bund.de).

Ministry of Finance, 97 Wilhelmstrasse, 10117 Berlin (tel: 682-0; fax: 682-4420; e-mail: poststelle@bmf.bund.de).

Ministry of Foreign Affairs, 1 Werderscher Markt, 10117 Berlin (tel: 500-000; fax: 500-3402; e-mail: poststelle@auswaertiges-amt.de).

Ministry of Health, 78a Am Propsthof, 53121 Bonn (tel: 941-0; fax: 941-4900; e-mail: info@bmg.bund.de).

Ministry of the Interior, 101 Alt-Moabit, 10559 Berlin (tel: 681-0; fax: 681-2926; e-mail: poststelle@bmi.bund.de).

Ministry of Justice, 37 Mohrenstrasse, 10117 Berlin (tel: 202-570; fax: 259-525; e-mail: poststelle@bmj.bund.de).

Ministry of Transport, Construction and Housing, 44 Invalidenstrasse, 10115 Berlin (tel: 200-80; fax: 200-81920; e-mail: buergerinfo@bmvbw.bund.de).

Deutsche Bundestag, Platz der Republik 1, 11011 Berlin (tel.: 227-0; fax:

2273-6878 or 2273-6979; internet: www.bundestag.de).

Other useful addresses

American Embassy, 4-5 Neustädtische Kirchstrasse , 10117 Berlin (tel: 830-50; fax: 238-6290).

Aussenhandelsvereinigung des Deutschen Einzelhandels (Ave) (foreign trade association of the German retail trade), 1 Mauritiussteinweg, 50676 Cologne 1 (tel: 921-8340; fax: 921-8346; e-mail: info@ave-koeln.de).

Ausstellungs-und Messe-Ausschuss der Deutschen Wirtschaft (Auma) (trade fair industry association), 9 Littenstrasse, 10179 Berlin (tel: 240-000; fax: 240-00263; e-mail: info@auma.de).

British Embassy, 70-71 Wilhelmstrasse, 10117 Berlin (tel: 201-840; fax: 201-84123; e-mail: info@britischebotschaft.de).

Bundesagentur für Aussenwirtschaft (bfai) (German Office for Foreign Trade), 87-93 Agrippastrasse, 50676 Cologne (tel: 205-70; fax: 205-7212; e-mail: info@bfai.de).

Bundesanstalt für Arbeit (federal labour office), 106 Regensburger Strasse, 90478 Nuremberg (tel: 179-0; fax: 179-3600; e-mail: zentralamt@arbeitsamt.de).

Bundesverband der Deutschen Industrie (Bdi) (industry federation), Haus der Deutschen Wirtschaft, 29 Breite Strasse, 10178 Berlin (tel: 202-80; fax: 202-82450; e-mail: info@bdi-online.de).

Bundesverband des Deutschen Gross-und Aussenhandels (wholesale and foreign trade federation), Haus des Handels, 1A Am Weidendamm, 10117 Berlin (tel: 590-09950; fax: 590-099519; e-mail: info@bga.de).

Bundesvereinigung der Deutschen Arbeitgeberverbände (BDA) (employers' associations federation), Haus der Deutschen Wirtschaft, 29 Breite Strasse, 10178 Berlin (tel: 203-30; fax: 203-31055; e-mail: info@bda-online.de).

Büro des Beauftragten für Auslandsinvestitionen in Deutschland (foreign investment in Germany), 34 Markgrafenstrasse, 10117 Berlin (tel: 206-570; fax: 206-57111; e-mail: office@fdin.de).

Deutscher Gewerkschaftsbund (DGB) (trades unions federation), 2 Henrietta Herz Platz , 10178 Berlin (tel: 240-600; fax: 240-60324; e-mail: info@bundesvorstand.dgb.de).

Deutsches Institut für Wirtschaftsforschung (DIW) (economic research institute), 5 Königin Luise Strasse, 14195 Berlin (tel: 879-890; fax: 897-89200; e-mail: postmaster@diw.de).

Deutsche Presse-Agentur (dpa) (news agency), 38 Mittelweg, 20148 Hamburg (tel: 411-30; fax: 411-32219; e-mail: info@hbg.dpa.de).

German Convention Bureau, 48 Münchener Strasse, 60329 Frankfurt am Main (tel: 242-9300; fax: 242-93026; e-mail: info@gcb.de).

German Embassy (US), 4645 Reservoir Road, NW, Washington DC 20007 (tel: (+1-202) 298-4000; fax: (+1-202) 298-4249; e-mail: ge-embus@ix.netcom.com).

Industrial Investment Council (IIC), 57 Charlottenstrasse, 10117 Berlin (tel: 209-45660; fax: 209-45666; e-mail: info@iic.de).

Presse- und Informationsamt der Bundesregierung (government press office), 84 Dorotheenstrasse, 10117 Berlin (tel: 272-0; fax: 272-1365; e-mail: InternetPost@bundesregierung).

Statisches Bundesamt (federal statistical office), 11 Gustav Stresemann Ring, 65189 Wiesbaden (tel: 752-405; fax: 724-000; e-mail: pressestelle@stba.bund400.de; internet site: www.statistik-bund.de/e_home.htm).

Wirtschaftsförderung Berlin (Berlin Business Development Corpration), Ludwig Erhard Haus, 85 Fasanenstrasse, 10623 Berlin (tel: 399-800; fax: 399-80239; e-mail: info@wf-berlin.de).

Zentralverband der Deutschen Werbewirtschaft (ZAW) (advertising industry federation), 17 Villichgasse, 53177 Bonn (tel: 820-920; fax: 357-583; e-mail: zaw@zaw.de).

National news agency: DPA (Deutsche Presse-Agentur), PO Box 13 02 82, 20102; Mittelweg 38 20148, Hamburg (tel: 404-113; email: info@dpa.com).

Other news agencies: Pressetext Deutschland (business news):www.pressetext.de

Internet sites

Gateway site to web directory (in German with translation facilities): www.dino-online.de/

German-British Chamber of Commerce: www.germanbritishchamber.co.uk

German Government Website: www.bundesregierung.de

Germany Business Finder: www.infospace.com/uk.telegr/intldb/bizfindint.htm?QO=DE

Germany Technical Corporation: www.gtz.de/home/english/index.html

Rentenbank: www.rentenbank.de

State Bank of Baden-Württemberg: www.l-bank.de

Tourist Board: www.germany-tourism.de

Yellow pages: http://english.branchenbuch.com

Ghana

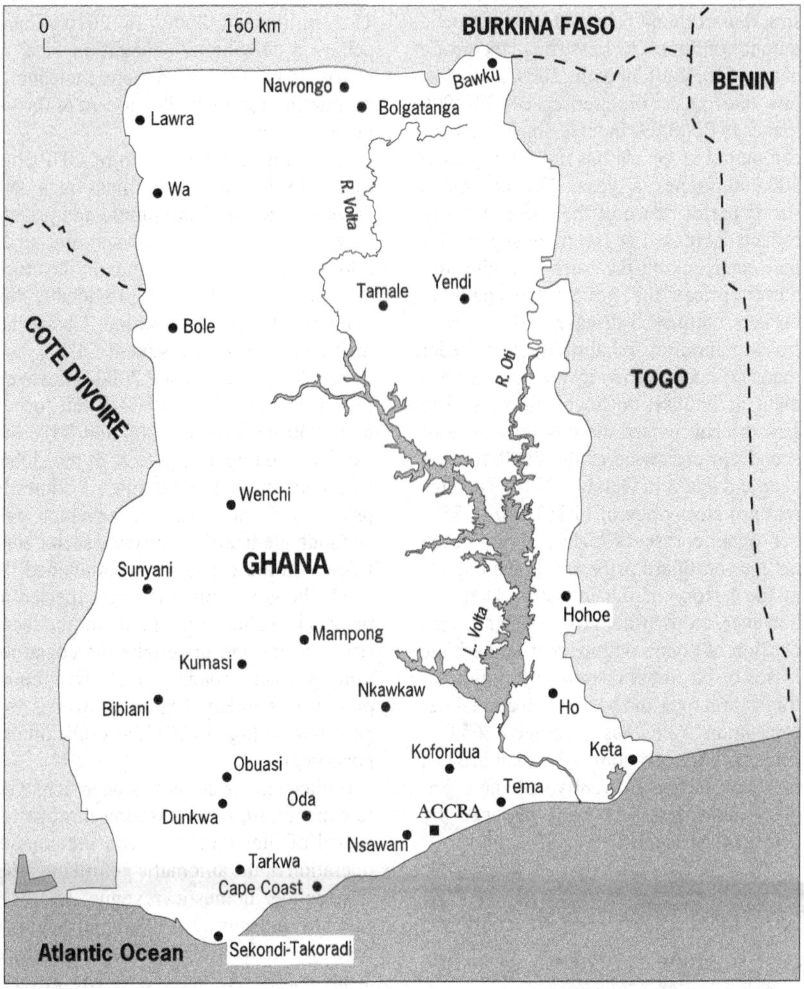

After one of Africa's closest ever presidential elections in December 2008 – John Evans Atta Mills (NDC) won 50.23 per cent and his rival, Nana Addo Dankwa Akufo-Addo (NPP) 49.77 per cent – the government of Ghana once again changed parties pretty smoothly.

According to the *African Economic Outlook 2011* (AEO), published jointly by the African Development Bank and the Organisation for Economic Co-operation and Development the Ghanaian economy has continued to perform well over the last decade, with consistently increasing annual growth rates from 4.2 per cent in 2001 to 7.3 per cent in 2008. However, in 2009 the growth rate dipped to 4.7 per cent, reflecting the fallout of the global economic crises. The change in political leadership and the inevitable sense of uncertainty in policy strategies and direction associated with elections, slowed investor activity only temporarily. In 2010 the economy recovered to achieve an estimated growth rate of 5.9 per cent. Growth is projected to surge to 12.0 per cent in 2011 as Ghana exports crude oil for the first time. Oil output is projected to contribute 5.3 percentage points to this growth. It is projected to be slightly lower at about 11.0 per cent in 2012, an election year, when increased uncertainty may dampen investor confidence, and after the initial surge generated by oil exports.

KEY FACTS

Official name: Republic of Ghana

Head of State: President John Evans Atta Mills (NDC) (from 7 Jan 2009)

Head of government: President John Atta Mills (NDC)

Ruling party: National Democratic Congress (NDC) (from 7 Jan 2008)

Area: 239,460 square km

Population: 24.22 million (2010; census figure)

Capital: Accra

Official language: English

Currency: Cedi (GH¢) = 100 pesewas (re-denominated 3 July 2007)

Exchange rate: GH¢1.60 per US$ (Oct 2011); (re-denominated 3 July 2007; 4 zeros removed)

GDP per capita: US$1,312 (2010)

GDP real growth: 5.70% (2010)

GDP: US$31.10 billion (2010)

Inflation: 10.70% (2010)

Balance of trade: -US$2.96 billion (2010)

Constitutional review

In 2010 the government set up a Constitutional Review Commission to review the 1992 constitution. The commission is expected to solicit and articulate the concerns of the public on amendments that may be required for a comprehensive review of the 1992 constitution, make recommendations to government for consideration and provide a draft bill for possible amendments. In 2010 public forums were held across the country on the public's views on the 1992 constitution. It is expected that a bill will be tabled in Parliament on the constitutional amendments in 2011.

The economy

Ghana's growth performance in 2010 was driven by the industrial sector with a 7 per cent growth rate, achieved largely through the impressive growth performance of the mining and energy sub-sectors which grew by 10.5 per cent and 13.3 per cent respectively compared with 8.2 per cent and 7.5 per cent respectively in 2009. The manufacturing sub-sector continued to record poor growth in 2010 with a provisional 1.0 per cent growth rate following the dismal -1.3 per cent growth rate recorded in 2009. Following years of poor performance by the manufacturing sector, its dominance in industry had been overtaken by the construction sub-sector in 2007. Indeed, Ghana's manufacturing continues to struggle with poor growth performance and renewed government effort at addressing the sub-sector's constraints is needed. Over the years tax increases on the sector and intensified import competition have continued to dampen prospects.

Agriculture

In 2010 agriculture grew at 4.8 per cent, lower than the 6.1 per cent in 2009. Crops output and livestock production suffered in 2010 from flooding in the northern regions of the country which caused the destruction of many farms. However, cocoa output continued to be strong, recording nearly 640,000 tonnes in 2009/10 to follow the peak production of 710,000 tonnes in 2008/09. Indeed, since 2004 cocoa output in Ghana has not fallen below 600,000 tonnes a year. The continued strong performance of the cocoa industry reflects increased government support for the sector, taking the form of higher domestic prices the government pays to farmers, improved disease and pest control programmes, rehabilitation of feeder roads in cocoa-growing areas, and payment of bonuses to cocoa farmers. The government revised the producer price of cocoa upward twice in the 2009/10 crop year and again in October 2010. The current producer price of GH¢3.200 (US$2) per tonne represents 75.15 per cent of the net free-on-board price and is the highest in the history of the industry. There is, however, a downside risk to Ghana's expansion of cocoa output, that is the huge losses of its forest resources through deforestation over the years. The annual deforestation rate has averaged 65,000 hectares per year, some of which are lost to cocoa farms. Currently, Ghana's primary rainforest has been reduced by nearly 90 per cent.

The services sector recorded a 6.1 per cent growth in 2010 compared with 5.9 per cent in 2009. Financial services and expansion in the telecommunications industry continued to spearhead growth of the sector in 2010. The telecommunications sub-sector expanded by 10.8 per cent in 2010 raising total telephone access lines to about 17 million in 2010 from 15.2 million in 2009. In 2010 Ghana achieved telephone penetration rate of nearly 74 per cent, with mobile telephony accounting for about 98 per cent of the total access lines.

The demand composition of GDP continues to indicate investment is a key driver of growth. Both public and private investments have remained strong since 2007, when sharp reductions in the stock of external public debt provided a big stimulus to capital formation. Ghana has maintained an investment-GDP ratio above 30 per cent since 2006. However, the investment share of GDP fell to just below 30 per cent in 2009 and 2010 because of the lingering effects of the global financial crisis. The volume of domestic private and public capital formation will be moderate in 2011 as private sector confidence in the economy is maintained. In 2011, the government is also expected to begin a huge housing scheme for the security services and undertake the construction of many roads, which will boost public investment. Export growth is expected to be high in 2011, as crude oil exports begin.

While some success has been achieved in expenditure rationalisation through removal of fuel subsidies with the smooth operation of the automatic petroleum pricing regime, domestic revenue mobilisation has not improved much, largely as a result of the lack of new measures aimed at increasing the tax effort. The government, therefore, continues to accumulate large domestic payment arrears. In 2010 these payment arrears were estimated at 12 per cent of GDP.

The payment arrears have a significant negative impact on the economy. They constrain private sector activities, thereby slowing down growth and employment creation. Indeed, many private entrepreneurs, especially in the construction sector, complain of an inability to revamp their businesses because of the government's failure to honour its payment obligations to them. In 2010 lower private capital formation was largely attributed to these arrears. Also, government arrears in transfers to statutory funds delay the provision of the economic infrastructure

KEY INDICATORS — Ghana

	Unit	2006	2007	2008	2009	2010
Population	m	21.42	21.97	22.53	23.11	24.22
Gross domestic product (GDP)	US$bn	12.89	15.00	16.70	15.50	31.10
GDP per capita	US$	593	683	739	671	1,312
GDP real growth	%	6.2	5.7	7.3	3.5	5.7
Inflation	%	10.9	10.7	16.5	19.3	10.7
Industrial output	% change	8.6	5.1	8.1	4.5	–
Agricultural output	% change	5.5	2.4	5.1	7.6	–
Exports (fob) (goods)	US$m	3,685.0	4,172.1	5,269.7	5,839.7	7,960.1
Imports (fob) (goods)	US$m	7,264.0	8,066.1	10,268.5	8,046.3	10,922.1
Balance of trade	US$m	-3,579.0	-3,894.0	-4,998.8	-2,206.6	-2,962.0
Current account	US$m	-1,381.0	-2,894.0	-3,543.1	-1,198.5	-2,700.5
Total reserves minus gold	US$m	2,090.3	–	–	–	–
Foreign exchange	US$m	2,089.1	–	–	–	–
Exchange rate	per US$	0.92	0.94	1.05	1.40	1.43

required to support growth and deliver much needed social services.

In 2010 both government revenue and expenditure fell. Government expenditure dropped from 41.5 per cent of GDP in 2009 to 39.7 per cent in 2010 reflecting a decline in recurrent expenditure. At the same time, all the revenue components declined in 2010. The overall budget deficit increased marginally in 2010 to 7.9 per cent of GDP from 7.6 per cent of GDP in 2009.

The government has made a more determined effort to enhance revenue mobilisation in 2011 with a number of proposed tax policies including review of exemptions, widening the tax base and increasing the marginal tax rate. Improving revenue mobilisation in 2011 is indeed critical to the implementation of the government's new wage policy – the Single Spine Salary (SSS) policy. This pay policy is a unified salary structure that places all public sector employees in one vertical structure and ensures that jobs within the same job category are paid within the same pay range. The SSS replaces the system of over 90 different salary structures as well as over 65 different types of allowances that has been in existence in the Ghana public service. Although, the implementation of this new wage policy is spread over a period of five years, the wage bill for fiscal 2011 is estimated to be one of the highest in sub-Saharan Africa. Also, over 75 per cent of the total wage bill and the associated increases resulting from the salary structure go to employees in only three ministries, departments and agencies (MDAs), namely education, health and local government. Thus, implementing the new pay policy could result in reducing social spending on a sustainable basis if no new additional resources are mobilised.

In spite of the new tax initiatives and the expectations of oil revenues the government's total revenue position is expected to stagnate in 2011 and 2012. Indeed, oil revenue is expected to contribute at least 6 per cent of total revenue. Fiscal revenues from crude oil exports are forecast at US$700 million in 2010 rising to US$3 billion by 2013. Overall, available estimates indicate that crude oil exports will be in the range of US$2 billion to US$3.2 billion between 2010 and 2030. The overall budget deficit is projected to fall to around 7.7 per cent of GDP in 2011 and further down to about 5.0 per cent in 2012 as government revenues benefit from oil receipts.

The Bank of Ghana's (BoG) primary monetary policy objective remains the reduction of inflation to single digits, within a formal inflation-targeting framework. The BoG also seeks to dampen exchange rate fluctuations. In 2010 the thrust of monetary policy was to deepen macroeconomic stability through lowering the rate of inflation.

International trade

The main aim of Ghana's trade policy is to enhance international competitiveness and secure greater market access for the country's products. The composition of Ghana's exports has not changed significantly for a long time. They have been dominated by gold and cocoa with about 41 per cent and 24 per cent shares respectively, reflecting a lack of significant progress at export diversification. However, with the export of oil from 2010, this structure will change but still reflect little diversification away from primary commodity exports.

The private sector

Ghana's effort to improve its business environment continues to yield positive results. Private sector response to the government's programme has been positive. In 2009 the change in political administration and the associated uncertainty regarding the direction of economic policy were largely responsible for a dip in Ghana's business climate with a slip of five places on the World Bank's *Doing Business* ranking. The situation, however, reversed in 2010 with a position change by ten places to 67th out of 183 countries. The improvement in the country's *Doing Business* ranking in 2011 was largely accounted for by improvement in access to credit where the country's ranking improved to 46th. Other improvements were in the areas of starting a business, paying taxes and enforcing contracts. Ghana, however, slipped in the areas of registering property, trading across borders, closing businesses, protecting investors and dealing with construction permits.

Financial sector

The banking sector's support for private sector development has been growing. In 2010 the banks extended more financing to the private sector. The banks allocated significant proportion of deposits to long-term investments, which is a good sign of their commitment to long-term development. The Ghana Stock Exchange (GSE) continues to develop with improved market turnover and market capitalisation. The GSE was ranked the most innovative African Stock Exchange for 2010 by the New York based *Africa Investor*. Market turnover, in terms of number of shares traded, increased by about 224 per cent with 94.4 per cent improvement in shares values. Market capitalisation also improved by about 25 per cent in 2010. The improved performance of the stock market in 2010 was largely driven by stocks in the banking and finance sector, agriculture, food and beverage, and energy sectors. The improved performance of the stock market in 2010 could also be explained by a possible shift of funds from the money market in favour of the capital market on account of the lowering of the Treasury bill rate in 2010. However, the fact that there were no new listings on the GSE in 2010 raises questions about the depth of the exchange. The outlook over the next few years hinges strongly on the continued improvement in the macro fundamentals.

Ghana's economic relations with the rest of the world have seen a remarkable shift in recent times from close ties with advanced economies to growing links with emerging ones in the areas of trade, aid and foreign direct investment (FDI). Between 2003 and 2009, the value of Ghana's exports to advanced economies dropped from 65 per cent to 50 per cent against an increase from 25 per cent to 36 per cent in those to emerging and developing economies. Similarly, the value of Ghana's imports from emerging economies has witnessed a significant increase from 50 per cent to 59 per cent and a drop of 8 percentage points to 40 per cent in those from advanced economies during the same period. The share of imports from countries in Africa averages 25 per cent.

During the past decade the destination of Ghana's exports has increasingly shifted away from countries such as the United States, Belgium, France, Germany and Japan to India, Malaysia, Mongolia and Ukraine. At the same time, imports from India, China, Brazil, Nigeria and Côte d'Ivoire have risen considerably while those from the United Kingdom, the United States, Belgium and France have either stagnated or declined. The major increase in imports value from emerging economies came from China which saw an increase in exports to Ghana from US$354.2 million in 2003 to US$1.78 billion in 2009 resulting in a rise in China's share of total import value to Ghana from 9 per cent to 17 per cent.

Unemployment

Unemployment and underemployment remain major problems, reflecting the failure of past economic growth to generate substantial formal employment in the private sector, and the lack of job-relevant skills of the majority of the workforce. Ghana's labour market is still characterised by the dominance of employment in agriculture and a large informal economy. Government figures indicate that currently two out of three working adults are employed. The national unemployment rate is estimated at only 3 per cent by government sources. The low rate of unemployment in the country disguises the high levels of unemployment and underemployment inherent in the large informal sector.

Indeed, the government's definition of unemployment excludes the large numbers of jobless people who may be available for work but do not necessarily seek work, for various reasons. Given the large informal sector where the genuine unemployed are engaging in any economic activity simply to survive, concerted effort is needed to reduce the numbers in employment that may be considered as vulnerable, as well as the 'working poor'.

Risk assessment

Politics	Good
Economy	Good
Regional stability	Fair

COUNTRY PROFILE

Historical profile

1482 A trading settlement was set up by the Portuguese at Elmina.
1821 The British Gold Coast was formed. The area under British influence grew with the addition of the Danish Gold Coast in 1850 and the Dutch Gold Coast in 1871. Four wars were fought with the Ashanti people between 1863 and 1896.
1874 The British proclaimed the coastal area a crown colony.
1914 The German Protectorate of Togoland (1884–1914) surrendered to British and French troops in August.
1916 Togoland was separated into French Togoland and British Togoland following the ratification of the Treaty of Versailles on 20 July 1922 when Togoland became a League of Nations Class B Mandate.
1925 First legislative council elections took place.
1945–1957 An independence movement grew under British rule.
1956 In a May plebiscite 58 per cent of residents of British Togoland voted to join Ghana on independence.
1957 Ghana (formerly The Gold Coast) was granted independence from Britain with Dr Kwame Nkrumah as prime minister.
1960 The country voted to become a republic. Dr Kwame Nkrumah of the People's Convention Party became president.
1964 Nkrumah declared the country a single political party state.
1966 The military overthrew Nkrumah and installed the National Liberation Council, a transitional government.
1969 Dr Kofi Busia secured victory in the parliamentary elections and became prime minister.
1972 After another military coup, Col Ignatius Acheampong took control of the country.
1978 Acheampong was deposed by the military and Lt-Gen F Akuffo, previously chief of the defence staff, became president.
1979 Akuffo's government was destabilised in an unsuccessful coup launched by Flt-Lt Jerry J Rawlings. Dr Hilla Limann of the People's National Party (PNP) was later elected as president. A new constitution was promulgated.
1981 Jerry J Rawlings took power through a second military coup, dissolved parliament and ruled through the Provisional National Defence Council (PNDC).
1983–89 Discontent with the regime and its economic ineffectiveness led to a series of attempted coups, student unrest and alleged anti-government conspiracies. The government attempted to impose fiscal and monetary discipline and bring the economy into alignment with market trends and influences. The cedi was devalued by 6,300 per cent in 1987. Over 1.1 million Ghanaians were expelled from Nigeria and returned home, placing great strain on limited resources.
1990 A national referendum on the restoration of multi-party politics was demanded.
1992 A referendum endorsed a new constitution to allow a multi-party system. Jerry Rawlings was elected president and his National Democratic Congress (NDC) secured an overall majority in legislative elections.
1993 The constitution came into force and the Fourth Republic was inaugurated.
1996 Jerry Rawlings won the presidential election and his party, the NDC, won the legislative elections.
1997 Ghanaian diplomat, Kofi Annan was appointed General Secretary of the United Nations.
2000 John Kufuor and the New Patriotic Party (NPP) took power. Kufuor became the first elected president in Ghana's history to succeed another elected president.
2002 Ethnic battles in the north led to the murder of Ghana's second most important tribal king, Ya Naa Yakubu Andani of the Dagbon people. His death led to the resignation of two senior government ministers.
2004 The former president, Jerry Rawlings, testified before the National Reconciliation Commission investigating human rights offences during the early years of his rule. Incumbent John Kufuor (NPP) and the ruling NPP retained power.
2005 The first fall in HIV/Aids infection rates in five years was reported.
2007 The cedi was re-valued when four zeros were removed. The new banknote was referred to as the Ghana Cedi. 'Substantial oil deposits' were found in Ghanaian territorial waters.
2008 Tribal violence between the Kusasi and Mamprusi people led to the deaths of 13 people in Bawku. A heavy military presence and a curfew were needed to bring peace, while the president called for talks over a contested chieftaincy to be resolved. In parliamentary elections the opposition NDC won 114 seats (out of 230), the ruling NPP 107; after two rounds of presidential elections opposition leader John Evans Atta Mills (NDC) won 50.23 per cent and his rival, Nana Addo Dankwa Akufo-Addo (NPP) won 49.77 per cent.
2009 President Atta Mills took office. US President Obama visited and addressed parliament, citing four key areas that were critical to Africa's success: democracy, opportunity, health and the peaceful resolution of conflict. The IMF agreed to a three-year loan of US$600 million, to help Ghana grappled with the global economic crisis.
2010 In March, the World Bank agreed to fund the US$258 million refurbishment of the 998.8km West African coastal corridor road, running through Ghana from Abidjan (Côte d'Ivoire) to Lagos (Nigeria). In July, Equatorial Guinea began export of two million barrels of crude oil a year to Ghana. Dividends from the operators of the Prestea-Bogoso and Wassa mines in the west of the country amounted to US$6.6 million by the second half of the year. The first oil from the offshore Jubilee Field was pumped on 15 December.
2011 On 13 July, the African Development Bank approved a US$70 million loan and US$41.3 grant to finance the poverty reduction and business environment support programme (PRBESP), with the intention of improving the private sector business environment and public financial management. Approval followed GDP growth figures for 2010 of 7.7 per cent.

Political structure

Constitution

The constitution came into force on 7 January 1993. It is based on the US model. It allows for a multi-party system.
Ghana has 10 administrative regions which are subdivided into districts.

Between 2000–04, 30 new constituencies were created.

Form of state

Unitary republic

The executive

Executive power is vested in the president, vice president and Council of Ministers; both the vice president and the Council of Ministers are appointed by the president. The president is elected by universal suffrage for a maximum of two four-year terms.

If no candidate receives more than 50 per cent of votes in the presidential election, a new election between the two candidates with the highest number of votes is to take place within 21 days.

National legislature

The unicameral Parliament of Ghana has 230 members directly elected in single-seat constituencies to serve four-year terms.

Legal system

The legal system is based on English common law and local customary law.

Last elections

7 December 2008 (parliamentary); 7 and 28 December 2008 (presidential and runoff)

Results: Parliamentary: National Democratic Congress (NDC) won 116 seats, New Patriotic Party (NPP) 107, Independents four, People's National Convention (PNC) two and Convention People's Party (CPP) one.

Presidential (first round): Nana Addo Dankwa Akufo-Addo (NPP) won 49.13 per cent, John Evans Atta Mills (NDC) 47.92 per cent; turnout was 69.5 per cent. No other candidate won more than 2 per cent of the vote. Second round: Atta Mills (NDC) won 50.23 per cent, Nana Akufo-Addo (NPP) 49.77 per cent; turnout was 72.9 per cent.

Next elections

December 2012 (parliamentary and presidential)

Political parties

Ruling party

National Democratic Congress (NDC) (from 7 Jan 2008)

Main opposition party

New Patriotic Party (NPP)

Population

24.22 million (2010; census figure)

Last census: March 2000: 18,912,079

Population density: 79 inhabitants per square km. Urban population: 36 per cent (1995—2001).

Annual growth rate: 2.3 per cent 1994–2004 (WHO 2006)

Ethnic make-up

Akan (including Ashanti) (44 per cent), Dagomba (16 per cent), Ewe (13 per cent), Ga-Adangbe (8.3 per cent), Guan (3.7 per cent), Gurma (3.5 per cent).

Religions

Christian (43 per cent), traditional religions (38 per cent), Muslim (12 per cent). There is complete freedom of worship in Ghana.

Education

Since the government removed school fees for primary education in 2005, record numbers of children have been enrolled. Over 600,000 more children of ages 5–13 were enrolled, with girls being the greater proportion of new students. The World Bank is due to give a grant of US$11 million in 2006, to provide more teachers, build new classrooms and purchase textbooks, in recognition for the government's efforts in achieving an objective of the UN Millennium Development Goals in education.

Government expenditure on education is about a quarter of total government spending.

Ghana boasts the oldest university in sub-Saharan Africa – at Legon in Accra.

Literacy rate: 74 per cent adult rate; 92 per cent youth rate (15–24) (Unesco 2005).

Enrolment rate: 69 per cent primary enrollment (2005–06 academic year, up from 59 per cent in 2004–05) (2006).

Pupils per teacher: 33 in primary schools.

Health

Around five million children were vaccinated against polio over three days in 2009, sponsored by the UN Children's fund, the World Health Organisation and the Ghana health ministry and costing US$2.5 million.

HIV/Aids

The fragile infection rate trend was down from 3.6 per cent in 2003 to 3.1 in 2004. Officials will not laud the result as a victory until the trend shows a three-year steady decline. In the meantime infection rates of other sexually transmitter deseases (STD) are showing a rise among young people indicating unprotected sex. Authorities are planning to switch emphasis A survey in 2003 indicated there were over 350,000 people living with HIV (UNAIDS).

HIV prevalence: 3.1 per cent aged 15–49 in 2004. Prevalence in the north is lower averaging 1.8 per cent, while in the south it is 6.5 per cent (government figures).

Life expectancy: 57 years, 2004 (WHO 2006)

Fertility rate/Maternal mortality rate: 4.2 births per woman, 2004 (WHO 2006)

Child (under 5 years) mortality rate (per 1,000): 59 per 1,000 live births; 25 per cent of children aged under five are malnourished (World Bank).

Head of population per physician: 0.15 physicians per 1,000 people, 2004 (WHO 2006)

Welfare

The government's policies of structural adjustment have hit urban Ghanaians hard as the contraction of industry and the removal of state subsidies have led to increased unemployment, crime and poverty. In a bid to dampen the impact of reform, the government adopted a US$100 million Programme of Action to Mitigate the Social Costs of Adjustment (Pamscad) in the late 1990s to help cushion the shock of redundancies or redeployment as a result of the ERP. It involves 23 projects under five main categories: community initiatives, employment (including food-for-work schemes), redeployment (compensation for those made redundant), basic needs (self-help schemes) and education. Medium-term strategies are centred on the provision of primary health care.

Main cities

Accra (capital, estimated population 1.6 million in 2004), Kumasi (649,652), Tamale (278,676) Tema (209,250), Ashiaman (170,143), Obuasi (163,349), Teshi (109,927), Bolgatanga (93,100).

Languages spoken

There are over 25 major languages with numerous dialects. The principal languages spoken are Twi and Fante (spoken by the Akans), Ga, Hausa, Dagbani, Ewe and Nzema.

There is an official policy to encourage Ghanaians to be multilingual so French is also taught in most schools.

Official language/s

English

Media

Press freedom is respected and Ghana has a reputation as 'one of the most unfettered' in Africa. A government appointed commission regulates all media.

Press

Dailies: There are many newspapers on offer, all chasing a constricted advertising market hampered by government advertising being limited to state-owned publications and other advertisers tending to do business with only the larger publications. In English, the *Daily Graphic* (www.graphicghana.com) and *Ghanaian Times* (www.newtimesonline.com) are state-owned; the *Daily Guide* (http://dailyguideghana.com) is a tabloid, the conservative publication *The Statesman* (www.thestatesmanonline.com) is one of the oldest (although with a broken record) newspapers with a full range of articles, and the *Accra Daily Mail* (http://news.accra-mail.com).

Weeklies: In English, independent publications include the *The Ghanaian Chronicle* (www.ghanaian-chronicle.com), *Ghana Palaver* (www.ghana-palaver.com), with news and current affairs, *Public Agenda* (www.ghanaweb.com/public_agenda) is published twice weekly with social stories and *The Spectator* (http://spectator.newtimesonline.com) is a weekend edition of entertainment news. *The Mirror* is state-owned.
Business: In English, the *Business and Financial Times* (http://bftghanaonline.com), provides comprehensive information. Major newspapers have sections on business and finance.
Periodicals: In English, *The Heritage* (www.theheritagenews.com) is a month political review and the *Christian Messenger* is a conservative Presbyterian monthly. The *Ghana Review International* (http://ghanareview.com) is a foreign publication of national news.

Broadcasting

The state-run Ghana Broadcasting Corporation (GBC) is the national public operator.
Radio: GBC Radio (www.gbcghana.com) has a network of three stations with radio service in English, Hausa and other African languages and an external radio service in English, French and Hausa.
Private, commercial stations include Vibe FM (www.vibefm.com.gh) Citi FM (www.citifmonline.com), Solid FM (www.mysolidonline.com) and Space FM (www.spacefmradio.com).
Television: GBC operates Ghana TV (GTV) (www.gbcghana.com), which produces 80 per cent of locally made programmes. There are several private TV stations including TV3 (www.tv3.com.gh), Crystal TV and Media TV.

News agencies

National news agency: Ghana News Agency

Economy

The economy is sustained by agriculture. Ghana is the world's second-largest producer of cocoa after Côte d'Ivoire and exports palm oil, timber, coffee and coconuts, as well as other, non-traditional produce including pineapples, cashews and peppers. Domestic crops include among others, cassava, yams, rice and plantains. Agriculture constitutes over 33 per cent of GDP and industry over 25 per cent. Ghana's natural resources in gold, oil, diamonds, bauxite and timber have resulted in an advanced extraction industry and the service industries that support them. The service sector constitutes over 40 per cent of GDP, led by government services, finance and energy production. The manufacturing sector, which is relatively small (over 6 per cent of GDP), processes agricultural produce into foodstuffs, as well as producing garments, steel (using scrap metal), timber products, simple consumer goods and vehicles assembly.
GDP growth was 7.2 in 2008 when global commodities prices were at a record high, but as prices fell later GDP growth also dropped to 4.1 per cent in 2009, but rising to an estimated 5 per cent in 2010. High inflation has been a long-term problem, spiking in 2009 at 19.3 per cent before falling back to a more typical 10.6 per cent in 2010.
In July 2009 the IMF agreed to a three-year general loan of US$600 million and a further US$450 through a special facility set up to help poor countries. The money was intended to reduce the budget deficit and support the currency. Ghanaian exports of cocoa and gold had left the economy 'relatively resilient' during the global economic crisis, but with oil production beginning in December 2010 and the expected US$1 billion and boost GDP by 5 per cent per year will support Ghana's request for funds.
The World Bank ranks Ghana as a low-income country and per capita income was US$732 in 2008, which fell to US$663 in 2009 before recovering to US$762 in 2010. The UN reported in 2010 that Ghana had a poverty headcount rate of 30.1 per cent and that 46.4 per cent of poor households were subject to three or more indicators of deprivation. Remittances were US$114 million in 2009 (0.7 per cent of GDP), rising to an estimated US$119 million in 2010.
With its modern port Ghana's importance as a trading hub has grown for foreign investors but it needs to improve roads and port efficiency before it can take full advantage of all that this facility can provide for the country.

External trade

Ghana is a member of the Economic Community of West African States (Ecowas), which was set up to promote economic integration among members. It is a member of the Anglophone, West African Monetary Zone (WAMZ), which is due to introduce a common currency. WAMZ will eventually be merged with the Francophone-members' currency to produce a single currency (the eco) for the region.

Imports

Principal imports are petroleum, manufacturing equipment, raw materials and foodstuffs.
Main sources: China (12 per cent total of total), Nigeria (9 per cent), US (8 per cent).

Exports

Principal exports are cocoa, gold, timber, tuna, bauxite, aluminium, manganese ore diamonds and agricultural produce.
Main destinations: South Africa (typically 44 per cent of total), The Netherlands (12 per cent), India (5 per cent).

Agriculture

Farming

Agricultural land – around 14,600 hectares (ha) – accounts for almost 65 per cent of the total land area. There is over 6330ha of arable and permanently cultivated land and around 8350ha of pastureland.
Ghana is a leading cocoa producer in the world, providing 19 per cent of the total. Cocoa still has major importance to the economy providing around 60 per cent of export earnings. Government monopoly on cocoa sales was removed in 1993; private trading companies purchase directly from farms.
Other cash crops for export include bananas, kola nuts, limes, coffee, copra and palm kernels.
Crops grown for the local agribusiness include rubber, sugar, cotton, and oil palms.
Subsistence farming of food crops (cassava, plantains, rice, maize, sorghum, millet, yams) has been affected by prolonged drought and shortages of fertilisers, but there has been a recovery, particularly in maize and rice production.

Fishing

The annual domestic fish catch averages 300,000 tonnes, satisfying over 75 per cent of domestic demand. Fish farms have been set up in the north in an effort to achieve total fish self-sufficiency.
Tuna is one of Ghana's non-traditional exports, but the maximum sustainable yield from the 28,000 square km territorial waters is far from being realised.

Forestry

Ghana has around 39 per cent of forest cover in addition to 37 per cent of woodland. There are over 200 species of tropical hardwood.
Most commercial forestry is concentrated in the south. The extent of productive forest reserves is put at 1.2 million hectares, containing 190 million cubic metres of potential wood volume in trees over 30cm in diameter. Timber is Ghana's third-largest export commodity. The current export level of commercially viable species and sizes (trees with diameters of 70cm or more) can only be maintained if reliance on popular hardwoods is lessened and exploitation of lesser known species is increased. Domestic demand for wood for fuel is far greater than the permissible cut of one million cubic metres.

The National Forests Protection Strategy resulted in decreasing deforestation during the 1990s. The strategy plans to make the private sector responsible for the costs of forest depletion. The Environmental Protection Agency (EPA) monitors developments and policy affecting wildlife, forests and mining activities.

A local non-government body is developing a bamboo and rattan industry instead of available timber.

In 2009 the European Union (EU) and Ghana signed an agreement that ensures only legally harvested timber is exported to Ghana's most valuable markets in the EU. Around 43 per cent of total exports and 33 per cent of total volume of Ghanaian timber is sold to the EU and the agreement is expected to further the country's reforms of its forestry sector, promoting investment, sustainability and poverty alleviation.

Industry and manufacturing

The industrial sector accounts for over 27 per cent of annual GDP, of which, manufacturing only contributes 9.0 per cent; services are the second largest sector in the country and accounted for over 30 per cent of the economy.

The privatisation and commercialisation of Ghana's public sector since the mid-1990s led to a severe contraction in manufacturing as jobs were shed, firms liquidated and the economy flooded by cheap imports. Officials believe foreign investment offers the key to the development of the sector.

Ghana's medium-sized manufacturing industries include aluminium smelting, paper and cement manufacturing and petroleum refining. The aluminium smelter at Tema, the Volta Aluminium Company (Valco), is the country's most capital-intensive enterprise. Potential production capacity is 200,000 tonnes, but only a fraction of this has been produced in recent years.

The government is seeking to expand important agri-based industries and textile manufacturing. It is also encouraging the establishment of more industries geared to processing local raw materials to replace imported inputs.

Tourism

Tourism has developed into a major foreign currency earner and the sector is one of the fastest-growing in Africa. An ambitious 15-year development plan, exploiting tourism as a means of improving the economy, aimed at increasing arrivals to one million by 2010. However, for this target to be achieved, more needed to be done to improve infrastructure and travel connections. Eco-tourism sites are being developed for European and the US markets, other amenities will cater for conventions, adventure holidays and the historical slave trade heritage sites.

Mining

Mining typically accounts for 18 per cent of GDP and employs 3 per cent of the workforce. Minerals resources include gold, manganese, diamonds, bauxite, iron ore, limestone, silica, columbite, tantalite and several rich clays.

Gold is the principal mineral export and Ghana is Africa's second-largest gold producer, after South Africa. Ashanti Goldfields Corporation (AGC) accounts for 85 per cent of total output. The other major producer is the State Gold Mines Corporation. Recoverable gold reserves are estimated at 57,000 tonnes. AGC has invested US$200 million in two new mines, while Newmont (the largest mining company globally) was given the go-ahead to begin the Ahafo South Project, a greenfields site, in 2005.

The US-based, World Food Association Organisation (WFAO) began purchasing the mineral rights to 300 acres of alluvial gold mines in 2009 as it expanded its farming operations in Ghana. The mines, some pre-existing and being refurbished, are in Kibi (in the southeast of the country) and each are expected to produce 10–20kg of gold dust per month. With the proceeds from the mines, WFAO intends to set up large farming entities with local people as co-operators.

Diamonds and manganese each account for 1–2 per cent of export earnings. Diamonds (mostly industrial) are mined by Ghana Consolidated Diamonds Ltd in the Birim Basin. Ghana is the eighth-largest diamond producer in the world. Manganese ore is mined at Nsuta by the National Manganese Corporation. Manganese production averages 280,000 tonnes per annum.

Ghana has vast bauxite reserves near Kibi, but heavy transport/extraction costs have limited commercial development of local bauxite for use by the Valco aluminium smelter.

Ghana granted mining licences in its protected forest reserves to attract new foreign investment.

Hydrocarbons

Proven oil reserves have rapidly grown since 2000 when joint government and commercial oil companies began exploring Ghanaian territory. In 2007 commercial quantities of oil were found offshore in the Tano Basin by a consortium of Kosmos Energy, Anadarko Petroleum and Tullow Ghana in partnership with Ghana National Petroleum Corporation (GNPC), estimated at 2 billion barrels, although analysts believe undiscovered reserves are even greater. The US oil and gas company, ExxonMobil acquired a US$4 billion stake in the Jubilee Field, Africa's biggest deepwater offshore oil field, in October 2009. Production began in December 2010, beginning at 55,000 barrels per day (bpd) rising to 120,000bpd by mid-2011 and a maximum 250,000bpd at full production. The US-Kosmos Energy company announced confirmation of oil in its Odum drilling site, discovered offshore in Ghana's territorial waters, in December 2009.

Until domestic supplies are online, a substantial proportion of Ghana's 46,000bpd oil requirement is generally imported from Nigeria. Petroleum products account for about a quarter of the country's energy requirements.

The Tema Oil Refinery has a capacity of 45,000bpd. A residual catalytic cracking (RCC) unit has been installed to boost productivity and produce petroleum and liquefied petroleum gas (LPG) for export.

Natural gas reserves totalled 23.8 billion cubic metres, primarily located in the Tano fields. Natural gas is not used in domestic consumption, but rather is used to produce electricity for use domestically and commercially. The West African Gas Pipeline Project (WAGP) which links Nigeria, Ghana, Togo and Benin, supplying gas from Nigeria's gas fields, began delivering natural gas to Ghana in December 2008.

Ghana does not produce coal but imports minimal amounts of around 3,000 tonnes annually.

Energy

Ghana's installed electricity generating capacity is 1.73 gigawatt (GW), producing 8.8 billion kilowatt hours (kWh) per annum, the majority of which is produced by hydropower, to a total of 1.2GW. The Volta River Authority (VRA) has responsibility for the development, generation and national distribution of electricity. The 912MW Akosombo hydropower plant and the 160MW Kpong plant are run at capacity. The Chinese-funded Black Volta River, 400MW hydroelectric dam at Bui, was agreed in 2007, to be completed by 2012. Construction of the US$600m dam continues despite concerns about the environmental and social effects of the dam.

The thermal power station near Takoradi produces 300MW and is linked to the (WAGP) natural gas pipeline from Nigeria. Ghana is a net exporter of electricity to the power grids in Benin and Togo, from the Akosombo Plant on the Volta River.

Around 60 per cent of the population has access to electricity. In September 2008 a US$350 million credit facility was granted by the US to fund the implementation of the latest rural electrification programme, which has been underway since the 1980s.

Financial markets

Stock exchange

Ghana Stock Exchange (GSE)

Banking and insurance

Stability in money markets and low inflationary expectations following petroleum deregulation, led to a reduction in the prime interest rate of 16.5 per cent on 30 May 2005, down from 18.5 per cent which had remained unchanged since May 2004.

It was announced in March 2005 that the introduction of the shared currency, the Eco, in Ghana, Guinea, Nigeria, Sierra Leone and The Gambia, which was due in July 2005, would be postponed. The currency was proposed to facilitate trade and growth with an ultimate plan to merge it with the CFA franc.

Central bank

Bank of Ghana

Main financial centre

Accra

Time

GMT

Geography

Ghana's southern border is the Gulf of Guinea. To the north, east and west lie the states of Burkina Faso, Togo and Côte d'Ivoire. From north to south the country extends a distance of about 680 km.

The River Volta, which flows from the north to the south-east, is the most conspicuous landmark. There is a coastal area of thicket and mangrove which gives way in the east and north-east to more open plains and semi-deciduous forest. To the west and north-west of the coastal strip is high forest, which still covers the greater part of Ashanti and part of the Northern Region. The forest gives way in the north to Guinea savannah woodland; the extreme north-eastern corner of Ghana forms part of the drier Sudan savannah woodland.

Hemisphere

Northern

Climate

Ghana lies entirely within the tropics. In the northern savannah the climate is hot and dry, with intermittent rainfall during March–September. In the hot and humid forest regions there are two rainy seasons, during March–June and September–November. At the coast, which is only 4.5 degrees from the Equator, the heat is intense.

The capital city, Accra, is only 65 metres above sea level. The capital's hottest month is March, with temperatures of 24–32 degrees Celsius (C); August is the coldest month, with temperatures of 21–27 C. The annual rainfall in the capital averages 865mm. The driest month is December when rainfall averages 18mm, and the wettest month is June when rainfall averages 235mm.

Dress codes

Western-style clothes are usually worn for business purposes, including shorts for outdoor occupations. On social or ceremonial occasions, traditional costume or Western-style clothes are equally acceptable.

Local dress includes the expensive, hand-woven Kente cloth for which Ghana is famous: this is worn by men like a toga. Wearing any military clothing, such as camouflage jackets or trousers, or any clothing or items that may appear military in nature, is strictly prohibited.

Entry requirements

Passports

Required by all, except by members of the Economic Community of West African States (Ecowas) with a valid travel certificate.

Visa

Required by all, except nationals of Ecowas countries, Kenya, Zimbabwe, Egypt, Mauritius, Singapore and Hong Kong.

Visas are valid for three-month periods. An application for a business visa must contain a letter of confirmation from the representative's employer and itinerary, plus an invitation from a local host. All visitors must have return/onward passage.

Currency advice/regulations

It is advisable to check the latest currency regulations prior to visit.

It is easy to exchange US dollar bills for cedis. Visa cards can be used to withdraw cedis from Barclays Bank automatic teller machines (ATMs).

Unlimited import of foreign currency, but it must be declared. Unused foreign currency, travellers cheques, etc, declared on arrival, can be exported. Foreign currency must be exchanged with authorised dealers only. Keep the foreign exchange form. Import of local currency is prohibited and export is limited to C5,000, which must be recorded in passport.

Unused cedis can be re-exchanged into foreign currency by local banks or the Bank of Ghana, but the declaration form T.5 must show that the monies were obtained while in Ghana from an authorised dealer in foreign exchange.

Health (for visitors)

Mandatory precautions

A yellow fever vaccination certificate must be presented on arrival. A cholera vaccination may be required, depending on local circumstances.

Advisable precautions

Cholera is seasonal. Typhoid, polio, tetanus, hepatitis A and meningitis vaccinations are recommended. A hepatitis B vaccination is recommended if staying in Ghana over six months. A vaccination for rabies is recommended if travelling to rural areas. Malaria prophylaxis should be taken as risk exists throughout the country. Water precautions are essential. There is a bilharzia risk and swimming in rivers is not advisable. HIV/Aids is present in Ghana. Guinea worm is rife and increasing in northern regions.

Emergency facilities are extremely limited. Insurance is vital and emergency evacuation should be included.

Hotels

Available in Accra, Kumasi, Takoradi and other regional capitals. Prices are high. A 10 per cent government tax is added. Tipping is permitted in hotels, restaurants, etc. It is rarely added to the bill.

Credit cards

The most widely accepted credit cards are American Express, Diners' and Visa. They may be used for payment at nearly all airlines, leading hotels and major supermarkets.

Many restaurants and airlines prefer to be paid in cash.

Public holidays (national)

Fixed dates

1 Jan (New Year's Day), 6 Mar (Independence Day), 1 May (Labour Day), 25 May (Africa Day), 4 Jun (1979 Coup Anniversary), 1 Jul (Republic Day), 25 Dec (Christmas Day), 26 Dec (Boxing Day), 31 Dec (Revolution Day).

Variable dates

Good Friday, Easter Monday, National Farmers' Day, Eid al Adha, Eid al Fitr.

Islamic year 1433 (26 Nov 2011–14 Nov 2012): The Islamic year contains 354 or 355 days, with the result that Muslim feasts advance by 10–12 days against the Gregorian calendar. Dates of feasts vary according to the sighting of the new moon, so cannot be forecast exactly.

Working hours

Banking

Mon–Thu: 0830–1400; Fri: 0830–1500.

Business

Mon–Fri: 0800–1200, 1400–1700. Sat: 0830–1200.

Government

Mon–Fri: 0800–1230, 1330–1700.

Shops

Mon–Tue and Thu–Fri: 0800–1200, 1400–1730. Wed and Sat: 0800–1300. Closed on Sundays.

Electricity supply

220V AC, 50 cycles

Social customs/useful tips

It is traditional to arrive with a gift when accepting private hospitality, particularly in rural areas. It is customary to use the right hand when presenting an object to another person, particularly in the case of food or a gift.

In northern Ghana, where the population tends to be Muslim, Islamic customs should be respected: it is considered unclean to eat or drink with the left hand; it is insulting to point the sole of your shoe at a Muslim. Older people are treated with special respect in Ghana.

It is inadvisable for foreigners to refer to tribalism or ethnic affiliations when discussing current affairs.

Body language differences include the custom of a greater degree of physical contact – touching and holding hands – between men and between women.

Business people need patience when dealing with bureaucracy. There are regular power cuts in Accra.

There are no unusual or particularly strict laws, but foreign visitors should observe all rules and regulations as Ghana does not take ignorance of the law as an excuse for non-observance. It is prudent to carry proof of identity.

Security

Violent crime has risen, particularly in and around Accra. Visitors are advised to exercise a high level of vigilance in public areas and when travelling in vehicles. If possible, avoid travelling alone in taxis after dark. Be wary when withdrawing cash from the few cash points in central Accra. Thefts of both luggage and travel documents occur at Kotoka International Airport. Ensure your documents are kept secured (particularly when leaving the airport) and never leave your baggage unattended.

Be wary of all offers of unsolicited assistance at the airport unless from uniformed porters or officials who, as with all other permanent staff, wear a current ID card bearing their name and photograph. ID cards without photographs are not valid.

Taking photographs near sensitive installations, including military sites and government buildings, is prohibited.

Permission should be obtained before taking photographs of anyone in uniform.

Getting there

Air

National airline: Ghana International Airlines

International airport/s: Accra-Kotoka International (ACC), 5km from city; duty-free shop, bar, buffet, restaurant, bank, post office, taxis.

Airport tax: International departures C22,000; domestic departures C500.

Surface

Road: The coastal road runs from Lagos (Nigeria) through Cotonou (Benin) and Lomé (Togo) to Accra. The condition of this road is variable. A generally good road links Abidjan (Côte d'Ivoire) with Kumasi.

Main port/s: The main ports are Tema and Takoradi. Ships connect Tema, 25km east of Accra, with ports in Nigeria, Côte d'Ivoire, Cameroon and South Africa.

Getting about

National transport

Transport in northern Ghana can be more difficult than in southern Ghana.

Air: Several airlines fly domestic routes from Kotoka to Kumasi and Tamale.

Road: There are over 30,000km of classified roads — 15,000km of these are trunk roads, the remainder being feeder roads. There are also around 6,000km of unclassified tracks. Of the total road network, approximately 6,000km are paved. There are reasonable roads between Accra and the main towns.

The main routes are Accra-Tema, Accra-Takoradi, Accra-Kumasi, Accra-Koforidua, Accra-Ho. Roads are often potholed and badly marked.

Buses: State-run bus services connect major centres. They are subject to delays and cancellation and are not recommended for business users.

Rail: The total network is about 1,000km, connecting Tema-Accra through Nsawam-Koforidua-Nkawkaw (Eastern Region) to Kumasi (Ashanti Region) through to Dunkwa and Prestea, Tarkwa and Sekondi-Takoradi (Western Region). Another line runs from Huni Valley (Western Region) to Kade (Eastern Region). Two classes; air-conditioning and restaurant cars not available; sleeping accommodation available on some services.

Water: A weekly ferry, the *Yapei Queen*, plies Lake Volta between Yeji in the north and Akosombo, more than 200km to the south, a two-day journey. Ferries connect Yeji with Makongo and Buipe.

City transport

Taxis: There are cheap and reliable taxis in Accra.

Tipping is not usual; taxis are unmetered – fare is by negotiation; rates are often posted in hotels.

Buses, trams & metro: The bus services in Accra are run by the city authority and private operators.

Car hire

Car hire is expensive. An international driving licence is recommended; this must be endorsed by Police Licensing Office if stay exceeds 90 days. Traffic drives on the right.

Driving at night is not advised.

BUSINESS DIRECTORY

The addresses listed below are a selection only. While World of Information makes every endeavour to check these addresses, we cannot guarantee that changes have not been made, especially to telephone numbers and area codes. We would welcome any corrections.

Telephone area codes

The international direct dialling code (IDD) for Ghana is +233, followed by area code and subscriber's number:

Accra	21	Takoradi	31
Koforidua	81	Tamale	71
Kumasi	51	Tema	22

Useful telephone numbers

Police, fire and ambulance: 999.

Chambers of Commerce

Accra District Chamber of Commerce, Trade Fair Centre, PO Box 2325, Accra (tel: 662-427).

British-Ghana Chamber of Commerce and Industry, PO Box GP 21101, Accra (tel: 674-762; fax: 296-836; e-mail: info@ghanabritishchamber.com).

Ghana National Chamber of Commerce, 65 Kojo Thompson Road, PO Box 2325, Accra (tel: 662-427; fax: 662-210; e-mail: gncc@ncs.com.gh).

Banking

Agricultural Development Bank, PO Box 4191, Cedi House, Liberia Road, Accra (tel: 662-758, 662-762; fax: 662-912, 662-846).

Amalgamated Bank Limited, PO Box C1541, C131/3 Farrar Avenue, Accra (tel: 249-690; fax: 249-697; e-mail: amalbank@ighmail.com).

Barclays Bank of Ghana Ltd, PO Box 2949, Barclays House, High Street, Accra (tel: 664-901/4, 665-382; fax: 667-420).

CAL Merchant Bank Ltd, PO Box 14596, 45 Independence Avenue, Accra (tel: 221-056, 231-098, 222-345, 221-091, 231-912-7; fax: 231-104, 231-913).

Ecobank Ghana Ltd, 19 Seventh Avenue, Ridge West, Private Mail Bag, GPO, Accra (tel: 229-532, 228-812, 221-103, 667-109; fax: 667-127, 232-086).

First Atlantic Merchant Bank Ltd, PO Box C1620, Atlantic Place, No. 1 Seventh Avenue, Ridge West, Cantonments, Accra (tel: 231-433-5, 245-647, 245-660, 232-566; fax: 231-399).

Ghana Commercial Bank Ltd, PO Box 134, Accra (tel: 664-914 (5 lines), 664-911, 664-918; fax: 662-168).

International Commercial Bank Ltd, PO Box 20057, Accra (tel: 666-190, 665-779; fax: 668-221).

Merchant Bank (Ghana) Ltd, PO Box 401, Merban House, 44 Kwame Nkrumah Ave, Accra (tel: 666-331/2, 666-336; fax: 663-398).

Metropolitan and Allied Bank (GH) Ltd, PO Box C 1778, Valco Trust House, Castle Road Branch, Cantonments, Accra (tel: 232-770, 232-776; fax: 232-728).

National Investment Bank Ltd, PO Box 3726, 37 Kwame Nkrumah Avenue, Accra (tel: 240-001, 240-024; fax: 240-030/34).

Prudential Bank Ltd, PO Box 9820, Airport, Accra (tel: 226-322, 226-803; fax: 226-803).

SSB Bank Ltd, 1 Cola Avenue, Kokomlemle, Accra (tel: 222-564/223-375/222-136; fax: 222-136).

Stanbic Bank Ghana Limited, PO Box CT 2344, Valco Trust House, Castle Road, Ridge, Accra (tel: 234-683-4, 234-679, 250-066-7, 250-070-5; fax: 234-685).

Standard Chartered Bank Ghana Ltd, PO Box 768, 3rd Floor, Accra High Street Building, Accra (tel: 664-591-8, 672-210; fax: 667-751, 663-560).

The Trust Bank Ltd, PO Box 1862, Re-insurance House, 68 Kwame Nkrumah Avenue, Accra (tel: 240-049–052; fax: 240-056, 240-059).

Central bank

Bank of Ghana, PO Box 2674, Thorpe Road, Accra (tel: 666-174; fax: 662-996; e-mail: secretary@bog.gov.gh).

Stock exchange

Ghana Stock Exchange (GSE): www.gse.com.gh

Travel information

Accra Kotoka International Airport, PO Box 87, Accra (tel: 776-171).

Ghana International Airlines, Silver Star Tower, PO Box 78, Kotoka International Airport, Accra (tel: 213-555; fax: 767-744).

Ghana Tourist Development Co Ltd, PO Box 8710, Accra (tel: 772-084; fax: 772-093).

Ministry of tourism

Ministry of Tourism, PO Box 4386, Accra (tel: 666-314, 666-426; fax: 666-826).

National tourist organisation offices

Ghana Tourist Board, PO Box 3106, Accra (tel: 238-330; fax: 231-779; e-mail: gtb@africa-on-line.com.gh).

Ministries

Ministry of Communications: PO Box M.41, Accra (tel: 229-870; fax: 229-786).

Ministry of Defence, Burma Camp, Accra (tel: 774-727; fax: 773-951).

Ministry of Education, PO Box M45, Accra (tel: 662-772; fax: 664-067).

Ministry of Employment and Social Welfare, PO Box M84, Accra (tel: 665-421; fax: 667-251).

Ministry of Environment, Science and Technology, PO Box M39, Accra (tel: 662-626; fax: 666-828).

Ministry of Finance and Economic Planning, PO Box M40, Accra (tel: 665-441, 665-587, 666-512; fax: 667-069; internet: www.finance.gov.gh).

Ministry of Food and Agriculture, PO Box M37, Accra (tel: 663-036, 665-421; fax: 663-250).

Ministry of Foreign Affairs, PO Box M53, Accra (tel: 664-008; fax: 665-363; internet: www.mfa.gov.gh/).

Ministry of Health, PO Box M44, Accra (tel: 665-323; fax: 663-810).

Ministry of Information, PO Box M41, Accra (tel: 228-0211).

Ministry of Interior, PO Box M42, Accra (tel: 665-421; fax: 662-688).

Ministry of Justice & Attorney General, PO Box M60, Accra (tel: 665-051).

Ministry of Land and Forestry, PO Box M212, Accra (tel: 665-949; fax: 666-801, 666-896).

Ministry of Local Government, Rural Development and Co-op, PO Box M50, Accra (tel: 664-763; fax: 667-911).

Ministry of Mines and Energy, PO Box 40, Stadium Post Office, Accra (tel: 667-090; fax: 668-262).

Ministry of Mobilisation (tel: 665-349; fax: 667-251).

Ministry of Roads and Transport, PO Box M43, Accra (tel: 666-465; fax: 667-911).

Ministry of Tourism, PO Box 4386, Accra (tel: 666-314; fax: 666-182; e-mail: MOT@ghana.com; internet site: http://www.estghana.gov.gh; www.africaonline.com.gh/Tourism).

Ministry of Trade and Industry, PO Box M47, Accra (tel: 663-327; fax: 665-114).

Ministry of Works and Housing, PO Box M43, Accra (tel: 662-242; fax: 663-268).

Ministry of Youth and Sports, PO Box M 252, Accra (tel: 664-71; fax: 663-927).

Other useful addresses

Accra International Conference Centre, PO Box C1054, Accra (tel: 669-600; fax: 669-825).

Ashanti Goldfields Co Ltd, Gold House, Patrice Lumumba Road, Roman Ridge, PO Box 2665, Accra (tel: 772-190, 776-224, 778-155; fax: 775-947).

Association of Ghanaian Industry, PO Box 8624, Accra (tel: 777-283; fax: 773-143).

Black Star Line, PO Box 2760, Accra (tel: 776-161; fax: 775-140).

British Diplomatic Mission, Accra (tel: 221-665).

Civil Aviation Authority, Kotoka International Airport, PO Box 87, Accra (tel: 773-283).

Coffee, Sheanuts Exporters' Association, c/o Mr J W Biney, Agrotrade Ltd., PO Box 226, Accra (tel: 224-820; fax: 224-564).

Customs, Excise and Preventive Service, PO Box 68, Accra (tel: 666-841; fax: 660-019).

Department of Co-operatives, PO Box M150, Accra (tel: 666-212).

Department of Urban Roads, Ministry of Roads and Transport, PO Box 38, Accra (tel: 230-381, 223-908; fax: 234-522).

Divestiture Implementation Committee, F35/5 Ring Road East, North Labone, PO Box CT102, Cantonments, Accra (tel: 772-049, 773-119, 760-281; fax: 773-126; e-mail: dicgh@ncs.com.gh).

Export Finance Company, Bank of Ghana, PO Box 2674, Accra (tel: 666-902; fax: 662-996).

Federation of Association of Ghanaian Exporters (FAGE), c/o Kiku Ltd., PO Box M378, Accra (tel: 223-215; fax: 776-755).

Finsap Implementation Secretariat, Private Mail Bag (PMB), Ministries Post Office, Accra (tel: 666-254, 664-976; fax: 667-448; e-mail: finsap@gh.com).

Ghana Assorted Foodstuffs Exporters Assocation, PO Box 16073, Airport - Accra (tel: 220-746; fax: 223-663).

Ghana Chamber of Mines, PO Box 991, Accra (tel: 665-355; fax: 662-926).

Ghana Civil Aviation Authority, Private Mail Bag, Kotoka International Airport, Accra (tel: 776-171; fax: 773-293; e-mail: centre-GCAA@ighmail.com; internet site: http://www.gcaa.com.gh).

Ghana Cocoa Board, PO Box 933, Accra (tel: 221-212; fax: 667-104, 665-076; e-mail: cocobod@africaonline.com.gh).

Ghana Export Promotion Council, Republic House, Tudu, PO Box M 146, Accra (tel: 228-813/830/623; fax: 668-263, 233-715; e-mail: gepc@ighmail.com).

Ghana Free-Zones Board, PO Box M626, Accra (tel: 670-532/5; fax: 670-536; e-mail: freezone@africaonline.com.gh; internet site: http://www.ghanaclassified.com.ghzb).

Ghana Furniture Producers/Exporters Association, PO Box 32, Trade Fair Centre, Accra (tel: 775-311).

Ghana Highway Authority, PO Box 1641, Accra (tel: 666-591; fax: 665-571).

Ghana Investment Promotion Centre (GIPC), PO Box M193, Accra (tel: 665-125/9; fax: 663-801; e-mail: gipc@ghana.com; internet site: http://www.gipc.org.gh).

Ghana Liaison Office, Cotecna Inspection S A, 10 Drake Avenue, Airport Residential Area, PO Box C2212, Cantonments, Accra (tel: 775-698; fax: 553-522).

Ghana National Petroleum Corporation (GNPC), Private Mail Bag, Tema (tel: 232-056; fax: 774-143).

Ghana National Procurement Agency, Ministries Post Office, Private Mail Bag, Accra (tel: 220-851; fax: 221-049).

Ghana Shippers Council, Private Mail Bag, Ministries Post Office, Accra (tel: 666-915; fax: 668-768).

Ghana Stock Exchange, Marketing Department, 5th Floor, Cedi House, Liberia Road, Accra (tel: 669-914; fax: 669-913; e-mail: stockex@ncs.com.gh; internet site; http://www.gse.com.gh).

Ghana Trade and Investment Gateway Project (GHATIG), PO Box M47, Accra (tel: 663-439, 664-074; fax: 665-423; e-mail: gateway1@ghana.com).

Ghana Yam Producers and Exporters' Association, PO Box 5233, Accra (tel: 775-311; fax: 668-263).

Ghanaian Embassy (USA), 3512 International Drive, NW, Washington DC 20008 (tel: (+1-202)-686-4520; fax: (+1-202)-686-4527; e-mail: hagan@cais.com).

Horticulturists' Association of Ghana, PO Box 9303, Accra (tel: 772-139; fax: 772-350).

Institute of Economic Affairs (tel: 776-641; fax: 776-724).

Internal Revenue Services, PO Box 2202, Accra (tel: 664-961; fax: 664-938).

Organisation for Export Development for Seafood, c/o Signotrade Ltd., PO Box 16851, Accra (tel: 712-762; fax: 668-263).

Precious Metals Marketing Corporation, PO Box M108, Accra (tel: 664-931; fax: 772-350).

Private Enterprises Foundation (PEF), PO Box C1671, Cantoments, Accra (tel: 222-313; fax: 231-487).

Registar-General's Department, PO Box 118, Accra (tel: 666-469).

US Diplomatic Mission, Accra (tel: 228-440).

Vegetables Exporters' Association, c/o Ghana Export Promotion Council, PO Box M146, Accra (tel: 221-212; fax: 668-263).

Volta River Authority, PO Box MB77, Accra (tel: 664-941, 221-124; fax: 662-610; e-mail: orgsrv@accra.vra.com).

National news agency: Ghana News Agency, PO Box 2118, Accra (tel: 662-381, 665-135/6/7; fax: 669-841; email: ghnews@ghana.com; internet: www.ghananewsagency.org).

Internet sites

Africa Business Network: http://www.ifc.org/abn

Ghana Forestry Commision: http://ghanatimber.org/

AllAfrica.com: http://allafrica.com

African Development Bank: http://www.afdb.org

Mbendi AfroPaedia (information on companies, countries, industries and stock exchanges in Africa): http://mbendi.co.za

Yellow Pages: http://www.ghanaforum.com/directory.htm

Gibraltar

KEY FACTS

Official name: Gibraltar

Head of State: Queen Elizabeth II, represented by Governor Sir Adrian Johns (from 26 Oct 2009)

Head of government: Chief Minister Fabian Picardo (GSL) (from 9 Dec 2011)

Ruling party: Gibraltar Socialist Labour Party-Liberal Party (GSL-LP) alliance (from 9 Dec 2011)

Area: 7 square km

Population: 29,431 (2010)*

Capital: Gibraltar

Official language: English

Currency: Pound sterling (£) = 100 pence (the euro also circulates and is accepted informally)

Exchange rate: £0.64 per US$ (Oct 2011)

GDP per capita: US$41,200 (2007)

GDP real growth: 6.00% (2008)

Inflation: 2.80% (2008)

Balance of trade: -US$193.90 million (2005)

Visitor numbers: 7.79 million (2005)

* estimated figure

The 8 December 2011 general elections resulted in a change from the Gibraltar Social Democrats (GSD), which had been in power since 1996, to an alliance of the Gibraltar Socialist Labour Party and Liberal Party (GSL-LP). Fabian Picardo became chief minister on 9 December. Before the election, the association of Spanish workers in Gibraltar (Citipeg), that represents Spanish cross-frontier workers, demanded assurances from Picardo and the GSL-LP, that if elected, Citipeg member's livelihoods would not be seriously challenged. Mr Picardo was swift in saying that while he will not be seeking confrontation with Spain, his 'first obligation will be to provide jobs for Gibraltar residents.' As the GSL is the oldest active political party with its roots in the trades union movement, one can be forgiven for saying his declaration may well have been a sound-bite for his party members.

Different guide, same route

The collective policies of both sides of parliament reject Spain's claims of sovereignty of Gibraltar. However, the GSL-LP are more hardline in their opposition to any British-Spanish negotiated settlement and remains steadfast in keeping Gibraltar's status as a British Overseas Territory (BOT), with a right of self-determination. In turn, the UK government has responsibility for Gibraltar's defence, foreign relations, internal security and financial stability. It also provides a lead in protecting Gibraltar's interests in European Union (EU) business that may have an effect on Gibraltar. In July 2011, the UK government reiterated its commitment to reverse a European Commission proposal to have a UK-Gibraltar declared marine habitat – a site of community importance (SCI) – being subsumed into a SCI administered by Spain. However, the European General Court (EGC) ruled against the UK, on technical grounds; the UK government has said it will appeal against the ruling.

The economy

Gibraltar's economy is underpinned by its financial services sector. The historic naval docks, which were sold in 2001 to Cammell Laird (Gibraltar) Limited – renamed Gibdock in 2009 – have had extensive upgrades and provide ship building and services to cruise liners.

The UK government ensured that Gibraltar phased out a corporate tax system for non-resident operated companies in January 2011 and replaced it with a flat-rate corporate tax of 10 per cent. The online gaming operators are expected to be most disadvantaged by this new regime. Gibraltar is already a signatory of the EU tax agreement whereby Gibraltar's financial authorities passes on, to the tax department of an EU citizen's country, information concerning the amount of money in savings accounts, to allow tax to be levied by the account holder's home country.

To maintain its market position as an offshore financial services destination, Gibraltar works hard to maintain its reputation for probity and for turning a profit. It is in competition with a number of tax havens within the EU and outside, and is subject to international limits on money transactions.

Risk assessment

Economy	Good
Politics	Good
Regional stability	Fair

COUNTRY PROFILE

Historical profile

1704 Gibraltar, commonly referred to as the Rock, was captured by the UK from Spain.

1713 Gibraltar was ceded to Britain in the Treaty of Utrecht. The Treaty stipulated that the Rock would become a part of Spain if Britain gave up sovereignty.

1830 Gibraltar became a crown colony.

1869 The opening of the Suez Canal increased Gibraltar's importance in guarding the route to India and the Far East.

1939–45 Gibraltar was a busy naval base in the Second World War. After the war, Spain continued to press for the return of Gibraltar, but rejected the UK's offer to refer the matter to the International Court of Justice.

1967 More than 12,000 Gibraltarians voted to remain British; only 44 opted for Spanish rule. The dispute continued to

disrupt friendly relations between Spain and UK; for a while, Spain closed the frontier. Both countries sought a peaceful settlement, and the Gibraltarian people maintained their wish to remain British.
1969 Gibraltar adopted a new constitution that devolved a measure of power from the UK to local ministers.
1975 The death of Spain's dictator, General Franco, led to more friendly relations with Spain, but there was still no resolution of the sovereignty issue.
1984 The Brussels Agreement was signed between Spain and the UK, establishing a negotiating process over the issue of Gibraltar's sovereignty.
1985 Spain lifted its border blockade.
1996 The Gibraltar Social Democrats (GSD) were elected; Peter Caruana became chief minister.
1998 Spanish proposals for joint sovereignty were rejected by the UK.
2000 The UK and Spain reached an agreement over Gibraltar's administrative status, which allowed Spanish recognition of documents and passports issued in Gibraltar.
2001 The Royal Navy dockyard was sold to Cammell Laird (Gibraltar) Limited.
2002 Spain and UK held talks to consider grounds for sharing sovereignty of Gibraltar.
2004 The 300th anniversary of the British occupation of Gibraltar was commemorated amid continued tensions with Spain. A trilateral forum, of the UK, Spain and Gibraltar, began talks on the territory's future.
2005 Gibraltarians took part in their first European Union (EU) elections.
2006 An agreement easing border controls allowed flights from Spain to land in Gibraltar.
2007 A constitution amendment required that a majority of 60 per cent of votes was requisite for changes to the constitution. The GSD were re-elected.
2008 Cammell Laird invested US$34.9 million in its shipyards to develop its market in super-yacht building and refitting.
2009 The foreign ministers of Spain and UK and Chief Minister Caruana held talks in Gibraltar over greater cross-border co-operation in maritime, financial and judicial matters. Sovereignty of the territory was not discussed. A move by Spain to denote the seas around Gibraltar as Spanish in an environmental directive submitted to the European Commission almost scuttled the visit before it began. This was the first visit by a Spanish minister since 1704. Sir Adrian Johns became the new governor.
2010 A new passenger ferry service to Algeciras (Cadiz) was launched in July. In August, the neighbouring Spanish town of La Línea de la Concepción (La Línea), Cadiz Province, announced plans to impose a road toll tax for all vehicles entering from Gibraltar. Residents of La Línea will be granted waivers to commute into Gibraltar but no reciprocating waiver for Gibraltarian commuters was proposed.
2011 The corporate tax system for non-resident operated companies was phased out in January and replaced with a flat-rate corporate tax of 10 per cent. Online gaming operators are expected to be disadvantaged by this new regime, introduced as a requirement of the UK tax authority. On 22 July, the owners of the Algeciras ferry announced that it would expand the service to carry freight; this will allow Gibraltarian exports to Spain to avoid the restrictive land-border crossing at La Línea. In parliamentary elections held on 8 December the opposition alliance of the Gibraltar Socialist Labour Party-Liberal Party (GSL-LP) won 48.9 per cent of the vote (10 seats of 17) and ousted the ruling GSD. Fabian Picardo (GSL) was sworn in as chief minister on 9 December.

Political structure

Constitution

A new constitution was promulgated on 2 January 2007, which modernises the UK-Gibraltar relationship. Some responsibilities undertaken by the governor are limited, particularly those areas of external affairs, defence, internal security and the public service. The house of Assembly became the Gibraltar Parliament, which determines its own size and new commissions were create to undertake the appointments to the judiciary and public service and a new police authority was created, which will undertake greater local input.

Form of state

British Overseas Territory (BOT)

The executive

The governor does not take an active role in governmental affairs.
The Chief Minister is the head of the Gibraltar government and holds much of the power.

National legislature

The unicameral Gibraltar Parliament is governed by the 2006 constitution. It has at least 17 elected members serving four-year terms plus a speaker, appointed by parliament, who does not have a casting vote. The governor appoints as chief minister the member of parliament (MP) most likely to command the largest political block.
There are no constituencies and all votes are cast for individual candidates that may make up block votes. Every voter has a maximum 10 votes, to cast among all candidates standing. Universal suffrage is at aged 18.

Legal system

It is based on English common law coupled to statutes. The civil courts in Gibraltar are the Court of First Instance, the Supreme Court, the Court of Appeal and ultimately, the Privy Council in the UK.

Last elections

8 December 2011 (parliamentary)
Results: Parliamentary: the Gibraltar Socialist Labour Party-Liberal Party (GSL-LP) alliance won 48.9 per cent of the vote (10 seats of 17), the Gibraltar Social Democrats (GSD) 46.8 per cent (7), and the Progressive Democratic Party (PDP) 4.4 per cent (0); turnout was 82.5 per cent.

Next elections

2015 (parliamentary)

Political parties

Ruling party

Gibraltar Socialist Labour Party-Liberal Party (GSL-LP) alliance (from 9 Dec 2011)

Main opposition party

Gibraltar Social Democrats (GSD)

Population

29,431 (2010)*
Last census: November 2001: 27,495
Annual growth rate: 0.2 per cent (2003)

Ethnic make-up

English, Italian, Maltese, Portuguese, Spanish.

Religions

Roman Catholic (77 per cent), Church of England (7 per cent), Muslim (7 per cent), Jewish (2 per cent).

Education

Gibraltar has a comprehensive system of education, based on the UK model. Bayside (merged with three separate schools), is the only secondary school for boys between the ages of 12 and 18. Westside School, the Gibraltar Girls' Comprehensive School caters for 900 students between the ages of 12 to 18. Many children are likely to receive third level education in the UK through several grant facilities, resulting in the high incidence of returning professional graduates.

Health

Health conditions are generally good and broadly comparable to most of Western Europe. Heart diseases and cancers account for most mortality. Gibraltar's health services are closely modelled on the UK's National Health Service, with which it maintains professional and service links. There is provision for a full range of primary care and secondary care services, available through the Primary Care Centre. Medical cases requiring tertiary care are usually referred to the UK or Spain. The St Bernard's Hospital is the

only general hospital, with 170 beds providing outpatient services, emergency facilities and investigative facilities.
Government expenditure towards healthcare amounted is around £30 million (US$45.2 million) per annum
Life expectancy: 79 years (estimate 2003)
Fertility rate/Maternal mortality rate: 1.7 births per woman (2003)
Birth rate/Death rate: 11 births per 1,000 population; nine deaths per 1,000 population (2003).
Child (under 5 years) mortality rate (per 1,000): Five per 1,000 live births (2003)

Welfare
A social insurance funds all state pensions and benefits, with contributions and other earnings on investments meeting the cost of the scheme. The government's investment in capital projects towards social and economic development is funded by the Improvement and Development Fund, 12 per cent of which is allocated for housing.

Languages spoken
Spanish, Italian, Portuguese and Malti; English is used in schools and for official purposes.
Official language/s
English

Media
Press
Dailies: Gibraltar's oldest daily newspaper is the *Gibraltar Chronicle* (www.chronicle.gi).
Weeklies: There are several magazines including *Panorama* (www.panorama.gi), *Vox* (www.vox.gi), which also publishes a Spanish section, *The New People* (www.thenewpeople.net) with political reports and the satirical *Gibraltar Inquirer* *(www.gibinquirer.net)*.
Business: The *Gibraltar International* (www.gibraltarfinance.com) is a quarterly magazine covering finance and business matters.
Periodicals: Magazines include the monthly *Insight* (www.insight-gibraltar.com) with lifestyle news and *The Gibraltar Magazine* (www.thegibraltarmagazine.com) with business and leisure articles.
Broadcasting
Public radio and television services are provided by the Gibraltar Broadcaster Corporation (GBC) (www.gbc.gi), funded partly by revenue from TV licence fees and also through advertising fees and the UK military broadcaster, BFBS (www.ssvc.com/bfbs).
Radio: Two station networks broadcast within the territory Radio Gibraltar (www.gbc.gi) and the BFBS Radio and Radio 2 (www.ssvc.com/bfbs). There are a number of external services from Spain that can be received.
Television: GBC (www.gbc.gi) operates one channel and BFBS offers access to pay-to-view TV and satellite services.
Advertising
All, typical media outlets offer the availability for advert.

Economy
Gibraltar has few natural resources, with almost no part of its land area capable of sustaining agriculture. It has a significant absence of heavy manufacturing activity, apart from ship repair. The economy is dependent on imports of food, consumer goods, building materials, construction equipment and fuel. As such, the economy is service-based, in particular financial, tourism (over 5 million tourists annually – including day-visitors from Spain); shipping services fees, and duties on consumer goods. The first three sectors contribute 25–30 per cent of GDP. Telecommunications accounts for another 10 per cent.
The gambling sector has been a growth industry since the first gambling business began operating in 1989. An agreement reached with Spain in 2006 finally broke a 30-year ban on flights between Gibraltar and Spain. Spain also agreed to recognise Gibraltar's Internet suffix .gi and mobile (cell) phone signals across the border.
Gibraltar has a small population, boosted by a large pool of foreign workers recruited for the financial sector. The economy is dependent on offshore financial services. It is in competition with a number of tax havens within the EU and outside, and is subject to international limits on money transactions, while maintaining a reputation for probity and turning a profit in order to continue to flourish.

External trade
Gibraltar is a member of the European Community as an overseas territory of the UK, however it does not participate in the customs union, common commercial policy (free movement of goods do not apply), and the levy of VAT. Nevertheless community rulings are implemented through UK local legislation.
Its regular trade deficit is largely offset by invisible earnings in financial services, ship-repairs, internet gambling and telecommunications.
Imports
Main imports are petroleum, manufactured goods, vehicles, machinery and foodstuffs.
Main sources: Spain (typically 24 per cent of total), Russia (12 per cent), Italy (12 per cent).
Exports
Manufactured goods.
Main destinations: UK (typically 30 per cent of total), Spain (23 per cent), Germany (14 per cent).
Re-exports
Petroleum (over 50 per cent of total), tobacco, manufactured goods and wine.

Industry and manufacturing
The shipbuilding company, Cammell Laird (Gibralter) Ltd ownes and operates the shipyard and dry dock. The port provides an important source of income. The Gibraltar government has encouraged the setting up of light industries there, by making available a package of incentives and other benefits to successful companies. Gibraltar also has a wine bottling plant and a satellite control system.
The New Harbours, a free-port zone where there are no duties or taxes on imported materials and low rates of tax on profits, comprises warehousing, industrial workshops and office space, available to rent or purchase for exporting companies.

Tourism
This tiny ex-British colony on the tip of the Iberian peninsular is staunchly independent of its Spanish neighbour. However, Spain does have a constricting influence on Gibraltar's tourism industry as visitors may not travel back and forth from Spain by road unimpeded. On 22 July 2011, the owners of the Algeciras ferry announced that it would expand the service to carry freight; this will allow Gibraltarian cars and passengers to Spain to avoid the restrictive land-border crossing at La Línea.
Never-the-less, travel and tourism is an important component and constitutes around 60 per cent of GDP. Gibraltar is a destination for the yachting enthusiast as it is within range of both the Atlantic Ocean and Mediterranean Sea. Cruise liner visitors, day-trip tax free shoppers and military history enthusiasts are also among the estimated seven million visitors annually.

Hydrocarbons
Gibraltar does not produce oil, gas or coal. It imports petroleum products to meet its energy needs of around 26,600 barrels per day; however it does not import either gas or coal.

Energy
The Gibraltar Electricity Authority is responsible for generation, transmission and supply of electricity. It had a total installed generating capacity of 15.75MW in 2008. It also takes electricity from a privately owned company. Total consumption was 142 million kilowatt hours (kWh) in 2007.

Banking and insurance

Gibraltar has a well-developed financial services sector, which has grown due to its independent jurisdiction under the EU's Treaty of Rome and its sound fiscal regime.

Gibraltar is a signatory of the EU tax agreement whereby it passes on, to the tax department of an EU citizen's country, information concerning the amount of money in savings accounts, to allow tax to be levied from the account holder's home country.

There are over 20 licenced banks and some 18 insurance companies operating.

Offshore facilities

There is a well established offshore banking sector in Gibraltar, although by 2008 the number of banks in operation dropped from 26 in 1996 to 17. Gibraltar complies with the European Union (EU) agreement on withholding tax for saving accounts held by EU citizens.

Time

GMT plus one hour (daylight saving, late-March to late-September, GMT plus two hours).

Geography

Gibraltar is situated at the southernmost tip of the Iberian Peninsula in southern Europe. The territory consists of a narrow peninsula running southwards from the south-west coast of Spain, to which it is connected by a sandy isthmus. About 8km (five miles) across the bay, to the west, lies Algeciras, the Spanish port, and 32km (20 miles) to the south, across the Strait of Gibraltar, is Morocco. The Mediterranean Sea is to the east.

Hemisphere

Northern

Climate

At the junction between the Mediterranean and Atlantic Ocean the climate in Gibraltar is heavily influenced by these and its local topography. Two local winds the *levanter* and *poniente* determine conditions. The easterly *levanter* produces warm, humid weather with sea fogs. The westerly *poniente* produces hot and mostly dry weather. Temperatures in summer average 25 degrees Celsius (C), although it can rise to over 30 degrees C; in winter it averages 14 degrees C.

Entry requirements

Passports

Required by all, except EU nationals travelling with valid national ID cards.

Visa

As an overseas territory of the UK, visa requirements are the same. Visas are required by all, except nationals of North America, Australasia, Japan and other EU members. For further exceptions and advice visit www.ukvisas.gov.uk/ (includes application forms). All visas must be applied for before travelling.

Gibraltar is outside the Schengen Agreement area. Visitors should ensure they have the right to return to Spain on their Schengen visa before entering Gibraltar from Spain.

Currency advice/regulations

There are no restrictions on the import or export of local or foreign currencies. Local bank notes are not accepted in the UK and should be exchanged before leaving Gibralter.

Travellers cheques are widely accepted and should be in pound sterling to avoid extra exchange fees.

Hotels

There is an official rating system in either stars or diamonds. Reservations should be made in advance, especially during summer (April–October).

Public holidays (national)

Fixed dates

1 Jan (New Year's Day), 8 Mar (Commonwealth Day), 1 May (May Day), 10 Sep (Gibraltar National Day), 25–26 Dec (Christmas).

Holidays that fall on the weekend are taken on the next Monday.

Variable dates

Good Friday, Easter Monday (Mar/Apr), Spring Bank Holiday (last Monday in May), Queen's Official Birthday (Jun), August Bank Holiday (last Monday in Aug).

Working hours

Banking

Mon–Thur: 0900–1530; Fri: 0900–1700.

Business

Mon–Fri: 0900–1700 (0800–1400, summer). Sat: 0900–1300.

Government

Mon—Fri: (winter) 0800—1615; (summer) 0730—1330.

Shops

Mon–Fri: Most shops open from 0900–1930 and some open from 0900–1300 and 1500–1900, Sat: 1000–1300.

Telecommunications

Mobile/cell phones

GSM 900 is available throughout the territory.

Electricity supply

240V AC, with UK style flat, thee-pin plugs.

Security

Violence and street crime is rare.

Getting there

Air

British Airways and Monarch Airlines operate daily direct flights from the UK.

National airline: GB Airways

International airport/s: Gibraltar (GIB) North Front airport, 1km from town centre. Facilities include duty-free shops, restaurants, bank and car hire. Taxis and hotel coaches are available. The airport is a ten minute walk from the centre of town.

Airport tax: None

Surface

Access is from Málaga, through the Spanish frontier at La Línea, which only opens 0900–1700 (Mon–Fri) and at weekends for longer hours.

Rail: There are no railways in Gibraltar but there are links to the Spanish national railway across the border, accessible within a few minutes.

Water: There are regular ferry services from Tangier in Morocco.

Getting about

National transport

Bus and taxi services are available. Taxi drivers are obliged by law to produce, on demand, a copy of the taxi fares. Gibraltar has a total of about 45km of roads. There is no railway network.

City transport

Taxis: Taxis are available from the airport to the town centre.

Buses, trams & metro: There is a bus service which operates from the airport to the town centre, journey time 15 minutes.

Car hire

Local car hire is available. A valid EU or international driving licence and evidence of insurance are required (third party). An age limit may be imposed usually 23–70 years. Traffic drives on the right. The speed limit is 50kph (31mph), except where indicated. Dipped headlights are compulsory at night time and seat belts are compulsory.

Additional conditions apply for travel into Spain.

BUSINESS DIRECTORY

The addresses listed below are a selection only. While World of Information makes every endeavour to check these addresses, we cannot guarantee that changes have not been made, especially to telephone numbers and area codes. We would welcome any corrections.

Telephone area codes

The international direct dialling code (IDD) for Gibraltar is +350 followed by subscriber's number. (The IDD for Gibraltar is not recognised by Spain).

Chambers of Commerce

Gibraltar Chamber of Commerce, Don House, 38 Main Street, PO Box 29, Gibraltar (tel: 78-376; fax: 78-403; e-mail: gichacom@gibnet.gi).

Banking

Abbey National (Gibraltar) Ltd, 237 Main Street (tel: 76-090; fax: 72-028).

ABN Amro Bank (Gibraltar) Ltd, PO Box 100, 2-6 Main Street (tel: 79-220/79-370; fax: 78-512).

Baltica Bank (Gibraltar) Ltd, 215a Neptune House, Marina Bay (tel: 42-670; fax: 42-676).

Banco Atlántico (Gibraltar) Ltd, Eurolife Building, 1 Corral Road (tel: 40-117; fax: 40-110).

Banco Bilbao Vizcaya International (Gibraltar) Ltd, 3rd Floor, Hadfield House, Library Street (tel: 79-420; fax: 73-870).

Banco Bilbao Vizcaya (Gibraltar) Ltd, 260/262 Main Street (tel: 77-797, 77-871, 77-896).

Banco Central Sa, 198/200 Main Street (tel: 73-625, 73-650, 73-675; fax: 73-707).

Banco Español de Crédito, 114 Main Street (tel: 76-518; fax: 73-947).

Banque Indosuez, 206/210 Main Street (tel: 75-090; fax: 79-618).

Barclays Bank plc, 84/90 Main Street (tel: 78-565; fax: 79-509).

Crédit Suisse (Gibraltar) Ltd, Neptune House, Marina Bay (tel: 76-606; fax: 76-027).

Gibraltar Private Bank Ltd, PO Box 407, 10th Floor, ICC, Casemates (tel: 73-350; fax: 73-475).

Hambros Bank Ltd, PO Box 375, 32 Line Wall Road (tel: 74-850; fax: 79-037).

Hispano Commerzbank (Gibraltar) Ltd, Suite 14, 30/38 Main Street (tel: 74-199; fax: 74-174).

Lloyds Bank plc, 323 Main Street (tel: 77-373; fax: 70-023).

Midland Bank Trust Corporation (Gibraltar) Ltd, PO Box 19, Hadfield House, Library Street (tel: 79-500; fax: 72-090).

National Westminster Bank, 57 Line Wall Road (tel: 77-737; fax: 74-557).

Republic National Bank of New York (Gibraltar) Ltd, Neptune House, Marina Bay, PO Box 5578 (tel: 79-374; fax: 75-684).

Royal Bank of Scotland (Gibraltar) Ltd, 1 Corral Road (tel: 73-200; fax: 70-152).

Varde Bank International (Gibraltar) Ltd, PO Box 476, Suite E, Regal House, 3 Queensway (tel: 42-455; fax: 42-456).

Travel information

GB Airways, Iain Stewart Centre, Beehive Ring Road, Gatwick Airport, West Sussex RG6 0PB, UK (tel: (1293)664-239; fax: (1293)664-218).

London Passport Office, Globe House, 89 Ecclestone Square, London SW1V 1PN, UK (tel: (0870) 521-0410 (24-hour UK national advice line); (+44-20) 7901-2150 (international visa enquiries for British Overseas Territories. Opening hours: Mon-Fri 0730-1900; Sat 0900-1600); internet: www.passport.gov.uk; www.ukpa.gov.uk).

National tourist organisation offices

Gibraltar Tourist Board, Duke of Kent House, Cathedral Square (tel: 74-950; fax: 74-943; e-mail: tourism@gibnet.gi; internet site: www.gibraltar.gi).

Ministries

Government of Gibraltar, UK Office, 179 Strand, London WC2R 1EL, UK (tel: (+44-20) 7836-0777; fax: (+44-20) 7240-6612; e-mail: info@gibraltar.gov.uk; internet site: www.gibraltar.gov.uk).

Government Secretariat, 6 Convent Place (tel: 70-071; fax: 74-524).

Governor's Office, The Convent, Main Street (tel: 45-440; e-mail: convent@gibnet.gi).

Ministry of Tourism and Transport, Duke of Kent House, Cathedral Square (tel: 74-950; fax: 74-943).

Ministry of Trade, Industry and Telecommunications, Suite 771, Europort (tel: 52-052; fax: 71-406; e-mail: dticomm@gibnet.gi; internet site: www.gibraltar.gov.gi).

Other useful addresses

Economic Planning and Statistics Office, 6 Convent Place (tel: 75-515, 70-071).

Gibraltar Finance Centre, Suite 771, Europort (tel: 50-011; fax: 47-677; e-mail: fsc@gibnet.gi).

Gibraltar Information Bureau, Arundel Great Court, 179 Strand, London WC2R 1EH (tel: (+44-20) 7836-0777; fax: (+44-20) 7240-6612).

Gibraltar Telecommunications International Ltd, Mount Pleasant, 25 South Barrack Road (tel: 59-609; fax: 59-644).

Gibtelecom, Suite 942, Europort (tel: 52-200; fax: 71-673; internet site: www.gibtele.com).

Internet sites

Audio site – Talking about Gibraltar: www.gibnynex.gi/info/gibtalk

Business in Gibraltar: www.Gibraltarian.com/Gibraltar_business.asp

Government of Gibraltar: www.gibraltar.gov.gi

Gibraltar Broadcasting Corporation (GBC): www.gbc.gi

Offshore facilities: www.Gibraltaroffshore.com/

Greece

As the Greek crisis wore on in October 2011, the Greek economy began to look worse and worse. What was on offer by way of a euro-zone bail-out looked, in the words of one Greek politician, as 'too little, too late'. Brussels and the euro-zone governments had taken so long to reach anything resembling a 'rescue' that the financial markets had already factored it into the equation before it had even been announced. The *troika* that would decide on future levels of Greek prosperity, or more likely levels of austerity – the International Monetary Fund (IMF), the European Central Bank (ECB) and the European Union (EU) – could not ignore the fact that although Greece's deficit might be reducing, its interest payments were still increasing. Secondly, unless structural changes and economic reforms were introduced quickly, investors would be unlikely to step forward in sufficient numbers. Unless the investment climate was both reformed and stabilised, it was unlikely that the economy could be re-activated. Third, as television newsreel footage confirmed almost nightly, Greek public opinion was increasingly angry at what it was being asked to put up with. This was not just an expression of pure anger, it was a combination of anger and fear. Greeks had seen their salaries decrease as street protests continued to increase. Many politicians saw a general election as the only option, enabling the government elected to benefit from a clear majority. The elephant in the room – and Greece was by no means alone in this respect – was the glaring absence of any obvious formula allowing euro-zone countries to leave the union.

Throughout the first six months of 2011 Greece found itself on the sharp end of uncomfortable scrutiny from the world's financial communities. To the outside observer, less well versed in the ways of international finance, a number of curious facts were surprisingly obvious. Of these

KEY FACTS

Official name: I Elliniki Dimokratia (The Hellenic Republic)

Head of State: President Karolos Papoulias (since 2005; re-elected Feb 2010)

Head of government: Prime Minister Lucas Papademos (from 11 Nov 2011)

Ruling party: Panellino Sosialistiko Kinima (Pasok) (Pan-Hellenic Socialist Movement) (from 7 Oct 2009)

Area: 131,957 square km

Population: 11.16 million (2009)

Capital: Athens

Official language: Greek

Currency: Euro (€) = 100 cents (from 1 Jan 2002; previous currency drachma, locked at Dr340.75 per euro)

Exchange rate: €0.75 per US$ (Oct 2011)

GDP per capita: US$27,302 (2010)

GDP real growth: -4.50% (2010)

GDP: US$305.40 billion (2010)

Labour force: 5.02 million (2010)

Unemployment: 12.50% (2010)

Inflation: 4.70% (2010)

Balance of trade: -US$37.54 billion (2010)

NOTA

11 November 2011, parliament selected Lucas Papademos as prime minister, following days of wrangling between the ruling the Pasok and opposition Nea Dimokratia (ND) (New Democracy) to find an acceptable candidate to replace Georgios Papandreou; Papademos took office on 11 November.

two stood out: first was that successive Greek governments had long been less than truthful about the state of their economy. Second, that Greeks at all levels of society, are simply averse to paying tax. Third was the increasing reluctance of European taxpayers – particularly those in Germany, Holland and Finland – to foot the bill for bailing out countries where, it appeared, taxes were not duly paid and where political corruption was endemic.

Rendering unto Caesar

In simple terms, Greece's tax aversion adds up to a shortfall of about a third of the total tax due. Perhaps ironically, this is more or less the size of the budget deficit. Which means that if Greeks simply paid their tax, the country would have no problems. On the contrary, compared to other European countries it would be a model of fiscal rectitude. Instead, the 'grey' economy adds up to over 25 per cent of the total national economy (compared, for example, to an estimated nine per cent in the US). An article on this subject entitled *Dodger Mania* by James Surowiecki in the *New Yorker* highlighted the hidden costs of tax avoidance; Greece apparently spends, per head, four times as much as the US on collecting taxes. In his article Mr Surowiecki observed that 'Greek officials were notoriously easy to bribe with a 'fakelaki' (small envelope) of cash. The fakelaki system also covered payments to doctors, contractors – even lawyers. Amazingly, even if those avoiding tax were apprehended, it could take as much as ten years to process their case. The Greek courts reportedly have a backlog of some 300,000 cases. According to Transparency International, the three most corrupt counries in Europe are Greece, Bulgaria and Romania. Mr Surowiecki concluded his article by quoting a study by the economist Martin Halla that concluded that 'tax morale' in the US could be traced back to countries of origin. Cynical observers might note that the three European countries in question all shared an Ottoman heritage.

What light? What tunnel?

As those Greeks that could afford to deserted their desks to take a summer vacation, others were left to ponder the home truths. If anything, the measures recommended by the trinity of the IMF, the EU and the ECB in July 2011 had managed to make matters worse. Greece was celebrating three years of recession, with a heart stopping gross domestic production (GDP) contraction of 6.9 per cent from the year before. In the first quarter of 2011 the contraction figure had actually reached 8.1 per cent. Cuts in state salaries and pensions had combined with the reduction in purchasing power as taxes increased and public investment fell, producing a dramatic decline in the size of the economy. Industrial production contracted by 11.3 per cent in the second quarter of 2011, almost double the rate of the first quarter. To make matters worse, despite the increase in value added tax (VAT) in bars and restaurants from 13 per cent to 23 per cent, between January and July 2011 the budget deficit had risen by an estimated 24 per cent. Meanwhile, the Greek government endeavoured to improve its tax collection rates by simplifying the tax system, abolishing the more obvious loopholes and strengthening its woefully weak enforcement system.

The real Greeks

The politicians and civil servants in Brussels and Washington who, in mid-2011, once again became the reluctant arbiters of Greek's economic fate, seemed to be in denial. The prospect of Greece ever being able to meet the payments it had signed up to was simply farcical. The farce centred on the plain fact, bravely recognised by some Greek economists, that Greeks don't like paying taxes. Greece's tax collection rate has long been the lowest in the EU, while its state pensions are among the highest.

Understandably, German taxpayers were less than enthusiastic to bail out their Greek counterparts who not only enjoyed higher pensions but also benefited from an earlier retirement age. Thus, a Greek postman retiring at the age of 60 would receive a higher pension than his German counterparts, already obliged to work until the age of 65 and soon until 67. According to some reports, a Greek postman who had worked in the postal service since leaving school, could expect to receive a monthly state pension of around €2,500 (US$3,498).

Salome the Greek?

It is difficult for modern scholars to ascertain the exact nationality of the biblical seductress Salome. However, she seemed to share certain Greek qualities, not least her ability to win support by slowly revealing herself to charmed observers. As the pressure on the Greek authorities rose in 2010 and 2011, it became apparent at each stage, that there was more bad news to follow. Underlying the general apprehension was the feeling that the Greek economy, Greek prosperity and stability were being sacrificed on the altar of a European political project that no longer had any validity and was even beginning to lose support in Europe's heartland of France, Germany and the Netherlands.

First, in its efforts to address its crises, it appeared to most observers and certainly to the world's financial wheelers and dealers, that there was no way in which the Greek government could both resolve its historic debt crisis and at the same time address current levels of debt. Greece's budget deficit in mid-2011 was put at 10.5

KEY INDICATORS **Greece**

	Unit	2006	2007	2008	2009	2010
Population	m	11.12	11.12	11.14	11.16	*11.28
Gross domestic product (GDP)	US$bn	268.69	310.40	351.90	330.80	305.40
GDP per capita	US$	24,157	27,930	31,602	29,635	27,302
GDP real growth	%	4.2	4.5	2.0	-2.0	-4.5
Inflation	%	3.3	3.0	4.2	1.4	4.7
Unemployment	%	8.9	8.3	7.7	9.5	12.5
Coal output	mtoe	9.3	8.1	8.3	8.1	8.8
Exports (fob) (goods)	US$m	20,300.0	23,991.0	29,163.0	21,361.0	22,628.0
Imports (fob) (goods)	US$m	64,585.0	81,041.0	94,209.0	64,187.0	60,165.0
Balance of trade	US$m	-44,285.0	-57,050.0	-65,046.0	-42,826.0	-37,537.0
Current account	US$m	-29,684.0	-44,587.0	-51,216.0	-37,043.0	-32,335.0
Total reserves minus gold	US$m	565.9	631.1	343.8	1,554.8	1,309.5
Foreign exchange	US$m	408.3	518.2	158.7	198.8	108.2
Exchange rate	per US$	0.75	0.69	0.68	0.78	0.76

* estimated figure

per cent of its GDP. At the same time, its public debt came in at a ringing 150 per cent of GDP. In May 2010 the IMF and the EU had accorded Greece a €110 billion (US$157.7 billion) loan. The original conditions of this loan foresaw a situation whereby Greece could begin to refinance on the world's markets in 2012. The rescue plan envisaged a drastic privatisation plan and massive budget cuts. However, come June 2011 when further aid was to be considered, the rescue plan had barely been drawn up, never mind been put into action.

In view of the Greek government's failure to get the reform show on the road by July 2011, discussion of the second stage of the rescue plan was initially deferred until September 2011. In an ideal world, this might well have worked; the intervening month of August would have seen most Greek bankers, politicians and civil servants away from Athens, preferably on a remote Aegean island without telephone or e-mail connection. But ideal worlds do not take into account predatory financial markets, where hungry hedge funds live to make a financial killing from sovereign default.

The second stage of the Greek rescue plan had originally envisaged a participation by the private financial sector – banks, pension funds and insurance companies – adding up to about 30 per cent. This was a condition imposed by Germany, where regional elections had shown the German electorate strongly opposed to their taxes being used to bail out profligate states such as Greece. German insistence on this point brought the whole deal to the point of collapse, since few German – or indeed other European institutions – were particularly keen to come to the rescue of a state that most of them already regarded as a busted flush, already easy prey to financial predators. Any forced participation in the Greek bail-out would represent a *de-facto* Greek collapse, a euro-zone first with consequences that were unimaginable. Not only for Greece, but for the euro-zone as a whole.

However serious the situation, in mid-July it seemed that the almost theological differences between the French and German governments, which apparently hinged on the nature of the role, if any, of the private sector, were proving intractable. The hitherto unmentionable word 'default' came increasingly into play. But a Greek default might still be avoided if the private sector's participation in the bail-out was voluntary, (the German option) rather than the result of government coercion (which seemed to be the French preference). Any Greek failure to make a re-payment on time would constitute default; as this seemed increasingly likely, the private sector throughout Europe was understandably reluctant to risk shareholder funds.

Peering in to the abyss that would accompany a Greek default, European markets could only see further doom and gloom. In the first instance, Greek banks would face substantial losses while at the same time the weakness of their balance sheets would make it difficult, even impossible, to borrow on the international markets. Consequently, the Greek government would face the prospect of rescuing the country's banks – which in turn posed the question – with what money? A default would inevitably prevent the Greek government from turning to the international markets for some time. The ECB would also catch a cold, left with substantial exposure to Greek obligations. As members of the ECB, the two countries with the largest exposure to a Greek default were – no surprises here – France (with loans to public and private sector borrowers totalling €57 billion (US$81.70) at the end of 2010) and Germany (a meagre €34 billion (US$47.7 billion)). Quite apart from the consequences for each country's banking sectors, in the view of many analysts, the ECB's own position would become less than straightforward. On the one hand, the ECB would be technically prevented from granting further loans to Greece; on the other it would be under pressure to restore order – which meant credit – to the struggling Greek economy.

Tsunami

Any Greek default would also leave other European economies facing the chill wind of the world's financial markets. The financial *tsunami* that had overtaken Ireland and Portugal would begin to lap at the shores of Belgium, Italy and Spain. All three have debt levels well over 90 per cent of their GDP and weak growth, inevitably attracting the attention of the predatory financial markets. In the case of Italy, the political uncertainties and lack of transparency of the Berlusconi régime cast doubts on the government's austerity plans. Thus Greece found itself at the epicentre of a crisis that risked not only dragging Greece down, but also those European banks and financial institutions with weakened balance sheets were also vulnerable.

In simple terms, if such they may be called, the initial failure of France and Germany to reach agreement managed to remind the markets that uncertainties abounded. Not least in the case of Italy, with a level of debt five times greater than Greece. The options appeared to boil down to an about-turn by Germany, agreeing to a 100 per cent public Greek rescue, which at least would calm market nerves, or the intervention of the private sector, which would almost certainly be interpreted as a default, not least by the credit rating agencies. The possibility of some intermediate solution being agreed upon had not been ruled out in mid-July, whether lower interest rates, extended re-payment periods or the purchase of Greek debt by the ECB. Re-arranging the deck-chairs on the Titanic came to mind. Were Greece to be seen to default, then the ECB would inevitably have to refuse to accept Greek bonds as collateral for loans, something that would bring many Greek financial institutions to their knees. But even if accepted, none of these were seen as a far-reaching solution to the problem. On the contrary, behind any façade of resolution lay the reality that the Greek economy was in such a dire state that only serious reform and surgery could possibly even begin and only begin, to take Greece out of penury.

Risk assessment

Economy	Poor
Politics	Poor
Regional stability	Good

COUNTRY PROFILE

Historical profile

1454 After the fall of Constantinople to Suleiman the Magnificent, Greece and most of the eastern Mediterranean were occupied by the Ottoman Empire.
1829 Following a war against the Ottomans lasting eight years, Greece declared its independence as a monarchy.
1913 The London Conference reduced the amount of ethnic Albanian-dominated territory of the former Ottoman Empire and Cameria (Chamouria) was granted to Greece.
1917 Greece entered the First World War on the side of the Allies and made territorial gains.
1923 Greece signed the Lausanne Peace Treaty with Turkey. The Treaty outlined the territory of each country and provided Greece with a number of islands in the Aegean Sea.
1939 Greece rejected Italy's ultimatum seeking free passage for its troops in the Second World War and repelled its attack, but was occupied by Germany. The government and the King went into exile.

Mass armed resistance grew out of various political groupings.
1944 Liberation from the Nazis. The returned National Unity government under George Papandreou fought a civil war against the Communists.
1949 Constitutional monarchy was re-established. There were territorial gains from the war, the last of which was the Dodecanese islands in the south-eastern Aegean Sea.
1967–72 A military coup led by right-wing army officers deposed King Konstantinos II. An attempted counter-coup by the King failed, and he went into exile. Colonel Georgios Papadopoulos appointed himself prime minister. The regime was brutal and repressive with all political activity banned.
1973 Greece was declared a republic with Papadopoulos as president. General Demetrios Ioannides led a bloodless coup; Papadopoulos was overthrown. Partial civilian rule was allowed. General Phaidon Gizikis was appointed president.
1974 Civil war in Cyprus and the Turkish invasion of the island brought Greece close to war with Turkey and caused the downfall of the military junta. Elections resulted in a decisive victory for Nea Dimokratia (ND) (New Democracy). A referendum rejected proposals for a return to constitutional monarchy.
1975 A republican constitution providing for a parliamentary democracy was promulgated and Konstantinos Tsatsos was elected president.
1977 The ND was re-elected with a reduced majority.
1980 In May, Constantine Karamanlis was elected president. Greece joined the EU.
1981 The Panellino Socialistiko Kinima (Pasok) (Pan-Hellenic Socialist Movement) gained an absolute majority in parliament in the elections. The Pasok government, led by Andreas Papandreou, was the first socialist government in Greek history.
1985 President Karamanlis resigned and Christos Sartzetakis became president. Pasok was returned to power and implemented proposed constitutional changes. The government's programme of economic austerity became very unpopular and resulted in widespread industrial unrest.
1986 Constitutional amendments limited the powers of the president.
1989 ND won the largest proportion of votes in the elections.
1993 The ND government was forced to resign after losing its one seat parliamentary majority. Pasok regained power.
1995 Costis Stephanopoulos was elected president.
1996 Prime Minister Papandreou resigned due to ill health and Costas Simitis became prime minister. Andreas Papandreou died, ending an era of authoritarian control over Pasok, which won the parliamentary elections.
2000 Incumbent president, Stephanopoulos, was re-elected. Pasok was re-elected, becoming the first party to win three successive elections. Greece's application to join the Economic and Monetary Union (Emu) was accepted.
2001 Greece officially joined the Emu.
2002 Euro currency replaced the drachma.
2004 The ND, led by Costas Karamanlis, won the parliamentary elections.
2005 Karolos Papoulias was elected president. Newly introduced labour laws ended 'jobs for life'.
2007 A series of forest fires swept through areas in southern Greece and killed over 60 people and destroyed over 4,500 homes. The prime minister called an early election and the ruling ND won but with a reduced majority. Karamanlis remained prime minister.
2008 Greece blocked the Former Yugoslav Republic of Macedonia's (FYROM) membership of NATO, due to the unresolved issue of FYROM using Macedonia in its name. Eight days of rioting in Athens resulted in the death of a youth during protests about the growing unemployment rate.
2009 GDP growth fell to 1 per cent; unemployment reached 9.4 per cent. Tourism, which typically employed 20 per cent of the working population, suffered due in most part to a strong euro and a drop in the number of visitors by 15–20 per cent. The former state-owned Olympic Airlines was privatised following an agreement with the EU to write-off US$3.87 billion (€2.6 billion) in accumulated debt; it was re-launched as Olympic Air. It began operations as a competitive, full-service airline for southern Europe and the east Mediterranean. In snap parliamentary elections the ruling ND lost to Pasok and Georgios Papandreou became prime minister. The credit rating agency Fitch reduced Greece's sovereign debt rating to BBB+.
2010 Parliament re-elected Karolos Papoulias as president in February. The government made further cuts in public spending. The domestic economic crisis grew into a eurozone problem when the government informed the European Central Bank (ECB) that its deficit was unsustainable and it was in danger of defaulting on its public debts. Several international rating agencies downgraded Greece's sovereign ratings to 'junk bond' status between March and May. The euro came under international pressure. Greece only just avoided insolvency when a US$147 billion three-year loan was arranged with the ECB and IMF in May, under a newly created European Financial Stability Facility (EFSF). The government implemented stringent austerity measures, including cuts in pensions and salaries of government workers, which resulted in widespread strikes and street protests. Greek truckers went on strike at the end of July, protesting against the government's move to liberalise road transport. The strike ended after a week (in August) when the government threatened to revoke their licences; armed forces were ordered to deliver fuel to petrol stations.
2011 Rioting broke out in Athens on 15 June as the prime minister announced the next phase in an economic austerity plan, required before further aid would be available. Over two days, 29–30 June, parliament voted to approve the five-year austerity plan, which would qualify Greece for €110 billion (US$80.3 billion) in external financial aid from the ECB and IMF, or risk defaulting on its debts. A 48-hour general strike was held at the same time to protest at measures that included raised taxes and salary cuts for public employees at a time when unemployment was over 16 per cent. The ECB restructuring plan was implemented but by 20 July money markets and investors were still concerned about Greece's ability to fund the debt. Germany appeared unsympathetic to Greece's continued financial needs. On 29 August the planned merger of Greece's second and third largest banks, Eurobank EFG and Alpha Bank, was announced. The merger created the biggest bank in south-east Europe, with assets of US$212 billion and around 1,300 branches. Prime Minister Papandreou caused consternation on 4 November when he declared that any agreement for further fiscal austerity measures, concluded with European Monetary Union leaders to allow the next instalment of the bailout (US$11 billion), would be put to a referendum. In parliament both his supporters and the opposition attacked his handling of the crisis and on 5 November he narrowly won a vote of confidence (153 to 145). Parliament agreed to pass austerity legislation on the proviso that Papandreou stepped-down as prime minister after the formation of a government of unity. The proposed referendum was abandoned. Parliament selected Lucas Papademos as prime minister following days of wrangling between the ruling the Pasok and opposition ND to find an acceptable candidate to replace Georgios Papandreou; he took office on 11 November. Mr Papademos is a technocrat and was a vice president of the European Central Bank (ECB). He will attempt to secure bailout-funds and implement budget cuts to avert economic collapse.

Political structure
Constitution
The constitution of 1975 has been revised on several occasions in line with contemporary circumstances. It sets out the rights and responsibilities of the parliament, judiciary, people and church. The constitution is enshrined in law.
In March 1986, parliament ratified changes to the 1975 constitution, limiting the president's power in relation to parliament.
Independence date
1921, declared independence
Form of state
Parliamentary democratic republic
The executive
The president of the republic is Head of State, and is elected by parliament for a five-year term, for a maximum of two terms. The president must be elected by a two-thirds majority, or on the third ballot by a three-fifths majority.
Since 1985 when presidential power was reduced, *de facto* executive power is wielded by the prime minister and cabinet. The cabinet is named by the prime minister.
National legislature
Legislative power rests with the 300-member unicameral Vouli ton Ellinon (parliament), elected for four years by universal and compulsory adult suffrage.
Legal system
Greek law is based on codified Roman law with the judiciary divided into civil, criminal, and administrative courts. Judicial independence is guaranteed under the constitution.
Last elections
4 October 2009 (parliamentary); 8 February 2005 (presidential)
Results: Presidential: Karolos Papoulias was elected president, receiving 279 votes in the 300-seat parliament.
Panellino Sosialistiko Kinima (Pasok) (Pan-Hellenic Socialist Movement) won 43.9 per cent of the vote (160 seats of 300), Nea Dimokratia (ND) (New Democracy) 33.5 per cent (91), Kommounistiko Komma Ellados (KKE) (Communist Party of Greece) 7.5 per cent (21), Laikos Orthodoxos Synagermos (LAOS) (Popular Orthodox Rally) 5.6 per cent (15), Synaspismos tis Rizospastikis Aristeras (SYRIZA) (Coalition of the Radical Left) 4.6 per cent (13); turnout was 70.9 per cent.
Next elections
2013 (parliamentary); 2015 (presidential)

Political parties
Ruling party
Panellino Sosialistiko Kinima (Pasok) (Pan-Hellenic Socialist Movement) (from 7 Oct 2009)
Main opposition party
Nea Dimokratia (ND) (New Democracy)

Population
11.16 million (2009)
Last census: March 2001: 10,964,020
Population density: 81 inhabitants per square km. Urban population: 60 per cent (1995–2001).
Annual growth rate: 0.5 per cent 1994–2004 (WHO 2006)
Ethnic make-up
Greece is a very homogenous state and the vast majority of its citizens regard themselves as ethnic Greek. However, there are also small numbers of Turks, Pomaks, Gypsies, Vlaks and an increasing numbers of illegal Albanian economic refugees (some 300,000 are believed to live in Athens).
Religions
Over 95 per cent of the population are baptised in the Greek Orthodox Church. There are small Muslim, Catholic and Jewish communities.

Education
Primary education lasts for six years. Secondary education generally lasts for six years and is divided into two equal periods. Approximately 47 per cent of the relevant age group participate in some form of tertiary education. Overcrowded classes at public high schools and a lack of facilities mean that students take private tuition or attend night school to improve their chances of going to university, for which entrance is fiercely competitive. Women comprise almost 60 per cent of Greek graduates.
Public education expenditure is equivalent to just over 3 per cent of GDP.
Literacy rate: 98 per cent, male; 96 per cent, female; adult rates (World Bank).
Enrolment rate: 93 per cent at primary level and 95 per cent at secondary level (of the relevant age groups).
Pupils per teacher: 14 in primary schools

Health
Although basic healthcare is provided free of charge, many Greeks find standards unsatisfactory and prefer to go to private doctors and clinics, or even to pay the high cost of treatment abroad.
HIV/Aids
HIV prevalence: 0.2 per aged 15–49 in 2003 (World Bank)
Life expectancy: 79 years, 2004 (WHO 2006)
Fertility rate/Maternal mortality rate: 1.2 births per woman, 2004 (WHO 2006)
Child (under 5 years) mortality rate (per 1,000): 5.0 per 1,000 live births (World Bank)
Head of population per physician: 4.38 physicians per 1,000 people, 2001 (WHO 2006)

Welfare
Social security is handled by more than 350 state-run or state-supervised social insurance funds, which together cover almost all the Greek population. The largest of these funds is the general social security scheme, run by the Idryma Koinonikis Asfalisis (IKA) (Social Security Institute). The scheme covers 1.8 million wage earners, pays pensions and operates a network of hospitals and out patient clinics.
Parliament approved the restructuring of the debt-burdened and complex state pension system in June. Greece has a growing aged population, which will become problematic.
At 9 per cent of the total labour force, the proportion of Greek employees living in conditions of poverty is one of the highest in the EU.

Main cities
Athens (capital, estimated population 721,477 in 2005), Piraeus (172,025), Thessaloniki (356,449), Patras (164,968), Iráklion (capital of Crete, 139,798), Corinth (31,377), Lárisa (129,661), Kallithéa (108,202).

Languages spoken
Macedonian, Albanian, Turkish, Aroumanian, Bulgarian and Pomak are spoken by their resident populations. Most people in the business community also speak English, French or German.
Official language/s
Greek

Media
Press
Although the media has considerable freedom, a public prosecutor may stop circulation of an edition of a newspaper on the grounds that it is blasphemous, offends public decency, reveals military or state secrets or offends the Greek president.
Dailies: There are 34 national daily newspapers and most publish Sunday editions. Most newspapers have political party affiliations.
In Greek, high circulation newspapers include *Ethnos* (*Nation*) (www.ethnos.gr), *Kathimerini* (*Daily*) (www.kathimerini.gr), *To Vima*, (*The Tribune*) (www.tovima.gr), *Eleftheros Typos* (*Free Press*) (www.e-tipos.com) and two evening publications include *Eleftherotypia* (*Press Freedom*) (www.enet.gr) and *Ta Nea*, (*The News*) (www.tanea.gr). Some offer online articles in English.
Weeklies: Many daily newspapers publish weekend editions. In Greek, *To Proto Thema* (www.protothema.gr) is a tabloid

newspaper and *Stochos* (www.stoxos.gr) is a nationalist publication. In English *Athens News* (www.athensnews.gr); Big News Network is an internet site (www.bignewsnetwork.com).

Business: In Greek, there are several business newspapers, *Naftemboriki* (www.naftemporiki.gr) is a financial daily, *Kerdos* (www.kerdos.gr), *Reporter* (www.reporter.gr) reports on financial markets, others include *Express* (www.express.gr), *Imerissia* (www.imerisia.gr), *Isotimia* (www.isotimia.gr) and *Oikonomikos Tachydromos* (http://oikonomikos.dolnet.gr), a magazine for economic and policy analysis. Regional publications include *Thrakiki Agora* (www.thrakikiagora.gr) and *Thrakiki Gi* (www.thrakikigi.gr) from Komotini in the north-east. Industry publications include *Naftika Chronika* (www.naftikachronika.gr) concerning Greek shipping. Some offer online articles in English.

Periodicals: In Greek, for women, monthly magazines include *Gynaika*, the oldest women's publication and *Praktiki* for articles on the home.

Broadcasting

Elliniki Radiophonía Tileórassi (ERT) (Hellenic Radio and Television) (www.ert.gr) is the state-owned, public broadcaster. It derives around 80 per cent of its funding through licence fees.

Radio: ERT (http://tvradio.ert.gr) operates five radio channels, ERA 1–5, with nationwide coverage. ERA5 is an overseas network called 'Voice of Greece', while Filia (Friendship) broadcasts to immigrants in 12 languages, mainly European but includes Arabic, providing news, information and entertainment. There are over 400 commercial radio stations, many unregulated by government, providing programmes of music, sport and news and talk.

Television: ERT (www.ert.gr) operates three TV channels; two, ET1 and NET are broadcast from Athens and ET3 broadcasts from Thessaloniki with regional programmes for Northern Greece. New technologies include ERT Digital and ERT World (via satellite) with programmes broadcast around the world.

There are dozen commercial, private, digital and satellite channels based regionally, including Mega Channel (www.megatv.com), Skai TV (www.skai.gr), ANT1 Gold (www.gold.antenna.gr), Nova Cinema (www.novacinema.gr) and Nova Sport (www.novasport.gr).

In 2008 there were no cable TV services, although two services are available via high-speed internet connections.

Advertising

Greece has a modern advertising market with a typical annual adspend of US$12.5 billion. Television and magazines account for around 30 per cent each of the total amount, with newspapers capturing around 15 per cent.

There are restrictions on advertising to children, with no ads targeting them on TV until 2200 hours. Alcohol cannot be advertised on radio or TV until 1800 and 1900 hours respectively, while tobacco advertising is completely banned on electronic media.

External poster panels are popular with an estimated 26,000 nationwide.

Economy

Greece's mixed economy is heavily dependent on tourism, agriculture and shipping. The service sector contributes over 75 per cent of GDP, industry around 20 per cent and agriculture less than 5 per cent. The tourist industry is based on Greece's ancient historic sites inland and its Mediterranean coastal resorts and islands. According to 2007 EU statistics, 59 per cent of all employment in Greece is related to the tourist accommodation sector and provides around 15 per cent of GDP. In 2009, Greece's commercial shipping fleet was second (after Japan) in size, with around 4,000 registered vessels, over 16 per cent of the world's carrying capacity; the sector contributed 5.7 per cent to GDP and employed around 160,000 people or 4 per cent of total employment.

GDP growth in 2007 was 4.5 per cent, which fell to 2.0 per cent in 2008 as the global economic crisis deepened; by 2009 Greece had fallen into recession with GDP growth of -2.0 per cent. The crisis resulted in a credit restriction, weakening world trade and a fall in domestic consumption and ultimately un-competitiveness. As a member of the eurozone, the Greek economy is supposed to remain within a 3 per cent deficit margin as set by the European Central Bank (ECB), but as the crisis depressed the economy government debt grew to 13.6 per cent of GDP and public debt burgeoned to 115.1 per cent of GDP. The government initiated a three-year reform programme, under pressure from the EU, that included spending cuts, higher taxes, reducing the size of the public sector while freezing wages and introducing fiscal measures such as tackling tax evasion, reducing welfare payments in health and pensions. By May 2010 the economy was in crisis as Greece was in danger of defaulting on its loans; the EU and IMF had to provide financial aid to support the government. The EU issued infringement notices against Greece for past official statistics detailing economic data on Greece's deficit and debt which were deemed 'false'. In April 2010 the credit rating agency Standard and Poor's took the lead in downgrading Greece's credit rating to junk status so that not only is the Greek population required to forego expansion it has to pay more for its daily borrowing to keep its economy afloat.

Over two days, 29–30 June 2011, parliament voted to approve the five-year austerity plan, needed to qualify Greece for €110 billion (US$80.3 billion) in external financial aid from the ECB and IMF, or risk defaulting on its debts. A 48-hour general strike was held at the same time to protest at measures that included raised taxes and salary cuts for public employees, at a time when unemployment was over 16 per cent.

Parliament selected Lucas Papademos as prime minister following days of wrangling between the ruling the Pasok and opposition ND to find an acceptable candidate to replace Georgios Papandreou; he took office on 11 November. Mr Papademos is a technocrat and was a vice president of the European Central Bank (ECB). He will attempt to secure bailout-funds and implement budget cuts to avert economic collapse.

External trade

As a member of the European Union, Greece operates within a community-wide free trade area, with tariffs sets as a whole. Internationally, the EU has free trade agreements with a number of nations and trading blocs worldwide. It is Europe's largest producer of tobacco and the fifth largest exporter of cotton worldwide. Exports account for almost 50 per cent of Greece's GDP.

Imports

Principal imports include raw materials, fuels and lubricants, chemicals, machinery and transport equipment, foodstuffs, basic manufactures and consumer goods.

Main sources: Germany (typically 12 per cent of total), Italy (11 per cent), Russia (7 per cent).

Exports

Principal exports include tobacco, electrical and manufactured goods, petroleum products, chemicals, textiles and agricultural products, fruit and vegetables and live animals.

Main destinations: Italy (typically 12 per cent of total), Germany (11 per cent), Bulgaria (7 per cent).

Agriculture

Farming

Agriculture is an important but diminishing sector of the economy, typically contributing, around 8.3 per cent to GDP and employing around 12 per cent of the labour force.

The government's agricultural policy is, to a large extent, shaped by the EU's Fundamental reform to the Common Agricultural Policy (CAP), which was introduced in Greece in 2005. The subsidies paid on farm output, which tended to benefit large farms and encourage overproduction, were replaced by single farm payments not conditional on production.
Main crops include wheat, barley, maize, fruit (especially olives), vegetables, oil seeds, tobacco, cotton and sugar beet.
Traditionally, farm co-operatives have played a large role in agriculture as a source of purchasing seeds, renting machinery and selling products. Larger co-operatives also handle basic processing and marketing. Attempts to restructure the co-operatives have largely failed, with weak management and widespread corruption preventing their modernisation and development.
The sector is also handicapped by weak infrastructure, low levels of technology and generally poor soil. However, with the exception of meat, dairy products and animal feeds, Greece is self-sufficient in foodstuffs.
During the summer of 2007 forest fires devasted large areas of southern Greece, with particular damage inflicted on the olive groves of Kalamata; an estimated 20 per cent of national production was lost. Production is not expected to recover fully until 2012.

Fishing

Fish production is important for domestic consumption and export. The annual freshwater fish catch is around 25,000 tonnes, with a marine catch of approximately 270,000 tonnes. Coastal fish farms produce sea bass and gilthead bream.
Although Greece has an expanding aquaculture sector, its processing and marketing sector remains underdeveloped. Following the EU's common fisheries policy, the country benefits from the EU structural fund that covers the whole sector and also includes the development of the processing and marketing of products.

Forestry

Forest and other wooded land accounts for half of the land area, with forest cover estimated at 3.5 million hectares (ha). Most of the forest is in the northern and western part of the mainland and about 90 per cent is available for wood supply. Significant quantities of roundwood production are used for fuel consumption. More than three-quarters of the forest and other wooded land is under public ownership, and only about 20 per cent is privately owned. The forest sector is rather small and all types of forest products are imported, mainly comprising sawnwood and paper products.

Industry and manufacturing

Industry typically accounts for 25 per cent of GDP and employs 26 per cent of the labour force. Within the industrial sector, manufacturing accounts for 57 per cent of output and construction 32 per cent. The remaining 11 per cent of industrial output is accounted for by the minerals and utilities sectors.
Manufacturing, which contributes around 15 per cent to overall GDP, is dominated by small family-owned companies, most of which are situated around Athens or in export-oriented zones around the port of Thessaloniki.
The number of mergers and acquisitions of Greek firms by foreign investors has increased in recent years, with greater numbers of companies making initial public offerings (IPOs) on the Athens Stock Exchange. However, production has been sluggish and relatively few industries are competitive on a European level.
Greek industry is also less competitive compared to its EU neighbours because it has no land boundaries with the Union.
The aluminium sector, which is facing a shortage of domestic raw material, represents more than 1.5 per cent of GDP and employs approximately 40,000 workers.

Tourism

Greece attracts not only sea and sun-worshipers to its many islands, it also has many other attractions including classical ruins, Byzantine monuments, many of which are on the UN World Heritage list. Greece is one of Europe's top-ten destinations for foreign travellers.
Tourism is an important component of GDP, which up until 2007 had represented over 17 per cent. Since then the global economic crisis has cut visitor numbers and the contribution of travel and tourism to GDP fell to 16.5 per cent in 2008 and further to just over 15 per cent in 2009–11. Likewise employment in the sector was at an all-time high of 20 per cent of total employment (2005–07), which fell to just over 17 per cent in 2009–10, but with an improvement to 18.4 per cent in 2011. Visitor numbers in 2010 fell by 7 per cent
In 2009, the former state-owned Olympic Airlines was privatised following an agreement with the EU to write-off US$3.87 billion (eur2.6 billion) in accumulated debt; it was re-launched as Olympic Air. It began operations as a competitive, full-service airline for southern Europe and the east Mediterranean.
In 2011 as Greece was experiencing political and economic turmoil, its tourist sector experienced mixed fortunes.
Greece signed a memorandum of tourism co-operation with the Province of Guangdong (China) aimed at boosting Chinese tourist numbers. Visitor numbers from Germany and Russia recorded significant increases of 11.8 per cent and 57.5 per cent year-on-year to August 2011 respectively. Tourist receipts for these were also higher than for others; Germans spent a total of eur1.2 billion (US$1.68 billion) and Russians eur546 million (US766.5 million). However, the international airport of Athens experienced a drop in passenger numbers and arrivals from former markets, particularly the UK, fell.
The new government, installed in November 2011, will look to tourism as an source of foreign exchange – net inflows of foreign direct investment was eur1.4 billion (US$1.96 billion) for the year up to August – and will treat the sector as an important part of its economic recovery programme.

Mining

There is a relative wealth of natural resources including large deposits of bauxite (aluminium ore), marble, lignite, magnesite, ferro-chrome, ferro-nickel, lead, zinc, uranium and manganese. Mining activity is small-scale and the sector typically contributes only 3 per cent to GDP and employs only 1 per cent of the workforce.
New gold resources have been found at Skouries (an ancient copper mine), estimated to contain five–seven million ounces of gold.

Hydrocarbons

Greek oil reserves fell below commercial levels before 2007, however consumption continued to rise to 372,000 barrels per day (bpd) by 2010. Hellenic Petroleum (HP) dominates the oil industry, operating three refineries and over 1,400 petrol stations, as well as interests in petrochemicals, natural gas supplies and electricity production. The government has a 35.49 per cent stake in HP.
In 2007, Russia, Greece and Bulgaria signed a US$1.2 billion pipeline deal. The pipeline will run inland, from the Bulgarian Black Sea port of Burgas to Alexandropoulos, on the Aegean Sea. Russian oil will be transported via the 285km pipeline to the huge EU market, avoiding the busy Bosphorus. A Russian consortium will hold a 51 per cent stake in the deal to build and operate the pipeline and a joint Greek/Bulgarian consortium 24.5 per cent each. The project had been expected to be completed by 2010, but in June 2011 only an environmental and social impact assessment (ESIA) had begun into the construction of the Trans-Adriatic Pipeline (TAP), providing a description of the preferred route and

potential risks with their mitigation measures. HP operates a 214km oil pipeline, with a capacity to carry about 50,200bpd, from the port of Thessaloniki to Skopje in Macedonia.
Natural gas amounts for over 10 per cent of Greece's energy mix. The natural gas sector is led by DEPA (Greek Public Gas Company), which despite liberalisation in the market still dominates, selling gas to commercial users and commercial suppliers to domestic users. The state and HP each own 35 per cent of DEPA.
Greece had coal reserves of 1.9 million tonnes in 2010. Reserves are comprised wholly of low quality lignite, with high extraction costs, high pollutants and used exclusively in thermal power stations.

Energy
Greece generates approximately 50 million MW of electricity annually, producing over 55.4 billion kilowatt hours (kWh) in 2006; around 75 per cent is thermal, 21 per cent hydro and 4 per cent solar. The majority of thermal power stations are fuelled by domestically produced lignite coal, with the remainder supplied by imported oil. Growth in electricity has increased by 50 per cent since 1995 and the energy authorities estimate that Greece will need an extra 6,000MW of additional capacity by 2015. Greece is the EU's second-largest solar collector (after Germany), with 20 per cent of households using solar powered water heaters. The national Public Power Corporation (PPC) is the country's largest energy company and sole power supplier, operating 34 electricity-generating stations in an interconnected power grid as well as 60 autonomous power plants on Greek islands. The government has sold its assets in PPC but retained statutory control of its operations. The national electricity grid is connected to the networks of Albania, Bulgaria, Macedonia and Kosovo.

Financial markets
Stock exchange
Athens Stock Exchange (ASE)
Commodity exchange
ADEX (Athens Derivatives Exchange)

Banking and insurance
Liberalisation of the banking system was initiated in 1987. Interest rates are fully freed and commercial banks permitted to handle forward dealing in foreign exchange. Companies can borrow in foreign exchange without restriction.
On 29 August 2011 the planned merger of Greece's second and third largest banks, Eurobank EFG and Alpha Bank, was announced. The merger created the biggest bank in south-east Europe, with assets of US$212 billion and around 1,300 branches.

Central bank
Bank of Greece; European Central Bank (ECB).

Time
GMT plus two hours (daylight saving, late-March to late-September, GMT plus three hours)

Geography
Greece lies in south-eastern Europe. The country consists mainly of a mountainous peninsula between the Mediterranean Sea and the Aegean Sea. It is bounded by Albania, Macedonia (FYROM) and Bulgaria to the north, Turkey to the north-east, the Aegean Sea to the east, the Sea of Crete to the south and the Ionian Sea to the west. To the south, east and west of the mainland are many Greek islands, the largest being Crete.
Hemisphere
Northern

Climate
Coastal regions and the islands have typical Mediterranean conditions, with mild, rainy winters and hot, dry, sunny summers. Rainfall comes almost entirely in the winter months, although amounts vary widely according to position and relief. Continental conditions affect the northern mountainous areas, with severe winters, deep snow cover and heavy precipitation, but summers are hot.
Athens: 9 degrees Celsius (C) (January); 28 degrees C (July); annual rainfall 414mm.

Dress codes
A suit and tie or formal clothing are necessary for business meetings, even during the hot summer months.
Women tend to dress smartly in the evening and men wear either suits or smart, casual clothes.

Entry requirements
Passports
Required by all, except nationals of EU/EEA countries, Switzerland and Monaco holding valid national identity cards. Passports must be valid for at least three months beyond length of stay.
Visa
Required by all, except nationals of Schengen agreement signatory countries and citizens of most of the Americas, Europe and many Asian countries. For confirmation of exceptions, contact the consular section of the nearest embassy. For those applying for a business visa, contact the consulate before travelling to determine requirements. A Schengen visa application (offered in several languages) can be downloaded from http://europa.eu/abc/travel/ see 'documents you will need'.

Currency advice/regulations
There are no restrictions on the import and export of local or foreign currency. Foreign currency over US$1,000 or equivalent must be declared on arrival.
Customs
Personal items are duty-free. There are no duties levied on alcohol and tobacco between EU member states, providing amounts imported are for personal consumption.
Strict regulations apply concerning the export of antiquities, including rocks from archaeological sites. Penalties range from large fines to prison terms.

Health (for visitors)
Nationals of the European Economic Area (EEA) countries and Switzerland can access reduced cost and sometimes free medical treatment using a European Health Insurance Card (EHIC) while visiting the EEA. Exceptions include nationals of the 10 countries which joined the EU in 2004 whose EHICs are not valid in Switzerland. Application for the EHIC should be made before travelling.
Mandatory precautions
Yellow fever vaccination certificate is required if travelling from infected area.
Advisable precautions
Long-term visitors should consider hepatitis A immunisation. Drinking water is not always purified .
Comprehensive travel insurance is advisable, in case of medical or other emergencies.

Hotels
Numerous hotels in all main towns, classified as de luxe, A,B,C,D and E. There is a 15 per cent service charge. A small tip will be expected. It is advisable to make reservations well in advance, especially between May and September.

Credit cards
All major credit cards are accepted.

Public holidays (national)
Fixed dates
1 Jan (New Year's Day), 6 Jan (Epiphany), 25 Mar (Independence Day), 1 May (Labour Day), 15 Aug (Assumption Day), 28 Oct (Ochi Day/National Day), 25 Dec (Christmas Day), 26 Dec (St Stephen's Day).
Variable dates
Greek Orthodox Shrove Monday, Greek Orthodox Good Friday, Greek Orthodox Easter Monday, Greek Orthodox Whit Monday, Greek Orthodox Pentecost.

Working hours
Banking
Mon–Fri: 0800–1400.
Business
Mon–Fri: generally 0800–1400 and 1700–2000; tend to close earlier during

summer and on Mon and Wed afternoons.

Government

Mon–Fri: usually 0800–1500.

Shops

Mon, Wed and Sat: 0800–1400; Tue, Thu and Fri: 0800–1400 and 1800–2100.

Telecommunications

Mobile/cell phones

There are GSM roaming facilities available in 900/1800 band widths, with coverage throughout the country, including the island territories.

Electricity supply

220V AC

Social customs/useful tips

Personal contact is an important way of conducting business in Greece.

Greek bureaucracy can be slow. Identification documents and various authorisation letters or seals are necessary.

It is forbidden to photograph military installations and aircraft. Penalties for breaking the law can be severe.

Security

Visitors should be alert to the presence of pickpockets and purse-snatchers in tourist sites, particularly in Athens. As with the rest of Europe, there is a threat from terrorist activity, but Greece has its own anarchists, who occasionally engage in violence.

Getting there

Air

Greece has a strong tourist industry that relies on 80 per cent of international visitors arriving by air. Airports are located on the mainland as well as the islands.

National airline: Olympic Air

International airport/s: Eleftherios Venizelos Airport (ATH), sited in Sparta, 27km north-west of Athens. Facilities include: business centre, shops, duty-free shops, restaurants and car hire. Further information can be obtained at www.aia.gr. Express bus routes carry passengers into Athens or the port of Pireaus.

Other airport/s: Alexandroupolis (AXD), 7km from city; Corfu (CFU), 1.6km from city; Heraklion (HER), 5km from city; Ioannina (IOA), 5km from city; Kos (KGS), 27km from city; Mykonos (JMK); Paros (PAS); Rhodes (RHO), 16km south-west of Rhodes; Thessaloniki Makedonia (SKG), 16km from city; Skiathos (JSI); Thira (JTR).

Airport tax: International €12.5; domestic €8.51

Surface

Road: The Greek road network is accessible via Italy, Bulgaria and Macedonia (FYROM) (border crossing at Medzitlija, near Bitola).

Rail: The Greek rail network is connected to most European routes via Italy, Bulgaria and Macedonia (FYROM). There is a daily service between Athens and Istanbul.

Water: Frequent passenger ferry services operate from Italy to Piraeus. A car ferry service runs between Ancona and Brindisi (Italy) and Igoumenitsa and Patras.

There is a ferry from Marmaris, Turkey, to the island of Rhodes.

Main port/s: Heraklion, Igoumenitsa, Patras, Piraeus, Rafina, Salonika and Volos.

Getting about

National transport

Air: As well as the international airports, there are a further 25 other airports all connected by regular services operated by Olympic Airways.

Road: There are 117,000km of roads in Greece, of which about 9,000km are unpaved. There are 470km of motorways, including a route from Athens to Thessaloniki.

Rail: Over 2,500km of track is operated by Hellenic Railways Organisation Ltd, with services to most towns.

Water: About 80km of navigable inland waterways are used, as well as several regular ferry services along the coast and connecting the various islands.

City transport

Taxis: Taxis are plentiful in Athens, but avoid rush hours. There is an extra charge for each piece of luggage, waiting time, journeys outside Athens/Piraeus and journeys after midnight. Yellow taxis run from the airport to downtown Athens.

Buses, trams & metro: There is a good, but often busy, bus network in Athens with a standard flat rate within city limits. Tickets are available at blue booths situated near the bus stops, or at many kiosks throughout the city. These tickets must be inserted into a machine inside the bus to be valid. Double-decker buses run between the airport and downtown Athens, operating every 20 minutes from 0600 until midnight.

The Attico Metro runs from 0530 to midnight daily, approximately every four minutes during rush hour and every 10 minutes at other times. Tickets must be purchased before entering the metro and must be cancelled upon entry.

An extension to the subway system was inaugurated in 2000 as part of the subway grid built for the 2004 Olympic Games.

Car hire

All major car hire companies have offices in Athens and some other main towns. Rates vary depending on size of car, length of hire and season. International driving licences are recognised, but UK, Belgian, Austrian and German full licences are also accepted. International insurance Green Card is valid, provided Greece is mentioned. The wearing of seatbelts is compulsory. Traffic drives on the right .

Extreme care is necessary if riding a motorbike.

BUSINESS DIRECTORY

The addresses listed below are a selection only. While World of Information makes every endeavour to check these addresses, we cannot guarantee that changes have not been made, especially to telephone numbers and area codes. We would welcome any corrections.

Telephone area codes

The international direct dialling code (IDD) for Greece is +30, followed by area code and subscriber's number:

Athens	210	Samos	273
Heraklion	81	Thessaloniki	31

Useful telephone numbers

Police: 100

Fire: 199

Hospitals: 106

Emergency services (24-hours; information in English, French and Greek, to request ambulances, fire department, police and coastguard): 112

Chambers of Commerce

American-Hellenic Chamber of Commerce, 109 Messoghion Avenue, 11526 Athens (tel: 699-3559; fax: 698-5686; e-mail: info@amcham.gr).

Athens Chamber of Commerce and Industry, 7 Akademias Street, 10671 Athens (tel: 360-4815; fax: 361-6408; e-mail: info@acci.gr).

British-Hellenic Chamber of Commerce, 25 Vassilissis Sophia Avenue, 10674 Athens (tel: 721-0361; fax: 722-2119; e-mail: info@bhcc.gr).

Heraklion Chamber of Commerce and Industry, 9 Koronaiou Street, 71202 Heraclion, Crete (tel: 022-9013; fax: 022-2914; e-mail: info@ebeh.gr).

Samos Chamber of Commerce and Industry, 19 Koundourioti Street, 83100 Samos (tel: 087-970; fax: 022-784; e-mail: samcci@otonet.gr).

Thessaloniki Chamber of Commerce and Industry, 29 Tsimiski Street, 54624 Thessaloniki (tel: 037-0100; fax: 037-0166; e-mail: root@ebeth.gr).

Union of Hellenic Chambers of Commerce and Industry, 7 Akademias Street, 10671 Athens (tel: 363-2702; fax: 362-2320; e-mail: hellas@uhcci.gr).

Banking

Agricultural Bank of Greece SA, Panepistimiou 23, 105-64 Athens (tel: 939-9911; fax: 323-9611).

Alpha Bank, 40 Stadiou Street, 102-52 Athens (tel: 326-0000; fax: 326-5438).

Commerical Bank of Greece, 11 Sophocleous Street, 102-35 Athens (tel: 328-4000; fax: 325-3746).

Egnatia Bank, Omirou 22, 106-72 Athens (tel: 360-6914; fax: 362-7945).

General Bank, Panepistimiou 9, 105-64 Athens (tel: 324-1289; fax: 322-2271).

National Bank of Greece, Aeolou 86, 150-51 Athens (tel: 334-1000; fax: 321-3119; internet site: www.nbg.gr).

Post-Office Savings Bank, Pesmazoglou 2-6, 105-59 Athens (tel: 323-0621; fax: 323-1055).

Central bank

Bank of Greece, 21 E Venizelos Avenue, GR 102-50 Athens (tel: 320-1111; fax: 323-2239; e-mail: secretariat@bankofgreece.gr).

European Central Bank (ECB), Kaiserstrasse 29, D-60311 Frankfurt am Main, Germany (tel: (+49-69) 13-440; fax: (+49-69) 1344-6000; e-mail: info@ecb.int).

Stock exchange

Athens Stock Exchange (ASE): www.ase.gr

Commodity exchange

ADEX (Athens Derivatives Exchange): www.adex.ase.gr

Travel information

Athens Airport (East), Helliniko, 167-00 Athens (tel: 969-9111; fax: 966-6162).

Athens Airport (West), Helliniko, 167-00 Athens (tel: 936-9111; fax: 936-3328).

Athens International Airport (Eleftherios Venizelos), 5th km Spata, Loutsa Ave, 190 04 Spata (tel: 369-8300; fax: 369-8883; internet site: http://www.aia.gr).

Hellenic Chamber of Hotels, 24 Stadiou Street, 10564 Athens (tel: 331-0022/33; fax: 323-6962, 322-5449).

Olympic Airways, Syngrou Ave 96-100, 117-41 Athens (tel: 926-9111; fax: 926-7154).

Ministry of tourism

Ministry of Tourism, Amerikis 2B, 105-64 Athens (tel: 322-3111; fax: 322-4148).

National tourist organisation offices

Ellinikos Organismos Tourismou (GNTO) (Greek National Tourist Organisation), Odos Amerikis 2, Athens 10564 (tel: 322-3111/9).

Ministries

Ministry of Aegean, Syngrou Ave 49, 117-43 Athens (tel: 923-7970; fax: 923-8200).

Ministry of Agriculture, Acharnon 2, 101-76 Athens (tel: 529-1111; fax: 524-0475).

Ministry of Commerce, Caningos Square, 106-77 Athens (tel: 381-6242; fax: 384-2642).

Ministry of Culture, Bouboulinas 20, 106-82 Athens (tel: 820-1100; fax: 820-1337).

Ministry of Education and Religious Affairs, Mitropoleos 15, 101-85 Athens (tel: 325-4221; fax: 324-8264).

Ministry of Environment, Town Planning and Public Works, Amaliados 17, 115-23 Athens (tel: 643-1461; fax: 644-7608).

Ministry of Finance, Karageorgi Servias 10, 101-84 Athens (tel: 331-3400; fax: 323-8657).

Ministry of Foreign Affairs, Academias 1, 106-71 Athens (tel: 361-0584; fax: 645-0028).

Ministry of Health, Welfare and Social Security, Aristotelous 17, 101-87 Athens (tel: 524-9010; fax: 522-3246).

Ministry of Industry, Energy and Technology, Michalakopoulou 80, 101-92 Athens (tel: 748-2770; fax: 770-8003).

General Secretariat for Energy and Technology, Mesogeion Ave 14-18, 115-10 Athens (tel: 775-2221; fax: 771-4153).

Ministry of Interior, Dragatsaniou 2, 105-59 Athens (tel: 322-3521; fax: 324-1180).

Ministry of Justice, Mesogeion 96, 115-27 Athens (tel: 775-7619; fax: 779-6055).

Ministry of Labour, Pireos 40, 101-82 Athens (tel: 523-3110; fax: 524-9805).

Ministry of National Defence, Papagou Camp, Mesogeion 227-229, 154-51 Athens (tel: 646-5201; fax: 646-5584).

Ministry of National Economy: Division for Foreign Capital and Attracting Investments, Syntagma Square, 101-80 Athens (tel: 333-2000; fax: 333-2130; internet site: http://www.dos.gr/welcome_en.htm).

Division for Private Investment Policy, Syntagma Square, 101-80 Athens (tel: 333-2252/3; fax: 333-2326).

Regional Development Divisions of Attica, Thiras 60, 112-52 Athens (tel: 862-9810; fax: 862-9742).

Ministry of Press and Mass Media, Zalokosta 10, 101-63 Athens (tel: 363-0911; fax: 360-6969).

Ministry of Prime Minister's Office, Vas Sofias, 106-74 Athens (tel: 339-3000; fax: 339-3020).

Ministry of Public Order, Pan Kanellopoulou 4, 101-77 Athens (tel: 692-8510; fax: 692-1675).

Ministry of Transport and Communications, Xenofontos 13, 105-57 Athens (tel: 325-1211; fax: 324-7400).

Prime Minister's Office, Maximos Mansion, Herod Atticus 19, 106-74 Athens (tel: 671-7071; fax: 671-5799).

Other useful addresses

Athenagence (ANA) (news agency), Odos Pindarou 5, Athens 10671 (tel: 363-9816).

Athens and Piraeus Electric Railways (ISAP), Athinas 67, 105-52 Athens (tel: 324-8311; fax: 322-3935).

Athens and Piraeus Trolleys (ILPAP), Admitou 17, 104-46 Athens (tel: 821-6305; fax: 883-7445).

Athens and Piraeus Water Company (EYDAP), Oropou 156, 111-46 Athens (tel: 253-3402; fax: 253-3124).

Athens Municipal Gas Corporation (DEFA), Orfeos 2, 118-54 Athens (tel: 346-1194; fax: 346-1400).

Athens Stock Exchange, Sofokleous 10, 105-59 Athens (tel: 321-1301; fax: 321-3938; internet site: www.ase.gr/).

British Embassy, I Ploutarchou Street, 106-75 Athens (tel: 727-2600).

Centre for Planning and Economic Research (KEPE), Hippokratous St 22, 106-80 Athens (tel: 362-7321; fax: 361-1136; e-mail: kepe@kepe.gr).

Cotton Organisation (OBA), Syngrou Ave 150, 176-71 Athens (tel: 923-4314; fax: 924-3676).

'Democritus' Nuclear Research Centre, Ag Paraskevi, 153-10 Athens (tel: 651-8911; fax: 651-9180).

Department of Press and Information, Ministry to The Prime Minister's Office, Odos Zalokosta 10, Athens (tel: 363-0911).

Economic and Industrial Research Institute (IOBE), Tsami Karatasi 11, 117-42 Athens (tel: 924-1378; fax: 923-3977).

Export Promotion Organisation (OPE), Mar Antippa 86-88, 163-46 Athens (tel: 996-1900; fax: 991-5392).

Federation of Greek Industry (SEB), Xenofontos 5, 105-57 Athens (tel: 323-7325; fax: 322-2929).

Geological and Mineral Research Institute (IGME), Mesogion Ave 70, 115-27 Athens (tel: 779-8412; fax: 775-2211).

Greek Atomic Energy Commission, Ag Paraskevi, 153-10 Athens (tel: 651-8911; fax: 651-9180).

Greek Embassy (USA), 2221 Massachusetts Avenue, NW, Washington DC 20008 (tel: (+1-202)-939-5800; fax: (+1-202)-939-5824; e-mail: greece@greekembassy.org).

Greek Post Offices (ELTA), Apellou 1, 101-88 Athens (tel: 324-3311; fax: 324-1228).

Greek Radio and Television (ET 1), Mesogion Ave 432, 153-42 Athens (tel: 639-0772; fax: 639-0652).

Greek Radio and Television (ET 2), Mesogion Ave 136, 115-62 Athens (tel: 770-1911; fax: 777-6239).

Greek Railways Organisation (OSE), Sina 6, 106-72 Athens (tel: 362-4402; fax: 362-8933).

Hellenic Aerospace Industry (EAB), Mesogion Ave 2-4, 115-27 Athens (tel: 779-9679; fax: 779-7670).

Hellenic Centre for Investment (HCI), 3 Mitropoleos Str, GR-105 57 Athens (tel: 324-2070; fax: 324-2079).

Hellenic Organisation for Small- and Medium-Size Enterprises and Handicraft Undertakings (EOMMEX), Xenias 16, 115-28 Athens (tel: 771-5002; fax: 771-5025).

Hellenic Organisation for the Promotion of Exports (HOPE), 1 Mitropoleos Street, 10557 Athens (tel: 324-7011/16).

Hellenic Standardisation Organisation (ELOT), Acharnon 313, 111-45 Athens (tel: 201-5025; fax: 202-0776).

Hellenic Telecommunications Organisation (OTE), Kifissias 99, 151-24 Athens (tel: 611-7466; fax: 681-0899).

Hellenic Tobacco Organisation (EOK), Kapodistriou 36, 104-32 Athens (tel: 524-7311; fax: 524-7318).

National Statistical Service , Lykourgou 14-16, 101-66 Athens (tel: 324-85118; fax: 324-1098; internet site: http://www.statistics.gr/).

Panhellenic Confederation of Farmers' Co-operatives (PASEGES), Kifissias 16, 115-26 Athens (tel: 770-4737; fax: 777-9313).

Panhellenic Exporters' Association, Kratinou 11, 105-52 Athens (tel: 522-8925; fax: 522-9403).

Public Materials Administration Organisation (ODDY), Stadiou 60, 105-64 Athens (tel: 324-4231; fax: 324;2970).

Public Petroleum Corporation (DEP), Mesogion Ave 357-359, 152-31 Athens (tel: 650-1340; fax: 650-1383).

Public Power Corporation (PPC), Halkokondyli 30, 104-32 Athens (tel: 523-4301; fax: 523-5307).

Union of Commercial Agents, Voulis 15, Athens (tel: 322-3148).

Urban Transport Organisation (OAS), Metsovou 15, 106-82 Athens (tel: 883-6077; fax: 821-2219).

Other news agencies: ANA-MPA: www.ana-mpa.gr

Internet sites

Bridge to Greece and Cyprus: http://greekvillage.com/bridge/bridge.htm

EFG Eurobank Ergasias: www.eurobank.gr

Greek telephone directory: www.hellasyellow.gr

Greenland

KEY FACTS

Official name: Greenland (Kalaallit Nunaat)

Head of State: Queen Margrethe II of Denmark, represented by High Commissioner Søren Hald Møller (since 1 Apr 2005)

Head of government: Prime Minister Jakob Edvard Kuupik Kleist (IA) (from 2 Jun 2009)

Ruling party: Inuit Ataqatigiit (IA) (Inuit Community) (from 2 Jun 2009)

Area: 2,166,086 square km, of which 410,449 square km is not covered by permanent ice

Population: 56,452 (2010; census figure)

Capital: Nuuk (Godthåb)

Official language: Greenlandic Inuit and Danish

Currency: Danish krone (Kr) = 100 ore

Exchange rate: Kr5.55 per US$ (Oct 2011)

GDP real growth: 1.50% (2008)

Labour force: 28,240 (January 2009)

Unemployment: 6.80% (2007)

Inflation: 9.70% (2008)*

* estimated figure

COUNTRY PROFILE

Historical profile

1940 During the German occupation of Denmark in the Second World War, Greenland came under US protection. Denmark re-assumed control of Greenland but with continued military use of bases by the US and later NATO.

1953 Greenland ceased to be a colony and became an autonomous province of the Danish Kingdom under the Home Rule Constitution. Native Inuit were expelled, by Danish officials, from their ancestral lands in the north to make way for expansion of the US airbase at Thule.

1973 Greenland joined the EEC (later EU) as part of Denmark.

1979 Full home rule was granted to Greenland; Denmark retained control of constitutional matters, foreign relations and defence.

1985 Greenland left the EEC following two referenda.

1987 A disagreement with Denmark over the presence of a US military radar system in Thule led to the fall of the coalition government.

1991 Parliamentary elections resulted in a coalition government composed of the Siumit (Forward) party and the Inuit Ataqatigiit (IA) (Inuit Brotherhood).

1995 The IA formed a coalition with Attasut. Lars Emil Johansen became prime minister.

1999 The Danish High Court concluded the Inuit were illegally removed from their land around Thule in 1953, but their right to return was denied.

2000 NASA scientists found that the ice sheet which covers 85 per cent of Greenland's territory was melting by one metre per year.

2002 A coalition government was formed comprising the Siumut and IA parties; Hans Enoksen, became prime minister.

2003 The short-lived coalition collapsed amid allegations of corruption and the use of a native shaman. A new coalition of Siumut and the Atassut party was formed, but it failed within months during a row over the budget. Siumut resumed its coalition with the IA. Inuits lost their appeal to the Danish Supreme Court for return of their land.

2004 Denmark signed an agreement with the US to refurbish the US airbase at Thule.

2005 Prime Minister Enoksen was returned to power in early elections, called in response to allegations of misuse of public funds by ministers and failure of budgetary discussions.

2006 Official studies declared the Greenland ice sheets were melting at an increased rate.

2007 Plans by Greenland Inuits to increase their quota for whale hunting deadlocked the International Whaling Commission negotiations. Critics accused Greenland of expanding for commercial reasons rather than for cultural and nutritional values of native whaling.

2008 The five countries surrounding the Arctic met in Greenland to discuss territorial claims. The talks were aimed at reducing the detrimental effect of unrestrained exploration for oil and gas and forming an agreement concerning access to the north-west passage between the Atlantic and Pacific oceans. A referendum on more autonomy from Denmark was agreed by 75 per cent. Under the new arrangement Greenlanders are recognised as a separate people under international law and the local government was given more control of resources, including a bigger share of oil revenues, and control of internal security.

2009 Early general elections were called so that a new administration would be in place to implement the new self-governing reforms. The left-wing opposition IA won 43.7 per cent of the vote, the ruling Siumut 26.5 per cent. Jakob Edvard Kuupik Kleist (IA) became prime minister.
2010 In July, the Scotland-based exploration company Cairn Energy began drilling for oil offshore between Greenland and Baffin Island. Following the hottest six months of global recorded temperatures, the biggest ice island to break from the Arctic ice sheet since 1962, broke away from northern Greenland in early August. Estimated at around 250 square kilometres and 180m deep the island slowly drifted into the Atlantic Ocean and melted down. In August Cairn Energy announced that it had found natural gas and oil-bearing sands (containing crude oil) off the coast of Greenland.
2011 The leader of the environmental activist group Greenpeace, Kumi Naidoo, was arrested on 17 June, having breached a court-imposed exclusion zone and scaled the Cairn Energy's Greenland exploration oil rig.

Political structure

Constitution

The Home Rule constitution, enacted on 2 June 1953, altered the status of Greenland from a colony to an autonomous province of Denmark. In 1979 full powers were granted with executive, judicial and legislative branches. Denmark retained control of constitutional matters, foreign relations and defence. Following a 26 November 2008 referendum, Greenlanders became recognised as a separate people under international law and the local government gained more control of resources, including a bigger share of oil revenues, and control of internal security. Self-government came into effect on 21 June 2009.
Greenland elects two members to the Danish parliament.

Form of state

Parliamentary democratic dependency

The executive

The Danish monarch is head of state and is represented by a High Commissioner appointed by the monarch.
Executive power is exercised by a prime minister who heads the government, which is composed by the majority political party or parties in parliament.
There are seven Landsstyremaend (ministers) headed by the Landsstyreformanden (prime minister).

National legislature

The unicameral Landstingets (parliament) has 31 members, elected by proportional representation for four-year terms.

Last elections

2 June 2009 (parliamentary)
Results: Parliamentary: Inuit Ataqatigiit (IA) (Inuit Community) won 43.7 per cent of the vote (14 seats out of 31), Siumut (Forward) 26.5 per cent (9), Demokraatit (Democrats) 12.7 per cent (4), Atassut (Community Spirit) 10.9 per cent (3), and Kattusseqatigiit (Candidate list (a grouping of independent candidates)) 3.8 per cent (1). Turnout was 71.3 per cent.

Next elections

2013 (parliamentary)

Political parties

Ruling party

Inuit Ataqatigiit (IA) (Inuit Community) (from 2 Jun 2009)

Main opposition party

Siumut (Forward)

Political situation

As warmer winters have melted more Arctic ice, the countries that surround the newly accessible land and waters free of ice may now allow exploitation. This has become an international bone of contention. The US was in disagreement with Canada concerning access to the Northwest Passage as free passage for all shipping in 2006. Russia, using a submarine, planted its national flag on the Arctic seabed and claimed an area of one million square kilometres in 2007. The five countries surrounding the pole – the US, Russia, Canada, Norway and Denmark (including Greenland) – finally sat down to discuss the future of the region in August 2009. No immediate resolution was agreed but Russia and Denmark were confident that each of their proposals would be ready for submission to the Arctic Council, within the UN Environmental Programme (UNEP), by 2014.
In July 2009, the Danish government had announced plans to set up a permanent military presents in the Arctic and establish a regional joint service command in the Faroe Islands, with troops also stationed in Greenland. In mid-2010, natural gas and oil deposits were discovered offshore in Greenland territorial waters, by the prospecting company, Cairn Energy, which described the find as 'North Sea-scale' and likely to be significant, with an estimated 20 billion barrels of oil.

Population

56,452 (2010; census figure)
Last census: 1 January 2008: 56,462
Population density: Seven inhabitants per square km (2001) (icecap excluded).
Annual growth rate: 0.2 per cent (2003)

Ethnic make-up

Eighty-eight per cent of the population are Inuit and Greenland-born whites and the remainder are primarily Danes.

Religions

Ninety-six per cent belong to the Evangelical Lutheran Church of Denmark.

Education

Pupils per teacher: 10 in primary schools.

Health

Life expectancy: 68.9 years (estimate 2003)
Fertility rate/Maternal mortality rate: 2.4 births per woman (World Bank)
Birth rate/Death rate: 16 births per 1,000 population; eight deaths per 1,000 population (2003).
Child (under 5 years) mortality rate (per 1,000): 17 per 1,000 live births (2003)

Main cities

Nuuk (Godthåb) (capital, estimated population 14,438 in 2005), Sisimiut (Holsteinsborg) (5,335), Ilulissat (Jakobshavn) (4,352).

Languages spoken

Danish and Greenlandic Inuit, which is an eastern branch of the East-Eskimo language categorised by linguists as Inupik, which is spoken on the northern coasts of Canada and Alaska and the eastern-most tip of Siberia. Greenlanders connected with tourism often speak English.

Official language/s

Greenlandic Inuit and Danish

Media

Press

In Greenlandic (although with Danish and sometimes English online editions), there are only two newspapers, Atuagagdliutit Gronlandsposten (www.ag.gl) is published twice weekly and Sermitsiak is published weekly; *Niviarsiaq* is published monthly.
Dailies: There are no daily newspapers.
Weeklies:
Grønlandsposten/Atuagagdliutit and *Sermitsiak*.
Periodicals: *Grønland* is a general interest periodical, published 10 times a year.

Broadcasting

The national public broadcaster is Kalaallit Nunaata Radioa (KNR) (Greenland Broadcasting Company) with overall responsibility for radio and television services. It is financed through government funding, advertising and sponsorship and broadcasts a range of cultural, news, music and entertainment programmes.
Radio: Greenland Radio (KNR) broadcasts in Greenlandic and Danish with both local productions and Danish programmes.
Private radio stations include Radio 50Z20, an affiliate of the Danish, Radio Nyhederne (www.radionyt.com), Radio Grønnedal and Nuuk FM

Television: KNR TV broadcasts in Greenlandic and Danish with domestic productions of cultural and youth programmes and imported (mostly Danish) shows.
Each local community has one or more private TV stations which are allocated a 15-minute broadcast daily on KNR-TV (30 minutes on Sunday).

Advertising

The most widely used means of advertising are the press and direct mail. The only cinema in Greenland also shows advertising. There is no advertising on radio, and poster sites are heavily regulated.

Economy

There are over 400 licensed fishing vessels operating in Greenland, where over 90 per cent of all exports are derived from fish products, and fishing is the primary industry. Around 2,700 whales are caught each year. Although Greenland draws on subsidies from Denmark, in the form of block grants, the government maintains a tight fiscal policy to create public budget surpluses and low inflation. The total financial package received from Denmark is around US$650 million annually, providing 60 per cent of government revenues.
The service sector is an important component of the economy, constituting 63.2 per cent of GDP, of which public service is a leading factor. Although not a mass-market destination, Greenland is a destination for particular travellers and has a growing tourism sector.
Greenland has abundant thermal and hydropower and investigation to utilise them as export elements is being undertaken. The US aluminium producer, Alcoa, has plans to build a smelter, using a thermal power facility. The smelter is expected to come into production at the end of 2014 and together with the related power station will employ some 1,200 workers.
Natural gas and oil deposits were discovered offshore in Greenland territorial waters in mid-2010. The prospecting company, Cairn Energy, described the find as 'North Sea-scale' and likely to be significant, with an estimated 20 billion barrels of oil.

External trade

Greenland is not a member of the European Union, despite being an overseas territory of Denmark. However, it has a fishing agreement with the EU, which allows it to sell its fish products as non-dutiable goods in the EU. It also has leased fishing rights to the EU.
While Canada provides Greenland with fresh fruit and vegetables Greenland does not produce anything that Canada does not already have, so trade is generally one-way.

Imports

Imports include machinery and transport equipment, food, manufactured goods and petroleum products.
Main sources: Denmark (typically 75 per cent of total), Sweden (12 per cent), Norway (2 per cent).

Exports

Exports consist mainly of fish (cod, halibut and crabs, which accounts for approximately 45 per cent) and shrimp, which makes up over 55 per cent.
Main destinations: Denmark (typically 61 per cent of total), Japan (14 per cent), China (6 per cent).

Agriculture

Farming

The agricultural sector, comprising around 60 farms, is largely confined to sheep farming in the south and small-scale reindeer farming. Livestock production is around 360 tonnes of mutton and lamb. The production of lamb and reindeer meat is mainly for domestic consumption. Arable areas mainly produce hay for fodder.

Fishing

Fishing is the mainstay of the economy, accounting for over 90 per cent of exports and giving employment to a quarter of the population. Principal products include shrimp, halibut, cod and seal. Typical annual catches include over 142,000 tonnes (t) shrimps and 197,000t fish. Halibut is increasingly important, while cod has declined in importance. Traditional sea mammal catches are typically over 2,500 whales and 115,000 seals annually.
The fishing industry employs around 6,000 people. The principal export markets are the EU, especially Denmark, and Japan.
Greenland lost the vote to have its whaling quota expanded to include 10 humpback whales, at the International Whaling Commission (IWC) meeting in 2008. Other members considered that too much of the whale meat, 25 per cent, was sold commercially, in contravention of the IWC qualification for aboriginal or subsistence whaling. The quota for Inuit whaling 2008–12 was agreed at 212 minkes, 19 fins and two bowhead whales.

Industry and manufacturing

Industry is centred on fish processing and packaging. Most of the sector is controlled by the government-owned Royal Greenland company, which manages factories and smaller plants in both Greenlnd and Denmark. Some tanning and leatherworking takes place in the south.
Infrastructure improvements have provided a boost to construction activity, in particular the development of new airstrips.

Tourism

The short tourist season limits the industry and most visitors make the journey to the Arctic and semi-Arctic country for its spectacular landscape of glaciers, icebergs, Arctic wildlife and the chance to see the *aurora borealis* (northern lights). Activities include dog-sledding, whale watching and experiencing a little of the ingenious Inuit culture.
Visitor numbers have grown to around 30,000 annually, mostly from Denmark.

Mining

There are known reserves of zinc, lead, copper, cobalt, uranium, iron ore, gold and diamonds. Mineral exploration is actively encouraged and the administration has reformed its mining regulations. Large quantities of two of the world's rarest metals, niobium and tantalum, exist in Greenland.

Hydrocarbons

Greenland still hopes that oil and gas might become one of the mainstays of its economy. However, currently it relies on imports of over 4,000 barrels per day. Oil exploration began in the 1970s and the government is encouraging further exploration offshore of West Greenland. Arctic climatatic conditions and deep waters make the task difficult. Greenland does not produce or import gas and coal.
Natural gas and oil deposits were discovered offshore in Greenland territorial waters in mid-2010. The prospecting company, Cairn Energy, described the find as 'North Sea-scale' and likely to be significant, with an estimated 20 billion barrels of oil.

Energy

Total installed generating capacity is some 106kW; electricity production was over 300 million kilowatt hours in 2007, the majority of which was produced by thermal power plants. There is a hydroelectric station in Buksefjorden, which supplies Nuuk; other hydroelectric plants are under construction or being planned.

Banking and insurance

NUNA Bank A/S is an independent bank that was formerly a subsidiary of the Danish bank Sparekasse Bikuben AS. The two banks share a strong business relationship. The other major bank in Greenland is Grønlandsbanken, which is owned by Danish banks.

Central bank

Monetary policy and administration is handled by the Danish central bank (Danmarks Nationalbank).

Time

Greenland has four time zones:

East Greenland and Scoresbysund – GMT minus one hour (daylight saving, end March to end September, GMT)
Central Greenland, Godthåb – GMT minus three hours (daylight saving, GMT minus two hours)
Western Greenland, Thule – GMT minus four hours (no daylight saving)
Danmarkshavn – GMT (no daylight saving)

Geography

Greenland is the world's largest island, although much of the surrounding seas are permently frozen forming the arctic shelf. Greenland lies in the North Atlantic Ocean, to the east of Canada and to the west of Iceland. Around 85 per cent of the landmass is permanently covered by ice up to 3,375 metres (m) thick. A snow peaked central range of mountains run north/south, with the highest peak reaching 3,200m above sea-level. There are 410,449 square km of coastland that is habitable.

Hemisphere
Northern

Climate

Arctic; temperatures at Nuuk/Godthåb vary between about minus 12 degrees Celsius (C) and 11 degrees C.

Entry requirements

Entry requirements are the same as for Denmark.

Passports
Required by all, except EU visitors travelling on national ID cards.

Visa
Even though a Danish territory, visas are not valid for Greenland unless specified in the permit. For a business visa, an original letter of invitation from a local company or organisation, giving details about purpose of visit and duration of stay must accompany an application, along with evidence of hotel reservations.
Approval must be obtained from the Greenland Home Rule administration, PO Box 1015, 3900 Nuuk, Greenland, for entry into the military defence areas including the gateways of Sondre Stromfjord and Thule (unless in direct transit to points outside the airport of Sondre Stromfjord) and entry for the purpose of mountain/glacier climbing or geological/archaeological research.

Health (for visitors)

Mandatory precautions
Vaccination certificates are not usually required.

Public holidays (national)

Fixed dates
1 Jan (New Year's Day), 6 Jan (Epiphany), 21 Jun (National Day), 24–26 Dec (Christmas).

Variable dates
Maundy Thursday, Good Friday, Easter Monday, Great Prayer Day (Apr/May), Ascension Day, Whit Monday.

Working hours

Banking
Mon–Fri: 0930–1600 (Thu 1800).

Business
Mon–Fri: 0800–1600 or 0830–1630.

Government
Mon–Fri: generally 0900–1700.

Shops
Mon–Fri: 0800–1700 or 0900–1730, Sat: close at 1300 or 1400.

Telecommunications

Mobile/cell phones
There is a 900 GSM service in populated areas only.

Electricity supply

220V AC, 50Hz.

Getting there

Air
National airline: Air Greenland
International airport/s: Kangerlussuaq (Sondre Stromfjord) (SFJ) international airport, on the west coast close to Sisimiut and the capital, Nuuk, has regular flights from Canada, Iceland and Denmark. Facilities include: bureau de change, restaurant, duty-free shops, post office and car rental.
Other airport/s: Narsarsuaq (UAK) is an airport for stopover flights between Europe and North America and internal flights, with few facilities.
Kulusuk (KUS), on the east coast receives some internal flights but most come from Iceland.
Airport tax: None

Surface
Water: Comfortable cruise ships sail during the summer season.
Main port/s: Nuuk/Godthåb

Getting about

National transport
Air: Air Greenland flies routes along the western coast from Pituffik and Qaanaaq in the north to Paamiut in the south and across to Kulusuk and Tasiilaq in the east. The regularity of services is dependent on the weather; reservations should be made well in advance. Helicopter services link other, more remote, settlements.
Road: There are virtually no roads connecting towns in Greenland. Only 60km of paved roads exist, realistically the best means of transport is the traditional sea and air travel where available.
Dog-sledges and snow mobiles can be hired for variable periods.
Water: Greenland Trade operates two passenger liners on the west coast. Villages are served by local boats, some of which are for private hire.

BUSINESS DIRECTORY

Telephone area codes

The international direct dialling (IDD) code for Greenland is +299, followed by the subscriber's number.

Banking

Grønlandsbanken (Bank of Greenland) 29 Skibshavnsvej, PO Box 1033, DK-3900 Nuuk (tel: 347-700; fax 347-706).

Central bank
Danmarks Nationalbank, Havnegade 5, DK-1093 Copenhagen (tel: (+45) 3363-6363; fax: (+45) 3363-7103; e-mail: info@nationalbanken.dk).

Travel information

Greenland Tourism Main Office, 29 Hans Egedesvej, PO Box 1615, Nuuk DK-3900 (tel: 342-820; fax: 322-877; e-mail: info@greenland.com).

National tourist organisation offices
Greenland Tourism a/s, Main Office, PO Box 1552, 3900 Nuuk (tel: 322-888; fax: 322-877; e-mail: info@visitgreenland.com).

Ministries

Grønlands Hjemmestyre (Greenland Home Rule administration), PO Box 1015, 3900 Nuuk (tel: 345-000; e-mail: info@gh.gl; internet site: www.gh.gl).

Greenland Home Rule Government Denmark Office, Sjaeleboderne 2, 1122 Copenhagen K, Denmark (tel: (+45) 3313-4224; fax: (+45) 3332-2024).

Prime Minister's Office, Greenland Department, 3 Hausergade, DK-1128 Copenhagen K, Denmark (tel: (+45) 3393-2200).

Other useful addresses

Ministry of Foreign Affairs, Asiatisk Plads 2, DK-1448 Copenhagen, Denmark (tel: (+45) 3392-0000; internet: www.um.dk/en).

Greenland Trade Shipping Department, Grønlandshavnen, DK-9220 Aalborg Ost (tel: (+45) 9815-7677).

Kalaallit Nunaata Radioa (Grønlands Radio) (KNR) (Radio Greenland), H J Rinksvej 35, PO Box 1007, 3900 Nuuk (tel: 321-172; fax: 324-703).

Internet sites

Bureau of minerals and petroleum: http://bmp.gl/

Greenland Radio: www.knr.gl/

Greenland Tourism: www.greenland-guide.gl

Grenada

KEY FACTS

Official name: Grenada

Head of State: Queen Elizabeth II, represented by Governor General Sir Carlyle Arnold Glean (since 27 Nov 2008)

Head of government: Prime Minister Tillman Thomas (took office 9 Jul 2008)

Ruling party: National Democratic Congress (NDC) (from 9 Jul 2008)

Area: 345 square km

Population: 104,000 (2010)*

Capital: St George's

Official language: English

Currency: East Caribbean dollar (EC$) = 100 cents

Exchange rate: EC$2.70 per US$ (fixed)

GDP per capita: US$6,543 (2010)

GDP real growth: -1.40% (2010)

GDP: US$674.00 million (2010)

Inflation: 5.00% (2010)

Balance of trade: -US$253.36 million (2010)

* estimated figure

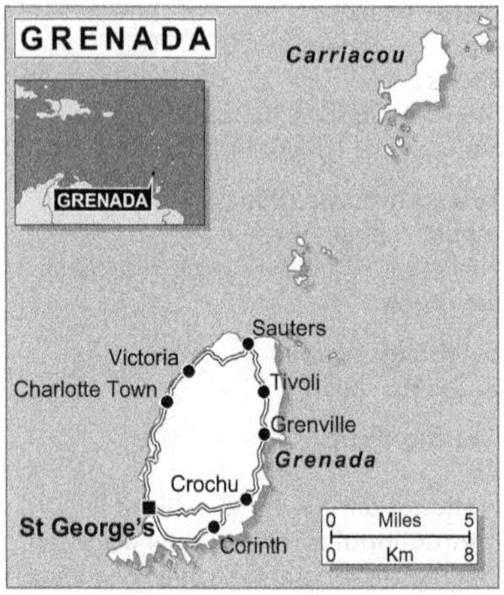

COUNTRY PROFILE

Historical profile

1762 Grenada was initially colonised by the French until captured by the British.
1783 British control of the islands was recognised.
1958 Grenada joined the Federation of the West Indies.
1967 Internal self-government was granted.
1974 Eric Gairy became prime minister of a newly independent Grenada.
1979 A coup deposed Gairy; Maurice Bishop, leading the socialist New Jewel Movement, took power.
1983 Civil disturbances, anti-government protests, media restrictions and a power struggle within the left-wing government resulted in a *coup d'etat*, led by General Hudson Austin, which deposed and then executed Prime Minister Bishop and nine members of his cabinet. A US-led invasion, backed by troops from Jamaica, Barbados and other members of the Organisation of Eastern Caribbean States (OECS), arrested Austin and reinstated the 1974 constitution.
1984 The general election was won by the New National Party (NNP) led by Herbert Blaize.
1987 The National Democratic Congress (NDC) was formed.
1996 Grenada signed anti-drug trafficking treaties with the US. The appointment of Sir Daniel Williams as governor general provoked controversy because of his links with the NNP.
1999 The NNP won the general election, winning every seat in the House of Representatives.
2001 Grenada was blacklisted by the Organisation for Economic Co-operation and Development (OECD)'s Financial Action Task Force (FATF) for not doing enough to combat money laundering. A review of offshore banking was begun.
2002 The government revoked the licences of 36 offshore banks in an attempt to secure Grenada's removal from the FATF blacklist. Grenada was hit by tropical storm Lili, causing damage estimated at around 2 per cent of GDP.
2003 Grenada was removed from the FATF's blacklist. The NNP was re-elected.
2004 Prime Minister Mitchell was accused of taking a US$500,000 bribe from a German citizen. Hurricane Ivan struck Grenada damaging 85 per cent of the island's housing.
2005 Grenada-born, army Private Johnson Beharry received Britain's highest military bravery awarded, the Victoria Cross, for his service in Iraq. Hurricane Emily struck the island, causing extensive damage.
2006 The EU granted around US$11 million for the rehabilitation of schools devastated by Hurricanes Ivan and Emily.
2008 Sir Eric Gairy was named as Grenada's first National Hero. He founded the Grenada United Labour Party in 1950 and steered the island to independence in 1974, becoming Grenada's first prime minister. The opposition NDC won the elections, ousting the former ruling party, the NNP. Tillman Thomas became prime minister. Sir Daniel Williams retired as governor general and was replaced by Carlyle Glean.
2009 The Point Salines international airport was renamed after former prime minister, Maurice Bishop, who had been executed in 1983 as a result of a *coup d'etat*, led by General Hudson Austin. A number of the perpetrators of the *coup d'etat* were released from jail after serving their 25 year sentences.
2010 In June the Organisation of Petroleum Exporting Countries (Opec) Fund for International Development approved a US$8.5 million loan for the second phase of an infrastructure programme of 25 agricultural feeder roads. The location of Grenada's new parliament and judiciary

was announced, to be at Mount Wheldale, St George; work to be funded by the Australian government. The 4,645 square metre building will house both chambers of parliament, separated since hurricane Ivan in 2004 damaged the previous parliament; work is scheduled to be completed by 2013.

2011 On 20 May, Grenada signed the Rome Statute of the International Criminal Court (ICC), the articles necessary to become a member. On 20 June the World Band agreed to a zero interest loan of US$5.6 million to fund an improved electricity distribution system and diversity of energy production (including renewable energy sources). On 15 July Grenada became a full member of the International Renewable Energy Agency (Irena). On 1 August citizens of the Organisation of Eastern Caribbean States (OECS) – Antigua and Barbuda, Dominica, Grenada, St Kitts and Nevis, St Lucia and St Vincent and the Grenadines – were granted freedom of movement, allowing them to reside, work, establish businesses and provide services throughout the organisation.

Political structure

Form of state

Independent state; it is a member of the Commonwealth.

The executive

The British monarch is the head of state, represented by the governor general appointed by the monarch. Executive power is vested in the cabinet, led by the prime minister. The cabinet is appointed by the governor general on the advice of the prime minister and is responsible to parliament. Following legislative elections, the leader of the majority party or the leader of the majority coalition is usually appointed prime minister by the governor general.

National legislature

The bicameral parliament consists of a 15-member House of Representatives (members are elected by popular vote to serve five-year terms) and an upper, 13-member, Senate (10 senators appointed by the government and three by the leader of the opposition)

Legal system

The legal system is based on English common law. Grenada is responsible for its own magistrate's courts. The regional Eastern Caribbean Supreme Court is responsible for the high court and the court of appeals. The final court of appeal is to the Privy Council in the UK.

Last elections

8 July 2008 (parliamentary)

Results: Parliamentary: The NDC won 50.9 per cent of the vote (11 seats out of 15), the NNP won 47.7 per cent (four); turnout was 80.3 per cent.

Next elections

2013 (parliamentary)

Political parties

Ruling party

National Democratic Congress (NDC) (from 9 Jul 2008)

Main opposition party

New National Party (NNP)

Political situation

Prime Minister Keith Mitchell has an apparent penchant for persistent misfortune. Firstly, in 2004 he was accused of accepting US$500,000 from a German citizen in return for the post of general ambassador to Grenada and a diplomatic passport. An accusation he denied and was never proven. The second accusation is not only more convoluted but also has a wider implication if proved true.

In 2007, in a US criminal trial Prime Minister Mitchell was sited as a recipient of US$1 million from a US swindler. In the documents submitted to court it was asserted that Mitchell was or had been a US citizen. The news of this resulted in a question mark over Mitchell's Grenadian citizenship and his legitimacy as a Grenadian politician (only Grenadian citizens may be politicians). As of March 2008 the prime minister had not revealed the circumstances regarding his citizenship and whether he had revoked US citizenship at the time of his first election to the parliament of Grenada.

Population

104,000 (2010)*

Last census: May 2001: 102,632

Population density: 285 inhabitants per square km. Urban population: 38 per cent (1995—2001).

Annual growth rate: 0.3 per cent 1994–2004 (WHO 2006)

Ethnic make-up

Black (82 per cent), mixed black and European (13 per cent), European and East Indian (5 per cent) and a small number of Arawak/Carib.

Religions

Roman Catholic (53 per cent), Anglican (13.8 per cent), other Protestants (33.2 per cent).

Education

Education in Grenada is based on the English GCSE and A level system. There are several excellent local schools and an international primary school.

In total, there are 79 schools, 59 primary, 19 secondary and one tertiary institution. TA Marryshow Community College has a school of agriculture and a teacher's training college.

The St George's University School of Medicine is run by a US firm and offers medical training as well as non-medical courses.

Compulsory years: Five to 16.

Enrolment rate: 95 per cent gross primary enrolment of relevant age groups (including repeaters) (World Bank 2003).

Health

Grenada is divided into seven health districts, six of which have a health centre responsible for primary care. In addition, there are several medical stations throughout the country.

Medical care is limited, but everyone has access to some form of healthcare, regardless of ability to pay.

Life expectancy: 68 years, 2004 (WHO 2006)

Fertility rate/Maternal mortality rate: 2.4 births per woman, 2004 (WHO 2006)

KEY INDICATORS — Grenada

	Unit	2006	2007	2008	2009	2010
Population	m	0.11	0.11	0.11	*0.10	*0.10
Gross domestic product (GDP)	US$bn	0.56	0.61	0.68	0.61	0.67
GDP per capita	US$	5,480	5,926	6,587	5,969	6,543
GDP real growth	%	-2.3	4.9	0.3	-7.7	-1.4
Inflation	%	4.3	3.9	8.0	-0.3	5.0
Exports (fob) (goods)	US$m	32.3	40.7	40.5	38.7	31.1
Imports (fob) (goods)	US$m	297.1	327.9	338.8	252.8	284.4
Balance of trade	US$m	-264.8	-287.2	-298.3	-214.1	-253.4
Current account	US$m	-232.8	-261.6	-268.7	-174.8	-218.2
Total reserves minus gold	US$m	100.0	110.6	105.3	129.1	119.2
Foreign exchange	US$m	100.0	110.5	104.1	112.4	102.8
Exchange rate	per US$	2.70	2.70	2.70	2.70	2.70

* estimated figure

Birth rate/Death rate: 23 births per 1,000 population; 7.5 deaths per 1,000 population (2003).
Child (under 5 years) mortality rate (per 1,000): 18.0 per 1,000 live births (World Bank)

Welfare
The social welfare department of the ministry of labour administers social work programmes to families and gives financial aid to three private children's homes. There is also a women's shelter in the northern part of the island. There are a number of government social service agencies that monitor the welfare of children, women and those with disabilities.

Main cities
St George's (capital, estimated population 3,680 in 2005)

Languages spoken
English and French patois
Official language/s
English

Media
Freedom of the press is guaranteed by law.
Press
The monthly *The Barnacle* publishes business news. There are no daily newspapers. *The Grenada Guardian* is sponsored by the Grenada United Labour political Party.
Weeklies: Weeklies include *The Grenadain Voice* (www.granadianvoce.com), *The Grenada Informer* (www.belgrafix.com) and *Grenada Today*.
Periodicals: *The Barnacle* (www.barnaclegrenada.com) is published monthly.
Broadcasting
The Grenada Broadcasting Network (GBN) (www.klassicgrenada.com) provides the national, public service, and is partly owned by the government and partly by the Caribbean Communications Network (CCN) (www.onecaribbeanmedia.net).
Radio: GBC operates two radio stations, Klassic Radio and Hott FM (www.klassicgrenada.com). Klassic Radio has 43 per cent of the audience listening figures and can be received by surrounding islands. Hott FM has a younger audience than its associate station. Commercial radio includes City Sound FM (www.citysoundfm.com) and Voice of Grenada (www.spiceislander.com/vog), religious stations include Harbour Light Radio (www.harbourlightradio.org) and the Catholic Radio Upgrade.
Television: GBC Television (www.klassicgrenada.com) operates one channel and Gayelle TV is a the private cable service from Trinidad and Tobago.
News agencies
Other news agencies: Caribbean Net News: www.caribbeannetnews.com

Economy
The economy is dominated by the service sector, in particular tourism, which attracts most foreign direct investment (FDI), particularly in construction of holiday facilities. The service sector is almost 75 per cent of GDP, with industry just over 20 per cent, of which manufacturing accounts for around 5 per cent and agriculture makes up just under 5 per cent of GDP. The St George's University, located in Grenada, but prized as the combined Caribbean islands' centralised university, offers medical, veterinarian and other science courses as well as business and arts courses to 11,000 students from 140 countries. The Caribbean islands are subject to damage inflicted by hurricanes and Grenada is no exception. It experienced a contraction in its agricultural sector after hurricanes Ivan and Emily in 2004 and 2005, which cut production and hastened the migration of farm workers into towns and other industries.
GDP growth was 4.9 per cent in 2007, after two consecutive years of negative growth, as reconstruction and the 2007 Cricket World Cup boosted demand. Growth fell to 2.2 per cent in 2008 before plummeting to -7.7 per cent in 2009 as the global economic crisis cut tourist numbers and petroleum reached record high prices. Unemployment rose to 25 per cent nationally and up to 40 per cent in rural areas.
The government invested more in the agricultural sector in 2009, with attention paid to neglected farms and access roads and assistance given to land clearance. These undertakings paid off as production of Grenada's principal agricultural exports – cocoa, nutmeg and mace – increased. And despite an overall decline in global trade these products sold well. Cocoa production was 463,000 tonnes in 2008/09, an increase of 30.2 per cent on the previous (financial) year, valued at US$1.5 billion. Nutmeg in the same period was 35.8 tonnes, an increase of 13.1 per cent and valued at US$3.1 billion. Livestock farming and the fishing industry both enjoyed increased output, but domestic food crops were adversely affected by bad weather and consumer's low purchasing power.
The government introduced fiscal measures to balance the economy, including replacing, in 2008, a general consumption tax, with a valued added tax (VAT). The International Monetary Fund (IMF) provided from April 2010, around US$13.3 million in a three-year extended credit facility to help Grenada recover from the economic crisis, boost growth, reduce poverty and strengthen the private sector and business climate, while reducing vulnerabilities in the financial sector.

External trade
As a member of the Caribbean Community and Common Market (Caricom), Grenada operates within the single market (Caribbean Single Market and Economy (CSME)), which it joined in 2006 and has a common currency as a member of the Eastern Caribbean Central Bank (ECCB). Caricom has a common external tariff and offers duty-free trade among its members. Grenada is a member of the Organisation of East Caribbean States (OECS); set up to promote region development and economic integration. It is also a member of the World Trade Organisation (WTO).
Imports
Main imports are food, manufactured consumer goods, machinery, chemicals, petroleum and construction materials.
Main sources: US (typically 31 per cent of total), Trinidad and Tobago (25 per cent), Venezuela (7 per cent).
Exports
Main agricultural exports include cocoa, nutmeg and mace, bananas, tropical fruit, vegetables, fish and meat products, manufactured goods include clothing, light industrial products and foodstuffs.
Main destinations: Dominica (typically 16 per cent of total), US (16 per cent), Saint Lucia (11 per cent).

Agriculture
Farming
The agricultural sector contributes around 8 per cent to GDP and accounts for around 65 per cent of exports.
Activity centres on the traditional farming of nutmeg/mace (the world's second-largest producer after Indonesia), cocoa and bananas. Nutmeg and cocoa exports have benefited from a decline in world supply due to political problems in global suppliers (Indonesia and Côte d'Ivoire), as opposed to improvements in output.
Agricultural development policy is geared towards the rehabilitation of the cocoa industry, the promotion of new export crops, greater provision of fertilisers and other inputs and privatisation of state farms.
Grenada was adversely affected by the loss of export markets in 2007, when WTO-led legislation opened up the EU banana market to worldwide suppliers.
Fishing
There is a small fishing industry.
The typical total annual fish catch is over 2,247t. Shellfish, molluscs and cephalopods account for another 39t per annum.

Industry and manufacturing
The industrial sector accounts for around 20 per cent of GDP, of which manufacturing constitutes around 7 per cent.

Manufacturing activities include the production of garments, beverages, flour, wheat-bran, animal feed, furniture, paints and varnishes, sugar, rum, coconut oil, lime juice and honey. Furniture, handicrafts and garments are also manufactured for export to the Caricom market. The government is committed to achieving growth in the manufacturing sector and to this end is endeavouring to attract foreign firms to use Grenada as a base for exports to extra-regional markets. Joint ventures are encouraged between local private sector and foreign investors in order to assist local manufacturers to access capital, technology and marketing channels.

Tourism

Tourism, which accounts for around 5 per cent of Grenada's GDP and 5 per cent of the total labour force, is an increasingly important element in the economy, particularly in terms of its foreign exchange-earning capacity. After several difficult years, the sector has recovered since in 2003. The cruise market is being actively developed and a newly-constructed cruise terminal was opened in December 2004 that is part of phase one of a redevelopment site for the city of St George. The damage to accommodation caused by Hurricane Ivan in September 2004 resulted in an overall contraction of stay-over numbers for the year. The cruise-ship sector, on the other hand, recovered very quickly, recording 226,944 visitors for 2004.

The majority of visitors originate in the US, other Caribbean countries and the UK. An increasing number of visitors are coming from the UK and Germany due to the expansion of charter flights.

Hydrocarbons

There are no known hydrocarbon reserves. Consumption of oil was 3,000 barrels per day (bpd) in 2008, all of which was imported. In 2005, Grenada, plus a number of other Caribbean states, signed an agreement with Venezuela to establish PetroCaribe, a multi-national oil company, owned by the participating states. PetroCaribe buys low-priced Venezuelan crude oil under long-term payment plans.

Any use of natural gas or coal is commercially insignificant. Trinidad and Tobago has had a plan to build a US$500 million, 965km natural gas pipeline linking the eastern Caribbean islands, which would open possibilities of importing natural gas into Grenada.

Energy

Thermal power plants produce a total installed electricity generating capacity of 32MW. The infrastructure damage caused during hurricane seasons has hampered the country's attempts at finding alternative sources of energy. The potential of solar and wind power are recognised but investment is constrained by their fragile characteristics. Providing energy through individual installations offers an option that could avoid wholesale public generating capacity devastation. Cuba already has a system of distributed generation (DG), whereby small-scale plants are located around the country and closer to their end users. This has allowed Cuba to recover from Caribbean hurricanes much more rapidly than countries which adopted more centralised power generation plants.

Plans for the commercial development of a geothermal-fuelled power plant, developed by the Eastern Caribbean Geothermal Development Project (ECGDP) (or Geo-Caraïbes), which is estimated will provide 60–120MW overall, will be operated by the West Indies Power Limited (WIPL), which is owned by ECGDP countries. On 20 June 2011, the World Band agreed to a zero interest loan of US$5.6 million to fund an improved electricity distribution system and diversity of energy production (including renewable energy sources).

Grenada became a full member of the International Renewable Energy Agency (Irena) in July 2011.

Financial markets

Stock exchange

Eastern Caribbean Securities Exchange (ECSE)

Banking and insurance

The seven members of the Organisation of Eastern Caribbean States (OECS), Antigua and Barbuda, Dominica, Grenada, Montserrat, St Kitts and Nevis, St Lucia and St Vincent and the Grenadines, share a common currency and central bank. The British Virgin Islands and Anguilla are associate members.

Central bank

Eastern Caribbean Central Bank, St Kitts and Nevis.

Offshore facilities

The strengthening of the regulatory framework by the Grenada International Financial Services Authority (GIFSA) led to significant improvement and in 2003 Grenada was removed from the blacklist drawn up by the Organisation for Economic Co-operation and Development (OECD).

Time

GMT minus four hours

Geography

Grenada is a mountainous, heavily forested island. It is the most southerly of the Windward Islands in the West Indies. The country also includes some of the small islands known as the Grenadines, which lie to the north-east of Grenada, the largest of these being the low-lying island of Carriacou.

Hemisphere

Northern

Climate

Tropical marine with an annual mean temperature of 28 degrees Celsius. Rain occurs mainly from June–December. Driest from February–May.

Entry requirements

Passports

Required by all and must be valid for six months from the date of departure. Proof of return/onward passage is necessary.

Visa

Not required by nationals of most of the Americas, Europe, Australasia and Japan, for both tourist and business trips, valid for three months. Business visitors should supply extra information: letter of introduction from foreign company and letter of invitation from a local host. For further details and exceptions contact the consular section of the nearest High Commission or Embassy.

Currency advice/regulations

The import and export of foreign currencies is unrestricted, however large amounts should be declared.

Travellers cheques are widely accepted. To avoid extra exchange fees US dollar denominations are advised.

Health (for visitors)

Mandatory precautions

Yellow fever certificate required if arriving from an infected area.

Advisable precautions

Immunisation against hepatitis A, B and diphtheria may be recommended.

Medical attention can cost several thousand dollars and doctors often expect immediate cash payments; insurance is advisable.

Hotels

There are a wide variety of hotels from luxurious to one star. Except for town hotels, most are located near beaches, all hotels should be booked well in advance. An 8 per cent sales tax on food and beverages and 10 per cent service charge are added to the bill.

Public holidays (national)

Fixed dates

1 Jan (New Year's Day), 7 Feb (Independence Day), 1 May (Labour Day), 25 Oct (Thanksgiving Day), 25–26 Dec (Christmas).

Variable dates

Good Friday, Easter Monday (Mar/Apr), Whit Monday, Corpus Christi (May/Jun),

Emancipation Day (first Mon in Aug), Carnival (two days, Aug).

Working hours
Banking
Mon–Thu: 0800–1400; Fri: 0800–1300, 1430–1700.
Business
Mon–Thu: 0800–1145, 1300–1600; Fri: 0800–1145, 1300–1700.
Government
Mon–Thu: 0800–1145, 1300–1600; Fri: 0800–1145, 1300–1700.
Shops
Mon–Fri: 0800–1145, 1300–1600; Sat: 0800–1145.

Telecommunications
Mobile/cell phones
GSM 850 900/1800/1900 services cover all of St George.

Electricity supply
220/240V AC, 50 cycles

Getting there
Air
International airport/s: Maurice Bishop International Airport (previously Point Salines, renamed in 2009) (GND), 8km from St George's; bureau de change, duty-free shops, restaurant, shops and car rental.
Taxis are available.
Airport tax: Departure tax EC$50, payable in local currency only.
Surface
Water: Many cruise lines call at Grenada. Regular boat services from St Vincent, Martinique and Trinidad. There is a ferry service to Carriacou Island.
Main port/s: St George's.

Getting about
National transport
Road: There are approximately 1,050km of roads, of which 650km are paved, although most main roads are narrow and winding.
Buses: Public transport is provided by small private operators, with a system covering the entire country. Cheap but often slow and few run during the late afternoons, evenings and Sundays.
City transport
Taxis: Widely available. Fares are regulated.
Car hire
International licence required or local permit obtained (valid national licence must be presented to local Traffic Department), a minimum age of 25 applies. Traffic drives on the left.

BUSINESS DIRECTORY

Telephone area codes
The international direct dialling code (IDD) for Grenada is +1 473, followed by subscriber's number.

Chambers of Commerce
Grenada Chamber of Industry and Commerce, PO Box 129, St George's (tel: 440-2937; fax: 440-6621; e-mail: gcic@caribsurf.com).

Banking
Bank of Nova Scotia, PO Box 194, Grand Anse, St George's (tel: 440-3274).

Barclays Bank, PO Box 37, Grand Anse, St George's (tel: 440-3232; fax: 440-3232).

Grenada Bank of Commerce, PO Box 4, Grand Anse, St George's (tel: 440-3521; fax: 440-4153).

Grenada Co-operative Bank, Church Street, St George's (tel: 440-2111, 440-3549; fax: 440-6600).

Grenada Development Bank, Halifax Street, St George's (tel: 440-2382/1620).

National Commercial Bank of Grenada, Halifax Street, St George's (tel: 440-3566/8).

Scotiabank, Halifax Street, St George's (tel: 440-3274).

Central bank
Eastern Caribbean Central Bank, Agency Office, Monckton Street, St George's (tel: 440-3016; fax: 40-6721).

Stock exchange
Eastern Caribbean Securities Exchange (ECSE): www.ecseonline.com

Travel information
Grenada Hotel Association, Ross Point Inn, Lagoon Road, St George's (tel: 444-1353; fax: 444-4847).

Ministry of tourism
Ministry of Tourism, Civil Aviation, Social Security, Culture, Gender and Family, Ministerial Complex, 4th Floor, St. George's, (tel: 440-0366; fax: 440-0443).

National tourist organisation offices
Grenada Board of Tourism, PO Box 293, The Carenage, St George's (tel: 440-2279; fax: 440-6637; internet: www.grenadagrenadines.com).

Ministries
Ministry of Agriculture, Ministerial Complex, 2nd and 3rd Floors, St George's (tel: 440-27008 fax: 440-4191).

Ministry of Carriacou and Petit Martinique Affairs, Beausejour, Carriacou (tel: 443-6026; fax: 443-6040).

Ministry of Communication & Works, Ministerial Complex, 4th Floor, St George's (tel: 440-2181; fax: 440-4122).

Ministry of Education, Botanical Gardens, St George's (tel: 440-2166; fax: 440-6650).

Ministry of Finance, Trade, Industry and Planning, Financial Complex, St George's (tel: 440-2731; fax: 440-4115).

Ministry of Foreign Affairs and International Trade, Ministerial Complex, 4th Floor, St George's (tel: 440-2640; fax: 440-4184).

Ministry of Health and Environment, Ministerial Complex, 1st and 2nd Floords, St George's (tel: 440-2649; fax: 440-4127).

Ministry of Housing, Social Services and Co-operatives, Ministerial Complex, 1st and 2nd Floors, St George's (tel: 440-6917; fax: 440-7990).

Ministry of Implementation, Ministerial Complex, 6th Floor, St George's (tel: 440-2255; fax: 440-4116).

Ministry of Labour and Local Government, Ministerial Complex, 3rd Floor, St George's (tel: 440-2532).

Ministry of Legal Affairs, Attorney General's Office, Church Street, St. George's (tel: 440-2050; fax: 440-6630).

Ministry of Youth, Sports and Community Development, Ministerial Complex, 2nd Floor, St George's (tel: 440-6917; fax: 440-6924).

Office of the Prime Minister, Ministerial Complex, 6th Floor, St George's (tel: 440-2225; fax: 440-4116).

Other useful addresses
Export Development Unit, Ministry of Trade, Lagoon Road, St George's (tel: 440-2101; fax: 440-4115).

Grenada Cocoa Board, Scott St, St George's (tel: 440-2234).

Grenada Co-operative Banana Society, Scott St, St George's (tel: 440-2117).

Grenada Co-operative Nutmeg Association, PO Box 160, St George's (tel: 440-2097).

Grenada Industrial Development Corporation, Frequente Industrial Park, True Blue, St. George's (tel: 444-1035; fax: 444-4828; e-mail: gidc@caribsurf.com; internet site: www.grenadaworld.com).

Grenada International Financial Services Authority (GIFSA), PO Box 39713, Carenage (tel: 440-8717; fax: 440-4780; e-mail: grenoffshore@caribsurf.com).

Grenada Manufacturers' Council, PO Box 129, St George's (tel: 444-4485/2937; fax: 440-6627).

Grenadan Embassy (US), 1701 New Hampshire Avenue, NW, Washington DC 20009 (tel: 202-265-2561).

Guadeloupe

COUNTRY PROFILE

Historical profile

Guadeloupe is situated within the Lesser Antilles. The first inhabitants were the Arawak Indians and Carib Indians. The Carib name for the island was Karukera (island of beautiful water).

1493–1600 Columbus was the first European visitor. Spain made two attempts to colonise the islands of Guadeloupe but was unsuccessful, due to strong indigenous resistance.

1635 France conquered the islands and established its first settlement.

1654 The French welcomed a small number of Dutch who settled in Guadeloupe. They proved vital to the turnaround of Guadeloupe's economy by developing its sugar industry. Black African slaves were brought to the island to work on plantations.

1674 Guadeloupe became part of the French Crown Colonies.

1700s Guadeloupe was the scene of many battles between the French and British, who repeatedly fought for possession.

1808–1814 Guadeloupe was occupied by the British.

1816 The islands were handed back to France by the Treaty of Vienna.

1854–1885 Following the abolition of slavery in 1847, workers were brought to Guadeloupe from India. During this period, blacks were allowed to participate in Guadeloupe's politics and Guadeloupe was allowed representation in the French parliament.

1946 Guadeloupe became a French Département d'Outre-Mer (DOM) (Overseas Department).

1974 Guadeloupe was further incorporated into the French political system and granted the status of region of France.

1983 Guadeloupe was granted devolution. A Regional Council was established under the French decentralisation policy.

1998 Hurricane Georges wreaked havoc on the islands

1999 The Basse Terre declaration by Guadeloupe, Martinique and French Guiana called for greater local control. The country was hit by hurricane Lenny.

2002 Guadeloupe adopted the euro as its official currency. In the French presidential elections, Guadeloupe's support for Jacques Chirac was overwhelming (91 per cent of the vote).

2003 A referendum in Guadeloupe and Martinique rejected a French government-backed reform plan to streamline the system of local government and give the islands a new status. Guadeloupe's dependencies, St Barthélémy and St Maarten, voted to become overseas collectives.

2004 Victorin Lurel took office as president of the regional council and Jacques Gillot as president of the general council. Paul Girot de Langlade took office as *préfet*.

2006 Jean-Jacque Brot became *préfet*.

2007 Emmanuel Berthier became *préfet*. A new desalination unit, capable of producing 4,000 cubic metres of drinkable water from seawater, was installed on St Barthélémy. Hurricane Dean destroyed 80 per cent of all banana plantations. St Barthélémy and St Maarten became French overseas collectives.

2008 Guadeloupe and Dominica agreed to develop and deliver geothermal energy from Dominica, via undersea electricity cables.

2009 There was civil unrest and a general strike in protest against low pay and rising prices. Riot police from mainland France were deployed, including four French military police units of 260 officers. The actions included roadblocks, un-cleared rubbish in streets and closed shops and schools. The France-based minister of overseas territories arrived to negotiate a solution. After 44 days the general strike ended with the promise of higher wages for workers. The protests affected tourism as a reported 10,000 tourists cancelled holidays.

2010 On 16 November, the French-based, Agence des Aires Marines Protégées (Marine Areas Protection Agency) announced the creation of a marine mammals' sanctuary (known as Agoa) in the territorial waters and economic exclusion zone of the French West Indies (Guadeloupe, Martinique, St Martin, and St Barthélémy). The 138,000 square km marine habitat will require any proposed development to include consideration of their impact on marine mammals, such as whales.

2011 Amaury de Saint-Quentin took office as *préfet* on 11 September. The new, year-round, Jeans Ferry Service operated by L' Express Des Il, between Dominica, St

KEY FACTS

Official name: Guadeloupe

Head of State: President of France (Nicolas Sarkozy), represented by *préfet* Amaury de Saint-Quentin (from 11 Sep 2011)

Head of government: President of Conseil Général Jacques Gillot (since 23 Mar 2001); President of Conseil Régional Victorin Lurel (since 2004; re-elected 21–22 Mar 2010)

Ruling party: Objectif Guadeloupe

Area: 1,780 square km

Population: 461,000 (2010)*

Capital: Basse Terre

Official language: French

Currency: Euro (€) = 100 cents (from 1 Jan 2002; previous currency French franc, locked at Ff6.56 per euro)

Exchange rate: €0.75 per US$ (Oct 2011)

* estimated figure

Lucia, Martinique and Guadeloupe will begin on 20 October.

Political structure

Constitution

28 September 1958 (French Fifth Republic).

Under the 1946 constitution of the French Fourth Republic, Guadeloupe became a Département d'Outre-Mer (DOM) (Overseas Department) of France. In 1974, it was granted additional status as a region of France.

Guadeloupe is represented in the French National Assembly by four deputies and in the Senate by two senators.

Since 1983, following the French government's policy of decentralisation, regional councils have been elected with powers similar to those of the regions.

Administration is by a *préfet* appointed by the government in Paris.

The local government comprises a Conseil Régional (Regional Council) of 39 members and a 42-member Conseil Général (General Council), both directly elected for six-year terms.

Dependencies: Marie Galante, Les Saintes, Désirade, St Barthélémy and St Martin, Grand Bourg (on Marie Galante).

In a 2003 referendum, voters on Guadeloupe's dependencies, St Barthélémy and St Martin, approved a referendum which streamlined the islands' local government and gave them a new status as French overseas collectives in 2007.

Form of state

Département d'Outre-Mer (DOM) (Overseas Department) of France, with additional status as a *région* (region) of France.

National legislature

The Conseil Régional (regional council) has 41 members elected for four-years by proportional representation. All members of the Conseil Général (general council) are elected for six-year terms in single seat constituencies. The two councils have diverging powers over local and departmental legislation.

Legal system

French legal system

Last elections

21–22 March 2010 (Conseil Général and Conseil Régional)

Results: General council: Parti Socialiste (PS) (Socialist Party) won 56.51 per cent (31 seats out of 41), Divers Gauche (DVG) (Miscellaneous Left) 14.01 per cent (four), Collectif Des Inkoruptibles (DdI) (The Incorruptible Party) 6.96 per cent (two); five other political parties each won less than 3 per cent of votes and gained no seats.

Next elections

2014 (Conseil Général and Conseil Régional)

Political parties

Ruling party

Objectif Guadeloupe

Main opposition party

Political situation

In a region dominated by either the English or Spanish language, official measures to support the Francophone West Indies now includes not only a French language training programme offered by the Université des Antilles et de la Guyane to students from the Organisation of Eastern Caribbean States (OECS) region but also a French-speaking mobile (cell) phone network set up in 2007–08, by the Digicel Group, for the French West Indies and French Guiana.

Population

461,000 (2010)*

Last census: 1 January 2006: 400,736

Population density: 250 inhabitants per square km.

Annual growth rate: 1 per cent (2003)

Ethnic make-up

Black or mixed race (90 per cent), white (5 per cent), East Indian and others (5 per cent).

Religions

Roman Catholic (95 per cent), other: Hindu, African animist, Protestant (5 per cent).

Education

Many students pursue higher education in the islands or in France. The islands have a teacher's training college, a school of law, and a school of science.

Literacy rate: Over 90 per cent

Compulsory years: 6 to 17.

Health

In addition to several hospitals, Guadeloupe has a Pasteur Institute for the study of tropical diseases. The consumption of crack cocaine has increased steadily with a large number of drug addicts being treated regularly by the health and social services.

Life expectancy: 77.5 years (estimate 2003)

Fertility rate/Maternal mortality rate: Two births per woman (2003)

Birth rate/Death rate: 16 births per 1,000 population; six deaths per 1,000 population (2003).

Child (under 5 years) mortality rate (per 1,000): Nine per 1,000 live births (2003)

Welfare

The existence of a state homecare policy and a traditional lifestyle enable most people aged 60 and over to live at home. The people are highly dependent on French social welfare programmes and development funds. About one-third of children under the age of 17 are brought up in single-parent families. Financial assistance is often available to needy families for their children's basic needs and to enable children to attend school at an early age.

Main cities

Basse-Terre (capital,on Basse Terre, estimated population 12,046 in 2005); Les Abymes (on Grande Terre, 65,700); Pointe-à-Pitre (commercial centre, straddles islands of Grande Terre and Basse Terre, 21,580); Capesterre (on Basse Terre, 20,400).

Dependencies include Marie Galante, Les Saintes, Désirade, St Barthélémy and St Martin, Grand Bourg (on Marie Galante).

Languages spoken

French (99 per cent); Creole patois is also spoken.

Official language/s

French

Media

Press

The only daily newspaper is the regional publication *France Antilles*. Local newspapers include *Le Journal de St Barth* (www.st-barths.com/jsb/headlinesfr.html), with a weekly edition.

Broadcasting

The French overseas broadcaster RFO (www.rfo.fr) provides locally produced radio and television news (http://guadeloupe.rfo.fr) and imported French programmes, as well as internet TV services.

Radio: Private radio stations include Radio Caraibes International (www.rci.gp), NRJ Antilles (www.nrjantilles.com) and Radyo Tanbou (www.radyotanbou.com).

Economy

Guadeloupe is heavily dependent on aid from France, which has prevented any significant macroeconomic adjustment to local conditions. The services sector dominates the economy, providing almost 70 per cent of GDP and over 60 per cent of employment. Tourism is the prominent sector with most visitors originating from the US; cruise ships are providing an increasing number of tourists. Agriculture is important; sugarcane has lost its dominance and has being replaced by bananas, aubergines (eggplants) and flowers. Industry includes light manufacturing and foodstuffs using mostly local ingredients. Unemployment, particularly among the young, is high at over 25 per cent.

External trade

As a département d'outre-mer (DOM) of France, Guadeloupe has the status within

the European Union as one of its members; overseas countries and territories (OCT) and has free trade within the EU and other trade agreements through the EU.
The rising trade deficit is only partially offset by earnings from tourism and aid flows from France aimed particularly at lowering the unemployment rate.

Imports

Principal imports are machinery and transport equipment, foodstuffs and live animals, basic manufactures, miscellaneous manufactures, road vehicles and parts, chemicals and related products.
Main sources: France (typically over 60 per cent of total), US (5 per cent), Germany (3 per cent).

Exports

Principal exports are bananas, aubergines (eggplants) and flowers, machinery and transport equipment, rum, basic manufactures and sugar.
Main destinations: France (typically over 60 per cent of total), Martinique (18 per cent), US (4 per cent).

Agriculture

Farming

Agriculture is the main sector of the economy, contributing 15 per cent to GDP and employing 15 per cent of the population. Guadeloupe is not self-sufficient, relying heavily on food imports from France.
An estimated 36 per cent of the total area is cultivated arable land, 10 per cent is pasture and 15 per cent woodland/forest (including national park land of around 3,000 hectares).
The export of bananas has been a prime acitivity accounting for around 50 per cent of foreign earnings. The future of the banana industry, which has relied on preferential access to the EU, is threatened by a World Trade Organisation (WTO) ruling that this access is illegal and will end. The EU has agreed new tariff quotas from 2006.
Sugar, flowers and melons are also cultivated.

Fishing

Offshore fishing is a traditional source of food. The main fish catch includes lobsters, crab and octopus. The sector is underdeveloped, although demand is growing.
The typical total annual fish catch is over 10,114t. Shellfish, molluscs and cephalopods account for another 714t per annum.

Industry and manufacturing

The industrial sector contributes around 17 per cent to GDP and employs 15 per cent of the workforce.
Manufacturing industries are small and centre on the processing of raw materials. Main activities include sugar refining, rum distilling, food processing, cement and brick manufacture, mineral water bottling and ship repair. The construction industry employs 12 per cent of the workforce and is the third-largest sector of activity.
There is an industrial freeport at Jarry.

Tourism

Tourism is estimated to account for over 8 per cent per cent of GDP and employ more than 25 per cent of the workforce. The sector is predicted to grow by 7.2 per cent year-on-year between 2006–15 with economic activity doubling from US$1,046 million in 2005 to US$2,004 million in 2015.
About 81 per cent of Guadeloupe's tourists come from France, 12 per cent from other European countries and 7 per cent from US.

Mining

Guadeloupe has no mineral resources.

Hydrocarbons

Guadeloupe relies entirely on imported petroleum products, which amount to around 15,000 barrels per day. It does not import coal or natural gas.
A proposed pipeline from Trinidad and Tobago to Guadeloupe and Martinique opens possibilities for the future import of natural gas; but the project still remained a scheme in 2008.

Energy

Total installed generating capacity is over 400MW, produced by thermal power stations.

Banking and insurance

Central bank

Caisse Centrale de Co-opération Economique; European Central Bank (ECB)

Time

GMT minus four hours

Geography

Guadeloupe is the most northerly of the Windward Islands group in the West Indies. Dominica lies to the south, and Antigua and Montserrat to the north-west. Guadeloupe is formed by two large islands, Grande Terre (mountainous) and Basse Terre, separated by a narrow sea channel, with two smaller islands, Marie Galante, to the south-east, and La Désirade, to the east. St Barthélémy and the northern half of St Maarten (the remainder being part of the Netherlands Antilles) Maarten became French overseas collectives in 2007 (they were previously French dependences).

Hemisphere

Northern

Climate

Sub-tropical with annual mean temperature of 27 degrees Celsius. Levels of humidity and rainfall highest around Basse-Terre. Refreshing trade winds all year round. Humid season – *hivernage* – is between September and November.

Entry requirements

Passports

Required by all.

Visa

As an overseas region of France entry requirements are the same as those for France.
Visas required by all, except citizens of EU, North America, Australasia and Japan, for stays up to one month; this includes business trips by representatives of foreign entities with an invitation from a local company or organisation. Proof of adequate funds for stay, an itinerary, a guarantee of repatriation if necessary and return/onward ticket are also required.
For further exceptions, full details and a copy of the application form visit www.diplomatie.gouv.fr/en/ and follow the path (going to France) on the legend.

Currency advice/regulations

There are no restrictions on the import and export of foreign currency but the amount imported must be declared. The amount of foreign currency, other than euros, that may be taken out must not exceed that imported.
ATMs are readily available. Travellers cheques in euros are accepted everywhere, however cheques in other currencies if accepted, may attract extra exchange fees.

Prohibited imports

Illegal drugs.

Health (for visitors)

Mandatory precautions

A yellow fever vaccination certificate is required if travelling from an infected area.

Advisable precautions

Hepatitis, typhoid, tetanus and polio vaccinations. Water precautions should be taken.

Hotels

There is a good range of quality hotels in Guadeloupe, as well as more basic accommodation. If a service charge is not added, a 15 per cent tip is usual.

Credit cards

Credit and charge cards are accepted in may places.

Public holidays (national)

Fixed dates

1 Jan (New Year's Day), 1 May (Labour Day), 8 May (Victory Day), 27 May (Abolition Day), 14 Jul (Bastille Day), 21 Jul (Schoelcher Day), 15 Aug (Assumption Day), ^1 Nov (All Saints' Day), 2 Nov (All Souls' Day), 11 Nov (Armistice Day), 25 Dec (Christmas).

Variable dates
Carnival (Feb, two days), ^Ash Wednesday (Feb/Mar), Good Friday (Mar/Apr), ^Easter Monday, ^Ascension Day, Whit Monday.
^ Religious holiday.

Working hours

Banking
Mon–Fri: 0800–1200, 1400–1600.
Some banks open Sat: 0800–1200, but these close 1200 Wed.
Banks close at noon on the day preceding a bank holiday.
Business
Mon–Fri: 0800–1200, 1400–1800.
Business visits are best between January–March and June–September.
Government
Mon–Fri: 0800–1300, 1500–1800.
Shops
Mon–Sat: 0800–1200, 1430–1700.

Telecommunications

Mobile/cell phones
GSM 900 and 1800 services are available on Basse Terre.

Electricity supply

220/380V AC, 50 and 60 cycles

Getting there

Air
National airline: Air Caraibes.
International airport/s: Pointe-à-Pitre Le Raizet International Airport (PTP), 3km from Pointe-à-Pitre; duty-free shop, restaurant, buffet, bank, post office, shops, hotel reservations, car hire.
Airport tax: None
Surface
Water: A new, year-round, 137-passenger, Jeans Ferry Service operated by L' Express Des Il, between Dominica, St Lucia, Martinique and Guadeloupe will begin on 20 October 2011.

Getting about

National transport
Air: Air Guadeloupe, Air St Barthélémy and Liat operate frequent services to all the dependent islands from Pointe-à-Pitre.
Road: The total network is around 3,000km – including about 500km of national highway; secondary roads can be tortuous.
Buses: There are several private bus lines that connect Pointe-à-Pitre or Basse Terre with all villages. There are no timetables; a hand gesture is needed to stop buses.
City transport
Taxis: Plentiful but generally regarded as expensive, particularly in rural areas.
Car hire
Reservations for car rental are advisable, especially between December and April. An international licence is required and one year's experience driving.

BUSINESS DIRECTORY

The addresses listed below are a selection only. While World of Information makes every endeavour to check these addresses, we cannot guarantee that changes have not been made, especially to telephone numbers and area codes. We would welcome any corrections.

Telephone area codes

The international direct dialling code (IDD) for Guadeloupe is +590, followed by another 590 and subscriber's number.

Chambers of Commerce

Basse Terre Chamber of Commerce and Industry, 6 Rue Victor Hugues, 97100 Basse Terre (tel: 994-444; fax: 812-117; e-mail: ccibt:ais.gp).

Pointe-à-Pitre Chamber of Commerce and Industry, Hôtel Consulaire, Rue Félix Eboué, 97159 Pointe-à-Pitre (tel: 937-600; fax: 902-187; e-mail: contacts@cci-pap.org).

Banking

Caisse Régionale de Crédit Agricole Mutuel de la Guadeloupe, BP 134, Zone Artisanale de Petit Perou, 97154 Pointe-à-Pitre (tel: 906-565).

Central bank
European Central Bank (ECB), Kaiserstrasse 29, D-60311 Frankfurt am Main, Germany (tel: (+49-69) 13-440; fax: (+49-69) 1344-6000).

Travel information

Air Caraibes, Morne Vergain, 97139 Abymes (tel: 824-747; fax: 824-749; e-mail: direction@aircaraibes.com).

Ministry of tourism
Bureau Industrie et Tourisme, Préfecture de la Guadeloupe, Rue de Lardenoy, 97109 Basse Terre (tel: 817-681).

Direction de la Promotion Touristique, Préfecture de la Guadeloupe, Rue Lardenoy, 97100 Basse Terre (tel: 811-560).

National tourist organisation offices
Office Départemental du Tourisme (Guadeloupe Tourism Board), 5 Square de la Banque, PO Box 1099, 97181 Pointe-á-Pitre (tel: 894-689, 820-930; fax: 838-922).

Other useful addresses

Agence pour la Promotion Industrielle de la Guadeloupe (APRIGA), BP 1229, 97184 Pointe-à-Pitre (tel: 834-897; fax: 902-187).

Chambre d'Agriculture de la Guadeloupe, 27 rue Sadi-Carnot, 97110 Pointe-à-Pitre (tel: 821-130; fax: 918-873).

Port Autonome de la Guadeloupe, Boulevard Pointe Jarry, Zone de Commerce International, Basse Terre (tel: 213-971; fax: 213-979).

Port Autonome de Pointe-á-Pitre, Gare maritime, 97165 Pointe-á-Pitre Cedex (tel: 213-900; fax: 213-969; internet site: http://www.port-guadeloupe.com).

Syndicat des Producteurs-Exportateurs de Sucre et de Rhum de la Guadeloupe et Dépendances, Zone Industrielle de la Pointe Jarry, 97122 Baie Mahault, BP 2015, 97191 Pointe-à-Pitre (tel: 266-212).

Internet sites

L' Express Des Iles ferry service: express-des-iles.com

Local government: http://guadeloupe.pref.gouv.fr

Guam

KEY FACTS

Official name: Territory of Guam (Guahan)

Head of State: President of the United States of America Barack Obama (from 20 Jan 2009)

Head of government: Governor Eddie Calvo (Republican) (from 3 Jan 2011)

Ruling party: Democratic Party (elected 4 Nov 2008)

Area: 549 square km

Population: 180,692 (2010)*

Capital: Agaña

Official language: Chamorro and English

Currency: US dollar (US$) = 100 cents

Exchange rate: US$1.00 per US$ (Oct 2011)

* estimated figure

COUNTRY PROFILE

Historical profile

Guam is the largest of the Marianas islands, which were occupied by the Chamorro Indians, a Malayo-Polynesian people, around 1500 BC.

1521 The Spanish seized control of Guam, which became a port of call for its galleons travelling between Mexico and the Philippines.

1898 Spain ceded Guam to the US after it lost the Spanish-American war. Guam was transformed into a strategic naval base.

1941 The US were forced out by the Japanese during the Second World War.

1944 US rule was reinstated after three years of fighting. Guam has remained an important military base since then.

1950 The Organic Act of Guam granted the island internal self-government and the islanders US citizenship, but not voting rights in US elections.

1962 The US passed the Naval Clearing Act which opened Guam's ports to foreign visitors.

1975 More than 100,000 evacuees from the fall of Vietnam were repatriated via Guam.

1996 Around 7,000 Kurdish refugees, fearing retaliation from Iraqi leader Saddam Hussein were housed on Guam.

1997 The strongest ever recorded typhoon ripped through Guam, leaving thousands homeless.

2002 Felix Camacho (Republican) was elected governor. Super-typhoon Pongsona struck in December.

2004 A state of emergency was declared after typhoon Tingting hit the island, leaving it almost completely flooded; weeks later super-typhoon Chaba struck. The Republicans won control of the legislature.

2006 Governor Camacho won re-election with 50 per cent of the vote.

2008 The Democratic Party won a majority in the legislature.

2009 The US launched marine protected areas (MPA), totalling 500,000 square km of sea and sea floor, around its Pacific islands. Mining and commercial fishing out to 50 nautical miles (54.26km) from shore was banned. A lost Chamorro-English dictionary was found on Guam and re-published to help preserve Guam's indigenous language. The dictionary had been compiled by Chamorro elders in the late 1970s, in longhand, then stored away and lost. The US Environmental Protection Agency (EPA) ordered the oil company Shell to clean up its site in the west of Guam, which had contaminated groundwater with hazardous waste.

2010 In February, Governor Camacho proposed that Guam's name should be changed to Guahan, a spelling, which he said, was a more indigenous spelling and pronunciation of the island. Official correspondence with the governor already uses the alternative spelling and other government departments are being encouraged to adopt the practice. The resident population took part in the United States census on 1 April, which, after personal details, included questions on race, housing and internet and mobile phone access. In July, the US decided to increase its military forces on Guam with the addition of an expanded dock for a nuclear-powered aircraft carrier and missile defence system. It was seen as a response to China's increased spending on its military. In gubernatorial elections held on 2 November, Eddie Calvo (Republican) won 50.6 per cent of the vote, Carl Gutierrez (Democrat) 49.4 per cent.

2011 Governor Eddie Calvo took office on 3 January. Following a proposal by the state authorities in Guam to include visitors from China and Russia in the visa-waiver programme, federal officials began evaluating the impact on US national security, in July.

Political structure

Constitution

Guam is represented by an elected non-voting delegate to the US House of Representatives; elections are every two years. Its inhabitants are US citizens but are not allowed to vote in US elections. In June 2004, a new process for the island's primary elections was approved, which prevents voters from crossing over between political parties on the ballot; voters can, however, keep their political affiliations confidential.

Form of state

Although it is administered by the department of the interior, Guam is virtually a self-governing unincorporated territory of the US.

The executive
Local executive power rests with a governor, elected by popular vote to a four-year term, who heads a cabinet made up of departmental directors.
National legislature
The unicameral, Liheslaturan Guåhan (in Chamorro) (Legislature of Guam) has 15 members, elected to a two-year term by popular vote, within one constituency that covers the whole island. It deals with legislation on local matters.
Last elections
4 November 2008 (parliamentary); 2 November 2010 (gubernatorial).
Results: Parliamentary: Democratic Party won 10 seats (out of 15), Republican Party 5.
Gubernatorial: Eddie Calvo (Republican Party) won 50.6 per cent of the vote, Carl Gutierrez (Democratic Party) 49.4 per cent.
Next elections
2 November 2010 (parliamentary and gubernatorial)

Political parties
Ruling party
Democratic Party (elected 4 Nov 2008)
Main opposition party
Republican Party
Political situation
The US House of Representatives passed an economic stimulus plan, whereby tax rebate cheques began to be sent to all tax payers in mid-2008, to stimulate the local economy and encourage consumer spending. Most households in Guam were looking forward to sums between US$300–600 for singles and US$1,200 for couples but 247 were disappointed when the Guam administration garnished their cheques for outstanding local tax duties.
The recovered US$100,788 was much needed, to cover costs for the Memorial Hospital, Guam Housing, an Urban Renew plan and child support.
In March 2011, the Republican controlled US-Congress voted to rescind the voting rites of representations of Guam effectively disenfranchising their electorate in policies that directly affect them.

Population
180,692 (2010)*
Last census: April 2000: 154,805
Population density: 276 inhabitants per square km.
Annual growth rate: 1.5 per cent (2003)
Ethnic make-up
Native Chamorros comprise 37 per cent of the population, Filipinos (26 per cent), white (10 per cent), Chinese, Japanese, Korean and others (27 per cent). There is tension between the Chamorros and guest workers from the Philippines and other Asian countries.

Religions
Roman Catholic (85 per cent)

Education
The education system is similar to that of the US but is poorly managed, with drop-out rates at around 50 per cent. Schools lack basic equipment and essential books.
Education is a high priority for parents and is considered the key to success in Chamorro life. Despite ongoing criticisms of the flaws in the system, the government has implemented no major reforms.
An agreement between the education departments of Guam and the Marshall Islands, signed in October 2010, will allow an exchange of students to study at the University of Guam and the College of the Marshall Islands.
Compulsory years: Five to 16

Health
With a young and growing population the government is faced with the challenge of developing a health care system that will meet their needs. Health services are funded by the US government and the World Health Organisation (WHO).
Health services are good but there is a shortage of adequately trained medical staff. Training of medical personnel was a government priority throughout 2002–05.
There are high incidents of mental retardation and thyroid cancers, blamed on nuclear contamination when naval ships were sent for decontamination to Guam.
Life expectancy: 77.9 years (World Bank)
Fertility rate/Maternal mortality rate: 3.7 births per woman (World Bank)
Birth rate/Death rate: 23 births and four deaths per 1,000 population (2003)
Child (under 5 years) mortality rate (per 1,000): 6.5 per 1,000 live births (2003)

Welfare
Welfare is unevenly distributed among the population. The Chamorros are the main beneficiaries of welfare while Filipinos receive less than 10 per cent of government money, however in a 2005 a survey over 50 per cent found to be homeless were Chamorros.

Main cities
Agaña (capital, estimated population 3,923 in 2005), Tamuning (11,361), Mangilao (9,116), Barrigada (4,860), Yigo (8,677)

Languages spoken
English, Chamorro, Chinese, Japanese and Korean.
Official language/s
Chamorro and English

Media
Press
The *Guam Business News* is a monthly publication.
Dailies: In English the *Pacific Daily News* (www.guampdn.com) is the only national newspaper. The US Navy has its own publication *Navigator* with news and stories relevant to its readership.
Weeklies: There are several weeklies available. In English, *Micro Call*, *Guam Shopper's Guide*, *Pacific Crossroads*, *Pacific Voice* (published on Sundays for the Catholic community), *Pacific Sunday News* and *Tropic Topics*. In Japanese, *Guam Shinbun* and *Guam Kyodo News Service*, which provides a facsimile news service twice daily for the Japanese community and tourists. In Korean, the *Korean Community News* and *Korean News*.
Business: *Guam Business News* is a monthly publication.
Periodicals: In English, *Latte Magazine* is a quarterly, featuring contemporary life and multiculturalism; *Micronesica* is a bi-annual and *Manila, Manila* is a glossy news and lifestyle magazine catering to the Filipino community.
Broadcasting
The US Federal Communications Commission is responsible for broadcasting regulations.
Radio: There are several radio stations, the largest are K57 (KGUM) (www.k57.com) and KAUM (www.kuam.com), with news and talk shows, and these are parts of larger broadcasting media enterprises. KTKB Mega Mixx (www.ktkb.com) and Loud Radio 88 (http://loudradio88.homestead.com) are private stations. Several Christian radio stations provide music and entertainment, Light 91, Joy 92 and Adventist World Radio.
Television: Commercial TV stations include K57 (www.k57.com) and KAUM (www.kuam.com), with locally produced news and imported entertainment programmes. A cable service is provided by MSNBC KUAM (www.msnbc.msn.com)
News agencies
ABC Pacific Beat: www.radioaustralia.net.au/pacbeat
Pacific Magazine: www.pacificmagazine.net
Pacific Islands New Association (Pina): www.pina.com.fj

Economy
Guam remains one of the most prosperous islands in the Pacific and has the second highest GDP per capita of the region, Hawaii having the highest. About 60 per cent of Guam's income comes from US federal spending, which has, since 2006, grown with the decision to open a new military base. The Marine's base is

planned to open in 2012, to be home to around 8,000 military personnel. US$1 billion per annum for 6–10 years (2006–16) has been allocated for the construction of the military base. An additional US$400 million has been allocated for Guam civil purposes and general infrastructure, which is expected to benefit from more investment.
Tourism is the single largest component of the service sector with Guam increasingly being seen as a reasonable destination for Japanese visitors on a limited budget. Tourism accounts for around 35 per cent of total employment.
Aside from tourism, the only other significant source of income is the fishing industry, although the cement and construction industries have continued to prosper due to the damage to buildings and infrastructure by natural disasters, as well as construction of the US military base.

External trade
Guam exports free of duty to a number of countries, including Australia, Japan and the US.
Imports
Main imports are petroleum and petroleum products, food and manufactured goods.
Main sources: Singapore (typically 50 per cent of total), South Korea (21 per cent), Japan (14 per cent).
Exports
Main exports are onstruction materials, fish, food and beverage products.
Main destinations: Japan (typically 67 per cent of total), Singapore (7 per cent), UK (5 per cent).
Re-exports
Food re-exports for distribution throughout the Pacific provide the mainstay of export income along with refined petroleum products.

Agriculture
Farming
The agriculture sector typically accounts for 7 per cent of gross island product (GIP). Most agricultural activity is part-time market gardening on smallholdings.
In March 2004, a fungus infected thousands of betel nut trees in the southern parts of Guam and scientists feared it could spread to other types of palm tree. More than 3,000 infected trees were destroyed.
Fishing
Fishing is an important source of protein. Future areas for growth include salmon and trout farming. Typical annual catches include 200t freshwater fish, 280t marine fish, and 28t of all other seafood.

Industry and manufacturing
Industry typically accounts for 15 per cent of GDP and employs about 3 per cent of the labour force. Most industrial goods are imported.
Main industries include US military, tourism, construction, transshipment services, concrete products, printing and publishing, food processing and textiles.
Government policy is attempting to focus on attracting foreign investment, particularly from Asian manufacturers, in order to develop the industrial base.

Tourism
Tourism is still Guam's most important economic activity. The government is seeking to expand into new markets in Europe and Asia, including China, and to diversify Guam's tourism product, especially into sports tourism.
Among Guam's natural attractions are it's unspoilt coral reefs, white sand beaches, lagoons and waterfalls. The brown tree snake, accidentally introduced in the 1940's has, however, decimated its bird-life and eradication programmes are carried out regularly. Guam is ideal for water sports including surfing, canoeing, jet skiing, and deep-sea fishing, in waters that are clear and warm. On the land, there are seven golf courses and good hiking tracks. It is one of the best diving destinations in the world with shipwrecks and coral reefs. On Cocos Island, two miles off the Southern tip of Guam there is a Spanish galleon wreck with billions of dollars worth of treasure that has still to be recovered.

Environment
In May 2005 a US research study confirmed that Guam had received measurable radioactive fallout during nuclear testing from 1946–62. The government confirmed that residents would be eligible under the Radiation Exposure Compensation Act. Radioactive polution was also acknowledged in Apra Habour, caused when military ships were decontaminated by washing down after testing.
Military expansion of the Andersen Air Force Base will cause the loss of some pristine native forest at a time when several endangered bird species are being reintroduced into the area.

Mining
Mining contributes less than 5 per cent to GDP. Rock and cement production supplies the construction industry.

Hydrocarbons
Guam does not produce or refine oil; it relies entirely on imports, which amounts to around 12,000 barrels per day.
Any use of import natural gas or coal is commercially insignificant.

Energy
Total installed electricity generating capacity is over 500MW, produced in thermal power station; consumption is around 1.7 billion kilowatt hours.

Banking and insurance
Central bank
Federal Reserve Bank of San Francisco

Time
GMT plus ten hours

Geography
Guam is the southernmost and largest of the Marianas, situated about 2,170km (1,350 miles) south of Tokyo, Japan, and 5,300km (3,300 miles) west of Honolulu, Hawaii.
The island consists of two ancient volcanoes of which the southern peak is 407 metres at its tallest. In the north and between the summits are limestone plateaux with deep gorges that drop to the narrow coastal shelf.
The world's deepest chasm in the deepest ocean, the Marianas Trench, lies around 400km south-west of Guam.
Hemisphere
Northern

Climate
Guam is warm and humid with temperatures averaging between 24–30 degrees Celsius. Dec–May is generally cooler and drier. Rainfall, up to 300mm per month, averages 2,000mm per annum. The heaviest rainfall is usually between Jul–Sep. There are occasional tropical storms. The tropical humidity is tempered somewhat by the prevailing north-westerly trade winds.

Dress codes
Informal, lightweight clothing is acceptable.

Entry requirements
Passports
Required by all.
Visa
US entry requirements apply. Visas required by all, except US citizens and foreign nationals of countries that have visa free entry to the US and are in possession of machine readable passports with biometric data, under the Visa Waiver Program (VWP) introduced in 2005. All other visitors and passport holders must apply for a visa. Visas, for both tourism and business, are valid for up to 90 days. A return/onward ticket is also required.
Further information can be found at http://travel.state.gov/ including information on temporary business visas. More detailed information can be found at http://uscis.gov/graphics/services/visa_info.htm.

Currency advice/regulations
There are no restrictions on import or export of foreign or local currency. However amounts over US$10,000 or equivalent must be declared.
Customs
Personal items are duty-free.
Prohibited imports
Plant material, meat products, illegal drugs and any material that breaches US copyright laws.

Health (for visitors)
Mandatory precautions
Vaccination certificates required for yellow fever if travelling from infected area.
Advisable precautions
Dengue fever is endemic; it is advisable to cover up at dawn and dusk and prophylaxis should be used. Vaccinations for diphtheria, tuberculosis, hepatitis A and B, tetanus, typhoid fever should be considered. No cases of polio have been reported since the 1990s. There is a rabies risk in rural areas.
Ciguatera poisoning is possible if eating tropical reef-fish – toxins are not removed through cooking – avoiding barracuda, grouper, snapper and amberjack will reduce the risk.
Medical insurance is necessary as all healthcare costs are high. All continuous medication should be carried along with its packaging and prescription.

Public holidays (national)
Fixed dates
1 Jan (New Year's Day), 4 Jul (US Independence Day), 21 Jul (Liberation Day), 2 Nov (All Souls' Day), 11 Nov (Veterans' Day), 8 Dec (Lady of Camarin Day), 25 Dec (Christmas).
Variable dates
Martin Luther King Day (third Mon in Jan), President's Day (second Mon in Feb), Guam Discovery Day (first Mon in Mar), Good Friday, Memorial Day (last Mon in May), Labour Day (first Mon in Sep), Columbus Day (first Mon in Oct), Thanksgiving Day (fourth Thu in Nov).

Working hours
Banking
Mon–Thu: 1000–1500; Fri: 1000–1800; Sat 0900–1200. ATMs are available.
Business
Mon–Fri: 0730/0830–1730/1800; Sat: 0830–1200.
Government
Mon–Fri: 0730/0830–1730/1800; Sat: 0830–1200.
Shops
Mon–Fri: 0800–1700; Sat: 0800–1300.

Telecommunications
Mobile/cell phones
GSM 1900 and 850 services cover most of the island.

Electricity supply
110V AC, 60Hz

Weights and measures
US system

Getting there
Air
Korean Air, Continental Micronesia, All Nippon Airlines, Japan Airlines and Palau Micronesia Air all serve Guam.
International airport/s: The Antonio B Won Pat International Airport (GUM), 11km from Agaña; duty-free shop, first-class lounge, restaurant, currency exchange, hotel reservations and car hire.
Airport tax: None
Surface
Main port/s: Apra Harbour.

Getting about
National transport
Road: The roads and highways are third-rate and bumpy, with some 600km surfaced.
Buses: A reasonable service connects almost all villiages, however services do not run on Sundays or public holidays.
Taxis: Are readily available and fares are metered.
City transport
Car hire
Available through most major companies. In general, charges are based on time, mileage and insurance. An international driving licence is required.

BUSINESS DIRECTORY

The addresses listed below are a selection only. While World of Information makes every endeavour to check these addresses, we cannot guarantee that changes have not been made, especially to telephone numbers and area codes. We would welcome any corrections.

Telephone area codes
The international direct dialling code (IDD) for Guam is +1 671, followed by subscriber's number.

Chambers of Commerce
Guam Chamber of Commerce, 173 Aspinall Avenue, Ada Plaza Center, PO Box 283, Agana 96932 (tel: 472-6311; fax: 472-6202; e-mail: gchamber@guamchamber.com.gu).

Banking
Bank of Hawaii, PO Box BH, Agaña 96910 (tel: 4779-781; fax: 4777-533).

First Commercial Bank, 1st Floor, 330 Hernan Cortes Ave, Agaña 96910 (tel: 4726-864/5; fax: 4778-921).

Union Bank of California NA, 194 Hernan Cortes Ave, Agaña 96910 (tel: 4778-811; fax: 4723-284).

Central bank

Federal Reserve System, 20th Street and Constitution Avenue, NW, Washington DC 20551 (tel: (202) 452-3000; fax: (202) 452-3819).

Travel information
Dive Rota, PO Box 941, Rota MP 96951 (email: mark@diverota.com; internet: www.diverota.com).

Freedom Air, PO Box 1578, Hagatna, 96932 (tel: 647-8360/1; fax; 472-8080; email: freedom@ite.net).

National tourist organisation offices
Guam Visitors Bureau, PO Box 3520; 401 Pale San Vitores Road, Tamuning 96913 (tel: 646-5278/9; fax: 646-8861: internet: www.visitguam.org).

Other useful addresses
Guam Economic Development Authority, Suite 911, ITC Building, 590 South Marine Drive, Tamuning, Guam 96911 (tel: 649-4141; fax: 649-4146).

Internet sites
The Pacific Daily News: www.guampdn.com

KUAM Broadcasting News: www.kuam.com

US Office of Insular affairs: www.doi.gov/oia

Guatemala

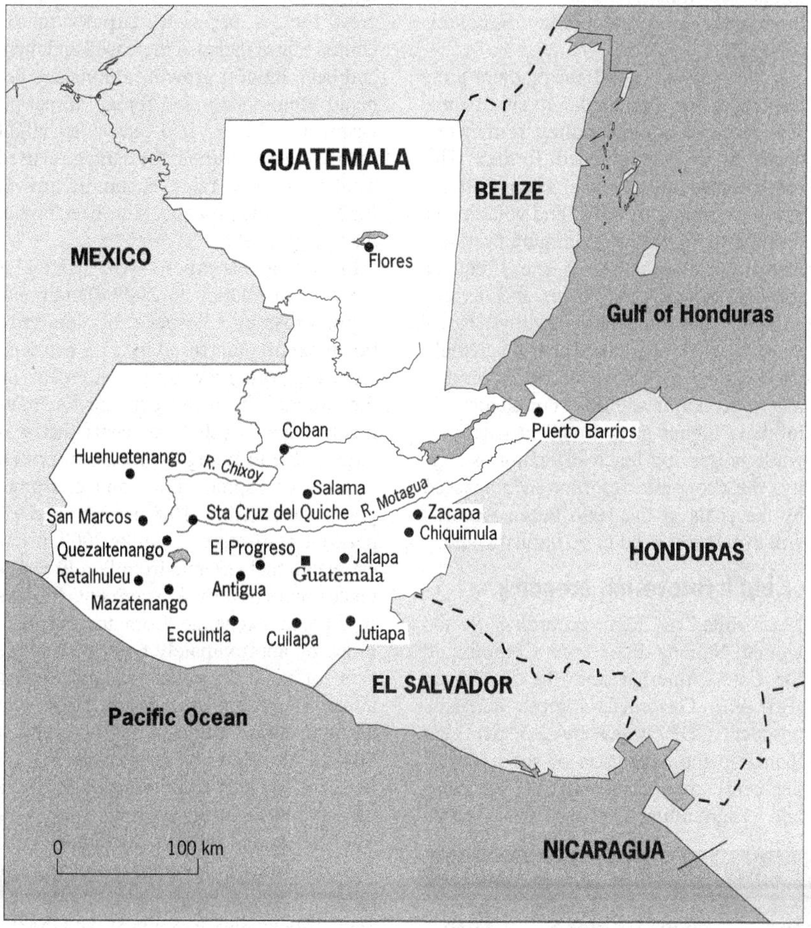

KEY FACTS

Official name: República de Guatemala (Republic of Guatemala)

Head of State: President Álvaro Colom (UNE) (from 14 Jan 2008); President-elect Otto Pérez Molina (PP) (to be installed on 14 Jan 2012)

Head of government: President Álvaro Colom (from 14 Jan 2008); Otto Pérez Molina (PP) (to be installed on 14 Jan 2012)

Ruling party: Coalition led by Partido Patriota (PP) (Patriotic Party (from 14 Jan 2012

Area: 108,890 square km

Population: 14.36 million (2010)*

Capital: Guatemala City

Official language: Spanish

Currency: Quetzal (Q) = 100 centavos

Exchange rate: Q7.87 per US$ (Oct 2011)

GDP per capita: US$2,888 (2010)

GDP real growth: 2.60% (2010)

GDP: US$41.50 billion (2010)

Inflation: 3.90% (2010)

Balance of trade: -US$4.29 billion (2010)

* estimated figure

Former army general Otto Pérez Molina, who vowed to pursue a hard line against violent crime, won Guatemala's presidential run-off election in November 2011. Mr Pérez Molina won some 54 per cent of the vote, with his rival, Manuel Baldizon, on 46 per cent, electoral officials said. Both candidates had promised to tackle growing insecurity and the presence of Mexican drug gangs in the country. Guatemala has become a key transit point for drugs from South America to the US. Mr Pérez Molina, the candidate of the right-wing Partido Patriota (PP) (Patriotic Party), will be the first former military leader to occupy the presidency since Guatemala restored democracy in 1986. 'We're going to fight very hard to bring peace, security, work opportunities and rural development,' he announced in his victory speech. His comments touched on two key issues facing Guatemala: rising insecurity and endemic poverty. The President has promised to hire 10,000 new police officers and deploy 2,500 more soldiers as part of his tough stance on crime.

The 60 year old Pérez Molina had been seen as the favourite after coming out on top in the first round against 41-year-old Mr Baldizon, the leader of the Libertad Democrática Renovada (Lider) (Renewed Democratic Liberty party). Critics claimed that Mr Pérez Molina's record was tarnished by his time in the army; human rights groups accused him of abuses as commander of troops during Guatemala's civil war. The newly elected President, who retired from the army in 2000, responded that there was no evidence to substantiate the claim. The 36-year-long conflict, in which more than 200,000 people are believed to have been killed, came to an end in 1996.

Despite Guatemala's painful and violent recent past, Mr Pérez Molina was able to persuade voters he was the best candidate to reduce the country's high murder rate. According to United Nations figures, Guatemala has a rate of some 41 murders per 100,000 – eight times that of the US. Mr Pérez Molina, who will take up the presidency in January 2012, narrowly lost four years ago to the current president, Alvaro Colóm, who was constitutionally limited to one term.

Diminished growth...

In its annual assessment of the Guatemalan economy, the International Monetary Fund (IMF) noted that although it has been negatively affected by the global crisis, the Guatemalan economy has maintained higher growth than other countries in the region. Nevertheless, growth in economic output has slowed considerably, diminished by declines in exports, remittances, tourism receipts, investment and capital inflows. Inflationary pressures have also eased. Yet, according to the IMF, the latest data suggest that the recovery is gaining steam. The government's policies, supported by an IMF Stand-By Arrangement (SBA), have helped preserve macro-economic stability and mitigate the impact of the global crisis. The government's strategy has focused on adopting moderately counter-cyclical fiscal and monetary policies, maintaining exchange rate flexibility, advancing reforms to further strengthen the financial sector and refocusing public expenditures toward social spending and infrastructure, as outlined in the National Programme of Emergency and Economic Recovery (PNERE).

In the view of the IMF the medium-term challenges for Guatemala are significant. The macro-economic policy framework needs to be strengthened further. The scope for counter-cyclical fiscal policies has been limited by a low and volatile tax revenue-to-GDP ratio stemming from political opposition to higher taxes, frequent recourse to temporary taxes and tax exemptions and budgetary rigidities. However, the IMF also noted that Guatemala has a strong record of low inflation and macro-economic stability. For Guatemala to attain higher growth and productivity while preserving macro-economic stability, the economic reforms encompassed by the goals of the 1996 Peace Accords will eventually need to be implemented.

...but a recovering economy

Meanwhile, in 2010 according to the United Nations Economic Commission for Latin America and the Caribbean (ECLAC), Guatemala's gross domestic product (GDP) grew by 2.5 per cent thanks to the expansion of services (3.5 per cent), manufacturing (2.2 per cent) and agriculture (1.6 per cent). Construction contracted by 12.2 per cent (similar to the figure for 2009), as the sector struggled to overcome financial uncertainty and oversupply. Mining fell by 0.4 per cent. Gross fixed investment declined by 5 per cent, compared with 15 per cent in 2009. Private investment saw a 2.8 per cent reduction, while public investment fell by 13.6 per cent. Total consumption grew by 1.9 per cent. Exports to the United States had also increased and there had been modest growth in domestic demand. Remittances and foreign direct investment (FDI) also saw a slight improvement. Without the damage caused by the torrential rains, economic growth for 2010 would probably have been higher than 2.5 per cent.

In 2010, goods exports were up by 11.8 per cent in relation to 2009. Traditional exports rose by 13.4 per cent; non-traditional exports increased by 11.2 per cent. Goods imports grew by 15.7 per cent, on the strength of greater demand for intermediate goods (20.3 per cent) that was largely due to rising hydrocarbon prices. Imports of capital goods and consumer goods increased by 10.8 per cent and 9.5 per cent, respectively. Unlike 2009, it was estimated that revenue from family remittances increased by 3.7 per cent. Inflows of foreign exchange from tourism also grew, by approximately 6 per cent as the flow of visits by Guatemalans residing abroad picked up. As a result, the current account deficit stood at 2.7 per cent of GDP. FDI inflows were equivalent to 1.8 per cent of GDP and the balances of the capital and financial accounts were positive. Net capital inflows (including errors and omissions) therefore exceeded the current account deficit, such that the balance of payments was a positive US$294 million.

It is estimated that the central government's total public debt was 24 per cent of GDP in 2010, which is one percentage point higher than in 2009. This figure does not take into account the central government's floating debt, the size of which is being calculated by the national authorities.

The government estimates that the rebuilding effort will require an investment of Q15.369 billion (US$1.95 billion) over a five-year period (2011–15) which is equivalent to 4.6 per cent of GDP in 2010. The funding gap was therefore expected to be close to Q12 billion (US$1.5 billion) (equivalent to 3.6 per cent of GDP in 2010). Of that amount, the authorities were expecting some Q6.2 billion (US$0.78 billion) in the form of

KEY INDICATORS **Guatemala**

	Unit	2006	2007	2008	2009	2010
Population	m	*12.98	*13.31	*13.69	*14.01	*14.36
Gross domestic product (GDP)	US$bn	30.21	34.00	39.10	37.30	41.50
GDP per capita	US$	2,322	2,550	2,862	2,662	2,888
GDP real growth	%	5.2	6.3	4.0	0.6	2.6
Inflation	%	6.6	6.8	11.4	1.9	3.9
Industrial output	% change	5.5	4.5	1.4	-1.4	–
Agricultural output	% change	1.8	5.9	2.0	1.7	–
Exports (fob) (goods)	US$m	6,025.2	4,489.5	7,846.4	7,330.5	8,565.9
Imports (fob) (goods)	US$m	11,068.7	10,981.1	13,421.2	10,621.9	12,858.2
Balance of trade	US$m	-5,043.6	-6,491.6	-5,574.8	-3,301.4	-4,293.3
Current account	US$m	-1,510.0	-1,769.0	-1,843.8	-267.4	-878.3
Total reserves minus gold	US$m	3,914.9	4,129.9	4,461.9	4,963.6	5,636.8
Foreign exchange	US$m	3,909.3	4,125.6	4,458.4	4,690.3	5,369.4
Exchange rate	per US$	7.69	7.60	7.56	8.16	8.06

* estimated figure

international co-operation. Total real central government revenue was estimated to have risen by 1.7 per cent in relation to 2009. Real total spending shrank by 0.3 per cent, owing mainly to the 9.4 per cent fall in capital expenditure, which was dragged down by the decline in real investment since current expenditure rose by 3.4 per cent in real terms. The tax burden stood at 10.6 per cent of GDP, which was similar to the level in 2009 but much lower than the target stipulated in the Peace Accords (13.2 per cent of GDP). The authorities were expecting the tax burden to reach at least 10.8 per cent of GDP in 2011, following the adoption of new tax evasion legislation in late 2010. However, more far-reaching fiscal reform is still needed.

The consumer price index rose by an estimated 5.3 per cent between December 2009 and December 2010, owing mainly to the economic recovery and to marked, though temporary, variations caused by the natural disasters. Food and beverages alone contributed an additional 0.2 per cent to inflation by year-end. An adjustment setting a uniform minimum wage of 56 quetzales in both agricultural and non-agricultural activities took effect in January 2010.

Guatemala's economy was forecast to grow by 2.5 per cent in 2011. One contributing factor being higher public investment in rebuilding from the damage caused by the 2010 eruption of

the Pacaya volcano, tropical storm Agatha and subsequent torrential rains. Another factor was moderate domestic and external demand, affected by the uncertainty surrounding the September 2011 presidential elections.

Inflation is expected to come in at about 5.5 per cent, as a result of stronger domestic demand and higher prices for imported goods. The central government's deficit looked likely to exceed its current level owing to an increase in social demands and the inevitably higher spending during the electoral process.

Risk assessment

Economy	Good
Politics	Fair
Regional stability	Good

COUNTRY PROFILE

Historical profile

1523–24 Pedro de Alvarado defeated the indigenous Mayan peoples and created Guatemala as a Spanish colony.
1821 The Central American provinces (Costa Rica, Guatemala, Honduras, Nicaragua and El Salvador) declared independence from Spain.
1822 Central American provinces annexed to the Mexican Empire, under General Agustín de Iturbde, later Emperor Agustín I.
1823 Agustín I was overthrown and Mexico became a republic. The Central American states formed the United Provinces of Central America.
1825 Costa Rica, Guatemala, Honduras, Nicaragua and El Salvador formed the Central American Federation (CAF).
1838 The CAF was dissolved and Guatemala became a fully independent republic.
1844–65 Guatemala was ruled by conservative dictator Rafael Carrera.
1873–85 Liberal, Rufino Barrios, became president, he attempted to modernise the country by developing an army and introducing coffee plantations.
1930 General Jorge Ubico began his repressive dictatorship.
1941 Guatemala declared war on the Axis Powers.
1944 Ubico was overthrown in a popular revolution. Juan José Arevalo headed a new government that introduced social reforms, including a social security system and land redistribution.
1951 Jacobo Arbenz Guzmán became president and stepped up the reforms.
1954 A US-backed *coup d'état*, led by Colonel Carlos Castillo Armas and prompted by the US United Fruit Company when disused land it owned was nationalised, overthrew the democratically elected government. A military dictatorship was installed.
1957 Castillo Armas was assassinated.
1958 Miguel Ramon Ydígoras Fentes took control and his autocratic rule led to a failed military revolt by junior officers in 1960. Most leaders of armed insurrection for the next 36 years of civil war were part of this group.
1963 Enrique Peralta became president following a coup and civilian administration was completely assumed by the military whose power and influence increased. Widespread repression of opposition groups increased as leaders were targeted for assassination or 'disappearance'. Insurgents countered with sabotage and violent guerrilla tactics.
1966 Civilian rule was restored when César Méndez of the Revolucionario Partido (PR) (Revolutionary Party) was elected president. Nevertheless, the military launched a major counterinsurgency campaign, which crippled the guerrilla movement in the countryside.
1970 Carlos Arena, backed by the military and the US, was elected president.
1976 An earthquake struck just south-west of Guatemala City killing around 27,000 people and leaving one million citizens homeless.
1978–1984 Over 90 per cent of all atrocities occurred during this time as government forces and insurgents battled. The most frequent victims were the ethnic Mayan population who were attacked by both sides and accused of being collaborators or sympathisers of the opposition.
1980 Thirty seven people died in the Spanish Embassy siege in Guatemala City, when Mayan peasant farmers were protesting about military repression.
1981 Left-wing insurgent groups unified to become Unidad Revolucionaria Nacional Guatemalteca (URNG) (National Guatemalan Revolutionary Unit).
1982 General Efraín Ríos Montt seized power in a military coup. His dictatorship was in power during the bloodiest period of the civil war.
1983 Montt was ousted by General Mejía Victores, who declared an amnesty on guerrillas.
1985 Marco Vinicio Cerezo was elected president and Democracia Cristiana Guatemalteco (DCG) (Guatemalan Christian Democracy) won legislative elections.
1989 An attempt to overthrow Cerezo failed.
1991 Jorge Serrano Elias was elected president.
1993 Serrano's attempt to impose an authoritarian regime led to mass demonstrations and he was forced to resign. Ramiro de Leon Carpio was elected president by the legislature.
1994 Peace talks began between the government and the URNG.
1995 The URNG declared a cease-fire. The UN and the US criticised the government for widespread human rights violations and the deaths of more than 200,000 civilians during the civil war.
1996 After a civil war lasting 36 years, a peace treaty was signed. Alvaro Arzú and his Partido de Avanzada Nacional (PAN) (National Advancement Party) won the subsequent presidential and National Congress elections. Arzú began a purge on senior military officers implicated in human rights violations.
1999 A UN-sponsored investigation found that the security forces were responsible for 93 per cent of all human rights atrocities committed during the civil war and that the military had overseen 626 massacres in Mayan villages. Alfonso Portillo of the Frente Republicano Guatemalteco (FRG) (Guatemalan Republican Front) was elected president.
2000 Portillo was sworn in as president.
2001 A foreign exchange law allowed the free circulation of US dollars; citizens and companies were allowed to hold US dollar bank deposits without prior authorisation. The government paid

US$1.8 million in compensation to the families of 226 victims killed by soldiers and death squads in the village of Las Dos Erres in 1982.
2003 The ruling FRG was defeated by the Gran Alianza Nacional (GANA) (Grand National Alliance) in the parliamentary elections. Óscar Berger Perdomo (GANA) became president.
2004 Former dictator, Ríos Montt, was put under house arrest on charges of inciting a riot, and genocide relating to atrocities carried out when he was in power. The State accepted responsibility for more human rights violations during the civil war; US$3.5 million was paid out to victims.
2005 The government signed the Central American Free Trade Agreement (Cafta) with the US and five other Central American and Caribbean states, amid anti-US demonstrations. Hurricane Stan hit the region causing 699 deaths; over 35,000 homes were destroyed and there were numerous landslides and extensive flooding. In the US, Guatemala's top anti-drugs investigator was arrested on drug trafficking charges.
2006 Manslaughter charges against Ríos Montt were dropped. A request by the Spanish government to extradite him to face charges of genocide was denied.
2007 In parliamentary elections the opposition Unidad Nacional de la Esperanza (UNE) (National Union of Hope) won 48 seats out of 158. After two rounds of presidential elections Álvaro Colom (UNE) won 52.82 per cent of the vote; his nearest rival Otto Pérez Molina (PP) won 47.18 per cent. The second round of the presidential election was won by Álvaro Colom Caballeros (53 per cent) over Otto Pérez Milina (47 per cent).
2008 Álvaro Colom Caballeros was sworn in as president. Former president Alfonso Portillo Cabrera was extradited from Mexico to face fraud charges over the loss of US$15 million of government money. Premium Guatemalan coffee reached a record US$80.20 per pound, the highest price offered in the world.
2009 The IMF approved a US$935 million credit line to Guatemala as a stand-by arrangement providing a liquidity cushion during the global economic crisis.
2010 Tropical storm Agatha, which struck in May, killed more than 90 people and around 4,000 people were forced to evacuate their homes, while a 30m-diametre, 60m deep sinkhole swallowed a three-storey building in Guatemala City. Many bridges were swept away and mudslides closed the traffic along 100km stretch of the Pan-American Highway. In September further heavy rains caused by Hurricane Frank, resulted in mudslides in the highlands that killed dozens and the Pan-American Highway was again cut, in over 30 places. Work carried out after the May storm was mostly undone. By 13 December, and at the end of a year of natural disasters that caused an estimated US$1.55 billion in damages and a loss of 4.1 per cent of GDP, the World Bank approved a US$100 million loan to provide emergency assistance and preserve health and education services in Guatemala.
2011 On 17 March US Secretary General Ban Ki-moon voiced anxiety at the deterioration in personal security in Guatemala, which has one of the World's highest rates of gun-crime and deaths as well as reported human rights abuses. In March, President Colom's wife, Sandra Torres de Colom, confirmed that she would be divorcing her husband so she could stand for election to succeed him. The constitution bans close relatives of the president from standing. On 2 April a court put the divorce on hold after complaints it was aimed at bypassing the constitution; nevertheless a family court granted the divorce on 8 April. On 8 June the Organisation of American States (OAS) called on member-states to co-operate to improve citizen security and endorse measures to stop drugs, arms and people trafficking. On 8 August, the Constitutional Court ruled that Sandra Torres was ineligible to run as president, despite her divorce from Álvaro Colom, which they regarded as a political ploy. Ten candidates took part in the first round of presidential elections held on 11 September in which Otto Pérez Molina (PP) won 31.1 per cent of the vote, Manuel Baldizón (Lider) 22.68 per cent and Eduardo Suger (CREO) 16.62 per cent; as none won more than 50 per cent of the vote a runoff was held on 6 November in which Molina won 53.74 per cent and Baldizón 46.26 per cent; turnout was 60.82 per cent.

Political structure

In addition to their unicameral national parliaments, El Salvador, Guatemala, Honduras, Nicaragua, Panama and Dominican Republic also return directly-elected deputies to the supranational Central American Parliament.

Constitution

The constitution, which came into effect in 1986 (replacing the 1966 constitution suspended in 1982), created a representative system of government in which power is exercised equally by the legislative, executive and judicial arms. Guatemala is divided into 22 provinces, subdivided into municipalities.

Form of state

Presidential democratic republic

The executive

Executive power is held by the president, directly elected for four years, assisted by a vice president and an appointed cabinet.

National legislature

The unicameral Congreso de la República (Congress of the Republic), has 158 directly elected deputies, of which 29 are elected from a nationwide list and the remainder from district lists (relating to departments, with the capital divided into two districts). All deputies serve for four-year terms. No political party can win outright power and must form a coalition. Congress is responsible for all legislative matters, including approving the budget and decreeing taxes by means of an absolute majority. All laws involving constitutional change or any international treaty or agreement affecting the sovereignty of the state must secure a two-thirds majority.

Legal system

Guatemala has a civil law system with judicial review of legislative acts. The Supreme Court serves as the highest appeal court in the country; there is also a separate Court of Constitutionality and a Supreme Electoral Tribunal. The country does not accept the compulsory jurisdiction of the International Court of Justice.

Last elections

11 September and 6 November 2011 (presidential, first round and runoff); 11 September 2011 (parliamentary)

Results: Presidential (first round): Otto Pérez Molina (PP) won 31.1 per cent of the vote, Manuel Baldizón (Lider) 22.68 per cent, Eduardo Suger (CREO) 16.62 per cent, Mario Estrada (UCN) 8.72 per cent; six other candidates each won less than 6.5 per cent of the vote. Runoff: Molina won 53.74 per cent and Baldizón 46.26 per cent; turnout was 60.82 per cent.

Parliamentary: Partido Patriota (PP) (Patriotic Party) won 26.62 per cent of the vote (56 seats out of 158), Unidad Nacional de la Esperanza – Gran Alianza Nacional (UNE-GANA) (National Union of Hope – Grand National Alliance) 22.57 per cent (48), Union del Cambio Nacionalista (UCN) (Nationalist Change Union) 9.5 per cent (14), (Libertad Democrática Renovada (Lider) (Renewed Democratic Liberty) 8.87 per cent (14), Compromiso, Renovación y Orden (CREO) (Commitment, Renewal and Order) 8.67 per cent (12); six other political parties and coalitions each won less than 8 per cent and shared the remaining 14 seats, three other political parties failed to win any seats. Turnout was 69.3 per cent.

Next elections

2015 (presidential and parliamentary)

Political parties

Ruling party

Coalition led by Partido Patriota (PP) (Patriotic Party (from 14 Jan 2012

Main opposition party

To be announced

Population

14.36 million (2010)*

Last census: November 2002: 11,237,196

Population density: 101.8 inhabitants per square km. Urban population: 40 per cent (1995–2001).

Annual growth rate: 2.3 per cent 1994–2004 (WHO 2006)

Ethnic make-up

A high proportion of the population belongs to 22 Mayan ethno-linguistic groups, conserving the cultural heritage of their ancestors. Their numbers are disputed but they constitute at least 45 per cent of the population and possibly as much as 60 per cent. Many of the inhabitants of the Caribbean coast are of Afro-Caribbean origin.

Religions

The constitution guarantees freedom of worship. Catholicism is the most widespread religion, although large numbers of conversions have been made in recent years by Protestant churches, including mainstream non-conformists and US-based fundamentalist sects. Protestant leaders claim to have converted some 30 per cent of the population and are playing an increasingly active role in the country's politics. Some indigenous communities hold services combining Catholicism with pre-Columbian rites.

Education

Elementary education is free and lasts for six years and secondary education, which begins at age 13, for a further six years, divided into two three-year courses.

There are five universities, three of which are private, located in Guatemala City and Quetzaltenango, the country's second-largest city.

Literacy rate: 70 per cent adult rate; 80 per cent youth rate (15–24) (Unesco 2005).

Compulsory years: Seven to 14 in urban areas only.

Enrolment rate: 90 per cent total primary enrolment of the relevant age group; 26 per cent total enrolment in secondary schools, of the relevant age group; enrolment in tertiary education is less than 10 per cent.

Pupils per teacher: 35 in primary schools.

Health

Healthcare remains inadequate with 80 per cent of spending and hospitals confined in the two major cities.

HIV/Aids

HIV prevalence: 1.1 per cent aged 15–49 in 2003 (World Bank)

Life expectancy: 68 years, 2004 (WHO 2006)

Fertility rate/Maternal mortality rate: 4.5 births per woman, 2004 (WHO 2006); maternal mortality 2.9 per 1,000 live births (World Bank).

Child (under 5 years) mortality rate (per 1,000): 35 per 1,000 live births; 44 per cent of children aged under five are malnourished (World Bank).

Welfare

Social security, which is compulsory, covers health and hospital care as well as industrial accidents, disability and widowhood for registered workers. All employers with five or more workers are required by law to register with the State Institute of Social Security.

Main cities

Guatemala City (capital, estimated population 964,823 in 2005), Mixco (297,039), Villa Nueva (218,513), Quezaltenango (112,121).

Languages spoken

Approximately 22 Indian languages are widely spoken throughout the highlands, including Quiché, Cakchiquel, Mam and Kekchi. About 40 per cent of all Guatemalan children enter school with no knowledge of Spanish.

English is spoken in almost all tourist areas.

Official language/s

Spanish

Media

The constitution guarantees freedom of the press. Private, independently owned media outlets dominate the market.

Press

Most of Guatemala's media is privately owned. Journalists have reported incidents of intimidation particularly following articles exposing corruption.

Dailies: In Spanish, national newspapers include *Prensa Libre* (www.prensalibre.com), *La Hora* (www.lahora.com.gt) and *El Periodico* and are broadsheets with articles on business and finance, while *Siglo Veintiuno* (www.sigloxxi.com) is a tabloid style newspaper.

Regional newspapers, in Spanish, include *El Metropolitano* (www.elmetropolitano.net) with local editions in five cities. Other local publications such as *Diario de Centroamérica* (www.dca.gob.gt), *Nuestro Diario* (www.nuestrodiario.com) and *El Qeutzalteco* (www.elquetzalteco.com.gt) are tabloid style newspapers.

In English, the Guatemala Times (www.guatemala-times.com) is an online publication.

Broadcasting

The state-owned Radiodifusión y Televisión Nacional operates public broadcasting.

Radio: The state-owned Radio TGW (www.radiotgw.gob.gt) operates a network of five radio stations, providing news, educational and cultural programmes, however it has low audience numbers. It competes with dozens of commercial stations, located regionally and locally and many of them broadcasting at least part of the time in indigenous languages. In Spanish, news and information stations include Emiroras Unidas (http://radio.emisorasunidas.com), a national network, Radio Sonora (www.sonora.com.gt) and Radio Punto (www.radiopunto.com).

Christian churches operate several radio stations which broadcast from rural areas, including Radio Cultural TGN (www.radiocultural.com), broadcasting in several languages.

Television: There is no public TV. The majority of commercial TV is owned by a few elites. TV channels broadcasting on terrestrial and satellite include Canal 3 (www.canal3.com.gt), Televisiete (www.canal7.com.gt), Vea Canal (www.veacanal.com), Guatevision (www.guatevision.com), TeleOnce, Trecevision and Latitud.

The Comtech cable TV channel operates Claro TV (www.comtech.net.gt) in Guatemala City.

News agencies

Other news agencies: Inforpress (in Spanish and English): www.inforpressca.com

Prensa Latina (from Cuba, in six languages): www.prensa-latina.com.ar

Economy

The economy is driven by the service sector, which represents over 55 per cent of GDP; agriculture constitutes around 12 per cent and industry over 30 per cent, of which manufacturing is 20 per cent. Cash crops for export include coffee, bananas and sugar and these are typically produced on commercial farms, while the majority of farming is subsistence, which is demonising as land is continually divided among the family. Multinational agri-businesses occupy much of the prime agricultural land. Industry is dominated by light manufacturing establishments, many of which are located in free-trade-zones, including textiles, general assembly of machinery and equipment, electronic equipment and electrical appliances.

GDP growth was a high of 6.3 per cent in 2007, falling to 3.3 per cent in 2008.

The economy did not fall into recession, although it fell to its lowest of 0.5 per cent in 2009 as the global economic crisis cut international trade. The economy grew by 2.4 per cent in 2010 and is predicted to maintain this at 2.6 per cent in 2011.

Inequality and social outcomes in Guatemala are particularly stark and in 2009, 50 per cent of children under the age of five suffered from chronic malnutrition and one in three do not complete primary education, according to the Central American Centre for Economic and Social Rights. Remittances are important not only to the general economy but also to household budgets. In 2009 remittances were US$4 billion (9.8 per cent of GDP), which is estimated to have risen to US$4.26 billion in 2010.

There were a series of natural disasters in 2010, including a volcanic eruption, a tropical storm and a gigantic sink hole that opened up and swallowed a multi-storey building, which did not unduly affect the economy, despite the loss of life, disruption to transportation and damage to infrastructure and agricultural crops. The World Bank and Inter-American Development Bank together estimated the total GDP loss was 2.4 per cent.

External trade

Guatemala is a member of the Central America Free Trade Agreement (DR-Cafta), which includes the Dominican Republic, Costa Rica, El Salvador and Honduras and the US. It is also a member of the Central American Common Market (CACM), along with Costa Rica, El Salvador, Honduras and Nicaragua.

Imports

Principal imports are foodstuffs including grain, petroleum, vehicles, clothing and other consumer goods, and construction materials.

Main sources: US (typically 36 per cent of total), Mexico (10 per cent), China (9 per cent).

Exports

Principal exports are coffee (typically around 40 per cent of annual total), light assembly products, processed food, textiles, sugar, rum, bananas, cardamom and cut flowers.

Main destinations: US (typically 41 per cent of total), El Salvador (11 per cent), Honduras (8 per cent).

Agriculture

Farming

Guatemala's most important economic sector is agriculture. The sector accounts for approximately 25 per cent of total GDP and employs about half of the country's total workforce. Despite the agricultural sector's high employment level, the number of jobs in the sector is falling due to increased mechanisation. Approximately 17 per cent of Guatemala's total land mass is cultivated arable land, 10 per cent pasture and 35 per cent forest.

Throughout the 1990s, Guatemala was relatively successful in establishing agricultural diversification, in an effort to buttress export earnings against commodity price fluctuations. It also sought to encourage the development of processing and packaging plants so as to upgrade the value of farm exports. Most of this took place in the highland areas where there is a good supply of land and labour. The production of fresh and frozen vegetables and ornamental plants and flowers has been particularly successful.

Production is mainly export-oriented, the major cash crops being coffee (the largest single earner of foreign exchange), sugar cane, bananas, cotton, cardamom (Guatemala accounts for over 90 per cent of world trade in cardamom) and tobacco.

Vegetables such as mangetout, broccoli and asparagus, as well as a wide variety of fruits, are exported to the US and Europe.

Coffee growers plan to double the country's production between 1998–2008. Coffee has suffered from poor global commodity prices, although rising output has helped offset some of the losses.

Maize is the main food crop, although rice and wheat are also grown. Agricultural produce also includes cocoa, beans and flowers.

Foreign investment has so far been limited as a result of the absence of a domestic land market. Land is regarded as an indication of wealth and most owners leave it fallow if they choose not to plant. Land distribution is uneven, with just under 80 per cent of all farms under 3.5 hectares (ha) and 1 per cent over 2,500ha. Most foreign participation is concentrated on the non-traditional agricultural crops now emerging as major export earners.

Fishing

Guatemala's typical catch is approximately 14,300 tonnes (t), 9,800t freshwater fish inclusive.

Forestry

Approximately 35 per cent of Guatemala's total land mass is covered by forests. Some 20 per cent of Guatemala's land area is protected against industrial exploitation.

Softwood conifers account for 22 per cent with broad-leaved species, including valuable hardwoods such as mahogany, cedar and rosewood, accounting for the rest. Other forest products include rubber and chicle, an important chewing gum base, which is extracted in the forested Petén region.

The majority of timber production is consumed as domestic fuel, while a modest amount of sawnwood is exported. Much of the domestic demand for paper is met by imports.

Industry and manufacturing

Guatemala has a well developed industrial sector and the sector as a whole contributes approximately one fifth to GDP in a typical year. Industry contributes around 20 per cent to GDP (manufacturing contributes around 14 per cent) and employs 15 per cent of the workforce. Industry is primarily involved in activities related to agricultural inputs for major firms involved in food and drink processing, rubber, textiles, pottery, paper and pharmaceuticals. Other important industries are the assembly of electronic products, manufacture of furniture, canned goods, oil refining, cement, metals (especially steel), electrical goods assembly, plastics, chemicals, fertilisers and cigarettes.

Social and industrial unrest, high energy costs, shortages of imported materials and a slump in private and public investment have severely hampered industrial production. However, major government house building and infrastructural repair plans since the end of the civil war seem to have given a signficant boost to the construction industry, although construction as a proportion of GDP has shrunk in recent years.

Tourism

The tourism industry of Guatemala has achieved steady growth in recent years. The sector now accounts for 6.9 per cent of total GDP and 6 per cent of total employment.

Guatemala relies on its ecology and Mayan ruins to attract visitors. The largest market for Guatemalan travel and tourism in recent years has been El Salvador, though the US and Canada overtook that country.

Mining

The Alta Verapaz copper mine represents the main mining operation in Guatemala. In addition to copper, tungsten and antimony there are also exploitable reserves of marble and sulphur. Deposits of lead, zinc, gold and silver are also known to exist.

Lead is mined at Ballena and Penasco by Cía Minas de Oriente SA (Minersa). Reserves are estimated at 2.2 million tonnes and contain 86 grammes per tonne of silver. Minas de Guatemala operates the Annabella and Los Lirios antimony and tungsten mines, producing about 1,800 tonnes per month of ore (6 per cent antimony, 0.5 per cent lead). The Oxec copper mine, worked by Transmetales in Alta Verapaz, has a capacity of 150,000 tonnes per year. The country's major

mineral resource is laterite, with the El Estor deposits estimated at 50 million tonnes.
In 2005 the World Bank was crtiticised for its role in funding a gold mining project in Guatemala. The Bank was criticised for not consulting the local community properly and for failing to evaluate the humanitarian or environmental implications of the proposed facility.

Hydrocarbons
Guatemala is one of only two oil-producing countries in Central America. Proven oil reserves were less than 83 million barrels in 2010, though actual reserves are thought to be as much as 1 billion barrels. Most production occurs in the northern jungle areas, near to the border with Mexico.
Gas reserves were less than 2.96 billion cubic metres (cum) in 2010, but Guatemala does not consume or import natural gas. Guatemala and Mexico signed a protocol for the construction of a natural gas pipeline from southern Mexico to Guatemala but by 2009 it had not become operational. The pipeline was to be part of a wider Central America gas pipeline network to meet an initial demand estimated at about 1.1 million cum per day, but which is still at the design stage. It should offer the potential to reduce the region's reliance on seasonally-dependent hydroelectric power.
Guatemala typically imports over 220,000 tonnes of coal annually. Coal is mainly used for primary energy production. Guatemala does not produce coal.

Energy
Guatemala has a total electricity generation capacity of approximately 1.8GW. The San José power station is Central America's largest coal-fired power plant. Net installed capacity of 739kW is supplied by hydropower.
Electricity consumption doubled between 1997–2005, from 3.2 billion kilowatt hours (kWh) to 6.4 billion kWh.

Financial markets
Stock exchange
BVN (Bolsa de Valores Naciónal) (Guatemala Stock Exchange)

Banking and insurance
The Guatemalan banking and financial services sector is organised under a central banking system, above which is the higher authority of the Monetary Board. There are 35 private commercial banks in Guatemala, but the banking market is dominated by a handful of large institutions. Some 40 per cent of total assets are in the hands of the five largest banks. Guatemala is no longer on the OECD Financial Action Task Force (FATF) list of non-co-operative countries regarding money laundering.
Central bank
Banco de Guatemala

Time
GMT minus six hours

Geography
Guatemala has five distinct geographical zones. The first is the lowland Pacific strip running the length of the coastline, where the climate is tropical and summer rains are heavy. Most of the country's large sugar, banana and cotton farms are based here. Some 50km in from the coast the land rises to form the first of two mountain ranges running north-west to south-east. This range includes a string of volcanoes. A plateau formed by a series of volcanic basins at an average height of 1,500 metres above sea level forms the third zone; the capital, Guatemala City, and most of the country's population are to be found here.
Another mountain range with peaks of over 4,000 metres forms the basis of the north-west highlands, tapering down to the border with Honduras and El Salvador at its south-east extremity, where most of the country's more than four million indigenous people live. Beyond the mountains the land falls rapidly into a flat expanse of tropical forest. This area, which accounts for the northern part of the departments of Izabal, El Quiche, and Alta Verapaz and all the 36,400 square km of El Petén department, remains one of the region's last wildernesses.
Hemisphere
Northern

Climate
The climate varies with altitude but is essentially sub-tropical with little variation between the seasons. The hottest month is May when the average daily minimum and maximum temperatures are 16 degrees Celsius (C) and 29 degrees C. The coldest month is January when the temperature varies between 12 degrees C and 23 degrees C. The driest month is February and the wettest June, when there is an average of 274mm of rainfall.

Dress codes
Guatemalans are generally conservative in dress. Tropical lightweight suits are the accepted dress in business circles in the capital. Extremes of fashion should be avoided.

Entry requirements
Passports
Required by all.
Visa
Visas are not required by most nationals of the Americas, EU, Australasia, and a few Asian countries, for between 1–3 months.
A business visa, requiring additional information to the visitor's visa, must be applied for before arrival. The application should include a company letter as proof of business intentions.
Currency advice/regulations
No restrictions on import/export of foreign currency. There is free circulation of US dollars.

Health (for visitors)
Mandatory precautions
Cholera and yellow fever vaccination certificates are required from citizens of infected countries.
Advisable precautions
Malaria is prevalent in the low-lying areas outside the city, prophylaxes are recommended. Dengue fever is endemic, although there is no preventive medication, mosquito repellent and clothing covering as much skin as possible at dawn and dusk should help. Inoculations are recommended against typhoid, hepatitis A and B and typhoid.
Guatemalan hospitals are reluctant to give medical treatment unless a patient has medical insurance, so evidence of insurance cover should be carried at all times. State-funded hospitals are regarded as understaffed, ill-equipped and often unhygienic. Private clinics should be used where possible.
Bottled water should be used. Milk is often unpasteurised and should be boiled; avoid dairy products which are likely to have been made from unboiled milk. Only eat hot well-cooked meat and fish. Pork, salad and mayonnaise carry increased risk. Vegetables should be cooked and fruit peeled. There is a rabies risk.

Hotels
In the main cities there are a range of good hotels, the range can be limited in provincial towns. Most charge 20 per cent room tax; 10 per cent is added where service charges are not levied.

Public holidays (national)
Fixed dates
1 Jan (New Year), 1 May (Labour Day), 30 Jun (Army Day), 15 Aug (Assumption Day), 15 Sep (Independence Day), 20 Oct (Revolution Day), 1 Nov (All Saints' Day), 24 Dec (half-day), 25 Dec, 31 Dec (half-day).
Variable dates
Easter (Wed–Fri; Mar/Apr)

Working hours
Banking
Generally Mon–Fri: 0900–1500.
Business
Mon–Fri: 0800–1600. Private companies Mon–Fri: 0800–1200, 1400–1800.

Government
Mon–Fri: 0800–1600.
Shops
Shopping centres (Mon–Sun) 0900–2000.

Telecommunications
Mobile/cell phones
GSM 850/1900 services are available.

Electricity supply
110V AC, 60 cycles

Social customs/useful tips
Customs and social mores tend to mirror those of Catholic Europe or the more conservative southern states of the United States. Punctuality is not one of most Guatemalans' strongest points, although Western propensity for good time keeping is recognised in their phrase 'English time'.

Security
Security in the capital has become much more of a problem in recent years as street crime and house break-ins have risen. Armed mugging and gratuitous violence is common and most companies have armed guards and watchmen.

Getting there
Air
National airline: TACA – an amalgamation of the flag airlines of Guatemala (Aviateca), Costa Rica (Lacsa) and Nicaragua (Nica).
International airport/s: Guatemala City-Aurora (GUA), 6km from the city; duty-free shop, bank, bar, restaurant, bank, hotel reservations, post office, shops, car hire.
Airport tax: Departures tax US$30; not applicable to 24 hour transit passengers.
Surface
Road: The Pan-American Highway runs through the country from Mexico to El Salvador, stretching 511km. There are other roads from El Salvador, Honduras and Mexico and there is a route via Melchor de Mencos from Belize. Plans for any journey should be made in the light of prevailing road conditions.
Rail: It is possible to use scheduled train services but some of these are often subject to suspension.
Main port/s: Champerico, Puerto Barrios, San José, Santo Tomás de Castilla and the Quetzal Port.

Getting about
National transport
Air: TACA operates a domestic service to major centres.
Road: Total network is 13,238km, only 26 per cent of which is paved; using unpaved roads can be difficult. Paved roads are of fair quality.
Buses: Bus services connect major towns.
City transport
Taxis: There is a good taxi service in Guatemala City. Fares are generally negotiated but there are set rates for journeys from the airport to certain destinations. Tipping (5–10 per cent) is discretionary.
Buses, trams & metro: Numerous services within Guatemala City – said to be (outside usual rush hours) less crowded than some cities.
Car hire
Any valid licence is usually acceptable. Many of the international rental agencies have offices both at La Aurora airport and in Guatemala City centre.

BUSINESS DIRECTORY

The addresses listed below are a selection only. While World of Information makes every endeavour to check these addresses, we cannot guarantee that changes have not been made, especially to telephone numbers and area codes. We would welcome any corrections.

Telephone area codes
The international direct dialling code (IDD) for Guatemala is +502, followed by subscriber's number. Telephones and faxes have been eight digits since Septermber 2004.

Chambers of Commerce
American Chamber of Commerce in Guatemala, Avenida las Americas 18-81, Zona 14, 01014 Guatemala City (tel: 2363-1774; fax: 2367-3414; e-mail: director@amchamguate.com).

Guatemala Chamber of Commerce, 10a Calle 3-80, Zona 1, 01001 Guatemala City (tel: 2253-5353; fax: 2220-9393; e-mail: info@camaradecomercio.org.gt).

Banking
Banco Nacional de Desarrollo Agrícola (BANDESA), 9 Calle 9-47, Zona 1, 01001.

Banco Nacional de la Vivienda (BANVI), 6 Ave 1-22, Zona 4, 01004.

Credito Hipotecario Nacional, 7 Ave 22-77, Zona 1, 01001.

Banco de Occidente, 7 Ave 11-15, Zona 1, 01001.

Banco del Agro, 9 Calle 5-39, Zona 1, 01001 (tel: 2251-4026; fax: 2230-0322).

Banco del Café SA, Ave La Reforma 9-00, Zona 9, 01009.

Banco del Quetzal SA, Plaza El Robel, 7 Ave 6-26, Zona 9, 01009.

Banco Granai & Townson SA, 7 Ave 1-86, Zona 4, 1004.

Banco Industrial SA, 7 Ave 5-10, Zona 4, 01004.

Citibank, Ave La Reforma 15-45, Zona 10, 01010.

Lloyds Bank International, 6 Ave 9-51, Zona 9, 01009.

Central bank
Banco de Guatemala, 7 Avenida 22-01, Zona 1, PO Box 365, 01001 Guatemala City (tel: 2230-6222; fax: 2253-4035; email: webmaster@banguat.gob.gt).

Stock exchange
BVN (Bolsa de Valores Naciónal) (Guatemala Stock Exchange): www.bvnsa.com.gt

Travel information
Asociación Guatemalteca de Agentes de Viajes (AGAV) (Guatemalan Association of Travel Agents), 6a Avenida 8-41, Zona 9, Apdo 2735, Guatemala City.

TACA, Avenida Hincapié 12-22, Aeropuerto La Aurora, Zona 13, Guatemala City (internet (including email) www.taca.com).

National tourist organisation offices
Instituto Guatemalteco de Turismo (INGUAT) (Guatemalan Tourism Institute), 7 Avenida 1-17, Zona 4, Centro Cívico 01004, Guatemala City (tel: 2331-1333; fax: 2331-8893; e-mail: inguat@guate.net; internet: www.visitguatemala.com).

Ministries
Ministry of Agriculture, Livestock and Food, Avenida Reforma 4-47, Zona 10, Guatemala City.

Ministry of Communications, Transport and Public Works, Avenida Reforma 4-47, Zona 10, Guatemala City (tel: 2362-6051; fax: 2362-6059).

Ministry of Culture and Sport, 5 Calle 4-33, Zona 1, Plaza Rabi, Guatemala City.

Ministry of Defence, Avenida Reforma 4-47, Zona 10, Guatemala City (tel: 2360-9907; fax: 2360-9909).

Ministry of Economy, 8 Avenida 10-43, Zona 1, Guatemala City (tel: 2238-3331/2/3; fax: 2251-5055).

Ministry of Education, Avenida Reforma 4-47, Zona 10, Guatemala City.

Ministry of Employment and Social Security, 14 Calle 5-49, Zona 1, Edificio Nasa, Guatemala City (tel: 2230-5592/4; fax: 2251-3559).

Ministry of Energy and Mines, Diagonal 17, 29-78, Zona 11, Guatemala City (tel: 2477-0382, 2476-0680).

Ministry of Finance, Entre 8 Avenida y 21 calle, Zona 1, Centro Cívico, Guatemala City (tel: 2230-5180, 2230-5202; fax: 2251-6514).

Ministry of Foreign Affairs, Avenida Reforma 4-47, Zona 10, Guatemala City.

Ministry of Health and Social Assistance, Avenida Reforma 4-47, Zona 10, Guatemala City (tel: 2232-4509).

Ministry of the Interior, Avenida Reforma 4-47, Zona 10, Guatemala City.

Other useful addresses

Agroindustrias de Exportación, 14 Calle 7-46, Zona 10, Guatemala City

Asociación de Gerentes de Guatemala, 10a Calle 3-17, Zona 10, Edificio Aseguradora General, Nivel 70, Apartado Postal 2373, Guatemala City, 01010.

Bolsa Agrícola Nacional, 4a Calle 6-55, Zona 9, Guatemala City.

Bolsa de Valores Global, Av La Reforma 9-76, Zona 9, Edificio SCI Centre, Nivel 70, Guatemala City, 01009.

Bolsa de Valores Nacional, SA, 7a Av 5-10, Zona 4, Centro Financiero, Torre II, Nivel 20, Guatemala City, 01004.

British Embassy, Edificio Torre Internacional, Nivel 11, 16 Calle 0-55, Zona 10, Guatemala City (tel: 2367-5425–9; fax: 2367-5430; email: embassy@intelnett.com).

Centro de Investigaciones Económicas Nacionales (CIEN), 5 Av 15-45, Zona 10, Centro Empresarial, Torre 1, Of 302, Apartado Postal 260-C, Guatemala City.

Centro Nacional de Promoción de las Exportaciones, 6A Avenida Torre Profesional, Zona 14, Apdo 1237, Guatemala City.

Comité Co-ordinador de Asociaciones Agrícolas, Comerciales, Industriales y Financieras (CACIF), Ruta 6 9-21, Zona 4, Nivel 90, Guatemala City.

Coperex (international marketing fair), 8 Calle 2-33, Zona 9, Parque de la Industria, Guatemala City.

Dirección General de Radiodifusión y Televisión Nacional, 5a Avenida Zona 1, Guatemala City.

Empresa Eléctrica de Guatemala (EEGSA), 8a Calle y 6a Avenida Esquina, Zona 1, Guatemala City.

Empresa Municipal de Agua (Empagua), 7a Avenida 1-20, Zona 4, Edificio Torre Café, Nivel 16, Guatemala City.

Fundación para el Desarrollo de Guatemala (FUNDESA), Parque Gerencial Las Margaritas, Diagonal 6, 10-65, Zona 10, Of 402, Guatemala City.

Guatemala–US Trade Association (GUSTA), 299 Alhambra Circle, Suite 207, Coral Gables, Florida 33134, USA (tel: (+1-305) 443-0343; fax: (+1-305) 433-0699).

Guatemalan Embassy (USA), 2220 R Street, NW, Washington DC 20008 (tel: (+1-202) 745-4952; fax: (+1-202) 745-1908; e-mail: info@guatemala-embassy.org).

Inforpress Centroamericana, 9a Calle A 3-56, Guatemala City 01001.

Instituto Centroamericano de Investigación y Tecnología Industrial (ICAITI), Avenida La Reforma 4-47, Zona 10, Guatemala City.

Instituto Nacional de Electrificación (INDE), 7a Avenida 2-29, Zona 9, Guatemala City.

International Investment Securities Corporation, Edificio Galerías Reforma 8-60, Zona 9, Torre 1, Nivel 90, Guatemala City.

Telgua (Empresa de Telecomunicaciones de Guatemala), 5 Calle Avenida Reforma, Zona 9, Guatemala City (tel: 2331-8999/6599, 2230-1050).

United States Department of Commerce, Guatemala Desk, Department of Commerce H3025, Washington DC 20230, USA (tel: (+1-202) 377-2627; fax: (+1-202) 377-3718).

US Embassy, Avenida La Reforma 7-01, Zona 10, Guatemala City.

Internet sites

Guatemalan portals:
http://mi-guatemala.tripod.com

http://www.elcafecito.com/Zonas_geograficas/Paises/Guatemala

Business information:
http://www.tradepoint.org.gt

KEY FACTS

Official name: République de Guinée (Republic of Guinea)

Head of State: President Alpha Condé (RPG) (from 21 Dec 2010)

Head of government: Prime Minister Mohamed Said Fofana (from 24 Dec 2010)

Ruling party: Le Conseil National de Défense et de Développement (CNDD) (the National Council for Defence and Development) (took control 24 Dec 2008)

Area: 245,857 square km

Population: 9.98 million (2010)*

Capital: Conakry

Official language: French

Currency: Guinean franc (Gf)

Exchange rate: Gf6,900.00 per US$ (Oct 2011)

GDP per capita: US$448 (2010)

GDP real growth: 1.90% (2010)

GDP: US$4.60 billion (2010)

Inflation: 15.50% (2010)

Balance of trade: US$66.30 million (2010)

* estimated figure

NOTA

29 December 2011, parliamentary elections scheduled to take place in 2011 were postponed indefinitely

Guinea

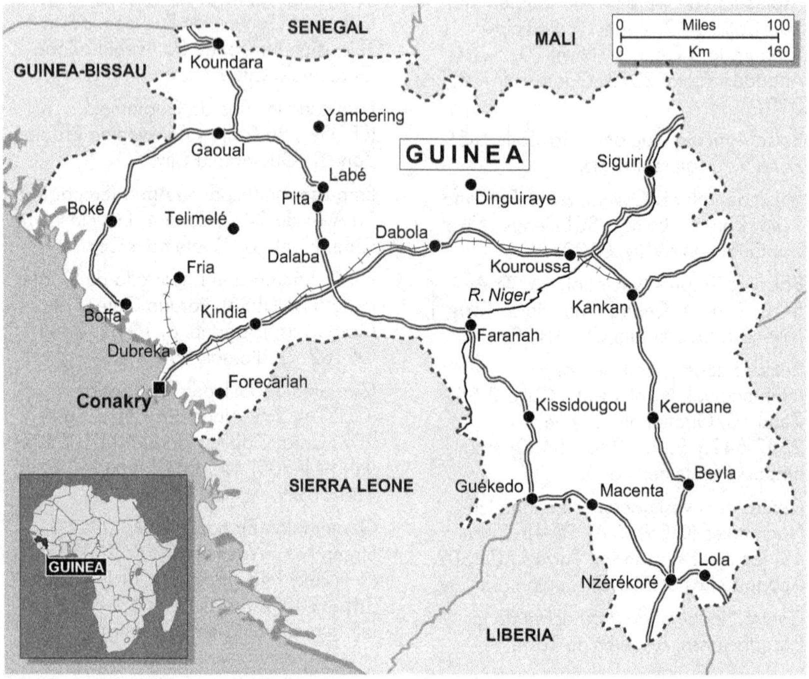

In 1958, when the French left Guinea in a fit of pique after Guineans had voted 'No' in a referendum on whether the country should remain as a member of the French community or not, they took everything they could with them, never mind it was Guinean tax payers who had paid for it. They even, it was said, threw the typewriters overboard as they sailed away.

Guinea has had its ups and downs since then. A potentially wealthy country – it has two-thirds if the world's bauxite, large reserves of iron ore and gold, and diamonds – it is never-the-less still a poor country with a gross domestic product (GDP) per capita of just US$448 in 2010. According to the *African Economic Outlook 2010* (AEO), published jointly by the African Development Bank and the Organisation for Economic Co-operation and Development, over the period of 1985 to 2002, Guinea engaged in a process of economic liberalisation and transformation that drove real GDP growth to an average of 4 per cent per year over the period (equal to a 0.8 per cent increase in per capita income), while stabilising prices and the exchange rate. But then problems in the implementation of reforms between 2003 and 2006 resulted in a 0.6 per cent fall in per capita income, and the economic slump subsequently worsened in 2007 as a result of the global crisis. In response to these difficulties, since 2007 Guinea has been conducting reforms under its second poverty reduction strategy (PRSP2), which is supported by the International Monetary Fund's (IMF) Poverty Reduction and Growth Facility (PRGF) and by other technical and financial partners. The reforms bore fruit in 2008, despite the difficult international context, as growth accelerated from 1.8 per cent in 2007 to 4.9 per cent in 2008. From 2009, however, the economic situation was marked by the combined effects of the economic and financial crisis and the socio-political crisis, resulting in a 0.3 per cent fall in GDP.

The economic situation remains difficult, as reflected in the 2010 indicators. The rate of economic growth is 1.6 per cent, too low to reduce poverty. The high rate of inflation (15.8 per cent) continues to undermine the population's purchasing power. The poverty rate, which stood at 49 per cent in 2002, reached 55 per cent in 2010. Foreign exchange reserves have dwindled to only 1.9 months of imports. Domestic and foreign arrears have rocketed, making it difficult to improve the macroeconomic situation. Added to all this is a substantial reduction in official development assistance (ODA), both bilateral and multilateral, and increased prices for the main imported products, such as food and oil. If these trends are not reversed soon, it will be difficult for Guinea to reach the completion point of the Heavily Indebted Poor Countries (HIPC) Initiative, even though it had nearly attained this important milestone at the end of 2008.

Political shinanigans

Over the last decade, Guinea has experienced recurring socio-political instability marked by state violence against the civilian population. After Lansana Conté's death on 22 December 2008, the country was led by a military junta, which suspended the constitution and dissolved the legislature. It set up a transitional body, the 32-member Conseil National pour la Démocratie et le Développement (CNDD) (National Council for Democracy and Development). The president, succeeded by an interim president from December 2009, of the junta governed the country with the assistance of the CNDD, led by a civilian prim minister. The Conseil National de Transition (CNT), (National Transitional Counci) a legislative-like body, was formed in February 2010. One of the duties of the CNT was drafting a new constitution, which was promulgated in May 2010. As a result of the new constitution presidential elections were scheduled.

The twice-postponed first round of the presidential elections were held on 27 June 2010, when 24 candidates, including four former prime ministers, took part. Cellou Dalein Diallo of the Union des Forces Democratiques de Guinee (UFDG) (Union of Democratic Forces of Guinea) won 39.72 per cent and his closest rival, Alpha Condé of the Rassemblement du Peuple Guinéen (RPG) (Rally of the Guinean People) 20.67 per cent. Condé challenged the results, claiming the election was 'flawed'. The run-off was set for August but later postponed until 19 September. However on 16 September, following a week of street violence between rival political supporters the elections were postponed again, until 24 October and then until 7 November. The result was a win for opposition leader Alpha Condé with 52.52 per cent of the vote, ahead of Diallo with 47.48 per cent. Parliamentary elections which had been scheduled originally for 11 October 2009, were first put off until after the presidential elections, and then after several postponements throughout 2010 and 2011 (after the already several times postponed presidential elections), on 29 December they were postponed indefinitely. The result is that the CNT continues to act as the country's legislative body.

On 22 February 2011, President Condé declared the previous ruling military junta (2008–10) had bankrupted the country, so that the economy was in tatters, with no agricultural production and unpaid customs officials. President Conde's private residence was attacked on 19 July. Up to 37 soldiers, some of who had been close to the members of the military junta who had handed over power in 2010, were arrested the following day. The president was not injured. Further clashes in September, when opposition supporters defied a ban on rallies and confronted large numbers of security forces, left two dead and some 40 injured.

International trade and development

The structure of external trade in goods is dominated by mining exports (14.5 per cent of GDP in 2010), made up mainly of bauxite, which accounted in 2010 for 34 per cent of total revenue from goods exports. Guinea's main customers are India, Spain, Russia, Germany, Ireland, the United States and France. Imports in 2010 were composed of intermediate and capital goods (46.8 per cent), food products and other consumer items (35.3 per cent) and petroleum products (25.9 per cent) from China, the Netherlands, France and the United Kingdom. Services exports (4.6 per cent of total goods and services exports) are the third greatest source of export revenue, ahead of agricultural products, and services imports (26 per cent of total goods and services imports) are the main import item. Since 2009, with the collapse of aluminium prices by more than 40 per cent, gold has taken over to become the main source of export revenue (more than 57 per cent).

In total, exports of goods increased by 34 per cent in value (fob) in 2010, up from 26 per cent in 2009. This raised the GDP share of exports by 6.8 percentage points to 30.8 per cent. Imports increased from 24.2 per cent of GDP to 27.5 per cent. The trade balance improved by 3.5 percentage points, owing to the rise in gold and diamond prices and the increase (relative to the downward trend in 2009) in those for bauxite and alumina. Consequently, the coverage rate increased by 130.9 per cent in 2009 and 142.1 per cent in 2010.

The flow of FDI from emerging countries to Guinea is rising fast, but the volume remains relatively low. Inward FDI originates mainly from China (the main source) and Russia. In 2005, the stock of Chinese FDI in Guinea accounted for 6.4 per cent of the total stock. In the medium term, China plans to finance the construction of a 750 megawatt hydroelectric dam in Guinea. In exchange, Guinea will guarantee China access to mining resources equivalent to 2 billion tonnes of bauxite. The Chinese private sector is involved in various areas of the Guinean economy:

KEY INDICATORS **Guinea**

	Unit	2006	2007	2008	2009	2010
Population	m	9.64	9.96	10.28	*10.61	*10.54
Gross domestic product (GDP)	US$bn	3.14	4.20	4.50	4.40	4.60
GDP per capita	US$	325	473	439	414	448
GDP real growth	%	2.1	1.8	4.9	-0.3	1.9
Inflation	%	34.7	22.9	18.4	4.7	15.5
Industrial output	% change	5.0	6.6	6.4	6.7	–
Agricultural output	% change	4.2	2.8	3.6	-28.4	–
Exports (fob) (goods)	US$m	1,073.6	1,203.2	1,342.0	1,049.7	1,471.2
Imports (fob) (goods)	US$m	939.8	1,217.6	1,366.1	1,060.1	1,404.9
Balance of trade	US$m	-89.4	-14.4	-24.1	-10.4	66.3
Current account	US$m	-185.0	-389.8	-440.1	-329.2	-329.2
Exchange rate	per US$	5,556.00	4,242.70	5,500.0	5,197.0	5,010.0

* estimated figure

wholesale and retail trade, restaurants and hotels, textiles, communication and construction.

The importance of China as Guinea's main emerging partner is also apparent in the area of official development assistance. Most of the co operative agreements between the two countries are in the form of interest-free loans, followed by economic and technical co-operation agreements and, lastly, commercial loans. In 2008, the Chinese ambassador to Guinea announced that in future Chinese aid to Guinea would focus on social projects. Projects that have recently been completed or are currently under way include the construction of a 50,000-seat stadium and technical assistance concerning the servicing and maintenance of the Guinean public broadcaster's equipment and the presidential palace.

Other non-traditional partners such as Iran, Saudi Arabia and Malaysia are also interested in Guinea. In addition to diplomatic relations, these countries are involved in mining and quarrying, transport and insurance.

Guinea could further develop its relations with its emerging partners by adopting a more active strategy and by focusing its efforts on developing relations with emerging countries, especially oil-producing countries.

The level of poverty, together with the country's dilapidated infrastructure (housing, transport, energy, water and telecommunications), constitute a real challenge in the context of political, economic and monetary instability. Huge additional resources are needed to support faster growth. In education, Guinea has made efforts to improve primary schooling, gender parity, and parity between regions and between towns, but the objectives set in the PRSP2 have not been achieved for various reasons: firstly the lack of funding for the sector (from 2000 to 2010, less than 12 per cent of the national budget was allocated to education), including the suspension of some international funding; and secondly the quality of expenditure, which has shown no notable improvement.

Guinea is nicknamed 'the water tower of West Africa, as it has many watercourses and the highest rainfall in the sub-region. Even so, much-desired structural and institutional reforms in the water and sanitation sector are proving hard to implement, and supply levels remain well below the regional average of 18.1 per cent for electricity and 73.8 per cent for drinking water.

Risk assessment

Economy	Poor
Politics	Poor
Regional stability	Fair

COUNTRY PROFILE

Historical profile

From the thirteenth to fifteenth centuries Guinea was part of the Mali Empire which covered a large part of West Africa.
1450s The coastal region began to be settled by European traders.
1849 The French declared the area around Boké a protectorate. France's influence grew as it took over most of the rest of the country calling it Rivières du Sud (rivers of the south).
1891 French Guinea was formally constituted a colony, separate from Senegal.
1956 In a referendum Guinea voted to opt out of the French Community.
1958 Guinea became independent under the leadership of Sekou Touré. France severed all financial and technical ties.
1960s Despite having the backing of the Soviet Union, Guinea expelled the Soviet ambassador for interference in internal matters. Guinea began to improve its relations with the West although it remained a non-aligned, Marxist, one-party state.
1977 Private trade had been banned until demonstrations by traders in the market women's revolt led to a change in government policy.
1984 Touré died. In a bloodless coup, Colonel Lansana Conté became president and introduced IMF-backed austerity measures as well as a new currency, the Guinean franc, which replaced the syli.
1990 A new constitution was approved.
1991 Union des Forces Démocratiques de Guinée (UFDG) (Union of Democratic Forces of Guinea) was formed.
1993 Conté won the presidency in multi-party elections, which were marred by killings and alleged fraud.
1995 The Parti de l'Unité et du Progrès (PUP) (Party of Unity and Progress), led by President Conté, won the multi-party legislative elections.
1996 As much as a quarter of the army mutinied due largely to low pay.
1998 President Lansana Conté was re-elected.
1999 Lamine Sidime (PUP) was appointed prime minister.
2001 The government accused neighbouring Liberia and rebels from Sierra Leone of aiding its army mutineers and attempting to destabilise the country. The number of displaced peoples, locally and from abroad, grew. There were rebel attacks along the borders between Guinea and Liberia, and Sierra Leone. A constitutional referendum permitted Conté to retain the presidency and run for a third and extended term (from five to seven years).
2002 The ruling PUP won parliamentary elections, delayed by two years allegedly due to the fighting between Guinea and Sierra Leone, and Liberia.
2003 Incumbent Lansana Conté won the presidential elections. The National Assembly voted unanimously for an amnesty for those convicted of political crimes, allowing them to stand for positions in national politics.
2004 Cellou Dalein Diallo was named prime minister.
2006 A general strike lasted five days. A power struggle among Conté's inner circle resulted in Prime Minister Diallo's sacking and the post of prime minister being dropped with its responsibilities given to other, expanded ministries. Fode Bangoura became minister of presidential affairs, with control of the military and the economy.
2007 An 18-day general strike disrupted the vital bauxite industry causing President Conté to dismiss his long-term supporter, Fode Bangoura, in an effort to placate the unions. Eugène Camara (a hard-line supporter of the president) was appointed to the vacant post of prime minister. Camara's appointment sparked riots. Martial law was imposed as another national general strike began and opposition and union leaders called on the president to resign. Lansana Kouyaté, a candidate acceptable to the opposition, was appointed prime minister, ending the general strike.
2008 President Conté sacked Prime Minister Kouyaté; Ahmed Tidiane Souaré became prime minister. Parliamentary elections were postponed by the electoral commission as voter registration was incomplete. President Conté died, of natural causes. The army launched a *coup d'état* and suspended the constitution. Coup leader Captain Moussa Dadis Camara seized the presidency, taking control through Le Conseil National de Défense et de Développement (CNDD) (the National Council for Defence and Development); he appointed Kabiné Komara as prime minister. Although the coup led to the African Union (AU) suspending Guinea from its organisation, the Economic Community of West African States (Ecowas) took a more positive attitude, trusting the transfer of power would allow 'democratic growth'.
2009 All mining operations, including Guinea's huge bauxite reserves and gold, diamond and ferrous metals, were suspended until 'renegotiations' of existing contracts had been agreed. Ousmane Conté, the son of the late president Lansana Conté, confessed to drug

trafficking on state television. Hundreds of opposition protesters were wounded and dozens were shot dead or trampled to death attempting to flee from a sport stadium in the capital, Conakry, after security forces had opened fire and used teargas. Thousands were attending a rally in the stadium demanding a return to civilian rule and objecting to Captain Camara standing in forthcoming presidential elections. President Camara received medical attention in Morocco following an assassination attempt by an *aide-de-camp*.

2010 In January, the Joint Ouagadougou Declaration confirmed Sékouba Konaté as interim president and the ruling military council appointed Jean-Marie Doré was as prime minister. Parliamentary elections, originally scheduled to take place in 2009 were, by agreement, postponed until after presidential elections took place. Presidential elections that had been postponed from March (and previously from December 2009) were held in June; 24 candidates took part including four former prime ministers. Cellou Dalein Diallo (UFDG) won 39.72 per cent and his closest rival, Alpha Condé (Rassemblement du Peuple Guinéen (RPG) (People's Party of Guinea) (a party mainly base among the Mandinka population) 20.67 per cent. As no candidate won 50 per cent of the vote, a second round was scheduled for July, but was postponed as Condé challenged the results, claiming the election was 'flawed'. The Supreme Court confirmed the results of the first round. The second round was scheduled for August but later postponed until 19 September. However on 16 September, following a week of street violence between rival political supporters the elections were postponed again, until 24 October and then until 7 November. In the run-off, opposition leader Condé won 52.52 per cent of the vote and Diallo 47.48 per cent; turnout was 68.87 per cent. Diallo conceded defeat on 3 December, after the Supreme Court had rejected his complaint of election fraud. Condé took office on 21 December.

2011 On 22 February, President Condé declared the previous ruling military junta (2008–10) had bankrupted the country, so that the economy was in tatters, with no agricultural production and unpaid customs officials. President Conde's private residence was attacked on 19 July. Up to 37 soldiers, some of who had been close to the members of the military junta who had handed over power in 2010, were arrested the following day. The president was not injured.

Political structure

Constitution

The constitution was promulgated in 1990. In 2001 a constitutional amendment revised the length of the presidential term from five years to seven, with no legal limit to the number of terms a president may sit.

Form of state

Republic

The executive

Prior to the constitutional amendments, made in 2001, the president was elected for a five-year term, renewable only once. Following the changes, the mandate increased to a seven-year term with no legal limit as to the number of times that it could be renewed.

The prime minister and the Council of Ministers are appointed by the president.

National legislature

The unicameral Assemblée Nationale Populaire (People's National Assembly) was dissolved in December 2008; it will be re-convened following new elections in 2009. Membership is 114, of which 76 are directly elected by proportional representation from party lists and 38 are elected in single seat constituencies by simple majority. All members serve five-year terms.

Legal system

The legal system is based on French civil law, customary law and decree.

Last elections

27 June and 7 November 2010 (presidential, first and second round); 30 June 2002 (parliamentary) (originally scheduled for November 2000).

Results: Presidential: (first round) Cellou Dalein Diallo (UFDG) won 39.72 per cent, Alpha Condé (Rassemblement du Peuple Guinéen (RPG) (People's Party of Guinea)) 20.67 per cent, Sidya Touré (L'Union des Forces Républicaines (UFR) (Union of Republican Forces)) 15.6 per cent, Lansana Kouyaté (Parti de l'Espoir pour le Développement National (PEDN) (Hope Party for National Development)) 7.75 per cent, 20 other candidates each won less than 5 per cent. Second round: Alpha Condé won 52.52 per cent, Cellou Dalein Diallo 47.48 per cent. Turnout was 67.87 per cent.

Parliamentary: the ruling Parti de l'Unité et du Progrès (PUP) (Party of Unity and Progress) won 61.5 per cent of the vote; Union pour le Progrès et le Renouveau (UPR) (Union for Progress and Renewal) 21.7 per cent; the opposition boycotted the election; the turnout was low.

Next elections

11 October 2009 (parliament) postponed indefinitely; 24 October 2010 (presidential).

Political parties

Political parties were legalised from 1992.

Ruling party

Le Conseil National de Défense et de Développement (CNDD) (the National Council for Defence and Development) (took control 24 Dec 2008)

Main opposition party

Rassemblement du Peuple Guinéen (RPG) (Rally of the Guinean People).

Population

9.98 million (2010)*

Last census: December 1996: 7,156,406 (provisional)

Population density: 28 per square km. Urban population: 28 per cent (1995–2001).

Annual growth rate: 2.4 per cent 1994–2004 (WHO 2006)

Internally Displaced Persons (IDP)

100,000 (UNHCR 2004)

Ethnic make-up

Fulani (35 per cent), Malinke (30 per cent), Soussou (20 per cent).

Religions

Islam (85 per cent), a small number of Roman Catholics (8 per cent) and traditional beliefs (7 per cent).

Education

Guinea shows an upward trend in gross enrolment rate with increasing demand for teachers, school facilities, and other resources. The government has initiated the third phase of the project Basic Education for All (2001—2012) focussing on increased access, improved quality and efficiency through decentralisation processes.

Despite significant urban/rural and gender disparities in enrolment ratios, there is overall improvement. The crisis in teacher supply persists despite the World Bank and the government's intensive teacher-training programme (FIMG), which had planned recruitment of approximately 6,000 teachers for the entire 1998-2001 period.

Government expenditure on education is about 25–26 per cent of the total national budget.

Enrolment rate: 45.2 per cent net enrolment in primary; 11.9 per cent net enrolment in secondary schooling (World Bank).

In rural areas the enrolment rate for girls remains at only 26 per cent.

Pupils per teacher: 49 in primary schools.

Health

Improved water sources and sanitation facilities are available to 48 per cent and 58 per cent of the population, respectively.

HIV/Aids

HIV/Aids infection is currently concentrated in urban areas. Overall 2.8 per cent of pregnant women, 42 per cent of sex workers and 2.5 per cent of young adults (aged 15–24) are HIV positive. With governmental initiatives and local

education, it is hoped to avert a potential pandemic if the rates in rural areas follow the urban trend.
HIV prevalence: 3.2 per cent aged 15–49 in 2003 (World Bank)
Life expectancy: 53 years, 2004 (WHO 2006)
Fertility rate/Maternal mortality rate: 5.8 births per woman, 2004 (WHO 2006); maternal mortality 620 per 100,000 live births (World Bank).
Child (under 5 years) mortality rate (per 1,000): 109 per 1,000 live births; 23 per cent of children under aged five are malnourished (World Bank).
Head of population per physician: 0.11 physicians per 1,000 people, 2004 (WHO 2006)

Welfare
Guinea's social insurance system provides coverage for unemployed people, pensions, old-age benefits and survivor benefits (payable to widows, orphans and dependant relatives). Old age pensions are applicable to all those aged 55 and over. The system also provides sickness and maternity benefits as well as allowance for those families with children under the age of 17.

Main cities
Conakry (capital, estimated population 1.4 million in 2005), Nzérékoré (177,855), Kankan (141,446), Kindia (160,884).

Languages spoken
African languages are in daily use. English is seldom used.
Official language/s
French

Media
The government maintains a tight control of the media, with censorship of newspapers and controls to close private radio stations and interrupt international relays, while the military has a secure hold of the national broadcaster.
Press
The high cost of printing hampers and restricts independent publishing and disrupts regular print runs.
In French, the only business publication is the *Sud Economic* (http://sud-economie.press-guinee.com), other general news publications include *Le Diplomate* (www.nouvelle-tribune.com), *L'Enqueteur* (http://enqueteur.boubah.com), *La Nouvelle Tribune* (www.nouvelle-tribune.com), *L'Observateur* (www.observateur-guinee.com) and *Le Populaire* (http://lepopulaire.press-guinee.com). The *Sanakou* (http://sanakou.press-guinee.com) is published in Labé. The *Le Lynx* (www.mirinet.net.gn/lynx) is an independent satirical weekly.
Broadcasting
Radio: The state-owned, commercial Radiodiffusion-Télévision Guinéenne (RTG) operates Radio Guinenne in several languages including French, English, Arabic, Portuguese and a series of Radio Rurale in local languages. Private stations include Familia FM, Liberte FM, Radio Nostralie Guinea and Soleil FM. Radio France Internationale and BBC World Service can both be received.
Television: The state-owned, commercial Radiodiffusion-Télévision Guinéenne (RTG) has one channel.
News agencies
National news agency: Agence Guineenne de Presse
APA: www.apanews.net
Panapress: www.panapress.com

Economy
Guinea has the potential to be a wealthy country, with extensive resources in minerals and fertile land, but it remains one of the world's poorest and Africa's more underdeveloped economies. The country possesses around 50 per cent of the world's bauxite reserves, also diamonds, iron ore, salt and uranium. The agriculture sector includes rice, coffee, bananas, palm oil, cattle, sheep and goats, fish and timber. It has greater potential for producing hydroelectricity then the 75MW being produced in 2009. The mining of bauxite and iron ore along with other minerals accounts for around 80 per cent of foreign earnings.
GDP growth was 4.9 per cent in 2008, as Guinea followed fiscal measures set out by the International Monetary Fund (IMF) when it had agreed to a three-year loan under the poverty reduction and growth facility in 2007 to secure debt relief. However when the government was overthrown in December 2008 the programme faltered and in 2009 the IMF suspended its programme and by February 2010 Guinea was US$16 million in loan arrears. GDP growth fell to –0.3 per cent in 2009 as trade in commodities dropped, caused by the global economic recession. Output of bauxite fell by 22.9 per cent in the first nine months of 2009; output of other minerals also fell although diamond mining rose by 30.5 per cent. As the global economy recovered so did the Guinean economy and GDP growth was 3 per cent in 2010.
Despite the potential for large-scale investment projects in agriculture, mining and hydroelectricity Guinea's political instability, corruption and poor resource management have blighted chances of foreign investment.

External trade
Guinea is a member of the Economic Community of West African States (Ecowas), which was set up to promote economic integration among members. It is a member of the Anglophone, West African Monetary Zone (WAMZ), which is due to introduce a common currency (although in January 2011 it had only just undertaken a feasibility study). WAMZ will eventually be merged with the Francophone-members' (Communauté financière d'Afrique (CFA) (Financial Community of Africa)) currency to produce a single currency (the eco) for the region.
Guinea has around 50 per cent of the world's reserves of bauxite and is the second largest supplier. Although diamond exports are rising, the balance of payments situation is precarious, especially since large volumes of concessionary assistance from the World Bank, IMF and foreign aid donors were suspended in 2009
Imports
Principal imports are petroleum products, metals, machinery, vehicles and parts, textiles, foodstuffs and grain.
Main sources: The Netherlands (typically 21 per cent of total), France (10 per cent), UK (8 per cent).
Exports
Exports are dominated by bauxite and aluminium ore, gold, diamonds, coffee, fish, fresh fruit, vegetables and timber.
Main destinations: France (typically 25 per cent total of total), Switzerland (20 per cent), Russia (11 per cent).

Agriculture
Traditional farming generates around 23 per cent of GDP and around 67 per cent of the population is engaged in subsistence farming.
Only 7 per cent of land is cultivated, although there is considerable potential for development.
Main cash crops are sugar cane, groundnuts, oil palm, cotton, citrus fruits and coffee. Main subsistence crops are rice (60 per cent of cultivated land), cassava, maize and vegetables.
Output has stagnated due to transport problems, low levels of mechanisation, poor marketing and a lack of vital inputs. Although infrastructural projects have rectified some problems, the country is in need of further investment to improve roads linking agricultural areas to domestic and foreign markets.
The fishing, forestry and livestock sectors are small. There is potential for lucrative fishing but the fishing fleet suffers from lack of funds.

Industry and manufacturing

The industrial sector contributes around 4 per cent to GDP and employs 5 per cent of the workforce.

Apart from aluminium smelting, it is small-scale and designed to meet local requirements. Aluminium smelting from locally mined bauxite is being modernised with French aid.

The other main industries, textiles, food processing and plywood, are handicapped by supply bottlenecks and shortages of skilled labour.

The investment code and economic liberalisation are expected to attract more foreign capital.

Tourism

Tourism is undeveloped, lacking appropriate infrastructure and attracting only small numbers of visitors. The potential importance of the sector is recognised by the authorities who plan to develop it.

Mining

Mining is the most dynamic sector of the economy, accounting for around 30 per cent of GDP and almost all export earnings. It is rich in uranium, titanium, copper, manganese, iron ore, gold and diamonds. Around 8 per cent of the workforce is employed in the sector. A mining code introduced in 1995 renewed foreign interest in the mining sector, offering a range of guarantees and tax incentives to foreign investors, who may own up to 85 per cent of any venture.

Bauxite accounts for around 20 per cent of GDP and around 90 per cent of exports. 650,000 tonnes of alumina are produced from the country's single refinery at Fria. The largest bauxite producer is the Sangarédi mine, operated by Compagnie des Bauxites de Guinée (CBG), a joint venture between the government (51 per cent) and Halco (49 per cent). CBG has an annual production capacity of 14 million tonnes.

Diamond reserves are estimated at 40 million carats (93 per cent gem quality). The Aredor diamond mine, near Banankore, is 50 per cent owned by the government and 50 per cent by a consortium led by Bridge Oil of Australia and produces around 25,000 carats per year. Diamond mining capacity in Guinea is far lower than recorded exports. It is thought that many gems exported from Guinea have been smuggled from neighbouring countries into Guinea. Key sites of precious stones include Siguiri, Mandiana, Dinguiraye, Kissidougou and Kérouané, and along the rivers of Baoulé, Milo and Diani.

In 2007, the Australian minerals exploration company, Murchison United, announced a significant deposit of uranium in the southeast of Guinea, near Firawa.

The Australian mining company Rio Tinto and Chinese state-owned Chinalco signed a partnership deal in March 2010 to develop one of the world's best, and Africa's least-developed, sources of iron ore. The development of the Simandou mine is worth US$2.3 billion. Hidalco paid US$1.3 billion for a 47 per cent stake in the project.

Hydrocarbons

There are no known hydrocarbon reserves and all petroleum needs must be imported, which amounted to 9,000 barrels per day in 2007, primarily for use in vehicles.

Any use of imported natural gas or coal is commercially insignificant.

Energy

There is considerable potential for hydroelectric power from several large rivers, but apart from the existing Garafiri Dam with a 75MW capacity there are currently no plans to expand. International finance has been deterred due to the estimated 50,000 people that would be displaced if the projects were implemented. Guinea mostly imports oil to run its power stations.

Banking and insurance

It was announced in March 2005 that the introduction of the shared currency, the Eco, in Guinea, Ghana, Nigeria, Sierra Leone and The Gambia, which was due in July 2005, would be postponed. The currency was proposed to facilitate trade and growth with an ultimate plan to merge it with the CFA franc.

Central bank

Banque Centrale de la République de Guinée

Main financial centre

Conakry

Time

GMT

Geography

Guinea lies on the west coast of Africa, with Sierra Leone and Liberia to the south, Senegal to the north, and Mali and Côte d'Ivoire inland to the east.

The country is curved in shape, with Sierra Leone occupying a large chunk of the central region. It can be divided into four geographic zones: the furthest from the coast is bio-diverse rain forest, which turns into savannah in the centre. There is a northern hill region and a coastal zone with an Atlantic coast of 320km. The highest mountain is Mont Nimba (1,752 metres), which is at the centre of an internationally recognised nature reserve, on the border with Côte d'Ivoire and Liberia. There are 22 rivers that begin life in Guinea, including the Senegal, Gambia and Niger rivers.

Hemisphere

Northern

Climate

The climate is tropical and humid. In the south the rainy season falls in June–October; rainfall is particularly heavy in Conakry, average temperatures range from 22–30 degrees Celsius (C). The dry season is from November–April, likely temperature range 24–35 degrees C. The north is generally cooler and drier.

Entry requirements

Passports

Required by all and must have six months validity from the date of departure.

Visa

Required by all except nationals of some African countries. Applications for visas must be made to a Guinea Consulate before travelling. Business visas should included proof of sufficient funds, a business letter with a full itenerary, and an invitation from a local company or organisation. Contact the nearest embassy for further details.

Currency advice/regulations

There are no restrictions on the import of foreign currency but the amount must be declared; export may not exceed the amount imported. It is a requirement to exchange an amount of foreign currency into Gf, depending on the length of stay. Local currency up to Gf1,000 may be imported provided a valid declaration for its previous export can be provided.

Traveller's cheques have limited outlets in banks and large hotels. To avoid extra exchange fees US dollars and Euros are recommended.

Health (for visitors)

Mandatory precautions

Yellow fever vaccination certificate.

Advisable precautions

Malaria prophylaxes are essential as risk exists throughout the country. Immunisations or booster shots are necessary for diphtheria, tetanus, polio, hepatitis A, typhoid and yellow fever. Vaccinations may be needed for hepatitis B, TB, meningitis and cholera. Rabies is a risk in rural areas.

Use only bottled or boiled water for drinks, washing teeth and making ice. Eat only well cooked meals, preferably served hot; vegetables should be cooked and fruit peeled. Avoid pork, salad and food from street vendors. A full first-aid kit would be useful.

Hotels

Limited first-class accommodation is available in Conakry and Kankan; good hotels are expensive. Hotel bills may be paid in foreign currency or by credit card. A service charge is usually included in the bill. Tipping is optional.

Public holidays (national)

Fixed dates

1 Jan (New Year's Day), 1 May (Labour Day), ^15 Aug (Assumption Day), 27

Aug (Anniversary of Women's Revolt), 28 Sep (Referendum Day), 2 Oct (Republic Day), 1 Nov (All Saints' Day), 25 Dec (Christmas).

Variable dates

^ Easter Monday, Eid al Adha, Birth of the Prophet, ^Ascension Day, Day after the Night's Vigil (Nov), Eid al Fitr (three days).

^ Christian holiday only

Islamic year 1433 (26 Nov 2011–14 Nov 2012): The Islamic year contains 354 or 355 days, with the result that Muslim feasts advance by 10–12 days against the Gregorian calendar. Dates of feasts vary according to the sighting of the new moon, so cannot be forecast exactly.

Working hours

Banking

Mon–Fri: 0800–1230, 1430–1700.

Business

Mon–Thu: 0830–1730; Fri: 0800–1300.

Government

Mon–Thu: 0800–1500; Fri: 0800–1300; Sat: 0800–1500.

Telecommunications

Mobile/cell phones

GSM 900 services are available.

Electricity supply

220V AC, 50 cycles

Social customs/useful tips

Showing respect for people will enhance your regard. Always greet people and never go straight into conversation without pleasantries beforehand. It is considered polite to use people's titles.

Security

Visitors are advised not travel to border areas where security is weak and there is a risk of kidnapping.

Always carry an identity card or passport, if stopped you are obliged to show ID. Pickpocketing, muggings and armed break-ins occur in the city; avoid carrying valuables in public and remain vigilant. There are numerous confidence tricksters typically attempting to dupe foreigners into buying precious gems (which, even if authentic, need export licences), gold and counterfeit goods.

Getting there

Air

National airline: Air Guinée (government owned) flies domestic routes only. International flights are regional or European.

International airport/s: Conakry (CKY), 13km from city, bank, and car hire. Taxis are to city.

Airport tax: None

Surface

Road: Best route is the coastal road from Sierra Leone (Freetown) to Conakry. Roads from Ganta (Liberia) to N'zérékoré and from Mali (to Kankan and Siguiri) can be difficult.

Getting about

National transport

Air: Air Guinée operates regular domestic service between Conakry, Boké, Kankan, Kissidougou, Labé, Macenta, N'zérékoré, Siguiri.

Road: A few main roads are surfaced, eg from Conakry north to Kindia and Kissidougou, and parts of the road east to Freetown in Sierra Leone. Most roads are laterite and become impassable during the rainy season (Jun–Oct).

Buses: Coach services include Conakry-Kindia-Gaoual and Dabola-N'zérékoré.

Rail: Narrow-gauge railway from Conakry to Kindia and Kankan, which is in poor condition.

City transport

Taxis: Available in Conakry, limited availability elsewhere; can be hired from hotels by the hour or day. Standard fares apply within towns, but for longer journeys fares should be agreed in advance. Tipping is optional.

Car hire

International and national driving licence required. Driving outside city limits with chauffeur and special authorisation only.

BUSINESS DIRECTORY

Telephone area codes

The international dialling code (IDD) for Guinea is + 224, followed by subscriber's number.

Chambers of Commerce

Guinea Chamber of Commerce, Industry and Handicrafts, PO Box 545, Conakry (email: cciag@sotelgui.net.gn).

Banking

Banque Internationale pour le Commerce et l'Industrie de la Guinée SA; PO Box 1484, Avenue de la République, Conakry (tel: 3041-2908/3643).

Banque Islamique de Guinee; PO Box 1247, 6è Avenue de la Republique, Conakry (tel: 3041-4581, 3046-2075).

Banque Populaire Maroco-Guineenne; PO Box 4400, Avenue de la Republique, Conakry-360 (tel: 3041-1599/2360/2552).

Ecobank-Guinee; PO Box 5687, Avenue de la Republique, Conakry (tel: 3045-5876).

International Commercial Bank; PO Box 3547, Cité Chemin de Fer, Conakry (tel: 3041-2590.

Société Générale de Banques en Guinée; PO Box 1514, Kaloum Coronthie Immeuble Boffa, Cité Chemin de Fer, Conakry (tel: 3041-1746).

Union Internationale de Banque en Guinée UIBG; PO Box 324, Angle 5è Boulevard, 6è Avenue de la République, Conakry (tel: 3041-2096/4309).

Central bank

Banque Centrale de la République de Guinée; PO Box 622, 3 Boulevard du Commerce, Conakry (tel: 3041-2651; fax: 3041-4898).

Travel information

Air France, BP 590, Ave de la Republique, Conakry (tel: 3046-4535)

Air Guinée, Route du Niger, BP 12, 12 Côte Commissariat Central, Conakry (tel: 3045-3662).

Other useful addresses

Bureau Veritas, BP 1451, Conakry (tel: 3044-1841, 3044-2202; fax: 3041-2112).

Chambre Economique de Guinée, BP 609, Conakry.

Comité d'Etat pour la Co-opération avec l'Europe Occidentale, Conakry.

Direction Nationale des Marchés Publics et du Portefeuille de l'Etat (privatisation office), La Division du Portefeuille du Ministère des Finances, avenue de la République, Face á l'Hôpital Ignace DEEN, BP 2006, Conakry (tel: 3041-3957; fax: 3041-4220).

ENTRAT (state forwarding firm), BP 315, Conakry.

Entreprise Nationale Import–Export (Importex), BP 152, Conakry (tel: 3044-2813, 3044-2809).

French Commercial Department, Ambassade de France, BP 373, Conakry (tel: 3041-1605, 3041-1655; fax: 3041-2708).

Guinea Embassy (US), 2112 Leroy Place, NW, Washington DC 20008 (tel: (+1-202) 483-9420; fax: (+1-202) 483-8688; e-mail: emgui@sysnet.net).

Office National des Hydrocarbures (Onah), Conakry.

L'Office de Promotion des Investissement Privés – Guichet Unique (OPIP) (assistance for foreign investors), BP 2024, Conakry (tel: 3045-1830, 3041-4985; fax: 3041-3990; e-mail: dg@opip.org.gn).

Port Autonome, BP 805, Conakry (tel: 3044-2728, 3044-2737; fax: 3041-4564).

Radio-Télévision Guinéenne (RTG), BP 391, Conakry.

Statistical Office, Bureau du Premier Ministre, Conakry (tel: 3044-2148).

National news agency: Agence Guineenne de Presse, BP 1535; Anciens locaux d'Enelgui, 2ème boulevard, 5ème avenue, Conakry (tel: 144-434; 430-549; email: info@agpguinee.net)

Guinea-Bissau

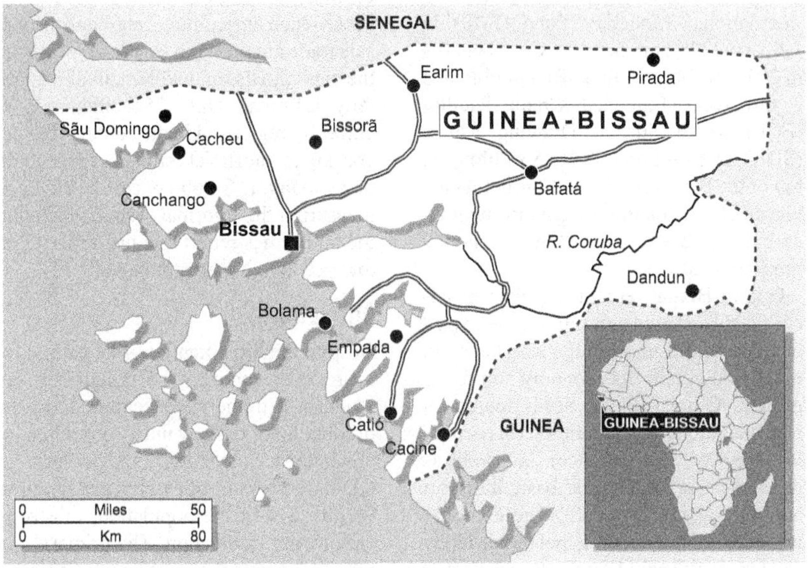

After almost a year of relative stability following President Malam Bacai Sanha's election in May 2009, a military mutiny broke out in April 2010. The mutineers opposed the security and defence sector reforms led by the head of the army, General Jose Zamora Induta. The deputy army chief of staff, General Antonio Indjai, led the mutiny that ousted the head of the army – who was eventually released from custody in January 2011 – and resulted in Prime Minister Carlos Domingos Gomes Júnior being briefly detained. The real mastermind is believed to have been the former navy chief Admiral José Américo Bubo Na Tchuto, a fugitive accused of plotting a coup in 2008 and of being a drug lord. The mutiny lacked popular support and civilians expressed their discontent in the streets of the capital, an unusual event in Guinea-Bissau. Throughout the mutiny, businesses, ministries and parliament operated normally.

Following these events, and rather surprisingly, President Sanha appointed General Indjai as the new head of the army and reinstated Admiral Na Tchuto, who had taken refuge inside the United Nations premises in Bissau on his return to the country in December 2009. These appointments and the mutiny in April led the European Union (EU) to suspend its mission to implement the security sector reform (SSR) as well as budget support. This freeze of donor funds is destabilising the government's efforts to improve the fiscal situation and clear arrears. Teachers' salaries were no longer being paid by December 2010, which could lead to unrest.

The future stability of the country largely depends on the SSR, which involves modernising the army and reinserting around 1,500 ex-liberation movement combatants into society. The legal framework for a pension fund for the military and security forces was approved in June 2010, but the suspension of financial assistance from the main donors halted its implementation.

The drug scene

Since 2006, the Bijagos islands have served as a transhipment point for Latin American drug cartels moving cocaine to Europe. President Sanha has declared the problem a top priority for his administration. However, cracking down on trafficking is almost impossible as the islands have no police and no communications or surveillance equipment. Furthermore, Guinea-Bissau has no prisons or forensics

KEY FACTS

Official name: República da Guiné-Bissau (Republic of Guinea-Bissau)

Head of State: President Malam Bacai Sanhá (PAIGC) (took office 8 Sep 2009)

Head of government: Prime Minister Carlos Domingos Gomes Júnior (25 Dec 2008)

Ruling party: Coalition government: Partido Africano da Independência de Guiné e Cabo Verde (PAIGC) (African Independence Party of Guinea and Cape Verde), Partido para a Renovaçao Social (PRS) (Party for Social Renewal) and Partido Unido Social Democrático (PUSD) (United Social Democratic Party) (from 17 Apr 2007)

Area: 36,125 square km

Population: 1.51 million (2010)*

Capital: Bissau

Official language: Portuguese

Currency: CFA franc (CFAf) = 100 centimes (Communauté Financière Africaine (African Financial Community) franc).

Exchange rate: CFAf488.90 per US$ (Oct 2011); CFAf655.95 per euro (pegged from Jan 1999)

GDP per capita: US$513 (2009)*

GDP real growth: 2.90% (2009)*

GDP: US$826.00 million (2009)*

Inflation: -1.70% (2009)*

Balance of trade: -US$70.66 million (2008)

* estimated figure

laboratory, the detention centre in Bissau has no guards and no administrative staff, the few courts are overburdened, and laws too complex to apply consistently. Trafficking poses a serious challenge to stability and governance, as it has exacerbated corruption in the government and armed forces. Observers fear drug money could finance sleeping terrorist cells in the western part of Africa.

The economy

The *African Economic Outlook 2011* (AEO), published jointly by the African Development Bank and the Organisation for Economic Co-operation and Development, reported that economic growth in Guinea-Bissau picked up slightly to 3.6 per cent in 2010 from 3.0 per cent in 2009 thanks to higher cashew nut prices, sustained construction of private housing and major infrastructure projects. The indirect impact of the global economic crisis, felt mainly through lower government export revenues and remittances, has been mitigated by a strong increase in the world demand for cashew nuts. Heightened political instability, however, resulted in the withdrawal of budget support from the EU, one of the country's main development partners. Economic growth is expected to increase to 4.5 per cent and 4.8 per cent in 2011 and 2012, sustained by increased agricultural production, cashew nut exports and foreign direct investment (FDI) in mining projects and infrastructure. The major downside risk is persistent political instability, which could result in a further decrease in donor funding, hampering the execution of the public investment programme in the coming years. In the medium term, inflation is expected to remain within the Banque Centrale des Etates de l'Afrique de l'Ouest's (BCEAO) (Central Bank of West African States) target of 3 per cent, maintaining the good performance of 2010.

The normalisation of relations with the International Monetary Fund (IMF) in January 2008 continued to yield benefits in 2010. In May, Guinea-Bissau obtained a three-year Extended Credit Facility (ECF) worth Special Drawing Rights (SDR) 22.4 million (US$13.8 million) on top of the Emergency Post Conflict Assistance (EPCA) facility to support the government's 2008 and 2009 economic programmes.

Guinea-Bissau remains highly dependent on subsistence agriculture, the export of cashew nuts and foreign assistance. In order to diversify its economy and foster growth, Guinea-Bissau needs major reforms in public administration (in particular security and defence), as well as investment in agriculture, basic transport and energy infrastructure. The exploitation of its large minerals potential, likely to start soon, could generate substantial resources to finance these investments.

In December 2010, Guinea-Bissau reached completion point under the Heavily Indebted Poor Countries (HIPC) debt relief initiative, which should result in a debt reduction of US$1.2 billion and qualifies the country for further debt relief under the Multilateral Debt Relief Initiative (MDRI).

KEY INDICATORS — Guinea-Bissau

	Unit	2006	2007	2008	2009	2010
Population	m	*1.51	1.54	*1.58	*1.61	*1.51
Gross domestic product (GDP)	US$bn	0.59	0.63	0.73	*0.83	–
GDP per capita	US$	*393	206	*461	*513	–
GDP real growth	%	*1.8	*2.5	*3.3	*2.9	–
Inflation	%	0.7	4.6	10.4	-1.6	–
Industrial output	% change	6.0	3.0	4.0	–	–
Agricultural output	% change	5.5	3.3	3.5	–	–
Exports (fob) (goods)	US$m	110.0	107.0	128.1	–	–
Imports (fob) (goods)	US$m	28.0	167.9	198.8	–	–
Balance of trade	US$m	82.0	-60.9	-70.7	–	–
Current account	US$m	-33.0	-66.0	-92.9	13.0	–
Total reserves minus gold	US$m	82.0	112.9	124.4	168.6	156.4
Foreign exchange	US$m	81.5	112.8	124.3	149.8	137.2
Exchange rate	per US$	496.60	454.40	418.59	472.19	495.28

* estimated figure

Creating political stability, implementing reforms in the defence sector and fighting the narcotics trade were the government's main political challenges in 2011. Economic performance will depend on the government's success in tackling these issues.

A very large part of Guinea-Bissau's economy is informal. Besides widespread subsistence agriculture, retail and wholesale trade are the main source of income in the capital, Bissau, and remain almost totally informal. Only 75 companies are currently registered in the country, but according to unofficial estimates there could be as many as 8 000 concerns. Although measuring the informal sector is difficult, the authorities report that the tertiary sector grew by 3.4 per cent in 2010.

Agriculture

Despite the big potential of its natural resources, the economy of Guinea-Bissau remains extremely concentrated on the production of cashew nuts. Agriculture as a whole accounts for 29.8 per cent of GDP, 81 per cent of exports and employs 90 per cent of the population, mostly in cashew nut production. The primary sector's performance remained stable in 2010, growing by around 2.7 per cent. The volume of cashew nut production dropped by an estimated 10 per cent, but was offset by increased output in other crops, notably rice. Cashew nut production should pick up gradually, as newly planted trees will start producing in the coming years, and existing trees are progressively reaching their most productive ages. Yet the sector operates below its potential. A transition from bartering to cash payments, extra storage capacity and modern production technologies could raise income for both farmers and the government. The sector suffers also from an opaque land regulation, a poor judicial system, and limited access to credit and insurance, although commercial banks are gradually starting to finance agricultural campaigns.

Economic diversification is a priority if the country is to increase its resilience to external shocks. The country could benefit from better development and marketing of the most competitive crops. The Rural and Agricultural Sector Rehabilitation Project (PRESAR), financed by the African Development Bank (AfDB) until the end of 2011, aims to increase rice production from 2.9 tonnes per hectare to 5 tonnes/ha through the transfer of technology, wider provision of public services such as energy, water and transport, and anti-pest programmes. The project, implemented in five out of the country's eight regions including Bissau, also focuses on improving horticulture and livestock. Other donors, such as India and Brazil, are supporting research projects aimed at increasing agricultural productivity using modified seeds. Spanish investors have invested heavily in modern machinery and storage facilities to increase rice production in the region of Bafata. The first crops should be marketed in 2011, targeting local and regional consumption.

Production of bauxite, phosphates and oil could double or triple Guinea-Bissau's foreign exchange and fiscal revenues. Phosphate exploration near Farim has the greatest mining potential, and production is likely to begin soon. Guinea-Bissau Phosphate Mining Company, which holds the lease, brought in an Italian company, Trevi, and a local firm, Alscon, to evaluate the project. Potential gross revenues are conservatively estimated at US$90 million annually. In addition, Bauxite Angola plans to invest US$321 million in a bauxite project in Boe, which has the potential to double GDP. The mine should reach full-scale production during 2011 and would be jointly owned by Bauxite Angola (70 per cent), and the governments of Angola (20 per cent) and Guinea-Bissau (10 per cent). Gold exploration also yielded promising results in 2010.

The oil potential is unclear, and territorial disputes between Guinea-Bissau and Senegal are affecting the sector's development. Current oil reserves are estimated at 1.1 billion barrels. According to Petroguin, the state-owned oil company, 14 offshore blocks are under exploration. Guinea-Bissau and Senegal are trying to create an agency to manage the sector.

The country has a huge but untapped tourism potential, starting with the Bijagos Archipelago, which UNESCO has declared a Biosphere Ecology Reserve. Political stability and basic infrastructure need to be in place for tourism to develop, however.

Millennium Development Goals

Guinea-Bissau ranked 164 out of 169 nations on the UNDP Human Development Index (HDI) in 2010. Economic growth was barely sufficient to keep pace with population growth, estimated at 2.4 per cent, making it unlikely to meet the Millennium Development Goal (MDG) on poverty reduction. According to the World Bank, GDP per capita declined by an average 2.6 per cent a year from 1990 to 2008. However, Guinea-Bissau is on track to achieve the goals of promoting gender equality and empowering women, and universal primary education.

Unemployment remains high, particularly for urban youth. The latest unemployment rate for young people aged between 15 and 24, for 2006, is 46.87 per cent in Bissau and 19.34 per cent in rural areas. The government will have to step up economic growth, targeting sectors that provide employment for the poor, in particular agriculture.

Risk assessment

Politics	Poor
Economy	Poor
Regional stability	Fair

COUNTRY PROFILE

Historical profile

1400s Until Portuguese traders first came to Guinea-Bissau, the country was part of the Mali Empire. It was administered as part of the Portuguese Cape Verde Islands, the Guinea area was important in the slave-trade.

1879 Guinea became a separate colony.

1951 Guinea declared a province of Portugal.

1915 The Portuguese had colonised only the coastal regions until the nineteenth century but finally gained control of the interior. Unlike its other colonies, Portugal made little attempt to develop the then Portuguese Guinea.

1956 The liberation movement, Partido Africano da Independência de Guiné e Cabo Verde (PAIGC) (African Independence Party of Guinea and Cape Verde), was founded by Amilcar Cabral.

1973 Amilcar Cabral was assassinated. PAIGC, which controlled much of the interior of the country, announced a unilateral declaration of independence. PAIGC dropped the name Portuguese from the country's name in favour of Guinea-Bissau.

1974 Portugal had long refused to relinquish power, extending Africa's longest war of independence, but it was finally granted after a *coup d'état* deposed the Portuguese prime minister, Marcello Caetano, in Lisbon, Portugal. Luis Cabral, (brother of the PAIGC founder, Amilcar Cabral), became president.

1980 PAIGC was committed to the unification of Guinea-Bissau and Cape Verde, but this aim was dropped when President Cabral was removed and replaced by his prime minister, João Bernardo Vieira (Nino).

1990 Parliament revoked the PAIGC sole legitimate party status.

1994 Vieira was elected president in the first free elections and PAIGC won the parliamentary elections.

1997 Formal entry to the Communauté Financière Africaine when the CFA franc replaced the peso as national currency.

1998 A civil war began. General Ansumane Mane attempted a coup against Vieira following an army uprising, when Vieira had tried to sack the general for smuggling arms into the neighbouring Senegalese province of Casamance. Senegalese and Guinea troops supported the government and after a month of fighting a cease-fire was agreed.

1999 Ecowas forces arrived to keep the peace, but fighting broke out again and President Vieira was ousted. Malam Bacai Sanhá became interim president. The Partido para a Renovaçao Social (PRS) (Party for Social Renewal) won the parliamentary elections.

2000 Kumba Ialá (Yala), leader of the PRS, was elected president.

2003 President Kumba Ialá was deposed in a bloodless coup.

2004 The opposition PAIGC won the parliamentary elections and Carlos Domingos Gomes Júnior (Carlos Gomes) was sworn in as prime minister.

2005 Former military leader and deposed president, João Bernardo 'Nino' Vieira, won presidential elections and almost immediately sacked Prime Minister Carlos Gomes; Aristides Gomes (no relation) was named as prime minister.

2006 The World Bank suspended a US$15 million funding for infrastructure, due to a lack of transparency in contracts.

2007 Prime Minister Aristides Gomes resigned, following a no-confidence vote in the legislature. Martinho Ndafa Kabi took office as prime minister. A law was enacted that guaranteed amnesty to the perpetrators of violence committed between 1980–2004 during the period of political unrest.

2008 The UN Office on Drugs and Crime (UNODC) declared Guinea-Bissau as the new hub for drugs from South America for onward distribution into Europe. The president appointed Carlos Correia as prime minister. The ruling PAIGC won 49.8 per cent of the votes (67 seats out of 100) in elections. President Vieira survived an attack by mutinous soldiers on his family compound. He appointed Carlos Gomes as prime minister.

2009 President João Bernardo Vieira was shot dead by soldiers loyal to the Army Chief of Staff, General Tagme Na Waie, who had been killed hours earlier in a bomb blast. Raimundo Pereira was sworn-in as acting president. Former president Luis Cabral died in Portugal; he had been the first post-independence president in 1974. Eleven candidates took part in presidential elections, but without any candidate reaching the minimum vote necessary, a run-off was held, which was won by Malam Bacai Sanhá with 63.31 per cent. EU observers declared the polling as 'calm and orderly'.

2010 In April, the prime minister was detained briefly by soldiers during a failed coup. The EU decided to end its security mission in September, which had been set up in 2008 to fund defence and security and sector reform (SSR) of the defence and police forces as well as the judiciary. Political instability and the deteriorating standards of law and order were cited as the reasons to end the mission following the appointment of one of the failed coup leaders, General Antonio Indjai, as head of the army. Head of the air force, Ibraima Papa Camara and former naval chief, Jose Americo Bubo Na Tchuto, were named by the US as 'drug kingpins'; their assets in the US were frozen and they were put on a US list of people with whom US citizens may not do business.

2011 On 10 May the Paris Club of international creditors cancelled US$256 million in debt, as a result of government efforts in tackling poverty and boosting growth. A further US$27 million of bilateral debt was also waived. Following agreements with donor countries to provide the funds, military pensions will be paid from September. The income is considered important in deterring military coups and uprisings.

Political structure

Constitution
The 1984 constitution has been revised five times. The 1999 amendment reserves the highest posts in the country for 'native Bissau-Guineans'.

Independence date
24 September 1973 (proclaimed unilaterally); 10 September 1974 (de jure from Portugal).

Form of state
Unitary republic

The executive
Executive power rests with the president, who is the head of state and serves a five-year term. The president appoints the prime minister, who presides over the Council of Ministers.

National legislature
The unicameral Assembleia Nacional Popular (National People's Assembly) has 102 members of which 100 are elected by proportional representation by party lists; two seats are reserved for expatriate citizens. All members serve for five-year terms.

Legal system
The legal system is based on the 1984 constitution, revised in 1993.

Last elections
16 November 2008 (parliament); 28 June/25 July 2009 (presidential, two rounds)

Results: Presidential: (first round) Malam Bacai Sanhá (PAIGC) won 37.6 per cent of the vote, Kumba Ialá (PRS) 27.9 per cent, Henrique Rosa (independent) 22.9 per cent, and Iaya Djaló (Partido Nova Democracia (PND) (New Democracy Party)) 2.9 per cent; turnout was 60 per cent. (Second round) Sanhá won 63.31 per cent, Ialá 36.69 per cent; turnout was 61 per cent.

Parliamentary: Partido Africano da Independência de Guiné e Cabo Verde (PAIGC) (African Party for the Independence of Guinea and Cape Verde) won 49.8 per cent of the votes (67 seats out of 100), the Partido para a Renovaçao Social (PRS) (Party for Social Renewal) 25.3 per cent (28), the Partido Republicano para Independência e Desenvolvimento (Prid) (Republican Party for Independence and Development) 7.5 per cent (3), the Partido da Nova Democracia (PND) (New Democracy Party) 2.3 per cent (1) and the Aliança Democrático (AD) (Democratic Alliance) 1.4 per cent (1); no other party won parliamentary seats. Turnout was about 82 per cent.

Next elections
2012 (parliament); 2014 (presidential)

Political parties

Ruling party
Coalition government: Partido Africano da Independência de Guiné e Cabo Verde (PAIGC) (African Independence Party of Guinea and Cape Verde), Partido para a Renovaçao Social (PRS) (Party for Social Renewal) and Partido Unido Social Democrático (PUSD) (United Social Democratic Party) (from 17 Apr 2007)

Main opposition party
Partido Unido Social Democrático (PUSD) (United Social Democratic Party)

Population
1.61 million (2009)*

Last census: December 1991: 983,367

Population density: 31 per square km. Urban population: 32 per cent (1995–2001).

Annual growth rate: 2.9 per cent 1994–2004 (WHO 2006)

Ethnic make-up
Balanta (30 per cent), Fula (20 per cent), Manjaca (14 per cent), Mandinga 13 per cent, Papel 7 per cent.

Religions
Some 65 per cent of the population are animist, 30 per cent Muslim and 5 per cent Christian.

Education
Literacy rate: 59 per cent, total; 26.2 per cent female adult rates (World Bank).

Health
Improved water sources are available to 49 per cent of the population.

HIV/Aids
HIV prevalence: 2.8 per cent (UNAIDS estimate 2004)

Life expectancy: 47 years, 2004 (WHO 2006)

Fertility rate/Maternal mortality rate: 7.1 births per woman, 2004 (WHO 2006); maternal mortality 910 deaths per 100,000 live births (World Bank).

Child (under 5 years) mortality rate (per 1,000): 126 per 1,000 live births (World Bank).

Head of population per physician: 0.12 physicians per 1,000 people, 2004 (WHO 2006)

Main cities
Bissau (capital, estimated population 452,640 in 2005), Bafatá (26,312), Gabú (12,255), Catió (7,279), Canchungo (6,282).

Languages spoken
Crioulo (a hybrid of medieval Portuguese and local words) is the common language. Balanta, Bijago and Fulani are also spoken. French is more widely spoken than English. All correspondence and documentation should be in Portuguese and French.

Official language/s
Portuguese

Media
Despite the constitution guaranteeing freedom of the press, the government has not always respected this and journalists are known to practice self-censorship. Journalists that have reported on drug trafficking have been subject to harassment.

The small and weak media scene is hampered by the country's financial constraints.

Press
Newspaper and magazines include *No Pintcha*, *Correio de Bissau Fraskera* and *Banobero*.

Broadcasting
The state-owned Radio Televisao de Guinea-Bissau (RTGB) is the public broadcaster.

Radio: RTGB operates the only Radiodifusão Nacional public radio station. International radio is provided by RTP in Portuguese and RFI in French. Private radio stations include Radio Pidjiquiti, Bombolom FM both very popular and Voice of Quelele.

Television: The state-owned RTGB broadcasts locally. RTP Africa (ww1.rtp.pt) is funded by Portugal, with donated equipment, but managed locally by Bissau-Guineans.

News agencies
National news agency: ABMP (Agência Bissau Media e Publiçacões)

Bissau Digital: www.bissaudigital.com

Guine-Bissau: www.guine-bissau.com

Economy

Guinea-Bissau is one of the poorest countries in the world with its economy heavily dependent on foreign aid. The main economic activity is farming, with crops including cashew nuts, peanuts, rice and palm kernels. Although fishing is another component of the economy, very little is undertaken by domestic fishermen, but rather fishing rights are licensed to foreign trawlers.

GDP growth was 3 per cent in 2009, down from 3.2 per cent in 2008, but predicted to grow to 3.5 per cent in 2010. Exports of cashew nuts 2006–10 doubled, from over 54,000 tonnes to a projected 109,000 tonnes, at the same time as global prices were rising. This was despite the sudden fall in sales in 2009 as the global economic crisis cut trade. However much of the revenue benefit from increased exports was offset by increased commodity import prices, particularly in petroleum and foodstuffs. The International Monetary Fund (IMF) stated in its December 2010 report that Guinea-Bissau's very low revenue collection, at 9 per cent of GDP (the lowest of all sub-Saharan countries), was the 'root cause' for its fiscal imbalance and that with a support programme Guinea-Bissau should be able to increase its collections.

GDP per capita in 2005 was US$221 and by 2010 it was estimated to have grown to US$497, according to the IMF. The majority of the population, around 75 per cent, live below the poverty line, surviving through subsistence farming. The informal economy has been estimated as larger than the legal market. Remittances in 2009 were US$28 million (9.1 per cent of GDP), but were estimated to have fallen to US$27 million in 2010. Remittances provide families with vital, focused income that may represent their only tangible means of livelihood.

The military conflict of 1998–99, which damaged the infrastructure and still impacts on production, has been eased through projects of repair and expansion. Investment in energy has also aided growth.

The IMF considered the efforts undertaken by the government to manage the economy, including an economic programme supported by a three-year extended credit facility (ECF), is likely to result in debt relief funds under the Heavily Indebted Poor Countries (HIPC) Initiative being extended from 2011.

External trade

Guinea-Bissau is a member of the Economic Community of West African States (Ecowas), and is also a member of the West African Economic and Monetary Union (WAEMU) using the common currency, the CFA franc.

Guinea-Bissau has a large trade deficit and heavy dependence on foreign aid and credits.

Imports

Principal imports are fuel and energy, foodstuffs, transport equipment, capital goods.

Main sources: Portugal (typically 17 per cent of total), Senegal (14 per cent), The Netherlands (9 per cent).

Exports

Principal exports are agricultural produce such as cashew nuts, shrimp (prawns), peanuts, palm kernels and sawn timber. Fish is harvested by foreign trawlers, who pay for fishing rights.

Main destinations: India (typically 62 per cent of total), Nigeria (31 per cent), Portugal (2 per cent).

Agriculture

Farming

The agricultural sector (including fishing) is the principal economic activity, accounting for around 60 per cent of GDP and over 70 per cent of total export earnings and employing 70 per cent of the workforce.

Only 9 per cent of total area is cultivated; inland areas are largely savannah, coastal areas are forest and mangrove swamps.

Construction of a bridge on the Mansoa river between Dakar and Bissau improved links between Cacheu and Oio regions (which produce half of the country's agricultural output) and markets.

There are chronic food shortages, despite the emphasis on food self-sufficiency and co-operative farming.

The main food crop is paddy rice (19 per cent of cultivated land); other food crops include millet, sorghum, plantains, root crops, some maize and groundnuts.

Guinea-Bissau is one of the world's largest producers of cashew nuts. Other cash crops include palm kernels, coconuts, tobacco, sugar.

Fishing

The fishing sector is important. Exports of fish and shellfish are expected to increase as the country's large marine resources are exploited. The European Development Fund gave US$35 million in aid to develop the fishing industry, including an ice-making plant. Fish worth between US$300–600 million are caught in the waters each year, but value added production on-shore is minimal.

More investment is needed to refurbish the main port, damaged during the civil war, to enable fish processing for export to Europe or to neighbouring countries for processing and re-export.

Industry and manufacturing

The industrial sector contributes around 12 per cent to GDP and employs 10 per cent of the workforce. Production is mostly agri-related: processing groundnuts, fish processing, rice dehusking, sugar refining. There is also a large brewery plant, a small Citroën assembly plant, brick making and textile industries. Since the end of the civil war, there has been a drive to modernise transport facilities.

Tourism

The sector is undeveloped, with only around 1,000 visitors per year, mostly for fishing or hunting.

Mining

There are some 200 million tonnes of bauxite reserves in the region of Boé, but exploration costs are too high to justify extraction. There are also known deposits of phosphate near Farim, as well as gold and possibly diamonds. The main barrier to investment in the mining sector is the country's poor infrastructure.

Test drilling at the Farim phosphate deposit indicated it was commercially viable with high phosphate recovery rates (84.1 per cent).

Hydrocarbons

There are no known commercially viable oil reserves although exploration is ongoing. Consumption of oil was 3,000 barrels per day in 2008, all of which was imported.

The state-owned PetroGuin (formerly called Petrominas) is the national oil company, which controls downstream facilities.

Neither natural gas nor coal are produced, any imports are commercially negligible.

Energy

Total installed generating capacity was 21MW in 2007, producing 6 billion kilowatt hours. Only 2.6 per cent of the population has access to electricity. Energy particularly in rural areas is mainly derived from charcoal and wood.

In June 2008 the UN reported on the condition of the parastatal utility Electricidade e Águas de Guiné-Bissau (EAGB) (Electricity and Water Company of Guinea-Bissau), in which it described the energy crisis as acute and reported that the lack of investment in the energy sector had caused a serious bottleneck in socio-economic recovery. EAGB is chronically under-funded and the UN provided emergency assistance to the energy sector by providing three 850KW and two 1.5MW generators for the capital; these replaced existing generators, so no additional energy was created.

The World Bank and the West African Development Bank is supporting the EAGB in restructuring and developing the sector with loans of US$20 million and US$5 million respectively. Integration with the West African Power Pool (WAPP), operated by the Economic Community of West African States (Ecowas), and the Gambia River Development Organisation project is expected to enhance EAGB's longer term prospects. Further aid from the EU was committed in 2009.

Financial markets

Stock exchange

Afribourse (Bourse Régionale des Valeurs Mobliéres) (BRVM)

Banking and insurance

Central bank

Banque Centrale des Etats de l'Afrique de l'Ouest

Main financial centre

Bissau

Time

GMT

Geography

Guinea-Bissau lies on the west coast of Africa, with Senegal to the north and Guinea to the east and south. The terrain is mainly low coastal plain with thick forest and mangrove swamps, rising to hills in the east, where savannah prevails; the highest elevation is approximately 300 metres. Guinea-Bissau also includes Bolama island and the Bijagós archipelago of 15 main islands, lying over 40km out in the Atlantic Ocean.

Hemisphere

Northern.

Climate

Tropical with rainy season from mid-May to November and dry season from December–April. Average temperatures range from 20–38 degrees Celsius (C) in April–May, and from 15–33 degrees C in December–January. High humidity from July–September.

Entry requirements

Passports

Required by all, valid for six months.

Visa

Required by all, except nationals of Ecowas countries for stay of one month. Applications for business visas should include a letter from the visitor's company accepting responsibility for any expenses incurred, and a full itinerary. For further details, contact the nearest embassy.

Currency advice/regulations

Import and export of local currency is prohibited. There is no restriction on the import of foreign currency, but amounts should be declared; export of foreign currency is allowed up to the declared amount.

Health (for visitors)

Medical facilities are limited.

Mandatory precautions

Yellow fever vaccination certificate.

Advisable precautions

Malaria prophylaxes are essential as risk exists throughout the country. Immunisations or booster shots are necessary for diphtheria, tetanus, polio, hepatitis A, typhoid and yellow fever. Vaccinations may be needed for hepatitis B, TB, meningitis and cholera. Rabies is a risk in rural areas.

Use only bottled or boiled water for drinks, washing teeth and making ice. Eat only well cooked meals, preferably served hot; vegetables should be cooked and fruit peeled. Avoid pork, salad and food from street vendors. A full first-aid kit would be useful.

Hotels

Accommodation is very limited and difficult to obtain at short notice. Reservations should be made well in advance, preferably through business contacts. Hotel tariffs are liable to change at short notice, therefore confirmation of booking is recommended.

Credit cards

Credit cards cannot be used.

Public holidays (national)

Fixed dates

1 Jan (New Year's Day), 20 Jan (Death of Amilcar Cabral), 8 Mar (Women's Day), 1 May (Labour Day), 3 Aug (Colonisation Martyrs' Day), 24 Sep (National Day), 14 Nov (Readjustment Movement Day), 25 Dec (Christmas Day).

Variable dates

Eid al Adha, Eid al Fitr

Islamic year 1433 (26 Nov 2011–14 Nov 2012): The Islamic year contains 354 or 355 days, with the result that Muslim feasts advance by 10–12 days against the Gregorian calendar. Dates of feasts vary according to the sighting of the new moon, so cannot be forecast exactly.

Working hours

Banking

Mon–Fri: 0830–1430.

Business

Mon–Fri: 0830–1430.

Government

Mon–Fri: 0830–1430.

Shops

Mon–Fri: 0730–1230, 1430–1830.

Telecommunications

Telephone/fax

Communications are poor.

Mobile/cell phones

GSM 900 roaming facilities are available.

Getting there

Air

International airport/s: Bissau-Osvaldo Vieira Airport (OXB), 8km from city. Taxis and minibuses are available to take visitors to the city.

Airport tax: None.

Surface

Road: The road from Guinea is mostly paved; however, that which is not, from the border to Labé, gets boggy in the rainy season. Petrol is readily available only in the cities.

A 720-metre bridge over the Mansoa river has improved the traffic flow on the trans-African coastal road between Dakar, Senegal and Bissau.

Water: There are sea links between Cape Verde and Guinea-Bissau.

Main port/s: Bissau

Getting about

National transport

Air: There are no mainland internal flights. Flights go between Bissau and Bubaque Island and a small plane flies to Orango Island from Bissau.

Road: Total road network is over 3,250km, of which about a third is all-weather.

Buses: Minibuses operate on the main roads.

Taxis: Long-distance taxis leave from the market square in Bissau.

Water: Boats serve most towns on the coast and up-river. Tickets available from the Guinémar Office.

City transport

Taxis: Taxis are available in Bissau and serve all main towns.

BUSINESS DIRECTORY

The addresses listed below are a selection only. While World of Information makes every endeavour to check these addresses, we cannot guarantee that changes have not been made, especially to telephone numbers and area codes. We would welcome any corrections.

Telephone area codes

The international dialling code (IDD) for Guinea-Bissau is + 245 followed by subscriber's number.

Chambers of Commerce

Guini-Bissau Associação Comercial, Industrial e Agricola, PO Box 88, Bissau (tel: 222-276).

Guini-Bissau Camara do Comercio, Industria e Agricultura, PO Box 361, Bissau (tel: 212-844; fax: 201-602).

Banking

Central bank

Banque Centrale des Etats de l'Afrique de l'Ouest, Direction Nationale, Avenue Amilcar Cabral 124, PO Box 38, Bissau (tel: 215-548; fax: 201-305).

Stock exchange

Afribourse (Bourse Régionale des Valeurs Mobliéres) (BRVM): www.brvm.org

Ministries

Ministry of Economy and Finance, Rua Justino Lopes 74A, Bissau (tel: 203-495; fax: 203-496).

Ministry of Finance, Avenue Domingos Ramos, Caixa Postal 67, Bissau (tel/fax: 201-037).

Ministry of Mines and Energy, Caixa Postal 387, Bissau.

Other useful addresses

Empresa Nacional de Comércio Geral, CP 5, Bissau (tel: 212-925).

Empresa Nacional de Pesquisas e Exploração Petroliferas e Mineiras (Petrominas), 58 Rua Eduardo Mondlane, Bissau (tel: 212-279).

Guinea-Bissau Embassy (USA), 15929 Yukon Lane, Rockville MD 20855 (tel: (+1-202) 947-3958).

Guinémar Office, 21A Rua Guerra Mendes, Bissau.

Petroguin, Caixa Postal 387 Bissau (tel: 221-155, 222-625; fax: 221-155, 222-625).

Radiodifusão Nacional da República da Guiné-Bissau, CP 191, Bissau.

National news agency: ABMP (Agência Bissau Media e Publiçacões), CP1069; Rua Euardo Mondlane 52, Bissau (tel: 206-147; email: agenciabissau@agenciabissau.com; internet: www.agenciabissau.com).

Internet sites

Africa Business Network: http://www.ifc.org/abn

AllAfrica.com: http://allafrica.com

African Development Bank: http://www.afdb.org

Africa Online: http://www.africaonline.com

Mbendi AfroPaedia (information on companies, countries, industries and stock exchanges in Africa): http://mbendi.co.za

KEY FACTS

Official name: Co-operative Republic of Guyana

Head of State: President Donald Ramotar (PPP/Civic) (from 3 Dec 2011)

Head of government: Prime Minister Samuel AA Hinds (since 1997; reappointed 5 Dec 2011)

Ruling party: People's Progressive Party/Civic (PPP/Civic) (from 1997; re-elected 28 Nov 2011)

Area: 214,970 square km

Population: 754,000 (2010)*

Capital: Georgetown

Official language: English

Currency: Guyana dollar (G$) = 100 cents

Exchange rate: G$200.70 per US$ (Oct 2011)

GDP per capita: US$2,868 (2010)

GDP real growth: 3.60% (2010)

GDP: US$2.21 billion (2010)

Inflation: 3.70% (2010)

Balance of trade: -US$394.40 million (2008)

* estimated figure

Guyana

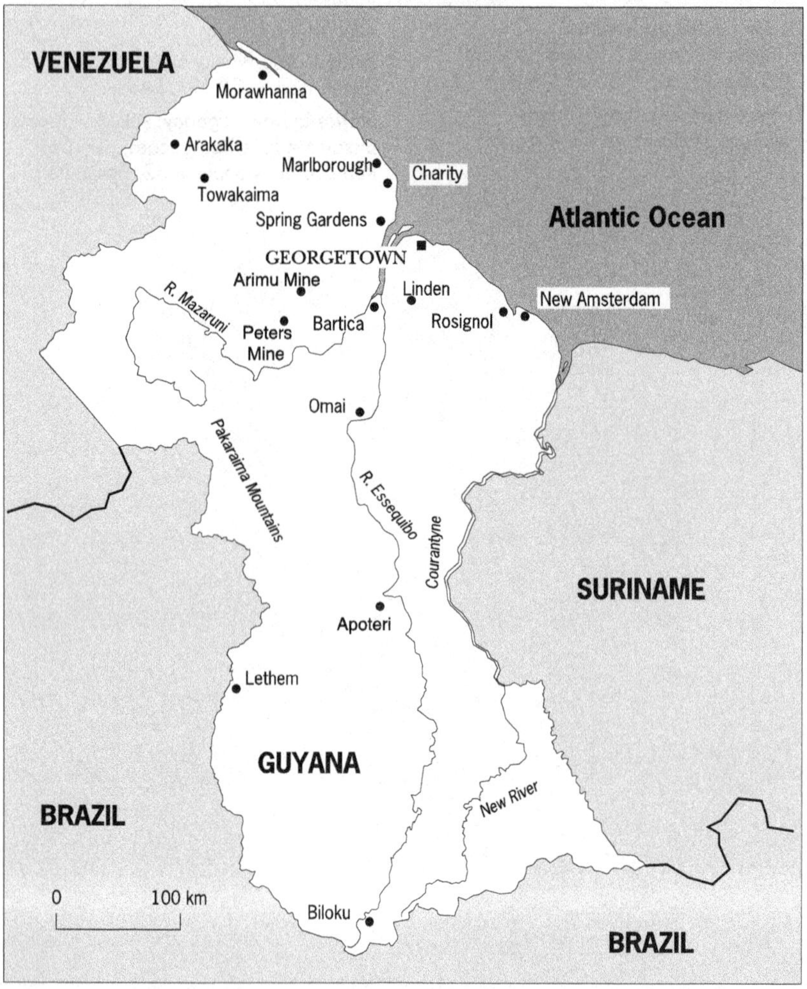

On 5 July 2011, President Jagdeo, at the close of his second and final term in office, addressed the conference of heads of government attending the Caribbean Community (Caricom) meeting in St Kitts. He urged the leaders to focus on outcomes rather than processes, 'people judge us by results' he said, and exhorted other leaders to 'always ascertain the value added to the process before plunging into new initiatives'. Parliamentary elections were held on 28 November, in which the People's Progressive Party/Civic (PPP/Civic) won 49 per cent of the vote (32 seats out of 65), the coalition of four parties called A Partnership for National Unity (APNU) won 41 per cent (26) and the Alliance for Change (AFC) seven seats. PPP/Civic appointed its candidate, Donald Ramotar, as president, who in turn reappointed Samuel A A Hinds as prime minister.

The economy

As global demand recovered, the economy of Guyana continued to grow in 2010, albeit at a slower pace (2.8 per cent) than the rate projected in the budget (4.4 per cent). According to the United Nations Economic Commission for Latin America and the Caribbean (ECLAC) the medium-term prospects for Guyana are very good thanks, in part, to the closer ties being forged with Brazil, of which the completion of the Takutu Bridge and the energy project at Amaila Falls are just two examples. In addition, expected transfers under its low-carbon development strategy, which commits Guyana to reducing emissions from deforestation in return for up to US$250 million in compensation over time, will boost foreign exchange inflows. An initial deposit of US$30 million was made to this fund by the government of Norway in October 2010.

The main drivers of economic growth in 2010 were the service, manufacturing, and construction sectors, while the agricultural sector experienced some setbacks. Rice output is expected decline by an estimated 0.9 per cent, while sugar grew by some 11.2 per cent. Such a sharp increase in sugar output was a remarkable turnaround in view of the 1.8 per cent decline in sugar production recorded at mid-year. Given that agriculture accounts for some 20 per cent of GDP, the performance of sugar sharply impacts overall growth. Livestock, which declined by 14.2 per cent at mid-year, ended the year with a fall of just over 13.0 per cent. Manufacturing, largely driven by sugar manufacturing, grew by 3.5 per cent in 2010. Meanwhile the services sector benefited from increased activity in information and communications (5.7 per cent) and wholesale and retail trade (7.0 per cent) and should exhibit continued growth in 2011. The construction sector recorded a 9.5 per cent expansion to mid-year and an improvement of 3 per cent is anticipated for the year as a whole.

The mining sector, on the other hand, has continued to struggle owing to faltering demand for bauxite: output declined by 4.1 per cent at mid-year and the overall contraction for 2010 is estimated to be 2.8 per cent.

The Georgetown Urban Consumer Price Index (CPI) experienced a 2.0 per cent rise in the first half of 2010, driven by rising food prices. Average annual inflation will be about 3.7 per cent in 2010 (up from 2.9 per cent in 2009). Inflation is expected to ease marginally in 2011, subsiding, as commodity prices stabilise, to 3.5 per cent at the end of the year.

The current account of the balance of payments showed a deficit of US$219.7 million in 2009 and an increase to US$255.9 million is forecast for 2010.

Although merchandise exports are expected to increase, imports will also expand. Net imports, which recorded a deficit of US$1.169 billion in 2009, should reach an estimated US$1.265 billion in 2010. The balance of payments surplus of US$234.4 million in 2009 is expected to give way to a deficit of US$9.3 million in 2010. The capital account recorded a surplus of US$454 million in 2009 and a smaller surplus of US$247 million is anticipated for 2010. Guyana will continue to run relatively large current-account deficits, backed by strong multilateral debt and investment inflows. For example, project grants increased in the first half of 2010 by 7.5 per cent to US$2 billion. The current transfers surplus of US$300 million should increase to US$310 million in 2010 with only a marginal improvement in remittance inflows since incomes in the industrialised countries are still depressed.

Risk assessment

Economy	Fair
Politics	Fair
Regional stability	Fair

COUNTRY PROFILE

Historical profile

The area before European settlement was inhabited by semi-nomadic, hunter-gatherer Amerindian tribes, notably Arawaks and Caribs.

1498 Christopher Columbus first sighted Guyana.

1616 The Dutch built the first fort.

1640 The first African slaves arrived to work on sugar plantations. Settlements grew up in Essequibo, Demerara and Berbice and were sustained by trade through the Dutch West India Company.

1763 The Berbice slave rebellion began on one plantation and spread to others along the Berbice River.

1781–1803 The Three colonies of Essequibo, Demerara and Berbice passed into the hands of the English, briefly to the French, back to the Dutch, then the English, then the Dutch and lastly back to the English.

1814 After the Napoleonic Wars the colonies of were ceded to Britain.

1831 The British administration merged the three colonies into British Guiana, but retained the Dutch administrative, legislative and legal system.

1834 Britain abolished slavery in all its territories. Many Indian and smaller numbers of Chinese and Japanese indentured labourers were brought to work on the estates.

1920 Indentured labour ended.

1953 The General election was won by the People's Progressive Party (PPP), led by Cheddi Jagan and Forbes Burnham. The British government deemed the government as pro-Communist and suspended the constitution. The PPP spilt and Burnham founded the People's National Congress/Reform (PNC) party.

1957 and 1961 The PPP won both general elections. Support began to grow for independence.

1964 Guyana's political system was generally viewed as fraudulent with Guyana a *de facto* one-party state and an 'administrative dictatorship'.

1965 The PPP won most seats in the general election; however a coalition of PNC and another minor, conservative, party formed a government. Burnham became prime minister and stayed in post in an increasingly authoritarian manner, until 1980

1966 Guyana gained independence.

1971 A UN tribunal convened to try and resolve the long-standing border dispute

KEY INDICATORS — Guyana

	Unit	2006	2007	2008	2009	2010
Population	m	0.76	0.76	0.76	*0.77	*0.75
Gross domestic product (GDP)	US$bn	0.89	1.07	1.92	2.02	2.21
GDP per capita	US$	1,201	1,405	2,497	2,629	2,868
GDP real growth	%	5.1	5.4	2.0	3.3	3.6
Inflation	%	6.6	12.2	8.1	2.9	3.7
Exports (fob) (goods)	US$m	594.8	689.3	789.0	–	–
Imports (fob) (goods)	US$m	792.4	977.6	1,183.4	–	–
Balance of trade	US$m	-197.6	-288.3	-394.4	–	–
Current account	US$m	-172.0	-112.3	-191.6	-172.0	-216.0
Total reserves minus gold	US$m	279.6	313.0	355.9	631.4	782.1
Foreign exchange	US$m	278.1	312.5	355.9	627.5	780.0
Exchange rate	per US$	201.69	204.20	203.60	204.00	203.60

* estimated figure

with neighbouring Venezuela concerning the oil-rich Essequibo region.
1980 A new constitution introduced the post of executive president, and Forbes Burnham became the first.
1985 President Burnham died. Desmond Hoyte became president. The one-party state and radical socialism was gradually replaced by a market economy. Austerity measures introduced in the late 1980s resulted in great civil unrest.
1992 The National Assembly and Regional Council were elected in the first free and fair general elections. Hoyte lost the presidency to former Marxist, Dr Cheddi Jagan (PPP).
1997 A PPP/Civic (PPC/C) coalition won the election, but PNC refused to accept the election results. Cheddi Jagan died in March. Samuel Hinds became president until December when Jagan's widow Janet was elected president.
1998 After boycotting parliament since the 1997 election, the PNC returned to the National Assembly, following intervention by the Caribbean Community (Caricom), which carried out an independent audit of the election results and brokered an accord with the PNC, which also catered for a new constitution and fresh elections.
1999 Janet Jagan resigned the presidency due to ill-health; she was succeeded by Bharrat Jagdeo.
2000 Guyana had an agreement with the Canadian oil company CGX Energy to drill within waters also claimed by neighbouring Suriname. Suriname gunboats raided the exploration oil-rig sparking international tension; diplomatic proposals for joint exploration and exploitation failed.
2001 The general election was won by President Jagdeo's ruling PPC/C.
2002 A high-profile television presenter, Mark Benschop, was charged with treason after he was accused of inciting demonstrators to storm the presidential offices compound. The demonstrators were complaining of discrimination against Afro-Guyanese.
2003 A UN tribunal convened and tried, without success, to resolve the maritime border dispute with Suriname.
2004 CGX Energy announced it had begun exploration of inshore waters along the Cortenyne Coast, with drilling in the disputed Berbice area about to begin. A key witness in the trial of home affairs minister Ronald Gajraj was shot dead before he could testify about allegations of extra-judicial killings. The minister had stepped down after several months of procrastination and opposition inquiry. Guyana joined 12 South American countries in the launch of an economic and political bloc called the South American Community of Nations.
2005 Severe flooding affected half the country's population. The economic effect was shown to be a 2.2 per cent reduction in the year's economic growth, costing the nation about US$65 million. Ronald Gajraj was reinstated as home affairs minister, following a ruling by a presidential commission acquitting him of any wrongdoing; however the decision to reinstall the minister provoked international criticism. Gajraj resigned his position.
2006 The agriculture minister, Satyadeow Sawh, was murdered. President Jagdeo was re-elected with 54.6 per cent of the vote while his PPP/C party won a majority in parliament.
2007 The UN ruled that both Suriname and Guyana should share the disputed, possibly oil-rich, offshore territory.
2008 Guyana signed a trade agreement with the EU.
2009 Local elections were postponed until 2010 due to revisions necessary in the voter list, new identification cards and the demarcation and delineation of electoral boundaries. The new Takutu River Bridge, across the border with Brazil, was opened.
2010 A new, flood-resistant rice, developed for the Guyana Rice Development Board (GRDB) in the Guyana-based Burma Rice Research Station, underwent testing in local conditions. It was designed to survive being completely submerged for up to 17 days. In July the government and the China Development Bank signed a loan agreement (for an undisclosed amount) to begin the Amaila Falls Hydro-Electric Project (AFHEP), for which the Inter-American Development Bank (IDB) also approved US$1.2 million for project preparation.
2011 On 5 July, at the close of President Jagdeo's second and final term in office, he addressed the conference of heads of government attending the Caricom meeting urging them to focus on outcomes rather than processes, 'people judge us by results' he said, and exhorted other leaders to 'always ascertain the value added to the process before plunging into new initiatives'. Presidential and parliament elections were tentatively set for 12 August. Parliamentary elections were held on 28 November, in which the PPP/Civic won 49 per cent of the vote (32 seats out of 65), the coalition of four parties called A Partnership for National Unity (APNU) won 41 per cent (26) and the AFC seven seats. PPP/Civic were given a mandate to appoint its candidate, Donald Ramotar, as president, and to operate a minority government.

Political structure

Constitution

The constitution was enacted in 1980, a decade after Guyana became a co-operative republic and 14 years after joining the Commonwealth.
Guyana is divided into 10 regions, each headed by a chairman who presides over a regional democratic council. Local communities are administered by village or city councils.

Independence date

26 May 1966

Form of state

Co-operative republic

The executive

Executive power rests with the president, who appoints and supervises the prime minister and other ministers. The president is the presidential candidate chosen by the major party in the National Assembly. Most cabinet ministers are also members of the National Assembly; the constitution limits non-member technocrat ministers to five. Technocrat ministers serve as non-elected members, allowing them to debate, but not to vote.

National legislature

The unicameral National Assembly comprises 65 members directly elected by proportional representation, of which 25 are elected in 10 geographic constituencies and 40 from national lists of political parties. The president may dissolve the Assembly and call new elections at any time, but no later than five years from its first sitting. All laws passed by the assembly must be endorsed by the president.

Legal system

Guyana's legal system is based on Roman Dutch law modified by English common law. The country has a series of magistrates' courts and further appellate courts, a Court of Appeal, headed by a chancellor of the judiciary, and a High Court, presided over by a chief justice. The chancellor and the chief justice are appointed by the president.
An ombudsman investigates complaints against government departments or other authorities.

Last elections

28 November 2011 (presidential and parliamentary)
Results: Presidential: candidates win depending on party list votes for parliamentary constituencies, in order of parliamentary voting, therefore the winner was Donald Ramotar (PPP/Civic); David Granger (APNU) and Khemraj Ramjattan (AFC) were runner's up.
Parliamentary (2011): People's Progressive Party/Civic (PPP/Civic) won 48.62 per cent of the vote (32 seats out of 65), A Partnership for National Unity (APNU) (coalition of four parties) 40.83 per cent (26), Alliance for Change (AFC) 10.33 per cent (seven), the United Force 0.26 per cent (none). Turnout was 72.9 per cent

Next elections
2015 (presidential and parliamentary)

Political parties
Ruling party
People's Progressive Party/Civic (PPP/Civic) (from 1997; re-elected 28 Nov 2011)
Main opposition party
Partnership for National Unity (APNU) (coalition of four political parties led by the People's National Congress/Reform (PNCR), Guyana Action Party (GAP), National Front Alliance (NFA) and Working People's Alliance (WPA).

Population
754,000 (2010)*
Last census: September 2002: 751,223
Population density: Four inhabitants per square km. Urban population: 38 per cent (1995–2001).
Overall population density is low although population distribution is very uneven with a high concentration of people along the coastal strip and many inland areas virtually uninhabited. More than one-quarter of the total population live in the capital, Georgetown.
Annual growth rate: 0.3 per cent 1994–2004 (WHO 2006)
Ethnic make-up
East Indian (51 per cent) (resident mostly in agricultural areas) and Afro-Guyanese (30 per cent) (resident mostly in towns) make up the majority. The remainder are of Chinese and European heritage, or Amerindians, most of whom live in the west and south or on reserves.
The main groups of Amerindians are Arawak, Carib, Wapisiana and Warao. The Caribs include Akawaio, Macushi, Patamona and Waiwai.
Religions
Christian (approximately 50 per cent), Hindu (35 per cent) and Muslim (10 per cent).

Education
Education includes primary school, four to six years of secondary school and between three to four years of higher academic or practical education. Students are usually expected to remain in the school system until the age of 16. There are around 900 schools in Guyana.
Increased access to secondary education is supported by two bilateral funded education projects – the Guyana Education Access Programme (GEAP) and the Guyana Building Equity Project (GBET).
The Minister of Labour announced on 29 June 2011 that the schedule to distribute one laptop computer per family by October 2011 was on target. Computer trainers were also being recruited to go into communities and target groups that were required to undertake coaching in the new technology.
Literacy rate: 98.7 per cent, total; 98.3 per cent, female: adult rates in 2002 (World Bank).
Compulsory years: Five to 14
Enrolment rate: 97.4 per cent net primary enrolment (World Bank).

Health
The government has stepped up provisions for drugs and medical supplies in all hospitals and health centres including facilities in the Georgetown Public Hospital Corporation (GPHC).
In June 2011, the Inter-American Development Bank approved a US$12 million loan to improve the water supply to Guyana's second city Linden. Overall, the plans include water pressure to be improved, quality sustained and a reduction in water loss achieved. Over five years (2011–16) the annual cost of water supply to Linden (100km inland from the coast) is estimated to fall from US$232,000 to US$140,000.
HIV/Aids
By 2001 46 per cent of sex workers were living with HIV/Aids and the probability of the virus passing into the wider population is considered by UNAID/WHO as high.
HIV prevalence: 3.2 per cent aged 15–49 in 2003 (World Bank)
Life expectancy: 63 years, 2004 (WHO 2006)
Fertility rate/Maternal mortality rate: 2.2 births per woman, 2004 (WHO 2006)
Birth rate/Death rate: 9 deaths and 18 births, per 1,000 population (World Bank).
Child (under 5 years) mortality rate (per 1,000): 52 deaths per 1,000 live births; 12 per cent of children aged under five are malnourished (World Bank).

Welfare
The government has been developing new housing schemes, including distributing over 20,000 housing lots for a Low Income Settlement Project. The private sector has also been encouraged to assist in the development of the housing sector.

Main cities
Georgetown (capital, estimated population 227,700 in 2003), Linden (44,300), New Amsterdam (32,500).

Languages spoken
Guyana is the only English-speaking country in South America. Urdu, Hindi, Amerindian languages and Creole are also spoken. Along the Brazilian border, many Guyanese also speak Portuguese.
Official language/s
English

Media
Press
Dailies: In English, the *Guyana Chronicle* (www.guyanachronicle.com) is state-owned, private newspapers include *Stabroek News* (www.stabroeknews.com) and *Kaieteur News* (www.kaieteurnews.com).
Weeklies: All daily newspapers publish a weekend edition. In English, other newspapers include The *Catholic Standard* and the *Mirror* (www.mirrornewsonline.com) published twice weekly.
Broadcasting
The state-owned National Communications Network (NCN) (www.ncnguyana.com) operates radio and television services.
Radio: The (NCN) (www.ncnguyana.com) operates two radio stations, Hot FM (http://98hotfm.co.gy) broadcasting modern music. The Voice of Guyana (http://voiceofguyana.com) broadcasts internationally (http://vog560am.co.gy).
Television: The (NCN) (www.ncnguyana.com) operates a public TV station (http://ncn.co.gy). A number of TV channels are received from neighbouring countries. There are international satellite TV channels available.
News agencies
National news agency: GINA (Government Information Agency)
Other news agencies: Caribbean Net News: www.caribbeannetnews.com
Guyana Journal: www.guyanajournal.com

Economy
Although the service sector is the major component of the economy, comprising over 50 per cent of GDP, agriculture is still an important factor within the economy at over 25 per cent of GDP. It represents a larger sector than the industry sector contributes, at over 20 per cent (of which manufacturing is a minor 5 per cent). Agriculture provides employment for around 30 per cent of the workforce and traditional produce of sugar and rice remain major exports, with development and investment in new enterprises, including sea and freshwater fish and shrimp and crawfish, raw timber and finished lumber. Mining of bauxite and gold constitutes the majority of industrial activity, with open cast mines operating for both minerals.
GDP growth was a record high of 7.0 per cent in 2007, falling to 2.0 per cent as the global economic crisis cut world trade, particularly in commodities. However, Guyana avoided the worst of the downturn and in 2009 GDP growth picked up and was 3.0 per cent and estimated to have grown to 4.4 per cent in 2010.
Guyana has since the early 1990s been working to transform itself from a

state-dominated economy to a largely free-market enterprise driven economy. In 2010, the government announced an Agricultural Export Diversification Programme (ADP), funded by US$21.9 million from a loan from the Inter-American Development Bank (IDB), with US$1.1 million of public funds, to develop non-traditional agricultural exports, including fruit and vegetables, livestock and farm and sea-caught fish. Despite the government priority of promoting foreign investment and membership of the Caribbean Community (Caricom), inward investment has been slow. Social and political unrest between ethnic divisions of the country has proved a deterrent to foreign investors.

According to the 2010 UN Development Programme (UNDP) data, the intensity of deprivation in Guyana was rated as 39.7 per cent with per capita income US$2,671, which tends towards the lower quartile when compared with other South American and Caribbean countries of similar size and GDP. Remittance, which not only stimulates the economy in general but also directly supports family budgets, was US$253 million (17.3 per cent of GDP) in 2009 and was estimated to have risen to US$280 million in 2010.

External trade

Along with 11 other members of the Caribbean Community and Common Market (Caricom), Guyana operates within the single market (Caribbean Single Market and Economy (CSME)), which became operational in 2006. CSME includes the free movement of goods and services, a common trade policy and external tariff.

Imports

Fuels and lubricants (typically up to 40 per cent of total), machinery and transport equipment, consumer goods, food and chemicals.

Main sources: US (typically 31 per cent of total), Trinidad and Tobago (18 per cent), Cuba (6 per cent).

Exports

Sugar, bauxite and alumina, shrimps, rice, rum, timber, diamonds and gold.

Main destinations: Canada (typically 28 per cent total of total), UK (15 per cent), US (13 per cent).

Agriculture

Farming

Agriculture is a very important economic activity in Guyana. The sector employs approximately 35 per cent of the workforce and contributes a similar amount to the country's total GDP.

The sugar industry is an important export earner, responsible for around 46 per cent of total exports. Rice accounts for 12 per cent of Guyana's export earnings and 19 per cent of its agricultural contribution to GDP.

About 2 per cent of the total land area is under cultivation. Cultivation of cash crops is confined to the alluvial coastal plain.

The main cash crops are sugar, rice and shrimps.

Guyana is self-sufficient in sugar, rice, vegetables, fish, meat and fruit and increased government investment in the sector has improved production of many other products. Cassava is the principal crop grown in the interior.

Emphasis is also being placed on the cultivation of oil palms, soya beans and corn, and on the development of dairy farming.

There is a national herd of livestock of between 200,000–250,000 head which are ranched on the Rupununi savannah in the south-east.

Fishing

The fishing industry represents a valuable source of income to the economy of Guyana. Produce is sold on both domestic and international markets and the industry employs approximately 5 per cent of the country's total workforce.

Guyana is the region's largest exporter of shrimp, which make up 14 per cent of total exports. Government initiatives in the fishing sector include the improvement of fisheries management and the encouragement of investment in unexploited marine stocks. The typical annual fish catch is over 55,000mt, of which 27,000mt is shellfish.

Forestry

Guyana is one of the most densely forested countries in the world. Approximately 95 per cent of the country's total land mass is covered by forest and woodland.

All the forests are state-owned. Sawnwood and plywood are the principal forest products; pulp and paper, however, are imported.

Industry and manufacturing

The expansion of the industrial sector has traditionally been hampered by a lack of domestic energy supplies together with a dearth of technical and managerial personnel. At present the sector contributed roughly 10 per cent of total GDP and employs approximately 10 per cent of the total work force.

Previously, a serious shortage of foreign exchange had also caused the closure of many firms relying on imported inputs. However, the government is trying to expand the country's industrial base with a policy of diversification and greater encouragement of foreign investors to work with the predominant state sector.

Guyana's manufacturing industry is dominated by the processing of raw materials. Activity related to the mining sector (predominantly bauxite, gold and diamonds) and the processing of agricultural products such as sugar, rice, coconuts and timber, together account for about three-quarters of manufacturing activity. The remainder is accounted for by small-scale import substitution production for the local market. A shortfall in investment is a recurring problem.

Tourism

The tourism industry in Guyana is growing relatively quickly, but the industry's potential remains to be fully exploited. The sector is increasing in importance as an economic activity and currently contributes 9.3 per cent to GDP while accounting for 7.7 per cent of total employment. Development is at an early stage with much work to be done to establish the necessary infrastructure and conditions. There are problems of safety and waste management. Eco-tourism is seen as the way forward. Most visitors are overseas Guyanese and Caribbean nationals.

Mining

Both mining and quarrying are of great importance to Guyana's economy. Both activities combined, amount to 25 per cent of total GDP and account for approximately 12 per cent of the country's total work force.

Annual gold production averages 440,000 ounces, 70 per cent of which comes from Omai Gold Mines, a US$300 million venture. Cambior and Golden Star Resources – Canadian companies – own 65 per cent and 30 per cent of Omai, respectively, and the Guyana government owns 5 per cent. In mid-2003, residents of western Guyana began legal action against Omai for allegedly allowing a dam to collapse on the Essequibo river in 1995, pouring 2.9 million cubic metres of cyanide-tainted slurry into the river. Around 23,000 residents supporting the writ want Omai to pay US$2 billion in damages and are demanding an end to the dumping of toxic waste into the river. A similar writ was issued in 2000, but was thrown out by the courts on technical grounds.

Royalties paid to Guyana's Gold Board are linked to world gold prices. An estimated one-fifth of gold production is smuggled across the borders to Venezuela, Brazil and Suriname by local miners. There is also inefficient alluvial mining by some 10,000 miners using dredgers and suctions.

Bauxite is the country's most important mineral, typically accounting for around a quarter of total export earnings. Production slumped in the early 1980s,

prompting the government to seek outside help for the management of the industry. There are known deposits of kaolin, molybdenum, uranium, copper, semi-precious stones, talc, soapstone and high-silica sand, which the government would like to develop.
In a typical year, Guyana's gold production is estimated to be 384,000 ounces.

Hydrocarbons
There are no proven hydrocarbon reserves. Consumption of oil was 11,000 barrels per day (bpd) in 2008, all of which was imported. In 2005, Guyana, plus a number of other Caribbean states, signed an agreement with Venezuela to establish PetroCaribe, a multi-national oil company, owned by the participating states. PetroCaribe buys low-priced Venezuelan crude oil under long-term payment plans.
In 2007, a UN tribunal decision settled a boundary dispute, which resulted in Guyana being granted 33,152 square kilometres of disputed oil-rich territory off the Atlantic coastline. An estimate of the recoverable oil is 2 billion cubic metres (15 billion barrels) and 1.19 trillion cubic metres of gas. Exploration continued into 2009.
Any use of natural gas or coal is commercially insignificant.

Energy
Total installed generating capacity was 226MW in 2007, the majority of which was produced by thermal power plants. Consumption is typically around 800 million kilowatt hours. Only 60 per cent of the population has access to an electricity supply and self-reliance on individual power sources is widespread. The country has two centres of generation, the Berbice and Demerara Systems; the government has plans to integrate them.
Guyana continues to be heavily dependent on imported oil from both Venezuela and Trinidad and Tobago in order to meet its energy needs. Guyana Electricity Corporation (GEC) is government-subsidised. The Inter-American Development Bank (IDB) has provided loans to rehabilitate a number of GEC's existing thermal stations, as well as expanding the power grid.
The GEC's commissioning of the US$17 million 22MW Wartsila generating plant has brought total capacity in the Demerara system up to 93MW, sufficient to meet peak demand in 2007, but which will need an additional 16MW by 2011 to meet needs. The entire generating system should be increased by 72MW by 2011. Renewable energy includes a new wind farm on the east coast supplying 4MW. The country has considerable potential for hydroelectric power generation, but significant investment remains dubious due to the lack of existing, extensive infrastructure.

Financial markets
Stock exchange
Gasci (Guyana Association of Securities Companies and Intermediaries Incorporated)

Banking and insurance
Guyana's banking and financial services industry is concentrated in the capital Georgetown. The Central Bank of Guyana regulates the industry.
Central bank
Bank of Guyana
Main financial centre
Georgetown

Time
GMT minus four hours.

Geography
A plain about 15km wide runs along the 320km northern (Atlantic) coast and extends west into Venezuela and east into Suriname. This strip, which lies some 1.5 metres below sea level and is protected by a system of dykes, is intensively farmed and contains 90 per cent of the population. To the south of this area the land is mountainous, heavily forested and covered with a network of fast-flowing rivers with numerous rapids and falls, including the Kaietur Falls on the Potaro River which is seven times higher than Niagara. There are substantial reserves of bauxite, gold and diamonds in this area. To the south-west along the border with Venezuela is a region of upland savannah, the Rupununi, where the rest of the population, predominantly Amerindian, engages in limited agriculture and cattle-raising.
Hemisphere
Northern.

Climate
The climate is tropical, with a mean monthly temperature of 26–28 degrees Celsius (C) throughout the year on the coast (28 degrees C in the interior). Temperatures of above 32 degrees C or below 24 degrees C at any time of day or any season are rare. Rainfall is between 200–280mm per year on the coast, mainly in two sharply defined wet seasons, May to August and November to January. In the south there is a single rainy season from April to September, but rainfall is lower – averaging 150mm per year.

Dress codes
Among local businessmen the *shirtjac suit* – based upon a civilian version of the bush jacket – is widely worn in preference to the traditional business suit. It is perfectly acceptable to wear an open-necked shirt without a jacket on all but the most formal of occasions, but shorts are frowned upon.

Entry requirements
Passports
Required by all and valid for at least six months beyond intended stay.
Visa
Visas are required by all, except nationals of North America, Western Europe, Australasia, some Asian and all Caricom countries. For full details see: www.guyana.org/govt/visa_requirements.html.
Currency advice/regulations
The import and export of local currency is limited to G$200. The import of foreign currency is unlimited, subject to declaration on arrival; export is limited to amount declared.

Health (for visitors)
Mandatory precautions
A yellow fever vaccination certificate is required if arriving from an infected area.
Advisable precautions
Vaccination against yellow fever is encouraged for travellers to rural areas. There is a risk of malaria in some areas of the interior, and adequate precautions should be taken. Water in urban areas is chlorinated, but typhoid is a risk in rural areas so drinking water should be boiled; bottled water is widely available. Dairy products are likely to be made from unpasteurised milk.
Various hepatitis strains are common. B and D stains are endemic in the Amazon basin and precautions are necessary. Tropical parasites, TB, and dengue fever all occur in certain areas. Professional advice concerning precautions should be sort before travelling to Guyana.
Hospital conditions may not match those in developed countries; health insurance, including repatriation is recommended. Travellers should carry enough prescription and medical supplies for the duration of their stay.

Hotels
Hotels are available in Georgetown, Linden and New Amsterdam. Rooms are generally in short supply. A 10 per cent tip is usual.

Public holidays (national)
Fixed dates
1 Jan (New Year's Day), 23 Feb (Republic Day), 1 May (Labour Day), 5 May (Arrival Day), 26 May (Independence Day), 25–26 Dec (Christmas).
When a public holiday falls on a Sunday, the following Monday is taken as the holiday.
Variable dates
Holi (Hindu, Mar), Good Friday, Easter Monday, Caricom Day (first Mon in Jul), Liberty Day (first Mon in Aug), Diwali

(Hindu, Oct/Nov), Eid al Adha, Birth of the Prophet.
Hindu and Muslim festivals are timed according to local sightings of various phases of the moon.

Working hours

Banking
Mon–Thu: 0800–1230; Fri: 0800–1230, 1500–1700.
Business
Mon–Thu: 0800–1600; Fri: 0800–1200.
Government
Mon–Thu: 0800–1200, 1300–1630; Fri: 0800–1200, 1300–1530.
Shops
Mon–Fri: 0800–1130, 1300–1600; Sat: 0800–1130.

Electricity supply

Electricity supply is not standardised; Georgetown generally 110V AC 60Hz, but some supplies are 220V AC, 50Hz. Elsewhere supply is 110V AC at either 50 or 60 cycles.

Weights and measures

The metric system is official, but imperial measures are often preferred.

Social customs/useful tips

Business is often conducted in a relaxed atmosphere and an emphasis is placed upon personal contact. At the same time, careful observance of polite formalities such as handshaking and formal use of titles (such as Mr, etc) is appreciated. All officials should be treated with careful respect. Attention to detail in the making and keeping of appointments is also appreciated, although punctuality may not be reciprocated.
Invitations to the homes of business contacts are regularly offered since Guyanese pride themselves upon their hospitality. It is customary for visitors to return the invitation in a hotel or to a restaurant.
Hotel and restaurant staff and taxi drivers customarily receive a 10 per cent tip; airport porters are tipped by the bag.

Security

The streets of Georgetown can be unsafe after dark due to street robbery, and the use of taxis is recommended. Ostentatious display of wealth such as expensive wristwatches or jewellery and the carrying of large amounts of cash should be avoided. As in all cities, it is unwise to leave articles unattended in parked cars or hotel rooms.

Getting there

Air
International airport/s: Cheddi Jagan International Airport (GEO), 40km from Georgetown; bank, duty free, restaraunts and car hire.
Airport tax: G$4,000 for international departures; not applicable to transit passengers.

Surface
Road: A coastal road runs from the Suriname border to Georgetown, via a ferry across the Berbice River at New Amsterdam.
Entry from Brazil is possible at Lethem where international border controls are in place. A bridge being constructed across the Takutu river will eventually connect Bonfim in Roraima State (Brazil) to Lethem. There are unsealed roads in current use. There are no road connections to Venezuela.
Water: There is a ferry service between Guyana-Suriname.
Main port/s: Georgetown, New Amsterdam and Springlands.

Getting about

National transport
Air: Air travel is the only efficient method of reaching the interior of the country. Trans Guyana Airways operates both regional and interior flights, but occasionally permits are needed from the ministry of the interior for non-nationals. Early booking is essential.
Charter facilities are available at Georgetown. Larger towns and mining companies have airports or landing strips.
Road: There are all-weather, asphalt roads along the coast and some brick roads inland. A coastal road links Georgetown, Rossignol, New Amsterdam and the Suriname border. Another coast road runs west from Georgetown, via the Demerara River, to Parika. A sealed highway to the Brazilian border via Lethem is in the initial stage of construction; only unsealed roads exist currently.
Buses: Buses are operated privately and run regularly and are generally reliable (although crowded). Services run along the coast. Private *tapir* minibuses, mine buses and bush buses (into the interior) are also available.
Rail: There is no passenger rail service, although some mining companies have private goods lines.
Water: Passenger and cargo vessels travel up the Demerara, Essequibo and Berbice rivers, and also along the coast between the rivers. Ferries link Parika-Bartica on the Essequibo River; Rosignol-New Amsterdam on the Berbice River; Corriverton-Suriname on the Corentyne River. These services include New Amsterdam-Ituni, Georgetown-Bartica, Rosignol-New Amsterdam. River taxis (small wooden boats) service the same areas as the ferries. The taxis are faster and more expensive, they may also be chartered.

City transport
Taxis: Taxis are widely available in major towns and can be found on ranks. They have standard fares for inner city journeys; fares for longer trips should be negotiated in advance. A 10 per cent tip is usual.
For early morning flights from Timehri, make taxi arrangements the previous day.
Buses, trams & metro: Minibuses are a cheap mode of transport. They connect Timehri airport with Georgetown and are safe in the day. At night it is wiser to use a taxi.
Car hire
Car hire facilities are limited. They are available in Georgetown but must be booked well in advance. An international driving licence is required. Traffic drives on the left.

BUSINESS DIRECTORY

The addresses listed below are a selection only. While World of Information makes every endeavour to check these addresses, we cannot guarantee that changes have not been made, especially to telephone numbers and area codes. We would welcome any corrections.

Telephone area codes

The international dialling code (IDD) for Guyana is +592, followed by subscriber's number:

Chambers of Commerce

Berbice Chamber of Commerce, 12 Chapel Street, New Amsterdam, Berbice (tel: 227-6340; fax: 226-4535).

Georgetown Chamber of Commerce and Industry, PO Box 10110, 156 Waterloo Street, North Cummingsburg, Georgetown (tel: 225-5864; fax: 226-3519; e-mail: info@georgetownchamberofcommerce.org).

Banking

Bank of Baroda, Avenue of the Republic & Regent Street, Georgetown (tel: 226-4005).

Bank of Nova Scotia, Regent & Hinck Streets, Georgetown (tel: 640-312; fax: 225-7985).

Citizens Bank Guyana Ltd, 201 Camp & Charlotte Sts, Georgetown (tel: 226-1705/6; fax: 226-1719).

Demerara Bank Ltd, 230 Camp St & South Rd, Georgetown (tel: 225-0610/9; fax 225-0601).

Guyana Bank for Trade & Industry, 47-48 Water Street, Georgetown (tel: 226-8430/9; fax: 227-1612).

Guyana Co-operative Agricultural & Industrial Development Bank, 126 Barrack & Parade Streets, Kingston, Georgetown (tel: 225-8806/9; fax: 226-8260).

Guyana National Co-operative Bank, Lombard & Cornhill Streets, Georgetown (tel: 225-7810/9).

National Bank of Industry & Commerce, 38-40 Water Street, Georgetown (tel: 226-4091/5; fax: 227-2921).

Central bank
Bank of Guyana, 1 Church Street & Avenue of the Republic, PO Box 1003, Georgetown (tel: 226-3250; fax: 227-2965; e-mail: comminications@bankofguyana.org.gy).

Stock exchange
Gasci (Guyana Association of Securities Companies and Intermediaries Incorporated): www.gasci.com

Travel information
Air Services Ltd, Wights Lane, Kingston, Georgetown (tel: 226-1767, 226-5759).

Guyana Overland Tours, PO Box 10173, 6 Avenue of the Republic, Robbstown, Georgetown (tel: 226-9876).

Roraima Airways, 101 Cummings Street, Georgetown (tel: 225-9647; fax: 225-9646).

Tourism Association of Guyana, 228 South Road, Lacytown, Georgetown (tel: 225-0807; fax: 225-0817).

Ministry of tourism
Ministry of Tourism, Industry and Commerce, 229 South Road, Lacytown, Georgetown (tel: 226-8629; fax: 225-9898; e-mail: ministry@mintic.gov.gy).

National tourist organisation offices
Guyana Tourism Office, Sophia Exhibition Complex, Georgetown (tel: 223-6351 fax: 231-6351).

Ministries
Ministry of Agriculture, Regent Road, Bourda, Georgetown (tel: 223-7844; fax: 225-0599; e-mail: moa@sdnp.org.gov.gy).

Ministry of Amerindian Affairs, 236 Thomas and Quamina Streets, Georgetown (tel: 227-5067; fax: 223-1616; e-mail: moaa@networksgy.com).

Ministry of Culture, Youth and Sports, 71 Main Street, Georgetown (tel: 227-7866; fax: 226-8549; e-mail: psmincys@guyana.net.gy).

Ministry of Education, 26 Brickdam, Stabroek, Georgetown (tel: 223-7900; fax: 225-8511; e-mail: moegyweb@yahoo.com).

Ministry of Finance, Main Street, Kingston, Georgetown (tel: 225-6088; fax: 226-1284; e-mail: guyanadmd@solutions2000.net).

Ministry of Fisheries, Crops & Livestock, Regent Road, Bourda, Georgetown (tel: 226-1565; fax: 227-2978; e-mail: minfci@sdnp.org.gy).

Ministry of Foreign Affairs, 254 South Road & New Garden Street, Georgetown (tel: 226-9080; fax: 223-5241; e-mail: minfor@sdnp.org.gy).

Ministry of Foreign Trade, 254 South Road & New Garden Street, Georgetown (tel: 226-1607; fax: 223-0900; e-mail: moftic@moftic.gov.gy).

Ministry of Health and Labour, Brickdam, Stabroek, Georgetown (tel: 226-1560; fax: 225-4505; e-mail: moh@sdnp.org.gy).

Ministry of Home Affairs, Brickdam, Stabroek, Georgetown (tel: 225-7270; fax: 227-4806).

Ministry of Housing and Water, 41 Brickdam, Stabroek, Georgetown (tel: 225-7192; fax: 227-3455; e-mail: housing@guyana.net.gy).

Ministry of Information, Area B Homestretch Avenue, Georgetown (tel: 226-8996; fax: 226-4003; e-mail: gis@sdnp.org.gy).

Ministry of Labour, Human Services and Social Security, 1 Water and Cornhill Streets, Stabroek, Georgetown (tel: 225-0655; fax: 227-1308; e-mail: nrdocgd@sdnp.org.gy).

Ministry of Legal Affairs, 95 Carmichael Street, Georgetown (tel: 223-7355; fax: 227-5419).

Ministry of Local Government and Regional Development, Fort Street, Kingston, Georgetown (tel: 225-8621; fax: 226-5070).

Ministry of Parliamentary Affairs, Office of the President, New Garden Street, Georgetown (tel: 226-6453).

Ministry of Public Service Management, 164 Waterloo Street, Georgetown (tel 227-1193; fax: 227-2700; e-mail: psm@sdnp.org.gy).

Ministry of Transport and Hydraulics, Wights Lane, Kingston, Georgetown (tel: 226-1875; fax: 225-8395; e-mail: minoth@networksgy.com).

Office of the President, New Garden Street, Bourda, Georgetown (tel: 225-1573; 227-3050; e-mail: op-iu@sdnp.org.gy).

Office of the Prime Minister, Wights Lane, Kingston, Georgetown (tel: 226-6695; fax: 226-7573; pmoffice@sdnp.org.gov.gy).

Other useful addresses
Association of Non-Traditional Exporters of Guyana (ANTEG), (tel: 226-0779; fax: 226-1063),

Bauxite Industry Development Co, 71 Main Street, Georgetown (tel: 225-7780; fax: 226-7413).

British High Commission, 44 Main Street, PO Box 10849, Georgetown (tel: 226-5881; fax: 225-0671; e-mail: bhcguyana@networksgy.com).

Caribbean Community Secretariat, PO Box 10827, Turkeyen, Georgetown (tel: 222-0001; fax: 222-0171; e-mail: info@caricom.org).

Consultative Association of Guyanese Industry, East Street, PO Box 10730, Georgetown.

Forest Products Association of Guyana (tel: 226-9848).

Forestry Commission, 1 Water Street, Georgetown (tel: 226-7271; fax: 226-8956; e-mail: forstry@sdnp.org.gy).

Geology and Mines Commission, PO Box 1028, Brickdam, Georgetown (tel: 225-3047; fax: 225-2274; e-mail: ggmc@sdnp.org.gy).

Guyana Broadcasting Corporation, PO Box 10760, Georgetown (tel: 226-9231).

Guyana Embassy (USA), 2490 Tracy Place, NW, Washington DC 20008 (tel: (+1-202) 265-6900; fax: (+1-202) 232-1297; e-mail: guyanaemb@aol.com).

Guyana Export Promotion Council, Sophia National Exhibition Park, Sophia, Georgetown (tel: 225-9443, 227-3394, 226-8526; fax: 226-3400).

Guyana Manufacturers' Association (GMA), 62 Main Street, Georgetown (tel: 227-4295; fax: 227-0670).

Guyana Mining Enterprise Ltd, Linden, Georgetown.

Guyana Office for Investment, Go-Invest, 190 Camp & Church Streets, Georgetown (tel: 225-0658, 227-0653; fax: 225-0655).

Guyana Rice Producers' Association (tel: 226-4411, 227-6957).

Guyana Rice Board, 1-2 Water Street, Georgetown (tel: 226-6822).

Guyana State Corporation, 45-47 Water Street, Georgetown (tel: 226-0530).

Guyana Sugar Corporation, 201 Camp Street, Cummingsburg, PO Box 10547, Georgetown (tel: 226-0571; fax: 225-7274).

Institute of Private Enterprise Development, (IPED), Georgetown (tel: 225-8949, 225-3067, 226-4765).

New Guyana Marketing Corporation, Robb Street, Georgetown.

Omai Gold Mines Limited, 176-D Middle Street, Cummingsburg, Georgetown (tel: 226-8129, 226-5898; fax: 226-6468).

Private Sector Commission (PSC), Georgetown (tel: 225-7170, 64-603; fax: 227-0725).

Public Corporations Secretariat, PO Box 1020, 45-7 Water Street, Georgetown (tel: 226-0536/9).

Shipping Association of Georgetown, 28 Main and Holmes Streets, Georgetown (tel: 226-2632).

United States Embassy, 31 Main Street, Georgetown (tel: 225-4900; fax: 225-8497).

National news agency: GINA (Government Information Agency), Area B Homestretch Ave, D' Urban Backlands, Georgetown (tel: 226-6715; fax: 226-4003; internet: www.gina.gov.gy).

Internet sites

Berbice online newspaper: http://www.berbicenews.com

Guyana News and Information: http://www.guyana.org/

Economic Commission for Latin America and the Caribbean: http://www.eclac.cl/index1.html

Inter-American Development Bank: http://www.iadb.org

Organisation of American States: http://www.oas.org

Latin World: http://www.latinworld.com

Latin Trade Online://www.latintrade.com

Local web directory: http://sdnp.org.gy/guylink.html

Haiti

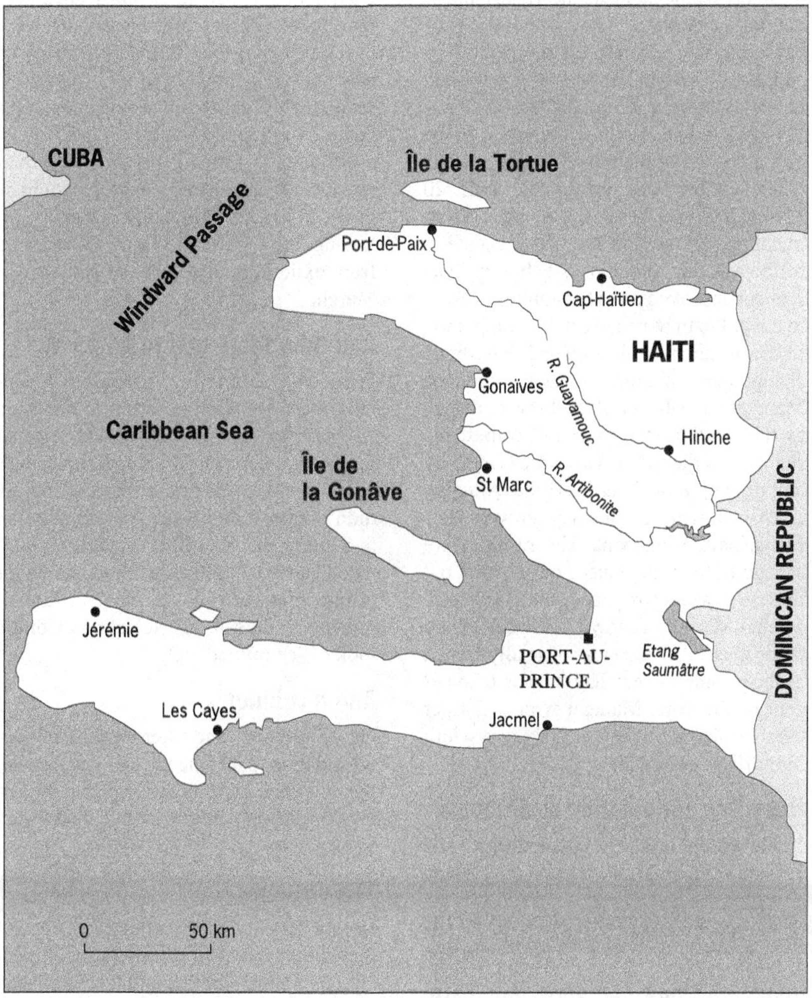

Almost two years after the massive 7.0 point magnitude earthquake struck Port-au-Prince on 13 January 2010, there were still several hundred thousand people camped out in displacement camps around the city, while NGOs and the government argued about whose fault it was and whose responsibility was it to sort it all out. On top of the earthquake, which killed anything from 45,000 to 360,000, depending on who you believed, an outbreak of cholera in refugee camps began in October and killed perhaps another 2,000 persons, with up to 90,000 infected. A row later developed about how the cholera had come to be there. A report published on 7 December 2011, by a French epidemiologist, concluded that UN Nepalese troops were the source of the cholera outbreak; the UN continued to deny a link between the arrival of these troops and the first outbreak of cholera in October 2010.

In December 2010 the Bureau des Avocats Internationaux (BAI), along with the Institute for Justice and Democracy in Haiti, began preparing to sue the UN for introducing the cholera. They are seeking US$100,000 for each person who died as a result of the cholera, and US$50,000 each for those who contacted the disease. As of the end of 2011, the BAI was acting on behalf of 15,000 Haitians. However, all told,

KEY FACTS

Official name: République d'Haiti (Republic of Haiti)

Head of State: President Michel Martelly (from 14 May 2011)

Head of government: Prime Minister Garry Conille (from 5 Sep 2011)

Ruling party: Coalition led by Fwon Lespwa (Front for Hope) (formed 7 June 2006)

Area: 27,750 square km

Population: 9.99 million (2010)*

Capital: Port-au-Prince

Official language: French and Creole

Currency: Gourde (G) = 100 centimes

Exchange rate: G40.35 per US$ (Oct 2011)

GDP per capita: US$373 (2010)

GDP real growth: -5.10% (2010)

GDP: US$6.60 billion (2010)

Inflation: 4.10% (2010)

Balance of trade: -US$1.48 billion (2009)

* estimated figure

there were some 6,900 deaths, and 500,000 who were infected, which would make this one of the largest claims for damages ever brought against the UN.

Rebuilding Haiti

By 17 March 2010, the government estimated that US$11.5 billion would be needed to rebuild the country. A donor meeting held on 31 March pledged US$9.9 billion in immediate and long-term aid for reconstruction in Haiti. Long-term plans included environmental reconstruction and agricultural recovery and services and help for the maimed. In July the IMF announced it had agreed to cancel Haiti's US$268 million debt and would lend a further US$60 million. Within months the estimated cost of rebuilding had risen to US$14 billion.

Elections

Election campaigning for parliament and the presidency got underway in August 2010. Presidential elections were held on 28 November, amid some international criticism that free and fair elections could not be ensured given the disruption caused by the earthquake in January; 12 of the 18 candidates denounced the elections as fraudulent. In the parliamentary elections held at the same time, political parties had formed and merged to back individual presidential candidates. The new Inité (Unity) won 33 seats (out of 99), Alternative pour le Progrés (Altnativ) (Alternative for Progress and Democracy) 14, Ansanm Nou Fò nine, L'Ayiti an Aksyon (AAA) (Haiti in Action) eight and Lavni Organisation (Lavni) seven. There were reports of general mismanagement, with vote stuffing by some officials, and violence in voting stations. However, on 29 November observers from the OAS declared the elections valid, despite 'serious irregularities' which were not reason enough to cancel the election.

On 7 December, election officials announced that Jude Celestin and Mirlande Manigat would contest the runoff presidential election. The announcement caused violent protests in the capital by supporters of Michel Martelly who had narrowly missed the runoff. On 26 January 2011 Jude Celestin withdrew from the second round of the presidential election.

The runoff was postponed until 20 March 2011, which meant an added complication as President Preval's mandate in office was due to end on 7 February. Parliament approved an extension to 14 May, to cover the time necessary for completion of the presidential election and the official change-over of administration. Mirlande Manigat and Michel Martelly were named as the candidates who would contest the runoff – neither of the two were backed by any of the political parties (Inité, Altnativ, AAA or Lavni) that had earlier won seats in the new parliament. The results were scheduled to be announced on 16 April, but these too were postponed, until 21 April. Michel Martelly (known as Sweet Micky in his musical career) was officially named as the president-elect, having won 67.6 per cent of the vote, Manigat won 31.74 per cent. President Michel Martelly was sworn into office on 14 May.

Baby Doc and Aristide come home

In the middle of all the electioneering and earthquake rebuilding, Jean-Claude 'Baby Doc' Duvalier returned to Haiti from exile in France on 16 January 2011, 25 years after being overthrown by a popular revolt. He was immediately charged with corruption and embezzlement on 18 January and a day later the former UN spokeswoman, Michele Montas, and three other Haitians brought a suit of torture against him. Duvalier denied all accusations. On 2 February, Swiss banks froze his assets – however he claimed the US$6 million involved was not his, but belonged to a foundation set up by his family and should be released and used to rebuild Haiti.

Officials said on 1 February that former president Jean-Bertrand Aristide would be given a Haitian diplomatic passport, allowing him to return to Haiti. He returned from exile in South Africa to Haiti on 18 March.

And then there had to be a PM

President Martelly proposed Daniel-Gerard Rouzier as prime minister on 21 May. On 21 June parliament rejected his nomination. On 4 July, Rouzier was again proposed as prime minister, but he didn't make it this time either. Finally, on 5 September, President Martelly nominated Garry Conille as his third choice for prime minister and parliament unanimously endorsed his selection. Conille took office immediately.

And a cabinet

On 15 October and after months of procrastination parliament finally approved the new cabinet proposed by Prime Minister Conille, and Haiti was able to get back to business.

The economy

Before the cholera epidemic, according to the United Nations Economic Commission for Latin America and the Caribbean (ECLAC), the economic prospects for 2011 looked good: GDP growth was expected to be 9 per cent; there was strong recovery in the farming, construction and maquila sectors; and larger disbursements of external aid. However, the public health challenge now facing the country may necessitate a reallocation of resources and thus affect the previous outlook.

The main macroeconomic indicators yielded less gloomy results for 2010 than had initially been expected. The public sector deficit, calculated on an accrual basis, stood at 2.9 per cent of GDP (0.3 per cent in 2009), and cumulative inflation in the 12 months to September was 4.7 per cent. A moderate increase in exports (3.2

KEY INDICATORS — Haiti

	Unit	2006	2007	2008	2009	2010
Population	m	8.48	*8.63	8.78	*8.94	*9.99
Gross domestic product (GDP)	US$bn	4.66	5.90	6.60	6.60	6.60
GDP per capita	US$	550	679	748	733	673
GDP real growth	%	2.3	3.3	0.8	2.9	-5.1
Inflation	%	14.2	9.0	14.4	3.4	4.1
Exports (fob) (goods)	US$m	384.0	522.1	490.2	551.0	–
Imports (fob) (goods)	US$m	1,329.0	-1,704.2	-2,107.8	-2,032.1	–
Balance of trade	US$m	-945.0	-1,182.1	-1,617.6	-1,481.1	–
Current account	US$m	-19.0	-477.4	-762.6	-626.6	-155.0
Total reserves minus gold	US$m	253.1	443.2	541.4	788.6	1,335.0
Foreign exchange	US$m	245.1	435.6	534.3	680.4	1,228.8
Exchange rate	per US$	37.65	36.75	39.11	41.20	39.80

* estimated figure

per cent) was offset by a surge in imports (33 per cent), considerably widening the trade deficit (by 48 per cent, to 43 per cent of GDP). However, current transfers in the form of remittances and grants (US$3.18 billion) yielded a surplus equivalent to 4.3 per cent of GDP on the balance-of-payments current account. The capital account benefited from external debt forgiveness programmes aimed at assisting the country's reconstruction effort. Government spending fell short of its mark owing in part to a deliberate cost-containment effort, but mainly because of administrative, physical and personnel constraints throughout the public sector. Start-up delays at some key bodies, among them the Interim Haiti Recovery Commission and the Multi-Donor Trust Fund, hindered programme and project implementation in a few instances. Another crucial factor was the relatively slow disbursement of international funds for the reconstruction work (just US$900 million, or 42 per cent of the amount agreed on for the 2010 fiscal year).

Public-sector initiatives, involving funds from the PetroCaribe programme and the government's own resources, prioritised the areas of agriculture, education and health care, with programmes totalling US$212 million. The education sector received two thirds of this amount, in the form of direct spending and subsidies that were used to reopen some schools in April, rebuild classrooms and set up alternative facilities. As many people had to relocate to provincial towns and rural areas, the government pursued a strategy of building capacity in the farm sector to prevent further deterioration of living conditions in these areas.

The positive performance of the agricultural sector (which had suffered little direct impact from the earthquake and benefited from recovery measures in 2008 and 2009), the rapid recovery of the *maquila* export industry and incipient debris removal, rehabilitation and reconstruction activities helped to avert a greater decline in GDP.

The international prices of greatest significance to the Haitian economy, i.e., those of hydrocarbons and food, rose by 19 per cent and 8 per cent, respectively, but those increases were not passed through in full to local consumers and were offset by the international humanitarian assistance received and the stronger exchange rate. Consequently, general inflation (September to September) stood at only 4.7 per cent, while food price inflation was 5 per cent.

Employment policy was oriented towards labour-intensive programmes having a humanitarian slant (such as the cash-for-work programme). These programmes, which were implemented by various international co-operation agencies, were designed to restore a minimum level of consumption in the most vulnerable households; they focused on low-skill activities and ensured a rotation of beneficiaries. Temporary jobs of a more formal nature were created in service provision areas associated with the activities financed by the international community. Nonetheless, it is quite likely that the earthquake has led to a net loss of skilled jobs as professional and technical workers emigrated abroad taking advantage of the facilities provided by different countries.

Risk assessment

Economy	Recovering
Politics	Fair
Regional stability	Good

COUNTRY PROFILE

Historical profile

1492 Christopher Columbus landed and named the island Hispaniola, or 'little Spain'.
1496 The Spanish established the first European settlement in the Western hemisphere at Santo Domingo, now the capital of the Dominican Republic.
1697 The island of Hispaniola was divided between France and Spain. The western half became Haiti (Land of Mountains).
1801 A former black slave, Toussaint Louverture, led a guerrilla rebellion, conquering Haiti, abolishing slavery and proclaiming himself governor general of all Hispaniola. He was captured by the French and died in their custody.
1804 Independence was declared by former slave Jean-Jacques Dessalines, who declared himself emperor. There were various monarchical periods until 1859.
1806 Dessalines was assassinated and Haiti became divided into the black-controlled north and the mulatto-controlled south.
1818–43 Pierre Boyer unified Haiti, but excluded blacks from power.
1915 The US invaded Haiti claiming it was protecting its property and investments threatened by clashes between blacks and mulattos.
1934 The US withdrew its troops.
1956 François 'Papa Doc' Duvalier, a voodoo physician, seized power in a military coup and became president in the following year.
1964 Duvalier declared himself president-for-life and established a dictatorship with the help of the violent Tontons Macoute militias.
1971 Duvalier died and was succeeded by his son, the 19-year-old Jean-Claude 'Baby Doc' Duvalier, who declared himself president-for-life.
1986 Baby Doc fled Haiti amid riots and a multitude of coup attempts. Lieutenant General Henri Namphy assumed power as the head of a governing junta.
1988 Leslie Manigat became president but was overthrown in a coup led by Brigadier General Prosper Avril, who installed a civilian government under military control.
1990 Jean-Bertrand Aristide was elected president.
1991 Aristide was expelled from the country following a military coup headed by Brigadier-General Raoul Cedras. The new junta promised elections at a future date. The US, France and Canada suspended aid to Haiti and refused to recognise the new government.
1993 The UN imposed sanctions on Haiti after the military regime rejected an accord designed to facilitate Aristide's return to power.
1994 After US forces removed the military government of General Raoul Cedras, Aristide returned from exile and was reinstalled as president. He was not permitted by law to stand for re-election in 1995.
1995 René Preval was elected to replace Aristide.
1997 US troops left Haiti. Prime Minister Rosny Smarth resigned.
1999 President Préval dissolved the legislature and a Provisional Electoral Council (CEP) was created to organise elections; Jacques Eduard Aléxis was appointed prime minister and a government was sworn in.
2000 The Fanmi Lavalas (FL) (Lavalas Family) party won control of the Senate and President Jean-Bertrand Aristide won the controversial presidential election.
2001 President Aristide appointed Jean-Marie Chéréstal as prime minister. Aristide agreed to hold new parliamentary elections in return for the OAS helping Haiti to receive the US$500 million of suspended aid. There was an unsuccessful coup attempt.
2002 Prime Minister Chéréstal resigned amid allegations of corruption and incompetence. Aristide appointed Yvon Neptune as prime minister. Government and opposition factions clashed violently, with attacks by government loyalists on civic groups and armed anti-government gangs.
2004 Opposition rebels, led by Guy Philippe, won control of several towns. President Aristide resigned and left the country; Chief Justice Boniface Alexandre was sworn in as caretaker president. The

UN approved a multi-national security force to restore law and order. Gérard Latortue became prime minister and a government of national unity was sworn in. Hurricane Mitch devastated large areas and left a death toll of around 2,000. UN forces assumed Haiti peacekeeping duties. Hurricane Jeanne swept through Haiti, killing as many as 1,500 Haitians.
2006 Presidential and legislative elections, postponed since 2005, finally took place and former president René Préval won. Fwon Lespwa (Lespwa) (Front de l'Espoir) won the largest share of votes in parliamentary elections in both the Senate and the Chamber of Deputies. Jacques-Edouard Alexis became prime minister and formed a six-party coalition cabinet under Lespwa leadership.
2008 Prime Minister Alexis lost support in the Senate following widespread rioting over soaring food prices and the perceived lack of government action to increase national food production. Both houses of parliament accepted President Préval's third nomine, Michèle Pierre-Louis, as prime minister. A series of two tropical storms, Hanna and Fay, and two hurricanes, Gustav and Ike, collectively killed over 800 Haitians and left more than one million homeless. The hurricanes were estimated to have caused almost US$1 billion in demage.
2009 Swiss banks agreed to return the frozen assets of former dictator Jean-Claude Duvalier. The US$6 million, sequestered since 1986, will be used on development projects. An aid package of US$324 million was agreed by international donors to help Haiti recover from the damage and food shortages caused by the 2008 storm damage. Prime Minister Pierre-Louis lost a vote of no-confidence in parliament and was dismissed; parliament unanimously voted for Jean-Max Bellerive as her replacement.
2010 A massive 7.0 point magnitude earthquake struck on 13 January, centred close to the capital, Port au Prince, causing extensive damage and loss of life. According to the Red Cross, around three million people were in need of initial aid. Officials reported that there were over 230,000 confirmed deaths and 1.5 million homeless. By 17 March, the government estimated that US$11.5 billion would be needed to rebuild the country. Following a donor meeting held on 31 March, US$9.9 billon was pledged in immediate and long-term aid for reconstruction in Haiti. The money to be provided in three stages, with the first focussing on rebuilding infrastructure, government buildings, hospitals and schools. Long-term plans included environmental reconstruction and agricultural recovery and services and help for the maimed. In July the IMF announced it had agreed to cancel Haiti's US$268 million debt and would lend a further US$60 million. Former prime minister, Marc Louis Bazin, who was known as 'Mr Clean' for his attempts to improve the lot of ordinary Haitians during his term as interim prime minister in 1992–93, died in August. Election campaigning for parliament and the presidency got underway in August. An outbreak of cholera in refugee camps began in October and officials confirmed it had reached Port au Prince by 10 November. The number of deaths and infection grew steadily and by December had killed over 2,000 people and infected a further 90,000. A cholera awareness campaign was initiated. Local people attacked UN and relief workers in November accusing them of bringing cholera to Haiti. Aid flights and water purification projects around the country were suspended until order could be restored. Presidential elections were held on 28 November, amid some international criticism that free and fair elections could not be ensured given the disruption caused by the earthquake in January; 12 of the 18 candidates denounced the elections as fraudulent. In the parliamentary elections held at the same time, political parties had formed and merged to back individual presidential candidates. The new Inité (Unity) won 33 seats (out of 99), Alternative pour le Progrés (Altnativ) (Alternative for Progress and Democracy) 14, Ansanm Nou Fò nine, L'Ayiti an Aksyon (AAA) (Haiti in Action) eight and Lavni Organisation (Lavni) seven. There were reports of voters unable to cast a vote as their names were missing from voter-lists, general mismanagement, with vote stuffing by some officials, and violence in voting stations. However, on 29 November observers from the OAS declared the elections were valid, despite 'serious irregularities' which were not reason enough to cancel the election. On 7 December, a French epidemiologist concluded that Nepalese troops were the source of the cholera outbreak; the UN continued to deny a link between the arrival of these troops and the first outbreak of cholera, in October. On 7 December, election officials announced that Jude Celestin and Mirlande Manigat would contest the runoff presidential election. The announcement caused violent protests in the capital by supporters of Michel Martelly who had narrowly missed the runoff.
2011 Jean-Claude 'Baby Doc' Duvalier returned to Haiti from exile in France on 16 January, 25 years after being overthrown by a popular revolt. On 18 January state prosecutors charged him with corruption and embezzlement. A day later the former UN spokeswoman Michele Montas and three other Haitians brought a suit of torture against him. Duvalier denied all accusations. Jude Celestin withdrew from the second round of the presidential election on 26 January. Officials said on 1 February that former president Jean-Bertrand Aristide would be given a Haitian diplomatic passport, allowing him to return to Haiti. On 2 February, Swiss banks froze the assets of Jean-Claude Duvalier, however he claimed the US$6 million involved was not his, but belonged to a foundation set up by his family and should be released and used to rebuild Haiti. Artistide returned from exile in South Africa to Haiti on 18 March. The elections were postponed until 20 March. As President Preval's mandate in office was due to end on 7 February, parliament approved an extension to 14 May, to cover the time necessary for completion of the presidential election and the official change-over of administration. Jude Celestin was dropped by Lespwa as its candidate. Mirlande Manigat and Michel Martelly were named as the candidates that would contest the runoff presidential election. Poling in some constituencies had been re-run, which caused further postponement of the run-off presidential elections, which were finally held on 20 March. The results were scheduled to be announced on 16 April but were finally declared on 21 April. Michel Martelly, (known as 'Sweet Micky' in his musical career) was officially named as the president-elect, having won 67.6 per cent of the vote, Manigat 31.74 per cent. None of the new political parties, Inité, Altnativ, AAA or Lavni that won seats in the new parliament had backed either of the two run-off presidential candidates. President Michel Martelly was sworn into office on 14 May. He proposed Daniel-Gerard Rouzier as prime minister on 21 May. A USAID report was leaked to the media in May, which stated that there had been significantly fewer deaths, of 46,000–85,000 during the 2010 earthquake and not 361,000 as previously estimated. However, it also stated that the majority of survivors were still living in tent cities 18 months later. The report used a door-to-door survey carried out over most of January. On 21 June parliament rejected Rouzier's nomination as prime minister. On 4 July, Rouzier was again proposed as prime minister. On 5 September, President Martelly nominated Garry Conille as his third choice for prime minister and parliament unanimously endorsed his selection. Conille took office immediately. Hundreds of demonstrators protesting in Port-au-Prince on 14 September against the UN peace-keeping force, demanding that it be removed, were dispersed by security forces. On 15

October and after months of procrastination parliament finally approved the new cabinet proposed by Prime Minister Conille.

Political structure

Constitution
Under the 1987 constitution, executive power is held by an elected president, serving a five-year term, and a cabinet of ministers.
Independence date
1 January 1804
Form of state
Republic
The executive
The president is elected for a five-year term by universal suffage. A president may be elected for a maximum of two, non-continuous terms. The prime minister is appointed by the president whose decision is ratified by the senate.
National legislature
The bicameral Assemblée Nationale (National Assembly) consists of the Chambre des Députés (House of Representatives) (lower house) with 99 members elected every four years in single-seat constituencies, and a 30-member Sénat (Senate) (upper house), elected for six years (one-third renewed every two years) in single-seat constituencies.
Legal system
Haiti's judicial system is based on the French Napoleonic Code. Judges are appointed by the president. The supreme court is the Court de Cassation, which may make rulings on constitutional matters. There is a court of appeal and civil courts in the major administrative centres.
Last elections
28 November 2010 (parliamentary and senate (10 seats), presidential, first round); 20 March 2011 (presidential runoff).
Results: Parliamentary: political parties formed and merged to back individual presidential candidates.
Chamber of Deputies: Inité (Unity) won 33 seats (out of 99), Alternative pour le Progrés (Altnativ) (Alternative for Progress and Democracy) 14, Ansanm Nou Fò nine, L'Ayiti an Aksyon (AAA) (Haiti in Action) eight, Lavni Organisation (Lavni) seven; 11 other political parties and two independent candidates shared the remaining 37 seats and none won more that four seats. Senate (10 seats in contention): Altnativ won three seats, Inity three, Lavni one (other seats unknown).
Presidential: Second round: Martelly won 67.57 per cent of the vote, Manigat 31.74 per cent.
Next elections
2015 (Chamber of Deputies and presidential); 2013 (senate 10 seats)

Political parties

Ruling party
Coalition led by Fwon Lespwa (Front for Hope) (formed 7 June 2006)

Population

9.99 million (2010)*
Last census: January 2003: 8,373,750
Population density: 283 inhabitants per square km. Urban population: 36 per cent (1994–2000).
Annual growth rate: 1.4 per cent 1994–2004 (WHO 2006)
Ethnic make-up
Approximately 95 per cent are Afro-Caribbean; the remainder are white or of mixed race.
Religions
Roman Catholic (80 per cent), Protestant (16 per cent). Around half the population also practices voodoo, an African-derived belief.

Education

Only 20 per cent of the population complete primary schooling which is theoretically compulsory and the pass rate for secondary school exams is 7–8 per cent. Secondary education is provided by the state and *lycées* (private secondary schools). There are also vocational training and domestic science establishments. There is a state-run university and an administration and management institute (which offers courses in medical subjects, agricultural and veterinary sciences, law, economics and ethnology) and an Institute of Administration and Management.
Literacy rate: 52 per cent adult rate; 66 per cent youth rate (15–24) (Unesco 2005).
Compulsory years: 6 to 15.
Enrolment rate: 64 per cent total primary school enrolment of the relevant age group (including repetition rates) (World Bank).
Pupils per teacher: 35 in primary schools.

Health

According to the UN's food aid agency, in 2006, over 50 per cent of women suffer from anaemia, most of which is often caused by insufficient iron in their generally poor diet, plus worm infestation and malaria. The percentage of pregnant women suffering from anaemia is even higher at two out of three and is the leading cause of spontaneous miscarriage and infant mortality during delivery.
An outbreak of cholera in refugee camps had, by December 2010, killed over 2,000 people and infected a further 90,000. A cholera awareness campaign was initiated, urging everyone to boil food and water, avoid raw vegetables and wash their hands regularly with soap. By January 2012, around 7,000 people were reported to have died of the disease.
HIV/Aids
HIV/Aids has become a leading cause of death, and urban infection rates are over twice the number of rural population infection rates.
For the first time, in June 2004, a joint mission was undertaken by the UN and UNAids, who have sent teams into the field with peacekeepers, in an attempt to limit HIV in a conflict zone. This initiative is designed to pre-empt the spread of the desease before the main contingent of peacekeepers arrive. There are fears that as 1 in 20 Haitians are HIV positive and with the arrival of a peacekeeping force with an almost inevitable sex-industry that will develop, Haiti could become a flashpoint of transmission. UNAids provides condoms, education and testing services to the peacekeepers.
HIV prevalence: 5.6 per cent aged 15–49 in 2003 (World Bank).
Life expectancy: 55 years, 2004 (WHO 2006)
Fertility rate/Maternal mortality rate: 3.9 births per woman, 2004 (WHO 2006)
Birth rate/Death rate: 34 births per 1,000 population; 13.4 deaths per 1,000 population (2003).
Child (under 5 years) mortality rate (per 1,000): 76 per 1,000 live births (World Bank)

Welfare

Since 80 per cent of Haiti's population live below the poverty line and its social and economic indicators remain far lower than the average for Latin America and the Caribbean, the country is not eligible for the IMF's Heavily Indebted Poor Countries (HIPC) debt relief initiative.
In the public sector, still only 20 per cent of resources go to rural areas, where approximately two-thirds of the people live. Poor welfare provision is one factor which causes migration both from the countryside to the capital and out of the country. As many as 330,000 Haitians are thought to be living in the US.
Incidences of crime and violence are very high in Haiti. The strengthening of the Haitian police force with improvements in the penal system is likely to improve the situation. The government will need to spread the cost of maintaining social welfare services including those on education, health, water, sanitation and family planning with private sectors.

Main cities

Port-au-Prince (capital, estimated population 1.2 million in 2005), Carrefour (438,057), Delmas (375,218), Cap Haïtien (134,163), Pétionville (106,369).

Languages spoken

Official language/s

French and Creole

Media

Freedom of the press was a casualty of political instability, nevertheless, as the situation improved self-censorship has remained as journalists avoided reporting on politicians and commercial sponsors.

Press

Dailies: In French, private newspapers include *Le Nouvelliste* (www.lenouvelliste.com) and *Le Matin* (www.lematinhaiti.com).

Weeklies: In French, *Haiti Progrès* (www.haiti-progres.com) has online editions in English and Creole. In English Haitian Times (www.haitiantimes.com).

Business: In French, *Haiti en Marche* (www.haitienmarche.com) is a weekly newspaper.

Broadcasting

The Conseil National des Télécommunications (www.conatel.gouv.ht) is responsible for broadcasting regulations. The national, public broadcaster is Radio Télévision Nationale d'Haiti (RTNH).

Radio: With a low literacy rate radio is the principal medium for news and information. There are over 250 radio stations in operation in both private and public service. The government-owned Radio Nationale d'Haiti (www.radionationalehaiti.net) broadcasts in French. Private, independent radio stations include Radyo Atlantik (www.atlantikhaiti.com), Radio Metropole Haiti (www.metropolehaiti.com) and Signal FM (www.signalfmhaiti.com).

Television: Télévision Nationale D'Haiti (www.tnh.ht) has a tie-in with the pay-to-view Jump-TV, the international TV cable and satellite service. Private, commercial TV stations include Télé-Haiti (www.telehaitionline.com), which is a cable station relaying captured satellite signals on four channels, Tele Quisqueya Saint-Marc (TQ) (www.haitipal.com/tq) and PVS Antenne.

News agencies

National news agency: Agence Haitienne de Presse

Other news agencies: Caribbean Net News: www.caribbeannetnews.com

Haiti Press Network (in French): www.haitipressnetwork.com

Economy

Before the devastating earthquake that struck close to the capital, Port au Prince, in the centre of Haiti on 13 January 2010, it was deemed the poorest country in the western hemisphere. After the massive 7.0-magnitude earthquake struck, the country lost vital infrastructure including parliament and government buildings, roads, bridges, the presidential palace and homes for around 1.5 million people, its prospects fell further. In the aftermath of the destruction that killed around 230,000 people and injured a further 311,000, international aid and assistance, spearheaded by the US, was quickly provided for the most immediately needy. Within weeks, a donor meeting was held on 31 March, where a total of US$9.9 billon was pledged in short and long-term aid for reconstruction of Haiti. The money was to be provided in three stages, with the first focussing on rebuilding infrastructure, government buildings, hospitals and schools. Long-term plans include environmental reconstruction and agricultural recovery and services and help for the maimed.

In July 2010 the World Bank reported that of the initial US$5.3 billion pledged for reconstruction by 2012, only US$103 million had been paid with pledges from 10 countries and the European Commission awaiting payment following approval from their budgetary systems. The Inter-American Development Bank and the Water and Sanitation Spanish Co-operation Fund are providing an initial US$35 million to repair reservoirs and pumping stations and refurbish and expand Port au Prince's drinking water and sanitation system, as well as construct water projects in rural communities. Further grants will be provided to combat waterborne diseases.

In July 2010 the IMF announced it had agreed to cancel Haiti's US$268 million debt and would lend a further US$60 million.

Before the earthquake, three-quarters of the population lived below the poverty line, of which 50 per cent subsisted on less than US$1 a day. Subsequently, the extreme poverty rate increased to 71 per cent, according to the March 2010 draft report by the United Nations Economic Commission for Latin America and the Caribbean (Eclac), which determined 15 per cent of the population were homeless and the total damage caused by the earthquake was estimated at US$7.8 billion, equivalent to over 120 per cent of 2009 GDP.

High unemployment has been a long-term problem, with a typical rate of 65 per cent. With the destruction of so many businesses, unemployment has inevitably grown. Remittances in 2009 were estimated at US$1.3 billion, down from US$1.4 billion in 2008 (20.3 per cent of GDP), as the global economic crisis limited the opportunities of workers aboard. Haiti's public sector was in disarray and the country's infrastructure network badly fragmented and in need of significant investment even before the earthquake, so that the work to be undertaken will provide the opportunity to provide a better environment for the population and economic growth. However, government has been disbanded and power contracted into the hands of the president and his cabinet; reconstruction was slow to begin and accusations of corruption and favouritism (with work seemingly only going to those with connections to the administration) have been levelled at the regime of President Préval as overcrowded refugee camps take-on a state of permanence.

External trade

Although Haiti is member of the Caribbean Community (Caricom), it did not adopt the single market and economy (CSME), which was ratified by 12 other member states in 2006.

The main Haitian port and secondary port facilities along the coast from Port-au-Prince were damaged in the January 2010 earthquake. Two piers in the capital's port collapsed and containers fell into the harbour. Imports and exports by sea will be hampered until work to clear-up and re-construct the damaged facilities are completed. Likewise, roads and bridges were damaged along with business premises and electrical installations, all of which need repair or replacement before Haiti returns to pre-earthquake productivity.

In May 2010 the US extended its conditions for favourable trade preferences for Haiti, giving it greater access to US markets and prolonging the current duty-free access.

Imports

Main imports are foodstuffs, manufactured goods, machinery and transport equipment, fuels and raw materials. Post-earthquake imports include construction materials, communications equipment and primary products, such as food and fuels.

Main sources: US (typically 34 per cent of total), Dominican Republic (23 per cent), Netherlands Antilles (11 per cent).

Exports

Main exports are clothing, mangoes, manufactured goods, leather and raw hides, seafood and cocoa.

Main destinations: US (typically 71 per cent of total), Dominican Republic (9 per cent), Canada (3 per cent).

Agriculture

Farming

Before the 2010 earthquake, agriculture accounted for around 27 per cent of GDP and employs two-thirds of the working population. The main cash crops are coffee, sisal and sugar.

An estimated 47 per cent of the total land area is cultivated and 20 per cent is pasture. Subsistence farming and animal husbandry predominate. Only 10 per cent of cultivation is carried out on large plantations. Maize, rice, sorghum, millet, beans, fruit and vegetables are grown. Production is largely outside the cash economy. Recurrent drought, insufficient irrigation, low producer prices and a weak infrastructure have kept production levels down and necessitated the import of foodstuffs, particularly cereals.

Fishing

The total annual fish catch is typically around 5,000 tonnes, three-quarters of which is through marine fishing. Around 10 per cent is exported.

Forestry

Forests cover around 88,000 hectares (ha) or 1 per cent of the total land area. This compares to around 40 per cent of land area in 1940. Deforestation is causing serious soil erosion and desertification. The rapid decline of the forests is partly due to the demand for fuel wood. There are no large-scale forest industries. The local demand for industrial wood and paper products is mainly met by imports.

Industry and manufacturing

Before the earthquake, there was production in traditional food processing, construction and textile industries, and there was an important artisan manufacturing sector producing handicrafts, such as baskets, leather goods, brushes, and rugs.

Manufacturing operations are concentrated in electronic and electrical equipment, sporting goods, toys and garments. Haiti was the world's leading producer of baseballs and one of the Caribbean's largest suppliers of garments and electronic components to the US market.

There is very little production for local consumption.

Mining

The mining and export of bauxite ceased in 1983 with the closure of Reynolds mine at Miragoane. There are known, but not commercially viable, deposits of copper, silver, gold, marble, lignite and natural asphalt.

Hydrocarbons

Haiti relies on imported petroleum products to meet domestic demand, which was over 12,000 barrels per day in 2007. Most of this is supplied by Mexico and Venezuela, which sell oil to 11 Caribbean and Central American countries on favourable terms under the San José Pact of 1980.

Any use of import natural gas or coal is commercially insignificant.

Energy

Total installed generating capacity is over 220MW, of which over two-thirds is produced by thermal power stations and the remainder by hydropower, although dry seasons can limit production. The electricity supply is restricted to main towns as the country lacks a national power grid. Power cuts are experienced on a regular basis, as the purchase of imported petroleum is restricted by foreign-exchange shortages. Local wood provides three-quarters of total domestic energy and is a major cause of deforestation and soil erosion.

Financial markets

Stock exchange

Haitian Stock Exchange

Banking and insurance

The banking sector is underdeveloped and in disarray. The crowding out of private sector credit has undermined the banks' ability to function as an important part of the economy. Few people have bank accounts and the large informal sector and black market tends to keep the savings ratio and therefore banks' capital at low levels.

Central bank

Banque Nationale de la République d'Haiti

Main financial centre

Port-au-Prince

Time

GMT minus five hours.

Geography

Haiti occupies the western part of the Caribbean island of Hispaniola (the Dominican Republic occupies the remaining two-thirds), and some smaller offshore islands. Cuba is to the west and is less than 80km away.

Much of Haiti's land area is covered by mountains, which rise up to about 3,000 metres. Environmental damage caused primarily by population pressure has reduced the area of forests to about 6–8 per cent of land area. A number of rivers flow vigorously during the rainy season only, and there are large lakes in the centre of the country close to the border with the Dominican Republic.

Hemisphere

Northern

Climate

Year-round temperatures in Port-au-Prince varies only slightly from 24–27 degrees Celsius (C). The rainy season is from May–November. The climate is tropical, with the rainy seasons in October–November and May–June. May is the wettest month (231mm average rainfall) and December to February the driest and coldest. Temperatures vary from around 22 degrees C on the coast in January to 34 degrees C in July.

Dress codes

Jackets (tropical weight) and ties are normally worn for business. Swimwear is only worn at beaches and pools. Dresses of at least knee-length are recommended for women.

Entry requirements

Passports

Passports are required by all and must have at least six months validity beyond the date of departure. Proof of return/onward passage is required.

Visa

Required by all. Business and tourist visas are not required by citizens of North America or Argentina.

Business visitors from other destinations should supply a letter of introduction from their company and proof of sufficient funds for length of stay. For further information contact the nearest embassy.

Currency advice/regulations

There are no restrictions on the import or export of foreign or local currency. Nevertheless, amounts over G200,000 should be declared.

Travellers cheques are widely accepted, however it is difficult in banks, hotels and shops to exchange foreign currency other than US dollars.

Health (for visitors)

The rate of HIV/Aids is high and precautions should always be taken.

Mandatory precautions

Yellow fever vaccination is required if arriving from an infected area.

Anti-malaria precautions are essential.

Tap water is not safe to drink, and therefore ice, salads, raw vegetables and unpeeled fruits are suspect.

Advisable precautions

Inoculations against typhoid, polio and tetanus are recommended. Malaria prophylaxis and a mosquito net may be necessary. There is a very high prevalence of HIV/Aids. Use only bottled or boiled water for drinks, washing teeth and be wary of ice in restaurants. Eat only well cooked meals, preferably served hot; vegetables should be cooked and fruit peeled.

Medical facilities are very limited and offer a poor standard of care. Adequate supplies of essential medicines should be carried by visitors, with their prescription details. Local emergency services are inadequate, so full travel insurance, which includes emergency medical evacuation, should be obtained.

Hotels

There is not a good range of accommodation, the best hotels are in the capital and in tourist resorts. Hotels are fully booked during Carnival. There is a government tax of 10 per cent and hotels add a 5 per cent service charge to bills.

Credit cards

Major credit cards are accepted.

Public holidays (national)
Fixed dates
1 Jan (Independence Day), 2 Jan (Ancestors' Day), 14 Apr (Pan American Day), 1 May (Labour Day), 18 May (Flag and University Day), 15 Aug (Assumption Day), 17 Oct (Dessalines Day), 24 Oct (United Nations Day), 1 Nov (All Saints' Day), 2 Nov (All Souls' Day), 18 Nov (Vertières Battle Day), 25 Dec (Christmas Day).
Variable dates
Carnival (two days, Feb), Ash Wednesday, Good Friday (Mar/Apr), Ascension Day, Corpus Christi (May/Jun).

Working hours
Banking
Mon–Fri: 0900–1300, 1500–1700; Sat: 0900–1300.
Business
Mon–Fri: 0800–1600. (Visits are best arranged between November–March).
Government
Mon–Fri: 0800–1400.

Telecommunications
Mobile/cell phones
There is a 850 GSM service in operation.

Electricity supply
110-220V AC

Weights and measures
Officially the metric system is in force but many US measures are also used.

Social customs/useful tips
Careful observance of polite formalities such as handshaking, direct eye contact, formal use of titles such as Monsieur, etc, is essential, and offence may be taken if they are not observed. All officials should be treated with careful respect.

Security
Crime is widespread and often violent. The kidnapping of foreign nationals for ransom money is increasingly common. Random shootings, during robbery, has become more common, and pickpockets are numerous. Do not leave property in vehicles and always travel with doors locked and windows up. Armed hold-ups of vehicles take place, even in daylight, in busy parts of Port-au-Prince.
Some areas of Port-au-Prince should be avoided at all times. Whenever possible avoid going out after dark.
Whenever possible leave documents in a safety deposit box.

Getting there
Air
National airline: Haiti Trans Air offers limited flights to the US.
International airport/s: Port-au-Prince International Airport (PAP), 10km from city; duty-free shop, bar, bank, car hire. Cap-Haitien (CAP), 10km from the city.
Airport tax: Departure tax US$30 and security charge G10, excluding transit passengers.
Surface
Road: Access is possible from Dominican Republic, although sometimes, bureaucratic delays can occur.
Main port/s: Port-au-Prince, Cap Haitien, Gonaives.

Getting about
National transport
Air: Caribintair flies to Cap Haitien. Other towns can be reached from Port-au-Prince by charter flights.
Road: The total road network is around 4,000km, although not all passable/practicable in wet weather. There are surfaced roads from Port-au-Prince to Cap Haitien, Jacmel and Les Cayes.
Camionettes (large, out-of-town taxis) are available.
Buses: Unscheduled services operate from Port-au-Prince to Les Cayes, Jacmel, Jérémie, Hinche, Port de Paix and Cap Haitien.
City transport
Taxis: *Publiques* (shared taxis) can be identified by red ribbon in the window and registration number beginning 'P'. Tipping is not usual.
Car hire
Cars can be hired in Port-au-Prince and Petionville, at the airport and from hotels. International licence is required. Petrol is hard to find outside cities. Hire cars have registration numbers beginning with 'L'.

BUSINESS DIRECTORY

Telephone area codes
The international direct dialling code (IDD) for Haiti is +509, followed by subscriber's number.

Chambers of Commerce
Haiti Chamber of Commerce and Industry, Boulevard Harry Truman, PO Box 982, Port-au-Prince (tel: 222-8661; fax: 222-0281; e-mail: ccih@acn2.net).

Banking
Banque Commerciale d'Haiti, Champ de Mars, Port-au-Prince.
Central bank
Banque de la République d'Haiti, Rues des Miracles et du Magasin de l'Etat et , PO Box 1570, Port-au-Prince (tel: 299-1200; fax: 299-1045; e-mail: webmaster@brh.net).
Stock exchange
Haitian Stock Exchange: www.haitianstockexchange.com

Travel information
Air Haiti, 35 ave Marie-Jeanne, Port-au-Prince.

Association Hotelière et Touristique d'Haiti, Hotel Montana, rue F. Cardozo, route de Pétionville, BP 2562, Port-au-Prince.
National tourist organisation offices
Office National du Tourisme d'Haiti, Avenue Marie Jeanne, Port-au-Prince (tel: 223-5631).

Ministries
Ministry of Economy and Finance, Palais des Ministères, Port-au-Prince.

Ministry of Information and Co-ordination, 300 Route de Delmas, Port-au-Prince.

Other useful addresses
Association des Industries d'Haiti (ADIH), Delmas 31 et 33, Etase Galeria 128, BP 2568, Port-au-Prince.

Association des Producteurs Agricoles (APA), c/o Chambre de Commerce et d'Industrie d'Haiti, blvd Harry S. Truman, Cite de l'Exposition, Port-au-Prince.

Centre de Promotion des Investissements et des Exportations Haitiennes (Prominex), Angle rue Lamarre et ave John Brown, Port-au-Prince.

Haitian Embassy (USA), 2311 Massachusetts Avenue, NW, Washington DC 20008 (tel: (+1-202) 332-4090; fax: (+1-202) 745-7215; e-mail: embassy@haiti.org).

Haitian International Business Center, 444 Brickell Avenue, Brickell Suite 650, Miami, Florida 33131, USA (tel: (+1-305) 374-8300).

National news agency: Agence Haitienne de Presse, 6 Rue Fernand, Port-au-Prince (tel: 245-7222; fax: 245-5836; internet: www.ahphaiti.org).

Internet sites
Embassy of Haiti: www.haiti.org

Haiti Business Directory: www.ascnet.net/haiti/directory.htm

Haiti website (in French): www.haitiwebs.com/

Latin America Network Information Center: www.lanic.utexas.edu

Honduras

For years Honduras was little known outside Central America, relying on its status as the leading exporter of men's underwear to the USA for recognition elsewhere. At least that was the case until June 2009 when Honduras made an unwelcome entry on to the world's stage when it deposed into exile abroad its civilian president, Manuel Zelaya. Although Honduras has had a civilian government since 1982, its military is still a powerful force. This became evident as soldiers stormed the presidential palace early in the morning of 28 June, disarming the presidential guard and marching Mr Zelaya out of his house in his pyjamas and taking him to an air force base, where he was unceremoniously dumped on a flight to Costa Rica.

Later that day, Congress voted Mr Zelaya out of office, replacing him with Roberto Michelotti the president of Congress. Mr Micheletti lost little time in telling the protesting Organisation of American States (OAS) member states simply to mind their own business. US concerns centred on Honduras' perversely fast deepening alliance with Venezuela's Hugo Chávez. Honduras was ejected from the OAS, but efforts to restore Mr Zelaya to office failed as Mr Micheletti refused to step down.

Friends and relations

The political crisis that followed created turmoil inside Honduras, with curfews and disruptive marches by Mr Zelaya's supporters paralysing Tegucigalpa. In October 2009 Honduras' political and presidential crisis still hung in the balance. Representatives of the deposed Manuel Zelaya met with officials of the 'new' President Roberto Micheletti to see if any (unlikely) deal could be struck whereby President Zelaya could be re-instated. To the embarrassment – and fury – of the new regime, in September Mr Zelaya had managed to slip back into Honduras, taking refuge in Tegucigalpa's Brazilian embassy. It was reported that agreement had been reached on the wording of an announcement; however, it later emerged that the agreement did not have Mr Micheletti's approval.

Amazingly, this had been the first military coup in Central America since the end of the cold war.

Elections were held in November 2009. Rumour had it that Zelaya might run again; failing that, it was also rumoured that, á la Evita, Zelaya's wife, Xiomara Castro, was preparing herself for a presidential bid. However, the election was

KEY FACTS

Official name: República de Honduras (Republic of Honduras)

Head of State: President Porfiro Lobo (elected November 2009; inaugurated January 2010)

Head of government: President Porfiro Lobo

Ruling party: Partido Liberal de Honduras (PLH) (Liberal Party of Honduras) (elected 27 Nov 2005)

Area: 112,088 square km

Population: 8.05 million (2010)*

Capital: Tegucigalpa

Official language: Spanish

Currency: Lempira (L) = 100 centavos

Exchange rate: L18.90 per US$ (Oct 2011)

GDP per capita: US$2,016 (2010)

GDP real growth: 2.80% (2010)

GDP: US$15.30 billion (2010)

Inflation: 4.70% (2010)

Balance of trade: -US$2.47 billion (2009)

* estimated figure

won by Porfirio Lobo Sosa (known as Pepe Lobo) of the Partido Liberal de Honduras (PLH) (Liberal Party of Honduras), allowing Mr Micheletti to hand over the government.

Overcoming the coup

In January 2010 Porfirio Lobo, a longtime conservative politician (the name means 'wolf'), was inaugurated as president. Despite the support of Washington, Mr Lobo had little room for manoeuvre. Rather ambitiously, he formed an international truth commission to look into the events of 2009, but the commission was condemned both by supporters of Mr Zelaya and by Mr Micheletti. Mr Lobo didn't do much better internationally: he was invited to attend the European Union (EU) Latin American summit meeting in Madrid in May 2010, but decided not to participate when several Latin American countries, notably Brazil and Venezuela, threatened to boycott the meeting if he participated.

Economic woes

In 2011 Mr Lobo still had a lot to contend with. Honduras remained stuck with the enormous debt levels run up during the period following the coup when international financial institutions had suspended loans and grants. On top of this, Honduras' drug industry, and the unwelcome satellite business it attracted, seemed to be steadily growing. An estimated 200 tonnes of cocaine are shipped through Central America each year, for the most part heading for Mexico. An unintended consequence of the drug trade has been Honduras' murder rate, which has reached 70 per 100,000 people, one of the highest in the world.

In 2009 the combination of internally generated political uncertainty and the knock-on effects of the international financial crisis had meant that the Honduran economy experienced its first recession since 1999. Gross domestic product (GDP) is estimated to have contracted by 3 per cent, with a 5 per cent decline in per capita GDP, owing to the effects of both the international financial crisis and the domestic political crisis. Inflation fell significantly, closing the year at 3.5 per cent.

Whatever its democratic legitimacy, the new government of Sr Lobo that took office in January 2010 faced, in the words of the United Nations Economic Commission for Latin America and the Caribbean (ECLAC) 'an extraordinarily difficult situation'. Among the items to be addressed were a poverty rate of over 60 per cent, few opportunities for formal employment for the vast majority, and even under-nutrition, particularly among children.

In 2010, the Honduran economy began to recover slowly from the effects of the international financial crisis and the country's domestic political crisis in 2009. GDP growth of 2.5 per cent in real terms was forecast (compared with the 1.9 per cent contraction of 2009), as consumption and investment gained strength along with the recovery of Honduras' main external markets (Costa Rica, Europe, Mexico and the United States), which boosted exports. The Banco Central de Honduras (central bank) estimated that annual inflation would be around 6 per cent at the end of December (compared with 0.9 per cent 12 months earlier), as a result of the economic upturn and higher prices for petroleum and staple foods, especially wheat and rice. In September 2010, Honduras reached an agreement with the International Monetary Fund (IMF), designed to expand access to international financial markets and help build a better business climate, thanks to a recognition of the country's efforts to achieve fiscal consolidation and stabilise the economy.

In September 2010 the monthly index of economic activity showed growth of 3.2 per cent, with a strong performance by transport and communications (8.1 per cent), manufacturing (3.9 per cent), and agriculture, livestock, forestry and fishing (3.2 per cent). In the primary sector, the production of bananas, coffee and farmed shrimp expanded, driven, in the latter two cases, by a strong rise in prices. In manufacturing, the highest growth was seen in textiles and clothing (*maquila*) and the food, beverages and tobacco sector, thanks again to recovering external markets and increased domestic consumption.

The government approved a minimum wage increase of between 3 per cent and 7 per cent for companies with more than 20 workers, which came into effect on 1 September 2010. The minimum wage for micro- and small enterprises with between 1 and 20 workers remained at 5,500 lempiras in urban areas and 4,055 lempiras in rural areas. A decree was published de-indexing the minimum wage established for the professional statutes.

In the first half of 2010, the Act for the Enhancement of Revenues, Social Equity and Rationalisation of Public Expenditure was adopted with a view to correcting the fiscal imbalance. The Act considerably reformed the tax system, including significant changes to income tax. For example, it provides for the temporary solidarity contribution to be raised to 10 per cent and then reduced annually until it is phased out completely in the 2015 fiscal year.

The Honduran authorities hoped the new legislation would help to reduce the central government deficit to 4.4 per cent of GDP by December 2010. The monetary programme for 2010–11 set an inflation target of 6 per cent with a one-percentage-point margin on either side, which the central bank managed through open market operations. In September, with year-on-year inflation standing at 5 per cent, the central bank

KEY INDICATORS — Honduras

	Unit	2006	2007	2008	2009	2010
Population	m	7.36	7.51	7.66	*7.83	*8.05
Gross domestic product (GDP)	US$bn	10.76	12.40	14.10	14.30	15.30
GDP per capita	US$	1,474	1,648	1,842	1,823	2,016
GDP real growth	%	6.3	6.3	4.0	-1.9	2.8
Inflation	%	5.6	6.9	11.4	5.5	4.7
Industrial output	% change	5.2	5.2	4.4	-6.9	–
Agricultural output	% change	8.1	5.7	3.4	-1.7	–
Exports (fob) (goods)	US$m	1,930.0	5,783.6	6,457.5	5,089.6	–
Imports (fob) (goods)	US$m	5,418.0	8,887.7	10,509.1	7,560.2	–
Balance of trade	US$m	-3,488.0	-3,104.1	-4,051.6	-2,470.6	–
Current account	US$m	-508.0	-1,116.1	-1,799.9	-448.6	-955.0
Total reserves minus gold	US$m	2,628.5	2,526.8	2,473.4	2,086.5	2,670.8
Foreign exchange	US$m	2,615.5	2,513.1	2,460.0	1,908.7	2,497.9
Exchange rate	per US$	18.89	18.89	18.90	18.89	18.90

* estimated figure

opted to leave the monetary policy rate unchanged.

In the year to September 2010, exports showed an annual growth figure of 13 per cent (compared with a 20.2 per cent contraction up to September 2009), which is attributable to strong growth in agricultural exports (14 per cent), particularly coffee (23.5 per cent) and agro-industrial products (8.8 per cent), especially African palm oil and sugar. Manufacturing exports posted a more moderate upturn of 7 per cent to September, driven by the recovery of *maquila* firms producing clothing and wiring assemblies for the automotive industry. Imports to September 2010 also picked up strongly, rising by 13.9 per cent after dropping by 32.7 per cent in 2009, thanks to more buoyant economic activity. Imports of capital goods for the manufacturing industry rose by 11.3 per cent (compared with a 50.2 per cent drop in 2009), while imports of raw materials and intermediate goods went up by 13.9 per cent (compared with a 29.5 per cent fall in 2009). Imports of consumer goods edged up 4.7 per cent. Imports of fuels, lubricants and electrical energy jumped 33.7 per cent (after a 47.6 per cent slump in 2009), on the strength of economic recovery, increased consumption and higher petroleum prices.

The cumulative trade deficit between January and September was US$3.145 billion, which was 14.6 per cent higher than that recorded 12 months earlier. The current account deficit was expected to deteriorate significantly and close the year at 7.2 per cent of GDP, more than double the previous year's figure of 3.2 per cent of GDP. In the first half of the year, foreign exchange inflows in the form of foreign direct investment (FDI) were up by 11 per cent.

In 2010, the country's relations with the various multilateral credit institutions regained a normal footing, enabling the resumption of external loan disbursements, which thus reached US$51.9 million in net terms in June. An IMF programme with resources totalling approximately US$202 million (which the government intends to treat as precautionary) was approved in early October, providing a macroeconomic setting which should be propitious to the restoration of stability and the strengthening of public finances. Economic growth of close to 2 per cent was projected for 2011, owing to a slowdown in external demand, while inflation was estimated to be about 6 per cent and the current account deficit around 7 per cent of GDP.

Risk assessment

Economy	Fair
Politics	Poor
Regional stability	Good

COUNTRY PROFILE

Historical profile

1821 The Central American provinces (Costa Rica, Guatemala, Honduras, Nicaragua and El Salvador) declared independence from Spain.
1822 The five provinces annexed themselves to the Mexican Empire, under General Agustín de Iturbde, later Emperor Agustín I.
1823 Agustín I was overthrown and Mexico became a republic. The Central American states formed the United Provinces of Central America.
1825 Costa Rica, Guatemala, Honduras, Nicaragua and El Salvador formed the Central American Federation (CAF).
1838 The CAF was dissolved and Honduras became a fully independent republic.
1840–1957 Honduras was ruled by a military and civilian élite.
1957 The first democratic presidential election was won by Ramon Villeda Morales, a popular moderate reformist.
1963 Morales was ousted by Colonel Osvaldo Lopez Arellano in a military coup. Military rule continued until 1980.
1969 Honduras and El Salvador fought what became known as the 'soccer war', which was prompted by land disputes and El Salvador's win in the World Cup play-offs between the two countries. Over 3,000 people died.
1981 Presidential elections were won by Roberto Suazo Cordova of the Partido Liberal de Honduras (PLH) (Liberal Party of Honduras), although real power remained in the hands of the army under General Gustavo Alvarez.
1985 José Azcona Hoyo (PLH) won the presidential election, following a change in the constitution which limited the presidency to a maximum of one term.
1989 Rafael Leonardo Callejas Romero of the Partido Nacional (PN) (National Party), the right-wing opposition party, was elected president.
1993 Carlos Roberto Reina Idiáquez (PLH) won the presidential election.
1997 Carlos Roberto Flores Facussé (PLH) was elected president.
1998 Hurricane Mitch killed around 11,000 people and left 1.3 million homeless.
1999 The constitution was amended to make the president the commander-in-chief of the armed forces.
2001 Ricardo Maduro Joest (PN) was elected president.
2002 Honduras renewed diplomatic ties with Cuba, with whom it had cut relations in 1961. Persistent drought and the decline in world coffee prices left around 300,000 Hondurans suffering from hunger.
2004 More than 100 prisoners, many of them gang members, were killed in a fire at San Pedro Sula prison. Honduras withdrew its troops from the coalition forces in Iraq.
2005 The PLH won the presidential and legislative elections.
2006 President Manuel Zelaya Rosales (PLH) was inaugurated. The Central American Free Trade Agreement (Cafta) came into effect.
2007 After eight years of conflict, the International Court of Justice ruled on a new maritime boundary between Honduras and Nicaragua. The result gave both countries equal access to the rich fishing grounds and oil and gas exploration waters in the area.
2008 Honduras signed a free trade agreement with Taiwan.
2009 Just hours before a referendum to change the constitution and allow an incumbent president to stand for a second term in office, the military deposed President Zelaya and flew him into exile in Costa Rica. Days later Zelaya attempted to re-enter the country but was refused. International condemnation of the coup was expressed by the UN, US and EU; Honduras was suspended from the Organisation of American States (OAS). Zelaya successfully returned, in secret, to take refuge in the Brazilian embassy in Tegucigalpa, which became a focal point for his supporters. A state of emergency was declared and lifted amid signs of reconciliation and negotiation. Porfirio Lobo Sosa (known as Pepe Lobo) (PNH) won the scheduled presidential election; Zelaya was constitutionally barred from standing
2010 President Lobo was sworn into office in January as ex-president Zelaya went into exile in the Dominican Republic. In July, the Central Bank of Economic Integration (BCIE) approved funds of US$288 million for social and welfare programmes, providing for education, health and nutrition, including school meals. The military was deployed in cities around the country to counter violent criminal gang activity (linked to Mexican drug cartels) in September, following the murder of 18 people in a shoe factory in San Pedro Sula.
2011 All charges of fraud and falsifying documents laid against former president Zelaya were dismissed on 3 May. Zalaya claimed the accusations of corruption had been politically motivated. The court ruling will allow international relations,

severed during the exile of former president Zelaya, to be resumed. Zelaya returned from exile on 29 May. The OAS lifted its suspension of Honduras on 1 June.

Political structure

In addition to their unicameral national parliaments, El Salvador, Guatemala, Honduras, Nicaragua, Panama and Dominican Republic also return directly-elected deputies to the supranational Central American Parliament.

Constitution

The constitution was promulgated in 1982 and amended in 1999, making the president the commander-in-chief of the armed forces.

Voting is by secret ballot and is compulsory for all citizens aged 18 or over. Members of the security forces are barred from voting. Municipal elections and elections of representatives in the 18 departments are held every two years.

Form of state

Presidential democratic republic

The executive

Power is divided between a strong executive, a unicameral national assembly and an independent judiciary. The president, three vice presidents and members of the national assembly serve parallel four-year terms. Presidents are not allowed to stand for re-election to a second term in office.

National legislature

The unicameral Congreso Nacional (National Congress) has 128 deputies directly elected by proportional representation by departments, to serve for four-year terms.

Legal system

The legal system is based on Roman and Spanish civil law. Honduran laws are set out in the 'Cordigoes' or codes. The civil code covers dealings between people. The business code covers all matters relating to business while the penal code covers crime and punishment. The legal system is in desperate need of reform.

Last elections

27 November 2005 (parliamentary); 29 November 2009 (presidential)

Results: Parliamentary: Partido Liberal de Honduras (PLH) (Liberal Party of Honduras) won 62 seats (out of 128); Partido Nacional de Honduras (PNH) (National Party of Honduras) 55; Partido de Unificación Democrática (PUD) (Democratic Unification Party) five; turnout was 45.97 per cent.

Presidential: Porfirio Lobo Sosa (PNH) won 55.91 per cent of the vote, Elvin Santos 38.16 per cent; three other candidates won less than 3 per cent each. Turnout was 61 per cent.

Next elections

2013 (presidential)

Political parties

Ruling party

Partido Liberal de Honduras (PLH) (Liberal Party of Honduras) (elected 27 Nov 2005)

Main opposition party

Partido Nacional de Honduras (PNH) (National Party of Honduras)

Population

8.05 million (2010)*

Last census: July 2001: 6,071,200 (provisional)

Population density: 56 inhabitants per square km. Urban population: 54 per cent of total (1995—2001).

Annual growth rate: 2.6 per cent 1994–2004 (WHO 2006)

Ethnic make-up

Around 90 per cent are *mestizos*, with minorities of Indians, blacks, whites and others. The largest indigenous group is the Garifuna, descendants of African slaves and Arawak Indian women from San Vicente, who live along the north coast. The Miskitos live in the Mosquitia – wetland, rainforest country – and the Lencas live around Copan.

Religions

More than 90 per cent of the population are Roman Catholics. There is freedom of worship.

Education

Primary education is compulsory and free of charge. Secondary education, from 13 years to 17 years, is not compulsory.

Literacy rate: 80 per cent adult rate; 89 per cent youth rate (15–24) (Unesco 2005).

Compulsory years: Seven to 12

Enrolment rate: 110 per cent gross primary enrolment, of the relevant age group (including repetition rate); 32 per cent gross secondary enrolment; 9 per cent gross tertiary enrolment (World Bank).

Pupils per teacher: 35 in primary schools

Health

In Honduras the quality of, and access to, healthcare is directly tied to income levels. Adequate health care is available to those able to pay the high cost. Health care for the urban and rural poor is limited.

The ministry of health manages 28 hospitals with 4,093 beds. There are also 31 hospitals managed by the private sector. The private sector generally concentrates on individual care and does not participate in general public sector health activities. A national policy was formulated to make sure people have access to safe, quality drugs. This policy however, has not been implemented.

The relatively young population places an extra burden on health facilities. Nearly two-thirds of the population have no access to essential drugs.

Infectious and parasitic diseases are the leading causes of death. Gastroenteritis and tuberculosis are serious problems. Approximately one-third of the population has no access to safe water or sanitation facilities.

HIV/Aids

The disease is spread predominantly through heterosexual intercourse. A study showed that the HIV prevalence in female sex workers was over 10 per cent (USCF – Centre for HIV Information, 2005).

HIV prevalence: 1.8 per cent aged 15–49 in 2003 (World Bank)

Life expectancy: 67 years, 2004 (WHO 2006)

Fertility rate/Maternal mortality rate: 3.6 births per woman, 2004 (WHO 2006); maternal mortality 110 per 100,000 live births (World Bank).

Child (under 5 years) mortality rate (per 1,000): 32 per 1,000 live births; 25 per cent of children aged under five are malnourished (World Bank).

Welfare

Honduras is classified as a low-income country by the World Bank – 50 per cent of its inhabitants live below the poverty line. Social security benefits, mainly for pensions and health care, cover around 12 per cent of the Honduran population and account for around 1 per cent of GDP. Social security is mainly limited to urban centres. About 80 per cent of those covered live either in the capital, Tegucigalpa, or in the northern city of San Pedro Sula.

Organised social security started operations in 1962. Contributors are covered for general illness, maternity, accidents at work, professional illnesses, invalidity, old age and funeral expenses. There is no unemployment benefit.

Dependants, who account for 60 per cent of those covered, get some access to health care and pensions. Children under five years get free health treatment and wives of contributors receive maternity care in hospitals run by the social security institute. The widows of contributors receive pensions and there are more restricted pensions for widowers. Orphans, usually up to the age of 14 years, receive some support.

Main cities

Tegucigalpa (capital, estimated population 1.3 million in 2010), San Pedro Sula (505,200), La Ceiba (116,700).

Languages spoken

English is common in some parts of the north coast and the Caribbean Islas de la Bahía.

Official language/s

Spanish

Media

While the constitution guarantees freedom of speech and the press, there are punitive defamation laws that tend to restrict journalism and journalists are known to practice self-censorship. Journalists reporting on corruption, drug trafficking and human rights abuses have been targeted not only for harassment but also by laws that require them to divulge their sources. Media outlets have been the object of political attacks with death threats issued to journalists and managers. Corruption of the media has also included bribes to journalists, selective government advertising and access and denial of public officials.

In 2005, the Supreme Court declared that defamation laws that protected public officials were unconstitutional.

Press

Ownership of newspapers in held by a few conglomerates with political and economic ties to the elite.

Dailies: The most popular newspapers are, in Spanish, *El Heraldo* (www.heraldohn.com) and *El Tiempo* (www.tiempo.hn), others include *La Tribuna* (www.latribuna.hn) and *La Prensa* (www.laprensahn.com). Articles include financial and business news.

Weeklies: In Spanish, government announcements are published in *La Gaceta*. In English, *Honduras This Week* (www.marrder.com/htw) covers news from Central America.

Broadcasting

Radio and television play a key role in Honduras, where literacy is around 60 per cent. Television is all privately owned and operated; there is one state-owned radio station.

Radio: There are five stations broadcasting nationally and over 280 local radio stations.

The biggest stations include Radio HRN (www.radiohrn.hn), Radio América (www.radioamerica.hn) and Power FM (www.powerfm.hn). The public radio network broadcasts under the collective name of Radio Corporación.

Television: There are six nationwide TV stations and some with more than one channel. The ones with the biggest market share are Televicentro (www.televicentrotv.net) with several channels and digital services and CBC Canal 6 (www.noti6.com), Vica TV (www.vicatv.hn) and Soptel Canal 11 (www.canal11.hn).

Economy

The service sector, at just over 55 per cent, constitutes the largest portion of the economy, with industrial activity at 31 per cent (of which manufacturing is over 20 per cent) and agriculture at less than 15 per cent. The importance of the *maquila* sector has grown since their introduction in the late 1980s, so that by 2009 it accounted for 55 per cent of merchandise exports, of which 90 per cent were textile products; around 80 per cent of *maquila* exports were destined for the US. Of the remaining exports, two-thirds are agricultural products, including coffee, bananas and crustaceans, and the remaining one-third are general manufactured goods, such as machinery and vehicle parts.

GDP growth was 6.2 per cent in 2007, which fell to 4.0 per cent in 2008 as the global economic crisis cut world trade and exports fell. Honduras entered recession in 2009 with growth of -1.9 per cent, but growth was positive by 2010 with a rate of 2.5 per cent and projected to grow to 3.5–4.0 per cent in 2011. Remittances in 2009 totalled US$2.55 billion (19.3 per cent of GDP), rising to an estimated US$2.66 billion in 2010. Inflation has been a long-term problem for Honduras and it reached a high of 11 per cent in 2008, before falling to 8.9 per cent in 2009 and further to 4.6 per cent in 2010.

According to the UN Human Development Index (HDI) in 2010, Honduras' intensity of deprivation was 48.9 per cent, with 18.19 per cent living below US$1.25 a day. It is one of the most impoverished countries in the western hemisphere and unemployment remains high.

The new administration of President Lobo has to address a difficult social and economic situation, not only with the global slowdown in trade but also the internal divisions created during the 2009 political crisis. The parliament approved the president's new budget, which included important tax reforms and full relations and co-operations with bilateral and multilateral financial donors and investment programmes.

External trade

Honduras is a member of the Central America Free Trade Agreement (DR-Cafta), which includes Dominican Republic, Costa Rica, El Salvador, Guatemala and the US; it is working to remove all tariffs and barriers between members by 2024. It is also a member of the World Trade Organisation (WTO). Honduras has free-trade agreements with Chile, Colombia, US, Mexico, Panama, the Dominican Republic and Taiwan.

A *maquila* industry, which began in the late 1980s, produces clothing for export, mainly to the US. Other non-traditional exports include cultivated cash-crops, farmed shrimps and melons.

Imports

Principal imports are petroleum, machinery and vehicles, pharmaceuticals, industrial raw materials and foodstuffs.

Main sources: US (typically 36 per cent of total), Guatemala (11 per cent), Mexico (7 per cent).

Exports

They include clothing, coffee, bananas and crustaceans, palm oil, fruit and vegetable, timber and gold and machinery and vehicle parts.

Main destinations: US (typically 48 per cent total of total), El Salvador (7 per cent), Germany (7 per cent).

Agriculture

Farming

Agriculture is one of the most important economic activities in Honduras. The sector accounts for around 80 per cent of total exports, constitutes 20 per cent of total GDP and employs 57 per cent of the country's workforce.

Sugar cane, bananas (grown on the northern lowland) and coffee are the main agricultural exports. The government is encouraging the growth of new banana varieties but it is likely to be a number of years before new crops become profitable exports.

The main food crops are maize, rice, sorghum and beans. Production of these staples has steadily risen, though food imports are still necessary to meet domestic demand.

Emphasis has been on land reform and the cultivation of new crops such as cocoa, allspice, cardamom, melons and citrus fruits.

Fishing

Honduras' annual fish catch is typically over 18,000mt, of which approximately 12,000mt is shellfish. The country's main fish export is lobster, harvested by divers who spend up to seven hours a day on the sea bed. The lobsters are mainly exported to the US. Legislation requires all divers to undergo specific instruction and boat owners to hold licences to carry trained divers only. The government is expected to promote the potential of Honduras' fishing industry in order to attract investment and curtail growing unemployment along the country's coasts which has forced fishermen to dive for lobsters. Improved regulation would benefit the lobster colonies which are in danger of being depleted. Honduras also has a well-established shrimp farming industry.

Forestry

Honduras does not have a great deal of energy resources and consequently wood is widely used as an inexpensive form of fuel. This has led to a widespread problem of deforestation in Honduras.

The government has promoted the protection of Honduras' forests by agreeing with foreign companies such as Stone Container Corporation (US), to establish a comprehensive forestry management plan enabling Honduras to increase the size of its forest coverage.
In a typical year, exports of forest materials amount to US$43.1 million, while imports amount to US$100 million.

Industry and manufacturing

Honduras's industrial sector is the smallest in Central America and contributes in the region of 27 per cent to total GDP. Approximately 15 per cent of Honduras' workforce is employed in the sector.
Government responsibility for the industrial sector has traditionally been divided between the ministry of economy's general directorate of industry, the central bank and various other official institutions.
In the late 1980s, government introduced policies aimed at stimulating Honduran labour-intensive industries, especially agro-industry, while boosting investment and exports to combat high unemployment. The authorities since then have continued to try and release Honduras from dependency on certain commodities such as bananas and coffee.
Virtually no production equipment is produced in Honduras and capital goods must be imported from foreign suppliers. The demand for capital goods cannot be funded without the government's help and the need to expand the country's industrial base is being frustrated by financial constraints.
Manufacturing remains heavily dependent on imports of capital goods, raw materials and foreign technology; the biggest growth in the sector has been the *maquiladora* (in-bond assembly and manufacturing) industries. The four main areas of manufacturing in Honduras are concentrated around food processing, agro-export, *maquila* and chemicals. However, capacity utilisation is still low on account of Honduras' narrow domestic market and lack of international competitiveness.
The key to helping the growth of the Honduran industrial sector has been the government-backed free trade zones (FTZ) and privately funded Export Processing Zones (EPZs). Roughly 90 per cent of all merchandise currently manufactured in the zones is clothing. Cloth is manufactured in the US and exported to Honduras from where it is then re-exported as garments, often duty free, to the US.

Tourism

The tourism industry of Honduras continues to expand. The sector now constitutes 10.4 per cent of the country's total GDP and accounts for 8.5 per cent of total employment.
Travel and tourism is an increasingly important economic activity, with the environment and Mayan remains as major attractions. Over half of the visitors come from other Central American countries.

Mining

At present the mining sector employs approximately 2 per cent of Honduras' total workforce. The country has large reserves of tin, iron, copper and coal. There are small reserves of gold, silver, lead and zinc that are extracted for export.

Hydrocarbons

Honduras does not produce oil at present, despite extensive offshore exploration aimed at locating deposits. Consumption was 47,000 barrels per day in 2007, all of which was imported. In 2007 a long-running maritime border dispute between Honduras and Nicaragua was resolved, whereby four small Caribbean islands, including any oil rights, were ceded to Honduras.
There are no refineries in Honduras.
There are no natural gas reserves and Honduras does not import natural gas.
Honduras imports around 3.4 million tonnes of coal per annum.

Energy

Total installed generating capacity was 1,568 megawatts (MW) in 2007, of which 38 per cent is publicly owned and the remainder privately. Of those in public ownership, 30 per cent are hydroelectric.
Only 69 per cent of the population has access to mains electricity, of which 94 per cent are in urban areas and 45 per cent in rural areas. Generating capacity is less than installed capacity due to aging and underperforming power plants. There are several expansion projects with a net addition of 1,479MW, of various energy mixes including hydro, coal, diesel, wind, geothermal, biomass and natural gas, to be installed by 2015.
Honduras does not possess an integrated electricity supply system as local and regional electricity companies vie for business. However it has a limited connection with El Salvador, Guatemala and Nicaragua from where it imports electricity.

Financial markets

Stock exchange

Bolsa Honduras de Valores (BHV) (Honduran Stock Exchange)

Banking and insurance

The regulators of the banking and financial services sector of Honduras retain tight restrictions on bank ownership of fixed assets and limits on buying corporate shares. Foreign banks wishing to set up in Honduras must obtain approval from the president. Domestic and foreign-owned banks operate under identical rules, and historically there has been little difference in the type of business they conduct.

Central bank

Banco Central de Honduras

Main financial centre

Tegucigalpa

Time

GMT minus six hours

Geography

Honduras is in the middle of the Central American isthmus. It has a long northern coastline on the Caribbean Sea and a narrow southern outlet to the Pacific Ocean. Guatemala is to the west, El Salvador to the south-west and Nicaragua to the south-east. Covering 112,088 square km, Honduras is the second largest country in Central America after neighbouring Nicaragua. Much of the country is covered by thick forests and mountains, while around a quarter of the land is suitable for farming. Apart from a low coastal plain in the north-east, the country is crossed by numerous ranges of mountains and hills. The highest peak is the Cerro de las Minas at 2,866 metres in the western Sierra de Celaque.

Hemisphere

Northern.

Climate

Honduras has a tropical climate on the coast and a temperate climate in the mountainous interior. Temperatures in the capital Tegucigalpa, at 960 metres, are usually between 15 degrees Celsius (C) and 30 degrees C. Rain falls throughout the year on the north coast, while the rest of the country has heaviest rains between May and November. The average rainfall is 3,037mm per year. During the rainy season, May–November, the climate is temperate; in March and April the warm days are punctuated by cool nights; and in December–February it is cool and dry during the day, but chilly at night. The best time to visit is April–May.

Entry requirements

Passports

Required by all, valid for three months on arrival.

Visa

Visas are not required by nationals of most of the Americas and Europe (excluding Schengen agreement states), Australasia, Japan and some other Asian countries. Business visas should be accompanied by a company letter as proof of business intentions, and a full itinerary. For confirmation and requirements, contact the local embassy.

Currency advice/regulations
There are no restrictions on the import and export of local and foreign currency. US dollars should be declared on arrival; re-export is allowed up to the declared amount.

Health (for visitors)
Mandatory precautions
A yellow fever vaccination certificate is required if arriving from an infected area.
Advisable precautions
Typhoid, tetanus and polio vaccinations are advisable. There is a risk of malaria, especially in rural areas – prophylaxis is recommended. Water precautions are essential throughout the country.

Hotels
Hotel standards are reasonable in Tegucigalpa and San Pedro Sula. Hotel bills are subject to 16 per cent sales tax.

Public holidays (national)
Fixed dates
1 Jan (New Year's Day), 14 Apr (Americas Day), 1 May (Labour Day), 15 Sep (Independence Day), 3 Oct (Morozán Day), 12 Oct (Columbus Day), 21 Oct (Armed Forces Day), 25 Dec (Christmas Day).
Variable dates
Maundy Thursday, Good Friday.

Working hours
Banking
Mon–Fri: 0900–1500.
Business
Mon–Fri: 0800–1200, 1330/1400–1700; Sat: 0800–1100.
Government
Mon–Fri: 0800–1200, 1330/1400–1700; Sat: 0800–1100.

Electricity supply
110 or 220V AC, 60 cycles.

Social customs/useful tips
Handshaking is the main form of greeting. Embracing is frowned upon by both men and women.
Mothers are regarded as the leading family figures. It is a grave offence to insult someone's mother. Women rather than men are often the principal family breadwinners. Grandparents and elders are highly respected. The extended family plays an important social role by providing a sense of unity.
It is customary to send flowers to the hostess if invited to dinner or as a guest to someone's home.
Professional persons should be addressed by their title. Graduates are known as *Licenciados*.

Security
There is widespread petty and violent crime, including armed robbery, car hijacking, burglary and sexual assaults. Visitors are advised to exercise vigilance and caution in all areas, not to carry large amounts of money, take only what is necessary, keep the rest deposited at the hotel and not to resist robbery attempts.

Getting there
Air
National airline: Sol Air.
International airport/s: Tegucigalpa-Toncontín (TGU), 5km from city; duty-free shop, bar, restaurant, bank, post office, vaccination centre, shops, car hire.
Airport tax: US$32.
Surface
Road: It is possible to reach Tegucigalpa via the Pan-American Highway from Goascorán (on the border with El Salvador) and from El Espino and Guasaule (on the border with Nicaragua). Bus services run from most Central American countries. Entry from Guatemala is possible via the Western Highway.
Main port/s: Ampala, La Ceiba, Cortés, Roatan, Castilla, Tela, Lorenzo.

Getting about
National transport
Air: Isleñas Airlines, Sosa Airlines and Rollins Air are the three local airlines, operating numerous flights between Tegucigalpa, San Pedro Sula, Roatan, La Ceiba, Trujillo and Tela. To reach more remote areas using other services, local enquiries should be made.
Road: Network of 10,468km, concentrated along coast (roughly San Pedro Sula to Trujillo) and the area between San Pedro Sula and Tegucigalpa and the Guatemalan border. The main highways are paved, although roads are of varying quality. Travel on unpaved roads is not recommended.
Buses: Frequent services San Pedro Sula to Tegucigalpa; also linking with Juticalpa, Danlí, Choluteca.
Rail: There are passenger train services in the north, running between San Pedro Sula, Puerto Cortés and Tela, although they are somewhat ramshackle and the service is slow.
Water: Water transport is commonly used to travel between Honduras, the Caribbean islands and the bay islands. In Mosquitia almost all transport is along the waterways due to poor road infrastructure.
City transport
Taxis: Can be hailed, ordered by telephone or found at ranks; also possible to hail and share a taxi; fares by negotiation (sometimes a flat rate). Tipping is not usual.
Buses, trams & metro: Buses stop outside the entrance to the Toncontín international airport. All buses in and around the capital operate between 0500 and 2100.

Car hire
A national or international licence is required. Rental cars are available in Tegucigalpa, San Pedro Sula, La Ceiba and on the island of Roatán.

BUSINESS DIRECTORY

The addresses listed below are a selection only. While World of Information makes every endeavour to check these addresses, we cannot guarantee that changes have not been made, especially to telephone numbers and area codes. We would welcome any corrections.

Telephone area codes
The international direct dialling code (IDD) for Honduras is +504 followed by the customer number.

Chambers of Commerce
American-Honduran Chamber of Commerce, Hotel Honduras Maya, PO Box 1838, Tegucigalpa (tel: 232-7043; fax: 232-2031; e-mail: amcham@t.hn2.com).

Cortes Camará de Comercio e Industrias, 17 Avenida Circunvalación, PO Box 14, San Pedro Sula (tel: 553-0761; fax: 533-3777; e-mail: ccic@ccichonduras.org).

Honduras Federación de Camarás de Comercio e Industrias, Edificio Castañito, Bulevar Morazan, Tegucigalpa, PO Box 3393 (tel: 232-6083; fax: 232-1870; e-mail: fedecamara@sigmant.hn).

Tegucigalpa Camará de Comercio e Industrias, Bulevar Centramérica, PO Box 3444, Tegucigalpa (tel: 232-4200; fax: 232-0159; e-mail: infoccit@ccit.hn).

Banking
Banco Atlantida SA, PO Box 3164, Plaza Bancatlan, Tegucigalpa (tel: 321-742; fax: 321-273).

Banco CentroAmericano de Integración Económico, Edificio Midence Soto, Nivel 10, PO Box 772, Tegucigalpa, M D C Honduras (tel: 372-230; fax: 311-906).

Banco Continental SA, PO Box 390, San Pedro Sula, Cortes (tel: 531-310; fax: 522-750).

Banco del Comercio SA (Bancomer), PO Box 160, San Pedro Sula, Cortes (tel: 533-600; fax: 533-128).

Banco de El Ahorro Hondureño SA, PO Box 3185, Tegucigalpa (tel: 375-161; fax: 374-638).

Banco de Honduras SA, PO Box 3434, Tegucigalpa (tel: 326-122; fax: 326-164).

Banco de la Exportación SA (Banexpo), PO Box 3988, Tegucigalpa (tel: 394-256; fax: 394-265).

Banco de las Fuerzas Armadas SA (Banffaa), PO Box 877, Tegucigalpa (tel: 312-051; fax: 313-832).

Banco de Los Trabajadores SA, PO Box 3246, Tegucigalpa (tel: 379-501; fax: 378-422).

Banco de Occidente SA, PO Box 3284, Tegucigalpa (tel: 370-310; fax: 370-486).

Banco del País SA, PO Box 314, San Pedro Sula, Cortes (tel: 525-202; fax: 525-229).

Banco Hondureño del Café (Banhcafe), PO Box 583, Tegucigalpa (tel: 328-370; fax: 328-332).

Banco Financiera Centroamericana SA (Ficensa), PO Box 1432, Tegucigalpa (tel: 381-661; fax: 381-630).

Banco La Capitalizadora Hondureña SA (Bancahsa), PO Box 344, Tegucigalpa (tel: 371-171; fax: 372-775).

Banco Mercantil SA (Bamer), PO Box 116, Tegucigalpa (tel: 320-006; fax: 323-137).

Banco Sogerín SA, PO Box 440, San Pedro Sula, Cortes (tel: 533-888; fax: 572-001).

Lloyds Bank, PO Box 3136, Tegucigalpa (tel: 366-864; fax: 366-417).

Central bank

Banco Central de Honduras, PO Box 3165, Tegucigalpa MDC (tel: 237-2270; fax: 237-1876; e-mail: webmaster@mail.bch.hn).

Stock exchange

Bolsa Honduras de Valores (BHV) (Honduran Stock Exchange)

Bolsa Centroamericana de Valores (BCV) (Central American Stock Exchange Securities): www.bcv.hn

Travel information

National tourist organisation offices

Instituto Hondureño de Turismo, Col San Carlos, Edificio Europa, PO Box 3261, Tegucigalpa (tel: 222-2124 ext 502; fax: 222-2124 ext 501; e-mail: tourisminfo@iht.hn).

Ministries

Ministry of Agriculture, Boulevard Miraflores, Tegucigalpa, MDC (tel: 32-8394; fax: 325-375).

Ministry of Culture, Arts and Sport, Ave La Paz, Tegucigalpa, MDC (tel: 369-738; fax: 369-738).

Ministry of Defence, 4c, 5a Tegucigalpa, MDC (tel: 380-065; fax: 380-238).

Ministry of Education, 1C 2-3A Comaguela (tel: 228-517; fax: 374-312).

Ministry of External Relations, Antigua Casa Presidencial, Centro Civico Gubernamental, Tegucigalpa, MDC (tel: 343-297; fax: 341-484).

Ministry of Health, 3C 4A Tegucigalpa, MDC (tel: 228-518; fax: 384-141).

Ministry of Industry, Trade and Tourism, 5A, 4C Edif Salame, Tegucigalpa, MDC (tel: 382-025; fax: 372-836).

Ministry of Labour and Social Security, 7C 2-3 Ave Comayaguela (tel: 379-778; fax: 223-220).

Ministry of Natural Resources and Environment, Barrio la Fuente, Tegucigalpa, MDC (tel: 375-664; fax: 375-726).

Ministry of Public Works, Transport and Housing, Barrio la Bolsa, Comayaguela (tel: 33-7690; fax: 252-227).

Presidential Office, Palacio José Cecilio del Valle, Bd Juan Pablo II, Tegucigapa, MDC (tel: 326-282; fax: 31-0097).

Other useful addresses

Asociación Nacional de Industriales, Boulevard los Proceres, 4a Avenida, Colonia Lara, Tegucigalpa.

Asociación Hondureña de Productores de Café (Coffee Producers' Association), 10a Avenida, 6a Calle, Apdo 959, Tegucigalpa.

British Embassy, Edif Palmira, 3rd Floor, Colonia Palmira, Tegucigalpa (tel: 320-612, 320-618; fax: 325-480).

Consejo Hondureño de la Empresa Privada, Barrio la Plozuela, 5th Floor, Edificio San Miguel, Tegucigalpa.

Corporación Nacional de Inversiones (CONADI), Apdo 842, Tegucigalpa (tx: 1192).

División Estudios Económicos, Banco Atlántida, Apdo 57-C, Boulevard Centroamérica, Tegucigalpa.

Home Office, Palacio Nacional, 2o Piso, Tegucigalpa, MDC (tel: 228-604; fax: 37-1121).

Honduran Embassy (US), 3007 Tilden Street, NW, Washington DC 20008 (tel: (+1-202) 966-7702; fax: (+1-202) 966-9751; e-mail: embassy@hondurasemb.org).

Honduras Stock Exchange, PO Box 161, San Pedro Sula (tel: 534-410; fax: 534-480).

Secretary of the Treasury, 3C, 5A Tegucigalpa, MDC (tel: 220-111; fax: 382-309).

Secretaria de Planificación y Presupuesto (SECPLAN), 2 Avenida 9 y 10 Calle Comayaguela, Tegucigalpa.

US Embassy, Avenida La Paz, Apdo 26-C, Tegucigalpa (tel: 323-120; fax: 320-027).

Internet sites

Cámara de Comercio e Industrias de Cortes (Cortes Chamber of Commerce and Industry) (local, national and international business issues in Spanish only): www.123.hn/

Honduras yellow pages: www.only-honduras.com

Latin America Network Information Center:www.lanic.utexas.edu/

Hong Kong

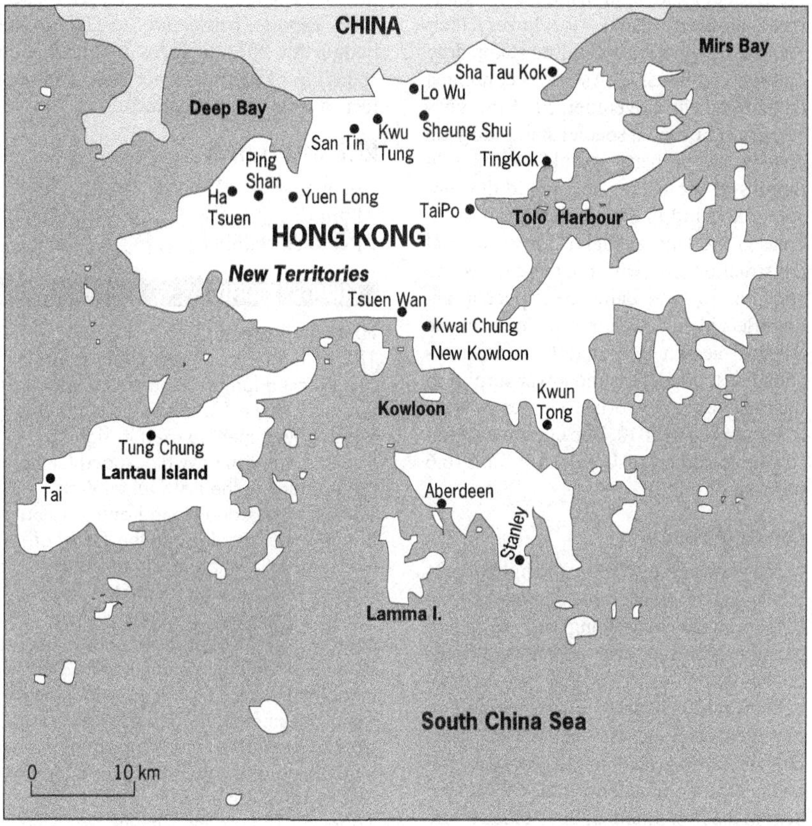

Hong Kong's services-driven economy made a strong comeback in 2010 as it recovered from the contraction in 2009. According to the Asian Development Bank, gross domestic product (GDP) picked up by 6.8 per cent. On the demand side, consumption, investment and net exports all contributed to growth. Private consumption grew by 5.8 per cent and was responsible for more than half the GDP growth. Consumption spending was supported by a pickup in employment and buoyant stock and property markets. Retail sales were boosted by a 22 per cent jump in visitor arrivals to 36 million.

Government spending

Government consumption made a small contribution to the expansion. Budget spending in the 2010 financial year (which ended on 31 March 2011) came in below allocation, while revenue burgeoned alongside the recovery in economic activity and asset prices. The budget was in surplus by an estimated 4 per cent of GDP. After two weak years, fixed investment rebounded by 8.1 per cent in 2010, accounting for about one-quarter of GDP growth. Private investment in machinery, equipment and computer software was strong, especially in the first half (reflecting the low starting point). Several large-scale projects boosted public construction, including the Guangzhou–Shenzhen–Hong Kong express rail and the Hong Kong–Zhuhai–Macao bridge.

With the revival of global trade, exports of goods bounced back to record 17.3 per cent growth in real terms, from a double-digit contraction a year earlier. Exports to the People's Republic of China (PRC) and other major Asian markets (

KEY FACTS

Official name: Xianggang Tebie Xingzhengqu (Hong Kong Special Administrative Region (SAR) of China)

Head of State: State President of China Hu Jintao (from 2003)

Head of government: Chief Executive Donald Tsang (from 2005, re-elected Jul 2007)

Ruling party: Coalition government (approved by the Zhongguo Gongchandang (Chinese Communist Party))

Area: 1,070 square km (including 235 islands)

Population: 7.07 million (2010)*

Capital: The Legislative Council building is situated in the central district of Victoria, on Hong Kong Island

Official language: Chinese (Mandarin, Beijing dialect *de jure*; Cantonese *de facto*) and English

Currency: Hong Kong dollar (HK$) = 100 cents

Exchange rate: HK$7.78 per US$ (Oct 2011)

GDP per capita: US$31,591 (2010)

GDP real growth: 6.80% (2010)

GDP: US$225.00 billion (2010)

Labour force: 3.68 million (2010)

Unemployment: 4.30% (2010)

Inflation: 2.40% (2010)

Balance of trade: -US$42.97 billion (2010)

Japan, the Republic of Korea, Singapore and Taiwan,) saw growth of 15–23 per cent. Exports to the United States and Europe also rose, but failed to reach 2008's pre-crisis peak. Imports of goods in real terms rose by 18.1 per cent, reflecting growth in private consumption and the pickup in investment. Services exports grew by 15.0 per cent in 2010 as financial and professional services, trade services, transport and tourism all benefited from the recovery in global trade and deepening integration with the rapidly growing PRC.

The important financial and insurance sub-sector grew by 7.5 per cent in 2010. Equity capital raised through initial public offerings rose to HK$449.5 billion (US$57.9 billion), making Hong Kong the world's biggest centre for such capital raising in 2010. The number of authorised financial institutions participating in yuan business increased from 61 to 115 and their total deposits increased almost five-fold.

Employment grows

A resumption of employment gains in 2010 (after net job losses in 2009) lowered the seasonally adjusted unemployment rate to 4.0 per cent in the fourth quarter. Real earnings grew by only 0.1 per cent during the year. Inflation quickened over the year to 3.1 per cent in December 2010 owing to rising domestic demand, a softer US dollar, higher prices for imported food and rising housing costs. Inflation averaged 2.4 per cent for the year.

Very low interest rates and abundant liquidity, coupled with strong underlying demand for housing, propelled prices of all categories of property in 2010. Residential property prices rose by 20.4 per cent in the 12 months to December 2010, following a gain of 28.5 per cent a year earlier. A housing affordability index shows that houses became more expensive in relation to incomes. Concerned that the sharp rise in prices was spilling over from the high-end property sector to the broader residential market, the authorities directed banks to lower their loan-to-value ratios and raised stamp duty on high-end housing. As prices continued to increase, in November 2010 the government imposed a special stamp duty on residential property resold within 24 months of acquisition. To add to the supply of housing in the medium term, it increased the land available for residential construction. By year-end, these measures appeared to have dampened speculation, as reflected in fewer transactions. In the external accounts, a sharply wider merchandise trade deficit and lower surplus in the income account offset a larger services trade surplus in 2010. The current account surplus declined to US$14.8 billion (6.6 per cent of GDP).

Looking ahead

In the view of the ADB, in the light of projected slower global trade and moderating PRC growth, Hong Kong will see its expansion ease this year and next. Private consumption is expected to remain healthy in 2011, based on growth in employment and incomes and be the main contributor to growth in the economy. Retail sales in volume terms rose by 23.6 per cent in the first month of 2011 aided by inbound tourism. Business investment will likely expand moderately in 2011, supported by low interest rates. Major public infrastructure projects begun in the past two years will continue contributing to growth in the forecast period and is expected to bring down growth in merchandise exports to about 7.5 per cent in nominal terms in 2011 from 22.4 per cent in 2010. Robust growth is foreseen for services exports, particularly to China. The budget for 2011 includes an increase in spending of nearly 25 per cent, and projects a small budget deficit.

Risk assessment

Economy	Good
Politics	See China
Regional stability	Good

KEY INDICATORS — Hong Kong

	Unit	2006	2007	2008	2009	2010
Population	m	6.86	6.97	7.01	7.07	*7.07
Gross domestic product (GDP)	US$bn	190.00	207.10	215.10	210.70	225.00
GDP per capita	US$	27,499	29,783	30,694	29,826	31,591
GDP real growth	%	7.0	6.4	2.5	-2.7	6.8
Inflation	%	2.0	2.0	4.3	0.5	2.4
Unemployment	%	4.8	4.1	3.5	5.2	4.3
Exports (fob) (goods)	US$m	317,600.0	345,979.0	365,236.0	321,836.0	394,015.0
Imports (fob) (goods)	US$m	331,634.0	365,679.0	388,353.0	348,698.0	436,980.0
Balance of trade	US$m	-14,033.0	-19,701.0	-23,117.0	-26,862.0	-42,965.0
Current account	US$m	22,936.0	25,532.0	29,296.0	18,278.0	13,936.0
Total reserves minus gold	US$m	133,170.0	152,640.0	182,470.0	255,770.0	268,649.0
Foreign exchange	US$m	133,170.0	152,640.0	182,470.0	255,770.0	268,649.0
Exchange rate	per US$	7.77	7.79	7.78	7.75	7.77

* estimated figure

COUNTRY PROFILE

Historical profile

1839 China impounded opium stocks and blocked further shipments. Major traders, Jardine Matheson, called on the British government to exert its right to trade. The British navy blockaded Chinese ports, sparking the first Opium War.

1842 China ceded Hong Kong to Great Britain under provision of the *Treaty of Nanking*, following defeat in the first Opium War, which it fought to wipe out the illicit smuggling of opium into the country. Hong Kong was already a sizeable local fishing community with 3,000 inhabitants and 2,000 fishermen. Hong Kong became an important British naval base and attracted merchants from mainland China; the colony became an important regional *entrepôt*.

1856–60 The second Opium War was fought in which the British and French defeated China.

1860 The Kowloon Peninsula was acquired under the *Convention of Peking*.

1898 The New Territories were leased from China for a period of 99 years.

1900s Immigration from the mainland increased as social turmoil due to the Boxer rebellion and general insecurity in China grew. The prospects of employment in Hong Kong's light industries increased.

1937 Outbreak of the Sino-Japanese War. As the Japanese army advanced further into China, more Chinese fled to Hong Kong. It is estimated that over 500,000 Chinese entered the territory at this time.

1941 Hong Kong fell to the Japanese.

1945 After Japan's defeat in the Second World War, Britain resumed control of the territory.

1984 The UK conceded that from July 1997, on the expiry of the lease on the New Territories, China would regain sovereignty over the whole of Hong Kong.

The Sino-British Joint Declaration contained detailed assurances on the future of Hong Kong.
1997 Hong Kong became a Special Administrative Region (SAR) of the People's Republic of China in an arrangement to last for 50 years. The Hong Kong stock market crashed; a fear that currency speculators would trade the Hong Kong dollar down in value prompted authorities to raise interest rates.
1998 Only 23 per cent of eligible voters turned out to choose an 800-member election committee with powers to nominate the chief executive and 10 legislators. The election process was criticised as complicated and undemocratic. Hong Kong International Airport on Lantau Island opened.
1999 Beijing redefined the constitution, ruling who had the right to live in Hong Kong. This constitutional change sparked protests.
2000 There was a low turnout in the LegCo elections; the Democratic Party (DP) lost a seat to the pro-Beijing Democratic Alliance for the Betterment of Hong Kong (DAB).
2001 Chief Secretary Anson Chan, holder of the SAR's second most powerful office, resigned, amid concerns that pressure from Beijing had made her position untenable. Donald Tsang replaced Chan as chief secretary.
2002 Chief Executive Tung Chee-hwa was appointed for a second five-year term.
2003 Around 500,000 people protested over a proposed anti-subversion law, which many believe threatened basic rights; another demonstration of 50,000 people called for universal suffrage and the dismissal of Chief Executive Tung Chee-hwa.
2004 Chinese legislators ruled out direct elections for a Hong Kong leader in 2007.
2005 Chief Executive Tung Chee-hwa resigned due to ill health; he was replaced by Chief Secretary Donald Tsang.
2007 Donald Tsang won a second term as chief executive. The former Chief Secretary, Ms Anson Chan, won a seat in the legislature with 55 per cent of the vote against China-backed Regina Ip (43 per cent) and six other candidates. Ms Chan campaigned for universal suffrage and full democracy. Donald Tsang submitted his report on democratic reform in Hong Kong to Beijing.
2008 In Legislative Council elections, pro-democrats won 58.99 per cent of the vote (23 seats out of 60), pro-Beijing parties 41.01 per cent (35) and independents 2.72 per cent (2). Hong Kong's economy officially fell into recession.
2009 The economy pulled out of recession in the second quarter. Construction of a new, six-lane bridge, linking Hong Kong and Macao to China's mainland province of Guangdong, began in December; when completed (2016) it will be the longest sea-crossing bridge in the world (almost 50kms).
2010 The air pollution level in March reached a record high, caused by severe sandstorms in Northern China, and prompting authorities to warn Hong Kong citizens to avoid going out. In April, to dampen a possible property bubble, stamp duty on properties of over US$2.6 million was increased by 0.50 per cent (up to 4.25 per cent). In May a by-election was held following the resignation of five pro-democracy party legislative councillors, in January. They had complained about the slow pace of democratisation, in particular the failure to introduce universal suffrage. All five members were re-elected; Beijing branded the elections 'illegal'. Protests in both Hong Kong and Guangdong took place in August over concerns that central government plans to insist that the regional dialect of Cantonese should be replaced by the national dialect of Mandarin in mainstream, primetime broadcasting. The worry for the protestors was that Cantonese will become marginalised.
2011 A minimum wage of HK$28 (US$3.60) per hour was introduced in Hong Kong on 1 May. Around 270,000 low-paid workers (10 per cent of the working population) were expected to benefit from the change. A voluntary minimum wage scheme had been introduced in 2006, but never achieved widespread success. The five-yearly national census began on 30 June, with completion on 24 July. Early results will be published by February 2012 and final results by March 2013. On 13 December, the Swiss-based, World Economic Forum voted Hong Kong as the world's leading financial centre in its annual survey of global financial development. This is the first time an Asian city has outstripped the traditional leading centres of Wall Street (New York) and the City of London (UK).

Political structure

Constitution

The Basic Law, promulgated by the People's Republic of China (PRC) in 1990, effectively became Hong Kong's constitution after sovereignty of the former British colony was handed over to mainland China in July 1997. The Basic Law pledges to maintain Hong Kong's economic, social and political distinctiveness for a period of 50 years after the handover to the PRC, under the principle of 'one country, two systems'. Foreign affairs and defence are the responsibility of the central government in Beijing.

Form of state

Special Administrative Region (SAR) of the People's Republic of China

The executive

Hong Kong is administered by a Beijing-appointed chief executive, who represents the Chinese Politburo. Tung Chee Hwa was appointed chief executive by a 400-member Selection Committee in 1996, assuming the role in July 1997. The 13-member Executive Council (ExCo) serves in an advisory role for the Chief Executive. Under the terms of the Basic Law, an 800-member 'election committee', mostly selected from the business community via functional constituencies, will nominate future chief executives.

National legislature

The 60-seat unicameral Legislative Council (LegCo) has 60 members, of which 30 are elected by proportional representation in geographical constituencies and 30 by majority voting in functional constituencies (trade unions, professional and business associations). All members serve four-year terms.

Legal system

Under the Basic Law, Hong Kong's legal system is guaranteed independence from the Chinese judiciary. A Hong Kong Court of Final Appeal replaced the Privy Council in the United Kingdom as the highest court. The autonomy of this institution was seriously undermined in 1999 after a bitter dispute between the executive and the court over the migration of dependants from mainland China, in which China's legislature, the National People's Congress (NPC), overruled the Court of Final Appeal. However, the government in Beijing declared that recourse to the NPC would be kept a rare and exceptional act, and has not been invoked since.

Last elections

7 September 2008 (Legislative Council); 25 March 2005 (chief executive).
Results: Legislative Council: pan-Democrats won 58.99 per cent of the vote (23 seats out of 60), the pro-Beijing parties won 41.01 per cent (35) and independents 2.72 per cent (2). Turnout was 45 per cent.
Chief executive: the 800-member election committee re-elected Donald Tsang by 649 votes to 123 for Alan Leong.

Next elections

September 2012 (Legislative Council)

Political parties

Ruling party

Coalition government (approved by the Zhongguo Gongchandang (Chinese Communist Party))

Main opposition party

There is no formal opposition.

Population
7.07 million (2009)
Last census: 14 March 2006: 6,864,958
Population density: 6,400 inhabitants per square km (2010), one of the highest densities in the world.
Annual growth rate: Projected growth 1 per cent per annum (2000–15).
Ethnic make-up
Approximately 98 per cent of the population is of Chinese descent. There are Caucasian, Indian and Filipino minorities, perhaps totalling more than 200,000, but many of these are seasonal migrant workers.
Religions
Buddhism and Taoism (74 per cent); Confucianism, Islam and Hinduism (17 per cent); Christianity (9 per cent). There are places of worship for most other religious groups. Falun Gong, the sect banned in mainland China, is legal in Hong Kong.

Education
Primary education is provided free in all government schools and in most government-assisted schools from the ages of six to 11 years. Secondary schools are divided into junior and senior levels, for 12–14-year-olds and 15–16-year-olds, respectively. The secondary school system consists of Anglo-Chinese grammar schools, Chinese middle schools, secondary technical schools and pre-vocational schools. There are a number of universities, several of which used to be technical colleges. After the British handover in 1997, 24 of Hong Kong's 124 secondary schools which taught in English were ordered to change to Cantonese.
Government expenditure on education amounts to over 20 per cent of the SAR government budget. The largest proportion of the budget is spent on basic education, accounting for 68.8 per cent of total spending on education.
Literacy rate: 93.8 per cent total, 90.1 per cent female; adult rates (World Bank).

Health
Government efforts have been mainly geared to the continuous development of the primary health care services.
Eighteen health centres and 18 visiting health teams provide services to the elderly and their carers. There are three types of hospital in Hong Kong: public, government-assisted and private. Provision of hospital service at nominal cost is made universally accessible to all people. Hong Kong's health care service faces a huge financial strain due to its ageing population and escalating medical costs.
Life expectancy: 80.1 years (estimate 2003)
Fertility rate/Maternal mortality rate: 1.0 birth per woman; maternal mortality 5.6 per 100,000 total births (World Bank).
Birth rate/Death rate: 7.9 births and 5 deaths and per 1,000 people (World Bank)
Child (under 5 years) mortality rate (per 1,000): 2.7 per 1,000 live births (World Bank)

Welfare
The social security schemes available in Hong Kong cover a broad range of developmental, support and remedial services, and financial assistance to those in need.
The Comprehensive Social Security Assistance Scheme is means-tested and non-contributory. The Scheme provides cash assistance to individuals and families to meet their basic and essential needs. The recipients are also helped through various initiatives to establish self-reliance. The Social Security Allowance Scheme aims to meet the special needs of the elderly and people with disabilities. The Accident Compensation Schemes provide short-term assistance to families or individuals in cases of reduced or lost earnings.

Main cities
Xianggang (Victoria, Hong Kong Island) (estimated population 1.0 million (m) in 2005); Juilong (Kowloon) (2.0m); Tuen Mun (522,370), Sha Tin (475,177), Fanling (321,650)

Languages spoken
Cantonese is the Chinese language spoken at home by more than 90 per cent of the population. Mandarin Chinese (Putonghua), the official language of the People's Republic of China, is widely understood.
English is universally understood in business and commerce.
Official language/s
Chinese (Mandarin, Beijing dialect *de jure*; Cantonese *de facto*) and English

Media
The freedom on the press is guaranteed in basic law.
Press
Hong Kong has retained its press freedom since being reunited with China and is a major centre for print journalism with one of the world's largest press industries. It does not impose prior censorship on its newspapers or television and radio news reports.
Dailies: There are over 50 daily newspapers, most of which are published in Chinese.
In English, the *South China Morning Post* (www.scmp.com) has the largest circulation, *China Daily* (www.chinadaily.com.cn) is published by the Chinese communist party.
In Chinese, broadsheets include *Ming Pao* (www.mingpaonews.com) and *Sing Tao* (www.singtao.com). Newspapers considered pro-Beijing include *Ta Kung Pao* (www.takungpao.com.hk), *Sing Pao* (www.singpao.com) and *Wen Wek Po* (www.wenweipo.com). The newspapers with the highest circulations are tabloid and informal, including *The Sun* (http://the-sun.on.cc), the *Oriental Daily* and *Apple Daily* (http://home.atnext.com).
Weeklies: In Chinese and with the highest circulation *Next Magazine* (http://next.atnext.com) is tabloid in style that not only covers entertainment but also current affairs, economic and business issues. Others include *Easy Finder* (http://face.atnext.com), *East Touch*, *East Week* and *Him Magazine* (www.him.com.hk). The only Chinese newsweekly, *Yazhou Zhoukan* (*Asia Weekly*) (www.yzzk.com) has broad contents of economic and international news.
Business: In English, the free-issue *The Standard* (www.thestandard.com.hk) covers financial markets and news and the *Far Eastern Economic Review* (Feer) (www.feer.com), is an influential monthly covering all aspects of the news throughout Asia. In Chinese newspapers include *Hong Kong Commercial Daily* (www.hkcd.com.hk) with the largest circulation in Mainland China, *Hong Kong Economic Journal* (www.hkej.com) and *Hong Kong Economic Times* cover financial news.
Periodicals: There are over 500 periodicals in circulation. In English, the monthly *Prestige Hong Kong* (www.prestigehk.com), is a glossy lifestyle and society magazine and *Muse* (www.musemag.hk) covers art and culture.
Broadcasting
The Hong Kong Broadcasting Authority (BA) is responsible for regulating and licensing all broadcasting outlets, while standards are maintained by the Television and Entertainment Licensing Authority (TELA).
The government-funded, but independent, Radio Television Hong Kong (RTHK) (www.rthk.org.hk) provides public broadcasting.
Radio: RTHK (www.rthk.org.hk) provides seven radio channels (RTHK Radio 1–6 and Radio Putonghua), with a full range of locally produced programmes in Cantonese, English and Mandarin. RTHK Radio 6 relays the BBC World Service. There are two private, commercial radio stations. Commercial Radio Hong Kong (CRHK) (www.crhk.com.hk) has three channels and a full range of programmes to rival RTHK. The other station is Metro (www.metroradio.com.hk) with three

channels, Metro- Finance, Showbiz and Plus.

Television: RTHK (www.rthk.org.hk) produces locally made educational, entertainment and news and current affairs programmes that are shown on other TV stations.

The two private, free-to-air TV stations are Asia Television (ATV) and Television Broadcasts (TVB), each with one channel in English and one in Chinese. There are several subscription networks which between them offer over 200 channels, showing locally produced and international programmes, the largest of which is Cable TV Hong Kong (www.cabletv.com.hk), which produces more programmes than any other broadcaster.

Advertising

Advertising is available in the press, on commercial radio and TV, in cinemas and on poster sites, with direct mail and news technology. Advertising expenditure is equivalent is typically over 1 per cent of GDP.

News agencies

National news agency: Xinhua News Agency, Hong Kong Branch

Hong Kong China News Agency (HKCNA): www.chinanews.com.hk

Economy

Hong Kong is one of the most densely populated islands in the world; it is also one of the most economically dynamic. The economy is founded on financial services, light engineering and assembly-line manufacturing, property and trading; Hong Kong has the world's third largest harbour and the world's largest container port (processing 21 million containers annually), which accords Hong Kong its status as a major transportation hub.

Although the global economic crisis affected all sectors, Hong Kong's economy only registered recession in the third quarter of 2008, as annual GDP growth fell from 6.4 per cent in 2007 to 2.1 per cent; it fell to -2.7 per cent in 2009. However the economy grew out of recession in the second quarter of 2009, when it grew by 3.3 per cent from April–June. The annual GDP growth is projected to rise to 5.0 per cent in 2010 as global trade recovers.

Hong Kong's relationship with China is mixed. At one end, it benefits from China's booming economy that sees inward investment by some of China's newly created wealthy buying property and investing in businesses in the region. In 2009 investment in the Hong Kong's residential rental market was depressed and rents were decreasing and unemployment rising. However, by 2010 property prices were rising rapidly, 47 per cent January 2009–August 2010, as mortgages rates fell to their lowest since the early 1990s – a result of the Hong Kong dollar's peg to a weakening US dollar. An estimated 20 per cent of buyers of new residential property were from mainland China. The risk of an overheated property market prompted the government to increase the equity-ratio at the beginning of the transaction in October 2010. At the other end of the relationship, China's vast manufacturing sector can out-perform anything Hong Kong has to offer the world if it chooses. Hong Kong could become subsumed into China's leviathan business machine, if it did not provide China with an interesting anomaly for a communist state – a fully functioning and energetic world-class stock exchange that processes not only currency and business transactions for China but also for many overseas entities. In August 2010, the Hong Kong Stock Exchange (KHEx) had a combined market capitalisation of US$2.3 trillion, ranking it second behind Tokyo (Japan) in Asian stock exchanges; KHEx is ranked sixth in world stock exchanges.

On 13 December 2011, the Swiss-based, World Economic Forum voted Hong Kong as the world's leading financial centre in its annual survey of global financial development. This is the first time an Asian city has outstripped the traditional leading centres of Wall Street (New York) and the City of London (UK).

External trade

Hong Kong, as an independent customs territory separate from the rest of China, can enter into international commercial and economic agreements on it own behalf. As an economic entity it participates in full membership of a number of international organisations including the Asia Pacific Economic Co-operation forum (APEC).

Under the Closer Economic Partnership Arrangement (CEPA), Hong Kong has a trade alliance with China's nine southernmost provinces and Macao through the pan-Pearl River Delta (PRD) trade bloc, which has been described as 'the largest and most export-oriented of China's regions' with a regional GDP of over US$270 billion. It has a free trade agreement with China, which allows the trade of goods of Hong Kong origin entry at zero tariff, as well as preferential treatment in 27 service sectors.

Hong Kong's manufacturing base has relocated to mainland China where raw materials are readily available and labour is cheaper. Its service industry has grown, in part to compete against China's own growing financial centres.

Imports

Main imports are petroleum, raw materials and semi-manufactures, capital goods and foodstuffs.

Main sources: China (typically 46 per cent of total), Japan (9 per cent), Taiwan (7 per cent).

Exports

Exports include electrical machinery and appliances – telecommunications, sound recording and electronic components – textiles, clothing, footwear, watches and clocks, toys, plastics, precious stones and printed material.

Main destinations: China (typically 50 per cent of total), US (11 per cent), Japan (4 per cent).

Re-exports

These include consumer goods, clothing, electrical machinery and appliances.

Agriculture

Agriculture accounts for around 0.1 per cent of GDP. The land area is mountainous, with fertile soils when they are watered. Agricultural land, including 600 hectares of orchards, accounts for 7 per cent of the total land area.

Main crops include sweet potatoes, yams, taro, sugar cane, white cabbage, flowering cabbage, lettuce, chinese kale, radishes and watercress.

Hong Kong has a fishing fleet of about 4,900 vessels, most of which are mechanised. The fishing sector employs about 24,000 fishermen, who are provided with training organised by the Agriculture and Fisheries Conservation Department (AFCD) in order to enhance the competitiveness of the sector. Pond and marine fish farming in the New Territories accounts for 3 per cent of total production. Seafood production can reach up to 200,000 tonnes per annum. Freshwater fish production is more limited, typically 4,000 tonnes or less per annum. In addition, Hong Kong imports in the region of 60,000 tonnes of freshwater fish per annum and some 500,000 tonnes of seafood, of which 300,000 tonnes are typically re-exported.

Industry and manufacturing

Industry accounts for around 11 per cent of GDP and employs 18 per cent of the workforce. The relocation of manufacturing operations from Hong Kong to mainland China is causing a long-term decline in the sector. The re-export sector, in contrast, has grown due to growing consumer demand and industrial production on the mainland.

Tourism

Tourism is one of the most important sector of the economy. Hong Kong is a blend of Chinese and Western cultures with the emphasis on shopping and oriental cuisine. The tiny island of Hong Kong is topped by The Peak from which most surrounding territories can be viewed. At night the neon and halogen lighted

cityscape offers a stunning vista best seen from tall skyscrapers.
Growth in tourism was 21.8 per cent in 2010, as 36 million visitors arrived, of which 20 millions stayed overnight. The majority of visitor came from mainland-China.

Environment
Hong Kong is suffering air pollution as a result of pollution from southern China; visibility has declined over the past 30 years and continues to worsen. Although Hong Kong has sharply reduced its own emissions, it lies at the southern end of a vast industrial conurbation that includes Guangzhou and Shenzhen.

Mining
Mining accounts for less than 0.05 per cent of GDP, producing mainly kaolin (around 44,500 tonnes) and feldspar (around 5,500 tonnes).

Hydrocarbons
Hong Kong relies entirely on imports of hydrocarbons. Consumption of petroleum products was 366,000 barrels per day in 2007. Natural gas is imported via a pipeline from the South China Sea offshore gas field and is used for power generation. Consumption was 3.8 billion cubic metres in 2010. Annual coal imports were 1.7 billion tonnes oil equivalent, meeting about 20 per cent of energy consumption.

Energy
Total installed generating capacity is around 10GW, with consumption at 37.7 billion kilowatt hours (kWh) in 2008. Two commercial companies own and operate the power stations located within Hong Kong. CLP Power uses diesel, natural gas and nuclear energy, while HK Electric uses natural gas, coal and operates the only wind turbine, which became operational in 2006. HK Electric is a public company, responsible for generation, distribution and sale of electricity; there are other, private companies also supplying electricity. The upgrade completed in 2007 had introduced gas-fired turbines, and the wind-turbine.

Financial markets
Stock exchange
HKEx (Hong Kong Exchanges and Clearing) operates Hong Kong Stock Exchange and Hong Kong Futures Exchange.

Banking and insurance
Domestic banks in Hong Kong have tended to rely on the property sector for their earnings. Mortgages and other property-related lending still account for 40 to 50 per cent of total loans. Banking practice codes were revised in 2001 to make banking more transparent and consumer friendly. In 2002, some of the criteria for entry to the banking sector were relaxed. The aim was to attract a wider range of domestic and international banks to become involved in the SAR.
Hong Kong is an excellent location for insurers and has the largest number of insurance companies in Asia. Mainland Chinese insurers are linking up with foreign insurers in Hong Kong to cater for China's insurance market. By 2003, there were around 7,000 insurance establishments in the SAR with a total premium income of US$7 billion. French AXA group, the world's biggest insurance company, has its regional headquarters in Hong Kong.
Central bank
Hong Kong has no finance ministry or official central bank. The Hong Kong Monetary Authority (HKMA) oversees the monetary and banking system.
Main financial centre
Central District

Time
GMT plus eight hours

Geography
Hong Kong comprises some 235 islands and islets and a portion of the Chinese mainland, adjoining China's southern province of Guangdong. It consists of three areas: Hong Kong Island, the Kowloon Peninsula and the New Territories, which account for 92 per cent of the territory. About 75 per cent of Hong Kong's land is unsuitable for food production, consisting of hills that rise from sea level to 900 metres.
Hemisphere
Northern

Climate
Hong Kong is subtropical and monsoonal. Summer (May to mid-September) is hot and humid with a risk of typhoons. July and August can be very hot. Autumn (September to December) is generally sunny, but drier, and the most pleasant time of year. Winter (December to February) is dry, but can get uncomfortably cold, with an average temperature of 15 degrees Celsius (C). Spring (March and April) is moderately warm and damp. The average annual temperature is about 23 degrees C, while rainfall averages 2,224mm per year, and humidity is often above 83 per cent.

Dress codes
Business dress is formal as appearance is taken seriously. Very smart dress is also *de rigueur* for ladies; skirts are advisable, rather than trousers.

Entry requirements
Passports
A valid passport is required by all. Passports must be valid for six months after arrival.
Visa
Visas required by all, with some exceptions see www.immd.gov.hk/ehtml/hkvisas.htm for further details.
Business and tourist visas are considered the same, up to the minimum time allowed to visit. For further clarification email: enquiry@immd.gov.hk; or contact the local Chinese embassy.
Regulations regarding entry into Hong Kong are extensive owing to the high level of illegal immigration. Travellers are advised to obtain up-to-date information before any journey.
Currency advice/regulations
There are no currency restrictions. Travellers cheques are readily accepted.
Customs
Personal effects are duty-free. Visitors wishing to purchase ivory products in Hong Kong will need an export licence from the Hong Kong authorities, and will also need to show an import licence for their final destination.
Prohibited imports
Illegal drugs, fireworks, firearms, counterfeit items, textiles, ivory products, animals and plants, game, meat and poultry. Live animals are strictly controlled. Antibiotics may not be imported without an accompanying doctor's letter .
Visitors entering from China should expect searches for fireworks.

Health (for visitors)
Mandatory precautions
Yellow fever and cholera inoculation if travelling from infected areas.
Advisable precautions
Vaccinations are recommended for diphtheria, tuberculosis, hepatitis A and B, polio, tetanus and typhoid. Dengue fever is increasing, however the risk of malaria has been reduced. Tap water is safe to drink.
A HK$580 fee is imposed on any visitor who has to use accident and emergency hospital services. Medical insurance is recommended.

Hotels
A wide range of hotels are available; advance bookings are recommended between May–November. A 10 per cent service charge and 5 per cent tax are added to hotel bills.

Credit cards
Major international credit cards are widely accepted, although cash prices may be lower.

Public holidays (national)
Fixed dates
1 Jan (New Year's Day), 5 Apr (Ching Ming/Tomb Sweeping Day), ^1 May (Labour Day), 1 Jul (HKSAR Establishment Day), 1 Oct (National Day), 25–26 Dec (Christmas).

^ Holidays falling on Sunday are taken on Monday.

Variable dates
Chinese New Year (Jan/Feb, three days), Good Friday and Easter Monday (Mar/Apr), Birth of Buddha (May), Tuen Ng (Dragon Boat festival, May/Jun), Chinese Mid-Autumn Festival (Sep/Oct), Chung Yeung Festival (Oct).

Working hours

Banking
Mon–Fri: 0900–1630; Sat: 0900–1230.

Business
Mon–Fri: 0900–1300, 1400–1700; Sat: 0900–1300.

Government
Mon–Fri: 0900–1300, 1400–1700; Sat: 0900–1230.

Shops
Central District 1000–1900; Causeway Bay and Wanchai 1000–2130; Tsimshatsui East 1000–1930; Tsimshatsui, Yaumatei and Mong Kok 1000–2100. Most department stores and shops open Sundays. Some Japanese stores close one day per week, and street markets operate all day and into the night.

Telecommunications

Mobile/cell phones
GSM 900/1800 services are available throughout the islands and territories.

Electricity supply

200V AC, 50Hz. No uniformity in plug design.

Weights and measures

Metric system (Imperial system and local units also in use).

Social customs/useful tips

Western influence in Hong Kong has produced ways of doing business that are similar to other major business capitals. However, behind the facade of modern office blocks and neon-lit shopping malls, ancient Chinese customs still survive and have become part of the life of the foreign community.
Business cards are handed out liberally as a method of developing a network of professional contacts. A Chinese translation on the reverse side is a worthwhile addition. Use both hands when offering a business card, as passing it with one hand is seen as impolite.
Appearances of wealth are considered important in a territory that is dedicated to making money. Business contacts are ostentatiously wined and dined. Most entertaining is done in restaurants. It is considered bad manners to divide the bill after a meal. If you go to a dinner as the guest of honour, you should rise and thank the host briefly for his hospitality.
Personal friendships and family ties oil the wheels of business. The wealthy keep a high social profile, donating large sums of money to charity.
Punctuality is helpful as most people have packed days, although some allowances are made for the heavy traffic.
Policemen who speak English have a red shoulder badge.

Security

The level of crime against visitors is relatively low. Theft, mainly by pickpockets, is a problem on the streets.

Getting there

Air
National airline: Cathay Pacific Airways
International airport/s: Hong Kong International (HKG), 34km from the centre. Post office, bank, bureau de change, restaurants/cafeterias, duty free shop, taxis.
Airport tax: HK$120, excluding transit passengers.

Surface
The business district and commercial centre of Hong Kong is located on Hong Kong island. Kowloon and the new territories across the harbour are part of the Asia mainland, with road links providing connections.
Road: Bus services link Guangzhou to the Hong Kong border.
Rail: The Kowloon-Canton Railway Corporation (KCR) is the main carrier of passengers to and from China, with express trains serving Kowloon-Guangzhou and Kowloon-Lowu.
Water: Hovercraft services operate four times a day to and from Guangzhou and several times daily to and from Zhuhai. There are frequent daily services to and from Macao by hovercraft (75 minutes), jetcats (75 minutes), high speed ferry (90 minutes) and jetfoil (60 minutes).
Main port/s: Victoria Harbour (Hong Kong Island) and Tolo Harbour (New Territories).

Getting about

National transport
Air: Dragonair flies to 23 mainland Chinese destinations, as well as other regional capitals in Asia.
Hong Kong maintains separate immigration and customs policies from the mainland and flights between them are treated as international and not domestic flights.
Road: Hong Kong's road network is extensive and of high quality but often congested in central areas.
Buses: Bus services are inexpensive and convenient.There are three main private bus companies, China Motor Bus (CMB), Citybus and Kowloon Motor Bus (KMB, Kowloon only), and private minibus services.
Rail: There are three rail systems which operate outside urban areas. The KCR runs a passenger service between Kowloon and Guangzhou (China) and a suburban service to the new towns of the north-eastern New Territories; KCR also operates the Light Rail Transit network in the north-western New Territories; a cable-hauled funicular railway operates on Hong Kong Island between Garden Road in the Central District to Victoria Gap on the Peak.
The Airport Express is a dedicated high-speed train link, with a journey time of 24 minutes from central Hong Kong to the airport. Operating hours: 0550–0115 daily.
Water: There are extensive ferry, hovercraft, hydrofoil and coastal services between the islands of Hong Kong.

City transport
Taxis: Metered taxis (that calculate time and distance) are readily available in most areas of the territory. They carry four to five passengers. Cabs are painted green and silver in the New Territories, and red and silver in town. Hong Kong taxis are reasonably priced. It is advisable to have the destination written in Chinese. Tips are discretionary. Taxi drivers retain odd cents of change as a matter of course. A ride to or from the airport–Central District will include an extra toll charge of HK$30 plus any tunnel tolls.
Buses, trams & metro: There are regular shuttle buses to and from the airport to both Central District (Hong Kong Island) and Tsimshatsui (Kowloon). They are cheaper than taxis and serve five routes every 12–15 minutes. Airport bus routes A11 and A12 operate 0600–2359 hours to Central District, journey time 70 minutes.
Trams: A flat fare system operates on Hong Kong Island's double-decker five-line tram system. The trams are crowded at rush hour, but afford good views of Hong Kong at other times.
Ferry: There are regular ferry services across the narrow strip of water from Star Ferry terminal at the north of Hong Kong Island to Kowloon.

Car hire
A valid driving licence issued in the country of origin may be used for up to 12 months. Parking difficulties and traffic congestion should be taken into account when planning to drive in Hong Kong. Chauffeur-driven and self-drive car hire is available.

BUSINESS DIRECTORY

Telephone area codes

The international direct dialling code (IDD) for Hong Kong is +852, followed by subscriber's number.

Useful telephone numbers

Emergencies	999
Directory enquiries	108
Problems	109
International calls	010

Calls to China 012
International direct dialling code enquiries 013

Chambers of Commerce

American Chamber of Commerce in Hong Kong, 1904 Bank of America Tower, 12 Harcourt Road, Central (tel: 2526-0165; fax: 2810-1289; e-mail: amcham@amcham.org.hk).

British Chamber of Commerce in Hong Kong, Emperor Group Centre, 288 Hennessy Road, Wan Chai (tel: 2824-2211; fax: 2824-1333; e-mail: info@britcham.com).

Banking

Bank of East Asia Ltd, GPO Box 31, 10 Des Voeux Road, Central (tel: 2842-3200; fax: 2845-9333).

Bank of China (Hong Kong) Ltd; Bank of China Tower, 1 Garden Road, Hong Kong (tel: 2826-6350; fax: 2530-3875).

DBS Bank (Hong Kong) Ltd, 99 Queen's Road Central, Central (tel: 2218-2706).

Hang Seng Bank Ltd, Hang Seng Bank Headquarters, 83 Des Voeux Road, Central (tel: 2825-5111; fax: 2845-9301).

HSBC, 1 Queen's Road, Central (tel: 2822-1111; fax: 2868-1646; internet: www.hsbcnet.com).

Nanyang Commercial Bank Ltd, 151 Des Voeux Road, Central (tel: 2852-0888; fax: 2815-3333).

Shanghai Commercial Bank Ltd, 12 Queen's Road, Central (tel: 2841-5415).

Wing Lung Bank Ltd, 45 Des Voeux Road, Central (tel: 2826-8333; fax: 2810-0592).

Central bank

Hong Kong Monetary Authority, 3 Garden Road, Central (tel: 2878-8196; fax: 2878-8197; e-mail: hkma@hkma.gov.hk).

Stock exchange

HKEx (Hong Kong Exchanges and Clearing): www.hkex.com.hk

Travel information

Cathay Pacific Airways, Swire House, 9 Connaught Road, Central (tel: 2747-5000; fax: 2810-6563).

Hong Kong Automobile Association, March Road, Wanchai (tel: 2574-3394).

Star Ferry Concourse, Kowloon; Shop 8, Basement Jardine House, Central (tel: 2801-7177 (visitor hotline); fax: 2810-4877).

National tourist organisation offices

Hong Kong Tourist Board (HKTB), 9-11th Floor, Citicorp Centre, 18 Whitfield Road, North Point (tel: 2807-6543, 2807-6177 (tourist information); fax: 2807-6582; internet: www.discoverhongkong.com).

Other useful addresses

Agriculture and Fisheries Department, 13/F Canton Road Government Offices, 393 Canton Road, Kowloon (tel: 2733-2174; fax: 2311-3731).

Banking, Securities, Insurance & Companies Division, 24th Floor Admiralty Centre, Tower II, Central (tel: 2527-8337; fax: 2865-6146).

Buildings Department, 3-12/F Murray Building Garden Road, Central (tel: 2848-2327; fax: 2840-0451).

Business and Industrial Trade Fairs Ltd, 51 Gloucester Road, Wanchai (tel: 2865-2633; fax: 2866-1770, 2865-5513).

Census and Statistics Department, Wanchai Tower 1, 12 Harbour Road, Wanchai (tel: 2823-4807).

Chinese Manufacturers' Association of Hong Kong, 3rd and 4th Floor CMA Bldg, 64 Connaught Road, Central (tel: 2545-6166).

Civil Aviation department, 46/F Queensway Government Offices, 66 Queensway (tel: 2867-4332; fax: 2869-0093).

Consumer Council, 22/F, K Wah Centre, 191 Java Road, North Point (tel: 2856-3113; fax: 2856-3611).

Department of Health, 17 & 21/F Wu Chung House, 213 Queen's Road East, Wan Chai (tel: 2961-8989; fax: 2836-0071).

Environmental Protection Department, 24-28/F Southorn Centre, 130 Hennessy Road, Wan Chai (tel: 2835-1018; fax: 2838-2155).

Exchange Fund Division, 24th Floor Admiralty Centre, Tower II, Central (tel: 2529-0024; fax: 2865-6146).

Federation of Hong Kong Industries, 4/F Hankow Centre, 5-15 Hankow Road, Kowloon (tel: 2723-0818).

Finance Branch, Government Secretariat, Central Government Offices, Lower Albert Road, Central (tel: 2810-2540; fax: 2810-1530).

Hong Kong Convention & Incentive Travel Bureau (trade fairs), 35th Floor Jardine House, Central (tel: 2801-7111; fax: 2810-4877).

Hong Kong Exporters' Association, Room 825 Star House, 3 Salisbury Road, Tsim Sha Tsui, Kowloon (tel: 2730-9851).

Hong Kong Government Industry Department, 'One-Stop' Unit, 14th Floor, Ocean Centre, 5 Canton Road, Kowloon (tel: 2737-2434; fax: 2730-4633).

Hong Kong Economic and Trade Office, 6 Grafton Street, London W1S 4EQ (tel: (+044-20) 7499-9821; fax: (+044-20) 7495-5033; email: general@hketolondon.gov.hk).

Hong Kong Industrial Estates Corporation, 107 Estate Centre Building, 19 Dai Cheong Street, Tai Po Industrial Estate, Tai Po, New Territories (tel: 2664-1183).

Hong Kong Productivity Council, 78 Tat Chee Avenue, HKCP Bldg, Kowloon (tel: 2788-5678).

Hong Kong Standards and Testing Centre, 10 Dai Wang Street, Tai Po Industrial Estate, Tai Po, New Territories (tel: 2667-0021).

Hong Kong Telecom Association, GPO Box 13461 (tel: 2881-2333; fax: 2881-2332).

Hong Kong Trade Development Council, Research Department, 36-39/F Office Tower, Convention Plaza, 1 Harbour Road, Wan Chai (tel: 2584-4333; fax: 2824-0249; internet site: http://www.tdc.org.hk).

Industry Department, 14/F Ocean Centre, 5 Canton Road, Tsim Sha Tsui (tel: 2737-2216; fax: 2377-0730).

Labour Department, 16/F Harbour Building, 38 Pier Road, Central (tel: 2852-3511).

Securities & Futures Commission, 38/F Two Exchange Square, 8 Connaught Place (tel: 2840-9202; fax: 2845-9553).

Stock Exchange of Hong Kong Ltd, 1/F, 1 and 2 Exchange Square, 8 Connaught Place, PO Box 8888 (tel: 2522-1122; fax: 2868-1308).

Telecommunications Authority, 29th Floor, Wu Chung House, 213 Queens Road East, Wan Chai (tel: 2961-6333; fax: 2803-5110).

Trade Department, Ocean Centre, 5 Canton Road, Kowloon (tel: 2722-2333).

US General Consulate, 26 Garden Road (tel: 2523-9011; fax: 2845-1598).

Visa Office, Ministry of Foreign Affairs, 5th Floor, Lower Block, 26 Harbour Road, Wanchai (tel: 2835-3794).

National news agency: Xinhua News Agency, Hong Kong Branch, 381 Queen's Road East, Hong Kong

Internet sites

Economic Services Bureau: www.info.gov.hk/esb/content.htm

Hong Kong Airport: www.hongkongairport.com

Hong Kong Shipping directory: www.info.gov.hk/mardep/sdfiles/shipdir.ht

Hong Kong Statistics: www.info.gov.hk/censtatd/eindex.htm

Hungary

In early April 2010 Hungary's largest opposition party Fidesz-Magyar Polgári Szövetség (Fidesz) (Fidesz-Hungarian Civic Union) had looked set to win the first round of the country's parliamentary elections comfortably. The incumbent, minority Magyar Szocialista Párt (MSzP) (Hungarian Socialist Party), government looked unlikely to remain in power according to the opinion polls. The 2010 elections came at a sensitive time for Hungary, the first European Union (EU) country to obtain the support of the International Monetary Fund (IMF) following the advent of the international financial crisis.

Orban in

In the event, Fidesz's Viktor Orban surprised even his harshest critics by winning an impressive two thirds majority with 283 of the 386 seats. The MSzP government received a mauling at the hands of the electorate. Mr Orban risked getting carried away with his reformist zeal. In his pre-election desire to be all things to all men, he proudly announced that: 'The Hungarian people today have ousted the regime of oligarchs who misused their power and the people have established a new regime of national unity.' Hungary's socialists were probably not accustomed to being labelled 'oligarchs'. Mr Orban vowed to create a modest one million new jobs within ten years and to cut through Hungary's often stifling bureaucracy. All good stuff, but the more cynical of his audience could be forgiven for raising an eyebrow at the scale of Mr Orban's promises.

Thanks to the IMF

In June 2010 Mr Orban's new centre right government set out its programme of additional spending cuts following the balance of payments crisis of 2008 that had required a ?20 billion (US$25.6 billion) aid package from the IMF, the EU and the World Bank. With theatrical exaggeration, Hungary's new government stated that Hungary could be the new Greece, struggling to service its debt. In fact, Hungary's debt levels were not considered by analysts to be too worrying. The national debt at the end of 2009 was

KEY FACTS

Official name: Magyar Köztársaság (Republic of Hungary)

Head of State: President Pál Schmitt (Fidesz) (from 6 Aug 2010)

Head of government: Prime Minister Victor Orbán (Fidesz) (from 29 May 2010)

Ruling party: Fidesz-Magyar Polgári Szövetség (Fidesz) (Fidesz-Hungarian Civic Union) (from 25 Apr 2010)

Area: 93,033 square km

Population: 10.00 million (2010)*

Capital: Budapest

Official language: Hungarian (Magyar)

Currency: Forint (Ft)

Exchange rate: Ft218.68 per US$ (Oct 2011)

GDP per capita: US$12,879 (2010)

GDP real growth: 1.20% (2010)

GDP: US$129.00 billion (2010)

Labour force: 4.25 million (2010)

Unemployment: 11.10% (2010)

Inflation: 4.90% (2010)

Balance of trade: US$6.21 billion (2010)

78.9 per cent of gross domestic product (GDP), almost exactly the same percentage figure as Germany and well below Italy's 118.2 per cent and Greece's 124.9 per cent. Growth in GDP for 2009 was exactly zero, but forecast to return to an annual 2.8 per cent in 2011.

Since the autumn of 2008 international investors had turned their backs on Hungary fearful that its excessive external debt and loose fiscal policies – or even the absence of them – would lead to default of one kind or another. Government austerity policies, which had inevitably lead to increased unemployment and diminished rates of consumption, in the view of many Hungarian voters, only made a bad situation worse. If the socialist lead coalition was both the cause and victim of the plot, the beneficiaries were the Fidesz party lead by hardened politician Orban and the more extreme right-wing parties such as Jobbik Magyarországért Mozgalom (Jobbik) (Movement for a Better Hungary), which in the run up to the first round of the elections had seen a surge in support. Pre-election polls put Fidesz support as high as 57 per cent of the vote, with Jobbik around 16 per cent and the Socialists at 19 per cent. The Socialist government had forecast a budget deficit of 3.8 per cent of GDP, a figure rejected by Fidesz. Mr Orban's party announced that it planned to cut taxes, create one million jobs in a ten year period and raise the 2010 budget deficit to 6.5 per cent of GDP. The IMF standby credit arrangement would, Fidesz had also announced, have to be re-negotiated. So far so good.

No thanks to the IMF

By late July 2010 that, however, was turning out to be about as good as it was likely to get. Better, looked like being replaced by worse. At first, Mr Orban seemed to be limiting his apportionment of blame for Hungary's stagnant economy and other problems to the Magyar Nemzeti Bank (MNB) (National Bank of Hungary) and its governor, Andras Simor. To make his point, Mr Orban – not a man for subtlety – decreed that Mr Simor's salary should be cut by a whopping 75 per cent. Responding, possibly over-responding, to the populist mood that had given him his substantial parliamentary majority, Mr Orban widened his criticism to take in the international banks and, critically, the IMF. In criticising the Washington based agency Mr Orban was, of course, preaching to the converted. As with other austerity-struck Southern European countries, the IMF was a sitting target for an electorate that had taken more than it wished of bleak economic times. A dispute with the IMF over exactly how Hungary's deficit was going to be brought under control ended up with relations being unceremoniously broken off. At the heart of the dispute was the government's plan to loosen its fiscal policy, making it more than likely that the national debt – which by the end of June 2010 had risen to 80 per cent of GDP – would rise still further. As long as debt re-payment remained an abstract, distant prospect, rather than an immediate objective and requirement, this was not too big a problem. However, in 2011 Hungary would have to start re-payments totalling some €30 billion (US$38.4 billion), plus a further €2 billion (US$2.5 billion) due to the IMF itself. The latter was, in fact, a problem of the government's own making, since if relations with the IMF had not been broken off, the IMF would have covered the repayment itself. Hungary was left with little option but to pin its hopes on the EU riding to the rescue. But without the participation of the IMF, this was unlikely. The cultural and political flavour to Mr Orban's attitude to the IMF in general and Mr Simor in particular enabled the prime minister to externalise Hungary's economic problems and maintain Fidesz's popularity at the same time. One analyst was quoted in the *International Herald Tribune* as saying that 'these guys are from the countryside'. They were 'opposed to the refined intellectual sensibilities of the Budapest elite', epitomised by the much pilloried Mr Simor.

In June 2010 Mr Orban endeavoured to spell out some of the fine print of his government's economic programme with a 29-point programme of cost-cutting measures, for the most part predictable: cuts in public sector wages, levies on an already unpopular banking sector and reduced benefits for state employees. Income tax was simplified to a standard 16 per cent rate; Mr Orban proposed a ban on the foreign currency loans much beloved by Hungarian investors – amazingly, in Hungary foreign currency loans constituted around 70 per cent of all consumer credit. Reactions to the budget proposals were mixed. But the elephant in the room remained Hungary's failure to maintain a dialogue with the IMF, a lapse which risked undermining and endangering all the new government's proposed measures.

The IMF reports

According to the IMF, in its March 2010 report on the Hungarian economy, the country had been rapidly affected by the global financial crisis largely because of its high levels of government and external debt. This vulnerability had been built up over several years, reflecting both the exaggerated risk appetite on the part of foreign investors during the boom years, mirrored by over-borrowing by both the public and private sectors in Hungary. The government had embarked on fiscal consolidation in 2006, but this adjustment was incomplete when the global financial crisis hit in late 2008. In the light of the sharp increase in global risk aversion, gross financing needs became more

KEY INDICATORS **Hungary**

	Unit	2006	2007	2008	2009	2010
Population	m	10.08	10.05	10.06	10.01	*10.00
Gross domestic product (GDP)	US$bn	112.92	138.40	155.50	129.40	129.00
GDP per capita	US$	11,206	13,746	15,477	12,927	12,879
GDP real growth	%	3.9	1.0	0.6	-6.3	1.2
Inflation	%	3.9	7.9	6.1	4.2	4.9
Unemployment	%	7.5	7.4	7.8	10.0	11.1
Coal output	mtoe	2.1	2.9	1.9	1.9	1.9
Exports (fob) (goods)	US$m	74,348.0	93,592.0	106,644.0	82,095.0	93,294.0
Imports (fob) (goods)	US$m	75,494.0	93,316.0	106,469.0	76,418.0	87,082.0
Balance of trade	US$m	-1,146.0	277.0	175.0	5,678.0	6,212.0
Current account	US$m	-7,352.0	-9,081.0	-11,172.0	441.0	3,049.0
Total reserves minus gold	US$m	21,527.0	23,970.0	33,788.0	44,074.0	44,849.0
Foreign exchange	US$m	21,316.0	23,773.0	33,620.0	42,479.0	43,581.0
Exchange rate	per US$	192.27	176.03	172.11	202.34	207.94

* estimated figure

difficult to meet, requiring not only strong government action, but also significant assistance from the IMF.

In the report the IMF also affirms that this combination of stronger policies, the availability of official financing and the easing of global financial conditions has anchored the stabilisation of the economy. The underlying fiscal position improved by 3 percentage points of GDP in 2009, while the fiscal deficit target was increased in the first half of 2009 to avoid exacerbating the economic contraction. In the financial sector, liquidity support was provided in a timely way and bank supervision and the remedial action framework were substantially enhanced. This strengthening of government policies alongside IMF support helped to limit both the depreciation of the exchange rate and possible increases in interest rates in early 2009, thus avoiding even worse macroeconomic outcomes and instead created room for reductions in interest rates. By March 2010 in the optimistic view of the IMF, investment was returning and the economy was on the road to recovery.

However, the IMF also noted that a further strengthening of government policies was required to ensure macroeconomic stability and growth in the medium term. Against the backdrop of fragile global conditions and high gross financing needs, any increase in financial strains could soon disrupt Hungary's stabilisation. In 2011, additional measures will be needed to reduce the general government deficit to below 3 per cent of GDP and put government debt firmly on a downward path.

The IMF report had been prepared against the backdrop of the imminent parliamentary elections. Fidesz representatives had advised the IMF of their intention to reduce the fiscal deficit over time, but had not discussed specific objectives or policies. Hungary's GDP had shrunk by a massive 6.3 per cent in 2009, although this was less than had been expected at the time of the IMF's previous review. The pace of economic contraction had eased in the fourth quarter of 2009, with real GDP falling by 4.0 per cent, down from 7.1 per cent in the third quarter of 2009. This was broadly in line with the performance of neighbouring economies. Private consumption remained weak as the unemployment rate increased and credit contracted.

Credit squeezed

Loans to households remained stable in 2009 as credit granted to corporations fell by 5 per cent. In the fourth quarter of 2009, credit to the private sector fell by more than anticipated. Inflation had received a temporary boost from mid-2009 by increases in the VAT rate and higher excise taxes. The headline inflation rate accelerated to 6.4 per cent in January 2010, due to the increases in excise taxes, higher food and energy prices. Private sector wage growth excluding bonuses fell to 3.5 per cent in December 2009. There were some pieces of good news: the current account was estimated to have been in surplus in 2009 for the first time in over 15 years (if only by about 0.5 per cent of GDP). The trade balance also increased significantly as the fall in domestic demand led to a more rapid decline in imports than exports. Hungary's income balance also improved as profits fell. As a result, the current account was estimated to have adjusted by over 7.5 percentage points of GDP.

Economic outlook

Hungary's macroeconomic outlook has, in the view of the IMF, improved. GDP was expected to decline by 0.2 per cent in 2010, an improvement of 0.5 percentage points since the organisation's last review. Stronger global demand has enabled export and investment growth to be revised upwards. However, private consumption was expected to be sluggish, due to the continued weakness of the labour market and slower-than-previously anticipated credit growth. This phenomenon is in line with previous episodes of prolonged increased household savings.

Credit to the economy was expected to contract further in early 2010, before picking up in the second half of the year. Weak demand and lack of risk appetite among lenders looked likely to restrict corporate credit in the first half of 2010, especially to small and medium-sized enterprises. A gradual recovery was projected to set in around mid-2010, in line with a general strengthening of economic activity. Credit to households was expected to remain subdued throughout 2010, reflecting weak demand.

Annual inflation was expected to fall to about 3 per cent in the second half of 2010 but was expected to remain high in the first half of 2010, due to the effect of indirect tax increases. In 2011, inflation was forecast to moderate further to 2.5 per cent, due to continued weak labour market conditions. The external current account balance was also expected to deteriorate modestly in 2010, to a deficit of 0.4 per cent of GDP. According to the IMF, Hungary's economic growth is projected to recover in 2011 and beyond.

Risk assessment

Economy	Poor
Politics	Fair
Regional stability	Good

COUNTRY PROFILE

Historical profile

The Hungarian (Magyar) peoples settled on the Hungarian plains in the seventh century AD, arriving from the Black Sea coast and southern Russia. The Hungarian language belongs to the Finno-Ugric family and is one of the few languages of the European Union that are not of Indo-European origin.

From the mid-eighteenth century, Hungary, together with Austria and a large area of central and eastern Europe, was part of the dual monarchy ruled by the Habsburgs.

1914–18 After the assassination of Archduke Ferdinand, the heir to the Austro-Hungarian throne, Austro-Hungary declared war on Serbia in June 1914, with the support of Germany. In November 1918, after the Austro-Hungarian Empire was defeated in the First World War, Hungary declared its independence, King Karl IV stood down as head of state of Hungary and the Entente powers carved-up Hungary as a punishment for its role in the First World War, taking two-thirds of its territory and nearly 60 per cent of its pre-war population.

1919 Communists seized power and declared the Hungarian Soviet Republic but were defeated by Admiral Miklos Horthy, who governed as Regent from 1920 until 1944.

1920 Hungary signed the *Treaty of Trianon*, confirming its territorial losses to Romania, Yugoslavia, Czechoslovakia and Austria.

1939–45 During the Second World War Hungary initially allied with Germany and acquired territory through the partitioning of Czechoslovakia and the Axis invasion of Yugoslavia. Having sought to break the alliance, Hungary was occupied by Germany in 1944 before being invaded by the Soviets later in the same year. Following the end of the Second World War, Hungary's territory was reduced to pre-war boundaries and severe reparations exacted.

1947 Communists were the largest single party in the general election.

1949 The Communist, People's Republic of Hungary was established. With Matyas Rakosi as prime minister, purges and political trials on the Stalinist model followed. Agriculture was collectivised along

the Soviet pattern and industry was nationalised.
1953 The more liberal Imre Nagy became prime minister, but fell out of favour with the Soviet politburo and was ousted in favour of András Hegedüs in 1955.
1956 During a period of anti-Soviet agitation, Imre Nagy returned, by popular demand, as prime minister. He moved to introduce multi-party politics and then announced Hungary's withdrawal from the Warsaw Pact. He appealed to the West for Hungary to be recognised as a neutral state. Soviet tanks rolled into Budapest and crushed the Hungarian Revolution. Nagy and others took sanctuary in the Yugoslav embassy but he was subsequently arrested by Russian forces and taken to Romania. The communist Magyar Szocialista Mukaspart Partja (MSzMP) (Hungarian Socialist Workers' Party), returned to power with János Kádár as prime minister.
1958 Nagy was executed in Romania. Árpád Szákasits, as chairman of the Presidential Council, became the Head of State.
1960s Kádár introduced a number of minor liberal reforms such as dismantling collective farms, raising wages and introducing some intellectual freedom.
1988 Dissatisfaction among party members with the remoteness of the leadership led to the resignation of Kádár and moves towards 'Socialist Pluralism'.
1989 In May the border with Austria was opened and thousands of East Germans fled to the West, breaching the 'Iron Curtain'. The Communist state of Hungary was dismantled and a transition to a multi-party democracy begun. The MSzMP was re-named the Magyar Szocialista Párt (MSzP) (Hungarian Socialist Party). Mátyás Szürös became Hungary's interim president.
1990 First free multi-party parliamentary elections for 43 years resulted in the formation of a coalition government led by József Antall of the Magyar Demokrata Fórum (MDF) (Hungarian Democratic Forum). Mátyás Szürös was replaced as president by Árpád Göncz
1994 The general election resulted in a coalition government led by Gyula Horn of the MSzP.
1998 The centre-right Fiatal Demokraták Szövetsége-Magyar Polgári Párt (Fidesz-MPP) (Federation of Young Democrats-Hungarian Civic Party), led by Viktor Orbán, unexpectedly won the general election.
1999 Hungary became one of the first former Soviet satellite states to join NATO.
2000 Ferenc Mádl was elected president by parliament, replacing Árpád Göncz.
2001 The government introduced the Status Law, giving the four million ethnic Hungarians in neighbouring countries the right to work and study in Hungary.
2002 Péter Médgyessy (MSzP) became prime minister of a coalition government, comprising MSzP and Szabad Demokratak Szovetsege (SzDSz) (Alliance of Free Democrats).
2003 In a referendum with a 46 per cent turnout, 84 per cent voted in favour of EU membership.
2004 Hungary joined the EU. After the ruling MSzP withdrew support for him, Prime Minister Péter Medgyessy resigned. Ferenc Gyurcsány became prime minister.
2005 László Sólyom became president.
2006 Prime Minister Gyurcsány was re-elected. Rioting followed his admission that he had lied about the economy during the election, but he defied demands for his resignation. He later won a vote of confidence in parliament.
2007 Hungary became a member of the European Union Schengen area whereby all travellers may cross borders without a passport or visa.
2008 An agreement for visa-free visits of citizens to the US was signed. The IMF led a consortium to lend Hungary US$25.1 billion to aid the economy.
2009 Prime Minister Ferenc Gyurcsány resigned. His government's popularity had plummeted and he declared that he was an obstacle to the changes necessary to rectify the economy and bring about social reforms. Gordon György Bajnai (an independent), became prime minster. A new political party, Lehet Más a Politika (LMP) (Politics Can Be Different), was founded, espousing environmental protection and sustainable development.
2010 In parliamentary elections held over two rounds in April, the opposition coalition of Fidesz won an overwhelming majority of 262 seats out of 386. This was enough to enact major changes without relying on the support of other political parties. The outgoing MSzP won 59 seats in total, and the far-right nationalist Jobbik Magyarországért Mozgalom (Jobbik) (Movement for a better Hungary) won 47 seats. Prime Minister Victor Orbán (Fidesz) took office in May and parliament voted for Pál Schmitt (Fidesz) as president by 263 votes (out of 386); he took office on 6 August.
2011 On 18 April, parliament voted to change the constitution and bring to an end the transitional government implemented after the fall of Communist rule in 1989. Two opposition political parties boycotted the vote, claiming the ruling Fidesz were imposing divisive right-wing ideology on the country. Other critics characterised the constitution as 'socially and fiscally conservative', while human rights campaigners opposed articles that limited freedoms, banned same-sex marriages (although partnerships may be legally registered) and awarded legal protection for foetuses from conception. Economic analysts, however, were supportive of the articles that provided for the national deficit to be kept below 50 per cent of GDP and an opening of government operations to private enterprise.

Political structure

Constitution

In 1989 the 1949 constitution was amended so that Hungary was formally re-titled the Hungarian Republic, concluding 40 years as a People's Republic. Under the amended constitution, Hungary has a multi-party system.
Supreme power is vested in parliament. The Constitutional Court has the power to overturn decisions or decrees that are considered unconstitutional.
On 18 April 2011, parliament voted to change the constitution and bring to an end the transitional government implemented after the fall of Communist rule (1989). Among the articles adopted were a limit on the powers of the Constitutional Court and the head of the central bank, any changes to tax and pension laws to require a two-thirds majority in parliament, government operations to be opened up to private enterprise, the national deficit to be kept below 50 per cent of GDP, legal protection for foetuses from the time of conception, a ban on same-sex marriages (although partnerships may be legally registered), discrimination to be outlawed (but excluded age and sexual orientation).

Form of state

Parliamentary democratic republic

The executive

The prime minister is chosen by the National Assembly and heads the executive Council of Ministers or cabinet. The prime minister's control of the cabinet has been enhanced by the creation of a minister for the prime minister's office.
The president is also elected by the National Assembly for a five-year term. The president has no executive power, and is not able to dissolve parliament.

National legislature

The unicameral Országgyüles (National Assembly) has 386 members in total, of which 176 are elected in single seat constituencies; 152 by proportional representation in multi-seat constituencies and 58 for what are called compensation seats. Voting for the national assembly is in two rounds. In the first, voters vote for an individual candidate and one from the party list. Any candidate failing to win 50 per cent in single seat constituencies must enter the second round. In round two, the process is repeated but the candidate who wins most votes wins the seat. Any constituency that has a less than 25 per cent vote for the leading candidate is added to the compensation seats.

Legal system

The legal system is based on the amended 1949 constitution.

Civil and criminal cases are brought before district and county courts and the Supreme Court in Budapest. District courts are courts of first instance whereas county courts may act either as courts of first instance or as appeal courts. The Supreme Court is usually an appeal court, but can also take cases submitted to it by the Public Prosecutor and act as a court of first instance. All courts of first instance have one professional judge and two lay assessors. Appeal courts have three professional judges. The district and county judges are elected by district or county councils. All members of the Supreme Court are elected by parliament.

Last elections

11 and 25 April 2010 (parliamentary, first and second round); 29 June 2010 (presidential – indirect)

Results: Presidential: Pál Schmitt won 263 votes, András Bologh 58.

Parliamentary (first round): Fidesz - Magyar Polgári Szövetség (Fidesz) (Fidesz - Hungarian Civic Union) won 52.73 per cent of the vote (206 seats), Magyar Szocialista Párt (MSzP) (Hungarian Socialist Party) 19.31 per cent (28), Jobbik Magyarországért Mozgalom (Jobbik) (Movement for a better Hungary) 16.67 per cent (26), Lehet Más a Politika (LMP) (Politics Can Be Different) 7.44 per cent (five); 15 other political parties failed to win enough votes to gain any seats. Turnout was 64.42 per cent. Second round: Fidesz 60 seats (total 262 seats out of 386), MSzP 29 (total 59), Jobbik 21 (total 47), LMP 11 (total 16) independent one. Turnout was 46.52 per cent.

Next elections

2015 (presidential); 2014 (parliamentary).

Political parties

Ruling party

Fidesz-Magyar Polgári Szövetség (Fidesz) (Fidesz-Hungarian Civic Union) (from 25 Apr 2010)

Main opposition party

Magyar Szocialista Párt (MSzP) (Hungarian Socialist Party)

Population

10.00 million (2010)*

Last census: February 2001: 10,198,315

Population density: 110 inhabitants per square km. Urban population: 65 per cent (1995–2001).

Annual growth rate: -0.2 per cent 1994–2004 (WHO 2006)

Ethnic make-up

The population is almost entirely made up of ethnic Hungarians. Small groups of Germans, Slovaks, Romanians, Serbs and Gypsies (Roma) make up about 4 per cent of the population. Roma are not recognised as an official ethnic group, although they are estimated to number between 360,000 and 600,000.

Religions

There is no official national religion. Roman Catholic (67.5 per cent), Calvinist (20 per cent) and Lutheran (5 per cent). There are approximately six million Roman Catholics, two million Calvinists, 430,000 Lutherans, and 80,000 Jews in Hungary.

Education

Compulsory education starts at six years of age and most children complete secondary education. There are four types of secondary school, offering either academic or vocational education. Apprentice training schools are attached to factories and agricultural co-operatives. There are 57 higher education institutes, including 10 universities and nine technical universities. Some privatisation of education is taking place as church and other private schools are created. Public expenditure on education is equivalent to around 5 per cent of annual gross national income (GNI), and includes subsidies to private education at the primary, secondary and tertiary levels.

Literacy rate: 99.4 per cent total, 99.2 per cent female, adult rates in 2002 (World Bank).

Compulsory years: Six to 18

Enrolment rate: 89.7 per cent net primary enrolment, 84.9 per cent net secondary enrolment (World Bank 2003).

Pupils per teacher: 12 in primary schools.

Health

The health system is run by the State Health Fund, an entity with substantial operational autonomy and no effective accountability. It is financed by payroll taxes of 15 per cent from employers and 4 per cent from employees, although transfers from the budget have been necessary due to a large funding gap.

Service delivery remains poor. Although healthcare is free in Hungary, patients regularly hand over cash bribes to poorly-paid medical staff in order to gain proper access. There are reports of doctors recommending dangerous treatments in exchange for bribes. A major area of concern is the heavy subsidisation of medicine, which patients often obtain freely and then sell on.

HIV/Aids

HIV prevalence: 0.1 per cent aged 15–49 in 2003 (World Bank)

Life expectancy: 73 years, 2004 (WHO 2006)

Fertility rate/Maternal mortality rate: 1.3 births per woman, 2004 (WHO 2006); maternal mortality 15 per 100,000 live births (World Bank).

Child (under 5 years) mortality rate (per 1,000): 7.7 per 1,000 live births (World Bank)

Head of population per physician: 3.33 physicians per 1,000 people, 2003 (WHO 2006)

Welfare

Economic reforms have included a pioneering reorganisation of the pension system, with a new 'multi-pillar' system launched in 1996, supported by a World Bank US$150 million loan. Employees make mandatory contributions to the existing pay-as-you-go (PAYG) system and to a fully funded second pillar, based on a system of personal savings accounts held in privately managed pension funds. Those joining the work force after June 1998 were obliged to participate in the new system. In 2001, the government made both systems voluntary. The new scheme has proved highly popular. The largest private pension fund is managed by Nationale-Nederlanden (NN), with 257,000 members and Ft4 billion (US$16.4 million) in managed assets. Social security contributions on salaries are paid by the employer (39 per cent) and by the employee (10 per cent). Employer contributions must also be made to the unemployment solidarity fund (4.5 per cent) and by the employee (1.5 per cent).

Main cities

Budapest (capital, estimated population 1.7 million in 2005), Debrecen (213,692), Miskolc (180,012), Szeged (169,198), Pécs (161,355), Györ (130,480), Nyíregyháza (120,880), Székesfehérvár (106,951).

Languages spoken

Slovak, Croatian, Serbian, Slovene, Romani are also spoken.

The main foreign language is German, followed by English, Russian and French.

Official language/s

Hungarian (Magyar)

Media

Press

Foreign ownership dominates the print media and all newspapers are privately owned. While the market in tabloid news is growing, quality newspapers are in decline.

Dailies: There are over 30 dailies of which 10 are national newspapers. Local newspapers have a strong market lead and national broadsheets are considered partisan.

In Hungarian, the most popular national newspaper is the free issue *Metro* (www.metro.hu); the most popular quality newspapers are the *Népszabadság* (www.nol.hu) and *Magyar Nemzet* (www.mno.hu), with *Magyar Hírlap* (ww.magyarhirlap.hu), *Népszava* (www.nepszava.hu) and *Reggel* (www.reggel.hu), which include articles on business and finance.

Weeklies: In Hungarian, magazines for news and current affairs include *168 Óra* (www.168ora.hu), *Hírek* (www.miep.hu), *Magyar Demokrata* (www.demokrata.hu) and *HVG* (http://hvg.hu); for women, *Hölgyvilág* (www.holgyvilag.hu), *Nok Lapja* (www.nlcafe.hu); *Hócipo* (www.hocipo.hu) is a satirical magazine.

Business: In Hungarian, the leading business and financial newspapers are the *Napi Gazdaság* (www.napi.hu), *Magyar Tokepiac* (www.magyartokepiac.hu) and *Világgazdaság* (www.vilaggazdasag.hu). Magazines include *Adó* (www.ado.hu) and *Bank & Tözsde* (www.bankestozsde.hu).

In English, the weekly *Budapest Business Journal* (www.bbj.hu), has a round up of news and comprehensive industry and company information.

Periodicals: In Hungarian the monthly *Közéleti Krónika* (www.kronika.matav.hu) covers general interest.

Broadcasting

The state-owned media has lost its monopoly and, since 1996, most of its market. Its reputation has been damaged with accusation of political interference by government.

Radio: The state-run Magyar Rádió (www.radio.hu) operates three national public stations, Bartok (www.mr3-bartok.hu), Kossuth (www.mr1-kossuth.hu) and Petofi (www.mr2.hu), which include specialist interest broadcasts of parliamentary proceedings and religion. The two private, national commercial stations Danubius (www.danubius.hu) and Sláger (www.slager.hu) are also those with the highest listener figures. There are many local radio stations, either private, public and community, with intense competition for listeners.

Television: Television is the most popular medium for news, information and entertainment.

Magyar Televízió (MTV) (www.mtv.hu) has two channels M1 and M2. Funding for these services is provided by government grants and advertising revenue. MTV is chronically under-funded and the quality and quantity of programming is weak. Private commercial TV is led by RTLKlub (www.rtlklub.hu) and TV2 (http://tv2.hu), which offer a wide range of locally produced programmes and well as imported TV shows. Hir TV (www.hirtv.net) is a 24-hour news channel. There are dozens of pay-to-view TV channels offering programmes in most genres.

Advertising

The professionalism of advertising has grown rapidly since the 1990s and services include traditional ad campaigns and new technologies.

Advertising space can be purchased directly on television and radio, in cinemas, newspapers, magazines and posters. The advertising of tobacco, alcohol and medicines is regulated under a code of ethics and edicts.

News agencies

National news agency: Magyar Távirati Iroda (MTI) (Hungarian News Agency): http://english.mti.hu

Economy

Hungary has an open market economy built up since the mid-1990s and could boast one of the most successful growth rates in Central Europe. It has a large industrial base including automobile manufacturing, mining and metallurgy, energy production and food processing. Agriculture benefits from the Great Hungarian Plain and Little Hungarian Plain, which together make up 75 per cent of the land available for cultivation, and from their rich farming soils which provide among other crops, grapes, fruit, grain and pastures for livestock. However over 60 per cent of Hungary's economy is based in the tertiary service sector, with tourism comprising a major component. The capital, Budapest, attracted 3.6 million visitors in 2008; the sector employs around 150,000 people. The private sector accounts for around 80 per cent of GDP, with a high level of foreign ownership and foreign investment.

GDP growth in 2007 was 1.0 per cent; growth was relatively low due to government spending cuts imposed in 2006 following the EU rejection of Hungary's deficit of almost 10 per cent of GDP, which lost Hungary its prospects of joining the eurozone in 2010. In 2008 when the global economic crisis struck GDP growth was 0.6 per cent and Hungary was in danger of defaulting on its short-term debt, so that in October 2008 the IMF led a consortium to lend Hungary US$25.1 billion to aid the economy. Exports, the backbone of the economy, weakened (exports of goods fell from 16.4 per cent of GDP in 2007 to 4.8 per cent in 2008 – with expectations of a further fall to -15.1 per cent in 2009)l Low domestic consumption and the government austerity measures meant the economy fell into recession in the first quarter of 2009 with GDP of -6.6 per for the year. Growth is predicted for 2010 as global trade recovers but Hungary's growth rate is expected to be some -0.2 per cent.

Despite Hungary's tribulations, investor confidence in the longer-term outlook remains high, while the economy continues to benefit from the financial benefits of EU membership, including balance of payment support amounting to €1.5 billion (US$2.1 billion) in 2009.

External trade

As a member of the European Union, Hungary operates within a community-wide free trade area, with tariffs set as a whole. Internationally, the EU has free trade agreements with a number of nations and trading blocs worldwide.

The economy is dependent on export trade, of which 75 per cent goes to the EU, mainly Germany. Major sectors include vehicle assembly and electronics which account for a third of exports. Hungarian wine and fruit are consumed throughout the EU.

Imports

Principal imports are capital goods, machinery and equipment, fuels and electricity, food products, raw materials, energy (natural gas and electricity).

Main sources: Germany (typically 23 per cent of total), China (6 per cent), Austria (6 per cent).

Exports

Principal exports are machinery and equipment, manufactured goods, foodstuffs and agricultural produce, raw materials, energy (refined oil and electricity).

Main destinations: Germany (typically 25 per cent of total), Romania (5 per cent), Italy (5 per cent).

Agriculture

Farming

The agricultural sector contributes 7 per cent to GDP and employs around 12 per cent of the workforce. Agriculture and animal husbandry dominate in the Great Plain in central and eastern Hungary. The western region of Transdanubia – which includes Lake Balaton, the largest lake in Central Europe – is dominated by intensive agriculture and animal husbandry.

Farming is largely socialised; co-operatives are the dominant form of production. The agriculture and food industry produces on average 50 per cent more food than is consumed domestically. Principal crops include wheat, maize, barley, sugar beet and potatoes. The livestock sector is also important. Crop cultivation, especially wheat, maize, potatoes, fruit and vegetables, accounts for around half of Hungary's agricultural output. Processed and unprocessed meat, dairy products and wine are the other main products.

The agriculture and food industry produces, on average, 50 per cent more than is needed for domestic consumption.

After EU accession in 2004, Hungary is eligible for EU agricultural subsidies and rural development through the Common Agricultural Policy (CAP). However, it will only receive the full amount by the end of a 10-year transition period in 2013. During its transitional entry stage Hungary has decided to implement the reform of the CAP in January 2009. The reform was introduced throughout most of the EU in 2005, when subsidies on farm output, which tended to benefit large farms and encourage overproduction, were replaced by single farm payments, not conditional on production. The change is expected to reward farms that provide and maintain a healthy environment, food safety and animal welfare standards. The changes are also intended to encourage market conscious production and cut the cost of CAP to the EU taxpayer.

Fishing

Hungary is a landlocked country and although there is some fishing from lakes and rivers, most of the country's consumption needs are met through imports. Fish production in Hungary is mostly concentrated in the available 140,000 hectares (ha) of natural water and 20,000ha of man-made fishponds. The fish production sector primarily involves common carp and African catfish and remains a small and special sub-sector of agriculture. The sector traditionally supports less than 0.5 per cent of the total labour force and contributes below 2 per cent of the total for agricultural production. Annual consumption per capita is typically less than 3kg.

Forestry

Forests account for a fifth of Hungary's land area but the industry amounts to only 0.3 per cent of GDP. Forestry agriculture largely concentrates on production using hardwood species of trees, mostly being used for energy purposes. Oak and black locust are most prevalent. The state owns about 58 per cent of forests and and employs 20,000 workers on this land. Hungary is a net importer of all primary forest products as a result of not undertaking softwood and pulp production.

Industry and manufacturing

Mechanical engineering, chemicals, pulp and paper industries, as well as the iron and steel industry and metal processing are particularly successful sectors. Other industries include building materials, food processing and textiles. One of the fastest growing sectors in Hungary, as the country moves away from heavy industry, is motor vehicle components and assembly. Foreign direct investment (FDI) has contributed greatly to industrial output in Hungary, concentrating in areas such as machinery, vehicles, computers, telecommunications equipment, electrical and electronic goods. These successes have been concentrated in a relatively small number of capital-intensive companies. Analysts warn that Hungary could be in danger of developing a two-tier economy, with a prosperous, predominantly foreign-owned sector of larger enterprises and a struggling, locally- owned sector of small- and medium-sized enterprises (SMEs).

In the past, government policy focussed on the development of heavy industry and agriculture. In the late-1990s, this shifted towards the development of SMEs. These account for 45 per cent of GDP and represent 69 per cent of employment. The main problem facing smaller enterprises is the growing black market. This is due to a constantly changing and, thus far, largely unfavourable tax system in which evasion is widespread. Law-abiding SMEs are finding it difficult to compete with black market labour. In order to help compensate for this, the government has tried to promote entrepreneurial SMEs through tax cuts and better access to credit.

Tourism

Since 1988, Hungary has seen an unprecedented tourist boom as package tourists and international convention delegates take advantage of competitive prices, relatively crime-free streets and a rich and varied cultural scene. Most visitors are from Germany and Austria, but there are increasing numbers from Poland, America and Japan. The sector accounts for almost 10 per cent of GDP and employs 10–13 per cent of the workforce. The sector has traditionally played an important role in Hungary's foreign exchange revenues.

Emphasis is on three fields of tourism – conference, spa, and exclusive tourism, particularly equestrian tourism.

Environment

Mining

The mining sector accounts for 5 per cent of GNP and employs 3 per cent of the workforce.

Hungary is a major European producer of bauxite, and also a small-scale producer of lignite and manganese ore. In the Northern Hills, iron ore and copper are mined.

Hydrocarbons

Hungary is a small-scale producer of coal, oil and natural gas. In the Great Plain in central and eastern Hungary, there are natural gas and oil deposits while brown coal is mined in the Northern Hills region.

Proven reserves were 102 million barrels of oil in 2007, producing around 33,000 barrels per day (bpd), with consumption at 163 billion bpd the balance is provided by imports. There is one oil refinery with a capacity of 161,000bpd; US$59 million has been invested to create a new hydro-desulphurisation unit in line with EU standards for low sulphur petrol and diesel.

Proven reserves of natural gas was 34.3 billion cubic metres (cum) in 2007. Consumption was 12 billion cum and production some 3 billion cum per annum. Imports of natural gas come primarily from Russia. Gas storage capacity is well developed and can hold 120 days of peak winter imports.

Coal reserves totalled 3.3 billion tonnes in 2007; coal production was 2 million tonnes oil equivalent. Hungarian coal is the less valuable sub-bituminous and lignite composition that is typically used in power stations, but is a large atmospheric pollutant.

Energy

Total electricity generating capacity was over 8,000MW in 2008. Electricity generation has moved away from large, central production sites to small to medium locally placed cogeneration plants, of less than 50MW, producing electricity and heat, which in 2008 provided 25 per cent of the country's total generating capacity. Power stations are predominately fuelled by natural gas, 3,000 million tonnes oil equivalent (mtoe) per annum, as lignite coal has fallen (from over 25,000mtoe in 2003 to less than 17,000mtoe in 2005). Hungary has one nuclear power plant, near Paks, producing 3.3mtoe in 2007. The plant provides 40 per cent of domestic energy needs and is dependent on enrichment and processing facilities from the Russian Federation. Renewable wind energy has been growing in use but in 2008 provided less than 600mtoe per annum; there are plans to implement geothermal energy.

Financial markets

Stock exchange

Budapesti Értéktőzsde (Budapest Stock Exchange) (BSE)

Banking and insurance

Hungary has the most developed financial sector in Eastern Europe, with the Magyar Nemzeti Bank (MNB) (National Bank of Hungary) (central bank) playing an important role in economic and financial management of the economy. The country privatised banking services from 1994–97 in order to attract foreign investment. About 30 of the 38 banks in Hungary are foreign-owned and are led by the OTP Bank (formely known as the National Savings Bank). Foreign-owned banks control 90 per cent of the country's total banking assets. OTP Bank, with an extensive

branch network, offers banking for the general public, and also foreigners needing foreign exchange accounts.
Foreign trade and currency transactions are conducted by the Magyar Külkereskedelmi Bank (MKB) (formerly the Hungarian Foreign Trade Bank) and by some other banks.
The Central-European International Bank is an internationally active offshore bank owned by the central bank and six foreign banks.
Hungary adopted a German model for the banking system in 1999, allowing banks to engage in both commercial and investment banking.

Central bank
Magyar Nemzeti Bank (MNB) (National Bank of Hungary)

Main financial centre
Budapest

Time
GMT plus one hour (daylight saving, late March to late October, GMT plus two hours)

Geography
Hungary is a landlocked country in central Europe surrounded by the Alps, the Carpathians and the Dinaric Mountains. The Danube and Tisza rivers run through the country, which is bounded by Slovakia to the north, Ukraine to the north-east, Romania to the east, Serbia, Croatia and Slovenia to the south and Austria to the west.
The River Danube forms Hungary's north-western border with Slovakia and then flows south through Budapest, bisecting the country. More than half of the land surface consists of plains less than 200 metres above sea level. The highest point is Kekes at 1,015 metres in the Matra hills to the north, while the lowest point is on the southern edge of Szeged along the River Tisza (the longest tributary of the Danube) at 77 metres.
The major regions of the country are: the Pannonian or Great Hungarian Plain (central and eastern Hungary), east of the River Danube and also drained by the Tisza; Transdanubia (western Hungary, including Lake Balaton, the largest lake in central Europe); the Little Hungarian Plains in the north-west between the mountains and the Danube; and along Hungary's northern border are the Matras, foothills of the Carpathian Mountains.

Hemisphere
Northern

Climate
The temperate continental climate of Hungary is under the varying influence of three climatic zones: continental, Atlantic and Mediterranean. The annual median temperature in Budapest is 11 degrees Celsius (C). The warmest month is July, with an average of 22 degrees C, the coldest January, with minus 1 degrees C. Averaging 1,988 hours of sunshine a year, Hungary experiences more sun than most of the countries in Western Europe. Average annual rainfall is 630mm, but distribution is unpredictable. Most rain usually falls in May and June, but the south-west regions may have more in October. May is the wettest month, and September the driest. The central parts of the Great Plains are the driest with 200–500mm, the hilly western area of Koeszeg and Sopron the wettest with 900–1,000mm.

Dress codes
Hungarians used to dress more formally than West Europeans, but blazers, sports coats and flannels are as acceptable as lounge suits for visiting businessmen. Do not be offended if Hungarians ask where you bought your clothes or how much they cost.
Advisable clothing: medium to heavyweight and heavy topcoat for winter; lightweight clothing for summer. A raincoat will be needed in spring and autumn.

Entry requirements

Passports
Passport required by all; must be valid for six months beyond date of departure.

Visa
Required by all, except nationals of EU and Schengen area signatory countries, North America, Australasia and Japan. For further exceptions contact the nearest embassy. A Schengen visa application (offered in several languages) can be downloaded from http://europa.eu/abc/travel/ see 'documents you will need'. Business trips may be made visa-free, or on short-term visas. For terms and conditions see: www.mfa.gov.hu/kum/en/bal/ and follow links to consular services.
Transit passengers must have onward/return passage.

Currency advice/regulations
The import and export of local currency is limited to Ft200,000, provided the amount is declared. The import of foreign currency is unlimited, although amounts over Ft1 million must be declared. The export of foreign currency cannot exceed the amount imported and must be exported no later than three months after import. There is no compulsory money exchange on departure, however only 50 per cent of a visitor's forints can be re-exchanged (up to a limit of US$450, and with exchange receipts) at any authorised *bureaux de change*, or branch of the National Savings Bank.

Customs
Personal items are duty-free. There are no duties levied on alcohol and tobacco between EU member states, providing amounts imported are for personal consumption.

Health (for visitors)
Nationals of the European Economic Area (EEA) countries and Switzerland can access reduced cost and sometimes free medical treatment using a European Health Insurance Card (EHIC) while visiting the EEA. Exceptions include nationals of the 10 countries, which joined the EU in 2004, whose EHIC is not valid in Switzerland. Applications for the EHIC should be made before travelling.

Mandatory precautions
There are no special requirements.

Advisable precautions
There are no specific precautions necessary although a hepatitis A immunisation might be useful.

Hotels
There is a full range of hotels in Budapest. Reservations can be made in advance directly or through IBUSZ.
All hotels charge a 1–2 per cent tourism tax for guests staying more than one night. Tipping usually 10–15 per cent. Good hotels are concentrated in Pest, the business half of Budapest.

Credit cards
Credit cards are accepted and can be used for cash advances.

Public holidays (national)

Fixed dates
1 Jan (New Year's Day), 15 Mar (National Day), 1 May (Labour Day), 20 Aug (National Constitution/St Stephen's Day), 23 Oct (Remembrance Day), 1 Nov (All Saints' Day), 25–26 Dec (Christmas).

Variable dates
Easter Monday, Whit Monday.

Working hours

Banking
Mon–Thu: 0800–1500; Fri: 0800–1300.

Business
Mon–Thu: 0800–1600.

Government
Mon–Fri: 0800–1630.

Shops
Mon, Tue, Wed & Fri: 1000–1800, Thu: 1000–2000, Sat: 1000–1300.
Shops may have varied opening hours. Food shops open at 0600–0700 and may not close until 2000.

Telecommunications

Mobile/cell phones
There is a GSM dual band of 900 and 1800 with coverage throughout the country.

Electricity supply
220V AC, 50 cycles

Social customs/useful tips
Business people are expected to dress smartly. Local business people are generally friendly and hospitable and it is usual for visitors to be invited to lunch or dinner in a restaurant. Business cards are widely distributed and visitors are advised to have a supply available in Hungarian. Best months for business visits are September to May and appointments should always be made. Interpreter and translation services may be booked through travel agents. In business Hungarians expect people to speak their mind. Giving and receiving gifts is very common; take promotional gifts with you.
Punctuality is appreciated.
If you are invited to a Hungarian home, take flowers for the hostess and wine or liquor for the host.
Hungarian law requires visitors to carry passports or other ID at all times.

Security
There has been an increase in street crime in Budapest, although levels are still below those in many Western capitals. Bag-snatching and pickpocketing are common in Budapest. Criminals at times pose as police officers, and credentials should be requested for inspection.

Getting there
Air
National airline: Malév (Hungarian Airlines)
International airport/s: Budapest-Ferihegy (BUD, 16km from city; duty-free shop, restaurants and bar, bank/bureaux de change, tourist information centre, post office and car hire. Scheduled bus services run to the city centre; minibuses run to and from any address in the city. The 93 bus runs an express service between the underground terminus at Kobánya-Kispest and the Ferihegy terminals; a pre-purchased or season ticket is required. Taxis are available at all times.
Airport tax: None
Surface
Hungary is included in the Pan-European Corridor 5 scheme. The project has some 3,270km of railways, linking Kiev in the Ukraine with western Europe via Italy, and 2,850 of new and upgraded roads.
Water: A hydrofoil service is available on the Danube between Vienna and Budapest in the summer. Ships provide regular passenger service and cruises starting at Passau and Regensburg (Germany) to Budapest, passing through Austria and Slovakia. There are also links with the rivers Rhine and Main and the Black Sea.

Getting about
National transport
Road: Generally the road system is good. Tolls are payable on some roads and all motorways for which season tickets can be purchased. There are eight arterial roads: all but the M8 start from central Budapest. From Budapest the two main highways are the M1 to Györ (then to Austria) and the M7 along Lake Balaton. The M3 connects Budapest with eastern Hungary.
Buses: Budapest is linked to all major towns. Tickets are available from Volán offices throughout the country.
Rail: Services are operated by MÁV. All cities are linked by efficient services, but facilities are often inadequate. Supplements are payable on intercity (IC) and express trains and reservations are compulsory on IC trains and recommended for express trains, particularly in summer. Tickets and seat reservations can be bought 60 days in advance at domestic railway stations.
Water: Ferries run several times daily between Budapest and Visegrád over the summer; one service extends to Esztergom.
City transport
Most government offices, business centres and main hotels are located in Pest, on the eastern side of the Danube. The public transport system is good and it is rarely necessary to take a taxi, especially as the city centre is quite compact.
Buda, the hilly, western part of the city, is more difficult to get around without a car.
Taxis: Taxis are available from ranks, by telephone or can be hailed in the street. Taxis are metered. Avoid all unmarked cabs as they not only demand payment for mileage covered, but also for the return journey to their starting point.
A taxi from the airport to the centre of Budapest takes between 40 minutes and one hour; always agree your fare in advance. Non-airport taxis are plentiful and inexpensive although rates vary widely (watch out for meters being on the 'night' rate during the day). Tipping of 15–20 per cent is expected.
Buses, trams & metro: There is good public transport in all the main towns, including tramways in some.
Budapest has bus, trolleybus, tramway, suburban railway (HEV), a three-line metro and boat services. The metro has ticket barriers at all stations. The bus-trolleybus-tramway system has pre-purchase flat fares with ticket puncher on board. Day passes and season tickets are available for all the transport modes in the city. Trams and buses generally run from 0430–2300. Some night services also operate. The metro runs from 0430–2310; stations are identified by a large 'M'.
Trains: Main railway stations: Déli Pu (Southern RW Terminal), Krisztina krt 37/a, Budapest I.
Keleti Pu (Eastern RW Terminal), Baross Tér (tel: 142-9150).
Nyugati Pu (Western RW Terminal), Teréz krt 111 (tel: 122-7860).
Ferry: The Danube provides a ready highway for ferries and sightseeing cruises.
Car hire
Hire cars are available from the airport, hotels and IBUSZ travel company. The speed limit is 50kph in built up areas, 90kph on main roads, 110kph on highways and 130kph on motorways. There is an absolute ban on drinking and driving, headlights must be kept dipped, mobile phones can only be used with headsets and seat belts are compulsory. An international driving licence is recommended. For travel on the M1 and M3 motorways, drivers require a motorway *vignette*, obtainable from the Hungarian Auto Klub, petrol stations, post offices, and some motorway access points; without one, drivers may be fined.

BUSINESS DIRECTORY

The addresses listed below are a selection only. While World of Information makes every endeavour to check these addresses, we cannot guarantee that changes have not been made, especially to telephone numbers and area codes. We would welcome any corrections.

Telephone area codes
The international direct dialling code (IDD) for Hungary is +36, followed by area code and subscriber's number:

Budapest	1	Pecs	72
Debrecen	52	Salgotarjan	32
Gyor	96	Szeged	62
Miskolc	46	Szekesfehervar	22
Nyiregyhaza	42	Szombathely	94

Useful telephone numbers
Ambulance, Police, Fire: 112
24-hour emergency service (English-speaking): 118-8212
24-hour multi-lingual crime reporting service: 0800—2000: 438-8080; after hours: 06-80-660-044
Fotaxi (tel: 222-2222)
City Taxi (tel: 211-1111)
Volantaxi (tel: 166-6666)

Chambers of Commerce
American Chamber of Commerce in Hungary, 10 Deak Ferencu utca, 1052 Budapest (tel: 266-9880; fax: 266-9888; e-mail: info@amcham.hu).

Borsod-Abauj-Zemplen County Chamber of Commerce and Industry, 1 Szentpali u, 3530 Miskolc (tel: 328-539; fax: 328-722; e-mail: bokik@mail.bokik,hu).

British Chamber of Commerce in Hungary, 6 Bank utca, 1054 Budapest (tel:

302-5200; fax: 302-3069; e-mail: bcch@bcch.com).

Budapest Chamber of Commerce and Industry, Krisztina krt 99, 1016 Budapest (tel: 488-2000; fax: 488-2119; e-mail: bkik@bkik.hu).

Czongrád Chamber of Commerce and Industry, 2-4 Tisza Lajos krt, 6701 Csongrád (tel: 426-343; fax: 426-149; info@csmkik.hu).

Fejér County Chamber of Commerce, 4-6 Hosszusetater, 8000 Székesfehérvár (tel: 510-310; fax: 510-312; e-mail: fmkik@mail.fmkik.hu).

Gyor-Moson-Sopron County Chamber of Commerce and Industry, 10/A Szent Istvan ut, 9021 Gyor (tel: 520-202; fax: 520-291; e-mail: kamara@gymskik.hu).

Hajdu-Bihar County Chamber of Commerce and Industry, 10 Petofi ter, 4025 Debrecen (tel: 500-721; fax: 500-720; e-mail: info@hbkik.hu).

Hungarian Chamber of Commerce and Industry, 6-8 Kossuth Lajos ter, 1055 Budapest (tel: 474-5101; fax: 474-5105; e-mail: mkik@mkik.hu).

Pecs-Baranya Chamber of Commerce and Industry, 36 Majorossy I ut, 7625 Pécs (tel: 507-149; fax: 507-152; e-mail: pbkik@pbkik.hu).

Pest County Chamber of Commerce and Inustry, 40 Vaci utca, 1051 Budapest (tel: 317-7666; fax: 317-7755; e-mail: titkarsag@pmkik.hu).

Sopron Chamber of Commerce and Industry, 14 Deak ter, 9400 Sopron (tel: 523-570; fax: 523-581; e-mail: k-kamara@sopron.hu).

Vas County Chamber of Commerce and Industry, 2 Honved ter, 9700 Szombathely (tel: 312-356; fax: 316-936; e-mail: vmkik@vmkik.hu).

Veszprem Chamber of Commerce, 3 Budapesti u, 8200 Veszprém (tel: 429-008; fax: 412-150; e-mail: vkik@iveszpremikamara.hu).

Zala County Chamber of Commerce and Industry, 24 Petofi Sandor ut, 8900 Zalaegerszeg (tel: 550-514; fax: 550-525; e-mail: zmkik@zmkik.hu).

Banking

General Banking and Trust Co Ltd, Markó ut 9, H-1055 Budapest (tel: 269-1450; fax: 260-1440).

Magyar Külkereskedelmi Bank (commercial bank), St István ter 11, H-1821 Budapest (tel: 269-0922; fax: 269-0959).

OTP Bank, Nádor ut 16, H-1876 Budapest (tel: 153-1444; fax: 112-6858).

Raiffeisen Bank, PO Box 173, H-1054 Budapest (tel: 484-4400; fax: 484-4444).

Central bank

Magyar Nemzeti Bank (National Bank of Hungary), 1054 Szabadság tér 8-9, 1850 Budapest (tel:428-2752; fax: 302-3000).

Stock exchange

Budapesti Értéktözsde (Budapest Stock Exchange) (BSE): www.bse.hu

Travel information

Ferihegy International Airport flight enquiries (tel: 157-7155); passenger service (tel: 157-8555; fax: 157-8993).

Hungarian Automobile Club, Francis ut 38, Budapest XIV (tel: 691-8310).

IBUSZ – Hungarian Travel Agency (main Budapest office), Tanács krt 3/c, Budapest VII (tel: 142-3140).

Lufthansa Airport Office (tel: 157-0290, 157-6506; fax: 157-6192); town office, V ci utca 19-21, Budapest (tel: 266-4511; fax: 266-8669).

Malév Hungarian Airlines, (headquarters), 1097 Könyves Kálmán Krt 12-14 (tel: 235-3535); (customer service) Váci út 26, Budapest 11532 (tel: 235-3222; fax: 235-3244; email: centrum@malev.hu).

Police Tourinfo Office (service in English and German), Vigado Utca 6, 1051 Budapest.

Secretariat of the Hungarian Tourist Council, 6th floor, Margit krt 85, H-1024 Budapest (tel: 1175-1682; fax: 1175-38190).

National tourist organisation offices

Tourinform (Hungarian Tourist Board), Suto ut 2, H-1052 Budapest (tel: 117-9800; fax: 117-9578; e-mail: tourinform@mail.hungarytourism.hu; internet site: www.hungarytourism.hu).

Ministries

Ministry of Agriculture and Regional Development, Kossuth Lajos tér 11, H-1055 Budapest (tel: 302-0000; fax: 302-0402).

Ministry of Defence, Balaton ut 7-11, H-1055 Budapest (tel: 332-2500; fax: 311-0182).

Ministry of Economic Affairs, Honved U 13-14, H-1055 Budapest (tel: 302-2355; fax: 302-2394; internet site: http://www.gm.hu/english).

Ministry of Education, Szalay U 10-14, H-1055 Budapest (tel: 302-0600; fax: 302-2002).

Ministry of Environmental Protection, Fo ut 44-50, H-1011 Budapest (tel: 457-3300).

Ministry of Finance, József Nádor tér 2-4, H-1051 Budapest (tel: 118-2066, 138-2633; fax: 118-2570).

Ministry of Foreign Affairs, Bem rkp 47, H-1027 Budapest (tel: 458-1000; fax: 155-9693).

Ministry of Health, Arany János u 6-8, H-1051 Budapest (tel: 332-3100; fax: 302-0925).

Ministry of Home Affairs, József Attila u 2-4, H-1051 Budapest (tel: 331-3700, 332-5790; fax: 118-2870).

Ministry of Justice, Kossuth Lajos ter 4, H-1055 Budapest (tel: 268-3003).

Ministry of Transport, Telecommunications & Water Management, Dob ut 74-81, H-1077 Budapest (tel: 322-0220, 341-4300; fax: 322-8695).

Office of the President, Kossuth Lajos Ter 3-5, Budapest (tel: 268-4000).

Pressinform (information bureau for foreign journalists), Budakeszi ut 41, H-1021 Budapest (tel: 175-1890; fax: 175-1178).

Prime Minister's Office, Kossuth Lajos tér 1-3, H-1055 Budapest (tel: 268-3000; fax: 268-3050).

Other useful addresses

Allami Biztositó (state insurance company), Ullöi ut 1, H-1813 Budapest (tel: 117-8566).

Amex, Deak Ferenc ut 10, 1050 Budapest (tel: 117-8008).

British Embassy, 6 Harmincad utca, Budapest 1051 (tel: 266-2888; fax: 429-6360).

Budapest Stock Exchange, Deak Ferenc ut 5, H-1052 Budapest (tel: 117-5226; fax: 118-1737; internet site: www.fornax.hu/fmon/index.html).

Central Statistical Office, International Relations Department, Keleti Károly utca 5–7, , PO Box 51, H-1525 Budapest (tel: 212-6136; fax: 212-6378; internet site: www.ksh.hu/eng/index.htm).

Federation of Scientific and Technical Societies (MTESZ), Kossuth Lajos tér 6–8, Budapest V (tel: 153-3333).

Hungarian Aluminium Industrial Co Ltd (Hungalu), Privatisation Directorate, Room 419, 85 Margit krt, Budapest 1024 (tel: 175-6528; fax: 175-5802).

Hungária Biztositó (Hungária Insurance Company), Bánk ut 17–6, H-1115 Budapest (tel: 182-0750).

Hungarian Embassy (USA), 3910 Shoemaker Street, NW, Washington DC 20008 (tel: (+1-202) 362-6730; fax: (+1-202) 686-6412; e-mail: office@huembwas.org).

Hungarian Foundation for Enterprise Promotion, Etele ut 68, Budapest H-1115 (tel: 203-0348/60; fax: 203-0377).

Hungarian Investment and Trade Development Agency (ITD), Euro Information Correspondence Centre, Dorottya ut 4, 1051 Budapest (tel: 118-1712/6064; fax: 118-6198; e-mail: itdheicc@mail.datanet.hu; internet site: www.itd.hu/index.htm).

Hungarian Privatisation and Foreign Investment, APV, Pozsonyi ut 56, H-1133 Budapest (tel: 269-8600; fax: 267-0079).

Hungary EU Energy Centre (Thermie), Konyves Kalman Krt 76, 1087 Budapest VIII (tel: 269-9067, 133-1304; fax: 269-9065).

Hungexpo International Fair Centre, Dobi Istvan ut 10, Budapest X.

Magyar Tavirati Iroda (Hungarian news agency) (MTI), Fem utca 507, 1016 Budapest (tel: 155-6722).

Mineralimpex Hungarian Oil and Gas Co, Benczur u 13, 1068 Budapest (tel: 131-6720; fax: 153-1779, 142-3584).

US Embassy, Szabadsag ter 12, 1054 Budapest (tel: 267-4400; fax: 269-9326 or 269-9337 (Consular Section).

National news agency: Magyar Távirati Iroda (MTI) (Hungarian News Agency): http://english.mti.hu

Other news agencies: Havaria Press (in Hungarian): www.havariapress.hu

Internet sites

Budapest Network: www.budapestnetwork.com

Budapest Sun: www.budapestsun.com

Hungary Network: www.hungary.com

Online financial journal: www.portfolio.hu/en

Virtual Hungary: virtualhungary.com

Iceland

KEY FACTS

Official name: Lyoveldio Island (Republic of Iceland)

Head of State: President Ólafur Ragnar Grímsson (since 1996; re-elected 1 Aug 2008)

Head of government: Prime Minister Jóhanna Sigurðardóttir (SDA) (appointed 1 Feb 2009; re-elected 25 Apr 2009)

Ruling party: Coalition led by Samfylkingin (Social Democratic Alliance) (SDA) with Vinstrihreyfingin-grænt frambod (VG) (appointed 1 Feb 2009; re-elected 25 Apr 2009)

Area: 103,100 square km

Population: 320,000 (2010)*

Capital: Reykjavík

Official language: Icelandic

Currency: Icelandic krona (Ikr) = 100 aurar

Exchange rate: Ikr118.24 per US$ (Oct 2011)

GDP per capita: US$39,026 (2010)

GDP real growth: -3.50% (2010)

GDP: US$12.60 billion (2010)

Labour force: 181,000 (2010)

Unemployment: 8.10% (2010)

Inflation: 5.40% (2010)

Balance of trade: US$983.00 million (2010)

* estimated figure

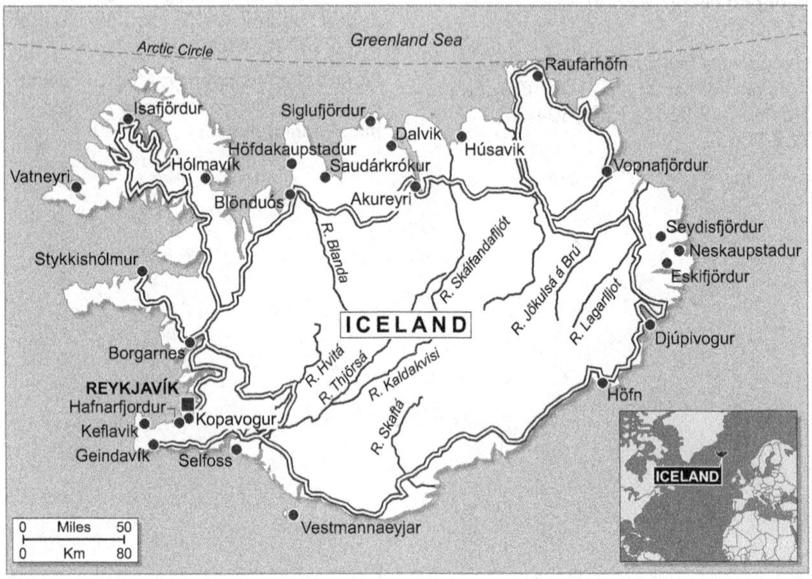

Iceland's silent revolution took a new turn in September 2011 when, after months of preparation a special court was convened to begin proceedings against former prime minister, Geir Haarde, for his role during the 2008 financial crisis. Mr Haarde thus became the first head of government in the world to be put on trial for his alleged negligence during the crisis and in the preceding years.

J'Accuse

Three years after the event, Icelanders were still reeling from the shock of their country's collapse. Mr Haarde, who during the crisis was the leader of Iceland's ironically named Sjálfstaeðisflokkurinn (SSF) (Independence Party) stood accused of breaking Iceland's law of ministerial responsibility and of ignoring the warnings that he received of the imminence of a crash in his country's overstretched financial system. If found guilty, Mr Haarde could face a two-year prison sentence. His legal team sought to dismiss the charges on the grounds that the reasons for his accusation were unclear. Mr Haarde's defence counsel, Andi Arnason, also claimed that the trial was unjust in that Mr Haarde was the only member of the former government who was being brought to trial.

The action against Mr Haarde was authorised in 2010 by Iceland's parliament, which in late 2010 had a left of centre majority. In bringing charges, parliament was following the advice of an investigative commission which had been created specifically to determine the responsibilities of Iceland's political and economic authorities during the crisis. When voting to proceed with the indictment of the former prime minister, parliament absolved three other members of Mr Haarde's government, two of whom were members of the ruling Samfylkingin (Social Democratic Alliance) (SDA). This decision called into question the independence of the proceedings. The tribunal responsible for hearing the case against Mr Haarde, the *Landsdómur*, was formed in 1905 with the specific objective of judging the behaviour of government ministers and members of parliament. Mr Haarde's case was the first time that the tribunal had sat in judgement.

Predictably, Mr Haarde had not been slow to dismiss the case against him as a 'farce', claiming that it was a purely political gambit by a left-leaning government to punish his party. He had asserted this in the preliminary hearings in June 2011. The former prime minister also claimed that his conscience was clear and that he would await the tribunal's verdict patiently.

Mr Haarde had been prime minister from 2006 until 2009, during which Iceland's economy boomed on a fragile foundation of credit which rapidly unravelled as the financial crisis took hold. In a matter of days Iceland's three major financial institutions were forced into bankruptcy, Iceland's currency – the krone – imploded, and soaring unemployment made Icelanders take to the streets in protest. Such was the persistency of the protesters that after months of demonstrations, Mr Haarde's ruling coalition comprising his own party (the SSF) and the SDA, fell apart. Politically, the SDA may have been winners, ending a twenty-year period of right-wing government, But economically, every Icelander was a loser.

Debt refusal

In April 2011 Icelanders rejected for a second time proposals put forward for their country to repay its debts to the Netherlands and the United Kingdom. The referendum result represented a dramatic act of defiance by Iceland's electorate. The government had warned that any rejection of the proposals could thwart the country's efforts to join the European Union (EU). The rejection left the two creditor nations with little option but to seek legal redress, taking their claim to international courts. The referendum outcome was a major setback for Iceland's SDA government which had been assiduously endeavouring to build domestic support for a repayment deal since taking office. At the centre of the dispute was the question of money deposited by British and Dutch customers in the Icesave subsidiary of the bankrupt Landesbanki. Although they had been reimbursed by state deposit insurance schemes, the British and Dutch treasuries had not been reimbursed.

Not only was it the British and Dutch governments who were closely following the referendum result. Although the international credit rating agencies' standing and reputation had suffered dramatically following the global financial crisis, which they had allowed to happen under their noses, they had managed none the less to retain some international clout; not least in a battered Iceland. The fear was that the rejection of any deal would lead to a downgrade of Iceland's sovereign debt. The Dutch authorities also saw fit to observe that the fulfilment of EU regulations on bank deposit guarantees was a prerequisite of EU membership.

In fact, the referendum rejection was not so dramatic in substance as it was in appearance. The government maintained that whatever its voters thought, the Netherlands and the UK would in fact recover their money. Iceland's President Olafur Ragnar Grimsson described the referendum result as 'absurd' since the bank's balance sheet would in any event allow it to begin reparations at the end of 2011. Estimates suggested that at least 90 per cent of the Icesave debt could be recovered from the Landesbanki estate, which – inter alia – included a majority holding in the major UK frozen food retailer, the appropriately named Iceland Food. Even before the second, and final, referendum vote, in December 2010 the Iceland government had reached agreement with the UK and Dutch governments to provide a sovereign guarantee to cover any shortfall in the amounts actually recovered from the Landesbanki fire sale. In February 2011 parliament voted 44–16 in favour of approving the deal to repay €4billion (US$5.4 billion) of the money lost in the Icesave collapse.

An earlier debt proposal had been even more roundly rejected, by over 90 per cent of the voters. But the long suffering President Grimsson had seen fit to allow the voters a second attempt. Following the second rejection, one of the 'Vote No' campaign leaders declared that ' Icelanders are honourable people who want to pay their bills but it is our civil right to have this tried in court to determine legal responsibility for the debt.'

Looking east

In mid-2011 Iceland's politicians seemed to have lost hope in restoring their country's depleted fortunes with help from within the EU. President Grimsson had accused the EU of 'turning its guns on Iceland'. To an outside observer, it rather looked as though Iceland, the first year pupil in the playground, had tried to mix it with the sixth year heavyweights, and having received a mauling, was now crying 'foul'. So instead, led by President Grimsson, discussions had been held with Chinese entrepreneurs; Iceland's President had visited China no less than five times in six years. He also claimed, improbably, that Iceland had received more Chinese delegations than 'the US, the UK, Germany, France, Italy and Spain combined.' These resulted in the proposed, if improbable, sale of an enormous extent of land – reportedly 300 square km – to Chinese entrepreneurs as an eco-tourism resort. Such was the scheme's improbability, that Icelandic critics suggested there might be a more strategic motive for the purchase.

China was known to be making energy related investments wherever possible. Iceland's mid-Atlantic location and its proximity to the Arctic ice cap offered new possibilities to both parties.

One unexpected effect of the financial crash was a renewed interest in the country's fishing industry. The larger Icelandic fishing companies were truly global in their scope, with operations in several continents. Fishing as an investment opportunity had suffered from the fraught

KEY INDICATORS — Iceland

	Unit	2006	2007	2008	2009	2010
Population	m	0.31	0.31	0.32	0.32	*0.32
Gross domestic product (GDP)	US$bn	16.68	20.00	17.50	12.10	12.60
GDP per capita	US$	54,205	64,833	55,462	37,853	39,026
GDP real growth	%	4.4	6.0	1.4	-6.9	-3.5
Inflation	%	6.8	5.3	12.4	12.0	5.4
Unemployment	%	1.3	1.0	1.6	8.0	8.1
Exports (fob) (goods)	US$m	3,477.0	4,792.0	5,399.0	4,051.0	4,603.0
Imports (fob) (goods)	US$m	5,716.0	6,181.0	5,699.0	3,318.0	3,620.0
Balance of trade	US$m	-2,239.0	-1,388.0	-300.0	733.0	983.0
Current account	US$m	-4,232.0	-3,125.0	-6,081.0	-270.0	-1,235.0
Total reserves minus gold	US$m	2,301.3	2,578.7	3,515.2	3,813.2	5,698.9
Foreign exchange	US$m	2,273.2	2,549.1	3,486.2	3,638.7	5,557.0
Exchange rate	per US$	69.53	62.93	87.95	123.64	122.24

* estimated figure

question of the EU's conservation driven Common Fisheries Policy, which in the view of most Icelanders would result in Iceland losing control of a major industry. Iceland's fishing industry receives no subsidy from the government, is efficient and well run. The fishing industry generates a massive 40 per cent of gross domestic product (GDP). Talks on membership began in mid-2010, but polls suggest some 58 per cent of the population would rather their government withdrew its application. One commentator attributed the application to join the EU to a 'national nervous breakdown'. Iceland, which only emerged as an independent nation after the Second World War had seen one of its dreams – that of becoming an international financial centre – come to an end, leaving the bruised Icelanders to give more constructive thought to the positive and negative elements of its economy. Fishing it seemed in mid-2011, was making a comeback.

Risk assessment

Economy	Poor
Politics	Fair
Regional stability	Good

COUNTRY PROFILE

Historical profile

Settled by Norwegians and Celtic (Scottish and Irish) immigrants during the late ninth and tenth centuries, Iceland boasts the world's oldest parliament, the Althingi. Iceland was under Norwegian, then Danish, rule from the thirteenth century. The severity of Iceland's terrain was frequently compounded by natural disasters leading, in the nineteenth century, to large-scale emigration to the USA and Canada. The island was granted its own constitution in the 1840s.

1903 Iceland was granted Home rule from Denmark.

1918 Iceland became a sovereign state in union with Denmark.

1940 Germany invaded Denmark. British troops were stationed in Iceland.

1944 Iceland terminated the convention linking it with Denmark and declared itself a republic.

1948 Iceland joined the International Whaling Commission (IWC).

1949 Iceland joined NATO and the Council of Europe. A large US airbase was established at Keflavík.

1953 Iceland became a founding member of the Nordic Council.

1959–71 The Coalition of Independence and Social Democratic Parties remained in power.

1960s–70s Iceland's unilateral extensions of its territorial waters to protect its fishing grounds led to the 'Cod Wars' with the UK, and in 1976, caused a temporary break in diplomatic relations, the first such break between NATO members.

1980 Vigdís Finnbogadóttir was elected president, the world's first popularly elected female head of state.

1985 Iceland was declared a nuclear-free zone, barring entry to all nuclear weapons.

1987 Thorsteinn Pálsson was appointed prime minister.

1991 Iceland quit the IWC after the organisation refused to consider Icelandic proposals for moderate catch quotas.

1996 Ólafur Ragnar Grímsson was elected president.

1999 The elections again returned a centre-right coalition of Sjálfstaeðisflokkurinn (SSF) (Independence Party) and Framsóknarflokkurinn (FSF) (Progressive Party).

2000 Ólafur Ragnar Grímsson was re-elected president unopposed.

2002 Iceland's bid to rejoin the IWC, without signing up to the moratorium on commercial whaling, was rejected.

2003 Prime Minister Oddsson's SSF won the parliamentary elections.

2004 Incumbent Ólafur Ragnar Grímsson was re-elected in the presidential elections. Halldór Ásgrímsson (FSF) became prime minister.

2005 The government granted Bobby Fischer, the chess grandmaster and US fugitive of 10 years, Icelandic citizenship.

2006 Halldór Ásgrímsson resigned as prime minister and Geir Haarde (SSF) replaced him. The US closed its naval base at Keflavík.

2007 In general elections, the SSF retained power.

2008 Former world chess champion and naturalised citizen, Bobby Fischer, died. President Grímsson was re-elected unopposed. Following the collapse of Iceland's largest bank, Landsbanki, the UK government made available a loan of £100 million (US$174 million) to help repay the bank's UK creditors. The Sedlabanki (central bank) rate was raised to 18 per cent from 12 per cent in a move to stave off the collapse of Iceland's banking system. Iceland came under IMF administration.

2009 The central bank rate was raised to a record high of 21 per cent. Prime Minister Haarde resigned, following the collapse of the coalition government. The president called on the Samfylkingin (Social Democratic Alliance) (SDA) and VG to form a minority coalition, interim government. Jóhanna Sigurðardóttir (SDA) became prime minister and was endorsed into office following early parliamentary elections. Iceland formally applied for European Union membership. Moody's Investors Service cut Iceland's credit rating to the lowest investment grade. A record 5,027 babies were born in Iceland.

2010 The Eyjafjallajökull volcano erupted in April; volcanic ash thrown up into the atmosphere as high as 20,000 feet caused the shutdown of air traffic in 11 western and northern European countries, leading to severe disruption of passengers and cargo. In May, former directors of the bankrupt bank Glitnir, including Jón Ásgeir Jóhannesson, a retail magnate, were sued for US$2 billion in a US lawsuit, accused of a 'sweeping conspiracy' and draining cash from its assets. The lawsuit followed a year of forensic accountancy of the bank's books that supported the allegation of robbery 'from the inside'. The interest rate was cut to 7 per cent on 18 August, as inflation fell and the currency strengthened. The annual unemployment rate reached 8 per cent, a jump from 1 per cent in 2009.

2011 On 20 February the President announced that a referendum would be held on the latest plan to repay the Dutch and UK governments the US$4 billion lost in 2009 when the Icesave Bank collapsed. Parliament voted to accept the plan, but narrowly voted against a referendum. President Grimmson was against the repayment plan and refused to sign the deal, thereby triggering the referendum on 9 April. The government lost the referendum by a vote of 59.77 to 40.22; turnout was 75.34. The Dutch and UK governments said they would go to court to recover the lost US$4 billion. In the High Court, on 11 May, former prime minister, Geir Haarde, had formal charges laid against him of failing to prevent the banking crisis and failing his ministerial duties of managing the repercussion of the collapse of the Icelandic economy while he was in charge of the country. Haarde denied the charges.

Political structure

Constitution

The constitution was adopted 17 June 1944.

The parliament and office of president jointly exercise legislative power, with due adherence to the constitution. The judiciary is guaranteed independence.

Elections are by proportional representation with universal direct suffrage over the age of 18.

The constitution recognises the Evangelical Lutheran Church as the state church.

Independence date

17 June 1944

Form of state

Parliamentary democratic republic

The executive
Executive power is vested jointly in the offices of the president as Head of State, directly elected for a four-year term, and the prime minister as head of government (appointed by the president); the prime minister appoints a cabinet, which is approved by parliament).
Any citizen aged over 35 may become president, by popular vote (if more than one candidate stands for the post; without a challenge a candidate is duly elected without a vote).
National legislature
The unicameral Althingi (parliament) has 63 members elected for a four-year term, by a two-tier proportional representation system. Six constituencies each elect nine members (54), based on party lists with rankings that may be changed or candidates rejected; the remaining nine members are allocated as weighting seats (one for each constituency) equalising all votes for a party, which ensure total national votes reflect the number of seats gained by a political party.
Legislative power is held jointly by the president and the Althingi.
Legal system
The legal system is based on the 1944 constitution; the civil law system is based on Danish law.
Last elections
1 August 2008 (presidential); 25 April 2009 (parliamentary)
Results: Presidential: Ólafur Ragnar Grímsson was re-elected unopposed.
Parliamentary: Samfylkingin (SF) (Social Democratic Alliance) won 29.8 per cent of the vote (20 seats out of 63), Sjálfstæðisflokkurinn (SSF) (Independence Party) 23.7 per cent (16), Vinstrihreyfingin – grænt framboð (VG) (Left-Green Movement) 21.7 per cent (14), Framsóknarflokkurinn (Progressive Party) (FSF) 14.8 per cent (9), Borgarahreyfingin (BF) (Citizen's Movement) 7.2 per cent (4). Two other parties won less than 3 per cent each and failed to gain any seats. Turnout was 85.1 per cent.
Next elections
2012 (presidential); 2013 (parliamentary)

Political parties
Ruling party
Coalition led by Samfylkingin (Social Democratic Alliance) (SDA) with Vinstrihreyfingin-grænt frambod (VG) (appointed 1 Feb 2009; re-elected 25 Apr 2009)
Main opposition party
Framsóknarflokkurinn (FSF) (Progressive Party)

Population
320,000 (2010)*
Last census: July 2000: 281,154
Population density: 2.7 per square km.
Urban population: 93 per cent (1995—2001).
Annual growth rate: 1.0 per cent 1994–2004 (WHO 2006)
Ethnic make-up
Almost the entire population are descendants of Norwegians and Celts.
Religions
Lutherans (96 per cent), Protestants and Catholics (3 per cent).

Education
Pre-schooling is offered to children aged between one and six years when compulsory primary education begins. This leads into lower secondary school until aged 16 when students choose upper secondary education – either academic grammar or comprehensive schooling or vocational industrial or specialised training. Upper secondary education covers four years and is open to anyone who has completed compulsory school. Grammar and comprehensive attainment leads to higher education facilities at age 20.
Icelandic municipalities are responsible for delivering education in different regions.
There are eight higher education institutions in Iceland, most of which are run by the state and require no tuition fees. Private parties with state support run three institutions that charge tuition fees. About 16 per cent of Icelandic students in higher education study abroad.
The total public expenditure in education is typically 5—6 per cent of GDP.
Compulsory years: Six to 16.
Enrolment rate: 99 per cent net primary enrolment; 85.3 per cent net secondary enrolment (World Bank 2003).

Health
The country is divided into health care regions, each with their own primary health care centres, some of which are run jointly with the local community hospital; hospitalisation is free of charge. The number of Icelandic physicians has increased steadily during the last decade.
HIV/Aids
HIV prevalence: 0.2 per cent aged 15–49 in 2003 (World Bank)
Life expectancy: 81 years, 2004 (WHO 2006)
Fertility rate/Maternal mortality rate: 2.0 births per woman, 2004 (WHO 2006)
Child (under 5 years) mortality rate (per 1,000): 3.0 per 1,000 live births (World Bank)
Head of population per physician: 3.62 physicians per 1,000 people, 2004 (WHO 2006)

Welfare
Iceland follows the Nordic social security system, which aims to provide universal social welfare and health services.
The social security system covers pension, occupational injury, health and maternity insurance. Most pensions are covered by private pension funds. There is generous coverage for maternity leave for both men and women.
Special attention has been given to women's employment and special grants have been provided to women for running businesses.

Main cities
Reykjavík (capital, estimated population 114,661 in 2005), Kópavogur (26,754), Hafnarfjörður (21,820), Akureyri (16,221).

Languages spoken
The Icelandic language belongs to the North Germanic branch of the Indo-European family.
Official language/s
Icelandic

Media
The constitution guarantees freedom of the press.
Press
Dailies: In Icelandic popular newspapers include *Morgunbladid* (www.mbl.is), *Frettabladid* (www.visir.is), *DV* (www.dv.is) is an evening newspaper.
Weeklies: In Icelandic, regional newspapers include *FréttirWO (www.sudurlandid.is/Eyjafrettir) from Sudland, Vikurfrettir* (www.vf.is), from Sudurnes, *Tidis* (www.patreksfjordur.is), from Vestfirdir and *Skessuhorn* (www.skessuhorn.is) from Vesturland. *Sed og Heyrt* is a tabloid magazine.
Business: In Icelandic, *Viðskiptablaðið* (www.vb.is), is a daily, *Markadurinn* (http://vefmidlar.visir.is), is published weekly. Marine industry publications include *Aegir* and *Fiskifrettir*.
Periodicals: In Icelandic, the monthly *Mannlíf* (www.mannlif.is) covers news and current affairs and for women, *Birtingur* (www.birtingur.is) is published 10 times a year.
Broadcasting
The Ríkisútvarpið (RÚV) (Icelandic National Broadcasting Service) is the public network providing services from a number of regional centres.
Radio: RÚV (www.ruv.is) operates two radio stations Rás 1 and Rás 2. The largest private commercial radio network is Bylgjan (http://lettbylgjan.is).
Television: Sjónvarpið/RÚV (www.ruv.is) operates the national television service and locally producing Icelandic language shows as well as transmitting imported TV shows. It transmits for around eight hours

per day during the week and 16 hours per day during the weekend. Private commercial TV stations includes Stöð 2 (www.stod2.visir.is) with five channels and Skjárinn (http://skjarinn.is) with three channels.

Advertising

Although the market is very small the advertising market is very dynamic with ads being placed in all media including new technologies. The print media typically accounts for over 50 per cent of the market. The quality of locally produced television advertising material is very high by international standards.

There is a total ban on advertising alcohol and tobacco and restrictions on advertising over the counter medicines. Outdoor advertising is limited by environmental laws, however billboards are popular. Information can be obtained from Association of Icelandic Advertising Companies.

Economy

The banking sector was privatised in 2003, from which time the banks increased their assets from just over 100 per cent of GDP to more than 1,000 per cent of GDP with the banks taking high risks, outstripping the government's ability to act as lender of last resort. As the global crisis struck in 2008, investors quickly withdrew their funds and three banks failed, which caused a crash of the Icelandic krona, which fell in value by over 70 per cent. The stock market lost 80 per cent of its value. Effectively the economy was left bankrupt. GDP growth fell from a healthy 6 per cent in 2007 to a painful -6.9 per cent in 2009; although the situation remained serious in 2010 the recession slowed to -3.5 per cent. In 2011, GDP growth was estimated to have risen to 2.5 per cent. Iceland crashed from an economy with one of the highest GDP per capita rates in Europe of US$64,833 in 2007, to US$55,462 in 2008 and then further still to US$37,853 in 2009; there was a rise in 2010 to US$39,026 as the situation improved.

Unemployment had begun rising shortly after the economy floundered in 2008, so that in 2009 around 1 per cent of the workforce (2,000 people), were unemployed; by 2010, 8 per cent (16,000 people) were unemployed.

The International Monetary Fund (IMF) approved an initial emergency financing loan of US$2.1 billion in 2008; the two-year Stand-By Arrangement was used to stabilise the krona as successive governments set about making swingeing cuts to public spending. The government, which had come to power in early 2009, quickly recapitalised two of the three largest failed domestic banks and introduced tighter banking regulations. Moody's Investors Service cut Iceland's credit rating to the lowest investment grade in November 2009. The interest rate was cut to 7 per cent on 18 August 2010, as inflation fell and the currency strengthened.

Iceland's non-financial economy is an open market economy based largely on fishing (although cod stocks are diminishing), tourism (expanding fast) and aluminium smelting (based on abundant geothermal power and water). The fishing industry typically makes up around 60 per cent of exports and contributes 10 per cent of GDP. However, the level of cod catches is falling and this has had a knock-on effect for the processing industry. The large fish processing company, Samherji, now has its operations in Grimsby (UK), rather than Dalvík. When the move was made in 2006 it took advantage of lower UK wages (30–40 per cent less), and also lower transport costs; however, by 2009 unemployment had become higher and wages lower in Iceland than in the UK. The Alcoa Fjaroaal aluminium smelting plant started operations in 2007 and when it reaches full capacity aluminium exports are expected to be 50 per cent of total exports.

External trade

Iceland is a member of the European Economic Area (EEA), which maintains an internal market with, although not actually joining, the EU. The EU consults EEA members before making its decisions on community legislation. The EEA agreement allows freedom of movement of goods (excluding, to a significant degree, agriculture and fisheries), persons, services and capital.

In an attempt to move away from primary industries, which are subject to world prices and dwindling stocks, Iceland has developed interests in software production and biotechnology.

Imports

Principal imports include capital goods, vehicles, consumer goods, petroleum, foodstuffs and clothing.

Main sources: Norway (typically 12 per cent of total), Germany (10 per cent), Sweden (9 per cent).

Exports

Fish and marine products (over 50 per cent), manufactured goods and minerals – aluminium, ferrosilicon, diatomite.

Main destinations: The Netherlands (typically 35 per cent of total), UK (11 per cent), Germany (11 per cent).

Agriculture

Farming

Some 20 per cent of Iceland's land area is suitable for the raising of livestock and for fodder production. Only 6 per cent of the area is used for the cultivation of, principally, hay and potatoes, and the rest is used for livestock.

Arable land is scarce, but good grazing allows for self-sufficiency in meat (mostly lamb), milk, poultry, eggs, cheese and butter.

The sector is small-scale, heavily subsidised and organised into co-operatives. High import tariffs protect domestic production from foreign competition.

Fishing

Fishing replaced farming early in this century as the dominant sector of the economy. The fishing industry (including processing) is the single most important export earner, accounting for 60 per cent of Iceland's exports. The large modernised trawler fleet supplies over 110 freezing plants, which produce white fish fillets, frozen shrimps, capelin, scampi, scallops, fish oil and fish meal.

The Icelandic Freezing Plants Corporation and Iceland Seafood Ltd are the leading fish exporters.

There is rapid growth of inland and offshore fish farming.

In 2007 fishing quotas for Atlantic cod were drastically reduced due to the falling number of young fish stocks. The decision by the government to cut back on the country's biggest export earner is expected to have a big impact, on not only fishermen's livelihoods but also the short- to medium-term outlook for the industry. While the measures should preserve the industry the long-term outlook will be of a reduced fishing fleet. New whaling quotas were issued in January 2009, increasing the number to be caught, the majority of which are expected to be exported to Japan.

Industry and manufacturing

The industrial sector contributes 26 per cent to GDP and employs 30 per cent of the workforce.

It is centred on fish and food processing. A salmon fish processing plant on Iceland's east coast is the first to use state-of-the-art technology to process salmon for export to the EU and US.

Other major industrial activity focusses on aluminium smelting, ferro-silicon alloys, diatomite production and light manufacturing. The demands of the fishing industry have lead to developments in the country's computer, software and electronics industries and have also encouraged developments in biotechnology and pharmaceuticals.

With abundant hydroelectric and geothermal power in Iceland has led to power-intensive industries, the largest of which is aluminium smelting. In June 2007 the US-owned Alcoa smelter opened in eastern Iceland, with a capacity of 314,000 tonnes annually when fully operational.

Tourism
Tourism is an increasingly important sector, accounting for 13 per cent of foreign exchange earnings and 4.5 per cent of GDP. A growing proportion of arrivalsare winter visitors. The Nordic countries, North America and particularly the UK are the main markets. The industry is well organised and expanding, catering largely to adventure and eco-tourists.
Whale-watching, which attracts around 25 per cent of tourists, is growing in popularity. The decision to resume whale-hunting in 2003 hurt Iceland's image abroad and has given rise to fears that it could undermine the more lucrative tourist sector.

Hydrocarbons
Iceland does not produce any hydrocarbons. Exploration of offshore sites proved unsuccessful. Imports of petroleum products were 21,120 barrels per day in 2007.
No natural gas is imported.
Over 4.0 million tonnes of coal is imported for electricity generation.
The government is committed to replacing as much as possible of the country's imported fossil fuels with renewable energy sources, so the consumption of oil and coal is likely to decrease as this industry grows.

Energy
Total installed generating capacity was 1.9 gigawatts (GW) in 2007; production amounted to around 12 gigawatts hours (GWh). The energy was produced in 11 hydroelectric stations, 63 geothermal stations and two oil fired-powered stations. Hydro-power produced 93.9 per cent of all electricity and geothermal power 6.1 per cent. Imported hydrocarbons are still used for spare power generation in emergencies.
Iceland is not only self-sufficient in energy requirements but has the potential to be a major exporter of electricity. It is estimated that only 12 per cent of Iceland's energy potential has been harnessed. Iceland aims to become the first fossil-fuel free economy by 2020 and plans to develop a fully hydrogen-powered transport system by 2035; new technology in hydrogen-fuelled buses began trials in 2000. Around 85 per cent of homes have geothermal heating. The fishing fleet remains dependent on imported oil.
Landsvirkjun is the national electricity company, responsible for production, transmission and sale of electricity to commercial and domestic customers.

Financial markets
Stock exchange
ICEX (Kauphöll Íslands) (Iceland Stock Exchange)

Banking and insurance
In addition to the central bank, there are four commercial banks operating: the Búnadarbanki Íslands (Agricultural Bank), Icebank Ltd, Islandsbanki Ltd and Landsbanki Íslands (National Bank of Iceland) are privately owned.
Kaupthing, an investment bank, and the Búnadarbanki merged in May 2003 to form the Kaupthing Búnadarbanki.
Central bank
Sedlabanki Íslands (Central Bank of Iceland)

Time
GMT

Geography
Iceland comprises one large island, with an area of 103,000 square km, and numerous smaller ones, situated near the Arctic Circle in the North Atlantic Ocean. The main island lies about 300km (190 miles) south-east of Greenland, about 1,000km (620 miles) west of Norway and about 800km (500 miles) north of Scotland. The Gulf Stream keeps Iceland warmer than might be expected.
A geologically young island, Iceland is volcanically and geothermally active. The largest volcanoes are Hekla and Snaefellsness. The terrain has a rugged aspect. As much as half of it is mountainous lava desert and wasteland. The central highlands are barren and interspersed with mountains and glaciers. 11 per cent of Iceland is covered by glaciers. The most extensive glacier, located in the south-east of the island, is Vatnajökull, which covers an area of 8,500 square km. The highest point in Iceland, Hvannadalshnúkur, which rises to 2,119m, is in this region. There are numerous lakes and fast-flowing, unnavigable rivers, some of which rise in the glaciers, while others are spring-fed. The coastline is irregular, with bays and fjords, affording good natural harbours, though some parts are sandy with lagoons. The populated areas are are restricted to less than a fifth of the land, around the coasts and in the valleys, especially in the Reykjavik area.
The largest islands are the Westmann Isles to the south, Hrísey to the north and Grímsey in the Arctic Circle.
Hemisphere
Northern.

Climate
Temperate, with mild but stormy winters and cool summers. Rainy in the south. Average temperatures vary between about minus 1 and 12 degrees Celsius.

Dress codes
Medium-weight throughout year, plus a topcoat and raincoat for winter.

Entry requirements
Passports
Required by all, except nationals of Nordic and Schengen Accord countries. Passports must be valid three months after date of departure.
Visa
Required by all, except nationals of EU/EEA and other European countries, North America, Australasia and some Latin American and Asian countries. For a full list of exceptions visit: www.utl.is/english. A Schengen visa application (offered in several languages) can be downloaded from http://europa.eu/abc/travel/ see 'documents you will need'.
Currency advice/regulations
There are no restrictions on the import and export of local and foreign currency.
Customs
Visitors may bring in personal effects and limited quantities of tobacco products and alcohol free of duty. Fishing and riding equipment must be accompanied by a certificate of disinfection issued by an authorised veterinary authority.

Health (for visitors)
Nationals of the European Economic Area (EEA) countries and Switzerland can access reduced cost and sometimes free medical treatment using a European Health Insurance Card (EHIC) while visiting the EEA. Exceptions include nationals of the 10 countries which joined the EU in 2005 whose EHIC is not valid in Switzerland. Applications for the EHIC should be made before travelling.
Mandatory precautions
There are no compulsory vaccinations.
Advisable precautions
Travellers should have up-to-date tetanus and polio immunisations.

Hotels
Most towns have hotels and guest houses. Between June and September university hostels and boarding schools are also used as hotels. Some hostels and many farms provide bed and breakfast service. The rating system is one-star (basic) to five -star (luxury). Tipping is not customary.

Credit cards
All major credit cards, such as American Express, Diners', Eurocard, Visa and Master Card, are accepted.

Public holidays (national)
Fixed dates
1 Jan (New Year's Day), 1 May (Labour Day), 17 Jun (National Day), 24 Dec (Christmas Eve, from mid-day), 25 Dec (Christmas Day), 26 Dec (Boxing Day), New Year's Eve (from mid-day).
Variable dates
Maundy Thursday, Good Friday, Easter Monday, First Day of Summer, Ascension

Day, Whit Monday, Commerce Day (first Mon in Aug).

Working hours

Banking

Mon–Fri: 0915–1600 (winter), 0800–1600 (summer), plus 1700–1800 on Thu (Co-operative Bank, National Bank, Agricultural Bank (Kringlam).

Business

Mon–Fri: usually 0900–1700.

Government

Mon–Fri: usually 0900–1700.

Shops

Mon–Fri: 1000–1800. Most also open Sat 1000–1400/1600 (winter only, Oct to end May). Kiosks remain open until 2330 or even later.

Telecommunications

Mobile/cell phones

GSM 900/1800 services are available in populated areas.

Electricity supply

220V AC

Social customs/useful tips

Icelanders are generally self-confident, self-reliant and reserved. However, once the initial contact has been made people are more than likely to be friendly. Handshaking is customary on arrival and departure.

Getting there

Air

National airline: Icelandair

International airport/s: Keflavík International Airport (KEF), 51km south-west of Reykjavík; bank, restaraunts, shops, car hire.

Airport tax: A security fee of Ikr620 (Ikr285 for children two to 12 years of age) is charged on departure.

Surface

Water: There are ferry services to Iceland from Denmark, Norway and the Shetland Isles.

Getting about

National transport

Air: Air Iceland and Landsflug operate domestic services throughout the island to destinations which link with regional carriers in the west, north and east of the country. Light aircraft readily available for charter and sightseeing.

Road: There are approximately 1,350km of roads. Main highways (approximately one quarter of total) follow the coastline and are hard-surfaced; the rest are gravel-surfaced. Regular coach services link even the remote inland areas.

Water: Regular cargo coastal services link all major ports. Passenger and car ferries sail several times a day between Reykjavík and Akranes and between Thorlakshöta and Vestmannaeyian.

City transport

Taxis: These are used extensively and usually summoned by telephone, although they can be hailed in the street. The journey time from the airport to the city centre is about 40 minutes.

Buses, trams & metro: There are excellent regular services covering the centre and suburbs of Reykjavík. There is a standard fare for any length of journey, even if it involves more than one bus route. Journey time from the airport to the city centre is about 45 minutes.

Car hire

Car hire is available in Reykjavík and several other towns. Rates vary depending on the type of car. Minimum age 20 years, and an international driving licence is usually required. Advance reservations are necessary between June and August. Self-drive cars not recommended as a method of national transport as road surfaces tend to be poor.

BUSINESS DIRECTORY

The addresses listed below are a selection only. While World of Information makes every endeavour to check these addresses, we cannot guarantee that changes have not been made, especially to telephone numbers and area codes. We would welcome any corrections.

Telephone area codes

The international direct dialling code (IDD) for Iceland is +354, followed by subscriber's number.

Chambers of Commerce

Iceland Chamber of Commerce, House of Commerce, Kringlan 7, 103 Reykjavík (tel: 510-7100; fax: 568-6564; e-mail: info@chamber.is).

Banking

Kaupthing Búnadarbanki, Austurstraeti 3, 101 Reykjavík (tel: 525-6000; fax: 525-6209).

Íslandsbanki (Bank of Iceland), Kringlunni, 155 Reykjavík (tel: 560-8000; fax: 560-8150).

Landsbanki Íslands (National Bank of Iceland), Laugavegur 77, 155 Reykjavík (tel: 560-6400; fax: 552-9882; internet site: http://www.landsbanki.is).

Central bank

Sedlabanki Íslands, Kalkofnsvegi 1, 150 Reykjavík (tel: 569-9600; fax: 569-9605; e-mail: sedlabanki@sedlabanki.is).

Stock exchange

ICEX (Kauphöll Íslands) (Iceland Stock Exchange): www.omxnordicexchange.com

Travel information

Airport Authority, Leifur Eiriksson Passenger Terminal, Keflavík Airport, 235 Keflavík.

BSI Travel (buses), Umferdarmidstödin v/Hringbraut, 101 Reykjavík.

Icelandair (Flugleidir), Reykjavík Airport, Reykjavík IS-101 (tel: 505-0200; fax: 505-0300; internet site: http://www.icelandair.com).

National tourist organisation offices

Icelandic Tourist Board, Laekjargotu 3, 101 Reykjavík (tel: 535-5500; fax: 535-5501; e-mail:info@icetourist.is).

Ministries

Ministry of Agriculture, 4th Floor, Sölvhólsgötu 7, 150 Reykjavík (tel: 560-9750; fax: 552-1160).

Ministry of Commerce and Industry, Arnarhváli, 150 Reykjavík (tel: 560-9070, 560-9420; fax: 562-1289).

Ministry of Communication, Hafnarhúsinu vio Tryggvagötu, 150 Reykjavík (tel: 560-9630; fax: 562-1702).

Ministry of Culture and Education, Sölvhólsgötu 4, 150 Reykjavík (tel: 560-9504; fax: 562-3068).

Ministry of the Environment, Vonarstraeti 4, 150 Reykjavík (tel: 560-9600; fax: 562-4566).

Ministry of Finance, Arnarhválli, 150 Reykjavík (tel: 560-9200; fax: 562-8280).

Ministry of Fisheries, Skúlagötu 4, 150 Reykjavík (tel: 560-9670; fax: 562-1853).

Ministry for Foreign Affairs, Rauoarásti\01g 25, 150 Reykjavík (tel: 560-9900; fax: 562-2373, 562-2386).

Ministry for Foreign Affairs, Trade Department, Hverfisgata 115, 105 Reykjavík (tel: 560-9930; fax: 562-4878).

Ministry of Health and Social Security, Laugavegi 116, 150 Reykjavík (tel: 560-9700; fax: 551-9165).

Ministry of Industry, Arnarhváli, 150 Reykjavík (tel: 560-9420; fax: 562-6859).

Ministry of Justice, Arnarhváli, 150 Reykjavík (tel: 560-9010; fax: 552-7340).

Ministry of Social Affairs, Hafnarhúsinu vio Tryggvagötu, 150 Reykjavík (tel: 560-9100; fax: 552-4804).

Office of the Prime Minister (Stjórnarráoshúsinu vio Laekjargötu), 150 Reykjavík (tel: 560-9400, 560-9403; fax: 562-4014, 562-8626).

Other useful addresses

Association of Icelandic Importers, Exporters & Wholesale Merchants, (Félag Islands Storkaupmanna), Húsi verslunarinnar, 103 Reykjavík (tel: 567-8910; fax: 468-8441).

British Embassy, Laufásvegur 31, PO Box 460, 101 Reykjavík (tel: 550-5100; fax: 550-5105; e-mail: britemb@centrum.is).

Customs Department, Tolhusid, Tryggvagata 19, 150 Reykjavík (tel: 560-0300; fax: 562-5826).

Embassy of the United States of America, Laufásvegur 21, Reykjavík (tel: 629-100; fax: 29-139).

Export Council of Iceland, Lagmuli 5, Box 8796, 129 Reykjavík (tel: 568-8777; fax: 568-9197).

Federation of Icelandic Co-operative Societies (Samband of Iceland), Import Division, v/Holtavegur, 104 Reykjavík (tel: 568-1266; fax: 568-0290).

Icelandic Embassy (USA), Suite 1200, 1156 15th Street, NW, Washington DC 20005 (tel: (+1-202)-265-6653; fax: (+1-202)-265-6656; e-mail: icemb.wash@utn.stjr.is).

Icelandic Energy Marketing Agency, Haaleitisbraut 68, 103 Reykjavík (tel: 515-9000; fax: 515-9003; e-mail: landsvirkjun@lv.is).

Iceland Management Association, Ananaust 15, 121 Reykjavík (tel: 562-1066).

Invest in Iceland Bureau (privatisation and foreign investment), Hallveigarstigur 1, PO Box 1000, IS-121 Reykjavík (tel: 511-4000; fax: 511-4040; internet site: http://www.invest.is/us/index.htm; e-mail: Invest@icetrade.is).

National Economic Institute (for information on economic development corporations), Thjodhagsstofnun, Kalkofnsvegi 1, Reykjavík (tel: 569-9500; fax: 562-6540).

Retailers' Association of Iceland, Hus Verslunarinnar, Kringlan 7, 103 Reykjavík (tel: 568-7811; fax: 568-5569).

Samband islenskra auglysingastofa (Association of Icelandic Advertising Companies), Borgartún 35, 105 Reykjavík (tel: 562-9588; internet: www.sia.is/SIA/English).

Statistical Bureau in Iceland, Hagstofa Islands, Skuggasund 3, 150 Reykjavík (tel: 560-9800; fax: 562-8865; internet site: http://www.statice.is/).

Internet sites

Iceland Reporter: www.centrum.is/icerev

Iceland websites: www.iceland.vefur.is

The Trade Council of Iceland: www.icetrade.is

India

KEY FACTS

Official name: Republic of India (also known as Bharat, local-language name)

Head of State: President (Rashtrapati) Pratibha Patil (from 25 Jul 2007)

Head of government: Prime Minister Manmohan Singh (Indian National Congress) (since 2004; re-elected May 2009)

Ruling party: United Progressive Alliance; led by the Indian National Congress (Congress) (from 2004; re-elected 16 Apr–13 May 2009)

Area: 3,287,590 square km

Population: 1.18 billion (2010)*

Capital: New Delhi

Official language: Hindi and English; 15 other languages are recognised for official use in regional areas.

Currency: Rupee (Rs) = 100 paisa

Exchange rate: Rs48.98 per US$ (Oct 2011)

GDP per capita: US$1,265 (2010)

GDP real growth: 10.40% (2010)

GDP: US$1,538.00 billion (2010)

Inflation: 13.20% (2010) (9.06% May 2011)

Oil production: 826,000 bpd (2010)

Balance of trade: -US$97.93 billion (2010)

* estimated figure

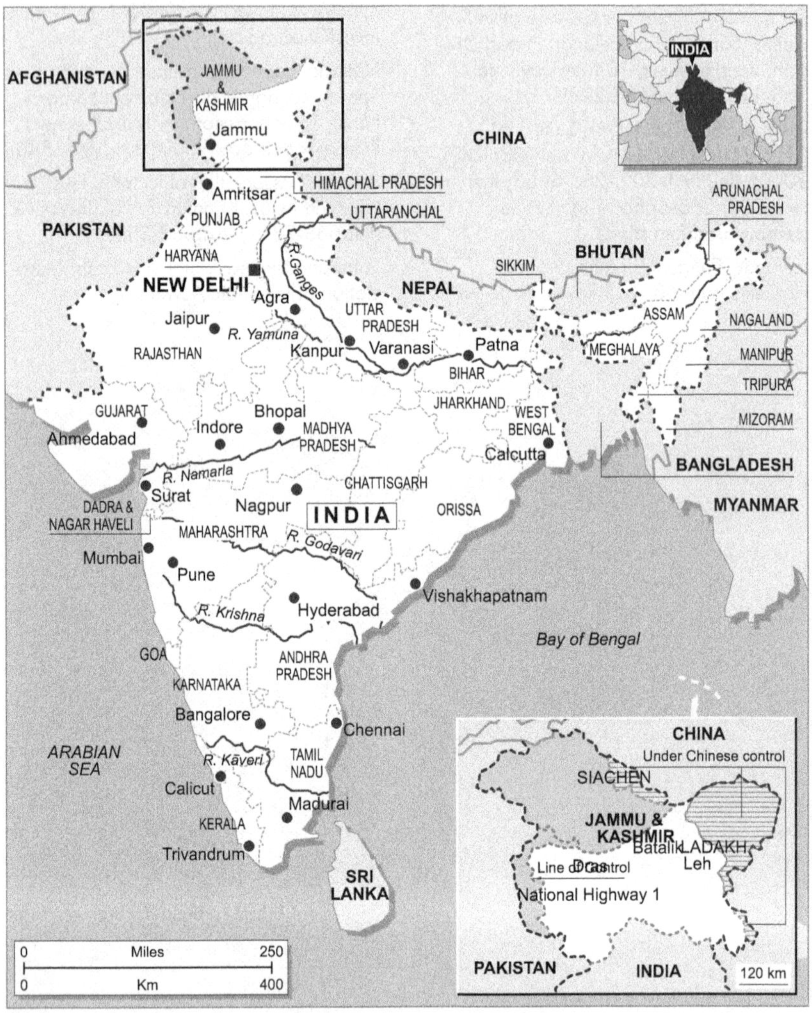

By 2050 (possibly earlier), on current population growth trends, India – with 1,690 million people – will have become the most populous country in the world, comfortably surpassing its nearest rival, China with only 1,390 million. India is a teeming, diverse, ex-colonial, secular, democratic, nuclear state. It has the second biggest population in the world, some 1.1 billion people, but only the seventh greatest land area. Its middle classes, already numbering 200 million people, are growing thanks to some extent to a booming software and IT sector. Hundreds of millions, however, remain in devastating poverty.

Relative growth

In late August 2011 the Reserve Bank of India (RBI) (central bank) warned government ministers that the country's impressive growth rate – that had averaged around nine per cent of gross domestic product (GDP) annually before the 2008 financial crisis – risked dropping below eight per cent. Most industrialised countries would be more than pleased to see growth at this rate: not so India.

Private investment has been falling in India since late 2010, tracking a gradual slide on stock exchanges, where indices have dropped by as much as 24 per cent. On top of this, inflation has been around the ten per cent mark for some time, despite the central bank's efforts to control it by raising interest rates more than ten times in a two year period. Reports prepared by independent analysts go further than the RBI in forecasting a slump in growth rates to less than seven per cent.

The Asian Development Bank (ADB) reported that India's economy grew by 8.6 per cent in the 2010 fiscal year (ending March 2011) according to the government's advance estimates. Growth in 2010 was broad-based, driven by a solid recovery in the agricultural sector and strong performances by both the industry and services sector. Agriculture was estimated to have grown by 5.4 per cent in 2010, after the weak 0.4 per cent registered in 2009, when the deep and widespread drought (and subsequent flooding) affected farming adversely. Grain production was estimated at 232 million tonnes in 2010, 6.4 per cent higher than in 2009 (though still lower than the record 234 million tonnes of 2008). Industry was estimated to have registered growth of 8.1 per cent in 2010, although the second half of the year saw a moderation of growth. According to the ADB, after growth of 10.1 per cent in the first half of the year, industrial output growth slowed to single-digits in the second. The main contributors to strong growth in the first half of 2010 were consumer durables and capital goods. The deceleration in the second half was driven, *inter alia*, by a slowdown in investment. While it is difficult to pin down the cause of the investment slowdown, delays in obtaining environmental clearances, difficulties with land acquisition, and the lack of progress on some expected policy reforms certainly played a part.

The services sector was estimated to have grown by 9.6 per cent in 2010, slightly lower than the 10.1 per cent growth registered in 2009. Key drivers included the trade, hotels, transport and communications and finance, insurance, real estate, and business sub-sectors. Given the dominance of the services sector, its performance is crucial for high overall growth. The services sector accounted for 64 per cent of overall GDP growth in 2010, down from 71 per cent in 2009.

Investment registered a significant increase from 34.5 per cent of GDP in 2008 to 36.5 per cent in 2009, driven by a rise in corporate sector investment of 1.7 percentage points of GDP. The overall investment rate is estimated by the Economic Advisory Council of the Prime Minister to have increased to 37 per cent. The savings rate recovered somewhat in 2009 to 33.7 per cent of GDP and appears to have risen marginally to 34 per cent in 2010. Both savings and investment remain below their pre-crisis highs.

Inflation was a major concern in 2010. While monthly year on year rates moderated from the double-digits reached in mid-2010, they are estimated to have been 9.2 per cent for the fiscal year. Food inflation was an important driver, accounting for between a quarter and a third of monthly wholesale price inflation in 2010. Food inflation in 2010 largely arose from the weak 2009 monsoon's impact on output and prices of cereals, pulses, and sugar. It was also driven by subcontinent-specific weather shocks and demand/supply mismatches, as rising incomes and shifting dietary patterns increased demand for vegetables, fruits, and high protein items. These factors have highlighted the need for dramatically improving production and distribution systems in agriculture.

The RBI recognises that monetary policy may not be the most effective instrument to deal with supply-side pressures on inflation. But its concern is that the repeated supply shocks that have affected the economy, along with recent petroleum price increases, have generated expectations of high inflation and may contribute to future inflation.

Merchandise exports were estimated have risen from US$175 billion in 2009 to US$230.3 billion in 2010, but rising oil prices and resurgent domestic demand have taken imports from US$295.5 billion to US$362.3 billion, pushing the trade deficit from US$120.5 billion to US$132 billion in 2010. The first half of 2010 also recorded sluggish performance of invisibles, largely due to the non-software component of services. As a result of these trends, the current account deficit was estimated to have increased from US$38.4 billion in 2009 to US$50.3 billion in 2010. But a stronger currency and high nominal GDP growth in 2010 meant that, as a share of GDP, the current account deficit was estimated to be around 3.0 per cent, a little higher than 2009/10's 2.8 per cent.

The upsurge in portfolio inflows reflected higher capital flows to emerging markets and interest shown in some public offerings. These flows helped the stock market to put on 30 per cent in May–October 2010, though it has since declined by about 12.7 per cent. In contrast, foreign direct investment (FDI) inflows slowed notably, from US$35.6 billion in 2009 to US$27.6 billion in 2010. Better than expected revenue from the sale of

KEY INDICATORS — India

	Unit	2006	2007	2008	2009	2010
Population	m	1,108.00	1,173.87	1,182.06	*1,199.06	*1,182.11
Gross domestic product (GDP)	US$bn	877.22	1,098.95	1,206.70	1,236.00	1,538.00
GDP per capita	US$	792	945	1,021	1,031	1,265
GDP real growth	%	9.7	9.2	7.3	5.7	10.4
Inflation	%	6.2	6.4	8.3	10.9	13.2
Industrial output	% change	10.6	8.1	3.9	8.0	–
Agricultural output	% change	2.7	4.9	1.6	0.4	–
Oil output	'000 bpd	807.0	801.0	766.0	754.0	826.0
Natural gas output	bn cum	31.8	30.2	30.6	39.3	50.9
Coal output	mtoe	209.7	208.0	194.3	211.5	216.1
Exports (fob) (goods)	US$m	127,090.0	149,314.0	187,912.0	168,219.0	225,502.0
Imports (fob) (goods)	US$m	191,995.0	208,024.0	283,720.0	247,883.0	323,435.0
Balance of trade	US$m	-64,905.0	-58,710.0	-95,808.0	-79,665.0	-97,934.0
Current account	US$m	-9,800.0	-11,284.0	-36,088.0	-25,885.0	-48,977.0
Total reserves minus gold	US$m	170,738.0	266,988.0	247,419.0	265,182.0	275,277.0
Foreign exchange	US$m	170,187.0	266,553.0	246,603.0	258,583.0	267,814.0
Exchange rate	per US$	44.50	39.34	43.50	48.40	45.73

* estimated figure

third-generation spectrum for high-speed telephony and broadband services, as well as robust GDP growth, helped to reduce the central government's fiscal deficit from 6.4 per cent of GDP in 2009 to 5.1 per cent in 2010, thereby restricting the combined deficit of the centre and states to around 8.1 per cent.

Despite India's strong resilience to the crisis and its ability to post robust growth rates, it has made little progress in some reforms. Moves to increase the limit of foreign investment in sectors such as retail and insurance stalled in 2010. Also, some major industrial projects faced difficulties in getting the required clearances from the environment ministry. Finally and critically, the move toward a unified goods and services tax (GST), which is an important step for fiscal consolidation, slowed, with the centre and states gridlocked in negotiations. The states have been concerned about losing their fiscal autonomy, which would follow from a loss of power to change tax rates. They also have anxieties that a GST would raise their dependence on central government transfers. The centre and states are also discussing GST rates, as some states view the proposed revenue-neutral rates as too low. Moreover, they disagree over the taxes to be subsumed under the GST system.

Recent months have, however, seen positive steps on some of these issues. A renewed effort is under way to allow greater FDI in retail and insurance in a phased manner. The environment ministry has allowed through (with conditions) some of the projects initially denied environmental clearance but has asked promoters for some of the others to apply afresh. Finally, the government on 21 March 2011 introduced to parliament a constitution amendment bill to facilitate implementation of the GST.

Corruption

While elephants may have an iconic importance for India and its people, the elephant in India's room has for some time been the question of corruption, which many estimates consider to account for an unacceptable percentage of GDP. In 2010 India fell three places on the Transparency International ranking, to 87th. India also fared badly on a regional comparison by Transparency International, coming 17 (out of 33) Asian nations. However, 2011 saw something of a sea change in public attitudes, as the biggest protests in some twenty years grabbed attention. The protests were led by a Gandhi-like figure, Anna Hazare, head of the anticorruption movement India Against Corruption. Mr Hazare's campaign caught the Indian establishment by surprise. On the back foot, the official response was to send plain clothes police to arrest Mr Hazare and lock him up in jail for a week. In essence, all that Mr Harare has sought is the creation of an anti-corruption ombudsman, or *lokpal*. Although corruption is at the core of the movement, it has also generated protests against India's high inflation rate (not helped, of course, by widespread corruption) and a lack of job opportunities in many parts of the country. Mr Hazare chose to force the issue by going on hunger strike in mid-August 2011, polarising his supporters and his opponents who saw Mr Hazare's movement as a distraction at a time when India needed to confront the possibility of a new recession in the US and Europe. Over half Mr Hazare's supporters were aged less than 25 and paid little heed to the constraints of India's political sensibilities as they donned Hazare T-shirts, baseball caps and badges.

Mr Hazare had opened a Pandora's box of resentment on the part of India's youth in protest against the political élite, amounting to a serious lack of confidence in Indian democracy itself. The Hazare crisis has shown up the Indian National Congress (Congress) Party's clumsy inadequacies as a political machine. The 74 year old Mr Hazare had simply out-manoeuvred it. The Congress Party had wheeled in all its big guns including Prime Minister Manmohan Singh who had appealed in parliament for Mr Hazare to end his hunger strike. India's prime minister in waiting, Rahul Gandhi had appealed to Parliament to consider carefully the implications of introducing the *lokpal* sought by Mr Hazare.

The notable absentee in the debate was Sonia Gandhi, the Congress Party's president, and leader of the ruling coalition, who was reported to be convalescing in the US following surgery. Mrs Gandhi's indecision and lack of leadership did not augur well for the Congress Party. Mr Hazare had managed to touch a very sensitive nerve among India's educated middle classes and its youth. Where he failed was to attract the support of India's lower castes and its Muslim community. At the end of August 2011 it remained to be seen whether Congress would embrace the *lokpal* development, and whether Mr Hazare and his supporters would turn out to be a one month wonder.

The odd couple

The absence of Mrs Gandhi from the political stage in India inevitably fuelled countless rumours, most of which surmised that she was suffering from some form of cancer. Her absence underscored the relative weakness of the ruling coalition. The absence of the headmistress has not only helped Mr Hazare, it has actually helped opposition parties to disrupt government by taking advantage of a government vacuum. India's next elections are planned for 2014. Whether the incumbent prime minister, Manmohan Singh, would be moved aside before the elections remains an open question. But the coalition's perceived lack of direction and purpose certainly does it no favours. After seven years in power, it had become apparent that the coalition is failing to deliver on a number of points.

Paradoxically, the strength of the coalition has rested in the rather non-Indian qualities of its two leaders. Prime Minister Singh is a reserved scholarly economist who has overseen the government and India's foreign policy. Mrs Gandhi is equally reserved, to the point of shyness; she has focussed more on internal politics and the Congress Party's election strategies. Although she has twice orchestrated an election victory, Mrs Gandhi has held back from appointing herself prime minister. She has been content with her position as an elected member of India's lower house, occupying almost an honorary head of state position, meeting visiting heads of state and heading up the National Advisory Council, which accords her cabinet minister rank. The 2011 celebration of India's Independence Day took place without Mrs Gandhi. Her son, and heir-apparent, Rahul returned from her bedside to attend the ceremonies as a member of the four man committee appointed by his mother to run the Congress Party in her absence.

Energy demands rise

With high economic growth rates and over 15 per cent of the world's population, India is a significant consumer of energy resources. In 2009, India was the fourth largest oil consumer in the world, after the United States, China, and Japan. Despite the global financial crisis, India's energy demand continues to rise. In terms of end-use, energy demand in the transport sector is expected to be particularly high, as vehicle ownership, particularly of four-wheel vehicles, is forecast to increase rapidly in the years ahead.

According to the International Energy Agency (IEA), coal/peat account for nearly 40 per cent of India's total energy consumption, followed by nearly 27 per cent for combustible renewables and waste. Oil accounts for nearly 24 per cent of total energy consumption, natural gas six per cent, hydroelectric power almost 2 per cent, nuclear nearly 1 per cent, and other renewables less than 0.5 per cent. Although nuclear power comprises a very small percentage of total energy consumption at this time, it is expected to increase in light of international civil nuclear energy co-operation deals. According to the Indian government, nearly 30 per cent of India's total energy needs are met through imports. According to the June 2011 issue of the *BP Statistical Review of World Energy* (BP11), India had approximately nine billion barrels of proven oil reserves as of December 2010, the second-largest amount in the Asia-Pacific region after China. India's crude oil reserves tend to be light and sweet, with specific gravity varying from 38 degrees API (American Petroleum Institute) in the offshore Mumbai High field to 32 degrees API at other onshore basins.

India produced roughly 826,000 barrels per day (bpd) of total oil in 2010 from over 3,600 operating oil wells. Approximately 680,000bpd was crude oil, the remainder was other liquids and refinery gain. In 2009, India consumed some 3.3 million bpd, making it the fourth largest consumer of oil in the world. The US government Energy Information Administration (EIA) expects approximately 100,000bpd annual consumption growth through 2011. The combination of rising oil consumption and relatively flat production has left India increasingly dependent on imports to meet its petroleum demand. In 2009, India was the sixth largest net importer of oil in the world, importing nearly 2.1 million bpd, or about 70 per cent, of its oil needs. The EIA expects India to become the fourth largest net importer of oil in the world by 2025, behind the United States, China, and Japan.

Nearly 70 per cent of India's crude oil imports come from the Middle East, primarily from Saudi Arabia, followed by Iran. The Indian government expects this geographical dependence to rise in light of limited prospects for domestic production. Though the government has taken steps in recent years to deregulate the hydrocarbons industry and encourage greater foreign involvement, the oil sector is dominated by state-owned enterprises. India's state-owned Oil and Natural Gas Corporation (ONGC) is the largest oil company and dominates India's upstream sector. State-owned Oil India Limited (OIL) is the next largest oil producer. Other major state-run players include the Indian Oil Corporation (IOC) and the Gas Authority of India Limited (GAIL). In addition, the private Indian firm, Reliance Industries Limited, is becoming a significant operator in the oil sector and is the largest private oil and gas company in the country. Cairn India, a branch of UK-based Cairn Energy, and BG Exploration are also important private sector operators in the industry.

As a net importer of oil, the Indian government has policies aimed at increasing domestic exploration and production (E&P) activities. As part of an effort to attract oil majors with deepwater drilling experience and other technical expertise, the ministry of petroleum and natural gas created the New Exploration License Policy (NELP) in 2000, which for the first time permits foreign companies to hold 100 per cent equity ownership in oil and natural gas projects. Despite this, international oil and gas companies currently operate a small number of fields.

India's downstream sector is also dominated by state-owned entities. The IOC is the largest state-owned company in the downstream sector, operating 10 of India's 18 refineries and controlling about three-quarters of the domestic oil pipeline transportation network. Reliance Industries opened India's first privately-owned refinery in 1999, and has gained a considerable market share in India's oil sector.

Exploration and production

Most of India's crude oil reserves are located offshore, in the west of the country, and onshore in the north-east. Substantial reserves, however, are located offshore in the Bay of Bengal and in Rajasthan state. India's largest oil field is the offshore Mumbai High field, located north-west of Mumbai and operated by ONGC. Another of India's large oil fields is the Krishna-Godavari basin, located in the Bay of Bengal

Overseas expansion

In recent years, Indian national oil companies have increasingly looked to acquire equity stakes in hydrocarbon projects overseas. The most active company abroad is ONGC Videsh Ltd (OVL), the overseas investment arm of ONGC. OVL conducts oil and natural gas operations in 13 countries, including Vietnam, Myanmar, Russia (Sakhalin Island), Iran, Iraq, Sudan, Brazil and Columbia.

Downstream/refining

According to the *BP Statistics Review, 2011 (BP 2011)* India had 3.7 million bpd of crude oil refining capacity at 18 facilities as of December 2010. India has the fifth largest refinery capacity in the world. Due to expectations of higher demand for petroleum products in the region, further investment in the refining sector is likely. As part of the country's 11th Five Year Plan from 2007 to 2012, the government has been promoting India as a competitive refining destination, and industry experts expect the country to be an exporter of refined products to Asia in the near future.

Refined fuel subsidies

The Market Determined Price Mechanism is notionally benchmarked to international oil prices, but the Indian government heavily subsidises domestic prices of oil products such as diesel, gasoline, kerosene and LPG. At the same time, taxes on crude and petroleum products imposed by different layers of Indian government often exceed the subsidies. According to industry analysts, though originally an attempt to protect economically disadvantaged Indian consumers, fuel subsidies distort India's domestic market by forcing India's state owned oil companies to accept 'under-recoveries' (ie losses) and encouraging India's private companies to orient their product sales internationally. With diesel prices significantly lower than other fuels, particularly gasoline, diesel consumption rose by nearly 20 per cent from 2007 through 2009. The IEA reports that losses from fuel price subsidies for the 2010–11 fiscal year are expected to exceed US$23 billion.

Strategic petroleum reserve

To support its energy security, India is constructing a strategic petroleum reserve (SPR). The first storage facility at Visakhapatnam will hold approximately 9.8 million barrels of crude (1.33 million tons) and is scheduled for completion by the end of 2011. The second facility at Mangalore will have a capacity of nearly 11 million barrels (1.5 million tons) and is scheduled for completion by the end of 2012. The third facility of Padur, also scheduled to be completed by the end of 2012, will have a capacity of nearly 18.3 million barrels (2.5 million tons).

The selection of coastal storage facilities was made so that the reserves could be easily transported to refineries during a supply disruption. The SPR project is being managed by the Indian Strategic Petroleum Reserves Limited (ISPRL), which is part of the Oil Industry Development Board (OIDB), a state-controlled organisation. India does not have any strategic crude oil stocks at this time.

According to the BP2011, India had approximately 1.5 trillion cubic metres (tcm) of proven natural gas reserves as of December 2010. *BP 2011* estimates that India produced approximately 50.9 billion cubic metres (bcm) of natural gas in 2010, a 29.7 per cent increase over 2009 production levels. The bulk of India's natural gas production comes from the western offshore regions, especially the Mumbai High complex, though the Bay of Bengal and its Krishna-Godavari (KG) fields are proving quite productive. The onshore fields in Assam, Andhra Pradesh, and Gujarat states are also significant sources of natural gas production.

In 2010, India consumed roughly 61.9bcm of natural gas, 21.5 per cent more than in 2009, according to BP2011 estimates. Natural gas demand is expected to grow considerably, largely driven by demand in the power sector. The power and fertiliser sectors account for nearly three-quarters of natural gas consumption in India. Natural gas is expected to be an increasingly important component of energy consumption as the country pursues energy resource diversification and overall energy security.

Despite the steady increase in India's natural gas production, demand has outstripped supply and the country has been a net importer of natural gas since 2004. India's total consumption was 55.7 million tonnes of oil equivalent (mtoe) in 2010, an increase of 21.5 per cent over consumption in 2009. The outlook for India's upstream natural gas sector is more positive than its upstream oil sector, although the IEA forecasts Indian natural gas to reach peak production between 2020 and 2030.

Risk assessment

Economy	Good
Politics	Fair
Regional stability	Fair

COUNTRY PROFILE

Historical profile

1200 The start of five-and-a-half centuries of Muslim rule over the region, beginning with the Sultanate era.
1757 The region gradually came under the influence of British rule after the battle of Plassey.
1858 India came under the direct rule of the British crown after a failed mutiny.
1885 The Indian National Congress was founded by Indian nationalists.
1920s Nationalist leader, Mohandas Karamachand Gandhi, launched a campaign of civil disobedience against British rule.
1942 Congress launched its 'Quit India' campaign.
1947 The Union of India was granted independence by Britain. The partition of the sub-continent into mainly Hindu India and the Muslim-majority state of Pakistan led to the death of hundreds of thousands as communal violence followed independence. Jawaharlal Nehru of the Congress became India's first prime minister. The Hindu ruler of Muslim-majority Jammu and Kashmir joined secular India rather than Islamic Pakistan when the subcontinent was partitioned at the end of British rule.
1948 Gandhi was assassinated by a Hindu fundamentalist. India and Pakistan went to war in Kashmir for the first time.
1950 India became a republic. It remained a member of the Commonwealth. The constitution of India was adopted. France transferred sovereignty of Chandernagore to India.
1951–52 Congress Party won first general elections under leadership of Jawaharlal Nehru.
1954 France ceded its four remaining Indian settlements (Pondicherry, Yanam, Mahe and Karaikal).
1961 Indian forces overran the Portuguese territories of Goa, Daman and Diu and they were annexed by India.
1962 India lost a border war with China.
1964 Nehru died and was succeeded by Lal Bahadur Shastri.
1965 India and Pakistan fought a second war over Kashmir.
1966 Shastri died and Nehru's daughter, Indira Gandhi, became prime minister.
1971 India-Pakistan war over East Pakistan (later Bangladesh). A Treaty of Friendship was signed with the Soviet Union.
1972 The Simla peace agreement set a new Line of Control (LoC) in Kashmir, separating India- and Pakistan-controlled areas.
1974 India exploded its first nuclear device in underground tests.
1975 Indira Gandhi was found guilty of instigating electoral malpractice and was barred from office.
1977 Congress lost elections for the first time.
1980 Indira Gandhi was reinstated as prime minister heading a Congress splinter group, Congress (Indira). There followed years of widespread political and religious disturbances in several states.
1984 Indira Gandhi was assassinated by her Sikh bodyguard after troops stormed the Golden Temple, the Sikhs' most holy shrine, to arrest Sikh separatists. Her son, Rajiv Gandhi, was sworn in as prime minister. Widespread violence continued. The world's worst industrial accident, a gas leak, killed thousands of people living around the US-owned and operated, Union Carbide pesticide plant in Bhopal.
1987 India deployed peace-keeping troops in Sri Lanka.
1989 After an election in which over 100 people died, VP Singh was sworn in as prime minister. His government was the first minority government in Indian history.
1990 The Indian army opened fire in Srinagar during a protest against a crackdown on separatism, killing 38 and giving impetus to rebel campaigns. Singh resigned and Chandra Shekhar was sworn in as prime minister. Indian troops withdrew from Sri Lanka. Muslim separatists, trained and armed by Pakistan, began a campaign of violence in Kashmir.
1991 Shekhar resigned, and the reformist government of PV Narashima Rao came to power. Former prime minister, Rajiv Gandhi, was assassinated by a supporter of the Sri Lankan Tamil separatists.
1996 Congress was defeated in elections and the largest single party in parliament became the Hindu fundamentalist Bharatiya Janata Party (BJP) (Indian Nationalist Party), which attempted and failed to form a government, after which the United Front (UF), a 13-party coalition, succeeded.
1997 Kocheril Raman Narayanan was elected president. He was the first Dalit (untouchable) to become president. The UF government was toppled after Congress withdrew its support in the lower house.
1998 BJP formed a coalition government and Atal Behari Vajpayee was appointed prime minister. Sonia Gandhi became leader of the opposition in the Lok Sabha on 19 March. India and Pakistan each conducted underground nuclear tests, leading to widespread international condemnation and US sanctions. Sonia Gandhi became president of the Indian National Congress Party.
1999 Prime Minister Vajpayee made a historic bus ride to Pakistan for a peace summit with Prime Minister Nawaz Sharif. Vajpayee lost a confidence vote, but was reaffirmed following general elections. Pakistan and India fought a brief war in Kargil in Indian-controlled Kashmir.
2000 India celebrated the birth of its one-billionth citizen. New states – Chattisgarh (part of Madhya Pradesh), Uttaranchal (in the north) and Jharkand (part of the eastern state of Bihar) – were created.
2001 The US lifted sanctions on Pakistan and India as a reward for supporting its attacks on Afghanistan.
2002 An attack on an Indian army camp in Kashmir killed more than 30 people. India threatened retaliation and moved

troops to the border with Pakistan. The tension eased when India lifted its five-month ban on direct flights to Pakistan and ordered its naval battleships back to port. A P J Abdul Kalam was sworn in as president.
2003 India and China reached a *de facto* agreement over the status of Tibet and Sikkim in a cross-border trade agreement. The Indian and Pakistani armies began a cease-fire across the LoC dividing the disputed state of Kashmir and the Himalayan glacier of Siachen.
2004 Prime Minister Vajpayee visited Pakistan. Kashmiri separatist leaders agreed that all violence in the Himalayan region should stop. The Congress Party won parliamentary elections and Manmohan Singh was named prime minister. An earthquake off the island of Sumatra caused a *tsunami* that devastated coastal areas in the region. The final toll for India was estimated to be 12,407 dead or missing, 647,599 displaced.
2005 The first bus-link for 57 years between cities in divided Kashmir began. India, along with Bangladesh, Bhutan, Maldives, Nepal, Pakistan and Sri Lanka, signed the South Asia Free Trade Agreement (Safta).
2006 The third bus link between India and Pakistan was launched, providing the first direct link across the divided Punjab since partition in 1947. Agreement was reached with the US giving India access to American civilian nuclear technology.
2007 Pratibha Patil became India's first female president and Head of State. She was elected by state and federal parliaments. Severe monsoon flooding in Bihar caused death and destruction and left around 11 million Indian villagers affected. India celebrated 60 years of independence from Britain.
2008 The first passenger train since 1965 began operations between Dhaka (Bangladesh) and Kolkata. A number of Indian cities were targeted by Islamist bombers, killing dozens and injuring many more. India launched an unmanned spacecraft to the moon. Pakistani Islamist terrorist teams attacked a series of famous and important targets in Mumbai, lasting 60 hours and killing around 52 people and injuring hundreds more.
2009 During his trial, the sole surviving terrorist of the 2008 attacks pleaded guilty to taking part. Parliamentary elections held for the Lok Sabha (lower house), were won by the United Progressive Alliance (UPA) with 262 seats (out of 543). The UPA's leading party, Congress, won 206 seats, an increase of 61 seats on the 2004 election. The National Democratic Alliance won 159 seats, losing 17 seats overall; its leading party the Bharatiya Janata Party (BJP) won 116 seats, a loss of 22 seats from 2004. On 11 December a new state of Telengana, with a population of 35 million people, was created from 10 districts of Andhra Pradesh, with Hyderabad as the new capital. L K Advani stepped down as leader of the BJP in December; Sushma Swaraj became leader of the party in parliament and Nitin Gadkari was chosen as party president.
2010 In January, the biggest military operation began in what is called the 'red corridor' of 164 contiguous districts of eastern states under the control of the Naxalite-Maoists. A force of 75,000 paramilitaries and thousands of police moved against the communist insurgency as violence by the Naxalite-Maoists increased. By September, over 828 people, mostly civilians had been killed, including 150 people in the derailment of the Gyaneshawari Express (in West Bengal) on 28 May. Since the insurgency began in 1989 a total of 10,529 deaths have been caused by violence on both sides of the conflict. On 1 April, the first phase of the population and house-listing census began. In May the only surviving terrorist of the 2008 Mumbai attacks was convicted of possessing explosives, murder and 'waging war on India'. He later appealed his sentence. In a move to defuse tension India began removing some of the 200 paramilitary bunkers in Kashmir's main city in October. The US-based Global Financial Integrity group reported in November that India had lost an estimated US$462 billion in 'illegal capital flows' (corruption) since independence in 1947. The report also estimated the underground economy at around 50 per cent of GDP (US$640 billion in 2008).
2011 On 30 March, Prime Minister Manmohan Singh and Pakistan Prime Minister Yousuf Raza Gilani together watched the Indian cricket team beat Pakistan in a World Cup Cricket, semi-final played in the Indian city of Mohali. In discussions the two premiers pledged to 'normalise relations'. The second phase of the census was undertaken (9–28 February), including, for the first time, collection of biometric information. The provisional population figure published on 31 March was 1,210,193,422, a 10-year growth rate of 17.64 per cent. Bangladesh and India held a joint census in July, in an attempt to determine just how many Indians there are in the 51 enclaves in Bangladesh and how many Bangladeshis in the 100 or so Indian enclaves. There are possibly as many as tens of thousands of people on the wrong side of each border in enclaves which are historical anomalies of the partition of the subcontinent in 1947. A change to the rules governing exporrt earnings was announced on 9 September, although the date the change would become effective was not given. The new rules will require companies to repatriate foreign currency earnings from exports, and to hold the earnings in domestic bank accounts. It is estimated that the amount concerned will be as high as US$33 billion. A earthquake of magnitude 6.9 struck on 18 September in the Himalayan regions of India, Nepal and Tibet. The epicentre was the Indian state of Sikkim, where at least 50 people were killed and 150 injured. India successfully launched a new satellite, called Megha-Tropiques, on 12 October, to study the patterns of the annual monsoon. Information from Megha-Tropiques will be shared with meteorological organisations in the US and Europe. The first section of the new metro service, Namma (Our), was launched in Bangalore in October, with an initial six stations in the business district, from MG Road in the west, to Baiyappanahalli Terminal in the east of the city.

Political structure

Constitution

The Constitution of India was inaugurated on 26 January 1950. The Preamble declares that the people of India solemnly resolve to constitute a 'sovereign socialist secular democratic republic' and to secure to all its citizens, justice, liberty, equality and fraternity. India has 28 self-governing states and seven union territories with a federal form of government. Any citizen aged 18 years and over is eligible to vote. India is the world's largest democracy.

Independence date

15 August 1947

Form of state

Secular, democratic republic

The executive

Executive power lies with the prime minister, who is appointed by the president, who has a largely ceremonial role and serves a five-year term. The prime minister nominates a 20-member Council of Ministers (cabinet).

National legislature

The bicameral parliament consists of the Lok Sabha (House of the People) (lower chamber) with a maximum 552 members (including up to 20 representatives of India's Union Territories and two representatives of the Anglo-Indian community appointed at the discretion of the president); all serve for five-year terms, and the Rajya Sabha (Council of States) (upper chamber), with a maximum 250 members, of which 238 are elected by state and territorial legislatures and 12 nominated members chosen by the president to provide cultural and scientific expertise. An alternate one third of the membership

is elected every two years. In March 2010 parliament voted to guarantee one-third of all seats of the Lok Sabha be reserved for women.
The legislative field is divided between the Union (central government) and the states. The Union possesses exclusive powers to make laws with respect to matters grouped under 97 headings in the constitution, including foreign affairs, defence, citizenship and trade with other countries. The Union territories are administered by the federal government based in New Delhi. Major legislation requires passage through both houses of parliament.
Each state has its own governor and elected state assembly, with a chief minister and council of ministers. Policy in areas such as agriculture, education and law and order are determined at the state level.

Legal system

The legal system is based on English common law. There is limited judicial review of legislative acts.
The judiciary is independent and known for delivering verdicts which may not necessarily please the government in power. The Chief Justice presides over the Supreme Court, which is the highest court in the land. Each state has its own high court.

Last elections

16 April–13 May 2009 (parliamentary); 21 July 2007 (presidential).
Results: Parliamentary: United Progressive Alliance won 261 seats (out of 543), National Democratic Alliance 159, Third Front 78, Fourth Front 27; the remainder were won by other parties. Turnout was around 60 per cent.
Presidential: Pratibha Patil won 65.8 per cent of the vote; Bhairon Singh Shekhawat won 34.2 per cent.

Next elections

2012 (presidential); 2014 (parliamentary)

Political parties

Ruling party

United Progressive Alliance; led by the Indian National Congress (Congress) (from 2004; re-elected 16 Apr–13 May 2009)

Main opposition party

The National Democratic Alliance led by Bharatiya Janata Party (BJP) (Indian People's Party)

Population

1.18 billion (2010)*
Last census: A census is conducted every ten years. The 2011 census began in 2010 with the fingerprinting and photographing of every individual over the age of 15 in order to build up a national biometric database. The information will be used to issue identity cards with a 16-digit identity number, beginning in November 2010. The process is expected to take one year and will classify gender, religion, occupation and education. The actual count will take place on 9–28 February 2011and the results issued mid-year.
March 2001: 1,028,610,328
Population density: 360 inhabitants per square km (2010)
Annual growth rate: 1.7 per cent 1994–2004 (WHO 2006)

Ethnic make-up

Indo-Aryan (72 per cent), Dravidian (25 per cent), Mongoloid and others (3 per cent).

Religions

Hindu (84 per cent), Muslim (13 per cent), Christian, Sikh, Buddhist, Jain.

Education

A Constitutional Amendment act passed in 2001 made education for all children aged six to 14 a fundamental right. The government earmarked 8 per cent of GNP for education, of which at least 50 per cent would be allocated to primary education. The government is also aiming for universal elementary education by 2010. Accordingly, the department of elementary education and literacy was allocated Rs4,900 crore (US$1,067 million) for 2002/03.
Primary education up to the age of 14 is compulsory in most states and lasts for eight years. Lower primary education between aged six and 11 is free in all states, but upper primary education from 11 to 14 years is free in only 12 states.
Secondary and higher education spending is forecast at Rs49.5 billion (US$1 billion) in 2003/04, of which, Rs17.7 billion (US$388 million) is allocated to higher education spending.
Gender differences, ethnic minorities, caste discrimination and regional disparities have contributed largely to wide inequalities in the development of basic education between Indian states. Independent surveys at the grassroots level show that despite the rhetoric of policy makers, expenditure in the education sector has been falling and typically 6,600,000 working children are still denied the right to primary education. Micro-level strategies for basic education in rural areas are developed through concerted co-operation between local communities, NGOs, government, and international donors.
In April 2010 the federal government introduced laws that gave all children aged six to 14 years the right to free education and announced that enough funds would be made available to ensure that the estimated eight million school-aged children can attend schools. A US$2 billion education fund was established by computer software tycoon Azim Premji in December 2010. The money will be used to found a university in Bangalore to produce 2,000 teaching and education graduates per year.
In September 2011 the Tamil Nadu State began a five-year programme of issuing free laptop computers to an estimated 6.8 million schoolchildren who attend government-funded schools and colleges. This was India's first such programme and is based in a state with a high use of information technology in general.
Literacy rate: 61 per cent adult rate (Unesco 2005)
Compulsory years: Six to 14. Compulsory education is enforced in eight States/Union Territories (UT) when it covers entirely primary schooling; in four States/UT compulsory education is only enforced between ages six to 11; while in March 2003, the ministry of education confirmed that as many as 20 States/UT had not introduced any measure of compulsion.
Enrolment rate: 92 per cent gross primary enrolment; 58 per cent for upper primary enrolment.
Pupils per teacher: 62 in primary schools.

Health

The size and complexity of the Indian population renders universal healthcare difficult to achieve.
India, with its large migrant workforce, is one of only two countries that exports polio (the other is Nigeria), according to the World Health Organisation – Global Polio Eradication Initiative (WHO – Polio Eradication). In particular the state of Uttar Pradesh, where the disease is endemic, saw an outbreak infecting over 400 people in 2006, which was spreading into neighbouring states. India represented 28 per cent of worldwide polio cases in 2006 an increase of 3 per cent from 2005.
In 2004 a new drug treatment for tuberculosis, the first in 40-years, which kills one million sufferers in India and 10 million worldwide, was announced. The medication was developed, and will be manufactured, in India as part of its positioning as a major location for cost-effective, bio-medical research.
In October 2007 the government launched a plan for insurance covering disability, health and life for India's 400m working poor. The plan is part of the government's 'New Deal' for rural India.

HIV/Aids

The World Bank warned India that without greater measures to prevent the spread of HIV through the use of condoms, infections rates and subsequent deaths from Aids could surpass all other pathogens. Indian authorities say infection rates are

falling, though critics claim that the factors that lead to high rates in sub-Saharan Africa are all present in India: large pools of migrant labour, large numbers of prostitutes and stigma about sex and the Aids disease. Condom use has levelled out at 50 per cent and without an increased use new infections could grow by 3 million before 2013. Nationwide policies to tackle the disease are not apparent, with each state tackling the threat locally and some seemingly unable to change old habits.
A UNAids report, published in May 2006, claimed that there were 5.7 million people HIV positive in India, overtaking the 5.5 million infected in South Africa.
In April 2005 the head of the UN backed Global Fund to Fight Aids, Tuberculosis and Malaria, Richard Feacham, said official Indian statistics on the disease were wrong. Stating that Indian had more infections than registered, due to underreporting and that India's infection rates had surpassed that of South Africa. He rejected India's estimate of 5.1 million HIV sufferers, saying that the etimate was a 'conservative figure based on limited data', and he did not believe that India had adequate surveillance measures. The Global Fund has contributed US$265 million for Aids control (2004–09). The government increased the Naco spending to US$95.8 million, however it is estimated that per capita spending on Aids control in India is only US0.29, half the rate spent in Thailand.
While India's infection rate is only 1 per cent, in some of its most populous states the infection rates are up to 20 per cent. The UK endorsed the Naco assertion that more foreign aid would be spent on HIV/Aids sufferers. Of the £123 million (US$219), donated by the UK to fight the disease, £95 million (US$169 million) is still scheduled to be spent by March 2007.
HIV prevalence: 0.9 per cent aged 15–49 in 2003 (World Bank)
Life expectancy: 62 years, 2004 (WHO 2006)
Fertility rate/Maternal mortality rate: 3.0 births per woman, 2004 (WHO 2006); maternal mortality 410 per 100,000 live births (World Bank).
Birth rate/Death rate: 9 deaths to 27 births per 1,000 head of population.
Child (under 5 years) mortality rate (per 1,000): 63.0 per 1,000 live births; 45 per cent of children aged under five are malnourished (World Bank).
Head of population per physician: 0.6 physicians per 1,000 people, 2005 (WHO 2006)

Welfare

The between 60–115 million children toiling as bonded workers in India. Most are agricultural labourers while others work in factories or as domestics. The majority of these children are *Dalit* caste (the untouchables) and may be bound to their employer for years to pay back loans incurred by their parents. While these children are working they do not attend school which perpetuates their deprivation in later life.
The are estimates of between 60–115 million children toiling as bonded workers in India. Most are agricultural labourers while others work in factories or as domestics. The majority of these children are *Dalit* caste (the untouchables) and may be bound to their employer for years to pay back loans incurred by their parents. While these children are working they do not attend school, which perpetuates their deprivation in later life.
Homeless children, widows, the elderly, and the disabled (who often occupy the strata of the most destitute people in India) do not have any explicit protection in the constitution, and consequently not enough demand for any government - (whether local, state or national) to extend care to them. The National Nutrition Mission, distributes food grains at subsidised prices to poor families.
World Bank estimates that India has 40 per cent of the World's poor. The government estimates that 85 per cent of the population is in need of some form of welfare support; 25 per cent of the population belongs to either scheduled castes (SC) or scheduled tribes (ST) and these people have been ascribed special welfare measures. The National SC and ST Finance and Development Corporation provides funds for developing entrepreneurial and other skills.
The central government's expenditure on social services accounts for 1.66 per cent of GDP. India's population suffers periodic problems of floods, droughts and other natural disasters.

Pensions

From 2004, new employees in the public and private sector stopped paying into state pensions and were made to pay into privately managed funds.
The public sector finance organisation, Life Insurance Corporation of India (LIC), also ran a new pension scheme, the The state-subsidised scheme will be available to workers above the age of 55, guaranteeing an annual return of 9 per cent and a maximum pension of Rs2,000 (US$43) per month.
An assurance scheme called *Janaraksha* has been designed by the LIC to provide life insurance for farmers and workers with irregular incomes.

Main cities

New Delhi (capital, estimated population 10.4 million (m) in 2004); Mumbai, capital of Maharashtra state (12.6m) (was Bombay, renamed 1995); Kolkata, capital West Bengal state (4.9m) (was Calcutta, renamed 1999); Bangalore (name changing to Bengaluru 1 Nov 2006), Karnataka state (4.6m); Chennai, capital of Tamil Nadu state (4.5m) (was Madras, renamed in 1995); Ahmadabad, Gujarat state (3.7m); Hyderabad, capital of Andhra Pradesh state (3.7m); Kanpur, Uttar Pradesh state (2.7m); Pune, Maharashtra state (2.7m), Sûrat (2.6m), Jaipur (2.5m), Lakhnau (2.3m), Nâgpur (2.2m).

Languages spoken

Hindi is spoken by almost a third of the population. English is widely spoken and is often the main language of business, with over 350 million Indians using it as the *lingua franca*. Most central government documents are in both Hindi and English. Government policy is to encourage wider use of Hindi.
There are 15 local official languages in the various states, of which the most widely spoken are Punjabi, Telugu, Bengali, Marathi, Tamil, Urdu and Gujarati. There are 1,652 languages spoken throughout the country.
In August a ruling by the mayor of Mumbai, Shubha Raul, made Marathi the official language of local government in Mumbai. Concern was expressed by a number of elected officials with a limited grasp of Marathi, who felt they would be put at a disadvantage. There was also concern that the move would hamper Mumbai's aspirations of becoming an international financial centre, and that it would encourage a resurgence of regional politics. All documents for the Municipal Corporation of Greater Mumbai (BMC) have to be written in Marathi.

Official language/s

Hindi and English; 15 other languages are recognised for official use in regional areas.

Media

The government guarantees the freedom of the press. The market is huge and has been expanding as the economy has grown.

Press

India has a large middle class and newspaper circulation has expanded with new titles being added.
Dailies: Newspaper titles may be published in English and a local language, editions in English have national readerships, whereas local language newspapers are often regionally limited.
Circulation figures for top newspapers are in the millions.
In English, *The Times of India* (http://timesofindia.indiatimes.com) is the leading broadsheet, followed by

Hindustan Times (http://timesofindia.indiatimes.com), *The Hindu* (www.thehindu.com), *New Delhi Times* (www.newdelhitimes.org) and *Early Times* (www.earlytimes.in).
Regional newspapers include *The Indian Express* (www.indianexpress.com) and *The Asian Age* (www.asianage.com) from New Delhi, *The Statesman* (www.thestatesman.net) and *The Telegraph* (www.telegraphindia.com) from Kolkata, *Kashmir Observer* (www.kashmirobserver.com) from Srinagar and *Deccan Herald* (www.deccanherald.com) from Bangalore.
Weeklies: There are no major national weeklies, but a huge number of all genre published at local level.
Business: There are several financial and business newspapers, including, in English, *Mint* (www.livemint.com), is a national newspaper, regional newspapers include *The Economic Times* (http://economictimes.indiatimes.com) and *The Financial Express* (www.financialexpress.com) are based in Mumbai and *Business Line* (www.blonnet.com) is based in Chennai. *Business Today* (http://businesstoday.digitaltoday.in) is a national magazine.
Periodicals: In English, the monthly *Diplomatist* (www.diplomatist.com) covers international relations and trade, *Frontline* covers news and current affairs, published fortnightly, the monthly *Verve* (www.verveonline.com) is the oldest publication for women.

Broadcasting

Radio: India has the largest radio network, worldwide. It has hundreds of FM radio stations, broadcasting, most music programmes, in local languages Only All India Radio (http://allindiaradio.org) the public network, with over 200 local stations may broadcast the news. Major commercial networks include Radio Mirchi (www.enil.co.in) with a network of 32 stations and Radio City (www.radiocity.in) with 18 stations. Meow FM is a talk radio station in Delhi and Mumbai for women.
Television: The national, public broadcaster is Noordarshan (www.ddindia.gov.in) with eight regional centres. There are large media groups that operate TV channels, including Zee TV (www.zeetelevision.com), Star TV (http://starnews.indya.com) and Sun Network (www.sunnetwork.org), which broadcast via satellite and cable, with schedules including locally produced and imported TV shows. India has the largest cable TV market in the world, with over 60 million subscribers.

Advertising

The Advertising Standards Council of India (ASCI) has codes of practice some of which are voluntary. Advertising is available throughout traditional media as well as new technologies. Outdoor advertising is subject to certain restrictions.

News agencies

There are over 40 domestic news agencies.
Press Trust of India: www.ptinews.com
United News of India: www.uniindia.com

Economy

India weathered the global economic crisis relatively well, compared to its neighbours in the Asian market, due mostly to the speedy intervention by the government and Reserve Bank of India (RBI). Policy changes included measures to increase liquidity in the rupee and foreign currencies, increasing the availability of credit and encouraging capital inflows supported by national fiscal measures. By June 2009 the International Monetary Fund (IMF) report was cautiously optimistic of India's prospects in the medium-term for economic growth, although it is expected to be sluggish and protracted, with high unemployment and credit constraints in the short-term. India is a member of the BRIC (Brazil, Russia, India and China) emerging economies, which have 40 per cent of the world's population, accounting for 25 per cent of global GDP and which do not rely on exports as there are sizeable domestic markets to maintain production. Merchandise trade accounts for one-third of India's GDP and trade between BRIC countries has grown, so that China is India's primary trading partner (accounting for 10.5 per cent of imports in 2008).
Economic growth fell from a record high of 9.8 per cent in 2006 to an estimated 7.3 per cent in 2008, with a projected reduction to 5.4 per cent in 2009, as manufacturing output was cut by a downturn in international trade. The current account for 2007/08 was 1.5 per cent of GDP which grew by 2.6 per cent in 2008/09. The Indian rupee depreciated by 23 per cent against the US dollar in 2008, and was one of the largest depreciations recorded in Asia. Unacceptable capital outflows resulted in a large foreign exchange intervention, undertaken up to November 2008, which exacerbated pressures on domestic liquidity and resulted in a large loss in reserves. Foreign exchange reserves declined to US$255 billion between May 2008 and January 2009 (US$281 billion in September 2009). Inflation rose from 6.4 per cent in 2007 to 11 per cent year-on-year in June 2008, the highest rate since 1995. Interest rates broke the government's target of 5.0–5.5 per cent per annum. The RBI raised key lending rates by 25 base points to 8 per cent in June 2008; rates are expected to remain at between 8–10.2 per cent until 2010; rising costs in fuel and food were responsible for the interest rate hikes. Although tax revenues grew by 15 per cent between April and November 2008, year-on-year, government revenue as a whole fell as tax collections slowed markedly in line with the slowdown in the domestic economy and the decline in imports.
Services provide over 50 per cent of GDP and agriculture over 15 per cent, whereas industry supplies around 30 per cent, of which manufacturing is over 16 per cent. Manufacturing companies have emerged as efficient, low cost producers through a large increase in the number of small- to medium-sized Indian companies that are competing on the world market, with Indian entrepreneurs buying internationally recognised companies. India is beginning to compete with the West for 'intellectual capital' by investing in value-added, technology intensive industries at home and abroad, which utilise the graduates of its new universities and the successful Indian diaspora. Per capita income has almost doubled from US$599 in 2004 to US$1,017 in 2008, but the country still has a large underclass of unemployed and underemployed workers. Agriculture employs around 60 per cent of the workforce and the government is attempting to increase growth, necessary to achieve food security, by providing farmers with cheap credit and an expansion of the rural jobs guarantee scheme.
Around 40 per cent of the population live below the poverty line (of US$1.25 per day) according to the World Bank, a significant decline from the 60 per cent of the 1980s. Using its own criteria, the Planning Commission of India estimates 28 per cent of the population lives in poverty, with the central province of Madhya Pradesh having the highest rate of malnutrition. India believes that with sustained growth it can reduce poverty to a low single digit number within two generations.
In April 2010, the Reserve Bank of India raised its key interest rate by 0.25 per cent to 5.25 per cent in a measure to curb inflation, which had peaked to 9.9 per cent. Even so in May the wholesale price index rose to 10.16 per cent. India calculates its inflation rate on wholesale prices, making the actual prices paid higher. India's GDP growth was higher than expected in the first quarter of 2010, rising to 8.9 per cent (up from the expected 8.8 per cent. In the second quarter it recorded growth of 8.9 per cent year-on-year, through strong agricultural production and vehicle sales. Manufacturing in the same period

was 9.8 per cent and construction 8.8 per cent year-on-year. Annual GDP growth could reach 8.5–8.75 per cent for 2010.

External trade

India is a member of South Asia Association for Regional Co-operation (SAARC), which operates the SAARC agreement on preferential trading arrangements (Sapta) that covers over 6,000 products. The South Asia Free Trade Area was agreed by to be implemented between the seven member states (India, Pakistan, Bhutan, Nepal, Bangladesh, Sri Lanka and Maldives) by 2012.

Traditional products such as jewellery and gems (around 80 per cent of cut diamonds worldwide were produced in India), textiles, clothes and footwear, foodstuffs, metal manufacture and leather products remain leading exports but the rapidly growing software sector, including IT services in outsourced call centres, have assumed a large proportion of export trade.

On 16 February 2011, Japan and India signed a free trade agreement (FTA), which will cut tariffs on 94 per cent of goods by 2020. Among the goods to benefit textiles, pharmaceuticals and vehicles, as well as services, are prominent.

Imports

Main imports include crude oil, machinery, precious stones, fertiliser and chemicals.

Main sources: China (typically 11.0 per cent total), Saudi Arabia (8 per cent), UAE (6 per cent).

Exports

Principal exports include textiles, gem stones and jewellery, engineering goods, organic chemicals and leather manufactures.

Main destinations: US (typically 12 per cent total), UAE (10 per cent), China (6 per cent).

Agriculture

Farming

Agriculture accounts for around 21 per cent of GDP. Main crops are wheat, rice, pulses, tea, sugar cane, cotton, jute, coffee, oilseeds, tobacco, rubber and potatoes. The southern state of Kerala accounts for 93 per cent of the natural rubber production. Dairy farming has made India self-sufficient in milk powder and butter (*ghee*).

Domestic demand and consumption patterns within the country have shifted from cereals to non-cereals including oilseeds, pulses, fruits, vegetables and dairy products. This shift calls for diversification of agricultural production and rural development to sustain future growth. While emphasis on minimum price support for rice and wheat has been beneficial, crop diversification and removal of restrictions on stock limits allowing greater flexibility in marketing are some of the key issues requiring more attention.

Of the 181 million hectares (ha) of argricultural land available, 162 million ha is arable and 11 million ha is permanent pasture. Land legislation has ensured that agriculture remains a fragmented sector, with the typical holding about one hectare. The land ceiling does not extend to farmland used for the cultivation of plantation crops, such as tea, coffee and rubber. Other problems for the sector include a lack of technological modernisation and infrastructural bottlenecks related to irrigation and rural electrification.

Use of improved seed varieties, irrigation and fertilisers has made India self-sufficient in most grains. Land for extending cultivation is limited, but there is scope for productivity improvements in other crops. The sector is dependent on annual monsoon levels and if rains are poor during the July sowing season production can suffer.

In a move to improve the income of the poorest farmers the government, in its 2008 budget, cancelled the debt of small farmers, in a scheme of loan cancellations costing US$15 billion.

During the 2007–08 winter, the heaviest snowfalls since the 1970s buried the desert habitat of the rare Himalayan pashmina goat that produces exceptionally fine wool. As winter stocks of fodder ran out the goats began to starve and by February official figures reported 600 had died, and many more in remote areas were endangered.

India's spice market rose to US$2.8 billion in 2010. Rises included a 150 per cent rise in tumeric futures over the January to November period, and an 80 per cent increase in pepper futures over the same period. Spices are staples of the Indian diet and an increase of 50% on some of the most commonly used in sweets and snacks (such as cimmamon and nutmeg) have been recorded as disposable incomes rise and more money is spent on extras.

Fishing

India's share in the world seafood market largely depends on its shrimp exports. The crustacea catch is typically around 600,000 tonnes, and the fish catch is typically around six million tonnes, the export value of which is approximately US$65 million and US$80 million respectively. The government has given increased attention to the development of other fishery resources including squid, cuttlefish and fin fish. Export of frozen items has enabled India to penetrate into markets of Western Europe, North America and South-east Asia.

About a third of exports comprise low-value fin fish varieties and another third are frozen shrimp. Japan remains the largest importer of Indian sea food, although the emergence of the South-east Asian market due to import liberalisation has boosted the industry. The US is also a major buyer of frozen seafood, accounting for around 15 per cent of the value of marine products exported.

The sector is likely to witness steady growth as the organised corporate sector has become increasingly involved in the preservation, processing and export of coastal fish. The introduction of several resource specific vessels will enlarge the scope of marine fish landings.

Forestry

India has vast and diverse forest resources, comprising around 22 per cent of the total land area and ranging from tropical moist and dry deciduous types to evergreen, alpine, thorn and mangrove forests. Forest cover is estimated at 64 million hectares (ha). India has more than 12 million ha of forest plantations, used mainly for fuel consumption. There are about 80 national parks and around 450 wildlife sanctuaries.

Wood is an important source of fuel: India is the world's largest consumer of fuelwood. India has a very low level of industrial wood consumption in per capita terms. The forestry industry consists of small production units with low operating efficiency. There is an acute shortage of raw material, particularly for the manufacture of pulp and paper.

Industry and manufacturing

Industry contributed 27 per cent to GDP in 2004. Heavy industry has traditionally been dominated by large state-controlled enterprises. With the steady removal of protection by the state since the early 1990s, these lost some ground to smaller enterprises. Main heavy industries include steel, chemicals, cement and heavy engineering. Further developments in petrochemicals and fertilisers are expected.

Textiles account for 35 per cent of India's export earnings.

Small companies are moving into high-technology products including computers, as well as traditional light engineering and textiles. Import controls have been relaxed on raw materials and services necessary for increased export trade. The entire system of industrial licensing has been revised to promote freer competition and many companies are now turning to private capital markets for expansion funding.

Tourism

Tourism is the third-largest foreign exchange earner and is growing at more than 6 per cent per year. The sector

accounted for 4.9 per cent of GDP in 2004. About six per cent of the workforce is employed in the sector.
There were 3.91 million arrivals in 2005, an increase of 13.2 per cent on 2004, despite the impact of the December 2004 *tsunami* on the region.

Environment
Since 2002 the number of Indian tigers has fallen drastically from 3,642 to 1,411, due to poaching and urbanisation. India is home to 40 per cent of the World's tigers and has 23 tiger reserves in 17 states. The government sponsored a protection unit in 2007, but wildlife experts have said that urgent efforts should be made to save more tigers with inviolate areas and well armed forest guards. The poaching is for body parts for Chinese medicine, with tiger pelts valued up to US$12,500 in China.

Mining
India is well-endowed with mineral resources, mainly iron ore, manganese, uranium, good-quality bauxite (an estimated 2.65 billion tonnes of reserves, the world's fourth largest) and chromite, but they are not fully exploited. Other minerals present include lead, zinc, tin, silver, mercury and cobalt.
Most of India's raw materials are for domestic consumption. The only exports of any significance are iron ore, mica and manganese ore. India's major markets for iron ore are Japan, South Korea and China. India's reserves of copper, zinc and lead are of relatively low quality.

Hydrocarbons
India had 5.5 billion barrels of oil reserves in 2007, produced 801,000 barrels per day (bpd) and consumed 2.7 million bpd, which was an increase of almost 7 per cent on the 2006 figure. Oil consumption has risen dramatically, from 1.7 million bpd in 1997 to 2.9 million bpd in 2008, in line with the country's economic growth. However oil production has remained relatively stable while growth has been mainly fuelled by imported petroleum products.
In an effort to reduce dependence on imports, India is encouraging further exploration and production. India had a refinery capacity of 2.9 million bpd in 2007. Most of the oil reserves are located in the Mumbai High, Upper Assam, Cambay, Krisha-Godavari and Cauvery basins.
India had proven natural gas reserves of 1.0 trillion cubic metres (cum) in 2007 and produced 30.2 billion cubic metres. Consumption rose from 20 billion cum in 1997 to 38 billion cum in 2007. Much of this increase is attributed to increased use of gas in electricity power generation. Consumption could be higher, but problems in financing liquefied natural gas (LNG) import projects have led to downward revisions of forecasts. Imports of LNG in 2007 were 9.98 billion cum. The government is improving and expanding the infrastructure to meet the growing demand for natural gas.
Over two-thirds of India's gas reserves are located in the Mumbai High basin and Gujarat.
Total proven coal reserves were 56.5 trillion tonnes in 2007 with production of 181 million tonnes oil equivalent (mtoe). India is the world's third-largest coal producer after China and the US. The main coal fields are in Bihar, West Bengal and Madhya Pradesh. Around 90 per cent of coal is produced by Coal India Ltd (CIL). Power generation accounts for around 70 per cent of coal consumption; the second-largest consumer is heavy industry.
A 360 mile-long (580km) heated pipeline from the Thar deserts of Rajasthan to the Gujarat coast was completed, by Cairn India, in June 2010. The pipeline will allow oil to be pumped direct to refineries; production from the Mangala is expected to increase as a result.

Energy
Total installed electricity generating capacity was 145.5GW in 2008. Conventional thermal power stations produce over 60 per cent of total capacity, of which coal powers over 53 per cent of the mix. Natural gas and hydroelectric power provide 8 per cent and 6 per cent respectively.
Although 80 per cent of the population has access to electricity, the supply is unreliable and interruptions are frequent. More efficient stoves, solar cookers and biogas plants are being developed to address the problem of energy shortages. Other renewable sources are being explored, including wind and solar generators.
In August 2009 the minister of power announced that India was considering building a 4,000 megawatt power station in Iran to take advantage of Iran's natural gas reserves. The cost would be some US$4.1 billion, excluding the cost of a transmission line that would need to transit Pakistan.
The government announced in September 2009 that it was preparing to build the world's largest photovoltaic (solar) panels power complex in Gujarat State. The 3,000MW project, estimated at US$10 billion, will be endorsed by the US-based Clinton Foundation, which will provide support in raising the funds necessary to complete the development. The demand for electricity is expected to grow five-fold by 2030 and India aims to install an additional 20,000MW of solar power by 2020.

Financial markets
Stock exchange
National Stock Exchange of India (NSE)
Commodity exchange
Multi-Commodity Exchange (MCX)

Banking and insurance
Indian banking has traditionally been strongly directed from the centre; even private sector banks (excluding foreign banks) are required to lend to national priority projects. In February 2005 the remaining 27 banks in government hands were given freedom to manage themselves, including the ability to acquire foreign assets and close down unprofitable accounts. The government had nationalised the country's 14 major domestic banks in 1969. Since the mid-1980s there has been a relaxation and improved profitability due to the deregulation of interest rates and the removal of credit allocation obligation, except for quotas for priority sectors. Reforms made since the mid-1990s have led to a growth in private sector banking activity.
Financial reforms implemented in 2001 focussed on tightening regulations on capital adequacy, income recognition, non-performing assets (NPAs), disclosure and transparency in accounting and risk management. The 2002 budget allowed foreign banks to establish subsidiaries in India for the first time, and sector caps on portfolio investments made by foreign institutional investors were eased.
Central bank
The Reserve Bank of India (RBI) controls India's financial system on a day-to-day basis.
Main financial centre
Mumbai is the main financial centre; New Delhi, Kolkata and Chennai are also important.

Time
GMT plus 5.5 hours

Geography
India is a bounded by Pakistan in the north-west, China in the north, the Himalayan Kingdoms of Nepal (administered by China) and Bhutan in the north and north-east. Bangladesh is surrounded on three sides by a bulge of Indian states that border China in the north-east and Myanmar in the east to south, with the Bay of Bengal separating it from the mainland. In the Indian Ocean India's neighbours are Sri Lanka and the Maldives.
India is a large landmass with four distinct regions. The northern Himalayan regions rise to a peak of 7,757 metres before falling away towards the east. The great rivers, Ganges and Brahmaputra begin

life in these mountains before draining through a flat alluvial plain into the Bay of Bengal. On the other side of the country, the Great Indian or Thar Desert separates India and Pakistan. In the south the Deccan tableland is bordered by ranges of hills, the Western and Eastern Ghats and Nilgiri Hills in the south, and their coastal belts.

Hemisphere

Northern

Climate

India's winter is January–February, with hot weather increasing from March–May, south-western monsoons from June–September, and post monsoons or north-east monsoons in the southern peninsula from October–December. Temperatures vary from sub-zero in the far north during winter to constant tropical heat in southern regions. Average summer temperatures on the plains are approximately 27 degrees Celsius.

Dress codes

Dress is mostly informal in India except in winter months in New Delhi, where suits and coats are more usually worn. Women are expected to dress with modesty even in very hot weather. Businessmen can expect to wear suits and ties to meetings all year as most buildings have air conditioning.

Entry requirements

Passports

Required by all.

Visa

Required by all, and must be obtained before travelling as visas cannot be issued on arrival. Foreign nationals arriving on long-term, multiple visas are required to register with the nearest Foreigners Regional Registration Officer within 14 days of arrival. Those overstaying their visa entitlement will be fined and may be prosecuted.

For business visas a letter, issued by the local host company or organisation, giving details of itinerary, and traveller's company, a summary of purpose of trip, and the acceptance of full responsibility for any expenses incurred during the term of stay, should be submitted with the application. Business visas, valid for 10 years with multiple entries, are available to foreign businessmen who have set up or intend setting up joint ventures in India. Long-term visa requirements were changed in December 2009; as a result all visitors on long-term visas (over 180 days) must leave the country and reapply for a visa from abroad.

For further details of various visas and restrictions see www.indianembassy.org or www.hcilondon.net. Nationals of Pakistan and Bangladesh are advised to seek further advice before travelling to, or via, India.

Currency advice/regulations

Import and export of local currency is prohibited; the exception is rupees that visitors may take to Nepal – notes must be less than Rs100, and Bangladesh and Sri Lanka – up to Rs20 per person.

Import of foreign currency is unlimited; amounts below US$1,000 (or equivalent) need not be declared, however, amounts over US$5,000 must be declared and registered on a *encashment certificate* on arrival. Export of foreign currency is limited to the amount declared, therefore all currency transaction receipts should be retained.

Travellers cheques are widely accepted. Currency may only be exchanged at banks or authorised money changers.

Customs

The export of products over 100 years old need a permit. Animal products from endangered species are illegal.

Health (for visitors)

Mandatory precautions

Vaccination certificates for yellow fever if travelling from an infected area.

Advisable precautions

Vaccinations for cholera, dysentery, Japanese B encephalitis and typhoid are recommended. Other vaccinations that may be recommended are diphtheria, tuberculosis, hepatitis A and B, meningitis and tetanus. Malaria, hepatitis B, dengue and chikungunya fever are caused by mosquitoes, precautions including mosquito repellents, nets and clothing covering the body, should be used, especially at night. There is a risk of rabies in rural areas. Polio is endemic in certain states and precautions, including booster shots, should be taken.

Use only bottled or boiled water for drinks, washing teeth and making ice. Eat only well cooked meals, preferably served hot; vegetables should be cooked and fruit peeled. Avoid pork and salad and food from street vendors. A full first-aid kit would be useful.

Locally manufactured Western proprietary medicines are easily obtainable, but visitors on regular medication should bring their own supplies – amounts for the length of the visit only.

Hotels

International-standard accommodation is widely available. Hotel bills must be paid in foreign exchange or in rupees proved to have been purchased in India with foreign exchange. Hotels in main cities are usually heavily booked, and it is advisable to book well in advance.

Extra charges may be applied to hotel bills, including variable service charges plus 10 per cent expenditure tax and 15 per cent luxury tax.

Credit cards

Major credit cards are accepted by larger hotels, travel agencies and airline offices, as well as some larger stores. The Central Card is issued by the Reserve Bank of India and is widely accepted.

Public holidays (national)

Fixed dates

1 Jan (New Year's Day), ^26 Jan (Republic Day), ^15 Aug (Independence Day), ^2 Oct (Mahatma Gandhi's Birthday), 26 Nov (Guru Nanak's Birthday), 25 Dec (Christmas Day).

Variable dates

Good Friday (Mar/Apr), Mahavira's Birthday (Feb/Mar), Holi (Hindu, Mar), Sri Rama's Birthday (Apr), Buddha Purnima (May), Vijaya Dasami/Dussera (Sep/Oct), Diwali (Hindu, Oct/Nov), Eid al Adha, Eid al Fitr, Islamic New Year, Birth of the Prophet Mohammed.

^ Recognised official national holiday.

All other holidays are either state, religious or informal holidays and may be observed at locally determined times dependent on sightings of various phases of the moon, or by adherents only.

Working hours

Banking

Mon–Fri: 1000–1400; Sat: 1000–1200, in New Delhi, Kolkata and Chennai.

Mon–Fri: 1100–1500; Sat: 1100–1300 in Mumbai.

Business

Mon–Fri: 1000–1700, in New Delhi and Chennai; 0930–1700 in Kolkata; 1000–1730 in Mumbai.

Government

Mon–Fri: 1000–1730, in New Delhi, Kolkata and Chennai; 0930–1630 in Mumbai.

Shops

Mon–Fri: 0930–1930 in New Delhi; 1000–1830 in Kolkata; 1000–1830 in Mumbai; 0900–1930 in Chennai.

Telecommunications

Mobile/cell phones

There are 900 and 1800 GSM services available, most are regionally based within cities and towns. A temporary ban imposed on imports of Chinese equipment was lifted in August 2010 when the government allowed Tata Teleservices and Reliance Communications to bring in equipment from Huawei and ZTA. In return the Chinese companies agreed to give Indian security agences access to their network source codes.

Electricity supply

Usually 220V AC, 50Hz; some areas have a DC supply for domestic use. Plugs used are of the round two- and three-pin type.

Weights and measures
Metric system

Social customs/useful tips
Namaste is the usual greeting (palms together as in prayer). Visiting cards are exchanged – use the right hand when giving or receiving items. It is not customary for business associates to be entertained at home. Hotels, which provide virtually the only bars in India, require non-resident foreigners to pay their bills in foreign currency.
Business and official contacts are addressed by their last name – *Sri* (Mr), *Srimati* (Mrs or Ms).
Cows are sacred to Hindus, and many Hindus are vegetarian. Sikhs and Parsees do not smoke tobacco. Muslims do not eat pig's flesh in any form, and orthodox Muslims do not drink alcoholic beverages. Officially the government follows a strictly secular policy, with religion considered a private affair.
Smoking is banned in public places, including all offices and restaurants (since October 2008).

Security
Generally, travel in India is quite safe, but travel to Jammu and Kashmir regions is not recommended. Mumbai is the safest city in India. Its police force is known to be the most efficient in the country. It is reasonably safe to travel by taxi until midnight anywhere in the city except slums and red-light districts.

Getting there
Air
National airline: Air India (Air India and Indian Airlines, which flies domestic routes, are to merge in mid-2007).
International airport/s: There are five international airports: Indira Gandhi International (DEL), 20km south of Delhi; Sahar International (BOM), 36km north of Mumbai; Netaji Subhas Chandra Bose International (CCU), 27km north-east of Kolkata; Meenambakkam (MAA), 14km south-east of Chennai; Patna (PAT), 8km from Patna. Dabolim (GOA) airport receives international chartered flights.
All international airports have duty-free shopping, bars, restaurants, currency exchanges, post offices and business centres that include telecommunications and rest facilities.
The Airport Metro rail link between Delhi's Indira Gandhi International airport and the city centre was opened in March 2011. Trains run every 20 minutes from 06.00 to 22.00 and take 20 minutes, compared to over an hour by car.
Airport tax: International flights, Foreign Travel Tax (FTT) Rs500; neighbouring countries only, FFT Rs150; excluding transit passengers.
Surface
Road: Overland access is possible through Nepal and Bangladesh, there is only one access point from Pakistan at Wagah – it may be dangerous crossing the border at any other place. The status of border crossing points and opening hours should be checked before travelling.
Rail: Rail connections exist between India and Bangladesh, although the journey is difficult.
The train service between Pakistan and India was restored in 2004 – one train a week between Lahore in Pakistan and Attari in India.
Water: Ferry services between Colombo and Tuticorin in Tamil Nadu state of India were resumed on 14 June after almost 30 years of having been suspended due to the security situation. There will be two round trips per week initially.
Main port/s: India has 12 major ports: five on the east coast, Kolkata-Haldia, Paradip, Visakhapatnam, Chennai and Tuticorin and seven on the west coast, Kandla, Mumbai, Jawaharlal Nehru, Mormugao, New Mangalore and Cochin.

Getting about
National transport
Air: The only time-efficient way to get between the large cities and even some smaller ones is by plane. The cost of air travel is reasonable and there are several domestic carriers. Airline tickets may now be bought at the airport, at least one hour before a flight.
Smoking and drinking are banned on board all internal flights.
Road: There are two million kilometres of road, including 833,000km of surfaced roads and 35,000km of national highways connecting main cities. Chauffeur driven cars can be hired in the big cities.
Buses: A number of long-distance express bus services operate, and air conditioning is becoming increasingly available. Poor roads make travel uncomfortable.
Rail: The Indian rail network covers over 64,000km and is the main form of domestic transport. Rail connections are available between all major towns and cities, with air-conditioned coaches and sleeper accommodation available on some routes. Some train journeys take 24 hours or more.
Water: There are coastal shipping and ferry services.
City transport
Taxis: Local taxis of varying standards are usually available. In main cities, metered taxis may not always show current rates, and fares should be negotiated in advance. Tipping is officially discouraged, but is practiced.
Other transport includes motorised trishaws.
Buses, trams & metro: There are over 40 stations in the New Delhi metro network, which will eventually cover 60km and is due to be completed by 2010. The first section of elevated track was opened in 2002 and in 2005 another 11km stretch of underground lines, from the government areas of the capital, via the commercial area, to the old city, was opened. A completed 32km section was opened in December 2005. When completed it is expected to cut a journey across the city from one hour at rush-hour, to 15 minutes.
There are surburban metro systems in Mumbai, Kolkata and Chennai (a monorail rapid transit system). The first section of the new metro service, Namma (Our), was launched in Bangalore in October 2011, with an initial six stations in the business district, from MG Road in the west, to Baiyappanahalli Terminal in the east of the city.
Car hire
Self-drive hire cars are available in Mumbai and chauffeur-driven car hire is available in main cities.

BUSINESS DIRECTORY

Telephone area codes
The international direct dialling (IDD) code for India is +91, followed by area code and subscriber's number:

Ahmedabad	79	Jammu	191
Amritsar	183	Kolkata	33
Bangalore	80	Lucknow	522
Bhopal	755	Madurai	452
Chandigarh	172	Mumbai	22
Chennai	44	Nagpur	712
Cochin	484	New Delhi	11
Goa	832	Patna	612
Hyderabad	40	Pune	212
Jaipur	141	Rajkot	281
Jallunder	181	Varanasi	542
Kanpur	512	Vishakhapatnam	891

Useful telephone numbers

Police:	100
Ambulance:	102
Fire:	101
Operator:	199
Directory enquiries:	197
International enquiries:	187
Call booking:	186

Chambers of Commerce
American Chamber of Commerce in India, Maurya Sheraton Hotel, Sardar Patel Marg, New Delhi 110021 (tel: 2302-3102; fax: 2302-3109; e-mail: usamcham@bol.net.in).

Associated Chambers of Commerce and Industry of India, 147B Gautam Nagar, Gulmohar Enclave, New Delhi 110049 (tel: 2651-2477; fax: 2651-2154; e-mail: assocham@sansad.nic.in).

Bengal National Chamber of Commerce and Industry, 23 RN Mukherjee Road, Kolkata 700001 (tel: 248-2951; fax: 248-7058; e-mail: bncci@bncci.com).

Bombay Chamber of Commerce and Industry, Mackinnon Mackenzie Building, Shoorji Vallabhdas Road, Mumbai 400001 (tel: 2261-4681; fax: 2262-1213; e-mail: bcci@bombaychamber.com).

Cochin Chamber of Commerce and Industry, Bristow Road, PO Box 503, Cochin 682003 (tel: 266-8650; fax: 266-8651; e-mail: chamber@md2.vsnl.net.in).

Federation of Indian Chambers of Commerce and Industry, Federation House, Tansen Marg, New Delhi 110001 (tel 2373-8760; fax@ 2332-0714; e-mail: ficci@ficci.com).

Goa Chamber of Commerce and Industry, Goa Chamber Building, Rua de Ormuz, Panaji-Goa 403001 (tel: 222-4223; fax: 242-9010; e-mail: gcci@sancharnet.in).

Gujarat Chamber of Commerce and Industry, Ashram Road, PO Box 4045, Ahmedabad 380009 (tel: 658-2301; fax: 658-7992; e-mail: gcci@gujaratchamber.org).

Indian Chamber of Commerce and Industry, Indian Chamber Road, Mattancherry, PO Box 236, Cochin 682002 (tel: 222-4335; fax: 222-4203; e-mail: mail@iccicochin.com).

Madras Chamber of Commerce and Industry, Karumuttu, 634 Anna Salai, Chennai 600035 (tel: 2434-9452; fax: 2434-9164; e-mail: mascham@md3.vsnl.net.in).

Mahratta Chamber of Commerce, Industries and Agriculture, 14 Tilak Road, Pune 411002 (tel: 444-0371; fax: 444-7902; e-mail: mccipune@vsnl.com).

PHD Chamber of Commerce and Industry, PHD House, opposite Asian Games Village, New Delhi 110016 (tel: 685-2416; fax: 686-3135; e-mail: phdcci@del2.vsnl.net.in).

Rajasthan Chamber of Commerce and Industry, Chamber Bhawan, MI Road, Jaipur 302003 (tel: 256-163; fax: 256-1419; e-mail: info@rajchamber.com).

Banking

Allahabad Bank, 2 Netaji Subhas Road, Kolkata 700 001 (tel: 220-0283; fax: 221-4598; email: homktg@allahabadbank.co.in).

Bank of Baroda, Suraj Plaza-1, Sayaji Ganj, Baroda 390 005 (tel: 361-852; 362-395).

Bank of India, Express Towers, Nariman Point, Mumbai 400 021(tel: 2202-3020; fax: 2202-3167; email: cmdboi@bom5.vsnl.net.in).

Canara Bank, Canara Bank Buildings, 112 Jayachamarajendra Road, PO Box 6648, Bangalore 560 002 (tel: 222-1581; fax: 222-2704; email: canbank@blr.vsnl.net.in).

Central Bank of India, Chandermukhi, Nariman Point, Mumbai 400 021 (tel: 2202-6428).

Corporation Bank, Mangalore 575 001 (tel: 426-416; fax: 441-208; email: corpho@corpbank.com).

ICIC, 163 Backbay Reclamation, Mumbai 400 020 (tel: 2202-5115; fax: 2204-6582).

Oriental Bank of Commerce, Harsha Bhawan, E-Block, Connaught Place, New Delhi 110 001 (tel: 2332-3444; fax: 2371-3244; email: obc@obcindia.com).

Punjab National Bank, 5 Sansad Marg, New Delhi 110 066 (tel: 2371-6032; fax: 2332-1305; email: pnbibd@ndf.vsnl.net.in).

State Bank of India, Madame Cama Road, PO Box 10121, Mumbai 400 021 (tel: 2202-2059; fax: 2204-0073).

Union Bank of India, Union Bank Bhavan, 239 Vidhan Bhavan Marg, Nariman Ponit, Mumbai 400 021 (tel: 2202-4647, 2202-6049; email: ibdhelpdesk@unionbankofindia.co).

Central bank

Reserve Bank of India, Central Office Building, Shahid Bhagat Singh Road, Mumbai 400 001 (tel: 286-1602; fax: 266-2105; e-mail: helpprd@rbi.org.in).

Stock exchange

National Stock Exchange of India (NSE): www.nse-india.com

Stock exchange 2

Bombay Stock Exchange (BSE): www.bseindia.com

Commodity exchange

Multi-Commodity Exchange (MCX): www.mcxindia.com

Commodity exchange 2

National Multi-Commodity Exchange of India Limited (NMCE): www.nmce.com

Travel information

Indian Airlines, Airlines House, 113 Gurdwara Rakabganj Road, New Delhi 110 001 (tel: 2335-7307; fax: 2371-9484).

Ministry of tourism

Department of Tourism of the Government of India, Ministry of Tourism, Transport Bhawan, 1 Parliament Street, New Delhi 110001 (tel: 371-0379; fax: 371-0518; internet: www.tourismindia.com).

National tourist organisation offices

India Tourism Development Corporation Ltd, SCOPE Complex, Core VIII, 6th Floor, 7 Lodi Road, New Delhi 110003 (tel: 436-0303; fax: 436-0233).

Ministries

Ministry of Agriculture, Krishi Bhavan, Dr Rajendra Prasad Road, New Delhi 110 001 (tel: 2378-2691; fax: 2338-8006).

Ministry of Chemicals and Fertilisers, Shastri Bhavan, Dr Rajendra Prasad Road, New Delhi 110 001 (tel: 2338-6519; fax: 2338-6364).

Ministry of Civil Aviation, Rajiv Ghandi Bhavan, Safdarjung Airport Complex, New Delhi 110 003 (tel: 2463-2991; fax: 2461-0354; e-mail: secy@civilav.delhi.nic.in).

Ministry of Commerce and Industry, Udyog Bhavan, Rafi Marg, New Delhi 110 001 (tel: 2301-0261; fax: 2301-4418; e-mail: commerce@hub.nic.in).

Ministry of Communications, Dak Bhavan, Parliament Street, New Delhi 110 001 (tel: 2371-0350; fax: 2371-2333).

Ministry of Consumer Affairs, Food and Public Distribution, Krishi Bhavan, Dr Rajendra Prasad Road, New Delhi 110 001 (tel: 2338-5723; fax: 2378-2213).

Ministry of Defence, South Block, New Delhi 110 011 (tel: 2301-6220; fax: 2301-5403).

Ministry of the Environment and Forests, Paryavaran Bhavan, CGO Complex, Lodhi Road, New Delhi 110 003 (tel: 2436-1896; fax: 2436-2222; e-mail: secy@menf.delhi.nic.in).

Ministry of External Affairs, South Block, New Delhi 110 011 (tel: 2301-6660; fax: 2301-0700).

Ministry of Finance, North Block, New Delhi 110 001 (tel: 2301-2810; fax: 2301-3289; internet: wwwmnic.in/finmin/).

Ministry of Health and Family Welfare, Nirman Bhavan, Maulana Azad Road, New Delhi 110 011 (tel: 2301-4751; fax: 2301-6648).

Ministry of Heavy Industries and Public Enterprises, Udyog Bhavan, Rafi Marg, New Delhi 110 001 (tel: 2301-4598; fax: 2301-3086; e-mail: nic-dpe@hub.nic.in).

Ministry of Home Affairs, North Block, New Delhi 110 001 (tel: 2301-1011; fax: 2301-5750).

Ministry of Human Resource Development, Shastri Bhavan, Dr Rajendra Prasad Road, New Delhi 110 001 (tel: 2378-2698; fax: 2338-1355; e-mail:ksm@sb.nic.in).

Ministry of Information and Broadcasting, Shastri Bhavan, Dr Rajendra Prasad Road, New Delhi 110 001 (tel: 2338-4782; fax: 2378-3513).

Ministry of Labour, Shram Shakti Bhavan, Rafi Marg, New Delhi 110 001 (tel: 2371-7515; fax: 2371-1708; e-mail: labour@lisd.delhi.nic.in).

Ministry of Law, Justice and Company Affairs, Shastri Bhavan, Dr Rajendra Prasad Road, New Delhi 110 001 (tel: 2338-7557; fax: 2338-4241; e-mail: lawmin@caselaw.delhi.nic.in).

Ministry of Mines, Shastri Bhavan, Dr Rajendra Prasad Road, New Delhi 110 001 (tel: 2338-3082; fax: 2338-6402; e-mail: dom@sb.nic.in).

Ministry of Ocean Development, Mahasagar Bhavan, CGO Complex, Lodhi Road, New Delhi 110 003 (tel: 2436-0874; fax: 2436-0779).

Ministry of Parliamentary Affairs, Parliament House, New Delhi 110 001 (tel: 2301-7798; fax: 2301-7726; e-mail: parlmin@sansad.nic.in).

Ministry of Petroleum and Natural Gas, Shastri Bhavan, Dr Rajendra Prasad Road, New Delhi 110 001 (tel: 2338-3100; fax: 2338-6550).

Ministry of Power, Shastri Bhavan, Dr Rajendra Prasad Road, New Delhi 110 001 (tel: 2371-4168; fax: 2371-7519).

Ministry of Railways, Rail Bhawan, Parliament Street, New Delhi 110 001 (tel: 2338-2323; fax: 2330-3871).

Ministry of Science and Technology, Technology Bhavan, New Mehrauli Street, New Delhi 110 016 (tel: 2301-4999; fax: 2686-3847).

Ministry of Space, Lok Nayak Bhavan, New Delhi 110 003 (tel: 2469-7130; fax: 2461-7377).

Ministry of Surface Transport, Transport Bhavan, Parliament Street, New Delhi 110 001(tel: 2371-4095; fax: 2373-1270).

Ministry of Textiles, Udyog Bhavan, Rafi Marg, New Delhi 110 001 (tel: 2301-3779; fax: 2301-3711).

Ministry of Tourism, Transport Bhawan, Parliament Street, New Delhi 110 001 (tel: 2338-4173; fax: 2338-5115).

Ministry of Urban Development and Poverty Alleviation, Nirman Bhavan, Maulana Azad Road, New Delhi 110 011 (tel: 2301-8495; fax: 2301-4459; e-mail: muae@urban.delhi.nic.in).

Ministry of Water Resources, Shram Shakti Bhawan, Rafi Marg, New Delhi 110 001 (tel: 2371-4200; fax: 2371-0253; e-mail: webmaster@mowr.delhi.nic.in).

Ministry of Youth Affairs and Sport, Shastri Bhavan, Dr Rajendra Prasad Road, New Delhi 110 001 (tel: 2338-4183; e-mail: web.yas.@sb.nic.in).

Prime Minister's Office, South block, New Delhi 110 011 (tel: 2301-2312; fax: 2301-6857).

Other useful addresses

Asian Development Bank, India Resident Mission, 37 Golf Links, New Delhi 110 003 (tel: 2469-2578; fax: 2463-6175; e-mail:adbinrm@mail.asiandevbank.org).

British Deputy High Commission, Maker Chambers IV, 222 Jamnalal Bajaj Road, PO Box 11714, Nariman Point, Mumbai 400021 (tel: 2283-0517, 2283-2330, 2283-3602; fax: 2202-7940).

British High Commission, Shanti Path, Chanakyapuri, New Delhi 110 021 (tel: 2687-2161; fax: 2687-2882).

British Deputy High Commission, 1 Ho Chi Minh Sarani, Kolkata 700016 (tel: 242-5171; fax: 242-3435).

British Deputy High Commission, 24 Anderson Road, Chennai 600006 (tel: 827-3136/7; fax: 826-9004).

British Trade Office, 37/7 Cunningham Road, Bangalore 560052 (tel: 2220-4844; fax: 2220-4855).

Delhi Stock Exchange Association Ltd, 3 and 4/4B Asaf Ali Rd, New Delhi 110 002 (tel: 2327-9000/1302; fax: 2332-6182).

Delhi Tourism and Transport Development Corporation Ltd, 18A DDA, SCO Complex, Defence Colony, New Delhi 24 (tel: 2461-4354; fax: 2469-7352).

Department of Atomic Energy, South Block, New Delhi 110 011 (tel: 2301-1773; fax: 2301-3843).

Department of Electronics, Electronics Niketan, 6 CGO Complex, New Delhi 110 003 (tel: 2436-3101; fax: 2436-3083).

Federation of Indian Exports Organisation (FIEO), 56 Asiad Village, New Delhi 110 016 (tel: 2649-3220).

Foreign Investment Promotion Board, Prime Minister's Office, South Block, New Delhi 110 011 (tel: 2301-7839; fax: 2301-6857).

India Investment Centre, Jeewan vihar Building, Sansad Marg, New Delhi 110 001 (tel: 2373-3673; fax: 2373-245).

Indian Airlines, Stores and Purchases Department, Safdarjung Airport, New Delhi 110 003 (tel: 2461-1293; fax: 2462-1776; e-mail: sinha.ial@gems.vsnl.net.in).

Indian Embassy (USA), 2107 Massachusetts Avenue, NW, Washington DC 20008 (tel: (+1-202) 939-7000; fax: (+1-202) 265-4351; e-mail: indembwash@indiagov.org).

Infrastructure Leasing and Financial Services, East Court, Zone VI, 4th Floor, India Habitat Centre, Lodhi Road, New Delhi 110 003 (tel: 2463-6637/41/42).

Power Grid Corporation of India Ltd, 10th Floor, Hemkunt Chambers 89, Nehru Place, New Delhi 110 019 (tel: 2622-2995, 2646-6806; fax: 2647-3332, 2642-8357).

Silk and Rayon Export Promotion Council, Resham Bhavan 78, Veer Nariman Rd, Mumbai 400020 (tel: 2294-792).

State Trading Corporation of India, Jawahar Vyapar Bhavan, Tolstoy Marg, New Delhi 110 001 (tel: 2331-3177; fax: 2332-6741).

The Stock Exchange (BSE), Phiroze Jeejeebhoy Towers, Dalal Street, Mumbai 400001 (tel: 2272-1233/4; fax: 2272-1552; e-mail: info@bseindia.com; internet site: http://www.bseindia.com).

Trade Development Authority, PO Box 767, Bank of Baroda Building, Parliament St, New Delhi 110 001 (tel: 2332-0214).

US Embassy, Shanti Path, Chanakyapuri, New Delhi 110 021(tel: 2687-6500; fax: 2687-6579, 2687-0031 (Consular Section)).

Internet sites

Explore India: http://www.exploreindia.com

General Information: http://www.hcidhaka.org

India Department of Commerce: http://www.nic.in/eximpol/

Indian business: http://www.indiamart.com/allindia/

Indian company information: http://www.tradeaccess.com/general.htm

Indian Economy and Business links: http://www.ib-net.com/links/economy.htm

India Opportunity: http://www.DocuWeb.ca/India

Indian Press Information Bureau: http://www.nic.in/India-Image/PIB/

Indian weather service: http://weather.nic.in

Indonesia

Indonesia is Asia's fifth largest economy and third most populous nation in the world after China and India. Yet somehow Indonesia seems to skate below the international radar; it is rarely realised that this group of over 17,000 islands is the only member of the Association of Southeast Asian Nations (Asean) – of which it assumed the rotating presidency in January 2011 – that is also a member of the prestigious Group of 20 leading industrial and developing nations (G20). It is also one of the few Islamic democracies.

While the threat of Islamic revolution and terrorism had subsided and the subversive Jemaah Islamiyah network looked to have been eradicated, in 2011 Indonesia still had to face persistent outbreaks of racial violence. In February 2011 it was reported that a group of Muslims had beaten to death three members of the Ahmadiyah sect in a village near Jakarta. Religious attacks of this sort on Ahmadis have become commonplace in parts of Indonesia. Coincidentally, a larger group of Muslims protested about the – in their view – light sentence given to a Catholic man accused of blasphemy. In fact the sentence was the maximum possible for his so called offence, but the protesters still torched three churches.

Broken promises

Barely two years into its second term, the government of Indonesia's President, Susilo Bambang Yudhoyono, was by mid-2011 perceived to be one of promises broken, rather than fulfilled. For Indonesia's emerging middle class, the promises to build schools and hospitals and to root out entrenched corruption simply hadn't been met, pushing the President's popularity ratings to all time lows. The failure to get to grips with corruption has meant that Indonesian institutions such as the judiciary and Dewan Perwakilan Rakyat (DPR) (the national parliament) are seen as weak and ineffective. In May 2010 Indonesia's respected finance minister Sri Mulyani Indrawati had resigned (been removed?) from office following allegations by the then in opposition Golkar Party that she had mis-managed the bail-out of an Indonesian bank. Ms Indrawati now works for the World Bank. In similar fashion, the Indonesian United Nations human rights representative, Jonathan Prentice, was obliged to leave after a dispute over prison inspections.

For the government, the nascent Indonesian middle class means not only a larger tax base, it also means a more articulate and informed electorate. In the government's two years in office, it was the linkage between these two factors, the perception that increased tax bills should mean improved basic services, that was causing President Yudhoyono to be perceived as in the mould of too many Indonesian politicians. At first glance, Indonesia's macro-economic performance would look to be a matter for congratulation, but being one of the world's fastest growing economies is not, in itself, enough. In Indonesia, increased gross domestic product (GDP) needs to go hand in hand with improved distribution of wealth. Mr Yudhoyono's government could take some credit for the fact that over half the population now earn more than US$2 per day, an increase of around 50 million since 2003. In development speak, the language of bodies such as the Asian Development Bank (ADB) and the World Bank, this makes them middle class. But one look at the affluent gated communities of Jakarta would suggest that the classification may need to be re-considered. Many NGOs and other independent development organisations would double the figure to US$4 dollars per day. In terms of international comparisons, US$4 doesn't get you very far in Paris or Tokyo; it certainly doesn't permit many middle class aspirations.

The World Bank Director for Indonesia has gone on record as stating that 'In future, this growing middle class will be consuming more and will demand better jobs and higher quality health services and tertiary education. Policymaking in the medium term will need to meet these new demands.' An article in the London *Financial Times* went further, pointing out that the government estimates that US$150 billion should be spent on basic infrastructure during Mr Yudhoyono's term up to 2014. In fact, only some US$50

KEY FACTS

Official name: Republik Indonesia (Republic of Indonesia)

Head of State: President Susilo Bambang Yudhoyono (from 2004; re-elected 8 Jul 2009)

Head of government: President Susilo Bambang Yudhoyono

Ruling party: Coalition of 10 political parties led by Partai Golongan Karya (Golkar) (Party of the Functioning Groups), Partai Demokrasi Indonesia-Perjuangan, (PDI-P) (Indonesian Democratic Party-Struggle) and Partai Keadilan Sejahtera (PKS) (Posperous Justice Party) (from 1 May 2009)

Area: 1,919,443 square km (17,508 islands)

Population: 237.64 million (2010; census figure)

Capital: Jakarta, on Java

Official language: Bahasa Indonesia

Currency: Rupiah (Rp) = 100 sen

Exchange rate: Rp8,790.00 per US$ (Oct 2011)

GDP per capita: US$3,015 (2010)

GDP real growth: 6.10% (2010)

GDP: US$706.70 billion (2010)

Inflation: 5.10% (2010)

Oil production: 986,000 bpd (2010)

Balance of trade: US$5.65 billion (2010)

billion has been allocated. Roughly 20 per cent of annual government expenditure goes on subsidies for the poor.

The fact that Indonesia has managed to maintain growth levels throughout the global financial crisis has made it a natural centre for foreign investment. In 2010, foreign direct investment (FDI) was US$16.1 billion, double the level of 2005 and almost four times the level of investment registered in 2000.The government target is for annual GDP growth to reach 9 per cent by 2025. Continuing its impressive performance during the global financial crisis, Indonesia's economy expanded 6.1 per cent in 2010 and accelerated to 6.5 per cent in the first half of 2011. Growth has also become more balanced, with investment adding to consumption and exports as the main engines of growth. In the absence of a significant further deterioration in global conditions, GDP growth is projected to remain robust at about 6-6.5 per cent in both 2011 and 2012, increasingly driven by investment, which is offsetting a lower contribution from net exports.

Headline inflation eased in mid-2011 according to the International Monetary Fund (IMF), due principally to softening food prices, but upward pressure on core inflation is expected to continue. At the end of 2010, rising food prices had pushed inflation up to 7 per cent; exceeding Bank Indonesia's (BI) (the central bank) 4–6 per cent target range. Headline inflation began to ease after February 2011, falling to 4.6 per cent in July 2011, as good local harvests and increased rice imports helped hold down food prices. Core inflation rose steadily through 2010 and into 2011, reaching 5.2 per cent in August 2011. The future path of food prices will clearly play a major role in inflation trends. Nevertheless, a closing output gap, accelerating credit growth and elevated inflation expectations from an anticipated reduction in energy subsidies were expected to push core inflation higher in the second half of this year and into 2012. The ADB expected inflation to average 6.3 per cent in 2011, subsiding in 2012 subject to food price fluctuations.

The current account surplus has declined, but capital inflows have increased. Exports have been robust, buoyed by higher commodity prices and growing demand from major emerging market partners. According to the ADB merchandise exports rose by an impressive 32 per cent in 2010, to US$158 billion. Exports of rubber more than doubled and exports of palm oil rose by one third. By value, metal and coal shipments also rose by 32 per cent. The ADB expects merchandise export growth to decelerate to about 15 per cent in 2011. Imports also rose rapidly, by 42 per cent to US$127 billion in line with the strengthening domestic demand. The ADB forecast import growth of 17 per cent for 2011, on the back of strong consumer demand and investment trends. Positive growth prospects, solid macro-economic fundamentals and the potential for a ratings upgrade to investment status have led to large portfolio inflows, boosting bond and equity prices to all time highs. The rupiah has appreciated about 5 per cent against the dollar from end 2010 to end August 2011 and external debt spreads have narrowed.

The IMF notes that Indonesian banks continue to be profitable and are generally well capitalised. In line with the findings of the 2010 Financial Sector Assessment Programme (FSAP), capital adequacy ratios remain high at 17.5 per cent and asset quality is satisfactory, with the non-performing loan ratio at about 3 per cent as of March 2011.

The Bank Indonesia raised its policy rate by 25 basis points to 6.75 per cent in February 2011, after holding it unchanged at a historical low of 6.5 per cent since August 2009. Reserve requirements on both local currency and foreign currency deposits have also been raised. The moderate fiscal stimulus provided in 2009 was reduced in 2010. The 2010 central government budget deficit was 0.6 per cent of GDP, well below the government's revised budget deficit target of 2.1 per cent, reflecting problems in implementing spending programmes. The public debt to GDP ratio fell to 27 per cent, one of the lowest among G20 countries. The overall budget deficit in 2011 is projected to increase slightly to about 1.25 per cent of GDP, reflecting higher energy subsidies.

Energy – the oil…

The boom in energy related commodity prices has certainly gone some way to create a genuinely prosperous middle class, with incomes well above the government's benchmark of US$2 per day. Although Indonesia has been a net importer of oil since 2004, it is the World's sixth largest net exporter of natural gas and the second largest net exporter of coal. However, as a result of inadequate infrastructure and Indonesia's complex business environment, Indonesia has struggled to attract investment sufficient to meet its energy development goals.

Indonesia is currently a net importer of both crude oil and refined products. Indonesia's crude oil production has been declining since 1998, due to the maturation of the country's largest oil fields and failure to develop new, comparable resources. Indonesia was a member of the Organisation of Petroleum Exporting Countries (OPEC) from 1962 to 2009 when in January it suspended its OPEC membership.

Indonesia's upstream oil sector is dominated by several international oil companies – in particular Chevron, Total, ConocoPhillips, ExxonMobil and BP. Chevron is the largest single oil producer in Indonesia, accounting for more than 40 per cent of the country's total crude production. PT Pertamina, Indonesia's state-owned integrated energy supply company, accounted for approximately 15 per cent of 2009 crude and condensate production, making it the second largest producer in the country.

According to *Oil & Gas Journal* (OGJ), Indonesia had 3.9 billion barrels of proven oil reserves as of January 2011. In 2010, total oil supply averaged just over one million barrels per day (bpd). Of this total, about 943,000bpd was crude oil and lease condensate production. Crude and condensate production has declined at an annual average rate of 4.1 per cent between 2000 and 2010. Indonesia's two largest producing oil fields are the Minas and Duri fields, located on the eastern coast of Sumatra. Chevron operates both fields with a 100 per cent working interest under the Rokan Production Sharing Agreement. Producing since 1952 and 1955 respectively, production at both fields is in decline, even with the employment of enhanced oil recovery techniques to bolster production.

The most significant recent discovery with the potential to counter some of Indonesia's production decline is the Cepu block of East and Central Java. Exxon Mobil is the operator of the Cepu production-sharing contract (PSC) (45 per cent interest), in a joint venture with PT Pertamina's exploration and production unit (45 per cent working interest) and four local government companies (10 per cent interest). Cepu is estimated to contain 600 million barrels of recoverable liquids and to have a peak production of 165,000bpd. Although discovered in 2001, the project has encountered several delays in the development process and Exxon recently revised its goal for peak production from 2012 to 2014. Banyu Urip is currently the only producing field in the Cepu PSC and as of January 2010, had reached a production level of about 18,000bpd.

... and the gas

Indonesia's geography presents a challenge to resource development, because the archipelago nation's most prolific blocks of conventional gas reserves are located far from its major demand markets.

According to the OGJ, Indonesia had 106 trillion cubic feet (tcf) of proven natural gas reserves as of January 2011. Indonesia is the fourteenth largest holder of proven natural gas reserves in the world and the third-largest in the Asia-Pacific region. Although domestic consumption of natural gas has nearly doubled since 2004, Indonesia continues to be a major exporter of pipeline and liquefied natural gas (LNG).

The regulatory structure that shapes Indonesia's upstream oil sector also forms the basis for the gas sector. BPMigas serves as the upstream regulator and state-owned PT Pertamina – although still active in upstream exploration and production – no longer plays a regulatory role. Pertamina accounts for about 15 per cent of natural gas production. International oil companies such as Total, ConocoPhillips and ExxonMobil dominate the upstream gas sector, while natural gas transmission and distribution activities are carried out by the state-owned utility Perusahaan Gas Negara (PGN).

In 2009, Indonesia produced 2.6tcf of dry natural gas. Production has grown at an average annual rate of about 1.5 per cent over the previous two decades and Indonesia's 2009 gas production was the eleventh-highest in the world. A little more than half of Indonesia's 2009 production came from offshore fields, although the government estimates that more than 70 per cent of the country's conventional gas reserves may be located offshore. An increasingly large majority of Indonesia's natural gas production has come from non-associated fields in recent years, with associated gas accounting for about 18 per cent of gross production in 2009.

In addition to expansion of current projects, there are several major new gas projects in development for the next decade. Total and Petronas (Malaysia) recently joined ExxonMobil and Pertamina to develop the Natuna D-Alpha field in the East Natuna Sea. Pertamina expects the project to start by 2021 and has estimated that East Natuna in total holds 46tcf of gas. However, the field contains about 70 per cent carbon dioxide, significantly tightening production margins for its developers. Chevron is pursing the deepwater Gendalo-Gehem project with partners Eni (Italy) and Sinopec (China). At its peak, the project – which spans four PSC blocks – may produce 400 billion cubic feet (bcf) per year. The project is Indonesia's first deepwater gas project. According to BPMigas, the first stage of the project will come from the Bangka field and may commence as early as 2014. Inpex (Japan)

KEY INDICATORS — Indonesia

	Unit	2006	2007	2008	2009	2010
Population	m	222.75	225.64	228.57	*231.55	237.64
Gross domestic product (GDP)	US$bn	364.38	432.20	511.50	539.40	706.70
GDP per capita	US$	1,640	1,916	2,238	2,329	3,015
GDP real growth	%	5.5	6.3	6.0	4.6	6.1
Inflation	%	13.1	6.0	9.4	4.8	5.1
Unemployment	%	10.3	9.1	8.4	–	–
Industrial output	% change	4.7	4.7	3.7	3.5	–
Agricultural output	% change	3.0	3.4	4.8	4.1	–
Oil output	'000 bpd	1,071.0	969.0	1,004.0	1,021.0	986.0
Natural gas output	bn cum	74.0	66.7	69.7	71.9	82.0
Coal output	mtoe	119.9	27.8	141.1	155.3	188.1
Exports (fob) (goods)	US$m	103,514.0	118,014.0	139,291.0	119,480.0	158,074.0
Imports (fob) (goods)	US$m	73,868.0	84,930.0	115,981.0	84,347.0	127,447.0
Balance of trade	US$m	29,646.0	33,083.0	23,309.0	35,133.0	30,628.0
Current account	US$m	10,836.0	11,009.0	126.0	10,746.0	5,654.0
Total reserves minus gold	US$m	41,103.0	54,976.0	49,597.0	63,563.0	92,908.0
Foreign exchange	US$m	40,866.0	54,737.0	49,339.0	60,572.0	89,970.0
Exchange rate	per US$	9,098.10	9,327.50	9,699.00	8,977.50	9,080.40

* estimated figure

received permission to begin development in its Masela block, which is estimated to hold about 14tcf of natural gas. This offshore block in the Arafura Sea will serve export markets through the planned associated LNG terminal and is expected to begin production in 2016.

Indonesia was the world's sixth largest net exporter of natural gas in 2009. Although the majority of Indonesia's gas exports are transported as LNG, Indonesia also exports about a quarter of its gas exports via pipeline to Singapore, with which it has two pipeline connections: one from its offshore fields in the West Natuna Sea and the other from the Grissik gas processing plant in Sumatra. These pipelines have a combined capacity of approximately 400bcf per year and deliver gas to Singapore under long-term contracts, both set to expire around 2020. However, as part of its efforts to secure its own domestic supply, the Indonesian government has expressed an interest in negotiating a reduction in the volumes of these contracts.

The remaining three-quarters of Indonesia's gas exports – excluding a small amount of pipeline exports to Malaysia – are exported as LNG. Japan is the major destination for Indonesia's LNG exports, accounting for about 65 per cent of the total, but South Korea and Taiwan are also significant importers. Indonesia was the third-largest exporter of liquefied natural gas in 2009, following only Qatar and Malaysia. There are three operational liquefaction terminals in Indonesia, with a combined production capacity of about 1.6tcf (32 million metric tons (MMT)) per year. In 2009, Indonesia exported about 950bcf of LNG.

Coal

In 2005 Indonesia became the world's largest thermal coal exporter. By 2015, 40 per cent of the world's coal shipments will come from Indonesia. In 2011 tax revenues from coal are expected to boost the government's coffers by some US$7 billion. Coal production in 2010 was 320 million tonnes, a figure that is expected to rise to 340 million tonnes in 2011.

According to the US Energy Information Administration (EIA) estimates, Indonesia has 4.8 billion short tons of recoverable coal, of which the vast majority is located in Sumatra and East and South Kalimantan. Government and industry estimates suggest that the resource base may be considerably higher than this amount. Indonesian coal production – which is primarily bituminous or sub-bituminous in rank – has approximately quadrupled between 2000 and 2009, reaching 333MMst in 2009. In the same year, Indonesia consumed 77MMst of coal, which was less than a quarter of its production, but more than three times the consumption level in 2000. Power plants accounted for nearly two-thirds of 2009 total coal sales. Electricity sector demand for coal is expected to more than double by 2014 as a result of coal-fired generation capacity additions.

Although coal consumption has grown significantly in the last decade, the majority of additional production has gone towards exports. In order to guarantee sufficient domestic supply, the Indonesian government has set a domestic market obligation of 24 per cent for producers. Indonesia is now the second-largest exporter of coal (after Australia) on the international market and is the largest exporter of thermal coal used for power plants. Indonesia's coal exports primarily serve Asian markets, with about 70 per cent of 2009 total exports being sent to China, Japan, Taiwan and other Asian markets. In 2010, Indonesia was the leading source of Chinese coal imports.

Risk assessment

Economy	Good
Politics	Fair
Regional stability	Good

COUNTRY PROFILE

Historical profile

It is thought that Negroid peoples came to Irian Jaya from East Africa around 30,000 years ago. Melanesians arrived later; the resultant population migrated throughout the islands of what is now Indonesia. Later settlers arrived from India, Burma and China. Islam spread to Indonesia as a result of strong trading links with the Arabian Peninsula.

1511 The Portuguese arrived in Indonesia, looking for spices. The Spaniards followed, bringing Christianity to the region.

1799 The Dutch spread control of the territory through the United East India Company. They gradually extended their control throughout the entire region. The Portuguese maintained East Timor.

1924 The Partai Kommunis Indonesia (PKI) (Indonesian Communist Party) was established. It was first active among trade unionists and rural villagers. The rural areas came to be the PKI's main power base.

1942-45 The islands of the Dutch East Indies were occupied by the Japanese. After the Second World War the Dutch regained control. Nationalist leader Ahmed Sukarno returned from internal exile and organised the fight for independence from Dutch colonial rule.

1945 In a speech in July Sukarno urged the adoption of the *Panca Sila* (Five Principles) as the ideological basis of the new state. The five principles were nationalism, internationalism (or humanitarianism), democracy, social justice, and belief in God.

1949 After four years of insurgency The Netherlands recognised the independence of Indonesia. A federal constitution was introduced, giving limited self-government to the 16 constituent regions. Ahmed Sukarno as leader of the Partai Nasional Indonesia (PNI) (Indonesian Nationalist Party), assumed the presidency. The Dutch retained control of West Papua; the Portuguese retained control of East Timor.

1950 The constitution was dissolved and the country adopted a unitary political structure. Sukarno was elected president.

1955 Sukarno won Indonesia's first general election. Political instability prompted Sukarno to dissolve parliament and a period of autocratic rule ensued.

1962 Dutch authority for West Papua was passed to UN administration.

1963 Authority for West Papua was transferred to Indonesia.

1964 Indonesia laid claim to areas of Borneo which had been granted to Malaysia on its independence, leading to a three-year guerrilla conflict on the Malaysian border, which severely damaged the Indonesian economy.

1965 A failed *coup d'état* by the PKI resulted in the deaths of hundreds of thousands of left-wing activists.

1967 Sukarno transferred full emergency power to General Suharto, commander of the Indonesian armed forces.

1968 General Suharto became president.

1975 Portugal granted independence to its colony of East Timor.

1976 East Timor was invaded by Indonesia and became a province. This annexation was never officially recognised by the UN.

1985 Australia recognised Indonesia's incorporation of East Timor.

1997 The South-East Asian economic crisis caused the rupiah to plummet in value.

1998 Suharto, re-elected in March, was forced to resign on 21 May after accusations of corruption and widespread public disturbances as the country's economy reached near collapse. He was succeeded by Bacharuddin Jusuf Habibie.

1999 A UN sponsored referendum on independence was supported by the population of East Timor. Anti-independence militia rampaged through East Timor until UN administration is imposed and the Indonesian government agreed to grant it independence. Abdurrahman Wahid was elected president of Indonesia by the People's Consultative Assembly.

2000 Ex-president Suharto's trial, on corruption charges, collapsed. Ethnic, religious and separatist violence in several provinces grew.
2001 The IMF halted further loans citing the government's inability to tackle corruption. Wahid was voted out of office for his alleged involvement in two financial scandals. Vice President Megawati Sukarnoputri (daughter of Indonesia's first president, Ahmed Sukarno) was sworn in as president.
2002 Indonesia, Malaysia and the Philippines signed a pact to counter terrorism. The government and separatist rebels in Aceh province signed a peace agreement giving greater autonomy and free elections to Aceh in exchange for disarmament by rebels. Constitutional changes included the posts of president and vice president to be by popular vote. A bomb planted by Islamic fundamentalists on the island of Bali, and targeted at Western tourists, killed 202 people. The International Court of Justice awarded the disputed islands of Sipadan and Ligitan to Malaysia.
2003 The Aceh peace accord failed; martial law was imposed. Three Bali bomb suspects were found guilty and sentenced to death.
2004 Susilo Bambang Yudhoyono won the presidential elections. An earthquake off the island of Sumatra caused a devastating tsunami that struck coastal areas throughout the region, particularly the peninsula of Aceh on Sumatra island. The final estimate for Indonesia was 167,000 dead or missing and 572,126 displaced.
2005 An agreement was signed between the leaders of Indonesia and Timor-Leste, recognising the location of their shared land border. The government withdrew the last troops from Aceh province, following the disbanding of the military wing of the Gerakan Aceh Merdeka (GAM) (Free Aceh Movement) a few days earlier.
2006 Legislation was introduced extending partial home rule to Aceh. Local elections were held in Aceh for a governor and other officials. The Partai Hati Nurani Rakyat (Partai Hanura) (People's Conscience Party) was founded by retired General Wiranto, formerly of the Golkar party.
2008 Former president (1967-98) Suharto died. The government was forced to raise fuel prices by around 30 per cent, in line with global prices; this lead to civil unrest. Global oil prices fell at the end of the year allowing subsidies to be re-introduced.
2009 In parliamentary elections, 38 political parties and 11,219 candidates (of which 30 per cent were required to be women candidates), took part. Incumbent, President Susilo Bambang Yudhoyono (commonly known as SBY) (DP coalition) was re-elected with 60.8 per cent of the vote. A 10-party coalition was formed from all political parties that won seats in the elections. An earthquake of 7.9 magnitude struck centred off the island of Sumatra, killing over 500 people, as buildings collapsed in the city of Padang.
2010 Darmin Nasution was approved as governor of Bank Indonesia (the central bank) in July. There had been no permanent governor for 14 months. Religious violence increased in secular Indonesia, as the hard-line Front Pembela Islam (FPI) (Islamic Defenders Front) targeted Christians and other minority religious minorities and popular night-time entertainment venues. In September, all illegally harvested wood and wood products were banned from export; official certificates, proving timber was legally sourced became mandatory. A *tsunami* struck the islands of Mentawai, off the west coast of Sumatra, on 25 October, killing over 400 people. On 26 October, the volcano Merapi erupted on the central island of Java, killing dozens of people.
2011 On 22 June, following the execution of an Indonesian domestic worker by Saudi Arabia, a ban was placed on all Indonesian citizens working as domestic servants in Saudi Arabia from 1 August. On 9 June, President Yudhoyono announced that neither he, nor his wife or sons would run in presidential elections in 2014.

Political structure

Constitution

The system of government is based on the 1945 constitution which underlines the unity of Indonesia as a republic, supplemented by the General Elections Law of 1969.
The constitution provides for five branches of government: the president, the Dewan Perwakilan Rakyat (DPR) (House of People's Representatives), the Supreme Audit Board, the Supreme Court and the Supreme Advisory Council. Despite geographic diversity and the limited reach of the political centre, Indonesia has not implemented a federal system, an option tarnished by association with the colonial era under Dutch rule. Instead, each of the 27 provinces is headed by a governor who is responsible to the president through the minister of home affairs, and represents the central government in his province. The north Sumatran province of Aceh, the territory of Jogjakarta in central Java, and the capital, Jakarta, have a special status.
Since 1985, by law, all major organisations, including political parties, religious groups and trade unions, must include acknowledgement of *Pancasila* (the Five Principles) as their sole guiding ideology in their constitutions. It emphasises tolerance among different religious groups and a political system based on consensus.
All Indonesian citizens over the age of 17 are eligible to vote, as well as those citizens under the age of 17 who are married. To stand for election, a citizen must be at least 21 years old.
In 2002, 14 amendments were made to the constitution, to take effect with the next elections. The revisions included the abolition of the reservation of 38 parliamentary seats for military personnel.
In 2003, parliament passed legislation setting the parameters for the first direct presidential election.

Independence date

17 August 1945

Form of state

Democratic republic

The executive

Supreme power is vested in the President of Indonesia, who is both head of state and head of government, directly elected for a term of five years with re-election allowed once. The president may appoint and dismiss ministers (which may be partisan or largely composed of technocrats without an independent power base) and create laws, in agreement with the legislature. The president is head of the military and has the power to declare war, peace and sign treaties.

National legislature

The bicameral Majelis Permusyawaratan Rakyat (MPR) (People's Consultative Assembly) consists of Dewan Perwakilan Rakyat (DPR) (house of representatives) and Dewan Perwakilan Daerah (DPD) (consultative assembly). Since 2009, the DPR has 560 members, directly elected by proportional representation in multi-seat constituencies, to serve for a five-year term. The DPD has 128 members, with each province directly electing four candidates to serve for a four-year term.
All statutes and the state budget must be approved by the DPR, which has the right to initiate legislation. All legislation relating to provincial matters is referred to the DPD for consideration and counsel.

Legal system

The judicial powers of the state are exercised by the Supreme Court.

Last elections

8 July 2009 (presidential); 9 April 2009 (parliamentary)
Results: Presidential: Susilo Bambang Yudhoyono (PD) won 60.8 per cent of the vote, Megawati Sukarnoputri (PDI-P) 26.79 per cent Jusuf Kalla (Golkar) 12.41 per cent.
Parliamentary: Partai Demokrat (PD) (Democratic Party) won 20.9 per cent of the vote (150 seats out of 560), Partai Golongan Karya (Golkar Party) (Party of

the Functioning Groups) 14.5 per cent (108), Partai Demokrasi Indonesia Perjuangan (PDI–P) (Indonesian Democratic Party-Struggle) 14 per cent (93), Partai Keadilan Sejahtera (PKS) (Prosperous Justice Party) 7.9 per cent (59), Partai Amanat Nasional (PAN) (National Mandate Party) 6 per cent (42), Partai Persatuan Pembangunan (PPP) (United Development Party) 5.3 per cent (39), Partai Kebangkitan Bangsa (PKB) (National Awakening Party) 4.9 per cent (26), Partai Gerakan Indonesia Raya (Gerindra) (Great Indonesia Movement Party) 4.5 per cent (30), Partai Hati Nurani Rakyat (Hanura) (People's Conscience Party) 3.8 per cent (15). Twenty-nine other political parties failed to win enough votes to gain any seats.

Next elections
2014 (parliamentary and presidential)

Political parties

Ruling party
Coalition of 10 political parties led by Partai Golongan Karya (Golkar) (Party of the Functioning Groups), Partai Demokrasi Indonesia-Perjuangan, (PDI-P) (Indonesian Democratic Party-Struggle) and Partai Keadilan Sejahtera (PKS) (Posperous Justice Party) (from 1 May 2009)

Main opposition party
The government is composed of all political parties that won seats in the general election. There is no official opposition

Population

237.64 million (2010; census figure)
Last census: June 2000: 206,264,595
Population density: 123 inhabitants per square km (2010)
Annual growth rate: 1.3 per cent 1994–2004 (WHO 2006)

Ethnic make-up
Although 95 per cent of the population are of Malay origin, there are some 300 minorities, including Melanesian, Proto-Austranesian, Polynesian and Micronesian; there are approximately four million ethnic Chinese. Indonesia encompasses the Islamic people of Aceh on the northern tip of Sumatra, the densely populated main island of Java, the tourist resorts of Bali, the island of Flores and the primitive tribes of Irian Jaya in the east.

Religions
Only six faiths are officially recognised in Indonesia - Islam (87 per cent), Catholic and Protestant Christianity (10 per cent), Hinduism (2 per cent, mainly in Bali), Buddhism (1 per cent), and Confucianism.
Indonesia has the world's largest Muslim population, although Hindu-derived and indigenous religious variations are common. Religious violence has spread in line with political uncertainty. Animist beliefs are held in remote areas.

Education

Free universal primary education has been a long-term aim of the government. Almost 100 per cent of eligible children attend such schools, compared to only 40 per cent when President Suharto came to power in 1968. The overall literacy rate has increased by 31 per cent, up from 54 per cent in 1970.
Secondary education consists of two three-year cycles; over 50 per cent of eligible students are in secondary education. Tertiary education has also expanded, with 11 per cent of eligible students in school, up from 1 per cent in the late 1960s. The vast majority of tertiary institutions are privately owned, although there is a network of state institutions around the country. The quality of these universities and colleges varies enormously and large numbers of Indonesian students go overseas for their tertiary education. Despite improvements, the Indonesian education system is not supplying enough technicians and scientists for the country's ambitious plans.
Public expenditure on education typically amounts to 1.4 per cent of annual GDP. In April 2003, the Islamic Development Bank approved a US$31 million loan to Indonesia to finance university expansion.
Literacy rate: 88 per cent adult rate; 98 per cent youth rate (15–24) (Unesco 2005).
Compulsory years: 7 to 16
Enrolment rate: 113 per cent gross primary enrolment of the relevant age group (including repeaters); 56 per cent gross secondary enrolment (World Bank).
Pupils per teacher: 22 in primary schools.

Health

While basic healthcare has improved immeasurably over the past 30 years, it remains an urban rather than rural phenomenon. Inadequate numbers of trained staff remain the rule. Expatriates and wealthier Indonesians usually go to Singapore or Australia for operations. State healthcare is rudimentary. According to government figures, there are about 1,350 hospitals in Indonesia with 110,200 beds. There are approximately 0.7 hospital beds per 1,000 people, which is low even by regional standards (India has 0.8 beds per 1,000).
Improved water sources are available to 74 per cent of the population.

HIV/Aids
Government health figures in December 2009 showed that at least 290,000 people in Indonesia are HIV positive.
HIV prevalence: 0.1 per cent aged 15–49 in 2003 (World Bank)
Life expectancy: 67 years, 2004 (WHO 2006)
Fertility rate/Maternal mortality rate: 2.3 births per woman, 2004 (WHO 2006); maternal mortality 230 per 100,000 live births (World Bank).
Child (under 5 years) mortality rate (per 1,000): 31 per 1,000 live births; 27.3 per cent of children aged under five are malnourished (World Bank).
Head of population per physician: 0.13 physicians per 1,000 people, 2003 (WHO 2006)

Welfare

Although poverty has been greatly reduced, the decline in living standards during the economic contraction of 1998 has yet to be reversed. The government has no plans to provide comprehensive welfare for the country's population of over 200 million. Instead, the government attempts to subsidise the cost of living of the poor through price controls, although these are being phased out in line with IMF commitments on goods such as kerosene. The state-run Workers' Accident Insurance and Provident Fund (*Jamsostek*) is the only form of social security in Indonesia. The insurance covers accident, sickness, pensions, unemployment, health and housing benefits. Outside *Jamsostek* there are other welfare programmes provided by private insurance companies, but they are not compulsory.

Main cities

Jakarta (capital, on island of Java, estimated population 9.0 million (m) in 2004); Surabaya (3.1m); Bandung (2.8m); Medan (2.2m) on Sumatra; Palembang (1.5m) on Sumatra; Tangerang (1.3m), Semarang on Java (1.3m); Ujung Pandang (Makassar) on Sulawesi (Celebes) (1.3m); Banjarmasin (568,800); Samarinda (508,900) and Pontianak (506,300) on Kalimantan (Borneo); Denpasar on Bali (502,100); Jogjakarta on Java (484,200).

Languages spoken

Bahasa Indonesia has existed as an official language for the past 70 years, and is still in the process of developing, with new words constantly being added. For simplicity's sake, the use of English words is common, particularly in the banking, insurance and technology sectors. However, the government wishes to promote Indonesian language development and reduce the use of foreign words.
English is widely spoken in government and business circles and by the younger generation. Many older Indonesians speak Dutch as a second language.
Each ethnic group has its own language. Altogether, more than 580 languages and

dialects are spoken, including Javanese, Sundanese, Arabic and Chinese.

Official language/s

Bahasa Indonesia

Media

The constitution provides for freedom of the press and speech, however, the government has occasionally restricted these rights. The Constitution Court struck down several laws in 2006–07 that criminalised defamation of the government, president and vice president, which had been used to curtail reporting. The government restricts the movement of journalist around the country and special permits must be obtained to visit, for example, West Papua.

Press

Dailies: In Indonesian, the largest newspapers include *Kompas* (http://kompas.com), *Media Indonesia* (www.mediaindonesia.com), *Koran Tempo* (www.korantempo.com), *Republik* (www.republika.co.id), *Pos Kota* (www.poskota.co.id) and *Rakyat Merdeka* (www.rakyatmerdeka.co.id) a tabloid. In English *The Jakarta Post* (www.thejakartapost.com), which includes business and financial news.

There are many more regional and local newspapers available.

Weeklies: In Indonesian, magazines include *Tempo* (www.tempointeractive.com) with English online edition, *Gatra* (www.gatra.com) for news and current affairs, *Tabloid Nova* (www.tabloidnova.com) and *Hanyawanita* (www.hanyawanita.com), is for women.

Business: In Indonesian, newspapers and magazines include *Bisnis Indonesia* (http://web.bisnis.com), *Bisnis Bali* (www.bisnisbali.com) and *SWA* (www.swa.co.id); the *JIEF Economic Monthly* (www.jief.biz) is also in Japanese and *Warta Ekonomi* (www.wartaekonomi.com). In English, publications include the *Standard Trade and Industry Directory of Indonesia Indonesian Commercial Newsletter*.

Periodicals: In Indonesian, the monthly *Femina* (www.femina-online.com) is for women. *Intisari* is a science monthly. In English, the quarterly *Inside Indonesia* (http://insideindonesia.org) has in-depth articles on politics and social issues and the monthly *Latitudes Magazine* has features on culture, travel and the arts.

Broadcasting

The government bans live news coverage and relayed international live news programmes on radio and television. However, digital news via the internet is a growing market.

Radio: There are many radio stations operating in FM and AM frequencies. A few digital audio broadcasting (DAB) stations have begun operations in Jakarta and Surabaya, since 2006.

The national public broadcaster is Radio Republik Indonesia (RRI) (www.rri-online.com), with six networks including the international channel, Voice of Indonesia. Private, commercial stations include Kiss FM (www.kissfm.co.id), Oz Radio Bali (www.ozradio.net) and Radio Otomotion (www.otomotionfm.com) for news.

Television: There are around a dozen national TV networks competing with the publicly owned Televisi Republik Indonesia (TVRI), (www.tvri.co.id), which broadcast free-to-air, cable and satellite TV. Major private TV channels include RCTI (www.rcti.tv) with a variety of locally produced shows including news, entertainment and religion. With similar content, SCTV (www.sctv.co.id) is known for its soap operas (entertaining serials?) and Indosiar (www.indosiar.com) known for its cultural programmes and foreign language dramas.

Advertising

With a population of over 220 million, advertising revenue per annum is around US$11.6 billion. All traditional outlets are available plus new technologies.

Television advertising must be 100 per cent Indonesian resourced, through agencies, actors and location, unless a government waver is agreed and the product or service is an international brand or icon.

News agencies

National news agency: Antara National News Agency

Indoexchange (for stock market news): www.indoexchange.com

Economy

The economy has prospered relatively well since 2006, when Indonesia repaid outstanding US$3.2 billion of the US$11.1 billion loan, incurred during the 1997 Asian financial crisis, four years ahead of schedule and just in time to contend with the next, and greater, global financial crisis. Indonesia is ranked 11 in the world by GDP, at over US$500 billion. It has a market economy in which the government plays an important role through state-owned entities and direct influence through regulation of prices of basic foodstuffs, utilities and fuel.

Within the structure of the economy, the service sector at 40 per cent of GDP vies with industry at 45 per cent. Commodity exports are dominated by oil, natural gas and minerals at over 38 per cent, with manufactured goods at around 15 per cent. Agriculture provides less than 14 per cent, a figure that has been steadily falling since 1985.

GDP growth was 6 per cent in 2008 as domestic consumption and fiscal stimulus counteracted the weak external conditions. In 2009, growth fell to 4.6 per cent reflecting the lack of domestic demand, however GDP growth rebounded in 2010 to 6.1 per cent as global trade resumed; the forecast for 2011 remained at a higher rate of 6.4 per cent.

The fiscal stimulus package introduced in 2008, as part of the global co-ordinated response to the financial crisis was US$6 billion. Total external debt in 2008 and 2009 was 29.3 per cent and 29.4 per cent of GDP respectively. Foreign direct investment grew by 9 per cent in 2009, due to its resilience in the face of the financial crisis; the Jakarta stock market (JSX Composite) grew by 44 per cent and the rupiah strengthened by 6 per cent against the US dollar in 2009. If growth continues as predicted, Indonesia expects to join the fast-growing developing economies (Brazil, Russia, India, China, the so-called BRIC countries) by 2011.

The International Monetary Fund (IMF) has been positive in its appraisal of Indonesia's economic prospects, as the government had instigated 'timely policy responses' which lessened the effects of the crisis on the economy, unlike so many of Indonesia's regional neighbours.

External trade

Indonesia is a member of the Asian and Pacific Economic Co-operation (Apec) and belongs to the Asian Free Trade Area (AFTA) operated by the Association of Southeast Asian Nations (ASEAN), which was set up to attract foreign direct investment (FDI) and the elimination of tariffs within the membership.

The US-owned Freeport-McMoran mine Grasberg, located in Papua province, contains the largest single reserves of copper and gold in the world.

Imports

Main commodities include machinery and equipment, petroleum and chemicals, foodstuffs.

Main sources: Singapore (typically 15 per cent total), China (10 per cent), Japan (10 per cent).

Exports

One of the most successful export sectors has been consumer electronics and home appliances. Indonesia is the world's leading exporter of coal for power stations, as well as palm oil. Major exports also include oil and gas, plywood, textiles and rubber, copper, gold and other minerals. Total exports increased by some 37 per cent between January and July 2011 (to US$116 billion).

A change to the rules governing export earnings was announced on 9 September 2011, although the date the change would become effective was not given. The new rules will require companies to repatriate foreign currency earnings from

exports, and to hold the earnings in domestic bank accounts. It is estimated that the amount concerned will be as high as US$33 billion.
Main destinations: Japan (typically 20 per cent total), US (10 per cent), Singapore (10 per cent).

Agriculture

Farming

Agriculture accounts for around 15 per cent of GDP and employs 48 per cent of the labour force. Agricultural products make up 25 per cent of non-oil export earnings.

After planting more high-yield varieties, investing in irrigation systems, doubling the use of fertilisers and trebling the use of pesticides, Indonesia has achieved self-sufficiency in rice. Poor harvests can still result in rice and other cereals having to be imported to rebuild stocks.

Cassava, maize, sugar, sweet potatoes, bananas and many other fruits and vegetables are grown for local consumption. Self-sufficiency in sugar is a government goal.

It is estimated that there are 1.2 million clove farmers. Indonesia consumes 95 per cent of worldwide clove production, used in the manufacture of *kretek* (clove/tobacco mix) cigarettes. The clove cigarette industry is one of the country's major employers and the government has tariffs in place to restrict the import of cloves, mainly from Madagascar and Zanzibar, in an attempt to maintain its sustainability when over 80 per cent of the cloves consumed is home grown.

Large estates that have undergone rehabilitation produce coffee, tea, rubber, coconuts and palm oil nuts, mostly for export.

Indonesia is the world's largest producer of coconuts and the second-largest of palm oil, copra and natural rubber. It is the third-largest in rice, coffee and cocoa.

Fishing

Foreign aid organisations have assisted the government in rehabilitating the fishing sector. Foreign fishing trawlers are not permitted to operate in Indonesian waters, as these would obstruct traditional coastal fishermen.

Indonesia's fishing industry is plagued by corruption and illegal fishing methods, such as the use of bottle bombs to increase the size of the catch. Ineffective monitoring of fishing techniques means that these practices are likely to continue.

Shrimp and tuna fish are important exports. Other species include scad, Indian mackerel and sea catfish. Indonesia is the fifth largest producer of tuna in the world and has become one of the world's biggest exporters of shrimps and prawns.

Following the annual meeting of the Commission for the Conservation of Southern Bluefin Tuna (CCSBT), held on Cheju Island, South Korea, all members agreed to a 20 per cut in the roughly 17,000 tonnes in 2009 bluefin tuna catches from 2010. Scientists had warned that without a cut fish stocks could crash as numbers had become dangerously low.

Forestry

Forest products are the third most important export earner. Indonesia has some of the world's largest remaining reserves of tropical hardwoods. Legislation aims to reduce the rate of felling and to ban the export of logs, and has increased the proportion used locally in timber processing. Illegal logging remains a problem and has doubled the deforestation rate. It is estimated that Indonesia is losing up to two million hectares (ha) of forest annually. It was estimated that 300,000cum of hardwood is illegally felled each year in the state of New Guinea and shipped to China for processing. Indonesia's decentralisation programme could worsen the situation since local governments do not have the ability to manage their resources effectively. The military have also been implicated in the illegal logging trade with corruption and entrenched interests underpinning the activity. Indonesia is under pressure from international organisations to reform its forestry policy and to control the unprecedented rate at which its forests are depleted.

Industry and manufacturing

Industry contributes around 44 per cent of GDP and employs 15 per cent of the workforce.

In the oil-rich 1970s, Indonesia operated a highly protected industrialisation policy with heavy state involvement on both a regulatory and investment front. Declining export revenues from oil and gas in the mid-1980s led to a reversal of this policy. Industry was progressively deregulated and foreign investment encouraged in previously protected areas. Non-traditional export industries were promoted – initially garments and shoes, later electronics, chemicals and minerals. The government also successfully encouraged investment in automobile manufacturing, air and sea transportation, power, communications and highways.

Tourism

The tourist sector, attracts over five million visitors from Asia alone. However Western visitors, particularly from Australia and the US were targetted by militant Islamists in 2005, which set back the industry for several years. The government, which recognises the importance of tourism to the economy, has actively promoted the sector, aiming to attract 10 million visitors regularly each year.

The biggest market is Singapore, which accounted for 1.6 million arrivals, followed by Malaysia, Japan, Australia and Taiwan.

Environment

Indonesia is ranked first in the world for its range and variety of corals, and together with the Philippines, Australia, Papua New Guinea and Solomon Islands for coral reef fish species.

In 2007 Indonesia was warned by Greenpeace that the drainage of peat wetlands in favour of plantations producing palm oil (used in foods and bio-fuel) was causing greater release of carbon dioxide (a greenhouse gas) than forest clearances by burning alone. Indonesia is planning to become the world's leading producer of palm oil, with a huge project planned for Borneo. In the face of international critisism of deforestation, and Indonesia's ranking as the world's third largest greenhouse emitter, around 80 million trees were planted nationwide in November.

In February 2011 the government admitted that rampant, illegal logging was beyond its control.

Mining

The archipelago of Indonesia produces tin, copper and chromium ore. Indonesia is the world's second-largest producer of tin (after China), producing typically 46,000 tonnes of tin concentrate. In addition to other precious metals, it is also a major producer of copper, bauxite and nickel.

Mining and quarrying typically account for around 13 per cent of GDP. Mining's share of GDP has fallen continuously in recent years as production has dropped in response to depressed world prices. Increasing world demand for copper and rising prices have encouraged mines to be restarted and new mines opened.

The government is eager to increase investment in gold, copper and nickel exploitation, although complex issues are involved in mineral exploitation throughout the archipelago. Indonesia is by far the largest gold producing nation in Asia and one of the top 10 producers in the world. Gold is mined at Lebong Tandai in Sumatra and is produced as a by-product from the Freeport copper mine in the highlands of Irian Jaya. Most of Indonesia's gold mines have a short life span. Instability, particularly in separatist areas such as Aceh and Papua, has halted exploration projects in the past. The majority of gold comes from PT Freeport's mining facility in Irian Jaya.

Nickel is mined from new, large deposits in central Sulawesi and Irian Jaya; much of it becomes ferro-nickel and nickel matte, primarily for export. Bauxite production is carried out at Asahan in north Sumatra, for export to Japan.

Tin mining is carried out by state-owned PT Tambang Timah and joint-venture company PT Koba Tin (25 per cent owned by PT Tambang Timah and 75 per cent owned by Iluka Mining Corporation). PT Tambang Timah is the world's largest tin producer, producing tin from Bangka Island, including dredging operations at Karimun and Kundur islands in the Riau Province. The company has tin reserves estimated at around 382,000 tonnes, of which 60 per cent is located offshore.

Hydrocarbons

The role of oil and gas peaked in the early 1980s when it contributed over four-fifths of total exports. Although oil and gas earnings are still significant, their contribution to GDP is declining. Nevertheless, the oil sector remains very important and Indonesia is the major oil producer in South-east Asia. Nevertheless, the country became a net importer of petroleum products in 2004.

Proven oil reserves were 4.2 billion barrels in 2010, with production of 986,000 barrels per day (bpd). The state-owned oil company, Pertamina, dominates the sector, although foreign involvement has steadily increased. In the downstream sector, Indonesia has eight refineries with a combined capacity of 1.16 million bpd in 2010. The refinery in Balikpapan, East Kalimantan, is to be upgraded in an estimated US$1.7 billion investment plan.

Proven natural gas reserves were 3.1 trillion cubic metres (cum) in 2010 and produced 82 billion cum. Natural gas is supplied from two very large fields at Arun in North Sumatra and Badak in East Kalimantan, although large offshore discoveries have been made around the Natuna Islands in the South China Sea. Exports of natural gas in 2010 were 41.25 billion cum, of which 31.36 was liquefied natural gas (LNG): 17 million cum of LNG was exported to Japan and 6.95 million cum was in gas flow to Singapore, via a pipeline.

In 2005 Indonesia became the world's largest thermal coal exporter. By 2015, 40 per cent of the world's coal shipments will come from Indonesia. In 2011 tax revenues from coal are expected to boost the government's coffers by some US$7 billion. Coal production in 2010 was 320 million tonnes, a figure which is expected to rise to 340 million tonnes in 2011. However, reserves are dominated by the less valuable 'brown coal' which is typically used in power stations and produces higher amounts of polluting gases. Coal is one of the country's top 10, non-oil exports.

Energy

Despite one of the largest populations in Asia, Indonesia has an installed electricity-generating capacity of only 25GW, and power shortage outside Jakarta (on Java) has grown due to underinvestment. Access to electricity was 57 per cent of the population in 2008 and an estimate US$25 billion is needed to provide electricity to the remainder and allow the projected 6 per cent per annum growth. Generation is mainly by oil-fired power plants and some hydro-power. Projects are planned to develop coal and gas-fired and hydro-electric power generation in order to preserve oil for export.

Financial markets

Stock exchange

Bursa Efek Indonesia (Indonesia Stock Exchange) (IDX)

Banking and insurance

In 2006 the central bank announced plans to restructure the banking system by limiting the number of banks investors may control to one. The Indonesia Bank Restructuring Agency (IBRA) was given the task of enhancing public confidence in the banking industry, which had reached a low in 2002, before the sale of Bank Central Asia (BCA), Indonesia's largest bank. Following the sale the IMF commended the government's restructuring policies, which restored solvency to the banking system with net earnings becoming positive for the first time since the 1998 Asia economic crisis. It also advised the government to strengthening standards of corporate governance within the sector.

Indonesia released its first Islamic bond, for individual or retail investors, in 2009. The government will invest the projected US$6 billion raised to stimulate the economy.

Central bank

Bank Indonesia

Main financial centre

Jakarta

Time

Indonesia has three time zones.

Java, Sumatra, west and central Kalimantan and Madura: GMT plus seven hours – West Zone

Bali, south and east Kalimantan, Sulawesi: GMT plus eight hours – Central Zone

Aru, Kai, Moluccas, Tanimbar, Irian Jaya: GMT plus nine hours – East Zone

Geography

The Indonesian archipelago has 17,508 islands and is the largest in the world, extending about 5,150km (3,200 miles) from Sumatra in the west to Irian Jaya, the western half of New Guinea, in the east. The main islands are Sumatra, Java, Bali, Sulawesi (the Celebes) and Timor. Kalimantan, the Indonesian part of Borneo island shared with Malaysia and Brunei, forms a major part of Indonesian territory. Now independent, the former Portuguese colony of East Timor became the youngest province in 1976. Indonesia's neighbours are Malaysia, Singapore, Papua New Guinea, the Philippines and Australia.

Part of the so-called volcanic 'ring of fire' on the Pacific rim, Indonesia has hundreds of volcanoes, 70 of them still active, and hardly a year passes without a major eruption. Earthquakes are also frequent, but rarely cause significant damage.

The country has the world's second largest area of primary rainforest after Brazil, with species of plant and animal life as diverse as anywhere on the planet. On Borneo alone, there are 3,000 different tree species. It also has an extraordinary diversity of animal life, with an estimated 500 species of mammals, including tigers, elephants, hairy rhinoceros, warthogs, small leopards, civets, mouse deer, orangutans, baboons and monkeys. Birds of Paradise, hornbills, peacocks and cockatoos are among the 1,500 species of known birds. The Komodo dragon is three metres long and weighs up to 150kg. It is the world's largest lizard and it is found only on the east Indonesian island of Komodo.

Hemisphere

Straddles the equator

Climate

All of the islands in the archipelago lie within the tropical zone, with average temperatures of 26 degrees Celsius (C). The dry season usually lasts from May to September, the wet season from October to April. In the hill regions west of Jakarta, average temperatures drop to a pleasant 21 degrees C. Indonesia straddles the equator and days are all the same length and rain is frequent. Yearly rainfall in Jakarta is about 300mm and humidity is more than 80 per cent. The islands east of Bali have a much drier climate, and tropical vegetation and jungles give way to rocky savannahs.

Dress codes

Foreigners are expected to dress for business as they would at home, despite the heat, although men can get away without ties and jackets during the day. Formal attire includes suits, or traditional *batik* shirts. Women are advised to dress conservatively as do their Indonesian counterparts. Although Indonesia is Muslim, there is little of the radicalism found elsewhere. At least in Jakarta, the only women wearing veils will be strict Islamic schoolgirls. The dress traditionally worn by men and women, is the *sarong*. This length of fabric wraps around the waist and is topped by elaborate blouses or shirts. Halter tops and shorts are frowned upon in most places except around sports facilities or on the beach. Proper decorum should especially be observed when visiting places of worship.

Entry requirements

Passports

Required by all and must have at least six months validity from date of entry, with proof of return/onward passage and sufficient funds for length of stay.

Visa

Required by all.

Nationals of Apec countries may obtain business visas for up to six months depending on the country of origin. Travellers should contact an Indonesian Consulate for details.

Business visitors arriving from countries with reciprical visa-free facilities on short-term visits need to supply an itinery, letter of business intent from their employer and a letter from a local sponsor. All other visitors should contact an Indonesian Consulate for visa details.

Currency advice/regulations

The import of local currency is limited to Rp50,000 and must be declared, amounts over Rp10 million must be authorised; export is limited to the amount declared on import. Import and export of foreign currency is unlimited.

Major currencies or travellers cheques may be exchanged at most banks, except in the provinces. It is advisable to carry rupiahs in sufficient amount before travelling to outer provinces or minor towns.

Customs

Personal effects are allowed entry; cameras must be declared. Video cameras, tape recorders, binoculars, portable radios, typewriters and sports equipment may be imported on condition that they are exported on departure.

Prohibited imports

These include illegal drugs and narcotics, firearms, ammunition, TV sets, pornography, publications in Chinese characters and Chinese medicine.

Health (for visitors)

Mandatory precautions

Vaccination certificates for yellow fever if travelling from infected area.

Advisable precautions

Vaccinations that are necessary include: cholera, diphtheria, tetanus, hepatitis A, polio and typhoid. Vaccinations that may be advised include: hepatitis B, tuberculosis, Japanese B encephalitis and rabies. Anti-malarial precautions should be taken; the use of mosquito nets and repellents and covering up the body after dark can help avoid malaria, hepatitis B and dengue fever. Only well-maintained and chlorinated swimming pools are safe in which to swim.

Use only bottled or boiled water for drinks, washing teeth and making ice. Eat only well cooked meals, preferably served hot; vegetables should be cooked and fruit peeled. Avoid dairy products, salad and food from street vendors. A full, first-aid kit would be useful.

Tap water must be treated as unsafe unless boiled and filtered (bottled water is available in the main cities). Eat only well cooked meals, preferably served hot; vegetables should be cooked and fruit peeled. Dairy products are unpasteurised and should be avoided

Medical insurance is essential, including emergency evacuation, and an adequate supply of personal medicines is necessary.

Hotels

International-standard hotels have air-conditioning and often business centres, where translation and secretarial services are normally available. A 10 per cent service charge is normally added to the bill, so tipping with small change is usual. Where no service charge has been added, a tip of 5–10 per cent would be appropriate.

Credit cards

Credit and charge cards are widely accepted and ATMs are available in city centres.

Public holidays (national)

Fixed dates

^1 Jan (New Year), ^17 Aug (Independence Day), ^25 Dec (Christmas Day).

Variable dates

^Chinese New Year (Jan/Feb), Nyepi (Hindu New Year, Mar/Apr), Waisak Day (Birth of the Lord Buddha, May), Good Friday (Mar/Apr), Ascension Day, Eid al Adha, Islamic New Year, Birth of the Prophet Mohammed, Ascent of Prophet Mohammed, ^Eid al Fitr (two days).

^Official national holidays, holidays that fall on Friday are taken the next day. The remainder, Muslim, Hindu and Christian, are informal holidays taken by adherents.

Islamic year 1433 (26 Nov 2011–14 Nov 2012): The Islamic year contains 354 or 355 days, with the result that Muslim feasts advance by 10–12 days against the Gregorian calendar. Dates of feasts vary according to the sighting of the new moon, so cannot be forecast exactly.

Working hours

Banking

Mon–Fri: 0830–1530/1730; Sat: 0930–1230. Hotel banks may remain open longer.

Business

Mon–Fri: 0800–1600; Sat: 0830–1230. Fri: it is difficult to make an appointment after 1100 although businessmen sometimes meet people in the late afternoon and early evening.

Government

Mon–Thu: 0800–1500; Fri: 0800–1130; Sat: 0800–1400.

Shops

0800/1000–2100/2200 (some close at 1730).

Telecommunications

Mobile/cell phones

There are limited 900/1800 GSM services around Jakata. A G3 system in planned.

Electricity supply

Generally 220V 50Hz, with two-pronged plug. However, some hotels in the provinces may still be using 110V AC, 50Hz. It is better to check before using an appliance.

Weights and measures

Metric system

Social customs/useful tips

Indonesia is predominantly Muslim and alcohol is not considered essential to social intercourse. Care should be taken to respect Muslim, Hindu and other religious conventions. Footwear should be removed before entering places of worship and temples and sometimes also private homes.

Handshaking with the right hand is customary both for men and women. It is conventional to shake hands and give a slight bow with the head on meeting and taking leave. Punctuality is appreciated on social occasions.

Pork is forbidden for the Muslim population and beef for the Balinese Hindus. Do not start to consume food or drink until invited by the host to do so.

Pribumi is used to describe anything indigenous or native to Indonesia, and occurs in commercial or business contexts with reference to local participation, local capital investment or local loans.

In Indonesia, Western-style beckoning is considered rude; instead, turn your hand palm down, and waggle your fingers – like an upside-down wave. Putting your hands on your hips is considered an overt sign of aggression or contempt.

The word 'no' is regarded as impolite; often people use the word *belum*, which means 'not yet'.

Security

Since 2000, Indonesia has been experiencing unrest and violence. There has been sectarian and ethnic strife in Aceh, Irian Jaya, Central and West Kalimantan, Maluku, North Maluku, Central and South Sulawesi and tension in West Timor.

Since 2002, terrorist attacks have deliberately targetted Western tourists.

Getting there

Air

National airline: Garuda Indonesia (GA) and Merpati Nusantara Airlines (MZ). *In July 2007 the European Union banned all Indonesian airlines from EU air space, due to safety concerns and warned its citizens*

not to use these airlines elsewhere in the world.
International airport/s: Soekarno-Hatta International (CGK), 28km north-west of Jakarta, banks/bureaux de change, a post office, duty-free shops, gift shops, 24-hour restaurants, snack bars, car hire and 24-hour medical/vaccination facilities; Denpasar Bali Ngurah Rai International (DPS), 13km south-west of the city, is the main airport on Bali; Bandung Husein (BDO); Cirebon Penggung (CBN); Ketapang (KTG); Pontianak Supadio (PNK); Semarang Uani (SRG); Surabaya Juanda (SUB).
Airport tax: International departures: Rp100,000.
Surface
Water: High-speed ferries run between Sumatra and Malaysia. Routes are either Medan–Penang or Dumai–Melaka. There are also services between Mandalo (Sulawesi) and the Philippines. Maritime piracy is a problem in some Indonesian waters.
Main port/s: Tanjung Priok, Jakarta; Tanjung Perak, Surabaya; Belawan, on Sumatra.

Getting about

National transport
Air: Garuda Indonesia operates extensive domestic services, including daily services between Jakarta, Surabaya and Medan. Other routes are also served by Sempati Air and Merpati Nusantara Airlines.
Road: Extensive road network includes over 370,000km of road, 25 per cent of which is surfaced. A 525km highway links key areas in Jambi and South Sumatra. Motorways and toll roads are good, but roads are narrower and poorly maintained in rural areas and remote regions. Secondary roads are frequently impassable in the rainy season. Driving outside major cities at night can be hazardous.
Buses: Express coach services link the main cities. Local bus services are inexpensive, but their use is complicated, they are often crowded, and service may be interrupted in the rainy season.
Rail: The rail network, limited to Java, Sumatra and Madura, comprises 8,600km of track. Java and parts of Sumatra have air-conditioned express rail services with sleeping and dining cars only between major cities. Fares are comparatively cheap but higher on air-conditioned trains. There are several trains daily from Jakarta to Bandung and Surabaya. Ordinary services can be slow, with many stops.
Water: There are extensive scheduled and non-scheduled inter-island sailings.
City transport
Roads in major cities are good.
Taxis: Taxis are plentiful but in various states of disrepair. Wherever possible, opt for Blue Bird or Silver Bird taxis and check the driver switches on the meter before starting the journey.
Taxis can be obtained at hotels, airports and railway stations. From Sukarno-Hatta airport to Jakarta, taxis add a surcharge and toll.
There are metered taxis only in Jakarta, Surabaya, Bandung, Solo, Semarang and Jogjakarta, but it may be necessary to insist on the use of the meter. Fares are very reasonable. Taxis may also be hired by the hour, which is less expensive for longer journeys.
In Jakarta it can be difficult to hail taxis, so engage one at the hotel and retain it until returning. A 10 per cent tip is usual.
There are also minicabs for two passengers, the *bemo* (small bus) which plies regular routes, and the *becak*, all of which need advance bargaining to come to a mutually accepted fare.
From city centre to Jakarta Soekarno-Hatta airport taxi journey times are about 45 minutes.
Buses, trams & metro: Journey time on the bus from city centre to Jakarta Soekarno-Hatta International Airport is about 60 minutes.
Trains: Women-only carriages (recognisable by their brightly covered pink seats) were introduced on busy commuter routes in Jakarta in 2010.
Car hire
Car hire, mostly chauffeur-driven, is available in major towns and cities. Except for international car hire operators which accept credit cards, full payment for car hire is made up-front. Traffic drives on the left. Driving at night can be dangerous outside major urban areas as it is common to encounter drivers who do not use their lights.

BUSINESS DIRECTORY

Telephone area codes

The international direct dialling (IDD) code for Indonesia is +62, followed by the area code and subscriber's number:

Balik Papan	542	Manado	431
Bandung	22	Medan	61
Banjarmasin	511	Padang	751
Denpasar	361	Palembang	711
Jakarta	21		

Useful telephone numbers

Police: 110
Ambulance:118
Fire:113
Directory (local):108
Directory (other Indonesian):106
International information102
International operator:101
Domestic connections:100

Chambers of Commerce

American Chamber of Commerce in Indonesia, World Trade Centre, Jalan Jend Sudirman Kav 29-31, Jakarta 12920 (tel: 526-2860; fax: 526-2861; e-mail: info@amcham.or.id).

Bali Chamber of Commerce and Industry, Gedung Merdeka, Jalan Surapati 7, Denpasar 80232 (tel: 233-053; fax: 227-020; e-mail: kadin_bali@balinetwork.com).

British Chamber of Commerce in Indonesia, World Trade Centre, Jalan Jend Sudirman Kav 31, Jakarta 12920 (tel: 522-9453; fax: 527-9135; e-mail: bisnis@britcham.or.id).

Indonesian Chamber of Commerce and Industry, Menara Kadin Indonesia, Jalan HR Rasuna Said X-5 Kav 2-3, Jakarta 12950 (tel: 916-5535; fax: 527-4485; e-mail: info@kadin.net.id).

Jakarta Chamber of Commerce and Industry, Majapahit Permai B21-23, Jalan Majapahit 18-22, PO Box 3077, Jakarta 10160 (tel: 380-8091; fax: 384-4549; e-mail: kadin_jkt@indosat.net.id).

Banking

Bank Dagang Nasional Indonesia (BDNI), Jl Hayam Wuruk No 8, Jakarta (tel: 231-1221/0530/0886; fax: 380-5725).

Bank Danamon, Jl Kebon Sirih No 15, Jakarta 10340 (tel: 231-1331, 230-1901/2; fax: 230-1883/5).

BankExim, Jl Lapangan Setasiun No 1, Jakarta 11110 (tel: 692-3122, 690-0991; fax: 692-3047, 690-5328).

Bank Internasional Indonesia (BII), Jl MH Thamrin Kav 22 No 51, Jakarta Pusat (tel: 230-0888/0666; fax: 230-1426).

Bank Mandiri, Jakarta (e-mail: corp.communications@bankmandiri.co.id; internet site: http://www.bankmandiri.co.id).

Bank Negara Indonesia (BNI), Jl Jend Sudirman Kav 1, Jakarta 10220 (tel: 251-1946; fax: 251-1214).

Bank Umum Nasional, 135 Jl Senen Raya, Jakarta 10410 (tel: 231-2828; fax: 231-2929).

Indonesian Bank Restructuring Agency, Komplek Bank Indonesia, Jl Budi Kemuliaan, Building D, 10th Floor, Jakarta (fax: 231-1478).

PT Bank Pembangunan Indonesia, JL RP Soeroso No 2-4, Jakarta 10011 (tel: 230-1908; fax: 230-1242/3, 230-0154).

PT Bank Bali Tbk, 17th Floor, Gedung Bank Bali, Jalan Jenderal Sudirman Kav 27, Jakarta 12920 (tel: 523-7899; fax: 250-0811).

PT Bank Buana Indonesia, Jalan Asemka 32-36, Jakarta 11110 (tel: 260-1051, 260-1055; fax: 260-1014).

Central bank

Bank Indonesia, 2 Jalan MH Thamrin, Jakarta 10110 (tel: 381-7187; fax: 350-1867; e-mail: humasbi@bi.go.id).

Stock exchange

Bursa Efek Indonesia (Indonesia Stock Exchange) (IDX): www.idx.co.id

Travel information

Bouraq Indonesia Airlines, PO Box 2965, Jalan Angkasa 1-3, Kernayoran, Jakarta 10720 (tel: 629-5289; fax: 629-5364).

Garuda Indonesia, Jl. Merdeka Selatan 13, Jakarta 10110 (tel: 380-1901; fax: 380-6652; internet site: http://www.garuda-indonesia.com).

Ikatan Motor Indonesia (IMI), Gedung KONI, Pusat Senayan, Kotakpos 609, Jakarta (tel: 591-102).

Merpati Nusantara Airlines, PO Box 323, Jalan Angkasa 2, Jakarta 10013 (tel: 413-608; fax: 420-7311).

Sempati Air Transport, Jalan Medan Merdeka Timur No 7, PO Box 2068, Jakarta 13610 (tel: 348-760; fax: 809-4420).

National tourist organisation offices

Direktorat Jenderal Pariwisata Indonesia (Directorate-General of Tourism), 16/19 Jalan Medan Merdeka-Barat, Jakarta 10110 (tel: 386-0934; fax: 386-0828; internet site: www.tourismindonesia.com).

Ministries

Ministry of Agriculture, Jalal Harsono RM 3, Ragunan, Pasar Minggu, Jakarta 12550 (tel: 781-5380; fax: 781-6385).

Ministry of Defence, Jalal Medan Merdeka Barat 13-14, Jakarta 10110 (tel: 384-0889; fax: 384-5178).

Ministry of Economy, Jalal Lapangan Banteng Timur 2-4, Jakarta 10310 (tel: 319-01152; fax: 319-01151).

Ministry of Education, Jalal Jend Sudirman, Senayan, Jakarta (tel: 573-1618; fax: 573-6870).

Ministry of Energy and Mineral Resources, Jalal Medan Merdeka Selatan 16, Jakarta 10110 (tel: 380-4242; fax: 384-7461).

Ministry of Finance, Jalall Lapangan Banteng Timur 2, Jakarta 10170 (tel: 344-9230; fax: 381-4324).

Minstry of Fisheries and Maritime Affairs, Jalal Veteran, 3rd Floor, Jakarta (tel: 385-7009; fax: 344-6733).

Ministry of Foreign Affairs, Jalal Taman Pejambon 6, Jakarta 10111 (tel: 344-1508; fax: 385-1193).

Ministry of Forestry and Estate Crops, Jalal Jend Gatot Subroto, Senayan, Jakarta (tel: 573-1820; fax: 570-0226).

Ministry of Health, Jalal HR Rasuna Said Blok X-5 Kav 4-9, Jakarta 12950 (tel: 520-1590; fax: 520-1591).

Ministry of Home Affairs, Jalal Medan Merdeka Utara 7, Jakarta 10110 (tel: 384-2222; fax: 385-1193).

Ministry of Justice and Human Rights, Jalal HR Rasuna Said Kav 4-5, Kuningan, Jakarta (tel: 525-3006; fax: 525-3090).

Ministry of Manpower and Transmigration, Jalal Taman Makam Pahlawan 17, Jakarta (tel: 798-9912; fax: 799-2629).

Ministry of Political, Social and Security Affairs, Jalal Medan Merdeka Utara 7, Jakarta 10110 (tel: 384-9453; fax: 345-0918).

Ministry of Religious Affairs, Jalal Lapangan Banteng Barat 3-4, Jakarta 10710 (tel: 381-1679; fax: 381-1436).

Ministry of Resettlement and Regional Infrastructure, Jalal Pattimura 20, Kebayoran Baru, Jakarta 12110 (tel: 720-3962; fax: 726-0769).

Ministry of Social Affairs, Jalal Rasuna Said blok X-5 Kav 4-9, Jakarta 12950 (tel: 310-3781; fax: 310-3783).

Ministry of Trade and Industry, Jalal Jend Gatot Subroto Kav 52-53, Jakarta 12950 (tel: 525-6548; fax: 522-9592).

Ministry of Welfare, Jalal Salemba Raya 28, Jakarta 10430 (tel: 310-3781; fax: 310-3783).

Other useful addresses

Asean Investment Promotion Agency, The Investment Co-ordinating Board (BKPM), Jalan Gatot Subroto No 44, PO Box 3186, Jakarta (tel: 512-008, 515-041, 517-022, 510-023; fax: 514-945).

Asean Secretariat, 70 A Jalan Sisingamangaraja, Jakarta 12110 (tel: 726-2991, 724-3372; fax: 724-3504, 739-8234; e-mail: asean.or.id).

Asian Development Bank, Indonesia Resident Mission, Gedung BRI II, 7th Floor, Jl. Jend Sudirman Kav. 44-46, Jakarta 10210 (tel: 251-2721; fax: 251-2749; e-mail: adbirm@mail.asiandevbank.org).

Badan Ko-ordinasi Penanaman Modal (BKPM) (Co-ordinating Board for Capital Investment), Jalan Jend Gatot Subroto 44, Jakarta Selatan (tel: 525-4981, 525-4619; fax: 525-4945).

Badan Pelaksana Bursa Komoditi (ICEB) (Indonesian Commodity Exchange Board), Bursa Building, 2nd and 4th floors, Jalan Medan Merdeka Selatan 14, Jakarta 10110 (tel: 371-921; fax: 380-4426).

Badan Pelaksana Pasar Modal (BAPEPAM) (Capital Market Operation Board), Jalan Medan Merdeka Selatan 14, Jakarta 10110 (tel: 365-509).

British Consular enquiries: British Embassy, Deutsche Bank Building, 19th Floor, 80 Jalan Imam Bonjol, Jakarta 10310, Indonesia (tel: (62 21) 390-7484; fax: (62 21) 316-0850; internet site: www.britain.in.indonesia.or.id).

Business Advisory Services, Kuningan Plaza Building, Jalan Rasuna Said Kav C-11-14, Jakarta (tel: 517-7295).

Central Bureau of Statistics, Jl Dr Sutomo 18, Jakarta (tel: 372-808; internet site: http://www.bps.go.id).

Commander-in-Chief of the Armed Forces, ABRI Headquarters, Mabes ABRI Cilangkap, Jakarta Timur (tel: 384-2679, 840-1243; fax: 380-6711).

Indonesia-British Business Association, C/O Ernst & Young International, Jakarta Stock Exchange Building 23rd Floor, J1 Jenderal Sudirman, Kav 52-53, Jakarta 12190 (tel: 515-1984; fax: 515-1985).

Indonesia Science Institute, Jl Jend. Gatot Subroto No. 10, Jakarta 12710 (tel: 525-1831).

Indonesian Bank Restructuring Agency, Komplek Bank Indonesia, JL Budi Kemuliaan, building D, 10th Floor, Jakarta (fax: 231-1478).

Indonesian Embassy (USA), 2020 Massachusetts Avenue, NW, Wasahington DC 20036 (tel: (+1-202) 775-5200; fax: (+1-202) 775-5365; e-mail: indonetsia@dgs.dgsys.com).

Jakarta Stock Exchange (JSE), Jalan Mendeka Selatan 14, Jakarta Pusat (internet site: http://www.jsx.co.id).

Office of the National Land Agency (BPN), Jl Sisingamangaraja 2, Jakarta Selatan (tel: 722-2420, 739-3939).

Subroto, Kav 52-53, Jakarta (tel: 520-1613; fax: 520-1606).

US Embassy, Medan Merdeka Selatan 5, Jakarta (tel: 344-2211; fax: 386-2259; e-mail: jakconsul@state.gov; internet site: http://www.usembassyjakarta.org).

National news agency: Antara National News Agency, Wisma Antara Building, Floor 3, 19, 20, Ji. Medan Merdeika Selatan 17, Jakarta (tel: 384-3051; fax 386-5577; internet: www.antara.co.id/en).

Internet sites

IndonesiaNet Business Centre: http://www.indonesianet.com/

Yellow pages: http://www.yellowpages.co.id/

Iran

Creating any form of consensus among Iranians is never easy. But the tenth anniversary of the 11 September 2001 terrorist attacks in the US is generally accepted by all Iranians to have improved their country's international influence – if not its moral standing. If the attacks proved to be a catalyst, the clumsy regional response of the West was all the more so. Add to this the war in Afghanistan and the stage was set for a dramatic rise in Iran's strategic importance, both regionally through alliances with Hamas in Gaza and Hezbullah in Lebanon, as well as on a nervous world stage. From being a bit-player in the twentieth century Iran began to play a far more important part in the region's affairs in the twenty-first, to the extent that by 2011 it had become – obsessively – the top strategic priority for both the US and for Israel. Whether this obsession would ever reach boiling point and express itself militarily is a moot point. The US's experience in Iraq and Afghanistan make it look less than likely.

The Iran of 2011 is a very different body politic from that of 2001. Then it was a country still ruled by the reformist wing; President Mohamed Khatami was one of the first heads of state to convey his condolences to the US. The day after the attacks thousands of Iranians took to the streets of Tehran with candles and flowers. These mourners were from Iran's middle classes, many of whose families had relatives in the US.

Nuclear

Iran's announcement that it planned to treble its capacity to produce highly enriched uranium and move its production facility underground didn't win it too many friends. Quoted in the London *Financial Times*, Mark Fitzpatrick of the International Institute for Strategic Studies, said that 'Iran has absolutely no need for any more 20 per cent enriched uranium, since any reactors that would conceivably use it have not been built.' The French foreign ministry said that the move 'reinforces the international community's concerns over

KEY FACTS

Official name: Jomhoori e Islami e Iran (Islamic Republic of Iran)

Head of State: Supreme Leader, Grand Ayatollah Seyyed Ali Khamenei (from 4 June 1989)

Head of government: President Mahmoud Ahmadinejad (from 2005; re-elected 12 June 2009)

Ruling party: Conservative coalition, led by the Combatant Clergy Society (elected 7 May 2004)

Area: 1,648,195 square km

Population: 74.30 million (2010)

Capital: Tehran

Official language: Farsi (Persian)

Currency: Rial (IR) 10 rials = 1 toman

Exchange rate: IR10,737.50 per US$ (Oct 2011)

GDP per capita: US$4,741 (2010)

GDP real growth: 1.00% (2010)

GDP: US$357.20 billion (2010)

Unemployment: 14.60% (2010)*

Inflation: 12.50% (2010)

Oil production: 4.25 million bpd (2010)

Balance of trade: US$20.93 billion (2010)

* estimated figure

Nota

Since this article was written, on 23 January 2012 the EU announced an oil embargo on Iran from 1 July over its nuclear progamme. In retaliation Iran threatened to block the Strait of Hormuz; following the threat a US aircraft carrier, French warship and Royal Navy frigate sailed through the Strait. Israel maintains a high level of preparedness and has said it will not inform the US in advance of any attack they might make on Iran's nuclear facilities.

the intransigence of the Iranian authorities and their persistent violation of international law.' Iran's nuclear programme is seen by the US as deeply destabilisng for the region, but the United Nations agency responsible – the International Atomic Energy Agency (IAEA) – has yet formally to find the Iranian programme to be militarily oriented. What the agency has – worryingly – said is that it is unable to find the programme to be exclusively peaceful. Despite international sanctions, Tehran has long continued to enrich uranium, a process capable of making both nuclear fuel and weapons-grade material.

Stand by your man?

Students new to the subtleties of the Iranian power structure can be forgiven for struggling with its complexities. At the top of the tree, Iran's highest political authority is the Supreme Leader, currently Grand Ayatollah Seyyed Ali Khamenei. To the Supreme Leader falls the responsibility of determining foreign policy and military decisions, including those relating to the sensitive area of nuclear weapons. A number of key political and military institutions report directly to the Supreme Leader; these include the Revolutionary Guards, the Guardian Council and state broadcast media. The Supreme Leader also exerts control over the ministries of foreign affairs, defence, the interior and intelligence. So the President is not left with that much to preside over; his role is that of 'number two'; with his principal lever of power being his access to state funding. Until 2011 President Ahmadinejad had had a close relationship with Iran's Supreme Leader. He owed his elevation to the position to the Supreme Leader who, in turn, saw the maverick President as his protégé. The nature of the relationship became very clear during the violent unrest that had followed the 2009 presidential election, won by Mr Ahmadinejad after a contest that most Iranians regarded as rigged in the incumbent's favour. The Supreme Leader stood by his protégé despite mounting criticism.

The relationship between the two men began to turn sour soon after the disputed election. The Supreme Leader perceived his protégé, after six years as President, to be getting too big for his boots. After the election, the strained relationship between the two men had become an all out power struggle. At stake was the shape and direction of Iranian politics, both at home and abroad. By mid-2011 most Iranians considered the President to be losing the battle. The final straw was his decision to simply ignore an order from the Supreme Leader not to sack the intelligence minister, Heydar Moslehi. In a fit of pique after being reprimanded for his disobedience (Mr Moslehi was sacked), Mr Ahmadinejad sulked in his official residence for ten days, during which time he was not seen in public at all. In mid-2011 efforts by the President and his coterie to sideline the Supreme Leader did not seem to be gaining ground. One commentator considered that if the President's men failed to contain the Supreme Leader's influence, then they might opt for straightforward elimination – whatever that might mean. Political battles in Iran are nothing like their Western counterparts. The religious dimension is almost overwhelming, with the Ahmadinejad camp claiming not to need the Supreme Leader to communicate with the Mahdi. The traditional belief is that the Supreme Leader is the missing link until the return of the Mahdi.

Corruption charges

In any event, Mr Ahmadinejad will have to step down in 2013. In 2011 it remained to be seen whether he would do so gracefully, or – á la Putin – would endeavour to engineer a continuing role for himself and those close to him. Both the middle classes and the fundamentalists are opposed to Mr Ahmadinejad, albeit for diametrically different reasons. The fundamentalists regard the President as a would be religious leader whose aim is to found a sect based on a confused mixture of religious beliefs. The middle classes regard Ahmadinejad as simply bent on maintaining – or even increasing – his political power. As Supreme Leader, Ayatollah Khamenei, has already dealt with challenges to his authority; in the case of Mr Ahmadinejad the threat appeared manageable, not least because a number of the President's allies were already facing, or about to face, corruption charges of one kind or another.

The most serious of these charges surfaced in September 2011, alleging that an associate of the President, Amir Mansour Khosravi, had in the period of Mr Ahmadinejad's presidency become a dollar billionaire. It was rumoured that Mr Khosravi was in fact a front man for the head of the President's private office and his chief strategist, Esfandiar Rahim-Mashaei. Rumours also circulated that senior government figures, including Mr Mashaei, had formed a circle of affiliated businessmen and bankers by granting them large loans and other favours in return for election funding. Allegations also circulated claiming in more general terms that Mr Ahmadinejad's government was the most corrupt since the creation of the Islamic Republic. This was put down to Iran's massive oil revenues, which during Mr Ahmadinejad's time in the presidency had generated some US$450 billion.

In June 2011 Mr Ahmadinejad had already been referred to the judiciary for sacking Mr Masoud Mir-Kazemi, the oil minister, and effectively taking over his ministry. The President had ignored calls by parliament to appoint a caretaker oil minister. It was rumoured that Mr Ahmadinejad had sacked the oil minister because he had complained to the Supreme Leader that the President had illegally spent bonds, earmarked for oilfield development, on vote-seeking handouts to compensate needy Iranians for lower energy and food subsidies. Additionally, a

KEY INDICATORS — Iran

	Unit	2006	2007	2008	2009	2010
Population	m	70.50	*70.88	*72.87	*74.10	*74.34
Gross domestic product (GDP)	US$bn	222.13	285.90	333.20	330.50	357.20
GDP per capita	US$	3,197	3,990	4,573	4,460	4,741
GDP real growth	%	5.8	10.8	0.6	3.5	3.2
Inflation	%	11.8	18.4	25.4	10.3	12.5
Oil output	'000 bpd	4,343.0	4,401.0	4,325.0	4,216.0	4,245.0
Natural gas output	bn cum	105.0	111.9	116.3	131.2	138.5
Exports (fob) (goods)	US$m	67,682.0	*83,000.0	*116,350.0	*78,050.0	*87,534.0
Imports (fob) (goods)	US$m	49,943.0	*45,000.0	*57,230.0	*51,450.0	*66,599.0
Balance of trade	US$m	17,739.0	*38,080.0	*15,120.0	*26,600.0	*20,935.0
Current account	US$m	20,650.0	34,081.0	23,987.0	7,931.0	*21,561.0
Exchange rate	per US$	9,230.00	9,332.00	9,428.53	9,864.00	10,254.00

* estimated figure

report by the parliamentary energy committee stated that the President, in failing to appoint an oil minister at a time when Iran held the OPEC Presidency, had brought the country into disrepute.

An under-performing economy

Iran is the second largest economy in the Middle East and North Africa (MENA) in terms of gross domestic product (GDP) – US$400 billion in 2011 (after Saudi Arabia) – and in terms of population – 74.3 million people (after Egypt). It is characterised by a disproportionately large hydrocarbon sector, small scale private agriculture and services and a large state presence in manufacturing and finance. Iran ranks second in the world in natural gas reserves and third in oil reserves. Iran is the second largest OPEC oil producer; with output averaging about 4 million barrels per day (bpd) in the first decade of the 21st century. Unsurprisingly, Iran's chief source of foreign exchange comes from oil and gas. Thus, aggregate GDP and government revenues are intrinsically volatile, fluctuating with international prices of these commodities. So far, macro-economic policies have typically failed to counteract these boom and bust cycles in economic performance which increase the uncertainty faced by the private sector, impeding investment and job creation.

Despite these structural weaknesses, Iran's economy is developing into a market-based economy. However, the Iranian state still plays a key role in the economy, owning large public and quasi-public enterprises which partly dominate the manufacturing and commercial sectors. Over 60 per cent of the manufacturing sector's output is produced by state-owned enterprises; the financial sector is also dominated by public banks despite the entrance of four private banks in the early 2000s. Moreover, Iran's June 2011 Ease of Doing Business ranking (published by the World Bank) is 15 out of 18 of the MENA region. However, the authorities have adopted a comprehensive strategy as reflected in their 20-year Vision document and the 5th Five-Year Development Plan (2010/11–15/16) to ensure the implementation of market-based reforms. Economic growth increased by 3.5 per cent in 2009/10 while prudent macro-economic policies reduced inflation to about 10 per cent and ensured a fiscal surplus. The initial impact of the removal of the substantial energy and food subsidies in December 2010 did not depress Iran's economic performance, despite stricter economic sanctions. Nevertheless, growth was projected to decline to 2.5 per cent and inflation to increase to above 20 per cent due to the impact of the substantial increase in energy prices. However, tight monetary and fiscal policies are expected to bring inflation back to 12 per cent in 2012/13. The medium term outlook for economic growth is positive (around 4.5 per cent) but crucially depended on sound macro-economic management and the capacity of the corporate sector to adjust to higher energy costs.

Iran's social indicators are relatively high by regional standards. Most human development indicators have improved noticeably based on the government's efforts to increase access to education and health. Virtually all children of the relevant age group enrolled into primary schools in 2008 while enrollment into secondary schools increased from 66 per cent in 1995 to 80 per cent in 2008. As a result, youth literacy rates increased from 86 per cent to 94 per cent over the same period, rising significantly for girls. Currently, the number of Iranian women enrolled at university (at the undergraduate level) is twice as high as the number of men. Similarly, Iranian women are playing an increasingly important role in the economy, though their market participation and employment rates remain limited. Iran's health outcomes have also improved considerably over the past twenty years. The mortality rate for children under five steadily declined from 73 (per 1,000) in 1990 to 32 in 2008. Similarly, the maternal mortality ratio per 100,000 live births declined from 150 to 30 during the same period. Consequently, health indicators are usually above regional averages. This success is based on the effective delivery of primary health care, which almost balanced health care outcomes in rural and urban areas. Iran's 5th Five-Year Development Plan continues to focus on social policies.

Subsidies...

The government has launched a major reform of its indirect subsidy system, which, if successful would markedly improve the efficiency of expenditures and economic activities. The overall subsidies were estimated to cost 27 per cent of GDP in 2007/08 (approximately US$77.2 billion). According to the World Bank the government has opted for a direct cash transfer programme while substantially increasing the prices of petroleum products, water, electricity, bread and a number of other products. Iran started implementing its major subsidy reform by raising sharply the prices of energy and agricultural products in December 2010, removing close to US$60 billion dollars (about 15 per cent of GDP) in annual product subsidies. The subsidy reform is expected to increase efficiency and competitiveness of the economy, improve income distribution, reduce poverty and help Iran unlock its full growth potential. The ongoing subsidy reform has reduced poverty and regional income disparities significantly.

... and sanctions

The fourth round of international sanctions imposed on Iran in 2010 increased the cost of doing business, limited access to foreign direct investments and foreign technologies and exacerbated international trade and financial transactions. The United Nations Security Council (UNSC) sanctions include a ban on financing and exports related to Iran's nuclear and military programmes. Additional sanctions beyond those called for by the UNSC pose constraints on some international financial transactions, particularly in the euro and US dollar. In late 2011 further sanctions by the EU and UNSC were threatened after an invasion of the British embassy in Tehran was widely condemned

Growth

Economic growth rebounded from the cyclical downturn in 2008/09 to reach 3.2 per cent for the year 2010/11 (better than the projected 2.5 per cent), spurred by a recovery in agriculture production and higher oil prices. Building upon its success in reducing inflation from 25.4 per cent in 2008/09 to 12.4 per cent in 2010/11, the Bank Markazi Jomhouri Islami Iran (central bank) was able to contain inflation in the aftermath of the subsidy reform. As a result, consumer price inflation only increased from 10.1 per cent in December 2010 to 14.2 per cent at the end of May 2011. The International Monetary Fund (IMF) noted that other key macro-economic indicators continued to improve in 2010/11. The overall fiscal surplus is estimated at 1.7 per cent of GDP in 2010/11, reflecting prudent spending policies. The current account surplus increased to 6 per cent of GDP in 2010/11, in line with the recovery of oil prices. While overall money growth has remained moderate, an increase in central bank credit to banks, mainly related to the financing of subsidised housing, led to the emergence of a wide spread between the inter-bank rate and the parallel rate, as well as a rapid increase in gold coin prices. Against the backdrop of high oil prices and expected efficiency gains resulting from the domestic subsidy reform, the outlook is positive with growth expected to rebound in the medium-term. Average inflation is expected to rise in 2011/12 because of a steep increase in prices, but should come down in 2012/13 if the Iranian authorities implement sufficiently tight credit and fiscal policies. The fiscal balance and the current account surplus are both projected to improve in line with the rise in oil prices in 2011/12.

Syriana

Mid-2011 saw Iran doing its best to prop up the failing regime of Syria's Bashar al Assad, while celebrating the fall of Egypt's Hosni Mubarak. Mubarak's fall was a tactical victory for Iran, inasmuch as any likely successor would be more favourably disposed towards Iran than the fallen despot. Iran could also derive some satisfaction from the fact that President Ahmedinejad's reputation and that of his country had, according to reports in the international press, improved immeasurably in the Gulf region following the end of the Gulf War 'proper'.

In the earlier part of 2011 Iran had called upon Syria to adopt a less brutal stance towards the protest movement. Distancing itself as far as it could from the Syrian leadership, Tehran had called on Damascus at least to talk to the protestors. President Ahmadinejad had gone so far as to suggest that Damascus should enter dialogue with the protestors, saying (without so much as a tongue in its cheek) that 'a military solution is never the right solution'. Such is the importance of its relationship with Damascus that any dilution would be perceived as a diminution of Iran's regional power and authority. Syria's ruling Alawi minority is Shi'a rather than Sunni, hence the strength of its links with Shi'a Iran. Elsewhere, Iran's client state by design, Bahrain, reflected similar Sunni-Shia imbalances as a Sunni monarchy endeavoured to bottle up the dissent spilling over from its Shi'a majority.

Iran has long been Syria's main strategic ally in the Middle East. The nature of that alliance began to change in the second half of 2011 as it became clear to Tehran that it needed to tread carefully if it was to keep its reputation as the champion of the region's oppressed and dispossessed. Were the Syrian regime to be toppled and replace with one less well disposed towards Tehran, it would be perceived as a major strategic defeat for Iran. Given Syria's sectarian structure and the fact that the minority ruling Alawites are themselves an offshoot of Shi'a Islam, it is unlikely that a Sunni Syrian government would wish to be on quite the same cosy terms with Iran. Mr Ahmadinejad had welcomed the Arab Spring simply because it represented a challenge to the region's Sunni governments. In Syria the same logic did not apply. The Syrian uprising did not fit comfortably into any pattern that Tehran could easily fit into. The Syrian protestors' anger was often directed at Iran and its Hizbollah offshoot.

Oil

According to the US based *Oil and Gas Journal* (OGJ), in January 2011, Iran had an estimated 137.6 billion barrels of oil reserves, roughly 10 per cent of the world's total. The US Government Energy Information Administration (EIA) reports that Iran has 40 producing fields (27 onshore and 13 offshore) with the majority of crude oil reserves located in the south-western Khuzestan region near the Iraqi border. Iran's crude oil is generally medium in sulfur content and in the 28°–35° API range. In 2009/10 Iran exported about 2.3 million bpd of oil (slightly down on the 2.4 million bpd in 2008), primarily to Asia and Organisation for Economic Co-operation and Development (OECD) Europe countries, making it the fourth largest exporter in the world.

The state-owned National Iranian Oil Company (NIOC) under the supervision of the Ministry of Petroleum, is responsible for oil and natural gas production and exploration. The National Iranian South Oil Company (NISOC), a subsidiary of NIOC, accounts for 80 per cent of oil production covering the provinces of Khuzestan, Bushehr, Fars and Kohkiluyeh and BoyerAhamd. Though private ownership of upstream functions is prohibited under the Iranian constitution, the government permits buyback contracts which allow international oil companies (IOCs) to enter into exploration and development contracts through an Iranian affiliate. The contractor receives a remuneration fee, usually an entitlement to oil or gas from the developed operation. Iran is OPEC's second-largest producer after Saudi Arabia. In 2010, Iran produced approximately 4.2 million barrels of oil per day (bpd) of total liquids, of which roughly 3.9 million bpd was crude oil, equal to about 5 per cent of global production. For most of 2009, it is estimated that Iran's crude production was approximately 3.8 million bpd, almost 500,000bpd above Iran's estimated 3.3 million bpd OPEC quota. Iran's 2009 crude oil production capacity was estimated to be 3.9 million bpd. Iran produced over 5 million bpd of oil in 1978, but since the 1979 revolution a combination of war, limited investment, sanctions and a high rate of natural decline in Iran's mature oil fields have prevented a return to such production levels. Iran's fields have a natural annual decline rate estimated at 8 per cent onshore and 11 per cent offshore, with recovery rates at 20–25 per cent. An estimated 400,000–700,000bpd of crude production is lost annually due to declines in the mature oil fields. To offset natural decline rates, Iran's oil fields require structural upgrades including enhanced oil recovery efforts such as natural gas injection.

Iran's oil consumption was approximately 1.8 million bpd in 2010. Iran has limited refinery capacity for the production of light fuels and consequently imports a sizeable share of its gasoline supply. Iranian domestic oil demand is mainly for diesel and gasoline. According to FACTS Global Energy, diesel consumption was roughly 570,000bpd in 2008, nearly 90 per cent of which was produced domestically. Domestic demand for other oil products is declining as natural gas is further integrated into Iran's energy consumption makeup. The Iranian government has subsidised the price of refined oil products over the years, but in January 2010 the Guardian Council approved measures with the aim of eliminating energy subsidies by 2015; an number of these reforms were put in place in December 2010. However, Iran is an overall net petroleum products exporter due to large exports of residual fuel oil.

Iran's total refinery capacity in 2010 was about 1.8 million bpd, with its nine refineries operated by the National Iranian Oil Refining and Distribution Company (NIORDC), another NIOC subsidiary. Iranian refineries are unable to keep pace with domestic demand, but Iran plans to increase refining capacity to around 3 million bpd by 2013. Increases through expansions at existing refineries as well as planned grass-root refinery construction could eliminate the need for imports by 2013. In addition, Iran has discussed joint ventures in Asia, including China, Indonesia, Malaysia and Singapore to expand refining capacity.

Natural gas

According to the OGJ, in January 2011 Iran's estimated natural gas reserves stand at 1,045 trillion cubic feet (tcf), second only to Russia. Over two-thirds of Iranian natural gas reserves are located in non-associated fields and have not yet been developed. Major natural gas fields include South and North Pars, Kish and Kangan-Nar. In 2010 Iran produced an estimated 138.5 billion cubic metres (bcm) of natural gas and consumed an estimated 136.9bcm. Natural gas consumption is expected to grow by around 7 per cent annually for the next decade. Both production and consumption have grown rapidly over the past 20 years and natural gas is often used for re-injection into mature oilfields in Iran. According to FACTS Global Energy, Iran's natural gas exports will be minimal due to rising domestic demand even with future expansion and production from the massive South Pars project.

The National Iranian Gas Company (NIGC) is responsible for natural gas infrastructure, transportation and distribution. Due to the poor investment climate, some international oil companies including Repsol, Shell and Total have divested from Iran's natural gas sector. In response, Iran has looked toward eastern firms, like state-owned Indian Oil Corporation, China Petroleum & Chemical Corporation and Russia's Gazprom to take an increased role in Iranian natural gas upstream development. Under Iran's buy-back scheme, foreign firms hand over operations of fields to the NIOC and after development they receive payment from natural gas production to cover their investment. NISOC is responsible for much of the southern natural gas production.

The most significant energy development project in Iran is the offshore South Pars field (known as the 'North Field' in Qatar), which is estimated to have 450tcf of natural gas reserves, or around 47 per cent of Iran's total natural gas reserves. Discovered in 1990 and located 62 miles offshore in the Persian Gulf, South Pars has a 25 phase development scheme spanning 20 years. The entire project is managed by Pars Oil & Gas Company also a subsidiary of the NIOC. The majority of South Pars natural gas development will be allocated to the domestic market for consumption and gas re-injection. The remainder will either be exported to South Asia or Europe, used for LNG production and/or used for gas to liquids (GTL) projects. Iran's annual LNG exports may peak around 1,462bcf once all projects are complete. LNG projects in Iran lag behind neighbouring Qatar, the world's largest LNG exporter.

Oman and Iran signed an agreement in 2008 to develop Iran's huge offshore Kish field. With estimated reserves of 50tcf, Oman will invest US$7 billion in developing Kish in the hopes of producing 3bcf/d of natural gas. Phase I of the project, tentatively scheduled for first delivery to Oman by 2013, will produce approximately 2bcf/d; 65 per cent of production will remain in Iran, the remaining 35 per cent goes to Oman. Phase II of the project will produce 1bcf/d to be used for Iranian purposes.

Risk assessment

Economy	Fair
Politics	Poor
Regional stability	Poor

COUNTRY PROFILE

Historical profile

1907 A constitution was introduced, limiting the royal absolutism of the ruler. An Anglo-Russian agreement (annulled after the First World War) divided Iran into spheres of influence, one Soviet and the other British.

1909–13 Following the discovery of a large oil field in Masjet Soleiman, the Anglo-Persian Oil Company (APOC) was founded in 1909. A licence to search for, refine, produce and export oil was granted to APOC in 1913.

1921–26 A Cossack officer, Reza Khan, carried out a military coup, becoming prime minister in 1923. Parliament subsequently proclaimed him the Shah, to be called Reza Shah Pahlavi, ushering in the Pahlavi era. His eldest son, Mohammed Reza was proclaimed crown prince.

1935 Persia was renamed Iran. APOC changed its name to the Anglo-Iranian Oil Company (AIOC); it was a British enterprise, owned jointly by the private sector and the British government. Later, the company was renamed British Petroleum (BP).

1941 In the Second World War, after Reza Shah demonstrated allegiance to Germany, the British and Soviets entered Iran and removed him from power. They permitted his son, Mohammad Reza Shah Pahlavi, to succeed to the throne.

1949 The power of the Shah was increased following an attempted assassination by the Tudeh communist party, which was then banned.

1950 Mohammed Mosaddeq, a leading advocate of oil nationalisation, was installed as prime minister, following the assassination of his predecessor.

1951 Iran's Assembly approved the nationalisation of the oil industry, which was formerly controlled by Britain. As a result, Britain boycotted the purchase of Iranian oil. A contest for control of the government began between the young Shah and the nationalistic Mosaddeq.

1953–54 Mainly due to oil interests, the British persuaded the US to help the Shah remove Mosaddeq. Large sectors of Iranian public opinion condemned the US and Britain for this coup and Mosaddeq became a folk hero of Iranian nationalism. Drilling concessions were granted to eight foreign oil companies.

1963 The Shah assumed complete control of the government and launched a programme of land reform and social and economic modernisation. He used the Secret Police (Savak) to control opposition to his reforms.

1978 Following several years of growing opposition to the Shah's rule, martial law was imposed.

1979 The Shah was overthrown by forces loyal to the exiled religious leader, Ayatollah Khomeini, who became *Valy e Faqih* (supreme spiritual leader) of Iran. The Shah and his family were forced into exile. The Islamic Republic of Iran was proclaimed following a referendum. Fifty-two staff members at the US Embassy in Tehran were taken hostage by Islamic militants, who demanded the extradition of the Shah from the US, where he was having medical treatment.

1980 Abolhassan Beni Sadr was elected president. The former shah died of cancer.

1980–88 The Iran-Iraq War broke out after Iraq invaded Iran over disputed border areas.

1981 The US Embassy hostages in Tehran were released.

1989 After Ayatollah Khomeini's death, Grand Ayatollah Seyyed Ali Khamenei was sworn in as Supreme Leader (Head of State).

1990 A peace agreement with Iraq was signed.

1995 Oil and trade sanctions were imposed by the US, which alleged that Iran had sponsored terrorist groups throughout the region, had sought to acquire nuclear arms and destabilised the Middle East peace process.

1996 The Combatant Clergy Society (CCS) remained the largest single political group in parliament.

1997 Moderate cleric Mohammad Khatami, was elected president.

2000 Elections to an expanded Majlis returned a majority for reformist candidates. Ayatollah Ali Khamenei halted a bill that would have revived Iran's banned reformist newspapers. The Oil Stabilisation Fund (OSF) was established, to use money accumulated when oil prices rise above a set level, to level out fluctuations in prices and to promote the private sector.

2001 President Khatami was re-elected for a second term. Saudi Arabia and Iran signed a security accord to combat terrorism, drug trafficking and organised crime.

2002 Iran released nearly 700 Iraqi prisoners held since the 1980–88 war.

President Bush included Iran in an 'axis of evil' due to its supposed development of weapons of mass destruction (WMD). Iran began construction of its first nuclear reactor.
2003 Parliament passed a bill guaranteeing free parliamentary elections. Iran came under pressure from the International Atomic Energy Agency (IAEA) over its nuclear energy programme. Subsequent IAEA inspections concluded there was no evidence of a weapons programme. A major earthquake hit the city of Bam in the southeast, killing 40,000 people and leaving the city in ruins.
2004 Over a third of parliament resigned after the Council of Guardians upheld the disqualification of more than 2,000 prospective reformist candidates hoping to stand in parliamentary elections, which were won by conservative candidates.
2005 Three villages were destroyed and 40 badly damaged when an earthquake struck central Iran. Mahmoud Ahmadinejad was elected president. He caused international concern when he suggested that Israel should be 'wiped off the map'.
2006 The UN Security Council voted to impose sanctions over Iran's refusal to stop uranium enrichment.
2007 The state-owned Bank Sepah was blacklisted by the US, accused of being the 'financial lynchpin' in Iran's efforts to procure material for its missile programme.
2008 President Ahmadinejad visited Iraq, the first visit by a president since the Iran/Iraq war in the 1980s. In parliamentary elections, candidates with a conservative affiliation won most seats. Iran test-fired nine missiles, including Shahab 3, which, with a range of over 2,000 kilometres, could reach Israel. The French oil company Total announced it would not be investing in Iran because the political situation was too risky. The company had been considering an investment in developing gas fields in the south of the country. Traders in Tehran's bazaar shut down for a month in protest at a new value added tax; traders in Isfahan, Mashad and Tabriz also shut down.
2009 Iran's first domestically produced telecommunications satellite was launched. Mahmoud Ahmadinejad won the presidential elections. There were immediate claims of vote rigging by opposition candidates but Iran's Supreme Leader Ayatollah Ali Khamenei endorsed the result and urged the defeated rivals against 'provocations'. Days of violence on the streets of Tehran followed, the Supreme Leader eventually ordered an inquiry into claims of vote rigging. However the Guardian Council, the top judicial body in Iran, confirmed Ahmadinejad as president. The government announced that there had been another successful test-fire of the Shahab-3 missile, at the same time as international condemnation was growing of Iran's nuclear programme, including the (suspected) enrichment of low-grade uranium into weapons-grade uranium. The government agreed to allow inspectors of the IAEA to visit its nuclear sites and to join negotiations with the six major nuclear powers (US, Russia, China, UK, France and Germany) concerning its nuclear programme. IAEA inspectors were allowed to view the, until recently secret, nuclear facility before inspecting the known site, near the holy city of Qom.
2010 In June, the highest denomination bank note was raised to IR100,000 (US$10). In June the UN Security Council voted to impose further sanctions against Iran, for its lack of compliance with earlier UN resolutions to ensure the peaceful nature of Iran's nuclear programme. To begin electricity generation, nuclear fuel rods were scheduled to be injected into the nuclear power plant of Bushehr in September. Foreign minister Manouchehr Mottaki was sacked by President Ahmadinejad in December while on an official visit to Senegal. Top nuclear official, Ali Akbar Salehi, was appointed as a temporary replacement. The government cut food and fuel subsidies in December as spending on such subsidies was put at around US$100 billion.
2011 Ali Reza Pahlavi, the younger son of the last Shah of Iran, committed suicide on 4 January. His sister Leila had also committed suicide, in 2001. Akbar Hashemi Rafsanjani was replaced as head of the Assembly of Experts by Ayatollah Mohammad Reza Mahdavi Kani. On 17 April intelligence minister Heydar Moslehi resigned unexpectedly. Although his resignation was accepted by President Ahmadinejed, he was rapidly reinstated by Ayatollah Ali Khamenei, (the highest authority in state affairs). In May Ahmadinejed declared himself 'acting' oil minister but said he would not attend the June Opec meeting in Vienna, even though Iran held the rotating chairmanship. Ahmadinejed supporter, Mohammad Sharif Malekzadeh, quit as deputy foreign minister three days after he took office. He was arrested a few days later, accused of corruption. The Iranian oil bourse, the Kish International Commodity Exchange, was officially launched on 13 July, with 600,000 barrels of heavy crude oil for sale. The opening ended the government's complete control of the country's oil trade. On 8 November the IAEA published its quarterly report that stated Iran appeared to be on a 'structured programme', which included computer models exclusively used to develop a trigger for a nuclear bomb. Iran rejected the report as 'unbalanced, unprofessional with political motivation...' The UK suspended all banking transactions with Iran on 21 November as part of a series of international sanctions; on 24 November France announced that it would no longer buy Iranian oil on a 'national basis', which typically amounts to 49,000 barrels per year. On 29 November, the British embassy in Tehran and a British diplomatic compound in northern Tehran were stormed by hundreds of protestors, angry at British sanctions against Iran. All UK diplomatic staff and their families were evacuated on 30 November; all Iranian embassy staff in London were told to quit the UK within 48 hours. The foreign minister called the UK action 'hasty' and that appropriate action would be taken against the protestors.

Political structure

Constitution

Iran became an Islamic Republic in April 1979, having previously been a monarchy under the Shah. The constitution of the Islamic Republic was formally adopted in December 1979. The constitution also provides for representation in the Majlis Shura-e-Islami (Islamic Consultative Assembly) of non-Islamic minorities, Zoroastrians, Jews and Christians. However, power is wielded mainly by the Shi'a clergy.

Form of state

Islamic republic

The executive

The Wali Faqih (Supreme Leader of the Islamic Revolution) retains overall control of all branches of government, including the judiciary and the revolutionary guard. He declares war and peace and can veto presidential nominations. His role combines spiritual leader, theological protector and supreme authority. The structure of the constitution is effectively split between the president, who is elected every four years, and the Supreme Leader, who has overall control. The Supreme Leader, in his role as theological protector, appoints the Council for the Protection of the Constitution. All legislation adopted by the Majlis Shura-e-Islami is scrutinised by the council to ensure that it is in keeping with Islamic principles and laws. The council consists of six religious lawyers. The Council of Guardians, composed of 12 jurists and clerics, has supervisory powers over elections and a right of veto over all legislation if it does not conform with Islamic law and the constitution. It is independent of the Supreme Leader.
In 1986, the Expediency Council was established to mediate between the Majlis and the Council of Guardians. It is designed to

resolve political decisions which cannot be solved through the main channels, but it is controlled by the spiritual leader.
A further adjunct to the Supreme Leader's power is the Assembly of Experts which consists of 83 clerics who elect the next Supreme Leader, interpret the constitution and approve Majlis decisions. The cumulative effect of this plethora of legislative institutions is that despite the enhancement of the president's power, following reform in 1989, he remains tightly constrained by these institutional checks and balances.

National legislature
The unicameral Majlis Shura e Islami (Islamic Consultative Assembly) has 290 members, elected for four-year terms. Although members of parliament are technically independent, the Majlis is now very loosely divided along party political lines between the conservative clergy groupings and reformists. The Majlis is elected by universal suffrage, with a voting age of 15.
The Majles e Khobregan (Assembly of Experts) is a body of 86 Islamic scholars who deliberate the election and dismissal of the Supreme Leader of Iran and supervise his activities. Members are popularly and directly elected from a government approved list, for eight-year terms in office.

Legal system
The judiciary is organised independently of the other branches of government. There are two types of courts: public and special. The Penal Courts, Special Civil Court and Islamic Revolution Courts adjudicate on the basis of Islamic laws, fixed since 1979 for a wide range of crimes.

Last elections
12 June 2009 (presidential); 16 March 2008 (parliamentary).
Results: Presidential: Mahmoud Ahmadinejad won 63.3 per cent of the vote, Hossein Moussavi 34.1 per cent, Mohsen Rezai 1.7 per cent and Mehdi Karroubi 0.9 per cent; turnout was 85 per cent.
Parliamentary: candidates with a conservative affiliation won most seats.

Next elections
2012 (parliamentary); June 2013 (presidential).

Political parties

Ruling party
Conservative coalition, led by the Combatant Clergy Society (elected 7 May 2004)

Main opposition party
May 23 Front, of which the largest grouping is the Mosharekat (Participation) Front

Population

74.30 million (2010)
Last census: 28 October 2006: 70,495,782
Population density: 65 per cent (1995–2001).
Annual growth rate: 1.2 per cent 1994–2004 (WHO 2006)

Ethnic make-up
The population is predominantly Persian (55 per cent), with the second largest group being Azeris, concentrated in the north-west. There are also Afghans (approximately two million Afghan refugees were repatriated by the UN refugee organisation in 2002), Kurds, Baluchis, Lurs, Turkmen, Arabs and nomads.

Religions
Islam of the Twelver Shi'a sect is dominant. A Sunni Muslim minority is concentrated in fringe areas of Iran. There are also small Baha'i, Christian, Jewish and Zoroastran communities.

Education

Education is compulsory for eight years from the ages of six. This is not fully effective in rural areas. Primary education is free and lasts for five years. Secondary education begins at 11 years and lasts for up to seven years, with a first course of three years and a second course of four years.
Secondary education is split between intermediate (or 'guidance') schools and secondary schools. There are also technical, business and other specialised vocational schools.
Iran has 116 higher education institutes, 23 of which are full universities. Enrolment in the universities accounts for 68 per cent of Iran's 123,000 students, with the remainder enrolled in other institutes of higher education. Secondary education (Reform system) covers three years and a one-year pre-university programme.
Higher education is provided by comprehensive universities, specialised universities, universities of technology, medical universities, teacher training centres and private institutions. The Islamic Open University was established in 1981. It has around 100,000 students in 70 Iranian cities and towns. In addition, there are 131 teacher-training colleges, 107 teacher colleges for rural areas, 10 colleges for technical and vocational teachers, and 19 institutes of technology.
Education became a state monopoly following the 1979 Revolution, but a law passed in 1987 provided for the creation of private schools under certain conditions. To keep pace with population growth, 10,000 new university educated teachers are required each year.
Literacy rate: 78.1 per cent total; 71.4 per cent female, adult rates in 2002 (World Bank).
Compulsory years: 6 to 14.
Enrolment rate: 98 per cent total primary enrolment of relevant age group; 77 per cent total secondary enrolment (World Bank).
Pupils per teacher: 30 in primary schools.

Health

The combined ministry of hygiene, medical care and education is the authority responsible for health and medical care, controlling all related offices and organisations in the private sector as well as those directly funded by the state. The Social Security Organisation (SSO) offers health insurance and runs 60 hospitals, 260 clinics and 30 medical record registration offices in the country.
Iran has adequate healthcare facilities in the cities, although it is generally insufficient in rural areas. The government has, however, created a large number of health clinics in small towns, as well as in villages, to serve the population of the surrounding area. The ministry has undertaken a national hygiene campaign by setting up 'hygiene houses' in many villages and towns.
Drug abuse is a serious problem in Iran, due to imports of cheap heroin and opium from Afghanistan, and there are an estimated two million drug addicts.

HIV/Aids
Intravenous drug users in Iranian prisons accounted for 65 per cent of HIV infections in the country. A programme has been implemented, by non-governmental agencies, working to reduce the harm of HIV/Aids among this group.
HIV prevalence: 0.1 per cent aged 15–49 in 2003 (World Bank)
Life expectancy: 70 years, 2004 (WHO 2006)
Fertility rate/Maternal mortality rate: 2.1 births per woman, 2004 (WHO 2006); maternal mortality 30 deaths per 100,000 live births (2008) (World Bank).
Child (under 5 years) mortality rate (per 1,000): 32 per 1,000 live births (2008); 11 per cent of children aged under five are malnourished (World Bank).
Head of population per physician: 0.45 physicians per 1,000 people, 2004 (WHO 2006)

Welfare

A large number of organisations, usually autonomous, are responsible for social welfare. Various foundations manage sequestered property worth billions of US dollars. They are responsible for the care of families of men killed in the war with Iraq, for war refugees and for rural development. At the local level in the cities and towns, mosque committees (*komitehs*) have funds, which are made available for poorer families. The country's rationing system, that includes giving coupons for limited quantities of staple foods and other items at heavily subsidised prices, is also run through mosques.

Iran's Social Security Organisation (SSO) provides a list of services, including survivor's pension, subsidies to large families, retirement, unemployment and disability benefits.

The social security scheme covers some 260,000 factories, workshops and offices.

The Foundation for the Refugees of the Imposed War operates under the authority of Iran's ministry of labour and social affairs. It is responsible for the welfare of over two million of the country's internal refugees, or displaced persons, from the Iran-Iraq war.

Main cities

Tehran (capital, estimated population 7.5 million (m) in 2005), Mashhad (2.3m), Esfahan (1.5m), Tabriz (1.2m), Shiraz (1.2m), Karaj (2.5m), Ahvaz (1.0m).

Media

The government maintains strict control of the media and imposes censorship, particularly of material with Western influence and any divergence from religious regulations. In 2007 the US-based human right's watchdog, Freedom House, rated Iran as 'not free', with one of the lowest scores worldwide, as all publications must be licensed and can be subject to closure, with criminal penalties for journalists for reporting 'propaganda against the state' and the intimidation of publishers, editors and journalist has included detaining, fines and in some cases torture.

Press

There are a large number of daily and weekly newspapers, which had a wide range of political stances; however since 2006 the government began a crack down on reformist publications. Newspapers are challenged by a falling readership, the small advertising market and the shortage of imported and locally produced paper.

Dailies: In Farsi, the main conservative newspapers include *Kayhan* (www.kayhannews.ir) the oldest and run by the office of the supreme leader, *Resalat* (www.resalat-news.com), favours a market economy, and *Jomhouri Eslami* (www.jomhourieslami.com), is linked to Ayatollah Ali Khamene'i with radical views on foreign policies. *Jaam e Jam* (www.jamejamonline.ir), has the largest circulation and is published by IRIB. Reformist newspapers include *Etemaad* (www.etemaad.com) and *Aftab e Yazd* (www.aftab-yazd.com). In English, *Iran News* (www.irannewsdaily.com), the *Tehran Times* (www.tehrantimes.com), is government-run, *Iran Daily* (www.iran-daily.com), is published by IRNA.

Weeklies: Magazines tend to be special interest publications. In Farsi, the *Chelcheragh* (www.40cheragh.org) is a social magazine and *Gozaresh* (www.gozaresh.com), covers computers and technology.

Periodicals: The quarterly *Azari Majedi* (www.azarmajedi.com) in Farsi, English and French, for articles on culture, the monthly *Donya e Bazi* (www.dbazi.com) covers computer games.

Broadcasting

The national public broadcaster is the Islamic Republic of Iran Broadcaster (IRIB) (www.irib.ir).

Radio: The state-run IRIB (www.irib.ir) has eight national networks with provincial services and an external service that broadcasts in 27 languages.

Television: Around 80 per cent of the population watch TV, with the youth TV having the largest audience. The state-run IRIB (www.irib.ir) has four national networks with provincial services, plus an international channel and three satellite channels. IRIB also has a motion picture production company, Sima Film. In 2007, an alternative, state-run TV network, Press TV (www.presstv.com), based in Tehran, with 24-hour news was introduced.

News agencies

National news agency: IRNA (Islamic Republic News Agency): www2.irna.ir

Other news agencies: IRIB: www.irib.ir
Iranian Students News Agency (ISNA): http://isna.ir
Press TV: www.presstv.com

Economy

Hydrocarbon exports are the mainstay of Iran's economy, accounting for around 25 per cent of GDP and 20 per cent of government revenue; it has the world's second largest reserves of oil, with production at over 4.3 million barrels per day (bpd). However, Iran's oil sector is severely hampered by its inability to increase production due to insufficient investment as a result of sanctions imposed by the UN. The economy as a whole registered a healthy GDP growth of 10.8 per cent in 2007, but this fell sharply in 2008 to 0.6 per cent before recovering in 2009 to register 3.5 per cent, which remained almost constant through 2010 with 3.2 per cent; the forecast rate for 2011 was 2.5 per cent.

Inflation has been a long-term problem for Iran, with an average yearly rate above 10 per cent since 2000, but reaching 25.4 per cent in 2008 due to an expansionary credit policy and fiscal stimulus. The medium-term forecast is for the consumer price index (CPI) to fall to around 15 per cent by 2011/12. In response the government indicated that it would focus on reducing expenditure growth and press banks not to lend to low-priority sectors. Subsidies on fuel and other items may be reduced, public administration will be streamlined and tax collection improved.

In 2006, the government, in retaliation to US pressure over Iran's nuclear development plans, announced that it would no longer trade its oil for US dollars but instead shift its foreign currency reserves to the euro. On-going international sanctions against a number of Iranian institutions have resulted in difficulties in trading and profitability of some financial entities and discouraged foreign investment. In 2009 the Norwegian state owned oil company, Statoil, announced it would no longer reinvest in Iran.

The ability of the Central Bank of Iran (CBI) to influence monetary policy decisions was curtailed in 2008 as the policy board which oversaw monetary and credit supply was integrated into the government's supreme council for economic management and planning. The government had planned to introduce a value added tax (VAT) in 2008, beginning at 3 per cent. However after days of political protests the president announced he would delay the VAT introduction until 2009/10. Months of opposition to VAT force a delay, but it was finally introduced in March 2011, at 4 per cent.

The economy is protected by high external tariffs, price controls and subsidies. The International Monetary Fund (IMF) advised, in 2008, that large state-owned banks and private smaller banks would have to be recapitalised and banking procedures aligned to World Trade Organisation (WTO) standards if Iran is to become integrated with the global banking sector. Anti-money laundering regulations were introduced in January 2008, but the IMF still regards the law as deficient in some aspects which will need detailed regulations.

Political and religious charities, *bonyads*, established at the founding of the Iranian Islamic state and that had appropriated assets of the former Shah to be used to provide welfare payments to disadvantaged groups in society, have evolved into huge private monopolies, which have no governmental oversight of their operations but contribute to the ideological and cultural needs of the Islamic state. They dominate the economy, particularly the non-oil sector. They are allocated around two-thirds of the budget each year and own or control all the country's transport, oil, petrochemical and mining companies.

The service sector accounts for 46 per cent of GDP, with industry 17 per cent and agriculture 10 per cent. Iran has to find employment for around 750,000 new

workers each year and unemployment consistently averages over 10 per cent. Among the noteworthy export products that do not belong to the petrochemical industry are highly prized carpets and motor vehicles. Pistachio nuts account for around 8 per cent of non-oil GDP with exports of over 200 tonnes per year.
The highest denomination bank note was raised to IR100,000 (US$10) in June 2010, due to inflation of 10 per cent (falling from a high of 29 per cent in 2008), with around 150 million bank notes being printed for distribution by September.

External trade

Iran belongs to the Economic Co-operation Organisation (ECO), with seven central Asia countries with Turkey and Pakistan. The ECO has plans to create a free trade zone. Iran also has bilateral trade agreements with, among others, Venezuela, Cuba, Iraq and South Africa.
Oil accounts for around 60 per cent of GDP and 80 per cent of export revenues. Shortages of foreign currency have produced a boom in counter (barter) trade, which obscures the extent of foreign trade.

Imports

Main imports include industrial raw materials (iron and steel) and intermediate goods, electrical and electronic equipment, foodstuffs and other consumer goods, technical services and military supplies.
Main sources: United Arab Emirates (typically over 20 per cent of total), Germany (10 per cent), China (7 per cent), France, South Korea and Switzerland (5 per cent), India (3 per cent).

Exports

Crude oil, petroleum products; non-oil items, include iron and steel, organic chemicals, carpets, pistachio nuts, dates and caviar.
Iran and Pakistan signed a deal to build a US$7.5 billion gas pipeline in 2008 and in May 2009 signed a trade agreement for an initial 30 million cubic metres per day of Iranian natural gas (increasing to 60 million cum) to by transferred to Pakistan.
Main destinations: Japan (typically over 20 per cent total), other Gulf states 25 per cent (non-hydrocarbons), China (8 per cent) India and Italy (5 per cent).

Agriculture

Since the 1979 revolution, land ownership has been in dispute. Meanwhile, people have moved from the countryside to the city. This has left a shortage of agricultural labour, despite high unemployment in the economy as a whole. On many farms, particularly those in the private sector near Tehran, immigrant Afghan workers have replaced Iranians.
Since it was set up in the 1980s, the Bonyad-e Mostazafin (Foundation for the Oppressed and Deprived) has brought new facilities, especially water, electricity and roads, to thousands of rural villages.
Government efforts to stimulate sluggish private investment in agriculture have made little headway. As half of Iran's farmers belong to 3,000 rural co-operatives, grouped into 180 unions and benefiting from cheap credit made available by the state, they are reluctant to embrace private sector competition.
The government wants to reduce the import bill for food and agricultural inputs. Iran imports large quantities of meat, rice, vegetables, oil, sugar and tea, as well as cattle fodder, fertilisers, machinery and tractors. It is encouraging the expansion of cotton and sugar cane plantations, livestock production and downstream processing industries for these products.

Fishing

There are few river systems in Iran, and most freshwater fishing is for subsistence purposes. There is commercial fishing on the Persian Gulf and the Caspian Sea. Iran produces around 444,000 tonnes of seafood per year. Main species are sturgeon, tuna, mackerel, shrimps, lobsters and crayfish. Iran produces around 90 per cent of the world's caviar. Fish farming is an increasingly important activity.

Forestry

There is some forestation in the north of the country, near the Caspian Sea, but limited commercial exploitation is generally for domestic purposes only.

Industry and manufacturing

The government's goal in the past has been to build up basic industries as a means of import substitution and to develop a broad industrial base to reduce reliance on oil. The government has also given priority to the development of downstream industries in the oil and gas sectors and to the development of mining and metals processing.
Tehran and Isfahan are the main industrial centres. The largest industrial conglomerate is the National Iranian Industries Organisation (NIIO), a state-owned group which is directly responsible for 90 companies in manufacturing, engineering and trading. The NIIO companies are in nine industrial groups: textiles and leather, chemicals, pharmaceuticals, food, electrical goods, construction and cellulose.

Tourism

Iran's potential as a major tourist destination has been impeded by inadequate accommodation standards and travel restrictions, as well as a generally poor image abroad.

Environment

Tehran is susceptable to severe air polution as the population has greatly increased and there is a growing number of cars on the roads – many of them old. The city is wedged between mountains, meaning dirty air can get trapped when there is no wind or rain.

Mining

Iran is one of the world's 15 major mineral-rich countries and the mining sector employs directly over 107,000 workers. Production has a market value of over US$4 billion. The government is trying to encourage private investment in mineral exploration and production.
The majority of the large-scale mines and major industries, including steelworks, copper, lead and zinc, are partially or totally state-owned. The government has sought to develop the country's abundant mineral resources as an alternative to oil- and gas-based industrial development. However, as in other sectors, expansion of mineral production has suffered from shortages of foreign currency for machinery and spare parts, power cuts, and the lack of mining experts. Consequently, Iran is still obliged to import many raw materials, which it could produce from its own resources, given appropriate investment and manpower skills.
The Iranian government has strongly encouraged foreign investment on 'buy-back' terms that enables foreign investors to recoup capital through receipt of the project's output. Substantial improvement is targetted for the non-ferrous metals sector including aluminium, copper and zinc. Iran has 60 lead and zinc mines, 30 coal mines, 20 copper mines and 40 deposits of chromite, fluorene and sulphur. It also has an important industrial mineral sector, and is the third largest producer of gypsum in the world.

Hydrocarbons

Proven oil reserves were 137.0 billion barrels 2010, which was around 10 per cent of the world's total petroleum reserves. Production in 2010 was 4.2 million barrels per day (bpd), a riseof 0.9 per cent from 4.1 million bpd. Although a new oil and gas field was discovered in 2009, in the Khorramabad block, in western Iran, with an estimated proven natural gas reserves to increased to 26.8 trillion cum (second only to Russia's gas reserves) the industry is still faced with maturing oil fields, limited investment and international sanctions imposed on the country.
Oil consumption is around 1.8 million bpd but mainly in light fuels, petrol and diesel. Iran increased its refining capacity to 1.86 million bpd in 2009, necessary to satisfy its domestic requirements.

Iran was a founding member of the Organisation of the Petroleum Exporting Countries (Opec) and is its second largest exporter (after Saudi Arabia). The Ministry of Petroleum has responsibility for oil and natural gas exploration and production through the state-owned National Iranian Oil Company (NIOC). International oil companies are involved in developing Iran's oil fields on a buyback basis, which entails the contractor funding all investment in return for an allocated production share from NIOC. The operation of the oil field is transferred to the NIOC once the contract is completed.

In the downstream sector, the government's strategy is to develop petrochemicals as part of a plan to add value to hydrocarbon exports; it is encouraging foreign investment into the industry.

Proven gas reserves were 29.6 trillion cubic metres in 2010, the world's second largest natural gas reserves (after Russia). Production was 138.5 billion cubic metres (cum), an increase of 5.6 per cent on the 2009 figure. Around 60 per cent of all reserves are undeveloped. Consumption was 136.9 billion cum in 2010, and shows a steady growth from 47 billion in 1997. The government is keen to expand export markets, particularly in Asia. The massive South Pars gas field, which is shared with Qatar, is being developed in 25 stages over 25 years.

Production of coal is less than one million tonnes per year (tpy) but with consumption at approximately 1.6 million tpy imports complete the supply. In 2009, Iran's first mechanised underground coal mine at Tabas was inaugurated. It is expected to produce around 1.5 million tonnes of coking coal for steel production each year.

Energy

Total installed generating capacity is 42.7GW; 98 per cent is produced by thermal power stations of which natural gas accounts for 53 per cent and oil 45 per cent; hydroelectricity makes up 2 per cent of the energy mix and coal 1 per cent. Iran's demand is growing rapidly at 7–9 per cent per annum and this will require a doubling of electricity generating capacity by 2012.

In February 2009 test runs on Iran's first nuclear power plant near the Iranian port of Bushehr began. The 1,000kw plant is expected to be operational by August. Since 2001 when Russia agreed to help develop this reactor the US has raised strong objections over the development of nuclear power in Iran, claiming that the technology will be used for military purposes and the construction of nuclear warheads. The Iranian government insists the Bushehr reactors are for domestic energy consumption and says it has stood by the terms of the Nuclear Non-Proliferation Treaty, of which it is a signatory.

Financial markets

Stock exchange

Tehran Stock Exchange (TSE)

Commodity exchange

Kish International Commodity Exchange

Banking and insurance

Before the revolution, Iran's banking system was handicapped by the small number of banks, by heavy indebtedness (both to the central bank and to foreign creditors) and by the high levels of non-performing assets, a legacy of the virtual absence of regulatory controls under the Shah's regime. After the reorganisation in 1979, the sector's weakness was further aggravated by economic recession, the freezing of Iranian assets held abroad and the long war with Iraq.

The government recognises that the state-owned banking system is unable to provide sufficient credit for economic growth. Non-banking credit institutions (NBCIs) will legally do what *bazaaris* have been doing for two decades. Foreign banks, a number of which have a representative office in Tehran, became more active as oil exports revived and financing became available for the reconstruction programme. Reconstruction requires imported goods and services. French banks are keen to regain the dominance they enjoyed in foreign trade financing in Iran before 1983, when France's supply of weapons to Iraq caused a breakdown in relations between France and Iran. Several French banks are on the approved list of the National Iranian Oil Company (NIOC). The most active are Banque Paribas, Société Générale and Banque Nationale de Paris.

As part of the 2000—04 economic development programme, the banking sector is being opened up to foreign participation and in 2002, Bank Markazi (the central bank) agreed to license the first fully foreign-owned banks since the 1979 revolution.

Bank Sepah was blacklisted by the US. The state-owned bank was accused of being the 'financial lynchpin' in Iran's efforts to procure material for its missile programme.

The Iran-Europe Commercial Bank (ICB) opened for business on the 27 May 2008, with the Iranian Bank of Industry and Mines (San'at va Ma'dan) as a major shareholder, and registered in Germany as a lender. The ICB was the first of six foreign banks allowed to operate in Iran (and not just on the island of Kish Free Trade Zone).

Central bank

Bank Markazi Jomhouri Islami Iran

Main financial centre

Tehran

Time

GMT plus 3.5 hours

Geography

Iran is a large and varied country. Much of it is desert wilderness, with mountainous regions along the western borders with Iraq and in the north with Turkey. Around 11 per cent of Iran is forested, notably in the northern regions of the Caspian Sea and Zagros mountains.

By the early part of the twentieth century, the majority of the population were villagers living in fertile fringes of Iran's great central plateau, which is made up of vast sand and salt deserts. However, rapid urbanisation, especially the growth of the capital Tehran, has changed the distribution of the population and the activities in which it is engaged.

Water is scarce in most of Iran and its availability dictates the density of the population in settled areas. There are very few towns of any size in central and eastern Iran, although there are lush oases scattered across the sand and salt deserts. There is a traditional system of subterranean water channels, cut from the water tables in mountains for irrigation.

Hemisphere

Northern

Climate

The climate for most of the country is dry and hot in summer before abruptly changing to a bitterly cold winter. The best season for visiting is around the Persian New Year (Nowruz). Temperatures range from 51 degrees Celsius (C) in summer at the head of the Gulf to minus 14 degrees C in winter in the interior. The mean temperatures are 3 degrees C in January and 29 degrees C in July. The Gulf area becomes very hot and humid in summer.

Dress codes

Since the 1979 Islamic Revolution, ties are shunned by Iranians but suits are acceptable. Informal dress is acceptable for men (not shorts). Women should always dress discreetly in public and avoid make-up.

Iranian women are required to cover all their hair and to disguise the shape of their bodies by wearing long, loose fitting clothes. Men can be stopped for having inappropriate hairstyles. Punishment can take the form of imprisonment, lashes or fines.

Entry requirements

Passports

Required by all, valid for six months beyond period of visit.

Visa
Visas are required by all, except nationals of Turkey and some other countries subject to change, and are valid for 30 days. Business visas must have an invitation letter from a local, sponsoring company, to be submitted to the foreign ministry in Tehran for approval. When authorised, the host company can obtain a reference number which is forwarded to the applicant. After one week, the visitor should contact the consulate quoting the reference number, and confirm the approval. Once confirmed, the application and documents can be submitted to the consular section for further action.

Prohibited entry
Israeli citizens or anyone with Israeli stamps in their passport will be rejected.

Currency advice/regulations
Import and export of local currency is limited to IR200,000. No restrictions on the import of foreign currency, but over US$1,000 must be declared on arrival; export is limited up to amount declared. Currency should be exchanged by authorised banks and exchange dealers and the receipts presented on departure.

Customs
The export of all antiques (over 50 years old) is prohibited, including gems, coins, handwritten manuscripts and other artifacts.

Prohibited imports
The import of all alcohol, firearms and ammunitions, video tapes and obscene publications.

Health (for visitors)

Mandatory precautions
A yellow fever certificate is required if travelling from an infected area. An AIDS certificate is required if staying more than three months.

Advisable precautions
Cholera is a high risk and precautions are required. Typhoid, dysentery and typhoid fever are common.

Hotels

The situation and status of hotels should be carefully checked. The use of the name of an international management chain does not imply a current connection with the chain, but may indicate only a previous link or the usual name by which the hotel is known. Most hotels are utilitarian. Evening entertainment is very rare.

Credit cards

Mastercard and visa are accepted in major locations.

Public holidays (national)

Fixed dates
11 Feb (Victory of Islamic Revolution, 1979), 20 Mar (Oil Nationalisation Day), 1 Apr (Islamic Republic Day), 2 Apr (Public Outing Day), 4 Jun (Death of Imam Khomeini), 5 Jun (Anniversary of Uprising against the Shah).

Variable dates
Nowruz (Persian New Year), Martyrdom of Imam Hassan Mojtaba, Martyrdom of Imam Reza, Martyrdom of Hazrat Fatemeh, Birthday of Imam Ali, Prophet Mohammad received his calling, Birthday of Imam Mahdi (12th Imam), Martyrdom of Imam Ali, Eid al Fitr, Martyrdom of Imam Sadegh, Eid e Ghorban (Eid al Ahda), Eid e Ghadir Khom, Tassoua, Ashura, Arbeen, Demise of Prophet Mohammad, Martyrdom of Imam Reza.
Iran uses the solar Persian calendar, which differs from the Gregorian calendar: there are 31 days in each of the first six months of the Persian calendar, 30 days in each of the next five months and 29 days in the last month, except in leap year when it has 30 days.
The Persian calendar dates from the Arab/Muslim invasion and the introduction of Islam into the country. The calendar (known as the *Hejrieh Shamsi*) is very precise; it was devised by the renowned Persian mathematician, Omar Khayyam. The months are: Farvardin, Ordibehesht, Khordad, Tir, Mordad, Shahrivar, Mehr, Aban, Azar, Day, Bahman, Esfand. The Iranian calendar year was briefly changed in commemoration of the 2,500th anniversary of the Persian Empire in 1971. The year was changed from 1350 Hejrieh Shamsi to 2530 Melli (national). This calendar was unpopular and the nation reverted to the old calendar soon afterwards.
Persian year 1390: 21 March 2011 to 22 March 2012.

Working hours

Friday is the Muslim day of religious observance (weekly holiday).

Banking
Sat–Wed: 0800–1700; Thu: 0800–1200; closed on Friday.

Business
Sat–Wed: 0700/0800–1300, 1600–1900. Closed on Thursday and Friday.

Government
Sat–Wed: 0700/0800–1300, 1600–1900. Closed on Thursday and Friday.

Shops
Sat–Wed: 0800–2000; Thu: 0800–1200; most bakeries and some food shops stay open on Fridays while the rest close.

Electricity supply

230V AC, 50 cycles

Weights and measures

Metric system

Social customs/useful tips

Visitors for business engagements are expected to arrive on time for appointments. However, it is by no means uncommon to be kept waiting, or even for appointments to be cancelled without notice. Tehran is susceptable to severe air polution as the population has greatly increased and there is a growing number of cars on the roads – many of them old. The city is wedged between mountains, meaning dirty air can get trapped when there is no wind or rain. The government can declare a public holiday when the polution is particularly bad.
The Gulf is never called Arabian, but is usually identified as Persian.
Normal Muslim customs prevail within most areas of the country. Alcohol is forbidden, although tolerance is shown to non-Muslims who may drink it at home.
Women must sit at the back of buses.
Men and women who are not married must not touch, therefore a business deal with a woman may not be sealed with a handshake.
Business negotiations can take a long time. A good lawyer and a detailed contract are essential.
Prostitution, casual sex and especially homosexual sex, are punishable with death or long prison sentences. Foreign visitors are not exempt from these laws.

Security

There is little violent street crime in Tehran, but visitors should take great care of their wallets and bags. Keep passports separate from other valuables.

Getting there

Air

National airline: IranAir
International airport/s: Mehrabad (THR), 5km west of Tehran, with duty-free shop, restaurant, bank, post office, shops; Shiraz (SYZ), 15km from city, with currency exchange, post office, shops.
Airport tax: Departure tax: IR70,000.

Surface

Road: There are roads from Iraq, Turkey, Armenia, Afghanistan and Pakistan, although these routes are not always passable.
Rail: There is a link with Turkey and Syria. A rail route runs nearly 300km from Mashhad into Turkmenistan, crossing the border at Sarakhs to join the Soviet-era Turksib railway at Tedzhen.
Water: Ferries run between Iran and United Arab Emirates, Manama (Bahrain) and Kuwait City.
Main port/s: The large ports on the Gulf include the country's main oil terminal at Kharg Island, the largest port Khorramshahr, Bandar Shahid Rajai, Bushehr, Bandar Khomeini and Chah Bahar. The main ports on the Caspian Sea are Bandar Anzali and Bandar Nowshahr.

Getting about

National transport

Air: IranAir and Aseman Airlines run frequent services between most cities and Tehran.

Road: Surfaced roads serve main centres; condition of secondary roads may vary.

Buses: There is an extensive, comfortable and cheap bus network that runs throughout the country. Scheduled long-distance coach services vary in their routes, but usually travel between all the main towns.

Rail: Rail services on the 5,500km network may vary, but there are usually various classes of service, with sleeping accommodation, air-conditioning and restaurant services available.

City transport

Taxis: Taxis are not metered and frequently shared. Those hired by telephone or by hotels are more expensive. Tipping is not expected.

Car hire

An international driving licence (along with two photographs) is required.

BUSINESS DIRECTORY

Telephone area codes

The international direct dialling (IDD) code for Iran is +98, followed by area code and subscriber's number:

Abadan	631	Isfahan	311
Ahvaz	611	Kerman	342
Arak	262	Mashad	511
Babol	111	Shiraz	711
Bakhtaran	431	Tabriz	411
Hamadán	811	Tehran	21

Useful telephone numbers

Ambulance: 123
Fire: 125
General emergencies: 123
Police: 110
Traffic accidents: 197

Chambers of Commerce

Iran Chamber of Commerce, Industries & Mines, 254 Taleghani Avenue, Tehran 15814 (tel:8884-6031; fax: 8882-5111; e-mail: info@iccm.org).

Irano-British Chamber of Commerce, Industries and Mines, 254 Taleghani Avenue, Tehran 15814 (tel 8881-0525; fax: 8881-0526; e-mail: info@ibchamber.org).

Shiraz Chamber of Commerce, Industries and Mines, Zand Street, Shiraz 71356-53564 (tel: 2230-4415; fax: 2233-1220; e-mail: info@sccim.com).

Tehran Chamber of Commerce, Industries and Mines, 254 Taleghani Avenue, Tehran 15814 (tel: 8884-6031; fax: 882-5111; e-mail: info@tccim.com).

Banking

Bank Maskan, Ferdowsi Avenue, PO Box 11365-3499, Tehran (tel: 6670-9658; fax: 6670-9684; e-mail: info@bank-maskan.ir).

Bank Mellat, Head Office Bldg, 327 Taleghani Ave, 15817 Tehran (tel: 8296-2700).

Bank Melli Iran, Ferdowsi Avenue, PO Box 11365-171, Tehran (tel: 3231; fax: 3391-2813).

Bank Refah Kargaran, 40 Northern Shirazi Street, Mollasadra Avenue, Tehran (tel: 8804-2926; fax: 8804-2926).

Bank Saderat Iran, Sepehr Tower, 43 Somayeh Avenue, PO Box 15745-631, Tehran (tel: 8829-9469; fax: 8883-9534).

Bank Sepah, Imam Khomeini Square, PO Box 11364-9569, Tehran (tel: 6674-3761; fax: 6674-3282; e-mail: info@banksepah.ir). (Bank Sepah was blacklisted by the US. The state-owned bank was accused of being the 'financial lynchpin' in Iran's efforts to procure material for its missile programme.)

Bank Tejarat, PO Box 11365-5416, 130 Taleghani Avenue, Nejatoullahie, 15994 Tehran (tel: 8882-6690; fax: 8889-3641).

Central bank

Bank Markazi Jomhouri Islami Iran,PO Box 11365-8551, Tehran (tel: 29-951; fax: 673-5674;e-mail: g.secdept@cbi.ir).

Stock exchange

Tehran Stock Exchange (TSE): www.iranbourse.com

Commodity exchange

Kish International Commodity Exchange

Travel information

Irpedia, 6 Kachouee Avenue, Chamran Highway, Tehran (tel: 200-8189; e-mail: info@irpedia.com).

Pars Tourist Agency, Zand Sreet 71358, Shiraz (tel: 222-3163; fax: 224-0645; e-mail: info@key2persia.com).

Ministry of tourism

Ministry of Culture and Islamic Guidance, Baharestan Square, Kamal-al-Molk Avenue, Avenue Kamalolmolk, Tehran (tel: 3851-2583; fax: 3311-7535).

National tourist organisation offices

Iran Tourist Co, 257 Motahari Avenue, Tehran 15868 (tel: 8873-6762/5; fax: 8873-6158; e-mail: info@irantouristco.com; internet site: http://www.irantouristco.com).

Ministries

Ministry of Commerce, 492 Valieasr Avenue, Tehran (tel: 8889-3553; fax: 8890-3943).

Ministry of Foreign Affairs, Imam Khomeini Square, Tehran (tel: 6673-9191; fax: 6674-3149; e-mail: matbuat@mfa.gov.ir).

Ministry of Information and Communication Technology (MICT), Sharlati St, PO Box 15875-4415, 16314 Tehran (tel: 8846 9000; fax: 8846 8131).

Ministry of Petroleum, Hafez Crossing, Taleghani Street, Tehran (tel: 6615-2606; fax: 6615-4977; e-mail: public-relations@mop.ir).

Ministry of Science, Research and Technology, Unit 2, Ostad Nejatollahi Street, Teheran (tel: 8890-2024; fax: 8890-2027; e-mail: msrt@mche.or.ir).

Other useful addresses

Export Promotion Centre of Iran, PO Box 11-48, Tajrish, Tehran (tel: 2205-1437; fax: 2205-1438; e-mail: epc-iran@epc-iran.com).

Iranian Interests Section (USA), 2209 Wisconsin Avenue, NW, Washington DC 20007 (tel:(+1-202)-965-4990; fax: (+1-202)-965-1073; e-mail: requests@daftar.org).

National Iranian Oil Company (NIOC), Taleghani Avenue, PO Box 1853, Tehran (tel: 6615-2275; fax: 6641-0916; e-mail: public-relation@nioc.com).

Statistical Centre of Iran, Dr Fatemi Ave, PO Box 14155-6133 Tehran (tel: 8896-5061; fax: 8896-5070; e-mail: sci@sci/org.ir).

Tehran Stock Exchange, 228 Hafez Avenue, Tehran (tel: 6670-4130; fax:6670-2524; e-mail: info@tse.ir).

National news agency: IRNA (Islamic Republic News Agency): www2.irna.ir

IRIB: www.irib.ir

Iranian Students News Agency (ISNA): http://isna.ir

Press TV: www.presstv.com

Internet sites

Customs Administration: http://www.irica.gov.ir

General information: http://www.salamiran.org

General political information: http://www.netiran.com

Iraq

In the period following the deposition of Saddam Hussein in 2003 until the withdrawal of US forces at the end of 2011, an estimated 100,000 Iraqis will have lost their lives. Some observers put the figure even higher. Alongside this sombre statistic, 4,500 US soldiers (not to mention those from other Coalition countries) also lost their lives. The military exercise was estimated to have cost one trillion US dollars, and again some estimates are even higher. The accepted budgeting figure was that it costs US$1 million a year to keep a single soldier in Iraq.

Withdrawal symptoms

In October 2011 President Obama announced to journalists in the White House briefing room that 'as promised, the rest of our troops in Iraq will come home by the end of the year – after nearly nine years, America's war in Iraq will be over.' The US had tried to extend the military presence of their troops past 31 December. However, according to Max Boot, a senior fellow in national security studies at the United States Council on Foreign Relations writing in the New York based *Wall Street Journal*, the deal breaker was the Iraqis refusal to grant legal immunity for US troops if they are accused of breaking Iraq's laws. Prime Minister Nouri al Maliki was quoted as stating that 'When the Americans asked for immunity, the Iraqi side answered that it was not possible.' So it seemed, the withdrawal was under way.

Criticisms of President Obama's handling of the withdrawal agreement suggested that, not for the first time, the President's aloofness had got the better of him. According to Mr Boot, the same reservations over immunity had loomed in 2008 during the negotiation of what was

KEY FACTS

Official name: Al Jumhouriya al Iraqia (The Republic of Iraq)

Head of State: President Jalal Talabani (PUK) (from 2005; re-elected 12 Nov 2010)

Head of government: Prime Minister Nouri al Maliki (Dawa) (from 2006; re-elected 11 Nov 2010)

Ruling party: National Alliance coalition, led by Al Iraqiya (Iraqi National Movement), with I'tilaf Dawlat al Qanon (State of Law Coalition) and Al Ittilaf al Watani al Iraqi (National Iraqi Alliance) (known as Watani List) (from 14 Jun 2010)

Area: 434,924 square km

Population: 32.10 million (2010) (Figure includes the UN estimated 4.6 million living in exile)

Capital: Baghdad

Official language: Arabic and Kurdish

Currency: New Iraqi dinar (ID) 1,000 fils

Exchange rate: ID1,166.00 per US$ (Oct 2011); (Iraqi Central Bank auction rate) (New Iraqi dinar since 2003)

GDP per capita: US$2,564 (2010)

GDP real growth: 0.80% (2010)

GDP: US$82.20 billion (2010)

Unemployment: 27.50% (2007)* (Average figure, does not include underemployment)

Inflation: 5.10% (2010)

Oil production: 2.46 million bpd (2010)

Balance of trade: US$1.65 billion (2010)

* estimated figure

to be the last Status of Forces Agreement (SFA). At the time there were many more US personnel in Iraq – almost 150,000, compared with less than 50,000 in 2011. It seemed that Mr Bush had spoken on a weekly basis with Mr Maliki by video teleconference. Mr Obama had not spoken with Mr Maliki for months before calling him in late October 2011 to announce the end of negotiations. Surprisingly, Mr Boot also claimed that Mr Obama and his senior aides did not even bother to meet with Iraqi officials at the United Nations General Assembly in September 2011. President Obama's officials had waited until mid-2011 before opening talks on renewing the Status of Forces Agreement, a matter of months before US troops would have to start closing their remaining bases to be able to pull out by the end of the year. The withdrawal from Iraq was thought to be the largest military logistical operation carried out by the US since the Second World War. Mr Boot also pointed out that while the SFA could authorise joint exercises between the two countries and even the presence of a small US Special Operations contingent in Iraq, it was no substitute for a robust US military presence.

Not in vain

President Obama, in a pre-election speech, had described the invasion of Iraq as a 'Dumb war'. As the date for the evacuation of all the US troops from Iraq had approached, the President found himself in a difficult position. The Iraq military intervention had not seen a Dunkirk or an Iwo-Jima: in Iraq there were no iconic images of US bravery, no more references to 'mission accomplished'. In their place were the embarrassing memories of the disgraceful treatment of prisoners at Abu Ghraib.

Obama was obliged to tell the troops, and more particularly the families of those servicemen and women who had died in Iraq, that it had not been in vain. That the US had left behind what it liked to describe as a 'self governing country'. Often described as having a freely elected parliament, Iraq still has some way to go before democratic institutions become institutional. Nearer the truth is the realisation that while Iraq is no longer a dictatorship, in the words of the London *Economist*, it is 'something of a violent police state'.

What was also certain was that in 2011, Iraq was plagued by violence, a lack of jobs and random arrests and imprisonment. Not all Iraqis were happy to see the US forces depart. Many of them had fallen into the habit of blaming the presence of US forces for virtually everything that had gone wrong with their country – putting them down either to a conspiracy or a cock-up by what they saw as an invasive force. Some go so far as to attribute the mess their country is in to a US policy to weaken Iraq.

'Self governing', however, may be a matter of interpretation. In the early part of 2011, inspired by events in North Africa, a wave of protests swept across Iraq. Rallies were held in Baghdad, protesting not so much against a lack of democracy, but against the lack of basic utilities such as a reliable electricity supply and medical services. The government's initial response was to describe the rioters (in the words of Prime Minister Nouri al Maliki) as 'Saddamist elements' in collusion with al Qaeda. It soon appeared, however, that the government had reconsidered this first response. The early accusations were soon replaced by promises to hold elections. Much of the crowds' anger was directed at Mr al Maliki himself, at alleged corruption and the failure to appoint a government during the nine month period following the 2010 elections, which had done little to inspire Iraqi confidence in their elected representatives. In late 2011 it still looked unlikely that Iraq's forces could keep their country secure. The US embassy in Baghdad would inevitably have to step up to the plate and organise a host of private contractors. The US bases may close, but countless companies will be involved in operating air defence systems and more mundane activities.

Iran

Iraq's foreign policy following the departure of the US forces, looked increasingly likely to grow more sympathetic towards Iran. Iranian influence in Iraq certainly seemed to be increasing, epitomised by the return of the controversial Shi'a cleric, Moqtada al Sadr to Iraq after a four year exile in Iran. In October 2010 Mr Sadr had decided to support fellow Shi'a Mr Maliki as prime minister in a deal brokered by Iran; this enabled the formation of an Iraqi government after a lapse of nine months during which time Iraq had no effective government at all. The political accommodation with Mr Sadr meant that his faction controlled at least eight ministries. This contrasted sharply with the circumstances surrounding his departure, when, fearing the consequences of an arrest warrant, he had felt it best to leave the country. He was charged with the murder of a rival Shi'a cleric in Najaf.

Triangulation

Iraq's Shi'ites have emerged from years of suppression by Iraq's ruling Ba'athist-Sunni minority to become the ruling majority. Post Saddam Iraq needed to come to terms with a new balance of power in which Shi'ites were the dominant community. The likely king-makers in a complex equation were thought, at intervals, to be either Iraq's prosperous Kurds or the Sadrist Movement, lead by the maverick Moqtada al Sadr. The Sadrists were the political wing of the al

KEY INDICATORS — Iraq

	Unit	2006	2007	2008	2009	2010
Population	m	27.50	*27.50	*30.41	*31.23	*32.10
Gross domestic product (GDP)	US$bn	49.30	62.40	91.50	65.80	82.20
GDP per capita	US$	1,714	2,109	3,007	2,108	2,564
GDP real growth	%	6.2	1.5	9.5	4.2	0.8
Inflation	%	53.2	30.8	2.7	-2.2	2.4
Oil output	'000 bpd	1,999.0	2,145.0	2,423.0	2,482.0	2,460.0
Natural gas output	bn cum	1.5	1.5	1.9	1.2	1.3
Exports (fob) (goods)	US$m	30,529.4	39,587.0	62,013.0	38,439.0	51,934.0
Imports (fob) (goods)	US$m	18,707.5	16,623.0	40,812.0	45,765.0	50,280.0
Balance of trade	US$m	11,821.9	22,965.0	21,201.0	-7,329.0	1,654.0
Current account	US$m	1,252.0	14,056.0	11,049.0	-12,762.0	-5,053.0
Total reserves minus gold	US$m	19,535.4	31,297.6	50,042.5	46,255.4	50,377.0
Foreign exchange	US$m	18,839.2	30,887.5	49,635.8	44,168.9	48,339.6
Exchange rate	per US$	1,314.65	1,216.70	1,155.05	1,170.00	1,170.00

* estimated figure

Mahdi army, drawing its support from less affluent Shi'a communities in Baghdad and the south of Iraq. In the north Iraqi Kurdistan's tribal politicians ruled a relatively secure and prosperous roost between the plains of Mesopotamia and Kurdistan's mountains, inhabited by only 2.5 million Kurds. The Kurds differ from both Sunni and Shi'a in that they are not Arabs. Competing Arab and Kurdish claims to the oil-rich areas around the Kurdish city of Kirkuk are unresolved. By mid-2010 the Kurds had seemed to have emerged as the key third party in the equation. However, it was certainly safe to assume that Mr Sadr's return and re-instatement represented an increase in Iranian influence. In January 2011 Iran's new foreign minister, Ali Akbar Salehi, had held meetings with Mr Maliki and a number of government officials. At the same time as its suspected rapprochement with Iran, Iraq had distanced itself from Arab League resolutions censuring the Ba'athist Syrian regime for the harsh repression of the street protests in Syria.

Among the risks that confronted President Obama's apparently implacable determination that the US should adhere to its timetable to step back from an active military role, one prevailed above all. As the US took a back seat, fears began to be expressed – within Iraq as well as in its Sunni neighbours –that a Shi'ite government would begin to align itself with Shi'a Iran. Iran's foreign policy certainly sought a closer alliance with Iraq. The alarming prospect of Iran, possibly nuclear armed, becoming the king-maker in Iraq caused sleepless nights not only in Washington, Riyadh and even Cairo. But precedents abounded: Syria had for over 20 years called the shots in Lebanon, only to be replaced by an Iranian backed Hezbollah.

President Obama had certainly shown a greater willingness to fudge other election promises, but the decision to withdraw combat forces by August 2010 and the remaining 50,000 'trainers and advisers' by December 2011 appeared inviolate. So much so, that it seemed as though Mr Obama had other fish to fry. Senior level meetings were handled by Vice President Joseph Biden, who also managed Iraq policy.

Poverty

The World Bank notes that poverty and human conditions in Iraq worsened in the 1990s and have not improved much in recent years. Overall unemployment is at 11.7 per cent but higher among younger adults (20–24 years old) at 16.9 per cent for men and 35.7 per cent for women. The provision of public services continues to be unreliable; only 12.5 per cent of persons whose dwelling is connected to the public network report their supply of water as stable. Additionally, only 22.4 per cent can rely solely on the public power network for electricity for their housing units. The government continues to provide large subsidies for food, fuel and utilities. In November 2009, the cabinet had approved a new National Strategy for Poverty Reduction (2010–14). Efforts are also underway to reform Iraq's Public Distribution System (PDS), the country's largest safety net programme for the poor.

Energy

In April 2011 Iraq managed to raise its oil output to the highest level for almost a decade, adding 350,000 barrels per day (bpd) to reach a level of 2.8 million bpd. The increase reflected the improved operating conditions in Iraq's oilfields. The government's production target is 11 million bpd by 2020, although most industry experts discount this as unrealistic simply because Iraq lacks adequate water supplies to pump such a quantity of oil. The International Energy Agency (IEA) forecasts that Iraq will add a further one million bpd by 2015.

According to the US government Energy Information Administration (EIA) Iraq was the world's 12th largest oil producer in 2009 and has the world's fourth largest proven petroleum reserves after Saudi Arabia, Canada and Iran. Only a fraction of Iraq's known fields are currently operational and Iraq may be one of the few inhabited places left where vast reserves, proven and unknown, have hardly been exploited. Iraq's energy sector is overwhelmingly based upon oil, with approximately 94 per cent of its energy needs met by petroleum. Crude oil export revenues accounted for over two-thirds of gross domestic product (GDP) in 2009. Iraq's oil sector had suffered in the Saddam Hussein days from both sanctions and wars and its oil infrastructure is still in need of wholesale modernisation and investment. Up to mid-2010, the US had allocated US$2.05 billion to the Iraqi oil and gas sector to begin this modernisation, although it had ended its direct involvement in 2008. According to reports by various US government agencies, multilateral institutions and other international organisations, long-term Iraq reconstruction costs could reach US$100 billion or higher. A draft of the proposed Hydrocarbons Law, which governs oil contracting and regulation, and which had been under review in the Council of Ministers since October 2008, was finally approved by the cabinet in August 2011. The law is key to the future of Iraq's industry with the main sticking point being who controls the oil from semi-autonomous Kurdistan. The Kurdistan Regional Presidency (KRP) condemned the cabinet for approving the draft as it failed to take into account previous agreement.

According to the *Oil and Gas Journal* (OGJ), Iraq's proven oil reserves are 115 billion barrels, although these statistics have not been revised since 2001 and are largely based on 2-D seismic data from nearly three decades ago. Geologists and consultants have estimated that relatively unexplored territory in the western and southern deserts may contain an estimated additional 45 to 100 billion barrels of recoverable oil. Iraqi oil minister, Hussain al Shahristani, said that Iraq is re-evaluating its estimate of proven oil reserves and expects to revise them upwards. A major challenge to Iraq's development of the oil sector is that resources are not evenly divided across sectarian-demographic lines. Most known hydrocarbon resources are concentrated in the Shi'ite areas of the south and the ethnically Kurdish north, with few resources in the control of the Sunni minority.

The majority of the known oil and gas reserves in Iraq form a belt that runs along the eastern edge of the country. Iraq has 9 fields that are considered super giants (over 5 billion barrels) as well as 22 known giant fields (over 1 billion barrels). According to independent consultants, the cluster of super-giant fields of south-eastern Iraq forms the largest known concentration of such fields in the world and accounts for 70 to 80 per cent of the country's proven oil reserves. An estimated 20 per cent of oil reserves are in the north of Iraq, near Kirkuk, Mosul and Khanaqin. Control over rights to reserves is a source of controversy between the ethnic Kurds and other groups in the area.

In 2009 and 2010, Iraq's crude oil production averaged 2.4 million barrels per day (bpd), about the same as 2008 levels and below its pre-war production capacity level of 2.8 million bpd in 2003. About two-thirds of production comes from the southern fields, with the remainder from the north-central fields near Kirkuk. At present, the majority of Iraqi oil production comes from just three giant fields: North and South Rumaila in southern Iraq and Kirkuk.

Currently, the ministry of oil has central control over oil and gas production and development in all but the Kurdish territory through its three operating entities, the North Oil Company (NOC), the South Oil Company (SOC) and the Missan Oil Company (MOC), which was split off from the South Oil Company in 2008. According to the NOC's website, their concession and jurisdiction extends from the Turkish borders in the north to 32.5 degrees latitude (about 100 miles south of Baghdad) and from Iranian borders in the east to Syrian and Jordanian borders in the west. The company's geographical operation area spans the governorates of Tamim (Kirkuk), Nineveh, Irbil, Baghdad, Diyala and part of Babil to Hilla and Wasit to Kut. The remainder falls under the jurisdiction of the SOC and MOC and though smaller in geographical size, includes the majority of proven reserves. MOC's oil fields hold an estimated 30 billion barrels of reserves. They include Amara, Halfaya, Huwaisa, Noor, Rifaee, Dijaila, Kumait and East Rafidain.

Iraq has begun an ambitious development programme to develop its oil fields and to increase its oil production. Passage of the proposed Hydrocarbons Law, which would provide a legal framework for investment in the hydrocarbon sector, remains a main policy objective. Despite the absence of the Hydrocarbons Law, the Iraqi ministry of oil signed 12 long-term contracts between November 2008 and May 2010 with international oil companies to develop 14 oil fields. Under the first phase, companies bid to further develop six giant oil fields that were already producing with proven oil reserves of over 43 billion barrels. Phase two contracts were signed to develop oil fields that were already explored but not fully developed or producing commercially. Together, these contracts cover oil fields with proven reserves of over 60 billion barrels, or more than half of Iraq's current proven oil reserves.

As a result of these contract awards, Iraq expected to boost production by 200,000bpd by the end of 2010 and to increase production capacity by an additional 400,000bpd by the end of 2011. When these fields are fully developed, they will increase total Iraqi production capacity to almost 12 million bpd, or 9.6 million bpd above current production levels. The contracts call for Iraq to reach this production target by 2017.

Energy infrastructure

Iraq faces many challenges in meeting this timetable. One of the most significant is the lack of an outlet for significant increases in crude oil production. Both Iraqi refining and export infrastructure are currently bottlenecks and need to be upgraded to process much more crude oil. Iraqi oil exports are currently running at near full capacity in the south, while export capacity in the north has been restricted by sabotage and would need to be expanded in any case to export significantly higher volumes.

Production increases of the scale planned will also require substantial increases in natural gas and/or water injection to maintain oil reservoir pressure and boost oil production. Iraq has associated gas that could be used, but it is currently being flared. Another option is to use water for re-injection and locally available water is currently being used in the south of Iraq. However, fresh water is an important commodity in the Middle East and large amounts of seawater will likely have to be pumped in via pipelines that have yet to be built. ExxonMobil has co-ordinated initial studies at water injection plans for many of the fields under development. According to their estimate, 10–15 million bpd of seawater could be necessary for Iraq's expansion plans, at a cost of over US$10 billion.

Furthermore, Iraq's oil and gas industry is the largest industrial customer of electricity, with over 10 per cent of total demand. Large-scale increases in oil production would also require large increases in power generation. However, Iraq has struggled to keep up with the demand for power, with shortages common across Iraq. Significant upgrades to the electricity sector would be needed to supply additional power. Iraq also plans to sign delineation agreements on shared oil fields with Kuwait and Iran. Iraq would like to set up joint committees with its neighbours on how to share the oil.

Natural gas

According to the OGJ, Iraq's proven natural gas reserves are 112 trillion cubic feet (tcf), the tenth largest in the world. An estimated 70 per cent of these lie in Basra governorate (province) in the south of Iraq. Probable Iraqi reserves have been estimated at 275–300tcf and work is currently underway by several international oil companies (IOCs) and independents to accurately update hydrocarbon reserve numbers. Two-thirds of Iraq's natural gas resources are associated with oil fields, including Kirkuk, as well as the southern Nahr (Bin) Umar, Majnoon, Halfaya, Nassiriya, the Rumaila fields, West Qurna and Zubair. Just under 20 per cent of known gas reserves are non-associated; around 10 per cent is salt dome gas. The majority of non-associated reserves are concentrated in several fields in the North including: Ajil, Bai Hassan, Jambur, Chemchemal, Kor Mor, Khashem al Ahmar and al Mansuriyah.

Iraqi natural gas production was 1.3 billion cubic metres (bcm) in 2010. Some is used as fuel for power generation and some is re-injected to enhance oil recovery. In 2008 over 40 per cent of the production had been flared due to a lack of sufficient infrastructure to utilise it for consumption and export, although Royal Dutch Shell estimated that flaring losses were even greater at 1bcf per day. As a result, Iraq's five natural gas processing plants, which can process over 773 billion cubic feet per year, had been mostly idle.

To reduce flaring, Iraq has been working on an agreement with Royal Dutch Shell to implement a 25-year project to capture flared gas and provide it for domestic use. Iraq's cabinet gave preliminary approval for the US$17 billion deal covering development of 25 – 30tcf of associated natural gas reserves in Basra province through a new joint venture, Basra Gas Company. The agreement, which originally was to cover all of Basra province, has been modified to include only the associated gas from the Rumaila, Zubair and West Qurna Phase I projects. Implementation of this agreement is necessary for the new oil development projects to go forward.

Plans to export natural gas remain controversial due to the amount of idle and sub-optimally-fired electricity generation capacity in Iraq – much a result of a lack of adequate gas feedstock. Prior to the 1990–91 Gulf War, Iraq exported natural gas to Kuwait. The gas came from Rumaila through a 105-mile, 400-MMcf/d pipeline to Kuwait's central processing centre at Ahmadi. In 2007, the oil ministry announced an agreement to fund a feasibility study on the revival of the mothballed pipeline.

Iraq has considered northern export routes such as the proposed Nabucco pipeline through Turkey to Europe and Prime Minister Maliki has suggested that Iraq could be exporting 530bcf per year to Europe by 2015.

Risk assessment

Economy	Fair
Politics	Poor
Regional stability	Poor

COUNTRY PROFILE

Historical profile

For 400 years, until the end of the First World War, the region was part of the Ottoman Empire.

1920 Iraq was placed under British mandate. The Great Iraqi Revolution began in May as a revolt against British rule. It united Sunnis, Shi'as and tribal groupings but by the end of the year had failed.

1921 Amir Faisal ibn Hussain (a member of the Arab Hashemite dynasty) was proclaimed Iraq's first King.

1932 Iraq became an independent state.

1933 King Faisal died and was succeeded by his son, Ghazi.

1939 King Ghazi was killed in a car crash and was succeeded by the infant Faisal II, whose uncle, Prince Abd al Ilah, acted as regent.

1953 King Faisal II assumed full powers.

1958 A military coup overthrew the monarchy and a republic was proclaimed.

1963 Pan-Arab elements in the armed forces staged a coup and formed a government under Colonel (later Field Marshal) Abd as Salem Muhammad Aref

1966 Aref was killed in an airplane crash and was succeeded by his brother, Major General Abd ar Rahman Muhammad Aref.

1968 Major General Aref was removed from office in a coup organised by the Hizb al Ba'ath al Arabiyah al Ishtiraki (Ba'ath) (Socialist Arab Rebirth Party). The Ba'ath government was headed by Major General Ahmad Hassan al Bakr (a former prime minister) and supreme authority was vested in the Revolutionary Command Council (RCC).

1970 The RCC and the leader of the Kurdistan Democratic Party (KDP) signed a peace agreement.

1972 Iraq nationalised the Iraq Petroleum Company (IPC).

1979 The vice president of the RCC, Saddam Hussein (already the real power in Iraq), replaced Al Bakr as president.

1980–88 The Iran-Iraq War broke out after Iraq invaded Iran over a disputed border area.

1988 A chemical attack ordered by Saddam Hussein on the northern Kurdish town of Halabja, killed 5,000 people.

1990 Iraq invaded Kuwait on 2 August. The invasion was condemned by the international community. Iraqi troops destroyed over 400 oil wells, causing environmental and economic havoc. Following the invasion, the United Nations Security Council (UNSC) imposed an arms embargo and economic sanctions on Iraq (Resolution 661) and passed Resolution 678, which authorised member states to use force if Iraq had not withdrawn from Kuwait by 15 January 1991

1991 The Gulf War started in the early hours of 17 January when coalition forces launched an aerial bombing campaign against Iraq and Iraqi forces in Kuwait. US-led ground forces (from around 30 countries, including Syria, Egypt and Morocco) moved into Kuwait on 24 February and drove the Iraqi forces there back into Iraq. The UN maintained the arms embargo and economic sanctions on Iraq after the end of the War in an attempt to force it to disarm of weapons of mass destruction (WMD). After a Kurdish and Shi'a Muslim-led uprising was brutally quashed by Saddam Hussein's regime, the US, UK and France imposed 'no-fly zones' on Iraq to protect the Kurds in the north and the Shi'as in the south. The UN administered the three northern provinces of Dahuk, Arbil and As Sulaymaniyah, which allowed the Kurds to develop their own semi-autonomous Kurdish enclave, with its own parliament.

1993 The US launched 24 cruise missiles at targets in Baghdad after an alleged Iraqi plot to assassinate former US president George Bush was uncovered.

1994 Saddam Hussein appointed himself prime minister as well as president.

1995 The population voted in a referendum on Saddam Hussein's presidency and, inevitably, supported him. The Iraq oil-for-food programme, administered by the UN, began.

1996 Saddam Hussein's son-in-law, his brother and their families, were granted asylum in Jordan; the two men were subsequently promised a pardon by Saddam Hussein, but were killed on their return to Baghdad. Saddam Hussein's eldest son, Uday, survived an assassination attempt.

1998 Various disputes arose between Iraq and the UN over UN inspections to verify the termination of Iraq's WMD programme; Saddam Hussein excluded the weapons inspectors from Iraq. As a result, the US and the UK launched their largest military attack against Iraq since the Gulf War, bombing installations throughout Iraq.

1999 The spiritual leader of the Shi'a community, Ayatollah Mohammed Sadiq al Sadr, was assassinated in Najaf.

2000 In his capacity as head of the Organisation of the Petroleum Exporting Countries (Opec), President Hugo Chávez Frías of Venezuela travelled overland to Baghdad – the first democratically elected head of state to enter Iraq since the Gulf War.

2001 Five UN officials working for the UN oil-for-food programme were expelled by Iraqi authorities on charges of spying.

2002 A presidential referendum extended Saddam Hussein's rule for a further seven years. US President Bush demanded that Hussein must prove to the UN weapons inspectors that all WMD had been destroyed, as stipulated in the UN resolution after the First Gulf War – if not the US would launch a war against Iraq. UN weapons inspectors returned to Iraq for the first time in four years, however the information they were shown was not sufficient to convince the US that there were no WMD. President Bush included Iraq, North Korea with Iran in a list of countries that supported terrorism as an 'axis of evil'.

2003 After diplomatic efforts to force Iraq to disarm failed and the expiry of an US ultimatum giving Hussein and his sons 48 hours to leave the country, US-led coalition forces invaded Iraq. Within 20 days central Baghdad was under US control and the Hussein government had collapsed. The Ba'ath party was abolished, together with institutions of the former regime. The UN Security Council lifted economic sanctions and a 25-member Iraq Governing Council (IGC) was appointed, with a rotating nine-member presidency. Hussein's sons, Uday and Qusay, were killed in a skirmish with US troops attempting to arrest them. The leader of the Shi'as, Ayatollah Mohammed Baqr al Hakim, was killed in Najaf. An amended US resolution on Iraq, legitimising the US-led administration, was approved by the UN, which stressed early transfer of power to the Iraqis. The security situation deteriorated as guerrilla warfare intensified. At the end of the year, Saddam Hussein was captured in Tikrit.

2004 After the president of the IGC was killed in a car bomb attack, Iyad Allawi (a Shi'a) was designated prime minister and Ghazi al Yawar (a Sunni tribal leader) was chosen as president. An interim 36-member cabinet was appointment to Transitional Government, until elections for a fully independent government could be held; it had power-sharing responsibilities with the US-led multinational forces in matters of security. The US handed over sovereignty to the Iraqi interim government. Hussein was transferred into Iraqi legal custody. There was heavy fighting for more than a week in an uprising against coalition troops by Shi'a militia loyal to radical cleric, Moqtada al Sadr, in the holy city of Najaf.

2005 The Transitional Government of Iraq recognised the Kurdish Autonomous Region, along with the sovereignty of its government. An estimated eight million people voted in the elections for a Transitional National Assembly. Many Sunni Moslems boycotted the elections, and the Shi'a United Iraqi Alliance won most seats. Iraq's first freely elected parliament in half a century began its opening session after a series of explosions targeted the gathering. Kurdish leader Jalal

Talabani was named president. Former president, and Sunni leader, Ghazi al Yawar, and Shi'ite leader, Adel Abdul Mahdi, were named as deputies. The Shi'ite leader, Ibrahim Jaafari, was named prime minister. The Kurdish parliament unanimously elected Massoud Barzani as president of the autonomous region of Kurdistan. In his trial, former president, Saddam Hussein, was accused, along with seven others, of murdering 148 people in 1982 in the Shi'a town of Dujail. Parliamentary elections were held.

2006 With little progress made in forming a new government, the interim prime minister, Ibrahim Jaafari, relinquished the office and was replaced by Nouri al Maliki (Islamic Dawa Party) (a leading party within the Shi'ite grouping, United Iraqi Alliance). The chief judge in Saddam Hussein's trial, Abdullah al Amiri, was removed as being 'no longer neutral', after he made court statements that Saddam had not been a dictator; he was replaced by Muhammad al Uraiybi. Saddam Hussein was executed by hanging on 30 December, after being found guilty of crimes against humanity. An unauthorised recording was broadcast on the Internet of the event, showing him being taunted by his captors.

2007 US President Bush dispatched a further 21,500 soldiers, specifically to police Baghdad. Civilian deaths in the four weeks before their arrival were 1,440, which dropped to 265 in the following four weeks. Iraqi-US forces targeted the followers of the Shi'a cleric, Moqtada al Sadr, known as the Mahdi army, as its leadership fled to Iran. Former vice president, Taha Yassin Ramadan, was executed for crimes against humanity. Seventeen Sunni government members either quit or suspended their involvement in the Unity Government, leaving it weak and vulnerable. The Kurdish government, in northern Iraq, signed four exploration and two refinery contracts, worth about US$800 million, with several international energy companies. The deals were signed ahead of Iraqi national oil and gas laws and increased tension between the central government and the Kurdish territory.

2008 Final approval by the Presidency Council allowed former Ba'ath party members to return to public life. Russia announced that it was writing off US$12 billion of debt which had built up under Saddam Hussein. President Ahmadinejad made the first official visit by an Iranian president since the Iran-Iraq war in the 1980s. The Christian Archbishop of Mosul, Paulos Faraj Rahho, was kidnapped and killed. The leader of al Qaeda in Iraq, Ahmed Ali Ahmed (known as Abu Omar) was sentenced to death for the murder of Archbishop Rahho. Parliament approved a draft law for provincial elections to be held, despite a boycott by the Kurdish bloc and a few Shi'a MPs. Anbar Province was officially handed over to Iraqi control by the US. The province had been one of the most militant and dangerous for US troops until the Sunni population took control of their own security by helping to fight al Qaeda insurgents. The Kuwaiti ambassador took up residence in Iraq, after an 18-year gap since the Iraqi invasion of Kuwait; diplomatic relations had been restored in 2003.

2009 The US embassy, its largest in the world, was officially opened in Baghdad, four days after responsibility for security for the central Baghdad Green Zone was handed over to Iraqi forces. Provincial elections were held in February and won by those candidates that supported the ruling administration of Prime Minister al Maliki. US military personnel withdrew from Iraqi cities, prior to a full re-deployment to the US. In elections for Iraqi Kurdistan, Massoud Barzini won the presidency and the Kurdistani List alliance won the leadership of the Kurdish National Assembly (KNA). The government released the first official estimate of violent deaths during 2004–08, of 85,694, based on death certificates issued by the ministry of health, including some 15,000 unidentified bodies. Barham Salih became prime minister of the Kurdistan autonomous region on 1 September.

2010 Ali Hassan al-Majid, Saddam Hussein's notorious cousin known as 'Chemical Ali', was hanged for crimes against humanity in January. In parliamentary elections held in March, the Al Iraqiya (Iraqi National Movement) won 25.87 per cent of the vote (91 seats out of 325) and the ruling I'tilaf Dawlat al Qanon (State of Law Coalition) 25.76 per cent (89). On 26 April the Iraq High Electoral Commission (IHEC) banned 52 members of the Watani Alliance from serving in parliament due to their links to the outlawed Ba'ath Party. The votes within constituencies were recalculated and allocated to other candidates of the Watani Alliance. In May, Iraqi Airways was declared bankrupt. In June the Supreme Court endorsed the April general election results and dismissed all demands for a recount. The Al Iraqiya won the right to begin negotiations to form a government. A new coalition formed in June, called the National Alliance, which included the two major Shi'a political parties – Al Iraqiya and I'tilaf Dawlat al Qanon – plus a number of other Shi'a parties including the Watani List. A new parliament was convened and the 325 members of parliament sworn in on 14 June, even though there was as yet no government. In August, Iraq's General Chief of Staff, Lieutenant General Babakir voiced his concern that Iraqi troops were not ready to take over security following the planned US troop withdrawal, which he considered premature. The last US combat troops left Iraq on 19 August, although 50,000 advisory troops were to remain until 2011. By 13 September no coalition government had been formed. On October 26 Tariq Aziz, the most senior Christian to serve Saddam Hussein, as deputy prime minister and foreign minister, was found guilty of the persecution of religious parties and sentenced to death. A power-sharing agreement was forged between former prime ministers Allawi and Maliki, so that Nouri al Maliki was re-appointed prime minister on 11 November, while Iyad Allawi was appointed head of the National Council for Strategic Policies; four Sunni politicians were reinstated, having been banned as former Ba'ath party members. In November President Talabani said he would refuse to sign the execution order on Tariq Aziz. After eight months delay, following the general elections, the new government began parliament's first session on 21 November. On 15 December the UN lifted the last sanctions against Iraq which had first been imposed in 1991.

2011 On 5 January, radical cleric Moqtada al Sadr returned from four years of self-imposed exile in Iran. Sheikh Nasser al Mohammed al Sabah became the first prime minister of Kuwait to visit Iraq since the 1990 invasion, arriving in Bagdad on 12 January. Prime ministerial discussions covered border issues, finance and security as well as the payment of war reparations said to amount to amount to billions of US dollars. The UK military operations in Iraq ended completely on 20 May, when 81 naval trainers of the Royal Navy left the country, having completed their training of Iraqi sailors, ready to defend Iraqi territorial waters and its shipping. On 7 July, in a ceremony held in Washington, some Babylonian antiquities that had been looted from the Iraqi Museum in 2003 and found in the US, were formally returned. The central bank announced on 4 August that the Iraqi dinar was to have three zeros removed. The authorities said 30 trillion (US$26 billion) banknotes were being printed to replace existing notes. In September, the CBI declared its intention of implementing the change in 2013. On 21 October, US-President Obama announced that all US troops (around 39,000) would leave Iraq in an orderly withdrawal by 31 December.

Political structure

Constitution

A public referendum approved a new permanent constitution on 15 October 2005. It came into effect when the elections for the Council of Representatives took place on 15 December 2005.

The constitution declares that the Republic of Iraq is an independent, sovereign nation, and its system of governance is democratic, federal, and representative (parliamentary). Islam is the official religion of the state and is a basic source of legislation. Iraq is part of the Arab nation and the Islamic world.

Universal suffrage begins at aged 18.

The country is divided into 18 provinces (*muhafazat*, singular *muhafazahW0): al Anbar, al Basrah, al Muthanna, al Qadisiyah, An Najaf, Arbil, As Sulaymaniyah, At Ta'mim, Babil, Baghdad, Dahuk, Dhi Qar, Diyala, Karbala', Maysan, Ninawa, Salah ad Din and Wasit.*

Independence date

3 October 1932, independent Kingdom; 14 July 1958, Republic.

Form of state

Republic, federal

The executive

Executive authority consists of the Presidency Council, the Council of Ministers, presided over by the prime minister.

The Presidency Council consists of the president and two deputies; they are elected by the national assembly.

National legislature

The unicameral Majlis al Watani (National Assembly), with 275 members (the constitution defines the number ratio as one representative per 100,000 Iraqi citizens), elected by proportional representation from party lists. All members serve for four-year terms.

Kurdish Autonomous Region (known as Iraqi Kurdistan): the unicameral Civata Nîstimanî Kurdistan (Perleman) (Al Majlis al Watani Li Kurdistan) (Kurdistan National Assembly) (KNA) has 111 members, elected by proportional representation from party lists, with each political party allocated seats in proportion to their share of the vote. By law, 25 per cent of membership must be female and 11 seats are reserved for minority people's candidates. Elections take place every four years. The KNA shares federal power with the Iraqi National Assembly but has a dominant role and responsibility for indigenous matters, including the economy and investment of the region.

Legal system

Under the constitution the Judiciary is independent and represented by courts of different kinds and levels, issuing their rulings according to law. No authority can interfere in the judiciary or in the affairs of justice.

The Federal Judiciary includes the Supreme Judiciary Council, and the Supreme Federal Court.The Iraqi court system is divided into the Civil Courts, Courts of Personal Status, and Criminal Courts.

Last elections

7 March 2010 (National Assembly); 25 July 2009 (Kurdistan National Assembly (KNA) and presidential)

Results: National Assembly: Al Iraqiya (Iraqi National Movement) won 25.87 per cent of the vote (91 seats out of 325); I'tilaf Dawlat al Qanon (State of Law Coalition) 25.76 per cent (89); Al Ittilaf al Watani al Iraqi (National Iraqi Alliance) (known as Watani List) 19.43 per cent (70); Lîstî Kurdistan (Kurdistan List) 15.27 per cent (43); Gorran (Movement for Change) 4.36 per cent (8); Al Tawafuq (Iraqi Accord Front) 2.72 per cent (six); three other political parties won less than five seats each and eight independents failed to win any seats. Turnout was 62.4 per cent.

On 26 April 2010 the Iraq High Electoral Commission (IHEC) banned 52 members of the Watani Alliance from serving in parliament due to their links to the outlawed Ba'ath Party. The votes within constituencies were recalculated and allocated to other candidates of the Watani alliance.

KNA: Kurdistani List alliance 57.34 per cent (59 seats out of 111), Change List 23.75 per cent (25), Service and Reform List 12.8 per cent (13), IMK List 1.45 per cent (2), Turkmen Democratic Movement 0.99 per cent (3), Social Justice and Freedom List 0.82 per cent (1), Chaldean Syriac Assryrian Popular Council 0.58 per cent (3), Reform Turkmen List 0.38 per cent (1), National Rafidain List 0.3 per cent (2), Aram Shahine Dawood (independent Armenian) 0.22 per cent (1) and Erbil Turkmen (independent Turk) 0.21 per cent; 13 other political parties failed to win any seats.

Iraqi Kurdistan presidential: Massoud Barzani won 69.6 per cent, Kamal Mirawdily 25.3 per cent, Halow Ibrahim Ahmed 3.5 per cent, Ahmed Mohammed Rasul 1.4 per cent, Hussein Garmiyani 0.6 per cent.

Next elections

21 January 2010 (presidential) postponed; 2014 (parliamentary)

Political parties

Ruling party

National Alliance coalition, led by Al Iraqiya (Iraqi National Movement), with I'tilaf Dawlat al Qanon (State of Law Coalition) and Al Ittilaf al Watani al Iraqi (National Iraqi Alliance) (known as Watani List) (from 14 Jun 2010)

Main opposition party

Hizb al Fadhila al Islamiyah (Islamic Virtue Party)

Population

31.23 million (2009) (Figure includes the UN estimated 4.6 million living in exile)

Last census: October 1997: 19,184,543 (excluding data for autonomous northern regions)

Population density: 49 inhabitants per square km. Urban population: 68 per cent (1995–2001).

Annual growth rate: 3.0 per cent 1994–2004 (WHO 2006)

Ethnic make-up

Arabs comprise 75 per cent of the population, with Kurds representing a further 20 per cent (mostly located in northern Iraq) and Turkmen, Assyrian and other minorities making up the remaining 5 per cent.

Religions

Shi'a (also known as Shi'ite, Shiite, Shi'is) Muslims are the largest religious group, comprising 54 per cent of the population. Sunni Muslims were politically dominant in the Saddam Hussein period, although accounting for only 42 per cent of the total. There is a significant number of Christians and a small number of Yazidis and others.

Education

After the 2003 Iraq War, attempts began to re-build Iraq's education system, as the US Agency for International Development (USAID) granted US$2 million to provide immediate educational needs.

Free education is provided for children between the ages of six and 18.

Literacy rate: 40.1 per cent total, 24.1 per cent female, adult rates in 2002 (World Bank).

Compulsory years: Six and 12

Enrolment rate: 46 per cent in primary education. Only 37 per cent of girls attend school. (Unicef, 2008)

Pupils per teacher: 20 in primary schools.

Welfare

Iraq is struggling to repair its social infrastructure, welfare and pensions are being administered in an *ad hoc* manner until the newly elected government can get to grips with the economy and implement nationwide policies.

Main cities

Baghdad (capital, estimated population 6.9 million (m) in 2005), Mosul (1.1m), Basra (1.1m), Arbil (910,381), Kirkuk (618,149), Sulaymaniyah (683,261).

Media

The media has been liberated from official sanctions and there has been a rapid growth in all mediums. Private media outlets are typically linked to political, religious and ethnic groupings.

Press

Dailies: In Arabic, newspapers with the highest circulations include *Al Mada* (www.almadapaper.com), *Al Sabah* (www.alsabaah.com), *Al Mashriq* (www.al-mashriq.net), *Al Ahali* (www.ahali-iraq.net). In Kurdish, *Al Ittihad* (www.alitthad.com) and *Khabat* (www.xebat.net), published by the Kurdistan Democratic Party. Iraqi newspapers with English online editions include *Al Sabah* and *Azzaman* (www.azzaman.com).

Broadcasting

The Iraqi Media Net (www.iraqimedianet.net) is the national public radio and television broadcaster.

Radio: The Republic of Iraq Radio (www.iraqimedianet.net), known as Iraqi Radio has two networks RI 1 and H Quraan. There are many local radio stations in operation, including Radio Annas (www.radioannas.com), Al Huda Radio (www.al-hodaonline.com), Radio Sawa (www.radiosawa.com) and Radio Nawa Kurdish (www.radionawa.com). There are international services provided by France, UK and the US available via local relays.

Television: Around 70 per cent of the TV audience watch satellite TV with pan-Arab stations taking the majority share of ratings. Iraqi Media Net (www.iraqimedianet.net) operates three channels of Al Iraqiya TV, TV2 and Sports TV. Private stations include *Al Sharqiya* (www.alsharqiya.com) and Al Sumaria (www.alsumaria.tv). In the semi-autonomous Kurdistan there are three satellite stations, Kurdistan Satellite Channel (www.kurdistan.tv), KurdSat (www.kurdsat.tv) and Zagros (www.zagrostv.com).

News agencies

Other news agencies: Nina (National Iraqi News Agency): www.ninanews.com Voices of Iraq: www.aswataliraq.info

Economy

With huge proven oil reserves, 137 billion barrels of oil and 3.2 trillion cubic metres of natural gas at the end of 2010, Iraq has the potential to have a modern well-funded economy. However, the problems created under the old regime and the destruction of the economy since 2003 have left a huge legacy of poverty, unemployment and underinvestment. The government has been addressing the country's problems and has begun to initiate change, rebuilding its infrastructure and providing commodities for its people.

As the economy has gradually been brought under control, inflation, which had been at a record 53.2 per cent in 2006, began to fall, so that by 2008 it was into single digits at 2.7 per cent. The rate then fell into a negative rate of -2.2 per cent in 2009, as the global economic crisis cut world trade. By 2010, inflation had picked up, and ran at 2.4 per cent, with a forecast of a rising rate of 5 per cent in 2011.

GDP growth has experienced wild fluctuations since 2005, as it jumped from -0.7 per cent to 6.2 per cent in 2006, before falling back to 1.5 per cent in 2007; in early 2008 global oil prices were at their highest and with rebuilding underway GDP growth was estimated at 9.5 per cent, before slowing down to 4.2 per cent and then almost stalling at 0.8 per cent in 2010. The forecast for 2011 indicated a return to positive growth of 9.6 per cent.

Oil typically provides over 99 per cent of all exports and in 2009 exports of oil was estimated at US$38.2 billion (down from US$61.1 billion in 2008), then as global trade picked up exports rose to a projected US$50.0 billion in 2010, rising to US$61.4 billion in 2011.

The government operates under a system whereby oil revenue is shared among the three principal ethnic/religious groups (Shi'a, Sunni and Kurds). It is hoped this measure will ensure unity and a cessation in sectarian bloodshed, as current oil fields are located in the predominately Shi'a region in the south while the best prospects for oil in the future are in the Kurdish region of the north.

The IMF agreed to extend to Iraq its largest loan, of US$3.6 billion, to be used to rebuild its infrastructure, in February 2010.

In July 2010, the government announced a US$186 billion five-year development plan, which will launch 2,700 projects planned to enhance economic growth, develop infrastructure – with an emphasis on the oil and electricity sectors, reduce regional differences and increase employment by 3.5 million jobs. Although US$100 billion will be funded through the state budget, the remainder will be provided by local and foreign investment.

The central bank announced on 4 August 2011 that the Iraqi dinar was to have three zeros removed. The authorities said 30 trillion (US$26 billion) banknotes were being printed to replace existing notes. In September, the CBI declared its intention of implementing the change in 2013.

External trade

In 2005 the Greater Arab Free Trade Area (Gafta) was ratified by 17 members, including Iraq, creating an Arab economic bloc. A customs union was established whereby tariffs within Gafta will be reduced by a percentage each year, until none remain. By late-2009 Iraq was still in negotiation with WTO for membership.

Iraq has an open trade investment regime whereby a customs duty of 5 per cent is levied on all import goods, except primary commodities such as food, medicines, clothing and humanitarian items.

Imports

Commodities include food, medicines and manufactured goods.

Main sources: Syria (typically 30 per cent of total), Turkey (20 per cent), US (10 per cent).

Exports

Main exports include crude oil (over 95 per cent), non-oil items include raw materials, food and live animals.

Main destinations: US (typically 45 per cent of total) Italy (10 per cent), South Korea (8 per cent).

Agriculture

Farming

The area of cultivatable land in Iraq is estimated to be around 12 million hectares (ha). About four million ha of this arable land consists of rain-fed agriculture and the remaining eight million depends on irrigation. Less than 50 per cent of this land is actually cultivated. However, irrigation systems are badly in need of repair and salinity is increasingly affecting large areas of arable land.

The most important crops are barley and wheat (yields of each exceed one million tonnes in a good year) and rice; and after cereals, which account for most of the arable land, cotton, dates, vegetables and fruit.

Historically, dates were the most valuable exports after oil (with an annual value of around US$75 million). Production plummeted due to the war with Iran (1980–88), and to pollution which affected millions of trees in the south, following the 1991 Gulf War.

Fishing

There is a small fishing industry, mostly based on the Tigris and Euphrates rivers. Without import and export activities it will remain insignificant.

Forestry

Forests cover around 800,000ha, or 1.8 per cent of the land area and are mainly confined to the northern part of the country. There is no significant commercial exploitation.

Industry and manufacturing

Iraq's major industries centre on the petroleum, chemical, textile, construction and food processing sectors. Much of Iraq's industrial base was affected by war and sanctions. Before the 1991 Gulf War, Iraq was second only to Saudi Arabia in

terms of oil production and reserves.
Iraq's oil industry was boosted and re-invested into by the UN oil-for-food programme, although it was far from pre-1991 levels. During 2004 and 2005 there were efforts to re-build Iraq's industrial and manufacturing base, particularly in oil production.

Mining

The mining sector contributes about 8 per cent to GDP and employs 4 per cent of the working population.
Iraq has huge resources of phosphates and its sulphur reserves are among the world's largest; there is significant potential for sulphur exports.
Other minerals include glass sand, raw materials for the construction industry, and modest quantities of iron ore, lead, copper and gypsum.

Hydrocarbons

Proven oil reserves were 115 billion barrels of oil at the end of 2010, with production of 2.46 million barrels per day (bpd). It is considered, by experts in the field, that Iraq has known and unknown reserves of oil yet to be exploited, which may contain anything from 45–100 billion bpd of recoverable oil. In 2007 most oil production was derived from just three giant fields (super giant fields yield 5 billion bpd, of which Iraq has nine; giant fields yield 1 billion bpd, of which there are 22 known). War damage to the northern oil fields around Kirkuk caused a significant drop in production from the pre-war level of 680,000bpd to 206,000bpd in 2007.
Oil revenues for the first quarter of 2010 reached US$17 billion, from the export of 222.7 million barrels of oil.
In 2009 the UK-based oil company Heritage announced it had discovered an oil field of 2.3–4.2 billion barrels in Kurdish Iraq. It announced on 26 January 2011 that a significant find of natural gas, estimated at 348 billion cubic metres (cum), in the Kurdistan region of northern Iraq. In June, following the completion of an oil pipeline exporting oil from the region, China's Sinopec out-bid South Korea's National Oil Company, with an offer of US$7.8 billion to purchase Addax Petroleum Corporation, which has large oil assets in Kurdish Iraq. In 2009, the minister of oil announced that oil capacity was predicted to reach 12 million bpd by 2015 following the signing of a number of contracts: the Russian Lukoil and Norwegian Statoil firms won a joint contract to exploit the supergiant West Quran field (with around 13 billion barrels of oil), the Anglo-Dutch Shell oil will develop the Majnoon field (with around 12.6 billion barrels of oil), and the Chinese state oil company CNPC now has the rights to the Halfaya field (with 4.1 billion barrels of oil). The Al Ahdab oil field in central Iraq began production on 1 July with 60,000bpd, according to its operator the CNPC. When fully operational, by December 2011, production will rise to 120,000bpd.
Refining capacity had grown to 856,000 bpd in 2010, an increase of 12.2 per cent on the 2009 figures.
Proven natural gas reserves were 3.2 trillion cum at the end of 2010. However, probable reserves are considerably higher with as much as 8.4 trillion cum. About 70 per cent of Iraq's natural gas supplies are by-products of oil production. Natural gas production was 1.3 billion cum in 2010, which has shown a steady decline since the 3.2 billion cum in 2000. The largest gas fields are in the north at Kirkuk, and in Rumaila and Zubair in the south and are all oil field associated gas.
Iraq signed a multi-million dollar purchase agreement for Iranian natural gas (25 million cum per day) on 7 June 2011, to be delivered to two Iraqi power plants in the north-east via a new gas pipeline, due to be completed in 2012.
Iraq has some small low-grade coal deposits, with some limited exploitation before 1990 supplying the domestic chemicals industry. These mines are thought to have fallen into disuse following the destruction of industrial capacity and imposition of UN sanctions in the 1990s.

Energy

Total installed generating capacity was 4,000MW in 2006, with a further 200–300MW imported daily. Consumption was 9,299MW, and the goal has been to increase generating capacity to 6,000MW. The electricity infrastructure is undergoing refurbishment and expansion; however an estimate US$20–25 billion will have to be spent to bring the system into full operation with electricity supplied to all. In the meantime, the government has been attempting to get Baghdad's electricity grid linked to neighbouring country power systems, so as to increase the city's 12–14 hours of power.
The International Monetary Fund (IMF) extended a US$5.5 billion loan to Iraq, which will be used to upgrade the electricity infrastructure. The loan will be repaid by 2014, at a 1 per cent interest rate per annum.
In May 2010 a new 31.5MW electricity sub-station in Kirkuk became operational. On 3 April 2011, the Kurdistan ministry of electricity signed a US$18 million contract with the Turkish energy company Shar to connect electricity power lines between the provinces of Sulaimaniya (Iraq) and Erbil (Turkey).
In February 2011, the ministry of electricity announced that to resolve the country's energy crisis a sum of US$6 billion was needed in the 2011 annual budget and that US$3–4 billion was necessary for several years in the future to allow for growth.
An electricity generating plant, build by Sunir, an Iranian energy development company, was opened on 1 May 2011, in the north-eastern Baghdad suburb of Sadr City. It has two 160MW turbines, which can be run on either oil or natural gas. One turbine went into operation immediately and was linked to the national grid, while the remaining turbine will become operational in June 2011. Plans to install a further two, gas-operated turbines should also be confirmed by June. However, poor infrastructure around the plant hampers operations as 80 fuel trucks must deliver 10,000 hectolitres (264,170 US-gallons) everyday, with poor roads, traffic jams and security checkpoints slowing progress. The installation of a natural gas pipeline to overcome the problems is under discussion.
At the peak of summer demand, Iraq requires over 15,000MW of electricity, but the scheduled generating capacity for 2011 was 7,000MW.

Financial markets

Stock exchange

Iraq Stock Exchange (ISX)

Banking and insurance

The banking systems, according to the IMF in 2005, is weak and barely functioning. It comprises the Central Bank of Iraq and 26 chartered banks. Two state-owned banks, the Rafidain and Rashid Banks, account for over 90 per cent of the commercial banking assets and 75 per cent of the local branch network. These institutions are heavily over-staffed with too many staff under-skilled and the government may invite foreign involvement in restructuring them. It may also amalgamate four of the smaller, and specialised banks into two regional development banks and well establishing new Islamic banks.
In 2003, the Trade Bank of Iraq (TBI) was established to provide financial and related services to facilitate imports and exports. It is independent of the Central Bank of Iraq.
The authorities will be implementing international accounting and auditing standards, and improving disclosure requirements, to adhere to recognised practices in good governance.
The Iraqi Central Bank (IBC) paid off a total of US$2.7 billion to 3,500 commercial creditors in February 2011, to ensure protection for the Iraqi dinar on foreign currency markets.

On 2 February 2011, the ICB confirmed that six private and publicly owned banks were using electronic banking systems and that it had allocated US$10 million to state banks to activate the system. By 2010, 85 per cent of government financial transactions were processed through state banks.
Parliament's Economic Commission announced on 20 March 2011 that it will introduce legislation to organise the work of private and publicly owned banks, to enhance financial and economic development and avoid the growth of irregular business practices.

Central bank
Central Bank of Iraq

Time
GMT plus three hours (daylight saving, April–September, GMT plus four hours)

Geography
Iraq is bounded by Turkey to the north, Iran to the east, Kuwait to the south-east, and Saudi Arabia, Jordan and Syria to the west. There is also a neutral zone between Iraq and Saudi Arabia administered jointly by the two countries with Iraq's portion covering 3,522 square km. The country's most fertile area and heartland is the flood plain of the Tigris and Euphrates rivers, which flow in parallel for most of their length from the Turkish and Syrian borders respectively, to the Gulf. The north-east of Iraq is mountainous while the large western desert area is sparsely populated and undeveloped.

Hemisphere
Northern

Climate
There is an excessively hot sub-tropical period with no rainfall from May–September (38–49 degrees Celsius (C)). Dry and pleasantly warm from October–April (20–25 degrees C), with occasional heavy rain. Continental conditions affect the northern mountainous areas which experience severe winters, but the southern plains have warm winters with some rain and very hot, dry summers. The temperature in Baghdad ranges from between 4 degrees C and 16 degrees C in January, to between 24 degrees C and 33 degrees C in July and August. Average annual rainfall is 300mm.

Dress codes
Conservative and modest dress should be worn in public in conformity with local Islamic traditions. Safari suits or short-sleeved suits are acceptable for men at work or at informal meetings; lounge suits in light materials are worn for formal meetings and in the evening.

Entry requirements
All requirements are subject to change and should be thoroughly checked before departure.

Passports
Passports are required by all.

Visa
There are only a few countries designated to issue visas and only to certain authorised visitors. See *Entry Visa Regulations* in the consular section at www.iraqembassy.org for a list.

Prohibited entry
Nationals of Israel and holders of passports with evidence of travel in Israel are denied entry.

Currency advice/regulations
A currency declaration form must be completed on arrival and departure. The import and export of local currency is restricted to small coins only. The import of foreign currency is unlimited but amounts must be declared. Export cannot exceed the amount declared on entry. Travellers cheques are little used.

Customs
Beyond the allotted duty-free allowance, the total value of imports must not exceed ID100. Electrial goods (not for personal use), commercial artifacts and fruits and plant material are subject to import duty. The export of antiques and artefacts is prohibited.

Health (for visitors)
Travellers should be aware of the poor capacity of Iraqi hospitals to extend medical care and that communications and essential services, including power and water cannot be relied on. Comprehensive medical insurance covering repatriation is essential. There are severe shortages of essential drugs. Detailed health advice should be sought before visiting Iraq.

Mandatory precautions
A certificate of vaccination against yellow fever, if travelling from an infected area.

Advisable precautions
Precautions should include vaccinations, or booster shots, for typhoid, diphtheria, tetanus, polio and hepatitis A; some vaccines may be advised including hepatitis B, TB, cholera and rabies. Anti-malarial precautions should be taken; the use of mosquito nets and repellents and covering up the body after dark can help avoid malaria and hepatitis B.
All water should be regarded as being potentially contaminated. Water used for drinking, brushing teeth or making ice should be boiled or otherwise sterilised. Dairy products are likely to be unpasteurised and should be avoided. Eat only well-cooked meat and fish, preferably served hot. Vegetables should be cooked and fruit peeled. Pork, salad and mayonnaise may carry increased risk.

Public holidays (national)

Fixed dates
1 Jan (New Year's Day), 17 Apr (FAO Day), 1 May (Labour Day), 14 Jul (Republic Day).

Variable dates
Eid al Adha (four days), Islamic New Year, Birth of the Prophet, Eid al Fitr (two days).
Islamic year 1433 (26 Nov 2011–14 Nov 2012): The Islamic year contains 354 or 355 days, with the result that Muslim feasts advance by 10–12 days against the Gregorian calendar. Dates of feasts vary according to the sighting of the new moon, so cannot be forecast exactly.

Working hours
The weekly closing day is Friday.

Banking
Sat–Wed: 0800–1230; Thur: 0800–1100. During Ramadan: 0800–1000.

Business
Sat–Wed: 0800–1400; Thursday: 0800–1300.

Government
Summer hours: Sat–Wed: 0800–1230; Thu: 0800–1100. Winter hours: Sat–Wed: 0830–1430 Thu: 0830–1330.

Shops
Small shops tend to open very early, close during the middle of the day and then re-open from around 1600–1900 or later. Food markets open around 0900 and close at mid-day or when supplies are exhausted.

Telecommunications

Mobile/cell phones
GSM 900 services are available. Numbers begin 7801/2/3/4, plus 6 digits.

Electricity supply
220V AC, 50 cycles

Weights and measures
Metric system.

Social customs/useful tips
Traditional Islamic culture predominates, with Quranic law playing an active role in the day-to-day life of the country. Visitors should be careful to respect this and act accordingly. They should always address their hosts by full name and title. Traditional Arab hospitality is generally offered. In business meetings formal courtesies are expected. Visiting cards are regularly exchanged and these should be printed in Arabic as well as English. Meetings may not always be on a one-to-one basis and it is often difficult to confine conversation to the business in hand, as many topics may be discussed in order to assess the character of potential business partners. Patience and good humour are required.

Always refer to the stretch of water south of Iraq as the Arabian Gulf or the Gulf – never the Persian Gulf.
It is unwise to discuss religion or politics, and desirable to have an informed view on contemporary issues (such as Israel) in case such subjects arise.
During the Ramadan fasting month, both smoking and drinking in public are forbidden.

Security

Visitors should keep in touch with developments in the Middle East as any increase in regional tension might affect travel advice. The security situation in Iraq remains dangerous with insurgent forces targetting coalition interests and personnel as well as international agencies, such as the UN and the Red Cross. There are daily bombings in central and southern Iraq.

Getting there

Air

National airline: Iraqi Airways
International airport/s: Baghdad International Airport (BGW), 18km west of Baghdad; Basra International Airport.
Other airport/s: Smaller airfields exist at Hadithah, Kirkuk and Mosul.
Airport tax: Departure tax: ID2,000.

Surface

Travel by road remains hazardous and is not recommended.
Rail: The line between Mosul and Aleppo, Syria was reopened, although the service was suspended.
Water: All ports remain closed to civilian traffic.
Main port/s: Umm Qasr and Khor al Zubair are the major commercial ports.

Getting about

National transport

Air: Services are subject to US military restrictions. Prior to 2003 Iraqi Airways flew from Baghdad to Basra. There are domestic airports at Mosul and Kirkuk.
Road: Despite the Iraq War, the country's 40,800km road system is in relatively good condition with 84 per cent paved.
Rail: Prior to 2003, the rail network included three-class services with sleeping accommodation, restaurant cars and air-conditioning. Rail links between most major centres include Baghdad-Mosul, Baghdad-Arbil and Baghdad-Basra.
In June 2011 a preliminary deal was signed by French engineering company Alstom to build a high-speed rail line linking Basra and Baghdad. The line would also connect with Karbala and Najaf in a total network of 650km.

City transport

Taxis: Prior to 2003, taxis were available in major cities and at hotels. There were shared and regular taxis. There was a standard fare system and taxis were meters. A surcharge was made after 2200 hours. Fares should be clearly agreed in advance. Tipping is not expected.

BUSINESS DIRECTORY

The addresses listed below are a selection only. While World of Information makes every endeavour to check these addresses, we cannot guarantee that changes have not been made, especially to telephone numbers and area codes. We would welcome any corrections. Readers should be aware that the details following may not be current. Telephone numbers probably won't work.

Telephone area codes

The international direct dialling code (IDD) for Iraq is +964, followed by area code and subscriber's number:

Baghdad	1	Mosul	60
Basra	40	Najaf	33
Erbil	66	Nasiriya	42
Kirkuk	50	Sulayimaniya	53
Kut	23	Tikrit	21

Useful telephone numbers

Police: 104
Fire: 115
Ambulance: 122
Emergency hospital: 719-5191
Operator: 537-2191
Directory enquiries: 102
International operator: 105

Chambers of Commerce

Federation of Iraqi Chambers of Commerce, Sadoon Street, PO Box 3388 Al-Alwia, Baghdad (tel: 718-7348; fax: 718-1115; e-mail: union@uruklink.net).

Baghdad Chamber of Commerce, Mustansir Street, PO Box 24168 Almsarif, Baghdad (tel: 887-6111; fax: 887-9563).

Basrah Chamber of Commerce, Al-Azizyah Street, Alashad, Basrah (tel: 211-343; fax: 212-478).

Mosul Chamber of Commerce, Khalid Ibn Al-Waleed, PO Box 35, Mosul (tel: 774-771; fax: 771-359).

Banking

Bank of Baghdad, PO 3192, Alawiyah (tel: 822-7083).

Credit Bank of Iraq, PO Box 3420, Baghdad (tel: 360-0494).

Dar Es Salaam Investment Bank, PO Box 3067, Alawiyah (tel: 360-4646).

Industrial Bank of Iraq, al Khullani Square, PO Box 5825, Baghdad (tel: 887-2181).

Iraq Middle East Investment Bank, PO Box 10379, Baghdad (tel: 360-4242).

Rafidain Bank, New Banks' Street, Massarif, PO Box 11360, Baghdad (tel: 887-0522: fax: 415-8616).

Rashid Bank, PO Box 7177, Tourism Building, Haifa Street, Baghdad (tel: 884-5287, 885-3433; fax: 882-6201).

Central bank

Central Bank of Iraq, PO Box 64, Rashid Street, Baghdad, Iraq (tel: 886-5171; fax: 886-6802).

Stock exchange

Iraq Stock Exchange (ISX): www.isx-iq.net

Travel information

Baghdad International Airport, Baghdad (tel: 887-2500, 886-3999; fax: 887-5808).

Ministries

Ministry of Foreign Affairs (email: press@iraqmofamail.net; internet: wwww.iraqmofa.net).

Directorate of Foreign Economic Relations, Ministry of Trade, Khulafa Street, al Khullani Square, Baghdad (tel: 887-2682).

Ministry of Industry and Military Industrialisation, Nidhal Street, near Sa'adoun Petrol Station, Baghdad (tel: 887-2006).

Ministry of Oil, al Mansour, PO Box 6178, Baghdad (tel: 541-0031).

Other useful addresses

Iraqi Embassy (in the USA), 1801 P Street, NW, Washington, DC 20036 (tel: (+1-202) 483 7500; internet: www.iraqiembassy.org).

Iraq National Oil Company, al Khullani Square, PO Box 476, Baghdad (tel: 887-1115).

Iraqi Federation of Industries, Iraqi Federation of Industries Building, al Khullani Square, Baghdad.

News agencies

Nina (National Iraqi News Agency): www.ninanews.com

Voices of Iraq: www.aswataliraq.info

Internet sites

Guide to Iraqi businesses: www.iraqdirectory.com

Iraq Stock Exchange: www.isx-iq.net

Ireland

KEY FACTS

Official name: Éire (Ireland)

Head of State: President Michael D Higgins (from 11 Nov 2011)

Head of government: Prime Minister (*Taoiseach*) Enda Kelly (FG) (from 9 Mar 2011)

Ruling party: Coalition led by Fine Gael (FG) (United Ireland Party) with Labour Party (LP) (from 9 Mar 2011)

Area: 70,283 square km

Population: 4.43 million (2009)

Capital: Dublin

Official language: Irish (Gaelic) and English

Currency: Euro (€) = 100 cents (from 1 Jan 2002; previous currency, punt, locked at IR£0.79 per euro)

Exchange rate: €0.76 per US$ (Oct 2011)

GDP per capita: US$45,689 (2010)

GDP real growth: -1.00% (2010)

GDP: US$204.30 billion (2010)

Labour force: 2.14 million (2010)

Unemployment: 13.70% (2010)

Inflation: -1.60% (2010)

Balance of trade: US$48.27 billion (2010)

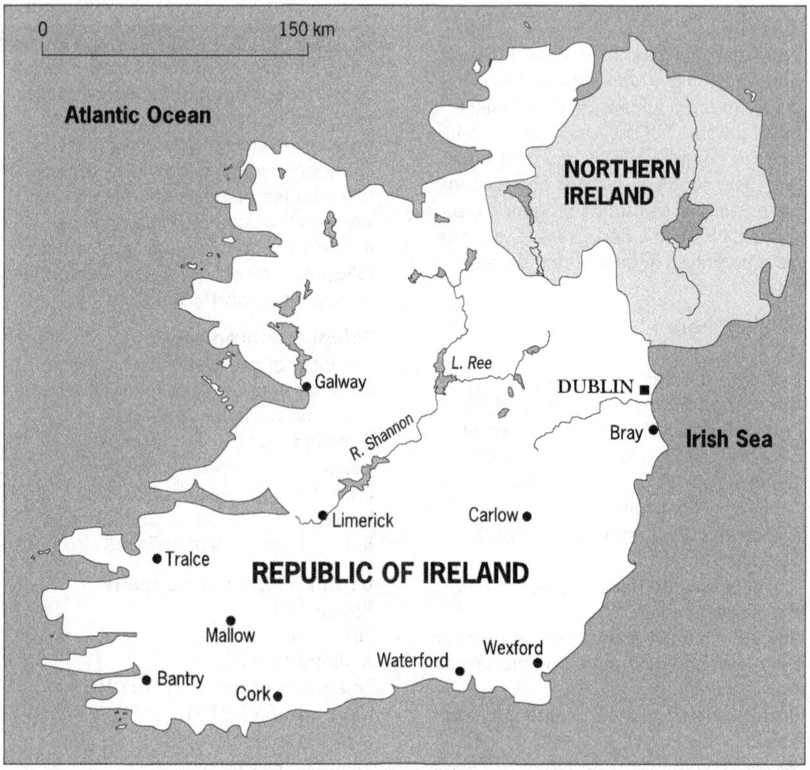

To go from Celtic Tiger to Gaelic lame duck in a matter of months is no mean achievement. In 2011 it was easy to be cynical about the Irish 'euro-enthusiasm' of the 1970s. Ireland had good reason to embrace the European vision – not least the €50 billion (US$67 billion) that flowed to Irish farmers from Brussels in the shape of agricultural subsidies. On top of this there also flowed some €17 billion (US$22.8 billion) from the European Union's (EU) infrastructure fund destined to improve Irish roads and bridges.

Bungalow bliss

Town planning has never been one of Ireland's stronger points. Throughout the property boom of the late 1990s and the early 'noughties' (that is to say from 2000 onwards) an uncontrolled building boom saw a bad planning situation get worse as often unattractive buildings sprouted willy-nilly, in many cases in completely inappropriate locations. The speed with which, in the second half of 2008, the financial *tsunami* swept over the EU's most westerly outpost took developers, real estate agents, banks and borrows all by surprise. As a result, unattractive buildings that had already been started were often simply abandoned in a half-finished state, making a bad situation worse.

If Ireland's 'Bungalow Bliss' was a symbol, it was a symbol, in the view of one commentator, of the way in which Ireland was selling its soul for Brussels gold. Prior to EU membership, Ireland was not seen as an investment opportunity. In 1972 total foreign direct investment (FDI) was a paltry €16 million. Thirty years on, the figure was €30 billion (US$40.2 billion). FDI, principally from the US, made Ireland the model for new and aspirant members of the EU. But for Ireland, EU membership went a lot further. It gave Ireland a means of gaining international importance and stature without having to depend on its neighbour to the east, Great

Britain. At the same time, EU inspired legislation reinforced Ireland's citizens sense of individuality.

A sense of European identity also made it easier for Ireland's government (and that of Great Britain) to resolve some of the thornier issues surrounding the future of Northern Ireland. This sense of belonging to something meant that Ireland appeared to prosper in a welcoming international environment. Differences no longer needed to be suppressed or killed, they could be lived with. For the most part, Ireland had learned to accept diversity, to a degree that made its own internal arguments seem all the more petty.

Thus, Ireland had benefited from EU membership when it was one of the poorer European nations. But the longer it basked in a prosperity founded on low taxation, light legislation and US investment, the more it acquired the business philosophy and methodology of North America rather than Europe. It was a while before the realisation dawned that it was following a business model that, at least in the European context, didn't work. By then, however, it was too late. Ireland woke up to face what was the most expensive bank bailout in history. In the 1970s Ireland's European dream had started with money; money received from Europe. The dream ended with money to be paid back to Europe. In between there had been a period when more noble European ideals were adopted and cherished.

Austerity

As the Celtic Tiger lost its teeth, Ireland's mid-2010 austerity package saw a number of swingeing measures that many observers had previously only considered appropriate for other European countries. Public sector wages were cut by as much as 20 per cent, alongside reductions in child benefits. Quite dramatically, many teachers, nurses and police officers were not even offered the 'luxury' of wage cuts. They were simply laid off and invited to join Ireland's ever-lengthening dole queues. The public response to their government's determination was a mixture of bitterness and stoicism. However, the international financial markets appeared to be sufficiently impressed by the Irish resolve to address the situation, which was in stark contrast to the reluctance in a number of other members of the euro-zone.

What had become clear as the effects of the financial crisis came to be evaluated, was that much, if not most, of the damage in the crisis was in fact caused by one single institution: the Anglo Irish bank. This bank had been taken into full private ownership in 2009 after discoveries of extensive 'doubtful' transactions emerged. By early 2010, meeting the liabilities of Anglo Irish had already cost the Irish taxpayer over €12 billion (US$16 billion), with dismal expectations that the likely further cost could be as much as €10 billion (US$13.4 billion). With hindsight, it was clear that the bank – which grew at a mind-boggling annual rate of 36 per cent for the ten years up to 2007 – was out of control.

Ireland's apparent progress to recovery and reform was, however, knocked sideways in mid-September 2010 by an article in the *Irish Independent* which claimed that the country was 'perilously close' to calling in the assistance of both the EU and the International Monetary Fund (IMF). The article created a widespread response from the IMF which refuted the newspaper's claims saying that it did not foresee that its aid would be needed for Ireland, adding that 'The Irish authorities have taken assertive measures to deal with the banking crisis.' The Irish government, through its department of finance, added that there was 'absolutely no truth to a rumour concerning external assistance'. It attacked the basis of the article, saying that it was 'based on a local misinterpretation of a research report'. The research report quoted was one published by the investment bank Barclays Capital which had observed that Iraland's liquidity position was 'comfortable' but that if unexpected banking losses emerged or economic conditions were to deteriorate, 'outside help might be needed'.

The IMF

While the Irish electorate were still in a state of shock, the Irish authorities pressed forward with their financial sector reform strategy while keeping the budget on track for the major fiscal consolidation targeted in 2011. All quantitative macro-economic targets were achieved and these efforts contributed to a notable decline in Ireland's bond spreads, which also benefited from EU interest rate cuts agreed at the July 2011 Euro Summit, participation by private investors in bank recapitalisation and from renewed confidence in Ireland's medium term growth potential following strong export-led growth in the first half of 2011.

However, sustaining this nascent economic recovery, despite adverse external developments, is key to ensuring debt sustainability and programme success. Trade partner growth prospects have deteriorated as the euro area crisis has outpaced the adoption and implementation of measures by the European authorities. In the face of this external drag on economic recovery, the Irish authorities are adopting additional consolidation measures to meet the original fiscal targets and they are implementing structural reforms in the labour market and sheltered sectors to enhance competitiveness. Strengthened euro area support for Ireland's growth and debt sustainability would greatly reinforce prospects for Ireland to regain market access at an early stage given these more adverse circumstances.

KEY INDICATORS **Ireland**

	Unit	2006	2007	2008	2009	2010
Population	m	4.24	4.34	4.42	4.43	*4.47
Gross domestic product (GDP)	US$bn	219.37	260.10	267.60	227.80	204.30
GDP per capita	US$	51,800	59,924	60,510	51,356	45,689
GDP real growth	%	5.7	6.0	-3.0	-7.1	-0.4
Inflation	%	2.7	2.9	3.1	-1.7	-1.6
Unemployment	%	4.4	4.6	6.1	11.8	13.7
Exports (fob) (goods)	US$m	104,667.0	115,517.0	119,620.0	106,978.0	109,856.0
Imports (fob) (goods)	US$m	72,779.0	84,226.0	81,134.0	62,018.0	61,583.0
Balance of trade	US$m	31,888.0	31,292.0	38,486.0	44,960.0	48,273.0
Current account	US$m	-9,136.0	-13,876.0	-13,886.0	-6,488.0	954.0
Total reserves minus gold	US$m	720.0	779.0	871.0	1,941.0	1,843.0
Foreign exchange	US$m	494.0	591.0	609.0	517.0	502.0
Exchange rate	per US$	0.75	0.69	0.68	0.78	0.76

* estimated figure

Since their peak in July 2011 Irish bond spreads fell markedly, but remained prone to tremors in the euro area. Reports suggested that investors were differentiating Ireland based on its policy implementation track record and growth prospects. Vulnerabilities persisted, however, as international demand for Irish bonds is sensitive to developments in the euro area.

Growth was stronger than anticipated in the first half of 2011, led by net exports and stock re-building. GDP rose by 1.9 per cent and 1.6 per cent in the first two quarters, bringing the annual growth rate to 2.25 per cent. While final domestic demand continued to weigh negatively on annual growth, by some 3.75 percentage points, the rate of decline in private consumption and investment moderated. Re-building of inventories after years of de-stocking contributed almost 2 percentage points to annual growth. Net exports remained the key driver, contributing almost 4.75 percentage points. The resulting large trade surplus was offset by income outflows, leaving the current account in a modest deficit.

But strong export growth has benefited from continued competitiveness improvements. Goods and services exports grew at annual rates of 4.25 and 5.5 per cent respectively in the second quarter, with the IT sector leading the expansion in services exports.

Pharmaceuticals continue to account for most of the rise in goods exports, but the indigenous food and beverage sector also registered strong annual growth of 17 per cent in the second quarter of the year. These developments partly reflect the almost 20 per cent decline in unit labour costs for the economy since the peak in 2008, relative to the euro area average and especially the 30 per cent decline seen in the export-oriented manufacturing sector. Recent data show continued growth in goods exports and industrial production, but by October there were signs of stagnation in new export orders in the manufacturing and services sectors going forward.

The second half of 2011 saw the employment climate appear to be stabilising after a severe fall, but unemployment remained high and emigration continued. Employment declined by 0.2 per cent annually in the second quarter, its lowest fall since 2008, with the decline concentrated in the public sector. The unemployment rate remained high at 14.4 per cent in October. Net outward migration of 34,100 persons in the year to April 2011 was broadly unchanged from the previous year, but within this total, emigration of Irish nationals rose from 27,000 to 40,200 persons. Headline inflation was an annual 1.5 per cent in October, mostly accounted for by rising energy and food prices. Eurostat estimated that the gap between Irish and euro area consumer prices had fallen from 25 to 13 per cent over 2008–10.

Anglo-Irish relations

If the positive notes being struck by the economy remained subdued, one brighter spot in 2011 was the May visit of Britain's Queen Elisabeth. This was the fist visit of a reigning British monarch to Ireland since the creation of the Irish Free State. In what was described as a 'diplomatically calibrated' suggestion of regret that the relationship between the two countries had been stained by so much bloodshed, to the surprise of all those attending the official dinner held in Dublin to mark the visit, Queen Elisabeth prefaced her address with a greeting in Gaelic. This prompted the Irish president, Mary Macaleese, to mouth the word 'wow' in appreciation of the unexpected gesture. Under British rule, Gaelic had been outlawed. For the British Queen, the state visit held some poignancy: her uncle, Lord Mountbatten had been murdered by the Irish Republican Army while on holiday in Ireland in 1979.

Risk assessment

Economy	Poor
Politics	Good
Regional stability	Good

COUNTRY PROFILE

Historical profile

In the twelfth century, the Norman invasion began a long period of foreign domination. Over the centuries, Irish Catholic hostility increased along with English control, following the seizure of land, the Protestant Reformation and the loss of religious and political freedoms.

1801 Ireland was united with Great Britain through the Act of Union.

1840s The potato crop suffered from blight over several years, leading to severe famine. Combined with emigration, this reduced the population by one-third. The decade also saw the beginnings of a republican movement.

1916 The British army suppressed the republican Easter Rising, provoking the formation of Sinn Féin (Ourselves Alone).

1919–21 The Anglo-Irish War was fought against British troops and police by the military arm of Sinn Féin, the Irish Republican Army (IRA).

1921 The Irish Free State was formed, under the British crown, by partition of 26 southern counties from six north-eastern counties that remained part of the UK.

1922 The Dáil Eireann (Irish parliament) ratified the treaty establishing the Free State, sparking a civil war with nationalists, led by Eamonn De Valera, who advocated full independence.

1927 De Valera entered parliament as the head of the newly-created Fianna Fáil (Soldiers of Destiny).

1932 Fianna Fáil won the elections. De Valera began to work towards full independence from Britain.

1937 The constitution was promulgated, abolishing the Free State and declaring Ireland as an independent state.

1938 Douglas Hyde became the country's first president, with De Valera as prime minister.

1939–45 Ireland remained neutral during the Second World War, although many Irish citizens fought in the British Army.

1948 Fianna Fáil lost the election and De Valera was replaced by John Costello as prime minister.

1949 A republic was proclaimed and Ireland left the Commonwealth. Partition remained contentious and the IRA mounted a terrorist campaign for reunification with the six northern counties.

1955 Ireland joined the UN.

1957 De Valera was voted back into office as prime minister; he said that the union of Northern Ireland with the Republic could not be achieved through violence.

1959 De Valera became president.

1971 Around 8,000 Catholics fled to Ireland from Northern Ireland, due to violence by sectarian paramilitaries following the introduction of internment of IRA suspects in the North.

1973 Ireland joined the forerunner of the EU, the European Economic Community (EEC). Fianna Fáil, the traditional party of government, lost power in the general election and Jack Lynch resigned. Liam Cosgrave formed a coalition between his party, Fine Gael, and the Labour Party. The IRA became active again after a long period of decline, as inter-communal fighting intensified in the north, under the Unionist-run regime and later, direct rule from London.

1977 Fianna Fáil won the general election and Jack Lynch again became prime minister.

1980s None of a succession of elections produced a single-party majority government.

1985 The Ango-Irish Agreement established regular participation by the Irish government in political, legal, security and cross-border matters in Northern Ireland.

1990 Mary Robinson was the first woman and the first left-winger to be elected president.
1992 In a referendum, Irish voters agreed to relax the abortion laws, enabling women to travel abroad to have an abortion.
1993 The Downing Street Declaration by the Irish and British governments offered talks to all parties in Northern Ireland if they renounced political violence.
1995 A referendum to change the 1937 constitution narrowly approved the lifting of the ban on divorce.
1997 Mary McAleese, (born in Northern Ireland), was elected president of the Irish Republic.
1998 In a referendum, nearly 95 per cent of voters approved the Good Friday Agreement, which entailed Ireland giving up its constitutional claim to Northern Ireland.
2002 The euro replaced the punt. After parliamentary elections, Bertie Ahern was confirmed as prime minister and formed a coalition government led by Fianna Fáil. At the second attempt, Ireland voted in favour of the EU's Treaty of Nice.
2003 The population of Ireland reached four million.
2004 President Mary McAleese was returned unopposed for a second term as president.
2005 Irish was adopted as an official working language of the EU.
2006 An official tribunal found that former prime minister, Charles Haughey, had 'accepted bribes and followed unethical business practices' and accepted 'cash from wealthy businessmen over a 17-year period, including eight years as *taoiseach*'.
2007 Fianna Fáil led a coalition government.
2008 Brian Cowen (FF) replaced Bertie Ahern following his resignation as prime minister. Voters rejected the Lisbon Treaty in a referendum held on reform of the EU. The Progressive Democrats disbanded, due to its low national support base. Ireland was the first of the eurozone economies to succumb to recession during the global economic crisis. GDP growth fell to -3.0 per cent as both government deficit and unemployment grew. An early budget introduced austerity measures.
2009 Over 120,000 people marched through Dublin city centre protesting at government austerity measures. The credit rating agency, Standard and Poor's (S&P) cut the Ireland debt rating from AAA to AA+. The government introduced an aggressive emergency budget; it cut government spending by €3.3 billion (US$4.3 billion) and raised taxes, which combined amounted to 5 per cent of GDP. After two referenda within 16 months, the Irish electorate sanctioned the EU *Lisbon Treaty*. A catalogue of sexual and physical assaults, mostly on children, perpetrated by Roman Catholic priests and church officials between 1975–2004 was published, causing widespread condemnation of those in authority for their failure to protect vulnerable youngsters while covering up abuse and suppressing investigations. A new, National Asset Management Agency (Nama) was set up to rehabilitate the banking sector by removing toxic debt from bank ledgers. Annual GDP growth was -7.1 per cent. There was a 24 per cent year-on-year increase in the suicide rate.
2010 In August, the credit ratings agency S&P downgraded Ireland's economy to AA-, following the US$63 million recapitalisation of the banking system and the strain it put on the economy; it warned that another downgrade was possible. The forecast annual GDP growth rate was -1.5 per cent. On 1 October the government announced that the total cost of bailing out the country's loss-making banks had to be revised upward to just under €50 billion (US$65.5 billion) and was likely to cost over 30 per cent of GDP. By December, Nama had paid banks €30.2 billion (US$42.4 billion) for 11,500 non-performing loans, belonging to 850 debtors, each with an average of 13 loans.
2011 Revelations that Prime Minister Cowan had had personal contact with Sean Fitzpatrick, former head of Anglo Irish Bank, during the period of maximum financial loss caused widespread controversy. Although Cowan won a vote of confidence from his political party (FF) on 18 January, several cabinet members resigned, resulting in Cowan calling an early general election; he announced that he would not stand for re-election. However, he was determined to see the passing of the finance bill, necessary for the December 2010 IMF loan to be paid, before stepping down. The Greens withdrew from the government coalition on 24 January, leaving Prime Minister Cowan in charge of a minority administration. The general election was held on 25 February, the opposition FG won 36.1 per cent (76 seats out of 166) and immediately began coalition talks, which were successfully concluded with the Labour Party on 6 March. The Greens lost all their seats from the previous election. On 31 March, the governor of the Bank of Ireland (BOI) announced that following 'stress tests' of the banking system a further €24 billion (US$33.65 billion) would have to be injected into the top four banks to ensure stability as a whole. This brought the total amount of recapitalisation by the Irish economy to €70 billion (US$98.13 billion). Loans to fund their bailout will come from the EU and IMF and the BOI will be forced to sell off €30 billion (US42.1 billion) in assets by 2013. The UK's Queen Elizabeth made a state-visit to the Irish Republic in May (17–20), the first by a British monarch since 1911. On 18 September Sinn Féin nominated former IRA commander Martin McGuiness as their candidate for the October presidential election. Presidential elections were held on 27 October in which five candidates took part. Following the ballot and elimination of the lesser candidates who transferred their votes to the two strongest candidates Michael D Higgins (LP) won a total of 56.8 per cent and Sean Gallagher (independent) 35.5 per cent; he took office on 11 November.

Political structure

Constitution

The constitution was drawn up in 1937. The Uchtarán na Eireann (president), directly elected every seven years, is guardian of the constitution, and may submit a bill to the people in a referendum or to the Supreme Court if it is felt that legislation might contravene the constitution. The constitution was amended three times by referendum in the 1990s, to loosen anti-abortion laws, legalise divorce and give up Ireland's territorial claim to Northern Ireland in favour of the principle of unity by consent.

Form of state

Parliamentary democratic republic

The executive

Executive power is exercised by the cabinet, led by the *Taoiseach* (prime minister) who is appointed by the president on the recommendation of the Dáil Eireann (House of Representatives).

National legislature

The bicameral Oireachtas (National Parliament), consists of the Seanad (Senate) and the Dáil.

The Dáil (House of Representatives) (lower chamber) has 166 members (known as Teachta Dála (TD)), elected by proportional representation, using single transferable votes (STV) in multi-seat constituencies. All members serve for up to five years. The Dáil has responsibility for electing the cabinet, consisting of between 7–15 members, proposing a budget, ratifying treaties and declaring war or permitting participation in a war.

The Seanad, with 60 members, is elected by a system of electoral colleges, its periods corresponding with that of the Dáil. The *taoiseach* (prime minister) nominates 11 members, 43 are elected by panels representing vocational and cultural interests and six are elected by Ireland's universities.

Legal system
The Irish constitution declares that every person living in Ireland has certain fundamental personal rights, listed in articles. Every constitutional right has the same status and value, however when a conflict arises between constitutional rights the courts have the prerogative to adjudicate which constitutional right is more important in which particular case. Much civil and criminal law is derived from English common law and remains in force if it is consistent with the Constitution.
The courts are made up of District, Circuit and the High Court. District Courts deal with summary offences and minor civil cases. Circuit Courts deal with civil cases of a more serious nature and criminal cases are presented before a judge with a jury of 12 citizens.
The High Court, has full jurisdiction in civil and criminal cases and can act as an appeal court from the Circuit Court. When exercising criminal jurisdiction, it is called the Central Criminal Court. Under the Offences Against the State Act 1939, Special Criminal Courts were set up; these sit without a jury.
The Supreme Court, the court of final appeal, consists of a Chief Justice and five other judges who can hear appeals on all High Court decisions. It is also the final arbiter on the interpretation of the constitution.
Last elections
27 October 2011 (presidential); 25 February 2011 (parliamentary).
Results: Presidential: Michael D Higgins (LP) won 39.6 per cent of the vote, Sean Gallagher (independent) 28.5 per cent, Martine McGuinness (Sinn Féin) 13.7 per cent, Gay Mitchell (Fine Gael) 6.4 per cent, David Norris (independent) 6.2 per cent; turnout was 56.1 per cent. After elimination, lesser candidates transferred their votes: Higgins won a total of 56.8 per cent and Gallagher 35.5 per cent.
Parliamentary: Fine Gael (FG) (United Ireland Party) won 36.1 per cent (76 seats out of 166), Labour Party 19.4 per cent (37), Fianna Fáil 19.4 per cent (20), Sinn Féin 9.9 per cent (14), United Left Alliance (ULA) per cent (five), Independents 5.7 per cent (14). Turnout was 70 per cent.
Next elections
2018 (presidential); 2016 (parliamentary).

Political parties
Ruling party
Coalition led by Fine Gael (FG) (United Ireland Party) with Labour Party (LP) (from 9 Mar 2011)
Main opposition party
Fine Gael (FG) (United Ireland Party)

Population
4.43 million (2009)
Last census: April 2006: 4,239,848
Population density: 54 inhabitants per square km. Urban population: 59 per cent of total (1995–2001).
Annual growth rate: 1.3 per cent 1994–2004 (WHO 2006)
Ethnic make-up
Ireland is predominantly white. Only recently has it seen non-white immigration.
Religions
Roman Catholic (95 per cent); Church of Ireland (2.8 per cent); Presbyterian (0.4 per cent) Jewish (0.1 per cent); others (0.3 per cent); no religion (1.2 per cent).

Education
Education is divided into three levels: primary, secondary and tertiary. Primary schooling (including, although not compulsory, infant pre-schooling from age four), lasts for eight years. Secondary schooling starts age 12 for either five or six years, and includes a junior and a senior cycle with examinations at the end of each. About 81 per cent of Irish students complete the senior cycle and almost 50 per cent go on to tertiary education, which can be either academic or vocational.
Ireland has a higher proportion of graduates with scientific skills in the 25–34 age group than any other OECD member, except Japan.
Compulsory years: Six to 15.
Enrolment rate: 105 per cent gross primary enrolment of relevant age group; 118 per cent gross secondary enrolment (including repeaters) (World Bank).
Pupils per teacher: 22 in primary schools.

Health
Eight regional health boards administer Ireland's health system, which is funded by the central government, through the department of health, which in turn is under the control of the minister of health. Various community welfare services operate for the chronically sick, the elderly and the disabled. Almost 38 per cent of the population – those on lower incomes – receive medical services free of charge. The remainder receive public hospital services for a minimum charge. Charges are also made to the better-off for visits to the family doctor and to hospital consultants.
HIV/Aids
HIV prevalence: 0.1 per cent aged 15–49 in 2003 (World Bank)
Life expectancy: 78 years, 2004 (WHO 2006)
Fertility rate/Maternal mortality rate: 1.9 births per woman, 2004 (WHO 2006); maternal mortality, 5 per 100,000 live births (World Bank).
Child (under 5 years) mortality rate (per 1,000): 5.1 per 1,000 live births (World Bank)
Head of population per physician: 2.79 physicians per 1,000 people, 2004 (WHO 2006)

Welfare
Social insurance is compulsory for employees and the self-employed. The principal benefits are unemployment, disability and maternity payments plus pay-related benefits to supplement those on low incomes, invalidity pension (for those on disability benefit), widows' payments (contributory and non-contributory), orphans' payments, deserted wives' payments, old age pensions (contributory and non-contributory), medical treatment benefits, including dental and optical, an occupational injuries scheme and certain free schemes for the elderly. Employees in the private sector contribute at the highest rate.

Main cities
Dublin (capital, estimated population 1.0 million in 2004), Cork (193,400), Limerick (84,900), Galway (67,200), Waterford (47,800).

Languages spoken
Official documents are printed in both English and Irish.
Five per cent of the population speak Irish as their first language.
Official language/s
Irish (Gaelic) and English

Media
Press
In 2007 less than 50 per cent of the population read a daily newspaper, however, access of newspaper websites rose by 27 per cent.
There are over 50 newspapers and over 100 magazines. The circulation figures for morning newspapers have remained stable but figures for evening newspapers have been falling.
Dailies: The newspapers with the highest circulations are the *Irish Independent* (www.independent.ie), *The Irish Times* (www.irishtimes.com) and the *Irish Examiner* (www.irishexaminer.com). The free issue *Metro* (www.metroireland.ie) has taken a lead in circulation figures in Dublin.
Weeklies: In Gaelic *Foinse* (www.foinse.ie) is published in Galway. In English, *Woman's Way* (www.harmonia.ie) is the leading woman's magazine, *An Phoblacht Republican* (www.anphoblacht.com) takes with an Irish Republican perspective on national and international affairs. A number of local or regional newspapers, owned by few conglomerates including North West of Ireland Printing and Publishing

(www.nwipp-newspapers.com) published weeklies such as *Donegal News* and *GaelicLife* and Independent News and Media. (www.independent.ie). Other smaller newspapers include *Waterford Today* (www.waterford-today.ie), *Limerick Post* (www2.limerickpost.ie) and *Anglo Celt* (www.anglocelt.ie) from Cavan. There are also many specialist, genre magazines available.

Business: Dublin has a small number of business publications. The weekly newspaper *Sunday Business Post* (www.sbpost.ie) provides Ireland's financial, political, The monthly *Marine Times* (www.marinetimes.ie) covers the fishing industry and aquaculture industries and communities and *ShelfLife* (www.mediateam.ie) for retail news. A magazine aimed at directors *Decision* (www.decisionireland.com) is published six times a year.

Periodicals: The monthly *Image* (www.image.ie) is a glossy women's magazine. *U* (www.harmonia.ie) is a tabloid, published fortnightly. Of general interest, the scholarly *History Ireland* (www.historyireland.com) and *Irish Roots Magazine* (www.irishrootsmedia.com) on genealogy and ZenthOptimedia (www.zenithoptimedia.com.sg) publishes entertainment guides *GV Magazine* and *Newsline*.

Broadcasting

The Broadcasting Authority is responsible for regulating public and private broadcasting. Broadcasting laws lay down rules regarding the balance of news and current affairs and culture in broadcasting, in addition to the prohibition of matters which the minister for telecommunications considers likely to promote or incite crime. Radio Telefís Éireann (RTE) (www.rte.ie) is the national public broadcaster, funded by a license fee and advertising revenue.

Radio: There are around 60 radio stations located around the country. Almost three million adults listen to the radio every day and of the top 20 shows, 18 are broadcast by RTE (www.rte.ie), which has four networks including popular music, classical and cultural, talk and an Irish-language station. Private, commercial radio includes Today FM (www.rte.ie), NewsTalk (http://newstalk.ie) and 98FM (www.dublins98.ie) from Dublin, Red FM (www.redfm.ie) from Cork and Galway Bay FM (www.galwaybayfm.ie).

Television: The RTE (www.rte.ie) has two television channels (RTE 1 and Network 2) and provides locally produced shows as well as imported programmes. It has a 57 per cent share of the advertising market and its main local competitor TV3 (www.tv3.ie) has 20 per cent, followed by TG4 (www.tg4.ie) the Irish language station. Overall, RTE's principal competition is from UK digital TV providers. Digital TV is received by 58 per cent of households, but free-to-air digital services is expected to begin in 2009. One-third of homes are cabled, however satellite TV is becoming popular, carrying further UK channels.

Advertising

Annual adspend is typically around US$19 billion. Promotion of tobacco products is banned, and the advertising of alcohol is strictly controlled. Commercials on TV and radio are limited to 10 per cent of transmission time. Newspapers, magazines, posters and films are also widely used. Information is available from the Advertising Standards Authority in Dublin.

Economy

Ireland has an open economy with principle exports in goods and services producing 50 per cent of GDP, of which tourism, as the major service industry, typically contributes over 4 per cent of GDP. Juxtaposed with high-tech industries is an agricultural sector that accounts for 8 per cent of GDP and 7 per cent of exports. Ireland has a highly skilled labour pool. A national development plan is focussed on IT, life-sciences, medical technologies, engineering, financial and international services, Internet based activity and digital businesses. Of the more than 1,100 foreign-owned companies operating in Ireland around 50 per cent are US, while the combined numbers of UK and German companies make up around 25 per cent. Those industries that have shown most growth in exports are computers and electrical machinery and chemical and pharmaceutical products.

Ireland's economy was one of the hardest hit by the 2008 global financial crisis and was the first EU country to enter recession, which became severe and is forecast not to be broken until 2011. The crisis exposed an ultimately unsustainable economy, fuelled as it was by expansionary bank credit, which promoted a boom in construction that led to rising property prices and excessive domestic spending. The annualised GDP growth from 1990–2007 was 10.37 per cent, according to UN statistics, but in 2008 it plunged to 3 per cent, as the current account lurched abruptly from surplus to deficit; GDP growth fell further to -7.1 per cent in 2009, at which point the government introduced an aggressive emergency budget, which in April 2009 cut government spending by €3.3 billion (US$4.3 billion) and raised taxes which, combined, amounted to 5 per cent of GDP. Salaries of private sector workers began falling, while public worker's salaries fell by 7 per cent. This produced the official end of the recession in the first quarter of 2010 with GDP growth of 2.7 per cent for the period; however, the annual rate was -0.4 per cent in 2010 and forecast to be 0.4 per cent in 2011.

According to the Organisation for Economic Co-operation and Development (OECD), annual unemployment jumped from 6.3 per cent in 2007 to 11.9 per cent in 2009 (particularly in the construction industry (the housing market slumped by 24 per cent in 2008, which at its most productive, in 2006, contributed 15 per cent to GDP); the highest ever number of registered unemployed, 326,100, was recorded in January 2009. Unemployment climbed to 13.7 per cent in 2010. The rate in 2011 was 14.3 per cent, peaking in March–May. There was an inevitable impact on government revenue with reduced tax returns, both corporate and personal. The rising unemployment rates sparked the historic curse of Ireland and prompted a rise in migration (particularly to the US and Australia), although immigration from other European nations maintained the level of the workforce until 2009–10.

The government established the National Asset Management Agency (Nama) in late 2009. The chief aims of the agency are to rehabilitate the banking sector by removing toxic debt from bank ledgers and channel credit to productive sectors of the economy, which should underpin activity and strengthen employment prospects. In November 2009, US$80 billion was made available for Nama to set up a bank to buy up the loans of defaulting borrowers held by other commercial banks. In March 2010 the Anglo Irish Bank reported the loss of US$17.2 billion in assets, making it the largest corporate loss in Irish commercial history. The Irish government agreed to inject €8.3 billion (US$11.2 billion) to recapitalise the bank as 'the least worst option'. Nama will take €10 billion (US$13.5 billion) in bad debts, while the European Union regulators began an investigation into the help offered by the government for the Anglo Irish Bank. The government committed a further €8.3 billion (US$10.9 billion) in October 2010.

On 1 October 2010, the government announced that the total cost of bailing out the country's loss-making banks had to be revised upward to just under €50 billion (US$65.5 billion) and was likely to cost over 30 per cent of GDP. On 21 November 2010, the government formally applied for a US$140 billion EU/IMF loan to guarantee its credit worthiness. On 24 November, a new austerity budget was introduced, slashing US$20 billion in public spending over four years, including

among other things, welfare cuts, public job losses, a drop in the minimum wage, an increased VAT rate to 23 per cent and a new property tax on homeowners.
On 31 March 2011, the governor of the Bank of Ireland (BOI) announced that following 'stress tests' of the banking system a further €24 billion (US$33.65 billion) would have to be injected into the top four banks to ensure stability as a whole. This brought the total amount of recapitalisation by the Irish economy to €70 billion (US$98.13 billion). Loans to fund their bailout will come from the EU and IMF and the BOI will be forced to sell off €30 billion (US42.1 billion) in assets by 2013. Restructuring of the banking system was begun in April 2011; the number of domestic banks was reduced from four to two core banks based around the Allied Irish Bank (AIB) and BOI. A rate cut was given to Ireland by the EU and IMF on the US$572 million emergency loan in May 2011.
On 5–6 December 2011, an interim, austerity budget reduced public spending by over €1 billion (US$1.34) and raised income through tax increases of €1.6 billion (US$2.14 billion). VAT will rise from 21 per cent to 23 per cent.

External trade

As a member of the European Union (EU), Italy operates within a community-wide free trade area, with tariffs set across the whole community. Internationally, the EU has free trade agreements with a number of nations and trading blocs worldwide.
International trade accounts for around 150 per cent of GDP. Ireland is an exporter of electronic and IT equipment and pharmaceutical and biotechnology products produced by multinational and start-up hi-tech companies utilising a highly educated workforce.
Ireland is the fourth largest producer of salmon in Europe and exports 60 per cent of its meat production.

Imports

Imports consist of data processing equipment, other machinery and equipment, chemicals, petroleum and petroleum products, textiles and clothing.
Main sources: UK (typically over 30 per cent of total), US (over 10 per cent), Germany (almost 10 per cent).

Exports

Exports consist mainly of machinery and equipment, computers, chemicals, pharmaceuticals, live animals and animal products and natural gas (to Northern Ireland).
Main destinations: US (typically around 20 per cent of total), UK (almost 20 per cent), Belgium (under 15 per cent).

Agriculture

Farming

Agricultural earnings equate to over 8 per cent of annual GDP and around 7 per cent of export earnings. The sector employs 7.5 per cent of the labour force.
With its temperate climate and relatively high levels of rainfall, Ireland is suited to stock raising, with the result that there is a predominance of livestock production in Irish agriculture. Approximately 70 per cent of all land is devoted to pasture while 10 per cent is tilled. Irish farms tend to be owner-occupied, with an average size of just over 25 hectares.
The EU's Fundamental reform to the Common Agricultural Policy (CAP) was introduced in Ireland in 2005. The subsidies paid on farm output, which tended to benefit large farms and encourage overproduction, were replaced by single farm payments not conditional on production.
Ireland is a net exporter of agricultural goods. Main exports include meat, vegetables, milk, butter and alcoholic beverages. Main agricultural imports include rice and maize.
The government announced in July 2009 that the cattle disease brucellosis (*Brucella abortus*) had been eradicated from the country.

Fishing

The sea fishing industry makes an important contribution to the agricultural economy. Mackerel accounts for about 35 per cent of total catch, and is the most important species landed.

Forestry

With forest cover estimated at 659,000 hectares (ha), it occupies less than a tenth of the total land area. Though Ireland is traditionally one of Europe's least forested countries, massive afforestation programmes have contributed to an annual average increase of 3.03 per cent, the equivalent of 17,000ha of forest cover. Private ownership in new planting areas has been rising with around two-thirds of the forest remaining under state ownership. Employment in the forest and wood products industry is about 13,000.
Most of the forest is available for wood supply. Roundwood production has considerably increased with the expansion of forest cover. Much of the production consists of softwood logs for the domestic sawn wood and panel industry. Ireland imports most of its paper and sawn wood.

Industry and manufacturing

The industrial sector accounts for 24 per cent of GDP, 80 per cent of the value of annual exports and approximately 27 per cent of employment.
Ireland's indigenous manufacturing base is relatively small. Traditional industries, such as food and beverages, textiles, paper, non-metallic minerals and machinery, dominate, although there has been rapid growth in new export-oriented chemicals as well as electronic engineering industries. Most of the new capital and skill-intensive industries are subsidiaries of large US and European multinationals and are heavily reliant on imported primary and intermediate inputs.
US Wyeth Pharmaceuticals is investing US$1 billion in a factory in the world's largest integrated biotechnology campus at Grange Castle in Dublin, which opened in September 2005. Wyeth will produce infant vaccines, antibiotics and an arthritis treatments.

Tourism

The sector contributes around 4.5 per cent of GDP and gives employment to 140,000 people. All parts of the Republic benefit from the expansion of tourism, which has become an important factor in regional development, bringing employment and business to otherwise economically-deprived areas. Dublin has become a major short city-break destination. The UK is the main source of visitors. US tourists is the next largest and the most lucrative market. Vastly improved air connections, as well as sea links, have assisted Ireland's tourist explosion. The authorities are concerned about the cost and quality of the tourism product and are seeking to sharpen the sector's competitiveness.

Mining

Mining accounts for about 1 per cent of GNP and 1 per cent of the workforce. Europe's largest zinc and lead deposits are located at Navan, County Meath, and are operated by Tara Mines. Production has continued since the mid-1970s.
Ireland is Europe's leading producer of zinc. There are also reserves of gypsum, barytes, dolomite, silica sand, limestone, coal, marble and small amounts of silver. Gypsum is extracted from an open-pit at Knocknacran, Co Monaghan. Gold and base metals have been discovered at Clontibret, County Monaghan.
A zinc mining project at Lisheen, county Tipperary, began production in 2000. The US$280.5 million project is a joint venture between Ivernia West, an Irish exploration company, and Anglo-American, the South African company. The two ore deposits, containing 19 million tonnes of recoverable reserves, have been producing 1.5 million tonnes of ore or 160,000 tonnes of zinc a year since 2000.

Hydrocarbons

Dependence on imported petroleum has been reduced due to the exploitation of domestic natural gas and peat reserves.

Consumption of oil was 158,000 barrels per day in 2010. Oil is imported for refinement and re-export. In 2009, the UK Serica Energy announced an oil find off the west coast; the size of the well was undetermined.
Ireland's total gas reserves were around 9.9 billion cubic metres (cum) in 2010. However, Ireland still continues to import natural gas, primarily from Britain, at 5.29 billion cum in 2010. Natural gas represents around 23 per cent of primary energy consumption. The government had plans to become self sufficient in gas but public pressure and environmental considerations hampered the progress of the Corrib and Sevens Head gas fields. Indigenous reserves of natural gas are located in the Kinsale Head gas field and the smaller Ballycotton field off the Cork coast. Other sites for exploration were opened up in 2009.
Coal is not produced in Ireland but is imported.

Energy
In 2007 the Single Electricity Market (SEM) became operational, between the Irish Republic and Northern Ireland, uniting the wholesale electricity market, with all generated power pooled and suppliers buying from it. Total installed generating capacity is over 5.5 gigawatts (GW); installed generating capacity in Northern Ireland is over 2.1GW. The largest power station is gas-fired and located in Country Antrim (Northern Ireland), producing 50 per cent of the North's energy and 17 per cent of the all-Ireland capacity.
A natural gas pipeline project linking the country to the UK will provide security of supply and meet growing demand from industry and power generation.
Dependence on imported petroleum has been reduced due to the exploitation of domestic gas and peat reserves. Peat continues to provide around 550MW of generated electricity and is also used in significant quantities as a domestic fuel.

Financial markets
Stock exchange
Stocmhalartán na hÉireann (Irish Stock Exchange) (ISE)

Banking and insurance
The governor of the Bank of Ireland (BOI) announced on 31 March 2011 that banks were to be restructured to 'put the banking system on a firm footing for the future...' This followed five attempts to recapitalise the system that cost the economy a total of €70 billion (US$98.13 billion). The number of domestic banks was reduced from four to two core banks based around the AIB (Allied Irish Bank) and BOI. The AIB will be merged with the EBS building society to form a second banking group.
The governor also said that 'significant contributions' would be sought from the bank's subordinate bondholders to aid recapitalisation and banking officials may re-examine the legitimacy of imposing losses on major bondholders at AIB, if the bank required additional capital.
The Irish Life and Permanent insurance company will be restructured and broken up as it sells its profitable pensions division, Irish Life.
In April 2011, the international credit ratings agency Moody's downgraded AIB and Irish Life and Permanents' long-term deposit ratings to Ba2; the Bank of Ireland was downgraded to Ba1
Central bank
Central Bank of Ireland; European Central Bank (ECB).

Time
GMT (daylight saving, end March to end October, GMT plus one hour)

Geography
Ireland is situated in the north-west of Europe, bordered in the east by the Irish Sea, in the west by the Atlantic Ocean and in the south by the Celtic Sea. The landmass is bounded by mountains and has a low-lying central plain.
The island of Ireland consists of 32 counties, of which six, in the north east, belong to Northern Ireland, part of the United Kingdom.
Hemisphere
Northern

Climate
Ireland is in the temperate zone, with moderate south-westerly winds, influenced by the warm waters of the Gulf Stream, which produce a mild climate with rain throughout the year and annual rainfall varying between 800–1,200mm. The driest months are May and June.
The coldest months are January and February, when temperatures average between 4 and 7 degrees Celsius (C); the warmest months are July and August, when temperatures average between 14 and 17 degrees C.

Dress codes
While dress tends to be informal, business people normally wear suits, and evening social events can be quite formal. A medium-weight raincoat is advised throughout the year.

Entry requirements
Passports
Required by all, except UK-born nationals, who require official photographic identification, and other EU visitors with a valid national ID card.
Visa
Visas are not required by nationals of the EU, the Americas, Australasia and many Asian countries. For confirmation see www.irlgov.ie/iveagh and see *Service*.
Other business travellers should contact the consulate of the nearest Irish Embassy for further information.
Currency advice/regulations
The import of local and foreign currency is unrestricted.
Travellers cheques are widely accepted.
Customs
Personal items are duty-free. There are no duties levied on alcohol and tobacco between EU member states, providing amounts imported are for personal consumption.
Prohibited imports
A wide range of items, including firearms, offensive weapons, ammunition and explosives, pornography, meat and meat products, live or dead animals (including birds and poultry), hay and straw (including used in packing) and endangered species.
UK residents only may be accompanied by a domestic dog, which has its necessary passport of health.

Health (for visitors)
Nationals of the European Economic Area (EEA) countries and Switzerland can access reduced cost and sometimes free medical treatment using a European Health Insurance Card (EHIC) while visiting the EEA. Exceptions include nationals of the 10 countries, which joined the EU in 2004, whose EHIC is not valid in Switzerland. Applications for the EHIC should be made before travelling.
Mandatory precautions
There are no requirements.
Advisable precautions
Travel insurance for those not entitled to free emergency cover.

Hotels
Classified into three categories: Star A, B and C. Reservations should be made in advance. Tipping: 10 per cent is customary.

Credit cards
All international credit and debit cards are widely accepted. ATMs are available in most town.

Public holidays (national)
Fixed dates
1 Jan (New Year's Day), 17 Mar (St Patrick's Day), 25–26 Dec (Christmas).
Variable dates
Good Friday, Easter Monday, May Bank Holiday (first Mon in May); June Bank Holiday (first Mon in Jun), Summer Bank Holiday (first Mon in Aug), Halloween Bank Holiday (last Mon in Oct).

Working hours

Banking
Mon–Fri: 0900–1600 (banks open later one evening a week, in Dublin on Thursdays until 1700, may vary in other cities).
Business
Mon–Fri: 0900–1700.
Government
Mon–Fri: 0915–1300, 1415–1715.
Shops
Mon–Fri: 0900–1730; late night shopping in city centres usually occurs once a week when shops are open to 2100. Supermarkets Mon–Wed: 0830–1900; Thu–Sat: 0830–2100/2000/1900; Sun: 1200–1800.

Telecommunications

Mobile/cell phones
GSM 900/1800 operate throughout the country.

Electricity supply

220V AC, with UK style, flat, three-pin plugs.

Social customs/useful tips

The hold of the Catholic Church over Ireland has diminished in recent years and the country now has an air of moderate social liberalism, although there are more conservative attitudes in rural areas. Smoking is banned in pubs and restaurants.

Getting there

Air
National airline: Aer Lingus
International airport/s: Dublin (DUB), 10km north of city. Airport express coaches and taxis are available to the city centre.
Shannon (SNN), 26 km from Limerick. Bus services are available every hour to and from both Limerick and Clare, (60 minutes duration). A daily express coach travels between both Shannon and Limerick, or Galway. A taxi service is also available to Limerick.
Airport facilities at both airports include duty-free shopping, bank, *bureau de change*, bar, restaurant and tourist information centre.
Other airport/s: Cork (ORK), 5 km from city; Horan (NOC) at Knock, Co Mayo, Connaught Province.
Airport tax: None
Surface
Road: Bus Éireann and National Express operate services from London, and many other UK centres, to Dublin and other destinations.
Rail: Most rail-ferry services to Ireland depart from London. There are a number of services across the Northern Ireland border including the regular, direct intercity Belfast-Dublin service (duration 2.15 hours).
Water: In addition to conventional ferry crossings, there are high-speed catamaran sailings. Routes include links with Scotland, England and Wales to alternative destinations in Ireland. Continental connections include routes to north-western France.
Rail links provide connections from the major seaports.
Main port/s: The main ports are Dun Laoghaire, Dublin, Rosslare and Cork.

Getting about

National transport
Air: Daily services between Dublin and Shannon, and Dublin and Cork operated by Aer Lingus. Also one flight daily between Dublin and Horan Airport, Knock. Charter services are available. Domestic airports include Waterford (WAT), Galway (GWY), Sligo (SXL), Carrickfinn (CFN) and Kerry (KIR). In addition, there are also various small airstrips which receive passenger services.
Road: The Irish road network carries the overwhelming part of Irish imports and exports. A good highway system links all cities.
Buses: Bus Éireann is the national bus line, with services all over the south and north. Winter bus schedule is often drastically reduced and many routes simply disappear after September.
Rail: Ireland's rail network is not extensive. Irishrail is the main operator, with routes which fan out from Dublin.
Water: There are ferry services to outlying islands off the west coast and across rivers.
City transport
Taxis: Taxis in Ireland tend to be expensive. There are metered taxis in Cork, Dublin, Galway and Limerick, but in other places fares must be agreed beforehand. If a taxi is booked by telephone there may be a small pick-up charge.
Buses, trams & metro: There are comprehensive bus services in all towns and cities, combined in Dublin with a fast, surburban rail service, the Dart.
Two tram services – the Luas – were inaugurated in 2004. The red line runs from Connelly Street in Dublin's city centre, west then south-west, to Tallaght. The green line runs from St Steven's Green, in the administrative district of Dublin, south to Cherrywood.
Car hire
Available in all main towns, but heavy demand during tourist season. All international hire companies are represented in Ireland. Drivers must be aged between 21 and 75. A national or international driving licence is required and the driver is generally required to have had at least two years experience. Speed limits 30mph (48kph) in built-up areas and 60mph (96kph) on main roads. Driving is on the left.

BUSINESS DIRECTORY

The addresses listed below are a selection only. While World of Information makes every endeavour to check these addresses, we cannot guarantee that changes have not been made, especially to telephone numbers and area codes. We would welcome any corrections.

Telephone area codes

The international direct dialling (IDD) code for Ireland is +353 followed by area code and subscriber's number:

Cork	21	Mullingar	44
Donegal	73	Shannon	61
Dublin	1	Sligo	71
Galway	91	Tipperary	62
Kilkenny	56	Waterford	51
Killarney	64	Wexford	53
Limerick	61	Wicklow	404

Chambers of Commerce

American Chamber of Commerce Ireland, 6 Wilton Place, Dublin 2 (tel: 661-6201; fax: 661-6217; e-mail: ifo@amcham.ie).

Chambers of Commerce of Ireland, 17 Merrion Square, Dublin 2 (tel: 661-2888; fax: 661-2811; e-mail: info@chambersireland.ie).

Cork Chamber of Commerce, Fitzgerald House, Summerhill North, Cork (tel: 450-9044; fax: 450-8568; e-mail: info@corkchamber.ie).

Dublin Chamber of Commerce, 7 Clare Street, Dublin 2 (tel: 644-7200; fax: 676-6043; info@dublinchamber.ie).

Dun Laoghaire Rathdown Chamber of Commerce, Kilcullen House, 1 Haigh Terrace, Dun Laoghaire (tel: 284-5066; 284-5034; e-mail: info@dirchamber.ie).

Dundalk Chamber of Commerce, Hagan House, Ramparts Road, Dundalk (tel: 933-6343; fax: 933-2085; info@dundalk.ie).

Limerick Chamber of Commerce, 96 O'Connell Street, Limerick (tel: 415-180; fax: 415-785; e-mail: info@limchamber.ie).

Mullingar Chamber of Commerce, ACC House, Dominick Street, Mullingar (tel: 44-044; fax: 44-045; e-mail: info@mullingar-chamber.ie).

Sligo Chamber of Commerce and Industry, 16 Quay Street, Sligo (tel: 916-1274; fax: 916-0912; e-mail: sligochamber@eircom.net).

Waterford Chamber of Commerce, Georges Street, Waterford (tel: 311-136; fax: 876-002; e-mail: info@waterfordchamber.ie).

Wexford Chamber of Industry and Commerce, The Ballast Office, Crescent Quay, Wexford (tel: 22-226; fax:241-70; e-mail: info@wexchamber.iol.ie).

Banking

Allied Irish Bank Ltd, Bankcentre, PO Box 452, Ballsbridge, Dublin 4 (tel: 660-0311; fax: 668-2508).

Allied Irish Investment Bank plc, Bankcentre, Ballsbridge, Dublin 4 (tel: 660-4733).

Bank of Ireland, Lower Baggot Street, Dublin 2 (tel: 661-5933; fax: 661-5671).

The Institute of Bankers in Ireland (banking association), Nassau House, Nassau Street, Dublin 2 (tel: 679-3311).

Investment Bank of Ireland Ltd, 26 Fitzwilliam Place, Dublin 2 (tel: 661-6433; fax: 661-6433).

National Irish Bank, 7/8 Wilton Terrace, Dublin 2 (tel: 678-5066; fax: 661-3324).

Ulster Bank, 33 College Green, Dublin 2 (tel: 677-7623).

Ulster Investment Bank Ltd, 2 Hume Street, Dublin 2 (tel: 661-3444; fax: 676-3021).

Central bank

Central Bank and Financial Services Authority of Ireland, PO Box 559, Dame Street, Dublin 2 (tel: 434-4000; fax: 671-6561; e-mail: enquiries@centralbank.ie).

European Central Bank (ECB), Kaiserstrasse 29, D-60311 Frankfurt am Main, Germany (tel: (+49-69) 13-440; fax: (+49-69) 1344-6000; e-mail: info@ecb.int).

Stock exchange

Stocmhalartán na hÉireann (Irish Stock Exchange) (ISE): www.ise.ie

Travel information

Aer Lingus, Head Office Block, Dublin Airport (tel: 705-2222; fax: 705-3832; internet site: www.aerlingus.ie).

Cork Airport (tel: 431-3131; internet: www.corkairport.com)

Dublin Airport (tel: 814-1111; internet: www.iol.ie).

Irishrail (internet: www.iarnrodeireann.ie and www.irishrail.ie)

Ryanair, Corporate Head Office Building, Dublin Airport (tel: 844-4489, 844-4400; fax: 844-4402; internet: www.ryanair.com).

Shannon Airport (tel:712-000; internet: www.shannonairport.com).

Ministry of tourism

Department of Arts, Sport and Tourism, 23 Kildare Street, Dublin 2 (tel: 631-3800; fax: 661-1201; internet: www.arts-sport-tourism.gov.ie).

National tourist organisation offices

Irish Tourist Board, Baggot Street Bridge, Dublin 2 (tel: 676-5871, 661-6500; fax: 676-4764, 676-4765; internet site: www.irland.ie).

Ministries

Department of Agriculture and Food, Agriculture House, Kildare Street, Dublin 2 (tel: 607-2000; internet: www.agriculture.gov.ie).

Department of Defence, Colaiste Caoimhin, Mobhi Road, Glasnevin, Dublin 9 (tel: 804-210; fax: 804-5000; email: info@defence.irlgov.ie).

Department of Education and Science, Marlborough Street, Dublin 1 (tel: 889-6400; email: info@education.gov.ie).

Department of Enterprise, Trade and Employment, 23 Kildare Street, Dublin 2 (tel: 631-2121; fax: 631-2827; email: info@entemp.ie).

Department of Environment, Heritage and Local Government, Custom House, Dublin 1 (tel: 888-2000; internet: www.environ.ie).

Department of Finance, Government Bldgs, Upper Merrion Street, Dublin 2 (tel: 676-7571; fax: 678-9936; email: webmaster@finance.irlgov.ie).

Department of Foreign Affairs, 80 St Stephen's Green, Dublin 2 (tel: 478-0822; fax: 478-1484; internet: http://foreignaffairs.gov.ie).

Department of Transport, Transport House, 44 Kildare Street, Dublin 2 (tel: 670-7444; email: info@transport.ie).

Department of Taoiseach, Government Buildings, Upper Merrion Street, Dublin 2 (tel: 662-4888; fax: 678-9791; email: webmaster@taoiseach.gov.ie).

Department of Arts, Sport and Tourism, 23 Kildare Street, Dublin 2 (tel: 631-3800; fax: 661-1201; internet: www.arts-sport-tourism.gov.ie).

Other useful addresses

Central Statistics Office, Skehard Road, Cork (tel: 359-000; fax: 359-090; internet site: www.cso.ie).

Confederation of Irish Industry, Confederation House, Kildare Street, Dublin 2 (tel: 660-1011).

Enterprise Ireland, Glasnevin, Dublin 9 (tel: 808-2000; fax: 808-2020; internet site: www.enterprise-ireland.com).

IDA Ireland (Industrial Development Agency), Wilton Park House, Wilton Place, Dublin 2 (tel: 668-6633; fax: 660-3703).

Irish Business and Employers' Confederation, 84 Lower Baggot Street, Dublin 2 (tel: 660-1011; fax: 660-1717).

Irish Embassy (USA), 2234 Massachusetts Avenue, NW, Washington DC 20008 (tel: (+1-202) 462-3939; fax: (+1-202) 232-5993; e-mail: embirlus@aol.com).

Provincial Newspapers' Association of Ireland, 33 Parkgate Street, Dublin 8 (tel: 679-3679).

RTÉ (Irish broadcasting), Donnybrook, Dublin 4 (tel: 208-3111; fax: 208-3080; internet: rte.ie)

The Stock Exchange, 24-28 Anglesea Street, Dublin 2 (tel: 677-8808; fax: 677-6045).

Internet sites

Access Ireland: www.visunet.ie

Business information: www.factfinder.ie

Doras web directory: www.doras.ie

Ireland On-Line: www.home.iol.ie

Irish Government website: irlgov.ie

Irish Times: www.irish-times.com

Irish trade web (information on Irelands' top 1000 companies): www.itw.ie

KEY FACTS

Official name: Medinat Israel (State of Israel)

Head of State: President Shimon Peres (Likud) (since July 15 2007)

Head of government: Prime Minister Benjamin Netanyahu (from 1 Apr 2009)

Ruling party: Coalition led by Likud (The Consolidation), with Yisrael Beiteinu (Israel is Our Home), Mifleget HaAvoda HaYisraelit (Israeli Labor Party) (Labor), Shas, HaBayit HaYehudi (The Jewish Home) and Yahadut HaTorah HaMeukhedet (United Torah Judaism) (UTJ) (from 1 Apr 2009)

Area: 20,700 square km (excluding occupied territories)

Population: 7.63 million (2010)

Capital: Jerusalem (Israel regards the entire city as its capital although it is not recognised by the UN); Tel Aviv, administrative and diplomatic centre

Official language: Hebrew

Currency: New shekel (NIS) = 100 agorot

Exchange rate: NIS3.75 per US$ (Oct 2011)

GDP per capita: US$28,686 (2010)

GDP real growth: 4.60% (2010)

GDP: US$213.10 billion (2010)

Labour force: 3.15 million (2010)

Unemployment: 6.70% (2010)

Inflation: 2.70% (2010)

Balance of trade: -US$2.37 billion (2010)

Israel

In August 2011 Prime Minister Benjamin 'Bibi' Netanyahu's government created a commission to look into the demands of thousands of Israelis who had taken to the streets calling for more comprehensive social policies and better access to subsidised housing. To the government's embarrassment Tel Aviv residents seemed more concerned with living conditions than with their nation's isolated state. If anything the demonstrators, who had been described as the Israeli Indignation Movement, avoided adopting a firm position on the question of the occupation of Palestinian territory. This was a case of pragmatism rather than policies, as the demonstrators' views on the question of the occupation of Palestinian territory were often at odds. Where they agreed, however, was that the policy of settlements was being carried out at the expense of the government's ability to provide decent, affordable housing for its residents.

Mr Netanyahu's fear was that the protests would distract Israelis from the then imminent threat of a United Nations' resolution in favour of the establishment of a Palestinian state. Stalling appeared to be Mr Netanyahu's answer to a number of the problems that faced him – not only that of Palestine, but also that of a fractious coalition which could easily fall apart. In essence, the only strategy that coalition members could agree upon was that of staying in power. But the Israeli Indignation protests certainly represented a new, disorienting challenge for the coalition, in the face of which Mr Netanyahu's chosen solution of a commission looked unlikely to resolve.

An October 2011 letter in *Time* magazine summed up Israel's foreign policy as one of little concern over what happens in Palestine, Egypt, Turkey or indeed anywhere else in the world as long as the Israeli tail continues to wag the American dog. In 2010 this might still have been thought to be the case. However, in 2011 another element emerged in the regional yard. The Palestinians decided to take matters into their own hands and disregard Israel's cosy relationship with the US.

Isolation?

In his May speech on the Middle East, President Obama had exhorted the countries associated with the Arab Spring to keep up the good work. This was fairly predictable stuff and those members of the Israeli cabinet that read the first few paragraphs of the transcript could find nothing to take exception to. The closing paragraphs, however, struck a different note. President Obama told the Israeli government that 'the borders of Israel and Palestine should be based on the 1967 lines, with mutually agreed swaps. The US

President allowed Israeli blood pressures to return to normal as he went on to deal with related questions such as the borders and demilitarisation issues. A furious Prime Minister Benjamin 'Bibi' Netanyahu, who was on the point of leaving for Washington where he would address the American Israel Public Affairs Committee (AIPAC – see below) responded by claiming that the 1967 border was 'indefensible'. Where Mr Obama had insisted that Israeli forces withdraw from the West Bank, Mr Netanyahu countered by saying that they would remain in the Jordan Valley indefinitely.

Israel's relations with Turkey sank to a new low with the publication by the United Nations, in September 2011, of its report on Israel's attack on a flotilla bringing aid to Gaza in May 2010. The report upheld the legality of Israel's blockade of Gaza, but declared Israel's methods 'excessive and unreasonable'. In the raid on the flotilla, Israeli commandos killed eight Turks and one Turkish American. Although Israel agreed to adopt the report 'with reservations', Turkey's President Abdullah Gul described the ruling as 'null and void'. Turkish Prime Minister Recep Tayyip Erdogan simply stated that 'it means nothing to us'.

It was later reported in the Israeli *Yediot Aharonot* newspaper that after months of negotiation involving US, Turkish and Israeli negotiators the two sides agreed that Israel would apologise for its 'operational mistakes' and, for their part, the Turks would not raise any legal claims. But at the eleventh hour, Mr Netanyahu rejected the agreement. The newspaper attributed the decision to reasons of national pride and fear that Israel's right wing foreign minister, Avigdor Lieberman, would be able to use the report against him. Depressingly, *Yediot Aharonot* also published the results of a poll which suggested that over sixty per cent of Israelis considered that there is no chance of peace with Palestinians, ever.

The worsening of relations with Turkey came at a time when Israeli diplomats were also withdrawn from Cairo and from Amman. An article by Aluf Benn in the respected Israeli newspaper *Haaretz* in September 2011 observed that 'The years-long diplomatic effort to integrate Israel as an accepted neighbour collapsed this week with the expulsion of Israeli ambassadors from Ankara and Cairo, and the rushed evacuation of embassy staff from Amman. The region is spewing out the Jewish state, which is increasingly shutting itself off behind fortified walls, under a leadership that refuses any change, movement or reform. Netanyahu demonstrated utter passivity in the face of the dramatic changes in the region and allowed his rivals to seize the initiative and set the agenda.'

At the same time, former US President Bill Clinton placed the blame for the failure of the Middle East peace process with Mr Netanyahu. In the midst of delicate negotiations concerning the Palestinian bid for UN membership, Mr Netanyahu announced the construction of a further 1,100 new houses in a part of Jerusalem outside its pre-1967 borders. Both the substance of the announcement and its timing were insensitive. The resolution of the two sides' positions on Jerusalem is accepted as being one of the thornier issues of the peace process. To ignore this reality is to commit any peace agreement to the waste bin at the outset.

The UN

Some analysts thought that although, in purely regional terms, Israel found itself more isolated than ever, the relationship with the US would see it through. It may have thrown away its friendship with Turkey, but the prospect of a Republican victory in the 2012 US presidential elections gave it new cause for optimism. That optimism was perhaps reflected in the late 2011 opinion poll which suggested that two-thirds of Israelis no longer hold out any hope of achieving a peaceful settlement with the Palestinians. Surprisingly, the same poll suggested that 88 per cent of Israelis consider their country a good place to live. Despite Israel's isolation, despite the continued threat from their closest neighbours, Israelis appeared prepared to settle for a strong economy and – at least for the moment – diminished terrorist threat. For most Israelis, that choice seemed preferable to many of the alternatives in Europe, North America or elsewhere.

Iran

Press reports in Israeli newspapers in late October and early November 2011 suggested that Mr Netanyahu and his experienced defence minister, Ehud Barak, have been drawing up plans for a nuclear strike against Iran's nuclear facilities. The press reports were prompted by a report published by the International Atomic Energy Agency (IAEA) expressing 'serious concerns regarding possible military dimensions to Iran's nuclear programme.' The report considered 'that Iran has carried out activities relevant to the development of a nuclear explosive device.' In the run-up to a presidential election, it seemed unlikely that President Obama would give any Israeli pre-emptive strike the green light. Without US approval and by extension, US involvement, it seemed equally likely that a unilateral Israeli attack on Iran would provoke an intense Iranian counter-attack on Israel. Whatever pre-election lip-service has been paid to supporting Israel, no American President would wish to, never mind know how to, deal with a Middle East conflagration that risked developing into a lengthy regional war, or worse.

An article in the US journal *Foreign Affairs* by Ronald Krebs of the University of Minnesota suggested that Israel's

KEY INDICATORS — Israel

	Unit	2006	2007	2008	2009	2010
Population	m	7.05	*6.96	*7.11	*7.27	*7.63
Gross domestic product (GDP)	US$bn	142.25	161.94	202.10	194.80	213.10
GDP per capita	US$	20,177	23,990	28,409	26,797	28,686
GDP real growth	%	5.2	5.3	4.0	0.7	4.6
Inflation	%	2.1	0.5	4.6	3.3	2.7
Unemployment	%	8.4	7.3	6.1	7.6	6.7
Exports (fob) (goods)	US$m	43,724.0	50,242.0	56,638.0	45,898.0	55,674.0
Imports (fob) (goods)	US$m	46,958.0	55,760.0	64,308.0	45,993.0	58,039.0
Balance of trade	US$m	-3,234.0	-5,518.0	-7,670.0	-96.0	-2,365.0
Current account	US$m	8,546.0	4,603.0	1,422.0	7,486.0	6,369.0
Total reserves minus gold	US$m	29,153.2	28,518.5	42,513.2	60,611.4	70,907.3
Foreign exchange	US$m	29,011.0	28,406.0	42,324.0	59,091.0	69,265.0
Exchange rate	per US$	4.19	3.99	3.59	3.93	3.74

* estimated figure

occupation of Palestine lands had 'fuelled an aggressive ethno-religious nationalism that has become increasingly prominent since the second *intifada*.' Professor Krebs considers that this sentiment had arisen precisely because Israelis have grown despondent over the prospects for peace. Traditional arguments rehearsed by Israelis are that their country has 'tried everything to end the conflict', to be repaid with increased terrorism, obstruction and 'global opprobrium'. The anxiety that accompanies these feelings has certainly benefited the reputation and political prospects of Avigdor Lieberman of the Yisrael Beitenu (Israel is our Home) party. Yisrael Beitenu forms part of Mr Netanyahu's governing coalition. It has sought to contain Israel's human rights NGOs. Of greater concern, perhaps, is the increased isolation of the Israeli Arabs, who constitute some 20 per cent of the population. Under the Netanyahu administration, the Knesset has tabled a number of implicitly anti-Arab bills, notably that requiring all Israeli immigrants to swear an oath of loyalty to Israel as a Jewish state. Another proposed piece of legislation would end Arabic's status as an official language. The trend away from liberal values and the once prevalent pioneer spirit of the Kibbutz, coupled with shifts in immigration patterns, has seen the emergence of the 'little Israeli' mentality, uninterested in and unaware of, the lands and peoples that surround his country. This ingrained cycle of mistrust and enmity certainly makes it unlikely that any Israeli government will revert to serious, thoughtful and sensitive negotiation with the Palestinians.

Anticipating trends towards the international recognition of Palestine, April 2011 saw the results of a poll seeking Israelis' views. As reported by the London *Economist*, the poll asked 'what should Israelis do, seeing that most of the world intends to recognise a Palestinian state in September?' Around 48 per cent thought that Israel should 'recognise a Palestinian state but keep the settlement blocks.' Only 41 per cent thought that Israel should 'vehemently oppose it, even at the price of directly confronting the United Nations (UN).' A majority 53 per cent thought that Prime Minister Netanyahu should, on a forthcoming visit to the US, 'present a diplomatic initiative in Washington that would include significant concessions.' In the same poll, the Kadima party, headed by former foreign minister Tzipi Livni, came ahead of Mr Netanyahu's Likud when it came to the question of re-engaging with the Palestinians. Mr Netanyahu (who studied in the US), had been put on the back foot by an agreement, signed in early May 2011, between the two Palestinian factions, Fatah (West Bank, moderate) and Hamas (Gaza, less than moderate). The Palestinian agreement, however precarious, was welcomed by an international community that was running out of patience with Mr Netanyahu, who was considered responsible for the initial failure and subsequent lack of peace talks. Mr Netanyahu's response was typically feisty: 'How is it possible to achieve peace with a government half of which calls for the destruction of the state of Israel and even praises the arch-murderer, Osama bin Laden?' Mr Netanyahu's response was seen by many as an attempt to play to Israel's political gallery, particularly its right wing, as well as to his US supporters and to AIPAC.

In May 2011, coinciding with Mr Netanyahu's visit to the US, AIPAC held its annual conference in Washington. No barn-dance this – with 10,000 attendees including an impressive 67 senators and 286 members of the House, a gala dinner, and an address from the President himself (who flew off to Europe immediately afterwards). President Obama, in a pre-election year unsurprisingly promised his undying support for the US Jewish Community. The President took the opportunity to back-track on proposals made in his speech of the preceding week where he had said that Israel would need to retreat to its pre-1967 borders. Instead, he said that Israel and Palestine would negotiate a border that is different than the one that existed on 4 June 1967. The 1967 border, in other words, was no more than a starting line.

The American Jewish community is supported by both American parties, although it traditionally votes Democrat. Opinion polls suggested that unlike his predecessor, Mr Obama sympathised more with the Palestinian community than the Jewish community. Opinion polls also suggested that AIPAC risked drifting out of sympathy with its younger US supporters who could no longer be counted on to endorse an 'Israel right or wrong' policy. AIPAC was seen by many to have become (in the words of Peter Beinart writing in *The New York Review of Books*) 'the intellectual bodyguards for Israeli leaders who threaten the very liberal values they profess to admire.' Mr Beinart went on to say that a Zionism that emphasised Jewish 'victimhood' and allowed no empathy for the Palestinians is losing its resonance with younger voters.

Gilad Shalit

In October 2011 Israel agreed to a rather lopsided prisoner exchange to secure the release of Sergeant Gilad Shalit, abducted by Hamas in 2006. Israel appeared to have paid a high price for Sgt Shalit's freedom. In return for Shalit, Isreal was to hand over 1,000 Palestinian male prisoners and 27 women. Of the 1,000, no less than 550 were labelled a 'gesture to Egypt' in recognition of its role in reaching agreement. Many of the Palestinians released were serving life sentences for killing Israelis. It was unclear quite why Mr Netanyahu, who had long opposed any such deal, had relented. In some degree, the Arab Spring and the chaos in Syria, came to Mr Netanyahu's rescue. Mr Netanyahu said that 'I don't know if the future would have allowed us to get a better deal – or any deal at all for that matter.' In a letter to the families of those killed by some of the released prisoners, Mr Netanyahu said: 'I understand the difficulty in accepting that the vile people who committed the heinous crimes against your loved ones will not pay the full price they deserve.'

Haredi

The Haredi, the ultra-orthodox wing of Israeli society, have certainly demonstrated a lack of interest and awareness in the challenges confronting Israel. They have received substantial benefits from those Israeli governments that have owed their election victories to Haredi support. Such is the size of the Haredi subsidies that they are considered by many secular Israelis to be an unacceptable drag on the Israeli economy. As long as Haredi parties can call the political shots, it looks unlikely that any negotiating consensus will arise in Israel.

The economy

Israel managed to pass through the global recession swiftly. The continuing challenge was to sustain growth and low inflation while boosting medium-term prospects – in a context of continued global uncertainty, appreciation of the shekel and a housing market that was overheating. Buoyant activity and employment alongside incipient inflation pressures called for the overall stance of economic policies to be tightened more quickly than planned. But the onus for the accelerated effort fell mainly on fiscal rather than monetary policy. This shift in the policy's centre of gravity helped to contain inflation, reduce upward pressure on the shekel and support the new fiscal rule. Monetary policy focussed on inflation and moved further towards a neutral stance. In so doing, it continued to respond to shocks to global demand and foreign exchange intervention became more symmetric. Steps to re-balance housing supply and demand were supported by these efforts. To secure Israel's medium term prospects, greater co-ordination between the authorities responsible for the stability of the financial system and enhanced procedures governing medium-term public spending appeared to be essential.

Economic output fell mildly and for only two quarters from the fourth quarter of 2008. Growth for 2009 as a whole was 0.8 per cent, projected to rise to around 4 per cent in 2010.

Despite public debt at around 80 per cent of GDP, initial market jitters over Israel in the wake of the Lehman Brothers crash soon subsided.

The recovery was led by consumption and exports. After falling with the onset of the 2008 global economic shock, consumer spending led the recovery from the second quarter of 2009. The strength of consumption was mainly in non-durables – spending on durables fell sharply (by 6 per cent in 2009) and recovered relatively slowly, but this primarily affected imports. Exports recovered in the second half of 2009, in part as world trade rebounded and they were already back at pre-crisis levels by 2010. Demand for housing construction also picked up strongly from the second quarter of 2009, a delayed supply response to the take-off in the housing market which began a year earlier. But in the third quarter of 2010, nascent falls in export volumes and a sharp deceleration in private consumption indicated that limits on the durability of output strength were being reached.

Oil and gas

According to the *Oil and Gas Journal* (OGJ) Israel's reserves of natural gas, now under development in the offshore Mediterranean, are poised to rise substantially in the near future. Israel's Natural Gas Authority (NGA) Director General Yehosua Stern is quoted as confirming that 'Israel's potential gas discoveries stand at 1,000 billion cubic metres (bcm),' General Stern added that Israel's proven gas reserves amount to 300bcm, most of it in the offshore Tamar field. Speaking at an international conference, General Stern told delegates that the reserves figure is expected to rise by a further 453bcm after production tests are completed at the Leviathan field.

General Stern also told conference delegates that the NGA expected an additional 550bcm of gas to be discovered in Israeli waters, which eventually will bring the country's total reserves to 1,300bcm. In 2014–15 there would be an additional entry from Tamar to Israel in the Ashkelon region. General Stern's remarks coincided with reports that Dolphin 1 gas field partners Noble Energy Inc, Delek Group Ltd. and Ratio Oil Exploration LP had found clear signs of gas at the Dolphin 1 exploratory well in the Hanna licence.

Israeli government officials said that Israel and neighbouring Cyprus were ready to co-operate on a joint project to tap potentially huge offshore gas deposits. 'We can co-operate in generating this new found energy and use it for the benefit of the entire region,' said Israel's President Shimon Peres, who added that the two countries have 'substantial economic co-operation potential' with the discovery of gas in the Mediterranean. Focus on the region's hydrocarbons picked up in 2010 when the US Geological Survey said that the Levant basin, which covers waters off Syria, Lebanon, Israel and Cyprus, contains 122 trillion cubic feet (tcf) of gas and as much as 4 billion barrels of oil.

In addition to Israel's offshore reserves The World Energy Council estimates Israel is sitting on enough shale to produce around 4 billion barrels of oil, enough at today's usage to keep the country in oil for more than 40 years. Despite the discovery of vast offshore reserves, Israel still imports much of its gas from Egypt. That supply is precarious. In 2010 it was interrupted by a string of attacks on gas pipelines running through the Sinai desert. These attacks continued into 2011 with the most recent in November when supplies to both Israel and Jordan were interupted. Concerns remain about future relations with Cairo after the fall of Hosni Mubarak.

Risk assessment

Economy	Fair
Politics	Fair
Regional stability	Poor

COUNTRY PROFILE

Historical profile

The struggle between the Israelis and the Palestinians over historic claims to land is one of the most enduring of all the world's conflicts.

1917 The Balfour Declaration suggested the establishment in Palestine of a national home for the Jewish people.

1922 The Council of the League of Nations assigned to Britain a mandate for the Ottoman Arab territory of Palestine, a region that covered present-day Israel and Jordan, plus the Golan Heights region (claimed by Syria). The British divided the mandate into two parts, designating all lands west of the Jordan River as Palestine and those east of the river as Transjordan. The League of Nations mandate also addressed the goal of restoring a Jewish homeland in Palestine.

1929 Riots in Jerusalem between Arab Palestinians and Jews were sparked by a dispute over the use of the western wall of the Al Aqsa Mosque (the site is sacred to Muslims, and Jews claim it as part of their temple).

1936–39 The Arab Higher Committee opposed Jewish immigration to Palestine and the Peel Commission concluded that the mandate in Palestine was unworkable. Legislation limiting the number of Jewish immigrants into Palestine was introduced by the British government.

1945–46 Many Jews who had survived the Nazi German Holocaust arrived in Palestine and Jewish extremists began to oppose Britain's immigration legislation. Transjordan became independent and was later re-named Jordan.

1947 The UN adopted Resolution 181, establishing Jewish and Arab states within Palestine. A partition plan was based solely on population, with Jerusalem as an international zone under UN jurisdiction. The Jews agreed to the partition; the Arabs refused. Britain withdrew from Palestine.

1948 Conflict ensued between Arabs and Jews. Jewish leaders announced the formation of the State of Israel, open to the immigration of Jews from all countries. Egypt, Iraq, Lebanon, Syria and Jordan joined Palestinian and other Arab guerrillas and invaded Israel. The armistice agreements extended the territory under Israel's control beyond the UN partition boundaries. Many Arabs fled Israel to become refugees in the surrounding Arab countries, ending the Arab majority in the new Jewish state.

1956 Egypt nationalised the Suez Canal and blockaded the Red Sea port of Eilat. Israeli forces attacked and occupied the Sinai Peninsula, later being joined by Britain and France, seeking to regain control of the Canal Zone. In the face of strong international opposition, particularly from the US, all three withdrew their forces.

1967 Egypt blockaded Eilat again. Israel launched and won the Six Day War taking control of the Sinai peninsular and the Gaza Strip, which had been Egyptian

territory, together with the Golan Heights, formerly claimed by Syria, and the West Bank, including East Jerusalem, which had been united with Jordan since 1950. Around 300,000 Palestinian Arabs fled to Jordan. Israel's settlement policy began with occupation of all territory seized including East Jerusalem, re-unifying the city; such areas became known as the occupied territories.
1968–70 The War of Attrition was a limited war fought between Egypt and Israel, initiated by Egypt as a way to recapture the Sinai from Israel. The war ended without changes to the borders.
1969 Golda Meir became prime minister.
1973 Lebanon was used by the Palestinians as a base for activities against Israel. In retaliation, Israeli commandos raided Beirut, killing three associates of Palestine Liberation Organisation (PLO) chairman, Yasser Arafat. In the 6 October War (also known as the Yom Kippur War), Egypt and Syria invaded Israel to reclaim some of the land lost in the Six Day War, but despite some early strategic gains by Egypt and Syria, Israel counter-attacked and repelled the invasion, re-conquering the Golan Heights from Syria.
1974 Golda Meir resigned and was succeeded as prime minister by Yitzhak Rabin. Jordan and other Arab countries recognised the PLO as the sole legitimate representative of the Palestinian people.
1977 President Sadat of Egypt visited Jerusalem.
1978 Prime Minister Menachim Begin and Egyptian Prime Minister Anwar Sadat signed peace accords at Camp David in the US. Israel agreed to withdraw from the Sinai.
1981 Israel annexed East Jerusalem and the Golan Heights.
1982–85 The Sinai peninsular was returned to Egypt in 1982. Israel launched a full-scale invasion of Lebanon. Despite subsequently withdrawing from most of the territory, Israel maintained some troops in Lebanon in order to help secure its own northern border.
1987 The Palestinians launched an *intifida* (uprising) against the Israelis.
1988 The Harakat al Muqawama al Islamia (Hamas) (Islamic Resistance Movement) was formed and began armed resistance to Israeli rule in the occupied territories of the West Bank and Gaza Strip.
1989 Mass immigration of Jews from the Soviet Union began; many settled in the occupied territories.
1991–93 Israel and the PLO conducted secret negotiations in Oslo (Norway), agreeing an interim peace accord, which was signed in the US. The Oslo Peace Accords laid the basis for transfer of authority from the Israeli military administration to the PLO in the Gaza Strip and an undefined area around the town of Jericho in the West Bank. President Ezer Weizman took office.
1995–96 A follow-up treaty, Oslo II, (known collectively, with the first, as the Accord), envisaged Palestinian autonomy, with Israeli troop units withdrawn from the West Bank. Yasser Arafat was elected president of the Palestinian Legislative Council (PLC), the assembly of the Palestinian National Authority (PNA).
2000 President Ezer Weizman resigned and Moshe Katsav, (Likud), was elected president. Israel withdrew from southern Lebanon without reaching an agreement with Syria on the future of the Golan Heights, still under Israeli control. The Camp David summit aimed at pushing forward the Accord failed when no agreement could be reached; the Palestinians claimed sovereignty over all of east Jerusalem, including Judaism's holiest place of Temple Mount. The right-wing opposition leader, Ariel Sharon, made a provocative visit to Palestinian controlled Temple Mount (called al Haram as Sharif by Arabs) and the second *intifada* was launched. A total blockade was imposed by Israel on the West Bank and Gaza.
2001 Ariel Sharon was elected prime minister. He declared the PNA a terrorist-supporting organisation and launched Operation 'Defensive Shield', invading the PNA-controlled West Bank and Gaza Strip, attacking its institutions and besieging Yasser Arafat's headquarters.
2002 Saudi Arabia proposed a peace initiative, whereby Israel could have normal relations, peace and security with the Arab world if Israel withdrew from captured territories and agreed to recognise a Palestinian state. Israel began building a 640km security barrier, claiming it was the only way to control the infiltration of militant terrorists.
2003 US President Bush unveiled the Middle East Road Map to Peace, to run between 2003–05, with a cease-fire, an end to Jewish settlements in the occupied territories and the creation of an independent Palestinian state. However neither side kept to its timetable and it, *de facto*, failed.
2004 The International Court of Justice ruled that the West Bank security barrier was illegal. Palestinian President Yasser Arafat died.
2005 Sharon and the newly elected Palestinian president, Mahmoud Abbas, signed a truce that planned to bring to an end four years of violence between the two states. Egypt and Jordan agreed to return their ambassadors to Israel. The cabinet approved the removal of Jewish illegal settlers from the Gaza Strip and part of the West Bank. Hamas bombed targets in Israel claiming it was not party to the truce. Abbas ordered a crackdown and sacked senior security chiefs. Israeli troops began clearing Jewish settlements from Gaza. Most commercial buildings were left standing but some homes and synagogues were destroyed. Sharon left Likud, a party he had helped found, to form a centrist party, Kadima, a right-of-centre party. Binyamin Netanyahu was elected leader of Likud.
2006 Sharon suffered a massive stroke and was hospitalised; Ehud Olmert became acting prime minister. Kadima won parliamentary elections. Olmert became prime minister after Sharon was declared 'permanently incapacitated' in a coma. Israel became a member of the International Red Cross, adopting a diamond-shaped red crystal as its symbol. Hezbollah paramilitary forces based in southern Lebanon crossed the border and captured two Israeli soldiers. Israel retaliated by invading Lebanon in an attempt to retrieve its soldiers; it inflicted massive damage, especially in the south, to infrastructure, with thousands of homes destroyed and hundreds of civilian casualties. The conflict lasted for 34 days. The Israeli soldiers were not recovered and the whole exercise was considered a failure on behalf of the Israeli Defence Force (IDF).
2007 Raleb Majadele (Labour) was the first Arab Muslim to hold office in Israel. The head of Israel's armed forces General Halutz resigned following an enquiry that criticised poor planning, strategy and execution of the 2006 invasion of Lebanon. A criminal inquiry into Ehud Olmert's role in the privatisation of Bank Leumi began. President Moshe Katsav resigned; Shimon Peres became president. Binjamin Netanyahu was re-elected leader of Likud.
2008 Ehud Olmert resigned as prime minister, due to a damaging corruption case. Tzipi Livni (Kadima) became acting prime minister but was unable to form a coalition government within a constitutionally set period. Israel launched an offensive into the Gaza Strip on 27 December, to deter ongoing Hamas rocket attacks on its territories. Despite Israel's claims of targeting Hamas weapons dumps, tunnels running between Gaza and Egypt and Hamas officials, casualties were highest among civilians. In August the government halted the immigration scheme which had allowed Ethiopians of Jewish descent to settle in Israel.
2009 An Israeli invasion of the Gaza Strip left over 1,000 Gaza Palestinians dead and 4,700 wounded, as well as 13 Israelis including two civilians killed by rocket attacks. UN and EU representatives called for a halt to the military action and humanitarian aid to be supplied to Gaza.

Israel agreed to a daily aid convoy during a three-hour cease-fire. Israel declared a cease-fire and Hamas announcement it would stop launching missiles into Israel. Early general elections were held. Although Kadima won the most seats in the Knesset it could not form a coalition and became the official opposition. President Peres asked Benjamin Netanyahu (Likud) to form a coalition government, which finally included nationalist and ultra-orthodox Jewish political parties. The UN investigated alleged violations of international law during Israel's conflict in the Gaza Strip and concluded Israeli military action had 'involved varying degrees of negligence or recklessness' and accused the military of war crimes and possible crimes against humanity. Israel rejected the report as showing bias and claiming that Hamas had hidden fighters among civilians in the vicinity of UN properties. The government confirmed that construction of Jewish settlements in the West Bank would resume, even if peace talks with the Palestinians were renewed.

2010 In May, the Organisation for Economic Co-operation and Development (OECD) voted unanimously to admit Israel as a member, despite strong opposition from the Palestinian government. Nine activists were killed by Israeli security forces when they stormed a ship in international waters, attempting to break the blockade of Gaza, resulting in US condemnation. Israel announced in June that it would ease the Gaza Strip blockade and allow more civilian items into the territory. In August Israel and Palestine agreed to resume peace talks after a two year gap. Talks began between Prime Minister Netanyahu and Palestinian President Mohmoud Abbas in Washington on 2 September, hosted by President Obama and chaired by Secretary of State, Hillary Clinton. The negotiations began with a dinner at the White House, which President Mubarak of Egypt and King Abdullah of Jordan also attended. President Obama criticised plans, announced on 9 November, to build a further 1,300 homes in East Jerusalem. In November, the government approved a scheme that would allow a further 8,000 Ethiopians of the Falash Mura community and of Jewish descent to settle in Israel by 2013. Construction of a barrier along the border with Egypt, agreed by the government in March, began in late November. The 250km barrier will cost an estimated US$232 million, and take a year to build. The government estimated that up to 700 illegal immigrants cross into Israel from Egypt each week.

2011 On 13 March, despite international disapproval and condemnation by Palestinian authorities, the government approved the construction of hundreds of Jewish settlers' homes in the occupied West Bank. The so-called 'Nakba' ('catastrophe') bill, which refuses funding to organisations that deny Israel's existence as a Jewish state, was passed in parliament by a majority of 37–25 on 23 March. The construction of a further 942 homes in the Jewish settlement of Gilo on the outskirts of Jerusalem was approved on 5 April, just days before President Peres was due to meet President Obama in Washington. A group of 21 prominent Israelis signed an open letter in May calling on the international community to recognise a Palestinian state in Jerusalem, the West Bank and Gaza. In a speech on 19 May, US President Obama said that any future settlement with Palestine must be based on 1967 borders, although 'with mutually agreed swaps, so that secure and recognised borders are established for both states.' Prime Minister Netanyahu rejected the proposal in a speech to the US Congress on 24 May, saying that 'Israel will be generous on the size of a Palestinian state but will be very firm on where we put the border'. His office had earlier said that President Obama should refrain from demanding Israel withdraw to 'indefensible' 1967 borders. On 11 July parliament passed, by 47 votes to 36, a law banning the boycotting of West Bank settlements. A legal challenge to the ban was announced on 14 July, by civil-rights groups that called it 'deeply undemocratic'. A prisoner swap deal between the government and Hamas involving the young Israeli soldier, Gilad Shalit, and 'hundreds' of Palestinian prisoners was agreed in the Knesset by 26–3 votes on 11 October. Sargeant Shalit had been held for five years.

Political structure

Constitution

Israel passed the Law and Administration Ordinance on attaining independence, in 1948. In the Declaration of the Establishment of the State of Israel that embodied the principals of law, it was recognised that these principals would evolve in time and circumstances.

Basic laws set out the powers of the executive, legislative and judicial branches. The country functions without a written constitution as Israel's founders wanted to avoid creating problems between religious and secular Jews and between Jews and the non-Jewish minority.

Independence date

14 May 1948

Form of state

Parliamentary democracy

The executive

Executive power rests with the government (a cabinet of ministers), headed by a prime minister as head of government. The government may determine its own agenda and executive procedures.

The prime minister is directly elected for four years and cannot be deposed from office without fresh elections.

The prime minister chooses members of the cabinet from either inside or outside the Knesset (parliament). The cabinet is responsible to the Knesset.

The president is Head of State and has a largely ceremonial role; elected every five years for a maximum of two terms.

National legislature

The 120-seat unicameral Knesset is elected by proportional representation for a maximum of four years. The country is divided into six *mezoh* (administrative districts).

Legal system

The law is based on English common law, components of Jewish religious law and some features of other systems, as appropriate.

The judiciary has constitutionally guaranteed independence. The court system has three levels: the Supreme Court, district courts and magistrates' courts. The court system does not employ juries in Israel. There is also a separate system of limited and specific tribunals that deal with military, labour law and religious, civil matters.

Last elections

10 February 2009 (parliamentary); 31 June 2007 (presidential).

Results: Parliament: Kadima won 28 seats (out of 120), Likud 27 seats, Yisrael Beiteinu 15, Labor Party 13 and Shas 11; seven other parties won five seats or less; 21 parties failed to reach the minimum 2 per cent threshold vote, necessary to secure seats.

Presidential: (first round) Shimon Peres won 58 votes (out of 120), Reuven Rivlin 37, Colette Avital 21. Second round: Rivlin and Avital withdrew and Peres won 86 votes.

Next elections

2012 (presidential); 2011 (parliamentary)

Political parties

Ruling party

Coalition led by Likud (The Consolidation), with Yisrael Beiteinu (Israel is Our Home), Mifleget HaAvoda HaYisraelit (Israeli Labor Party) (Labor), Shas, HaBayit HaYehudi (The Jewish Home) and Yahadut HaTorah HaMeukhedet (United Torah Judaism) (UTJ) (from 1 Apr 2009)

Main opposition party

Kadima (Forward)

Population

7.27 million (2009)

Last census: November 1995: 5,548,523 (including residents of East

Jerusalem and Israelis in Palestinian territories).
Population density: 302 inhabitants per square km. Urban population: 92 per cent (1995–2001).
Annual growth rate: 2.4 per cent 1994–2004 (WHO 2006)
Ethnic make-up
European, Middle Eastern and North African Jews, Arabs and Druze.
Religions
The Jewish, Muslim, Catholic, Greek Orthodox, Druze, Protestant and Baha'i faiths are all represented. Non-Jews make up 18 per cent of the population. They include 635,000 Muslims, 105,000 Christians (almost all Arabs) and 78,000 Druze. The ultra-orthodox Jewish, or charedi, population has nearly doubled since 1990 to about 600,000, or 10 per cent of Israel's population.

Education
Education is provided free of charge and is organised by the state. Primary schooling lasts until aged 11.
Secondary schools are divided into four groups: state schools, which are attended by the majority, state religious schools, Arab and Druze schools and Torah schools for ultra-orthodox Jews. Youth Aliya schools specialise in educating new immigrants.
Demand for tertiary education consistently outstrips domestic supply, so that more Israelis study at universities abroad than at home, giving the country a ratio of graduates that is one of the highest in the world.
Public expenditure on education typically amounts to around 8 per cent of GDP.
Literacy rate: 95 per cent adult rate; 100 per cent youth rate (15–24) (Unesco 2005).
Compulsory years: Five to 16
Enrolment rate: 98 per cent total primary enrolment, of relevant age group (including repeaters); 88 per cent total secondary enrolment (World Bank).
Pupils per teacher: 14 in primary schools

Health
The ministry of health, the large municipalities, private, non-profit institutions and health insurance funds cater to different medical facilities. Companies are required to contribute to insurance for their employees to cover hospital treatment.
The Histadrut (General Federation of Labour) whose members include 90 per cent of Jewish workers, provide sickness benefits and medical care. About 95 per cent of the population are covered by a health insurance plan.
Smoking is prevalent among 45 per cent of men and 30 per cent of women causing health hazards. It is estimated that 99 per cent of the population have access to safe water and sanitation facilities are universal.
HIV/Aids
HIV prevalence: 0.1 per cent aged 15–49 in 2003 (World Bank)
Life expectancy: 80 years, 2004 (WHO 2006)
Fertility rate/Maternal mortality rate: 2.8 births per woman, 2004 (WHO 2006); maternal mortality 5 per 100,000 live births (World Bank).
Birth rate/Death rate: 6 death and 21 births per 1,000 people (World Bank)
Child (under 5 years) mortality rate (per 1,000): 5.0 per 1,000 live births (World Bank)
Head of population per physician: 3.82 physicians per 1,000 people, 2003 (WHO 2006)

Welfare
There is a state-sponsored social welfare system, the National Insurance Institute, which covers the entire population. It is largely financed by compulsory monthly fees collected under the National Insurance Law, with the government providing the remaining funds. The system provides pensions, general disability payments, work injury compensation, child support and other allowances. The Institute also reimburses employers for salaries paid to employees during annual military reserve duty. Citizens disabled during military service are entitled to additional benefits from the defence ministry.

Main cities
Jerusalem (capital, estimated population 700,745 in 2005). Israel regards the entire city as its capital, but its claim to East Jerusalem, captured by Arab forces in 1948 but recaptured by Israel in 1967, is disputed by Palestinians and a number of other countries.
The diplomatic centre is Tel Aviv (estimated population 365,677 in 2005). Other cities include Haifa (273,877), Ashdod (207,268), Bersheva (191,349) and Netanya (170,332).

Media
Press
The press has more freedom than in any of its neighbours and the government respects its media.
The mix of newspapers reflects the diversity of the population with Hebrew national dailies vying with Arabic, English and the Russian language newspapers for their readership, although non are exclusive and crossover readership is common.
Dailies: In Hebrew *Yediot Aharonot* (www.ynet.co.il), a tabloid has the largest circulation, *Haaretz* (www.haaretz.co.il), has a reputation for quality reporting, *Maariv* (www.nrg.co.il) is a popular tabloid. In English *The Jerusalem Post* (www.jpost.com), is a broadsheet and *Vesti* is a popular Russian language newspaper.
Weeklies: In Arabic *Kul al Arab* (www.kul-alarab.com) is a popular publication of news and current affairs.
Business: In Hebrew, *Globes* (www.globes.co.il), with an English online edition, is a weekly publication along with *The Marker* (www.themarker.com). An online site *Bull* (www.bull.co.il) covers news from the stock market.
Periodicals: In English and German, *Challenge* (www.challenge-mag.com), is a magazine concerning the Israeli-Palestinian conflict, published six times a year.
Broadcasting
The Israel Broadcasting Authority (IBA) (www.iba.org.il) is the national, public broadcaster, which is funded by licence fees, sponsorship and radio adverts.
Al Jazeera broadcasts were restricted in Israel in February 2009 following Qatar's decision to cut ties with Israel. Visas for al Jazeera correspondents were not renewed and access to news briefings were curtailed.
Radio: The IBA (www.iba.org.il) operates a network referred to as Kol Yisrael (Voice of Israel), of eight different stations, the four popular, domestic services include in Hebrew (Network A, B and C) broadcasting news, talk radio, music and (Network D) is an Arabic service. There is also a station for recent immigrants to Israel broadcasting in 13 languages, predominantly Russian. The other three are devoted to classical music, education and Jazz.
Independent radio stations include Arutz 7 (www.inn.co.il) a national network, all other stations are locally based including 90FM (www.90fm.co.il) in Jerusalem, Galgalatz (http://glz.msn.co.il) in Beersheva and Radio Haifa (http://1075.fm).
Television: The IBA (www.iba.org.il) has two channels, one broadcasting in Hebrew and the other in Arabic. There are other, pubic commercial stations including Channel 2, with weekly schedules operated by Keshet TV (www.keshet-tv.com) and Reshet TV (www.rashet.tv), Channel 10 (www.nana10.co.il) and Israel Plus (www.israel-plus.com) which broadcasts in Russian. There are several cable services and one local satellite service, Yes (www.yes.co.il). Other, international satellite services are available.
Advertising
Besides television, radio and press, there is cinema screen advertising, as well as limited poster and illuminated sign facilities. Newspapers accounts for the single largest share of adspend although revenues are falling as TV's share is increasing. New technologies are beginning to

claim their own share of advertising venue.

News agencies

Other news agencies: Israel National News: www.israelnationalnews.com
Israel News Agency (INA): www.israelnewsagency.com
Israeli News Now: www.israelinewsnow.com
PR Newswire: www.prnewswire.co.il

Economy

Israel has a thriving modern economy, based on high technology and communications industries, which is orientated towards exports. The markets for its products lie outside the Middle East, mainly in North America, Western Europe and east Asia. The US is the principal market. As well as high technology equipment, the main exports are cut diamonds, agricultural produce and pharmaceuticals. Israel is reliant on imports for raw materials and oil. Grains also have to be imported, although Israel is otherwise self-sufficient in other agricultural produce. In 2009, the International Monetary Fund (IMF) considered Israel's economy to be robust, strong, sustainable and balanced.
The IMF judged Israel's banking sector to have come through the global economic crisis relatively unscathed, due to its conservative establishment practices and supervisory regulations that saw much of the selling of asset-backed securities (ABS) in early 2008 before the critical peak of the crisis stuck later that year.
GDP growth in 2008 was 3.9 per cent, a fall from 5.4 per cent in 2007; growth in 2009 is forecast to be -1.7 per cent in line with the global economic downturn. Inflation rose sharply from 0.5 per cent in 2007 to 4.7 per cent in 2008, and is expected to fall back to 1.4 per cent in 2009. Since a high of around 11 per cent in 2002, unemployment has steadily fallen to around 6 per cent in 2008.
Israel is a leading trader in raw diamonds with around half of all polished diamonds worldwide processed in Israel. The industry accounted for US$7 billion in exports in 2007 and along with fuel, shipping and aircraft was the only sector of the economy not to fall in growth in 2008.
Israel benefits from strong overseas investment, despite the instability of the region, as well as tax revenues, high personal consumption levels and substantial aid from the US.

External trade

Israel had bilateral free trade agreements with, among others, the EU, Turkey, the US, Canada and Mexico.
Exports provide over 95 per cent of GDP, of which 40 per cent are hi-tech industry output and pharmaceutical companies producing generic medicines; cut and dressed precious and semi-precious gems and pearls provide over 35 per cent. The trade and processing of diamonds accounted for US$7 billion in exports in 2007; the industry is one of the country's largest. Israel has a free trade agreement with the US and is also a signatory of the Euro-Mediterranean Partnership agreement, which provides for the introduction of free trade between the EU and 10 Mediterranean countries by 2012.

Imports

Principal exports are machinery and equipment, software, cut and polished diamonds, agricultural products, chemicals, textiles and clothes.
Main sources: US (typically 35 per cent of total), Belgium (7 per cent), Hong Kong (5 per cent)

Exports

Principal imports include raw materials, military equipment, investment goods, rough diamonds, fuels, grain and consumer goods.
Main destinations: US (typically 15 per cent of total), Belgium (10 per cent), Germany (6 per cent).

Agriculture

Farming

The agricultural sector contributes around 2 per cent to GDP and employs 5 per cent of the working population.
Israel is largely self-sufficient in food, importing some cereals, sugar beet and animal feeds. Food, beverages and tobacco are exported.
Farms are relatively small but mostly part of *kibbutzim* (larger co-operatives) or *moshavim* (co-operative smallholder villages), sharing machinery etc. The *kibbutz* and *moshav* movement formed the backbone of early Jewish settlement in Palestine before the State's creation in 1948. The *Keren Kayemeth Le Yisrael* (Jewish National Fund) was created in 1901 to buy land for the settlers. Since 1948 it has become involved in land development, especially land reclamation and forestry.
Israel's agricultural miracle of the 1950s and early 1960s, with annual growth levels of around 12 per cent, was based on intensive irrigated farming, the rise in domestic demand from new immigrants and the expansion of export markets. From the late 1960s, growth slowed to stagnation by the 1980s. Many blamed the bureaucratic marketing organisations for stifling incentives and others blamed an overemphasis on heavily irrigated cash crops, such as cotton, which have become increasingly costly to produce and are vulnerable to international competition.
The major crops are fruits (30 per cent of total production), vegetables (14 per cent) and livestock (42 per cent).
About 40 per cent of farm produce is sold locally, 26 per cent to industry for processing and another 26 per cent is exported directly.
Of the total cultivated land area (4,400 square km), over half is under irrigation. The general trend in agriculture is towards greater mechanisation and many agricultural workers have transferred to industry.

Fishing

There is some fish farming; approximately 85 per cent of the total catch of fish is consumed locally.

Forestry

Between 60,000–70,000 tonnes of timber are harvested annually.

Industry and manufacturing

The sector contributes around 17 per cent to GDP and employs 28 per cent of the working population.
The growth sectors are the capital intensive, science-based industries, such as aircraft (executive jets and fighters), electronics (telecommunications equipment), biotechnology, agricultural technology, chemicals and mining.
A wide range of goods are made or assembled for the domestic market, including cars, commercial vehicles, electrical goods, paper and paper products.
Israeli governments have historically worked with trade unions and employers to plan economic policy. Key policy elements have been to build up basic industry with state or trade union funds and high-tech industries that are either state-owned (a spin-off from the important arms industry) or privately-owned, but which benefit from government incentives aimed specifically at attracting foreign technology. Industry has long been supported with protective tariffs and subsidies, but Israel is progressively exposing its domestic market to competition from abroad as a result of growing trade with the EU and the US. Exports are vitally important to Israeli industry on account of the small size of the domestic market.
The strength of the Israeli manufacturing industry is increasingly in high technology. Traditional industries, such as food processing, textiles, metals, rubber and plastics and chemicals, are well developed but the future manufacturing base is likely to be in heavy and hi-tech industries, particularly the defence industry. Government policy is to shift from low value labour intensive industries to high value hi-tech industries. These have become increasingly important as labour-intensive industries such as the textile industry relocate to more competitive economies such as Jordan, Egypt and Turkey where labour costs are lower.
In 2005 the government embarked on its largest privatisation programme since the

late 1990s. A stake of 30 per cent of Bezeq Israel Telecom was sold to a private consortium headed by media mogul Haim Saban, for US$970 million.

Tourism

The tourism industry is affected by the ongoing domestic terrorism since 2000. It has been estimated that up to 2 out of 3 anticipated visitor arrivals failed to arrive. Luxury hotels, built in anticipation of the greater numbers, have been standing empty as the industry restructures itself. Numbers are increasing as the focus of marketing has turned to Jewish and Christian pilgrims, cultural tourists and secular visitors who now see the destination as a country with localised violence.

Israel belongs to the Euromed Heritage Programme, a computerisation project, sponsored by the EU, which focusses on cultural tourists of archaeology, arts and history, promoting sites through the internet. Israel and Jordan have a joint marketing arrangement to package resorts for overseas visitors, such as cruise ships visiting the Gulf of Aqaba.

Mining

The mining sector typically contributes 1 per cent to GDP and employs 1 per cent of the workforce.

There are vast reserves of potash, bromine and periclase in the area of the Dead Sea, the world's most saline lake, and deposits of 600 million tonnes of phosphate rock in the Negev Desert. These evaporites are produced for fertilisers and industrial minerals. Phosphates are mined at Oron (around 1.2 million tonnes per annum); potash is extracted from the Dead Sea at Sodom (approximately 3.5 million tonnes per annum). Israel is the world's second-largest producer of bromine and produces 20 per cent of world output.

Hydrocarbons

Israel has no oil production of its own and for political and security reasons is reluctant to obtain its hydrocarbons from one single source, particularly one from the Middle East. Currently, Israel obtains most of its oil from Russia and central Asia – Turkmenistan and Kazakhstan. Other sources include Mexico, Egypt, Angola and the UK. It imports around 230,000 barrels per day (bpd) and it is estimated to have around four million barrels of oil reserves, located underneath gas reserves. There has been significant oil exploration onshore and in the Mediterranean (with the drilling of over 350 wells). In 2004 a deposit to the east of Kfar Saba was discovered with an estimated billion barrels of oil.

Israel has two oil refineries, at Haifa and Ashdod, with a joint capacity of 220,000bpd, which is sufficient for all of the country's refined oil needs. If the Israeli-Palestinian conflict is resolved then Israel could provide an alternative route for Middle Eastern oil exports from the Gulf to the West. At present, oil exports travel by tanker through the Suez Canal or around southern Africa.

Israel has an estimated 600 million tonnes of recoverable oil shale, producing around 9,000bpd. This reserve is located mainly in the Rotem basin region.

Proven natural gas reserves were 38.9 billion cubic metres (cum) in 2007, found in deposits off the Israeli coast and Gaza Strip coast. In January 2009, a significant natural gas deposit was discovered offshore in the region of Haifa. The deposit had been estimated to hold up to 5.6 billion cum of natural gas, although production may not begin until 2014. An agreement for the start of 1.7 billion cum of natural gas imports (over 20 years) from Egypt via the el Arish-Ashkelon pipeline began in 2008.

Imports of coal were 217.9 tonnes in 2007, providing approximately 32 per cent of Israel's energy requirements. All coal imports come primarily from South Africa, Columbia, Australia and Indonesia.

Energy

Total installed generating capacity was 10.1 gigawatts in 2006, with production at 46.8 billion kilowatt hours (kWh) and consumption at 43.2 billion kWh. Around 70 per cent of electricity comes from coal-fired power stations, 25 per cent from oil-fired stations and the remainder by gas-oil and independent power producers (IPPs). Approximately 97 per cent of fuel requirements are met from imports. Israel's energy security is severely compromised by the lack of peace between Israel and its Arab population and neighbours. The energy infrastructure, including offshore exploration, onshore installations and proposed pipelines connecting Central Asia with Europe are vulnerable to continued attacks.

The Israel Electric Corporation (IEC) is responsible for generating and supplying energy. The government hopes to increase the participation of the private sector, with the aim of 10 per cent of electricity to be generated by IPPs. A programme of converting oil and coal-fired power stations to natural gas has begun. The delivery of Egyptian gas is subject to production problems and political opposition. Renewable energy supplies include primarily solar which is widely used for domestic hot water heating, although not in commercial generation of electricity.

Financial markets

Stock exchange

Tel Aviv Stock Exchange (TASE)

Banking and insurance

The government introduce structural reforms to the banking system in 2005 with the legislation to break the dominance of the largest banks over capital markets. It is intended to open up the banking sector to foreign competition. The top two banks, Hapoalim and Leumi, will be required to sell their mutual funds before 2009 and provident funds by 2008. Smaller institutions have longer to do the same.

Central bank

The Bank of Israel (BOI), Jerusalem. It has the sole right to issue currency, create and implement monetary policy, regulate and supervise commercial and other banks, control foreign exchange, maintain foreign currency reserves and publish the only representative exchange rate for the shekel versus foreign currencies.

Main financial centre

Tel Aviv

Time

GMT plus two hours (daylight saving GMT plus three hours)

Geography

Israel is at the eastern end of the Mediterranean Sea, with a coastline of about 270km from the Lebanese border in the north to the north-eastern tip of the Sinai Desert in the south. Israel has borders with Lebanon in the north, Syria in the north-east, Jordan in the east and south-east and Egypt is in the south west. There is a short coastline on the Gulf of Aqaba in the south

Within these internationally recognised borders there are disputed borders between Israel and State of Palestine. Gaza is a strip (around 40km wide) of coastline in the south-west and the West Bank is an area west of the Jordan River, containing Jerusalem and areas west and north of the city, the borders of which have been in dispute since the Six Day War in 1967.

The country can be divided into four regions, the coastal plain, the central highlands, the Jordan Rift Valley (which includes Lake Tiberias (also known as the Sea of Galilee in the bible and Lake Kinneret by Israelis) and the Negev Desert (an area including the Dead Sea, the lowest land point on the planet at 399 metres below sea level). The desert comprises over half the country's landmass and is an extension of the greater Sinai Desert.

Hemisphere

Northern

Climate

Two climates exist, Mediterranean in the north and an arid sub-tropical in the south. Jerusalem, situated in the central highlands, has summer temperatures in July–August of 19–29 degrees Celsius (C) and 6–14 degrees C in winter (December–January). Tel Aviv on the coast has a more humid climate with summer temperatures of 24–35 degrees C and 19–30 degrees C in winter. Eilat, on the Gulf of Aqaba, records the hottest average summer temperatures of 40 degrees C.

Dress codes

Business dress is fairly relaxed, except on formal occasions. In Jerusalem even in the height of summer a sweater is often necessary at night. Tel Aviv, along the coast, is far more humid and evenings are warmer.

It is recommended that business women should wear respectable clothing; bare arms, trousers and short skirts may cause offence to some community members.

Entry requirements

Passports

All travellers require passports with at least six months validity from the date of entry; proof of return/onward passage and sufficient funds for stay are also required.

The Israeli Ministry of the Interior insists that Israeli citizens holding dual nationality must enter and leave Israel on their Israeli passport.

NB When crossing into Israel from any border other than the West Bank, it is important to note that an Israeli stamp, or exit stamp from any of the neighbouring countries, will mean entry is barred to almost any other Arab country. It is possible to request that the passport should not be stamped and a separate form is stamped instead and attached to the passport; the form can be removed when exiting the country.

Visa

Israel has agreements with 65 countries for visa-free travel, including most citizens from Europe, the Americas, Australasia and some Asian countries. Transit passengers with onward passage within 24 hours do not require visas. Contact the nearest Israeli consulate for further information.

Prohibited entry

Persons carrying a Palestinian identity number will not be permitted to enter Israel through Ben Gurion International Airport if their last departure was through the Allenby Bridge or Rafah border crossings.

Currency advice/regulations

There are no restrictions on the import of local and foreign currencies but amounts to be exported should not exceed the amount imported.

Money should only be changed at authorised exchanged outlets.

Travellers cheques are widely accepted.

Customs

Video cameras and other electronic items must be declared on entry.

Prohibited imports

Fresh meat and fruit and vegetables from Africa.

Health (for visitors)

Mandatory precautions

There are no vaccinations required.

Advisable precautions

Inoculations and boosters should be current for tetanus and hepatitis A. There may be a need for vaccinations for typhoid, tuberculosis, diphtheria and hepatitis B. Rabies is a risk.

Mains water is normally safe to drink but readily available bottled water is advised for the first few weeks of a visit.

A supply of any regular medicines required should be carried, with their prescription details; medical insurance, which includes emergency evacuation, is recommended.

Hotels

There are plenty of hotels in business and tourist centres. Service charge of 15 per cent usually added to bill. Settlement of bills in foreign currency will avoid payment of local taxes. Many hotels quote prices in US dollars.

Credit cards

All major credit and charge cards are widely accepted. ATMs are widely available.

Public holidays (national)

Fixed dates

Variable dates

Purim (Mar), First day of Passover (Apr), Last day of Passover (Apr), Independence Day (May), Shavuot (Pentecost) (Jun), Tisha B'Av (Aug), Rosh Hashanah (Jewish New Year) (Sep/Oct), Yom Kippur (Day of Atonement) (Oct), First day of Succoth (Feast of Tabernacles) (Oct), Last day of Sukkot (Oct), Shemini Atzeret (Celebration of Renewal and Thanksgiving) (Oct).

The Jewish calendar is based on the lunar and solar cycle. Each month begins with a new moon and runs for either 29 or 30 days; this results in years that are either 12 or 13 months long. The Jewish new year begins in March or April.

The Jewish religious day is Saturday – the *Sabbath* – which begins at nightfall on Friday until nightfall on Saturday. Most public services and shops close early on Friday.

Muslim and Christian holidays are also observed by their respective populations. Thus, depending on the district, the day of rest falls on Friday, Saturday or Sunday.

Jewish year – 5767 (23 Sep 2006–12 Sep 2007): the Jewish calendar is lunar and loses approximately 12 days per year against the Gregorian calendar, therefore every three years a leap or intercalary month is inserted to re-align the calenders.

Working hours

Banking

Sun–Fri: 0830–1200; Sun/Tue/Thu: 1600–1800.

Business

Sun—Thu: 0800–1730. On Fridays, some businesses stay open until 1230, but most close all day.

Government

Sun–Thu: 0730–1430 (Jun—Oct); 0730–1300, 1345–1600 (Nov–May). All government offices close on Friday afternoon and all day on Saturday.

Shops

Sun—Fri: 0800—1900; some shops close 1300—1600. Jewish shops observe closing time near sunset Friday evenings; Arabic stores are closed on Friday; Christian shops are closed on Sunday. Shops in hotels are often open until midnight.

Telecommunications

Mobile/cell phones

There are GSM 900/1800 roaming facilities available, with coverage throughout Israel and the West Bank.

Electricity supply

220V AC, 50 cycles. Most sockets are round and three-pronged so a European adaptor is necessary.

Weights and measures

Metric system, but area is usually measured in dunam (1,000 sq metres).

Social customs/useful tips

People are hospitable and informal and culturally diverse. Jewish traditions and customs are generally adhered to.

Israel is largely secular in character and Mediterranean in style. The Jewish *Sabbath*, from Friday dusk until Saturday dusk is, however, widely observed. Shops close on Friday and do not open again until Sunday morning. Most cinemas and restaurants are closed on Friday night. In most cities over the *Sabbath* there is no public transport (except for taxis), postal service, or banking service. Some religious sections in Jerusalem and the Tel Aviv suburb of Bnei Brak, as well as Tel Aviv's main street, Rehov Dizengoff, are closed to traffic. The same is true on six Jewish religious holidays.

Punctuality is not a strong point and business visitors should not be surprised to be kept waiting. Business meetings are less formal in character than in northern Europe but the normal courtesies are observed.

It is considered by many a violation of the *Sabbath* to smoke in public places such as restaurants and hotels.

Security

Security is tight owing to the threat of terrorist activity, and delays in the ongoing peace process have increased tensions. Business travellers often encounter delays because of security alerts. Prolonged questioning and detailed searches may take place at the time of entry and/or departure. Do not leave bags unattended. In Jerusalem, tourists should exercise caution at religious sites on holy days. Visitors are advised to avoid demonstrations and areas where large crowds are gathering. The theft of passports, credit cards and valuables from public beaches is commonplace. Visitors should carry passports at all times as a form of identity. Money and valuables should be kept out of sight.

Getting there

Air

National airline: El Al

El Al has an intensive security check and passengers are advised to arrive for flights in plenty of time.

International airport/s: Ben Gurion International (TLV), 20km south-east of Tel Aviv (50k west of Jerusalem); duty-free shop, ATMs, currency exchange, bar, restaurant, hotel reservations, post office, shops, car hire. A rail service to Tel Aviv operates between 0300–0000, journey time 15 minutes. Taxis and buses are available to Jerusalem and Tel Aviv.

Other airport/s: Eilat Central Airport (ETH)

Airport tax: None

Surface

Road: Tourists from Jordan can cross into Israel after obtaining a 'bridge pass' from the Jordanian Interior Ministry in Amman. It is also possible to cross the border at Eilat on the Red Sea coast. The road and bus route, via Cairo and Rafa (Gaza Strip), has been closed.

There is an exit tax of US$16 at all land border crossings.

Water: There are ferry services from Piraeus (Greece) and Larnaca (Cyprus) to Haifa.

Main port/s: Haifa, Ashdod and Eilat.

Getting about

National transport

Air: Arkia operate daily services from Tel Aviv to Jerusalem, Haifa, Eilat, and other major cities.

Road: Main roads are good. Maximum speed 90km per hour.

Buses: Buses connect all centres of population; they are frequent and cheap but can be crowded. Buses do not operate from sunset on Friday to sunset on Saturday.

Rail: Services between Tel Aviv and Haifa (hourly). Seats can be reserved. No service Friday evenings or Saturday.

City transport

Taxis: Taxis are metered but flat rates often apply so it is advisable to check before any long trips.

From Ben Gurion airport to Tel Aviv centre takes about 30 minutes.

Many offices close on Fridays and consequently traffic flows are better.

For inter-city travel (including Saturdays), *sherut* (share taxis) run between central points in main cities and are not expensive. Some *sherut* companies, including Arieh and Aviv, will accept advance bookings.

Car hire

International companies have offices in main cities and at Ben Gurion airport. Drivers must be over 21 years and have an international credit card and national or international licence. Seat belts are compulsory for drivers and front-seat passengers. Most road signs on major roads are in English.

BUSINESS DIRECTORY

The addresses listed below are a selection only. While World of Information makes every endeavour to check these addresses, we cannot guarantee that changes have not been made, especially to telephone numbers and area codes. We would welcome any corrections.

Telephone area codes

The international direct dialling (IDD) code for Israel is +972, followed by area code and subscriber's number:

Afula	4	Kfar Saba	9
Ashdod	8	Natanya	9
Ashkelon	8	Nazareth	4
Beersheva	8	Raanana	9
Briei Brak	3	Ramat Gan	3
Eilat	8	Rehovot	8
Haifa	4	Safed	4
Holon	3	Tel Aviv	3
Jerusalem	2		

Useful telephone numbers

International operator: 188
Directory enquiries: 144
Collect calls: 142
Overseas operator: 188
Ambulance: 101
Fire: 102
Police: 100
Correct time: 155

Chambers of Commerce

America-Israel Chamber of Commerce and Industry, 35 Shaul Hamelech Boulevard, PO Box 33174, Tel Aviv 61333 (tel: 695-2341; fax: 695-1272; email: amcham@amcham.co.il).

British-Israel Chamber of Commerce, 29 Hamered Street, PO Box 50321, Tel Aviv 61502 (tel: 510-9424; fax: 510-9540; email: isrbrit@bezeqint.net).

Federation of Israeli Chambers of Commerce, 84 Ha'ashmonaim Street, PO Box 20027, Tel Aviv 61200 (tel: 563-1020; fax: 561-9027; chamber@chamber.org.il).

Haifa and the North Chamber of Commerce and Industry, 53 Ha'atzmaut Road, PO Box 33176, Haifa 31331 (tel: 862-6364; fax: 864-5424; email: main@haifachamber.org.il).

Banking

Bank Hapoalim BM, 50 Rothschild Blvd, Tel Aviv 66883 (tel: 567-5777; fax: 567-6015; internet site: www.bankhapoalim.co.il).

Bank Leumi Le-Israel BM, 24-32 Yehuda Halevi St, Tel Aviv 65546 (tel: 514-8111; fax: 566-1872).

The First International Bank of Israel Ltd, Shalom Tower, 9 Ahad Haam St, Tel Aviv 65251 (tel: 519-6111; fax: 510-0316).

Investec Bank (Israel) Ltd; PO Box 677, 38 Rothschild Boulevard, Tel Aviv 61006 (tel: 564-5645; fax: 564-5210).

Israel Discount Bank Ltd, 27-31 Yehuda Halevi Street, Tel Aviv 65136 (tel: 514-5555; fax: 514-5346; internet site: www.discountbank.net).

Union Bank of Israel Ltd, 6-8 Ahuzat Bayit Street, Tel Aviv 65143 (tel: 519-1111; fax: 519-1421).

Central bank

Bank of Israel, PO Box 780, Kiryat Ben-Gurion, Jerusalem 91007 (tel: 655-2211; fax: 652-8805; e-mail: webmaster@bankisrael.gov.il).

Stock exchange

Tel Aviv Stock Exchange (TASE): www.tase.co.il

Travel information

Arkia Israeli Airlines Ltd, (Charter Airline), Sde Dov, PO Box 39301, Tel Aviv, 61392 (tel: 690-2222; fax: 699-1512).

Automobile and Touring Club of Israel (MEMSI), 20 Harakevet Street, PO Box 65144, Tel Aviv 65117 (tel: 564-1122; fax: 566-0493).

Bus Station, Levinsky and Levanda intersection, Nava Sha'anan, Tel Aviv.

Dan Co-operative Society for Public Transport Ltd. (City buses), 39 Shaul Hamelech Blvd., Tel Aviv, 64928 (tel: 693-3333; fax: 693-3511).

Egged Israel Transport Co-operative Ltd (Intercity buses), 142 Petach Tikvah Road, Tel Aviv, 64921 (tel: 692-2211; fax: 696-5354).

El Al Israel Airlines Ltd, Ben Gurion Airport, Lod, 71285 (tel: 971-6111; fax: 972-1442; internet site: www.elal.co.il).

Israel Airports Authority, Ben Gurion Airport, PO Box 137 70100 (tel: 975-5555; fax: 973-1650; www.iaa.gov.il).

Israel Ports and Railway Authority, 74 Derech Petach Tikva, POB 20121, Tel Aviv, 61201 (tel: 565-7000; fax: 512-1048).

Israel Railways, PO Box 18085, Tel Aviv, 61180 (tel: 542-1515; fax: 695-8176).

Ministry of tourism

Ministry of Tourism, 24 King George Street, PO Box 1018, Jerusalem 94262 (tel: 675-4811; fax: 625-3407; e-mail: doar@tourism.gov.il; internet site: www.travelnet.co.il).

Ministries

Prime Minister's Office, 3 Kaplan Street, PO Box 187, Kiryat Ben-Gurion, Jerusalem 91919 (tel: 670-5555; fax: 651-2631; email: markal@pmo.gov.il).

Ministry of Agriculture, Agricultural Centre, PO Box 50200, Bet-Dagan (tel: 948-5555; email: pniot@moag.gov.il).

Ministry of Communications, 23 Jaffa Street, Jerusalem 91999 (tel: 670-6320; fax: 670-6372; email: intmocil@moc.gov.il).

Ministry of Construction and Housing, Kiryat Hamemshala, PO Box 18110, Jerusalem 91180 (tel: 584-7211; fax: 581-1904).

Ministry of Defence, Kaplan Street, Hakirya, Tel-Aviv 61909 (tel: 569-2010; fax: 691-6940).

Ministry of Education, 34 Shivtei Israel Street, PO Box 292, Jerusalem 91911 (tel: 560-2222; fax: 560-2223; email: info@education.gov.il).

Ministry of the Environment, 5 Kanfei Nesharim Street, Givat Shaul, PO Box 34033, Jerusalem 95464 (tel: 655-3777; fax: 653-5934).

Ministry of Finance, 1 Kaplan Street, Kyriat Ben-Gurion, PO Box 13195, Jerusalem 91008 (tel: 531-7111; fax: 563-7891; email: webmaster@mof.gov.il).

Ministry of Foreign Affairs, Hakirya, Romema, Jerusalem 91950 (tel: 530-3111; fax: 530-33367; email: markal@mofa.gov.il; internet site: (Information) www.israel.org).

Ministry of Health, 2 Ben-Tabai Street, PO Box 1176, Jerusalem 91010 (tel: 670-5705; fax: 623-3026).

Ministry of Industry and Trade, 30 Agron Street, PO Box 299, Jerusalem 91002 (tel: 622-0220; fax: 624-5110).

Ministry of the Interior, 2 Kaplan Street, PO Box 6158, Kiryat Ben-Gurion, Jerusalem 91061 (tel: 670-1411; fax: 670-1628).

Ministry of Justice, 29 Salah A-din Street, Jerusalem 91010 (tel: 670-8511; fax: 628-8618; email: feedback@justice.gov.il).

Ministry of Labour and Social Welfare, 2 Kaplan Street, PO Box 915, Kiryat Ben-Gurion, Jerusalem 91008 (tel: 675-2311; fax: 675-2803).

Ministry of National Infrastructure, 216 Jaffa Street, Jerusalem 91130 (tel: 500-6777; fax: 500-6888).

Ministry of Public Security, Kiryat Hamemshala, PO Box 18182, Jerusalem 91181 (tel: 530-9999; fax: 584-7872).

Ministry of Religious Affairs, 236 Jaffa Street, PO Box 13059, Jerusalem 91130 (tel: 531-1171; fax: 531-1183; email: tsibor@religinfoserv.gov.il).

Ministry of Science, Culture and Sport, Kiryat Hamemshala Hamizrahit, POB 49100, Jerusalem 91181 (tel: 541-1111).

Ministry of Transport, 97 Jaffa Street, Jerusalem 91000 (tel: 622-8211; fax: 622-8693).

Office of the President, 3 Hanassi Street, Jerusalem 92188 (tel: 670-7211; fax: 561-0037).

The Knesset, Kiryat Ben-Gurion, Jerusalem 91950 (tel: 675-3333; fax: 652-1599).

Other useful addresses

Administration of Rabbinical Courts, 9 Koresh Street, Jerusalem 91012 (tel: 624-8603; fax: 624-5019).

British Embassy, 192 Hayarkon Street, Tel Aviv 63405 (tel: 524-9171; fax: 524-3313).

Central Bureau of Statistics, 3 Kaplan Street, PO Box 187, Kiryat Ben-Gurion, Jerusalem 91919 (tel: 655-3553; fax: 655-3325).

Israeli Academy of Sciences and Humanities, Albert Einstein Square, Talbieh, PO Box 4040, Jerusalem 91040 (tel: 563-6211).

Israel Airports Authority, Ben Gurion Airport (tel: 971-2804; fax: 971-2436). For information on taxes and tariffs (tel: 971-5596).

Israeli Broadcasting Authority, Klal Building, 97 Jaffa Street, PO Box 6387, Jerusalem 91063 (tel: 529-1888).

Israel Chemicals Ltd, 123 Hahashmonaim Street, Tel Aviv, 67133 (tel: 563-0232; fax: 561-5391).

Israel Electric Corporation Ltd, 2 Hahagana Boulevard, Haifa, 35254 (tel: 854-8548; fax: 853-8149).

Israel Fuel Corporation Ltd (Delek), Prof. Y. Kaufman Street, PO Box 50250, Tel Aviv, 61500 (tel: 591-5555; fax: 510-2072).

Israel Land Administration (part of the National Infrastructure Ministry), 6 Shamai Street, POB 2600, Jerusalem 94631 (tel: 520-8422; fax: 523-4960).

Israel Shipyards Ltd, Po Box 10630, Haifa Bay, 26118 (tel: 846-0245; fax: 841-0572).

Israel Telecommunication Corporation, PO Box 1088, Jerusalem, 91010 (tel: 539-5333; fax: 625-2506).

Israel Trade Fairs Centre/Israel Convention Centre, PO Box 21075, 61210 Tel Aviv (tel: 422-422).

Israeli Embassy (US), 3514 International Drive, NW, Washington DC 20008 (tel: (+1-202) 364-5500; fax: (+1-202) 364-5560; email: ask@israelemb.org).

Manufacturers' Association of Israel, Industry House, PO Box 50022, 29 Hamered Street, Tel Aviv (tel: 650-121).

National Coal Supply Corporation Ltd, 155 Bialik Street, Ramat Gan, 52523 (tel: 751-2261; fax: 751-0119).

National Insurance Institute, 13 Weizmann Blvd, Jerusalem 91909 (tel: 670-9211; fax: 670-9792).

National Water Company (Mekorot), 9 Lincoln Street, Tel Aviv, 67134 (tel: 623-0555; fax: 623-0833).

Pama Development for Energy and Sources, PO Box 20118, 14 Kalman Magen Street, Tel Aviv, 61200 (tel: 695-8129; fax: 695-8131).

Postal Authority, 237 Jaffa Street, Jerusalem 91999 (tel: 629-0800; fax: 629-0921).

State Comptroller, POB 1081, Jerusalem 91010 (tel: 531-5111).

Tahal Consulting Engineers Ltd (Water), PO Box 11170, 54 Ibn Gvirol Street, Tel Aviv, 61111 (tel: 692-4434; fax: 696-9969).

The Tel Aviv Stock Exchange (TASE), 54 Ahad Ha'am Street, Tel Aviv 65202; PO Box 29060, Tel Aviv 61290 (tel: 567-7411; fax: 510-5379; internet site: www.tase.co.il).

Zim Israel Navigation Co. Ltd, 7-9 Pal Yam Avenue, Haifa, 31000 (tel: 865-2111; fax: 865-2956).

Israel National News: www.israelnationalnews.com

Israel News Agency (INA): www.israelnewsagency.com

Israeli News Now: www.israelinewsnow.com

PR Newswire: www.prnewswire.co.il

Italy

KEY FACTS

Official name: Repubblica Italiana (Italian Republic)

Head of State: President Giorgio Napolitano (elected 10 May 2006)

Head of government: Prime Minister Mario Monti (from 13 Nov 2011)

Ruling party: Coalition led by Popolo della Libertà (PdL) (People of Freedom) with Partito Democratico (PD) (Democratic Party) and Lega Nord (LN) (Northern League) (from 14 Apr 2008)

Area: 301,277 square km

Population: 60.48 million (2010)

Capital: Rome

Official language: Italian

Currency: Euro (€) = 100 cents (from 1 Jan 2002; previous currency lira, locked at L1,936.27 per euro) (Campione d'Italia, an Italian enclave near Lake Lugano in Switzerland, uses the Swiss franc, although the euro also circulates)

Exchange rate: €0.76 per US$ (Oct 2011)

GDP per capita: US$34,059 (2010)

GDP real growth: 1.30% (2010)

GDP: US$2,055.10 billion (2010)

Labour force: 24.98 million (2010)

Unemployment: 8.40% (2010)

Inflation: 1.60% (2010)

Oil production: 106,000 bpd (2010)

Balance of trade: -US$27.28 billion (2010)

November 2011 was the end of an era in Italian politics. Silvio Berlusconi had endeavoured to rule the Italian political roost since 1994, but by 2011 he was viewed by a majority of the Italian electorate as simply no longer up to the job. Italy faced overwhelming economic problems and risked being declared in default of its financial obligations.

Mr Berlusconi had, throughout his political career, been a populist showman. His political career may have been a long one, but it had always been tainted with corruption. Questions had often been asked, but never properly answered, as to how he had amassed his considerable fortune. It had always seemed that his political power existed to strengthen his economic interests and conversely, that his economic strength served to advance political power. He certainly broke the Italian political mould, introducing right wing government to a country that for over 30 years had grown accustomed to weak, for the most part, Christian Democrat, governments that rarely saw out their elected terms. Mr Berlusconi's populist Forza Italia (FI) (Go Italy!) – the name was inspired by a football supporters' chant – enjoyed considerable electoral support for a period. But even when it seemed to have lost its touch and was voted out of power, Mr Berlusconi refused to accept defeat, preferring to go on the offensive. In his personal dealings, the same applied. Right up to the moment of his resignation, he was continually defending himself against accusations that often reeked of petty corruption and tawdriness. He himself claimed to have faced over 10 accusations of wrongdoing of one sort or another. These charges did little to create the image of probity and integrity he desperately sought to acquire. Taking a leaf out of former French President Jacques Chirac's book, Berlusconi succeeded in introducing legislation rendering Italy's prime minister and other senior officials immune from prosecution during their time in office.

Monti's the Man

As had been expected, President Giorgio Napolitano appointed technocrat Mario Monti as Berlusconi's successor as prime minister. The acute debt crisis that threatened the euro-zone had been a mountain too high for even Mr Berlusconi. He lost his parliamentary majority and finally accepted the inevitable, promising to go once parliament had approved new austerity measures. The political – as well as the economic – climate had changed radically. Crowds celebrated outside the presidential palace, shouting 'buffoon' as he entered the building to tender his resignation. Mr Berlusconi's last journey as prime minister was an undignified one. The police struggled to control a large, hostile crowd which booed and jeered as his convoy swept by and after his resignation he ignominiously left by a side exit to avoid the protesters.

Promises, promises

As the European financial crisis gathered speed in mid-2011, Berlusconi, the ageing Lothario simply had not looked like the leader Italy needed to sort out its fiscal woes. And woes there were – Italy's borrowings of US$2.6 trillion were larger than any other euro-zone country. Although a large proportion of Italy's debt was in Italian hands, some estimates put the amount held by foreign entities at a frightening €700 billion (US$938 billion). Its borrowing costs were over 6.00 per cent – levels dangerously near those which forced bail-outs upon Greece, Ireland and Portugal. Mr Berlusconi's behaviour through the crisis had not been that of a threatened man, rather that of a man unaware of the storms that surrounded him. Storms that, in mid-2011, finally sank Mr Berlusconi, his fragile government and Italy's struggling economy.

Mr Berlusconi's promises to accelerate fiscal tightness and 'overhaul' the economy had looked empty, all the more so as they came from a man whose word few Italians could still trust. Not that the promises in themselves represented a new departure – all that had changed was the speed of their implementation. In early August 2011 Mr Berlusconi had agreed to bring forward €48 billion (US$62.9 billion) of austerity measures originally planned to take effect in 2013 and 2014. He also, optimistically, promised to balance the budget earlier. The budget balancing act was not actually within Mr Berlusconi's gift, but as parliament had approved an earlier plan as recently as July 2011, it was unlikely to prove an obstacle.

Like many European economies, however, plans to reduce the deficit were more than likely to impair economic growth, calling into question forecast tax revenues and unemployment benefits. The government's forecast growth figures for 2012 and 2013 were 1.3 per cent and 1.5 per cent respectively. Independent forecasts hovered around figures of 0.8 per cent for 2012 and 0.6 per cent for 2013.

The joker in Italy's pack is what is politely referred to as the 'grey' economy. This and the quickening pace of a realisation that – if the yields on Italian bonds are anything to go by – Italy has very little room for manoeuvre. If the scope for the Italian economy was constrained, that available to Mr Berlusconi was even more so. Even such a seasoned politician as Mr Berlusconi must have felt imperilled as neighbouring heads of government – Spain's Zapatero and Portugal's José Socrates – fell on their swords and called general elections. In an address to parliament Mr Berlusconi had vowed to remain in office until 2013 – to the obvious dismay of his finance minister, Giulio Tremonti, himself dangerously close to a financial scandal involving the use of an apartment in a fashionable quarter of Rome which he had paid for in cash. Mr Tremonti had admitted to the arrangement, but as the apartment's owner – Marco Milanese, a former political adviser and member of parliament – had himself been arraigned for accepting bribes, the murky affair did not bode well for Mr Tremonti.. In a *mea culpa* letter published in Rome's *Corriere Della Serra*, the finance minister acknowledged that: 'I made a mistake. There was nothing under the table, nothing irregular.' Mr Tremonti claimed that he had chosen not to have a formal rental contract 'not for economic convenience, but for privacy'.

As the austerity measures were being discussed in parliament, it emerged in newspaper reports that the Italian parliament's resident barber earned as much as the US vice president and that the subsidies given to the parliament canteen enabled members to enjoy cordon bleu cuisine lunches for as little as eight euros

KEY INDICATORS **Italy**

	Unit	2006	2007	2008	2009	2010
Population	m	58.44	58.67	59.34	59.78	*60.48
Gross domestic product (GDP)	US$bn	1,858.34	2,104.67	2,313.90	2,118.30	2,055.10
GDP per capita	US$	31,802	35,872	38,996	35,435	34,059
GDP real growth	%	1.8	1.5	-1.3	-5.2	1.3
Inflation	%	2.2	2.0	3.5	0.8	1.6
Unemployment	%	6.7	6.0	7.8	7.8	8.4
Oil output	'000 bpd	111.0	122.0	108.0	95.0	106.0
Natural gas output	bn cum	11.0	8.9	8.4	7.4	7.6
Exports (fob) (goods)	US$m	418,074.0	502,384.0	546,857.0	407,160.0	448,374.0
Imports (fob) (goods)	US$m	430,585.0	498,142.0	546,908.0	403,900.0	475,652.0
Balance of trade	US$m	-12,510.0	4,242.0	-51.0	3,259.0	-27,278.0
Current account	US$m	-47,566.0	-51,574.0	-66,252.0	-41,004.0	-71,986.0
Total reserves minus gold	US$m	25,662.0	28,385.0	37,088.0	45,770.0	47,684.0
Foreign exchange	US$m	24,413.0	27,319.0	35,306.0	34,521.0	35,678.0
Exchange rate	per US$	0.75	0.69	0.68	0.78	0.76

* estimated figure

and a dish of lunchtime pasta for only one euro. The scope for cuts and savings in the Italian legislature alone is enormous. Italy has a total of 945 legislators – 630 in the Lower House, 315 in the Senate. This is more than is the case in the US, for a population of four times the size. Members of Parliament earn €11,700 (US$15,700) a month pre-tax, with an additional €7,200 (US$9,600) in allowances to cover expenses and the cost of aides and secretaries, who may be their wives, lovers or just friends. A book on the subject: *The Caste* by Sergio Rizzo alleges that while US citizens pay an annual €5.00 (US$6.70) per annum on the cost of politicians, in Italy the figure is over €25.00 (US$33.50).

By July 2011 the political whirlwind surrounding an apparently complacent Mr Berlusconi meant that instead of offering any solution to the problem, he had become a central part of it. But a lethargic Italian public – in an 'it'll be alright on the night' mode – often seemed as complacent as their prime minister. Messrs Berlusconi and Tremonti seemed to agree on very little, making it even less likely that the government would survive until 2013. Perhaps holding back a more immediate move to shift Mr Berlusconi was the question the succession, which would become critical. In mid-2011 two options had existed – a wider coalition government lead by a politician commanding greater respect than Berlusconi, or new elections. But to hold elections in the midst of an economic crisis seemed at the time to risk being counter-productive, creating increased market nervousness.

The economy struggles

In mid-2011, according to the International Monetary Fund (IMF) Italy was experiencing a weak recovery, mainly driven by exports. Overall, the picture painted by the IMF was not a bright one. The economy grew by 1.3 per cent year-on-year in 2010, less than the euro-zone average of 1.7 per cent. The trend continued in the first quarter of 2011, with growth at 0.1 per cent quarter-on-quarter. Domestic demand was weak. Household spending remained cautious on the back of rising unemployment and declining real disposable income. Investment rebounded significantly in the first half of 2010 but weakened following the termination in June of the tax incentives for investment. Government consumption was flat. The current account deficit worsened despite robust export growth, owing to rising energy prices and high import growth. Inflation increased moderately to 1.6 per cent in 2010 from 0.8 per cent in 2009 due to rising energy and commodity prices. Inflation rates were comparable to those in the euro area, mainly because of non-core components, while the inflation differential on core prices remained relatively stable.

Perhaps surprisingly, the Italian authorities comfortably achieved the 2010 fiscal target. The overall fiscal balance declined from 5.3 per cent of GDP in 2009 to 4.5 per cent of GDP in 2010, well below the target of 5.0 per cent of GDP. The improvement reflected both good revenue performance and contained budget expenditure. The increase in indirect taxes partly offset the decline in capital revenues. The introduction in 2010 of more stringent value added tax (VAT) refund rules reduced reimbursements by about 0.4 per cent of GDP. Real primary current expenditure grew at the lowest rate since the mid-1990s. The structural balance improved by about one percentage point of GDP in 2010, among the largest improvements in the euro area. However, payment delays increased. Still, the positive budgetary trends continued in the first months of 2011 and the government enacted a fiscal adjustment package identifying the measures to reach a near-balanced budget target by 2014.

The IMF reported that Italian banks had been adversely affected by the recession, with their asset quality worsening over the last two years due to the economic slowdown. Earnings were hampered by low net interest income and high loan-loss provisions, but Italy's banks had remained profitable. While the deterioration in credit quality was likely to slow, loan-loss provision costs remained elevated, given the high level of accumulated non-performing loans. Profitability was undermined by rising funding costs. A large and stable retail funding base and ample collateral to access Eurosystem refinancing helped Italian banks to face liquidity and funding risks, which have intensified with the euro-zone sovereign crisis.

The IMF noted that while Italy was experiencing a modest recovery, mainly driven by exports, public debt was high and growth was expected to remain constrained because of long-standing structural bottlenecks. The main policy goals should be to continue pursuing fiscal consolidation to reduce the large public debt, maintain financial sector stability and boost growth potential through structural reforms.

The IMF welcomed the authorities' commitment to reduce the fiscal deficit to below 3 per cent of GDP by 2012 and close to zero by 2014. The medium-term fiscal package enacted by the government was seen as an important step towards making these goals achievable. The IMF stressed that decisive implementation of the package was key and that more frontloaded spending measures would have a positive effect on market sentiments. The IMF also noted that the adjustment appeared to rely also on measures at the sub-national level and that the tax reform envisioned in the package was still to be defined.

In the view of the IMF sustainable fiscal consolidation should rely first and foremost on expenditure rationalisation based on clear priorities. In this regard, the IMF was encouraged by the government's intention to undertake comprehensive public expenditure reviews, emphasising that such reviews should result in major public expenditure contraction and improve public sector's efficiency. Containing the public sector wage bill within a broader public administration reform would also generate positive spillovers for the private sector. While important pension reforms have already been implemented, there was scope for further measures to boost employment and generate savings. More generally, the IMF stressed that the large fiscal retrenchment requires structural changes in public expenditure.

Turning to the revenue side, the view was that the tax system should be simplified to support growth and enhance tax compliance. The government's ongoing review of preferential tax regimes was welcomed. Careful execution of fiscal federalism should not undermine fiscal discipline.

The Italian authorities' preemptive call for bank capital increases and the banks' prompt response was welcomed, as was the swift completion of the recapitalisation plan. Bank funding costs and equity prices remained sensitive to market sentiment about the Italian sovereign debt, underscoring the need for fiscal consolidation. Scope was also seen for improving governance and transparency in some local banks. At the same time the IMF

stressed the need for decisive progress on structural reforms. While the National Reform Programme identified several key priorities, a comprehensive package of reforms was necessary to further raise productivity and enhance growth potential. In the product market, measures should aim at establishing a more efficient regulatory environment, opening up further services and network industries and reducing public ownership. In the labour market, policies should address duality and the low participation rate. Reducing the labour tax burden, in a fiscally prudent way, could also boost employment. More decentralised bargaining would better align wages with productivity and boost competitiveness. The IMF welcomed the flexibility introduced by the recent labour market agreement.

Risk assessment

Economy	Fair
Politics	Fair
Regional stability	Good

COUNTRY PROFILE

Historical profile

1796–1806 The French, under Emperor Napoléon Bonaparte, occupied Italy. The country was carved up and ruled by Napoléon, his relatives and Pope Pius VII.
1814–15 Following Napoléon's defeat by the Austrians, British, Prussians and Russians, Italy returned to its feudal status under the terms of the Congress of Vienna. Regions of northern Italy were also handed to Austria.
1848 A rise in nationalism and rebellion against Austrian rule began, known locally as the Risorgimento (Revival). A key figure in this process was Giuseppe Garibaldi.
1859–61 A partially unified Italy (Sardina, Piedmont, Genoa and Savoy) was created under the King of Sardina, Vittorio Emmanuelle II.
1870. Italian nationalists liberated Rome from French rule and proclaimed it the capital of a unified Italy under Vittorio Emmanuelle II.
1889–90 Italy established colonies in Africa (Somalia and Eritrea) through military conquests.
1901 Italy secured a territorial concession in the Chinese city of Tientsin
1911–12 Italy gained Tripolitania and Cyrenaica (later Libya) and the Dodekanesa (Dodecanese) Islands from the Ottoman Empire.
1916–18 Italy eventually fought alongside the Allies in the First World War. Ensuing disorder and economic weakness fostered the rise of Benito Mussolini and the Partito Nazionale Fascista (PNF) (National Fascist Party).
1919 Italy gained Trentino-Südtirol (South Tyrol), the Istrian peninsula and Trieste, which had been parts of the Austro-Hungarian Empire, under the terms of the Treaty of Versailles. Italian nationalists later seized control of the former Austro-Hungarian city of Fiume (now Rijeka), in the face of Yugoslav claims.
1922 After Italian fascists marched on Rome, Mussolini and the PNF were invited to form a government by King Vittorio Emmanuele III.
1924–26 Mussolini increased his prime ministerial powers, effectively making his rule a dictatorship.
1929 Three Lateran Treaties granted Roman Catholicism special status in Italy. The Vatican City state, under the rule of the Pope, was created within Rome.
1935–36 Italy invaded Abyssinia (now Ethiopia).
1936 Italy supported General Franco's nationalists in the Spanish Civil War, until they won in 1939.
1940–42 Italy was part of the Axis powers, assisting Nazi Germany's military campaigns in Europe and Africa. It also invaded British Somaliland in East Africa in 1940.
1943 Allied forces invaded southern Italy and its African colonies. Mussolini was removed from government, imprisoned, and Pietro Badoglio was appointed prime minister. After escaping from prison, Mussolini declared the creation of the Repubblica Sociale Italiana (Social Republic of Italy) in German-controlled northern Italy.
1945 The fascist regime collapsed as the allies liberated the whole of Italy. Mussolini was executed by Italian partisans.
1946 In May, Vittorio Emmanuele III abdicated from the Italian throne and was temporarily replaced by Umberto II. After a referendum the Italian monarchy was abolished and a republic was declared. Enrico De Nicola was appointed as temporary head of state.
1948 De Nicola was elected the Republic's first president. The constitution, which established a parliament, was promulgated.
1949–82 A succession of short-lived coalitions followed, involving the Democrazia Cristiana (DC) (Christian Democrats) and up to four other major parties, frequently producing several regroupings and new cabinets in a year.
1978 Former prime minister and then president of the DC, Aldo Moro, was assassinated by the Red Brigades.
1983–87 Bettino Craxi, of the Partito Socialista Italiano (PSI) (Italian Socialist Party), headed what was then the longest-running post-war Italian government.
1989 The DC returned to government and Giulio Andreotti became prime minister for the third time.
1992–93 Italy had two prime ministers in two years, Giuliano Amato and Carlo Azeglio Ciampi. Both were forced to resign after political and corruption scandals.
1994 Silvio Berlusconi, of the Forza Italia (FI) (Go Italy!) – a party he largely created and funded, was elected prime minister for nine months. A transitional government was formed led by Lamberto Dina (independent).
1996 The centre-left Ulivo (Olive Tree) coalition won the parliamentary elections and Romano Prodi, was appointed prime minister.
1997 A constitutional reform commission, drawn from both houses of parliament, altered the Italian political system by introducing direct elections for the office of president.
1998 The Democratici di Sinistra's (DS) (Democrats of the Left) Massimo d'Alema succeeded Romano Prodi.
1999 The government fell and d'Alema resigned. He was reinstated by the newly-elected president, Carlo Ciampi.
2000 D'Alema resigned and was replaced by Giuliano Amato, heading a new centre-left 12-party coalition government.
2001 The Casa delle Libertà (House of Freedom) coalition won elections and Silvio Berlusconi became prime minister for a second time. Voters approved a referendum on constitutional changes to give more power to the regions.
2002 The euro currency replaced the lira. A controversial bill, allowing Berlusconi to retain control of his media empire, was passed in parliament.
2003 The Parmalat dairy food-manufacturing giant – one of Italy's blue-chip companies – was declared insolvent when a US$11 billion-plus accountancy fraud was discovered.
2004 The Constitutional Court threw out the immunity from prosecution law granting Mr Berlusconi and other top state post holders immunity from prosecution and Berlusconi's trial on corruption charges resumed; he was found not guilty.
2005 Romano Prodi became leader of the renamed centre-Left bloc, L'Unione (The Union), formerly Ulivo. Reform of the electoral system was passed: in future all parliamentary seats will determined by proportional representation and only parties winning a minimum of 2 per cent of the vote will be allocated seats
2006 Romano Prodi and the coalition L'Unione won national elections. Giorgio Napolitano was elected president by the Electoral College; he was the first former Communist to be elected president of Italy.
2007 Prodi resigned as prime minister, following a defeat in the senate on his foreign policy of enhancing NATO's deployment in Afghanistan. Prodi won a vote of confidence and was reinstated
2008 FI merged with Alleanza Nazionale (AN) (National Alliance) to form Il Popolo della Libertà (PdL) (The People of Freedom) and formed a three-party coalition

with Partito Democratico (PD) (Democratic Party) and Lega Nord (LN) (Northern League) and won the national elections with a combined 46.81 per cent of the votes (340 seats out of 630). Silvio Berlusconi became prime minister for a second time. Italy apologised for damage inflicted during its occupation of Libya and agreed to invest US$5 billion as compensation. The state-owned Alitalia airline filed for bankruptcy.

2009 Prime Minister Berlusconi was stripped of his immunity from prosecution by the Constitutional Court, which rejected legislation that gave immunity to top government officials while they are in office, on the grounds that all Italians must be equal before the law and that the legislation had not been subject to greater scrutiny before being enacted.

2010 In July Futuro e Libertà (FLI) (Future and Freedom), a new political party, was formed by followers of its founder Gianfranco Fini, who broke away from Berlusconi's PdL-led coalition government.

2011 From January, thousands of migrants and refugees from Africa made the Mediterranean Sea crossing to reach the EU and landed on the Italian island of Lampedusa, overwhelming local resources and immigration procedures. Italy called on the EU for increased funds to deal with the influx. On 19 March, Italy joined in a five-country coalition (with Canada, France, the UK and the US) to impose a no-fly zone over Libya. On 4 April Italy became the third country (after France and Qatar) to recognise the Transitional National Council (TNC) as the legitimate government of Libya. In April, Italy granted 20,000 Tunisians temporary residence permits allowing free access to other EU countries and prompting France to call for the suspension of the Schengen agreement. On 14 April Silvio Berlusconi confirmed that he would not run for office again when his current term as prime minister expires in 2013. Investors in the Italian economy were losing confidence in its viability as, on 15 July, the government's austerity budget, designed to cut the deficit by □47 billion (US$65.98 billion) by 2014, was adopted by parliament. However on 28 July, unforgiving bond markets forced the Italian treasury to pay more for sovereign bonds than previous rates. On 20 September, Standard & Poor's downgraded Italy's sovereign debt rating from A+ to A, and added an economic outlook for the country of 'negative', saying it feared for the government's ability to cut state spending and reduce the deficit. The government responded by saying the downgrade was 'politically motivated'. Moody's cut Italy's credit rating from Aa2 to A2, with a negative outlook. Italy's sovereign debt crisis came to a head on 10 November following weeks when the government failed to implement agreed austerity measures (on 15 July and 14 September) aimed at saving eur124 billion (US$174.7 billion) in government spending. Italian government bonds were sold at an interest rate of 6.087 per cent (for one year) meaning the government will have to pay an extra eur28 billion (US$38.5 billion) to service the new debt. Prime Minister Berlusconi narrowly won a vote of confidence on 5 November but his support and position were critically undermined and he announced he would step-down once the key austerity package, as demanded by leaders of the EU, had been passed. Silvio Berlusconi resigned on 13 November and on 14 November the president appointed Mario Monti, a technocrat, as prime minister.

Political structure

Constitution

Under the terms of the 1948 constitution, Italy's legislative power is held by a bicameral parliament.

Italy is divided into 20 regions which enjoy a large degree of autonomy. Each region has a regional council elected every five years by universal suffrage.

In 2001, the constitution was amended by the federalist reform bill which increased the decision-making power of the regions. In 2005 proportional representation was introduced to elect both houses of parliament.

Form of state

Parliamentary democratic republic

The executive

Executive power is held by the prime minister, who is usually the leader of the largest party in the lower house of the parliament, and by a cabinet of ministers chosen by him.

The president, who must be more than 50 years old, holds a seven-year term of office and is elected by an electoral college consisting of both chambers of parliament and regional representatives. From the presidential term due to start in 2006, presidents will be directly elected. The president nominates a number of Supreme Court judges and has the power to dissolve parliament but has no other executive powers.

National legislature

Parliament consists of the *Camera dei Deputati* (Chamber of Deputies) and the Senato della Repubblica (Senate of the Republic). The chamber of deputies comprises 630 members, of which 475 are directly elected and the remainder are elected be proportional representation. The senate has 315 members, of which 83 are elected be proportional representation and the remainder by direct popular vote. In addition there are several senators-for-life who are former presidents of the Republic. Members of both houses are elected for five-year terms.

Legal system

The legal system is based on the constitution of 1948.

The Constitutional Court, set up in 1955, is the final arbiter of the constitutionality of laws and decrees. It defines the powers of the state and regions and passes judgements in disputes between them. It can also try the president and government ministers. The court consists of 15 judges. Five are appointed by the president, five by parliament and the remainder by the highest law and administrative courts.

The highest court of cassation is divided into 23 appeal court districts, with three other sections. These are then further divided into 159 tribunal districts which, together, are divided into 899 magistracies. There are 90 first degree assize courts and 26 assize courts of appeal.

Last elections

13-14 April 2008 (parliamentary); 10 May 2006 (presidential).

Results: Presidential: Giorgio Napolitano, elected president by the Electoral College, with 543 votes (out of 1009).

Parliamentary (Chamber of Deputies): the three-party coalition supporting Silvio Berlusconi won 46.81 per cent of the votes (340 seats out of 630), the two-party coalition supporting Walter Veltroni won 37.54 per cent (239), the Unione di Centro (UdC) (Union of the Centre) won 5.62 per cent (36), the Südtiroler Volkspartei (SVP) (South Tyrolean People's Party) 0.4 per cent (two). No other party won enough votes to achieve any seats.

Senate: Silvio Berlusconi's coalition won 47.32 per cent of the votes (171 seats out of 309), Walter Veltroni's coalition won 38.01 per cent (130), the UdC won 5.69 per cent (three), others including SVP won 2.78 per cent (five). Turnout was around 80 per cent.

Next elections

April 2013 (parliamentary); 2011 (presidential).

Political parties

Ruling party

Coalition led by Popolo della Libertà (PdL) (People of Freedom) with Partito Democratico (PD) (Democratic Party) and Lega Nord (LN) (Northern League) (from 14 Apr 2008)

Main opposition party

Opposition in the chamber of deputies and the senate – coalition led by Partito Democratico (PD) (Democratic Party) with Italia dei Valori (IdV) (Italy of Values)

Population

60.48 million (2010)

Last census: October 2001: 57,110,144
Population density: 196 inhabitants per square km (2000). Urban population: 67 per cent.
Annual growth rate: 0.1 per cent 1994–2004 (WHO 2006)
Ethnic make-up
Centuries of colonisation have meant that Italy has many ethnic heritages and groups, including Arberesh (Albanian) (around 100,000, mainly in southern Italy), French (around 100,000, mainly in Valle d'Aosta), German (around 290,000, mainly in Trentino-Alto Adige), Friulian (around 600,000, mainly in Friuli-Venezia Giulia), and Greek (around 4,000, mainly in Calabria). The country has been a destination for immigrants from all over the world. There are an estimated one million foreigners residing in Italy.
Religions
97.5 per cent Roman Catholic.

Education
Schooling is free of charge and compulsory from age six. Primary schooling lasts until age 11 years, and lower secondary schools from age 11 to 14 years. Only the first year of upper secondary schooling is compulsory.
Higher secondary schools, from age 14, provide five-year courses in the arts, sciences and teacher training. Specialised secondary schools run four-year courses, and vocational and professional training programmes lasting for three and five years, respectively.
Graduation from higher secondary school automatically gives a student a place at university. Besides universities, a wide range of professional training establishments also provide higher education. Most of the existing universities were directly established by the state, although some private institutions are recognised. There are 51 state universities and three technical universities.
Public expenditure on education typically amounts to 4.9 per cent of annual gross national income.
Literacy rate: 98.5 per cent total; 98.2 per cent female, adult rates (World Bank).
Compulsory years: Six to 15
Enrolment rate: 101 gross primary enrolment of relevant age group (including repeaters); 95 per cent gross secondary enrolment (World Bank).
Pupils per teacher: 11 in primary schools

Health
The healthcare system is regionally based, providing universal coverage free of charge at the point of service. There are deep regional inequalities in healthcare expenditure and in supply and utilisation of healthcare services.
Healthcare is financed through general taxation collected centrally, various other regional taxes and users' payments, which replaced the previous system of social health insurance contributions. The National Solidarity Fund was developed to transfer funds to the regions unable to raise sufficient resources. The Fund was authorised to spend 10 per cent of the overall regional funding.
HIV/Aids
HIV prevalence: 0.5 per cent aged 15–49 in 2003 (World Bank)
Life expectancy: 81 years, 2004 (WHO 2006)
Fertility rate/Maternal mortality rate: 1.3 births per woman, 2004 (WHO 2006); maternal mortality 11 per 100,000 live births (World Bank).
Birth rate/Death rate: 10 deaths to nine births per 1,000 people (World Bank)
Child (under 5 years) mortality rate (per 1,000): 4.3 per 1,000 live births (World Bank)
Head of population per physician: 4.2 physicians per 1,000 people, 2004 (WHO 2006)

Welfare
Italy has a fully comprehensive social security system with benefits covering unemployment, retirement pensions, disability, family allowances and health services.
The social security system is financed by contributions made by the state, employers and employees, and forms part of the government's overall budget.
The pension system is contribution-based calculated on the basis of the social security contributions paid over the course of working life. The system assures equal benefits for both public and private sector employees. There is increasing government expenditure on old-age pensions and survivorship annuities due to its ageing population.
There have been promising developments in the regulation of family allowances and income maintenance programmes. The Family Allowance fund, replaced by the Family Unit Allowance, differentiates the allowance in relation to the number of members of the family and the make-up of the family unit's income.
Pensions
The long-awaited pension reform bill was passed in July 2004. Italy was spending 14 per cent of GDP on pensions and the bill is expected to save 0.7 per cent of GDP annually from 2013–30.
The requirements for employees will be that they must pay 40 years of contributions into the fund before receiving benefits at aged 57, or retire later at aged 60 with a minimum 35 years contributions. This reform will be implemented by 2008.

Main cities
Rome (capital, estimated population 2.5 million in 2004), Milan (1.2 million), Naples (991,700), Turin (856,000), Palermo (651,500), Genoa (602,500), Bologna (369,300), Florence (351,600), Bari (311,900), Catania (305,900), Venice (265,700).

Languages spoken
German is spoken in South Tyrol on the Austrian border. Slovene is spoken by a minority in Trieste. French is spoken in the Val d'Aosta, bordering France and Switzerland. Albanian is spoken in some areas of Basilicata, Calabria and Sicily. An increasing number of business people also speak English, replacing French as the second commercial language.
Official language/s
Italian

Media
Press
There are approximately 125 newspapers, which reach 42.5 per cent of the adult population, and an estimated 10,000 magazines.
Italy's press is highly regionalised and controlled directly or indirectly by either major media groups, political parties or corporate entities. The Agnelli family (which owns Fiat) controls the Turin-based *La Stampa*, Milan's *Corriere della Sera* and the sports daily *Gazzetta dello Sport*; the multinational, Ferruzzi group owns *Il Messagero in Rome* and *Italia Oggi*; Fininvest controls the Milan-based *Il Giornale*; Carlo de Benedetti, chairman of Gruppo Editoriale L'Espresso, owns *La Repubblica* and over 12 regional newspapers.
Dailies: There are around 150 dailies newspapers, of which 20 are distributed nationally. In Italian, those with the highest circulations include, *Il Corriere della Sera (Evening Courier)* (www.corriere.it), *La Repubblica* (www.repubblica.it), *La Stampa (The Press)* (www.lastampa.it) and *Il Messaggero* (www.ilmessaggero.it). All regions produce their own dailies including *Barisera* (www.barisera.it) in Puglia, *L'Arena* (www.larena.it) in Verona, *Gazzetta del Sud* (www.gazzettadelsud.it) in Sicily and *In Umbria* (www.inumbria.it) in Perugia. Free issue newspapers have become popular and many centres have their own editions within a national format (www.epolis.sm). Italy does not have tabloid newspapers but the sports newspaper *La Gazzetta dello Sport* (www.gazzetta.it) has one of the largest circulations.
Weeklies: There are over 50 weekly magazines, with an average of 15 million copies produced. In Italian, general interest weeklies and special interest magazines include *Gente (People)*, *Panorama*, *Famiglia Cristiana* (www.sanpaolo.org/fc),

for Roman Catholic views and *Oggi* (Today), *Panorama* (http://www.panorama.it) and *L'Espresso* (http://espresso.repubblica.it) for news and current affairs.
Business: In Italian, there are several newspapers from Milan, including the respected *Milano Finanza* (www.milanofinanza.it), *Il Sole 24 Ore* (www.ilsole24ore.com), *24 Minuti* (www.24minuti.ilsole24ore.com) and *Affari Italiani* (www.affaritaliani.it), which also offers tabloid news and from Naples *Il Denaro* (www.denaro.it) and in German *Sudtiroler Wirtschaftszeitung* (www.swz.it) from South Tyrol. In Italian, weekly magazines include *Il Mondo* (www.ilmondo.rcs.it) concerned with the economy, business and politics and a supplement of *La Repubblica* (www.repubblica.it), *Affari & Finanza*.
Periodicals: There are around 100 monthly magazines published catering for all genres. In recent years 'gossip' magazines such as, in Italian, *Gossip News* (www.gossipnews.it) and *Kiss Me* (www.kissme.it), have grown in popularity. Mondodori Media (www.mondadori.it) publishes a range of general periodicals on life-style, consumer, cuisine, entertainment and commercial interests including *Grazia*, and *Cucina*, other publications include *Donna Moderna* (www.donnamoderna.com).

Broadcasting

The national public broadcaster is Rai (Radiotelevisione Italiana) (www.rai.it).
Radio: There are numerous radio stations, of which over a dozen form national networks. Rai (www.rai.it) has three stations which offer entertainment, culture and news from parliament. National commercial stations include 105 Classic (www.105classics.net), CNR (www.radiocnr.it), a news network, Radio Cuore (www.radiocuore.it) and Radio Italia (www.radioitalia.it) is a community radio station.
Television: Rai (www.rai.it) has three channels (Rai Uno, Due, Tre) and has a market share of around 50 per cent, with funding derived from public funding (through TV licences, general taxes and donations) and advertising, providing locally produced and imported programmes. The main competitors are Mediaset (www.mediaset.it), owned by Silvio Belusconi, the biggest national, commercial network with three channels and La7 (www.la7.it).
Analogue transmissions are due to end in 2010, in favour of digital terrestrial transmission. There are many cable TV and Satellite, pay-to-view broadcasting is almost entirely provided by US-based Sky; , ing locally produced and imported programmes.

Advertising

Typical annual expenditure on advertising is US$10.7 billion, of which over 50 per cent is spent on television ads, with newspapers only accounting for 20 per cent. There are regulations restricting advertising during children's programmes and cartoons of less than 30 minutes, nor must children appear in broadcast adverts. Tobacco is banned completely. There are a range of regulations that allow advertising for alcohol and pharmaceuticals on TV.

News agencies

National news agency: ANSA (Agenzia Nazionale Stampa Associata)

Economy

According the International Monetary Fund (IMF) and the World Bank, Italy was ranked eighth in the world and fourth in Europe, by gross domestic product (GDP), at around US$2.3 trillion in 2010 (but down from seventh in the world in 2008). Italy is a leading industrialised country with an economy that is driven by the manufacture of high-quality goods. Export of these goods is crucial to the health of the economy so that Italy's fortunes have been hard hit by the worldwide recession that cut exports as demand fell in all sectors. In 2009, exports were particularly hard hit in specialised machines with the loss of billions of euros to the economy. In 2009, the service sector constituted an estimated 73.1 per cent of GDP, with industry accounting for 25 per cent and agriculture 1.8 per cent. Italy's largest companies include businesses in energy, banking and insurance, utilities, telecommunications, aerospace and defence and manufactured, consumer durables.
GDP growth was 1.5 per cent in 2007, but Italy quickly succumbed to recession with negative growth of -1.3 per cent in 2008. The Italian government was the first of the G8 countries to instigate a stimulus package, of US$102 billion, in 2008, that included public works, mortgage relief and tax cuts for poorer families, which in turn left it with the world's third-largest debt burden, estimated at over 110 per cent of GDP. However, the recession deepened to -5.2 per cent in 2009 as the global economic crisis worsened. As world trade picked up, GDP growth returned to a positive 1.3 per cent. Inflation did not spiral out of control during this period, it rose from 2 per cent in 2007 to 3.5 per cent as the global price of energy and food reached record highs, but as domestic spending was cut so too inflation fell to 0.8 per cent in 2009, rising to 1.6 per cent in 2010.
The country's south, the Mezzogiorno, has much lower per capita income levels and higher unemployment rates than the more industrialised north, despite many years of heavy government subsidies; the severe regional imbalances in Italy's labour market causes on-going problems for the economy. Unemployment was forecast to reach 7.8 per cent in 2009, rising to 8.4 per cent in 2010. Remittances in 2009 were US$2.68 billion (less than 0.1 per cent of GDP) and are estimated to have risen to US$3.39 billion in 2010.
The services sector, particularly tourism, is important to overall economic performance; in 2008 tourist numbers fell by 25 per cent as the economic situation in home countries limited discretionary spending, plus the euro remained relatively strong against other currencies, so making holidays costlier. The sector experienced a fall in hotel occupancy of -6 per cent in 2009; in 2010 the industry began to revive as tourists returned.
An austerity budget was passed on 14 July 2011, including cuts to public spending of US$67 billion. The measure is to reduce the national deficit, which had grown to 115 per cent of GDP in 2010.
On 20 September 2011, Standard & Poor's downgraded Italy's sovereign debt rating from A+ to A, and added an economic outlook for the country of 'negative', saying it feared for the government's ability to cut state spending and reduce the deficit. The government responded by saying the downgrade was 'politically motivated'. Italy's sovereign debt crisis came to a head on 10 November following weeks when the government failed to implement agreed austerity measures (on 15 July and 14 September) aimed at saving €124 billion (US$174.7 billion) in government spending. Italian government bonds were sold at an interest rate of 6.087 per cent (for one year). Financial markets were worried at Italy's public debt, of €1.9 trillion (US$2.6 trillion), for which €173.3 billion (US$238 billion) in short- and long-term debt was coming to maturity in 2011; between 2011–14 €656.4 billion (US$901.8 billion) will mature. As of 10 November 2011, Italy will have to pay an extra €28 billion (US$38.5 billion) over three years to service the newly rated debt. Silvio Berlusconi resigned on 13 November and on 14 November the president appointed Mario Monti, a technocrat, as prime minister.
On 19 December 2011, Mario Monti's €30 billion (US$39.7 billion) austerity budget was presented to parliament and gained approval. The economic package is intended to balance the budget by 2013.

External trade

As a member of the European Union (EU), Italy operates within a community-wide free trade area, with tariffs set across the whole community. Internationally, the EU has free trade agreements with a number of nations and trading blocs worldwide. Exports provide over 50 per cent of GDP, with manufactured goods representing around 97 per cent, despite lacking most raw materials and energy needed to sustain the trade; nevertheless it is renowned for its luxury goods and quality manufactures. Italy is the world's second largest exporter of wine and Europe's premier exporter of rice, fruit and vegetables.

Imports

Main imports are capital goods, consumer products, chemicals, transport equipment, energy products, minerals and non-ferrous metals, textiles and clothing, food, wine, tobacco and raw materials.

Main sources: Germany (typically 16 per cent total), France (10 per cent), China (5 per cent).

Exports

Main exports are engineered and electrical products, textiles and fashion clothing, precision machinery, armaments, vehicles and transport equipment, pharmaceuticals and chemicals; food, beverages and tobacco; minerals, plastics and non-ferrous metals.

Main destinations: Germany (typically 15 per cent total), France (10 per cent), US (5 per cent).

Re-exports

Re-fined oil and petroleum products

Agriculture

Farming

Italian farming is characterised by substantial regional differences. Farms in the north are closer to their counterparts in north European countries – in terms of technology, culture and economy – than Italian farmers in the south. Italy's programme for developing the south of the country includes drainage and irrigation schemes, and building up co-operatives and integrated agribusiness ventures to improve trading opportunities.

The EU's Fundamental reform to the Common Agricultural Policy (CAP) was introduced in Italy in 2005. The subsidies paid on farm output, which tended to benefit large farms and encourage overproduction, were replaced by single farm payments not conditional on production. Only 20 per cent of Italy is fertile arable land and farms are mostly small-scale. Regions with the most labour intensive farms are Sicily and Apulia. Capital intensive farms are most common in the northern province of Emilia Romagna, but the overall proportion of agricultural employment is the same in the north and south. In mountain areas, which stretch throughout the peninsula and on the islands, agricultural activity concentrates on forestry and livestock. The climate is ideal for vineyards and Italy vies with France as one the world's biggest wine producers. The plains of the north and of Apulia, the heel of Italy, are also important areas for wheat, olives and fruit. Half of total agricultural income is generated in the Po valley and the plains in the north. The area produces the entire rice crop, cereals such as wheat and corn, fodder and livestock. In central Italy, wine-making and wheat-growing are the main activities. Most citrus fruit and olives are grown in the south, where vegetables and cereals are also grown.

Fishing

The fishing industry has a turnover of around US$4 billion, but it remains a neglected sector of the economy. Sicily and the Adriatic coast produce 76.4 per cent of the country's fish. The most important fish commercially are sardines and anchovies.

Forestry

Forest and wooded land account for less than 40 per cent of land area. Sixty per cent of the forest is available for wood supply. Broadleaved species account for 66 per cent of the growing stock, the main species being beech, deciduous and evergreen oaks, poplars and chestnut. Common coniferous species include pine, Norway spruce and European larch.

Italy is one of the major consumers, producers and traders of forest products in the EU. It accounts for nearly ten per cent of EU total paper and wood-based panel production.

Industry and manufacturing

The industrial sector contributes approximately 32 per cent to GDP and employs 33 per cent of the labour force. Subdivided by sector, manufacturing contributes approximately 26 per cent to annual GDP, with construction accounting for a further 6 per cent.

Problems in the sector include growing competition in traditional products from developing countries, and the small share of the export market taken by value added high technology products. Efforts to attract industrial investment to the depressed southern region have met with only partial success, despite large subsidies.

Tourism

Italy has one of the world's largest collections of UN World Heritage Sites, containing a wealth of ancient, classical, medieval and Renaissance art, artefacts and architecture. It is a destination for pilgrims as the centre to a major religion and home to the origins of many institutions of the Catholic Church.

The global economic crisis, which began in 2008, impacted on the tourist sector as growth fell from 0.9 per cent in 2007 to -7.7 per cent in 2008, and -8.2 per cent in 2009. It rebounded with a modest 0.5 per cent growth rate in 2010, as tourism improved throughout Europe. The forecast for 2011 was 3.0 per cent, but this figure was given before the Italian economic crisis struck in November and had followed months of uncertainty and a lower than expected GDP growth. Tourism is a major component of GDP; in 2008 tourism receipts were a high of US$46.23 billion, but this fell to US$40.74 in 2009 and only increased marginally to US$40.853 billion in 2010. Around 1 per cent of employment is related to tourism with the impact of the recession swift and heavy with negative growth in employment of -5.7 per cent in 2008, which only returned to positive growth in 2011.

In 2009, the regions of Venice and Emilia-Romagna were the top destinations for visitors staying overnight. These destinations include the established holiday regions on the Adriatic Sea of Rimini and Pesaro, favoured by Italians and foreign visitors alike. Most visitors are from other European countries, followed by North America.

Mining

The mining sector accounts for only 0.5 per cent of GDP and employs a similar percentage of the workforce. Italy has relatively poor mineral resources, although large quantities of iron ore and pyrites, mercury, lead, zinc, bauxite, aluminium, sulphur, gravel, alabaster and marble exist.

Sardinia (Cagliari, Sassari and Iglesias) is the main mining area and holds the only large sulphur deposit in Europe, but mining it is not economically viable. Bauxite is mined mainly in Abruzzi, Campania and Apulia, though output has dropped due to falling demand from the aluminium industry. Output of lead, zinc and particularly copper have all increased. Quarrying activity is strong, with marble and gravel much in demand for the construction and road building industries.

Hydrocarbons

Italy relies heavily on energy imports although there is a plan under way to develop indigenous hydrocarbon resources, which are scattered along its peninsula, offshore, and on Sicily.

Proven oil reserves were 800 million barrels in 2007 with production at 122,000 barrels per day (bpd); it is expected that output will peak in 2010 at 180,000bpd. Italy consumes 1.9 billion barrels a year and is one of the largest oil importers in Europe with 90 per cent of its consumption dependent on imports. Italian refining capacity was 2,399,000bpd in 2007. The most important oil reserves are in Val d'Agri (Potenza) southern Italy and Villafortuna-Trecate (Novara) northern

Italy. The Italian multinational energy company ENI let a contract in 2009 to purchase two of the world's largest refinery reactors for its refinery in Sannazzaro (Sicily), which will increase production of middle distillates. Delivery is planned for 2011 and production by 2012.
Proven natural gas reserves were 90 billion cubic metres (cum) in 2007, with production at 8.9 billion cum, a fall of 11.5 per cent on the 2006 figure. Natural gas use has increased significantly from the 1990s and accounts for 30 per cent of the country's total energy consumption.
ENI owns Snam Rete Gas which operates a major gas supply network in Italy and has the country's only re-gasification of liquefied natural gas operation. A call for tenders for the Italian section of the Trans-Adriatic Pipeline (TAP) was issued in May 2011. Existing international pipelines deliver gas from Norway, The Netherlands, Algeria and Russia.
Most domestic coal production is used in electricity generation; coal accounts for 14 per cent of total domestic energy consumption.

Energy

Total installed electricity generating capacity is 77.3GW, producing around 292 billion kilowatt hours (kWh). Natural gas accounts for around 60 per cent of electricity generation.
Enel, the former state-owned energy monopoly, is the largest power company in Italy, producing over 50 per cent of domestic electricity needs. It produces and sells electricity throughout Italy and operates an international power grid trading energy Italy-France and Italy-Slovenia.
Enel began a programme of converting its huge oil-fired power plant in Civitavecchia to coal, and to increase the role of coal in Italy's energy mix from 14 per cent in 2008 to 50 per cent by 2013.
Italy had four nuclear power stations but they are not currently in operation nor expected to be reopened.

Financial markets

Stock exchange
Borsa Italiana (Italian Stock Exchange)

Banking and insurance

Scandal hit the Central Bank in July 2005 when the governor, Antonio Fazio, refused to allow a cross-border banking takeover and was subsequently placed under investigation in two criminal inquiries. He refused to resign for several months, receiving strong support from one of Italy's governing parties, the Lega Nord, and the Catholic Church, but was eventually replaced by Mario Draghi in December. Unlike Mr Fazio, who held an open-ended mandate, Mr Draghi will serve a six-year term, renewable once.

Central bank
Banca d'Italia; European Central Bank (ECB).

Time

GMT plus one hour (daylight saving, late March to late October, GMT plus two hours)

Geography

Italy consists of a peninsula stretching from southern Europe into the Mediterranean and includes a number of adjacent islands, including Sicily in the south-west and Sardinia in the west. The country stretches 1,200km from north to south and has 7,456km of coastline.
The distinctive boot-shaped peninsula is dominated by two extensive mountain ranges, accounting for about 75 per cent of the land area. The Alps form a natural barrier separating Italy from Slovenia in the north-east, Austria and Switzerland in the north and France in the north-west. The Apennines form the backbone of the peninsula.
Italy experiences frequent minor earthquakes, especially in the south, and its active volcanoes include Vesuvius in the Naples district, Etna in Sicily and Stromboli in the Aeolian Islands.
Two autonomous countries lie within Italy's frontiers, the Vatican City in Rome, home of the Holy See, and the tiny republic of San Marino in the north-east.

Hemisphere
Northern

Climate

While Italy lies in a temperate zone, the climates of the north and south vary. Summers are uniformly hot, although summers in the south can be extremely hot and dry. In the winter, the south is generally mild, while the north can be extremely cold – particularly near the Alps and Po Valley. Temperatures range from about 4–30 degrees Celsius.

Dress codes

Particular attention is paid to dress, although dress codes are not rigid. Most businessmen wear suits and ties during business hours.

Entry requirements

Passports
Required by most; passports must be valid for three months from arrival. Nationals of countries which are signatories of the Schengen Accords, which includes most EU/EEA member states, San Marino and Croatia, may visit on national IDs.

Visa
No visa requirements for citizens of most of Europe, the Americas, Australasia and some Asian countries, visiting for up to 90 days. For a full list, and further information for those citizens not included on the list of visa-free travel, visit www.ambwashingtondc.esteri.it and see consular services. A Schengen visa application (offered in several languages) can be downloaded from http://europa.eu/abc/travel/ see 'documents you will need'.
Business travel is also allowed for those enjoying visa-free travel. Those who do not have visa-free arrangements must provide a letter from their employer guaranteeing travel expenses, including full itinery and purpose of the trip. Letters of invitation from all Italian companies to be visited, and a current (not over 90 days) *Visura Camerale* issued by the Italian Chamber of Commerce should be attached; a return/onward ticket must be produced before collection of the passport and visa from the issuing consulate; which may request any additional documents at its discretion.
Within eight days of arrival in Italy the visa traveller must appear before local police authorities to receive a Residency Permit and will also need to show proof of health insurance.

Currency advice/regulations
Import and export of local and foreign currency up to eur12,000 (or foreign equivalent) is permitted. Imports and export of amounts greater than this must be declared within 48 hours of arrival or departure.
Travellers cheques are widely accepted.

Customs
Personal items are duty-free. There are no duties levied on alcohol and tobacco between EU member states, providing amounts imported are for personal consumption.

Health (for visitors)

Nationals of the European Economic Area (EEA) countries and Switzerland can access reduced cost and sometimes free medical treatment using a European Health Insurance Card (EHIC) while visiting the EEA. Exceptions include nationals of the 10 countries, which joined the EU in 2004 whose EHIC is not valid in Switzerland. Applications for the EHIC should be made before travelling.

Mandatory precautions
None.

Advisable precautions
No special immunisations are needed. Pharmacists are usually open from 0830 to 1300 and 1600 to 2000.

Hotels

Classified into five star categories. Rates are fixed by the Provincial Tourist Board, and vary according to class, season, services available and locality. A service charge of 15–18 per cent is added to bills, but additional tips are also expected for individual services. Restaurants expect 15 per cent on top of the bill.

Credit cards
International credit cards are widely accepted.

Public holidays (national)
Fixed dates
1 Jan (New Year's Day), 6 Jan (Epiphany), 25 April (Liberation Day), 1 May (Labour Day), 2 Jun (National Day), 15 Aug (Assumption Day), 1 Nov (All Saints' Day), 8 Dec (Immaculate Conception), 25–26 Dec (Christmas).
Variable dates
Easter Monday

Working hours
Business travellers would do best to avoid August when Italians desert the stifling heat of the big cities for the beaches and mountains. The mass exodus usually begins in mid-July and lasts at least until after the *Ferragosto* festival (August 15). Most factories, government offices, shops and restaurants close for all of August or are run by minimal staff.
The afternoon siesta is still very much part of the Italian way of life in Rome and the south. In northern Italy, there is a trend towards standard European business hours of 0900 to 1700, at least in offices.
Banking
Mon–Fri: 0830–1300; 1500–1600.
Banks in tourist areas may not close for lunch.
Business
Northern Italy: 0930–1300 and 1400–1800.
Central and southern Italy: 0830–1245 and 1630–2000.
Government
Post offices: Mon–Fri: 0830–1345 and Sat: 0830–1200; central city post offices stay open until 2100.
Government offices: Mon–Sat: 0830–1345.
Shops
Mon–Sat: 0830–1230, 1500–1800; Sat: 0900–1230.

Telecommunications
Mobile/cell phones
There are 3G, 900/1800 GSM services throughout the country.

Electricity supply
220V AC, 50Hz

Social customs/useful tips
Italians always shake hands on meeting and leaving. Exchanging business cards is also normal practice as it helps to reinforce the informal network of personal contacts which permeates Italian business. Businessmen prefer that written communication, either by e-mail, facsimile or letter, be sent before a telephone discussion. Personal titles are considered important, although often more prestigious than professionally accurate. Small luxury goods are frequently exchanged as gifts in business. Smoking is still fashionable, with fewer restrictions than in many other Western countries.
Italians are required to carry identification on them at all times and foreigners are recommended to do likewise.

Security
Handbag snatching and pickpocketing are widespread, particularly in popular tourist spots in Rome and Naples. It is advisable not to wear conspicuous jewellery or carry personal valuables. In general the level of violent crime is low, but drug-related crime is on the increase in Milan, Rome and Naples. With this in mind, visitors to Rome are advised to avoid the streets around the central railway station at night.

Getting there
Air
National airline: Alitalia
International airport/s: Leonardo da Vinci (Fiumicino) Rome (FCO) 26km south-west of Rome. There is a direct rail link to the central railway station (duration 35 minutes), and express buses into Rome. Licensed, metered taxis are also available to the city.
Milan Malpensa (MXP) 45km north-west of Milan. Both airport facilities include duty-free shops, bar, restaurant, car hire, bank, *bureau de change* and business centre.
Other airport/s: Pisa (PSA), 2km from city, (an hour by train from Florence); Turin International (TRN), 16km north-west of city; Venice Marco Polo (VCE), 13km north-west of city; Bologna G Marconi (BLQ); Milan Linate (LIN); Naples Capodichino (NAP); Genoa Cristoforo Colombo (GOA); Palermo (PMO).
Airport tax: None
Surface
Italy is included in the Pan-European Corridor 5 scheme. The project has some 3,270km of railways, linking Kiev in the Ukraine with western Europe via Italy, and 2,850 of new and upgraded roads.
Road: Italy can be entered by road from France, Switzerland, Austria and Slovenia. However, several passes are closed during winter. In addition to the Riviera coastal motorway, access from France and Switzerland is maintained via the St Bernard, Mont Blanc and Fréjus tunnels.
Rail: There are daily services, run by Ferrovie dello Stato (FS) (Italian State Railways) that run from France, Switzerland and Austria, which are linked to the European rail network.
The high-speed Lyon-Turin Ferroviaire rail link, consisting of two linked tunnel sections, which are due to join the north-south, east-west transport network hub in Lyon, is expected to be completed by 2012.
Water: There are regular ferry service connections to Greece, Albania, North Africa, Croatia and France.
Main port/s: Genoa, Trieste, Augusta, Taranto, Leghorn, Savona, Ancona, Bari, Brindisi, Civitavecchia, Venice, La Spezia, Naples, Palermo (Sicily), and Cagliari and Porto Torres (Sardinia).

Getting about
National transport
Air: Alitalia and Aero Transporti Italiani (ATI) operate services connecting Rome to most major towns. Alisarda operates services connecting Rome, Milan and Turin with Sardinia.
Road: There is a road network of over 300,000km, of which 6,000km are motorways (*autostrade*) with tolls, connecting most cities.
Buses: Extensive bus services, operated by several companies, link all major towns.
Rail: Trenitalia operates an extensive network in all regions. Express trains, which provide buffet carriages, have seats to be booked in advance. Larger railway stations provide left luggage, banks, ATMs and refreshment facilities.
Water: Ferryboat and hydrofoil services linking the mainland with Sicily, Sardinia and the smaller islands are operated by several lines including the State Railways.
City transport
Taxis: Available in all towns and tourist resorts, usually in ranks at railway stations, or can be called by phone. Fares vary considerably, and unmetered cabs should be avoided. Drivers round up their fares; gratuities are not necessary.
Buses, trams & metro: All major cities have bus services with one standard fare. Day and monthly tickets are available. Bus tickets can also be bought in packs of five and then fed into a machine upon boarding.
There are metros in Rome and Milan with standard single fares as for buses. In Milan tickets last for 70 minutes and can be used on both metro lines and all bus routes. A daily or monthly ticket usable for all Rome services is available. The metro journey from Malpensa international airport, Milan, to the city centre takes around 30 minutes.
Tram services are available in Milan, Naples and Turin.
Car hire
Self-drive cars are available; the daily rate depends on the engine size, plus an additional charge per kilometre. Special weekly tariffs are available. VAT is charged. Official translation of driving licence required. Driving is on the right. Maximum speed is 50kph in towns,

90/110kph on country roads and 130kph on motorways. There are legal obligations for wearing seat belts while driving and warning waistcoats (fluorescent jackets) when leaving a vehicle during a breakdown or emergency.
Road signs are international.

BUSINESS DIRECTORY

The addresses listed below are a selection only. While World of Information makes every endeavour to check these addresses, we cannot guarantee that changes have not been made, especially to telephone numbers and area codes. We would welcome any corrections.

Telephone area codes

The international direct dialling code (IDD) for Italy is +39, followed by area code, including the first zero:

Bologna	051	Pisa	050
Capri	081	Rome	06
Florence	055	Trieste	040
Genoa	010	Turin	011
Milan	02	Venice	041
Naples	081	Verona	045

Useful telephone numbers

Police, fire and ambulance: 113

Chambers of Commerce

American Chamber of Commerce in Italy, 1 Via Cantù, 20123 Milan (tel: 869-0661; fax: 805-7737; email: amcham@amcham.it).

Bergamo Camera di Commercio, 16 Largo Belotti, 24121 Bergamo (tel: 422-5111; fax: 226-023; email: info@bg.camcom.it).

Bologna Camera di Commercio, Palazzo Mercanzia, 4 Piazza Mercanzia, 40125 Bologna (tel: 609-3111; fax: 609-3451; email: segreteria.generale@bo.camcom.it).

Brescia Camera di Commercio, 3 Via Orzinuovi, 25125 Brescia (tel: 351-41; fax: 351-4222; email: brescia@bs.camcom.it).

British Chamber of Commerce for Italy, 12 Via Dante, 20121 Milan (tel: 877-798; fax: 8646-1885; email: bcci@britchamitaly.com).

Ferrara Camera di Commercio, 11 Via Borgoleoni, 44100 Ferrara (tel: 783-711; fax: 240-204; email: cciaa.ferrara@fe.camcom.it).

Florence Camera di Commercio, 3 Piazza dei Giudici, 50122 Florence (tel: 2795-1; fax: 2795-259; email: info@fi.camcom.it).

Genoa Camera di Commercio, 4 Via Garibaldi, 16124 Genoa (tel: 270-41; fax: 270-4300; email: camera.genova@ge.camcom.it).

Mantua Camera di Commercio, 28 Via Pietro Fortunato Calvi, 46100 Mantua (tel: 234-1; fax: 234-234; email: mantova@mn.camcom.it).

Milan Camera di Commercio, 9b Via Meravigli, 20123 Milan (tel: 8515-1; fax: 8515-4232; email: infohighway@mi.camcom.it).

Naples Camera di Commercio, 2 Via S Aspreno, 80133 Naples (tel: 760-7111; fax: 552-6940; email: segretaria.generale@na.camcom.it)

Padua Camera di Commercio, 34 Via E Filiberto, 35122 Padua (tel: 820-8111; fax: 820-8290; email: info@pd.camcom.it).

Parma Camera di Commercio, 2 Via Verde, 43100 Parma (tel: 210-11; fax: 282-168; email: segretaria.generale@pr.camcom.it).

Pavia Camera di Commercio, 27 Via Mentana, 27199 Pavia (tel: 393-1; fax: 304-559; email: pavia@pv.camcom.it).

Rome Camera di Commercio, 147 Via De' Burrò, 00186 Rome (tel: 520-2630; fax: 520-82617; email: info@rm.camcom.it).

Siena Camera di Commercio, 30 Piazza Matteotti, 53100 Siena (tel: 202-511; fax: 270-981; email: cciaa@si.camcom.it).

Treieste Camera di Commercio, 14 Piazza della Borsa, 34121 Trieste (tel: 670-1111; fax: 670-1321; email: info@ts.camcom.it).

Turin Camera di Commercio, 24 Via San Francesco da Paola, 10123 Turin (tel: 571-6405; fax: 571-6404; email: urp@to.camcom.it).

Unione Italiana delle Camere di Commercio, Industria, Artigianato e Agricoltura, 21 Piazza Sallustio, 00187 Rome (tel: 470-41; fax: 470-4240; email: segretaria.generale@unioncamere.it).

Venice Camera di Commercio, 2032 Via XXII Marzo, San Marco, 30124 Venice (tel: 786-111; fax: 786-330; email: segretaria.generale@ve.camcom.it).

Verona Camera di Commercio, 96 Corso Porta Nuova, 37122 Verona (tel: 808-5011; fax: 594-648; email: cciaavr@vr.camcom.it).

Banking

Banca Commerciale Italiana, Via del Corso, 226 C.A.P. 00186 Rome (tel: 67-121; fax: 6712-4925).

Banca di Napoli, Via Toledo 177–188, 80132 Naples (tel: 791-1111).

Banca Nazionale del Lavoro, Via Vittoro Veneto 119, 00187 Rome (tel: 47-021; fax: 4702-6263).

Banca Nazionale dell'Agricoltura SPA, Via Salaria 231, 00199 Rome (tel: 85-881; fax: 8588-3396).

Banca Popolare Commercio E Industria Scarl, Via Casifina 1790, 00132 Rome (tel: 207-1712; fax: 207-2676).

Banca di Roma, Via del Corso 320, 00186 Rome (tel: 67-071; fax: 6707-3783).

Cassa di Risparmio delle Provincie Lombarde, Piazza Barberini 21, 00167 Rome (tel: 46-781; fax 486-884).

Cassa di Risparmio di Roma, 320 Via del Corso, 00186 Rome (tel: 67-071; fax: 6707-3783).

Cassa di Risparmio di Torino, 31 Via XX Settembre, 10121 Torino (tel: 57-661; fax: 638-203).

Credito Italiano, 00144 Piazzale dell'Industria 46 (tel: 54-631; fax: 5423-7006).

European Investment Bank, via Saroagna 36, 100187 Rome (tel: 47-191; fax: 487-3438).

Istituto Centrale Delle Banche Di Credito Cooperativo, Via Torino 146, 00184 Rome (tel: 47-161; fax: 4716-5583).

Istituto Di Credito Delle Casse Di Rigparmio Italiane, Via San Basilo 15, 00187 Rome (tel: 47-151).

Mediocredito Centrale, Via Piemonte 51, 00187 Rome (tel: 47-911; fax: 479-1626).

Monte dei Paschi di Siena, Piazza Salimbeni, Siena (tel: 294-111).

Nuovo Banco Ambrosiano, Piazza Paolo Ferrari 10, 20121 Milan (tel: 85-941).

UBAE Arab Italian Bak SpA, Piazza Venezia 11, 00187 Rome (tel: 67-5921; fax: 678-4606).

Central bank

Banca d'Italia, Via Nazionale 91, 00184 Rome (tel: 47-921; fax: 479-22983; internet: www.bancaditalia.it).

European Central Bank (ECB), Kaiserstrasse 29, D-60311 Frankfurt am Main, Germany (tel: (+49-69) 13-440; fax: (+49-69) 1344-6000; email: info@ecb.int).

Stock exchange

Borsa Italiana (Italian Stock Exchange): www.borsaitaliana.it

Travel information

Alitalia (Linee Aeree Italiane), Centro Direzionale, Viale Alissandro Marchetti, 111, Rome 100148 (tel: 709-2780; fax: 709-3065).

Leonardo da Vinci (Fiumicino) Airport, Via dell'Aeroporto di Fiumicino 320, PO Box 68, 00050, Fiumicino (tel: 5951; fax:

595-5707; email: info@adr.it; internet: www.adr.it).

Milan Malpensa Airport, 21010 Varese (tel: 7485-2200; fax: 7485-4010: email: communication@sea-aeroportimilano.it; internet: www.sea-aeroportimilano.it/eng).

Trenitalia, 1 Piazza della Croce Rossa, Rome (tel: 892-021; internet: www.trenitalia.com).

Ministry of tourism

Ministry of Industry and Tourism, Via Molise 2, 00187 Rome (tel: 47-051; fax: 4705-2215).

National tourist organisation offices

Ente Nazionale Italiano per il Turismo (ENIT), 2/6Via Marghera, 00185 Rome (tel: 49-711; fax: 446-3379; email: sedecentrale@cert.ent.it; internet: www.enit.it).

Ministries

Ministry of Agriculture and Forests, Via XX Settembre 20, 00187 Rome (tel: 46-651; fax: 592-314).

Ministry of Defence, Via XX Settembre 8, 00187 Rome (tel: 488-2126; fax: 474-7775).

Ministry of Education, Viale Trastevere 76/A, 00153 Rome (tel: 58-491; fax: 580-3381).

Ministry of Employment and Social Welfare, Via Flavia 6, 00187 Rome (tel: 46-831; fax: 4788-7174).

Ministry of the Environment, Piazza Venezia 11, 00187 Rome (tel: 70-361; fax: 678-3844).

Ministry of Equal Opportunities, c/o Presidenza del Consiglio dei Ministry, Palazzo Chigi, 00187 Rome (tel: 67-791; fax: 678-3998).

Ministry of Finance, Viale Europa 242, 00144 Rome (tel: 59-971; fax: 501-5714).

Ministry of Foreign Affairs, Piazzale della Farnesina, 00194 Rome (tel: 36-911; fax: 323-6258).

Ministry of Foreign Trade, Viale America 341, 00144 Rome (tel: 59-931; fax: 5964-7504).

Ministry of Health, Viale dell'Industria 20, 00144 Rome (tel: 59-941; fax: 5964-7649).

Ministry of Industry and Tourism, Via Molise 2, 00187 Rome (tel: 47-051; fax: 4705-2215).

Ministry of the Interior, Piazzale del Viminale, 00184 Rome (tel: 6451; fax: 482-5792).

Ministry of Justice, Via Arenula 71, 00186 Rome (tel: 68-851; fax: 5227-8550).

Ministry of Posts and Telecommunications, Viale America 201, 00144 Rome (tel: 59-581; fax: 594-274).

Ministry of Public Administration, Palazzo Vidoni, Corso Vittorio Emanuele 116, 00186 Rome (tel: 680-031).

Ministry of Public Works, Piazza Porta Pia 1, 00198 Rome (tel: 44-121; fax: 4426-7275).

Ministry of Transport, Piazza della Croce Rossa 1, 00161 Rome (tel: 84-901; fax: 4424-1539).

Ministry of the Treasury and Budget, Via XX Settembre 97, 00187 Rome (tel: 47-611; fax: 488-2146).

Ministry for University, Scientific and Technological Research, Piazzale Kennedy 20, 00144 Rome (tel: 59-911; fax: 591-5493).

Office of the President, Palazzo del Quirinale, 00187 Rome (tel: 4699).

Prime Minister's Office, Palazzo Chigi, Piazza Colonna 370, 00187 Rome (tel: 67-791; fax: 678-3998).

Other useful addresses

Agenzia Nazionale Stampa Associata (news agency), Via della Dataria 94, 00187 Rome (tel: 678-6161).

Borsa Valori di Milano, Piazza Degli Affari, 20100 Milan (tel: 8534).

British Embassy, Via XX Settembre 80/A, 00187 Rome (tel: 482-5551, 482-5441; fax: 487-3324).

Commissione Nazionale per le Società e la Borsa (Commission for Companies and the Stock Exchange), Milan (tel: 877-841).

Confederazione Generale dell'Industria Italiana (General Confederation of Italian Industry), Viale dell'Astronomia 30, 00144 Rome (tel: 59-031).

Confederazione Generale Italiana del Commercio (General Confederation of Italian Commerce), Piazza G.C. Belli 2, Rome (tel: 588-783, 580-192).

Ente Nazionale Idrocarburi (ENI), Piazzalo E. Mattei, 00144 Rome (tel: 59-001).

Ente Partecipazioni e Finanziamento Industria Manifatturiera (EFIM), Via XXIV Maggio 43–45, 00187 Rome (tel: 47-101).

Istituto Nazionale di Statistica (ISTAT) (national statistics office), Via Cesare Balbo 16, 00100 Rome (tel: 46-731; fax: 4673-4177).

Istituto per la Ricostruzione Industriale (IRI) Via Vittorio Veneto 85, 00187 Rome (tel: 47-271).

Istituto Nazionale per il Commercio Estero (Italian government agency for promotion of foreign trade), 21 Via Liszt, 00100 Rome (tel: 59-921).

Italian Embassy (US), 3000 Whitehaven Street, NW, Washington DC 20008 (tel: (+1-202) 612-4400; fax: (+1-202) 518-2154; email: stampa@itwash.org).

US Embassy, Via Vittorio Veneto 119A, 00187 Rome (tel: 46-741; fax: 4674-2356).

National news agency: ANSA (Agenzia Nazionale Stampa Associata)

Via della Dataria 94, 00187 Rome (tel: 677-41; fax: 677-4638; internet: www.ansa.it).

Other news agencies: AGI (Agenzia Giornalistica Italia) (in Italian): www.agenziaitalia.it

Internet sites

City of Venice Gateway: www.venetia.it

City of Florence information: www.aboutflorence.com

Gateway site of servers listed by city (launches into Italian language sites): www.cilea.it/WWW-map

Italian Central Bank: www.bancaditalia.it

Italian Statistics: www.istat.it

Italian Embassy in the US (includes economic and trade data) www.italyemb.org

Ministry of Foreign Affairs: www.esteri.it/eng/index/htm

The Uffizi Museum: www.uffizi.firenze.it

Yellow pages Online: www.paginegialle.it

KEY FACTS

Official name: Jamaica

Head of State: Queen Elizabeth II (since 1952); represented by Governor General Patrick Allen (from 26 Feb 2009)

Head of government: Prime Minister Andrew Holness (JLP) (from 23 Oct 2011)

Ruling party: Jamaica Labour Party (JLP) (from 3 Sep 2007)

Area: 10,989 square km

Population: 2.74 million (2010)*

Capital: Kingston

Official language: English

Currency: Jamaican dollar (J$) = 100 cents

Exchange rate: J$85.78 per US$ (Oct 2011)

GDP per capita: US$5,039 (2010)

GDP real growth: -1.10% (2010)

GDP: US$13.70 billion (2010)

Labour force: 1.25 million (2010)

Unemployment: 12.40% (2010)

Inflation: 12.60% (2010)

Balance of trade: -US$3.09 billion (2009)

* estimated figure

NOTA

23 October 2011, Andrew Holness took office as prime minister, following the resignation of Bruce Golding.

29 December 2011, in parliamentary elections the People's National Party (PNP) won 53.3 per cent of the vote (42 seats of 63) and the Jamaica Labour Party (JLP) 46.6 per cent (21); turnout was 52.8 per cent. Portia Simpson Miller became prime minister on 5 January 2012.

Jamaica

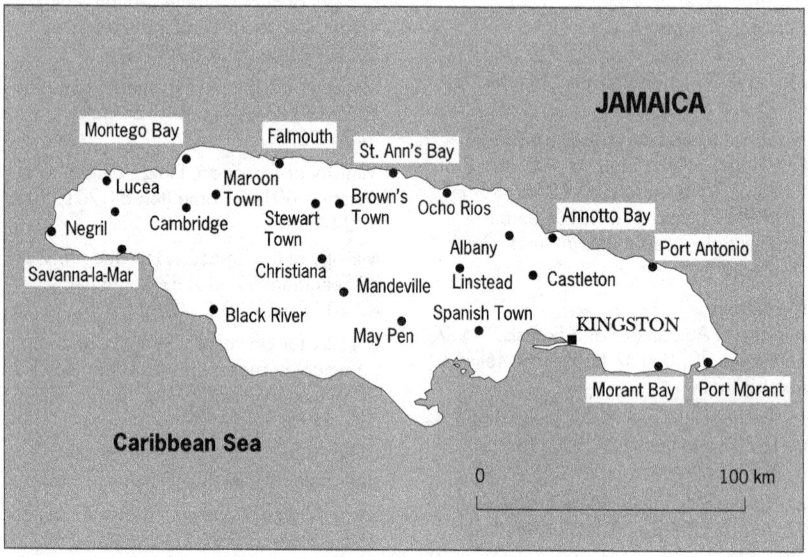

During her inaugural speech on 6 January 2012, newly elected Prime Minister Portia Simpson Miller, Jamaica's first female prime minister, declared that Queen Elizabeth should be removed as Head of State and that Jamaica should become a republic. Mrs Simpson Miller considers 2012, when Jamaica celebrates its golden jubilee since independence, to be an appropriate date to break with the United Kingdom. The royal answer to any such declaration is a magnanimous and uncontroversial 'it is a matter for the people to decide'.

Political victory

Portia Simpson Miller led the People's National Party (PNP) to victory in parliamentary elections on 29 December 2011, winning 53.3 per cent and a majority of 42 seats out of 63 with a promised 'growth and development with job creation' as a platform for her election. This triumph came three months after Bruce Golding resigned suddenly as prime minister, leaving his Jamaican Labour Party (JLP) having to find a new leader at a time when the country was deeply dissatisfied with his handling of the economy. Golding was also embroiled in an on-going scandal over his management of the US request for the extradition of Jamaican drugs lord, Christopher 'Dudus' Coke, which ended with the death of 76 bystanders, as the police raided Coke's hideout in a Kingston slum. The onerous task of leading the country and the JLP fell to Andrew Holness, who quickly found the task of picking up the reins of premiership too much and called for early general elections. The electorate was unforgiving and didn't consider the JLP's new face a good enough replacement to reassure them.

The economy

The service sector accounts or over 60 per cent of GDP. Tourism, remittances and bauxite/alumina provide the majority of foreign exchange. Since 2007, global prices for all commodities have risen and bauxite/alumina is no exception, with revenue up by 10 per cent in 2011. Tourism constitutes around 10 per cent of GDP, but high crime rates deter some visitors and hampers expansion of the industry. Remittances were US$2.0 billion in 2010 (15.2 per cent of GDP) and estimated to have been US$2.1 billion in 2011.

Jamaica is one of the most indebted countries in the world – 129 per cent of GDP in 2009/10. Interest payments alone have averaged 13 per cent of GDP (2007–11) and were as high in 2009/10 as 17 per cent of GDP. An agreement has been reached with the International Monetary Fund (IMF) in 2011 for a US$1.27 billion loan to underwrite government spending; an austerity budget was agreed as a condition of the loan.

The IMF recognised that due to the heavy debt burden Jamaica's social progress has suffered considerably, especially in education and infrastructure. This is likely to have a long-term consequence on development prospects.

Honeymoon blues?

The new administration has much to do, with an economy so heavily indebted and unemployment running at 13 per cent, the austerity measure that have to be implemented could quickly dishearten and alarm all but the most loyal supporters of either tight fiscal monetary policies or the PNP and Portia Simpson Miller, a leader with big plans for a republican Jamaica, which could be enough to boost the spirit of enterprise.

Risk assessment

Economy	Poor
Politics	Good
Regional stability	Good

COUNTRY PROFILE

Historical profile

1494 Jamaica was sighted by members of an expedition led by Christopher Columbus.
1509 Jamaica was occupied by Spaniards. Most of the indigenous Arawak community died from exposure to European diseases. African slaves were brought in to work on the sugar plantations.
1655 The British captured the island. Jamaica became a slave-based economy producing sugar and some coffee for export.
1692 Jamaican capital, Port Royal, sunk into the sea after an earthquake and Spanish Town became the new capital.
1834 Slavery was abolished.
1865 A major revolt against Jamaican landowners among freed slaves living in hardship was brutally put down by the British. The local legislature surrendered its powers and Jamaica became a crown colony.
1870 Plantations began to replace sugar cane with banana production, due to increased sugar beet production in Europe.
1884 A new constitution marked the revival of Jamaican autonomy.
1930s The worldwide economic depression and greater international competition further undermined the Jamaican sugar industry.
1938 Popular uprisings caused by unemployment and resentment of racial British policies led to the establishment of the People's National Party (PNP) by Norman Manley.
1943 The Jamaica Labour Party (JLP) was founded.
1944 Universal adult suffrage was introduced and a new constitution allowed for the election of the House of Representatives.
1958 Jamaica became part of the attempted West Indies Federation.
1962 At the insistence of Prime Minister Alexander Bustamante, Jamaica left the West Indies Federation and gained separate independence. It became a member of the Commonwealth. Kingston became the capital city.
1968–69 Protests against poor housing conditions turned into serious riots in Kingston.
1972 Michael Manley became prime minister and pursued a policy of economic self-reliance.
1976 The PNP won another term following elections marked by violence and proceeded to nationalise businesses and build closer ties with Cuba.
1980 The JLP won the elections and Edward Seaga became prime minister reversing the nationalisation policies of the previous government. The US granted the Seaga government substantial aid after it distanced itself from Cuba.
1988 Hurricane Gilbert caused an estimated US$3 billion damage to much of the island.
1989 The PNP ousted the JLP in elections, returning Michael Manley as prime minister. Manley, however, chose to continue Seaga's policies.
1992 Manley retired on health grounds and was succeeded by Percival Patterson.
1993 The PNP was returned to office with an increased majority.
1997 The PNP won a third term in office.
1999 Protests against a new fuel tax spilled over into rioting in several areas. The Jamaican Defence Force (JDF) was ordered onto the streets to tackle the high rate of crime.
2001 Violence broke out in Kingston. There were gun battles between the police and gangs with political links. The army was called out after 25 people had been killed.
2002 The ruling PNP won parliamentary elections.
2004 Extra police were drafted into St James, the island's tourism capital, to tackle an escalating crime wave. Ivan, the worst hurricane since 1988, struck Jamaica, damaging thousands of homes and killing 15 people.
2005 Jamaica and Venezuela signed a US$200 million agreement to modernise and expand the Petrojam oil refinery in Kingston.
2007 In parliamentary elections, the opposition JLP won 50.1 per cent, 33 seats (out of 60); the ruling PNP won 49.8 per cent (27). Bruce Golding became prime minister.
2008 Parliament voted to continue the death penalty; Jamaica has one of the world's highest murder rates.
2009 Governor General Sir Kenneth Hall retired and was replaced by Dr Patrick

KEY INDICATORS — Jamaica

	Unit	2006	2007	2008	2009	2010
Population	m	2.67	*2.68	*2.70	*2.71	*2.74
Gross domestic product (GDP)	US$bn	10.39	13.00	14.00	11.90	13.70
GDP per capita	US$	3,887	4,836	5,199	4,390	5,039
GDP real growth	%	2.5	1.5	-0.9	-3.0	-1.2
Inflation	%	8.6	9.3	22.0	9.6	12.3
Unemployment	%	10.3	9.9	10.6	11.4	12.4
Industrial output	% change	–	–	-3.0	-12.0	–
Agricultural output	% change	–	–	-5.0	13.7	–
Exports (fob) (goods)	US$m	1,984.0	2,362.6	2,743.9	1,387.7	–
Imports (fob) (goods)	US$m	4,868.0	6,203.9	7,546.8	4,475.7	–
Balance of trade	US$m	-2,884.0	-3,841.3	-4,802.9	-3,087.9	–
Current account	US$m	-1,197.0	-2,038.1	-2,793.3	-1,125.6	-1,110.0
Total reserves minus gold	US$m	2,318.4	1,878.5	1,772.7	2,075.8	2,501.1
Foreign exchange	US$m	2,318.2	1,878.2	1,772.6	1,729.4	2,171.4
Exchange rate	per US$	66.92	69.19	72.75	87.89	87.20

* estimated figure

Linton Allen, pastor and president of the Adventist Church's West Indies Union.
2010 A state of emergency was declared in parts of the capital in May after several police stations were attacked. Security forces stormed the Kingston suburb of Tivoli Gardens, in an operation to arrest an alleged drugs baron, Christopher 'Dudus' Coke. The resulting gun-battle killed 73 people. The US had issued an international arrest warrant for Coke for drugs smuggling and gang-related offences. Coke was arrested in June and extradited, without opposition, to the US. The state of emergency was ended in mid-July after the government failed to get enough votes in Parliament to extend it. All suspects arrested during the disturbances had to be released. In July, Jamaica announced it was establishing an embassy in Kuwait.
2011 On 11 May Prime Minister Golding announced that Jamaica was officially out of recession, following modest GDP growth in the first quarter. On 27 June parliament approved the increase of fees charged to airline passengers visiting Jamaica from US$10 to US$20 (to take effect in October). Prime Minister Golding announced his resignation in September and, on 19 October, the JLP voted for Andrew Holness as his replacement as both leader of the party and therefore the country. Holness took office on 23 October. During the Commonwealth Heads of Government summit, on 28 October, the 16 countries in which the British monarch is Head of State unanimously agreed to change the royal line of succession from that of first born son to the first born child (regardless of its gender). The change will be enacted after the succession of Prince William (currently second in line to the throne, after his father Prince Charles).

Political structure

Constitution

Jamaica is a parliamentary democracy and independent state within the Commonwealth. The British monarch is the titular head of state and is represented by a governor general appointed on the advice of the prime minister. The governor general's role is mainly ceremonial and is guided in most cases by the prime minister, who as head of government effectively exercises executive power. Duties include appointing the leader of the opposition from among members of parliament who do not support the government. The governor general must have no affiliation with any political party while holding office.
Local governments in the 14 parishes are due for election every three years. The minimum voting age is 18. Voting is by secret ballot and the candidate who wins the most votes in each constituency is elected in a first-past-the-post electoral system.

Form of state

Constitutional monarchy

The executive

The head of state is the British monarch who is represented by the Governor General of Jamaica. The prime minister is selected by the governor general from the House of Representatives as the member best able to command the support of the House. Executive power rests with the cabinet – made up of the prime minister and at least 11 ministers. Cabinet ministers are chosen by the prime minister.

National legislature

The legislature is a bicameral parliament. It consists of a 60-member House of Representatives, elected every five years, and a 21-member Senate, appointed to a parallel term. The prime minister, who is also leader of the majority in the House of Representatives, appoints 13 senators, while the remaining eight are named by the leader of the opposition. The Senate mainly reviews legislation passed by the House of Representatives, although it can also initiate legislation, except on financial matters.
Voting must be held within three months of the dissolution of parliament. There have been eight parliaments since 1962, when Jamaica became the first English-speaking West Indian island to gain independence from the UK.

Legal system

The judiciary is headed by a Supreme Court and a Court of Appeal. The governor general, acting under the guidance of a six-member Privy Council based in London, UK, can grant pardons to convicted criminals. The final appeal is to the Judicial Committee of the Privy Council in the UK.

Last elections

3 September 2007 (parliamentary)
Results: Parliamentary: the Jamaica Labour Party (JLP) won 50.1 per cent (33 seats out of 60), People's National Party (PNP) won 49.8 (27 seats). Turnout was 60.4 per cent.

Next elections

2012 (parliamentary)

Political parties

Ruling party

Jamaica Labour Party (JLP) (from 3 Sep 2007)

Main opposition party

Jamaica Labour Party (JLP)

Population

2.74 million (2010)*
Last census: September 2001: 2,607632
Population density: 209 inhabitants per square km. Urban population: 56 per cent of total population.
Annual growth rate: 0.7 per cent 1994–2004 (WHO 2006)

Ethnic make-up

Afro-Caribbean (90.9 per cent), East Indian (1.3 per cent), European (0.2 per cent), Chinese (0.2 per cent), mixed (7.3 per cent) and other (0.1 per cent).

Religions

Jamaica is home to a number of Christian denominations, mostly Protestant (over 61 per cent of the population). These include the Church of God (21 per cent), Baptist (9 per cent), Anglican (6 per cent) and Seventh-Day Adventist (9 per cent) churches. Roman Catholics (4 per cent) and spiritual cults (35 per cent) make up the other principal religious groups.

Education

The quality of schooling has slowly deteriorated over the last 20 years as debt reduction and other fiscal issues take higher priority. Jamaica's education system is based on the British system. Schooling consists of a two year pre-primary from aged 4, then a compulsory primary cycle of six years. Secondary schooling is divided into three phases, at the end of each, students either leave or move up to the next grade. They enter a 'first cycle' secondary school for three years, then a sixth form education of two-years and finally a 'second cycle' secondary school of two years; GSE 'O' and 'A' level examinations conclude the latter two. The education system accommodates a variety of public and private schools.
The main beneficiary of the government's spending on education is the primary school system, which enjoys a higher per capita expenditure than secondary and tertiary education.
Free places are offered in secondary schools through an annual common entrance examination, but a shortage of places has meant that not all children who qualify can be accommodated.
Post-secondary education is available at three universities and a number of community and teacher-training colleges. Opportunities for tertiary education remain limited, with only 8 per cent of high school graduates going to university or other higher institutions.
The primary and secondary education system was affected by the structural adjustment programme agreed with the IMF during the 1990s, which resulted in general cutbacks in social services expenditure. However, education has also benefitted from direct support from multilateral institutions. In 1996, the World Bank initiated a US$28 million student loan project, and has sponsored reform of secondary education. In 2000, the Inter-American Development Bank (IDB) approved a US$31 million loan to

support the development of the primary school system.
Literacy rate: 88 per cent adult rate; 95 per cent youth rate (15–24) (Unesco 2005).
Compulsory years: Six to 12
Enrolment rate: 101 per cent gross primary enrolment, of relevant age group (including repeaters) (World Bank)
Pupils per teacher: 31 in primary schools.

Health
Jamaica's health care is affordable and improving dramatically; increasing life expectancy and lowering infant mortality rates to some of the best figures in the Caribbean. Unfortunately, money has been taken out of the funding for the public education system.
Improved water sources and sanitation facilities are available to 71 per cent and 84 per cent of the population, respectively.
HIV/Aids
HIV prevalence: 1.2 per cent aged 15–49 in 2003 (World Bank)
Life expectancy: 72 years, 2004 (WHO 2006)
Fertility rate/Maternal mortality rate: 2.4 births per woman, 2004 (WHO 2006)
Birth rate/Death rate: 17.4 births per 1,000 population; 5.4 deaths per 1,000 population (2003).
Child (under 5 years) mortality rate (per 1,000): 17 per 1,000 live births (World Bank)
Head of population per physician: 0.85 physicians per 1,000 people, 2003 (WHO 2006)

Welfare
Welfare is provided under the National Insurance Scheme (NIS) and the Social Assistance Programme. The NIS is contributory and provides protection against loss of income for men aged 18 to 70 years and women aged 18 to 65 years. There has also been multilateral involvement in welfare provision, including a US$20 million Jamaica Social Investment Fund (JSIF) initiated by the World Bank in 1996. JSIF is part of a national programme aimed at eliminating poverty and generating social funds. The Bank has initiated a social assessment programme for the inner cities, to allow the JSIF to target poverty more effectively. The Jamaican government has mobilised support from several non-governmental organisations and other charities towards the administration of social security and welfare measures. It is open to collaboration and partnership with stakeholders, both locally and abroad to improve the quality of services delivered to the poor. Such organisations include, Food for the Poor, which was involved in a massive programme to build 2,000 homes for poor families across Jamaica.

Main cities
Kingston (capital, estimated population 701,063 in 2005), Portmore (124,050), Montego Bay (108,968), Spanish Town (97,729).

Languages spoken
English and a local patois, influenced by Elizabethan English.
Official language/s
English

Media
The media is free from censorship, athough the government has wide involvement in television, it has little control over radio and none in the print media.
Press
Dailies: There of the three dailies, two are published in the morning, *The Jamaica Gleaner* (www.jamaica-gleaner.com) and *The Jamaica Observer* (www.jamaicaobserver.com), *The Jamaica Star* (an afternoon tabloid) (www.jamaica-star.com).
Weeklies: There are several publications for local communities as well as one national newspaper, *Sunday Herald* (www.sunheraldja.com), *North Star Times* and *Mandeville Weekly*. The *Xtra-News* (www.xnewsjamaica.com) is an entertainment magazine.
Business: The monthly *Investor's Choice* magazine serving a diverse audience. Daily and weekly newspapers have local business news articles.
Periodicals: A monthly magazine, *The Commentator* (www.thecommentatorjm.com) publishes submitted articles on a variety of historical and current topics.
Broadcasting
Radio: All radio stations are independently owned and commercially operated. RJR Communications Group (www.rjrgroup.com) operates Radio Jamaica with a network of three stations including RJR (www.rjr94fm.com) for news and talk radio, Fame FM (www.famefm.fm) for innovative music and Hitz 92. Other stations include NewsTalk (www.newstalk.com.jm), Kool 97 FM (http://kool97fm.com) and Irie FM (www.iriefm.net).
Television: There are three TV stations in operation, of which TVJ (www.televisionjamaica.com) and CVM TV (www.cvmtv.com) are the other major broadcasters providing locally produced and imported TV programmes, Love TV (www.love101.org) is a religious broadcaster. Cable and satellite TV is available for subscribers, including CETV, Hype TV and RJR (http://rjrgroup.com).
Advertising
Radio, television, the press and billboards are the major advertising media. Although radio and local TV provide the widest ranging of media options, new technologies such as the internet are attracting more advertisers and advertising revenue.
News agencies
National news agency: Jamaica Information Service
Other news agencies: Caribbean Net News: www.caribbeannetnews.com
Jamaica New Bulletin: (www.jamaicanewsbulletin.com)

Economy
The economy is primarily based on services (over 60 per cent of GDP in 2008), centred on tourism, while remittances and bauxite exports also provide valuable foreign earnings. Agricultural exports include bananas, coffee, sugar, rum and spices.
The economy has a history of low economic growth and high public debt, which has been exacerbated by the global economic crisis. Average GDP growth since 1991 was 1 per cent per annum and in 2008 public debt was 128.3 per cent of GDP. However, in mitigation for a seeming profligate economy, damage from hurricanes and tropical storms create economic shocks and adverse have caused continued impacts on the Jamaican economy. Tropical storm Gustav, which struck in August 2008, destroyed many plantations and halted all exports. This, along with costlier imports, was a major reason for the current account deficit in 2008 being 21.9 per cent of GDP.
GDP growth in 2008 was 1.0 per cent, down from 2.4 per cent in 2007. Inflation for the first half of 2008 was 11.5 per cent, sharply higher than the 4.7 per cent for the previous six months, accelerated by sharp increases in international commodity prices. Although inflation fell to 4.8 per cent in the last half of 2008, the depreciation in the exchange rate affected domestic prices so that inflation rose and the December year-on-year rate was 16.8 per cent from 2007.
Foreign exchange earnings are generated by agricultural products, tourism and the bauxite-alumina industry. As global commodity prices rose Jamaica benefited from increased earnings from its alumina, ethanol and mineral fuel exports. However as the global economic crisis deepened three of the four bauxite companies suspended operations in 2009 as worldwide demand fell.
Remittances in 2009 were US$1.9 billion and was estimated to have risen to US$2.0 billion in 2010; however, these figures are less than the US$2.18 billion that flowed into Jamaica in 2008. Tourist numbers increased in 2008, but only

through a greater number of stopover visitors, with a 3.1 per cent reduction in the average length of stay and a reduction of 7.7 per cent in cruise visitor arrivals.
The International Monetary Fund (IMF) advised the government in 2008 that Jamaica should reduce its public debt to GDP ratio to around 100 per cent by 2013; it should also tighten its monetary policy and let the Jamaican dollar find its own level in the world market, close fraudulent investment schemes which could have an adverse affect on macro-economics and take more control of supervision of financial conglomerates. The business environment continues to be affected by high levels of petty and organised crime, with observers monitoring the murder rate as closely as more orthodox indicators.

External trade

Along with 11 other members of the Caribbean Community and Common Market (Caricom), Jamaica operates within the single market (Caribbean Single Market and Economy (CSME)), which became operational in 2006. CSME includes the free movement of goods and services, a common trade policy and external tariff. There is a heavy reliance on commodity exports while its dependency on energy imports continues to cause severe balance of payments difficulties, although the PetroCaribe Energy Co-operation Agreement with Venezuela helps to ease these difficulties.

Imports

Principal imports are foodstuffs, petroleum, capital goods and industrial supplies, vehicles, machinery and transport equipment, construction materials and consumer goods.
Main sources: US (typically 40 per cent of total), Trinidad and Tobago (20 per cent), Venezuela (10 per cent).

Exports

Principal exports are alumina, bauxite and chemicals, rum, coffee, sugar, bananas and yams, manufactured clothes. An ethanol plant exported seven million barrels to the US in 2008 and earning around US$60 million in 2007.
Main destinations: US (typically 40 per cent of total), Canada (10 per cent), China (10 per cent).

Re-exports

Re-exports including chemicals, machinery, transport equipment and miscellaneous manufactures represent 3.5 per cent of total value.

Agriculture

Farming

The agricultural sector, including forestry and fishing, typically contributes 6.9 per cent to GDP and employs approximately 19 per cent of the workforce. Agricultural production is often affected by adverse weather conditions. Blue Mountain coffee, one of the most expensive in the world, is grown in Jamaica.

Fishing

Although most fishing is for domestic consumption, inland commercial fishing could be developed. The local freshwater fish industry has been able to increase production of fish in smaller ponds and cut its production cost by 30 per cent, thanks to new technology. Traditional ponds which occupy vast acreages, produce a negligible 6.25 fish per square metre. Latest technology put to use at the Longville Park fish farm, which consists of four concrete-lined ponds approximately 250 square metres in size with automated systems to monitor oxygen levels in the water and feeding, is likely to increase production up to 125 fish per square metre. Estimates show that annual output could increase to 6.6 million pounds of freshwater fish, enabling Jamaica to compete on the world market.
The typical annual marine fish catch is 4,660mt and 560mt shellfish.

Industry and manufacturing

The industrial sector typically contributes 35 per cent to GDP, of which manufacturing contributes 12 per cent. The sector employs around 8 per cent of the workforce.
The growth in cement production, in line with increased construction, and food processing were 2004 production leaders. Agro-industries dominate the manufacturing sector, particularly textiles, sugar refining, paper products, cigarettes and alcohol, particularly rum and beer. Of these the textile industry has declined under the impact of competition from producers with freer trade links to the US, such as Mexico.
Other important manufacturing industries (most of which are foreign-owned and heavily dependent on imported materials and components) include chemicals, machinery and tools, glass, cement and metal products. Industry in Jamaica has suffered from difficulty in competing with more efficiently produced imports. Other problems include the high cost of security due to instances of drug contamination of exports by smugglers.
The main capital-intensive industries are petroleum refining at Kingston (capacity 34,200 barrels per day), and the refining of bauxite for export. The emphasis of industrial policy during the 1990s was on expanding facilities at the Kingston and Montego Bay free zones, encouraging foreign investment in export-based manufacturing and exploiting opportunities offered under the Caribbean Basin Initiative (CBI).
In 2003, Alcoa Inc, the world's leading supplier of alumina, completed a 250,000 tonne expansion project at the Jamalco refinery at a cost of US$115 million. The revised tax arrangements, along with the expansion, lowered costs at the refinery by approximately 30 per cent. Further expansion of the Jamalco's Clarendon refinery was announced in July 2005 when a plan was agreed by Alcoa and the Jamaica government. This will add 1.5 million tonnes per year (mtpy) of capacity at a cost of US$1.2 billion, bringing the total capacity to 2.8 mtpy. The construction costs include a new power station and high hurricane wind and earthquake protection.

Tourism

Jamaica has been a leading Caribbean holiday destination for decades and has an established tourism infrastructure. It offers a wide range of accommodation and cultural and sports activities such as carnivals, yachting regattas and sports fishing. Jamaica was the home of the creator of James Bond, Ian Fleming and Noel Coward, whose home Firefly Estate is a national heritage site.
Jamaica's tourism sector is an important component of the economy and typically constitutes around 25 per cent of GDP, which despite the fall in visitor numbers due to the global economic crisis has remained relatively constant. In 2011, from January–August, visitor arrivals increased by 5.7 per cent over the same period in 2010; in August 2011 2,098,964 people had arrived compared to 1,985,784 in August 2010. Over 60 per cent of visitors come from the US and over 15 per cent from Canada. Europe accounts for 15 per cent of all visitors, of which the UK represents 10 per cent. Employment in the travel and tourism sector is typically 22.2–24.5 per cent. Foreign exchange earnings were US$2.128 billion in 2010 and was projected to be US$2.293 billion.
In October 2011 the tourism minister called on his Caribbean counterparts to address the adverse effect of the UK-applied Air Passenger Duty (APD) that levies an average of US$478 on a family of four flying economy class from the UK to the region.
Legislation was passed in October 2011 for gaming regulation and the opening of two casinos.
China has designated Jamaica as an approved destination for its holidaying citizens; Chinese visitors could swell arrival numbers by many thousands.

Mining

The mining sector generates around half of export earnings and contributes approximately 9 per cent to GDP. Mining and quarrying employs approximately 1 per cent of the workforce.

Activity is centred on the extraction of bauxite and alumina refining. Known reserves of bauxite are around two billion tonnes, although most is of relatively low quality. Other minerals exploited include gypsum, marble, silica and clays.

in 2005 a bilateral agreement was signed between China and Jamaica to, establish a bauxite mining and alumina refinery facility, projected to process 1.4 million tonnes of alumina a year.

Hydrocarbons

There are no known oil or natural gas reserves. Consumption of oil was 78,000 barrels per day (bpd) in 2008, all of which was imported. In 2005, Jamaica, plus a number of other Caribbean states, signed an agreement with Venezuela to establish PetroCaribe, a multi-national oil company, owned by the participating states. PetroCaribe buys low-priced Venezuelan crude oil under long-term payment plans. The state-owned Petroleum Corporation of Jamaica (PCJ) is responsible for the management, exploration and importation of oil. Around 48 per cent of all imported oil is used in the bauxite refining and alumina processing industry. A refinery is located in Kingston, which processes 36,000bpd of oil, all of which is consumed locally.

Coal imports were 44,000 tonnes in 2008, used in power generation.

Energy

Total installed generating capacity was 1,161MW in 2007, producing over 7.04 billion kilowatt hours (kWh). The commercial company, Jamaica Public Service Company (JPS) is the sole distributor of electricity and owns four power stations and an additional eight-hydropower stations producing only 23.8MW of electricity, but which have a further installed potential of 100MW. There are five alternative, private independent power producers.

Almost all the country's energy needs are imported, with an estimated 70 per cent of foreign exchange earnings spent on oil. Oil is supplied at concessionary rates by Mexico and Venezuela. The major consumer is the alumina industry, where energy accounts for around 48 per cent of production costs. There is a strategy to move from oil to liquefied natural gas as the country's main source of energy for electricity generation; however this is dependent on the construction of either an undersea gas pipeline from Trinidad and Tobago, or a liquefied national gas processing plant for supplies from elsewhere. Other renewable sources of power are being considered.

Financial markets

Stock exchange

Jamaica Stock Exchange (JSE)

Banking and insurance

The banking sector has undergone extensive restructuring since 1997, when the government intervened to prevent a complete collapse of the country's financial institutions. The sector's problems arose from a lack of proper risk management which created inherent weaknesses. These were exposed when the monetary authorities raised interest rates to stem the tide of inflation causing asset values to plummet. The restructuring of the financial sector was completed by the Financial Sector Adjustment Company (Finsac) in 2002 at an estimated cost of around 30 per cent of GDP. In the restructuring process, Finsac merged banks and sold them to the Royal Bank of Trinidad and Tobago. Consequently, foreign banks have a high presence in Jamaica, controlling around 80 per cent of total bank deposits.

Central bank

The Bank of Jamaica

Time

GMT minus five hours

Geography

Jamaica, with an area of 10,989 square km, is the third largest island in the Caribbean. Covered with dense tropical vegetation, it is 234km long and 82km across at the widest point. The island lies about 145km south of Cuba and 160km west of Hispaniola. Mountain ranges snake across the island from south-east to north-west, with many long spurs to north and south. The highest summits are at the eastern end of the island, with the Blue Mountain Peak the tallest at 2,256 metres. The longest river, the Rio Minho, flows south from its source in the centre of the country, and is 92km long.

Hemisphere

Northern

Climate

Jamaica is around 5 degrees south of the Tropic of Cancer and has a maritime tropical climate characterised by warm trade winds. Average coastal and lowland temperatures are around 27 degrees Celsius, with little seasonal variation. Mean annual rainfall is about 200mm, with the main rainy season in October and a second one in May. Jamaica may be subject to the tropical storms and hurricanes typical of the Caribbean basin weather system.

Dress codes

Dress codes are mainly informal. Officials wear a jacket and tie or loose-fitting lightweight clothes when the climate is hot and humid. A sweater is rarely needed, even on cooler evenings. Light rainwear is useful. On social occasions, dress as for business meetings unless otherwise indicated.

Entry requirements

Passports

Required by all, valid for six months from date of departure, except nationals of the US and Canada, who require only proof of identity and nationality, (all US and Canadian nationals require a passport for re-entry to their country from 2007).

Visa

No visa requirements for nationals of EU/EEA countries, North America, Australasia, and some Latin American and Asian countries. For details, see www.jhcuk.com/newguide-fr.html. Business visas require a letter from the employer, an itinerary and evidence of sufficient funds.

Currency advice/regulations

The import and export of local currency is prohibited. The import and export of foreign currency is allowed, subject to declaration.

Prohibited imports

Obscene images and publications. The following items are restricted and require permits: meat, ground provisions, fruit and vegetables, pharmaceuticals, firearms, used tyres, two-way radios, coconut derivatives, motor vehicles, explosives, bulk alcohol, sugar, human remains, pesticides and live animals.

Health (for visitors)

Mandatory precautions

A yellow fever vaccination certificate is required if arriving from an infected area.

Advisable precautions

Hepatitis A and B, tetanus, TB, typhoid and polio vaccinations are recommended. Drinking water from the public supply is safe.

Foreigners visiting the island can use public health services, but are advised to seek private medical attention. Insurance to cover the latter which can be expensive is highly recommended.

Hotels

Hotels and guest houses are graded and mostly geared towards holidaymakers. There are also numerous resort villas and apartments.

Public holidays (national)

Fixed dates

1 Jan (New Year's Day), 23 May (Labour Day), 1 Aug (Emancipation Day), 6 Aug (Independence Day), 25–26 Dec (Christmas).

Variable dates

Ash Wednesday, Good Friday, Easter Monday, National Heroes' Day (third Mon in Oct).

Working hours
Banking
Mon–Thu: 0900–1400; Fri 0900–1500. Branches of some banks open on Sat.
Business
Mon–Fri: 0830–1630/1700. Some offices open Sat.
Government
Mon–Fri: 0830–1630/1700. Some offices open Sat.
Shops
Mon–Sat: 0830–1630/1700.

Telecommunications
Mobile/cell phones
There are several GSM 850, 900, 1800 and 1900 services available throughout the country.

Electricity supply
110/220V AC, 50 cycles

Social customs/useful tips
Appointments should be made in advance. Punctuality is appreciated. An additional 10 per cent tip is usual, even where a 10–15 per cent service charge is billed automatically. Penalties for drug offences are severe, with possession of even small quantities possibly leading to imprisonment. Luggage should be packed without the help of others and only your own should be carried through customs.

Security
It is advisable not to walk around after dark due to street crime. Some parts of Kingston are considered dangerous even during the daytime, avoid exploring nightlife away from main hotels and restaurants, unless accompanied by Jamaican friends. Only taxis, authorised by the Jamaica Union of Travellers Association (Juta) should be used and preferably ordered through hotels.

Getting there
Air
National airline: Air Jamaica.
International airport/s: Kingston-Norman Manley International (KIN), 17km south-east of city, duty-free shop, bars, restaurants, bank, post office, car hire.
Other airport/s: Montego Bay-Sangster International (MBJ), 3km north of Montego Bay.
Airport tax: J$1,000.
Surface
Water: The island has several ports catering for international shipping and local ferries.
Main port/s: Kingston, Montego Bay, Ocho Rios and Port Antonio.

Getting about
National transport
Air: Air Jamaica serves several destinations. TimAir Ltd and International Air Link provide charter services.
Road: There is an extensive network of surfaced, all-weather roads, accounting for 70 per cent of the total of around 18,000km.
Buses: Minibuses in towns are generally cheap but crowded; in the country they are often considered slow, crowded and sometimes dangerous. There are regular, scheduled services over longer distances (eg Kingston-Montego Bay; journey time varies, to some extent dependent on route).
Rail: Jamaica has 272km of track. Passenger services have been suspended since 1992. A privately-owned portion of the network is used for transport of bauxite.
City transport
Taxis: All taxis have red PPV plates. It is advisable to negotiate fares (J$) in advance. Taxis in Kingston no longer use meters. A 10 per cent tip is usual.
Car hire
Widely available. International or national licence accepted; traffic drives on the left.

BUSINESS DIRECTORY
The addresses listed below are a selection only. While World of Information makes every endeavour to check these addresses, we cannot guarantee that changes have not been made, especially to telephone numbers and area codes. We would welcome any corrections.

Telephone area codes
International direct dialling code (IDD) for Jamaica is +1 876, followed by subscriber's number.

Chambers of Commerce
American Chamber of Commerce of Jamaica, Le Méridien Jamaica Pegasus Hotel, 81 Knutsford Boulevard, Kingston (tel: 929-7866; fax: 929-8597; e-mail: info@amchamjamaica.org).

Jamaica Chamber of Commerce, 85a Duke Street, Kingston (tel: 922-0150; fax: 924-9056; e-mail: jamcham@cwjamaica.com).

Montego Bay Chamber of Commerce and Industry, 4-7 Overton Plaza, PO Box 213, Montego Bay (tel: 952-6045; fax: 952-2784).

Banking
National Investment Bank of Jamaica, 32 Trafalgar Road, Kingston 10 (tel. 929-9050).

Bank of Nova Scotia Jamaica, Scotia Centre, Port Royal Street, Kingston (tel: 922-1000).

CIBC Jamaica, 23-27 Knutsford Boulevard, Kingston 5 (tel: 929-9310).

Citibank N.A., 63-67 Knutsford Boulevard, Kingston 5 (tel: 926-3270/3285; fax: 929-3745).

National Commercial Bank of Jamaica, The Atrium, 32 Trafalgar Road, Kingston 10 (tel: 929-9050).

RBTT Bank Jamaica, 17 Dominica Drive, Kingston 5 (tel: 960-2340; e-mail: rbtt@cwjamaica.com).

The Financial Sector Adjustment Company, PO Box 54, 76 Knutsford Boulevard, Kingston 5: (tel: 906-1809; fax: 906-1822; info@FINSAC.com).

Trafalgar Commercial Bank, 60 Knutsford Boulevard, Kingston 5 (tel: 929-3383, 929-3511, 929-3521; fax: 929-3654).

Central bank
Bank of Jamaica, Nethersole Place, PO Box 621, Kingston (tel: 922-0750; fax: 922-0854; e-mail: info@boj.org.jm).

Stock exchange
Jamaica Stock Exchange (JSE): www.jamstockex.com

Travel information
Air Jamaica Ltd, 72–76 Harbour St, Kingston (tel: 922-3460; fax: 967-3125; pr@airjamaica.com).

Jamaica Hotel and Tourist Association, 2 Ardenne Road, Kingston 10 (tel: 926-3635; fax: 929-1054; e-mail: info@jhta.org).

National tourist organisation offices
Jamaica Tourist Board, Knutsford Boulevard, Kingston 5 (tel: 929-9200; fax: 929-9375; e-mail: info@visitjamaica.com).

Ministries
Office of The Prime Minister, Jamaica House, 1 Devon Road, Kingston 6 (tel: 927-9941/3; fax: 929-0005).

Ministry of Agriculture, Hope Gardens, Kingston 6 (tel: 927-1731/45; fax: 927-1904).

Ministry of Education and Culture, 2 National Heroes Circle, Kingston 4 (tel: 922-1400/19; fax: 967-1837).

Ministry of Finance and Planning, 30 National Heroes Circle, Kingston 4 (tel: 922-8600/15; fax: 922-7097).

Ministry of Foreign Affairs and Foreign Trade, 21 Dominica Drive, Kingston 5 (tel: 926-4220/8; fax: 929-5112; e-mail: mfaftjam@cwjamaica.com).

Ministry of Health, Oceana Hotel Complex, 2 King Street, Kingston (tel: 967-1092; fax: 967-7293).

Ministry of Industry, Commerce and Technology, 36 Trafalgar Road, Kingston 10 (tel: 929-8990/9; fax: 960-1623; e-mail: gojmii@infochan.com).

Ministry of Labour and Social Security, 1f North Street, Kingston (tel: 922-9500, 967-1900; fax: 922-6902).

Ministry of Land and Environment, 2 Hagley Park Road, Kingston 10 (tel: 926-1590, 926-7008; fax: 926-2591; e-mail: mehsys@hotmail.com).

Ministry of Local Government, Youth & Community Development, 85 Hagley Park, Kingston 10 (tel: 754-0994; fax: 960-0725).

Ministry of Mining and Energy, 36 Trafalgar Road, Kingston 10 (tel: 926-9170/7; fax: 968-2082; e-mail: hmme@cwjamaica.com).

Ministry of National Security and Justice, Mutual Life Building, North Tower, 2 Oxford Road, Kingston 5 (tel: 906-4908/33; fax: 906-1724; e-mail: inform@infochan.com).

Ministry of Tourism and Sports, 64 Knutsford Boulevard, Kingston 5 (tel: 920-4956; fax: 920-4944; e-mail: opmt@cwjamaica.com).

Ministry of Transportation and Works, 1c-1f Pawsey Place, New Kingston (tel: 754-1900; fax: 927-8763).

Ministry of Water and Housing, 7th Floor, Island Life Building, 6 St Lucia Avenue, Kingston 5 (tel: 754-0973; fax: 754-0975; e-mail: prumow@cwjamaica.com).

Attorney General's Department, Mutual Life Building, North Tower, 2 Oxford Road, Kingston 5 (tel: 906-2416/7) and 79-83 Barry Street, Kingston (tel: 922-6140; fax: 922-5109).

Other useful addresses

All-Island Jamaica Cane Farmers' Association, 4 North Ave, Kingston 4 (tel: 922-3010; fax: 922-077).

Banana Export Co (BECO), 10 South Ave, Kingston 4 (tel: 922-5490).

British High Commission, Trafalgar Road, PO Box 575, Kingston 10 (tel: 926-9050; fax: 929-7869).

Cabinet Office, 1 Devon Road, Kingston 10 (tel: 927-9941/3; fax: 929-8459).

Cocoa Industry Board, Marcus Garvey Drive, PO Box 68, Kingston 15 (tel: 923-6411).

Coffee Industry Board, Marcus Garvey Drive, Kingston 15 (tel: 923-7211).

Jamaica Bauxite Institute, Hope Gdns, PO Box 355, Kingston 6 (tel: 927-2073; fax: 927-159).

Jamaica Exporters' Association (JEA), 13 Dominica Drive, PO Box 9, Kingston 5 (tel: 929-1292; fax: 929-831).

Jamaica Information Service, Kingston (tel: 926-3740, 926-3590; fax: 926-715).

Jamaica Manufacturers' Association, 85a Duke Street, Kingston (tel: 922-8880/2).

Jamaica Promotion Corporation (Jampro Limited), 35 Trafalgar Road, Kingston 10 (tel: 929-9450, 929-9452/6; fax: 924-9650; e-mail: jamprouk@investjamaica.com).

Jamaica Stock Exchange, 40 Harbour Street, Kingston (tel: 922-0806; fax: 922-6966; e-mail: info-jse@jamstockex.com).

Jamaican Embassy (USA), 1520 New Hampshire Avenue, NW, Washington DC 20006 (tel: (+1-202)-452-0660; fax: (+1-202)-452-0081; e-mail: emjam@sysnet.net).

Kingston Free Zone, Lot 27, Shannon Drive, Kingston 15 (tel: 923-5274).

The Planning Institute of Jamaica, 39 Barbados Ave, Kingston 5 (tel: 926-1480; fax: 926-4670).

US Embassy, Mutual Life Centre, 2 Oxford Road, Kingston 5 (tel: 929-4850).

National news agency: Jamaica Information Service, 58a Half Way Tree Road, Kingston 10 (tel: 926-3740; fax: 926-6715; email: jis@jis.gov.jm; internet: www.jis.gov.jm).

Internet sites

Export Jamaica: http://www.exportjamaica.org

Jamaica Stock Exchange: http://www.jamstockex.com

CVM Television: http://www.cvmtv.com/top_news1.htm

Jamaica and Jamaican Top 5 Sites: http://www.top5jamaica.com

Jamaicamarket (business gateway): http://www.jamaicamarket.com

Jamaica Promotions Corporation (Jampro) (export and investment promotion agency): http://www.investjamaica.com

Japan

KEY FACTS

Official name: Nippon or Nihon (Japan)

Head of State: Emperor Tsegu no Miya Akihito (since 1989)

Head of government: Prime Minister Yoshihiko Noda (DPJ) (from 30 Aug 2011)

Ruling party: Democratic Party of Japan (DPJ) (elected 30 Aug 2009)

Area: 377,728 square km (3,900 small islands)

Population: 128.06 million (2010; census)

Capital: Tokyo

Official language: Japanese

Currency: Yen (¥)

Exchange rate: ¥77.08 per US$ (Oct 2011)

GDP per capita: US$42,851 (2010)

GDP real growth: 4.20% (2010)

GDP: US$5,458.90 billion (2010)

Labour force: 65.90 million (2010)

Unemployment: 5.10% (2010)

Inflation: -0.70% (2010)

Balance of trade: US$90.97 billion (2010)

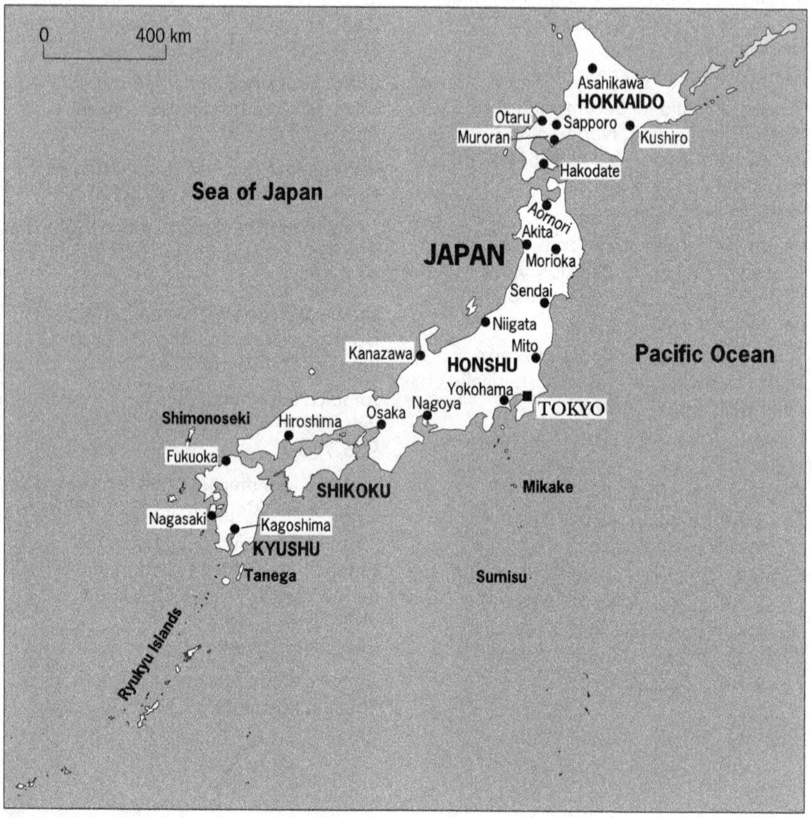

It came as no surprise when, in late August 2011 the Japanese prime minster, Naoto Kan, announced his resignation after only 15 months in office. The average length of tenure for a Japanese prime minister in the twenty-first century was 407 days. Mr Kan had managed 444 days. The uncertainty surrounding his departure had more to do with the possible identity of his successor. Mid-2011 Japan was still coming to terms with the consequences of the March earthquake, the resultant *tsunami* and the continuing crisis at the Fukushima Dai-ichi nuclear power plant.

Earthquake and *tsunami*

On Friday, 11 March, a 9.0 magnitude earthquake struck off the coast of Sendai, Japan, triggering a large *tsunami*. The earthquake and ensuing damage resulted in a shutdown of 6,800MW of electric generating capacity at four nuclear power stations that have a total capacity of 12,000MW (some plants were already offline for maintenance). Other energy infrastructure such as the electrical grid, refineries and gas and oil-fired power plants were also affected by the earthquake. Japan will likely require additional natural gas and oil to provide electricity, although power demand may be dampened at least in the short term as a result of the destruction of homes and businesses. The early radiation releases corresponded to about ten per cent of those emitted by the Chernobyl discharge.

If history is any guide, economic growth will be negatively affected until around mid-2011. The World Bank thought it likely that growth would pick up in subsequent quarters as reconstruction efforts, which could last five years, accelerate. The intensity of these efforts is likely to impact on the final cost of the disaster. While it is too early to estimate accurately, the cost of the damage is likely to be greater than the damage caused by the 6.9 magnitude Kobe earthquake in 1995. Private insurers are likely to bear a relatively small portion of the cost, leaving a substantial part to be borne by households and the government. After the Kobe earthquake, Japan's trade slowed only for a few quarters before recovering. Within a year, imports had recovered fully and exports had rebounded to 85 per cent of pre-quake levels.

Since 2006, developing East Asia's trade with Japan has accounted for about 9 per cent of the region's total external trade. On average, assuming Japanese real gross domestic product (GDP) growth slows by 0.25–0.5 percentage points by mid-2011, exports from developing East Asia may slow by 0.75–1.5 per cent. But this time around, disruption to production networks, especially in automotive and electronics industries, could continue to pose problems. Japan is a major producer of parts, components and capital goods which supply East Asia's production chains. In Thailand, exporters of cars initially reported that current supplies of components imported from Japan would last through to April. Some plants in Japan experienced shortages in parts sourced from the north-east quite soon after the earthquake. In electronics, Korean firms faced higher prices for memory chips, in part because Japan accounts for up to 36 per cent of global production and that production is now disrupted. Prices quickly rose by more than 20 per cent in some categories. China and the Philippines are more connected to developments in Japan than the rest of East Asia; in the Philippines, electronics exports account for two-thirds of total exports. In the short to medium-term, energy producers, such as Indonesia, Malaysia and Vietnam, could benefit from higher energy prices, as Japan begins to rebuild and tries to close the energy gap caused by the loss of nuclear capacity.

Growth shrinks

Japan's growth had begun to show signs of shrinking in late 2010, a trend that was dramatically accentuated by the earthquake. In April 2011, one month after the earthquake, Japan's consumer confidence index had plummeted down to 33.1; any reading below the level of 50 indicates consumer pessimism. At the end of March 2011, Japan's GDP had shrunk by 0.9 per cent for the first quarter of the year, pushing the annual contraction rate to 3.7 per cent. The end March figures meant that Japan was 'officially' in recession, after two quarters in decline. Reflecting the immediate effects of the earthquake, the contraction was inevitably bigger than most analysts had expected; average forecasts had put it at around 2 per cent. JP Morgan analysts forecast that the economy would contract by one per cent in the April–June quarter and by 3.5 per cent in the following three months. Takahide Kiuchi at Nomura calculated that a ten per cent cut in electricity usage by big companies could reduce industrial production by as much as 1.5 per cent. Perhaps whistling in the wind, economics minister, Kaoru Yosano, claimed that 'The economy has the strength to bounce back.'

Although both exports and private consumption were adversely affected by the earthquake, it was the latter that gave most cause for concern. Private consumption accounts for almost 60 per cent of the Japanese economy. Exports only account for 13.5 per cent of GDP, but were seriously affected by the earthquake; the cost of imports was already rising due to high commodity prices. This swing meant that Japan's trade surplus dropped by one third in March 2011 compared to the 2010 figure. Damaged production lines and supply chains in Japan's sophisticated 'just in time' economy meant that assembly lines soon came to a halt. At the same time extra imports of fossil fuels were urgently needed to offset the loss of nuclear generated electricity.

Kan-Can?

Mr Kan's approval ratings had sunk steadily as the crisis unwound. Many Japanese considered Mr Kan's move to break away from nuclear power a positive step. But the 'Yes We Kan' days were soon over, replaced by a perceived lack of leadership. Mr Kan certainly deserved some sympathy for the daunting array of problems that faced his premiership. An estimated 20,000 people were killed in the *tsunami* and the subsequent nuclear crisis brought unprecedented challenges. The divisions that arose within the ruling Democratic Party of Japan (DPJ) and Parliament were largely intractable. Unable to build any kind of consensus, Mr Kan appeared to have attracted the opprobrium of politicians, pundits and journalists alike. It was doubtful that his successor would be able to re-direct the course of Japanese politics. Some observers surmised that Mr Kan could remain in power for some months before actually stepping down, simply because his political opponents were happy for him to continue carrying the can for the administration's manifest failure to deal effectively with the crisis.

In May 2011 Mr Kan faced a divided parliament and what amounted to open revolt among some senior members of the ruling DPJ. Bravely, Mr Kan announced that he saw Japan's problems as going further than restoring the *status quo ante*: 'For the 20 years before this great earthquake disaster, our nation has seemed in many ways to be at an impasse. As we overcome the crisis created by this disaster, we must also overcome the preceding crisis, what could be called Japan's structural crisis.' Mr Kan went on to exhort the

KEY INDICATORS — Japan

	Unit	2006	2007	2008	2009	2010
Population	m	127.74	*127.76	*127.69	*127.56	128.06
Gross domestic product (GDP)	US$bn	4,377.05	4,383.76	4,887.00	5,068.10	5,458.90
GDP per capita	US$	34,150	34,268	39,731	39,731	42,850
GDP real growth	%	2.4	2.1	-1.2	-6.3	4.0
Inflation	%	0.3	0.1	1.4	-1.1	-0.7
Unemployment	%	4.1	3.9	4.0	5.1	5.1
Coal output	mtoe	0.7	0.8	0.7	2.8	0.5
Exports (fob) (goods)	US$m	615,810	678,090	746,470	545,280	730,080
Imports (fob) (goods)	US$m	534,510	573,340	708,340	501,650	639,100
Balance of trade	US$m	81,300	104,750	38,130	43,630	90,970
Current account	US$m	170,437	210,490	157,079	141,190	195,754
Total reserves minus gold	US$bn	879.7	952.8	1,009.4	1,022.2	1,061.5
Foreign exchange	US$bn	874.9	948.4	1,003.7	996.9	1,036.3
Exchange rate	per US$	117.24	113.35	103.36	93.57	87.78

* estimated figure

Japanese to mend their ways: 'We have to make new communities with greater dreams and more hope than they used to have.'

Tepco

In addition to his parliamentary problems, Prime Minister Kan had to defend his administration's handling of the nuclear crisis. At pains to dismiss allegations that his administration had played down problems at Fukushima, Mr Kan said that he had 'not once' sought to prevent the release of information. However much the administration appeared to be failing, it was as nothing compared to the disastrous performance of the power utility Tokyo Electric Power Company (Tepco). With unequalled ham-fistedness, two weeks after the March disaster, Tepco had submitted a proposal to the Tokyo ministries for the construction of two more reactors sited at the plant that was happily melting down. Tepco has form when it comes to a failure to come clean about disasters. Following an earthquake in Niigata prefecture, Tepco's president Masataka Shimizu (later to resign following the announcement of a US$15.3 billion loss, a record for a Japanese non-financial firm) was hauled over the coals for being economical with the truth over the release of radioactive material into the atmosphere at the Kashiwazaki-Kariwa nuclear reactor, one of the world's largest. Mr Shimizu had avoided earlier press conferences due to illness, but eventually made an appearance in mid-April 2011. His April appearance was only the second time he had faced the music since the earthquake; press comments later described his appearance at what is known in Japan as an *o-wabikaiken* (apology news-conference) as inadequate. Mr Shimizu talked of 'the situation gradually progressing toward stability' and claimed that Tepco had 'done its best'. He admitted that 'There may have been some things that were not adequately transmitted and for that I apologise.'

Described by the London satirical magazine *Private Eye* as having a 'semi-adjacent relationship with the truth', Tepco appears to have often sailed close to the wind. In 2000 Japanese nuclear safety inspectors were told by US engineers that Tepco had been hiding safety violations at its nuclear plants. The Japanese safety regulator promptly appointed Tepco as the investigating body. The same *Private Eye* article reported that as many as 21 problems had been reported at the Fukushima-Dai'ichi plant in a four year period. Whistle-blowers, it was reported, had complained directly to the then governor of the Fukushima prefecture (later forced into resignation) as they were concerned that Tepco and Japan's Nuclear and Industrial Safety Agency (NISA) would attempt to hush matters up. Part of the problem has been the long accepted practice of *amakudari* (literally 'descent from heaven') whereby senior civil servants secure director level positions at electric utilities after they retire. Data prepared by Japan's Communist Party suggest that Japan's ten electric utilities have hired a total of 45 retired civil servants to director level positions, including six who in 2011 held senior executive positions. Japan's opponents of nuclear power have also demanded the banning of *amakudari*.

When Tepco announced a loss of US$15.3 billion for the previous financial year (2010/11) the company's president, Masataka Simizu, resigned, to be replaced by Managing Director Toshio Nishiwaza. Discreet press announcements by Tepco indicated that some heads had rolled. One such announcement was to the effect that from 'December 1, 2011 commissioned work of executive officer will be changed as stated below since Mr Masao Yoshida (General Manager, Fukushima Dai'ichi Nuclear Power Station, Fukushima Dai'ichi Stabilisation Centre, Nuclear Power & Plant Siting Division) will be on sick leave.'

Tepco's overall output had fallen by as much as 40 per cent immediately after the earthquake and *tsunami* disaster. But to its credit, the company was able to recover about half the lost capacity by repairing *tsunami* swamped thermal generators and reinstating plants that had been closed for inspection. Even before the losses were announced and before the full scale of the damage at the Fukushima plant had emerged, Tepco had sought emergency funding of US$25 billion from three of Japan's largest banks.

Lights out

The spillover from the earthquake and *tsunami* meant that not just northern Japan, but also the capital city were placed on what resembled a wartime footing. Lights were dimmed or turned off completely. Entertainment events curtailed. Government buildings lacked heating and lighting, lifts and escalators immobilised. Rolling blackouts and power shortages meant closure for enterprises such as Disneyland. The power shortages may well have been a catalyst for social change in Japan. The concept of home working had never really been adopted in Japan, but companies quickly saw the advantages and adjusted their internal e-mail systems to allow it. As the summer approached and air conditioning looked like becoming a discarded luxury, for the first time Japan's 'salarymen' were allowed to work in their shirtsleeves.

Shadow Shogun

In most industrialised democracies, it is the ability, accomplishments and acceptance of the candidates that determines the selection of political leaders. Were that the case in Japan, the choice of the DPJ would probably have been the impressive Seiji Maehara, a former foreign minister, who at the age of 49 was surprisingly young by Japanese standards. Mr Maehara was certainly the front runner, who – as far as is possible in Japan – seemed to be in tune with his country's post earthquake mood. He advocated phasing out nuclear power over a twenty year period and increasing taxes to pay for earthquake relief and reconstruction schemes. But Mr Maehara lacked one critical element of support, that of the so-called 'Shadow Shogun' Ichiro Ozawa. Ironically, Mr Ozawa – an old school DPJ baron – was barred from standing following irregularities in the political donations he had received in earlier elections. But Mr Ozawa saw Mr Maehara as a rival and swung his significant support behind another of the four party candidates, trade and industry minister, Banri Kaieda. Finance minister, Yoshihiko Noda, was also seen as a moderniser.

Noda knows

In the event, it was the 54 year old Yoshihiko Noda that the Japanese parliament selected to be its sixth prime minister of the century. Mr Noda only narrowly edged out Mr Kaieda, winning after two votes by only 38 votes. Perhaps his biggest challenge was to repair the fractures of the DPJ, without which the electorate would be unlikely to regain confidence. The DPJ had only existed for thirteen years, during only two of which it had been in power. It had, however, already managed to disappoint the Japanese electorate. Alongside the priority of repairing his party and of greater importance to the electorate, came the question of Japan's nuclear plants. Following the March earthquake, Japan had lost an estimated 400 million kilowatt hours of daily electricity production as a result of the shutdown of all but 15 of the county's 54 nuclear generating plants. The cost to the

Japanese exchequer of this energy replacement programme did not bear thinking about. Annual fuel costs were quoted by government sources as rising by as much as US$39 billion. Any energy replacement programme was going to be costly and not just in money terms. Pollution would inevitably rise, delays would be inevitable however fast planning applications were pushed through. It was more than likely, in the post earthquake political climate that all the functioning nuclear plants would be closed down as their inspection dates arrived. The crisis has inevitably led to additional government spending which is pushing the country's public debt to higher levels. The world's third largest economy must consolidate its fiscal position over the medium term if it is to continue being a positive force in the region, said the International Monetary Fund (IMF) in its regular assessment of the country's economy. 'Japan needs to implement fiscal and structural reforms to strengthen the resilience and growth prospects of its own economy if it is to continue with its existing important, positive role,' said Mahmood Pradhan, the IMF mission chief for the north-east Asian country.

Japan's public debt is over 220 per cent of the country's GDP in gross terms – the highest level among advanced economies. In their report on the state of the Japanese economy, IMF economists proposed reforms to bolster confidence in public finances, including reining in social security spending, increasing the country's tax revenue and boosting growth through structural reforms.

An uncertain near term

Economic activity began to recover tentatively following the March earthquake and *tsunami*, but a high degree of uncertainty remained with the recovery dependent on the easing of supply bottlenecks, a stable long-term supply of electricity and the recovery of sentiment. Reconstruction spending was likely to further increase Japan's sizable public debt and the IMF predicted that Japan's GDP growth was likely to slow to -0.7 per cent in 2011 before rising to 2.9 per cent in 2012. The IMF also suggested that Japan's reconstruction spending could be financed by a modest increase in the consumption tax from 5 to 7–8 per cent in 2012, with a greater and continued increase up to 15 per cent thereafter. In the IMF's opinion, increased taxation of one sort or another was also needed to bring down Japan's high level of public debt.

Taxation reform

Given the limited scope for spending cuts, any fiscal adjustment would, in the view of the IMF, depend on limiting existing spending and finding new sources of revenue. Tax revenues could provide one such source. Japan has one of the lowest tax revenue levels in the world – about 17 per cent of GDP – thus creating ample space to use taxes as a way of consolidating the country's fiscal position. Japan's authorities have outlined plans to double the sales tax to 10 per cent to help meet its target of halving the primary deficit. This forms part of a package of measures unveiled in June 2011 which included reforms to social security spending, a proposal to raise the retirement age and adjustments to pension benefits.

In 2010, before the earthquake, Japan had looked on as China aggressively usurped its position as Asia's major power. In stark contrast to China's strong economic fundamentals, Japan's demotion to third place had followed the publication of growth figures for the second quarter of 2010 indicating that Japan had notched up a dismal 0.1 per cent advance over the previous quarter, well below even the most pessimistic forecasts and suggesting that in Japan the engines of recovery had simply stalled. Economists admitted to some degree of puzzlement over the response of the Japanese economy to the global crisis. Japan had been the first major economy to enter recession and was thought to have been the first to emerge from recession in 2009. The sustainability of the recovery appeared to have been jeopardised by the relentless appreciation of the yen, reaching a 15-year peak against the US dollar in mid-2010.

An opportunity in the face of disaster

In 2011 IMF economists welcomed the government's plan for fiscal consolidation, but called for more vigorous action to reduce public debt levels at a faster rate within the next five years. They believed the economic slowdown prompted by the earthquake provided an opportunity to kick-start much-needed structural reforms. The IMF reported that: 'Notwithstanding the large but temporary shock, the earthquake provides an opportunity to broaden and accelerate reforms in several areas.' Although in the short term, fiscal adjustment could reduce domestic demand, over the longer term, lowering the level of public savings would help improve confidence, spur investment and boost household incomes, suggested the IMF.

The IMF also considered that fiscal consolidation would also benefit Japan's partners by releasing a pool of savings for other countries to borrow and reducing risks from a disruption in the Japanese government bond market. On top of the cost to the exchequer of the earthquake, the Japanese economy was already battling a shrinking labour force and the priorities identified by the economists include boosting employment by raising labour participation among the elderly, young and women, pursuing trade liberalisation and promoting small-and medium sized company restructuring. Despite Japan's economic slowdown in recent years and the disaster in March, the IMF maintained the view that, as one of the largest and richest economies in the world, Japan remained an important contributor to regional growth and stability.

Energy

Japan was the third-largest net importer of oil in the world after the United States and China in 2009, having imported 4.3 million barrels per day (bpd). The country is primarily dependent on the Middle East for its oil imports, as roughly 80 per cent of Japanese crude oil imports originate in the region, up from 70 per cent in the mid-1980s. Japan is currently looking towards Russia, south-east Asia and Africa to geographically diversify its oil imports.

Japan has few domestic energy resources and is only 16 per cent energy self-sufficient. It is the third largest oil consumer in the world behind the United States and China and the third-largest net importer of crude oil. It is also the world's largest importer of both liquefied natural gas (LNG) and coal. In light of the country's lack of sufficient domestic hydrocarbon resources, Japanese energy companies have actively pursued participation in upstream oil and natural gas projects overseas and provide engineering, construction, financial and project management services for energy projects around the world. Japan is one of the major exporters of energy-sector capital equipment and has a strong energy research and development programme that is supported by the government, which pursues energy efficiency measures domestically in order to increase the country's energy security and reduce carbon dioxide emissions.

Japan's limited domestic oil reserves, were 44 million barrels in January 2011, according to the *Oil and Gas Journal*

(OGJ), well down from the 58 million barrels reported by OGJ in 2007. These oil reserves are concentrated primarily along the country's western coastline. Offshore areas surrounding Japan, such as the East China Sea, also contain oil and gas deposits; however, development of these zones is held up by competing territorial claims with China. While a preliminary accord was reached between the two governments in May 2008 over two fields – Chunxiao/Shirakaba and Longjing/Asunaro – in September 2010, Japan urged China to implement the agreement as tensions rose over the contested area.

Japan relies heavily on imports to meet its consumption needs. It maintains government-controlled oil stocks to ensure against a supply interruption. Total strategic oil stocks in Japan were 596 million barrels at the end of December 2010, with 54 per cent being government stocks and 46 per cent commercial stocks, according to the US government Energy Information Administration (EIA). Japan consumed 4.4 million bpd of oil in 2010, making it the third largest petroleum consumer in the world, behind the United States and China. However, oil demand in Japan has been declining since 2005. This decline stems from structural factors, such as fuel substitution, an aging population and government-mandated energy efficiency targets. In addition to the shift to natural gas in the industrial sector, fuel substitution is occurring in the residential sector as high prices have decreased demand for kerosene in home heating.

Japanese oil companies have also sought participation in exploration and production projects overseas with government backing. The government's 2006 energy strategy plan encourages Japanese companies to increase energy exploration and development projects around the world to secure a stable supply of oil and natural gas. The Japan Bank for International Co-operation supports upstream companies by offering loans at favorable rates, thereby allowing Japanese companies to bid effectively for projects in key producing countries. Such financial support helps Japanese companies to purchase stakes in oil and gas fields around the world, reinforcing national supply security while guaranteeing their own financial stability. The government's goal is to import 40 per cent of the country's total crude oil imports from Japanese-owned concessions by 2030, up from the current estimated 19 per cent.

Japan's overseas oil projects are primarily located in the Middle East and South-east Asia. Japanese oil companies involved in exploration and production projects overseas include Inpex, Cosmo Oil, Idemitsu Kosan Company, Japan Energy Development Corporation, Japex, Mitsubishi, Mitsui, Nippon Oil and others. Many of these companies are involved in small-scale projects that were originally set up by Japan National Oil Corporation. However, many are involved in high-profile upstream projects involving major investments in overseas ventures in recent years.

Risk assessment

Economy	Poor
Politics	Fair
Regional stability	Fair

COUNTRY PROFILE

Historical profile

1600 The unification of Japan began in the Tokugawa period (1600–1868), during which a national administrative hierarchy was formed.

1868 The restoration of the imperial family from political obscurity ended the Tokugawa Shogunate and began the Meiji era. Key reforms were initiated to orient Japan to the West and end centuries of isolation.

1894 Japan defeated imperial China in a brief war.

1895 China ceded Taiwan to Japan and allowed Japan to trade in China.

1904–05 Japan went to war with Russia and won.

1910 After three years of fighting, Japan annexed Korea.

1914–19 Japan had limited participation in the First World War on the side of Britain and the allies. The Treaty of Versailles gave Japan some territory in the Pacific.

1920–32 Since the late 1920s, extreme nationalism had increased. In 1931, Japan invaded Manchuria (northern China), renaming it and installing a puppet regime. The Japanese prime minister was assassinated in 1932 by ultra-nationalists. The military held increasing influence in the country.

1938–41 Japanese forces occupied large parts of China and south-east Asia, forcing the British out of Singapore, Malaysia and Hong Kong.

1945 Following its defeat in the Second World War, the subsequent armistice ceded control over many of Japan's outer islands, and the country was placed under US military occupation.

1947 Under direction and influence of the US occupying administration a new democratic constitution was enacted, with many aspects based on the US constitution. Foremost of which had Japan renouncing all military activity outside Japan and the Emperor being stripped of all political power; women were enfranchised and civil liberties were enshrined in law.

1951 Following the signing of the peace treaty, Japan regained its sovereignty. Sovereignty over the Tokara Archipelago and the Amami islands were also restored.

1955 The Liberal-Democratic Party (L-DP) was formed by a coalition of centre-right groups.

1956 Japan joined the UN.

1964 Prime Minister Hayato Ikeda was succeeded by Eisaku Sato, who was to become the longest-serving prime minister in Japanese history, remaining in office until 1972.

1972 The Bonin Islands and the remainder of the Ryukyu Islands (including Okinawa), which had been under US administration since 1945, were finally returned to Japan. Kakuei Tanaka became prime minister; he resigned in 1974.

1976 Kakuei Tanaka was arrested on charges of accepting bribes. The scandal damaged the L-DP, which, in the elections, lost its overall majority for the first time.

1983 Following seven years of judicial proceedings, Tanaka was found guilty of accepting bribes. He began appeal proceedings and refused to resign his legislative seat, forcing a premature general election.

1986 The L-DP recovered its absolute majority in the Diet

1987 The high court upheld the 1983 decision, finding Tanaka guilty of accepting bribes.

1989 The Showa era ended with the death of Emperor Hirohito, who had reigned since 1926. He was succeeded by his son, Akihito, beginning the Heisei era.

1993 The L-DP lost its majority in the lower house in the national elections and a coalition government was formed.

1994 Tomiichi Murayama, leader of the Social Democratic Party of Japan (SDPJ), became Japan's fourth prime minister in a year.

1997 Ryutaro Hashimoto of the L-DP were elected for a second term. The economy entered a severe recession.

1998 Keizo Obuchi succeeded Hashimoto.

2000 Obuchi died and was replaced by Yoshiro Mori. The L-DP lost its parliamentary majority, forcing Mori to rely on coalition partners.

2001 Mori, rocked by scandals and an unpopular image, resigned as prime minister and party leader. Junichiro Koizumi became prime minister and leader of the L-DP. He helped turn around the fortunes of the L-DP.

2002 Koizumi's opinion poll ratings plummeted as his 'reform' agenda prove unpopular.
2003 The L-DP was re-elected in the parliamentary elections.
2004 The opposition won the upper house partial elections; however, the L-DP-led coalition retained its majority in both houses. Japanese non-combat troops were sent to Iraq. Huge earthquakes killed 30 people in the north.
2005 Early elections were called after the prime minister's proposal to privatise Japan Post was defeated in the upper house. The L-DP won an increased majority in the Diet (parliament). Relations with China were strained as a result of controversial Japanese textbooks, Koizumi's visits to a war shrine commemorating war criminals and China's exploration of disputed areas of the East China Sea.
2006 Shinzo Abe won the L-DP's party presidency. Koizumi resigned from the premiership and was replaced by Abe. The Japan Defence Agency became the Ministry of Defence.
2007 Satsuki Eda (Democratic Party of Japan) (DPJ) became the first opposition politician to be president of the upper house. Shinzo Abe resigned as prime minister and Yasuo Fukuda (L-DP), was appointed as his successor.
2008 Indigenous people of the northern island of Hokkaido, the Ainu, were granted full recognition. A four-year bilateral dispute was settled when Japan and China agreed to the joint development of a gas field in the East China Sea. Fukuda resigned as prime minister and was replaced by Taro Aso.
2009 Following a decisive defeat for L-DP in local elections, Prime Minister Aso called early general elections, in which the opposition DPJ won a landslide victory with 42.4 per cent of the vote (308 seats of 480). Yukio Hatoyama (DPJ) was elected prime minister.
2010 Japan Airlines (JAL) filed for bankruptcy in January; it was the largest corporate failure in Japan's business history. The government decided to revitalise JAL with funds for reorganisation of US$3.3 billion, debt waivers of US$8 billion and a line of credit of over US$6.5 billion. It was estimated that around one-third of the workforce (of 45,000) would be make redundant due to the failure. Prime Minister Yukio Hatoyama resigned in June, following his inability to close the unpopular US military base in Okinawa, which had been an election campaign pledge, and a funding scandal involving government aides. Days later parliament elected Naoto Kan (DPJ) as prime minister. The state-funded deposit insurance agency announced that only the first US$120 million of depositor's money in the insolvent Incubator Bank of Japan (IBJ) was guaranteed to be refunded, while around US$130 million of 3,423 depositor's money was uninsured. The IBJ was a private lender to small businesses and the first bank failure since 2003.
2011 A massive earthquake, the biggest since 1871, of magnitude 8.9, struck offshore of the north-eastern coast of Honshu on 11 March. A *tsunami* that followed caused extensive damage onshore, not only killing thousands of people and leaving hundreds of thousands homeless, but also causing explosions in the Fukushima nuclear power station. Another earthquake of 7.1-magnitude hit on 11 April, causing localised damage. The severity rating of the nuclear crisis for the Fukushima nuclear plant was raised to the highest level for such accidents (seven) on 12 April. However officials said radiation leakage were a tenth of that from the 1986 Chernobyl disaster. On 21 April the government made it illegal to enter a 20km evacuation zone around the stricken Fukushima nuclear reactor. The government announced an emergency budget of 4 trillion yen (US$48.9bn) on 22 April. Monies intended for pension funds, child allowances and reducing highway tolls were diverted to the emergency budget. Analysts estimated that the final cost to the economy of the disaster could be US$309 billion. By the beginning of 1 May, 14,704 people were confirmed dead and 10,969 people were still missing and tens of thousands of people were in need of re-housing. The disaster was estimated to have cost Japan the equivalent of 6 per cent of its 2010 economic output and forced the economy to fall back into recession in the first quarter of 2011. In July, children that were living in Fukushima City (60km from the damaged Fukushima nuclear power plant) tested positive for trace amounts of radioactive substances. The sluggish economy and slow clean-up and recovery undermined the authority of Prime Minister Kan, who resigned on 27 August. He was replaced by Yoshihiko Noda (DPJ) on 30 August. Japan confirmed in early October that it would be sending its whaling fleet back to the Antarctic. The move was condemned by the New Zealand government while the anti-whaling campaiging group, Sea Shepherd, said they would continue to hassle the boats.

Political structure

Constitution

The Japanese constitution came into force in 1947. It may be amended only if the proposed alteration is passed with a two-thirds majority by the Diet (parliament) and then submitted to the people for ratification, either in a referendum or by election. Religion and state are constitutionally separate.
The imperial succession crisis caused by the lack of any male heir being born for over 40 years was eased following the birth of Prince Hisahito in 2006 (son of the Emperor's cousin), however since 2005 there has been much discussion about amending the constitution to allow equal primogeniture to allow the Emperor's daughter Princess Aiko to ascend to the imperial throne.

Form of state

Constitutional monarchy

The executive

Executive power is vested in the cabinet, which consists of the prime minister and not more than 20 ministers of state (including ministers without portfolio and the chief cabinet secretary) and is collectively responsible to the Diet.
By convention, the chosen president of the majority party becomes prime minister; the Emperor appoints the prime minister, who must already have been approved by the Diet. The prime minister appoints the cabinet, the majority of whom must be members of the Diet; the cabinet remains collectively responsible to the Diet.
The Emperor is the head of state under the constitution, but is primarily a national figurehead

National legislature

The bicameral Kokkai (National Diet) (parliament) is the highest organ of state power and the sole lawmaking authority, comprising two chambers, both directly elected by independent and separate voting systems. The Sangi-in (House of Representatives) (lower house), has 480 members, of which 300 members are directly elected in single-seat constituencies and 180 are elected by proportional representation within 11 multi-member constituencies; all members serve for four-year terms.
The Shugi-in (House of Councillors) (upper house) has 242 members, of which 96 are elected by proportional representation in a single nationwide electoral district. The remaining 146 are elected in 47 constituencies each returning 2–10 members. All candidates must be aged at least 30 years and voters must by aged at least 20 years. All members serve for a fixed six-year term, with an alternate half the number elected every three years. This chamber cannot be dissolved by the prime minister.
Both houses must be in agreement for legislation to be enacted, although when the Diet is in deadlock the lower house takes precedence.
Universal adult suffrage is from aged 18.

Legal system

The judiciary is independent, but the role of bureaucratic interpretation and the

reluctance of the Japanese to get involved in litigation mean that judges are less influential than in Western democracies. All judicial power is vested in the Supreme Court and four types of inferior court – High, District, Family and Summary Courts.
The judges of the Supreme Court, except the chief judge, who is appointed by the Emperor, are appointed by the cabinet. The judges of inferior courts are also appointed by the cabinet, but only from a list of persons nominated by the Supreme Court.
Last elections
30 August 2009 (parliamentary: lower house); 11 July 2010 (parliament: 50 per cent of upper house)
Results: Parliamentary (lower house): Democratic Party of Japan won 42.4 per cent of the vote (308 seats of 480), Liberal-Democratic Party 26.7 per cent (119), New Komeito Party 11.5 per cent (21), Japanese Communist Party 7 per cent (9), Social Democratic Party 4.3 per cent (7). Turnout was 69.3 per cent.
Parliamentary (upper house – 50 per cent of membership): the coalition of LDP, NKP and New Renaissance Party (NRP) won 105 seats overall (out of 242 in house); LDP won 51 seats (to achieve an overall 84); the NKP nine (19 overall), NRP 1 (2 overall), the coalition of DJP, PNP and New Party Nippon won 44, out of 110 overall (out of total 242 in house) DPJ 44 overall, PNP nil (three overall), NPN nil (one overall); Your Party (YP) 10 (11 overall), JCP three (six overall), SDP two (four overall), Sunrise Party of Japan (SPJ) one (three overall), Happiness Realisation Party one (one overall), independents two (two overall). Turnout was between 48–73 per cent.
Next elections
2013 (parliamentary: 50 per cent of upper house); August 2013 (parliamentary: lower house)

Political parties
Ruling party
Democratic Party of Japan (DPJ) (elected 30 Aug 2009)
Main opposition party
Liberal-Democratic Party (L-DP)

Population
128.06 million (2010; census)
Last census: 1 October 2010: 128,056,000
Population density: 337 inhabitants per square km. Urban population: 79 per cent (1995—2001).
Annual growth rate: 0.2 per cent 1994–2004 (WHO 2006)
Ethnic make-up
Japan is generally recognised to be racially homogenous, however there are small numbers of Ainu (indigenous people) and almost one million Koreans. The 1980s saw an influx of illegal immigrants into Japan, notably from the Philippines. Immigration levels have remained low relative to other industrialised countries, with non-Japanese making up only 2 per cent of the population.
Religions
Shintoism and Buddhism (majority), Christianity (minority). Many people profess both Shintoism and Buddhism, observing Shinto rites for birth and marriage and Buddhism for funerals. Both religions continue to play a significant role in cultural, philosophical and even business and political spheres. There are approximately 1.7 million Christians.

Education
Japan follows the American educational cycle of 6-3-3-4 years, where the six, elementary (primary) years and three junior high school years are free of charge and mandatory.
Even though competition is fierce, 97 per cent of students enrol for non-compulsory high school at aged 15. Valued places in prestigious high schools virtually guarantee a direct path into universities and other institutes of higher education. High school lasts for three years. There are a number of private international schools. At 62.6 per cent, Japan has the highest rate, of any industrialised country, for students going into higher education. There are three types of institutes of higher education: university, junior college and technical college.
There are also kindergartens for pre-school children, and miscellaneous schools for vocational and practical training, and special education schools for the physically and mentally handicapped.
Admission is highly competitive at every stage of schooling and there have been many critics who question whether the intensive school curriculum enables students to confront a dynamic, modern world. Changes have been introduced to encourage a greater flexibility in both teaching and learning. The academic year has been amended to five days a week and 210 days a year.
Public expenditure on education typically amounts to 3.6 per cent of annual gross national income.
Compulsory years: Six to 15
Enrolment rate: 101 per cent gross primary enrolment, 103 gross secondary enrolment; of the relevant age groups (including repeater) (World Bank).
Pupils per teacher: 19 in primary schools

Health
Medical facilities in Japan are excellent, with around 97 per cent of all medical services covered by plans such as National Health Insurance, which is also available to foreigners with residence or work visas.
Japan has a low fertility rate reflecting trends in all developed countries as its population ages rapidly. In a 2005 study the recorded number of Japanese men fell by 0.01 per cent, as the population rose by 0.05 per cent, these figures are the smallest seen (apart from the war years when statistics of military deaths were withheld) since records began in 1920. The fall in the number of men could be explained by many working abroad, however what is sure is the number of Japanese aged over 65, in 2004, reached a record high of 19.5 per cent, as those aged under 14 fell to an all-time low of 13.9 per cent. The concerns in the changing demographics has prompted reform of the state pension where amendments implemented in 2004 steadily reduce benefits, as premiums increase.
HIV/Aids
There are signs that the sexual behaviour of youth in Japan could be changing significantly and putting this group at greater risk of HIV infection.
HIV prevalence: 0.1 per cent aged 15–49 in 2003 (World Bank)
Life expectancy: 82 years, 2004 (WHO 2006)
Fertility rate/Maternal mortality rate: 1.3 births per woman, 2004 (WHO 2006); maternal mortality eight per 100,000 live births (World Bank)
Birth rate/Death rate: 1.26. In 2007 forecasters said the population could fall by 20 per cent by 2050.
Child (under 5 years) mortality rate (per 1,000): 3.1 per 1,000 live births (World Bank)
Head of population per physician: 1.98 physicians per 1,000 people, 2002 (WHO 2006)

Welfare
Japan's social security system is divided into five parts: public assistance, welfare services, social insurance (medical care, pensions, child allowances, unemployment insurance and workers' accident compensation), public health, public service pensions and assistance for war victims.
There are some 26,000 social welfare institutions (excluding day nursery facilities), of which around 16,600 are public and 9,400 private.
Pensions
The falling birth rate and ageing population has increased the pressure on the pension scheme, which relies on contributions paid by those working, too many of whom have opted out.

The welfare ministry estimates that social security costs will increase fourfold by 2025, from ¥65 trillion (US$608 billion) in 1995 to ¥274 trillion (US$2.6 trillion) in 2025. To compound the problem, the stagnating economy in the 1990s resulted in a huge pension liabilities gap – underfunded pension liabilities are thought to total ¥419 trillion (US$3.9 trillion). To fill the gap, the government has raised corporate taxes and scaled back the benefits.
The pension reform bill was opposed by those who claimed that the underlying assumptions on which it was based were flawed. About 40 per cent of self-employed workers are said to have failed to pay contributions, many believe they would be unlikely to see any retirement benefits. Without a unified pension, which covers all workers, the funding remains problematic, although a sales tax has been proposed to add to the funding.

Family support

A social security reform bill was passed in June 2004, in which corporate tax will be increased gradually from 13.58 per cent in 2004 to 18.3 per cent in 2017, while benefits will be reduced, with payments at only 50 per cent of the average take-home pay. Opposition say increased tax will encourage employers to hire part-time workers who are covered by another scheme.

Main cities

Tokyo, on Honshu, (capital, estimated population 8.3 million (m) in 2004); Yokohama, (3.5m); Osaka (2.6m) Nagoya, (2.2m), Sapporo (1.9m), Kobe (1.5m), Ome (1.5m), Kyoto (1.5m), Fukuoka (1.4m), Kawasaka (1.3m), Hiroshima (1.1m), Sendai (1.0m), Kitakyushu (1.0m).

Languages spoken

It is hard to operate in Japan without some knowledge of Japanese or the services of an interpreter.
Pupils are taught English in school for seven years but this involves a formal grammatical knowledge rather than spoken English.

Official language/s

Japanese

Media

Press

Around 80 per cent of the population read a daily newspaper, of which there are over 120 to choose from, with a combined publish run of around 70 million. In the largest markets, such as Tokyo, there can be three editions published per day. Nevertheless, the number of subscribers is declining and this trend is expected to continue.
Dailies: In Japanese (with English online editions) the major nationals include *Yomiuri Shimbun* (www.yomiuri.co.jp/dy), the leading newspaper with a circulation of around 10 million and is affiliated to Nippon TV, *Asahi Shimbun* (www.asahi.com/english) is affiliated to Asahi TV and *Mainichi Shimbun* (http://mdn.mainichi.jp) is affiliated to TBS. Other major newspapers are regionally based including *Hokkaido Shimbun* (www.hokkaido-np.co.jp), *The Kyoto Shimbun* (www.kyoto-np.co.jp) and *Sankei Shimbun* (www.sankei-kansai.com) from Osaka.
The *Japan Times* (www.japantimes.co.jp) is the only exclusively English language newspaper published, while Japan Today (www.japantoday.com) is a comprehensive online publication.
Weeklies: Some Japanese newspapers publish an English weekly edition. The *Tokyo Journal* (www.tokyo.to), *Tokyo Weekender* (www.weekender.co.jp) and *Metropolis* (www.metropolis.co.jp), are published for foreigners living in Japan, and in particular the capital.
There are weekend or Sunday editions of daily newspapers, including. *Aera* (www3.asahi.com) and *Sekai* (www.iwanami.co.jp).
Business: In Japanese, the *Nikkan Kogyo Shimbun* (www.nikkan.co.jp) and *Nihon Keizai Shimbun* (www.nikkei.co.jp) are leading financial newspapers from Tokyo of which *The Nikkei Weekly* (www.nikkei4946.com) is the English-language weekly edition of the latter. All quality newspapers cover business and economic news.
A trade-press of 7–8,000 publications covers most aspects of business and the economy.
The Japan Economic Institute of America (www.jei.org) publishes articles and analysis of the business environment from a US perspective.
Periodicals: Japanese Anime and Manga magazines featuring illustrative, cartoon stories are very popular and cater for all ages.

Broadcasting

NHK (Nippon Hoso Kyokai) (www.nhk.or.jp) is only one of five national terrestrial broadcasters all of which compete strenuously for audiences. TBS (www.tbs.co.jp) provides national radio and television services.
Radio: NHK (www.nhk.or.jp) has a network of three stations, Radio 1 for news a talk radio, Radio 2 for cultural and educational programmes and FM Radio for classical music. It also operates an external network, Radio Japan; the First Services broadcasts in Japanese and English to Asia and the Second Service which broadcasts in 20 other languages throughout Asia. There are numerous commercial radio stations located regionally including Tokyo FM (www.tfm.co.jp) TBS Radio (www.tbs.co.jp/radio), FM Cocolo (www.cocolo.co.jp) from Osaka, Zip FM (http://zip-fm.co.jp) from Nagoya and FMii (www.fmii.co.jp) from Morioka.
The American Forces Network (AFN) operates from US military bases, offering English-language programmes from Yokata Air Base (www.yokota.af.mil/afn).
Digital radio services are available, provided by all major broadcasters.
Television: NHK (www.nhk.or.jp) is the only public TV service, funded largely by a licence fee. It is at the forefront in providing new technological transmissions and analogue signals will be completely replaced by digitals signals by 2011. Japan was the first country to introduce high definition (HD) TV services and NHK has a channel exclusively for these transmissions. Of the other major national TV networks all are commercial, including Nippon Television Network (NTV) (www.ntv.co.jp), the Tokyo Broadcasting System (TBS) (www.tbs.co.jp), Fuji Television (www.fujitv.co.jp) and TV Asahi (www.tv-asahi.co.jp).
Locally produced TV programmes dominate the schedules and foreign shows may have an influence on production although they do not get screened.
Millions of viewers subscribe to cable and satellite TV.

Advertising

The advertising industry is governed by self-regulations. All the traditional advertising outlets are available through the press, commercial radio, TV and cinemas as well as outdoor advertising sites. New technologies are an important source of new advertising revenue.

News agencies

Jiji Press (in Japanese): www.jiji.com
Kyodo News: http://home.kyodo.co.jp
Nikkei Net (business and stock market news): www.nni.nikkei.co.jp

Economy

Japan's advanced industry-led economy is dependent on exports and between 2002, when it came out of a decade-long recession, and late 2007 the economy has grown steadily. However, the shock of the global financial crisis of 2008–09 left it in a precarious state, with a return to negative GDP growth in 2008 of -1.2 per cent; in 2009 growth contracted further falling to -6.3 per cent, before pulling out of recession in 2010 with growth of 4.0 per cent.
Inflation matched this trend, falling from 1.4 per cent in 2008 to -1.1 per cent in 2009. The government, in concert with other G8 countries, committed US$100 billion in a fiscal stimulus plan to fight deflation. The package followed three

months of the fastest ever contraction in the economy, with the trade deficit in January (US$9.9 billion) the worst since records began in 1980; exports of automobiles fell by 69 per cent (Toyota, the world's largest vehicle manufacturer, made its worst annual loss in 2008/09, losing a net US$4.4 billion, compared to record profits in 2007/08; as a result production was cut across a number of its manufacturing sites both in Japan and overseas). Exports in general dropped by 45.7 per cent. Industrial production fell by 10 per cent in January 2009, the fourth consecutive monthly drop in factory output. By August 2009 the economy had begun to pick up and GDP growth rose to 0.9 per cent in the second quarter. Deflation continued in 2010, at -0.7 per cent and, before the earthquake in March 2011, was expected to continue this trend.

On 26 January 2011, the international rating agency, Standard & Poor's, downgraded Japan from AA to AA-. The 2010/11 debt is almost twice the annual economic output and has been rising steadily since the mid-1990s.

The trend in unemployment continues to be upward with the annual average rate of 4.0 per cent in 2008 rising to 5.1 per cent in 2009 and remaining constant in 2010. However, as global trade has picked up the rate was forecast to fall to 4.9 per cent by 2011. There has been a corresponding change in work patterns, from long-term, full-time employment, to part-time, casual or contract employment. An emergency social safety net was introduced in 2009 to help alleviate the plight of newly unemployed workers, including measures to cover pensions, medical services and re-employment.

The Bank of Japan reacted to the economic crisis by implementing measures to reduce interest rates, ensure stability in financial markets and engender corporate financing, as well as buying up stocks held by banks and providing subordinate loans to banks.

An earthquake, the biggest since 1871, with a magnitude of 8.9, struck offshore of the north-eastern coast of Honshu on 11 March 2011, followed by a massive *tsunami* that caused extensive damage onshore not only killing thousands of people and leaving hundreds of thousands homeless but also causing explosions in the Fukushima nuclear power station. In response, the government announced an emergency budget of 4 trillion yen (US$48.9bn) on 22 April. Monies intended for pension funds, child allowances and reducing highway tolls were diverted to the emergency budget. On 21 March, the World Bank estimated that Japan may need up to five years to recover from the earthquake and *tsunami* that damaged industrial output, wrecking ports, steel works and vehicle parts and electronic manufacturing. Analysts estimated that the final cost to the economy of the disaster could be US$309 billion. By the beginning of May, 14,704 people were confirmed dead and 10,969 people were missing and tens of thousands of people were in need of re-housing. The disaster is estimated to have cost Japan the equivalent of 6 per cent of its 2010 economic output and forced the economy to fall back into recession in the first quarter of 2011. On 24 October 2011, the government approved a ¥12.1 trillion (US$157 billion) budget for the reconstruction of the area devastated by the March earthquake and *tsunami* and to decontaminate the damaged Fukushima nuclear power station. This was the third supplementary budget (and the second largest) ever to be presented to parliament.

Economic growth rebounded in the third quarter of 2011, recording 1.5 per cent after the previous three quarters of contraction.

External trade

Japan is a member of the Asia-Pacific Economic Co-operation (Apec) which is a forum for discussing regional economic, investment and trade matters. It does not belong to any free trade zone but does have bilateral trade agreements with several countries and regional blocs worldwide.

The open market economy is predicated on external trade, which provides around 25 per cent of GDP, allowing for the purchase of the raw materials that Japan does not produce; the majority of exports are finished goods. Japan is highly dependent on imported energy and minerals.

Japan has the world's largest fishing fleet which accounts for around 15 per cent of the global catch; the Japanese consume more seafood than any other nation. Japan is the second largest producer of paper (after the US).

On 16 February 2011, Japan and India signed a free trade agreement (FTA), which will cut tariffs on 94 per cent of goods by 2020. Among the goods to benefit textiles, pharmaceuticals and vehicles, as well as services, are prominent.

Imports

Principal imports are fuels, industrial raw materials, machinery and equipment, textiles, foodstuffs – rice, other grains, fish products, meat products, chemicals and non-ferrous ores and ash.

Main sources: China (typically 20 per cent total), US (10 per cent), Saudi Arabia (5 per cent).

Exports

Principal exports are vehicles and transport equipment, semiconductors, electronic and electrical machinery, optical and measuring equipment.

Main destinations: US (typically 20 per cent total), China (15 per cent), South Korea (10 per cent).

Agriculture

Farming

The agricultural sector accounts for approximately 1.5 per cent of GDP and employs around 7 per cent of the workforce (down from 50 per cent at the end of the Second World War). Most people in farm employment supplement their income with non-farm employment.

Only about 15 per cent of the land area is available for agriculture and stock-rearing and this is constantly in demand for residential use. Agriculture is highly intensive, making considerable use of technology and capital investment.

Wet cultivation of rice is the main activity (virtually self-sufficient), with a trend toward production of beef, citrus fruits and tobacco. Wheat, barley, soya beans, potatoes, sweet potatoes, vegetables, fruit, tea and silkworms are also produced.

The price of rice has declined and it is difficult for the paddy farmers to make a profit. In addition, consumers' tastes have changed and they are eating more potatoes, bread, pasta and noodles instead of rice.

Japanese farming is heavily protected by government subsidies and high import tariffs, despite the fact that Japan is dependent on food imports. The political influence of farmers has frequently stalled free trade negotiations with other countries which are deemed as competitors to the Japanese farming sector.

Fishing

Japan is one of the world's great fishing nations and there are some 3,000 fishing ports dotted around its coasts. Its methods of driftnet fishing, which drags up sea fauna indiscriminately from the ocean, have been criticised throughout the world. The establishment of 200-mile economic zones at sea by a number of countries has meant that Japan has had to go further afield for fishing grounds: half the catch now comes from outside Japanese waters and Japanese boats have increasingly been accused of predatory practices.

Fishing contributes substantially to domestic food supply and export earnings. Japanese fishermen catch pollack, pilchards, cod, salmon, mackerel and other fish throughout the north and central Pacific, and are second only to the former USSR in whaling. The total annual marine catch can be up to seven million tonnes per year, with a further 5 per cent of demand imported. Aquaculture is well developed and there are inshore fisheries for squid, clams, crustaceans, shallow-water fish and dolphins.

Japan remains a whaling nation and has been criticised for using overseas aid to manipulate countries into voting in favour of maintaining whaling in international waters. The typical import value of aquatic mammals amount to over US$176 million yearly, while total fish imports average over US$2 billion.

The Japanese whaling fleet set sail in 2007, with a quota to kill up to 1,000 whales. There was considerable international condemnation, especially from the US, Australia and New Zealand, of the inclusion of humpback and fin whales in the numbers to be killed. There had been a moratorium on commercial whaling since 1986, and on the killing of humpback whales 1963. The Japanese maintain that they are whaling in the name scientific research. By April 2008, the fleet had failed to reach its quota due to interference by anti-whaling activists, who took direct action to disrupt whaling.

Following the annual meeting of the Commission for the Conservation of Southern Bluefin Tuna (CCSBT), held on Cheju Island, South Korea, all members agreed to a 20 per cut in the roughly 17,000 tonnes in 2009 bluefin tuna catches from 2010. Scientists had warned that without a cut fish stocks could crash as numbers had become dangerously low.

Forestry

Japan is heavily forested, with forests covering around 66 per cent of the total land area. The variation in climate across Japan means that the country enjoys a diverse range of forests. Plantations account for around 44 per cent of total forested area. About 42 per cent of forests are in public ownership.

Japan is a major consumer of wood and paper products. Despite being heavily forested, Japan is one of the world's largest importers of forest products and by far the largest importer of tropical logs and wood products. The production costs involved in the extraction of Japanese wood are high, so the country is forced to rely on imports.

Industry and manufacturing

The industrial sector contributes approximately 40 per cent of GDP. Manufacturing employs nearly 24 per cent of the workforce, compared to 16 per cent in the US and an average of 18 per cent in OECD countries. In the past, industry has benefited from innovative technology and, in some less competitive sectors such as chemicals, aircraft and software, from considerable financial backing from the government. Japan has also traditionally led the world in automated production processes, which has helped to reduce the industrial workforce and redeploy workers into the tertiary sector.

Factory production shrank by 2 per cent in January 2008, from a 1.6 per cent growth in 2007. The recession in the US and a slower demand for electronics in Asia and Europe were blamed for the fall. Japan's export driven economy could suffer further from falling global demand, which may result in a fall in wage growth and less domestic consumption.

One of the main long-term problems in Japanese industry is its productivity. The Nikkei-300 non-financial companies have typically had a return on equity of just 4 per cent, compared to 20 per cent in the US. Since the mid-1990s, Japanese industry has failed to produce a positive spread between cost of capital and return on capital.

Part of the root cause of inefficiency is the prevailing culture. The Japanese are admired for their discipline and patience, but these qualities have not resulted in increased productivity; and whereas Japanese product innovation and development is excellent, sales and marketing have lagged behind. In uncompetitive, protected sectors, firms have paced their development to keep step with the slowest. Although the government, as well as companies themselves, is coming round to seeing the benefit of alliances with foreign firms in order to compete on the international stage, the process is slow. Moreover, communication issues surrounding Japan's complex corporate culture can act as something of a barrier to merger and acquisition activities between Japanese and foreign firms. Nevertheless, as the cross-holding structure typical of Japan's famous *keiretsu* groups (business networks which own stakes in one another as a means of mutual security) unravels, Japanese firms in general are coming under pressure to prioritise profits over their traditional relationships. Firms kept alive by their banks after they have lost all hope of financial viability – often termed the 'zombies' by Asian business journalists – will need to be closed or merged in order to restore investor confidence in the industrial sector.

The world's largest vehicle manufacturer, Toyota, made its worst annual loss in 2008/09, losing a net US$4.4 billion, compared to record profits in 2007/08. Production was cut across a number of its manufacturing sites both in Japan and overseas. However, Nintendo, the video games manufacturer, recorded its biggest profits in 2008/09 of US$2.79 billion, following the introduction of its successful Wii interactive console.

Tourism

Taiwan and Korea are the main sources of tourists to the country. Tourist arrivals number over 5.5 million, while the tourism sector was worth 3.5 per cent of GDP and provides over 2.5 million jobs and involving around 5 per cent of the workforce.

Mining

Mining accounts for 0.5 per cent of GDP and 1 per cent of total employment. There are few exploitable mineral resources. Molybdenum, manganese, zinc, copper and iron are mined on a small scale. Japan is self-sufficient in sulphur and limestone.

Hydrocarbons

Japan has virtually no domestic hydrocarbon reserves and must rely on imports for its needs; it is the world's third highest oil consumer (after the US and China) at 5.0 million barrels per day in 2007. Most of Japan's oil is sourced from the Middle East, however as this area is politically volatile and supplies may be subject to outside interference, Japan has been looking elsewhere for supplies. It entered into negotiations with Russia to buy Russian oil, via the as yet incomplete East Siberian-Pacific Ocean (ESPO) pipeline. An agreement for buying this oil would have included investment in completing the pipeline, but during the 2008–09 financial crisis, when Japan's economy contracted, China jumped in and signed a deal, on 18 February 2009, whereby the pipeline will be routed from its Russian terminal in Yakutia and south into China.

In June 2008, Japan and China agreed to jointly develop and share the profits of gas fields in the East China Sea, when production was 17.7 million cubic metres per day. Japan imported almost 89 billion cubic metres of liquefied natural gas from 13 different countries in 2007, the bulk of which was from other Asian countries.

All of Japan's coalmines are closed; there are reserves of 355 million tonnes of black coal. Coal imports account for 25 per cent of the country's electricity generation and most of it is imported from Australia.

Energy

Japan has a total generating capacity of around 238GW, producing over 1 trillion kilowatt hours (kWh). Around 60 per cent of total generation is produced by conventional thermal plants, 20 per cent by nuclear reactors, 19 per cent by hydroelectric dams and the rest from geothermal, solar and wind power. With 53 nuclear power plants, Japan is the world's third largest nuclear power consumer but plans to increase the number of reactors were suspended following public opposition, radiation leaks and faults found following an earthquake at Kashiqazaki, the major plant close to the capital.

Following the earthquake of 11 March 2011 and subsequent damage to the Fukushima nuclear power plant, its owners, Tokyo Electric Power (Tepco), announced on 30 March that it would decommission reactors 1–4, due to harmful levels of radioactivity detected in the power plant's location.

Liquefied natural gas (LNG) is also likely to become an important source of energy for electricity generation in the long-term. Japan's electricity prices are among the highest in the world, but prices are falling due to cuts in capital investment. The country is served by 10 vertically integrated utility companies which have monopolies over different regions; Japan has no national grid. The regional organisation of grids has a limited number of inter-connections. The utilities market has been de-regularised and made more efficient, leading to significant price cuts.

The Japanese government signed the Kyoto Protocol on reducing greenhouse gases and is committed to energy efficiency.

In July 2011 electricity supply was cut to large businesses in Tokyo by 15 per cent of their 2010 consumption, due to the fall in energy supply following damage to the Fukushima nuclear power plant.

Financial markets

Stock exchange

Tokyo Shoken Torihikisho (Tokyo Stock Exchange) (TSE)

Commodity exchange

The Tokyo Grain Exchange

Banking and insurance

In the 1990s the bubble burst in the Japanese economy and banks were the major casualties. They became burdened with huge amounts of non-performing loans (NPL) and bad debt.

In efforts to bounce back and also to prevent future risk, a series of mergers and takeovers took place in the banking sector. The fifteen banks that had existed during the financial crash were reduced to four. The biggest bank, Mizuho Bank, was created when Dai-Ichi Kangyo Bank, Fuji Bank and the Industrial Bank of Japan merged. The other three are: Mitsubishi Tokyo Financial Group, Sumitomo Mitsui Banking and the United Financial of Japan Group (UFG). However, the biggest 'bank' in the world is the Japanese post office, which is in the process of privatisation.

The Bank of Japan (BoJ) was granted independence from the government in 1998. However, in 2005 the government applied acute pressure to the BoJ to ensure that it did not raise interest rates above zero before economic growth was proven to be steady. The finance ministry reacted to the BoJ's reluctance by threatening to rescind its independence. The government's distrust of the Bank's monetary policy stems from 2000 when the Bank prematurely raised interest rates against the will of domestic finance officials and the IMF.

Central bank

Bank of Japan.

Main financial centre

Tokyo, Osaka and Nagoya.

Time

GMT plus nine hours

Geography

Japan lies off the north-east coast of Asia and consists of four main islands – Hokkaido, Honshu, Shikoku and Kyushu – and thousands of smaller islands running in an arc from north (latitude 45 33'N) to south (latitude 24 25'N). Japan is mainly mountainous with only 29 per cent of the national land area consisting of plains and basins. It has about 10 per cent of the world's active volcanoes and its highest mountain, Mount Fuji (3,776 metres), is a dormant volcano. Japan occupies less than 0.3 per cent of the earth's total land area: it is only 4 per cent of the size of the United States and one and a half times bigger than the United Kingdom.

Climate

The general climate is temperate, except for part of Hokkaido in the north and some of the southernmost islands. Spring is March–May, with average temperatures of 6 degrees Celsius (C) (minimum) and 21 degrees C (maximum). The rainy season is mid-June–mid-July. Summer is June–August, with temperatures between 20 degrees C and 28 degrees C. Autumn is September–November, with temperatures ranging from 10 degrees C to 24 degrees C. Rainfall is heaviest June and August–September. Winter is December–February, with temperatures from minus 5.1 degrees C to 16 degrees C. Annual rainfall is 1,000–2,500mm. South and central Japan can be subject to typhoons in late summer and early autumn.

Dress codes

In modern Japan, dark business suits and Western dress are the normal rule. Traditional Japanese dress consisted of kimonos for both men and women. On for formal occasions women often wear kimonos, while men usually wear morning dress, but occasionally also wear kimonos for weddings etc.

Entry requirements

Passports

Required by all. Passports must be valid for the duration of stay.

Visa

No visa requirements for citizens of most of Europe, the Americas, Australasia and some Asian countries, visiting for up to 90 days. For a full list, and application form, plus further information for those citizens not included on the list of visa-free travel, see www.mofa.go.jp/j_info/visit/visa/index.html.

Business travel is allowed for those enjoying visa-free travel for the minimum period. Those who do not must provide business letters, itinerary and invitations from Japanese hosts.

Foreigners arriving in Japan (both visitors and residents) are fingerprinted and photographed. The move was introduced in November 2007 as an anti-terrorist measure.

Currency advice/regulations

There are no restrictions on currency import or export. However, amounts in excess of ¥1 million (or equivalent) must be declared. All money exchanged must be through authorised banks and money changers. The money exchange counter at Narita airport is open from 0900–2300.

Travellers cheques are accepted in larger bank branches, hotels and duty-free shops. To avoid extra exchange fee, US dollars and Japanese yen are best.

Customs

Personal effects duty-free. Visitors may purchase souvenir items (pearls, cameras, transistor radios) free of sales tax at designated shops, but they must be taken out of the country within six months.

Prohibited imports

Firearms, ammunition, illegal drugs, pornography including films. Counterfeit or altered currencies. Animal, plant/soil and food products.

Health (for visitors)

There are no mandatory precautions. Japan has extensive health facilities with high standards, although medical services are expensive and insurance is essential. The International Association of Medical Assistance to Travellers provide English speaking doctors.

Advisable precautions

Inoculations may be useful for the occasional occurrence of typhoid hepatitis A and C and TB.

Hotels

Hotels should be booked well in advance. Service charges and taxes are added to the bill, and tipping is not customary. In addition to Western-style hotels, there are traditional Japanese-style inns (*ryokan*) in Tokyo and Osaka.

Credit cards

International credit and charge cards are widely accepted. ATMs, may not accept foreign cards, although Citbank ATMs do and are open 24 hours.

Public holidays (national)

Fixed dates

31 Dec–3 Jan (New Year holidays), 11 Feb (Foundation Day), 29 Apr (Greenery

Day), 3–5 May (Constitution Day/Citizens' Day of Rest/Children's Day), 20 Jul (Marine Day), 15 Sep (Respect for the Aged Day), 23 Sep (Autumnal Equinox), 3 Nov (Culture Day), 23 Nov (Labour Thanksgiving Day), 23 Dec (Emperor's Birthday).

With the exception of New Year's Day, if a holiday falls on a Sunday, the following day is treated as a holiday instead. When there is a single day between two national holidays, it is also taken as a holiday.

Avoid visits during Golden Week (Apr–May) and the Obon festive season (late Jul–third week in Aug), when everywhere is very crowded.

Variable dates

Coming of Age Day (Seijin-no-hi) (Jan), Vernal Equinox (Shunbun-no-hi) (Mar), Physical Fitness Day (Oct).

Working hours

Banking

Mon–Fri: 0900–1500.

Business

Mon–Fri: 0900–1700; Sat: 0900–1200 (most companies close on Saturdays).

Government

Mon–Fri: 1000–1700; Sat: 1000–1200.

Shops

1000–1900 (many closed on Wed or Thu).

Telecommunications

Mobile/cell phones

3G services are available in most cities.

Electricity supply

100V AC, 60 cycles in west Japan (Osaka) and 100V AC, 50 cycles in east Japan (Tokyo), with flat two-pin plug fittings.

Weights and measures

Metric system

Social customs/useful tips

The Japanese are a polite and reserved people. They do not expect overseas visitors to understand or adopt their customs – but they do value courtesy and friendliness and efforts to follow their customs are appreciated. The suffix san is added to the surname (ie Suzuki-san instead of Mr Suzuki) in polite conversation.

In most Japanese homes, in Japanese-style inns and frequently in traditional restaurants, it is taboo to wear outdoor shoes; instead slippers are provided. It is considered bad etiquette to step on the door sill or the borders of the *tatami* mats.

Japan has become thoroughly Westernised on the surface but the people still celebrate numerous traditional festivals. These range from the informal – cherry blossom viewing in the spring and kite flying – to formal festivals such as celebrating a person's coming of age.

The Japanese insist on punctuality and punctiliousness in business behaviour. It is essential to carry *meishi* or name cards (preferably with your name in Japanese on the reverse). When receiving name cards at formal meetings, the correct procedure is to study them carefully and then place them in front of you on the table.

Seating arrangements are particularly important in Japan. The place of honour is generally that furthest from the door.

Gift giving is a pleasant Japanese custom and for Japanese businessmen the exchange of gifts at New Year is very important. Ideally, gifts should consist of something personal, and be given, unopened, at the start of meetings. Whisky is now so widely sold and discounted in Japan that it is not a particularly attractive gift. When receiving gifts the Japanese practice is to treat them as objects of great reverence, but never to open them in front of the donor.

Late night business entertainment is common, but being invited to a Japanese home is rare. Restaurants are the usual venue for private social entertaining.

Drinking has its own rituals: it is bad manners for a visitor to pour a drink for himself. It is impolite to blow your nose in public. Kissing in public, standing too close to someone while talking and eating while walking down the street are also considered impolite. Do not point with your index finger – use the whole hand, palm turned upwards, in a flowing movement.

Security

Japanese cities are safe despite recent increases in crime. Burglaries are uncommon. Late night travel is usually perfectly safe, even for unaccompanied women, though drunks are to be avoided.

Getting there

Air

National airline: Japan Airlines (JAL); Japan Air System (JAS); All Nippon Airways (ANA)

International airport/s: Tokyo International, Narita (NRT), 60km east of Tokyo, with duty-free shops, bank/bureau de change (0900–2300), car hire, restaurants and tourist information centres with multilingual staff. There is a free shuttle bus connecting the two terminals.

Osaka Kansai International (KIX), 50km south-west of city; duty-free shops, car hire, banks/bureaux de change, tourist information (0900–2100) and bar/restaurant. Travel time by Nankai Express to Nama station in central Osaka 29 minutes. Tickets for trains, which connect with the Shinkansen Bullet train network, must be pre-booked.

Fukuoka, Itazuke (FUK), 10km from city; Nagoya, Komaki (NGO), 18km from city; Kagoshima (KOJ), 6km from city; Kumamoto (KMJ), 8km from city; Okinawa (OKA) 3km from Naha; Osaka International (OSA); Kobe; Kyoto.

Limousine bus services link Kansai International Airport with Osaka city centre and various other points including Kobe, Hikone and Nara.

Other airport/s: Haneda (HND), the former international airport, serves largely as a domestic airport, 19km south of Tokyo. China Airlines flights from Taipei, Taiwan, arrive here.

Airport tax: Tokyo Narita International Airport levies a tax of ¥2,040, which is usually included in the ticket price.

Getting about

National transport

Air: Most domestic flights from Tokyo to Osaka and other Japanese cities are from Haneda, 19km from Tokyo. Extensive air services provided by a number of local airlines link all main cities and provincial towns. Tickets can be purchased by automatic machines at Tokyo and Osaka International Airports' domestic departure counters.

Road: Road transport is the main form of domestic access. The network consists of 1.2 million km of road. There are good motorways linking Tokyo, Osaka, Kobe, Hiroshima, Yamaguchi, Shimonoseki, Moji, Fukuoka, Kumamoto and Morioka. Tolls are payable on certain roads.

Long-distance travel by road is not recommended (travel time from Tokyo to Nagasaki by car is 18 hours, by train 9 hours and by plane less than 2 hours), road signs are in Japanese and roads are frequently very crowded outside main cities.

Buses: An extensive network of frequent coach services link main centres via express motorways, but visitors are advised against coach travel in view of language difficulties and the complexity and number of routes available.

Rail: Japan Railways run national routes from the terminal located beneath the airport.

It is easy to travel by rail to all regions. Express and limited express trains are best for intercity travel with very frequent services run on the main routes. *Shinkansen*, the *Bullet Trains*, are the fastest, with compartments for wheelchair passengers, diners and buffet facilities. Supplements are payable on the three classes of express train and in green (first-class) cars of principal trains, for which reservations must be made well in advance; two pieces of ordinary luggage may be carried free, but there are restrictions on size and weight. Other types of train include *Tokkyu* (Limited Express), *Kyuko* (Express), *Kaisoku* (Rapid Train) and *Futsu* (Local Train). For short-distance trains, tickets can only be bought at vending machines outside train stations.

Long-distance one-way tickets generally do not permit stopovers and ticket refunds are not made after the time of the planned journey. Foreign visitors can make considerable savings by buying a Japan Rail exchange voucher, which is sold only outside Japan.

All Japan Railways (JR) stations display station names in both Japanese and Roman letters. The station's name is at the top centre of the signboard, in large letters; the names of the previous station and the next station are at the bottom of the signboard, in smaller letters.

Water: Jetfoil services to Kobe. There is also a jetfoil from Kansai International Airport to Osaka Port, with a journey time of around 40 minutes.

City transport

Taxis: Metered taxis can be easily hired in large cities at hotel entrances or by flagging them down in the street, but do not try to open or close the driver-controlled passenger door. Tipping is not required. Journey times: from Narita International Airport to Tokyo city centre around 90 minutes; from Kansai International Airport to Osaka city centre about 60 minutes. There is a surcharge after 2200 and an additional time charge is levied for traffic jams. Taxis are five times more expensive than trains.

Few taxi drivers understand foreign languages or read Roman lettering, so it is advisable to have your destination, including the name of a nearby landmark, written down in Japanese, along with the telephone number if possible. Hotels can often help with this. A map showing the location of the destination is also helpful.

Buses, trams & metro: Limousine buses depart several times an hour from Narita airport to city-centre hotels; journey time is about two hours. There is also a bus to the Tokyo City Air Terminal (TCAT). Tickets for all services can be bought in the terminals. Buses can be confusing and are best used with someone who knows the system.

Efficient underground railway services operate in Tokyo, Yokohama, Osaka, Kyoto, Kobe, Nagoya, Sapporo and Fukuoka, with station names displayed in Roman as well as Japanese lettering.

Trains: JR and Keisei railway lines provide frequent services from Narita airport to the city centre, journey time 60—90 minutes.

Car hire

An international driving licence is required. Driving is on the left. Chauffeur-driven cars are often recommended for visitors without command of Japanese and knowledge of the area, as traffic and navigation can be difficult. Symbolic road signs have the expected international meanings, but few signs are written in the Roman alphabet. A red triangle with white script means 'stop', while a white triangle with a red border and blue script means 'proceed slowly'.

BUSINESS DIRECTORY

Telephone area codes

The international direct dialling (IDD) code for Japan is +81, followed by area code and subscriber's number:

Fukuoka	92	Nagoya	52
Hiroshima	82	Okayama	862
Kawasaki	44	Osaka	66
Kobe	78	Sapparo	11
Kyoto	75	Tokyo	3
Nagasaki	958	Yokohama	45

Useful telephone numbers

Emergency
Police: 110.
Ambulance/Fire: 119
Overseas calls
Tokyo to south-east Asia: 3211-4211.
Tokyo operator: 0051.
Tokyo telegraph office: 3211-5588.
Nagoya telegraph office: 203-3311.
Osaka telegraph office: 228-2151.

Chambers of Commerce

American Chamber of Commerce in Japan, Masonic 39 MT Building, 2-4-5 Azabudai, Minato-ku, Tokyo 106-0041 (tel: 3433-5381; fax: 3433-8454; e-mail: info@accj.or.jp).

British Chamber of Commerce in Japan, Kenkyusha Eigo Centre Building, 1-2, Kagurazaka, Shinjuku-ku, Tokyo 162-0825 (tel: 3267-1901; fax: 3267-1903; e-mail: info@bccjapan.com).

Fukuoka Chamber of Commerce and Industry, 2-9-28 Hakata-ekimae, Hakata-ku, Fukuoka 812-8505 (tel: 441-1110; fax: 474-3200; e-mail: fksomu@fukunet.or.jp).

Kobe Chamber of Commerce and Industry, 6-1 Minato-jima Naka-machi, Chuo-ku, Kobe 650-8543 (tel: 303-5801; fax: 303-2312; e-mail: info@kcci-iic.ne.jp).

Nagoya Chamber of Commerce and Industry, 2-10-19 Sakae, Naka-ku, Nagoya (tel: 223-5611; fax: 231-6768; e-mail: info@nagoya-cci.or.jp).

Yokohama Chamber of Commerce and Industry, 2 Yamashita-cho, Naka-ku, Yokohama 231-8524 (tel: 671-7400; fax: 671-7410; e-mail: info@yokohama-cci.or.jp).

Banking

Mitsubishi Tokyo Financial Group, 1-3-2 Nihonbashi-Hongkucho, Chuo-ku, Tokyo (tel: 3245-1111; fax: 3246-1708); 7-1 Marunouchi 2-chome, Chiyoda-ku, Tokyo 100 (tel: 3240-1111; fax: 3211-6645).

Mizuho Bank, 1-1-5 Uchisaiwaicho, Chiyoda-ku, Tokyo 100 (tel: 3596-111).

Sumitomo Mitsui Banking Corporation, 1-2 Yurakucho, 1-chome, Chiyoda-ku, Tokyo 100-0006 (tel: 2501-1111).

Central bank

Bank of Japan (Nippon Ginko), 2-1-1 Nihonbashi-Hongokucho, Chuo-ku, Tokyo 103 (tel: 3279-1111; fax: 3277-1473).

Stock exchange

Tokyo Shoken Torihikisho (Tokyo Stock Exchange) (TSE): www.tse.or.jp

Stock exchange 2

Kabushiki-gaisha Osaka Shoken Torihikijo (Osaka Securities Exchange) (OSE): www.ose.or.jp

Commodity exchange

The Tokyo Grain Exchange: www.tge.or.jp

Commodity exchange 2

Tokyo Commodity Exchange (Tocom): www.tocom.or.jp

Travel information

Japan Airlines (JAL), Tokyo Building, Marunouchi 2-7-3, Chiyoda-ku, Tokyo 100 (tel: 3284-2610; fax: 3284-2659; internet: www.spin.ad.jp/jal/home-e.html).

Japan Automobile Federation, Shiba-Koen, 3-5-8 Minato-ku, Tokyo 105 (tel: 3436-2811).

Tourist Information Centre, 1-6-6 Yurakucho 1-chome, Chiyoda-Ku, Tokyo 100 (tel: 3502-1461); Kyoto Tower Building, Higashi-Shiokojicho, Shimogyo-ku, Kyoto 600 (tel: 371-5649).

Japan Travel Phone is a nationwide telephone service for English-language assistance and travel information. Available from 0900–1700 daily, the service is toll-free from outside Tokyo or Kyoto: information on eastern Japan: 0088-222-800 (or 0120-222-800); information on western Japan: 0088-22-4800 (or 0120-444-800). Tokyo: 3503-4400. Kyoto: 371-5649. Tokyo; French-language assistance: 3503-2926.

Tokyo: Japan Railways (JR) English-language information service, (Mon–Fri, except holidays) 1000–1800; reservations cannot be accepted by telephone service: 3423-0111. (Narita Express has a free phone connection to this service).

National tourist organisation offices

Japan National Tourist Organisation, 2-10-1 Yuraku-cho, Chiyodaku, Tokyo (tel: 3201-3331; fax: 3201-3347; internet: www.jnto.go.jp).

Ministries

Ministry of Agriculture, Forestry and Fisheries, 1-2-1 Kasumigaseki, Chiyoda-ku, Tokyo 100-8950 (tel: 3502-8111; fax: 3592-7697; e-mail: white56@maff.go.jp).

Ministry of Education, Culture, Sports, Science and Technology, 3-2-2

Kasumigaseki, Chiyoda-ku, Tokyo 100-8959 (tel: 3581-4211; fax: 3595-2017).

Ministry of the Environment, 1-2-2 Kasumigaseki, Chiyoda-ku, Tokyo 100-8975 (tel: 3581-3351; e-mail: MOE@eanet.go.jp).

Ministry of Foreign Affairs, 2-2-1, Kasumigaseki, Chiyoda-ku, Tokyo 100-8919 (tel: 3580-3311; fax: 3581-2667; e-mail: webmaster@mofa.go.jp).

Ministry of Health, Labour and Welfare, 1-2-2 Kasumigaseki, Chiyoda-ku, Tokyo 100-8916 (tel: 5253-1111; fax: 3501-2532).

Ministry of Justice, 1-1-1 Kasumigaseki, Chiyoda-ku, Tokyo 100-8977 (tel: 3580-4111; fax: 3592-7011; e-mail: webmaster@moj.go.jp).

Ministry of Land, Infrastructure and Transport, 2-1-3 Kasumigaseki, Chiyoda-ku, Tokyo 100-8918 (tel: 5253-8111; fax: 3580-7982; e-mail: webmaster@mlit.go.jp).

Ministry of Public Management, Home Affairs, Posts and Telecommunications, 2-1-2 Kasumigaseki, Chiyoda-ku, Tokyo 100-8926 (tel: 5253-5111; fax: 3504-0265; e-mail: feedback@mpt.go.jp).

Defence Agency, 5-1 Ichigaya, Honmura-cho, Shinjuku-ku, Tokyo 162-8801 (tel: 3268-3111; e-mail: info@jda.go.jp).

National Public Safety Commission, 2-1-2 Kasumigaseki, Chiyoda-ku, Tokyo 100-8974 (tel: 3581-0141).

Prime Minister's Office, 1-6-1, Nagata-cho, Chiyoda-ku, Tokyo 100-8914 (tel: 3581-2361; fax: 3593-1784).

Other useful addresses

Asian Development Bank, Japanese Representative Office, Second Floor, Yamato Seimei Building, 1-7 Uchisaiwaicho 1-Chome, Chiyoda-ku, Tokyo 100 (tel: 3504-3160; fax: 3504-3165; E-mail: adbjro@mail.asiandevbank.org).

Association for the Promotion of International Trade, Nihon Building, 6-2 Otemachi 2-chome, Chiyoda-ku, Tokyo (tel: 3245-1561).

British Embassy, No 1 Ichiban-cho, Chiyoda-ku, Tokyo 102 (tel: 3265-6340; fax: 5275-0346).

Council of All-Japan Exporters' Association, Kikai Shinko Kaikan Building, 5-8 Shibakaen 3-chome, Minato-ku, Tokyo.

Defence Agency, 9-7-45 Akasaka, Minato-ku, Tokyo 107-0052 (tel: 3408-5211; fax: 3408-6480).

Economic Planning Agency, 3-1-1 Kasumigaseki, Chiyoda-ku, Tokyo 100-0013 (tel: 3581-0261; fax: 3581-0838).

Environment Agency, 1-2-2 Kasumigaseki, Chiyoda-ku, Tokyo 100-0013 (tel: 3581-3351; fax: 3502-0308).

Fair Trade Commission, 2-2-1 Kasumigaseki, Chiyoda-ku, Tokyo 100-0013 (tel: 3581-5471; fax: 3581-1963).

Federation of Economic Organisations (Keidanren), 9-4 Othe-machi 1-chome, Chiyoda-ku 100, Tokyo (tel: 3279-1411; fax: 5255-6250).

Hokkaido Development Agency, 3-1-1 Kasumigaseki, Chiyoda-ku, Tokyo 100-8922 (tel: 3581-9111; fax: 3581-1208; e-mail: info1@had.go.jp).

House of Councillors, 1-7-1 Nagata-cho, Chiyoda-ku, Tokyo 100-0014 (tel: 3581-3111; fax: 3581-2900).

House of Representitives, 1-7-1 Nagata-cho, Chiyoda-ku, Tokyo 100-0014 (tel: 3581-5111; fax: 3581-2900).

Imperial Household Agency, 1-1 Chiyoda, Chiyoda-ku, Tokyo 100-0001 (tel: 3213-1111; fax: 3282-1407).

Japan Commercial Arbitration Association, Tosho Building, 2-2 Marunouchi 3-chome, Chiyoda-ku, Tokyo (tel: 3214-0641).

Japan Committee for Economic Development, Kogo Club Building 4-6 Marunouchi 1-chome, Chiyoda-ku, Tokyo (tel: 3211-1271).

Japan External Trade Organisation (JETRO), 2-5 Toranomon 2-chome, Minato-ku 105, Tokyo (tel: 3582-5511).

Japan Federation of Economic Organisations (Keidanren), 9-4 Otemachi 1-chome, Chiyoda-ku, Tokyo (tel: 3279-1411).

Japan Federation of Importers' Organisation, Nihombashi Daiwa Building, 1-6-1 Nihombashi Hon-Cho, Chuo-ku, Tokyo (tel: 3270-2020).

Japan Federation of Smaller Enterprise Organisation, 8-4 Nihonbashi Kayaba-cho 2-chome, Chuo-ku 103, Tokyo (tel: 3669-6862; fax: 3668-2957).

Japan Foreign Trade Council, World Trade Centre Building, 4-1 Hamamatsu-cho 2-chome, Minato-ku 105, Tokyo (tel: 3435-5952; fax: 3435-5979).

Japan Guide Association (interpreter and translation services), Shin Kokusai Building, 4-1 Marunouchi 3-chome, Chiyoda-ku, Tokyo (tel: 213-2706).

Japan International Co-operation System, 5th Floor, Shinjuku Sanshin Bldg, 4-9 Yoyogi 2-chome, Shibuya-ku, Tokyo 151 (tel: 5981-5988; fax: 5981-5994).

Japan Productivity Centre, 1-1 Shibuya 3-chome, Shibuya-ku 150, Tokyo (tel: 3409-1111; fax: 3409-4128).

Japan Securities Dealers Association, 5-8 Nihombashi Kayabacho 1-chome, Chuo-ku, Tokyo (tel: 3667-8459; fax: 3666-8009).

Japanese Embassy (USA), 2520 Massachusetts Avenue, NW, Washington DC 20008 (tel: (+1-202) 238-6700; fax: (+1-202) 328-2187).

Kansai Economic Federation, Nakanoshima Centre Bldg, 2-27 Nakanoshima 6-chome, Kita-ku, Osaka 530 (tel: 253-2351; 253-1678).

Management and Co-ordination Agency, 3-1-1 Kasumigaseki Chiyoda-ku, Tokyo 100-0013 (tel: 3581-6361; fax: 3593-1620).

Okinawa Development Agency, 1-6-1 Nagata-cho, Chiyoda-ku, Tokyo 100-0014 (tel: 3581-2361; fax: 3581-4783).

Science and Technology Agency, 2-2-1 Kasumigaseki, Chiyoda-ku, Tokyo 100-8966 (tel: 3581-5271; fax: 3593-1371; e-mail: www@sta.go.jp).

Statistics Bureau & Statistics Centre Management & Coordination Agency, 19-1 Wakamatsu-cho, Shinjuku-ku, Tokyo 162 (tel: 3202-1111; fax: 5273-1180).

Supreme Court, 4-2 Hayabusa-cho, Chiyoda-ku, Tokyo 102-0092 (tel: 3264-8111; fax: 3221-8975).

Tokyo International Trade Fair Commission, 7-24 Harumi 4-chome, Chuo-ku, Tokyo 103 (tel: 3666-0141, 3531-3371; fax: 3663-0625).

Tokyo Stock Exchange, 2-1 Nihombashi Kabutocho 1-chome, Chuo-ku, Tokyo (tel: 3666-0141; fax: 3663-0625, 3666-0141; internet: www.tse.or.jp).

West Japan Railway Company, 4-24 Shibata 2-chome, Kita-ku, Osaka 530-8341 (tel: 375-8981; fax: 375-8919).

World Trade Centre of Japan, 4-1 2-chome Hamamatsu-cho, Minato-ku, Tokyo (tel: 3435-5651).

Internet sites

Japan Company Record: www.japancompanyrecord.com/

Japan Hotel Association: www.j-hotel.or.jp

Japan Information Network: http://jin.jcic.or.jp

Japan Statistics: www.stat.go.jp/1.htm

JETRO Homepage (Japanese Trade Promotion): www.jetro.go.jp

Sanwa Bank: www.sanwabank.co.jp

Jordan

KEY FACTS

Official name: Al Mamlaka al Urduniya al Hashemiya (The Hashemite Kingdom of Jordan)

Head of State: King Abdullah II (crowned 1999)

Head of government: Prime Minister Awn al Khasawneh (from 23 Oct 2011)

Ruling party: National Constitutional Party (NCP) (pro-monarchy coalition formed from a union of independent members of parliament and nine centrist parties)

Area: 91,860 square km

Population: 6.11 million (2010)

Capital: Amman

Official language: Arabic

Currency: Jordanian dinar (JD) = 1,000 fils

Exchange rate: JD0.71 per US$ (Oct 2011)

GDP per capita: US$4,500 (20100

GDP real growth: 3.10% (2010)

GDP: US$27.50 billion (2010)

Inflation: 5.00% (2010)

Balance of trade: -US$6.65 billion (2010)

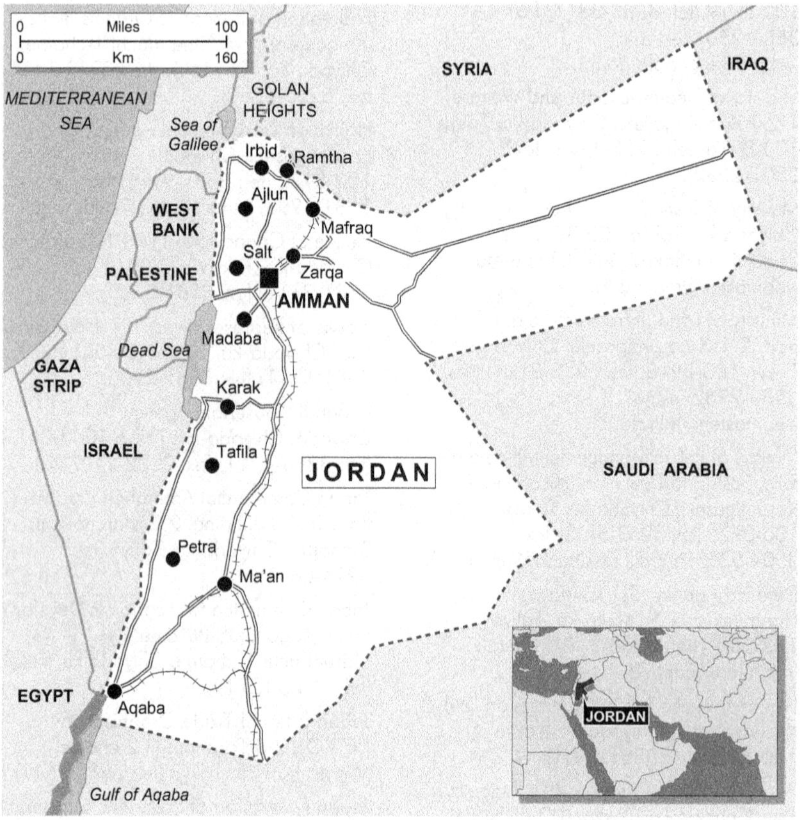

By regional standards, Jordan is not a wealthy country. It depends heavily on foreign financial support, making the importance of fostering good international relations primordial. To attract loans, grants in aid and foreign direct investment (FDI), Jordan also needs to address the perennial problem of a lack of transparency in its governance. This can be described as an occupational hazard in modern monarchies such as the Hashemite Kingdom. Lines of power – allegiances and loyalties – often need to be kept confidential.

Electoral system?

Thus when, in May 2010, the Kingdom of Jordan unveiled its new electoral system, it was met with an optimistic curiosity. Writing in *Foreign Policy*, Curtis Ryan noted that the response from advocates of reform was less than enthusiastic, the new law being variously described as 'disappointing' and even 'a disaster'. The underlying problem was that the new legislation touched a raw nerve in the ruling Jordanian elite. It risked both triggering domestic change in Jordan and at the same time whatever hopes remained for resolving the broader Israeli Palestine conflict. The law failed to address the question of proportional representation. Mr Ryan speculated that one of the possible objectives underlying the government's strategy was to secure the regime against challenges to the identity of Jordan as a Hashemite kingdom.

The protests that broke out in Jordan in January 2011, were both prompted and inspired by the waves of unrest – the Arab Spring – that was spreading across the Arab world in the wake of revolution in Tunisia. Paradoxically, the electoral reforms went some way to meeting the protestors' demands. In an initial response, at the beginning of February, King Abdullah II dismissed his cabinet and prime minister in a surprise move meant to calm the protests that have also been fuelled by Jordan's worst economic crisis in years. Fortunately, by luck or by effective policing, the demonstrations and counter-demonstrations that ensued were for the most part peaceful. At least until March, when at least one man died when government supporters attacked a tent camp that pro-democracy protesters had set up in the centre of Amman. The violence stopped when security forces intervened and a week later a new round of demonstrations went off peacefully.

As one observer correctly pointed out, changing cabinets is nothing new for King Abdullah. He has done so eight times in his 12 years on the throne. But this was the first time that he had done so in reaction to public pressure, seeking to undermine a growing protest movement across a broad spectrum of society and to pre-empt further unrest. It came after four weeks of unusual public demonstrations. In June 2011, King Abdullah finally confirmed that the government would henceforth be elected, not appointed, responding to a demand by protesters calling for democratic change. No timetable for the change was suggested. However, under pressure to accelerate political reform and introduce transparency measures, in October 2011 King Abdullah sacked his government yet again. In a statement announcing the change, King Abdullah said, 'We have accepted the resignation of Prime Minister Marouf al Bakhit, taking into consideration the views of the various sectors of society as well as a letter we have received from the parliamentary majority.' Mr Marouf's successor was the reform-minded Awn Khasawneh, a judge who had worked at the Hague-based International Court of Justice.

Faultline

Described by one Lebanese journalist writing in the *The Daily Star*, Beirut, as Jordan's 'faultline', the division between its East Bank and Palestinian citizens also poses something of a threat. To head off civil unrest, under the obvious guidance of King Abdullah, the Jordanian authorities expanded subsidies to the tune of US$1.4 billion and channeled tens of millions of dollars to develop provincial areas and offer more handouts to the East Bank citizens used to preferential treatment in state jobs. The moves defused some of the protests, but appeared not to stop East Bankers from seeking a bigger share of state munificence. The state's support of East Bankers, who exert political power in areas such as budget allocations and subsidies, has also revealed tensions between them and the majority population of Palestinian origin.

According to the article in the *The Daily Star*, East Bank Jordanian tribes, who form the bedrock of support for King Abdullah's Hashemite monarchy, felt threatened by falling state benefits brought about by the global financial crisis and economic reforms of previous governments, as well as any prospect for political empowerment of Palestinian Jordanians. The Palestinians dominate business but are under-represented in politics. The street protests centred on East Bank tribal strongholds as well as around Amman, where Palestinians – and Islamists, who form the most popular political force – are concentrated.

East Bank protests appeared to be motivated largely by concerns over state jobs and benefits that go to pro-state tribal leaders, rather than any sense of injustice in Jordan's electoral laws.

The economy

To head off the unrest, in 2011 the government had introduced extra social spending packages and subsidies from January, ranging from salary rises for civil servants to a freeze in gasoline price rises and lower taxes on basic commodities. The extra spending inflated the projected 2011 budget deficit to a forecast 6.2 per cent of gross domestic product (GDP). Officials hope that Gulf aid, especially from Saudi Arabia, will partially offset lower revenues and sluggish business. However, economic sanctions on neighbouring Syria, a major business partner, have reportedly had an inflationary effect, raising costs and dealing another blow to Jordan's already stagnant economy. Rising demands from Jordan's powerful state bureaucracy, combined with anticipated civil service salary rises, also looked more than likely to test the ability of the government to reduce spending. This has sent negative signals to Jordan's relatively vibrant private sector, which the treasury relies on to generate jobs and taxes, jeopardising the modest growth target of around 3 per cent in 2012, up from the lower forecast of 2.3 per cent for 2011.

In its early 2011 assessment of the Jordanian economy, the International Monetary Fund (IMF) noted that the global economic downturn had adversely affected economic activity in Jordan. GDP growth fell from almost 7.33 per cent in 2008 to 2.33 per cent in 2009, mainly due to weaker activity in the finance, manufacturing and trade sectors. Inflation declined steadily through 2009 to near zero, in line with lower commodity prices worldwide, although core inflation remained stable at around 3 per cent year-on-year by December 2009. For 2010 headline inflation increased to 5.0 per cent, roughly in line with imported commodity (energy and food) prices.

The Jordanian banking system remains sound and has proven resilient to the global financial crisis. The CBJ's prudent banking

KEY INDICATORS — Jordan

	Unit	2006	2007	2008	2009	2010
Population	m	5.60	*5.75	*5.85	5.99	6.11
Gross domestic product (GDP)	US$bn	14.10	17.00	21.20	22.90	27.50
GDP per capita	US$	2,519	2,971	3,262	3,829	4,500
GDP real growth	%	6.3	8.9	7.9	5.5	2.3
Inflation	%	6.3	5.4	14.9	-0.7	5.0
Industrial output	% change	11.4	8.4	8.5	1.0	–
Agricultural output	% change	5.4	1.0	1.4	18.4	–
Exports (fob) (goods)	US$m	5,204.4	5,700.0	6,365.6	6,365.6	7,028.3
Imports (fob) (goods)	US$m	10,260.2	12,021.0	12,497.5	12,497.5	13,678.7
Balance of trade	US$m	-5,055.9	-6,321.6	-6,131.9	-6,131.6	-6,650.4
Current account	US$m	-1,598.0	-2,933.0	-1,250.7	-1,250.0	-1,311.4
Total reserves minus gold	US$m	6,722.0	7,542.0	8,561.6	11,689.3	13,056.7
Foreign exchange	US$m	6,720.4	7,539.4	8,558.0	11,458.8	12,830.5
Exchange rate	per US$	0.71	0.71	0.95	0.71	0.71

* estimated figure

regulation and supervision and banks' conservative funding practices (with loan/deposit ratios near 75 per cent) have shielded domestic banks from exposure to troubled international banks, structured products and wholesale financial markets. The banking sector's macro-prudential indicators remain strong – banks remain profitable and well capitalised, deposits continue to be the major funding base, liquidity ratios and provisioning remain high, while non-performing loans (NPL) ratios increased modestly to 6.66 per cent of outstanding loans at the end of 2009.

Risk assessment

Economy	Fair
Politics	Poor
Regional stability	Poor

COUNTRY PROFILE

Historical profile

1928 Transjordan obtained qualified independence in a treaty with Britain.
1946 Transjordan achieved full independence as the Hashemite Kingdom of Jordan under the Emir, who took the title of King Abdullah.
1948 Jewish leaders announced the formation of the State of Israel in British-mandate Palestine and thousands of Palestinian Arabs fled to Jordan and the West Bank.
1950 A post-war agreement united Jordan with the part of Palestine remaining in Arab hands (the West Bank, including East Jerusalem, but excluding the Gaza Strip).
1951 King Abdullah was assassinated and was succeeded by his son, Talal bin Abdullah.
1952 Hussein bin Talal formally took power as King Hussein after his father, Talal bin Abdullah, stepped down due to mental illness.
1956 King Hussein banned political parties.
1957 British troops completed their withdrawal from Jordan.
1967 Six Day War with Israel. Israel occupied the West Bank and Gaza Strip and re-unified Jerusalem; around 300,000 Palestinian Arab refugees entered Jordan.
1970 Civil war (Black September) between the Jordanian army and Palestinians followed airplane hijackings by the Palestine Liberation Organisation (PLO) resistance group. The PLO was forcefully expelled from its bases in Jordan and moved to Lebanon
1972 An attempted military coup was thwarted.
1974 Jordan and other Arab countries recognised the PLO as the sole legitimate representative of the Palestinian people.
1978–84 The House of Representatives (parliament) was temporarily replaced during these years by a National Consultative Council appointed by the King.
1986 King Hussein severed political links with the PLO and ordered its main offices to shut.
1988 The House of Representatives was dissolved, prior to King Hussein's announcement of the severance of all administrative and legal ties with the West Bank. The King publicly backed the Palestinian *intifada* against Israeli rule.
1989 The first general elections since 1967 were contested only by independent candidates.
1992 Parliament authorised political parties for the first time since they were banned by King Hussein 36 years previously.
1993 Multi-party elections were held.
1994 The Jordan-Israel Peace Treaty was signed at Wadi Araba, Jordan, following the opening of the first border crossing between Aqaba (Jordan) and Eilat (Israel).
1997 The parliamentary elections were boycotted by nine opposition parties, led by the Islamic Action Front (IAF). The Islamists said the electoral law favoured the rural constituencies, where support for the King was strong, over the towns, where nearly half of Jordan's population lived. The elections were won by the National Constitutional Party (NCP), a pro-monarchy coalition formed from the union of nine centrist parties.
1999 King Hussein appointed his eldest son, Abdullah bin Hussein, as crown prince and heir, replacing Prince Hassan, the King's brother, who had been appointed crown prince in 1965. King Hussein, who had been treated for cancer for many years, died, and Abdullah bin Hussein was sworn in as King.
2000 King Abdullah II made a historic visit to the state of Israel. Jordan joined the World Trade Organisation (WTO).
2002 Senior US diplomat, Laurence Foley, was shot dead outside his home in Amman. Many political activists were arrested.
2003 King Abdullah II ratified an amended law adding six women members to the women's share in parliament. Independent candidates, allies of the King, won two-thirds of the seats in the parliamentary elections. The King appointed Faisal al Fayez as prime minister and three female ministers.
2005 Jordan returned its ambassador to Israel after a truce was signed by Israel and Palestine.
2006 The joint Jordanian-Syrian Wahdah Dam project was completed.
2007 New entry regulations stemmed the flow of refugees from Iraq; over one million Iraqis had taken up residence since 2003.
2008 George Habash, the (founder of militant Popular Front for the Liberation of Palestine) (PFLP) died in Amman. King Abdullah became the first Gulf-Arab leader to visit Iraq.
2009 By royal decree, Hussein bin Al Abdullah, eldest son of King Abdullah II, became Crown Prince and when he ascends to the throne, to become King Hussein II. Pope Benedict XVI visited, holding an open air mass for some 25,000 celebrants. The unemployment rate was estimated at 30 per cent. King Abdullah dissolved parliament and called for early elections. Prime Minister Dahabi resigned and Samir al Rifai was appointed as his replacement.
2010 In September, linguists warned that the Arab text was being side-lined in favour of Roman text, due to the increased use of internet and mobile (cell) phone text messages, where Arabic speech is transliterated into, typically, English. In September, talks with a French-Japanese consortium regarding Jordan's nuclear power programme entered its second stage, concerning commissioning the plant and logistics. The main opposition IAF boycotted parliamentary elections held on 9 November, one-year earlier than planned, calling them unfair, due to election laws that gave undue weight to votes from rural, sparsely populated areas. Of the 763 candidates standing for election, three-quarters were previous members of the legislature; all stood as independents. Only 17 candidates elected (out of 120 seats) were members of political parties; 78 elected candidates were new to parliament. Prime Minister Samir al Rifai and his new government were sworn in on 24 November.
2011 On 1 February, King Abdullah dismissed his cabinet and appointed a new prime minister, Marouf al Bakhit. On 12 June he announced that he will relinquish his right to appoint prime ministers, and future government cabinet posts will be formed by an elected parliamentary majority. On 25 July, Prince Rashid Bin El Hassan (son of the former Crown Prince El Hassan bin Talaal) married Zeina Shaban. On 17 October, Prime Minister Maarouf al Bakhit resigned and King Abdullah appointed a former judge of the International Court of Justice (ICJ), Awn al Khasawneh as prime minister.

Political structure

Constitution

Under a revised constitution of January 1952, the throne passes by male descent to heirs above the age of 18. A Regent or Council of Regency exercises power on behalf of the heir if he is below the age of

18 on succeeding to the throne. King Hussein's youngest brother, Prince Hassan, was Crown Prince between 1964–99, but in January 1999, a change was made to the constitution. The constitution previously required the meeting of a 'family council' to discuss a change of succession. Under the revision, King Hussein directly appointed his eldest son, Abdullah bin Hussein, as the new Crown Prince.
Jordan is divided into eight governorates, each headed by a governor and consisting of districts, sub-districts and counties. At local government level there are 152 municipalities, including Greater Amman, and 340 village councils. Local affairs are managed by city or village councils. Councils are under the supervision of the ministry of municipal and rural affairs.
A national charter, published by King Hussein in 1991, enshrined the principle of political freedom. It also underscored the ultimate power of the monarchy.
In February 2003, King Abdullah II ratified an amended law adding six women members to the parliament. This number was increased to 12 in the 2010 electoral law. The new law also increased the total number of parliamentary seats to 120, including adding four seats each to Amman, Irbid, and Zarqa. Nine seats are reserved for Christians and three more for Jordan's Circassian or Cherkess minority.

Independence date

25 May 1946

Form of state

Monarchy with limited parliamentary democracy.

The executive

The King is head of state and commander-in-chief of the armed forces.
The King has the power to declare war or conclude peace treaties, order elections, inaugurate, adjourn and prorogue the lower house of parliament as well as to appoint the prime minister, cabinet and speaker of the upper house of parliament.

National legislature

The bicameral Majlis al Umma (National Assembly) consists of the Majlis al-Nuwab (Chamber of Deputies) (lower house) with 110 members of which 104 are directly elected in single-seat constituencies including 13 seats reserved for Christians and Checkens/Circassians (nine and three respectively); six female members are selected by electoral college; and the Majlis al A'ayan (Assembly of Senators) (upper house) with 40 members appointed by the King.
Individual ministers or governments may be removed from office on a vote of no-confidence by the Chamber of Deputies.

Legal system

Judges are appointed by royal decree and are independent of the legislature and the executive. The King has the right of clemency and must confirm death sentences.

Last elections

9 November 2010 (parliamentary)
Results: Parliamentary: all candidates stood as independents.

Next elections

2011 (parliamentary)

Political parties

Ruling party

National Constitutional Party (NCP) (pro-monarchy coalition formed from a union of independent members of parliament and nine centrist parties)

Main opposition party

Islamic Action Front (IAF) (the political wing of the Muslim Brotherhood)

Population

6.11 million (2010)
Last census: October 2004: 5,100,981
Population density: 53 inhabitants per square km. Urban population: 79 per cent (1995—2001).
Annual growth rate: 3.1 per cent 1994–2004 (WHO 2006)

Ethnic make-up

The population is predominantly Arab, with small minorities of Circassians, Armenians and Kurds. No official figures are kept but it is generally accepted that Palestinians constitute 60 to 70 per cent of Jordan's population.

Religions

Over 80 per cent of the population are Sunni Muslims. There is a Christian minority, mainly Roman Catholic, Coptic and Greek Orthodox, and smaller numbers of other Muslims.

Education

The government has instituted a programme to revise and upgrade the state school system, involving teacher retraining, new curricula and substantial school construction. University students tend to concentrate on science, mathematics and computer programming. Consequently, Jordan has a steady supply of young people with the necessary skills in computer programming, as well as those with training in basic technical education.
Literacy rate: 91 per cent adult rate; 99 per cent youth rate (15–24) (Unesco 2005).
Compulsory years: 6 to 14; elementary aged 6–11 and preparatory 12–14.
Enrolment rate: 70 per cent for boys and 72 per cent for girls total primary school enrolment, (including repetition rates) of the relevant age group (World Bank estimates 1994–2000).
Pupils per teacher: 21 in primary schools.

Health

Improved water sources and sanitation facilities are available to 99 per cent and 96 per cent of the population, respectively.

HIV/Aids

HIV prevalence: 0.1 per cent aged 15–49 in 2003 (World Bank)
Life expectancy: 71 years, 2004 (WHO 2006)
Fertility rate/Maternal mortality rate: 3.4 births per woman, 2004 (WHO 2006); maternal mortality 41 per 100,000 live births (World Bank).
Birth rate/Death rate: 4 deaths and 30 births per 1,000 population.
Child (under 5 years) mortality rate (per 1,000): 23 per 1,000 live births (World Bank)
Head of population per physician: 2.03 physicians per 1,000 people, 2004 (WHO 2006)

Welfare

Social security in Jordan has few beneficiaries relative to contributing workers and it only first started paying benefits in 1995.
All workers in non-government establishments that employ more than five persons are obliged to contribute to the state social security fund. Those in smaller establishments may contribute voluntarily.
Lump-sum payments and hospital expenses are made in the case of work-related injury, death and retirement pensions. The Social Security Corporation (SCC) provides two types of insurance — old age disability and work-related injuries insurance. It collects revenues directly from wages and is not reliant on the government budget. It covers both the private sector and any public employees hired after 1995.

Main cities

Amman (capital, estimated population 1.3 million in 2004), Zarqa (512,200), Irbid (267,200), Aqaba (100,700), Salt (66,200), Mafraq (67,400).

Media

Press

A press and publications law was passed in late 1992. The law banned a wide range of items including those which harm the King or his family or reveal information about the armed forces. The ban on hurting national unity, insulting Arab or Muslim heads of state or transgressing so-called 'public ethics' caused the most controversy.
The law also forced all Jordanian journalists to become members of the Jordan Press Association and denies them the right to protect their sources. The law came as media activity surged with a dozen newspapers licensed or applying for licences and the legalisation of domestic satellite dishes opening Jordanians to uncensored world television.

The Jordan News Agency (Petra) provides news to local and foreign media. The Ministry of Information, which Petra had been a part of, ceased to exist in early 2002. A new media policy is being drawn-up by the Jordanian Media Higher Council, which was established in December 2001.

Dailies: Jordan has both Arabic and English dailies, all published nationally. The Arabic newspapers are *Sawt al Shaab*, *al Ra'i Daily* (both government-owned), *al Dustour*, *al Aswaq* and *al Arab Alyawm*. The English newspapers are *Arab Daily*, *Assabeel Jordan Times* and *Jordan Times*.

Weeklies: There are several weeklies in Arabic, including *Akhbar al Usbu*, *Amman al Masa*, *Assabeel Weekly* and *al Hawadith*. English language weeklies include *The Star* and there is also a French weekly supplement to *The Jordan Times*.

Broadcasting

Broadcasting is run by state bodies and the press is licensed by the government. Restrictions on the press eased considerably in the early 1990s and many areas have been opened to active discussion. A certain amount of self-censorship remains and some subjects – including information on military and security establishments and criticism of the royal family – are strictly taboo.

Radio: The state radio service broadcasts domestic and external programmes in Arabic and English.

Television: The state television service runs one Arabic channel and one foreign channel which broadcasts programmes in English, French and Hebrew.

Advertising

Advertising is handled through the private sector, and appears in newspapers and on the television and radio.

Economy

Jordan is poor in resources: unlike its neighbours it has no oil, water is scarce and agricultural land is limited. Its geographic location at the centre of the Middle East means that its fortunes are strongly influenced by regional circumstances. Unlike many Arab states, Jordan has strong trade links with its neighbours. Intra-Arab trade and remittances from overseas workers, especially those in the Gulf States, make a significant contribution to the economy. Jordan has long served as a transit route for goods destined for Iraq, from which it formerly received subsidised oil.

In 2008 the government removed subsidies on oil and foodstuffs which reduced its overall fiscal deficit and allowed for an increase in spending in 2009. GDP growth averaged 6 per cent over 2000–07 and despite the global economic recession growth was still 5.5 per cent in 2009. However, in line with the weaker global outlook, it dropped to 2.3 per cent in 2010. Inflation, jumped to 14.9 per cent in 2008, up from 5.4 per cent in 2007, but fell to -0.7 per cent in 2009; by 2010 inflation was 5 per cent.

In addition to substantial remittances from expatriate workers, tourism is a major earner of foreign exchange. Visitor numbers increased in 2006 by 13 per cent to 6.5 million. Jordan exports potash and phosphate, which are its only available natural resources, as well as fertilisers, pharmaceuticals, clothing and fruit. It is however, dependent on imports, especially for basic foodstuffs and oil and runs a large trade deficit.

The Islamic Development Bank (IDB) and the World Bank announced in October 2010, that they were setting up a regional initiative of up to US$1 billion to help close the infrastructure gap in the Middle East and North African region (Mena) and help boost economic growth. The World Bank considers that the Mena region requires US$75–100 billion per year to sustain the growth of recent years and boost economic competitiveness. Private sector investment is limited and the new initiative should address the shortfall in investment, through Shari'a-compliant and conventional investment. The initiative should benefit Egypt, Morocco, Jordan and Tunisia in particular.

Saudi Arabia has also agreed to give grants to Jordan to help its budget deficit. The grants were paid in two tranches of US$400,000 in June 2011 and US$1 billion in July, with more help provided through the supply of crude oil at a discounted price.

External trade

Jordan has signed the Agadir Agreement which proposes to set up a free trade zone (FTZ) between Egypt, Jordan, Tunisia and Morocco. In 2005 the Greater Arab Free Trade Area (Gafta) was ratified by 17 members, including Jordan, creating an Arab economic bloc. A customs union was established whereby tariffs within Gafta will be reduced by a percentage each year, until none remain. A new free-trade zone, including visa-free travel for their nationals, was agreed in June 2010, between Turkey, Lebanon, Jordan and Syria. A co-operation council will be established to 'develop a long-term strategic partnership' to encourage free movement of goods and persons.

It is also a signatory of the Euro-Mediterranean Partnership agreement, which provides for the introduction of free trade between the EU and 10 Mediterranean countries, including Jordan, by 2012.

Imports

Main imports are crude oil, textiles, machinery, vehicles, capital goods and manufactured goods.

Main sources: Saudi Arabia (typically over 20 per cent of total), China (10 per cent), Germany (5 per cent).

Exports

Main exports are manufactured clothing, phosphates, fertilisers and potash, vegetables, manufactured goods and pharmaceuticals.

Main destinations: Iraq (typically 15 per cent of total), India (15 per cent), US (10 per cent).

Agriculture

Farming

Jordan became a net importer of foodstuffs when it no longer had access to its principal growing areas on the West Bank of the River Jordan. More than 91 per cent of the total land area is classified as desert and only 6 per cent is cultivable. The sector is vulnerable to drought. Extreme variations in seasonal rainfall in the highland areas lead to severe fluctuations in yields from year to year. Highland farmers are one of the poorest groups in the country. Irrigated farming in the Jordan Valley has been a success in production terms, but marketing has suffered from periods of overproduction and fluctuations in exports.

Jordan has two distinct agricultural zones: the irrigated Jordan Valley and the rain-fed highlands. Government policy has been to encourage intensive fruit and vegetable growing in the Jordan Valley, both for local consumption and as a major export earner, and to boost cereal and fodder production in the highlands in an effort to reduce a high food import bill.

Farming is a private sector activity, but the state-owned Agricultural Marketing and Processing Company (AMPC) plays a regulatory role in fresh produce imports. The government buys cereal and fodder crops at fixed prices, with prices of other crops set according to supply and demand.

Since 1986, state land in southern Jordan has been leased to private farmers for sophisticated irrigation projects conceived at a time when the Arab world was placing heavy emphasis on food self-sufficiency. The projects rely on ground water reserves and there is increasing concern that the benefits of increased production are outweighed by the depletion of scarce water supplies.

Fishing

Jordan's only seaboard is in the south at Aqaba, on the Red Sea. The number of fishermen and vessels is negligible and the catches are consumed locally for the most part. A number of fish farming projects have been started, but with little success. The level of the Jordan river is frequently very low, contributing to the difficulties of fish farming. The majority of Jordan's fish for consumption is imported.

Forestry

Active afforestation programmes are under way in some areas in an effort to control soil erosion and desertification. There is little commercial exploitation of forests.

Industry and manufacturing

Jordan's geographical location has affected its trade and industrial development. The Iran-Iraq war (1980–88) and the Gulf War (1991), as well as the Israeli-Palestinian crisis, have restricted Jordan's trade. It is therefore understandable that the government believes that industrial expansion depends on developing new overseas markets beyond the region. The minerals sector has successfully developed secure markets in the Indian sub-continent and in South-East Asia. Most other Jordanian industry relies on highly volatile Arab markets. State industries have become a particular burden, with the Jordanian Water Authority accumulating debts of US$113 million.

Tourism

Tourism is the most important sector of the economy. The sector accounts for about 10 per cent of GDP and is the second highest earner of foreign exchange. Jordan has been experiencing a growth in tourism inspite of the regional conflicts. New resorts are being built along the Dead Sea and Gulf of Aqaba with luxury hotels, international retail outlets, sports facilities, entertainment centres and private residences. The resort of Ras al Yamaniya in Aqaba has been designated a duty-free zone to attract both visitors and investment. Urban regeneration has also been included in plans, by the antiquities ministry, to market Jordan, with Amman and Petra rivalling its coastal resorts as top holiday destinations.

Jordan joined the Euromed Heritage Programme, a computerisation project, sponsored by the EU, which focuses on cultural tourists of archaeology, arts and history, promoting sites through the internet.

Environment

Water is the single greatest challenge to Jordan's long-term well-being. The available figures on supply and demand present a disturbing picture. Agriculture remains the largest consumer of water resources, accounting for over 70 per cent of total water use. The acute water shortage means that Jordan is heavily reliant on ground water, of which 45 per cent is irreplaceable. In the long-term, water consumption at the present rates cannot be sustained. With an increasing population rate in Jordan, the government has estimated that per capita water supply will fall from the current 200 cubic metres per person to only 91 cubic metres by 2025.

A programme of dam building has improved supply but it is clear that a solution to the problem will have to come from better regional arrangements for water sharing. Jordan receives 215 million cubic metres annually from Israel through dams and pipelines. The Israeli-Palestinian conflict has not disrupted these water supplies and the government has done its utmost not to offend Israel over the conflict in order to prevent a repeat of Israel's decision in 1999 to cut water supplies to Jordan . The building of the Wahdeh (formerly known as Maqarin) dam on the Jordanian-Syrian border cannot proceed without the agreement of Israel, which stands to lose water as a result of the project.

The water and irrigation ministry has invested some US$5billion to boost supply, which will be invested in a number of projects until 2010.

Mining

The Jordanian government earmarked the mining and minerals industry as a priority sector for investment and development. The Natural Resources Authority (NRA) is the main policy-making body in the mineral sector, which promotes investment and undertakes operations. The agency has benefited from the UN Conference on Trade and Development's (Unctad) technical assistance and is able to attract foreign investment into the sector. The NRA has identified a range of metallic and non-metallic minerals, of which Jordan has substantial reserves. The EU is funding a project to identify the economic potential of non-oil mineral resources, including copper, a granitoid complex and ornamental stone.

The phosphate and potash industries in Jordan are key contributors to the economy. The Eshidiya deposit owned by Jordan Phosphate Mining Corporation (JPMC) has a proved phosphate reserve of 1,200 million tonnes. The Arab Potash Company (APC), which accounts for 4.4 per cent of the world's total potash production, produces 1.8 million tonnes of potash annually in Jordan. Almost 1.4 million tonnes is exported to 28 countries (mostly Asian).

The Jordan Safi Salt Company (Jossco) produces 1.2 million tonnes per year of industrial salt. Jordan is also an important exporter of calcium carbonate to other Middle Eastern states. Mineral production is largely of industrial minerals derived from the overlying sediments and volcanics. The most important mineral resources, which merit development and provide investment opportunities, are silica sand, tripoli, gypsum, ornamental stone (Ajlun limestone) and zeolite.

Hydrocarbons

Jordan, unlike its neighbours Iraq and Saudi Arabia, is not blessed with huge gas or oil reserves and has to import the bulk of its oil requirements to meet domestic demand. Imports were 106,000 barrels per day (bpd) of oil in 2007, costing the country US$4.3 billion.

Proven oil reserves are small and there is no oil production. The rise in global oil prices encouraged the consideration of production from oil shale, located in west central Jordan and amenable to open cast mining. The Dutch-oil company Shell signed an oil shale exploration agreement in July 2008 and was expected to invest US$20 billion within a period of 20 years. However, in November the government put an 18-month moratorium on such activity, in favour of uranium exploration.

Jordan had 6.2 billion cubic meters (cum) of natural gas reserves in 2007; production was 623,000 cum of natural gas from the Risheh field, for both domestic consumption as well as to a thermal power station. Jordan receives natural gas from Egypt, through the Arab Gas Pipeline (AGP), running from Egypt through Jordan and Syria and extending, by end-2008, to the border with Turkey. Jordan does not produce or import coal.

Energy

Total installed generating capacity was 1.9 gigawatts (GW) in 2006. Consumption has grown steadily from 5.7 billion kilowatt hours (kWh) in 1997 to 8.5 billion kWh in 2007. This is despite government policy which has been to restrain energy consumption while increasing efforts to develop domestic energy sources and lessen dependence on costly oil imports. The state-owned National Electric Power Company (Nepco) is split into three independent operating companies, responsible for generation, distribution and sales. The majority of electricity generated is supplied by three power plants, the Hussein Thermal Power Station outside Amman, the Aqaba Thermal Power Station in the south and at Rihab in the west. By late 2007, 85 per cent of all electricity generated was fuelled by Egyptian natural gas received via the Arab Gas Pipeline (AGP). The power grids of Jordan, Syria and Egypt are linked.

Other options for producing electricity are being considered, including solid waste, wind and biomass.

In January 2010 the government signed a US$178 million contract with a South Korean consortium to build a 5MW nuclear reactor by 2014, which will be used for scientific research before Jordan embarks on building its own nuclear power plants.

Financial markets
Stock exchange
Amman Stock Exchange (ASE)

Banking and insurance
Central bank
Central Bank of Jordan (CBJ)
Main financial centre
Amman

Time
GMT plus two hours (daylight saving GMT plus three hours)

Geography
Jordan is bounded by Syria to the north, Iraq to the east, Saudi Arabia to the south and Israel, the West Bank and Gaza Strip to the west. The only access to the sea is at Aqaba at the northern tip of the Gulf of Aqaba and about 400km south of the capital Amman.
There are three major geographical regions – the Jordan Rift Valley, the Eastern Uplands and the desert. Settlement is concentrated in northern and central sections of the uplands which run in a narrow strip from the Syrian border in the north to the Shubak/Petra area in the south.
Hemisphere
Northern

Climate
The climate is Mediterranean with dry, warm to hot summers and wet, mild to cool winters. There are noticeable variations due to altitude with temperatures in the Jordan Valley and Aqaba region around 10 degrees Celsius (C) higher on average than the highlands area throughout the year. Daytime temperatures in the highlands range from 25 to 32 degrees C in summer and from 7 to 15 degrees C in winter. Rainfall ranges from 40cm annually in the northern highlands to 10cm in the south and 20cm in the Jordan Valley.

Dress codes
Lightweight clothing is needed during the hottest months and warm clothing in winter when snow is not uncommon. Both men and women should dress discreetly in public.

Entry requirements
Passports
Required by all and must have at least six months validity.
Visa
Required by all, except most citizens of the Middle East. Many nationals may obtain a visa at the port of entry (for stays up to 14 days) and all others must apply in advance. Visit www.mfa.gov.jo and follow path from Ministry to Consular Affairs Department, for a full list of each category. Business visas should be applied for in advance and require a business letter outlining purpose of visit and an itinerary. Visas are not issued at the King Hussein Bridge across the Jordan River from Israel.
Currency advice/regulations
There are no restrictions on the import or export of foreign or local currency. Travellers cheques are accepted in banks.
Prohibited imports
Illegal drugs. Firearms require export permission for country of origin and prior approval for import into Jordan. Permitted weapons must be transported as baggage.

Health (for visitors)
Mandatory precautions
There are no automatic health checks at entry points, but travellers arriving from areas with infectious diseases such as cholera are expected to have had appropriate vaccinations. Travellers coming from an infected area require a yellow fever vaccination certificate.
Advisable precautions
Vaccination against typhoid, polio and hepatitis is advisable. Tap water is generally of a good standard, but short-stay visitors may prefer bottled water.

Hotels
There is a good selection of hotels in Amman. A number of new hotels are being built in Amman, around the Dead Sea and in Aqaba. The main tourist centres are Aqaba and the ancient city of Petra. A service charge of 10–12 per cent is usually added to the bill plus a government tax of 10 per cent on all services at three-, four- and five-star hotels and restaurants.
Extra tips are discretionary. Porters' and drivers' tips are about 8 per cent.

Credit cards
Major credit cards are accepted at hotels and restaurants.

Public holidays (national)
Fixed dates
1 Jan (New Year's Day), 30 Jan (King Abdullah II's Birthday), 1 May (Labour Day), 25 May (Independence Day), 14 Nov (King Hussein's Birthday), 25 Dec (Christmas Day).
Variable dates
Eid al Adha (four days), Islamic New Year, Birth of the Prophet, Ascent of the Prophet, Eid al Fitr (three days).
Islamic year 1433 (26 Nov 2011–14 Nov 2012): The Islamic year contains 354 or 355 days, with the result that Muslim feasts advance by 10–12 days against the Gregorian calendar. Dates of feasts vary according to the sighting of the new moon, so cannot be forecast exactly.

Working hours
Friday is the official day of rest.
Banking
0830–1230 (Sat–Thu); some banks open for two hours in the afternoon, generally from 1500–1700.
Business
Summer: 0800–1300, 1500–1900 (Sat–Thu); winter: 0800–1330 (Sat–Thu). During Ramadan, most firms operate only from 0900–1600. Christian businesses may close on Sunday afternoon.
Government
0800–1400 (Sat–Thu).
Shops
0800–2000/2100 or 0930–1330, 1530–1800 daily. Some shops close Fridays and public holidays.

Telecommunications
Mobile/cell phones
GSM 900 and 1800 services cover almost all of the country.

Electricity supply
Domestic 220V, 50 cycles AC. Industrial 220–380V 50 cycles AC.
Lamp sockets are screw-type, and there is a wide range of wall sockets. Bring a universal adapter.

Weights and measures
Metric system. Land is measured in dunums (1,000sq metres).

Social customs/useful tips
Jordanian society operates a mixture of traditional and modern attitudes and habits, and a foreigner needs to be aware which apply in any given situation. Business appointments are usually respected, though most people keep an open door and interruptions must be expected. All meetings are prefaced by an extended exchange of pleasantries allowing both sides the chance to assess each other. Tea and coffee are offered in all offices, and should be accepted; however, on the third or fourth appointment during a morning it is acceptable to excuse oneself and accept just a glass of water. It is still not customary to refer directly to a man's wife unless you have actually met her; it is safer to enquire after the welfare of 'the family'. It is forbidden to eat, drink or smoke in public in daylight hours during Ramadan.
Handshaking is the customary form of greeting. Jordanians are proud of their Arab culture and are hospitable and courteous. A small gift is quite acceptable in return for hospitality.
Islam plays an important role in society. Be discreet when drinking alcohol and do not drink in public places. Women are expected to dress modestly, and for both women and men beachwear must only be worn on the beach or by the poolside.

Security
Visitors should keep in touch with developments in the Middle East as any increase in regional tension might affect travel advice.
Street crime is rare in Jordan, with mugging virtually unheard of. However, housebreaking and car theft is on the increase and reasonable precautions must be observed. There are occasional small-scale bomb attacks against cinemas and nightclubs in Amman. Women do not usually walk alone in Amman after about 2200, but driving alone is safe. A woman alone wanting a taxi late at night is advised to telephone a taxi office with which she is familiar.

Getting there
Air
National airline: Royal Jordanian Airlines
International airport/s: Amman-Queen Alia International (AMM), 32km east of Amman (35 minutes from city centre).
Airport tax: Departure tax: JD4
Surface
Road: King Hussein Bridge is the only way to cross the Jordan river from Israel, and only the official minibus services are allowed to cross it. There are also buses and taxis from Syria, where the only border crossing point is at Ramtha/Der'a. There are a number of routes into Jordan from Jeddah and Riyadh in Saudi Arabia.
Rail: There is an elderly and decrepit rail link between Damascus (Syria) and Mecca (Saudi Arabia), via Amman but the journey time can be two–three times the length of time taken to drive the same route.
Water: There are ferry services, including car ferries, between Aqaba and Nuweiba in Egypt.
Main port/s: Aqaba is the country's only port.

Getting about
National transport
Air: The only internal air route is between Amman and Aqaba. Royal Jordanian Airlines operate regular flights. Arab Wings offer a charter service.
Road: The road network is good, with well-surfaced main roads connecting all the major towns and cities.
Buses: The Jordanian Express Tourist Transport Company (Jett) runs extensive services.
Rail: The rail network is no longer viable for the traveller.
Water: There are no passenger services along the Jordan river.
City transport
Taxis: Metered taxis are readily available in Amman and other cities (do not let your driver forget to switch on his meter). Can be hired for the journey or the day for an agreed sum. Do not use a taxi without a meter before agreeing the fare with the driver. There are also many service taxis offering a standard charge for any journey. Since there are few street names outside Amman, destinations are generally described in relation to landmarks.
Tipping is approximately 10 per cent.
Car hire
National or international driving licence required. Driver must be at least 25 years old and not over 60. Speed limit is 100kph. Insurance is compulsory.

BUSINESS DIRECTORY

The addresses listed below are a selection only. While World of Information makes every endeavour to check these addresses, we cannot guarantee that changes have not been made, especially to telephone numbers and area codes. We would welcome any corrections.

Telephone area codes
The international direct dialling (IDD) code for Jordan is +962 followed by the area code:

Amman	6	Madaba	8
Aqaba	3	Mafraq	4
Balga (Salt)	5	Zarqa	9
Irbid	2		

Useful telephone numbers

Ambulence	193
Fire	193
Police	192

Chambers of Commerce
American Chamber of Commerce in Jordan, 23 Salem Al-Hindawi Street, Shmeisani, PO Box 840817, Amman 11184 (tel: 565-1860; fax: 565-1862; e-mail: mail@jaba.org.jo).

Amman Chamber of Commerce, Al-Sharif Shaker Bin Zaid Street, PO Box 287, Amman 11118 (tel: 566-6151; fax: 566-6155; e-mail: info@ammanchamber.org.jo).

Amman Chamber of Industry, 2nd Circle Amman, PO Box 1800, Amman 11118 (tel: 464-3001; fax: 464-7852; e-mail: aci@aci.org.jo).

Aqaba Chamber of Commerce, PO Box 12, Aqaba 77110 (tel: 201-2235; fax 201-3070; e-mail: ask@index.com.jo).

Federation of Jordanian Chambers of Commerce, Al-Sharif Shaker Bin Zaid Street, PO Box 7029, Amman 11118 (tel: 566-5492; fax: 568-5997; e-mail: fjcc@nets.com.jo).

Irbid Chamber of Commerce, PO Box 13, Irbid (tel: 724-2077; fax: 724-2072; e-mail:icc@go.com.jo).

Jerash Chamber of Commerce, PO Box 195, Jerash (tel/fax: 635-1278).

Madaba Chamber of Commerce, PO Box 120, Madaba (tel: 544-120; fax: 545-878).

Mafraq Chamber of Commerce, PO Box 21, Mafraq (tel: 623-4197; fax: 623-1135).

Zarqa Chamber of Commerce, PO Box 77, Zarqa (tel: 385-3307; fax: 385-4617).

Banking
Arab Bank Plc, PO Box 950545, 11195 Amman (tel: 560-7231; fax: 560-6793; e-mail: international@arabbank.com.jo).

Arab Banking Corporation (Jordan), PO Box 926691, 11190 Amman (tel: 5 66-4183; fax: 568-6291; e-mail: info@arabbanking.com.jo).

Arab Jordan Investment Bank, PO Box 8797, 11121 Amman (tel: 560-7126; fax: 568-1482; e-mail: info@ajib.com).

Bank of Jordan, PO Box 2140, 11181 Amman (tel: 569-6277; fax: 569-6291; boj@go.com.jo).

Cairo Amman Bank, PO Box 950661, 11195 Amman (tel: 461-6910; fax: 464-2890; e-mail: cainfo@ca_bank.com.jo).

Export and Finance Bank, PO Box 941283, 11194 Amman (tel: 569-4250; fax: 569-2062; e-mail: info@efbank.com.jo).

Housing Bank for Trade and Finance, PO Box 7693, 11118 Amman (tel: 560-7315; fax: 567-8121; e-mail: quality@hbtf.com.jo).

Jordan Gulf Bank, PO Box 9989, 11191 Amman (tel: 5 60-3931; fax: 566-4110; e-mail: jgb@jkbank.com.jo).

Jordan Investment and Finance Bank, PO Box 950601, 11195 Amman (tel: 566-5145; fax: 568-1410; e-mail: jifbank@jifbank.com.jo).

Jordan Kuwait Bank, PO Box 9776, 11191Amman (tel: 568-8814; fax: 569-5604; e-mail: webmaster@jkbank.com.jo).

Jordan National Bank, PO Box 3103, 11181 Amman (tel: 562-2282; fax: 562-2281; ingo@inb.com.jo).

Union Bank for Saving and Investment, PO Box 35104, 11180 Amman (tel: 560-7011; fax: 566-6149; e-mail: info@unionbankjo.com).

Central bank
Central Bank of Jordan , PO Box 37, 11118 Amman (tel: 463-0301–10; fax: 463-8889; e-mail: banksuper@cbj.gov.jo).

Stock exchange
Amman Stock Exchange (ASE): www.ase.com.jo

Travel information

Royal Jordanian Airlines, PO Box 302, Amman (tel: 672-872).

Ministry of tourism

Ministry of Tourism & Antiquities, PO Box 224, Amman (tel: 464-2311/4; fax: 464-8465; e-mail: tourism@mota.gov.jo).

National tourist organisation offices

Jordan Tourism Board, PO Box 830688, Amman 11183 (tel: 567-8294; fax: 567-8295; e-mail: jtb@nets.com.jo; internet: www.see-jordan.com).

Ministries

Ministry of Agriculture, University of Jordan Street, PO Box 2099, Amman (tel: 568-6431, 568-6151; fax: 568-6310).

Ministry of Awqaf and Islamic Affairs, POB 659, Amman (tel: 566-141; fax: 560-2254).

Ministry of Communications and Postal Affairs, PO Box 35214 (tel: 560-7111; fax: 560-6233).

Ministry of Culture, PO Box 6140, Amman (tel: 463-6392/3569-6588; fax: 569-6598).

Ministry of Defence, PO Box 80, Amman (tel: 464-1211, 462-2131; fax: 464-2520).

Ministry of Development Affairs, PO Box 1577, Amman (tel: 464-361; fax: 464-8825).

Ministry of Education, PO Box 1646, Amman (tel: 847-671; fax: 566-6019).

Ministry of Energy and Mineral Resources, PO Box 2310 (tel: 586-3326/9; fax: 586-5714, 581-5615).

Ministry of Finance, PO Box 85, Amman (tel: 463-6321, 463-6502, 463-7781/2; fax: 464-3132, 464-3121).

Ministry of Foreign Affairs, 3rd Circle, PO Box 35217, Amman (tel: 464-4361, 464-4311; fax: 464-8825; internet www.mfa.gov.jo/).

Ministry of Health, PO Box 86, Amman (tel: 566-5131; fax: 568-8373).

Ministry of Industry and Trade, PO Box 2019, Amman (tel: 560-7191; fax: 560-3721).

Ministry of Information, PO Box 1794, Amman (tel: 464-1467; fax: 464-8895).

Ministry of the Interior, PO Box 100, Amman (tel: 463-8849, 566-3111, 569-1141; fax: 560-6908).

Ministry of Justice, PO Box 6040, Amman (tel: 566-3101; fax: 568-0238).

Ministry of Labour, PO Box 9052, Amman (tel: 560-7481; fax: 566-7193).

Ministry of Municipal, Rural and Environmental Affairs, 3rd Circle, PO Box 1799, Amman (tel: 464-1393/7; fax: 467-2135).

Ministry of Parliamentary Affairs, Jabal, Amman (tel: 464-1211; fax: 464-2520).

Ministry of Planning, PO Box 555, Amman (tel: 464-4466/7; fax: 464-9341).

Ministry of Public Works and Housing, PO Box 1220, Amman (tel: 585-0470, 585-0479; fax: 585-7590).

Ministry of Social Development, PO Box 6720, Amman (tel: 593-1391; fax: 567-3198).

Ministry of Supply, PO Box 830, Amman (tel: 560-2121, 560-2135; fax: 560-4691).

Ministry of Tourism & Antiquities, PO Box 224, Amman (tel: 464-2311/4; fax: 464-8465; e-mail: tourism@mota.gov.jo).

Ministry of Trade and Industry, PO Box 2019, Amman (tel: 663-191; fax: 603-721).

Ministry of Transport, PO Box 35214, Amman (tel: 551-8111; fax: 552-7233).

Ministry of Water and Irrigation, PO Box 2412, Amman (tel: 568-0100, 568-0117; fax: 567-9143).

Ministry of Youth, PO Box 1794 (tel: 604-701; fax: 604-717).

Prime Minister's Office, PO Box 80, Amman (tel: 641-211; fax: 642-520).

Other useful addresses

Amman Financial Market (AFM), PO Box 8802, Amman (tel: 660-170; fax: 686-830).

Amman World Trade Centre, PO Box 962140, Amman (tel: 560-5791/2; fax: 560-5793).

Arab Potash Company (APC), PO Box 1470, Amman (tel: 566-6165; fax: 567-4416).

British Embassy, PO Box 87, Abdoun, Amman (tel: 592-3100; fax: 592-3759; e-mail: british@nets.com.jo).

British Embassy, Commercial Section, PO Box 6062, Amman (tel: 592-3100; fax: 592-3759; e-mail: becommercial@nets.com.jo).

Chief of the Royal Court, PO Box 80, Amman (tel: 464-1211, 462-7421; fax: 464-2520).

Civil Aviation Authority, PO Box 7547, Amman (tel: 92-282; fax: 891-653).

Customs Department, PO Box 90, Amman (tel: 463-8358; fax: 464-7791; internet site: www.customs.gov.jo).

Indo-Jordan Chemicals Company, PO Box 926787, Amman (tel: 568-5732; fax: 568-5730).

Institution for Standards and Metrology, PO Box 941287, Amman 11194 (tel: 568-0139; fax: 568-1099).

Investment Promotion Council, PO Box 893, Amman 11821 (tel: 553-1081/2/3; fax: 552-1084; e-mail: ipc@amra.nic.gov.jo).

Jordan Dead Sea Industries Company (JODICO), PO Box 941260, Amman (tel: 569-941; fax: 569-5939).

Jordan Europe Business Association, PO Box 910751, Amman (tel: 568-5433; fax: 566-6550).

Jordan Export Development and Commercial Centres Corporation (JEDCO), PO Box 7704, Amman (tel: 560-3507; fax: 568-4568; internet site: www.jedco.gov.jo).

Jordan Fertilisers Industrial Company, PO Box 409, Aqaba (tel: 201-4156; fax: 201-7008).

Jordan Magnesia Company (JORMAG), PO Box 941260, Amman (tel: 569-5941; fax: 569-5939).

Jordan Phosphate Mines Company (JPMC), PO Box 30, Amman (tel: 560-7141; fax: 568-2290).

Jordanian Business Association, PO Box 926182, Amman (tel: 568-0855; fax: 566-0663).

Jordanian Embassy (USA), 3504 International Drive, NW, Washington DC 20008 (tel: (+1-202) 966-2664; fax: (+1-202) 966-3110; e-mail: hkjembassydc@aol,com).

National Electric Power Company (NEPCO), PO Box 2310, Amman 1181 (tel: 558-615; fax: 518-336).

Nippon Jordan Fertilisers Company Ltd., Po Box 926861, Amman (tel: 569-1708; fax: 568-4127).

US Embassy, PO Box 354, Jabal, Amman 11118 (tel: 592-0101; fax: 592-0163).

Internet sites

Arabia On-line: www.arabia.com

ArabNet: www.arab.net

Global Chamber of Commerce: www.gcc.net

Jordan information site: www.kinghussein.gov.jo

Kazakhstan

The US State Department has for some time seen Kazakhstan as a successful 'corridor of reform'. In 2002 the US Department of Commerce granted it the accolade of market-economy status. Not everyone would agree with these rose-tinted descriptions. Some critics claim that Kazakhstan is just another corrupt petroleum-dominated republic, with President Nazarbayev as a repressive, authoritarian ruler. Partisan critics would even volunteer that in Kazakhstan 'it's all about oil' and probably about Halliburton as well. Oil has certainly got a lot to do with it. Kazakhstan has oil and a lot of it. Russia and China are both customers, as are Europe and the United States. The same critics allege widespread corruption. Certainly in the years following the Soviet collapse, corruption was endemic in Kazakhstan as in many other 'new' states. But in fairness, Kazakhstan has made serious efforts to promote transparency. Amongst other initiatives it has signed up for the UK's rigorous Extractive Industries Transparency Initiative.

According to the Asian Development Bank (ADB) the poverty rate was cut by half in five years. A large middle class is rapidly forming, thanks in part to tax code reforms that favour small- and medium-size enterprises (SMEs). Kazakhstan spends 4 per cent of gross domestic product (GDP) on education and each year foots the bill to send its top 3,000 high school graduates to study in the United States, Europe, Japan and other developed countries. The Organisation for Security and Co-operation in Europe (OSCE) has drawn the same negative assessment of Kazakh elections that it has for all elections in the former Soviet Union except for the three Baltic countries: they fail to meet European standards. But the OSCE has acknowledged that revisions in Kazakhstan's electoral law represent 'significant progress'.

Birthday boy

The 'big event' of 2010 was the 70th birthday of President Nursultan Nazarbayev. In fact, although every man, woman and child in Kazakhstan was aware of their president's age, in a continuing effort to play down any suggestions that he was encouraging a Korean style personality cult, birthday festivities were banned. Not that Mr Nazarbayev was putting up too much of a struggle. In June 2010 the one-party had given him the title of 'Leader of the Nation'. Warned by events in neighbouring Kyrgyzstan, where President Bakiyev was deposed and forced into a very rapid exile, the new title went alongside new legislation granting the president immunity from prosecution as well as protecting all the presidential family's assets (of which there were quite a few).

The economy recovers

The World Bank notes that Kazakhstan enjoyed strong economic performance

KEY FACTS

Official name: Kazakstan Respublikasy (Republic of Kazakhstan)

Head of State: President Nursultan Äbishuly Nazarbayev (Nur Otan) (from 1990; re-elected 3 Apr 2011)

Head of government: Prime Minister Karim Masimov (appointed Jan 2007)

Ruling party: Nur-Otan (Fatherland's Ray of Light) (since 1999; re-elected Aug 2007) (re-named from Otan 2006)

Area: 2,717,300 square km

Population: 15.90 million (2010)*

Capital: Astana (seat of government) (renamed 1998; formerly called Akmola; inaugurated as the new capital 1997); Almaty (formerly Alma Ata, commercial capital)

Official language: Kazakh

Currency: Tenge (T) = 100 tein (introduced Nov 1993)

Exchange rate: T148.16 per US$ (Oct 2011)

GDP per capita: US$8,883 (2010)

GDP real growth: 7.00% (2010)

GDP: US$138.40 billion (2010)

Labour force: 8.12 million (2010)

Unemployment: 5.80% (2010)

Inflation: 7.40% (2010)

Oil production: 1.76 million bpd (2010)

Balance of trade: US$28.88 billion (2010)

* estimated figure

from 2000 to 2007, with average GDP growth of 10 per cent. The government maintained a healthy fiscal surplus during that period, accumulating about 21 per cent of GDP in the National Fund of the Republic of Kazakhstan (NFRK). However, the economy was and remains highly resource-dependent, with manufacturing accounting for 11 per cent and agriculture 5 per cent of GDP in 2008. In contrast, minerals, oil and gas, accounted for 73 per cent of exports and 39 per cent of GDP. Consequently, the government has made diversification of the economy a development priority.

Despite the strong overall economic trends in Kazakhstan, a spiral of unsustainable growth in commercial lending and foreign borrowing in 2005–07 set the stage for difficulties in the financial and construction sectors. Since mid-2007, problems in the global financial markets have blocked local banks' access to cheap external financing. The deepening of the world economic crisis since September 2008 has had further negative repercussions on the country. Kazakhstan faced a short but very sharp terms-of-trade shock and large capital outflows, which forced a 20 per cent devaluation of the tenge in February 2009. GDP growth had decelerated to 3.2 per cent in 2008.

Responding to the crisis, government has tapped the NFRK to deploy a large fiscal stimulus programme (US$8 billion in 2008–09), focusing on supporting SMEs, agriculture, construction and banks. The latest data suggest that the stimulus may have had an impact on preventing a more severe recession. Going forward, the stimulus will need to be reduced, since NFRK cannot be tapped at the same pace as in 2008 and Kazakhstan intends to contain the build up of sovereign foreign debt.

At present, it appears that an economic recovery has begun in Kazakhstan, with the strengthening of commodity prices being the most important factor supporting it. Positive trends in the real sector of the economy have boosted the confidence of investors, increased profitability in key sectors like mining and strengthened domestic demand. In the view of the Bank, Kazakhstan remains highly vulnerable to commodity price fluctuations. When oil fell to 40 dollars a barrel in early 2009, the economy dived into recession and the currency depreciated. Since then, economic prospects have improved enormously on the back of strong commodity prices. But reducing resource dependence is a key development challenge for the country, for which close to 90 per cent of exports are resource-related. Critically, the banking sector continues to face serious problems and will recover only gradually even in the best case scenario. The share of non-performing loans in the portfolios of Kazakhstan banks continues to grow, reflecting the cumulative effects of the recession, real estate price declines and depreciation of the tenge in February 2009. Overall, the foreign debt position of the Kazakhstan banking sector has been reduced from US$46 billion in mid-2007 to US$25 billion and was expected to fall below US$20 billion by the end of 2010.

Disregarding the prospect of another world economic slowdown and associated sharp decline in commodity prices, the Kazakhstan economy is expected to continue to grow, although at a modest pace. The financial and construction sectors are expected to remain depressed for some time. The surge in oil output growth in 2009 reflected increased capacity that will most likely not appear again until Kashagan oil comes on line, which is expected in 2014. The absence of abundant cheap commercial credit will also be a general constraint on the pace of growth.

KEY INDICATORS — Kazakhstan

	Unit	2006	2007	2008	2009	2010
Population	m	15.40	15.54	15.55	*15.57	*15.90
Gross domestic product (GDP)	US$bn	81.00	104.90	135.60	109.30	138.40
GDP per capita	US$	5,363	6,748	8,719	7,019	8,883
GDP real growth	%	10.6	8.9	3.2	1.2	7.3
Inflation	%	8.6	10.8	17.2	7.3	7.4
Unemployment	%	7.4	7.3	6.6	6.6	–
Industrial output	% change	13.4	8.5	1.9	0.4	–
Agricultural output	% change	6.0	8.9	-6.2	13.2	–
Oil output	'000 bpd	1,426.0	1,490.0	1,554.0	1,682.0	1,757.0
Natural gas output	bn cum	23.9	27.3	30.2	32.2	33.6
Coal output	mtoe	49.2	29.9	58.8	51.8	56.2
Exports (fob) (goods)	US$m	38,762.0	48,439.1	71,970.8	43,961.1	60,837.9
Imports (fob) (goods)	US$m	24,120.0	33,208.4	38,452.0	28,773.9	31,956.5
Balance of trade	US$m	14,642.0	15,140.7	33,518.8	15,187.3	28,881.4
Current account	US$m	-1,795.0	-6,851.0	6,978.0	-3,405.0	4,319.0
Total reserves minus gold	US$m	17,750.8	15,776.8	17,871.5	20,719.8	25,222.7
Foreign exchange	US$m	17,749.5	15,775.4	17,870.1	20,179.6	24,692.1
Exchange rate	per US$	125.33	120.75	120.30	147.36	147.36

* estimated figure

The importance of having oil

According to the US Energy Information Administration (EIA) Kazakhstan has the Caspian Sea region's largest recoverable crude oil reserves and its production accounts for over half of the roughly 2.8 million barrels per day (bpd) currently being produced in the region (the other major regional oil producers being Azerbaijan, Uzbekistan and Turkmenistan). The growing petroleum industry accounts for roughly 30 per cent of Kazakhstan's GDP and over half of its export revenues. Combined onshore and offshore proven hydrocarbon reserves have been estimated at between 9 and 40 billion barrels – somewhere between Algeria at one end of the scale and Libya at the other. According to the June 2010 issue of the BP *Statistical Review of World Energy* (BP10) Kazakhstan produced approximately 1.68 million barrels per day (bpd) of oil in 2009 and only consumed 260,000bpd, resulting in petroleum net exports of around 1.4 million bpd. Oil production in Kazakhstan was 1.54 and 1.48 million bpd in 2008 and 2007, respectively.

The increased oil production of recent years has been the result of an influx of foreign investment into Kazakhstan's oil sector. International projects have taken the form of joint ventures with Kazmunaigaz (formerly Kazakhoil), the national oil company, as well as production-sharing agreements and exploration/field concessions. Kazakh oil exports are growing rapidly, with current infrastructure delivering it to world markets through the Black Sea (via

Russia), the Arabian Gulf (via swaps with Iran), to the north via pipeline and rail (through Russia) and now to the East to China. According to the EIA during 2007 Kazakhstan exported around 1.2 million bpd of petroleum on average. The connections to ports on the Black Sea and the Gulf have allowed some Kazakh oil (or proxy oil from Iran) to be traded on the world market. Efforts are underway to expand the country's export infrastructure (especially to the east) over the next decade as Kazakhstan's oil production increases. The 613-mile-long, 813mm and 200,000bpd capacity pipeline from Atasu, in north-west Kazakhstan to Alashankou in China's north-western Xinjiang region is exporting Caspian oil to serve China's growing energy needs. PetroChina's ChinaOil is the exclusive buyer of the crude oil.

Following maintenance at Tengiz and Karachaganak in the last couple years, Kazakhstan became a net exporter of gas in 2008. The Kazakhstan energy ministry estimated that production during 2009 totalled 32.2 billion cubic metres (Bcm), over 70 per cent of which was produced by international consortia at the Tengiz and Karachaganak fields. 2009 gas production decreased by just over 2 per cent from 2008. In 2007, the US *Oil and Gas Journal* revised upwards its estimate of proved natural gas reserves in Kazakhstan to 100 trillion cubic feet (Tcf), putting the country on par with Turkmenistan. Most of Kazakhstan's natural gas reserves are located in the west of the country, with roughly 25 per cent of proven reserves situated in the Karachaganak field.

Risk assessment

Economy	Fair
Politics	Fair
Regional stability	Good

COUNTRY PROFILE

Historical profile

1854 The Russian garrison town of Verny, now Almaty, was established. Russian and Ukrainian peasants were brought in to settle the Kazakh lands and the first industrial enterprises were set up.

1916 A major anti-Russian rebellion was suppressed, with about 150,000 people killed and more than 300,000 fleeing abroad.

1917 After the October Revolution in Russia, the Russian ruler, Lenin, gave the peoples of Central Asia the right of self-determination.

1920s–30s Kazakhstan was granted autonomous status as part of the USSR in 1920. Soviet nationalities policy under the direction of Joseph Stalin saw Soviet rule enforced from Moscow by Red Army troops who put down Muslim revolts throughout Central Asia after the Russian civil war. Industrialisation and collectivisation of agriculture began. One million mainly nomadic Kazakhs died of starvation in the central government's campaign to enforce permanent settlements and build collective farms.

1930s–40s Kazakhstan was granted full Soviet Socialist Republic status in 1936. The country was transformed into a major producer of non-ferrous metals, coal and oil, as well as a region of developed agriculture.

1940s–50s Koreans, Crimean Tatars, Germans and others were forcibly moved to Kazakhstan. The first nuclear test explosion was carried out in 1949 at Semipalatinsk in eastern Kazakhstan.

1950s–60s Russian President Nikita Khruschev's 'Virgin Lands' scheme began. It brought agriculture to much of the Kazakh steppe and made the Kazakhs a minority in their own republic, as Russian and Ukrainian settlers were sent to run the collective farms. In 1961, the first manned spacecraft took off from Baykonur cosmodrome in central Kazakhstan.

1986 Riots in Almaty over the replacement of Dinmukhamed Kunayev (an ethnic Kazakh) with Gennady Kolbin (an ethnic Russian) as head of the Kommunisticheskaya Partiya Kazakhstana (KPK) (Communist Party of Kazakhstan) were the first signs of ethnic and nationalist unrest in Central Asia.

1989 Nursultan Nazarbayev, an ethnic Kazakh, was appointed leader of the KPK. Kazakh was declared an official language and Russian a language of inter-ethnic communication.

1990 Kazakhstan's Supreme Soviet appointed Nazarbayev as the country's first president and declared state sovereignty.

1991 Nazarbayev won uncontested presidential elections. President Nazarbayev had supported Gorbachev's efforts to keep the Soviet Union intact and Kazakhstan was the last Soviet Republic to declare full independence. Kazakhstan joined the Commonwealth of Independent States (CIS), an association which grew out of the remnants of the Soviet Union. The President signed a decree closing the Semipalatinsk nuclear testing ground.

1992 Kazakhstan became a member of the UN.

1993 A programme of national privatisation began.

1994 The first multi-party parliamentary elections were held for a full-time professional legislature, the Kenges (parliament). Results returned a predominantly pro-Nazarbayev assembly. Kazakhstan signed an economic, military and social co-operation treaty with Uzbekistan and Kyrgyzstan.

1995 President Nazarbayev dissolved parliament following a ruling by the Constitutional Court that the 1994 parliamentary elections were invalid. The president's term of office was extended to 2000 and a referendum endorsed the introduction of a new constitution.

1996 Uzbekistan, Kazakhstan and Kyrgyzstan agreed to create a single economic market.

1997 Oil agreements were signed with China. Kazakhstan's capital was moved from Almaty to Akmola, formerly known as Tselinograd.

1998 The new capital was renamed Astana. The constitution was amended to extend the presidential term from five to seven years and to remove the upper age limit for a president.

1999 In early presidential elections Nazarbayev was re-elected after his main rival was barred from standing. International observers claimed there were serious irregularities in the parliamentary elections. An attempt by ethnic Russians in north-east Kazakhstan to form a separate state failed.

2000 A law was passed granting Nazarbayev life-long powers and privileges. Belarus, Kazakhstan, Kyrgyzstan, Russia and Tajikistan (formerly the Customs Five) established the Eurasian Economic Community (EEC). Internal security and border controls were increased following incursions by Islamic militants from Kyrgyzstan and Uzbekistan.

2001 The country's first major pipeline running from the large Tengiz oil field to the Black Sea was opened. Nazarbayev purged the government of officials accused of joining the newly formed Qazaqstannyn Demokratiyalyk Tandau (QDT) (Democratic Choice (of Kazakhstan)) reform movement. Pope John Paul II paid his first visit to Kazakhstan. Tajikistan, China, Russia, Kazakhstan, Kyrgyzstan and Uzbekistan formed the Shanghai Co-operation Organisation (SCO) and agreed to fight ethnic and religious militancy, while promoting investment and trade.

2003 A bill allowing private ownership of land was passed. Russia, Ukraine, Kazakhstan and Belarus signed an economic union treaty.

2004 A deal was signed with China on the construction of an oil pipeline to the Chinese border. Nazarbayev's Otan (Fatherland) party was re-elected in the Majlis elections; international observers considered them flawed.

2005 Nursultan Nazarbayev was re-elected president. Democratic Choice was ordered by the supreme court to be dissolved because it had encouraged

protests against the parliamentary election results.
2006 Galymzhan Zhakiyanov, one of the founders of Democratic Choice, was released from prison. Asar (All Together), the small political party of President Nazarbayev's daughter, merged with the president's ruling party, Otan; two other small parties merged with Otan, which was re-named Nur-Otan (Fatherland's Ray of Light).
2007 Karim Masimov replaced Daniyal Akhmetov as prime minister. The constitution was amended so that a president may serve an unlimited number of terms. The ruling Nur-Otan won early parliamentary elections and ratified the constitution.
2008 Newly elected Russian president, Dmitry Medvedev, made his first state visit to Kazakhstan and obtained agreement that Kazakhstan-produced oil should be routed through Russia to the energy hungry markets in Europe.
2009 President Nazarbayev offered to site a nuclear fuel bank on Kazakh territory.
2010 At the beginning of the year, the Organisation for Security and Co-operation in Europe (OSCE) elected Kazakhstan, its first ex-Soviet republic, to take the chair as president. Talks between the IAEA and Kazak authorities on siting a low enriched uranium fuel bank began in January. A lawsuit was filed in June, in the UK, by a subsidiary of the Russian company, Polyus, which had bought a 50.1 per cent share of KazakhGold for US$254 million, claiming that the previous owners, a prominent Kazakh family, the Assaubayevs, had inflated the assets of the goldfield. The claim demanded US$450 million in compensation. While the court case was on-going, the UK-assets of the Assaubayevs were frozen. Export of wild caviar began again in July, but under a strict quota agreement.
2011 On 14 January, the lower house of parliament voted to hold a referendum to extend the term in office of President Nazarbayev until 2020. On 31 January, the constitutional court dismissed the grounds for the referendum. President Nazarbayev, who had not supported the referendum, called early presidential elections on 3 April, in which four candidates took part. The incumbent Nursultan Nazarbayev (Nur Otan) won 95.55 per cent of the vote and the three other candidates won less than 2 per cent each. Observers from the OSCE declared that there had been a lack of transparency and competition in the vote and that more was needed to improve election laws, strengthen media freedoms and the right to free assembly before the 2012 parliamentary elections. On 1 July the upper house of parliament agreed to hold a referendum on extending President Nazarbayev's term in office. On 18 November, the presidents of Russia, Belarus and Kazakhstan signed an agreement to set targets for setting up an internal market, the Eurasian Union, by 2015. A Eurasian Commission will begin an overseeing role for integration on 1 January 2012.

Political structure

Constitution
On 21 May 2007 amendments to the constitution were approved by parliament. Some presidential power was transferred to parliament, whereby it now influences the formation of government, the constitutional court and the central election committee. The number of Majilis (lower house) members was increased to 154: 98 deputies by proportional representation (with 10 per cent reserved for women), nine seats exclusively reserved for ethnic representatives. Elections for the Majilis are to be five-year terms. The president can now become involved with political parties during his time in office. Parliament voted to allow President Nazarbayev an exception from the two-term restriction and allow him to stand for a third term, while presidential terms will be reduced from seven years to five, from 2012. The majority parliamentary party will determine the government. State funding of political parties was introduced for parties that received over 7 per cent of the popular vote in previous elections. Political candidates may only use specifically allocated election funds but media coverage will be granted to all candidates. The role of the Senate (upper house) will assume full powers when the Majilis is in recess. The president shall appoint 15 senators (instead of seven). The power and independence of the judiciary was increased.

Independence date
16 December 1991

Form of state
Secular democratic republic

The executive
The power of the executive was redistributed in 2007. The president is elected for seven years (to be reduced to five-year terms from 2012). The prime minister and the Council of Ministers are appointed by the president and approved by parliament.

National legislature
The bicameral parliament consists of the Majilis (lower house) with 77 members, of which 67 are popularly elected in single seat constituencies and 10 are elected from party lists, members serve four-year terms; the Senate (upper house) has 39 members, as each regional legislature elects two members as their representative senators (32 in total) and the remaining seven senators are appointed by the president; members serve six-year terms. All former presidents and *ex officio* members are senators for life.

Legal system
The legal system is based on the civil law system. The country has a Supreme Court (44 members), and a Constitutional Council (seven members).

Last elections
18 August 2007 (parliamentary); 3 April 2011 (presidential).
Results: Parliamentary: (Majilis) the Nur-Otan won 88.1 per cent and all available seats (98); Zhalpyulttyk Sotsial-Demokratiyalyk Partiya (Nationwide Social Democratic Party) 4.6 per cent; Qazaqstan Demokratiyalyk Partiya Ak Zhol (Democratic Party of Kazakhstan Bright Path) 3.2 per cent; turnout was 64.6 per cent.
Presidential: Nursultan Äbishuly Nazarbayev (Nur Otan) won 95.55 per cent of the vote, Ghani Qasymov 1.94 per cent, Zhambyl Akhmetbekov 1.36 per cent, Mels Eleusizov 1.15 per cent; turnout was 89.99 per cent.

Next elections
2011 (parliamentary); 2016 (presidential).

Political parties
President Nazarbayev's ruling party, Otan (Fatherland), merged with the small Asar (All Together), Civic and Agrarian parties in 2006, and was re-named Nur-Otan (Fatherland's Ray of Light). The defunct Civic Party and Agrarian Party had jointly contested the 2004 election as the Agrarian and Industrial Union of Workers Bloc.

Ruling party
Nur-Otan (Fatherland's Ray of Light) (since 1999; re-elected Aug 2007) (re-named from Otan 2006)

Main opposition party
No opposition political party sits in parliament.

Population
15.90 million (2010)*
Last census: February 1999: 14,953,126
Population density: Six inhabitants per square km (one of the most sparsely populated countries in the world) (2010).
Annual growth rate: -0.8 per cent 1994–2004 (WHO 2006)

Ethnic make-up
Kazakh (Qazaq) (45 per cent, principally in the south), Russian (36 per cent, principally in the north), Ukrainian (5 per cent), German (4 per cent), Uzbek (2 per cent), Tartars (2 per cent), Uighur (1 per cent), Korean (0.6 per cent).

Religions
Muslim (47 per cent), Russian Orthodox (44 per cent), Protestant (2 per cent) and other (7 per cent). Kazakhstan is officially

a secular state along Turkish lines. Kazakhs are predominantly Islamic (Sunni), while Russians belong to the Orthodox Church. Islam, not of a fundamentalist nature, is strongest in the countryside. North American and European evangelical organisations are very active throughout the country.

Education

Although the 99 per cent literacy rate claimed by the Soviet authorities for Central Asia was exaggerated, particularly in rural areas, education in Central Asia surpasses that of neighbouring countries to the south.

Primary education starts from the age of six and lasts for four years followed by basic secondary education for five years and general secondary, which is not compulsory, lasting for another two years. Secondary professional education is offered in special professional or technical schools, lyceums or colleges and vocational schools. The Academy of Sciences in Almaty is the republic's principal college of higher education. Several private institutions offering higher education have been licensed. The Academy of Sciences is the republic's principal college of higher education.

All classes are now officially conducted in Kazakh, but many schools have been allowed to continue teaching in Russian after strong Russian protests. The argument is somewhat academic, however, as most educated Kazakhs converse in Russian and all ethnic groups are eager to learn English. Plans to introduce the Latin script, bringing the republic closer to Turkey, are unlikely to be realised for some years.

Literacy rate: 99 per cent adult rate; 100 per cent youth rate (15–24) (Unesco 2005).

Compulsory years: Six to 15

Enrolment rate: 89 per cent, total primary school enrolment of the relevant age group, including repetition rates (World Bank estimates 1994–2000).

Pupils per teacher: 18 in primary schools.

Health

Kazakhstan's healthcare system is highly decentralised with a separate development model for every region. Public funds available for reforming the system are limited and do not cover the basic needs of the population, including access to primary healthcare services.

The healthcare services sector consists of public and private providers, including hospitals, offices and clinics of medical doctors, other specialised healthcare facilities and health insurance providers. The number of public hospitals has fallen leaving 63.8 beds available per 10,000 people. This reduction corresponded to a growth of small out-patient facilities (so-called family healthcare units); with the network numbering 1,752 facilities. The number of private hospitals has increased by over 30 per cent since 2000. More than half of private clinics and hospitals concluded contracts with regional healthcare departments to provide certain medical services to be paid from regional state budgets.

In the Semipalatinsk area in northern Kazakhstan, a former nuclear testing area, cases of cancer and birth defects are widespread. During the Soviet era, the military tested the local population before and after nuclear tests to assess the consequences of exposure to radiation. The high levels of plutonium in the soil stem from the numerous tests and cause, among other things, immune-deficiency which is passed from generation to generation.

Respiratory diseases are the most common illnesses because of the republic's myriad environmental problems.

Improved water sources are available to 91 per cent of the population. Funds to provide improved water supplies to over 500,000 people, in four regions of Kazakhstan, was jointly provided by the Asian Development Bank (ADB), the Islamic Development Bank and the government – US$34.6 million, US$9.5 million, US$20.9 million respectively. The average per capita investment for water services is US$125 for surface facilities such as construction of pumping stations and treatment facilities and US$90 for groundwater services, including repairing pipes, sewage and wastewater drainage. In 2009, hygiene and sanitation education programmes were run along with the infrastructure programme and works.

HIV/Aids

HIV prevalence: 0.2 per cent aged 15–49 in 2003 (World Bank)

Life expectancy: 61 years, 2004 (WHO 2006)

Fertility rate/Maternal mortality rate: 1.9 births per woman, 2004 (WHO 2006); maternal mortality 70 per 100,000 live births (World Bank).

Child (under 5 years) mortality rate (per 1,000): 63 per 1,000 live births; 4.2 per cent of children aged under five are malnourished (World Bank).

Head of population per physician: 3.54 physicians per 1,000 people, 2003 (WHO 2006)

Welfare

The former Soviet Union developed an extensive welfare system, but price liberalisation has rendered pensions, unemployment benefit and money paid out to single parent families virtually worthless. Most Kazakhstanis hold down two or three jobs and rely heavily on privately grown food. The government has said it intends to cushion low-income groups from the heaviest blows of economic reform, but is under pressure not to stretch the budget for fear of hyperinflation.

Kazakhstan has emerged as a role model in pension reform in the Commonwealth of Independent States (CIS). In January 1998, a pay-as-you-go (PAYG) system was replaced with a privately managed and fully-funded system (similar to that introduced by Chile in the 1980s). Under the new system, employees pay a compulsory 10 per cent of their wages into a personal retirement account. This is in addition to existing pension liabilities funded through a 15 per cent payroll tax which will be cut to 5 per cent by 2009. The reform initially increased the pension fund deficit, as the state had to make up for the contributions that were diverted to the private funds. In 1998, the World Bank approved a US$300 million loan to support the government's efforts to finance the transition to a fully-funded pension system by financing part of the estimated 1.7 per cent of GDP fiscal deficit. Nevertheless, the programme is regarded as highly successful, with participation levels and the yields on investments remaining high.

Main cities

Astana (capital, estimated population 343,250 in 2005); Almaty (commercial capital, 1.2 million); Karaganda (404,881); Shymkent (373,658); Taraz (352,769); Pavlodar (309,723), Semey (269,759).

Media

Although the constitution guarantees freedom of the press, private owned and opposition media outlets are subject to harassment and censorship. Presidential prerogative includes his private life, health and financial dealings being designated state secrets and criminal charges can be incurred for 'insulting' the president and public officials. The government has control of most printing presses and transmission facilities for radio and television.

Press

According to government statistics, there are 990 privately owned newspapers and 418 privately owned magazines. Most are supportive of the government with members of President Nazarbayeva's family owning some of the largest circulating newspapers.

Dailies: There are several daily and weekly newspapers in both Russian and Kazakh including: *Kazakhstanskaya Pravda* (www.kazpravda.kz), *Karavan* (www.caravan.kz), *Ekspress-K* (www.express-k.kz), *Vremya* (www.time.kz), *Liter* (www.liter.kz) and *Zhas Alash* (www.zhasalash.kz).

Business: In Cyrillic, *Delovaya Nedelya* (www.dn.kz), *Panarama* (www.panorama.vkkz.com) are Russian-language publications. The US-based news agency EIN News (www.einnews.com) also provides business and economic news, in English.

Broadcasting

A law was introduced in 2002 requiring that at least 50 per cent of all television and radio broadcasts must be in the Kazakh language other languages include Russian and Chinese. The Turkish Radio and Television Corporation (TRT) also broadcasts programmes for Kazakhstan.

Radio: Kazakh Radio is state-run, private stations including Europa Plus (www.europaplus.kz) with a nationwide network, Khabar Hit FM and Russkoye Radio-Aziya are owned by President Nazarbayeva's daughter. Other, private stations include Radio 31 (www.31.kz/radio31), Radio Tekc (www.radiotex.net) and Auto Radio (www.avtoradio.kz).

International radio networks including the BBC (www.bbc.co.uk/worldservice) and Radio Free Europe (www.rferl.org) are available.

Television: Of there are five television channels available all are either government owned by family members of President Nazarbayeva. The state-run Kazakh TV has two channels. The Khabar news agency owns Khabar TV (www.khabar.kz), Yel Arna (for cultural programmes) and Caspionet (www.caspionet.kz) a satellite station. KTK (www.ktk.kz) is a commercial channel. Other private stations include Channel 31 TV (www.31.kz), Alma TV, the first cable TV station in Almaty and Perviy Kanal Evraziya a local channel.

Imported US TV programmes are popular.

News agencies

National news agency: Kazinform

Other news agencies:

Interfax-Kazakhstan: www.interfax.kz

Economy

Kazakhstan's economy is characterised as being resource-rich, with a large oil fund (US$23 billion in 2009, 22 per cent of GDP). It has a largely domestically-owned banking system and external debt at almost 100 per cent of GDP, of which 40 per cent is internal company debt within the mining and hydrocarbon sectors. It remains an attractive destination for international investment. The principal challenge for Kazakhstan in the latter stages of the global recession was the impact of the fall in world commodity prices, particularly oil, on its economy.

The crisis in banking in 2008–09 impacted on the rest of the economy, causing a contraction in credit, so that GDP growth fell from a high of 8.9 in 2007 to 3.2 per cent in 2008 and further still to 1.2 per cent in 2009. However as world trade picked up in 2010, so too growth rose to 7.3 per cent. Foreign direct investment (FDI) mirrored GDP growth trends. In 2008 FDI was a record high of US$14.3 billion, but fell to US$13.7 billion in 2009 and US$9.9 billion in 2010.

There are significant deposits of petroleum, gas, and minerals including coal, iron ore, copper, zinc, uranium, and gold. The global price of a barrel of oil peaked at over US$140 in 2008 and provided a welcome buffer for the economy. Oil production was 1.69 million barrels per day (bpd) in 2009, rising to 1.76 million bpd in 2010 – oil and natural gas products provide around 30 per cent of GDP.

Agriculture products include dairy goods, leather, meat, wool and grain (Kazakhstan is the seventh-largest producer of wheat in the world, typically producing 15–16 million tonnes per annum).

Although Kazakhstan faces a challenging future and is subject to potentially damaging external influences – oil and gas prices determined abroad, FDI subject to market forces – the IMF recommended in its report in 2009 that it should remain focussed on managing the impact of the crisis, with a developed strategy for the banking sector and macroeconomic policies that remain supportive of growth.

In July 2010 Russia launched a customs union with Belarus and Kazakhstan, looking to further integrate with the former Soviet bloc. The customs union plans a single currency in the next ten years.

External trade

In 2009 Kazakhstan was still in negotiations to join the World Trade Organisation (WTO). It belongs to the Eurasian Economic Community (EurAsec or EAEC), which was set up in 2000 to promote a customs union between its six member states (Belarus, Kazakhstan, Kyrgyzstan, Russia, Tajikistan and Uzbekistan) and, among other objectives, to introduce a standardised currency exchange and rules for trade in goods and service. The EAEC evolved out of the Commonwealth of Independent States (CIS) Customs Union and has begun the process of merging with the Central Asian Co-operation Organisation (CACO). On 19 October 2011, a free trade agreement (FTA) was signed by Russia with seven of its former Soviet republics: Armenia, Belarus, Kazakhstan, Kyrgyzstan, Moldova and Tajikistan. The FTA must be ratified by all relevant parliaments before its instigation in 2012.

On 18 November 2011, the presidents of Russia, Belarus and Kazakhstan signed an agreement to set targets for setting up an internal market, the Eurasian Union, by 2015. A Eurasian Commission will begin an overseeing role for integration on 1 January 2012.

Kazakhstan has plentiful natural resources, including oil and gas, coal, copper, silver, uranium and zinc, all of which are export commodities. Around 50 per cent of all exports is oil, which provides 30 per cent of GDP. As the manufacturing sector is underdeveloped imports are dominated by capital and consumer goods.

Imports

Principal imports include machinery and equipment (over 40 per cent), typically for the extractive industries; vehicles, machinery, iron and steel, appliances and electronic products and fuel.

Main sources: Typically Russia (40 per cent total, 2006), China (15 per cent), Germany (10 per cent)

Exports

Principal exports are dominated by primary products including oil and oil products (over 50 per cent), ferrous metals (around 25 per cent), chemicals, machinery, grain, wool, meat and coal.

Main destinations: Typically Italy (20 per cent total), Switzerland (15 per cent), China (10 per cent).

Agriculture

Farming

Agriculture contributes approximately 8.5 per cent to GDP and employs a quarter of the working population.

Kazakhstan's farming area constituted 16 per cent of the former Soviet Union's farm land. The cultivation of the 'Virgin Lands' in the north during the Soviet period introduced a high level of mechanisation and Kazakhstan used to provide around 14 per cent of Soviet grain.

There are still many problems in the agricultural sector, including weaknesses in input supply (such as fertilisers), poor incentives for farm production and failure to restructure farm enterprises. Privatisation is proceeding slowly. Small-scale private farming has been introduced in the south, while production in the north remains more centralised. While agricultural land may be leased long-term, attempts to introduce private land ownership is unpopular.

Irrigated land in the south and east produces fruit, vegetables, sugar beet, rice, tobacco, mustard and natural rubber. Wheat, cotton and oilseeds are the main crops produced. Dairy farming, horse breeding and sheep breeding are also undertaken.

Fishing
In the north-eastern part of Kazakhstan cold water fish are found in the River Ob catchment area, including the Altai Mountains drainage of the Irtysh River, mountain rivers of the Tien Shan range and in Lake Balkhash, which has a mix of cold water and temperate water fish stocks.The fishing of streams and rivers is largely unmanaged, but considerable effort has been put into maintaining reasonably high fish catches in some lakes and reservoirs. Kazakhstan has concentrated largely on the exploitation of indigenous fish stocks. The typical annual fish catch is over 31,000mt.

Forestry
Forest and other wooded land account for a small part of the total. Forests cover around 12.1 million hectares, which has increased by an average of 2.22 per cent per annum.
The increasing demand for forest products is met by imports, mainly from the Russian Federation.

Industry and manufacturing
Kazakhstan inherited a well-developed industrial base from the Soviet era. The principal activities are in minerals, petrochemicals, food processing, machinery and light industry.

Tourism
Kazakhstan's considerable tourist potential is being actively developed by the government, which has accorded it priority status. A Law on Tourism Activities was promulgated and a five-year Tourist Development Plan adopted in 2001, with the object of presenting a positive image of the country, building essential infrastructure and ensuring visitor safety. Visitor numbers and revenues have risen. Tourism contributes around 1.5 per cent to GDP. Attractions include the Silk Road, adventure and eco-tourism. Air connections are being improved — Air Astana has opened direct routes to major European cities as well as Seoul and Bangkok.

Environment
The Aral Sea was subject to a loss of up to 50 per cent of its water, dropping by up to 19 metres, due to the overuse of water from the two main rivers which fed into it. A UN study published in 2004 reported that there was no possibility of restoring the water and the need must be on preserving what is left. A World Bank funded project to build, reconstruct and rehabilitate waterworks along the river Syr Darya has reversed the damaged in the northern section of the sea. A sluice will be installed to supply water to the parched southern section.
Plans are underway to improve irrigation in the farmland around the sea.
Potentially, revenue may be earned from the sale of hydroelectic power.
A meeting was held in April 2009 to determine water sharing between Tajikistan, Kyrgyzstan, Uzbekistan, Turkmenistan and Kazakhstan failed, as negotiators were unable to find a trade in water for energy and hydrocarbons. Tajikistan and Kyrgyzstan hold around 80 per cent of the water in the Aral Sea but suffer from lack of electricity during freezing winters, while the remaining three states downstream are semi-arid and need water for their cotton industries and agriculture.

Mining
Mining contributes around 15 per cent to GDP and employs 8 per cent of the workforce.
Rich in mineral resources, Kazakhstan produces some 40 per cent of the world's chrome ore, second only to South Africa. There are also important deposits of iron ore, nickel, cobalt, vanadium, titanium, copper, lead, wolfram, zinc, gold, silver, tin, tungsten, molybdenum, uranium (Kazakhstan overtook Canada and Australia as the world's biggest uranium miner in 2009), cadmium, bismuth, pyrophyllite, barite, phosphorites, magnesium, phosphorous, asbestos, rare earths and sizeable manganese deposits in eastern and northern Kazakhstan. There are significant bauxite reserves in southern Kazakhstan.

Hydrocarbons
Kazakhstan is believed to have the world's largest untapped oil and gas reserves. Since the 1990s the government has concentrated its efforts on attracting foreign investment to the hydrocarbons sector. Upstream production is funded by foreign oil companies in association with the government. However, in 2007 an amendment was passed into law whereby the government could unilaterally break contracts with oil companies, either by forcing a renegotiation of contracts or the outright termination of contracts. The new law was seen as a move to stimulate greater urgency for production and a greater return on royalties.
There were 39.8 billion barrels of proven oil reserves in 2010, with production at 1.75 million barrels per day (bpd). Production in the country's main oil field, Tengiz, is expected to double and an additional 1 million bpd is anticipated from the Kashagan field (the largest outside the Middle East), as long as construction in vital infrastructure is maintained. Around 75 per cent of production is exported and accounts for around a quarter of GDP.
There are three major refineries, at Pavlador, Atyrau and Shymkent, all largely owned by the state and lacking in any significant foreign direct investment, so that be 2010 their joint capacity had fallen below commercially recorded levels.
Oil from the Tengiz oilfield was first pumped down the Caspian Pipeline Consortium (CPC) pipeline in 2001. The oil was sent to a Russian marine termial on the Black Sea near Novorossiysk. This effectively stopped Kazak hydrocarbons from becoming a direct competitor to Russian oil and gas. In December 2010 CPC shareholders agreed a further investment of US$4.5 billion to increase capacity to 1.5 million bpd. The US and Europe had originally been negotiating to build a pipeline beneath the Caspian Sea to avoid Russia altogether. There is another pipeline supplying oil to China, jointly owned by the China Nation Petroleum Corporation (CNPC) and KazMunaiGas.
Kazakhstan had proven natural gas reserves of 1.8 trillion cubic metres in 2010 and produced 33.6 billion cubic metres, an increase of 3.3 per cent on the figure for 2009. The largest gas field is Karachaganak in the north. The gas reserves in the Tengiz and Kashagan fields are almost entirely 'associated gas' produced by drilling for oil and as the country has insufficient pipeline infrastructure excess production that is not exported or used locally is being re-injected into crude oil bore holes to maintain pressure for oil extraction. Eventually, this gas can be recovered, when commercial exploitation is viable. In the meantime Kazakhstan is the world fifth-largest flarer of excess gas.
The government has targeted the sector for expansion – the country became a net exporter of natural gas as late as 2008. Distribution in 2008 was divided, with natural gas from the northern Karachaganak fields being exported to Russia, via the Karachaganak-Atyrau pipeline, while gas from the other fields is used domestically or exported via the Baku-Tibilisi-Ceyhan pipeline to Europe.
Kazakhstan has Central Asia's largest reserves of recoverable coal, of 33.6 trillion tonnes in 2010, the majority of which is the higher quality anthracite. Production in 2010 was 56.2 million tonnes of oil equivalent (toe), an increase of 5 million toe on the 2009 production level. Russia is a major importer of Kazak coal.
Coal is the largest domestic source of energy; production is hampered by the lack of investment in new and existing mines. Many of the high-cost underground coalmines have been closed, and the more competitive open (surface) mines are owned and operated by international energy companies.

Energy
Total electricity generating capacity was 17.4GW in 2007. Of the 71 power plants in operation, coal accounted for

49.8 per cent of primary energy, followed by natural gas at 29.6 per cent, with 17.6 per cent from oil and 3 per cent hydropower. The sector is faced with large amounts of inefficient or redundant equipment and needs considerable investment if it is to reverse the decline in output and halt the frequent power stoppages experienced since the 1990s. There are government plans to renovate 23 power stations and build 22 new bones y 2015 in order to develop a reliable electricity grid to supply growing economic needs.
Kazakhstan closed down its only nuclear station in 1999 and government plans for constructing a new 1,500MW nuclear power plant in the south-east near Lake Balkash remain long-term.

Financial markets

Stock exchange
Kazakhstan Stock Exchange (KASE)

Banking and insurance

The National Bank of Kazakhstan was given powers, from late 2007, to undertake measures to strengthen regulations and improve corporate governance over banks as they were restructured and re-capitalised. Nevertheless the banking system was still caught up in the crisis and the International Monetary Fund (IMF) said in 2009 that, since 2007, total losses to the banking system had been US$40 billion (in foreign debt). In October 2009 the state news agency Interfax reported that the total net loss to the banking system between January–September 2009 was T2.8 trillion (about US$19 billion). In October 2009 the government secured a deal with creditors of the Alliance Bank for US$4 billion of gross debt in exchange for equity in the Alliance Bank's reconstruction.

Central bank
National Bank of Kazakhstan
Following the National Bank of Kazakhstan's transition to international accounting standards, it announced on 29 January 2003 that it will no longer set the exchange rate for the tenge for accounting purposes.

Time

Western Kazakhstan: GMT plus four hours
Central Kazakhstan, Astana: GMT plus five hours
Eastern Kazakhstan, Almaty: GMT plus six hours

Geography

Kazakhstan, in Central Asia, is a land-locked country but with a coastline on the Caspian Sea, (the largest lake in the world). It is the second-largest country in the region, extending some 1,900km (1,200 miles) from the Volga river in Europe, in the west, to the Altai mountains, in the east, and about 1,300km (800 miles) from the Siberian plain in the north to the Central Asian deserts in the south. Kazakhstan's 2.7 million square km are equivalent to the size of Western Europe and comprise rolling steppes to the north, desert to the south and part of the western edge of the Tien Shan mountains to the south-east.
Kazakhstan is bordered by the Russian Federation to the north, China to the east, Kyrgyzstan, Uzbekistan and Turkmenistan to the south. In the south-west there is almost a 1,000km coastline on the Caspian Sea. Half of the Aral Sea lies within Kazakhstan, the other half in Uzbekistan.

Hemisphere
Northern

Climate

The temperature varies greatly from temperate steppe in the north to desert in the south. Temperatures in southern Kazakhstan average minus 3 degrees Celsius (C) in January and 29 degrees C in June. Average temperatures in Almaty range from minus 5 degrees C to 35 degrees C. Rainfall averages 200–300mm per annum in the north of the country and 400–500mm in the south.

Dress codes

Not overly formal during business hours, although women must dress modestly. Formal wear may be expected when visiting the theatre or attending a dinner party. Shorts should not be worn except in a sporting environment.

Entry requirements

Passports
Required by all visitors, valid for six months beyond intended length of stay.

Visa
Required by all, except nationals of CIS countries and Turkey. Business visas are issued after an invitation from a local company has been registered with the consular department of the Ministry of Foreign Affairs in Kazakhstan. When authorised, the host company obtains a reference number which is forwarded to the applicant who submits the application form along with a business letter of intent, a full itinerary and an undertaking of financial responsibility for expenses incurred by the representative. Details can be obtained from the consular section of the nearest embassy.
Tourist visits over five days require registration by the local authorities on arrival.

Currency advice/regulations
There are no restrictions on the import and export of local currency. Import of foreign currency is allowed subject to declaration on arrival; export is limited to amount declared.

Customs
A customs declaration form must be completed on arrival and retained until departure. Items for declaration are articles intended for personal use (currency, jewellery, cameras, computers, etc), which must be exported when leaving. It is advisable to keep receipts for goods purchased locally.

Prohibited imports
Military weapons and ammunition, illegal drugs, pornography, live animals, photographs or printed material detrimental to the image of Kazakhstan, loose pearls or anything carried for a third party.

Health (for visitors)

Mandatory precautions
Vaccination certificates are required for yellow fever if travelling from an infected area. For stays over one month and applications for visas for stays over three months, an AIDS certificate is required.

Advisable precautions
It is advisable to be in date for the following immunisations: polio (within 10 years), tetanus (within 10 years), typhoid fever, TB, hepatitis A, tick-borne encephalitis. Anti-malarial precautions advisable. Any medicines required by the traveller should be taken by the visitor, and it could be wise to have precautionary antibiotics if going outside major urban centres. A travel kit including a disposable syringe is a reasonable precaution. Water precautions recommended: water purification tablets may be useful or drink bottled water. Rabies is a health risk.

Hotels

Advisable to book at least a month in advance through Intourist or other specialist travel agents. There are many luxury Western-style hotels in Almaty. Gratuities are becoming more customary, particularly in international hotels.

Credit cards

More widely accepted than anywhere else in Central Asia; as well as being welcomed in shops and hotels, they can be used for cash advances.

Public holidays (national)

Fixed dates
1–2 Jan (New Year), 8 Mar (Women's Day), 22 Mar (Nauryz Meyrami/Traditional Spring Holiday/Persian New Year), 1 May (Unity Day), 9 May (Victory Day), 30 Aug (Constitution Day), 25 Oct (Republic Day), 16 Dec (Independence Day).

Variable dates
Eid al Adha

Working hours

Banking
Mon–Fri: 0930–1730.

Business
Mon–Fri: 0900–1800.

Government
Mon–Fri: 0900–1730.
Shops
Mon–Sat: 0900–1700.

Electricity supply
220V AC.

Social customs/useful tips
Kazakhistanis are very hospitable and courteous. It is best to book appointments for meetings in the morning. Cancellation, even at the last minute, is fairly common. Russian is the everyday business language. Business and politics are intertwined, with negotiations and deals often 'arranged'.

Security
It is unwise to venture out on the streets alone at night. Dress inconspicuously as wealthy-looking foreigners can be a target for muggers.
It may be preferable to travel by intercity bus rather than train, as robberies are making rail travel increasingly hazardous.

Getting there
Air
Almaty is the principal gateway to the country and well-served, with the most developed air routes through Turkey and Russia.
National airline: Air Astana.
International airport/s: Almaty International (ALA), 10km north-east of the city; hotel, car hire, duty-free shops, cafeterias. Atyrau International (GUW), 8km west of the city; bank, post office, restaurant, car hire. Astana (TSE), 17 km south of the city; facilities include duty-free shop and restaurant. Buses and taxis connect to the city centre.
Other airport/s: There are fifteen other airports.
Airport tax: None
Surface
Road: There are generally good international road connections to the surrounding countries. The north-east area is well served by roads to the Urals and the North Caucasus.
The Regional Road Corridor Improvement Project, estimated at US$18 billion, to improve Central Asian roads, airports, railway lines and seaports and provide a vital transit route between Europe and Asia was agreed, on 3 November 2007. Six new transit corridors, between Afghanistan, Azerbaijan, China, Kazakhstan, Kyrgyzstan, Mongolia, Tajikistan and Uzbekistan, of mainly roads and rail links, will be constructed, or existing resources upgraded, by 2013. Half the costs with be provided by the Asian Development Bank and other multilateral organisations and the other half by participating countries.
Rail: A railway line was completed in 1991 between Almaty and Urumchi in China. There are also rail connections to Russia, Kyrgystan and Turkmenistan. A new railway line is being built to connect Iran and Turkey with Kazakhstan.
Foreign visitors should use caution when travelling by train, other than the Almaty-Moscow line, as violent crime against westerners is on the increase.
Main port/s: Aktau (formerly Shevchenko) on the Caspian Sea is the main oil port and trans-shipment centre.

Getting about
National transport
Air: There are fifteen domestic/local airports located around the regions that are served by scheduled internal flights. It should be noted that maintenance procedures for aircraft on internal flights may not conform to internationally accepted standards.
Planes and helicopters can be chartered for nominal prices provided you have a good local contact.
Road: Primary and secondary roads are of poor quality, particularly in desert and semi-desert regions. However, the Oral region is well served by road links to the Urals, European Russia and the North Caucasus. Road transport is subject to cancellation and delay. Passengers are advised to travel in groups. Petrol supplies are adequate. Kazakhstan has 189,000km of paved and gravelled roads, 108,100km of unpaved roads and 80,900km of earth roads.
Buses: There are regular bus services between all the main cities.
Rail: Rail links are extensive but slow. There are 14,460km of railway, excluding industrial lines, in Kazakhstan. The Turksib railway connects Almaty with the Trans-Siberian line to the north at Novisibirsk, while the principal rail connection with Moscow runs through Chimkent and Uralsk.
City transport
Taxis: Unless Russian or Kazakh is spoken, ensure any taxi taken is booked through the hotel reception desk and that the price is agreed beforehand.
Buses, trams & metro: Swift and cheap trolley-bus and bus network in Almaty.
Car hire
A national driver's licence with an authorised translation or an international driving permit is required.

BUSINESS DIRECTORY

The addresses listed below are a selection only. While World of Information makes every endeavour to check these addresses, we cannot guarantee that changes have not been made, especially to telephone numbers and area codes. We would welcome any corrections.

Telephone area codes
The international direct dialling code (IDD) for Kazakhstan is +7, followed by area code and subscriber's number:

Almaty	3272	Shimkent	3252
Astana	3172	Uralsk	3112
Karaganda	3212	Ust-Kamenogorsk	3232
Petropavlovsk	3152	Zhezkazgan	3102

Useful telephone numbers
Police: 02
Fire: 01
Ambulance: 03

Chambers of Commerce
Almaty Chamber of Commerce and Industry, 45 Tole bi Street, Almaty 480091 (tel: 620-301; fax: 611-404; e-mail: alcci@nursat.kz).

American Chamber of Commerce in Kazakhstan, 531 Seifullina Prospect, Almaty 480091 (tel: 587-938; fax: 587-939; e-mail: information@amcham.kz).

East Kazakhstan Chamber of Commerce and Industry, PO Box 177, 3 Novatorov Street, Ust-Kamenogorsk 492000 (tel: 265-310; fax:267-247; e-mail@cci@ustk.kz).

Kazakhstan Union of Chambers of Commerce and Industry, 26 Masanchi Street, Almaty 480091 (tel: 920-052; fax: 507-029; e-mail: tpprkaz@online.ru).

North Kazakhstan Chamber of Commerce and Industry, 112 Mira Street, Petropavlovsk 642015 (tel: 460-568; fax: 465-443; e-mail: tpp@petropavl.kz).

Semipalatinsk Chamber of Commerce and Industry, 92/22 Abai Street, Semipalatinsk 490050 (tel/fax: 627-887; e-mail: tpp@relcom.kz).

South Kazakhstan Chamber of Commerce and Industry, 31 Tauke khan Street, Shimkent 486050 (tel: 211-405; fax: 211-403).

West Kazakhstan Chamber of Commerce and Industry, 67 Kuibyshev Street, Uralsk 417000 (tel: 504-440; fax: 513-537; e-mail: zktpp@kaznet.kz).

Banking
ATF Bank, 100 Furmanov Str, 480091 Almaty (tel: 503-765; fax: 501-995).

Bank Centercredit, 100 Shevchenko Street, 480072 Almaty (tel: 634-605, 680-140; fax: 507-813).

Central Asian Bank for Co-operation and Development, 115-a Abay Ave, Almaty (tel: 422-737; fax: 428-627).

Demir Kazakhstan Bank, 61A Kurmangazy Street, 480091 Almaty (tel: 508-550, 508-527; fax: 508-525).

Export-Import Bank of Kazakhstan, 118 Pushkin Street, 480021 Almaty (tel:

622-815, 633-767, 634-300; fax: 631-985).

Halyk Savings Bank of Kazakhstan; 97 Rozybakieva St, 480046 Almaty (tel: 509-991; fax: 679-738).

Kazkommertsbank, 135 Gagarin Avenue, 480060 Almaty (tel: 585-101; fax: 585-281; internet site: http://www.kkb.kz).

Temirbank, 68/74 Abay Ave, 480008 Almaty (tel: 587-888; fax: 590-529; e-mail: board@temirbank.kz; internet site: http://www.temirbank.kz).

Central bank

National Bank of Kazakhstan, 21 Koktem-3, 480090 Almaty (tel: 504-631; fax: 506-090; e-mail: info@nationalbank.kz).

Stock exchange

Kazakhstan Stock Exchange (KASE): www.kase.kz

Travel information

Aeroflot, 111 Zhibek Zhola Street, Almaty (tel: 390-594).

Air Kazakhstan, 59 Mira Street, 480003 Almaty (tel: 335-518; fax: 335-506).

Flight information (24 hours) (tel: 541-555).

Intourist, Hotel Ostrar, Gogolya 65, Almaty (tel: 330-045, 330-076).

Almaty Airport, Mailin Street 2B, 480040 Almaty (tel: 571-300; fax: 571-281).

Astana International Airport, PO Box 1968, 473026 Astana (tel: 333-709; fax: 333-741).

Kazakhstan Tourist Agency, 22 Kosmonautov Street, 480083 Almaty (tel: 390-318; fax: 390-257).

Travel Bureau, Hotel Irtysh, Ulitsa Abai 97, Semipalatinsk, Almaty (tel: 447-529, 447-531).

National tourist organisation offices

Department of Tourism, 4 Republic Square, Almaty 4860065 (tel/fax: 620-030; e-mail: dep_tour@nursat.kz; internet: www.kaztour.kz).

Ministries

Ministry of Agriculture, 49 Abai Street, 473000 Astana (tel: 323-763; fax: 324-541).

Ministry of Culture, Information and Public Accord, 22 Beibitshilik Street, 473000 Astana (tel: 322-495; fax: 326-203).

Ministry of Defence, 49 Auezova Street, 473000 Astana (tel: 337-845;fax: 337-892).

Ministry of Economy and Trade, 2 Beibitshilik Street, 473000 Astana (tel/fax: 333-003).

Ministry of Education and Science, 83 Kenesary Street, 473000 Astana (tel: 322-540; fax: 326-482).

Ministry of Employment and Social Security, 2 Manasa Street, 473000 Astana (tel: 153-602; fax: 341-270).

Ministry of Energy and Mineral Resources, 37 Beibitshilik Street, 473000 Astana (tel: 337-133; fax: 337-164).

Ministry of Finance, 60 Republic Avenue, 473000 Astana (tel: 334-186;fax: 280-321).

Ministry of Foreign Affairs, 10 Beibitshilik Street, 473000 Astana (tel: 327-669; fax: 327-667).

Ministry of Internal Affairs, 4 Manasa Street, 473000 Astana (tel: 343-601; fax: 341-738).

Ministry of Justice, 45 Pobeda Street, 473000 Astana (tel: 391-213; fax: 321-554).

Ministry of Natural Resources and Environmental Protection, 81 Karl Marx Street, 475000 Kokshetau (tel: 54-265; fax: 50-620).

Ministry of State Revenues, 48 Abai Avenue (tel: 326-951;fax: 326-963).

Ministry of Transport and Communications, 49 Abai Street, 473000 Astana (tel: 326-277; fax: 321-058).

Prime Minister's Office, 11 Beibitshilik Street, 473000 Astana (tel: 320-985;fax: 152-028).

Other useful addresses

Atomic Energy Agency, 13 Republic Square, 480013 Almaty (tel: 637-626; fax: 633-356).

Board for Investment Projects, Department of Transport, Room 124, Gogol Str 86, 480091 Almaty (tel: 323-661, 324-769; fax: 322-679, 324-449).

Business Communication Centre, 89 Michurina Street, Almaty 480059 (tel: 476-803, 347-549; fax: 347-798).

Centre for Economic Reforms, 4 Republic Square, Almaty (tel: 621-836).

Committee for the use of Foreign Capital, 152 Bogenbai Batyr, 3rd Floord, Ablay Khan Street 97, 480091 Almaty (tel: 627-326; fax: 696-152).

Kazakh Centre of Business Co-operation 'Atakent', 42 Timiryazeve Street, Almaty 480058 (tel: 473-113; fax: 509-238).

Kazakh Embassy (USA), 1401 16th Street, NW, Washington DC 20036 (tel: (+1-202)-232-5488; fax: (+1-202)-232-5845; e-mail: kazakh@intr.net).

Kazakhgas, 521 Seifullin Street, Almaty (tel: 324-288; fax: 325-442).

Kazakhstan Caspishelf, 211 Mukhanov Street, Almaty (tel: 416-034; fax: 416-430).

Kazakhstan Commerce (import-export), Zhibek Zholy 64, 480002 Almaty (tel: 333-871; fax: 331-483).

Kazakhstan Foreign Trade Organisation, v/o Kazakhintorg, Gogolya 111, Almaty (tel: 328-381).

Kazakhstanmunaigas (oil and gas refining), 458 Seifullin Street, Almaty (tel: 695-800; fax: 626-630).

Kazakh Academy of Sciences Engineering Institute, 80 Bogenbay Batyr Street, Almaty 480100 (tel: 541-281; fax: 695-769).

Kazakhstan Stock Exchange, Ulitsa Timipiazeva 42, Almaty (tel: 441-043; fax: 447-809).

Kazakh State TV and Radio, Ulitsa Mira 175, Almaty (tel: 633-716).

Kazchrome Transnational Corporation, 56 Kunaev Street, Almaty, 480002.

KazMunayGaz, 142 Bogenbai Batyr Street, 470091 Almaty (tel: 626-080; fax: 695-405).

Kazpisprom (a joint-stock company representing food producers), 92 Internatsionalnaya Street, Almaty (tel: 629-482; fax: 628-652).

Kaztag (state news agency), 77 Ablai Han Street, Almaty (tel: 625-037).

Kazvetmet (represents metal producers), 111 Gogol Street, 480003 Almaty (tel: 622-318; fax: 328-488).

Market Economy Group (privatisation committee), President's Office, Government House, Almaty (tel: 621-022).

State Property and Privatisation Committee, Ministry of Finance, 36 Auezov Street, 473024 Astana (tel: 334-397; fax: 320-937).

Union of Manufacturers and Businessmen, 4/450 Republic Square, Almaty (tel: 622-307; fax: 665-490).

National news agency: Kazinform, Interfax-Kazakhstan: www.interfax.kz

Internet sites

Kazakhstan local navigator: http://reenic.utexas.edu/reenic/countries/kazakhstan/kazakhstan/html

Kazakhstan government website: http://www.president.kz/

Kenya

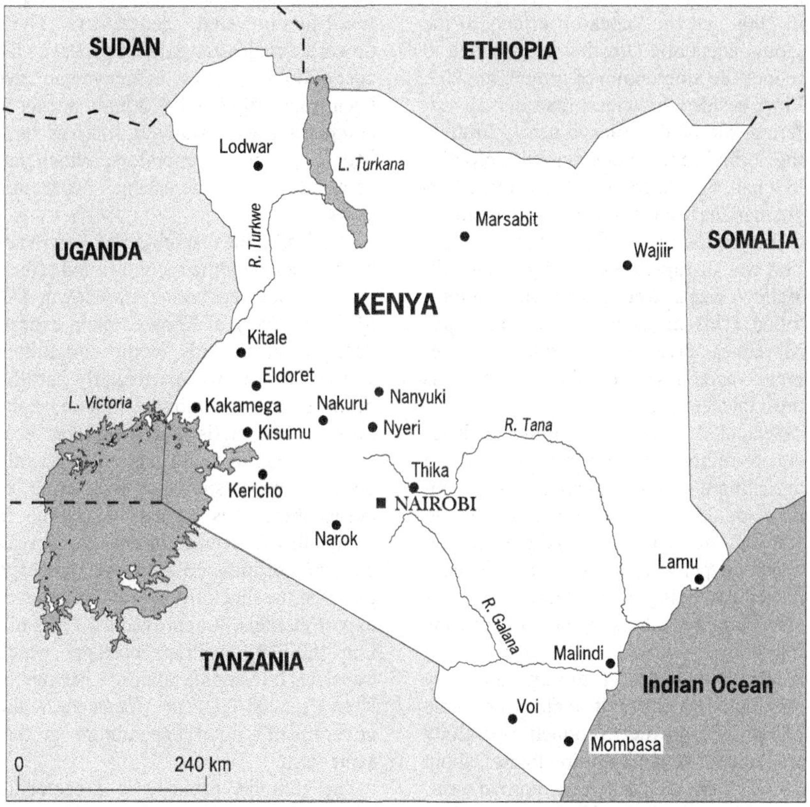

KEY FACTS

Official name: Jamhuri ya Kenya (Republic of Kenya)

Head of State: President Mwai Kibaki (Narc) (re-elected 27 Dec 2007)

Head of government: Prime Minister Raila Odinga (ODM) (from 13 Apr 2008)

Ruling party: Coalition led by Orange Democratic Movement (ODM) with Party of National Unity (PNU) (elected 27 Dec 2007)

Area: 582,646 square km

Population: 40.40 million (2010)*

Capital: Nairobi

Official language: KiSwahili and English

Currency: Kenyan shilling (Ksh) = 100 cents (convertible with currencies of Tanzania and Uganda)

Exchange rate: Ksh100.40 per US$ (Oct 2011)

GDP per capita: US$809 (2010)

GDP real growth: 5.00% (2010)

GDP: US$32.20 billion (2010)

Inflation: 4.1% (2010)

Balance of trade: -US$4.99 billion (2009)

* estimated figure

Kenya suffered a rude awakening in January 2008 when violence flared up after the December 2007 elections. As many as 1,500 people were killed and approximately 650,000 persons fled their homes. Operation 'Rudi Nyumbani' (which means 'Return Home'), initiated by the government in May 2008, enabled most families to return home, or built new houses. Nonetheless, it is estimated that approximately 20,000 families were still in camps in December 2009. Relocating those internally displaced persons will remain a challenge in 2010.

At last, a new constitution

However, the extent of the violence had shocked the international community and the European Union (EU) and US both imposed travel restrictions on senior government officials and members of parliament. Donor agencies threatened to withdraw aid on top of the general global slow down. On the positive side, the international pressure had galvanised the body politic and after some 20 years of often acrimonious debate the Kenyan parliament finally approved a draft constitution in April 2010. A referendum was held on 4 August and the constitution was passed by a vote of almost two to one. Voting was largely along tribal lines with the Kikuyu, Kenya's largest tribe, voting in favour, supported by the Luo, Luhya and coastal Muslims and Somalis. The Kalinjin voted against, fearful that they would loose rights to their land in the Rift Valley.

The new constitution puts greater checks on presidential powers while at the same time ensuring the president draws wider support. In future a presidential candidate will require 50 per cent of the national vote and over 25 per cent of the vote in more than half of the electoral constituencies. There will be a greater devolution of power to a senate and network of local counties while a member of parliament who is appointed to the cabinet will have to give up their parliamentary seat. President Mwai Kibaki and Prime Minister Raila Odinga, along with every other government office-holder, were sworn in under the new constitution on 27 August 2010.

The *African Economic Outlook 2010* (AEO), published jointly by the African Development Bank and the Organisation for Economic Co-operation and Development reports that the Mau Forest, which is the key water catchment area in Kenya, has been allocated to private entities by previous governments and local authorities. Some of it was also acquired illegally. In 2009, the government decided to reclaim the Mau Forest land. Families that resided on the land were evicted in preparation for the rehabilitation of the forest. Although this decision is a positive development for environmental protection, in the short run it poses unique challenges for those who were evicted and in turn creates discontent.

Aid and corruption

In early 2010, one donor expressed concerns about the allocation and use of resources in the education sector and suspended a US$7 million capacity-building programme to the ministry of education, citing corruption. This suspension is an indication that failure to tackle reported repeated allegations and occurrences of corruption will damage the country. Finally, 2010 may see the financiers and organisers of the post-election violence brought to justice following investigations by the International Criminal Court.

The economy falters

The ongoing negative fallout from the 2008 post-election violence, poor rainfall in 2009 and the knock-on effects of the global economic slowdown combined to reduce the momentum of growth in 2009. First, besides the widespread human suffering, the 2008 violence nearly brought the normal conduct of economic activities to a halt. Goods could not reach their target markets because the level of insecurity disrupted transport. Agricultural production was disrupted, especially in the Rift Valley, crops were burnt and animals killed. This all lead to food shortages. Moreover, investors' confidence plummeted and is yet to climb back to its pre-violence level.

Second, five years of continuously inadequate rainfall has severely affected the agricultural sector and had a negative impact on power generation owing to Kenya's reliance on hydroelectricity: about 60 per cent of national-grid connected power is generated through hydroelectric sources. In 2009, not only was the long rainy season late by one to four weeks, it was also erratic and unevenly distributed. As a result, maize (the staple of the Kenyan diet) production in 2009 was estimated at 1.8 million tonnes, about 30 per cent less than in a normal year. Lower maize production translated into higher prices, affecting the poor especially hard. The government allowed millers to import maize duty free to alleviate the tensions on the maize market and implemented a food-subsidy scheme in urban areas. Another consequence of the inadequate rainfall was that it forced the ministry of energy to adopt a power-rationing schedule and increase the use of fossil-fuel-powered generators. These power shortages had a direct impact on the cost of doing business in Kenya and have been frequently cited as a main barrier to competitiveness. Many businesses have had to purchase generators, which has contributed to increasing production costs.

Third, as in the rest of Africa, Kenya has been affected by the second-round effects of the global economic slowdown. Demand for many of Kenya's main exports declined, particularly in the horticulture sector. Tourism was particularly hard hit because of the combined impact of the post-election crisis and the global economic slowdown and has only recently been showing signs of recovering to pre-election-crisis levels. Similarly to many other African countries, the Kenyan government initiated a stimulus package to soften the shock from the contraction of export markets. It approved a KSh22 billion (US$300 million) package which translates into approximately 1 per cent of Kenya's 2008 GDP or 3 per cent of the government's total expenditure in that same year.

The stimulus package is expected to have had little effect in 2009, however, owing to delayed disbursement. The money was in fact blocked when parliament deferred voting on an Appropriations Bill, which included the package. The funds were released only in November 2009, and the effects of the stimulus package will be felt mostly in 2010. Given the time taken to tender for services, however, and bearing in mind that additional time is required between the purchasing of the services and their delivery, some of the effects of the 2009 stimulus are likely to be delayed until 2011.

Agriculture accounts for about one-fourth of Kenya's GDP and employs more than 50 per cent of the labour force. The performance of Kenya's economy is therefore dependent to a large extent on the agricultural sector. Kenya's main agricultural products include cereals (maize and wheat), horticulture, industrial crops (sugar cane and pyrethrum), permanent crops (coffee and tea) and livestock. Although the agricultural sector posted

KEY INDICATORS — Kenya

	Unit	2006	2007	2008	2009	2010
Population	m	34.05	*34.65	*35.27	*35.88	*40.40
Gross domestic product (GDP)	US$bn	22.82	27.10	29.60	32.70	32.20
GDP per capita	US$	661	782	1,712	912	809
GDP real growth	%	6.1	7.1	1.7	2.6	5.6
Inflation	%	14.4	9.8	13.1	10.6	4.1
Industrial output	% change	2.0	7.1	4.8	3.6	–
Agricultural output	% change	3.0	2.1	-5.0	-2.4	–
Exports (fob) (goods)	US$m	3,502.0	4,132.2	5,039.8	4,502.3	–
Imports (fob) (goods)	US$m	6,768.4	8,388.2	10,689.0	9,491.6	–
Balance of trade	US$m	-3,266.4	-4,256.0	-5,649.2	-4,989.3	–
Current account	US$m	-525.7	-1,032.0	-1,982.6	-1,661.1	–
Total reserves minus gold	US$m	2,415.8	3,355.0	2,878.5	3,849.0	4,320.2
Foreign exchange	US$m	2,396.0	3,334.6	2,855.7	3,478.1	3,981.7
Exchange rate	per US$	69.55	62.95	69.17	77.35	79.23

* estimated figure

positive growth from 2004 to 2008, variance in the growth rate was high. From 1.7 per cent in 2004, the agriculture growth rate increased to 7 per cent in 2005, dropping to 4.6 per cent in 2006 and falling even further to 2.2 per cent in 2007. The main reason for this uneven agricultural growth is inadequate rainfall. The high cost of agricultural inputs, in particular fertilisers, also played an important role. In addition, the agricultural sector contracted by 5.4 per cent in 2008, the worst year on record, owing to the added impact of post-election violence.

While the prices of tea and coffee increased in 2009, Kenya's production of these and other agricultural products in 2009 was uneven because of adverse weather conditions. In the case of tea, on the one hand, its price grew slowly during the first five months of 2009, increasing from US$2.30 per kilogram (kg) in January to US$2.49 per kg in May. It returned to its January 2008 high in September 2009. On the other hand, poor weather reduced Kenya's tea harvest by 9.1 per cent from 345,818 tonnes in 2008 down to 314,194 tonnes in 2009. Over the same one-year period, horticultural production declined by 6.4 per cent.

Coffee performed better. Production from January to December 2009 increased by 26 per cent to reach 48,900 tonnes, higher than in 2008 (38,705) but lower than in 2007 (52,288) . Coffee prices also increased steadily from US$2.01 per kg in January 2009 to a year-high US£3.39 per kg in August, the highest price since January 2007. After August, prices fell in September and October to US$3.19 per kg. However, the outlook for the 2009/10 harvest is less positive. The Coffee Board of Kenya predicts that output may fall by 13 per cent to 47,000 tonnes in spite of the heavy rains at the beginning of 2010.

Tourism accounts for approximately 5 per cent of Kenya's GDP. The December 2007 violence took a heavy toll on the tourism sector, which has yet to recover its pre-violence performance. In the 2000_07 period, the number of tourist arrivals increased from 1 million to 1.8 million. In 2008, the number of arrivals plummeted because of the post-election violence. In 2009, the sector hoped to reach the million-tourist mark but by end-December 2009 the number of visitors was 952,481. Tourism earnings in 2009 fell by US$29 million to US$630 million.

While Kenya's trade deficit as a share of GDP improved by 3.1 percentage points in 2009, this was largely the consequence of the global economic slowdown, which led to a larger contraction in imports than in exports. The value of imports as a share of GDP fell by 3.8 percentage points, largely because of a lower oil bill, which dropped by approximately one-third thanks to the decline in world oil prices. Exports are estimated to have fallen by close to 10 per cent in 2009, mainly because of lower revenue from manufactured goods, raw materials and horticulture. Kenya's coffee exports grew in 2009 by roughly 13,000 tonnes to reach 64,574 tonnes, the highest level since 2001. Relative to 2008, the higher coffee exports translated into a KSh6.5 billion (US$890 million), or 64 per cent, increase. Tea exports in 2009 fell, on the other hand, by 71000 tonnes to 319,000 tonnes relative to 2008. As a result, revenue in Kenyan shillings from tea exports contracted by 2.5 per cent. Fresh horticulture exports also performed poorly in 2009, when export revenue fell by 8 per cent.

Doing business

The 2010 World Bank Doing Business report ranked Kenya 95 out of 183 economies, down from a ranking of 84 in 2009. According to the AEO Kenya's performance worsened in all 10 sub-categories of the report, except in the Getting Credit category, where Kenya maintained its excellent fourth rank, and in the Trading Across Borders category, where Kenya moved up two positions but is still 147 out of 183 countries. Perceived corruption remains a challenge, as Kenya ranked 146 out of 180 worldwide according to Transparency International's 2009 Corruption Perception Index.

Risk assessment

Economy	Improving
Politics	Poor
Regional stability	Fair

COUNTRY PROFILE

Historical profile

1944 The Kenyan African Union (KAU) was formed to voice local demands for the return of native lands.
1947 KAU was led by Jomo Kenyatta, a prominent member of the Kikuyu tribe.
1952 A state of emergency was announced in response to guerrilla activity by the Kikuyu-led secret society, the Mau Mau. More than 13,500 Africans were killed during the uprising, compared to less than 100 Europeans.
1953 The KAU was suspended. Kenyatta was detained.
1957 Africans were elected to the Legislative Council and offered ministerial posts.
1960 A new constitution gave Africans a majority in the Legislative Council. The KAU split; the Kenya African National Union (Kanu) (which had a strong Kikuyu and Luo membership) and the Kenya African Democratic Union (Kadu) were established.
1961 Kenyatta was freed and became president of Kanu and leader of an all-party African government.
1963 The Republic of Kenya was proclaimed and Kenyatta became president.
1964 Kadu was dissolved.
1978 Jomo Kenyatta died and was succeeded as president by Daniel arap Moi.
1979, 1983 and 1988 Only Daniel arap Moi stood in presidential elections and was elected unopposed.
1992 After a lengthy period as, effectively, a one-party state, multi-party elections were held and President Moi was re-elected.
1997 President Moi and Kanu won the presidential and parliamentary elections.
1998 Terrorists blew up the US embassy in Nairobi; 244 people were killed and over 4,000 people were injured.
2001 President Daniel arap Moi appointed the opposition National Development Party (NDP) leader, Raila Odinga, to his 26-member cabinet, forming Kenya's first coalition government. International aid was withheld by the IMF when the government failed to implement anti-corruption measures.
2002 The NDP and Kanu announced a merger in the run-up to the general election. Uhuru Kenyatta became Kanu's presidential candidate, leading to a wave of defections, including Raila Odinga. Emilio Mwai Kibaki of the opposition, National Rainbow Coalition (Narc), won the presidential elections with 62.3 per cent of the vote.
2003 A draft constitution was presented to parliament, proposing a number of reforms.
2004 The deadline for the enactment of the long-awaited new constitution, which proposed restricting presidential powers and creating a post of prime minister, was missed. In a corruption survey Kenya was rated 129, out of 146, by the watchdog Transparency International, which said the problem remained 'rampant'.
2005 Justice and constitutional affairs minister, Martha Karua, was asked to prepare a bill for a new constitution. The Orange Democratic Movement (ODM) was formed, led by Raila Odinga and Kalonzo Musyoka.
2006 Finance minister, David Mwiraria, resigned in a corruption scandal. The police raided and closed down the premises of the Standard Media Group (publishers

of the daily *The Standard* newspaper), drawing widespread international condemnation. The Chinese president, on a visit to Kenya, signed an offshore oil exploration agreement with Kenya. Uhuru Kenyatta was replaced as Kanu chairman by Nicholas Biwott; the High Court blocked the elections, pending a hearing of a challenge by Kenyatta.

2007 A new political party was formed, the Party of National Unity (PNU) out of the ruling Kanu coalition and other pro-Kibaki political parties. In presidential elections the incumbent Mwai Kibaki (PNU coalition) won 46.6 per cent of the vote and his closest rival Raila Odinga (ODM) won 44.3 per cent. Widespread rioting broke out following the results and while international observers reported that polling had been 'relatively orderly and generally positive', the chief EU monitor said the Electoral Commission of Kenya had 'not succeeded in establishing the credibility of the tallying process'.

2008 An estimated 1,500 people died and 600,000 people were displaced in the violence following the presidential elections, as distrust increased between the main tribal groups. President Kibaki opened parliament and called for members to become 'ambassadors of peace' in their constituencies and urged them to pass the four bills (the National Accord and Reconciliation Bill, the Constitutional Amendment Bill, the Truth Justice and Reconciliation Bill and the Ethnic Commission Bill) which formed part of the Kofi Annan-brokered agreement, whereby the ODM shared power with the PNU. President Kibaki announced a new cabinet, naming Raila Odinga (ODM) as prime minister. The formation of a tribunal to consider the violence during the last general elections was announced and parliament was given a deadline of 45 days to enact the tribunal or a sealed list of accused ringleaders would be given to the International Criminal Court (ICC). Some prominent politicians were thought to be on the list, making parliament wary of instigating further inquiries.

2009 A national emergency was declared as drought in the east threatened almost 10 million people with food shortages. Martha Karua, the first coalition minister, resigned as minister of justice. She had been a close ally of President Kibaki and resigned after he had appointed a number of judges without consulting her. After two years of low annual rainfall the Masinga dam hydroelectric power station was shut down for only the second time in the plant's 28-year history. The government decided to use local courts rather than a special tribunal to deal with post-election violence. However, the ICC confirmed it would proceed with prosecution of the leaders of post-election violence, saying Kenya had failed, for the third time, to set a deadline to establish the agreed tribunal. The ICC accused the police force, judiciary and Attorney General of failure to prosecute suspects locally. The US and EU imposed restrictions on senior officials travelling to the US and Europe.

2010 In January the US suspended US$7 million of funding for free primary schools. On 15 February, Prime Minister Odinga suspended William Ruto and Sam Ongeri, the ministers of agriculture and education for alleged corruption, only for President Kibaki to reinstate them a few hours later. On 4 August, 68.55 per cent of voters agreed to a new constitution and the new Second Republic was inaugurated on 27 August. Although both political parties within the coalition government supported the new constitution, voting was generally along tribal lines with Kenya's largest tribe, the Kikuyu, voting 'yes', supported by the Luo, Luhya and coastal Muslims and Somalis. The Kalenjin voted against. In future a presidential candidate will require 50 per cent of the national vote and over 25 per cent of the vote in more than half of the electoral constituencies to succeed to the presidency. This was designed to achieve greater acceptance and appeal from a more diverse electorate for any presidential winner. The new constitution also includes significant reform to the judiciary. On 15 December the ICC named six people they suspected of being behind the violence after the 2007 elections. The six included deputy prime minister and finance minister, Uhuru Kenyatta.

2011 One of the ministers named by the ICC, Henry Kosgey, resigned on 4 January; he said he was stepping down to allow the accusations to be 'fully investigated'. Another of the accused, William Ruto, had already resigned. On 8 March the ICC issued summonses for six persons accused of being behind the violence after the 2007 elections; they were ordered to attend the court in The Hague on 7 April. On 9 March, Kenya announced that it would challenge the ICC's right to prosecute six of its nationals, summoned to appear before it. On 24 March, the General Service Union of the Kenyan police force crossed into Somalia at the border town of Liboi, to confront the militant forces of the al Shabab. It was the first time that Kenyan forces had directly fought al Shabab, which was accused of raids into Kenya. Four Kenyans who allege they were tortured during the suppression of the Mau Mau uprising of 1952–61 started legal proceedings against the UK government on 6 April. Deputy Prime Minister Uhuru Kenyatta appeared at the ICC on 8 April, along with two other supporters of the president. The three supporters of Raila Odinga had already appeared on 7 April. Three refugee camps at Dadaab on Kenya's northern border were inundated by Somalis and Ethiopians seeking help as a two-year drought (the worst since late-1940s) caused widespread failure in crop and animal production. The camps, designed to house 90,000 people, had by 1 July grown to 350,000. The UN estimated that 10 million people in the Horn of Africa were affected by drought and food insecurity. The first African woman to win the Nobel Peace Prize, Wangari Maathai , died in Nairobi on 25 September. A conservationist, she founded the Green Belt Movement which has planted 20–30 million trees across the continent.

Political structure

Constitution

The constitution was promulgated in 1963. In 1997, a number of constitutional changes took place; these allowed the formation of a coalition government, the review of the constitution by an independent commission and increased the number of directly elected seats in the Kenyan National Assembly from 188 to 210. A further 12 seats are nominated by the government.

A constitutional amendment affirming the National Assembly's supremacy and curbing the powers of the presidency was approved in 1999. This removed the president's right to appoint the clerk of the house, enabling the legislature to appoint and dismiss the clerk, who is no longer answerable to the president's office. The clerk manages everything from the National Assembly's agenda to its budget.

The country is divided into seven provinces run by provincial commissioners appointed by the president. The provinces are divided into districts run by district commissioners. Towns and districts have municipal and country councils, which are partly elected and partly nominated, but the commissioner has wider powers than the councils. The Nairobi area has a separate government-appointed city commission.

The referendum on constitutional amendments, held on 4 August, passed by a majority of around two to one. In future a presidential candidate will require 50 per cent of the national vote and over 25 per cent of the vote in more than half of the electoral constituencies to succeed to the presidency. This is expected to achieve greater acceptance and appeal from a more diverse electorate for any presidential winner. The new constitution also includes significant reform to the judiciary.

Form of state
Republic
The executive
Executive power in Kenya is in the hands of the president, assisted by the vice president and cabinet, both named by the president.
National legislature
The unicameral National Assembly has 224 members, of which 210 are elected in single-seat constituencies for five-year terms and 12 members are appointed by the president with two *ex officio* members, who are the speaker of the parliament and the attorney general.
Legal system
Kenya's legal system is based on English common law, Islamic law and tribal law, with a High Court and Court of Appeal. The Chief Justice of the Court of Appeal is appointed by the president.
Last elections
27 December 2007 (presidential and parliamentary)
Results: Presidential: Mwai Kibaki won 46 per cent of the vote, Raila Odinga won 44 per cent, all other candidates won less than 10 per cent. These results were published by the Electoral Commission on 8 January 2008.
Parliamentary: Orange Democratic Movement (ODM) won 99 seats (out of 224); Party of National Unity (PNU) 43, Orange Democratic Movement-Kenya (ODM-K) 16, Kenya African National Union (Kanu) 14, Safina 5, all other parties won less than 5 seats.
Next elections
2012 (presidential and parliamentary).

Political parties
Ruling party
Coalition led by Orange Democratic Movement (ODM) with Party of National Unity (PNU) (elected 27 Dec 2007)
Main opposition party
Kenya African National Union (Kanu)

Population
40.40 million (2010)*
Last census: August 1999: 28,686,607
Population density: 52 inhabitants per square km. Urban population: 31 per cent (1995–2001).
Annual growth rate: 2.4 per cent 1994–2004 (WHO 2006)
Internally Displaced Persons (IDP)
350,000 (UNHCR 2004)
Ethnic make-up
Kenya is a multi-cultural society. Most of Kenya's people belong to 13 ethnic groups although there are a further 27 smaller groups. The majority of Kenyans belong to Bantu tribes such as the Kikuyu (22 per cent), Luhya (14 per cent) and Kamba (11 per cent). The Luo (13 per cent) are of Nilotic origin, as are the smaller Kalenjin (12 per cent), Maasai, Turkana and others.
The Kikuyu live in the central highlands and have traditionally been dominant in commerce and politics, although this is changing. A small European settler population remains in the highlands, involved in farming and commerce. In the north live the Somalis and the nomadic Hamitic peoples (Turkana, Rendille and Samburu); Kamba and Maasai peoples are concentrated in the south and eastern lowlands, and the Luo live around Lake Victoria.
Religions
Protestant (38 per cent), Roman Catholic (28 per cent), animist (26 per cent), Muslim (6 per cent), others (including small Hindu, Sikh and Jain minorities) (2 per cent).

Education
Education has expanded rapidly since independence in 1963. The number of primary schools has more than doubled, while that of secondary schools has increased eighteen-fold. Enrolment at primary schools has declined by 20 per cent since 1980, when the gross enrolment rate was 115 per cent (including repeaters).
Primary education begins at the age of six and is provided free of charge at state schools, however the lack of state funds compels schools to charge fees for books, electricity, water and upkeep, forcing children of poor families to either abandon learning early on or develop an erratic attendance record.
It has been estimated by Oxfam that 75 per cent of children aged six to 11 will enrol for school by 2015.
Secondary school enrolment has grown since 1980, when it was 20 per cent, but still covers only a small proportion of the relevant age group.
The present government, elected in December 2002, has pledged to introduce universal, free and compulsory primary education, an aim which will require higher levels of expenditure then currently spent.
Literacy rate: 84 per cent adult rate; 96 per cent youth rate (15–24) (Unesco 2005).
Enrolment rate: Unicef says the primary school population jumped from 5.9 million in 2002 to 7.6 million in 2005.
Pupils per teacher: 31 in primary schools.

Health
Improved water sources are available to 48 per cent of the population.
There were cases of polio reported to the World Health Organisation – Global Polio Eradication Initiative (WHO – Polio Eradication) in 2006; the country had previously been free of the disease and its re-emergence was due to infected travellers. In a synchronised campaign with Ethiopia and Somalia, inoculation began for under fives by WHO – Polio Eradication and the country's health authorities in 2006.
In 2007, it was estimated that around 10 per cent of the population were suffering from diabetes, but only 3.5 per cent were diagnosed. Around 85 per cent of the cases were type II diabetes, linked to an unhealthy diet of too much starchy food, high in sugars, salts and fats, and lack of exercise.
HIV/Aids
The number of HIV positive cases have fallen from a high of 4.5 million in 2000 to 2.1 million in 2004. HIV testing also improved with a 10-fold increase between 2002–04. Kenyan businesses were rated as best in the region for having HIV prevention programmes and providing their workers with condoms. In 2006 the fee for anti-retroviral (ARV) drugs was removed in hospital and public clinics; this is expected to boost the number of Aids sufferers who undertake the course of treatment.
The national level of HIV/Aids infections is mixed, in urban areas rates have declined, however, infection figures for rural areas have yet to peak. Added to which, food shortages due to East Africa's worst drought in a decade, hampers Aids patients with their ARV treatment.
The annual loss in terms of GDP per capita growth was projected to be 1.3 per cent per annum between 2000–10. Households, in which one family member dies of Aids, are estimated to lose between 49–78 per cent of their annual income.
Kenya's Population Council has reported that many women surveyed, knowing they were HIV positive had not disclosed their condition to their partners for fear of violence or abandonment.
The Kenyan government's annual expenditure on HIV/Aids amounts to 6.5 per cent of the annual healthcare budget.
HIV prevalence: 4 per cent (2006), down from 14 per cent in 1997 (UNAids 2006).
Life expectancy: 51 years, 2004 (WHO 2006)
Fertility rate/Maternal mortality rate: 5.0 births per woman, 2004 (WHO 2006); maternal mortality 590 per 100,000 live births (World Bank).
Child (under 5 years) mortality rate (per 1,000): 79 per 1,000 live births (World Bank)
Head of population per physician: 0.14 physician per 1,000 people, 2004 (WHO 2006)

Welfare

Approximately 47 per cent of the total population is under 15 years. Around 50 per cent of the population is thought to live on less than US$1 a day. Around 80 per cent of the population is at risk from drought, famine and HIV/Aids.

A social security system, administered separately from the government budget, covers only government employees and workers in the small modern sector of the economy. The welfare system is financed by the National Social Security Fund (NSSF), set up in 1965. The NSSF has approximately 2.7 million members. In theory, social security contributions are compulsory and are deducted from wages at source. Deductions range from one-thirtieth to one-tenth of earnings. The employer pays half of each employee's contribution. In practice, few families or small businesses enrol their servants or workers. In November 2001, President Moi announced the establishment of a mandatory National Social Health Insurance (NSHI) scheme that would cover all Kenyans.

Social security benefits are limited to survivor's benefit (paid on the death of contributor), invalidity benefit, withdrawal benefit (a fixed sum paid on retirement) and an emigration grant. There is no unemployment benefit. Every Kenyan is entitled to supplementary health benefit under the National Hospital Insurance scheme, founded in 1966.

Main cities

Nairobi (capital, estimated population 2.8 million in 2005, some 1,650 metres above sea-level), Mombasa (795,174), Nakuru (276,263), Kisumu (394,684), Eldoret (230,351), Ruiru (225,794)

Languages spoken

KiSwahili is the lingua franca. In addition, most tribes have their own language. English is universally used in business and spoken by most people in the tourist industry. Other languages are Gikuyu, Kiluhya, Dholuo, Kikamba, Maasai and Somali.

Official language/s

KiSwahili and English

Media

The press is lively and mostly free but can be subjected to extra-legal intimidation if it incurs the wrath of the authorities.

In August 2007 President Kibaki refused to sign a bill which could have forced reporters to reveal their sources. The bill was returned to parliament. Kenya has a lively media which has exposed corruption in government in the past.

Press

Dailies: The Nation Media Group publishes the independent *Daily Nation* (www.nation.co.ke) in English and in KiSwahili *Taifa Leo*, other private publications include, in English, *The Standard* (www.eastandard.net) which is the oldest newspapers; the *Kenya Times* (www.timesnews.co.ke) and *The People Daily* are owned by political entities.

Weeklies: Some daily newspapers publish weekend editions, others include *Coastweek* (www.coastweek.com) from Mombassa and the *Weekly Advertiser*.

Business: The Nation Media Group publishes the *Business Daily* (www.bdafrica.com) and the weekly *The East African* (www.theeastafrican.co.ke). The *Business Mirror* is a fortnightly, promotional trade publication. The Centre for Business Information in Kenya (CBIK) (www.epckenya.org) publishes a number of specific marketing, sales, exports and business information pamphlets.

Periodicals: There are a number of general and specialised periodicals.

Broadcasting

The Kenya Broadcasting Corporation (KBC) (www.kbc.co.ke) is the state-run radio and television provider.

Radio: With high levels of poverty radio is the principal medium for news and information and with the significant expansion of FM radio, particularly ethnic stations which have increased public participation through call-in programmes radio provides an important medium for public debate. KBC (www.kbc.co.ke) operates extensive national services in English, Hindi, KiSwahili and 14 other local languages. Private radio stations include Capital FM (www.capitalfm.co.ke), Kiss FM (www.kissfm.co.ke) and a Christian station Family FM (www.familykenya.com). Coro FM and Radio Citizen in Kikuyu and East FM in Hindi.

Television: KBC (www.kbc.co.ke) operates one channel with programmes in KiSwahili and English it also runs Metro TV with a younger target audience. The satellite channel, Kenya Television Network (KTN) (www.ktnkenya.tv) broadcasts imported and locally produced programmes. Other, private TV stations include the Christian Family TV (www.familykenya.com), Stella TV and NTV (http://politics.nationmedia.com) run by Nation Media Group.

The Africa-wide Business Africa (www.business-africa.net) broadcasts news and business items over the internet in French and English.

News agencies

National news agency: Office of Public Communications

Economy

Kenya has East Africa's largest economy. It maintained strong GDP growth of 4.6 per cent in 2004 to a high of 7.1 per cent in 2007 before plummeting to 1.7 per cent in 2008. The global recession forced the government to introduce its biggest ever budget in June 2009 (a 24 per cent increase over 2008) to boost the economy through government spending. The government forecast that the US$11 billion stimulus package would expand GDP growth, which it did by 2.6 per cent in 2009 and 5.6 per cent in 2010. The budget had specifically allocated a larger than previous proportion of development spending on roads, energy and water supplies, including irrigation schemes.

Kenya is a predominantly rural, low-income economy and although heavily indebted to international lenders, managed to reschedule its Paris Club debts, to be paid within 20 years with 10-years grace, from 2004. The global recession hit key sectors of the economy at risk from external influence, with losses in tourism, horticulture and remittances. Inflation rose in 2008 into double digits of 13.1 per cent, and began to fall, to 10.6 per cent in 2009 and 4.1 per cent in 2010. Industrial activity provided over 20 per cent of GDP in 2009–10, but with a falling share of manufacturing (3.5 per cent in 2008 down to 2 per cent in 2009). The industrial sector is more diversified than in neighbouring countries and includes more private sector involvement. Industries include food processing, tobacco, beverages and transport. There is a strong service sector, which accounts for over 55 per cent of GDP in mainly tourism and financial services and is a major source of employment and foreign exchange.

Kenya's tourism industry was rocked in 2011 as Somali Islamic insurgents and pirates targeted wealth visitors to Kenya's coastal resorts.

Agriculture in 2008–09 provided over 20 per cent of GDP, falling from almost 25 per cent of GDP in 2007. With 75 per cent of the land area arid or semi-arid there is a high urban population, notably in the large shanty towns that skirt the major cities such as Nairobi. Unemployment remains high and around 40 per cent of the population lives on less than US$2 per day.

In May 2009 the International Monetary Fund (IMF) approved a US$209 million loan to boost Kenya's foreign exchange reserves. In July 2009 the international credit ratings agency Standard & Poor's graded Kenya's sovereign credit rating as B+B with transfer and convertibility to foreign exchange at BB-.

A serious obstacle to Kenya's development is the level of corruption and nepotism, in both government and business. It has resulted in the suspension of aid from several international donors, led by the

US which, in 2009 warned that tighter scrutiny would be given to all proposed projects, loans and assistance programmes provided for Kenya until an agreed tribunal, charged with reviewing the violence during the 2007 elections, was finally inaugurated.

External trade

Kenya is a member of the East African Community (EAC) (with Burundi, Rwanda, Tanzania and Uganda). The East African Community Common Market Protocol (EACMP) was launched on 1 July 2010, which will lead to the free movement of labour, capital, goods and services between member states as well as employment opportunities and easier flow of investment capital. The signed protocol now requires that legislation in all states must be harmonised to conform to its jurisdiction.

Kenya is also a member of the Common Market for Eastern and Southern Africa (Comesa), which operates a free trade zone with 13 of the 19 member states and belongs to the InterGovernmental Authority on Development (IGAD), which offers regional help to members during times of drought and natural disasters as well as economic co-operation and integration.

Around 65 per cent of all exports are fresh flowers, fruit and vegetables which are flown to European markets hours after harvesting. Around 50 per cent of all agricultural produce, valued at over US$200 million are exported to the UK; horticulture provided the second largest foreign earnings after tourism.

Imports

Principal imports are machinery and vehicles, petroleum, iron and steel, resins and plastics.

Main sources: UK (typically over 15 per cent of total), UAE (13 per cent), India (10 per cent).

Exports

Principal exports are tea (typically over 25 per cent of total), horticultural products and coffee. Other exports include petroleum products, fruit and vegetables, cement and sisal.

Main destinations: UK (typically over 15 per cent of total), Uganda (10 per cent), The Netherlands (5 per cent).

Agriculture

Farming

The agriculture sector generates some 60 per cent of export earnings and gives employment to 62 per cent of the workforce. Less than 20 per cent of Kenya's land surface is arable. There is an acute shortage of arable land and uneven distribution has resulted in most farmers working plots of two hectares or less. Population growth and rapid urbanisation place increasing pressure on food production and distribution to meet demand at affordable prices. In addition, there is an ecological risk to some of the most fertile areas of western and central Kenya, which are already severely overpopulated. Given the pressure on the land, increased food production depends on the development of new high-yielding crops.

The principal cash crops are tea, coffee (mainly arabica grown by smallholders), sugar, cotton, sisal, tobacco, pineapples and wattle. Kenya produces high quality coffee, an average of one million bags per annum. Horticultural production has increased in importance and it is the second-largest export earner after tea with flowers making up the largest share (close to 40,000 tonnes).

Kenya's 200,000 or so farmers who used to grow the natural pesticide, pyrethrum, have been badly let down over the years. The once globally dominant industry (as much as 70 per cent of world production) has dwindled as mismanagement of the Pyrethrum Board of Kenya (PBK) has forced farmers, many of whom haven't been paid for three years, to uproot their crops. In 2011 there was a move towards liberalisation of the industry, which would provide an alternative to the PBK, which currently has a monopoly on buying, processing and marketing the plant.

Primary and processed agricultural products account for over 55 per cent of export earnings. Subsistence farming comprises more than half of output.

Maize is the most important food crop. Sorghum, cassava, beans and fruit are also grown. Inadequate storage facilities, little irrigation, recurrent drought and lack of incentives and land have restricted growth.

Kenya's growers of fresh flowers and vegetables are vunerable to disruption of airfreght. For instance, the shutdown of air travel in Europe in April 2010, caused by the Icelandic volcanic ash cloud, resulted in the horticultural sector losing around US$3–4 million per day over the six-day period of closure. Millions of flowers and hundreds of tonnes of vegetables had to be discarded. From one refrigeration plant alone, in a two-day period, almost 65 tonnes of vegetables and 400,000 roses were dumped.

Despite the insecurity and harrassing from bandits, a booming trade in livestock has thrived for more than two decades along the borders between Somalia, Ethiopia and Kenya. However, in 2011, this trade was badly affected by the drought which covered the Horn of Africa region and the resultant high numbers of refugees who fled south from Somalia and Ethiopia into Kenya.

Fishing

Kenya has a coastline of 680km, as well as territoral waters in Lake Victoria and Lake Takana. Some 20,000 small fishermen along the coast complained in 2008 that large foreign boats were depriving them of their living. Although 60 boats, mostly from Europe and the Far East, have been licensed to fish, local fisherman estimate that some 200 boats are fishing in a single season. Most of the ships target prawns, yellow fin tuna and sharks. A report by the UK's Department for International Development (DFID), shows that Kenya losses about US$5m through illegal fishing by foreign boats each year.

In a meeting of African ministers in Namibia, held on 2 July, members discussed illegal and unregulated fishing, which is estimated to cost Africa US$1 billion per annum in lost revenue and the threat to stocks and local artisan fishing.

Forestry

Kenya has only 2 per cent of forest cover. Deforestation is a major problem along with desertification in northern regions. Fuel wood and charcoal meet more than 75 per cent of the domestic energy requirement, however, the government is attempting to protect timber resources which are being depleted from excessive demands. The government estimates that only 70 per cent of Kenya's wood fuel demands are met by regenerative growth. The need for land is placing increasing pressure on Kenya's forestry reserves.

Industry and manufacturing

Foreign investment, particularly from the UK, Japan and US, plays a significant role. Emphasis is on developing joint venture, export-oriented industries and encouraging greater utilisation of local raw materials and other inputs. Large sections of industry continue to operate well below full capacity as a result of import controls, rising costs and marketing difficulties. Rainfall can also have an impact on the sector's performance, with power shortages and reduced agricultural production during drought causing knock-on effects for manufacturing.

The manufacturing sector has been affected by power shortages, a fall in the growth of foreign direct investment (FDI) and rising costs of fuel imports. However, it remains the most developed manufacturing sector in East Africa.

Principal industries include food and tobacco processing, beverages, chemicals, machinery and transport equipment, textiles, glass, vehicle assembly and construction materials.

The public sale of shares in the mobile/cell phone company Safaricom, which was set at Ks5, when they went on sale on 9 June 2008, rose by 60 per cent in one day to Ks8. It was Kenya's record biggest stock market flotation and earned

the government around US$833 from its 25 per cent stake in the company. The sale was over-subscribed by more than 500 per cent, with those successful receiving around 20 shares. Safaricom, with profits of US$370 million in 2007, is East Africa's most profitable company.
Kenya's mobile/cell phone market has only a take-up of 33 per cent, with further room for growth.

Tourism
Tourism is the country's largest foreign exchange earner and its assets include its wildlife, mostly accessible through a system of parks and reserves, extensive white sand beaches protected by coral reefs, and dramatic scenery from deserts to tropical rain forest.
Tourism is recognised as a means of poverty reduction and private sector growth. To this end, Kenya and the EU formed the Kenya Trust Fund to finance tourism development and the marketing and promotion of tourism.
The growth of the market during the 2000s has exceeded the availability of accommodation. Attention is being turned to developing Kenya from a mass market to a high-value destination.
The violence following the presidential elections in early 2008 impacted badly on tourism as an estimated one million visitors cancelled their holidays. Tourism is the country's premier foreign income earner – providing more than the combined amount from tea and horticulture. Visitor numbers had doubled between 2004–07, but in January 2008, 85 per cent of the usual number was lost, which had a direct impact on employment with the loss of 20,000 jobs and a further 80,000 indirect jobs by March. An estimated US$1 billion was lost, with a fall in investor confidence, according to the finance minister.
Kenya's tourism industry was rocked in 2011 as Somali Islamic insurgents and pirates targeted wealth visitors to Kenya's coastal resorts. The government's response was to send a military force into Somalia to raid likely insurgency camps.

Environment
Almost five tonnes of confiscated elephant ivory tusks, worth US$16 million, were destroyed on 20 July 2011. President Kibaki set the torch that burned the tusks, which were seized in Singapore, in a public display of combating the illegal poaching trade.

Mining
Mining accounts for just 1 per cent of GDP. The sector is dominated by the production of industrial minerals such as soda ash, flourspar, kaolin and some gemstones. Gold is also produced in small quantities by artisanal gold miners. The government's policy is to encourage private sector participation in further exploration, prospecting and development of the mineral resources sector.
The most promising mining prospects are within the licences held by the Canadian mining company Tiomin Resources for deposits covering four areas – Mambrui, Sokoke, Vipingo and Kwale – which hold 12 per cent of the world's rutile and ilmenite resources.

Hydrocarbons
There has been limited exploration, but without tangible results. Interest has been ignited by discoveries in Sudan, which shares Kenya's geology, and by the rise in world oil prices. Companies from a number of countries, including China, are becoming increasingly involved in the possibility of locating reserves of oil and also gas and the search is also being extended offshore to the Lamu basin.
Kenya does not produce or import natural gas.
In 2008 the government invited mining companies to bid for a tender to extract coal from the Kitui and Mwingi districts and the last phase of exploration for the Mui basin to determine its commercial viability.

Energy
Total generating capacity is 1,200MW. KenGen, the former government-owned entity, is the leading electricity generating company, supplying around 80 per cent of the electricity consumed. It generates power through hydro-, thermal-, wind- and geothermal-power, of which hydropower provides 72.3 per cent of the company's installed capacity of 677MW. There are hydroelectric plants in the Tana River basin, a geothermal station at Olkaria, and at Kipevu, on the coast and a 75MW oil-fired plant, which was opened in 1999. In June 2008, the president announced that a plan to install around 1,700MW of geothermal energy by 2018 would begin and increase capacity by 150 per cent.

Financial markets
The NSE is small and somewhat speculative. It was established in 1954 and is sub-Saharan Africa's fourth-largest bourse. It originally operated as an association of stockbrokers with no trading floor until October 1991. The introduction of the trading floor has led to a substantial increase in trading volumes and dramatic upward movement in the various indexes. In 1995, foreign investors were allowed back into the NSE for the first time in 30 years. The NSE has been instrumental in enabling the public and private sectors in Kenya to raise large amounts of capital for expansion projects and for the financing of new businesses.
The public sale of shares in the mobile/cell phone company Safaricom, which was set at Ks5, when they went on sale on 9 June 2008, rose by 60 per cent in one day to Ks8. It was Kenya's record biggest stock market flotation and earned the government around US$833 from its 25 per cent stake in the company. The sale was over-subscribed by more than 500 per cent, with those successful receiving around 20 shares.

Stock exchange
Nairobi Stock Exchange (NSE). The Nairobi Stock Exchange was formed in 1954. It became fully automated in 2007.

Banking and insurance
Kenya contains a thriving community of foreign banks, which were attracted during the 1970s and 1980s by its reputation for political and commercial stability, good telecommunications infrastructure and the large number of multinationals based in the country. However, the sector is plagued by high levels of non-performing loans which threaten to undermine banking liquidity, affecting the wider economy.

Central bank
Central Bank of Kenya

Main financial centre
Nairobi

Time
GMT plus three hours

Geography
Kenya lies on the east coast of Africa. It is bounded by Ethiopia and Sudan to the north, Uganda and Lake Victoria to the west, Tanzania to the south and Somalia and the Indian Ocean to the east.
From the Indian Ocean, the land rises gradually through dry bush to the arable land of the highlands. The highest peak is Mount Kenya at 5,200 metres. The west of the country is dissected by the Great Rift Valley, partly filled by a chain of lakes.

Hemisphere
Straddles the equator

Climate
The climate is tropical in low-lying districts, especially along the coast, but is more temperate on the plateau and in the highlands. Kenya has two rainy seasons when temperatures can fall sharply: the long rains from April to June and the short rains in October and November. The hottest month is February, with temperatures of 20–30 degrees Celsius (C), while the coolest month is July, with temperatures of 11–22 degrees C. Nairobi, at an altitude of 1,661 metres, has a mean annual temperature of 17 degrees C and annual rainfall averaging 864mm.

Dress codes

A lightweight suit, collar and tie or other formal clothing should be worn for business meetings. Despite a hot tropical climate, nights can be cool and it is advisable to have a sweater to cover day wear, which should be light cotton casual at the coast. Warmer clothing is needed especially in June and July. Evening dress should normally be smart casual. Nairobi is considerably cooler than Mombasa.

Entry requirements

Passports

Required by all, valid for three months from date of entry.

Visa

Required by all, with the exception of nationals of some Commonwealth and other countries. Visas may be obtained from Kenyan missions or at the port of entry, although nationals of certain specified countries nationals must apply well in advance for referral to Nairobi. For a full list of each category and further details, visit www.kenyaembassy.co.uk.

Currency advice/regulations

There are no restrictions on the import and export of local and foreign currencies, subject to declaration of amounts in excess of Ksh100,000.

US dollar or other hard currency travellers cheques are recommended.

Health (for visitors)

Mandatory precautions

Yellow fever vaccination certificate if arriving from an infected area.

Advisable precautions

Yellow fever, typhoid, tetanus, hepatitis A, meningitis and polio vaccinations. Malaria prophylaxis necessary for coastal and other lower altitude regions. Water precautions should be taken – bilharzia is present. Rabies is a risk in rural areas and vaccinations must be administered following a bites from any mammal.

Hotels

There is a wide range available in main centres. It is advisable to book well in advance during peak season (November–April).

Credit cards

Major cards are widely accepted.

Public holidays (national)

Fixed dates

1 Jan (New Year's Day), 1 May (Labour Day), 1 Jun (Madaraka Day), 10 Oct (Moi Day), 20 Oct (Kenyatta Day), 12 Dec (Independence/Jamhuri Day), 25–26 Dec (Christmas).

Holidays falling on a Sunday are observed the following Monday.

Variable dates

Good Friday, Easter Monday, Eid al Fitr.

Working hours

Banking

Mon–Fri: 0900–1400. Open first and last Sat in each month 0900–1100.

Barclays Bank, Kenyatta Avenue, Nairobi, open daily for foreign exchange until 1600.

Airport banks are open until midnight every day.

Business

Mon–Fri: 0800–1300, 1400–1700; Sat: 0830–1200/1230. Mombasa offices normally open and close half-an-hour earlier.

Government

Mon–Fri: 0800–1300, 1400–1700; Sat: 0830–1200/1230. Mombasa offices normally open and close half-an-hour earlier.

Shops

Mon-Fri: 0800–1700; Sat: 0830–1300. Many shops open outside these hours.

Telecommunications

Mobile/cell phones

GSM 900/1800 services are available, particularly in the south of the country.

Electricity supply

230/240V AC, 50 cycles. Subject to power surges outside main centres. Sockets are usually three-pin square (British type).

Social customs/useful tips

Personal contact is an important way of doing business in Kenya.

Bureaucracy can be frustratingly slow, although persistence pays. Going in person to the relevant office is often the best way of getting things done. Government and commercial offices are within easy walking distance of the main hotels.

Outside the major towns local customs vary from place to place. In the game parks and bush, some tribes do not like being photographed, although in areas where tourism is more developed, some tribe members will allow photographs for a fee. Visitors to game parks should not leave their vehicles without permission from the guide. There is a large Arab influence on the coast and most hotels display government signs saying nudity is banned. Topless bathing for women is, however, tolerated in areas where there are large concentrations of hotels.

Kenyans are friendly and open, and the greeting, *jambo*, will be returned with a smile.

It is prohibited to photograph the president or his residence, military, police or related installations.

Security

Security is not a problem in the major towns during the day but flashy displays of jewellery are not recommended. Do not carry large amounts of cash.

Nairobi is practically deserted after 2200. Walking around the African quarters of town without a guide or in the shanty towns around the capital is not advised.

Visitors are advised to avoid political meetings and demonstrations.

Incidents of armed car-hijacking are prevalent in Nairobi and Mombasa.

Do not attempt to escape from hijackers or resist their demands.

Getting there

Air

National airline: Kenya Airways

International airport/s: Nairobi – Jomo Kenyatta International (NBO), 17km from city, duty-free shop, bar, restaurant, buffet, bank, post office, shops, car hire.

Other airport/s: Mombasa – Moi International (MBA), 13km south-east of city, duty-free shop, bar, restaurant, bank, post office, shops, car hire. Medium-sized airports have also been developed at Eldoret, Kisumu and Malindi.

Airport tax: US$20, usually included in ticket price.

Surface

Road: Entry by road from Uganda, Ethiopia, Sudan and Tanzania can be difficult. Regulations and conditions should be checked with Kenyan authorities before travelling.

An all-weather road links Nairobi to Addis Ababa (Ethiopia) and there is a 590km road link between Kitale and Juba (Sudan).

In rural areas, some of the unsurfaced roads can be difficult in wet weather.

Rail: A 1,085km main line runs from the port of Mombasa through Nairobi, Nakuru and Eldoret to Uganda. There is also a link to Moshi (Tanzania).

Main port/s: Mombasa

Getting about

National transport

Air: Kenya Airways operates regular services linking Mombasa, Malindi, Kisumu and other major centres with Nairobi.

Local light aircraft companies fly regular services to smaller airfields, such as Lamu, a tourist attraction on the coast.

Charter flights are also available to game reserves, such as Maasai Mara, and main centres.

Road: The growth in road transportation has led to overloading of some highways, and both the maintenance and improvement of these routes have been neglected. This also applies to roads which come under the jurisdiction of town authorities.

Nearly all main towns are connected by good surfaced roads. In rural areas some of the unsurfaced roads can be difficult in wet weather.

Long-distance (Peugeot) taxi service operates between towns. Cars can be shared, although it is not generally recommended.

Buses: Coach services operate on all major routes between towns and cities and into Tanzania, Ethiopia and Uganda.

Rail: The Kenya Railways system comprises approximately 1,920km of one metre gauge single track.

There are departures daily, with first- and second-class service, from Nairobi to Mombasa; the overnight service is popular. Journey time is approximately 14 hours. Trains often run late, but are fairly comfortable. It is advisable to book sleeping compartments in advance.

Two Uganda-Kenya railway agreements were signed in April 2006. In Uganda a concession agreement covers the freight services of Uganda Railways Corporation (URC), while an Interface agreement covers matters common to the Kenya freight and passenger concession and the Uganda freight concession. The Rift Valley Railways Consortium (RVRC) will invest US$15 million over the first five years and a further US$75 million over the remainder of the agreement in Uganda and US$45 and US$300 million respectively in Kenya.

City transport

Taxis: Available in most major towns. Some licensed taxis are metered and often shared, with fares according to time and distance. Fares for long trips should be agreed in advance.

Buses, trams & metro: Good and fairly cheap services operate regularly in Nairobi and Mombasa and between towns and cities, as well as across the borders to Tanzania, Ethiopia and Uganda. Minibuses and vans (*matatu*) are unregulated and can be overcrowded; they are not recommended for visitors.

Car hire

Can be hired from travel operators and hotels in Nairobi, Mombasa and Malindi. A national or international driving licence which has been held for at least two years without endorsements, including the period of visit to Kenya, is required .

BUSINESS DIRECTORY

The addresses listed below are a selection only. While World of Information makes every endeavour to check these addresses, we cannot guarantee that changes have not been made, especially to telephone numbers and area codes. We would welcome any corrections.

Telephone area codes

The international direct dialling (IDD) code for Kenya is +254, followed by area code and subscriber's number:

Eldoret	53	Malindi	42
Garissa	46	Mombasa	41
Kajiado	45	Nairobi	20
Kericho	52	Naivasha	50
Kisumu	57	Nakuru	51
Kwale	40	Voi	43

Chambers of Commerce

Kenya National Chamber of Commerce & Industry, Ufanisi House, Haile Selassie Avenue, PO Box 47024, Nairobi (tel: 220-867; fax: 334-2934; e-mail: kncci@swiftkenya.com).

Banking

African Banking Corporation Ltd, PO Box 46452, Mezzanine Floor, ABC-Bank, Koingange Street, Nairobi (tel: 223-922, 251-540/1, 226-712, 248-978; fax: 222-437).

Barclays Bank of Kenya Ltd, PO Box 30120, Barclays Plaza, Loita St, Nairobi (tel: 214-270, 313-405; fax: 213-915, 215-418).

The Co-operative Bank of Kenya Ltd, PO Box 48231, Union Towers, Kenya-Re Plaza - Taifa Rd, Moi Ave, Nairobi (tel: 225-579, 228-453/7, 251290/9; fax: 229-38, 246-635, 227-747).

Commercial Bank of Africa Ltd, Commercial Bank Building, Standard/Wabera Streets, Nairobi (tel: 228-881; fax: 335-827, 340-157).

Development Bank of Kenya Ltd, PO Box 30483, Finance House, Loita Street, Nairobi (tel: 340-401, 340-402, 340-403; fax: 338-426).

Imperial Bank Ltd, PO Box 44905, 8th Floor, IPS Bldg, Kimathi St, Nairobi (tel: 252-175/6/7/8, 252-184/5, 225-060; fax: 230-994, 250-137).

Investments & Mortgages Bank Ltd, PO Box 30238, I & M Bank House, 2nd Ngong Avenue, Nairobi (tel: 711-994-8, 310-105-7; fax: 713-757, 716-372).

Kenya Commercial Bank Ltd, PO Box 48400, Moi Avenue, Nairobi (tel: 339-441; fax: 215-565).

National Bank of Kenya Ltd, PO Box 72866, National Bank Building, Harambee Avenue, Nairobi.

Standard Chartered Bank Kenya Ltd, PO Box 30003, Stanbank House, Moi Avenue, Nairobi (tel: 330-200, 331-210; fax: 214-086).

Central bank

Central Bank of Kenya, Haile Selassie Avenue, PO Box 60000-0200 Nairobi (tel: 286-1000; fax: 340-192; e-mail: info@centralbank.go.ke).

Stock exchange

Nairobi Stock Exchange (NSE): www.nse.co.ke

Travel information

Automobile Association of Kenya, AA House, Embakasi, PO Box 40087, Nairobi (tel: 825-060; fax: 825-068; e-mail: aakenya@africaonline.co.ke).

Air Kenya, Wilson Airport, PO Box 30357, Nairobi (tel: 605-745; fax: 602-951; e-mail: resvns@airkenya.com).

Kenya Airways, Airport North Road, Embakasi, PO Box 19142, Nairobi (tel: 642-2000; fax: 823-488).

Kenya Railways, PO Box 30121, Nairobi (tel: 221-211; fax: 340-049).

Ministry of tourism

Ministry of Tourism and Wildlife, Utalii House, Uhuru Highway, PO Box 30027, Nairobi (tel: 333-555; fax: 318-045; e-mail:info@tourism.go.ke).

National tourist organisation offices

Kenya Tourist Board, Kenya-Re Towers, Ragati Road, PO Box 30630, Nairobi (tel: 711-262; fax: 719-925; e-mail: info@kenyatourism.org).

Ministries

Ministry of Agriculture, Livestock Development and Marketing, Kilimo House, Cathedral Road, PO Box 30028, Nairobi (tel: 718-870; fax: 725-774).

Ministry of Commerce and Industry, Co-operative House, Haile Selassie Avenue, PO Box 30430, Nairobi (tel: 340-010, 340-224; fax: 218-845).

Ministry of Energy, Nyayo House, Kenyatta Avenue, PO Box 30582, Nairobi (tel: 333-551).

Ministry of the Environment and Natural Resources, Kencom House, Moi Avenue, PO Box 30126, Nairobi (tel: 229-261).

Ministry of Finance, Treasury House, Harambee Avenue, PO Box 30007, Nairobi (tel: 338-111; fax: 330-426).

Ministry of Information and Broadcasting, Jogoo House 'A', Taifa Road, PO Box 30025, Nairobi (tel: 334-688; fax: 340-659).

Ministry of Planning and National Development, PO Box 3007, Nairobi (tel: 338-111; fax: 330-426).

Ministry of Transport and Communications, Transcom House, Ngong Road, PO Box 52692, Nairobi (tel: 729-200; fax: 726-362).

Office of the President, Harambee House, Harambee Avenue, PO Box 30510, Nairobi (tel: 227-411; fax: 723-666).

Other useful addresses

Africa Growth Fund, PO Box 34045, Nairobi (tel: 721-566; fax: 722-240).

African Project Development Facility, International House, PO Box 46534, Nairobi.

Agricultural Development Corporation, PO Box 30367, Nairobi (tel: 338-530).

Attorney-General's Office, State Law Office, Harambee Avenue, PO Box 40112, Nairobi (tel: 227-461; fax: 211-082).

British High Commission, Bruce House, Standard Street, PO Box 30465, Nairobi (tel: 335-944; fax: 333-196); Commercial Section, Upper Hill Road, PO Box 30133, Nairobi (tel: 714-699; fax: 719-082; e-mail: bhctrade@users.africaonline.co.ke).

Capital Markets Authority (CMA), Re-Insurance Plaza, Taifa Rd, PO Box 74800, Nairobi (tel: 221-910/869; fax: 216-681).

Central Police Station, University Way, Nairobi (tel: 222-222).

Central Reference Library, Ministry of Information, Department of Information, PO Box 8053 or 30025, Nairobi (tel: 223-201).

Communications Commission of Kenya (CCK), 5th Floor, Longonot Place, Kijabe Street, PO Box 14448, Nairobi 00800 (tel: 240-165, 250-173, 310-083/4; fax: 252-547; internet site: www.cck.go.ke).

Customs and Excise, PO Box 40160, Nairobi.

Development Finance Company of Kenya, Finance House, Loita Street, PO Box 30483, Nairobi (tel: 340-401; fax: 338-246).

East African Report on Trade and Industry, PO Box 30339, Nairobi.

Economic Development for Equatorial and Southern Africa, PO Box 56038, Nairobi (tel: 822-920/4; fax: 822-925/907).

Executive Secretariat and Technical Unit (ESTU), Anniversary Towers, University Way, 7th Floor, PO Box 34542, Nairobi (tel: 222-127/57/68; fax: 216-945).

Export Processing Zones Authority (EPZA), British American Centre, Mara Rd, PO Box 50563, Nairobi (tel: 712-800/6; fax: 713-704).

Export Promotion Council (EPC), Anniversary Towers, 1st Floor, University Way, PO Box 40247, Nairobi (tel: 228-534/5; fax: 218-013).

Federation of Kenya Employers (FKE), Argwings Kodhek Road, PO Box 48311, Nairobi (tel: 721-929; fax: 721-948).

General Post Office, Kenyatta Avenue, Nairobi.

Horticultural Crops Development Authority (HCDA), Uniafric House, Koinange St, PO Box 42601, Nairobi (tel: 337-381/3).

Industrial and Commercial Development Corporation, Uchumi House, Nkrumah Avenue, PO Box 45519, Nairobi (tel: 229-213; fax: 333-880).

Industrial Promotion Services Ltd, IPS Building, PO Box 30500, Nairobi (tel: 228-026, 728-207; fax: 214-563).

International Finance Corporation, View Park Towers, PO Box 30577, Nairobi (tel: 224-726; fax: 219-980).

Kenya Association of Manufacturers (KAM), Mpaka Rd, Westland, PO Box 30225, Nairobi (tel: 746-005/7; fax: 746-028).

Kenya Association of Tour Operators (for information on conference facilities throughout Kenya), PO Box 48461, Nairobi (tel: 227-005).

Kenya External Trade Authority, PO Box 43137, Nairobi (tel: 226-016).

Kenya Investment Authority, National Bank of Kenya Building, Harambee Avenue, PO Box 55704, Nairobi (tel: 221-401; fax: 243-862; e-mail: info@investmentkenya.com).

Kenya Power Company Limited, Stima Plaza, Kolobot Road, PO Box 47936, Nairobi (tel: 741-181/9; fax: 337-351).

Kenya Revenue Authority, Tax Programmes and New Business Initiatives, Nairobi (tel: 715-428; fax: 715-432).

Kenya Tea Development Authority, Commonwealth House, Moi Avenue, Nairobi (tel: 221-441).

Kenyan Embassy (USA), 2249 R Street, NW, Washington DC 20008 (tel: (+1-202)-387-6101; fax: (+1-202)-462-3829; e-mail: info@kenyaembassy.com).

Kenyatta International Conference Centre, PO Box 30746, Nairobi (tel: 332-383).

Nairobi Stock Exchange, Kimathi Street, IPS Building, 2nd Floor, PO Box 43833, Nairobi (tel: 230-692; fax: 224-200).

US Embassy, Corner Moi and Haile Selassie Avenues, PO Box 30137, Nairobi (tel: 334-141; fax: 340-838).

National news agency: Office of Public Communications, PO Box 45617; KICC Building, 3 Floor, 8 Harambee Ave, 00100 Nairobi (tel: 202 224-0488; fax: 202 240-600; email: comms@comms.go.ke).

Internet sites

Africa Business Network: http://www.ifc.org/abn

AllAfrica.com: http://allafrica.com

African Development Bank: http://www.afdb.org

Africa Online: http://www.africaonline.com

KenyaWeb: http://www.kenyaweb.com/

Mbendi AfroPaedia (information on companies, countries, industries and stock exchanges in Africa): http://mbendi.co.za

Kiribati

KEY FACTS

Official name: Ripaberikan Kiribati (Republic of Kiribati) (pronounced Kiribas)

Head of State: President (Beretitenti) Anote Tong (BTK) (elected 2003; re-elected Oct 2007)

Head of government: President (Beretitenti) Anote Tong

Ruling party: Boutokan te Koaua (BTK) (Pillars of Truth) (since 2003; re-elected Aug 2007)

Area: 810 square km (33 islands and atolls)

Population: 100,000 (2010)*

Capital: Bairiki (on Tarawa)

Official language: I-Kiribati, English

Currency: Australian dollar (A$) = 100 cents)

Exchange rate: A$1.03 per US$ (Oct 2011)

GDP per capita: US$1,479 (2010)

GDP real growth: 1.80% (2010)

GDP: US$147.00 million (2010)

Inflation: -1.40% (2010)

Balance of trade: -US$1,000,000 (2008)*

* estimated figure

NOTA

29 December 2011, parliament will hold a delayed presidential election on 30 January.

Kiribati has had to draw on its wealth fund in the last four years as the economy has faltered. The fund fell from A$637 million (US$618 million) in 2007 to A$571 million (US$554 million) in 2009; it has contributed around 19 per cent of gross domestic product (GDP) since 2007. The fund's investments, having made losses over the 2007–09 period, recovered in 2010.

The Asian Development Bank (ADB) reported that the economy performed better in 2010, after two years of contraction, while growth in 2011 is forecast to be 2 per cent. A number of donor-funded projects, including improving the international airports at Tarawa and Kiritimati, will contribute to this growth.

On the down side, remittances from seafarers, which account for some 7 per cent of GDP, dropped by 13 per cent in 2010 as demand fell away and workers of other nationalities replaced the men from Kiribati. Income from copra also declined, mostly due to bad weather.

COUNTRY PROFILE

Historical profile

1892 Kiribati became part of the British colony of the Gilbert and Ellice Islands and was administered by the West Pacific High Commission in Fiji.

1942 The islands were occupied by the Japanese during World War II.

1963 Transition to independence began, with the formation of legislative and executive councils under the supervision of a British governor general.

1975 Ellice Islands seceded and formed the separate entity of Tuvalu.

1979 Became the fully independent Republic of Kiribati.

1982–91 Iremia Tabai won the first three post-independence presidential elections in 1982, 1983 and 1987. Constitutional restrictions prevented Tabai contesting the 1991 elections which were won by Teatao Teannaki.

1994 Teburoro Tito of the Mwaneaaban te Mauri Party (MMP) was elected president.

1995 The government unilaterally moved the International Date Line eastwards to ensure the country's collection of islands were all designated as being within the same day.

1997 China built a satellite-tracking base on Kiribati's main atoll on a 15-year lease.

1998 President Tito was elected to his second term.

2000 Caroline Island was the first inhabited place to greet the new century, the name of the island was changed in celebration of the event to New Millennium.

2001 The Pacific Islands Forum, of which Kiribati is a member completed its negotiations to bring 14 Pacific island countries into a free trade agreement, known as the Pacific Islands Countries Trade Agreement (PICTA). The government of President Tito suffered heavy losses in the second round of parliamentary elections.

2002 Parliament passed newspaper registration laws, giving powers to ban the publication of newspapers that face complaints.

2003 Teburoro Tito (MMP) won presidential elections. President Tito lost a motion of no confidence and parliament was dissolved. In the resulting general elections the ruling MMP won 16 seats, the Boutokaan te Koaua (BTK) (Pillars of Truth) won 17. Anote Tong (BTK) was elected president. Kiribati established diplomatic relations with Taiwan, but also offered to honour the lease of the satellite tracking station with China; however, China rejected the offer, dismantled the station and severed diplomatic relations.

2005 Kiribati joined the International Whaling Commission.

2006 Kiribati designated an area of 184,700 square km in the Phoenix Islands as the world's third largest marine reserve. Kiribati appealed to the United Nations for action on global warming amid concerns about rising sea levels.

2007 The BTK won parliamentary elections with 18 seats. MTM won seven and independents 19 seats. In presidential elections, incumbent Anote Tong won about 65 per cent of the vote, his next closest rival, Nabuti Mwemwenikarawa, won about 33 per cent.

2008 The Phoenix Islands Protected Area was increased to 410,500 square kilometres to become the world's largest marine reserve.

2010 Air Pacific resumed its services (cancelled in 2008) following the upgrade

of the airstrip on the island of Kiritimati. In June, the UK's *The Sunday Times* alleged that Kiribati (among other countries) was bribed by Japan to vote in favour of Japan's killing of whales for scientific reasons at the International Whaling Commission. The denial by Kiribati of the allegation was based on the government's stance that 'everything has to be harvested in a sustainable manner' and all travel expenses were paid for from a fund provided by donor countries.
2011 The World Bank provided US$2 million in emergency funding for importing food for 60,000 people (60 per cent of the population) due to food shortages that resulted from a government funding shortfall for shipping costs. Since 2008, Kiribati has experienced both extreme weather and adverse financial conditions that had drained public coffers so that rising shipping costs reduced the quantity of affordable foods. The grant will pay for shipping costs, specifically to outer islands.

Political structure
Constitution
The 1979 constitution created an independent republic with a president as head of state, executive government, judicature and public service. A provision for citizenship of Kiribati also includes special status of Banaba and Banabans, as well as fundamental rights of freedom for individuals.
Form of state
Independent democratic republic; it is a member of the Commonwealth.
The executive
Executive power is exercised by a popularly elected *beretitenti* (president), for a four-year term, limited to three terms. The president is elected by the people from among three candidates nominated by the Maneaba (house of assembly) from its ranks. The president is head of state and head of government and appoints a cabinet composed of a president, vice president, 10 ministers from the house of assembly and an *ex officio* attorney general.
National legislature
The unicameral Maneaba Ni Maungatabu (house of assembly) consists of 46 members elected for four-year terms in multi-seat constituencies. One appointed member represents the Banaban community (most of whose inhabitants were evacuated from the Banaba Island during phosphate mining and now live on Rabi Island in Fiji). The speaker is an appointed post from outside the membership of the house of assembly and the attorney general is an *ex officio* post.
Universal suffrage begins at aged 18.
Last elections
17 Oct 2007 (presidential); 22/30 August 2007 (parliamentary).
Results: Parliamentary: (the combined result of rounds one and two) the BTK won 18 seats, MTM seven and independents 19 seats.
Presidential: incumbent Anote Tong (BTK) won 65 per cent of the vote; Nabuti Mwemwenikarawa won 43.5 per cent; and Banuera Berina (Maurin Kiribati Pati) (MKP)) won 9.1 per cent. Turnout was around 50 per cent.
Next elections
2011 (presidential and parliamentary)

Political parties
Ruling party
Boutokan te Koaua (BTK) (Pillars of Truth) (since 2003; re-elected Aug 2007)
Main opposition party
Maneaban te Mauri (MTM) (Protect the Maneaba)

Population
100,000 (2010)*
Last census: 7 December 2005: 92,533
Population density: 124 inhabitants per square km (2010)
Annual growth rate: 2.2 per cent 1994–2004 (WHO 2006)
Ethnic make-up
Predominantly Micronesian, with some Polynesian.
Religions
Roman Catholic (52 per cent), Protestant (Congregational) (40 per cent), Seventh-Day Adventist, Islam, Baha'i Faith, Latter-day Saints and Church of God.

Education
The Junior Secondary School (JSS) programme aims to provide universal access to basic secondary education. Almost all the outer islands (except Teraina and Tabuaeran) and South Tarawa have junior secondary schools.
Higher education, including both university level programmes and post-secondary vocational/technical training, is provided by the government and the regional institution, University of the South Pacific (USP). The government also operates two tertiary institutions on South Tarawa: Tarawa Technical Institute and Kiribati Teachers College.
Literacy rate: 92.2 per cent, adult rate.
Compulsory years: six to 15
Enrolment rate: 67.8 per cent gross school enrolment.

Health
The government has collaborated with the World Health Organisation (WHO) to strengthen its primary healthcare services. WHO's technical support has brought down the infant mortality rate and increased life expectancy.
Improved water sources are available to 47 per cent of the population.
There is one general hospital in Tarawa and a number of health centres in the more populated islands. There are few doctors. Medical facilities are of the most basic kind and there are no pharmacies. Excessive alcohol consumption has become a very severe problem both socially and medically. Diabetes linked to a western diet is widespread.
HIV/Aids
There has been a significant increase in infections on Tarawa.
Life expectancy: 65 years, 2004 (WHO 2006)
Fertility rate/Maternal mortality rate: 4.1 births per woman, 2004 (WHO 2006)
Birth rate/Death rate: 31 births per 1,000 population; 8.6 deaths per 1,000 population (2003).
Child (under 5 years) mortality rate (per 1,000): 49 per 1,000 live births (World Bank)

Welfare
The government has instituted a bonding system requiring all trained personnel to serve the country for at least the same number of years that it has funded their training. The retirement age, which was previously 50 years for all government employees, has been increased to 60 years for doctors and 55 for other categories.

KEY INDICATORS **Kiribati**

	Unit	2006	2007	2008	2009	2010
Population	m	0.10	0.10	0.10	*0.10	*0.10
Gross domestic product (GDP)	US$bn	0.11	0.13	0.14	0.13	0.15
GDP per capita	US$	1,147	1,312	1,304	1,304	1,479
GDP real growth	%	1.9	0.4	-1.1	-0.7	1.8
Inflation	%	-1.5	4.2	11.0	8.8	-1.4
lCurrent account	US$m	-3.0	-1.0	-1.0	-5.0	-34.0
Exchange rate	per US$	1.27	1.16	1.05	1.12	1.09

* estimated figure

Main cities
Bairiki, (capital, on Tarawa, estimated population 30,600 in 2005), Bikenibeu (on Tarawa, 7,704).

Languages spoken
English is used for official communications and is widely understood in the capital, Tarawa. It is used less on the outer islands where i-Kiribati is the norm. In the i-Kiribati language the letters 'ti' are pronounced 's' (Kiribati is pronounced Kiribas).

Official language/s
I-Kiribati, English

Media
Despite the lack of independent news outlets the government-owned radio and newspaper provide an appropriate level of press freedom.

Press
Since 2002, the Newspaper Registration Amendment Bill allows publications to be deregister and stopped when faced with complaints.
Weeklies: The government-owned *Te Uekera* is published in I-Kiribati and English. An independent newspaper, *Kiribati New Star*, began publication in 2004.
Periodicals: There are no newsagents and only limited copies of overseas papers and magazines are sold in shops. Religious organisations publish newsletters and periodicals in I-Kiribati with local news and stories relevant to their readership. *Te Itoi ni Kiribati* and *Kaotan te Ota* for Catholic and Protestant communities respectively.

Broadcasting
Kiribati is a member of the Commonwealth Broadcasting Association (www.cba.org.uk), which promotes best practices in broadcasting.
Radio: The only radio stating in operation is Radio Kiribati broadcasting in AM and FM, which provides a national, public network. External services from the BBC and VOA may be received on short-wave radios.

News agencies
ABC Pacific Beat: www.radioaustralia.net.au/pacbeat
Pacific News: www.pacificmagazine.net
Pacific Islands New Association (Pina): www.pina.com.fj

Economy
Kiribati lacks both human and natural resources; the infrastructure is weak, the islands remote and the soil poor, with frequent droughts. This, together with a traditional land tenure structure, makes the islands unattractive to large-scale agricultural activity. The principal source of foreign exchange comes from the Revenue Equalization Reserve Fund (RERF), which was set up to invest funds from the now depleted phosphate mining operation on Banaba Island. Income from the RERF enables the government to cover fiscal deficits and to buffer year-to-year movements on the current account. As the global economy slowed in 2008–09, so has the value of the RERF assets (more than 40 per cent below the peak in 2000), which has led to jump in annual drawdowns from 3.0 per cent of GDP in 1997–2001 to 14.5 per cent (2002–07) and 15.7 per cent in 2008, to offset larger fiscal deficits. The RERF balance was A$561.6 million (US$660 million) in 2008.
GDP growth in 2008 was 3.5 per cent, however the trend since the 1990s has been declining from 5 per cent to 2 per cent 2000–08, with unemployment averaging 30 per cent throughout this time. Although agricultural production rose in 2008, higher priced imports pushed up inflation to around 19 per cent. According to the International Monetary Fund (IMF) external risks have increased for Kiribati, as the three main sources of income – investments, fishing license fees and remittances – which together account for one-third of GNP, can be adversely affected by the global economy. Between them, the public sector and external grants account for 60 per cent of GDP.
Almost all manufactured goods are imported – US$76.4 million (fob) in 2008. Commodity exports include copra (coconut flesh), seaweed and fish (US$4.8 million (fob) in 2008), while the agricultural sector is mostly subsistence farming.
Kiribati's large (around 3.5 million square kilometres – some six times the area of France) Exclusive Economic Zone (EEZ) is a major source of fishing licence revenue.
Tourism could be a major source of foreign earnings but its isolation in the Pacific Ocean and the lack of infrastructure limits development. Game fishing and bird-watching are an attraction for visitors to the island.
Kiritimati (Christmas) Island has been used for landings of unmanned space shuttles operated by the Japan Aerospace Exploration Agency (Jaxa). Japan is leasing land on Kiritimati to build a spaceport, and according to the agreement will spend US$12.9 million over the period 1999–2012. Japan is also funding the building of storage and handling areas at the island's fishing port.

External trade
Kiribati is a member of the South Pacific Regional Trade and Economic Co-operation Agreement (Sparteca) along with 12 other regional nations, which allows products duty free access by Pacific Island Forum members to Australian and New Zealand markets (subject to the country of origin restrictions).
Much of Kiribati's foreign revenue is provided through leased fishing rights, remittances and international aid and operates with a trade deficit that is not balanced by export trade.

Imports
Principal imports are fuel, vehicles, machinery, food, manufactured goods, miscellaneous manufactures and chemicals.
Main sources: Australia (typically over 30 per cent total), Fiji (over 25 per cent), Japan (20 per cent).

Exports
Principal exports are copra (over 60 per cent), aquarium fish, dried shark fins and seaweed. Tuna is exported from Kiribati waters by foreign fleets under license.
Main destinations: US (typically over 25 per cent total), Belgium (around 25 per cent), Japan (over 15 per cent).

Agriculture

Farming
The agricultural sector accounts for about 15 per cent of GDP and around 60 per cent of exports.
Agricultural development is limited by poor soil quality. There are commercial and government-owned copra plantations on Teraina (Washington) and Tabuaeran (Fanning) islands, but peasant smallholdings are more usual. Most copra is exported to Europe by the Copra Co-operative Society (CCS).
Flour, sugar and rice are replacing the traditional breadfruit and taro in the national diet, increasing reliance on imports.

Fishing
There are programmes to upgrade subsistence fisheries to small commercial enterprises.
Deep-sea fishing is carried out by foreign fleets under licence in the immense Kiribati Exclusive Economic Zone (EEZ).
In September 2006, a second Kiribati and EU contract under which Spanish, French and Portuguese purse seine and long-line fishing boats are to be allowed to catch tuna in the EEZ. The latest deal emphases the promotion of sustainable and responsible fishing.
Typically, the annual catch for home consumption is over 32,000t including both fish and other seafood.
In April 2010 the Parties to the Nauru Agreement (PNA) (eight island states including Kiribati) collectively agreed to close to *purse seine* fishing in 4.55 million square kilometres of high seas in their area, from 1 January 2011, to vessels licensed to fish in their waters. The area involved stretches from Palau and Papua New Guinea in the west to Kiribati in the east, from the Marshall Islands in the north to Tuvalu in the south; it holds an

estimated 25 per cent of the world's tuna supply.

On 12 April 2011, a summit of the Parties to the Nauru Agreement (PNA) concluded its strategy for a policy of sustainable fishing in the Pacific. The PNA treaty, which was established in 1989 and expires in 2012, is seen as in need of an overhaul. As a collective region (FSM, Kiribati, Marshall Islands, Nauru, Palau, PNG, Solomon Islands and Tuvalu) control around 25–30 per cent of world stocks of tuna. Only 5 per cent of sales revenue is returned to the PNA and ministers called for specific changes, including an increased share of profits, PNA crews on-board *purse seine* vessels (minimum 10 per cent), conservation and management measures including a limit to fish trapping (fish aggregating devices (FADs)), net mesh rules and the establishment of an observer agency and fisheries information management system.

Industry and manufacturing

Small-scale manufacturing industries include clothing, furniture and handicrafts.

Tourism

Tourism plays a minor role in the Gilbert Islands but in the northern Line Islands tourism has a high priority. A growing number of tourists visit the rare seabird colonies situated on Kirimati (Christmas Island).

Attractions include World War Two battle sites, game fishing, ecotourism, and the Millennium Islands, situated just inside the International Date Line and the first place on earth to celebrate the New Year. There are also opportunities for fishing, surfing and diving, although there are not many organised activities.

Access to Kiritimati has been aided by a weekly charter flight from Honolulu.

Environment

The South Pacific Regional Environment Programme (SPREP) reported in 1999 that, due to global warming, two uninhabited islands in the Kiribati group, Tebua Tarawa and Abanuea, had disappeared beneath the waves, others have almost gone, and the main islands suffer severe floods from high tides.

The Phoenix Islands Protected Area, the world's largest marine reserve of 410,500 square kilometres was created by Kiribati in 2008. It includes the planet's biggest intact coral archipelagos with an estimated 120 species of coral, 520 species of fish, some of which have only recently been discovered, large sea turtle populations and important seabird nesting sites.

Kiribati is one of the low lying islands with most to loose through global warming and the government was unhappy at the lack of commitment by countries worldwide to limit their emission of greenhouse gases, outlined by the Kyoto agreement and the UN-backed conference in Copenhagen (Denmark) in December 2009. Two uninhabited islands in the Kiribati group, Tebua Tarawa and Abanuea, disappeared beneath the waves in 1999 and others have almost gone, the main islands suffer severe floods at high and king tides.

Hydrocarbons

There are no known hydrocarbon reserves and Kiribati does not import natural gas or coal. It relies entirely on imported oil products, of distillate, jet fuel and gasoline, to meet its fuel requirements at around 230 barrels per day.

Energy

There are publicly owned generators on Tarawa and Christmas Island and private generators on Banaba and others, producing annually around 6.5 million kilowatt hours.

Banking and insurance

There is no central bank in Kiribati and the sole commercial bank is the Bank of Kiribati. The government does not buy and sell foreign exchange.

Time

GMT plus twelve hours

Geography

Kiribati comprises 33 atolls in three principal groups, within an area of about 3.6 million square km (two million square miles) in the mid-Pacific Ocean. The country extends about 3,870km (2,400 miles) from east to west and about 2,050km (1,275 miles) from north to south. Nauru lies to the west and Tuvalu and Tokelau to the south.

Most islands are low-lying coral outcrops covered in poor soil, except for Banaba, which rises to 80m with good planting. Kiribati has no hills or freshwater streams on any of its islands and relies on wells and stored rainwater.

Hemisphere

Straddles the equator, with most islands in the southern hemisphere.

Climate

Temperatures range from 25–33 Celsius. The wet season extends from Dec–May and rainfall variation is high in most of the islands. A gentle breeze from the easterly quarter is predominant. The westerly gale (Oct–Mar) can be unpleasant.

Entry requirements

Passports

Required by all and must have six months validity from date of arrival.

Proof of return/onward passage and sufficient funds are also required.

Visa

Required by all, except citizens of UK and most Commonwealth countries and Pacific Islanders, for up to either 20 or 30 days, dependent on business, tourist and nationality criteria. Contact the nearest consulate for further information (some details are given at www.embassy-avenue.jp/kiri/visa/index.html). Citizens of Australia, Japan and US require visas.

Currency advice/regulations

There are no restriction on the import or export of foreign or local currencies Travellers cheques in Australian dollars avoid extra exchange fees; they are accepted in main banks and some shops.

Customs

Personal effects are allowed duty-free. Strict quarantine laws govern the import of plants, or parts of plants, vegetable matter or soil, clay or earth, animals and/or animal products.

Visitors are not allowed to take out of the country human remains, artefacts over 30 years old, traditional fighting swords, traditional tools, dancing ornaments or suits of armour.

Prohibited imports

Firearms, ammunition, explosives and indecent publications.

Health (for visitors)

Mandatory precautions

Vaccination certificate for yellow fever is required if travelling from an infected zone.

Advisable precautions

Vaccination for diphtheria, tuberculosis, hepatitis A and B, polio, tetanus, typhoid are recommended. There is also a rabies risk. It is advisable to boil water before drinking. Dengue fever is occasionally reported.

Hotels

In addition to the islands' four hotels, there are rudimentary rest houses. All hotels provide laundry services. Travellers cheques are seldom accepted.

A 10 per cent service charge is added to all hotel bills. Tipping is not customary.

Public holidays (national)

Fixed dates

1 Jan (New Year's Day), 8 Mar (Women's Day), 18 Apr (Health Day), 12 Jul (Independence Day – three days), 7 Aug (Youth Day), 7 Oct (Education Day), 25–26 Dec (Christmas).

Variable dates

Good Friday and Easter Monday (Mar/Apr) Gospel Day (Jul), Human Rights Day (Dec).

Working hours

Banking

Mon–Fri: 0930–1500 for all branches of Bank of Kiribati except Bikenibeu which opens from 0900–1400 and Kiritimati

Island branch which opens between 1230 and 1330.

Business

Mon–Fri: 0800–1230, 1330–1615.

Government

Mon–Fri: 0800–1230, 1330–1615.

Shops

Shopping on Tarawa is very limited. Mon–Sat: 0700–1900 (some shops open until 2030).

Telecommunications

Telephone/fax

Radio telephone links available to most outer islands.

Mobile/cell phones

There is a limited GSM 900 service available.

Electricity supply

240V AC, 50 cycles. Appliances with the standard Australian type three-pin plug will operate within South Tarawa.

Weights and measures

Metric system (Imperial units also used).

Social customs/useful tips

In official correspondence i-Kiribati adopt the western convention of signing their names with initials and surname, but it is customary (and more polite) to address people by their first name.

Women should not go out in shorts or short dresses especially on the outer islands. Bikinis should not be worn.

Getting there

Air

National airline: Air Kiribati

International airport/s: Bonriki International (TRW) on Tarawa.

Other airport/s: An upgrade to the airstrip on the island of Kiritimati in 2010 resulted in the resumption of an air service by Air Pacific, which had been cancelled since 2008.

Airport tax: Departure tax A$20; except transit passengers.

Surface

Government ships operate between Fiji and Kiribati. The remoteness of the islands restricts the number of large vessels which call. The international ports are Betio (on Tarawa), Banaba and Kirimati.

Getting about

National transport

Air: Air Kiribati provides inter-island plane connections several times a week to most of the islands. Charter flights can be arranged.

Road: There are 30km of asphalt road on Tarawa and Christmas Island.

Buses: A large fleet of privately owned buses operates an efficient and inexpensive mode of public transport from the airport to the main centres on South Tarawa. They may be flagged down anywhere on the main road; users may get off anywhere they wish. Buses operate daily from Betio to Buota 0600–2100.

Water: Passenger ferries operate between the islands.

City transport

Taxis: Taxis are available on Tarawa but cannot be booked, nor do they have meters. Charges are high.

Car hire

An international driving licence is required. Driving is on the left side of the road. In general, car hire is available on urban Tarawa and Kiritimati only.

BUSINESS DIRECTORY

Telephone area codes

The international direct dialling (IDD) code for Kiribati is +686, followed by subscriber's number.

Useful telephone numbers

Fire, police, ambulance: 999

Tungaru Central Hospital, Nawerewere, South Tarawa: 28-100.

Chambers of Commerce

Kiribati Chamber of Commerce, PO Box 550, Betio, Tarawa (tel: 26-351; fax: 26-332; e-mail: kcc@tski.net.ki).

Banking

Bank of Kiribati Ltd, PO Box 66, Bairiki, Tarawa (tel: 21-095; fax: 21-200; e-mail: bankofkiribati@tksl.net.ki).

Development Bank of Kiribati, PO Box 33, Bairiki, Tarawa (tel: 81-224; fax: 81-444; e-mail: bokxmas@tksl.net.ki).

Travel information

Air Kiribati, PO Box 274, Bikenibeu, Tarawa (tel: 28-088/093; fax: 26-204).

Air Marshall, PO Box 104, Bairike, Tarawa (tel: 21-578; fax: 21-579).

Air Nauru, Tobaraoi Travel, Tarawa (tel: 26-567; fax: 26-000).

Air Tungaru Corporation, PO Box 274, Bikenibeu, Tarawa (tel: general 28-088; reservations 21-214).

Authentic Atoll Tours, PO Box 296, Bangantebure, Bikenibeu, Tarawa (tel and fax: 28-454).

Tarawa Agency, PO Box 274, Bikenibeu, Tarawa (tel: 28-088, 28-165; fax: 28-216).

National tourist organisation offices

Kiribati Visitors Bureau, PO Box 261, Bikenibeu, Tarawa (tel: 28-287/288; fax: 26-193).

Ministries

Ministry of Commerce, Industry and Tourism, PO Box 510, Betio, Tarawa (tel: 26-157, 26-158; fax: 26-233).

Ministry of Education, Bikenibeu, Tarawa (tel: 28-091; fax: 28-222).

Ministry of Environment, Bairiki, Tarawa (tel: 21-099; fax: 21-120).

Ministry of Finance and Economic Planning, PO Box 67, Bairiki, Tarawa (tel: 21-082; fax: 21-307).

Ministry of Foreign Affairs, PO Box 68, Bairiki, Tarawa (tel: 21-342; fax: 21-466; email: mfa@tskl.net.ki).

Ministry of Health and Family Planning, Bikenibeu, Tarawa (tel: 28-081; fax: 28-152).

Ministry of Line and Phoenix Group, Bairiki, Tarawa (tel: 21-449).

Ministry of Trade, Industry and Labour, Bairiki, Tarawa (tel: 21-097; fax: 21-167).

Ministry of Transport and Communications, Betio, Tarawa (tel: 26-435; fax: 26-193).

Ministry of Works and Energy, Betio, Tarawa (tel: 26-192; fax: 26-343).

Other useful addresses

Abamakoro Trading Ltd, PO Box 492, Betio, Tarawa (tel: 26-568; fax: 26-415).

Asian Development Bank (ADB), South Pacific Regional Mission, La Casa di Andrea, Fr. Dr. W. H. Lini Highway; PO Box 127, Port Vila (tel: (+678-2) 23-300; fax: (+678-2) 23-183; email: adbsprm@adb.org; internet: www.adb.org/SPRM).

British High Commission, PO Box 61, Bairiki, Tarawa (tel: 21-327; fax: 21-488).

Broadcasting and Publications Authority, PO Box 78, Bairiki, Tarawa.

General Post Office, Bairiki (tel: 21-080).

Kiribati Co-operative Wholesale Society (tel: 26-092; fax: 26-224).

Kiribati National Library and Archives, PO Box 6, Bairiki, Tarawa (tel: 21-245; fax: 28-222).

Kiribati Shipping Corporation, PO Box 495, Betio, Tarawa (tel: 26-195; fax: 26-204).

Office of the Attorney General, Bairiki, Tarawa (tel: 21-242).

Philatelic Bureau, Ministry of Transport and Communications, PO Box 494, Betio, Tarawa (tel: 26-515; fax: 26-193).

Telecom Kiribati Ltd, PO Box 72, Bairiki, Tarawa (tel: 21-287; fax: 21-010).

Tungaru Central Hospital, Bikenibeu, Tarawa (tel: 28-081).

Internet sites

South Pacific Tourism Organisation: http://www.tcsp.com/kiribati/index.html

Kiribati homepage: http://www.trussel.com/f_kir.htm

North Korea

For most of the period following the Korean war, that had ended in 1953, and the separate establishment of North and South Korean republics, Korea watchers gave North Korea at most 'ten more years' before the regime collapsed. But, against all the odds, it has not collapsed. The Communist republic's founder, Kim Il-sung, was succeeded by his son, Kim Jong-il in 1994 and in the first decade of the 21st century it was rumoured that President Kim Jong-il would hand power to his youngest son, 27 (or is it 28?) year old Kim Jong-un. If the strength of a family dynasty such as this is one of trust, its weakness has to be its rigidity and the likelihood that eventually one family member will prove to be a link too weak.

Not entirely to everybody's surprise, Kim Jong-il died, on 17 December 2011, apparently of a heart attack brought on by fatigue and while on board a train. His health had reportedly been poor since he suffered a stroke in 2008.

Even without Kim's demise, which added another dimension, 2012 was lining up as a year of above average interest in the Korean Peninsula. South Korea will have a presidential election, as will the US. And North Korea, the world's most politically isolated republic (although in many respects it is beginning to resemble a remote medieval kingdom) is getting itself ready for the 100th anniversary of the birth of the new leader's grandfather and North Korea's almost deified leader, President for Life, Kim Il-sung. And now there will also be a leadership transition with the country, and the world, watching to see what changes, if any, there will be.

Military advisers on both sides of the 38th Parallel have been factoring in the

KEY FACTS

Official name: Chosun Minchu-chui Inmin Konghwa-guk (Democratic People's Republic of Korea) (DPRK)

Head of State: Kim Jong-il formally assumed power and was elected General Secretary of the KWP in 1997. In 1998, his father, Kim il-Sung, who died in 1994, was named President of North Korea for life.

Head of government: Premier Choe Yong-Rim (from 7 Jun 2010)

Ruling party: Chosun Rodongdang (Korean Workers' Party) (KWP)

Area: 122,400 square km

Population: 22.80 million (2010)*

Capital: Pyongyang

Official language: Korean

Currency: Won (W) = 100 chon)

Exchange rate: W1.30 per US$ (Oct 2011)

GDP per capita: US$1,065 (2008)

GDP real growth: 3.70% (2009)

GDP: US$25.50 billion (2006)*

Labour force: 11.70 million (2004)

Balance of trade: -US$1.38 billion (2005)

* estimated figure

risk that North Korea – under whatever leadership – might decide to make a 'military gesture', leading to an inevitably greater conflagration. A study by the US Centre for Strategic and International Studies suggested that North Korea might feel compelled to take military action if ignored by the US. On previous form, however, North Korea does not revert to military 'shows' while talks are under way.

The handover from father to son had been designed to avoid the protracted succession process that had characterised the years following Kim Il-sung's death. Kim Jong-il's scheme had been to put off choosing a successor from among his sons to prevent them building up their own independent support base. His successor, Kim Jong-un, had been confirmed as the heir apparent in 2010. His education at expensive private schools in Switzerland hardly constituted a leadership training course. Some North Korea watchers considered it likely that Kim Jong-un's uncle, Jang Song-thaek, would be his Richelieu, his *éminence grise*. As with the succession from Kim Il-sung to Kim Jong-il, there will be winners and disgruntled losers in the process.

The sixty-four thousand dollar question was whether the North Korean military would be among the losers. Kim Jong-un is officially the Vice Chairman of the Central Military Commission of the Workers Party of Korea and in preparation for leadership was made a four-star general. North Korea's military would, if kept on the inside of the leadership tent, remain loyal to the new leadership. However, the chilling thought remained that if in this nuclear armed state, the military feel sidelined, they could feel provoked into making a military gesture of some sort. Kim's death put increased pressure on China to restrain and guide its neighbour. However pressured North Korea may feel by its growing dependence on China, that dependence remained the most reassuring element in a very variable and volatile equation.

Attacks

Nervousness on the Korean Peninsula had risen to its highest level in decades when, in November 2010 North Korea bombed the South Korean island of Yeonpyeong in the Yellow sea, killing two South Korean soldiers and injuring a number of civilians. South Korea returned artillery fire and scrambled its F-16 fighter jets to cover the areas of the attack. The United Nations Secretary General Ban Ki-moon described the North Korean attack as 'one of the gravest incidents since the end of the Korean war'. The seemingly random choice of target by North Korea followed the revelation days earlier that North Korea possessed an advanced uranium enrichment plant near the town of Yonbon, hitherto hidden from overseas observers. In principle, the plant was able to produce not only nuclear fuel, but also fissile material capable of use in a nuclear weapon. North Korea appeared to be riding roughshod over United Nations resolutions, but US officials were quoted as accepting that additional sanctions would have minimal, if any, effect. The South Korean *Chosun Ilbo* newspaper reported that both Seoul and Washington believed that North Korea had 'three or four' enrichment sites, not including the Yongbon site. The report continued: 'We have established that the uranium enrichment tests that the North has been conducting for some time are at separate locations.' North Korea, alongside Iran, has maintained that its nuclear development is solely for peaceful purposes. Pakistan's military establishment had faced embarrassment in mid-2011 when revelations surfaced claiming to provide proof of a deal between senior Pakistani army officers and representatives of the North Korean government for the sale of nuclear arms technology. An article in the *Washington Post* suggested that the former director of Pakistan's nuclear weapons programme, Abdul Qadeer Khan, had released documents from his house arrest endorsing his claims that senior Pakistani military officials had received bribes of US$3 million in cash, as well as expensive jewellery. The army officers in question were General Jehangir Karamat, a former Chief of Army Staff and Lieutenant General Zulfiqar Khan. The two Generals issued denials of the claims, but the US newspaper claimed that the article had the support of US officials. Reports in 2010 had confirmed that North Korea had an active uranium enrichment programme designed to make fissile material for nuclear weapons.

There'll be some changes made?

As 2011 began, Korea-watchers detected a subtle change in North Korea's attitude to its neighbours and the other countries with a vested interest in future relations with the rogue state. North Korea had not only hinted at the restoration of the six nation negotiation procedure on nuclear disarmament, but had also made overtures to South Korea on re-establishing some sort of a dialogue. The countries and organisations involved in formally attempting to disarm North Korea (China, the US, N Korea, S Korea, Russia and Japan) had not met since late 2008. North Korea claimed that it was prepared to resume the six-party talks on its nuclear programme 'at an early date' and 'without preconditions'. A North Korean foreign ministry statement said North Korea remained 'unchanged' in its desire to restart the talks. The North Korean statements followed two days of 'exploratory' talks – known by diplomats as 'track two' talks – between the US and North Korea in New York. In anticipation North Korean officials met counterparts from the South while attending a security conference in Indonesia. The North Korean statement also said that the government was ready to fulfil commitments it signed up to in 2005 to end its nuclear programme in return for energy and economic aid.

South Korean President Lee Myung-bak had vowed not to allow Pyongyang any room for manoeuvre until it had apologised for March 2010 sinking of the corvette *Cheonan* with the loss of 46 South Korean sailors, and provided undertakings of good faith to downgrade its nuclear activities.

Keeping it in the family

The changes in North Korea's foreign policy, if such it can be called, were as nothing compared to the rumours, hints and clues emanating from Pyongyang relating to domestic politics. At face value, the anointment of Kim Jong-un as successor to Kim Jong-il seemed at best surprising, at worst, frightening. His mother, who died of cancer in 2004, had been Kim Jong-il's third wife, Koh Yong-hee, a dancer. The prospect of an inexperienced 27 year old with his finger on the nuclear trigger would be enough to give both Barack Obama and Vladimir Putin sleepless nights. Their concerns, however, were as nothing compared to those of Japan, Taiwan and even China. Little is known about the chubby Kim Jong-un except that he had been to school for a short time in Switzerland – first at a private international school in Bern and later at the Liebfeld-Steinhoelzi school, where it was thought he had learnt both English and German. Apart from his apparent liking for basket ball, nothing much is known about the new leader. To strengthen Kim Jong-un's position, his father had made him up to a four-star general. This, in theory, secured the loyalty of the army who, it was hoped, will see him as one of their own.

Close knit?

But Kim Jong-un's rise to prominence coincided with other behind the scenes promotions. Kim Jong-il's sister, Kim Kyong-hui, thought to be Kim's confidante and possibly the only one of his entourage who enjoyed his complete trust, was also promoted to the rank of four-star general. Korea watchers consider it likely that in the event of Kim Jong-il's death Kim Kyong-hui would step into the limelight, holding the hand of her nephew as he learned the ropes. Kim Kyong-hui had, in 2011, already become a far more familiar face, attending public ceremonies with her brother. Her husband, former bandleader, Chang Sung-taek, is considered to be the second most powerful figure in the North Korean hierarchy. Among other positions, in 2010 he was appointed vice chairman of the National Defence Commission, North Korea's highest military body. It is not known how many children Kim Kyong-hui and Chang Sung-taek have, but in 2006 their daughter committed suicide while in Paris, causing the couple's political fortunes to be under a cloud for a while. Kim Jong-il may well have been seeking from his sister and her husband some form of tutelage role for his youngest son. Whether his sister and brother-in-law see it the same way is another matter.

Which may well be where China comes into the frame. For reasons best known to himself, Kim Jong-il had visited China three times in less than a year in 2010 and 2011. China is North Korea's most important ally, by a long chalk. North Korea provides a useful buffer between China and South Korea which hosts over 20,000 US troops. Trade between the two countries is by no means insignificant, running at just under US$3 billion annually. Following North Korea's 2006 missile tests China had little option but to sign up to UN sanctions on North Korea, but it has traded this off with a steadfast refusal to criticise North Korea's attack on the *Cheonan*. China remains the only country that North Korea can cosy up to when seeking international recognition. The two countries have a notional plan to develop the area around the two cities of Dandong (China) and Sinuiji (Korea) that straddle the lower reaches of the River Yalu. Schemes to set the region up as a Special Administrative Region (SAR) a mechanism successfully developed by China elsewhere, had, in 2011, turned out to be something of a failure. In June 2011 the scheme was re-launched, this time on two special economic zones with officials from the two countries announcing 'government led' initiatives including the construction of a highway from China to the Northern border city of Rajin-Sonbong (Rason). The Rason Economic and Trade Zone includes an area that North Korea had already designated as an investment zone in the 1990s. In his role as leader of the Korean Workers' party, the ceremony was attended by Chang Sung-taek. However, Chinese government enthusiasm for the project did not seem to be shared by its business community, leaving the project a wasteland three months after the launch ceremony. The only obvious economic advantage for China was the provision of a link to the Sea of Japan for Northern Chinese industry. North Korean hopes seemed to focus on striking a closer rapprochement with China not only to confer some sort of legitimacy on a new leadership, but also to make any pre-emptive US-backed South Korean military action less likely. China's concerns probably lay elsewhere, not least in wondering just how safe the North Korean nuclear installations were.

The North Korean diplomatic offensive also reached Russia, whence Kim Jong-il travelled by train in August 2011. A Russian source was quoted in the *Financial Times* as describing the North Korean leader's visit as indicating that 'they want to show that they have countries to talk to and that they are realistic'. In the view of Russian sources, international sanctions were affecting North Korea severely and that 'They need a respite from the tensions.' North Korea owes Russia a crippling US$11 billion for debts contracted during the Soviet period. In 2011 this thorny issue had already been under discussion with Russia for months; Russia has sought to use the debt issue to provide strategic leverage on other projects, particularly those allowing Russian energy supplies to be transported more efficiently.

Risk assessment

Economy	Poor
Politics	Poor
Regional stability	Poor

COUNTRY PROFILE

Historical profile

1910 Japan formalised its annexation of Korea after gaining responsibility for its security following victory in the Russo-Japanese war of 1905.
1919 Japan suppressed the mass March First movement for self-determination.
1930s–1940s Japan imposed measures designed to assimilate the Korean population, including the outlawing of the Korean language and family names. Korea suffered under military occupation but gained the benefits of forced industrialisation.
1945 Liberation at the hands of Allied forces was a prelude to partition of the peninsula as the victorious powers encouraged friendly governments north and south of the 38th parallel. The US occupied the south while the north was taken over by the Soviet Union. As the two powers did not wish to give independence to Korea, feeling that the Korean people needed political and social re-education, a line of demarcation was established.
1947 The Chosun Rodongdang (Korean Workers' Party) (KWP) was established by Kim il-Sung (known as the 'Great Leader').
1948 The Democratic People's Republic of Korea (DPRK) was established as an independent communist state.
1950 North Korea, backed by Soviet and Chinese Communist forces, invaded South Korea after it had declared independence. War ensued.
1953 A cease-fire was signed on 27 July; a peace treaty was never signed.
1972 A constitution was laid down.
1990s Ten years of famine began after the fall of the Soviet Union, which had been supporting the DPRK regime. It lasted for most of the decade and due to lack of verifiable statistics it killed anywhere between 800,000 and 3.5 million people from starvation and hunger-related illness; deaths peak in 1997. At the height of the famine, the UN estimated one-third of the population received food aid and half the population were malnourished.
1994 Kim il-Sung, who spent his last two decades in power, died. He was succeeded by his son Kim Jong-il (, he did not take the title of president but became known as the 'Dear Leader').
1995–96 Floods destroyed 16 per cent of arable land.
1997 Kim Jong-il formally assumed power. He was elected general secretary of the KWP.
1998 Kim il-Sung, who died in 1994, was named president of North Korea for life.
2000 Australia, the Philippines and Italy restored diplomatic ties with DPRK. South Korea President Kim Dae-Jung visited Pyongyang and met Kim Jong-il in an unprecedented and much fêted meeting of the two Korean leaders. The then US secretary of state, Madeleine Albright, visited Kim Jong-il. North Korea and the UK established diplomatic relations.
2001 An EU delegation held talks with Kim Jong-il. Talks started by the US administration in 2000 were suspended. Talks on opening the first land route between the Republic of Korea and Korea DPR broke down. After the worst winter in

50 years and a summer drought harvests were devastated, the UN WFP called for over US$300 million in food aid.
2002 North Korea was included on the list of countries that were an 'axis of evil' due to their development of weapons of mass destruction (WMD). Inter-Korean relations progressed, as the two sides agreed to resume the engagement process after the South Korean envoy, Lim Dong-won visited DPRK. The accord included plans for economic co-operation, continuing family reunions and a revival of a cross-border railway project linking the two countries.
2003 China began talks in an effort to persuade North Korea to end its nuclear arms programme. All 687 KWP candidates, standing unopposed, won 100 per cent of the votes in elections to the National Assembly. Pak Pong Ju became premier.
2004 A train carrying volatile materials exploded killing at least 161 people and injuring over 1,000. South and North Korea temporarily opened their borders. The Gyeongui railway line was under refurbishment and a new line, Donghae Bukbu (Tonghae Pukpu), began construction.
2005 A short-range missile was test-fired in the general direction of Japan. International talks led to an agreement whereby the nuclear weapons programme would be terminated in return for aid and security guarantees. Further negotiations were vetoed due to international sanctions that had frozen DPRK assets in a Macau bank, which the US alleged was responsible for laundering millions of US dollars' worth of counterfeit and illegally earned money and which effectively denied DPRK access to the international banking system.
2006 The North Korea government listed its central bank on the London Stock exchange in an attempt to circumvent financial sanctions and sold an estimated US$28 million in gold bullion on international markets. A limited nuclear explosion of less than one kiloton was detonated in DPRK, resulting in international financial sanctions.
2007 The UN suspended all aid until an audit was completed, following US accusation that the aid was 'perverted for the benefit of the Kim Jong Il regime' instead of being spent on the people of DPRK. An agreement was reached whereby two contentious nuclear reactors would be closed down, to be verified by international inspectors, in return for the supply of 50,000 tonnes of heavy fuel oil, plus food and other aid. It would also allow DPRK access to the international banking system and a formal end to the 1950–53 Korean War. North and South Korea resumed ministerial meetings. Pak Pong Ju was replaced as prime minister by Kim Yong Il. UN inspectors confirmed that the Yongbyon nuclear reactor had been shut down. Floods killed over 100 people and left 300,000 people temporarily homeless. A summit of leaders of North and South Korea took place in Pyongyang. The South Korea delegation included industrialists, bureaucrats, poets and clerics. US technicians began the process of disabling the Yongbyon nuclear complex. The end-of-year deadline to disclose its nuclear programme was missed.
2008 North Korea was offered its removal from the US-list of state sponsors of terrorism and told it could be exempt from the Trading with the Enemy Act if it disabled its nuclear facilities. President Kim did not appear at the military parade to celebrate the country's 60th birthday, leading to reports that he had suffered a stroke; he did, however, attend a football match later in the year. International negotiations on the nuclear weapons programme ground to a halt, as verification of work cessation could not be agreed.
2009 All political and military agreements with South Korea were scraped, due to what the DPRK saw as 'hostile intent' by South Korea. Legislative elections were announced, with the supreme leader picking one candidate for each constituency, to be voted on by the electorate. The ill-health of Kim Jong-il was considered the reason for changes in the cabinet in what observers considered a move to re-invigorate the government and stimulate the economy at a time when there is no clear successor. In the parliamentary elections, 687 candidates were elected unopposed; turnout was said to be 99.98 per cent. The US called the launch of a DPRK satellite rocket 'provocative', even though the US and South Korea said the launch had been unsuccessful. Contrary to all agreements a large nuclear test took place, estimated at 20 kilotons; the UN Security Council condemned the test. North Korea declared that it was 'no longer bound by the 'armistice' of 1953, following South Korea's participation in the Proliferation Security Initiative (PSI) which includes measures to search ships suspected of carrying nuclear materials. North Korea considers such searches 'hostile' acts against its 'peaceful vessels' and an infringement of its sovereignty. New, UN sanctions were imposed on named North Korean citizens and businesses, as well as some foreign firms doing business with DPRK. A decree was issued ordering all bank notes be exchanged for new, lower re-valued bank notes. The re-valuation was reasoned to be a move by the government to counter black-market money traders.
2010 The finance official overseeing the re-valuation of the won in 2009, Pak Nam-ki, was sacked in January due to the chaotic process which wiped out many people's savings and caused food shortages; he was executed in March. The report by an international investigation team, led by South Korea, concluded that DPRK torpedoed a South Korean warship in March, with the loss of all 46 sailors aboard. North Korea angrily denied the accusation as condemnation by UN members followed. China, North Korea's principal ally, and Japan agreed to impose financial sanctions on DPRK. Choe Yong-Rim became premier (head of government) on 7 June, replacing Kim Yong-il, who stepped down following bungled currency reforms begun in 2009. South Korea staged five days of military drills off its west coast in August. The move infuriated the North Koreans, who in retaliation fired off over 100 rounds of artillery close to the disputed sea border between the two countries. On 8 August a South Korean fishing vessel, which may have strayed across the border, was seized by North Korea; the government in South Korea demanded the vessel's immediate and safe return. Kim Jong-il and his son, Kim Jong-un, travelled to China again in August (first visit was in May). There was speculation that Kim Jong-il was looking for approval of Kim Jong-un as his successor. Four people, including two civilians, were killed after North Korea fired artillery shells at the island of Yeonpyeong in South Korea on 23 November. Damage to homes and businesses was widespread and hundreds of people fled the island. Korean observers consider the aggression by North Korea could be seen as endorsing the succession of Kim Jong-un and a measure of the significance the North places on fishing rights in the rich seas around the island. The attack on the island came just days after news that North Korea had completed the building of a modern plant to enrich uranium, for possible use in nuclear weapons, in secret in Yongbyon. In November, the UN warned of food shortages and continued hunger, following poor harvests due to bad weather.
2011 An outbreak of foot and mouth struck livestock and weakened an already fragile food supply. On 10 February, the government appealed for foreign aid to feed its people. The 'Elders' a group of four international statesmen, (former presidents Jimmy Carter (US), Martti Ahtisaari (Finland) and Mary Robinson (Ireland), with prime minister Gro Brundtland (Norway)) paid a three day visit in April, in an effort to revive the six-party talks on North Korea's nuclear programme, and to ease tensions with South Korea. In June the government closed all universities and sent students to factories, farms and

construction sites in an attempt to rebuild the economy, but also to limit any opposition moves caused by uprisings elsewhere in the world. On 1 August DPRK called for a resumption of the six-party nuclear negotiations 'without preconditions'. President Jong-il travelled by train to the Russian border town of Khasan on 20 August. He held talks with the Russian president, Dmitry Medvedev and visited a dam north of Vladivostock. Kim Jong-un made a rare public appearance when he stood with his father at the national celebrations to celebrate North Korea's 63rd anniversary of its founding on 9 September.

Political structure

Constitution

Under the terms of the 1972 constitution, nominal political authority is held by a unicameral Supreme People's Assembly (SPA).

Local government is vested in nine provincial and three municipal elected people's assemblies.

Government at all levels is dominated by the Chosun Rodongdang (Korean Workers' Party) (KWP).

The executive

The head of state holds executive power and governs in conjunction with a Central People's Committee and an appointed Administrative Council (cabinet).

The head of state is no longer president since the title was given to Kim il-Sung, after he had died, for life.

Kim Jong-il was given administrative powers in 1994 and formally assumed power as head of state after being elected general secretary of the ruling KWP in 1997.

National legislature

A unicameral, Supreme People's Assembly (SPA) exercises nominal legislative power. Its 687 members are elected every four years from a single list of candidates, sanctioned by the General Secretary of the KWP.

The SPA, which elects a standing committee to represent it when not in session, also elects the head of government.

Legal system

The legal system is based on the German civil law system with Japanese influences and Communist legal theory.

Last elections

8 March 2009 (parliamentary)

Results: All 687 candidates, chosen by the ruling Chosun Rodongdang (Korean Workers' Party) (KWP), were elected unopposed; turnout was 99.98 per cent.

Next elections

March 2013 (national legislature)

Political parties

No political parties, other than the KWP, are permitted to operate.

Ruling party

Chosun Rodongdang (Korean Workers' Party) (KWP)

Population

22.80 million (2010)*

Last census: 1 October 2008: 24,051,403 (provisional)

Population density: 186 inhabitants per square km.

Annual growth rate: 0.8 per cent 1994–2004 (WHO 2006)

Ethnic make-up

The Korean DPR (DPRK) has a highly homogeneous population descended from migratory groups who entered the Korean Peninsula from Siberia, Manchuria and inner Asia. There is a small Chinese community and a few ethnic Japanese.

Religions

The constitution provides for 'freedom of religious belief' but, in practice, organised religious activity is discouraged, except for certain government-sponsored religious groups. Traditional religions are Buddhism, Confucianism, Daoism, Shamanism and Chondogyo.

Education

The is a national Education for All Forum (EFA) that organises consultations with organisations such as the Youth League, the Women's Union and the Academy of Educational Science.

Education in Korea consists of six years of elementary education, three years of junior high school, three years of senior high school, and four years of college education. The government has established a free educational system and plans to extend this to the remote areas of the country. However, school attendance in some areas has reportedly dropped to between 60—80 per cent, due to extreme economic hardship not only, in families through lack of food, but also in school facilities with inadequately trained teachers, poor heating and scarce learning materials.

Competition for college entry is fierce. There are three universities. These are the Kim Il-Sung, Kim Chaek Polytechnic and Korryo-Songgyungwan. There are also around 280 colleges.

It is common for students to opt for military service after graduation. This is not compulsory, but can positively affect an individual's future career.

Literacy rate: 95–99 per cent, adult rate.

Health

There is an extensive, free medical care system, but the quality of care has declined.

Water and sanitation sector, one of the key priority areas, remains poorly funded at only 18 per cent of the requirement.

A nutrition survey conducted by Unicef, in 2002, indicated that 40 per cent of children under five were chronically malnourished or stunted (a fall from the previous high of 45 per cent in 2000) and in 2003 nationwide, 5 million people, especially children, the elderly and pregnant females were dependent on foreign food aid. The mortality rate for those aged under 5 was 55 per 1,000 children; maternal mortality continues to increase as estimates show that the nutritional status of some 480,000 pregnant and nursing women is poor.

Life expectancy: 66 years, 2004 (WHO 2006)

Fertility rate/Maternal mortality rate: 2.0 births per woman, 2004 (WHO 2006)

Birth rate/Death rate: 17.6 births per 1,000 population; seven deaths per 1,000 population (World Bank 2003).

Child (under 5 years) mortality rate (per 1,000): 42 per 1,000 live births (World Bank 2004)

Welfare

A large segment of the civilian population rely on the government-run public distribution system. In 2003 the meagre food ration was further reduced to 250–380 grammes per person daily – half the minimum daily energy requirement. People are required to rely on independently procured supplements; families in urban, industrial areas have fared worst.

Main cities

Pyongyang (capital, estimated population 3.5 million (m) in 2005), Kaesong (1.9m), Hamhung (724,720), Ch'ongjin (705,850), Namp'o (2.3m), Sunch'on (423,790), Wonsan (350,179).

Languages spoken

English, amoung other international languages, is used in business.

Official language/s

Korean

Media

Despite a constitution that guarantees freedom of the press, media is a severely restricted as the government prohibits and controls information and the means of distribution. In 2008 the Paris-based Reporters Without Borders condemned North Korea as isolating its population from the world and subjecting it to 'propaganda worthy of a bygone age'. Criticism of the state leader and government is not tolerated as news is heavily censored; typically all media reinforces the personality cult of the leader, Kim Jong-il.

Press

All publications are state-owned or controlled, including *Rodong Shinmun* (*Labour Daily*), *Minju Choson* (*Democratic Korea*), *Joson Inmingun* (*Korean People's*

Army Daily) and *Rodongja Sinmum* (*Worker's Newspaper*). In English, *People's Korea* (www.korea-np.co.jp/pk) is a government online publication.
Dailies: These include *Rodong Shinmun*, *Minju Choson*, *Rodong Chongnyon* and *Pyongyang Times*. The Korean News Service in Tokyo also provides an internet service *Korean News* at www.kcna.co.jp/index-e.htm.
Business: The Foreign Trade Publishing House publishes a monthly journal, *Foreign Trade of the DPRK*, which includes listings of specialised corporations, giving telegraphic and telex addresses.
Periodicals: A semimonthly, Tokyo-based unofficial mouthpiece of the Korea DPR government, *The People's Korea*, reports on Korean affairs.

Broadcasting

All radios and television sets are pre-tuned to state-run stations and there are heavy penalties for anyone caught listening to a foreign broadcast.
There are two radio stations, the Korean Central Broadcasting Station and the external service Voice of Korea, both are state-run. The Korean Workers' Party operates Korean Central TV; Mansudae TV is a cultural service.
Radio: National and locally-produced programmes are widely disseminated (factory, outdoor loudspeakers); there are external services in several languages.
Television: There are two stations, plus a third channel at weekends. Viewing foreign channels is illegal for Korean DPR nationals.

News agencies

National news agency: Korean Central News Agency (KCNA): www.kcna.co.jp

Economy

North Korea has probably the world's most highly centralised planned economy; the regime is highly secretive and does not publish national accounts which may reflect poorly on its dogmatic political philosophy. The concentration of economic policy on the development of heavy industry reflects the continued implementation of outdated Soviet-style priorities, wholly unsuited to present conditions which is characterised as under-invested and outmoded and which has led to a moribund industrial sector that is considered beyond rescue. Energy output is, likewise, declining.
GDP growth in 2007 was -2.3 per cent due to severe flooding that devastated harvests and forced North Korea to petition for food aid. However, following a *rapprochement* with South Korea in 2008 the economy grew by an estimated 3.7 per cent largely due to the inter-Korean economic co-operation, whereby South Korea provided investment and collaboration in setting up the Kaesong Industrial Region, in the border region of North Korea. By December 2009 there were 117 South Korean companies manufacturing goods in North Korea and employing over 42,000 local workers.
Economic sanctions have been in force since 1989 and have either been renewed or added to since then, due in most part to North Korea's belligerent military stance and its vacillation concerning ending its nuclear programme.
Industry accounted for 46.2 per cent of GDP, services 21.6 per cent and agricultural and fisheries 21.6 per cent of GDP in 2008.
Foreign investment in industry, construction, technology and tourism is officially encouraged, but there have been few firms willing to invest in North Korea. Without investment in infrastructure, North Korea, with its low-cost, relatively educated workforce, cannot become the centre for competitively-priced exports to Russia and China that its geographic location could provide.

External trade

North Korea's foreign trade accounts for less than 10 per cent of GDP. There is a special economic zone, Rajin-Sonbong, near Rason on the north-eastern border with China and Russia, allowing free trade access in return for investment.
The Kaesong Industrial Region is an economic development zone where South Korean companies have set up manufacturing facilities. The zone is expected to be completed by 2012 and employing around 700,000 people.
Two-way trade between the two countries amounted to US$1.68 billion in 2009.
The trade in illicit drugs is thought to be an important source of foreign currency within the grey economy.

Imports

Vital supplies of food aid are still required. Main imports are petroleum and coking coal, crude rubber, alloying elements, sulphur, halite, grain, cotton, sugar and palm oil.
Main sources: China (typically 47 per cent of total), South Korea (26 per cent), Algeria 13 per cent).

Exports

Commodity exports are clothing, iron and steel, armaments, machinery and equipment, non-ferrous metals, manufactured goods, fireproof bricks, anthracite, magnetite cakes, cement, magnesia clinker and machine tools.
Main destinations: China (typically 33 per cent of total), South Korea (25 per cent), Venezuela (15 per cent).

Agriculture

Farming

The agriculture sector accounts for an estimated 30 per cent of GDP and is thought to employ 43 per cent of the workforce.
Agriculture is mostly practised on large-scale collective and state farms, which have been fatally mismanaged. Main crops are rice, maize and potatoes. Other crops include wheat, barley, rape, sugar, millet, sorghum, pulses, sweet potatoes, vegetables, tobacco and silkworms. Extra grain supplies are necessary. Since the mid-1990s, North Korea has been affected by adverse climatic conditions, with a series of floods and droughts destroying crops. Other problems affecting the sector include severe deforestation, which has caused silting of rivers, a lack of fertilisers and pesticides and low levels of mechanisation. This has led to a serious food deficit at a time when North Korea's increasing political isolation has affected aid flows.

Industry and manufacturing

The industrial sector accounts for an estimated 20 per cent of GDP and is thought to employ a similar percentage of the workforce.
Major manufacturing activities have been diversified to include production of steel, iron, non-ferrous metals, machinery and equipment, fertilisers, plastics and cement. Light industrial products include silk, cotton and rayon textiles, chemicals, processed food, machine tools, hardware and machinery.
Development projects in western and eastern industrial zones have included a vinalon factory in Sunchon with productive capacity of 100,000 tonnes per annum, a potash fertiliser complex in Sariwon, a coal mining complex in Anju, steel complexes in Nampo and Chongjin and synthetic rubber plants in Hamhung and Namhung.
Two production centres are planned at the port cities of Nampo and Wonsan to supplement a free-trade zone in the Rajin-Sonbong area bordering China and Russia, which has little infrastructure to support its industry. The new centres will specialise in consumer product exports by foreign companies and will be located near population centres.
Hyundai, South Korea's largest conglomerate, has developed DPRK's largest industrial complex, costing US$5 billion and located in Kaesong.
The Korean Friendship Association organises business trips to DPRK (see internet sites)

Tourism

Tourism is recognised as a means of earning foreign exchang although the

sector is undeveloped. Infrastructure is lacking, entry procedures are protracted, the cost, which includes mandatory minders, is high, and movements are tightly controlled. Arrivals, organised as package tours, are mainly by cruise ships, but a land route, via the Demilitarised Zone, opened in 2003. The main markets are South Korea, China and Japan. South Korea is actively engaged in consolidating tourism between the two countries for political reasons.
In January 2010 it was announced that an increased number of US visitors would be allowed to visit throughout the year, instead of only at the time of the Arirang mass games (when thousands of performers create slogans and mosaics with colourful cards).

Mining
The mining sector is thought to account for some 10 per cent of GDP and to employ 5 per cent of the workforce. North Korea is well-endowed with mineral resources, including refractory clays, phosphates, sulphur and graphite and ores of iron, magnesium, tungsten, copper, lead, zinc, silver, gold, magnesite and nickel. Non-ferrous metals are an important foreign exchange earner, with 70 per cent of zinc, lead and copper production in the Hamhung district.

Hydrocarbons
There are no known oil or natural gas reserves. North Korea relies entirely on imports of oil for its requirements, which were 16,000 barrels per day in 2008; it does not import natural gas.
Coal reserves are conservatively estimated at around 1.0 billion tonnes, with annual production at over 100 million tonnes, and small amounts imported. Coal provides over 85 per cent of domestic primary energy.

Energy
Total installed generating capacity was 9.5GW, two-thirds of which is provided by hydropower and the rest by coal-fired plants. Capacity is under-utilised and consumption has declined over the years. Infrastructures, including power plants and the transmission grid, have deteriorated due to lack of investment causing frequent outages and falls in transmissions (brownouts).
North Korea's first nuclear power plant, producing a maximum 5MW at peak periods, but which produced fissile material in 2006, has been a cause of intense negotiations in bringing North Korea under the regulation of the International Atomic Energy Agency. There was international condemnation when North Korea disregarded agreements made for its closure.

Banking and insurance
There are no private banks in North Korea. The euro is the official foreign exchange currency; the Japanese yen is an unofficial exchange currency.
Central bank
Central Bank of the Peoples' Repubic of Korea
Main financial centre
Pyongyang

Time
GMT plus nine hours

Geography
North Korea occupies the northern part of the Korean peninsula, bordered to the north by the People's Republic of China and to the south by South Korea. It has a series of mountain ranges, covering up to 80 per cent of the land, across the Korean peninsula and includes all the tallest peaks of over 2,000 metres. A ridge of mountains, the Nangnim Range, runs north-south and makes communication between the east and west coast difficult. Most of the habitable areas are either in the lowlands or the coastal plains, which are, in turn, limited; the two largest plains – P'yongyang and Chaeryng – are only 500 square kilometres each. Most rivers run in a westerly direction due to the lie of the mountains. The Yalu River is the longest at 790km and flows west into Korea Bay in the Yellow Sea.
Hemisphere
Northern

Climate
Winters are cold, with temperatures ranging from minus 3 degrees Celsius (C) to minus 8 degrees C in January and falling as low as minus 20 degrees C at night. Summers are warm and humid, with an average temperature in August of 25 degrees C. Most rainfall is from June–September.

Entry requirements
Passports
Required by all.
Visa
Required by all. Applications for visas should be made well in advance. It is impossible to visit Korea DPR except by official invitation or by joining group tours from certain countries. Contact the nearest embassy for further details.
Currency advice/regulations
Import and export of local currency is prohibited. Import and export of foreign currency is unlimited, but must be declared. The euro has replaced the US dollar as the official foreign exchange currency; all other currencies will be exchanged at unfavourable rates.
Customs
Single shot cameras, laptop computers (without internet connections) and personal electronic music players are allowed but must be declared.
Prohibited imports
Illegal drugs, firearms and explosives, animals, plants, video cameras, camera lens over 150mm and pornography. Any mass printed documents, literature, audio and videotapes, compact discs and letters deemed political or intended for religious proselytising are also prohibited.
Mobile telephones and global positioning satellite systems and radios are not permitted and must be deposited on entry and collected on departure at the Customs checkpoint.

Health (for visitors)
Mandatory precautions
No compulsory vaccinations.
Advisable precautions
Malaria and cholera are a risk and precautions are essential. Vaccinations against diphtheria, hepatitis A and B, Japanese B encephalitis, polio, tuberculosis, tetanus and typhoid are recommended. Rabies is a risk.
There is a foreigners' hospital in Pyongyang, with higher standards then elsewhere in North Korea where hospitals often lack heat, medicine and supplies and suffer from frequent power loss and outbreaks of infection. In these hospitals one should avoid any invasive surgery. It is strongly recommend that visitors obtain comprehensive health insurance before travelling to DPRK, including emergency medical evacuation as necessary.
All medication necessary should be taken (in their original packaging) in sufficient quantities, as it is not possible to purchase supplies locally.
Drink only bottled or sterilised water, avoid dairy products, which are probably unpasturised. Eat only hot, cooked meat, fish and vegetables, or peeled fruit, and avoid pork, salads and mayonnaise.

Credit cards
The main hotels in Pyongyang will take credit and debit cards (Visa and Mastercard but not American Express).
Travellers' cheques are not accepted. Hotels generally insist on full payment in advance when checking-in.
Tipping is officially frowned upon, but is increasingly expected by some hotel staff.

Public holidays (national)
Fixed dates
1 Jan (New Year's Day), 16–17 Feb (Kim Jong-il's Birthday), 15 Apr (Kim il-Sung's Birthday), 25 Apr (Army Day), 1 May (Labour Day), 27 Jul (Victory Day), 15 Aug (Liberation Day), 9 Sep (Independence Day), 10 Oct (Foundation of the Korean Workers' Party), 27 Dec (Constitution Day).

Working hours
Banking
0900–1700. The Trade Bank of the DPRK situated near Kim Il-Sung Square in Sungni Street, Pyongyang, is open in the morning every day except Sunday.
Business
0800–1200, 1300–1700.
Government
0800–1200, 1300–1700.
Shops
1000–1800.

Electricity supply
The electric current on the national grid is 220V AC and 60Hz. 220V and 110V power points are available in hotels.

Weights and measures
Metric system

Social customs/useful tips
Koreans give a short bow or nod as a sign of respect when greeting or departing, although foreigners are usually greeted with a handshake.
When anything is handed over to or received from another person, including business cards, it is polite to use both hands. The card should be read and not immediately put away.
The surname precedes the given name in Korean, but may be transposed for the benefit of foreigners.
Chopsticks should never be placed upright in rice: this is only done at funerals.
In homes and traditional restaurants, shoes are removed and slippers worn.
The Korean word for 'four' is similar to that for death and considered unlucky. Many public buildings and all hospitals omit the fourth floor.
Names should never be written in red ink, a traditional symbol of death.

Security
Government agencies closely supervise visitors to North Korea. Hotel rooms, telephones and fax machines may be monitored, and personal possessions in hotel rooms may be searched. Photographing roads, bridges, airports, railway stations, or anything other than designated public tourist sites may be perceived as espionage and could result in confiscation of cameras and film or even detention.

Getting there
Air
It is essential to reconfirm ticket bookings for a journey some days in advance, as an issued air ticket does not guarantee a seat, unless it has been confirmed and endorsed prior to travel. For most travellers this will be done by their travel agents or inviting organisation in the DPRK.
National airline: Air Koryo
International airport/s: Sunan (FNJ), 24 km from Pyongyang.
Airport tax: None.
Surface
Rail: Rail services operate to/from Beijing and Moscow. Cargo trains started running between North and South Korea on 11 December 2007.
Main port/s: Chongjin, Haeju, Hungnam, Najin, Nampo, Wonsan. The two Koreas are discussing expansion of shipping routes. Nampo and Wonsan may become special import-export zones.

Getting about
National transport
It can be difficult to reach many areas of the interior, although the system is developing.
Air: Air Koryo operates domestic services.
Road: The road network (75,112km) includes motorways between Pyongyang and Wonsan and Pyongyang and Nampo.
Rail: The rail network is estimated at 8,533km, 89 per cent of which is electrified, with two classes of accommodation. Rail travel is slow.
Water: Rivers, canals and sea transport provide important internal links.
City transport
Taxis: Taxis are available and should be booked through the hotel.
Buses, trams & metro: There is a four-line underground system in Pyongyang with a hub at Jonu Station.

BUSINESS DIRECTORY

Telephone area codes
The international direct dialling (IDD) code for PDR Korea is +850, followed by area code and subscriber's number.

Pyongyang	2	Hamchon	9

Banking
Changgwang Credit Bank Chukzen 1-dong, Mangyongdae District, Pyongyang (fax: 381-4793).

Credit Bank of Korea, Chongryu 1-Dong, Munsu Street, Otan-dong, Central District, Pyongyang (tel: 381-8285; fax: 381-7806).

Foreign Trade Bank of the Democratic People's Republic of Korea, FTB Building, Jungsong dong, Central District, Pyongyang (tel: 381-5270; fax: 381-4467).

The International Industrial Development Bank, Mansu-dong, Central District, Pyongyang (tel: 381-8610).

Korea Daesong Bank, Segori-dong, Gyongheung Street, Pyongyang.

Korea Joint Bank, Ryugyong 1 dong, Pothonggang District, Pyongyang (tel: 381-8151; fax: 381-4410).

Koryo Bank, Pong-Hwa Dong, Potonggang District, Pyongyang (tel: 381-8168; fax: 381-4033).

Central bank
Central Bank of the Democratic People's Republic of Korea, Mansu-dong, 58-1 Sungri Street, Central District, Pyongyang, (fax: 381-4624).

Travel information
Air Koryo, Sunan Airport, Sunan District, Pyongyang (fax: 381-4410 ext 4625).

Kumgangsan International Tourist Company, Central District, Pyongyang (fax: 381-2100).

Tourist Advertisement and Information Agency, Songuja-dong, Mangyongdae District, Pyongyang

National tourist organisation offices
State General Bureau of Tourism of the DPRK, Central District, Pyongyang.

Other useful addresses
Committee for the Promotion of International Trade of the Democratic People's Republic of Korea, Central District, Pyongyang.

Foreign Languages Publishing House, Sosong District, Pyongyang.

Foreign Trade Publishing House, Pyongyang District, Pyongyang.

Korea-Europe Technology & Economy Services, 15 Sojae-chon, Konguk-dong, Potonggang District, Pyongyang (e-mail: ketes@ketes.org).

Korean Central News Agency (KCNA), Potonggang District, Pyongyang.

Korean Committee for Solidarity with World People, 8-120 Yonggwang Street, Central District, Pyongyang.

Korean General Company for Economic Co-operation, Central District, Pyongyang.

Korean General Merchandise Export and Import Corporation, Central District, Pyongyang.

Korean Publications Exchange Association, PO Box 222, Pyongyang 20691.

Korean Publications Export and Import Corporation, Central District, Pyongyang.

Permanent Representative of the DPRK to the United Nations, 515 East 72nd Street, 38-F, New York, NY 10021 (tel: (+1-212) 972-3106; fax: (+1-212) 972-3154; email: prkun@undp.org).

National news agency: Korean Central News Agency (KCNA): www.kcna.co.jp

Internet sites
Korean Friendship Association (for business trips): www.korea-dpr.com

Koryo Group, British company in Beijing, China, arranging tourism to North Korea: www.koryogroup.com

South Korea

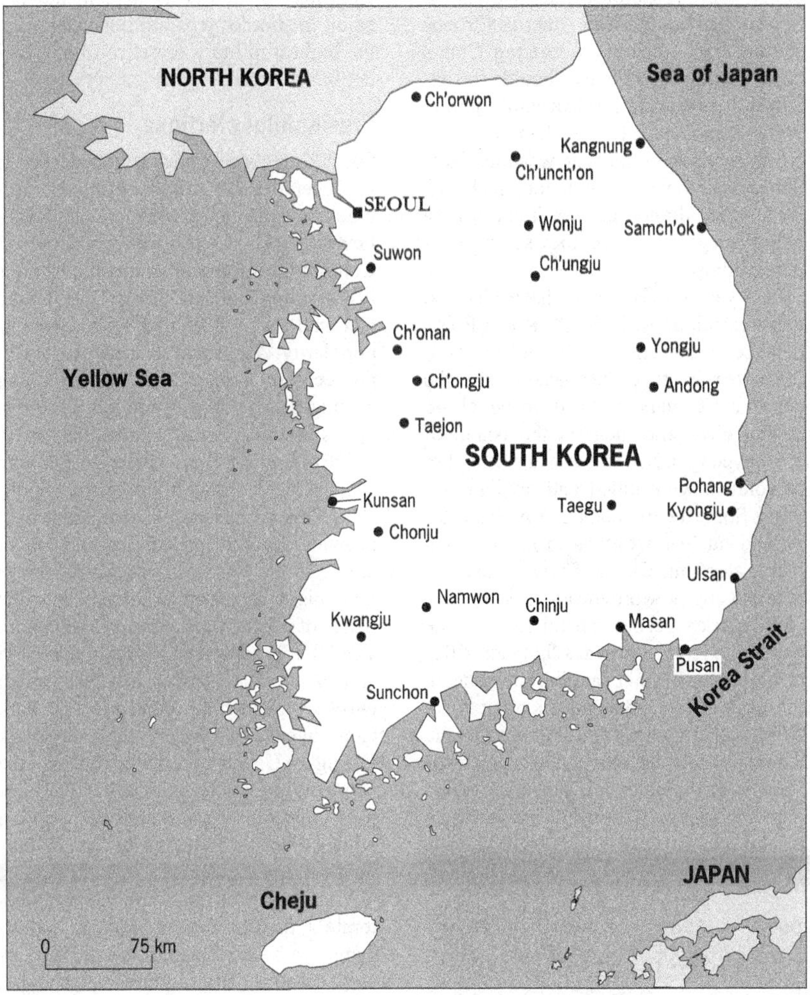

KEY FACTS

Official name: Daehan Min-kuk (Republic of Korea) (ROK)

Head of State: President Lee Myung-bak (HD) (sworn in 25 Feb 2008)

Head of government: Prime Minister Kim Tae-ho (HD) (from 8 Aug 2010)

Ruling party: Hannara Dang (HD) (Grand National Party) (since 9 Apr 2008)

Area: 99,091 square km

Population: 48.90 million (2010)*

Capital: Seoul

Official language: Korean

Currency: Won (W) = 100 chon

Exchange rate: W1,178.05 per US$ (Oct 2011)

GDP per capita: US$20,591 (2010)

GDP real growth: 6.10% (2010)

GDP: US$1,007.10 billion (2010)

Labour force: 24.75 million (2010)

Unemployment: 3.70% (2010)

Inflation: 3.00% (2010)

Balance of trade: US$41.88 billion (2010)

* estimated figure

The sudden death of North Korea's president, Kim Jong-il, in December 2011 posed an array of problems for the South Korean government. Events over the preceding few years had created a climate of mistrust and fear. But if Kim Jong-il was a mystery, his 29 (or is it 28?) year old successor Kim Jong-un was ten times so. As the world watched newsreel clips of weeping thousands in a snowy Pyongyang, the chilling realisation was that, some 160 kilometres to the north of Seoul decisions were being made that could well affect not just the livelihoods, but the lives of South Koreans.

With a little help from our friends

South Korea had probably never felt more reassured by the 40,000 or so United States military personnel stationed in its half of the Korean Peninsula. The common enmity towards and suspicion of, North Korea, meant it could also count on the support of Japan, despite the sensitivity over Japan's colonial presence in Korea in the twentieth century. In 2010 China had disappointed South Korea by failing to condemn either the sinking by North Korea of a South Korean naval vessel in March, or the shelling in November of a South Korean island. Now, however, Chinese scholars and officials do indeed seem to be sending strong signals to North Korea that enough is enough.

In June Liang Guanglie, China's defence minister, told a regional-security forum in Singapore that China had done much more in communicating with North Korea 'than you can imagine'. At another conference, in Kuala Lumpur, Zhu Feng, a professor at Peking University, pointed out to a North Korean participant that the security issue on the Korean peninsula was a result of the unchanged nature of the North Korean regime and its behaviour. Tougher talking indeed.

Reported in the London *Economist*, another Chinese academic, You Ji, a former Chinese foreign ministry official now teaching at the University of New South Wales in Australia, suggested that Kim Jong-il never forgave China for its disapproval of the hereditary succession in which he took over from his father, Kim-il Sung. Taking umbrage at the slight, President Kim Jong-il did not visit China once between 1983 and 2000. Between May last year and his death in December this year, however, he visited China no less than three times. That is a symptom of North Korea's greater dependence on China, which accounts for four-fifths of its trade and energy needs and most of the food aid it gets to avert renewed famine.

The corollary of greater North Korean dependence should be greater Chinese influence. But in the past the North Korean regime has always managed to fend off unwelcome pressure by silently playing on two big Chinese strategic fears. One is that a spurned North Korea might provoke South Korea and America, triggering a cycle of retaliation and even war. The second is that it might collapse in chaos with a mass exodus of refugees into China. Any collapse would presumably be followed by reunification of the Korean peninsula under the prosperous, American-allied South. That could mean American troops stationed in a country bordering China, complicating its strategy should, for example, it ever find itself in a confrontation with America over Taiwan. Until now, the North's primitive nuclear weapons have not seemed to worry China too much. After all, they do not threaten it and if they help the regime survive, they serve a Chinese purpose.

Last year's events may have changed these calculations. In South Korea President Lee faced criticism for not responding more robustly to the attacks on first the corvette *Cheonan* in April, in which 46 sailors died, and then on the island of Yeonpyeong in November when a number of soldiers were killed and civilians injured. Some have called for American battlefield nuclear weapons to be stationed there, alarming China. There is also the risk that any new provocation, or mishap, could quickly get out of hand. In mid-June two South Korean marines shot their rifles at a civilian airliner landing at Incheon, the airport for Seoul, mistaking it for a North Korean plane. You Ji thinks that the Korean peninsula may have supplanted Taiwan as the potential war most worrying China. China's North Korea-watchers also fret that the dynastic succession, from Kim Jong-il to the plump but callow Kim Jong-un, may be more than the system can stand, leading to a military junta or civil war

Communist North Korea and booming South Korea are technically warring enemies: the Korean War ended in 1953 with an armistice not a peace agreement. As a result the border separating the states has the highest military presence of any border in the world.

KEY INDICATORS — South Korea

	Unit	2006	2007	2008	2009	2010
Population	m	48.30	48.55	48.55	*48.80	*48.90
Gross domestic product (GDP)	US$bn	888.44	957.05	947.00	832.50	1,007.10
GDP per capita	US$	18,395	19,751	19,505	17,074	20,591
GDP real growth	%	5.1	4.9	2.2	0.2	6.1
Inflation	%	2.2	2.5	4.7	2.8	3.0
Unemployment	%	3.5	3.3	3.2	3.6	3.7
Coal output	mtoe	1.3	1.3	1.3	5.3	0.9
Exports (fob) (goods)	US$m	331,842.0	378,982.0	433,472.0	373,584.0	464,301.0
Imports (fob) (goods)	US$m	303,937.0	349,573.0	427,421.0	317,457.0	422,425.0
Balance of trade	US$m	27,905.0	29,409.0	6,051.0	56,128.0	41,876.0
Current account	US$m	5,385.0	5,954.0	-6,406.0	42,668.0	28,214.0
Total reserves minus gold	US$m	238,882.3	262,150.2	201,144.5	269,932.9	291,491.1
Foreign exchange	US$m	238,387.9	261,770.7	200,479.1	265,202.3	286,926.4
Exchange rate	per US$	925.14	930.10	1,102.05	1,276.90	1,156.10

* estimated figure

Presidential elections

South Korea's next presidential election is in December 2012. South Koreans' attitudes towards their present clutch of politicians range from apathy to disgust. Continuous infighting among the factions of the ruling Hannara Dang (HD) (Grand National Party) does nothing to boost its popularity. According to one poll, only 30 per cent of voters think President Lee Myung-bak is doing a good job. The main opposition United Democratic Party (UDP) is faring even worse: 26 per cent support it, according to Realmeter, a pollster. This comes despite concerns over growing income inequalities and an increase in the price of basic goods, issues that might be expected to play into the hands of a left-of-centre opposition party. The UDP is hampered by poor leadership and a confused message. The ruling party's presidential contender is Park Geun-hye. Her father, the late Park Chung-hee, was president during the economy's miracle years. Miss Park enjoys apparently unshakeable support among older voters and is the firm favourite for the next election.

A large part of the South Korean electorate's disillusionment with its politicians can be attributed to the perceptions and rumours of corruption that abound. The republic ranks a lowly 43rd on the Transparency International Corruption Perceptions Index. South Korea may take comfort from the fact that it is ahead of China, India, Indonesia, Malaysia and Thailand, but should note that Singapore is ranked 5th.

The electorate's fears seemed to be borne out in mid-June 2011 when – as reported by the London *Financial Times*, President Lee Myung-bak, announced that a banking scandal had suggested that there was endemic corruption in some official quarters that put at risk South Korea's metamorphosis from a fast developing economy to one that could begin to claim 'developed' status. Events appeared to focus on a double whammy level of deception, as weary prosecutors looked in to allegations that the Republic's state regulators had turned a blind eye to corruption at a number of savings banks in return for tens of thousands of dollars in cash filled envelopes and, in one case, a diamond.

South Korea's economy heads North

The Asian Development Bank (ADB), in its April 2011 report on the South Korean economy reports that its economic recovery gained traction in 2010. Gross domestic product (GDP) rose by 6.1 per cent, the sharpest increase since 2002. The exceptional growth largely reflects a rebound from below-trend growth of 2.3 per cent in 2008 and 0.2 per cent in 2009. The recovery was broad-based and rested on both external and domestic drivers. Externally, exports surged in tandem with the rebound in the world economy and trade. Domestically, private demand replaced fiscal and monetary policy stimuli pushed through during the global recession.

Among the different sources of growth in 2010, according to the ADB, robust investment played a dominant role, accounting for over two-thirds of the year's expansion. Resurgent exports of manufactured goods generated a sharp rise in investment. Private consumption accounted for the rest of GDP growth. Government consumption contributed less than a tenth, mirroring a transformation from 'policy-led' recovery to growth based on private demand. The impact on GDP of the stronger total demand was offset to a degree by a surge in imports of goods and services.

Exports up...

As global trade volume swung from sharp contraction in 2009 to expansion in 2010, it propelled a 29.6 per cent rise in merchandise exports in US dollar terms. Exports were strong throughout the year. Information technology-related products such as semiconductors and liquid crystal displays performed particularly well. Exports of autos, auto parts and general machinery also grew rapidly. In terms of export destinations, demand from the People's Republic of China (PRC) and south-east Asia drove growth in the first half and held up well in the second. Demand from Japan and the United States also picked up in 2010 over 2009.

... Imports too

Mirroring the strong recovery of demand, imports rose sharply, by 31.9 per cent. The merchandise trade surplus rose to about US$42 billion, but the deficit in services trade nearly doubled to US$11 billion. The current account surplus fell to 2.8 per cent of GDP, from 3.9 per cent in 2009.

The ADB reports that an outstanding feature of growth in 2010 was the acceleration of equipment investment, which soared by 24.5 per cent, though it partly reflects a base effect from 2009, when such investment fell by 9.1 per cent. Companies in export-oriented industries regained their appetite for investment as global demand for their products recovered. Companies were also spurred to expand facilities by a rise in manufacturing capacity utilisation from an average of 74.6 per cent in 2009 to 81.8 per cent in 2010. The ADB notes that the won appreciated against the US dollar in the second half of the year, lowering the cost of imported capital goods. Imports of machinery rose sharply, although those of transport equipment grew much less quickly.

Construction suffers, consumption rises

Construction investment contracted by 2.3 per cent in 2010, after growing by 4.4 per cent in 2009 on the back of public works. The weakness in construction reflected the sluggish housing market, where the inventory of unsold housing continued to build. Private consumption bounced back to grow by 4.1 per cent in 2010, after feeble growth in 2009, supported by a stronger labour market. In terms of economic sectors, manufacturing stood out with a 14.6 per cent increase in production last year, fuelled by surging export demand. The services sector expanded by a healthy 3.5 per cent. None the less, despite the strong economic growth, average inflation rose only slightly in 2010, to average 2.9 per cent, well within the Bank of Korea (central bank)'s target band of 2.0–4.0 per cent. As economic recovery gained traction, the Bank started to edge up its interest rate from the record low 2.0 per cent set during the global recession. From July 2010 to March 2011, the Bank raised the rate in four steps to 3.0 per cent.

... Employment too

Employment rose by 323,000, even as the government scaled back its job creation programmes. Real wages increased by more than 3 per cent, after contracting by 6 per cent in 2009. Gross domestic income rose by 5.8 per cent, the fastest pace in 8 years. An upturn in the stock market and appreciation of the won contributed to stronger consumer sentiment. The unemployment rate nudged up to 3.7 per cent from 3.6 per cent in 2009, mainly a result of more Koreans looking for work in light of the improved outlook.

Strong growth to continue?

The exceptionally strong growth seen in 2010 was in part due to the contrast with the weak performance registered in 2009. The ADB expected the economy to decelerate in 2011 to more sustainable levels. The growth rate was forecast around an annual 4.3–4.9 per cent. These figures were drawn up long before the European debt crisis, as well as that of the euro. The generally benign global climate once expected looked to be disappearing fast, with inevitable consequences for the South Korean economy into late 2011 and 2012. Merchandise exports had originally been set to grow by more than 10 per cent in 2011.

In the second half of 2011, demand from industrial economies looked likely to be subdued, while developing countries were forecast to grow rapidly and provide a more certain source of demand. South Korea has diversified its export markets in recent years, with PRC in particular providing an important export market during the global recession, Exports to the PRC have traditionally been dominated by high-tech parts and components for assembly and re-export to industrialised countries. Increasingly, however, the PRC is becoming a direct consumer of final goods, which helps to explain why South Korea's exports to that market held up so well in 2009–10. Faltering Chinese demand and GDP growth in late 2011 risked endangering the hypothesis, however.

On the domestic front, strong consumer and business confidence will – at least in the short term, support growth in private consumption and investment. High corporate profits in 2010 and prospective foreign capital inflows have enabled firms to invest. However, as pent-up demand for investment postponed during the global slump was largely satisfied in 2010, equipment investment looked likely to moderate to a more sustainable level of about 8 per cent in 2011.

Private consumption is projected to expand by 4.0–4.5 per cent in 2011, bolstered by growth in incomes. The labour market looks set to remain strong (up to 250,000 jobs will likely be generated, down a bit from last year owing to the expected moderation in growth in exports industries).

The decline in housing prices that bottomed out in the second half of 2010 should support consumer confidence, although the inflation pressures that became apparent in late 2010 were expected to intensify in 2011. Major price indicators were rising with inflation breaching the central bank's target band in January and February 2011. Inflation in 2011 was forecast at 3.5 per cent. It was expected to ease a little in 2012, when monetary policy will be tighter and global prices for oil and food are expected to moderate. Factors such as higher global oil and food prices have contributed to the rise in inflation, though aggregate demand is also putting upward pressure on prices. Additionally, as actual output has surpassed potential output since the first quarter of 2010, it looked more than likely that monetary policy will be tightened further to contain inflation.

Risk assessment

Economy	Good
Politics	Fair/poor
Regional stability	Poor

COUNTRY PROFILE

Historical profile

1910 Japan formalised its annexation of Korea after gaining responsibility for its security following victory in the Russo-Japanese war of 1905.
1919 Japan suppressed the mass March First movement for self-determination.
1930s–1940s Japan imposed measures designed to assimilate the Korean population, including the outlawing of the Korean language and family names. Korea suffered under military occupation but gained the benefits of forced industrialisation.
1945 Liberation at the hands of allied forces was a prelude to partition of the peninsula as the victorious powers encouraged friendly governments north and south of the 38th parallel. The US occupied the south while the north was taken over by the Soviet Union. As the two powers did not wish to give independence to Korea, feeling that the Korean people needed political and social re-education, a line of demarcation was established.
1948 Political divisions in the peninsula deepened. In the south, the Republic of Korea became independent after UN-supervised elections were held. Dr Syngman Rhee, leader of the Liberal Party, became the country's first president. The declaration of the Democratic People's Republic of Korea (DPRK) in the north followed, with Kim il-Sung as premier and Head of State.
1950 North Korea invaded the South with backing from China and the Soviet Union, prompting US-led intervention under a UN mandate.
1953 A cease-fire was agreed, but a peace-treaty was not signed.
1960 President Rhee was forced to resign.
1961 The government was deposed by a military coup led by General Park Chung-Hee.
1963 After the military dictatorship, a new constitution was enacted. General Park Chung-Hee became president.
1980 Demonstrations by students led to martial law being imposed throughout the country. The National Assembly was closed and all political activity banned.
1981 Martial law was lifted and political parties were formed.
1985 The election results transformed the political scene with the emergence for the first time of a relatively powerful parliamentary opposition.
1986 The opposition launched a campaign demanding constitutional reform.
1987 Roh Tae-Woo was elected president.
1988 The Constitution of the Sixth Republic was adopted, following sustained popular unrest during 1987.
1993 President Roh was succeeded by Kim Young-Sam.
1994 President of DPRK, Kim il-Sung died
1997 The Asian financial crisis precipitated the near collapse in South Korea's economy, as its credit rating plunged from A1 to BAA2; the won was devalued and the IMF and G-7 countries provided a US$57 billion loan. The resultant political upheaval led to the defeat of the Hannara Dang, (Grand National Party) (GNP) as opposition leader Kim Dae-Jung was elected president.
2000 President Kim Dae-Jung visited Pyongyang, DPRK (North Korea) and met President Kim Jong-il, in an unprecedented and much-f?ted meeting of the two Korean leaders. President Kim Dae-Jung won the Nobel peace prize. Family reunions were allowed between the north and south for the first time since the Korean War.
2001 The government resigned after a vote of no-confidence threatened Lim Dong-Won, the unification minister and chief architect of the 'Sunshine' policy promoting engagement with North Korea. The president subsequently returned Lim to government as a presidential advisor and appointed five new ministers and retained Lee Han-Dong as prime minister.
2002 Key inter-Korean relations developed after the South Korean envoy Lim Dong-Won visited North Korea. Kim Suk Soo became prime minister. Roh Moo-Hyun won the presidential elections.
2003 Goh Kun became prime minister. President Roh resigned from the ruling Saecheonnyeonminju Dang (SMD) (Millennium Democratic Party) for the Uri Dang (UD) (Our Party). Hundreds of South Koreans crossed the demilitarised zone into North Korea in a declaration of unity.
2004 The National Assembly impeached President Roh; Prime Minister Goh Kun became acting president. The left-leaning liberal UD won National Assembly elections. The Constitutional Court overturned President Roh's impeachment. Prime Minister Goh Kun resigned and Lee Hai Chan became prime minister. South and North Korea agreed to open cross-border roads and to make test runs on two railways. The Yeongi-Kongju region, in the central south province of Chungchong, was chosen as the site of the new capital city, to be completed by 2030.
2005 Street protests in Seoul followed Japan's confirmation of its claim to a small group of uninhabited islands called Dokdo, which South Korea also claimed. Chairman of Daewoo, Kim Woo-chong was convicted on fraud charges and ordered to pay back US$22 billion, for his part in the company's US$70 billion collapse.
2006 Han Myung-sook of the Daetongham Minjusin-dang (DM) (United New Democratic Party) became the first female prime minister. Ban Ki-moon was appointed secretary general of the United Nations. Five spies for the DPRK were convicted, the biggest case of espionage since the North and South Korean reconciliation in 2000.
2007 North and South Korea resumed ministerial meetings following the DPRK's nuclear closure deal. The chairman of Hyundai was convicted of embezzlement. South Korea agreed to assume operational control of its military forces, in the event of a war, after 2012. A US-South Korea FTA was signed. The first passenger trains since 1953 crossed the north-south border. A summit of leaders of North and South Korea took place, the first in 15 years. They agreed to formally end the Korean War. The South Korean delegation included industrialists, bureaucrats, poets and clerics. Lee Myung-bak (GNP) won the presidential election with 48.7 per cent. The UD collapsed and broke into splinter groups.
2008 One of the country's great cultural treasures, the Namdaemun Gate, was destroyed by fire. The Minju-dang (Democratic Party) (DEP) political party was formed from a merger between the DM and the UD. Relations between DPRK and South Korea deteriorated after DPRK expelled managers of joint industrial enterprises and test fired short-range missiles. In parliamentary elections the GNP won a slim majority of 153 seats (out of 299).

2009 All political and military agreements with South Korea were scrapped by DPRK, due to what DPRK saw as 'hostile intent' by South Korea. Former president Roh Moo-Hyun committed suicide while under investigation for alleged corruption. President Lee appointed Chung Un Chan as prime minister, to carry forward his planned programme of reforms.
2010 In February the Constitutional Court, South Korea's highest court, ruled that the death penalty does not violate the constitution and should continue. A report by an international investigation team, led by South Korea, concluded that North Korea torpedoed a South Korean warship in March, with the loss of all 46 sailors aboard. North Korea angrily denied the accusation, as condemnation by UN members followed swiftly. In a major cabinet re-shuffle in August, President Lee replaced seven ministers and nominated Kim Tae-ho as prime minister after Prime Minister Chung Un-Change resigned, citing parliament's failure to endorse his policy to found a science-business park in a central region. South Korea staged five days of military drills off its west coast in August. The move infuriated the North Koreans, who, in retaliation, fired off over 100 rounds of artillery close to the disputed sea border between the two countries. On 8 August a South Korean fishing vessel, which may have strayed across the border, was seized by North Korea; the government in South Korea demanded the vessel's immediate and safe return. On 15 August, Liberation Day, President Lee called for a fund to be started towards the cost of unification with the north. Four people, including two civilians, were killed after North Korea fired artillery shells at the island of Yeonpyeong in South Korea on 23 November. Damage to homes and businesses was widespread and hundreds of people fled the island. Korean observers consider the aggression by North Korea could be seen as endorsing the succession of Kim Jong-un and a measure of the significance the North places on fishing rights in the rich seas around the island. The attack on the island came just days after news that North Korea had built a modern plant to enrich uranium, for possible use in nuclear weapons.
2011 North and South Korean military talks collapsed on 9 February within hours of commencing, following South Korea insistence that North Korea must apologise for shelling Yeonpyeong island in November 2010. North Korea had agreed to talks under pressure from China and by its need to secure food and fuel aid. On 6 July Pyeongchang was awarded the 2018 Winter Olympics. On 1 July the EU signed a free trade agreement with South Korea, its biggest with any Asian country, as South Korea agreed to end the 20 per cent import duty on alcohol and its complicated rules on labelling and storage. On 1 August DPRK called for a resumption of the six-party nuclear negotiations 'without preconditions'. A trade agreement with the US was agreed by both houses of the US congress on 12 October.

Political structure

Constitution

A new constitution, allowing direct presidential elections and thus providing a framework for civilian rule, took effect in 1988 after receiving overwhelming approval in a referendum. The constitution removed the president's sweeping emergency powers that included the right to dissolve parliament. It also enhanced the authority of the legislature and judiciary. It provided for more civil liberties, including restoration of *habeas corpus*, while the National Assembly was empowered to supervise and investigate state affairs. Free presidential elections replaced the electoral college system, which had favoured the ruling party candidate. In addition, the constitution requires that the armed forces must maintain political neutrality.
The constitution provides for greater checks and balances among the executive, legislative and judiciary powers. A Board of Audit and Inspection was set up to monitor all government expenditure, revenue and agencies. The chairperson is appointed by the president but only with the National Assembly's approval.
A constitutional court has judgement on the constitutionality of any legislation.

Form of state

Democratic republic

The executive

Executive power is held by the president, who is popularly elected for a single term of five years and governs with the assistance of the State Council, normally composed of 15–30 ministers and headed by the prime minister. The State Council is appointed by the president on the advice of the prime minister. It does not have to be composed entirely of members of the National Assembly. No active member of the armed forces may serve on the State Council.
The president has veto power over legislation, but the National Assembly can override this by a two-thirds vote.
Other presidential powers include the appointment of officials such as judges, ministers, the mayors of five cities (Seoul, Pusan, Taegu, Inchon and Kwangu) and the governors of nine provinces.

National legislature

The unicameral Kuk Hoe (National Assembly) has 299 members, of which 245 are directly elected in single-seat constituencies and 54 are elected by proportional representation; all serve for four-year terms.

Legal system

There is a three-tier legal system, headed by a Supreme Court. This Court is composed of a chief justice (for a six-year term) and 13 justices (on recommendation by the chief justice), all appointed by the president, with the consent of the National Assembly. Below the Supreme Court are High Courts (intermediate appelate courts) and, below these, District Courts. High Courts and District Courts are divided into geographic districts. Korea also has a number of specialised courts, such as a Family Court and an Administrative Court.

Last elections

9 April 2008 (parliamentary); 19 December 2007 (presidential).
Results: Parliamentary: Hannara Dang (HD) (Grand National Party) won 153 seats (out of 299), the United Democratic Party (UDP) 81, the Liberty Forward Party (LFP) 18, pro-Park Geun-hye coalition 14, Creative Korea Party 3, independents 25. Presidential: Lee Myung-bak (HD) won 48.7 per cent of the vote, ahead of Chung Dong-young (Daetonghap Minju Sindang, (United New Democratic Party) (UNDP)) with 26.1 per cent and Lee Hoi Chang (independent) with 15.1 per cent.

Next elections

December 2012 (presidential); 2012 (National Assembly).

Political parties

Ruling party

Hannara Dang (HD) (Grand National Party) (since 9 Apr 2008)

Main opposition party

United Democratic Party (UDP)

Population

48.90 million (2010)*
Last census: 1 November 2005: 47,278,951
Population density: 490 inhabitants per square km (2010)
Annual growth rate: 0.7 per cent 1994–2004 (WHO 2006)

Ethnic make-up

Koreans, although apparently homogeneous, have complex ethnic origins, with much genetic input from the nomadic tribes of Mongolia and Central Asia. There are over 25,000 Chinese, the only major foreign ethnic community besides the 37,000 US troops stationed in South Korea. In addition, there are some 230,000 migrant labourers from a variety of countries such as Kazakhstan, Morocco and China. There is also a growing number of refugees who have escaped from the harsh conditions of North Korea.

Religions

There is no state religion and the country is tolerant of various religious faiths.

Although census and churchgoing data conflict, the most recent information available indicates that up to 49 per cent of the population professes to be Christian, 47 per cent Mahayana Buddhist, 3 per cent Confucianist.

Education

Public expenditure on education amounts to 3.6 per cent of GDP. Universal primary education and gender parity, at this level and in secondary schools, have been achieved.

Primary schooling lasts until a child is 12, middle secondary schooling lasts for three years, these constitute compulsory education. Upper secondary high schools offer either, an academic, special purpose (combined academic and vocational courses), or a wholly vocational programme, lasting for three years.

There are five types of public and private teriary institutions including junior colleges and universities.

Literacy rate: 98 per cent, male; 96.8 per cent, female; adult rates (World Bank).

Compulsory years: 6 to 15

Enrolment rate: 110 per cent, gross primary enrolment, of relevant age group (including repeaters); 102 per cent, gross secondary enrolment (World Bank).

Pupils per teacher: 31, in primary schools

Health

There are around 19,500 private clinics complementing the country's hospitals, of which a significant number are university-affiliated. Improved water sources and sanitation facilities are available to 92 per cent and 63 per cent of the population resectively.

Life expectancy: 77 years, 2004 (WHO 2006)

Fertility rate/Maternal mortality rate: 1.2 births per woman, 2004 (WHO 2006); maternal mortality 20 deaths per 100,000 live births (World Bank).

Birth rate/Death rate: 6 deaths and 14 births per 1,000 population (World Bank estimates).

Child (under 5 years) mortality rate (per 1,000): 5 per 1,000 live births (World Bank)

Welfare

The National Basic Livelihood Protection Law makes social assistance a legal right for the unemployed, based on a concept of 'productive welfare' which combines means-testing with self-support plans to facilitate re-entry to the workforce.

Public pensions provision, introduced in 1988, is set to increase as the system confronts an ageing population with a 12-fold increase in the expected number of beneficiaries by 2010. Contributions will have to double to 18 per cent of salary to maintain an actuarial balance, according to the Organisation for Economic Co-Operation and Development (OECD). The South Korean government may consider alternative options, such as privately-managed pensions funds, paid into by the allowances firms are obliged to award departing employees.

Main cities

Seoul (capital, estimated population 10.1 million (m) in 2005), Pusan (3.7m), Inch'on (2.7m), Taegu (2.6m), Taejeon (1.5m), Kwangju (1.4m), Seongnam (1.0m), Ulsan (1.1m), Koyang (1.0m).

In 2007, the government will start building a new administrative capital in Chungcheongnam-do province, to the south of Seoul; the first ministries and government departments will move in 2012; the city should be complete by 2030.

Languages spoken

The Korean language is a member of the Altaic family with origins in Mongolia. Approximately 60 per cent of the vocabulary is borrowed from Chinese. The written language employs its own phonetic character system, Hangul.

English is spoken to a limited extent in government and business circles. The older generation often speak Japanese.

Official language/s

Korean

Media

The Korean media, reputedly notorious for their appetite for influence, are thought, by civic campaigners, to be a constituency in need of urgent reform. Efforts made in the past to curtail publishers and their various backers have not succeeded. The sector has a long tradition of collaborating with South Korea's authoritarian regimes and is sensitive about criticism of bias.

Press

Much of the Korean press is controlled by industrial conglomerates. Readership is high and there are over 100 national and local dailies to choose from.

Dailies: The 'Big Three' nationals published in Seoul are *Chosun Ilbo* (http://english.chosun.com) is considered a conservative publication, *JoongAng Ilbo* (http://joongangdaily.joins.com) and *Donga Ilbo* (http://english.donga.com), take an independent line. In Korean, other regional publication include from Pusan *Pusan Ilbo* (www.busanilbo.com), *Kookje Shinmun* (www.kookje.co.kr); from Inch'on *Inchon Ilbo* (http://news.itimes.co.kr); from Taegu *Kyongbuk Ilbo* (www.kyongbuk.co.kr), *Maeil Shinmun* (www.imaeil.com) and *Morning News* (www.morningnews.co.kr). In English, *The Seoul Times* (www.theseoultimes.com).

Weeklies: Many foreign magazines have Korean sections, local news magazines include *Korea Newsreview*, which publishes articles from the government-owned *Korea Herald* (www.koreaherald.co.kr), in English.

Business: In Korean, *Hankyung* (www.hankyung.com), *Financial News Daily* (www.fnnews.com), *Seoul Economic Daily* (www.hankooki.com) and *Maeil Business Newspaper* (http://news.mk.co.kr, with online English edition. Most national newspapers also provide business news some with online English editions.

Periodicals: *Dong-A Herald* is a bimonthly student newspaper. *The Granite Tower* is a monthly English language tabloid.

Broadcasting

Radio: The public service is the Korea Broadcasting System (http://english.kbs.co.kr), which operates six networks including Radio Korea International (http://world.kbs.co.kr) offering programmes in 11 languages.

There are over 200 local radio stations some of which are relayed nationwide. Around 30 per cent of all stations are privately owned and commercial. There are national networks that are educational and religious. The American Forces Network (AFN) Korea (http://afnkorea.net) is operated by the US military.

Television: There are over 30 television stations run by the country's networks, of which the most important are Korea Broadcasting System (KBS) and Munwha Broadcasting Corporation (MBC). The longest-running stations are KBS 1, 2, 3 (an educational station), MBC and AFKN-TV (operated by the US military for its personnel and their dependants). Other networks operating in South Korea include Asia-Pacific broadcaster Arirang TV, which provides English-language programming, the youth-oriented Mnet, Korea Music Television, Seoul Broadcasting System (SBS) and the News Channel of Korea. Around 90 per cent of the population subscribe to cable TV.

Advertising

Commercial advertising may be placed in the press, on radio and television and in cinemas, as well as on public billboards and posters. The Korea Broadcasting Advertising Corporation (Kobaco) is authorised as the sole media representative responsible for over 50 broadcasting stations in television, radio and digital services. It publishes a document setting out all advertising requirements *Introduction to broadcast advertising in Korea*.

News agencies
Yonhap News Agency, 85-1, Susong-dong, Jongro-gu, Seoul (fax: 398-3463/3567; internet: http://english.yonhapnews.co.kr).

Economy
South Korea, which was Asia's fourth largest economy in 2010, is open and mixed and heavily geared to exporting its manufactured goods, particularly vehicles and shipbuilding, textiles, steel, electronics and computers, bioengineering, fine chemistry and aerospace items. However with its lack of hydrocarbons and an economy dependent on exports South Korea is vulnerable to external shocks, as it requires the import of oil and natural gas, while being subject to the vagaries and changing market needs of international trading.
GDP growth in 2007 was 5.1 per cent, which fell to 2.3 per cent in 2008 as global trade was hit in the worldwide economic crisis and South Korea experienced its worst drop in exports since 2001, falling in January 2008 by 35 per cent year-on-year from the same period in 2007. Investment and domestic consumption fell as a result and the South Korean economy suffered one of the sharpest contractions of any country. However, as South Korea had experienced two recessions (following the Asian economic crisis of 1997 and the 'dotcom' bubble of 2001) within 11 years (1997–2008), which had been characterised by massive capital outflows and a slump in exports, lessons had been learned. The government swiftly adopted measures to curtail serious damage to the economy by initially setting aside US$55 billion in foreign exchange reserves to provide loans to banks and trade-related businesses, and administered major monetary and fiscal stimuli (to stop any slide in confidence). To shield the banking sector it established a bank to buy up toxic assets and recapitalise bank funds.
By 2009 GDP growth was 0.2 per cent, but South Korea avoided falling into recession with the Bank of Korea revising its GDP growth prediction to 5.9 per cent as exports increased and oil imports were less expensive than previously anticipated. It also lifted its key interest rate to 2.25 per cent, the first increase since August 2008 when it was dropped to a record low of 2 per cent.
As government sponsored initiatives were discontinued the unemployment rate hit a 10-year high of 4.8 per cent in January 2010, which when seasonally adjusted recorded 3.5 per cent in June.

External trade
South Korea is a member of the Asia-Pacific Economic Co-operation (Apec) forum, which is a group of 21 countries that border the Pacific. The objective of Apec is to facilitate trade, economic growth and investment in the region.
A revised, Korea-US Free Trade Agreement (Korus FTA) was announced on 3 December 2010; the original had been signed in 2006. US exports to South Korea were expected to rise to US$11 billion annually. The agreement allows the import of vehicle-parts that had been, until the revision, blocked but denied import of beef aged over 30-months.
Main export sectors include semiconductors, telecommunications, computers, steel making, shipbuilding, vehicle assembly, organic chemicals and textile manufacturing. In 2008, electronics accounted for 26 per cent of all exports, with ships and other vessels accounting for 10 per cent and road vehicles 8 per cent.
Imports
Principal imports are petroleum and natural gas, machinery, electronics and electrical equipment, petroleum, steel, plastics, transport equipment, iron and steel.
Main sources: China (typically 17 per cent of total), Japan (15 per cent), US (9 per cent).
Exports
Principal exports are semiconductors, telecommunications equipment, vehicles, computers, steel, ships and petrochemicals.
Main destinations: China (typically 24 per cent of total), US (10 per cent), Japan (6 per cent).

Agriculture
Farming
The agricultural sector accounts for around 3.7 per cent of GDP and employs 15 per cent of the workforce. Farming remains essentially subsistence-based and is inherently uncompetitive. While, by comparison, farmers are richer than their counterparts elsewhere in Asia, the average farm holding is big enough to support only a small family and the disparity in incomes between the urban and rural populations is growing.
Price-support policies for farmers are being reduced in line with South Korea's international commitments. Increasing the average size of farms and decoupling production decisions from government aid are likely to be vital in promoting efficiency in farming.
The main crops grown are rice, sweet potatoes, barley, soya beans and a wide range of fruit and vegetables. Despite considerable efforts, the country depends on imports for animal feed grains. Ginseng, tobacco, pears and processed noodles are among South Korea's exports.
Fishing
The fishing industry is an important source of export earnings but international restriction of fishing zones has limited potential growth. South Korean fishing vessels are mostly active in the South Pacific. The annual catch, of which some 60 per cent is marine fish, totals up to 2.6 million tonnes.
Following the annual meeting of the Commission for the Conservation of Southern Bluefin Tuna (CCSBT), held on Cheju Island, South Korea, all members agreed to a 20 per cut in the roughly 17,000 tonnes in 2009 bluefin tuna catches from 2010. Scientists had warned that without a cut fish stocks could crash as numbers had become dangerously low.
Forestry
Forests, around half of which are conifer, cover some 65 per cent of the total land area. Much of the forest owes its existence to large-scale replanting programmes implemented after the Second World War and since the end of the Korean War in 1953. The latter conflict, together with logging under the Japanese occupation, and demand for fuelwood, badly degraded the native forest.
South Korea and Indonesia have an agreement for forestry co-operation. This involves projects such as tree planting, fighting forest fires, skills development and eco-tourism investment.

Industry and manufacturing
Korea's industrialisation programme made it the world's eleventh richest economy during the 1990s, when it became the world's largest shipbuilder and producer of DRAM memory chips, the fourth biggest car exporter and the sixth largest steelmaker. The industrial sector accounts for around 40 per cent of GDP and employs around a fifth of the workforce.
The manufacture of iron and steel products, the automobile industry, shipbuilding, petrochemicals and electronics continue to be central to export-led growth. Other main products include fertilisers and other industrial chemicals, rubber, synthetic and natural textiles, garments, footwear and processed foods.
The industrial structure continues to be haunted by the legacy of rapid state-guided industrialisation protected from overseas competition. The government has struggled to limit the economic power of the 30 largest leading companies (*chaebol*), which still dominate national industry.

Tourism
Tourism is an important and growing industry. New hotels, both deluxe and budget class, have opened and more are

being built throughout the country. New resort complexes are under construction.

Mining

There are no significant mineral resources. South Korea relies mainly on imports to meet its increasing domestic demand. The major mineral imports are iron ore, copper and zinc ore concentrates. Cement is a major export commodity to the US, as there is surplus in the domestic market.

LG-Nikko Copper Incorporated, a joint venture established by LG and Japan Korea Joint Smelting Company, a Japanese consortium, is the only copper smelting and refining operation in South Korea. Each company was obliged to invest US$20 million in the joint venture that took control of LG's Changhang and Onsan copper smelting and refining operations, which had an estimated value of US$830 million.

Domestic iron ore supplies only about one per cent of South Korea's needs. The Pohang Iron and Steel Company (Posco), the largest crude steel producer in South Korea and the only integrated iron and steel producer, formed a strategic alliance with Nippon Steel Corp, to expand research and development, and also encouraged other Asian companies to join the alliance. Posco employs more than 5,000 employees at production plants in Pohang and Kwangyang, producing more than 23.4 million tonnes of steel products annually for customers in over 60 countries. Its products range from electrical steel sheets to stainless steel products.

The only lead and zinc mine, at Kumba, supplies about 10 per cent of the demand for lead and zinc concentrates. Korea Zinc, which is one of the largest primary zinc producers in the world, completed the expansion of its zinc plant complex at Onsan, and is able to produce over 350,000 tonnes per year. Young Poong Corporation, its parent company, increased zinc metal output at the Sukpo zinc refinery, in the North Kyongsang Province, by over 198,300 tonnes per year.

The non-metal mineral sector accounts for 51.9 per cent of the total mining industry. Other industrial mineral production includes limestone, silica stone, kaolin, serpentine, feldspar and zeolite. Major imports consist of potash, asbestos and manganese ores and concentrates.

Hydrocarbons

There are no domestic oil reserves. Oil consumption was 2.2 million barrels per day (bpd) in 2007, making it the world's ninth largest consumer and fifth largest importer of oil, of which 20 per cent is exported as refined. The country has a strategic petroleum reserve of over 110 million barrels of oil, which covers 90 days of imports, in order to offset any disruption to supply; in 2009 the reserve is expected to total over 146 million barrels. The state-owned Korea National Oil Corporation (KNOC) has, in an effort to secure the country's oil supply, bought up stakes in oil companies throughout the world and is involved in 32 foreign exploration and production projects, of which six are producing oil. South Korea has an oil refining capacity of 2.6 million bpd, from six facilities, with plans for another 480,000bpd plant in Sosan.

Domestic gas production has ceased and in 2009 South Korea was the world's second largest importer of liquefied natural gas (LNG) importing 88.8 billion cubic metres in 2007 mostly provided by Qatar, Oman, Malaysia and Indonesia.

Proven coal reserves were 135 million tonnes in 2007, all of which is the less valuable brown coal typically used in power plants. Domestic production has declined from 10 million tonnes in the mid-1980s to less than 1.3 million tonnes in 2007. Metallurgical coal for steelmaking come mainly from China and Australia, where the Korean Electric Power Corporation (Kepco) has invested in a number of mines.

Energy

Total installed electricity generation was 62 gigawatts (GW) in 2007, of which 63 per cent was produced by conventional thermal power stations, with nuclear reactors producing around 36 per cent of all energy. There are four nuclear power stations with plans for two more.

The privatisation of the state-owned electricity utility, Korean Electric Power Corporation (Kepco), has moved at a slow pace but Kepco has been broken into six generating companies with the government retaining control of the Korea Hydro and Nuclear Power Company (KHNPC). Auctioning off of the other five companies has been repeatedly postponed. Foreign ownership is limited to 30 per cent of any single power company.

Financial markets

Stock exchange

Koria Exchange (KRX)

Banking and insurance

The 1997/98 financial crisis revealed underlying structural problems in South Korea's banking system. The crisis led to the creation of the Financial Restructuring Committee (FRC), which reported a large ratio of non-performing loans (NPLs) to total loans and poor accounting standards. The government was forced to nationalise the country's five largest banks so that by 2002/03 at 7.5 per cent, South Korea had the second-lowest NPL ratio in East Asia after Hong Kong. The estimated recovery rate on South Korean NPLs is 35 per cent, compared to Singapore and Hong Kong at 75 per cent and 50 per cent respectively.

Although the financial system is in better health, controversies linger over bank privatisation. Arguments also surround banking regulation, with President Roh reluctant to allow the *chaebol* to regain their influence over the sector. Roh favours increasing the powers of independent directors and shareholders as well as encouraging greater foreign ownership, although there is little foreign interest in South Korea's banking sector which is seen as risky.

Another pressing concern for the government is consolidating the banking sector into three or four large banks.

Central bank

Bank of Korea

Main financial centre

Seoul

Time

GMT plus nine hours

Geography

South Korea forms the southern part of the Korean peninsula, in north-east Asia, with the Democratic People's Republic of Korea to the north. To the west is the Yellow Sea, the East China Sea is to the south and the Sea of Japan is to the east. The Korea Strait separates the peninsula from Japan in the south-east. The country's portion of the peninsula is dominated by rugged terrain and mountains, culminating in the T'aebaek-sanmaek mountain range which runs from north to south along the eastern coast. Two major rivers originate in this range, the Naktong flowing to the Korea Strait and the Han river to the Yellow Sea. Plains are few and far between, mostly concentrated in the west, with the coastal strips in the east and south typically narrow. There are a number of islands off the southern and western coasts. Of these the largest is Cheju, over 1,800 square km in size and home to South Korea's highest peak, Mount Hallasan (1,950 metres).

Hemisphere

Northern

Climate

Winters are dry and very cold, with temperatures well below 0 degrees Celsius (C) between December–February. Korean summers are typically hot and humid, with monsoon rains, tropical storms and occasional typhoons from June–September. The average July temperature range is 22–29 degrees C. The narrow southernmost coastal plain has the mildest climate and is home to vegetation such as bamboo and evergreen oak.

Entry requirements

Passports

Required by all and must be valid for six months from the date of departure.

Visa

Not required by tourists from North America, Japan, Australia and many citizens of EU for up to 60 days. See http://english.tour2korea.com and the link to *Entry Info* for a full list and entitlements. For business travellers and those not eligible for visa-free travel, visit www.mofat.go.kr/me/index.jsp and see *visa control*. Applications must be submitted to the nearest Korean consulate.

Currency advice/regulations

The import of local and foreign currency greater than US$10,000 must be declared; permission for the export of local and foreign currency larger than US$10,000 (or equivalent, including travellers cheques) must be obtained from customs or the Bank of Korea; export is limited to the amount declared on arrival. Exchange receipts should be retained for verification.

Travellers cheques are accepted in banks, hotels and larger shops in major towns.

Customs

Personal effects are duty free, including high-value items (cameras, watches etc) which should be recorded on a baggage declaration form on arrival.

A certificate from the Cultural Properties Preservation Bureau is necessary for exporting antiques. Permission for trade imports or exports must be obtained from the trade and industry ministry or from authorised foreign exchange banks, and certain items may be restricted or prohibited (such as ginseng and cuttlefish).

Prohibited imports

Illegal drugs and pornography. Firearms and ammunition, fruit, vegetables soil and seeds all require licences, obtained before arrival.

Health (for visitors)

Health facilities in South Korea are generally good. The high level of pollution may be a serious problem for those suffering from respiratory conditions.

Mandatory precautions

An HIV/Aids-free certificate is required for stays of over three months.

Advisable precautions

Vaccinations are recommended for diphtheria, tuberculosis, hepatitis A and B, Japanese B encephalitis, polio, tetanus and typhoid. There is rabies risk and travellers should avoid stray animals.

Hotels

Luxury hotels include a 10 per cent service charge in the bill. Tipping is not usual, although it is on the increase in Western-style hotels.

Credit cards

Major hotels accept credit cards, but check when booking which ones are accepted for settlement of hotel bills. Also accepted in major department stores, supermarkets etc.

The Korea Travel Card, a pre-paid debit card allows visitors to pay for goods and services throughout the country at favourable rates. The card is obtained through tourist outlets.

Public holidays (national)

Fixed dates

1 Jan (New Year's Day), 1 Mar (Independence Movement Day), ^ 1 May (Labour Day), 5 May (Children's Day), 6 Jun (Memorial Day), 17 Jul (Constitution Day), 15 Aug (Liberation Day), 3 Oct (National Foundation Day), 25 Dec (Christmas Day).

^ Bank and business organisations holiday.

The summer vacation is the last week in July and the first week in August.

Variable dates

Soellal (Lunar New Year, Jan/Feb, three days), Birth of Buddha (May), Chu'seok (Harvest Moon Festival, Sep/Oct, three days).

Working hours

Banking

Mon–Fri: 0900–1700.

Business

Mon–Fri: 0900–1800.

Government

Mon–Fri: 0900–1800.

Shops

Sun–Sat: 1030–2000 (department stores, closed one day per month, typically Mon, different stores choose different days).

Small shops open from early morning till late evening every day of the week.

Telecommunications

Mobile/cell phones

There are 3G GSM services available.

Electricity supply

220V AC, 60 cycles, with round two-pin plugs.

Weights and measures

Metric system used in commerce; local system also in use, especially relating to land and buildings.

Social customs/useful tips

Korean surnames precede given names, and given names are never used alone, except by intimates. The family names, 'Kim', 'Lee' and 'Park', cover more than half the population and may have variant spellings. Business associates are normally addressed by title (eg Director Kim or Manager Lee).

Business entertaining usually takes place in restaurants and wives do not participate. Business visitors should carry a good supply of business cards, which are exchanged on introduction. Hotels can provide bilingual business cards overnight.

Note the official romanisation of Korean words has been altered to more accurately reflect pronunciation (eg Gimpo international airport rather than Kimpo, Busan instead of Pusan and Gimchi instead of Kimchi, Korea's signature spiced cabbage dish). However, the former romanisations are still widely used, with some major newspapers declaring a complete boycott of the new system.

Business etiquette is very formal. Punctuality and a smart appearance are important. Jackets and ties are required, even in summer. However, the ritual of getting drunk with a potential business partner may be expected. You should appear respectful at all times and keep smiling even if negotiations are slow. Business associates like to spend time getting to know you. Confirm agreements in writing.

It is impolite to refuse food or drink. Use the right hand when giving or receiving. Outdoor shoes should never be worn inside a house.

There are certain areas, particularly near the demilitarised zone, where entry and photography are forbidden.

Getting there

Air

National airline: Korean Air and Asiana Airlines

International airport/s: Seoul-Inchon International Airport (ICN), 40km west of Inchon and 52km from Seoul. Facilities include, duty-free shopping, restaurant, bar, banks, business centre, medical services and car hire. It is connected to the city by rail, taxi (30–60 mins) buses and ferry. Pusan (PUS) 27km from city, with flights arriving mainly from Japan. Cheju (CJU) on the island of Cheju.

Airport tax: Departure tax: W10,000, not applicable to transit passengers.

Surface

Road: There are no land borders with any other country except North Korea; all border crossing are closed.

Rail: Cargo trains started running between North and South Korea in 2007.

Water: There is a daily ferry service between Pusan and Shiminoseki, Japan.

Main port/s: Pusan, Inchon, Masan, Ulsan, Mokpo, Kunsan, Yosu.

Getting about

National transport

Air: Gimpo Airport, located close to Gimpo, west of Seoul, is used for all domestic flights. Korean Air operates daily services between Seoul and Pusan (50 minutes), Taegu, Cheju, Ulsan and Kwangju, with less frequent services to other centres. Other services are provided by Asiana Airlines. Expect to be searched for firearms when embarking on internal flights.

Road: The road network contains more than 60,000km of highways and lesser roads. More than half of roads are paved. Major cities are linked by motorways, but minor roads may be poorly maintained. Pusan is over five hours distant from Seoul by road, compared to four hours by rail.

Buses: Air-conditioned express *Chwasok* buses operate between major cities, in competition with trains. Villages are often connected by a network of local buses.

Rail: Korean National Railroads offers normal and super-express trains between major cities. The super-express train (*Saemaul-ho*) runs between Seoul and Pusan, Chongju, Yosu and Inchon. Timetables and station signs are often in English. Many trains have sleeping and dining cars.

Water: Various services are available. Mokpo and Pusan are linked by a steamer service twice weekly. The *Angel Line*, a hydrofoil service, runs between Pusan and Yosu five times daily, via Chongmy. The island of Cheju is linked to the mainland by daily ferries, including car ferries, three times per week.

City transport

Public transport in Seoul is well-developed, but becomes crowded at rush-hour.

Taxis: Registered taxis carry meters and are clearly marked on the roof. Taxis are plentiful, and available at ranks, by telephone or hailed in the steet. A 20 per cent surcharge applies between 0000–0400. Taxi drivers suspend use of meters for journeys outside town, so negotiate the fare for such trips in advance. It is advisable to carry written instructions in Korean if possible.

Buses, trams & metro: The Korean Air limousine shuttle bus calls at 20 Seoul locations, including major hotels.

City buses, though cheap and convenient, are crowded. Purple and white buses have few seats. Green and beige 'seat buses' make fewer stops and are more comfortable and air-conditioned. Tokens are available at most stops. There are English-language signs on city-centre buses only.

Seoul has an extensive metro system with eight lines accessing most parts of the city and provides a rapid means of travelling between places. First and last trains are around 0500–2400 depending on individual lines. Comprehensive information is given at www.seoulmetro.co.kr/eng/ with maps and related links. Signs are in English and Korean.

Pusan, Daegu and Incheon have metro systems and Gwangju and Daejeon have systems under construction.

Car hire

International driving licences are acceptable, but chauffeur-driven car hire is recommended in the main cities.

BUSINESS DIRECTORY

The addresses listed below are a selection only. While World of Information makes every endeavour to check these addresses, we cannot guarantee that changes have not been made, especially to telephone numbers and area codes. We would welcome any corrections.

Telephone area codes

The international direct dialling (IDD) code for the Republic of Korea, is +82, followed by area code and subscriber's number:

Inchon	32	Seoul	2
Pusan	51	Taegu	53

Useful telephone numbers

Police: 112
Fire: 119
Medical emergency 1339
Directory inquiries: 114
International calls: 1035/1037
Tourist helpline: 1330

Chambers of Commerce

American Chamber of Commerce in Korea, 4501 Trade Tower, 159-1 Samsung-dong, Kangnam-gu, Seoul 135-729 (tel: 564-2040; fax: 564-2050; e-mail: info@amchamkorea.org).

British Chamber of Commerce in Korea, 21/F Seoul Finance Centre, 84 Taepyoung-ro 1-ga, Chung-gu, Seoul 100-101 (tel: 720-9406; fax: 720-9411; e-mail: bcck@bcck.or.kr).

European Union Chamber of Commerce in Korea, Kyobo Building, 1 Chongro 1-ga, Chongro-gu, Seoul, 110-714 (tel: 725-9880; fax: 725-9886; e-mail: eucck@eucck.org).

Inchon Chamber of Commerce and Industry, 447 Nonhyon-dong, Namdong-gu, Inchon 405-300 (tel: 810-2800; fax: 810-2807; e-mail: ebiz@incci.co.kr).

Korea Chamber of Commerce and Industry, 45 Namdaemunro 4-ga, Chung-gu, Seoul 100-743 (tel: 316-3114; fax: 771-3267; e-mail: info@korcham.net).

Pusan Chamber of Commerce and Industry, 853-1 Pomchon-dong, Pusanjin-gu, Pusan 614-021 (tel: 645-7771; fax: 645-3003; e-mail: julyjang@pcci.or.kr).

Taegu Chamber of Commerce and Industry, 107 Sinchon 3-dong, Tong-gu, Taegu 701-023 (tel: 755-0041; fax: 795-5774; e-mail: mrlee@dcci.or.kr).

Banking

Bank of Seoul, 10-1, 2-ka, Namdaemun-ro, Chung-gu, Seoul (fax: 756-6389).

Cho Hung Bank Ltd., 14, 1-ka, Namdaemun-ro, Chung-gu, Seoul (tel: 733-2000; fax: 732-0835).

Citizens National Bank, 9-1, 2-ka, Namdaemun-ro, Chung-gu, Seoul (fax: 757-3679).

Commercial Bank of Korea, 111-1, 2-ka, Namdaemun-ro, Chung-gu, Seoul (tel: 754-3920; fax: 754-9203).

Export-Import Bank of Korea, 16-1, Yoido-dong, Youngdungpo-gu, Seoul 150-010 (tel: 779-6114; fax: 784-1030).

Hanil Bank, 130, 2-ka, Namdaemun-ro, Chung-gu, Seoul (fax: 754-0479).

Hana Bank, 101-1, 1-ga Ulchiro, Chung-gu, Seoul 100-191 (tel: 754-2121; fax: 756-6358).

Korea Development Bank, 10-2, Kwanchul-dong, Chongro-gu, Seoul (tel: 398-6369; fax: 720-0015).

Korea Exchange Bank, 181, 2-ka, Ulji-ro, Chung-gu, Seoul.

Korea First Bank, 100 Kongpyong-dong, Chongro-gu, Seoul (tel: 733-0070; fax: 736-8092).

Shinhan Bank, 120, 2-ga, Taepyung-ro, Chung-gu, Seoul (tel: 756-0505; fax: 774-7013).

Central bank

Bank of Korea, 110, 3-KA Namdaemun-ro, Chung-ku, Seoul 100-794 (tel: 759-4114; fax: 759-4060; e-mail:bokdplp@bok.or.kr).

Stock exchange

Koria Exchange (KRX): www.krx.co.kr

Travel information

Korea Automobile Association, 1, PO Box 2008, Seoul (tel: 785-5051).

Korean Air, 41-3 Seosomun-Dong, Chung-gu, Seoul (tel: 755-2221; fax: 751-7799; internet: www.koreanair.com).

Ministry of tourism

Ministry of Culture and Tourism, 82-1 Sejongno, Chongno-gu, Seoul (tel: 736-7946; fax: 736-8513).

National tourist organisation offices

Korean National Tourism Organisation (KNTO), 40 Cheongyecheonmo, Chung-gu, Seoul 100-180 (tel: 729 9497; fax: 319 0086; e-mail: webmaster@mail.knto.or.kr; internet site: www.tour2korea.com).

Ministries

Ministry of Agriculture and Forestry, 1 Jungang-dong, Kwachon, Kyongki-do 427-760 (tel: 500-1587; fax: 503-7249; e-mail: webmaster@maf.go.kr).

Ministry of Construction and Transportation, 1 Jungang-dong, Kwachon, Kyongki-do 427-712 (tel: 504-9031; fax:

504-6825; e-mail: webmaster@moct.go.kr).

Ministry of Culture and Tourism, 82-1 Sejongno, Jongno-gu, Seoul 110-703 (tel: 3704-9114; fax: 3704-9119; e-mail: webmaster@mct.go.kr).

Ministry of Defence, 1 Yongsan-dong, Yongsan-gu, Seoul 140-701 (tel: 795-0071; fax: 703-3109; e-mail: cyber@mnd.go.kr).

Ministry of Education and Human Resources Development, 77-6 Sejong-no, Jongno-gu, Seoul 110-760 (tel: 3703-2114; fax: 2100-6133; e-mail: webmaster@moe.go.kr).

Ministry of Environment, 1 Jungang-dong, Kwachon, Kyongki-do 427-729 (tel: 2110-6546; fax: 504-9206; e-mail: shinae@me.go.kr).

Ministry of Finance and Economy, 1 Chungang-dong, Kwachon City, Kyonggi-Do, Seoul (tel: 503-7171; fax: 502-0193; internet site: www.mofe.go.kr/mofe/eng).

Ministry of Finance, Jungang-dong, Kwachon, Kyongki-do 427-725 (tel: 503-9032; fax: 503-9033; e-mail: fppr@mofe.go.kr).

Ministry of Foreign Affairs and Trade, Doryeom-dong Jongno-gu Seoul 110-787 (tel: 100-2114; fax 100-7999:email: web@mofat.go.kr; internet: www.mofat.go.kr/me/index.jsp).

Ministry of Gender Equality, 77-6 Sejong-no, Jongno-gu, Seoul 110-760 (tel: 3703-2500; fax: 2106-5145; e-mail: webadmin@moge.go.kr).

Ministry of Government Administration and Home Affairs, 77-6 Sejong-no, Jongno-gu, Seoul 110-760 (tel: 3703-2114; fax: 3703-5502; e-mail: webmaster@mogaha.go.kr).

Ministry of Government Legislation, 77-6 Sejong-no, Jongno-gu, Seoul 110-760 (tel: 3703-2114; fax: 738-2649; e-mail: lawinfo@moleg.go.kr).

Ministry of Health and Welfare, 1 Jungang-dong, Kwachon, Kyongki-do 427-760 (tel: 503-7524; fax: 504-6418; e-mail: m_mohw@mohw.go.kr).

Ministry of Information and Communication, 100 Sejong-no, Jongno-gu, Seoul 110-777 (tel 750-2114; fax: 750-2915; e-mail: webmaster@mic.go.kr).

Ministry of Justice, 1 Jungang-dong, Kwachon, Kyongki-do 427-760 (tel: 503-7023; fax: 2110-3079; webmaster@moj.go.kr).

Ministry of Labour, 1 Jungang-dong, Kwachon, Kyongki-do 427-716 (tel: 2110-2114; fax: 503-9772; e-mail: webmaster@molab.go.kr).

Ministry of Maritime Affairs and Fisheries, 50 Chungjeongno, Saedaemun-gu, Seoul 120-715 (tel: 3148-6114; fax: 3148-6044; e-mail: webmaster@momaf.go.kr).

Ministry of Planning and Budget, 520-3 Banpo-dong, Seocho-gu. Seoul 137-756 (tel: 3480-7990; fax: 3480-7600; e-mail: nara@mpb.go.kr).

Ministry of Science and Technology, 2 Jungang-dong, Kwachon, Kyongki-do 427-715 (tel: 503-7600; fax: 503-7673; e-mail: webadmin@most.go.kr).

Ministry of Trade, Industry and Energy, 1 Jungang-dong, Kwachon, Kyongki-do 427-760 (tel: 2110-5061; fax: 503-9496; e-mail: webmocie@mocie.go.kr).

Ministry of Unification, 77-6 Sejong-no, Jongno-gu, Seoul 110-760 (tel: 3703-2433; fax: 739-5047; e-mail: webmaster@unikorea.go.kr).

Other useful addresses

Association of Foreign Trading Agents in Korea, 218 Hangangro 2-ka, Youngsan-gu, Seoul (tel: 792-1581; fax: 749-1830).

Board of Audit and Inspection, 25-23 Samchong-dong, Jongno-gu, soul (tel: 721-9114; fax: 721-9299).

British Embassy, 4 Chung-dong-Chung-gu, Seoul (tel: 735-7341/3; fax: 736-6241).

Customs Administration, 71 Nonhyun-dong, Kangnam-gu, Seoul (tel: 512-0011; fax: 512-2322).

Economic Planning Board, 1 Chungang-dong, Kwach'on City, Kyonggi, Seoul (tel: 503-7171).

Emergency Planning Committee, 1 Chungang-dong, Kwachon-City, Kyonggi-Do (tel: 503-7723; fax: 503-7727).

Fair Trade Commission, 1 Chungang-dong, Kwachon-City, Kyonggi-Do (tel: 503-7171; fax: 504-5144).

Foreign Investment Policy Division, Rm 203, Complex No 3, 1 Chungang-dong, Kwacheon City, Kyongki-do (tel: 503-9276/7; fax: 503-9324).

Institute of Foreign Affairs and National Security, 1376-2 Seocho-dong, Seocho-gu, Seoul (tel: 571-1020; fax: 571-1019).

Invest Korea, Kotra Bldg 300-9 Yomgok-dong, Seocho-gu, Seoul 137-70 (tel: 3460-7545; fax: 3460–7946; internet: www.investkorea.org).

Korean Exhibition Centre, 65 Samsung-dong, Gangnam-gu, Seoul (tel: 553-7907/8; fax: 557-5784).

Korean Foreign Trade Association, TCPO Box 100, Seoul (tel: 551-5114; fax: 551-5100/5200).

Korean Information Service, 82-1 Sejongno, Jongno-gu, Seoul 110-703 (internet site: www.korea.net).

Korean Republic Embassy (US), 2450 Massachusetts Avenue, NW, Washington DC 20008, USA (tel: (+1-202) 939-5600; fax: (+1-202) 797-0595; e-mail: information_usa@mofat.go.kr).

Korea Stock Exchange, 33, Yoido-dong, Youngdeungpo-gu, KR-Seoul 150-010 (tel: 780-2271; fax: 786-0263; internet site: www.kse.or.kr/e_index.html).

Korean Trade Promotion Corporation, CPO Box 1621 10-1, 2-ka Hoehyun-dong, Chung-gu, Seoul (tel: 753-4180/9; internet site: www.kotra.or.kr/eng/index.php3).

Meteorological Administration, 1 Songwall-dong, Jongno-gu, Seoul (tel: 738-0345; fax: 723-8731).

National Statistical Office, Hanta Building, 645-15 Yoksam-dong, Kangnam-gu, Seoul (tel: 222-1901; fax: 538-3874; internet site: www.nso.go.kr/eindex.htm).

National Tax Administration, 108-4 Susong-dong, Jongno-gu, Seoul (tel: 397-1200; fax: 720-0278).

Overseas Aircargo Service Inc, 1–6 Fl. Daishin Bldg, 93–62 Bukchang-dong, PO Box 2757, Chung-gu, Seoul (tel: 753-8374/6; fax: 756-9400).

Rural Development Administratin, 250 Socun-dong, Suwon-City, Kyonggi-Do (tel: 292-4370; fax: 292-4163).

Securities Exchange Commission, 28-1 Yoido-dong, Yongdongpo-gu, Seoul (tel: 785-7593; fax: 785-3475).

Small and Medium Business Administration, 2 Chungang-dong, Kwachon-City, Kyonggi-Do (tel: 509-7114; fax: 503-7941).

Internet sites

Asiana Airlines: http://us.flyasiana.com

EC21 (Internet trade site): www.ec21.net

Korea Air: www.koreanair.com

Korea Asset Management Corporation: www.kamco.or.kr/eng/index.htm

Korea Infogate: www.koreainfogate.co.kr

Korean Travel: http://english.tour2korea.com/).

Inchon International Airport, www.airport.or.kr/eng/airport/

Samsung Economic Research Institute: www.koreaeconomy.org

Kosovo

KEY FACTS

Official name: Republic of Kosovo

Head of State: President Atifete Jahjaga (from 7 Apr 2011)

Head of government: Prime Minister Hashim Thaçi (PDK) (from 11 Nov 2007)

Ruling party: Coalition led by Partia Demokratike e Kosovës (PDK) (Democratic Party of Kosovo), Lidhja Demokratike e Kosovës (LDK) (Democratic League of Kosovo) and Aleanca Kosova e Re (AKR) (New Kosovo Alliance) (from 11 Feb 2011)

Area: 10,887 square km

Population: 1.73 million (2010: preliminary census figure)

Capital: Pristina

Official language: Albanian, Serbian (English was the official language of the UN Interim Administration Mission in Kosovo (UNMIK))

Currency: Euro (€) = 100 cents

Exchange rate: €0.71 per US$ (Jul 2009)

GDP per capita: US$1,303 (2008) (eur1,886 2010*)

GDP real growth: 4.00% (2010)*

GDP: US$5.35 billion (2009)*

Unemployment: 40.00% (2010)*

Inflation: 3.50% (2010)*

Balance of trade: -US$2.28 billion (2010)

* estimated figure

Kosovo's Prime Minister Hashim Thaçi reluctantly found himself in the news in 2011 as his party was accused of vote rigging in the December 2010 parliamentary elections, the first to be organised by the Kosovo government. The allegations against Mr Thaçi gave rise to a renewed interest in Kosovo in the media and a number of articles questioning the intervention of the North Atlantic Treaty Organisation (NATO) in 1999 and the wisdom of supporting Kosovo independence. Recent commentaries have questioned whether the NATO intervention and Western support for independence were misguided.

The European Union

The European Union (EU) has its largest ever civilian mission in Kosovo. The European Union Rule of Law Mission, known as Eulex, it is a police and justice mission designed to help build the rule of law. Kosovo is rife with corruption and organised crime and is a major source of drug trafficking, as well as the smuggling of people and arms into the EU. In addition to paying for this mission, European taxpayers have also funded a huge aid programme totalling several billion euros over the past decade aimed at reconstructing Kosovo after the conflict between Serbian Security Forces and the rebel Kosovo Liberation Army (KLA) in the late 90s and Nato's intervention in 1999.

Kosovo's declaration of independence from Serbia in 2008 was supported by the United States, Britain, France and Germany. But such is the precariousness of Kosovo's independence, and so many are the vested interests and pressure groups endeavouring to have their own ideologies, tribes, clans and religions prevail, that – in the words of one BBC journalist – it is unfinished business. The EU is (perhaps forlornly) 'attempting to supervise the development of a functioning state along European lines', but despite the support of the US and leading EU countries, Kosovo as an independent state has struggled to achieve international acceptance. In late 2011, 88 countries had actually recognised Kosovo. The rest of the world's 193 United Nations members (including, for different reasons generally related to domestic issues concerning breakaway regions, five EU countries – Cyprus, Greece, Romania, Slovakia and Spain) still regard Kosovo as part of Serbia, including most of the world's major emerging countries from China to Brazil to South Africa.

Albanians and Serbs have been involved in a struggle for control of Kosovo on and off for well over a century. When NATO intervened to stop ethnic cleansing in 1999, it was perceived in the region to be siding with the Albanians. The unwelcome publicity surrounding Mr Thaçi looks likely to damage Kosovo's prospects of achieving full international recognition. Kosovo has been cast in a negative light, which will probably delay further the process of international recognition.

The Economy

The International Monetary Fund (IMF) noted in 2011 that Kosovo enjoyed robust economic growth in the 2000s and weathered the global financial crisis well, owing to its limited integration into global financial and goods markets. The economy was expected to grow by more than 5 per cent in 2011, up from 4 per cent in 2010, supported by continued large remittance inflows from the Kosovar diaspora, robust credit growth, especially to households, and higher public spending, including on infrastructure projects. In Kosovo, inflation closely follows price developments for imported food and gasoline, triggering deflation in 2009 and double-digit inflation in early 2011; core inflation, however, has remained well-behaved. While credit growth has moderated, banks' portfolio quality has deteriorated only modestly and profits have remained high. Large capital buffers suggest that Kosovo's banks – which are mostly foreign owned – have ample shock-absorbing capacity.

While Kosovo pursued a conservative fiscal policy during most of the 2000s, since 2008 the government has moved to an increasingly expansionary stance, financing the resulting deficits from accumulated savings, the sale of assets and donor support. As a result, the general government balance shifted from a surplus of more than 7 per cent of gross domestic product (GDP) in 2007 to a deficit of 2.6 per cent in 2010. Capital spending has been the main driver of this expansion. In 2010, construction started on a highway connecting Pristina with Albania's border, with total costs estimated at more than 20 per cent of annual GDP spread over a period of 4 years. In 2011, the government increased public sector wages and benefits for war invalids and their families by 30 to 50 per cent.

An 18-month Stand-By Arrangement (SBA) was approved by the IMF Executive Board on 21 July 2010. The programme supported by the SBA was built around, first, restraint on current spending, higher revenues and privatisation receipts to contain the impact on the investment programme on the overall deficit, and second, bolstering the government's deposits with the Banka Qendrore e Repubukës së Kosovës (BQK) (Central Bank of Kosovo) to build buffers for fiscal and financial contingencies. The 2011 budget adopted by the newly constituted Assembly deviated from the budget agreed in the context of the SBA, notably the large public sector wage increases.

The IMF has welcomed the progress made by the Kosovar authorities in building key social and economic institutions. Nevertheless, further efforts are necessary to enhance competitiveness, ensure fiscal sustainability and safeguard financial stability. In the view of the IMF there remained a need to revise Kosovo's growth model, especially to address the uncertain prospects of remittances and foreign direct investment (FDI), which have so far supported growth. Economic policies are needed to focus on enhancing competitiveness to drive economic development and self-sustained growth and help reduce unemployment. While the *de facto* adoption of the euro had initially provided a strong monetary anchor, it also both increased demands on macro-economic management and meant that areas of monetary policy were beyond the Kosovar authorities' control. Kosovo's shift to an expansionary fiscal stance since 2008 has been unsustainable. In the near term, disciplined budget execution and public financial management are essential.

Risk assessment

Economy	Fair
Politics	Fair
Regional stability	Poor

COUNTRY PROFILE

Historical profile

1389 The battle of Kosovo was lost by the Serbian people and the Turkish Ottoman Empire began a 500-year rule. During this time the population changed from Christian Serbs to Muslim Albanians.

1912 During the Balkan Wars Serbia regained control of Kosovo.

1918 Kosovo became part of the Kingdom of Serbs, Croats and Slovenes.

1941 During World War II the Italian army controlled the entire region.

1945 The Federal People's Republic of Yugoslavia was formed into a communist republic by Josip Broz Tito, and included the province of Kosovo with its own constitutional rights.

1974 Yugoslavia increased the autonomy of constituent republics, allowing Kosovo *de facto* self-government.

1980 Tito died.

1987 Serbian nationalist politician, Slobodan Milosevic, incited Serbian Kosovans to protest at alleged harassment by the majority ethnic Albanians.

1989 Yugoslav president Milosevic stripped Kosovo of its constitutional rights.

1990 Ethnic Albanians declared Kosovo independent. The Yugoslav government dissolved the Kosovo government and sacked 100,000 workers, which led to a general strike.

1991 Two major Yugoslav republics (Slovenia and Croatia) declared their independence. Slovenia became independent with little dispute. Croatia with its 12 per cent Serbian population fought the remaining Yugoslav army and evicted its Serbs to gain its independence. The Yugoslav government in Belgrade began a process of disenfranchising Albanian Kosovans by closing down schools and marginalising the Albanian language.

1992 Macedonia and Bosnia and Hercegovina (BiH) declared their independence. Nationalist and ethnic tensions in BiH, the most ethnically diverse Yugoslav republic, strained until the territory erupted into war. Thousands died in 'ethnic cleansing' as one faction tried to clear a region of civilians of another faction; a million people were displaced. Ibrahim Rugova was elected president of the self-proclaimed Republic of Kosovo.

1996 The Ushtria Çlirimtare e Kosovës (UÇK) (Kosovo Liberation Army) began attacking Serbian police.

1998 Confrontation between Serbian forces and the UÇK increased, culminating in a brutal crackdown by Serbian police and paramilitary units which resulted in massacres and thousands of civilians being driven from their homes. NATO gave the Milosevic government an ultimatum to halt the crackdown or risk air attacks.

1999 An international peace deal failed and NATO began air attacks on Serbia, which finally agreed to withdraw troops and the UN Kosovo Peace Implementation Force (Kfor) began peace-keeping operations. The UN Interim Administration Mission in Kosovo (UNMIK) came into operation, charged with determining the future of Kosovo. The UÇK agreed to disarm, while Serb civilians fled the province in the face of revenge attacks.

2000 Local elections were won by the Lidhja Demokratike e Kosovës (LDK) (Democratic League of Kosovo), led by Ibrahim Rugova.

2002 The parliament elected Ibrahim Rugova as president and Bajram Rexhepi

KEY INDICATORS — Kosovo

	Unit	2006	2007	2008	2009	2010
Population	m	–	–	*2.00	*2.00	1.73
Gross domestic product (GDP)	US$bn	–	–	2.81	*5.35	–
GDP per capita	US$	–	–	1,303	–	–
GDP real growth	%	–	–	5.4	–	*4.0
Inflation	%	–	–	9.3	-2.4	*3.5
Unemployment	%	–	–	–	–	*40.0
Exports (fob) (goods)	US$m	–	–	115.0	242.0	403.0
Imports (fob) (goods)	US$m	–	–	1,254.1	-2,608.0	2,679.0
Balance of trade	US$m	–	–	-1,139.0	-2,367.0	-2,276.0
Current account	US$m	–	–	-494.1	-882.0	860.0
Total reserves minus gold	US$m	–	–	892.1	830.2	846.4
Foreign exchange	US$m	–	–	892.1	721.2	739.6
Exchange rate	per US$	–	–	0.68	0.72	0.76

* estimated figure

of the Partia Demokratike e Kosovës (PDK) (Democratic Party of Kosovo) was elected prime minister of a power-sharing 10-member cabinet.

2003 Official negotiations between Kosovo and Serbia began. Conditions for the talks to determine Kosovo's final status were announced by the UN in December.

2004 The LDK won parliamentary elections and incumbent President Ibrahim Rugova was re-elected. Ramush Haradinaj became prime minister. Serbian Kosovans boycotted the elections. The worst inter-ethnic violence since 1999 erupted in Mitrovica, with up to 22 people killed and hundreds injured.

2005 Prime minister Haradinaj resigned and Adem Salihaj replaced him.

2006 President Ibrahim Rugova died; as a moderate Kosovan leader his death just as negotiations on Kosovo's future were about to start, was a setback. He was succeeded by Fatmir Sejdiu. Agim Çeku became prime minister. Joachim Rucker took office as the head of UNMIK.

2007 The UN Special Envoy Martti Ahtisaari submitted a *Comprehensive Proposal for the Kosovo Status Settlement* (the Ahtisaari Plan) for the independence of Kosovo which also focused on protecting the rights, identity and culture of Kosovo's non-Albanian communities, including establishing a framework for their active participation in public life. Ahtisaari also proposed that Kosovo become independent, subject to a period of international supervision. Agim Çeku said that no unilateral declaration of independence would be made (by ethnic Albanian leaders) without the support of the EU and US. No agreement was reached during the first round of talks concerning the future of Kosovo: Serbian authorities offered broad autonomy while the province's ethnic Albanians demanded full independence. Parliamentary elections were won by the PDK with 34.3 per cent of the vote (37 seats out of 120), led by Hashim Thaçi, former leader of the UÇK.

2008 President Sejdiu resigned and took part in fresh elections, held on the same day, under Kosovo's new constitutional framework. After three rounds he won a simple majority of 61 votes to become president for a second time. The Kosovo Assembly issued a unilateral declaration of independence (UDI), in line with the Ahtisaari Plan. The new constitution came into force and the Kosovo government took over most of the powers previously held by the UN. Although Russia initially rejected the deployment of the EU Law and Order Mission (Eulex), a 2,200 policing force, it was eventually used after UN agreement. Ethnic Serbs insisted that the new constitution did not apply to them. and as a last act of the outgoing government in Serbia, the Serbian minister for Kosovo set up a new parliament in the divided city of Mitrovica for minority Serbs. The new Kosovan Serb Assembly may challenge the legitimacy of the Kosovan Assembly and entrench *de facto* partition of Kosovo. The issuing of Kosovan passports began. Kosovo's UDI was referred to the International Court of Justice (ICJ) by the UN General Assembly to give its opinion.

2009 A new 2,500-strong Kosovo Security Force (KSV), trained by the UN, became operational. Members of the KSV were drawn from all members of the community to undertake civil protection and crisis response. Serbian President Boris Tadic attended a religious service at the Serb Orthodox monastery of Visoki Decani. Kosovo was offered membership of the International Monetary Fund (IMF). The number of NATO (Kfor) troops was reduced from around 14,000 to 10,000.

2010 Former prime minister Haradinaj was ordered to stand trial for a second time, as his earlier acquittal on murder and torture charges was ruled to have been a miscarriage of justice, due to the intimidation of prosecution witnesses. In July, the ICJ ruled that Kosovo's UDI from Serbia did not violate international law. The ruling should allow more countries to recognise Kosovo as a sovereign state. Serbia rejected the ruling and called for fresh talks at the UN over Kosovo's status. The number of Kfor troops was reduced from around 10,000 to 6,300. By September, 70 countries had recognised Kosovo's sovereignty. In September, the constitutional court ruled that the leader of a political party may not serve as president. This caused Fatmir Sejdiu (LDK) to step down as president on 27 September and for him to withdraw the LDK from the coalition government in October. On 2 November Prime Minister Hashim Thaçi lost a vote of no-confidence by 66–1, which resulted in a snap general election, held on 12 December. The PDK won the largest block of seats (36 out of 120) and began coalition negotiations.

2011 The PDK agreed a coalition negotiations with LDK and Aleanca Kosova e Re (AKR) (New Kosovo Alliance) on 11 February. On 22 February, Hashim Thaçi (PDK) was re-elected as prime minister by parliament, which, after three rounds, also voted for Behgjet Pacolli as president, despite most opposition members boycotting the vote. He replaced Jakup Krasniqi who had been acting-president since former president Sejdiu had been forced to step down. On 28 March the Constitutional Court ruled that the election of President Pacolli was unconstitutional as there was not a quorum in parliament when the vote to elect him was taken. On 7 April, parliament elected Atifete Jahjaga president by 80 votes (with 10 for Suzanna Novoberdaliu); he was sworn in the same day. Kosovo's first state census was completed on 15 April and preliminary results published in July showed a total population of 1,733,872 with 295,070 households. The Kosovo police attempted to replace Kosovan-Serbs manning the border crossing between Kosovo and Serbia on 27 July, but were repelled by the Kosovan-Serbs. NATO-led peacekeepers were required to restore order. The EU and US criticised Kosovo for this unannounced move to assert its authority in Northern Kosovo. Ramush Haradinaj re-appeared before the ICJ on 18 August, along with two other defendants, on charges of joint criminal enterprise during the civil war. Forces, led by NATO-peacekeepers, dispersed Kosovan-Serb protestors and dismantled their barricades on 20 October. On 2 December, an EU-mediated agreement was reached between Serbia and Kosovo to jointly manage and to 'gradually set up the joint, integrated, single and secure posts at all their common crossing points.'

Political structure

Constitution

An interim constitutional framework was ratified in 2001 providing legitamacy for the provisional institutions of self-government, with deferral to the UN Special Representative based on the UN Security Council Resolution 1244.

A draft constitution was being prepared in February 2008.

Independence date

17 February 2008

Form of state

Parliamentary democracy

The executive

The president is elected by parliamentary members for a term of three years. The president represents the country in foreign affairs and in domestic matters acts on the advice of the prime minister and cabinet. The executive branch of government is headed by the prime minister, deputy prime ministers and all other ministers.

National legislature

The unicameral Assembly of Kosovo (Kuvendi i Kosovës) has 120 members; 100 seats directly elected by the Albanian majority population, 10 seats are reserved for Serbs and 10 seats for all other nominated ethnic groups. Legislative power is vested in the assembly and government.

Last elections

17 November 2007 (parliamentary); 9 January 2008 (presidential).

Results: Parliamentary: the Partia Demokratike e Kosovës (PDK) (Democratic Party of Kosovo) won 34.3 per cent of the vote (37 seats out of 120), the

Lidhja Demokratike e Kosovës (LDK) (Democratic League of Kosovo) 22.6 per cent (25), the Aleanca Kosova e Re (AKR) (New Kosovo Alliance) 12.3 per cent (13), the Lidhja Demokratike e Dardanisë-Unioni Shqiptare DemoKristiane LD-USDK (Democratic League of Dardania-Albanian Union of Christian Democrats) 10 per cent (11), and the Aleanca për Ardhmërinë e Kosovës (AAK) (Alliance for the Future of Kosovo) 9.6 per cent (10); 20 seats were reserved for minorities. Turnout was 40.1 per cent.
Presidential: round one, Fatmir Sejdiu won 62 votes (percentage not enough for an outright win), Naim Maloku won 37 votes. Round two (a simple majority for a win), Sejdiu won 61 votes, Maloku won 37 votes.

Next elections
2011 (parliamentary)

Political parties

Ruling party
Coalition led by Partia Demokratike e Kosovës (PDK) (Democratic Party of Kosovo), Lidhja Demokratike e Kosovës (LDK) (Democratic League of Kosovo) and Aleanca Kosova e Re (AKR) (New Kosovo Alliance) (from 11 Feb 2011)

Main opposition party
Lidhja Demokratike e Kosovës (LDK) (Democratic League of Kosovo)

Population

1.73 million (2010: preliminary census figure)

Last census: 1991: 1,956,000 (during political troubles)
2001: 2,400,000 (estimate: Office for Security and Co-operation in Europe)

Population density: 202 per square km

Internally Displaced Persons (IDP)
Internal Displacement Monitoring Centre

Ethnic make-up
Estimated demographics: Albanian (92 per cent) Serbian (5.3 per cent) and others (Croats, Roma, Turks) (2.7 per cent).

Religions
Muslim 90 per cent, the majority of which are Sunni, Christian Orthodox 5 per cent.

Education

Before 1991 educational institutions were administered independently of Serbian influence by Kosovan authorities, which were at liberty to construct a national curriculum and system of education. All levels of education were provided in the Albanian and Serbian languages and schools were charged with maintaining levels of instruction for all minority communities. Enrolment rates where typically almost 100 per cent and this resulted in literacy levels that matched the average of surrounding territories. From 1991, the independence of Kosovo's education service was abolished by Serbian authorities, which closed down schools and dismissed over 14,000 primary and 4,000 secondary school teachers plus over 860 university lecturers of Albanian ethnicity and required all teaching to be in the Serbian language. A parallel schooling system developed whereby Serbian schools were enhanced at the expense of Albanian schools which began to lag behind in books and equipment. Albanian students were denied access to Serbian libraries and so took up informal learning provided by sacked teachers. However, at this time Serbian investment was cut due to the economic crisis following the conflict in Croatia and even the Serbian schools became poorly stocked and maintained. The University of Pristina was badly damaged by vandalism and looting during the NATO attacks on Serbia in 1999, but was finally reopened to all students by 2000. Around 45 per cent of all schools were severely damaged or destroyed and many were within minefields which prevented their use until cleared. When the 2000/01 school-year began only around 50 per cent of school students attended remedial classes; the percentage began to rise as facilities improved. Apart from war damage, the previous nine years of under-investment also added to the problems of rehabilitation for the UN Administration authorities (UNMIK).
UNMIK began the reconstruction of the educational system with a three-way split into priority areas of consideration, which included the physical (buildings, books and equipment), legal aspects (new teaching structures that provided for or moderated opposing orthodoxy) and academic reform (curricula development and educational management). Teacher training was implemented under UN-sponsored programmes from 2004/05.
Finding an ongoing consensus was hampered in 2006 following the Serbian constitutional referendum (that excluded Kosovans), which voted to enshrine the Cyrillic alphabet as the official script for all territories; Albanians use the Latin script.
In 2007 Unesco stated that less than 10 per cent of 3–6 year olds had access to early childhood education, with the majority of facilities located in larger urban areas.
The conflict with Serbia led to a massive population shift from the country to towns and resulted in the overcrowding of many primary schools, which have had to operate at least a two shift system.

Literacy rate: 89.8 per cent female rate; 97.7 per cent male. Around 14 per cent of rural females are illiterate (Unesco 2007).

Compulsory years: Six to 14

Enrolment rate: 97.5 per cent (Albanian), 99 per cent (Serbian), 77 per cent (all others, of which only 69 per cent female) (Unesco 2007).

Pupils per teacher: The average was 19 per class (in primary schools) before 1999; the average has increased to 35 students per class.

Health

Kosovo, as one of the poorest territories in Europe has, as a UN report in 2007 reported, 37 per cent of the population living in poverty and 15.2 per cent in absolute poverty. The healthcare system is chronically under funded with a lack of medical equipment and drugs. Poorly educated mothers and lack of access to facilities has resulted in Kosovo having the highest fertility rate in Europe, and also the highest maternal mortality rate, despite 95 per cent of all births taking place in medical facilities. Measures to reach UN Millennium Development Goals (MDG) have been included in necessary restoration policies since 1999. Childhood immunisation reached levels of 90 per cent by 2007, although parents in some minority ethnic communities delayed vaccinations.
In 2005 a total of 72.4 per cent of the population had access to clean water, of which 96 per cent were urban dwellers, around 70 per cent of total households were connected to the sewage system, of which 95 per cent were urban dwellers.

HIV/Aids
The young have not been or are poorly informed about HIV/Aids, sex education and the risks of drugs. Less than 41 per cent of sexually active young people used a condom, according to a 2007 Unesco report.

Life expectancy: 68.8 years (67.8 male; 69.9 female) (2006 Kosovo Government)

Fertility rate/Maternal mortality rate: Separate figures from Serbia for Kosovo are unavailable.

Child (under 5 years) mortality rate (per 1,000): 69 per 1,000 (estimated, Unicef 2006)

Head of population per physician: 1 doctor per 840 head of population (2004, Kosovo Statistics Office)

Welfare

At a time when Europe's populations are ageing Kosovo's average age is 22–23 years, with around 33 per cent less than 15 years old. This group will be an ongoing burden of responsibility for the government to educate, find work and house at a time of economic hardship. There is no social welfare although international donors provide funds for programmes to aid the vulnerable. There are high levels of unemployment and poor prospects for improvement.

Main cities
Pristina (capital, 600,000 population), Mitrovica (67,900), Caglavica.

Languages spoken
Albanian, Serbian, Bosniak and Turkish. Since the arrival of the UN English has increased in popularity.

Official language/s

Albanian, Serbian (English was the official language of the UN Interim Administration Mission in Kosovo (UNMIK))

Media
Press

Periodicals: UNMIK started the publication of a quarterly *Focus* (www.euinkosovo.org) with a variety of background articles on people and events in Kosovo.

Broadcasting

The national, public broadcaster is RTK (www.rtklive.com).

Radio: RTK operates two stations, Radio Kosova and Radio Blue Sky. Other, private radio stations in operation include Radio Dukagjini (www.radio-dukagjini.com), Radio Kim (www.kimradio.net) and Radio Tema (www.radiotema.net).

News agencies

National news agency: Kosova Press

Economy
Since independence in 2007, the fledgling economy has had to contend with the severe downturn in the global economy. It has begun to set up the infrastructure to provide financial services necessary. The Central Bank of Kosovo (CBK) began work in 1999 and by 2009 there were eight commercial banks, 19 micro-financial institutions, 11 insurance companies and two pension funds in operation.
Kosovo became a member of the International Monetary Fund (IMF) in June 2009, with an initial capital subscription of US$91.5 million, which amounted 0.027 per cent of the total fund membership quota.
GDP growth was 5.0 per cent in 2007, rising to an estimated 5.4 per cent in 2008; in 2009 growth was forecast to fall to 3.8 per cent, indicated by the contraction in imports and remittances; it is expected to rise to 5.0 per cent by 2012. Government revenues average 25 per cent of GDP, while expenditure is due to have risen to almost 30 per cent in 2009, as the government assumes more responsibility for loss of earnings. From mid-2007 inflation rose from 4.4 per cent to a peak of 9.3 per cent in 2008, but is projected to have fallen back to around 3 per cent in 2009.
Investment is a priority for Kosovo. The political relations with Serbia and the tensions between the majority ethnic Albanian and minority Serbian populations have dampened the prospects of much foreign direct investment (FDI) (€2.5 billion (US$3.6 billion) in 2008) and risks leading to a stagnating economy. Donor countries pledged €1.2 billion (US$1.65 billion) in 2009, but with little prospects of domestic-driven growth the worry is that loans and aid will hide systemic problems.
With the world's fifth largest stock of lignite coal, Kosovo is planning to privatise two existing coal plants, to realise around US$4.8 billion, and construct another. Sales of other assets are also under consideration, such as the mobile/cell operator Vala. Around 300 national entities had been privatised by 2009, although the sale of the state-owned Kosovo Energy Corporation (KEK) had been unsuccessful.
Around 60 per cent of the population live in rural areas and agriculture contributes 25 per cent of GDP; it is also an important sector for employment. Industrial production is centred on mining, agribusiness, including wood processing, and manufacturing of textiles and automotive components. Tourism is still nascent, but has the potential for strong growth when the infrastructure is brought up to international standards.

External trade
Kosovo has a customs-free access to the European Union market, based on an EU Autonomous Trade Preference (ATP) regime. It also has free trade agreements (FTA) with Albania, Croatia, Bosnia and Hercegovina and Macedonia (FYROM).
Around 20 per cent of all exports are agricultural, including wheat, meat and wine.
Major trading partners include the European Union, Balkans region, Turkey and US.

Exports

Principal exports are base metals (including scrap) (50 per cent), leather goods (18 per cent), food stuffs (15 per cent), plastics and rubber (10 per cent).

Main destinations: Balkans region (typically 50 per cent), Turkey (20 per cent), US (15 per cent) and rest of the world (15 per cent).
Of the 1.1 million hectares (ha) of Kosova land, 53 per cent (577,000ha) is arable. Over 85 per cent is privately owned, however the average size of land per rural household in 3ha. Of the arable land 51 per cent is grain, 45 per cent pastures and meadows, 2 per cent orchards and less than 1 per cent vineyards. Principal crops are wheat, corn, potatoes, watermelons and lucerne (animal fodder).
The government regards small farms as less than 5ha and large farms over 5ha, around 96 per cent of farming households work small farms. Many farms were abandoned in 1999 and rural infrastructure is in disrepair. There is an urgent need to modernise traditional practices that provide little more than subsistence production. Around 65 per cent of the working population is employed in agriculture, providing 30 per cent of GDP. Kosovo has fallen from being a net exporter of agriculture products to foodstuffs accounting for around 30 per cent of all imports, the largest single import segment.
Since the early 1990s the number of livestock has fallen and the trend has continued. From 2003 small farms have mostly invested in beef cattle, donkeys and bee hives; larger farms have invested in breeding pigs and donkeys, all other farm animals have fallen in number. Government statistics acknowledge that all but the largest of farms fail to keep records and the number of animals reported may be incorrect.
Forests represent an important resource but historic mismanagement has resulted in heavy degradation; the high demand for timber following the conflict with Serbia has increased the pressure on forestry's long-term sustainability.
Timbered areas make up 47 per cent of all land, of which forests are 460,800ha. Around 62 per cent of forests are publicly owned. Forest products, before the break-up of Yugoslavia, were a significant export sector. In 2007 manufactured products included doors, window frames and furniture, although exports remain limited.

Industry and manufacturing
Industrial development was historically dictated by the economic interests of firstly Yugoslavia and later Serbia, with widespread exploitation of natural resources. Mining and forestry products formed the majority of intra-exports.
Due to war damage and the lack of investment in what were state-owned industries and manufacturing, food processing, tobacco, wood processing and textiles were all disrupted and non-productive by 2006. Privatisation was begun but the problems may be long term as poor transport infrastructure, with 25 per cent of the road network in serious need of remedial work, a serious impediment to redevelopment.
Kosovo has limited water resources, as most rivers run out of the country, any process that requires water to facilitate production will be severely hampered.

Tourism
There is little opportunity for tourism.

Environment
The US committed an initial US$15.5 million to repairing war damage, which included water contamination, minefields and unexploded ordinance (UXO). In 2007, the ongoing clearance programme concentrated on unmarked minefields and UXO in forested areas.
Archaic communist industrial practices degraded land, water and air quality and until production plants are either upgraded or closed the pollution is likely to continue. A government environmental plan was proposed in 2006 to introduce legislation to develop policies and guidelines for international funding and donor communities to deal with the problems and plan for the future. It was also recognised that a full inventory of fauna and flora for Kosovo was needed.
Kosovo, in 2006, had one national park and 11 natural reserves, 37 natural monuments and two protected landscapes totalling 46,000ha (4.27 per cent of the country). The richest area for wildlife is the Sharr Mountains and the Bjeshkët e Nemuna area.
Rivers around industrial regions are heavily polluted and denuded of aquatic life. Energy production is the major polluter in Kosovo, producing acid rain and contaminated water with high concentrates of phenols.

Mining
The large industrial complex of Trepca, near the town of Mitrovica, is a conglomerate of 40 mines, foundries, refineries and subsidiary plants. It has one of Europe's richest deposits of lignite, lead, zinc and non-ferrous ores, as well as gold, silver and over 1.6 billion tonnes of coal, valued at an estimated eur13 billion (US$18.9 billion). However, the only railway capable of transporting coal is through Serbia and an alternative route through Albania or Macedonia is not expected for many years. Trepca had previously been the source of much of former Yugoslavia's mining wealth and after the 1999 conflict was realised as Kosovo's principal economic asset, despite the need for investment to revitalise its infrastructure.
Geophysical studies undertaken in 2007 showed a high potential for larger than already known gold, nickel and chrome deposits.
There are large stocks of decorative stone, including onyx, white, grey and black marble, gray granite and other stone such as gneiss, magnesite, quartzite and porphyry which may have an important as export goods, but have yet to be fully exploited.
Kosovo has no hydrocarbon resources or refineries. All petroleum products must be imported from neighbouring countries, where refining capacity allows. An estimated 600,000 tonnes (4.4 million barrels) of oil will be imported in 2010, but the global price of oil and the transport costs will keep the level of imports low.
There are large deposits, estimated at around 18 billion tonnes, of lignite coal typically used in power stations.

Energy
The Kosovo Energy Corporation (KEK), operates two large coal-fired power plants and was scheduled to produce 4,483GW of electricity and import 497GW in 2008. These power stations are close to the open cast lignite mines of Bardhi and Mirash and burn 7 million tonnes of per annum. Energy production is the major polluter in Kosovo, producing acid rain and contaminated water with high concentrates of phenols. Two new 2100MW coal-fired power plants are being construction and scheduled to be operational by 2012.
Long-term energy development and electricity supply is also being provided for as Kosovo's national power grid is brought up to international standards.

Banking and insurance
The World Bank is providing grants and technical assistance to the Central Banking Authority to oversee the financial system and provide stability and development, including supervision of banks and non-bank financial institutions (insurance and pension funds).
Central bank
Banka Qendrore e Repubukës së Kosovës (BQK) (Central Bank of Kosovo)
Main financial centre
Pristina

Time
GMT plus one hour (daylight saving, late March to late October, GMT plus two hours)

Geography
This land-locked country, roughly square in shape standing on a corner is surrounded by Serbia from the north to the south-east, Macedonia (FYROM) in the south, Albania to the west and Montenegro in the north-west. The average altitude is 800 metres above sea level, however, there are several mountain ranges encircling the country, with the highest ranges in the south-west, north-west and north. The highest mountain, Gjeravica, in Peja in the south-west, is 2,656 metres high, with deep, wide valleys and the largest river, the White Drin at 122 km, flowing down into the central plain, on which most of the urban areas are located. The largest lake, Gazivoda, in Mitrovica, is 9.1 square km.
Hemisphere
Northern

Climate
With a continental climate summers in Kosovo are warm and winters are cold. Temperature ranges average from +30 degrees Celsius (summer July–August) to -10 degrees C (winter December–January). Snowfalls are typical between November and March even on the lowland flat plains. The large mountain ranges also produce local variations and rainfall distributions.

Entry requirements
Passports
Required by all and must be valid for up to 90 days from date of entry.
Serbian authorities will not allow entry to Serbia from Kosovo, unless as a through journey from Albania or Macedonia, or as part of a return journey.
Visa
As of February 2008, for visits of less than 90 days, visitors with US passports do not require visas. EU citizens from countries that recognised Kosovo's independence also do not require visas. All other visitors and those staying over 90 days must provide documentary evidence for purpose of visit, such as employment or education. A 90-day entry stamp will be issued at the border.
For further information see www.unmikonline.org/regulations/ADMDIRECT/2005/ADE2005_08.pdf or visitors should contact the consular section of their own ministry of foreign affairs for advice.
Currency advice/regulations
The banking system is embryonic and a cash economy exists so visitors should expect to travel with enough cash for their stay. There are a few ATMs in Pristina; credit cards are not widely accepted.
The Serbian dinar is in use in Serbian-populated regions.
Customs
UNMIK has been responsible for customs, before trained Kosovan officials are deployed.
Consumer items are limited and should be declared, including jewellery, only two cameras (including a video camera allowed), binoculars, one bicycle and camping equipment, electronic equipment such as laptops and musical players.
Sporting equipment may have added restrictions and further information should be obtained.
Prohibited imports
Regulations may be altered with little notice, check details before travelling.
Weapons and ammunitions. Animals may be imported with a vet certificate and proof of healthy condition.

Health (for visitors)
Mandatory precautions
None

Advisable precautions
It is advisable to be in date for the following immunisations: diphtheria, polio and tetanus (within 10 years), typhoid fever, hepatitis A (moderate risk only), hepatitis B and tuberculosis; rabies is a risk. Crimean Congo Haemorrhagic Fever (CCHF) is endemic, particularly in the central Kosovo region and visitors suffering from flu-like systems with a red rash or bleeding in the mouth should seek medical advice.
The health system is severely under funded and care may not reach visitors expectations, so comprehensive travel insurance, including medical evacuation, should be purchased before travelling. There is a shortage of medicines and visitors should travel with all necessary medications for the duration of their stay.

Hotels
There are no four- or fire-star hotels, Pristina has the largest stock of hotels, but elsewhere there is little choice beyond mid-range and budget accommodation.

Credit cards
Are not widely accepted.

Public holidays (national)
Public holidays that fall at the weekend are taken on the following Monday.
Fixed dates
1–2 January (News Year), 7 January (Orthodox Christmas), 17 February (Independence Day), 1–2 May (Labour Day), 28 November (Flag Day), 25 December (Christmas Day)
Variable dates
Orthodox Christmas, Easter Monday, (first Monday in May), Start of Ramadan, Eid al Fitr, Eid al Adha.

Working hours
Banking
Mon–Fri 0800–1900; Sat 0800–1500; a few open on Sun.
Business
Mon–Fri: 0700/0800–1500/1600.
Government
Mon–Fri: 0700/0800–1500/1600.
Shops
Mon–Fri: 0800–1200, 1500–2000; Sat: 0800–1500. Supermarkets and food shops open for longer.

Telecommunications
Mobile/cell phones
There is an uneven coverage of GSM 900/1800 services.

Electricity supply
220 volts AC, 50Hz.

Social customs/useful tips
A 10 per cent tip is expected.
Avoid taking photographs of military installations and obvious war damage.

Security
In 2008, landmines and unexploded ordinance (UXO) still posed a threat, particularly in border areas with Albania, the Dulje Pass area (in central Kosovo) and in the west and south of the country. All roads and tracks have been cleared.
Political demonstrations have been known to spill over into violence and should be avoided. Criminal activity is largely centred on pickpockets and theft of vehicles, particularly four-wheel drive and luxury cars.

Getting there
Air
National airline: Kosova Airlines (HHI)
International airport/s: Pristina International Airport (PRN), 18km south-west of the capital, with a business lounge, duty free, restaurants, car hire and banking. Taxis from the airport are available between 0500–2230 for a 20 minute journey; airport buses start running two hours before the first flights at 0500 up to 2300. It handled 1.2 million passengers in 2008, and 14,000 aircraft operations. In 2009 the government announced it was looking to agree a design-build-finance-operate-transfer (DBFOT) contract with a private operator to expand the infrastructure, including a new landmark terminal, and thereafter manage and maintain the airport.
Airport tax: A eur15 departure tax is typically included in the price of a ticket.
Surface
Road: There are several frontier posts between Serbia, a few between Albania and Macedonia of which delays are common due to the poor road conditions.
Rail: The railway system operates an irregular service and should not be considered reliable.

Getting about
National transport
Road: There is a 1,925km network of two-lane main and secondary roads of which 1,576km is paved, but even the standard of this is fair to poor and conditions deteriorate in rural areas and after bad weather.
Rail: The railway system operates an irregular service and should not be considered reliable. A 300km single-track railway runs north-south and from the north to the east-west. These are part of the railway that ran from Serbia to either Macedonia or Albania through Kosovo. Domestic services are poor and slow in winter and prone to delays.
City transport
Taxis: As most people's first choice for any distance most taxis are marked and have metres. The destination should be written in Albanian, as English is not spoken by all and the condition of taxis and standard of driving varies.
Buses, trams & metro: Public transport is limited.
Car hire
International car hire firms offer modern vehicles from Pristina and its airport. The European Green Card vehicle insurance is not valid in Kosovo and vehicle insurance, preferably comprehensive, is necessary and should be purchased before driving. It is unlikely that credit cards or travellers cheques will be accepted everywhere so sufficient euro should be carried to pay for insurance and petrol.
Traffic and local drivers may pose a hazard to unwary foreign drivers and travelling at night can be risky. Fuel, although widely available, varies in quality.
In summer during dry hot weather there is a danger of forest fires and care must be taken when driving through wooded areas and lighted cigarette ends should not be thrown away.
Note that Serbian car hire firms do not permit their rented vehicles to enter Kosovo.

BUSINESS DIRECTORY

Telephone area codes
The international direct dialling code (IDD) for Kosovo is +381, followed by 38 area code for Pristina and then the subscriber's number. *In 2008, area codes for the rest of Kosovo were still being determined.*

Useful telephone numbers

Emergency number	112
Police	92
Fire service	93
First aid	94

Chambers of Commerce
Kosovo Chamber of Commerce, Mother Theresa No 20, Pristina 10000 (tel: +381 224-741; fax: +381 224-299; email: info@oek-kcc.org; internet: www.oek-kcc.org).

Banking
Bank for Business, UÇK Street No 41, 10000 Pristina (tel: 244-666).

Economic Bank, Migjeni Street No 1, 10000 Pristina (tel: 244-396).

KASA Bank, Rexhep Luci Street No 5, 10000 Pristina (tel: 246-180).

New Bank of Kosova, Nëna Terezë Street No 49a, Pristina 10000 Pristina (tel: 223-976).

ProCredit Bank, Skenderbeu Street, 10000 Pristina (tel: 240-248).

Raiffeisen Bank Kosovo UÇK Street No 51, 10000 Pristina (tel: 226-400/1

Central bank

Central Bank of Kosovo, 33 Garibaldi Street, Pristina (tel: 222-055; fax: 243-763; email: publicrelations@bpk-kos.org; internet: www.cbak-kos.org).

Travel information

Kosova Airline, Vellusha e Poshtme 17, Te Kino Rinia (tel: 249-184/5; fax: 249-186; email: info@kosovaairlines.com; internet: www.flyksa.com).

Kosovo Railways, Sheshi i Lirisë pn, Fushë Kosovë (tel: 536-355; fax: 536-307; email: info@kosovorailway.com; internet: www.kosovorailway.com).

Ministries

Ministry of Trade and Industry, Perandori Justinian Street, Pejton Square, 3–5 Pristina (tel: 38 20 036-015; internet: www.mit-ks.org)

Other useful addresses

Auditor General, Gazmend Zajmi No 59, 10000 Pristina (internet: www.ks-gov.net/oag).

Community Development Fund Rruga Perandori Justinian No 4, Pristina (tel: 249-677/8; fax: 249-679; internet: www.kcdf.org).

Constitutional Secretariat, New Bld, 8th Floor, Office 803, Skenderbeg Square, 10000 Pristina (tel: email: info@kushtetutakosoves.info; internet: www.kushtetutakosoves.info).

Economic Initiative for Kosovo (ECIKS), Nussdorfer Strasse 20–23, A-1090 Vienna, Austria (+43 1-890-5026; internet: www.eciks.org).

British Consulate, Ismail Qemajli 6, Arbëri Dragodan, Pristina (tel: 254-700; fax: 249-799; email: britishoffice.pristina@fco.gov.uk).

Independent Media Commission, Gazmend Zajmi Street, No 1 Pristina (tel: 245-031; fax: 245-034; email: info@imc-ko.org; internet: www.imc-ko.org).

Investment Promotion Agency of Kosovo, Perandori Justinian No 3-5, Qyteza Pejton, Pristina (tel/fax: 38 200-360; email: infor@invest-ks.org; internet: www.invest-ks.org).

National Assembly (Media Office), Mother Theresa No 20, Pristina 10000 (tel: 211-186/189; fax: 211-188; internet: www.assembly-kosova.org).

Statistics Office of Kosovo, Zenel Salihu Street No 4, Pristina (tel: 235-111; fax: 235-545; email: esk@ks-gov.net; internet: www.ks-gov.net/esk).

United Nations Development Programme (UNDP), (internet: www.ks.undp.org).

National news agency: Kosova Press, No 20, Mother Teresa Square, 10000 Pristina (tel/fax: 38 248-721; internet: www.kosovapress.com).

Other news agencies: Kosovalive: www.kosovalive.com

Kosova Information Center: www.kosova.com

Internet sites

Department of Tourism, Visit Kosovo, (internet: www.visitkosova.org).

Hotel Pristina: www.hotelprishtina.com

Grand Hotel Pristina: www.grandhotel-pr.com

Kosovo Force (KFOR): www.nato.int/KFOR

Kosovo map: http://kosova.org/maps/atlas/index.asp

Kosovo postal codes: http://kosova.org/docs/pdf/Kodet_Postare.pdf

Kosova Tourism Association: www.kotas-ks.org

Ministry of Trade and Industry, (internet: www.mti-ks.org).

OSCE: http://www.osce.org/kosovo

Republic of Kosovo Assembly: www.assembly-kosova.org

UNMIK: www.unmikonline.org

Kuwait

KEY FACTS

Official name: State of Kuwait

Head of State: Sheikh Sabah al Ahmed al Jabir al Sabah (since 25 Jan 2006)

Head of government: Prime Minister Jabir Mubarak al Hamad al Sabah (from 4 Dec 2011)

Ruling party: 15-member Council of Ministers (re-appointed 20 May 2009)

Area: 17,818 square km (including neutral zone)

Population: 3.58 million (2010)*

Capital: Kuwait City

Official language: Arabic

Currency: Kuwaiti dinar (KD) = 1,000 fils

Exchange rate: KD0.28 per US$ (Oct 2011)

GDP per capita: US$36,412 (2010)

GDP real growth: 2.00% (2010)

GDP: US$131.30 billion (2010)

Inflation: 4.10% (2010)

Oil production: 2.51 million bpd (2010)

Balance of trade: US$36.82 billion (2010)

* estimated figure

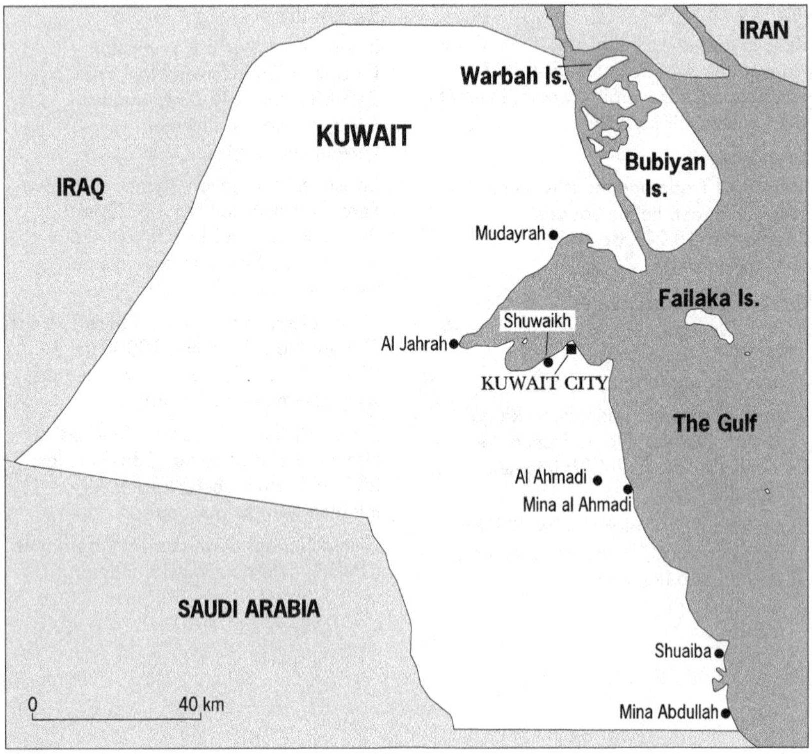

Kuwait's brief history as an independent state has certainly been eventful. After a number of false starts, the lingering threat of Iraqi invasion became a reality in 1990 leaving the Arabian Gulf's most northerly state battered but, with international assistance, not beaten. Twelve years later, Kuwait played a key role in the invasion of Iraq by the coalition forces overwhelmingly led by the US.

On the international map

Since the 1950s Kuwait has developed what is by Gulf standards, a sophisticated education system. In anticipation of English school certificate examinations, bright, middle class male Kuwaiti students found themselves studying Shakespeare and the subtleties of Pythagoras long before they had seen a train or traffic light, not to mention Trafalgar Square. Kuwait was the first Gulf state to have its own airlne, which not only flew (and still flies) to Tehran, Bahrain, Dubai and other regional airports, but also to Bombay, London and New York. Kuwait has also long hosted embassies of every political hue. Thus, in the days of the Soviet Union, it was the only Gulf state to have diplomatic links not only with the USSR, but also with China and even North Korea, alongside the US and the UK.

This maturity, however, has encountered difficulties in properly establishing itself in the framework of domestic politics. In late 2010 Sheikh Nasser al Mohammed al Sabah, Prime Minister and nephew to the ruling Emir, stood before the Kuwaiti National Assembly to face intensive questioning from representatives of Kuwait's three main opposition groupings. The parliamentary 'grilling' came in response to his government's use of force to break up a meeting of academics and parliamentarians, a gathering which itself was called to protest alleged constitutional violations by the government. Eight days later, the premier managed, narrowly, to escape a vote of no-confidence by the Kuwaiti parliament which would have forced the Emir either to relieve him of his post or dissolve parliament and call for new elections.

This legislative scrutiny and accountability is virtually unheard of in the Arab Middle East. Yet few Kuwaitis saw fit to celebrate this significant step toward a genuine constitutional monarchy and few Gulf citizens looked to Kuwait in envy. Sadly, in an era of oil prosperity, Kuwait – once the envy of the Gulf – appears to have become viewed as a mess. This grilling of the Prime Minister was the eighth of his tenure, a tumultuous five year period which has seen six different governments and three elections, two after constitutional dissolutions of the parliament due to repeated conflict between parliamentarians and the executive.

Political instability has had an adverse effect on Kuwait's development: while Qatar, the UAE and even Saudi Arabia have forged ahead with infrastructure projects, economic and social development, Kuwait seems to have marked time. The constitutional role of its parliament and the dynamism of its civil society organisations and media are accepted, but the question remains as to what really is their value? In short, what, when push comes to shove, has this degree of political involvement actually achieved for Kuwait and its people? This climate of doubt had ended up delivering a defeat for most of Kuwait's organised opposition movements in the May 2009 election, returning the most pro-government parliament since liberation. Yet just a year and a half later, this same parliament fell just a few votes short of voting a standing Prime Minister and royal family member out of office. How did this reversal of fortune happen?

One theory is that the core support for the opposition has moved from Kuwait's urban center to the more populous and once reliably pro-government, 'tribal' outer districts. These relatively late-arriving citizens, most of whom were naturalised after Kuwaiti independence in part as a ruling family strategy to dilute the influence of urban Arab nationalist movements are (ironically as a result of Kuwait's educational system and policies) becoming better educated and less willing to accept purblind loyalty to their rulers. While politically organised as tribes, economically they have long been sedentary and, like so many of Kuwait's inhabitants, are mostly dependent on state employment. They have seen fit to protect their perceived economic interests in parliament where their represenatives now have a numerical advantage, looking to prevent privatisations which they see as benefiting the already prosperous urban merchants while endangering their stream of state benefits. This urban-rural division very much characterises Kuwaiti politics today.

The ruling family has been using this political cleavage to its own advantage, playing on urban resentment against tribal nepotism and obstructionism toward large development projects. Indeed, the May 2009 elections for the National Assembly delivered more pro-government MPs from the *hadhar* inner constituencies of Kuwait city based on just such sentiments. Their stronger position in parliament allowed the ruling al Sabah family to change tactics. Confident of majority support, the Emir opted to have the prime minister stand for votes of no confidence when necessary, rather than shuffling the cabinet or forcing new parliamentary elections. There have been worrying features of government efforts to control the situation. One such was the arrest and prosecution of a popular journalist, Mohammad Abdulqader al Jasem, who has been sharply critical of the government and the prime minister. Events such as Mr al Jasem's arrest prompted the creation of a 'defense of the constitution' movement, made up of opposition tribal and Islamist MP's supporting their colleague's attempt to keep his parliamentary immunity, but with broader support from liberal MP's fearing government encroachment on political freedoms. The violent December 2010 attack of special forces on a meeting of this group united all the parliament's opposition groupings in criticism of the government. Subsequently, a broader opposition coalition fell only three votes short of dissolving parliament losing a no confidence vote by only three votes. This impressive showing belies the fragility of the coalition. However, in one respect there is a sharp contrast to later events in Bahrain and the Arab Spring undercurrent running through the region. In Kuwait, as opposition tribal MPs pledge to continue their campaign to oust the Prime Minister through street protests, they risk alienating their urban allies in parliament, who face constituents who see the rise of tribal populism as an even greater threat to civil liberties than the strong arm tactics of the government.

There is another dimension to political developments in Kuwait. Those viewing the rise of tribal populism as a threat are, paradoxically, the Shi'a, concerned at the rising influence of Salafi anti-Shi'a thought in Kuwait. Increasingly, the Kuwaiti government has come to rely upon the Shi'a, who did well in the past election and form a key supportive voting bloc for the al Sabah ruling family. The Sunni tribal opposition, have been quick to impugn the al Sabah with this alliance, adding, for the first time in Kuwait, a disturbing sectarian dimension to a potentially volatile situation.. In 2011 the relationship between the government and parliament remained tense. After a short-lived improvement in relations in 2010, tensions re-ignited in the latter part

KEY INDICATORS — Kuwait

	Unit	2006	2007	2008	2009	2010
Population	m	3.18	*3.31	*3.44	*3.54	*3.58
Gross domestic product (GDP)	US$bn	98.72	111.80	158.10	111.30	131.30
GDP per capita	US$	31,014	33,760	45,920	31,482	36,412
GDP real growth	%	6.2	2.5	6.3	-5.2	3.4
Inflation	%	3.0	5.5	10.5	4.7	4.1
Oil output	'000 bpd	2,704.0	2,626.0	2,784.0	2,481.0	2,508.0
Natural gas output	bn cum	12.9	12.6	12.8	12.5	11.6
Exports (fob) (goods)	US$m	58,638.0	62,526.0	86,944.0	50,344.0	66,973.0
Imports (fob) (goods)	US$m	14,350.0	19,117.0	22,939.0	17,081.0	19,065.0
Balance of trade	US$m	44,288.0	43,409.0	64,004.0	33,263.0	47,908.0
Current account	US$m	50,996.0	42,175.0	60,242.4	28,605.0	36,822.0
Total reserves minus gold	US$m	12,566.0	16,660.0	17,112.8	20,267.5	21,236.7
Foreign exchange	US$m	12,177.6	16,285.0	16,611.0	17,608.4	18,623.0
Exchange rate	per US$	0.28	0.27	0.26	0.28	0.28

* estimated figure

of the year and pressures on the government led to its resignation in late March 2011 the sixth cabinet resignation in the past five years. A new government was formed by the re-appointed prime minister but disputes on economic and political issues have persisted and led to the resignation of the deputy prime minister for economic affairs in mid-June. Several members of parliament have also voiced their intention to go ahead with earlier plans to question key ministers.

The economy

Kuwait has a strong economy. Its stock market performs relatively well, it currently benefits from continuously high oil prices and it enjoys relative, if fragile, political stability. With all of the pieces of the economic puzzle in place, this could be the perfect time for the country to start diversifying away from oil in order to limit dependence on this limited natural resource and ensure future growth. However, as noted above, political preocccupations have often hindered economic progress.

In a report on the Kuwaiti economy, the Swiss Bank Crédit Suisse once noted that in the 1990s, Kuwait was faced with three potentially serious situations: the Iraqi invasion, the drop of oil prices and the securities market crash, all of which had taken their toll on the country's economy. In its characteristic way, Kuwait had quietly set about addressing problems that would probably have overwhelmed some of its Gulf neighbours. By 2011 Kuwait appeared to have fully recovered from these issues and the economic forecast for the country remains good. The relatively long history of the Kuwaiti stock market has produced experienced investors who are not interested in a quick buck. On the contrary, many Kuwaiti investors are extraordinarily sophisticated. They are very competently advised and tend to think long-term and invest accordingly, which creates stability. Kuwait's stock market has a good record of paying solid dividends to investors. Kuwait's current account balance is 50 per cent of its GDP – unlike almost any other market in the region and certainly one of the largest in the world. In the early part of the 21st century Kuwait broke away from the fixed link to the US dollar. The move enabled Kuwait to mitigate the risk of import inflation due to the weakening of the US dollar.

Further mitigation is provided by Kuwait's sovereign-wealth fund, the Kuwait Investment Authority, which oversees all state expenditures and international investments. Kuwait also allocates 10 per cent of all state revenues into the Reserve Fund for Future Generations (RFFG), for the day when oil income starts to decline. Article 21 of the Kuwaiti constitution specifically allocates all natural resources and revenue they generate to the state. However, the Foreign Direct Capital Investment Law passed by the National Assembly in March 2001, has facilitated some foreign investment and development in those sectors, causing significant controversy in Kuwait.

Kuwait emerged from the global financial crisis in a position of strength. The government posted large saving rates during the pre-crisis boom years, which had allowed it to accumulate large external buffers in the form of foreign assets; this placed it in a relatively strong fiscal and external position to address the impact of the crisis. The government launched a four year development plan (DP) in early 2010 – which emphasised much needed investment in health, education and infrastructure with the lofty objective of transforming Kuwait into a regional trade and financial centre, while expanding the role of the private sector in the economy. Kuwaiti nationals only account for 1.1 million, just over 30 per cent of the country's 3.6 million population and are predominantly employed in the public sector while the private sector is largely dependent on expatriate, for the most part unskilled or semi-skilled, labour.

Gross domestic product (GDP) growth in 2010 was estimated at 3.3 per cent, comprising oil growth of 3.2 per cent and non-oil growth of 3.4 per cent. According to the International Monetary Fund (IMF) economic activity has been driven mostly by government expenditure. Credit growth in 2010 was small with lending growth of 3.3 per cent to the productive sectors (industry, services and trade) partially offset by a reduction in credit to the real estate. Regional unrest characterised as the Arab Spring has had a negative effect on equity prices, which declined by over 8 per cent in the year up to May 2011.

The IMF notes that Kuwait's fiscal stance has been expansionary. Government expenditure in the fiscal year 2010/11 (April to March) excluding energy-related subsidies and recapitalisation of social security, is estimated to have increased by 21.5 per cent. Half of this growth was attributable to a recent Emiri grant (including KD1,000 (US$3,500) to each Kuwaiti citizen and a food basket for every family for 14 months, amounting to a total cost to the budget of some US$5.3 billion), which offset the under-implementation of the budget. Higher international oil prices bolstered revenue with oil export receipts increasing by 19 per cent. In 2010, fiscal and external surpluses are estimated at about 21 and 28 per cent of GDP, respectively, compared to 28 and 24 per cent in 2009. Inflation increased in 2010, primarily due to higher international food prices. Average food inflation reached about 8.2 per cent in 2010 (9.8 per cent at end-April 2011), compared to 3.4 per cent in 2009, but its impact on Kuwaiti citizens was to some extent mitigated by the Emiri grant. Non-food inflation remains subdued at around 3.6 per cent as of April 2011, reflecting moderate increases in rents.

Kuwait's banking sector remained strong in 2010 and into 2011, but continued weaknesses in investment companies persisted. The banking sector's profitability and capitalisation have improved but the purely investment sector continued to post losses. Profits of local banks increased by 70 per cent in 2010 and capitalisation strengthened further.

The performance of the non-financial corporate sector improved in 2010, notwithstanding the continued drag by the real estate sector. The corporate sector's net profits increased by 170 per cent in 2010, but the real estate sector continued to post losses at levels similar to those seen in 2009.

The economy is expected by the IMF to grow steadily in 2011 and over the medium term as the government implements the development plan and global recovery supports the demand for oil. Kuwait's GDP is projected to increase by about 5 per cent in 2011, reflecting an increase in oil. GDP of about 3.25 per cent and non-oil GDP of 6 per cent, spurred by government spending. Inflation is projected to pick up in 2011 to about 6.25 per cent, driven by imported inflation.

Hydrocarbons

It is simply impossible to discuss any aspect of Kuwaiti life without making reference to its hydrocarbon resources. According to the *Oil & Gas Journal* (OGJ), in January 2011, Kuwait's territorial boundaries contained an estimated 101.5 billion barrels of proven oil reserves, roughly 7 per cent of the world total. Additional reserves are held in the Partitioned Neutral Zone (aka Divided Zone), which Kuwait shares on a 50-50 basis with Saudi Arabia. According to the US government Energy Information Administration (EIA) the Neutral Zone holds an additional 5 billion barrels of proven reserves, bringing Kuwait's total oil reserves to 104 billion barrels. These reserve estimates have been openly questioned by some analysts and a number of Kuwaiti parliamentarians, with some putting reserves as low as 48 billion barrels.

The government of Kuwait owns and controls all development of the oil sector. The Supreme Petroleum Council (SPC) oversees Kuwait's oil sector and sets oil policy. The SPC is headed by the prime minister. The rest of the council is made up of six ministers and six representatives from the private sector, all of whom serve three-year terms and are selected by the emir. The ministry of petroleum supervises all aspects of policy implementation.

The Kuwait Petroleum Corporation (KPC) manages domestic and foreign oil investments. Kuwait Oil Company (KOC), the upstream subsidiary of KPC, was taken over by the Kuwaiti government in 1975 and manages all upstream development in the oil and gas sectors. Various subsidiaries of KPC control Kuwait's oil sector. The Kuwait National Petroleum Company (KNPC) controls the downstream sector, while the Petrochemical Industries Company (PIC) is in charge of the petrochemical sector. Export operations are overseen by both KNPC and the Kuwait Oil Tanker Company (KOTC). Foreign interests of KPC are handled by the Kuwait Foreign Petroleum Exploration Company (Kufpec) and international upstream development and downstream operations are controlled by Kuwait Petroleum International (KPI). The Partitioned Neutral Zone (PNZ) has its own management companies, separated into onshore and offshore activities. The onshore sector was originally developed by the American Independent Oil Company (Aminoil), which was nationalised in 1977. Getty Oil, which would eventually be subsumed by Chevron, was brought in to develop the onshore PNZ fields. Chevron remains a participant along with KPC, although management of all KPC PNZ interests were later transferred to the Kuwait Gulf Oil Company (KGOC).

In 2010, according to EIA figures, Kuwait's total oil production was approximately 2.5 million barrels per day (bpd), including its share of approximately 250,000bpd production from the PNZ. Of the country's 2010 production, approximately 2.3 million bpd was crude and 200,000bpd was non-crude liquids. Slightly over half of Kuwaiti crude production in 2010 came from the south-east of the country, largely from the Burgan field; production from the north has increased to approximately 800,000bpd. As a member of Organisation of the Petroleum Exporting Countries (Opec), Kuwait's total production is constrained by the organisation's production targets, which in 2010 meant the country maintained about 320,000bpd of spare crude oil production capacity. In early 2011, as one of the few Opec members with spare capacity, Kuwait increased oil production to compensate for the loss of Libyan supplies.

KPC has initiated a US$90 billion expansion plan encompassing both upstream and the downstream activities. Included in this are plans to upgrade Kuwait's production and export infrastructure and its tanker fleet, expand exploration and build downstream facilities, both domestically and abroad, which are expected to boost oil production capacity to 4 million bpd by 2020. Largely as a result of the political impasse, exploration in Kuwait has not made significant inroads in the recent past. Discoveries of lighter crudes in the center of the country have been successful, but progress has not moved beyond the planning stages.

Much of Kuwait's reserves and production are concentrated in a few mature oil fields discovered in the 1930s and 1950s. The Greater Burgan oil field, which comprises the Burgan, Magwa and Ahmadi reservoirs, makes up the dominant portion of both reserves and production. Burgan is widely considered the world's second largest oil field, surpassed only by Saudi Arabia's Ghawar field. Greater Burgan was discovered in 1938, but did not become fully developed until after World War II. Northern Kuwait holds the majority of Kuwait's larger fields other than Greater Burgan. Kuwait's second largest source of crude production is from the northern Raudhatain field, with a capacity of 350,000-400,000bpd.

A focal point of Kuwait's aspirations to attain a production capacity of 4 million bpd is Project Kuwait. Proposed in 1998, Project Kuwait was an asserted effort to create proper incentives for attracting foreign participation. The contract structure that resulted was challenged as unconstitutional and the National Assembly impeded progress of Project Kuwait for a number of years. In May 2007, the Kuwaiti ruling family conceded the responsibility to approve each Project Kuwait contract to parliament, which has caused further delays.

Kuwaiti exports of total oil in 2010 amounted to some 1.8 million bpd, of which 1.7 million bpd was crude oil. Most Kuwaiti crude oil is sold on term contracts. Kuwait's crude exports are all a single blend of all its crude types. In 2010, the Asia-Pacific region received approximately 1.4 million bpd, while exports to the United States totaled 196,000bpd and Western Europe around 100,000bpd.

Natural gas

According to the OGJ, in January 2011, Kuwait had an estimated 63 trillion cubic feet (tcf) of proven natural gas reserves. Kuwait's reserves are not significant and this has spurred an extensive drive in natural gas exploration. Vast discoveries of non-associated gas in the north of the country attracted interest from international oil companies (IOCs). However, unattractive contract structures and political uncertainty remain principal impediments to any rapid expansion of both reserves and production. Additionally, new discoveries are geologically more complex, being mainly tight and sour gas deposits which require more sophisticated and costly development.

Risk assessment

Economy	Good
Politics	Fair
Regional stability	Fair

COUNTRY PROFILE

Historical profile

1600s The north-east Arabian peninsula, including what is now Kuwait, was part of the Ottoman Empire.

1756 The Al-Sabah family took control of Kuwait and there was a degree of semi-autonomy from Ottoman Turkey.

1899 Sheikh Mubarak 'the Great' accepted British protection in order to counter the spread of Turkish influence. Kuwait became a British protectorate but control of external relations remained with Britain.

1918 The end of the First World War saw the end of what was already only nominal Turkish control over Kuwait.

1938 Oil was first discovered by the US-British Kuwait Oil Company. Further exploration was interrupted by the Second World War.

1940s–50s Drilling resumed after the War and Kuwait soon developed into a thriving commercial centre. The government began using oil revenues to develop the country's infrastructure and a modern and comprehensive welfare system.

1961 Kuwait's status as a British protectorate ended and it became an independent country. The ruling Sheikh became the Emir and assumed full executive power. Iraq claimed Kuwait as part of its territory,

but backed down after British military intervention.
1963 The constitution was promulgated and National Assembly elections were held.
1976 The Emir suspended the National Assembly; he said it was not acting in the country's best interests.
1977 Sheikh Jaber al Ahmad al Sabah succeeded his cousin, Sheikh Sabah al Salem al Sabah as Emir.
1980 In the Iran-Iraq War, Kuwait supported Iraq.
1981 The political and economic union, Co-operation Council for the Arab States of the Gulf (CCASG) (known as Gulf Co-operation Council (GCC)) was formed by Bahrain, Kuwait, Oman, Qatar, Saudi Arabia and the United Arab Emirates (UAE). The National Assembly was recalled, but was again dissolved in 1986.
1985 The Emir survived an assassination attempt.
1990 Iraq invaded Kuwait and the Emir and cabinet fled to Saudi Arabia. The invasion was condemned by the international community which, led by the US, deployed armed forces to Saudi Arabia. UN Resolution 678 authorised member states to use force if Iraq did not withdraw by 15 January 1991.
1991 When Iraq did not withdraw, in the early hours of 17 January coalition forces launched an aerial bombing campaign against Iraq and Iraqi forces in Kuwait. US-led ground forces (from around 30 countries, including Syria, Egypt and Morocco) moved into Kuwait on 24 February and drove the Iraqi forces there back into Iraq. Iraq agreed to accept all UN resolutions concerning Kuwait.
1992 The Emir was pressurised into allowing National Assembly elections, in which the opposition fared well.
1999 Islamists and liberals swept to victory in parliamentary elections. A draft law granting women full political rights, including the right to vote, was narrowly rejected by parliament. The National Assembly was suspended by the Emir, following a dispute over a misprinted state edition of the Quran.
2001 The Constitutional Court refused to grant women the vote.
2002 The Emir suffered a brain haemorrhage; he received treatment in London.
2003 US troops and allies massed in the border area of Kuwait before invading Iraq. Islamist and pro-government candidates were successful in parliamentary elections; liberal candidates suffered heavy losses. Emir Sheikh Jaber appointed his brother, Sheikh Sabah al Ahmad al Jaber al Sabah, as prime minister, separating the post from the role of heir to the throne for the first time since independence.
2005 A constitutional amendment gave women the right to vote and stand for parliament from 2007. For the first time, two women were named as members of the national assembly.
2006 Sheikh Sabah al Ahmed al Jaber al Sabah became Emir instead of ailing Crown Prince Sheikh Sa'ad al Abdullah al Sabah, who had been heir apparent since 1978. Sheikh Nasser al Mohammad al Ahmad (nephew of the Emir) was appointed prime minister. Women voted for the first time, in a council by-election. The Emir dissolved parliament and scheduled new elections; members opposed to the government's stance on electoral reform won 33 elected seats out of 50. A new reform bill reduced the number of parliamentary constituencies from 25 to five.
2007 The cabinet of Prime Minister Sheikh Nasser al Mohammad al Ahmad resigned and was re-appointed to form another cabinet. As a counter-inflationary measure, the central bank ended the dinar's peg to the US dollar (adopted in 2003) in favour of a basket of currencies.
2008 A GCC common market was created by the six wealthiest Gulf States. Citizens of these countries are allowed to travel between, and live in any of the six states, where they may find employment, buy properties and businesses and use the educational and health facilities freely. Early elections were called as Prime Minister Nasser al Sabah's cabinet resigned. Sheikh Saad al Abdullah al Salim al Sabah, who had been prime minister and Emir for six days in 2006, died. In parliamentary elections, Sunni Islamists won 21 seats, Shi'ite Islamists five, the National Action Bloc (liberals) seven, and independents 17. Incumbent Prime Minister Sheikh Nasser al Sabah formed a new government, but with no change from the previous cabinet in the key portfolios. After an 18-year gap the Kuwaiti ambassador took up residence in Iraq; diplomatic relations had been restored in 2003. The prime minister and other cabinet members walked out of parliament just as the questioning of the prime minister, concerning a visiting Iranian cleric accused of insulting Sunni Muslims, was set to begin. This led to the government resigning.
2009 Prime Minister Nasser al Sabah formed a new government with members of his previous cabinet retaining key posts. The prime minister and cabinet resigned again. Critics said this allowed the administration to avoid questions of alleged misuse of public funds. In early parliamentary elections independents won 21 seats (out of 50), Sunni Islamists 13, Liberals 7, Shi'a Islamists 6, and the Popular Bloc 3; turnout was 50 per cent. Two of the successful candidates were women, the first females to win entry to parliament. The Emir re-appointed Nasser al Sabah as prime minister.
2010 In June, around 93,000 people (including about 31,000 Kuwaiti nationals) were banned from travel by the authorities due to outstanding debts to the state; the total owed was some KD784 million (US$2.7 billion). On 8 September, the first chairman of the Capital Market Authority, the first independent regulatory body to oversee the stock exchange, was appointed.
2011 On 12 January, Sheikh Nasser al Mohammed al Sabah arrived in Bagdad and became the first prime minister of Kuwait to visit Iraq since the 1990 invasion. Discussions covered border issues, finance and security as well as the payment of war reparations said to amount to amount to billions of US dollars. Kuwait's entire government resigned on 2 March over a row with parliament that wanted to question three senior cabinet ministers and Al Sabah family members concerning allegations of corruption and failure to perform their duties. Sheikh Nasser Mohammad al Ahmad al Sabah was appointed prime minister on 5 April. On 29 June parliament voted to spend around US$70 billion, of which 90 per cent will go on fuel subsidies for Kuwaiti citizens. Observers considered this a measure to placate any opposition to the Al Sabah family rule as protests during the Arab Spring pressured and undermined Bahrain. On 16 November, a group of campaigners stormed the parliamentary chamber in protest at the leadership of the prime minister and corruption; hundreds more protested outside. Prime Minister Nasser Mohammad al Ahmad al Sabah resigned on 28 November and Jabir Mubarak al Hamad al Sabah was appointed as prime minister, he took office on 4 December. On 6 December, the Emir dissolved parliament, citing 'deteriorating conditions'. New elections will be held by 4 February 2012.

Political structure

Constitution

The constitution was enacted on 29 January 1963. It authorises the ruling al Sabah family to choose an Emir, who holds executive power and can proclaim legislation by decree.

The constitution ascribes the political system as democratic, with sovereignty residing in the people. Impartial personal liberty and equality of rights and duties before the law are guaranteed.

The Emir or one-third of the national assembly may propose amending the Constitution by deleting or adding new ones, except for the Emiri System and the principles of liberty and equality unless to increase provisions. Approval by a

two-thirds majority is required for such a bill to succeed.
Males aged over 21 may vote; to include women aged over 21 from 2007.

Independence date
19 June 1961

Form of state
Constitutional monarchy (Emirate)

The executive
Executive power resides with the Emir, who is Head of State and appoints a prime minister, acceptable to the national assembly. In consultation with the prime minister the Emir appoints the Council of Ministers, who may not be members of parliament, although they assume *ex officio* membership during their term of office.
The Emir rules by decrees agreed by the Council of Ministers and, approved by parliament. He is also supreme commander of the armed forces.
Since 2003, the office of prime minister has been separated from the office of the Crown Prince, allowing greater independence of the legislature.

National legislature
The unicameral Majlis al Umma (National Assembly) has 50 members; five constituencies each return 10 members who are directly elected by proportional representation in block voting (electorate has 10 votes to chose any candidate available, voted in order of preference; not all votes need to be cast). All members serve for four-year terms. Legislation must be confirmed by two-thirds of the National Assembly membership before being endorsed by the Emir.
There is a cabinet with a total of 15 members which may be elected from the National Assembly membership or appointed *ex officio*.

Legal system
The Judiciary is based on Egyptian laws, derived from French law. The legal system is a mix of *Sharia* (Islamic law) and Napoleonic law.
In 1960, a unified judicial system was adopted, establishing different levels of courts. There are three separate divisions including the Courts of First Instance subdivided into criminal, commercial and civil boards, the Constitutional Court and the Court of State Security. The judiciary is administered by a council of seven senior judges and minister.

Last elections
16 May 2009 (parliamentary)
Results: Parliamentary: independents won 21 seats (out of 50), Sunni Islamists 13, Liberals 7, Shia Islamists 6, and the Popular Bloc 3. Turnout was 50 per cent.

Next elections
2013 (parliamentary)

Political parties
No political parties are allowed, although informal groupings exist. Candidates standing for election to the National Assembly do so as individuals, although they maybe a member of a political group. The largest such groupings are the Islamic Patriotic Coalition (a Shi'a fundamentalist group), two Sunni fundamentalist groups, the Islamic Constitutional Movement and the Islamic Popular Grouping (also known as the Salafi). The Kuwait Democratic Forum is the largest secular political group and has liberal and Arab nationalist opinions.

Ruling party
15-member Council of Ministers (re-appointed 20 May 2009)

Population
3.58 million (2010)*
Last census: April 2005: 2,213,403 (880,774 Kuwaitis; 1,332,629 expatriates)
Population density: 102 inhabitants per square km. Urban population: 96 per cent (1995–2001).
Annual growth rate: 4.1 per cent 1994–2004 (WHO 2006)

Ethnic make-up
Kuwaiti (37 per cent), other Arab (35 per cent), south Asian (9 per cent) and Iranian (4 per cent).

Religions
Sunni Muslim (45 per cent), Shi'ite Muslim (30 per cent), other Muslims (10 per cent); others, including Christian, Hindu and Parsi (15 per cent).

Education
There is state and private education at all levels; state schools are single-sex and only private schools may be co-educational. Tuition in the state sector is in Arabic.
Compulsory schooling begins at aged six and lasts until students have completed two four-year cycles in, first, elemental then intermediate schools. The last four-year cycle is not compulsory; as with the previous two stages, it is free of charge.
Pre-primary schools (also funded by the state) cater for four- to six-year-olds.
Public expenditure on education is typically equivalent to around 5 per cent of annual GNP and included subsidies to private education at primary, secondary and tertiary levels. Average public expenditure was estimated at 39.6 per cent of GDP per capita for primary level students, 5.5 per cent for secondary level and a higher expenditure of 87.9 per cent for tertiary level students.
Literacy rate: 83 per cent adult rate; 93 per cent youth rate (15–24) (Unesco 2005).
Compulsory years: Six to 14
Enrolment rate: 77 per cent gross primary enrolment of relevant age group (including repeaters); 65 per cent gross seconday enrolment (World Bank).
Pupils per teacher: 14 in primary schools

Health
Kuwait offers free, high quality health services through its clinics and hospitals, but charges for certain medical services for some residents and expatriates. The Ministry of Public Health (MPH) manages the health system and provides care on a referral basis through a network of local clinics, general and specialised services.
Life expectancy: 77 years, 2004 (WHO 2006)
Fertility rate/Maternal mortality rate: 2.3 births per woman, 2004 (WHO 2006); maternal mortality 5 per 100,000 live births (World Bank).
Birth rate/Death rate: 3 deaths and 20 births per 1,000 people (World Bank)
Child (under 5 years) mortality rate (per 1,000): 8.0 per 1,000 live births; 2 per cent of children aged under five years are malnourished (World Bank).
Head of population per physician: 1.53 physicians per 1,000 people, 2001 (WHO 2006)

Welfare
The social insurance system was set up as a basic scheme to include all employees with an addition supplementary scheme covering only those employees with an average monthly income above KD1,250.
Disability benefits are provided up to 60-years of age. The survivor pension amounts to 33.3–100 per cent of the deceased person's earnings according to number of widows and family dependants. A widow or widower receives a minimum monthly benefit.

Pensions
The old age pension is calculated on the number of years of contribution, the age at retirement and average earnings. It is set at a minimum of 65 per cent, and by a maximum benefit of 95 per cent, of the last monthly earnings.

Main cities
Kuwait City (capital, 502,099 in 2008), Farwaniya (908,360), Hawali (738,881), Armaid (648,313), Jahra (420,674), Mubarak al Kabeer (210,475).

Media
In 2008 Kuwait was ranked first for press freedom among all Arab states, by the Amman Centre of Human Rights Studies.
A press law prohibits references to God and the prophet Mohammed. Criticism of the Emir, the constitution, the judiciary and the 'tenets and mores of the society' can be prosecuted and imprisoned thus self-censorship is practised.

Press
The Ministry of Information issues licences to newspaper publishers.
Dailies: In Arabic, *Al Qabas* (www.alqabas.com.kw), *Al Rai al Amm* (www.alraialaam.com), *Al Watan* (www.alwatan.com.kw), *Annarar* (www.annaharkw.com), *Al Anba (www.alanba.com.kw), Al Seyassah* and *Al Taleea*. In English *Al Watan Daily* (www2.alwatan.com.kw), *Kuwait Times* (www.kuwaittimes.net) and *Arab Times* (www.arabtimesonline.com).
Weeklies: In Arabic, *Al Nahda* (www.al-nahda.com) and *Al Mujtammaa* (www.almujtamaa-mag.com) cover for current affairs.
Business: There are three regional business magazines which provide local and regional news on financial and business news, the Lebanon-based *Al Iktissad Wal Aamal* (www.iktissad.com), the UAE based *Zawya* (http://www.zawya.com) and the monthly *Investors* (http://mosgcc.com/english) published by the Gulf Co-operation Council. Local daily newspapers also publish business news.
Periodicals: In Arabic, the cultural review magazines *Dar al Yaqza* (www.alyaqza.com), *Al Arabi* (www.alarabimag.com) and *Anhar* (www.anhaar.com) are published monthly. The Quarterly *Thouq* (www.thouq.com) is a glossy magazine on fashion and lifestyles.
Broadcasting
State-run radio and television is operated by the Ministry of Information.
Radio: Radio Kuwait is the national public radio station providing several services of news, sports, religion, traditional and pop music and programmes in English. The only other local radio station is the private Marina FM (www.marinafm.com). Foreign radio stations available include the UK's BBC and BFBS, the US AFN and the French Monte Carlo Doualiya. There are numerous satellite radio stations available.
Television: The state-run Kuwait Televion has four channels, KTV1–4. Other, private broadcasters include the Al Watan (www.watan.tv), Al Resalah (www.alresalah.net), a religious channel and the first satellite TV service Al Rai, funded by the Al Rai Media Group (www.alraimedia.com) which has nationwide interests in TV, radio, publishing and advertising. Minority satellite TV interests include Bahry TV (www.bahry.com) with marine programmes and CNBC Arabiya (www.cnbcarabia.com) for business programmes. There are other smaller, local TV services available.

Advertising
Foreign firms must work through local agents and distributors, or joint ventures to advertise in Kuwait. In April 2007, 70 per cent of all advertising revenue was channelled through newspapers. Direct marketing through the mail has become popular along with internet sites. Satellite television is an effective tool for reaching conservative Kuwaiti and expatriate women in the privacy of their own homes.
News agencies
National news agency: Kuwait News Agency (Kuna): www.kuna.net.kw

Economy

Once described as 'an oil well masquerading as a country', Kuwait has vast oil reserves (101.5 billion barrels of oil in 2010, the fourth largest reserves in the world). The economy is centred on the oil and natural gas extraction industries. In May 2010, the government announced a provisional budget surplus of US$28.2 billion for 2009/10.
GDP growth in 2008 was 6.3 per cent, but in 2009 the economy fell into a short-lived recession with growth of -5.2 per cent, however positive growth returned in 2010, at 3.4 per cent. Inflation jumped in 2008 to 10.5 per cent as the price of imports, particularly food, were high, but returned to its typical 3–4 per cent per annum in 2009–10.
The Kuwaiti dinar (KD) was uncoupled from the US dollar in 2006 and pegged against a basket of currencies in 2007. Following the beginning of the global economic slowdown the dinar appreciated in value by 7 per cent in real terms. The windfall income from oil at its high price led to substantial fiscal and current account surpluses. The government sets aside 10 per cent of all oil revenue, to be paid into the Reserve Fund for Future Generations (RFFG). The reserves are managed by the state-owned asset management company, Kuwait Investment Authority (KIC), which invests in projects aimed at diversifying Kuwait's economy.
Arab finance ministers launched a US$2 billion Arab Development Fund (ADF) on 18 October 2010, to be administered by the Arab Fund for Economic and Social Development (AFESD). The Fund will finance small and medium investments in the 11 donor countries and is aimed at improving the circumstances of the some 140 million Arabs living below the poverty line.

External trade

Kuwait is a member of the Gulf Co-operation Council (along with Bahrain, Oman, Qatar, Saudi Arabia and the UAE), and the Greater Arab Free Trade Area (Gafta), which operates a customs union whereby tariffs within Gafta will be reduced by a percentage each year, until none remain, expected in 2010.
Around 90 per cent of all exports are oil and gas, while 90 per cent of all imports are consumer commodities and goods.
Imports
Food, construction materials, vehicles and parts, consumer goods and clothing.
Main sources: US (typically 10 per cent of total), Japan (10 per cent), Germany (8 per cent).
Exports
Petroleum, refined oil-related and by-products, predominately plastics and fertilizers and electrical and electronic equipment.
Main destinations: Japan (typically 20 per cent of total), South Korea (15 per cent), Singapore (10 per cent).

Agriculture

Kuwait remains dependent on food imports. The sector as a whole accounts for only 0.4 per cent of GDP.
Fishing
Fish stocks have recovered after war-related pollution reduced stocks in the early 1990s. Fish forms a relatively major part of the national diet, and domestic production can satisfy only 40 per cent of domestic requirements.

Industry and manufacturing

Industrial areas are located in Shuaiba, Mina Abdullah (both in south Kuwait) and Shuwaikh. Efforts to foster growth of non-oil industries have been hindered by the small size of the domestic market and a lack of natural resources other than hydrocarbons. Industry has been growing very slowly as a proportion of GDP, to between 11 and 13 per cent of total output.

Tourism

Kuwait adopted a long-term strategy in 2004 to develop tourism as part of its economic diversification objectives. The sector has been dominated by official and business visitors and entry has been difficult. The priority is to improve domestic tourism (73 per cent of Kuwait residents travel abroad each year) and increase arrivals from other Gulf states. Visa regulations were eased in 2004 to make Kuwait more accessible to overseas tourists. Kuwait has few tourist attractions, but is engaged on an ambitious programme to expand resort and leisure facilities, including the development of Failaka Island and the Sulaibikhat coast.
Travel and tourism is estimated to have contributed 1.5 per cent of GDP and employ 7.6 per cent of the work force.The sector generates around US$2.6 billion in export revenue.

Hydrocarbons

In 2010, proven oil reserves were 101.5 billion barrels, with production at 2.5

billion barrels per day (bpd). Kuwait was the third largest oil producer in the Middle East and had the fifth largest oil reserves worldwide in 2010.

Kuwait has three refineries with capacity of 905,000bpd in 2007; Amec won a five-year, US$8 billion contract to modernise them, to increase total domestic processing capacity and to allow for environmentally cleaner products. In 2010 refinery capacity had risen to 931,000bpd.

Proven natural gas reserves were 1.8 trillion cubic metres (cum) in 2010; production totalled 11.6 billion cum. Currently all domestic natural gas production is consumed locally and to meet demand, Kuwait imported 2.8 billion cum in 2010. Kuwait has plans to convert as much domestic consumption of energy as possible from oil to natural gas. This will free up more oil for foreign export earnings. Kuwait used to import natural gas from Iraq and had also signed a memoranda of agreement with Qatar and Iran to import natural gas, following the completion of the necessary gas pipelines. However by early 2009 these plans were stalled and was subject to international boundary considerations. Kuwait relies on imported liquefied natural gas (LNG) from a variety of sources.

Any coal imported or used is commercially insignificant.

Energy

Total installed generating capacity is 9.4 gigawatts (GW), produced in five power stations. Kuwait has one of the world's largest per capita electricity consumption rates at 14,000 kilowatt hours (kWh) and is growing by 7–9 per cent annually. Not only is there heavy demand due to air conditioning and water desalination but electricity prices are subsidised. Total generating capacity will be increased by a further 1,000MW following the completion of the new Al Zour South power plant. Another 3,000MW will be added when the Al Zour North power plant is constructed, plus a further nine independent power stations to be built in 2010–17.

In August 2009, the US-manufacturing company General Electric, was chosen to build a new 2,000MW (six gas turbines and six steam turbines) electricity generating plant by 2011, for KD700 million (US$2.6 billion). As demand is set to grow, Kuwait is planning to increase generating capacity to around 16,000MW by 2012.

A Gulf Co-operation Council (GCC) project to link the six member states (Saudi Arabia, Qatar, Bahrain, Kuwait, Oman and the United Arab Emirates) to an integrated power-grid began in 2005. The first phase of the GCC power grid was completed in 2009 at a cost of US$1,095 million, linking Saudi Arabia, Bahrain, Kuwait and Qatar through 800km of transmission lines. Kuwait and Saudi Arabia will each receive an extra 1,200MW of power capacity and later, the UAE will receive 900MW, Qatar 750MW, Bahrain 600MW and Oman 400MW. In the first phase, a 400kV overhead line links Kuwait's Al Zour power station with Doha, and a 400kV submarine line to Saudi Arabia with Bahrain. The second phase will link the UAE with Oman. The resulting two mega-grids will be joined in the final phase.

The new, US$2.65 billion, Sabiyya electric power plant, capable of producing 1,400MW with six generating turbines, came on stream in July 2011. When fully operational in 2012, the plant will produce 2,000MW and ensure that Kuwait's peak electricity demand in summer is met.

Financial markets

On 8 September 2010, the first chairman of the Capital Market Authority, the first independent regulatory body to oversee the stock exchange, was appointed.

Stock exchange

Kuwait Stock Exchange (KSE)

Banking and insurance

The IMF, Financial System Stability Assessment (FSSA), reported that the banking system was well capitalised with no immediate threat of instability. The capital adequacy ratio (CAR) was positive and quality assets were improving profits and returns on equity, which were increasing significantly. The financial institutional framework has been strengthened.

An agreement was reached between Saudi Arabia, Kuwait, Bahrain and Qatar to establish the Gulf Co-operation Council (GCC) Monetary Council to be established (originally in 2009), marking plans to set up a regional central bank, to be based in Riyadh (Saudi Arabia). The GCC Monetary Council will oversee the introduction of a monetary union, due to be in operation by 2013.

By June 2010, the Kuwaiti-owned Burgan Bank had completed the purchase of Tunis International Bank from the United Gulf Bank as part of its regional expansion strategy. The US$725 million purchase will allow the Burgan Bank access to other North African markets, to offer specifically investment banking and asset management.

Central bank

Central Bank of Kuwait

Main financial centre

Kuwait City

Time

GMT plus three hours

Geography

Kuwait lies at the north-west corner of the Gulf. To the south and south-west it shares a border with Saudi Arabia, and to the north and west with Iraq.

Kuwait is mainly flat desert with a scattering of oases. From east to west, the country is about 208km and from north to south, 185km. The al Mutla ridge is the only significant geographic feature. The desert is generally gravelly.

Hemisphere

Northern

Climate

Kuwait is less humid than other Gulf countries. However, the coast is more humid than inland, although the temperatures are lower.

Kuwait has four seasons. Mid-February to mid-April is spring; April to September (summer) is very hot (up to 49 degrees Celsius (C) in the shade); autumn is around mid-September to mid-November. The winter months are usually pleasant, with daytime temperatures around 18 degrees C and cold nights. Sandstorms occur, particularly in spring. Kuwait has an annual rainfall ranging from 10mm to 370mm which falls almost entirely between the months of November and April.

Dress codes

Lightweight or tropical clothes are worn in the summer, although in winter months a medium-weight jacket and a jumper are advisable. Women should dress modestly. A long-sleeved shirt and tie should be worn at business meetings but a jacket may be carried. On social occasions dress as for business meetings, unless otherwise indicated.

Entry requirements

Passports

Passports are required by all, and must be valid for six months from date of entry.

Visa

Required by all, except citizens of Gulf Co-operation Council countries. All other visitors should contact the nearest Kuwaiti Consulate for current exceptions and requirements.

Business visas, obtained before travelling, require an invitation from a sponsor in a local company or organisation. When completed it should be submitted to the issuing embassy, along with a business letter from the employer giving an account of the visitor's position and role within the foreign company, and full itinerary with purpose of visit and length of stay.

Tourist visas can be obtained at ports of entry, by nationals of the US, Western Europe, South East Asia and Australasia.

Currency advice/regulations
There are no restrictions on local and foreign currency imports or exports.
Customs
Personal effects and a limited supply of tobacco are duty-free.
Prohibited imports
Alcohol, illegal drugs, pornographic and/or politically subversive materials; pork products in any form; all non-tinned food and fresh fruit, vegetables and shellfish. Products that originate from Israel.

Health (for visitors)
Health facilities are excellent.
Mandatory precautions
There are no compulsory vaccinations.
Advisable precautions
Recommended immunisations are hepatitis A, polio and tetanus. There is a risk of rabies.

Hotels
Most visitors are business travellers. Five-star hotels have swimming pools and exercise/gymnasium facilities. Small tip for porters is customary. There is usually a 15 per cent service charge.

Credit cards
Major credit cards (American Express, Diners Club, Visa and Mastercard or Access) accepted at all hotels and many restaurants and shops.

Public holidays (national)
Fixed dates
1 Jan (New Year's Day), 25 Feb (National Day), 26 Feb (Liberation Day), 1 Jul (Bank Holiday).
Variable dates
Eid al Adha (four days), Islamic New Year, Birth of the Prophet, Ascent of the Prophet, Eid al Fitr (three days).
Islamic year 1433 (26 Nov 2011–14 Nov 2012): The Islamic year has 354 or 355 days, with the result that Muslim feast advance by 10–12 days against the Gregorian calendar each year. Dates of the Muslim feast vary according to sightings of the new moon, so cannot be forecast exactly.

Working hours
Friday is the Muslim day of religious observance (weekly holiday).
Banking
Sun–Wed: 0800–1200; Sun–Wed, Ramadan: 0900–1230.
Business
Sat–Wed: 0830–1400; some businesses work 1700–2000.
Government
Sat–Wed, winter: 0700–1430; Sat–Wed (summer): 0700–1400; Ramadan: 0900–1300.
Shops
Sat–Thu: 0800–1230, 1630–2100.

Telecommunications
Mobile/cell phones
There are GSM roaming facilities available, with coverage throughout the country. The ministries of communications and commerce announced their intention to auction a 26 per cent share in the Third Mobile Telecommunications Company in 2007.

Electricity supply
240V AC; plug fittings normally three-pin flat type (British).

Weights and measures
Metric system (local units are also in use).

Social customs/useful tips
Appointments should be made in advance. Punctuality is appreciated. Personal introductions are advantageous. If the visiting executive is a woman, this must be clearly stated in initial correspondence. On the street, women should not respond to approaches by men and should avoid eye contact.
Men shake hands on meeting and taking leave. Conference visits are an accepted way of doing business and other visitors may be present. The host may hold several conversations at the same time. It is not customary to start talking business immediately. Business cards should have an Arabic translation on the reverse side.
Islamic conventions apply. At meetings it is polite to drink coffee or tea when offered. It is the convention to use the right and not the left hand when shaking hands, eating, and passing or receiving anything. Almost everything may stop five times a day for prayers. Some people prefer not to shake hands with those of the opposite sex. When sitting cross-legged on sofas or cushions, soles of the feet must not be shown. A man should not enquire about another man's wife, only about the children. Pork and alcohol are forbidden.
Gratuities are around 10 per cent. Bargaining is not as common as in other countries. There are many restrictions on photography.

Security
Visitors should keep in touch with developments in the Middle East as any increase in regional tension might affect travel advice.
Kuwait is relatively safe but take normal travel precautions. Like the rest of the Middle East, there is a threat to westerners from possible terrorist attacks. Mines remain a problem outside Kuwait City.

Getting there
Air
National airline: Kuwait Airways.
International airport/s: Kuwait International (KWI), 16km south of city; duty-free shop, restaurant, banks, hotel reservations, post office, car hire. Taxis and hotel courtesy buses are available.
Airport tax: Departure tax: KD2, except transit passengers remaining in the airport.
Surface
Road: There are excellent roads from the Saudi Arabian and Iraqi borders.
Main port/s: Several commercial shipping lines call in at Kuwait City.

Getting about
National transport
Road: A network of 3,800km of good paved roads and expressways link towns.
Buses: Nationwide service operated by Kuwait Transport Company, generally rated good and inexpensive.
Rail: In February 2008 a plan to build a US$11 billion rail network was announced. The plan includes a metro system for Kuwait city.
City transport
Taxis: Taxis are not metered. Both private and shared taxis, which are orange and operate on set routes, are available. Taxis are more expensive from hotel ranks. There is a standard taxi fare in Kuwait City and drivers do not expect a tip. If hiring a taxi for a day or half-day agree the fare in advance. Call taxis are reliable and widely used.
Car hire
Locally approved/inspected international driving licence (valid for duration of entry permit) and insurance with Gulf Insurance Company or Kuwait Insurance Company are essential. Driving is on the right.

BUSINESS DIRECTORY

The addresses listed below are a selection only. While World of Information makes every endeavour to check these addresses, we cannot guarantee that changes have not been made, especially to telephone numbers and area codes. We would welcome any corrections.

Telephone area codes
The international direct dialling code (IDD) for Kuwait is +965, followed by subscriber's number.

Useful telephone numbers
Ambulance: 777
Telephone enquiries: 101
Directory enquiries: 023 or 244-4777

Chambers of Commerce
American Business Council of Kuwait, PO Box 29992, Safat 13159 (tel: 564-3149; fax: 563-8012; e-mail: abckuwait@hotmail.com).

Banking
Al-Ahli Bank of Kuwait KSC, PO Box 1387 Safat-13014, Mubarak Al-Kabir St,

Kuwait City (tel: 241-1101/2; fax: 242-4557).

Commercial Bank of Kuwait SAK, PO Box 2861 Safat-13029, Mubarak Al-Kabir St, Kuwait City (tel: 241-1001; fax: 245-0150).

Gulf Bank KSC, PO Box 3200 Safat-13032, Raed Centre next to Awadi Tower, Kuwait City (tel: 244-9501; fax: 244-5212).

Industrial Bank of Kuwait KSC, PO Box 3146, Safat 13032, Kuwait City (tel: 245-7661; fax: 246-2057).

National Bank of Kuwait SAK, PO Box 95 Safat-13001, Ali Awadi Tower, Ahmed Al-Jaber St, Kuwait City (tel: 242-2011; fax: 246-4156).

Central bank

Central Bank of Kuwait, PO Box 526, Abdulla Al-Salem Street, Safat 13006, Kuwait City (tel: 244-9200; fax: 244-0887; cbk@cbk.gov.kw).

Stock exchange

Kuwait Stock Exchange (KSE): www.kuwaitse.com

Travel information

Gulf Automobile Association, PO Box 827, Safat, Kuwait City (tel: 242-3864, 243-8640).

Kuwait Airways, PO Box 394, Safat, Kuwait International Airport, Safat 13004, Kuwait (tel: 434-5555; fax: 431-9204; internet site: www.kuwait-airways.com).

Kuwait International Airport (tel: 473-3625).

Touristic Enterprises Co (TEC), PO Box 23310, Safat 13094, Kuwait City (tel: 806-806, 565-0111; fax: 565-0514; internet: www.kuwaittourism.com).

Ministry of tourism

Tourism Department, Ministry of Information, PO Box 193, Safat, Kuwait City (tel: 242-7141).

Ministries

Ministry of Awqaf and Islamic Affairs, PO Box 13, 13001 Safat, Kuwait City (tel: 248-0000; fax: 243-3750).

Ministry of Communications, PO Box 318, 13004 Safat, Kuwait City (tel: 481-9033; fax: 484-7058).

Ministry of Defence, PO Box 1170, 13012 Safat, Kuwait City (tel: 484-8300; fax: 483-7244).

Ministry of Education, PO Box 7, 13001 Safat, Kuwait City (tel: 483-6800; fax: 483-7829).

Ministry of Electricity and Water, PO Box 12, 13001 Safat, Kuwait City (tel: 537-1000; fax: 537-1420).

Ministry of Foreign Affairs, PO Box 3, 13001 Safat, Kuwait City (tel: 242-5141; fax: 241-2169; e-mail: info@mofa.org).

Ministry of Health, PO Box 5, 13001 Safat, Kuwait City (tel: 246-2900; fax: 243-2288).

Ministry of Higher Education, PO Box 27130, 13132 Safat, Kuwait City (tel: 240-1300; fax: 245-6319).

Ministry of Information, PO Box 193, 13002 Safat, Kuwait City (tel: 241-5300; fax: 241-9642; e-mail: info@moinfo.gov.kw).

Ministry of Interior, PO Box 12500, 71655 Safat, Kuwait City (tel: 243-3804; fax: 243-6570).

Ministry of Justice, PO Box 6, 13001 Safat, Kuwait City (tel: 248-0000; fax: 243-3750).

Ministry of Oil, PO Box 5077, 13051 Safat, Kuwait City (tel: 241-5201; fax: 241-7088).

Ministry of Planning, PO Box 15, 13001 Safat, Kuwait City (tel: 242-8200; fax: 240-7326).

Ministry of Public Works, PO Box 8, 13001 Safat, Kuwait City (tel: 538-5520; fax: 538-0829).

Ministry of Social Affairs & Labour, PO Box 563, 13006 Safat, Kuwait City (tel: 248-0000; fax: 241-9877).

Other useful addresses

British Embassy, PO Box 300, 13003 Safat (tel: 240-3334; fax: 240-7395).

Central Tenders Committee, PO Box 1070, 13011 Kuwait City (tel: 243-1719; fax: 241-6574).

Council of Ministers, PO Box 1397, 13014 Safat (tel: 245-5333; fax: 245-5002).

General Secretariat, PO Box 1397, Safat 13014 (tel: 245-5333; fax: 245-5002).

Kuwait Foreign Trading, Contracting & Investment Co, PO Box 5665, Kuwait 13057 (tel: 244-9031).

Kuwait International Fair Co, PO Box 656, Safat, Kuwait City (tel: 245-8560/1/2/3/4/5).

Kuwait National Industries Co, PO Box 417, Safat, Kuwait City (tel: 815-466, 812-455).

Kuwait National Petroleum Company, PO Box 70, 13001 Safat (tel: 326-2616; fax: 326-0280).

Kuwait Oil Company (KOC), PO Box 9758, 61008 Ahmadi (tel: 398-9111; fax: 398-3661).

Kuwait Parliament, The National Assembly (tel: 245-5422; fax: 243-9032).

Kuwait Petroleum Corp, PO Box 26565, Safat, Kuwait City (tel: 245-5455; fax: 246-7159).

Kuwaiti Embassy (USA), 2940 Tilden Street, NW, Washington DC 20008 (tel: (+1-202)-966-0702; fax: (+1-202)-364-2868).

National Housing Association, PO Box 23385, 13094 Safat (tel: 471-7844; fax: 242-8801).

Petrochemical Industries Board Co, PO Box 1084, Safat, Kuwait City (tel: 242-2141; fax: 246-0224).

Shuaiba Area Authority, PO Box 4690, Safat (tel: 960-903).

National news agency: Kuwait News Agency (Kuna): www.kuna.net.kw

Internet sites

Business News, Arabia online: www.arabia.com

Gulf Business Explorer: www.igulf.com

Kuwait Information: www.kuwait-info.org

Kyrgyzstan

KEY FACTS

Official name: Kyrgyz Respublikasy (Kyrgyz Republic)

Head of State: President Almazbek Sharshenovich Atembayev (SDPK) (took office 1 Dec 2011)

Head of government: Prime Minister Omurbek Babanov (SDPK) (from 1 Dec 2011)

Ruling party: Coalition led by Sotsial-Demokraticheskaya Partiya Kyrgyzstana (SDPK) (Social Democratic Party of Kyrgyzstan), with Respublika (Republican Party) and Ata-Zhurt (Fatherland) (from 17 Dec 2010)

Area: 198,500 square km

Population: 5.33 million (2010)*

Capital: Bishkek (formerly Frunze)

Official language: Kyrgyz, Russian

Currency: Som (S) = 100 tyin

Exchange rate: S45.15 per US$ (Oct 2011)

GDP per capita: US$863 (2010)*

GDP real growth: -1.40% (2010)*

GDP: US$4.62 billion (2010)*

Inflation: 7.80% (2010)*

Balance of trade: -US$1.20 billion (2010)

* estimated figure

The protests in Bishkek in April 2010 that ousted the former President Bakiyev, followed by ethnic violence in the south in June, did little to boost the Kyrgyz economy. The widespread disruption was further exacerbated by border closures with Kazakhstan and Uzbekistan, the main transport conduits for trade. The crisis placed public finances under severe stress, alleviated by a July 2010 US$1.1 billion pledge of assistance from donors. The time taken to return to normality will very much depend on the new government's ability to bring about and maintain political and social stability.

Wobbling along

Kyrgyzstan's geography does little to give it a national peace of mind. Claiming to be the home of the apple and the walnut (both grow wild in Kyrgyzstan's mountains) the former Soviet satellite borders international heavyweights such as China and high risk countries such as Afghanistan as well as its fellow ex-USSR sub-states Tajikistan, Uzbekistan and Kazakhstan. In the twenty years since 1991 and freedom from Soviet rule, Kyrgyzstan's domestic politics have hardly been stable or even benevolent. To make matters worse, Kyrgyzstan finds itself pulled in different directions by its own minority ethnic groups, notably a number of Uzbek enclaves. Added to the mix is Kyrgyzstan's almost unique international position of playing host to both US and Russian air bases. However important Kyrgyzstan may be to the global powers, both the US and Russia were less than forthcoming in providing aid and assistance in June 2010 as thousands of Kyrgyzstan's ethnic Uzbek's were forced to flee the country.

Not only is Kyrgyzstan divided geographically by its high mountain ranges. There are ethnic divisons as well, although to the outside world these had not appeared to be on the brink of violence. The larger part of Kyrgyzstan's estimated 800,000 Uzbeks live in the southern part of the country, to the west of Osh and centred on Andijan. In the fertile Fergana valley, Uzbeks are generally thought to be in a majority. One of the few advantages of Soviet rule was the tight grip maintained by the (essentially Russian) troop presence.

Northern Kyrgyzstan was the most distinctly Russian part of the country. In 2005 Kyrgyzstan experienced its first post Soviet revolution with the toppling of the country's Soviet placeman president, Askar Akayev. He was replaced by Kurmanbek Bakiyev who turned out not to be much of an improvement. Mr Bakiyev followed in what had now become a Kyrgyz tradition of extending presidential powers and self enrichment. His departure was triggered by the protests that arose after police and army units opened fire on Uzbek demonstrators in

April 2010. Mr Akayev had ended up in Moscow, Mr Bakiyev in Minsk, the capital of Belarus. According to a report in the London *Economist* Mr Bakiyev's son was detained on arrival in Great Britain, where he was apparently seeking political asylum.

Following the resignation of President Bakiyev in April 2010, Roza Otunbayeva became interim president; she appointed Almazbek Atambayev of the Sotsial-Demokraticheskaya Partiya Kyrgyzstana (SDPK) (Social Democratic Party of Kyrgyzstan) as interim prime minister. The interim government drafted a new constitution, which was adopted in a nationwide referendum in June, changing the country's political system into a parliamentary republic.

On 3 July 2010, Roza Otunbayeva was sworn in as president, under the terms of the new constitution, with a term in office to last until 31 December 2011. She headed a cabinet until a new government could be formed following the elections scheduled for October.

In parliamentary elections held on 10 October, using the newly adopted system of proportional representation from political party lists, no party won overall power and talks on a coalition government began immediately. Parliament approved the new government coalition led by Sotsial-Demokraticheskaya Partiya Kyrgyzstana (SDPK) (Social Democratic Party of Kyrgyzstan), with Respublika (Republican Party) and Ata-Zhurt (Fatherland) on 17 December; Almazbek Atambayev (SDPK) became the country's first prime minister as Kyrgyzstan became Central Asia's first parliamentary republic.

On 23 September 2011, in a move to allow him to run for president, Prime Minister Atambayev temporarily transferred his authority to First Deputy Prime Minister Omurbek Babanov. Presidential elections were held on 30 October in which five candidates took part. Former prime minister and supporter of Russia, Almazbek Atambayev (SDPK) won an overwhelming majority with 62.9 per cent of the vote, his closest rivals Adahan Madomarov (Butun Kyrgyzstan (United Kyrgyzstan)) and Kamchybek Tashiev (Ata-Zhurt) won just over 14 per cent each. On 14 November, Almazbek Atambayev resumed his duties as prime minister, prior to taking office as president on 1 December when Omurbek Babanov takes over as prime minister.

The economy

According to the Asian Development Bank (ADB) in its *Asian Development Outlook* publication, after modest growth of 2.9 per cent in 2009, Kyrgyzstan was recovering well from the global economic crisis as gross domestic product (GDP) growth bounded to 16.4 per cent in the first quarter of 2010. But the closures of international borders following the April and June events stopped imports and exports at times, intensifying the impact of the internal disruptions on the economy. For the whole of 2010, GDP dropped by 1.4 per cent. All sectors contracted in 2010, except for gold and other industrial production, which grew by 8 per cent and 11.3 per cent, respectively. Gold output climbed mainly because of a higher ore yield. Expansion in industrial production was largely attributable to a low 2009 base, reflecting the impact of global and regional recession. Some sub-sectors, however, showed strong outturns: garments were up by an estimated 50 per cent and electricity, gas and water services were together 11 per cent higher.

Agricultural output for 2010 fell by 2.8 per cent largely due to delays in sowing crops (a knock-on effect of the disturbances) and an ensuing lower harvest in part caused by shortages of imported fuel. Construction output fell by 22.8 per cent, as unrest and supply disruptions curtailed work, including that on large investment projects in the hydropower and mining sub-sectors.

The ADB noted that the contraction in GDP would have been more severe without expanded gold production. Also of help was an estimated 25 per cent increase in workers' remittances (from the Russian Federation and Kazakhstan, the country's main economic partners) that boosted a major source of income for the population, helping to ease the downward pressure on aggregate demand.

The imposition of duty by the Russian Federation on oil exports to the Kyrgyz Republic raised domestic oil-product prices by about 35 per cent. This and increasing imported food prices, combined with lower domestic wheat production, have significantly added to inflationary pressures. In the second half of 2010, inflation accelerated steadily and reached 19.2 per cent at year-end, with food prices up by 27 per cent. The April 2010 reversal of electricity and heating tariff increases to their 2009 levels (tariffs were doubled on 1 January 2010) helped to mitigate price escalation. Low inflation early in the year kept annual average inflation to 8.0 per cent.

The April and June 2010 events significantly increased budgetary expenditure on compensation to the families of victims; unplanned spending for the constitutional referendum and elections; outlays associated with rehabilitating damaged infrastructure and buildings; security expenditure; and subsidies for utility companies due to the tariff rise reversal. On the revenue side, improved tax administration in the second half of the year helped to offset the negative impact of the crisis and border closure on value-added tax and customs collections. The budget deficit for 2010 widened to an estimated 6.5 per cent

KEY INDICATORS **Kyrgyzstan**

	Unit	2006	2007	2008	2009	2010
Population	m	5.20	*5.25	*5.31	*5.37	*5.33
Gross domestic product (GDP)	US$bn	2.84	3.75	5.13	*4.57	*4.62
GDP per capita	US$	546	726	966	*851	*863
GDP real growth	%	3.1	8.5	7.6	*-0.1	*-1.4
Inflation	%	5.6	10.2	24.5	*6.4	*7.8
Unemployment	%	8.3	8.2	–	–	–
Industrial output	% change	-7.4	12.5	7.6	–	–
Agricultural output	% change	1.5	1.6	0.7	–	–
Exports (fob) (goods)	US$m	906.0	1,337.0	1,846.9	1,700.4	1,782.6
Imports (fob) (goods)	US$m	1,792.4	2,635.5	3,753.5	2,813.6	2,980.9
Balance of trade	US$m	-886.5	-1,298.5	-1,906.6	1,113.2	-1,198.3
Current account	US$m	-87.0	-261.3	-413.0	30.0	-269.8
Total reserves minus gold	US$m	764.3	1,107.2	1,152.9	1,494.0	1,603.6
Foreign exchange	US$m	731.1	1,093.4	1,097.6	1,331.9	1,431.9
Exchange rate	per US$	38.25	34.54	36.57	46.65	45.96

* estimated figure

of GDP. Assistance from both bilateral and multilateral donors as well as use of the US$300 million Russian loan proceeds (received in 2009) covered financing needed for the enlarged deficit. Since some of the recent spending increases were one off items (for rehabilitation and social protection, resettlement and reconstruction), they could be unwound as the situation improved in 2011, though much rebuilding will still be needed in 2012. Reconstruction, alongside the government's planned increase in salaries of teachers and other social sector workers from May 2011, further widened the budget deficit. Government estimates of the budget deficit for 2011 were around 9 per cent.

In July 2010, the donor community pledged US$1.1 billion assistance over 30 months. External support will be critical in helping the authorities to deal with the consequences of the crisis. External – mainly concessional – borrowing increased publicly guaranteed external debt to an estimated 62 per cent of GDP in 2010. The external debt ratio was forecast to reach 67 per cent by end-2011. Although the International Monetary Fund (IMF) rates the country's risk of debt distress as moderate, the government will need to follow prudent policies to ensure external debt sustainability.

In response to the crisis, the National Bank of the Kyrgyz Republic (NBKR) (central bank) eased its monetary stance by lowering the reserve requirement by 1.5 percentage points to 8.0 per cent in May 2010 and adjusted the sale of its notes to changing monetary circumstances. Nevertheless, credit to the economy increased by only 2.7 per cent due to weak demand and troubled banking conditions. The public's preference to increase its cash holdings at the expense of deposits surged after the April events, pressuring banking system liquidity and complicating the central bank's monetary operations. In 2010, the ADB noted, Kyrgyzstan's money supply rose by 18.6 per cent, primarily due to increased foreign assets. However, the global economic crisis shook financial stability. Loan quality has worsened dramatically – the ratio of non- performing loans rose from 7.9 per cent before April to an estimated 16 per cent at year-end. The deterioration in quality has been mainly concentrated in loans for trade and commerce. The NBKR introduced temporary administration at seven banks (later reduced to four), including Asia Universal Bank – the largest bank, with over 20 per cent of bank deposits – after it experienced a large nonresident deposit outflow, allegedly linked to the previous regime. To mitigate deposit-run risks, the authorities nationalised the bank and created a new bank based on the old one. Despite these difficulties, the banking system remains adequately liquid and capitalised.

Over 2010 the som depreciated by around 7 per cent against the dollar. In view of the continued large expected inflows of external assistance in 2011, the NBKR planned to intervene to forestall an unwarranted appreciation of the exchange rate and reduce excess bank liquidity created by these operations.

Kyrgyz exporters did not fully benefit from the economic recovery in the Russian Federation and Kazakhstan in the wake of internal unrest and periods of closed borders. Further, the introduction of a customs union among the Russian Federation, Kazakhstan and Belarus in July 2010 decreased the volume of Chinese goods that are re-exported, as they now face higher duties into the union. Increased production of gold, the country's main export commodity and rising gold prices helped to bolster export revenue that was estimated to have increased by 7.0 per cent for the year.

Despite the border disruptions, imports were estimated to have increased by 15.0 per cent. This expansion reflected higher import prices of food and fuel, though imports financed by donors and workers' remittances were also factors. The current account deficit was estimated at 5.0 per cent of GDP in 2010, up from 2.4 per cent a year earlier.

The economy is expected to pick up with GDP growing at around 5 per cent in 2011 and 2012. The forecasts rest on expectations of a normal security environment, continued reconstruction works, full resumption of trade and services flows and improved investor confidence. They also rely heavily on construction growing by about 40 per cent, mainly due to large scale reconstruction works in the south. Services and industry are seen growing by 6 per cent and 4 per cent, respectively. The economic expansion of the Russian Federation and Kazakhstan will also contribute to growth through increased demand for the Kyrgyz Republic's exports and higher remittances from workers in those two countries.

Risk assessment

Economy	Poor
Politics	Poor
Regional stability	Fair

COUNTRY PROFILE

Historical profile

1700s–1800s After being invaded by the Arabs, Mongols and the Chinese, Kyrgyzstan was ruled by the Khanate of Kokand (part of modern-day Uzbekistan).

1876 Tsarist troops conquered Kokand and incorporated Kyrgyzstan into the Russian Empire.

1916–17 Following the suppression of rebellion in Central Asia against Russian rule and the outbreak of civil war after the October Revolution in Russia, many Kyrgyz crossed the eastern border into China.

1918 Parts of Kyrgyzstan were absorbed into Russian-controlled Turkestan.

1920s–30s Soviet nationalities policy under the direction of Joseph Stalin saw Soviet rule enforced from Moscow by Red Army troops who put down Muslim revolts throughout Central Asia after the Russian civil war. All arable and grazing lands were consolidated into large state-owned farms, upsetting the traditional Kyrgyz way of life, based on nomadic livestock-herding. The Kyrgyz Communist Party was established as the sole legal party.

1924 Kyrgyzstan was designated the Kara-Kyrgyz Autonomous Region (renamed Kyrgyz Autonomous Region in 1925) and absorbed into the Russian Socialist Federated Soviet Republic (RSFSR).

1926 The Kyrgyz Autonomous Region was upgraded to an Autonomous Soviet Socialist Republic (ASSR).

1936 Kyrgyzstan became a constituent republic within the Union of Soviet Socialist Republics (USSR).

1940s–80s Kyrgyzstan was an important source of raw materials to the Soviet Union.

1990 Leaders of the Kyrgyz Communist Party opposed changes to the Soviet constitution as they would have allowed non-Communist parties to take part in political life. The Kyrgyz and Uzbek populations rioted in ethnically-divided Osh in southern Kyrgyzstan and a state of emergency was declared after several hundred people were killed. Askar Akayev, a liberal academic on the reform wing of the Kyrgyz Communist Party, was elected by the legislature to the newly created post of president of the Kyrgyz Socialist Republic.

1991 Kyrgyzstan was the first Central Asian republic to declare independence from the USSR. Akayev stood alone in the country's presidential elections. Kyrgyzstan joined the Commonwealth of Independent States (CIS).

1992 An economic reform programme was launched. Kyrgyzstan joined the United Nations and the Conference on Security and Co-operation in Europe, the predecessor of the Organisation for Security and Co-operation in Europe (OSCE);

1993 Kyrgyzstan adopted its first post-Soviet constitution allowing for a parliamentary system of government. The som replaced the rouble as the unit of currency.
1994 Akayev won a resounding referendum victory, giving him the mandate to make the legislature a bicameral body. Uzbekistan signed an economic, military and social co-operation treaty with Kazakhstan and Kyrgyzstan.
1995 Akayev was re-elected for a second five-year term.
1996 A referendum gave the president the authority to appoint all top officials; parliamentary approval is only required for prime ministerial candidates. Uzbekistan, Kazakhstan and Kyrgyzstan agreed to create a single economic market.
1998 Constitutional changes were approved to change former communist farm collectives to private land ownership – the first time this was attempted by a Central Asian state. Kyrgyzstan became a member of the World Trade Organisation (WTO), the first of any former Soviet Union republics to join.
2000 President Akayev was elected for a third term, contrary to the constitution and amid allegations of electoral irregularities. The elections were followed by the harassment and imprisonment of opposition leaders and the closure of opposition newspapers. The presidents of Belarus, Kazakhstan, Kyrgyzstan, Russia and Tajikistan (formerly the Customs Five) established the Eurasian Economic Community (EEC).
2001 Tajikistan, China, Russia, Kazakhstan, Kyrgyzstan and Uzbekistan formed the Shanghai Co-operation Organisation (SCO) and agreed to fight ethnic and religious militancy, while promoting investment and trade.
2002 Prime Minister Kurmanbek Bakiyev resigned and Nikolai Tanayev was named as his replacement. Opposition protesters marched in the capital, demanding the President's resignation.
2003 President Akayev's constitutional reforms, which included extending the president's term of office were endorsed by 80 per cent of voters; the opposition said they restricted civil liberties and consolidated power in the hands of the president. Widespread voting irregularities were reported by international observers. Parliament granted President Akayev and two other Soviet era Communist leaders lifelong immunity from prosecution.
2005 Numerous independent and opposition candidates were barred from standing in parliamentary elections, sparking widespread demonstrations. Protests increased during the second round of voting as demonstrators occupied government buildings and calls were made for President Akayev to resign. When protesters occupied official buildings in the capital Akayev fled to Moscow. The supreme court cancelled the results of the elections, although later elected members took their seats. The acting president, Kurmanbek Bakiyev, won a landslide victory in presidential elections. Feliks Kulov became prime minister.
2006 President Bakiyev signed a new constitution after a week of mass protests for constitutional reforms and action to combat crime and corruption. Kyrgyzstan became a member of the World Trade Organisation (WTO). Bakiyev accepted the resignation of the entire cabinet in his long-running dispute with parliament. Parliament revised the latest constitution, reinstating some presidential powers concerning government appointments.
2007 Almazbek Atambayev became prime minister. A constitutional referendum agreed to a change in voting laws from first-past-the-post to party-list voting; it also endorsed constitutional changes, which had been invalidated by the Constitutional Court. Prime Minister Atambayev and his cabinet resigned; Iskenderbek Aidaraliyev became acting prime minister. In early parliamentary elections, the ruling Ak Zhol Eldik Partiyasy (Ak Zholor) (Bright Path Popular Party) won over 48 per cent of the vote. A presidential ruling required any political party to achieve a threshold 5 per cent of the national vote, of which 0.5 per cent of the vote had to be in every district in the country, to win seats. As no other party managed this, Ak Zholor would have had a clean sweep and taken all 90 seats. However, the Supreme Court revoked the 0.5 per cent aspect of the presidential ruling and Ata Menken Socialist Party (Fatherland Socialist Party) won several seats.
2008 Fourteen medical professionals were charged with malpractice and negligence, following the infection of 42 children with the HIV virus as a consequent of injections and blood transfusions.
2009 Following an offer of US$1.4 billion in aid from Russia, the president asked parliament to terminate the US lease on its Manas air base, which the Americans used to transport material and personnel into Afghanistan. In presidential elections Kurmanbek Bakiyev won overwhelmingly with 77.8 per cent of the vote. Opposition candidate Almaz Atambaev withdrew from the election citing electoral fraud. The OSCE considered the elections to be flawed. Prime Minister Igor Chudinov resigned and Daniyar Üsönöv was appointed as his replacement.
2010 After a series of mass protests throughout the country, President Bakiyev was ousted in April and retreated to his home in the south of the country. He initially refused to step down as president but eventually fled to Kazakhstan and resigned from there. In April, the interim government extended the American's lease on the Manas air base. Communal violence in the city of Osh in early June between ethnic Kyrgyz and Uzbeks resulted in the killing of 470 mainly Uzbeks, and with hundreds injured. An estimated 400,000 fled into neighbouring Uzbekistan; the UN launched an aid appeal to raise US$71 million to help the refugees. In a constitutional referendum held in June, 90 per cent voted in favour of proposals to remove a number of presidential powers and turn the country into a parliamentary republic, with a single six-year presidential term of office and parliamentary elections to be held every five years. International observers declared the referendum as 'largely transparent and peaceful'. The amendments included a new political system that prevents concentration of power in the executive, and a limit of 50 on the number of parliamentary members for any one political party; the president will be banned from deriving income from any source other than the presidential salary; the president and family will lose their immunity from the law and their personal lives will not be subsidised by the state. On 3 July, Roza Otunbayeva was sworn in as president, under the terms of the new constitution, with a term in office to last until 31 December 2011. She has the responsibility of heading a cabinet until a new government is formed in elections scheduled for October. The state of emergency, imposed in the southern region in June, was lifted in August. In parliamentary elections held on 10 October, using the newly adopted system of proportional representation from political party lists, no party won overall power and talks on a coalition government began immediately. In November, a military court sentenced Sanzhar Bakiyev, nephew of ousted president Kurmanbek Bakiyev, to 10 years in jail for plotting rebellion. Parliament approved the new government coalition led by Sotsial-Demokraticheskaya Partiya Kyrgyzstana (SDPK) (Social Democratic Party of Kyrgyzstan), with Respublika (Republican Party) and Ata-Zhurt (Fatherland) on 17 December; Almazbek Atambayev (SDPK) became the country's first prime minister as Kyrgyzstan became Central Asia's first parliamentary republic.
2011 The Kyrgyzstan Inquiry Commission (KIC) report into the ethnic violence in Osh in 2010 was published on 2 May. It concluded that political fanaticism mixed with ethno-nationalism had resulted in violence and that the minority Uzbek community was the overwhelming victim of

attack. The report also said that there was evidence of official complicity. It also determined that some acts could be considered crimes against humanity, but not genocide. The official response was of acceptance of the KIC, but that the report was rushed and subjective. In early July, the Criminal Code was amended, whereby libel was removed as a criminal offence, a move expected to strengthen press freedom. In a move to allow him to run for president, Prime Minister Atambayev temporarily transferred his authority to First Deputy Prime Minister Omurbek Babanov on 23 September. Presidential elections were held on 30 October in which five candidates took part. Former prime minister and supporter of Russia, Almazbek Atambayev (SDPK) won an overwhelming majority with 62.9 per cent of the vote, his closest rivals Adahan Madomarov (Butun Kyrgyzstan (United Kyrgyzstan)) and Kamchybek Tashiev (Ata-Zhurt) won just over 14 per cent each. On 14 November, Almazbek Atambayev resumed his duties as prime minister, prior to taking office as president on 1 December when Omurbek Babanov took over as prime minister.

Political structure

Constitution

The constitution was adopted in 1993 (amended in 1998, 2003, 2007 and 2010). It defines Kyrgyzstan as a sovereign, unitary, parliamentary democratic and secular republic. All land, airspace and natural resources are the property of the state unless assigned for private usage. Discrimination on the grounds of language is forbidden. There is universal direct adult suffrage by secret ballot. There are six administrative *oblasts* (regions): Chu, Issyk-Kul, Osh, Talas, Jalal-Abad and Naryn. The capital, Bishkek, has special status and is not included in any oblast.

The 2003 consitutional amendment gave local authorities more power.

The 2007 consitutional amendment changed voting laws from first-past-the-post to party-list voting, as well as the constitutional changes, agreed in 2005, but which had been invalidated by the Constitutional Court.

The first 2010 consitutional amendment prevented authoritarianism and included a new political system that prevents concentration of power in the executive, a limit of 50 to the number of parliamentary members any one political party may have. The president must not derive income from any source except the presidential salary. The president and his family will lose their immunity from the law and his family's personal lives will not be subsidised by the state. The status of the country was changed to a parliamentary republic, with a single six-year presidential term of office and parliamentary elections to be held every five years.

Independence date

31 August 1991

Form of state

Parliamentary republic

The executive

The president is directly elected with a single six-year presidential term of office. The constitution states that the president must be able to speak the Kyrgyz language. In 2010 executive power was ceded to parliament, under the leadership of the interim president.

National legislature

There are 120 seats in the unicameral, Jorgorku Kenesh (Supreme Council). All seats are elected by proportional representation from party lists. Seats are allocated to political parties obtaining over 5 per cent of the national vote and more than 0.5 per cent within each of the nine provinces and capped at 65 seats per party.

Legal system

The legal system is based on a civil law code. There are three ultimate legal authorities: the Constitutional Court, the Supreme Court and the Higher Arbitration Court. All are composed of judges with a 15-year term of office who must be approved by the national legislature and the executive. The Constitutional Court rules on the constitutionality of central and local government legislation and on the validity of elections. The Supreme Court is the highest court of appeal for civil, criminal and administrative cases previously heard in oblast, district, city and military courts. The Higher Arbitration Court oversees and rules on the operation of the regional and City of Bishkek arbitration courts.

Last elections

30 October 2011 (presidential); 10 October 2010 (parliamentary)

Results: Presidential: Almazbek Atambayev (SDPK) won 62.9 per cent of the vote, Adakhan Madomarov (Butun Kyrgyzstan (United Kyrgyzstan)) 14.9 per cent, Kamchybek Tashiev (Ata-Zhurt) 14.4 per cent; 14 other candidates each won less than 1 per cent. Turnout was 57 per cent.

Parliamentary: Ata-Zhurt (Fatherland) won 16.1 per cent of the vote (28 seats out of 120), Sotsial-Demokraticheskaya Partiya Kyrgyzstana (SDPK) (Social Democratic Party of Kyrgyzstan) 14.55 per cent (26), Ar-Namys (Dignity) 14.02 per cent (25), Respublika (Republican Party) 13.12 per cent (23), Ata-Meken (Fatherland Socialist Party) 5.6 per cent (18); over four other parties failed to win enough votes to win any seats.

Next elections

2015 (parliamentary); 2016 (presidential)

Political parties

Ruling party

Coalition led by Sotsial-Demokraticheskaya Partiya Kyrgyzstana (SDPK) (Social Democratic Party of Kyrgyzstan), with Respublika (Republican Party) and Ata-Zhurt (Fatherland) (from 17 Dec 2010)

Population

5.33 million (2010)*

Last census: March 1999: 4,822,938

Population density: 27 inhabitants per square km (2010)

Annual growth rate: 1.4 per cent 1994–2004 (WHO 2006)

Ethnic make-up

Kyrgyz (54.0 per cent, originally a nomadic people of Turko-Mongolian origin who still dominate in rural areas), Russians (12.0 per cent), Ukrainians (2.5 per cent), Germans (2.0 per cent), Kazakh, Uighurs and others (29.5 per cent).

Religions

Predominantly Muslim (Sunni) (70 per cent of the population). There are also Russian Orthodox and Baptist churches.

Education

Primary education lasts for three years between the ages of seven and 10. Secondary education comprises of compulsory basic secondary (five years) and non-compulsory complete secondary (two years) which gives access to higher education. Vocational education is provided by professional schools which lasts for one-and-a-half years for those with complete secondary education.

There are 51 higher education institutions, of which 26 are run by the government. There are 13 non-governmental and 12 private higher education institutions.

Compulsory years: Seven to 15

Enrolment rate: 104 per cent gross primary enrolment of relevant age group (including repeaters); 79 per cent gross seceondary enrolment (World Bank).

Pupils per teacher: 20 in primary schools.

Health

The healthcare system in Kyrgyzstan continues to be based on practices developed in the Soviet era, which concentrate on primary care and are cost-inefficient. The primary health sector has been supported by international donors, including the International Development Association (IDA), Asian Development Bank (ADB) and the German and Swiss governments, to resist the tide of an overall decline. Primary healthcare has slowly been re-formed, by local people identifying their own needs and devising methods to improve health generally. Despite the best efforts of local committees, a scandal in the hospital system resulted in a known 78 babies and some of their nursing mothers being infected with the HIV virus during to poor hygiene and corrupt practises in 2006. It has been recognised that the millions of dollars spent in international aid in prevention programmes in Kyrgyzstan the health system was of more danger than the disease.

A mandatory medical health insurance fund provides for 70 per cent of the population, covering 65 hospitals and 350 groups of family doctors. In-patient treatment is provided through a system of referrals throughout several levels of the system. Patients are entitled to essential drugs free of charge. Medical equipment supplies only 20 per cent of the needs of medical institutions. Kyrgyzstani clinics and hospitals use outdated equipment, 75 per cent of which needs to be replaced or upgraded. There is a shortage of affordable drugs and vaccines and most of the drugs are imported by small traders who do not conform to strict safety rules.

HIV/Aids

HIV prevalence: 0.1 per cent aged 15–49 in 2003 (World Bank)

Life expectancy: 63 years, 2004 (WHO 2006)

Fertility rate/Maternal mortality rate: 2.6 births per woman, 2004 (WHO 2006); maternal mortality 65 per 100,000 live births (World Bank).

Child (under 5 years) mortality rate (per 1,000): 59 per 1,000 live births; 7 per cent of children aged under five are malnourished (World Bank).

Head of population per physician: 2.51 physicians per 1,000 people, 2003 (WHO 2006)

Welfare

Like many other former Soviet countries, Kyrgyzstan has a large and complex social benefit system. Social spending, including expenditures of the social fund, makes up 28 per cent of the government budget and 7 per cent of GDP. Although the government budget subsidises the social fund, the payroll tax and the total costs of pensions are high. Pensions are often below subsistence level and the government believes that the current pension system is financially unsustainable. It is looking at cutting costs, preferably by reducing the number of beneficiaries, and aims to move to a system with a minimal state pension and a service pension based on payments into a pension insurance scheme.

Around 44.5 per cent of the population live below the poverty line. The aim of the Participatory Poverty Alleviation Programme (PPAP), set up by the UN Development Programme (UNDP), in co-operation with President Akayev's administration, is to reduce poverty in the country by 10 per cent by 2010.

Main cities

Bishkek (formerly Frunze) (capital, estimated population 843,240 in 2005); Osh (207,078).

Languages spoken

Kyrgyz is a Turkic language. Russian is widely spoken, even among ethnic Kyrgyz.

Official language/s

Kyrgyz, Russian

Media

A rise in pressure on the media in recent years from informal government censorship and large fines from legal action for slander has resulted in self-censorship in editorial content and a financial burden on media entities.

Press

Several daily and weekly newspapers include in Russian, *Slovo Kirgyzstana*, *Vecherni Bishkek* (www.vb.kg), *Komsomolskaya Pravda* (KP) (www.kp.kg), *Moya Stoltisa Novosti* (MSN) (www.msn.kg), *Obshchestvennyy Reyting* (www.pr.kg). In English *The Times of Central Asia* (www.timesca-europe.com) with regional news.

Broadcasting

Kyrgyz National TV and Radio Broadcasting Corporation is state-run. The government maintains control of broadcasting through licenses which can be revoked if political comment becomes provoking. Live broadcasts are restricted in what can be reported.

Radio: The state-run Kyrgyz Radio Broadcasting Corporation operates Radio 1 and 21 Vek. Most private stations operate from Bishkek, including AutoRadio, Europa Plus, Radio Max (www.max.kg) Ekho Bishkeka and Russkove Radio.

Television: There Kyrgyz National TV operates two channels. Other private stations include NTS (www.nts.kg), Piramida, Independent Bishkek TV and Broadcasts are in Kyrgyz and Russian. Osh TV is an independent TV company broadcasting in the southern regions of the country mostly in the Uzbek language.

Advertising

There is an active advertising sector using print media and billboards in particular, but services are also available in broadcast media.

News agencies

National news agency: Kabar: http://en.kabar.kg

AKIpress: www.akipress.com

24.Kg: http://eng.24.kg

Economy

As a poor, essentially rural country that relies on exports of its natural resources, when the former Soviet Union collapsed it experienced a severe economic shock as trading links were severed and exports of its natural resources were markedly reduced. However, as trade began to grow again, with Russia and Kazakhstan and other new markets, the economy picked up from 2000 and experienced relatively high GDP growth for a number of years. GDP growth was 7.6 per cent in 2008, falling to 2.9 per cent in 2009 and further still, to -1.4 per cent in 2010. The IMF forecasts that GDP growth will be 6 per cent in 2011.

In October 2009, the governor of the Bank of Kyrgyzstan (BoK) characterised the effect of the global crisis on the economy as having struck in three waves. Beginning in 2007, as global commodity prices rose, Kyrgyzstan was threatened with a severe shortage of foodstuffs, typically imported from other countries, which resulted in a sharp rise in inflation to over 20 per cent in late 2007. In 2008, a steep rise in fuel costs increased inflation to over 30 per cent before falling back to 14.4 per cent in 2009 as oil prices moderated. The current account in 2008 was -US$413 million, rising to US$30 million in 2009, due to increasing exports of gold, strong remittance inflows (30 per cent of GDP in 2008) and increased tourist receipts. However, in 2010, the current account fell again to -US$269 million. The balance of trade narrowed from -US$1.9 billion in 2008 to US$1.1 billion in 2009, before expanding again in 2010 with an estimated -US$1.19 billion.

With its mountainous terrain and plentiful water resources, Kyrgyzstan has the potential to produce and export large quantities of electricity. However, it currently suffers from a shortfall in energy and water, which typically impacts on industrial output.

External trade

Kyrgyzstan is a member of the World Trade Organisation (WTO). It also belongs to the Eurasian Economic Community (EurAsec or EAEC), which was set up in 2000 to promote a customs union between its six member states (Belarus, Kazakhstan, Kyrgyzstan, Russia, Tajikistan and Uzbekistan) and among, other objectives, to introduce standardised currency exchange and rules for trade in goods and service.

Imports

Main imports are food, oil and gas, machinery and equipment, chemicals and foodstuffs.

Main sources: China (typically 40 per cent of total), Russia (20 per cent), Kazakhstan (10 per cent), Turkey (5 per cent)

Exports

Principal exports are primary minerals, including mercury, antimony and rare-earth

metals, chemicals, electricity and engineering goods, paper and timber products, agricultural products including woollens, vegetable oil, rice and meat.
Main destinations: UAE (typically 35 per cent of total), Russia (20 per cent), China (15 per cent), Kazakhstan (10 per cent)

Agriculture

Farming

Agriculture is one of Kyrgyzstan's main sources of wealth, accounting for around 37 per cent of GDP and employing approximately 48 per cent of the labour force.
The total area of agricultural land is 10 million hectares (ha), but only 7 per cent is cultivated.
The main products are tobacco (55,000 tonnes per annum), wool, cotton, leather, silk, meat, grain (especially barley), fruit and vegetables.
Livestock production accounts for about 60 per cent of gross agricultural income.
Kyrgyzstan is the third-largest wool producer in the former Soviet Union. Only 15 per cent is processed locally. Vegetable oil, milk products and baby foods are imported.
There are no price regulations and there is no duty on export products. Since the amendment of the constitution in 1998 to allow for the full private ownership of land, the government has worked on a plan to auction land under the Land Redistribution Fund (which administers about 25 per cent of all arable land) and to implement a scheme to eliminate the state monopoly on seed production.

Fishing

Fishing remains important for domestic consumption, but fish stocks have been drastically reduced by irrigation, pollution and a lack of investment. The typical annual catch is 200million tonnes.

Forestry

Forests cover four per cent of Kyrgyzstan's land area, or 7,000 square km. Conifers account for 40 per cent of forest composition. Almost half of the forests are mature and over-mature stands. All forests are state-owned. Despite commercial potential, there are no significant forest industries, although Kyrgyzstan has a co-operation agreement with Switzerland for forestry development.
The total forested area has remained stable for several decades and could probably absorb higher levels of exploitation. The government aims to increase production, both to meet domestic needs and to export to other Central Asian countries.

Industry and manufacturing

The industrial sector contributes around 21 per cent to GDP, with manufacturing accounting for 13.6 per cent.
Prior to independence, Kyrgyzstan was a significant producer of agricultural machinery, military equipment and medical supplies. Since fundamental manufacturing inputs came from other parts of the former Soviet Union, independence severely impacted upon the size of the industrial base.

Tourism

The geographical remoteness of Kyrgyzstan is an immediate obstacle to growth in the tourist sector, but the country's attractions should encourage international tourist demand. In 2001, the government initiated measures to develop the potentially lucrative tourist sector, but has been slow to build on them. Internal unrest and unsatisfactory infrastructure and services have also impeded significant progress. Despite its immediate shortcomings, Kyrgyzstan tourism should benefit from the country's natural beauty, historical sites and some of the highest mountains in the world.

Environment

The Aral Sea is drying up due to the overuse of water from the two main rivers which feed into it and has lost 40 per cent of its water, dropping by up to 19 metres. This has resulted in desertification of the surrounding land. A UN study published in 2004 reported that there was no possibility of restoring the water and the need must be on preserving what is left.
A meeting was held in April 2009 to determine water sharing between Tajikistan, Kyrgyzstan, Uzbekistan, Turkmenistan and Kazakhstan failed, as negotiators were unable to find a trade in water for energy and hydrocarbons. Tajikistan and Kyrgyzstan hold around 80 per cent of the water in the Aral Sea but suffer from lack of electricity during freezing winters, while the remaining three states downstream are semi-arid and need water for their cotton industries and agriculture.

Mining

Kyrgyzstan has deposits of gold, mercury, antimony, wolfram, tungsten, lead, zinc, uranium, rock salt and gypsum. Uranium oxide and molybdenum are produced at the Kara-Balta combine (Chu Valley). Metallic antimony (7,800 tonnes per year (tpy)) and antimony oxide (6,000 tpy) produced at the Kadamzhay combine (Osh Region), account for 13 per cent of world supply. Mercury is produced at the Khaidarkan combine (Osh Region), accounting for 21 per cent of world output. Kyrgyzstan has impressive reserves of tin and tungsten, which are concentrated in the Sary-Dzhaz river basin, in the east of the country, and have been prospected and prepared for commercial development.
Kyrgyzstan attracts foreign mining and metallurgical companies due to its lax environmental laws. Large mining and metallurgical plants have failed to take into account the hazards of mercury, cyanide, acids and other toxic substances used in the ore refining and enrichment process. This has caused environmental disasters and poses a threat to the health of workers and the local population.
Antimony manufactured at the Kadamzhay combine suffers from high production costs and is unable to compete with relatively cheap antimony available from Chinese producers. Three other undeveloped reserves include Nichkesu (with estimated reserves of 100,000 tonnes), Savoyardy (90,000 tonnes) and Aktyub (30,000 tonnes).
The Russian, Kyrgyzstani and Kazakhstani governments have co-operated to step up the extraction and processing of raw uranium. The state-owned Khaidarkan combine in the Osh region is the only mercury producer in Kyrgyzstan. It is responsible for the improvement of ore enrichment technology and the development of the Novoye deposit, which has a high concentration of mercury, antimony and fluoride.
Most of the gold reserves are concentrated in lode deposits. With substantial deposits in the Talas mountains in the north and the Batken region in the south, together with relatively low production costs, gold is a key export for Kyrgyzstan.
The Kumtor gold mine is one of the 10 largest in the world, accounting for around 30 per cent of exports and 11 per cent of GDP. Kumtor has reserves of 514 tonnes of gold. The mine typically has an annual production of 18.9 tonnes of gold; this level of production will be sustainable until 2010–13. The Kumtor Gold Company, a joint venture between Canada's Cameco and state-owned Kyrgyzaltyn, provides around 95 per cent of Kyrgyzstani gold.

Hydrocarbons

Proven oil reserves were 40 million barrels in 2007, with production a 1,000 barrel per day (bpd). Consumption, however, was 14,000bpd and imports of 13,000bpd were required. The downstream industry consists of one crude oil refinery at Dzhalal-abad, south of Bishkek, which has a capacity of 10,000bpd, although supplies of crude are unreliable and the refinery operates below capacity.
Oil and Natural Gas exploitation has begun in the Naryn Basin in the centre of the country. By 2009 there had been a few descoveries, but any evaluation had yet to be determined.
Proven natural gas reserves were 5.6 billion cubic metres (cum) in 2007, with production at 28 million cum. Consumption was 27 million cum and was made up from imports, mainly from Uzbekistan.
Coal reserves are estimated at 1.3 billion tonnes. There are sizeable coal deposits

in Shurab, Kyzyl-Kiya, Naryn and Kok-Yangak. Further coal could be extracted from the Kara-Keche deposit in the north, but it would need foreign investment to cover the development costs.

Energy

Kyrgyzstan has an electricity generating capacity of 3.72GW. Hydropower account for over 80 per cent of electricity generated. If the country were to utilise its full hydropower potential it could produce 160 billion kilowatt hours (kWh) per year, whereas currently it uses only 10 per cent of this amount. There are 15 hydropower stations, of which five major plants are located on the Naryn River below the Tokogul dam, providing 97 per cent of hydroelectricity. There are two thermal power stations. Another two thermal power plants, with construction begun in 1980 but left incomplete in 1991, are being considered for addition to the production capacity.

The Electric Stations Open Joint Stock Company (OJSC) controls all major power stations and has a monopoly in electrical generation. The National Electric Network operates all power lines. Both companies are government-owned but in 2008 plans were initiated to privatise the hydro power plants.

A report in February 2009 by Eucam (EU Central Asia Monitoring) highlighted the energy emergency facing Kyrgyzstan. The country is reliant on hydropower but the 'outdated' and 'barely functioning' energy infrastructure is faced with collapse following the recent cycles of drought and harsh winters. The lack of energy threatens food security and could destabilise the country through social upheaval.

Kyrgyzstan has the second largest water resource in Central Asia and conflicts have arisen over the water taken for hydropower which is also vital downstream in neighbouring countries.

Financial markets

Stock exchange

Kyrgyz Stock Exchange (KSE)

Banking and insurance

During the final years of the Soviet Union, the banking sector was one of the first economic activities to be liberalised.

Upon independence in 1991, Kyrgyzstan had a large number of small banks, many of which offered limited services and had poor ratios of reserves to deposits. Of the Central Asian countries, Kyrgyzstan has made the best progress towards tighter regulation and supervision of banks, although it continues to fall short of the progress made by the Baltic states and Eastern European countries.

Kyrgyzstan adopted the Basle capital requirements in 1995, since when the minimum capital requirement has been increased in stages. As regulation of the system has tightened, so the number of banks has fallen. Simultaneously, privatisation has progressed in Kyrgyzstan to the extent that less than 10 per cent of the banking market is controlled by state banks. Furthermore, 16–17 per cent of the market is controlled by the three foreign banks with a presence in the country. The largest investment bank is the Kairat Bank.

The Law on Banks and Banking Activity, enacted in 2003, strengthened the regulatory powers of the central bank to ensure good management and corporate governance in banks, improve financial disclosure, and control insider dealing.

Central bank

National Bank of the Kyrgyz Rebublic

Time

GMT plus five hours

Geography

Kyrgyzstan is a relatively small, landlocked country situated in eastern central Asia. There are border crossings with the People's Republic of China to the east and south-east, Kazakhstan to the north, Tajikistan to the south and south-west and Uzbekistan to the west.

The Tian Shan mountains, with glaciers, fast flowing rivers and deep lakes, account for most of the country's high alpine terrain, except for the eastern edge of the steppe bordering Kazakhstan and the fertile Osh Valley to the west. Lake Issyk-Kul in the north-east of the country is the second deepest crater lake in the world.

Hemisphere

Northern

Climate

Temperature varies from the temperate steppe to sub-zero temperatures in the mountains (Bishkek: minus 5–35 degrees Celsius). Depending on terrain, annual rainfall varies from 170mm and 265mm.

Dress codes

Dress in the business community is informal, European style.

Entry requirements

Passports

Passports are required by all and must be valid for a minimum of six months at the time of entry.

Visa

Required by all except some nationals of former communist states. For tourist purposes, it is advisable to obtain visas in advance even though some nationals can obtain a visa on arrival, without a letter of invitation.

For most visitors tourist and business visas require an invitation from a local sponsor or company or government organisation. Business visas require confirmation of the contacts to be met and their business addresses and telephone numbers. These should be submitted to the issuing embassy, along with a business letter from the employer giving an account of the visitor's position and role within the foreign company, and full itinerary with purpose of visit and length of stay. For individual business travellers, visa support is required from the Ministry of Foreign Affairs. More information should be gathered from the nearest consulate.

CIS transit visas are no longer valid to enter neighbouring countries; a visa for each state should be obtained in advance.

Currency advice/regulations

Only Kyrgyz residents may import and export local currency.

The import of foreign currency is unlimited but must be declared; export is limited to the amount declared.

Travellers cheques, in US dollars, have limited acceptance in banks in the capital.

Customs

A customs declaration form is issued on arrival and must be surrendered on departure; declare all foreign currency and valuable items such as jewellery, cameras, computers, etc.

Prohibited imports

Illegal drugs, precious metals and artefacts, fur, fruit and vegetables and printed material, including photographs, which are detrimental to Kyrgyzstan.

Firearms, ammunition, works of art and antiques and live animals are subject to special permits.

Health (for visitors)

A reciprocal health agreement for urgent medical treatment exists with the UK. Proof of UK residence will be required.

Mandatory precautions

Vaccination certificates are required for yellow fever if travelling from an infected area.

Advisable precautions

Water precautions are recommended: water purification tablets may be useful or drink bottled water. It is advisable to be in date for the following immunisations: polio (within 10 years), tetanus (within 10 years), typhoid fever, tuberculosis, hepatitis A (moderate risk only), hepatitis B, tick-borne encephalitis.

Any medicines required by the traveller should be stocked by the visitor, and it would be wise to have precautionary antibiotics if going outside major urban centres. A travel kit including a disposable syringe is a reasonable precaution. There is a risk of rabies.

Hotels

It is advisable to book in advance through specialist travel agents. Tips are becoming customary.

Credit cards
Credit cards are accepted in larger hotels and banks in Bishkek.

Public holidays (national)
Fixed dates
1 Jan (New Year's Day), 7 Jan (Orthodox Christmas Day), 8 Mar (Women's Day), 21 Mar (Noruz/Persian New Year), 24 Mar (National Day), 1 May (Labour Day), 5 May (Constitution Day), 9 May (Victory Day), 31 Aug (Independence Day), 7 Nov (Socialist Revolution Day).
Variable dates
Eid al Adha, Eid al Fitr.
Islamic year 1433 (26 Nov 2011–14 Nov 2012): The Islamic year contains 354 or 355 days, with the result that Muslim feasts advance by 10–12 days against the Gregorian calendar. Dates of feast vary according to the sighting of the new moon, so cannot be forecast exactly.

Working hours
Banking
Mon–Fri: 0930–1730.
Business
Mon–Fri: 0900–1800.
Government
Mon–Fri: 0900–1800.
Shops
Mon–Fri: 0900–1700.

Telecommunications
Mobile/cell phones
GSM 900 and 1800 services are available in populated areas only.

Electricity supply
220V AC

Social customs/useful tips
There are many customs and traditions to be understood. Alcohol is available and smoking is widespread. Gratuities are becoming more customary, particularly in international hotels.

Security
Western nationals have been advised to be vigilant if staying in Kyrgyzstan. Close proximity to Afghanistan and the presence of Western troops in the country could make foreign travellers a target of Islamic rebels. Travellers have been particularly advised to stay away from the southern provincial capital of Osh and especially the surrounding area.
It is unwise to venture out on the streets alone at night. Keep expensive jewellery, watches, cameras, etc, out of sight. Avoid parks at night and use registered taxis only.

Getting there
Air
National airline: Kyrgyz Aba Zholdoru (Kyrgyzstan Airlines)
International airport/s: Bishkek-Manas airport (FRU), 30km north of city, *bureau de change*, duty-free shops, post office, restaurants.
Almaty International Airport (ALA), 10km north-east of the city. Facilities include VIP lounge, car hire, duty-free shops, restaurant and post office.
Airport tax: US$10
Surface
Road: There are roads and border crossings with China, Kazakhstan, Tajikistan and Uzbekistan. Roads can be hazardous in winter. The border crossings in the south-west of the country are considered insecure due to the activity by Islamic rebels.
The Regional Road Corridor Improvement Project, estimated at US$18 billion, to improve Central Asian roads, airports, railway lines and seaports and provide a vital transit route between Europe and Asia was agreed, on 3 November 2007. Six new transit corridors, between Afghanistan, Azerbaijan, China, Kazakhstan, Kyrgyzstan, Mongolia, Tajikistan and Uzbekistan, of mainly roads and rail links, will be constructed, or existing resources upgraded, by 2013. Half the costs with be provided by the Asian Development Bank and other multilateral organisations and the other half by participating countries.
Rail: Bishkek is linked by rail to Central Asia's transport hub, Tashkent, in Uzbekistan.

Getting about
National transport
Air: Kyrgyz Aba Zholdoru operates domestic services. There are regular flights from Bishkek to Osh.
Road: There are 21,000km of roads, only about 50 per cent of which are in reasonable condition. Travel by road is generally difficult because of the terrain and in spring, landslides are common in mountain areas, especially around Osh. Travel by horseback in the mountains. There are few garage facilities on the main roads to and from Bishkek. Care should be taken when travelling by road, especially if a breakdown is involved. Driving during the winter months in private vehicles can be hazardous and some routes could be closed at times. Taxis and private drivers are often willing to provide inter-city services at reasonable prices.
Buses: There are regular and convenient bus services between major towns and cities.
Rail: The only line in use for passenger services is the 340km line in the north of the country, which connects to the Kazakhstani border at both ends and passes through Bishkek. The service is unreliable and is not widely used.
City transport
Taxis: Few taxis have meters and a price should be agreed beforehand. It is sometimes possible to hire private cars, but visitors are recommended to travel only in official taxis.
Buses, trams & metro: Cheap trolley-buses. Service 153 from Bishkek-Manas airport to city centre, every 15 minutes.
Car hire
A national licence with authorised translation or an international driving permit is required. A rented car is often accompanied by a driver.

BUSINESS DIRECTORY

The addresses listed below are a selection only. While World of Information makes every endeavour to check these addresses, we cannot guarantee that changes have not been made, especially to telephone numbers and area codes. We would welcome any corrections.

Telephone area codes
The international direct dialling (IDD) code for Kyrgyzstan is +996, followed by area code and customer's number:

Bishkek	312	Osh	322

Useful telephone numbers
Fire: 101
Police: 102
Ambulance (free): 103
Ambulance (private): 151

Chambers of Commerce
Bishkek Chamber of Commerce, Industry and Hanicraft, 539 Jibek-Jolu, Bishkek (tel: 670-113; fax: 660-048; e-mail: bishkekchamber@netmail.kg).

Kyrgyzstan Chamber of Commerce and Industry, 107 Kievskaya Street, Bishkek 720001 (tel: 210-565; fax: 210-575; e-mail: cci-kr@imfiko.bishkek.su).

Banking
Bakai, 75 Isanov Street, Bishkek 720001 (tel: 660-610; 660-612; e-mail:bank@bakai.kg).

Demir Kyrgyz International, 245 Chui Boulevard, Bishkek 720040 (tel: 610-610; fax: 610-444; e-mail: dkib@demirbank.com.kg).

Eridan, 57 Kalyk-Akieva Street, Bishkek 720001 (tel: 650-610; fax: 650-654; e-mail: eridanbank@infotel.kg).

Kairat, 390 Frunze Street, Bishkek 720033 (tel: 218-932; fax: 218-955; e-mail: kairat@kairatbank.kg).

Kurulush, 28 Manas Street, Bishkek 720391 (tel: 219-736; fax: 219-743; e-mail: kurulush@bank.kg).

Kyrgyzstan, 54 Togolok Moldo Street, Bishkek 720001 (tel: 219-598; fax: 610-220; e-mail: akb@elcat.kg).

Central bank
National Bank of Kyrgyz Republic, 101 Umetalieva St, 720040 Bishkek (tel:

669-011; fax: 669-176; internet: www.nbkr.kg).

Stock exchange

Kyrgyz Stock Exchange (KSE): www.kse.kg

Travel information

Airport 'Manas', Bishkek 720062 (tel: 313-593; fax: 313-040; e-mail: manas@ch2m.bishkek.su).

AKC Kyrgyz Concept, 1000 Razzakova Street, Bishkek 720001 (tel 210-556; fax: 660-220; e-mail: akc@mail.elcat.kg).

Kyrgyzstan Aba Joldoru (national airline), Airport 'Manas', Bishkek 720062 (tel: 257-755; fax: 257-162; e-mail: mana@ch2m.bishkek.su).

Kyrgyzstan Airlines (domestic services), Airport 'Manas', Bishkek 720062 (tel: 696-600).

National tourist organisation offices

Kyrgyz State Agency for Tourism and Sport, 17 Togolok Moldo Street, Bishkek 720033 (tel: 220-657; fax: 212-845).

Ministries

Ministry of Agriculture and Water Resources, 96a Kievskaya Street, Bishkek 720040 (tel: 221-435; fax: 226-784).

Ministry of Environmental Protection, 131 Isanova Street, Bishkek 720033 (tel: 219-737; fax: 216-763).

Ministry of Finance, 58 Erkindik Boulevard, Bishkek 720002 (tel: 228-922; fax: 227-404, 620-955).

Ministry of Foreign Affairs, 59 Razzakopva Street, Bishkek 720040 (tel: 220-545; fax: 263-639).

Ministry of Foreign Trade and Industry, 106 Chui Boulevard, Bishkek 720002 (tel: 223-866; fax: 220-793, 252-747).

Ministry of Justice, 37 Orozbekova Street, Bishkek 720040 (tel: 228-489; fax: 261-115).

Ministry of Transport and Telecommunications, Isanova Street, Bishkek 720017 (tel: 216-672; fax: 213-667).

Other useful addresses

British Embassy, 173 Furmanova Street, Alma Ata, Kazakhstan (accredited to Kyrgyzstan) (tel: (7-3272) 506-191; fax: (7-3272) 506-260).

Free Economic Zone General Directorate, 303 Manas Street, Bishkek 720026 (tel: 670-511; fax: 670-512).

Goskominvest (State Committee on Foreign Investments and Economic Co-operation), 58A Erkindik Boulevard, Bishkek 720002 (tel: 223-292; fax: 620-017; e-mail:satc@imfiko.bishkek.su).

Kyrgyzstan Embassy (USA), 1732 Wisconsin Avenue, NW, Washington DC 20007 (tel: (+1-202) 338-5141; fax: (+1-202) 338-5139; e-mail: embassy@kyrgyzstan.org).

Kyrgyzvneshtorg (Foreign Trade Association), 276 Abdymomunova Street, Bishkek 720033 (tel: 215-701; fax: 620-836).

National Statistical Committee of the Kyrgyz Republic, 374 Frunze Street, Bishkek 720033 (tel: 226-363; fax: 220-759; e-mail: zkudabaev@nsc.bishkek.su).

State Property Fund, 57 Erkindik Boulevard, Bishkek 720002, (tel: 227-706; fax: 660-236; e-mail: spf@imfiko.bishkek.su).

Stock Exchange, 172 Moskvskaya Street, Bishkek 720010 (tel:665-059; fax: 661-595; e-mail: kse@kse.kg).

US Embassy, 171 Mira Boulevard, Bishkek 720016 (tel: 551-241; fax: 551-264; e-mail: mukambaevaibx@state.gov).

National news agency: Kabar: http://en.kabar.kg

Internet sites

The Times of Central Asia: http://www.times.kg

Government of Kyrgyzstan (list of departments in Cyrillic script, email addresses in Latin script): http://kenesh.bishkek.gov.kg/

Laos

KEY FACTS

Official name: Saathiaranarath Prachhathipatay Prachhachhon Lao (Lao People's Democratic Republic)

Head of State: President Choummaly Sayasone (since Jun 2006; re-elected 15 Jun 2011)

Head of government: Prime Minister Thongsing Thammavong (from 23 Dec 2010; re-elected 15 Jun 2011)

Ruling party: Phak Paxaxôn Pativat Lao (Lao People's Revolutionary Party) (LPRP) (since 1975; re-elected 30 April 2011)

Area: 236,800 square km

Population: 6.31 million (2010)*

Capital: Vientiane

Official language: Lao (English is the business language of the Lao government)

Currency: New kip (Nk) = 100 at

Exchange rate: Nk7,980.00 per US$ (Oct 2011)

GDP per capita: US$984 (2010)

GDP real growth: 7.70% (2010)

GDP: US$6.30 billion (2010)

Inflation: 5.40% (2010)

Balance of trade: -US$407.80 million (2009)

* Estimated figure

In late December 2010 Laos announced that it had a new prime minister after the surprise resignation of Bouasone Bouphavanh. Mr Bouasone, 56, who had spent more than four years in office, is replaced by Thongsing Thammavong in the communist-dominated Sapha Heng Xat (National Assembly). After accepting the resignation of Mr Bouasone, the National Assembly unanimously voted Mr Thongsing Thammavong in as the new prime minister. Mr Bouasone referred to 'family issues' as the reason for his resignation but rumours suggested that the reasons for his resignation were more likely to be internal factional re-alignments. A government spokesman announced that Mr Bouasone would remain a member of the central committee of the Phak Paxaxôn Pativat Lao (Lao People's Revolutionary Party) (LPRP), which holds a near monopoly on power. Unsurprisingly, the new prime minister was approved unanimously by the National Assembly's 101 members present.

Careful choreography

Political shifts are carefully choreographed in the People's Democratic Republic of Laos, a large but underpopulated, land-locked state bordering Vietnam, China and Thailand. Quoted by the BBC in London, Damien Kingsbury, chair professor in the School of International and Political Studies at Deakin University in Melbourne, Australia took the view that 'sifting the tea leaves, this is a shift in the internal factional alignments, a shifting in the balance of power within the politburo. It is certainly not transparent, but it happens from time to time.' Professor Kingsbury went on to say that there was unlikely to be any major shift in policy as a result of the change in leadership, adding that China's growing prominence in the country was likely to continue. China has made huge investments in Laos, building roads and agricultural and industrial estates across the country, which has long been politically close to Vietnam. A high-speed railway is planned to run from China to Laos.

The tea leaves shift again

The Ninth Congress of the LPRP, held in March 2011, dropped former prime minister, Bouasone Bouphavanh, from both the Politburo and the Central Committee. On the other hand, his successor, Thongsing Thammavong, was elevated to number two in the politburo, behind General Secretary Choummaly Sayasone.

Elections

Some three million Laotians went to the polls at the end of April 2011 to elect a new National Assembly. No real surprises here, as it was common knowledge before a vote was cast that the whole show was controlled by the ruling communist party. 190 candidates had already been through a rigorous selection process before being able to stand for election. The candidates were 'competing' for 132 seats.

Very much in the manner of Pyongyang (North Korea), government announcements of the results were similarly stage-managed, praising the 'joyful atmosphere' of the elections and congratulating the 'multi-ethnic' character of the electorate. The government's self congratulation sat uncomfortably with the general awareness that Laos is a country where no opposition is tolerated and even peaceful displays of dissent or criticism are harshly suppressed.

Official sources also announced that 99.6 per cent of the electorate had taken part in the elections (3.23 million out of 3.24 million registered voters). Voting is compulsory in Laos. A visiting Australian academic described the situation thus : 'Everything is decided in secret by the Communist Party's hierarchy. Even subjects debated in parliament have already been decided by the party.' For the record, of the 132 seats, only four were not taken by the Communist Party. The number of female deputies was unchanged (25 per cent of seats). Ethnic minorities were allocated 51 seats – 9 per cent were from the Khmu community (12 seats) and only 5.3 per cent (7 deputies) were from the Hmong community (see below).

There exist those observers who optimistically consider that the National Assembly has made some progress in recent years, going from its traditional rubber stamp role to intervening with modifications to laws pasing through the Assembly. However, the Assembly is unable to decide on anything without the prior approval of the Party. In true Soviet style, real political power lies with the 61 member Central Committee and 10 man Political Bureau (politburo) the latter headed up by the conservative General President Choummaly Sayasone holding the 'number one' position in the régime. These two powerful vestiges of the Soviet-style system were adopted after the Pathet Lao takeover in 1975.

Few outside the inner sanctum really understand the political scene, but it is accepted that the LPRP is loosely split between an older, more conservative guard and younger members pushing for limited reform. Cynical observers note that the infighting is mainly for the control of the lucrative kickbacks available to those who control the rights to Laos's rich natural resources. Others say the reformers' primary motivation is to alleviate poverty more quickly by speeding up development. The reality most likely lies somewhere in-between.

The Hmong

Outside Laos, little is known about the ethnic Hmong people and even less about those rumoured to be fighting a low-level war against the Lao government. But according to BBC reports, what seems certain, is that many of the Hmong in Laos have a poor standard of living and often feel marginalised by the authorities. Human rights group Forum Asia describe a 'fault line which separates the Hmong from the rest of the population. They are treated like traitors by the authorities and are blamed for siding with the foreign imperialists.' The origins of the problem stem from the Vietnam War, when large numbers of ethnic Hmong sided with the United States army, as the conflict spread from Vietnam into neighbouring Laos and Cambodia. The Hmong became an integral part of a secret CIA-trained militia that helped dismantle communist supply lines. But at the end of the war, the US government abruptly stopped its support for the Hmong. Things worsened for the Hmong when, in 1975, the communist Pathet Lao Movement ousted the US-backed Lao royal family and took control of the country.

Fearing the worst, as many as a third of the Hmong population are thought to have left Laos. Many settled in the United States, while others went to Thailand, Vietnam, France and Australia. But the 300,000 left in Laos have had to deal with the consequences of backing the losing side.

KEY INDICATORS — Laos

	Unit	2006	2007	2008	2009	2010
Population	m	6.03	6.14	6.26	6.38	*6.31
Gross domestic product (GDP)	US$bn	3.46	4.30	5.30	5.60	6.30
GDP per capita	US$	594	696	856	878	984
GDP real growth	%	8.1	7.5	7.2	7.6	7.9
Inflation	%	6.8	4.5	7.6	0.0	6.0
Industrial output	% change	16.5	2.9	8.2	–	–
Agricultural output	% change	2.0	8.4	3.7	–	–
Exports (fob) (goods)	US$m	996.0	922.7	*16.4	*107.0	–
Imports (fob) (goods)	US$m	1,384.0	1,064.7	*28.2	*1,430.0	–
Balance of trade	US$m	-388.0	-142.0	*-11.8	*-1,323.0	–
Current account	US$m	-367.0	-107.3	*-887.0	-921.0	-647.0
Total reserves minus gold	US$m	328.4	532.6	628.7	702.5	706.4
Foreign exchange	US$m	313.7	517.1	613.6	622.5	624.7
Exchange rate	per US$	9,721.00	9,401.50	8,744.10	8,516.00	8,258.80

* estimated figure

According to Forum Asia, the Lao government often accuses the Hmong of being the cause of many of the country's problems, such as the high levels of deforestation and widespread cultivation of opium. But many Hmong are also being forced to relocate from their highland homes to areas with poor agricultural potential. Amnesty International has claimed that Hmong people in detention were often treated unfavourably compared with other prisoners.

There are, however, signs that the Hmong are fighting back. Over the last few decades, there have been persistent rumours of Hmong rebel fighters living in remote jungle areas. It is very difficult to get accurate information about the number of rebels in Laos, or the activities they are engaged in, but diplomatic sources have said that the Lao authorities believe the rebels are behind a spate of recent ambush attacks on buses in the region. The government has found it difficult to blame the Hmong for the attacks, as this would imply the authorities were no longer in control of the situation. The attacks are instead blamed on 'bandits' or 'bad people'.

The economy

In recent years the biggest development catalyst came when China started spending some of its enormous surplus in Laos. Apart from the obvious investment in infrastructure such as roads, dams and plantations, there have been two significant effects. First, Chinese aid comes with few strings attached, meaning for example that roads, plantations and dams are built by Chinese companies with little or no concern for local people or environments. Significant reform appears not to be on the Lao government's agenda, but emulating China certainly will not help get it there.

After decelerating a little during the global recession, economic growth picked up to 7.5 per cent in 2010, returning to the average expansion rate for 2004–08. According to the Asian Development Bank (ADB), this prolonged period of growth mainly reflects substantial investment in mining and hydropower. Industry, representing about one-quarter of gross domestic product (GDP), grew by 18.0 per cent in 2010 and contributed most of the growth. Output of electricity more than doubled when the Nam Theun 2 hydropower plant, the biggest in the country at 1,070 megawatts, had reached full capacity in April 2010. Some smaller new plants also started generating power. Most of their output is exported to Thailand.

Mining production rose by 19.0 per cent in 2010, spurred by higher global metal prices. Output of copper from the two main mines rose by 21.0 per cent to 147,500 tons. Gold production rose by 7.0 per cent to 173,000 ounces and silver by 13.5 per cent to about 500,000 ounces. Construction activity benefited from expansionary fiscal moves while the global recovery in travel lifted the number of tourists by about 25 per cent to 2.5 million in 2010, after a strong rebound in tourism from Europe and the United States. This increase in visitors lead to growth of 6.0 per cent in the hotel and restaurant industry. Other services to grow by at least 6 per cent were financial services, wholesale and retail trading and transport and communications (boosted by the introduction of third-generation mobile telephone and Internet services). The services sector as a whole grew by 5.0 per cent.

Agriculture, in contrast, which accounts for a third of GDP but employs about three-fifths of the workforce, suffered from bad weather (droughts followed by floods) as well as from diseases in pigs and cattle. Production of rice, the main crop, increased by about 4 per cent to 3.26 million tons and fisheries recorded solid growth of 7.0 per cent. The sector as a whole, though, grew by just 2.0 per cent.

Consumer prices rose in 2010, pushing annual inflation to 6.0 per cent. Higher global oil prices pushed up the cost of fuel and transport and bad weather and animal diseases disrupted food supplies, raising food prices. Strengthening domestic demand, the rollout of a value-added tax from April 2010 and growth in credit also fuelled inflation. Bank credit expanded by 46 per cent over the year, moderating from over 80 per cent, in 2008 and 2009. Moving to counter inflation pressures, the Banque de la RDP Lao (Bank of Lao PDR) in September 2010 raised the interest rate, from 4.0 per cent to 5.0 per cent for loans of less than one week. It phased out direct lending for off-budget infrastructure projects, which had been a cause of high rates of growth in credit. Disbursement of central bank lending committed in 2009 continued to feed credit growth.

Strong growth in government revenue, in part a result of high global prices for copper and gold, helped to rein in the budget deficit in the 2010 fiscal year (which ended on 30 September 2010). Growth in spending moderated relative to 2009, when the government had lifted outlays to cushion the impact of the global recession. The budget deficit, including grants but excluding off-budget spending, narrowed to an estimated 3 per cent of GDP from 5.1 per cent in 2009. Including off-budget spending, it was close to 5 per cent.

Higher metal production and prices helped raise the US dollar value of merchandise exports by an estimated 30 per cent to US$1.9 billion in 2010. Mineral exports exceeded US$1 billion for the first time and electricity exports rose to US$375 million. Shipments of clothing increased in value by about 14 per cent to US$184 million, mainly on better demand from Japan and the Republic of Korea.

Merchandise imports rose by an estimated 13.5 per cent to US$2.8 billion. The trade and current account deficits narrowed, the latter to an estimated 9 per cent of GDP from 12 per cent in 2009. After accounting for capital inflows, gross international reserves climbed to US$727 million at end-2010, sufficient for about 3.5 months of imports.

The government's Seventh Socio-Economic Development Plan (2011–15) strongly emphasises growth, targeting annual average GDP expansion of 8 per cent and moving the country from least developed country (LDC) status by 2020. Scheduled hydropower and mining activity in 2011 and 2012 will underpin growth. Nam Theun 2 will contribute to GDP for a full year from this year and another relatively large new plant, Nam Ngum 2 (615 megawatts) was expected to be running at full capacity from April 2011. Construction is set to start on a Nam Ngum 3 plant by mid-year.

Services and construction are expected to maintain solid growth, bolstered by expansion of domestic demand and of tourism. Export orders suggest that clothing shipments will increase by about 10 per cent in 2011. Agriculture is expected to return to trend growth of about 2 per cent, if weather permits. Taking these factors into account, the ADB expects GDP growth to edge higher to 7.7 per cent in 2011 and to 7.8 per cent in 2012.

Risk assessment

Economy	Good
Politics	Poor
Regional stability	Good

COUNTRY PROFILE

Historical profile

Between the fourth and eighth centuries, communities along the Mekong River began to form into townships, called muang. 1353 This development culminated in the formation of the Lane Xang (the million elephants) Kingdom by King FaNgum and established Xieng Thong, now known as Luang Prabang as capital of Lane Xang Kingdom.

1548–71 During the reign of King Setthathirat, the capital was moved to Vientiane. During this period the That Luang Stupa, a venerated religious shrine and a temple to house the Phra Keo, the Emerald Buddha, were constructed.
1641 A Dutch merchant of the East India Company, Geritt Van Wuysthoff established the first European contact with the Kingdom. Later, Italian missionaries visited.
1893 Laos was put under French administration.
1945 Laos was briefly occupied by the Japanese towards the end of the Second World War.
1950 Laos was granted semi-autonomy as an associated state within the French union.
1954 Laos gained independence and became a constitutional monarchy. Civil war began between monarchists and communists of the Pathet Lao.
1960s Laos was subjected to intensive bombing by the US in its war against the North Vietnamese in one of the worst aerial bombardments in world history.
1973 The Vientiane cease-fire agreement led to renewed divisions between royalists and communists.
1975 The Pathet Lao (the Lao Communist movement) won the civil war. The Lao People's Democratic Republic (LDPR) was proclaimed by a National Congress of People's Representatives. Pathet Lao was renamed the Lao People's Revolutionary Party (LPRP), which became the sole legal political party. Kaysone Phomvihane was appointed prime minister and began a policy of socialist transformation of the economy.
1979 The government modified its approach following widespread food shortages and an exodus of Laotian refugees to Thailand.
1986 Laos introduced market reforms, encouraged by Soviet leader Mikhail Gorbachev.
1989 The first elections since 1975 were held, although all candidates had to be vetted by the LPRP. The LPRP retained power.
1991 A security and co-operation pact was signed with Thailand. A new constitution was promulgated. Kaysone Phomvihane became president and General Khamtai Siphandon became prime minister.
1992 President Phomvihane died. Siphandon became head of the LPRP.
1995 A 20-year aid embargo was lifted by the US.
1997 Laos became a member of the Association of Southeast Asian Nations (Asean). The Asian financial crisis undermined the value of the kip.
1998 Khamtai Siphandon became president.
2000 Anti-government demonstrations erupted and a series of terrorists bomb blasts killed over a dozen people. Laos celebrated 25 years of communist rule in December.
2001 Boungnang Vorachith was appointed prime minister and Khamtai was re-elected president. The death penalty was introduced for the possession of more than 500 grams of heroin. The UN's World Food Programme (WFP) launched a three-year programme to feed 70,000 malnourished children in Laos.
2002 The LPRP was re-elected; Khamtai Siphandon was re-elected president.
2003 As part of reforms pledged to foreign donors in 2000, Laos' one-party parliament began a process of amending its constitution, to decentralise power.
2005 The World Bank approved funds for the construction of the US$1.2 billion Nam Theun Two hydroelectric dam. According to a UN report, the poppy crop in Laos has been reduced by 73 per cent since 1998 and the number of opium addicts has fallen by 42,000 to 21,000.
2006 President of the ruling LPRP Khamtay Siphandone resigned and was succeeded by Choummaly Sayasone; Bouasone Bouphavanh was appointed prime minister. A new bridge was opened across the Mekong River in the central region of Savannakhet.
2007 Former General Vang Pao, a leader among the ethnic Hmong people was arrested in the US, accused of planning a coup to overthrow the Lao government. The Hmong people backed the US in the Vietnam War during the 1960s and aid agencies in the region have reported that they have been subjected to human right's abuses since then.
2008 The government confirmed plans to increase the area of forest to 18.7 million hectares. Deforestation has reduced natural forests from 41 per cent of the country in 2002 to 35 per cent in 2008, due to changes in agriculture, hydroelectric projects, mining and illegal logging.
2009 A rail link was established between Thailand and Laos with a freight and passenger service officially opened.
2010 In January, a ministerial conference of 13 countries in the south-east Asian region, including Laos, discussed conservation and co-ordinated measures, with targets set to boost the numbers needed to protect the indigenous wild tiger from extinction. Laos held the first official international convention on cluster munitions between 9–12 November in Vientiane. Delegates from governments, the UN and non-governmental agencies as well as survivors of such bombs discussed a treaty on clearance and limited use. Prime Minister Bouasone Bouphavanh resigned on 23 December and parliament elected Thongsing Thammavong as his replacement. The new Lao Securities Exchange Market building was opened on 29 December.
2011 In parliamentary elections held on 30 April the LPRP won 131 seats (out of 132), five independent candidates were allowed to stand and one won the remaining seat. The number of members of parliament (MPs) had increased by 17, due to the rise in population. A decision, by the four-country Mekong River Commission, to implement plans to build the controversial Mekong Xayaburi dam in Laos was due to be taken on 19 April, but following ecologically and socially adverse reports the decision was postponed. The Mekong River is a food source for millions of people along its length; the dam would reduce food production in favour of electricity production. On 15 June, President Choummaly Sayasone and Prime Minister Thammavong were re-elected by parliament.

Political structure

Constitution

The first constitution was endorsed in August 1991, enshrining the single-party rule of the Lao People's Revolutionary Party (LPRP).
The country is divided into provinces, municipalities, districts and villages. Each of these has a local administrative structure that is subject to the laws and policies of the national government.
Laos' one-party parliament is in the process of amending its constitution in a move towards decentralisation.

Independence date

12 October 1954

The executive

The president, elected by the National Assembly every five years, is the head of state.
The head of government is the prime minister, who is appointed by the president. The Council of Ministers is also appointed by the president.

National legislature

The unicameral Sapha Heng Xat (National Assembly) has 115 members, directly elected for a five-year term.

Last elections

30 April 2011 (parliamentary); June 2011 (presidential, indirect)
Results: Parliamentary: Phak Paxaxôn Pativat Lao (Lao People's Revolutionary Party) (LPRP) (the only legal party allowed) won 131 seats (out of 132), five independent candidates were allowed to stand and one won the remaining a seat.
Presidential: parliament re-elected Choummaly Sayasone, unopposed.

Next elections
2016 (parliamentary and presidential)

Political parties
Effective political power is exercised by the leadership of the sole legal political organisation, the Lao People's Revolutionary Party (LPRP).
Ruling party
Phak Paxaxôn Pativat Lao (Lao People's Revolutionary Party) (LPRP) (since 1975; re-elected 30 April 2011)

Population
6.31 million (2010)*
Last census: 1 March 2005: 5,621,982
Population density: 26 inhabitants per square km (2010)
Annual growth rate: 2.4 per cent 1994–2004 (WHO 2006)
Ethnic make-up
There are three main ethnic groups: the Lao Loum (lowlanders), the Lao Theung (semi-nomadic people who live mainly on the mountain slopes) and the Lao Soung (hill tribes and minority elements).
Religions
The Lao Theung and the Lao Soung are animist, but the great majority of Lao are Theravada Buddhists; there are some Christians.

Education
Nearly 60 per cent of teachers in primary and secondary schools are underqualified.
Secondary education starts at the age of 11 and is divided into three-year lower secondary school and three-year upper secondary school. Higher education is provided by the National University of Laos, which has merged with 10 higher education institutions located in Vientiane. There are also higher technical institutes and teacher training colleges.
Public expenditure on education typically amounts to 2.1 per cent of annual gross national income. In 2001, the Asian Development Bank approved a US$20 million loan to support a project partly that will enable over 550,000 children, especially girls and ethnic minorities to receive better primary education. The government is expected to fund the balance with the help of other international donors and complete the project by end-2007./10/04
Literacy rate: 66 per cent adult rate; 79 per cent youth rate (15–24) (Unesco 2005).
Compulsory years: Primary education is compulsory between the ages of six and 11.
Enrolment rate: 112 per cent gross primary enrolment of the relevant age group (including repeaters); 29 per cent gross secondary enrolment (World Bank).
Pupils per teacher: 30 in primary schools.

Health
Laos had one of the highest rates of maternal deaths in 2010, at 1 death per 33 births, due largely to a lack of skilled healthcare workers and emergency obstetric services. In a measure to reduce the rate the authorities, with the backing of the UN Population Fund, re-introduced midwifery training courses that were stopped in 1987. It also agreed that affordable and reliable antenatal services were needed and would be introduced in due course.
Improved water sources and sanitation facilities are available to 90 per cent and 46 per cent of the population, respectively.
HIV/Aids
HIV/Aids infection is one of the major public health challenges in the country, affecting almost all provinces and populations and is expected to triple in the next 20 years, unless preventive measures are undertaken.
HIV prevalence: 0.1 per cent aged 15–49 in 2003 (World Bank)
Life expectancy: 59 years, 2004 (WHO 2006)
Fertility rate/Maternal mortality rate: 4.7 births per woman, 2004 (WHO 2006); maternal mortality 650 per 100,000 live births (World Bank).
Child (under 5 years) mortality rate (per 1,000): 82 deaths per 1,000 live births; 40 per cent of children under aged five are malnourished (World Bank).

Welfare
About 40 per cent of the population live in poverty. The country is covered under the Asian Development Bank (ADB's) poverty reduction strategy that focusses on rural development, regional integration, human resource development, sustainable environmental management and private sector development. To achieve this, the ADB has lent Lao PDR about US$45—55 million annually on concessional terms for the period 2002–04, in addition to other technical assistance grants. Another US$1 million grant is provided by the Japan Fund for Poverty Reduction to help the landless poor increase their participation in farm-based production.

Main cities
Viangchan (Vientiane) (capital, estimated population 287,579 in 2005), Savannakhet (155,974), Louangphrabang (110,380).

Languages spoken
The adopted business language of the Lao government is English. Widely spoken languages other than Lao are: Thai, English, Vietnamese, Chinese, Russian, German, and to a much lesser extent, French; plus tribal languages.

Official language/s
Lao (English is the business language of the Lao government)

Media
Press
Dailies: In Lao, the *Vientiane Mai* (www.vientianemai.net) is state-run; *Pasason* (www.pasaxon.org.la) is owned by the Laos Communist Party. In English *Vientiane Times* (www.vientianetimes.org.la) is published biweekly and in French *Le Renovateur* (www.lerenovateur.org.la) are both state-owned.
Broadcasting
Lao National Radio (www.lnr.org.la) operates two nationwide stations FM1–2, relayed by satellite on FM and AM frequencies. Foreign radio can also be received. Although all domestic Lao National TV (TVNL) is owned by the state viewers have unrestricted access to foreign TV via satellite and internet channels.
News agencies
National news agency: KPL (Khaosan Pathet Lao)

Economy
Laos is one of the poorest countries in the world. A third of the population exists outside the money economy and 80 per cent depend on subsistence agriculture, which produces some 40 per cent of GDP; rice is the main crop. Despite over twenty-five years of post-communist government (since 1986) when the previously centrally planned economy was dropped in favour of a free market economy and monetary reforms were adopted along with fiscal expansion, the pace of change has been slow so that Laos still remains heavily dependent on international aid.
Despite the economic reforms, the economy is still burdened by low productivity, poor infrastructure and a dominant public sector. Tourism is beginning to have an impact as its share of GDP increases and the sector becomes an important source of foreign exchange.
GDP growth in 2008 was 7.2 per cent and remained constant at 7.6 per cent in 2009 and 7.9 per cent in 2010. Inflation reacted to the high prices of world commodities and rose to 7.6 per cent in 2008, before falling back to 0.0 per cent in 2009 as domestic spending slowed; in 2010 inflation again rose, to 6 per cent.
The export of electricity to neighbouring countries is another major foreign exchange earner, along with mined ores which have benefited from rising global prices.
The Greater Mekong Sub-Region development project, of which Laos is a part, is supported by the Asian Development Bank (ADB). The project includes all the riparian countries of the Mekong River

Delta and provides a forum and platform for co-operative programmes such infrastructure development, energy sharing and economic relations.

External trade

Laos belongs to the Association of South-east Asian Nations (Asean) Free Trade Area (Afta) which maintains a list of goods with preferential import duties between members and a programme of tariff reductions due to be introduced in the next few years. In 2009, Laos was in negotiation with the WTO for membership.

There are transit agreements with Vietnam, Cambodia and Thailand allowing cargo, by bonded customs carriers, to travel by cross-border highways from the coast to landlocked Laos.

Imports

Principal imports are vehicles, capital goods, food and consumer goods.

Main sources: Thailand (typically 69.0 per cent of total), China (11 per cent), Vietnam (5 per cent).

Exports

Principal exports are electricity (typically 40 per cent of total), garment and small-scale manufacturing, timber products, coffee and mined ore including gold, silver, tin, copper, nickel and zinc.

Main destinations: Thailand (typically 35 per cent of total), Vietnam (13 per cent), China (9 per cent).

Agriculture

Agriculture contributes around 47 per cent of GDP and employs over 80 per cent of the workforce.

Rice, the main crop, is cultivated in irrigated lowland paddies and on drier hill farms.

Other crops include maize, sweet potatoes, cassava, pulses, groundnuts, fruit, vegetables, sugar cane, coffee, tobacco and cotton. Livestock raised includes cattle, buffaloes, pigs, goats and poultry.

Forestry

Plans to increase the area of forest to 18.7 million hectares were confirmed by the government in 2008. Deforestation had reduced natural forests from 41 per cent of the country in 2002 to around 35 per cent, due to changes in agriculture, hydroelectric projects, mining and illegal logging.

Industry and manufacturing

The industrial sector accounts for around 27 per cent of GDP and employs over 10 per cent of the workforce.

There is no heavy industry. The production of tin concentrates is the main industrial activity. Other major industries include textiles, bricks, cement, minerals and hydroelectricity.

Small-scale manufacturing industries produce beer, cigarettes, detergents, rubber footwear, plywood, matches, salt, animal feed, veterinary products, handicrafts, alcoholic beverages and soft drinks.

The growth sectors are garments, wood products, handicrafts and light industry, including vehicle assembly.

In June 2009 the US removed Laos from its economic black list and opened up opportunities for bilateral trade.

Tourism

Tourism is an increasingly important contributor to GDP and the balance of payments. The sector has strengthened steadily since the mid-1990s. Around three-quarters of visitors came from the region, with Thailand in the lead.

Mining

Mining together with hydrocarbons contributes around 5 per cent to GDP. The sector employs 1 per cent of the workforce.

As with other economic sectors in Laos, resources have not been optimised because of bureaucracy, lack of infrastructure and inefficiency.

Principal minerals include tin, high-grade iron ore, gold, copper, potash, limestone, manganese, lead, zinc, gypsum and bauxite.

There is great potential for the extraction of gold, and explorations have been conducted by Pan Australian and CRA Exploration of Australia (a subsidiary of Rio Tinto Zinc), both in joint ventures with the Laos government. Commercial interest in gold mining has surged following the success of the Sepon project – 80 per cent Oxiana Resources and 20 per cent Rio Tinto – which started gold and copper production in 2003.

Hydrocarbons

Laos does not produce any hydrocarbons. It relies on imports of petroleum products to meet domestic consumption levels.

Laos does not import either coal or natural gas. Imports of oil are typically 3,000 barrels per day.

Exploration for oil in 2008 was carried out by two companies from Vietnam and the UK. Large deposits of oil and natural gas are expected, but if found commercially viable production would take years to begin.

Energy

Laos has installed generating capacity of 700MW, supplied mainly by hydropower, producing 1.64 billion kilowatt hours in 2006. Electricity supplies are restricted mainly to the capital and other large urban areas.

The potential for expansion of hydropower is enormous due to plentiful water and a mountainous terrain. An estimated 30,000MW could be developed, given the investment in plant and infrastructure.

In 2005, construction began on the World Bank-supported, but controversial, Nam Theun 2 Hydropower Project, which will add 1,070MW to capacity when fully operational and of which 95 per cent will be exported to Thailand; the export of energy began in 2009.

Financial markets

On 11 January the new Lao Securities Exchange Market opened, with two companies listed. It is expected that the stock exchange will raise US$8 billion in equity and bond sales to help fund investment in the country. Trading details are available through the website of Banque pour le Commerce Laos (www.bcel.com.la) and Laos' first brokerage firm, Lane Xang Securities Public Company.

Stock exchange

Laos Securities Exchange

Banking and insurance

Since the early 1990s, the number of banks in Laos has more than doubled, with a corresponding rise in business. There are eight state-run commercial banks, two joint venture banks, seven foreign banks and 32 private non-bank foreign exchange bureaux operating in Laos. Banks have adopted commercial lending practices. Restructuring from September 2002 included the phased recapitalisation of the state commercial banks, the merger of two smaller banks and a rationalisation of banking operations.

Central bank

Banque de la RDP Lao (Bank of Lao PDR)

Time

GMT plus seven hours

Geography

Laos is a landlocked country in south-east Asia, bordered by the People's Republic of China to the north, Vietnam to the east, Cambodia to the south, Thailand to the west and Myanmar (Burma) to the north-west.

It is largely a mountainous country with the Annam Range running like a spine down the length of the country producing a natural barrier, with only three mountain passes into Vietnam. The highest mountain is Pou Bia at 2,817m in the northern central region. In the south and west, along the Mekong River, large alluvial plains provide much of the country's agricultural produce. The Mekong runs for 1,805km through Laos and provides much of its border with Thailand.

Hemisphere

Northern

Climate

Most of the year is hot and humid. The climate is monsoonal and has three distinct seasons. The hot dry season begins in February, with temperatures up to 40 degrees Celsius (C), only broken by the odd shower of rain. A build-up of storm activity in April–May with increasing humidity heralds the wet season during June–October, typified by a more consistent pattern of rain and cloudy days through June, July and August. There can be as much as 250mm rainfall per month. Temperatures average 29 degrees C. During this time, the Mekong River rises and flooding of the surrounding area is not uncommon. The cool, dry season arrives in November with lower temperatures and reduced humidity. Average temperature may drop to 14–15 degrees C. The cool weather can continue until February. Always cooler in the mountains, especially at night.

Entry requirements

Passports

Required by all, valid for six months beyond departure date.

Visa

Tourist visas are only obtained abroad through a Laotian consulate or accredited tour operator and must be used within two months. However they can be issued for immediate use at most ports of entry for periods of up to 15 days. Business visas are only issued from Laos and require a completed application form with a letter of invitation from a local company or entity. Further information should be sought through the nearest embassy.

Currency advice/regulations

Import and export of local currency is prohibited; there are no restrictions on foreign currency but amounts over US$2,000 must be declared.

Travellers cheques are not widely accepted, the Thai baht and US dollar are easiest to exchange.

Customs

It is forbidden to take any antiques or Buddha images over 50-years-old out of the country. Such items brought into Laos from other countries have to be declared at Customs.

Health (for visitors)

Laos has few hospitals and medical facilities.

Mandatory precautions

Vaccination certificates for yellow fever if travelling from an infected area.

Advisable precautions

Anti-malaria precautions; malaria is endemic in many areas of Laos but is not found in Vientiane. Mosquito repellent is recommended as dengue fever can be caught in Vientiane all year round. Immunisations against diphtheria, hepatitis A and B, Japanese B encephalitis, TB, tetanus, polio and typhoid. Rabies is a health risk.

Comprehensive health insurance, including provision for air evacuation, is strongly advised.

Hotels

The hotel sector is at an early stage of development and is at present restricted mainly to Vientiane, Luang Prabang and Vang Vieng, where there are a number of tourist-standard and luxury hotels. Visitor accommodation around the country is in short supply, the main resource being village hostels and guesthouses, where available.

Credit cards

Major credit cards are accepted by main hotels and some restaurants. The handling fee of 1.5–3.0 per cent is generally passed on to the customer.

Public holidays (national)

Fixed dates

1–2 Jan (New Year's Day/National Day), 6 Jan (Pathet Lao Day), 20 Jan (Army Day), 8 Mar (Women's Day), 22 Mar (People's Party Day), 13–15 Apr (Lao New Year), 1 May (Labour Day), 1 Jun (Children's Day), 13 Aug (Day of the Free Laos), 12 Oct (Day of Liberation), 2 Dec (Republic Day).

Variable dates

Chinese New Year (Feb), Birth of Buddha (May), Buddhist Fast begins (Jun/Jul), Buddhist Fast ends (Oct).

Working hours

Banking

Mon–Fri: 0800–1200, 1330–1730.

Business

Mon–Sat: 0800–1200, 1300–1600.

Government

Mon–Sat: 0800–1200, 1400–1700.

Some ministries close at 1130 for lunch; others work a half-day Saturday.

Shops

(Mon–Sun) 0900–1700.

Telecommunications

Mobile/cell phones

There are GSM 900/1800 services available in major cities only.

Electricity supply

220V 50Hz. Power outlets are two-prong round or flat sockets.

Weights and measures

Metric system (local units also in use).

Social customs/useful tips

The generally accepted form of greeting among Lao people is the *nop*, performed by placing one's palms together in a position of praying at chest level, but not touching the body. The higher the hands, the greater the sign of respect. Nonetheless, the hands should not be held above the level of the nose. The *nop* is accompanied by a slight bow to show respect to persons of higher status and age. It is also used as an expression of thanks, regret or saying goodbye. But with Western people, it is acceptable to shake hands.

Since the head is considered the most sacred part of the body and the soles of the feet the least, one should not touch a person's head nor use one's foot to point at a person or any object. It is forbidden for a woman to touch a Buddhist monk.

Men and women rarely show affection in public.

Getting there

Air

National airline: Lao Airlines

International airport/s: Vientiane-Wattay International Airpirt (VTE), 4km from city centre.

Airport tax: Departure tax US$10

Surface

Road: The Mitraphap (Friendship) Bridge over the Mekong River at Nong Khai, situated 14km east of Vientiane, provides the first modern road link with Thailand. It also gave Laos road access to a port for the first time.

There are road crossings from all surrounding countries, although the roads via Cambodia and Myanmar are not recommended due to poor security. Road No 1 runs from Thailand, through Laos, to China; road No 9 runs from Thailand, through Laos, to Vietnam.

Major infrastructure and construction of the Chiang Rai-Kunming Road Improvement Project is underway. When complete, it will involve over 1,220km of road along the north axis of the subregion, and will provide road links from Yunnan Province, Laos, to Bangkok in Thailand.

Rail: A railway line runs up to the border of Laos near Vientiane, although it does not run in Laos.

Water: From Kunming or Xishuangbanna, China, it is possible to travel by boat along the Mekong river south into Bokeo Province.

Getting about

National transport

It is relatively easy to travel in northern Laos but in the south, public transport is extremely erratic.

Air: Travel by air is the most convenient means of transportation within Laos. Lao Aviation flies daily from Vientiane to Luang Prabang, Savannakhet, Xieng Khouang, Pakse and Oudomsay. There are several flights a week to Luang Namtha, Sayaboury, Houeixay, Sam Neua, Saravane, Lak Xao, Muangkhong and Attapeu.

Road: Laos has 18,153km of national roads, 2,500km of which are paved. The most important road is route No 13 which runs north-south from China to Cambodia. It links Pak Mong in the north with Khong in the south, passing through

major urban areas of Luang Prabang, Vientiane, Savannakhet and Champassack.
Buses: There are services between main centres.
Rail: A line from Vientiane to Nong Khai is operating, including air-conditioned coaches.
Water: River transport is important, especially on the Mekong River, which flows through 1,865km of Laos.

City transport
The easiest way to travel around town is with a car and driver, usually arranged through your hotel.
Taxis: Three-wheeled *tuk-tuk* (motorcycle taxis) are easily found.
Taxis are available in Vientiane, but often operate along certain routes in the manner of buses. Individual hire may require negotiation. Tipping is discouraged.

Car hire
Arrangements are generally made through hotels.

BUSINESS DIRECTORY

Telephone area codes
The international dialling code (IDD) for Laos is +856 followed by area code (Vientiane only) and subscriber's number:
Vientiane 21

Useful telephone numbers
Police: 191
Police (Immigration Office) emergency number: 212-520
Fire: 190
Ambulance: 195
International Medical Clinic: 214-018, 214-022, 214-025

Chambers of Commerce
Lao National Chamber of Commerce, Phonphanao village Saysettha, PO Box 4596, Vientiane (tel: 452-579, 453-311; fax: 452-580; e-mail: laocci@laotel.com).

Banking
Acleda Bank Lao Ltd, P O Box 1555, #372, Corner of Dongpalane and Dongpina Road, Unit 21, Phonesavanh Neua Village, Sisattanak District, Vientiane (tel: 264-994; fax: 264-995).

Banque de la République Democratique Populaire Lao, PO Box 19, Rue Yonnet, Vientiane (tel: 213-109, 213-110; fax: 213-108).

Banque Pour Le Commerce Exterieur La; PO Box 2925, N 1 Pang Kham Rd, Vientiane (tel: 213-200; fax: 213-202).

Joint Development Bank Ltd; 75/15 Lane Xang Ave, Vientiane (tel: 213-536; fax: 213-530).

Lane Xang Bank Ltd; 6-80 Setthathiilath, Vientiane (tel: 213-400, 212-186, 212-108, 212-105; fax: 213-404).

Vientiane Commercial Bank Ltd; 33 Lane Xang Ave, Hatsady, Chanthaboury, Vientiane (tel: 222-700; fax: 213-513).

Central bank
Banque de la République Democratique Populaire Lao, PO Box 19, Rue Yonnet, Vientiane (tel: 213-109; fax: 213-108; e-mail: bol@pan-laos.net.la).

Stock exchange
Laos Securities Exchange

Travel information
Lao Aviation, 2 Pangkham Road, PO Box 4169, Vientiane (tel: 212-055; fax: 212-056).

Ministry of tourism
Ministry of Trade and Tourism, Vientiane (tel: 412-003, 412-436; fax: 412-434).

National tourist organisation offices
National Tourism Authority of Lao PDR, PO Box 3556, PO Box 3556, Lane Xang Avenue, Vientiane (tel: 212-248, 212-251; fax: 212-769).

Ministries
Department of Foreign Trade, Ministry of Industry and Commerce, Vientiane.

Ministry of Agriculture and Forestry, Vientiane (tel: 412-358).

Ministry of Commerce and Tourism, Vientiane (tel: 107-484).

Ministry of Communications, Transport, Post and Construction, Vientiane (tel: 412-281); Foreign Relations Department (tel: 412-267).

Ministry of Defence, Vientiane (tel: 412-803); Foreign Relations Departments (tel: 412-805, 412-810).

Ministry of Education, Vientiane (tel: 216-000); Foreign Relations Department (tel: 216-005).

Ministry of External Economic Relations, Foreign Investment Adviser, Vientiane (tel: 169-804).

Ministry of Finance, Vientiane (tel: 412-142, 412-404, 412-417).

Ministry of Foreign Affairs, Vientiane (tel: 414-002, 414-003).

Ministry of Industry and Handicrafts, Vientiane (tel: 413-000, 413-004, 413-006); (Electricity Division) (tel: 413-010; fax: 413-013); (Industry Division) (tel: 414-332); (Geology and Mines Division) (tel: 212-080, 212-082; fax: 222-539).

Ministry of Information and Culture, Vientiane (tel: 212-898, 212-402); (Foreign Relations Director) (tel: 212-409).

Ministry of the Interior, Vientiane (tel: 212-503, 212-501); (Foreign Relations Division) (tel: 212-554).

Ministry of Justice, Vientiane (tel: 414-101).

Ministry of Labour and Social Welfare, Vientiane (tel: 213-001, 213-002).

Ministry of Public Health, Vientiane (tel: 412-985, 214-046).

Other useful addresses
ASEAN Investment Promotion Agency, Foreign Investment Management Committee in charge of Promotion Administration and Investment Services, Luang Prabang Road, Vientiane (tel: 216-663; fax: 215-491).

ASEAN Secretariat, 70 A J1 Sisingamangaraja, Jakarta 12110, Indonesia (tel: (+62-21) 726-2991, 724-3372; fax: (+62-21) 724-3504, 739-8234; e-mail: asean.or.id).

British Embassy, Commercial Section, 1031 Wireless Road, Bangkok 10330, Thailand (tel: (+66-2) 253-0191; fax: (+66-2) 255-8619).

British Trade Office, Vientiane, Pandit J Nehru Road, PO Box 6626, Vientiane (tel: 413-606; fax: 413-607).

Foreign Investment Management Committee, Luang Prabang Road, Vientiane (tel: 216-662, 216-663, 217-009, 217-018); fax: 215-491, 217-007, 217-013).

Lao Embassy (USA), 2222 S Street, NW, Washington DC 20008 (tel: (+1-202) 332-6416; fax: (+1-202) 332-4923).

Lao Import-Export Company, 43-47 Lanexang Road, Vientiane.

Lao National Radio, Vientiane (tel: 212-428, 212-429, 212-431, 212-430).

Lao National Television Channel 9, Vientiane (tel: 412-182).

Lao Water Authority, Commercial Division, Vientiane (tel: 412-885; fax: 414-378).

United Nations Development Programme (UNDP), Phon Kheng Road, PO Box 345, Vientiane (tel: 4101, 5605; fax: 5001).

US Embassy, Thatdam Bartholonie Road, Bane Thatdam, Vientiane (tel: 213-966, 212-581, 212-582, 212-585).

National news agency: KPL (Khaosan Pathet Lao), 80 Setthathirath Rd, Vientiane (tel: 215-402; fax: 212-446; internet: www.kpl.net.la).

Internet sites
Asian Development Bank: http://www.adb.org/lrm

Laos Business Centre: http://www.asiadragons.com/

Laos website: http://laos.asiaco.com/

Web directory: http://www.angelfire.com/ca/laoscom/

Web directory: http://www.laoworld.com/

Worldwide Gazeteer — Laos: http://www.c-allen.dircon.co.uk/Countries/Laos.htm

Latvia

KEY FACTS

Official name: Latvijas Republika (Republic of Latvia)

Head of State: President Andris Berzinš (from 8 Jul 2011)

Head of government: Prime Minister Valdis Domrovskis (from 2009; re-elected 27 Oct 2011)

Ruling party: Coalition of Vienotiba (Unity) (coalition of three parties) with Zatlera Reformu Partija (ZRP) (Zatlers' Reform Party) and), Nacionala Apvieniba (NA) (National Alliance) (coalition of two parties) (from 27 Oct 2011)

Area: 64,589 square km

Population: 2.24 million (2010)*

Capital: Riga

Official language: Lettish

Currency: Lats (Ls) = 100 santims

Exchange rate: Ls0.53 per US$ (Oct 2011)

GDP per capita: US$10,695 (2010)

GDP real growth: -0.30% (2010)

GDP: US$24.00 billion (2010)

Labour force: 1.16 million (2010)

Unemployment: 18.70% (2010)

Inflation: -1.20% (2010)

Balance of trade: -US$1.55 billion (2010)

* Estimated figure

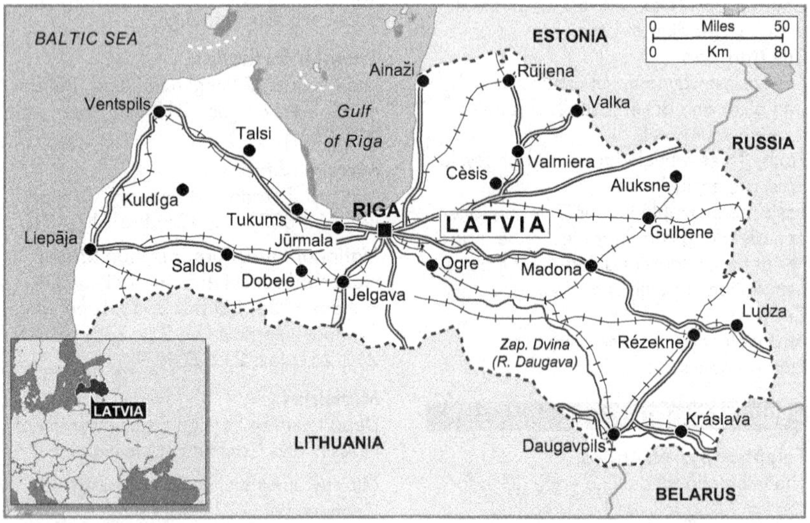

Latvia's twentieth century history was anything but tranquil, with fourteen governments in as many years before the establishment of authoritarian rule in 1934. In his excellent study *The Baltic World* David Kirby notes that 'although four of the ten men who occupied the post of *Riigivanem* (prime minister, although the literal translation is 'senior statesman') between 1919 and 1934 did so more than once, almost half of those holding ministerial office were not invited to do so a second time.' Surprisingly, fourteen of the nineteen between 1918 and 1934 represented farmers' parties.

Election surprises

October 2010's elections had returned Prime Minister Valdis Dombrovskis to office. A coalition government of the Prime Minister's Vienotiba (Unity, coalition of three parties) won 33 seats and together with the Zalo un Zemnieku Savieniba (ZZS) (Union of Greens and Farmers, coalition of two parties) which won 22, held a majority in the 100-seat parliament. Despite having a parliamentary majority and fewer coalition partners than before, garnering political support for further fiscal adjustment (even though much smaller than in previous years) became increasingly challenging.

So much so that on 29 May constitutional powers were used for the first time when President Valdis Zatlers dissolved parliament, following a political crisis when the government failed to endorse a law to limit the immunity of one of its members accused of corruption. Parliament, in retaliation, replaced Zatlers with Andris Berzinš in an indirect presidential election on 2 June – in the second round of voting Berzinš of the Zemnieku Savieniba (Farmers Union) won 53 votes (out of 100) and Valdis Zatlers 41.

Zatlers formed a new political party, Zatlera Reformu Partija (ZRP) (Zatlers' Reform Party), on 23 July, to coincide with a national referendum to endorse the dissolution of parliament and hold an early general election. He declared that ZRP would not co-operate with the three leading political parties.

In the 17 September 2011 parliamentary elections the pro-Russia party the Saskanas Centrs (Harmony Centre, coalition of three parties) won 28.36 per cent (31 seats out of 100), the strongest showing for an ethnic Russian party since the former Soviet state's independence. The ZRP won 20.82 per cent (22 seats) while the Unity bloc of Prime Minister Valdis Dombrovskis could only manage 18 per cent (20 seats) as it was seen to be the instigator of an austerity regime and a government with three, alleged, corrupt politicians at its centre.

After weeks of unsuccessful coalition talks, undertaken by Nils Usakovs the leader of Harmony Centre, on 19 October the President invited Valdis Dombrovskis to form a new government. President Berzinš also suggested that a coalition be formed to include politicians from all political parties that had won seats in the elections.

However, the other political parties are wary of the Harmony Centre party's ties with Russian leaders so that in the end the Unity bloc and the ZRP formed a coalition to ensure that the Harmony Centre was sidelined. This means that the quarter of Latvia's population that is Russian-speaking is largely unrepresented. During the Soviet period, which ended in 1991, Latvia had experienced a big influx of immigrants from other parts of the USSR, mainly Russia.

The other two parties who crossed the 5 per cent threshold needed to enter parliament were the Greens and Farmers Union with 12 per cent and the right-wing National Alliance with 14 per cent. As the Greens and Farmers Union is led by Aivars Lembergs, a fierce political opponent of Mr Zatlers, it was unlikely that it would join a Zatlers-Unity coalition.

The economy

Despite the corruption scandal and its ramifications, by 2011 Latvia's economy was recovering after the sharp contraction of 2008–09. Gross domestic product (GDP) started to increase in late 2009, with annual growth forecast at 3.3 per cent for 2011 and 4 per cent in the medium term. Net exports supported the initial recovery, but domestic demand was expected to drive growth from 2011 onwards as improving confidence and investment outweigh continued fiscal consolidation, the weak labour market and contracting credit.

Rising food and energy prices have led to an increase in inflation. Unemployment, while falling, is still high (17 per cent), underscoring the continuing need for an effective social safety net. Latvia's financial indicators suggest growing confidence; in March the Fitch rating agency raised Latvia's credit rating to investment grade status. T-bill rates remain close to historic lows, 10-year lats bonds were issued in February 2011 and bank deposits are above pre-crisis levels. Though repayment of banks' foreign liabilities has led to some decline in international reserves, they remain at comfortable levels.

Latvia's fiscal performance has been better than expected. Strong spending discipline enabled Latvia to lower its 2010 deficit to 7.7 per cent of GDP, well below the 8.5 per cent target. The December 2010 budget and April 2011 supplementary budget should cut the 2011 deficit to below 4.5 per cent of GDP. Much less adjustment than previously expected is needed to reduce the 2012 deficit below the 3 per cent Maastricht level. Latvia met all its September and December 2010 quantitative performance criteria and continued to perform well in 2011, meeting most structural benchmarks, although some with delay. In discussions with the International Monetary Fund (IMF) Latvia agreed to aim at a 2012 deficit of 2.5 per cent of GDP to try and meet the Maastricht criterion convincingly, consistent with their strategy for euro adoption in 2014.

The overall risks facing Latvia are, in the view of the IMF, much lower, but the exit strategy for euro adoption could well be affected by politics and 'reform fatigue' complicating a 2012 deficit reduction; further global commodity price increases could also raise inflation above the Maastricht reference value.

The IMF expressed the view that a delay in euro adoption, after massive adjustment and when Latvia is so close to meeting the Maastricht criteria, would be a tremendous lost opportunity. Although as the euro-zone crisis wore on in 2011 there were dissenting voices in Latvia on this.

Risk assessment

Economy	Good
Politics	Good
Regional stability	Good

COUNTRY PROFILE

Historical profile

Before being occupied by the Germans in the thirteenth century, Latvia had been part of an important Baltic-trading route and was a largely feudal and tribal society.

1561 Latvia came under Polish rule after the Livonian Order appealed to Poland-Lithuania for protection from Russia's Ivan the Terrible.

1620s Following the Polish-Swedish war, most of Latvia came under Swedish rule, except Courland in western Latvia where the dukes of Jelgava maintained allegiance to Poland until 1709.

1700–21 Russia's Peter the Great destroyed Swedish power in the Great Northern War. Latvia became part of the Russian empire.

1795 Apart from a brief period of French occupation in 1812, Courland was under Russian control until 1915 when the Germans occupied the province.

1914–18 During the First World War, Latvia alternated between Russian and German control five times. It was under Bolshevik Russian control in late 1918 by which time Latvian independence had been declared by nationalists.

1919 Joint British and German forces expelled Bolshevik Russian forces and democratic rule was introduced.

1922 Latvia's first constitution, including proportional representation, was adopted.

1934–39 Prime Minister Karlis Ulmanis declared a state of emergency, suspended parliament and banned all political parties. In 1936, he assumed the title of president, becoming an autocratic ruler.

1939 Through the German and Soviet Ribbentrop-Molotov pact, Latvia was

KEY INDICATORS — Latvia

	Unit	2006	2007	2008	2009	2010
Population	m	2.29	2.28	2.27	2.26	*2.24
Gross domestic product (GDP)	US$bn	20.10	28.80	34.00	26.20	24.00
GDP per capita	US$	8,760	12,622	14,964	11,607	10,695
GDP real growth	%	12.2	10.0	-4.6	-18.0	-0.3
Inflation	%	6.5	10.1	15.3	3.3	-1.2
Unemployment	%	6.8	6.0	7.5	17.2	18.7
Exports (fob) (goods)	US$m	6,140.0	8,143.0	9,559.0	7,387.0	8,989.0
Imports (fob) (goods)	US$m	11,271.0	14,822.0	15,343.0	9,209.0	10,535.0
Balance of trade	US$m	-5,131.0	-6,679.0	-5,784.0	-1,822.0	-1,546.0
Current account	US$m	-4,479.0	-6,231.0	-4,492.0	2,284.0	873.0
Total reserves minus gold	US$m	4,353.4	5,553.4	5,027.6	6,631.8	7,256.2
Foreign exchange	US$m	4,353.1	5,553.3	5,027.2	6,445.0	7,069.5
Exchange rate	per US$	0.56	0.51	0.48	0.50	0.53

* estimated figure

forcibly incorporated back into the Soviet Union.
1940 Latvia was incorporated as a constituent republic of the USSR.
1941 The Germans invaded and occupied Latvia.
1944 The Soviet Union liberated Latvia from German rule.
1945–80s Mass deportation to Siberia of Latvian citizens by Stalin, following the war and resulting in an influx of Russian nationals as the Soviet Union introduced collective farming and developed heavy industries in Latvia.
1990 The Supreme Court declared *de jure* independence from the Soviet Union. The Latvijas Komunistiska Partija (LKP) (Latvian Communist Party) lost office.
1991 Elite Soviet troops were deployed in Riga, but were withdrawn following international pressure. Anatolijs Gorbunov of the Latvijas Tautas Fronte (LTF) (Latvian Popular Front) became head of state as chairman of the Latvian Supreme Council. Ivars Godmanis (LTF) became head of government as the chairman of the Council of Ministers, which declared Latvia's independence. Lativia joined the United Nations. Latvian citizenship was reinstated for all those who held it before 1940, including their dependents.
1993 A coalition led by Latvijas Cels (LC) (Latvia's Way) formed a government with the Latvijas Zemnieku Savienîa (LZS) (Latvian Farmers' Union). The 1922 Satversme (constitution) was fully reinstituted. Guntis Ulmanis (LZS) was elected the first post-Soviet Latvian president. Valdis Birkavs (LC) was appointed prime minister.
1995 Parliamentary elections led to political turmoil as the ruling LC lost its dominant position and no single party held a majority. A six-party coalition government was eventually formed, dominated by the two largest parties, the centrist LC and the left-wing Democrâtiskâ Partija 'Saimnieks' (DPS) (Master Democratic Party). After a lot of wrangling, Andris Skele (LC) became prime minister.
1996 President Ulmanis was re-elected by parliament for a second term in office.
1998 Latvians narrowly backed the liberalisation of the country's citizenship laws in a referendum held alongside general elections. A centre-right coalition was formed, with Vilis Kristopans (LC) as prime minister.
1999 Latvia became a member of the World Trade Organisation (WTO), the first of the Baltic states to join. Independent Vaira Vike-Freiberga was elected president. The minority centre-left coalition headed by Vilis Kristopans fell and a majority coalition government was formed under Prime Minister Andris Skele.
2000 Skele's coalition collapsed over plans to privatise the Latvian Shipping Company (Lasco).
2002 The president invited Einars Repše and his Jaunais Laiks (JL) (New Era) to form a coalition government following the general elections. It included Latvijas Pirmâ Partija (LPP) (Latvia's First Party), Zalo un Zemnieku Savieniba (ZZS) (Green and Farmers Union) (coalition of two parties) and the Apvienîba Tçvzemei un Brîvîbai'/Latvijas Nacionala Konservativa Partija (TB/LNNK) (Union for the Fatherland and Freedom/Latvian National Conservative Party).
2003 President Vaira Vike-Freiberga was re-elected. In a referendum 67 per cent voted to join the European Union (EU).
2004 The ruling coalition collapsed; Repše resigned. Indulis Emsis (ZZS) became prime minister and formed a minority coalition government. Latvia joined NATO and the EU. The government's draft budget was rejected and Emsis resigned. Aigars Kalvitis became prime minister.
2006 Citizenship laws were seen as more pressure on the minority Russian community. The ruling coalition won a majority in parliamentary elections.
2007 Latvia signed a treaty with Russia defining their mutual border. The parliament elected Valdis Zatlers as president with 59 votes, Aivars Endzins won 39 votes. Aleksijs Loskutovs, a leading anti-corruption investigator was sacked; large street demonstrations forced his reinstatement. Prime Minister Kalvitis resigned amid allegations of corruption and Ivars Godmanis was appointed prime minister. Latvia became a member of the EU Schengen area, whereby all travellers may cross borders without a passport or visa.
2008 An agreement for visa-free visits by citizens to the US was signed. The parliament approved the EU's Lisbon Treaty for community constitutional reforms.
2009 Prime Minister Ivars Godmanis and his government resigned, amid political turmoil caused by the global economic crisis. Parliament approved the appointment of Valdis Dombrovskis as prime minister. EU regulators began an investigation into the rescue of Latvia's second largest bank, JSC Parex Banka. The government had agreed to US$401 million in loan guarantees, which together with a loan from the European Bank for Reconstruction and Development (EBRD) may have given Parex Bank undue commercial advantage, contrary to EU trading regulations.
2010 Latvia's economy fell some 24 per cent over 2007–09, and GDP is expected to fall by another 4 per cent in 2010. The government coalition lost two constituent parties on 19 February, following street riots in January, protesting at the country's severe economic state and the introduction of austerity measures that avoided devaluing the lat through a US$9.5 billion loan agreed by the International Monetary Fund (IMF) in 2009. In April, EU investigators passed the government's rescue plan for JSC Parex Banka. Prime Minister Gadmanis resigned but the president rejected his resignation and Gadmanis invited other, smaller political parties to join his coalition. In parliamentary elections held on 2 October, the incumbent Vienotiba (Unity) coalition won 31.22 per cent of the vote (33 seats out of 100), which was not enough to hold power unaided. Partnership talks began immediately to form a government. On 7 November a coalition government was formed led by Par Labu Latviju! (For a Good Latvia) (a coalition which includes the prime minister's party Tautas Partija (People's Party), with ZZS and Tevzemei un Brivibai/LNNK (For Fatherland and Freedom/LNNK) of the Nacionala Apvieniba (NA) (National Alliance)).
2011 Constitutional powers were used for the first time when President Valdis Zatlers dissolved parliament on 29 May, following a political crisis when the government failed to endorse a law to limit the immunity of one of its members accused of corruption. Parliament, in retaliation, replaced Zatlers with Andris Berzins in an indirect presidential election on 2 June; Andris Berzinš (Zemnieku Savieniba (Farmers Union)) won 50 votes (out of 100) and Valdis Zatlers 48. In the second round Berzinš was elected with 53 votes, while Zatlers won 41. Zatlers formed a new political party, Zatlera Reformu Partija (ZRP) (Zatlers' Reform Party), on 23 July, to coincide with a national referendum to endorse the dissolution of parliament and hold an early general election. Valdis Zatlers declared that ZRP would not co-operate with the three leading political parties. In the 17 September parliamentary elections, the pro-Russian, centre-left, Harmony Centre won 28.36 per cent of the vote (31 seats out of 100) and with 20.82 per cent ZRP won the next largest number (22). Unity, the previous ruling party, won 20 seats and lost 13, as it was seen to be the instigator of an austerity regime and a government with three, alleged, corrupt politicians at its centre. After weeks of unsuccessful coalition talks, undertaken by Nils Usakovs the leader of Harmony Centre, the president invited Prime Minister Dombrovskis (TP) to form a new government on 19 October, President Berzinš also suggested that a coalition be formed to include politicians from all political parties that had won seats in the 17 September parliamentary elections.

A coalition was formed between Unity with ZRP and NA, following Valdis Dombrovskis re-appointment as prime minister; the government took office on 27 October.

Political structure

Constitution

In 1993, the Constitutional Law supplemented the 1922 constitution. The constitution provides for basic rights and freedoms.

Latvian citizens 18 years and over and those resident in Latvia before 27 June 1940, are eligible to vote.

Form of state

Parliamentary democratic republic

The executive

Executive powers are vested in the Cabinet of Ministers, nominated by the prime minister and appointed by and accountable to, parliament. The Cabinet of Ministers is led by the prime minister, who is appointed by the president.

The president is elected by parliament for a four-year term.

National legislature

The unicameral Saeima (parliament) has 100 members, directly elected for a four-year term by proportional representation in seats allocated to political parties which gain at least 5 per cent of the popular vote.

The president may dissolve parliament earlier than scheduled. General elections are held on the first Saturday of October.

Legal system

The legal system is based on a civil law system. The appointment of judges to the Supreme Court is confirmed by the Saiema.

Last elections

2 June 2011 (presidential, indirect); 23 July 2011 (referendum); 17 September 2011 (parliamentary)

Results: Presidential: Andris Berzinš (Zemnieku savieniba) won 50 votes (out of 100), Valdis Zatlers (independent) 48. Second round: Berzins won 53 votes, Zatlers 41.

Referendum: In the motion to dissolve parliament and hold another general election, 94.3 per cent voted yes; 5.48 per cent no.

Parliamentary: Saskanas Centrs (Harmony Centre) won 28.36 per cent of the vote (31 seats out of 100), Zatlera Reformu Partija (ZRP) (Zatlers' Reform Party) 20.82 per cent (22), Vienotiba (Unity) (coalition of three parties) 18.83 per cent (20), Nacionala Apvieniba (NA) (National Alliance) (coalition of two parties) 13.88 per cent (14), Zalo un Zemnieku savieniba (ZZS) (Green and Farmers Union) (coalition of two parties) 12.22 per cent (13); eight other political parties each won less than 3 per cent and failed to win any seats. Turnout was 59.49 per cent.

Next elections

2015 (parliamentary)

Political parties

Ruling party

Coalition of Vienotiba (Unity) (coalition of three parties) with Zatlera Reformu Partija (ZRP) (Zatlers' Reform Party) and), Nacionala Apvieniba (NA) (National Alliance) (coalition of two parties) (from 27 Oct 2011)

Main opposition party

Saskanas Centrs (Harmony Centre)

Population

2.26 million (2009)

Last census: March 2000: 2,377,383

Population density: 37.5 inhabitants per square km. Urban population: 69 per cent (1995–2001).

Annual growth rate: -0.9 per cent 1994–2004 (WHO 2006)

Ethnic make-up

Latvian (56 per cent), Russian (32 per cent), Belarussian (4 per cent), Ukrainian (3 per cent), Polish (2 per cent), Lithuanians (1 per cent). The Latvian parliament revised naturalisation laws in 1998 to speed up the integration of Latvia's 680,000 non-citizens, mostly ethnic Russians. Citizenship is granted to stateless children, even if their parents are not citizens, provided they have lived in Latvia for at least five years. Most ethnic Russians must still pass language examinations to become citizens.

Religions

Predominantly Protestant (Lutheran), with a Roman Catholic minority in the east of the country. Orthodox Christianity is the most common religious denomination among Russians in Latvia.

Education

Education has traditionally been important in Latvia and a high level of education enabled Latvia to become a centre of the Soviet communications and electronics industries.

For those who live in rural Latvia, educational opportunities are limited. About 25 per cent in the 18–24 age group receive only a basic education.

Basic education lasts for nine years. From this, students are channelled into either 1) a basic vocational school for a two-year course from age 16; or 2) a vocational school from age 15 for three years; or 3) a vocational secondary school at age 15 for four years. Each vocational school course has its relevant qualifications. Students undertaking academic study progress to a general secondary school from age 16 for four years. Students who graduate from either the general or vocational secondary school may undertake higher education.

There are four universities and a number of other higher education institutions in Latvia. All universities and 17 other higher education institutions are state-run. In addition, there are a number of private institutions of which 10 are state-recognised. Higher education institutions confer academic degrees and professional higher education qualifications.

Latvia has a higher proportion of undergraduates than many countries (including Japan, Poland and the Czech Republic). Engineering and science courses are well established, while commercial courses such as law, accountancy and business management, although in their infancy, are growing in popularity.

Annual total expenditure on education is around 7 per cent of GDP.

Literacy rate: 100 per cent adult rate; 100 per cent youth rate (15–24) (Unesco 2005).

Compulsory years: Seven to 18.

Enrolment rate: 96 per cent gross primary enrolment of the relevant age group (including repeaters); 84 per cent gross secondary enrolment (World Bank).

Pupils per teacher: 13 in primary schools.

Health

The Latvian healthcare system is set to become more expensive with the introduction of more payment-based services. However, the country has one of the highest ratios of doctors to population in the world.

Healthcare has largely deteriorated in Latvia. This has been due to a lack of primary healthcare provision, an over-stretched network of small hospitals, overstaffing and over-specialisation, the lack of modern management systems and the use of hospitals as dumping grounds for people with social rather than medical problems.

HIV/Aids

HIV prevalence: 0.6 per cent aged 15–49 in 2003 (World Bank)

Life expectancy: 71 years, 2004 (WHO 2006)

Fertility rate/Maternal mortality rate: 1.3 births per woman, 2004 (WHO 2006); maternal mortality 45 per 100,000 live births (World Bank).

Child (under 5 years) mortality rate (per 1,000): 10 per 1,000 live births (World Bank)

Head of population per physician: 3.01 physicians per 1,000 people, 2003 (WHO 2006)

Welfare

The social security system provides a state pension. There is provision for a social insurance fund. The pension system is a fund-based one, with three tiers composed of a modified pay-as-you-go (PAYG) system stronger links with contributions, a mandatory state-funded system of privately managed savings accounts and voluntary privately managed pensions.

A private pension fund law came into effect at the beginning of 1998. The legislation regulates private pension funds, which are supervised by the state insurance inspection department. Banks, life insurance companies, brokerages and investment companies are permitted to operate private pension funds, which allow saving in addition to the state pension scheme.

In 2001, the government introduced mandatory contributions for those who are subject to state pension insurance and under the age of 30, but optional for those aged between 30—49 years; the scheme is likely to be transferred to private companies. Annual total expenditure on social welfare is around 14 per cent of GDP.

Main cities

Riga (capital, estimated population 753,478 in 2005), Daugavpils (115,430), Liepaja (86,114), Jelgava (63,063), Jurmala (56,384), Ventspils (43,180), Rezekne (40,242).

Languages spoken

Russian, English and German are widely spoken (over 80 per cent of Latvians speak both Lettish and Russian); Lettish is required for citizenship. Belarusian, Ukrainian, Polish and Yiddish are also spoken. Some 150,000 Latvians speak Latgalian. A law passed in February 2004 requires at least 60 per cent of teaching at minority schools to be in Latvian.

Official language/s

Lettish

Media

Press

After spectacular growth since 1995, consolidation became the typical development. The small press market is separated into two languages Latvian and Russian.

Dailies: In Latvian, *Diena* (www.diena.lv) is a prestigious, independent newspaper, which owns several local newspapers, as does *Neatkariga Rita Avize* (NRA) (www.nra.lv) which owns the evening tabloid *Vakara Zinas* among others, *Latvijas Avize* (www2.la.lv) is a daily tabloid. The free newspaper *5 Min* (published by *Diena*) has been steadily increasing its circulation since 2005.

In Russian *Vesti Segodnja* (*Today's News*) (http://rus.delfi.lv/news/press/vesti), is the largest circulating newspaper; *Chas* (www.chas-daily.com) from Rida and *Ventspils* (www.ventspils.lv) from Ventspilis.

Weeklies: In English, the independent weekly *The Baltic Times* (www.baltictimes.com) provides news from the region; *Tovary Optum* is published in Russia.

Business: In Latvian, the newspapers *Dienas Bizness* (www.db.lv), and in Russian *Biznez I Baltiya* (www.bb.lv), plus the magazine *Kapitals* (www.kapitals.lv) in Latvain provide comprehensive news and views on business and financial matters. Some daily newspapers include business articles.

Periodicals: There are around 190 magazine titles on offer of which *Lilit* (www.lilita.lv) is a leading women's monthly magazine.

Broadcasting

Radio: The national, public Latvian Radio (www.radio.org.lv) operates four stations, including Radio 1 and 2, plus Klasika and Latvia International. Private, commercial stations includes Gold FM (www2.goldfm.lv) and Radio Naba (www.naba.lv) from Riga, the public Saldus Radio (www.saldus.lv) and Alise Plus (www.aliseplus.lv) from Daugavpils in Russian.

Television: Private, commercial television dominates the market. TV3 Latvis (www.tv3.lv), launched in 1998, with programmes in Latvian, became the leading TV station in September 2007 overtaking the previous leader, Latvian Independent Television (LNT) (www.lnt.lv). The national, public Latvian Television (LTV) (www.ltv.lv) operates LVT 1 and 7, with 70 per cent funding provided by the government and the remainder by advertising and sales. Russian-based channels, although popular with large parts of the population, have increasingly faced opposition as the government – through its control of transmission rights – attempts to limit Russian influence on Latvia.

Advertising

Television advertising accounts for around 35 per cent of adspend with the print media accounting for over 40 per cent, of which newspapers account for 30 per cent. All tobacco advertising in banned and alcohol may only be advertised through printed material.

News agencies

National news agency: LETA (Latvian News Agency)

Economy

Latvia's principal export commodity is timber, with domestic production at around 5 per cent of GDP and 70 per cent of all production exported; in 2009, 10–11 million square metres of timber was harvested. Industry in general is diverse and largely geared to serve local markets. Latvia's financial services are growing.

Latvia successfully transformed its economy from an integrated part of the former-Soviet Union's centrally planned economy to a free market economy, despite a couple of setbacks in the 1990s, and became the European Union's fastest growing economy after joining in 2004. However, it experienced a severe deterioration of its economy beginning in late 2007, in line with the global economic crisis. GDP growth, which had been in double digits since 2005, with a peak of 12.2 per cent in 2006 and 10 per cent in 2007, plummeted in 2008 to negative -4.6 per cent and in 2009 as the recession deepened growth fell further to -18 per cent. The recession slowed in 2010 to -0.3 per cent. Inflation rose from 6.6 per cent in 2006 to 10.1 per cent in 2007 and 15.3 per cent in 2008, before falling to 3.3 per cent in 2009 as domestic spending virtually stopped – retail sales dropped by around 30 per cent and moved into deflation of -1.2 per cent in 2010. Latvia's unemployment rate in 2009 became one of the worst in the EU at almost 23 per cent and GDP per capita fell from US$14,833 to US$11,448 in 2009.

The booming economy had been driven by consumer demand, personal debt and unsustainable property values but the global financial crisis rapidly stopped this as investors withdrew funds. The recession for Latvia was predicted to be long and deep, due not only to underlying fiscal weaknesses leading to unsustainable deficits but also because Latvia failed to transform its product base. Over 35 per cent of all exports are timber products from the huge forests that cover around 45 per cent of the land. Exports that were concentrated in high resource and labour intensive products (30 per cent timber) and utilising low-technology and low skilled workers have been reduced, but still outpace highly skilled workers and value added production techniques. The move to increase the degree of skills and performance has not kept pace with other Baltic economies.

In 2010, the government introduced stringent austerity measures to cut public spending, including the loss of 20–30 per cent of central government administrative positions, as well as raising taxes in a €700 million (US$929.3 million) budget. Standard and Poor's upgraded Latvia's rating to BB+ on 7 December 2010 for its faster than expected rebound from recession; although this is still below an investment grade. By November 2011, the BB+ rating had been given an appendage 'positive', but with the warning that the banking system was still recovering from the shock of non-performing loans at 20 per cent of lending and the high private sector leverage given Latvia's modest per capita income.

External trade

As a member of the European Union, Latvia operates within a community-wide free trade area, which sets import tariffs as a whole. The EU has free trade agreements with a number of nations and trading blocs worldwide.
Latvia has to import all of its energy and raw material; timber is Latvia's sole natural resource and is the single largest export, as either logs, finished panels or charcoal. External trade accounts for over 75 per cent of Latvia's GDP.

Imports

Principal imports are fuels and vehicles, iron ore, steel and capital goods.
Main sources: Lithuania (typically 17 per cent of total), Germany (13.0 per cent), Russia (10 per cent).

Exports

Principal exports are timber (typically over 35 per cent of total), machinery, electrical and electronic and equipment, iron and steel, textiles and foodstuffs.
Main destinations: Lithuania (typically 16 per cent of total), Estonia (14 per cent), Russian Federation (10.1 per cent).

Agriculture

Farming

Latvia's agricultural sector still has remnants of the old Soviet central planning system and has suffered during the transition to a capitalist economic environment. With the majority of output going to the food processing sector, demand has fallen considerably. With agriculture employing over 15 per cent of the workforce, its problems are becoming increasingly significant politically. The agriculture sector is also hugely disadvantaged by the subsidies that the EU pays to its own farmers under the Common Agricultural Policy (CAP). Latvia itself is not due to benefit from CAP policies until 2013.
During its transitional entry stage Latvia has decided to implement the reform of CAP in 2009. The reform was introduced throughout most of the EU in 2005, when subsidies on farm output, which tended to benefit large farms and encourage overproduction, were replaced by single farm payments, not conditional on production. The change is expected to reward farms that provide and maintain a healthy environment, food safety and animal welfare standards. The changes are also intended to encourage market conscious production and cut the cost of CAP to the EU taxpayer.
The sector is dominated by dairy farming, pig-breeding, grain production and potatoes. Latvia is self-sufficient in the production of cattle and dairy products, pork, sugar beet, flax and potatoes. Any surplus is exported to Russia, other republics of the CIS and the EU.
The reform of the agricultural sector has proceeded at a faster rate than in either Lithuania or Estonia and 95 per cent of agricultural production comes from the private sector. Crops cover about 28 per cent of the total land area and permanent pastures about 13 per cent.
Decreases in agricultural output have been caused by the structural reforms in the sector, a lack of modern technology and the money to buy it, problems in the distribution of produce – particularly from the small private farms – and an absence of bank credit combined with high interest rates.
Stock-breeding contributes over 50 per cent of gross agricultural production; however, this means that large amounts of fodder must be imported. Consequently the structure of the agricultural sector is changing with greater emphasis placed on grain production.

Fishing

Latvia's extensive coastline provides large fish catches. Principal catches include sprat, Baltic Sea pilchards, Riga Gulf pilchards, cod and salmon. Typical annual catches amount to some 145 million tonnes per year (tpy).
Thirty per cent of total fish production is used domestically while 70 per cent is exported. Latvia held discussions with Joe Borg, EU Commissioner for Fisheries, about conservation methods to protect overexploited and depleted cod stocks in the Baltic Sea.

Forestry

With forests covering approximately 40 per cent of total land area, forestry has the potential to become one of the most important sectors of the economy. About 60 per cent of the forest is classified as soft wood (66 per cent pine forest and 34 per cent spruce) with the remaining hardwood mainly birch. Reforestation following cutting is compulsory.
Latvia's rich and extensive forests are mainly in areas of low population, making the felling, processing and export of timber relatively easy. There is potential to harvest 8.3 million cubic metres of timber a year, half of which would be available for pulp production. The timber and furniture industry accounts for about 8 per cent of GDP and employs around 51,000 people. Timber and furniture exports grew substantially in the 1990s and currently comprise around 25 per cent of total exports. In particular, growth in exports to the EU is the result of higher wood exports.
There are about 2,500 forest industry companies in Latvia, all but a few in private ownership; the majority concentrate on sawn wood milling, wood panel production and furniture. Progress in the timber industry has been made since independence, although there is still a lack of finance, management and design skills and many production techniques remain inefficient. Pulp and paper production does not meet domestic demand. Even though Latvia is one of the top five countries in Europe in terms of forest resources per capita, it lacks a large processing plant for pulp and paper production, and consequently a large proportion of raw timber produce is exported to the pulp mills of Sweden.

Industry and manufacturing

The industrial sector accounts for 25.3 per cent of GDP and employs around 30 per cent of the work force.
Total manufacturing output declined in the late 1990s with food-processing hit particularly. Many Latvian food producers do not yet meet EU specifications and are therefore limited to less lucrative domestic or CIS markets such as Russia. Machinery and equipment manufacture also suffered.
Latvia is one of the most heavily industrialised areas of the former Soviet Union. A well-developed infrastructure and a broadly diversified industrial base includes both light and heavy industries including high-technology manufacturing and shipbuilding. Main industries are mechanical engineering, metal working, textiles and the food industry. Forestry, paper, chemicals, petrochemicals and communications are also important. The textiles sector is successful and export-focussed (82 per cent).
The manufacturing industry is concentrated on the production of railway carriages, buses, mopeds, washing machines and telephone systems. Mineral fertilisers are also produced. Riga, Liepaja and Ventspils are the principal industrial centres.
IT and telecommunications are expanding sectors, with a growth rate averaging 25 per cent over the past ten years. Banking, transport and logistics services also contribute significantly to the ecomony.

Tourism

Interest in tourism grew again after Latvia's independence in 1991 and there has been substantial investment. However, the sector is still underdeveloped. The sector employs around14,000 people, which amounts to about1.2 per cent of the total workforce. The short summer season is a barrier to development.

Mining

Mineral resources include limestone, clay for cement industry, dolomite, gypsum, sand for glass, clay for pottery, sand for silicate products, sand and gravel. The

few minerals found in Latvia are used as building materials.
Mining and the quarrying of mineral resources account for approximately 0.5 per cent of annual GDP and have a negligible impact on the economy.

Hydrocarbons
Latvia has proven oil reserves of 297 million barrels; consumption was 37,000 barrels per day in 2007, mostly imported, largely from Belarus, Russia and Lithuania. As it has no refining capacity it imports all petroleum products necessary.
Proven natural gas reserves were 22.6 billion cubic metres (cum) in 2007; consumption was over 1.8 billion cum. Latvia relies on Russian imports to meet domestic demand.
Latvia does not produce coal but does produce around 500,000 tonnes of peat per annum. Coal imports come mostly from Poland.

Energy
Total installed generating capacity was over 2.1 gigawatts in 2007, of which hydroelectric power provided 68 per cent. However, hydroelectric and thermal power plants do not provide the country with enough power to meet requirements and the country must rely on imports to meet its needs. While the energy market was opened up to competition in 2005 little progress has been made as the state-owned Latvenergo has a monopoly on the distribution of electricity and operates the generating hydro- and thermal-power plants, which provide 93 per cent of production.
The Estlink project, an underwater cable linking the Baltic States with the Scandinavian and Nordic power grids, was partly funded by the EU and became operational in 2007. The cable will reduce Latvia's dependency on Russian supplies.
Latvia has the largest wind energy station in the Baltic, with a peak output of 2.5 million kilowatt hours of electricity per year (enough for over 1,500 households). The German energy company Preussen Elektra funded 70 per cent of the plant, which has a minimum operating life of 20 years. Over 500MW of wind energy is technically possible in the country, with only 20MW installed so far. National legislation facilitates investment in renewable energy.

Financial markets
Stock exchange
Rigas Fondsbørs (Riga Stock Exchange) (RSE)

Banking and insurance
The Bank of Latvia, the national central bank, is independent and manages the monetary supply and instigates governmental financial policy. The Financial Capital Markets Commission audits commercial banks. In the early 1990s most state banks were privatised and the sector proliferated. 1995 and 1998 saw major crises in the sector, involving mass insolvency and closures. Since then, regulation has been improved to stabilise Latvian banking and encourage investment by the West. Western owned banks control much of the country's finances. There are over 20 banks in operation.
Central bank
Latvijas Banka (Bank of Latvia)
Offshore facilities
Riga is popular with Russians seeking safe dollar accounts. Russian-linked banks have become influential in the sector.

Time
GMT plus two hours (daylight saving, late March to late September, GMT plus three hours)

Geography
Latvia is situated in north-eastern Europe on the east coast of the Baltic Sea. It is slightly larger than Switzerland at 64,589 sq km and is bordered by Estonia to the north, the Russian Federation to the east, Belarus to the south-east and Lithuania to the south and south-west. With rolling plains and gentle hills, half the country is less than 90 metres above sea level. There are over 2,300 lakes and 12,000 rivers; the longest is the River Daugava. The largest lake is Lake Lubans which stretches over 81 square km. Latvia's highest point is in the south-east of the country where Latgale Upland reaches 289 metres.
Hemisphere
Northern

Climate
Temperate climate, but with considerable temperature variations. Mildest areas along the Baltic coast. Summer is warm with relatively mild weather in spring and autumn. Summer sunshine may be nine hours a day. Winter, which lasts from November to mid-March, can be very cold. Rainfall is distributed throughout the year with the heaviest rainfall in August. Snowfalls are common in winter months.

Dress codes
Warm clothing is essential in winter as are a raincoat and umbrella during spring and summer. Business dress is conservative but relatively informal, with a jacket and tie expected for meetings.

Entry requirements
Passports
Required by all and must be valid for at least six months. For identification purposes, a photocopy of the passport should be carried at all times.
Visa
Required by all, except nationals of EU and Schengen area signatory countries, North America, Australasia and Japan. For further exceptions contact the nearest consulate or see www.am.gov.lv/en/service/ for a full list. A Schengen visa application (offered in several languages) can be downloaded from http://europa.eu/abc/travel/ see 'documents you will need'. All visitors must have valid travel health insurance, including emergency repatriation cover.
Currency advice/regulations
There are no restrictions on import and export of local and foreign currency. Travellers cheques, in freely convertible currencies, preferably US dollars and euros, are accepted.
Customs
Personal items are duty-free. There are no duties levied on alcohol and tobacco between EU member states, providing amounts imported are for personal consumption.
It is advisable to declare valuable items such as jewellery, cameras, computers and musical instruments. Ensure that the declaration is stamped by the customs officials.
A certificate must be obtained to export of art objects over 50 years old.
Prohibited imports
Illegal drugs; guns and ammunition (without a police import permit); fresh meat.

Health (for visitors)
Nationals of the European Economic Area (EEA) countries and Switzerland can access reduced cost and sometimes free medical treatment using a European Health Insurance Card (EHIC) while visiting the EEA. Exceptions include nationals of the 10 countries, which joined the EU in 2004, whose EHIC is not valid in Switzerland. Applications for the EHIC should be made before travelling.
Mandatory precautions
There are no special requirements.
Advisable precautions
It is advisable to be in date for the following immunisations: tuberculosis, hepatitis A and diphtheria.
Any medicines required by the traveller should be taken by the visitor, and it could be wise to have precautionary antibiotics if going outside major urban centres. Rabies is endemic.
A travel kit including a disposable syringe is a reasonable precaution. It is recommended to drink bottled water. The tap water is occasionally yellow.

Hotels
Riga has business-class hotels. Tips are included in restaurant bills.

Credit cards

Credit and charge cards are accepted in large hotels and restaurants and some shops. ATMs are widely found in towns and cities.

Public holidays (national)

Fixed dates

1 Jan (New Year), 1 May (Labour Day), 4 May (Restoration Day), 23 Jun (Ligo Day/Midsummer's Eve), 24 Jun (St John's Day/Summer Solstice), 18 Nov (National Day), 25–26 Dec (Christmas/Winter Solstice).

Variable dates

Good Friday, Easter Monday.

Working hours

Banking

Mon–Fri: 0900–1700. Some banks are open between 0900–1300 on Saturdays.

Business

Mon–Fri: 0830/0900–1730/1800.

Government

Mon–Fri: 0900–1700.

Shops

Mon–Fri: 1000–1900, Saturday: 1000–1600. Grocery and department stores are usually open from 0800 until 1900. There are quite a few food stores in Riga that provide 24-hour service.

Telecommunications

Mobile/cell phones

GSM 900/1800 services are available throughout most of the country.

Electricity supply

220V AC, 50 Hz. European-style two-pin plugs are in use.

Social customs/useful tips

Latvians can be reserved and formal, but hospitable. When meeting, shake hands and slightly nod your head. If invited to a private home, it is usual to bring flowers for the hostess. Business cards are widely used.

The informal custom of overcharging foreigners (particularly by taxi-drivers) has developed since 1991.

Taxi fares do not usually include a tip, whereas restaurant bills usually do. Tipping is generally expected. Carry small-denomination US dollar bills as well as local currency for tips, taxis etc.

Reference to Russia and Russians should be avoided, at least until you are sure of the ethnic background of your host. Many Latvians have strong feelings about Russia as many have relatives who were sent to Siberia during the Soviet period. It is also wise not to ask your host what they did before independence, as they may think you are asking whether they were in the Communist Party or even if they were sent to Siberia.

Security

As living standards have dropped, so the crime rate has risen since independence. Care should be taken not to display valuables when walking around the city.

When walking, travellers should be alert to the threat of pickpocketing and other forms of theft. Always avoid unlit streets and parks at night, and be extra vigilant if walking alone.

Wherever possible, guarded car-parks should be used and valuables kept out of sight.

Getting there

Air

National airline: Air Baltic (ABC)

International airport/s: Riga International (RIX) 8km west of Riga; facilities include currency exchange, car hire, post office, business lounge and duty-free. A courtesy shuttle bus and the number 22a bus (tickets available from the post office) run to city centre hotels; alternatively taxis are located in front of the terminal building, and the journey takes about 15 minutes.

Airport tax: None

Surface

Road: There are roads leading from all the surrounding countries, however not all have customs control and it is advisable to determine which border crossing has this facility before undertaking a fruitless journey. Visit http://www.transit.lv/ for details of the country's road network.

Rail: The Berlin to St Petersburg service passes through Daugavpils in south-eastern Latvia. Trains also link Riga with Moscow, St Petersburg and Minsk.

Water: There are direct ferries to Riga from Travemünde in Germany and Stockholm in Sweden.

Main port/s: Warm-water ports at Riga and Ventspils and Liepaja, (designated a Special Economic Zone (SEZ)).

Getting about

National transport

Air: Daily flights operate between Riga and Liepaja regional airport in the west.

Road: Latvia has a good road network, although secondary roads are in a variety of conditions.

Buses: The extensive bus network is a better form of transport than trains.

Rail: Riga is connected to all major towns and there are some cross country services. The railway terminal in Riga is Stacijas Laukums.

City transport

Taxis: Taxis can be flagged down or hired from taxis stands. All taxis have metres that should be used; there is a surcharge between 2200–0600. Some taxis accept credit cards and display a credit card sticker. Tipping is not usual.

Buses, trams & metro: There is an economic and extensive transport system, including buses, trams and trolley buses operating between 0530–2330 in Riga. In addition, some trolley bus and tram routes run an hourly night service. Tickets can be purchased from the driver or conductor. Routes are displayed on the Riga city map, available from most city kiosks.

Car hire

There are a number of international car hire firms in Riga. Either an international driving licence or an EU pink format licence is necessary and drivers have to be over 21 years old. Cars with drivers are also available. Traffic drives on the right, seat belts must be worn and car headlights must remain on at all times. Alcohol consumption and mobile phone use by drivers is strictly prohibited. Speed limits are 50kph in urban areas and 90kph on open roads.

BUSINESS DIRECTORY

The addresses listed below are a selection only. While World of Information makes every endeavour to check these addresses, we cannot guarantee that changes have not been made, especially to telephone numbers and area codes. We would welcome any corrections.

Telephone area codes

The international direct dialling (IDD) code for Latvia is +371, followed by area code

Daugavpils	54	Rezekne	46
Jelgava	30	Riga	not required
Liepaja	34	Ventspils	36

Useful telephone numbers

Fire brigade: 01

Police: 02

Ambulance: 03

National telephone operator: 116

International telephone operator: 115

Train information: 1181

Chambers of Commerce

American Chamber of Commerce in Latvia, 4 Torna iela, Riga 1050 (tel/fax: 721-2204; e-mail: amcham@amcham.lv).

British Chamber of Commerce in Latvia, Valdemara Centres, 21 Kr Valdemara iela, Riga 1010 (tel: 703-5202; fax: 703-5318; e-mail: info@bccl.lv).

Latvian Chamber of Commerce and Industry, 35 Kr Valdemara iela, Riga 1010 (tel: 722-5595; fax: 782-0092; e-mail: info@chamber.lv).

Banking

Hansabank, 26 Kalku Street, Riga LV-1050 (tel: 702-44444; fax: 702-4400; e-mail: info@hansabanka.lv).

Latvijas Krājbanka, 1 Palasta Street, Riga LV-1954 (tel: 709-2020; fax: 721-2083).

Parex Banka, 3 Smilsu Street, Riga LV-1522 (tel: 701-0000; fax: 701-0001; e-mail: inquiry@parex.lv).

Saules Bank, 16 Smilsu Street, Riga (tel: 702-0500; fax: 702-0505; e-mail: office@saules.com).

Unibanka, 23 Pils Street, Riga (tel: 721-5555; fax: 721-5566; e-mail: atsauksmes@unibanka.lv).

Central bank

Latvijas Banka, K Valdemara iela 2a, LV-1050, Riga (tel: 702-2300; fax: 702-2420; e-mail: info@bank.lv).

Stock exchange

Rigas Fondsbørs (Riga Stock Exchange) (RSE): www.omxnordicexchange.com

Travel information

Air Baltic Corporation (ABC), Riga International Airport, Riga LV-1053 (tel: 207-777; fax: 207-505); Kalku iela 15, Riga LV-1050 (tel: 207-777; fax: 722-8284).

LDZ (Latvian Railways), 3 Gogola Street, Riga, LV-1547 (tel: 723-1181; fax: 782-0231; International booking: 721-664; internet: www.ldz.lv).

Latvian Tourism Development Agency, Pils laukums 4, Riga (tel: 722-9945; fax: 750-8468; e-mail: tda@latviatourism.lv).

Lidosta Airport flight enquiries (tel: 207-009; fax: 348-654).

Lufthansa Airport Office (tel: 207-183; fax: 207-026); city centre, Kr Barona iela 7-9, Riga LV-1442 (tel: 728-5614; fax: 782-8199).

Polish Airlines, Maza Pils iela 5, Riga LV 1863 (tel: 724-2870; fax: 724-2869).

Riga International Airport Information (tel: 720-7009; internet site: http://www.riga-airport.com).

Riair (Rigas Aeronavijas), 1 Melluzu Street, Riga LV-1067 (tel: 720-7325; fax: 786-0189).

Riga Bus Station (Autoosta) (tel: 721-3611, 721-3826).

Riga Tourist Information Centre, 22 Skarnu iela (tel: 722-1731; fax: 722-7680; internet: www.rigatourism.com).

SAS, Kalku iela 15, Riga LV 1050 (tel: 721-6139; fax: 722-4282).

Ministry of tourism

Ministry of Environmental Protection and Regional Development, Peldu iela 25, Riga (tel: 702-6492; fax: 782-0442; e-mail: tourism@varam.gov.lv).

National tourist organisation offices

Latvian Tourist Board, Riga 800 Office, Torna iela 4, 1B-103, Riga LV-1050 (tel: 732-0550; fax: 732-0609; e-mail: ltboard@latnet.lv; internet: www.latviatourism.lv).

Ministries

Department of Citizenship and Immigration, 6 Raina Blvd, Riga LV-1181 (tel: 721-9181; fax: 782-0156).

Latvian Customs Department Kr Valdemara iela 1a, Riga LV-1841 (tel: 732-0928; fax: 732-2440).

Ministry of Agriculture, Republikas Laukums 2, Riga LV-1981 (tel: 702-7107; fax: 702-7512).

Ministry of Culture, Kr Valdemara iela 11a, Riga LV-1364 (tel: 722-4772; fax: 722-7916).

Ministry of Defence, Kr Valdemara iela 10-12, Riga LV-1010 (tel: 721-0124; fax: 783-0236).

Ministry of Economics, Brivibas Boulevard 55, LV 1519 Riga (tel: 701-3109; fax: 728-0882); Department of Energy Development (tel: 728-7730, 722-0151; fax: 733-8026, 722-4794).

Ministry of Education, Vajnu iela 2, 1098 Riga (tel: 722-2415; fax: 721-3992; e-mail: vetpmu@com.latnet.lv).

Ministry of Environmental Protection and Regional Development, Peldu St 25, 1494 Riga (tel: 722-3612; fax: 782-0442; e-mail: Saule@varam.gov.lv).

Ministry of Finance, Smilsu iela 1, Riga LV-1919 (tel: 722-6672; fax: 721-1140); World Bank Technical Unit (tel: 722-0348; fax: 782-0168).

Ministry of Foreign Affairs, 36 Brivibas bulv, Riga LV-1395 (tel: 701-6210; fax: 728-2121; e-mail: info@info.gov.lv; internet site: http://www.mfa.gov.lv).

Ministry of the Interior, Raina bulv 6, Riga LV-1533 (tel: 728-7260; fax: 721-2255).

Ministry of Justice, Brivibas bulv 34, Riga LV-1536 (tel: 728-2607; fax: 728-5575).

Ministry of Transport, Gogola iela 3, 1743, Riga (tel: 702-8214; fax: 721-7180).

Ministry of Welfare, Skolas iela 28, Riga LV-1331 (tel: 729-2800; fax: 727-6445).

State Property Fund (privatisation), Ministry of Economics, 36 Brivibas Boulevard, LV 1519 Riga (tel: 213-501; fax: 280-882); external department (tel: 722-5426; fax: 828-223).

Other useful addresses

Association of Insurers, Valnu iela 1, Riga LV-1912 (tel: 722-4375, fax: 724-3286).

Baltic Data House Ltd (marketing research), Akas iela 5/7, Riga LV-1050 (tel: 227-6144; fax: 227-6246, 934-6442).

British Council, Blaumena iela 5a, LV-1050 Riga (tel: 232-0468; fax: 883-0031).

British Embassy, 5 Alunana iela, Riga LV-1010 (tel: 733-8126/31; fax: 733-8132).

Business Centre (to use fax, telex, xerox, e-mail, typing, international telephone) 55 Elizabetes, Hotel 'Latvia' (tel: 722-2211).

Central Statistical Bureau of Latvia, Lacplesa Str, 1 Riga (tel: 727-0126; fax: 782-0166; internet site: www.csb.lv/avidus.cfm).

Commercial Port of Riga, Eksporta iela 6, Riga LV-1242 (tel: 732-5350; fax: 783-0051).

Commercial Port of Ventspils, Dzintaru iela 22, Ventspils LV-3602 (tel: 22-821; 21-231).

Committee for Television & Radio Broadcasting, Doma Laukums 8, Riga LV-226935 (tel: 227-906; fax: 200-025).

Consular Department, Elizabetes iela 57, Riga (tel: 728-6815; 928-7398 (24 hours); fax: 782-8274).

Department of Customs, Kr Valdemara iela 1a, Riga LV-1181 (tel: 721-9639; fax: 733-1123; e-mail: pmlp@pmlp.gov.lv).

Enterprise Support Centre, Perses Str 2, 1011 Riga (tel: 722-7623, 728-9328; fax: 782-0442); External Adviser (tel: 701-3161; fax: 782-8251, 728-0882).

Fire Protection Agency, 5 Maskavas Street, Riga (tel: 220-1322).

Government Information Agency, 36 Brivibas bulv, Riga LV-1070 (tel: 728-2828; fax: 728-4450).

Interlatvija Foreign Trade Association, Komunaru Bulv 1, 226010 Riga (tel: 332-952, 333-597; fax 226-070).

International Advertising Association, Liela Pils iela 9, Riga LV-1755 (tel: 722-8361; fax: 722-9252).

Komunalprojekts AS, 148A Brivibas Blvd, Riga LV 1012 (tel/fax: 237-6920).

Latvian Association of Civil Construction Engineers, 22/24 Grecinieku Street, Riga LV 050 (tel: 721-2661; fax: 722-4832).

Latvian Association of Traders, Kr Barona 48/50, LV-1011 Riga (tel: 721-7372; fax: 782-1010).

Latvian Business Consultants' Association, Jauniela 24, Riga LV-1050 (tel: 722-0320, 782-0076; fax: 722-8926).

Latvian Business Union (commercial information), Bungada PO Box 475, 226001 Riga (tel: 320-888; fax: 217-633).

Latvian Development Agency, Business Information Institute, 2 Perses Street, Riga LV-1442 (tel: 728-3425; fax: 782-0458; e-mail: invest@lda.gov.lv; internet site: www.lda.gov.lv).

Latvian Embassy (USA), 4325 17th Street, NW, Washington DC 20011 (tel: (+1-202) 726-8213; fax: (+1-202) 726-6785; e-mail: embassy@latvia-usa.org).

Latvian Foreign Trade Centre, 2 Elizabetes Street, Riga (tel: 732-0619, 732-1818, 732-2816; fax: 783-0035, 732-3313).

Latvian Privatisation Agency, Kr Valdemara Street 31, Riga LV-1887 (tel: 732-2281, 733-2082; fax: 783-0363; e-mail: lpa@mail.bkc.lv).

Latvian Retailers' Association, Kr Barona iela 48/50, Riga LV-1011 (tel: 721-7372; fax: 782-1010).

Latvian State Radio, 8 Doma Laukums (tel: 720-6722; fax: 720-6709, 782-0216).

Liepaja Special Economic Zone Authority, 4 Feniksa iela, LV-3401 Liepaja (tel: 26-605; fax: 80-252).

Main Post Office, Brivibas Bulvaris 21, Riga (tel: 224-155; fax: 733-1920).

National Environmental Health Centre, 7 Klijanu Street, Riga (tel: 237-7473; fax: 237-5940).

Port of Liepaja, Feniksa iela 4, Liepaja LV-3400 (tel: 342-5887; fax: 789-3418).

Public Investment Unit, Brivibas Blv. 36, 1519 Riga (tel: 701-3122; fax: 782-0458).

Riga City Council, 3 kr Valdemara Street, Riga LV-1539 (tel: 232-0680; fax: 222-0785).

Riga Fairs, Conferences & Exhibitions (tel: 213-637).

Riga Commercial Port, 5a Katrinas Street, Riga LV-1227 (tel: 732-9224; fax: 783-0215; e-mail: rto@mail.bkc.lv).

Rigas Ostas Parvalde (Riga Port Authority), 6 Eksporta St, Riga LV-1010 (tel: 732-2644; fax: 783-0051).

Riga Stock Exchange, Doma Laukums 6, Riga LV-1885 (tel: 721-2431, 722-9449; fax: 722-4515).

Saeima (Parliament), 16 Jekaba (tel: 732-2938; fax: 721-1611).

US Embassy, Raina Bulvaris 7, LV-1050 Riga (tel: 721-0005, 722-0367, 722-9709; fax: 722-6530).

Ventspils Free Port Authority, 8 Uzavas Str, Ventspils LV3601 (tel: 362-2586; fax: 362-1297).

Ventspils Tirdznecibas Osta (Ventspils Commercial Port), 20a Dzintaru Street, Ventspils LV-3602 (tel: 366-8778; fax: 362-1231).

World Trade Centre, Elizabetes iela 2, Riga LV-1340 (tel: 322-242; fax: 7830-0385).

National news agency: LETA (Latvian News Agency), 2 Marijas Street, Riga (tel: 6722-2509; fax: 6722-3850; internet: www.leta.lv).

Other news agencies: BNS: www.bns.lv

Delfi (in Latvian and Russian):www.delfi.lv

Internet sites

Baltic News Service: http://www.bns.ee

Business in the Baltic States: http://www.binet.lv/english/database

Latvian information: http://www.ciesin.ee/LATVIA/

Pirma banka: http://www.rkb.lv

Trasta Komercbanka: http://www.tkb.lv

Lebanon

KEY FACTS

Official name: Jumhouriya al Lubnaniya (Republic of Lebanon)

Head of State: President Michel Suleiman (from 25 May 2008)

Head of government: Prime Minister Najib Mikati (from 25 Jan 2011)

Ruling party: A coalition government led by 14 March Alliance

Area: 10,452 square km

Population: 4.30 million (2010)*

Capital: Beirut

Official language: Arabic

Currency: Lebanese pound (LL) = 100 piastres

Exchange rate: LL1,506.00 per US$ (Oct 2011)

GDP per capita: US$10,044 (2010)

GDP real growth: 7.50% (2010)

GDP: US$39.20 billion (2010)

Inflation: 4.50% (2010)

Balance of trade: -US$12.26 billion (2010)

* Estimated figure

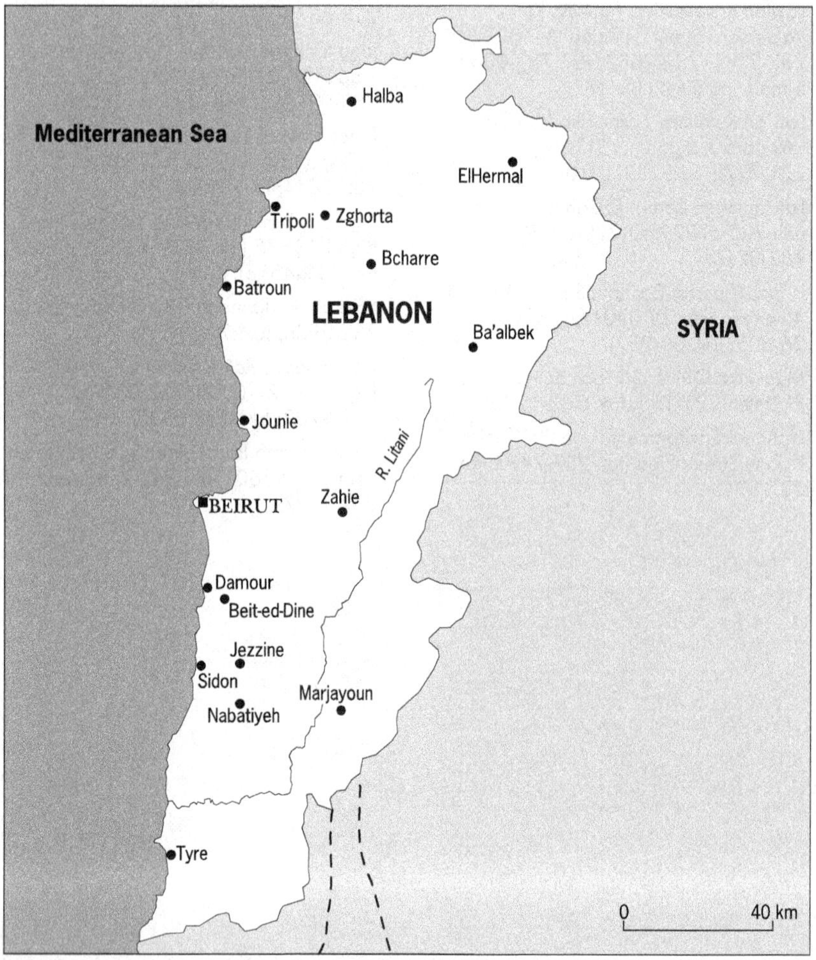

Like a number of flashpoint countries, Lebanon's biggest problem is that of its neighbours. Long seen by Syria as a vassal state, Lebanon has also had to cope with the mistrust of its neighbour to the south, Israel. As if that were not enough, Lebanon also had to come to terms with the volatile presence of Hezbollah in its midst. Although the Shi'ite grouping was thought to be governed and directed from Syria, its operational base and the country within which it has exercised greatest political influence, is Lebanon.

Fault lines

In January 2011 the inevitable happened when, after a period of deepening instability, Lebanon's government, led by the pro-Western 14 March Alliance collapsed. In many ways, given the obstacles that confront any form of government in Lebanon, the surprising thing was that it had lasted as long as it had. The government's collapse was brought about by the resignation of no less than 11 of the cabinet's 30 ministers, 10 of whom were Hezbollah. The opposition 8 March Alliance had been shanghaied into government in 2008 with the promise of a vote-blocking third of cabinet posts. The government set about reviving the economy, in which (see Economy below) it succeeded. Where it failed, however (as had so many before it) was in reconciling the complex mosaic of often antagonistic political and religious interests that makes up the Lebanon.

Expressed in its simplest terms, the struggle that dominates Lebanese politics sets the pro-Western forces linked to the son of assassinated former Prime Minister Rafik al Hariri, and Lebanon's current prime minister, Saad al Hariri, against Hezbollah and its allies, backed by Syria and Iran. All are represented in the national unity government set up under Qatari mediation in the wake of the 2008 street battles, but they are generally unable to agree on much.

In late 2010 a tense meeting of Lebanon's deeply-divided national unity government had agreed to halt public disagreements and resume some sort of dialogue to resolve their bitter internal differences. However the meeting failed to settle any of the issues which had looked certain to prompt sectarian violence and even, according to the London BBC the collapse of the government. Each side had accused the other of trying to take over the Lebanese state. All the elements of the Lebanese political clash can be traced back to the 2005 assassination al Hariri. A special international tribunal was set up under UN auspices to investigate the killing. There have long been unconfirmed reports that the tribunal was close to indicting members of Hezbollah for their role in the assassination, although it first focussed its attention on alleged Syrian involvement. Unsurprisingly, Hezbollah has denied any role in the Hariri killing, dismissing the tribunal as an 'Israeli instrument'. Inevitably, the tension over the assassination had generated derivative tensions leading, in an established pattern of Lebanese politics, to increasingly inflammatory rhetoric and accusations.

The extent of the tensions became clear in late 2010 following a news conference by the former head of general security, Brigadier General Jamil al Sayyid. General Sayyid accused Prime Minister Hariri of manipulating events in order to inculpate Syria. The General, who had been accused of involvement in the assassination, demanded redress, a claim supported by Hezbollah. The general called on the Lebanese to revolt against Mr Hariri's government. He then disappeared to France, returning to Beirut to face a summons to explain his statements. He was met at Beirut's airport by a large group of armed Hezbollah 'supporters'. Meanwhile, Mr Hariri's supporters accused Hezbollah of invading the airport and flouting official state security and authority. In response Hezbollah loyalists claimed that the prime minister's followers had already carried out a coup from within by taking control of state institutions. General Sayyid had also demanded the dismissal of a number of Hariri allies, insisting that the assassination should be investigated and properly prosecuted as a priority, before dealing with the reports of the international tribunal and any indictments it may produce.

As Saudi Arabia attempted to preserve the peace in Lebanon, Prime Minister Hariri had appeared to admit that the accusations which he and others had voiced against Syria were 'political' and withdrew them. Mr Hariri also admitted the existence of what he described as 'false witnesses' who had misled the tribunal and upset Lebanon's relations with Syria. This seemed to be something of a volte-face and a confusing one at that. Mr Hariri had made vociferous public accusations that the Syrians were behind his father's death. The UN-backed tribunal looking into the assassination handed its report to the Lebanese government in June. The deal was that it should remain confidential for at least 30 days. Lebanese officials said four arrest warrants were issued for Hezbollah members, including senior leader Mustafa Badreddine, but refused to confirm any names.

This reflected a major shift in the regional balance of power, suggesting that Syrian influence was again a factor in Lebanese politics. Coincidentally or otherwise, one of Mr Hariri's erstwhile allies, the Druze leader Walid Jumblatt, (who had also accused the Syrians of killing his father, in 1977), had restored relations with both Hezbollah and Syria, at the same time distancing himself from Mr Hariri's 14 March Alliance. Mr Jumblatt, who has been mediating between the two factions, has suggested that there should be a consensus decision to drop the international tribunal if it is likely to produce an inflammatory situation on the ground in Lebanon.

The fault line at the heart of Lebanese politics risked leading to a conflagration between the Sunni community (who largely support Mr Hariri) and Hezbollah's Shi'a community. The Lebanese government agreement to cool down the rhetoric may also help to keep the lid on things for the moment. But the issues underlying the tension and the deep divisions they signal, have not gone away.

The Syria question

A year later and the matter of Lebanese relations with Syria had taken on a different aspect. In simple terms, the question boiled down to whether the incumbent Syrian régime, which United Nations reports suggested had killed upwards of 5,000 protesters, was to be supported or not. In late 2011, the head of Hezbollah's Shura Council, Sheikh Mohammad Yazbek, announced that the group would remain supportive of Syria in the face of conspiracies. Quoted in the Beirut *Daily Star* the Sheikh said that: 'Syria's only guilt is the support it has given to those who resist and we will stand by this country, its army, leadership and people so that

KEY INDICATORS — **Lebanon**

	Unit	2006	2007	2008	2009	2010
Population	m	3.70	3.76	3.81	3.86	*4.30
Gross domestic product (GDP)	US$bn	22.40	25.00	29.40	33.60	39.20
GDP per capita	US$	5,969	6,663	7,708	8,707	10,044
GDP real growth	%	0.6	7.5	9.3	3.5	7.5
Inflation	%	5.6	4.1	10.8	1.2	4.5
Industrial output	% change	-1.0	12.9	2.0	3.0	–
Agricultural output	% change	-6.0	-4.6	2.5	3.5	–
Exports (fob) (goods)	US$m	3,207.0	4,077.0	5,251.0	4,716.0	5,466.0
Imports (fob) (goods)	US$m	9,345.0	11,926.0	16,261.0	15,895.0	17,728.0
Balance of trade	US$m	-6,138.0	-7,850.0	-11,010.0	-11,179.0	-12,263.0
Current account	US$m	-1,372.0	-2,634.0	-4,103.0	-7,555.0	-8,797.0
Total reserves minus gold	US$m	13,376.4	12,909.9	20,244.5	29,102.9	31,514.1
Foreign exchange	US$m	13,313.3	12,844.1	20,181.8	28,744.5	31,163.3
Exchange rate	per US$	1,512.00	1,512.00	1,512.00	1,512.00	1,507.50

* estimated figure

it would remain in the face of all conspiracies aimed at tearing the [Arab] nation.' Hezbollah, headquartered in Damascus has repeatedly voiced its support for President Bashar al Assad's government and repeated Damascus' views that the country is facing a foreign conspiracy to topple Assad.

At the other end of the political spectrum, Lebanese Forces (LF) leader Samir Geagea announced that Lebanon would begin a process of state building following the collapse of President Assad's government, which he predicted would happen in 2012. 'Following the fall of the Syrian regime, we will enter a complicated political process before we create another political system that is well defined and capable of building relations between Lebanon and Syria as two [separate] states,' Mr Geagea advised. Mr Geagea had been a staunch critic of both of Bashar al Assad's government and of Damascus' relations with Beirut. The LF leader, with his allies in the 14 March Alliance, had repeatedly voiced support for the uprising in Syria.

The economy

In its October 2010 report on the Lebanese economy, the International Monetary Fund (IMF) was fulsome in its praise for the government's economic management. Lebanon's economy may be booming, but to sustain growth and translate economic expansion into jobs and broader social gains, Lebanon needs to strengthen public finances, upgrade its infrastructure and improve the business environment, according to IMF economists.

The IMF found that domestic economic and financial conditions remained favourable, possibly more so than at any point since the civil war ended in 1990. After two years of relative political stability, the country had shown an 'exceptional 'resilience in the face of the global financial crisis and a capacity to rebound and thrive. Led by a dynamic private sector, Lebanon grew an estimated 9 per cent in 2009 dropping slightly, to 8 per cent in 2010.

To sustain the rebound in growth and to achieve durable job creation, in the view of the IMF, a major effort is needed to upgrade the country's infrastructure (mainly electricity and water supply, telecommunications and transport) and improve the business environment. Growth is currently concentrated in a few sectors – retail trade, tourism services and construction – in and around Beirut. To achieve more widespread and durable growth, electricity and water must be provided around the clock; energy, telecommunication and transportation costs reduced; and internet services improved.

But the government will need to reconcile plans for a substantial increase in infrastructure investments with the need to maintain macro-economic stability and reduce the country's debt burden. While significantly reduced in recent years, Lebanon's public debt – at about 148 per cent of gross domestic product (GDP) – still ranks among the highest in the world and drains about half of the annual budget revenues in interest payments, leaving little room for productive public spending. The need to refinance this large stock of debt from time to time is a source of vulnerability, despite Lebanon's dedicated and resilient investor base.

A determined strategy to reduce the debt-to-GDP ratio is thus essential, the IMF said. Such a strategy should not rely solely on economic growth but also focus on creating fiscal space to reduce the deficit while increasing social spending and public investment in infrastructure. This will require increasing tax revenues – in an efficient and equitable manner, by broadening the tax base and possibly raising some tax rates – and cutting inefficient public spending, including through electricity sector reforms to reduce the need for large untargeted transfers from the budget.

In the near term, a key issue is to manage the buoyant economy so as to avoid excessive pressures on consumer and real estate prices and a widening of the external current account deficit, among other things. In the view of the IMF this will require a prudent fiscal policy stance as well as monetary and prudent policies aimed at tempering deposit inflows and avoiding excessive credit growth. At the same time, risks of a slowdown in growth – for example, from the recent rise in political tensions – must also be monitored.

In the medium term, the main challenges are to address the sizeable remaining macro-financial vulnerabilities and implement growth-enhancing structural reforms. This involves taking decisive measures to gradually reduce the budget deficit (which reached over 8 per cent of GDP last year) and re-launching the structural reform agenda to maintain high and sustainable rates of growth.

The Banque du Liban (BDL) (Bank of Lebanon) (central bank) has so far been successful in shielding Lebanon from the global financial turmoil. Attractive interest rates promoted continued deposit inflows, thereby supporting the exchange rate peg and allowing an unprecedented accumulation of foreign exchange reserves during the past two years. Now that BDL reserves have reached a comfortable level, interest rates have been lowered to moderate deposit inflows to a pace that can be more readily absorbed by the economy. Lebanon's banking sector is thriving but the authorities need to continue to strengthen bank regulation and supervision and to prevent excessive risk taking. Prudent regulation helped prevent Lebanese banks from being overly exposed to risky assets, a strategy that proved far-sighted during the global financial crisis. Now, with a thriving economy and real estate sector, care should be taken to prevent any weakening in credit standards and excessive leverage. Domestic banks are expanding abroad to diversify their business and take advantage of growth opportunities in other markets. This is a welcome development, but also requires a sharp focus on cross-border supervision to ensure that the banking sector remains strong.

Risk assessment

Economy	Good
Politics	Poor
Regional stability	Poor

COUNTRY PROFILE

Historical profile

1926 The constitution was approved and the Lebanese Republic declared.
1940 Lebanon came under the control of the Vichy French government.
1941 After occupation by Free French and British troops, independence was declared.
1943 France agreed to the transfer of power to the Lebanese government with effect from 1944.
1948 A major influx of Arab refugees from Palestine built tensions between Christian Maronites and Muslim Shi'as.
1958 The first civil war erupted between Muslim and Christian groups
1964 Yasser Arafat established a Palestine Liberation Organisation (PLO) stronghold in Lebanon.
1970 Anti-Israeli terrorist attacks from Lebanese bases increased after the PLO was expelled from Jordan. Israeli retaliations further alienated leftist Muslims from conservative Maronites (the largest Christian sect) and undermined governmental legitimacy, with nine changes in three years.
1975 Full-scale civil war erupted between Muslims (with PLO aid) and Christians. Southern Lebanon and the western half of

Beirut became bases for the PLO and other Muslim militias, while the Christians controlled East Beirut and the Christian section of Mt Lebanon.
1976 A 30,000-strong Arab Deterrent Force was established to restore peace.
1978 In reprisal for an attack by Palestinians based in Lebanon, Israel invaded and occupied the south of the country; the UN called on Israel to withdraw its troops; it handed over the territory to the mainly Christian Lebanese militia.
1982 Hezbollah (Party of God) was formed by Muslim clerics, backed by Iran and Syria, to respond to the Israeli invasion of Lebanon and to advocate the establishment of an Islamic government (it became a political movement in 1985 and entered parliament in 1992). Israel launched a full-scale invasion after an assassination attempt on Shlomo Argov, its ambassador to the UK. Syria, which maintained a large army in Lebanon, unsuccessfully fought Israel. Christian Phalangist militiamen, with Israeli compliance, massacred more than 1,000 Palestinian refugees in the Sabra and Shatila camps. A Western multinational force monitored the evacuation of the PLO to Tunis.
1983 Hostilities between Israel and Lebanon ended. Syrian forces remained in Lebanon.
1985 Despite withdrawing from most of the territory, Israel maintained some troops in support of the mainly Christian South Lebanon Army (SLA) (a militia set up and supported by Israel) in order to help secure its own northern border.
1986–90 Factional conflict worsened as various efforts at national reconciliation failed. Lebanon had two governments – one mainly Muslim in West Beirut, headed by Salim al Huss, the other, Christian, in East Beirut, led by the Maronite Commander-in-Chief of the Army, General Michel Aoun.
1989 Under the Ta'if Accord, a government of national reconciliation was formed with an equal number of Christian and Muslim members. Elias Hrawi was elected president.
1990 The civil war ended and General Aoun fled.
1992 President Hrawi appointed Rafik al Hariri as prime minister, heading a cabinet of technocrats. Al Hariri, a rich businessman, born in Sidon but with Saudi Arabian nationality, became the mastermind behind the reconstruction of Lebanon.
1993–97 The Oslo Peace Accords laid the basis for transfer of authority from the Israeli military administration to the PLO in the Gaza Strip and an undefined area around the town of Jericho in the West Bank. A follow-up treaty, Oslo II, envisaged Palestinian autonomy, with Israeli troop units withdrawing from the West Bank. Yasser Arafat was elected president of the Palestinian Legislative Council (PLC), the assembly of the Palestinian National Authority (PNA). Attacks and reprisals continued between Hezbollah and Palestinian guerrillas, and Israel.
1998 The National Assembly elected army chief of staff, General Émile Lahoud, as president, replacing Elias Hrawi. Following the resignation of Prime Minister al Hariri, Salim al Huss was appointed to the post.
2000 The Israeli army withdrew from southern Lebanon and the SLA disbanded. Sporadic clashes continued between Hezbollah and Israeli forces. Rafik al Hariri won convincingly at the elections and was re-appointed prime minister.
2003 Israeli warplanes and artillery attacked suspected Hezbollah positions in the disputed Shebaa Farms area in south Lebanon in retaliation for guerrilla attacks.
2004 Syria insisted that President Lahoud's term in office be extended until 2007, which was approved by parliament. UN Security Council resolution 1559 demanded that Syrian soldiers leave Lebanon and that Hezbollah disarm. Rafik al Hariri opposed the extension of Lahoud's term and stood down as prime minister; Omar Karami was nominated for the post.
2005 Former prime minister Rafik al Hariri was assassinated. Syria was accused of supporting the perpetrators. Thousands of protesters gathered in Beirut, demanding the withdrawal of Syrian troops; the pro-Syrian government resigned. Syria agreed to withdraw its troops to the Bekaa valley in eastern Lebanon. Najib Mikati became prime minister of a mixed pro- and anti-Syrian cabinet. Syrian troops pulled out of Lebanon. In parliamentary elections, Hariri-Jumblatt, the bloc led by Sa'ad al Hariri (son of Rafik al Hariri), won 72 seats, the Shi'a Muslim bloc of Amal and Hezbollah won 35 seats and the anti-Syrian Michel Aoun and allies won 21 seats. Fouad Siniora became prime minister. He formed a cabinet which mostly included those opposed to Syrian involvement in Lebanon but also included – for the first time – ministers of the Hezbollah and Amal movements. Four pro-Syrian generals were charged with the assassination of Rafik al Hariri, following the findings of the UN's chief investigator.
2006 Israel bombed southern Lebanon after Hezbollah kidnapped two Israeli soldiers while raiding Israel. Israel invaded the south attempting to retrieve its soldiers but after 34 days of fighting without a conclusive victory and the death of approximately 1,000 Lebanese, the Israelis agreed to a truce. Israeli troops withdrew and the Lebanese army deployed along the border. Hezbollah claimed the war was 'a strategic and historical victory for Lebanon against the Israeli enemy'. Plans for a UN tribunal to prosecute the suspects in the Rafik al Hariri assassination led to the resignation of ministers of Hezbollah and the Amal.
2007 International donors pledged US$7.4 billion in aid towards reconstruction and the repayment of war debt at a conference held in Paris. The anti-Syrian politician, Antoine Ghanim, was assassinated. Syria denied responsibility. The death of Ghanim plus several more assassinations of anti-Syrian members of parliament reduced the government's majority and with the lack of a quorum forced the first presidential vote in parliament to be postponed. A compromise candidate for president, Michel Suleiman, won backing from all political parties. However, as a serving military officer, the constitution had to be amended to allow his candidacy. In order to gain enough support Suleiman had to agree a shortened presidential term in office, to end in 2009 instead of 2013, and an appointed prime minister with neutral allegiances. Presidential elections were postponed several more times.
2008 The Lebanese National Dialogue Conference between religious blocs and political parties agreed to new electoral laws, whereby the128-seat Majlis al Nuwab (parliament) was allocated equally between Christians and Muslims with 64 seats each; while individual constituencies were elected by proportional representation among religious communities (confessionally distributed). Elections for president were again postponed until General Michel Suleiman was finally elected president; he received 118 votes out of 127 and was sworn in immediately. Prime Minister Siniora announced the formation of a national unity government with members from all political and religious blocs. An agreed common border was formally demarcated between Lebanon and Syria, in a move to improve diplomatic relations. Syria opened an embassy in Beirut.
2009 President Suleiman approved the appointment of Mr Ali Abdul Karim Ali as Syrian ambassador to Lebanon, thereby re-establishing full diplomatic relations for the first time since the 1940s. A former Syrian security officer suspected of assassinating Rafik al Hariri was detained in Dubai on an international arrest warrant. Before he could be extradited to Denmark to the Special Tribunal for Lebanon (STL) at the International Court of Justice (ICJ) he absconded. In parliamentary elections, within the 14 March Alliance (Christians), the Maronites won 34 seats, the Greek

Orthodox 14; within the 8 March Alliance (Muslims) the Shi'a (Hezbollah) and Sunni each won 27 seats. Sa'ad al Hariri was nominated as prime minister by President Suleiman; 86 members of parliament confirmed his appointment. Hezbollah agreed to join a unity government under Prime Minister Hariri, breaking a four month deadlock over the appointment of a government; 15 ministers were nominated from the 14 March Alliance and 10 from the 8 March Alliance; the president nominated five appointees for the remaining ministries.

2010 Prime Minister Hariri visited Syria in July to discuss bilateral relations and closer ties. On 6 September, Hariri said his accusation that Syria was responsible for the murder of his father was an error and that it was a 'political accusation'. Water shortages are predicted for 2010–11 due to the lack of investment in 11 new dams proposed by the ministry of energy and water, despite foreign aid totalling US$44 million being pledged to support the programme.

2011 On 12 January, the Hezbollah group of 10 cabinet ministers resigned and therefore the whole cabinet was considered resigned. On 25 January the president, with agreement of 68 of 125 members of parliament, appointed Hezbollah-backed candidate, Najib Mikati, as prime minister. On 30 June, the chief prosecutor of the STL issued indictments for four, senior members of Hezbollah – Assad Sabra, Hassan Issa, Salim Ayachhe and Moustaf Badredine, accused of the assassination of former prime minister Rafiq Hariri in 2005. In August, the authorities asked Hezbollah to hand over the suspects for trial; failing that they will be tried *in absentia*.

Political structure

Constitution

The constitution was enacted in May 1926, and has since been amended on five occasions. A key amendment agreed under the Ta'if Agreement of 1989 reduced the authority of the president by transferring executive power to the cabinet. The prime minister must be a Sunni Muslim, with the cabinet made up of equal numbers of Muslims and Christians. An amendment to the constitution was introduced in 2000, reducing the minimum age of a president from 40 to 34 years. Following the Lebanese National Dialogue Conference, in 2007, between religious blocs and political parties, an agreement was reached for new electoral laws, whereby the128-seat parliament is allocated equally between Christians and Muslims at 64 seats each; while individual constituencies are elected by proportional representation among religious communities (confessionally distributed).

Independence date

22 November 1943.

Form of state

Republic

The executive

As head of state, the president is elected for a single six-year term by parliament and should be a Maronite Christian. Since 1990, however, Syria has effectively chosen the president and thereby alienated large parts of the Christian community. Under the consitution, the president chooses the prime minister upon recommendation from the parliament. In reality, Syria decides who is appointed to the position. The prime minister, who must be a Sunni Muslim, is responsible for choosing members of the 30-member Council of Ministers (cabinet). Ministers may be selected from inside or outside parliament. President General Émile Lahoud's six-year term of office, which was due to end in November 2004, was extended by parliament by three years.

National legislature

The Majlis al Nuwab (unicameral National Assembly) has 128 parliamentary members (MP), elected for a five-year term, by a religious community into allocated seats: Maronites (34), Sunnites (27), Shi'ites (27), Greek Orthodox (14), Greek Catholics (eight), Druzes (eight), Armenian Orthodox (five), Alaouites (two), Armenian Catholics (one), Protestants (one), Christian Minorities (one).

Parliament reduced the voting age from 21 to 18 on 19 March 2009; a national referendum must ratify the decision.

Legal system

The legal system is based on the 1926 constitution and the Commercial Code, the Civil Procedure Code, the Criminal Procedure Code and the Penal Code. French law has had a lasting impact on local legislation, while Ottoman law and Islamic law have also influenced Lebanon's legal system. Civil law is based on the Code of Obligations and Contracts and the Land Ownership Law. Various branches of the legal framework are being revised and updated. Lebanon has an independent judiciary.

Last elections

7 July 2009 (parliamentary); 25 May 2008 (presidential)

Results: Parliamentary: 14 March Alliance including Tayyar Al Mustaqbal (Future Movement) (Future) (Maronite), Hizb al Taqadummi al Ishtiraki (Progressive Socialists Party) (PSP) (Druze), Al Quwat al Lubnaniyya (Lebanese Forces) (LF) (Maronite), Hizb al-Kataeb (Kataeb Party) and others won 71 seats (out of 128). The 8 March Alliance, including Hezbollah (Shi'a); Harakat Amal (Amal Movement) (Sunni); Al Hizb al Qawmi al souri al ijtima'I (Syrian Social Nationalist Party), Ba'arth (Arab Socialist Ba'arth Party) and others won 29 seats. Change and Reform alliance, including Tayyar Al Watani Al Horr (Free Patriotic Movement) (FPM) (Maronite), Marada Movement, Armenian Revolutionary Federation and Lebanese Democratic Party won 28 seats.

Presidential: Michel Suleiman was elected president by the National Assembly.

Next elections

2013 (parliamentary and presidential)

Political parties

Ruling party

A coalition government led by 14 March Alliance

Main opposition party

Population

4.30 million (2010)*

Last census: 3 March 2007: 3,759,134 (excluding Palestinian refugees in camps)

Population density: 90 per cent (1995—2001).

Annual growth rate: 1.4 per cent 1994–2004 (WHO 2006)

Ethnic make-up

The Lebanese belong to a single ethnic grouping, Levanto Arab, which encompasses the people of the Levant coast from northern Syria to southern Palestine. Armenians and Kurds have settled in Lebanon and there are Syrian troops and many Syrian workers.

Religions

There are 17 recognised religious groupings in Lebanon. Five predominate: Shi'a Muslims, Sunni Muslims, Maronite (Catholic) Christians, Greek Orthodox Christians and Druze.

Education

Education is mainly run by private enterprises and the religious sector. State schools exist and are free of charge. Primary education lasts for nine years.

The civil war severely disrupted state education at all levels and by the end of the civil war in 1990, 1,270 schools throughout the country needed rehabilitation at an estimated cost of US$65 million. Public expenditure on education is equivalent to approximately 2.5 per cent of annual GNP.

There is a government-run Lebanese National University, but the major universities continue to be operated by the US, France and Egypt. There are over 10 universities in Beirut.

Literacy rate: 86.1 per cent total, 81.4 per cent female, adult rates (World Bank).

Compulsory years: None

Enrolment rate: 111 per cent total primary enrolment of the relevant age group (including repetition rates); 81 per cent total secondary enrolment (World Bank).

Health

A Social Security Fund covers the health expenses of workers.

HIV/Aids

HIV prevalence: 0.1 per cent aged 15–49 in 2003 (World Bank)

Life expectancy: 70 years, 2004 (WHO 2006)

Fertility rate/Maternal mortality rate: 2.3 births per woman, 2004 (WHO 2006); maternal mortality 100 per 100,000 live births (World Bank).

Child (under 5 years) mortality rate (per 1,000): 27 per 1,000 live births; 3 per cent of children aged under five are malnourished (World Bank).

Head of population per physician: 3.25 physicians per 1,000 people, 2001 (WHO 2006)

Welfare

Since 1963, Lebanon has operated a social insurance system offering lump sum benefits only. Social insurance covers employees in industry, commerce and agriculture, but excludes temporary agricultural employees and those previously entitled to special benefits under the labour code.

In 1999, old age pensions were available to men aged over 60, but compulsory for those aged over 64. The benefit included a lump sum amount equivalent to the average monthly earnings during the last 12 months or the final month. The rate for disability benefit is a lump sum equal to the final month's earnings multiplied by the number of years in service. Widows receive 25 per cent of their former spouse's benefit. There are no sickness or maternity benefits. Workers receive medical benefits for up to 26 weeks or 52 weeks in special cases. Family allowances are employment-related and are available to employees with a non-working wife or with one to five children. The maximum monthly allowance is equivalent to 75 per cent of the minimum wage.

Main cities

Beirut (capital, estimated population 2.1 million in 2007), Tripoli (212,900), Sidon (149,000), Zahlé (76,600).

Media

Freedom of the press is practiced but there are laws forbidding defaming the president and other heads of states and inciting sectarian strife.

Press

Dailies: In Arabic *An Nahar* (www.annahar.com), *Al Safir* (www.assafir.com), *Al Anwar* (www.alanwar.com), *Al Diyar* (www.journaladdiyar.com), *Al Mustaqbal* (http://almustaqbal.com) with affiliation to the Future Movement. In Armenian *Aztag Daily* (www.aztagdaily.com). In French *L'Orient-Le Jour* (www.lorient-lejour.com.lb) is the country's fifth-largest newspaper. In English *The Daily Star* (www.dailystar.com.lb).

Weeklies: In Arabic, *Al Shiraa Magazine* (www.alshiraa.com) and *Al Afkar* (www.alafkar.net) for politics; *Al Noujoum* (www.alnoujoum.com) for celebrity news and *Al Jaras* (www.aljaras.com) for entertainment news. In French, *L'Hebdo Magazine* (www.magazine.com.lb) for news and current affairs and *La Revue du Liban* (www.rdl.com.lb) is a news review In English *Monday Morning* (www.mmorning.com) for general news.

Business: In Arabic *Al Markazia* (www.immarwaiktissad.com) with articles on finance and current affairs and the monthly *Al Iktissad Wal Aamal* (www.iktissad.com) covers Arab business and economic news. In English, the UK-based monthly magazine *Executive* (http://executive-magazine.com) offers articles on Lebanese world of commerce in major sectors.

Periodicals: Monthly women's magazines include *Snob Magazine* (www.snobmagazine.com) in Arabic, is aimed at a young female audience and in French, *Femme* (www.femmemag.com.lb) is aimed at an older readership while *Noun* (www.noun.com.lb) is aimed at a sophisticated female market. In Arabic, *Al Mustiqbal Al Arabi* (www.caus.org.lb) is an academic publication on Arab matters.

Broadcasting

The Lebanese Broadcasting Company (LBCI) is privately owned. In 1996, Lebanon banned broadcasts of political programmes and news by about 50 private television stations and 150 radio stations and ordered them to close. Political broadcasting is restricted to four TV stations and three radio outlets controlled by the pro-government establishment.

Radio: The government gives permission to operators to broadcast and limits which station may broadcasts the news.

Radio Liban (www.96-2.com) is state-run with nationwide reception. There are many private, commercial stations including Mix FM (www.mixfm.com.lb), NBN (www.nbn.com.lb) and NRG Beirut (www.nrjlebanon.com). International broadcasts are relayed through local stations.

Television: Viewing of satellite and cable television is widespread.

Tele-Liban is the state-run channel. Other, private, commercial channels include the Lebanese Broadcasting Corporation (LBC) (www.lbcgroup.tv) the market leader with regional and international coverage through satellite transmissions. Its political stance is towards the Christian community. Future Television (www.future.com.lb) is affiliated to a Sunni Muslim political movement (Tayyar Al Mustaqbal (Future Movement). Orange TV (www.otv.com.lb) is a publicly owned station which began broadcasting in 2007. Al Manar (www.almanar.com.lb) is a station affiliated to the Hezbollah. The Lebanon-based news station Al Jaheed (www.akjadeed.tv) broadcasts throughout the region.

Cable Vision (www.cablevision-leb.net) is the largest of the cable TV services.

Advertising

The local advertising and marketing industry is well developed. Television accounts for around 60 per cent of adspend; print media accounts for 30 per cent, with the majority being channelled into national newspapers and radio and billboards accounting for the remainder.

News agencies

National news agency: NNA (National News Agency): www.nna-leb.gov.lb

Other news agencies: Central News Agency: www.almarkazia.com

Economy

Lebanon has a strong tradition as an open market, trade-orientated economy. Coupled with strong banking rules and a high ratio of 50 per cent liquid assets to short-term loans its banking system has not been subject to the high level of toxic debts prevailing elsewhere. Thus, while the world experienced a global economic crisis and world trade fell, Lebanon experienced GDP growth of 0.6 per cent in 2006, rising to 7.5 per cent in 2007 as rebuilding after the Israeli invasion began. In 2008, GDP growth was at a decade-high 9.3 per cent before falling back to 8.5 per cent in 2009 and further still to 7.5 per cent in 2010.

Lebanon is one of the world's largest recipients of remittances, which in 2009 were US$7.56 billion (22.4 per cent of GDP) and an estimated US$8.18 billion in 2010. Over 50 per cent of all remittances originate in Gulf Co-operation Council (GCC) states. The service sector is by far the dominant component of the economy at over some 78 per cent of GDP (mainly banking and tourism), industry provides 17 per cent, of which manufacturing accounted for 8.8 per cent, with the remainder provided by agriculture.

A law allowing Palestinian refugees to work legally was passed by parliament in August 2010. There are some 400,000 Palestinians in Lebanon.

External trade

Lebanon belongs to the Greater Arab Free Trade Area (Gafta), which has 17 members, creating an Arab economic bloc. A customs union was established whereby tariffs within Gafta will be reduced by a percentage each year, until none remain. Lebanon is also a signatory of the Euro-Mediterranean Partnership agreement, which provides for the introduction of free trade between the EU and 10 Mediterranean countries by 2012. A new free-trade zone, including visa-free travel for their nationals, was agreed in June 2010, between Turkey, Lebanon, Jordan and Syria. A co-operation council will be established to 'develop a long-term strategic partnership' to encourage free movement of goods and persons.

In 2009 Lebanon was close to full membership of the WTO, having progressed to the outline phase for terms of membership.

Around 65 per cent of GDP is provided by foreign trade, with recent growth in the IT (information technology) sector, although financial services still provide the lion's share.

Imports

Major imports include petroleum products, vehicles, medicine, clothing, meat and live animals, consumer goods, paper, textiles, tobacco.

Main sources: Syria (typically 12 per cent of total), Italy (9 per cent), France (8 per cent).

Exports

Commodity exports include gems and jewellery, electrical and electronic equipment, minerals such as salt and sulphur, iron and steel, consumer goods and construction materials.

Main destinations: Syria (typically 25 per cent of total), UAE (12 per cent), Switzerland (8 per cent).

Agriculture

The agricultural sector has still not recovered from the effects of the civil war. While agricultural exports have shown signs of recovery, they earn only around US$233 million compared with expenditure of US$1.5 billion on imports of agricultural produce. Main goods for export are surplus products such as apples, citrus fruit and potatoes.

Agricultural and farming activities are in private hands. The land tenure system and difficult terrain have resulted in the majority of farmland being divided into small relatively uneconomic units. This has acted as a disincentive to investment in irrigation and mechanisation. The government provides little aid to the sector, which has had to compete with heavily subsidized produce from other countries. Lebanon's membership of the Greater Arab Free Trade Agreement (Gafta), which came into effect in 2005, could expose the sector to further pressures.

The relatively mild climate allows for diversified agricultural production. Main crops: wheat, barley, maize, vegetables, potatoes, fruit, olives, tobacco. Farmers have started the cultivation of advanced cash crops, such as avocados and flowers.

Goats, cattle and sheep are the main types of livestock raised in Lebanon.

One-third of Lebanon's land is cultivable with 400,000 hectares of arable land, of which 25 per cent is irrigated. The main agricultural areas are the Beka'a valley, the Akkar plain, the coastal plain and the foothills of the central mountain range. Most of these areas were badly affected by war. Agriculture in the south and in the Beka'a valley was particularly affected. Agriculture remains an important source of income in rural areas, and although it is difficult to estimate the number of full-time farmers, most families conduct or participate in agriculture as a part-time activity.

Fishing

Despite Lebanon's extensive coastline, commercial fishing remains a minor activity, contributing less than one per cent to GDP annually.

Forest cover amounts to less than 8 per cent of total land area.

Industry and manufacturing

Industry and manufacturing is small to medium scale. The sector accounts for around 12.6 per cent of GDP and employs 18 per cent of the workforce. The main products are building materials, textiles and clothing, food processing and furniture.

Construction employs about 6 per cent of the workforce. Industry provides more than 40 per cent of Lebanon's merchandised export earnings.

Tourism

Over one million arrivals are recorded each year and the sector's contribution to GDP continues to increase, although, at around 12 per cent, it is still short of the 19.4 per cent attained in 1974 (before the civil war).

The sector suffered a setback in 2005, precipitated by the assassination early in the year of Rafik al Hariri and the subsequent political instability. However, the longer-term prospects for the sector are expected to improve, although there is a growing need for lower-cost accommodation and better air connections.

The main market is Saudi Arabia, followed by Kuwait and Jordan, but increasing numbers of Europeans are rediscovering Lebanon. Asia is another growing market for the Lebanon.

The sector is concentrated on Beirut and the surrounding region. The attractions and infrastructure of the rest of the country remain to be developed.

Mining

Lebanon has few natural resources. There are minor deposits of high-grade iron ore, asphalt, coal, lignite, phosphates and salt, all of which are exploited for internal consumption. There are also quarries for building-stone, and sand and lime suitable for use in construction.

Hydrocarbons

Lebanon relies on the import of refined oil to meet domestic demand. In 2007 it imported 94,000 barrels per day (bpd) of oil. Explorations for oil remain unsuccessful and in 2007 Lebanon agreed with Cyprus to a seabed demarcation of their boundary to what are considered to be potentially rich oil and natural gas fields.

Lebanon does not produce natural gas. The 1,200km Arab Gas Pipeline (AGP) runs from Egypt to Jordan anf Syria and by November 2008 had reached the border with Turkey; it has a spur to Lebanon, via Syria, which was completed in 2004, and able to deliver over 1.5 million cubic metres (cum) of gas per day to the Beddawi power station in northern Lebanon. However supplies have been subject to political and commercial problems and gas has never been delivered. Natural gas is expected to arrive by early-2009 although at 60 million cum it will be less than half the amount originally intended.

Lebanon has no coal, but imports around 5.6 million tonnes per annum.

Energy

Total installed generating capacity is over 1.5 gigawatts (GW), which produces around 10 billion kilowatt hours (kWh) per annum. However demand at 2.5GW outstrips supplies; Lebanon signed an agreement in 2008 to buy Egyptian surplus energy, which will initially only deliver 125MW and 450MW in off-peak periods. Electricity rationing is widespread and power cuts common. The electricity supply is highly inefficient and expensive. Electricité du Liban (EDL), the state-owned electricity provider, operates at an annual loss of US$400 million a year. Electricity is produced using imported fuel oil, which accounts for around 70 per cent of EDL's total costs.

Lebanon is seeking to convert from fuel oil to natural gas for electricity generation. Like oil, natural gas has to be imported. A pipeline giving access to Egyptian gas, via Syrian, at preferential prices was completed in 2004. However supplies have been subject to political and commercial problems and gas was never delivered. Egyptian natural gas was scheduled to begin flowing to the Lebanese Beddawi gas-fired power plant in September 2009. When at full capacity around 850,000cum of natural gas will operate two turbines.

Financial markets

Stock exchange

Beirut Stock Exchange (BSE)

Banking and insurance

Before the civil war, Lebanon was the unrivalled financial centre in the Middle East. Lebanon's free exchange system, strict secrecy laws, and strong currency all served to attract regional and international institutions and customers. Favourable economic and financial conditions following the end of the civil war initially led to an improved monetary and banking situation. However, lack of dynamism in the sector has since discouraged most foreign investors.

Central bank

Banque du Liban (BDL) (Bank of Lebanon)

Main financial centre

Beirut

Time

GMT plus two hours (daylight saving GMT plus three hours)

Geography

Lebanon stretches approximately 140km along the eastern shore of the Mediterranean, bounded by Syria to the north and east and Israel to the south. Its terrain is mountainous, dominated by the parallel ranges of the Lebanon in the west and the Anti-Lebanon in the east, which run north-east to south-west. Between these ranges lies the Beka'a valley, broad in the north, narrowing in the south. The coastal plain is defined by the Lebanon range which in places plunges into the sea, dividing the coastal strip into segments. The major cities are: Tripoli in the north, Beirut on one of the wider segments halfway down the coast and Sidon and Tyre in the south.

Hemisphere

Northern

Climate

In the summer, temperatures range between 20–30 degrees Celsius (C); Beirut averages 27 degrees C. The coastal region is humid in the summer months. In the winter, temperatures in the coastal region range between 10–16 degrees C and it becomes colder inland. Snow is usual on mountains. Most rain falls between November and March. Lebanon enjoys an essentially Mediterranean climate with mild, rainy winters and long warm summers. It almost never rains between June and October, and there is an average of 300 sunny days every year. In summer it is possible to escape the heat and humidity of the coast and go to the mountains. Average annual rainfall is 893mm in Beirut, mostly occurring in winter.

Dress codes

Formal clothing is required for business meetings. Women should dress modestly.

Entry requirements

Passports

Required by all and must have six months validity from date of visit.

Visa

Required by all, with a few exceptions for regional nationals. Contact the nearest consulate for confirmation. Those who apply for a business visa must submit a business letter from the visitor's company with a letter or fax from a local business contact stating the purpose of the trip.

Prohibited entry

Entry is refused to holders of Israeli and Palestinian passports, holders of passports containing a visa for Israel, valid or expired, used or unused, and passports with entry stamps to Israel.

Currency advice/regulations

There are no restrictions on the import and export of local or foreign currencies. Travellers cheques are not suitable for Lebanon as it takes two weeks for cheques to clear.

Customs

Duty-free allowances include amounts of alcohol, tobacco and perfume. Personal belonging may not exceed LL200,000. Antiques require export permits.

Prohibited imports

Firearms, ammunition, illegal drugs and pornography.

Health (for visitors)

Mandatory precautions

Vaccination certificates for yellow fever are required if travelling from an infected area. There are no other mandatory vaccinations required to enter Lebanon.

Advisable precautions

It is recommended that visitors have preventative vaccinations for polio, typhoid, tetanus and hepatitis A.

Lebanon's medical services are generally modern, with most doctors speaking French or English. The private hospitals are the best, but more expensive, and it is recommended that insurance is taken out by all visitors.

Hotels

The ministry of tourism assesses the quality of hotels and publishes an annual report. A full range of hotels were available before the Lebanese/Israeli conflict of 2006.

A 15 per cent service charge is usually added to the bill, with additional tipping optional.

Credit cards

International credit cards are accepted throughout the capital, and in the more developed areas across the country. ATMs are plentiful

Public holidays (national)

Fixed dates

1 Jan (New Year's Day), ^9 Feb (Feast of St Maroun), 1 May (Labour Day), 6 May (Martyrs' Day), ^15 Aug (Assumption Day), ^1 Nov (All Saints' Day), 22 Nov (Independence Day), ^25 Dec (Christmas Day).

^ Observed by adherents only.

Holidays that fall at the weekend are taken on the Monday following.

Variable dates

Orthodox Christmas (Jan), Orthodox Easter (Mar/Apr, Fri–Mon), Eid al Adha (three days), Islamic New Year, Ashura (two days), Birth of the Prophet, Eid al Fitr (three days).

Islamic year 1433 (26 Nov 2011–14 Nov 2012): The Islamic year contains 354 or 355 days, with the result that Muslim feasts advance by 10–12 days against the Gregorian calendar. Dates of feasts vary according to the sighting of the new moon, so cannot be forecast exactly.

Working hours

Banking

Mon–Fri: 0800–1230; Sat: 0800–1200.

Business

Mon–Fri: 0900–1600.

Government

Mon–Fri: 0800–1400; Sat: 0800–1300.

Shops

Mon–Sat: 0800–1900. Some shops open on Sundays.

Telecommunications

Mobile/cell phones

GSM 900 services cover the entire country.

Internet/e-mail

Electricity supply

110V or 220V AC, 50 cycles. Supply is subject to fluctuations and blackouts. It is advisable to use a stabiliser when operating more advanced electronic equipment.

Weights and measures

Metric system

Social customs/useful tips

Punctuality is expected for business appointments but is less strictly observed for social engagements. The usual form of greeting is to shake hands. It is the custom to offer coffee or tea to visitors and it is considered rude to refuse. Muslim traditions are observed.

During Ramadan (the four weeks prior to the Eid al Fitr holiday) employees tend to work shorter hours. It is advisable to avoid business trips at this time.

Security

Visitors should keep in touch with developments in the Middle East as any increase in regional tension might affect travel advice.

Security in Lebanon is likely to remain hostage to the regional tensions over the Israeli-Palestinian and Iraqi conflicts. Visitors are advised to carry their passports.

Getting there

Air

Runways at Beirut airport sustained damage during the conflict in 2006. It is estimated that repairs will be completed by November 2006.

National airline: Middle East Airlines (MEA).

International airport/s: The Rafik Hariri International Airport (renamed in June 2006) (BEY), is 16km from Beirut, with duty-free shops, VIP lounge, post office, restaurant *bureau de change*, hotel reservation and car hire.

Airport tax: Departure tax: LL100,000 first class, LL75,000 business class, LL50,000 economy class passengers

Surface

Road: Road access is possible through Turkey via Aleppo and Syria via the Bekaa valley. No access is possible via Israel.

Water: A ferry operates between Larnaca in Cyprus and Beirut.

Main port/s: Beirut, Tripoli, Saida (Sidon), Jounieh, Tyre and Byblos.

Getting about

National transport

Air: There are no domestic flights.

Road: Some 6,000km of roads and highways, excluding municipal roads. There are two international motorways with a total length of 570km. Some 40 per cent of the road network is in poor condition. New routes were under construction prior to the 2006 conflict with Israel.

Buses: Buses travel between Beirut and other major towns around the country. There are only limited daily departures.

Rail: There is no passenger railway network in Lebanon.

City transport

Taxis: There are taxis available throughout Beirut and most of the country. Service taxis usually follow established routes where one person will often share the taxi with up to four other passengers. Share taxis will stop on request. Ordinary taxis are not restricted to a set route and will take passengers anywhere in the country. The government has fixed charges for airport taxis.

Buses, trams & metro: A few buses are available to certain destinations. Not recommended for foreign visitors.

Car hire

There are several international car hire companies in Beirut, usually offering competitive rates. Rental companies can also provide drivers with their cars.

BUSINESS DIRECTORY

The addresses listed below are a selection only. While World of Information makes every endeavour to check these addresses, we cannot guarantee that changes have not been made, especially to telephone numbers and area codes. We would welcome any corrections.

Telephone area codes

The international direct dialling (IDD) code for Lebanon is +961, followed by area code:

Grand Beirut	1	Tripoli	6
Kerswan / Jbeil	9	Tyre	7
Sidon	7	Zahle	8

Chambers of Commerce

American Lebanese Chamber of Commerce,1153 Foch Street, PO Box 175093, Beirut (tel: 985-330; fax: 985-331; e-mail: amchamlb@cyberia.net.lb).

Beirut and Mount Lebanon Chamber of Commerce, Industry and Agriculture, Sanayeh, 1 Justinien Street, PO Box 11-1801, Beirut (tel: 353-390; fax: 353-395; e-mail: info@ccib.org.lb).

Federation of the Chambers of Commerce, Industry and Agriculture in Lebanon, Sanayeh, 1 Justinien Street, PO Box 11-1801, Beirut (tel: 745-288; fax: 341-328; e-mail: fccial@cci-fed.org.lb).

Sidon and South Lebanon Chamber of Commerce, Industry and Agriculture, Boulevard Maarouf Saad, PO Box 41, Sidon (tel: 720-123; fax: 722-986; e-mail: chamber@ccias.org.lb).

Tripoli and North Lebanon Chamber of Commerce, Industry and Agriculture, Bechara Khoury Street, PO Box 47, Tripoli (tel: 425-600; fax: 442-042; e-mail: comindeg@adm.net.lb).

Banking

ABN-AMRO Bank Lebanon, ABN AMRO Tower, Charles Malek Avenue, Achrafieh, Beirut (tel: 219-200; fax: 217-756/7).

Arab African International Bank, Riad El Solh, beirur (tel: 980-162/3, 980-264/5; fax: 633-912).

Bank of Beirut; PO Box 11-7354, Bank of Beirut sal Bldg, Foch Street, Beirut Central District, Beirut (tel: 738767/68; fax: 602166).

Banque Audi, Banque Audi Plaza, Bab Idriss, 2021 8102 Beirut (tel: 200-250, 331-600; fax: 339-220).

British Arab Commercial Bank Ltd, ARESCO Centre, Banque du Liban Street, PO Box 113-5495, Hamra, Beirut (tel: 602-437; fax: 602-438).

HSBC Bank Middle East Ltd, PO Box 11-1380, St Georges Bay, Minet el Hosn, Beirut (tel: 377-477, 369-900; fax: 372-362).

Banque Libano-Française, PO Box 11808, Beirut Liberty Plaza Bldg, Roma Street, Ras Beirut, Beirut (tel: 791332; fax: 340355).

BLOM Bank, BLOM Banks's Bldg, Rashid Karami St, Verdun, Beirut, Lebanon (tel: 743-300, 738-938; fax: 738-946).

Banque de la Méditerranée; Méditerranée Group Building, Clemenceau Street, Kantari Beirut, 2022 9302 Beirut (tel: 373-937; fax: 362-706).

Central bank

Banque du Liban, PO Box 11-5544, Masraf Loubane Street, Beirut (tel: 750-000; fax: 478-2740; e-mail: bdlit@bdl.gov.lb).

Stock exchange

Beirut Stock Exchange (BSE): www.bse.com.lb

Travel information

Middle East Airlines, PO Box 206, Beirut International Airport.

Tourist Police (343-209).

Trans Mediterranean Airways, PO Box 11-3018, Beirut International Airport.

Ministry of tourism

Ministry of Tourism, Information Services, 550 Central Bank Street, PO Box 11-5344, Beirut (tel: 354-764; fax: 343-279; e-mail: mot@lebanon-tourismgov.lb; internet: www.destinationlebanon.gov.lb).

Ministries

Ministry of Agriculture, Georges Jaber Building, Badaro Street, Beirut (tel: 455-613; fax: 455-475; e-mail: ministry@agriculture.gov.lb).

Ministry of Defence, Yarzé, Beirut (tel: 452-963; fax: 457-920).

Ministry of the Displaced, Old Sidon Road, Damour (tel: 840-474; fax: 840-476; e-mail: mod@dm.net.lb).

Ministry of Economy and Trade, Assaf Building, Rue Artois, Beirut (tel: 340-504; fax: 354-640; e-mail: postmaster@economy.gov.lb).

Ministry of Education and Higher Education, Rue Georges Piko, Beirut (tel: 744-251; fax: 371-079).

Ministry of Electricity and Water Resources, Shiah, Beirut (tel: 565-040; fax: 449-639).

Ministry of the Environment, 550 Central Bank Street, Beirut (tel: 524-999; fax: 524-555).

Ministry of Finance, MOF Building, Riyad el Solh Square, Beirut (tel: 981-001; fax: 642-762; e-mail: infocenter@finance.gov.lb).

Ministry of Foreign Affairs, Rue Sursock, Beirut (tel: 334-400; fax: 584-098).

Ministry of Health, Museum Street, Beirut (tel: 615-701; fax: 645-099).

Ministry of Industry, Rue Sami Solh, Beirut (tel: 427-247; fax: 427-112).

Ministry of Information, Rue Hamra, Beirut (tel: 351-032; fax: 423-189).

Ministry of the Interior, Rue des Arts et Métiers, Sanayeh, Beirut (tel: 981-270; fax: 751-622).

Ministry of Justice, Rue Sami Solh, Beirut (tel: 425-670; fax: 422-957).

Ministry of Labour, Shiah, Beirut (tel: 556-831; fax: 556-832).

Ministry of Posts and Telecommunications, Rue Sami Shoh, Beirut (tel: 888-100; fax: 423-005; e-mail: webmaster@mpt.gov.lb).

Ministry of Public Works and Transport, Fiyadieh, Hazmieh, Beirut (tel: 458-975; fax: 459-434).

Ministry of Social Affairs, Rue Badaro, Beirut (tel: 395-561; fax: 396-148).

Ministry of Sports and Youth, Campus of Unesco, Beirut (tel: 790-529; fax: 840-440).

Ministry of Tourism, 550 Central Bank Street, Beirut (fax: 340-940; e-mail: mot@lebanon-tourism.gov.lb).

Office of the President, Presidential Palace, Beirut (tel: 220-0000; fax: 425-395).

Office of the Prime Minister, Riyad el Sol Square, Beirut (tel: 862-001; fax: 869-630).

Other useful addresses

Assocation of Lebanese Industrialists, PO Box 1520, Chamber of Commerce and Industry Building, Justinian Street, Beirut (tel: 350-280; fax: 351-167).

Board for Foreign Economic Relations, PO Box 11-5344, Beirut (tel: 483-391/5

British Embassy, Commercial Section, PO Box 60180, Coolrite Building, Autostrade, Jal El Dib, Beirut (tel: 406-330, 405-033, 402-035; fax: 402-033).

Council for Development and Reconstruction (CDR), Tallet El Serail, Beirut Central District (tel: 643-981; fax: 647-947, 864-494, 865-630).

Electricité du Liban, Nahr Street, Beirut (tel: 442-720; fax: 583-084).

Higher Council for Privatisation, Grand Serail, Beirut Central District, Beirut (tel: 987-500; fax: 983-061).

International Fairs and Promotions, SARL, PO Box 55576, Beirut.

Investment Development Authority of Lebanon, Presidency of the Council of Ministers, Liberty, Lyon Street, PO Box 113-7251, Sanayeh, Beirut (tel: 344-676, 344-403; fax: 344-463, 347-397).

Lebanese Embassy (USA), 2560 28th Street, NW, Washington DC 20008 (tel: (+1-202) 939-6300; fax: (+1-202) 939-6324; e-mail: info@lebanonembassy.org).

Solidére (development company for rebuilding Beirut), Industry and Labour Bank Building, Riyadh El-Solh Street, PO Box 11-9493, Beirut (tel: 346-891, 646-137/8/9; fax: 646-136).

National news agency: NNA (National News Agency): www.nna-leb.gov.lb

Central News Agency: www.almarkazia.com

Internet sites

Investment Development Authority of Lebanon (IDAL): www.idal.com.lb

Lebanon Online: www.lebanon.com

Ministry of Economy and Trade: www.economy.gov.lb

Ministry of Tourism: www.lebanon-tourism.gov.lb

Lesotho

KEY FACTS

Official name: Kingdom of Lesotho

Head of State: King Letsie III (since 7 Feb 1996)

Head of government: Prime Minister Bethuel Pakalitha Mosisili (LCD) (since 1998; re-elected Feb 2007)

Ruling party: Lesotho Congress for Democracy (LCD) (re-elected Feb 2007)

Area: 30,355 square km

Population: 1.89 million (2010)*

Capital: Maseru

Official language: Sesotho and English

Currency: Loti (maloti, plural) (L) = 100 lisente; has parity with the South African rand, which is legal tender.

Exchange rate: L8.04 per US$ (Oct 2011)

GDP per capita: US$837 (2010)

GDP real growth: 2.40% (2010)

GDP: US$2.13 billion (2010)

Inflation: 3.80% (2010)

Balance of trade: -US$1.15 billion (2010)

* estimated figure

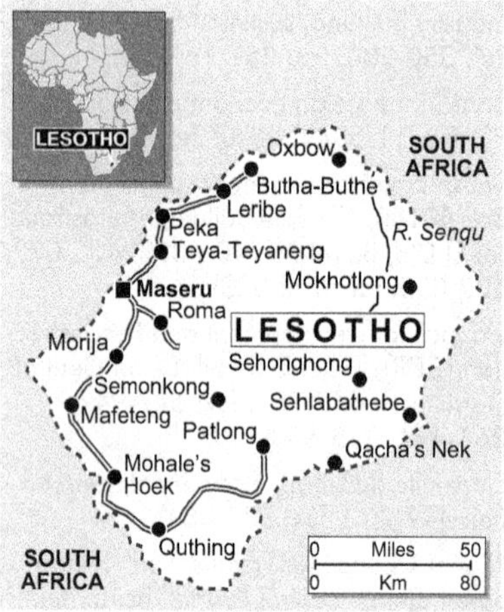

In early 2011 there were signs of a slow economic recovery in Lesotho, although the damage caused to this small and open economy may last longer than elsewhere in Africa. According to the *African Economic Outlook 2011* (AEO), published jointly by the African Development Bank and the Organisation for Economic Co-operation and Development, Lesotho's dependency on exports has left it vulnerable to the global economic downturn. Lesotho's close ties to South Africa, a country that was also affected by the collapse in commodity prices, exacerbated Lesotho's problems. Lesotho's gross domestic product (GDP) declined by about 4.4 per cent in 2008 and fell further, to 1.9 per cent, in 2009. In 2010 growth recovered to an estimated 3.8 per cent. This recovery is due to both firming commodity prices and high government capital expenditures. The government's focus on infrastructure development is driving activity in the construction sector.

Recent efforts by the government to diversify the economy are beginning to take effect. The development of manufacturing, services and the export of water resources has meant the economy is relying less on subsistence agriculture and remittances. Even so, the country's growth is forecast to be lower in 2011 as no major investments are expected, while recovery in the global economy remains weak. In addition, growth in 2011 is likely to be dampened because of a projected high current account deficit resulting from higher imports to meet requirements for projects in the construction sector, compounded by continued low Southern Africa Customs Union (SACU) revenues. The government has taken measures to reduce its current expenditure, including a freeze on government jobs, and has also committed not to fund new projects during the current fiscal year, 2010/11.

Although Lesotho's government is making efforts to reduce its budget deficit, it has maintained infrastructure development as a priority, particularly to link remote areas to markets and to enable new investments that would provide opportunities for value addition, especially in the agriculture sector. The country's poor business environment has curtailed the expansion of private-sector activities, and government still accounts for nearly 50 per cent of Lesotho's GDP. Current efforts to improve the business environment are likely to increase private-sector activities. The passing of the Land Act (2010) and the establishment of the land register, with the pilot phase completed in 2010, will go a long way to address the challenges of financing small- and medium-scale enterprises (SMEs) and improve the country's attractiveness for foreign investment. The government has also made substantial progress in drafting and completing its industrial and competition policies.

Diamonds recover...

Significant recovery in the volume and prices of diamonds helped to increase export revenues in 2010. The Liqhobong and Kao mines, which had suspended operations during the financial crisis, have resumed operations, and new mines, Mothae and Lemphane, have started up. Recovery in the mining sector has helped absorb returnees from South Africa's mining sector. However, growth in export receipts from this sector is not expected to offset the decline in remittances, which have been a major source of income for many Basotho families for decades.

... textiles fall

Recent investments in industry, especially in the textiles and clothing sub-sector have generated new job opportunities in the country. Textiles and clothing, which accounts for over 80 per cent of all manufacturing jobs, was hit by the global financial crisis. Employment in the textiles and clothing sector declined as a result, shedding about 13 per cent of jobs in 2009 compared with the 2008 level. A slight recovery in employment occurred in 2010, from just over 31,000 jobs to 32,000. Current total employment in the sector remains significantly low compared with the peak of about 48,000 jobs in 2004. Women, who constitute more than 80 per cent of the textiles-sector workforce, have been most affected by these job losses. With about 87 per cent of manufacturing jobs being provided by the textiles sector, job losses in this sector are more visible than in others despite the fact that wages in it are lower than in others. Moreover, the increasing competition from producers in Asia is making the clothing-sector contribution to future economic growth uncertain.

Exports from the textiles sector are likely to remain weak because of competition from Asia and slow recovery in the United States. Lesotho is a relatively high-cost source for American buyers compared with its Asian and South American competitors. This is partly explained by the unit costs faced by Lesotho's producers, which in 2010 were almost 80 per cent higher than those of Pakistan, the lowest-cost supplier. Appreciation of the South African currency, the rand, to which the loti is pegged, has also reduced the competitiveness of the textiles and clothing sector. The rand is reported to have appreciated by more than 8 per cent in 2010.

SACU revenues fall

Low SACU revenues are putting pressure on the current account balance. This is worsened by the fact that Lesotho is due to repay an estimated L2.9 billion (US$360,000) to the SACU Common Revenue Pool (CRP) in 2010 and 2011. Net SACU revenue flows are therefore expected to fall by 57 per cent, from L4.9 billion (US$610,000) in 2009/10 to just L2.1 billion (US$250,000) in 2010. The current-account balance is estimated to worsen from its 2009 US$7.9 million deficit by nearly US$400 million more in 2010, widening the deficit from 0.2 per cent to 14.9 per cent of GDP during this period.

Despite economic recovery in South Africa and in the global economy, SACU revenues, which averaged 37 per cent of GDP in 2006–08, are not expected to recover to pre-crisis levels in the short term. Continuing trade liberalisation in the region, in particular the institution of a Southern African Development Community (SADC) customs union and other bilateral arrangements, along with a possible change in the revenue sharing formula may result in a decline in trade taxes as a share of total tax revenue. Projections suggest that SACU revenues will stabilise at around 20 per cent of GDP in the medium term.

The worsening fiscal and current account deficits have led the government of Lesotho to embark on policy- and structural-reform processes aimed at fostering private-sector activity. Such reforms include the enactment of a new Land Act and revisions to the Financial Institutions Act. The need for a vibrant private sector is even more critical in a context of fiscal constraints, which argue against increasing the role of government in propelling economic growth in the medium term, especially given its current high share of GDP.

The focus on improving the business environment to a level similar or better than that of neighbouring countries is important for Lesotho to attract foreign capital. This would compensate the policy limitations that the country is facing given the existing arrangements in the Common Monetary Area (CMA), in which the South African Central Bank determines monetary policy for the region.

Inflation in 2010 stood at 7.3 per cent, the same as in 2009, but increases in electricity tariffs and the projected depreciation of the rand in the year ahead are likely to push up inflation in 2011 before declining to 6.8 per cent in 2012.

Agriculture

Although the agricultural sector is vital for the rural livelihoods of the Basotho, its importance as a growth driver has been superceded by services and industrial activities. Almost 74 per cent of the rural population depends on agriculture for its livelihood, but at the sectoral level, agriculture currently constitutes less than 8 per cent of total GDP compared with more than 42 per cent for services and about 19 per cent for manufacturing. Agriculture is largely based on small-scale farming with little mechanisation. This is explained by the land-tenure system and to some extent by the terrain of the country. Moreover, the sector is vulnerable to seasonal rainfall levels. As a consequence, productivity in the agriculture sector is low. Income derived from agriculture is therefore minimal, partly explaining the high poverty rates in the rural areas. In response, the government is promoting block farming, where land holdings belonging to different owners are combined into larger blocks that would allow single-crop production so that it becomes viable to use machinery and benefit from extension services.

Water for export

Growth in the construction sector has been supported by investments in infrastructure, especially in the Metolong Dam, which is also receiving joint

KEY INDICATORS — **Lesotho**

	Unit	2006	2007	2008	2009	2010
Population	m	2.36	*2.41	*2.45	*2.50	*1.89
Gross domestic product (GDP)	US$bn	1.49	1.67	1.62	1.60	2.13
GDP per capita	US$	632	694	660	642	837
GDP real growth	%	4.7	4.5	4.3	3.1	3.6
Inflation	%	6.3	9.2	10.7	5.9	3.8
Industrial output	% change	11.4	10.1	1.7	-4.4	–
Agricultural output	% change	1.7	-8.6	-0.6	4.0	–
Exports (fob) (goods)	US$m	693.6	829.7	882.4	734.1	851.8
Imports (fob) (goods)	US$m	1,360.6	1,506.2	1,618.4	1,587.2	1,998.3
Balance of trade	US$m	-656.2	-676.5	-736.0	-853.0	1,146.5
Current account	US$m	66.0	98.5	143.7	-2.4	-421.4
Total reserves minus gold	US$m	658.4	–	–	–	–
Foreign exchange	US$m	652.7	–	–	–	–
Exchange rate	per US$	7.23	6.84	8.26	7.32	7.32

* estimated figure

financing from the Millennium Challenge Account (MCA) and the Lesotho Highlands Water Project II (LHWP II), a Lesotho and South Africa bi-national water project. The Metolong Dam, which is expected to cost about US$413 million is scheduled to be completed by 2013 and will help to meet the increasing domestic demand for water resulting from rapid urbanisation.

Phase 2 of the LHWP includes the construction of the Polihali Dam at Tlokoeng in the Mokhotlong District. The Polihali Dam involves the construction of a 165-metre-high dam wall and a 2.2 billion cubic metre reservoir. Water harvested from Polihali will flow into South Africa through a series of transfer tunnels via the Ash river in Free State and then into the Vaal river system. When completed, this project is expected to generate significant revenues for Lesotho.

Given that Lesotho is a landlocked country, inadequate infrastructure, coupled with a poor regulatory environment, presents a challenge for business operators, especially in the transport sector. With Lesotho facing the highest costs for doing business in the SACU region, its ability to attract investment, which is critical for growth and job generation, is limited. In the World Bank's *Doing Business* report for 2011, the country is ranked 138th out of a total of 183 countries and territories for *Ease of Doing Business*, comparing poorly to Swaziland's 118th or Namibia's 69th ranking.

Banking

Lesotho's financial sector is underdeveloped. As access to finance remains a critical constraint for businesses in the country, measures have been implemented to strengthen and enhance access to financial services in conjunction with improvements in the prudential regulation framework. In this regard, in 2010 the Central Bank of Lesotho submitted to parliament the revised Financial Institutions Act and amended the Co-operative Societies Act. These measures were meant to address issues related to the supervision of non-bank financial institutions such as savings and credit co-operatives, and unlawful operations such as Ponzi schemes. In addition, the central bank finalised preparations of the Anti-Money Laundering Act and regulations intended to guide the Financial Intelligence Unit.

Changing economic realities are impacting not only the country's economic development but its diplomatic relations as well. The increasing importance of China as an economic partner has resulted in Lesotho severing diplomatic relations with Chinese Taipei. China has since opened an embassy in Maseru. According to a Chinese embassy official in Maseru, China-Lesotho relations are a friendship co-operation that values the strengthening of economic and political relations. Lesotho has had access to the Chinese market on a duty-free basis since 2008. Almost 95 per cent of Lesotho's exports, made up of 45 products, but mainly of wool, are allowed into China duty-free. Data on Chinese investments are not readily available, but estimates put the current figure at more than US$80 million, up from US$8 million in 1990.

Civil society organisations in Lesotho have viewed China's approach to aid in Africa with suspicion, especially the fact that there is very little transparency and that most discussions have taken place at the highest levels of government. In the private sector, there is increasing resistance to the low wages paid to local workers. In Lesotho, for instance, the lowest paid textile worker in 2010 was paid L790 (about US$95) per month compared to about US$148 in South Africa.

Parliamentary elections are scheduled for 2012, when the ruling Lesotho Congress for Democracy (LCD) will face competition from the two main opposition parties (National Independent Party and All Basotho Convention). Lesotho has had some political scares in the recent past, such as the attempted assassination of the prime minister in 2009, but 2010 has been stable.

Risk assessment

Economy	Poor
Politics	Poor
Regional stability	Fair

COUNTRY PROFILE

Historical profile

1600s Modern-day Lesotho was settled by the Sotho people; the area was already home to the San people.

1800s European traders and missionaries arrived in the area, and were soon followed by the Boers on their Great Trek. The Boer trek coincided with the expansion of the Zulu state. King Moshoeshoe the Great ensured the survival of his people by taking them to a mountain stronghold in about 1820. The policy of assisting refugees on condition that they help in defence proved successful – by 1842 the King's people numbered around 40,000 and were protected by outlying refugee settlements.

1870 By the time King Moshoeshoe died, a Basuto nation of 150,000 had been established.

1910 After annexing Basutoland, the British established the Basutoland National Council comprising members nominated by chiefs.

1960 After a new constitution was introduced, elections were held, which were won by the Basutoland Congress Party (BCP) ahead of the Basutoland National Party (BNP) led by Chief Leabua Jonathan.

1965 The BCP lost the election to the BNP; Chief Jonathan became the first prime minister of the Kingdom of Lesotho. King Moshoeshoe II was stripped of most of his powers.

1966 Independence was granted.

1970 The constitution was suspended and opposition political parties banned.

1986 The government of Chief Leabua Jonathan was overthrown in a military coup by Major General J M Lekhanya. A military government chaired by Lekhanya ruled Lesotho in co-ordination with King Moshoeshoe II and a civilian cabinet appointed by the King. The new regime was more amenable to South Africa's wishes.

1990 A constituent assembly was set up to frame a new constitution; a timetable was announced for a return to civilian rule. King Moshoeshoe II was stripped of his executive and legislative powers and exiled by Lekhanya.

1991 Lekhanya was overthrown by a group of military officers led by Major General Elias Ramaema who took control. Because Moshoeshoe II initially refused to return under the new rules of the government, in which the King was given only ceremonial powers, Moshoeshoe's son was installed as King Letsie III.

1992 King Moshoeshoe returned from exile as a common citizen, in a deal with the military regime.

1993 A new constitution was adopted leaving the King as ceremonial head of the country. Elections signalled a return to democracy; the BCP won a convincing victory. King Letsie III became a purely constitutional monarch.

1994 After growing unrest, King Letsie III suspended the constitution. King Moshoeshoe, in collaboration with military supporters staged a coup but it was thwarted within a month. The settlement eventually negotiated allowed for both the re-establishment of parliamentary rule and King Letsie abdicated in favour of King Moshoeshoe.

1996 King Moshoeshoe II was killed in a road accident and was again succeeded by his son, who was sworn in as King Letsie III.

1997 King Letsie III was formally crowned.

1998 The Lesotho Congress for Democracy (LCD) won the elections. The result was rejected by opposition groups. After riots broke out in Maseru and reports circulated of an imminent military coup, 800 South African and Botswanan soldiers entered Lesotho with the aim of restoring order. Pakalitha Mosisili (LCD) became prime minister. The Interim Political Authority (IPA) was created to work alongside the government to prepare for elections.
2000 King Letsie III married Karabo Motsoeneng.
2001 President Thabo Mbeki of South Africa visited Lesotho to mend diplomatic relations and develop economic links. Twenty-seven LCD members of parliament quit the party to form the Lesotho People's Congress (LPC).
2002 The first chamber of parliament was enlarged from 80 seats to 120.
2003 Families displaced by the Lesotho Highlands Water Project (LHWP), and resettled in the Maseru district, won a ruling that improvements to their schools should be made by the project's authority.
2004 Prime Minister Mosisili declared a state of emergency and appealed for food aid. The first phase of the LHWP was officially opened.
2006 Foreign Minister Monyane Moleleki was shot and wounded by a gunman. The Lesotho Promise, one of the world's largest diamonds, was sold uncut for US12.4 million. To celebrate 40 years of independence, Lesotho adopted a new flag to show it was 'at peace with itself and its neighbours' and replaced the one adopted in 1986 after a coup.
2007 In parliamentary elections, the ruling LCD won 61seats (out of 120) in the national assembly. The most severe drought since the 1970s caused widespread hunger, exacerbated by a drop in food production due to HIV/Aids. A state of emergence was announced to avert famine, as the UN World Food Programme called for international aid. The annual cereal harvest was less than 25 per cent of the country's needs.
2008 The European Investment Bank (EIB) agreed a loan of US$22 million for 50 per cent of the cost of the expansion and rehabilitation of wastewater and sanitation facilities in the capital.
2009 The home of Prime Minister Mosisili was attacked and he was wounded by firearms.
2010 In June, as South Africa closed its borders to Lesotho ahead of the Soccer World Cup, a petition was handed to the government and South African High Commission calling on South Africa to integrate Lesotho into its country. The reason for the petition was that signatories considered Lesotho to be a ruined state. HIV/Aids has decimated the country, with up to 400,000 Aids orphans among the population of 2.5 million; life expectancy has fallen to 44.9 years and the population growth rate of 0.8 per cent is the lowest in Africa. The economy only survives through international aid and employment in South Africa. In July, the UNAids stated that the HIV infection rate for 15–24 year olds in Lesotho had fallen by over 30 per cent, due to prevention campaigns.
2011 On 20 April, seven suspected mercenaries were remanded in custody, charged with attempting to assassinate Prime Minister Pakalitha Mosisili in 2009. In July, health workers were trained to use motorbikes to reach remote and rural areas that were unlikely to receive medical help otherwise.

Political structure

Constitution

A new constitution was adopted in 1993, which redefined the role of the monarchy and altered the legislative branch of the government.

The King, who is head of State, has no executive or legislative authority.

Form of state

Constitutional monarchy

The executive

Executive power is vested in the prime minister, leader of the majority parliamentary party, and the cabinet appointed by the prime minister.

National legislature

Legislative power is held by a bi-cameral National Assembly.

The first chamber, the Assembly has 120 seats, 80 of which are elected by a simple majority in single-member constituencies, while 80 seats are chosen by proportional representation through party lists.

The second chamber (Senate) is made up of 22 hereditary principal chiefs and 11 members are appointed by the King, on advice from the prime minister.

All members serve for a maximum 5-year term.

Legal system

The legal system is based on English common law and Roman-Dutch law.

Last elections

17 February 2007 (parliamentary)

Results: Parliamentary: the LCD won 61out of 120 seats; National Independent Party (NIP) 21; the All Basotho Convention (ABC) 17; Lesotho Workers' Parthy 10; all other parties won less than five seats.

Next elections

2012 (parliamentary)

Political parties

Ruling party

Lesotho Congress for Democracy (LCD) (re-elected Feb 2007)

Main opposition party

All Basotho Convention (ABC)

Population

1.89 million (2010)*

Last census: 9 April 2006: 1,880,661 (provisional)

Population density: 66 inhabitants per square km. Urban population: 29 per cent of the total population (1995–2001).

Annual growth rate: 0.7 per cent 1994–2004 (WHO 2006)

Ethnic make-up

The Basotho nation is an amalgam of mainly Sesotho-speaking people. Some 45 per cent of the population is of Nguni origin. A number of smaller groups, including San Griqua, Indian and European, have also become naturalised Basotho.

Religions

Christianity (approximately 80 per cent, mainly Roman Catholic), various traditional beliefs and others (20 per cent).

Education

Primary education is free from the age of six.

Public expenditure on education typically amounts to around 8.5 per cent of gross national income (GNI). Lesotho has one university, located in the capital, Maseru.

Literacy rate: 81 per cent adult rate (Unesco 2005)

Compulsory years: Six to 13

Enrolment rate: 108 per cent gross primary enrolment, of the relevant age group (including repeaters); 31 per cent gross secondary enrolment (World Bank).

Pupils per teacher: 46 in primary schools.

Health

HIV/Aids

The HIV prevalence is one of the highest in the world. The government has undertaken a scheme to offer HIV counseling and testing for every household by 2007; seven thousand people will be trained in medical care and for the purpose of the campaign.

Lesotho has record success by exceeding epectations in its participation of the UN sponsored '3 by 5' campaign (worldwide, providing three million HIV sufferers with antiretroviral drugs by 2005).

HIV prevalence: 25 per cent in 2005

Life expectancy: 41 years, 2004 (WHO 2006)

Fertility rate/Maternal mortality rate: 3.5 births per woman, 2004 (WHO 2006); maternal mortality 530 per 100,000 live births (World Bank).

Child (under 5 years) mortality rate (per 1,000): 79 per 1,000 live births; 16 per cent of children aged under five are malnourished (World Bank).

Head of population per physician: 0.05 physicians per 1,000 people, 2003 (WHO 2006)

Main cities
Maseru (capital, estimated population 267,652 in 2005), Maputsoa (97,296), Mafeteng (75,939), Teyateyaneng (37,239).

Languages spoken
English becomes the medium of instruction from the fifth year of primary education.

Official language/s
Sesotho and English

Media
Press
Journalists and the print media are frequently subject to defamation lawsuits, which hampers their freedom to report. High publishing costs keep the number of publications limited and all on offer are weeklies.
In English, *Informative News* (www.informativenews.co.ls) is a business magazine published on Friday. For general news, *The Mirror* and *Public Eye* (www.publiceye.co.ls). In Sesotho *Makatolle*, *MoAfrica* and *Mohlanka*. *Mopheme (The Survivor)* is published in Sesotho and English.

Broadcasting
Radio: Radio provides the majority of the population with news, information and entertainment.
The national, state-run Radio Lesotho (www.radioles.co.ls) has programmes in Sesotho and English (in educational shows during the school year). There are several private radio stations including Lesotho NBS (www.radiolesotho.co.ls), PC FM (www.pcfm.co.ls), Joy Radio, Mo Afrika FM and Catholic Radio.
Television: The national, state-run Lesotho Television has a limited service. The South African Broadcasting Corporation (SABC) (www.sabc.co.za) is available.

News agencies
National news agency: LENA (Lesotho News Agency)

Economy
Lesotho's economy is fuelled by the sale of water and electricity to South Africa. It is a small, land-locked country, surrounded by South Africa, with few natural resources beyond its rivers. The Lesotho Highlands Water Project (LHWP) is one of the largest and most ambitious multi-purpose water schemes anywhere in the world, which, once completed, will provide South Africa with 79 cubic metres of water a second, by diverting the flow of the Senqu River and its tributaries northwards to South Africa. The first phase was completed when the Katse Dam began supplying the Muela hydroelectric power station in 1998, since when Lesotho has been self-sufficient in electricity. The Mohale Dam was completed in 2002, also supplying water to Muela power station and the Katse Dam. The final phase, scheduled for completion in 2016, includes three more dams but is still in its feasibility study stage.
Other exports include manufactured goods, diamonds, mohair and wool and agricultural products including livestock. The textile industry has dwindled to a cottage industry, although in November 2011 the government announced plans to spend 100 million maloti (US$12.7 million) over the next two years in an effort to breathe life into the once crucial industry.
GDP growth remained relatively constant at 4 per cent for the last half of 2000s, despite a fall in industrial production by -4.4 per cent. GDP growth was 3.1 per cent in 2009 at a time of maximum downturn in global trade, however, in 2010 growth picked up at 3.6 per cent and was projected to rise to 5.2 per cent in 2011.
Inflation jumped from 6.3 per cent in 2006 to 9.2 per cent in 2007, rising to 10.7 per cent in 2008 in a year of record high energy and food costs, before falling back in 2009 to 5.9 per cent and 3.4 per cent in 2010 as domestic spending shrank.
Although the majority of the population live in rural areas, agriculture's share of the economy has declined in recent decades to around 12 per cent of GDP. There has also been a loss of man-power and farming skills due to the spread of HIV/Aids. Almost one in three people suffers from HIV/Aids in Lesotho, which adversely affects both domestic and public economies. The industrial sector accounts for over 45 per cent of GDP, of which manufacturing accounts for around 20 per cent; services account for just of 40 per cent.
The main support of the economy has been remittances from migrant workers employed in South Africa, but this source of revenue is declining, as South Africa reduces its reliance on imported labour. Social indicators remain poor with around two-thirds of the population living below the poverty line.

External trade
Lesotho 's economy is heavily influenced by South Africa; all foreign trade is either with South Africa or has to pass through it to reach other markets. Lesotho is a member of the Southern African Customs Union (Sacu), with South Africa, Namibia, Swaziland and Botswana. Sacu sets customs duties for commodities passing between member states and members share the common pool of customs and excise revenue on all external trade.
Lesotho is also a member of the Southern African Development Community (SADC), the objectives of which include reduction in trade barriers, achieving regional development and economic growth and evolving common systems and institutions.
Lesotho produces more denim jeans (over 26 million pairs each year) than any other country in Africa. This is despite the fall in sales and the temporary loss of jobs following the end of the Multi-Fibre Agreement (MFA) in 2005, which saw world sales of Asian garments eliminate many markets for African manufacturers. Trade picked up later as the clothing industry was revitalised, mainly by new markets for ethical clothing.

Imports
Principal imports include petroleum, food, building materials, machinery and vehicles, pharmaceuticals and medical products.
Main sources: Middle East, South Africa, US

Exports
Principal exports are electricity and water (to South Africa), garment manufactures, vehicles parts, wool and mohair, food and live animals.
Main destinations: South Africa, US, Hong Kong

Agriculture
The agricultural sector has traditionally been a major contributor to the economy. A series of programmes were implemented from 1996 to boost agricultural development through commercialisation and privatisation. Progress has been slow and the IMF reported in 2005 that agriculture suffered from structural weaknesses that included poor farming techniques, soil erosion, lack of water in lowland areas and lack of access to agri-finance.
There are a number of factors constraining development such as the government's heavy involvement in production, marketing and processing of the sector. This involves controlling commodity prices as well as containing imports and exports. These policies have deterred private sector involvement and hampered growth. The country also faces a severe lack of land suitable to arable farming as well as poor soil fertility and unreliable rainfall. Poverty is widespread in rural areas, where households rely on miners' remittances to remain in operation. As more workers are being laid off in South African mines the agricultural sector is finding it hard to maintain production levels enough to feed the population.
Moreover, the construction of the Mohale dam as part of the Lesotho Highlands Water Project (LHWP) has meant flooding the most fertile land area, the only region producing a food surplus. The World Bank maintains that the US$55 million earned from water

sales to South Africa will far exceed the US$2 million value of Mohale valley crops. Farmers from the Katse Dam area have been given food aid and skills training and communities have been resettled. Environmental organisations expressed concern over increased unemployment, food insecurity and water shortages downstream due to dams.

Industry and manufacturing

The industrial sector as a whole typically contributes around 40 per cent of GDP and employs around 26 per cent of the labour force.

Most firms are small and are in joint ventures with the Lesotho National Development Corporation (LNDC). Production is largely for export (clothing, footwear, textiles) or import substitution (food processing, bricks). Other enterprises include handicrafts, ceramics and furniture making. Pharmaceuticals and leather/hide processing are under development.

Tourism

The Lesotho Tourism Development Corporation (LTDC) provides the direction for the tourism sector. It's strategy is to develop village based facilities where visitors can experience traditional customs and lifestyles. The country is also being marketed for the eco-tourist and those enjoying activity holidays.

The Lesotho highlands are the main tourist attraction as well as the world heritage site of Maloti/Drakensberg, which has been given a US$15 million grant, by the World Bank, to protect its bio-diversity.

Mining

The diamond industry is mainly based on the Letseng la Terae mine. Letseng Diamonds and the New Mining Corporation each have a 38 per cent share in the project while the government retains a 24 per cent share. The mine produces just three carats per 100 tonnes, compared to the global average of 50–100 carats per 100 tonnes. Production costs are at least 10 times greater than the world average. However, Letseng la Terae continues to be in operation due to the high number of large diamonds produced.

Hydrocarbons

Lesotho does not produce any hydrocarbons. Explorations for oil took place in 1970. These proved unsuccessful and no further attempts have been made. Currently it imports around 2,000 barrels per day of refined oil, primarily from South Africa.

Energy

Installed generating capacity was 76MW in 2008, supplied by the Lesotho Highlands Water Project (LHWP); an increase of 2MW is anticipated by 2011. However consumption was 126MW, which had to be imported from South Africa, which since it began experiencing its own shortages reduced supplies to Lesotho. Blackouts have resulted at times of maximum overload. In 2008, electricity supply reached 16 per cent of the population. Production is projected to be 288MW in 2020.

The, government and African Development Bank have initiated plans to invest in the electricity system. Studies began in 2009, to ascertain the feasibility of installing, distributing and storing power by 2012.

Until electricity is supplied to a majority of homes the urban population will reply on paraffin, and the rural population on biomass, for primary energy.

Banking and insurance

Restructuring of the banking sector in the 1990s has strengthened the position of Lesotho's banking sector by improving asset management and the capital base of domestic banks. Along with the liberalisation of interest rates, restructuring has enabled domestic banks to respond to interest rate movements in South Africa and strengthened the Central Bank's ability to influence the money supply.

Central bank

Central Bank of Lesotho

Time

GMT plus two hours

Geography

Lesotho is a landlocked country, entirely surrounded by South African territory. It is a mountainous land situated at the highest part of the Drakensberg escarpment on the eastern rim of the South African plateau.

To its west, the land falls through foothills to a lowland area where the majority of the population lives. Three large rivers, the Orange, the Caledon and the Tugela, rise in the mountains and flow through it.

Hemisphere

Southern

Climate

Temperate climate with well-marked seasons.

More than 85 per cent of the country's rainfall – averaging 700mm in mountain areas – falls from October to April. Spring comes in August. Summer from November–January with average temperature 27 degrees Centigrade (C), rising to 32 degrees C in lowland areas.

Autumn days are warm. Winter from May–July with temperatures as low as minus 7 degrees C in lowlands and minus 18 degrees C in highlands.

Snowfalls can occur on the highlands at any time of the year.

Dress codes

In summer, light, loose clothing is most comfortable, but include a raincoat.

Spring and autumn clothing should include a jersey for the cool evenings. Heavy woollens, vests, windcheaters, socks and jackets are a must in winter. Warm clothing is also essential for a journey into the Maloti where severe weather conditions can be encountered any time of the year.

Entry requirements

Passports

Required by all.

Visa

Required by all, except those (mostly Commonwealth) countries listed on the internet at www.lesotholondon.org.uk, in the consular section. Further information may be requested through the consulate, or application forms downloaded from consulate websites, within applicant's country.

Currency advice/regulations

There are no restrictions on the import or export of local or foreign currency. The South African rand is interchangeable with the loti in Lesotho, but the loti cannot be used in South Africa.

Travellers cheques are widely accepted.

Customs

Personal items are exempt from duty.

Prohibited imports

Alcohol and firearms

Health (for visitors)

Mandatory precautions

Yellow fever vaccination for visitors from infected areas.

Advisable precautions

Immunisation and booster shots are advised for diphtheria, tetanus, typhoid and hepatitis A. Tuberculosis, polio and hepititis B may be advised. Malaria is not common. There is a rabies risk in rural areas. There is a very high prevalence of HIV/Aids.

Sun-burning is a problem for visitors at higher altitudes and sunscreens are recommended.

All medication necessary should be brought by a visitor.

Hotels

There are a number of comfortable, international-class hotels in Maseru. Throughout the rest of the country, accommodation ranges from medium-sized hotels to smaller tourist lodges.

Credit cards

Major credit and charge cards have acceptance.

Public holidays (national)

Fixed dates

1 Jan (New Year's Day), 11 Mar (Moshoeshoe's Day), 1 May (Workers' Day), 25 May (Heroes' Day), 17 Jul (King

Letsie III's Birthday), 4 Oct (Independence Day), 24–25 Dec (Christmas).

Variable dates

Good Friday, Easter Monday, Ascension Day.

Working hours

Banking

Mon, Tue, Thu, Fri: 0830–1530; Wed: 0830–1300; Sat: 0830–1100.

Business

Mon–Fri: 0800–1245, 1400–1630; Sat: 0800–1300.

Government

Mon–Fri: 0800–1245, 1400–1630.

Shops

Mon–Fri: 0800–1700; Sat: 0800–1300.

Telecommunications

Mobile/cell phones

GSM 900 services are available in larger populated areas.

Getting there

Air

National airline: South African Airways provide regular scheduled flights via Johannesburg.

International airport/s: Maseru-Moshoeshoe I (MSU), 18km south of Maseru. All international flights are via South Africa.

Airport tax: International departures M20; transit passengers are exempt.

Surface

Road: There are three good tarred roads from South Africa into the western region, via the Maseru Bridge, Ficksburg Bridge (both open 24 hours) and Caledonspoort (open daytime only). With the implementation of the Highlands Water Project, the road network has being expanded.

There are several other border crossings but with limited opening hours.

A road tax of M5 exists for visitors leaving Lesotho by light vehicles.

Rail: Only freight traffic is carried on the rail system that links to the South African system via Maseru.

Getting about

National transport

Air: Charter flights are difficult to find. South African companies may provide a service.

Road: Over 3,500km of tarred, gravel and dirt roads. Approximately 500km are tarred.

Roads are being continuously upgraded, and tarred roads connect main towns in seven out of 10 districts.

Buses: A good service provided by mainly privately owned buses. Coach services operate Maseru-Welkom; Maseru-Qacha's Nek.

Car hire

Drivers must hold an international driving licence. Driving is on the left and seat belts are compulsory.

In winter, antifreeze is a wise precaution for all cars with watercooled engines. Chains are useful in mud and snow. Petrol can be obtained in all District Headquarter towns but is not easily obtainable elsewhere.

For visitors using their own vehicles information should be obtained from Lesotho Tourist Board Information Office (www.lesotho.gov.ls).

BUSINESS DIRECTORY

The addresses listed below are a selection only. While World of Information makes every endeavour to check these addresses, we cannot guarantee that changes have not been made, especially to telephone numbers and area codes. We would welcome any corrections.

Telephone area codes

The international dialling code (IDD) for Lesotho is +266 followed by the subscriber's number.

Useful telephone numbers

Queen Elizabeth II Hospital:	312-501
Police:	123
Fire brigade:	122
Ambulance:	121

Chambers of Commerce

Lesotho Chamber of Commerce & Industry, PO Box 79, Fairways Centre, Kingsway Avenue, Maseru 100 (tel: 2232-3482; fax: 2231-0414; e-mail: lcci@lesoff.co.za).

Banking

Lesotho Bank Ltd; PO Box 1053, Kingsway, Maseru 100 (tel: 2231-4333; fax: 2231-0348).

Barclays Bank plc, PO Box 115, Kingsway, Maseru (tel: 2231-2423; fax: 2231-0068).

NedBank, 1st Floor, Standard Bank Bldg, Kingsway, PO Box 1001, Maseru 100 (tel: 2232-2696; fax: 2231-0025).

Central bank

Central Bank of Lesotho, PO Box 1184, Corner Airport and Moshoeshoe Roads, Maseru 100 (tel: 2231-4281; fax: 2231-0051; email: cbl@centralbank.org.ls).

Travel information

Ministry of tourism

Ministry of Tourism, Environment and Culture, PO Box 52, Maseru 100 (tel: 2231-3034).

National tourist organisation offices

Lesotho Tourist Development Corporation, PO Box 1378, Maseru 100 (tel: 2231-2427; fax: 2232-3674; email: touristinfo@ltdc.org.ls; internet: www.ltdc.org.ls).

Ministries

Minister to the Prime Minister, PO Box 527, Maseru 100 (tel: 2231-1000; fax: 2231-0102).

Ministry of Agriculture, Co-ops, Marketing and Youth Affairs, PO Box 24, Maseru 100 (tel: 2232-3561; fax: 2231-0349).

Ministry of Defence and Public Service, PO Box 527, Maseru 100 (tel: 2231-1000; fax: 2231-0102).

Ministry of Education and Manpower Development, PO Box 47, Maseru 100 (tel: 2231-3045; fax: 2231-0206).

Ministry of Finance and Economic Planning, PO Box 395, Maseru 100 (tel: 22311-101; fax: 2231-0157).

Ministry of Foreign Affairs, PO Box 1378, Maseru 100 (tel: 2231-1150; fax: 2231-1150).

Ministry of Health and Social Welfare, PO Box 514, Maseru 100 (tel: 2232-4404; fax: 2231-0467).

Ministry of Home Affairs and Local Government, Rural and Urban Development, PO Box 174, Maseru 100 (tel: 2232-3771; fax: 2231-0319).

Ministry of Information and Broadcasting, PO Box 36, Maseru 100 (tel: 2232-3561; fax: 2231-0003).

Ministry of Justice, Human Rights, Law and Constitutional Affairs, PO Box 402, Maseru 100 (tel: 2232-2683).

Ministry of Labour and Employment, Private Bag A116, Maseru 100 (tel: 2232-2565).

Ministry of Natural Resources, PO Box 426, Maseru 100 (tel: 2231-3632).

Ministry of Trade and Industry, PO Box 747, Maseru 100 (tel: 2232-2138; fax: 2231-0326).

Ministry of Transport and Telecommunications, PO Box 413, Maseru 100 (tel: 2232-3691).

Ministry of Works, PO Box 20, Maseru 100 (tel: 2231-1362; fax: 2231-0125).

Other useful addresses

British High Commission, PO Box 521, Maseru 100 (tel: 22313-961; fax: 2231-0120).

Lesotho Embassy (USA), 2511 Massachusetts Avenue, NW, Washington DC 20008 (tel: (+1-202) 797-5533; fax: (+1-202) 234-6815).

Lesotho National Development Corporation, Private Mail Bag A96, Maseru 100 (tel: 2231-2012; fax: 22310-038; internet site: www.lndc.org.ls).

Lesotho National Insurance Corporation, Private Bag A96, Maseru 100 (tel: 2231-3031; fax: 2231-0007).

Livestock Marketing Corp, PO Box 800, Maseru (tel: 2232-2444) (sole marketing concern for all livestock and products, including mohair).

Multilateral Investment Guarantee Agency (MIGA), 1818 H Street NW, Washington DC 20433, USA (tel: (+1-202) 473-1079; fax: (+1-202) 334-0265).

Radio Lesotho, PO Box 552, Maseru (tel: 2232-3561).

Statistics Bureau, PO Box 455, Maseru (tel: 2232-3852).

Trade Promotion Unit, Ministry of Trade and Industry, PO Box 747, Maseru (tel: 2232-3414; fax: 2231-0121).

National news agency: LENA (Lesotho News Agency), PO Box 36; Lerotholi Street, Maseru 100 (tel: 2232-5317; fax: 2232-6408; internet: www.lena.gov.ls).

Internet sites

Africa Business Network: www.ifc.org/abn

AllAfrica.com: http://allafrica.com

African Development Bank: www.afdb.org

Africa Online: www.africaonline.com

Public Eye (on-line edition of daily newspaper): www.publiceye.co.ls

Lesotho news agency: www.lena.gov.ls/news.htm

Mopheme newspaper: www.lesoff.co.za/news/

Lesotho Council of Non-Governmental Organisations (LCN): www.lecongo.org.ls/

Lesotho Government online: www.lesotho.gov.ls

Liberia

KEY FACTS

Official name: Republic of Liberia

Head of State: President Ellen Johnson-Sirleaf (from 2005; re-elected 8 Nov 2011)

Head of government: President Ellen Johnson-Sirleaf

Ruling party: Coalition led by the Unity Party (UP) (re-elected 11 Oct 2011)

Area: 111,370 square km

Population: 4.10 million (2010)*

Capital: Monrovia

Official language: English

Currency: Liberian dollar (L$) = 100 cents

Exchange rate: L$71.00 per US$ (Oct 2011)

GDP per capita: US$239 (2009)*

GDP real growth: 5.60% (2010)*

GDP: US$990.00 million (2010)*

Inflation: 6.60% (2010)*

Balance of trade: -US$379.00 million (2010)

* estimated figure

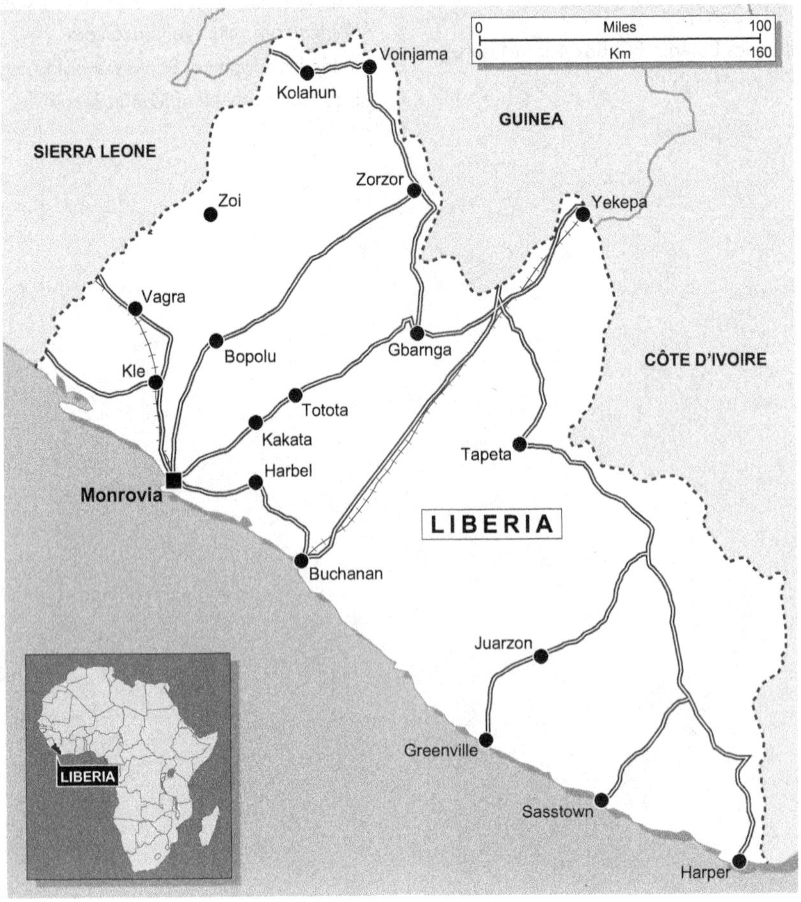

In January 2011 the controversial 30-year ban from politics imposed on President Ellen Johnson Sirleaf and a number of politicians and individuals by the now dissolved Truth and Reconciliation Commission (TRC), for their alleged roles in the country's war, was declared unconstitutional by the Supreme Court. This enabled Mrs Johnson to announce that she would stand for re-election in the coming presidential elections.

Parliamentary elections were held on 11 October, all seats in the lower house were in contention and half the seats in the Senate were up for re-election. The Unity Party (UP) won most seats in the lower house with 24 (out of 73). The opposition Congress of Democratic Change (CDC) won 11 seats. Presidential elections were also held on 11 October in which 16 candidates took part. Incumbent Ellen Johnson Sirleaf (UP) won 43.9 per cent of the vote and her closest opponent, Winston Tubman (CDC) won 32.7 per cent. Tubman withdrew from the runoff elections on 7 October, alleging fraud; he called on his supporters to boycott the election. President Sirleaf accused Tubman of violating the constitution by urging Liberians not to take part in the elections and advised all to participate. A runoff election was scheduled for 8 November between these two candidates and despite the appeal by the President for voters not to boycott the election turnout was only 33 per cent; Sirleaf won 90 per cent and Tubman around 9 per cent.

On 7 October President Sirleaf and Liberian activist Leymah Gbowee were announced as two of the three women to win the 2011 Nobel Peace Prize – the third was Tawakkul Karman of the Yemen. The three women were honoured for 'their non-violent struggle for the safety of women and for women's rights to full participation in peace-building work.'

The security situation is generally stable, though fragile, and a sizeable United Nations Mission in Liberia (UNMIL) peacekeeping force remains in the country. Regional instability caused by the political stalemate (until being resolved in 2011) in neighbouring Côte d'Ivoire made the situation in Liberia increasingly precarious as the UN reported that former fighters from Liberia were being recruited in Côte d'Ivoire. Over 10,000 refugees from Côte d'Ivoire are in Liberia. Finally, there is some concern that Liberia could become a transit point for drugs to Western Europe and the United States.

The economy

Liberia's economy is recovering from the global economic downturn in the view of the *African Economic Outlook 2010* (AEO), published jointly by the African Development Bank and the Organisation for Economic Co-operation and Development. Growth in 2010 was estimated at 6.1 per cent, up from 4.6 per cent in 2009, driven by an increase in exports and foreign direct investment (FDI). Growth is projected to reach 7.3 per cent in 2011 and 8.9 per cent in 2012. The rise in exports was thanks to an increase in commodity prices, particularly rubber, palm oil and minerals. In 2010, the government also began receiving royalty payments (of US$1.57 million) from the extractive industries sector and these are projected to grow to US$30 million by 2015. Inflation is estimated at 7.6 per cent in 2010 and is projected to be 4.4 per cent in 2011 before picking up to 4.8 per cent in 2012. The dollarisation of the Liberian economy helps keep inflation under control.

Liberia made significant progress by reaching the Completion Point under the Enhanced HIPC Initiative in June 2010 resulting in debt relief of US$4.6 billion. Reforms required to reach the Completion Point also had the additional benefit of creating a positive reform dynamic in many sectors including public financial management, implementation of the Extractive Industries Transparency Initiative, health services and harmonisation of the education payroll. In 2010, the government also reached an out-of-court settlement with two 'vulture funds' – Hamsah Investment and Wall Capital – agreeing to repay just over 3 per cent of the US$43 million it owed on a 1970s debt.

The overall challenge for Liberia is to make the transition from a period of post-conflict reconstruction to sustainable development. This will require not only a long-term vision as articulated in the Liberia Rising 2030 development plan, but also strong emphasis on regional integration. The Liberia Rising 2030 strategy, currently being elaborated, will emphasise projected large-scale foreign investment in enclave sectors – mainly iron ore, rubber and palm oil. Revenues will be invested in infrastructure to create growth corridors, which should be linked to international markets. Under this strategy, royalty revenues could finance infrastructure investments and improve the business climate.

As Liberia is a small country with limited purchasing power, a strong export policy to regional markets and shared regional infrastructure projects would boost development. Such a policy could be integrated into the next cycle of the country's poverty reduction strategy.

Non-African and African emerging partners are active in Liberia. Non-African countries are mainly active in the private sector and extractive industries, including iron ore and palm oil plantations. Clearly, recent high commodity prices provide an additional incentive to invest in Liberia's relatively risky business environment. Of the non-African emerging partners group, China is the largest public donor giving an estimated US$20 million annually to Liberia, mainly in the form of tied aid. This aid – which is primarily bilateral – is being used to build infrastructure, and to improve healthcare and education. China is also an observer on various donor co-ordination frameworks and is a member of the country's Economic Management Team, the highest body that reviews development projects managed by the ministry of planning and economic affairs. The comparatively good co-ordination between China and Liberia's other development partners has been attributed by traditional donors to the absence of competition or strategic interests in Liberia compared with other resource rich African countries.

In terms of African emerging partners, Nigeria leads the group and Nigerian banks are planning on introducing mobile phone banking to Liberia on the back of the innovation's success in East Africa. A rubber processing plant is also planned that will produce tyre-grade rubber for export as well a project to improve food security.

Revenues from rubber production have increased in conjunction with the rebound in world prices, while FDI has increased with the inflow of investment related to the Bong Mines and Yekepa iron ore operations. In 2010, large-scale extraction commenced and the government should also receive its first US$1.57 million royalty payment from the mines in 2010; these are projected to grow to US$30 million by 2015.

The economy is dominated by agricultural activities. As a share of GDP, agriculture, forestry and fisheries accounted for 62.7 per cent of the economy in 2010 reflecting the weakness of other sectors after decades of civil war and economic mismanagement. Liberia's agricultural production is mainly subsistence as the country suffers

KEY INDICATORS — Liberia

	Unit	2006	2007	2008	2009	2010
Population	m	3.58	3.75	3.94	*3.67	*4.10
Gross domestic product (GDP)	US$bn	0.61	0.75	0.85	*0.88	*0.99
GDP per capita	US$	171	199	242	*239	–
GDP real growth	%	7.8	13.7	*7.1	4.6	*5.6
Inflation	%	7.2	11.2	17.5	*7.4	*6.6
Exports (fob) (goods)	US$m	157.8	196.2	255.3	180.0	*215.0
Imports (fob) (goods)	US$m	401.4	498.5	954.7	559.0	*674.0
Balance of trade	US$m	-243.6	-302.3	-699.4	-379.0	*-459.0
Current account	US$m	-368.7	-233.0	1,451.2	-541.1	–
Total reserves minus gold	US$m	72.0	119.4	160.9	372.5	–
Foreign exchange	US$m	71.9	119.3	139.0	171.0	–
Exchange rate	per US$	58.00	59.15	63.20	71.55	*70.88

* estimated figure

from low agricultural yields and the main staple food is rice. Rubber is the biggest cash crop, although there have been recently large investments in palm oil.

In the near future, palm oil production is expected to increase with two major investments by the Malaysia company Sime Darby and the UK's Equatorial Palm Oil, which were awarded concessions of 220,000 and 169,000 hectares, respectively. Another Malaysian company Golden Veroleum, is currently negotiating with the government over a US$1.6 billion investment for a 30,000 hectare palm oil concession that would employ 10,000 people in full operation. The project is anticipated to include value-added processes to transform palm oil into biodiesel and other fuels.

Manufacturing accounted for about 5.3 per cent of the economy in 2010, mostly from small-scale industrial activities such as the manufacture of cement, bricks, tiles, wooden and metal furniture. There are a few limited opportunities to expand the manufacturing sector to support investments in the extractive industries, road and railway construction and small- and medium-sized enterprises (SMEs). Private sector development however requires the creation of an enabling environment, which remains a challenge in this post-conflict country lacking human resources, physical infrastructure and banking services as it is.

Structural growth in the manufacturing sector is restricted due to the smallness of the domestic market, lack of purchasing power and limited public consumption. Long-term growth will likely depend on further regional integration, in particular the Mano River Union economic grouping of Liberia, Guinea and Sierra Leone. The immediate priority here is to expand regional infrastructure to facilitate cross border trade.

The service sector contributed 25.9 per cent to GDP in 2010 and includes wholesale and retail trade, hotels and restaurants (6 per cent), transport, storage and communication (4.2 per cent), finance and real estate and business services (2.8 per cent), general government services (9.5 per cent) and other services (3.4 per cent). These services mainly cater to the international community as well as UNMIL and are often supplied by Lebanese-owned and operated companies. As such, profits and employment tend not to trickle down to the wider Liberian population.

International trade

Liberia is a member of Economic Community of West African States (Ecowas). The country also applied for World Trade Organisation membership in 2007, but it is still in the first stages of the admission process and must submit a memorandum on its foreign trade regime.

As a member of Ecowas, Liberia is party to ongoing negotiations with the EU regarding an Economic Partnership Agreement. At the same time, Liberia has market access to the EU on terms similar to the Everything But Arms initiative for least developed countries. Since 2006, Liberia has benefited from the American Growth and Opportunity Act and some textiles are exported to the United States. However, overall the country has difficulty benefiting from these preferential access schemes due to structural and supply constraints, such as poor infrastructure, intermittent energy supplies and a paucity of companies with export networks. Liberia will also benefit from preferential market access in China under engagements arising from the 2009 Forum on China-Africa Co-operation.

FDI flows have picked up since the effects of the 2008 financial crisis subsided. A large share of FDI is linked to the extractive industry and represents private-sector investments from emerging partners, most notably China and India. These have respectively committed to investing US$2.6 billion and US$1.5 billion. Their investments include building road and rail infrastructure such as the 80km Bong Mine and 250km Lamco iron-ore railroads to the port of Buchanan. Across the border in Guinea, similar private-sector infrastructure projects have been implemented but as the parties could not reach an agreement, the two systems are not compatible. Consequently, Guinea will be unable to use Liberian rail and port infrastructure to access overseas markets, highlighting the drawbacks of private-sector driven regional infrastructure projects.

Private sector

The overall business climate in Liberia remains challenging. Liberia has low human capital, poor physical infrastructure and limited access to financial services. Despite a recent transparency drive, corruption is also a major concern. The weak business climate will hamper export processing and import substitution remains very limited, even for many basic commodities.

Liberia was ranked 155th out of 183 countries in the 2010 World Bank *Doing Business* report. This marked an improvement by three places over previous years although it still takes 20 days to start a business in Liberia, 77 days to obtain a construction permit and 50 days to register a property. The registration of property and land titles is particularly challenging, as ownership shifted rapidly during the civil war. From an economic perspective, the absence of land titles poses a barrier to accessing credit, and from a peace-building perspective, disputed claims are a source of tension.

As part of achieving the Heavily Indebted Poor Countries (HIPC) Completion Point, a range of reforms have been implemented in public finances aimed at improving the performance of the public sector and which range from debt management to budget preparation. This latter includes a medium-term context, a budget framework paper, and state enterprise reporting. The public wage bill was estimated to have increased by 1.7 per cent of GDP in 2010 due to the inclusion of education, health and some security salaries in the payroll for the first time.

Liberia's infrastructure is limited, posing a critical bottleneck for economic growth. The government has prioritised public works, education and health infrastructure investments, and capital expenditure is projected to increase from 3.4 per cent of GDP in 2010 to 4.3 per cent in 2011. The implementation of investment programmes may be hampered however if budget support operations are not approved in a timely manner causing capital expenditures to reduce.

The management of natural resources is a key component of Liberia's development strategy and is set to be financed by licence fees in the short term, and by royalty payments in the longer term. A number of forestry laws have been introduced aiming at balancing sustainable development and social responsibility. Eight new companies received logging licences limited to no more than 5,000 hectares each.

Social sector expenditure

Decades of civil war and economic mismanagement have resulted in very poor socio-economic indicators. Achieving the Millennium Development Goals (MDGs) is therefore a daunting challenge as the war destroyed the country's infrastructure and eroded the human capital base. Liberia's Human Development Index value for 2010 was 0.300, which ranks it 162nd out of 169 countries. Up to 68 per cent of Liberians live below the poverty line and 38 per cent of the population is undernourished.

Because of these challenges, the government has prioritised social sector expenditure and free primary education is being introduced. Net enrolment for primary, secondary and tertiary education in 2010 was 605,236 (up 10 per cent) for primary, 117,507 (up 12 per cent) for secondary and 65,367 (up 15 per cent) for tertiary. These increases will be mainly attributed to private sector education establishments and while these developments are commendable, it should be noted that annual population growth is about 2.5 per cent, meaning that enrolment would increase naturally. The overall gross enrolment rate remains less than 50 per cent.

According to the most recent ILO labour market survey (2008), half of the adult Liberian population is engaged in unpaid family work and only a third are engaged in paid work. The informal economy employs 84 per cent of Liberians, who do not have access to sufficient income, regular work, acceptable working conditions, social security or assets. Another major challenge is youth unemployment due to lack of education and vocational skills. Finally, there also seems to be gender bias as 80 per cent of the new jobs created in the public sector were for men.

Risk assessment

Economy	Improving
Politics	Fair
Regional stability	Fair

COUNTRY PROFILE

Historical profile

1822 Liberia was created by a number of US philanthropists with the idea that freed American and Caribbean slaves would be resettled in Africa. Many refused to go and those who did were met with hostility from the majority indigenous population.
1847 Liberia was established as an independent state with a constitution modelled on that of the United States.. The US did not formally recognise this status until 1862.
1944–71 Under President William Tubman of the True Whig party (which monopolised power from early in Liberia's existence), the country received massive foreign investment, but this only exacerbated tension between the descendants of the settlers and the indigenous people.
1963 The local people were enfranchised – around 97 per cent of the total population.
1971 Tubman was succeeded by William Tolbert.
1980 Following protests against the government the previous year, Tolbert's government was overthrown in a coup led by Master Sergeant Samuel Doe, who survived several coup attempts and won an 'election' held in 1985. His government proved widely unpopular.
1984 A new multi-party constitution was introduced.
1985 Samuel Doe was elected president.
1989 Charles Taylor led the National Patriotic Front of Liberia (NPFL) in an uprising.
1990 Opposition groups, led by Prince Johnson and Charles Taylor overran most of Liberia and captured Monrovia. With Johnson and Taylor both claiming the presidency, the West African peacekeeping force, the Economic Community of West African States Monitoring Group (Ecomog), installed Amos Sawyer as head of an Interim Government of National Unity (IGNU). The NPFL controlled around 90 per cent of Liberia; the remnants of Doe's supporters and Johnson's forces were both encamped within the capital. President Doe was executed by NPFL.
1993 After a period of heavy fighting, a UN-sponsored peace accord was signed, calling for the creation of a six-month transitional government representing the IGNU, the NPFL and Doe's supporters and the United Liberation Movement for Democracy (Ulimo).
1994–95 Several agreements were reached, none of which brought a final peace.
1996 An attempt to arrest one faction leader for breaking the truce led to two weeks of serious street fighting in Monrovia until Ecomog regained control. Following the renewed conflict, both the faction leaders and Ecowas agreed to hold elections in 1997.
1997 Charles Taylor and his NPFL won a landslide victory.
1999 The Ghanaian and Nigerian troops, who were part of Ecomog, withdrew from Liberia.
2000 President Charles Taylor announced that his government was forming a new army.
2001 There were rebel attacks on the border between Guinea and Liberia and Liberia closed its border with Sierra Leone.
2002 A state of emergency was declared after rebels (Liberians United for Reconciliation and Democracy (LURD)) attacked a town near the capital, Monrovia.
2003 The UN Security Council extended its arms embargo against Liberia for 12 months and added an export ban on raw timber. Foreign nationals were evacuated from Monrovia amid fighting by LURD rebels in their campaign against President Taylor, who initially refused to resign. President Taylor finally accepted Nigeria's asylum offer. West African peacekeepers entered Monrovia as President Taylor resigned and named Moses Blah as president. The government and two rebel groups selected Gyude Bryant, chairman of the Liberia Action Party (LAP), to head Liberia's interim post-war administration.
2004 International donors pledged more than US$500 million in reconstruction aid. The UN Security Council voted to freeze the assets of former president, Charles Taylor.
2005 The first elections since the end of the civil war were held; in the presidential run-off Ellen Johnson-Sirleaf (Unity Party) (UP) defeated George Weah (Liberal Party) (LP), becoming the first woman president in Africa. The UN Security Council extended its ban on arms sales to Liberia for a further 12 months and the sale of diamonds and timber for a further six months.
2006 Ellen Johnson-Sirleaf took office as president. A Truth and Reconciliation Commission began work. Former president Charles Taylor was extradited from Nigeria into UN custody in Sierra Leone and indicted for war crimes before the UN-backed Special Court in The Hague (The Netherlands). The government concluded a mineral concession agreement with Indian-based, Mittal Steel.
2007 Personal banking arrived in the north-east border region of Ganta, with the opening of the first bank after 16 years of civil war, when most banks outside the capital region were looted and left defunct. Liberia inherited debts of US$3.7 billion – an unsustainable amount the World Bank said was 30 times the country's annual export earnings and eight times greater than its GDP. The US granted US$500 million in aid and agreed to cancel US$391 million in debt, then pledged US$200 million in further funds. The UN lifted a ban on the export of diamonds. The government lifted the moratorium on the mining, sale and export of diamonds. The vital Mano River Bridge, connecting Sierra Leone with Liberia, was officially re-opened.
2008 US President George W Bush became the first US president to visit in 30 years. The first census since 1984 was undertaken, which recorded a population of 3,489,072.
2009 A US court convicted Charles 'Chuckie' Taylor, son of former president Taylor, and sentenced him to 97 years in prison for torture and *ex officio* executions. Liberia reduced its foreign debt by a significant amount when it bought back US$1.2 billion in government debt at 97 per cent of its face value. The World Bank provided 50 per cent of the necessary payment and Germany, Norway, the UK and US provided the other 50 per cent between them. Former president, Charles Taylor, began his testimony in his trial, in The Hague, on charges of terrorism,

murder, rape and torture. The Liberian Truth and Reconciliation Commission recommended that a 30-year ban should be placed on President Johnson-Sirleaf, and many other senior politicians, for backing Charles Taylor when he overthrew the previous administration in 1989. President Johnson-Sirleaf apologised for her support of Charles Taylor in 1989. In August, the members of parliament (MPs) said they would take one year to consult their constituent's views of President Johnson-Sirleaf, before making a decision about her future.
2010 In January, despite a pledge not to seek another term in office, Ellen Johnson-Sirleaf announced her nomination for president in the November 2011 elections. By August, President Johnson-Sirleaf had received a number of plaudits by leading international publications, claiming she was one of the best leaders in the world and the best in Africa. Opposition parties and candidates claim her progress has been too little and too slow.
2011 In January the controversial 30-year ban from politics imposed on President Ellen Johnson Sirleaf and a number of politicians and individuals by the now dissolved Truth and Reconciliation Commission (TRC), for their alleged roles in the country's war was declared unconstitutional by the Supreme Court. Mrs Johnson said that she would stand for re-election in the coming presidential elections. On 8 February, one of Charles Taylor's lawyers, Courtenay Griffiths, walked out of Taylor's war trial, after Griffiths' final written brief, submitted 20 days late, was rejected by the judges. Griffiths was later brought before a disciplinary hearing in Sierra Leone. Two Liberians, found guilty of defrauding World Vision (funded by USAid) of food and construction materials for Liberia, valued at US$2 million, were jailed in the US for over 11 years. The first official announcement of GDP since 1987 was published on 2 August. President Sirleaf and Liberian activist Leymah Gbowee were announced as two of the three women (the third was Tawakkul Karman from the Yemen) to win the 2011 Nobel Peace Prize on 7 October. The three women were honoured for 'their non-violent struggle for the safety of women and for women's rights to full participation in peace-building work'. Parliamentary elections were held on 11 October, all seats in the lower house were in contention and half the seats were up for re-election in the Senate. The UP won most seats in the lower house, with a return of 24 candidates. The opposition CDC won 11 seats. Presidential elections were also held on 11 October in which 16 candidates took part. Incumbent Ellen Johnson Sirleaf (UP) won 43.9 per cent of the vote and her closest opponent, Winston Tubman (CDC) won 32.7 per cent. Winston Tubman withdrew from the runoff elections on 7 October, alleging fraud; he called on his supporters to boycott the election. President Sirleaf accused Tubman of violating the constitution by urging Liberians not to take part in the elections and advised all to participate. A runoff election was scheduled for 8 November between these two candidates and despite the appeal by the president for voters not to boycott the election turnout was only 33 per cent; Sirleaf won 90 per cent and Tubman around 9 per cent.

Political structure

Constitution

The multi-party 1984 constitution, approved by referendum, replaced the 1847 constitution which was suspended in April 1980.

The executive

Executive power rests with the president, elected by universal adult suffrage for a term of six years; the maximum number of terms is two. The president is head of state, head of government and commander-in-chief of the armed forces.
The president must be a natural-born Liberian citizen of not less than 35 years of age, the owner of unencumbered property valued at not less than US$25,000 and resident in Liberia 10 years prior to the elections.

National legislature

The bicameral Legislature of Liberia consists of the House of Representatives (lower house) with 64 members directly elected by popular vote for six-year terms, and the Senate (upper house) with 30 members; each county (constituency) returns two candidates each (the winner is the senior senator and second placed is the junior senator). Senior senators serve for nine-year terms and junior senators for six-year terms.

Legal system

Liberia has a dual system of statutory law based on Anglo-American common law for the modern sector and customary law based on unwritten tribal practices for the indigenous sector.

Last elections

11 October and 8 November 2011 (parliamentary, presidential and runoff)
Results: Parliamentary (lower house): Unity Party (UP) won 24 seats (out of 73), Congress of Democratic Change (CDC) 11, Liberty Party (LP) seven, National Union for Democratic Progress (NUDP) six, National Democratic Coalition (NDC) five, National Patriotic Party (NPP) three, Alliance for Peace and Democracy (APD) three, Movement for Progressive Change (MPC) two, independents nine; three other political parties each won one seat. Senate (50 per cent of membership): UP four (out of 15), NPP four, CDC two, four other parties and one independent each won one seat.
Presidential: Ellen Johnson Sirleaf (UP) won 43.9 per cent of the vote, Winston Tubman (CDC) 32.7 per cent, Prince Yormie Johnson (NUDP) 11.6 per cent, Charles Brumskine (LP) 5.5 per cent; 12 other candidates each won less that 1.5 per cent. Turnout was 71.64 per cent.
Runoff: Sirleaf won 90 per cent, Tubman (boycotting runoff) around 9 per cent. Turnout was 33 per cent.

Next elections

2011 (presidential and House of Representatives); 2014 (Senate)

Political parties

Ruling party

Coalition led by the Unity Party (UP) (re-elected 11 Oct 2011)

Main opposition party

Congress of Democratic Change (CDC)

Population

4.10 million (2010)*
Last census: 21 March 2008: 3,476,608
Population density: 32 inhabitants per square km. Urban population: 45 per cent.
Annual growth rate: 4.6 per cent 1994–2004 (WHO 2006)

Internally Displaced Persons (IDP)

500,000 (UNHCR 2004)

Ethnic make-up

Indigenous tribes (95 per cent), Americo-Liberians (5 per cent).

Religions

Christianity (68 per cent), traditional beliefs (18 per cent), Muslim (14 per cent).

Education

Primary education lasts for six years ending at age 12. Junior secondary school last for three years before successful students can progress onto senior secondary school for a further three years.
Higher education is provided principally by the Uninversity of Liberia in Monrovia, the African Methodist Episcopal University and Cuttington University College.
Literacy rate: 56 per cent adult rate; 71 per cent youth rate (15–24) (Unesco 2005).
Compulsory years: Six to 16.

Health

In 2007, the health minister estimated that the country had only one-tenth of the doctors needed for its post-conflict society. Of the 120 doctors in post, 70 were foreign doctors serving with international medical organisations and charities. Other healthcare professionals needed included nurses, midwives and laboratory technicians. Under-funding and lack of opportunity has led most trained healthcare workers to emigrate and many doctors resident in Liberia prefer to live in the coastal region leaving rural areas without medical cover. The government has offered a gratuity of US$1,000 (five times the current average salary) for any doctor who accepts assignments inland.

HIV/Aids

Altogether there were 96,000 adults, of which 54,000 women, and 8,000 children under the age of 15, living with HIV/Aids in 2003. Deaths from Aids totalled 7,200 and there were 36,000 orphans aged 0–17 created in 2003 (UCSF).

HIV prevalence: 5.9 per cent aged 15–49 in 2003 (World Bank)

Life expectancy: 42 years, 2004 (WHO 2006)

Fertility rate/Maternal mortality rate: 6.8 births per woman, 2004 (WHO 2006)

Child (under 5 years) mortality rate (per 1,000): 157 per 1,000 live births (World Bank).

Head of population per physician: 0.03 physicians per 1,000 people, 2004 (WHO 2006)

Main cities

Monrovia (capital, estimated population 550,200 in 2003), Zwedru (35,300), Buchanan (27,300).

Languages spoken

English is the business language. There are three main Liberian dialects – Golla, Bassa, Kpelle, Kru and Vai.

Official language/s

English

Media

The state of media in Liberia is still struggling to repair not only the damaged technology but also the proficiency and of the profession. Installations were either destroyed or looted during the civil war and the professionalism of journalists was corrupted as patronage was bestowed on only those that supported the former regime of Charles Taylor.

Press

Since the former president Taylor's departure, several independent newspapers have started publication.

Dailies: In English *The Inquirer* (www.theinquirer.com.lr), *The News* (www.thenews.com.lr), *The Analyst* (www.analystliberia.com), *Daily Observer* (www.liberianobserver.com) and *Poll Watch* are all published in Monrovia.

Weeklies: The private publication, *The Heritage*, is published in Monrovia.

Broadcasting

State-owned TV and radio suffered particularly from looting in the civil war and lost its TV and FM radio transmitters in 1991. The Liberia Broadcasting System (LBS) has one FM small transmitter that can reach only Monrovia, and no television.

The LCN controls a TV and radio network which uses the frequency 89FM, previously used by LBS, and which, by law, belongs to the state.

Radio: The public, Liberia Broadcasting System (ELBS) (www.liberiabroadcastingsystem.com) has a limited service but provides programmes in local languages, English and French. Others radio services include Star Radio (www.starradio.org.lr), Unmil Radio (http://unmil.org) operated by the United Nations mission, Sky FM and two Christian stations. Community radio services are operated, supported by international entities.

Television: There are three, private TV stations, Clar TV, Power TV and Real TV.

News agencies

APA: www.apanews.net

Panapress: www.panapress.com

Economy

Liberia has a number of marketable natural resources including iron ore, gold, diamonds, rubber, timber and recently discovered oil off its Atlantic coastline. It also has the world's second largest registered fleet (after Panama), licensing over 1,700 maritime vessels, including 35 per cent of the global tanker fleet. This has the potential to provide a reasonable standard of living for its people; however, in 2011 the UN Human Development Index (HDI), ranked Liberia 182 out of 187 for health, education and income development. The level of poverty was 57.7 per cent (2000–10), with 83.7 per cent living below a purchasing equivalent of US$1.25 per day.

Many years of mismanagement, before the end of the civil war in 2003, left Liberia with unsustainable debt of around US$3.7 billion, or 800 per cent of GDP, or 3,000 per cent of total export earnings. Under the Paris Club's April 2008 agreement Liberia was granted debt relief to clear US$1.5 billion. As it complies with economic reforms to attract investment it also aims at further debt relief through the Highly Indebted Poor Country (HIPC) initiative. In 2009 a British court ordered Liberia to pay US$20 million to two investment funds based in Caribbean tax-havens for debts dating back to 1978, an amount equivalent to 5 per cent of the government's 2009 budget. Liberia referred to these as 'vulture funds' (finance companies that buy up defaulted debts of poor countries and either harass the country or any entity trading with, or investing in, the country, demanding prompt repayment or risk seizure of monies through legal channels) and declared it had no money to pay the debt.

In September 2010 the 19-nation Paris Club of creditors wrote-off a further US$1.2 billion in Liberian debt, a sum that had until then accounted for most of debt servicing within the national budget. In November the government came to an agreement with two 'vulture funds', to repay 3 per cent of US$43 million, to clear the debt. This follows rulings in the US and UK court rulings, both of which said Liberia must repay the debt. The finance minister said that since 2006 the government had 'not borrowed a dime from any country'.

Liberia is a large recipient of international aid, used to fund both public spending and social projects. GDP growth since 2006 has been consistently high at 8.9 per cent, rising to 9.1 per cent in 2007. Despite a downturn in the global economy real growth was still buoyant at an estimated 7.1 per cent in 2008, although in 2009 growth slowed to 4.6 per cent as world trade was cut. In 2010, GDP growth picked up to an estimated 5.6 per cent, with a projected growth in 2011 of 6.8 per cent.

As Liberia tried to rebuild, the cost of imports far outstripped exports, resulting in an annual trade deficit of around -US$379 million in 2009 and -US$459 million in 2010 (with a projected -US$630 million in 2011) of which the largest components were imported oil and rice. Rubber accounted for over US$200 million in export revenue in 2008, falling to US$93 million in 2009 before returning to earlier levels, with exports of US$156 million in 2010 and a projected US$202 million in 2011.

Although unemployment is estimated to be over 50 per cent and an IMF programme objective in 2011 included plans to improve broad-based employment, Liberia suffers from a lack of educated and trained workers, many of whom left the country during the civil war.

External trade

Liberia is a member of the Economic Community of Western African States (Ecowas), which was set up to promote economic integration among members. It has expressed an interest in joining four other Anglophone-members in setting up a single currency, which will eventually be merged with the Francophone-members' currency to produce a single currency (the eco) for the region.

The government has encouraged foreign direct investment (FDI) in mining with a US$1 billion deal negotiated with Arcelor Mittal Steel in 2007. Natural rubber is the largest export product.

Imports

Principal imports include petroleum, rice and other foodstuffs, medicines and

pharmaceuticals, machinery and transport equipment and manufactured goods.
Main sources: South Korea (typically 35 per cent of total), Japan (20 per cent), Singapore (15 per cent)

Exports

Principal exports rubber, timber, iron, diamonds, cocoa and coffee.
Main destinations: Germany (typically 40 per cent of total), Poland (10 per cent), US (10 per cent)

Agriculture

Farming

Hit by hostilities and migration from rural areas, production has been reduced from pre-war levels. Agriculture is still the most important sector of the economy, contributing approximately 35 per cent to GDP and employing 55 per cent of the workforce.

One of the country's principal cash crops is rubber, which provides a large proportion of exports. Although mostly grown in foreign-owned plantations, smallholders are responsible for over half the total acreage planted.

Coffee, cocoa and timber are also grown for export, but, as with rubber, earnings have been reduced due to falling world prices. The main food crops are rice, cassava and sweet potatoes, followed by eddoes and yams. The government has attempted to improve production to reduce the need for imports of rice which have become necessary to meet domestic demand.

Palm oil has been produced mostly for the domestic market, but since 2009 a number of Asian companies have shown an interest in investing in the industy. Sime Derby (Malaysia) was granted a 220,000 hectare (ha) concession in 2009, Equatorial Palm Oil (UK) have a 169,000ha development and in 2010 Golden Agri Resources (Singapore) were 'actively evaluating' investing in another 220,000ha project. These three developments alone would signicantly contribute to Liberia's exports.

A national emergency was declared in January 2009 following an infestation of the caterpillar of the *Achaea catocaloides* moth, which consumed crops and spoiled drinking water; 20,000 families were evacuated from the overrun regions.

Commercial ocean fishing is a growing activity, particularly fishing for shrimps.

Forestry

Despite international sanction prohibiting timber exports, imposed in 2001, revenue from the trade in timber played a vital role in providing funding to ex-president Charles Taylor, for illicit arms imports during the civil war. Following his defeat, all sanctions were lifted in 2006; at which time steps were undertaken to control the exploitation of forest recourses, including the cancellation of all previous logging concessions. The Forestry Development Authority began by introducing new, transparent contracts and a forestry reform programme.

Industry and manufacturing

The small industrial sector contributes 4.9 per cent to GDP. The manufacturing sector is relatively underdeveloped, contributing 4 per cent to GDP. Activity is mainly confined to textiles, food and rubber processing, wood products, cement and chemicals.

The sector has been weakened by the country's upheavals, which damaged infrastructure and deterred investment. Growth in the sector is in any case constrained by the small size of the domestic market, the need to import practically all raw materials, shortage of skilled labour and financial problems.

Tourism

Although Liberia requested the UN Scientific and Cultural Organisation (UNESCO) to add two Liberian sites, Sarpo National Park and Providence Island, to The World's Cultural Heritage, by January 2012 no decision had been made.

Environment

Liberia is involved in the Great Apes Survival Project (Grasp), in concert with Unesco, in the first concerted programme developed to counter a major extinction crisis of great apes. Liberia requested the UN Scientific and Cultural Organisation to add two Liberian sites, Sarpo National Park and Providence Island, to The World's Cultural Heritage.

Mining

Prior to the civil war, Liberia was one of the world's major producers of iron ore (mainly extracted from mines at Mount Nimba, Mano River and Bong), which accounted for around 30 per cent of GDP. Production ceased completely as a result of the war. Efforts are being made to revive the sector. In August 2005, an agreement was entered into with the Mittal Steel Company to develop reserves and associated infrastructure in western Liberia.

Diamonds are mined, previously earning Liberia an estimated US$300 million annually. During the war, factions exploited production. Current production figures are hard to gauge due to the allegations of diamond smuggling with Sierra Leone, Guinea and Côte d'Ivoire. Liberia's diamond exports, along with timber, have been subject to UN economic sanctions since 2001, because of misuse of the revenues. Foreign investors, anticipating future stability, are showing interest in the sector.

A deal between the Israeli Diamond Institute (IDI) and the government was signed, whereby diamond experts from IDI will help in the search for local diamonds. The agreement was the first since a moratorium on mining, sales and export of Liberian diamonds was lifted by the UN, imposed in 2001 in an effort to halt the trade in 'blood diamonds' used to fund the civil war.

Hydrocarbons

There are no known oil or gas reserves in Liberia although there is potential in the territorial waters in the Gulf of Guinea. Investigations are at an early stage, in a second round of offshore exploration bids, opened in July 2008. The National Oil Company of Liberia is responsible for the oil industry.

Oil consumption remained fairly constant at between 3.5–4.0 million barrels per day over the period 2004–07, but is likely to increase as development picks up since the end of the civil war.

Any uses of natural gas and coal imports are commercially insignificant.

Energy

The electricity generation and supply infrastructure was wrecked early in the civil war. Total installed generating capacity in 2006, by the state-owned Liberian Electricity Corporation (LEC) was 2MW. In 2007 the emergency power program (EPP), in partnership with international donors, supplied emergency generators for use in Monrovia. Funds for development will add 7MW to Monrovia's power supply by 2009; neighbourhood deliveries will be provided via pre-pay meters and rural electricity will be provided by solar panels and other renewable sources.

A technical study was undertaken to determine sites for seven hydroelectricity plants, plus the development of a new 100MW facility at the existing Mount Coffee hydro location. Mini-hydro power plants are also being considered, throughout the country. When completed the country's generating capacity should be around 1.2 gigawatts.

Banking and insurance

The civil war has led to a virtual collapse of the banking system and lending services have declined dramatically. The country's five commercial banks have found it hard to attract capital savings, as the public and businesses have tended to hoard money rather than put it in banks due to a general crisis of confidence in the banking system. The subsequent lack of liquidity in the banking sector has led to a wide spread between the average deposit and lending rates. Lack of affordable bank credit has hampered growth across the economy, particularly the agricultural sector. Unless the government can ensure political stability and security and a policy is instituted to increase bank savings, Liberia's banking sector will remain in the doldrums.

Central bank

In 1999 the National Legislature enacted a law creating the Central Bank of Liberia, which replaced the National Bank of Liberia. Monetary authority functions are undertaken by the central government.

Main financial centre

Monrovia

Time

GMT

Geography

Liberia lies on the west coast of Africa, with Sierra Leone and Guinea to the north and Côte d'Ivoire to the east.

Liberia's coastline extends for about 580km, over half of which comprises sandy beaches. The terrain is generally low-lying. Lagoons, creeks and mangrove swamps punctuate the low coastal plain, behind which the land rises to a gently rolling, grassy plateau. Further inland, in the north-east, is mountainous, where the highest point in the country at 1,380m is Mount Wuwve. The plateau and mountain regions are home to approximately 40 per cent of Africa's rainforest.

Hemisphere

Northern

Climate

Hot and tropical with high levels of humidity (85–90 per cent) and there is little temperature variation throughout the year. Average temperatures range between 20–22 degrees Celsius (C) at night and 28–32 degrees C during the day. Wet season lasts from May–October with especially heavy rain June–July.

Entry requirements

Passports

Required by all, valid for six months from date of entry.

Visa

Required by all, except nationals of Ecowas countries, Israel, South Korea and Thailand.

Currency advice/regulations

There are no restrictions on import and export of local or foreign currencies. US dollars are legal tender.

Health (for visitors)

Mandatory precautions

Yellow fever vaccination certificate is required.

Advisable precautions

Typhoid, hepatitis A, tetanus and polio vaccinations are recommended. Malaria prophylaxis should be taken as risk exists throughout the country. There is a rabies risk. Drinking water should be boiled and filtered.

Hotels

The airport hotel and other major hotels in Monrovia should be booked in advance. Rates are expensive and tipping is optional.

Credit cards

There is limited acceptance of credit cards.

Public holidays (national)

Fixed dates

1 Jan (New Year's Day), 11 Feb (Armed Forces Day), 15 Mar (J J Roberts' Birthday), 12 Apr (National Redemption Day), 14 Apr (Fast and Prayer Day), 14 May (National Unification Day), 26 Jul (Independence Day), 24 Aug (Flag Day), 29 Nov (President Tubman's Birthday), 25 Dec (Christmas Day).

Variable dates

Decoration Day (Mar), Fast and Prayer Day (Apr), Thanksgiving Day (Nov)

Working hours

Banking

Mon–Thu: 0900–1200; Fri: 0800–1400.

Business

Mon–Fri: 0800–1200, 1400–1600.

Government

Mon–Fri: 0800–1200, 1300–1600.

Shops

Mon–Sat: 0800–1300, 1500–1800.

Telecommunications

Telephone/fax

The service is 100 per cent automatic but limited outside Monrovia.

Mobile/cell phones

Cell phone numbers (seven plus seven digits, six plus five digits) are working.

Weights and measures

Imperial system

Security

Crime is high in the capital, Monrovia, with theft and assault prevalent, particularly at night.

Getting there

Air

International airport/s: Monrovia-Roberts International (ROB), 60km from city; duty-free shop, bar, restaurant, buffet, post office, shops.

Airport tax: US$25

Surface

Road: The vital Mano River bridge connecting Sierre Leone with Liberia was officially reopened in June 2007.

Getting about

National transport

Air: Air taxi companies charter planes between Monrovia and airfields throughout the country.

Road: A network of 10,000km covers most areas, although many roads are untarred. Main highways are: Monrovia-Sanniquellie (with a branch Ganta-Harper) and Monrovia-Buchanan.

Rail: There are no passenger railways.

Water: Freight/passenger services between Monrovia and Buchanan.

City transport

There are buses and taxis available from the airport to the city centre.

Taxis: Zoning system in operation. Negotiate fares in advance for long-distance journeys. Tipping is not usual.

Car hire

Chauffeur-driven or self-drive cars are available in Monrovia. International driving licence or national driving licence with permit (valid for up to 30 days) accepted. Traffic drives on the right. Self-drive cars are not generally recommended.

BUSINESS DIRECTORY

The addresses listed below are a selection only. While World of Information makes every endeavour to check these addresses, we cannot guarantee that changes have not been made, especially to telephone numbers and area codes. We would welcome any corrections.

Telephone area codes

The international dialling code (IDD) for Liberia is +231, followed by subscriber's number.

In late-2006 land-line telephone numbers (6 digits beginning with a 2) were still not functioning. Cell phone numbers (7 + 7 digits and 6 + 5 digits) were working.

Chambers of Commerce

Liberia Chamber of Commerce, Capitol Hill, PO Box 92, Monrovia (tel: 223-738).

Banking

Liberian Bank for Development and Investment (LBDI), Corner of Randall and Ashmun Streets, PO Box 547, Monrovia (tel: 227-140; fax: 226-939).

International Bank (Liberia) Limited; 64 Broad Street, Monrovia (tel: 227-438; fax: 226-092/3).

Liberian Trading and Development Bank Ltd, PO Box 293, Tradevco Building, Ashmun Street, 1000 Monrovia 10 (tel: 226-072, 226-074; fax: 226-471).

Central bank

Central Bank of Liberia: PO Box 2048, Warren and Carey Streets, Monrovia (tel: 226-991; fax: 226-144).

Travel information

Ministry of tourism

Ministry of Information, Cultural Affairs and Tourism, United Nations Drive, Capitol Hill, PO Box 10-9021, 1000 Monrovia 10 (tel: 226-269; fax:

226-069; e-mail: webmaster@liberia.net).

Ministries

Ministry of Commerce, Industry, PO Box 10-9041, 1000 Monrovia 10 (tel: 226-283).

Ministry of Finance, Bureau of Customs and Excise, PO Box 10-9013, 1000 Monrovia 10.

Ministry of Foreign Affairs, PO Box 10-9002, 1000 Monrovia 10 (tel: 226-763, 221-029, 221-751).

Ministry of Information, Culture and Tourism, PO Box 10-9021, Capitol Hill, 1000 Monrovia 10 (tel: 226-045, 226-269, 227-349; fax: 226-045).

Ministry of Justice, Bureau of Immigration, PO Box 10-9006, Broad Street, 1000 Monrovia 10.

Ministry of Lands, Mines and Energy, PO Box 10-9024, 1000 Monrovia 10 (tel: 226-281, 221-580, 221-488, 221-460).

Ministry of Planning and Economic Affairs, PO Box 10-9016, 1000 Monrovia 10 (tel: 226-962, 227-987, 222-121, 222-331, 223-208, 221-971).

Ministry of Youth and Sports, PO Box 10-9040, 1000 Monrovia 10 (tel: 226-284).

Other useful addresses

ELTV (Liberian television system), PO Box 594, Monrovia.

Liberian Development Corporation, PO Box 9043, Monrovia.

Liberian Embassy (USA), 5201 16th Street, NW, Washington DC 20011 (tel: (+1-202)-723-0437; fax: (+1-202)-723-0436; e-mail: info@liberiaemb.org).

Liberian News Agency (LINA), Ministry of Information, PO Box 9021, Capitol Hill, Monrovia (tel: 222-229).

National Investment Commission, PO Box 10-9043, 1000 Monrovia 10 (tel: 226-685, 226-575).

National Ports Authority, PO Box 14, Monrovia.

Statistics Bureau, PO Box 9016, Monrovia (tel: 222-622).

Internet sites

Africa Business Network: www.ifc.org/abn

African Development Bank: www.afdb.org

Africa Online: www.africaonline.com

AllAfrica.com: http://allafrica.com

Mbendi AfroPaedia (information on companies, countries, industries and stock exchanges in Africa): http://mbendi.co.za

Libya

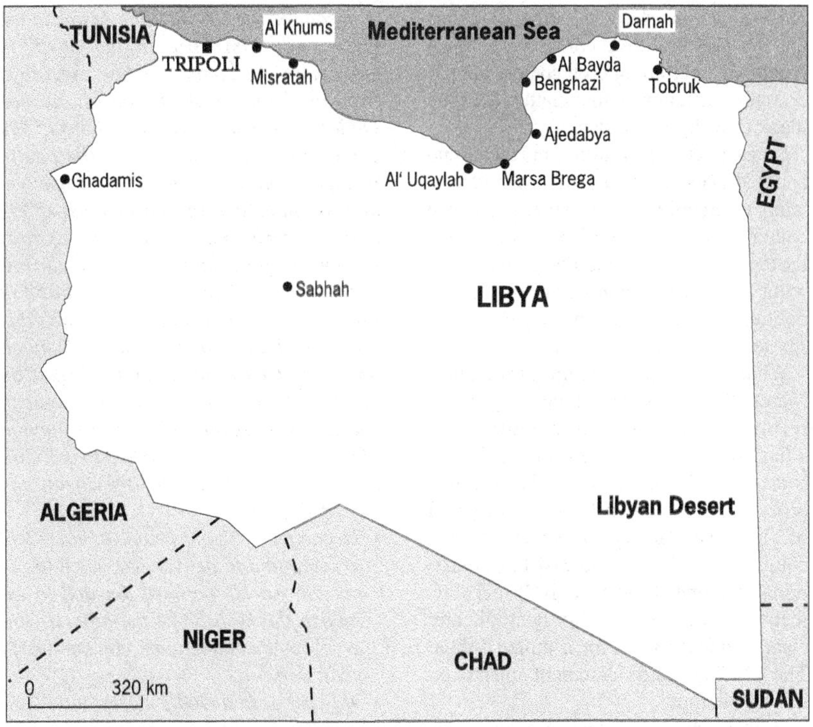

The violent death of Libya's ruler Muammar al Qadafi in December 2011 brought a sudden end to the Libyan uprising. The challenge for the rag-tag army that was the military wing of the Benghazi based Transitional National Council (TNC) was whether they were capable of forming a credible government and a properly functioning body politic. Justin Marozzi, writing in the London *Spectator* in August 2011 had noted that 'where Libyans talk of creating a new Dubai on the shores of the Mediterranean, sceptics mutter about another Somalia.'

Fears had been expressed over the possible presence of al Qaeda operatives within the protestors' ranks, but little concrete evidence appeared. Although the TNC had drawn up a 'route map' towards democratic elections, the start date had very much hinged on the eventual downfall of Qadafi. However homogenous Libya may have appeared in contrast to, say, Egypt or Syria, the traditional differences that existed between western Tripolitania and eastern Cyrenaica were thought likely to resurface. Estimates put at around eighteen months the time needed to restore oil production to pre-uprising levels.

And restoring oil production was pretty straightforward stuff compared to the tensions and uncertainties that were likely to beset post Qadafi Libya.

Any overview of Libyan politics and economics prepared, as is the case here, in mid-2011 is a foray into uncharted territory. Western media have largely reflected the views of their governments in depicting the Qadafi regime as broadly corrupt and ill-intentioned. This is probably a reasonable enough assessment, although such has been the chaos prevalent since March 2011 that the dictum 'truth is the first casualty of war' has probably been more appropriate than ever. What emerged was a *de facto* civil war between the regime and an assorted group of largely under-organised rebels, between East and West Libya – a curious

KEY FACTS

Official name: Al Jamahiriya al Arabiya al Libiya ash Shabiya al Ishtirakiya al Uzma (The Great Socialist People's Libyan Arab Jamahiriya)

Head of State: Leader of First of September Revolution Colonel Muammar al Qadafi (since Sep 1969)

Chairman Transitional National Council (TNC) Mustafa Muhammad Abdul Jalil

Head of government: Secretary of the General People's Congress Muftah Mohammed Kaiba (from 3 Mar 2008)

TNC Prime Minister Mahmoud Jibril

Ruling party: All political parties are banned by law.

Area: 1,775,500 square km

Population: 6.36 million (2010)*

Capital: Tripoli

Official language: Arabic

Currency: Libyan dinar (LD) = 1,000 dirhams

Exchange rate: LD1.23 per US$ (Oct 2011)

GDP per capita: US$11,314 (2010)

GDP real growth: 4.20% (2010)

GDP: US$74.20 billion (2010)

Inflation: 2.40% (2010)

Oil production: 1.66 million bpd (2010)

Balance of trade: US$40.29 billion (2009)

* estimated figure

NOTA

20 October 2011, Muammar al Qadafi was caught and killed in his home town of Sirte, following weeks of intense fighting.

throwback to the desert country's Roman antecedents, and something resembling a tribal conflict.

The tribal mosaic

The importance of a country's history has never been more evident than in Libya. Most countries represent a commonality of history and geography. Libya can best be described as a buffer zone between the Arab east (the Mashreq) and the Arab west (the Mahgreb). In the east, Cyrenaica was historically Greek or Hellenistic. In the west, Tripolitania was Roman. However, there are obvious dangers in simplifying and generalising Libya's social make-up. It is also misleading to attribute political (rather than simply democratic) motivation to the warring factions. Col Qadafi's main support appears to come from three major sources: the Warfalla, based 180km south-west of Tripoli, the largest tribe in the country and with sizeable communities within Tripoli. The Warfalla also comprise the majority of well-educated Libyans. Qadafi's own tribe, the Gaddafa, is centred in Sirte, 500km east of Tripoli, and is another pillar of his support. The allegiance between the Gaddafa and the Warfalla has been described as a 'blood link'. Their ties pre-date Col Qadafi's rise to power and will be slow to change now. Prejudice against other tribes in Libya, particularly against the Misrata, make many Warfalla more hardline than Col Qadafi himself. Sizeable support for Col Qadafi also exists deep into Libya's south, notably around Sebha, the capital of the southern region.

This tribal mosaic still counts for a lot in Libya. Under the rule of King Idris, the east of the country, with Benghazi as its capital, was the country's political and commercial capital. With Qadafi, this changed: Tripoli became the capital. Libya has not had political parties for more than four decades; tribal loyalties are the closest Libya comes to politics. Anything resembling civil society simply does not exist, nor for that matter, does the idea of loyalty to the state.

Libya lacks a constitution, and there is no nationally-accepted rule of law and certainly no practical mechanisms to guide the country in the event of a power vacuum at the top. Qadafi himself is always at pains to point out that he has no official role. US politicians would no doubt suggest that he 'try telling that to the marines'.

What has taken place in Libya since March 2011 is more of an uprising than a revolution. Perhaps because of tribal loyalties, there is no obvious leader (a feature shared with Tunisia and even Egypt). It is difficult to see how, if Qadafi is defeated or flees the country, a power vacuum could be avoided. In the east the Transitional National Council (TNC) lacks effective leadership, not to mention any clear political vision for a united Libya. The TNC's mission statement appears on its website thus:

'In this important historical juncture which Libya is passing through right now, we find ourselves at a turning point with only two solutions. Either we achieve freedom and race to catch up with humanity and world developments, or we are shackled and enslaved under the feet of the tyrant Mu'ammar Qadafi where we shall live in the midst of history. From this junction came the announcement of the Transitional National Council, a step on the road to liberate every part of the Libyan lands from Aamsaad in the east to Raas Ajdair in the west, and from Sirte in the north to Gatrun in the south. To liberate Libya from the hands of the tyrant Mu'ammar Qadafi who made lawful to himself the exploitation of his people and the wealth of this country. The number of martyrs and wounded and the extreme use of excessive force and mercenaries against his own people requires us to take the initiative and work on the Liberalization of Libya from such insanities. To reach this goal, the Transitional National Council announced its official establishment on 5th March 2011 in the city of Benghazi, stating its perseverance towards the aim of relocating its headquarters to our capital and bride of the Mediterranean, the city of Tripoli.

- *To connect with our people at home and abroad, and to deliver our voice to the outside world, we have decided to establish this website as the official window of communication via the world wide web.*
- *May peace and God's mercy and blessings be upon you*
- *Long live Libya, free and dignified.'*

These were bold statements, but if asked exactly who was represented on the TNC, most diplomats and foreign ministries could only guess. Some of the TNC members could probably be described as democrats, others as Islamists. Rumours – probably originating from Tripoli – persisted that the TNC had been hi-jacked by al Qaeda activists. This was an unlikely scenario, not least because the Libyan uprising appeared to be a nationalist, rather than internationalist, and would-be democratic phenomenon. The TNC members did not seem inclined towards the al Qaeda vision (or delusion) of restoring the Caliphate. It was probably the case that some of those fighting with the rebels had once been involved with al Qaeda in one form or another. But they seemed a long way from hi-jacking the nascent, if rather erratic, political body.

Keep it in the family – if we can

As the civil war dragged on, the defection of many of his senior aides left Colonel Qadafi increasingly reliant on members of

KEY INDICATORS — Libya

	Unit	2006	2007	2008	2009	2010
Population	m	5.97	6.09	6.21	*6.33	*6.36
Gross domestic product (GDP)	US$bn	49.72	71.70	100.10	60.40	74.20
GDP per capita	US$	8,327	11,773	14,479	9,529	11,314
GDP real growth	%	5.2	7.5	3.4	1.8	4.2
Inflation	%	3.4	6.2	10.4	2.7	2.4
Oil output	'000 bpd	1,835.0	1,848.0	1,846.0	1,652.0	1,659.0
Natural gas output	bn cum	14.8	15.2	15.9	15.3	15.8
Exports (fob) (goods)	US$m	37,473.0	46,970.0	61,950.0	–	–
Imports (fob) (goods)	US$m	13,219.0	17,701.0	21,658.0	–	–
Balance of trade	US$m	24,254.0	29,269.0	40,292.0	–	–
Current account	US$m	25,646.0	24,278.0	35,702.0	9,481.0	11,897.0
Total reserves minus gold	US$m	59,289.0	79,405.0	92,313.0	104,026.0	99,645.0
Foreign exchange	US$m	57,907.0	77,897.0	90,803.0	100,917.0	96,800.0
Exchange rate	per US$	1.28	1.22	1.17	1.28	–

* estimated figure

his family. Most visible in the war of words was his second son, Saif al Islam ('Sword of Islam'). Once seen as the dictatorship's more acceptable face, the 39 year old Saif 'studied' at the London School of Economics and was generally perceived to hold the contradictory roles of moderniser and heir apparent. Qadafi's third son, Saadi was the commander of Libya's special forces; little is known of his military training as for some years he lived in Italy and had tried to become a professional footballer. Two other sons, Mutassim – the National Security Adviser – and Khamis, commander of the 32nd reinforced Brigade, also appeared to be playing important roles in the régime's defence strategy. A 2002 interview with son Saif in the London *Spectator* magazine was headlined 'Son of Mad Dog'; certainly, if madness can be described as persisting in an interpretation of reality that no one else accepts, then Qadafi could fairly be described as mad. Writing in the *Spectator* some nine years later, the author in the interview, Justin Marozzi, observed that Qadafi had always sought to be the region's clown, in contrast to his fellow dictator, Iraq's darkly sinister Saddam Hussein. Mr Marozzi pointed out that in most respects, Qadafi was just a sinister a figure. In 1996 the régime murdered 1,200 inmates at the Abu Salim prison, apparently as a punishment for dissent. Certainly, most Libyans lived – and many continue to live – in a state of fear; a fear caused by their ruler's brutality and unpredictability.

UN Security Council Resolution 1973

On 17 March 2011 United Nations Security Council Resolution 1973 was adopted by a vote of 10 in favour to none against, with 5 abstentions (Brazil, China, Germany, India and Russia). The resolution authorised Member States, 'acting nationally or through regional organisations or arrangements, to take all necessary measures to protect civilians under threat of attack in the country.' The resolution, principally orchestrated by France and the United Kingdom, significantly ruled out any 'foreign occupation force of any form on any part of Libyan territory.' In the run up to the resolution's adoption, US President Obama initially appeared to be a reluctant participant, allowing his European allies to make the running. This approach continued after the implementation of the resolution as US frontline aircraft were steadily withdrawn to be replaced by their French and British counterparts. In contrast to France and the UK, the German government did not support the United Nations resolution. This, despite strong (but as it turned out, empty) words from the German Ambassador to Libya, Peter Wittig, who went on record as saying that 'their (I e Qadafi's) time is over and they must relinquish power immediately. The people of Libya who have so clearly expressed their aspirations for democracy should be supported.' Former German foreign minister Joschka Fischer drily noted that 'What use are German leaders' lofty speeches about international law being exercised if Germany refuses to endorse a resolution for the protection of Libya's citizens from a brutal regime?' Other German politicians described their country's failure to endorse the resolution as 'an historic blunder' and 'historic cynicism'.

The initial phase of the Nato offensive was directed by the US, but the US command soon shifted to Nato command, allowing a hesitant US to take something of a back seat. France and the UK became the leaders in the pack. Notwithstanding the Arab League's overt support for Resolution 1973, the only Arab countries whose support amounted to more than signatures and words were Qatar, the UAE and Kuwait. Algeria remained the lone Qadafi supporter, in apparent contradiction of the African Union's support for resolution 1973. The Benghazi based 'rebel' Transitional National Council (TNC) was recognised not only by the US, UK, Canada, Spain, Portugal, France and Italy, but also by Senegal and The Gambia. Russia, having abstained on Resolution 1973, hedged its bets by establishing relations with Benghazi, but maintaining those with Qadafi. Russia's special envoy to Africa, Mikhail Margelov, stated that Russia was 'ready, if it is possible, to act as a middleman'. Mr Margelov described a visit to Libya as 'an attempt to help the Libyan elite find a national consensus', adding that 'Russia has a unique opportunity to become a bridge between those parts of the Libyan political elite which see the future of their country as one united state. Mr Margelov made no mention of any possible commercial or even strategic opportunities for Russia, but his June 2011 visit coincided with concerns over the future viability of Russia's Mediterranean port facilities in the recently renovated Syrian base of Tartus.

The IMF – getting it wrong

In February 2011 the International Monetary Find (IMF) executive board (the Washington based organisation's highest authority) commended the Libyan government for its 'ambitious reform agenda'. Reforms? The IMF encouraged the Qadafi government to continue on its promising path. As the *New York Times* observed at the time, the IMF's mission to Tripoli had omitted to check whether the reform agenda had anything that amounted to popular support. No doubt the IMF mission was well looked after by their Libyan hosts, inspiring them to report that 'Libya's economic growth and financial position are expected to strengthen over the medium term as a result of higher oil receipts and investment in the oil sector, the upgrading of infrastructure, the implementation of reforms, and continued interest of foreign investors. Oil production is projected to increase to about 2.5 million barrels per day by 2015 on account of large investments and the utilisation of advanced technologies by foreign partners. The non-hydrocarbon sector is also expected to remain buoyant, boosting growth to a projected 8 per cent by 2015. Taking into account the authorities' intention to continue to prioritise spending, the growth of public expenditure is expected to remain moderate at about 7 per cent a year in nominal terms. This would also allow for nominal import growth of about 10 per cent a year while maintaining current account surpluses of about 20 per cent of GDP. Such large surpluses imply correspondingly large increases in foreign assets, with the Libyan Investment Authority (LIA) and the Central Bank of Libya (CBL)'s portfolio projected to reach over US$250 billion by 2015.'

In October 2010 the IMF had actually managed to praise the Libyan government for having previously transferred to a central labour office for retrenchment (I e made redundant) no less than 340,000 civil servants, noting that 'about a quarter (of those losing their jobs) have reportedly found other sources of income and are no longer receiving transfers from the state budget. The mission recommends that the retrenchment programme be accelerated.' If the IMF delegates had taken the trouble to talk to the Libyan in the street, their assessment of the situation might have been differently coloured. Instead, the IMF noted that 'Recent developments in neighbouring Egypt and Tunisia have had limited economic impact on Libya so far.' The IMF went on to report that 'An ambitious programme to privatise banks and develop the nascent financial sector is under way. Structural reforms in other areas have progressed.' The IMF, apparently unaware that they were dealing with a non-democratic, unrepentant dictatorship of the kind that were already toppling in the region, went on to say that 'they welcomed Libya's strong macro-economic performance and the progress on enhancing the role of the private sector and supporting growth in the non-oil economy.' The IMF concluded that 'the outlook for Libya's economy remains favourable.'

The oil and the gas

The Libyan economy has long been heavily dependent on its oil and gas industries which, according to the IMF accounted for a massive 95 per cent of export earnings in 2010. According to the US based *Oil and Gas Journal* (OGJ), Libya holds around 46.4 billion barrels of oil reserves, the largest in Africa, and close to 55 trillion cubic feet (Tcf) of natural gas reserves. In 2010, total oil production (crude plus liquids) was close to 1.8 million barrels per day (bpd). The US Energy Information Administration (EIA) in its last report on the Libyan energy industry dated (with felicitous timing) February 2011 states that the country continues to recover from over a decade of US and international sanctions. The United Nations and the United States lifted sanctions on Libya in 2003 and 2004, respectively. In 2006, the United States rescinded Libya's designation as a state sponsor of terrorism. Since then, international oil companies have stepped up investments in hydrocarbon exploration and production despite some degree of regulatory and contractual uncertainty. The next update of the report on Libya will no doubt expand on the theme of 'contractual uncertainty'. The weeks before the June 2011 meeting of the Organisation of the Petroleum Exporting Countries (Opec) saw the organisation divided between those members supporting the rebels, notably Qatar, Kuwait and the United Arab Emirates, and the Qadafi camp, clinging to the wreckage of Africa's largest crude petroleum and gas reserves. Abdelaziz Belkhadem, Algerian Minister of State sided with Qadafi, denouncing 'foreign interference' in Libya. Whatever members thought about the Libyan conflict, Opec 's constitution prevented itself from recognising the rebel government. Opec members were left with little alternative but to turn a deaf ear to representations from government and rebels.

The conflict has, according to Opec, blocked the export of some 1.4 million bpd. Opec estimated that its members would have to produce in the region of an extra 500,000bpd simply to meet demand. The UK based Petroleum Policy Intelligence research analysts expected Saudi Arabia to increase its output by ten per cent. Unfortunately, Opec itself was not at its strongest – the organisation's rotating presidency for its June meeting was held by Iran. The leader of the Iranian delegation was initially announced as the former head of Iran's Physical Education Organisation. In early June however, the situation appeared even more confused when Press TV, the state television station announced that Iran would be represented by Mohammad Aliabadi, who had been appointed acting oil minister. The former minister, Masoud Mir-Kazemi, had been summarily fired by President Ahmadinejad in mid-May 2011 in a ministerial re-shuffle. Not that the Qadafi camp looked able to field a strong team either; Libya's senior oil official, Shokri Ghanem, defected to join the rebels at the beginning of June, leaving his country to be represented in international meetings by Mosbah Ali Matoug, a member of the management committee of the National Oil Corporation.

In mid-2011 it was difficult to assess the severity of the consequences of the civil war. Some oil was still being exported, but only a fraction of former levels. Money due for oil exported from eastern Libya was being paid. Whether the same was the case in Qadafi controlled western Libya was less certain. According to the EIA Libyan crude oil production in 2010 was approximately 1.65 million bpd, about 150,000bpd below capacity but still above the production quota set by Opec, currently at 1.47 million bpd. Prior to the civil war most of the short-term oil production increases were expected to come from enhanced oil recovery (EOR) processes. Any major new production in Libya would require additional pipeline capacity for exports. As reported by the EIA, according to Wood Mackenzie analysts, about two-thirds of Libyan oil production comes from the Sirte Basin, with about 25 per cent also coming from the Murzuq basin and most of the remainder coming from the offshore Pelagian Shelf Basin near Tripoli.

In 2010 Libya's net exports (including all liquids) were slightly over 1.5 million bpd. According to the IEA the vast majority (around 85 per cent) of Libyan oil exports were shipped to European countries, notably Italy, Germany, France and Spain. Following the lifting of sanctions against Libya in 2004, the United States had increased its imports of Libyan oil. According to the EIA estimates for the period from January to November, the United States imported an average of 71,000bpd from Libya in 2010 (of which, 44,000bpd was crude oil), up from 56,000bpd in 2005 but a decline from the 2007 highs of 117,000bpd.

The OGJ put Libya's proven natural gas reserves at 54.7 trillion cubic feet (Tcf) in January 2011 (again before the advent of the civil war). Recent new discoveries and investments in natural gas exploration were expected to raise these estimates in the near-term. The Libyan government had planned to increase the country's natural gas production. Libya's natural gas production has grown substantially in the last few years. According to EIA, Libya produced 1,034 billion cubic feet (Bcf) of gross natural gas in 2009 of which 562Bcf was marketed dry natural gas – the remainder was vented, flared or re-injected to enhance oil recovery. Again prior to the outbreak of the civil war, natural gas accounted for 45 per cent of generated electricity. Despite plans to increase natural gas use for electricity generation, project delays and infrastructure limitations kept consumption in this sector relatively stable over the past decade. However, the IEA had originally estimated that by 2012, domestic consumption might increase by as much as 50 per cent if planned pipelines and gas-fired power plants were to come on stream.

Risk assessment

Economy	Chaotic
Politics	Chaotic
Regional stability	Uncertain

COUNTRY PROFILE

Historical profile

1510 During the struggle between Hapsburg Spain and the Ottoman Turks for supremacy in the Mediterranean, Spanish forces captured and largely destroyed Tripoli.

1524 Tripoli was entrusted to the Knights of St John of Malta.

1551 The Knights were driven out of Tripolitania by the Turks who began consolidating their control over the Maghreb region. The three provinces of Tripolitania, Cyrenaica and Fezzan were combined into one regency in Tripoli by the Ottomans.

1711–1835 Although nominally part of the Ottoman empire, the Turks in effect gave way to the local Karamanli dynasty until 1835, when the Turks strengthened their control again. The local rulers levied a toll on every Christian fleet using the Mediterranean.

1870–1911 The area was dominated by the Sanusi religious order, although the

Turks and the Italians continued to invade periodically.
1911–42 By the time of the First World War in 1914, an Italian force had taken control of the coastal towns. After the War, Italy captured the Libyan nationalist hero, Omar Mukhtar, hanging him in 1931. Italy introduced an Italianisation programme. Italy's colonisation of Libya ended when the Italians and Germans lost the war in the Western Desert. The British took over Tripolitania and Cyrenaica and the French took over the Fezzan.
1951 Libya was granted independence under King Idris (originally Mohammed Idris al Sanusi, a member of the Sanusi religious order).
1955 Oil exploration started.
1959 Oil was discovered.
1961 King Idris opened a 167km pipeline, which linked important oil fields in the interior to the Mediterranean Sea, making it possible for Libya to export oil.
1969 As pan-Arabism swept the Arab world, Colonel Muammar al Qadafi seized power as Leader of the Revolution. Most economic activities were nationalised, including the oil industry.
1970 The government closed the British airbase in Tobruk and the US Air Force base in Tripoli. Property belonging to Italian settlers was nationalised.
1971 The Federation of Arab Republics (FAR), comprising Libya, Egypt and Syria, was approved by national referendum, but was never realised.
1972 Libya and Egypt agreed to merge into a single state; but the plans were abandoned.
1973 Qadafi announced a cultural revolution in which people's committees were established throughout the country. Libyan forces invaded the Aozou Strip in northern Chad.
1974 A plan to unify Libya and Tunisia was agreed, but never implemented.
1977 Qadafi set up the General People's Congress (GPC) and the country was renamed the Great Socialist People's Libyan Arab Jamahiriya.
1981 The US shot down two Libyan aircraft which challenged its warplanes over the Gulf of Sirte, claimed by Libya as its territorial waters.
1984 Police Constable Yvonne Fletcher was killed during demonstrations outside the Libyan embassy in London. The UK suspended diplomatic relations with Libya.
1986 An attempt to overthrow the Qadafi regime was unsuccessful. The US launched a major air strike on Tripoli, causing substantial damage. The US claimed its raids were in response to an alleged Libyan involvement in the bombing of a nightclub in Berlin, which was used by US military personnel. The US imposed economic sanctions on Libya.
1988 Libyan terrorists were blamed for the bomb which destroyed a Pan Am passenger aircraft over Lockerbie in Scotland.
1989 Algeria, Libya, Mauritania, Morocco and Tunisia formed the Arab Maghreb Union.
1992 UN sanctions were imposed on Libya for refusing to hand over two men suspected of the Lockerbie bombing.
1994 Libya returned the Aozou Strip to Chad.
1995 Qadafi ordered the expulsion of 30,000 Palestinians in protest at the Oslo accords signed by the Israeli government and the Palestine Liberation Organisation (PLO).
1999 UN and EU sanctions were suspended after Libya agreed to arrest and extradite Lockerbie bombing suspects. The UK re-established diplomatic links with Libya.
2000 Qadafi visited Arab states in North Africa and the Middle East, seeking to promote Arab co-operation. Libya was one of the key signatories for the creation of the African Union (AU) to replace the Organisation of African Unity (OAU).
2001 Abdelbaset Ali Mohmed al Megrahi, a Libyan intelligence agent, was found guilty of the Lockerbie bombing in a Scottish court based in The Netherlands, while his co-accused, al Amin Khalifa Fhimah, was acquitted. The US imposed a five-year extension to sanctions against Libya.
2002 Megrahi's appeal failed and he was sentenced to life imprisonment in a Scottish jail.
2003 Libya was chosen to chair the UN Human Rights Commission. The Libyan government and lawyers representing families of Lockerbie bombing victims signed a compensation agreement worth US$2.7 billion. Libya formally took responsibility for the bombing before the UN Security Council. The UN Security Council voted to lift the 11-year-old sanctions against Libya (already suspended). Libya announced that it would abandon its programmes to develop weapons of mass destruction (WMD).
2004 Libya agreed to compensate families of victims of the 1989 bombing of a French passenger aircraft and to pay US$35 million to victims of the bombing of a Berlin nightclub in 1986. The UK prime minister, Tony Blair, met Colonel Qadafi, the first visit of this kind since 1943. UN sanctions were finally lifted and the US and Libya restored diplomatic relations after a break of 24 years as US economic sanctions were lifted. President Chirac of France visited Libya, the first by a French president since 1951.
2005 Libya officially opened to tourist visitors. Leases on 26 oil fields were allocated to foreign companies.
2006 The US restored full diplomatic relations with Libya and rescinded Libya's designation as a state sponsor of terrorism.
2008 Muftah Mohammed Kaiba became secretary of the General People's Congress. Italian Prime Minister Silvio Berlusconi apologised for the damage caused to Libya during Italy's colonial reign and signed a US$5 billion investment plan to fund a coastal highway.
2009 Muammar al Qadafi was elected chairman of the African Union and later proposed a United States of Africa. Abdelbaset Ali Mohmed al Megrahi, imprisoned in Scotland since 2002 for the bombing of Pan Am Flight 103 over Lockerbie, was released, due to his failing health, to serve his prison term in Libya. Qadafi made an official visit to Italy.
2010 In a speech in March, Leader al Qadafi proposed that Nigeria should be split into two countries, one Muslim and the other Christian. The suggestion was vigorously rejected by Nigeria. In June, the UN High Commission for Refugees (UNHCR) agency was told to quit Libya, with no reason given. The agency considered its work with asylum-seekers and migrants trying to reach Europe as the source of friction with the authorities.
2011 Following the fall of authoritarian regimes in neighbouring Tunisia and Egypt in January, on 14 February there was a call on the social network, Facebook, for peaceful demonstrations against the regime of Muammar Qadafi. A number of demonstrations, triggered by the arrest of a lawyer acting for the families of prisoners believed to have been murdered in the Abu Salim prison in Tripoli, began in the east, centred on the second city of Benghazi, from 15 February. Police countered the demonstrations and there were a number deaths reported. On 18 February protesters gained control of Benghazi, while pro-government demonstrators held enthusiastic gatherings in Tripoli. By 20 February, a reported 173 people had been killed by security forces and anti-government protests had spread to Tripoli. Qadafi's son, Saif al Islam, broadcast a warning to protesters that their actions could lead to a civil war in Libya. On 22 February, Abdel Fattah Younis, considered Qadafi's number two in his government, resigned and sided with the rebel movement. The Transitional National Council (TNC) was established in Benghazi on 26 February, on the same day as the UN Security Council (UNSC) unanimously voted for an arms embargo, travel bans and asset freezes on Libyan regime leaders. The actions of Colonel Qadafi were referred to the International Criminal Court (ICC). Foreign workers began to leave the country as the

fighting grew more widespread. Libyan observers said that security forces had been supplemented by 'African mercenaries' and both had fired indiscriminately on protestors. On 23 February thousands of Egyptian workers fled home across the border as other nationals either crossed into Egypt or Tunisia for evacuation by the international community. The battle for Misrata, the third city and most important business centre, began on 24 February. On 26 February, the EU imposed sanctions against the regime of Qadafi. NATO and its allies discussed a no-fly zone over Libya on 27 February; the Indian government began evacuating its nationals. There were estimated to be 18,000 Indian nationals working in Libya, of which 3,000 were in Benghazi working for car companies and hospitals. On 28 February, the US froze US$30 billion in assets belonging to the Libyan government. Qadafi launched a combined air and armoured ground assault on Misrata on 1 March. While other rebel leaders were debating whether to ask for Western military support, Abdul Fattah Younis said he would welcome foreign intervention by air strikes, but not a ground invasion. Four senior military commanders defected from Qadafi to the rebels. Qadafi sent food and medical supplies to Benghazi as a demonstration of national unity. On 2 March, the TNC formally requested that the UN impose a no-fly zone over Libya. On 3 March the chief prosecutor of the ICC announced that he would investigate Qadafi, his sons and senior aids for crimes against humanity. Qadafi's forces attempted to retake the oil refineries of Zawiya on 4 March but were repelled with heavy losses on both sides. On 7 March, in the UNSC, France and the UK proposed a no-fly zone. Hundreds of Qadafi's forces, supported by tanks, entered Zawiya; following heavy fighting they were beaten off. On the 8 March the TNC told Qadafi that if he stopped his offensive, and he and his family left Libya, they would not face any future prosecution. On 9 March the European Parliament called on all European countries to recognise the TNC as Libya's legitimate government. The EU agreed to extend sanctions against the Qadafi regime to include Libya's sovereign wealth fund and central bank. The measures would deny Qadafi funds from oil sales, used to buy armaments. The sanctions also included a weapons ban; any equipment that could be used for 'internal repression' had already been banned. On 10 March, Qadafi's forces began a concerted effort to retake cities along the coast from Tripoli, starting with Zawiya. On 12 March, Arab League foreign ministers meeting in Cairo endorsed calls for a UN no-fly-zone and formally recognised the TNC. Human rights observers accused Qadafi's security forces of arbitrary arrests, disappearances and torture following the fall of rebel towns. On 17 March the UNSC approved, by 10 votes (with five abstentions), UN Resolution 1973 which imposed a no-fly-zone over Libya, with 'all necessary measures' to protect civilians. An immediate ceasefire and an end to attacks on civilians were also demanded. On 18 March Qadafi called a ceasefire and invited foreign observers to witness his actions. However, on 19 March his forces shelled the outer suburbs of Benghazi. At 1300 GMT, the first military flights by a five-country coalition (Canada, France, Italy, the UK and the US) attacked Libya's air defence systems and Libyan 'command and control' centres to impose the UN-sanctioned no-fly zone. On 19 March the TNC designated the Central Bank of Benghazi (CBB) as its monetary authority and a governor was appointed. It also set up the Libyan Oil Company (LOC) as the supervising authority for oil policy and production. From 23 March, LOC was able to sell all oil and natural gas within its control on international markets and deny profits to the Qadafi treasury. All oil income from LOC, headquartered in Benghazi, will be deposited in the CBB. Qadafi forces continued their assault on Misrata and coalition fighters struck airfields and the road to Tobruk on 21 March. Coalition air attacks followed for several days, while rebel forces took advantage of the safety being provided and began another campaign to capture towns between Benghazi and Tripoli. NATO took command of the no-fly zone and naval operations against Qadafi on 24 March. Thousands of migrants and refugees from Somalia and Eritrea and other sub-Saharan African migrants caught up in the Libyan crisis, as well as Libyan citizens fleeing a regime change, made the Mediterranean Sea crossing to reach the EU, and landed on the Italian island of Lampedusa, overwhelming local resources and immigration procedures. Malta also registered a steep rise in Libyans reaching its territory. On 3 April an envoy from Qadafi's, deputy foreign minister Abdelati Obeidi, left for Athens on an apparent peace mission. On 4 April Italy became the third country (after France and Qatar) to recognise the TNC. In a television broadcast on 29 April Qadafi vowed not to leave Libya. He also called for talks with NATO. The chief prosecutor for the ICC announced on 4 May that there were reasonable grounds for charges against Colonel Qadafi and international arrest warrants could be issued by July. NATO damaged eight warships in three ports on 20 May; they were being used by Gaddafi's forces to target civilians in Misrata and other towns. On 30 May, South African President Jacob Zuma visited Colonel Qadafi in an attempt to mediate a cease-fire. Qadafi agreed to the cease-fire but would not relinquish power, as called for by the TNC. As a result the TNC rejected the agreement. The ICC issued an arrest warrant for Qadafi on 27 June, accusing him of crimes against humanity. Warrants were also issued for Saif al Qadafi and intelligence chief Abdullah al Sanusi. On 29 June a supply of weapons (including assault rifles, machine guns and rocket launchers) was parachuted into rebel held territory of Libya by the French military. The AU condemned the move saying it puts the whole region at risk. The French stated that this was a one-off decision to re-arm a town cut off from supplies from its allies. On 3 July Turkey recognised the rebel TNC as the legitimate representatives of the Libyan people. US officials confirmed that they had held talks with representatives of Qadafi in mid-July, reiterating the US demand that Qadafi should step down. The TNC's military leader Abdel Fattah Younis, was killed on 28 July. At first his death was blamed on Islamist-linked militia, within TNC forces that did not trust Younis and thought he still had ties to Qadafi. On 1 August, France agreed to release US$259 million of frozen funds, banked by Qadafi, to the TNC for the express purchase of humanitarian materials (food and medicine). By 2 August, 63 people suspected of links to Qadafi had been arrested for murdering Younis. Forces of the TNC took control of Tripoli on 23 August. Mass graves began to be found around the city. A large convoy of heavily armed and armoured vehicles crossed the Sahara and entered Niger on 6 September. It was rumoured to be carrying high-ranking members of Qadafi's regime, although Qadafi himself was not among those fleeing, and Tuareg fighters. On 11 September Mustafa Abdel Jalil, head of the TNC, arrived in Tripoli. He delivered his first public speech, in Martyrs' Square (the re-named Green Square where Qadafi used to harangue the nation) on 13 September. Although he said that *Sharia* (Islamic law) would be the main source of the law, he also said the TNC would not 'accept any extremist ideology, on the right or the left. We are a Muslim people, for a moderate Islam, and will stay on this road.' He also warned against reprisals by rebel forces against elements of the Qadafi regime. UK Prime Minister David Cameron and French President Nicolas Sarkozy visited Libya on 15 September. Both leaders promised financial and practical support. A mass grave thought to contain the remains of over

1,200 prisoners from the Abu Salim prison murdered by the Qadafi regime in 1996 was found in Tripoli on 25 September.

Political structure

Constitution

Libya has no constitution. In 2000, 14 ministries were abolished and their powers devolved to provincial committees or other bodies.

Independence date

24 December 1951

Form of state

Jamahiriya, or state of the masses.

The executive

Libya has no official head of state, but Colonel Muammar al Qadafi exercises absolute authority in his role as Leader of the First of September Revolution. Federal executive power is exercised by the General People's Committee (GPC) (council of ministers). The Secretary General of the GPC is a post broadly equivalent to that of prime minister.

National legislature

Political power is vested in the Mu'tammar al sha'ab al 'âmm (General People's Congress) (GPC); Libya is officially run by popular committees and congresses. As political parties are banned, other means of civic representation is often through professional associations where participants are nominated to serve on various committees and congresses. Delegates to the GPC approve laws and sets policy guidelines. There are 300 congresses, each having an executive popular committee, which can effectively take some decisions at a local level.

Legal system

The Libyan legal system is based on *Sharia* (Islamic law) and the Italian civil law system. There are separate religious courts and no constitutional provision for judicial review of legislative acts. The judicial system consists of the Supreme Court, courts of appeal, courts of first instance and summary courts. Libya has not accepted compulsory International Court of Justice (ICJ) jurisdiction.

Political parties

Ruling party

All political parties are banned by law.

Main opposition party

Until 2011 the two most active internal opposition movements were the Islamic Liberation Party and the Muslim Brotherhood. The main exiled opposition is the US-based National Front for the Salvation of Libya (NFSL).

Population

6.36 million (2010)*

Last census: August 1995: 4,404,986

Population density: Three inhabitants per square kilometre. Urban population: 88 per cent (1995–2001).

Annual growth rate: 2.0 per cent 1994–2004 (WHO 2006)

Ethnic make-up

Berber-Arab (97 per cent). There are small communities of Greeks, Maltese, Italians, Egyptians, Pakistanis, Turks, Indians and Tunisians.

Religions

Sunni Muslim (97 per cent). A third of Libya's Muslims are affilitated to the Sanusi religious sect, which had fought against European colonialism in the first half of the twentieth century.

Education

Libya has paid particular attention to its education system, with the aim of reducing illiteracy and improving the education available to women.

Education is free for all children during the compulsory years. Secondary schooling begins at aged 15 and the curriculum is divided into three- or four-year courses and comprises a number of secondary school types including both academic and specialised or vocational centres. English and Arabic are the main languages for instruction.

Higher education is offered in 14 universities and 54 higher vocational institutes.

Literacy rate: 82 per cent adult rate; 97 per cent youth rate (15–24) (Unesco 2005).

Compulsory years: 6 to 15.

Health

The government provides free health services to all its citizens. UN sanctions had a detrimental impact on the quality and access to healthcare provision and many medical services and pharmaceutical products became unavailable. With the lifting of sanctions in 2004, these shortcomings were overcome to a certain extent. Many Libyans typically seek medical treatment in Tunisia, Egypt or in Western Europe. There are two large hospitals in Tripoli and Benghazi.

HIV/Aids

HIV prevalence: 0.3 per cent aged 15–49 in 2003 (World Bank)

Life expectancy: 72 years, 2004 (WHO 2006)

Fertility rate/Maternal mortality rate: 2.9 births per woman, 2004 (WHO 2006); maternal mortality 0.75 per 1,000 live births (World Bank).

Child (under 5 years) mortality rate (per 1,000): 13 per 1,000 live births; 5 per cent of children aged under five are malnourished (World Bank).

Welfare

The government is theoretically committed to full provision of welfare services to all Libyan nationals. In reality, parts of the population are often not covered by welfare provisions. The most common welfare benefit is housing to those in need. The government provides a national social security system covering pensions and other social insurance, but the availability of such services regularly depends on annual oil receipts, which make up a large proportion of total government revenues.

Main cities

Tripoli (capital, estimated population 1.2 million in 2004), Benghazi (734,900), Al-Khums (Homs) (195,000), Misratah (Misurata) (345,566), Al-Marj (164,700), Tobruk (152,200).

Media

The France-based media watchdog, Reporters Without Borders (RWB) assessed Libya's attitude to its news gathering, reporting and broadcasting services in 2006 and considered that the government 'maintains its monopoly of power, and the press continues to be just a propaganda tool'. In 2008 RWB noted that non-government media were allowed to operate but were firmly kept under its control, only foreign internet and satellite radio and television stations, particularly Al Jazeera, provide an independent viewpoint.

Change has begun, as the market is less tolerant of the political cant provided by the official media. Self-censorship by journalists is widespread.

Press

Private newspapers were only introduced in 2006, although censorship limits their news contents and no criticism of Colonel Qadafi is allowed.

In Arabic, newspapers controlled by the ministry of information include *Al Shames* (www.alshames.com), *Al Jamahiriya* (www.aljamahiria.com), *Al Fajr Al Jahideed* (www.alfajraljadeed.com) a bi-monthly and *Al Zahf Al Akhdar* (www.azzahfalakhder.com) which is controlled by the Revolutionary Committees Movement. Private newspapers produced by One Nine Media, owned by Saif al Islam Qadafi, include *Oea* (www.oealibya.com) and *Quryna* (www.quryna.com). In English, *The Tripoli Post* (www.tripolipost.com) is a weekly newspaper. The women's magazine *Kul Alfonoon* (www.kulalfonon.com) is a government publication.

Broadcasting

The state-owned, Libyan Jamahiriya Broadcasting Corporation (LJBC) (http://en.ljbc.net) is the national domestic broadcasting organisation.

Radio: The state-run Great Jamahiriya Radio operates four stations from major cities and includes a religious station. Its external service, Voice of Africa (www.voiceofafrica.com.ly), broadcasts in

Arabic, French, Hausa and KiSwahili to countries in Africa with Muslim communities. The private, Allibya Radio broadcasting from Tripoli is operated by the organisation One Nine Media owned by Saif al Islam Qadafi.
Television: The state-run Great Jamahiriya Television operates several networks, with national coverage, providing different contents such as sport and entertainment. The only local, private TV station is Al Libiyah (www.allibiya.tv), provided via satellite and is operated by the organisation One Nine Media, owned by Saif al Islam Qadafi.
News agencies
National news agency: Jamahiriya News Agency (Jana): www.jananews.ly

Economy

The economy is heavily dependent on oil revenues, which provide 95 per cent of all export earnings (the remaining exports are primary mining products) and around 25 per cent of GDP. Following a global high in oil prices in 2007 Libya's current account balance was given a significant boost to US$35 billion in 2008, up from US$24 billion in 2007, even though oil production was stable over three years from 2006 at 1.8 million barrels per day (bpd) each year. However, according to an International Monetary Fund (IMF) report (in February 2011) the current account fell dramatically to US$9.4 billion (15.6 per cent of GDP) in 2009, as the global economic crisis caused worldwide trade and the demand for oil to slump. GDP growth which had been around 6.0 per cent in 2006 and 2007, began falling in 2008 to 2.8 per cent before falling into recession in 2009 with GDP growth of –1.6 per cent. Preliminary estimates of GDP growth for 2010 were of 10.3 per cent, as the world demand for oil rebounded. However the civil unrest since January 2011 has had a negative effect on growth, not only because international sanctions halted oil exports, but also because the rebel, Transitional National Council (TNC) (based in Benghazi) set up its own Libyan Oil Company (LOC) to export crude oil from wells within its region of influence.
Agriculture is the second-largest sector of the economy, although Libya is still reliant on imported foodstuffs as it only produces around 25 per cent of its needs. Output is limited by poor soil and extreme climatic conditions that produce low rainfalls. To aid irrigation, the Great Manmade River (GMR) project, begun in 1991, consists of more than 1,300 wells, most over 500 metres deep, and supplies 6.5 million square metres of fresh water per day to the capital and other major cities. The project supplies much needed water from underground aquifers beneath the Sahara to the Mediterranean coast and to some 135,000 hectares of cultivatable land. However, large resources are also spent on desalinisation research to meet growing demand.
The non-oil sector, including construction accounts for over 20 per cent of GDP, with significant foreign direct investment (FDI) in the tourism and real estate sectors – over US$435 million for three projects in 2008.
Some problems within the economy have yet to be addressed. It is still, largely, state controlled with minimal diversification with around 75 per cent of all employment in the public sector. Nevertheless Libya has liberalised its banking sector, given more independence to the Central Bank of Libya, with authority to allow foreign banks to operate, and enacted anti-money laundering laws. A privatisation programme has been broadened to include health, insurance, transport and downstream oil activities.

External trade

Libya is a member of the Common Market of Eastern and Southern Africa (Comesa) with 18 other country members.
Comesa's objective is to formulate a large economic and trading union which will be able to promote the interests of all members. Libya led the move towards a customs union, which became operational in 2009, in which all non-members are charged a common external tariff (CET).
Libya is also a member of the Arab Maghreb Union (AMU) and the Greater Arab Free Trade Area (Gafta) which operates a customs union whereby tariffs within Gafta will be reduced by a percentage each year, until none remain.
Libya applied for membership of the World Trade Organisation (WTO) in 2004 but by early 2011 was still undergoing economic and trade alignment required for full membership.
Imports
Goods imported include machinery, vehicles, semi-finished goods, food and consumer products.
Main sources: Italy (typically 20 per cent of total), Germany (10 per cent), China (10 per cent).
Exports
Principal commodities are crude oil, refined petroleum products and natural gas, gypsum, limestone and salt.
Main destinations: Italy (typically 40 per cent of total), Germany (10 per cent), Spain (10 per cent).

Agriculture

Farming
Agriculture is estimated to account for 5 per cent of GDP and to employ 18 per cent of the labour force.
The cultivated land is only 1.2 per cent of the total land area and over 80 per cent of all agricultural production is concentrated around oases and the northern coastal regions, especially near Benghazi and Tripoli. Less than 1 per cent of land is irrigated.
Climatic conditions and irrigation problems limit output. Over 70 per cent of food requirements are imported. Libya is self-sufficient in fruit and vegetables, dairy products and poultry. The main crops are potatoes, wheat, barley, dates, tomatoes, almonds, oats, olives, citrus fruits and groundnuts.
The huge Great Man-Made River (GMR) phased project delivers 3.68 million cubic metres of water from underground reservoirs in the Sahara to Libya's main cities and 135,000 hectares of cultivatable land. The irrigation will allow an increase in the land available for agriculture. Small farms for food for local comsumption are encouraged along with large farms that grow wheat and corn and fruits for export markets.
Fishing
The total annual catch is typically 33,000 tonnes, of which up to 6,000 tonnes are exported with a total value of between US$15–30 million. Most of the catch is taken by artisanal boats with nets or hooks. There is negligible freshwater fishing, although the government has attempted to stock reservoirs with fish. Libya has a number of fish canning plants, which can tuna and sardines. Fishmeal is also produced.
Small quantities of fish are exported to Greece, Malta and Tunisia. There is a tuna cannery at Zanzur, and sardine canneries at Zuara and Khoms.
Forestry
Libya is very lightly forested, with less than 1 per cent of total land area covered by forest and woodland, from which small quantities of sawn timber and paper are produced. The majority of domestic demand for industrial wood products is met by imports. Experiments have been undertaken into tree planting, to halt the advance of the desert, but with mixed success; there has been some development of orchards.

Industry and manufacturing

The industrial sector is estimated to contribute 18 per cent to GDP and to employ 15 per cent of the workforce. Virtually all industry was state-owned until the privatisation of state entities – excluding utilities and the gas and oil sectors – began in 2004.
Traditionally the industrial sector was limited to small-scale processing operations, mostly in food, wood and paper, textiles and soap. However, traditional

small-scale agri-allied industries have given way to the growth of import substitution industries (such as building materials manufacture) and heavy industries (such as petrochemicals, iron and steel, concrete pipes and vehicle assembly). The National Petrochemicals Company (Napectco) has built up a substantial petrochemicals capacity since the late 1970s using local feedstock. The large Marsa Brega complex is owned by Napectco which hosts a number of plants producing petrochemicals, ethanol, ammonia and urea. Much industrial investment has gone into expanding capital intensive chemicals capacity as a means of increasing the value added content of exports. Major metal smelting projects have been impeded by low incomes and depressed world prices in recent years. Other constraints to development are insufficiently trained Libyan manpower and the small domestic market.

Tourism

After the rapprochement with the West achieved in 2003 and the lifting of US sanctions in February 2004, Libya officially opened to tourism on 26 February 2005.

Travel sanctions and political isolation was an obstacle to the revival of Libya's tourism sector. Its tourist infrastructure had been neglected for many years and, while new resort and hotel projects have been initiated, more investment is needed to upgrade old resources. The Mediterranean beaches and ancient historical sites, together with its proximity to Europe and other developed North African tourist destinations, provide the country with good potential for expanding visitor numbers.

Prior to the civil war in 2011, travel and tourism had been forecast to directly contribute 1.6 per cent of GDP in the year, and 7.5 per cent through indirectly. Direct employment in the sector was predicted to be 1.6 per cent of total (26,000 jobs) and 3.1 per cent of indirect employment (53,000 jobs). Tourist exports were expected to generate LD221.2 million (US$182.8 million) and the industry to have had direct investment of LD231.7 million (US$191.4 million), 2.6 per cent of total investment, committed for 2011.

Mining

Major mineral deposits include iron ore (which supplies the steel complex at Misrata), potassium, magnesium, sulphur, gypsum and phosphate. There are also potential uranium deposits. Commercial exploitation of minerals is restricted by high development costs.

Salt and construction materials are produced, but large reserves of iron ore at Wadi Shatti remain undeveloped, although this is being reconsidered.

Hydrocarbons

Proven oil reserves were 346.4 billion barrels at the end of 2010; Libya has one of the world's top ten highest oil reserves. Production was 1.6 million barrels per day (bpd), with domestic consumption at 261,000bpd; hydrocarbon exports represent 95 per cent of total merchandised exports and over 50 per cent of GDP. Oil production is expected to increase by 40 per cent to reach 3.0 million bpd in 2013.

Libya has Africa's largest proven oil reserves, but requires foreign investment of billions of US dollars in production and infrastructure to exploit its resources. The state-owned National Oil Company (NOC) is responsible for the oil industry, including exploration, production and distribution.

There are five domestic refineries, with a combined capacity of approximately 378,000bpd, in 2007. They produce for the domestic market as well as the export of refined products. Libya also has oil refining operations overseas, mainly in Europe, operated by the state-owned Tamoil.

Proven gas reserves were at 1.5 trillion cubic metres (cum) at the end of 2010, with production at 15.8 billion cum. Production remained no higher than 6.2 billion cum from 1997–2004, but following the lifting of sanctions in 2004 gas production had surged to 11.3 billion cum in 2005.

The government is expanding gas production as it attempts to replace oil with natural gas, so that more oil is available for export. Plus, Libya, with its huge gas reserves is looking to Europe to build a market while using European energy companies to provide investment.

Any use of coal is commercially insignificant.

Energy

Electricity production capacity was 6.3GW in 2008, producing 25.5 gigawatts hours (gWh) and supplying around 100 per cent of the population; there is a totally interconnected system. While the vast majority of the 27 electricity-generating plants are gas-fired and steam-driven, some are still oil-fired but are located in rural, desert, areas. Crude oil is used in power plants located close to oil fields in remote desert areas.

The General Electricity Company of Libya (Gecol) has sole responsibility for generating and distributing electricity.

Power demand is growing rapidly at 9 per cent per annum, the government hopes to double generating capacity by 2020 as new, smaller power plants are opened in local areas. Gecol has allocated US$2.8 billion to upgrade the transmission system and construct sub-stations.

Banking and insurance

Central bank

Central Bank of Libya

Main financial centre

Tripoli

Time

GMT plus three hours

Geography

Libya is the fourth-largest country in Africa. It extends along the Mediterranean coast of North Africa with Tunisia and Algeria to the west, Niger and Chad to the south, Egypt to the east, and Sudan to the south-east. Most of the country is part of the Sahara Desert. Only the narrow coastal strip receives sufficient rainfall to be suitable for agriculture and it is here that 90 per cent of the population live.

In 1984, the Great Man-Made River Project was begun and when completed will transport daily 6.5 million cubic metres of fresh water, drawn from Sahara Desert aquifers in the south, to the coast in the north. The aquifer water is estimated to be over 40,000 years old. The irrigation will allow an increase in the land available for agriculture.

Hemisphere

Northern

Climate

The coastal areas enjoy a temperate Mediterranean climate. Summer (May–September) temperatures are up to 40 degrees Celsius (C), while winter (November–April) temperatures reach 25–32 degrees C during daytime but can fall to 4–5 degrees C at night. Otherwise, with 90 per cent of the country desert, very hot days (to 50 degrees C), cold nights and sandstorms are likely in May–June. There is low rainfall, mainly between October and March, in the highlands and semi-desert.

Dress codes

A lightweight suit or jacket and trousers are advised. A tie and a long-sleeved shirt should be worn at business meetings, but a jacket is not essential. Women should dress modestly, covering their arms and knees.

Entry requirements

Passports

Required by all. From 11 November 2007 all foreign passports require an Arabic translation. Visitors are advised to contact a Libyan consulate or tourist office for the latest official ruling before travelling.

Visa

Required by all and valid for three months. Exceptions granted for citizens of most Middle East countries, and a few other, African, states. For further information contact the nearest Libyan consulate. All visitors must have an invitation from a Libyan contact – these can be obtained from a Libyan travel agent or Embassy – and essential information on the documentation must have Arab translations. Business visitors should be sponsored by a Libyan company, which will organise the issue of a business visa.

Prohibited entry
Nationals of Israel and passport holders with Israeli visas may be refused entry, check status with a Libyan Consulate.

Currency advice/regulations
Import and export of local currency is prohibited. The import of foreign currency is unlimited but must be declared; export is limited to the amount declared.
Travellers cheques are not readily accepted. Carrying cash is the only realistic option, and the favoured currency is the US dollar. Penalties for the use of unauthorised currency dealers are severe.

Customs
There are strict customs regulations about the import or export of firearms, religious materials, antiquities and medications.

Prohibited imports
Alcohol and illegal drugs

Health (for visitors)

Mandatory precautions
Yellow fever vaccination certificate is required if travelling from an infected areas.

Advisable precautions
Vaccinations or booster shots are advised for typhoid, tetanus and hepatitis A. Other immunisation that may be advised are polio, TB, diphtheria, and hepatitis B. Malaria prophylaxis is recommended for visits to certain areas.
Avoid drinking tap water.
All necessary medication brought in by a visitor should be accompanied by a letter of explanation. A first-aid kit would be useful.

Hotels

Tripoli has a range of hotels.

Credit cards

Credit cards are not accepted.

Public holidays (national)

Fixed dates
9 Feb (Ashura), 3 Mar (Declaration of the People's Authority Day), 11 Jun (Evacuation Day), 1 Sep (Revolution Day), 7 Oct (Friendship Day), 26 Oct (Day of Mourning).

Variable dates
Eid al Adha (two days), Islamic New Year, Eid al Fitr (two days).
Islamic year 1433 (26 Nov 2011–14 Nov 2012): The Islamic year contains 354 or 355 days, with the result that Muslim feasts advance by 10–12 days against the Gregorian calendar. Dates of feasts vary according to the sighting of the new moon, so cannot be forecast exactly.

Working hours

Friday is the Muslim holy day and all offices, businesses and banks are closed. The oil industry is also closed on Saturday.

Banking
Sat–Wed: 0800–1500 (winter); Sat–Wed: 0800–1200 and 1600–1700, Thu: 0800–1200 (summer).
Hours may be reduced during Ramadan.

Business
Sat–Thu: 0800–1600 (winter); Sat–Thu: 0700–1400 (summer).

Government
Sat–Thu: 0730–1430 (winter); Sat–Thu: 0700–1400 (summer).

Shops
Shops are mainly open 0800–1800, often closing for a few hours during the middle of the day.

Telecommunications

Mobile/cell phones
GSM 900 services are limited to populated areas.

Electricity supply

110 or 220V AC

Social customs/useful tips

Alcohol is banned throughout Libya and visitors arriving with alcohol will have it confiscated. Women often do not attend Arab social or business meetings, despite gender equality enshrined in the constitution.
Photography of public buildings and anything of military or security interest is not permitted. It is best to avoid criticism of the country, its leadership or Islam while in Libya since this could potentially result in a heavy-handed response from the authorities.
During Ramadan, eating, drinking and smoking in public is banned throughout the hours of daylight. Islamic and Arab customs prevail and must be respected by visitors. Pork is forbidden by Muslim law. Food is traditionally eaten with the right hand only.

Security

Crime is growing in Libya. The most common crimes are car theft and theft of items left in vehicles. Muggings have occurred on the beaches. Travel to remote areas is best undertaken in groups.

Getting there

Air
National airline: Libyan Arab Airlines.
International airport/s: Tripoli International airport (TIP), 35km from the city, facilities include duty-free shops, restaurants, post office and bank.
Benina International (BEN), 19km from Benghazi; Sebha (SEB), 11km from town.
Airport tax: Departure tax LD6, except for transit passenger. It may be included in the price of the ticket.

Surface
Road: There are entry points via Tunisia and Egypt by the main coast road, Algeria (via Sabhah and Ghat) and Niger and Chad (via Sabhah).
Water: There are ferry services from Malta to Tripoli. There are also occasional services from Casablanca (Morocco) and Alexandria (Egypt).
Main port/s: Benghazi, Misratah, Marsa Brega and Tripoli (free port).

Getting about

National transport
Air: Libyan Arab Airlines operates an hourly shuttle between Tripoli and Benghazi. Other scheduled routes include all major centres. Buraq Air also provides internal flights.
Road: There is a surfaced road system comprising an estimated 32,000km linking all main centres. The main roads include the 1,820km national coast road from the Tunisian border to the Egyptian border; Sabhah-Ghat; Tripoli-Sabhah; Agedabia-Kufra; Sabhah-Chad and Niger borders. Many rural roads have improved due to the infrastructure work carried out for the Great Man-Made River project.
Buses: There are services between main centres.
Rail: There has been no railway in operation since 1965 when the network was broken-up. There are plans to construct a new east-west railway line from the Tunisian border to Tripoli, extending it along the coast to Misratah and then on to Egypt via Tobruk. Another railway line is planned to run north-south from Misratah to Sabhah, and then on to Chad, however these projects are still little beyond their planning stages and may take several years before fruition. Meanwhile Libya has let contracts with private foreign companies to supply crossing and pointwork for the proposed east-west line.

City transport
Taxis: Yellow government taxis are generally cheaper than private taxis. It is advisable to negotiate the fare in advance. Taxis are often on a shared basis.
Buses, trams & metro: State-run bus services operate in Benghazi and Tripoli. They can be unreliable and overcrowded.

Car hire
There are car hire agencies in Tripoli and Benghazi, although rates can be quite high. Cars with drivers can be hired.

BUSINESS DIRECTORY

The addresses listed below are a selection only. While World of Information makes every endeavour to check these addresses, we cannot guarantee that changes have not been made, especially to telephone numbers and area codes. We would welcome any corrections.

Telephone area codes

The international direct dialling code (IDD) for Libya is +218, followed by area code and subscriber's number:

Benghazi	61	Tobruk	87
Misratah	51	Tripoli	21

Chambers of Commerce

Benghazi Chamber of Commerce, Trade, Industry and Agriculture, Issabri Street, PO Box 208, Benghazi (tel: 80-971; fax: 80-761; e-mail: benghaziccia@netscape.net).

Misurata Chamber of Commerce, Trade, Industry and Agriculture, Souweihli Street, PO Box 84, Misurata (tel: 616-497; fax: 620-340; e-mail: info@ccimisrata.org).

Tobruk Chamber of Commerce, Industry and Agriculture, Alfadel Abu Omar Street, PO Box 868, Tobruk (tel/fax: 24-835).

Tripoli Chamber of Commerce, Trade, Industry and Agriculture, 6 Najd Street, PO Box 2321, Tripoli (tel: 333-6855; fax: 333-2655).

Union of Chambers of Commerce, Trade, Industry and Agriculture, PO Box 12556, 26 Bandong Street, Tripoli (tel: 444-1613; fax: 444-1457; e-mail:unionchamber@hotmail.com).

Banking

Libyan Arab Foreign Bank, PO Box 2542, That al-Imad Administrative Complex, Tripoli (tel: 335-0155, 335-0160, 335-0086/7; fax: 335-0164/8).

Sahara Bank, PO Box 270, 10 First of September Street, Tripoli (tel: 333-9804; fax: 333-7922).

Wahda Bank, PO Box 452, Sharia Gamal Abd an-Naser, Benghazi (tel: 222-4122; fax: 222-4122, 222-4709).

Umma Bank Sal, PO Box 685, 1 Giaddat Omar El-Mokhtar Street, Tripoli (tel: 333-4031/35, 444-2541, 444-2544; fax: 333-2505, 444-2476).

Central bank

Central Bank of Libya, PO Box 1103, Tripoli (tel: 333-3591; fax: 444-1488; e-mail: info@cbl-ly.com).

Travel information

Libyan Arab Airlines, PO Box 2555, Haiti Street, Tripoli (tel: 602-093, 608-860; fax: 2-230-970; internet: www.libyanarabairline.com).

National tourist organisation offices

General People's Committee of Tourism, PO Box 82063, Tripoli (tel: 333-6452, 333-7576; fax: 334-2709; internet: www.libyan-tourism.org).

Other useful addresses

General National Organisation for Industrialisation, PO Box 4388, Tripoli (tel: 44-680, 34-995).

Kufrah & Serir Authority, Council of Agricultural Development, Benghazi.

National Oil Corporation, PO Box 2655, Tripoli (tel: 46-180).

National Trade Union Federation, PO Box 734, Tripoli.

National news agency: Jamahiriya News Agency (Jana): www.jananews.ly

Internet sites

Africa Business Network: www.ifc.org/abn

African Development Bank: www.afdb.org

Africa Online: www.africaonline.com

AllAfrica.com: http://allafrica.com

Buraq Air: www.buraqair.com

Libya on the Web: www.libyaweb.com/news.htm

Libyans Online: www.libyaonline.com

Libyan Mission at United Nations: www.un.int/libya/

Azar Libya Travel and Tour Company: www.angelfire.com/az/azartours/index.html

Juddaim Tourism Service: www.libya-juddaim.com/eng/index.html

Caravanserai Tours: www.caravanserai-tours.com

Liechtenstein

KEY FACTS

Official name: Fürstentum Liechtenstein (The Principality of Liechtenstein)

Head of State: Prince Hans-Adam II (titular), (since 1989; on 15 Aug 2004, Crown Prince Alois became acting Head of State)

Head of government: Prime Minister Klaus Tschütscher (from Feb 2009)

Ruling party: Coalition led by Fortschrittliche Bürgerpartei (FBP) (Progressive Citizens' Party) with Vaterländische Union (VU) (Patriotic Union) (FBP since 2001; re-elected 2005, VU since 2005)

Area: 160 square km

Population: 36,023 (2010)*

Capital: Vaduz

Official language: German

Currency: Swiss franc (Swf) = 100 centimes/rappen (the euro also circulates informally)

Exchange rate: Swf0.91 per US$ (Oct 2011)

* estimated figure

COUNTRY PROFILE

Historical profile

Independence in 1719 was followed in the early nineteenth century by a period of French domination, then close connection with Austria until 1918.

1938–70 Fortschrittliche Bürgerpartei (FBP) (Progressive Citizens' Party) was the majority party in the coalition government.

1970–74 Vaterländische Union (VU) (Fatherland Union) was the majority party in coalition, followed by FBP in the 1974 elections.

1978 Liechtenstein was admitted to the Council of Europe. A VU-led coalition was formed.

1984 Prince Hans-Adam II took over executive power from his father. Women were granted the vote in national elections, but not in local elections.

1986 Women were given to right to vote in all elections.

1989 The VU gained a majority of one seat.

1993 FBP became the largest party

1997 The VU gained an outright majority in the elections, the first by any party for over 60 years, and Mario Frick became prime minister.

2001 FBP was elected and Otmar Hasler became prime minister.

2002 The Organisation for Economic Co-operation and Development's (OECD) included Liechtenstein on a list of seven states that were failing to meet international standards on financial transparency and information exchange. An agreement was signed with Monaco over the prevention of money laundering and terrorist financing.

2003 In a referendum, 64 per cent of voters agreed to give Prince Hans-Adam II more power, including the right to dismiss any government deemed incompetent. The vote followed a long-standing dispute between parliament and the monarch, who had threatened to leave the country if his constitutional reform proposals were not adopted.

2004 Liechtenstein adopted a new aubergine-coloured flag. Prince Hans-Adam II handed over day-to-day responsibility for running the country to his son, Prince Alois, while remaining head of state himself.

2005 Otmar Hasler of the ruling FBP was re-elected with 48.7 per cent of the vote (12 seats out of 25). A coalition with the VU was formed.

2006 Liechtenstein celebrated the bi-centenary of its admission to the Confederation of the Rhine in 1806. After its borders were re-measured the size of the country was found to be greater than previously thought at 160 square km,

2007 The Swiss army, on night manoeuvres, accidentally treked up to 2km into Liechtenstein before the error was noticed and the 171-man company returned to their own lands.

2008 An international arrest warrant was issued for the former employee of the LGT Bank, who allegedly sold client details to foreign governments. Germany, the UK and several other countries, have used these records to pursue tax evasion by their citizens. Liechtenstein announced it would modify its banking rules to allow 'comprehensive co-operation' with foreign finance ministries on tax issues. However, 'a culture of privacy' would still be maintained.

2009 In parliamentary elections, the VU won 47.6 per cent of the votes (13 seats out of 25). Otmar Hasler resigned as prime minister and was succeeded by Klaus Tschütscher. Liechtenstein was removed from the OECD's list of countries considered unco-operative tax havens.

2011 A rental scheme for the entire principality was launched in April for US$70,000 per night, with the offer of accommodation for 150 people, customised street signs and temporary currency. The marketing opportunities were identified following a refusal in 2010 by authorities in hiring the country as a backdrop to a music video for the Rap-star Snoop Dogg. On 19 December, Liechtenstein became a member of the European Union Schengen area, whereby all travellers may cross borders without a passport or visa.

Political structure

Constitution

The constitution dates from 1921.Voting rights for women on national issues were granted in 1984, and on local matters two years later.

In 2003, 64 per cent of voters were in favour of constitutional changes, which gave Prince Hans-Adam II power to veto the decisions of parliament and to sack the government, and powers over the appointment of judges, but it took away his right to rule by emergency decree for an unlimited period and to nominate government officials.

Form of state

Absolute monarchy (since 2003)

The executive

The head of state is the monarch. The 2003 referendum conferred on the monarch the power to veto the decisions of parliament and to sack the government.

National legislature

The constitution provides for a unicameral Landtag (parliament) with 25 seats, elected by proportional representation in two multi-seat constituencies, for a four-year term. The Landtag elects a five-member government, which is thereafter officially approved by the head of state.

Legal system

The monarch appoints the country's judges.

Last elections

7–8 February 2009 (parliamentary)

Results: Parliament: Vaterländische Union (VU) (Fatherland Union) won 47.6 per cent (13 seats out of 25), the Fortschrittliche Bürgerpartei (FBP) (Progressive Citizen's Party) won 43.5 per cent (11) and Freie Liste (FL) (Free List) won 8.9 per cent (1).

Next elections

2013 (parliamentary)

Political parties

Ruling party

Coalition led by Fortschrittliche Bürgerpartei (FBP) (Progressive Citizens' Party) with Vaterländische Union (VU) (Patriotic Union) (FBP since 2001; re-elected 2005, VU since 2005)

Main opposition party

Fortschrittliche Bürgerpartei in Liechtenstein (FBP) (Progressive Citizens' Party in Liechtenstein)

Political situation

Following Liechtenstein's signing of tax disclosure agreements from March 2009, it was removed from the Organisation for Economic Co-operation and Development's (OECD) blacklist of non-co-operative tax havens, in April. This followed two years of concerted effort and international pressure from EU and US tax departments, in their attempt to find and curb their citizens' tax evasion schemes. Liechtenstein banking, always a secretive sector, was undermined in its capacity to conceal when in 2007 an employee of the Liechtenstein Global Trust had sold account details to interested tax operations worldwide.

Population

36,023 (2010)*

Last census: December 2000: 33,307

Population density: 200 per square km.

Annual growth rate: 1.3 per cent (2003)

Ethnic make-up

Alemannic (87.5 per cent), Italian, Turkish and other (12.5 per cent).

Religions

Roman Catholic (80 per cent), Protestant (7.4 per cent).

Education

Primary education lasts for five years. Secondary education, starting at aged 12, is provided through three school types: *Oberschule, Realschule* and *Gymnasium*. Each is geared to the attainment outcomes expected of their students.

On completing four years (compulsory) secondary education, a lower secondary school certificate is awarded. *Realschule* students either undertake a one year technical or vocational course leading to specialised schools of further education, or an academic course to attain the lower level Matura Certificate. Students of the *Gymnasium* complete a four year academic course, attaining the higher grade Matura Certificate which is recognised for university entrance either at home or in Switzerland, Austria and Germany.

Compulsory years: Seven to 16.

Health

Life expectancy: 79 years (estimate 2003)

Child (under 5 years) mortality rate (per 1,000): 10 deaths per 1,000 live births.

Main cities

Vaduz (capital, estimated population 4,999 in 2005), Schaan (5,717), Triesen (4,787), Balzers (4,486), Eschen (4,090).

Languages spoken

Allemannish – a dialect of German – is also spoken.

Official language/s

German

Media

Press

There two dailies newspapers are *Liechtensteiner Vaterland* (www.vaterland.li) and *Liechtensteiner Volksblatt* (www.volksblatt.li) and one weekly *Liewo Sonntagszeitung* which is published on Sunday.

Dailies: Two main dailies include the *Liechtensteiner Vaterland* (Vaduz) and *Liechtensteiner Volksblatt* (Schaan).

Weeklies: *Liechtenstein News* is the official weekly newspaper, providing tourist and hotel information in the principality.

Broadcasting

Radio Liechtenstein (www.radio.li) has a network of seven stations. Swiss radio signals are readily received in Liechtenstein including RTSI (www.rtsi.ch) and DSR, with seven stations. RTSI also broadcasts TV programmes.

Advertising

The Media Commission has the authority to implement the Television and Radio Act. While there are few restrictions, tobacco advertising is banned and alcohol restricted in all media outlets and advertising must not be misleading or aggressive.

Economy

Liechtenstein has a highly industrialised, export-based economy with a well-developed banking sector. It ranks as one of the wealthiest countries by GDP per capita in the world. There is close economic interdependence with Switzerland through a customs and currency union.

Financial services contribute about 30 per cent of GDP. It is home to 17 banks, including Liechtenstein Global Trust (LGT), owned by the royal family. The tourism sector is an important foreign exchange earner and together with the services sector enjoyed rapid expansion during the latter part of the 1990s to provide over 55 per cent of GDP. Around 40 per cent of the workforce is employed in the service sector, with a large proportion of cross-border workers from Switzerland and Austria. Around 30,000 businesses are registered in Liechtenstein, which is not far short of one business per resident. There is an extremely high ratio of self-financing enjoyed by domestic businesses plus their ability, if necessary, to fall back on private wealth. A number of companies are research-focussed and are considered world leaders in their particular specialties.

External trade

Liechtenstein is one of the four members of the European Free Trade Association (EFTA) and European Economic Area (EEA) which allows access to the internal EU market and takes around 70 per cent of Liechtenstein's exports.

While the industrial sector produces goods of high value it is the financial services and tourism that make the most significant contributions to the balance of payments.

Imports

Main imports include agricultural products, raw materials, machinery, metal goods, textiles, foodstuffs and vehicles.

Main sources: EU, Switzerland

Exports

Principal commodities include small speciality machinery, audio, video and vehicles parts, dental and optical products, prepared foodstuffs, ceramics, hardware and electronic equipment.

Main destinations: EU (typically over 60 per cent in total – Germany (24 per cent) Austria (10 per cent), France (9 per cent),

Italy (7 per cent), UK (5 per cent)), US (18.9 per cent), Switzerland (15.7 per cent)

Agriculture

Farming

Agriculture is small-scale, employing only about 1.7 per cent of the population (350 workers). Activity is concentrated on dairy farming and farming of fodder cereals although vegetable cultivation and wine production are also undertaken. Utilising methods such as technical rationalisation and intensive cultivation, yields have been steadily increasing. Production typically includes 150 tonnes (t) grapes and 12,000t milk.

Forested land accounts for 42 per cent of the principality and 0.3 per cent of the agicultural sector are employed in forestry. The forestry industry has grown since the late 1990s, doubling production to 22,167 cubic metres (cum) industrial roundwood and 18,000cum sawlogs and veneer logs and maintaining production of 4,000cum fuel wood annually.

Industry and manufacturing

Industry and trade employs about 45 per cent of the workforce. Owing to lack of raw materials and a small domestic market, the sector is export-based and centred on specialised and high-technology production. Manufacturing is centred on machine building, precision engineering and metal working industries. There are also traditional industries such as chemicals (mainly pharmaceuticals), textiles, ceramics and food processing. The production of materials for dental medicine, of microsections for optics and electronics, the manufacture of preserves and deep-frozen products, upholstery, and varnishes, have all attained growing importance. Liechtenstein is the world's largest exporter of false teeth.

Tourism

Liechtenstein receives around 50,000 tourist arrivals each year, mainly from Germany and Switzerland. The royal art collection includes over a thousand works including some by Van Dyck and Rubens. A portion of the £300 million collection is on display to the visiting public.

Hydrocarbons

Liechtenstein does not produce any hydrocarbons. Over 90 per cent of energy imports are acquired from Switzerland and 46 per cent of Liechtenstein's primary energy consumption is met by oil imports. Gas contributes 27 per cent of energy consumption.

Energy

Liechtenstein is dependent on imported energy from Switzerland, which supplies over 90 per cent of the energy needed. The remainder is sourced from domestically generated hydropower (75 per cent) and wood (25 per cent). The country has ratified the Kyoto Protocol. The government has pledged to source 10 per cent of domestic energy requirements from renewable sources particularly biomass and solar.

Banking and insurance

Three main banks are in operation: Liechtensteinische Landesbank, LGT Bank in Liechtenstein and Verwaltungs und Privat-Bank (VP Bank) AG. These have a close association with the Swiss banking system. Secrecy laws are strict although new legislation has put an end to the old anonymous numbered accounts.

There is a total of 17 banking institutes in operation.

Liechtenstein is a signatory of an EU tax agreement introduced in 2005 in a number of non-EU countries. Liechtenstein will impose a withholding tax, up to 35 per cent, to be passed to the tax department of an EU citizen's country, but retaining the anonymity of the saver. This means that the relevant EU country will not be informed about the amount of money in its citizens' bank accounts. In an effort to avoid joining the global list of non-co-operative tax havens, held by the Organisation of Economic Co-operation and Development (OECD), Liechtenstein eased its banking laws to allow the sharing of bank data that cracks down on offshore tax evasion.

Liechtenstein has also agreed to supply information on tax fraud, for criminal or civil trials, and notify EU member states about additional malpractices.

In 2005, a banking ombudsman was appointed in Liechtenstein, ending years of reliance on the Swiss banking ombudsman.

The insurance sector is a recent development. Eight companies make up the Liechtenstein Insurance Association, formed in 1998.

Central bank

Centrum Bank AG

Offshore facilities

Liechtenstein is a major international offshore financial centre, and the largest single supplier of fiduciary funds in Europe.

Time

GMT plus one hour (daylight saving, late March to late October, GMT plus two hours)

Geography

Liechtenstein is a tiny, land-locked country, surrounded by Switzerland (to the west and south) and Austria (to the east). The area of the principality is 160 square km. The river Rhine forms Liechtenstein's western frontier.

The western part of Liechtenstein is lowland, situated in the Rhine flood-plain. This has been drained, providing a wide range of soil types suitable for agriculture. The eastern half of the country is in the foothills of the Rhätikon mountains (Raetian Alps), which rise to snowy Alpine peaks. The highest point is the Grauspitz at 2,599m. Coniferous forests and alpine meadows cover the lower slopes. There are three main valleys in the mountains. The river Samina crosses the range south to north to join the Ill river in Austria.

Hemisphere

Northern

Climate

Varies with altitude, generally mild and often windy. Average summer temperature 17 degrees Celsius (C). Average winter temperature 1 degree C.

Dress codes

Medium-weight throughout the year, with a topcoat for winter.

Entry requirements

Passports

Swiss regulations apply. Passports are required by all, except nationals of EU countries. Passports must be valid for three months beyond intended stay.

Visa

Visas are required by all, except nationals of EU/EEA countries, Australasia, North America, Japan and some other countries. Contact the nearest embassy or consulate for details. A business visa for a citizen of a non-exempt country requires a letter of invitation from or evidence of correspondence with a Liechtenstein company.

Currency advice/regulations

There are no restrictions on the import and export of local and foreign currencies.

Customs

Restricted amounts of alcoholic beverages, tobacco and gifts (up to value of Swf300) may be imported duty free.

Health (for visitors)

Nationals of the European Economic Area (EEA) countries and Switzerland can access reduced cost and sometimes free necessary medical treatment using a European Health Insurance Card (EHIC) while visiting the EEA. Applications for the EHIC should be made before travelling.

The EHIC of nationals of the 10 countries which joined the EU in 2005 are not valid in Switzerland.

Mandatory precautions

None

Advisable precautions

Up-to-date tetanus and polio immunisations.

Hotels
Tips are included in hotel and restaurant bills.

Public holidays (national)
Fixed dates
1 Jan (New Year's Day), 2 Jan (St Berchtold's Day), 6 Jan (Epiphany), 2 Feb (Candlemas), 19 Mar (Feast of St Joseph), 1 May (Labour Day), 15 Aug (Assumption Day), 8 Sep (Nativity of Our Lady), 1 Nov (All Saints' Day), 8 Dec (Immaculate Conception), 24–26 Dec (Christmas), 31 Dec (New Year's Eve).
Variable dates
Shrove Tuesday, Good Friday, Easter Monday, Ascension Day, Whit Monday, Corpus Christi (May/Jun).

Working hours
Banking
Mon–Fri: 0800–1630.
Business
Mon–Fri: 0800–1200 and 1330–1730.
Government
Mon–Fri: 0800–1630.
Shops
Mon–Fri: 0800–1200, 1330–1830; Sat: 0800–1600.

Getting there
Air
International airport/s: There are no airports in Liechtenstein. The nearest international airport is Zürich-Unique (ZRH), Switzerland, approximately 130km from Vaduz. Travel to Liechtenstein can then be continued by road, rail or bus; an autoroute connects Zürich with Liechtenstein.
Surface
Road: Good road access from Switzerland and to a lesser extent Austria. Autoroute (N13) extends along Liechtenstein's Rhine border to Lake Constance, Austria and Germany in the north, continuing southwards towards St Moritz. In the west there are autoroutes to Zürich, Bern and Basel.
Motorway connections: Balzers, Vaduz, Schaan, Bendern, Ruggell.
Rail: The nearest rail stations to Vaduz are at Sargans and Buchs, in St Gallen, Switzerland. Another rail station is at Feldkirch in Austria.

Getting about
National transport
Buses: All villages can be reached by bus service.
Rail: Restricted rail network, with stations at Nendelny and halts at Schaan and Schaanwald.
Nearest main rail stations are at Buchs and Sargans in St Gallen, Switzerland, and Feldkirch in Austria.
City transport
There are regular and inexpensive bus services, and easily obtainable taxi services. Tipping is not customary.
Car hire
Service offered by Avis (Vaduz), Europcar (Eschen-Nendeln) and Nolo (Balzers). Driver must have held a valid driving licence for at least one year and be over 20 years of age. Speed limit 50kph in city, 80kph outside. Traffic drives on the right.

BUSINESS DIRECTORY

The addresses listed below are a selection only. While World of Information makes every endeavour to check these addresses, we cannot guarantee that changes have not been made, especially to telephone numbers and area codes. We would welcome any corrections.

Telephone area codes
The international direct dialling (IDD) code for Liechtenstein is +423, followed by subscriber's number.

Chambers of Commerce
Liechtenstein Chamber of Commerce and Industry, Altenbach 8, 9490 Vaduz (tel: 237-5511; fax: 237-5512; e-mail: info@lihk.li).

Banking
Centrum Bank AG, Heiligkreuz 8, FL-9490 Vaduz (tel: 235-8585; fax: 235-8686).

LGT Bank in Liechtenstein AG (prior to Jan 1996, known as BIL GT Group), Herrengasse 12, FL-9490 Vaduz (tel: 235-1122; fax: 235-1522).

Verwaltungs und Privat-Bank AG, Im Zentrum, Aeulestrasse 6, FL-9490 Vaduz (tel: 235-6655; fax: 235-6500).

Central bank
Liechtensteinische Landesbank, 44 Städtle, PO Box 384, FL-9490 Vaduz (tel: 236-8811; fax: 236-8822; e-mail: llb@llb.li).

Travel information
National tourist organisation offices
Liechtenstein Tourism, Städtle 38, PO Box 139, FL-9490 Vaduz (tel: 239-6300; fax: 239-6301; e-mail: info@tourismus.li).

Other useful addresses
Amt für Volkswirtschaft (national statistics office), Kirchastrasse 7, FL-9490 Vaduz (tel: 236-6871; fax: 236-6889).

Liechtenstein Embassy (USA), 633 Third Avenue, 27th Floor, New York, NY 10017 (tel: (+1-202)-599-0220; fax: (+1-202)-599-0064).

Postillion-Reisen AG, Landstrasse 9, FL-9494 Schaan (tel: 26-565; fax: 27-037).

Presse-und Informationsamt, Regierungsgebäude, FL-9490 Vaduz (tel: 236-6111; fax: 236-6460).

Internet sites
Liechtenstein News: http://www.news.li

Tourism information: http://www.tourismus.li/

KEY FACTS

Official name: Lietuvos Respublika (Republic of Lithuania)

Head of State: President Dalia Grybauskaitė (from 12 Jul 2009)

Head of government: Prime Minister Andrius Kubilius (TS) (LSDP) (since 27 Oct 2008)

Ruling party: Coalition led by Tevynes Sajunga-Lietuvos Krikšcionys Demokratai (Homeland Union-Lithuanian Christian Democrats) (TS-LKD) with Tautos Prisikelimo Partija (TPP) (National Resurrection Party) and Lietuvos Respublikos Liberalu Sajudis (LRLS) (Liberals' Movement of Republic of Lithuania) (from 27 Oct 2008)

Area: 65,200 square km

Population: 3.29 million (2010)*

Capital: Vilnius

Official language: Lithuanian

Currency: Litas (plural Litai) (Lt) = 100 cents

Exchange rate: Lt2.57 per US$ (Oct 2011)

GDP per capita: US$11,044 (2010)

GDP real growth: 1.30% (2010)

GDP: US$36.40 billion (2010)

Labour force: 1.64 million (2010)

Unemployment: 17.80% (2010)

Inflation: 1.20% (2010)

Balance of trade: -US$1.56 billion (2010)

* estimated figure

Lithuania

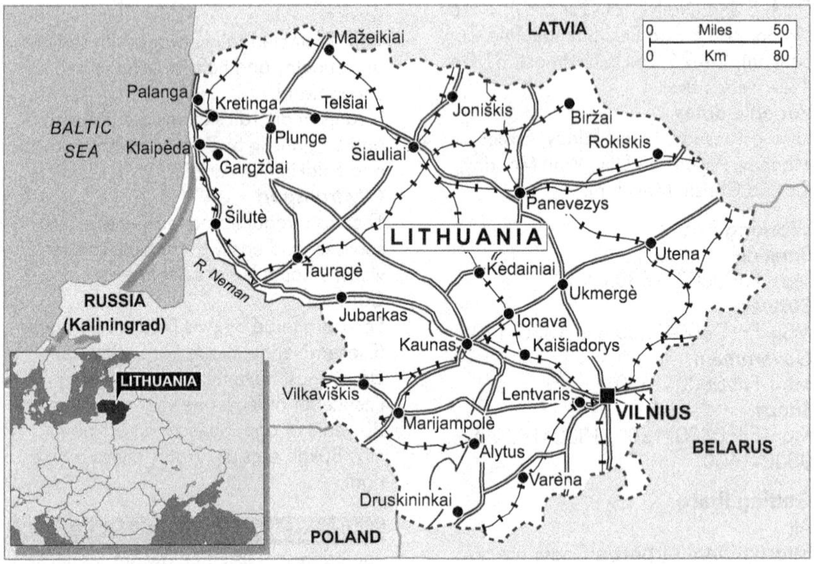

When Lithuania gained independence from the former Soviet Union in 1990, it soon became clear that unlike political independence, the social and economic changes did not immediately bring greater well being for the general good. On the contrary, the poles of wealth and poverty became more distant from each other. While the *nouveau* rich and successful became even richer state employees and public servants risked becoming the new *lumpenproletariat*.

The shadow of Russia

Lithuania has for a very long time lived in the shadow of Russia, the big bear on its doorstep. However, recent years have seen the former soviet satellite state break free from the shackles of Moscow, by and large, though remnants of the Russian regional power's iron fist remain to this day. Lithuania's embrace of the West and in particular the European Union (EU), has allowed the small state to look forward to charting its own future course in the world.

Lithuania was the first of the Soviet republics to breakaway from the then USSR, declaring its independence first in March 1990 and then again in 1991 when a referendum was held, overwhelmingly in favour of independence. Moscow refused to recognise the new state until after its own change of government in 1991. The last Russian troops withdrew from Lithuania in 1993. Lithuania has subsequently restructured its economy and joined both NATO and the EU in the 2004. A slow starter in the Westernisation and modernisation of its economy, Lithuania has caught up rapidly.

Polish relations

Ceremonies in 2011 to commemorate Lithuania's freedom from Soviet rule twenty years ago were marred by Poland's decision to be represented by a low-level delegation. Poland appeared to be angered by Lithuanian delays over the restitution of pre-war Polish property, allegedly broken promises on language rights for Lithuania's ethnic Polish minority, attempts to undermine its schools and ill-treatment of a Polish-owned oil refinery. As is often the way with small countries, Lithuanians feel they are being pushed around by their neighbour. Lithuania is the only country outside Poland to offer Polish-language education from infancy to adulthood, they point out. Latvia's arrangements for its Polish minority are broadly similar to their own nationals. Ethnic Lithuanians in Poland have problems, too.

Many Lithuanians and Poles consider that the row has gone too far. Polish newspapers have criticised the decision to downgrade the Lithuanian anniversary ceremonies. As far as it has any concerns over the matter, the US wants both countries to co-operate, not least in regional military exercises. Neighbouring Estonians and Latvians fear the dispute may block better road, rail and power links to the south-east that would end their isolation from the rest of Europe.

The economy

By 2011 Lithuania's economy had staged an impressive recovery, based on a supportive global environment and determined policy adjustment. After contracting sharply in 2008–09, economic activity grew by 1.5 per cent in 2010 and a robust 6.25 per cent in the first half of 2011. The main driver of the recovery was export growth, underpinned by strong external demand and sharp nominal wage declines that restored competitiveness. There are early signs of a reallocation of resources towards tradable sectors, such as rapid growth of employment in the transport sector and an increase in the share of foreign direct investment going to manufacturing.

The export-led recovery has over the past year broadened to domestic demand, lowered unemployment and stabilised wages. With higher domestic demand stimulating imports, the current account has moved from a slight surplus in 2010 to a small deficit in 2011. External debt has fallen since 2009, as foreign-owned banks have reduced liabilities to their parents, but is still relatively high. Higher energy and food prices pushed up inflation in early 2011, but inflation has slowed recently in line with international commodity price trends.

The fiscal deficit narrowed from 9.2 per cent of gross domestic product (GDP) in 2009 to 7.1 per cent of GDP in 2010 and continued to contract in 2011. Fiscal consolidation reflected mostly reductions in wages and social benefit payments. The government has fully financed its needs in 2011, but has some 8 per cent of GDP in gross financing needs in 2012.

The banking system as a whole is on the mend, but pockets of weakness remain. Non-performing loans have stabilised, net interest margins have risen, the average capital adequacy ratio is above the pre-crisis level and liquidity has increased. However, a few banks have set aside lower provisions for losses than others despite having higher non-performing loan ratios.

The International Monetary Fund (IMF) commended the Lithuanian authorities for their country's impressive economic recovery, noting in particular the sizeable fiscal consolidation, the maintenance of confidence in the banking system and the significant wage adjustment that underpinned gains in competitiveness. The export-led recovery has broadened to domestic demand and reduced unemployment. Given heightened uncertainty in the external environment, the IMF underlined the importance of continued vigilance and sustained progress in strengthening fiscal, financial and structural policies.

The IMF endorsed the government's goal of further reducing the fiscal deficit, thereby putting government debt on a downward path. The measures adopted included the expansion of wealth taxation and broadening tax bases, while protecting spending on public investment and the most vulnerable people from further cuts. Over the medium term, the IMF recommended further strengthening tax compliance, the fiscal framework, the pension and health care systems and the governance of state-owned enterprises.

In the view of the IMF the banking system as a whole is liquid and well capitalised. Addressing remaining pockets of weakness is a priority, including through conservative risk assessments, appropriate loan loss provisions and further capital increases where necessary. There also exists a need for a broader range of bank resolution tools and more effective personal and corporate insolvency regimes, along the lines of European and global initiatives.

Enhancing labour participation and facilitating labour reallocation to tradable sectors are key to sustainable growth. Lithuania proposed expanding the use of fixed-term contracts and making full use of EU structural funds to overcome skill mis-matches. The IMF called for a cautious approach to increasing the minimum wage, consistent with productivity developments. Further efforts to improve the business environment are also crucial.

Risk assessment

Economy	Good
Politics	Good
Regional stability	Good

COUNTRY PROFILE

Historical profile

The Grand Duchy of Lithuania was in union with Poland from 1569; it was annexed by Russia between 1772 and 1795.

1795–1914 Lithuania became part of the Russian empire.

1914–18 The Russians were driven out of Lithuania by the Germans in the First World War.

1918 Lithuania declared independence.

1922 A constitution declared Lithuania a parliamentary republic with the Seimas as the parliamentary organ.

1926 In a military coup, Antanas Smetona came to power as the head of an authoritarian regime.

1940 Lithuania was invaded and occupied by the Soviet Union.

KEY INDICATORS — Lithuania

	Unit	2006	2007	2008	2009	2010
Population	m	3.39	3.38	3.36	3.34	*3.29
Gross domestic product (GDP)	US$bn	29.76	38.90	47.30	37.30	36.40
GDP per capita	US$	8,768	11,520	14,084	11,056	11,044
GDP real growth	%	7.7	9.8	2.9	-14.7	1.2
Inflation	%	3.8	5.8	11.1	4.2	1.2
Unemployment	%	3.8	4.3	5.8	13.7	17.8
Industrial output	% change	7.0	9.8	1.0	–	–
Agricultural output	% change	4.0	13.3	0.4	–	–
Exports (fob) (goods)	US$m	14,150.6	17,162.0	23,768.3	16,480.6	20,815.8
Imports (fob) (goods)	US$m	18,359.8	23,035.8	29,507.1	17,558.0	22,375.7
Balance of trade	US$m	-4,209.3	-5,873.8	-5,738.7	-1,077.4	-1,560.0
Current account	US$m	-3,218.0	-5,692.4	-5,626.6	1,491.6	667.2
Total reserves minus gold	US$m	5,654.4	7,565.8	6,279.7	6,453.2	6,572.6
Foreign exchange	US$m	5,654.3	7,565.6	6,279.6	6,237.9	6,362.0
Exchange rate	per US$	2.67	2.39	2.36	2.48	2.61

* estimated figure

1941 Lithuania was occupied by the Germans, until it was re-annexed by the Soviets in 1944.
1988 A nationalist movement, the Lithuanian Reform Movement (Sàjudis), was set up by a group of writers and intellectuals; at a mass rally in Vilnius, the leaders declared that the USSR occupied Lithuania illegally.
1989 Parliament approved the declaration of Lithuanian sovereignty, stating that Lithuanian laws take precedence over Soviet laws.
1990 Sàjudis won the elections (the first free elections for 50 years). Vytautas Landsbergis was elected chairman of parliament, which declared Lithuania's independence. Fearing the impact that this would have on nationalist demands in the other Baltic republics, the Soviet Union immediately imposed an economic blockade; Lithuania agreed to suspend independence, pending talks.
1991 Talks with Moscow failed and the economy faced turmoil; Landsbergis ended the suspension of the declaration of independence. A referendum was held, resulting in an overwhelming vote for independence. Following a failed coup in Moscow, the USSR recognised Lithuania's independence. Lithuania, together with Latvia and Estonia, were admitted to the UN.
1992 A new constitution introducing a presidency was adopted by referendum. The Lietuvos Demokratine Darbo Partija (LDDP) (Democratic Labour Party of Lithuania) won more seats than Sàjudis in the elections – the LDDP was the first former communist party to return to power in central and eastern Europe.
1993 Algirdas Brazauskas, the former Lietuvos Komunistu Partija (LKP) (Lithuanian Communist Party) first secretary, won direct presidential elections and appointed Adolfas Slezevicius prime minister. Following the defeat of the Sàjudis organisation in the 1992 elections, the Homeland Union was established.
1996 Allegations of corruption led to the removal of Slezevicius and Mindaugas Stankevicius was appointed prime minister. After elections, the Tevynes Sajunga (TS) (Homeland Union) formed a centre-right coalition government with the Lietuvos Kricioniu Demokratu Partija (LKDP) (Lithuanian Christian Democratic Party) and the Lietuvos Centro Sajunga (LCS) (Centre Union of Lithuania). Gediminas Vagnorius was appointed prime minister.
1998 Valdas Adamkus was elected president.
1999 Vagnorius resigned, Rolandas Paksas substituted until a new government, under the leadership of Andrius Kubilius, came to power.
2000 Following the parliamentary elections, a minority coalition government was established, which included the Lietuvos Liberalu Sajunga (LLS) (Lithuanian Liberal Union), LCS and the Modernuju Kriscioni Demokratu Sajunga (MKDS) (Modern Christian-Democratic Union) with the support of other smaller parties. Rolandas Paksas, leader of the LLS, was again appointed prime minister.
2001 Prime Minister Rolandas Paksas' coalition government was brought down over differences about energy sector privatisations. A coalition government was formed, led by the Lietuvos Socialdemokratu Partija (LSDP) (Social-Democratic Party of Lithuania). The LSDP's Algirdas Brazauskas was appointed prime minister.
2002 The litas was re-pegged from the US dollar to the euro.
2003 Rolandas Paksas won the presidential election. Algirdas Brazauskas was re-appointed prime minister. In a referendum on membership of the European Union (EU), 90 per cent voted in favour; turnout was 60 per cent.
2004 Lithuania joined NATO and the EU. Parliament impeached President Paksas following an inquiry that concluded his alleged links with Russian organised crime was a threat to national security. Valdas Adamkus was re-elected president. In parliamentary elections, the Darbo Partija (DP) (Labour Party) formed a coalition government including the DP, LSDP, Naujoji Sajunga (NS) New Union and non-aligned members of parliament; Algirdas Brazauskas was re-appointed prime minister.
2005 The president declined an invitation to attend the ceremony in Moscow celebrating the end of the Second World War.
2006 Prime Minister Brazauskas's government resigned after the DP withdrew its support in protest against the president's statement that he did not trust two DP cabinet members. Gediminas Kirkilas became prime minister.
2007 Lithuania missed the start date for joining the European Monetary Union (Emu), due to a higher than planned inflation rate. Lithuania became a member of the EU Schengen area whereby all travellers may cross borders without a passport or visa.
2008 An agreement for visa-free visits by citizens to the US was signed. Parliament passed a law making it an offence to display Soviet or Nazi images, including flags, emblems and badges with swastikas or the hammer and sickle. In general elections, Tevynes Sajunga-Lietuvos Krikšcionys Demokratai (Homeland Union-Lithuanian Christian Democrats) (TS-LKD) won the highest number of seats (45 out of 141), the ruling LSDP won 25. An alliance of TS, Tautos Prisikelimo Partija (TPP) (National Resurrection Party) and Lietuvos Respublikos Liberalu Sajudis (LRLS) (Liberals' Movement of Republic of Lithuania) formed a government led by Andrius Kubilius.
2009 Dalia Grybauskaité became Lithuania's first female head of state following presidential elections in which she won 68.18 per cent of the vote; her closest rival Algirdas Butkevicius won 11.8 per cent.
2010 Former president Algirdas Brazauskas died in June.
2011 On 6 January, the European Court of Human Rights ruled against Lithuania for violating articles on free elections when former president Paksas had been prevented from standing for re-election. Lithuania will be required to prevent any future, similar violation. On 2 August the government ratified a visa-free agreement for local residents of Lithuania and Belarus to cross the border with the minimum documentation. New, long-term travel permits replaced costly and time consuming to attain visas. In a publicity campaign to deter illegal parking, on 3 August, the mayor of Vilnius was photographed crushing an expensive car parked in a cycle-lane with a military tank.

Political structure

Constitution

The constitution was adopted on 25 October 1992.
The written constitution has precedence over all subsequent laws unless amended by referendum. The office of the president, parliamentary democracy and an independent judiciary are all guaranteed under the constitution, along with specific citizens' rights.

Independence date

16 February 1918, statehood; 11 March 1990 – from the USSR.

Form of state

Parliamentary democratic republic

The executive

The head of state is the president, who is directly elected for a maximum of two five-year terms. The president can dissolve parliament if it refuses to appoint a new government or, at the latter's request, if the parliament passes a vote of no confidence. The president cannot use this power during the last six months of the presidential term of office, or if an early election has taken place during the previous six months.
The prime minister is appointed or dismissed by the president, with the approval of the Seimas. Ministers are appointed and dismissed by the president on the recommendation of the prime minister.

National legislature

The unicameral Seimas (parliament) has 141 members, of which 71 are elected by

in single-seat constituencies and 70 are elected by proportional representation in a nationwide constituency. All members serve for four-year terms.
The Seimas, on a two-to-three majority vote of its members, can decide to hold early elections.

Legal system
The Lithuanian legal code is based on civil law system with no judicial review of legislative acts. The court system consists of district and county courts, the Court of Appeal and the Supreme Court as well as the Administrative Court. The president participates in the process of appointment and dismissal of judges. Moreover, the president has the right to apply to the Constitutional Court concerning the conformity of the legal acts passed by the government. Judges are independent in administering justice.

Last elections
17 May 2009 (presidential); 27 October 2008 (parliamentary).
Results: Presidential: Dalia Grybauskaité won 68.18 per cent of the vote, Algirdas Butkevicius 11.8 per cent, Valentinas Mazuronis 6.2 per cent, Valdemar Tomasevski 4.7 per cent, Kazimiera Prunskiene 3.9 per cent, and Loreta Grauziniene 3.6 per cent. Turnout is 51.7 per cent.
Parliamentary: Tevynes Sajunga-Lietuvos Krikšcionys Demokratai (Homeland Union-Lithuanian Christian Democrats) (TS-LKD) won 19.7 per cent of the votes (45 seats out of 141), LSDP 11.7 per cent (25), Tautos Prisikelimo Partija (TPP) (National Resurrection Party) 15.1 per cent (16), Tvarka ir Teisingumas (TiR) (Order and Justice) 12.9 per cent (15), Lietuvos Respublikos Liberalu Sajudis (LRLS) (Liberals' Movement of Republic of Lithuania) 5.7 per cent (11), coalition of Darbo Partija (DP) (Labour Party) and Jaunimas (Youth) 9.0 per cent (10), Liberalu ir Centro Sajunga (LCS) (Liberal and Centre Union) 5.34 per cent (8), Lietuvos Lenku Rinkimu Akcija (LLRA) (Electoral Action of Poles in Lithuania) 4.8 per cent (3), Lietuvos Valstieciu Partija (LVP) (Lithuanian Peasant Party) 3.74 per cent (1). Turnout was 48.5 per cent.

Next elections
October 2012 (parliamentary); 2014 (presidential)

Political parties

Ruling party
Coalition led by Tevynes Sajunga-Lietuvos Krikšcionys Demokratai (Homeland Union-Lithuanian Christian Democrats) (TS-LKD) with Tautos Prisikelimo Partija (TPP) (National Resurrection Party) and Lietuvos Respublikos Liberalu Sajudis (LRLS) (Liberals' Movement of Republic of Lithuania) (from 27 Oct 2008)

Main opposition party
Lietuvos Socialdemokratu Partija (LSDP) (Social-democratic Party of Lithuania)

Population
3.29 million (2010)*
Last census: April 2001: 3,483,972
Population density: 56.7 inhabitants per square km. Urban population: 69 per cent (1995–2001).
Annual growth rate: -0.6 per cent 1994–2004 (WHO 2006)

Ethnic make-up
Lithuanian (80.1 per cent), Russian (9.1 per cent), Polish (7 per cent), Belarussian (1.5 per cent) and others (2.3 per cent). There are long-standing cultural and political links with Poland, and many Poles live in the southern Vilnius region where they are in the majority, and have their own schools and newspapers.

Religions
Roman Catholic (primarily), Lutheran, Russian Orthodox, Protestant, Evangelical Christian Baptist, Muslim, Jewish.

Education
Primary school starts at age seven and is compulsory. There are three types of school, run by the state: primary (attended for four years), middle (five years) and secondary (three years). There are 17 higher education institutions in Lithuania. Vilnius University, founded in 1579, is the oldest university in Eastern Europe and also the largest in Lithuania.
Literacy rate: 100 per cent adult rate; 100 per cent youth rate (15–24) (Unesco 2005).
Compulsory years: Seven to 14
Enrolment rate: 98 per cent gross primary enrolment of relevant age group (including repeaters); 86 per cent secondary enrolment and 31 per cent at tertiary level (World Bank).
Pupils per teacher: 16 in primary schools.

Health
Lithuania is suffering from a lack of primary healthcare provision and an overstretched network of small hospitals and large polyclinics. Over-specialisation of staff, low-quality equipment and a lack of investment have also put a strain on the health system.
The private sector accounts for only 2–3 per cent of total healthcare in Lithuania. Private clinics can charge 60 per cent more for any treatment than those funded by the state. The Lithuanian government sees these clinics as a threat to the state health care system.

HIV/Aids
HIV prevalence: 0.1 per cent aged 15–49 in 2003 (World Bank)
Life expectancy: 72 years, 2004 (WHO 2006)
Fertility rate/Maternal mortality rate: 1.3 births per woman, 2004 (WHO 2006); maternal mortality 18 per 100,000 live births (World Bank).
Child (under 5 years) mortality rate (per 1,000): 8.0 per 1,000 live births (World Bank).
Head of population per physician: 3.97 physicians per 1,000 people, 2003 (WHO 2006)

Welfare
The government is introduced a multi-pillar pension system, with voluntary public pension contributions for workers in 2004. A 2000 law enforces private voluntary pension funds.
The social security system provides pensions, sickness allowance, maternity and child care benefits and unemployment benefit. Small family grants are also provided that are not subject to means-testing. Contributions to the Lithuanian Social Insurance Fund are tax deductible. Employers contribute 30 per cent of the payroll of the company and employees pay 1 per cent of their wages.

Main cities
Vilnius (capital, estimated population 556,723 in 2005), Kaunas (367,483), Klaipeda (190,722), Siauliai (131,071), Panevezys (117,732).

Languages spoken
By law, all transactions, contracts and company returns must be in Lithuanian. English is widely spoken by business people. Other languages spoken include Russian, Polish, Belarusian, Ukrainian, German and Yiddish.

Official language/s
Lithuanian

Media

Press
All newspapers are privately owned.
Dailies: There are over a dozen daily newspapers, of which the majority are published in Lithuanian; other languages include Russian, Polish and German.
In Lithuanian, major newspapers include *Lietuvos Rytas* (www.lrytas.lt), *Lietuvos Žinios* (www.lzinios.lt) and *Respublika*; tabloids include*Vakaro Zinios* (www.vakarozinios.lt) and *15 Min* (www.15min.lt) which was first published in 2005 and as a free issue newspaper quickly captured around 30 per cent of the readership to became the leading tabloid.
Weeklies: There are over 450 magazines published in various languages and covering all interests.
In Lithuanian, magazines with news and political analysis include *Ekstra* (www.lrytas.lt/ekstra), *Atgimimas* (www.atgimimas.lt) and *Veidas* (www.veidas.lt). Women's magazines

include *Moteris* (www.moteris.lt) and *Panele* (www.panele.lt). In English, *The Baltic Times* (www.baltictimes.com), in Russian, *Litovskiy Kurier* (www.kurier.lt), in Polish, *Tygodnik Wilenszczyzny* (www.tygodnik.lt) and, in German, *Baltische Rundschau* (www.baltische-rundschau.eu) provide general local and international news.

Business: In Lithuanian, *Verslo Zinios* (http://vz.lt) is a comprehensive newspaper with local and international finance and business news. The agro-business magazine *Mano Ukis* (www.manoukis.lt) is published monthly; *Archiforma* is a quarterly architectural review. Verslo Savaite (www.verslosavaite.lt) is an online business publication with an English edition.

Broadcasting

The Radio and Television Commission of Lithuania (www.rtk.lt/en) has power to regulate and supervise all broadcasters, including satellite and internet providers. The national, public broadcaster is Lietuvos Radio ir Televizijos Centras (LRTC) (www.lrt.lt), which is funded by 57 per cent by government and the remainder by commercial sales.

Radio: LRTC (http://www.lrt.lt), operates three radio channels, LR, Klasika and Pus 3,— which includes Radijas. There are around 50 private, commercial radio stations, which include several national networks, Pukas (www.pukas.lt) with two channels broadcasting traditional and jazz music, Radio Centras (www.radiocentras.lt) and Ziniu Radijas (www.ziniur.lt).

Television: LRTC (http://www.lrt.lt), operates two TV stations (LTV1 and LTV2). Major, commercial channels includes LNK (www.lnk.lt), BTV (www.btv.lt) and TV3 (www.tv3.lt). Most programmes are locally produced by some foreign imports are included.

Advertising

The advertising market has grown rapidly since liberalisation in the 1990s. Annual expenditure is typically around US$400 million, of which television advertising takes the greatest share of over 70 per cent and newspapers and magazines accounting for 20 per cent, all other media share the remaining amount.

Restrictions in advertising include limited broadcasting hours for alcohol, with tobacco advertising at point of sales only. Adverts for prescription medications are banned and across the counter drugs must warn of possible harmful side effects. Political advertising in outdoor locations are banned.

Economy

The economy grew rapidly during the 1990s, moving from a centrally planned economy within the now defunct Soviet Union to an independent open market economy, characterised by rising productivity, investment and innovation. Following Lithuania's accession to the European Union in 2004 there was a sharp rise in investment and capital inflow, which were channelled into the non-tradable sector (services) and real estate. With a consistently high GDP growth rate 6.5–7.6 per cent (2004–06), rising to 9.8 per cent in 2007 it led to an expansion in credit and a rise in external indebtedness. In 2008, the global economic crisis knocked the economy off-balance and GDP growth slumped to 2.9 per cent, before falling into a serious recession of -14.7 per cent, in 2009. Inflation which had been relatively low began to increase in 2007 at 5.8 per cent and jumped to 11.1 per cent in 2008, before falling back to 4.2 in 2009, and lower still in 2010 to 1.2 per cent. As rapid wage growth eroded competitiveness, unemployment in the first quarter of 2009 rose to 11.9 per cent and for the year was 17.8 per cent. Salaries were cut by 12.3 per cent in 2009 as GDP per capita fell from US$14,084 in 2008 to US$11,056 in 2009.

In response the government implemented a US$2.3 billion stimulus plan along with severe budget cuts. The international credit ratings agency Standard and Poor's cut Lithuania's credit rating to BBB (the second lowest investment grade) in 2009 as the country's outlook deteriorated, with falling exports and a weakened banking system. At the same time Lithuania signed a US$1.45 billion loan with the European Investment Bank (EIB) to support EU-backed infrastructure, utilities, health and education sector projects.

Almost all of Lithuania's state-owned entities have been privatised, including the banks (of which 90 per cent are foreign controlled, mainly by Scandinavian interests); around 80 per cent of economic output is generated by the private sector. Around 12 per cent of GDP comes from fees for transit of oil from Russia to Western Europe.

External trade

As a member of the European Union, Lithuania operates within a communitywide free trade area, with tariffs set as a whole. Internationally, the EU has free trade agreements with a number of nations and trading blocs worldwide.

Despite the poor balance of trade, exports account for 60 per cent of GDP, of which around 10 per is provided by forest and timber products. Industrial production is in food processing, shipbuilding and manufacturing, with a growing interest in information technology (IT).

Imports

Principal imports include fuels and oil, vehicles, machinery and equipment, chemicals, textiles and clothing and metals.

Main sources: Russia (typically 30 per cent in total), Germany (12 per cent), Poland (10 per cent), (EU, combined total, 57 per cent).

Exports

Principal exports are mineral products (over 20 per cent), textiles and clothing, machinery and electronic equipment, chemicals, timber products and foodstuffs.

Main destinations: Russia (typically 16 per cent in total), Latvia (12 per cent), Germany (7 per cent), (EU combined total, 60 per cent).

Re-exports

Oil (from Russia) around 150,000 barrels per day (bpd).

Agriculture

Farming

Agricultural land constitutes 53.4 per cent of total land area, estimated at 3.4 million hectares (ha). The industry employs about 18 per cent of the total labour force and contributed 6.2 per cent of GDP in 2004. Main products include grain, potatoes, sugar beet and dairy products, meat and silk.

Land restitution began soon after independence in 1990, with the creation of 104,000 private family farms. The break up of state-owned farms into small plots, the limited availability of capital and a lack of business skills have slowed the recovery and development of the agricultural sector.

The agriculture ministry has embarked on the EU's Special Accession Programme for Agriculture and Rural Development (SAPARD) programme covering the period to 2007 and is intending to utilise EU funds to restructure the sector. Lithuania will not be eligible for full EU agricultural subsidies and rural development aid through CAP until 2013. During its transitional entry stage Lithuania has decided to implement the reform of the CAP on 1 January 2009. The reform was introduced throughout most of the EU in 2005, when subsidies on farm output, which tended to benefit large farms and encourage overproduction, were replaced by single farm payments, not conditional on production. The change is expected to reward farms that provide and maintain a healthy environment, food safety and animal welfare standards. The changes are also intended to encourage market conscious production and cut the cost of CAP to the EU taxpayer.

Lithuania's European and transatlantic integration will significantly increase competitive pressures on its agriculture, with a large proportion of exports heading to the US. It has adopted the Swedish model of organic farming with policies that draw heavily on bilateral international projects.

Environmental factors continue to affect agricultural reforms – 50 to 70 per cent of nitrogen and 10 to 20 per cent of phosphorus found in surface waters originated in farming activities.

Fishing

The opportunity to export fishery products to the EU market without any tariff barriers has attracted the interest of its seafood processing industry.

Redfish, mackerel, cod, red plaice, black halibut and shrimp are caught in the high seas. Baltic Sea catches include cod, sprat, Baltic sprat, plaice, turbot, salmon and smelt.

Forestry

Forest and other wooded land accounts for a third of the land area, with forest cover estimated at 1.9 million hectares (ha). Most of the forest is available for wood supply. About 80 per cent of the forest area is owned by the state, although private ownership has been rising since the early 1990s. Consumption of forest products per capita is below the European average level.

The sawmill industry, which exports half of its production, contributes largely to the national economy. Large volumes of roundwood, comprising mostly pulpwood, are exported mainly to Sweden and Germany. Although pulp and paper production is one of the oldest industries in Lithuania, most of the internal demand for high quality paper is met by imports. Chemical timber, furniture, wood-fibre and wood-chipboards are also produced, with chipboard materials in particular having strong export potential. Sawn hardwood is also used in the domestic furniture industry.

Industry and manufacturing

The industrial sector accounts for over 30 per cent of GDP of which, over f5 per cent is manufacturing; it employs around 40 per cent of the workforce. Main industries are shipbuilding, consumer electronics, metalworking, machine building, machine tools, scientific instruments, sulphuric acid, paper, meat, dairy products, food processing, textiles, clothing and furniture. One of Lithuania's priorities is the development of light industry, particularly furniture, using natural wood products.

The principal branches of existing light industry in Lithuania are textiles and knitwear, with the largest leather and footwear enterprises in Vilnius, Kaunas and Siauliai. Other areas offering potential for growth include electronics.

The EU has stressed the need for Lithuania to speed-up restructuring of the industrial sector, particularly food processing and agricultural industries.

Tourism

Lithuania's tourist facilities are improving and around 1.2 million tourists visit Lithuania annually. Travel and tourism is expected to contribute US$431 million, or 1.6 per cent to GDP. While total exports in tourism is expected to earn US$1 billion, it is only expected to attract US$656 or 10 per cent of total capital investment. The country's main foreign tourism markets are neighbouring countries from the former Soviet bloc – Russia, Latvia and Poland. The fastest growing markets are Latvia, Germany, Scandinavian and Asian countries.

There are a number of tourist centres, including Trakai, the medieval capital of Lithuania, in the country's lake district. Apart from the castle, there is potential for watersports. The coastal resort of Palanga boasts sandy beaches as well as health and spa facilities. Birstonas on the bank of the Nemunas River is also a centre for spa treatments. Five national and nearly 30 regional parks are classified as protected areas.

Mining

Lithuania is famous for its high quality deposits of amber which supply the local jewellery industry. Amber deposits have been found in the coastal region of Curonian Bay and Juodkrante. The Juodkrante site covers 82 hectares; amber deposits are estimated at 112 tonnes. Lithuania also has large reserves of high-quality iron ore in the south, but extraction is not economically viable.

Other raw materials found in small quantities include limestone, dolomite, gypsum, clay, sand and gravel.

Hydrocarbons

Lithuania reserves have been falling since the 1990s. Total, proven oil reserves were 10 million cubic metres (cum) (12 million barrels) of oil in 2007. Exploration has found only two new, small oilfields, in 2004 and 2005, close to existing oilfields; by 2008 exploration had ceased. The oil in production and the country's reserves so far are high quality, light crude, which is easy to convert into refined products.

The country imports most of its domestic consumption oil needs of approximately 70,000 barrels per day (bpd) from Russia, via the Druzhba pipeline, which terminates in Butinge, the site of the country's only oil refinery – Mazeikiu Nafta. It has a capacity of over 260,000bpd producing petrol, diesel and jet fuel. A major fire disrupted production in 2006; repairs had been completed by 2008.

Lithuania's natural gas situation is similar to that of oil: the country has scarce reserves and is heavily dependent on Russian imports to meet the country's domestic consumption demand of 2.9 billion cubic metres per annum.

Germany and Russia have agreed to build a gas pipeline, to supply Russian gas to Western Europe, which will be built under the Baltic Sea, bypassing Lithuania. Relations between Russia and Lithuania have been strained and West European countries are keen that their supplies of gas are not impeded by any such tensions. For Lithuania's part, any plan to become the hub for gas supplies to the EU is threatened by this arrangement, as well as the implicit risk to its own supplies from Russia. Nevertheless major infrastructure upgrading projects are under way at several Lithuanian ports.

Lithuania does not produce coal and has reduced its consumption, but still imports small quantities from Poland and Russia.

Energy

Total installed generating capacity was over 3,9000MW, producing 9.7 terawatt hours in 2007.

The Lithuanian energy sector is dominated by Lietuvos Energija, the largest electric power company in the country. It is 96.2 per cent state-owned, with a minority stake held by Sweden's Vatenfall. The company is structured into separate companies, responsible for generation, distribution and transmission. A privatisation programmed is due to be completed by 2010.

The Estlink project, an underwater cable linking the Baltic States with the Scandinavian and Nordic power grids, was partly funded by the EU and became operational in 2007. Lithuania has plans to interlink its power grid with those of Poland, Karliningrad (Russia) and eventually Western Europe.

The ageing Ignalia nuclear power plant, similar in construction to the Chernobyl facility is being decommissioned in 2009 as part of Lithuania's EU accession agreement. There are plans to build a replacement. Finland supplied technical expertise during the environmental assessment and by 2008 the new nuclear power plant (NNPP) project was at the procurement documentation stage.

The potential for geothermal energy production has been identified in west Lithuania, close to existing oil fields.

Financial markets

Stock exchange

Vilniaus Vertybiniu Popieriu Birza (Vilnius Stock Exchange) (VSE)

Banking and insurance

Lithuania has a two-tier banking system whereby the commercial and central bank functions of the state bank are separated. Foreign-owned banks may operate in the country. Commercial banking operations have been removed from the central bank, which has assumed the government's responsibility for setting interest policy. The Lietuvos Zemes Ukio Bankas (LZUB) (Lithuanian Agricultural Bank) was sold by the government in early-2002 — the end of state involvement in commercial banking.

Central bank

Lietuvos Banka (LB) (Bank of Lithuania)

Main financial centre

Vilnius

Time

GMT plus two hours (daylight saving, late March to late October, GMT plus three hours)

Geography

Lithuania is the largest of the three Baltic states, situated on the eastern coast of the Baltic Sea in north-eastern Europe. It is bordered by Latvia to the north, Belarus to the south-east, Poland to the south-west and the Russian Federation to the west. There is a dense network of waterways, the main river being the Nemunas, which flows south to north into the Baltic Sea. There are many lakes in the northern regions of the Baltic Highlands. The highest point is Juozapine Hill (294 metres) in the east of the country.

Hemisphere

Northern

Climate

Lithuania enjoys one of the mildest climates along the Baltic coast. Summer sunshine may last nine hours a day, but winters can be very cold. Annual rainfall averages 490mm and humidity 80 per cent.

Dress codes

Warm clothing is necessary in winter. Business dress is conservative but relatively informal, with a jacket and tie expected for meetings. A raincoat is useful during spring and autumn.

Entry requirements

Passports

Required by all.

Visa

Required by all, except nationals of EU and Schengen area signatory countries, North America, Australasia and Japan. For further exceptions contact the nearest embassy. A Schengen visa application (offered in several languages) can be downloaded from http://europa.eu/abc/travel/ see 'documents you will need'.

Business visas for all other nationals must be applied for with an invitation from a local company or organisation and certified by the migration authorities in Lithuania (stamped and signed by a migration officer). A business letter, by the visitor's company, giving purpose of visit and full itinerary should also be included.

Currency advice/regulations

Import of local currency is unlimited but export is limited to Lt5,000. Import and export of foreign currency is unlimited although any amount over the equivalent of Lt40,000 must be declared.

Travellers cheques are not widely accepted.

Customs

Personal items are duty-free. There are no duties levied on alcohol and tobacco between EU member states, providing amounts imported are for personal consumption.

Prohibited imports

Military and hunting firearms, ammunition, fishing equipment require a permit. Meat and dairy products; illegal drugs are prohibited.

Health (for visitors)

Nationals of the European Economic Area (EEA) countries and Switzerland can access reduced cost and sometimes free medical treatment using a European Health Insurance Card (EHIC) while visiting the EEA. Exceptions include nationals of the 10 countries, which joined the EU in 2004, whose EHIC is not valid in Switzerland. Applications for the EHIC should be made before travelling.

Mandatory precautions

Vaccination certificates are required for cholera or yellow fever if travelling from an infected area.

Advisable precautions

It is advisable to be in date for the following immunisations: polio (within 10 years), tetanus (within 10 years), typhoid fever, hepatitis A (moderate risk only).

It is recommended that bottled water is used for drinking; tap water is occasionally brown.

Hotels

There are many hotels in Vilnius. Some have been restored or taken over. Most ask for payment in hard currency. Western-class hotels charge Western prices. Tipping is not widely practised.

Credit cards

Major credit cards are accepted in hotels, restaurants and shops. ATMs are found in many centres.

Public holidays (national)

Fixed dates

1 Jan (New Year), 16 Feb (Independence Day), 11 Mar (Restoration Day), 1 May (Labour Day), 8 May (Mother's Day), 26 May (Jonines), 6 Jul (Statehood Day), 15 Aug (Assumption Day), 1 Nov (All Saints' Day), 25–26 Dec (Christmas).

Variable dates

Easter (two days)

Working hours

Banking

Mon–Fri: 0900–1700. Some banks open on Sat: 0900–1300.

Business

Mon–Fri: 0900–1300 and 1400–1800; lunch break 1300–1400.

Shops

Mon–Fri: 1000–1400 and 1500–1900; Sat: 1000–1600.

Telecommunications

Mobile/cell phones

A GSM network covers the republic's eight largest cities.

Electricity supply

220V AC, 50Hz. European plugs are required.

Social customs/useful tips

Social behaviour is fairly informal. Lithuanians are open and hospitable. Straight professional questions receive straight answers. Business cards are used widely and shaking hands is the common form of greeting and farewell. Most Lithuanians are punctual – being late for a meeting can be a bad start.

Tipping has become more widespread, with waiters often expecting generous tips from westerners – avoid leaving hard currency.

Lithuanian-Russian relations are not as tense as those between Estonians and Latvians and Russians, although care should be taken when discussing Russia and its role in the region. Lithuanians also dislike being described as members of the Baltic states, rather than Lithuanian.

Security

Compared to other European capitals, the crime rate in Vilnius is relatively low, but street crime does occur. Make use of hotel safe deposit boxes and be careful not to show valuables when walking around the city. Car theft is common.

Getting there

Air

National airline: FlyLAL (Lithuanian Airlines)

International airport/s: Vilnius International (VNO), 5km from city; facilities include business and VIP lounges, duty-free shops, car hire, post office, *bureau de change*, restaurants, first aid. Taxis and buses are available.

Airport tax: Departure tax Lt60

Surface

Road: Lithuania has a good network of interconnecting roads, providing links to neighbouring countries.

Rail: There is a well developed rail network with Vilnius as the hub for rail connections in the region. There are train connections with Poland through Grodno in Belarus. There are regular trains to

Russia (Moscow and St Petersburg). Rail travel between Lithuania, Latvia and Estonia can be slow.
Water: There are several regular ferry services from the main port of Klaipeda to UK, Russian Federation, Germany, Poland and Sweden. There are also many more irregular sea links to other foreign ports.

Getting about

National transport

Air: There are three domestic airports at Palanga, Kaunas and Siaulai but they have limited services.
Road: Paved roads are generally in good condition, however rural unpaved roads can be hazardous. There is a modern four-lane motorway connecting Vilnius with Kaunas, Laipeda and Panaeveys.
Buses: Buses are convenient and the cheapest way to travel as trains do not serve every town and village.
Rail: The rail system is being upgraded. Twice daily trains connect Vilnius with the Baltic coast.
Water: There is a coastal ferry linking Klaipeda and the Curonian Spit. There is also a dense network of rivers, the longest of which is the Nemunas River – total length 973km, 475km of which is in Lithuania – which is suitable for navigation in parts.

City transport

Taxis: Taxis display an illuminated *Taksi* sign and can be flagged down in the street or found at taxi-stands or booked by telephone. Meters should be in operation and visitors can insist that they be used. If not, fares must be negotiated and avoided being paid for in hard currency. Taxis are always more expensive from the airport, railway station, cathedral and the Vilnius Department Store.
Buses, trams & metro: There is a choice of buses and trolley buses within the city. Tickets can be purchased from kiosks (*spaudos kioskas*) and drivers; they must be inserted into a validating machine on board. Services operate from 0600 to 0030 or 0100.
The Vilnius railway station is a cosmopolitan marketplace and terminus, but it is not safe for visitors at night.

Car hire

Many of the major car rental companies operate in Lithuania. There are winter (Oct–Mar) and summer (Apr–Sep) speed limits on motorways: 110kph (winter), 130kph (summer); 90kph (all year) on open roads and 60kph on urban roads. National driving licences with photo IDs are required. Seat belts are compulsory and drink/driving is prohitited. Traffic drives on the right. It is advisable to make sure hire vehicles have an alarm and steering lock.
Drivers must pay a fee to use any road leading to Vilnius old town.

BUSINESS DIRECTORY

The addresses listed below are a selection only. While World of Information makes every endeavour to check these addresses, we cannot guarantee that changes have not been made, especially to telephone numbers and area codes. We would welcome any corrections.

Telephone area codes

The international direct dialling code (IDD) for Lithuania is +370, followed by area code and subscriber's number:

Kaunus	37	Panevezys	45
Klaipeda	46	Siauliai	41
Palanga	460	Vilnius	5

Useful telephone numbers

Directory enquiries: 09
International operator: 8-194
Fire: 01
Police: 02
Ambulance (greitoji pagalba): 03
Vilnius City Road Police, Giraites 3: 631-168

Chambers of Commerce

American Chamber of Commerce in Lithuania, 5 Lukiskiu Street, 2600 Vilnius (tel: 261-1181; fax: 212-6128; e-mail: acc@acc.lt).

Association of Lithuanian Chambers of Commerce, Industry and Crafts, 9 J Tumo-Vaizganto Street, 2001 Vilnius (tel: 261-2102; fax: 261-2112; e-mail: info@chambers.lt).

British Chamber of Commerce in Lithuania, 21 T Sevcenkos Street, 2009 Vilnius (tel: 239-2316; fax: 239-2301; e-mail: info@bccl.lt).

Kaunas Chamber of Commerce, Industry and Crafts, PO Box 2111, 8 K Donelaicis Street, 3000 Kaunas (tel: 229-212; fax: 208-330; e-mail: chamber@chamber.lt).

Klaipeda Chamber of Commerce, Industry and Crafts, 17 Danes Street, 5800 Klaipeda (tel: 390-861; fax: 410-626; e-mail: klaipeda@chambers.lt).

Panevezys Regional Chamber of Commerce, Industry and Crafts, 34 Respublikos Street, 5319 Panevezys (tel: 463-687; fax: 462-227; e-mail: panevezys@chambers.lt).

Siauliai Regional Chamber of Commerce, Industry and Crafts, 88 Vilniaus Street, 5400 Siauliai (tel: 525-504; fax: 523-903; siauliai@chambers.lt).

Vilnius Regional Chamber of Commerce, Industry and Crafts, 31 Algirdo Street, 2600 Vilnius (tel: 213-5550; fax: 213-5542; e-mail: vilnius@chambers.lt).

Banking

Bankas Snoras, 7A Vivulskio Street, 2600 Vilnius (tel: 216-2795).

Lietuvos Zemes Ukio Bankas (Lithuanian Agricultural Bank), Totoriu 4, 2600 Vilnius.

Lithuanian Commercial Banker's Association, Vilniaus 4/35, Vilnius 2001.

Lithuanian Development Bank, Stulginskio 4-7, 2600 Vilnius.

Lietuvos Taupomasis Bankas (Lithuanian Savings Bank), Savanoriu pr 19, 2015 Vilnius.

Lietuvos Valstybinis Komercinis Bankas (Lithuanian State Commercial Bank), Jogailos 14, 2001 Vilnius.

Vilniaus Bankas (commercial bank), Gedimino Avenue 12, 14, 2600 Vilnius.

Central bank

Lietuvos Bankas (Bank of Lithuania), 6 Gedimino Avenue, LT-01103 Vilnius (tel: 268-0029; fax: 262-8124; e-mail: info@lb.lt; internet: www.lb.lt).

Stock exchange

Vilniaus Vertybiniu Popieriu Birza (Vilnius Stock Exchange) (VSE): www.omxnordicexchange.com

Travel information

FlyLAL, 4 Gustaicio Avenue LT-02512 Vilnius (tel: 252-5555; email: info@flylal.com).

Krantas Travel Operator, 5 Teatro Street, LT-91247 Klaipeda (tel: 395-215)

Lithuanian Tourism Association, Pylimo 6, 2001 Vilnius.

Travel Bureau, Lietuva Hotel, Ukmerges 20, Vilnius.

Vilnius International Airport, Rodunios kelias 10A, LT- 02189, Vilnius (tel: 230-6666; fax: 232-9122; email: airport@vno.lt).

Vilnius Tourist Information Centre, (J-3) Didzioji 31, Town Hall, Vilnius (tel: 262-6470; email: turizm.info@vilnius.lt).

National tourist organisation offices

Lithuanian State Department of Tourism, A Juozapaviciaus 13, LT-09311 Vilnius (tel: 210-8796: fax:210-8753; email: vtd@tourism.lt; internet: www.tourism.lt).

Ministries

Ministry of Agriculture, Gedimino Avenue 19, LT-2025 Vilnius (email: zum@zum.lt).

Ministry of Culture, J Basanaviciaus Street 5, LT-5683 Vilnius (email: culture@muza.lt).

Ministry of Defence, Tortoriu 25/3, LT-2001 Vilnius (email: vis@kam.kam.lt).

Ministry of the Economy, Gedimino Avenue 38/2, LT-2600 Vilnius (email: pr@po.ekm.lt).

Ministry of Education and Science, A Volano Street 2/7, LT-2691 Vilnius (email: smmin@smm.lt).

Ministry of the Environment, A Jaksto Street 4/9, LT-2694 Vilnius (email: info@aplinkuma.lt).

Ministry of Finance, J Tumo-Vaizganto Street 8a/2, LT-2600 Vilnius (email: finmin@finmin.lt).

Ministry of Foreign Affairs, J Tumo-Vaizganto Street 2, LT-2600 Vilnius (email: urm@urm.lt).

Ministry of Health, Vilniaus Street 33, LT-2001 Vilnius (email: ministerija@sam.lt).

Ministry of the Interior, Sventaragio Street 5, LT-2600 Vilnius (email: infoskyrius@vrm/lt).

Ministry of Justice, Gediminio Avenue 30/1, LT-2600 Vilnius.

Ministry of Social Welfare and Labour, A Vivulskio Street 11, LT-2693 Vilnius (email: post@socmin.lt).

Ministry of Transport, Gediminio Avenue 17, LT-2679 Vilnius (email: transp@transp.lt).

Office of the President, S Daukanto Square 3, LT-2008 Vilnius (email: info@president.lt).

Office of the Prime Minister, Gedimino Avenue 11, LT-2039 Vilnius (email: kanceliarija@lrvk.lt).

Other useful addresses

Association of Light Industry Enterprises of Lithuania, Saltonishkiu 29/3, 2677 Vilnius.

Association of Lithuanian Entrepreneurs, A Jakshto 9, 2600 Vilnius.

BNS (English-language Baltic news service), Konarskio 49, Vilnius.

British Embassy, Antakalnio 2, Vilnius 2055 (tel: 222-070/1; fax: 727-579; e-mail: BE-VILNIUS@post.omnitel.net).

Central Post Office, Gedimino 7, Vilnius.

Commercial Court of the Republic of Lithuania, Gedimino pr 39/1, 2640 Vilnius.

Confederation of Lithuanian Industrialists, Saltonishkiu 19, 2600 Vilnius.

Construction Production Certification Centre, Linkmenu 28, 2600 Vilnius.

Department of Customs, A. Jaksto 1/25, 2600 Vilnius (internet: (foreign trade database) www.cust.lt/).

Department of Statistics, Gedimino pr 29, 2746 Vilnius.

ELTA Lithuanian News Agency, Gedimino Ave 21/2, Vilnius 2600.

Energy Agency, A Vienuolio 8/4, 2600 Vilnius.

Lithuanian Builders' Association, Vytauto 14/2, 2000 Vilnius.

Lithuanian Building Industry Association, Sevcenko 19, 2000 Vilnius.

Lithuanian Construction Association, Raugyklos 15, 2600 Vilnius.

Lithuanian Development Agency, Investment, Marketing and Public Relations Departments, Sv Jono Str 3 2600 Vilnius (email: lda@lda.lt; internet: www.lda.lt); Export Department, Algirdo 31, 2600 Vilnius (email: lda@lda.lt).

Lithuanian Economic and Foreign Investment Development Agency (FIDA), J Jasinskio 9, 4th floor, 2600 Vilnius.

Lithuanian Embassy (USA), 2622 16th Street, NW, Washington DC 20009 (tel: (+1-202) 234-5860; fax: (+1-202) 328-0466; email: info@ltembassyus.org).

Lithuanian Export Promotion Agency, J Tumo-Vaizganto 8a/2, 2739 Vilnius (email: lepa.epd@post.omnitel.net).

Lithuanian Free Market Institute, Birutes 56, 2600 Vilnius.

Lithuanian Information Institute, Kalvariju 3, 2659 Vilnius.

Lithuanian International Trade Agency, V Kudirkos st 18, 2600 Vilnius (email: LAITA@post.omnitel.net).

Lithuanian Investment Agency (LIA), Sv Jono 3, 2600 Vilnius.

Lithuanian Manufacturers' Confederation, Saltonishkiu 19, 2687 Vilnius.

Lithuanian Privatisation Agency, Gedimino 38/2, 2600 Vilnius.

Lithuanian Road Administration, State Property and Service Division, 36/2 Basanaviciaus Street, Vilnius LT-2009.

Lithuanian Standardisation Board, A Joksto g 1/25, 2600 Vilnius.

Lithuanian Television & Radio Broadcasting, Konarskio 49, 2674 Vilnius.

Privatisation Agency, Gedimino Prosp 38/2, Vilnius.

Securities Commission, Ukmerges g 41, 2600 Vilnius.

State Competition and Consumer Protection Office, Gedimino pr 38/2, 2600 Vilnius.

State Patent Bureau, Algirdo g 31, 2600 Vilnius.

State Quality Inspectorate, Gedimino pr 19, 2600 Vilnius

State Tax Inspection, Sermuksniu st 6, 2600 Vilnius.

Vilnius City Administration, Gedimino ave 9, 2600 Vilnius.

Other news agencies: ELTA (Lithuanian News Agency): www.elta.lt

Baltic News Service (BNS): www.bns.lt

Delfi: www.delfi.lt

Internet sites

Lithuania on-line: www.aiva.lt/lol

Official travel guide: www.travel.lt

Port of Klaipeda: www.portofklaipeda.lt/en.php

Yellow pages: www.yellowpages.lt

Luxembourg

With the highest per capita income in the world, neighbours and general observers quizzically look at the small Grand Duchy of Luxembourg and ask, 'how come?'

It's not our money!

Luxembourg's wealth was founded on steel, but as Western Europe evolved into a post-industrial economy, Luxembourg's financial service industry grew to become paramount. Eventually, Luxembourg became Europe's most powerful investment management centre. In 2009, Luxembourg was required to rehabilitate the reputation of its banking system, which had suffered by being castigated in the eyes of the G8 group of countries as a tax haven. But by signing agreements to exchange tax information on citizens of a dozen countries its reputation was restored. The European Investment Bank has its headquarters in Luxembourg. On 17 January 2011, the Industrial and Commercial Bank of China (ICBC), the world's largest bank (by market

KEY FACTS

Official name: Groussherzogtom Lëtzebuerg, Grossherzogtum Luxemburg, Grand-Duché de Luxembourg (The Grand Duchy of Luxembourg)

Head of State: Grand Duke Henri of Luxembourg (acceded Oct 2000)

Head of government: Prime Minister Jean-Claude Juncker (CSV) (from 1995; re-elected 7 Jun 2009)

Ruling party: Coalition led by Chrëschtlich Sozial Vollekspartei (CSV) (Christian Social People's Party) (from 2004; re-elected 2009), with Lëtzebuerger Sozialistesch Arbechterpartei (LSAP) (Luxembourg Socialist Workers' Party) (from 2009)

Area: 2,586 square km

Population: 507,000 (2010)*

Capital: Luxembourg-Ville

Official language: Lëtzebuergish (Luxembourgish); French and German are the administrative languages.

Currency: Euro (€) = 100 cents (from 1 Jan 2002; previous currency Luxembourg franc, locked at Lf40.34 per euro)

Exchange rate: €0.75 per US$ (Oct 2011)

GDP per capita: US$108,832 (2010)

GDP real growth: 3.20% (2010)

GDP: US$55.00 billion (2010)

Labour force: 363,000 (2010)

Unemployment: 6.00% (2010)

Inflation: 2.30% (2010)

Balance of trade: -US$5.29 billion (2010)

* estimated figure

capitalisation) announced that Luxembourg would be its European headquarters.

Luxembourg is home to the Secretariat of the European Parliament and, for three months each year (April, June and October), is host to the Council of the European Union, with its attendant, well paid, bureaucracy of ministers and their entourage. Some senior courts are also located in Luxembourg, as well as other EU governing entities. As they would say down the east end of London, 'what a nice little earner'.

Employees of these institutions may not live in Luxembourg and may make a daily commute from larger cities close by, such as Paris (France), Brussels (Belgium) and Frankfurt (Germany). However their costs impact on the living standards of Luxembourgers, so that in 2010 per capita income was estimated to be US$108,952; (per capita income using the purchasing power parity (PPP) method was US$81,466). In 2008 and before the global economic crisis weakened Luxembourg's economy, the per capita income had been a record US$119,534 (or using PPP, US$79,258). GDP growth in 2008 had been 1.4 per cent, however, in 2009, GDP growth slipped into recession with a rate of -3.6 per cent. In 2010, as world trade picked up, there was a recovery and the GDP growth rate rose to 3.5 per cent.

Of the 263,000 total local workforce in 2010, 6 per cent were unemployed; there were also over 100,000 cross-border workers.

Risk assessment

Politics	Good
Economy	Good
Regional stability	Good

COUNTRY PROFILE

Historical profile

Modern-day Luxembourg was occupied by the Burgundians, Prussians, Spanish and French until the nineteenth century, when it came under German and Dutch control.
1867 Luxembourg was granted independence.
1914–18 Luxembourg was occupied by the Germans.
1921 The Belgian-Luxembourg Economic Union (BLEU) was formed.
1940–45 Nazi Germany occupied Luxembourg.
1948 The Benelux Economic Union (Benelux) was inaugurated between Belgium, Luxembourg and the Netherlands and became effective in 1960, establishing the three countries as a single customs area in 1970.
1949 Luxembourg became a founding member of NATO.
1957 Luxembourg became one of the founder members of the forerunner to the EU, the European Economic Community (EEC).
1964 Grand Duchess Charlotte abdicated after a reign of 45 years and was succeeded by her son, Prince Jean.
1974 After being in power since 1918, the Chrëschtlich Sozial Vollekspartei (CSV) (Christian Social People's Party) was defeated by the Demokratesch Partie (DP) (Democratic Party) in general elections.
1979 The CSV regained power.
1990 Luxembourg was an original signatory of the Schengen Agreement to remove all border controls.
1994 Jean-Claude Juncker became prime minister.
1999 A CSV/DP coalition government was formed after the CSV failed to win enough seats in the parliamentary elections to have an outright majority. Juncker remained as prime minister.
2000 Grand Duke Jean abdicated and was succeeded by his son, Prince Henri.
2002 Euro currency replaced the Luxembourg franc. Luxembourg was named by a French parliamentary committee as a haven for tax evasion and money laundering.
2003 After EU talks on new rules for the taxation of savings invested abroad, Luxembourg won the right to decide when they would drop the withholding tax and begin exchanging information.
2004 The CSV was re-elected.
2005 Voters approved the European Union constitution by 57 per cent to 43 per cent.
2006 Arcelor, Luxembourg's premier steel manufacture was sold to the Indian-owned Mittal Steel, for US$34 billion, which created one the world's largest steel manufacturers.
2008 President Chavez of Venezuela announced that the Luxembourg-based and Argentine-owned steel maker, Ternium, would be nationalised to bring a key industry under state ownership and drive its socialist economy.
2009 In parliamentary elections, the ruling CSV won 26 seats (out of 60), and formed a coalition with Lëtzebuerger Sozialistesch Arbechterpartei (LSAP) (Luxembourg Socialist Workers' Party). Prime Minister Juncker remained in office.
2010 Luxembourg became Russia's third largest source of foreign investment by volume in the first half of the year with US$30.38 billion, up 5.5 per cent compared to the same period in 2009.
2011 A new law was introduced in January whereby households were required to pay a realistic price for their drinking water and removal of sewage. The general cost increase was aimed at achieving a good ecological status for clean water and such services by 2017, when a parity between cost and usage is due to be achieved. On 3 August the government agreed to pay three-months of outstanding salaries of 477 employees of the bankrupt construction company Socimmo, following a court decision that it was liable as guarantor for the bank-backed employment fund.

Political structure

Constitution

The constitution was adopted in 1868 and has been amended on four occasions

KEY INDICATORS — Luxembourg

	Unit	2006	2007	2008	2009	2010
Population	m	0.47	0.48	0.48	0.50	*0.51
Gross domestic product (GDP)	US$bn	42.51	51.40	57.90	51.70	55.00
GDP per capita	US$	89,923	106,983	119,534	104,512	*108,952
GDP real growth	%	6.1	6.5	0.1	-3.6	3.5
Inflation	%	2.7	2.3	3.4	0.8	2.3
Unemployment	%	4.0	4.4	4.4	5.7	6.0
Exports (fob) (goods)	US$m	16,383.0	18,418.0	21,431.0	15,501.0	16,798.0
Imports (fob) (goods)	US$m	20,795.0	23,131.0	27,729.0	19,760.0	22,084.0
Balance of trade	US$m	-4,411.0	-4,712.0	-6,298.0	-4,259.0	-5,286.0
Current account	US$m	4,389.0	4,746.0	3,104.0	2,985.0	4,385.0
Total reserves minus gold	US$m	218.1	143.6	334.6	730.5	747.1
Foreign exchange	US$m	156.0	93.8	258.4	267.5	270.6
Exchange rate	per US$	0.75	0.69	0.68	0.72	0.76

* estimated figure

(1919, 1994, 1996 and 1998). It can be amended when at least two thirds, of a minimum 75 per cent of parliamentary members, vote in agreement. A plebicite must ratify the amendment.
The constitution sets out the role of the hereditary crown as Head of State, and the rights of citizens before the law.
Universal direct suffrage for all those registered and over the age of 18.

Independence date
1814

Form of state
Parliamentary democratic monarchy

The executive
Executive power is vested in the Grand Duke and exercised through the constitution and the law.
The Council of Ministers is led by the prime minister, who is chosen by the Grand Duke, and must have the support of the Chamber of Deputies.

National legislature
Legislative power is exercised by a unicameral 60-member Châmber vun Députéirten / Chambre des Députés (Chamber of Deputies), which is elected for a five-year term by proportional representation in four multi-seat constituencies.
A 21-member Council of State, chosen by the Grand Duke, acts as an advisory body and has some legislative functions.

Legal system
Loosely based on Napoleonic code, of inquisitorial justice. The highest court is th Superior Court of Justice. Justices of the peace, district court judges and members of the Superior Court are appointed for life by the Grand Duke. Special laws regulate military tribunals. Administrative courts have jurisdiction over tax and administrative matters. There is a Constitutional Court that decides on the conformity of laws within the constitution.
The Grand Duke has the authority to revoke or reduce penalties awarded by judges.

Last elections
7 June 2009 (Parliamentary)
Results: Parliamentary: Chrëschtlech Sozial Vollekspartei (CSV) (Christian Social People's Party) 38.0 per cent (26 seats, out of 60), Lëtzebuergesch Sozialistesch Arbechterpartei (LSAP) (Luxembourg Socialist Workers' Party) 21.6 per cent (13), Demokratesch Partei (DP) (Democratic Party) 15.0 per cent (9), Déi Gréng (Gréng) (The Greens) 11.7 per cent (7), Alternativ Demokratesch Reformpartei (ADR) (Alternative Democratic Reform Party) 8.1 per cent (4), Déi Lénk (Lénk) (The Left) 3.3 per cent (1); turnout was 85.2 per cent.

Next elections
June 2014 (parliamentary).

Political parties

Ruling party
Coalition led by Chrëschtlich Sozial Vollekspartei (CSV) (Christian Social People's Party) (from 2004; re-elected 2009), with Lëtzebuerger Sozialistesch Arbechterpartei (LSAP) (Luxembourg Socialist Workers' Party) (from 2009)

Main opposition party
Lëtzeburger Sozialistesch Arbechterpartei or Parti Ouvrier Socialiste Luxembourgeois (LSAP/POSL) (Luxembourg Socialist Workers' Party)

Population
507,000 (2010)*
Last census: February 2001: 439,539
Population density: 166 inhabitants per square km. Urban population: 92 per cent of total (1995—2001).
Annual growth rate: 1.4 per cent 1994–2004 (WHO 2006)

Ethnic make-up
The inhabitants of Luxembourg are mostly of German and French origin, but have a distinct national consciousness. From just under 20 per cent in 1970, the percentage of foreign residents has risen to over 30 per cent. The Portuguese, who account for over 10 per cent of the total population, form the largest foreign community. The second largest immigrant community comes from Italy (5 per cent).

Religions
Approximately 97 per cent of the population is Roman Catholic.

Education
Primary education lasts for six years, until the age of 12. Instruction is initially given in German, and French is added in the second year. Secondary education can be obtained through either a lLycé, or *Lycé Technique*. The first offers general and technical schooling, for up to seven years with an initial period of three years then an advanced (and non-compulsory) programme of four years. The *Lycé Technique* offers complete seven-year courses. French replaces German in the classroom at secondary schooling.
Higher education in the Grand Duchy is limited in scope. Approximately 4,000 students attend foreign universities, predominantly in Belgium and France.
Compulsory years: Six to 15.
Enrolment rate: 85 per cent net primary enrolment (Unicef).

Health

HIV/Aids
HIV prevalence: 0.2 per cent aged 15–49 in 2003 (World Bank)
Life expectancy: 79 years, 2004 (WHO 2006)
Fertility rate/Maternal mortality rate: 1.7 births per woman, 2004 (WHO 2006)
Child (under 5 years) mortality rate (per 1,000): 4.9 per 1,000 live births (World Bank)
Head of population per physician: 2.66 physicians per 1,000 people, 2003 (WHO 2006)

Welfare
The social security system was built in several stages. It has been extended to include both the socio-professional categories and at risk groups. The minimum wage, which functions as a mechanism to guarantee resources, consists of a supplementary benefit paid up to a threshold determined according to the composition of the household. The benefit is awarded irrespective of the causes of the situation of need. Sickness benefits, in which patients pay only a small part of medical costs, as well as birth, family and unemployment payments, are included in the plans. Housing conditions are generally comparable to those found in other Western European countries. There has been some difficulty in assimilating the many thousands of foreign workers and their families.
Luxembourg conforms to the EU provisions dealing with social security based on the principle of free movement of workers within the EU that enables its workers to accept a job in another member state without suffering any inequality with regard to social security. The EU social security arrangements aim to co-ordinate the national social security schemes in all the member states of the EU and the European Economic Area (EEA).
The social security system covers benefits for sickness and maternity, pensions, insurance against accidents at work and occupational diseases, unemployment benefits and family allowances. The scheme is compulsory and covers all persons in paid employment as well as self-employed workers in the country. Half of the contribution due is payable by the worker and half by the employer. There is no contribution towards industrial accident insurance, family benefits or unemployment benefit. Contributions are payable for sickness and maternity insurance, disability insurance, old-age and survivor's pension, amounting to a certain percentage of his/her remuneration.

Main cities
Luxembourg-Ville (capital, estimated population 76,258 in 2005), Esch-sur-Alzette (27,559), Dudelange (18,036), Differdange (18,477).

Languages spoken

Official language/s
Lëtzebuergish (Luxembourgish); French and German are the administrative languages.

Media

Press

The high level of newspapers per readership is based on subsidies provided by public money and political affiliates. The market is dominated by the Imprimerie Saint Paul (www.isp.lu) media group which controls around 90 per cent of the daily newspaper market.

Newspapers are published in the predominant language (either French or Germany) of the region in which they sold with an edition in the alternative language.

Dailies: The most popular newspaper the *Luxemburger Wort* (www.wort.lu) is owned by the Roman Catholic Church and has close ties to the Christian socialist political party. The newspaper with the second highest circulation is *Tageblatt* (http://news.tageblatt.lu), published by the trade unions and is closely linked the the socialist political party. Other publications include *Lëtzebuerger Journal* (www.journal.lu), *Zeitung vum Letzebuerger Vollek* (www.zlv.lu) and *La Voix du Luxembourg* (www.lavoix.lu). The French newspaper *Le Républicain-Lorrain* (www.republicain-lorrain.fr), which has an extensive Luxembourg section, is also widely read.

Weeklies: Those featuring general interest, news and current affairs include *Revue* (www.revue.lu), *d'Letzebuerger Land* (www.land.lu), and *Letzebuerger Gemengen* (www.gemengen.lu) and, in English, *352* (www.352.lu) provides general news for the expatriate community. *Den Neie Feierkrop* (www.feierkrop.lu) is a satirical magazine.

Business: In French with an online German edition *l'Echo de l'Industrie* (www.fedil.lu/Echo) is published by the Federation of Luxembourg Industrialists (Fedil) and *Le Jeudi* (http://hebdo.le-jeudi.lu) is a weekly publication of financial and business news.

Broadcasting

Luxembourg has a long tradition of broadcasting to huge audiences in Europe including France, Germany and the UK. The RTL Group (www.rtlgroup.com) is Europe's largest media organisation with over 40 television and 30 radio stations throughout Europe plus production companies in the US and elsewhere, producing gameshows and long-running domestic dramas. While RTL is a private entity it has a government agreement whereby RTL keeps certain operations located in Luxembourg plus provide television and radio programmes for local audiences in exchange for freeing RTL from franchise fees and no third party being granted a licence by the government to broadcast if it competed with RTL international activities. The agreement runs until 2010.

Radio: There are a range of radio stations dedicated to the various official languages. Domestic radio is dominated by Radio Lëtzebuerg RTL (http://rtl.lu) with around 50 per cent of the audience share. Radio Ara (www.ara.lu) broadcasts alternative programming for marginal groups and foreign residents.

Television: Luxembourg was the first European country to switch completely from analogue signals to digital terrestrial television (DTT) signals, in 2006. Télé Lëtzebuerg RTL (http://rtl.lu) dominates with around 40 per cent of the audience in the local market and operates TV channels is each of the local languages.

Other, commercial stations include Nordliicht TV (www.nordliicht.lu) and Satmode for interactive TV.

Advertising

The typical advertising spend per annum is over US$110 million following the liberalisation, which opened up opportunities for commercial broadcasting, in the 1990s. However, restrictions do remain in the print media and free issue newspapers, largely sponsored and supported by advertising revenue are still excluded.

Economy

Luxembourg's financial sector is large by international standards and contributes substantially to GDP growth and trade. However, since the onset of the global economic recession GDP growth has contracted severely from 6.6 per cent in 2007 to 1.4 per cent in 2008, falling again, to -3.6 per cent, in 2009. In 2010, the economy recovered with the growth rate at 3.5 per cent, which should remain constant through 2011. As a member of the European Union euro-zone Luxembourg undertook recapitalisation of its banks in 2008, while the European Central Bank (ECB) reduced interest rates and initiated 'supportive fiscal' policies that included unlimited term funding at fixed rates. The euro-zone moved out of recession by mid-2009.

The other mainstay of Luxembourg's economy is steel production and as global trade fell European crude steel production dropped by 39.9 per cent in 2009. However, following the merger of Luxembourg's largest steelmaker Acelor with India's Mittal Steel in 2006, becoming the world's largest steelmaker, production of steel in Luxembourg in 2009 rose 7.6 per cent.

The service sector (dominated by banking) typically contributes 80 per cent of GDP with industry providing around 20 per cent of which manufacturing is about 12 per cent; agriculture provides less than 1 per cent.

Employment in Luxembourg is dynamic with cross-border workers living in neighbouring countries and returning each day, many employed in the financial sector. Of the 363,000 total workforce in 2010, 6 per cent were unemployed and over 100,000 were cross-border workers.

External trade

As a member of the European Union, Luxembourg operates within a community-wide free trade union, with tariffs set as a whole. Internationally, the EU has free trade agreements with a number of nations and trading blocs worldwide.

The traditional steel industry provides around 10 per cent of GDP, despite depleted domestic iron ore reserves. Hi-tech industries have grown in importance; nevertheless, the financial services sector is a major provider of external revenue, which provides around 80 per cent of GDP.

Imports

Imports include petroleum, gas, vehicles, iron ore, minerals, metals, foodstuffs and quality consumer goods.

Main sources: Belgium (typically 30 per cent of total), Germany (25 per cent), France (12 per cent).

Exports

Commodities include iron and steel, electrical and electronic equipment, machinery, glass, ceramics and plastics.

Intermediate manufactured products account for around 80 per cent of total exports.

Main destinations: Germany (typically 25 per cent of total), France (17 per cent), Belgium (12 per cent).

Agriculture

Farming

The country has gradually adapted and delegated much of its farm policy to the EU, through the Common Agricultural Policy (CAP). The EU's Fundamental reform to the CAP was introduced in Luxembourg in 2005. The subsidies paid on farm output, which tended to benefit large farms and encourage overproduction, were replaced by single farm payments not conditional on production.

Farming is concentrated on barley, oats and potatoes in the north, and fruit and grapes in the east.

Although agricultural output has tripled since the 1980s, its contribution to GDP has in the same period declined from 4 per cent in mid-1970s to around 1 per cent in late 1990s. The number of farms declined from 5,173 in 1980 to 2,950 in 1998 as high agricultural production costs and high employment in Luxembourg caused more people to leave the farming industry and farmland has subsequently been converted to other uses. This trend slowed in 2003–04 as the economy slowed and jobs were not so readily

available. Three-quarters of the land is cultivated. Pasture accounts for 55 per cent of all cultivated farmland.
Food and wine account for about 1.9 per cent of exports.

Fishing
Luxembourg does not have any significant freshwater fishing industry.

Forestry
Largely driven back to the least productive soil and escarpments where viable development is precluded, woods cover some 89,000 hectares or around a third of the country. Extending over 4,500 hectares, the forest of Gruenwald is the largest continuous wooded area in the Grand Duchy. Forestry only plays a very modest role in the overall economy, the commercial explotation of private forests and those subject to the system of forest tenure only represent on average between 0.1 per cent and 0.2 per cent of GDP.

Industry and manufacturing
As with the agricultural sector, Luxembourg's industrial base has declined in proportion to the dominant services sector and accounts for only 30 per cent of GDP. The country's principal industries include steel, chemicals, rubber, plastics, processing, glass, aluminium, metalworking and vehicle spares manufacture.

Tourism
The Grand Duchy of Luxembourg is a small land-locked country that is a major crossroads between France, Germany and Belgium which surround it and from which it draws many of its influences. The old quarters and fortification of the capital of Luxembourg-ville are included on the UN list of World Heritage Sites.
Luxembourg is home to a large community of wealthy residents and has one of the world's highest per capita incomes. Although the travel and tourism sector is an important component of GDP, its contribution is only around 5 per cent of the total, generating annually over US$2.26 billion since 2007. Total employment in the industry has been over 6 per cent since 2008, although most workers employed are from outside Luxembourg.
A new terminal was completed at Findel International Airport in 2008 to encourage more passengers to take direct flights to Luxembourg rather than to Frankfurt (Germany) or the other smaller, surrounding airports in Belgium and France.

Mining
Iron ore, discovered around 1850, made the fortune of modern Luxembourg's economy. The steel industry still serves as one of the most important sector of the economy, although its share of GDP fallen has since the early 2000s.

Hydrocarbons
Luxembourg does not have any oil, natural gas or coal reserves. The country imports all its hydrocarbons, totalling 60,000 barrels per day (bpd) of refined oil products, 1.3 billion cubic metres of natural gas and 153,000 tonnes of coal. These imports come primarily from within the EU.

Energy
Domestic production of electricity supplies 54.9 per cent of consumer needs; 45.1 per cent of supplies are imported from Germany, via a connection to its network. Installed generating capacity is over 1.16 gigawatts (GW); consumption in 2007 was 6,777 gigawatt hours (GWh).
The hydroelectric dam at Vianden is one of the largest hydro-power plants in Europe, producing 1.1GW. The biggest power company is Cegedel, supplying 69 per cent of all electricity consumed.

Financial markets
Stock exchange
Bourse de Luxembourg (Luxembourg Stock Exchange)

Banking and insurance
Luxembourg has a large banking sector. Activity is oriented towards wholesale banking services, with a large concentration of German and Scandinavian banks serving corporate customers in Europe. Private banking has rapidly increased. Banking accounts for around 16 per cent of GDP and employs 10 per cent of the workforce. Luxembourg's banking secrecy laws were a source of complaint abroad, however new rules allow authorities to investigate as necessary. There is concern that EU requirements for the deduction of a withholding tax from all foreign accounts will adversely affect the sector.
In an effort to avoid joining the global list of non-co-operative tax havens, held by the Organisation of Economic Co-operation and Development (OECD), Luxembourg eased its banking laws to allow the sharing of bank data that cracks down on offshore tax evasion.

Central bank
The European Central Bank (ECB) acts as the central bank, issuing notes and coins and determining interest rates.

Time
GMT plus one hour (daylight saving, late March to late October, GMT plus two hours)

Geography
Luxembourg is a landlocked country in Western Europe, bounded by Belgium on the north and west, Germany to the east and France to the south. Luxembourg consists mainly of the upper basins of the Sauer (Sûre) and Alzette rivers. The highest point is Buurgplaatz (559 metres), in the Ardennes Plateau in the north. The southern two-thirds of the country is a rolling plateau, the Bon Pays.

Hemisphere
Northern

Climate
Luxembourg's climate is temperate, without extremes. Sea winds (south-west and north-west) shed a great part of their moisture before reaching the Luxembourg frontiers. May to mid-October is suitable for vacations; July and August are the warmest; May and June are the sunniest months; in September and October there is often an 'Indian summer'.

Dress codes
Medium-weight clothing is required throughout the year. A raincoat is useful.

Entry requirements
Passports
Passports are required by nationals of most countries. Exceptions include holders of national identity cards issued to nationals of some European countries.

Visa
Required by all, except nationals of Europe, North America, Australasia, or Japan. For a full list of visa-free citizens visit www.luxembourg-usa.org/consindex.html. Schengen visas cover all entry needs; for those requiring a business visa, a letter of business references and proof of sufficient funds to cover the cost of your intended stay should accompany the application. A Schengen visa application (offered in several languages) can be downloaded from http://europa.eu/abc/travel/ see 'documents you will need'.

Currency advice/regulations
There are no restrictions on the movement of local or foreign currencies.

Customs
Personal items are duty-free. There are no duties levied on alcohol and tobacco between EU member states, providing amounts imported are for personal consumption.
Passengers carrying weapons and transiting Luxembourg must hold an *Autorisation de Transit d'Armes* certificate issued by the Luxembourg Ministry of Justice.

Health (for visitors)
Nationals of the European Economic Area (EEA) countries and Switzerland can access reduced cost and sometimes free medical treatment using a European Health Insurance Card (EHIC) while visiting the EEA. Exceptions include nationals of the 10 countries, which joined the EU in 2004, whose EHIC is not valid in Switzerland. Applications for the EHIC should be made before travelling.

Mandatory precautions
None
Advisable precautions
It is recommended that travellers have up-to-date tetanus and polio immunisations.

Hotels
A one-to five-star rating system is partially in operation. Bills include the service charge. Tipping is optional.

Credit cards
All main credit cards are accepted.

Public holidays (national)
Fixed dates
1 Jan (New Year's Day), 1 May (May Day), 23 Jun (National Day), 15 Aug (Assumption Day), 1 Nov (All Saints' Day), 25-26 Dec (Christmas).
If a holiday falls on a Sunday, the Monday following is usually a holiday as well (maximum two per annum).
Variable dates
Carnival (Feb), Good Friday, Easter Monday, Ascension Day, Whit Monday, Luxembourg City Fair Day (Luxembourg City only, Sep).

Working hours
Banking
Mon–Fri: 0900–1630.
Business
Mon–Fri: 0800–1800, lunch 1200–1400.
Government
Mon–Fri: 0800–1800, lunch 1200–1400.
Shops
There are large variations in shop hours, but they are generally open 0900–2000, closed Mon morning.

Electricity supply
220V AC

Weights and measures
Metric system

Social customs/useful tips
Punctuality is appreciated. Business people are expected to wear suits. It is advisable to make prior appointments and business cards are widely used.

Security
Luxembourg has a low crime rate. However, during the tourist season pickpocketing and theft from vehicles do occur.

Getting there
Air
National airline: Luxair
International airport/s: Luxembourg-Findel (LUX), 5km east of city; restaraunts, post office shops, car hire.
Airport tax: None

Surface
Road: There are good road links with Brussels, Trier, Paris, Frankfurt and Saarbrücken. Luxembourg has open borders with all its immediate neighbours, namely Germany, France and Belgium.
Rail: There are rail connections with Brussels, Frankfurt, Amsterdam, Basle and Paris.

Getting about
National transport
Network tickets (*billets réseaux*), which allow unlimited travel for one day on all forms of transport throughout Luxembourg, are also available.
Road: Luxembourg has an extensive network of roads and motorways, all of which are paved.
Buses: Bus services link most towns and villages.
Rail: There are 280km of railway track. State-run railway services link the capital with most main towns.
City transport
Taxis: There is a metered taxi service with a minimum charge. Tipping is usually 10 per cent.
Buses, trams & metro: Regular flat-fare bus service operates in Luxembourg city. Tickets are valid for one hour or 10km and also allow connections with out-of-city connections.
Car hire
Car hire is available from the airport and hotels.

BUSINESS DIRECTORY

The addresses listed below are a selection only. While World of Information makes every endeavour to check these addresses, we cannot guarantee that changes have not been made, especially to telephone numbers and area codes. We would welcome any corrections.

Telephone area codes
The international direct dialling (IDD) code for Luxembourg is +352, followed by subscriber's number.

Chambers of Commerce
American Chamber of Commerce in Luxembourg, 6 Rue Antoine de Saint Exupéry, PO Box 542, L-1432 Luxembourg (tel/fax: 431-756; e-mail: info@amcham.lu).

British Chamber of Commerce for Luxembourg, 6 Rue Antoine de Saint Exupéry, L-1432 Luxembourg (tel: 465-466; fax: 220-384; e-mail: info@bcc.lu).

Luxembourg Chamber of Commerce, 7 Rue Alcide de Gaspari, L-2981 Luxembourg (tel: 423-939; fax: 438-326; e-mail: chamcom@cc.lu).

Banking
Association des Banques et Banquiers, 59 Boulevard Royal, PO Box 13, L-2010 Luxembourg (tel: 29-501, 463-6601; fax: 460-921).

Banque Continentale du Luxembourg SA, 2 Boulevard Emmanuel Servais, L-2535 Luxembourg (tel: 474-491; fax: 477-688-333).

Banque de Luxembourg SA, 80 Place de la Gare, BP 2221, L-1022 Luxembourg (tel: 499-241; fax: 494-820).

Banque et Caisse d'Epargne de l'Etat, 1 Place de Metz, PO Box 2105, L-2954 Luxembourg (tel: 4015-1; fax: 4015-2099; e-mail: info@bcee.lu).

Banque Générale du Luxembourg, Boulevard JF Kennedy, L-2951 Luxembourg (tel: 47-991, 42-421; fax: 4799-2579).

Banque Internationale à Luxembourg SA BIL), 2 Boulevard Royal, L-2953 Luxembourg (tel: 45-901; fax: 4791-2010).

Banque Nationale de Paris SA, 22-24 Boulevard Royal, L-2952 Luxembourg-Ville (tel: 47-641; fax: 26-480).

Caisse Centrale Raiffeisen SC, 28 Boulevard Royal, BP 111, L-2011 Luxembourg (tel: 462-151).

Fortuna, Société Co-opérative de Credit et d'Epargne, 128-132 Boulevard de la Pétrusse, BP 1203, L-1012 Luxembourg (tel: 488-888).

Kredietbank SA Luxembourgeoise, 43 Boulevard Royal, L-2953 Luxembourg (tel: 47-971; fax: 472-667).

Société Générale Bank and Trust, 11 Avenue Emile Reuter, PO Box 1271, L-2420 Luxembourg (tel: 479-3111; fax: 228-859; e-mail:sgbt.lu@socgen.com).

Société Nationale de Credit et d'Investissement, 7 Rue du St Esprit, BP 1207, L-1012 Luxembourg (tel: 461-9711).

Central bank
Banque Centrale du Luxembourg, 2 Boulevard Royal, L-2983 Luxembourg (tel: 4774-1; fax: 4774-4910; email: info@bcl.lu).

European Central Bank (ECB), Kaiserstrasse 29, D-60311 Frankfurt am Main, Germany (tel: (+49-69) 13-440; fax: (+49-69) 1344-6000; email: info@ecb.int).

Stock exchange
Bourse de Luxembourg (Luxembourg Stock Exchange): www.bourse.lu

Travel information
Luxair, Luxembourg Airport, 2987 Luxembourg (tel: 798-2311; fax: 443-2482e-mail: information@luxair.lu).

Luxembourg Airport, PO Box 635, L-2016 Luxembourg (tel: 2464-1; fax: 2464-2464; e-mail: mail@lux-airport.lu).

Luxembourg City Tourist Office, Place d'Armes, L-1136 Luxembourg (tel: 222-809; fax: 474-818; e-mail: touristinfo@luxembourg-city.lu).

Ministry of tourism
Department of Tourism, 6 Avenue Emile Reuter, L-2937 Luxembourg (tel: 478-4751; fax: 474-011; e-mail: info@mdt.public.lu).

National tourist organisation offices
Office National du Tourisme, Gare Centrale, Box 1001, L-1010 Luxembourg (tel: 4282-821; fax: 4282-8238; e-mail: info@visitluxembourg.lu).

Ministries
Ministère des Affaires Etrangères, du Commerce Extèrieur et de la Coopèration, 5 Rue Notre-Dame, L-2913 Luxembourg (tel: 4781; fax: 461-720).

Ministère de l'Agriculture, de la Viticulture et du Developpement Rural, 1 Rue de la Congrègation, L-2913 Luxembourg (tel: 4781; fax: 464-027).

Ministère de l'Amenagement du Territoire, 18 Montèe de la Pètrusse, L-2946 Luxembourg (tel: 4781; fax: 408-970).

Ministère de la Culture, 20 Montée de la Pétrusse, L-2912 Luxembourg (tel: 4781; fax: 402-427).

Ministère de l'Economie, 19-21 Boulevard Royal, L-2914 Luxembourg (tel: 478-4100; fax: 460-448).

Ministère de l'Education Nationale et de la Formation Professionnelle, 29 rue Aldringen, L-2926 Luxembourg (tel: 4781; fax: 478-5113).

Ministère de l'Education Physique et des Sports, 66 route de Treves, L-2916 Luxembourg (tel: 4781; fax: 434-599).

Ministère de l'Energie, 19 Boulevard Royal, L-2449 Luxembourg (tel: 4781).

Ministère de l'Environnement, 18 Montèe de la Pètrusse, L-2918 Luxembourg (tel: 4781; fax: 400-410).

Ministère de la Famille, 14 Avenue de la Gare, L-2919 Luxembourg (tel: 4781; fax: 478-6570).

Ministère des Finances, 3 rue de la Congregation, L-2931 Luxembourg (tel: 4781; fax: 475-241).

Ministère de la Fonction Publique et de la Réforme Administrative, Plateau du St Esprit, L-2011 Luxembourg (tel: 4781; fax: 478-3122).

Ministère de la Force Publique, Plateau du St Esprit, Bâtiment Vauban, L-2915 Luxembourg (tel: 4781; fax: 462-682).

Ministère de l'Intèrieur, 19 Rue Beaumont, L-2933 Luxembourg (tel: 4781; fax: 418-46).

Ministère de la Jeunesse, 26 Rue Zithe, L-2943 Luxembourg (tel: 4781; fax: 467-454).

Ministère de la Justice, 16 Boulevard Royal, L-2934 Luxembourg (tel: 4781; fax: 227-661).

Ministère du Logement, 6 Avenue Emile Reuter, L-2942 Luxembourg (tel: 4781; fax: 478-4840).

Ministère de la Promotion Féminine, 33 Boulevard Prince Henri, L-2919 Luxembourg (tel: 4781; fax: 41-886).

Ministère de la Santé, 57 et 90 Boulevard de la Pétrusse, L-2320 Luxembourg (tel: 4781; fax: 484-903).

Ministère de la Sécurité Sociale, 26 Rue Zithe, L-2936 Luxembourg (tel: 4781; fax: 478-6328).

Ministère des Transports, 19-21 Boulevard Royal, L-2938 Luxembourg (tel: 4781; fax: 464-315).

Ministère des Travail et de l'Emploi, 26 rue Zithe, L-2939 Luxembourg (tel: 4781; fax: 478-6325).

Ministère des Travaux Publics, 4 Boulevard FD Roosevelt, L-2940 Luxembourg (tel: 4781; fax: 462-709).

Other useful addresses
Bourse de Luxembourg SA (stock exchange), 11 Avenue de la Porte-Neuve, L-2227 Luxembourg (tel: 477-9361; fax: 22-050; internet site: http://www.bourse.lu/).

Board of Economic Development, 19-21 Boulevard Royal, L-2914 Luxembourg (tel:478-4135/4141; fax: 460-448).

Confédération du Commerce Luxembourgeois, 23 Allée Scheffer, L-2520 Luxembourg (tel: 473-125).

Fédération des Industriels Luxembourgeois, 7 Rue Alcide de Gasperi, L-1615 Luxembourg (tel: 435-366; fax: 438-326).

Foires Internationales de Luxembourg, L-2088 Luxembourg (tel: 043-991; fax: 0439-9315).

Groupement des Industries Sidérurgiques Luxembourgeoises (Federation of Iron and Steel Industries in Luxembourg), 3 Rue Goethe, PO Box 1704, L-1637 Luxembourg (tel: 480-001).

Luxembourg Embassy (USA), 2200 Massechusetts Avenue, NW, Washington DC 20008 (tel: (+1-202)-265-4171; fax: (+1-202)-328-8270; e-mail: info@luxembourg-usa.org).

Offshore Company Registration Agents (Luxembourg) SA, PO Box 878, 19 Rue Aldringen, L-1118 Luxembourg (tel: 224-286; fax: 224-287).

Press and Information Service of the Government, 43 Boulevard Roosevelt, L-2450 Luxembourg (tel: 478-224, 478-321; fax: 470-285, 20-090).

Radio Télé-Luxembourg (RTL), Villa Louvigny, L-2850 Luxembourg (tel: 476-6242; fax: 4766-2737).

Service Central de la Statistique et des Etudes Economiques (STATEC), 6 Boulevard Royal, L-2013 Luxembourg (tel: 4781; fax: 464-289; internet site: http://statec.lu/).

Société Européenne des Satellites (SES), Château de Betzdorf, L-6815 Luxembourg (tel: 710-725/1; fax: 725-227; internet site: http://www.astra.lu).

Internet sites
Complete list of banks in Luxembourg: http://www.bank.lu

Government statistics: http://statec.gouvernement.lu

Luxembourg weekly publication (in English): http://www.352.lu

Luxembourg government: http://gouvernement.lu

The Station Network, online information (in English): http://www.station.lu

Web directory: http://Luxembourg.lu/

Macao (China)

KEY FACTS

Official name: Macao Special Administrative Region of China (Macao SAR)

Head of State: President Hu Jintao (in Beijing) (since Mar 2003)

Head of government: Chief Executive Edmund Ho Hau Wah (from 1999; re-elected 2004); Chief Executive elect Chui Sai On (takes office 20 Dec 2009)

Ruling party: An executive committee of technocrats, policymakers and business representatives provide a government cabinet.

Area: 29 square km (Macao peninsula, Taipa and Coloane islands)

Population: 544,000 (2010)*

Capital: Macao City

Official language: Chinese (Mandarin, Beijing dialect *de jure*; Cantonese *de facto*) and Portuguese

Currency: Pataca (Pa) = 100 avos

Exchange rate: Pa8.01 per US$ (Oct 2011); (the pataca is pegged to the Hong Kong dollar at Pa1.03)

GDP per capita: US$50,838 (2010)*

GDP real growth: 26.4.00% (2010)*

GDP: US$27.80 billion (2010)

Labour force: 328,000 (2010)

Unemployment: 2.80% (2010)

Inflation: 2.80% (2010)

Balance of trade: -US$4.96 billion (2009)

* estimated figure

Macao is a small island that typically relies on gambling and tourism for its revenue. The annual, Macao Grand Prix Motorcycle Race, held in November 2011 attracted an average 65,000 spectators but this is small in comparison to the total visitor arrivals for the first half of 2011 of 13,246,656, recording a year-on-year increase of 8.3 per cent. Total gambling revenue for 2011 was US$33.48 billion, providing Macao with one of the region's highest per capita incomes estimated at US$50,838.

The central Chinese government in Beijing has plans to develop the island as more than just an attraction for niche tourism. It will expand manufacturing facilities on the reclaimed land as part of the Pearl River Delta Region of southern China, which includes the cities of Guangzhou, Shenzhen and Zhuhai with a combined population of over 25 million.

Shipping facilities were upgraded following the construction of the Ka Ho port with its container terminal and an oil terminal. A number of enterprises, particularly textile manufacturers, have shifted out of Macao to Zhuhai, but new hi-tech manufacturing such as telecommunications and more sophisticated, capital-intensive processes have tended to remain in Macao.

Risk assessment

Economy	Good
Politics	Good
Regional stability	Good

COUNTRY PROFILE

Historical profile

1513 The first group of Portuguese arrived at the entrance to the Pearl River, the area that is now Macao.

1557 The colony of Macao was founded by the Portuguese with the apparent approval of the Chinese authorities.

1845 After years of Chinese rule, the Portuguese expelled the Chinese and announced Macao a free port. The territory enlarged to include the islands of Taipa and Coloane.

1860 The Portuguese introduced gambling licences to the territory.

1887 Macao's status was recognised by the Treaty of Amity and Commerce, signed between Portugal and China.

1939–45 Macao remained neutral during the Second World War and its economy prospered.

1976 The Portuguese government declared Macao a special territory and granted it a high degree of independence.

1987 The Sino-Portuguese Joint Declaration on the Question of Macao was signed.

1999 China resumed control over the territory. Edmund Ho Hau Wah became the first chief executive, as Macao became a Special Administrative Region (SAR) of China.

2001 The Associação de Novo Macau Democrático (ANMD) (New Democratic Macao Association), won two of the 10 directly elected seats in the legislature.

2002 As part of the move to liberalise the gambling sector, Macao issued three casino licences to private operators. This broke the monopoly of self-made billionaire and the world's most successful casino operator, Stanley Ho Hung San.

2004 Edmund Ho was re-elected chief executive. The American owned and operated Sands Macao Casino opened with more gaming tables than any other single casino in the world.

2005 The Banco Delta Asia had accounts of around US$7 million linked to North Korea frozen by the US, after the bank was branded a 'primary money-laundering concern' as having dealt in counterfeit and illicitly earned money. For almost a year before the suspension over US$49 million were transmitted through the bank on behalf of North Korean Daedong Credit Bank.

2009 A new security law prohibiting acts of treason, secession, sedition and subversion against China's central government was enacted. It also banned foreign political organisations from activities in Macao as well as Macao political organisations from establishing links with overseas bodies. Fernando Chui Sai On was the overwhelming winner of the vote for chief executive with 282 votes out of 296. There were no changes in the distribution of seats in legislative assembly elections (the pro-business block five seats (out of 29), pro-democracy block four, Traditionalists block three and others 17 seats. Construction of a new six-lane bridge linking Hong Kong and Macao to China's

mainland province of Guangdong began, to be completed by 2016; when completed it will be the longest sea-crossing bridge in the world (almost 50kms).
2010 In September Macao denied the Internet site Google permission to gather and photograph street views, while the Macao Office of Personal Data Protection investigated the legitimacy of Google's image collecting activities.
2011 Statistics released on 28 July showed Macao's fiscal surplus as US$4.53 billion in the first half of the year, while its deficit reached US$560 million by June. Merchandise imports in June were US$77.9 million a year-on-year increase of 40 per cent. Exports in June fell year-on-year by 6.3 per cent to US$425 million, of which re-exports declined by 10.4 per cent. Total visitor arrivals for the first half of the year were 13,246,656, recording a year-on-year increase of 8.3 per cent.

Political structure

Constitution

The Basic Law, promulgated by the People's Republic of China (PRC) in 1993, effectively became Macao's Constitution after sovereignty of the former Portuguese Special Territory was handed over to PRC in December 1999. The Basic Law pledges to maintain Macao's economic, social and political distinctiveness for a period of 50 years after the handover to the PRC, under the principle of 'one country, two systems'.
Under the Basic Law, members of the executive and legislature must be permanent Macao residents. Private property, free speech and freedom of conscience are guaranteed.

Form of state

Special Administrative Region (SAR) of the People's Republic of China.

The executive

Under the terms of the Basic Law of Macao SAR (MSAR), executive power is vested in the chief executive, except in foreign affairs and defence, which are the responsibility of the People's Republic of China (PRC) government.
The chief executive, appointed by PRC after local consultation and who must have been a resident for at least 20 years, serves a five-year term, limited to two consecutive terms. An Executive Council of 10, appointed by the chief executive, consists of five MSAR departmental heads, three MSAR legislators and two other representatives.

National legislature

The Assembleia Legislativa da Região Administrativa Especial de Macau (Legislative Assembly to the Macao Special Administrative Region) has 29 members, of which 12 are directly elected, 10 are indirectly elected by business associations and seven are appointed by the chief executive. All serve for a fixed four-year term. Among other responsibilities, the assembly may enact, amend, suspend or repeal laws, review and approve the budget, decide on taxes and review the conduct of the chief executive.
The chief executive has the power to remove members and dissolve the Legislative Council under conditions of political deadlock.

Last elections

20 September 2009 (legislative assembly); 26 July 2009 (chief executive)
Results: Legislative assembly: the pro-business block won 38.58 per cent of the vote (five seats out of 29), pro-democracy block 33.83 per cent (four), Traditionalists block 27.58 per cent (three), others 17 seats.
Chief Executive: Chui Sai On won 282 votes (out of 296) in the Assembly

Next elections

Unknown (parliamentary)

Political parties

There are no formal political parties. However, pro-Chinese associations control a majority of the Assembly's elective seats. A number of civic associations exist. The Associacao de Novo Macao Democratio (ANMD) (New Democratic Macao Association) has a significant presence in the Assembly.

Ruling party

An executive committee of technocrats, policymakers and business representatives provide a government cabinet.

Main opposition party

Associação de Novo Macao Democrático (ANMD) (New Democrat Macao Association); Associação dos Cidadãos Unidos de Macao (ACUM) (United Citizens Association of Macao); União para o Desenvolvimento (UPD) (Union for Development); União Promotora para o Progresso (UNIPRO) (Union for Promoting Progress).

Population

544,000 (2010)*
Last census: 19 August 2006: 502,113
Population density: Over 20,000 inhabitants per square km. Urban population: 99 per cent.
Annual growth rate: 1 per cent (2003)

Ethnic make-up

Approximately 96 per cent of the territory's inhabitants are Chinese (mostly Cantonese from Guangdong province); the remainder are Mavanese (mixed Portuguese and Chinese).

Religions

Chinese Buddhism (45 per cent), Christianity (Roman Catholicism) (15 per cent).

Education

Primary education begins at age six and lasts until age 12. There are three stages of secondary schooling, beginning with junior, lasting for three years, then senior for two years and finally a pre-university one-year course. The first 10 years of education are free of charge.
Teaching may be given in Chinese, English or Portuguese.
Some 25 per cent of Macao's inhabitants attend any of 83 primary schools, 40 secondary schools, nine vocational technical colleges or nine institutes of higher education. The University of Macao has approximately 3,500 students in 80 undergraduate and post-graduate degree subjects.
Literacy rate: 94.3 per cent total, 91.7 per cent female, adult rates (World Bank).

KEY INDICATORS **Macao (China)**

	Unit	2006	2007	2008	2009	2010
Population	m	0.52	0.54	0.45	*0.54	*0.54
Gross domestic product (GDP)	US$bn	14.40	18.70	21.40	21.20	27.80
GDP per capita	US$	30,013	36,357	40,829	39,264	*50,838
GDP real growth	%	17.0	14.4	3.4	1.6	*26.4
Inflation	%	5.2	5.6	8.6	1.1	2.8
Unemployment	%	3.8	3.1	3.0	3.6	–
Exports (fob) (goods)	US$m	2,559.0	2,544.0	2,004.0	962.0	–
Imports (fob) (goods)	US$m	6,496.0	7,348.0	7,228.0	5,921.0	–
Balance of trade	US$m	-3,937.0	-4,804.0	-5,224.0	-4,959.0	–
Current account	US$m	2,735.0	5,625.0	5,755.0	7,828.0	*12,233.0
Total reserves minus gold	US$m	9,132.0	13,230.0	15,930.0	18,350.0	23,726.0
Foreign exchange	US$m	9,132.0	13,230.0	15,930.0	18,350.0	23,726.0
Exchange rate	per US$	8.00	8.03	8.02	7.98	8.00

* estimated figure

Enrolment rate: 84.1 per cent net primary enrolment; 62.3 per cent net secondary enrolment (government statistics, 2005).
Pupils per teacher: 21.2 in primary/secondary schools; 9.3 in higher education.

Health
Macao's population is young, with around 60 per cent between the ages of 15 and 50. Approximately 9 per cent of the government budget is allocated to healthcare.
Life expectancy: 79.3 years (estimate 2003)
Fertility rate/Maternal mortality rate: 1.2 births per per woman (World Bank)
Child (under 5 years) mortality rate (per 1,000): Six per 1,000 live births (World Bank).

Welfare
Unemployment benefits, old age pensions and invalid benefits are administered by the Social Security Fund, which is financed through employer and employee contributions as well as government subsidies.
Public assistance centres are co-ordinated by the Macao Social Welfare Institute in conjunction with the Church and other civilian organisations.

Main cities
Macao City (capital, estimated population 421,662 in 2005).

Languages spoken
Only 1.8 per cent of the population speak Portuguese. English is widely spoken and used in business and tourist circles.
Official language/s
Chinese (Mandarin, Beijing dialect *de jure*; Cantonese *de facto*) and Portuguese

Media
Freedom of the press is guaranteed under the law and the government respects this. China's official Xinhua state news agency operates as the Liaison Offices of the Central People's Government for Macau and regulates broadcasting media.
Press
Dailies: In Portuguese, publications include *Hoje Macau* (www.hojemacau.com), *Jornal Tribuna de Macau* (www.jtm.com.mo) and *Ponto Final*. In Chinese, publications include *Macao Daily News* (www.macaodaily.com), with the highest circulation, the privately owned *Va Kio* (www.vakiodaily.com) and *Jornal Va Kio*, *Ou Mun*, *Si Man*, *Tai Chung Pou* and *Seng Pou*. The *Macau Post Daily* (www.macaupostdaily.com) is the oldest English language newspaper.
Weeklies: There are several magazines catering for all interests.
Business: In English, *Macau Business* (www.macaubusiness.com) is a monthly publication with sections dedicated to specific business interests such as banking, gaming and property. In Chinese *Business Intelligence* (www.bizintelligenceonline.com).
Periodicals: In Portuguese *Revista Macau* (www.revistamacau.com) is a quarterly magazine covering cultural matters. *Inside Asian Gaming* (www.asgam.com) is a monthly publication concerned with industry development.
Broadcasting
Teledifusão de Macau (TDM) (www.tdm.com.mo) is the public broadcaster.
Radio: TDM (www.tdm.com.mo) operates Radio Macau in Cantonese and Portuguese. Radio Villa Verde (www.am738.com) is an independent station.
Overseas radio stations from China and Hong Kong are available.
Television: TDM (www.tdm.com.mo) operates two channels, broadcasting in Cantonese and Portuguese. There are several private TV stations broadcasting, via digital cables or satellite, which provide international programmes, including Macao Cable (www.macaucabletv.com) and Villa Verde Ltd.

Economy
Macao, as determined by its former island status, has an economy heavily dependent on tourism principally based around gambling. While the emphasis on the tourist sector remains at the heart of all future plans for development by the governments of Macao and China, as part of the Pearl River Delta Region of southern China, which includes the cities of Guangzhou, Shenzhen and Zhuhai with a combined population of over 25 million, Macao is looking to diversify its economy. There is potential for greater scope in development into fields of not only existing enterprises such as textile manufacturing (despite lower operating costs in Zhuhai), but particularly in labour-intensive processes. A number of enterprises, particularly textile manufacturers, have shifted to Zhuhai, but new hi-tech manufacturing such as telecommunications and more sophisticated, capital-intensive processes have tended to remain in Macao. Shipping facilities were upgraded following the construction of the Ka Ho port with its container terminal and an oil terminal. Macao has physically grown – by 2.9sq km of reclaimed land in 2006 which was joined with the island of Coloane to become one landmass, thereby increasing Macao's area by 18 per cent. The Cotai Strip is a large development of hotels and casinos, with some of the world's largest casino operators building state-of-the-art gambling facilities. The American owned and operated Sands Macao Casino is the largest casino in the world with more gaming tables than any other single casino. Casino operators must pay 35 per cent of gross revenue, as a special gaming tax, and a premium for their gaming concession. They also pay 1.6 per cent of their gross revenue to the Macao Foundation (a social fund to promote cultural activities). Over 70 per cent of the SAR government's total revenue is garnered from gaming taxes.
Macao offers tax and other incentives for investment in tourism and hotels, the electronics manufacturing industry, fishing industry and property development. It has certain competitive advantages over Hong Kong, for example, wage costs, factory rentals, office space and residential accommodation cost about half – in some cases a third – of Hong Kong equivalents.
Macao's GDP in 2008 had fallen from 14.4 per cent in 2007 to 3.4 per cent in and fell further to 1.6 per cent in 2009 as the two major revenue earners, gambling and tourism, were severely cut. The Beijing government had limited the trips to Macao, the only Chinese territory with legal gambling, by Chinese citizens. There was also a drop in foreign exchange, due to the cut in visitors' discretionary spending as they reacted to the global economic downturn. However, in 2010, when world trade picked up, the economy experienced a resurgence with an estimated GDP growth rate of 26.4 per cent. The inflation rate was 8.7 per cent in 2008, which fell to 1.1 per cent in 2009 as domestic consumption declined, it picked up in 2010 to 2.8 per cent, but remained lower than the average 5.4 per cent of 2006-07.
Data released on 28 July 2011 showed Macao's fiscal surplus as US$4.53 billion in the first half of the year, while its deficit reached US$560 million by June. Merchandise imports in June were US$77.9 million a year-on-year increase of 40 per cent. Exports in June fell year-on-year by 6.3 per cent to US$425 million, of which re-exports declined by 10.4 per cent.

External trade
Under the Closer Economic Partnership Arrangement (CEPA), Macau has a trade alliance with China's nine southernmost provinces and Hong Kong through the pan-Pearl River Delta (PRD) trade bloc.
Imports
Principle imports include raw materials and semi-manufactured goods, foodstuffs, tobacco, capital goods, mineral fuels and oils and alcohol.
Main sources: China (typically 35 per cent of total), Hong Kong (10 per cent), Japan (8 per cent).

Exports
Principal exports include clothing, textiles, footwear, toys, electronics, machinery and parts and textile yarns.
Main destinations: US (typically 40 per cent of total), Hong Kong (20 per cent), China (10 per cent).

Agriculture
The agriculture and fishing sectors typically account for 0.1 per cent of GDP and 0.2 per cent of the workforce.
Soils are generally meagre and there is little agricultural production. Macao imports its food and water requirements, mainly from China.
Fish, prawns and other sea foods are trawled for local consumption and export.

Industry and manufacturing
The textile and garment industries provide the bulk of Macao's exports, although they are subject to limitations such as EU quotas and some producers have been moving to Zhuhai. Other main products include toys, printing and packaging, leather products, electronics and opticals, food and beverages, furniture, woodware and ceramics.

Tourism
Macao has become a premier destination for all lovers of gaming and gambling in the new state of the art casinos that have been built since 2002. It is also home to the Macao Formula Three Grand Prix (held annually in November) and is the only street circuit racing event for both cars (including touring cars) and motorcycles. The historic centre of Macao, with a fusion of Chinese and Portuguese architecture, has been placed on the UN list of World Heritage Sites. The statue of the Buddhist Goddess, Kun Lam, is described as 'dainty but gigantic' it is a carving representing the mother goddess and is an attraction for many practicing Buddhists and other tourists.
Travel and tourism are vital components of GDP, constituting over 80 per cent since 2006, it also provides a similar share of total employment. In 2010, revenue from visitors amounted to US$18 billion, of which almost US$2 billion was spent on business. Total visitor arrivals for the first half of 2011 were 13,246,656, recording an year-on-year increase of 8.3 per cent.

Hydrocarbons
There are no known hydrocarbons reserves. Consumption of oil was 16,000 barrels per day in 2008, all of which was imported.
Any imports of coal are commercially insignificant.

Energy
Total installed generating capacity was 488MW in 2007, producing over 1.59 billion kilowatt hours. The private utility company Companhia de Electricidade de Macao (Cem) (Macao Electricity Company) remains the energy monopoly in Macao, responsible for generating, transmitting, distributing and selling electricity. It operates two thermal power stations on Coloane Island, which meet about 80 per cent of the total requirements; the remainder is imported from neighbouring Zhuhai City in China.

Banking and insurance
Since China took control of Macao in 1999, new banking laws intended to attract more foreign banks and allow a full range of offshore banking services have been enacted to ensure participation in financing the development of southern China. Macao enjoys some of the most liberal financial systems in the world.
Central bank
There is no central bank. The Monetary Authority of Macao (known as Autoridade Monetária e Cambial de Macao until 2000) is the monetary and foreign exchange authority of the territory.
Main financial centre
Macao City

Time
GMT plus eight hours

Geography
Macao comprises the peninsula of Macao and two nearby islands: Taipa, linked to the mainland by a bridge, and Coloane, which is connected to Taipa by a causeway. The territory lies opposite Hong Kong on the western side of the mouth of the Xijiang (Sikiang) river.
Hemisphere
Northern

Climate
Subtropical and monsoonal. Winter (November–April) is cool and dry, with an average temperature of 14–23 degrees Celsius (C). Summer (May–September) is hot, humid and rainy, with an average temperature of 27 degrees C. October and November are somewhat less humid. Average annual rainfall ranges from 1,000–2,000mm; monsoon rains from May–October.

Entry requirements
Passport and visa regulations are liable to change at short notice.
Passports
Valid passport required by all except holders of a Hong Kong Identity Card (HKIC) and nationals of China with a China Identity Card.
Visa
Required by all, except citizens of many European and Asian countries, North America and Australasia, arriving as tourists. Requirements for business visas should be obtained from the nearest Chinese consulate, well in advance of a business visit.
Currency advice/regulations
There are no restrictions on the import and export of local and foreign currencies.
Customs
Personal effects are allowed duty-free.
Macao is a free port and there are no import duties, except on electrical appliances and equipment, which are subject to a 5 per cent *ad valorem* duty. Registration is required for all imports and an import licence for goods subject to consumption tax, such as beverages, coffee, rice, salt, sugar, wheat, matches, tobacco, bricks, cement and mineral oils, gases, vehicles. There are no export duties on articles purchased in Macao.
As inward and outward travel is generally through Hong Kong, export/import regulations of Hong Kong must be observed.

Health (for visitors)
Mandatory precautions
No compulsory vaccinations are required.
Advisable precautions
Vaccinations for diphtheria, tuberculosis, hepatitis A and B, Japanese B encephalitis, polio, tetanus and typhoid. Rabies is a risk.

Hotels
There are around 9,000 hotels rooms. A 10 per cent service charge and 5 per cent tax are added to the bill. It is customary to leave a small tip.

Credit cards
Most major credit cards are widely accepted.

Public holidays (national)
Fixed dates
1 Jan (New Year's Day), 5 Apr (Qing Ming Festival), 1 May (Labour Day), 1 Oct (National Day of China), 2 Nov (All Souls' Day), 8 Dec (Immaculate Conception), 20 Dec (Macao Special Administrative Region Establishment Day), 22 Dec (Winter Solstice), 24–25 Dec (Christmas).
Variable dates
Chinese New Year (Jan/Feb), Easter, Birth of Buddha (Apr/May), Dragon Boat Festival (May/Jun), Mid-Autumn Festival (Sep/Oct), Chung Yeung Festival (Oct).

Working hours
Banking
Mon–Fri: 0930–1600; Sat: 0930–1230.
Business
Mon–Fri: 0900–1300, 1500–1730; Sat: 0900–1230.

Government
Mon–Fri: 0930–1800.
Shops
Mon–Sat: 1000–1900.

Electricity supply
220V AC, 50Hz in new buildings and 110V AC for most domestic supply, with various types of plug fittings.

Weights and measures
Metric system

Social customs/useful tips
It is customary to shake hands on meeting and taking leave.

Getting there
Air
National airline: Air Macau
International airport/s: Macao International (MFM), on Taipa Island, seven km south of the city.
The airport is linked to Macao via a four-lane motorway and to mainland China via a dual-lane highway. Estimated travelling time into central Macao is 10 minutes and 20 minutes to the Chinese border.
Airport tax: Pa90, paid in local currency.
Surface
Road: Macao is connected to mainland China by a short causeway. Two bridges, the Friendship and Lotus, the latter carrying a six-lane highway, link the island of Taipa with the Zhuhai Special Economic Zone.
Water: Most visitors enter via Hong Kong. There are over 100 scheduled sailings both ways during the day, and jetfoils operate round the clock (journey time 55 minutes). It is advisable to book in advance.
Main port/s: Macao harbour.

Getting about
National transport
Buses: Bus services operate 0700–2400, with services between the ferry pier and the city centre and the islands.
Rail: The proposed light rail system will connect all major ports and tourist attractions along the coast of the Macao Peninsula and the new town, Cotai, terminating at Macao International Airport. The light rail system will also connect to the inter-city express railway transport system proposed by mainland China.
City transport
Central Macao is tiny and easily walkable. It is possible to hire two-passenger *triciclos* (pedal rickshaws), although they are unsuitable for climbing the hills. It is advisable to agree the fare before starting the journey.
Taxis: Taxis are inexpensive and readily available. Licensed, metered taxis are mostly painted black with cream-coloured tops. Radio taxis are painted yellow.
Buses, trams & metro: Good local bus services. Transmac AP1 service runs from airport to city centre every 30 minutes, journey time 30 minutes; STCM service 21 runs every 20 minutes, journey time 30 minutes.
Car hire
Car hire is available. Driving is on the left. An international driving permit is required. The minimum driving age is 21.

BUSINESS DIRECTORY

Telephone area codes
The international direct dialling code (IDD) for Macao is +853, followed by subscriber's number.

Useful telephone numbers
Medical emergencies: 999
Police tourist hotline: 112
Fire: 999

Chambers of Commerce
Macao Chamber of Commerce, Edificio ACM, 175 Rua de Xangai, Macao (tel: 576-833; fax: 594-513; e-mail: acm@macauweb.com).

Banking
Banco Comercial de Macau SA, Rua da Praia Grande No 22, PO Box 545, Macao (tel: 569-622; fax: 580-967).

Banco Delta Asia SARL, 79 Avenida Conselheiro Ferreira de Almeida, Macao (tel: 559-898; fax: 570-068).

Banco Weng Hang SARL, 241 Avenida de Almeida Ribeiro, Macao (tel: 335-678; fax: 576-527).

Luso International Banking Ltd, 47 Avenida Dr Mário Soares, Macao (tel: 378-977; fax: 578-517).

Tai Fung Bank Ltd, Tai Fung Bank Headquarters Building, 418 Alameda Dr Carlos d'Assumpção, Macao (tel: 322-323; fax: 570-737).

Central bank
Monetary Authority of Macao, Calçada do Gaio 24-26, Macao City (tel: 568-288; fax: 325-432; e-mail: general@amcm.gov.mo).

Travel information
Administração de Aeropoertos (tel: 711-808; fax: 711-803).

Air Macao (tel: 396-5555; fax: 396-6866).

East Asia Airlines (tel: 790-7040).

Far East Jetfoils (tel: 790-7093).

Flight information (24 hours) (tel: 2886 1111).

Macao International Airport, R Dr Pedro Jose Lobo, 1—3, Edif Luso Internacional, 26 o andar, Macao (tel: 511-213; fax: 338-089; e-mail: aacm@aacm.gov.mo; www.macau-airport.com/en).

Sociedade de Turismo e Diversoes de Macao, 9 Largo do Senado, Macao (tel: 315-566; fax: 510-104).

National tourist organisation offices
Macau Government Tourist Office, PO Box 3006, 9 Edifício Largo do Leal Senado (tel: 375-156, 561-167, 555-424, fax: 510-104; internet: www.macoutourism.gov.mo).

Other useful addresses
Coastal International Exhibition Co Ltd, Room 3808, China Resources Building, 26 Harbour Road, Wanchai, Hong Kong (tel: (+852) 2827-6766; fax: + 852 2827-6870; e-mail: general@coastal.com.hk).

Macao Business Support Centre (tel: 728-212; fax: 727-123, 728-213; e-mail: mbsc@ipim.gov.mo).

Macao Commercial Association (Associacão Comercial de Macão), Edifício ACM, Rua da Xanghai, 5th Floor (tel: 576-833; fax: 594-513).

Macao Export Promotions Department, 1-3 Rua Pedro José Lobo, International Building (tel: 78-221).

Macao Importers and Exporters' Association, Av do Infante D Henrique No 60-62, 30 o andar, Centro Comercial Central, Macao (tel: 553-187, 375-859; fax: 512-174; e-mail: aeim@macau.ctm.net).

Macao Industrial Association, PO Box 70, Travessa da Praia Grande No. 56 (tel: 574-125; fax: 578-305).

Macao Statistics Department, PO Box 3022, Ground Floor, Rua Inácio Baptista, 4D-6, Seaview Garden (tel: 550-935; fax: 307-825; internet: www.dsec.gov.mo).

Macao Trade and Investment Promotion Institute, 1—3 Rua Dr Pedro Jose Lobo (7th/8th Floor) (e-mail: ipim@ipim.gov.mo); Investment Promotion (tel: 340-090, 712-660; fax: 712-659; internet : www.ipim.gov.mo); Trade Promotion: (tel: 378-221, 710-528; fax: 590-309).

Internet sites
Customs formalities: www.customs.gov.mo

Immigration formalities: www.fsm.gov.mo

Macao Environment Council: www.ambiente.gov.mo

Macao government: www.macau.gov.mo

Macao Tower Convention and Entertainment Centre: www.gaming-exhibition.com

Macedonia

Surprisingly few non-Macedonians – other than scholars – are aware of the fact that Alexander the Great was rumoured to be Macedonian. Alexander was the young King of Macedon who, in the eleven years between 334 and 323BC not only reached Persia and conquered the Persian King Darius III, but pressed on to Northern India. Alexander died in Babylon on the way back from this epic trip, aged only 32. No wonder he had gained hero-status in remote Macedonia.

The Greeks, however, think differently. Possibly feeling devoid of heroes in these straightened times, in late 2009 no less than 2,000 Greek academics had signed a letter to President Obama endeavouring to correct Macedonia's claims on Alexander's nationality, counter-claiming that Alexander was 'thoroughly and indisputably Greek'. The dispute over the exact nationality of Alexander looked likely to drag on indefinitely in 2011, but one thing was certain – Macedonia, once a minor part of hybrid Yugoslavia – could stake as legitimate a claim to this particular hero as could Greece.

EU Membership

Macedonia applied for full European Union (EU) membership in March 2004. It was confirmed as a candidate in December 2005 when the European Commission recommended that the EU open membership talks, noting that the former Yugoslav republic had made 'convincing progress' in police reform, tackling corruption and bolstering human rights. Since December 2009 Macedonians have not needed visas to visit EU member states in the Schengen zone. Hopes that Macedonia's accession talks would open in 2008 were setback by election violence and a subsequent boycott of parliament by ethnic Albanian opposition parties.

At the same time, a dispute with Greece over Macedonia's name continued to interfere with the country's bids to join both the EU and North Atlantic Treaty Organisation (NATO). Macedonia was admitted to the United Nations in 1993 using the unwieldy and temporary name of the Former Yugoslav Republic of Macedonia (FYROM). Rather strangely, the UN website lists it under 'T', for 'The', unlike

KEY FACTS

Official name: Republika Makedonija (Former Yugoslav Republic of Macedonia) (FYROM)

Head of State: President Gjorgje Ivanov (VMRO–DPMNE) (from 12 May 2009)

Head of government: Prime Minister Nikola Gruevski (from 2006; re-elected 5 Jun 2011)

Ruling party: Coalition, led by Vnatrešno-Makedonska Revoluciona Organizacija-Demokratska Partija za Makedonsko Nacionalno Edintsvo (VMRO-DPMNE) (Internal Macedonian Revolutionary Organisation-Democratic Party for Macedonian National Unity) (from 2006; re-elected 5 Jun 2011)

Area: 25,713 square km

Population: 2.06 million (2010)

Capital: Skopje

Official language: Macedonian and Albanian.

Currency: Macedonian denar (Md) = 100 deni

Exchange rate: Md45.38 per US$ (Oct 2011); (pegged to the euro; trades around Md60 per euro)

GDP per capita: US$4,431 (2010)

GDP real growth: 0.70% (2010)

GDP: US$9.10 billion (2010)

Labour force: 938,000 (2010)

Unemployment: 32.10% (2010)

Inflation: 1.50% (2010)

Balance of trade: -US$1.95 billion (2010)

The Gambia or The Netherlands – a Greek plot to make it difficult to find, perhaps? Greece argues that the name 'Macedonia' cannot be monopolised by one country and that doing so implies a territorial claim over the northern Greek region of the same name. In a November 2008 interview, Macedonian foreign minister, Antonio Milososki said 'we remain firm on our stance that only the Republic of Greece has a problem with Macedonia's constitutional name.'

The economy

Macedonia's economy strengthened in 2010, but in 2011 faced a worsening external environment that created new risks and barriers to growth. Sound overall macro-economic policies, low public debt and limited cross-border financial linkages should help shield Macedonia from the impact of adverse external conditions. Nonetheless, in the view of the International Monetary Fund (IMF) the authorities should be prepared to respond to slowing growth and heightened risks.

The IMF expected Macedonia's growth to be 3 per cent in 2011, based largely on the strong performance in the first half of the year. Weak growth in trading partners and heightened financial stress in the euro area were expected to affect adversely prospects for growth in 2012. External factors were expected to reduce demand for Macedonia's exports and contribute to tighter domestic financial conditions. The IMF expected growth to be 2 per cent in 2012, with risks veering towards the downside. Inflation was expected to decline to 2 per cent in 2012, as the effects of higher food and commodity prices faded and in response to slowing domestic demand.

The current account deficit was expected to be around 5.5 per cent of gross domestic product (GDP) in 2011 and 6 to 6.5 per cent of gross domestic product (GDP) in 2012. This reflected a slowing of both exports and imports in 2012 in response to weaker growth externally and in Macedonia. Foreign direct investment (FDI) and external borrowing by the government were expected to provide adequate financing, allowing a modest accumulation of international reserves. Over the medium term the current account was expected to stabilise at levels that could largely be financed by FDI.

Macedonia's financial sector indicators continued to suggest sound overall conditions in 2011. The capital adequacy ratio climbed to nearly 17 per cent, with tier one capital at 14 per cent. Non-performing loans rose somewhat in the third quarter of the year, but remained below their post-crisis peak and were fully covered by bank provisions. Profitability was low but positive and profits were being used largely to strengthen capital buffers. Loans continued to be financed predominantly by local deposits, with limited reliance on external financing.

The possibility of an accelerated economic downturn continuing and the intensification of financial stress in the euro-zone pose significant risks for Macedonia. Demand for Macedonian exports would contract sharply and external financing for the public and private sectors, including FDI, could become more scarce. The inflow of private transfers, which continued to be an important source of support to the economy in 2011, could also be affected. In such a scenario, economic growth could fall considerably below forecasts and balance of payments pressures might arise. Several factors could help shield Macedonia from adverse external developments. First, the lack of reliance on external financing for the banking and corporate sectors reduced the likelihood of bank funding pressures or asset sales. Moreover, bank credit has grown moderately, so is less vulnerable to a rapid slowdown than in the run-up to the 2008 crisis. Second, the current account deficit was much lower than in 2008, lessening the scale of adjustment needed in the event of external shocks. Further, a strong pipeline of projects that are planned or already underway should provide a base for FDI in the coming year.

The IMF considered the government's deficit target of 2.5 per cent of GDP in 2012 as appropriate in the light of economic prospects. Over the medium term, it will be important to reduce deficits to preserve debt sustainability and to maintain space to respond to future economic cycles. The expected slowdown in economic growth would translate into a reduction in revenues relative to the 2012 budget assumptions. The IMF welcomed the authorities' intention to respond by reducing expenditure if necessary to achieve the deficit target in the 2012 budget. Compared to other countries in the region and elsewhere, the size of Macedonia's domestic public debt is small, suggesting there is significant room for growth. Moreover, the ample liquidity of the domestic banking system, including significant holdings of Narodna banka na Republika Makedonija (NBRM) (National Bank of the Republic of Macedonia) debt instruments, points to room for increased domestic public debt without crowding out private investment.

The NBRM kept its reference interest rate unchanged at 4 per cent over the course of 2011. International reserves were at broadly adequate levels and there was little evidence of significant pressures in the balance of payments. Inflation was contained and the growth of bank credit and domestic demand has been moderate. Conservative and independent regulation and supervision by the NBRM has contributed to the stability of the banking system.

KEY INDICATORS **Macedonia**

	Unit	2006	2007	2008	2009	2010
Population	m	*2.04	*2.05	*2.05	*2.06	*2.06
Gross domestic product (GDP)	US$bn	6.34	7.90	9.60	9.20	9.10
GDP per capita	US$	3,102	3,874	4,658	4,482	4,431
GDP real growth	%	3.7	5.9	4.9	-0.7	0.7
Inflation	%	3.2	2.3	8.3	-0.8	1.5
Unemployment	%	36.0	34.9	33.8	32.2	32.1
Industrial output	% change	2.8	7.6	6.7	7.5	–
Agricultural output	% change	0.6	-1.5	7.0	6.5	–
Exports (fob) (goods)	US$m	2,396.3	3,391.5	3,970.9	2,685.5	3,295.6
Imports (fob) (goods)	US$m	3,681.5	5,030.0	6,522.7	4,842.3	5,241.0
Balance of trade	US$m	-1,285.2	-1,638.5	-2,551.8	-2,156.9	-1,945.4
Current account	US$m	-23.7	-605.7	-1,252.0	-645.6	-261.8
Total reserves minus gold	US$m	1,750.6	2,082.3	1,920.3	2,050.9	1,970.0
Foreign exchange	US$m	1,747.6	2,080.8	1,918.9	1,959.8	1,968.8
Exchange rate	per US$	47.12	42.43	41.86	44.10	46.48

* estimated figure

The IMF stressed that Macedonia should be prepared for weak growth in its trading partners, with downside risks, in the coming year. A record of sound macro-economic and financial policies and limited imbalances provide important buffers. Nonetheless, the authorities should plan in advance for a slowdown in growth and remain vigilant to heightened risks, says the IMF.

Risk assessment

Economy	Good
Politics	Fair
Regional stability	Fair

COUNTRY PROFILE

Historical profile

1371 The Ottoman Turks conquered the area and retained control until the nineteenth century.
1893 The Vnatrešno-Makedonska Revoluciona Organizacija (VMRO) (Internal Macedonian Revolutionary Organisation) was founded to gain independence from the Ottoman Empire.
1912–13 During the Balkan conflicts, the Turks were driven out and the area was divided between Serbia and Greece, with a small section being retained by Bulgaria.
1918 Macedonia became part of the new Kingdom of Serbs, Croats and Slovenes along with parts of Bosnia-Hercegovina, Croatia, parts of Dalmatia, Montenegro, Serbia, Slavonia and Slovenia.
1929 The Kingdom was renamed Yugoslavia.
1941–45 Macedonia was occupied by Bulgaria, under German direction. The Partisans, led by Josip Broz Tito – also leader of the Communist Party of Yugoslavia (CPY) – eventually liberated the whole of Yugoslavia.
1945 Following the end of the Second World War, Macedonia became one of the constituent republics of a federated Yugoslavia. Tito assumed power and a Soviet-style constitution was adopted. The other republics were Bosnia-Hercegovina, Croatia, Slovenia, Montenegro, Serbia and the two autonomous regions of Vojvodina and Kosovo.
1953 Constitutions adopted in 1953, 1963 and 1974 increased the autonomy extended to the constituent republics.
1990 Following the collapse of communism in Yugoslavia, Macedonia held its first multi-party elections and the VMRO became the largest party in parliament.
1991 The first multi-party National Assembly was officially constituted. After a referendum in which the people voted overwhelmingly in favour of Macedonian sovereignty and independence, Macedonia declared its independence.
1992 Kiro Gligorov, the former communist leader, was elected president. A new currency, the denar, was adopted on 26 April.
1993 Greece showed consternation over Macedonia's choice of name and flag which the Greek government argued were a claim on its northern province of Macedonia. To accommodate Greek concerns, Macedonia eventually agreed to join the UN with the temporary prefix of 'Former Yugoslav Republic (of Macedonia (FYROM))' and an alternative national flag design was introduced.
1994 Kiro Gligorov was re-elected president. Greece imposed a partial trade embargo on Macedonia.
1995 An accord resulting in a normalisation of relations between Greece and Macedonia ensured that Macedonians had access to the northern Greek port of Thessaloniki, their nearest outlet to the sea.
1998 A coalition government under the leadership of Ljubco Georgievski was formed after elections.
1999 Amid accusations of electoral irregularities from the opposition, Boris Trajkovski of the Vnatrešno-Makedonska Revoluciona Organizacija-Demokratska Partija za Makedonsko Nacionalno Edintsvo (VMRO-DPMNE) (Internal Macedonian Revolutionary Organisation-Democratic Party for Macedonian National Unity) was elected president.
2000 A coalition government was formed, led by Prime Minister Georgievski.
2001 Ethnic Albanian guerrillas and police clashed in Tetovo and other parts of Macedonia. A cease-fire was brokered and a NATO force was sent to Macedonia to supervise the collection of arms handed in by ethnic Albanian rebels. The Ohrid Agreement was signed, paving the way for political reforms to enhance the status of the ethnic Albanian population within Macedonia. The government signed a Stabilisation and Association Agreement (SAA) with the EU, aimed at bringing Macedonia into line with EU political, economic and social norms.
2002 After parliamentary elections, the Socijaldemockratski Sojuz na Makedonija (SDSM) (Social Democratic Alliance of Macedonia) leader, Branko Crvenkovski, became prime minister, heading a multi-ethnic, 10-member coalition government.
2003 The EU took over NATO's military mission in Macedonia, overseeing the implementation of the Ohrid Agreement. Macedonia joined the World Trade Organisation (WTO).
2004 President Boris Trajkovski died in a plane crash; Ljupco Jordanovski became acting president. Macedonia formally submitted its application to join the EU. Branko Crvenkovski won the presidential elections. Hari Kostov became prime minister but later resigned following disputes within the ruling coalition; Vlado Buckovski became prime minister.
2005 Local elections were held, the first under redrawn electoral boundaries, as stipulated in the Ohrid Agreement. Despite fears of inter-communal tension, EU observers reported a high turnout and few irregularities. EU member states agreed to grant EU candidate status to Macedonia.
2008 The Skopje airport was renamed Skopje-Aleksandar Makedonski (Alexander of Macedonia, or Alexander the Great) Airport. Greece, unhappy with the exploitation of what it saw as its heritage and cultural iconography, criticised the decision and threatened to block Macedonia's membership of NATO unless it dropped the name. However, NATO believes membership for Macedonia will avert divisions within Macedonia, whereby the Slav majority in the east splits from the Albanian minority in the west. Following months of deadlock concerning the rights of the country's minority Albanian community, parliament was dissolved and early parliamentary elections held. For a Better Macedonia, a coalition (of 19 political parties), led by VMRO-DPMNE won 48.3 per cent of the vote (64 seats out of 120), the Sun–Coalition for Europe (coalition of eight parties), won 23.4 per cent (28 seats); turnout was 58 per cent. Nikola Gruevski (VMRO-DPMNE) remained as prime minister.
2009 Branko Crvenkovski decided not to stand in the presidential election. After two rounds George Ivanov (VMRO-DPNME) won the presidential elections with 63.41 per cent of the vote against Ljubomir Frckoski (SDSM) with 36.56 per cent. In the International Court of Justice (ICJ), Macedonia accused Greece of breaching the 1995 UN-brokered interim accord concerning the use of the name Macedonia, following Greece's blocking of Macedonia's membership of NATO.
2010 By June, 127 UN member countries recognised Macedonia by its constitutional name. However, Greece stubbornly required the UN to officially refer to Macedonia as FYROM until such time as Greece and Macedonia resolved their disagreement. Macedonia signed a protocol in September to jointly found a new company, called Cargo 10, with Serbia, Croatia and Slovenia to incorporate their railway companies.
2011 All opposition parties boycotted parliament on 28 January, accusing the

prime minister of authoritarian rule and curbing media freedom, and called for early elections. President Ivanov convened a meeting on 4 February to resolve the political crisis. On 21 February, the opposition SDSM walked out of parliament, accusing the government of interference in the media. On 30 March, Prime Minister Gruevski finally set a date for new elections. For the first time, three parliamentary seats were established for representatives of expatriate Macedonians (one each for those living in Europe, Americas and Asia), bringing the total number of parliamentary seats in contention to 123. In the elections, held on 5 June, the VMRO-DPMNE ruling coalition won 39.0 per cent of the vote (56 seats out of 123), which was less than the 64 seats won in 2008, and not enough to rule outright. The SDSM won 32.78 per cent which at 42 was a higher number of seats than in 2008 (27), but still not enough for the right to form a coalition government.

Political structure

Constitution

Under the constitution, adopted on 17 November 1991, the Former Yugoslav Republic of Macedonia (FYROM) is a sovereign, independent, democratic and socially responsive state. There is universal suffrage from age 18. The constitution guarantees the free expression of national identity, the rule of law (including international law) and the legal protection of property. The principles of a free commercial market, urban and rural planning and environmental protection are also enshrined in the constitution.

Constitutional amendments to give the ethnic Albanian minority more rights were endorsed by parliament in November 2001.

Form of state

Parliamentary democratic republic

The executive

The executive is headed by the president, directly elected every five years. The prime minister appoints a cabinet of 20 ministers, who must be approved by a majority of the country's national assembly.

National legislature

The unicameral Sobranje (National Assembly) has 120 members elected by proportional representation in multi-seat constituencies (six electoral districts returning 20 delegates each), for four-year terms.

In 2011, for the first time, three parliamentary seats were established for representatives of expatriate Macedonians (one each for those living in Europe, Americas and Asia), bringing the total number of parliamentary seats in contention to 123.

Legal system

Judicial powers are vested in courts which are nominally independent of government under the terms of the 1991 constitution. In practice, the judiciary remains politicised, especially in cases involving ethnic Albanians and other minorities. All civil and criminal cases are dealt with by courts of general jurisdiction. The Supreme Court is the highest court. Elected by parliament, the Judicial Council appoints and dismisses all judges and other judicial officials. The judicial system is the administrative responsibility of the justice ministry. There is a public prosecutor. The Constitutional Court decides on the conformity of national legislation with the 1991 constitution.

Macedonia is aiming to harmonise its laws and judicial standards with those of the EU and the Council of Europe, but progress is slow.

Last elections

22 March / 5 April 2009 (presidential and runoff); 5 June 2011 (parliamentary).

Results: Presidential: (first round) Gjorgje Ivanov (VMRO–DPMNE) won 33.95 per cent, Ljubomir Frckoski (Socijaldemokratski sojuz na Makedonija) (SDSM) (Social Democratic Union of Macedonia) 19.81 per cent, Imer Selmani (Demokracia E Re) (New Democracy) 14.51 per cent, Ljube Boškoski (Independent) 14.4 per cent. Four other candidates each won less than 10 per cent. (Runoff): Ivanov 63.41 per cent of the vote; Frckoski 36.56 per cent. Turnout was 42 per cent.

Parliamentary: Vnatrešno-Makedonska Revoluciona Organizacija-Demokratska Partija za Makedonsko Nacionalno Edintsvo (VMRO-DPMNE) (Internal Macedonian Revolutionary Organisation-Democratic Party for Macedonian National Unity) won 39 per cent of the vote (56 seats out of 123), Socijaldemockratski Sojuz na Makedonija (SDSM) (Social Democratic Alliance of Macedonia) 32.8 per cent (42), Bashkimi Demokratik për Integrim (BDI) (Democratic Union for Integration) 10.2 per cent (15), Partia Demokratike Shqiptare (PDS) (Democratic Party of Albania) 5.9 per cent (8); turnout was 63.5 per cent.

Expatriate Macedonians living in Europe, the US and Australia each elected one candidate as their Member of Parliament (MP).

Next elections

2014 (presidential); June 2015 (parliamentary)

Political parties

Ruling party

Coalition, led by Vnatrešno-Makedonska Revoluciona Organizacija-Demokratska Partija za Makedonsko Nacionalno Edintsvo (VMRO-DPMNE) (Internal Macedonian Revolutionary Organisation-Democratic Party for Macedonian National Unity) (from 2006; re-elected 5 Jun 2011)

Main opposition party

Socijaldemokratski sojuz na Makedonija (SDSM) (Social Democratic Union of Macedonia)

Population

2.06 million (2010)

Last census: November 2002: 2,022,547

Population density: 79 inhabitants per square km. Urban population: 62 per cent of total (1994–2000).

Annual growth rate: 0.4 per cent 1994–2004 (WHO 2006)

Internally Displaced Persons (IDP)

3,000 (UNHCR 2004)

Ethnic make-up

Macedonian (63 per cent), Albanian (30 per cent), Turkish (4 per cent), Romanian (3 per cent). The Albanians are concentrated in Tetovo, Gostivar and other parts of the north-west.

Religions

The official religion is Macedonian Orthodox Christianity, which is practised by approximately two-thirds of the population. Muslims (over a quarter of the population) and Roman Catholics practise openly.

Education

The educational system is entirely state-controlled. During the 1990s, independence from Yugoslavia meant an end to federal subsidies, resulting in declining educational provision in Macedonia. Politically, the issue of ethnic Albanian access to higher education in the Albanian language has been the cause of great controversy and even violence in Macedonia.

Primary schooling lasts for eight years and is followed by attendance at either a general secondary school for academic students or at a variety of technical, specialist or vocational schools. After four years, in whichever mode of school, students must undertake examination before advancement to the second, three-year stage. Courses may last until students are aged 19.

There are three universities in Macedonia: Skopje, Bitola and Tetovo. The Albanian-language University at Tetovo is legalised and classified by parliament as an accredited private institution.

Compulsory years: Seven to 15.

Enrolment rate: 99 per cent total primary enrolment of relevant age group (including repetition rates); 63 per cent total secondary enrolment (World Bank).

Health

The standard of state healthcare is low compared to the rest of the former Yugoslavia, the basic healthcare infrastructure has declined mainly due to the lack of funds to replace essential equipment and retain doctors in the state sector.
Healthcare provision has increasingly involved extra charges, notably for medication, leading to a large black market in healthcare services. Most healthcare professionals are either in semi-private or private practice and some parts of the healthcare system have been privatised.
Externally, Macedonia received considerable international aid for local healthcare during the 1990s.
Improved water sources and sanitation facilities are available to 99 per cent of the population.

HIV/Aids

HIV prevalence: 0.1 per cent aged 15–49 in 2003 (World Bank)
Life expectancy: 72 years, 2004 (WHO 2006)
Fertility rate/Maternal mortality rate: 1.5 births per woman, 2004 (WHO 2006); maternal mortality three per 100,000 live births (World Bank).
Child (under 5 years) mortality rate (per 1,000): 10 per 1,000 live births; and 5.9 per cent of children aged under five are malnourished (World Bank).
Head of population per physician: 2.19 physicians per 1,000 people, 2001 (WHO 2006)

Welfare

Welfare provision was heavily subsidised by budgetary transfers from outside Macedonia during the Yugoslav period, when retirement pensions and other welfare benefits were relatively generous at around 80 per cent of average monthly income. Consequently, the state pension fund experienced major financial problems after independence. Welfare benefits declined sharply, aggravated by spells of high inflation. The IMF and other official creditors have made loans available in recent years for the state pension fund and unemployment benefit outlays. The foreign exchange remittances of emigrants plays a major role in the economic support of many Macedonians.

Main cities

Skopje (capital, estimated population 460,239 in 2005), Bitola (70,423), Kumanovo (80,173), Prilep (68,472), Tetovo (51,258).

Languages spoken

Macedonian (Slavic) is written using the Cyrillic alphabet.
The Albanian minority campaigned successfully to have its language officially recognised as the country's second language. Turkish, Serbian, Croatian and Romani are also spoken.
English, French and German are often understood.

Official language/s

Macedonian and Albanian.

Media

The constitution guarantees freedom of the press and access to information, there are laws that back up these rights although specific regulation concerning media can be loosely implemented, including the non-transparency of media ownership.

Press

The newspaper market is dominated by three major media groups; the German Westdeutsche Allgemeine Zeitung (WAZ), A1-Vreme and Vecer-Sitel-Cetis.
Dailies: In Macedonian, the most widely read newspapers are *Utrinski Vesnik* (www.utrinski.com.mk), *Dnevnik* (www.dnevnik.com.mk), *Vest* (www.vest.com.mk), other publications include *Vreme* (www.vreme.com.mk), *Nova Makedonija* (www.novamakedonija.com.mk), and the state-subsidised *Vecer* (www.vecer.com.mk) which is a tabloid.
Weeklies: In Macedonian, general interest publications include *Forum* (www.forum.com.mk) and *Makedonsko Sonce* (www.makedonskosonce.com), *Aktuel Start* and *Focus*.
Business: In Macedonian, *Kapital* (www.kapital.com.mk) is an economic weekly magazine.

Broadcasting

The national, public broadcaster is Makedonska Radiotelevizija (MRT) (www.mrt.com.mk).
Radio: MRT (www.mrt.com.mk) operates three stations providing programmes in Macedonian, eight foreign languages of the region and English. There are many licensed and unlicensed local radio stations in a market that is highly fragmented. Private, commercial stations include City FM (www.cityradio.com.mk), Radio Antenna 5 (www.antenna5.com.mk) and Radio Vati (www.vati.com.mk).
Television: MRT (www.mrt.com.mk) operates three stations providing national coverage. Although two channels provide programmes for the majority Macedonian population the last channel broadcasts in local, ethnic languages. Alsat-M (www.alsat-m.tv) provides programmes for the large minority Albanian population. Sitel (www.sitel.com.mk) is the leading commercial channel, followed by A1 (www.a1.com.mk) and Kanal 5 (www.kanal5.com.mk). English language programmes provided by cable and satellite broadcasters are becoming increasingly popular.

News agencies

National news agency: MIA (Macedonian Information Agency

Economy

Macedonia's economy is small with gross domestic production (GDP) of over US$9 billion per annum (2008–10). It had a GDP growth rate of 6.2 per cent in 2007 which fell to 5 per cent in 2008 as the global economic crisis struck and it was affected by falling exports and higher priced imports. GDP growth in 2009 had fallen into recession of -0.9 per cent; however, it rose in 2010 as global trade picked up achieving 1.8 per cent.
The structure of the economy in 2009 was 52.3 per cent services sector, 36.3 per cent industrial sector in iron and steel as well as manufacturing in clothing, footwear and 11.3 per cent agriculture, particularly tobacco for export. Structural reforms to Macedonia's industrial sector have increased production and prosperity.
Unemployment has been a long-term problem with rates of over 30 per cent for all of the last half of 2000s and the prospects for the medium-term does not indicate any improvement. However, many work in the grey economy, which is estimated to be 20 per cent of GDP, with production consequently lost to the official economy. The lack of employment opportunities has also encouraged many skilled workers to seek work abroad. Remittances in 2009 were US$401 million (4.5 per cent of GDP), rising to an estimated US$414 million in 2010.

External trade

Macedonia has signed a Stabilisation and Association Agreement with the EU and has duty free access to EU markets. It is expected to become a full EU member by 2010. It belongs to the World Trade Organisation and has free trade agreements with Turkey and Ukraine as well as membership in the Central European Free Trade Agreement (Cerfta).
Macedonia is set to earn annual transit fees from the new 895km Balkan oil pipeline (AMBO), from Burgas, on the Black Sea (Bulgaria) to the port of Vlore, in southern Albania. The trilateral agreement contract was signed in 2007; the project is estimated to cost is US$1.2 billion and has a supply target of 750,000 barrels per day. It will allow Caspian oil to by-pass Turkey's increasingly congested Bosporus and Dardanelles shipping lanes.

Imports

Principal imports are hydrocarbons, machinery iron, steel and chemicals, foodstuffs and vehicles.

Main sources: Germany (typically 13 per cent of total), Greece (12 per cent), Bulgaria 10 per cent).

Exports

Principal exports are clothing and footwear, tobacco, food and beverages, machinery and equipment, iron and steel and chemicals.

Main destinations: Serbia and Montenegro (typically 20 per cent of total), Germany (15.0 per cent), Greece (12 per cent).

Agriculture

Farming

The agricultural sector accounts for 13 per cent of GDP and employs 30 per cent of the workforce.

Agricultural land totals 1.3 million hectares (ha), of which approximately half is cultivable and half is pasture. Macedonia has propitious conditions for agriculture and is nearly self-sufficient in food production. The private sector accounts for over 75 per cent of agricultural production.

The government has allowed a systematic break-up of the old *agrokombinats*, or collectivised farms. As a result, privately owned farms now account for 90 per cent of annual output, although each farm is rarely more than 25ha. New private company formation in agriculture is also growing rapidly.

On the negative side, the state still directly controls 30 per cent of all arable land, or around 300,000ha. Markedly less productive than the private sector, state farms and co-operatives are scheduled to be privatised in due course, although this remains politically controversial. Local agriculture is one of the few sectors of interest to potential foreign investors due to the cultivation of higher value cash crops (particularly tobacco) with ready markets in the EU, and cheap labour costs. Economically, the government now regards agriculture as a major area for future growth and development, including increased foreign direct investment (FDI).

Macedonia has a small fishing industry, which catches freshwater fish for domestic consumption.

Forestry

Forest and other wooded land account for about two-fifths of the land area, equivalent to approximately 906,000ha. More than four-fifths of the forest is available for wood supply. Forest resources supply an active forestry industry producing approximately 774,000 cubic metres (cum) of timber per annum.

Forest wood is mainly used for fuel, while hardwood processed in local sawmills is largely exported. Domestic demand for softwoods and paper is met by imports.

Industry and manufacturing

Industry and manufacturing account for nearly 35 per cent of GDP. Macedonia retains a relatively industrialised economy inherited from the Yugoslav period. During the 1990s, the collapse of the Yugoslav market and subsequent regional conflict, the loss of former Soviet markets, the Greek economic blockade and resultant energy shortages all had devastating consequences for Macedonian industrial output.

Although privatisation of smaller industries has been largely completed, sell-offs of larger industries are still at an early stage. State industries suffer from overstaffing, slow growth, a slow rate of change in the structure of production and ailing technology.

Tourism

Macedonia's nascent tourist industry is primarily based at the lakeside town of Ohrid. Summer tourism is concentrated around the lakes and the national parks. Lakes Ohrid, Prespa, Dojran and Mavrovo cover a total water surface of 679 square km.

Winter tourism is developing in several ski resorts; there are 14 mountain massifs with peaks over 2,000 metres and perpetual Alpine climatic conditions. Both summer and winter tourism offer good potential for development.

Interesting archaeological sites exist, as well as numerous mosaics, frescoes and icons, the earliest dating from Roman times, in monasteries, churches and mosques. The old part of Ohrid town is a UN Educational, Scientific and Cutural Organisation (Unesco)-protected World Heritage Site, as is the lake itself.

Environment

The Vardar, Macedonia's main river, collects the waste from several towns with no treatment facilities before flowing through Greece to the Aegean Sea. A system for monitoring the waterways and a project for communal water treatment for six towns have been initiated by the Macedonian government.

Macedonia and Albania participate in the Lake Ohrid Conservation Project (LOCP) which is a bilateral project supported by the World Bank.

Mining

Macedonia is an important producer of metals and mines significant quantities of copper and lead-zinc ores, ferroalloys and some silver. There is also some chromium production from reserves that overlap with those of nearby Albania. The aluminium and copper ore production is centred on Alumina AD in Skopje and 'Bucim' Radovis DM in Radovis respectively. There is also significant quarrying of decorative and architectural building stone.

The mining sector in Macedonia has had little chance for growth due to regional instability and depressed market conditions. The various conflicts in the former Yugoslavia have created a regional dislocation of transportation of cargoes on the Danube river, shifting the route of exports through the port of Thessaloniki in Greece at a huge cost. This financial burden has diminished Macedonia's production of hot and cold rolled steel to about 30 per cent of capacity, and the export of finished products by Balkan Steel International (BSI).

However, it was not regional dislocation that affected some companies that have traditionally exported through Greece. Their production fell or ceased due to shortage of foreign investment and adverse market conditions. Foreign investment and participation has been restricted to the steel industry (Duferco and BSI), petroleum refining (Hellenic Petroleum) and cement (Titan Cement and Holderbank Financiere Glaris).

Hydrocarbons

There are no commercial oil or gas reserves although exploration is ongoing. Consumption of oil in 2008 was 21,000 barrels per day (bpd) and consumption of natural gas was 113.2 million cubic metres (cum) all of which was imported. There is one oil refinery, located outside Skopje, with production of 50,000bpd.

Although Macedonia signed a US$1.8 billion agreement with Bulgaria and Albania in 2004 to construct a trans-Balkans oil pipeline, it was not until 2007 that an agreement to begin construction in 2008 had been signed. Even so in 2009 planning work was still ongoing. The 984km pipeline will connect the Black Sea with the Adriatic, via the Bulgarian port of Burgas and the Albanian port of Vlores, and will transport Russian and Caspian oil that would otherwise have to be shipped through the Bosphorus.

Plans to use natural gas as a main source of energy include reconstruction of the existing Skopje-Oblic (Pristina) gas pipeline. Macedonia also has a gas pipeline of 100km from Deve Bair to Skopje with a connection to the international gas pipeline in Bulgaria. This pipeline transfers over 800 million cum per annum as part of a wider Russian gas export pipeline network in the Balkan region that supplies Greece with natural gas.

Macedonia has large reserves of coal, estimated at more than one billion tonnes, with an annual production rate of 8.9 million tonnes. Most output is low-grade coal used extensively in domestic energy production. Higher quality anthracite coals and coke (approximately 130,000 tonnes per annum) have

Energy
Total installed generating capacity was 1,550MW in 2008 producing 6.67 billion kilowatt hours. In 2009, 70 per cent of energy needs were met by domestic production, with hydropower supplying most; 30 per cent of annual electricity need is imported. The Austrian EVN company bought 90 per cent of the formerly state-owned Elektrostopanstvo na Makedonija (ESM) in 2006.
There are six hydroelectric dams, the latest power station, at Cebren, has a total capacity of 255WM, whereas all but the Vrutok power plant, with a capacity of 245MW, are older and have capacities of no greater than 92MW. Thermal power stations are typically old and due for upgrading or decommissioning.
A number of new hydroelectric power plants are being built and plans are being considered by the government to modernise some of Macedonia's older power plants.

Financial markets
Stock exchange
Makedonska Berza (Macedonia Stock Exchange) (MSE)

Banking and insurance
There are seven major public lending and savings banks in Macedonia, as well as several smaller private commercial credit banks. The sector is dominated by Stopanska Banka, which has approximately 65 per cent of domestic banking assets and 50 per cent of banking deposits.
The republic has a tiered banking structure. The Narodna banka na Republika Makedonija (NBRM) (National Bank of the Republic of Macedonia) is responsible for the money supply, the liquidity of financial institutions and foreign currency transactions and reserves. The banking system requires a major overhaul. Competition is being introduced with the emergence of private credit institutions such as Uniprokom. International institutions are providing loans.
Central bank
Narodna banka na Republika Makedonija (NBRM) (National Bank of the Republic of Macedonia)

Time
GMT plus one hour (daylight saving, late March to late September, GMT plus two hours)

Geography
Situated in south-eastern Europe on the Balkan peninsula, Macedonia, or Vardar Macedonia, is part of a wider historical and geographical region of the same name. Part of this ancient territory, known as Pirin Macedonia, is situated in modern-day Greece. Roughly rectangular in shape, Macedonia is bordered by Serbia to the north (Kosovo province to the north-west and Serbia to the north-east), Albania to the west, Bulgaria to the east and Greece to the south. Geographically, the republic is dominated by the Balkan Mountains and the Vardar River, which flows north-west to south-east.
Macedonia's strategic importance is out of all proportion to its small size, population and economic resources. On the negative side, its small size and lack of direct access to the sea makes Macedonia very vulnerable to its stronger neighbours in the southern Balkans.
Macedonia's major geographic characteristics are two large inland lakes, Ohrid and Prespa, which are shared with Albania and Greece. Lake Ohrid is a Unesco-designated World Heritage Site.
Hemisphere
Northern

Climate
The river valleys of Vardar and Strumica are temperate Mediterranean, as is the eastern region. Western and northern regions are temperate continental. However, temperatures may vary from 40 degrees Celsius (C) in the summer to minus 30 degrees C in the winter. Rainfall averages 742 millimetres annually, but around 450 millimetres in Skopje which has about 100 days of rain annually. Skopje can be very hot in the summer and shrouded in mist in the winter.

Dress codes
Informal dress is tolerated in Macedonia, but should be avoided in business contexts, notably in Skopje.

Entry requirements
Passports
Required by all, with three months validity beyond date of stay.
Visa
Required by all, except nationals of EU/EEA and most CIS countries, US, New Zealand, Japan, Malaysia, Israel, Botswana, Argentina, Cuba and Barbados. Visitors should contact the nearest consulate to confirm their visa status and requirements before travelling.
Business visas require a letter of invitation from a local company, submitted with the application.
Prohibited entry
Currency advice/regulations
There are no restrictions on the import and export of local or foreign currency.

Health (for visitors)
Medical care in private facilities or by private practitioners is not covered by insurance. Foreigners are entitled to medical care in state medical facilities and those staying for a year or more have a right to full medical coverage. Temporary visitors and those in transit are entitled to basic necessities and emergency first-aid treatment, but payment in cash is expected, regardless of insurance cover.
Mandatory precautions
None
Advisable precautions
Vaccinations are recommended for hepatitis A and, if expecting to eat or drink outside main hotels and restaurants, typhoid. Food and water precautions should be observed. Public health is poor in certain parts of Macedonia.

Hotels
There are around 90 hotels in Macedonia. There is one first-class hotel, in Skopje.

Public holidays (national)
Fixed dates
1–2 Jan (New Year), 6-7 Jan (Orthodox Christmas), 14 Jan (Orthodox New Year's Day), 8 Mar (Women's Day), 1 May (Labour Day), 24 May (SS Cyrilus and Methodius Day), 2 Aug (Ilinden Day), 8 Sep (Independence Day), 11 Oct (National Day).
Variable dates
Orthodox Easter Monday, Eid al Adha, Eid al Fitr.

Working hours
Banking
Mon–Fri: 0730–1930; Sat: 0800–1300.
Business
Mon–Fri: 0800–1600 or 0830–1630.
Government
Mon–Fri: 0700–1500 or 0730–1530.
Shops
Mon–Fri: 0800–1200 and 1700–2000/2100, but many shops open throughout day; Sat: 0800–1500.

Telecommunications
Mobile/cell phones
GSM 900 roaming facilities are available with coverage throughout the country. Services are provided by Cosmofon and MobiMak.

Electricity supply
220V AC 50Hz with two large round prongs.

Weights and measures
Metric system.

Social customs/useful tips
Macedonians are a friendly people, although less gregarious then their Serbian neighbours in the Balkans. Similar to the Bulgarians, they are also practically minded.
Political discussions of any sort are best avoided altogether by foreigners. There are strict laws against drinking and

driving, speeding and other traffic offences. They are rigorously enforced.

Security
Car theft is very common. Local ownership of firearms is high. Visitors are advised to keep themselves informed of political developments.

Getting there
Air
National airline: Makedonski Aviotransport (MAT) (Macedonian Airlines)
International airport/s: Skopje (SKP), 25km from city, post office, restaurants, duty-free shop; Ohrid (OHD, 10km from city.
Air traffic control systems are not up to European standards and the airports are by-passed by many international carriers and used primarily by regional airlines.
Airport tax: None.
Surface
Road: Bus services operate along the main routes connecting Albania, Bulgaria, Greece and Serbia.
Rail: Several international railway lines pass through Skopje, including the Ljuljan-Athens and Budapest-Athens services. Intercity trains provide connections between Skopje and Belgrade (Serbia) and Thessaloniki (Greece).

Getting about
National transport
Air: There are no regular scheduled flights, although occasional flights between Ohrid and Skopje are available.
Road: There are 4,876km of modernised roads. The main road is between Ohrid and Tetovo.
Rail: There are 922km of railway lines, of which 231km are electrified. The main terminals are at Skopje, Bitola and Gevgelija on the Greek border, Kicevo in the west of the country and Kriva Palanka on the Bulgarian border.
City transport
Taxis: Good service operating in all main cities. Licensed taxis are metered, but the fare should be agreed before the journey. A 10 per cent tip is usual. Unmarked taxis should be avoided.
Buses, trams & metro: Most city centres are served by trams, and the suburbs by buses. The service is generally cheap and regular.
Car hire
Limited availability in Skopje, but very expensive. Special insurance is required for travel to certain parts of the country. An international driving licence is required. Hired cars generally have to be paid for in foreign exchange.

BUSINESS DIRECTORY

The addresses listed below are a selection only. While World of Information makes every endeavour to check these addresses, we cannot guarantee that changes have not been made, especially to telephone numbers and area codes. We would welcome any corrections.

Telephone area codes
The international direct diallng code (IDD) for Macedonia is +389 followed by the area code and subscriber's number:

Gostivar	42	Prilep	48
Kicevo	45	Skopje	2
Kochani	33	Tetovo	44
Kumanovo	31	Veles	43

Useful telephone numbers
Police: 92
Fire: 93
Ambulance: 94
Time: 95
Telegrams: 96
Telephone service: 977
Report emergencies: 985
Emergency road service: 987
Telephone information: 988

Chambers of Commerce
American Chamber of Commerce in Macedonia, 13 Juli Street 20, 1000 Skopje (tel: 3123-873; fax: 3123-872; e-mail: contact@amcham.com.mk).

Economic Chamber of Macedonia, Dimitrie Cupovski Street 13, PO Box 324, 1000 Skopje (tel: 3118-088; fax: 3116-210; e-mail: ic@ic.mchamber.org.mk).

Skopje Regional Chamber, Partizanski Odredi Boulevard 2, PO Box 509, 1000 Skopje (tel: 3112-511; fax: 3116-419; e-mail: regkomsk@regkom.org.mk).

Banking
Balkanska Banka, 6 Maksim Gorki, Skopje (tel: 3127-155; fax: 3132-186).

Eksport Import Banka, Dame Gruev 14, PO Box 836, Skopje (tel: 3133-411; fax: 3112-744; e-mail: info@eximpb.com.mk).

Invest Banka , Makedonija 9/11, Skopje (tel: 3114-166; fax: 3135-528).

Izvozna i Kreditna Banka, 11 Oktomvri 8, Skopje (tel: 3122-207; fax: 3122-393).

Komercijalna Banka, Kej Dimitar Vlahov 4, PO Box 563, Skopje (tel: 3112-077; fax: 3111-780; e-mail: international@kb.com.mk).

Kreditna Banka Skopje, Dame Gruev, Skopje (tel: 3116-433; fax: 3116-830).

Makedonska Banka, Bul. VMRO 3-12/2, Skopje (tel: 3117-111; fax: 3117-191; e-mail: info@makbanka.com.mk).

Radobank, Jurij Gagarin 17, Skopje (tel: 3393-300; fax: 3380-453; e-mail: radobank@radobank.com.mk).

Sileks Banka, Gradski Zid, Blok 9, Lokal 5, Skopje (tel: 3115-288; fax: 3114-891).

Stopanska Banka, 11 Oktomvri 7, Skopje (tel: 3191-191; fax: 3114-503; e-mail: sbank@stb.com.mk).

Teteks Bank, Naroden Front 19a, Skopje (tel: 3127-449; fax: 3131-419).

Tutunska Banka, 12 Udarna brigada bb, PO Box 702, Skopje (tel: 3105-600; fax: 3164-068; e-mail: tbanka@tb.com.mk).

Zemjodelska Banka, Vasil Glavinov 28/2, Skopje (tel: 3112-699; fax: 3224-844).

Central bank
National Bank of the Republic of Macedonia, PO Box 401, Kompleks banki bb, 1000 Skopje (tel: 3108-108; fax: 3108-357; e-mail: governorsoffice@nbrm.gov.mk).

Stock exchange
Makedonska Berza (Macedonia Stock Exchange) (MSE): www.mse.com.mk

Travel information
Macedonian Airlines (MAT), Vasil Glavinov 3, Skopje (tel: 3292-333; fax: 3229-576; e-mail: mathq@mat.com.mk).

Ohrid Airport, PO Box 134, Ohrid (tel: 252-820; fax: 252-840; e-mail: ohdap@airports.com.mk).

Skopje Airport, Skopje (tel: 148-300; fax: 148-360; e-mail: skpap@airports.com.mk).

Tourist Association of Skopje, Dame Gruev Gradski, Blok 3, PO Box 399, Skopje (tel: 3118-498; fax: 3230-803; e-mail: info@skopjetourism.org).

Ministries
Ministry of Agriculture, Forestry and Water, Leninova 2, Skopje (tel: 3134-477; fax: 3211-997).

Ministry of Culture, Bul. Ilinden bb, Skopje (tel: 3118-022; fax: 3127-112).

Ministry of Defence, Orce Nikolov bb, Skopje (tel: 3119-872; fax:3 221-808; e-mail: info@morm.gov.mk).

Ministry of Economy, Bote Bocevski bb, Skopje (tel: 3113-705; fax: 3111-541; e-mail: ms@mt.net.mk).

Ministry of Education and Science, Dimitrija Chupovski 9, Skopje (tel: 3117-277; fax: 3118-414; e-mail: contact@mofk.gov.mk).

Ministry of Environment and Urban Planning, Drezdenska 52, Skopje (tel: 3366-930; fax: 3366-931; e-mail: info@moe.gov.mk).

Ministry of Finance, Dame Gruev 14, Skopje (tel: 3117-288; fax: 3117-280).

Ministry of Foreign Affairs, Dame Gruev 6, Skopje (tel: 3110-330; fax: 3115-790; e-mail: mailmnr@mnr.gov.mk).

Ministry of Health, Vodnjanska bb, Skopje (tel: 3147-147; fax: 3113-014).

Ministry of Internal Affairs, Dimce Mircev bb, Skopje (tel: 3117-222; fax: 3112-468).

Ministry of Justice, Dimitrija Chupovski 9, Skopje (tel: 3117-277; fax: 3226-975).

Ministry of Labour and Social Policy, Dame Gruev 14, Skopje (tel: 3117-288; fax: 3118-242).

Ministry of Local Self-Government, Dimitrija Chupovski 9, Skopje (tel: 3117-288; fax: 3211-764)

Ministry of Transport and Communications, Crvena Skopska Opstina 4, Skopje (tel: 3128-200; fax: 3118-144).

Prime Minister's Office, Bul. Ilinden bb, Skopje (tel: 3115-389; fax: 3113-512).

Other useful addresses

Bank Rehabilitation Agency, Kompleks banki bb, Skopje (tel: 3126-323; fax: 3121-250).

British Embassy, Dimitrija Chupovski 26, 4th Floor, Skopje (tel: 3116-772; fax: 3117-005; e-mail: beskopje@mt.net.mk).

Customs Administration, Lazar Licenovski 13, Skopje (tel: 3224-467; fax: 3237-832).

Fund for National and Regional Roads, Dame Gruev 14, Skopje (tel: 3118-044; fax: 3220-535; e-mail: tanjam@.mpt.net.mk).

Macedonia Telecommunications, Orce Nikolov bb, Skopje (tel: 3141-000; fax: 3120-244).

Macedonian Embassy (USA), 3050 K Street, NW, Washington DC 20007 (tel: (+1-202)-337-3063; fax: (+1-202)-337-3093; e-mail: rmacedonia@aol.com).

Macedonian Stock Exchange, Mito Hadzivasilev 20, Skopje (tel: 3122-055; fax: 3122-069; e-mail: mse@unet.com.mk).

Privatisation Agency of the Republic of Macedonia, PO Box 410, Nikola Vapcarov 7, Skopje (tel: 3117-564; fax: 3126-022; e-mail: agency@mpa.org.mk).

Skopje Fair, Belasica bb, PO Box 356, Skopje (tel: 3118-288; fax: 3117-375; e-mail: skfair@mt.net.mk).

Skopje Free Economic Zone, Salvador Allende 73, Skopje (tel: 3176-170; fax: 3177-101; e-mail: sfez@mol.com.mk).

US Embassy, Bul. Ilinden bb, Skopje (tel: 3116-180; fax: 3117-103).

National news agency: MIA (Macedonian Information Agency, PO Box 4; Bojmija K-2, 1000 Skopje (tel: 246-1600; fax: 246-4048; email: mia@mia.mk; internet: www.mia.mk).

Other news agencies: Makfax: www.makfax.com.mk

Internet sites

Privatisation Agency of the Republic of Macedonia: http://www.mpa.org.mk

Economic Chamber of Macedonia: http://www.mchamber.org.mk

Government of FRY Macedonia: http://www.gov.mk/english

Agency of Information: http://www.sinf.gov.mk/defaulten.htm

National Bank of the Republic of Macedonia: http://www.nbrm.gov.mk

Macedonian Stock Exchange: http://www.mse.org.mk

Republic of Macedonia News Collection: http://b-info.com/places/Macedonia/republic/news/

Madagascar

KEY FACTS

Official name: Repoblikan'i Madagasikara (Republic of Madagascar)

Head of State: President Andry Rajoelina (The High Transitional Authority) (from 17 Mar 2009)

Head of government: Prime Minister Jean Omer Beriziky (from 2 Nov 2011)

Ruling party: The High Transitional Authority (provisional executive body of appointed members and dominated by Tanora malaGasy Vonona (TGV) (Young Malagasies Determined) (from Mar 2009)

Area: 592,000 square km (the world's fourth-largest island)

Population: 20.10 million (2010)*

Capital: Antananarivo

Official language: Malagasy, French, English (from 2007)

Currency: Ariary (MGA) = 5 iraimbilanja

Exchange rate: MGA2,080.50 per US$ (Oct 2011)

GDP per capita: US$412 (2009)

GDP real growth: -5.00% (2009)

GDP: US$8.60 billion (2009)

Labour force: 8.31 million (2004)

Inflation: 9.00% (2009)

Balance of trade: -US$2.26 billion (2008)

* estimated figure

The AFP headline 'New national unity government appointed in Madagascar' could have been written anytime since March 2009. In fact it was 26 March 2011 and it could have been used again later in the year. Then it had been Prime Minister Camille Vital's turn to appoint a new government of 'national unity transition' in an effort to resolve the two-year long crisis in the country.

The AFP report points out that the huge (592,000 square km, the world's fourth-largest island) island nation has been in political limbo since opposition leader Andry Rajoelina toppled president Marc Ravalomanana with the army's backing on 17 March 2009 but failed to muster the domestic and foreign backing necessary to set up an internationally recognised transitional government.

Rajoelina dismissed previous deals brokered by the African Union and the Southern African Development Community to share power with the man he ousted and two other ex-presidents. His own plans to form a unity government have been rejected by his opponents.

The latest bid by the southern Africa bloc saw Rajoelina and several small political groupings initial a deal on 8 March calling for the appointment of a consensus prime minister to head a unity government.

Rajoelina's re-appointment earlier in March 2011 of Vital, who almost immediately resigned again, sparked criticism by some opponents, but the strongman said he had sufficiently consulted. The new government is supposed to mirror all the political groups that signed up to a roadmap proposed by international mediators.

Vital said it should 'act as a caretaker administration and head with all speed to the elections.'

The three movements associated with former presidents are not in the new government though a younger brother of one has a ministerial job.

The appointment on 28 October 2011 of Jean Omer Beriziky as the new prime minister and a government of national unity after many months of hesitation by the President of the High Authority for Transition (HAT), Andry Rajoelina, known as TGV (after either the party he leads, the Tanora malaGasy Vonona (Young Malagasies Determined), or France's famous high speed train – the *train à grande vitesse*), could pave the way for a solution to the Malagasy crisis. It also marks a start of normalising TGV's relations with international institutions and embassies, who have shunned him since his violent accession to power in March 2009. Legitimised at last, the President of the HAT is preparing for the presidential elections to be held in 2012. However, that headline could still come in handy.

The economy

According to the *African Economic Outlook 2011* (AEO), published jointly by the African Development Bank and the Organisation for Economic Co-operation and Development, Madagascar inched back to growth in 2010, with the country still suffering in the political fallout from the 2009 coup that ousted president Marc

Ravalomanana and compounded the impact of the 2008-09 global slump. The economy expanded 0.3 per cent last year after shrinking 3.7 per cent in 2009. This was achieved despite donor countries cutting the development aid that has traditionally funded public investment in infrastructure. The international community does not recognise the political normalisation programme of the current government and so development aid is not expected to return to pre-crisis levels in the short term, with growth expected to be slower as a result.

Growth in 2010 was driven by the extractive industries, with production scaling up at large foreign-owned mines, and by a recovery in tourism. Agricultural output expanded slowly despite good weather while construction and the textile industry continued to contract. Agriculture, forestry and fishing accounted for 28.8 per cent of GDP in 2009, with the main food crops being rice, maize, beans, manioc and sweet potato.

Despite favourable climatic conditions, the sector registered slow growth in 2010. In 2011, the government plans to maintain tax exemptions on agricultural inputs and capital goods. Jointly with the expansion of arable land area, the emergence of new entrepreneurs and the rehabilitation of irrigation systems, this is expected to produce 2 per cent growth in the sector.

The government has adopted a tight fiscal policy. As revenues fell due to the slowdown in economic activity and aid flows, most ministries suffered cuts that helped contain the budget deficit at a remarkably low 1.6 per cent of gross domestic product (GDP). However, this was achieved at the expense of infrastructure development and maintenance, and threatens to compromise growth prospects in the medium term. At the same time, the Central Bank of Madagascar adopted a prudent monetary policy stance, holding inflation at 9.6 per cent despite a 14 per cent rise in food prices and keeping its key interest rate unchanged in spite of the sluggish economy. In coming years, the main challenge will be to ease constraints on economic growth without generating unsustainable fiscal deficits and excessive inflation.

Economic activity in the private sector remains constrained by the lack of clarity on future political developments. Foreign investment suffers from concerns over the ultimate legal standing of contracts and concessions signed by the current government and from the revision of contracts signed by the previous government. In addition, with political efforts concentrated on establishing the Fourth Republic, very little is being done to reform the business environment.

The informal sector of the economy has grown as the government cut public spending, private investment remained low and companies in export processing zones closed. Although updated estimates on progress towards the Millennium Development Goals (MDGs) are not available, it is most likely that the incidence of poverty has increased since the coup of 2009.

As a consequence of the slowdown in development aid flows, there has been no infrastructure development over the past two years and maintenance has been kept to a minimum. Installed power capacity remains incredibly low at 160MW, especially when set against a hydro-power potential of several million MW. All development projects remain on hold.

Poverty grows

More than two-thirds of Madagascar's population of over 20 million lives in extreme poverty – less than US$1.25 per day. The incidence of malnutrition is particularly high, at 35 per cent of the population, while Madagascar's GDP per capita is very low, at US$972 on a purchasing power parity basis. Over the last 40 years, there has been a steady deterioration in living standards as the economy has grown more slowly than the population. Despite this, Madagascar's human development index reading of 0.435 is higher than sub-Saharan Africa's average of 0.389 and the country compares favourably with other African countries on life expectancy at birth, 61 years, and on infant mortality, 106 per thousand live births.

HIV prevalence is relatively low but it is believed that official statistics underestimate the real number of cases as the incentive for testing is reduced by the poor healthcare available to HIV-positive individuals. Supplies of anti-retroviral treatments are not consistent and there have been cases of distribution of medications past their expiry date.

Employment

Those aged under 15 make up 47 per cent of the population, presenting a huge challenge for the future as they come onto the labour market. Among other acute problems, some 400,000 people enter the labour market each year. Madagascar faces a lack of formal sector jobs; low skills, labour mobility and productivity; insufficient support for job seekers and poor working conditions. Poverty is often associated with subsistence farming or informal non-agricultural employment. Poverty reduction is therefore dependent on increasing earnings in these areas as the public sector is unlikely to be able to take up the slack in the near future while wage employment in the formal sector is the preserve of highly skilled individuals.

Risk assessment

Economy	Poor
Politics	Improving, maybe
Regional stability	Fair

KEY INDICATORS Madagascar

	Unit	2006	2007	2008	2009	2010
Population	m	19.16	*19.68	*20.22	*20.75	*20.10
Gross domestic product (GDP)	US$bn	5.47	7.32	9.50	8.60	8.30
GDP per capita	US$	288	374	468	412	392
GDP real growth	%	5.0	6.2	7.1	-3.7	0.6
Inflation	%	10.8	10.4	9.2	9.0	9.3
Industrial output	% change	2.7	9.8	6.8	-8.5	–
Agricultural output	% change	2.2	2.2	2.8	8.5	–
Exports (fob) (goods)	US$m	975.0	*542.4	*532.1	–	–
Imports (fob) (goods)	US$m	1,684.0	*819.7	*1,231.6	–	–
Balance of trade	US$m	709.0	*-277.3	*-699.6	–	–
Current account	US$m	*-476.0	*-380.2	*-81,772.4	-1,433.0	-1,120.0
Total reserves minus gold	US$m	583.2	846.7	982.3	1,135.5	1,171.6
Foreign exchange	US$m	583.1	846.6	982.0	982.3	1,022.9
Exchange rate	per US$	2,142.30	1,873.90	1,708.40	1,956.20	2,090.00

* estimated figure

COUNTRY PROFILE

Historical profile

1500 The first Europeans landed in Madagascar.
1790s King Andrianampoinimerina unified the Merina tribe which soon became the island's dominant tribe, controlling nearly half of Madagascar.
1820 Britain signed a treaty recognising Madagascar as an independent state under Merina rule.
1890 An Anglo-French treaty gave control of the island to France.
1894 Queen Ranavalona III was forced to abdicate and Madagascar was declared a French colony.
1946 Madagascar became a Territoire d'Outre-Mer (TOM, overseas territory).
1947 After several decades of growing resentment and resistance to French rule, there was an armed rebellion. France crushed the revolt with the loss of several thousand lives.
1960 The Republic of Madagascar (known between 1960–72 as the Malagasy Republic) gained full independence on 26 June. Philibert Tsiranana became president.
1972 Tsiranana was forced from office; he dissolved parliament and was replaced by General Gabriel Ramanantsoa as head of a provisional government. He moved the country away from ties with France towards the Soviet Union.
1975 After a short tussle between pro- and anti-government forces a military coup replaced Ramantsoa with Didier Ratsiraka. The country was renamed the Democratic Republic of Madagascar; Ratsiraka was elected president for a seven-year term.
1976 Large parts of the economy were nationalised. The Andry sy Riana Enti-Manavotra an'i Madagasikara (Arema) (Association for the Rebirth of Madagascar) party was formed. Ratsiraka increased state control over the economy until 1986 when a market economy was encouraged.
1992 Following three years of protests and civil disturbances after Ratsiraka's third presidential election victory, a referendum endorsed a multi-party constitution which enshrined a unitary state and reduced the powers of the president.
1993 In the presidential election Ratsiraka was defeated by Albert Zafy.
1996 Zafy was impeached.
1997 Didier Ratsiraka beat Albert Zafy in the presidential election.
2000, Local elections were boycotted by 70 per cent of the electorate and Ratsiraka and his party retained considerable political power.
2001 The Senate reopened in May after 29 years, completing the government framework provided for in the 1992 constitution, which replaced the socialist revolutionary system.
2001 Both candidates, Ratsiraka and Marc Ravalomanana, declared themselves winners in the presidential election.
2002 Civil disturbance accompanied heated debate about the prospective winner of the presidential election. Ravalomanana was declared the winner by the Constitutional High Court, following a recount. Ravalomanana was recognised by the US as Head of State. Didier Ratsiraka fled to the Seychelles. President Marc Ravalomanana's Tiako i Madagasikara (TIM) (I Love and Care for Madagascar) won parliamentary elections.
2003 Prime Minister Jacques Sylla announced a new cabinet.
2004 The IMF agreed to write off debts of US$2 billion. Madagascar joined the Southern African Development Community (SADC).
2006 The president's plane was shot at as he returned home from France as General Andrianafidisoa (Fidy) attempted a military coup claiming the 2001 presidential election was illegitimate. President Ravalomanana won a second term in office.
2007 The president appointed General Charles Rabemananjara as prime minister. Constitutional amendments were agreed by referendum to increase presidential powers. Parliamentary elections were won by the ruling TIM. A US$3.3 billion nickel cobalt mine was opened in Tamatave.
2008 The UN launched an appeal to help the 332,391 people left homeless by Cyclone Ivan, one of the largest ever recorded. The first barrels of crude oil since the 1940s were produced. Madagascar issued 19 offshore exploration licences.
2009 Anti-government protests and political confrontation between the mayor of Antananarivo, Andry Rajoelina, and the president increased until the president sacked Rajoelina and appointed a city official as his replacement. Dissident soldiers joined Rajoelina and refused to take orders from the president and government. Police attempted to arrest Rajoelina, who took refuge in the French embassy. Troops stormed the presidential palace forcing Ravalomanana to resign and replacing him with Andry Rajoelina, who became president of the High Transitional Authority (HTA). The African Union (AU) suspended Madagascar, calling the regime change an 'unconstitutional coup'. The SADC said it would not recognise Rajoelina as the new president. An arrest warrant was issued by the HTA for former president Ravalomanana, who was living in exile in Swaziland. He was charged with misuse of government funds. Ravalomanana was sentenced, *in absentia*, to a four-year jail sentence and fined US$70 million for alleged abuse of office. UN-backed mediation talks began with HTA to reintroduce democratic principles and a unity government. President Rajoelina postponed parliamentary elections and appointed Brigadier General Albert Camille Vital as prime minister.
2010 The US and AU imposed sanctions on President Rajoelina and 108 of his supporters in March, following Rajoelina's failure to meet a deadline to set up a unity government despite earlier agreements. Foreign assets were frozen and travel restrictions were imposed in the hope that further negotiations would take place. In June the European Union (EU) confirmed that its substantial aid programme would remain frozen until Madagascar returned to democratic rule. In August, following agreement at a mediated forum, and despite the boycott by three major opposition parties, the date for a constitutional referendum was set to take place on 17 November, and the presidential election for mid-2011. Although opposition political parties called for voters to boycott the referendum, 74.19 per cent voted yes. The referendum endorsed the presidency of Andry Rajoelina and lowered the age of a presidential candidate from 40 to 36 years (thus allowing Rajoelina to stand in new presidential elections). On 6 December, the Constitutional High Court rejected all opposition objections to the results and validated the referendum. The fourth Malagasy Republic was declared.
2011 President Rajoelina dismissed Prime Minister Albert Camille Vital on 10 March, but on 16 March Vital was re-appointed and asked to form a new cabinet. In March, the presidential and parliamentary elections scheduled for May were postponed until September. On 22 July the UN *rapporteur* called for international sanctions on Madagascar to be reconsidered, as they were threatening more of the population with food insecurity. An agreement was reached between politicians allowing elections to take place in 2012. The agreement will also allow exiled former president Ravalomanana to return to Madagascar. Prime Minister Vital and his government resigned on 17 October. Former president, Didier Ratsiraka returned from exile in France (since 2002) on 24 November. In 2003, a court had convicted Ratsiraka, *in absentia*, of corruption. He was sentenced to 10 year's hard labour. President Rajoelina consented to his return, without penalty. His return followed the formation of a unity government on 21 November and a possible end to the political deadlock. President Rajoelina appointed Jean Omer Beriziky as prime minster on 28 October. Beriziky took office on 2 November.

Political structure

Constitution

The Fourth Malagasy Republic was declared in December 2010, following a constitutional referendum on 17 November, which reduced the age restriction of presidential candidates.
Constitutional reforms in 1995 and 1998 gave the president the power to appoint or dismiss the prime minister and presidential terms in office were limited to three.

Independence date

26 June 1960

Form of state

Republic

The executive

National legislature

The bicameral parliament consists of the Antenimieram-Pirenena (Assemblée Nationale) (National Assembly) (lower chamber) with 127 members elected in single and multi-seat constituencies, and the Antenimieran-Doholona (Sénat) with 33 members of which 22 are elected (one from each district) and 11 appointed.

Legal system

The constitution guarantees judicial independence. The single judicial system is tiered, including in the first instance civil, criminal and military courts. Above these are the Court of Appeal, High Court of Justice, which tries high officials, and a High Constitutional Court. Finally overseeing all is the Supreme Court. *Dian* (traditional courts) handle some civil disputes, among rural peoples only, and decisions are not subject to formal procedural protection of the formal court system. Both parties must agree to abide by the *dian's* authority and ruling.

Last elections

23 September 2007 (parliamentary); 3 December 2006 (presidential)
Results: Parliamentary: the Tiako i Madagasikara (TIM) (I Love and Care for Madagascar) won 106 seats out of 127, Fanjava Velogno won 2, independents 11; nine other minor parties won one seat each.
Presidential: Marc Ravalomanana won 54.8 per cent of the vote (a majority large enough to avoid a second round), Jean Lahiniriko 11.68 per cent, Roland Ratsiraka 10.9 per cent. Turnout was 61.45 per cent. These results were made void by a coup led by Andry Rajoelina in 2009.

Next elections

March 2010 (parliamentary) postponed; 2011 (presidential)

Political parties

Ruling party

The High Transitional Authority (provisional executive body of appointed members and dominated by Tanora malaGasy Vonona (TGV) (Young Malagasies Determined) (from Mar 2009)

Population

20.10 million (2010)*
Last census: August 1993: 12,238,914
Population density: 24 inhabitants per square km. Urban population: 25 per cent (2003).
Annual growth rate: 3.0 per cent 1994–2004 (WHO 2006)

Ethnic make-up

The population comprises 18 separate ethnic groups, all deriving in varying degrees from Malayo-Indonesian origin, with African and Arab influences a particular feature in coastal areas. The Merinas (central highlands) represent about 26 per cent of the total, while the Betsimisaraka on the east coast account for 15 per cent and the Betsileo (southern highlands) 12 per cent. The other main groups are the Antankarana (north), Sakalava (west) and Mahafaly and Antandroy (far south).
There is long-standing rivalry between the highland groups (particularly the Merina) and those of the coastal regions.

Religions

Traditional beliefs (45 per cent), Christianity (about 45 per cent), Islam (7 per cent).

Education

Primary education lasts for five years. Secondary schooling is divided into two, beginning with a four-year programme. When completed students may continue in either an acedemic or technical programme, for a further three years. Education may be given in either French or Madagasy.
The majority of those who do not attend school or who withdraw early come from the poorest sections of the population and those living in rural areas; illiteracy rates in women are a higher among the youngest; and nearly half of school age children are not enrolled in schools.
Public expenditure is around 3 per cent of GDP, of which around 40 per cent is spent on primary and 35 per cent on secondary education. Higher education expenses amount to only 0.5 per cent of GDP.
Literacy rate: 68.1 per cent total, 61.6 per cent female; adult rates (World Bank).
Compulsory years: Six to 11.
Enrolment rate: 120 per cent gross primary enrolment of relevant age group (including repeaters), World Bank.
Pupils per teacher: 47 in primary schools.

Health

About 60 per cent of the population live within 5km of, or about one hour's walk from, a public health centre.
Vaccination facilities remain poor with only 61 per cent of children immunised against measles, before aged one year. More than three-quarters of the people have no ready access to drinking water.

HIV/Aids

The government has a national Aids policy that covers all economic sectors.
HIV prevalence: 1.7 per cent aged 15–49 in 2003 (World Bank)
Life expectancy: 57 years, 2004 (WHO 2006)
Fertility rate/Maternal mortality rate: 5.3 births per woman, 2004 (WHO 2006); maternal mortality 488 per 100,000 live births (World Bank).
Child (under 5 years) mortality rate (per 1,000): 78 per 1,000 live births (World Bank)
Head of population per physician: 0.29 physicians per 1,000 people, 2004 (WHO 2006)

Welfare

In 2004, three separate cyclones, including Cyclone Gafilo, estimated to have been the worst cyclone in 20 years, killed over 100 people and damaged more than 117,000 hectares of farmland as well as many schools and healthcare centres. Total damage from Cyclone Gafilo was estimated, by Government, at US$250 million.

Main cities

Antananarivo (capital, and principal business centre, estimated population 1.6 million in 2005); Toamasina (Tamatave), (200,568); Antsirabé (176,933); Fianarantsoa (160,550); Mahajanga (Majunga) (134,600), Majunga (149,863); Toliara (formerly Tuléar) (113,014); Antsiranana (formerly Diégo-Suarez) (80,001).

Languages spoken

French is the usual business language and the medium for all documentation.
Very little English is spoken.

Official language/s

Malagasy, French, English (from 2007)

Media

National state radio and television is controlled by the office of the president. National broadcasting is a state monopoly.

Press

Most newspapers are privately owned and are published in French, with a minority number published in Malagasy.
Dailies: In French, *Midi-Madagasikara* (www.midi-madagasikara.mg), *Madagascar Tribune* (www.madagascar-tribune.com), *Les Nouvelles* (www.les-nouvelles.com), *L'Express* (www.lexpressmada.com) and *La Gazette de la Grande Ile* (www.lagazette-dgi.com) and in Malagasy *Gazetiko*; all are published and circulated in Antananarivo.

Weeklies: In French, *Dans les Media Demain* www.dmd.mg) is a privately owned news digest, with a large circulation in the Madagascan Diaspora. In Malagasy, *Lakroa* (Cross) is a Roman Catholic publication reaching rural and remote areas, *Feon'ny Merina* (Voice of the Merina) promotes the interests of Merina people of Malay origin.
Periodicals: In French, the monthly *Jureco* has articles on legal and economic issues while *Madagascar Magazine* (www.madagascarmagazine.com) is a quarterly publication that covers politics and economic issues as well as tourist features. The news magazine *Revue de l'Ocean Indian* (www.madatours.com/roi) covering issues of Indian Ocean islands.
Broadcasting
Radio: Radio-Télévision Malagasy (RTM) operates the only national radio service. Private, local, commercial stations include Radio MBS (www.mbs.mg) owned by President Ravalomanana, Radio Don Bosco (www.radiodonbosco.mg) owned by the Catholic Church, Radio Feon'ny Merina, which promotes the interests of the Merina people and Radio Fahazavana.
Television: Radio-Télévision Malagasy (RTM) operates the only national TV station. Other, private local TV stations include Radio-Television Analamanga (RTA) (www.rta.mg), MBS TV (www.mbs.mg) and Madagascar TV (MATV).
News agencies
APA: www.apanews.net
Panapress: www.panapress.com
Reuters Africa: http://africa.reuters.com

Economy
Madagascar was ranked 151 (out of 187) in the UN Human Development Index (HDI) in 2011. Madagascar has 67.8 per cent of its population living on the equivalent of US$1.25 per day, and 53.3 per cent who experience multiple deprivations in the same household. Madagascar has reached the conditions for aid under the IMF Enhanced Heavily Indebted Poor Countries (HIPC) Initiative, which allows it to borrow funds backed by the Initiative's guarantee.
Oil was discovered offshore in 2006, and with projected production of 60,000 barrels per day by 2010, energy analysts were predicting annual revenue of US$1 billion. Madagascar joined the Extractive Industries Transparency Initiative (EITI) a 'forum of oil producers and consumers seeking to promote accountability in oil revenue' which should supply the necessary support in Madagascar's efforts to strengthen public financial management.
GDP growth was 6.2 per cent in 2007 and 7.1 per cent in 2008, which suddenly plummeted to -3.7 in 2009 as political turmoil undermined the economy. In 2010, as a fragile stability was re-established, GDP growth picked up and reached 0.6 per cent, with a projected rise to 1 per cent in 2011. Inflation which had been in double digits for most of the 2000s, dipped to around 9 per cent in 2008 and remained fairly constant until 2010, before showing signs of rising to double digits again in 2011.
The service sector is the major generator of the economy at 54.9 per cent in 2009, with industry accounting for 16 per cent, of which manufacturing was 14.1 per cent; agriculture contributed 29.1 per cent. Madagascar overtook Nigeria as Africa's largest rice producer in 2099, but still needs to import a further 10 per cent to meet domestic demand. Other agricultural produce includes livestock, coffee, cotton, tobacco, and sugar. It also produces around 1,800–2,000 tonnes of vanilla a year as an important cash crop, although overseas competition comes from new plantations and synthetic vanilla. Its industries consist of food processing, textiles and clothing, refined petroleum products, mining and manufactured goods.
On 4 March 2011, the minister for mines and hydrocarbons announced that all planned licensing for oil exploration had been suspended indefinitely for around 225 blocks across three basins. These sites had attracted major international exploration companies, some of which had discovered oil and were awaiting an improvement in the political situation before increasing their investment. On 28 June it was announced that the French oil company Total had been given a one-year extension on its exploration licence.

External trade
Madagascar was one of the founding members of the Common Market of Eastern and Southern Africa (Comesa) and since June 2009 operates a customs union whereby the goods and services of non-members attract a common external tariff (CET).
Madagascar is one of the World's largest exporters of vanilla (it lost its pre-eminence in 2000 when a cyclone destroyed much of its production). It has significant reserves of minerals and ores; investment in mineral extraction was bolstered in May 2007 when the African Development Bank agreed to a US$150 million loan to develop the Ambatovy nickel plant.
Imports
Principal imports are petroleum, capital goods, consumer goods and foodstuffs and vehicles.
Main sources: China (typically 20 per cent of total), France (10 per cent), Bahrain (8 per cent).
Exports
Principal exports are coffee, vanilla, textiles, sugar, metals and minerals and petroleum products.
Main destinations: France (typically 45 per cent of total), US (20 per cent), Germany (6.0 per cent).

Agriculture
The agricultural sector dominates the economy.
Madagascar has a wide range of soil types and its main cash/export crops are prawns, coffee, cotton, cloves and vanilla, production of which has fluctuated due to recurrent droughts and cyclones. Vanilla used to be the country's main export crop but increased competition worldwide has reduced exports. Around 1,800–2,000 tonnes of vanilla a year is produced, but its cultivation has suffered a drop in value due to overseas competition from new plantations and synthetic vanilla.
Main food crops are rice, maize, bananas and sweet potatoes. Groundnuts, pineapples, coconuts and sugar are also grown, mostly for internal use. The decline in coffee prices led to many growers switching production to rice, increasing production by 5 per cent, and making Madagascar self-sufficient in rice (the staple diet of the country) for the first time since the mid-1970s, with annual production at around 3.0 million tonnes per year.
Divestiture of vanilla, cotton and sugar parastatals was expected to encourage greater foreign investment. However, as vanilla prices fell from US$450—500 per kilo in 2003, to US$30 in 2007, financial co-operatives kept several thousand vanilla farmers afloat.
The livestock sector is dominant in the west and south of the country.
Fishing
Since 1996, prawns have been the number one export earner, with around 7,000 tonnes of prawn exports earning revenues of over US$60 million per annum.
In a meeting of African ministers in Namibia, members discussed illegal and unregulated fishing, which is estimated to cost Africa US$1 billion per annum in lost revenue and the threat to stocks and local artisan fishing.
Forestry
Only 15 per cent of Madagascar's ancient forest remains. Deforestation has left the hills exposed to the wind and rain which strips away the soil. Forest preservation and the creation of national parks are receiving large-scale international support.

Industry and manufacturing
The industrial sector contributes around 16 per cent of GDP and employs around 9 per cent of the workforce.

Industry is dominated by food processing and the manufacture of textiles for international markets. Other major sectors include rice milling, sugar refining, distilling, oil-seed crushing, meat, fruit and vegetable canning, processing of cashew nuts, fruit juices, milk products and jams, cigarettes, soap and rope manufacturing, cotton spinning and brewing. Major capital-intensive industries are oil refining, fertiliser and cement production. There are 150 firms based in industrial free zones, representing mainly textile, food processing and information technology, and creating 6,000 jobs in the Antananarivo area alone. Many textile companies in Mauritius are relocating to Madagascar due to the cheaper labour rates.

Tourism

Tourism is the second most important foreign exchange earner, after textile exports. The sector is expected to earn US$152.7 million, contribute 3 per cent of GDP in 2005, and attract 11.6 per cent of all capital investment. Travel and tourism is predicted to employ over 450,000 people, or provide one in every 18 jobs. France is the main market and adventure and eco-tourism are the main attractions. There is considerable potential for expansion of the sector in these and other activities, such as coastal resorts, but inadequate infrastructure and low investment are a hindrance to becoming truly competitive with more established Indian Ocean destinations.

Environment

Madagascar has plants and wildlife found nowhere else on earth, and growth of both tourism and mining needs to be controlled to protect the fragile ecosystems. Evidence from satellites, in 2009, showed sediment flowing into the Mozambique Channel from the west coast of Madagascar. Deforestation for cultivation and pastureland since the 1960s has resulted in massive annual soil loss, estimated at 250 tonnes per hectare in some regions and the largest amount recorded anywhere in the world.

Mining

Excluding gold and gem production by artisinal miners, mining contributes less than 1 per cent of GDP and employs 1 per cent of the workforce. If the informal sector is included, the contribution to GDP is around 3 per cent.

Madagascar is rich in mineral resources, although it is still only a minor mineral producer by regional standards. There are sizeable deposits of a number of minerals, industrial ores and precious and semi-precious gemstones including chrome ore, mica, graphite, gold, bauxite, uranium, iron ore, ilmenite/titanium, quartz, nickel, copper, lead, platinum, labradorite, rock-crystal, rhodolite, marble, garnets, emeralds, rubies and sapphires. There are known deposits containing 100 million tonnes of bauxite and 400 million tonnes of iron ore, although these have not been developed due to the country's poor infrastructure.

Only chrome, mica and graphite have been exploited to any great extent, and export earnings from these are limited due to lack of demand. The world's largest known emerald cluster was discovered in Madagascar in 1996.

The region of Ilakaka in the southern interior has around 50 per cent of the world's sapphire reserves, while there are small quantities of semi-precious stones (garnets and amethysts) mined for export.

The state-owned Société Kraomita Malagasy (Kraoma) is Madagascar's main chromite producer. It extracts around 40,000 tonnes of concentrates and 80,000 tonnes of lumpy ore per year from the Andriamana complex and a further 20,000 tonnes from the Behandrinana mine.

There are some 100,000 individual gold miners and small syndicates. Although the government tolerates this form of mining, it is worried about its ecological effects which include a high level of mercury leaking into streams and rivers.

The country also produces graphite, 66 per cent of which comes from the Gallois mine. It exports up to 15,000tpy, mostly to UK, US and Germany.

Hydrocarbons

No oil was being produced in 2010. However, oil exploration by international oil companies has been underway since the mid-2000s. Finds are expected to yield 9.8 billion barrels of recoverable reserves from the Bermolanga, and another 1.3 billion barrels from the Tsimiroro, oil fields.

On 4 March 2011, the minister for Office des Mines Nationales et des Industries Strategiques (Omnis) announced that all planned licensing for oil exploration had been suspended indefinitely for around 225 blocks across three basins. These sites had attracted major international exploration companies, some of which had discovered oil and were awaiting an improvement in the political situation before increasing their investment. On 29 March 2011, the US-based Madagascar Oil declared *force majeure* under its contractual agreements for four production-sharing blocks that it believes would be slated for expropriation by the government. Conditions deteriorated as Omnis failed to instruct the state regulatory authority to proceed with the 2011 Madagascar works programme and discussions with the government had not improved the situation.

Consumption in 2008 was 20,000 barrels per day, all of which was imported. Since the only oil refinery, in Toamasina, was privatised in 2000, it was upgraded and processes 540,000 tonnes of crude per year and provides 85 per cent of the country's refined oil needs.

Omnis is a government organisation responsible for policy, implementation and managing the country's hydrocarbons and mining assets.

Proven coal reserves were 137 million tonnes in 2008, but commercial production was limited as old facilities became uncompetitive. However renewed interest by foreign energy companies ready to invest in coal mining for power generation may invigorate the industry over the next decade.

Madagascar does not produce or import natural gas.

Energy

Total installed generating capacity was 227MW in 2007, producing 980 million kilowatt hours. Around 60 per cent of all energy is generated by hydropower, however only 15 per cent of the population have access to electricity; the majority rely on biomass, including fuel wood, for cooking and lighting. With demand rising by 7 per cent per annum, government policy is to encourage growth in hydroelectric power, and it intends to increase hydropower to 70 per cent of the energy mix. Recent thermal power plants have been built by foreign companies using local coal, with all output used in the nickel mining industry.

There is no integrated power grid and each centre of population is served by its own power station, which either provides enough energy as needed or fails, resulting in outages. The state-owned national power and water utility Jiro sy Rano Malagasy (Jirama) is responsible for the provision of electricity and drinking water for the population of Madagascar. It is overseeing the installation of a mid-voltage transmission line between power plants. Solar-photovoltaic panels have been installed in rural communities to provide for localised energy needs.

Banking and insurance

Moves to strengthen banking supervision have been enhanced through the IMF backed Financial Sector Assessment Program.

Central bank

Banque Centrale de la République Malgache

Time

GMT plus three hours

Geography

Madagascar is situated in the western Indian Ocean, about 500km east of Mozambique in southern Africa. It comprises the island of Madagascar itself and several much smaller offshore islands. Madagascar is the fourth-largest island in the world. The terrain is dominated by a chain of mountains running the length of the island, with broad lowlands to the west and a narrow strip of lowlands to the east. The highlands, which occupy around half of the total area, rise to 1,800m. A rift valley runs from north to south and includes lake Alaotra, which, at 40km in length, is the largest body of water in the country. The capital, Antananarivo, is located on the plateau.The highest elevations face east, forming an escarpment above the eastern lowlands. The east coast is narrow, averaging about 50km in width, and is heavily forested. The mountains slope gradually down towards the broad west coast, which is given over to savannah; unlike that of the east coast, the coastline is indented and provides harbourage.

The highest point of the island (2,880m) is in the Tsaratanana Massif at the northern end of the island. The coastline is contoured and is home to the natural harbour of Antsiranana. The southern end of the island is semi-desert with cactus-like plant species, which are unique to Madgascar.

Rivers flowing east from the highlands are short and fast with waterfalls. Those flowing down the gentler western terrain are longer and slower-moving.

Hemisphere

Southern

Climate

Tropical, cooler in highlands. The summer period spans the months of November to April. Numerous areas have their own micro-climates – the highlands are subject to mild freshness in the winter, while the eastern parts of the island experience high temperatures and humidity, with barren and arid conditions dominating the western sector.

In Antananarivo, the hottest month is December (15–28 Celsius (C)), coldest July (9–19 C). The wettest month is January. Winter in the capital lasts from April to October, when it is cold and dry. Madagascar falls within the cyclone belt and cyclones tend to occur during the rainy season December–March, which is hotter than the rest of the year. It is rainy until June or July on the east coast and is very hot throughout the year. It is drier on the west coast.

Dress codes

In Antananarivo, in the winter months, normal weight clothing is suitable, with a woollen sweater/cardigan recommended. In the summer men should wear tropical suits and women, cotton dresses. On the coast, tropical clothing is recommended all year round.

Entry requirements

Passports

Required by all, valid for six months after date of entry.

Visa

Required by all, along with proof of return/onward passage. A business visas requires a letter of recommendation from the employer, confirming the traveller's business activity and financial responsibility, to be submitted with the application.

Currency advice/regulations

Import of local currency is limited to MGA1,000; visitors are not allowed to export local currency. There is no limit on import of foreign currency, subject to declaration on arrival, and export is allowed up to the declared amount.

Health (for visitors)

Mandatory precautions

Yellow fever vaccination certificate required if arriving from an infected area.

Advisable precautions

Typhoid, polio, tetanus and hepatitis A vaccinations recommended. Malaria risk exists throughout the country and prophylaxis is necessary. There is a rabies risk. Water precautions should be taken.

Hotels

Good hotels are available in Antananarivo, Toamasina, Nosy Be, Ste Marie and Taolanaro. A service charge is added to bills at some hotels. Discretionary tipping is usual.

Credit cards

Credit cards are of limited use in Madagascar and few establishments accept them.

Public holidays (national)

Fixed dates

1 Jan (New Year's Day), 29 Mar (Commemoration Day – 1947), 1 May (Labour Day), 26 Jun (Independence Day), 15 Aug (Assumption Day), 1 Nov (All Saints' Day), 25 Dec (Christmas Day), 30 Dec (Republic Day).

Variable dates

Easter Monday, Ascension Day, Whit Monday.

Working hours

Banking

Mon–Fri: 0800–1100, 1400–1600.

Business

Mon–Fri: 0830–1200, 1400–1800.

Government

Mon–Fri: 0800–1200, 1400–1800.

Shops

Mon–Fri: 0800–1200, 1400–1800.

Electricity supply

110 or 220V AC, 50 cycles; also 380V AC, 50 cycles

Getting there

Air

National airline: Air Madagascar

International airport/s:

Antananarivo-Ivato (TNR), 14km from the city; restaurant, currency exchange.

Airport tax: None.

Surface

Water: There are few scheduled sea passages.

Main port/s: Toamasina (Tamatave), on the east coast, is the island's main port. It is used by numerous foreign shipping lines. Mahajanga (Majunga) is the west coast's main port. Antseranana (Diégo-Suarez) is in the extreme north of the island, and Toliara (Tuléar) is on the south-west coast.

Getting about

National transport

Air: Air Madagascar and TAM airlines fly more than 60 domestic routes. There are connections between all major towns, apart from Antsirabe. Air travel is the most used and generally recommended form of transport. There are over 100 airfields on the island, although many are just airstrips.

Road: Generally poor and in need of repair, and only passable in good weather (the dry season).

Fairly well-maintained main roads leave Antananarivo – the N4 to Mahajanga (Majunga), the RN2 to Toamasina (Tamatave), and the RN7 plateau route south to Fianarantsoa.

Rail: Two classes; light refreshments may be available; air-conditioning available on first-class trains.

Routes are: between Toamasina and Antsirabe, via Antananarivo, incorporating a connection between Moramanga and Lake Alaotra; and between Fianarantsoa and Manakara on the east coast. Daily services operate on most routes.

City transport

Taxis: Flat fare system for short journeys in most towns, otherwise by negotiation; tipping is not usual.

Car hire

Available in main centres. International driving licence required.

BUSINESS DIRECTORY

The addresses listed below are a selection only. While World of Information makes every endeavour to check these addresses, we cannot guarantee that changes have not been made, especially to telephone numbers and area codes. We would welcome any corrections.

Telephone area codes
The international dialling code (IDD) for Madagascar is +261 20 followed by operator and area codes and subscriber's number:

Antananarivo	22	Nosy-Be	86
Antsiranana	82	Toamasina	53
Fianarantsoa	75	Toliara	18
Mahajanga	62		

Useful telephone numbers
Police: 17
Fire: 18
Ambulance: 357-53

Chambers of Commerce
Antananarivo Chamber of Commerce, Industry and Agriculture, 20 Rue Paul Dussac, PO Box 166, 101 Antananarivo 101 (tel: 202-11; fax: 20213).

Antsiranana Chamber of Commerce, Industry and Agriculture, 3 Rue Colbert, PO Box 76, Antsiranana 201 (tel: 223-72; fax: 294-03).

Madagascar Federation of Chambers of Commerce, Industry and Agriculture, 20 Rue Paul Dussac, PO Box 166, Antananarivo 101 (tel: 20-211; fax: 20-213).

Mahajanga Chamber of Commerce, Industry and Agriculture, Boulevard Poincaré, PO Box 52, Mahajanga 401(tel: 226-21).

Nosy-Be Chamber of Commerce, Industry and Agriculture, Cours de Hell, PO Box 11, Nosy-Be 207 (tel: 610-26; fax: 610-56).

Toamasina Chamber of Commerce, Industry, Handicrafts and Agriculture, 4 Rue de Commerce, PO Box 108, Toamasina 501 (tel: 323-45; fax: 320-25).

Banking
BMOI, Place de l'Indépendence, BP 25 bis, Antananarivo 101 (tel: 346-09; fax: 346-10; e-mail:bmoi.sm@simicro.mg).

Bank of Africa-Madagascar, 2 Place de l'Independance, BP 183, Antananarivo 101 (tel: 391-00/; fax: 294-08).

Banque SBM Madagascar, 1 Rue Andrianary Ratianarivo Antsahavola, Antananarivo 101 (tel: 666-07; fax: 666-08).

BFV-Société Générale, 14 Lalana Jeneraly Rabehevitra, BP 196, Antananarivo 101 (tel: 206-91; fax: 345-54).

BNI-Crédit Lyonnais Madagascar, 74 Rue du 26 Juin 1960, BP 174, Antananarivo 101 (tel: 228-00; fax: 337-49).

Investco Southern Investment Bancorp, Immeuble NIAG, 8 Lalana Rainizanabololona, BP 8510, Antanimena, Antananarivo 101 (tel: 648-20; fax: 613-29).

Union Commercial Bank SA, 77 Rue Solombavambahoaka Frantsay, Antsahavola, BP 197, Antananarivo 101 (tel: 272-62; fax: 287-40).

Central bank
Banque Centrale de Madagascar, Avenue de la Révolution Socialiste, PO Box 550, Antananarivo (tel: 234-65; fax: 345-32; e-mail: b.c.m@simicro.mg).

Travel information
Air Madagascar, 31 Avenue de l'Indépendance, Analakely, Antananarivo 101 (tel: 222-22; fax: 337-60; e-mail: commercial@airmadagascar.com)

Association des Agences de Voyages de Madagascar, 5 Rue Ravveloary, Antananarivo (tel: 656-31; e-mail: aavm@wanadoo.mg).

Air Mauritius, 77 lalana Solombavabahoaka, Frantsay, Antsahavola, Antananarivo (tel: 359-00; fax: 357-73).

Réseau National des Chemins de Fer, BP 259, Soarano, Antananarivo (tel: 205-21).

Ministry of tourism
Ministry of Culture and Tourism, Rue Fernand Kasanga, BP 610, Tsimbazaza, Antananarivo (tel: 668-05; fax: 789-53; e-mail: mct@tourisme.gov.mg).

National tourist organisation offices
Maison du Tourisme de Madagascar (Madagascar Tourist Office), Place de l'Indépendance, Antaninarenina, PO Box 3224, Antananarivo (tel: 351-78; fax: 695-22; e-mail: mtm@simicro.gov.mg).

Ministries
Ministry of Private Sector Development and Privatisation, Comité de Privatisation, Zone III 1er étage, Ampefiloha, Antananarivo (tel: 666-67; fax: 601-38; e-mail: magpriv@dts.mg).

Other useful addresses
Agence Nationale d'Information 'Taratra' (ANTA), 3 rue du R P Callet, BP 386, Antananarivo (tel: 211-71).

Association of the Hotel Industry of Madagascar (SIHM), c/o Sofitrans – Soarano, Antananarivo (tel: 223-30).

Comité de Privatisation, Secrétariat Technique á la Privatisation Immeuble FIARO, Zone III 1er étage, Ampefiloha, 101 Antananarivo (fax: 2260-138).

Customs Services, Ivato Airport, Antananarivo (tel: 440-32).

Institut National de la Statistique et de la Recherche Economique (DGBDE), Direction Générale, BP 485, Antananarivo (tel: 216-52).

Madagascan Embassy (US), 2374 Massachusetts Avenue, NW, Wasghington DC 20008 (tel: (+1-202)-265-5525; fax: (+1-202)-265-3034; e-mail: malagasy@embassy.org).

Office Militaire National pour les Industries Stratégiques (monitors major industrial projects), 21 Lalana Razanakombana, Antananarivo.

Société d'Etude et de Réalisation pour le Développement Industriel, BP 3180, Antananarivo (tel: 213-35).

Syndicat de l'Industrie Hôteliére de Madagascar, BP 341, Antananarivo (tel: 202-02).

Internet sites
Africa Business Network: www.ifc.org/abn

African Development Bank: www.afdb.org

Africa News Online: www.allafrica.com

Africa Online: www.africaonline.com

Mbendi AfroPaedia (information on companies, countries, industries and stock exchanges in Africa): http://mbendi.co.za

Malawi

KEY FACTS

Official name: Dziko la Malawi (Republic of Malawi)

Head of State: President Bingu wa Mutharika (DPP) (from 2004; re-elected 19 May 2009)

Head of government: President Bingu wa Mutharika

Ruling party: A coalition led by United Democratic Front (UDF) with the Mgwirizano (Unity) coalition, National Democratic Alliance (NDA), Alliance for Democracy (AFORD) and 38 non-partisan parliamentary members (elected 2004; re-elected 19 May 2009)

Area: 118,484 square km

Population: 14.90 million (2010)*

Capital: Lilongwe

Official language: English

Currency: Kwacha (K) = 100 tambala

Exchange rate: K165.50 per US$ (Oct 2011)

GDP per capita: US$322 (2010)

GDP real growth: 6.50% (2010)

GDP: US$5.10 billion (2010)

Labour force: 5.35 million (2004)

Inflation: 7.40% (2010)

Balance of trade: -US$753.6 million (2008)

Foreign debt: US$894.00 million (2007)

* estimated figure

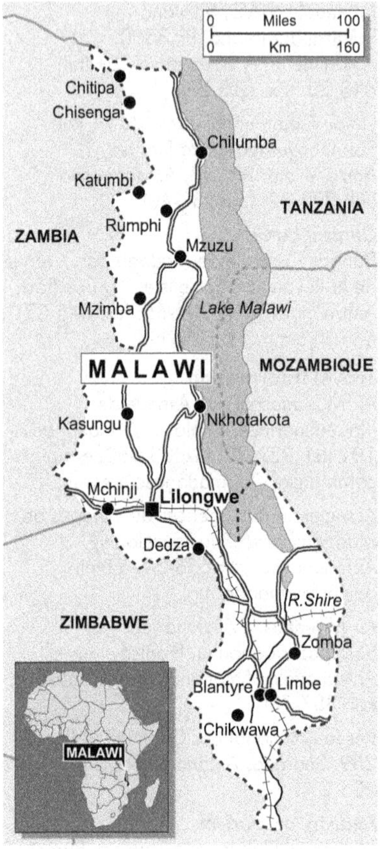

The fully risen sun of Malawi's new flag, launched in 2010 to signify a fully developed country, looked a bit pale in 2011. One former president went on trial for 'misappropriating' some US$11 million of international donor funds, a former vice president had his trial delayed, the UK High Commissioner (Ambassador) was expelled for accusing President Mutharika of being arrogant, both the UK and the International Monetary Fund (IMF) cut their aid funds, there were riots in July, the kwacha was devalued by 10 per cent, the President sacked his cabinet, running the whole show for several weeks before appointing new foreign, financial and domestic portfolios and Malawi slipped from 85 to 100 (out of 183 countries) on Transparency International's 2011 Corruption Index. In fact good news is pretty hard to find in Malawi.

The economy

Gross domestic product (GDP) growth in 2010 was a respectable 6.5 per cent, even though down from the 7.9 per cent of 2010. According to the *African Economic Outlook 2011* (AEO), published jointly by the African Development Bank and the Organisation for Economic Co-operation and Development, agriculture is the mainstay of Malawi's economy, accounting for around 32 per cent of GDP with 60 per cent of the total exports coming from tobacco alone. This revealed clearly that the economy of the country is largely undiversified. The agriculture sector recorded a growth rate of 13.9 per cent in 2009 following bumper yields on account of good weather during the 2008/09 season and the Farm Input Subsidy Programme. Growth in the agricultural sector slowed down to 1.5 per cent in 2010 as a result of dry spells that affected most parts of the country at the onset of the 2009/10 crop season. The sector is expected to grow by 6.4 per cent in 2011 subject to good weather and further expansion expected in the sugar sub-sector. One threat for the country, however, is the current global campaign against the use of additives to burley tobacco in cigarette manufacturing. Burley tobacco, the main type of tobacco grown in Malawi, is naturally bitter and manufacturers need to use additives to make it palatable to smokers. Since tobacco is the main foreign exchange earner for the country, a ban on these additives to burley tobacco would have serious repercussions on the foreign exchange availability.

Mining and quarrying is gradually taking a greater share of Malawi's economy. The sector is expected to grow by 83 per cent in 2010 compared to about 9 per cent in 2009. This is driven by uranium production at the Kayelekera Uranium Mine in Karonga and high demand for coal for tobacco processing and industrial use. For the same reason, the mining and quarrying sector is forecast to grow by 72 per cent in 2011. The on-going road, Nsanje in-land port and other public construction works are expected to drive growth in the construction sector by about 17 per cent in 2010.

Following country-wide expansion of the mobile phone industry (especially by the country's largest operator, Bharti Airtel) as well as innovations in the electronic finance and telecommunications sub-sectors, the information and communications sector is projected to grow by 15.3 per cent in 2010 and 11.1 per cent in 2011. Similarly, the financial and insurance services sector is estimated to grow by 11.5 per cent in 2010, from 7.5 per cent in the preceding year, on account of expansion of ATM services and introduction of mobile banking.

Manufacturing accounted for about 10 per cent of GDP in 2009. The main activities are in agro-processing which is expected to grow by 7.5 per cent in 2010 from 4.7 per cent in 2009. Energy and foreign exchange shortages continued to undermine operations in the manufacturing sector as some firms are scaling down operations. This situation may degenerate with serious negative effects on Malawi's economy if the problems are not addressed quickly.

Private sector development

Economic development in Malawi is constrained by several infrastructural and structural inadequacies, not least its long, skinny shape – 853km (530 miles) north to south and 257km (160 miles) east to west – which makes transportation both expensive and time consuming. Inadequate infrastructure in transportation, telecommunications, power and water supply all hamper private sector growth. Other challenges to growth are foreign exchange shortages, fuel shortages and multiple taxation and administrative barriers to trade.

Road transport is the main method for imports and exports, but its high cost affects the competitiveness of Malawian products and consumer prices. A lack of capital investment restrains the potential of rail and air transportation

As a net oil importer and landlocked country, Malawi is vulnerable to volatility in international oil prices. Perennial fuel shortages have, at times, either paralysed or severely inhibited the operations of different sectors of the economy. They have caused a decline in output by manufacturers, making Malawian exports uncompetitive. The fuel shortages have been blamed on both the rehabilitation work on the Tete bridge in Mozambique and a shortage of foreign exchange needed to import fuel.

Malawi's Emerging Partners (EPs) have concentrated on infrastructural development, agriculture, education and health. The EPs' investment has generated employment especially for Malawi's youth and their goods are found to be cheaper than western alternatives on the market. The overall advantage is that they are complementing traditional partners and not substituting them. The increasing importance of EPs notwithstanding, the share of traditional partners such as the UK, the USA and the European Union (EU) in trade, Overseas development aid (ODA) and foreign direct investment (FDI) flows to Malawi are still significant. However, the increasing presence of China and India in Malawi comes with a number of challenges including flooding the market with cheaper Chinese and Indian goods which make local industries uncompetitive.

Millennium Development Goals

The government suggests that Malawi is making progress on all eight Millennium Development Goals (MDGs). However, the Malawi MDG report for 2010 reveals that the country is on track only in five MDGs. These include eradicating extreme poverty; reducing infant mortality; combating HIV and AIDS, malaria and other diseases; ensuring environmental sustainability; and developing global partnerships for development. The remaining three MDGs on achievement of universal primary education; promotion of gender equality and empowering women; and reducing maternal mortality are unlikely to be attained by 2015.

Risk assessment

Politics	Poor
Economy	Poor
Regional stability	Good

COUNTRY PROFILE

Historical profile

In the eighth century, the Bantu people of Nyasaland began trading with Portuguese merchants on the east African coast. The slave trade expanded rapidly over the period of 1790–1860.

1850 After David Livingstone, a Scottish missionary, visited the area he was followed by other missionaries and traders.

1891 The Nyasaland and District Protectorate was established by Britain. In the wake of David Livingstone's explorations an increasing number of Europeans went to Nyasaland, particularly missionaries. The settlers expropriated land and imposed taxes which led to ever growing numbers of Africans working on the coffee plantations or moving to the then Rhodesia or South Africa.

1893 Name was changed to the British Central African Protectorate.

1907 The Central African Protectorate became Nyasaland.

1944 Nationalists establish the Nyasaland African Congress (NAC).

1950s Opposition to colonial rule, which had begun in the southern highlands, became more widespread. The NAC opposed the planned Central African Federation (CAF) with Northern and Southern Rhodesia, and the heavy-handed interference by white settlers in traditional agricultural methods. The CAF came into being on 1 August 1953.

1954 The NAC grew rapidly upon the return from Britain of Dr Hastings Kamuzu Banda; within a year the colonial authorities had jailed him and other leaders.

KEY INDICATORS — Malawi

	Unit	2006	2007	2008	2009	2010
Population	m	*13.12	*13.39	*13.66	*13.93	*14.90
Gross domestic product (GDP)	US$bn	3.16	3.60	4.30	4.60	5.10
GDP per capita	US$	236	268	313	328	322
GDP real growth	%	2.1	9.5	9.3	9.0	6.5
Inflation	%	13.9	8.0	8.7	8.4	7.4
Industrial output	% change	10.1	8.5	6.0	5.1	–
Agricultural output	% change	10.9	5.9	5.2	14.4	–
Exports (fob) (goods)	US$m	467.0	731.7	969.2	–	–
Imports (fob) (goods)	US$m	906.0	1,182.0	1,722.8	–	–
Balance of trade	US$m	-439.0	-450.3	-753.6	–	–
Current account	US$m	-195.0	-58.0	-331.0	-360.0	-66.0
Total reserves minus gold	US$m	133.8	216.6	242.8	149.4	–
Foreign exchange	US$m	129.6	212.9	239.1	143.6	–
Exchange rate	per US$	139.45	139.40	139.95	141.17	150.49

* estimated figure

1959 The NAC was banned after violence flared between supporters and government authorities. Banda and several other leaders were arrested and a state of emergency declared.
Malawi Congress Party (MCP) was founded as a successor to the NAC.
1961 Dr Banda was released and invited to London for a constitutional conference, at which Nyasaland was promised eventual independence regardless of constitutional developments in the rest of the CAF. Elections followed, which Dr Banda's MCP won.
1963 The CAF was officially dissolved, paving the way for independence in Nyasaland.
1964 Dr Banda became prime minister after independence was declared on 6 July.
1966 On 6 July Nyasaland became a republic and was renamed Malawi; Dr Banda became president. The constitution established a one-party state.
1971 Banda declared himself president for life.
1975 Zomba was replaced as the capital by Lilongwe
1978 Dr Banda and the MCP won the first election since independence. All candidates had to be members of the MCP and approved by Dr Banda.
1992 Catholic bishops condemned Banda and the one-party state and sparked mass demonstrations; humanitarian aid to the country was cut off.
1993 A referendum overwhelmingly backed a multi-party option and political parties began to develop.
1994 The United Democratic Front (UDF) beat the MCP in multi-party legislative elections and Bakili Muluzi became president. Dr Banda retired.
1995 Banda was acquitted of ordering the murder of three government ministers, he later apologised for any suffering he may have 'unknowingly caused'.
1997 Hastings Banda died in South Africa, where he was being treated for pneumonia.
1999 The UDF won the parliamentary elections and Muluzi retained the presidency for his last, five-year term.
2000 Corruption scandals began to threaten aid flow. Muluzi was forced to dismiss his government.
2002 Malawi's bishops condemned Muluzi's rule, warning that it was becoming a dictatorship. International aid was suspended due to a lack of reform and transparency. A drought caused widespread hunger; food aid was supplied by the UN.
2004 The government offered free anti-retroviral drugs to HIV/Aids sufferers. Bingu wa Mutharika (UDF), won presidential elections, while the MCP won most seats in the parliamentary elections. The elections were not considered free and fair by observers. A coalition government was formed, led by the UDF.
2005 President Mutharika founded the Democratic Progressive Party (DPP). Impeachment proceedings began against the president for corruption; he survived and many of the UDF-sponsors resigned from the party. As a rebuke to the UDF, the DPP won a number of by-elections in its support for the president.
2006 Vice President Cassim Chilumpha was arrested and charged with treason; it was alleged that he had hired a South African assassin to kill the president. Former president Bakili Muluzi was arrested for corruption, fraud and theft during his time in office.
2007 The 2007/08 budget debate by parliament started late after 60 members of the opposition parties UDF and MCP defected to the ruling DPP. The Supreme Court gave the Speaker powers to expel the defecting MPs.
2008 The government ended diplomatic relations with Taiwan, in favour of ties with China, stating it recognised Taiwan as 'an inalienable part of China's territory'. Aid worth several billion US dollars offered by China was thought to have persuaded Malawi to transfer its endorsement.
2009 In presidential elections, incumbent President Bingu wa Mutharika (DPP) won 2.7 million votes, against 1.3 million for John Zenus Ungapake Tembo (popularly known as JZU) (MCP). In parliamentary elections the DPP won 114 seats (out of 193) and remained in power.
2010 President Bingu wa Mutharika became chairman of the African Union (AU) for the year. In February, Japan sponsored the distribution of photovoltaic (solar) panels for electricity generation in Kamuzu International Airport, in a programme to introduce 'green-energy' to Malawi. In May international condemnation was heaped on Malawi for the conviction of a homosexual couple who had declared their betrothal (in 2009). A presidential pardon was granted to the couple in June. Malawi's new flag was unveiled in August. The new flag consists of three broad bands of red, black and green, with a stylised white, fully risen sun with sun rays in the centre. The president said the change from red half-sun to white full-sun symbolised Malawi's progress from under-developed country to developed one.
2011 The trial of former president, Bakili Muluzi, began on 8 March. He was accused of misappropriating some US$11 million of international donor funds. The UK's high commissioner was expelled in April after he was quoted in a leaked communication to London as saying President Mutharika was 'becoming ever more autocratic and intolerant of criticism'. In July the UK cut aid to Malawi; the IMF has also cut its aid. The recently passed austerity budget did not include any aid finance. In July riots broke out in a number of cities after a court ruled that protests against the high cost of living, and President Mutharika's government in general, were banned. The trial of Vice President Chilumpha, delayed since 2006, was scheduled to begin in July but Chilumpha sacked his second legal team, resulting in a further delay. The kwacha was devalued by 10 per cent on 8 August. On 19 August, President Mutharika sacked his entire cabinet and took over the running of every ministry himself. On 7 September, President Mutharika appointed new ministers for foreign, financial and domestic portfolios; the defence ministry was abolished.

Political structure

Constitution
The constitution dates from 1966. A multi-party political system was adopted in 1994.
Malawi is divided into 24 administrative divisions.

Form of state
Republic

The executive
The president is both the head of state and the head of government. The president names the 36-member Cabinet and is elected by popular vote for a five-year term.

National legislature
The unicameral 193-member National Assembly is elected by popular vote to serve a five-year term.

Legal system
The legal system is based on English common law.

Last elections
19 May 2009 (presidential and parliamentary)
Results: Presidential: Bingu wa Mutharika (UDF) won with 35.9 per cent of the vote, followed by John Tembo (MCP) with 27.1 per cent, Gwanda Chakuamba of the Mgwirizano Coalition with 25.7 per cent and Brown Mpinganjira (NDA) with 8.7 per cent.
Parliamentary: the Democratic Progressive Party (DPP) won 114 seats (out of 193), the Malawi Congress Party (MCP) 26, United Democratic Front (UDF) 17 and independents 32; four seats undetermined.

Next elections
2014 (presidential and parliamentary)

Political parties

Ruling party
A coalition led by United Democratic Front (UDF) with the Mgwirizano (Unity) coalition,

National Democratic Alliance (NDA), Alliance for Democracy (AFORD) and 38 non-partisan parliamentary members (elected 2004; re-elected 19 May 2009)

Main opposition party

Malawi Congress Party (MCP)

Population

13.93 million (2009)*

Last census: 5 June 2008: 13,066,320 (provisional)

Population density: 87 inhabitants per square km. Urban population: 15 per cent (1995–2001).

Annual growth rate: 2.4 per cent 1994–2004 (WHO 2006)

Ethnic make-up

Chewa (60 per cent), Lomwe (18 per cent), Yao (13 per cent), Ngoni (7 per cent).

Religions

Christianity (80 per cent), Islam (13 per cent), traditional beliefs (7 per cent).

Education

Primary education lasts for eight years. Junior secondary school follows, and if successful, students may progress to the senior secondary school, of which each stage lasts for two years. Instruction is given in English.

Educational attainment, defined as completion of standard eight (at the end of primary school), is only 11.2 per cent. While education is free, provision has not kept up with demand. In some rural areas children have to walk up to 13km to the nearest school. The government's decision to provide free primary education has brought a crisis in the system, placing severe restrictions on its education budget. Secondary schools have less than half the teachers they need and about two-thirds of these are not trained to teach at secondary level. The government proposes to convert Malawi Distance Education Centres (DECs) into Community Day Secondary Schools (CDSS) in order to alleviate the shortage of secondary school teachers.

The University of Malawi typically has approximately 3,000 students, with roughly 1,000 new enrolments every year.

Literacy rate: 62 per cent adult rate; 73 per cent youth rate (15–24) (Unesco 2005).

Compulsory years: 5 to 13.

Enrolment rate: 134 per cent gross primary enrolment, of relevant age group (including repeaters); 29 per cent gross secondary enrolment (World Bank).

Pupils per teacher: 59 in primary schools; in some classes the ratio has increased to 96:1 due to Aids related illness among teachers.

Health

Malaria is endemic; around four million new cases are reported each year.

Malaria accounts for 18 per cent of all hospital deaths and 40 per cent of all outpatients visits. A programme to reduce the effect of the disease includes the provision of insecticide treated nets, more access to prompt treatment for children and increased availability of insulin potentiation therapy for pregnant women.

Malawi experienced a severe drought and locust plagues in 2004–05 that left in 2005, over 4.6 million people short of food. The UK has provided around US$18 million in food aid and in September 2005 announced it will provide an extra £5 million (US$9.1 million) to feed those affected by food shortages. The aid will provide 60,000 tonnes of maize from South Africa, and funds for Unicef to feed 3,500 severely malnourished children as well as subsidies for farmers to buy high-yield maize seed for next year's harvest.

Both the president and the UN World Food Programme have declared Malawi, to be in crisis. Funds required for food-aid are put at US$88 million but only US$28 million, has been pledged by international donors.

HIV/Aids

There were over one million children and adults infected, of which over 50 per cent are females (2005).

With the most productive section of the population at the highest risk from HIV infection in one of Africa's poorest countries, there is concern at the long-term effect on the country's political stability, social cohesion and economic growth. Women, are the country's subsistence farmers, have been hard hit by the disease, which has had a catastrophic impact on agricultural output. It has been estimated that between a quarter and a half of civil servants may die from Aids by 2010, and the government's ability to implement health policies will be severely hampered in coming years.

Aids is the leading cause of death for those aged 20–49, with an estimated 50,000–70,000 adult and child deaths annually, and has left thousands of child-led households. Up to 70 per cent of hospital beds are occupied by patients who are HIV positive. The growing impact of Aids related deaths has driven up the state's health spending on the army and civil service by an estimated 50 per cent, diminishing the amount available to other section of the population.

In 2004 long-term funding was provided, by international donors, to provide more health workers, disease control, HIV testing, mother-to-child infection reduction and to dispense free antiretroviral drugs to HIV/Aids sufferers. Foreign donors had suspended aid funding in 2001 due to corruption and mismanagement and new funding is offered with the proviso of independent vetting.

HIV prevalence: 15 per cent of 15–49 year olds; 8.4 per cent national prevalence and 24 per cent females of reproductive age (The Global Fund).

Life expectancy: 41 years, 2004 (WHO 2006)

Fertility rate/Maternal mortality rate: 6.0 births per woman, 2004 (WHO 2006)

Child (under 5 years) mortality rate (per 1,000): 112 deaths per 1,000 live births (World Bank)

Head of population per physician: 0.02 physicians per 1,000 people, 2004 (WHO 2006)

Welfare

Around 65 per cent of the population lives below the poverty line and deaths from Aids has killed many family breadwinners, fractured families and left communities vulnerable to social disintegration.

In 2002, the government launched a Poverty Reduction Strategy Paper (PRSP) to gain unqualified relief on its US$2.5 billion foreign debt under the controversial Highly Indebted Poor Countries (HIPC) initiative. Malawi launched its war on poverty at a time when the country was facing a severe food shortage. Two subsequent years of poor harvests and a drought in 2005 increased food shortages and threatens millions of people with starvation.

Main cities

Lilongwe (capital, estimated population 656,549 in 2005), Blantyre (691,348), Mzuzu (130,205), Zomba (97,663).

Languages spoken

English is the primary language in business. Chewa (or Chichewa, literally, language of the Chewa) is the major national language; Nyanja, Yao and Tumbuka are also spoken.

Official language/s

English

Media

Press

The government has a range of among others, libel laws, to curb journalists and newspapers from publishing hostile stories.

In English, there are two daily newspapers *The Nation* (www.nationmw.net) and *The Daily Times* (www.dailytimes.bppmw.com), which is owned by Blantyre Newspapers Limited, which also publishes the weekly *Sunday News* (ww.sundaytimes.bppmw.com) and *Malawi News* (www.malawinews.bppmw.com). In Chichewa, *Boma Lathu* is a monthly publication.

Broadcasting
The Malawi Broadcasting Corporation (MBC) operates the state-owned, public radio and television services.
Radio: Radio services are the main medium of mass communication and sources of news and information for most of the population.
MBC operates two national, radio stations, Radio One and Radio 2FM. Private, national networks include, Star FM (www.starradiomw.com), Power 101 and Capital Radio Malawi (www.capitalradiomalawi.com). Radio Maria Malawi (www.radiomaria.mw) is operated by the Catholic Church.
Television: MBC operates TV Malawi (www.tvmalawi.com), which is the only domestic TV channel. It transmits programmes over 24 hours and broadcasting via satellite signals.
News agencies
National news agency: Mana (Malawi News Agency): www.malawi.gov.mw/information1/malawi_News_Agency.htm
APA: www.apanews.net
Panapress: www.panapress.com
Reuters Africa: http://africa.reuters.com

Economy
The country's economy is heavily dependent on agriculture for around 35 per cent of gross domestic production (GDP) and 80 per cent of all exports. The sector also contributes around 64 per cent of total rural income as almost 90 per cent of the population are engaged in subsistence farming. This means, however, that Malawi is vulnerable to external shocks due to global commodity prices as well as adverse weather conditions. Tobacco, tea and sugar are the principal cash crops and uranium is the main mineral exported.
GDP growth in 2008 was 8.3 per cent, which rose to 9 per cent in 2009, buoyed by a large rise in export goods, which are around 20 per cent of GDP (2007–09). Growth in 2010 was estimated at 6.5 per cent and projected to fall to 4.6 per cent in 2011. National development is hampered by poor road infrastructure and a low-skilled labour force, which has deterred foreign investment. High transport costs for this landlocked country can represent around 50 per cent of its import bill, impeding economic development and trade. There are few exploitable mineral resources (except uranium, which is profitable but has a limited and controlled market). Industry accounts for over 20 per cent of GDP (of which manufacturing represents 15 per cent) and the service sector 45 per cent. Structural adjustment has not yet led to an increase in private domestic savings, which have diminished partly due to the HIV/Aids pandemic. Wealth is concentrated within a small elite.
Malawi was ranked 171 (out of 187) in the UN Human Development Index (HDI) in 2011. Of its population of just under 14 million, 52.8 per cent experience multiple deprivations in the same household.
Malawi met the Heavily Indebted Poor Countries (HIPC) completion point in 2006 and became eligible for further relief.
Malawi's creditors allowed debt relief of US$646 million under the enhanced HIPC initiative, an amount equivalent to US$3.1 billion in nominal terms of actual dollar value over a period of time. The IMF believes this initiative will save an average of US$50 million per year in debt service payments by 2020, an amount equivalent to around 2.5 per cent of annual GDP for 2001–09 and 1.2 per cent of annual GDP for the period 2010–20. The country's annual service payments on outstanding debt are estimated to average US$5 million (2005–25).
The government passed an austerity budget in 2011, making no allowance for aid monies. In July 2011 the UK (Malawi's leading aid donor) announced it was cutting its government to government financial support to Malawi, following a diplomatic row. The kwacha was devalued by 10 per cent on 8 August 2011.

External trade
Malawi was one of the founding members of the Common Market of Eastern and Southern Africa (Comesa), which operates a free trade area (FTA) with eight out of the 20 Comesa members and a customs union (CU), which was launched in June 2009, with common external tariffs. Malawi is also a member of the Southern African Development Community (SADC), the objectives of which include reducing trade barriers, achieving regional development and economic growth and evolving common systems and institutions.
Malawi's major exports are tobacco (newly industrialising countries are increasingly important destinations for tobacco) and tea, which are susceptible to external shocks such as droughts and fluctuating world prices.
In April 2009 international donors pledged US$1 billion to upgrade transport links across eastern and southern Africa, in an initiative to speed up and reduce the cost of carrying goods to market. Not only will roads and rail links be improved, but also time-consuming official procedures will be streamlined for efficiency.
Imports
Principal imports are petroleum, food, products, semi-manufactures, consumer goods and vehicles.
Main sources: South Africa (typically 25 per cent of total), Mozambique (20 per cent), Tanzania (6.0 per cent).
Exports
Principal exports are tobacco (60 per cent), tea, sugar, cotton, coffee, peanuts, wood products and garments.
Main destinations: Belgium (typically 20 per cent of total), South Africa (15 per cent), UK (10 per cent).

Agriculture
Farming
The agricultural sector is the most important single sector of the economy, accounting for 39.1 per cent of GDP in 2004 and employing over 85 per cent of the workforce. The sector consists of two modes of production: smallholders, growing mainly food crops such as maize and groundnuts but also tobacco, and estate farmers, growing cash crops for export. Other food crops include cassava, millet, sorghum and rice. Tobacco production generates about 70 per cent of the country's exports.
Formerly a food exporter, Malawi has become a net importer due to the rising population, adverse weather conditions (especially drought), a decline in farming subsidies and smallholders switching to tobacco as their preferred crop.
In the long term, the country needs more investment in food production. Much of the investment in agriculture in the past has been directed at improving export-oriented production, while food production has been neglected.
Donors have been reluctant to give aid for investment due to the lack of transparency in previous years. The government and donor agencies will need to work together to ensure a more even pattern of investment in farming.
Fishing
Malawi has the western and southern shores of Lake Malawi, one of the world's largest lakes. The fishing industry is an important sector, providing much needed protein. Production can vary between 50–65,000 tonnes per year although catches have been falling since 1990 and as a consequent fish imports have increased.
The African Development Fund (ADF) has released US$10.5 million to increase fish resources in five Lake Malawi districts. Part of the money has been used to fund the Lake Malawi Artisanal Fisheries Development Project to assist local fishermen.
Forestry
Around 35 per cent of Malawi's land area is forested and there are significant areas of plantation forests. There are nine national parks and game reserves and a large number of forest reserves which provide varying levels of protection against

deforestation. However, during 1990–2000, forest cover disappeared at a rate of 2.41 per cent per year, one of the highest rates of deforestation in the world. This is largely due to the use of wood for fuel for domestic and industrial uses.

Industry and manufacturing
The industrial sector contributes around 15 per cent to GDP and employs 15 per cent of the workforce. The industrial sector is centred on agri-processing.
The major constraints on growth are the country's relatively limited resource base, small domestic market and difficulties in importing raw materials and intermediate goods.

Tourism
Tourism is being developed with foreign involvement. The country has much to offer the tourist with various landscapes including forests, lakes and mountains. There are several national parks, game reserves, and a friendly population. However attractive the country may be, Malawi's infrastructure is poor and off-putting to all but the most intrepid. The Department of Tourism has been criticised for being ineffective and lacking a national plan to market Malawi, which means that much revenue is being lost.

Mining
The sector is underdeveloped, but has potential in the extraction of heavy mineral sand, bauxite, phosphate, uranium and rare earth elements.
There are three heavy mineral sand deposits with considerable titanium resources: Tengani with over 100 million tonnes of heavy minerals, Mpyukyu/Kachulu with over four million tonnes of ilmenite, 300,000 tonnes of zircon and 10,000 tonnes of rutile and beach deposits along the shores of Lake Malawi.
The Australian owned Kayelekera uranium deposits has reserves of 11,000 tonnes of uranium ore at 0.16 per cent grade. The mine's total capital costs are estimated at up to US$65 million, while the revenue from the mine's 10-year lifespan is estimated to average between US$30–34 million per year.

Hydrocarbons
There are no known oil or natural gas reserves. Consumption was 8,000 barrels per day of oil in 2008, all of which was imported. Most of the country's fuel imports are supplied via Tanzanian and South African ports and delivered by tanker.
The possibility of oil reserves beneath Lake Malawi has been considered since 2000 but with little interest by foreign oil companies.
Any imported natural gas is used exclusively in the Blantyre power plant.
There are very small coal reserves; the main coal mine in Mchenga produces around 60,000 tonnes per annum of bituminous or brown coal, typically used in power stations.

Energy
Total installed generating capacity was 310MW in 2007, producing 1.13 billion kilowatt hours. Over 90 per cent of all generation is provided by hydropower, of which the majority of plants are concentrated on the Shire River in the south of the country; a mini-hydro plant (4.5MW) exists on the Wovme River in the north. Thermal power plants are used as back-up for hydro plants. Less than 10 per cent of the population has access to electricity, the majority of which live in urban areas. The majority of the population relies on non-commercial biomass, mostly fuel wood, for cooking, lighting and power, which has led to deforestation. A planting programme was implemented to replace dwindling resources with shortages becoming acute in the southern region. As oil prices rise there is a corresponding increased pressure on wood resources.
The parastatal, Electricity Supply Corporation of Malawi (Escom), is responsible for generation, transmission, distribution and sale of electricity. Malawi is a member of the Southern African Development Community (SADC) and the Southern African Power Pool (Sapp), set up to provide reliable and economical energy supplies to all 12 members in the region. Imports of energy come from Tanzania and Mozambique.

Financial markets
Stock exchange
Malawi Stock Exchange (MSE)

Banking and insurance
The banking system is underdeveloped and the vast majority of lending is to the government and parastatals. There is little lending to private individuals. There are five commercial banks in operation in Malawi. Although the sector is open to foreign participation, few foreign banks have shown an interest in establishing operations in Malawi.
Central bank
Reserve Bank of Malawi
Main financial centre
Blantyre and Lilongwe

Time
GMT plus two hours

Geography
Malawi is a landlocked country in southern central Africa, with Zambia to the west, Mozambique to the south and east, and Tanzania to the north.
A fifth of the country is covered by lakes, including one of the largest in Africa, the 580km-long Lake Malawi (formerly Lake Nyasa), which borders on Tanzania and Mozambique. The lake is situated in the north-south Rift Valley and is drained by the Shire river, which flows south to meet the Zambezi in Mozambique. The terrain beyond the Rift Valley comprises plateaux and mountains, ranging from 1,000m to 3,000m high, with lower-lying land in the south. There are forests in the northern mountain areas. The Mulanje Massif, at 3,002m (Sapitwa Peak) the highest point in Malawi and central Africa, lies in the southern area, near Blantyre.
Hemisphere
Southern

Climate
On the shores of Lake Malawi and upper Shire River, the weather is pleasantly warm most of the year, hotter in the rainy season. It is more temperate in the highlands and on the plateaux, with cool nights all year. Around the lower Shire River and the south, it is more tropical and very hot during the rains.
The May–August period is cool and dry (the *Chiperoni* wind can be chilly during July and August). The hottest months are September–November. The rainy season is November–April.

Dress codes
There are no restrictive dress codes and resort wear is informal. Travellers are advised to respect local sensibilities, especially when visiting remote areas. Formal attire is usual for business.

Entry requirements
Passports
Required by all, valid for six months beyond date of departure.
Visa
Required by all, except nationals of most EU and Commonwealth countries, Japan and US. For further details contact the nearest consulate.
All travellers must have return/onward passage.
Currency advice/regulations
There are no restrictions on the import of local currency, but export is limited to K200. There are no restrictions on the import of foreign currency, subject to declaration, and export is limited to the amount declared on arrival.
Travellers cheques and all major currencies are accepted by banks, authorised hotels and other institutions. Recommended travellers cheques are South African rand, UK sterling, euros and US dollars.

Health (for visitors)

Healthcare and facilities are basic and expatriate residents usually travel to South Africa when in need of anything but the most straightforward medical care. Medical insurance including emergency evacuation should be arranged prior to travel.

Mandatory precautions

Yellow fever vaccination certificate is required if arriving from an infected area.

Advisable precautions

Typhoid, polio, tetanus and hepatitis A vaccinations. HIV/Aids is endemic and precautions must be taken. Take malaria prophylactics and use mosquito nets at night when provided, as well as insect repellents, especially in lower-lying areas. Cholera and rabies are a risk in some areas; vaccinations are only recommended for those at particularly high risk. Bilharzia is an increasing problem, visitors should only swim in designated areas or in swimming pools.

Although tap water is safe to drink in Lilongwe, Blantyre, Limbe and Zomba, water should be boiled or purifying tablets used in rural areas.

It is advisable to carry a sterile first aid kit including syringes, as well as any prescribed medicines.

Hotels

Good hotels available in all main commercial centres. However, space can be limited so reservations should be made well in advance and a booking confirmation obtained. A 10 per cent service charge and government tax are added to bills, and a small tip is occasionally expected.

Credit cards

Credit cards are accepted in major hotels, restaurants and car hire companies in Blantyre and Lilongwe.

Public holidays (national)

Fixed dates

1 Jan (New Year's Day), 15 Jan (John Chilembwe Day), 3 Mar (Martyrs' Day), 1 May (Labour Day), 14 Jun (Freedom Day), 6 Jul (Republic Day), 25–26 Dec (Christmas).

If a public holiday falls on a Saturday, the preceding day will be a holiday; if on a Sunday, the next day will be a holiday.

Variable dates

Easter, Mothers' Day (second Mon in Oct), Arbor Day (second Mon in Dec).

Working hours

Banking

Mon–Fri: 0800–1400.

Business

Mon–Fri: 0730–1700, with one-hour lunch break 1200–1300.

Government

Mon–Fri: 0730–1700, with one-hour lunch break 1200–1300.

Shops

Mon–Fri: 0800–1700; Sat: 0800–1200.

Telecommunications

Telephone/fax

The telephone system is poor.

Mobile/cell phones

GSM 900 services are available throughout much of the country.

Electricity supply

230V/50Hz.

Security

Normal precautions should be taken. Travel after nightfall should be avoided.

Getting there

Air

National airline: Air Malawi.

International airport/s:

Lilongwe-Kamuzu International (LLW), 26km north of the city; bars, restaurants, bank, post office, shops, car hire.

Airport tax: US$30, paid in US dollars.

Surface

The lake-ship-road-rail Northern Corridor route to Dar es Salaam (Tanzania) carries half of Malawi's fuel imports. It has the potential capacity to carry up to two-thirds of foreign freight.

Road: Road border points with Zambia, Mozambique and Tanzania open 0600—1800. To bring a vehicle into Malawi, either a *carnet de passage* is required, or a temporary import permit (TIP) which can be obtained at border posts for a small fee. There are two main routes from Zambia: via Chipata on the Lilongwe to Lusaka road and, further north, via Chitipa on the Karonga to Nakonde road. Entry from Tanzania is via the Songwe river bridge, north of Kaporo. Roads also link with Mozambique.

Rail: Link with Nacala (Mozambique), but capacity is severely limited by poor track condition.

Getting about

National transport

Air: Air Malawi flies regular services linking Lilongwe, Blantyre, Mzuzu, Karonga, Nyika National Park and the southern lakeshore. There are also charter services to several locations.

Road: There are around 28,000km of roads with major highways linking main centres. The standard of the surfaces is variable and can be poor.

Buses: The bus network covers most of the country. Luxury coaches operate on the Blantyre-Zomba-Lilongwe route.

Rail: There is a limited rail network, largely used for freight. Passenger services are slow and crowded and not suitable for tourists.

Water: A passenger ferry boat operates on Lake Malawi travelling between Monkey Bay in the south and Chilumba in the north, stopping regularly in between. The round trip operates weekly.

City transport

Taxis: Taxis operate in the main towns, but are scarce. Fares should be agreed in advance of journey.

Buses, trams & metro: There are regular bus services in and between the main centres, including luxury services between Lilongwe and Blantyre and Lilongwe and Mzuzu.

Car hire

Car hire is available in main cities. Demand is high so cars should be booked in advance. Self-drive cars are hired at a daily rate, which includes the first 40km. A full international driver's licence is required and a minimum age of 25 with two years' driving experience. Seat belts must be worn in the front seats. Traffic drives on the left. General speed limit of 80kph, and 60kph in urban areas.

Chauffeurs charge a daily rate plus overtime after 1600 and at lunch-time.

BUSINESS DIRECTORY

The addresses listed below are a selection only. While World of Information makes every endeavour to check these addresses, we cannot guarantee that changes have not been made, especially to telephone numbers and area codes. We would welcome any corrections.

Telephone area codes

The international direct dialling code (IDD) for Malawi is +265, followed by the subscriber's number.

Useful telephone numbers

International operator: 102

Domestic operator: 0

Directory enquiries: 191

Emergencies (Blantyre, Lilongwe): 199

Chambers of Commerce

Central Region Chamber of Commerce, PO Box 31357, Lilongwe (tel: 1759-593; fax: 1758-982; e-mail: crcci@sdnp.org.mw).

Malawi Confederation of Chambers of Commerce and Industry, Masauko Chipembere Highway, Chichiri Trade Fair Grounds, PO Box 258, Blantyre (tel: 1671-988; fax:1671-147; e-mail: mcci@eomw.net).

Northern Region Chamber of Commerce, Private Bag 135, Mzuzu (tel: 3133-415; fax: 1334-619; e-mail: nrcci@sdnp.org.mw).

Southern Region Chamber of Commerce, PO Box 258, Blantyre (tel/fax: 1675-113; e-mail: srcci@sdnp.org.mw).

Banking

CBM Financial Services Limited, PO Box 2619, Victoria Avenue, Blantyre (tel: 1621-280; fax: 1624-525).

Stanbic Malawi, PO Box 1111, Capital City, Blantyre (tel: 6120-144; fax: 1620-117).

Finance Bank of Malawi, PO Box 421, Finance House, Victoria Avenue, Blantyre (tel: 1624-799; fax: 1622-957; email: makhan@malawi.net).

First Merchant Bank Limited, PO Box 122, First House, Glyn Jones Road, Blantyre (tel: 1622-787; fax: 1621-978).

Investment & Development Bank of Malawi, PO Box 358, Indebank House, Kaushong Road, Top Mandala, Blantyre (tel: 1620-055; fax: 1623-353).

Loita Investment Bank Ltd, Loita House, Victoria Avenue; Private Bag 389, Chichiri, Blantyre 3 (fax: 1622-683).

Malawi Savings Bank, PO Box 521, Umoyo House, Blantyre (tel: 1625-111 fax: 1621-929).

National Bank of Malawi, PO Box 945, Victoria Avenue, Blantyre (tel: 1620-622; fax: 1620-464).

Central bank

Reserve Bank of Malawi, Convention Drive, City Centre, PO Box 30063, Lilongwe 3 (tel: 1770-600; fax:1 772-752; e-mail: webmaster@rbm.mw).

Stock exchange

Malawi Stock Exchange (MSE): www.mse.co.mw

Travel information

Air Malawi, PO Box 84,4 Robins Road, Blantyre (tel: 1820-811; fax: 1820-042; e-mail: it@airmalawi.net).

Malawi Railways, PO Box 5492, Limbe (tel: 1640-844; fax: 1640-683).

Ministry of tourism

Ministry of Information and Tourism, Tourism House, Convention Drive, PO Box 326, Lilongwe (tel: 1775-499; fax: 1770-650; e-mail: psinfo@sdnp.org).

National tourist organisation offices

Malawi Tourism Association, Aquarius House, PO Box 1044, Lilongwe (tel: 1770-010; fax: 1770-131; e-mail: mta@malawi.net).

Ministries

Ministry of Economic Planning and Development, PO Box 30136, Capital City, Lilongwe 3 (tel: 1782-300; fax: 1782-224).

Ministry of Energy and Mining, Private Bag 309, Lilongwe 3 (tel: 1784-178; fax: 1784-236).

Ministry of Lands and Valuation, Tikwere House, Private Bag 311, Lilongwe 3 (tel: 1780-755; fax: 1780-727).

Ministry of Physical Planning and Surveys, PO Box 30385, Capital City, Lilongwe 3 (tel: 1784-655).

Ministry of Trade and Industry, PO Box 30366, Lilongwe 3 (tel: 1732-711; fax: 1732-551).

Other useful addresses

Agricultural Development & Marketing Corporation (ADMARC), PO Box 50512, Limbe (tel: 1640-500; fax: 1640-486).

Civil Service Commission, PO Box 30133, Capital City, Lilongwe 3 (tel: 1783-811).

Electricity Supply Commission of Malawi, PO Box 2047, Blantyre (tel: 1622-000; fax: 1622-008).

European Development Fund, Lingadzi House, PO Box 30102, Lilongwe 3 (tel: 1730-255).

Geological Survey Department, PO Box 27, Zomba (tel: 1522-166; fax: 1522-716).

Immigration Office, PO Box 331, Blantyre (tel: 1623-777; fax: 1623-065).

Malawi Broadcasting Corporation, PO Box 30133, Chichiri, Blantyre 3 (tel: 1671-222; fax: 1671-257).

Malawi Bureau of Standards, PO Box 946, Blantyre (tel: 1670-488; fax: 1670-756).

Malawi Development Corporation, Development House, PO Box 566, Blantyre (tel: 1620-100; fax: 1620-584).

Malawi Embassy (USA), 2408 Massachusetts Avenue, NW, Washington DC 20008 (tel: (+1-202)-797-1007; fax: (+1-202)-265-0976; e-mail: embassy@malawi.org).

Malawi Export Promotion Council, Delamere House, Victoria Avenue, PO Box 1299, Blantyre (tel: 1620-499).

Malawi Investment Promotion Agency, Private Bag 302, Lilongwe 3 (tel: 1780-800; fax: 1781-781).

Malawi Iron and Steel Corporation, PO Box 2165, Blantyre (tel: 671-455).

National Statistical Office, PO Box 333, Zomba (tel: 1522-377; fax: 1523-130).

Registrar General's Department (Companies etc), Private Bag 100, Blantyre (tel: 1635-077; fax: 1640-877).

United Nations Development Programme, Resident Representative, PO Box 30135, Capital City, Lilongwe 3 (tel: 1783-500; fax: 1783-637).

National news agency: Mana (Malawi News Agency): www.malawi.gov.mw/information1/malawi_News_Agency.htm

Internet sites

Africa Business Network: http://www.ifc.org/abn

AllAfrica.com: http://allafrica.com

African Development Bank: http://www.afdb.org

Africa Online: http://www.africaonline.com

MalawiBiz.com: http://www.malawibiz.com/complist.html

Mbendi AfroPaedia (information on companies, countries, industries and stock exchanges in Africa): http://mbendi.co.za

Malaysia

KEY FACTS

Official name: Persekutuan Tanah Malaysia (Federation of Malaysia)

Head of State: Yang di Pertuan Agong (traditional ruler) Tuanku Abdul Halim Muadzam Shah ibni al Marhum Sultan Badlishah (from 13 Dec 2011)

Head of government: Datuk Seri Mohamed Najib bin Tun Hj Abd Razak (UNMO) (appointed 3 Apr 2009)

Ruling party: Barisan Nasional (BN) (National Front) multi-racial coalition of 14 parties, led by Pertubuhan Kebangsaan Melayu Bersatu (United Malays National Organisation) (UMNO) (re-elected 8 Mar 2008)

Area: 330,434 square km

Population: 28.25 million (2010)*

Capital: Kuala Lumpur; Putrajaya (administrative capital)

Official language: Bahasa Malaysia

Currency: Ringgit (also known as Malaysian dollar) (M$) = 100 sen

Exchange rate: M$3.19 per US$ (Oct 2011)

GDP per capita: US$8,423 (2010)

GDP real growth: 7.20% (2010)

GDP: US$238.00 billion (2010)

Labour force: 11.38 million (2009)

Unemployment: 3.30% (2010)

Inflation: 1.70% (2010)

Oil production: 716,000 bpd (2010)

Balance of trade: US$40.25 billion (2009)

* estimated figure

Malaysia's cherished ambition of becoming a 'developed' country by 2020 looked a little elusive by mid-2011. In the previous year inward investment had dropped by 80 per cent and foreign reserves by 25 per cent. At the same time, the national debt had risen by 50 per cent. One pessimistic minister had expressed the view that by 2019 Malaysia would be bankrupt. The economy decelerated over the first half of 2011, with gross domestic product (GDP) expanding by 4.4 per cent. Private consumption growth continued at a healthy pace but solid domestic demand was not enough to offset a weakening external environment. Malaysia's highly open economy is expected to slow further during the remainder of 2011 and may pick up only in the second half of 2012.

In late 2011, Annette Dixon, the World Bank's Country Director for Malaysia, said in a report that 'In order to achieve high income country status by 2020, Malaysia needs to start creating the environment for 'smart' cities today... Malaysia's goal to become a high income economy by 2020 can be supported by co-ordinated policies addressed at making its cities smarter. Smart cities are skilled and innovative, green and sustainable and resilient to natural hazards. A key challenge for Malaysia will be to increase the volume and quality of skilled workers in its cities. This will require improving higher education and quality of life in cities to retain local talent and attract foreign skilled labour that can contribute to innovation.' Ms Dixon's report notes that the 10th Malaysia Plan (2011–15), which outlines the country's push towards becoming a high income economy, recognises the importance of density and cities to economic growth. Frederico Gil Sander, the World Bank's Senior economist for Malaysia added that 'GDP growth is projected at 4.9 per cent for 2012. This forecast hinges on the implementation of the government's reform agenda as the global economic environment will offer little help.'

The World Bank

In Malaysia, for a long period, the World Bank found itself with a higher than normal profile for all the wrong reasons, depicted as an agent of evil by the government of former prime minister, Dr Mahathir Mohamad. Dr Mahathir had accused the then World Bank president, James Wolfensohn, of using former deputy prime minister, Anwar Ibrahim, of being a proxy not only of Mr Wolfensohn, but also of the US government. Introducing an element of anti-semitism into the slander, according to an article by Ian Buruma in the *New Yorker* in mid-2009, Mahathir had claimed that Wolfensohn, alongside US officials Robert Rubin, William Cohen and Paul Wolfowitz were 'the people behind Anwar'. Mahathir's apparent anti-semitism reflected the sensitivity of Malaysian politics and the latent paranoia of the indigenous Malay community. Malaysia's population is more than half Malay, followers of the Muslim faith. The Chinese community represents a quarter of the population, with the Indians accounting for seven per cent. The Malays, *Bumiputra* as defined in Dr Mahathir's 1970 book *The Malay Dilemma*, are unable 'for genetic reasons' to compete with the Chinese. Hence pro-Bumiputra policies were introduced by successive Pertubuhan Kebangsaan Melayu Bersatu (United Malays National Organisation) (UMNO) governments. UMNO has held power in Malaysia since independence.

Corruption

The Malay community's perception that its interests must be protected at all costs was inevitably a recipe for corruption. As a result Malays were protected by something resembling affirmative action which granted them senior positions, ownership of companies and what Mr Buruma aptly describes as 'preferential treatment in public schools, universities, the armed forces and the government bureaucracy.' Rumours and allegations abounded that Dr Mahathir's family and cronies were enriching themselves illegally. Anwar Ibrahim was a lone voice in demanding transparency and the adoption of the recommendations of the International Monetary Fund (IMF). For this he was not only thrown out of the UMNO cabinet, but also himself charged with corruption and, even

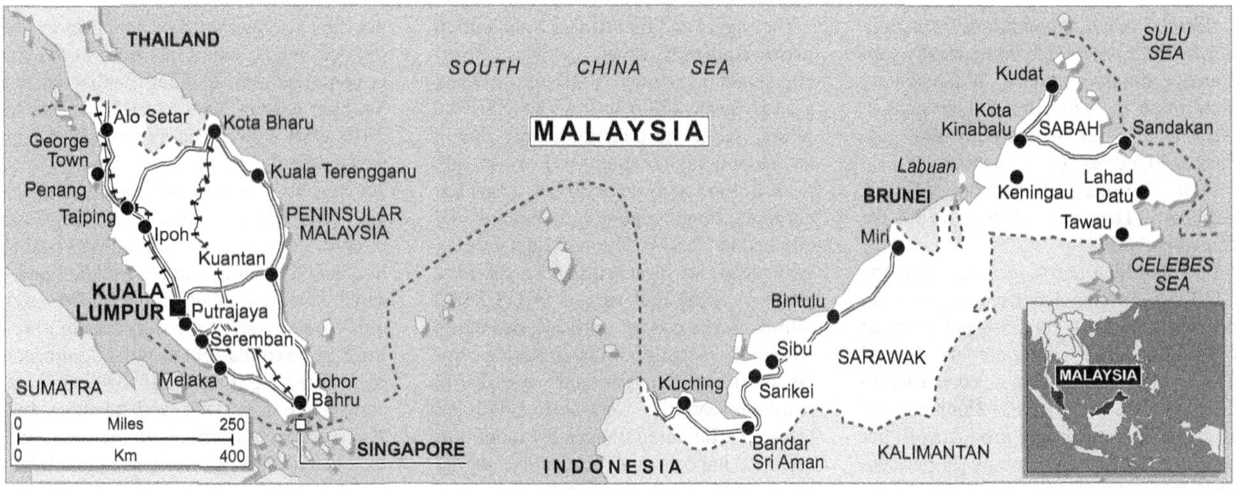

worse, convicted of sodomy. He was eventually released in 2004 having spent six years in solitary confinement. He was returned to parliament in 2008 on a coalition ticket including a secular Chinese minority party, the Pan-Malaysian Parti Islam Se Malaysia (PAS) (Islamic Party of Malaysia) and Anwar's own Parti Keadilan Nasional (National Justice Party). Mr Buruma attributed the steady Islamisation of the Malay community to their general paranoia. Gradually, Muslims were not supposed to drink alcohol (freely available in Malaysia) and women encouraged to wear head scarves.

In 2011, perhaps the highest profile corruption case in Malaysia was that relating to the government's purchase of two French submarines, an order which had created a far reaching and long lasting scandal. Apart from rumours that the submarines, which were delivered in mid-2010, failed to perform satisfactorily, matters worsened, when the remains of a young Mongolian model, Altantuya Shaaribu, were discovered outside Kuala Lumpur. Ms Shaaribu's murder was blamed on two police officers attached to Prime Minister Najib Razak. A third man, Razak Baginda, also linked to Mr Najib, was later arrested for abetting the murder. Following Malaysia's longest ever trial the two policeman were sentenced to death. Ms Shaaribu, it emerged, not only had been 'romantically' linked to Mr Baginda, but was pregnant at the time of her death. It was reported that in 2002 Ms Shaaribu had been promised no less that US$500,000 for her 'assistance' with the submarine contract.

The submarine's French manufacturers, Thales and DCNS, were under investigation following allegations that illegal 'payments for co-ordination and support services' had been made. Mr Baginda's company, Perimekar, had been paid a commission as high as US$150 million. When news of this reached Ms Shaaribu she decided to press for payment of US$150,000, a decision which probably led to her death.

The economy

According to the Asian Development Bank (ADB) strong domestic demand and a recovery in exports created a 7.2 per cent rebound in GDP in 2010, after the global recession had pushed the economy into a 1.7 per cent contraction in 2009. Private consumption rose by 6.6 per cent in 2010, buoyed by positive consumer sentiment, favourable labour market conditions and rising credit to households and businesses. Public consumption was flat, reflecting reductions in operational expenditure as part of the government's fiscal consolidation efforts, which resumed (after a recession-related hiatus) in 2010.

Investment, as measured by gross fixed capital formation and including public investment, surged by 9.4 per cent and contributed most of the total growth in GDP in 2010. Private investment benefited from an expansion in production of domestically oriented manufacturing. The increase in exports of goods and services (9.8 per cent in real terms) was more than offset by stronger growth of imports of goods and services (14.7 per cent). On the supply side, growth was supported by a relatively strong recovery in manufacturing output (11.4 per cent) and by strong growth in services (6.8 per cent) and construction (5.2 per cent). The recovery in manufacturing, which accounts for just over a quarter of total output, was driven by the strong growth in domestically oriented industries, notably those supplying construction and consumers. Export-oriented manufacturing was led by a surge in electrical and rubber products and a more moderate expansion in chemical products. Services, which account for 57 per cent of GDP, experienced broad-based growth. The strongest gains were in real estate and business services, transport and storage and wholesale and retail trade.

Malaysia's construction activity reflected the recovery in residential building, expansion in office and retail spaces and progress in infrastructure projects. Agriculture, however, was subdued, as a rise in natural rubber production was largely offset by declines in crude palm oil and cocoa, while mining output was stagnant largely as a result of a 3.3 per cent decline in crude oil production. Inflation rose to average 1.7 per cent in 2010, mainly owing to higher

prices of food and drink and non-durable goods. Rising global commodity and energy prices lifted inflation to 2.4 per cent year-on-year in January 2011. An increase in the 'official' price of sugar in late 2010 contributed to inflation. Core inflation, which excludes the more volatile food and drinks, has been edging up steadily since February 2010.

Bank Negara Malaysia (the central bank), dismantled a good part of the monetary stimulus injected in 2009. It raised the overnight interest rate three times during March–July 2010, by a cumulative 75 basis points, to 2.75 per cent and kept it there through the rest of the year. The economy's output was still below its potential and there were no strong signs that rising inflation stemmed from demand pressures. The appreciation of the ringgit against trading partner currencies, of around 10 per cent in 2010, helped to damp imported inflation.

Labour market conditions generally mirrored the rebound in domestically generated economic activity. While the labour force increased by 2.2 per cent in 2010, to 11.7 million, the number of people employed rose by 2.5 per cent, to 11.3 million. The unemployment rate fell to 3.2 per cent in December 2010, from 3.4 per cent at end-2009.

In US dollar terms, according to the ADB, total merchandise exports rebounded in 2010, by 26.4 per cent, to US$198.6 billion – after a contraction of 21.1 per cent in 2009 – recovering to 2008's level of exports. Shipments of electrical and electronic products (40 per cent of total exports) rose by 20 per cent and other manufactured exports by about 30 per cent. Exports of petroleum products, palm oil, liquefied natural gas and crude petroleum (together a quarter of total exports) recorded surges of between 33 and 44 per cent. The top five export destinations – Singapore, the People's Republic of China, Japan, the US and Thailand – represented just over half of total exports. Imports rebounded faster than exports, surging by 33.6 per cent to US$156.2 billion, more than offsetting the 21.0 per cent contraction in 2009. Imports of intermediate goods, which account for over two-thirds of the total, rose by about 34 per cent. The trade surplus of US$42 billion remained broadly unchanged from 2009 in US dollar terms.

The capital and financial account deficit narrowed greatly, owing to lower net foreign direct investment (FDI) outflows and a surge in portfolio inflows of US$14.0 billion, reflecting a strengthening ringgit and sharply higher equity inflows, mostly from Europe, into government securities, corporate bonds and stocks. Inward FDI climbed to US$8.6 billion, with a particularly steep rise in investment in services, while outward FDI surged to US $13.2 billion. Other capital outflows decreased slightly, on account of lower private capital outflows. International reserves at end-February 2011 were up to US$109.8 billion, sufficient to finance 8.1 months of retained imports and equivalent to 4.3 times short-term external debt. Following the expansionary fiscal policy adopted in 2009, consisting of two fiscal stimulus packages that widened the overall federal budget deficit to 7.0 per cent of GDP, preliminary figures indicate that the deficit narrowed in 2010 to 5.6 per cent of GDP, as budgeted. This outcome was achieved mostly through a modest increase in revenue and restrained operational spending.

By mid-2010, direct subsidies had risen to nearly 11 per cent of federal government operating expenditure, with over half going for fuel subsidies. Moving to rein in this cost to the budget, three times in 2010 the government raised fuel prices (they are still lower than in neighbouring countries) and sugar prices by just over 10 per cent. Reflecting the reduction in the federal budget deficit, the ratio of federal government debt to GDP declined from 54.0 per cent in 2009 to 51.3 per cent in 2010. Only 3.5 per cent of the public debt was external.

The ADB's outlook is predicated on two key assumptions. First, the surge in mostly short-term capital inflows stabilises and does not generate inflation pressures. Second, the government can quickly start carrying out its structural reform programme which will require not only effective horizontal co-ordination across line ministries and agencies but also vertical co-ordination between the federal and state governments. On this basis and against the backdrop of slowing growth in external demand from major industrial countries, continuing domestic fiscal consolidation and dissipating base effects GDP growth is projected to moderate to 5.3 per cent in 2011.

Domestic demand is likely to be the key driver of growth, reflecting broadly positive consumer and investor sentiment. Net exports are expected to exert a continued (though lightening) drag as the rate of growth of imports of goods and services stabilises following the rebound in 2010. Private consumption is seen staying robust and benefiting from relatively favourable employment, good real wages in manufacturing, rising commodity prices and the accommodative financing environment.

KEY INDICATORS — Malaysia

	Unit	2006	2007	2008	2009	2010
Population	m	26.39	26.84	27.30	27.76	*28.25
Gross domestic product (GDP)	US$bn	156.09	186.48	22.16	191.50	238.00
GDP per capita	US$	5,951	6,942	8,118	6,897	8,423
GDP real growth	%	5.9	6.2	4.8	-1.6	7.2
Inflation	%	3.6	2.1	5.4	0.6	1.7
Unemployment	%	3.3	3.2	3.3	3.6	3.3
Industrial output	% change	–	–	0.8	-6.6	–
Agricultural output	% change	–	–	4.3	0.4	–
Oil output	'000 bpd	747.0	755.0	754.0	739.0	716.0
Natural gas output	bn cum	60.2	60.5	62.5	64.1	66.5
Exports (fob) (goods)	US$m	160,842.0	176,403.0	199,733.0	157,655.0	–
Imports (fob) (goods)	US$m	124,144.0	139,075.0	148,472.0	117,402.0	–
Balance of trade	US$m	36,698.0	37,328.0	51,261.0	40,253.0	–
Current account	US$m	25,313.0	26,045.0	38,914.0	31,801.0	28,119.0
Total reserves minus gold	US$m	82,132.0	101,019.0	91,149.0	95,432.0	104,884.0
Foreign exchange	US$m	81,724.0	100,635.0	90,605.0	92,865.0	102,325.0
Exchange rate	per US$	3.55	3.44	3.33	3.52	3.22

* estimated figure

Energy

Malaysia's national oil and gas company, Petroleam Nasional Berhad (Petronas), holds exclusive ownership rights to all oil and gas exploration and production projects in Malaysia and is the single largest contributor of Malaysian government revenues, almost half in 2009, by way of dividends and taxes. As Malaysia's oil fields are maturing, the government is focused on enhancing output from existing fields and from new offshore developments of both oil and gas, which are expected to increase aggregate production capacity in the near- to mid-term.

Since its incorporation, Petronas has grown to be an integrated international oil and gas company with business interests in 31 countries. It was ranked by the US *Fortune* magazine as the 80th largest corporation in the world in 2009 but had slipped to the 86th largest by 2011. All foreign and private companies must operate through production sharing contracts (PSCs) with Petronas. ExxonMobil is the largest foreign oil company by production volume; other major foreign oil producers operating in Malaysia include Shell, Murphy Oil and Talisman Energy (Canada).

Malaysia's strategic seaboard location on its western coast runs alongside the Strait of Malacca, an important route for maritime energy trade that links the Indian and Pacific Oceans. Malaysia's position in the South China Sea makes it a party to the various disputes among neighbouring countries over competing claims to under-sea resources. Although Malaysia has bilaterally resolved competing claims with Vietnam, Brunei and Thailand, a potential problem is the fact that China claims almost all of the South China Sea, including the Spratly Islands, which are close to oil and gas producing basins.

According to the *Oil & Gas Journal* (OGJ), Malaysia held proven oil reserves of 5.8 billion barrels as of December 2010. Nearly all of Malaysia's oil comes from offshore fields. The continental shelf is divided into 3 producing basins: the Malay basin in the west and the Sarawak and Sabah basins in the east. Most of the country's oil reserves are located in the Malay basin and tend to be of high quality. Malaysia's benchmark crude oil, Tapis Blend, is very light and sweet with an API gravity of 44° and sulphur content of 0.08 per cent by weight.

Energy policy in Malaysia is made and overseen by the government's Economic Planning Unit (EPU) and the Implementation and Co-ordination Unit (ICU), which report directly to the Prime Minister. Malaysia's energy policy has historically focused on maintaining the reserve base to ensure long term supply security while providing affordable fuel supplies to its population. In July 2010, the government introduced subsidy reductions for gasoline, diesel and liquid petroleum gas (LPG).

According to the OGJ, Malaysia held proven oil reserves of 4 billion barrels as of January 2010. Nearly all of Malaysia's oil comes from offshore fields. The continental shelf is divided into 3 producing basins: the Malay basin in the west and the Sarawak and Sabah basins in the east. Most of the country's oil reserves are located in the Malay basin and tend to be of high quality. Malaysia's benchmark crude oil, Tapis Blend, is very light and sweet with an API gravity of 44° and sulphur content of 0.08 per cent by weight.

Exploration and production

Total oil production in 2010 was 716,000 barrels per day (bpd), of which 83 per cent was crude oil. More than half of total Malaysian oil production currently comes from the Tapis field in the offshore Malay basin. Malaysian oil production has been gradually decreasing since reaching a peak of 862,000bpd in 2004 due to its maturing offshore reservoirs. Malaysia consumes the majority of its production – domestic consumption has been rising as production has been falling. Exports in 2009 were 157,000bpd. However, the government is focussed on opening up new investment opportunities by enhancing output from existing fields and developing new fields in deepwater areas offshore Sarawak and Sabah.

Exxon-Mobil's enhanced oil recovery project at the Tapis field, which lies 118 miles off Terengganu in 210 feet of water, will start up in 2013, with an estimated gross investment of more than US$1 billion. Tapis is one of seven mature fields offshore peninsular Malaysia that ExxonMobil and Petronas have agreed to develop as part of a 25-year PSC that was finalised in June 2009. Under the agreement, which includes provisions for the deployment of enhanced oil recovery and further drilling to boost output, work will be carried out on all seven fields, including Seligi, Guntong, Tapis, Semangkok, Irong Barat, Tebu and Palas.

The Commercial Arrangement Area (CAA) in the Malay Basin, which Malaysia shares with Vietnam, also contributes to the country's oil production. Talisman Energy holds operating interests in the Northern and Southern oil fields in the CAA. While the Southern Fields are still under exploration, the Northern Fields development reportedly began producing at 25,000bpd in August 2009, reportedly rising to 50,000bpd in early 2010.

The over-20-years dispute between Malaysia and Brunei over land and sea boundaries had been resolved when the two countries signed a boundary agreement in April 2009. Blocks L and M were ceded to Brunei while Limbang, a popular tourist site on the Sarawak-Brunei border, was ceded to Malaysia. In September 2010, Petronas and the Brunei government reportedly agreed to jointly develop the 2 blocks offshore Borneo Island, signing a 40-year PSC for newly named Block CA1; an agreement on Block CA2 is expected.

Deepwater oil production projects under development are all offshore Sabah: The Kikeh oil field is currently Malaysia's only producing deepwater oil field. It is offshore Sabah in 4,400 feet of water and was discovered and is operated by Murphy Oil in partnership with Petronas. It came on-stream in 2007 at an initial rate of 20,000bpd; estimated production in 2010 is 68,000bpd of oil and 62 mcf/d of gas. Murphy Oil is carrying out more developmental drilling in order to boost output to 120,000bpd in the near term. The nearby Kakap and Siakap fields, discovered in mid-2009 in the same block, will be tied into Kikeh in 2011 and 2013, respectively, to maintain steady production through 2015.

Natural gas

According to the June 2011 issue of the *BP Statistical Review of World Energy* (BP11), Malaysia held 2.4 trillion cubic metres (tcm) of proven natural gas reserves as of December 2010. Most of the country's natural gas reserves are in its eastern areas, predominantly offshore. As in the oil sector, Malaysia's state-owned Petronas dominates the natural gas sector. The company has a monopoly on all upstream natural gas developments and also plays a leading role in downstream activities and the LNG trade. Most natural gas production comes from production sharing agreements operated by foreign companies in conjunction with Petronas.

Natural gas production has been rising steadily, reaching 66.5 billion cubic metres (bcm) in 2010, while domestic natural gas consumption has also increased steadily, reaching 35.7bcm in 2010. There are several important ongoing projects that are expanding natural gas production in Malaysia over the near term. Exploration and development activities in Malaysia continue to focus on offshore Sarawak and Sabah. One of the most active areas for natural gas exploration and production is the Malaysia-Thailand Joint Development Area (JDA), located in the lower part of the Gulf of Thailand. The area is divided into three blocks, Block A-18, Block B-17 and Block C-19 and is administered by the Malaysia-Thailand Joint Authority (MTJA), with each country owning 50 per cent of the JDA's hydrocarbon resources.

Risk assessment

Economy	Fair
Politics	Fair
Regional stability	Good

COUNTRY PROFILE

Historical profile

1511 The Portuguese took control of Malaysia's south-western state, Malacca, as part of their plans to monopolise the south-east Asian spice trade.

1641 Control of Malacca fell to the Dutch who came to control the entire spice trade.
1786 A port was established in Malacca as part of the British East India Company.
1795 The British took full control of Malacca.
1824 The Anglo-Dutch treaty peacefully divided rule of the peninsula between the Dutch and the British, with the British in control of Malacca.
1826 The states on Malacca, Penang and Singapore were combined to form the Straits Settlements.
1870's Britain brought the Malay states under direct rule. The Pangkor agreement signed with Malay leaders gave the British more control of the territory.
1895 Four Malay states combine to form the Federated Malay States.
1896 The Malay states were grouped together under a British general. During British control, public services, rubber and tin production were developed. The British brought Indian and Chinese labourers to the country to help with construction projects, altering the country's ethnic make-up.
1939–45 Malaysia was overrun by the Japanese. After their defeat, the British resumed control, but the Straits Settlements were abolished.
1948 The Federation of Malaya, comprising the 11 states of Peninsular Malaysia, was formed.
1951 Pressured by strong Malay nationalism, the British were forced to introduce elections.
1955 The first federal elections were held.
1957 Malaya was granted independence from the British. It remained part of the Commonwealth. Tunku Abdul Rahman became prime minister.
1963 The state changed its name to the Federation of Malaysia when Singapore, Sabah and Sarawak joined.
1965 Singapore withdrew from Malaysia. A communist insurgency began in Sarawak.
1969 Increasing frustration over the economic success of the ethnic Chinese lead to anti-Chinese riots by Malays.
1970 Abdul Rahman resigned and Tun Abdul Razak became prime minister. The Barisan Nasional (BN) (National Front) coalition was formed.
1977 Expulsion of the chief minister of Kelantan from the Parti Islam se Malaysia (PAS) (Islamic Party of Malaysia) resulted in violent demonstrations. Direct rule was imposed in Kelantan and PAS was expelled from the ruling BN coalition.
1981 Dr Mahathir Mohamad succeeded Hussein Onn as leader of the BN coalition and was formally elected as prime minister.
1986 Mahathir Mohamad was re-elected in the general election, despite internal party conflict caused by the resignation of the deputy prime minister, Musa Hitam.
1988 Constitutional amendments limiting the power of the judiciary to interpret laws were approved. The Security Law was introduced removing the right of persons detained under the Internal Security Act to have recourse to the courts.
1990 Mahathir Mohamad was re-elected.
1995 Mahathir Mohamad was elected for a third term.
1997–98 The ringgit plunged on worldwide money markets during the Asian financial crisis. The authorities imposed capital controls and a selective exchange rate regime, against the advice of the International Monetary Fund (IMF). Mahathir sacked his chosen successor; finance minister Anwar Ibrahim, after disagreements regarding economic management and political manoeuvring by some of Anwar's supporters. Anwar was arrested for corruption and sexual misconduct.
1999 Anwar was imprisoned. General elections returned the Pertubuhan Kebangsaan Melayu Bersatu (UMNO) (United Malay National Front)-controlled BN to power and brought Mahathir Mohamad's fourth election as prime minister, avowedly his last.
2001 The new federal territory of Putrajaya was created. Malaysian King, Sultan Salahuddin Abdul Aziz Shah of Selangor, one of nine hereditary rulers, died. The Conference of Rulers chose Syed Sirajuddin, the Raja of Perlis state, as the new King and head of state.
2002 King Syed Sirajuddin formally took office. Indonesia, Malaysia and the Philippines signed a pact to counter terrorism and to stop a network that is believed to be trying to turn all three into a single Islamic state.
2003 Mahathir Mohamad, who had been prime minister for 22 years, retired. The deputy prime minister, Abdullah Ahmad Badawi, was immediately appointed to be his successor.
2004 The ruling BN coalition was re-elected in parliamentary elections. An earthquake off the island of Sumatra caused a *tsunami*, which devastated coastal areas in the region. The final estimate for Malaysia was 75 dead or missing, 5,000 displaced.
2005 Malaysia's large population of illegal foreign workers was targeted for identification and removal, leaving the country short of labourers. A state of emergency was declared as the worst pollution since 1997, emanating from forest fires in Indonesia, spread over the country.
2006 Sultan Mizan Zainal Abidin ibni Almarhum Sultan Mahmud al Muktafi Billah Shah of Terengganu took office as the thirteenth *Yang di Pertuan Agong* (traditional ruler), and Head of State, a position he will hold until 2011 when the next Conference of Rulers choses another candidate.
2008 Early elections were called, a year before required. The ruling BN coalition (of 14 parties) was re-elected with 50.3 per cent of the vote (140 seats out of 222); the opposition Barisan Rakyat (People's Front) coalition (of three parties), led by Parti Keadilan Rakyat (PKR) (People's Justice Party, whose leader, Anwar Ibrahim, had been unable to contest the elections) won 46.75 per cent (82 seats). Abdullah Ahmad Badawi remained as prime minister. In what many claimed was a politically motivated police action, Anwar Ibrahim was arrested and charged with sodomy. Nevertheless, he won a landslide victory in the Penang by-election and maintained his innocence during months of investigations.
2009 Abdullah Badawi resigned as prime minister and leader of UNMO, Mohamed Najib Razak replaced him in both positions. Malaysia, was removed from the OECD's blacklist of secretive tax havens, and placed on a grey list of countries that have agreed to adhere to tax disclosure standards, although without legislation enacting it. The government instigated plans to build a new city at the southern tip of Malaysia in Johor State. The 20-year project is expected to cost over US$13 billion. The 2,217 square km area is planned to become the home and commercial centre for three million people. The high court refused to strike out the sodomy charge against Anwar Ibrahim.
2010 Tuanku Mahmud Iskandar ibni al Marhum Sultan Ismail, sultan of Johor died in January and his son Ibrahim Ismail Ibni Almarhum Sultan Mahmud Iskandar al Haj became the new Sultan. In February Anwar Ibrahim went on trial for a second time charged with sodomy; by September the trial continued as Anwar accused former prime minister Ahmad Badawi of political conspiracy.
2011 A bilateral agreement was signed on 7 May between the governments of Australia and Malaysia for irregular maritime arrivals (IMAs) (asylum seekers and unauthorised migrants) attempting to land in Australia to be held in camps in Malaysia while their applications for settlement are processed. Around 900 IMAs are expected to be held in Malaysia annually. In July, the Vatican and Malaysia agreed to establish diplomatic ties. On 14 July, a rally by supporters of PKR demanding electoral reforms turned violent as police cordoned off the centre of Kuala Lumpur and used tear gas and water cannon. The trial of Anwar Ibrahim continued in August

with earlier DNA evidence supporting his claim of innocence dismissed by the trial judge. On 15 September, Prime Minister Razak said that the *Internal Security Act*, a law that had been used to detain indefinitely opposition leaders, union activists and students since the colonial era, would be abolished to ensure a modern and functioning democracy. On 14 October, the Sultan of Kedah, Tuanku Abdul Halim Muadzam Shah ibni al Marhum Sultan Badlishah, was named as the next paramount ruler (from 13 December), by the Conference of Rulers.

Political structure

Constitution

In 1992, the powers granted to the country's traditional rulers upon independence were modified to the advantage of the federal government.

In 1994, a Constitutional Amendment Bill reduced the power of the monarchy.

Each of the 13 states of the federation has its own constitution and legislative assembly. Malacca, Penang, Sabah and Sarawak are each headed by a governor appointed for a four-year term by the King. A Council of State or cabinet has executive authority in the state, and each state has a legislature which legislates on matters not reserved for the federal parliament.

Independence date

31 August 1957

Form of state

Federative republic; constitutional elective monarchy.

The executive

The supreme head of state, the Yang di-Pertuan Agong (King), is elected every five years by a Conference of Rulers (nine hereditary state rulers). The non-executive Conference of Rulers is made up of the Sultans of Kedah, Perak, Johor, Selangor, Pahang, Trengganu and Kelantan, the Besar of Negeri Sembilan and the Raja of Perlis.

Power is concentrated at the federal level of government in Kuala Lumpur, where a Federal Executive Council, or cabinet, is formed by the party or parties with a working majority in the Dewan Rakyat, the lower house of the federal parliament.

The federal government and its premier deal with all federal matters.

National legislature

The bicameral parliment (the federal parliament) consists of the 222-member Dewan Rakyat (House of Representatives), elected every five years by universal suffrage, and the 69-member Dewan Negara (Senate) with two elected members from each state and 43 appointed by the King; senators serve a six-year term. Legislative power rests with the federal parliament, although the Dewan Negara can delay ordinary bills for up to a year. Supply bills, such as the budget, can be delayed for up to one month. The head of state can delay assent to legislation.

Legal system

The basis of the legal system is English common law.

The judiciary underwent major changes in the 1990s. By 1995, the jury system had been completely abolished. Constitutionally, judicial powers have been reduced to the advantage of the Executive. A code of conduct has been established for judges. Controversy has surrounded Malaysia's retention of the death penalty for certain offences.

Two states, Kelantan and Terengganu, have tried to implement a moderate form of Sharia (Islamic law). This move has been blocked by the federal government.

The Federal Court is Malaysia's highest judicial authority, although the King may grant pardons.

Last elections

8 March 2008 (parliamentary)

Results: Parliamentary: the ruling Barisan Nasional (BN) (National Front) coalition (of 14 parties) was re-elected with 50.3 per cent of the vote (140 seats out of 222); the opposition Barisan Rakyat (People's Front) coalition (of three parties) won 46.75 per cent (82 seats).

Next elections

March 2013 (parliamentary)

Political parties

Ruling party

Barisan Nasional (BN) (National Front) multi-racial coalition of 14 parties, led by Pertubuhan Kebangsaan Melayu Bersatu (United Malays National Organisation) (UMNO) (re-elected 8 Mar 2008)

Main opposition party

Barisan Rakyat (People's Front) coalition led by Parti Tindakan Demokratik (PTD) (Democratic Action Party), with Parti Islam se Malaysia (PAS) (Islamic Party of Malaysia) and Parti Keadilan Rakyat (PKR) (People's Justice Party).

Population

28.25 million (2010)*

Last census: July 2000: 23,274,690

Population density: 84 inhabitants per square km (2010)

Annual growth rate: 2.3 per cent 1994–2004 (WHO 2006)

Ethnic make-up

Malaysia is a multi-racial country, including Malay (50 per cent), Chinese (27 per cent) and Indian (9 per cent).

The political dominance of Malays, the 'bumiputeras' prominent in the civil service, military, and education, is accepted by the Chinese and Indian communities in exchange for relative freedom in the private sector. The Kadazans are the principal ethnic group in the state of Sabah, while the Ibans, Bidayuhs and Melanaus predominate in the state of Sarawak. Approximately one million Indonesians work in Malaysia.

Religions

The official religion is Islam (55 per cent), although Malaysia is constitutionally committed to being a secular state. Buddhism, Taoism, Confucianism, Ancestor Worship, Hinduism, Christianity and Sikhism are also practised. The constitution guarantees freedom of religion.

Malays are generally Muslim. Most of the Chinese are Buddhist or Taoist, a few are Christian. The majority of Indians are Hindu, but some are Muslim, Christian or Sikh. Eurasians are predominantly Christian.

Education

Compulsory education covers six years of primary education and three years of lower secondary education.

There is selective entry for upper secondary school that lasts two years for both academic schools and vocational training. Pre-university education lasts for a further year. Higher education is provided by universities, polytechnics and colleges. There are a few private universities with three foreign universities in the country including the Monash University, Curtin University and Nottingham University-Malaysian campus.

Public expenditure on education typically amounts to 4.9 per cent of annual gross national income.

Literacy rate: 89 per cent adult rate; 97 per cent youth rate (15–24) (Unesco 2005).

Compulsory years: 6 to 16.

Enrolment rate: 98.7 per cent net primary enrolment; 69.9 per cent net secondary enrolment (World Bank).

Pupils per teacher: 19 in primary schools.

Health

The Ministry of Health estimates that expenditure on health will reach 7 per cent of GDP by the year 2020. The World Health Organisation's (WHO) assistance to Malaysia for technical co-operation and improving national health strategies amounted to US$1.7 million.

Public hospitals treat about 24.3 million outpatients and 1.5 million inpatients yearly. 55 per cent of doctors are engaged in private practice although only 30 per cent of the population seek medical attention from them. There are 111 public hospitals with seven private medical institutions nationwide with a total of 33,338 beds. Public sector doctors are generally concentrated in urban areas.

The government has also made a special allocation of M$1.74 billion (US$46 million) towards improving the rural health services. There is increasing pressure on consumers to draw up individual financing plans through health insurance schemes and managed care organisations.

HIV/Aids

HIV prevalence: 0.4 per cent aged 15–49 in 2003 (World Bank)

Life expectancy: 72 years, 2004 (WHO 2006)

Fertility rate/Maternal mortality rate: 2.8 births per woman, 2004 (WHO 2006)

Child (under 5 years) mortality rate (per 1,000): 7 deaths per 1,000 live births; 19 per cent of children aged under five were malnourished (World Bank)

Welfare

Malaysia's system of social welfare is not comparable to Western standards, but considerable legislation exists in health and safety, and protection for workers against arbitrary dismissal. The Employees Provident Fund (EPF) and Social Security Organisation (SSO) each have approximately 8.5 million contributors. There are also non-profit-making voluntary organisations and ethnic associations that do much community work among Malays, Chinese and Indians.

Main cities

Kuala Lumpur (capital, estimated population 1.4 million in 2005); Kelang (859,864); Johor Bahru (capital of Johor, 416,364); Ipoh (capital of Perak, 690,118); Kelang (859,864), Petaling Jaya (576,077), Kuantan (338,790), Kuching (capital of Sarawak, 154,652); Kota Kinabalu (capital of Sabah, 201,218).

Languages spoken

Bahasa Malaysia is the national language; it is almost identical to Bahasa Indonesia, the official language of Indonesia. English is common in commerce and industry. Chinese dialects (Cantonese, Mandarin and Hokkien) are widely used in Malaysia, and Tamil and Punjabi among Indians. Other languages include Itan Dusan and Bajau.

Official language/s

Bahasa Malaysia

Media

The state exercises a great deal of control over print and broadcast media through the workings of the internal security ministry. In the 2008 annual report, by Reporters without borders, it stated the ministry censored articles and arrested journalists under the internal security law, while pressure was applied to media outlets to under-report or ignore opposition events and their contrary stances.

Press

Censorship laws constrain journalistic freedom and each year newspapers must renew their publication licence.

Dailies: There are many newspapers published in major cities and regionally. In English, *New Straits Times* (www.nst.com.my), *The Star* (http://thestar.com.my) and from the eastern provinces, the *Daily Express* (www.dailyexpress.com.my) and *Borneo Post* (www.theborneopost.com). In Malay, *Utusan Malaysia* (www.utusan.com.my) and *Berita Harian* (www.bharian.com.my). In Chinese *China Press* (www.chinapress.com.my) and *International Times* (www.intimes.com.my). In Tamil *Tamil Nesan* (www.tamilnesan.com.my).

Weeklies: ACP Publishing has several international magazines titles adapted for Malaysia, including *The Malaysian Women's Weekly*.

Business: In English, daily newspapers include *Business Times* (www.btimes.com.my) and *The Edge Daily* (www.theedgedaily.com). The Institute of Bankers publishes *Banker's Journal Malaysia* (www.ibbm.org.my) (see knowledge resources) as a quarterly and SME (www.smemagazine.com.my) is a monthly magazine for small and medium enterprises. Other industry publications include *Malaysian Industry* and *The Planter*.

The Malaysia External Trade Development Corporation (Matrade) has a website for international trade: www.matrade.gov.my.

Periodicals: Berita Publishing (www.beritapublishing.com.my) has several magazines within its house, including *Anjung Seri* for interior design and women's magazines *Iremaia* and *Jelita*.

Broadcasting

The state-owned, national public broadcaster is Radio Television Malaysia (RTM) (www.rtm.net.my).

Radio: The multi-lingual population has stations broadcasting in community languages only including, Malay, Iban, Chinese, Tamil, Arabic and English with content also targeting interest groups such as the business community (BMF www.bfm.my), women (WFM) and the Iban community of east Malaysia (Cats FM www.cats.fm).

RTM (www.rtm.net.my) operates over 30 radio stations nationally, regionally and locally, plus the external service, Voice of Malaysia. There are a number of private and commercial stations operated by media groups providing national networks including Era (www.era.fm) Hitz (www.hitz.fm), Ai FM (www.aifm.net.my) and Minnal FM (www.minnalfm.com).

Television: Digital TV trials are expected to end in 2009 and a full launch of digital services should be completed by 2015 when the analogue signal is terminated. RTM (www.rtm.net.my) operates two TV channels, RTM1 and RTM2 broadcasting domestic and import TV shows. Other, free-to-air TV stations include TV3 (www.tv3.com.my), NTV7 (www.ntv7.com.my) 8TV (www.8tv.com.my) and TV9 (www.tv9.com.my). Pay-to-view TV is operated by Astro satellite TV (www.astro.com.my) with 19 channels. Political parties broadcast programmes over the internet.

Advertising

The Malaysian Advertising Code, implemented by the Ministry of Information (MoI), and the Code of Ethics, implemented by the commercial department of the MoI, forms the framework for radio and television, the two most important advertising mediums. There are a number of restrictions that are culturally and politically based as the government insulates the large Islamic population from foreign influences. Content considered unacceptable includes, among others, nudity, indecent language and sexist images and the ban on commercials that promote a foreign lifestyle. There is a limit of 20 per cent foreign content on all advertising material.

The majority of the print media accept advertising. Outdoor and cinema advertising is widespread although it is restricted to consumer goods; direct mail is available, but the multi-lingual population can restrict its use. Direct marketing via the internet and mobile/cell phones is growing.

News agencies

National news agency: Bernama

Bernama: www.bernama.com

Economy

Malaysia is abundantly endowed with natural resources including oil and gas, and has a climate conducive to growing export crops including rubber, palm oil, pepper and timber. It has a stable and fast-growing economy, with wealth from basic resources including tin channelled into diversification through a rapidly expanding industrial sector. The Malaysian economy is the third largest in Asia and is geared towards attracting foreign investment, especially in the expanding knowledge-based industries. Malaysia has a high level of technological development, including e-commerce and has a high level of manufacturing for export. Foreign direct investment (FDI) in 2010 was US$9.102 trillion. Production was hit hard when the global economic crisis struck, but Malaysia had built up sufficient foreign exchange reserves to allow it to commit US$20 billion in a series of stimulus

packages between October 2008–November 2009. These packages were intended to create jobs, provide tax incentives and access funds for business. Nevertheless, GDP growth fell from 6.2 per cent in 2007 to 4.8 per cent in 2008, before falling into negative growth of -1.6 in 2009 as global trade weakened. However, in 2010 GDP growth surged back into life at 7.2 per cent as the Asian economies quickly recovered from the global crisis. Inflation followed the economic trend, jumping from 2 per cent in 2007 to 5.4 per cent in 2008, before dropping to 0.6 per cent in 2009 as domestic spending all but ceased; inflation rose again in 2010, to 1.7 per cent.
Malaysia relies heavily on oil and natural gas revenue; high world prices boosted its trade and current account balances to US$38.6 billion 2008, around US$10 billion more each than had been forecast. In 2010, Malaysia had proven reserves of 5.5 billion barrels of oil and 2.38 trillion cubic metres of natural gas.
The government's priority is to improve its human capital in order to remain regionally competitive.

External trade
Malaysia belongs to the Association of Southeast Asian Nations (Asean) Free Trade Area (Afta) and maintains a list of goods that have preferential import duties between members and a programme of tariff reductions due to be introduced in the next few years.
It is a major exporter of manufactured goods, including semiconductor devices and electrical goods and appliances; the government is encouraging the expansion of hi-technology and software products to provide more skilled employment.
Rubber product exports reached US$8.9 billion (M$10 billion), the highest since the 1980s. Malaysia is the world's largest rubber glove manufacturer, producing around 65 per cent of total worldwide rubber glove production. It became a key industry, matching palm oil for its importance along with tropical timber.
Imports
Main imports include electrical and electronic equipment, machinery, petroleum products and plastics, vehicles, iron and steel products and chemicals.
Main sources: China (typically 13 per cent of total), Japan (13 per cent total), Singapore (10 per cent).
Exports
Main exports are appliances and equipment, petroleum and liquefied natural gas, timber and wood products, palm oil, rubber, textiles and chemicals.
Main destinations: Singapore (typically 15 per cent total of total), US (13 per cent), Japan (10 per cent).

Agriculture
Farming
Agriculture contributes around 9.5 per cent to GDP. Labour shortages and migration from rural to urban areas are contributory factors in the decline of the sector in recent decades. Over 20 per cent of the total land area is cultivated. Malaysia is the world's largest producer of palm oil and natural rubber, the latter accounting for around 25 per cent of world production. Most rubber production (97 per cent) occurs in Peninsular Malaysia. Smallholders account for 69 per cent of output. The government is looking to upgrade the sector from small-scale farming to high-scale farming involving the use of technology.
The government has encouraged diversification away from rubber, the colonial-era staple export, into palm oil production; Malaysia now accounts for over half of world output. World Bank aid has supported government initiatives to improve productivity, increase diversification and alleviate poverty in the agricultural sector. In line with the government's emphasis on new sources of growth within the sector, the production of selected Malaysian tropical fruits and flowers has made a particular contribution. Production and export of cocoa and pepper have increased, as newly planted areas have improved yields. Other main crops are coconuts, sugar cane, tobacco, vegetables, coffee, tea, maize and groundnuts. Sugar cane and tea are grown as plantation crops; for the rest, smallholders account for most cultivation.
The government is trying to encourage higher yields in rice, the main subsistence crop. The formerly state-owned Bernas group, a monopoly rice importer, has entered into joint ventures with Marditech, the commercial arm of the Malaysian Agricultural Research and Development Institute (Mardi), in a drive to produce high-class rice that could rival Thai varieties. The dominance of smallholdings in rice cultivation remains the biggest barrier to advanced rice cultivation.
The state-run Palm Oil Research Institute of Malaysia (Porim) is attempting to genetically modify the oil palm, in order to create more palm olein, used as refined cooking oil in India and China.
In 2008 the government announced that more rice would be grown in Sarawak to boost domestic supplies in the face of global price rises of 70 per cent. Malaysia imports over 20 per cent of its rice needs and will divert land assigned for palm oil cultivation to make up national shortfalls.
Fishing
Malaysia typically produces 1.5 million tonnes of fish and other aquatic life per year. It imports about 100,000 tonnes and exports over twice this amount, but the bulk of production is destined for domestic consumption. The main species of fish catch are freshwater fish, marine fish, squid, cuttlefish, octopus, shrimps and prawns. Malaysia is also experimenting with fish-farming.
Forestry
Around 58 per cent of Malaysia is covered by natural forest. Some 14 million hectares (ha), or 43 per cent of total land area, are within designated Permanent Forest Estates, designed to ensure sustainable forestry. Of these some 10.5 million ha are productive forest, the remainder being protected. More than three million ha are designated as conversion forests, which will eventually be cleared and put into alternative use.
Malaysia is one of the world's largest exporters of tropical hardwood; Sarawak is the most important timber-producing area. New markets have been found in the Middle East. The sector is moving away from upstream operations into those with more value added, including furniture making (25 per cent of total exports), plywood (23 per cent), and sawn timber (17 per cent).
Malaysia is a member of the International Tropical Timber Organisation (ITTO) and is committed to sustainable forest management. Rattan, rubber and bamboo are alternatives to logging.

Industry and manufacturing
Manufacturing makes the largest contribution to the economy, accounting for over 30 per cent of GDP and 80 per cent of export earnings. Heavy industries based on the country's natural resources have been developed. The promotion of small- and medium-sized firms has been ephasised and measures taken to disperse industries to less developed states.
Conglomerate groups, often politically well-connected, used to control large parts of Malaysian industry.
The recession tamed some of the excesses of this system. Many have been restructured and the old management replaced.

Tourism
The sector is the second most important foreign exchange earner, after industry. Tourism has been accorded priority status by the government to improve foreign exchange earnings, and to provide employment opportunities. The majority of visitors to Malaysia traditionally come from other Asean nations. The government wants to attract more long-haul tourists from Europe and Australia.

Mining
The leading minerals mining firm, the Malaysia Mining Corporation (MMC), is trying to diversify away from tin and is

prospecting for base and precious metals on the east coast of peninsular Malaysia. Gold mining has been revived and the Penjom mine accounts for 70 per cent of annual gold production. Malaysia produces around 4,000kg of gold per year. Other resources mined include iron ore, bauxite and copper.

There are undisclosed reserves of gold and antimony in Bau in Sarawak. MMC has also found reserves of copper, silver, gold and bismuth in Pahang state and deposits of alluvial gold in Kelantan state. The mining sector output is declining, mainly as a result of falling tin, copper and petroleum output.

Hydrocarbons

Proven oil reserves were 5.8 billion barrels in 2010, with production at 716,000 barrels per day (bpd). Consumption was 556,000bpd in 2010 and the surplus was exported mainly to Japan, Singapore, South Korea and Thailand. There were 53 oil fields in production in 2009 concentrated offshore around the Malaysian peninsula, with several others under development.

The state-owned Petronas has exclusive rights to all Malaysian petroleum reserves and is responsible for all oil and gas exploration and production undertaken through production sharing contracts (PSC) with international oil and gas companies. It currently undertakes exploration outside Malaysia in over 25 countries, through a subsidiary company. Oil reserves are in decline and analysts consider the construction of a new Sabah Oil and Gas Terminal (SOCT) near the first deep-water oil and natural gas field, which will handle around 300,000bpd of oil and 30 million cubic metres of natural gas destined for export worldwide.

On 15 November Petronas reported a 'significant' oil find offshore of Sabah (Borneo). The initial estimate of reserves for this field was 227 million barrels of oil equivalent. The find is important for Malaysia as productivity is falling in existing ageing fields and it is forecast that Malaysia will be a net importer of oil by 2013.

Malaysia, along with China, Taiwan, Brunei, The Philippines and Vietnam, claims the potentially oil-rich Spratly Islands. In June 2010, an agreement was reached between the governments of Brunei and Malaysia to share the revenue of two disputed oil blocks in territorial waters. The dispute had led to international oil companies declining to invest in exploration within the offshore waters while the countries haggled over its sovereign ownership.

There are six refineries in operation, with a total refining capacity of 545,000bpd, sufficient to meet domestic needs.

Proven natural gas reserves were 3.00 trillion cum in 2010; production was 66.5 billion cum, located in the east, especially offshore Sarawak; consumption was 35.7 billion cum and all surplus was exported. Malaysia is the world's second largest liquefied natural gas (LNG) exporter (after Qatar), with the bulk of LNG exports going to Japan, then South Korea, Taiwan and China. Malaysia supplies almost 2 billion cum annually to Singapore, via a natural gas pipeline.

Proven coal reserves were 274 million tonnes in 2009, with a further 347 million tonnes estimated and 1 billion tonnes indicated, given the geological locations. Reserves are mainly located on Sarawak and Sabah. The sector has been subject to underinvestment, but government plans for expanding domestic energy production through the use of coal, so that more oil and natural gas can be exported, will enhance future production.

Energy

Total installed generating capacity was 23.33GW in 2006, of which 86 per cent is supplied by thermal plants and the rest by hydropower. Around 50 per cent of demand comes from the industrial sector, 25 per cent from transportation, 10 per cent from commercial sectors and 10 per cent from residential users.

Development of the coal reserves and hydropower potential is intended to diversify sources of energy and reduce the use of natural gas needed for export. Five independent power producers (IPPs) supply power alongside the established utilities in Sarawak, Sabah and Peninsular Malaysia.

Financial markets

Stock exchange

Bursa Malaysia (Malaysia Exchange)

Banking and insurance

Bank Negara Malaysia ordered a major consolidation programme in 2001. This involved creating 10 institutions from 31 commercial banks, 19 financial companies and 12 merchant banks. By end-2001, 51 financial institutions had successfully merged. As a result, Malaysia's banking system is well-capitalised to meet future demands for capital expenditure.

Central bank

Bank Negara Malaysia

Offshore facilities

Measures to enhance development of Labuan island, Malaysia's offshore banking centre, are planned. Approximately 1,000 financial institutions already have a presence in Labuan.

Time

GMT plus eight hours

Geography

Malaysia comprises 13 states in the Malay Peninsula situated south of Thailand, including Sabah and Sarawak states on the north coast of the island of Borneo, which is separated from the Peninsula by the South China Sea. Peninsular Malaysia extends 740km from Perlis state in the north to Johor state in the south. Sabah and Sarawak stretch some 1,120km from Tanjung Datu (Sarawak) in the west to Hog Point (Sabah) in the east.

Malaysia has a land frontier with Thailand to the north, is bordered by the Republic of Singapore to the south and by the Indonesian island of Sumatra across the Straits of Malacca to the west. Other important neighbours are the Philippines and Brunei which separates Sabah and Sarawak.

Hemisphere

Northern

Climate

The climate is tropical with high temperatures and high humidity throughout the year. Relative humidity averages about 80 per cent annually.

Average daily temperatures 21–32 degrees Celsius (C) in the lowlands; in the hill resorts they average 18–24 degrees C but can be as low as 16 degrees C.

November–February is the rainy season for the east coast of Peninsular Malaysia, the north-eastern part of Sabah and western part of Sarawak. In some years, rainfall is concentrated in short periods and some flooding can occur.

During the months of April, May and October, the west coast of the peninsula experiences occasional thunderstorms in the afternoons. Showers are heavy but they clear up as quickly as they come.

Rainfall averages around 2,300mm a year.

Dress codes

Lightweight clothing is worn all year. The dress code tends to be conservative and although jackets are not usually worn in offices, a tie and long-sleeved shirt are normal. For formal meetings, a full suit is required. Government officials often wear a safari-style short-sleeved suit. In deference to the Islamic culture, western business women should dress modestly at all times.

Entry requirements

Passports

Required by all, and must be valid six months from date of departure.

Visitors must have proof of return/onward passage and enough money to finance their stay.

Visa

Social visas are not required by nationals of most countries although the length of

stay permitted varies by nationality. There are a number of exceptions, particularly African countries, and for a full list go to http://malaysia.embassyhomepage.com/malaysia_visa_malaysian_embassy_london_uk.htm
There are two categories: a visa with reference (VWR), issued in Malaysia and appropriate for business travellers, and a visa without reference (VWTR), issued in overseas countries. All visitors with a VWTR must enter Malaysia through an airport only.
A visitor's pass issued for entry into the Malaysia peninsular is not valid for entry into Sabah and Sarawak.

Prohibited entry
Holders of Israeli passports.

Currency advice/regulations
The import of local currency is limited to M$1,000, the import of foreign currency in amounts over M$1,000 or equivalent must be declared using a Travellers Declaration Form (TDF), which can be obtained from airports, tourist offices or Malaysian diplomatic missions. Export of local and foreign currency is limited to the amount declared on arrival.

Customs
Personal items and a limited amount of tobacco and alcohol may be imported duty-free.

Prohibited imports
Illegal drugs, firearms and ammunition, daggers and knives and pornographic materials. Malaysia enforces a very strict drug trafficking policy that includes capital punishment.

Health (for visitors)

Mandatory precautions
Valid certificate of vaccination against yellow fever if travelling from infected area.

Advisable precautions
Vaccinations are advisable for diphtheria, tuberculosis, typhoid, hepatitis A and B, Japanese A encephalitis, tetanus and polio. Tap water is boiled by many people before drinking, although it is generally regarded as safe.
There is a malaria risk in Sabah (northern Malaysia) and the eastern Malaysia province of Sarawak. There is a rabies risk. Visitors with respiratory problems may be put at risk from the poor air quality caused by pollution.

Hotels
There are a range of good hotels in all main cities. A 5 per cent tax and 10 per cent service charge is added to hotel and restaurant meals. Tipping is not encouraged.

Credit cards
Extensive acceptance of all major cards, particularly in urban centres and hotels. Travellers cheques are also widely accepted.

Public holidays (national)

Fixed dates
1 Jan (New Year's Day), 1 May (Labour Day), 31 Aug (National Day), 25 Dec (Christmas Day).
Holidays falling on Sunday are celebrated the next day.
Malaysia's multi-ethnic and multi-religious population celebrates a variety of holidays – federal, Muslim, Christian, Buddhist, Hindu and others.
In addition to federal holidays, each state has 3–4 additional holidays, one of which is the birthday of its ruler.
1 Feb (City Day) is a holiday in the Federal Territory of Kuala Lumpur.

Variable dates
Chinese New Year (two days, Jan/Feb), Birth of Buddha (Apr), The King's Birthday (first Sat in Jun), Divali (Hindu, Oct/Nov), Eid al Adha, Islamic New Year, Birth of the Prophet Mohammed, Eid al Fitr (two days).

Islamic year 1433 (26 Nov 2011–14 Nov 2012): The Islamic year contains 354 or 355 days, with the result that Muslim feasts advance by 10–12 days against the Gregorian calendar. Dates of feasts vary according to the sighting of the new moon, so cannot be forecast exactly.

Working hours
The Muslim weekly holiday is Thursday afternoon and Friday and is observed in the states of Johor, Kedah, Kelantan, Perlis and Terengganu. Other states have a Saturday–Sunday weekend.

Banking
Mon–Fri: 0930–1600, Sat: 0930–1130 (second and fourth Sat only).
Mon–Fri: 0800–1200, 1400–1600; Sat: 0800–1100 in Sabah only.

Business
Mon–Fri: 0900–170; Sat: 0900–1300, Malaysia Peninsular, times vary in East Malaysia.

Government
Mon–Fri: 0830–1630 in most provinces. Sat–Wed: 0830–1630; Thu 0830–1230 in Kedah, Kelantan and Terengganu.

Shops
Usually 1000–2200 (department stores and supermarkets), 0930–1900 (shops) in Peninsular Malaysia; Mon–Sat: 0800–1830 in Sabah; Mon–Fri: 0900–1800, Sat: 0900–1300 in Sarawak.

Telecommunications

Mobile/cell phones
There are 3G, 900 and 1800 GSM services available in most populated areas.

Electricity supply
220V AC, 50Hz. Three-pin square plug fittings and bayonet-type light fittings are generally used.

Weights and measures
Metric system

Social customs/useful tips
Appointments should be made in advance and punctuality is important. It is customary to shake hands on meeting and taking leave, although Muslim women avoid shaking hands with men and vice versa. Business cards are exchanged after introduction. By tradition, Malaysians are hospitable, open people and prefer to avoid arguments, which are seen as distasteful. Avoiding loss of face is an important consideration in business negotiations. Malaysians place great importance on the correct use of titles. *Tunku* or *Tengku* indicates hereditary royalty; *Tun* denotes membership of a high order of chivalry. *Tan Sri an Datuk* (or *Datuk Seri* or *Dato*) indicate knighthood. *Tuan* or *Encik* is the equivalent of Mr, *Puan* of Mrs, *Cik* of Miss.
Visitors should be aware of the conventions of Muslims, Buddhists and Hindus, and other religious and ethnic groups. Muslims are not permitted to drink alcohol or eat pork. The fasting month of Ramadan is strictly observed. Use right hand only for receiving anything (food, drink, money etc) and for eating. Refusal of offered refreshment is considered discourteous. It is customary to bargain when shopping, except in department stores. Tipping is officially discouraged but is seen in the capital.
The authorities have a very strict attitude to drug abuse and there can be a mandatory death sentence for anyone, including foreigners, who is convicted of possession of even a very small amount of narcotics. Other punishments include whipping, in addition to any custodial sentence. Warning notices about *dadah* (drugs) are prominently displayed at the airport.

Security
Street crime is low compared with European cities, but is increasing. Bag snatching is becoming common generally, as is passport theft on aircraft and in airport buildings. Possessions should not be left unattended, even in vehicles with a locked boot. Credit card fraud is becoming more common, and care should be taken when paying by this method.
Visitors are advised to avoid street gatherings and demonstrations which could place them at risk, especially if gatherings lack police permission.

Getting there

Air

National airline: Malaysian Airlines (MAS).

International airport/s: Kuala Lumpur International Airport (KUL), 55km south of the city, near Putrajaya, duty-free shop, restaurant, ATMs, bank, business facilities, post office, shops, car hire. Taxis must be pre-paid in the airport arrivals area (travel time 40 minutes). There is also a 24-hour express bus service to and from the city centre (journey time 60 minutes). A high speed rail service, (the KLIA Ekspres), provides access to the city in 28 minutes. Tickets can be purchased onboard or at the KL air terminal office.

Kota Kinabalu (BKI), 7km from city, situated on the northern coast of Sabah state is the principal international airport of Sabah on the north-eastern part of Borneo Island of East Malaysia. Facilities include duty free, bank, restaurant and bars. Taxis have prices for zoned trips.

Other airport/s: Penang (Bayan Lepas) (PEN), 16km south of Georgetown, capital of small island off the north-west coast of the peninsula, duty-free shop, bar, restaurant, currency exchange, hotel reservations, shops, car hire; Kuantan (KUA), 16km from city; Kuching (KCH), 11km from the city, (situated in the west of Sarawak on the island of Borneo) and receives a limited number of international flights.

Airport tax: International departure tax: M$45

Surface

Road: There are two Asian highways that pass through Malaysia. The AH2 and AH18 combined, runs north-south along the eastern seaboard, from Thailand to Singapore.

The state of Johor is linked to Singapore by a causeway.

It is also possible to cross the land border between Malaysia and Indonesia between Pontianak in Kalimantan and Kuching in Sarawak.

Rail: A railway line runs from Singapore to Kuala Lumpur, Butterworth, and on into Thailand.

Water: The main ferry crossing from Singapore is between North Changi and Tanjung Belungkor. High-speed ferries run between Sumatra and Malaysia; routes are either Medan–Penang or Dumai–Melaka. A ferry from Port Kelang, Kuala Lumpur's port, goes to Belawan, on Sumatra. Yachts sail irregularly between Langkawi in Malaysia and Phuket in Thailand.

There are ferry connections between Brunei and Sabah.

Getting about

National transport

Air: There are over 20 domestic airports. MAS operates extensive network services to main centres and, particularly in Sabah and Sarawak, smaller towns.

Road: About 80—90 per cent of the 43,818km road network in Peninsular Malaysia is paved. All major cities and towns are linked by roads although in the monsoon season driving can be difficult.

Buses: Most long-distance bus services operate from Kuala Lumpur to all major cities and town. The buses are fast, economical and reasonably comfortable. Seats can be reserved. On many routes buses are air-conditioned, which cost a little more than the regular buses. In Sabah and Sarawak rural services are provided by four-wheel-drive vehicles.

Taxis: In almost every town there are long-distance taxi offices or *teksi* (taxi) ranks. They wait for the full complement of four passengers before leaving.

Rail: The capital city is the hub of the national railway system, which is modern, comfortable and economical. Day and night services link major cities in Peninsula Malaysia.

There is a line which branches off the Singapore-Kuala Lumpur-Butterworth-Thailand line at Gemas and runs through Kuala Lipis up to the north-east corner of Malaysia, near Kota Baharu. There are other branch lines which are not used very much.

There are express and ordinary trains. Express trains are air-conditioned and are generally first- and second-class only, and on night trains there is a choice of sleepers or seats.

Rail passes are only available to foreigners and can be purchased at a number of main railway stations.

Water: The Straits Steamship Company operates a passenger service between Port Kelang and Sabah and Sarawak every nine to 10 days. There are frequent ferry services between Penang and Butterworth. There are boats between the Peninsula and offshore islands, and along the rivers of Sabah and Sarawak.

City transport

Taxis: Travel vouchers for airport taxis are available at the airport counters at fixed rates.

Between midnight and 0600, an extra surcharge of 50 per cent applies. There is an extra charge for telephone bookings. Taxi coupons at fixed prices to various destinations in the city and its vicinity are available at Platform Four of the Kuala Lumpur railway station.

There are bicycle rickshaws in many towns.

Buses, trams & metro: Kuala Lumpur has a 29km, fully automated, driverless, three line, light rail transit (LRT) system (known locally as the Putra, after its original operators): the Kelana Jaya Line, the Ampang Line and the Sri Petaling Line. There are other rail services within the city, including a monorail, a commuter service and two high-speed airport rail links.

Trains: The express rail link between central Kuala Lumpur and the international airport opened in April 2002.

Car hire

Car hire is available in all main cities. Driving is on the left-hand side of the road, and the use of seat belts in front seats is obligatory. International driving licences are required. Chauffeur-driven cars are available.

BUSINESS DIRECTORY

The addresses listed below are a selection only. While World of Information makes every endeavour to check these addresses, we cannot guarantee that changes have not been made, especially to telephone numbers and area codes. We would welcome any corrections.

Telephone area codes

The international direct dialling (IDD) code for Malaysia is +60, followed by area code and subscriber's number:

Ipoh	5	Melaka	6
Johor Bahru	7	Penang	4
Kota Kinabalu	88	Port Dickson	6
Kuala Lumpur	3	Sandakan	89
Kuantan	9	Sibu	84
Kuching	82	Taiping	5

Useful telephone numbers

Emergency: 999

Operator (trunk call enquiries): 102

Directory: 103

International service: 108

Tourist Police: 243-5522

Chambers of Commerce

American Malaysian Chamber of Commerce, Amoda Building, 22 Jalan Imbi, 55100 Kuala Lumpur (tel: 2148-2407; fax: 2148-8540; e-mail: info@amcham.com.my).

British Malaysian Chamber of Commerce, c/o British High Commission, 185 Jalan Ampang, 50450 Kuala Lumpur (tel: 2163-1784; fax: 2163-1781; e-mail: britcham@bmcc.org.my).

Kuala Lumpur Chamber of Commerce, 79 Kompleks Damai, Jalan Datuk Haji Eusoff, Kuala Lumpur (tel: 4042-4711; fax: 4042-1540; e-mail: dpmmbkl@tm.net.my).

Malay Chamber of Commerce Malaysia, Plaza Pekeliling,2 Jalan Tun Razak, 50400 Kuala Lumpur (tel: 4041-8522; fax: 4041-4502; e-mail: wmaster@dpmm.org.my).

Malaysian International Chamber of Commerce and Industry, Plaza Mont' Kiara, 2 Jalan Kiara, 50480 Kuala Lumpur (tel: 6201-7708; fax: 6210-7705; e-mail:micci@micci.com).

Banking

Affin Merchant Bank Berhad, PO Box 1124, 27th Floor, Menara Boustead, 69 Jalan Raja Chulan, 50200 Kuala Lumpur (tel: 2070-8080; fax: 2070-7592).

Bumiputra-Commerce Bank Berhad, 6 Jalan Tun Perak, 50050 Kuala Lumpur, (tel: 2693-1722; fax: 2698-6628).

Bank Kerjasama Rakyat Malaysia Bhd, Bangunan Bank Rakyat, Jalan Tangsi, 50480 Kuala Lumpur (tel: 2612-9600; fax: 2612-9576).

Bank Muamalat Malaysia Berhad, Menara Bumiputra, 21, Jalan Melaka, PO Box 10407, 50913, Kuala Lumpur (tel: 2698-8787; fax: 2692-2000).

Bank Pembangunan & Infrastruktur Malaysia Berhad, PO Box 12352, Menara Bank Pembangunan, Jalan Sultan Ismail, 50774 Kuala Lumpur (tel: 2615-2020; fax: 2692-8520).

Bank Islam Malaysia Berhad, Level 11, Darul Takaful, Jalan Sultan Ismail, 50734 Kuala Lumpur (tel: 2616-8000; fax: 2698-0587).

Bank Simpanan Nasional, Wisma BSN, 117 Jalan Ampang, 50450 Kuala Lumpur (tel: 2162-3222; fax: 2710-7252).

Citibank Berhad, PO Box 10112, 165 Jalan Ampang, 50450 Kuala Lumpur (tel: 232-5334; fax: 232-8763).

Malayan Banking Berhad, PO Box 12010, 100 Jalan Tun Perak, 50050 Kuala Lumpur (tel: 2070-8833; fax: 2070-2611).

Bank Negara, Jalan Dato Onn, 50480 Kuala Lumpur (tel: 2698-8044; fax: 2691-2990).

Sabah Development Bank, PO Box 12172, 88824 Kota Kinabalu; SDB Tower, Wisma Tun Faud Stephens, Km 2.4, Jalan Tuaran, Sabah (tel: 232-177; fax: 261-852).

Southern Bank Bhd, Wisma Genting, Jalan Sultan Ismail, Peti Surat 12281, Kuala Lumpur (tel: 263-7000; fax: 232-5008).

Standard Chartered Bank, 2 Jalan Ampang, 50450 Kuala Lumpur (tel: 232-6555; fax: 238-3295).

Central bank

Bank Negara Malaysia, Jalan Dato' Onn, PO Box 10922, Kuala Lumpur 50929 (tel: 2698-8044; fax: 2691-2990; e-mail: info@bnm.gov.my).

Stock exchange

Bursa Malaysia (Malaysia Exchange): www.bursamalaysia.com

Travel information

Automobile Association of Malaysia, E-7-4, Megan Avenue 1, 189 Jalan Tun Razak, 50400 Kuala Lumpur (tel: 2162-5777; fax: 2162-5358; email: mru@aamhq.po.my; internet: www.aam.org.my).

KLIA Ekspres, Express Rail Link Sdn Bhd, L2, KL City Air Terminal, KL Sentral Station, 50470 Kuala Lumpur (tel: 2267-8088, customer enquiry: 2267-8000; fax: 2267-8910; email: air-rail@KLIAekspres.com; internet: www.kliaekspres.com).

Malaysia Airlines, Main Ticket Office, Bangunan MAS, Jalan Sultan Ismail, 50250, Kuala Lumpur (tel: 7846-3000; fax: 2162-9025; email customer@mas.com.my; internet: www.malaysiaairlines.com).

Rapid KL (Public Transport) 1 Jalan PJU 1A/46, Off Jalan Lapangan Terbang, Sultan Abdul Aziz Shah, 47301 Petaling Jaya, Selangor (tel: 7650-7788; fax: 7625-6667; email: suggest@rapidkl.com.my; internet: www.putralrt.com.my).

National tourist organisation offices

Malaysia Tourism Promotion Board, 17th Floor, Menara Dato' Onn, Putra World Trade Centre, 45, Jalan Tun Ismail, 50480 Kuala Lumpur (tel: 2615-8188; fax: 2693-5884; email: enquiries@tourism.gov.my; internet: www.tourism.gov.my).

Ministries

Ministry of Agriculture, Wisma Tani, Jl Sultan Salahuddin, 50624 Kuala Lumpur (tel: 2617 -5000; fax: 2691-3758; email: matdaud@agri.moa.my).

Ministry of Culture, Arts and Heritage, TH Perbadanan Tower, Maju Junction, 10110 Jl Sultan Ismail , 50694 Kuala Lumpur (tel: 2612-7600; fax: 2693-5114, 2697-6100; email: info@heritage.gov.my).

Ministry of Defence, Jl Padang Tembak, 50634 Kuala Lumpur (tel: 292-1333, 230-1033; fax: 298-4662, 298-5372).

Ministry of Domestic Trade and Consumer Affairs, Lot 2G3, Presint 2, Federal Goverment Administrative Centre, 62623 Putrajaya (tel: 8882-5500 ; fax: 8882-5763; email: nsuzana@kpdnhep.gov.my).

Ministry of Education, Level 5, Block E8 Parcel E, Federal Goverment Administrative Centre, 62604 Putrajaya (tel: 8884-6000; fax: 8889-5235; email: julina@bdpk.moe.gov.my).

Ministry of Energy, Water and Communications, Block E4/5, Government Complex, Parcel E , Federal Government Administrative Centre, 50668 Kuala Lumpur (tel: 8883-6000; fax: 8889-5235; email: norliza@ktak.gov.my).

Ministry of Entrepreneur Development and Co-operative Development, Lot 2G6, Precint 2, Federal Goverment Administrative Centre, 62100 Putrajaya (tel: 8880-5100; fax: 8880-5106; email: webmaster@mecd.gov.my).

Ministry of Federal Territories, Level 3, West block , Perdana Putra Building , Federal Government Administrative Centre, 62502 Putrajaya (tel: 8889-7844 ; fax: 8888-9140; email: admin@kwp.gov.my).

Ministry of Finance, Finance Ministry Complex, Precint 2, Federal Government Administrative Centre, 62592 Putrajaya (tel: 8882-3000; fax: 8882-3892/3894; email: webmaster@treasury.gov.my).

Ministry of Foreign Affairs, Wisma Putra , No 1, Jl Wisma Putra, Precint 2, 62602 Putrajaya (tel: 8887-4000/ 4570, 8889-2476; fax: 8889-1717/2816; email: webmaster@kln.gov.my; internet: www.kln.gov.my).

Ministry of Health, Block E1, E6, E7 and 10, Parcel E, Federal Government Administrative Centre, 62590 Putrajaya (tel: 8883-3888; fax: 2698-5964; email: iadam@moh.gov.my).

Ministry of Home Affairs, Block D2, Parcel D, Federal Government Administrative Centre, 62546 Putrajaya (tel: 8886-3000; fax: 8889-1613; email: pro@moha.gov.my).

Ministry of Human Resources, Level 6-9, Block D3, Parcel D, Federal Government Administrative Centre, 62502 Putrajaya (tel: 8886-5000; fax: 8889-2381; email: ksm@mohr.gov.my).

Ministry of Housing and Local Government, Level 3-7, Block K, Pusat Bandar Damansara, 50782 Kuala Lumpur (tel: 2094-7033; fax: 2094-9720; email: pro@kpkt.gov.my).

Ministry of Information, Angkasapuri, Bukit Putra, 50610 Kuala Lumpur (tel: 2282-5333; fax: 2282-1255; email: webmaster@kempen.gov.my).

Ministry of Internal Security, Level 3, Block D1 and D2, Parcel D, Federal Government Administrative Centre, 62546 Putrajaya (tel: 8886 8000; fax: 8889 1730; email: pro@mois.gov.my).

Ministry of Natural Resources and Environment, 13th Floor, Wisma Tanah,, Jl Semarak, 50574 Kuala Lumpur (tel:

2692-1566; fax: 2693-2166; email: webmaster@nre.gov.my).

Ministry of Plantation Industries and Commodities, Level 6–13, Lot 2G4, Precinct 2, Federal Government Administrative Centre, 62654 Putrajaya (tel: 8880-3300; fax: 8880-3482; email: info@kppk.gov.my).

Ministry of Rural and Regional Development, Level 5-9, Block D9, Parcel D, Federal Government Administrative Centre, 62606 Putrajaya (tel: 8886-3500/3700; fax: 8886-3801; email: webmaster@rurallink.gov.my).

Ministry of Science, Technology and Innovations, Level 1-7, Block C5, Federal Government Administrative Centre, 62662 Putrajaya (tel: 8885-8000; fax: 8888-9070; email: webmaster@mosti.gov.my).

Ministry of Transport, Level 5-7, Block D5, Parcel D, Federal Government Administrative Centre, 62502 Putrajaya (tel: 8886-6000/2597; fax: 8889-1569; email: saptuyah@mot.gov.my).

Ministry of Works, Level 4, Block B, Kompleks Kerja Raya, Jl Sultan Salahuddin, 50580 Kuala Lumpur (tel: 2711-1100/ 9309; fax: 2711-6612; email: pro@kkr.gov.my).

Ministry of Women, Family and Community Development, Level 1-6, Block E, Government Office Complex , Kompleks Pejabat Kerajaan Bukit Perdana, Jl Dato' Onn, 50515 Kuala Lumpur (tel: 2693-0095, 2693-0401; fax: 2693-4982; email: info@kpwkm.gov.my).

Ministry of Youth and Sports, Lot G4, Precinct 4, Federal Government Administrative Centre, 62570 Putrajaya (tel: 8871-3333; fax: 8888-8767; email: webmaster@kbs.gov.my).

Prime Minister's Department, Perdana Putra Building, Federal Government Administrative Centre, 62502 Putrajaya (tel: 8888-8000; fax: 8888-3444; email: ppmnun@pmo.gov.my).

Other useful addresses

Advertising Standards Authority of Malaysia, c/o Coopers and Lybrand, Hong Kong Bank Building, Leboh Pasar, Kuala Lumpur.

Asean Investment Promotion Agency, Malaysian Industrial Development Authority, 6th Floor, Wisma Damansara, Damansara Heights, PO Box 10618, 50720 Kuala Lumpur.

Asean Secretariat, 70 A Jl Sisingamangaraja, Jakarta 12110, Indonesia (tel: (+62-21) 726-2991, 724-3372; fax: (+62-21) 724-3504, 739-8234; internet: www.asean.or.id).

British Council, Jalan Bukit Aman, PO Box 10539, 50916 Kuala Lumpur.

British High Commission, PO Box 11030, 50732 KL; 185 Jalan Ampang, 50450 Kuala Lumpur (tel: 2170-2200; (Consular Section, tel: 2170-2345; email: consular2.kualalumpur@fco.gov.uk)).

British Malaysian Industry & Trade Association (BMITA), PO Box 12574, 50782 Kuala Lumpur.

Capital Issues Committee, Kementerian Kewangan, 11th Floor, Block 9, Khazanah Malaysia, Jl Duta, Kuala Lumpur.

Department of Immigration, Level 1-7 (Podium) Block 2G4, Precinct 2, Federal Government Administration Centre, 62550 Putrajaya, Federal Territory (tel: 8880-1000; fax: 8880-1200; internet: www.imi.gov.my).

Federal Land Development Authority, (FELDA), Wisma Felda, Jalan Perumahan Gurney, 54000 Kuala Lumpur (tel: 2693-5066; fax: 2692-0087; email: unitit.felda@felda.net.my).

Federation of Malaysian Manufacturers, Tingkat 7 Balai Felda, Jalan Gurney Satu (1), 54000 Kuala Lumpur (tel: 2698-7772; fax: 2693-0018; email: tohit.1@felda.net.my).

Foreign Investment Committee, Economic Planning Unit, Prime Minister's Dept, Jl Dato' Onn, Kuala Lumpur (tel: 230-0133).

Bursa Malaysia, (Kuala Lumpur Stock Exchange), Exchange Square, Bukit Kewangan, 50200 Kuala Lumpur (tel: 2034-7000; fax: 2732-0069; email: enquiries@bursamalaysia.com).

Malaysian Embassy (US), 2401 Massachusetts Avenue, NW, 20008 (tel: (+1-202) 328-2700; fax: (+1-202) 483-7661; email: mwwashdc@erols.com).

Malaysian Export Trade Centre, Ministry of Trade and Industry, Wisma PKNS, Jl Raja Laut, 50350.

Malaysian Industrial Development Authority (MIDA), Blk 4, Plaza Sentral, Jalan Stesen Sentral 5, Kuala Lumpur Sentral, 50470 Kuala Lumpur (tel: 2267-3633; fax: 2274-7970; email: promotion@mida.gov.my; internet: www.mida.gov.my).

Sarawak Economic Development Corporation, PO Box 400; 6-11th Floor, Menara SEDC, Jalan Tunku Abdul Rahman, 93902 Kuching, Sarawak, (tel: 416-777; fax: 424-330; email: ssedc@po.jaring.my; internet: www.sedc.com.my).

Securities Commission, 3 Persiaran Bukit Kiara, Bukit Kiara, 50490 Kuala Lumpur (tel: 6204-8510; fax: 6201-5078; internet: www.sc.com.my).

National news agency: Bernama, Malaysian National News Agency, Wisma No 28, Jalan 1/65A, Off Jalan Tun Razak, 50400 Kuala Lumpur (tel: 03-2693-9933; fax: 03-2698-2332; internet: www.bernama.com).

Internet sites

Malaysia Homepage: www.jaring.my

Malaysia portal: www.mycen.com.my

Malyasia yellow and white pages: www.tpsb.com.my/thome.htm

Maldives

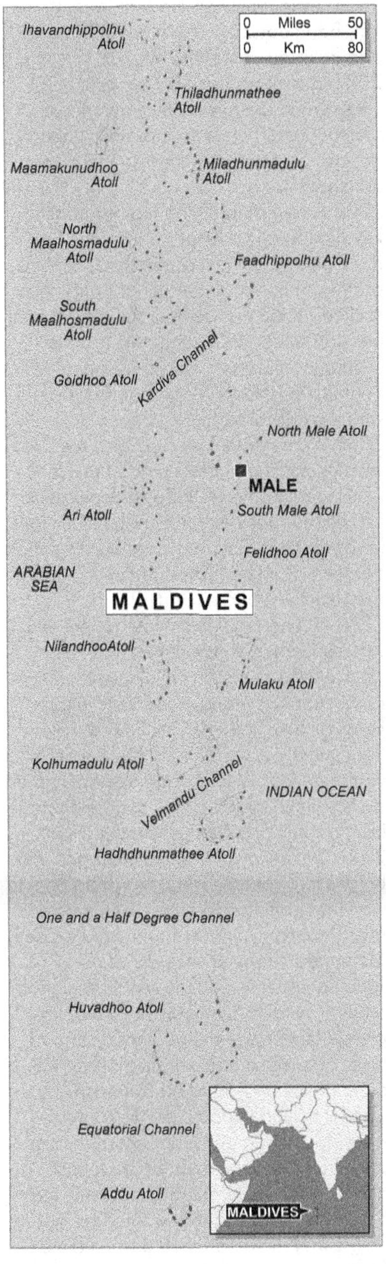

Tourism is both the Maldives' main income source and its biggest problem. As one of the world's top holiday destinations, the string of over 1,190 small islands grouped into 26 atolls, set in the Indian Ocean, typically attracts over 500,000 visitors annually. Sustainable tourism, however, is not possible as natural resources, particularly water, are being overwhelmingly consumed by visitors. Erosion of the fragile environments of Maldives' low-lying islands has also become a serious problem, as global warming begins to raise the level of the seas.

User pays – user gains

The tourist industry constitutes around 35 per cent of GDP, and provides over 60 per cent of all employment. The sector attracts the lion's share of foreign direct investment (FDI) – US$163.8 million in 2010. The capital investment also benefits the local population, even though it is principally used to provide for visitors' needs. Tourism drives investment in infrastructure, education and, by extension, social welfare; but for this the local population of 315,885 in 2010 must welcome a large influx of visitors.

In return for a standard of living largely gained through tourism (the islands are ranked as middle income by the World Bank) the culture of the Maldives has been under pressure from foreign forms of dress and behaviour that sometimes clash with the Islamic customs of the country. Over 70 per cent of all visitors come from Europe, with visitors from UK, Italy and Germany pre-eminent.

The reputation of the Maldives suffered a damaging public relations incident in 2010, when a hotel staff member, in the local language, abused a Swiss tourist couple renewing their wedding vows. The president of the country personally apologised to the couple, but not before the event was posted worldwide on YouTube.

In December 2011, all spas and health centres were closed down, on the orders of the government, following protests by the conservative Islamic, Adhaalath Party (AP) (Justice Party), that accused the establishments of being used as brothels. The President ordered their re-opening on 4 January 2012, pending a decision by the supreme court on whether they violate Islamic mores.

New taxes

In January 2011, a new goods and services tax (GST) was introduced which, with a

KEY FACTS

Official name: Divehi Raajjeyge Jumhooriyyaa (Republic of Maldives)

Head of State: President Mohamed Nasheed (MPP) (from 11 Nov 2008)

Head of government: President Mohamed Nasheed

Ruling party: Maldivian People's Party (MPP) (from 9 May 2009)

Area: 298 square km (1,190 tiny atoll islands) – Malé: 1.5 square km

Population: 315,885 (2010)

Capital: Malé, on Malé Island

Official language: Dhivehi (Maldivian)

Currency: Rufiyaa (MRf) = 100 laari

Exchange rate: MRf15.39 per US$ (Oct 2011)

GDP per capita: US$5,841 (2010)

GDP real growth: 8.00% (2010)

GDP: US$1.87 billion (2010)

Inflation: 5.00% (2010)

Balance of trade: -US$798.00 million (2010)

new business profit tax levied later in the year, are expected to provide an increase in government revenue of around 25 per cent. The Malé International Airport (MLE) was renamed Ibrahim Nasir International Airport on 26 July 2011 following its privatisation in 2010 and sale to a joint Indian and Malaysian entity. The energy sector was also part-privatised in 2011, while the government is heavily promoting the building of new island resorts.

Risk assessment

Politics	Good
Economy	Fair
Regional stability	Good

COUNTRY PROFILE

Historical profile

1887 The islands were placed under British protection, with internal self-government.
1932 The first democratic constitution was proclaimed. The sultanate became an elected position.
1953 The Maldives became a republic and a member of the Commonwealth as the sultanate was abolished. However, the sultanate was restored within months.
1965 Gained full independence as a sultanate and left the Commonwealth.
1968 Following a referendum, the country reverted from a sultanate back to a republic. Ibrahim Nasir became president.
1975 The UK pulled out of its military base on Addu atoll. A proposal from the USSR to take over the base was rejected.
1978 Nasir retired and Maumoon Abdul Gayoom was elected president.
1980s The expansion in the tourist industry resulted in economic growth. An industrial zone was established on Gan.
1982 Rejoined the Commonwealth.
1988 An attempt by Sri Lankan Tamil mercenaries to depose the government was thwarted with the help of Indian army forces.
1994 Non-party elections to the Majlis (parliament) were held.
1997 A new constitution was passed.
1998 President Maumoon Abdul Gayoom was re-elected for a fifth consecutive term in office.
1999 Forty non-partisan members were elected to the Majlis. Over 120 candidates had stood in the November elections.
2002 The Maldivian and Indian governments began working together to implement a plan for poverty reduction in the Maldives.
2003 Amnesty International accused the government of political repression and torture. Riots broke out in Malé when prison inmates protested at alleged torture. President Gayoom won a sixth term with over 90 per cent of the vote.
2004 A special Majlis was formed to consider constitutional changes proposed by the President, including limiting his powers and allowing the formation of political parties. A referendum agreed to a presidential and parliamentary style of government. A state of emergency was declared after violence during a pro-democracy demonstration. An earthquake off the island of Sumatra caused a *tsunami* that devastated coastal areas in the region, including 20 inhabited islands of the Maldives. The final toll in the Maldives was estimated at 108 dead or missing and 29,577 displaced.
2005 In parliamentary elections, all candidates for the 42 seats ran officially as independents; parliament unanimously voted in favour of introducing multiparty politics. Five new political parties were registered: Dhivehi Rayyithunge Party (DRP) (Maldivian Peoples Party); Islamic Democratic Party (IDP); Adhaalath Party (AP) (Justice Party); Maldivian Democratic Party (MDP). Mohamed Nasheed (known as Anni) returned from exile to register the MDP; he was later arrested for terrorism and sedition.
2006 The South Asia Free Trade Agreement (Safta) between the Maldives, Bhutan, Bangladesh, India, Nepal, Sri Lanka and Pakistan came into effect.
2007 In a referendum, 60 per cent of the vote agreed to a presidential and parliamentary government system, while endorsing President Gayoom's continued administration.
2008 A new constitution that introduced key democratic changes, including multi-party presidential elections, the separation of power and a bill of rights, was ratified. In the first democratic presidential election since 1978, after two rounds Mohamed Nasheed won 54.2 per cent beating incumbent Maumoon Gayoom who won 45.8 per cent.
2009 In parliamentary elections, the DRP won 28 seats (out of 77), and President Nasheed's party, MDP 26, independents 13, the People's Alliance (PA), led by former president Gayoom's brother Abdullah Yameen, 7, the Republican Party 1 and the Dhivehi Qaumee Party 2.
2010 In June, a 25-year lease agreement was signed by the government with the GMR-Malaysia Airport Holdings consortium to develop and manage the Male International Airport. In August a US$180 million agreement was signed with the US energy company Merciel to provide electricity for all islands (three atolls) in the upper north province, using bio-fuelled generators.
2011 On 1 May police used tear gas and batons to disperse several thousand people who had gathered to protest at the deteriorating economy and demand that President Mohamed Nasheed should quit. On 3 June Bangladesh and the Maldives signed a memorandum of understanding to implement free trade between them. Import taxes on medicines from Bangladesh will be removed. In August Sri Lanka gave a US$10 million import credit to the Maldives, to encourage the import of, particularly, fruit and vegitables for the tourist hotels. India has granted more credit than Sri Lanka, which felt they would lose out unless they increased their own credit. Sri Lanka also agreed to construct a road to help preparations of the South Asian Association for Regional Cooperation (SAARC) summit in Maldives in November.

Political structure

Constitution

The constitution dates from 1997, which provides power to the executive, the

KEY INDICATORS — Maldives

	Unit	2006	2007	2008	2009	2010
Population	m	0.30	0.34	0.34	*0.34	0.32
Gross domestic product (GDP)	US$bn	0.91	1.05	1.26	1.36	1.87
GDP per capita	US$	2,629	3,040	3,651	3,932	5,841
GDP real growth	%	19.1	6.6	10.9	-7.3	7.1
Inflation	%	3.7	5.0	11.9	4.0	5.0
Exports (fob) (goods)	US$m	215.9	228.8	330.5	169.0	180.0
Imports (fob) (goods)	US$m	815.3	964.7	1,221.0	851.3	978.0
Balance of trade	US$m	-599.5	-736.8	-890.8	-682.2	-798.0
Current account	US$m	-369.0	-437.8	-651.3	-418.7	-462.7
Total reserves minus gold	US$m	231.4	308.4	240.6	261.0	364.3
Foreign exchange	US$m	228.5	305.3	237.6	246.4	350.2
Exchange rate	per US$	12.80	12.80	12.80	12.80	12.80

* estimated figure

legislature and the judiciary, while these powers are vested from the people. The president also derives influence from the constitutional role as 'supreme authority to propagate the tenets of Islam'.
However critics argue that supreme power under the constitution is held by the president, who can appoint and dismiss the top posts in all branches of the administration. The constitution, it is argued, does not provide a guarantee that individuals' rights are not subject to subordinate laws and government practices.
In 2007 constitutional changes included the introduction of a US-style presidential form of government, where the president can only hold office for two terms and the introduction of a multiparty parliament.
In January 2008 the gender bar that allowed women to serve in the Majlis but not become a presidential candidate, was removed. A new constitution was ratified on 7 August which introduced key democratic changes, including multi-party presidential elections, the separation of power and a bill of rights.
Voting: universal suffrage over 21 years.
Local authority is vested in atoll chiefs and island headmen appointed by the president.

Independence date
26 July 1965

The executive
Executive power is held by the president, who is head of state and head of government, commander-in-chief of the armed forces, minister of defence and national security, and minister of finance and treasury.
The president is nominated by the legislature, who is the only candidate offered in a yes/no referendum to the people, for a renewable five-year term. The president has the sole power to summon the Majlis which can alter the constitution by majority vote. A government is appointed and chaired by the president; cabinet ministers are not required to be members of the Majlis.

National legislature
The unicameral Majlis (parliament) has 50 members; each atoll (20) directly elects two representatives, as does the capital, Malé; a further eight members are appointed by the president. All members serve for five-year terms. The Majlis must ratify all legislation introduced by the government or parliamentary members (MP).

Legal system
The legal system is based on Islamic law with admixtures of English common law, primarily in commercial matters.

Last elections
9 May 2009 (parliamentary); 28 October and 11 November 2008 (Presidential).

Results: Parliamentary: the Dhivehi Rayyithunge Party (DRP) (Maldivian Peoples Party) won 27.5 per cent of the vote (28 seats out of 77), the Maldives Democratic Party (MDP) 35.3 per cent (26), independents 24.9 per cent (13), the People's Alliance (PA) 5.3 per cent (7), the Republican Party (RP) 4.2 per cent (1), and the Dhivehi Qaumee Party (DQP) 2.7 per cent (2).
Presidential: in first round, Maumoon Gayoom won 40.3 per cent of the vote, Mohamed Nasheed 24.9 per cent, Hassan Saeed 16.7 and Qasim Ibrahim 15.2 per cent; turnout was 85.5 per cent.
Second round: Nasheed won 54.2 per cent and Gayoom 45.8 per cent; turnout was 86.6 per cent.

Next elections
2013 (presidential); 2014 (parliamentary)

Political parties

Ruling party
Maldivian People's Party (MPP) (from 9 May 2009)

Population

315,885 (2010)
Last census: 21 March 2006: 298,968
Population density: 1,066 inhabitants per square km (2010)
Annual growth rate: 2.8 per cent 1994–2004 (WHO 2006)

Ethnic make-up
The majority of the population are Sinhalese or Dravidian, with significant Arab and smaller African minorities.

Religions
Islam (Sunni majority)

Education

Primary education is provided through either private or state schools; lessons are given in English, Arabic and Dhivehi.
The curriculum, for segregated (by gender) secondary education, is based on the British system and many schools prepare students to sit the General Certificate of Education at 'O' level and a few for 'A' level examinations. Students have to travel abroad for higher education.
President Gayoom has made improving education levels his top priority. There is an ongoing teacher training programme due to the shortage of qualified teachers. Typically 2.4 per cent of the GNP is spent on primary education.
Literacy rate: 97.2 per cent total; adult rates (World Bank).
Enrolment rate: 98 per cent net primary enrolment (Unicef).
Pupils per teacher: 24 in primary schools.

Health

The Maldives has significantly improved health services and severe diseases such as malaria, childhood tuberculosis and leprosy have been eradicated.
There are two hospitals on the main island and six regional hospitals serving all the remaining islands. In addition, there are 45 health centres and 36 health posts serving the islands.

HIV/Aids
The first Maldivian with HIV was identified in 1991. There have been six deaths as a result of Aids. Although the HIV rate is very small, the Maldives is particularly vulnerable to the spread of the virus due to the high number of migrant workers that pass through the islands. Drug usage among young people is also on the rise.
Life expectancy: 67 years, 2004 (WHO 2006)
Fertility rate/Maternal mortality rate: 4.1 births per woman, 2004 (WHO 2006)
Child (under 5 years) mortality rate (per 1,000): 55 per 1,000 live births; 45 per cent of children aged under five are malnourished (World Bank).
Head of population per physician: 0.92 physicians per 1,000 people, 2004 (WHO 2006)

Welfare

Due to the highly dispersed character of the country, it is difficult for the government to ensure that everyone receives benefits. The ministry of women's affairs and social welfare has responsibility for administering the welfare programme that covers women, children, the disabled and unemployed.

Main cities

Malé (capital, estimated population 82,726 in 2005).

Languages spoken

The Maldivian language is Indo-Aryan.

Official language/s
Dhivehi (Maldivian)

Media

The government retains the power to close media outlets critical to its regime which has resulted in media self-regulation.

Press
There are several newspapers publishing in the Divehi language, and some with English online editions, including *Haveeru* (www.haveeru.com.mv) and *Miadhu* (www.miadhu.com.mv), *Aafathis Daily News* (www.aafathisnews.com.mv), is one of the oldest local newspapers and *Haama Daily* (www.haamadaily.com).

Broadcasting
Radio: There are only four radio stations broadcasting, two government owned, Voice of Maldives (www.vom.gov.mv) and Radio Eke and two private DhiFM (http://dhifm95.com) and Capital Radio (http://capital956.fm). An overseas radio operated by expatriates opposed to the government of President Gayoom

broadcasts over the internet, Radio Minivan (www.minivannews.com).
Television: The only local television service, TVM Maldives, is government-run. Satellite TV is available.

Economy

The economy is based on tourism and commercial fishing. The service sector in 2009 constituted 77.5 per cent of GDP, with the tourist industry the single largest component at around 35 per cent of GDP. Industry accounted for 17 per cent, of which manufacturing was 7 per cent and agriculture 5 per cent of GDP.
The global economic crisis of 2008 had an impact on GDP growth as it cut visitor numbers, which fell from 455,423 (January–August) in 2008, to 415,443 for the same period in 2009. GDP growth was 10.9 per cent 2008, but with a fall in foreign earnings from tourism, it fell sharply to -7.5 per cent in 2009. Growth recovered strongly in 2010 to 7.1 per cent, as promotional programmes stimulated tourism and the economies of the host countries recovered and tourists had time and money to spend.
There was a change of government in November 2008, when long-term President Gayoom retired and a new political regime took over the direction of the economy. Government expenditure had doubled between 2004–08 and would have represented 69 per cent of GDP by 2008 if the new government's reforms had not been implemented. Reforms included, in particular, a cut of around 9,000 public workers with a reduction in the public service wage bill, which had increased fourfold and grown to represent 28 per cent of GDP. These measures were welcomed by the International Monetary Fund (IMF) which extended Maldives a loan of US$93.5 million in 2009, to allow the government to manage its large external debt and shore up its foreign reserves. However, by 2010, the IMF reported that tax reforms had been delayed and public wages had increased, which had resulted in 'significant fiscal slippages', which would need adjustments to the exchange rate and fiscal strategy to achieve a reduction in public debt.
The largest project undertaken by the Maldives has been the Hulhumalé infrastructure project, which has reclaimed land close to the capital Malé, on Kafuul Atoll, for domestic, commercial and industrial expansion. By 2008, 504 housing units had been completed and facilities, including roads and waste management for the development had been completed by 2010, while other facilities such as a hospital, sports buildings and more housing were under construction in 2011.

External trade

The Maldives is a member of the South Asia Association for Regional Co-operation (SAARC), which operates a preferential trading arrangement that covers 6,000 products. It is also a member of the South Asia Free Trade Area (Safta) along with seven other member states (India, Pakistan, Bhutan, Nepal, Bangladesh and Sri Lanka), that by 2012 intends to have a customs union.
Fishing is a major industrial sector, which provides foreign exchange, as well as revenue from licensing fishing rights to foreign fleets. Manufactured garments and boat building are important sectors. The agriculture sector is unable to feed the population and staple foods must be imported.

Imports

Main imports are petroleum, commodities and foodstuffs, intermediate and consumer goods, capital machinery and vehicles.
Main sources: Singapore (typically 23 per cent of total), UAE (18 per cent), India (10 per cent).

Exports

Main exports include fish, garments and boats.
Main destinations: Thailand (49 per cent of total), Sri Lanka (10 per cent), France (9 per cent).

Agriculture

Agriculture, including fishing, accounts for around 15 per cent of GDP and employs 40 per cent of the labour force. Farming is at subsistance level on small-holdings, confined to field crops and fruit trees, with no livestock. Main crops are coconuts, bananas, watermelon, sweet potato, cucumber, cassava, pumpkin, cabbage and yam. Approximately 6 per cent of the total land area is under cultivation. The soil is shallow and highly alkaline, with poor water-retaining properties.

Fishing

The fishing sector, providing 11 per cent of GDP, is second to tourism in importance in the economy. Fish provide the main source of protein for the population with a 126,000mt annual catch. Fishing employs over 20 per cent of the workforce.
The 2004 *tsunami* caused US$14 million worth of damage or destruction to boats, harbours and jetties.

Tourism

The service sector is the most important component of the economy, constituting over 70 per cent of GDP, of which the tourist industry constitutes around 35 per cent, while providing over 60 per cent of all employment. The Maldives has promoted its tropical beauty to tourists from around the world with the islands receiving over 500,000 visitors each year. The global economic crisis of 2008 had a detrimental impact on the tourist industry as it cut visitor numbers, which fell from 455,423 (January–August) in 2008, to 415,443 for the same period in 2009, the corresponding fall in foreign earnings impacted on GDP growth and employment. Following a promotional programme that reduced prices, or extended a package stay from two weeks to three for the same price, tourism recovered. Over 70 per cent of all visitors come from Europe, with visitors from UK, Italy and Germany pre-eminent.
The government is attempting to balance the interests and the long-term requirements of the people of the Maldives with the needs and expectations of visitors. However, sustainable tourism may not be possible as fragile environments and natural resources, particularly water, are being overwhelmingly consumed by many tourists.
The reputation of Maldives was damaged in 2010 following an incident when a hotel staff member, in the local language, abused a tourist couple renewing their wedding vows. The president of Maldives personally apologised to the couple, but not before the event was posted worldwide on YouTube.

Environment

It has been reported that the beaches of one-third of the Maldives' 200 inhabited islands could be swept away by rising sea levels, as global warming melts the fringes of polar ice caps. Another issue affecting the Maldives is the depletion of fresh water aquifiers which threatens water supply.

Hydrocarbons

There are no known hydrocarbon reserves and all domestic energy requirements are met by imports. Oil consumption was 6,000 barrels per day in 2008. Any natural gas or coal imports are commercially negligible.

Energy

Total installed generating capacity was 106MW, produced by imported oil, of which around half the capacity is concentrated in tourist resort areas. The State Electricity Company (Stelco) generates a third of the supply; the rest is supplied by Island Development Committees and private generators.

Financial markets

Stock exchange

Maldives Stock Exchange (MSE)

Banking and insurance

Central bank

Maldives Monetary Authority

Time

GMT plus five hours

Geography

The Republic of Maldives is one of the smallest countries in the world. Situated in the Indian Ocean, it lies about 675km (420 miles) south-west of Sri Lanka. The northern tip of the Maldives is about 600km south of India. Over 99 per cent of the territory is sea.
The Maldives consists of around 1,190 small islands grouped into 26 atolls, running north to south in a double chain 823km long and 129km wide. The total land area is around 298 square km. Most of the islands are coral outcrops perched on a submarine mountain range, although some are only sandbars. They are low-lying, reaching no higher than two metres above sea level. They are at risk of flooding from natural causes, most recently the *tsunami* of December 2004.
The geography of the country can be affected in that islands can disappear as a result of flooding, as well as from erosion. The potential effects of global warming on sea levels puts the continued physical existence of the archipelago at risk.
Around 200 islands are inhabited. Many of these are covered by tropical vegetation, including coconut palms and breadfruit trees, while the uninhabitated islands are given over to scrub. Few islands in the archipelago are longer than 2km, the longest being Hithadhoo, which is 8km long. While most form atolls enclosing shallow lagoons, several are single islands with coral beaches.

Hemisphere

Northern

Climate

There is year-round sunshine, with temperatures ranging 26–30 degrees Celsius. Most rainfall occurs during the south-west monsoon season from April–October.

Entry requirements

Passports

Required by all, valid for six months.

Visa

Visas are issued free to all visitors on arrival at the airport in Malé for visits of up to 30 days (visas may be extended for a minimum of three months on payment of a fee). Proof of return/onward passage is necessary.

Currency advice/regulations

There are no restrictions on the import and export of local and foreign currencies.

Customs

Personal effects are allowed duty-free. Tortoise and articles produced using tortoise shells may not be exported.

Prohibited imports

Alcohol, pork, pharmaceuticals and goods at variance with Islamic culture are prohibited or subject to restrictions. Pornographic material may not be imported.

Health (for visitors)

Mandatory precautions

Vaccination certificate required for yellow fever if travelling from an infected area.

Advisable precautions

Anti-malarial precautions, outside Malé. Hepatitis A and B, tetanus and typhoid. There is a rabies risk.
Visitors are advised to use mosquito repellent, a mosquito net at night, and wear clothing covering as much skin as possible.

Hotels

The Maldives are a popular tourist destination. There are numerous first class hotels and island resorts.

Credit cards

All major credit cards, including American Express, Visa and MasterCard, are widely accepted on the islands.

Public holidays (national)

Fixed dates

1 Jan (New Year's Day), 26–27 Jul (Independence Days), 3 Nov (Victory Day), 11–12 Nov (Republic Day).

Variable dates

Hajj Day (Jan), Eid al Adha, Islamic New Year, National Day, Birth of the Prophet, Start of Ramadan, Eid al Fitr (End of Ramadan), Huravee Day (Jul), Martyrs' Day (Sep).

Islamic year 1433 (26 Nov 2011–14 Nov 2012): The Islamic year contains 354 or 355 days, with the result that Muslim feasts advance by 10-12 days against the Gregorian calendar. Dates of feasts vary according to the sighting of the new moon, so cannot be forecast exactly.

Working hours

Banking

Sun–Thu: 0800–1330.

Business

Sun–Thu: 0730–1430. During the month of Ramadan 0900–1300.

Government

Sun–Thu: 0730–1430.

Shops

Sat–Thu: 0930–2300; Fri: 1400–2300.

Weights and measures

Metric system

Social customs/useful tips

Alcohol can only be consumed in holiday resorts.

Getting there

Air

National airline: Island Aviation Services
International airport/s: Malé International Airport (MLE), (renamed Ibrahim Nasir International Airport) on Hulule Island, 2km north-east of Malé; post office, bank, restarurants, duty-free shop.
Airport tax: US$12, usually included in price of ticket.

Surface

Main port/s: Gan, Uligamu and Malé.

Getting about

National transport

Air: Island Aviation Services operates regular domestic flights between Malé and island airports at Gan, Kaadedhdhoo, Kadhdhoo and Hanimaadhoo. Charter planes are also available.
Water: There is a public boat service from the airport to Malé city centre, with a journey time of 15 minutes. Resort islands have regular ferry services. Local boats can be hired; rates are negotiable. Charter vessels are available.

City transport

Due to the small size of the islands, there is little need for transportation. It is possible to walk to all places within the small area of Malé.
Taxis: Taxis are available in Malé.

Car hire

BUSINESS DIRECTORY

The addresses listed below are a selection only. While World of Information makes every endeavour to check these addresses, we cannot guarantee that changes have not been made, especially to telephone numbers and area codes. We would welcome any corrections.

Telephone area codes

The international direct dialling code (IDD) for the Maldives is +960, followed by subscriber's number.

Useful telephone numbers

Police: 119
Fire: 118
Ambulance: 102

Chambers of Commerce

Maldives National Chamber of Commerce and Industry, G Viyafaari Hiya, Ameenee Magu, PO Box 92, Malé 2004 (tel: 332-6634; fax: 331-0233; e-mail: mncci@dhivehinet.net.mv).

Banking

Bank of Ceylon, 2 Boduthakurufaanu Magu, Malé (tel: 332-3045; fax: 332-0575; e-mail: bcmale@dhivehinet.net.mv).

Bank of Maldives, 11 Boduthakurufaanu Magu, Malé (tel: 333-0100; fax: 332-8233; e-mail: bmla@dhivehinet.net.mv).

Habib Bank Ltd, Ground Floor, Ship Plaza, 1/6 Orchid Magu , Malé (tel: 332-2051; fax: 332-6791; e-mail: hbmale@dhivehinet.net.mv).

State Bank of India, Boduthakurufaanu Magu, Malé (tel: 332-0860; fax: 332-3053; e-mail: sbimale@dhivehinet.net.mv).

Central bank
Maldives Monetary Authority, 3rd Floor, Umar Shopping Arcade, Chandhanee Magu, Malé 20156 (tel: 3312-343; fax: 3323-862; e-mail: mail@mma.gov.mv).

Stock exchange
Maldives Stock Exchange (MSE): www.maldivesstockexchange.com.mv

Travel information
Island Aviation Services, Malé (tel: 333-5566; fax: 331-4806; e-mail: sales@island.com.mv).

Maldives Tourism Promotion Board, 12 Boduthakurufaanu Magu, Malé (tel: 332-328; fax: 332-3229; e-mail: mtpb@visitmaldives.com).

Malé International Airport, Malé (tel: 332-5511; fax: 333-1515; e-mail: info@macinet.net).

Ministry of tourism
Ministry of Tourism, 2/F Ghazi Building, Orchid Magu, Henveiru, Malé (tel: 313-461).

Ministries
Ministry of Atolls Development, Faashanaa Bdg, Boduthakurufaanu Magu, Malé (tel: 332-3070; fax: 332-7750; e-mail: info@atolls.gov.mv).

Ministry of Communication, Science and Technology, 12 Boduthakurufaanu Magu, Malé (tel: 333-1695; fax: 333-1694; e-mail: secretariat@mcst.gov.mv).

Ministry of Economic Development and Trade, Ghazee Bdg, Ameeru Ahmed Magu, Malé (tel: 332-3668; fax: 332-3840; e-mail: contact@trademin.gov.mv).

Ministry of Fisheries, Agriculture and Marine Resources, Ghazee Bdg, Ameeru Ahmed Magu, Malé (tel: 332-2625; fax: 332-6558; e-mail: it@fishagri.gov.mv).

Ministry of Health, Ameenee Magu, Malé (tel: 332-5311; fax: 332-7793; e-mail: moh@dhivehinet.net.mv).

Ministry of Higher Education, Employment and Social Security, Haveeree Hingun, Malé (tel: 331-7172; fax: 333-1578; e-mail: admin@employment.gov.mv).

Ministry of Women's Affairs and Social Security, Umar Shopping Arcade, Chandhanee Magu, Malé (tel: 332-5956; fax: 331-6237; e-mail: info@urcmaldives.gov.mv).

Other useful addresses
Attorney General's Office, Huravee Bdg, Malé (tel: 332-3809; fax: 331-4109).

Maldives National Ship Management Ltd, 2/F, Ship Plaza, Male (tel: 332-3871; fax: 332-4323; e-mail@ mnfl@dhivehinet.net.mv).

Maldives Association of Tourism Industry, Gadhamoo Bdg, Boduthakurufaanu Magu, Malé (tel: 332-6640; fax: 332-6641).

Maldives Traders' Association, G Viyafaari Hiyaa, Meenee Magu, Malé (tel: 332-6634; fax: 332-1889).

State Trading Organisation, Haveeree Higun, Malé (tel: 332-3279; fax: 332-5218; e-mail: sto@dhivehinet.net.mvo).

Internet sites
Maldives Consular Information: http://www.travel.state.gov/maldives.html

Maldives news online: http://maldivesculture.com

Maldives Yellow Pages: http://www.maldivesyellowpages.com

Mali

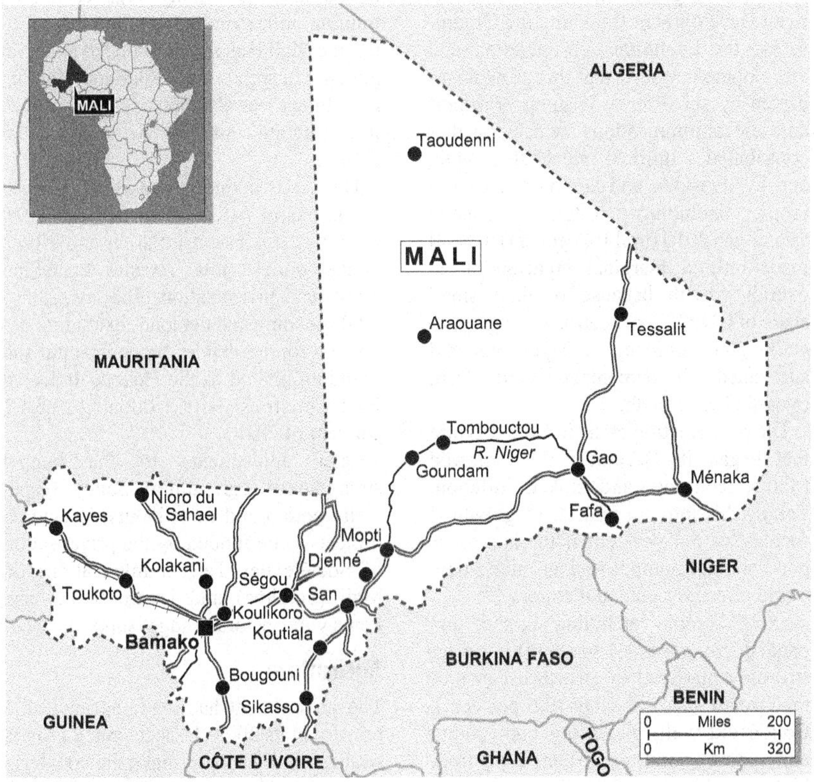

Politics are set to get interesting in Mali in 2012, with presidential elections scheduled for April, followed by parliamentary elections in July. President Amadou Toumani Touré is constitutionally barred from standing again, having had his two terms in office. Although not a member of any political party President Touré has been largely supported by one of the party coalitions, the Alliance pour la Démocratie et le Progrès (ADP) (Alliance for Democracy and Progress). The Alliance pour la Démocratie au Mali (ADEMA) (Alliance for Democracy in Mali), the biggest party in the ruling ADP coalition, says it will put up a presidential candidate.

The three main political groupings who will be competing in the July parliamentary elections are the ADP, Rassemblement pour le Mali (RPM) (Rally for Mali) and the Union pour la République et la Démocratie (URD) (Union for the Republic and Democracy).

A number of new parties were formed in 2010 in preparation for the elections and these could upset the current, already complicated, alliances and coalitions. The new parties include the Parti pour le Développement Economique et Social (PDES) (Party for Economic and Social Development), which has already attracted 17 (of the 147) members of parliament belonging to other parties and hopes to draw voters who agree with President Touré's non-partisan stance.

Meanwhile, impending reforms expected to strengthen the democratic system include creation of a senate, a government audit office, a single media monitoring council, a permanent elections office and a new code of conduct for political parties, all measures to be approved by referendum. Also planned is an administrative reorganisation of the country into 19 administrative regions and a capital district (Bamako) to replace the eight existing ones.

KEY FACTS

Official name: République du Mali (Republic of Mali)

Head of State: President Amadou Toumani Touré (since 2002; re-elected Apr 2007)

Head of government: Prime Minister Cissé Mariam Kaïdama Sidibé (from 3 Apr 2011)

Ruling party: The Congrès pour la Démocratie et le Progrès (CDP) (Alliance for Democracy and Progress) coalition led by Alliance pour la Démocratie en Mali-Parti Pan-Africain pour la Solidarité et la Justice (ADEMA-PASJ) (Alliance for Democracy in Mali-African Party for Solidarity and Justice) with Union pour la République et la Démocratie (URD) (Union for the Republic and Democracy) and Rassemblement National pour la Démocratie (RND) (National Assembly for Democracy) (from 22 July 2007)

Area: 1,241,238 square km

Population: 15.37 million (2010)*

Capital: Bamako

Official language: French

Currency: CFA franc (CFAf) = 100 centimes (Communauté Financière Africaine (African Financial Community) franc).

Exchange rate: CFAf588.90 per US$ (Oct 2011); CFAf655.95 per euro (pegged from Jan 1999)

GDP per capita: US$692 (2010)

GDP real growth: 4.50% (2010)

GDP: US$9.30 billion (2010)

Inflation: 1.20% (2010)

Balance of trade: -US$212.60 million (2009)

* estimated figure

Security in the north

On 1 August the government announced that the threat of attacks on tourists had cost Mali around CFAf50 billion (US$108.8 million) in lost tourism receipts and 8,000 jobs since 2009. Tourists are drawn to spectacular desert-scapes and the ancient trading town of Timbuktu, but the risk of kidnapping has grown. Several Western hostages had been seized in 2010 by rebels linked to the Al Qaeda in the Islamic Maghreb (AQIM) extremist group. Most were kidnapped in neighbouring countries (Niger and Mauritania), then taken to northern Mali. The Malian army does not have sufficient means to chase AQIM out of the north, despite the support of France and the United States and help from Algeria, Mauritania and Niger.

The partner-backed peace and development plan Programme Spécial pour la Paix, la Sécurité et le Développement dans le Nord du Mali (Special Programme for Peace, Security and Development in the North of Mali) is regarded by the government as very important for national stability. The plan is to introduce sustainable development and improve the security and social challenges. Development programmes such as the new Strategic Framework for Growth and Poverty Reduction 2012–17 (SFGPR), will have to take it into account, as the government sees peace in the north as a key to growth and a development driver. The state has strengthened its presence there by reopening military bases and building schools and clinics. This new link between security and development is accompanied by aid for local people and encouragement to the local economy.

The economy

Real gross domestic product (GDP) growth in 2010 (4.5 per cent) was the same as in 2009, though lower than expected. The *African Economic Outlook 2011* (AEO), published jointly by the African Development Bank and the Organisation for Economic Co-operation and Development reports that this growth was driven by subsistence farming, transport and telecommunications, which together contributed a third of real GDP growth, and by livestock and commerce. Export crops, including cotton, expanded strongly in 2010 (up 11.4 per cent) but still made only a marginal contribution to overall growth because of their small share of GDP (2.6 per cent). Mining, especially gold, slumped 16.2 per cent and subtracted 1.1 percentage points from overall GDP growth.

The post-election crisis in Côte d'Ivoire that began in December 2010 slowed Mali's economy, and stoked inflation. Taking this into account, 2011 growth is forecast as 5.4 per cent if the harvest is good and gold output revives, along with world prices for gold and cotton.

Export crops, including cotton, expanded strongly (11.4 per cent) but were still only marginal to growth because of their small share of GDP (2.6 per cent). Cotton did well, increasing both output and export volumes and benefiting from higher world prices. This should continue in 2011, with good international prospects and government incentives to revive production and speed up privatisation of the state cotton firm Compagnie Malienne de Développement Textiles (CMDT).

Gross investment rose 6.4 per cent in 2010 and gross capital formation increased to 22 per cent of GDP (from 20 per cent in 2009), due to higher public investment, including modernisation of Bamako's airport, building a third bridge in Bamako, university and vocational training infrastructure, community clinics, the Mali Hospital in Bamako and a regional hospital in Sikasso. Private investment was also boosted by improved infrastructure and a better business climate.

The 2010 budget is based on the assumptions of 6.4 per cent nominal GDP growth, 1.9 per cent inflation and a base budget deficit (total revenue excluding grants and privatisation proceeds, minus total spending and net loans excluding donor and foreign lender-funded capital and spending related to the Heavily Indebted Poor Countries [HIPC] Initiative) of 1.1 per cent of GDP.

Later adjustments to the budget strengthened agricultural policy (especially cotton and farm inputs), including projects to be funded by the privatisation of Société des Télécommunications du Mali (Sotelma) and incorporating new items with sectoral budget support.

Agriculture

The government has made agriculture a priority in its 2008–12 accelerated growth strategy and wants to make the country a sub-regional agro-pastoral centre through the agricultural guidelines law, which governs the drafting and implementation of sector laws. Agricultural development policy and the national agricultural investment programme in turn ensure application of the guidelines law. These measures are fully in step with the detailed agricultural development programme of the New Partnership for Africa's Development. The government wants the country to be producing 10 million tonnes of cereals by 2012 and to improve 103,356 hectares of land, rendering 61,910 fit for cultivation.

International trade and development

Mali has worked hard to strengthen its international links with emerging partners, especially China, which is involved in nearly all aspects of economic, social and cultural life. India, Russia, Brazil, Venezuela and Malaysia have also increased their economic and trade ties with Mali, especially in agro-industrial, chemical and construction sectors. Emerging-partner countries' interests are the same as

KEY INDICATORS — Mali

	Unit	2006	2007	2008	2009	2010
Population	m	13.90	13.06	13.36	*13.67	*15.37
Gross domestic product (GDP)	US$bn	6.22	7.20	8.80	9.00	9.30
GDP per capita	US$	487	548	657	656	692
GDP real growth	%	3.3	4.3	5.1	4.5	4.5
Inflation	%	1.9	1.5	9.1	2.2	1.2
Exports (fob) (goods)	US$m	1,550.4	1,556.3	2,097.2	1,773.7	–
Imports (fob) (goods)	US$m	1,475.4	1,846.0	2,735.9	1,986.3	–
Balance of trade	US$m	75.0	-289.7	-638.7	-212.6	–
Current account	US$m	-302.0	-581.1	-1,066.4	-654.9	-786.0
Total reserves minus gold	US$m	969.5	1,087.1	1,071.1	1,604.5	1,344.4
Foreign exchange	US$m	955.4	1,071.9	1,056.1	1,473.9	1,215.9
Exchange rate	per US$	496.60	454.40	447.81	514.03	495.28

* estimated figure

those of traditional partners: they seek access to local and West African regional markets and to natural resources. They are barely active for the moment in the mining sector. The government finds these new partners faster and less formal than traditional partners in carrying out projects. They are, however, not always in tune with the country's debt policy or anti-poverty programme, the SFGPR.

Mali participates in regional integration initiatives as a member of Economic Community of West African States (Ecowas) and West African Economic and Monetary Union (Waemu) and continues efforts to bring its trade and customs policies into line with regional agreements. Negotiations for an Economic Partnership Agreement (EPA) with the European Union (EU) are led by Ecowas with help from the Waemu. Mali wants to avoid making a temporary bilateral agreement of its own and will continue trade liberalisation, especially under a future EPA. The government hopes the economy will become more competitive but knows this could also mean loss of revenue. As a result, the Malian authorities, along with the rest of the region, are calling for assistance, financial and otherwise, to offset the effects of liberalisation before an EPA is signed.

Doing business

Mali moved up in 2010 from 155th to 153rd place out of 183 countries surveyed in the World Bank's *Doing Business* report. Its ratings improved for registering property (up 10 places), closing a business, starting a business, dealing with construction permits, trading across borders and enforcing contracts. Reducing the number of start-up procedures to six (the sub-Saharan average is 8.9) and the time taken to eight days (sub-Saharan average 45.2) also helped business creation.

Nevertheless, the private sector still faces obstacles, including lack of confidence in the legal system, flaws in the investment and mining laws, low worker productivity, a rather rigid labour law, under-developed physical infrastructure, expensive water and electricity, an undeveloped financial sector, problems getting medium- and long-term loans, and poor corporate governance. A law setting general policy for the private sector was passed in December 2010 to bring together the resources of all parties to ensure the sector's viability and help it to contribute more to economic growth.

Lack of infrastructure hinders growth

Mali's access to foreign markets is also hampered by sub-regional political conflicts and poor transport links to neighbouring countries. Mali's landlocked situation is aggravated by the shortage of basic social and economic infrastructure, including transport, energy, telecommunications, water and sanitation, which continues to prevent the economy from being competitive and living standards from improving, despite good progress in recent years.

The road network consists of 3,619 kilometres of paved roads in good condition, 5,772 kilometres of good unsurfaced roads and 719 kilometres of track roads. Upkeep of the network is the main problem for the road transport sector. Other forms of transport remain little developed, despite efforts to modernise airports, of which the country has six of international grade (Bamako, Gao, Kayes, Mopti, Sikasso and Tombouctou).

The government's priority remains to provide as many people as possible with cheap and sustainable energy under its national energy programme; currently less than 30 per cent of the country has an electricity supply.

Natural resource management

Mali faces enormous environmental challenges: desertification, disappearing plant cover, silting up of the Niger River, water shortages, loss of biodiversity and deterioration of living conditions. It will have to take steps to meet them and ensure sustainable development, including improving the operation of environmental bodies, giving more weight to the environmental aspects of its strategies and policies (such as the new SFGPR and sectoral programmes), raising public awareness, especially about the international conventions signed by Mali, ensuring their implementation and finding the necessary funding.

Risk assessment

Economy	Fair
Politics	Fair
Regional stability	Fair

COUNTRY PROFILE

Historical profile

900 Modern-day Mali was part of the empire of Ghana.
1250s Sundiata Keita, leader of the Mandinka people, established the Empire of Mali, which stretched from the Atlantic to the present-day borders of Nigeria and controlled most trans-Sahara trading routes by the fourteenth century.
1464 The Songhai Empire, centred around Gao, overwhelmed the Mali Empire and began to conquer the Sahel.
1591 After a Moroccan invasion, the Songhai Empire collapsed.
1890s Mali became a French colony.
1960 Mali gained independence from France as part of the Federation of Mali, which was dissolved a few weeks later when Senegal broke away. The Republic of Mali was established and Modibo Keita became the country's first president.
1968 Keita was overthrown by a military coup, led by Moussa Traoré, who became president.
1977 Protests erupted following Keita's death in prison.
1979 A new constitution provided for elections in which Traoré was elected as president.
1985 A border war erupted between Mali and Burkina Faso, but was ended after intervention by other African states.
1991 Following pro-democracy demonstrations, Traoré was deposed by a military coup. A 25-member military/civilian Transitional People's Salvation Committee came to power, led by Lieutenant Colonel Amadou Toumani Touré.
1992 Touré resigned and did not stand in the elections he organised. Alpha Oumar Konaré was democratically elected president.
1995 A peace agreement with Tuareg rebels led to the return of thousands of refugees from neighbouring African states.
1997 President Konaré was re-elected.
1999 Traoré was sentenced to death for corruption, but his sentence was commuted to life imprisonment by Konaré, who announced that he would not contest the next presidential election
2000 Mande Sidibe, a former International Monetary Fund (IMF) official, was appointed prime minister.
2001 Konaré announced the indefinite postponement of a constitutional referendum which proposed granting him immunity from prosecution.
2002 Amadou Toumani Touré (popularly known as ATT) won the presidential election and named Ahmed Mohamed Ag Hamani as prime minister. The Constitutional Court reversed the outcome of the parliamentary elections. The government resigned without explanation and a new government of national reconciliation took over.
2003 The IMF announced that Mali was to benefit from debt relief amounting to approximately US$675 million under the enhanced Heavily Indebted Poor Countries (HIPC) initiative.
2004 Ousmane Issoufi Maïga replaced Hamani as prime minister.
2006 Tuareg rebels, demanding greater autonomy, attacked government barracks in the north. The government signed a peace agreement, mediated by Algeria, with the rebels.

2007 President Amadou Toumani Touré was re-elected with 71.20 per cent of the votes; Ibrahim Boubacar Keïta, president of the national assembly, was runner-up with 19.15 per cent. In the two rounds of parliamentary election, the Congrès pour la Démocratie et le Progrès (CDP) (Alliance for Democracy and Progress) coalition led by Alliance pour la Démocratie en Mali-Parti Pan-Africain pour la Solidarité et la Justice (ADEMA-PASJ) (Alliance for Democracy in Mali-African Party for Solidarity and Justice) won 92 seats (out of 160). The ruling Espoir 2002 (Hope 2002) renamed Front pour la Démocratie et la République (FDR) (Front for a Democratic Republic) won 11 seats. Prime Minister Ousmane Issoufi Maïga resigned and Modibo Sidibé was appointed as his replacement.

2009 In an official ceremony to mark a return to the peace process, around 700 Tuareg insurgents surrendered their arms, with an expectation of joining the regular army. The rebels had been fighting for greater political influence and economic development for their traditional Sahel homeland. The government agreed to more regional autonomy and investment. Ibrahim Ag Bahanga, the rebel leader, fled into exile; he could pose a future threat to peace.

2010 In February, the IMF agreed to the disbursement of US$3.1 million under its Extended Credit Facility, after Mali successfully completed the IMF's second review of its economic performance. According to the International Organisation of Migration (IOM), Mali has lost 13 per cent of its population to emigration since 2000, an estimated 1.5 million people. In June, the mining ministry announced that 80.47 per cent of export earnings in 2009 were from gold. However with relatively low taxation, the export earnings only account for 8 per cent of GDP. A prolonged drought in the north forced nomad herders to move further south and into neighbouring Niger and Burkina Faso. By November another leg of the Sahel Highway north of Timbuktu was under construction.

2011 The president appointed Cissé Mariam Kaïdama Sidibé as prime minister on 3 April. On 1 August the government announced that the threat of attacks by Al Aqaeda on tourists had cost Mali around CFAf50 billion (US$108.8 million) in lost tourism receipts and 8,000 jobs since 2009. Many tourists are drawn to spectacular desert-scapes and the ancient trading town of Timbuktu but the risk of kidnapping, sponsored by Al Aqaeda, has grown.

Political structure

Constitution

A referendum held in January 1992 approved a constitution establishing multi-party rule.

A two-round voting system for electing parliamentarians was established.

In 1997, a new electoral code introduced an Independent National Electoral Commission (CENI) comprising 34 members: 10 representatives of government services, 10 from civil society and 14 from the political parties (seven from the opposition and seven from the parliamentary majority).

Other changes included the authorisation of independent candidacies, the reduction in the number of voters per polling station to 700 and an increase in the number of deputies in the National Assembly from 116 to 147. The principle of sponsoring presidential candidates was ended, and correspondence or proxy voting and eligibility for other African nationals were annulled.

Administratively, Mali is divided into eight regions and the capital district of Bamako, each under the authority of an appointed governor.

Form of state

Republic

The executive

The directly-elected president serves a five-year term, with a limit of two terms. The president is head of state and commander-in-chief of the armed forces. The president appoints the prime minister and chairs the Council of Ministers.

National legislature

The unicameral National Assembly has 160-members in total, of which 147 are directly elected in single or multi-member constituencies through two rounds ending in a run-off election. Expatriate Malians are represented by 13 representatives. All members serve for five-year terms.

Legal system

Based on French civil law system and customary law. The legal system is constitutionally independent of the executive.

Last elections

1/22 July 2007 (parliamentary); 29 April 2007 (presidential).

Results: Parliamentary: the Alliance pour la Démocratie en Mali-Parti Pan-Africain pour la Solidarité et la Justice (Adema-PASJ) (Alliance for Democracy in Mali-African Party for Solidarity and Justice) won 55 seats; the Union pour la République et la Démocratie (URD) (Union for the Republic and Democracy) 36; Rassemblement National pour la Démocratie (RND) (National Assembly for Democracy) one (these parties form the Congrès pour la Démocratie et le Progrès (CDP) (Alliance for Democracy and Progress) coalition. The Rassemblement Pour le Mali (RPM) (Party for Mali) won 11 seats; the Parti pour la Renaissance Nationale (Parena) (Party for a National Rebirth) four, (these parties form the coalition Front pour la Démocratie et la République (FDR) (Front for a Democratic Republic) formerly called Espoir 2002 (Hope 2002); the Solidarité Africaine pour la Démocratie et l'Indépendance (Sadi) (African Solidarity for Democracy and Independence) four; independents 12 and undecided 37 seats. Turnout was 33.39 per cent.

Presidential: Incumbent Amadou Toumani Touré won 71.20 per cent of the vote; Ibrahim Boubacar Keïta won 19.15 per cent. Turnout was 36.2 per cent.

Next elections

July 2012 (parliamentary); April 2012 (presidential)

Political parties

Ruling party

The Congrès pour la Démocratie et le Progrès (CDP) (Alliance for Democracy and Progress) coalition led by Alliance pour la Démocratie en Mali-Parti Pan-Africain pour la Solidarité et la Justice (ADEMA-PASJ) (Alliance for Democracy in Mali-African Party for Solidarity and Justice) with Union pour la République et la Démocratie (URD) (Union for the Republic and Democracy) and Rassemblement National pour la Démocratie (RND) (National Assembly for Democracy) (from 22 July 2007)

Main opposition party

Coalition: Front pour la Démocratie et la République (FDR) formed by 16 independent political parties led by Rassemblement pour le Mali (RPM) (Rally for Mali) and Le Parti pour la Renaissance Nationale (Parena) (Party for National Rebirth).

Population

15.37 million (2010)*

Last census: April 1998: 9,790,492

Population density: Eight inhabitants per square km. Urban population: 31 per cent (1995–2001).

Annual growth rate: 2.9 per cent 1994–2004 (WHO 2006)

Ethnic make-up

Mande (50 per cent), Peul (17 per cent), Voltaic (12 per cent).

Religions

Muslim (90 per cent), indigenous beliefs (9 per cent), Christian (1 per cent).

Education

Primary schooling is divided into two stages, with the first and compulsory stage lasting until aged 13, followed by three years of basic education. At age 16 students may follow either an academic path in a general secondary school, for three years, or specialisted education through a technical secondary school, for either two or three years. Four year vocational courses are also available.

Mali has one of the highest pupil-teacher ratio in the world, with an average of around 80 pupils per teacher.

Literacy rate: 19 per cent adult rate; 24 per cent youth rate (15–24) (Unesco 2005).
Compulsory years: Seven to 13
Enrolment rate: 29 per cent net primary enrolment (Unicef)
Pupils per teacher: 80 in primary schools.

Health

Improved water sources and sanitation facilities are available to 65 per cent and 30 per cent of the population respectively.
HIV/Aids
There are an estimated 100,000 people living with HIV/Aids in Mali – 5,000 are under the age of 15. Mali has so far escaped much of the African pandemic.
The African Development Fund (ADF) provided US$12.1 million for a programme to reduce the prevalence rate from 1.9 per cent in 2003 to 1 per cent by 2008. The money will be used to improved testing for the disease, antiretroviral drugs and training medical and research workers to monitor and manage the pandemic.
HIV prevalence: 1.9 per cent aged 15–49 in 2003 (World Bank)
Life expectancy: 46 years, 2004 (WHO 2006)
Fertility rate/Maternal mortality rate: 6.8 births per woman, 2004 (WHO 2006)
Child (under 5 years) mortality rate (per 1,000): 122 per 1,000 live births; 25 per cent of children aged under five are malnourished (World Bank).
Head of population per physician: 0.08 physicians per 1,000 people, 2004 (WHO 2006)

Welfare

In the mid-1990s, it was estimated that 72.8 per cent of the population lived on less than US$1 per day and over 90 per cent lived on less than US$2 per day. The distribution of wealth in Mali is highly unequal and the highest 10 per cent of the population owns 56.2 per cent of the wealth.
In over 70 districts in Mali, one million people were affected by swarms of locust and suffered acute food shortages. Emergency food aid was provided from reserves while government officials estimated over 440,000 tonnes of the 2004 harvest to have been destroyed.

Main cities

Bamako (capital and main business centre, estimated population 1.5 million in 2005); Sikasso (160,904); Gao (152,265), Ségou (149,530), Mopti (131,530).

Languages spoken

Tamazight (the Berber language) is recognised as a national language. Tamazight belongs to the Afro-Asiatic family and is related to ancient Egyptian and Ethiopian. Arabic, Bambara, Fulani, Senoufo and Dogon are commonly spoken. Very little English is spoken.
Official language/s
French

Media

Although harsh penalties exist for slandering public officials they are rarely invoked so that Mali's media enjoys widespread freedom to report.
Press
Dailies: In French, *L'Essor* (www.essor.gov.ml) is state-owned, *Info-Matin* (www.info-matin.com), *Le Républicain* (www.lerepublicain.net.ml) *Le Ségovien* (www.lesegovien.com), *Les Echos* (www.jamana.org) and *L'Aurore*.
Weeklies: In French, *Courrier*. In Bambara, Fulani, Songhai and Arabic *Cauris* is a training pamphlet for farmers.
Broadcasting
The Office de Radiodiffusion Télévision Malienne (ORTM) (www.ortm.ml) is the national public broadcaster.
Radio: ORTM (www.ortm.ml) operates Radio Mali, which has a nationwide network of stations to provide national and local programming. There are many privately operated radio stations throughout the country, including Radio Canal 2000 and Radio Liberté from Bamako, Radio Kene from Sikasso and Radio Ania from Gao.
Television: ORTM (www.ortm.ml) operates one channel broadcasting locally produced programmes in 10 locally languages of news, culture and entertainment and well as imported TV shows (typically French). The private satellite channel, Africable is also available.
News agencies
National news agency: Agence Malienne de Presse and de Publicité

Economy

The majority of the population is engaged in subsistence farming. Nevertheless the agricultural sector provides cash crops, primarily cotton and rice and livestock, for export and a range of foods for domestic consumption; it constitutes over 30 per cent of GDP. The industrial sector constitutes around 25 per cent of GDP, of which gold mining in particular constituted 80 per cent of exports in 2009. Manufacturing comprises less than 10 per cent of GDP, with the processing of foodstuffs and other agricultural products such as tobacco, ground nuts and shea butter. Historically Mali's climate has been subject to drought, which has severely damaged the economy as herds and crops have failed. In 2010 a prolonged drought in the north forced nomad herders to move further south and into neighbouring Niger and Burkina Faso. According to the International Organisation of Migration (IOM), Mali has lost 13 per cent of its population to emigration since 2000, an estimated 1.5 million people.
GDP growth was 5 per cent in 2008, which fell to 4.4 per cent in 2009 when world commodity prices fell. However, as global food prices had been at a record high in 2008 inflation peaked at 9.1 per cent before falling back to 2.2 per cent in 2009. GDP growth was 5.1 per cent in 2010. The mining ministry announced in 2010 that 80.47 per cent of export earnings in 2009 were due to gold mining. However with Mali's relatively low taxation, the export earnings only accounted for 8 per cent of GDP. Global prices of gold rose from US$309.97 per ounce in 2002 to US$871.71 per cent in 2008 and in 2009 an IMF working paper concluded that the mining industry has 'very limited positive spillovers to the Malian economy'.
Mali is one of the world's poorest countries in the world and is heavily dependent on foreign aid. Remittances in 2009 were US$405 million (4.8 per cent of GDP) and were estimated to have fallen to US$385 million in 2010.
In December 2009 the International Fund for Agricultural Development (Ifad) introduced a new US$25.04 million, microfinance fund, to expand the existing rural microfinance network of credit unions and to expand their reach.
In 2008 legislation was passed to privatise the Malian Textile Development Company, which was replaced by four new companies. In 2007–08 a drought affected the cotton crop and many farmers planned to switch to other crops in 2009. In 2010 world prices of cotton were at a record high as US and Chinese stocks had been depleted and farmers were able to claim higher prices at the farm gate.

External trade

Mali is a member of the Union Économique et Monétaire Ouest Africaine (UEMOA) (West African Economic and Monetary Union) (WAEMU). As a member of the Communauté financière d'Afrique (CFA) (Financial Community of Africa), it uses the CFA franc currency along with the seven other CFA members. It is also a member of the Economic Community of West African States (Ecowas).
Its primary exports, gold and cotton are subject to world prices and along with livestock sales provide 80–90 per cent of export earnings. Remittances constitute an important portion of foreign revenue.
Imports
Principal imports are petroleum products, vehicles, machinery and equipment,

pharmaceuticals, construction materials, foodstuffs and textiles.
Main sources: Senegal (typically 17 per cent of total), France (14 per cent), Côte d'Ivoire (10 per cent).
Exports
The main exports are gold, cotton, livestock and foodstuffs.
Main destinations: South Africa (typically 73 per cent of total), Senegal (7 per cent), Côte d'Ivoire (3 per cent).

Agriculture
Farming
Agriculture is the mainstay of the economy, contributing around 35 per cent of GDP, employing 73 per cent of the workforce (largely at subsistence levels) and accounting for about 45 per cent of agricultural exports. Only about 2 per cent of the total land area is cultivated, but approximately 20 per cent of the total land area along the Niger River is suitable for cultivation, with the most productive areas lying between Bamako and Mopti.
Principal food crops are millet, sorghum, paddy rice, maize and groundnuts. Supported by foreign aid, the government has co-ordinated a programme to expand production of rice as a staple food. There is a regular food deficit due to recurrent drought, crop smuggling and an inefficient marketing and distribution system.
The main export crops are cotton, groundnuts, cereals, fresh fruit and vegetables. Mali is Africa's second-largest cotton producer. Livestock exports have experienced growth in recent years following the abolition of export taxes on livestock. The livestock sector is a mainstay of the economy in the northern half of the country and contributes 20 per cent to GDP. Recent desertification caused by deforestation and global warming has shifted herding activity southwards.
Fishing
Fishing is an important livelihood along the Niger River. The annual fish catch is around 100,000 tonnes, of which 20 per cent is exported, mainly to Côte d'Ivoire. Production, through artisanal fishing, is vulnerable to drought, pollution and man-made obstructions across the river. Inland fisheries have been targeted for development as part of the national poverty reduction strategy. Fish processing and packaging centres and 10,000ha fish ponds plus supporting developments are among the undertakings.

Industry and manufacturing
Manufacturing is concerned mainly with agricultural processing for domestic consumption and export. Other industries include soft drinks, textiles, soaps, plastics, cigarettes, cement, bricks and agricultural tools and equipment. Activity is concentrated in Bamako.
Around 90 per cent of production is accounted for by state enterprises, although rationalisation and privatisation plans are likely to continue.

Tourism
Toursim is an increasingly important sector of the economy, third only to gold and cotton. On 1 August 2010 the government announced that the threat of attacks by Al Aqaeda on tourists had cost Mali around CFAf50 billion (US$108.8 million) in lost tourism receipts and 8,000 jobs since 2009. Many tourists were drawn to spectacular desert-scapes and the ancient trading town of Timbuktu but the risk of kidnapping, sponsored by Al Aqaeda, has grown. In 2010, the annual musical event, 'Le Festival au Désert' had to be relocated, as a safety precaution, from a remote region, north of Timbuktu, closer to the town.

Environment
In June 2010 the African Union backed a proposal to build the 'Great Green Wall' project, of a 15km wide, 7,775km long, continuous belt of trees from Senegal in the west to Djibouti in the east (traversing 11 countries) in an effort to halt the advance of the Sahara Desert. The trees to be used would be drought-adapted, preferably native to the area from a list of 37 possible species, and should help to slow soil erosion and filter rain water.

Mining
The mining sector typically contributes around 10 per cent to GDP and employs 0.5 per cent of the workforce. Gold is Mali's principal mineral resource and since the late 1990s has replaced cottojn and livestock as the country's largest export earner .
Following the introduction of new mining laws in 1991, which helped expand gold production, Mali has become Africa's third largest gold producer after Ghana and South Africa. Total gold reserves are estimated at up to 700 tonnes and geologists claim there is potential for further discoveries. However, commercial exploitation is hampered by the lack of adequate physical infrastructure. Gold represents 80 per cent of the country's total mineral production.
The first privately owned gold mine was opened by BHP-Utah at Syama in 1990, but following operational difficulties it was sold to Randgold of South Africa in 1996. The mine underwent an investment programme and production peaked at 6.1 tonnes in 1999. However, in January 2001, Randgold decided to mothball Syama after extensive flooding led to financial losses.
Opened in 1997, the Sadiola Hill open-cast mine, owned by AngloGold, IAMGold and the Mali government, has estimated reserves of around 130 tonnes. With average annual production estimated at around 10 tonnes per annum until 2010, it is the second largest gold mine in Africa and one of the biggest and lowest cost gold mines in the world.
The Yatela gold mine – owned jointly by AngloGold (40 per cent), IAMGold (40 per cent) and the Mali government (20 per cent) – lies 35km to the north of Sadiola, and was officially opened in September 2002. It has reserves of over 72 tonnes with estimated average annual production of 6 tonnes over a period of 12 years. In 2002, it produced 6.8 tonnes of gold.
The Morila gold mine, opened in early 2001, is forecast to produce an average of 10 tonnes per year over a period of 14 years and is jointly owned by Rangold (40 per cent), AngloGold (40 per cent) and the Mali government (20 per cent). In 2002, Morila produced 15.2 tonnes of gold. Feasibility studies are being conducted on the re-opening of the Kalana gold mine which could produce an estimated 430kg per annum. There are also large unexploited deposits at Kodieran (43 tonnes), Loulo (30.1 tonnes), Segala (15.4 tonnes) and Tabakto (1 tonne).
Artisanal gold mining has been practised in Mali for around 1,000 years and represents 0.6 per cent of GDP and employs around 150,000 seasonal workers. Much of this kind of mining is performed without permits and is generally dangerous.
Phosphate production is around 10,000 tonnes per annum. Small quantities of salt, limestone and uranium are also mined. There are known deposits of bauxite, manganese, iron and tin, and prospecting for lithium, diamonds and copper is under way. Lack of adequate infrastructure has deterred commercial exploitation.

Hydrocarbons
Although there are no proven oil or gas reserves, in February 2009 Algeria's Sonatrach and Canada's Selier Energy signed exploration deals for the Taoudeni basin. Oil and gas reserves were indicated from seismic and drilling tests undertaken in the 1970s, but civil unrest prevented earlier exploration.
Petroleum products (5,000 barrels per day in 2008) are imported from Côte d'Ivoire and Senegal. Mali has no oil refining capacity.

Energy
Total installed generating capacity was 280MW in 2007, producing 510 million kilowatt hours. The Manantali Dam located in Mali on the Senegal River, is operated by Senegal, Mali and Mauritania, it has five hydroelectric generators

supplying around 200MW in a three-way split: Mali 52 per cent, Senegal 33 per cent and Mauritania 15 per cent. The energy from this facility meets the demand of the capital's population. There are small-scale, isolated diesel generators providing power for community facilities but the majority of the population relies on non-commercial biomass, mostly fuel wood for cooking, lighting and power. Mali has the capacity to use 200,000 tonnes of agricultural waste to produce biogas.

Financial markets

Stock exchange

Afribourse (Bourse Régionale des Valeurs Moblières) (BRVM)

Banking and insurance

Mali has an undeveloped banking sector with just nine banks and two financial institutions. Three of the banks are majority owned by the state while the state owns a minority share in three others. There are three privately owned banks. In recent years, the sector has undergone liberalisation.

Central bank

Banque Centrale du Mali

Main financial centre

Bamako

Time

GMT

Geography

Mali is a landlocked country in West Africa, with Algeria to the north, Mauritania and Senegal to the west, Guinea and Côte d'Ivoire to the south, and Burkina Faso and Niger to the east.

Mali is a landlocked country in West Africa, with Algeria to the north, Mauritania and Senegal to the west, Guinea and Côte d'Ivoire to the south, and Burkina Faso and Niger to the east.

There are three distinct topographic regions. The north is the arid Saharan zone, the semiarid Sahel (an Arab word to describe a border or margin) of savannah and scrubland in the centre, and in the south the fertile and cultivated Sudanese zone. The land rises from the south, typically flatland, through rolling plains to high plateaux in the north. Rugged hills no higher than 1,000 metres line the north-east boundary with Mauritania. The Niger River is 1,693 kilometres long and runs through most of the central and southern region and is considered by Malians as the country's lifeblood as it provides drinking water, aquaculture, irrigation and transport.

Hemisphere

Northern

Climate

There is considerable variation between southern, central and northern areas, rain being rare and sporadic in the far north, Sahara region. Bamako's rainy season runs from June to October with humidity reaching 80 per cent and temperatures ranging from 20 degrees Centigrade (C) to 36 degrees C. The warm, dry season runs from November to February followed by a hot, dry season between February and May with average temperatures of 35 degrees C.

Entry requirements

Passports

Required by all. Passport must be valid six months from date of entry.

Visa

Required by all; there are a few exceptions such as citizens of Ecowas countries. For further details and exceptions visit www.maliembassy-addis.org with its link to consular services. Business visas also require a covering company letter declaring the purpose of the trip and proof of return/onward passage.

Currency advice/regulations

The import and export of local currency is unlimited. Import and export of foreign currency is unlimited however amounts over the equivalent of CFAf25,000 must be declared.

Travellers cheques are accepted in banks.

Customs

Personal belongings and a small amount of tobacco and alcohol are permitted duty free. Cameras and films must be declared.

Sporting firearms and plants, excluding fruit and vegetables, need a certificate of import.

Health (for visitors)

Mandatory precautions

Yellow fever vaccination certificate is required by all.

Advisable precautions

Typhoid, tetanus, hepatitis A and polio vaccinations are recommended. Malaria prophylaxis should be taken as risk exists throughout the country. There is a rabies risk. Water precautions must be taken.

Hotels

There are only a few good hotels available and these can be expensive.

Credit cards

Major international credit and charge cards have limited acceptance in major hotels in the capital.

Public holidays (national)

Fixed dates

1 Jan (New Year's Day), 20 Jan (Armed Forces Day), 26 Mar (Day of Democracy), 1 May (Labour Day), 25 May (Africa Day), 22 Sep (Independence Day), 25 Dec (Christmas Day).

Variable dates

Easter Monday, Eid al Adha, Birth of the Prophet, Eid al Fitr.

Islamic year 1433 (26 Nov 2011–14 Nov 2012): The Islamic year contains 354 or 355 days, with the result that Muslim feasts advance by 10–12 days against the Gregorian calendar. Dates of feasts vary according to the sighting of the new moon, so cannot be forecast exactly.

Working hours

Banking

Mon–Fri: 0730–1300; Mon–Thur 1400–1630; Fri 1500–1730.

Business

Mon–Thu: 0730–1230, 1300–1600. Fri: 0730–1230, 1430–1730.

Government

Mon–Thu, Sat: 0730–1430, Fri: 0730–1230.

Telecommunications

Telephone/fax

The internal service is unreliable.

Mobile/cell phones

GSM 900 services are available in the larger urban areas only.

Electricity supply

220V AC, 50 cycles.

Getting there

Air

National airline: Air Mali.

International airport/s: Bamako (BKO), 15km from city.

Airport tax: CFAf2,500 is payable on domestic flights; CFAf8,000 on international flights within Africa; and CFAf10,000 is payable for flights outside Africa. The airport tax may be collected at time of ticket sale and does not apply to transit passengers on the same flight and for children under two years.

Surface

Road: Good road from Niger (Niamey); condition of routes from Côte d'Ivoire and Burkina Faso varies; those from Senegal and Algeria are not generally recommended.

Rail: There is a regular twice weekly rail service from Senegal (Dakar) to Bamako (with sleeping and restaurant cars and facility for conveying vehicles). Journey takes up to 29 hours.

Main port/s: River ports of Bamako, Mopti, Tombouctou and Gao on the Niger.

Getting about

National transport

Air: There are no scheduled services between Bamako and other towns. Charter of light aircraft available from Société des Transports Aériens (STA). Tombouctou Air Service provides domestic flights.

Road: Main roads run from Sikasso and Bougouni in the south to Bamako, and from Bamako to Mopti and on to Gao via a tarred road. Conditions of roads are variable and secondary roads can be difficult.

Buses: Cheap but generally uncomfortable. Services run from Bamako to all main towns.

Rail: Main routes: Bamako-Koulikoro (59 km); Bamako-Kayes (494km). There are two classes: sleeping and restaurant facilities. Some air-conditioned cars are available.

Water: Three river steamers operate up and down the River Niger betwen August and late December, linking Koulikoro, Mopti, Tombouctou and Gao. Four classes are available, but first-class cabins must be booked in advance through SMERT, the tourist organisation.

City transport

Taxis: Cheap and widely available but not metered. Official standard fare system in Bamako. Tipping is not usual.

Car hire

International driving licence recommended. Hired cars are usually Renaults or Peugeots.

BUSINESS DIRECTORY

The addresses listed below are a selection only. While World of Information makes every endeavour to check these addresses, we cannot guarantee that changes have not been made, especially to telephone numbers and area codes. We would welcome any corrections.

Telephone area codes

The international dialling code (IDD) for Mali is +223, followed by subscriber's number.

Useful telephone numbers

Police: 17

Fire: 18

Ambulance: 225-002

Chambers of Commerce

Mali Chamber of Commerce and Industry, Place de la Liberté, BP 46, Bamako (tel: 222-9645; fax: 222-2120; e-mail: ccim@cefip.com).

Banking

Bank of Africa Mali, BP 2249, 418 Avenue de la Marne, Bamako (tel: 222-4672, 222-4088; fax: 222-4653).

Banque Commerciale du Sahel; BP 2372, 127 Rue, Bozola, Bamako (tel: 210-195/97, 225-536; fax: 222-5543, 222-0135).

Banque de Développement du Mali, BP 94, Ave Modibo Keita, Quartier du Fleuve, Bamako (tel: 222-2050, 222-4088; fax: 222-5085, 222-4250).

Banque de l'Habitat du Mali, BP 2614, Rue de Métal Soudan, Quartier du Fleuve, Bamako (tel: 222-9190, 222-9342; fax: 222-9350).

Banque Internationale du Mali; BP 15, Blvd de l'Indépendance, Bamako (tel: 222-5111, 222-5066; fax: 222-4566).

Banque Internationale pour le Commerce et l'Industrie du Mali; BP B72, Bd du Peuple, Immeuble Nimagala, Bamako (tel: 223-3370; fax: 223-3373).

Banque Malienne de Crédit et de Dépôts, BP 45, Avenue Modibo Keïta, Bamako (tel: 222-5336; fax: 222-7950).

Banque Nationale de Développement Agricole - Mali; BP 2424, Immeuble Dette Publique, Bamako (tel: 222-6464, 222-6611 fax: 222-2961).

Ecobank-Mali; BP 1272, Quartier du Fleuve, Place de la Nation, Bamako (tel: 223-3300; fax: 223-3305).

Central bank

Banque Centrale des Etats de l'Afrique de l'Ouest, Direction Nationale, PO Box 206, Avenue Moussa Travele, Bamako (tel: 222-3756; fax: 222-4786).

Stock exchange

Afribourse (Bourse Régionale des Valeurs Moblières) (BRVM): www.brvm.org

Travel information

Air Mali, Immeuble Scif, Square Lumumba, BP 27, Bamako (tel: 225-741/42; fax: 222-349).

Commissariat au Tourisme, BP 191, Bamako (tel: 225-673).

Delta Voyages SA, Immeuble Gamby (ex BNDA), BP 5005, Bamako (fax: 231-272).

Timbuctours, BP 222, Bamako (tel: 225-315).

Ministry of tourism

Ministry of Crafts Industry and Tourism, BP 2211, Bamako (tel: 223-6344, 223-6450; fax: 223-8201).

Ministries

Ministry of Agriculture, Breeding and Fishing, BP 61, Bamako (tel: 222-2979, 222-2785, 222-3006).

Ministry of Economy and Finances, BP 776, Bamako (tel: 222-9918, 222-8353; fax: 229-4440).

Ministry of Education, BP 71, Bamako, (tel: 222-2450; 222-2125; fax: 223-0545).

Ministry of Foreign Affairs, Bamako (fax: 230-327, 225-226).

Ministry of Industry and Trade, BP 1759, Bamako (tel: 221-6399, 222-8353; fax: 221-3114).

Ministry of Labour and Public Works, BP 80, Bamako, (tel: 222-4819; 222-1117; fax: 222-6548).

Ministry of Overseas Aid and International Co-operation, Bamako, (tel: 222-5092; 223-0056).

Other useful addresses

Direction Nationale du Plan et de la Statistique, Koulouba, Bamako (tel: 222-2753).

Government Press Office, Bamako, (tel: 222-0733).

Radiodiffusion-Télévision Malienne, BP 171, Bamako (tel: 222-2474).

Mali Embassy (USA), 2130 R Street, NW, Washington DC 20009 (tel: (+1-202) 332-2249; fax: (+1-202) 332-6603; e-mail: info@maliembassy-usa.org).

National news agency: Agence Malienne de Presse and de Publicité, BP 141 Bamako (tel: 222-2346; fax: 222-4774; internet: www.essor.gov.ml).

Internet sites

Africa Business Network: http://www.ifc.org/abn

African Development Bank: http://www.afdb.org

AllAfrica.com: http://www.allafrica.com

Africa Online: http://www.africaonline.com

Mbendi AfroPaedia (information on companies, countries, industries and stock exchanges in Africa): http://mbendi.co.za

Malta

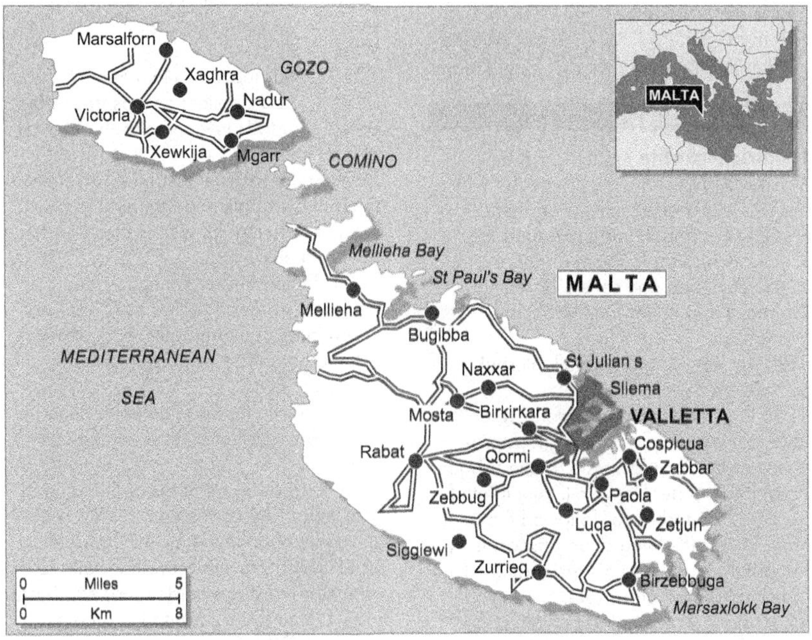

KEY FACTS

Official name: Republic of Malta

Head of State: President George Abela (from 4 Apr 2009)

Head of government: Prime Minister Lawrence Gonzi (from 2004; re-elected 12 Mar 2008)

Ruling party: Partit Nazzjonalista (PN) (Nationalist Party) (since 1998; re-elected 8 Mar 2008)

Area: 316 square km

Population: 415,990 (2010)*

Capital: Valletta

Official language: Malti and English

Currency: Euro (€) = 100 cents (from 1 Jan 2008; previous currency Maltese lira, locked at MI0.43 per euro)

Exchange rate: €0.75 per US$ (Oct 2011)

GDP per capita: US$19,746 (2010)

GDP real growth: 3.70% (2010)

GDP: US$8.30 billion (2010)

Labour force: 176,000 (2010)

Unemployment: 6.80% (2010)

Inflation: 2.00% (2010)

Balance of trade: -US$1.23 billion (2010)

* estimated figure

Malta, the last European country to ban divorce, finally put the question to the people in a close run referendum held on 28 May 2011. The issue had long provoked bitter arguments on both sides. The Catholic Church was most vociferous in its opposition to the proposal, echoing the Pope's 2010 praise of Malta's hitherto firm stance against abortion and divorce. A Catholic member of parliament even invoked the name of the 'Blessed Virgin' to secure a favourable outcome. But by 2011 there was such a groundswell of opinion that the government considered it was time to deal with the problem of failed marriages. The vote was 52.67 per cent in favour of the proposal with 46.4 per cent against, on a 72 per cent turnout. Parliament voted on 25 July to pass the law, which came into effect in October.

Good news for some

The Arab Spring, which brought so much freedom and joy to thousands of North Africans, also brought an influx of migrants to Malta. Although there were Libyans and Tunisians fleeing the violence in their countries, by far the largest body of migrants was from sub-Saharan Africa, as people took advantage of the chaos to pass through to the Mediterranean. By 2011, Malta had the highest per capita level of 'irregular migrants', including asylum seekers, in Europe. Under European Union (EU) rules Malta has a requirement to provide a minimum standard of accommodation and an official level of processing of a migrant's entry to the EU. The cost of this service rose to such an extent that the small island of Malta couldn't cope. It called on the EU Commission to not only provide more subsidies to run the migration operation, but to tackle the source of the problem and negotiate an agreement with African states to curb illegal immigration.

The economy

As a member of the euro-zone Malta has been adversely affected by the European economic chaos caused by the Greek debt crisis. However, according the Central Bank of Malta, annual GDP growth was over 2.0 per cent for the first half of 2011, spurred by net exports as domestic demand slowed. Unemployment edged up to over 6.7 per cent by mid-year. The general government deficit increased on an annual basis during the second quarter of 2011, as revenue declined while expenditure rose. The stock of general government debt also continued to increase, to stand at €4.53 million (US$6.52 million) at the end of June. On 7 September, the credit ratings agency Moody's downgraded Malta's foreign and domestic currency government bonds from A1 to A2 and revised its outlook to 'negative'. Moody's justified the downgrade by what it saw as the decline in potential output growth, which would leave the economy vulnerable to further economic shocks.

Ship repairing is an important foreign exchange earner. Malta is a maritime nation and operates a flag of convenience, so that it has a larger shipping fleet than other countries of larger sizes. At the end of 2010, a total of 5,249 ships (of which 2,440 were yachts) were registered under the Maltese Merchant Shipping Act.

Tourism

The wave or political unrest in North Africa and a strike by staff of Air Malta early in 2011, affected the tourist trade, with fewer visitors and a slowdown in bookings. However, later in the season (mid-year) numbers had grown and registered year-on-year growth of 11 per cent. Tourism constituted over 12 per cent of GDP in 2011; the sector typically employs 25 per cent of the total workforce. A growing number of cruise ships dock at the Port of Valetta, at newly refurbished historic buildings that once belonged to the Knights Hospitaller of Malta. The total number of cruise passengers arriving from January–November 2011, was 540,827, an increase of 15.8 per cent on the same period in 2010. Cruise liners made 303 calls to Malta in 2011, 40 more than in 2010.

Risk assessment

Economy	Fair
Politics	Good
Regional stability	Good

COUNTRY PROFILE

Historical profile

1814 Malta became a crown colony of the UK, with limited self-government.
1942 The islanders were awarded the George Cross for heroism during a three-year siege and severe bombing by Germans and Italians in the Second World War.
1947 Malta was granted full internal self-government.
1956 In a referendum, a majority voted in favour of integration with the UK as proposed by the Partit Laburista (Malta Labour Party) (MLP) under Dominic (Dom) Mintoff.
1959–62 Disturbances followed the rejection of Mintoff's integration proposals by the British, leading to his resignation. The British reinstated direct rule.
1964 Malta was granted full independence. It became a member of the Commonwealth, reinforced by defence and aid treaties with UK.
1971 A Labour government was elected under Dom Mintoff , who signed co-operative treaties with Eastern and Western countries and established close relations with Libya.
1974 Malta declared itself a republic.
1981 The MLP gained more seats but fewer votes than the Partit Nazzionalista (PN) (Nationalist Party), which mounted a campaign of civil disobedience and boycotted the House of Representatives for over a year.
1987 Following constitutional amendments, the PN, led by Eddie Fenech Adami, worked to maintain non-aligned status, while seeking closer ties with the West.
1990 Malta applied to join the EU.
1996 The EU application was frozen by Alfred Sant (MLP) when he took office as prime minister.
1998 Prime Minister Adami (PN) renewed the island's application to join the EU.
2003 The ruling PN won the parliamentary elections.
2004 Prime Minister Fenech Adami stepped down and Lawrence Gonzi was sworn in as prime minister. Eddie Fenech Adami took office as president. Malta joined the EU.
2005 The Maltese parliament ratified the European constitution in a unanimous vote.
2006 Increasing numbers of illegal immigrants from Africa forced Malta to seek stronger commitment from EU partners.
2007 The EU formally invited Malta to join the third stage of the European Monetary Union (EMU). Malta became a member of the European Union Schengen area whereby all travellers may cross borders without a passport or visa.
2008 Malta adopted the euro as its official currency. In parliamentary elections the PN won 49.3 per cent of the vote (35 seats out of 69), the MLP 48.8 per cent (34); turnout was 93 per cent.
2009 By unanimous approval, parliament elected George Abela as president.
2010 Former president Guido de Marco died on 12 August.
2011 A referendum held on 27 March was won by pro-divorce supporters. A bill was presented to parliament, and passed (by 52 votes to 11) on 25 July, making divorce legal so long as the couple have been separated for at least four years, that there was no chance of reconciliation, and adequate maintenance was agreed and the children were protected. It came into effect in October. Malta's call for a suspension of the 'Dublin regulation' and more help from the EU to cope with the unprecedented number of migrants and refugees arriving from North Africa since January was given limited approval at the 23–24 June summit meeting. Malta argued that as the 'Dublin regulation' requires all EU members to return migrants and refugees to the first country of entry and as Malta was a frontline country of the EU it was likely to be

KEY INDICATORS — Malta

	Unit	2006	2007	2008	2009	2010
Population	m	0.41	*0.41	*0.41	*0.42	*0.42
Gross domestic product (GDP)	US$bn	6.39	7.42	8.40	8.00	8.30
GDP per capita	US$	15,716	18,376	20,281	19,111	19,746
GDP real growth	%	3.4	3.8	2.1	-3.3	3.1
Inflation	%	2.6	0.7	4.7	1.8	2.0
Unemployment	%	7.3	6.5	6.0	6.9	6.8
Exports (fob) (goods)	US$m	2,948.2	3,237.9	3,177.0	2,383.0	3,088.0
Imports (fob) (goods)	US$m	4,154.3	4,541.1	4,844.0	3,594.0	4,317.0
Balance of trade	US$m	-1,206.1	1,303.2	-1,667.0	-1,211.0	-1,229.0
Current account	US$m	-426.0	-523.0	-469.0	-491.0	-415.0
Total reserves minus gold	US$m	2,876.8	3,785.4	368.3	532.1	535.8
Foreign exchange	US$m	2,865.0	3,662.0	288.3	329.7	340.5
Exchange rate	per US$	0.32	0.30	0.68	0.78	0.76

* estimated figure

disproportionately hit hard by the numbers to be processed. However, the summit did agree to a 'safeguard mechanism' which allowed the temporary re-introduction of border controls in exceptional circumstances in individual cases.

Political structure

Constitution

The independence constitution of 1964 was amended on 13 December 1974, to provide for the creation of the office of president to replace that of governor general.

Independence date

21 September 1964

Form of state

Parliamentary democratic republic; it is a member of the Commonwealth.

The executive

The House of Representatives elects the president as constitutional head of state for a five-year term. The president appoints the prime minister and, on the latter's advice, the cabinet, which holds executive power.

National legislature

The unicameral Kamra tad-Deputati (House of Representatives) has 65 members elected by proportional representation in multi-seat constituencies, to serve for five-year terms. Should a party polling a majority of votes fail to gain a majority of seats in the House, extra seats are allocated until a majority of one seat is achieved.

Legal system

The judiciary is independent. Public law is based on English common law.

Last elections

1 April 2009 (presidential); 8 March 2008 (parliamentary).

Results: Presidential: George Abela was unanimously voted into office by the House of Representatives.

Parliamentary: PN won 49.3 per cent of the vote (35 seats out of 69); PL won 48.8 per cent (34). Turnout was 93 per cent.

Next elections

2013 (parliamentary); 2014 (presidential).

Political parties

Ruling party

Partit Nazzjonalista (PN) (Nationalist Party) (since 1998; re-elected 8 Mar 2008)

Main opposition party

Partit Laburista (PL) (Labour Party)

Population

415,990 (2010)*

Last census: 27 November 2005: 404,962

Population density: 1,184 inhabitants per square km. Urban population: 91 per cent.

Annual growth rate: 0.7 per cent 1994–2004 (WHO 2006)

Ethnic make-up

Most Maltese are descendants of Phoenicians, with strong elements of Italian and other Mediterranean influences.

Religions

Roman Catholic (98 per cent).

Education

Primary education lasts for six years; secondary schooling lasts for five years, divided into a three-year orientation cycle and a two-year cycle of specialisation. There are two types of secondary education schools – junior Lyceums and area secondary schools; following either of these leads to a choice between academic or technical courses. Over 54 per cent of students continue with their education and training after the age of 16. Church schools are funded through the government and tuition is free.

Higher education is mainly provided by the University of Malta. The quality of education in Malta is high and attracts students from the Mediterranean and the Middle East.

Literacy rate: 92.6 per cent total; 93.4 per cent female, adult rates (World Bank).

Compulsory years: Five to 16.

Enrolment rate: 108 per cent (boys); 107 per cent (girls) gross primary enrolment of the relevant age group (including repetition rates) (World Bank).

Health

Public hospital services are adequate although there have been concerns over the long waiting times. Total bed capacity is around 2,000. An increasing number of doctors are resigning due to poor working conditions and wages. Due to the low numbers of doctors, some health centres have stopped operating on a 24-hour basis.

A programme of refurbishment and modernisation was undertaken in all government hospitals.

HIV/Aids

HIV prevalence: 0.2 per cent aged 15–49 in 2003 (World Bank)

Life expectancy: 79 years, 2004 (WHO 2006)

Fertility rate/Maternal mortality rate: 1.5 births per woman, 2004 (WHO 2006)

Child (under 5 years) mortality rate (per 1,000): 5.0 per 1,000 live births (World Bank).

Head of population per physician: 3.18 physicians per 1,000 people, 2003 (WHO 2006)

Welfare

The Maltese welfare system is poised for reform. There is a significant welfare gap in society.

The social security contribution rate paid by every Maltese employer is 10 per cent. The self-employed pay a rate of 15 per cent.

A Care Allowance was introduced for children living in institutions and was later extended to foster parents.

Main cities

Valletta (capital, estimated population 7,170), Birkirkara (22,685), Mosta (18,416), Qormi (18,100), Mosta (18,416), Sliema (12,380), Zabbar (15,452).

Languages spoken

Malti, English and some Italian; most business correspondence is in English.

Official language/s

Malti and English

Media

Press

Dailies: Bilingualism has resulted in 50 per cent of the number of newspapers published in either Maltese or English. In Maltese, *L-orizzont* (www.l-orizzont.com) has the highest circulation, followed by *In-Nazzjon* (www.nazzjon.com.mt). While *The Times* (www.timesofmalta.com), *The Malta Independent* (www.independent.com.mt) and *Malta Today* (www.maltatoday.com.mt), are popular English newspapers.

Weeklies: In Maltese, *It Torca* (www.it-torca.com), published on Sunday, has the highest circulation followed by *Kull Hadd* (www.kullhadd.com) and *Lehen is-Sewwa* a Catholic publication. English dailies publish Sunday editions.

Business: Two publications include, in English, the daily *Business Today* (www.businesstoday.com.mt) and *The Malta Business Weekly* (www.maltabusinessweekly.com.mt).

Broadcasting

The Public Broadcasting Service (PBS) (www.pbs.com.mt) is funded by both a television license and advertising.

Radio: There are dozens of local stations broadcasting; however the market is dominated by those operated by either the government, political parties or the Catholic Church. PBS (www.pbs.com.mt) operates three stations including Radju Malta, Radju Parlament and Majic FM. Super One Radio (www.one.com.mt) is owned by the Maltese Labour Party, Radio 101 (www.radio101.com.mt) is operated by the Nationalist Party, RTK (www.rtk.org.mt) is owned by the Catholic Church and Campus FM (http://campusfm.um.edu.mt) is operated by the University of Malta.

Television: For revenue, television companies lease airtime to independently production houses which provided programmes of agreed topics. The TV market is diverse with broadcasts from Italian television received and over 80 per cent of homes subscribing to cable services.

PBS (www.pbs.com.mt) operates TVM, which mainly broadcasts externally produced programmes in both Maltese and English. Super One TV (www.super1.com) is owned by the Maltese Labour Party and Net TV (www.nettv.com.mt) is operated by the Nationalist Party.

Advertising

All traditional forms of media accept advertising and new technologies are available as well.

Economy

The economy is largely structured on trade, tourism and financial services of which the latter two account for over 70 per cent of GDP and give employment to over 65 per cent of the workforce. However, the global economic crisis has affected trade and tourism since 2008, not only because they are both subject to external pressures, but also because Malta had adopted the euro as its currency on 1 January, which made exports costlier and visitor's currencies (unless from the euro-zone) less valuable.

GDP growth in 2008 was 5.4 per cent, falling into recession in 2009 with a rate of -3.3 per cent, but bouncing back in 2010 as tourism and global trade picked up so that annual growth was 3.1 per cent. Inflation in 2008 was 4.7 per cent as imports of energy and food had risen, by 2009 it had dropped to 1.8 per cent as domestic demand fell; inflation in 2010 was recorded at 2 per cent.

The government introduced a financial stimulus package in 2009, which included support for the manufacturing and tourism sectors and increased public investment. Female participation in the workforce is the lowest in the European Union at just over 30 per cent (typically the highest enrolment rates are over 60 per cent) and a personal income tax regime was modified to encourage their uptake of paid employment. Foreign direct investment (FDI) peaked in 2006 at US$1.84 billion (around 30 per cent of GDP), and much of the investment was directed towards the innovation-driven sectors, specifically semiconductor manufacturing. FDI declined steadily to US$753 million in 2009, before picking up in 2010 to US$998 million.

The financial sector remained relatively stable through the economic crisis as Malta's banks had limited exposure to international operations. In 2011, the international ratings agency Standard & Poor's re-confirmed Malta's sovereign credit ratings as A/A1 for its long and short-term (respectively), while the transfer and convertibility assessment remained AAA, due to the country's stable financial outlook.

Transport-related services, such as trans-shipment and ship repair, are important to the economy. Malta is a flag of convenience state and has been under pressure from the European Union (EU) to comply with EU maritime standards.

External trade

As a member of the European Union, Malta operates within a communitywide free trade union, with tariffs sets as a whole. Internationally, the EU has free trade agreements with a number of nations and trading blocs worldwide.

Manufactured commodities provide 75 per cent of total exports, while the tourist sector provides 30 per cent of GDP. Malta's has the world's fourth largest merchant fleet in the world and is actively encouraging growth in international banking and financial services and developing an offshore tax haven.

Imports

Principal imports are petroleum and vehicles, foodstuffs, electrical and electronic components, machinery, beverages and tobacco, manufactured and semi-manufactured goods.

Main sources: Italy (typically 26 per cent of total), UK (12 per cent), France (8 per cent).

Exports

Major exports include manufactured electrical and electronic items, general machinery, clothing and footware, stationery and books and building materials.

Main destinations: France (typically 14 per cent of total), Germany (13 per cent), Singapore (12 per cent).

Re-exports

Agriculture

Farming

The agricultural sector accounts for around 2.5 per cent of GDP and employs less than 2 per cent of the population. Agricultural production supplies only about 20 per cent of Malta's food needs. There is a limited area of land available for agriculture and freshwater supplies are scarce. Potatoes and onions are the largest vegetable crops; potatoes are also the largest export crop. Grapes are the largest fruit crop and flower cultivation is flourishing. Malta has decided to implement the reform of the EU Common Agricultural Policy (CAP) on 1 January 2007. The reform was introduced throughout most of the EU in 2005, when subsidies on farm output, which tended to benefit large farms and encourage overproduction, were replaced by single farm payments, not conditional on production. The change is expected to reward farmers who provide and maintain a healthy environment, food safety and animal welfare standards. The changes are also intended to encourage market conscious production and cut the cost of CAP to the EU taxpayer.

Fishing

Around 1,000 tonnes of marine fish are landed annually, while acquaculture produces 2,000 tonnes. Around 370 people are registered as full-time fishermen, with 300 registered fishing vessels in operation. Another 1,500 boats are owned by part-time fishermen.

Industry and manufacturing

The industrial sector contributes approximately 30 per cent to GDP and employs 35 per cent of the labour force.

Manufactures include textiles, clothing, synthetic fibres, footwear, wines and beer, furniture, electronic goods, automobile components, measuring/controlling equipment and tobacco products.

Ship-repairing is an important foreign exchange earner, but the Malta Drydocks company suffered falling revenues during the 1990s as worldwide shipping activity declined. As a result, the government has decided to end subsidies to both the Malta Drydocks and Malta Shipbuilding companies by 2008.

Tourism

Malta, strategically located in the middle of the Mediterranean, has been occupied or colonised down the ages by the Phoenicians, the Romans, Byzantines, Arabs, Normans, Crusaders, Napoleonic troops and the British. Each succeeding occupation left behind evidence of their passing. The Germans were the last to attack the islands, in the 1940s, subjecting the people to a blockade the privations of which earned the islands a Victory Cross (the highest award for bravery given by the UK). The capital Valetta is a UN World Heritage Site, which includes 320 monuments within an area of 55 hectares (one of the most concentrated historic areas in the world). Malta and Gozo's megalithic temples are also on the UN list.

With tourist numbers of over one million annually, for a population of some 415,000, the travel and tourism industry is a major component of the economy, which constituted over 12 per cent of GDP in 2011 and typically employs 25 per cent of the total workforce. The downturn in the world economy had the effect of depressing the tourist trade by -0.3 per cent in 2008 and further still in 2009 to -8.3 per cent before recovering strongly to 6.4 per cent in 2010, as most countries came out of recession and travel plans were reinstated.

Malta invests in its tourism industry and of total capital investment, travel and tourism has consistently attracted between 10–15 per cent per annum. Cruise ships dock at the Port of Valetta at newly refurbished buildings that once belonged to the Knights Hospitaller of Malta.

Malta's long association with the UK provides elderly Britons with a winter destination for longer stays. However, in 2010 the market saw an increase in younger visitors (up to 24 years) attracted by competitive prices in a euro-zone country.

Mining

Malta has no exploitable natural resources.

Hydrocarbons

There are no known oil or gas reserves although oil and gas exploration is ongoing. All hydrocarbon needs are met by imports; consumption of oil was 19,000 barrels per day in 2008.
The Enemalta Corporation is responsible for imports, storage and distribution of oil and liquefied petroleum gas (LPG), as well as liquefied natural gas (LNG). In 2007 and 2008 Heritage Oil and Malta Oil were given exclusive rights to explore in Malta's territorial waters up to 2010 and 2011 respectively.
What little reserves of coal Malta may have is not commercially recorded.

Energy

Total installed generating capacity was 570MW in 2007, producing 2.13 billion kilowatt hours. The Enemalta Corporation generates and distributes electricity nationwide. There are three traditional thermal power stations supplying electricity throughout Malta and by sub-marine cables to Gozo and Comino.
Many households buy bottled supplies of liquefied natural gas (LNG) for cooking and heating.
The government set a target of 5 per cent of total generating capacity to be supplied by renewable energy sources (RES) by 2010, and agreed to an EU target of 10 per cent by 2020. However by 2008 solar power and biofuels were only in minimal use.

Financial markets

Stock exchange
Borza ta' Malta (Malta Stock Exchange) (MSE)

Banking and insurance

There are two major commercial banks — Bank of Valletta and the HSBC Bank Malta plc.
Central bank
Central Bank of Malta

Time

GMT plus one hour (daylight saving, late March to late October, GMT plus two hours)

Geography

The largest and only inhabited islands of the Maltese archipelago in the Mediterranean are Malta, Gozo and Comino. The main island, Malta, lies 93km (58 miles) south of the Italian island of Sicily and 290km (180 miles) north of the Libyan coast, with Tunisia to the west.
Malta is typically limestone rock with a series of low hills and slopes running toward the north-west and low-lying land to the south-east. The soil can be thin producing heathland, while terraced hills produce much of Malta's agricultural produce.
Hemisphere
Northern

Climate

Mediterranean, with hot summers and warm winters. Temperatures range from about 29 degrees Celsius (C) down to about 10 degrees C. January and February are the coldest months, July and August the hottest. August and September tend to be hot and humid, but usually with sea breezes in evening.

Dress codes

European clothing is suitable for winter, spring and autumn; tropical weight for summer.

Entry requirements

Passports
Required by all, excepted for citizens of EU and EEA with national ID cards. Passports must be valid for three month beyond the length of stay.
Visa
Required by all, except nationals of EU and Schengen area signatory countries, North America, Australasia and Japan. For further exceptions contact the nearest embassy or see www.foreign.gov.mt and follow the link to travel advice. A Schengen visa application (offered in several languages) can be downloaded from http://europa.eu/abc/travel/ see 'documents you will need'.
Currency advice/regulations
The import and export of local currency is limited to Lm5,000; the import of export of foreign currency is unlimited.
Travellers cheques are widely accepted.
Customs
Personal items are duty-free. There are no duties levied on alcohol and tobacco between EU member states, providing amounts imported are for personal consumption.

Health (for visitors)

Nationals of the European Economic Area (EEA) countries and Switzerland can access reduced cost and sometimes free medical treatment using a European Health Insurance Card (EHIC) while visiting the EEA. Exceptions include nationals of the 10 countries, which joined the EU in 2004, whose EHIC is not valid in Switzerland. Applications for the EHIC should be made before travelling.
Advisable precautions
There are no special requirements.

Hotels

Classified from five-star to one-star. All hotel staff speak English and many are multi-lingual.

Credit cards

All major credit and debit cards are accepted; ATMs are widely available.

Public holidays (national)

Fixed dates
1 Jan (New Year's Day), 10 Feb (St Paul's Shipwreck), 19 Mar (St Joseph's Day), 31 Mar (Freedom Day), 1 May (Labour Day), 7 Jun (Commemoration of the 1919 Uprising), 29 Jun (Feast of St Peter and St Paul), 15 Aug (Assumption Day), 8 Sep (Victory Day), 21 Sep (Independence Day), 8 Dec (Immaculate Conception), 13 Dec (Republic Day) and 25 Dec (Christmas Day).
Variable dates
Good Friday

Working hours

Banking
Mon–Fri: 0830–1230; Sat: 0830–1200. Summer and winter opening hours may vary.
Business
Mon–Fri: 0830–1245 and 1430–1730.
Government
Mon–Fri: 0745–1230 and 1315–1715 (Jun to Sep Mon–Fri: 0730–1330).
Shops
Mon–Sat: 0900–1300 and 1600–1900.

Telecommunications

Mobile/cell phones
GSM 900 and 1800 services are available throughout the islands.

Electricity supply

240V AC

Weights and measures

The metric system is the main one in use. Sometimes the imperial system is also used and, on rare occasions, the old local measures.

Getting there

Air
National airline: Air Malta.
International airport/s: Malta (MLA) at Luqa, 5km from Valletta, facilities include *bureau de change*, duty-free shops, car hire and restaurant. Taxis and buses are available.
Airport tax: None
Surface
Water: There are regular car ferry services from Sicily and the Italian mainland.

Getting about

National transport
Air: Internal flights (by helicopter) operate between Malta and Gozo.
Buses: Regular bus services run from Valletta to most towns and villages on Malta and Gozo.

Water: Gozo Channel Company operates a regular round-the-clock daily ferry service between Malta and Gozo.

City transport

Metered taxis are available.

Car hire

Self-drive cars are available at daily, weekly and monthly rates with unlimited mileage and fully comprehensive insurance. A national or international driving licence is required, which must be endorsed at the Police Licensing Office, Floriana. Speed limits are 40kph in built-up areas and 64kph elsewhere. Driving is on the left.

BUSINESS DIRECTORY

Telephone area codes

The international direct dialling (IDD) code for Malta is +356 followed by subscriber's number.

Useful telephone numbers

Police: 191
Ambulance: 196
Fire brigade: 199
Directory enquiries: 190
Overseas operator: 194
Time check: 195

Chambers of Commerce

Malta Chamber of Commerce and Enterprise, Exchange Buildings, Republic Street, Valletta VLT 05 (tel: 2123-3873; fax: 2124-5223; e-mail: admin@chamber.org.mt).

Maltese-American Chamber of Commerce, Exchange Buildings, Republic Street, Valletta VLT 05 (tel: 2124-7233; fax: 2124-5223; e-mail: president@malta-uschamber.com).

Banking

APS Bank ltd, 275 St Paul Street, Valletta VLT 07 (tel: 247-547; fax: 238-698).

Bank of Valletta Ltd, 58 Zachary Street, Valletta VLT 04 (tel: 243-261/7; fax: 230-894).

Bank of Valletta Group, BOV Centre, High Street, Sliema, SLM 16 (tel: 336-224; fax: 346-160; internet site: www.bov.com).

HSBC Bank Malta (Overseas) plc, 15 Republic Street, Valletta VLT 05 (tel: 249-801/4; fax: 249-805).

Investment Finance Bank Ltd, 168 Strait Street, Valletta VLT 07 (tel: 232-017, 233-349; fax: 242-014).

Lombard Bank (Malta) Ltd, Lombard House, 67 Republic Street, Valletta VLT 05 (tel: 248-411/8; fax: 246-600).

Valletta Investment Bank Ltd, 144 St Christopher Street, Valletta VLT 02 (tel: 2235-246; fax: 234-419).

Central bank

Central Bank of Malta, Pjazza Kastija, Valletta CMR 01 (tel: 2550-0000; fax: 2550-2500; e-mail: info@centralbankmalta.com).

Stock exchange

Borza ta' Malta (Malta Stock Exchange) (MSE): www.borzamalta.com.mt

Travel information

Air Malta, Head Office, Malta International Airport, Gudja (tel: 2299-9984, 2299-9885; fax: 2299-9368; internet site: www.airmalta.com).

Malta International Airport Ltd, Luqa LQA 05 (tel: 249-600; fax: 243-042; internet site: www.maltairport.com).

National tourist organisation offices

Malta Tourism Authority, 280 Republic Street, Valletta CMR 02 (tel: 224-444, 225-048/9; fax: 220-401; e-mail: info@visitmalta.com; internet: www.visitmalta.com).

Ministries

Ministry of Investment, Industry and Information Technology, 168 Triq id-Dejqa, Valletta CMR 02 (tel: 2122-6808; fax: 2125-0700; email: miti@gov.mt).

Ministry of Foreign Affairs, Palazzo Parisio, Merchants Street, Valletta CMR 02 (tel: 2124-2853; fax: 2123-5032; email: info.mfa@gov.mt).

Ministry of Finance, Maison Demandols, South Street, Valletta CMR 02 (tel: 2124-9640/6; fax: 2122-4667; email info.mfin@gov.mt).

Ministry of Resources and Infrastructures, Block B, Floriana CMR 02 (tel: 2122-2378; fax: 2124-3306).

Other useful addresses

British High Commission, Whitehall Mansions, Ta'Xbiex Seafront, Ta'Xbiex, MSD 11, (tel: 2323-0000; fax: 622-001).

Department of Industry, St George's, Canon Road, St Venera (tel: 446-259).

Department of Information, Auberge de Castille, Valletta (tel: 225-241, 224-901; fax: 237-170).

Department of Trade, Lascaris, Valletta (tel: 224-411).

Embassy of the United States of America, PO Box 535, Valletta CMR O1 (tel: 2561-4000; fax: 2124-3229; email: usembmalta@state.gov).

Hotels and Restaurants Association, 7 Frederick Street, Valletta (tel: 336-843; fax: 237-253).

Malta Broadcasting Authority, National Rd, Blata 1-Bajda (tel: 221-281).

Maltacom (telecommunications), Spencer Hill, Marsa HMR12 (postal address: PO Box 40, Qormi, QRM01) (tel: 240-000; e-mail: mcintrel@maltacom.com; internet: www.maltacom.com).

Malta Development Corporation, PO Box 141, Marsa GPO 01; head office: Triq l-Industrija, Qormi (tel: 441-888; fax: 441-887; e-mail: info@mdc.com.mt; internet site: www.investinmalta.com).

Malta Drydocks, The Docks (tel: 822-451, 822-491; fax: 800-021).

Malta Export Trade Corporation, Trade Centre, PO Box 8, San Gwann SGN 01 (tel: 446-186/7/8; fax: 496-687; internet site: www.metco.com.mt/main.htm).

Malta Federation of Industry, Development House, St Anne Street, Floriana VLT 01 (tel: 222-074, 234-428; fax: 240-702).

Malta Financial Services Centre (MFSC), Attard (tel: 441-155; fax: 441-188).

Malta Freeport Corporation Ltd, Freeport Centre, Port of Matrsaxlokk, Kalafrana BBG 07 (tel: 650-200; fax: 684-814).

Malta Investment Management Co Ltd (MIMCOL), Trade Centre, San Gwann Industrial Estate, Birkirkara SGN09 (tel: 497-970; fax: 499-568).

Malta Maritime Authority, Maritime House, Lascaris Wharf, Valletta VLT 01 (tel: 250-360/4; fax: 250-365).

Malta Shipbuilding Co Ltd, Marsa (tel: 220-051, 237-297; fax: 240-930).

Malta Stock Exchange, Pope Pius V Street, Valletta VLT 11 (tel: 244-051/5; fax: 244-071).

Malta Trade Fairs Corporation, The Fair Grounds, Naxxar NXR 02 (tel: 410-371/4; fax: 414-099).

Maltese Embassy (US), 2017 Connecticut Avenue, NW, Washington DC 20008 (tel: (+1-202) 462-3611; fax: (+1-202) 387-5470; e-mail: malta_embassy@compuserve.com).

Parliamentary Secretariat for Maritime and Offshore, House of Four Winds, Valletta (tel: 241-570).

Privatisation Unit, Ministry of Finance and Economic Affairs, Trade Centre, San Gwann Industrial Estate, San Gwann SGN 09 (internet site: www.maltacom.com).

Sea Malta Co Ltd, Sea Malta Building, Flagstone Wharf, Marsa HMR 12 (tel: 232-230/9; fax: 225-776).

Internet sites

Malta Government: www.magnet.mt/

Marshall Islands

The Marshall Islands government is implementing tax reforms in 2011, in preparation for the ending of the grants under its Compact of Free Association with the US in 2024. The government has also made efforts to trim expenditure, although more will be needed, including allowances for civil servants and public officials and assistance to state enterprises.

The Asian Development Bank forecasts a small growth of 1.0 per cent for 2011, and a slight increase to 1.2 per cent in 2012. Fisheries, a key source of income could benefit from a planned sub-regional collaboration on managing fish stocks.

COUNTRY PROFILE

Historical profile

The Marshall Islands comprise over a thousand flat coral islands of white sand beaches and lagoons.

1788 The Marshall Islands were named after Captain John Marshall, who visited the islands on his way to China from Botany Bay.

1886 Germany established a protectorate over the Marshall Islands.

1914 The islands were captured from Germany by Japan.

1935 The Japanese transformed the islands into a military base.

1944 Allied troops occupied the islands.

1945 After the end of the Second World War, control of the Marshall Islands was granted to the US.

1946 The Marshall Islands were used as a nuclear testing ground by the US.

1947 Marshall Islands became one of six entities in the Trust Territory of the Pacific Islands (TTPI) established by the UN with the US as the Trustee.

1962 The US ended nuclear testing on the islands.

1965 The Congress of Micronesia was established, with representatives from all TTPI islands.

1978 The Marshall Islands' first constitution was adopted.

1979 The government of the Marshall Islands was officially established and the islands became self-governing. Amata Kabua was elected president.

1982 The official title of the islands became the Republic of the Marshall Islands (RMI).

1983 RMI voters approved the Compact of Free Association (CFA) with the US.

1986 The US Congress approved the CFA. The RMI was granted sovereignty, aid and US defence, in return for continued US military missile testing.

1990 The UN Security Council formally ended the trusteeship.

1991 The RMI joined the UN.

1995 President Kabua was re-elected for the fourth time.

1996 Amata Kabua died. He was succeeded by his cousin, Imata Kabua

1999 The United Democratic Party (UDP) won the general election.

2000 Kessai Note (UDP) was elected president.

2001 Former inhabitants of Bikini and the Enewetak atolls were awarded over US$1 billion in compensation for hardship suffered when they were evacuated and resettled in the 1940s to allow US nuclear tests on the islands.

2003 The RMI concluded negotiations with the US on the provisions of the CFA.

2004 Kessai Note was re-elected as president.

2006 Justin deBrum, a leading politician and presidential candidate died.

2007 In general elections the ruling UDP won 14 seats (out of 33) and the opposition coalition United People's Party (UPP) and Aelon Kein Ad (AKA) (Our Islands) won 17, independents won the remaining seats. The OECD removed RMI from the blacklist of unco-operative tax havens.

2008 Parliament elected Litokwa Tomeing (UPP/AKA) as president by 18 to 15 votes, replacing incumbent Kessai Note. A state of emergency was declared following high tidal surges and a storm which flooded low-lying areas resulting in the evacuation of over 300 people.

2009 Taiwan and Australia provided emergency funding and assistance to the Marshall Islands. The government-run retirement fund was declared to have a serious funding shortfall of US$231 million (a sum greater than the CMNI budget for 2009/10 of US$162 million). The superior court declared the government must fund the missing amount. President Litokwa Tomeing lost a vote of no-confidence in parliament (17–15). A vote between Ruben Zackhras and former president Kessai Note for the presidency was won by Note by 17 votes to 15.

2010 In August, the first black pearls to be harvested since 2005 prompted

KEY FACTS

Official name: Republic of the Marshall Islands

Head of State: President Ruben Zackhras (from 2 Nov 2009)

Head of government: President Ruben Zackhras

Ruling party: A loose coalition of the United People's Party (UPP) and Aelon Kein Ad (AKA) (Our Islands) (14 Jan 2008)

Area: 183 square km consisting of 29 atolls and 1,225 islets

Population: 54,305 (2010)*

Capital: Majuro (on Majuro atoll)

Official language: Marshallese, English

Currency: US dollar (US$) = 100 cents)

GDP per capita: US$3,130 (2008)

GDP real growth: 0.50% (2010)

GDP: US$250.50 million (2009)

Inflation: 2.80% (2009)

Balance of trade: -US$19.10 million (2009*

* estimated figure

NOTA

3 January 2012, parliament elected Christopher Loeak as president.

renewed interest in the pearl fishing industry. A 1,300 unit haul, as part of a government-backed three-year project of growing oysters on a remote outer atoll, was valued at US$20,000. An expansion of the industry is planned to provide an annual 50,000 pearls.

2011 On 23 February, the Director of the US Office of Insular Affairs conducted a joint US-Marshall Islands investigation into allegations of fraud involving US federal funds, which resulted in the arrest of 10 people who were charged with misappropriation of over US$500,000. The national census, postponed since 2009, due to lack of funds to undertake the work, was concluded in April. Preliminary results recorded a population of just over 52,000. In October, an existing shark sanctuary was enlarged, to encompass an ocean area of almost two million square km around the Marshall Islands. At the same time, a new law was enacted, banning commercial shark fishing and the trade in shark products.

Political structure

Constitution

The constitution was adopted in 1979. Under the Compact of Free Association (CFA), the Marshall Islands have control over all domestic and foreign affairs with the exception of defence which is the responsibility of the US.

Universal suffrage begins at aged 18.

Form of state

Self-governing territory in free association with the US.

The executive

Executive power rests with the president and the cabinet. The president is both head of state and head of government, elected by parliament for a four-year term. The president appoints the cabinet from members of the Nitijela (parliament).

National legislature

The bicameral system of government includes the Nitijela (lower house), with 33 senators of the Nitijela elected from 24 constituencies, for four-year terms. The Nitijela holds legislative power and elects the president.

The upper house, Council of Iroij (council of chiefs) is an advisory body, of 12 tribal chiefs, with consultative authority on matters relating to land and customs, who serves four-year terms.

Last elections

7 January 2008 (presidential); 19 November 2008 (parliamentary).

Results: Presidential: Litokwa Tomeing (UPP/AKA coalition) won 18 votes, Kessai Note won 15.

Parliamentary: UDP won 14 seats (out of 33) and the opposition coalition of United People's Party (UPP) and Aelon Kein Ad (AKA) (Our Islands) won 17, independents won the remaining.

Next elections

2011 (parliamentary and presidential)

Political parties

Ruling party

A loose coalition of the United People's Party (UPP) and Aelon Kein Ad (AKA) (Our Islands) (14 Jan 2008)

Main opposition party

United Democratic Party (UDP)

Political situation

The 2007 parliamentary elections resulted in two firsts. For the first time an unprecedented number of independent members were elected, leaving the government to be formed by a coalition, also for the first time. The result was determined to be a reaction by many landowners to the previous government's agreement with the US to lease, long-term, Kwajalein Atoll for missile testing. The landowners had consistently rejected the agreement for leasing the atoll until 2086 and said that unless there was an improvement in terms of conditions the agreement must end in 2016.

However by 2010 when a land use agreement (LUA) was thought to be ready for signing, in which landowners could be entitled to share the US$30 million from the leasing deal with the US military the LUA was found to be in abeyance since the landowners had included provision for funding a US$570 million infrastructure programme for the atoll. Neither the US military nor the RMI government were ready to sign the LUA, leaving all sides in need of further negotiations.

KEY INDICATORS **Marshall Islands**

	Unit	2006	2007	2008	2009	2010
Population	m	*0.06	*0.06	*0.06	*0.06	*0.06
Gross domestic product (GDP)	US$bn	0.15	0.16	166.00	250.50	–
GDP per capita	US$	2,770	2,696	3,130	–	–
GDP real growth	%	2.4	3.5	1.5	0.0	–
Inflation	%	4.3	2.4	14.8	2.8	–
Exports (fob) (goods)	US$m	16.0	13.6	*-16.0	*14.0	–
Imports (fob) (goods)	US$m	99.0	87.4	*90.9	*85.0	–
Balance of trade	US$m	-83.0	-73.8	*-74.9	*-71.0	–
Current account	US$m	7.0	-43.2	-43.1	-19.0	–
Exchange rate	per US$	1.00	1.00	1.00	1.00	1.00

* estimated figure

Population

54,305 (2010)*

Last census: June 1999: 50,848

Population density: 302 inhabitants per square km (2010)

Annual growth rate: 1.7 per cent 1994–2004 (WHO 2006)

Ethnic make-up

Micronesian

Religions

Christian (mostly Protestant).

Education

In 2009 the government announced that it would join the 'one laptop per child' programme (OLPC).

An agreement between the education departments of Guam and the Marshall Islands, signed in October 2010, will allow an exchange of students to study at the University of Guam and the College of the Marshall Islands.

Enrolment rate: 134 per cent (boys); 133 per cent (girls), gross primary enrolment of the relevant age group (including repetition rates) (Unicef).

Health

Over 80 per cent of children are immunised against measles. RMI has the highest per capita rate of leprosy in the world.

Life expectancy: 62 years, 2004 (WHO 2006)

Fertility rate/Maternal mortality rate: 4.4 births per woman, 2004 (WHO 2006)

Child (under 5 years) mortality rate (per 1,000): 53 per 1,000 live births (World Bank)

Main cities

Majuro (capital, on Majuro atoll, Dalap-Uliga-Darrit Municipality, estimated population 25,400 in 2004), Ebeye, on Kwajalein, (9,935), Darrit (7,263), Rairok (5,409).

Languages spoken

There are two main Marshallese dialects from the Malayo-Polynesian family. Marshallese is used by the government. English is taught in the schools and is widely spoken. Japanese is also spoken.

Official language/s
Marshallese, English

Media
Press
The *Marshall Islands Journal* (www.marshallislandsjournal.com) containing items in both Marshallese and English, is published every Friday and the government published *Marshall Islands Gazette* has official news.
Broadcasting
The government-owned radio station V7AB and MBC Television station are the only national broadcasters. Micronesia Heatwave is a commercial radio station and V7AA is a religious station. Pay-to-view, cable TV is available in some areas.
News agencies
ABC Pacific Beat:
www.radioaustralia.net.au/pacbeat
Pacific Magazine:
www.pacificmagazine.net
Pacific Islands New Association (Pina):
www.pina.com.fj

Economy
The Marshall Islands has a limited revenue base; most income is derived from payment by the US under the Compact of Free Association (CFA), the latest of which came into effect in 2004, and which commits the US to long-term financial support, international aid and a few commercial ventures. Following an initial US$29 million, the US contributes US$7 million a year to the Intergenerational Investment Fund (IIF) until 2023. Together with government contributions the Fund should be able to provide investment for the islanders' future. However, in December 2009 the International Monetary Fund (IMF) warned that if the government persisted in deficit spending while at the same time denying substantial money to the fund, as seen over the past years, the country will end up with a major financial crisis by 2023.
The government employs over 45 per cent of the salaried workforce; unemployment is as high as 34 per cent. Agriculture, a small sector of GDP, is largely subsistence products such as breadfruit, taro and pandanus; small quantities of commercial copra are processed but with limited means of trade. The Marshall Islands licenses ships as a flag of convenience and has around 1,200 ships registered, making it the fifth largest fleet in the world and earning about US$1 million annually.
GDP growth had been project to reach 1.5 per cent in 2008, but the impact of the global economic downturn forced the economy to negative growth of -2 per cent, with growth of less than 1 per cent projected for 2009.
The Chinese fishing company Shanghai Deep Sea Fisheries invested US$8.5 million in a processing plant in Manuro in 2007. The plant is for skipjack tuna processing for the Asian market. In February 2009 the Marshall Islands Service Corporation went ahead with plans to buy and operate modern fishing vessels for the island's tuna industry.

External trade
The Marshall Islands (RMI) is a member of the South Pacific Regional Trade and Economic Co-operation Agreement (Sparteca) along with 12 other regional nations, which allows products duty free access by Pacific Island Forum members to Australian and New Zealand markets (subject to the country of origin restrictions).
Semi-manufactured goods, assembled in the islands, enjoy preferential access to US markets under the Compact of Free Association. Light manufacturing includes soap, cooking oil, salad oil, margarine and cosmetics, using local processed coconut oil.
Imports
Principal imports, which far outstripping exports, are foodstuffs, petroleum, machinery and equipment, beverages and tobacco.
Main sources: US, Japan, Australia, New Zealand, Singapore, Fiji, China, Philippines.
Exports
Principal exports are copra cake, coconut oil, handicrafts and fish
Main destinations: US, Japan, Australia, China.

Agriculture
Farming
Subsistence farming of taro, breadfruit, bananas, yams, sweet potatoes and vegetables, along with pig and poultry raising, is the main occupation. Large areas of potentially arable land remain uncultivated.
Fishing
Fishing, particularly tuna, is important, supplying the principal source of protein as well as export revenues. A dozen longline tuna boats built with Asian Development Bank money almost doubled the fleet in the mid-1990s. Tuna is supplied to the country's tuna processing factory, located at Majuro.
A Hawaiian company, Black Pearl Inc, noted after extensive research the potential for breeding black pearl oysters. Some farms have opened but it will be several years before they can compete with world market leaders. Seaweed farming may offer an alternative. Typical pearl and shell harvest production is 100,000 units per annum.
In April 2010 the Parties to the Nauru Agreement (PNA) (eight island states including the Marshall Islands) collectively agreed to close to *purse seine* fishing in 4.55 million square kilometres of high seas in their area, from 1 January 2011, to vessels licensed to fish in their waters. The area involved stretches from Palau and Papua New Guinea in the west to Kiribati in the east, from the Marshall Islands in the north to Tuvalu in the south; it holds an estimated 25 per cent of the world's tuna supply.
On 12 April 2011, a summit of the Parties to the Nauru Agreement (PNA) concluded its strategy for a policy of sustainable fishing in the Pacific. The PNA treaty, which was established in 1989 and expires in 2012, is seen as in need of an overhaul. As a collective region (FSM, Kiribati, Marshall Islands, Nauru, Palau, PNG, Solomon Islands and Tuvalu) control around 25–30 per cent of world stocks of tuna. Only 5 per cent of sales revenue is returned to the PNA and ministers called for specific changes, including an increased share of profits, PNA crews on-board *purse seine* vessels (minimum 10 per cent), conservation and management measures including a limit to fish trapping (fish aggregating devices (FADs)), net mesh rules and the establishment of an observer agency and fisheries information management system.
Forestry

Industry and manufacturing
Small-scale industries include handicrafts, fish processing, copra processing, bakeries and boat building and repairs. A tuna processing factory which opened in 1999 was a significant addition to industry.
The Marshall Islands Ports Authority agreed with the Ching Fu Shipyard of Taiwan to locate a floating drydock in Majuro in 2005, which is the largest ship repair facility in the central Pacific.

Tourism
Tourism is relatively undeveloped, although there is potential for growth.

Environment
In October 2011, an existing shark sanctuary was enlarged, to encompass an ocean area of almost two million square km around the Marshall Islands. At the same time, a new law was enacted, banning commercial shark fishing and the trade in shark products.

Mining
Small mineral deposits exist, but exploitation is hampered by a shortage of land to accommodate the displaced population and doubts about economic viability. Extraction of phosphate occurs at Ailinglaplap.

Hydrocarbons
There are no known hydrocarbon reserves; all petroleum products are imported to meet domestic needs.

Energy
The Marshall Energy Company is responsible for generation and supply of electricity on all but Ebeye where the Kwajalein Atoll Joint Utility Resource provides energy.
In 2008, as the implementation of national electrification, based on solar-photovoltaic systems, was about to begin Marshall Island utilities participated in technical training workshops run by Pacific Power Association (PPA) and E8 (utility companies from G8 countries offering help and sponsorship in renewable energies).

Banking and insurance
Growth in the Marshall Islands' banking sector is limited by the size of its population. Commercial bank lending in 2004 was some US$45 million while deposits were substantially greater at US$81 million.

Time
GMT plus twelve hours

Geography
The Marshall Islands are located in the area of the Pacific Ocean known as Micronesia (which includes Kiribati, Tuvalu and other territories). The islands lie about 3,200km (2,000 miles) south-west of Hawaii and about 2,100km (1,300 miles) south-east of Guam.
The Marshall Islands comprises around 1,200 coral islands and islets, of which five are single islands, the rest combining into 29 atolls. The territory extends over 750,000 square km of sea area in two parallel chains: Ratak (Sunrise) to the east and Ralik (Sunset) to the west. Total land mass of the system is around 183 square km. The mean height is two metres. The atolls are narrow and encircle large lagoons. Beaches are white sand.
Hemisphere
Northern

Climate
Tropical climate. Warm and humid, temperatures 23–30 degrees Celsius, humidity around 80 per cent. High temperatures are cooled by trade winds. Rainfall variable, minimum 250mm per year, can occur in downpours. Hurricanes are possible.

Entry requirements
Passports
Required by all, valid for six months beyond date of departure.
Visa
Required by all, except nationals of the US, Federated States of Micronesia and Palau. Tourist and business visas are issued on arrival for stays up to three months.
All visitors must have proof of adequate funds and return/onward passage. Special regulations may apply to some non-tourist destinations. Further information can be obtained through www.rmiembassyus.org.

Health (for visitors)
Advisable precautions
Vaccinations for hepatitis A and B and typhoid are recommended; those for tetanus and diphtheria should be updated as needed.

Hotels
There are a number of first class and other hotels, mainly on Majuro and Ebeye, and guesthouses, which are more widely distributed.

Credit cards
Visa, Mastercard and American Express are accepted by most major businesses.

Public holidays (national)
Fixed dates
1 Jan (New Year's Day), 1 Mar (Nuclear Survivors Day), 1 May (Constitution Day), 21 Oct (Compact Day), 17 Nov (President's Day), 25 Dec (Christmas Day). Some dates vary from island to island.
Variable dates
Fishermen's Day (first Fri in Jul), Rijerbal/Labour Day (first Fri in Sep), Manit/Customs Day (last Fri in Sep), Gospel Day (first Fri in Dec).

Working hours
Banking
Mon–Fri: 1000–1500; Fri: 1000–1800.
Business
Mon–Fri: 0800–1700.
Government
Mon–Fri: 0800–1700.
Shops
Mon–Sat: 0800–2000; (Sun) 0800–1800.

Telecommunications
Mobile/cell phones
Cellular service is available on Maburo, Ebeye and Kwajalein.

Social customs/useful tips
In business an informal attitude prevails. Appointments should be made. Business cards are exchanged. Business is usually conducted in English. Permission should be sought before taking photographs of people. The minimum drinking age is 21 years. Swimsuits, shorts or short skirts should not be worn in urban areas. Tipping is optional.

Getting there
Air
National airline: Air Marshall Islands.
International airport/s: Amata Kabua International International (MAJ), 25km from Majuro. There are buses, taxis and hotel transport from the airport to the city.
Airport tax: US$15.
Surface
Main port/s: Majuro and Kwajalein.

Getting about
National transport
Air: Air Marshall Islands flies services to most of the atolls.
Road: The main roads on the major islands are paved. Others are stone-, coral- or laterite-surfaced roads and tracks.
Water: The government operates several vessels, which link the islands on an irregular schedule. Inter-island cruises are available and boats can be hired privately.
City transport
Taxis: Taxis are plentiful and relatively cheap, but usually operate on a shared basis.
Car hire
There are many car hire operators. Driving is on the right.

BUSINESS DIRECTORY

Telephone area codes
The international direct dialling (IDD) code for Marshall Islands is +692 followed by area code and subscriber's number:

Ebeye	329	Majuro	625.

Chambers of Commerce
Majuro Chamber of Commerce, PO Box 1318, Majuro 96960 (tel: 625-3051; fax: 625-3343; e-mail: majurochamber@hotmail.com).

Banking
Bank of Marshall Islands, PO Box J, Majuro 96960 (tel: 625-3636; fax: 625-3661; e-mail: bankmar@ntamar.com).

Travel information
Air Marshall Islands, PO Box 1319, Majuro 96960 (tel: 625-3731; fax: 625-37; e-mail: amisales@ntamar.net).

Marshall Islands Visitors Authority, PO Box 5, Majuro 96960 (tel: 625-6482; fax: 625-6771; e-mail: tourism@ntamar.com).

Ministry of tourism
Ministry of Resources and Development, Tourism Office, PO Box 1727, Majuro 96960 (tel: 625-6482; fax: 625-3218).

Other useful addresses
Marshall Islands Embassy (USA), 2433 Massachusetts Avenue, NW, Washington DC 20008 (tel: (+1-202)-234-5414; fax: (+1-202)-232-3236: e-mail: info@rmiembassyus.org).

Internet sites
Website of the Marshall Islands: http://www.rmiembassyus.org/

The Pacific business centre: http://cba.hawaii.edu/pbcp/

Martinique

KEY FACTS

Official name: Martinique

Head of State: President of France, (Nicolas Sarkozy, from 16 May 2007), represented by *Préfet* Ange Mancini (since 18 Jul 2007)

Head of government: President of Conseil Général Claude Lise (since 22 Mar 1992); President of Conseil Régional Serge Letchimy (from 26 Mar 2010)

Ruling party: Coalition led by Mouvement pour l'Indépendence de la Martinique (MIM), with Conseil National des Comités Populaires (CNCP) (since Mar 2004)

Area: 1,100 square km

Population: 406,000 (2010)

Capital: Fort-de-France

Official language: French

Currency: Euro (€) = 100 cents (from 1 Jan 2002; previous currency French franc, locked at Ff6.56 per euro)

Exchange rate: €0.75 per US$ (Oct 2011)

COUNTRY PROFILE

Historical profile

1493 Columbus was the first European visitor.
1635 The island was settled by the French – in the face of indigenous Indian hostility.
1700s The island was seized by the British several times.
1763 Marie-Josephe Rose Tascher de la Pagerie – Napoleon's Empress Josephine – was born at Les Trois Ilets.
1814 The British gave up their attempts to control the island and it became a French possession under the Treaty of Paris.
1848 The Emancipation Proclamation abolished slavery in the West Indies.
1902 St Pierre was destroyed by an eruption of the volcano Mount Pelée.
1946 Martinique became a French Département d'Outre-Mer (DOM) (Overseas Department).
1974 Martinique was further incorporated into the French political system and granted the status of region of France.
1983 Martinique was granted devolution. A Regional Council was established under the French decentralisation policy.
1999–2001 The presidents of the regional assemblies of Martinique, Guadeloupe and French Guiana called for more autonomy from France.
2002 Martinique adopted the euro as its official currency.
2003 A referendum in Guadeloupe and Martinique rejected a French government-backed reform plan to streamline the system of local government and give the islands a new status.
2004 Martinique was the first port of call for Cunard's newest, and largest, cruise ship, *Queen Mary II*. Yves Dassonville took over as *Préfet*, replacing Michel Cadot.
2007 Nicolas Sarkozy became head of state and president of the French Republic. Ange Mancini was appointed *Préfet*.
2008 The poet, Aime Cesaire, a leading figure of not only the local but also the wider, international black empowerment and cultural community, died. President Sarkozy led the mourners in a state funeral in Fort-de-France.
2009 Civil unrest following a workers' strike in protest against low pay and rising prices resulted in the deployment of riot police from mainland France. As a result a reported 10,000 tourists cancelled their holidays. The France-based minister of overseas territories arrived to oversee negotiations.
2010 By 80–20 per cent (on a turnout of 55 per cent), voters rejected a referendum proposal to devolve more power to local government and grant more autonomy. Serge Letchimy was elected president of the Regional Council in March.
2011 In July, the EU agreed to allow Martinique to impose import duties from 1 July 2014, to protect local production of food and manufactured goods.

Political structure

Constitution

28 September 1958 (French Fifth Republic)
Under the 1946 constitution of the French Fourth Republic, Martinique became a Département d'Outre-Mer (DOM) (Overseas Department) of France. In 1974, it was granted additional status as a region of France.
Martinique is represented in the French National Assembly by four deputies and in the Senate by two senators.
Administration is by a préfet appointed by the government in Paris.
Since 1983, following the French government's policy of decentralisation, regional councils have been elected with powers similar to those of the regions.
Local administration is through a Conseil Régional (Regional Council) of 41 members and a 45-member Conseil Général (General Council), both directly elected for six-year terms.

Form of state

Département d'Outre-Mer (DOM) (Overseas Department) of France, with additional status as a région (region) of France.

The executive

The island is administered by a *préfet* (commissioner), appointed by the central government in Paris.

National legislature

The Conseil Régional (Regional Council) provides legislative administration for the island; it has 41 members elected by proportional representation for four-year terms.

Legal system

French law applies. The country has no supreme court but this role is filled by a nine-member Conseil Constitutionel (Constitutional Council). Its task is to ensure that law treaties and regulations are in keeping with the constitution and that elections are conducted in a regular manner. The highest court of appeal is the Cour de Cassation, which can overrule decisions in all lower courts, but not government legislation. Since the signing of the Single European Act in 1986, the European Court of Justice (ECJ) has been the highest authority in certain areas of French law.

Last elections

28 March 2004 (Conseil Régional).

Results: Regional council: Parti Progressiste Martiniquais (PPM) (Martinique Progressive Party) 48.35 per cent of vote (26 seats out of 41), Mouvement Indépendantiste Martiniquais (MIM) (Martinique Independent Movement) 41.03 per cent (12), Comité de Liaison de la Majorité Présidentielle (Liaison Committee for the Presidential Majority) (Presidential Majority) 10.63 per cent (three); six other political parties each won less than 7 per cent and no seats. Turnout was 53.69 per cent.

Next elections

2014 (Regional council)

Political parties

Ruling party

Coalition led by Mouvement pour l'Indépendence de la Martinique (MIM), with Conseil National des Comités Populaires (CNCP) (since Mar 2004)

Main opposition party

Parti Progressiste Martiniquais (PPM) (Martinican Progressive Party)

Political situation

A referendum on a French government proposal held in Martinique in 2003 seemed straightforward. The proposal was twofold. First, it would streamline the local government apparatus and reduce the number of elected offices. The second effect would be a change in Martinique's relationship with France, which would effectively reduce its standing as a region of France. The proposal was made in response to a call made in 1999—2000 for more independence.

However, the proposal was rejected and the failure was thought to be due to voters' worry that any change in their status would ultimately result in a withdrawal of French central government funds needed, most particularly, for social security.

Population

406,000 (2010)

Last census: 1 January 2006: 397,732

Population density: 282 inhabitants per sq km.

Annual growth rate: 0.6 per cent (2003)

Ethnic make-up

African and mixed race (90 per cent), white (5 per cent), East Indian and others (5 per cent).

Religions

Roman Catholic (85 per cent), Protestant (10 per cent), Islam, Hindu, pagan African (5 per cent).

Education

There is 42 per cent enrolment in education for the 20- to 24-year age groups with a high rate of unemployment among them.

Literacy rate: 98 per cent, adult rate (2003)

Health

Water for consumption is subject to intensive controls and is of high quality.

There are three public hospitals including one teaching hospital, and three private clinics.

HIV/Aids

Martinique has a departmental Aids control scheme.

Life expectancy: 79 (estimate 2003)

Birth rate/Death rate: 15 births per 1,000 population; 6.4 deaths per 1,000 population (2003).

Child (under 5 years) mortality rate (per 1,000): 7.4 per 1,000 live births (2003)

Welfare

With unemployment ranging between 30 and 35 per cent among the youth, there has been a noticeable increase in the number of people calling for independence from France. The French social security system guarantees a high minimum wage, a 35-hour working week, five-week vacations, a 40 per cent incentive on salary and other social benefits.

Main cities

Fort-de-France (capital (prefecture), estimated population 96,400 in 2003), Le Lamentin (36,400), Le Robert (21,800), Schoelcher (21,400), Sainte Marie (20,600, Le Francois (19,000).

Languages spoken

French and Creole patois (developed from French, English, Spanish and some African languages). English is widely understood.

Official language/s

French

Media

Press

In French, *France Antilles* is the only daily newspaper, which belongs to a French-based publishing house. Weekly publications include *Le Progressiste, Aujourd'hui Dimanche, Justice, Le Naif* and *Antilla*.

Broadcasting

The French overseas broadcaster RFO (www.rfo.fr) provides locally produced radio and television news (http://martinique.rfo.fr) and imported French programmes, as well as internet TV services.

Radio: Apart from the public RFO Martinique radio broadcasts, Radio Caraibes International (http://rci.fm) and NRJ Antilles (www.nrjantilles.com) are private radio stations.

Economy

Martinique has an open market economy, with the service sector providing three out of four jobs and tourism providing 7 per cent of GDP. The tourist sector is a major employer and key source of foreign exchange; Martinique has not only increased its share of the cruise ship industry but has also become a leading provider of luxury holiday venues. Agriculture accounts for almost 40 per cent of export earnings, of which bananas account for 49.5 per cent.

The local economy represents no more than 25 per cent of GDP, with French funding accounting for the remaining 75 per cent.

A French government 15-year economic development plan for the dependent territories, published in 2002, has led to greater improvements in infrastructure and has improved the island's investment climate.

Among the improvements is the construction of a land and sea transport terminal, next to Pointe Simon Cruise Terminal, which integrates water taxis and public transport at the Cap Est lagoon resort and spa.

External trade

As a département d'outre-mer (DOM) of France, Martinique is integrated as an outermost region of the European Union, which includes all EU trade agreements. The large trade deficit is only partly offset by invisible earnings from tourism, workers' remittances from abroad, and French aid aimed at developing the tourist trade and reducing unemployment.

Imports

Principal imports are petroleum products, crude oil, foodstuffs, construction materials, vehicles, clothing and other consumer goods.

Main sources: France (typically 60 per cent), Venezuela (6.0 per cent), Germany (4.0 per cent), Italy (4.0 per cent), US (3.0 per cent).

Exports

Principal exports are refined petroleum products, bananas, rum and pineapples.

Main destinations: France (typically 45 per cent), Guadeloupe (28 per cent).

Agriculture

Farming

Once the mainstay of economy, the agricultural sector has declined in recent years. It employs 10 per cent of the

workforce and contributes 7 per cent to GDP. Around 48 per cent of total land area is cultivated, 25 per cent is forest and 19 per cent savannah. The majority of farms are privately run by smallholders. Activity is centred on the production of pineapples and bananas, mainly for industrial processing and export.
Crops such as sweet potatoes, yams, manioc, beans, cabbages and tomatoes are grown primarily for domestic consumption. Small quantities of aubergines and limes are exported. Virtually all the island's meat requirements are met by imports.
The future of the important banana industry, which has relied on preferential access to the EU, is threatened by a World Trade Organisation ruling that this access is illegal and must end.

Fishing
Fishing (lobster, crayfish, crab, clams) is undertaken all year round. The typical total annual fish catch is over 6,250t. Shellfish, molluscs and cephalopods account for another 909t per annum.

Industry and manufacturing
Major industries include an oil refinery (capacity 17,000 barrels per day (bpd)), a cement works, rum distilling, sugar refining, dairy produce, fruit canning, soft drinks manufacture, mineral water bottling and a polyethylene plant.
Industrial development has been poor and centres mainly on the manufacture of consumer goods for the local market. Five industrial zones have been set up and tax exemptions introduced to encourage light industrial development.

Tourism
Martinique offers a French culture in a Caribbean setting, which attracts around 500,000 visitors each year. However over 60 per cent of all visitors arrive by cruise liners (112 cruise liners in 2008 and 2009). The majority of visitors are from France (80 per cent), with citizens of other regional French departments (Guadeloupe, French Guiana) representing 9 per cent, but with no other nationality representing more than 2 per cent.
Travel and tourism typically represents over 10 per cent of GDP, with total employment also over 10 per cent.
A new passenger ferry was launched at the beginning of the 2011–12 tourist season, with links to other French departments, Dominica and St Lucia.

Mining
Martinique has no mineral resources.

Hydrocarbons
There are no known hydrocarbons reserves. Oil imports were 17,000 barrels per day (bpd) in 2008 all of which was refined on the island by Sara (Société Anonyme de Raffinerie des Antilles) in the only refinery. Consumption was 16,000bpd.
Any imports of coal or natural gas are commercially insignificant. A proposed pipeline from Trinidad and Tobago to Martinique and Guadeloupe could open up possibilities for the future import of natural gas.

Energy
Total installed generating capacity was 396MW in 2007, producing over 1.2 billion kilowatt hours, from two thermal power stations. The state-owned EDF (Electricité de France) is responsible for generation and distribution of electricity.

Banking and insurance
Central bank
Caisse Centrale de Co-opération Economique; European Central Bank (ECB)

Time
GMT minus four hours

Geography
Martinique is one of the Windward Islands in the West Indies, with Dominica to the north and St Lucia to the south. The island, which has an area of 1,100 square km, is bounded to the west by the calm Caribbean Sea and to the east by the choppier Atlantic Ocean.
The terrain rises from the south to the mountainous centre and the north. The highest point in the island, situated in the north, is an active volcano, Mount Pelée, which reaches 1,397m. The mountain areas are covered with rainforest. The Lamentin Plain, an area of hills and valleys, occupies the centre of the island. The northern beaches consist of volcanic ash and are grey, while those in the south, where the Salines Beach is located, are sandy and white. The southern Atlantic coastline is protected by coral reefs.

Hemisphere
Northern

Climate
Sub-tropical with an annual mean temperature of 26 degrees Celsius. Rain heaviest in the north. Rainy season from June–October. The island's temperature is moderated by trade winds.

Entry requirements
Passports
Required by all, valid for three months beyond the date of departure.
Visa
Required by all, except citizens of EU, North America, Australasia and Japan. Business visas require an invitation from a local company or organisation. Proof of adequate funds for stay, an itinerary, a guarantee of repatriation if necessary and return/onward ticket are also required.
Currency advice/regulations
There are no restrictions on the import and export of local and foreign currencies, but amounts in excess of eur7,600 must be declared.

Health (for visitors)
Mandatory precautions
A yellow fever vaccination certificate is required if travelling from an infected area.
Advisable precautions
Hepatitis, typhoid, tetanus and polio vaccinations. Water precautions should be taken.

Hotels
There is a 5 per cent room tax. If service charge is not added, 15 per cent tip is usual.

Public holidays (national)
Fixed dates
1 Jan (New Year's Day), 1 May (Labour Day), 8 May (Victory Day), 22 May (Abolition of Slavery), 14 Jul (Bastille Day), 21 Jul (Schoelcher Day), 15 Aug (Assumption Day), 1 Nov (All Saints' Day), 11 Nov (Armistice Day), 25 Dec (Christmas Day).
Variable dates
Carnival (four days, Feb), Good Friday, Easter Monday, Ascension Day, Whit Monday.

Working hours
Banking
Mon–Fri: 0800–1200, 1400–1700.
Banks close at noon on day preceding a bank holiday.
Business
Mon–Fri: 0800–1200, 1430–1700; Sat: 0800–1200.
Government
Mon–Fri: 0730–1300, 1500–1730.
Shops
Mon–Fri: 0900–1300, 1500–1800; Sat: 0900–1300.

Telecommunications
Mobile/cell phones
There are several GSM 850, 900, 1800 and 1900 services available throughout the country.

Electricity supply
220V AC, 50 cycles

Getting there
Air
National airline: Air Caraibes.
International airport/s: Lamentin (FDF), 11km from Fort-de-France; restaurant, banks, shops, car hire.
Airport tax: None.
Surface
Main port/s: Fort-de-France is the only commercial port; other ports of entry include St Pierre, Anse Mitan and Le Marin.

Getting about

National transport

Road: Well-developed network of more than 2,000km of roads, three-quarters of which are paved and the rest gravel and earth.

Water: There are regular ferry services (*vedettes*) from Fort-de-France to Pointe de Bout and Anse Mitan.

Car hire

There are ample car rental facilities. A valid driving licence is required and also, for periods beyond 20 days, an international licence.

BUSINESS DIRECTORY

The addresses listed below are a selection only. While World of Information makes every endeavour to check these addresses, we cannot guarantee that changes have not been made, especially to telephone numbers and area codes. We would welcome any corrections.

Telephone area codes

The international direct dialling code (IDD) for Martinique is +596, followed by subscriber's number.

Useful telephone numbers

Ambulance: 15

Fire brigade: 18

Police: 17

Chambers of Commerce

Martinique Chamber of Commerce and Industry, 50 Rue Ernest Deproge, PO Box 478, Fort-de-France 97241 (tel: 552-800; fax: 606-668; e-mail: info@martinique.cci.fr).

Banking

Banque des Antilles Françaises, 34 rue Lamartine, BP 582, 97200 Fort-de-France (tel: 739-344; fax: 635-894).

Banque Française Commerciale, 6-10 rue Ernest Deproge, 97200 Fort-de-France (tel: 638-257).

Banque National de Paris, Avenue des Caraibes, 97200 Fort-de-France (tel: 737-111).

Chase Manhattan Bank, Place de Monseigheur Romero, 97200 Fort-de-France (tel: 602-424).

Crédit Martiniquais, rue de la Liberté, Fort-de-France (tel: 701-240).

Institut d'Emission des DOM (IEDOM), Boulevard General de Gaulle, BP 512, 97206 Fort-de-France (tel: 594-400; fax: 594-404).

Société Générale de Banque aux Antilles, rue de la Liberté, BP 408, 97200 Fort-de-France (tel: 716-983).

Central bank

European Central Bank (ECB), Kaiserstrasse 29, D-60311 Frankfurt am Main, Germany (tel: (+49-69)-13-440; fax: (+49-69)-1344-6000; e-mail: info@ecb.int).

Travel information

Agence Régionale pour le Développement du Tourisme de la Martinique (ARDTM), 4 Rue de l'école Hotellière, Anse Goureaud, 97233 Schoelcher (tel: 616-177; fax: 612-272).

Air Caraibes, Morne Vergain, 97139 Abymes (tel: (0590)-824-747; fax: (0490)-824-749; e-mail: direction@aircaraibes.com).

Délégation Régionale au Tourisme, 41 Rue Gabriel Péri, 97200 Fort-de-France (tel: 393-767; fax: 730-096).

Fort-de-France Office du Tourisme, 76 rue Lazare Carnot, 97206 Fort-de-France (tel: 602-773; fax: 602-795; e-mail: info@tourismefdf.com).

Lamentin Airport, 97200 Lamentin (tel: 421-600; fax: 421-877).

National tourist organisation offices

Comité Martiniquais du Tourisme, Immeuble Le Beaupré, Pointe de Jaham, 97233 Schoelcher (tel: 616-177; fax:612-272; e-mail: infos.cmt@martiniquetourisme.com).

Other useful addresses

Agence pour le Développement Economique de la Martinique, Immeuble Nayaradou, Plateau de Cluny, 97233 Schoelcher (tel: 734-581; fax: 724-138).

Bureau del'Industrie de l'Artisanat, Préfecture, 97262 Fort-de France (tel: 713-627).

Chambre Départementale d'Agriculture, Place D'Armes, BP 312, 97286 Lamentin Cedex (tel: 517-575; fax: 519-342).

Chambre des Métiers, 2 Rue du Temple, Morne Tartenson, BP 1191, 97249 Fort-de-France (tel: 713-222; fax: 704-730).

Post Office, 132 boulevard Pasteur, Fort-de-France (tel: 599-600).

Préfecture, rue Victor Severe, BP 647-648, 97262 Fort-de-France (tel: 631-861; fax: 714-029; internet site: www.martinique.pref.gouv.fr/pages/somangl.html).

Internet sites

Regional Council of Martinique: http://www.cr-martinique.fr/anglais/accueil_anglais.html

Martinique Promotion Bureau: http://www.martinique.org

Martinique Shipping Services: http://www.marship.fr

Mauritania

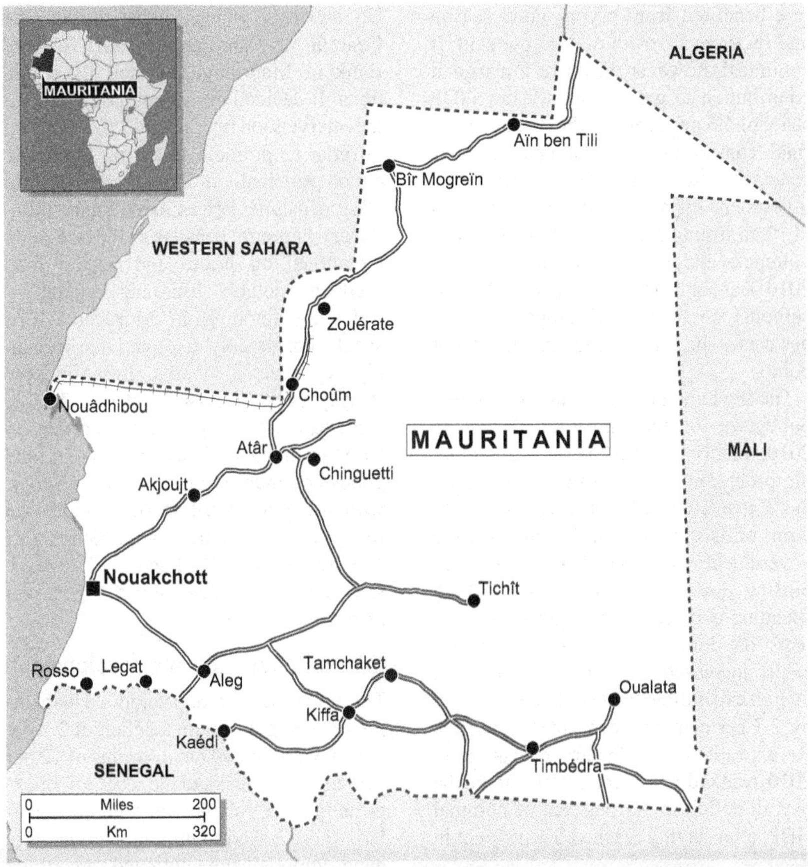

KEY FACTS

Official name: République Islamique Arabe et Africaine de Mauritanie (Islamic Republic of Mauritania)

Head of State: President Mohamed Ould Abdel Aziz (from 5 Aug 2009)

Head of government: Prime Minister Moulaye Ould Mohamed Laghdaf (appointed 14 Aug 2008)

Ruling party: All members of parliament are independents

Area: 1,030,700 square km

Population: 3.40 million (2010)*

Capital: Nouakchott

Official language: Hassani Arabic and Wolof

Currency: Ouguiya (UM) = 5 khoums

Exchange rate: UM285.40 per US$ (Oct 2011)

GDP per capita: US$1,141 (2010)

GDP real growth: 5.20% (2010)

GDP: US$3.80 billion (2010)

Unemployment: 30.00% (2008)*

Inflation: 6.10% (2010)

Balance of trade: -US$497.00 million (2008)

* estimated figure

The biggest cultural event of 2011 was probably the celebration of 50 years of independence on 28 November. The most important political event in 2010 was probably the first ever live television interview given by President Mohamed Ould Abdel Aziz with Mauritanian media. The President addressed the general conditions in the country, terrorism, corruption, national education, as well as the issue of national languages.

In June and July 2011 there were a number of skirmishes in the desert between government troops and fighters of Al-Qaeda in the Islamic Maghreb (AQIM). The numbers wounded or killed varied according to sources. Meanwhile a dialogue had been initiated with the supposed Islamic terrorists detained in the central prison in Nouakchott, after which several dozen were granted a presidential pardon.

Census

The national census that was undertaken from 20 June 2011 sparked protests from the black African community in Mauritania and abroad. It was branded as 'discriminatory' as it not only noted citizens within racial groupings (which, it was suspected, could be used to discriminate against various groupings in the future), but also required a set of civil documents (including identity papers of parents and grandparents, which excluded anyone born outside Mauritania before 1945), before a person could be recorded (or 'enrolled').

The economy

Gross domestic product (GDP) in Mauritania is dominated by the secondary (34.7 per cent of GDP) and tertiary (44.8 per cent) sectors, remaining almost entirely unchanged between 2009 and 2010. After a fall in GDP of 1.2 per cent in 2009, the economy rebounded in 2010, with GDP expanding by 5.2 per cent. This is expected to become stronger in the coming years with a slight decline in the tertiary sector to the advantage of the primary and secondary sectors. This performance is the outcome of the combined effects of the implementation of the public finances reform programme agreed with the International Monetary Fund (IMF) and the substantial rise in international minerals prices.

Mauritania should build on these results by achieving growth of 5.3 per cent in 2011 and 5.5 per cent in 2012. The authorities are relying on the maintenance of prices of mineral products, notably of iron, copper and gold. They are equally counting on the rationalisation of public expenditure, on an increase in private investment in the mining sector and on the ongoing support of donors. This optimism is reinforced by the close monitoring of the IMF which is aimed at seeing the policy of fiscal consolidation through to a successful conclusion in the framework of a coherent macroeconomic policy. This policy should enable Mauritania to further unblock domestic resources and maintain its debt at a sustainable level.

On the supply side, growth was sustained particularly by the metallic minerals mining sub-sector, which accounted for a quarter of real GDP growth, as well as by the trade and livestock sub-sectors, with contributions of 11.2 per cent and 10.7 per cent respectively. Mining activity grew slightly in 2010 (0.8 per cent), whereas prices on international markets rose significantly. Thus, the prices of iron, copper and gold rose by 60.4 per cent, 46.3 per cent and 25.9 per cent respectively, between 2009 and 2010. Agriculture benefited from a very good season and registered growth of 11.7 per cent. It continued, however, to make a marginal contribution to growth, with a low GDP share of 4.6 per cent. On the demand side, final consumption contributed 6.3 percentage points to growth in 2010. Gross investment expanded by 9.3 per cent in 2010, to around 26.4 per cent of GDP. The volume of exports remained unchanged in 2010 leaving imports (primarily hydrocarbons) to rise by an uncompensated 3.6 per cent, which penalised growth by 4.4 points.

The implementation of macroeconomic policy was on the whole satisfactory in 2010. Mauritania performed well under the programme of reforms supported by the Extended Credit Facility (ECF). In terms of fiscal policy implementation, the government also succeeded in better mobilising domestic resources, controlling spending and reducing instances and arrears on domestic debt. Budgetary receipts increased by 6.9 per cent while overall expenditure and net loans declined by 2.7 per cent between 2009 and 2010. As a result, the budgetary execution in 2010 resulted in an improvement in the overall deficit to 3.7 per cent of nominal GDP, after having reached 5.1 per cent in 2009. The deficit on the current account also improved by almost 4 per cent of GDP, falling from 12.6 per cent to 8.8 per cent of GDP. This improvement was due to the value increase in exports by more than 11 per cent and by the fall in the value of imports by more than 8 per cent.

The Mauritanian ouguiya has experienced a sharp depreciation since the start of 2010, of around 9 per cent against the US dollar, so much so that the Banque Centrale de Mauritanie (CBM) (Central Bank of Mauritania) limited its operations. It decided on a three-point drop in the intervention rate, from 12 to 9 per cent in order to promote financing by credit, aimed principally at the private sector. In 2010 consumer prices came under inflationary pressure, because of the rise in international oil prices and certain food products (notably fruit and vegetables, following flooding in Morocco). This shock considerably disrupted market supply for several months. Inflation rose sharply over 2009 (when it was 2.2 per cent) to reach 6.1 per cent according to CBM estimates. If the prices of food goods continue on an upward trajectory, with the gradual lifting of subsidies on food staples, inflationary pressures risk continuing during 2011 and 2012, to reach rates of 5.7 per cent and 5.4 per cent respectively.

International trade and development

The trade balance registered a clear improvement, going from a deficit of 2.7 per cent of GDP in 2009 to a surplus of 12 per cent in 2010, thanks to the recovery of exports in both volume and value, particularly those linked to mining. On the other hand, imports have continued to contract since 2009 to reach 40.9 per cent of GDP. In 2010, this was mostly attributable to the prolonged break in Moroccan exports of food products following the floods.

The services deficit deepened significantly in 2010 to represent -23.3 per cent of GDP in 2010, versus -15.9 per cent in 2009, driven by rising expenditure on external services and increased prospecting fees for mineral and oil companies.

The CBM's reserves fell to very low levels in 2008, reaching the equivalent of just 1.7 months of imports. They increased in 2009 to the level of 2.5 months of import cover and according to forecasts should reach the equivalent of 3 months in 2010.

While the EU continues to dominate the Mauritanian market in terms of trade and foreign direct investment (FDI), trade with new emerging partners has

KEY INDICATORS **Mauritania**

	Unit	2006	2007	2008	2009	2010
Population	m	*2.89	*2.96	*3.03	*3.11	*3.40
Gross domestic product (GDP)	US$bn	2.71	2.80	3.20	3.00	3.80
GDP per capita	US$	933	952	1,042	975	2,093
GDP real growth	%	11.7	1.0	3.5	-1.2	5.2
Inflation	%	6.2	7.2	7.3	2.2	6.1
Exports (fob) (goods)	US$m	1,812.0	–	–	–	–
Imports (fob) (goods)	US$m	1,205.0	–	–	–	–
Balance of trade	US$m	607.0	-573.0	-497.0	–	–
Current account	US$m	-36.0	-321.0	-497.0	-387.0	-187.0
Total reserves minus gold	US$m	187.2	197.8	188.6	225.4	271.7
Foreign exchange	US$m	187.1	197.8	188.5	225.2	271.6
Exchange rate	per US$	270.80	252.54	258.58	262.36	275.89

* estimated figure

proliferated over the past years. Russia, Brazil, Turkey and China, especially, are considered the most active in Mauritania.

Employment

Unemployment in Mauritania is high – 31 per cent of the population in 2008 (latest available figure) and under-employment of 14 per cent in 2008. There is, however, a highly developed informal sector (85 per cent of jobs in 2008). The growth of the modern sector generates little work (particularly the mining sector). It primarily feeds the informal sector, which does not provide 'decent' jobs in the International Labour Organisation sense of the word. The movement of economic units from the informal sector to the formal remains exceptional. In terms of strategy, the Poverty Reduction Strategy Framework (PRSF) 2006–10 highlighted one of the key lessons taken from the implementation of the 2001–04 framework, that is, the absence of a link between employment and the strategy's major thrust of accelerating growth and concentrating it on the poor.

Risk assessment

Politics	Fair
Economy	Fair
Regional stability	Fair

COUNTRY PROFILE

Historical profile

1800s France took control first of southern Mauritania, ruling it from Senegal.
1904 Mauritania became a colonial territory of France.
1920 Mauritania became part of French West Africa.
1946 Mauritania became a Territoire d'Outre-Mer (TOM, overseas territory) of France.
1957 Limited self-government was granted under the Loi cadre. Nouakchott became the capital.
1960 Mauritania gained full independence from France on 28 November, under the regime of the Mauritanian People's Party. Mokhtar Ould Daddah became president.
1974 Mauritania withdrew from the CFAf currency zone and introduced the ouguiya.
1975 An agreement between Mauritania, Morocco and Spain led to the division of the Spanish Sahara (a Spanish colony and the present-day Sahrawi Arab Republic (Western Sahara)) between Mauritania and Morocco.
1978 After fighting a largely unsuccessful war against the Frente para la Liberación de Saguia al Hamra y Río de Oro (Frente Polisario) (Popular Front for the Liberation of Saguia al Hamra and Río de Oro) rebels of the Western Sahara, President Daddah was overthrown.
1979 The government of President Haidallah agreed to renounce all territorial claims to Western Sahara.
1981 Slavery was banned in Mauritania.
1984 Haidallah was removed from office by Colonel Maaouya Ould Sid'Ahmed Taya.
1992 Multi-party elections were held in which President Taya was returned to office.
1996 The governing Parti Républicain Démocratique et Social (PRDS) (Social and Democratic Republican Party) won the elections.
1997 President Taya was re-elected.
1999 Full diplomatic relations were established with Israel. After criticism by Iraq, the foreign ministry announced that Mauritania had severed its relations with Iraq.
2001 The PRDS was re-elected.
2002 Famine increased due to three years of drought.
2003 The OPEC Fund for International Development donated US$300,000 to support an emergency operation by the World Food Programme (WFP). A coup attempt by rebels in Nouakchott was foiled by the President's troops. President Taya named Sghair Ould M'Bareck as the new prime minister. Incumbent Maaouya Ould Sid'Ahmed Taya was re-elected president. Prime Minister Sghair Ould M'Bareck was re-appointed.
2005 Mauritania lost its annual crop production after it was attacked by locust swarms. The UN called for food aid. While President Taya was out of the country, a military coup overthrew his regime. Colonel Ely Ould Mohamed Vall (leader of the military *Junta*) was declared president and head of the Military Council for Justice and Democracy.
2006 A referendum was held approving limitations on future presidential powers. Parliamentary and municipal elections took place.
2007 Sidi Mohamed Ould Cheikh Abdallahi won presidential elections and Zeine Ould Zeidane became prime minister.
2008 Prime Minister Zeine Ould Zeidane resigned and was replaced by Yahya Ould Ahmed El Waghef. A *coup d'etat* led by General Mohamed Ould Abdel Aziz removed President Abdallahi and Prime Minister El Waghef from power. Within a week, two-thirds of members of parliament had signed a document in support of the coup. A High Council of State was established, led by General Abdel Aziz. Moulaye Ould Mohamed Laghdaf was appointed prime minister. Former prime minister El Waghef was arrested, released and then rearrested a few days later and put on trial for malfeasance and later corruption.
2009 General Abdel Aziz resigned as president and chairman of the ruling High Council of State and Ba Mamadou dit M'Baré became interim president. The opposition agreed to participate in presidential elections on the condition that former prime minister El Waghef was released from gaol. Presidential elections were postponed but later Mohamed Ould Abdel Aziz (Union pour la Republique (UPR) (Union for the Republic)) won 52.58 per cent of the vote, his closest rival Messaoud Ould Boulkheir (APP) won 16.29 per cent. A unity government, headed by President Aziz, was formed to include opposition members.
2010 A *fatwa* (religious opinion), banning the practice of female genital mutilation was signed by 34 Islamic scholars in January. On 19 October, the UN-sponsored repatriation scheme for Mauritanian refugees in Senegal resumed.
2011 In June and July, there were a number of skirmishes between government troops and fighters of Al-Qaeda in the Islamic Maghreb (AQIM). The numbers wounded or killed varied according to sources. A national census was undertaken from 20 June, which sparked protests from the black African community in Mauritania and abroad. The census was branded as 'discriminatory' as it not only noted citizens within racial groupings (which, it was suspected, could be used to discriminate against various groupings in the future), but required a set of civil documents (including identity papers of parents and grandparents, which excluded anyone born outside Mauritania before 1945), before a person could be recorded (or 'enrolled').

Political structure

Constitution

A new constitution was approved in 2006; a president is limited to two consecutive terms in office, which are cut from six to five years and there is a presidential age limit of 75 years. The oath of office includes a vow not to alter these changes.

Form of state

Islamic republic

The executive

The president is the head of state and is elected by universal suffrage for five-year terms. The president appoints the prime minister and presides over the Council of Ministers, who are recommended by the prime minister and appointed by the president. The president is the supreme chief of the armed forces.
The president, after consultation with the prime minister and the presidents of the

assemblies, may pronounce the dissolution of the National Assembly.

National legislature

The bicameral Barlamane (parliament) is comprised of the Al Jamiya al Wataniyah (National Assembly), with 81 members, directly elected in single-seat constituencies for five-year terms and the Majlis al Shuyukh (Senate) with 56 members, of which 53 are elected by municipal councils for six-year terms. Three members are elected by expatriated Mauritanians. An alternate one-third of senators are re-elected every two years.

The prime minister, under the authority of the president, defines the policy of the government, divides the tasks among the ministers and directs and co-ordinates the action of the government.

Legal system

The legal system is based on the 1991 constitution and is strongly influenced by *Sharia* (Islamic law).

Last elections

18 July 2009 (presidential); 19 November/3 December 2006 (parliamentary)

Results: Presidential: Mohamed Ould Abdel Aziz (Union pour la Republique (UPR) (Union for the Republic)) won 52.58 per cent of the vote, Messaoud Ould Boulkheir (APP) 16.29 per cent, Ahmed Ould Daddah (RFD) 13.66 per cent; seven other candidates won less than 5 per cent of the vote.

Parliamentary: Regroupement des Forces Démocratiques (RFD) (Rally of Democratic Forces) won 15 out of 95 seats; Union des Forces du Progrès (UFP) (Union of Forces for Progress) won eight seats; Parti Republicain Démocratique et Renouvellement (PRDR) (Republican Party for Democracy and Renewal) seven seats; other parties, including Alliance Populaire pour le Progrès (APP) (Alliance for Popular Progress) 24 seats, and independents 41seats.

Next elections

2011 (parliamentary); 2014 (presidential)

Political parties

Political parties were legalised in July 1991 but were forbidden to be organised on racial or regional lines, or to be opposed to Islam.

Ruling party

All members of parliament are independents

Population

3.40 million (2010)*

Last census: November 2000: 2,548,157

Population density: Two inhabitants per square km. Urban population: 59 per cent.

Annual growth rate: 2.9 per cent 1994–2004 (WHO 2006)

Ethnic make-up

The population comprises a majority of Arabised Moors. The rest are ethnically linked with the peoples of Senegal and Mali. Moor-black (40 per cent), Moor (30 per cent), black (30 per cent).

Religions

Islam (99 per cent) is the state religion.

Education

Primary schooling lasts for six years. Progression to secondary education is through a competitive entrance examination. Secondary schooling lasts for six years, divided into two three-year cycles. Each stage requires further examination and students may graduate from either with academic or technical qualifications. Public expenditure on education typically amounts to around 5 per cent of gross national income (GNI).

Literacy rate: 41 per cent adult rate; 50 per cent youth rate (15–24) (Unesco 2005).

Compulsory years: Six to 16.

Enrolment rate: 87 per cent (boys); 82 per cent (girls) gross primary enrolment of the relevant age group (including repeaters), (Unicef).

Pupils per teacher: 50 in primary schools.

Health

Improved water sources and sanitation facilities are available to 37 per cent and 33 per cent of the population, respectively.

HIV/Aids

HIV prevalence: 0.6 per cent aged 15–49 in 2003 (World Bank)

Life expectancy: 58 years, 2004 (WHO 2006)

Fertility rate/Maternal mortality rate: 5.7 births per woman, 2004 (WHO 2006)

Child (under 5 years) mortality rate (per 1,000): 77 per 1,000 live births; 32 per cent of children aged under five are malnourished (World Bank).

Head of population per physician: 0.11 physicians per 1,000 people, 2004 (WHO 2006)

Main cities

Nouakchott (administrative capital, estimated population 719,167 in 2005); Nouadhibou (formerly Port-Etienne, 89,772), Rosso (59,592), Adel Bagrou (58,429).

Languages spoken

French is usually spoken in business circles; English is rarely spoken. Hassani Arabic, Pulaar, Soninke and Wolof are the major languages in everyday use.

Official language/s

Hassani Arabic and Wolof

Media

Since 2006 freedom of the press has been generally respected by two revolutionary regimes and has been described as 'partly free' by US-based human rights watchdog, Freedom House. Nevertheless, journalists are prohibited from publishing material that is anti-Islamic or threatens national security.

Press

There are three daily newspapers published by the state, two in Arabic *Chaab* (www.ami.mr/chaab) and *Akhbar Nouakchott* (www.ani.mr/anifr.php) and one in French, *Horizons* (www.ami.mr/horizons). Private dailies include, in French *Le Caleme* (www.lecalame.mr), *Le Quotidien de Nouakchott* (www.quotidien-nouakchott.com) and *Al Mourabit* (www.almourabit.mr); in Arabic *El Bedil Athalith*.

Broadcasting

The government operates the only national public broadcaster, operating Radio Mauritanie and Télévision de Mauritanie (TVM) (www.tvm.mr), which broadcast in Arabic and French.

News agencies

National news agency: Mauritanian News Agency (in Arabic): www.ami.mr
APA (African Press Agency): www.apanews.net

Economy

Mauritania began producing oil in 2006 and while there was an initial production of 75,000 barrels per day (bpd), this rapidly dropped to 30,000bpd by the end of the year, largely due to technical difficulties offshore in the Chinguetti oil field. Following challenges to the legality of the initial developer to drill for this oil the Chinguetti oil field was sold to the Malaysian state-owned energy company, Petronas. Further discoveries of oil and natural gas were announced in 2008, but commercial production is still under development. Exploration and drilling of new wells was also granted, under a memorandum of understanding (in 2006), to the China National Petroleum Corporation (CNPC). Mauritania joined the Extractive Industries Transparency Initiative (EITI) – a forum of oil producers and consumers seeking to promote accountability in oil revenue – as part of the International Monetary Fund (IMF) sponsored growth programme in 2005. The IMF advised that oil funds should be used in accordance with Mauritania's own poverty reduction strategy plans, with a fund for investment in future generations.

GDP growth was 3.5 per cent in 2008, but as the global economic crisis in 2008 cut world trade and iron ore exports dropped from US$828.4 million in 2008 to US$521.6 million in 2009, so GDP growth fell into recession at -1.2 per cent. However as global trade picked up growth surged back to 5.2 per cent in 2010.

The trade balance in 2009 was a deficit of US$26.7 million (-0.9 per cent of GDP), which turned around in 2010 with a balance of US$81.3 million (2.3 per cent of GDP). Around 40 per cent of total exports comes from iron ore. Foreign earnings are also generated from oil, gold and fish caught within Mauritania's territorial waters by licensed foreign vessels. Mauritania has been warned that its sea will become over-fished without strict monitoring.

The service sector accounted for 44.8 per cent of GDP in 2009, industry constituted 34.7 per cent of which manufacturing amounted to 4.1 per cent and agriculture contributed 20.6 per cent of GDP.

Around 50 per cent of the population depend on agriculture for a livelihood; a series of droughts since the 1980s have forced nomads and subsistence farmers into urban areas. Mauritania was ranked at 159 (out of 187) on the UN Human Development Index (HDI) in 2011. According to indicators, 57.1 per cent of people experience at least one of three levels of deprivation in health, education and income; 21.2 per cent of the population live on the equivalent of US$1.25 per day.

External trade

Mauritania is a member of the Arab Maghreb Union (AMU) (with Morocco, Tunisia, Algeria and Libya); however no economic integration or free trade agreement has been achieved between members.

Exports of crude oil averaged only 17,000 barrels per day in 2007, earning US$310 million. An agreement was signed with the European Union (EU) to allow EU fishing fleets access to Mauritanian waters for □516 million (US$700 million) over 2006–12.

Imports

Principal imports are capital machinery and equipment, petroleum products, vehicles, foodstuffs and consumer goods.

Main sources: France (typically 15 per cent of total), Russian Federation (10 per cent), The Netherlands (8 per cent).

Exports

Principal exports are fish and fish products, crude oil, iron ore and gold.

Main destinations: France (typically 15 per cent of total), Germany (10 per cent), China (8 per cent).

Agriculture

Farming

Production of food crops is restricted to irrigated land in the south along the north bank of the Senegal River. International aid and imported cereals have been vital in supplementing the main food crops – millet, sorghum, rice, maize, potatoes and dates.

Most of Mauritania consists of arid and semi-arid land and although it is unsuitable for crops, livestock rearing is an important sector. Nomadic herders comprise around 10 per cent of the population, although their numbers are dwindling. In 2005 Oxfam stated intermittent droughts since 2000 have affected nomadic herders and northern farming families, leading to food crises and a need of food and farming aid.

Fishing

Fishing contributes up to 10 per cent of GDP and provides around 45 per cent of export earnings as well as being an important source of food for Mauritanians. The coastal waters are among the richest in the world and joint venture fishing is one of the most important foreign exchange earners. The catch is mainly deep sea species and shellfish – particularly shrimp for the Japanese market.

Forestry

The majority of timber production is used as domestic firewood.

Industry and manufacturing

The industrial sector contributes around 10 per cent to GDP and employs 5 per cent of the workforce.

The most important activities are fish freezing and processing and the treatment of locally mined iron ore. There are also various small import substitution industries (brewing, footwear, dairy processing etc), oil refining and a sugar refinery in Nouakchott.

Tourism

The tourism sector is underdeveloped. Revenues from the sector are estimated at an annual US$20 million. Most foreign visitors are business travellers to Nouakchott, drop-in visitors crossing the border from Senegal or occasional desert safari enthusiasts.

Environment

In June 2010 the African Union backed a proposal to build the 'Great Green Wall' project, of a 15km wide, 7,775km long, continuous belt of trees from Senegal in the west to Djibouti in the east (traversing 11 countries) in an effort to halt the advance of the Sahara Desert. The trees to be used would be drought-adapted, preferably native to the area from a list of 37 possible species, and should help to slow soil erosion and filter rain water.

Mining

The mining sector contributes around 13 per cent to GDP, employs 5 per cent of the working population and generates 42 per cent of export earnings.

The annual output of iron ore is around 12 million tonnes, of which about 11 million tonnes is exported – 36 per cent to France, 26 per cent to Italy, 16 per cent to Belgium, 8 per cent to Germany, 4 per cent to Spain and 4 per cent to the UK.

The iron mines are located in the Tiris region in the north and are owned and operated by Société Nationale Industrielle et Minière (SNIM). Other mineral resources include copper (at Akjoujt); gold (also near Akjoujt); phosphates (deposits at Bofal), diamonds and uranium.

Hydrocarbons

Proven oil reserves were 100 million barrels in 2008, with production at 12,830 barrels per day (bpd). Consumption was 21,000bpd with the shortfall covered by imports. Oil production began in 2006 from the small offshore Chinguetti oil field; the Tiof oil field, which is not under production, has reserves estimated at 350 million barrels. Exploration of offshore sites is ongoing.

The Société Mauritanienne des Hydrocarbures (SMH) is responsible for all matters dealing with exploration, production and marketing of oil and gas in Mauritania, with exclusive rights to negotiate on behalf of the state any exploitation of the country's hydrocarbon resources.

The Somir oil refinery in Nouadhibou, is the only refinery in operation. Owned by an Algerian company, it processes Algerian crude oil, with a capacity of 20,000bpd.

Proven natural gas reserves were 28.3 billion cubic metres (cum) in 2008, but production remains negligible. In January 2009 the government signed an agreement with Shell Gas and Power to evaluate the potential for developing the natural gas reserves.

Any imports of coal are insignificant and reserves are negligible.

Energy

Total installed generating capacity was 180MW in 2007, producing 410 million kilowatt hours (kWh). Hydropower accounts for around 50MW of primary energy; Mauritania receives around 30MW from the Manantali hydroelectric dam in Mali.

The Société Mauritanienne d'Electricité (Maurelec) is responsible for electricity generation, transmission and supply. The electricity network serves only a few people in urban areas. There is small-scale thermal electricity (generating capacity 110MW), most of which is provided by isolated diesel generators. The majority of the population relies on non-commercial biomass, mostly fuel wood for cooking, lighting and power.

Banking and insurance

In recent years, Mauritania's banking sector has undergone liberalisation with the government selling its equity stake in commercial banks, making the sector more competitive. Reform of the banking sector has led to limits on bank lending and to new laws on debt recovery.

Domestic confidence in the banking sector remains low and 60 per cent of cash is still not placed in banks. However, this represents an enormous opportunity for the banking sector to increase savings and improve liquidity. An increase in the number of bank branches and the introduction of micro-banking schemes may transform the sector in coming years.

Central bank

Banque Centrale de Mauritanie

Main financial centre

Nouakchott

Time

GMT

Geography

Mauritania lies in north-west Africa, with the Atlantic Ocean to the west, Algeria and Western Sahara/Morocco to the north, Mali to the east and south, and Senegal to the south.

Mauritania extends over an area of 1,030,700 square km, around 75 per cent of which is covered with sand and scrub. South-west-facing scarps in the huge plains are home to oases. The general flatness is relieved by rocky plateaux, which rise to 500–600m. These are cut by ravines and punctuated by isolated peaks. The country's highest point is Kediet Ijill, which reaches 915m. The plateaux drop gradually north-eastwards to the Empty Quarter, heralding the onset of the Sahara. Westwards, between the plateaux and the Atlantic Ocean, the terrain alternates between areas of plains and dunes, which increase in size and movement to the north. The only area of permanent vegetation is in the south along the Senegal river, which forms the frontier with Senegal.

Hemisphere

Northern

Climate

The climate is hot and dry. The hottest month in Noukachott is September (24–34 degrees Celsius (C)); the coldest is December (12–29 degrees C); the wettest month is August.

Entry requirements

Passports

Required by all.

Visa

Required by all, except citizens of neighbouring states, contact the consular section of the nearest embassy for confirmation of exclusions. Business travellers may visit with a tourist visa, obtained in advance. An application should include a bank letter showing sufficient funds for the length of trip, an employer's letter of accreditation and an invitation from a local company or organisation. All travellers must have return/onward passage.

Currency advice/regulations

Unlimited foreign currency may be imported, but the amount must be declared on arrival. Unexchanged foreign currency may be exported. Declaration forms must be produced on departure. Import and export of local currency is strictly forbidden. Controls are constantly subject to modification.

Health (for visitors)

Mandatory precautions

Yellow fever vaccination certificate required if arriving from an infected area.

Advisable precautions

Yellow fever, hepatitis A, tetanus, typhoid and polio vaccinations. Malaria prophylaxis should be taken.

Water precautions are advisable. There is a rabies risk.

Hotels

Accommodation is limited and visitors should book well in advance. A service charge is normally included in the bill, otherwise a 15 per cent tip is usual.

Credit cards

Only accepted in main hotels.

Public holidays (national)

Fixed dates

1 Jan (New Year's Day), 1 May (Labour Day), 25 May (Africa Day), 10 Jul (Armed Forces Day), 28 Nov (Independence Day).

Variable dates

Eid al Adha, Islamic New Year, Birth of the Prophet, Eid al Fitr.

Islamic year 1433 (26 Nov 2011–14 Nov 2012): The Islamic year contains 354 or 355 days, with the result that Muslim feasts advance by 10–12 days against the Gregorian calendar. Dates of feasts vary according to the sighting of the new moon, so cannot be forecast exactly.

Working hours

Banking

Sun–Wed: 0800–1115; 1430–1630; Thu: 0800–1500.

Business

Sat–Wed: 0800–1500; Thu: 0800–1300. Some stop for a lunch-time break (usually 1200–1300 or 1500).

Government

Sat–Wed: 0800–1500; Thu: 0800–1300.

Shops

Sat–Thu: 0800–1200; 1430–1800.

Electricity supply

127/220V AC, 50 cycles. Plugs and sockets mostly two-pin (round).

Getting there

Air

National airline: Air Mauritanie

International airport/s: Nouakchott (NKC), 4km from city; Nouadhibou (NDB), 4km from city.

Airport tax: UM270.

Surface

Road: Crossing the Mali and Western Sahara/Morocco borders may present difficulties and the Algerian frontier is closed. The best route is via Senegal. A surfaced road exists from Dakar (Senegal) to Nouakchott.

Main port/s: Nouadhibou and Nouakchott

Getting about

National transport

Air: Air Mauritanie provides mainly weekly services between most main centres.

Road: Most roads linking major centres are adequate, although four-wheel drive vehicles are recommended. Minor roads are usually impassable after the rainy season. There is a paved road between Rosso (on the Senegal River, where a ferry connects with the road to Dakar) and Akjoujt, via Nouakchott, and another, *La Route de l'Espoir*, running from Nouakchott to Mali.

Rail: A track runs inland from the coast (Nouakchott-Zouerate), mainly for freight, but there are some passenger services (single-class) scheduled; motor vehicles are sometimes carried.

City transport

Taxis: Taxis are numerous in the main towns. They are not metered, but the fares are standardised, although they should be checked before departure. A small tip is usual. Taxis can be rented by the hour.

Car hire

Cars can be rented in Nouakchott, Nouadhibou and Atar. An international or national driving licence is required. Out of town, a four-wheel drive vehicle with chauffeur, although expensive, is recommended.

BUSINESS DIRECTORY

The addresses listed below are a selection only. While World of Information makes every endeavour to check these addresses, we cannot guarantee that changes have not been made, especially to telephone numbers and area codes. We would welcome any corrections.

Telephone area codes

The international dialling (IDD) code for Mauritania is +222, followed by subscriber's number.

Chambers of Commerce

Mauritania Chamber of Commerce, Industry and Agriculture, Avenue de la République, PO Box 215, Nouakchott (tel: 525-2214; fax: 525-3895; e-mail: ccia@mauritel.mr).

Banking
Banque Mauritanienne pour le Commerce International, PO Box 622, Immeuble Afarco, Avenue Gamal Abdel Nasser, Nouakchott (tel: 525-4349; fax: 525-2045).

Banque Nationale de Mauritanie; PO Box 614, Avenue Gamal Abdel Nasser, Nouakchott (tel: 525-2602; fax: 525-3397).

Central bank
Banque Centrale de Mauritanie, PO Box 623, Avenue de l'Indépendence, Nouakchott (tel: 525-2206; fax: 525-2759; e-mail: info@bcm.mr).

Travel information
Air Mauritanie, Avenue Gamal Abdel Nasser, PO Box 41, Nouakchott (tel: 525-2721; e-mail: resa@airmauritanie.mr).

Ministry of tourism
Ministry of Trade, Handicrafts and Tourism, Directorate of Tourism, PO Box 246, Nouakchott (tel: 525-1367; fax: 525-1057).

National tourist organisation offices
Office National du Tourisme, PO Box 2884, Nouakchott (tel: 529-0344; fax: 529-0528; e-mail: ont@mauritel.mr).

Ministries
Ministry of Economic Affairs and Development, BP 238, Nouakchott (tel: 525-1612; fax: 525-5110; e-mail: infomaed@mauritania.mr).

Ministry of Education, PO Box 227, Nouakchott (tel: 525-8445; fax: 525-1222).

Ministry of Finance, PO Box 197, Nouakchott (tel: 525-4397; fax: 525-3114; e-mail: sidahd@mauritania.mr).

Ministry of Fishing and Maritime Economy, PO Box 137, Nouakchott (tel: 525-9970; fax: 525-3146).

Ministry of Foreign Affairs and Co-operation, PO Box 230, Nouakchott (tel: 525-2682).

Ministry of Health and Social Affairs, PO Box 169, Nouakchott (tel: 525-2052).

Ministry of Infrastructure and Transport, PO Box 237, Nouakchott (tel: 525-3337).

Ministry of the Interior, Post and Telecommunications, PO Box 195, Nouakchott (tel: 525-2020).

Ministry of Mines and Industry, PO Box 199, Nouakchott (tel: 525-3086; fax: 525-6937; e-mail: mmi@mauritania.mr).

Ministry of Trade, Artisans and Tourism, PO Box 182, Nouakchott (tel: 525-1057).

Ministry of Rural Development and Environment, PO Box 366, Nouakchott (tel: 525-1500; fax: 525-7574).

Prime Minister's Office, PO Box 237, Nouakchott (tel: 525-3337).

Other useful addresses
Centre d'Information Mauritanien pour le Developpement Economique et Technique, PO Box 2119, Nouakchott (tel: 525-8738; fax: 525-8648; e-mail: cimdet@pacdet.org).

Confédération Générale des Employeurs de Mauritanie (CGEM), PO Box 383, Nouakchott (tel: 525-2160; fax: 525-3301).

Fédération des Industries et Armement de Pêche (FIAP), PO Box 43, Nouadhibou (tel: 574-5089; fax: 574-5430).

Fédération des Industries et des Mines (FIM), PO Box 5501, Nouakchott (tel: 525-0304; fax: 525-6955).

Mauritanian Embassy (USA), 2129 Leroy Place, NW, Washington DC 20008 (tel: (+1-202)-232-5700; fax: (+1-202)-319-2623).

Mauritanienne d'Entreposage des Produits Pétroliers (MEPP), Nouakchott (tel: 525-2646; fax: 525-4608; e-mail: mepp@mauritel.mr).

National Statistics Office, BP 240, Nouakchott (tel: 525-5031; fax:525-5170; e-mail: webmaster@)ons.mr).

National news agency: Mauritanian News Agency (in Arabic): www.ami.mr

Internet sites
Africa Business Network: http://www.ifc.org/abn

AllAfrica.com: http://allafrica.com

African Development Bank: http://www.afdb.org

Africa Online: http://www.africaonline.com

Mbendi AfroPaedia (information on companies, countries, industries and stock exchanges in Africa): http://mbendi.co.za

Mauritius

KEY FACTS

Official name: Republic of Mauritius

Head of State: President Sir Anerood Jugnauth (from 2003; re-elected 19 Sep 2008)

Head of government: Prime Minister Navin Ramgoolam (Parti Travailliste (PT) (Labour Party)) (5 Jul 2005)

Ruling party: Coalition Alliance de L'Avenir (Alliance of the Future) led by Parti Travailliste (PT) (Labour Party), with Parti Mauricien Social-Démocrate (Mauritius Social Democratic Party) and Mouvement Socialiste Mauricien (Militant Socialist Movement

Area: 1,865 square km

Population: 1.30 million (2010)*

Capital: Port Louis

Official language: English and French

Currency: Mauritian rupee (MR) = 100 cents

Exchange rate: MR29.00 per US$ (Oct 2011)

GDP per capita: US$7,593 (2010)

GDP real growth: 4.00% (2010)

GDP: US$9.70 billion (2010)

Labour force: 581,000 (2010)

Unemployment: 7.70% (2010)

Inflation: 2.90% (2010)

Balance of trade: -US$1.90 billion (2010)

Visitor numbers: 980,000 (2010)*

* estimated figure

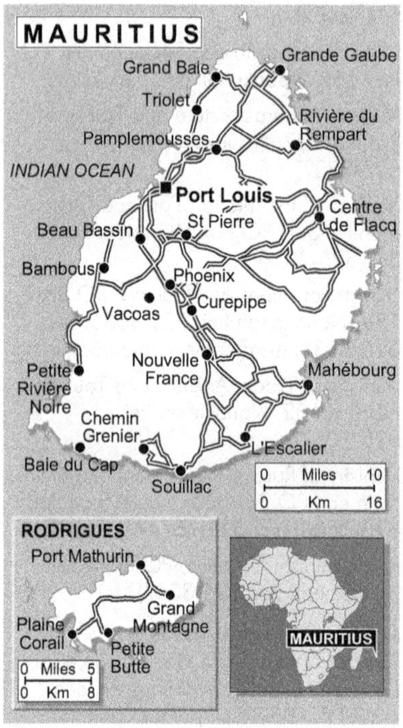

On 4 July 2011 Air Mauritius launched its first scheduled flight service to Shanghai, a sure sign that in Mauritius too China has become one of the country's main emerging economy partners. Prime Minister Navin Ramgoolam proposed in November 2010 that the National Assembly vote to appoint Monique Ohsan-Bellepeau, a prominent member of the Creole community, as the country's first female vice president. The proposal was supported by the opposition and she was duly appointed on 13 November. Analysts see her appointment as an astute move to consolidate the ethnic balance of Mauritian politics. The next general election is in 2015, although the next president (a ceremonial position) will be elected by the National Assembly in 2013.

The economy

Mauritius' economy is based on its 'four-pillars' – sugar, textiles, tourism and financial services. It is striving to diversify in order to make it more resilient to shocks, enhance productivity and competiveness, and support growth and job creation. The 2010 budget focused on job creation, social development and the environment. It maintained previous support measures taken by the government. For 2011, the three main thrusts of the budget are rebalancing growth, boosting productivity and consolidating social justice.

According to the *African Economic Outlook 2011* (AEO), published jointly by the African Development Bank and the Organisation for Economic Co-operation and Development real gross domestic product (GDP) grew by 4.1 per cent in 2010, up from 3.1 per cent in 2009 but lower than the 5.5 per cent in 2008. Despite challenges at home and abroad, the government has maintained a growth path. In 2011, GDP growth is projected to remain around 4 per cent. However, this will depend on the recovery in the country's main European trading partners, but could be faster if Mauritius reduces its dependence on sending exports to slow-growing traditional markets and looks instead to new markets in emerging economies. Projections for 2012 put economic growth at 4.1 per cent. The overall 2010 budget deficit was estimated at 4.7 per cent of GDP against 6.6 per cent in 2009. It is projected to fall back to 4.4 per cent in 2011 and 4.3 per cent in 2012. The relatively high fiscal deficits are caused by rapidly increasing government expenditure (including capital repayments) compared to revenues.

Estimates indicate that primary sector activities, mainly related to agriculture, grew by 2.5 per cent in 2010, down from 8.7 per cent in 2009. Sugarcane grew by only 0.6 per cent while other agriculture expanded 3.7 per cent in 2010. As part of efforts to make the economy more resilient, an agricultural production and marketing information system is being set up for planters and breeders to optimise revenue. Sugar co-operatives are being helped to get the European Union's Fair Trade accreditation. This will enable them to obtain a premium of US$60 per tonne of sugar. The government has provided liberal tax regimes for agriculture in the 2011 budget. In addition, the Leasing for

Equipment Modernisation Scheme is being extended to December 2012 to cover heavy duty agricultural equipment.

AEO figures show that headline inflation for 2010 stood at 2.9 per cent up from 2.5 per cent in 2009. There were higher prices for food, cigarettes and alcohol, some clothing and footwear, electricity, bus and taxi fares, motor vehicles, gasoline and diesel. Inflation is predicted to rise to 3.0 per cent in 2011 and 3.9 per cent in 2012. Pressure will come from predicted rising international commodity prices, imported inflation from major trading partners, weak export activity, expected high public spending, rising producer prices for manufactured products, higher labour costs, loss of productivity and high food prices.

Apart from infrastructure development, Mauritius is giving priority to the small- and medium-enterprise (SME) sector, which has been the main source of employment creation during the financial and economic crises. The government is also increasing support to export-oriented industries, especially textiles and clothing, which have been under severe stress in the crisis.

Gross foreign direct investment (FDI) stood at MR10.6 billion (US$0.37 billion) at the end of September 2010 against MR8.8 billion (US$0.30 billion) for the same period in 2009, a 20 per cent gain. The investment went mainly to health and social work activities, real estate, finance and insurance.

Tourism

In 2010, tourist arrivals were estimated at about 934,000 compared to 871,000 the previous year and 2010 tourism earnings were estimated at about MR39.5 billion (US$1.36 billion), up from MR35.7 billion (US$1.23 billion) in 2009.

On top of the 7.3 per cent increase in tourist arrivals and 10.5 per cent growth in tourism earnings in 2010, already noted, for the second consecutive year Mauritius was voted the World's Best Island Destination at the World Travel Awards ceremony in London in November 2010. The awards for the Indian Ocean's leading airline and airport went to Air Mauritius and Mauritius' Sir Seewoosagur Ramgoolam International Airport, respectively. These are a valuable boost for the tourism sector.

International trade and development

Britain and France in Europe remain the main trade partners for Mauritius but its most important new allies are India, for trade and investment, and China, for trade and future investment, though they could also be regarded as traditional partners given their historical links. Other emerging partners for investment are Malaysia, United Arab Emirates and Singapore.

Total exports of goods and services were estimated to have risen from MR1.38 billion (US$47.58 million) in 2009 to MR1.49 billion (US$51.4 million) in 2010, an 8 per cent increase. In real terms, exports grew 11 per cent after 3.4 per cent in 2009. Total imports of goods and services were estimated to have increased to MR1.86 billion (US$64 million) from MR1.64 billion (US$57 million) in 2009, a 13 per cent gain. In real terms, imports grew by 5.9 per cent following a decline of 9.2 per cent in 2009.

The deficit in net exports of goods and services had been estimated to have grown from MR2.6 billion (US$89 million) in 2009 to MR3.7 billion (US$127 million) in 2010, taking the deficit up to 12.4 per cent of GDP, at 2010 market prices, compared to 9.2 per cent in 2009.

The 2010 current account deficit stood at 7.9 per cent of GDP and this is projected to rise to 9.2 per cent in 2011 and stay at 9 per cent in 2012. The higher deficit is due to an expected higher merchandise trade deficit as imports grow and become more expensive. Exports growth is projected to be restrained by the UK's muted economic performance and the euro area debt crisis.

Ranking well

Mauritius does well in the international rankings industry. The 2011 World Bank *Doing Business* index put Mauritius in 23rd place out of 183 countries, top position in sub-Saharan Africa, ahead of South Africa and Botswana, showing it as a strong reformer. The country ranks particularly strongly for starting a business, protecting investors, and paying taxes but needs improvement in getting credit, closing a business, and registering property. The World Economic Forum ranked Mauritius 55th among 139 countries in its 2010–11 global competitiveness index. In Africa, only Tunisia and South Africa finished higher. It does particularly well in financial market development and goods market efficiency.

Its ranking in the Transparency International corruption index for 2010 is 39 out of 178 countries globally, with only Botswana ahead among African nations.

Apart from infrastructure development, the government is giving priority to small- and medium-sized enterprises (SMEs), the key creator of employment throughout the financial and economic crisis. Mauritius is also increasing support to export industries, especially textiles and clothing, which have been under severe stress in the crisis. To improve competiveness and the business environment, the government is streamlining and modernising licensing systems while developing an impact assessment framework for all new regulations to ensure that public interest is protected in a business friendly manner.

KEY INDICATORS — Mauritius

	Unit	2006	2007	2008	2009	2010
Population	m	1.25	1.26	1.27	*1.28	*1.30
Gross domestic product (GDP)	US$bn	6.31	6.96	8.70	8.80	9.70
GDP per capita	US$	5,043	5,520	6,872	6,838	7,593
GDP real growth	%	3.7	4.6	5.5	3.0	4.2
Inflation	%	5.6	10.7	8.8	2.5	2.9
Unemployment	%	9.2	8.5	7.3	7.2	7.7
Industrial output	% change	-0.1	1.9	5.0	2.4	–
Agricultural output	% change	-3.9	2.1	3.1	10.6	–
Exports (fob) (goods)	US$m	2,263.0	2,237.9	2,399.5	1,942.0	2,261.5
Imports (fob) (goods)	US$m	3,329.0	3,655.7	4,398.9	3,498.8	4,157.3
Balance of trade	US$m	-1,066.0	-1,417.8	-1,999.4	-1,556.9	-1,895.8
Current account	US$m	-336.0	-433.9	-761.0	-674.5	-799.6
Total reserves minus gold	US$m	1,269.9	1,780.3	1,742.7	2,178.8	2,441.8
Foreign exchange	US$m	1,226.3	1,739.9	1,693.4	2,001.5	2,254.2
Tourist numbers	'000	788.3	–	930.5	871.4	–
Exchange rate	per US$	32.57	28.80	28.45	31.96	30.78

* estimated figure

Financial sector

Financial services represent a significant 12 per cent of Mauritius' GDP. Banks are healthy, profitable, well-capitalised, resilient, and ready to move to Basel III requirements. The overall capital adequacy ratio of banks in 2010 was around 16 per cent on average under Basel II, which was higher than the minimum required. This suggests that reforms undertaken by the Basel Committee on Banking Supervision (BCBS), which involves new global regulatory standards under the Basel III framework may not be difficult to meet. With continued enhancement of its regulatory and supervisory framework, the country enjoys financial stability and has gained international praise for its policies, especially the exchange rate policy.

In 2010, the monetary authorities sharpened and streamlined their supervision of banks and other financial institutions, moving towards greater risk-based financial sector supervision. The authorities issued new guidelines to ensure that banks follow international best practices, while strengthening monitoring.

The Stock Exchange of Mauritius capitalisation increased by 17.9 per cent between 2009 and 2010. Annual turnover rose by 12.5 per cent over the same period.

Apart from infrastructure development, Mauritius is giving priority to the small- and medium-enterprise (SME) sector, which has been the main source of employment creation during the financial and economic crises. The government is also increasing support to export-oriented industries, especially textiles and clothing, which have been under severe stress in the crisis.

The Mauritius government is trying to improve the labour market through structural policies and increased public infrastructure development. The unemployment rate rose from 7.3 per cent in 2009 to 7.5 per cent in 2010. The average age of the unemployed is about 29 years and most have not reached the Certificate of Primary Education level and do not possess the Cambridge School Certificate. It is also high among women, at 12 per cent against only 4.8 per cent for men. The government has set up a support unit for those who have lost their jobs and a National Employment Policy aims to implement innovative practices to promote employment creation and social dialogue.

Risk assessment

Politics	Fair
Economy	Fair
Regional stability	Poor

COUNTRY PROFILE

Historical profile

1598 A Dutch squadron landed at Grand Port and named the island Mauritius.
1638 Mauritius was settled by the Dutch. The island became an important port of call for Dutch, English and French trading ships. The Dutch introduced sugar cane and imported slaves to harvest it.
1710 The Dutch abandoned their settlement.
1721 France claimed the island; it also imported large numbers of slaves to harvest sugar cane, cotton and other crops.
1810 Britain defeated a French naval squadron and the island was ceded to Britain at the end of the Napoleonic Wars.
1835 Slavery was abolished. Most freed slaves left the plantations and settled in coastal towns; workers had to be imported from the Indian sub-continent to take their place, most of whom opted to remain on the island at the end of their contracts.
1936 The Labour Party (LP) was formed and organised strikes and protests between 1937–45.
1953 A group of Mauritians under Seewoosagur Ramgoolam rose to the leadership of the LP, which won the elections to the Legislative Council. Most Creoles joined the Parti Mauricien Social-Démocrate (PMSD) (Social Democratic Party of Mauritius).
1959 New political parties emerged including the Muslim Committee of Action (CAM). CAM formed an alliance with the LP.
1968 Mauritius gained independence from Britain.
1969 Ramgoolam's LP-CAM (Muslim) ruling alliance was strengthened when a coalition with the PMSD was formed. In response, the Mouvement Militante Mauricien (MMM) (Mauritian Militant Movement) was established.
1982 The LP lost power as the MMM, in alliance with the Parti Socialiste Mauricien (PSM), gained power under the premiership of Anerood Jugnauth.
1983 The MMM split and Jugnauth formed the Mouvement Socialiste Mauricien (MSM) (Mauritian Socialist Movement) which formed a government with the LP.
1990 The MMM and the MSM formed a political alliance.
1991 In December the Legislative Assembly approved the transition to a republic within the Commonwealth.
1992 Cassam Uteem was elected president.
1995 An alliance of the LP and the MMM, led by Navinchandra (Navin) Ramgoolam (son of the late Sir Seewoosagur Ramgoolam) and Paul Berenger, won the parliamentary elections. Ramgoolam became prime minister.
1997 The LP-MMM coalition broke up when the MMM left government and became the official opposition. Even so, the LP continued to hold an outright majority in the legislature and for the first time since independence, Mauritius was governed by a single party. Cassam Uteem was re-elected president.
2000 The opposition, MSM/MMM, won the parliamentary election. Sir Anerood Jugnauth, leader of the MMM, became prime minister for the second time. Mauritius revived a claim to sovereignty over Diego Garcia, the British Indian Ocean Territory.
2001 The WTO trade policy review encouraged Mauritius to further liberalise and diversify its economy. A constitutional amendment was introduced, allowing Rodrigues Island to have two representatives in the National Assembly and its own regional assembly.
2002 President Uteem resigned and Vice President Angidi Chettiar became interim president, but he also resigned; both men had refused to sign into law controversial anti-terrorism legislation. The National Assembly elected Karl Offman as president. On Rodrigues Island, the Rodrigues People's Organisation (RPO) won 10 seats out of 18 and the Mouvement Rodriguais (MR) (Rodrigues Movement) won eight seats in the first Rodrigues Regional Assembly election. The Rodrigues Regional Assembly opened with Jean Daniel Spéville as chief commissioner.
2003 Serge Clair became chief commissioner of Rodrigues Island. Sir Anerood Jugnauth resigned and Paul Bérenger replaced him as prime minister. Parliament elected Jugnauth as president.
2005 In parliamentary elections the opposition Alliance Sociale (AS) (Social Alliance) won 49 per cent of the vote (38 out of 62 constituencies) and the incumbent coalition MSM and MMM won 43 per cent (22). Turnout was 81.5 per cent. Navin Ramgoolam (Parti Travailliste (PT) (Labour Party)) became prime minister.
2006 Former residents of Diego Garcia in the Chagos Archipelago, evicted by the British for the island to be turned into a US military air base in the 1960s and living since in Mauritius, which also claims Diego Garcia, won the right to visit their island.
2007 The British High Court ruled that families of the expelled Diego Garcia islanders could return home.
2008 Le Morne Mountain was added to the list of Unesco World Heritage sites. The mountain was an important site of shelter and became a symbol of freedom

for runaway slaves fleeing the eastern slave trade in the eighteenth and nineteenth centuries. Anerood Jugnauth was unanimously re-elected president by the national assembly. Chagos residents lost their rights to return to Diego Garcia in a legal battle with the UK government.
2009 The United States and Mauritius began negotiations towards a bilateral investment treaty. The intention was to strengthen investor protection in Mauritius and encourage market-oriented economic reforms.
2010 The world's largest marine reserve, around the Chagos Islands, was created in April by the British government. The 545,000 square kilometre reserve will protect a rich marine ecosystem, including 220 coral species and over 1,000 species of reef fish. It will exclude commercial fishing. There were objections from the Chagossian diaspora as the banning of commercial fishing will make it almost impossible for exiled Chagossians to return and earn a living from fishing. In parliamentary elections, held on 5 May, the Alliance de L'Avenir (Alliance of the Future) a coalition of three political parties led by the ruling PT, won 41 seats (out of 62). Prime Minister Ramgoolam remained in office.
2011 The Central Statistics Office announced that GDP growth for 2010 was 4.3 per cent, which had risen to a record 4.5 per cent by 3 July. Economic activity was centred on tourism (4 per cent) with an estimated 980,000 visitors, transport and communications (5.5 per cent) and financial services (5.7 per cent); construction fell from 4.3 per cent in 2010 to 1 per cent of GDP. A national census took place between 20 June–31 July; the first results are expected to be published in mid-June 2012. On 4 July Air Mauritius launched its first scheduled flight service to Shanghai (China).

Political structure

Constitution

Mauritius is a republic with a president as head of state.
The president is elected by a simple majority of all the members of the National Assembly for a five-year term. The National Assembly is the supreme body that votes laws. The president's agreement and signature is required to sign legislation into law.

Form of state

Republic

The executive

Executive power is vested in the prime minister, leader of the majority parliamentary party.
There is a Council of Ministers consisting of the prime minister and not more than 24 other ministers.

National legislature

The unicameral National Assembly has 70 members in total, of which 62 seats are elected in single seat constituencies for five years terms; eight members are appointed by the Supreme Court to represent minority ethnic and religious groups. The official language of the National Assembly is English but any member may address the Chair in French.

Last elections

5 May 2010 (parliamentary); 19 September 2008 (presidential)
Results: Presidential: the National Assembly re-elected Sir Anerood Jugnauth. Parliamentary: Alliance de L'Avenir (Alliance of the Future; three political parties) won 41 seats (out of 62), Alliance du Coeur (Alliance of the Heart; three political parties) 18; three other political parties won less than three seats each, 29 other political parties and an independent failed to win any seats. Turnout was 78 per cent.

Next elections

2015 (parliamentary)

Political parties

Ruling party

Coalition Alliance de L'Avenir (Alliance of the Future) led by Parti Travailliste (PT) (Labour Party), with Parti Mauricien Social-Démocrate (Mauritius Social Democratic Party) and Mouvement Socialiste Mauricien (Militant Socialist Movement

Main opposition party

Coalition of Mouvement Socialiste Mauricien (MSM) (Mauritian Socialist Movement) and Mouvement Militante Mauricien (MMM) (Mauritian Militant Movement)

Population

1.30 million (2010)*
Last census: July 2000: 1,178,848
Population density: Population density: 588 per square km. The population densities of the island of Mauritius and the island of Rodrigues are 624 and 345, respectively. Urban population: 42 per cent (1995—2001).
Annual growth rate: 1.1 per cent 1994–2004 (WHO 2006)

Ethnic make-up

Indentured workers were brought from India to work on sugar estates and their descendants form a majority of the population, followed by Creoles (of mixed, predominantly African, origin), Muslim Indians, Chinese and Europeans. Hindu Indo-Mauritian (51 per cent), Creole (27 per cent), Muslim Indo-Mauritians (17 per cent), Chinese (2 per cent).

Religions

Hinduism (51 per cent), Christianity (Roman Catholic) (31.3 per cent), Muslim (16.6 per cent).

Education

Education is modelled on the English school system. Primary schooling lasts for six years until the age of 12; lower secondary schooling lasts for five years and upper secondary schooling for a further two years. Examinations are undertaken at each transition.
The expenditure allocated to education by central government was 16 per cent (Unicef estimates 1992–1999).
Literacy rate: 85.3 per cent total; 82.3 per cent female, adult rates (World Bank).
Compulsory years: Five to 12.
Enrolment rate: 93.6 per cent net primary enrolment, of the relevant age group; 62.9 per cent net secondary enrolment (World Bank).
Pupils per teacher: 24 in primary schools.

Health

Life expectancy: 72 years, 2004 (WHO 2006)
Fertility rate/Maternal mortality rate: 2.0 births per woman, 2004 (WHO 2006)
Child (under 5 years) mortality rate (per 1,000): 16 deaths per 1,000 live births; about 15 per cent of children aged under five are malnourished (World Bank).
Head of population per physician: 1.06 physicians per 1,000 people, 2004 (WHO 2006)

Main cities

Port Louis (capital, estimated population 147,251 in 2005), Beau Bassin/Rose Hill (107,716), Vascoas-Phoenix (118,421), Curepipe (84,057), Quatre Bornes (79,504).

Languages spoken

Creole and Bhojpuri are the predominant languages in everyday life.

Official language/s

English and French

Media

Freedom of the press is guaranteed by the constitution.

Press

Two media groups, Le Mauricien and La Sentinelle are dominant in the market. The French language predominates in newspapers but most either have online editions in English or have locally produced editions in other languages. There are several dailies including *l'Express* (www.lexpress.mu), *Le Matinal* (www.lematinal.com), *L'Hebdo* (www.defimedia.info) and *Le Mauricien* (www.lemauricien.com), which also publishes a Sunday edition. Weekly newspapers include, in English *Mauritius Times* (www.mauritiustimes.com), *Sunday Vani* (http://sundayvani.intnet.mu) also in Creole and in French *Star* (www.mauriweb.com/star) and *Weekend* (www.lemauricien.com/weekend).

Broadcasting

The state-owned Mauritius Broadcasting Corporation (MBC) (mbc.intnet.mu), which is funded by both a license fee and advertising. Locally produced and imported programmes are broadcast in French, English, Hindi, Creole, Chinese and a number of indigenous Indian languages.

Radio: MBC (mbc.intnet.mu) operates seven stations including Radio Maurice (RM) 1 and 2, Taal FM and Kool FM. Other private, commercial radio stations include Radio One (www.r1.mu), Top FM (www.topfmradio.com) and Radio Plus.

Television: Digital TV services have become operational ahead of the total switch over from analogue to digital signals in 2011. MBC (mbc.intnet.mu) operates 12 TV channels, two of which are digital and free-to-air.

News agencies

APA: www.apanews.net

Panapress: www.panapress.com

Reuters Africa: http://africa.reuters.com

Economy

Mauritius' economy, one of the most vibrant in Africa, is founded on tourism, financial services, textiles and sugarcane. GDP growth was 5.5 per cent in 2008, falling to 3.0 per cent in 2009 as the global economic crisis cut visitor numbers and recovering in 2010 GDP to 4.2 per cent.

The government, in response to globalisation, initiated a reform strategy over 2006–09 to correct fiscal weaknesses and open up the economy, to facilitate business and improve the investment climate by encouraging foreign direct investment and expertise. The information and communication technology (ICT) and software development sector has expanded to over 350 ICT business entities, including French-speaking call centres. In 2012 the World Bank ranked Mauritius as 23 (of 183) countries in the world for ease of doing business.

Building on existing freeport facilities of logistics and distribution, Mauritius is also promoting itself as a seafood hub for the region. With the end of textile quotas and preferential sugar sales these sectors have been restructured and modernised. The number of sugar plantations has been increased to 50–80 per cent of total land cultivated so that sugar can be processed into ethanol and other by-products to alleviate the islands' energy needs.

The service sector constitutes over 66 per cent of GDP, agriculture around 5 per cent and industry almost 30 per cent, of which manufacturing is 20 per cent. Tourism is an important sector and one the government regards as a growth industry. It has increased the number of airlines allowed to arrive in high-season, while encouraging conference and retail investment.

External trade

Mauritius was one of the founding members of the Common Market of Eastern and Southern Africa (Comesa), and operates a free trade area (FTA) with eight out of the 20 Comesa members. Internal duties were eliminated in 2000 and common external tariffs were introduced in June 2009 for some member states. Mauritius is also a member of the Southern African Development Community (SADC), the objectives of which include reducing trade barriers, achieving regional development and economic growth and evolving common systems and institutions.

The importance of sugar as an export commodity has been replaced by services, which generate more than 33 per cent of total foreign exchange earnings; tourism contributes the largest share and is growing.

Imports

Principal imports are manufactured goods, manufacturing equipment, foodstuffs, petroleum products and chemicals.

Main sources: India (typically 25 per cent of total), China (10 per cent), South Africa (8 per cent).

Exports

Principal exports are clothing and textiles, sugar, cut flowers and molasses.

Main destinations: UK (typically 32 per cent of total), France (17 per cent), USA (7 per cent).

Agriculture

Farming

The agricultural sector contributes around 6 per cent to GDP and employs 13 per cent of the workforce.

Sugar cane cultivation dominates the sector. Approximately 70 per cent of all cultivated land is devoted to the crop, and the sugar industry as a whole employs the majority of the workforce and accounts for 3 per cent of GDP. Cultivation is undertaken both on large plantations and by smallholders.

The other major export crop is tea, grown by tenant farmers. Mauritius is the fourth-largest producer of tea per capita in the world. Around 75 per cent of tea production (green leaf) is controlled by the Tea Development Authority, whose commercial activities are privately run.

Tobacco is grown for the home market.

Main food crops include potatoes and other vegetables, output of which is sufficient to meet domestic demand.

Much of the island's meat requirement is imported. Around 75 per cent of food requirements are also imported.

Fishing

All fish-farming production and 90 per cent of marine fishing provides about 40 per cent of the nutritional requirement of the Mauritian population. Commercial aquaculture includes cultivation of giant freshwater prawns and oysters. Mauritius is a hub for longline tuna fishing fleets that dock to offload their cargo on to freezer ships for transhipment and provides the local economy with foreign currency.

Total fish catches amount to over 10,000 tonnes per year with another 70 tonnes of other sea food. Over 70,000 cultivated oysters are produced each year.

Sports fishing has become a major influence, along with reef diving, which not only drives the local tourist industry but also employs boats and crews formerly used in fishing that were less capable of competing with modern replacement ships and mechanisation.

Forestry

Annual estimated production: 13,500 cubic metres (cum) roundwood, 3,000cum sawnwood, 5,000cum sawlogs and veneers, 6,000cum woodfuel, 100mt charcoal.

Industry and manufacturing

The industrial sector contributes around 30 per cent to GDP and employs 28 per cent of the workforce.

The industrial sector is based on the Export Processing Zones (EPZ) which were opened in the 1970s to take advantage of the preferential treatment which Mauritius receives under the Cotonou Agreement.

Production of textiles, and in particular knitwear, has become the most significant EPZ industry, and Mauritius is the world's third-largest exporter of pure new wool products. The EPZ textiles industry employs 91 per cent of the industrial workforce, accounts for 68 per cent of EPZ enterprises and 80 per cent of EPZ exports. The EPZs generate 23 per cent of GDP. In 2001, the knitwear industry moved towards high-fashion apparel as part of the effort to modernise.

Diversification is being encouraged to help get over the loss of preferential treatment in textiles. Other industries include the manufacture of watches and clocks, jewellery, spectacle frames and leather goods.

Informatics Park for foreign companies specialising in information technology was opened in 1994. Mauritius has plans to develop into a 'cyber island' and will receive assistance from the IMF as part of its upgrade.

Tourism

There are around 105 registered hotels with around 11,000 total room capacity.

Twenty new hotels are planned by 2016 at the total cost of US$450 million. Saturation point is near and there is a risk of environmental damage if development is not managed and contained accordingly. Europe is the main market, especially France, which accounts for more than a quarter of visitors, followed by South Africa.

Hydrocarbons

There are no known oil or natural gas reserves. Consumption of oil was 23,000 barrels per day (bpd) in 2008, all of which was imported. The State Trading Corporation has a monopoly on importing strategic products, including petroleum.
Any use of natural gas is commercially insignificant.
Over 300,000 tonnes of coal is typically imported for use in power generation.

Energy

Total installed generating capacity was 688MW in 2007, producing over 2.2 billion kilowatt hours. Around 75 per cent of power is produced by conventional thermal stations using fossil fuels, the remainder is largely produced from bagasse (waste material from the sugar cane crop). Renewable sources, including hydro and wind generation, account for a very small percentage of production,
The state-owned Central Electricity Board is responsible for generation, transmission, distribution and sales of electricity.

Financial markets

Stock exchange
The Stock Exchange of Mauritius

Banking and insurance

In 1989 tax and duty incentives were introduced for foreign banks licensed to engage in offshore banking. Mauritius launched Africa's first offshore banking centre at the end of 1989 which continues to expand.
Central bank
Bank of Mauritius.
Main financial centre
Port Louis.

Time

GMT plus four hours

Geography

Mauritius lies in the Indian Ocean. The principal island, from which the country takes its name, lies about 800km (500 miles) east of Madagascar. The other main islands are Rodrigues, the Agalega Islands and the Cargados Carajos Shoals (St Brandon Islands).
The island of Mauritius is volcanic with a coastal plain sharply rising to a plateau of 275–580 metres (m). Piton de la Rivière Noire is the highest peak, at 828m and the Grand River South East is the longest river. Coral reefs surround the island from hundreds of metres to several kilometres off the coast.
Hemisphere
Southern

Climate

Maritime – tropical in summer (November–April), and sub-tropical for the rest of the year. High humidity especially in inland areas. Summer temperatures average 25–30 degrees Celsius (C) with maximum 35 degrees C in February. Highest rainfall occurs in summer (when cyclones are likely). From May–November, drier and warm with temperatures 19–27 degrees C. Lowest rainfall from September–November. Inland areas generally 5 degrees C cooler than coast and with higher rainfall.

Entry requirements

Passports
Passports must be valid for six months from date of entry.
Visa
Required by all except citizens of most Commonwealth countries, plus EU, US and others. For a full list and further information see www.gov.mu/portal/site/passportSite and follow link from *passport and visa requirements*. From May 2009 EU citizens may make a short-stay visit, for up to three months, without a visa. Business travellers may visit with a tourist visa, obtained in advance. An application should include details of sufficient funds for the length of trip, an employer's letter of accreditation and an invitation from a local company or organisation.
All travellers must have return/onward passage.
Currency advice/regulations
The import and export of local and foreign currency is unlimited.
Travellers cheques are accepted in banks, hotels and authorised dealers.
Prohibited imports
Sugar cane, invertebrates and soil micro-organisms and illegal drugs.
Firearms and ammunition require import permits and must be declared on arrival.

Health (for visitors)

Mandatory precautions
Yellow fever and cholera vaccination certificates are required if arriving from infected areas.
Advisable precautions
Typhoid, tetanus, hepatitis A and polio vaccinations. Water precautions should be taken.

Hotels

There is a wide choice available but relatively expensive. A value added tax of 15 per cent is added to hotel and restaurant bills. Tip is not compulsory.

Credit cards

International credit and charge cards are acceptable in many establishments. ATMs are available.

Public holidays (national)

Fixed dates
1–2 Jan (New Year), 1 Feb (Abolition of Slavery Day), 12 Mar (National Day), 1 May (Labour Day), 2 Nov (Arrival of Indentured Labourers), 25 Dec (Christmas Day).
Variable dates
Thaipoosam Cavadee (Jan/Feb), Chinese New Year (Jan/Feb), Maha Shivaratri (Feb/Mar), Ougadi (Mar/Apr), Ganesh Chaturthi (Aug/Sep), Diwali (Oct/Nov), Eid al Fitr.
There are a diversity of cultures, each with their own set of holidays. Muslim, Buddhist and Hindu festivals are timed according to local sightings of the moon and its phases.

Working hours

Banking
Mon–Thu: 0915–1515; Fri: 0915–1530; Sat: 0915–1115. Some banks open Mon–Fri: 0900–1700.
Business
Mon–Fri: 0830–1615, Sat: 0900–1200.
Government
Mon–Fri: 0900–1600; Sat 0900–1200 (minimal staff only).
Shops
Mon–Sat 0930–1930.

Telecommunications

Mobile/cell phones
GSM 900 and 3G services cover almost the entire area of Mauritius and Rodrigues.

Electricity supply

220V AC, 50 cycles.

Weights and measures

The metric system is in general use, but certain obsolete French measures are still used in connection with the measurement of land.

Getting there

Air
National airline: Air Mauritius.
International airport/s: Sir Seewoosagur Ramgoolam International (MRU) 3km from Mahébourg, 48km south-east of Port Louis; duty free, currency exchange, post office, shops, car hire, banks.
Airport tax: Departure tax: MR500
Surface
Main port/s: Port Louis is the island's only commercial port with five deep water quays. Its free port status underpins the island's offshore banking system.

Getting about

National transport
Air: Air Mauritius operates inter-island service between Mauritius and Rodrigues

and Réunion. Two Air Mauritius Bell Jet helicopters are available for transfer from airport to hotel and tours.

Road: There is an extensive network throughout the island. About 93 per cent of the road network is paved. Occasional congestion. A dual highway links Port Louis and Phoenix, Port Louis and Mapou/Pamplemousses.

Buses: Good bus services cover the main island.

City transport

Taxis: Operate in all towns, villages and resorts. Generally unmetered so it is advisable to agree a fare before starting the journey. Tipping is not usual.

Car hire

Widely available. International or foreign licence accepted; traffic drives on the left.

BUSINESS DIRECTORY

The addresses listed below are a selection only. While World of Information makes every endeavour to check these addresses, we cannot guarantee that changes have not been made, especially to telephone numbers and area codes. We would welcome any corrections.

Telephone area codes

The international dialling code (IDD) for Mauritius is +230, followed by subscriber's number.

Useful telephone numbers

Emergency	999
Fire	995
Police	208-7018

Chambers of Commerce

Mauritius Chamber of Commerce and Industry, 3 Royal Street, Port Louis (tel: 208-3301; fax: 208-0076; e-mail: mcci@intnet.mu).

Banking

African Asian Bank Limited, Office 5, 8th Floor, Max City Building, Corner Louis Pasteur & Remy Ollier Streets, Port Louis (tel: 240-7002, 240-7350; fax: 240-7009).

Bank of Baroda, African Asian Bank Limited, PO Box 553, Sir William Newton Street, Port Louis (tel: 208-1504; fax: 208-3892).

Bank of Mauritius, PO Box 29, Sir William Newton Street, Port Louis (tel: 202-3800; fax: 208-9204).

Banque Nationale de Paris Intercontinentale, 1 Sir William Newton Street, Port Louis (tel: 208-4147/8/9, 208-4151/2; fax: 208-8143).

Delphis Bank Limited, 16 Sir William Newton Street, Port Louis (tel: 208-5061; fax: 208-5388).

Development Bank of Mauritius Ltd, PO Box 157, Chaussée, Port Louis (tel: 208-0241; fax: 208-8498).

Indian Ocean International Bank Ltd, 34 Sir William Newton Street, Port Louis (tel: 208-0121; fax: 208-0127).

Mauritius Commercial Bank Ltd, 9-15 Sir William Newton St, Port Louis (tel: 202-5000; fax: 208-7054).

South East Asian Bank Ltd, 26 Bourbon Street, PO Box 13, Port Louis (tel: 208-8826/7/8, 212-2884/6/7; fax: 208-8825).

State Bank of Mauritius Ltd, PO Box 152, State Bank Tower, 1 Queen Elizabeth II Ave, Port Louis (tel: 202-1111; fax: 202-1234).

Central bank

Bank of Mauritius, Sir William Newton Street, Port Louis (tel: 208-4164 fax: 208-9204; e-mail: bomrd@bow.intnet.mu).

Stock exchange

The Stock Exchange of Mauritius: www.stockexchangeofmauritius.com

Travel information

Air Mauritius, Rogers House, 5 President John F. Kennedy Street, PO Box 441, Port Louis (tel: 208-7700; fax: 208-8331).

Ministry of tourism

Ministry of Tourism, Emmanuel Anquetil Bldg, Sir Seewoosagur Ramgoolam St, Port Louis (tel: 201-2286).

National tourist organisation offices

Mauritius Tourism Promotion Authority, 11th Floor, Air Mauritius Centre, President John Kennedy Street, Port-Louis (tel: 210-1545; fax: 212-5142; e-mail: mtpa@intnet.mu; Internet: www.mauritius.net).

Ministries

Ministry of Agriculture and Natural Resources, NPF Bldg, 9th Floor, Port Louis (tel: 212-7946; fax: 212-4427).

Ministry of Arts, Culture, Leisure and Reform Institutions, Government Centre, Port Louis (tel: 201-2032).

Ministry of Civil Service Affairs and Employment, Government Centre, Port Louis (tel: 201-1035; fax: 212-9528).

Ministry of Co-operatives and Handicraft, Life Insurance Corporation of India Bldg, 3rd Floor, John Kennedy St, Port Louis (tel: 208-4812; fax: 208-9265).

Ministry of Economic Planning and Development, Emmanuel Anquetil Bldg, Sir Seewoosagur Ramgoolam St, Port Louis (tel: 201-1576; fax: 212-4124).

Ministry of Education and Science, Sun Trust Bldg, Edith Cavell St, Port Louis (tel: 212-8411; fax: 212-3783).

Ministry of Energy, Water Resources and Postal Services, Government Centre, Port Louis (tel: 201-1087; fax: 208-6497).

Ministry of the Environment and Quality of Life, Barracks St, Port Louis (tel: 212-8332; fax: 212-9407).

Ministry of External Affairs, Government Centre, Port Louis (tel: 201-1416; fax: 208-8087).

Ministry of Finance, Government Centre, Port Louis (tel: 201-1145; fax: 208-8622).

Ministry of Fisheries and Marine Resources, Port Louis.

Ministry of Health, Emmanuel Anquetil Bldg, Sir Seewoosagur Ramgoolam St, Port Louis (tel: 201-1910; fax: 208-0376).

Ministry of Housing, Lands and Town and Country Planning, Moorgate House, Port Louis (tel: 212-6022; fax: 212-7482).

Ministry of Industry and Industrial Technology, Government Centre, Port Louis (tel: 201-1221; fax: 212-8201).

Ministry of Information, Government Centre, Port Louis (tel: 201-1278; fax: 208-8243).

Ministry of Internal and External Communications, Emmanuel Anquetil Bldg, 10th Floor, Sir Seewoosagur Ramgoolam St, Port Louis (tel: 201-1089; fax: 212-1673).

Ministry of Justice, Jules Koenig St, Port Louis (tel: 208-5321).

Ministry of Labour and Industrial Relations, Ming Court, cnr Eugène Laurent and GMD Atchia Sts, Port Louis (tel: 212-3049; fax: 212-3070).

Ministry of Local Government, Government Centre, Port Louis (tel: 201-1215).

Ministry of Manpower Resources and Vocational and Technical Training, Jade House, Remy Ollier St, Port Louis (tel: 242-1462).

Ministry for Rodrigues Island, Fon Sing Bldg, Edith Cavell St, Port Louis (tel: 208-8472; fax: 212-6329).

Ministry of Social Security and National Solidarity, cnr Maillard and Jules Koenig Sts, Port Louis (tel: 212-3006).

Ministry of Trade and Shipping, Government Centre, Port Louis (tel: 201-1067; fax: 212-6386).

Ministry of Women's Rights, Child Development and Family Welfare, Rainbow House, cnr Edith Cavell and Brown Sequard Sts, Port Louis (tel: 208-2061; fax: 208-8250).

Ministry of Works, Treasury Bldg, Port Louis (tel: 208-0281; fax: 212-8373).

Ministry of Youth and Sports, Emmanuel Anquetil Bldg, Sir Seewoosagur Ramgoolam St, Port Louis (tel: 201-1242; fax: 212-6506).

Prime Minister's Office, Government Centre, Port Louis (tel: 201-1001; fax: 208-8619).

Other useful addresses

British High Commission, Commercial Section, 7th Floor, Les Cascades Building, Edith Cavell Street, Port Louis (tel: 208-9850/1; fax: 212-8470).

Export Processing Zone Development Authority, 5th Floor, Les Cascades, Edith Cavell St, Port Louis (tel: 212-9760; fax: 212-9767).

Mauritius Embassy (USA), Suite 441, 4301 Connecticut Avenue, NW, Washington DC 20008 (tel: (+1-202) 244-1491; fax: (+1-202) 966-0983; e-mail: mauritius.embassy@prodigy.net).

Mauritius Employers' Federation, Cerné House, Chausse, Port Louis (tel: 212-1599; fax: 212-6725).

Mauritius Export Processing Zone Association, 42 Sir William Newton St, Port Louis (tel: 208-5216; fax: 212-1853).

Mauritius Free Port Authority, 2nd Floor, Deramann Tower, Sir William Newton St, Port Louis (tel: 212-9627; fax: 212-9629).

Mauritius Industrial Development Authority, Level 2, BAI Bldg, 25 Pope Hennessy St, Port Louis (tel: 208-7750; fax: 208-5965; e-mail: mida@media.intnet.mu).

Mauritius Offshore Business Activities Authority, 1st Floor, Deramann Tower, 30 Sir William Newton St, Port Louis (tel: 212-9650; fax: 212-9459).

Mauritius Standards Bureau, Ministry of Industry and Industrial Technology, Réduit (tel: 454-1933; fax: 464-7675).

Internet sites

Africa Business Network: www.ifc.org/abn

AllAfrica.com: http://allafrica.com

African Development Bank: www.afdb.org

Business Directory: www.mauritius.co.uk/

Mbendi AfroPaedia (information on companies, countries, industries and stock exchanges in Africa): http://mbendi.co.za

Mexico

KEY FACTS

Official name: Estados Unidos Mexicanos (United Mexican States)

Head of State: President Felipe de Jesús Calderón Hinojosa (took office on 1 Dec 2006)

Head of government: President Felipe Calderón (PAN) (from 1 Dec 2006)

Ruling party: Coalition, led by Partido Revolucionario Institucional (PRI) (Institutional Revolutionary Party), with Partido Acción Nacional (PAN) (National Action Party) (from 2000; re-elected 2009)

Area: 1,958,201 square km

Population: 112.34 million (2010; census figure)

Capital: Mexico City (DF)

Official language: Spanish

Currency: Mexican peso (Mex$) = 100 centavos

Exchange rate: Mex$13.83 per US$ (Oct 2011)

GDP per capita: US$9,566 (2010)

GDP real growth: 5.50% (2010)

GDP: US$1,039.10 billion (2010)

Labour force: 46.20 million (2009)

Unemployment: 5.40% (2010) (plus additional underemployment)

Inflation: 4.20% (2010)

Oil production: 2.96 million bpd (2010)

Balance of trade: -US$3.01 billion (2010)

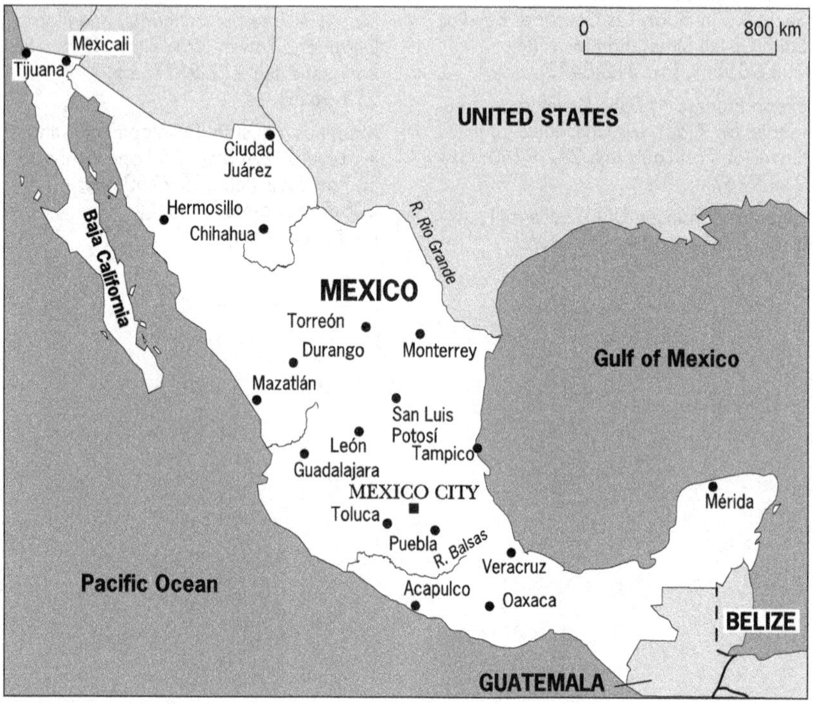

In an article entitled *Mexistan* the former US Commissioner of Customs (1981–89), William von Raab, quoted from Alan Riding's book *Distant Neighbours* in which he set out a litany of the factors that made Mexico 'More like Afghanistan than America.' 'There is unbridled violence, financing of corrupt activities through drug trafficking, control of what should be governmental authority by brigands or worse and corruption all the way through the social and political hierarchy.'

Mr von Raab makes the point that in the 1980s the US authorities had driven air and sea drug traffic out of the south-eastern US. The cartels' response was to move their reception areas across the border into Mexico and to smuggle the drugs by land across the length of the border with the US. The *fuerza motriz* behind this trend were the Colombian drug cartels, who had enlisted the support of local Mexican criminal organisations in their efforts to defeat the US Customs' controls. Mr von Raab quotes a White House source as saying that 'Drugs were not on the agenda in the West Wing.' He draws the inevitable conclusion that such is the size of the problem, that before long the US may have to get tough with Mexico, adopting a comparable response to the cartels as it has to al Qaeda in Afghanistan.

The Mexican government, under President Felipe Calderón has looked less than able to come up with any sort of cogent answer. Over 40,000 people have been killed in drug violence since the government began its offensive against the cartels in 2006. Tourism revenues have fallen by 10 per cent from US$13.3 billion in 2008. Overall numbers may have perked up a little but income has lagged behind. It is hardly surprising that American tourists are hesitant about visiting their neighbour to the south. In February 2011 a US agent was killed and 52 Mexicans died in an arson attack on a Monterrey casino. In September, on a highway in downtown Veracruz, 35 corpses were dumped in front of rush-hour traffic. Veracruz is on one of the main routes for both drugs and migrants heading northwards. The US government has warned against non-essential travel to Mexico. In March 2011 the Texas department of public safety warned students not to travel to Mexico for their spring break with the blunt message 'Stay Alive'.

The death, in early December 2010 of Nazario Moreno the head of Michoacan's *La Familia* cartel brought an end to a year in which senior members of virtually every major drug gang in Mexico had been killed. Cartel leader Arturo Beltrán Leyva was shot dead by marines in Mexico City and shortly afterwards, Victor Mendoza of the Zetas' hierarchy was assassinated by a hit squad from the Gulf cartel. In turn, the Gulf cartel's co-leader Antonio Cárdenas was killed by the Mexican army in November 2010.

In mid-2011 Mexico's presidential elections may have been little less than a year away, but candidates from the three major parties were already getting their acts together. No less than seven aspiring candidates to succeed President Felipe Calderón were from his own party, the ruling Partido Acción Nacional (PAN) (National Action Party). But the outgoing President appeared to have placed his succession onto the back burner, preoccupied with the drug related violence that had claimed the lives of so many Mexicans since he took office in 2006. Initially, the Calderón administration had claimed that the casualties were, for the most part, criminals involved in inter-cartel feuding. Most Mexicans knew that this was not the case. 'Collateral' casualties such as the April 2011 discovery of 183 corpses discovered in mass graves near San Fernando in Tamaulipas state near the US frontier were reported to include a car salesman and a social worker, as well as a Guatemalan migrant. San Fernando appeared to be on a fault line: the bodies of 72 migrants were discovered there in 2010. In each case the killings were attributed to the Zetas cartel. The involvement of officialdom in the San Fernando drug smuggling activities was alleged when 17 local police officers were among the 74 people arrested. However preoccupied he was, Mr Calderón had little success to show; on the contrary, Mexico's free-fall into violence was beginning to give it the attributes of a failed state. Although the *Distrito federal* (DF – the area including and immediately surrounding Mexico City) claims to be safer than most parts of Mexico, in 2010 the murder rate had increased by 25 per cent since 2006. But in Mexico no-one trusts official statistics. When murders are described as 'mis-classified' then it is almost certain that the figures have been manipulated.

Calderón's failure to deal with the drug violence showed itself in the opinion polls, as voters appeared to favour the return of the Partido Revolucionario Institucional (PRI) (Institutional Revolutionary Party) which had governed Mexico for 70 years until 2000 when the PAN's Vicente Fox won the presidential election. In 2011 the PRI governed in 19 of Mexico's 32 states after winning a number of key gubernatorial elections in mid-2011. Enrique Peña Nieto, the outgoing governor of Mexico state has been seen as the PRI's candidate-in-waiting. Andrés Manuel López Obrador, the former presidential candidate for the Partido de la Revolución Democrática (PRD) (Party of the Democratic Revolution) was in November again selected as the PRD candidate. Mr López Obrador narrowly lost to Mr Calderón in 2006 and refused to accept the election result, resulting in an extended stand-off that saw his supporters take to the streets. Despite having already – and very nearly successfully – competed in one election campaign, Mr López Obrador at 56 is still relatively young. Most opinion polls showed the PRI with a clear lead over the PAN. The two determining factors seemed to be the government's manifest failure to deal with the drug problem (serious enough for some observers to suggest that Mexico was close to becoming a failed state), and the parlous state of the economy. As it turned out, Mexico's economy was very much on the mend in 2011. In 2010 gross domestic product (GDP) had grown by an impressive 5.3 per cent (see Economy below).

The PRI's likely candidate, Enrique Peña Nieto, had a lot going for him. Good looking and young (46) he is now married to *Telenovela* (soap opera) star Angélica Rivera. PRI supporters saw the possibility of regaining the presidency as the restoration of their rightful position in Mexican politics. In contrast to the slick professionalism of Mr Nieto, the other two parties looked to be almost in disarray. The governing PAN lacked anyone of stature and risked coming third in the election, behind the left leaning PRD. The PRI's lead would seem to be one of image more than substance. Across the political spectrum, no party has been able to come up with anything resembling a plausible strategy for returning order to Mexico's streets and ridding it of pervasive corruption.

The drug problem

The government's handling of the drug problem has, unsurprisingly, been heavy-handed and inept. In its defence, few countries have ever had to tackle a problem as widespread, vicious and insidious. Faced with the inability of its police force to cope with heavily armed opposition,

KEY INDICATORS **Mexico**

	Unit	2006	2007	2008	2009	2010
Population	m	103.26	105.79	106.68	107.55	112.34
Gross domestic product (GDP)	US$bn	840.01	893.37	1,090.00	874.90	1,039.10
GDP per capita	US$	8,060	9,649	10,217	8,135	9,566
GDP real growth	%	4.8	3.3	1.5	-6.5	5.5
Inflation	%	3.6	3.9	5.1	5.3	4.2
Unemployment	%	3.2	3.4	4.0	5.5	5.4
Industrial output	% change	5.0	1.9	0.5	-7.3	–
Agricultural output	% change	4.8	2.1	3.1	1.8	–
Oil output	'000 bpd	3,683.0	3,477.0	3,157.0	2,979.0	2,598.0
Natural gas output	bn cum	43.4	46.2	54.9	58.2	55.3
Coal output	mtoe	5.3	9.2	5.5	5.3	4.5
Exports (fob) (goods)	US$m	250,292.0	271,875.0	291,343.0	229,783.0	298,473.0
Imports (fob) (goods)	US$m	256,131.0	281,949.0	308,603.0	234,385.0	301,482.0
Balance of trade	US$m	-5,839.0	-10,074.0	-17,261.0	-4,602.0	-3,009.0
Current account	US$m	-2,220.0	-8,687.0	-15,889.0	-5,734.0	-5,640.0
Total reserves minus gold	US$m	76,271.0	87,109.0	95,126.0	99,589.0	120,262.0
Foreign exchange	US$m	75,448.0	86,309.0	93,994.0	94,103.0	114,884.0
Exchange rate	per US$	10.85	10.82	11.12	13.51	12.64

the government had little option but to resort to the military. This has lead to the arrest and even summary killing, of large numbers of people suspected of involvement in Mexico's drug gangs. This in turn has lead to inevitable and by international standards largely justified, criticism from the US and numerous human rights bodies. In 2010 the US did not hand over a part of its aid funding for Mexico in protest over military abuses. The funding withheld was not insignificant – US$26 million from a total aid budget (under the so called Mérida Initiative) of US$1.4 billion. In April 2011 the United Nations asked Mexico to think again over its use of the military in the light of what were termed 'involuntary disappearances'. An estimated 45,000 troops have been deployed, charged with confronting the drug barons. US academics at the University of San Diego researching the use of the Mexican military were quoted in the *International Herald Tribunel* as saying that 'Its role has shifted from eradicating drug crops in remote rural areas to its current urban deployments to restore order and reclaim lost spaces in Mexico's largest cities.' Despite the murder of innocent victims and other recognised abuses, the involvement of the military against the drug cartels appears to be popular with most Mexicans, glad to see any opposition to the otherwise steady encroachment of the cartels.

The economy

In the view of the World Bank, in mid-2011 Mexico, the second largest economy in Latin America, was recovering from a brief but very deep recession – resulting mostly from its heavy reliance on oil exports and its trade with the United States. According to the Consejo Nacional de Evaluación de la Política de Desarrollo Social (CONEVAL) (National Council on Evaluation of Social Development Policy) the number of Mexicans living in poverty increased by 3.2 million from 2008 to 2010, following the global economic crisis. It implies that around 46.2 per cent of Mexico's total population (52 million people) live in poverty, mainly in urban areas. Meanwhile, extreme poverty reduced slightly from 10.4 to 10.2 per cent (11.5 million people). The fact that extreme poverty held steady over that period is attributed to targeted social protection programmes such as the *Oportunidades* Conditional Cash Transfer initiative and the *Seguro Popular* universal health insurance.

Real GDP in Mexico increased by 5.3 per cent in 2010 after contracting by 6.1 per cent in 2009. According to the United Nations Economic Commission for Latin America and the Caribbean (ECLAC) this partial recovery in economic activity was mainly sustained by the dynamism of exports. Consumption picked up moderately owing to a fall in real wages and weakness in the labour market, while gross fixed investment experienced only a slight expansion. Inflation was about 4.2 per cent at year's end, down on the 5.3 per cent of a year earlier. The urban open unemployment rate improved to 6.6 per cent in the third quarter of 2010 from 7.7 per cent in the same quarter of 2009. The current account deficit declined slightly as a percentage of GDP to 0.6 per cent from the 0.7 per cent recorded in 2009, as exports grew strongly. The public-sector fiscal deficit, including investment by Petróleos Mexicanos (Pemex), ended 2010 at 2.7 per cent, an increase on the 2009 figure of 2.3 per cent.

ECLAC estimates that the economy will expand by 3.5 per cent in 2011, as export growth tails off and domestic demand remains slack. The Bank of Mexico (central bank) expects its annual inflation target of 3 per cent to be met in late 2011, which is feasible if there are no new external shocks and the trend towards higher international commodity prices seen in late 2010 does not persist. Expectations are for a fiscal deficit of 2.3 per cent, including Pemex investment.

Mexico's 2011 Revenue Act provided for minor changes, most notably an increase in special taxes, leaving for later a comprehensive fiscal reform to make fiscal revenues less heavily dependent on oil. The new law assumes an average exchange rate of 12.9 pesos to the dollar in its estimates of fiscal revenue associated with oil exports.

Public-sector budgetary revenues grew by 0.1 per cent in real terms between January and September 2010 compared to the previous year. Tax revenues were 10 per cent of GDP and total oil revenues grew by 4.9 per cent in real terms (see Energy below), as lower volumes were offset by higher prices. Value added tax (VAT) revenue increased by 19.9 per cent in real terms thanks to an increase in the VAT rate from 15 per cent to 16 per cent and renewed economic growth. Similarly, an increase from 28 per cent to 30 per cent in the top income tax rate produced real-term growth of 12.5 per cent in the yield from this tax. This is explained by the substantial non-recurring revenues received in 2009 from the Bank of Mexico operating surplus and the recovery of Fondo de Estabilización de los Ingresos Petroleros (FEIP) (Oil Revenues Stabilisation Fund) resources, while in 2010 special fiscal benefits had been granted to the areas affected by Hurricane Alex.

Budgeted spending increased by 2.2 per cent in real terms between January and September 2010 compared with the same period in 2009, with particularly large rises in social development spending (5.7 per cent) and transfers to the states (14 per cent). Domestic borrowing was the main source of financing for the fiscal deficit (about two thirds of the total). Conversely, physical investment fell by 4 per cent in real terms. At the close of the third quarter, net federal public sector debt was worth 30.7 per cent of GDP (0.6 percentage points above the closing figure for 2009), which was lower than the average for the member countries of the Organisation for Economic Co-operation and Development (OECD) but higher than the Latin American average. Of this total, domestic debt represented 21.1 per cent of GDP and net external debt 9.6 per cent of GDP (0.5 and 0.1 percentage points more than at the close of 2009, respectively).

In the general environment of low inflation, the Bank of Mexico kept its reference interest rate, the one-day interbank rate, unchanged at 4.5 per cent for the first 11 months of the year.

With a view to strengthening the economy against possible external shocks, the Foreign Exchange Commission, comprising the Bank of Mexico and the Secretariat of Finance and Public Credit, decided to increase the pace of its international reserves build-up. Accordingly, these reserves grew strongly over the year – from US$91 billion at its start to US$110.54 billion towards its end. A flexible credit line of US$48 billion was renewed with the International Monetary Fund (IMF) in March for the same purpose.

November 2010 saw the announcement of the formal start of negotiations between Brazil and Mexico on a strategic economic integration agreement. This agreement between the two largest economies of Latin America is expected to include not just tariff reductions but also matters relating to services, investment, government procurement and intellectual property, among other things.

ECLAC noted that economic activity expanded strongly in the first three quarters of 2010, with average growth of 5.8 per cent. There was a slowdown in the third quarter (5.3 per cent) because of softer external demand. In the same period, agriculture recorded average growth of 4.4 per cent. The manufacturing industry staged a remarkable recovery, with average growth of 11.2 per cent. Nonetheless, preliminary figures to September 2010 reflected the beginnings of a slowdown in manufacturing, associated with the slackening of growth in the United States economy.

Formal employment grew steadily in the first 10 months of the year and by 31 October had exceeded its pre-crisis level (14.8 million workers). Nonetheless, the proportion of people who were under-employed or working in the informal economy remained high at 8.4 per cent and 27.3 per cent of the economically active population, respectively. The real minimum wage was down by 1.2 per cent in October on its level at the start of 2010.

Goods exports totalled US$243 billion between January and October, 32 per cent up on the same period in 2009, while those of manufactures had increased by a substantial 31.9 per cent. Mexico replaced Canada to become the second-largest exporter of manufactures to the United States after China. Nonetheless, growth began to slow in September, doubtless because of the loss of dynamism in the United States economy.

Imports were 30.4 per cent higher in the first 10 months of the year than in the same period the year before. Imports of consumer goods were up by 27.8 per cent and those of intermediate goods by 36.7 per cent, while capital goods imports were 2 per cent lower. By contrast with earlier upturns and thanks to the dynamism of exports, recovery was not accompanied on this occasion by any marked deterioration in the current account balance.

Energy

In 2010, Mexico was the seventh-largest oil producer in the world and the third-largest in the Western Hemisphere. State-owned Petróleos Mexicanos (Pemex) is one of the largest oil companies in the world. Oil production has decreased in recent years as production at the giant Cantarell field continues to decline. The oil sector is a crucial component of Mexico's economy: while its relative importance to the general Mexican economy has declined in the long term, the oil sector still generated 14 per cent of the country's export earnings in 2010, according to Mexico's central bank. Any decline in oil production has a direct effect upon the country's overall fiscal balance. In early 2011, Mexico held licensing rounds for performance-based contracts on oil blocks allowing participation to foreign oil companies for the first time since the nationalisation of the oil industry in 1938. The foreign firms will have no ownership rights over any oil they produce, but they are expected to provide Mexican fields with badly needed technological improvements According to the *Oil and Gas Journal* (OGJ), Mexico had 10.4 billion barrels of proven oil reserves as of 1 January 2011. Most reserves consist of heavy crude oil varieties, with the largest concentration of reserves occurring offshore in the southern part of the country, especially in the Campeche Basin. There are also sizable reserves in Mexico's onshore basins in the northern parts of the country. The country produced an average of 3.0 million barrels per day (bpd) of total oil liquids during 2010, down from 3.2 million bpd in 2008. Of Mexico's oil production, 86 per cent was crude oil and condensate, the rest consisting of natural gas liquids (NGL) and refinery gain. Investment by foreign oil companies from current and future licensing rounds will likely be required to develop Mexico's deep offshore reserves in the Gulf of Mexico and shale oil deposits in the north. Mexico is a net importer of refined petroleum products, with 447,000bpd coming from the United States alone in 2010.

Mexico nationalised its oil sector in 1938, creating Pemex as the sole oil operator in the country. Pemex has four operating subsidiaries: Exploration and Production, Gas and Basic Petrochemicals, Petrochemicals, and Refining. Pemex is the largest company in Mexico and one of the largest oil and natural gas companies in the world.

In 2008, Mexico enacted legislation that sought to reform the country's oil sector. The goal of these reforms was to enable Pemex to curb the slide in oil production experienced over the previous several years. The measures included several administrative changes, such as adding new seats to Pemex's administrative board for outside industry experts, creating a new advisory board designed to provide independent co-ordination of long-term energy strategy and establishing a new hydrocarbons agency to regulate the sector. The reforms permit Pemex to create incentive-based service contracts with foreign oil companies. Pemex also received greater autonomy under the reforms, including the ability to establish more flexible mechanisms for procurement and investment. In March 2011 Pemex announced Mexico's first production licensing round in more than 70 years, with 20 blocks to be tendered to international bidders.

Most of Mexico's oil production occurs in the Gulf of Campeche, located off the south-eastern coast of the country. The two main production centers in the area include Cantarell and Ku-Maloob-Zaap (KMZ), with smaller volumes also coming from the fields off the coast of Tabasco state. In 2010, Cantarell and KMZ represented 54 per cent of Mexico's total crude oil production. Due to the concentration of Mexico's oil production in the Gulf of Campeche, any tropical storms or hurricanes passing through the area can disrupt oil operations. In 2008, Pemex developed a new onshore field in the north at Aceite Terciario, which produced 41,000bpd in 2010.

The Cantarell oil field was once one of the largest oil fields in the world, but production there has declined dramatically in the past several years. In 2010, Cantarell produced 558,000bpd, down 19 per cent from the 2009 level and down 74 per cent from the peak production level of 2.14 million bpd in 2004. As production at the field has declined, so has its relative importance to Mexico's oil sector: Cantarell contributed 22 per cent of Mexico's total crude oil production in 2010, compared with 63 per cent in 2004, while other, more prolific fields have emerged. KMZ is now the highest producing field in Mexico. Another offshore field, Litoral Tabasco, has increased production from 212,300bpd in 2009 to 248,100bpd in 2010, partially offsetting the losses at Cantarell.

The US Government Energy Information Administration (EIA) forecasts that Mexico will produce 2.85 million bpd of oil in 2011 and 2.83 million bpd in 2012. The decline is driven mainly by falling production at the super-giant Cantarell field, which has only been partially offset by higher production from other areas. The EIA forecasts that Mexico will become a net oil importer by 2020, with net imports of over 1 million bpd by 2035. As one of the largest oil exporters to the United States, this has important implications for future US energy supplies. From Mexico's perspective, changing into a net oil importer would have important repercussions on the overall economy, due to the dependence of the federal government on Pemex for a sizable share of its revenues.

In 2010, Mexico exported 1.3 million bpd of crude oil, up from 1.2 million bpd in 2009. The United States receives the vast majority of Mexico's crude oil exports, which mostly arrive via tanker at the Gulf Coast. In 2010, the US imported

1.14 million bpd of crude oil from Mexico and about 140,000bpd of refined products, mostly residual fuel oil, naphtha and other unfinished oils.

Natural gas

According to OGJ, Mexico had 12.0 trillion cubic feet (tcf) of proven natural gas reserves as of January 2011. According to Pemex, the southern region of the country contains the largest share of proven reserves. However, the northern region is likely will be the center of future reserves growth, as it contains almost ten times as much probable and possible natural gas reserves as the southern region.

Mexico's natural gas production has grown in recent years, following steady declines during the late 1990s. Since 2007, natural gas consumption has also grown steadily, driven mostly by the electricity sector, whose share of total natural gas consumption increased from 29 per cent in 2000 to 48 per cent in 2009. According to Pemex, the company itself is the single largest consumer of natural gas, representing around 40 per cent of domestic demand in 2010.

In 2010, Mexico produced 2.1tcf of natural gas, while consuming 2.2tcf, with imports coming both via pipeline from the United States and liquefied natural gas (LNG).

Pemex holds a monopoly on natural gas exploration; however, private participation is permitted in non-associated gas production. The Mexican government opened the downstream natural gas sector to private operators in 1995, though no single company may participate in more than one industry function (transportation, storage, or distribution). It also created the Energy Regulatory Commission (CRE) to monitor the sector.

Mexico's natural gas production is spread throughout the country. Onshore fields in the northern part of the country represented 36 per cent of Mexico's natural gas production in 2010, while onshore fields in the south contributed 25 per cent and offshore fields in the Gulf of Campeche represented the remainder. While crude oil production at the Cantarell field has fallen in recent years, natural gas production has risen dramatically: natural gas production at the field increased from 278 billion cubic feet (bcf) in 2005 to 457bcf in 2010. However, the increase in natural gas production at Cantarell also has led to an increase in natural gas flaring, as there isn't adequate capacity to capture and process all of the new growth in production. According to NOAA, flaring of natural gas in Mexico increased from 75bcf in 2006 to 126bcf in 2008. However, gas flaring did decline to 88bcf in 2010, likely due to decreases in oil production. The Burgos Basin in northern Mexico has been a center for natural gas exploration and production and it currently represents about one-quarter of total natural production.

Risk assessment

Economy	Good
Politics	Fair
Regional stability	Good

COUNTRY PROFILE

Historical profile

The Olmecs inhabited the country around 3,500 years ago, their civilisation reaching its peak about 1200 BC. By AD 500–600, the Mayas had risen to prominence and Teotihuacan (where Mexico City now stands) was thriving, with 200,000 inhabitants.

1519 The Spanish, and Hernan Cortés, arrived. The Aztecs were the dominant culture.

1810–21 The Spanish colony became independent. Conflicts with the US and France ensued.

1876–1910 The Porfirio Díaz dictatorship, known as the *Porfiriato*, led to a series of revolutions and coups.

1910 The Epic Revolution, led by Emiliano Zapata, began

1911 Porfirio Diaz was overthrown. Francisco Madero, a liberal and one of the revolutionary leaders, became president. He introduced land reform and labour legislation. Political unrest continued with Zapata leading a peasant revolt in the south.

1913 Madero was assassinated. Victoriano Huerta seized power.

1914 Huerta resigned. He had been viewed with suspicion by the United States for his alleged pro-German sympathies. Huerta is succeeded by General Venustiano Carranza, preventing the re-emergence of the *Porfiriato*.

1917 Mexico's modern liberal constitution was adopted, enshrining land reform and labour rights.

1920 Carranza was assassinated. Civil war broke out.

1929 President Plutarco Elías Calles created the Partido Nacional Revolucionario (PNR) (National Revolutionary Party), a multi-class party that developed institutionalised mechanisms which enabled and controlled popular participation in government.

1934 General Lázaro Cárdenas became president and restructured the PNR, renaming it the Partido de la Revolución Mexicana (PRM) (Party of the Mexican Revolution). He also created official unions for workers and peasants, which were controlled by the official party.

1939 Disenchanted middle-class conservatives launched the Partido de Acción Nacional (PAN) (National Action Party).

1940 Leon Trotsky was assassinated in Mexico.

1946 Miguel Alemán became president and renamed the ruling party the Partido Revolucionario Institucional (PRI) (Institutional Revolutionary Party), signifying the final transition from the ideals of the revolution to liberal capitalism and a corporatist state.

1968 Growing disenchantment with authoritarian politics and rising urban poverty led to a series of mass demonstrations, culminating in a massacre of several hundred peaceful demonstrators, most of them young students.

1970 Luis Echeverría Alvarez became president, seeking to calm political turbulence through increased state spending and bolstering the power of trade unions.

1976 José López Portillo was appointed president. Oil revenues were used to borrow additional capital to initiate a rapid transition towards industrial development.

1982 A debt crisis was sparked by an economic recession in the US which left Mexico unable to obtain enough loans to service existing debts. A programme of economic stabilisation and structural adjustment was initiated under the administration of President Miguel de la Madrid.

1988 The PRI split. The left-wing *corriente democrática* joined a coalition of minor parties to back the presidential candidacy of Cuauhtémoc Cárdenas, son of former president, Lázaro Cárdenas. Despite massive electoral fraud, Cárdenas still managed to come second behind the PRI's Carlos Salinas de Gortari.

1992 As part of Mexico's commitments in the run-up to the signing of the North American Free Trade Agreement (Nafta), Salinas effectively repealed Article 27 of the Mexican Constitution which had guaranteed land reform.

1994 The Zapatistas led an uprising in Chiapas state in response to the treatment of indigenous peasants and neo-liberal economic policy. The Zapatistas attracted worldwide sympathy and attention was fixed on the effects of Mexico's economic policy and Nafta on the growing number of Mexican poor. The PRI's presidential candidate, Luis Donaldo Colosio, was murdered; many believed the killing was carried out by members of his own party.

1994 Ernesto Zedillo of the PRI won the presidential election amid accusations of dirty tricks and vote buying.

2000 PAN won parliamentary elections, the PRI lost the presidency and its majority in the Senate, as well as its status as the party with the largest number of seats in the lower house. The break with PRI rule was historic, as the party, including its previous incarnations, had enjoyed continuous office since 1929.

2001 The Senate unanimously approved a constitutional bill granting autonomy to indigenous people.

2002 Roberto Madrazo won the elections for the leadership of PRI.

2005 Six prison officers were murdered and all high security jails were put on alert, following an escalation of tension between the authorities and drug gangs.

2006 Felipe de Jesús Calderón Hinojosa (PAN) narrowly won the presidential election. The president declared war on drug cartels, with a new federal police force and thousands of troops deployed to the western state of Michoacán.

2007 Over 75,000 people protested in Mexico City and more in other locations, at the rapid rise in prices of basic foodstuffs. Tortillas, the staple food particularly among the poor, had risen by 40 per cent in the previous months and at a rate far faster than inflation in general. The price increases were largely due to the cost of maize imports from the US where such produce has been redirected for use in bio-fuel.

2008 There were 1,400 deaths due to organised drug cartels recorded in the first five months, bringing to 4,000 the number of drug trafficking related deaths since the beginning of the police crackdown in 2006. The navy seized a makeshift submarine smuggling almost six tonnes of cocaine to the US, while the army seized 12 tonnes of marijuana in Tijuana.

2009 The first case of a worldwide flu virus (H1N1) epidemic, characterised as a 'mild' strain, was reported in Mexico. The virus rapidly infected over 1,500 people in 20 countries and killed 26 people. The PRI made impressive gains by winning 241 seats in elections for the Chamber of Deputies, and became the leading political party in the coalition government.

2010 Amid an upsurge in drug-related gang violence gubernatorial and mayoral elections were held in 14 out of the 31 states of Mexico in July. The PRI won the majority of states in contention.

2011 The 31 January governorship election in Guerrero was won by Angel Aguirre of the left wing Partido de la Revolución Democrática (PRD (Democratic Revolutionary Party); Manuel Añorve of the opposition PRI was runner-up. Thousands of demonstrators joined marches in over 20 cities around the country on 6 April. They were protesting against the drug related violence that has estimated to have killed over 35,000 people since President Calderón began deploying the army to fight the cartels in December 2006. The PRI retained the governorship of Mexico State in the 3 July election. General elections were set for 2012 and voter frustration at the slow rate of economic reform under PAN is expected to make the election a close one. A drought, the worst since 1930s, left lakes and reservoirs low by the end of 2011. Agricultural output was affected as communities and farms became dangerously low on water, with the risk of food insecurity for many of the most vulnerable in Mexico. The drought was forecast to last into 2012.

Political structure

Constitution

The political system established by the 1917 constitution emphasises presidential power.

Mexico is a federal republic of 31 states and one federal district (Mexico City). States are divided into municipalities. State governors are directly elected every six years. Deputies of state legislatures hold office for three years. The states are empowered to raise taxes and introduce and enforce state laws.

In order to register for federal elections, political parties must have a total of at least 65,000 party members and must have 3,000 supporters per state in at least 16 states or 300 party members per constituency in at least half of the constituencies which return deputies elected by majority vote. Alternatively, a party may be allowed conditional registration if it has been active for four years. This conditional registration can be converted to official registration if the party then obtains at least 1.5 per cent of the vote. In 1989, a law was adopted giving a party obtaining 35 per cent of the vote in a general election an absolute majority in the chamber of deputies.

Form of state

Federal presidential democratic republic

The executive

The president is directly elected by majority vote for a period of six years and takes office on 1 December of the election year, but is unable to stand for a second term. The president is assisted by a cabinet (usually 19 members), one of whom is the governor of the Federal District (the administrative area which includes the capital, Mexico City), the attorney general for the country as a whole and the attorney general for the Federal District. The cabinet is appointed by the president.

The president also appoints the judges of the supreme court and higher courts of justice, the senior officers of the armed forces and diplomats, but these appointments are subject to approval by the Senate.

National legislature

The Congreso de la Union (Congress (of the Union)) is a bicameral legislature comprising the Chamber of Deputies and the Senate. Membership of the Chamber of Deputies is per 200,000 citizens and in 2009 there were 500 *diputado federal* (federal deputies), of which 300 are directly elected in single-seat districts. The remainder are elected by proportional representation from party lists and not tied to districts. All members of the Chamber of Deputies are elected for only one three-year term.

The Senate (upper chamber) has 128 members. Each state (31) and the federal district elects senators by relative majority (64 in number) based on a winning vote; an additional 32 senators are elected as runners up in the vote and a further 32 seats are divided among the parties in proportion to their share of the national vote. All members of the Senate are elected for only one six-year term.

Legal system

Under the 1917 constitution, the judiciary is independent of the executive and legislative bodies, but in practice the judiciary tends not to oppose the president.

The judicial system is divided into federal and state judiciaries.

The federal system has both ordinary and constitutional jurisdiction. It consists of the 21-member supreme court (which deals with penal, administrative, civil and labour cases), collegiate circuit courts (cases regarding an individual's constitutional rights) and unitary circuit courts (appeals). There are 12 collegiate circuits and nine unitary circuits. There are 68 district courts.

Last elections

2 July 2006 (presidential); 5 July 2009 (parliamentary).

Results: Chamber of Deputies: Partido Revolucionario Institucional (PRI) (Institutional Revolutionary Party) won 36.68 per cent of the vote, (241 seats (out of 500)), Partido Acción Nacional (PAN) (National Action Party) 27.98 per cent (147), Partido de la Revolución Democrática (PRD) (Democratic Revolutionary Party) 12.20 per cent (72), Partido Verde Ecologista de México (PVEM) (Ecologist Green Party of Mexico) 6.71 per cent (17), Partido del Trabajo (PT) (Labor Party) 3.68 per cent (nine), Partido Nueva Alianza (PNA) (New Alliance Party) 3.41 per cent (eight), Convergencia (Convergence) 2.49 per cent (six).

Senate: PAN won 34.1 per cent (11 seats out of 128); ABT 29.8 per cent (36), AM 27.4 per cent (38), PNA 4.2 per cent (1), PASC 2.0 per cent (1).

Presidential: Felipe de Jesús Calderón Hinojosa narrowly won with 35.88 per cent of votes; Manuel López Obrador won 35.31 per cent.

Next elections

2012 (presidential and parliamentary)

Political parties

Ruling party

Coalition, led by Partido Revolucionario Institucional (PRI) (Institutional Revolutionary Party), with Partido Acción Nacional (PAN) (National Action Party) (from 2000; re-elected 2009)

Main opposition party

Partido de la Revolución Democrática (PRD) (Democratic Revolutionary Party)

Population

112.34 million (2010; census figure)

Last census: 17 October 2005: 103,263,388

Population density: 51 inhabitants per square km (2000). Urban population: 74 per cent (1995–2001).

Annual growth rate: 1.5 per cent 1994–2004 (WHO 2006)

Ethnic make-up

Mestizo (mixed Indian-European) (55 per cent), Amerindian (29 per cent), European origin (16 per cent).

Religions

Roman Catholic (89 per cent), Protestant (6 per cent).

Education

Compulsory education is provided free of charge. Primary schooling lasts for six years; secondary education (which begins at age 12), is divided into two cycles of three years. Students either follow an academic or technical programme of education, which can lead on to higher education or specialised training.

In 1985, the government reorganised state education with priority given to literacy. A high proportion of spending has traditionally gone into higher education, with much of this devoted to adult literacy. While higher education has received relatively strong funding, the school system suffers from low teachers' pay, a consequent lack of teacher motivation and poor equipment. There is a high student drop-out rate from schools. Legal restrictions on religious education have reduced the willingness of the Catholic Church to provide education on a fee-paying basis. However, the falling birth rate has relieved some pressure on the school system. The student-teacher ratio, which reached a high point of 35.67 in 1964, improved during the 1980s and 1990s and was 27 by 2002.

At university level the private sector is active, although most Mexicans still attend state universities where fees are low. Standards are variable but often good. However, only a minority of students attending university complete their studies.

Literacy rate: 91 per cent adult rate; 97 per cent youth rate (15–24) (Unesco 2005).

Compulsory years: Six to 16

Enrolment rate: 106 per cent gross primary enrolment of relevant age group (including repeaters); 64 per cent gross secondary enrolment; 16 per cent in tertiary education (World Bank).

Pupils per teacher: 27 in primary schools (World Bank)

Health

Access to clean drinking water is available to over 80 per cent of the population. About half of the hospitals belong to the Instituto Mexicano del Seguro Social (IMSS) (Mexican Institute for Social Security).

HIV/Aids

HIV prevalence: 0.3 per cent aged 15–49 in 2003 (World Bank)

Life expectancy: 74 years, 2004 (WHO 2006)

Fertility rate/Maternal mortality rate: 2.3 births per woman, 2004 (WHO 2006)

Child (under 5 years) mortality rate (per 1,000): 23 per 1,000 live births; about 7.5 per cent of children aged under five are malnourished (World Bank).

Welfare

Social welfare is administered primarily by the IMSS and financed by contributions from employees, employers and the government. Some institutions, such as Petróleos Mexicanos (Pemex) (Mexican Petroleum), the military and the Federal Electricity Commission, have their own systems. About half of the working population is covered by social security. There is no unemployment benefit.

Since 1997, Mexicans have been able to sign up with private pension fund administrators, bypassing the IMSS, notorious for its inefficiencies as a state operator. The previous government led by the Partido Revolucionario Institucional (PRI) (Institutional Revolutionary Party) transferred the pension system from a state-funded pay-as-you-go basis to a scheme where private fund administrators compete for workers' pension contributions.

Main cities

Mexico City (capital, estimated population 8.5 million in 2005; 2,240 metres above sea-level), Ecatepec (2.0m), Guadalajara (1.6m), Puebla (1.4m), Ciudad Juárez (1.4m), Tijuana (1.5m), Nezahualcóyotl (1.2m), Monterrey (1.1m), León (1.2m), Zapopan (1.2m), Naucalpan (865,256), Tlalnepantla (699,847), Guadelupe (776,098), Acapulco (743,112), San Luis Potosí (721,619), Aguascalientes (707,964), Chihuahua (751,100), Merida (750,855).

Languages spoken

Native American languages spoken include Náhuati, Maya and Zapoteco. Some English is spoken in business centres.

Official language/s

Spanish

Media

The French-based Reporters Without Borders stated in 2008 that Mexico was the worst country in the Americas for violence against journalists reporting on organised crime. The authorities and the judiciary were considered hostile and unsupportive.

Press

With a population of over 100 million people the daily readership of newspapers is only around three million, which reviewers have ascribed to the politically biased nature of the press.

Dailies: In Spanish, the most influential newspapers include *Reforma* (www.reforma.com), *Excélsior* (www.exonline.com.mx), *La Jornada* (www.jornada.unam.mx) and *Diario de México* (www.diariodemexico.com.mx). The Organización Editortial Mexicana (www.oem.com.mx) publishes many newspapers throughout the country including *El Sol de Mexico*, *La Prensa* and one of the mass circulation newspapers on sport *Ovaciones*.

Weeklies: In Spanish, *Milenio* (www.milenio.com), *Proceso* (www.proceso.com.mx) and *Transición* (www.grupotransicion.com.mx) are influential political and analytical magazines. Other general interest magazines include *Siemprele* (www.siempre.com.mx) and *Vértigo* (www.revistavertigo.com).

In English, *Baja Times* (www.bajatimes.com), *Guadalajara Reporter* (http://guadalajarareporter.com), *Gringo Gazette* (www.gringogazettenorth.com) published in northern Mexico and from Mexico City *The News* (www.thenewsmexico.com).

Business: There are several publications available, which although carry a majority of business and financial news also cover more tabloid stories, including, in Spanish *El Economista* (http://eleconomista.com.mx), *Mundo Ejecutivo* (http://ejecutivo.mundoejecutivo.com.mx), *Expansion* (www.cnnexpansion.com), *Siglo 21* (www.siglo21.com.mx), *El Financiero* (www.elfinanciero.com.mx) and *Biz News* (www.biznews.com.mx) of North Mexico.

Periodicals: In Spanish, *Etcétera* (www.etcetera.com.mx) is a current affairs magazine.

Broadcasting

The huge, multinational, media group, Televisa (www.televisa.com.mx) was the first Latin American oligopoly producing

Spanish language programmes for transmission worldwide. Since the introduction of modern media technology from satellite, internet and digital platforms Televisa's dominant hold has been broken.

Radio: There are well over 1,200 local radio stations, of which many are operated by the 35 regional networks in operation.

Grupo Radio Centro (http://radiocentro.com.mx) is one of the largest networks, broadcasting from Mexico City; Grupo ACIR (www.grupoacir.com.mx) is another, as is W Radio (www.wradio.com.mx) operated by the Televisa Group. Instituto Mexicano de la Radio (IMER) (www.imer.com.mx) is the state-run radio station, with an external service via short-wave.

Television: The popularity of watching television has become a leading pastime. There are over 400 television stations with a complex structure of interaction between regulators and TV providers, which critics have said has disadvantaged the interests of the masses.

Televisa (www.televisa.com.mx) a national network, with many affiliates, has the highest ratings. TV Azteca (www.tvazteca.com) is the seconded rated TV network. Public TV includes Once TV (http://oncetv-ipn.ne) is an educational channel and Televisión Metropolitana (Canal 22) (www.canal22.org.mx) is a cultural network.

Digital broadcasting began in 2004 and analogue television is expected to be closed down in 2022. Most TV stations broadcast via satellite providing hundreds of channels from which to choose.

Advertising

Television attracts around 70 per cent of annual adspend, with newspapers and magazines achieving around 12 per cent. Annual advertising expenditure is equivalent to approximately 1.5 per cent of GDP. Most international advertising companies have offices in Mexico City.

News agencies

National news agency: NTMX (Notimex)

Other news agencies: El Universal (in Spanish): www.agenciaeluniversal.com.mx Agencia Mexicana de Noticias (in Spanish): www.agenciamn.com

Economy

Mexico's economy is a diverse mixture of modern hi-tech, an interdependent manufacturing base that relies on trade with the US, and subsistence agriculture that is not part of the formal economy. Exports are the mainstay of the economy providing around 60 per cent of GDP with over 75 per cent of all commodities exported to the US. In return Mexico derives around 40 per cent of all foreign direct investment (FDI) from the US; total FDI was US$18.67 billion in 2010. The downturn in the US economy impacted on Mexico in two ways – first as the US reduced its imports, and secondly, with 10 per cent of its population living and working abroad, mostly in the US, remittances, which are an important factor in Mexico's GDP fell from US$26.30 billion in 2008 to US$22.15 billion in 2009 (2.5 per cent of GDP). The figure for 2010 was estimated to have risen slightly to US$22.57 billion in 2010.

As a member of the North American Free Trade Agreement (Nafta) Mexico's manufacturing base serves not only its large domestic market but also the huge US market. A large number of the world's major companies are present in Mexico, using the cheaper labour market for manufacturing-based industries, driven by the initial growth of the *maquiladoras* (in-bond assembly lines) and the development of import-export business, particularly in the car and light manufacturing industries. Asian electronics companies, for instance, proliferate in the west coast state of Baja California, which is host to a multitude of operations run by companies based in the Far East. Ironically the rise of Chinese exports direct to the US has begun to have an adverse effect on Mexican exports.

GDP growth in 2008 was 1.2 per cent, falling from 3.3 per cent in 2007, but in 2009 the economy fell into recession with negative growth of -6.2 per cent. A recovery was achieved in 2010 with GDP growth of 5.4 per cent as world trade expanded. Government revenue is typically 22 per cent of GDP, of which hydrocarbons account for around 8 per cent; the non-oil sector remains constant at around 14 per cent.

An outbreak of the pandemic flu virus H1N1 (swine flu) in 2009 rocked the economy, closing down much of Mexico City (the country's economic powerhouse, which generates around 20 per cent of GDP) for a week, losing US$88 million per day and deterring tourists. The tourism sector typically provides 8 per cent of GDP and was the hardest hit with revenue down by 50 per cent for 10 days in May. The government estimated the country as a whole lost around US$100 million per day during the height of the crisis.

Inflation ranged from its lowest 3.6 per cent in 2006 to 5.3 per cent in 2009, the highest rate over 2000–10, due to economic reforms undertaken by the Partido Acción Nacional (PAN) government and the reduction in external public debt. Unemployment in the formal sector remained fairly constant at around 3.5 per cent since 2004, but as the recession struck unemployment rose to 4 per cent in 2008 and rose further to 5.5 per cent in 2009 and then 5.4 in 2010. Informal and underemployment is much higher at around 25 per cent and could go higher as the global economic crisis undermines the economy.

Proven oil reserves were 11.4 billion barrels at the end of 2010, with production of 2,958 million barrels of oil per day; production is, however, falling – oil fell by 0.8 per cent between 2009–10. Natural gas production rose by 0.7 per cent in the same period.

External trade

Mexico is a member of the North American Free Trade Agreement (Nafta), with the United States and Canada. Mexico has also signed free trade agreements with the European Union, the Central American Free Trade Agreement (DR-Cafta) and Japan.

The economy is heavily dependent on trade, and foreign trade accounts for around 60 per cent of GDP, of which 80 per cent is carried on with the US. There are free economic zones, *maquiladoras*, where semi-manufactured and duty-free goods are assembled and shipped directly to the US. A leading *maquiladoras* product was finished garments but heavy competition from Asian manufacturers has resulted in a drop in production since 2005.

Mexico is a leading world exporter of many minerals and agricultural products as well as petroleum and natural gas.

Imports

Principal imports are metalworking machines, steel mill products, agricultural machinery, electrical equipment, capital machinery for car assembly and aircraft building and parts.

Main sources: US (typically over 55 per cent of total), Brazil (30 per cent), China (5.0 per cent), South Korea (5.0 per cent).

Exports

Principal exports are manufactured and assembled goods, petroleum and oil products, vehicles and auto parts, silver, cotton, corn, oranges and other fruits, vegetables and coffee, mercury, zinc and fluorite.

Main destinations: US (typically over 75 per cent of total), Canada (10 per cent)

Agriculture

Farming

Approximately 5 per cent of Mexico's total GDP is attributable to the agricultural sector. Despite this relatively low percentage contribution to GDP, the labour intensive nature of the agricultural sector ensures that it employs up to a quarter of the total workforce.

Farming is small-scale and frequently inefficient. About 50 per cent of total cultivatable land (estimated at 19 million

hectares) is held by *ejidos*, rural communities farming on small individual/collective lots. There are few large commercial farms except in export-oriented vegetable-producing regions of the north-west.
The principal food crops are maize (over 50 per cent of harvested area and 60 per cent of total grain production), sorghum, wheat, rice, barley, potatoes, soya beans and dry beans. The production of basic foodstuffs can be severely affected by drought, insufficient irrigation (less than 30 per cent of cultivated land is irrigated) and underdeveloped marketing and infrastructural back-up. Supplies of food grain in particular have not kept up with the demands imposed by rapid population growth. Principal export crops are coffee, cotton, fresh fruit, honey, sugar, tobacco and tomatoes. Exports of cattle are also important.
Mexico's membership of the North American Free Trade Agreement (Nafta) has affected the farming sector, with the US dominating trade.
A sharp frost in February 2011 caused the loss of around four million tonnes of corn (16 per cent of the annual national harvest) in Sinaloa State in northern Mexico. Efforts to re-sow the crops were undertaken within two weeks, but the loss could increase the price of corn tortillas, the staple diet for the majority of the population; increases that had caused food riots in previous years.
A drought, the worst since 1930s, left lakes and reservoirs low by the end of 2011. Agricultural output was affected as communities and farms became dangerously low on water, with the risk of food insecurity for many of the most vulnerable in Mexico. The drought was forecast to last into 2012.

Fishing

Mexico's level of fish production is relatively high, with demand being met almost entirely by domestic production. Imports represent only 8.2 per cent of total seafood consumption.
Shrimps, tuna, mackerel, bass, perch, bonito, shark, oysters have risen in importance in the Mexican fishing sector. The leading fish producing states – Sinaloa, Sonora, Baja California, Veracruz and Baja California Sur – contribute to approximately 65.2 per cent of the country's total catch. Annually 70 per cent of the total catch comes from the Pacific Ocean compared to 30 per cent from the Gulf of Mexico, Caribbean and non-coastal states.

Forestry

Approximately 55.2 million hectares of Mexico's total landmass is covered by forests and the country is endowed with vast resources of soft and hard woods. Around 4 per cent of the country's total forested area is protected.
Most forestry products are produced for domestic consumption, mainly softwood sawnwood and wood-based panels.

Industry and manufacturing

The industrial sector is an important economic activity in Mexico, accounting for a significant proportion (29 per cent) of total GDP. About one fifth of total employment is accounted for by the sector.
The *maquiladoras* (in-bond assembly lines) make, assemble or process components and raw materials bought 'in-bond' from the US which are then re-exported duty-free. The growing importance of *maquiladora* exports to the US has made the Mexican economy more exposed to US demand.

Tourism

Mexico's tourism industry continues to grow strongly and the country remains Latin America's premier tourist destination. Travel and tourism now accounts for 14.5 per cent of total GDP and 14.2 per cent of total employment. Capital investment in the industry has also increased significantly in recent years and now accounts for 10.4 per cent of total capital investment in the economy.
Americans, wishing to avoid overseas travel and to holiday closer to home, visit Mexico, many by cruise ships.

Mining

Mining is an important industry in Mexico and the country is a major producer of gold, silver and base metals. Mexico accounts for approximately 17 per cent of total world production of silver, 38 per cent of celestite production and 29 per cent of bismuth production. The mining sector continues to attract significant foreign investment, the vast majority of which comes from the US and Canada.
There are four major domestic producers: Industrias Peñoles, Grupo Industrial Menera Mexico, Empresas Frisco and Luismin. The main mining states are Sonora, Coahuila, Zacatecas, Chihuahua, Baja California Sur, San Luis Potosí, Durango and Guanajuato.

Hydrocarbons

Proven oil reserves were 11.4 billion barrels in 2010, with production at 2.9 million barrels per day (bpd). Mexico is a significant oil producer and the oil sector is vital to the country's economy, providing around 40 per cent of government revenue. However, oil production in Mexico's largest oil field, Cantarell (located offshore in the Gulf of Mexico) which in 2003 was 2.1 million bpd, had plummeted to 772,000bpd by 2009. Without new sources of oil, not only will the economy be adversely affected but Mexico could become a net importer of oil by 2020.
The state-owned Petróleos Mexicanos (Pemex) is one of the world's largest multinational oil corporations. It has exclusive rights to oil exploration and production and is the sole supplier of petroleum products in Mexico. The majority of oil exports are taken by the US, supplied either by pipeline or tanker.
Although Mexico is not a member of the Organisation of the Petroleum Exporting Countries (Opec), government policy has often been to cut production in line with OPEC targets in an effort to increase world prices.
Mexico has the eleventh-largest refining capacity in the world, which has improved the country's export potential, with six refineries and a total capacity of 1.46 million bpd in 2010. Despite government plans to increase refinery capacity by 350,000bpd hurricane damage has led to unscheduled shut-downs and static annual capacity.
Petroleos Mexicanos (Pemex) lost around US$350,000 every day in 2010 from lost production of natural gas due to threats and violence from drug gangs operating in northern Mexico, centred on the Burgos gas field near the east Texas border.
Proven gas reserves were 500 billion cubic metres (cum) in 2010, with production at 55.6 billion cum. However, consumption was 68.9 billion cum and Mexico had to import the balance, either by natural gas pipelines from Canada and the US or by liquefied natural gas (LNG) from Egypt, Trinidad and Tobago and Nigeria.
Most gas production is associated with oil extraction. Although Pemex dominates the upstream gas industry, the downstream sector has undergone liberalisation which allows private companies to participate in gas transportation, storage and distribution. There are two LNG re-gasification plants in operation with another under construction and more, smaller facilities planned. In June 2011, TransCanada Corporation completed the Guadalajara Pipeline, to carry up to 14.2 million cubic metres of natural gas 310 kilometres from the LNG regasification terminal near Manzanillo (Colima State) to the city of Guadalajara (Jalisco State). The gas will be used primarily to run a series of gas-fired electricity generators in the city.
Mexico has proven coal reserves of 1.2 billion tonnes, mostly located in Coahuila in the north-east. Over 850 million tonnes are made up of anthracite, mainly used for steel production, with around 350 million tonnes in electricity generation.

Energy

Total installed generating capacity was 53.8 gigawatts in 2007, generating 243

billion kilowatt hours (kWh). Around 80 per cent of total electricity generated comes from conventional thermal sources, in particular from natural gas, with coal providing 10 per cent; hydropower accounts for around 10 per cent, while fuel oil and diesel have fallen in use. Alternative sources of energy, such as wind, solar and biomass, make up the remainder.
A contract to upgrade the sole nuclear power plant was let in 2007 and should provide 20 per cent of generating capacity when completed.
Independent power producers (IPPs) have become a major source of investment in the Mexican electricity sector. The government shut down the state-owned Luz y Fuerza del Centro energy company in October 2009, following losses of US$32.5 billion over 2003–08. Around 25 million customers were hastily transferred to other electricity providers across the country.
Mexico exports electricity to the US and is a participant of the Sistema de Interconexion Electrica para America Central (Siepac) to connect power grids with Guatemala and Belize and an integrated Central American electric power market.
In June 2011, TransCanada Corporation completed the Guadalajara Pipeline, to carry up to 14.2 million cubic metres of natural gas 310 kilometres from the LNG regasification terminal near Manzanillo (Colima State) to the city of Guadalajara (Jalisco State). The gas will be used primarily to run a series of gas-fired electricity generators in the city.

Financial markets

Stock exchange

Bolsa Mexicana de Valores (BMV) (Mexico Stock Exchange)

Commodity exchange

Mercado Mexicano de Derivados (Mexican Derivatives Exchange) (MexDer)

Banking and insurance

Mexico's banking and financial services sector is now well established, following privatisation in 1990. The sector had previously been nationalised in 1982. There are three main types of account held in Mexican banks; peso denominated checking accounts, US dollar checking accounts and certificates of deposit
Banco de México issues currency, controls monetary policy and is responsible for exchange rates and national reserves. Participation of the private sector is encouraged in a capital market involving leasing, mutual funds, insurance and brokerage. The banking crisis of 1995 caused by the turmoil of peso devaluation, resulted in the closure of several banks. The government was forced to inject huge amounts of emergency capital into the system. Mexico had 44 banks, 13 of which were government-owned.
Banamex is the country's largest bank, and comprises the operations of Citigroup and Banacci, which merged in August 2001.

Central bank

Banco de México

Main financial centre

Mexico City

Time

Central Mexico: GMT minus six hours (daylight saving, minus five hours)
Northern Mexico: GMT minus seven hours (daylight saving, minus six hours)
Sonora State: GMT minus seven hours (no daylight saving)
Baja State: GMT minus eight hours (daylight saving minus seven hours)

Geography

Mexico has a northern frontier of 2,400km with the US and a southern frontier of 885km with Guatemala and Belize. It has a coastline of 2,780km on the Gulf of Mexico and the Caribbean and of 7,360km on the Pacific and the Gulf of California.
Mexico comprises a great variety of terrain, ranging from swamp to desert, from tropical lowland jungle to high alpine vegetation and from thin, arid soils to others so rich that they can support three crops a year. More than half the country is at an altitude of over 1,000 metres and much is over 2,000 metres.
The centre is flanked by an eastern and a western range of mountains running roughly parallel to the coasts. The northern part of the plateau is low, arid and thinly populated. The southern section of the central plateau is crossed by a volcanic range of mountains. The mountainous southern end of the plateau, the heart of Mexico, has ample rainfall and although comprising only 14 per cent of the land, it holds nearly half the country's population. Mexico City lies in a small high basin measuring 50 square km.

Hemisphere

Northern

Climate

Varies with altitude. Tropical southern region and coastlands are hot and wet, while the highlands of the central plateau are temperate. Temperature in Mexico City ranges from 5–25 degrees Celsius (C) with occasional sharp frosts in winter (December–February).
Climate and vegetation depend on altitude. The *tierra caliente* (hot area) takes in the coastal and plateau lands below 750 metres. The *tierra fria* (cold zone) is from 2,000 metres upwards. The climate of the inland highlands is mostly mild, but with sharp changes of temperature between day and night, sunshine and shade.
Generally, winter is the dry season and summer the wet season. There are only two areas where sufficient rain falls all year round. The first lies south of Tampico, the capital of Tamaulipas state, along the lower slopes of the Sierra Madre Oriental and across the isthmus of Tehuantepec into Tabasco state, and the second along the Pacific coast state of Chiapas. The two areas represent about 12 per cent of the total surface area. Apart from these favoured regions, the rest of Mexico is arid.

Dress codes

People generally dress smartly in Mexico City. Shorts are worn only at holiday resorts. Dress codes for business and leisure are usually the same as those of Europe. There is little central heating and moderately warm clothing is needed in the winter, particularly at night. The capital, Mexico City, is 2,240 metres above sea level. At lower altitudes temperatures can be very high and lightweight clothing is essential.

Entry requirements

Requirements for Mexico are complex and comprehensive guidance should be obtained from consular sections of local embassies before departure, any infringement of regulations can result in fines and expulsion.

Passports

Required for all.

Visa

The regulations for entry into Mexico are complex and visitors are advised to confirm all aspects of visa requirements before travelling. Visas are not required by those using a tourist card, which are issued only to tourists and are valid for 30 days. All other visitors require visas. Business visas are divided into two, 'lucrative' and 'non-lucrative', and applications must be accompanied by a business letter of accreditation stating the nature of business, proof of sufficient funds for length of stay and a full itinerary, plus an invitation from a local company. See www.inm.gov.mx and follow the links, in English, to *I would like to visit Mexico* for full details, or www.mexonline.com for more general information.

Currency advice/regulations

The import and export of local currency is unrestricted up to the equivalent amount of US$10,000; amounts greater than this must be declared. The import of foreign currency is unlimited but must be declared as export is limited to the amount declared on arrival. The export of gold coins is prohibited.
Many establishments in cities or tourist areas accept payment in US dollars.

Travellers cheques in US dollars are readily accepted in most banks, hotels and commercial outlets.

Customs

There are sometimes rigorous searches for drugs, firearms or large sums of currency, and expensive jewellery or electronic equipment may attract attention and demands for customs duty. There are restrictions on the import of motor vehicles.

Prohibited imports

Fresh meat, particularly pork, fish, fruit, vegetables, flowers and seeds are prohibited unless a permit is obtained before travelling. Firearms and ammunition require an import licence.
Archaeological artifacts may not be exported.

Health (for visitors)

Mandatory precautions

A yellow fever vaccination certificate is required if arriving from an infected area.

Advisable precautions

Diphtheria, tuberculosis, hepatitis A and B, typhoid, tetanus and polio vaccinations. Malaria risk exists in some rural areas – prophylaxis recommended. There is a rabies risk. Dengue fever is endemic in northern regions.
Bottled water and water supplied from taps marked 'drinking/sterilised water' in hotels can be drunk without precautions. All other water should be regarded as potentially contaminated.
Mexico City is at 2.250 metres (7,400ft), and visitors may take some time to acclimatise to the altitude. The levels of pollution in Mexico City are extremely high and cab be a health threat.
Health insurance is advised. Medical facilities are good and pharmacies are permitted to diagnose and treat minor ailments.

Hotels

There are six classified types of hotels, of five stars and an additional *Gran Turismo*, with maximum rates set by the government.
Mexico City is one of the biggest cities in the world, so location is very important. The main hotels are in the business, financial and commercial area along Reforma Avenue. It is advisable to book in advance expecially during the high season and to confirm the booking in writing. There is a levy of 15 per cent VAT and 2 per cent accommodation tax added to bills – unless the visitor is from overseas travelling for meetings and conventions and fairs, who have confirmed their migatory status, use a credit card and make their arrangements through the event's organisers then VAT is exempt. Tipping is usually 10 per cent.

Credit cards

Visa and Mastercard are readily accepted, however there is a government tax of 6 per cent on transaction. ATMs are widely available.

Public holidays (national)

Fixed dates

1 Jan (New Year's Day), 5 Feb (Constitution Day), 21 Mar (Birthday of Benito Juárez), 1 May (Primero de Mayo), 5 May (Battle of Puebla Day), 1 June (Navy Day), 20 Nov (Revolution Day), 25 Dec (Christmas Day).
Religious holidays are celebrated by adherents.

Variable dates

Carnival (Jan/Feb, five days)

Working hours

Hours of business in Mexico City are variable and hours in other parts of the country vary considerably according to the climate and local custom.

Banking

Mon–Fri: 0900–1600; larger branches in Mexico city may opened Mon–Fri: 0800–1900; Sat 0800–1200. Small town branches may only open Mon–Fri 0800–1330.

Business

Mon–Fri: 0800–1800; lunch is taken anywhere between 1300–1500, for up to two hours.

Government

Mon–Fri: 0800–1500.

Shops

Mon–Sat: 1000–1800/1900.

Telecommunications

Mobile/cell phones

GSM 900 and 1900 services are available in highly populated areas only.

Electricity supply

120V AC, 60 cycles. Two-pin flat plugs (as in USA) are used.

Social customs/useful tips

During the working day moderate punctuality is appreciated although some lateness is tolerated. It is acceptable to arrive late for evening social occasions which often continue well into the night.
Mexicans are patient, courteous and hospitable and will often treat visiting foreigners with polite reserve. An effort to speak Spanish is much appreciated. Otherwise it is advisable not to presume too much until you know the people concerned fairly well.
Tipping in hotels, restaurants and bars is expected since service charges are not added to the bill. A normal tip is 15 per cent. If service has been very good, 20 per cent should be given.

Security

It is unwise to carry large sums of money or valuables in Mexico City, where the number of assaults is rising.
Visitors should be wary of walking through neighbourhood streets during festivities. Many Mexicans own guns and they tend to fire them in the air to celebrate, especially towards evening.
Armed robbery in urban areas is a risk. Short-term opportunistic kidnapping is common. Visitors should exercise care when using ATMs.

Getting there

Air

National airline: Aeroméxico (AM) and Mexicana (MX)

International airport/s: Mexico City-Benito Juárez (MEX), 13km south of city; duty-free shops, restaurants, bank, *bureau de change*, 24-hour refreshments, chemist, tourist information, 24-hour left luggage, post office, first aid (with vaccinations for cholera and yellow fever available) car hire.
A taxi to the city takes about 45 minutes. Prepaid taxi tickets are available from the 'Authorised Taxi Service' booth in baggage reclaim; authorised taxis are white and mustard yellow with an aeroplane logo. Travellers are strongly advised to take an authorised, prepaid taxi and to always lock taxi doors when inside.
Major hotels run shuttle minibuses from the airport. There is also a train and regular airport bus to the city centre.

Other airport/s: Acapulco (ACA) 26km from city; Guadalajara (GDL) 20km from city; Monterrey (MTY) 24km from city. All include restaurant, bank and car hire facilities; and access by taxi and bus.

Airport tax: Approximately US$21, which may be included in the ticket price, transit passengers are exempt.

Surface

Road: There are roads into Mexico from the US, Belize and Guatemala. Drivers should note that permission is required to bring a car into Mexico for longer than 72 hours.

Rail: Connections with Mexico can be made from any city in the US or Canada. All trains are provided with pullman sleepers, restaurant cars and club cars and most are air conditioned.

Water: Regular passenger ships run from the US and South America. There are also riverboat services from Flores and Tikal (Guatemala) to Palenque, Chiapas in Mexico. Enquire locally for further details.

Main port/s: Gulf of Mexico coast: Altamira, Cd del Carmen, Coatzacoalcos, Pto Madero, Tampico, Veracruz; Pacific coast: Acapulco, Ensenada, La Paz, Lázaro Cardenas, Mazatlán, Manzanillo,

Puerto Vallarta, Salina Cruz, Santa Rosalia.

Getting about

National transport

Air: There is a comprehensive network of daily scheduled services between main commercial centres.

Road: There are 95,000km of paved roads, about half of which are operated by the federal government, and the other half by the state governments. There are also more than 5,600km of toll roads, which are operated by private companies. Mexico's roads carry more than 85 per cent of the nation's overland freight and almost all intercity passengers.

Buses: There are three kinds, first- and second-class and local. It is advisable to book seats in advance in Baja California. Buses with odd numbers run north-south, while even numbered run east-west. Peribus services circulate Mexico City.

Rail: Rail services include special first-class, regular first-class and second-class. Routes include Guadalajara to Mexico City; Monterrey to Mexico City; Mexico City to Veracruz to Tapachula; Cuidad Juárez to Chihuahua. Services are slower than buses but electrification is in progress. There are sleeper services between Mexico City and Guadalajara, Monterrey, Veracruz, Ciudad Juárez, Chihuahua, Mérida. It is advisable to book well in advance.

Water: There are regular ferries from the mainland at Quaymas in Sonora, to Santa Rosalía in Baja California Sur. There are services to the Caribbean Islands of Isla Mujeres and Cozumel.

City transport

Taxis: Taxis are usually fitted with meters, but these are often not used. Agree fare in advance. No tip is necessary.

Fixed route taxis can be identified by lime-green colour, rank taxis by coral and those with no fixed route by yellow. There are around 17 fixed routes. The number of fingers held out of a taxi window indicates the number of seats left.

Special tourist taxis, *turismo*, have English-speaking drivers.

The safest means of transport is a *taxi de sitio* – dial-a-cab services which charge about double the metered street taxi rates, but which are still cheap by international standards. These can be found outside every hotel.

It is best to carry a map of Mexico City as taxi drivers cannot be relied on to know their way around the huge city.

Buses, trams & metro: The Mexico City Metro, with eight lines, is excellent, but often crowded. Runs 0500–0000 Mon–Sat; opens 0700 (Sun). Maps are not displayed at all stations, but can be obtained at Insurgentes station.

There is also a small tramway network, and extensive bus and trolley bus services. The latter system has been modernised, and also has a flat fare. There is a state-run bus and trolley bus service in Guadalajara, with trolley buses running in tunnels, and also extensive private bus services.

The Monterrey City metro system (called *Metrorrey*) has two lines with 25 stations, with more under construction, which runs from Sun–Sat: 0500–2400.

Car hire

Car hire is widely available, with or without a driver, but often expensive. A foreign licence is acceptable. Car hire is not recommended for business travellers or tourists because of excessive traffic, aggressive drivers, and counter-pollution measures which mean that on certain days of the week, driving is off limits.

BUSINESS DIRECTORY

Telephone area codes

The international direct dialling (IDD) code for Mexico is +52, followed by area code and subscriber's number:

Acapulco	744	Mexico City	55
Chihuahua	614	Monterrey	81
Ciudad Juárez	656	Oaxaca	951
Durango	618	Puebla	222
Guardalajara	33	Tampico	833
León	477	Torreón	817
Mérida	999	Veracruz	229

Useful telephone numbers

Police: 060

Fire/ambulance: 078

Highway emergency: 078

Locatel (service to locate missing persons or stolen cars): (55) 5658-1111.

Sectur (24-hour help to tourists in trouble): (55) 5250-0123

Chambers of Commerce

American Chamber of Commerce Mexico, Lucerna 78, Colonia Juarez, 06600 México, DF (tel: 5141-3800; fax: 5703-3908; e-mail: amchammx@amcham.com.mx).

British Chamber of Commerce in Mexico, 30 Río de la Plata, 6500 México, DF (tel: 5256-0901; fax: 5211-5451; e-mail: britchamexico@britchamexico.com).

Chihuahua Cámara Nacional de Comercio, Servicios y Turismo, 1800 Avenida Cuauhtemoc, 31020 Chihuahua (tel: 416-0000; fax: 415-1928; e-mail: cfn@infosel.net.mx).

Confederación de Cámaras Nacionales de Comercio, Servicios y Turismo, 144 Balderas, Colonia Centro, 06079 México, DF (tel/fax: 5722-9300; e-mail: sistemas@concanacored.com).

Guadalajara Cámara Nacional de Comercio, Servicios y Turismo, 4095 Avenida Vallarta, Fraccionamiento Camino Real, 45000 Guadalajara (tel: 3880-9090; fax: 3880-9097; e-mail: direccion@canacogdl.com.mx).

Juarez Cámara Nacional de Comercio, Servicios y Turismo, 4505 Avenida Henry Dunant y Avenida M Diaz, 32315 Ciudad Juarez (tel: 113-707; fax: 112-674; e-mail: canacojr@hotmail.com).

Mexico City Cámara Nacional de Comercio, 42 Paseo de la Reforma, Colonia Centro, 06048 México, DF (tel: 535-2502; fax: 703-2958; e-mail: presidencia1@ccmexico.com.mx).

Puebla Cámara Nacional de Comercio, Servicios y Turismo, 2704 Avenida Reforma, 72160 Puebla (tel: 480-705; fax: 480-800; e-mail: canacopu@axtel.net.mx).

Banking

Banamex, Actuario Robero Medellin 800, Colonia Santa Fé, 01219 México, DF (tel: 1226-2639; tel: 5999-2888).

Bancomer, Montes Urales 620,Colonia Lomas de Chapultepec, 11000 México, DF (tel: 5201-2264; fax: 5238-7790).

Banorte, Periférico Sur 4355, Colonia Jardines en la Montaña, 14210 México, DF (tel: 5169-9300; fax: 5169-9460).

Bital, Paseo de la Reforma 156, Juarez, 06600 México DF (tel: 5721-5715; fax: 5721-3846).

Santander Mexicano, Prolongación Paseo de la Reforma 500, Colonia Lomas de Santa Fé, 01210 México, D F (tel: 5257-8000; fax: 5629-4742).

Central bank

Banco de México, Avenida 5 de Mayo 1, Colonia Centro, Delegación Cuauhtémoc, 06059 (tel: 5237-2000; fax: 5237-2070; e-mail: sidaoui@banxico.org.mx; internet: www.banxico.org.mx).

Stock exchange

Bolsa Mexicana de Valores (BMV) (Mexico Stock Exchange): www.bmv.com.mx

Commodity exchange

Mercado Mexicano de Derivados (Mexican Derivatives Exchange) (MexDer): www.mexder.com

Travel information

Benito Juárez International Airport, Av Capitán Carlos León s/n Col Peñón de los Baños Del Venustiano Carranza, México, DF CP 15620 (tel: 5571-3600; fax: 5726-0107).

Fondo Nacional de Fomento al Turismo (FONATUR) 22nd Floor, Insurgentes Sur 800, Colonia del Valle, 03100 México DF (tel: 5687-0567/8; fax: 5687-5058, 5682-5058; email:

ibotas@fonatur.gob.mx; internet: www.fonatur.gob.mx).

Infotour, Zona Rosa, Amberes 54, Mexico City (tel: 5525-9380).

Ministry of tourism
Secretaría de Turismo (SECTUR) Presidente Mazaryck 172, Colonia Polanco, 11570 México DF (tel: 5250-8555; fax: 5250-4406 (general enquiries), 5254-0942 (marketing), email: correspondencia@mexico-travel.com; internet: www.mexico-travel.com).

National tourist organisation offices
Consejo de Promoción Turística de México, Mariano Escobedo 550, 11580 Mexico DF (tel: 5258-1090/2; email: cptmex@infosel.net.mx; internet: www.visitmexico.com).

Ministries
Ministry of Agrarian Reform (SRA), Tepozteco 36, 1er Piso, Col Vertiz Narvarte, 03020 Mexico (tel: 5579-6094; fax: 5579-3767).

Ministry of Agriculture, Rural Development and Livestock (SAGAR), Av Insurgentes Sur 476, 50. piso, Col Roma Sur, 06700 Mexico (tel: 5584-0808; fax: 5584-1177).

Ministry of Communication and Transport (SCT), Xola y Av Universidad, Cuerpo C, PB, Col Narvarte, 03028 Mexico (tel: 5538-5148; fax: 5519-9748).

Ministry of Defence (SEDENA), Blvd Manuel Avila Camacho y Av Industria Militar, Col Lomas de Sotelo, 11600 Mexico (tel: 5395-6766; fax: 5557-1370).

Ministry of Education (SEP), Brasil 31, PB oficina 115, Col Centro, 06029 Mexico (tel: 5329-6827; fax: 5329-6822).

Ministry of Energy (SE), Av Insurgentes Sur 552, 1er. Piso, Col Roma Sur, 06769 Mexico (tel: 5584-4304; fax: 5564-9782).

Ministry of Finance and Public Credit (SHCP), República de El Salvador 47, PA, Col Centro, 06080 Mexico (tel: 5709-6675; fax: 5709-3272).

Ministry of Fishing, Environment and Natural Resources (SEMARNAP), Anillo Periférico Sur 4209, 3er Piso, Col Jardines en la Montaña, 14210 Mexico (tel: 5628-0891; fax: 5628-0780).

Ministry of Foreign Affairs (SRE), Eje Central Lázaro Cardenas 257, ala 'A', 1er Nivel, Col Guerrero, 09600 Mexico (tel: 5782-3660; fax: 5327-3025).

Ministry of Health (SSA), Lieja 8, 50 piso, Col Juárez, 06600 Mexico (tel: 5553-7670; fax: 5286-5497).

Ministry of the Interior (SG), Abraham Gonzalez 48, PB, Col Juárez, 06699, Mexico (tel: 5535-2718; fax: 5535-9952).

Ministry of Labour and Social Welfare (STPS), Periférico Sur 4271, Edificio A, 1er Nivel, Col Fuentes del Pedregal, 14149, Mixico (tel/fax: 5645-3715).

Ministry of Naval Affairs (SM), Eje 2 Oriente 861, Tramo Heroica Escuela Naval Militar, Col Los Cipreses, Coyoacan, 04830 Mexico (tel: 5684-8188; fax: 5679-6411).

Ministry of Social Development (SEDESOL), Av Constituyentes 947-B, PB, Col Belén de las Flores, 01110 Mexico (tel: 5515-4508; fax: 5272-0118).

Ministry of Trade and Industry (SECOFI), Av Alfonso Reyes 30, 20 piso, Col Condesa, 06140 Mexico (tel: 5729-9193; fax: 5729-9314).

Other useful addresses
Asociación Nacional de importadores y Exportadores de la República Mexicana, Monterrey 130, Col Roma Sur, 06700, Mexico, DF (tel: 5564-9379; fax: 5584-5317).

Asociación Nacional para el Fomento de las Exportaciones Mexicanas, Ed de las Instituciones 702, Ocampo 250 Poncente Apartado 64100, Monterrey NL (tel: 5428-010, 422-143, 422-154; fax: 528-207).

Asociación de Personal Técnico para Conferencias Internacionales AC, Universidad 1855-502, Mexico 20, DF (tel: 5550-0170).

British Embassy, Lerma 71, Col. Cuauhtemoc, 06500 Mexico City (207-2569, 207-2089/2149; fax: 5207-2593, 207-7672).

Comptroller General (SECOGEF), Av Insurgentes Sur 1735, PB Ala Norte, Oficina 39, Col Guadalupe Inn, 01020 Mexico (tel: 5662-2762; fax: 5662-4511).

Confederación de Cámaras Industriales de los Estados Unidos Mexicanos, Manuel Maria Contreras 133, 8, Cuauhtemoc, 06597, Mexico DF (tel: 5546-9053; fax: 5535-6871).

Consejo Nacional de Comercio Exterior, Tiaxcala 177 Desp 803, Apartado 06100, Mexico DF (tel: 5286-8744, 286-8798; fax: 5211-8465).

Dirección General de Telecommunicaciones, Lázaro Cárdenas 567 11 Piso Ala Norte, Col Navarate, 03020 Mexico, DF (tel: 5519-4049, 530-3492, 519-0908; fax: 5559-9812).

Instituto de Intérpretes y Traductores SA, Rio Rhin 40, 06500 Mexico 5, DF (tel: 5566-7722, 566-8312).

Instituto Mexicano del Petróleo, Avenida Eje Central Lázaro Cardenas 152, 07730 Apartado 14-805, Mexico 14, DF (tel: 5567-6600).

International Telegraph Office, Balderas 14-18 Colon, Mexico DF.

Mexican Embassy (USA), 1911 Pennsylvania Avenue, NW, Washington DC 20006 (tel: (+1-202) 728-1600; fax: (+1-202) 728-1698; e-mail: mexembusa@aol.com).

Mexican Investment Board MIB, Paseo de la Reforma No. 915, Lomas de Chapultepec, 11000 Mexico (tel: 5202-7804; fax: 5328-9930).

Mexican Stock Exchange, Paseo de la Reforma 255, Colonia Cuauhtemoc, 06500 Mexico (tel: 5726-6600; fax: 5726-6805).

Pemex (Petróleos Mexicanos), Avenida Marina Nacional 329, Mexico 17, DF (tel: 5250-2611, 254-2044).

Public Telex Office, Vallejo y Norte 45, Mexico 2, DF/San Bartolo Naucaplan, Mexico 16, DF.

Secretariat of State for Commerce and Industrial Development, Alfonso Reyes 30, Mexico, DF (tel: 5286-1823, 211- 0036; fax: 5286-0804).

Secretariat of State for Energy, Mines and Federal Industry, Insurgentes Sur 552, 3, 06769 Mexico, DF (tel: 5564-9790; fax: 5574-3396).

Secretariat of State for Finance and Public Credit, Palacio Nacional, 1 Patio Mariano, 06066 Piso ofna 3045, Mexico, DF (tel: 5518-5420; fax: 5542-2821).

US Embassy, PO Box 3087, Paseo de la Reforma 305, Colonia Cuauhtemoc, 06500 Mexico City, DF (tel: 5211-0042; fax: 5207-8938).

National news agency: NTMX (Notimex), Morena 110, Col del Valle, Delg. Benito Juárez CP 03100 México DF (internet: www.notimex.com.mx).

Internet sites
Comprehensive information site: http://www.mexonline.com

El Heraldo newspaper http://www.heraldo.com.mx

General directory http://www.mexicoweb.com.mx

General guide http://www.mexconnect.com

Mexicana: airline http://www.mexicana.com

Mexican government agencies, chambers of commerce and other trade institutions (English) http://www.mexicosi.com

Statistics: http://www.inegi.gob.mx

Federated States of Micronesia

Growth in the Federated States of Micronesia (FSM) for the financial year October 2009/September 2010 was 0.5 per cent, thanks in part to projects including the extension of Pohnpei airport and the expansion of the fibre-optic communications network. There was also an increase in small-scale agriculture as commodity prices rose, and the fish processing plant at Kosrai was re-opened.

Planning for 2014 when grants under the Compact of Free Association with the US will cease, the FSM government trimmed expenditure by 3.6 per cent in 2010, cutting capital expenditure by almost 20 per cent, while raising current spending by 2.1 per cent, according to the Asian Development Bank. The government is also improving revenue collection.

Improved direct flights after the Pohnpei airport extension is completed in mid-2011 will expand opportunities for tourism and exports. Other than tourism, development in the private has been sluggish, held back by a lack of skilled labour and an inadequate infrastructure. GDP growth in 2012 is forecast at 0.8 per cent.

COUNTRY PROFILE

Historical profile

The Federated States of Micronesia (FSM) comprises four island states – the capital state of Pohnpei (formerly Ponape), Chuuk (known until 1990 as Truk), Yap and Kosrae. These were formerly Japanese League of Nations mandated islands.

1947 The islands became part of the UN's Trust Territory of the Pacific Islands (TTPI), administered by the US under a UN mandate.

1978 The FSM gained sovereignty following a constitutional convention and referendum.

1979 On implementing the FSM constitution, former districts became States of the Federation.

1982 FSM signed a 15-year Compact of Free Association (CFA, referred to as the Contract) with the US, which would retain responsibility for foreign affairs and defence.

1986 The Contract was implemented.

1990 The US Trusteeship was ended by the UN Security Council.

1991 FSM joined the UN.

1999 Talks on the relationship between the US and FSM following the ending of the Contract began.

2001 The Contract was extended for a further two years

2002 The super-typhoon Chata'an devastated the island of Chuuk, killing 37 people and destroying homes and crops. US federal funds were provided to help recovery and rebuilding.

2003 In FSM congressional elections, Joseph J Urusemal was elected.. A US$3.5 billion, 15-year, Contract was signed with the US.

2004 The super-typhoon Sudel devastated the island of Yap destroying 1,500 homes and utility facilities.

2006 China pledged around US$3.0 million in grant assistance to FSM. The first project to be undertaken with the funds is the Pohnpei State Administration building.

2007 FSM and the US Peace Corps celebrated 40 years of partnership in regional development. Parliamentary elections were held and congress elected Manny Mori as president.

2008 The Australian conman, Peter Foster, was jailed in Brisbane, Australia for money laundering and defrauding the Bank of FSM of around US$580,000.

2009 Foreign donations provided a photovoltaic (solar)-powered groundwater supply system and desalination units.

2010 FSM mourned the loss of two eminent persons: Chief Justice Andon L Amaraich, a founding father of the nation and an influential negotiator for the Compact of Free Association with the US, and Mau Piailug, a native navigator who taught how to navigate the vast Pacific Ocean using traditional knowledge and naturally occurring elements, such as tides, winds, stars, bird migrations and the position of the moon. They died on 26 January and 12 July respectively. The Chinese government granted FSM a concessionary loan of US$22 million in August, for use in refurbishing the main ports and adding facilities to include fish processing plants.

2011 In parliamentary elections held on 8 March, 14 non-partisan candidates were elected. In May 2011, the Federated State of Micronesia (FSM) challenged Czech

KEY FACTS

Official name: Federated States of Micronesia

Head of State: President Immanuel Manny Mori (from 11 May 2007)

Head of government: President Manny Mori

Ruling party: All parliamentary members sit as independents

Area: 607 Volcanic islands and coral atolls with land area of just over 700 square km

Population: 111,000 (2010)*

Capital: Palikir (in Pohnpei state)

Official language: English (nationwide); each state has its own official language including Pohnpeian, Ulithian, Woleaian, Yapese, Kosraean and Chuukese.

Currency: US dollar (US$) = 100 cents

Exchange rate: US$1.00 per US$ (fixed)

GDP per capita: US$2,497 (2009)

GDP real growth: 0.50% (2010)

GDP: US$269.70 million (2009)

Inflation: 3.50% (2010)

Balance of trade: -US$50.00 million (2008)*

* estimated figure

Republic government plans to expand its coal-fired Prunerov Two power plant, Europe's second-largest, which FSM reasoned such expansion, and the resulting increase in carbon dioxide output, could exacerbate problems of rising sea levels. FSM will use a legal instrument of the UN Convention on Environmental Impact Assessment in a Transboundary Context (known as the EIA convention) in Czech Republic courts and if successful will challenge similar projects in other signatory countries where the EIA convention applies. Parliament re-elected Manny Mori unopposed as president on 11 May. A grant from the European Union began construction of the Pohnpei State Emergency Operations Centre on 2 May. Legislation allowing for a controversial hotel and casino resort to be built on Pohnpei was passed on 29 May.

Political structure

Constitution
The constitution was promulgated in 1979, it guarantees fundamental human rights and established a separation of powers. Each state has a constitutional government with an elected governor and lieutenant governor. The US is responsible for defence and security issues.
Each state has its own constitution with a elected legislature, governor and power for implementing its own budget.
Form of state
A Federation of four states – Pohnpei, Chuuk, Kosrae and Yap; a self-governing territory in free association with the US.
The executive
The president and vice president are elected from a group of four senators, one nominated from each state, for a four-year term. The president is Head of State and head of government but does not exercise executive power, which is retained by the congress.
The president appoints a cabinet of supporters and technocrats.
National legislature
The unicameral congress has 14 non-partisan members; 10 members are elected in single seats constituencies for two-year terms (five from Chuuk, three from Pohnpei, one from Yap and one from Kosrae), four members are elected by proportional representation, one from each state, for four-year terms – these members provide the pool from which a president and vice president are chosen by congress members.
The congress exercises executive and legislative power.
Last elections
8 March 2011 (parliamentary); 11 May 2011 (presidential, in congress).
Results: Parliamentary: 14 non-partisan candidates were elected.
Presidential: Immanuel 'Manny' Mori was elected unapposed by parliament.
Next elections
2015 (parliamentary and presidential, in congress).

Political parties

There are no political parties; political allegiances follow family and island-related dynamics.
Ruling party
All parliamentary members sit as independents
Political situation
In an effort to find other revenue streams and reduce the reliance of FSM on the funding by the Compact of Free Association (with the US), President Mori set up a National Trade Facilitation Committee (NTFC) in 2008. One of the committee's first objectives was to formulate a comprehensive trade police to be used when FSM participates in international trade negotiations. Mori is also targeting FSM's need for foreign direct investment and China is rapidly become the country's high-profile donor. Self sustaining development would also include the world's most productive tuna resources and tourism. Construction of an extension to the airport runway in Pohnpei, should boost tourist numbers as larger jet aircraft, particularly from Japan, are able to land.
The project for an underwater, telecommunications optic cable had, by early 2008, secured the US$15 million necessary for phase one of the project. At the same time Mori has his eye on making FSM the agricultural centre of the region, not only to feed the growing domestic population but also the US military bases in Guam. The plans include investment in infrastructure and education with the re-opening of an abandoned agricultural and technical college on Pohnpei.

Population

111,000 (2010)*
Last census: April 2000: 107,008
Population density: 154 inhabitants per square km (2010)
Annual growth rate: 0.4 per cent 1994–2004 (WHO 2006)
Ethnic make-up
The population is composed of nine Micronesian and Polynesian groups.
Religions
Roman Catholic (50 per cent), Protestant (47 per cent).

Education

The education system is modelled after the US educational system. Over 30 per cent of the population attend secondary schools. Private elementary and secondary schools also exist, sponsored by religious groups. Although the College of Micronesia-FSM provides two- and three-year programmes, most students prefer to enrol in US tertiary educational institutions.
The Micronesia Maritime and Fisheries Academy in the State of Yap was set up to provide effective training in maritime and fisheries technologies, to cater for the growing demand for trained personnel in the expanding fishing industry.
Compulsory years: 6 to 14.
Enrolment rate: 142 per cent gross primary enrolment, of relevant age groups (including repeaters) (World Bank 2003).

Health

There are inadequate primary health care facilities, with little secondary and tertiary-level treatment facilities. In some states there are shortages of essential medical supplies including contraceptives. As a result patients have little choice but to travel to health facilities overseas. Government funds are channelled towards curative services rather than preventative and primary health care. The Asian Development Bank has granted loans for training health workers, improving medical supplies and extending a limited health insurance scheme to provide broader and universal coverage.
The number of cases of leprosy has increased; 124 new cases were reported in 2008.
Life expectancy: 70 years, 2004 (WHO 2006)
Fertility rate/Maternal mortality rate: 4.3 births per woman, 2004 (WHO 2006)
Birth rate/Death rate: 25.1 births per 1,000 population; 4.9 deaths per 1,000 population (2005).
Child (under 5 years) mortality rate (per 1,000): 30.2 per 1,000 live births (2005)

Welfare

Although the FSM does not produce a poverty profile as such, recent household income and expenditure surveys suggest that around 40 per cent of households could be considered as low income. Despite some remittances from overseas migrants, the number of low income households is still high. The lowest income households are on the outer islands where opportunities for formal sector employment and commercial activities are few.

Main cities

Palikir (capital, in Pohnpei State, estimated population 6,645 in 2005), Weno (on Chuuk) (13,758), Nett (7,365), Kitti (7,049), Tol (on Chuuk) (4,747), Tonoas (4,140), Kolonia Town (on Pohnpei) (5,360).

Languages spoken

English is the *lingua franca* of the country. Yap has four languages: Yapese, Ulithian,

Woleaian, and Satawalese; Pohnpei languages are Pohnpeian, Nukuoroan and Kapingamarangian, Chuukese in Chuuk and Kosraean in Kosrae. Other spoken languages include: Pingelapese, Ngatikese, Mokilese, Puluwatese and Mokilese.

Official language/s

English (nationwide); each state has its own official language including Pohnpeian, Ulithian, Woleaian, Yapese, Kosraean and Chuukese.

Media

Press

There are no daily newspapers but various weeklies, the *Pohnpei Business News*, *The Island Tribune* and *Micronesia Weekly* cover a range of subjects. The federal government publishes *The National Union*, with information bulletins, every fortnight, while state governments produce their own newsletters.

Broadcasting

Radio: There is a radio stations in each state, operated by both the government and a religious organisation through FSM Telecommunications (www.fm/radio.htm). Broadcasts are transmitted in English and the main local dialects.

Television: The government runs the only TV coverage on the islands KPON TV (on Pohnpei), TTKK TV (on Chuuk) and WAAB TV (on Colonia).

News agencies

ABC Pacific Beat:
www.radioaustralia.net.au/pacbeat
Pacific Magazine:
www.pacificmagazine.net
Pacific Islands New Association (Pina):
www.pina.com.fj

Economy

Fishing and subsistence farming are the main economic activities. Marine products generate almost all export revenues. Tourism is being developed, but the remoteness of the islands and the lack of air access are impediments.

The economy is dependent on US financial support, provided through the Compact of Free Association (CFA), which provided FSM with US$1.3 billion between 1986–2001. However this was modified in 2003 under a new agreement whereby both the US and FSM government contribute to a trust fund annually until 2023. All earnings from the trust fund will remain untouched until 2023 and thereafter will provide for FSM through payouts from the trust fund. However, the International Monetary Fund (IMF), in its November 2010 statement, advised that if FSM were to avoid a large revenue gap from 2024 then the government must increase its savings substantially, as well as the contributions to the trust fund. These payments should be achieved through tax reforms, expenditure cuts and improved governance and structural reforms to support the private sector. GDP growth was 0.5 per cent in 2009, following three years of negative growth. However the IMF also warned that activity in the private sector remained weak and the economy was dependent on public sector infrastructure projects for growth. It was also concerned that emigration in the near to medium-term could cause future contraction in the economy as active members of the community are lost. Capital investment in people, the infrastructure and telecommunications and IT were suggested as a means for FSM to provide long-term prosperity.

External trade

The FSM is a member of the South Pacific Regional Trade and Economic Co-operation Agreement (Sparteca) along with 12 other regional nations, which allows products duty free access by Pacific Island Forum members to Australian and New Zealand markets (subject to the country of origin restrictions).

FSM has an exclusive economic zone of almost 3 million square km of the Pacific Ocean and fish exports account for 80 per cent of export trade, mainly to Japan; it also has a bilateral trade agreement with the European Union regarding tuna fisheries.

Imports

Principal imports are petroleum, food, manufactured goods, machinery, equipment and beverages. Imports are approximately three times larger than exports.

Main sources: US (typically 40 per cent of total), Japan (10 per cent), Australia (4 per cent).

Exports

Principal exports are fish, garments, bananas and black pepper. Some beef, fruit and vegetables are also exported.

Copra was formerly Yap's principal export, but this has been overtaken by betel nut and pepper leaf, traditionally, used in chewing. A 'chew' consists of a betel nut wrapped in pepper leaf with a touch of lime powder made from burned coral; the combination stains teeth red and betel nut is described as mildly narcotic.

Main destinations: Japan, US, Guam

Agriculture

Farming

The agricultural sector contributes approximately 17 per cent to GDP. Subsistence farming is the main occupation and provides most of the food consumed in the territory.

Fishing

Fishing is the mainstay of the economy and generates most of the country's export revenues. International fishing fleets pay to fish in FSM's rich territorial waters, including one of the world's best tuna grounds. However, the sector is dominated by foreign owned companies operating offshore and so employs few local people.

The Pohnpei State government expanded its local fishing industry, using vessels which had been donated by the government of the Republic of Korea.

Fishing provides a primary source of protein for the local population.

FSM also typically harvests 150,000 pearls annually.

In April 2010 the Parties to the Nauru Agreement (PNA) (eight island states including FSM) collectively agreed to close to *purse seine* fishing in 4.55 million square kilometres of high seas in their area, from 1 January 2011, to vessels licensed to fish in their waters. The area involved stretches from Palau and Papua New Guinea in the west to Kiribati in the east, from the Marshall Islands in the north to Tuvalu in the south; it holds an estimated 25 per cent of the world's tuna supply.

On 12 April 2011, a summit of the Parties to the Nauru Agreement (PNA) concluded its strategy for a policy of sustainable fishing in the Pacific. The PNA treaty, which was established in 1989 and expires in 2012, is seen as in need of an overhaul. As a collective region (FSM, Kiribati, Marshall Islands, Nauru, Palau, PNG, Solomon Islands and Tuvalu) control around 25–30 per cent of world stocks of tuna. Only 5 per cent of sales revenue is returned to the PNA and ministers called for specific changes, including an increased share of profits, PNA crews on-board *purse seine* vessels (minimum 10 per cent), conservation and management measures including a limit to fish trapping (fish aggregating devices (FADs)), net mesh rules and the establishment of an observer agency and fisheries information management system.

Industry and manufacturing

Small-scale industries include handicrafts, fish processing, bottling, copra processing, bakeries and boat building. The Pohnpei Agricultural and Trade School runs a small coconut products plant, which makes 'Oil of Ponape' toiletries.

Most private sector activity is in retail and wholesale trade which are dependent on demand generated by government spending.

Tourism

Tourism accounts for only 6 per cent of GDP, but is a significant foreign exchange earner. The Asian Development Bank has identified tourism as one of FSM's highest potential growth industries, although the cost of airfares is seen as a hiderance to expansion. Tourist numbers have been

down, a trend that began in 2000 and although there was a recovery with 14,038 tourist arrivals in 2002 by 2004 numbers were as low as 10,000 people.
FSM is particularly attractive to divers and in 2004 tourist hotels related to the activity had an 80 per cent occupancy rate while general resorts reported typical occupancy rates of around 40 per cent.
The region's most spectacular scenery is underwater. The island of Chuuk has an underwater-wreck-museum where more than 60 Japanese ships, as well as planes, that were sunk during the Second World War are open to divers to view.

Environment
In May 2011, the Federated State of Micronesia (FSM) challenged Czech Republic government plans to expand its coal-fired Prunerov Two power plant, Europe's second-largest. Low-lying FSM is threatened by submersion as global warming adds to rising sea levels. It feels this expansion, and its resulting increase in carbon dioxide output could exacerbate its problems. FSM will use a legal instrument of the UN Convention on Environmental Impact Assessment in a Transboundary Context (known as the EIA convention) in Czech Republic courts and if successful will challenge similar projects in other signatory countries where the EIA convention applies.

Mining
Small mineral deposits exist, but there are doubts about the economic viability of commercial exploitation, which would be hampered by a shortage of land to accommodate any displaced population.
The FSM, Solomon Islands and Papua New Guinea will submit a joint proposal to the United Nations in 2009 to develop the Ontong Java Plateau, which is part of their extended continental shelf, for mineral prospecting.

Hydrocarbons
There are no known hydrocarbon reserves; all petroleum products are imported to meet domestic needs.

Energy
Each state has its own generating authority including the Chuuk Public Utility Corporation, Kosrae Utility Authority, Pohnper Utility Corporation and the Yap State Public Service Corporation, which are responsible for electricity generation and supply.
In 2008, as the implementation of national electrification based on solar-photovoltaic systems, was about to begin FSM utilities participated in technical training workshops run by Pacific Power Association (PPA) and E8 (utility companies from G8 countries offering help and sponsorship in renewable energies).

Banking and insurance
There are three commercial banks which serve the four states: Bank of the Federated States of Micronesia, Bank of Guam and the Bank of Hawaii. A government chartered FSM Development Bank is the main financial institution used to foster the growth of new business ventures and private sector development.

Time
GMT plus 12 hours

Geography
The Federated States of Micronesia (FSM), together with Palau, form the archipelago of the Caroline Islands, about 800km east of the Philippines. It is a group of 608 small islands, only four large islands are inhabited, in an area over 2.5 million square kilometres of Pacific Ocean.
Most of the islands are little more than sandy coral outcrops, while others are high rise volcanic peaks covered with forests, or mangroves along shorelines and lagoons.

Hemisphere
Northern

Climate
Warm and humid, temperatures 23–30 degrees Celsius with humidity around 80 per cent. Rainfall is variable, but the minimum is generally 250mm per annum.
Hurricanes are possible.

Entry requirements
Passports
Required by all except US citizens with proof of citizenship. Passports must be valid for 120 days beyond date of entry.

Visa
Not required by US citizens with proof of adequate funds. Entry permits granted to all others with proof of return/onward passage and adequate funds for stays up to 30 days. Business visits need an entry permit, (see www.visit-fsm.org/visitors/permit.pdf).

Currency advice/regulations
No restrictions on import and export of local or foreign currency.
Travellers cheques and credit/charge cards are accepted in visitor orientated businesses.

Health (for visitors)
Mandatory precautions
Vaccination certificates required for yellow fever if travelling from infected area.

Advisable precautions
Vaccinations for diphtheria, tuberculosis, hepatitis A and B, polio, TB, tetanus, typhoid and paratyphoid are advisable.
Leprosy has been endemic for generations.
Water precautions are necessary. There is a cholera risk due to lack of access to safe water.
There is a rabies risk.

Hotels
Hotels tend to be low rise, resort style. There is no star ratings. There is a 6 per cent accommodation tax on Pohnpei and 10 per cent on Yap; Chuuk and Kosrae do not levy a tax.

Credit cards
Limited to certain businesses and hotels in the state centres.

Public holidays (national)
Fixed dates
1 Jan (New Year's Day), 10 May (FSM Constitution Day), 24 Oct (United Nations Day), 3 Nov (National Day), 25 Dec (Christmas Day).

Variable dates
Good Friday (Mar/Apr)

Working hours
Banking
Mon–Thurs: 0930–1430; Fri: 0930–1600.

Business
Mon–Fri: 0800–1700.

Government
Mon–Fri: 0800–1700.

Shops
Mon–Sat: 0800–2000; Sun 0900–1030.

Telecommunications
Mobile/cell phones
A GSM 900 service exists on the inhabited islands.

Internet/e-mail

Electricity supply
110 volt and US type outlets are used.

Social customs/useful tips
Tips are neither expected nor encouraged.

Getting there
Air

National airline: None but the US owned Continental Micronesia Airlines operates throughout Micronesia with connections to Hawaii and Guam.
International airport/s: Pohnpei (PNI), 5km south of Kolonia Town.
Other airport/s: Chuuk (TKK), Yap (YAP), Kosrae (KSA).
Airport tax: Departure tax: Pohnpei US$10, Chuuk US$15, Kosrae US$10, Yap none.

Getting about
National transport
A trip to the outer islands can be complicated and arrangements should be made at least several months in advance.
Air: Pacific Missionary Aviation (PMA) in Yap State and in Pohnpei State provide domestic air services. There are airstrips in the outer islands of Ulul and Ta in Chuuk State.

Road: The road network has been upgraded in many areas through a resurfacing programme begun in the late 1990s.
Taxis: Inexpensive and readily available in most centres.
Water: Passenger and freight services between the islands and atolls are provided by state-owned vessels. The frequency of inter-island services is governed by weather conditions; it is best to contact the FSM visitor's board for current information (www.visit-fsm.org).
City transport

BUSINESS DIRECTORY

The addresses listed below are a selection only. While World of Information makes every endeavour to check these addresses, we cannot guarantee that changes have not been made, especially to telephone numbers and area codes. We would welcome any corrections.

Telephone area codes

The international direct dialling (IDD) code for the FSM is +691, followed by area code and subscriber's number:

Chuuk	330	Pohnpei	320
Kosrae	370	Yap	350

Useful telephone numbers

Pohnpei
Police: 320-2221

Fire: 320-2223

Ambulance: 320-2213

Chuuk
Police: 330-2223

Fire: 330-2222

Ambulance: 330-2444

Kosrae
Police: 911

Fire: 370-3333
Ambulance: 370-3012

Yap
Police: 911

Fire: 350-2415

Ambulance: 350-3446

Chambers of Commerce

Chuuk Chamber of Commerce, PO Box 700, Weno, Chuuk 96942 (tel: 330-2318; fax: 330-2314).

Kosrae Chamber of Commerce, PO Box 1075, Tofol, Kosrae 96944 (tel: 370-2044; fax: 370-2066; e-mail: kosraecci@mail.fm).

Pohnpei Chamber of Commerce, PO Box 405, Kolonia, Pohnpei 96941 (tel: 320-2452; fax: 320-5277).

Banking

Bank of the Federated States of Micronesia, PO Box BF, Tofol, Kosrae, 96944 (tel: 320-2850; fax: 370-3568; email: bofsmhq@mail.fm).

FSM Development Bank, Box M, Kolonia, Pohnpei State, 96941 (tel: 320-2840; fax: 320-2842)

Bank of Guam, Chuuk Office (tel: 330-2567; fax: 330-2640).

Bank of Hawaii, Kosrae Office (tel: 370-3230; fax: 370-2027).

Travel information

Chief of Immigration, Office of the Attorney General, Palikir, Pohnpei 96941 (tel: 320-5844; fax: 320-2234).

Pohnpei International Airport, PO Box 1150, Kolonia Town, Pohnpei 96941 (tel: 320-2682/2793/3999; fax: 320-2798).

National tourist organisation offices

National Visitors Board, PO Box PS-12, Palikir, Pohnpei, 96941 (tel: 320-5133; fax: 320-3251; email: fsminfo@visit-fsm.org; internet: www.visit-fsm.org).

Ministries

Department of Foreign Affairs and Trade, Pacific Islands Branch, R G Casey Building, John McEwan Crescent, Barton ACT 0221, Australia (fax: (+62-2) 6261-2332).

Secretary for Foreign Affairs, Pohnpei (tel: 320-2641; fax: 320-2933).

Secretary for Economic Affairs, Pohnpei (tel: 320-2646; fax: 320-5854).

Other useful addresses

British Embassy, PO Box No 61, Bairiki Tarawa (tel: 21-327; fax: 21-488).

Chuuk State Government, Weno, Chuuk State, 96942.

FSM Embassy (US), 1725 North Street, NW Washington 20036 (tel: (+1-202) 223-4383; fax: (+1-202) 223-4391; email: fsmamb@aol.com).

FSM Public Information Office, FSM Government, Box P.S. 34, Palikir, Pohnpei, 96941.

Kosrae State Government, Tofol, Kosrae, 96944.

Office of the Governor, Yap State Government, PO Box 39, Colonia, Yap, 96943.

Pohnpei State Government, Kolonia, Pohnpei, 96941.

The Secretary of Finance, PO Box P.S. 158, Palikir, Pohnpei, 96941 (tel: 320-2640; fax: 320-2380).

Internet sites

FSM Telecom: http://www.telecom.fm

Government website: http://www.fm.org

Tourist information: www.visit.micronesia.fm

US Office of Insular affairs: http://www.doi.gov/oia

Moldova

KEY FACTS

Official name: Republica Moldoveneasca (Republic of Moldova)

Head of State: President (acting) Marian Lupu (PLDM) (from 30 Dec 2010)

Head of government: Prime Minister Vladimir (Vlad) Filat (PLDM) (from 2009; re-appointed 31 Dec 2010)

Ruling party: Coalition: Alliance for European Integration (AEI), led by Liberal Democrat din Moldova (PLDM) (Liberal Democratic Party of Moldova), with Partidul Democrat din Moldova (PDM) (Democratic Party of Moldova) and Partidul Liberal (PL) (Liberal Party) (from 2009; re-elected 28 Nov 2010)

Area: 33,700 square km

Population: 4.89 million (2010)*

Capital: Chisinau (Kishinev)

Official language: Moldovan (in latin script)

Currency: Leu (L) = 100 bani

Exchange rate: L11.80 per US$ (Oct 2011)

GDP per capita: US$1,630 (2010)

GDP real growth: 6.90% (2010)

GDP: US$5.80 billion (2010)

Labour force: 1.24 million (2010)

Unemployment: 7.50% (2010)

Inflation: 7.40% (2010)

Balance of trade: -US$2.22 billion (2010)

* estimated figure

Moldova had become part of the Soviet Union at the close of the Second World War and Russian troops were stationed in the country thereafter. At the time of the break-up of the USSR and the creation of the Russian Federation in 1991, Moldova, along with the other Russian satellite states, became independent.

A landlocked republic on the borders of what used to be the Soviet Union, Moldova was once ruled by Romania. Indeed, to the present day Moldovans retain close linguistic, cultural and historic ties with the Romanian nation. Romania lies to the east and to the west is Ukraine, but in truth it is the influence of Russia that predominates. The largest successor state to emerge from the former Soviet Union remains all-powerful in the region and its heavy hand is still felt throughout Moldovan political and economic life on a day-to-day basis.

Government?

Moldova's political situation remained unsettled at the end of 2011 in the absence of an elected President. After the 5 April 2009 parliamentary elections the winning party, the Partidul Comunistilor din Moldova (PCM) (Communist Party of Moldova), had nominated Zinaida Greceanîi as president. However, she twice failed to win the necessary 61 votes so that under the constitution there had to be a re-run of the elections. This time (in the 29 July elections) the PCM failed to win a majority of seats and a coalition – the Alliance for European Integration (AEI), led by Liberal Democrat din Moldova (PLDM) (Liberal Democratic Party of Moldova), with Partidul Democrat din Moldova (PDM) (Democratic Party of Moldova) and Partidul Liberal (PL) (Liberal Party) – became the ruling party.

Once Vladimir Voronin found himself with a party other than his own leading parliament, he resigned, on 31 August. He said that 'As chairman of the Communist Party (PCM) I am not going to remain in the dubious and odd position of acting president at this critical time for the motherland and our party.' Voronin, who had run the country since 2001, said that he had 'no moral or political reasons to continue performing this high state role as a formality. I am strongly opposed to the way the country is going to be led. Therefore, I am joining parliament as an ordinary member, so that I could be with the party.'

Mihai Ghimpu (PL) became acting president. He nominated, and parliament endorsed, Vlad Filat of the PLDM as prime minister. Parliament, in its turn, then had to find a president. Filat nominated Marian Lupu (PDM), but parliament failed to elect him. Mihai Ghimpu, therefore agreed to continue as acting president after a new election for president within parliament was postponed until late 2010. In the meantime a constitutional amendment to return presidents to being directly elected by popular vote was put to the people in the form of a referendum.

Although the vote was overwhelmingly in favour of the proposal (87.83 per cent) there was an insufficient turnout of just 30.29 per cent so the motion failed. After months of legal wrangling and the failure of parliament to elect a new president, on 21 September the Constitutional Court ordered fresh parliamentary elections. These were held on 28 November 2010 when the PCM won 42 seats and APIE 59. The result was once again a stalemate with neither side winning the required 61 votes necessary to elect their candidate as president. Parliament appointed Marian Lupu to replace Mihai Ghimpu as acting president on 30 December. Acting President Lupu in his turn re-appointed Vlad Filat as prime minister on 31 December, and Mr Filat attempted to get him confirmed in position. But once again parliament refused to accept the prime minister's nomination.

Still with only an acting president, on 3 January 2011 Prime Minister Filat offered two cabinet posts to the opposition PCM in return for two votes to break the political deadlock and formally accept Marian Lupu as president. On 8 February, the Constitutional Court ruled that parliament was the only institution that could decide when new presidential elections should take place; the current government could therefore prolong its sitting by simply not setting a date for presidential elections.

There were more attempts at electing Mr Lupu president during 2011, each of which failed. The failure was put down to the refusal by the PCM to support him – Mr Lupu is a former member of the party. On 28 December, Vladimir Voronin, the last elected president (back in 2009) and leader of the PCM, was reported as saying that his party would be willing to put an end to the crisis by voting for a non-partisan candidate 'who is not from parliament'. The inability to elect a president and secure a four-year mandate, combined with strained relations within the governing coalition, generates unwelcome political uncertainty. The next election is scheduled for 15 January 2012, after publication of this edition, but don't hold your breath.

The economy

The International Monetary Fund (IMF), in its 2011 report on the Moldovan economy noted that growth remained strong in 2011, while core inflation was contained. After a rebound of 6.9 per cent in 2010, gross domestic product (GDP) grew by 8.4 per cent year-on-year in the first quarter of the year, one of the highest rates in Central and Eastern Europe. This growth was driven by private domestic demand (spurred by recovering inflows of remittances and capital and rising credit) and very strong exports (aided by buoyant external demand and favorable agricultural prices). Exports and imports surged by 63 and 44 per cent respectively in the period January–April 2011 when compared to a year earlier. Headline inflation inched upward to 7 per cent in May due mainly to rising energy prices, but core inflation remained contained at around 3 per cent as wages grew moderately and the exchange rate appreciated slightly. Unemployment, however, was still above its long-term average.

Growth was expected to settle at 5 per cent in 2011–12 as the period of expansion began to mature. Domestic demand financed by external inflows looked likely to underpin medium term growth, with exports, supported by market liberalisation and closer integration with the European Union (EU) making a steadily increasing contribution. Accordingly, the current account deficit was expected to first widen to 11.25 per cent of GDP in 2011, also reflecting higher costs of energy imports and to decline gradually thereafter to 8 per cent by 2016. Inflation was expected to reach 8 per cent at end-2011, before easing towards the National Bank of Moldova's (NBM) (the central bank) 5 per cent inflation target in early 2013.

Volatile commodity prices and a still fragile global economy pose risks to the outlook. Higher energy prices could reignite inflation pressures and further widen the current account deficit. Sovereign debt problems in Europe could also affect Moldova through slowing demand in some of its trading partners. Political uncertainty remains a constant risk for the structural reform agenda. On the upside, the robust growth momentum evident in the last three quarters could carry on for longer than currently expected.

The Transdniestr issue

With the dissolution of the USSR Moldova's Slavic population seized the opportunity to declare a breakaway territory east of the Dniestr River – the Republic of Transdniestr. Although Russian troops pulled out of Moldova, they remain in the breakaway territory, which is under the *de facto* rule of an elected pro-Russian 'president', Igor Smirnov. Mr Smirnov's term in office, however, is under threat as he failed to win the necessary 50 per cent of the vote in the 2011 presidential election. A run-off was scheduled for 25 December but on 16 December was put off until January 2012. Yevgeny Shevchuk (independent) had won 38.6 per cent while Mr Smirnov had come in third with 24.7 per cent. Transdniestr remains internationally unrecognised, except by Russia.

The economy of the Transnistrian region stagnated despite continued massive public support financed by accumulation of external arrears. In 2010, the local output contracted by nearly 2 per cent and consumer prices increased by almost 13 per cent.

Approximately US$500 million of new arrears were accumulated on payments for imported natural gas from Russia, with total arrears reaching US$2.5 billion. The domestic-currency proceeds from gas deliveries were partly used to finance the large budget deficit.

KEY INDICATORS **Moldova**

	Unit	2006	2007	2008	2009	2010
Population	m	3.59	3.58	3.57	3.57	*4.89
Gross domestic product (GDP)	US$bn	3.36	4.40	6.10	5.40	5.80
GDP per capita	US$	949	1,227	1,693	1,514	1,630
GDP real growth	%	4.0	3.0	7.8	-6.0	6.9
Inflation	%	12.7	12.4	12.7	0.0	7.4
Unemployment	%	7.6	5.1	4.0	6.4	7.5
Industrial output	% change	-10.0	-1.2	0.5	-22.5	–
Agricultural output	% change	2.0	-34.8	35.0	-10.5	–
Exports (fob) (goods)	US$m	1,044.0	1,360.7	1,646.7	1,329.2	1,590.4
Imports (fob) (goods)	US$m	2,684.0	3,676.7	4,870.0	3,272.7	3,810.0
Balance of trade	US$m	-1,640.0	-2,316.0	-3,223.4	-1,943.6	-2,219.5
Current account	US$m	-404.0	-746.9	-1,071.0	-508.6	-631.0
Total reserves minus gold	US$m	775.5	1,333.6	1,672.4	1,480.3	1,717.7
Foreign exchange	US$m	775.3	1,333.5	1,672.3	1,476.7	1,717.3
Exchange rate	per US$	13.03	12.14	10.39	11.11	12.37

* estimated figure

Moldova's risk of debt distress remained low at the beginning of 2011. Public debt at the end of 2010 was moderate at 30 per cent of GDP and is projected to decline thereafter. Moreover, public external debt largely consists of low-interest debt extended by international development partners. However, private external debt is high at 45 per cent of GDP, raising the economy's vulnerability to shocks. The public debt dynamics worsen if to Moldova's liabilities is added the debt of the gas importing company Moldovagaz (majority-owned by Russia's Gazprom), stemming from the gas arrears accumulated by Transdniestr is included. Even so, Moldova's risk of debt distress increases only to 'moderate' under this highly hypothetical scenario.

Risk assessment

Politics	Poor
Economy	Good
Regional stability	Poor

COUNTRY PROFILE

Historical profile

1940 The Moldovan Soviet Socialist Republic (SSR) was established within the Soviet Union. The Moldovan SSR included land annexed from Romania and the Ukraine, providing much of the basis for the inter-communal strife.

1989 Achieved *de facto* independence from the former Soviet Union.

1990 Moldova's attempts to become an independent republic were hindered by the country's economic weaknesses and its strained relations with Russia. Ethnic Russians proclaimed the Transdniestr Republic on the left bank of the Dniestr River.

1991 Civil war erupted between the Transdniestr separatists and Moldova. Russian troops were deployed in Moldova to oversee a cease-fire agreed between the warring factions. Moldova formally declared its independence, with Mercea Snegur as the country's first president; it joined the Commonwealth of Independent States (CIS).

1992 Moldova was recognised by the UN. The Partidul Popular Crestin-Democrat (PPCD) (Christian-Democrat People's Party) resigned in favour of a new coalition government.

1994 Moldova pursued a pro-Western policy and joined NATO's Partnership for Peace (PfP) programme. The extreme left Partidul Democrat Agrar din Moldova (PDAM) (Agrarian-Democratic Party of Moldova) won elections. A new constitution was introduced.

1996 Petru Lucinschi won the presidential elections.

1998 The Partidul Comunistilor din Moldova (PCM) (Communist Party of Moldova) won the biggest share of the vote in the parliamentary elections, but was unable to form a government as it was short of an absolute majority in the Parlamentul (Parliament). Right-wing parties, which had finished behind the PCM in the elections, joined together and formed a coalition government, led by Ion Ciubuc.

1999 There were three governments in one year as coalitions collapsed. A non-affiliated government emerged, led by Dumitru Braghis.

2000 Against President Lucinschi's wishes, Moldova was transformed into a parliamentary republic – giving the parliament the opportunity to elect the president instead of election by popular vote. Parliament failed to elect a new president when neither candidate received the 61 votes required for outright victory.

2001 The PCM won elections and Vasile Tarlev was appointed prime minister. Vladimir Voronin, leader of the PCM, was elected president by parliament. An Organisation for Security and Co-operation in Europe (OSCE) sponsored agreement committed Russia to removing troops from Moldova by 2002. Moldova joined the World Trade Organisation (WTO). Igor Smirnov was re-elected as self-styled president of the breakaway Transdniestr region.

2002 The announcement of plans to make Russian an official language and compulsory in schools sparked months of mass protests which ended only when the scheme was shelved. The OSCE deadline for Russian troops to withdraw from Transdniestr was extended until the end of 2003, then 2004.

2004 Moldova imposed economic sanctions on Transdniestr (the Russian and Ukrainian-speaking autonomous territory) after it closed several schools using the Moldovan language and Latin instead of Cyrillic script

2005 Vasile Tarlev's ruling PCM and President Voronin were re-elected. During the winter Gazprom doubled the price of gas and temporarily cut off supplies when Moldova refused to pay.

2006 The halted gas supplies also affected the flow through Moldova to Germany. An agreement was reached with phased price increases. Transdniestr reacted badly to a new law that all goods entering Ukraine through Transdniestr must have Moldovan custom stamps, to foil smuggling. In reprisal, Russia suspended imports of Moldovan meat and wine, claiming a lack of quality, but lifted the ban after Moldova threatened to block Russia's bid for membership of the WTO. A referendum in Transdniestr voted for independence from Moldova and eventually to become a region of Russia.

2008 Vasile Tarlev resigned as prime minister; Zinaida Greceanîi, became the first Moldovan woman prime minister.

2009 In parliamentary elections, the PCM won 49.5 per cent of the vote (60 seats out of 101), the Partidul Liberal (PL) (Liberal Party) 13.1 per cent (15), the Partidul Liberal Democrat din Moldova (PLDM) (Liberal Democrats (of Moldova)) 12.4 per cent (15), and the Partidul Alianta Moldova Noastra (PAMN) (Our Moldova Alliance) 9.8 per cent (11). The PCM nominated Zinaida Greceanîi as president but parliament twice failed to give her the minimum 61 votes necessary to take office. This automatically triggered another round of parliamentary elections, which were won by a coalition, called the Alianta Pentru Integrare Europeana (APIE) (Alliance for European Integration) (comprising PLDM, PL and PAWM) with a combined 53 seats, which outnumber the PCM's 48 seats. President Vladimir Voronin resigned and Mihai Ghimpu became acting president; he nominated, and parliament endorsed, Vlad Filat (PLDM) as prime minister. Parliament failed to elect Filat's nomination of Marian Lupu as president and a new presidential election was postponed until the third quarter of 2010.

2010 A referendum was held on 5 September to amend the constitution and return presidents to being directly elected by popular vote. Although the vote was overwhelmingly in favour of the proposal (87.83 per cent) there was an insufficient turnout of just 30.29 per cent so the motion failed. After months of legal wrangling and the failure of parliament to elect a new president, on 21 September the Constitutional Court ordered fresh parliamentary elections. These were held on 28 November when the PCM won 42 seats and APIE 59. The result was once again a stalemate with neither side winning the required 61 votes necessary to elect their candidate as president. Parliament appointed Marian Lupu (PLDM) as acting president on 30 December. Acting President Lupu re-appointed Vlad Filat (PLDM) as prime minister on 31 December.

2011 On 3 January, Prime Minister Filat offered two cabinet posts to the opposition PCM in return for two votes to break the political deadlock and formally accept Marian Lupu as president. On 8 February, the Constitutional Court ruled that parliament was the only institution that could decide when new presidential elections should take place. The current government could therefore prolong its sitting by not setting a date for presidential elections. On 29 July the EU agreed to provide around €200 million (US$281 million) in financial assistance, to be used in the energy sector, strengthening institutional capacities, measures to mitigate conflict in Transdniestr, legal reforms and support for the government's budget.In presidential elections held in Transdniestr, Yevgeny Shevchuk (independent) won 38.6 per cent of the vote, Anatoly Kaminsky (Obnovleniye (Renewal)) 26.3 per cent, and incumbent Igor Smirnov (independent) 24.7 per cent; three other candidates each won less than 6 per cent. Turnout was 60 per cent. As no candidate won over 50 per cent, a runoff was scheduled for 25 December. On 16 December, the national parliament failed to elect a president and a new ballot will be held in January. According to the constitution, if no candidate is chosen, then presidential elections must be held.

Political structure

Constitution

The 1977 constitution was replaced in August 1994, establishing the country as a 'presidential, parliamentary republic' based on political pluralism and 'the preservation, development and expression of ethnic and linguistic identity'. The constitution enforces the separation of judicial, legislative and executive powers.
Moldova's independence and neutrality are enshrined in the constitution, as are the rights of all ethnic minorities.
For administrative purposes Moldova is divided into 40 districts (*raioane*) and 10 cities. Gagauz-Yeri and Transdniestr are guarenteed autonomous status, although the unrecognised separatist government of Transdniestr also claims outright independence.

Independence date

27 August 1991

Form of state

Parliamentary democratic republic

The executive

Executive power is held by the president of the republic, who must approve legislation and may also propose it. The president nominates the prime minister and government.
Candidates for the presidency must be over 35 years of age, resident in the country for at least 10 years and speakers of the national language. The president is elected for a term of four years by the parliament. The president is limited to two consecutive terms of office.

National legislature

The unicameral Parlamentul (parliament) has 101-members elected by proportional representation for a term of four years. The legislative body appoints the president. It can also approve or reject presidential nominations for the prime minister and government. The government must be appointed within 30 days of parliamentary elections or fresh elections must be called.

Legal system

The legal system is based on civil law. The Constitutional Court is the highest legal authority. It reviews the legality of legislative acts and must validate the election of the president and all members of parliament. Its independence is guaranteed by the constitution and judges, once selected, cannot be removed without their consent. The Constitutional Court consists of six judges, two each appointed by the president, parliament and Higher Council of Magistrates, all for a six-year term.
The rest of the justice system is administered by the Supreme Court, Appeals Court and lesser courts. Following recommendation by the Higher Council of Justice, the judges of the Supreme Court are appointed by parliament, and those of all lesser courts by the president of the republic, all for a renewable term of five years.
The Higher Council of Magistrates consists of 11 members, of which five (the minister of justice, the president of the Supreme Court, the president of the Court of Appeal, the president of the Court of Business Audit and the prosecutor general) are automatic members, a further three are judges appointed by the Supreme Court and three are academic lawyers appointed by parliament.

Last elections

3 June 2009 (presidential; indirect by parliament); 5 April/29 July 2009 (parliamentary and re-run); 28 November 2010 ((early) parliamentary).
Results: Presidential: Zinaida Greceanîi was nominated by the PCM, but failed to gain 61 votes to attain the office.
Parliamentary: Partidul Comunistilor din Moldova (PCM) (Communist Party of Moldova) won 49.5 per cent of the vote (60 seats out of 101), the Partidul Liberal (PL) (Liberal Party) 13.1 per cent (15), the Partidul Liberal Democrat din Moldova (PLDM) (Liberal Democrats (of Moldova)) 12.4 per cent (15), and the Partidul Alianta Moldova Noastra (PAMN) (Our Moldova Alliance) 9.8 per cent (11). Turnout was 59.5 per cent.
Parliamentary: (re-run) PCM won 44.69 per cent the vote (48 seats out of 101), the PLDM 16.57 per cent (18), PL 14.68 per cent (15) and the PAMN 7.35 per cent (seven). Turnout was 58.8 per cent.
Parliamentary (early): PCM won 39.29 per cent of the vote (42 seats out of 101), PLDM 29.38 per cent (32), PDM 12.72 per cent (15), PL 9.96 per cent (12); 16 other political parties and various independents failed to win the threshold percentage of the votes necessary to gain parliamentary seats. Turnout was 59.1 per cent.

Next elections

2014 (presidential and parliamentary).

Political parties

Ruling party

Coalition: Alliance for European Integration (AEI), led by Liberal Democrat din Moldova (PLDM) (Liberal Democratic Party of Moldova), with Partidul Democrat din Moldova (PDM) (Democratic Party of Moldova) and Partidul Liberal (PL) (Liberal Party) (from 2009; re-elected 28 Nov 2010)

Main opposition party

Partidul Comunistilor din Moldova (PCM) (Communist Party of Moldova)

Population

4.89 million (2010)*
Last census: October 2004: 3,388,071 (provisional)
Population density: At 132 people per square km, Moldova is the second smallest republic of the Newly Independent States (NIS) but has the highest population density. Urban population: 45 per cent (1995—2001).
Annual growth rate: -0.3 per cent 1994–2004 (WHO 2006)
Internally Displaced Persons (IDP)
1,000 (UNHCR 2004)

Ethnic make-up

The high number of ethnic Ukrainians and Russians in Moldova stems from the former Soviet Union's forced emigration policies in an attempt to dilute the ethnic Moldovan population. There are internal disputes with ethnic Russians and Ukrainians in the separatist Transdniestr region and with Gagauz Turks in the south.
Ethnic groups in Moldova include: Moldovan/Romanian (64.5 per cent); Ukrainian (13.8 per cent); Russian (13 per cent); Gagauz (3.5 per cent); Bulgarian (2 per cent); and others (3.2 per cent).

Religions

Christianity is the majority religion in Moldova, the principal denomination being the Eastern Orthodox Church (98.5 per cent). The Gagauz also adhere to Orthodox Christianity despite their Turkic roots. There are Romanian and Turkish liturgies in Moldova, but the Russian Orthodox Church (Moscow Patriarchy) has jurisdiction.
Although there are an estimated 20,000 Roman Catholics in Moldova, the Moldovan branch of the Roman Catholic Church, founded in 1848, has few active congregations. Approximately 1.5 per cent of the population is Jewish.

Education

Primary education lasts for four years, at aged 10 students move on to secondary school for seven or eight years. This is divided into five years of lower secondary school and may be followed by two or

three years of upper secondary school, following either technical or academic programmes, leading to either higher education or further training. Lessons may be given in either Romanian or Russian. There are several private higher education institutions.
Before the collapse of the Soviet Union, Moldova's education system was completely integrated into the Soviet system. This meant that most teaching was in the Russian language. Since independence, the curriculum has become much more focussed on Moldovan history and culture. The Moldovan government has restored the Romanian language in schools and added courses in Romanian literature and history to the curriculum. The governments of Romania and Moldova established strong ties between their education systems. Several thousand Moldovan students have attended school in Romania, and the Romanian government has donated textbooks to replace Soviet-era books.
The government's decision to introduce Russian in primary schools as a mandatory subject in 2002 was a cause of much controversy, later however, the government announced that the Russian language lessons would be optional.
Literacy rate: 99 per cent adult rate; 100 per cent youth rate (15–24) (Unesco 2005).
Compulsory years: 6 to 15.
Enrolment rate: 97 per cent total primary enrolment of the relevant age group (including repetition rates); 81 per cent secondary enrolment (World Bank).
Pupils per teacher: 23 in primary schools.

Health

HIV/Aids
HIV prevalence: 0.2 per cent aged 15–49 in 2003 (World Bank)
Life expectancy: 67 years, 2004 (WHO 2006)
Fertility rate/Maternal mortality rate: 1.2 births per woman, 2004 (WHO 2006)
Birth rate/Death rate: 15.27 births and 12.79 deaths per 1,000 people (2005 estimates)
Child (under 5 years) mortality rate (per 1,000): 40.42 per 1,000 live births (2005)
Head of population per physician: 2.64 physicians per 1,000 people, 2003 (WHO 2006)

Welfare

A social insurance system covers old age pensions, worker's disability, survivors, sickness and maternity benefit and family allowance, plus unemployment payments. Contributions are obtained from workers at 1 per cent of earnings (23 per cent for self-employed); 29–30 per cent employer's payroll, dependent on industry or enterprise; central government pays *ad hoc* flat-rate payments; regional (Republics), local authorities and employers can also provide supplementary benefits, from their own budgets, for specific needs.
Moldova remains one of the poorest countries in the region and pensioners remain particularly disadvantaged, accounting for 20 per cent of the population. The government intends to introduce private pensions to supplement the current state pension system. In 1999, legislation on private pensions allowed for the establishment of both open and closed pension funds based on voluntary contributions.
Pensions
The minimum retirement age is 62 years with a full pension dependent on 32 years of insurance cover.

Main cities

Chisinau (Kishinev) (capital, estimated population 664,325 in 2005), Tiraspol (183,678), Balti (143,630), Tighina (123,038).

Languages spoken

The 1994 constitution states that Moldovan is the country's official language, although it allows for the use of other languages in the country's ethnic minority areas. Officially known as 'limba moldoveneasca' (language of Moldova), Moldovan is a dialect of Romanian. Russian is the first language of about one-third of the population, and is more universally spoken than Moldovan. Most people are bilingual.
The government attempted to introduce a language law in 1989 which would force government officials to speak both Moldovan and Russian. Since many Russian-speakers could not speak Moldovan and needed time to learn the language, the parliament decided in 1994 to postpone the law indefinitely. The law was a major factor in accelerating the separatist movements of the Russian-speaking Transdniestr region and of the Gagauz-Yeri minority who speak Gagauz (a Turkish dialect). Other minority languages include Ukrainian and Bulgarian. The government's decision, although later annulled, to introduce Russian in primary schools as a mandatory subject in 2002 was the cause of much controversy.
Official language/s
Moldovan (in latin script)

Media

Despite freedom of the press guaranteed under the constitution, press laws and a penal code can be used by the state to curb the reporting powers of the press. There is little real independence, particularly within the state-owned media. Editorial interference in privately or publicly owned media by political and business interests is commonplace.
Press
Dailies: In Moldovan Romanian, top newspapers include *Timpul* (www.timpul.mdl.net), *Moldova Suverana* (www.moldova-suverana.md) and *Jurnal de Chisinau* (www.jurnal.md), while *Flux* (www.flux.md) is an influential publication. In Russian, *Nezavisimaya Moldova* (www.nm.md) is a government publication, *Moldavskie Vedomosti* (www.vedomosti.md) is a conservative newspaper.
In Transdniestr, in Moldovan Romanian *Ziarul de Garda*, with an online English edition (http://garda.com.md/english/), is funded by the US government.
Weeklies: In Moldovan Romanian, *Saptamina* is a centrist publication. In Transdniestr, in English, *The Tiraspol Times* (www.tiraspoltimes.com) is a news review magazine.
Business: In Russian, publications include *Delovaya Gazeta* and *Ekonomicheskoe Obozrenie* (http://logos.press.md) and in Romanian *Observator Economic*.
Periodicals: In Moldovan Romanian, the arts magazine *Sud-Est* (www.sud-est.md) is published monthly.
Broadcasting
Teleradio Moldova (TRM) (www.trm.md) is the national broadcaster.
Radio: TRM (www.trm.md) operates Radio Moldova, which includes an international station. Other, private stations include Fresh FM (www.freshfm.md), which is a national network, Radio Noroc (www.radionoroc.md), Radio 7 (www.radio7.md), Russkoye Radio (www.rusradio.md) in Russian and Vocea Basarabiei (www.voceabasarabiei.net) a Christian content station.
Television: TRM (www.trm.md) operates Moldova One and TV Moldova International. Other, private digital channels include Pro TV (www.protv.md), TV7 (www.tv7.md) and Perviy Kanal Moldova (www.prime.md) which re-broadcasts the Russian federal channel from Moscow.

Economy

Moldova is one of the poorest countries in Europe, with an economy that was underdeveloped during the period of the Soviet Union's centrally planned economic control. In 2011 it was ranked 111 (out of 187) on the UN Human Development Index (HDI), for national development in health, education and income.
GDP growth was reduced from a steady 7.5 in 2004–05 to an average 3.9 per cent in 2006–07 as first a year-long ban was imposed by Russia on Moldovan wine imports and then a major drought in 2007 severely reduced agricultural

production. Despite a recovery of GDP growth in 2008 to 7.8 per cent, the economy fell into recession of -6.0 per cent in 2009 as Moldova was affected by the global economic recession and as remittances declined and FDI dropped off sharply; exports fell by 36 per cent in the first six months of 2009. GDP growth was grew to 6.9 per cent in 2010.

Agriculture still plays a large role in the economy, although its importance has decreased from 17 per cent in 2005–06 to 10 per cent of GDP in 2009. Moldova's long established viniculture sector typically provides 30 per cent of all exports. The service sector has steadily grown to 77 per cent of GDP in 2009, with manufacturing representing 12.5 per cent. Now that foreign direct investment (FDI) and international economic aid is being applied Moldova has embraced a free market economy. In 2011, Moldova increased its ranking from 99 to 81 (out of 183) on the World Bank's ease of doing business survey. FDI was US$712.7 million in 2008 which plummeted to US$127.8 million in 2009, before increasing to a modest US$194.3 million in 2010.

Emigration is around 14 per cent per annum, with over 85 per cent of migrants working in Europe. Remittances fell from a high of US$1.8 billion in 2008 to US$1.2 billion in 2009 (23.1 per cent of GDP), and was estimated at US$1.3 billion in 2010.

Inflation had been in double digits since before 2004, averaging 12 per cent, but in 2009 a sharp increase in imported natural gas and higher food prices cut domestic spending so that inflation fell to 0.0 per cent; it rose to 7.4 per cent as world trade began to pick up in 2010.

In 2009 the International Monetary Fund (IMF) agreed to a three-year loan of around US$588 million to cover government budgetary financing needs.

External trade

Moldova has a free trade agreement with the Central European Free Trade Agreement (Cefta). It has traditional ties with Russia which were, following the break-up of the Soviet Union, formalised through the Commonwealth of Independent States (CIS).

On 19 October 2011, a free trade agreement (FTA) was signed by Russia with seven of its former Soviet republics: Armenia, Belarus, Kazakhstan, Kyrgyzstan, Moldova and Tajikistan. The FTA must be ratified by all relevant parliaments before its instigation in 2012.

Imports

Natural gas and petroleum, machinery and equipment, chemicals, textiles and consumer goods.

Main sources: Ukraine (typically 17 per cent of total), Russian Federation (14 per cent), Romania (12 per cent).

Exports

Romania (typically 21 per cent of total), Russian Federation (20 per cent), Ukraine (11 per cent).

Main destinations: Russia (17.3 per cent total, 2006), Romania (14.8 per cent), Ukraine (12.2 per cent).

Agriculture

Farming

Agriculture remains a key sector of the national economy. The sector contributes around a fifth of GDP and is a considerable source of export revenue. It employs over 40 per cent of the working population. Moldova's main resources are its climate and the rich black *chernozem* soil covering 75 per cent of the land, making it ideal for growing wine grapes, tobacco, sugar beet and for raising dairy cattle. Grains, vegetables and fruits are also important. The animal husbandry sector specialises in the breeding of livestock, pigs and poultry.

The majority of production continues to be from state farms and co-operatives, although as the land reform programme progresses this is expected to change. Agro-industrial complexes are dominant in meat and dairy production. Pork is the main domestic protein source. A quarter of total meat production is exported. There are around 150 wineries in Moldova and 170,000 hectares (ha) of vineyards. The wine making industry has attracted foreign investment and is dependent upon markets in the CIS. The majority of annual sugar exports go to former Soviet republics. Moldova is also a major tobacco producer.

Fishing

Only 20 fish species, including crucian carp, perch, bream and soodak, are of any commercial importance. Most of the fish resources are concentrated in natural and artificial lakes devoted to fish breeding.

Forestry

Forest and wooded land account for about one-tenth of the land area, with forest cover estimated at 325,000 hectares (ha). All forests in Moldova are state-owned. About two-thirds of the forest is available for wood supply, while the rest is protected and conserved. Timber includes oak, beech and ash.

Production is mostly for domestic consumption. More than half of all wood consumed is used as fuel or processed into charcoal. The forestry industry faces a shortage of raw materials and is not sufficient to meet the domestic markets. Moldova imports sawnwood and paper.

Wood and wood products account for around four per cent of annual GDP. Moldova typically produces approximately 500,000 cubic metres of timber per annum.

Industry and manufacturing

Industry accounts for around 25 per cent of GDP. A large proportion of industrial production is concentrated in the breakaway Transdniestr region, where most of Moldova's electricity, metallurgy and metallurgical equipment are produced.

The agro-industrial complex is at the heart of the economy, carrying out the production, transportation, processing, storage and sale of agricultural products. Other industries include electronics, machine tools, tractors, agricultural engineering, building materials, chemicals and furniture manufacture.

Tourism

Tourism is at an early stage of development. The economic value of tourism is recognised and efforts are being made to entice visitors from outside the traditional east European market. Visitor numbers have fallen in recent years. Moldova lacks obvious tourist attractions, so the country's rural charms are being exploited with village holidays, hunting and vineyard tours. The small size of the country is presented as an advantage, allowing all of it to be toured in a short time. Conference and other business tourism is also being encouraged. New infrastructure is being constructed and old stock renovated.

Hydrocarbons

There were no commercially exploited oil or gas reserves by 2008. Consumption of oil was 17,000 barrels per day in 2008, all of which was imported. The potential for oil and gas is high, as Moldova has contiguous geology with known deposits of oil in neighbouring Ukraine. However, exploration is still hampered by limited foreign investment. The Valenskoye field has reserves of around 73 million barrels, with potential production estimated at 732,000 barrels per year.

A new, US$38 million, oil terminal was opened in 2007 in the south of Moldova at Giurgiulesti, on the Danube, reducing Moldova's overall reliance on Russian oil. Natural gas imports were 2.4 billion cubic metres (cum) in 2008, all of which was imported from Russia. Although breakaway Transdniestr has only 15 per cent of Moldova's population it consumes around 50 per cent of total natural gas imports for industrial production. The monopoly domestic gas distributor Moldovagaz, is heavily indebted to Russian gas monopoly Gazprom, amounting to in total US1.8 billion in 2008. Following the loss of a court case in Russia in 2008, it was

decided that Moldovagaz was responsible for debts accrued by the Transdniestr's gas distributor Tiraspoltransgaz, which owes US$1.46 billion of the total debt.
A major pipeline, the Moldova-Balkans Gas Transit Pipeline (MBGTP) runs through Moldova and the break-away Transdniestr region. In April 2009 the MBGTP was crushed by a landslide, in the Transdniestr region, cutting supplies by around 50 per cent and affecting customers in Romania, Bulgaria, Macedonia, Greece and the European part of Turkey.
Exploration for natural gas reserves is ongoing, with Gazprom leading the way.
There are an estimated 10 million tonnes of bituminous coal; however production is only around 100,000 tonnes per annum.

Energy
Total installed generating capacity was 1,029MW in 2007, producing over 3.8 billion kilowatt hours. The majority of energy is produced in three power stations. However, most capacity is produced in the disputed province of Transdniestr. Hydropower produced around 60MW of energy. Moldova is trying to conserve energy and to develop alternative power sources – solar, wind and geothermal.

Financial markets
Stock exchange
Bursei de Valori a Moldavie (Moldova Stock Exchange) (MSE)

Banking and insurance
Central bank
Banca Nationala a Moldovei (BNM) (National Bank of Moldova)

Time
GMT plus two hours (daylight saving, late March to late October, GMT plus three hours)

Geography
Moldova is a landlocked country in south-eastern Europe, bordered to the north, east and south by Ukraine and to the west by Romania. Most of the country consists of flat plains with low hills. Approximately 11 per cent of Moldova is forested.
Moldova is a fertile plain with small areas of hill country in the centre and north. The main rivers are the Dniestr, which flows through the eastern regions and on into the Black Sea, and the Prut, which marks the western border with Romania and which joins the Danube at the southern tip of Moldova.
The separatist Republic of Transdniestr (not officially recognised) lies between the eastern Ukrainian border and the Dniestr River.
Hemisphere
Northern

Climate
With a temperate, continental climate Moldova has long hot summers and chilly winters. Average temperatures vary between minus 2 degrees Celsius (C) and 22 degrees C. Extremes of temperature can reach 35 degrees C during summer and minus 25 degrees C (with a good deal of ice and snow) in the winter. Average annual rainfall is 500–550mm in the northern and central areas and 450mm in the south.

Dress codes
Business dress is usually quite conservative, but not excessively formal.

Entry requirements
Passports
Required by all. Passports must be valid for at least six months after the date of departure.
Visa
Required by all except CIS nationals. Visit www.consularassistance.com/consular.html for the requirements and a visa application form, to be submitted to the nearest consulate for processing. Limited stay visas can be obtained at Chisinau airport and some major road crossings from Romania; however, these cost more than those organised in advance. Arrival by train requires a visa before travelling.
Currency advice/regulations
The import and export of local currency is unlimited; the import of foreign currency is unlimited but the amount must be declared and export is limited to the amount declared.
Travellers cheques are not in general use, although some banks may exchange them.
Customs
A small amount of personal goods are allowed in duty-free. On arrival declare all valuable items such as jewellery, cameras, computers and musical instruments.

Health (for visitors)
Mandatory precautions
Vaccination certificates for cholera and yellow fever are mandatory if travelling from an infected area. Any person applying for a visa for a stay of more than three months must present a certificate showing that the individual is HIV negative. Only tests performed at clinics approved by the Moldovan government are accepted.
Advisable precautions
It is advisable to be in date for the following immunisations: diphtheria, polio and tetanus (within 10 years), typhoid fever, hepatitis A (moderate risk only), hepatitis B, tuberculosis and tick-borne encephalitis. Healthcare is free in Moldova (although medicines must be purchased). There are chemists where you can buy basic drugs (aspirin, etc), but it is wise to take a supply of frequently used medicines with you, including precautionary antibiotics if travelling outside main urban areas. A travel kit, including disposable syringes, is a reasonable precaution. There is a rabies risk. Water precautions are recommended and water purification tablets may be useful.

Credit cards
Credit cards are not in general use, some banks may accept them.

Public holidays (national)
Fixed dates
1 Jan (New Year's Day), 8 Mar (Women's Day), 1 May (Labour Day), 9 May (Victory Day), 27 Aug (Independence Day), 31 Aug (Limba Noastra/National Language Day), 14 Oct (Chisinau City Day).
Variable dates
Religious holidays are celebrated by adherents (Orthodox Christmas and Easter).

Working hours
Banking
Mon–Sat: 0930–1730 for banks; 0900–1800 for *bureau de change*.
Business
Mon–Fri: 0900–1800.
Government
Mon–Fri: 0900–1800.
Shops
Mon: 0800–1700, Tue–Sat: 0800–2100.

Telecommunications
Mobile/cell phones
GSM 900 services available throughout most of the country.

Electricity supply
220V AC 50 Hz.

Weights and measures
Metric system

Social customs/useful tips
Business appointments are essential and punctuality appreciated. Business cards are usually exchanged. There are many customs and traditions to be understood. Gratuities are becoming more customary, particularly in international hotels.
Take flowers if invited to someone's home and leave shoes at the door.

Security
Although safer than many Western cities, the streets of Chisinau have become more dangerous since independence, particularly after dark. Care should be taken to avoid unlit areas, even in the city centre. There are few embassies in Chisinau (no British Embassy, for instance). Before departure to Moldova, visitors are advised to check with their own ministry of foreign affairs for information on who to contact in the case of an emergency. The British Foreign & Commonwealth Office (FCO), for example, advises its nationals to contact

the British Embassy in Bucharest in Romania.
Avoid all travel in the eastern region of Transdniestr.

Getting there

Air

National airline: Air Moldova; services are not extensive with international flights to Europe only.
International airport/s: Chisinau International (KIV), 13km south-east of the city with duty-free and bank. Taxis and a regular bus service are available to the city (travel time 15–25 minutes).
Airport tax: Departure tax: US$12.

Surface

Road: The principal route runs from Odessa in the Crimea into Moldova through Tiraspol, north to Chisinau, Bel'tsy and then back into Ukraine.
Buses run to Chisinau from Bucharest, Romania.
Rail: The Moldovan rail network is connected to that of Ukraine, Romania and Russia. The principal rail routes connect Chisinau with Tiraspol and Ukraine to the east, and Lasi in Romania to the west. The journey time to Bucharest is approximately 11.5 hours, to Moscow 22 hours and Sofia 23 hours. First-class sleeping carriages, booked in advance from Chisinau station, are recommended.
Water: The Dniestr River flows into the Black Sea in Ukraine, near the port of Odessa. It is used more for industrial transportation than for passengers.

Getting about

National transport

Road: The road network, although extensive, is in need of significant investment and repair. The main routes run from Kagul to Chisinau via Komrat and from Chisinau to Lipkany via Bel'tsy. Roads from Tiraspol in Transdniestr to Chisinau and other destinations in the rest of Moldova may be subject to closure due to conflict in the breakaway region.
Buses: There are buses between larger towns.
Taxis: Can be hired by the hour, prices should be negotiated before travelling.
Rail: Most larger towns are connected by rail. Lines run north-south from Kagul and the southern border with Ukraine to Lipkany and the northern border with Ukraine. Owing to the Transdniestr conflict, routes from Chisinau and Kagul to Tiraspol and Bendery are liable to disruption.
Water: The Dniestr River runs parallel to Moldova's eastern border, and is extensively used, although mostly for industrial rather than passenger transport.

City transport

The names of streets are in both Moldovan and Russian.
Taxis: Taxis are widely available and can be picked up at stands or hailed anywhere in the city.

Car hire

Vehicles with a driver or for self-drive are readily available; an international driving permit is required.

BUSINESS DIRECTORY

The addresses listed below are a selection only. While World of Information makes every endeavour to check these addresses, we cannot guarantee that changes have not been made, especially to telephone numbers and area codes. We would welcome any corrections.

Telephone area codes

The international direct dialling (IDD) code for Moldova is +373, followed by the area code and subscriber's number:

Chisinau	22	Bendery	282
Bel'tsy	231	Tiraspol	284

Useful telephone numbers

Ambulance: 903
Fire: 901
Police: 902
Operator assistance for international telephone calls: 071

Chambers of Commerce

American Chamber of Commerce in Moldova, Joly Alon Hotel, 37 Maria Cebotari Street, Chisinau 2012.

Moldova Chamber of Commerce and Industry, 151 Stefan cel Mare Street, Chisinau 2004 (tel: 221-552; fax: 234-425; e-mail: president@chamber.md).

Banking

Banca Comerciala Romana SA Sucursala, 32A Tricolorului Street, Chisinau 2012 (tel: 220-549; fax: 223-509; email: bcr@cni.md).

Banca Sociala, 61 Banulescu-Bodoni Street, Chisinau 2006 (tel: 221-481; fax: 224-230).

BTR Moldova, 18 Renasterii Street, Chisinau 2005 (tel: 201-100; fax: 201-101; e-mail: office@btr.md).

Businessbanca, 9 Alexandru cel Bun Street, Chisinau 2012 (tel: 223-338; fax: 222-370).

Chisinau Municipal Bank, 83 Stefan cel Mare Avenue, Chisinau 2012 (tel/fax: 228-090).

Comertbank, 63 Columna Street, Chisinau 2001 (tel: 541-356; fax: 543-151; e-mail: combank@chmoldpac.md).

Energbank, 78 Vasile Alexandri Street, Chisinau 2012 (tel: 544-377; fax: 253-409).

Export - Import, 6 Stefan cel Mare Avenue, Chisinau 2001 (tel: 272-583; fax: 546-234; e-mail: exim@eximbank.com).

Finance and Trade Bank, 26 Pushkin Street, Chisinau 2012 (tel: 227-435; fax: 228-253; e-mail: fincom@fcb.mldnet.com).

International Commercial Bank (Moldova), 108 Mitropolit Dosoftei Street, Chisnau 2012 (tel: 226-025; fax: 225-053; e-mail: info@icbsb.md).

Investprivatbank, 34 Sciusev Street, Chisinau 2001 (tel: 274-386; fax: 540-510; email: bnc@ipb.mldnet.com).

Mobiasbanca, 65 Tighina Street, Chisinau 2001 (tel/fax: 541-974; email: info@bcmobias.moldova.su).

Moldindconbank, 38 Armeneasca Street, Chisinau 2012. (tel: 225-521: fax: 279-195; email: computer@micb.net.md).

Moldova - Agroindbank, 9 Cosmonautilor Street, Chisinau 2006 (tel: 222-770; fax: 242-454).

PetrolBANK, 33 Ismail Street, Chisinau 2001 (tel: 500-101; fax: 548-827; email: juri@petrolbank.com).

Savings Bank, 115 Columna Street, Chisinau 2012 (tel: 244-722; fax: 244-731; email: bem@cni.md).

Unibank, 26 Pushkin Street, Chisinau 2012 (tel: 225-586; fax: 220-530).

Universalbank, 180 Stefan cel Mare Avenue, Chisinau 2004 (tel: 246-406; fax: 246-489; email:stabil@mail.universalbank.md).

Victoriabank, 141 August 31 Street, Chisinau 2004 (tel: 233-065; fax: 233-933; email: mail@victoriabank.md).

Central bank

Banca Nationala a Moldovei, 7 Renasterii Avenue, Chisinau 2006 (tel: 221-679; fax: 220-591; e-mail: webmaster@bnm.org).

Stock exchange

Bursei de Valori a Moldavie (Moldova Stock Exchange) (MSE): www.moldse.md

Travel information

Air Moldova, Aeroportul Chisinau, MD 2026, Chisinau (tel: 529-356; fax: 525-064; internet: www.mdv.md).

Ministry of tourism

Ministry of Culture and Tourism, Piata Marii Adunari 1, MD-2033, Chisinau (tel: 227-620; fax: 232-388).

National tourist organisation offices

National Tourism Agency, 180 Stefan cel Mare Street, Office 901 Chisinau MD 2004, (tel: 210 774; internet www.turism.md).

Ministries

Ministry of Agriculture and Food Industry, 162 Stefan cel Mare Boulevard, Chisinau (tel: 233-427; fax: 232-368).

Ministry of Culture, 1 Piata Marii Adunari Nationale, Chisinau (tel: 227-620; fax: 232-388).

Ministry of Defence, 84 Vasile Alexandri Street, Chisinau (tel: 781-156; fax: 233-507).

Ministry of Economy and Reforms, Piata Marii Adunari Nationale 1, 277033 Chisinau (tel: 221-133; fax: 234-064).

Ministry of Education, 1 Piata Marii Adunari Nationale (tel: 233-151; fax: 233-474).

Ministry of Finance, Cosmonautilor Street, 277012 Chisinau (tel: 233-575; fax: 228-610).

Ministry of Foreign Affairs, 1 Piata Marii Adunari Nationale, Chisinau (tel: 233-940; fax: 232-302).

Ministry of Foreign Economic Relations, Piata Marii Adunari Nationale 1, Chisinau 277033 (tel/fax: 234-628).

Ministry of Health, 1 Vasile Alexandri Street, Chisinau (tel: 721-010; fax: 738-781).

Ministry of Industry and Trade, 69 Stefan cel Mare Boulevard, Chisinau (tel: 233-556; fax: 227-346).

Ministry of Internal Affairs, 75 Stefan cel Mare Boulevard, Chisinau (tel: 221-201; fax: 222-723).

Ministry of Justice, 82, 31 August Street, Chisinau (tel: 233-340; fax: 234-797).

Ministry of Labour, Social Protection and Family, 1 Vasile Alexandri Street, Chisinau (tel: 737-572; fax: 723-000).

Ministry of National Security, 166 Stefan cel Mare Boulevard, Chisinau (tel: 239-454; fax: 242-018).

Ministry of Privatisation and State Property Administration, 26 Puskin Street, Chisinau (tel: 234-350; fax: 234-336; internet site: http://privatization.md).

Ministry of Territorial Development, Public Utilities and Construction, 3 Gheorghe Tudor Street, Chisinau (tel: 259-111; fax: 259-499).

Ministry of Telecommunications and Informatics, 134 Stefan cel Mare Boulevard, Chisinau (tel: 221-001; fax: 241-553).

Ministry of Transport and Road Construction, 12/A Bucuriei Street, Chisinau (tel: 629-450; fax: 624-875).

Other useful addresses

British Embassy (there is no British representative in Moldova but the British Embassy in Moscow has some responsibility), Commercial Department, Kutuzovsky Prospeckt 7/4, Moscow 121248 (tel: 956-7477; fax: 956-7480).

Business Centre of Moldova Ltd., Stefan cel Mare 180, Room 303, 277004 Chisinau (tel: 247-914; fax: 247-915).

Department of Civil Protection and Exceptional Situations, 69 Cheorghe Asachi Street, Chisinau (tel: 233-430; fax: 233-430).

Department of Customs Control, 65 Columna Street, Chisinau (tel: 549-460; fax: 263-061).

Department of Energy Resources and Fuel, 50 Eminescu Street, Chisinau (tel: 221-010; fax: 222-264).

Department of Environmental Protection, 73 Stefan cel Mare Boulevard, Chisinau (tel: 226-161; fax: 233-806).

Department of National Relations, 109/1, Alexei Mateevici Street, Chisinau (tel: 240-292; fax: 243-610).

Department of Publishing, Polygraphy and Trade of Books, 180 Stefan cel Mare Boulevard, Chisinau (tel: 246-525).

Department of Standards, Metrology and Technical Control, 48 Serghei Lazo Street, Chisinau (tel: 247-991; fax: 222-321).

Department of Statistics, 124 Stefan cel Mare Avenue, Chisinau 227001 (tel: 233-549; fax: 545-162).

MoldEnergo, 78 Vasile Alexandri Str, 277012 Chisinau (tel: 221-065; fax: 253-142).

Moldexpo International Exhibition Centre, 1 Ghioceilor, 277008 Chisinau (tel: 627-416; fax: 627-420).

Moldovan Foreign Trade Organisation, ul Sadovaya 65, 277018 Chisinau (tel: 244-436; fax: 223-226).

Moldova-Gaz, 38 Albisoara Str, 277005 Chisinau (tel: 256-778; fax: 240-014).

Moldova Stock Exchange, 73 Stefan cel Mare, 277001 Chisinau (tel: 265-554; fax: 228-969).

Moldovan Embassy (USA), 2101 S Street, NW, Washington DC 20008 (tel: (+1-202) 667-1130; fax: (+1-202) 667-120-4; e-mail: moldova@dgs.dgsys.com).

Moldsilva (Forestry Association), 124 Stefan cel Mare Blvd, 277012 Chisinau (tel: 262-256; fax: 223-251).

National Association of Banks, 7 Renasterii Str, 277006 Chisinau (tel: 225-177; fax: 229-382).

National Foreign Trade Company (Moldova-EXIM), 65 Mateevici Str, 277012 Chisinau (tel: 223-226; fax: 244-436).

National Fuel Association, 90 Columna Str, 277001 Chisinau (tel: 223-078; fax: 240-509).

State Company Teleradio Moldova National TV and Radio, 64 Hincesti Highway, 277028 Chisinau (tel: 721-077, 721-863).

Other news agencies: Basa-press: www.basa.md

Infotag: www.infotag.md

Interlic: http://en.interlic.md

Moldpres: www.moldpres.md

Internet sites

Business information: http://www.infomarket.md

Business network: http://www.mbinet.md

Chamber of Commerce: http://www:chamber.md

Freezone and export processing: http://www:moldova-freezone.com

General information (in Moldovan - Romanian): http://www.moldova.md

General government and economy: http://www.moldova.org

IMF Moldova office: http://www.imf.md

Internet resources directory: http://www.ournet.md

Ministry of Economy - Trade department: http://www.trade.moldova

Moldovan parliament: http://www.parlament.md

National Bank rates: http://www.mldnet.com

Monaco

COUNTRY PROFILE

Historical profile

1297 Francois Grimaldi, at the time in exile from Genoa, led a group of partisans into Monaco, which has been ruled by the family ever since.
Honore II signed a treaty of friendship with France, guaranteeing the independence of the principality.
1524–1641 The Grimaldi family was allied with Spain and Monaco came under Spanish protection.
1793 After the French Revolution the Grimaldis were deposed and Monaco was unified with France.
1814 The principality was re-established after its abolition during the French Revolution.
1861 Its independence was guaranteed under French protection. The first constitution was introduced.
1918 Louis, the heir to the throne, was a bachelor and the next male in line to succeed if Louis died without an heir was a German prince, the Duke of Urach. France would not countenance a German monarch and therefore imposed a constitutional provision that only the monarch's own children could inherit the throne.
1949 Prince Rainier III succeeded to the throne.
1956 Prince Rainier married the American actress, Grace Kelly.
1962 A constitution was enacted that allowed for sharing of legislative powers between the monarch and elected national council; principle of divine right was abolished.
1982 Princess Grace was killed in a car accident.
1988 The Union Nationale et Démocratique (UND) (National and Democratic Union) won the elections.
1993 The UND was defeated by two lists of candidates, known as Liste Campora and Liste Medecin.
1993 Monaco was admitted to the UN.
1998 UND won the elections.
2000 France threatened to take legislative measures against Monaco unless it clamped down on money laundering activities.
2001 France and Monaco reached an agreement on money laundering. Monaco agreed to work more closely with the Financial Oversight Commission (FOC) to revise rules governing investment management companies.
2002 Monaco adopted the euro as its official currency. Parliament changed the 1918 law of succession, allowing succession through the female line (distaff side) if Prince Albert died without a legitimate heir. Liechtenstein concluded an agreement with Monaco over the prevention of money laundering and terrorist financing.
2003 The Union pour Monaco (UPM) (Union for Monaco) alliance, led by Stephané Valeri, won a landslide majority in the parliamentary elections, ending the 40-year rule of the UND.
2004 Prince Rainier was diagnosed with heart problems.
2005 Prince Rainier III died. He had been the longest serving monarch in Europe. Prince Albert II was enthroned and Jean-Paul Proust was appointed as minister of state.
2008 In parliamentary elections, the ruling Union pour Monaco (Union for Monaco) coalition won 21 out of 24 seats, the Rassemblement et Enjeux pour Monaco (REM) (Rally and Issues of Monaco) won three seats and the Monaco Ensemble (Monaco Together) failed to win any. Turnout was 76.9 per cent.
2009 The Organisation for Economic Co-operation and Development (OECD) removed Monaco from its list of non-co-operative tax havens, after Monaco declared that it would comply with OECD requirements.
2010 In March, Jean-Paul Proust retired as minister of state and Michel Roger was appointed by Prince Albert as his replacement
2011 Prince Albert married Charlene Wittstock (a South African Olympic swimmer) on 30 June.

Political structure

Constitution

Under the 1962 constitution, Monaco is governed under the authority of the monarch, a minister of state and a unicameral National Council.
Only Monégasques may vote.
In 2002, parliament passed a change to the 1918 law of succession. Princesses Caroline or Stephanie may inherit if Prince Albert dies without a legitimate heir. The line of succession will pass down through the line of whichever Princess assumes the title. An agreement with France allows

KEY FACTS

Official name: Principauté de Monaco (The Principality of Monaco)

Head of State: Prince Albert II (acceded to the throne 6 Apr 2005)

Head of government: Minister of State Michel Roger (took office 29 Mar 2010)

Ruling party: Coalition of the Union pour Monaco (Union for Monaco), led by Union pour la Principauté (UP) (Union for the Principality), with Union Nationale pour l'Avenir de Monaco (UNAM) (National Union for the Future of Monaco) and Promotion de la Famille Monégasque (PFM) (Promotion of the Monegasque Family (since 2003; re-elected February 2008)

Area: 2 square km

Population: 35,000 (2010)*

Capital: Monaco-Ville

Official language: French and Monégasque

Currency: Euro (eur) = 100 cents

Exchange rate: eur0.75 per US$ (Oct 2011)

Unemployment: 3.10%

* estimated figure

Monaco to remain an independent country in the event of a lack of heir to succeed to the Principality.

Form of state

Parliamentary democratic monarchy

The executive

The monarch is the head of state. The monarch nominates the minister of state from a list of three French diplomats submitted by the French government. As head of the Council of Government (three members appointed by the monarch), the minister of state exercises executive power under the monarch.

The laws are initiated by the monarch; the Council of Government prepares draft legislation in his name; the National Council passes laws and the national budget (in public session); the monarch alone promulgates laws which are then published in the *Journal de Monaco*.

The government is assisted by two consultative bodies: the Council of State and the Economic Council.

National legislature

The unicameral Conseil National (national council) has 24-members, elected from lists to serve for five years. The national council has no power to topple the government, although it may act independently of the monarch.

Legal system

Although judicial authority is vested in the monarch, it is delegated to the courts and tribunals, which dispense justice in the monarch's name, but completely independently (there is no minister of justice in the Principality).

Last elections

3 February 2008 (parliamentary)

Results: Parliamentary: The Coalition of the Union pour Monaco (Union for Monaco), led by Union pour la Principauté (UP) (Union for the Principality), with Union Nationale pour l'Avenir de Monaco (UNAM) (National Union for the Future of Monaco) and Promotion de la Famille Monégasque (PFM) (Promotion of the Monegasque Family) won 52.2 per cent of the vote (21 seats out of 24), the Rassemblement et Enjeux pour Monaco (REM) (Rally and Issues of Monaco) 40.49 per cent (three seats), Monaco Ensemble (Monaco Together) 7.31 per cent (no seats). Turnout was 76.9 per cent.

Next elections

2013 (parliamentary)

Political parties

Ruling party

Coalition of the Union pour Monaco (Union for Monaco), led by Union pour la Principauté (UP) (Union for the Principality), with Union Nationale pour l'Avenir de Monaco (UNAM) (National Union for the Future of Monaco) and Promotion de la Famille Monégasque (PFM) (Promotion of the Monegasque Family (since 2003; re-elected February 2008)

Main opposition party

Rassemblement et Enjeux pour Monaco (REM) (Rally and Issues of Monaco)

Political situation

There was a landslide majority for the UPM alliance, led by Stephané Valeri, in the 203 parliamentary elections that ended the 40-year rule of the UND. The UND, which had held all the seats in the previous parliament, only managed to hold on to three seats. The swing in favour of the UPM was largely due to the increasing unpopularity of the UND leader, Jean-Louis Campora, who had served as parliamentary speaker for 30 years. Campora lost his seat in the election. Turnout was 80 per cent, but only around 20 per cent of the total population is eligible to vote due to the constitutional nationality requirements.

Population

35,000 (2010)*

Last census: June 2000: 32,017 (provisional)

Population density: 16,410 inhabitants per sq km.

Annual growth rate: 1.1 per cent 1994–2004 (WHO 2006)

Ethnic make-up

According to the 2000 census, around 7,000 of the total population are Monégasques, 11,000 French, 7,000 Italian and some 2,000 British.

Religions

The state religion is Catholicism, but religious freedom is guaranteed by the constitution. Other religions practised are Anglicanism, Baha'i, Judaism, Protestantism.

Health

Life expectancy: 82 years, 2004 (WHO 2006)

Fertility rate/Maternal mortality rate: 1.8 births per woman, 2004 (WHO 2006)

Child (under 5 years) mortality rate (per 1,000): 4.0 per 1,000 live births (World Bank)

Main cities

Monaco-Ville (capital, estimated population 1,400 in 2003), Monte Carlo (15,400), La Condamine (14,600).

Languages spoken

Italian and English are widely spoken and understood. The traditional Monégasque language is spoken by the older generation of Monégasques and is taught in schools. Ligurian and Occitan are also spoken.

Official language/s

French and Monégasque

Media

Press

The official *Journal de Monaco* is a journal published weekly by the ministry of state,

The independent, Mediterraneum Editions (www.mediterra.com), publishes newspapers in several languages, including the in-house publications, in English *The Monaco Times* (www.mctimes.com) in Italian, *Il Corriere di Monaco* (www.corrieremonaco.com) and in German *Monaco Zeitung*. In French, *Monaco Hebdo* covers current affairs. Regional newspapers with sections devoted to Monaco include *Nice-Matin, Gazette Monaco-Côte d'Azur, Monaco Actualité* and *Monte Carlo Méditerranée*.

Broadcasting

The influence of Monaco on media broadcasting is high due, not only to its extensive radio network, but also as host to one of the oldest television awards festival.

Radio: Radio Monte Carlo (RMC) (www.rmc.fr) broadcasts throughout France and northern Italy with external services in 12 languages. The service it began, transmitting to the Arab world, Monte Carlo Doualiva, was taken over by Radio France Internationale. Riviera Radio (www.rivieraradio.mc), based in RMC studios, broadcasts in English 24 hours per day. Evangelical programmes are broadcast by shortwave in numerous foreign languages by Trans World Radio (www.twr.org).

There are also a number of private, commercial FM stations including Nostalgie (www.nostalgie.fr), Radio Monaco (www.radio-monaco.com) and Radio Classique (www.radioclassique.fr).

Television: The commercial station TMC Monte Carlo (www.tmc.tv) broadcasts popular imported films and shows as well as local news programmes. The government also operates a localised TV station, Monaco Info, showing cultural and magazine style programmes, for a limited number of hours each week.

Economy

Monaco enjoys a small, open and diversified economy based on tourism, the convention business, banking and insurance, but with a significant industrial sector. The government does not publish primary economic information and such information is typically derived from secondary sources. Government revenue is derived from value added tax (VAT) levied on hotel, banking and commercial services (55 per cent) and state monopolies such as telecommunications, the post office and tobacco industry (16 per cent); gambling revenue accounts for 4 per cent. It is thought that financial services accounts for 25 per cent of GDP. In 2008, the country's gross domestic production (GDP) was estimated to be US$976 million.

Although Monaco is not a member of the EU, France's membership gives it access to the European marketplace. Monaco adopted the euro as its official currency at the same time as France.

The base of the local economy was broadened notably through the Fontvieille development of 22 hectares of reclaimed land to the west of the old town, which is now a centre for light industry and low-cost housing. Monaco's total area was increased by one-tenth by this project.

Monaco is diversifying into the knowledge-based industry, aiming to become a European leader in multimedia, the Internet and telecommunications.

Monaco and France have a joint economic and customs union to regulate customs, postal services, telecommunications and the banking sector.

External trade

Monaco has a free trade and customs union with France, which operates within the European Union and, by extension, effects Monaco. France collects and rebates Monegasque trade duties. Virtually all foreign trade is within the service sector including financial, commercial and tourism. Many companies are registered, for tax reasons, in Monaco, which does not publish official statistics.

Imports

Fuels, food, vehicles and consumer goods.

Exports

Financial services

There is no commercial agriculture in Monaco.

Industry and manufacturing

Around 200 firms employing 4,000 people typically account for about 33 per cent of GDP. Main products are cosmetics, healthcare, pharmaceuticals, precision instruments, glass, plastics, electrical goods, electronics, textiles and food processing. Also important are construction and public works.

Tourism

Tourism contributes around 25 per cent of GDP. Monaco attracts around 260,000 tourists annually. Most visitors are day trippers. The casino and the annual Grand Prix motor race are major attractionons. The oceanographic museum, formerly directed by Jacques Cousteau, is one of the most renowned institutions of its kind in the world.

Monaco is expanding its conference and exhibition activities to enhance its appeal to the business travel market.

Hydrocarbons

There are no known hydrocarbon reserves. All oil, natural gas and coal imports are provided through France.

Energy

Monaco is entirely reliant on imports from France to meet its energy requirements. The Société Monégasque de l'Electricité et du Gaz is responsible for distribution and has a contract for electricity supply with Electricité de France (EDF).

Banking and insurance

There are nearly 50 banks and around 20 other financial institutions catering to 130,000 clients worth US$78 billion. In addition to commercial and retail services, Monaco has in recent decades increasingly provided private banking and wealth management services. Monaco's banking system operates under French banking law and is subject to regulation by the Banque de France.

Monaco's reputation as a tax haven with a secretive banking system has made enemies in other jurisdictions, which accuse Monaco of abetting money-laundering and tax evasion. Monaco has been resistant to pressure to be more be more rigorous and transparent in its dealings, but does take action against money-laundering under existing legislation. In addition, mutual assistance agreements to exchange information on money-laundering have been concluded since 2001 with several countries, including France, Spain, Belgium, and Switzerland .

Monaco was obliged to accede to the EU Savings Tax Directive, which took effect in July 2005. Under the withholding tax option, Monaco's banks and financial institutions will automatically deduct tax, initially 15 per cent rising to 35 per cent by 2011, from income earned on interest and other savings of EU citizens and transfer it to the national tax departments. Monaco will be able to retain its banking secrecy by being allowed to withhold information on non-residents' savings. Monaco has also agreed to supply information on tax fraud, for criminal or civil trials, and notify EU member states about additional malpractices.

Central bank

European Central Bank

Monaco does not have a central bank, but monetary links to France have included acceptance of French currency and subsequently the euro as legal tender, while financial institutions located in Monaco have access to the Banque de France on the similar terms to French banks.

Main financial centre

Monaco-Ville

Time

GMT plus one hour (daylight saving, late March to late September, GMT plus two hours)

Geography

The Principality of Monaco is a small enclave in south-eastern France, close to the French-Italian frontier. It comprises a narrow, 4km stretch of Mediterranean coastline with an area of 1.9 square km, situated at the foot of the Alpes Maritimes, which gives it a rocky aspect on the landward side. The highest point is Mont Agel, which reaches 140m.

Monaco is divided into four main localities: the old fortified town of Monaco-Ville, where the palace and cathedral are located; La Condamine, the harbour and business area; Monte Carlo, the resort and main residential area; and Fontvieille, an area of 0.33 square km recovered from the sea in recent years for light industry and residential development.

Hemisphere

Northern

Climate

The climate is Mediterranean with mild winters and warm summers. The hottest months are July and August, with average temperatures of 25 degrees Celsius.

Entry requirements

Passports

Required by all, except nationals of EU/EEAcountries, Switzerland, Andorra and San Marino, valid for three months beyond date of departure.

Visa

Not required for visits up to three months provided visitors arrive from France and adhere to French entry requirements.

French visas are required by all, except citizens of EU, North America, Australasia and Japan, for stays up to three months; this includes business trips by representatives of foreign entities with an invitation from a local company or organisation.

Proof of adequate funds for stay, an itinerary, a guarantee of repatriation if necessary and return/onward ticket are also required.

Currency advice/regulations

There are no restrictions on the import or export of local and foreign currencies.

Health (for visitors)

Mandatory precautions

None

Advisable precautions

Up-to-date tetanus and polio immunisations.

Hotels

Classified into one- to four-star and predominantly four-star/luxury categories. Monaco has around 2,500 hotel rooms, most of which are four-star. The occupancy rate is around 50 per cent.

Credit cards
All credit cards are accepted.

Public holidays (national)
Fixed dates
1 Jan (New Year's Day), 26–27 Jan (Feast of St Dévote), 1 May (Labour Day), 31 May (Prince Albert Day),15 Aug (Assumption Day), 1 Nov (All Saints' Day), 19 Nov (National Day/ Fête du Prince), 8 Dec (Immaculate Conception), 25 Dec (Christmas Day).
Variable dates
Easter Monday, Ascension Day, Whit Monday, Corpus Christ (May/Jun).

Working hours
Banking
Mon–Sat: 0900–1200 and 1400–1630 (except Saturday afternoons preceding Bank Holidays). Banque Franco-Portugaise, Monte Carlo, is open on Saturdays.
Business
Mon–Fri: 0900–1200 and 1400–1700.
Government
Mon–Fri: 0930–1230 and 1330–1700.
Shops
Mon–Sat: 0900–1230 and 1500–1830.

Telecommunications
Mobile/cell phones
GSM 900 serivice is available throughout the territory with a 3G service planned.

Security
Monaco has relatively low rates of crime. Pickpockets operate in train stations and subways.

Getting there
Air
The nearest international airport is at Nice (NCE) in France, 22km from Monaco. There is a heliport in Monte Carlo (MCM), from which Heli-Air Monaco and Monacair operate.
Airport tax: None.
Surface
Road: There are good road links between Monaco and France. No formalities are required to cross the border.
Rail: Monaco is well-served by rail links between and to cities in France, Italy and Switzerland. Daily and over-night through trains transit the Principality. The *TGV Méditeranée* operates between Monaco and Paris
Water: Harbours at Condamine (Hercule port) and Fontvieille can accommodate yachts. Larger vessels can anchor in the bay of Monaco.

Getting about
National transport
There are around 50km of roads and 1.6km of railways (operated by Société Nationale des Chemins de Fer Français).
Buses: There are regular bus services within Monaco, as well as to neighbouring French centres. A direct service is available from Nice Airport to Monaco, stopping at a number of hotels.
City transport
Taxis: Taxis are available around the clock in the Avenue de Monte Carlo and from the railway station. There are taxi ranks at Fontvieille, Place des Moulins, Avenue de la Costa and Beach Plaza.
Buses, trams & metro: Buses operate every five minutes from Monaco-Ville to the casino and every 10 minutes to the railway station and the beaches.

BUSINESS DIRECTORY
The addresses listed below are a selection only. While World of Information makes every endeavour to check these addresses, we cannot guarantee that changes have not been made, especially to telephone numbers and area codes. We would welcome any corrections.

Telephone area codes
The international direct dialling (IDD) code for Monaco is +377, followed by an eight-digit number.

Useful telephone numbers
Police (emergencies):	17
(switchboard):	9315-3015
Ambulance/ Fire services (emergencies):	18
(switchboard):	9330-1945
Medical/paramedic team/ ambulance:	9375-2525
Doctor or chemist on duty:	9325-3325
Princess Grace General Hospital, Av Pasteur (emergencies):	9325-9869
(switchboard):	9325-9900
Main Post Office, Palais de la Scala:	9325-1111
Car pound (Parking des Ecoles car park), Av des Guelfes, Monte Carlo:	9315-3084

Chambers of Commerce
Monaco Economic Development Chamber, 11 Rue du Gabian, BP 653, MC 98013 Monaco (tel: 9798-6868; fax: 9798-6869; e-mail: info@cde.mc).

Banking
Banque Franco Portugaise (BFP), 5 Av Princesse Alice, MC 98000 (tel: 9350-1115; fax: 9350-1921).

Banque Générale du Commerce, 2 Av des Spélugues, Monte Carlo (tel: 9350-1762).

Banque Internationale de Monaco, Sporting d'Hiver, 2 Av Princesse Alice, Monte Carlo (tel: 9216-5757; fax: 9216-5750).

Barclays Bank plc, 31 Av de la Costa, Monte Carlo (tel: 9315-3535; fax: 9325-1568).

Crédit Foncier de Monaco, 11 Bd Albert 1er, MC98000 (tel: 9310-2000; fax: 9310-2350).

Société Générale, 16 Ave de la Costa (tel: 9315-5700); also at 17 Bd Albert 1er (tel: 9350-8692).

Société Monégasque de Banque Privée, 9 Boulevard d'Italie, MC 98000 (tel: 9315-2323).

Central bank
European Central Bank (ECB), Kaiserstrasse 29, D-60311 Frankfurt am Main, Germany (tel: +49(69)13-440; fax: +49(69)1344-6000; e-mail: info@ecb.int).

Travel information
Automobile Club of Monaco, 23 Boulevard Albert 1er, Monaco (tel: 9315-2600; fax: 9325-8008; e-mail: info@acm.mc).

Gare de Monaco, 26 Avenue Prince Pierre, Monaco (tel: 9310-6015; e-mail: info@monaco-gare.com).

Heli-Air Monaco, Héliport de Monaco, Quartier de Fontvieille, Monaco (tel: 9205-0050; fax: 9205-0051; e-mail: helico@heliairmonaco.com).

Monacair, Héliport de Monaco, Quartier de Fontvieille, Monaco (tel: 9797-3900; fax: 9797-3909; e-mail: accueil@monacair.mc).

Compagnie des Autobus de Monaco (CAM), 3 Avenue Président J F Kennedy, Monaco (tel: 9770-2222; fax: 9770-2223).

Service de la Marine, Direction des Ports, 6 Quai Antoine, PO Box 468, Monaco (tel: 9315-8678; fax: 9315-3715; e-mail: marine@gouv.mc).

National tourist organisation offices
Direction du Tourisme et des Congrès, 2a Boulevard des Moulins, Monaco (tel: 9216-6116; fax: 9216-6000; e-mail: dtc@monaco-tourisme.com).

Other useful addresses
Centre de Congrès, Bd Louis II, Monaco (tel: 9310-8400).

Centre d'Informations Administratives, 23 Av Prince Héréditaire Albert, Monaco (tel: 9315-4026).

Centre de Presse, 4 Rue des Iris, Monte Carlo (tel: 9330-4227).

Centre de Rencontres Internationales, Ave d'Ostende, Monaco (tel: 9310-8600).

Comité des Fêtes, Monaco-ville (tel: 9330-8004).

Direction de l'Expansion Economique, 'Le Concorde', 11 Rue du Gabian, PO Box 665, Monaco (tel: 9798-6868; fax: 9798-6869; e-mail: info@cde.mc).

Directorate of Fiscal Services, 57 Rue Grimaldi, MC98000 (tel: 9315-8122; fax: 9205-8155).

Douanes, 7 Av Président JF Kennedy, Monaco (tel: 9330-2600).

Mairie de Monaco, Monaco-ville (tel: 9315-2863).

Ministère d'Etat, Monaco-ville (tel: 9315-8000).

Monte Carlo Casino, Place du Casino, Monaco (tel: 9216-2000; fax: 9216-3862; e-mail: mrk.jeux@sbm.mc).

Monte Carlo Main Post, Square Beaumarchais (Palais de la Scala) (tel: 9350-6987).

Radio Monte Carlo (RMC), 16 Bd Princesse Charlotte, Monte Carlo (tel: 9315-1617).

Service du Contrôle Technique et de la Circulation (traffic control service), 23 Av Prince Héréditaire Albert, Monaco (tel: 9315-8000).

Service de l'Urbanisme et de la Construction, 23 Av Prince Hérditaire Albert, Monaco (tel: 9315-8000).

Télé Monte Carlo, 16 Bd Princesse Charlotte, Monaco (tel: 9315-1415).

Internet sites

Banking and investment advice: www.cmb.mc

Monaco online: www.monaco.mc/

Monte Carlo web directory: http://monte-carlo.mc/

Mongolia

KEY FACTS

Official name: Mongol Uls (The State of Mongolia)

Head of State: President Tsakhiagiyn Elbegdorj (since 18 Jun 2009)

Head of government: Prime Minister Batbold Sukhbaatar (from 30 Oct 2009)

Ruling party: Mongol Ardyn Khuv'sgalt Nam (MAKN) (Mongolian People's Revolutionary Party) (since 2006; re-elected May 2008)

Area: 1,565,000 square km

Population: 2.80 million (2010)*

Capital: Ulaanbaatar (Ulan Bator) (formerly Urga)

Official language: Khalkha Mongolian

Currency: Tugrik (Tug)

Exchange rate: Tug1,287.50 per US$ (Oct 2011)

GDP per capita: US$2,267 (2010)

GDP real growth: 6.10% (2010)

GDP: US$6.10 billion (2010)

Inflation: 10.20% (2010)

Balance of trade: -US$180.40 million (2010)

Aid flow: US$700.00 million (2009)

Annual FDI: US$1.45 billion (2010)

* estimated figure

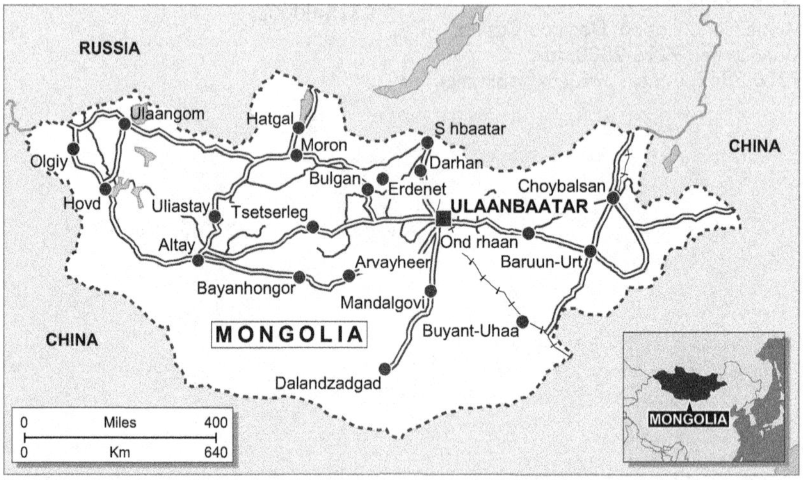

Astride huge quantities of untapped mineral wealth, Mongolia can looked forward to substantial foreign investment in the massive mining projects that are expected to transform an economy that in recent years has languished rather than prospered. A third of Mongolia's population lives in the capital, Ulan Bator, while around forty per cent of the workforce continues to herd livestock in Mongolia's extensive pasturelands. This centuries-old nomadic lifestyle is under pressure from climate change and greater urbanisation. China invests more money into Mongolia than any other country. While much of it can be classed as investment capital, a proportion of it is simply aid for its distressed neighbour. In 2010 the China's People's Liberation Army gave almost US$3 million in aid funds to the Mongolian military. But many Mongolians suspect their powerful neighbour's motives. A BBC report highlighted the signs of their resentment: swastikas and slogans are daubed on walls across the city. Human rights groups blame extreme nationalists for dozens of attacks on women, foreigners and others.

Mineral boom

If all goes to plan, by 2013 the mining of some of the world's largest unexploited mineral deposits will begin. In 2008, Mongolia's gross domestic product (GDP) was US$5.3 billion. By 2022, that could well have tripled. Mongolia has virtually every desirable mineral resource – gold, copper, coal, uranium, iron ore and oil are all to be found. It is the development of the gold and copper mine at Oyu Tolgoi in the south Gobi region that attracts most attention. The reported size of the gold and copper deposits is as large as the island of Manhattan, enough to keep mining there for the next 60 years. In October 2009, Ivanhoe Mines (Canada) and Rio Tinto (UK) signed a long-term Investment Agreement with the government of Mongolia for the construction and operation of the Oyu Tolgoi copper-gold mining complex. The agreement created a partnership between the Mongolian government – which acquired a 34 per cent interest in the project – and Ivanhoe Mines, which retained a controlling 66 per cent interest in Oyu Tolgoi. Rio Tinto has a 49 per cent interest in Ivanhoe Mines.

Harshest winter

The third of Mongolia's population that depends on livestock for a living had a testing time in the period 2010–11. The harshest winter for years was followed by the failure of the grasslands (badly affected by the sub-zero temperatures) to provide adequate pasture leading to widespread livestock decimation (see below). In April 2010 some 5,000 people took to the streets of Ulan Bator to demand that their politicians fulfill the promises they made during the 2008 election campaign. Both the main political parties – Mongol Ardyn Khuv'sgalt Nam

(MAKN) (Mongolian People's Revolutionary Party) and the Ardchilsan Nam (Democratic Party) (DP) – pledged to distribute cash handouts of around US$1,000 to every Mongolian citizen based on mining revenues. Government coffers were hardly bursting at the seams, as Mongolia faced not only the aftermath of winter, but also the lingering effects of the global recession. However, Mongolians knew that billions of dollars of new revenue from mining was set to fill the state's coffers.

In fact, there was a 6.1 per cent recovery in GDP in 2010, driven by growth in the minerals sector, high prices for mineral exports and support from development partners. According to the Asian Development Bank (ADB) the outcome represented a dramatic turnaround from the 1.3 per cent contraction of the economy in 2009. Mining benefited from a rebound in copper prices, strong external demand for coal and iron ore and construction at Oyu Tolgoi. Copper prices returned to 2008 levels and rose to over US$9,000 a ton in December 2010. Copper export volumes in 2010 were little changed from 2009, but their value jumped by more than 50 per cent; export volumes of coal and iron ore more than doubled in 2010. Strong economic growth in the People's Republic of China, Mongolia's major trading partner, underpinned the increase in mineral exports.

Industry as a whole contributed nearly half the growth in GDP in 2010 as construction and manufacturing expanded, along with mining. Services accounted for the rest of GDP growth: wholesale and retail trade recovered strongly as the economy bounced back. Agriculture, however, which directly supports about one-third of the population of 2.8 million, was hit by severe winter conditions (the *dzud*) that drastically reduced livestock numbers by about a quarter. The sector's overall output contracted by nearly 17 per cent. An estimated 10,000 households headed by livestock herders lost their livelihood and migrated to urban areas. The livestock losses also hurt the cashmere industry, reducing production of raw cashmere by 13.2 per cent and output of cashmere sweaters by 20 per cent.

Mongolia's economic recovery was supported by an SDR153.3 million (US$229 million) 18-month stand-by arrangement with the International Monetary Fund (IMF), completed in September 2010. Under this arrangement, Mongolia borrowed US$185.4 million from the Fund and received commitments for US$184 million for budget support from development partners. These financing and associated policy actions taken by the government bolstered both the budget and external positions and restored confidence in the togrog.

In 2010 external trade rebounded from a sharp slump in 2009. Merchandise exports and imports in US dollar terms both jumped by about 53 per cent, exports were propelled by higher copper prices and increased coal and iron ore volumes and prices. Higher imports stemmed from the need for equipment in the mining industry, as well as rising prices of oil and food.

A surge in foreign direct investment (FDI) to US$1.6 billion, largely into mining and in portfolio investment, boosted gross international reserves to US$2.2 billion at end-2010, equivalent to about 8 months of imports (reserves were just US$637 million at end-2008). Inflation accelerated to nearly 13 per cent by end-2010 and averaged 10.1 per cent for the year. The loss of livestock during the *dzud*, coupled with an outbreak of foot-and-mouth disease, caused a sharp rise in food prices.

Inflation would have been higher had it not been for a 13 per cent appreciation in the togrog against the US dollar in 2010. As the economy recovered and inflation quickened, so the Bank of Mongolia in May 2010 raised its interest rate from 10.0 per cent to 11.0 per cent. Higher commodity prices and cash prepayments from the Oyu Tolgoi mine contributed to a 54.5 per cent surge in government revenue in 2010. Government spending went up by 31.7 per cent, largely the result of cash transfers and increases in public sector wages and pensions. The budget was roughly in balance.

The ADB notes that Mongolia's economic recovery generated jobs and lowered the unemployment rate, though it was still high at 8.6 per cent at end-2010. Poverty continued to be widespread, with about one-third of the population living below the national poverty line.

Growth was expected to accelerate in 2011 and 2012, supported by high global mineral prices, the development of new mines and fiscal spending. Mining is the key driver. Investment in the Oyu Tolgoi copper and gold mine is projected to total more than US$4 billion in 2011–12. Preparations are also being made to develop the coal deposits of one of the largest undeveloped coalfields in the world, Tavan Tolgoi. Like Oyu Tolgoi, these deposits are near the border with China, the obvious potential market for the minerals. The government has ambitious plans for a new rail line linking into the Russian Federation's rail network and so through to its Pacific ports.

Risk assessment

Politics	Fair
Economy	Fair
Regional stability	Good

COUNTRY PROFILE

Historical profile

1206-63 Mongol tribes were unified under the leadership of Temujin, later called Genghis Khan. With his cavalry army, he invaded China and occupied Peking and built the largest land empire ever. His offspring increased the empire by invading much of Russia and defeating the armies of most of Eastern Europe, including

KEY INDICATORS — Mongolia

	Unit	2006	2007	2008	2009	2010
Population	m	2.58	2.62	2.69	*2.69	*2.80
Gross domestic product (GDP)	US$bn	3.16	3.90	5.20	4.20	6.10
GDP per capita	US$	1,216	1,503	1,975	1,530	2,267
GDP real growth	%	8.6	10.2	8.9	-1.3	6.4
Inflation	%	5.0	8.2	26.8	6.3	10.2
Industrial output	% change	7.3	7.0	4.7	-4.1	–
Agricultural output	% change	9.7	15.8	5.0	2.3	–
Exports (fob) (goods)	US$m	1,543.0	1,949.0	2,539.3	1,885.4	2,908.5
Imports (fob) (goods)	US$m	1,486.0	2,003.0	3,615.8	2,074.2	3,088.9
Balance of trade	US$m	57.0	-54.0	-1,076.8	-188.8	-180.4
Current account	US$m	222.0	265.0	-687.0	-341.8	-886.5
Total reserves minus gold	US$m	926.0	1,195.6	561.5	1,294.5	2,196.7
Foreign exchange	US$m	925.8	1,195.4	561.2	1,217.8	2,123.8
Exchange rate	per US$	1,165.00	1,169.30	1,165.74	1,437.80	1,357.10

* estimated figure

Hungary and Poland. The onslaught stopped just 40 miles short of Venice when the Mongol commander Subutai was ordered to return home.
1368 The Mongols were forced out of Peking by Chinese troops as the Mongol empire collapsed.
1380 The Golden Horde (troops of Genghis Khan's oldest son, Juchi) was defeated by the Russian, Prince Dmitriy Donskoy, in Russia. Chinese troops destroyed Karakorum, the Mongol capital.
1636 Inner Mongolia was formed by the conquest of the southern Mongols by the Chinese Manchu empire.
1691 Outer Mongolia was formed when the Manchu empire offered protection to the northern Mongols.
1911 Following the republican revolution, Mongolian princes declared the province's independence.
1921 The Mongolian People's Party was founded and a Provisional People's government was established.
1924 The Mongolian People's Republic was proclaimed.
1928–1960 The Soviet Union (USSR) influenced the governing of Mongolia as ideological and repressive communist rule was instigated. Historical and cultural heritage were undermined, family names were prohibited, monasteries destroyed and lamas murdered.
1961 Mongolia became a member of the UN, and was accorded diplomatic recognition by West European states.
1987 Mongolia was finally granted diplomatic recognition by the US.
1991 Mongolia's main backer, the USSR, disintegrated, ending decades of economic and political support for the country.
1992 A new constitution was introduced, establishing Mongolia as a democratic parliamentary state. Mongolia's official title became the State of Mongolia.
1997 Natsagiin Bagabandi of the Mongol Ardyn Khuv'sgalt Nam (Mongolian People's Revolutionary Party) (MPRP) (formerly the Mongolian People's Party), was elected president.
1999 Rinchinnyamiyn Amarjargal became prime minister.
2000 The MPRP won the parliamentary elections and Nambariin Enkhbayar (MPRP), was elected prime minister.
2001 The incumbent president, Natsagiin Bagabandi of the MPRP, was re-elected.
2002 Prime Minister Mikhail Kayanov of Russia visited Mongolia to boost economic co-operation between the two countries.
2004 The World Bank endorsed a new Country Assistance Strategy (CAS) and US$18 million urban water credit. Parliament elected Tsakhiagiyn Elbegdorj (Ekh Oron-Ardchilan (Motherland Democratic Coalition) (MDC)) as prime minister and parliament approved his cabinet.
2005 Nambaryn Enkhbayar (MPRP) won the presidential elections.
2006 Ten ministers, members of the MPRP, resigned accusing the coalition government of not doing enough to counter corruption and poverty. Parliament voted to dissolve the coalition government. Miyeegombo Enkhbold (MPRP) was endorsed by parliament as the new prime minister.
2007 Parliament elected Sanjaagiin Bayar as prime minister.
2008 A new voting system was used in parliamentary elections. The ruling MPRP won 46 seats (out of 76) and Prime Minister Bayar remained in office. The elections were widely contested and although election observers reported no major problems the results sparked violent protests over claims that they had been rigged. After four deaths and hundreds injured, a four-day state of emergency was imposed. At the opening of parliament, the 27 Democrat members staged a walkout and brought the session to a halt.
2009 In presidential elections opposition leader, Tsakhiagiyn Elbegdorj (Ardchilsan Nam) (Democratic Party) (DP) (formerly the MDC), won 51.2 per cent of the vote on a campaign of anti-corruption and proposed use of revenue from the country's rich resources. Incumbent Nambaryn Enkhbayar (MPRP) won 47.4 per cent and said he would abide by the result. Tsakhiagiyn Elbegdorj took office as president in June. Mongolia and Russia signed a five-year agreement which transferred the management of Mongolia's railways to Russia – they had previously been jointly managed. Prime Minister Bayar resigned due to ill health and Batbold Sukhbaatar (MPRP) replaced him.
2010 A moratorium on the death penalty was imposed by the president in January, while parliament discussed its use. A number of privatisations of Mongolia's extensive mineral assets began in January. The minister for mineral resources and energy, Dashdorj Zorigt, said that the government would welcome investment 'from our neighbours and third neighbours'. It is hoped these 'third neighbours' would balance the Chinese and Russian partners that are currently dominant. In April, parliament unanimously approved the building of a 5,000km east–west railway. The plans involve six lines, with construction of 1,800km beginning immediately, followed by 1,400km constructed in 2011 and the remainder by 2015.
2011 In March the government announced it was planning to send 1,500 troops as part of the UN peacekeeping force to Côte d'Ivoire (UNOCI). In May Russia, which supplies over 90 per cent of all oil to Mongolia, increased its export duty on oil by 40 per cent, citing domestic shortages; the imposition quickly caused shortages as prices doubled overnight. The government later announced plans to stockpile petrol reserves and construct the country's first modern oil refinery to mitigate future energy shocks. On 28 June, Unesco added the 12,000-year-old petroglyphs (rock carvings) of Altai Mountains to its list of world heritage sites.

Political structure

Constitution

The constitution entered into force on 12 February 1992. A January 1998 constitutional amendment stated that legislators were eligible to serve concurrently as prime minister or as other ministers. The January amendment was later effectively nullified by the Constitutional Court ruling of 24 November 1998 that prohibited members of the People's Great Hural from holding cabinet posts. On 15 March 2000, the Constitutional Court cancelled amendments to the 1992 constitution, which had been approved by the People's Great Hural, and later vetoed by the president.

Independence date

11 July 1921

Form of state

Parliamentary republic

The executive

The head of state is the president, nominated by parties in the People's Great Hural, and elected by popular vote for a four-year term.

National legislature

The unicameral Ulsyn Ikh Khural (State Great Khural or Hural (Assembly)) has 76 members elected in 26 multi-seat constituencies by proportional representation, to serve for four-year terms. The Assembly elects the prime minister and appoints a cabinet, in consultation with the president.

Legal system

A mixture of Russian, German and US law.

Last elections

24 May 2009 (presidential); 29 June 2008 (parliamentary)

Results: Presidential: Tsakhiagiyn Elbegdorj (DP) won 51.2 per cent of the vote, Nambaryn Enkhbayar MPRP 47.4 per cent; turnout was 73.5 per cent. Parliamentary: Mongol Ardyn Khuv'sgalt Nam (Mongolian People's Revolutionary Party) (MPRP) (46 seats out of 76), Ardchilsan Nam (Democratic Party) (DP) 27 seats; two other parties and an independent won the remaining three seats.

Next elections

June 2012 (parliamentary); 2013 (presidential)

Political parties

Ruling party

Mongol Ardyn Khuv'sgalt Nam (MAKN) (Mongolian People's Revolutionary Party) (since 2006; re-elected May 2008)

Main opposition party
Ardchilsan Nam (Democratic Party) (DP)

Population
2.80 million (2010)*
Last census: January 2000: 2,373,493
Population density: Two inhabitants per square km, one of the lowest densities in the world (2010).
Annual growth rate: 1.0 per cent 1994–2004 (WHO 2006)
Religions
Tibetan Buddhist Lamaism and Shamanism, Islam (4 per cent) – there is no state religion.

Education
Primary schooling lasts for four years until aged 12. Secondary education is divided into four years compulsory lower secondary schooling for students aged 12–16 years and two years upper secondary for those aged 16–18 years. Only students of upper secondary schools progress to higher education. Technical and vocational schools admit graduates of both lower and upper secondary schools. Government and private institutions provide higher education and offer BA, MA and PhD degrees.
Public expenditure on education typically amounts to 5.7 per cent of annual gross national income.
Literacy rate: 98 per cent adult rate; 98 per cent youth rate (15–24) (Unesco 2005).
Compulsory years: Eight to 16.
Enrolment rate: 88 per cent gross primary enrolment, of relevant age group (including repeaters); 56 per cent gross secondary enrolment (World Bank).
Pupils per teacher: 31 in primary schools.

Health
About 98 per cent of infants aged less than one year are immunised against measles.
HIV/Aids
HIV prevalence: 0.1 per cent aged 15–49 in 2003 (World Bank)
Life expectancy: 65 years, 2004 (WHO 2006)
Fertility rate/Maternal mortality rate: 2.4 births per woman, 2004 (WHO 2006); maternal mortality 150 per 100,000 live births (World Bank).
Child (under 5 years) mortality rate (per 1,000): 56 per 1,000 live births; 12.5 per cent children under aged five were malnourished (World Bank).
Head of population per physician: 2.63 physicians per 1,000 people, 2002 (WHO 2006)

Welfare
Growing unemployment and a weak social safety net remain the country's prime concern. About 36 per cent of Mongolia's population still live below the official poverty line. Many poor are unable to work and rely on social security to meet their basic needs. More than 100,000 people are registered as disabled by Mongolia's Ministry of Social Welfare and Labor. About 40,000 disabled people, who are capable of working, remain jobless.

Main cities
Ulaanbaatar (which translates as 'Red Hero') (Ulan Bator) (formerly Urga) (capital, estimated population 904,802 in 2005), Erdènèt (88,243), Darhan (62,696).

Languages spoken
Russian is the principal foreign language, although English is being encouraged. Kazak is also spoken in western Mongolia.
Official language/s
Khalkha Mongolian

Media
Although media is generally free to criticise, journalists are still governed by laws of defamation and state security.
Press
The newspapers with the largest circulations are the government *Odriyn Sonin*, successor to the state-owned *Ardyn Erh* (established in 1990) and *Zasgiyn Gazryn Medee* (weekly), *Nügel Buyan* (police) and *Ulaanbaatar* (local government). The party newspapers *Ardchilal* (MNDP), *Ug* (MSDP) and *Unen* (MPRP) appear less frequently.
English-language weekly newspapers include the *Mongol Messenger* and the on-line publication *Mongolia This Week* (http://www.mongoliathisweek.mn).
Broadcasting
The Mongolian National Broadcaster (MNB) (www.mnb.mn) is the only national, public network via satellite transmissions.
Radio: Radio services are important to the large nomad community. MNB (www.mnb.mn) operates the Voice of Mongolia, transmitting in Chinese, English, Russian and Japanese. Other, private radio stations include Radio Ulaanbaator, New Century 107FM and Info Radio.
Television: MNB (www.mnb.mn) broadcasts locally produced and imported programmes. There are several private and international TV services provided by both satellite and cable, including TV5 (www.tv5.mn), TV9 (www.tv9.mn) and TM Television.
News agencies
Most newspapers are owned by the government or political parties. Dailies include, in Mongolian, *Odriyn Sonin* (*Daily news*) (www.dailynews.mn), *Unen* (*Truth*) (www.unen.mn), *Zuuny Medee* (www.zuuniimedee.mn) and *Onoodor*. Weeklies include, in English, *Mongol Messenger* (www.mongolmessenger.mn), *The UB Post* (http://ubpost.mongolnews.mn).
National news agency: Montsame Agency

Economy
Mongolia not only has extensive deposits of minerals that include gold, copper, coal, tin, tungsten and molybdenum, it also has huge unspoiled areas of land. In the western region around 30 per cent of the national livestock herd, which is being raised in traditional methods, could supply meat to most of Central Asia, as well *niche* markets for organic meat in the West.
The economy was largely dominated by industrial production until 2009, when the service sector outstripped it at 43.8 per cent, compared to the 32.7 per cent for the industrial sector. Mining, particularly copper and gold, accounts for around 50 per cent of the sector. Agriculture is also an important component of the economy, constituting 23.5 per cent of GDP in 2009 and employing 40 per cent of the population. Remittances in 2009 were US$194 million (4.6 per cent of GDP), rising to an estimated US$211 million in 2010, which provide a significant proportion of foreign exchange earnings, along with international aid.
Following a severe winter in 2009–10, when 15 out of 21 provinces were declared disaster zones, around 20 per cent (over 8.5 million head of livestock) of the national herd died through hunger or by freezing to death in -45 degrees Celsius temperatures and heavy snows. Those that survived the winter were left weak, threatening the nomadic nature of herders in Mongolia, who may be forced to relinquish their lifestyle. The brutal winter, called a *zhud*, was blamed on climate change. The UN called on donor countries to provide US$21 million to help clean up and re-build the lives of the nomads, while analysts pointed out that an increase in animal numbers and inexperienced herders contributed to the poor winter's outcome.
Mongolia still has close ties to China and the Russian Federation, established when it was a dependent state of the former Soviet Union, and both still have an influence on the economy. Mongolia buys around 80 per cent of its petroleum needs from Russia while China is Mongolia's principal export partner. The 2007 National Development Strategy (NDS) lays down development objectives and strategies, including human development, the environment and a public investment programme, to be implemented over the 15 years to 2022.
GDP growth in 2007 was 10.2 per cent; it fell to 8.9 per cent in 2008 but

continued expanding on the back of export commodities and planned lending by the government to the private sector. In 2009 the economy weakened and GDP growth fell to -1.3 per cent, as the global economic crisis cut trade and foreign exchange fell. Growth picked up and registered 6.4 per cent in 2010. Inflation escalated from 8.2 per cent in 2007 to 26.8 per cent in 2008 as food imports and energy reached all-time highs. A fall in imports and consumer spending in 2009 meant that inflation fell back to around 3.6 per cent in 2009, before rising to 10.2 per cent in 2010

Mongolia has done much to embrace the practices of a free-market economy by privatising state-owned enterprises, but it also has a substantial grey economy, estimated to be as much as 50 per cent of GDP. The authorities have much more to do to bring this into the financial system, at a time of growing concern regarding money laundering through its banking system.

External trade

Mongolia belongs to the World Trade Organisation (WTO), but does not belong to any regional trade community; it has bilateral agreements with India, Russia and the US.

The economy is underpinned by sales in primary products, in particular copper, gold, molybdenum, tin and tungsten, which together represent 20 per cent of GDP.

Imports

Main imports are petroleum, electricity, machinery and equipment, vehicles, food products, consumer goods, chemicals, building materials, sugar and tea.

Main sources: Russia (typically 35 per cent of total), China (30 per cent), Korea (6 per cent).

Exports

The main export products are copper, gold, cashmere, livestock, animal products, wool, hides, fluorspar and other non-ferrous metals.

Main destinations: China (typically 75 per cent of total), Canada (10 per cent), US (4 per cent)

Agriculture

Farming

Major crops include barley, potatoes and wheat. Primary meat products include beef and veal, chicken, horse, camel, lamb and pork. The major agricultural exports are carded hair, wool sheepskins, beef and fine animal hair.

Following a severe winter in 2009–10, when 15 out of 21 provinces were declared disaster zones, around 20 per cent (over 8.5 million head of livestock) of the national herd died through hunger or by freezing to death in -45 degrees Celsius temperatures and heavy snows. Those that survived the winter were left weak, threatening the nomadic nature of herders in Mongolia, who may be forced to relinquish their lifestyle. The brutal winter, called a *zhud*, was blamed on climate change. The UN called on donor countries to provide US$21 million to help clean up and re-build the lives of the nomads, while analysts pointed out that an increase in animal numbers and inexperienced herders contributed to the poor winter's outcome.

Industry and manufacturing

The industrial sector contributes around 28 per cent to GDP and employs 12 per cent of the workforce. Industrial activity is centred on Ulaanbaatar and other main cities and is based mainly on agricultural products and mining. Products include bricks, cement, lime, sawn timber, scoured wool, felt, felt boots, woollen fabric, leather footwear, soap, flour, garments, matches, bakery goods, confectionery, meat products, beer and vodka.

Mining

Since 2004 mining has become the major component of the Mongolian economy. In 2008 the sector contributed 28.2 per cent of GDP and represented 64.3 per cent of industrial output and 80.7 per cent of total exports.

Mongolia boasts one of the richest reserves of mineral resources in the world, but economic mismanagement and a shortage of infrastructure have hindered exploitation. There are plans for 1,800km of track to start construction in 2010. The six rail lines will be followed in 2011 by a further 1,400km and in 2015 by another 2,000km. The lines will have a Russian gauge, necessitating a change of chassis as trains transit into China.

The Erdenet copper-molybdenum complex, an open-pit mining and concentrating development 340km from Ulaanbaatar, accounts for a large proportion of exports by value. Copper reserves are large enough for another 60 years.

Other mines include fluorspar at Bor-Ondör and gold at Ih-altat. Gold mining has increased significantly since 1990. Mongolia has approximately 2,000 tonnes of gold reserves. Major gold-producing areas are Naran, Tolgoi and Zamar.

Other minerals present include iron, zinc, silver, tungsten, tin, lead and graphite, but production levels are limited by inefficient extraction methods.

Mineral products account for around 40 per cent of the country's total exports. Almost all of Mongolia's copper concentrates are exported to Russia and China.

A law passed in 1995 permits full foreign ownership of mining ventures in Mongolia, including those involving precious metals. Gold producers are no longer forced to sell to the Mongolian central bank at prices below the prevailing international price.

The first foreign investment gold mine, Boroo Gold, opened in 2004 and immediately pushed up Mongolia's output by 40 per cent. The government signed a number of agreements with multinational mining companies to develop Mongolia's large copper deposits 80km from its border with China. When fully expanded the copper mining sector could provide around one-third of government revenue. The estimate is that deposits could produce 450,000 tonnes of copper ore by 2018.

Hydrocarbons

There are only small reserves of oil which have been identified and no known natural gas reserves. However international oil companies are interested in investing in Mongolia as a country with no drilling history and contiguous geological features, which have produced hydrocarbon reserves in neighbouring countries.

The Swiss company, Manas Petroleum Corporation, signed a production deal with the Petroleum Authority of Mongolia (PAM) in April 2009 to explore in licensed blocks in the south. The US company, Canoil International Energy Limited, signed a production deal with the PAM in May 2009 to explore in south-eastern Mongolia in the East Gobi basin, close to China's currently productive oil field in the Erlian basin.

Domestic consumption of oil was around 15,000 barrels per day in 2008, all of which was imported, mainly from Russia. There are no oil refineries.

There are sizeable deposits of coal reserves most of which is lignite. Production was 8.4 million tonnes in 2007. Coal accounts for around 80 per cent of primary energy consumption. The Mineral Resources Authority of Mongolia (MRAM) is responsible for policymaking and managing national coal assets.

Energy

Total installed generating capacity was 832MW in 2007, the majority of which is derived from coal-fired thermal power stations.

Financial markets

Stock exchange

Mongolyn Khöröngiin Birj (Mongolian Stock Exchange) (MSE)

Banking and insurance

There is a two-tier banking system.

Central bank

Bank of Mongolia

Main financial centre

Ulaanbaatar

Time

GMT plus eight hours

Geography
Mongolia is a landlocked country in central Asia, with Russia to the north and the People's Republic of China to the south, east and west.
The land consists of a plateau that rises to between 914–1,524 metres with mountain ranges running from the west to north-east. The tallest mountains are the Altai Mountains in the south-west, which rise to 4,267 metres. The large, flat plains of the centre, east and south-east include untracked Steppes and the arid Gobi desert. The largest rivers are the Selenge Mörön and its tributary, the Orhon Gol, which crosses the border into Russia in the north.
Hemisphere
Northern

Climate
Summers are warm and wet, and winters extremely cold. In Ulaanbaatar, winter temperatures range from minus 4 degrees Celsius (C) to minus 50 degrees C, with an average of minus 26 degrees C in January; in summer temperatures range from 0–40 degrees C, with an average of 17 degrees C in July. Relative humidity ranges from 65 per cent (July–August) to 75 per cent (November–February). Rainfall is low, with an average of 233mm per year in Ulaanbaatar (two-thirds of which falls June–August) and 116–344mm per year elsewhere. On average, there are 250 cloudless days a year.

Entry requirements
Passports
Required by all and must have six months validity from the date of entry to Mongolia.
Visa
Required by all, with some exceptions see: www.un.int/mongolia and follow the link to *visa and travel* for further information. Business and tourist visitors staying for more than 30 days are referred to as temporary residents and apply with a non-tourist visa; a local contact or business partner will increase the chance of visa approval. When granted, visitors must register with the Foreign Citizens Bureau in Ulaanbaatar within seven days of arrival. Visitors who need to register must de-register before leaving Mongolia, at the Office of Immigration, Naturalization and Foreign Citizens. After de-registering, an 'exit visa' from the consular department of the Mongolian Ministry of Foreign Affairs will be issued.
Contact the nearest consulate for further advice and to confirm all aspects of visa requirements before travelling.
Currency advice/regulations
The import of local currency is limited to Tug815 and must be declared. The import of foreign currency is limited to US$2,000 or its equivalent. The export of local and foreign currency is limited the amount declared on arrival.
Travellers cheques have limited use in the capital, cheques in US dollars are easiest to exchange.
Customs
Importation of pornography and export of valuable antiques is strictly prohibited. Customs regulations are enforced by strict examinations. Firearms for sporting purposes require a licence. Import allowances included 200 cigarettes and two litres of alcohol.

Health (for visitors)
Mandatory precautions
No vaccination certificates are required.
Advisable precautions
Immunisations for typhoid, TB, hepatitis A and B are necessary while tetanus, diphtheria and polio vaccinations should be up-to-date. Rabies is a risk, particularly in rural areas.
There is a shortage of routine medications and visitors should take all necessary medicines with them. A first aid kit that includes disposable syringes, is a reasonable precaution. Use only bottled or boiled water for drinks, washing teeth and making ice. Eat only well cooked meals, preferably served hot; vegetables should be cooked and fruit peeled. Dairy products are unpasteurised and should be avoided, unless cooked.
Healthcare is not to Western standards and medical insurance, including emergency evacuation, is necessary.

Hotels
There are a number of suitable hotels for foreign visitors in Ulaanbaatar, but in the provinces facilities are basic.

Credit cards
International credit and charge cards are accepted in major city centres.

Public holidays (national)
Fixed dates
1 Jan (New Year's Day), 8 Mar (Women's Day), 1 Jun (Mothers' and Childrens' Day), 11–13 Jul (Naadam), 26 Nov (Independence Day).
Variable dates
Bituum and Tsagaan Sar (Lunar New Year) (Jan/Feb/Mar, three days)

Working hours
Banking
Mon–Fri: 0930–1230; 1400–1500.
Business
Mon–Fri: 0900–1800.
Government
Mon–Fri: 0900–1800.
Shops
Mon–Sat: 1000–1800 (some food shops stay open later). Some open Sunday.

Telecommunications
Mobile/cell phones
GSM 900 services are available in large urban areas only.

Electricity supply
240V AC, 50Hz

Weights and measures
Metric system.

Getting there
Air
National airline: MIAT (Mongolian Airlines)
International airport/s: Ulaanbaatar Buyant-Ukhaa (ULN), 15km from city, facilities include duty-free shops, bank, restaurant and car hire. Taxis and buses provide access to the city, travel time 15–30 minutes.
Airport tax: Departure tax of US$12
Surface
Road: While there are many roads that cross the borders from China and Russia only a few are designated for international visitors and permission must be obtained from Mongolian authorities to cross, before travelling.
The Regional Road Corridor Improvement Project, estimated at US$18 billion, to improve Central Asian roads, airports, railway lines and seaports and provide a vital transit route between Europe and Asia was agreed, on 3 November 2007. Six new transit corridors, between Afghanistan, Azerbaijan, China, Kazakhstan, Kyrgyzstan, Mongolia, Tajikistan and Uzbekistan, of mainly roads and rail links, will be constructed, or existing resources upgraded, by 2013. Half the costs with be provided by the Asian Development Bank and other multilateral organisations and the other half by participating countries.
Rail: Ulaanbaatar is served by the Trans-Mongolian Railway connecting Moscow and Beijing, with an express train that runs once a week. International trains have restaurant and sleeping cars.
There are frequent delays on the routes to Beijing and Siberia. Trains operate on summer and winter schedules, alternating in May and October.

Getting about
National transport
Air: MIAT operates an extensive domestic network. Regular air services provide the only feasible means of long-distance internal travel, although delays and cancellations are frequent. There are officially 21 airports, but only eight have paved runways.
Road: There are 46,700km of roads and tracks. Only 3 per cent of roads are paved (mainly around the cities). Many of the unpaved roads and cross-country tracks are impassable during the summer, because of flooding or waterlogging. The

poor railway network dictates that roads provide the only access routes to 16 of Mongolia's 21 provinces.

Buses: Inter-urban bus services are available, with many long-distance bus routes, but their use is unfeasible due to the distances involved.

Rail: In addition to the cities served by the Trans-Mongolian Railway (Sühbaatar, Darhan, Ulaanbaatar, Dzamyn-Uüd and Saynshand), there are branch lines to various industrial centres and mining towns, including Erdenet, Baganuur and Bor-Ondör. Total network 1,815km.

City transport

Taxis: Taxis are available for journeys from the airport to the city centre, with a journey time of 15 minutes.

Buses, trams & metro: There are trolley-buses and buses. Service 11 operates 0600–2200 from airport to city centre, journey time 30 minutes.

Car hire

A hire car with driver is the only option as local knowledge of conditions is vital; hires can be arranged by most hotels or tourist organisations in Ulaanbaatar. Rates vary from fixed hourly, daily, weekly or monthly hire.

Off-road vehicles can be hired from specialist suppliers but a local licence is required, this can be obtained, for a fee, using a valid national or international licence.

BUSINESS DIRECTORY

Telephone area codes

The international direct dialling code (IDD) for Mongolia is +976, followed by area code and subscriber's number:

Ulaanbataar 11

Useful telephone numbers

Police: 102

Fire: 101

Ambulance: 103

Car hire

Ulaanbaatar

Car Base: (tel: 379-965).

Chambers of Commerce

Mongolian National Chamber of Commerce & Industry, 11 J Sambuu Street, Ulaanbaatar 38 (tel: 312-501; fax: 324-620; e-mail: info@mongolchamber.mn).

Ulaanbaatar Chamber of Commerce, Box 254, Ulaanbaatar 210136 (tel; 329-912; fax: 311-385; e-mail: ubcc@magicnet.mn).

Banking

Agricultural Bank, PO Box 185, Peace Avenue, Ulaanbaatar (tel: 457-880; fax: 458-670); e-mail: haab@magicnet.mn).

Anod Bank of Mongolia, PO Box 361, 18 Commerce Street, Chingeltei, Ulaanbaatar (tel: 327-566; fax: 313-070); e-mail: anod@magicnet.mn).

The Bank of Mongolia, Baga Toiruu-9, Ulaanbaatar (tel: 322-166; fax: 311-471).

Credit Bank, Suknbaatar Square, 20A, Ulaanbaatar (tel: 321-897; fax: 321-897).

Erelbank Ltd, Chingis Avenue, Khan-uul District, Ulaanbaatar (tel: 343-387; fax: 343-567).

Golomt Bank of Mongolia, PO Box 22, 4th Floor, Sukhbaatar Square 3, Central Place of Culture, Ulaanbaatar (tel: 311-530; fax: 312-307).

Mongol Post Bank, PO Box 874, Kholboochdiin Street 4, Ulaanbaatar (tel: 310-301; fax: 328-501).

Savings Bank, 6 Commerce Street, Ulaanbaatar (tel: 327-467; fax: 327-467).

Trade & Development Bank of Mongolia, 7 Commerce Street, Ulaanbaatar (tel: 327-020; fax: 312-418).

Ulaanbaater City Bank, PO Box 370, Baga toiruu 15, Ulaanbaatar (tel: 312-155; fax: 311-067).

Zoos Bank, 6 Choimbalin, Chingeltei, Ulaanbaatar (tel: 329-537; fax: 329-537).

Central bank

Bank of Mongolia, Baga Toiruu 9, Ulaanbaatar 46 (tel: 310-392; fax: 311-417; email: feprmd@mongolbank.mn).

Stock exchange

Mongolyn Khöröngiin Birj (Mongolian Stock Exchange) (MSE): www.mse.mn

Travel information

Flight information (0800-2200 hours) (tel: 119).

Juulchin, Ulaanbaatar (tel: 320-246, 328-428).

MIAT Head Office, MIAT Building, Buyant-Ukhaa 45, Ulaanbaatar 210134 (tel: 379-935, 984-070; fax: 379-919; email: contact@miat.com; internet: www.miat.com).

Ulaanbaatar Buyant-Ukhaa Airport, Ulaanbaatar 34 (tel: 379-986; fax: 379-744).

National tourist organisation offices

Mongolian Tourism Association, Room 318, Trade Union Building, Sukhbaatar Square 11, Ulaanbaatar 38 (tel/fax: 327-820; internet: www.travelmongolia.org)

Ministries

Ministry of Finance, Ulaanbaatar 46.

Ministry of Foreign Relations, Ulaanbaatar 11.

Ministry of Trade and Industry, 11 Sambuu St, Ulaanbaatar 46 (tel: 706-146; fax: 326-325).

Other useful addresses

British Embassy, 30 Enkh Taivry Gudamzh, PO Box 703, Ulaanbaatar 13 (tel: 458-133; fax: 458-036; email: britemb@mongol.net).

Mongol An Corporation, Baigal Ordon, Ulaanbaatar 38 (tel/fax: 360-067).

Mongolian Business Development Agency (MBDA), U Barsbold (fax: 311-092; email: mbda@magicnet.mn).

Mongolian Embassy (US), 2833 M Street, NW, Washington DC 20007 (tel: (+1-202) 333-7117; fax: (+1-202) 298-9227; email: monemb@aol.com).

Mongolian Stock Exchange, Sukhbaatar Square 14, Ulaanbaatar (tel: 310-501; fax: 325-170; email: msebatj@magicnet.mn).

The Permanent Mission of Mongolia to the United Nations, 6 East 77th street, New York, NY10021-1704 (tel: (+1-212) 861-9460; fax: (+1-212) 861-9464; email: mongolia@un.int).

School of Economic Studies (Economic Institute), National University of Mongolia (fax: 325-349; email: suvd@magicnet.mn).

State Statistical Board, Ulaanbaatar 11 (fax: 324-518).

National news agency: Montsame Agency, PO Box 1514, 8 Jigiidjav Street, Ulaanbaatar (tel: 314-507; fax: 327-857; internet: www.montsame.mn).

Internet sites

Guide to Mongolia (with links): http://www.mongoliaonline.com

Mongolian Stock Exchange: http://mse.com.mn

Parliament of Mongolia: http://www.parl.gov.mn/english.htm

School of Economic Studies: http://www.ses.edu.mn

State Property Committee: http://www.spc.gov.mn

Montenegro

In December 2010 Montenego's Prime Minister Milo Đukanovic resigned. At a news conference in December he announced his decision to step down as prime minister saying he would still play an important role in the ruling Demokratska Partija Socijalista (DPS) (Democratic Party of Socialists). Djukanovic emphasised he was stepping down after serving in top posts for two decades and not because he was being forced to. 'This decision of mine is not sudden or rash and was not reached, as certain irresponsible individuals claim for reasons known only to themselves, under anyone's pressure, either from the inside or from the outside,' he announced. 'Today, conditions have become ripe for my withdrawal from the executive authority'.

Mr Djukanovic said the time was right for a change and that his party's leadership had already proposed deputy prime minister and finance minister, Igor Luksic, to lead the new government. Djukanovic also said he wanted to continue his professional life 'in a more relaxing business environment'. Referring to the Balkan cigarette smuggling case for which he faced charges in the 1990s, Djukanovic said 'I am withdrawing from the executive authority with a clean conscience.'

Igor Lukšic (DPS) replaced Mr Đukanovic as prime minister on 29 Dec 2010, after being nominated by the President and confirmed in office by the Skupština Republike Crne Gore (Parliament of Montenegro).

Solid basics

Nearly 85 per cent of the capital value of Montenegran companies has already been privatised. The banking sector, telecommunications, oil distribution and import services are all privately owned. Nevertheless, Montenegro's business environment is still weak if measured by its international ranking, despite a significant improvement since independence. Montenegro ranks a lowly 81st (out of 183) in the world according to the World Bank's *Ease of doing business* index. Long licensing procedures, the severe difficulties faced when registering a property, a bureaucratic trading environment and a high level of difficulty in enforcing commercial contracts, remain significant disadvantages in Montenegro's business environment. Economic reforms, such as the privatisation of state-owned assets and a greater freedom of foreign trade and investment, have at least contributed to a stable macro-economic position.

Economic progress

In 2010 a tentative recovery looked to be taking hold, following the global crisis that dealt heavy blows on the economy. A good tourism season was followed by resumed metal production, while heavy rains in the region boosted electricity production and exports. The International Monetary Fund (IMF) noted that after contracting for almost two years, industry began to grow again in the second half of 2010. Nevertheless, industrial production at end-2010 was still considerably below its pre-crisis peak. Expected large-scale infrastructure foreign direct investment (FDI) has so far not materialised and construction activity remains depressed. Overall 2010 gross domestic product (GDP) growth was estimated at 1.1 per cent, keeping output below its 2008 level.

A rebalancing of the economy has begun. Inflation and wage growth have decelerated sharply and the current account deficit halved to around 26 per cent of GDP in 2010. While most of the improvement was due to a weather related boost in electricity exports and rebounding metals production, the nascent adjustment in costs has also improved competitiveness. The improved fundamentals have also contributed to the September 2010 debut eurobond issuance of €200 million (US$268 million), subsequent spread tightening and a further €180 million (US$241 million) issuance in April 2011.

Fiscal consolidation has commenced. Reflecting mainly significant capital expenditure cuts, the 2010 fiscal deficit is estimated to have declined by 1.5 per cent of GDP to 3.9 per cent. Loan guarantees, though, of 3.6 per cent were extended to industrial companies. Going forward, the authorities aim at balancing the budget in 2012 and achieving a sizeable surplus thereafter in order to bolster

KEY FACTS

Official name: Republika Crna Gora (Republic of Montenegro) (ROM)

Head of State: President Filip Vujanovic (since 2002; elected 2003, 6 Apr 2008)

Head of government: Prime Minister Igor Lukšic (DPS) (from 29 Dec 2010)

Ruling party: Koalicija za Evropsku Crnu Goru (KECG) (Coalition for European Montenegro, comprising Demokratska Partija Socijalista (DPS) (Democratic Party of Socialists), Socijaldemokratska Partija (SDP) (Social Democratic Party) and Demokratska Unija Albanaca (DUA) (Democratic Union of Albania) (from 2006; re-elected 2009)

Area: 14,026 square km

Population: 633,000 (2010)*

Capital: Podgorica (administrative); Cetinje (cultural)

Official language: Montenegro Serbian (Lekavian dialect)

Currency: Euro (€) = 100 cents (from 1 Jan 2002; previous currency Deutsche mark, locked at DM1.96 per euro)

Exchange rate: €0.75 per US$ (Oct 2011)

GDP per capita: US$6,070 (2010)

GDP real growth: 1.10% (2010)

GDP: US$4.00 billion (2010)

Labour force: 194,000 (2010)

Unemployment: 16.50% (2010)

Inflation: 0.50% (2010)

Balance of trade: -US$1.03 billion (2010)

Annual FDI: US$760.44 million (2010)

* estimated figure

sustainability, lower financing risk and boost the economy's resilience to shocks.

In the banking sector, confidence has begun to return, as evidenced by increasing deposits, though they were still below their levels of the third quarter of 2007. However, non-performing loans have not yet leveled off and Financial Soundness Indicators have continued to deteriorate. Stagnant lending at the current juncture primarily reflects the dearth of credit-worthy projects.

The IMF noted that, although Montenegro's recovery is gaining momentum, limited scope for policy implementation and incomplete reforms posed risks to the outlook. The IMF encouraged the Montenegran authorities to step up efforts to reconstitute fiscal, external and financial buffers and to address rigidities in product and labour markets.

The IMF also welcomed the start of fiscal consolidation and supported the government's plan to balance the central government budget by 2012 and run surpluses thereafter. It also considered that a durable fiscal adjustment should encompass both revenue and expenditure measures, including steps to increase the yield from property taxes and curb the public sector wage bill. An early implementation of pension reform would also strengthen the public finances, as would further efforts to avoid expenditure arrears and direct budget support to private companies.

The IMF stressed the importance of restoring the soundness of the banking system to bolster the resilience of the economy and promote private sector-led growth. It welcomed recent steps to reinforce the legal and prudential frameworks and encouraged stronger supervisory practices. In particular, noting that full 'euroisation' limits the ability of the central bank to provide liquidity support to banks, the IMF called for conservative capital and liquidity requirements and an early unwinding of regulatory forbearance. Noting the importance of strengthened competitiveness for securing external stability, it also agreed that structural reforms should remain a top policy priority. Greater flexibility in wage setting and employment protection would support job creation in the private sector, while addressing unemployment and poverty traps that would boost labour participation and market attachment. Improvements in the business environment and investment climate were also part of the unfinished agenda. It was noted that long-standing weaknesses in economic statistics (partly because of the way data was handled under the previous regime of Yugoslavia) hamper policy design and evaluation.

Risk assessment

Economy	Fair
Politics	Fair
Regional stability	Fair

COUNTRY PROFILE

Historical profile

1878 Following the collapse of the Ottoman Empire, of which Montenegro had been an autonomous region, the independence of the principality of Montenegro was recognised under international treaties.

1910 Prince Nikola became king and helped lead the Balkan forces that pushed the European boundaries of the Ottoman Empire back to north of Constantinople.

1914–18 As a supporter of the Allies (*Entente* Powers), Montenegro was occupied by Austro-Hungarian troops.

1918 The defeat of the Austro-Hungarian empire during the First World War saw the creation of the Kingdom of the Serbs, Croats and Slovenes, encompassing Bosnia and Hercegovina (BiH), Croatia, parts of Dalmatia and Macedonia, Montenegro, Serbia, Slavonia and Slovenia. King Nikola was deposed when, during the Podgorica People's Assembly, Montenegro voted for a union with the Kingdom of Serbia.

1919 The Kingdom of Serbs, Croats and Slovenes became a semi-autonomous region of Hungary.

1929 Following disputes between Serbs and Croats, King Alexander assumed dictatorial powers and the country was renamed Yugoslavia.

1941–45 During the Second World War parts of Yugoslavia were occupied by the Germans, Italians, Hungarians and Bulgarians.

1945–46 Following the end of the war, Serbia and Montenegro became two of the constituent republics of a federated Yugoslavia. The other republics were Bosnia and Hercegovina (BiH), Croatia, Macedonia, Slovenia and the two autonomous regions of Vojvodina and Kosovo. As the leader of the Yugoslav Communist Party (YCP), Josip Broz Tito became head of state and a Soviet-style constitution was adopted. The Serbian state and Belgrade, as the federation's capital, were the primary focus of economic and political control and the majority of the officers of the Yugoslav military were from Serbia and Montenegro.

1980 Tito died. A system of collective (rotating) presidency was adopted; ethnic tensions began to re-surface.

1989 The Serbian nationalist, Slobodan Milosevic, became president of the Republic of Serbia.

1991 Slovenia and Croatia and later Macedonia declared their independence from Yugoslavia.

1992 BiH declared its independence. Bosnian Serbs (who made up 30 per cent of the population) backed by the remaining Yugoslav federation, declared their own independence from BiH, claiming 65 per cent of the territory. The degree of inter-ethnic violence that followed, including 'ethnic cleansing', had not been seen in Europe since the Second World War. The UN imposed economic sanctions against Serbia and Montenegro, the only two Yugoslavian republics remaining.

1997 Milo Djukanovic (prime minister of Montenegro since 1994) became

KEY INDICATORS — Montenegro

	Unit	2006	2007	2008	2009	2010
Population	m	6.54	0.66	0.66	*0.66	*0.63
Gross domestic product (GDP)	US$bn	48.46	3.80	4.80	4.10	4.00
GDP per capita	US$	0	6,208	7,819	6,635	6,070
GDP real growth	%	5.7	10.7	6.9	-5.7	1.1
Inflation	%	2.1	3.4	8.5	3.4	0.5
Unemployment	%	22.3	18.0	15.1	14.0	16.5
Exports (fob) (goods)	US$m	594.0	744.0	760.0	412.0	472.0
Imports (fob) (goods)	US$m	1,342.0	2,330.0	2,942.0	2,317.0	2,217.0
Balance of trade	US$m	-748.0	-1,587.0	-2,182.0	-1,906.0	-1,745.0
Current account	US$m	*-755.0	-880.0	-1,473.0	-1,245.0	-1,031.0
Total reserves minus gold	US$m	432.7	732.6	478.4	572.6	556.2
Foreign exchange	US$m	432.7	722.0	467.8	521.3	505.7
Exchange rate	per US$	0.75	0.69	0.68	0.78	0.76

* estimated figure

president of Montenegro, after defeating a pro-Milosevic candidate. Milosevic was named president of what remained of Yugoslavia.
1998 NATO began air-strikes against military targets. NATO peace-keepers moved into Kosovo.
1999 NATO extended air-strikes to include mainly Serbian infrastructure. Politically, Montenegro began to distance itself from Serbia declaring it was not a party to the conflict in Kosovo.
2002 Demokratska Lista za Evropsku Crnu Goru (DLECG) (Democratic List for a European Montenegro) coalition, led by the Demokratska Partua Socualista Crne Gore (DPS) (Democratic Socialist Party), won the parliamentary elections. Milo Djukanovic (DPS) resigned from the presidency to become prime minister while former prime minister, Filip Vujanovic, took over as acting president. The euro was adopted as the official currency.
2003 Yugoslavia was abolished and replaced with a looser federation of its two member states, Serbia and Montenegro. Yugoslav President Kostunica stepped down and was replaced as Head of the State of Serbia and Montenegro by Svetozar Marovic, a Montenegrin. Filip Vujanovic was elected president of Montenegro.
2006 In a referendum on independence, 55 per cent voted to sever ties with Serbia. Montenegro formally declared itself an independent state and also became a member of the United Nations. In the first independent parliamentary elections the ruling coalition claimed victory. Prime Minister Djukanovic resigned and Zeljko Sturanovic (DPS) was appointed as his replacement. Montenegro joined NATO.
2007 A Stabilisation and Association Agreement (SAA) between the European Union and Montenegro, the first step in the process for accession to the EU, was signed. The agreement required constitutional and judicial reforms to comply with EU membership.
2008 Prime Minister Sturanovic resigned due to ill health; Milo Đukanovic took over. In presidential elections, incumbent Filip Vujanovic (DPS) won 51.89 per cent of the vote, while his nearest rival Andrija Mandic (Serb List) polled 19.55 per cent.
2009 In early parliamentary elections held in March, incumbent KECG won 51.94 per cent of the vote (48 seats (out of 81)); Prime Minister Đukanovic continued in office. The EU approved Montenegro's application to become a candidate for membership. Visa-free travel for all citizens of Montenegro within the EU's Schengen area became operable.
2010 In January, Montenegro was designated as .me on internet domain sites. A government-backed Eurobond of €200 million (US$254.9 million) was issued on 8 September, in a measure to cover the public deficit and avoid borrowing the amount from the International Monetary Fund (IMF). The Montenegrin bond, the first issued since independence, was set at ten years with a fixed interest rate of 7.85 per cent. Prime Minister Milo Đukanovic resigned on 21 December and Igor Lukšic (DPS) became prime minister on 29 December.
2011 A national census took place between 1–15 April, with preliminary results published in July. The population was 625,266, of which 44.98 per cent were designated Montenegrins, 28.73 Serbian, and 11.96 per cent Bosniaks (Bosnian Muslims). On 21 June, EU officials announced that Montenegro could apply for EU membership by the end of the year.

Political structure

Constitution

Passed in 1992.
The constitution may be amended if 10,000 voters, not less than 25 deputies or the president and prime minister submit a proposal, which is subsequently agreed by two-thirds of the Assembly members.

Independence date

3 June 2006 (from Serbia); 27 April 1992 (from Yugoslavia)

Form of state

Democratic, social and ecological state

The executive

The president of the republic is elected by universal suffrage for a term of five years. A president is limited to two terms in office.
The president has the right to refer adopted laws back to the Assembly for review; if the new legislation is passed for a second time the president must promulgate the law. The president names a successor if a prime minister loses the confidence of the Assembly.
A new law governing presidential elections was enacted in December 2007. All candidates must collect signatures from 1.5 per cent of registered voters to achieve a place in the ballot.

National legislature

The unicameral Skupština Republike Crne Gore (Parliament of Montenegro), has 81 members elected by proportional representation through party lists, to serve for four-year terms. The total number of deputies may vary dependent on population numbers of one deputy elected per 6,000 votes.
The president nominates the prime minister and parliament confirms the appointment, plus the proposed cabinet. All government policies and laws must be agreed by parliament; without agreement the prime minister must resign and be replaced by another candidate.

Legal system

The rule of law is mandated in the constitution.
The legal system is independent and autonomous. The law is administered by a judge and jury in public, where citizens have the right to legal assistance. The Supreme Court is the highest court of law. Capital punishment is reserved for the most serious offences.

Last elections

6 April 2008 (presidential); 29 March 2009 (parliamentary)
Results: Presidential: Filip Vujanovic (DPS) won 51.89 per cent of the vote, Andrija Mandic (Srpska lista (Serb List, coalition)) 19.55 per cent, Nebojša Medojevic (PzP) 16.64 per cent, Srdan Milic (SNP) 11.92 per cent.
Parliamentary: Koalicija za Evropsku Crnu Goru (KECG) (Coalition for European Montenegro) led by the Demokratska Partija Socijalista (DPS) (Democratic Party of Socialists), won 51.94 per cent of the vote (47 seats out of 81), Socijalisticka Narodna Partija Crne Gore (SNP) (Socialist People's Party (of Montenegro)) 16.83 per cent (16), Nova Srpska Demokratija (NSD) (New Serb Democracy) 9.22 per cent (8), Pokret za Promjene (PzP) (Movement for Change) 6.03 per cent (5), Demokratski Centar Crne Gore (DC) (Democratic Centre of Montenegro) (4), Demokratska Srpska Stranka (DSS) (Democratic Serb Party (2), Narodna Stranka (NS) (People's Party) (1); four ethnic Albanian parties, including Demokratska Unija Albanaca (DUA) (Democratic Union of Albania) one seat each. Turnout was 66.2 per cent.

Next elections

2013 (presidential and parliamentary)

Political parties

Ruling party

Koalicija za Evropsku Crnu Goru (KECG) (Coalition for European Montenegro, comprising Demokratska Partija Socijalista (DPS) (Democratic Party of Socialists), Socijaldemokratska Partija (SDP) (Social Democratic Party) and Demokratska Unija Albanaca (DUA) (Democratic Union of Albania) (from 2006; re-elected 2009)

Main opposition party

Socijalisticka Narodna Partija Crne Gore (SNP) (Socialist People's Party (of Montenegro))

Population

633,000 (2010)*
Last census: 1–15 April 2011: 620,029 (preliminary)

Ethnic make-up

Montenegrin (43.2 per cent), Serbian (32.0 per cent), Bosniak (7.7 per cent), Albanian (5.3 per cent), Croats (1.1 per cent) all others (10.7 per cent).

Religions
Orthodox Christian, Muslim and Roman Catholic.

Education

Compulsory education is provided free by the state. Lessons are taught in Serbian and Albanian, although under the constitution lessons may be taught in the language of any ethnic group.
Cyrillic and Latin text have equal standing under the constitution.
Secondary education may continue from three–four years and culminates in a *matura* graduation certificate, which allows acceptance at a university. There is only one university, in Podgorica, that provides higher education and post-graduate education.
Compulsory years: 7 to 16

Health

Healthcare is publicly financed for children, expectant mothers and the elderly, under the constitution.
Since 1992, the extent and quality of healthcare provision has sharply deteriorated. However, a well-developed private healthcare system has emerged for the better-off. Largely free at the point of delivery and funded by a universal social insurance tax levied on all employees and employers, public healthcare provision require all kinds of charges, most notably for imported medications.

HIV/Aids
There have been few cases of HIV/Aids recorded since the first case was diagnosed in Montenegro in 1989. Nevertheless, the Global Fund to Fight Aids provided US$2.9 million, for a national strategy to combat the disease including prevention measures and diagnostic and antiretroviral treatment for the years 2006–2010.

Welfare

The constitution declared that a mandatory insurance scheme provides all employees and their family all forms of social security. The state is required to provide for the old, infirm and incapable.

Main cities

Podgorica (capital, 141,854 in 2005), Nikšic (58,031), Pljevlja (18,943), Bijelo Polje (17,460).

Languages spoken

Serbian and Albanian
Official language/s
Montenegro Serbian (Lekavian dialect)

Media

Press freedom is guaranteed in law.
Press
Dailies: There are several newspapers published in Montenegro Serbian including *Pobjeda* (www.pobjeda.co.me) *Vijesti* (www.vijesti.cg.yu), *Dan* (www.dan.cg.yu) and *Republika* (www.republika.cg.yu); *Monitor* (www.monitor.cg.yu) is a weekly publication. Newspapers in other languages include *The Montenegro Times* (www.themontenegrotimes.com) in English and *Koha Javore* (www.kohajavore.cg.yu) in Albanian.

Broadcasting
Media laws allowed the transformation of the state-funded broadcaster Radio Televizija CRNE Gore (RTCG) (www.rtcg.cg.yu) into an independent commercial public broadcaster in 2002.
Radio: Most radio stations operate from Podgorica. RTCG (www.rtcg.cg.yu) operates Radio Crne Gore with two stations. Other, private stations include Radio Antena M (www.antenam.net), Corona Radio (www.corona-radio.com) and City Radio (www.cityradio.fm).
Television: RTCG (www.rtcg.cg.yu) operates two, national, terrestrial channels and a satellite channel, broadcasting domestic and imported programmes. Other private channels include TV IN (www.rtvin.com), ntv Montena (www.montena.cg.yu), Elmag RTV and TV Pink M (www.rtvpink.com) a relay from a Serbian station. There are small local TV channels located in larger cities.

News agencies
National news agency: Mina (MNNews): http://mnnews.net

Economy

Since disengaging from Serbia in 2005, the economy has strengthened as Montenegro adopted a fully open market, joined the European Monetary Union (EMU) and adopted the euro as its currency. By June 2009 over 85 per cent of state-owned commercial entities had been privatised, while the banking, telecommunications and oil import and distribution sectors had been fully privatised. This was achieved mainly through a steady increase in foreign direct investment (FDI), so that by 2009 FDI had reached US$1,527 billion (over 10 times the amount of FDI in 2004) and investment per capita was one of the highest in Europe. FDI began to weaken in the aftermath of the global economic recession and was only US$760 million in 2010.
The primary industries in Montenegro are bauxite mining and tourism. However, industry only accounted for around 20.1 per cent of the economy (high production costs have hampered growth in bauxite mining) in 2009, while the service sector accounted for 65.9 per cent, with tourism providing the largest share. In 2006 the government reduced the amount of value added tax (VAT) for all tourism related goods and services (down from the typically 17 per cent for all other goods and services) to encourage growth in tourism.
To encourage domestic spending the government decreased personal tax to a flat rate of 9 per cent in January 2010. GDP growth in 2007 was 10.7 per cent, which fell to 6.9 per cent in 2008 and then fell into recession in 2009 with a negative growth of -5.7 per cent, before rising to 1.1 per cent in 2010. Inflation rose from 4.2 per cent in 2007, which peaked at an official revised rate of 8.5 per cent in 2008, which fell to 3.4 per cent in 2009 and further still to 0.5 per cent in 2010.
High unemployment, typically in double digits, is still characteristic of an earlier economic regime when Montenegro was integrated with Serbia. However, unemployment has steadily fallen from 19.7 per cent in 2005 to 15.1 per cent in 2008 and 14 per cent in 2009 before rising to 16.5 per cent in 2010.

External trade

Montenegro has bilateral free trade agreements with the EU, European Free Trade Association (Efta), Russia and countries of Central and South-Eastern Europe (Cefta). On 16 December 2011, Montenegro was given approval to join the World Trade Organisation (WTO).
While Montenegro has an established industrial sector based on bauxite mining and aluminium production, tourism has become the principal foreign exchange earner.

Imports
Main imports include petroleum and lubricants, vehicles and machinery, capital machinery, manufactured goods, chemicals, food and live animals and raw materials.
Main sources: Serbia (typically 32 per cent of total), Italy (8 per cent), Slovenia (7 per cent).

Exports
Principal exports include aluminium, manufactured goods, food and live animals and raw materials.
Main destinations: Italy (typically 24 per cent of total), Serbia (22 per cent), Greece (22 per cent).

Agriculture

Farming
Around 1 per cent of the workforce is employed in the fishing industry.
Fishing
Around 1 per cent of the workforce is employed in the fishing industry.
Forestry
Montenegro, when it committed itself to eco-friendly development in its 1992 constitution, reflected what is a coincidence of history and geography. Its forests had not been plundered during eras of autocracy so that a largely pristine ecosystem is available for sustainable development including tourism and timber production.

Forest and woodland cover over half the total area of land – 743,609 hectares (ha), of which forest cover is 620,872ha. The majority of forests are state-owned – 500,041ha – while 243,568ha are privately owned. There is an estimated 72.1 million square metres of standing stock, of which conifers amount to 30 million square metres.
State ownership protects forests from over-exploitation, with sustainable objectives for timber production.

Industry and manufacturing
The manufacturing industry is one of the largest employers, followed by retail and transport.

Tourism
Montenegro has been successful in attracting European visitors and headed the list of the worlds fastest growing tourist destinations, by the World Travel and Tourism Council. Tourism accounts for 14.8 per cent of GDP, providing more than 22,000 jobs.

Environment
The constitution mandates that the environment is protected from exploitation.

Mining
There are large deposits of bauxite; aluminium accounts for around 25 per cent of Montenegro's industrial output and almost 75 per cent of export earnings. The first and largest bauxite mines are in Nikšic, employing about 1,400 workers. There are coal mines in Plijevlja but they are chronically underfunded and in need of investment to increase production. There are shale deposits but Montenegro does not have the technology to exploit them.

Hydrocarbons
There are no known oil and gas reserves; oil consumption is typically over 450 barrels per day, all of which is imported. Natural gas is not produced; any consumption is commercially negligible. Consumption of lignite coal is some 1.30 million tonnes for domestic and industrial needs and an additional 1.38 million tonnes for electricity generation. Coalmines, containing lignite, are mainly based in Plijevlja and have been chronically under funded and in need of investment to increase production. There are shale deposits but Montenegro does not have the technology to exploit them.

Energy
Total installed generating capacity was 1,550MW in 2007, producing 6.67 billion kilowatt hours per annum. The energy market has been privatised and the once state-owned Elektroprivreda Crne Gore (EPCG) was broken up. In May 2009, Italy's energy company A2A bought a 15 per cent share in the utility. Although EPCG is responsible for generation, distribution and supply of electricity, it no longer has a monopoly and transmission has been unbundled into a separate company. It runs the two hydroelectric power stations of Piva and Perucica with capacities of 342MW and 302MW respectively, plus the coal-fired power station at Plievlja, producing 210MW.
The Djerdap (Iron Gate) Gorge, located on the Danube, provided 2,532MW shared between Serbia, Montenegro and Romania, but since Montenegro split with Serbia the supply of electricity is subject to international commercial considerations. Montenegro has the potential to be a major exporter of electricity to neighbours and beyond the Balkans from its hydropower reserves. It is currently constructing new hydroelectric dams, including a controversial plan in the world heritage site of the Tara Gorge.

Financial markets
Stock exchange
Montenegro Berza (Montenegro Stock Exchange) (MSE)

Banking and insurance
Central bank
Centralna Banka Crne Gore
Main financial centre
Podgorica

Time
GMT plus two hours, (daylight saving GMT plus one hour, end March to end of October).

Geography
Montenegro is somewhat diamond in shape with a tiny, 25km, border with Croatia in the west. It has a much longer, 225km, border with Bosnia and Herzegovina from the west to the north. Serbia has a 203km border on its east to south east and Albania has a 172km border along the south. Lastly, it has a 294km coastline along the Adriatic Sea from the south west to west.
The name Montenegro (*Crne Gora*) means black mountain and, from the sea, must seem like a solid rock formation. High limestone mountains overshadow the shoreline, rising sharply from the narrow coastal plain (no wider than 10km), which is dotted with many bays and coves. The mountains form a tableland that lacks the soil to sustain much life as rainwater is quickly drained through porous rocks. At 2,522m the highest peak is Bobotov Kuk, in the north west of the country, in high mountains, that stretch along the border with Bosnia and Hercegovina. A matching mountain range lies along the Albanian border. These mountain ranges generally rise to over 2,000m in height, but then 60 per cent of the country is above 1,000m, nevertheless the northern region is futile pasturelands. Over 80 per cent of the country is forest, much of it primeval. There are three main rivers running north/south – Piva, Tara and Lim – added to which are 40 lakes, the largest of which is Skadar, which spans the border with Albania. The river Tara has a 82km long, 1300m deep canyon, which is the world's second deepest chasm (after the US Grand Canyon).
Hemisphere
Northern

Climate
The climate is dictated by the geography. Mediterranean climate allows coastal summer temperatures to reach 26 degrees Celsius (C), falling to 12 degrees C in winter. The tableland has a continental climate, when summer temperatures can reach 40 degrees C and drop during winter as low as 5 degrees C. In the alpine, snowcapped northern mountains winters are cold, temperatures can fall to minus 7 degrees C and summers cool at 20 degrees C.

Entry requirements
Passports
Required by all
Visa
Requirements for Montenegro have yet to be published – the following were appropriate for the union of Serbia and Montenegro and should only be considered as guidelines. Contact a Montenegro Consulate for further information.
Visas are required by all, with the exception of most European, North American and Australasian visitors for both business and tourist reasons. Visitors arriving via Serbia require a visa.
Those visitors that require visas should contact the nearest embassy or consulate for an application form. Business travellers in this category will require a letter of invitation from a local company giving the nature of business, duration of visit and a full itinerary, plus a letter from the employing company confirming details; and proof of sufficient funds for living expenses and medical insurance.
Currency advice/regulations
The import of local and foreign currency is unlimited but must be declared; export is limited to the declared amount.

Hotels
There are a wide range of hotels ranging from luxury to family-run *pensions*. The ministry of tourism began a system of star rating.
Hotel reservations should be made in advance, especially during summer.

Credit cards
Major international credit and charge cards are accepted.

Public holidays (national)

Fixed dates
1 Jan (New Year), 1 May (Labour Day), 9 May (Victory Day), 13 Jul (National Day), 29 Nov (Republic Day).
Variable dates
Orthodox: Christmas (three days), and Easter (two days); Bayram (Feast of the Sacrifice, first day of Ramadam)
These religious holidays are based on the lunar calendar.

Working hours

Banking
Mon–Fri: 0830–1630
Business
Mon–Fri: 0800–1500.
Government
Mon–Fri: 0730–1530.
Shops
Mon–Fri: generally in larger towns: 0800–2000 (some shops may close between 1200–1700); Sat: 0800–1500.

Telecommunications

Mobile/cell phones
There are GSM 900/1800 services that cover almost all of the country.

Electricity supply

220V, 50Hz with European flat and round, two-pin plugs.

Weights and measures

Metric system

Getting there

Air
National airline: Montenegro Airlines
International airport/s: Podgorica International airport (TGD), 12km from the city. A new terminal, opened in May 2006, includes *bureau de change*, restaurant, shops and an information centre. Taxis and buses are available to the city.
Other airport/s: Tivat Airport, on the Adriatic Coast, caters largely for tourist flights from Europe.
Airport tax: Departure tax: eur16, in cash.
Surface
Road: There are border crossings from Croatia at Debeli and Brijeg, from Albania at Bozaj, several from Bosnia and Hercegovina at Vilusi, Vracenovici, Scepan Polje and Metaljka and from Serbia at Bijelo Polje.
Vehicle owners must pay a toll on entering Montenegro.
Rail: There are links to Serbia via Belgrade and Albania via Skadar.
Water: There are regular ferry services from Italy.
Main port/s: Bar, Kotor and Zelenika

Getting about

National transport
Road: There are over 5,000km of roads but only 60 per cent are paved and are not maintained to a high standard. Two major roads that provide access around the country are the Adriatic Highway which runs along the coast from Ulcinj to Igalo and the motorway, with tolls, from Petrovac to the Serbian border at Bijelo Polje, via Podgorica.
Buses: Bus services link most towns and cities.
Rail: There are almost 250km of railways, with most lines running from the coast in the south west to the Serbian border in the north east. All lines run into Podgorica, of which one rail link terminates at Nikšic.
City transport
There are bus services in Podgorica.
Taxis: City taxis have meters, although if not in use negotiate a price before travelling.
Car hire
There are several local and international car hire firms in Montenegro, with cars available at the airport and in large towns.
An international driving licence is necessary, along with insurance. Traffic drives on the right, with speed limits at 120kph on motorways, 100kph on other main roads. Road signs are likely to be in Cyrillic script.

BUSINESS DIRECTORY

The addresses listed below are a selection only. While World of Information makes every endeavour to check these addresses, we cannot guarantee that changes have not been made, especially to telephone numbers and area codes. We would welcome any corrections.

Telephone area codes

The international direct dialling (IDD) code is +381, followed by area code and subscriber's number:

Podgorica	81

Useful telephone numbers

Ambulance	94
Fire	93
Police	92

Chambers of Commerce

Montenegro Chamber of Economy, 29 Novaka Miloseva, 81000 Podgorica (tel: 230-545; fax: 230-943; e-mail: pkcg@cg.yu).

Banking

Atlasmont Banka, 4 Stanka Dragojevica St, Podgorica (tel: 407-200; fax: 665-451; e-mail: office@atlasmont.cg.yu).

Crnogorska Komercijalna Banka (Commercial Bank of Montenegro), Moskovska bb, 81000 Podgorica (tel: 404-232; fax: 404-277: email: info@ckb.cg.yu).

NLB Montenegrobanka, 46 Bulevar Stanka Gragojevica, 81000 Podgorica (tel: 402-212; fax: 402-212; e-mail: info@montenegro-banka.com).

Podgoricka Banka, 8a Novaka Miloseva Street, 81000 Podgorica (tel: 224-555; fax: 405-100; email: pgbanka@cg.yu).

Central bank
Centralna Banka Crne Gore (CBCG) (Central Bank of Montenegro), Bulevar Svetog Petra Cetinjskog 7, Podgorica (tel: 403-191; fax: 664-140; e-mail: info@cb-cg.org).

Stock exchange
Montenegro Berza (Montenegro Stock Exchange) (MSE): www.montenegroberza.com

Stock exchange 2
Nova Berza Hartija od Vrijednosti Crne Gore (New Securities Exchange of Montenegro) (NEX Montenegro): www.nex.cg.yu

Travel information

Automobile Association of Montenegro, Podgorica (AMSCG), (tel: 225-493, 224-467).

Montenegro Airlines, Slobode 23, Podgorica (tel: 664-411/433/455; email: office.podgorica@mgx.cg.yu).

National Tourist Organization of Montenegro, Omladinskih Brigada 7, 81000 Podgorica (tel: 230-959; fax: 230-979; e-mail: tourism@cg.yu)

Zeljeznica Crne Gore (Montenegro railways), Trg Golootockih Zrtava 13, 81000 Podgorica (tel: 441-302; fax: 633-957; email: zcq-uprava@cg.yu).

Tivat Airport, PP24, 85320 Tivat (tel: 670-960; fax: 670-950; internet: www.aptivat.com).

Ministry of tourism
Ministry of Tourism, Rimski trg 46, Kancelarija br 8 Podgorica (tel: 482-145; e-mail: ministarstvo.turizma@mn.yu; internet: www.mturizma.cg.yu; www.visit-montenegro.org).

National tourist organisation offices
National Tourism Organisation, Omladinskih Brigada 7, 81000 Podgorica (tel: 230-959, 230-981; fax: 230-979; email: tourism@cg.yu; internet: www.visit-montenegro.com

Ministries

Ministry of Agriculture, Forestry and Water Management, Podgorica (tel: 482-109; fax: 234-306; email: milanm@mn.yu).

Ministry of Culture and Media, Podgorica (tel: 231-561; fax: 231-540; email: marinko_vorgic@min-kulture.mn.yu).

Ministry of Economics, Podgorica (tel: 242-104, 482-112; fax: 242-028; email: minprivrede@mn.yu).

Ministry of Education and Science, Podgorica (tel: 405-301; fax: 405-334; email: mpin@cg.yu).

Ministry of Environmental Protection and Physical Planning, Podgorica (tel: 482-220; fax: 34-131; email: milenaz@mn.yu).

Ministry of Finance, Stanka Dragojevica br 2, Podgorica (tel: 242-835; fax: 224-450; email: mf@mn.yu).

Ministry of Foreign Affairs, Stanka Dragojevica 2, Podgorica (tel: 246-357, 201-530; fax: 224-670; email: mip.ministar@mn.yu).

Ministry of Health, 46 Romas Square, Podgorica (tel: 234-056, 482-346; fax: 242-762; email: tijanak@mn.yu).

Ministry of Interior, Podgorica (tel: 241-252, 349-000; email: mup.kabinet@cg.yu).

Ministry for International Economic Relations, Stanka Dragojevica br 2, 81000 Podgorica (tel: 225-568; 225-591; email: mierei@mn.yu).

Ministry of Justice, Vuka Karadzica 3, 81000 Podgorica (tel: 507-552; fax: 407-522; email: pravda@cg.yu).

Ministry of Labour and Social Welfare, Podgorica (tel: 234-252; fax: 482-443).

Ministry of Maritime Affairs and Transportation, Rimski trg 46, 81000 Podgorica (tel: 234-179; fax: 234-331; email: mps@mn.yu).

Ministry of Minority Protection, Podgorica (tel: 482-126; fax: 234-198; email: min.manj@cg.yu).

Other useful addresses

Agency of Montenegro for Economic Restructuring and Foreign Investment, Jovana Tomasevica bb, 81000 Podgorica, Montenegro (tel: 242-640; fax: 245-756; email: anaz@mn.yu).

Aluminium Industry of Montenegro (tel: 620-616; fax: 620-955; e-mail: kap.board@cg.yu).

Vektra Montenegro (management, transportation, storage, international trade), Vuka karadzica 10, 81000 Podgorica (tel: 624-500; fax: 625-335; e-mail: office@vektra.cg.yu; internet: www.vektra.cg.yu).

Directorate for Construction of Highways in Montenegro, Podgorica (tel: 625-110, 625-102; fax: 624-353).

Montenegro Development Fund, Bulevar Rvolucije 9, 81000 Podgorica (tel: 245-973; email: fzcrg@cg.yu; internet: www.fzrcg.cg.yu).

Montenegrin Investment Promotion Agency (MIPA), Podgorica (e-mail: info@mipa.cg.yu; internet: www.mipa.cg.yu).

Montenegro Stock Exchange, Cetinjski put 2a (Zgrada Vektre) 81000 Podgorica (tel: 205-940, 205-960; fax: 205-920; internet: www.montenegroberza.com).

National Statistics Office, Proleterske No 2, Street IV, Podgorica (tel: 241-206; fax: 241-270; email: statistika@cg.yu; internet: www.monstat.cg.yu).

New Securities Exchange Montenegro (NEX Montenegro), Miljana Vukova bb, 81000 Podgorica (tel: 230-670, 230-690, 210-170; fax: 230-640; internet: www.nex.cg.yu).

National news agency: Mina (MNNews): http://mnnews.net

Other news agencies: Media Club: www.mediaclub.cg.yu

Internet sites

Customs Administration: www.djp.gc.yu

Government of Montenegro: www.vlada.cg.yu/eng

Official Gazette: www.sllrcg.cg.yu

Montenegro tourism: www.visit-montenegro.com

Montenegro Business Alliance: www.visit-mba.org

Montserrat

KEY FACTS

Official name: Montserrat

Head of State: Queen Elizabeth II; represented by Governor Adrian Davis (from 8 Apr 2011)

Head of government: Premier Reuben Meade (from 27 Sep 2011) (was Chief Minister from 10 Sep 2009)

Ruling party: Movement for Change and Prosperity (MCAP)

Area: 102 square km

Population: 6,000 (2010)* (An estimated 8,000 citizens left the island when volcanic eruptions began in 1995; numbers have yet to return to former levels).

Capital: Plymouth – destroyed by volcano in 1997; temporary headquarters at Brades while Little Bay is being developed as the new capital.

Official language: English

Currency: East Caribbean dollar (EC$) = 100 cents

Exchange rate: EC$2.70 per US$ (fixed)

GDP per capita: US$7,485 (2004)

GDP real growth: -2.83% (2006)

Labour force: 4,520 (pre-1997 eruption)

Inflation: 1.00% (2006)

Balance of trade: -US$18.77 million (2010)

Visitor numbers: 15,700

* estimated figure

COUNTRY PROFILE

Historical profile

1493 Montserrat was first sighted by Columbus.
1632 Britain gained possession of the island and English and Irish Catholic settlers from the Protestant island of St Kitts and Nevis colonised Montserrat.
1648 There were some 1,000 Irish families on the island.
1651 The first slaves were brought to the island to work in the sugar-based economy.
1871–1956 Montserrat was part of the Leeward Islands, and then became a British Dependent Territory.
1958–62 Montserrat was part of the Federation of the West Indies. From 1960 the island had its own administrator (the title was changed to governor in 1971).
1990 A new constitution was adopted.
1995 The Soufriere Hills volcano began to erupt.
1997 Massive volcanic eruptions destroyed the capital Plymouth, the airport and the port, and left the southern half of the island uninhabitable. Nineteen people were killed, thousands were left homeless and the population fell to around 4,000 as many fled to Britain and nearby Caribbean islands. David Brandt replaced Bertrand Osborne as chief minister.
1998 Reconstruction work began under the UK's Sustainable Development Plan.
1999 The UK government announced volcanic activity had dropped to safe levels. Evacuees began to return. With the loss of four and a half of the original seven constituencies, new election rules were introduced, and all national legislature seats became single-seat, first-pass-the-post constituencies.
2000 The growth of a new lava dome at the Soufriere Hills volcano once again threatened the island.
2002 A constitutional review was begun.
2003 There was another major eruption at the Soufriere Hills volcano.
2004 Deborah Barnes-Jones was sworn in as governor. The US Department of Homeland Security removed the temporary protected status of US-based Montserratians.
2005 The new airport was opened allowing access for international visitors.
2006 Although the Movement for Change and Prosperity (MCAP) won most seats In parliamentary elections, it did not win enough for an outright majority. The New People's Liberation Movement (NPLM) and the Montserrat Democratic Party (MDP) coalition formed the government. Lowell Lewis (MDP) was elected chief minister by his coalition colleagues.
2007 Peter Waterworth was sworn in as governor.
2008 The Soufriere Hills volcano exploded again without warning, scattering ash and debris over an area of many kilometres.
2009 Government plans to rebuild the capital were displayed in the cultural centre in Brades. In a pre-emptive move to derail coalition partners' plans to form an alternative government without him, Chief Minister Lewis sacked two ministers and called early general elections. The UK extended conditional aid, with the proviso that the Montserrat government agreed to the reform of public service pensions, the enactment of legislation for integrity in public office, the demonstration of good governance and the appointment of a co-ordinator to oversee improved transport services. It also required the government to provide plans to reduce public expenditure, reduce the size of the public service and increase revenues to the treasury by 2012. In parliamentary elections, MCAP won six seats out of nine and independents three; three other political parties each won less than 11 per cent and failed to win any seats, including Lowell Lewis (MDP). Reuben Meade (MCAP) took office as chief minister; he also became finance minister.
2011 Adrian Davis was sworn in as governor on 8 April. Chief Minister Reuben Meade was appointed annual chairman of the Monetary Council of the Eastern Caribbean Central Bank (ECCB) on 15 July. On 27 September the chief minister, Reuben Meade, was sworn in as premier under the new constitution.

Political structure

Constitution

The 1989 Constitution sets out the legal framework for all executive and legislative power, which came into force in 1990. Montserrat is an internally self-governing British Overseas Territory.

Form of state

British Caribbean dependency

The executive
The British monarch is Head of State and is represented by a governor, who is responsible for defence, internal security (including the police force), external affairs, the public service and international financial services.
The governor chairs meetings of the Executive Council (ExCo), which consists of the governor, attorney general, financial secretary, chief minister and three other ministers, elected from the LegCo.
National legislature
The Legislative Council (LegCo) has nine members, elected for a five-year term in single-seat constituencies.
Last elections
8 September 2009 (parliamentary)
Results: Parliamentary: Movement for Change and Prosperity (MCAP) won 52.64 per cent (six seats out of nine), independents won 31.24 per cent (three); three other political parties each won less than 11 per cent and failed to win any seats.
Next elections
2014 (parliamentary)

Political parties
Ruling party
Movement for Change and Prosperity (MCAP)
Main opposition party
Opposition members sit as independents
Political situation
In parliamentary elections held on 8 September 2009, the Movement for Change and Prosperity (MCAP) won six seats out of nine and independents candidates the remaining three. Reuben Meade took office as chief minister on 10 September, when he also became finance minister. His priority in office was to secure the economy in the face of the global economic downturn and the condition of the island. For over a decade the value of land has been depressed and local residents are beginning to notice that foreign visitors are buying up land for redevelopment as holiday homes despite ongoing seismic disturbances, locals are worrying that if this trend continues those in exile will never be able to afford to return home.
The UK extended conditional aid, with the proviso that the Montserrat government agreed to the reform of public service pensions, the enactment of legislation for integrity in public office, the demonstration of good governance and the appointment of a co-ordinator to oversee improved transport services. It also required the government to provide plans to reduce public expenditure, reduce the size of the public service and increase revenues to the treasury by 2012.
The Montserrat Development Corporation (MDC) was formed to facilitate the building of a new central town at Little Bay, in the north of the island. The MDC will form partnerships with private and public sector organisations to redevelop the island, the first to be the new capital. Local businesses have already begun to relocate and what began as temporary accommodation is quickly becoming permanent.

Population
6,000 (2010)* (An estimated 8,000 citizens left the island when volcanic eruptions began in 1995; numbers have yet to return to former levels).
Last census: May 2001: 4,491
Population density: 94.1 inhabitants per square km, prior to the volcanic eruptions in 1995.
Annual growth rate: 4.2 per cent (2003)
Ethnic make-up
Afro-Caribbean (95 per cent), white (5 per cent).
Religions
Anglican, Methodist, Roman Catholic, Pentecostal, Seventh-Day Adventist.

Education
Montserrat has a high level of literacy. Primary education formally begins at the age of five and continues until the age of 11. The state provides for a full five-year secondary education. Secondary schools offer programmes for academic entry courses to higher education and technical, vocational skills training. The University of the West Indies School of Continuing Studies offers university level courses.
The Montserrat Community College project, which is jointly funded by the EU and the UK-based Department for International Development (DfID), will cost EC$6 million (US$1.8 million). The new college will include classrooms, laboratories, library and offices.
Compulsory years: 2 to 16.

Health
Periodic volcanic eruption has wreaked havoc with health service maintenance, record keeping, and the overall collection of information. The immunisation programme continued to operate well throughout the volcanic emergency.
Life expectancy: 78 years (estimate 2003)
Fertility rate/Maternal mortality rate: 1.8 births per woman (2003)
Birth rate/Death rate: 17.6 births per 1,000 population; 7.3 deaths per 1,000 population (2003).
Child (under 5 years) mortality rate (per 1,000): 7.8 per 1,000 live births (2003)

Welfare
Montserrat remains dependent on the British government for budgetary aid and to finance its capital programmes. Previous Public Sector Investment Programmes were aimed at developing critical infrastructure in the habitable North. The emphasis was on accommodating the displaced population on the island and providing housing for a number of migrant workers from neighbouring Caribbean islands. The British Government has approved £10 million (US$ 14 million) for housing over a period of five years (2001–06).
The Social Welfare System in Montserrat has developed a comprehensive Poverty Protection Programme providing various forms of assistance to its people.

Main cities
Plymouth (estimated population 3,500 before being evacuated in 1996 (due to volcanic activity); by the end of 1997, the city had been destroyed by volcanic eruptions).
Interim government buildings have been built at Brades Estate, in the Carr's Bay/ Little Bay vicinity at the north-west end of Montserrat.

Languages spoken
Official language/s
English

Media
Press
The only newspaper is the weekly *The Montserrat Reporter* (www.themontserratreporter.com).
Broadcasting
Radio: The public radio service ZJB (www.zjb.gov.ms) has a full range of programmes with news, music and regular reports on volcanic activities.
Television: There are two private, cable TV channels, both operated by foreign services.
News agencies
Other news agencies: Caribbean Net News: www.caribbeannetnews.com

Economy
Volcanic activity between 1995–97 left around half of the island uninhabitable as two-thirds of the population fled and the economy fell into ruin. Intensive reconstruction efforts have helped pull the island out of a deep and prolonged recession, aided by US$33 million in funds from the UK Department for International Development (DfID).
GDP growth registers typically in reconstruction work to replace or relocate infrastructure and new construction of facilities for the recovering and strengthening tourism sector, including completion of the new airport, support for private sector development, tourism, housing,

improvements to the road network and developing Little Bay as the new capital. The Montserrat Development Corporation (MDC) was formed in 2007 to facilitate the building of a new central town at Little Bay, in the north of the island. The MDC forms partnerships with private and public sectors organisations to redevelop the island, the first being the new capital. Local businesses are relocating to Little Bay and what began as temporary accommodation has become permanent.
Local seismic predictions stated in 2008 that, in the short-term, further eruptions from the still active volcano are likely to remain localised and relatively small. For a decade the value of land has been depressed but local residents are beginning to notice that foreign visitors are buying up land for redevelopment as holiday homes and worrying that if this trend continues those in exile will never be able to return home.

External trade
As a British Overseas Territory, Montserrat is a member of the association of overseas countries and territories (OCTs) with formal relations with the European Union, which provides, among other things, investment in economic and sustainable development.
Remittances and tourism provide the majority of foreign earnings. There is, however, a large trade deficit, caused by the need to import most basic commodities.
Imports
Main imports include petroleum, lubricants and related materials, machinery and vehicles, foodstuffs and manufactured goods.
Main sources: US, UK, Trinidad and Tobago.
Exports
Commodity exports include light manufactures, agricultural produce and quarried stone.
Main destinations: US, Antigua and Barbuda, UK.

Agriculture
The agricultural sector was declining prior to the volcanic eruptions (1995–97), when approximately 25 per cent of land area was cultivated. There was a further setback when the Soufriere Hills volcano erupted again in 2004, covering 95 per cent of planted crops with ash. Agriculture used to contributed around 4 per cent to GDP, employing 5 per cent of the labour force. The main crops have traditionally been potatoes, tomatoes, carrots, cabbages, cucumbers, sweet potatoes and string beans.
The evacuation order issued in 1996 forced farmers to abandon fields in the danger zone, which was still in place in 2005; those entering the area face legal action.
Output in the agricultural sector has been reduced to merely producing goods for domestic consumption. With the south of the island destroyed by the volcano, land has become a precious commodity. Much of the land in the north is unsuitable for farming. Development efforts now focus on high-yield crops and restoring self-sufficiency in vegetables and livestock.
The typical total annual fish catch is 50t.

Industry and manufacturing
The industrial sector used to account for around 19 per cent of GDP and 10 per cent of employment and included rum, textiles and electronic appliances. After the electronic component assembly plant and the rice milling factory were forced to close due to the volcanic eruptions, the manufacturing sector's share of GDP fell from 5.9 per cent to less than 1 per cent. Manufacturing output is concentrated on two small furniture businesses.
Construction is the largest sector of the economy – mainly due to the demand for housing and basic infrastructure. This has been bolstered by substantial grants from the British government.
Discussions are being held with an Irish company with a view to establishing a factory to utilise volcanic ash in manufacturing roofing slates and other building construction materials for export.

Tourism
The tourism sector used to contribute around a fifth of GDP and was a major foreign exchange earner. After the volcanic eruptions began in 1995, the sector virtually disappeared, mainly due to the destruction of Plymouth, the island's capital, and the main airport. Despite continued volcanic activity, reconstruction of the infrastructure and marketing of the island's attractions have been a priority. A new airport opened in Gerald in 2005. Scheduled, daily flights to Antigua and St Maarten connect with international flights from North America and Europe. The airport is open to charter flights from other Caribbean islands.
Growing numbers of tourists are attracted to Montserrat by the live volcano. The main viewing point is the Montserrat Volcanic Observatory where the pyroclastic flows of lava can be observed. Total visitor arrivals are increasing, albeit from a low start base. Visitors from the English-speaking Caribbean make up around 40 per cent of stay-over tourist arrivals.

Hydrocarbons
There are no known hydrocarbon reserves. Consumption of oil was 1,000 barrels per day (bpd) in 2008, all of which was imported.
Any natural gas or coal used is commercially insignificant.

Energy
Total installed generating capacity was 6MW in 2007, producing 20 million kilowatt hours. The state-owned Montserrat Utilities Limited (MUL) is responsible for electricity and water supplies. While currently all generation is produced by diesel turbines renewable energy sources are being considered.

Financial markets
Stock exchange
Eastern Caribbean Securities Exchange (ECSE)

Banking and insurance
The banking sector was severely effected by the volcano eruption, which destroyed the buildings of the country's main banks. Barclays Bank pulled out of the island while the Royal Bank of Canada reduced its range of services. The locally-owned Bank of Montserrat continues to operate.
The seven members of the Organisation of Eastern Caribbean States (OECS), Antigua and Barbuda, Dominica, Grenada, Montserrat, St Kitts and Nevis, St Lucia and St Vincent and the Grenadines, share a common currency and central bank. The British Virgin Islands and Anguilla are associate members.
Montserrat has implemented the new EU tax directive, introduced in July 2005, as a British Caribbean Dependency. Details of all EU nationals' deposits will be forwarded to the tax department of the relevant EU country, allowing tax to be levied in their home country.
Montserrat has also agreed to supply information on tax fraud, for criminal or civil trials, and notify EU member states about additional malpractices.
Central bank
The Eastern Caribbean Central Bank, St Kitts & Nevis
Offshore facilities
The government is trying to promote offshore banking on the island.

Time
GMT minus four hours

Geography
Montserrat is one of the Leeward Islands in the West Indies. It is a mountainous, volcanic island, which lies about 55km (35 miles) north of Basse Terre, Guadeloupe, and about 43km (27 miles) south-west of Antigua.
Hemisphere
Northern

Climate
The island has tropical weather with a mean temperature of 30 degrees Celsius and low humidity due to tradewinds. There is little variation throughout the

year. The wettest months are from September–November, and the driest from February–June.

Dress codes

Casual lightweight clothing, and during the winter months a light jacket or sweater for the late evening is advisable.

Entry requirements

Passports

Required by all and valid for six months.

Visa

Required by all, except nationals of most EU and Commonwealth countries, North America, Japan and a number of other countries and territories. An onward/return ticket, proof of accommodation and sufficient funds for the stay are required.

Currency advice/regulations

There are no restrictions on import and export of local or foreign currencies, subject to declaration on arrival and limited to declared amount on departure.

Health (for visitors)

Mandatory precautions

Yellow fever vaccination certificate if arriving within six months from an infected area.

Those arriving from areas of known epidemics, including cholera must have vaccination certificates.

Advisable precautions

Typhoid and polio vaccinations are recommended. Tap water is considered safe.

Credit cards

Few shops, hotels or restaurants accept credit cards.

Public holidays (national)

Fixed dates

1 Jan (New Year's Day), 17 Mar (St Patrick's Day), 25–26 Dec (Christmas), 31 Dec (Festival Day).

Variable dates

Good Friday, Easter Monday, Labour Day (first Mon in May), Whit Monday, August Monday (first Mon in Aug).

Working hours

Banking

Bank of Montserrat: Mon, Tue, Thurs: 0800–1400; Wed 0800–1300; Fri: 0800–1500.

Royal Bank of Canada: Mon–Thurs: 0800–1400; Fri 0800–1500.

Business

Mon–Fri: 0800–1200, 1300–1600. Some businesses close early Wed: 0800–1200, and some open Sat: 0800–1230.

Government

Mon–Fri: 0800—1600.

Shops

0800–1600. Most shops close early in the afternoon on Wednesday and Saturday.

Telecommunications

Mobile/cell phones

There is a GSM 850 services available throughout the country.

Electricity supply

220V AC, 60 cycles; also 400V, three-phase.

Social customs/useful tips

A tip of 10 per cent, in hotels and restaurants, is usual.

Getting there

Air

International airport/s: Gerald's Airport (MNI), 2km from Little Bay; restaurant, shop, car hire.

Airport tax: Caricom nationals US$13; other nationals US$21.

Surface

Water: The ferry service between Montserrat and Antigua was discontinued following the opening of Gerald's Airport in July 2005.

Getting about

National transport

Due to volcanic activity, much of the south of the island is designated as an Exclusion Zone, to which entry is banned. Maps of affected areas are available on arrival.

Road: Before the eruption of Soufriere Hills volcano in 1995, there were 269km of roads, of which 203km were paved. The roads in the Exclusion Zone in the south were ruined and many in the rest of the island suffered considerable damage.

Buses: Buses are privately owned and readily available.

City transport

Taxis: Readily available. Legal fixed-rate system.

Car hire

Temporary licences can be obtained on production of national licence. Traffic drives on the left.

BUSINESS DIRECTORY

Telephone area codes

The international direct dialling code (IDD) for Montserrat is +1 664, followed by subscriber's number.

Chambers of Commerce

Montserrat Chamber of Commerce and Industry, PO Box 384, Brades (tel: 491-3640; fax: 491-3639; e-mail: chamber@candw.ag).

Banking

Bank of Montserrat, PO Box 10, St Peters (tel: 491-3843; fax: 491-3163; e-mail: bom@candw.ag).

Royal Bank of Canada, PO Box 222, Brades (tel: 491-2426; fax: 491-3391; e-mail: rbcmont@candw.ag).

Central bank

Eastern Caribbean Central Bank, Agency Office, PO Box 484, 2 Farara Plaza, Brades (tel: 491-6877; fax: 491-6878; e-mail: eccbmni@candw.ms).

Stock exchange

Eastern Caribbean Securities Exchange (ECSE): www.ecseonline.com

Travel information

Carib Aviation, VC Bird International Airport, PO Box 318, St Johns, Antigua (tel: (+1-268) 481-2401; fax: (+1-268) 481-2405; email: operationsmanager@carib-aviation.com).

Carib World Travel, Redcliffe Street, PO Box W122, Antigua (tel: (+1-268) 460-6103; fax: 480-2995; email: info@carib-world.com).

Montserrat Aviation Services, PO Box 257, Brades (tel: 491-2533; fax: 491-7186; email: monair@candw.ms).

National tourist organisation offices

Montserrat Tourist Board, 7 Farara Plaza, Buildings B&C: PO Box 7, Brades (tel: 491-2230 fax: 491-7430; e-mail: info@montserrattourism.ms).

Ministries

Governor's Office Lancaster House, Olveston (tel: 491-2688/9; fax: 491-8867; e-mail: govoff@cnadw.ag).

Ministry of Finance, Government Headquarters, Brades (tel: 491-2356/2777/3057; fax: 491-2367; e-mail: minfin@candw.ag).

Other useful addresses

British High Commission, 11 Old Parham Road, Box 483, St John's, Antigua (tel: (+1-268) 462-0008; fax: (+1-268) 562-2124; e-mail: britishh@candw.ag).

Development Unit, Government Headquarters, Brades (tel: 491-2066/2557; fax: 491-4632; e-mail: devunit@candw.ag).

Financial Services Commission, Phoenix House, PO Box 188, Brades (tel: 491-6887/8; fax: 491-9888; e-mail: fscmrat@candw.ag).

Montserrat government in UK, 7 Portland Place, London W1B 1PP. (tel: (+44-(0)20) 7031-0317; fax: (+44-(0)20) 7031-0318; e-mail: j.panton@montserratgov.co.uk).

National Development Foundation Montserrat Ltd, PO Box 337, Davy Hill (tel: 491-3070; fax: 491-6566; e-mail: mon;ndf@candw.ag).

Internet sites

Montserrat info: www.volcano-island.com.

Montserrat Volcano Observatory (MVO): www.mvo.ms

Morocco

KEY FACTS

Official name: Al Mamlaka al Maghrebia (The Kingdom of Morocco)

Head of State: King Mohammed VI (since 1999)

Head of government: Prime Minister Abdelilah Bankirance (appointed 29 Nov 2011)

Ruling party: Coalition, led by Parti de la Justice et du Développement (PJD) (Hizb al Adala wa at Tanmia) (Justice and Development Party)

Area: 711,000 square km

Population: 31.85 million (2010)*

Capital: Rabat (official, diplomatic) Casablanca (commercial centre)

Official language: Arabic and Berber

Currency: Dirham (Dh) = 100 centimes

Exchange rate: Dh8.68 per US$ (Oct 2011); (roughly pegged at Dh10 per euro, which circulates widely)

GDP per capita: US$3,249 (2010)

GDP real growth: 3.20% (2010)

GDP: US$103.50 billion (2010)

Labour force: 11.45 million (2010)

Unemployment: 9.10% (2010)

Inflation: 1.00% (2010)

Balance of trade: -US$15.06 billion (2010)

Annual FDI: US$1.24 billion (2010)

* estimated figure

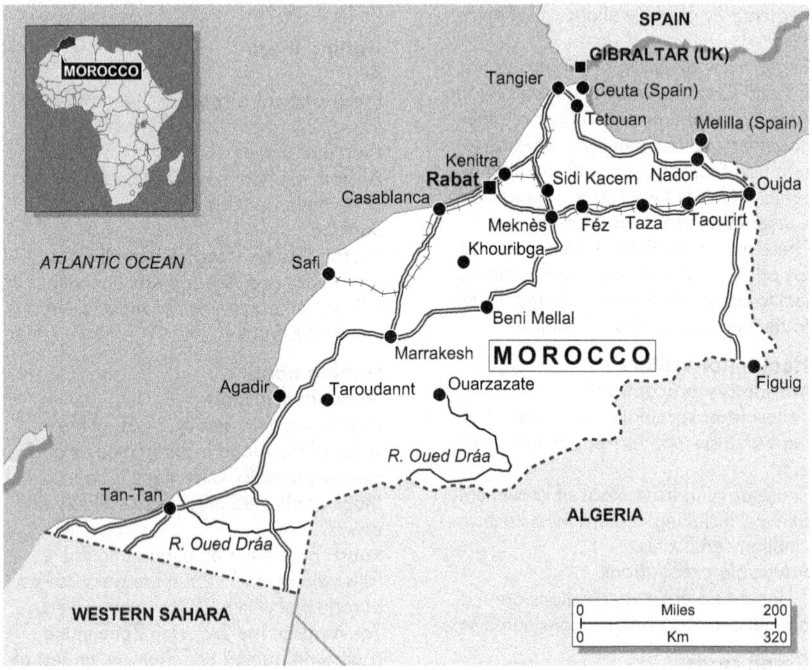

In the wake of the Arab Spring, King Mohammed VI proposed a broad and comprehensive package of political reforms through constitutional amendments. Put to the people in a referendum on 1 July 2011 it garnered the over-whelming support of the population. The 'Yes' vote in favour of the proposed reforms was 98.5 per cent on a turnout of 73 per cent. The heads of political parties, opinion leaders and civil society representatives reacted positively to the proposed reforms and there are high expectations amongst the population that these reforms will have to be implemented in a credible manner. Legislative elections are planned for 25 November and the new government formed thereafter will be responsible for implementing many of the reforms.

Constitutional changes

The new Constitution introduced important changes in Morocco's governance system both at central and regional level. Most notably it strengthens the following: the role of parliament and the existence of a multi-party system (ensuring a fair representation of the opposition); the role of the prime minister who will now be appointed by the party winning the most seats in Parliament and which will have the status of government; the independence of the judiciary; and the functions of the regions, which will now have directly elected and empowered regional councils. The new reforms need now to be translated more concretely into substantial revisions of the regulatory and administrative framework to reinforce accountability and to clarify roles of the government, especially in the context of the proposed regionalisation which encompasses the devolution of power to the 16 regions, strengthening the accountability of institutions and establishing constitutional rights on access to information and to quality public services.

PAM's People

The announcement of the new constitution and its implications were to an extent overshadowed by other developments in Moroccan politics; this was the formation, just before the 2011 elections, of an alliance with seven other political parties by the Parti Authenticité et Modernité (Authenticity and Modernity Party) known by its French acronym, PAM, a notionally centrist grouping. Surprisingly the opinion polls suggested that PAM was likely to to win the 2012 general election. In the 2009 municipal poll, PAM had emerged as the party with the most support, with 22 per cent of the vote. The strange thing about the PAM party was that its founder Fouad Ali El Himma was known to be a close political adviser to King Muhammad. PAM seemed to garner a good deal of its support from members of other political parties. In its early days, the PAM had parted company with the ruling coalition led by the prime minister, Abbas El Fassi, which left the government in a minority. One 2009 report on the PAM's significance, published by the London *Economist* appeared to suggest that the PAM might be no more than a re-shuffling of the *makhzen*, the informal establishment grouping that has traditionally dominated Moroccan politics.

King Mohammed has long said that the fight against poverty is a priority, earning him the name 'guardian of the poor'. Officials cite improved access to basic services in shanty towns and among the rural poor. But some non-government organisations say little has changed beyond the statistics, with poverty still widespread and unemployment remaining high. One of the King's key reforms has been the *Mudawana*, a family law which grants more rights to women. The king maintains it is in line with Koranic principles but it has been opposed by religious conservatives.

The economy

Morocco has enjoyed macro-economic stability since the early 1990s. Inflation has remained low. The external current account has been in surplus since 2001 and external reserves have increased to a comfortable level. However, fiscal deficits have remained large and the authorities have used part of the privatisation receipts to finance increased expenditures.

The World Bank in its 2011 assessment of the Moroccan economy noted that the economy continued to 'fare relatively well'. Growth was estimated at 4.5 per cent in the first half of 2011, mostly driven by domestic demand, and was expected to keep its momentum for the rest of the year, with the annual figure for 2011 estimated at 4.5–5 per cent. Inflation seemed to be under control at less than one per cent by end July (food inflation was higher at 1.4 per cent). However, the low inflation is mainly explained by the insulation of domestic prices from high world prices of food and fuels through the costly universal subsidy system. Unemployment, especially youth unemployment, remains a critical concern. Urban unemployment increased to 13.5 per cent in the second quarter of 2011, up from 12.7 per cent a year earlier. In particular, youth joblessness in urban areas worsened by almost 2.5 percentage points to reach 33.4 per cent, while that of the so called 'educated' jobless increased by one percentage point to 18.2 per cent.

High world prices of basic commodities placed substantial pressures on the subsidy system and, in consequence, on public finances. The budget deficit was expected by the World Bank to increase to between 5.5 per cent and 6 per cent of gross domestic product (GDP) for 2011 instead of the budgeted 3.6 per cent of GDP. The deficit might worsen further in case of higher world prices of fuels and food and the inability of the government to curtail other non-priority recurrent budgetary spending. While Morocco's indebtedness remained under control (the central government debt was projected to rise to around 52 per cent of GDP in 2011 from 50.3 per cent in 2010), the current universal subsidy system threatened medium term fiscal sustainability. The budget deficit needed to converge to its medium term target of 3 per cent of GDP to stabilise the debt-to-GDP ratio.

The slowing growth of Morocco's main trading partners has exacerbated the weaknesses of the balance of payments. The structurally high trade deficit was expected to deteriorate further in 2011, to 22 per cent of GDP, from 19.5 per cent in 2010. Although tourism receipts and workers' remittances were expected to evolve favourably over 2011 (up by 9.3 per cent and 7.4 per cent by the end of June 2011, respectively), the current account deficit was expected to worsen to around 6.7 per cent of GDP (compared to 4.3 per cent of GDP in 2010). External financing pressure was exacerbated by a sharp decline in foreign direct investment (FDI) -16.2 per cent by the end of June 2011). As a result, Morocco's net international reserves had declined by US$786 million since the beginning of 2011 and stood at US$22.3 billion at the end of June 2011, the equivalent of 5.2 months of imports of goods and services.

The government began preparation of its Budget Law 2012 before the elections,

KEY FACTS

Official name: Western Sahara

(The legal status of the territory and the issue of sovereignty are unresolved; they are contested by Morocco and the Polisario, which in Feb 1976, formally proclaimed a government-in-exile of the Sahrawi Arab Democratic Republic (SADR)).

Head of State: President Mohammed Abdelazziz (Frente Polisario) (since 1982) (based in Tindouf Refugee camp, Algeria)

Head of government: Prime Minister Abdelkader Taleb Oumar (from Oct 2004) (based in Tindouf Refugee camp, Algeria)

Ruling party: Independence movement – Frente para la Liberación de Saguia al Hamra y Río de Oro (Polisario) (Popular Front for the Liberation of Saguia al Hamra and Río de Oro) (based in Tindouf Refugee camp, Algeria)

Area: 266,000 square km

Population: 491,519 (2010)*

Capital: Laayoune (El Aaiún)

Official language: Arabic and Spanish

Currency: Moroccan dirham (Dh) = 100 centimes; the currency used in the Occupied Zone

Exchange rate: Dh8.01 per US$ (Jan 2009); (roughly pegged at Dh11 per euro, which circulates widely)

Labour force: 12,000 (2005)*

Aid flow: US$10.00 million (annually)*

* estimated figure

although its implementation would be the responsibility of the next government to be elected in November 2011. Noteworthy were the objectives to contain internal and external deficits at manageable levels with a clear decision to set a ceiling of 3 per cent of GDP on food and fuel subsidies. There are four main priorities set out: first, institutional reforms and good governance. The proposed advanced regionalisation as enshrined in the new constitution was seen as a strategic pillar for a model of economic and social development. Second, job creation by increasing the pace of investment in public and private sectors. In particular, new measures were proposed to improve the employability of young people and their integration into the labour markets. New arrangements reflecting the economic strengths of the regions would be highlighted with the aim of widening employment opportunities in areas such as agribusiness, the medical industry, the services sector, automotive assembly, media and filmmaking. Third, structural and sectoral reforms to improve the attractiveness of the national economy. Finally, improved efficiency in delivering education, health and social housing services, as well as promoting income-generating activities.

In the view of the World Bank, Morocco's medium term economic prospects were generally good, provided the government moved forward with the reforms needed to improve economic productivity and consolidate public finance. The government's objectives for 2012 included a GDP growth rate of 5 per cent, budget and current account deficits of less than 5 per cent of GDP, with the ceiling on subsidies set at 3 per cent of GDP. Sound monetary and budget policies should help maintain inflation at relatively low levels of around 2 per cent, a little more than that expected for 2011 (1.6 per cent). Meanwhile, the government has to better control recurrent expenditures to ensure macro-economic stability and regain budget balance as required now by the new Constitution.

Youth and educated joblessness remain a worrying issue, despite the recent active employment policies benefiting small and very small businesses and in addition to policy measures to help engage the private sector and large state-owned enterprises (SOEs) in employment promotion. Current account deficits were expected to improve over the medium term, based on the assumption that the government will scale up its reforms to enhance economic productivity and diversification, while progressively shifting to a more flexible exchange regime. Higher current account deficits could put pressure on external financing, but should remain manageable, as it is expected that FDI would continue to flow, attracted by efforts to improve the business environment. In this regard, the confirmation of investment grade from the major credit rating agencies will also encourage FDI and help the government access financing on more favourable conditions.

Restructuring

Many of Morocco's large SOEs have been privatised and remaining public enterprises are being restructured or prepared for privatisation. In the area of trade liberalisation, the implementation of the association agreement with the European Union (EU), Morocco's main trading partner, is proceeding as scheduled. Most Favoured Nation tariffs have been reduced to a maximum of 10 per cent for goods freely traded with the EU. Morocco is bidding for membership of the EU, but there appears to be little enthusiasm for the idea within Europe itself. It has been accorded the status of non-Nato ally by Washington, which has praised its support for the US-led war on terrorism. After deadly suicide bombings in Casablanca in 2003, Morocco launched a crackdown on suspected Islamic militants. The financial sector is also being strengthened. The promulgation of new central bank and banking laws should further enhance the autonomy of the Bank al Maghrib (central bank) and its supervisory power. The new labour code was expected to improve labour relations and flexibility in the labour market. Overall, the government is pursuing its efforts to fight poverty, improve social conditions and enhance the rights of the female population. The impact of these reforms on Morocco's growth rates should be observed in the medium-term.

Risk assessment

Economy	Fair
Politics	Fair
Regional stability	Fair

KEY INDICATORS — Morocco

	Unit	2006	2007	2008	2009	2010
Population	m	30.65	31.00	31.44	31.70	*31.85
Gross domestic product (GDP)	US$bn	65.41	75.20	88.90	90.80	103.50
GDP per capita	US$	2,142	2,427	2,827	2,865	3,249
GDP real growth	%	8.0	2.7	5.6	4.9	3.7
Inflation	%	3.3	2.0	3.9	1.0	1.0
Unemployment	%	9.6	9.5	9.6	9.1	9.1
Industrial output	% change	4.6	6.6	2.6	-0.8	–
Agricultural output	% change	23.0	-20.4	16.4	29.8	–
Exports (fob) (goods)	US$m	11,913.0	15,146.0	20,173.0	13,915.0	17,584.0
Imports (fob) (goods)	US$m	23,534.0	29,316.0	19,175.0	30,546.0	32,646.0
Balance of trade	US$m	-11,621.0	-14,170.0	998.0	-16,632.0	-15,062.0
Current account	US$m	1,856.0	-224.0	-4,821.0	-4,958.0	-4,209.0
Total reserves minus gold	US$m	20,341.0	24,123.0	22,104.0	22,797.0	22,613.0
Foreign exchange	US$m	20,182.0	23,980.0	21,976.0	21,924.0	21,762.0
Exchange rate	per US$	8.44	7.83	7.75	8.06	8.42

COUNTRY PROFILE

Historical profile

1777 Morocco was the first country to recognise the newly sovereign USA. The Treaty of Peace and Friendship between the two countries (negotiated in 1787) is the longest unbroken US treaty relationship.
1860 Spain declared war in a dispute over the Ceuta enclave and temporarily occupied Tetuán (later relinquished) and won an enlarged Melilla and Ceuta.
1884 Spain created a protectorate in coastal areas of Morocco.
1904 France and Spain agreed on respective zones of influence in the country.
1912 Morocco became a French protectorate under the Treaty of Fez. Spain continued to operate its coastal protectorate.
1923 France, Spain and Britain set up the international zone of Tangier.
1921–26 A rebellion in the Rif Mountains, led by Abdel Krim, was eventually quelled by French and Spanish troops.
1943 The Istiqlal (Parti de l'Istiqlal) (Independence Party) was founded and an independence struggle began.
1956–57 Independence was granted by France and Spain. Tangier became

Moroccan once more. Spain kept its two coastal enclaves. Sultan Sidi Mohammed ben Youssef adopted the title of King Mohammed V and established an hereditary monarchy.
1961 Mohammed V died and was succeeded by King Hassan II. He introduced political liberalisation.
1963 The first general elections were held.
1965 Following student riots and civil unrest, the King declared a state of emergency and suspended parliament.
1971 There was a failed attempt to depose the King and to establish a republic.
1972 A constitution was adopted.
1973–76 The Frente Popular para la Liberación de Saguia el Hamra y Río de Oro (Polisario) (Popular Front for the Liberation of Saguia el Hamra y Río de Oro), formed with Algerian support, aimed at an independent state in Spanish Sahara, a territory south of Morocco, controlled by Spain. King Hassan ordered a 350,000-strong Green March into the territory, attempting to annex it for Morocco. Spain agreed to withdraw from the region (later to become Western Sahara) and to transfer it to joint Moroccan-Mauritanian control. Polisario announced the formation of the Saharawi Arab Democratic Republic (SADR) and formed a government-in-exile. Western Sahara was divided between Morocco and Mauritania. Fighting continued between Moroccan military and Polisario forces.
1977 Morocco left the Organisation of African Unity (OAU) in protest at the SADR's admission to the body.
1983 Relations between Morocco and Algeria improve.
1988 Full diplomatic relations with Algeria were resumed.
1991 A UN-monitored cease-fire began in Western Sahara.
1998 The moderate Union Socialiste des Forces Populaires (USFP) (Socialist Union of Popular Forces) won the elections and formed a government.
1999 King Hassan II died suddenly and his son, Mohammed VI acceded to the throne.
2000 King Mohammed VI began a process of modest political liberalisation.
2002 King Mohammed married Salma Bennani, a 24-year-old computer engineer; the marriage to a commoner was a break with Royal Moroccan tradition. Morocco occupied the tiny, uninhabited island of Leila or Isla del Perejil (Parsley Island) off its coast and owned by Spain, prompting an international spat. After the general election, the two main parties – the USFP and Istiqlal – formed a coalition government. Driss Jettou was appointed prime minister.
2003 Senegal and Morocco signed agreements on closer co-operation. There were suicide bombings in Casablanca killing 41 and injuring many more. Anti-terrorism laws were enacted and a campaign against extremists undertaken. Crown Prince Moulay Hassan was born.
2004 An earthquake in the north killed over 500 people. A free trade agreement was signed with the US after Morocco had been designated a major non-NATO ally.
2005 Prime Minister Jettou announced that Morocco wanted to establish a TGV (French high-speed train) service, from Tangier to Casablanca (by 2013), Casablanca to Marrakech (by 2015) and Casablanca to Agadir (by 2020). Hundreds of migrants from sub-Saharan Africa attempted to force their entry into the Spanish enclaves of Melilla and Ceuta. Once repelled they were later deported from Morocco. An official commission reported that human rights abuses during the rule of King Hassan II included almost 600 deaths.
2007 Morocco proposed the Sahara autonomy plan which would allow Morocco and the Polisario to discuss the future of Western Sahara without pre-conditions, but later failed to achieve agreement. In parliamentary elections, 33 parties and 6,600 candidates participated; the Istiqlal won most votes, to retain power and become the governing coalition party. Its partner in the outgoing government, the USFP lost 12 seats. The turnout, at 37 per cent, was the lowest in Morocco's history.
2009 Christopher Ross was named as the UN's Special Envoy in mediation talks over the future of Western Sahara. Over US$10.3 billion was committed to modernising the energy sector, including 11 wind-generated electricity turbines. The tourism minister announced the government would invest US$37.3 million in its tourist industry.
2010 New talks with Polisario, concerning the future of Western Sahara, began in February. The minister of transport announced in April that the motorway network will total 1,417km by June 2011 following US$3.4 billion in investment. In Western Sahara, on 8 October 11 people were killed and hundreds reported missing in an operation by Moroccan security forces to clear the Gadaym Izik, Frente Polisario, protest camp close to Laayoune. Morocco defended its security forces, saying police had intervened in a peaceful manner and that they only defended themselves. Polisario called on the UN to investigate the incident that they claim killed 36 Sahrawis with 163 detained.
2011 On 28 April a remote controlled bomb in a café in Djemaa el-Fna square, Marrakesh, killed 15 people, including a number of tourists. King Mohammed VI announced proposed constitutional amendments on 17 June, to be put to a referendum on 1 July. The amendments included giving the prime minister more executive authority, reducing the powers of the monarch, making Berger an official language and boosting the independence of the judiciary. The king would remain supreme commander of the armed forces. There was scepticism within the opposition who said the reforms did not go far enough. However, 98.49 per cent of voters voted in favour, on a turnout of 72.65 per cent. Early elections were set for 7 October. In May, Morocco was being considered for membership of the political and economic union, Co-operation Council for the Arab States of the Gulf (CCASG) (known as Gulf Co-operation Council (GCC)). The recorded unemployment rate was 8.7 per cent by 30 June. Unemployment for those aged under 34 was 30.2 per cent. On 29 September King Mohammed and French President Sarkozy jointly launched the 350km high-speed railway project between the cities of Rabat and Casablanca in the south. The joint Moroccan-French, US$4.1 billion, Tangiers-Casablanca line development is due for completion in 2015, with a journey time cut from over six hours to two. The French engineering company Alstom will provide 14 high-speed trains for the new line. Early general elections were held on 25 November. The moderate Islamist, Hizb al Adala wa at Tanmia (Parti de la Justice et du Développement) (PJD) (Justice and Development Party) won the single largest block of seats of 107 (out of 395), while the pro-monarchy, Alliance pour la Démocratie (Coalition for Democracy), an eight party bloc, won 159 seats and Koutla, an alliance of three parties led by Istiqlal, won 117 seats, other minor parties won the remaining seats. On 29 November, King Mohammed appointed Abdelilah Bankirance (Hizb al Adala wa at Tanmia) (Parti de la Justice et du Développement) (PJD) (Justice and Development Party) to be prime minister. The PJD began coalition talks with Koutla.

Political structure

Constitution

Adopted 10 March 1972; amended 1992 and 1996.
The constitution prohibits a one-party political system.
The King is *Amir al Moumineen* (Commander of the Faithful), hereditary head of state and supreme commander of the armed forces.
A constitutional referendum held on 1 July 2011 was approved by 98.49 per cent of voters. The changes included: requiring the King to name a prime minister from

the largest political party in parliament; transferring some rights of government from the King to prime minister (including the dissolution of parliament); allowing parliament to grant amnesties (a privilege previously held by the King alone); promoting Berber to be an official language of Morocco.

Independence date
1956

Form of state
Constitutional monarchy

The executive
The King holds executive power, which is delegated to the prime minister and cabinet.

National legislature
The bicameral Barlaman (parliament) consists of the Majlis al Nuwab (assembly of representatives, lower house) with 325 members, of which 295 are elected in multi-seat constituencies and 30 from national lists of exclusively women candidates. All are elected to serve for five-year terms. The Majlis al Mustasharin (assembly of counsellors) has 270 members indirectly elected by two separate electoral colleges, of local councils (162 seats) and representatives of the working population (118 seats). All serve for nine-year terms with one-third elected every three years. The lower house debates legislation presented to it by the government; approved legislation is automatically promulgated after one month. The upper house has the power to caution or censure the government, which if successful requires the government to resign.

Legal system
The legal system is based on Islamic law and a combination of French and Spanish civil law codes. The Supreme Court is responsible for reviewing government legislation.

Last elections
1 July 2011 (constitutional referendum); 25 November 2011 (parliamentary)
Results: Referendum: approval was given by 98.49 per cent of voters, 1.5 per cent opposed; turnout was 72.65 per cent.
Parliamentary: (Hizb al Adala wa at Tanmia) (Parti de la Justice et du Développement) (PJD) (Justice and Development Party) won 107 seats (out of 395), Hizb al Istiqlal (Istiqlal) (Indpendence Party) 60, Rassemblement National des Indépendents (National Rally of Independent) 52, Parti Authenticité et Modernité (PAM) (Authenticity and Modernity Party) 47, Union Socialiste des Forces Populaires) (Socialist Union of Popular Forces) 39, Mouvement Populaire (Popular Movement) 32, Union Constitutionelle (Constitutional Union) 23, Parti du Progrès et du Socialisme (Party of Progress and Socialism) 18, Parti Travailliste (Labour Parti) four; four other political parties each won two seats and five other parties each won one seat. 13 other parties fail to win any seats. Turnout was 45.4 per cent.

Next elections
2016 (parliamentary)

Political parties

Ruling party
Coalition, led by Parti de la Justice et du Développement (PJD) (Hizb al Adala wa at Tanmia) (Justice and Development Party)

Main opposition party
Alliance pour la Démocratie (Coalition for Democracy), an eight party bloc, led by Mouvement Populaire (Popular Movement).

Population

31.85 million (2010)*
Last census: September 2004: 29,680,069
Population density: 68 inhabitants per square km (2001). Urban population: 55.1 per cent of the total (2004 census).
Annual growth rate: 1.4 per cent (2004 census); 1.6 per cent 1994–2004 (WHO 2006)

Ethnic make-up
Mostly Berbers and Arabs. There is a small Jewish minority and an estimated 60,000 foreign residents, mainly of French, Spanish and Italian origin.

Religions
Islam is the state religion. Sunni Muslim (98 per cent). There are small minority Jewish and Roman Catholic communities.

Education

The illiteracy rate is as high as 83 per cent among women in rural areas. The government aims to increase the literacy to 76 per cent by 2010. Public expenditure on education is about 5 per cent of annual Gross National Income (GNI) and includes subsidies to private education at all levels.
Primary, or first stage education lasts until the age of 12, then students move onto second stage until aged 15, when they choose between an academic general secondary school or a technical secondary school for three years. At aged 18 the academic students undertake the *Baccalauréat* for progression to higher education. Technical students may undertake a further two years study in their specialised skill.
Higher education is provided by 13 universities, specialised schools and institutes under the supervision of the National Ministry of Education. Besides a traditional system of higher education, there are 28 executive training institutes (Etablissements de Formation des Cadres), which provide specialised training under the direct control of ministerial departments. There are also eight Grandes Ecoles d'Ingénieurs (engineering schools). A private university opened in September 1994. Universities are mainly public institutions with budgetary autonomy.
In 2003, schools began to teach Tamazight, the Berber language which predates Arabic in north Africa; children will have to learn using Arabic, Latin and Berber scripts.
Literacy rate: 51 per cent adult rate; 70 per cent youth rate (15–24) (Unesco 2005).
Compulsory years: 7 to 14.
Enrolment rate: 86 per cent gross primary enrolment of relevant age group (including repeaters); 39 per cent gross secondary enrolment (World Bank).
Pupils per teacher: 28 in primary schools.

Health

It is estimated that less than 20 per cent of Moroccans have access to healthcare. Public hospitals are free, but patients must buy medicine and pay for certain services, such as X-rays. Medical fees are reimbursed only for children. There are basic health services in rural areas, including local dispensaries, rural hospitals and provincial hospitals. Government policy specifically targets the reduction of infant deaths, the provision of family planning services, nutrition awareness programmes and campaigns against malaria and tuberculosis.

HIV/Aids
HIV prevalence: 0.1 per cent aged 15–49 in 2003 (World Bank)
Life expectancy: 71 years, 2004 (WHO 2006)
Fertility rate/Maternal mortality rate: 2.7 births per woman, 2004 (WHO 2006); maternal mortality 230 per 100,000 live births (World Bank).
Birth rate/Death rate: Seven deaths and 25 births per 1,000 head of population (World Bank).
Child (under 5 years) mortality rate (per 1,000): 36 per 1,000 live births (World Bank)
Head of population per physician: 0.51 physicians per 1,000 people, 2004 (WHO 2006)

Welfare

There is a stark contrast between the living standards of the rural and urban population. In 2004, 19 per cent of the population lived below the poverty line. In rural areas over a third of the population are classified as poor.
Morocco's social security system is based on the Caisse Nationale de la Sécurité Sociale (CNSS) (National Social Security Fund), which is funded by subscribers' contributions and interest on investments.

All salaried workers in industry, commerce and services must belong to the CNSS. Civil servants belong to a similar scheme, run by the Caisse Nationale des Organismes de Prévoyance Sociale (CNOPS).

In cases of illness or accident, an employee can receive 50 per cent of salary after the eighth day. The employee can claim this benefit for up to 52 weeks every two years. Maternity benefit, equal to 50 per cent of salary, is paid for up to 10 weeks. The invalidity pension is equal to 50 per cent of salary for someone who has worked between five and 15 years. If a worker dies, the family is entitled to a payment equal to two months' salary. Old age pensions, equal to 50 per cent of salary, are payable to employees who have contributed for at least 15 years. The retirement age is 60. A pension is paid to the family of a deceased retired worker, provided they had worked for more than 15 years.

Main cities

Rabat (capital, estimated population 1.9 million (m) in 2005), Casablanca (commercial centre, 3.5m), Fez (1.2m), Marrakesh (969,420), Agadir (2.0m), Tangier (851,321), Meknès (587,315), Oujda (456,524), Kenitra (428,181).

Languages spoken

Business literature and correspondence should be in French or Arabic.

Arabic is spoken in general. French is taught in school and is more commonly spoken in government, business and among the Moroccans elite.

There are three main dialects of Tamazight (the Berber language) spoken all over the country. Tamazight belongs to the Afro-Asiatic family and is related to ancient Egyptian and Ethiopian.

Berber groups and their dialects: Shleuh (Ishalhiyan), in the High Atlas, Tashalhit dialect; Imazighen (Imazighen), Middle Atlas/Eastern High Atlas, Tamazight dialect; Rifans (Irifiyan), Northern Morocco, Tarifit dialect.

In the north, Spanish is widely spoken, while in the bigger cities like Casablanca, English is very common.

Official language/s

Arabic and Berber

Media

The government has a continued interest in the countries media with a participating role in newspapers, television and radio. Through a degree of liberalisation the private press has an expanded remit to report on previously prohibited topics. However there remains a stringent press code that could be used to curb journalist, who still exercise self-censorship.

In November 2008 the Ministry of Information banned the French *L'Express International* magazine, which was deemed to have insulted Islam and was in breach of the country's press code. The magazine had discussed the relationship between the Christian and Muslim faiths, ahead of the meeting of scholars and officials being held in the Vatican.

Press

Dailies: In Arabic, *Al Anbaa* is an official publication, other private newspapers include *Al Alam* (www.alalam.ma), *Assabah* (www.assabah.press.ma) and *Bayane al Yaoume* (www.bayanealyaoume.ma). In French, *Libération* (http://liberation.press.ma), *Maroc Hebdo* (www.maroc-hebdo.press.ma) and *Aujourd'hui Le Maroc* (www.aujourdhui.ma). In English, *Morocco Today* (www.moroccotoday.net).

Weeklies: In French *Telquel* (www.telquel-online.com), *La Gazette du Maroc* (www.lagazettedumaroc.com) and *La Nouvelle Tribune* (www.lanouvelletribune.com) report on news and current affairs.

Business: There are several publications, in French, including *l'Economiste* (www.leconomiste.com) *Finances News Hebdo* (http://menara.ma/fr/Finance), *La Vie Éco* (www.lavieeco.com). Daily newspapers also have financial news sections.

Broadcasting

The national public broadcaster is Société Nationale de Radiodiffusion et de Télévision (SNRT) (www.snrt.ma) and is state-run.

Radio: SNRT (www.snrt.ma) has five stations which broadcast news, religious and regional programmes. The national, commercial broadcaster 2M (www.2m.ma) is partly government owned and operates Radio 2M (www.radio2m.ma), and Hit Maroc (www.hitmaroc.com). Other stations include the bilingual French and Arabic Medi 1 Radio (www.medi1.com), Chada FM and Radio Atlantic.

Television: SNRT (www.snrt.ma) has several channels that provide programmes of news, culture, sport and entertainment. 2M (www.2m.ma) is the second national, commercial network with a range of imported and domestic news programmes. Cable and satellite TV has grown in popularity with many overseas broadcasters reaching Morocco.

News agencies

National news agency: Maghreb Arabe Presse (MAP)

APA (African Press Agency): www.apanews.net

Reuters Africa: http://africa.reuters.com

Economy

The economy has been steadily liberalised since the early 1990s, with many state-owned entities privatised through government policies of diversification. Morocco is the world's third largest producer of phosphorous (after China and the US) and mining and industry provides around 15 per cent of GDP, agriculture (including fish and seafood) around 16 per cent and the service sector 55 per cent, of which tourism is the major component. GDP growth in 2007 was 2.7 per cent; down from 7.8 per cent in 2006, following a year of severe drought when imported grain affected growth. Growth in 2008 rebounded to 5.6 per cent following a bumper harvest of cereals, before falling to 4.9 per cent in 2009 as global trade slumped. Growth in 2010 was 3.7 per cent.

In 2008, the Department of Tourism launched its *2010 Vision and Future*, to attract 10 million visitors by 2010, with a strategy to expand the sector from 160,000 beds to 230,000 beds and create 600,000 new jobs. However, despite a good start in 2008 when eight million visitors arrived, primarily from France and Spain, (over three million visitors were expatriates returning home on vacation), the downturn in the global economy reduced the number of visitors to 7.7 million in 2009. The Federation of Tourism forecast a 10 per cent increase in visitor numbers in 2010.

In 2008 the government implemented its seven-year *Plan Maroc Vert* with two main strategies: to develop high value and productive agriculture and fight poverty by increasing revenues to small-farmers.

Unemployment and underemployment are still problems, particularly for the young, leading many choose to work abroad. Foreign remittances were a record US$6.89 billion in 2008, falling to US$6.27 billion in 2009 (6.6 per cent of GDP) as the global economic crisis cut the amount and value of remittances from host countries. The estimate for remittances in 2010 was US$6.44 billion.

The Islamic Development Bank (IDB) and the World Bank announced in October 2010, that they were setting up a regional initiative of up to US$1 billion to help close the infrastructure gap in the Middle East and North Africa (Mena) and help boost economic growth. The World Bank considers that the Mena region requires US$75–100 billion per year to sustain the growth of recent years and boost economic competitiveness. Private sector investment is limited but it is hoped the new initiative will help address this shortfall in investment through both Shari'a-compliant and conventional investment.

External trade

Morocco is a member of the Greater Arab Free Trade Area (Gafta) along with

16 other countries, within an Arab economic bloc. A customs union was established whereby tariffs on locally produced items within Gafta are zero. It is also a signatory of the Euro-Mediterranean Partnership agreement, which provides for the introduction of free trade between the EU and 10 Mediterranean countries by 2012. Morocco belongs to the Arab Maghreb Union (AMU) with Algeria, Libya, Mauritania and Tunisia. However internal disputes have hampered the implementation of a free trade or customs union. It also has a free trade agreement with the US.

Imports

Principal imports are crude oil, textiles, electronic and telecommunications equipment, wheat, gas and electricity, plastics.

Main sources: France (typically 15 per cent of total), Spain (10 per cent), Italy (6 per cent), Saudi Arabia (6 per cent).

Exports

Principal exports are clothing, fish, fruits and vegetables, chemicals (including petrochemicals), transistors, unrefined minerals, fertilisers (including phosphates) and petroleum products.

Main destinations: France (typically 25 per cent of total), Spain (20 per cent), UK (5 per cent).

Agriculture

Farming

Around 70 per cent of the 7.9 million hectares (ha) of arable land is cultivated, mainly by subsistent farmers.

Principal crops are wheat, barley, maize (grown in the rain-fed areas), citrus fruits, beans, chick peas and other pulses, tomatoes (mainly for export), potatoes, olives and oilseeds. Important agri-export crops are sugar cane, sugar beet (the production of which is being developed to cut down on sugar imports) and cotton.

Livestock productivity and crop yields have remained low and regular food imports of grain are necessary to meet domestic cereal requirements. Agricultural development has also been hampered by the small size of the majority of holdings and restricted access to EU markets. Many long-term government projects are under way, including irrigation schemes, development of new techniques and financial incentives to farmers.

As the increasing population puts pressure on available resources, access to water will become more difficult. The World Bank has estimated that Morocco will become a water deficit country by 2020.

Some 32,500 tonnes of cannabis is grown annually in the deprived north of Morocco for the European market. King Mohammed has made developing the north a priority in government policy in order to combat illicit crop cultivation.

Fishing

The fishing sector offers considerable potential, although export markets for the main catch, sardines, are restricted by strong competition from Spain, Portugal and France. The total catch is estimated at around one million tonnes a year, of which 150,00 tonnes is shellfish and 930,000 tonnes is marine fish.

Morocco's fleet fishes in both Atlantic and Mediterranean waters and has an agreement to fish in the Gulf of Guinea. As well as its own ports, some of Morocco's catch is landed in Portugal. Fish frozen at sea is landed at Agadir and Tan-Tan.

The government is modernising the fishing fleet and ports to exploit the rich potential of local fishing grounds. The EU donated US$22.2 million to build four new fishing villages on Morocco's Mediterranean coast. A US$13 million expansion programme at Sidi Ifni fishing port, enabled catches in excess of 50,000 tonnes per annum.

After pursuing a policy of leasing fishing rights to foreign countries such as South Korea, Japan, the former Soviet Union, Spain and Portugal, the government is now encouraging national private enterprises in the sector.

Morocco has an agreement with Norway concerning co-operation on fishery issues, exchange of expertise and data and bilateral investment promotion.

Forestry

Only 9 per cent of land area is forested and most of Morocco's wood needs are imported.

Industry and manufacturing

The industrial sector accounts for 30–35 per cent of GDP and employs 37 per cent of the workforce. Most activity is concentrated in the Casablanca area.

The main industry is the processing of phosphates into phosphoric acid and fertilisers. Food processing is another major industry. Other significant industries include oil refining, steel, cement, chemicals, pharmaceuticals, toiletries, metallurgy, textiles, leather, paper and timber, metals, rubber, plastics and vehicle assembly. The textile and leather industries employ one quarter of the industrial workforce, and export successfully.

Industrial development has switched in recent years away from import substitution and towards encouraging the manufacture of goods for export, support for small- and medium-sized producers, devolution of spending powers to local authorities and investment in other areas of the country away from Casablanca.

Tourism

The tourism sector is active as a competitive destination for European tourists. To further encourage tourism, the prices of accommodation, restaurants and service charges have been reduced. Police checks on tourists have also been relaxed. The private sector has pooled resources to set up a National Tourism Federation to plan renovation of hotels, development of infrastructure and coastal resorts. The continuing privatisation of state-owned hotels should contribute to the growth of the sector.

The government's tourist strategy was to attract 10 million visitors by 2010. A new beach resort at Taghazout, tthe fifth resort in a string of six, as contained in The Azur Plan began in 2006.

The government has launched a campaign to triple the number of Arab tourists visiting, at a time when Western destinations have been less welcoming to them.

Mining

Government policy has been to open up the mining sector to investments by both minor and major mining companies.

There are more than 90 mining companies producing 20 different mineral products. The sector contributes approximately 15 per cent to GDP and employs 4 per cent of the workforce.

Although phosphates account for 92 per cent of mineral production, smaller quantities of other minerals are produced, including 500,000 tonnes of anthracite.

Morocco has large deposits of lead, zinc, copper, iron, fluorine, silver, manganese, cobalt, antimony, barytine, salt and other minerals.

Phosphate mining and the production of phosphoric acid are of vital importance to the Moroccan economy, although a large proportion of reserves is located in the disputed Western Sahara area occupied by Morocco since 1975. The sector is controlled by the state through the country's largest company, Office Chérifien des Phosphates (OCP). OCP is the world's largest exporter of phosphate rock. With reserves of approximately 110 billion tonnes, Morocco is estimated to contain three-quarters of the world's phosphate reserves.

Iron ore deposits in the northern Rif region, 25km from the port of Beni Eznar, include 18.2 million tonnes of magnetite ore, which could bring in 700,000–800,000 tonnes of ore per year. Silver, copper, zinc and lead are also mined.

Hydrocarbons

Proven oil reserves were one million barrels in 2008, with production at 500 barrels per day (bpd) from Morocco's Sidi Rhelem oil field. With total consumption of around 187,000bpd, the country is heavily reliant on imported oil. Oil accounts for over 80 per cent of total energy

requirements, mainly imported from Saudi Arabia. Exploration projects are under way onshore, mainly in the south-west and north-east, as well as offshore.
Morocco has two oil refineries, Samir and Sidi Kacem, with a combined capacity of 155,000bpd.
Although Morocco contains only limited natural gas reserves at 1.6 billion cubic metres in 2007, the country is a major transit centre for Algerian gas exports to Europe. The Maghreb-Europe pipeline transports Algerian gas to Spain via Morocco and the Straits of Gibraltar. Ultimately it is planned to carry 20 billion cubic metres of gas per year to Europe via Spain.
A new gas find in the Atlantic Ocean, off the northern coast of Morocco, was announced on 30 March 2009, with 28 billion cubic metres of recoverable natural gas.
Although there is one coal mine, at Jerada, with 91 million tonnes of reserves no production is undertaken and all coal is imported from South Africa and Poland.
Western Sahara currently does not produce any hydrocarbons and relies entirely on imports to meet domestic demand; it imported 2,000 barrels per day (bpd) of petroleum products in 2008.
Despite the UN's legal counsel to the Security Council, which said that Morocco should not have issued oil-exploration rights of the Western Sahara's 210,000 square km of territorial waters without the consent of the Polisario (Western Sahara's independence movement), seismic exploration offshore by contracted international oil and gas companies has continued since 2001. The legality of these contracts can only be settled after the status of Western Sahara is internationally recognised.
Western Sahara does not produce nor import natural gas and any coal in use is in insignificant amounts.

Energy

Total installed electricity generating capacity was over 5 gigawatts (GW) in 2006, producing 21.9 billion kilowatt hours (kWh). There are plans to increase capacity to cater for Morocco's expanding population and economic growth; contracts for new natural gas-fired power plants, sited in the north, have been let since 2007, including an 800MW station in the Sidi Kacem Province and a 300MW plant in Mohammedia.
To avoid blackouts and government expenditure the private sector is increasing its market share of electricity generation. The Office National de l'Electicité (ONE) is solely responsible for electricity transmission and distribution. The entire energy sector is in the process of being liberalised and observers consider the state's share of electricity generation will decline to around 40 per cent by 2020.
Morocco has completed 40 per cent of the construction of a nuclear reactor and is looking to other non-fossil fuel energy sources to provide 10 per cent of its energy needs by 2011, including wind turbines and hydro- and solar power.
The Programme d'Electrification Rural Global (PERG) (global rural electrification programme) began in the 1990s and through the use of distribution lines or photovoltaic panels most rural homes and villages have access to electricity. Around 10 per cent of homes are powered by solar energy.
In November 2011, the World Bank agreed to loan US$297 million to back the 500MW photovoltaic power plant in the southern city of Ouarzazate. The World Bank support will fund generation of the first 160MW before a commercial return of the investment provides the remainder.
Western Sahara's total installed generating capacity was 58MW in 2007, producing 90 million kWh.

Financial markets

Stock exchange
Borse de Casablanca (Casablanca Stock Exchange) (CSE)

Banking and insurance

The Banque Marocaine du Commerce Extérieur (BMCE) was the first Moroccan bank and has grown steadily since 1995. It has broadened its international shareholder base and opened new branches throughout Morocco and abroad. At 8 per cent it has the largest capitalisations on the stock exchange, and around 25 per cent of that of the banking sector.
The Banque Commerciale du Maroc (BCM) holds the sector's best return on equity. It has a bad debt reduction strategy, and lower levels of bad debts than its competitors.
The Banque Centrale Populaire (BCP), the Banque Nationale pour le Développement Economique (BNDE) and the Crédit Immobilier et Hôtelier (CIH) are scheduled for privatisation. They are criticised for being burdened with high levels of bad debt and may need radical restructuring if they are to survive and compete in an adverse economic climate.
Central bank
Bank al Maghrib
Main financial centre
Casablanca

Time

GMT

Geography

Morocco is situated in the extreme north-west of Africa. It has a long coastline on the shores of the Atlantic Ocean and, east of the Strait of Gibraltar, on the Mediterranean Sea, facing southern Spain. Morocco's eastern frontier is with Algeria, while to the south lies the disputed territory of Western Sahara.
There are four distinct geographical regions, from the low-lying arid Saharan desert in the south to the Rif mountains in the north. A wide, fertile, coastal plain runs in an arc along the western seaboard and around to the Mediterranean Coast, bounded by the Rif and Atlas mountains. The Atlas mountains bisect the country from south-west to north-east and contain the highest peak in North Africa, Jebel Toubkal (4,165 metres) in the main range called the Great Atlas. The two main rivers, the Moulouya flows into the Mediterranean sea and the Sebou flows into the Atlantic.
Western Sahara is typical semiarid Sahel (an Arab word to describe a border or margin) of savannah and scrubland with low hills in the north and south.
Hemisphere
Northern

Climate

Varies widely with area; while Mediterranean on the coast, it is hotter and drier inland and Alpine in the High Atlas, yet Saharan in the south. Summer is from May–October. It is dry and hot, with temperatures between 23–28 degrees Celsius (C) on the coast, 30–45 degrees C inland. Winter runs from November–April, with light rain on the coast, average temperature 15–21 degrees C, and dry inland with temperatures between 20–30 degrees C.

Dress codes

Lightweight suits are best for formal wear. Women should dress modestly. Some visitors adopt the traditional *jellaba*, which is more comfortable in both hot and cool weather and is usually worn by men. It can get cool quickly after dark, so a light overcoat or wrap is advised.

Entry requirements

Passports
Required by all. Passports must be valid for at least six months from the date of entry.
Visa
Required by all, except citizens of EU, North America and Australasia, for visits including business trips up to three months, for further exceptions and information see: www.maec.gov.ma and follow link from *Consular* to *Formalities and procedures for international visitors*.
Currency advice/regulations
The import and export of local currency is prohibited. The import and export of

foreign currency is unlimited but all amounts over Dh15,000 must be declared.
Up to half (and a greater percentage for visits of less than 48 hours) of the Moroccan dirham purchased by a visitor may be re-exchanged for foreign currency, on the production of bank sales vouchers, when departing.
Travellers cheques are accepted in banks and to avoid additional exchange fees, cheques in US dollars and pounds sterling are best.

Prohibited imports
Import restrictions apply to firearms and ammunition, permits must be obtained before travelling.

Health (for visitors)

Mandatory precautions
Vaccinations against yellow fever are required if arriving from an infected area.

Advisable precautions
Typhoid, tetanus and polio vaccinations are recommended. Anti-malaria precautions should be taken. Water may be contaminated. Milk is unpasteurised and should be boiled.

Hotels

Inexpensive and widely available. Two main types: graded hotels (which are given a one- to five-star rating by the Tourist Board) and small (and usually old) unlisted hotels. A service charge and local tax is normally added to bill.

Credit cards

Major credit cards widely accepted. ATMs can be found in cities and large towns.

Public holidays (national)

Fixed dates
1 Jan (New Year's Day), 11 Jan (Independence Day), 1 May (Labour Day), 30 Jul (Feast of the Throne), 14 Aug (Oued Eddahab Allegiance Day), 20 Aug (The King and the People's Revolution Day), 21 Aug (King Mohammed's Birthday), 6 Nov (Anniversary of the Green March), 18 Nov (Independence Day).
Holidays that fall at the weekend are not transferred to another day.

Variable dates
Eid al Adha (two days), Islamic New Year, Birth of the Prophet (two days), Eid al Fitr (two days).
Islamic year 1433 (26 Nov 2011–14 Nov 2012): The Islamic year contains 354 or 355 days, with the result that Muslim feasts advance by 10–12 days against the Gregorian calendar. Dates of feasts vary according to the sighting of the new moon, so cannot be forecast exactly.

Working hours

Banking
Mon–Thu: 0815–1215 and 1415–1715, Fri: 0815–1115 and 1430–1730; Sat 0900–1300. Ramadan: Mon–Fri: 0900–1530.

Business
Winter: Mon–Fri: 0800–1200 and 1400–1800/2000. Summer hours vary, some work Mon–Fri: 0800–1500/1600, others revert to winter hours. Ramadan: Mon–Fri: 0900–1500/1600.

Government
Winter: Mon–Fri: 0800–1200 and 1430–1800. Summer: Mon–Sat: 0800–1600. Ramadan: Mon–Sat: 0900–1500.

Shops
Shops are usually open between 0800 and 1800, often closing for a few hours in the middle of the day.

Telecommunications

Mobile/cell phones
GSM 900 services are available for most of Morocco and northern Western Sahara.

Electricity supply

220V AC, 50 cycles; sockets are typically the European two-pronged variety.

Social customs/useful tips

Business visits during the Muslim month of Ramadan are best avoided, as many businesses close during part or all of this period. During Ramadan, visitors should respect Muslim traditions and avoid drinking, eating and smoking in public during daylight hours.
Pork and alcohol are forbidden to Muslims at all times, so these should not be offered, although in practice alcohol is widely available and its consumption not considered an insult to Islam.
Business practices in most respects are similar to those in France and Spain.
Tipping is common for most services, including hotel porters, cinema usherettes, cloakroom attendants, railway porters, and so on. In hotels and restaurants a service charge is normally added to the bill. Taxi drivers (in *grand* taxis only) will expect a 10 per cent tip.

Security

Street crime is a problem, especially in the larger cities where petty theft is rife. Women may also encounter sexual harassment on the streets at any time, especially when walking alone.

Getting there

Air
National airline: Royal Air Maroc
International airport/s: Casablanca-Mohammed V (CMN), 30km south of the city, duty-free shops, restaurant, bank, post office, car hire and business centre. There are taxis to Casablanca and a rail link to Rabat.
Tangier-Boukhalef Souahel (TNG), 11km from city, with duty-free shops, restaurant, bank, post office, shops, car hire.
Other airport/s: Agadir-Inezgane (AGA), 6.5km south of city, bar, buffet, bank, car hire; Fez-Sais (FEZ), 10km from city; Rabat-Salé (RBA), 10km from city, restaurant, bank, car hire; Marrakesh (RAK), 6km from city.
Airport tax: None

Surface
Road: Road access is possible from Algeria via Oujda.
Rail: There are good rail connections to Tunisia, France and Spain (via rail-ferry link). The international rail link is via Oujda. In 2002, rail links to Algeria were suspended.
Water: Regular car ferry and hydrofoil services connect Spain, France and Gibraltar with Tangier and the Spanish administered ports of Ceuta and Melilla.
Main port/s: Agadir, Casablanca (major freight port), Jorf Lasfar, Kenitra, Mohammedia, Nador, Safi, Tangier (main passenger port).

Getting about

National transport
Air: Royal Air Maroc operates domestic services to main centres. Regional Airlines is another domestic carrrier.
Road: Morocco has approximately 30,000km of surfaced roads. The links between main centres are generally good. Some of the 30,000km country roads need care and/or local knowledge.
The Atlas Mountains may be impassable in winter.
Buses: There are frequent, cheap services between towns. Long-distance services include: Tangier-Oujda, Fez-Marrakesh; Agadir-Casablanca and Tangier-Casablanca. It is advisable to book in advance.
Rail: A limited (1,893km) but efficient network is operated by Office National des Chemins de Fer (ONCF). Fares are cheap. Three classes are available. Air-conditioning, air-conditioned sleeping cars – couchettes and restaurant cars are available; supplements may be payable. Routes include: Oujda-Fez-Rabat-Casablanca, Marrakesh-Casablanca-Rabat and Casablanca-Rabat-Tangier.

City transport
Taxis: The *grand* taxis (Moroccan bus-taxis), seating up to six persons, operate along specific routes and can be arranged at hotel receptions, or can be found outside bus and train stations and the airport. They are cheaper than a conventional taxi for long journeys and more comfortable and convenient than a bus. The *petit* taxis are metered and operate within cities. Fares vary considerably; drivers prefer to set fares in advance, rather

than use the meter, so each journey is preceded by a negotiation. A 10 per cent tip is usual.

Buses, trams & metro: Agadir, Casablanca, Tangier and other main towns have good bus services. Tickets can be bought in advance of journeys. There is a shuttle bus service from the Casablanca rail station to the CTM Gare Routière (bus station) which takes at least 45 minutes, depending on traffic.

Trains: Train service every 30 minutes connects Casablanca's Mohammed V Airport with the city's main railway stations, Voyageurs and Port.

Car hire

Car hire is widely available but expensive. Major hire companies operate from Agadir, Casablanca and Tangier. National or international driving licences are accepted. Driving is on the right.

BUSINESS DIRECTORY

The addresses listed below are a selection only. While World of Information makes every endeavour to check these addresses, we cannot guarantee that changes have not been made, especially to telephone numbers and area codes. We would welcome any corrections.

Telephone area codes

The international dialling code (IDD) for Morocco is +212, followed by area code and subscriber's number:

Agadir	48	Mohammedia	232
Casablanca	22	Rabat	37
Fes	55	Tangier	39
Marrakech	44		

Chambers of Commerce

American Chamber of Commerce in Morocco, Hyatt Regency Casablanca, Place des Nations Unies, Casablanca (tel: 293-028; fax: 481-597; email: amcham@amcham-morocco.com).

British Chamber of Commerce for Morocco, 65 Avenue Hassan Seghir, Casablanca (tel: 448-860; fax: 448-868; email: britcham@casanet.net.ma).

Casablanca Chambre de Commerce, d'Industrie et des Services, 98 Boulevard Mohammed V,PO Box 423, Casablanca (tel: 264-327; fax: 268-436; email: ccisc@cciscx.gov.ma).

Chambre de Commerce Internationale, Boulevard de Bordeaux, Casablanca (tel: 225-111; fax: 225-119; email: icc@casanet.net.ma).

French Chambre de Commerce et d'Industrie du Maroc,15 Avenue Mers Sultan, PO Box 15810, Casablanca (tel: 209-090; fax: 200-130; email: cfcim@cfcim.org).

Marrakech Chambre de Commerce, d'Industrie et de Services, Djnan El Harti Gueliz, Marrakech (tel: 431-951; fax: 430-950; email: ccismar@iam.net.ma).

Morocco Fédération des Chambres de Commerce et d'Industrie, 6 Rue Erfoud, Rabat (tel: 766-108; fax: 767-076; e-mail: fccjsm@maghrebnet.net.ma).

Rabat Chambre de Commerce, d'Industrie et de Services, 6 Rue Ghandi, PO Box 131, Rabat (tel: 703-185; fax: 703-166; email: ccisrs@ccisrs.org.ma).

Tangiers Chambre de Commerce, d'Industrie et de Services, Angle Rue Ibn Taymia et Rue El Hariri, Tangier (tel: 946-026; fax: 942-954; email: cciswtg@iam.net.ma).

Banking

ABN Amro Bank (Maroc) SA, PO Box 13478, 47 Rue Allal Ben Abellah, Casablanca 20000 (tel: 266-027; fax: 222-514).

Banque Centrale Populaire, 101 Boulevard Mohamed Zerktouni, Casablanca (tel: 222-589; fax: 222-699; e-mail: aslamti@cpm.co.ma).

Banque Commerciale du Maroc, 2 Boulevard Moulay Youssef, Casablanca (tel: 224-169; fax: 469-916).

Banque Marocaine du Commerce Extérieur SA, PO Box 13.425, 140 Avenue Hassan II, Casablanca 01 (tel: 220-0325, 220-0467; fax: 220-0005, 220-0060).

Crédit du Maroc SA, PO Box 13579, 48-58 Boulevard Mohammed V, Casablanca 20000 (tel: 477-000; fax: 277-127, 206-076/77).

Crédit Immobilier et Hôtelier, 187 Avenue Hassan II, Casablanca 20000 (tel: 222-7863; fax: 248-7537, 227-8631).

Groupement Professionel des Banques du Maroc (Moroccan Banking Association), 71 Avenue des Forces Armées Royales, Casablanca (tel: 311-624; fax: 311-911).

Société Marocaine de Dépôt et de Crédit, 79 Avenue Hassan II, Casablanca (tel: 224-114; fax: 271-590).

Wafabank, 163 Avenue Hassan II, Casablanca (tel: 220-0200, 227-1091, 226-5151, 222-4105; fax: 226-3621).

Central bank

Bank al Maghrib, PO Box 445, 277 Avenue Mohammed V, Rabat (tel: 702-626; fax:706-677).

Stock exchange

Borse de Casablanca (Casablanca Stock Exchange) (CSE): www.casablanca-bourse.com

Travel information

Casablana Airport, Office National des Aéroports, Casa-Oasis, BP 8101 Casablanca (tel: 539-040, 539-140; fax: 539-051, 539-901; internet: www.ondo.org.ma).

Office National des Chemins de Fer (ONCF) Tourist Office, 98 Boulevard Mohammed V, Casablanca (tel: 221-524).

Royal Air Maroc, 44 Avenue des Forces Armées Royales, Casablanca (tel: 311-122; fax: 442-409).

Ministry of tourism

Ministry of Economy, Finance and Tourism, Quartier Administratif, Chellah, Rabat (tel: 760-147; 760-509; fax: 761-575; e-mail: ministre@mfie.gov.ma; internet site: http://www.tourisme-marocain.com/frame/infos.htm).

National tourist organisation offices

Morocco National Tourist Board (ONMT), Rue Oued Fes, Angle Avenue Al Abtal, Agdal, Rabat (tel: 681-531; fax: 777-437; e-mail: visitemorocco@mbox.azure.net).

Ministries

Prime Minister's Office, Palais Royal, Le Méchouar, Rabat (tel: 762-709; fax: 769-995).

Ministry of Agriculture and Rural Development, Place Abdallah Chefchaouni, Quartier Administratif, Rabat (tel: 760-933; fax: 763-378).

Ministry of Communication, 10 Rue de Béni Mellal, Place de la Grande Poste, Avenue Mohammed V, Rabat (tel: 766-016; fax: 766-908; internet site: www.mincom.gov.ma).

Ministry of Economic Forecasts and Planning, Avenue Al Haj Cherkaoui, Agdal, Rabat (tel: 761-415; fax: 760-771).

Ministry of Economy, Finance and Tourism, Quartier Administratif, Chellah, Rabat (tel: 760-147; 760-509; fax: 761-575; email: ministre@mfie.gov.ma; internet site: www.finances.gov.ma).

Ministry of Education, Bab Rouah, Rabat (tel: 771-822; fax: 772-042).

Minister of Employment, Vocational Training, Social Development and Solidarity (tel: 760-695; fax: 766-633).

Ministry of Equipment, Quartier Administratif, Chellah, Rabat (tel: 762-811; fax: 765-505).

Ministry of Foreign Affairs and Co-operation, Avenue Roosevelt, Rabat (tel: 762-841; fax: 764-679; email: mail@maec.gov.ma; internet site: www.maec.gov.ma).

Minister of Habous and Islamic Affairs, Le Méchouar, Rabat (tel: 766-801; fax: 765-257; e-mail: webmaster@habous.gov.ma).

Ministry of Health, 335 Boulevard Mohammed V, Rabat (tel: 761-121; fax:

768-401; e-mail: webmaster@sante.gov.ma).

Ministry of Higher Education and Scientific Research, Charia Bouregreg, Rabat (tel: 707-496; fax: 737-236).

Ministry of Human Rights (tel: 673-131; fax: 671-967).

Ministry of Industry, Commerce, Energy, and Mines, Quartier Administratif, Chellah, Rabat (tel: 761-868; fax: 766-265; email: ministre@mcinet).

Ministry of Interior, Quartier Administratif, Rabat (tel: 761-861; fax: 762-056).

Ministry of Justice, Place Mamounia, Rabat (tel: 732-941; fax: 730-772).

Minister of Land Management, Urban Affairs, Housing and the Environment (tel: 763-539; fax: 763-510).

Ministry of Parliamentary Relations, Quartier Administratif, Agdal, Rabat (tel: 775-170; fax: 775-468).

Ministry of Public Service and Administrative Reform (770-894; fax: 775-690).

Ministry of Public Sector and Privatisation (internet site: www.minpriv.gov.ma).

Ministry of Sea Fisheries, Quartier Administratif, Rabat (tel: 770-154; fax: 778-540).

Ministry of Transport and Merchant Marine (tel: 774-266; fax: 779-525).

Ministry of Youth and Sport, Boulevard Ibn Sina, Agdal, Rabat, (tel: 680-045; fax: 680-916).

Other useful addresses

Bourse de Casablanca (Stock Exchange), Avenue de l'Armée Royale, Casablanca (tel: 452-626; fax: 452-625; email: contact@casablanca-bourse.com).

British Consulate-General, 43 Boulevard d'Anfa, Casablanca (tel: 221-653; fax: 265-779; email: british. consulate@casanet.net.ma).

British Embassy, 17 Boulevard de la Tour Hassan, Rabat (tel: 729-696; fax: 704-531; email: britemb@mtds.com).

Confédération Générale des Enterprises du Maroc (CGEM), Angle Avenue des Forces Armées Royales et Rue Mohamed Errachid, Casablanca (tel: 252-696; fax: 253-839).

Fédération des Industries Chimiques et Parachimiques (FICP), 36 Rue Chaouia, Casablanca (tel: 229-215; fax:225-613).

Fédération des Industries de la Conserve des Produits Agricoles du Maroc (FICOPAM), 77 Rue Mohamed Smiha, Casablanca (tel: 303-953; fax: 303-534).

Fédération des Industries Métallurgiques, Mécaniques, Electriques et Electroniques (FIMME), 147 Rue Mohamed Smiha, Casablanca (tel: 301-683; fax: 940-587).

Moroccan Centre for Export Promotion, 23 Rue Bnou Majed El Bahar, Casablanca (tel: 522 302 210; fax: 522 301-793; email: info@marocexport.ma).

Moroccan Embassy (USA), 1601 21st Street, NW, Washington DC 20009 (tel: (+1-202) 462-7979; fax: (+1-202) 265-0161; email: sifarausa@erols.com).

National Telecommunications Regulatory Agency (ANRT), Boulevard Ennakhil, Rabat (tel: 717-312; email: webmaster@anrt.net.ma).

Office pour le Développement Industriel (ODI), 10 Rue Ghandi, Rabat (tel: 708-460; fax: 707-695).

ONAREP (national oil company), 34 Avenue Al Fadila, Rabat (tel: 281-616; fax: 281-634; email: benkhadr@onarep.com).

United States Embassy, 2 Avenue de Mohamed El Fassi, Rabat (tel: 762-265; fax: 765-661).

National news agency: Maghreb Arabe Presse (MAP), BP1049, 122 Ave Allal Ben Abdellah, Rabat (tel: 764-083; email: webmap@map.co.ma; internet: www.map.ma/eng).

Internet sites

Africa Business Network: www.ifc.org/abn

AllAfrica.com: http://allafrica.com

African Development Bank: www.afdb.org

Information on Morocco – historical events, cities, economy, culture and media: www.dsg.ki.se/maroc/

Mbendi AfroPaedia (information on companies, countries, industries and stock exchanges in Africa): http://mbendi.co.za

Menara Yellow Pages (in French): www.menara.co.ma/pagejauneHome.asp

Mozambique

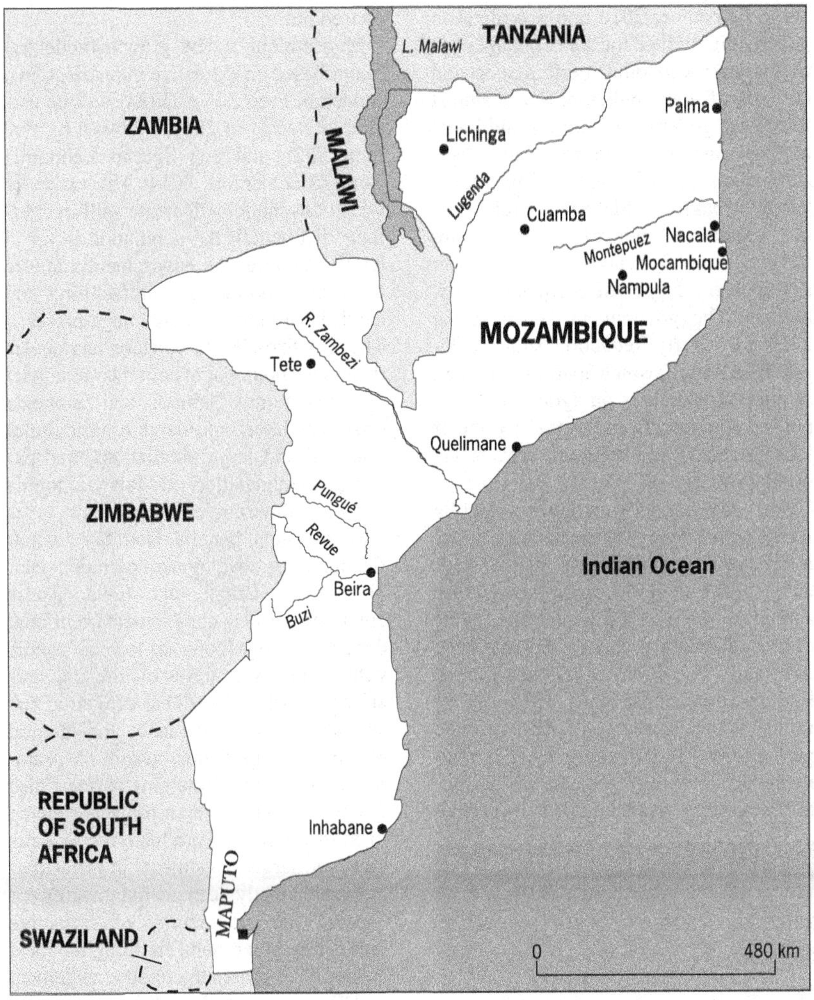

KEY FACTS

Official name: República de Moçambique (Republic of Mozambique)

Head of State: President Armando Guebuza (Frelimo) (from 2005; re-elected 28 Oct 2009)

Head of government: Prime Minister Aires Bonifácio Ali (from 16 Jan 2010)

Ruling party: Frente de Libertação de Moçambique (Frelimo) (Front for the Liberation of Mozambique) (since 1975; re-elected 28 Oct 2009)

Area: 799,380 square km

Population: 21.85 million (2010)*

Capital: Maputo

Official language: Portuguese

Currency: Metical (MT) = 100 centavos (New notes were issued in 2006 as part of a reform of the currency, which dropped three zeros).

Exchange rate: MT26.65 per US$ (Oct 2011)

GDP per capita: US$440 (2010)

GDP real growth: 6.70% (2010)

GDP: US$9.90 billion (2010)

Inflation: 12.70% (2010)

Balance of trade: -US$997.10 million (2010)

Annual FDI: US$788.85 million (2010)

* estimated figure

The euphoria of the late 1980s and early 1990s when Frente de Libertação de Moçambique (Frelimo) (Front for the Liberation of Mozambique) formally abandoned Marxism-Leninism in favour of democratic socialism and a market economy, a new constitution allowed for a multi-party electoral system and a cease-fire was agreed, followed by a full peace agreement, with Resistencia Nacional de Moçambique (Renamo) (Mozambique National Resistance), had dissipated rather by 2011.

Frelimo is said to be centralising political power, relegating Renamo to a marginal role as the democratic process is gradually being eroded, straining government relations with the donor community. New kid on the block, Movimiento Democratico de Moçambique (MDM) (Mozambique Democratic Movement), formed by a group of disaffected Renamo members, has yet to make much of an impression although it did win eight seats in the 2009 elections. This concentration of power is the result of closely intertwined political and economic interests, estranging the government from what was its natural constituency. The ostentatious behaviour of the present government and president stand in sharp contrast to the high levels of poverty in rural Mozambique. Another worrying issue is that it is believed Mozambique has become a major African hub for drugs from South Asia.

The economy

Mozambique's economy, reports the *African Economic Outlook 2011* (AEO), published jointly by the African Development Bank and the Organisation for Economic Co-operation and Development, continued to perform well in 2010, growing by an estimated 8.1 per cent. Growth in 2009 had been achieved despite a drop in aluminium prices, offset by massive inflows of foreign direct investment (FDI) in coal projects, whereas in 2010 the economy benefited from both FDI and recovering aluminium prices. In addition, coal extracted from the 'mega-projects' in Tete province will start adding to exports in late 2011. Exports are therefore expected to increase, although the current account balance will remain structurally negative due to the country's dependence on imports of food, oil and manufactured products. Mozambique is expected to maintain high growth rates in the medium term, driven by mega-projects.

The inflation rate hit double digits in 2010, as a result of the scrapping of fuel subsidies in March–August 2010, the rise in international oil and food prices, the depreciation of the currency against the US dollar and the South African rand, a poor agricultural year and loose monetary policies. Inflation should decline to single digits in 2011, contained by urban transport and wheat flour subsidies, a tighter monetary policy and reinforcement of the domestic food production strategy. The main risk in the growth forecast is that the recovery of international oil and food prices and poor weather will result in failure to control inflation.

However impressive the growth rate, riots in September 2010 and new data on poverty highlighted the weak linkages between macroeconomic performance and the bulk of the population. Social unrest forced the government, donors and international institutions to reconsider Mozambique's growth model. This model has been based on FDI mega-projects in the extractive industries, which are largely exempt from taxation, with human development supported by donor contributions. The government launched the 2010–14 Poverty Reduction Strategy Paper (PARPA) III, which apart from human development focuses on agricultural output and productivity and on the creation of jobs in small- and medium-sized enterprises (SMEs).

The government's ambitious public works programme over the next few years is expected to result in a substantial widening of the deficit. Capital expenditure should rise by over 1.5 percentage points of gross domestic product (GDP) between 2008 and 2012. Public investment funded by non-concessional loans will focus on infrastructure based on public-private partnerships (PPPs) along the development corridors. Such projects will absorb all fiscal space over the 2011–13 period, favouring in a first stage large foreign investments linking extractive areas with the coast. Agriculture and SME jobs are expected to benefit through spill-over effects along the development corridors. Donors continue to support human development, although their budget contribution, which accounted for almost 50 per cent of revenues in 2010, will start being phased out.

Mozambique's new growth model remains based on extractive industries. Two Industrial Free Zones (IFZs) will be created in Nacala in 2011, followed by five more IFZs and one Special Economic Zone (SEZ) before 2014. The extent to which this model will create spill-over effects that benefit the population is yet to be proven, after the government's failure to promote domestic manufacturing and services around existing mega-projects. The Moatize-Nacala corridor has nevertheless the potential to have a large impact on the economy. Nampula and Zambezia provinces have considerable agricultural potential and large populations, and exchanges with landlocked Malawi, Zambia and Zimbabwe could be exploited.

Mozambique benefits from the diversification of its development partners, notably China, Brazil and India. These emerging partners complement traditional donors' strong focus on social sectors with an interest in infrastructure and agriculture. During the global economic crisis, their rising demand for natural resources helped to sustain Mozambique's economy. Emerging partners also finance various research projects seeking to boost agricultural productivity. To date, however, large investments in infrastructure have mostly been geared towards enhancing the productivity of extractive industries, rather than benefiting the local economy. A more structured engagement with emerging and traditional partners alike is required to embed future projects in the national development plan.

KEY INDICATORS — Mozambique

	Unit	2006	2007	2008	2009	2010
Population	m	19.94	20.34	20.75	*21.16	*21.85
Gross domestic product (GDP)	US$bn	6.78	7.56	9.90	9.80	9.90
GDP per capita	US$	362	369	479	465	440
GDP real growth	%	7.9	7.0	6.8	6.3	6.7
Inflation	%	13.2	7.9	10.3	3.3	12.7
Industrial output	% change	9.7	5.0	3.5	5.6	–
Agricultural output	% change	9.0	7.7	9.5	10.7	–
Exports (fob) (goods)	US$m	2,391.0	2,412.1	2,653.3	1,852.6	2,243.1
Imports (fob) (goods)	US$m	2,878.0	2,811.1	3,457.8	3,243.1	3,240.2
Balance of trade	US$m	-487.0	-399.0	-804.6	-1,390.5	-997.1
Current account	US$m	1,335.0	-713.0	-1,165.0	-1,171.3	-1,517.6
Total reserves minus gold	US$m	1,155.7	1,444.7	1,577.7	2,099.3	2,159.4
Foreign exchange	US$m	1,155.5	1,444.5	1,577.6	1,929.9	1,992.3
Exchange rate	per US$	25.83	24.84	24.30	37.30	32.96

* estimated figure

Doing business

The business environment continued to improve, as reflected in the World Bank's 2011 *Doing Business* report, which ranked Mozambique four places higher than the previous year, at 126th out of 183 countries reviewed. In 2010, Mozambique introduced reforms that facilitated starting a business, registering property and closing a business. A simplified licensing process lowered the total number of days required to register a business to 13 days, compared to an average of 45.2 days in sub-Saharan Africa. The high cost of capital, with higher nominal and real interest rates than in neighbouring countries, remains a challenge, however. Further reforms are needed to reduce transaction costs and speed up the ongoing land reform, as land titles still cannot be used as collateral to obtain credit.

International trade and development

Despite the global downturn, net FDI inflows rose from US$587 million in 2008 to US$878 million in 2009 and US$917 million in 2010 (a figure roughly equivalent to the US$895.2 million in foreign grants received in 2010), primarily as a result of coal mega-projects. The government will almost double net non-concessional foreign borrowing, though remaining under the US$900 million annual ceiling, over the 2011–14 period compared to 2008–09, in order to fund massive infrastructure programmes under PPP arrangements. While the debt service to exports ratio remains well below the 20 per cent threshold, the present value of debt to GDP could exceed the 40 per cent limit set by the International Monetary Fund (IMF) in the event of an extreme shock within the 2011–20 horizon.

Mozambique is highly dependent on external partners to provide basic public services and infrastructure. Whereas traditional donors (the US and the European Union, for instance) emphasise social sectors, including education and health, emerging partners (China, Brazil) tend to focus on agriculture and infrastructure projects. Data on such emerging bilateral co-operation and investments are not captured through traditional information channels; they remain scarce and highly inaccurate, in particular with respect to Chinese activities.

Mozambique's three main non-traditional partners are China, Brazil and India, although other countries are increasingly active as well. Vietnam acquired the third mobile telephony licence and promotes agricultural research. Saudi Arabia plans to invest US$100 million in an upscale tourism resort. Sectors of interest to the private sector do not differ strongly between traditional and emerging partners: all aim to acquire a stake in the extractive industries and the construction sector. China has a strong interest in tropical hardwood and fisheries, whereas Brazilian and Indian conglomerates are extracting coal. India's priority, in particular, for the coming years is to secure access to sufficient coal from southern Africa, including Mozambique, where it has already acquired two coal mines. The aluminium sector's output is already captured by the EU, mainly the Benelux countries and Italy.

China's presence dates back to Mozambique's struggle for independence. Over the last decade, China's bilateral co-operation increased its activities in major public works, including transport, water and sanitation. China also supports the government's efforts to boost agricultural productivity through experimental research centres, focusing on increasing yields for rice production. The Mozambican government is now trying to encourage the Chinese private sector, already heavily involved in the logging industry, to further invest in the country, notably in the energy sector. In 2011, Chinese companies will construct a car assembly line and a cement factory.

Poverty and employment

Although the three days of serious civil disturbances in September 2010 were sparked by rising food and utilities prices, they were rooted in a deeper problem of eroding purchasing power. Although the riots involved a minority of the population, they reflected a general sentiment of discontent. They were repressed brutally by the police, resulting in 18 casualties. Although the government subsequently introduced wheat flour subsidies, further unrest is possible if food prices continue to increase.

Poverty remains widespread in Mozambique, notwithstanding sustained GDP growth over the past decade. The poverty rate declined from 69.4 per cent of the population in 1997 to 55 per cent in 2010, but poverty is now stagnating and regional disparities remain acute. Growing inequality could lead to further social tension if food prices remain high and the government out of touch with ordinary Mozambicans.

Development indicators have improved in recent years, but most of the Millennium Development Goals (MDGs) will not be attained unless the government and donors reinforce their commitment over the next five years. Basic challenges, such as improving the quality of education and health services and the fight against HIV/Aids, remain daunting.

Risk assessment

Economy	Fair
Politics	Fair
Regional stability	Good

COUNTRY PROFILE

Historical profile

1498 Portuguese explorer Vasco da Gama landed on the shores of what is now Mozambique. Portuguese settlements were quickly established, but full-scale colonisation did not begin until the seventeenth century. In the eighteenth and nineteenth centuries, Mozambique served as a major slave-trading centre.

1842 Portugal abolished the slave trade, although the practice continued.

1891 Mozambique's southern and western borders were defined by the British and Portuguese.

1932 Portugal broke up the companies which owned the land and controlled trade and imposed direct rule over Mozambique.

1962 The Frente de Libertação de Moçambique (Frelimo) (Front for the Liberation of Mozambique) was established and launched a military campaign for independence.

1975 Mozambique gained independence. A one-party system was implemented with Frelimo as the sole legal party. Mozambican support for the independence war in Rhodesia (Zimbabwe) and the African National Congress (ANC) in South Africa led to frequent reprisals from the governments of those countries. Independence was followed by 16 years of civil war against the rebels of the Resistencia Nacional de Moçambique (Renamo) (Mozambique National Resistance), a guerrilla army supported first by Rhodesia and later by South Africa and the US.

1977 Frelimo adopted Marxism-Leninism as its official doctrine.

1984 Frelimo reached a deal with South Africa in which it would halt its support for the ANC in return for an end to South Africa's aid to Renamo.

1986 President Machel was killed in an airplane crash; Joaquim Chissano became president.

1989 Frelimo formally abandoned Marxism-Leninism in favour of democratic socialism and a market economy. Renamo's support faltered as the civil war was already turning in the government's favour.

1990 A new constitution was promulgated to allow for a multi-party electoral system.

1992 A cease-fire was agreed, followed by a full peace agreement.

1994 In the first multi-party elections, Frelimo won an absolute parliamentary majority. Joaquim Chissano was re-elected president.

1995 Mozambique joined the Commonwealth, the only member not to have been a British colony.

1998 Low turnout for local elections, which were boycotted by Renamo, due to flaws in voter registration, prompted the government to overhaul the voting procedures for the national elections.

1999 Joaquim Chissano was re-elected president and Frelimo increased its parliamentary majority.

2000/01 Mozambique was devastated by a tropical cyclone and severe flooding. There was rioting over Renamo allegations that the 1999 elections were rigged; international observers claimed the elections were free and fair.
2003 Cyclones Delfina and Japhet caused extensive damage.
2004 Armando Guebuza won the presidential elections and Frelimo was re-elected in parliamentary elections.
2005 Guebuza (Frelimo) became president. A new bridge spanning the Zambezi between Sofala and Zambezia provinces began construction.
2006 The World Bank cancelled most of Mozambique's foreign debt. New bank notes bearing the face of independence leader and first president Samora Machel were issued as part of a reform of the currency, which dropped three zeros. The government announced a 13 per cent increase in the minimum wage for industry and services.
2007 Severe flooding in the Zambezi valley, caused by 340mm of rain falling within 24 hours, displaced over 50,000 people and more than 3,500 people had to seek shelter in government accommodation centres in the provincial city of Quelimane.
2008 Violence in South Africa towards foreign workers forced thousands of Mozambican workers to return home.
2009 According to the UN, 350,000 people were at risk of hunger due to meagre rains and poor harvests. In presidential and parliamentary elections, incumbents President Guebuza and Frelimo were returned to office.
2010 The president appointed Aires Ali as prime minister in January. The cashew nut crop was the largest since 2007, at over 95,000 tonnes, due to favourable weather conditions. A new bridge across the Ruvuma River in the north was inaugurated by the presidents of Mozambique and Tanzania in May. The US$35 million investment in the bridge is shared between the two countries and will link new roads already either constructed or under construction. In July the new US$132 million bridge spanning the Zambezi River was inaugurated. It will replace the existing single-file bridge that links the coal fields (the world's largest) of Tete Province to central Mozambique. Construction contracts were agreed with the Brazilian-Portuguese mining consortium Estradas do Zambeze. Bread prices were increased by 30 per cent in September. There were demonstrations in Maputo against the rising price of food in which six people were killed by police bullets. US diplomatic communiqués published by *Wikileaks* in December, accused two senior businessmen of being drug-traffickers and that they were being protected by President Guebuza. They also stated that Mozambique had become a major African hub for drugs from South Asia.
2011 On 9 February, the US-exploration company Anadarko Petroleum Corporation announced that it had found large quantities of 'high quality' natural gas offshore of Northern Mozambique.

Political structure

Constitution
The 1975 independence constitution was replaced by the 1990 constitution, which provides for a multi-party system, direct elections and a free market economy.

Form of state
Unitary republic

The executive
The head of state is the president, directly elected for a five-year term, who can be re-elected on only two consecutive occasions, and who governs with his appointed prime minister and Council of Ministers.

National legislature
The unicameral Assembleia de la República (Assembly of the Republic) has 250 members, directly elected by proportional representation from party lists. Members serve for five-year terms.

Legal system
Based on Portuguese/Roman law and the 1990 constitution. Since 1996, there has been a Law Reform Commission which has the responsibility for revising legislation.

Last elections
28 October 2009 (presidential and parliamentary)
Results: Presidential: Armando Guebuza (Frelimo) won 75 per cent of the vote, Afonso Dhlakama (Renamo) 16.4 per cent, Daviz Simango (Movimento Democrático de Moçambique (MDM) (Democratic Movement of Mozambique)) 8.6 per cent.
Parliamentary: Frelimo won 191 seats (out of 250), Renamo 51, MDM 8. Turnout was 44.6 per cent.

Next elections
October 2014 (presidential and parliamentary)

Political parties

Ruling party
Frente de Libertação de Moçambique (Frelimo) (Front for the Liberation of Mozambique) (since 1975; re-elected 28 Oct 2009)

Main opposition party
Resistencia Nacional de Moçambique (Renamo) (Mozambique National Resistance)

Population
21.85 million (2010)*

Last census: 1 August 2007: 20,530,714 (provisional)
Population density: 22 inhabitants per square km. Urban population: 38 per cent (1994–2000).
Annual growth rate: 2.4 per cent 1994–2004 (WHO 2006)

Ethnic make-up
Indigenous tribal groups, including Ronga, Shangaan, Chokwe, Manyika, Sena and Makua (99 per cent); European (1 per cent).

Religions
Some 300 registered religions, including traditional beliefs (50 per cent), Christianity (majority Roman Catholic) (30 per cent), Muslim (20 per cent).

Education
Primary education lasts until the aged 13. At this point students attend either a general or technical secondary school. The general school lasts for five years when students graduate for progression into higher education. Technical secondary school lasts for three years with a further two years for advanced courses.
The war devastated the education sector. However, by the end of the 1990s, the primary school network had recovered to levels seen in 1983. In 1999, there were 6,600 first-level primary schools (first to fifth years) attended by 2.1 million children. A third of primary school children attend schools that are so crowded that classes are oversubscribed by over 300 per cent. Educational provision is far worse in the second-level primary schools (sixth and seventh years), with only 440 operating in the entire country. The secondary school sector consists of 81 schools, with fewer than 64,000 students receiving basic secondary education. There are around 7,000 students enrolled in Mozambique's six university-level institutions and 15,000 in vocational colleges.
Literacy rate: 47 per cent adult rate; 63 per cent youth rate (15–24) (Unesco 2005).
Compulsory years: 6 to 13
Enrolment rate: 60 per cent gross primary enrolment, 7 per cent gross secondary enrolment; of relevant age group (including repeaters) (World Bank).
Pupils per teacher: 58 in primary schools

Health
With resources targetted at the growing problem of HIV/Aids, other healthcare needs are increasingly neglected. Moreover, the IMF forced the government to abandon its commitment to free healthcare provision and it is estimated that rural Mozambicans must walk an average of 46km to reach the nearest doctor. While modern health services reach

around 40 per cent of the population the maternal mortality rate is high, and cholera has been rampant due to poor sanitation. However, mobile medical brigades have formed the backbone of the government's inoculation campaign, with polio virtually eradicated.

HIV/Aids

Mozambique has been one of the countries worst affected by the Aids pandemic which is sweeping Africa. Central provinces are more affected than southern and northern provinces with infection trends following the major transport routes and areas bordering Zimbabwe, Malawi and Zambia. In the cities of Chimoio and Tete, HIV seroprevalence in pregnant women is over 20 per cent.

HIV prevalence: 12.2 per cent aged 15–49 in 2003 (World Bank)

Life expectancy: 45 years, 2004 (WHO 2006)

Fertility rate/Maternal mortality rate: 5.4 births per woman, 2004 (WHO 2006); maternal mortality 1,100 per 100,000 live births (World Bank).

Birth rate/Death rate: 20 deaths and 40 births per 1,000 head of population (World Bank 2002).

Child (under 5 years) mortality rate (per 1,000): 101 per 1,000 live births (World Bank)

Head of population per physician: 0.03 physicians per 1,000 people, 2004 (WHO 2006)

Welfare

World Bank figures show 69 per cent of the population live in poverty.

Economic liberalisation, hailed as the driving force behind Mozambique's high growth levels, has also removed the safety nets that existed under the command economy. The minimum wage of US$30 per month is paltry and in many companies even the minimum is not paid and workers often receive their wages weeks or months late. There is no longer a basic ration of subsidised food, leaving many in the growing informal economy with little to eat.

Main cities

Maputo (capital, estimated population 1.1 million in 2004), Matola (464,669), Beira (503,874), Nampula (405,308), Chimoio (246,080), Nacala (212,650), Quelimane (173,100).

Languages spoken

Portuguese is spoken by less than 30 per cent of the population. English is widely spoken in business circles.

There are three main African language groups: Tsonga, Sena-Nyanja, Makua-Lomwe.

Official language/s

Portuguese

Media

Freedom of the press is guaranteed under the constitution; however there are libel laws that result in penalties under criminal law which may encourage self-censorship.

Press

Dailies: In Portuguese, from Muputo *Noticias* (www.jornalnoticias.co.mz) with the largest circulation and, from Beira, *Diario de Mozambique* are both government supported. The cost of printing severely hampers distribution of newspapers and has resulted in a limit of two dailies published in different cities. Privately owned newspapers have resorted to faxing copies of newssheets around the country or via the internet; as such these newspapers arrive in an A4 format. MediaCoop, which owns the successful *Mediafax*, operates in this method to hundreds of direct subscribers.

Weeklies: In Portuguese *Fim de Semana* (www.fimdesemana.co.mz), *Savana*, *Domingo*, *Folha Universal* and *Demos* are independent magazines.

Periodicals: In English, the fortnightly *Mozambique Inview* is an independent publication.

Broadcasting

Radio: Radio services, particularly through community radio, are the main medium of mass communication and sources of news and information for most of the rural population.

The state-owned, Rádio Moçambique operates the Antena Nacional (www.rm.co.mz) network with stations throughout the country, with programmes in Portuguese, English and local languages. Other, private stations include Radio 99FM (www.99fm.co.mz) and Radio Maria Mozambique (www.radiomaria.org.mz) operated by the Catholic Church. Foreign services are provided by the South African TWR (www.twrafrica.org), the Portuguese RTP (http://tv.rtp.pt) and the French FRI (www.rfi.fr).

Television: The state-owned Televisão de Moçambique (TVM) (www.tvm.co.mz) is the only national network with one, commercial channel. Private TV stations include Radio televisão Klint (RTK), Soico Televisão (www.stv.co.mz) and TV Miramar (www.redemiramar.co.mz). Transmission coverage outside the region surrounding Maputo is poor, but there are moves to improve the situation.

News agencies

National news agency: Agência de Informação de Moçambique (AIM)

APA (African Press Agency): www.apanews.net

Reuters Africa: http://africa.reuters.com

Economy

Mozambique has shown a consistently strong macroeconomic performance since the mid-1990s, with output growth averaging 8 per cent since 1999. This performance is based on a strong trade sector with commodity exports and capital inflows. The economy has diversified rapidly and transport, metallurgy, manufacturing, hydroelectricity, tourism, timber and fishing are all growth areas. In 2009, the service sector accounted for 44.9 per cent of GDP, industry was 23.6 per cent, of which manufacturing constituted 13.6 per cent and agriculture 31.5 per cent. In 2011 the Human Development Index (HDI) ranked Mozambique as 184 (out of 187) for its development in health, education and income. In 2010, 60 per cent of the population were living on an equivalent of US$1.25 per day and 64.6 per cent experienced deprivation in at least one of the development criteria.

The main agricultural cash crops include sugar and cotton, although these products face problems competing on the international market. The manufacturing sector employs up to 10 per cent of the population, mainly in food processing (maize and wheat flour, sugar and salt) and beverages. Light industry includes textiles, soap, batteries, radios and bicycles.

Heavy industrial production includes mega-projects (those that attract large direct foreign investment) such as the Mozal aluminium smelter, the 900km Sasol pipeline from Beira, the Maputo Corridor project (to develop infrastructure between southern Mozambique and South Africa) and the Chibuto heavy sand project.

GDP growth was 6.8 per cent in 2008, which fell marginally to 6.3 per cent in 2009 and returned to 6.7 per cent in 2010, despite the cut in world trade as the global economy slowed. GDP per capita did not reflect the steadiness of growth, even though it steadily rose from US$362 in 2006 to a high of US$479 in 2008, before falling back to US$440 in 2010.

In November 2011, the US energy company, Anadarko Petroleum Corporation announced that its exploration offshore for natural gas had been successful, with a find of up to 849 billion cubic metres of natural gas. It will be sometime before production becomes commercially viable and the export of liquefied natural gas (LNG) begins.

External trade

Mozambique was one of the founding members of the Common Market of Eastern and Southern Africa (Comesa), but withdrew to concentrate on commercial opportunities with membership in the Southern African Development

Community (SADC), the objectives of which include reducing trade barriers, achieving regional development and economic growth and evolving common systems and institutions. A free trade agreement is operation between 12 of the 14 members.

Mozambique provides a major transit route for landlocked areas and countries in southern Africa. Its ports and transfer services provide a significant amount of foreign earnings. An aluminium smelter processes local bauxite using domestically produced electricity.

In April 2009 international donors pledged US$1 billion to upgrade transport links across eastern and southern Africa, in an initiative to carry goods to market cheaper and faster. Not only will roads and rail links be improved, but also time-consuming official procedures will be streamlined for efficiency.

Imports

Principal imports are petroleum, capital machinery and equipment, vehicles, pharmaceuticals, consumer goods, foodstuffs and textiles.

Main sources: South Africa (typically 30 per cent of total), The Netherlands (20 per cent), Bahrain (5 per cent).

Exports

Principal exports are hydroelectricity, aluminium, cashews, minerals, fish and shellfish, sugar, citrus, cotton, timber and natural gas.

Main destinations: The Netherlands (typically 55 per cent of total), South Africa (10 per cent), Zimbabwe (3 per cent).

Agriculture

Farming

The agricultural sector is the mainstay of the economy, employing 80 per cent of the workforce, mainly engaged in subsistence farming, and accounting for around a quarter of GDP. The main cash crops are cashew nuts, tea, sugar, sisal, cotton, copra, tobacco, oil seeds and some citrus fruits. Maize is the main subsistence crop, but cassava, millet, sorghum, groundnuts, beans and rice are also grown.

Some 45 per cent of the land area is considered suitable for agriculture, but only 4 per cent of that is under cultivation. Most production is carried out through rain-fed farming in the north, and much continues to be done by hand, with only 7 per cent of farmers using traction (animal or mechanical) and only 2 per cent using fertilisers and pesticides. The agricultural sector is dominated by peasant family smallholdings, which occupy 90 per cent of the total cultivated area. Only 5 per cent of cultivated land is used by commercial operations, which grow cash or export crops. There is significantly large potential for foreign investment in the agriculture sector due to the fertility and availability of unused cultivatable land.

Peace, good rains and an increase in the area under cultivation have resolved the chronic food deficit seen in the 1980s. However, food stocks are low and most families do not produce enough to build up a reserve of food and money that would see them through a bad harvest. Nevertheless, the sector is in need of ongoing structural improvement particularly in the fragile marketing systems and poor infrastructure. The state marketing body intervenes in the market in order to pay farmers for crops they have been unable to sell, either due to low prices on the open market or because the transport infrastructure is too poor. However, with bank credit scarce and with a reluctance of international financial institutions to support marketing boards, the state has been unable to fulfil its role completely. This has encouraged the growth of unscrupulous middlemen who demand lower farm gate prices.

Fishing

Fishing is of increasing importance. Prawns have become one of the sector's main exports. Mozambique's sustainable fish catch is estimated at 500,000 tonnes, including 300,000 tonnes of anchovy. The sustainable catch of prawns is estimated at 14,000 tonnes. Inland fish farming, especially of prawns, expanded. Over-fishing, particularly in the shallow coastal waters, has left the majority small-scale fishermen, who do not have the boats or engines for deep-water fishing, without an income. The over-fishing is mostly caused by large international fishing boats.

In a meeting of African ministers in Namibia, held on 2 July, members discussed illegal and unregulated fishing, which is estimated to cost Africa US$1 billion per annum in lost revenue and the threat to stocks and local artisan fishing.

Forestry

There is an important forestry sector, based on the exploitation of hardwoods from Zambezia, Sofala, Nampula, Manica and Niassa provinces. Almost 50 per cent of land is categorised as other wooded land. Wood fuel comprises almost 80 per cent of the country's energy needs. A wide variety of non-wood forest products includes grass, bamboo, medicinal plants and other wild edible plants. Forestry resources are exploited on a more systematic basis than previously and the government compels timber concerns to initiate reforestation programmes.

Overall, Mozambique has an estimated one million hectares (ha) of productive woodland. The government-owned Industrias Florestais de Manica (Ifloma), which manages 20,000ha of forest, has established a sawmill and particle-board factory with Swedish government and Arab fund assistance.

Industry and manufacturing

During the 1980s and 1990s, government policy emphasised the production of consumer goods, especially food, beverages and textiles, where supplies can be locally sourced, in an attempt to reduce import dependency and strengthen the market for peasant farmers producing cash crops. However, industry suffered from capital shortages, poor infrastructure and the high cost of credit. Manufacturers rely largely on internal funding from operating profits or owner savings. Recent metallurgical investments promise a dramatic departure from Mozambique's import substituting industrialisation strategy.

The greatest problems have occurred in the food processing industry, with cashew nut and sugar production particularly hit. Cashew nut prices have plummeted due to increased output in India, where production is more cost-effective and tree-planting has increased. India intends to become self-sufficient in cashew nuts, dealing a big blow to this important sector in Mozambique. The situation has been exacerbated by the damaging policy of trade liberalisation demanded by the World Bank, which had originally advised Mozambique to stop processing cashew nuts domestically, close down the processing factories and export unshelled nuts to India.

Sugar refining is another industry which was in the doldrums. Mozambican sugar mills were severely affected by the civil war, which virtually wiped out the industry. Foreign investment, mostly from South African companies such as Illovo, has been the driving force behind the rehabilitation of the sector.

By far the most important industrial project in Mozambique is the Mozal aluminium smelter. The plant is owned by BHP-Billiton (the leading shareholder), Mitsubishi, South Africa's Industrial Development Corporation (IDC) and the Mozambican government. The US$1.2 billion smelter is one of the largest industrial projects in sub-Saharan Africa and began production in June 2000, six months ahead of schedule. Mozal is already the world's cheapest producer of aluminium, and costs will fall as capacity is increased. The completion of the project will lead to around US$800 million in aluminium exports per year, increasing total exports by over 300 per cent of 2000 levels and adding up to 20 per cent to GDP. However, most of the profits from the smelter will be repatriated by its foreign investors and since it is highly capital intensive, it will not have a significant impact on employment. Although Mozal appears as a success story for Mozambique's development, it will have a limited long-term role in alleviating poverty and generating growth in other sectors.

Tourism

The sector has not played a significant role in the economy, due to the impact of the war. There is potential for the development of tourism in the south-eastern coastal region, where the beaches are attracting visitors as well as investment, especially from South Africa. The government is interested in developing high-value, low volume tourism and is rehabilitating the national parks. The first to reopen, the Maputo Elephant Park, is intended to with nature reserves and parks in neighbouring countries to form a trans-frontier conservation and tourism zone.

Environment

Unexpectedly high rainfall caused severe flooding in January 2008, forcing around 100,000 people living along the Zambezi River to be displaced. By February when waters had begun to receed the authorities for the Kariba Dam in Zambia announced that for safety reasons they had to release more water. The overflow was estimated to have displaced another 40,000 people as the water from the upper reaches of the river arrived downstream.

Mining

Mining is limited to gold in Manica province, pegmatites, ilmenite, zircon, rutile, monazite, tantalum, copper, marble and semi-precious stones. The sector is small and typically contributes to 1.4 per cent of exports and less than 0.25 per cent of GDP.

There are around 50,000 artisan miners who concentrate their operations on gold and gemstone extraction. Kenmare Resources has two gold licences in Niassa, with reserves of 200,000 ounces. Kenmare also has a licence for the titanium reserves at Congolone, which is considered one of the most valuable undeveloped titanium mines in the world. In mid-2003, the company announced it was investing US$200 million in developing the reserves to produce ilmenite, rutile and zircon by 2005. The titanium reserves near Xai-Xai, about 250km north of Maputo, have the potential to develop a second large mineral smelter project in the region. There are considerable secondary mineral resources, including iron, graphite, fluorites, mica, lime clays, tin, nickel and bauxite. There has been little foreign interest in developing these resources.

Hydrocarbons

There are no known reserves of oil, although the government believes that there is oil in the Rovuma basin and has appealed to major petroleum companies to engage in exploration. Mozambique relies entirely on refined oil imports, mainly from South Africa, with consumption of 8,200 barrels of oil per day.

Several announcements of three new oil and natural gas deposits, discovered offshore, were made by the US-based Anadarko Petroleum Corporation in 2010. In November, it stated that the latest natural gas find exceeded the threshold necessary to sustain a new liquefied natural gas (LNG) plant, the development of which was underway. Further exploration for offshore hydrocarbons continued in the Rovuma Basin.

There are substantial reserves of gas, estimated at 127.4 billion cubic metres (cum) in 2007, with production at 1.6 million cum. There are three onshore gas fields: Pande, Temane and Buzi-Divinhe, and offshore exploration in the Zambezi delta region. Mozambique is becoming a major gas producer in the region, with an 865km pipeline exporting natural gas to South Africa. Several announcements of new oil and natural gas deposits, discovered offshore, were made by the US-based Anadarko Petroleum Corporation in 2010.

Proven coal reserves are approximately six billion tonnes, mined at Moatize in Tete province. A US$1.3 billion coal mining project was launched in 2009 by the Brazilian, Companhia Vale do Rio Doce (CVRD), mining company. It will produce 8.5 million tonnes annually of metallurgical (anthracite) coal for steel making and 2.5 million tonnes of brown coal (bituminous), for use in thermal power plants. In July 2010, plans for a new US$132 million bridge to span the Zambezi River, to replace the existing single-file bridge that links the coal fields (the world's largest) of the Tete Province to central Mozambique, were agreed with the Brazilian-Portuguese mining consortium Estradas do Zambeze. Construction work is expected to begin in 2010. The 670km Sena Railway line, running from the coal-rich mines of northern Moatize to the Indian Ocean port of Kacala, will be restored by 2015, following an agreement for funding by the Dutch and Danish governments and the EU in October 2009. Although the line was cleared of unexploded ordnance in 2006, it was unserviceable and the port silted up. When fully modernised the line will become a regional transshipment route.

Energy

Total installed generating capacity was 2.38 gigawatts in 2007, a large proportion of which is produced by coal-fired power stations. Mozambique is one of the largest energy producers in the Southern African Development Community (SADC) and a member of the Southern African Power Pool (Sapp), set up to provide reliable and economical energy supplies to all 12 member countries in the region.

The state-owned Electricidade de Moçambique (EDM) is responsible for generation, transmission and distribution. A joint Portuguese and Mozambique energy company Hidroelectrica de Cahora Bassa, owns the biggest hydroelectric scheme in Southern Africa, which exports electricity to South Africa from the Cahora Bassa hydroelectric dam. There are a number of ongoing proposals to increase output based on the considerable potential in hydroelectric power and thermal power stations. These include the Moatize thermal power station (1,000MW), the expansion of the Cahora Bassa hydroelectric plant and a new, 2,000MW coal-fired power station, which is planned in conjunction with a new coalmine at Moatize, to be built by the Brazilian Companhia Vale do Rio Doce (CVRD), mining company.

The construction of new dams is facing mounting domestic and international opposition, though, with flooding becoming a regular occurrence. Many ecologists believe dams pose a significant threat to farming communities, particularly when dams release floodwaters.

In May 2009, an announcement was made of the construction of the US$2 billion Mpanda Nkuwa hydroelectric dam to begin in 2010, with a capacity of 1,350MW. The project will be financed by the Export-Import Bank of China (China Exim Bank), which will also finance the US$300 million transmission line from the dam to Maputo. Although some of the capacity will be used domestically, most will be exported to other SADC members.

Financial markets

The listing of enterprises has seen slow and modest growth, although the privatisation programme will provide potential for growth.

Stock exchange

The Bolsa de Valores de Moçambique (BVM) (Mozambique Stock Exchange) opened in October 1999.

Banking and insurance

All banks in Mozambique are privately owned, with more foreign competition entering the sector with the completion of the bank privatisation.

Central bank

Banco de Moçambique, with branches throughout the country.

Main financial centre

Maputo

Time
GMT plus two hours

Geography
Mozambique lies on the east coast of Africa, south of the equator. It is bordered by Tanzania to the north; Malawi, Zambia and Zimbabwe to the west; South Africa and Swaziland to the south and south-west; and by the Indian Ocean to the east (2,470km of coastline).
The country is divided into the coastal lowlands and plateaux (200–600 metres over most of the central region and north, reaching 1,000 metres in the north-west). The country is crossed by a large number of rivers, including the Zambezi (navigable for 460km), the Limpopo and the Save.
Hemisphere
Southern

Climate
Mozambique has two main seasons: a hot, normally wet season from October to March and a cooler, mostly dry season from April to September.
In the extreme south the mean annual temperature is around 23 degrees Celsius (C), with a difference of about 8 degrees C between the hottest and coldest months. In the north the mean annual temperature is about 25 degrees C. The temperature in Maputo is influenced by the direction of the wind and wide variations are experienced, especially during the cool season. Temperatures in Maputo can reach as high as 45 degrees C.
Most rain falls in the second half of the hot season. Northern regions receive 640–1,280mm and southern regions may receive 260–1,540mm. The average is 770mm.

Dress codes
During the hot wet season (October–March) light cotton clothes are advisable. During the temperate dry season (April–September) light or medium weight clothing should suffice. Warmer clothing is required for frequent cold spells.

Entry requirements
Passports
Required by all, valid for a minimum of six months beyond the intended date of departure.
Visa
Required by all. Business visas require a letter from the visitor's company and should include an itinerary.
Currency advice/regulations
The import and export of local currency is prohibited. Unlimited import of foreign currency is allowed, subject to declaration on arrival; export of foreign currency is limited to the amount declared on arrival. It is advisable to take travellers cheques or currency in sterling, US dollars or South African rands. Travellers entering Mozambique have to fill out a statement detailing the amount of currency in bank notes, cheques and travellers cheques being brought into the country. The declaration is passed over to the Exchange Control Office at the point of entry.
A new 'family' of bank notes came into circulation on 1 July 2006. This was part of wider currency reforms which also dropped three zeros, making 50,000 old meticais 50 meticais. The new notes (1,000, 500, 200, 100, 50 and 20 meticais) all bear the face of Samora Machel, who was Mozambique's first president after independence.
Prohibited imports
Illegal drugs and pornography. A permit is required for firearms.

Health (for visitors)
Mandatory precautions
Yellow fever certificate if arriving from an infected area.
Advisable precautions
Typhoid, polio, tetanus and hepatitis A and B vaccinations are recommended. Malaria prophylaxis is essential as risk exists throughout the country, and cerebral malaria occurs in some places. There is a risk of rabies.
Water precautions are advisable, especially in the rural areas where bilharzia is present. Some milk is unpasteurised and should be boiled. Avoid dairy products and only eat well-cooked hot meat and fish. Vegetables must be cooked and fruit peeled.
Medical facilities are minimal and many medicines are not available. Basic medical supplies, medicines and sterile syringes should be carried. Full medical insurance is essential. Insurance cover which provides for medical evacuation by air to South Africa is advisable.

Hotels
Good accommodation is available in Maputo and Beira, but of lower quality elsewhere. Bills must be paid in hard currency, travellers cheques or credit cards.

Public holidays (national)
Fixed dates
1 Jan (New Year's Day), 3 Feb (Heroes' Day), 7 Apr (Women's Day), 1 May (Workers' Day), 25 Jun (Independence Day), 7 Sep (Victory Day), 25 Sep (Armed Forces' Day), 25 Dec (National Family/Christmas Day).

Working hours
Banking
Mon–Fri: 0745–1130.
Business
Mon–Thu: 0730–1230, 1400–1730; Fri: 0730–1230, 1400–1700.
Government
Mon–Thu: 0730–1230, 1400–1730; Fri: 0730–1230, 1400–1700.
Shops
Mon–Fri: 0800–1230; 1400–1800; Sat: 0800–1330.

Electricity supply
220 V AC, 50 cycles.

Social customs/useful tips
The courtesies and modes of address customary in Portugal and other Latin countries are still observed. Visitors are normally addressed as *O Senhor*. Occasionally *camarada* (comrade) is used, but this is not correct outside the circles of the ruling party, Frente de Libertaçao de Moçambique (Frelimo), and is discouraged.

Security
Street crime is an increasingly serious problem, with armed robbery prevalent in Maputo. Visitors should not carry or display cash or jewellery, and are advised not to venture outside well-lit, busy streets. Female visitors should not walk unaccompanied along any beaches in Mozambique.
Visitors should check conditions with the local authorities before travelling outside major urban areas and should be aware that Mozambique has a severe problem with landmines left over from the conflict between Frelimo and Renamo.
Identity documents should be carried at all times.

Getting there
Air
National airline: Linhas Aéreas de Moçambique (LAM) (Mozambique Airlines)
International airport/s: Mavalane International (MPM), 3km north of Maputo; bank, restaurant, bar, car hire and post office. Beira (BEW), 13km from the city; restaurant, shops, car hire and post office.
Airport tax: US$20 destinations outside Africa; US$10 destinations within Africa.
Surface
Road: Road access is possible from all neighbouring countries except Tanzania; there are good paved roads from South Africa and Zimbabwe. The condition of roads in Mozambique is poor and banditry along major highways threatens the safety of road travellers. Travel outside Maputo often requires four-wheel drive vehicles.
Rail: Rail services can be unreliable. A daily service runs from Johannesburg to the border at Komatipoort where there is a connection to Maputo. There is also an overnight train from Durban to Maputo. A service runs from Harare to Beira. There are connections from Malawi to Beira but the border has to be crossed on foot.

Water: There are no regular passenger services.
Main port/s: Beira, Maputo, Nacala and Quelimane.

Getting about

National transport

Mozambique acts as a corridor between the ports of the Indian Ocean and the landlocked countries of the African hinterland with both rail and road tending to run east-west, with very few north-south connections.
Air: Travel between cities within Mozambique is best by air. LAM and Air Corridor operate domestic service to main towns. Local and charter flights can also be arranged with companies with offices at Maputo Airport.
Road: There are around 30,000km of roads in Mozambique. Good roads connect Maputo to main centres. Many roads are unpaved and are impassable in the rainy season (November–April).
In July 2010 the government announced plans to build a new bridge across the Zambezi river to improve access to Tete province and the coal deposits there. There are also plans to construct a forth deep water port to ease traffic on Maputo, Beira and Nacala.
Buses: There are services covering most parts of the country but are restricted by the state of the roads.
Rail: There are three separate networks: in the south (Maputo to Swaziland, South Africa and Zimbabwe), in the centre (Beira to Zimbabwe and Malawi) and in the north (Nacala to Malawi and to Lichinga). There is no link between Maputo and Beira. There are some branch lines (Xai-Xai to Manjacase; Inhambane to Inharrime; and Quelimane to Mocuba). Services are unreliable. In 2009 the government announced it had funding to build a new line to link the port of Nacala with mines in the north by 2015.
Water: There are plans to construct a forth deep water port to ease traffic on Maputo, Beira and Nacala.

City transport

Taxis: Available in cities, taxis are metered but for long journeys fares should be negotiated. A 10 per cent tip is usual.

Car hire

Car rental is available at airports and hotels. Only hard currency will be accepted. International licence required. Traffic drives on the left. Driving after dark can be hazardous due to other vehicles travelling without headlights.

BUSINESS DIRECTORY

The addresses listed below are a selection only. While World of Information makes every endeavour to check these addresses, we cannot guarantee that changes have not been made, especially to telephone numbers and area codes. We would welcome any corrections.

Telephone area codes

The international dialling code (IDD) for Mozambique is +258 followed by the area code and subscriber's number.

Beira	23	Maputo	21
Chokwe	221	Nampula	26

Chambers of Commerce

American-Mozambique Chamber of Commerce, Rua Mateus Sansão Muthemba 452, Maputo (tel: 492-904; fax: 492-779; e-mail: mail@mail.ccmusa.co.mz).

Mozambique Camara de Comercio, Rua Mateus Sansão Muthemba 452, Maputo (tel: 491-970; fax: 492-211).

Portugal-Mozambique Chamber of Commerce, Hotel Rovuma Centro de Escritórios, Rua da Sé 114, Maputo (tel: 300-229; fax: 300-232; e-mail: ccpmoc@teledata.mz).

South Africa-Mozambique Chamber of Commerce, FACIM, Avenida 10 de Novembro, Maputo (tel/fax: 431-621).

Banking

Banco Comercial do Moçambique, PO Box 865, Av 25 de Setembro 1800, Maputo (tel: 307-533, 307-471, 307-532; fax: 307-564/557/543).

Banco Internacional de Moçambique SARL, Av Zedequias Manganhela 478, Maputo (tel: 429-390/3; fax: 429-389).

Banco Standard Totta de Moçambique SARL, PO Box 2086, Praça 25 de Junho Nr 1, Maputo (tel: 423-041/5, 424-405, 301-616; fax: 426-967, 423-029).

Banco de Fomento SARL; Av. Julius Nyerere 1016, Maputo (tel. 494-010/1; fax: 494-401).

Banco de Moçambique, PO Box 423, Av 25 de Setembro 1679, Maputo (tel: 428-150/9; fax: 429-721).

BIM Investimento SARL, Av Kim Il Sung 961, Maputo (tel: 490-085/7; fax: 490-212; e-mail: bimi@vircom.com).

BNP Nedbank (Mocambique) SARL, PO Box 1445, Prédio 33 Andares; Av 25 de Setembro 1230, Maputo (tel: 306-700; fax: 306-305; e-mail: bnpnebank@bnpnedbank.co.mz).

Novo Banco SARL, Av.do Trabalho, 750-Sede, Maputo (tel: 407-755/6, 408-209; fax: 407-755/6, 408-210; e-mail: novobanco@teledata.mz).

Uniao Comercial de Bancos (Moçambique) SARL, Av. Fredrich Engels 400, Maputo (tel: 499-900, 495-221-5 fax: 498-675; e-mail: banque_fc@teledata.mz).

Central bank

Banco de Moçambique, Avenida 25 de Setembro 1695, PO Box 423, Maputo (tel: 318-001; fax: 323-712; e-mail: cdi@bancomoc.mz).

Stock exchange

The Bolsa de Valores de Moçambique (BVM) (Mozambique Stock Exchange) opened in October 1999.

Travel information

Empresa Nacional de Turismo (ENT) (Mozambique National Tourism Company), PO Box 2446, Avenida 25 de Setembro 1203, Maputo (tel: 420-324; fax: 421-795).

Linhas Aereas de Moçambique, Avenida Karl Marx 220, PO Box 2060, Maputo (tel: 326-001; fax: 496-105; e-mail: commercial@lam.co.mz).

Ministry of tourism

Ministry of Tourism, Avenida 25 de Setembro 1018, PO Box 4101, Maputo (tel: 313-755; fax: 306-212; e-mail: info@turismo.imoz.com).

National tourist organisation offices

Fundo Nacional do Turismo-FUTURA, Avenida de 25 Setembro 1203, PO Box 4758, Maputo (tel: 307-320; fax: 307-324; e-mail: info@futur.org.mz).

Ministries

Ministry of Commerce, Industry and Tourism, Praça do 25 Junho 37, Maputo (tel: 426-091/7).

Ministry of Finance and Planning, Praça da Marinha Popular, CP 272, Maputo (tel: 420-648; fax: 425-240).

Ministry of Industry and Energy, Avenida 25 de Setembro, PO Box 2904, 1502 Maputo (tel: 420-963, 492-011).

Ministry of Trade, PO Box 1831, Maputo (tel: 426-091/7; fax: 421-305).

Other useful addresses

Agência de Informação de Moçambique (AIM), CP 896, Maputo (tel: 430-795).

Agência Nacional de Frete e Navegação (ANFRENA) (main national shipping agency), Rua Consiglieri Pedroson 366, CP 1430, Maputo (tel: 427-064, 428-111).

BP Mozambique, PO Box 854, Maputo (tel: 425-021/5; fax: 426-042).

British Council, Travessa da Catembe 21 (corner of Av Martires de Inhaminga 1421), CP 4178, Maputo (tel: 421-571; fax: 421-577).

British Embassy, Av Vladimir I Lenine 310, CP 55, Maputo (tel: 420-111/2/5/6/7; fax: 421-666).

Commonwealth Development Corporation, Maputo (tel: 421-325; fax: 422-150).

Direcção Nacional Portos e Caminhos de Ferro (railways), PO Box 276, Maputo (tel: 420-748, 424-133, 430-151).

Empresa Nacional de Minas, PO Box 1152, Maputo (tel: 423-933).

Empresa Nacional de Portos e Caminhos de Ferro de Moçambique, Maputo (tel: 427-173).

Empresa Nacional Petroleos de Moçambique (Petromoc), PO Box 417, Maputo (tel: 427-191/7).

FACIM, PO Box 1761, Maputo (tel: 423-713, 427-151/2; fax: 427-129) (annual international trade fair).

Hidroelectrica de Cabora Bassa (HCB) (operators of Cabora Bassa power complex), Head Office, CP 263, Songo, Tete (tel: 82-221/4; fax: 82-364); PO Box 4120, Maputo (tel: 400-551, 400-647, 491-346, 492-976).

Imprensa Nacional de Moçambique (publishes statistical bulletins, census information etc), PO Box 275, Maputo.

Maputo Development Corridor, Maputo (tel: 426-359; fax: 430-159).

Mozambique Embassy (USA), Suite 570, 1990 M Street, NW, Washington DC 20036 (tel: (+1-202)-293-7146; fax: (+1-202)-835-0245; e-mail: embamoc@aol.com).

Mozambique Institute of Export Promotion (IPEX) (Government agency for export promotion), Av 25 de Setembro 1008, PO Box 4487, Maputo (tel: 423-343).

Office for Foreign Investment Promotion (GPIE), Av 25 de Setembro 2049, 2 andar, PO Box 2049, Maputo (tel: 422-456/7; fax: 422-459).

Radio Moçambique, PO Box 2000, Maputo (tel: 434-041/5, 432-591; fax: 421-816).

Technical Unit for Enterprise Restructuring (UTRE) (information on company tenders for privatisation and investment opportunities), Ministry of Planning and Finance, Rua da Imprensa No 256, 7th Floor, Suites 704-708, PO Box 4350, Maputo (tel: 426-514/6; fax: 421-541).

Televisão de Moçambique, Av Julius Nyerere 942, PO Box 2675, Maputo (tel: 491-198).

World Bank, Maputo (tel: 492-841; fax: 492-893).

National news agency: Agência de Informação de Moçambique (AIM)

Internet sites

Africa Business Network: http://www.ifc.org/abn

AllAfrica.com: http://allafrica.com

African Development Bank: http://www.afdb.org

Africa Online: http://www.africaonline.com

Mbendi AfroPaedia (information on companies, countries, industries and stock exchanges in Africa): http://mbendi.co.za

Myanmar

Myanmar's constitution rings with impressive phrases establishing the equality of men and women before the law. One whole chapter is devoted to fundamental rights and duties. It guarantees that 'all citizens are equal before the law irrespective of race, status, official position, wealth, culture, birth, religion or sex.' The Achilles Heel of this weighty document is the one clause that tilts the government of Myanmar away from any kind of Western democracy. It (Article 11) says that 'The state shall adopt a single-party system.' So, whatever its constitution may say, for forty years Myanmar has been a military dictatorship, guilty of some of the most prolific human rights abuses and ostracised by most of the international community. The US which for many years used the country's former name of Burma, once named it as an 'outpost of tyranny' and is one of the most vocal critics of the military regime. Former US secretary of state Condoleezza Rice lamented in July 2005 that 'there seems never to be progress' in the country's human rights arena and called on neighbouring South-east Asian countries to help press the need for peace and democracy. While America has tried to freeze Myanmar out of the international community and has imposed economic sanctions, Thailand has co-operated in the hope of facilitating an eventual adoption of democracy. And also happily buys vast quantities of gas.

While the US and the European Union (EU) have maintained and re-imposed sanctions, the same is not always the case of Myanmar's Asian neighbours. Rather surprisingly, the Association of Southeast Asian Nations (Asean) had welcomed Myanmar into its membership in 1997. But in 2005 when the rotating chairmanship should have gone to Myanmar, the association got cold feet and Myanmar backed down. By 2011, however, the country was considered to have made sufficient democratic and social improvements for it to be successfully nominated the chairmanship for 2014. China's commercial links grow stronger by the day, to the extent that many Burmese would like to see some sort of political and commercial counterweight to China emerge, either from Europe or from the US. Plans to build a high-speed rail link from China to Myanmar merely strengthen fears that it will end up a vassal state.

In sharp contrast, the US bans all new investment and votes against Myanmar's loan applications from international financial institutions. The EU imposes an arms embargo, a visa ban on senior officials and refuses all non-humanitarian aid. European companies and citizens are banned from importing gems, timber and minerals.

There'll be some changes made

2011 will, it is hoped, go down in history as the year in which Myanmar's post war history really began to change. This was best symbolised by the December 2011 visit to Yangon (Rangoon) and Naypyidaw by US Secretary of State Hillary Clinton, closely followed by her counterpart from the UK, William Hague. This was the first visit by such a senior American official for 50 years (the last being John Foster Dulles) and the most high-profile visitor received by Ms Suu Kyi in Myanmar. The two had a private dinner followed the next day by a meeting with Ms Suu Kyi and senior officials from her National League for Democracy party (NLD). The NLD has committed itself to re-entering mainstream politics, having boycotted general elections in 2010 and will contest by-elections in 2012. At their meeting Ms Suu Kyi was thought to have explained to Mrs Clinton how the US could help the reform process, possibly by giving small, gradual concessions to the regime to encourage change, while keeping up the pressure for long-term democratic transformation.

After their meeting, Ms Suu Kyi expressed herself 'happy' with the US' engagement. For Mrs Clinton the meeting, unthinkable at the beginning of the year, justified the administration's new policy of engagement with discredited regimes like that of Myanmar. For Ms Suu Kyi, the visit showed how much the regime needed her support if Myanmar is to change. It still has to be remembered that the original cause of Ms Suu Kyi's house arrest was the régime's inability to accept the NLD's landslide victory.

KEY FACTS

Official name: Myanmar Naingngandaw (The Union of Myanmar)

Head of State: President Thein Sein (from 4 Feb 2011)

Head of government: President Thein Sein

Ruling party: State Peace and Development Council (SPDC) (19-member military *junta* since 1997)

Area: 676,552 square km

Population: 53.40 million (2010)*

Capital: Naypyidaw (Abode of Kings) (from 2005)

Official language: Myanmar (Burmese)

Currency: Kyat (Kt) = 100 pyas

Exchange rate: Kt6.41 per US$ (Oct 2011)

GDP per capita: US$702 (2010)

GDP real growth: 5.30% (2010)

GDP: US$43.00 billion (2010)

Unemployment: 5.00% (2005)

Inflation: 7.30% (2010)

Balance of trade: US$892.00 million (2008)*

Annual FDI: US$756.32 million (2010)

* estimated figure

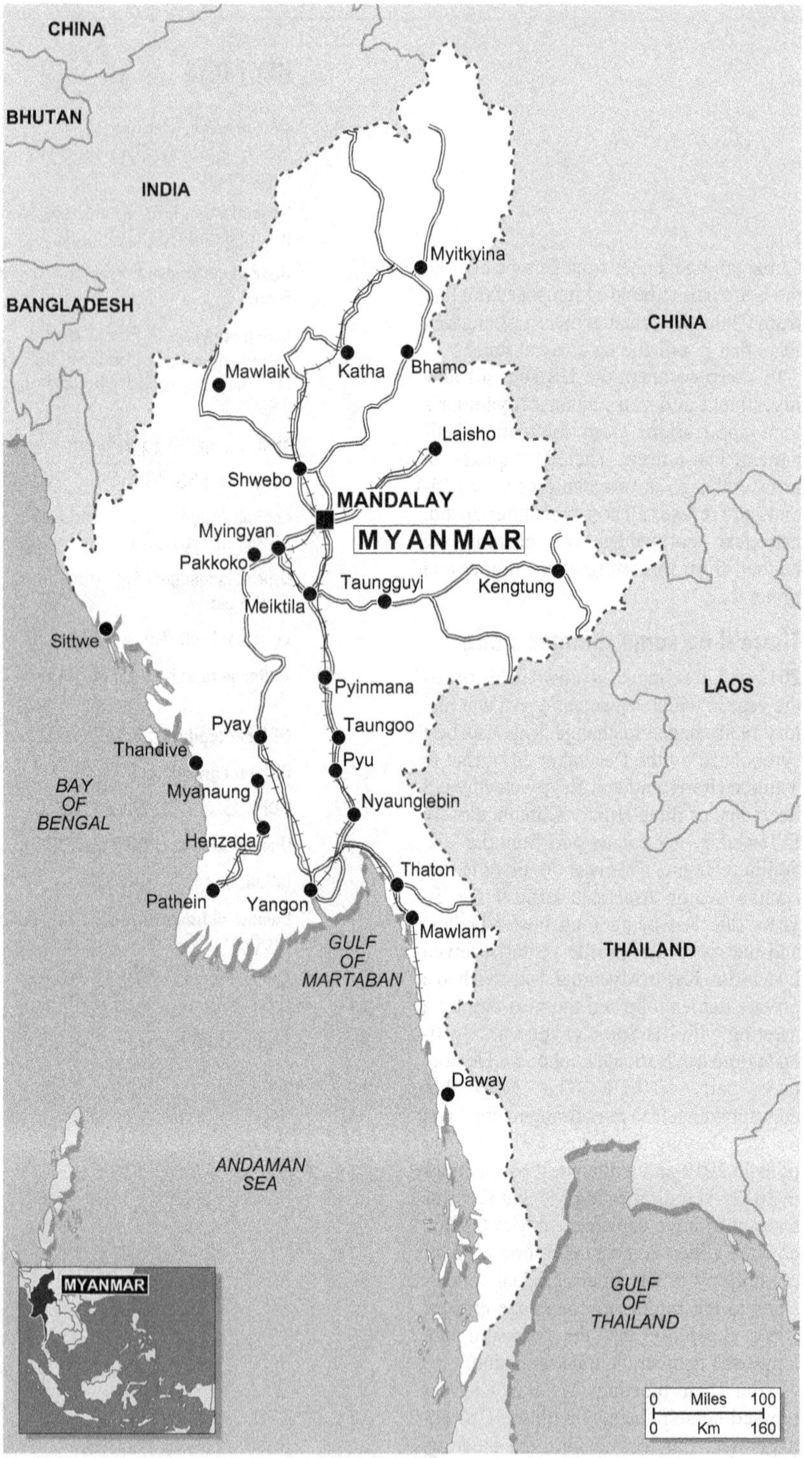

As important as Mrs Clinton's visit, and no doubt related to it, was the decision by the newly elected civilian government in October 2011 to release more than 6,300 prisoners under an amnesty aimed at improving Myanmar's disastrous human rights record. It was expected that many of the country's estimated 2,000 political prisoners would be among those freed, but the amnesty announcements did not give any names. Freedom for political detainees had been expected as part of the new liberalising measures introduced since the military government handed power in March 2011 to a (albeit military-backed), civilian administration.The NLD welcomed the amnesty as a step in the right direction. President Thein Sein, a former army officer who took office as President in March 2011, has begun a dialogue with the NLD led by Aung San Suu Kyi and promised other reforms that could start to reverse the harsh policies of decades of military rule. An earlier amnesty amounted to little more than a prison wide sentence reduction of one year, whether held on political or criminal charges.

Elections

The pro-junta Union Solidarity and Development Party (USDP) won the 2010 elections after winning 76.5 per cent of the seats across the three parliaments. The results of Myanmar's first elections in two decades were hardly a surprise: the USDP had the tacit support of the ruling junta, which, according to one local website, 'choreographed election conditions that appeared to favour the party.' Trailing the USDP, which won 883 of the total 1,154 seats, is the National Unity Party (NUP), which was also runner-up in the previous election. Also with close ties to the ruling junta, the NUP won only 63 seats. The next four minority parties all fell into the 'opposition' bracket, despite fears before the polls that any pro-democracy candidates would be altogether sidelined. However, the total amount of seats won by these parties made up only nine per cent of the total. They were, in order: the Shan Nationalities Democratic Party (SNDP), with 57 seats; the Rakhine Nationalities Development Party (RNDP) with 35 seats and the National Democratic Force (NDF) and All Mon Region Democracy Party (AMRDP), each with 16 seats. The presence of three ethnic-based parties in the top five was a symbolic victory for Myanmar's long-marginalised ethnic groups, although their potential clout post-election was likely to be very limited.

The three parliaments – the Pyithu Hluttaw (People's Assembly (lower house)), the Amyotha Hluttaw (Nationalities Assembly (upper house)) and the Regions and States Parliament – were set to convene within 90 days of the vote. An indication of the régimes attitude to the election was provided by the fact that a quarter of the seats for each had already been reserved for the military prior to the vote. It was the winning USDP that was the target of much of the controversy surrounding the polls. A number of parties considered making a formal complaint to the Electoral Commission about the USDP, a move that is both expensive and dangerous, with complainants risking jail terms if unsuccessful. If there were chinks in the regime's armour, they were less than significant. The supposedly civilian régime did not differ in any major way from its military predecessor. Parliaments sit spasmodically in Naypyidaw, the new capital, far from effective public scrutiny. Questions are put to the government – but answers are there none.

The economy

According to the Asian Development Bank (ADB) Myanmar's annual gross domestic product (GDP) growth recovered to an estimated 5.1 per cent in the fiscal year ended 31 March 2010 (FY2009), after slowing in the previous year owing to the impact of Cyclone Nargis and weakness in demand for imports from neighbouring economies. The recovery in FY2009 was led by improved results from agriculture, mining, manufacturing and the transport and communications sub-sectors. The ADB notes that living standards remain low, however.

Agriculture, including fisheries, forestry and livestock, accounts for over half of employment and about 40 per cent of GDP. Production from this sector picked up in FY2010 as areas damaged by the cyclone, mainly in the Ayeyarwady (formerly Irrawaddy) and Yangon divisions, were gradually rehabilitated. More recently, economic growth edged up to an estimated 5.3 per cent in FY2010 (ending 31 March 2011), with a solid contribution from construction, particularly in Naypyidaw, the new capital and Mandalay (a highway connecting these cities was under construction). Economic recovery in neighbouring countries that import goods including food and natural gas from Myanmar contributed to the increased growth in FY2010. Agriculture in FY2010 was sluggish, however, a result of persistent drought in the central region and residual soil salinity in cyclone-affected areas. (Official GDP growth figures, which are considerably higher than these unofficial estimates, are inconsistent with variables that are closely correlated with economic growth, such as energy use. Economic data are not timely either, making it difficult to assess economic developments.)

The government has financed part of its fiscal deficit through Treasury bond issues in the past 3 years, rather than relying completely on money creation to finance the fiscal gap. This approach has contributed to lowering annual inflation from over 20 per cent to single digits in that period. Average inflation was estimated at 8.2 per cent in FY2009 and 7.3 per cent in FY2010. Export income from natural gas continued to support the external accounts. Export prices for gas fell by about 20 per cent in FY2009, dragging down earnings from this source, but receipts recovered. Imports of construction materials and equipment widened the current account deficit to the equivalent of 2.2 per cent of GDP in FY2010, from 1.3 per cent in FY2009.

Inflows of foreign direct investment (FDI) into the hydrocarbon sector helped to lift international reserves to about US$5.3 billion at end-FY2010, equivalent to seven months of imports. The market exchange rate of the kyat appreciated from about MK1,000 to the US$1 to MK830 to the US$1 in the year to January 2011.

Estimates of the consolidated fiscal deficit, covering the central government and state economic enterprises, indicate it widened to 5.7 per cent of GDP in FY2010 from 5.4 per cent in FY2009. Expenditure on the construction of Naypyidaw remained a drain on the budget, while revenue growth was sluggish. The practice of valuing exports of state enterprises at the official exchange rate of MK5.5 to the US$1 (as opposed to the market rate) undervalues revenue available for spending. The government privatised several state assets in 2010, including an airline, 243 gasoline stations, public buildings and rice distribution operations. Further asset sales are expected.

Forecasts assume both normal weather patterns and a start to gradual economic reforms by the government that took office in March 2011. A modest increase in rural incomes, owing to increased exports and prices of cash crops, is expected to underpin private consumption in FY2011.

The Myanmar Agriculture Bank doubled credit to farmers in 2010. Further increases are planned in the next two years, going some way to addressing severe shortages of credit to agriculture. These moves, coupled with the gradual easing of controls on agriculture over recent years, are expected to stimulate production.

Investment is projected to rise in the forecast period, notably in construction. Projects planned or under way include new hydropower plants, gas fields and oil and gas pipelines to the People's Republic of China, largely financed by foreign investment. A Thai company agreed in 2010 to build a port, power plant and industrial estate in Dawei in southern Myanmar starting in 2011, and a company from the People's Republic of China signed a contract to build an airport at Naypyidaw.

Gas production is projected to be fairly flat in the forecast period, before new projects come on stream in about three years. Gas export prices will likely rise, together with global energy prices and solid demand from Thailand. (This will have a limited impact on GDP because gas income is converted at the official exchange rate rather than the market rate.) On the balance of these factors, GDP is forecast to grow by about 5.5 per cent in the period 2012–13. Inflation is projected at 8.0 per cent in the forecast period, reflecting higher domestic demand and increased global prices of food and fuel. The

KEY INDICATORS — Myanmar

	Unit	2006	2007	2008	2009	2010
Population	m	56.51	*57.64	*58.80	*59.98	*53.40
Gross domestic product (GDP)	US$bn	13.12	20.20	28.20	27.60	43.00
GDP per capita	US$	232	350	479	459	702
GDP real growth	%	12.8	11.9	3.6	4.8	5.3
Inflation	%	25.7	32.9	22.5	7.9	7.3
Natural gas output	bn cum	13.4	14.7	12.4	11.5	12.1
Exports (fob) (goods)	US$m	4,554.7	–	–	–	–
Imports (fob) (goods)	US$m	2,343.4	–	–	–	–
Balance of trade	US$m	2,211.3	–	–	–	–
Current account	US$m	802.0	112.0	-679.0	-272.0	-856.0
Total reserves minus gold	US$m	1,235.6	–	–	–	–
Foreign exchange	US$m	1,235.4	–	–	–	–
Exchange rate	per US$	6.42	6.42	5.38	6.41	5.58

* estimated figure

domestic price of rice surged in early 2011. A government decision to suspend rice exports in March 2011 is expected to moderate price increases, but much rice is still exported illegally.

The current account deficit is seen widening to 4.1–4.7 per cent of GDP. Increases in export earnings from gas and food crops will likely be offset by stronger imports of capital equipment and construction.

Risk assessment

Economy	Fair
Politics	Poor
Regional stability	Good

COUNTRY PROFILE

Historical profile

Burma was annexed to British India in the nineteenth century.
1824–26 Burma ceded the Arakan coastal strip (Chittagong to Cape Negrais) to the British at the end of the first Anglo-Burmese war
1852 At the end of the second Anglo-Burmese war Britain annexed lower Burma, including Rangoon.
1885–86 Britain captured Mandalay after a brief battle; Burma became a province of British India.
1937 Burma became a separate British dependency, with limited self-government.
1942 Japan invaded and occupied the country. The Burma Independence Army sided with the Japanese although it later transformed itself into the Anti-Fascist People's Freedom League (AFPFL) and fought against the invaders. A Provisional Administration was set up led by Dr Ba Maw.
1945 The AFPFL nationalists, led by Aung San, helped Allied forces to re-occupy the country.
1947 Aung San and six members of his interim government were assassinated. U Nu, foreign minister in Ba Maw's government, was asked to head the AFPFL and the government.
1948 The Union of Burma became independent outside the Commonwealth, with U Nu as the first prime minister.
1960 The ruling AFPFL party split and a caretaker government was formed, lead by army Chief of Staff General Ne Win.
1962 U Nu was overthrown in a coup led by Ne Win. The Revolutionary Council suspended the constitution and instituted authoritarian control through the Burma Socialist Programme Party (BSPP). Under the 'Burmese Way to Socialism' the economy was nationalised, the BSPP became the single political party and independent newspapers were banned.
1964 Political parties were outlawed.
1973 A new constitution was approved. BSPP became the only authorised political party and the country's name was changed to the Socialist Republic of the Union of Burma.
1974 The revolutionary council was dissolved and Ne Win was elected president by the state council. Secretary General of the UN, U Thant died and was buried in Rangoon without official state recognition.
1978 An election gave Ne Win the mandate for four more years in power.
1988 A military government, the State Law and Order Restoration Council (SLORC), took power in September, ending months of unrest. It took over the function of the former ruling party, the BSPP, and the parliament (Pyithu Hluttaw).
1989 Burma was renamed Myanmar.
1990 The government fulfilled its promise to hold multi-party elections, but said a new constitution must be brought into effect before power could be transferred to the victorious National League for Democracy (NLD), led by Aung San Suu Kyi (daughter of Aung San, who had lead the AFPFL).
1992 General Than Shwe became SLORC chairman, prime minister and defence minister, replacing Saw Maung.
1996 The law and order situation deteriorated and open conflict erupted. SLORC closed the universities and detained protesters.
1997 Bomb attacks were aimed at leading SLORC figures. Several thousand Karen National Union (KNU) ethnic minority refugees were forced across the Thai border leading to international protests when refugees were killed by SLORC forces. The US imposed economic sanctions, banning investments by US companies. The Association of Southeast Asian Nations (Asean) admitted Myanmar as a full member of the Association. A governing military *junta*, formed by the top four SLORC leaders, was named the State Peace and Development Council (SPDC).
1998 The SPDC detained some 110 leading members of the NLD.
1999 Madame Aung San Suu Kyi was put under house arrest and isolated from the world. The authorities refused her dying husband a visa to come and visit her for the last time. The International Labour Organisation (ILO) banned Myanmar from its activities until it ceased using forced labour.
2001 The military *junta* approached Aung San Suu Kyi to arrange talks – the first contact in five years. President Jiang Zemin of China visited – the first Chinese head of state to visit since the military *junta* seized power in 1988.
2002 Aung San Suu Kyi (NLD) was released from house arrest. Former president, military leader and BSPP chairman, Ne Win died. He was considered to have had *sub rosa* influence on national political machinations for decades.
2003 Aung San Suu Kyi was re-arrested and Japan suspended aid in protest. General Khin Nyunt was appointed prime minister.
2004 The government and the Karen National Union, the most significant ethnic insurgency group, agreed to end hostilities. A constitutional convention began, despite a boycott by the NLD. General Khin Nyunt resigned and was replaced by Lt General Soe Win. An earthquake off the island of Sumatra caused a *tsunami* that damaged coastal areas, particularly in the Irrawaddy Delta. The final estimate for Myanmar was 61 dead or missing and 5,000 displaced.
2006 The military *junta* renewed Aung San Suu Kyi's detention order. Her plight was the first case submitted to the newly established UN Human Rights Council. Thousands of ethnic Karens fled to Thailand in the face of the construction of the new capital, Naypyidaw, which had forced them from their homes.
2007 Russia agreed to provide the technology and train technicians to build and operate a 10MW light-water nuclear reactor to power Pyinmana. The International Committee of the Red Cross formally accused the government of abusing the rights of its citizens. A major civil rights protest developed, led by Buddhist monks, calling for a return to democratic rule. The protest was sparked by an increase in the price of domestic fuel. As demonstrations grew the government retaliated by arresting hundreds of monks and firing on protesters; internet and mobile telephone connections were cut by the authorities to prevent pictures and details of the demonstrations being sent to media outlets overseas. Scores of monks were forced to flee from Yangoon as thousands of civilians including three prominent activists were arrested. A UN special envoy met General Than Shwe in an effort to stem the repression. Prime Minister Soe Win died and was succeeded by Thein Sein. The government began to release detained protesters at the end of the year, as monks again marched, although in fewer numbers.
2008 Cyclone Nargis struck the southern region of the Irrawaddy Delta; relief efforts were hampered by the seeming indifference and obstruction of authorities to accept and distribute the huge international aid on offer to Myanmar. Despite disruption from the national disaster the constitutional referendum was held and within five days the government claimed 92 per cent of voters had approved the constitutional changes. Aung San Suu

Kyi's house arrest was extended for another year. An official estimate put 84,500 deaths following Cyclone Nargis with hundreds of thousands of people at risk from disease, homelessness, lack of food and clean water. UN President Ban Ki-moon criticised President General Than Shwe, who had refused to meet him to discuss the crisis. It was estimated by the UN and Asean that relief and reconstruction work following Cyclone Nargis would cost over US$1 billion, for food, agricultural and housing needs. They also estimated that as many as 134,000 had died during the cyclone.

2009 The UN stated that international and domestic law was being flouted by the military regime in the continued detention of Aung San Suu Kyi. She was formally arrested again for 'violating the terms of her house arrest', following an incident when an uninvited US citizen swam across a lake to her residence. The military regime's decision to prosecute, just two weeks before Suu Kyi's house arrest was due to end, drew international condemnation. Suu Kyi was convicted and sentenced to a further 18 month's house arrest; as a result she was unable to campaign in the 2010 elections. Despite the ruling, Suu Kyi had diplomatic meetings with representatives of the UK, Australia and the US, focussing on sanctions imposed by Western nations on Myanmar. The government removed a ban on the use of mobile telephones in the capital, Naypyidaw. At the Asean summit, Prime Minister Thein Sein was quoted as saying Aung San Suu Kyi could contribute to an unspecified 'process of national reconciliation'. The supreme court agreed that it would hear an appeal into Suu Kyi's sentence of a further 18 month's house arrest.

2010 Tin Oo, vice president of the NLD opposition party led by Suu Kyi, was released on 14 February, after serving six years under house arrest. New election laws introduced in March banned candidates with criminal records from standing in elections; the law drew international condemnation. On 29 March, Suu Kyi's political party (NLD) announced it would not expel Suu Kyi as leader nor register for the parliamentary elections, declaring the law 'unjust'. The NLD was disbanded in May after the election registration deadline expired. The *junta* carried out a military reshuffle on 27 August, ahead of the November elections. On 7 November 37 political parties took part in elections for the two houses of parliament, plus 14 regional state assembly elections. However, due to the boycott by, and deregistration of, the NLD, plus the high fee for entering the contest, virtually all parties taking part were proxy parties for the ruling military *junta*, in particular the Union Solidarity and Development Party (USDP), which contested all 1,157 seats nationally, and the National Unity Party (NUP), which contested 990. The National Democratic Force (a splinter of NLD) contested 163. As predicted the USDP won an overwhelming majority in both houses of parliament. The government released Aung San Suu Kyi on 13 November. She said that she would aim for a peaceful revolution and was sure that democracy would be achieved, but not when. On 19 November the UN human rights committee condemned the elections as being neither free nor fair.

2011 On 17 January, following an Asean meeting of foreign ministers, a call was made to drop all international sanctions against the military regime in Myanmar. This was in line with a similar declaration from five of the ethnic minority groups within Myanmar, urging an end to sanctions, which they said disadvantaged their people disproportionately. The first legislative session to be held since 1988 was opened on 31 January in the newly built parliament in Naypyidaw. The first order of business was to vote in speakers for both houses and the nomination of five candidates for the post of vice president. A presidential election, within parliament, began on 2 February, with three nominated candidates. All candidates nominated and chosen were drawn from the military-backed political party; President General Than Shwe did not stand for the post. On 4 February, former prime minister, Thein Sein, was elected as Myanmar's first civilian president (albeit a retired military officer) by parliament with 408 votes (out of 659). On 30 March the military government was officially dissolved after the new president of a civilian-led parliament was sworn in, the first civilian government since 1962. Than Shwe retired on 4 April, having ruled Myanmar for the last 19 years. The ethnic Kachin Independence Army (KIA) attacked the area close to the site of a hydroelectric power plant being built by the Chinese in northern Myanmar on 9 June. The government responded by mounting a military offensive against the rebels. A truce, which had been in place before the attack, had been broken when the KIA refused to become state border guards. On 18 August, President Thein Sein invited home Myanmar's diaspora that fled after the 2008 uprising. However following the speech, he was also quoted saying that those who had 'committed a crime' during the demonstrations would still be punished. The government issued an invitation to Aung San Suu Kyi to visit Naypyidaw, where she met President Thein Sein on 19 August. The government set up a National Human Rights Commission (NHRC) on 6 September, to investigate reported abuses within the country. On 3 October, the government unexpectedly suspended further construction of the Chinese-funded hydroelectric power plant on the Irrawaddy River; no reason was given. On 12 October, 200 political prisoners were freed as part of a government sanctioned general amnesty. Two prominent detainees, the Buddhist monk who had led the 2007 civil unrest and a popular comedian and dissident called Zarganar, plus other monks, minority ethnic group activists and journalists.

Political structure

Constitution

Since 1997, the principal organs of power are the State Peace and Development Council (SPDC), headed by a chairman, and the 40-strong military-dominated cabinet.

Politically, Myanmar is spread over seven divisions where the ethnic Burmans are in the majority, and seven states where the non-Burmans, the ethnic minority groups, are in the majority.

A constitutional referendum was held on 10 May 2008 in advance of multi-party elections scheduled for 2010. Among the articles to change were: the military commander in chief will assume full executive, legislative and judicial powers in the event of a state of emergency, including the power to suspend the constitution if they see fit; a guarantee of 25 per cent of parliamentary seats for the military; the military would be fully in control of the Ministry of Home Affairs; Myanmar citizens married to foreigners will be barred from the presidency; the military to be immune from prosecution for past crimes. According to the military junta which drew up the amended constitution it will ensure the creation of a 'discipline-flourishing democracy'.

Independence date

4 January 1948

National legislature

The bicameral national legislature, was constituted in 2010, consisting of the Amyotha Hluttaw (Nationalities Assembly (upper house)) with 224 members (of which 56 are reserved for military officers as members) and the Pyithu Hluttaw (People's Assembly (lower house)) with 440 members (of which 110 are reserved for military officers).

Last elections

7 November 2010 (parliamentary); 10 May 2008 (referendum on constitution); 4 February 2011 (president, indirect)

Results: Parliamentary (Upper house): Union Solidarity and Development Party (USDP) won 129 seats (out of 168), Rakhine Nationalities Development Party

(RNDP) seven, National Unity Party (NUP) five, Shan Nationalities Democratic Party (SNDP) three; two other political parties failed to win any seats.
Lower house: USDP 259 seats (out of 330), SNDP 18, NUP 12, RNDP nine; two other political parties failed to win any seats.
Referendum on constitution: government announcement declared 92 per cent of voters had approved the changes to introduce a bicameral parliament.
President: Thein Sein won 408 votes (out of 659), Tin Aung Myint Oo 171, Sai Mauk Kham 75 (four votes unaccounted).

Next elections

Not known

Political parties

Ruling party

State Peace and Development Council (SPDC) (19-member military *junta* since 1997)

Main opposition party

National League for Democracy (NLD)

Population

53.40 million (2010)*
Last census: March 1983: 35,307,913
Population density: 89 inhabitants per square km (2010)
Annual growth rate: 1.3 per cent 1994–2004 (WHO 2006)

Ethnic make-up

The indigenous population is Mongoloid. More than two-thirds are Burmans, racially akin to the Tibetans and the Chinese. There are also several indigenous minorities with their own language and culture – the Karen, Shan, Mon, Chin and Kachin; each group has its own state. The population includes immigrant minorities from India and China.

Religions

Theravada Buddhism (88 per cent), Christianity (7 per cent), Islam (3 per cent), Hinduism (0.5 per cent).

Education

Schooling begins in kindergarten for one year, then on to junior school for four years.
Secondary education is not compulsory and is divided into two phases: middle school, for four years, where all students undertake a general programme of learning; then upper secondary school where they elect to undertake either an academic course leading to higher education, or technical school, each lasting for two years. Technical education prepares students for admission to the government technical institutes or trade schools, or advancement on to university engineering courses.
All universities and colleges are financed by the state, although a nominal fee is charged for studies.
Literacy rate: 85 per cent adult rate; 91 per cent youth rate (15–24) (Unesco 2005).
Compulsory years: Five to 10.
Enrolment rate: 121 per cent gross primary enrolment of the relevant age group (including repetition rates); 30 per cent gross secondary enrolment (World Bank).
Pupils per teacher: 46 in primary schools.

Health

Each year an estimated 150,000 children aged less than five die of malaria, acute respiratory infections and diarrhoea.
Access to clean drinking water is available to over 68 per cent of the population.
Malaria and Tuberculosis are widespread.

HIV/Aids

Stories of emigrant Burmese labour in Thailand uniformly infected with hepatitis and/or HIV/Aids are commonplace. Foreign estimates place some 2 per cent of the population as HIV positive. The proportion is many times higher in the army and areas crossed by the 'needle trail' of heroin exports into Manipur, India, and Yunnan, China, among others. This is a clear legacy of neglect of basic human development under the *junta*, in favour of internal and external security expenditures, and will be a dangerous and pressing cost to the Burmese economy over the long term, possibly on a sub-Saharan African level.
Without official statistics published, it can only be estimated by aid workers that there are over 660,000 people with HIV/Aids, making Myanmar the centre of one of south-east Asia's worst epidemics.
In August 2005 the Global Fund to Fight Aids, Tuberculosis and Malaria announced that is was withdrawing from its US$98 million health programme due to government restrictions on health workers in the country. The HIV/Aids epidemic is one of the worst in Asia.
HIV prevalence: 1.2 per cent aged 15–49 in 2003 (World Bank)
Life expectancy: 59 years, 2004 (WHO 2006)
Fertility rate/Maternal mortality rate: 2.3 births per woman, 2004 (WHO 2006); maternal mortality 230 per 100,000 live births (World Bank).
Birth rate/Death rate: 10 deaths to 26 births per 1,000 people (World Bank).
Child (under 5 years) mortality rate (per 1,000): 76 per 1,000 live births (World Bank)
Head of population per physician: 0.36 physicians per 1,000 people, 2004 (WHO 2006)

Welfare

The department of social welfare (DSW) under the ministry of social welfare, relief and resettlement implements social welfare services in eight different areas of social needs by both direct and indirect means covering the aged, children, youths and women welfare services. There is provision for the rehabilitation of ex-drug addicts and the disabled. It provides grants-in-aids to voluntary organisations.
In Myanmar, all government servants retire at the age of 60, and are entitled to gratuity and pension.
There are approximately 45 homes for the aged throughout the country, which provide food, clothing, shelter and healthcare services to the aged. The traditional family structures also provide ample care for the aged. Several religious organisations donate large sums of money towards social welfare.

Main cities

Yangon (formerly Rangoon) (capital, estimated population 4.5 million in 2004), Mandalay (1.2 million), Mawla Myaing (formerly Moulmein, 395,900), Pathein (formerly Bassein, 212,600), Bago (198,000), Monywa (161,000), Sittwe (formerly Akyab, 159,200), Meiktila (157,900), Taung-gyi (149,600).

Languages spoken

English is used in business circles.

Official language/s

Myanmar (Burmese)

Media

In 2008, Freedom House, the US human rights watchdog, assessed Myanmar as not free and has the most tightly restricted media environment in the world. The government is the only broadcaster allowed and owns all daily newspapers. Private weekly and monthly printed material is subject to censorship. Self-censorship by journalists is widespread.

Press

In Burmese, with online editions in English, official publications include the daily *Kyehmon (The Mirror)* (www.myanmar.gov.mm), *Myanmar Alin* (www.mrtv3.net.mm), *The New Light of Myanmar* (www.myanmar.com/nim) is government owned and reports officially sanctioned news, *Pyaw Pyaw Shwin Shwin* is a humorous magazine and, in English, the *Myanmar Times* (www.myanmar.com/myanmartimes) is a weekly.
Dailies: In Yangon, *The New Light of Myanmar*, the multi-language official daily newspaper of the military junta was previously called *The Working People's Daily*. Other newspapers in Myanmar include *Burma Daily*, *Loktha Pyithu Nesin*, *Kyemon* (The Mirror), *Myotaw* (evening tabloid) and *Yadanabon* (Mandalay).
Periodicals: *Burma Focus* is a bi-monthly newsletter.

Broadcasting

Broadcasting is strictly controlled by the government. Due to the high level of illiteracy and the poor circulation of newspapers, radio and television are the main medium of mass communication and sources of news and information for most of the population. Listeners to foreign radio and television stations are subject to arrest.

Radio: The state-run stations include Radio Myanmar and City FM, which offers entertainment.

Popular, broadcasts that provide independent news include the Voice of America, Radio Free Asia and, from Norway, The Democratic Voice of Burma (http://english.dvb.no) which is run by Burmese exiles who provide unfettered and objective news, plus a platform for public opinion and political debate.

Television: TV Myanmar broadcasts in nine local languages plus English. MRTV-3 (www.mrtv3.net.mm) is the state-owned international service. Myawady TV is a military network and TV5 is the first, pay-to-view TV service in a joint state-private venture.

Advertising

Advertising is subject to tight censorship. There are limited outlets for modern advertising as mobile/cell phones are tightly regulated along with the internet which can only be accessed by 1 per cent of the population. Traditional methods are hampered by censorship and a stagnant economy.

News agencies

Mizzima News (by Burmese exiles): www.mizzima.com

Economy

Myanmar is a secretive society that does not publish extensive details of its economy.

The economy is centrally planned and because of international sanctions somewhat isolated, although never-the-less unable to avoid the detrimental effects of the global economic crisis. The government maintains a multiple exchange rate (MER) system, which consists of an official exchange rate that co-exists with informal, parallel market exchange rates. MER is supported by various exchange controls to limit the use of foreign exchange.

In theory, the use of foreign currencies is forbidden. Foreign Exchange Certificates (FEC) have a limited use and are available to purchase only against receipts for exports; the official rate is Kt6.51 per US$1 (March 2010), which is well below the informal rate of over Kt1,200. The informal sector uses the *Hundi* (*Hawala*) system to pay for unrecorded trade, the repatriation of profits and US dollar cash remittances.

The International Monetary Fund (IMF) considers the MER as producing economic distortions that cause a loss of over 10 per cent of GDP.

Foreign exchange reserves were at an all time high of US$3.6 billion in 2008 due to the record production of natural gas (12.5 billion cubic metres (cum)), earning US$2 billion in sales to Thailand alone. However, sales fell by around 50 per cent in 2009. Capital inflows are limited to direct foreign investment in the gas and energy sectors only.

Agriculture typically provides 45 per cent of GDP, but following the disastrous 2007 cyclone that killed around 135,000 people, much of the southern rice growing area was destroyed along with equipment and livestock, leaving already indebted faming families unable to replace their loss. The price of exported beans to India also fell, along with domestic prices so that many farmers have been unable to recover the full cost of production. Analysts predict a significant drop in rice planting as farmers attempt to reduce costs.

Myanmar has rich natural resources including forestry, minerals and fresh water and marine reserves; however it is only able to trade with neighbouring countries while UN imposed sanctions remain in force. The poverty rate is estimated at 26.6 per cent, with high unemployment and falling remittances from Myanmar's two million overseas workers – falling by 30 per cent from Thailand alone in 2009. Inflation, which had been at 32.9 per cent in 2007 fell to 22.5 in 2008 and was predicted to drop to 6.9 per cent in 2009, due to falling commodity prices.

In a report in 2009, the IMF described the economy as 'bleak', with a slowdown in GDP growth to around 4.5 per cent. With the lowest social spending rate in Asia the government appears to be leaving the general population of Myanmar to cope with the global financial crisis on their own.

By the second quarter of 2011, foreign direct investment (FDI) was a record US$20 billion, which vastly exceeded the last highest level of US$302 million in 2010 and the US$16 billion for the combined total 1990–2009. China was the biggest investor of US$8.27 billion in energy projects, followed by Hong Kong (US$5.39 billion) and Thailand (US$2.94 billion).

External trade

Myanmar belongs to the Association of Southeast Asian Nations (Asean) Free Trade Area (Afta) and maintains a list of goods that have preferential import duties between members. A programme of tariff reductions is due to be introduced in the next few years.

There are a number of international trade sanctions, led by the United Nations, the US and EU, although trade continues with China, India and Thailand

Most imports and exports originate with trade corporations and state boards. Trade is handled by the Myanmar Export Import Services using the Myanmar Five Star Line for shipping. The picture of external trade presented by official statistics does not reflect the considerable amount of smuggling and black market trading. Myanmar is a major centre for the production of illegal heroin, estimated at around 2,000 tonnes annually, and amphetamines. Heroin is by far the largest export commodity.

Imports

Principal imports textiles, crude oil and petroleum products, plastics, machinery, transport equipment, construction materials and foodstuffs.

Main sources: China (typically 30 per cent of total), Thailand (20 per cent), Singapore (20 per cent).

Exports

Principal exports are natural gas, timber, jade and precious stones, garments and agricultural produce including pulses, beans, fish and rice.

Main destinations: Thailand (50 per cent of total), India (12 per cent), China (10 per cent).

Agriculture

Farming

Agriculture accounts for around 60 per cent of GDP and provides around 56 per cent of employment. About 15 per cent of the total land area is cultivated.

Myanmar is usually self-sufficient in rice, although adverse weather conditions and an uninvested farming sector can cause shortages. Other main crops are sugar cane, wheat, maize, jute, cotton, beans, wheat and vegetables. Cattle, pigs, buffaloes, sheep, goats and poultry are raised for domestic consumption. Oil palm and rubber plantations are replacing forest in some areas.

Forestry

Around 50 per cent of the land area is forest, containing about 75 per cent of world teak resources. Heavy logging is carried out, mostly of export hardwoods, bamboo and fuel, leading to fears of rapid deforestation.

Industry and manufacturing

The industrial sector accounts for around 7 per cent of GDP and employs around 9 per cent of the workforce.

Small enterprises predominate.

Manufacturing industries include food processing (sugar, tobacco, palm oil, rice), cement, textiles, beverages, cigarettes, aluminium products, paper and nails, steel, cotton yarn, soap, pharmaceuticals and fertilisers. Textile and jute production is being expanded. There are 20 industrial zones. Foreign direct investment (FDI) is weak.

Tourism
Some liberalisation of the tourist industry has occurred. Tourists may now stay in licensed private hotels and travel on specially licensed buses from which they were previously prohibited. Tourism revenue is the second largest legal source of foreign exchange.

Mining
Mining accounts for around 4 per cent of GDP and employs around 3 per cent of the workforce.
Minerals mined include ores of zinc, lead, tin and copper, silver, gypsum, limestone and gems such as rubies, sapphires and jade.
In 2006 international sales of precious gems earned around US$300 million in foreign exchange. However the military crackdown of democracy demonstrations of 2007 prompted not only the French firm Cartier, US's Tiffany and Italy's Bulgari jewellers, but other Western jewellers as well, to halt purchases of rubies (prized for their rich red), jade and other gemstones. Myanmar supplies around 90 per cent of the world's rubies and 98 per cent of jade.

Hydrocarbons
Proven oil reserves were 50 million barrels in 2008, with production at 22,120 barrels per day (bpd). However, with consumption at 41,000bpd imports were required to cover the difference. The Chinese state-owned oil company began construction of a large oil port in Kyaukpyu City (Rakhine State) for importing oil from the Middle East to be transported by a new 771 km pipeline across Myanmar to China. The new port will have a storage capacity of 600,000 cubic metres and the pipeline, when fully operational, will carry 84 million barrels per year of oil.
Proven gas reserves were 300 billion cubic metres (cum) in 2010 with production at 12.1 billion cum. Export of natural gas was 8.81 billion cum to Thailand, with the remainder consumed domestically.
Coal production was around 1.5 million tonnes in 2008, used in energy and industrial production.

Energy
Total generating capacity was 1,616MW in 2007, producing 5.96 billion kilowatt hours (kWh). Myanmar is seeking to develop its considerable hydroelectric generating potential, but is constrained by the cost factor. Electricity services are not available for much of the population, who rely on traditional methods of cooking, lighting and power.

Financial markets
Stock exchange
The Myanmar Securities Exchange Centre opened in 1996.

Banking and insurance
Since 1995, the government has allowed foreign banks to operate in Myanmar which have opened representative offices, to set up joint ventures with private local banks.
Myanmar is on the Organisation for Economic Co-operation and Development (OECD) Financial Action Task Force (FATF) list of non-co-operative countries on money laundering.
In early 2003, there was trouble in the financial sector with the collapse of some private finance companies, which had taken deposits from the public. The problem spread to some private banks and large amounts of cash were withdrawn by depositors. A stronger regulatory framework for the banking system and a strategy to identify and resolve the problem banks are necessary to restore confidence in the sector.
Central bank
Central Bank of Myanmar

Time
GMT plus 6.5 hours

Geography
Myanmar lies in the north-west region of south-east Asia between the Tibetan plateau and the Malay peninsula. It is bordered by Bangladesh and India to the north-west, the People's Republic of China and Laos to the north-east and by Thailand to the south-east.
Myanmar covers an area of 676,552 square km. It is dominated by mountains, rivers and forests. The Ayeyarwady (Irrawaddy) river, which rises in Tibet, flows southwards through the country, dividing it in two, and opening out into a vast delta region. The system is extremely fertile. Other important rivers are the Chindwin and Sittaung. There are several high mountain ranges ringing the country and providing almost impassable barriers against neighbouring countries. These and other interior mountains make land travel difficult within Myanmar. The highest point in the country and in south-east Asia is Mount Hkakabo Razi, which reaches 5,881m. Much of the country is covered in thick, tropical forests.
Hemisphere
Northern

Climate
There are three seasons: the rainy season May/June–October with high humidity and monsoon rains; the hot season February/March–May with likely temperatures of 37 degrees Celsius (C) (coastal and delta areas) to 40 degrees C (central region); and the cool, dry season November–February with temperatures of 16 degrees C (central region) to 21 degrees C (coastal and delta areas). Average rainfall varies from 5,000mm (northern hills and coastal areas) to 2,500mm (delta areas) to 750mm (central region).

Dress codes
Revealing or sloppy clothing is not advisable on any occasion. There are no strict rules regarding business attire.

Entry requirements
Passports
Required by all, valid for six months beyond date of departure.
Visa
Required by all. Tourist and business visas, applied for well in advance of arrival, are valid for 28 days; they may be extended. For a business visa a letter of introduction and an invitation are required, with a full itinerary.
Currency advice/regulations
The import and export of local currency is not allowed. There are no restrictions on the import of foreign currency, subject to declaration; export is restricted to the amount declared on arrival. Exchange controls are strictly enforced and all foreign exchange receipts should be safeguarded.
Customs
Personal effects are allowed duty-free, but customs regulations are restrictive and it is best to travel light. Jewellery, cameras and electric goods must be declared on entry. Video cameras are not allowed into the country.

Health (for visitors)
Mandatory precautions
Yellow fever certificate if arriving from infected area.
Advisable precautions
It is advisable to be in date for polio (within 10 years), tetanus (within 10 years), hepatitis A and B, rabies (within one to three years, depending on exposure to risk), Japanese B encephalitis (within three years if travelling June to September), tuberculosis (children should be immunised at any age, although it is less important for adults), diphtheria (within 10 years). Dengue fever occurs intermittently, especially in the northern Mandalay division.
If travelling through the country it is advisable to be vaccinated against cholera.
Only Yangon (Rangoon) city and areas above 1,000m are malaria free; if in doubt, take malaria prophylaxis.

It is advisable to carry a pack of sterilised needles, and to take any medicines required – they can be in short supply. Water should be boiled and filtered before drinking. It is advisable to drink bottled water.
There is a rabies risk.

Hotels
Accommodation has been described as 'decrepit almost to the extent of charm'. There is no official rating system. Main Yangon (Rangoon) hotels can arrange an interpreter or translation services if necessary. Some Yangon hotels require payment in foreign currency. A 10 per cent service charge and a 10 per cent government tax are included in the bill.

Credit cards
American Express, Diners Club, Master, Visa, JCB are accepted at airlines, major hotels and supermarkets.

Public holidays (national)
Fixed dates
4 Jan (Independence Day), 12 Feb (Union Day), 2 Mar (Peasants' Day), 27 Mar (Armed Forces Day), 13–16 Apr (Maha Thingyan/Water Festival), 17 Apr (Myanmar New Year), 1 May (May Day), 19 Jul (Martyrs' Day), 25 Dec (Christmas Day).
Variable dates
Eid al Adha, Full Moon of Tabaung (Feb/Mar), Full Moon of Kasone (Apr/May), Full Moon of Waso/Beginning of Buddhist Lent (Jul/Aug), Full Moon of Thadingyut/End of Buddhist Lent (Oct), Diwali/Deepavali (Oct/Nov), Tazaungdaing Full Moon Day (Nov), National Day (Dec), Kayin New Year (Dec). In general, Hindu and Buddhist festivals are declared according to local astronomical observations.

Working hours
Banking
Mon–Fri: 1000–1400.
Business
Mon–Fri: 0930–1630.
Government
Mon–Fri: 0930–1630.
Shops
Mon–Sun: 0600–2200.

Electricity supply
230V AC, 50 cycles single-phase; five or 15 amp plugs with three round pins for power.

Weights and measures
Imperial system (the metric system and local units are also in use).

Social customs/useful tips
Shoes and socks must be removed before entering any religious building, and visitors should not wear shorts.
The title 'U' (pronounced 'oo') is the equivalent of 'Mr' in English. When addressing people always use the appropriate prefix and family name. Many people do not have a first name.
The head is considered the temple of the body and should not be touched by other people. It is also considered the ultimate in bad manners to put one's feet on the table or cross one's legs so that the sole of the shoe points at someone. This is because the feet are considered to be the least clean part of the body.
The code of standard behaviour is referred to as *bamahsan chin*. According to this mode of conduct, people are expected to respect elders, exhibit discretion in dealing with the opposite sex, be aware of Buddhist sayings and have an ability to recite some Buddhist verses. Additionally, one should maintain a reserved and indirect approach to another person and not be direct at all. This can lead to misunderstandings, especially in business dealings.

Getting there
Air
National airline: Myanmar Airways International .
International airport/s: Yangon International (RGN), 19km from city centre; duty-free shop, bar, restaurant, buffet, bank, post office and hotel reservations. Mandalay International (MDL), 25km from city; post office, bank, duty-free shop, car rental.
Airport tax: US$10, payable in Foreign Exchange Certificates (FEC).
Surface
Road: There are overland entry points on the borders with China and Thailand. A border pass is required for entry.
Water: Cruise vessels stop at Yangon.
Main port/s: Yangon.

Getting about
Not all parts of the country are open to visitors, and some are subject to guerrilla or bandit activity.
National transport
Tourists are required to keep to officially designated tourist areas and all arrangements for internal travel must be made well in advance via Myanmar Travel and Tours. Travel outside Yangon (Rangoon) is difficult to arrange. No attempt should be made to travel to restricted areas.
Air: Flying is the best and generally only permitted method of traversing the country and visiting tourist destinations. Flight schedules are restricted and subject to change without warning.
Road: There is a large network of roads all over the country, which are being upgraded, and new roads are being built.
Buses: There are a number of privately-owned bus companies which operate air-conditioned coaches between main centres. The main routes are from Yangon to Meiktila, Pyay, Mandalay and Taunggyi.
Rail: There is an extensive rail network. Myanmar Railways operates services to main centres. The Yangon-Mandalay express service runs four trains daily, with a branch line to Shwenyaung and Taunggyi. A service from Yangon to Bagan runs every other day.There are services from Mandalay to Lashio, Monywa and Bagan. Standards of equipment, service and safety are not high.
Water: There is extensive river and coastal traffic. Trips can only be made as part of an organised tour.
City transport
Taxis: In Yangon the government operates blue taxis with standard fares; otherwise, fares are by negotiation. Taxis can be shared or hired on a time basis.
Buses, trams & metro: There are antiquated and overcrowded bus services in all cities; they are not recommended for visitors. Yangon has a circular rail system.
Car hire
Tourists are not permitted to drive. Cars are hired with driver.

BUSINESS DIRECTORY
The addresses listed below are a selection only. While World of Information makes every endeavour to check these addresses, we cannot guarantee that changes have not been made, especially to telephone numbers and area codes. We would welcome any corrections.

Telephone area codes
The international direct dialling (IDD) code for Myanmar is +95 followed by area code:

Bassein	42	Moulmein	32
Mandalay	2	Prome	53
Monywa	71	Yangon (Rangoon)	1

Useful telephone numbers
Ambulance: 192, 71-111
Red Cross: 295-133
Police (emergency): 199
(headquarters): 282-541, 284-764
Telephone enquiries: 100
Booking (inland): 101
Booking (overseas): 130, 131, 667-444, 667-555, 667-601/2
Airport Security: 662-677
Customs: 284-533
Immigration: 286-434

Chambers of Commerce
Myanmar Federation of Chambers of Commerce & Industry, 504 Merchant Street, Kyauktada Township, Yangon (tel: 243-150; fax: 248-177; e-mail: ird@umfcci.com.mm).

Banking

Asia Wealth Bank, Ahlone, River View Housing Project, Olympic Tower II, Yangon (tel: 212-701; fax: 212-704).

First Private Bank Ltd, 619-621 Merchant Street, Pabedan T/S, Yangon (tel: 251-748; fax: 242-320).

Innwa Bank Ltd; 554-556 Corner of Merchant Street & 35th Street, Yangon (tel: 254-641, 254-647; fax: 254-431).

Kanbawza Bank Ltd; 1st Floor, Lanmadaw Condo Centre, No. 02/06, 02/07 Lanmadaw Street, Latha T/S, Yangon (tel: 212-780; fax: 212-778).

Myanmar Agricultural Development Bank, No. 1/7 Corner of Latha St & Kanna Rd, Latha T/S, Yangon (tel: 253-180, 250-569; fax: 245-119).

Myanmar Economic Bank, 1-19 Sule Pagoda Rd, Pabedan T/S, Yangon (tel: 289-329; fax: 283-679).

Myanmar Foreign Trade Bank, PO Box 203, 80-86 Maha Bandoola Garden Street, Kyauktada T/S, Yangon (tel: 284-911; fax: 289-585, 254-585).

Myanmar Industrial Development Bank Ltd, 26/42 Pansodan Street, Kyauktada T/S, Yangon (tel: 249-536; fax: 249-529).

Myanmar Investment and Commercial Bank, 170/176 Bo Aung Kyaw Street, Botataung Township, Yangon (tel: 250-509; fax: 281-775).

Myanmar Livestock & Fisheries Development Bank Ltd, 654-666 Corner of Merchant Street & Shwe Bon Tha Street, Pabedan T/S, Yangon (tel: 249-620; fax: 243-240).

Myanmar Citizens Bank Ltd, 383 Maha Bandoola St, Kyauktada T/S, Yangon (tel: 283-209, 283-719; fax: 245-932).

Myanmar May Flower Bank Ltd, Yadana Housing Project, 9 Mile, Pyay Rd, Mayangon T/S, Yangon (tel: 661-261; fax: 661-262).

Myanmar Oriental Bank Ltd, 166-168 Pansodan Street, Yangon (tel: 246-596; fax: 251-831).

Myanmar Universal Bank Ltd, 81 Theinbyu Rd, Botataung T/S, Yangon (tel: 297-337; fax: 245-449).

Yoma Bank Ltd, 1 Kun Gyan Road, Mingalar Taung Nyunt Township, Yangon (tel: 703-493; fax: 246-548).

Central bank

Central Bank of Myanmar, PO Box 184, 26(A) Sethmin Road, Yankin Tsp, Yangon (tel: 543-751; fax: 543-621; e-mail: cbm.ygn@mptmail.net.mm).

Stock exchange

The Myanmar Securities Exchange Centre.

Travel information

Myanmar Airways International , Sakura Toer, 339 Bogyoke Aung San Road, Yangon (tel: 255-260; fax: 255-305; e-mail: management@maiair.com).

Myanmar Tourism Promotion Board, Traders Hotel, 223 Sule Pagoda Road, Yangon (tel: 242-828; fax: 242-800; e-mail: mtpb@mptmail.net.mm).

Ministry of tourism

Ministry of Hotels and Tourism, 77-91 Sule Pagoda Road, Kyauktada Tsp, Yangon (tel: 285-689; fax: 289-588; e-mail: mtt.mht@mptmail.net).

National tourist organisation offices

Myanmar Travels and Tours, 77-91 Sule Pagoda Road, PO Box 559, Yangon (tel: 382-243; fax: 254-417; e-mail: mtt.mht@mptmail.net.mm).

Ministries

Ministry of Agriculture and Irrigation, Thiri Mingala Lane, Kaba Aye Pagoda Road, Yankin Tsp, Yangon (tel: 665-587; fax: 664-493).

Ministry of Commerce, 228-240 Strand Road, Pabedan Tsp, Yangon (tel: 289-660; fax: 289-578).

Ministry of Communications, Post and Telecommunications, 80 Corner of Merchant St & Theinbyu Street, Botahtaung Tsp, Yangon (tel: 292-019).

Ministry of Construction, 39 Nawaday Street, Botahtaung Tsp, Yangon (tel: 283-938).

Ministry of Co-operatives, 259-263 Bogyoke Aung San Street, Kyauktada Tsp, Yangon (tel: 277-096, 280-280; fax: 287-919).

Ministry of Culture, 26-42 Pansodan Street, Kyauktada Tsp, Yangon (tel: 243-235).

Ministry of Defence, Ahlanpya Phaya Street, Yangon (tel: 281-611).

Ministry of Education, Theinbyu Street, Botahtaung Tsp, Yangon (tel: 285-588).

Ministry of Energy, 23 Pyay Road, Yangon (tel: 221-060; fax: 222-964).

Ministry of Finance and Revenue, 26 Setmu Road, Kyauktada Tsp, Yangon (tel: 284-763).

Ministry of Foreign Affairs, Pyay Road, Dagon Tsp, Yangon (tel: 222-844; fax: 222-950).

Ministry of Forestry, Thirimingala Lane, Kabe Aye Pagoda Road, Mayangon Tsp, Yangon (tel: 289-184; fax: 664-459).

Ministry of Health, Theinbyu Street, Botahtaung Tsp, Yangon (tel: 277-334; fax: 282-834).

Ministry of Home Affairs, Corner of Saya San Street & No 1 Industrial Street, Yankin Tsp, Yangon (tel: 549-208).

Ministry of Immigration & Population, Theinbyu Street, Botahtaung Tsp, Yangon (tel: 249-215).

Ministry of Industry (I), 192 Kaba Aye Pagoda Road Yangon (tel: 566-066).

Ministry of Industry (II), 56 Kaba Aye Pagoda Road, Yangon (tel: 661-140; fax: 667-156).

Ministry of Information, 365-367 Bo Aung Kyaw Street, Kyauktada Tsp, Yangon (tel: 245-631; fax: 289-274).

Ministry of Labour, Theinbyu Street, Botahtaung Tsp, Yangon (tel: 278-320; fax: 256-185).

Ministry of Livestock Breeding and Fisheries, Theinbyu Street, Botahtaung Tsp, Yangon (tel: 280-398; fax: 289-711).

Ministry of Mines, 90 Kanbe Road, Yankin Tsp, Yangon (tel: 577-316).

Ministry of National Planning and Economic Development, Theinbyu Street, Botahtaung Tsp, Yangon (tel: 280-816; fax: 282-101).

Ministry of Development of Border Areas and National Races and Development Affairs, Theinbyu Street, Botahtaung Tsp, Yangon (tel: 280-032; fax: 285-257).

Ministry of Rail Transport, 88 Theinbyu Street, Botahtaung Tsp, Yangon (tel: 292-769).

Ministry of Religious Affairs, Kaba Aye Pagoda Precinct, Mayangon Tsp, Yangon (tel: 665-620; fax: 665-728).

Ministry of Science and Technology, 6 Kaba Aye Pagoda Road, Yangon (tel: 665-686).

Ministry of Social Welfare, Relief & Resettlement, Theinbyu Street, Botahtaung Tsp, Yangon (tel: 282-610).

Ministry of Sports, Office of the Ministrers, Yangon (tel: 553-958).

Ministry of Transport, 363/421 Merchant Street, Yangon (tel: 296-815; fax: 296-824).

Office of the Prime Minister, Minister's Office, Yangon (tel: 283-742).

Other useful addresses

ASEAN Investment Promotion Agency, 653/691 Merchant Street, Pabedan, Yangon (tel: 372-855; fax: 254-660; e-mail: dica.nped@mptmail.net.mm).

British Embassy, Commercial Section, 80 Strand Road, Box No 638, Yangon (tel: 281-700; fax: 289-566).

Central Statistical Organisation, New Secretariat, Yangon (tel: 270-578; e-mail: cso.stat@mptmail.net.mm).

Livestock Foodstuff & Milk Products Enterprise, Pyay Road, 10th Mile, Mayangon Tsp, Yangon (tel: 664-244; fax: 240-109).

Myanmar Embassy (US), 2300 S Street, NW, Washington DC 20008 (tel: (+1-202)-332-9044; fax: (+1-202)-332-9046; e-mail: thuriya@aol.com).

Myanmar Export and Import Services, 622-624 Merchant Street, Yangon (tel: 280-260; fax: 289-587).

Myanmar Fisheries Enterprise, 654 Merchant Street, Latha Tsp, Yangon (tel: 20-710; fax: 222-951).

Myanmar General Industries, 192 Kaba Aye Pagoda Road, Yankin Tsp, Yangon (tel: 660-521; fax: 56-066).

Myanmar Investment Commisssion, 653/691 Merchant Road, Yangon (tel: 272-912; fax: 282-101).

Myanmar Oil and Gas Enterprise, 604 Merchant Street, Pabedan Tsp, Yangon (tel: 282-121; fax: 222-964).

Myanmar Petrochemical Enterprise, 23 Pyay Road, Lanmadaw Tsp, Yangon (tel: 222-816; fax: 222-960).

Myanmar Ports Authority, 10 Pansodan Street, Yangon (tel: 283-122).

Myanmar Post & Telecommunications, 43 Bo Aung Gyaw Street, Kyauktada Tsp, Yangon (tel: 285-840; fax: 290-429).

Myanmar Railways, Bogyoke Aung San Street, Pabedan Tsp, Yangon (tel: 274-027; fax: 282-267).

Myanmar Textile Industries, 192 Kaba Aye Pagoda Road, Yankin Tsp, Yangon (tel: 566-320; fax: 566-053).

Post & Telecommunications Department, 125 Pansodan Street, Kyauktada Tsp, Yangon (tel: 283-737; fax: 286-365).

US Embassy, 581 Merchant Street, Yangon (tel: 282-055; fax: 280-409).

News agency: Mizzima News (by Burmese exiles): www.mizzima.com

Internet sites

Myanmar Resources: http://www.myanmars.net

Official Website of Myanmar: http://www.myanmar.com

Myanmar Business Information: http://www.myanmarpyi.com

Radio Free Myanmar: http://users.imagiware.com/wtongue/dvb2.html

Namibia

KEY FACTS

Official name: Republic of Namibia

Head of State: President Hifikepunye Pohamba (Swapo) (since 2005; re-elected 28 Nov 2009)

Head of government: Prime Minister Nahas Angula (appointed by the President 21 Mar 2005)

Ruling party: South West African People's Organisation (Swapo) (re-elected 16 Nov 2004)

Area: 824,269 square km

Population: 2.14 million (2010)*

Capital: Windhoek

Official language: English

Currency: Namibian dollar (N$) = 100 cents; at par with the South African commercial Rand

Exchange rate: N$8.04 per US$ (Oct 2011)

GDP per capita: US$5,652 (2010)

GDP real growth: -4.40% (2010)

GDP: US$11.90 billion (2010)

Inflation: 4.20% (2010)

Balance of trade: -US$983.50 million (2009)

Annual FDI: US$857.64 million (2010)

* estimated figure

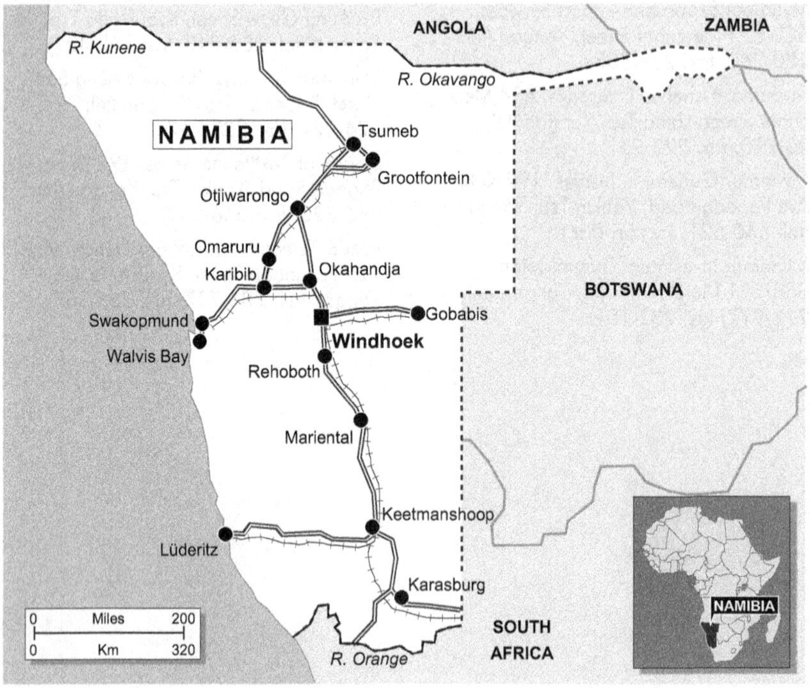

In 2011 the Namibian economy was looking good after the global economic downturn in 2010. Diamond and uranium mining, in particular, were recovering rapidly. The gross domestic product (GDP) is expected to expand further in 2011 and 2012, due primarily to sustained improvement in global demand for mineral products and improvements in credit extension. However, the risk of a sovereign debt crisis in the euro-zone poses a threat to domestic mining and tourism industries; a euro-zone debt crisis could derail the current recovery process.

In 2010, according to the *African Economic Outlook 2010* (AEO), published jointly by the African Development Bank and the Organisation for Economic Co-operation and Development, agricultural production expanded by 1.6 per cent due to favourable weather conditions. Namibian agricultural production has benefited from exceptionally high levels of rains during the past three years and this trend is predicted to continue during 2011 and 2012. The agriculture, fishing, forestry and hunting sectors contributed 9.4 per cent to GDP in 2009. The recovery in the sector is driven primarily by livestock farming anchored by the Combating Bush Encroachment for Namibia's Development (CBEND) project, or debushing programme. Good harvests are also expected in the crop farming sector mainly due to the expansion of land for crop production, the governments' Green Scheme programme and the Millennium Challenge Account (MCA) investment to increase crop production and business capacity. However, access to land remains one of the biggest challenges to boost rural productivity and reduce the current high levels of unemployment.

The mining sector, the backbone of the economy, was hit severely by the 2008–09 global recession. In 2009, production in total mining and quarrying declined by 45 per cent; diamond mining declined by 49.7 per cent and other mining and quarrying by 22.5 per cent. The mining and quarrying sector contributed 10.8 per cent to GDP in 2009. In 2010 there was some recovery in the mining sector, which expanded by an estimated

20.3 per cent as a whole, while diamond mining output grew by 25 per cent. Diamond, gold and zinc production increased by 71.8 per cent, 38.1 per cent and 5.6 per cent year-on-year during the third quarter of 2010, respectively, while uranium output declined by 5.4 per cent. Namibia is the fourth largest producer of uranium in the world; an increase in uranium prices – due to increased demand from China and India – is expected to anchor economic growth in the future. Uranium is poised to overtake diamonds as the main export commodity; nonetheless, the latter still contributes 15 per cent of the foreign exchange earnings.

Four investments, worth a total of about US$714 million, were undertaken in the mining and exploration sector in 2010. Between 2006 and 2009, the country received several investments in the mining and exploration sector due to the discovery of significant deposits of uranium. For instance, gross fixed investment in mining and quarrying increased by 139 per cent from N$1.8 billion (US$224 million) in 2005 to N$4.3 billion (US$53.5 million) in 2008. In spite of the recovery in global demand, a strong currency exchange rate remained a serious challenge for the sector during 2010.

On 8 March 2011, China's state-owned Guangdong Nuclear Power Holding Corporation (CGNPC) (nuclear energy producer) offered US$1.2 billion for the mining company, Kalahari Minerals, which has rights to mine uranium in Namibia. The deal fell through after the 11 March disaster in Japan when three Fukushima Daiichi nuclear reactors were hit by a *tsunami*; talks were on again in November.

Manufacturing remained resilient amid the global economic downturn in 2009, expanding by 6.5 per cent, while the sector is likely to grow by an estimated 6.2 per cent in 2010. The main drivers of growth in the manufacturing sector are fish processing onshore and processing of other food, excluding meat processing. The estimated growth rate for fish processing is 9.7 per cent, while 6.5 per cent growth is anticipated in the processing of other foodstuffs in 2010. Manufacturing contributed 14.7 per cent to GDP in 2009 and employed approximately 6 per cent of the total labour force.

The construction sector declined by an estimated 3.7 per cent in 2010, following a more severe contraction of 7.2 per cent in 2009 compared to 2008. The decline was driven mainly by the fall in residential building construction owing to a tightening of credit and high levels of household indebtedness. During the third quarter of 2010, the value of buildings completed fell by 35.5 per cent year-on-year, compared to the corresponding quarter of 2009.

The service sector, whose growth remained resilient during the 2009 global financial and economic crises, slowed down in 2010 with the exception of hotels and restaurants, transport, storage and communications. Growth in wholesale and retail trade slowed down by an estimated 2.5 per cent in 2010 from 3.1 per cent in the previous year, while growth in financial intermediation declined by 5.2 per cent in 2010 from 6.6 per cent in 2009. Real estate and business services grew by an estimated 2.1 per cent in 2010 compared to 6.0 per cent in 2009.

One of the strategic goals of the Namibian government is for the country to become a fully industrialised nation by the year 2030. One plan for achieving this is through import substitution by creating the capacity to process raw materials and hence, become a competitive goods manufacturing nation.

Doing business in Namibia

Namibia's private business regulatory environment deteriorated during 2009 and 2010. The country's overall rank in the World Bank *Doing Business* report declined to 69 in 2011 from 66 in 2010. The country remains, nonetheless, the seventh-best performer in the African continent in 2011. Structural bottlenecks that negatively affect the efficiency and competitiveness of the private sector include: high levels of concentration in key economic sectors; regulations that undermine competitiveness; energy shortages; lack of skilled workers; high transport costs, due to the large size of the country and low population density; bureaucratic inefficiencies, which affect the time taken to start businesses and register property; and rigid labour laws. The private sector remains divided into a small number of large, profitable businesses, and a large number of very small, unproductive and low-skilled businesses.

In 2010, the government took a number of measures to improve the overall business climate, and enhance productivity and competitiveness and is devising appropriate strategies to promote the development of small and medium enterprises (SMEs), which are needed crucially to curb the current high level of unemployment in the economy.

International trade and partners

China is the most important emerging economic partner of Namibia. Namibia and China marked 20 years of diplomatic relations in March 2010. The two countries signed a bilateral agreement for Economic and Technical Co-operation in 2009 and a number of other co-operation agreements. Namibia-China bilateral co-operation involves both trade and aid, including grants, interest-free loans and business partnerships. Namibia also signed two specific bilateral agreements on energy and mineral explorations with China in November 2010.

KEY INDICATORS — **Namibia**

	Unit	2006	2007	2008	2009	2010
Population	m	1.99	2.03	2.06	*2.08	2.14
Gross domestic product (GDP)	US$bn	6.94	8.80	8.80	9.50	11.90
GDP per capita	US$	4,008	4,355	4,278	4,543	5,652
GDP real growth	%	7.1	5.5	2.9	-0.7	4.8
Inflation	%	5.1	6.7	10.0	9.1	4.2
Industrial output	% change	6.1	6.0	0.8	-12.4	–
Agricultural output	% change	0.6	-6.7	-1.3	-3.1	–
Exports (fob) (goods)	US$m	1,503.0	2,921.6	3,116.4	3,535.3	–
Imports (fob) (goods)	US$m	2,090.0	3,101.6	3,833.2	4,518.8	–
Balance of trade	US$m	984.0	-180.0	-716.9	-983.5	–
Current account	US$m	1,106.0	692.6	44.9	-161.0	-126.0
Total reserves minus gold	US$m	449.6	896.0	1,292.9	2,050.9	1,695.7
Foreign exchange	US$m	449.4	895.9	1,292.8	1,846.4	1,494.7
Exchange rate	per US$	7.23	7.04	8.26	8.47	7.32

* estimated figure

China has invested in a number of sectors, including social services, construction and mining. In the 2009/10 fiscal year, China provided approximately N$109 million (US$13.56 million) in bilateral development assistance for 'green scheme' and aquaculture projects, construction, capacity building, education, health, defence and other sectors compared to N$1.29 billion (US$160 million) provided by all development partners. China also provided just over N$424 million (US$53 million) in concessional loans to the technology, transport, health and sanitation, youth, and government services and public administration sectors during the same period.

China is the third largest provider of bilateral development assistance after the United States and Germany, and the second largest provider of concessional loans after Germany. China provided nearly 33 per cent of the total concessional loans the country received in the 2009/10 financial year. Moreover, the total volume of bilateral trade between the two countries grew by 20 per cent in 2010 compared to 2009 to reach US$750 million.

India is the second most important emerging partner; it has an increasingly important role in the education and health sectors. In 2009, Namibia and India signed two bilateral agreements: one in the communication field and the other for co-operation in peaceful uses of nuclear energy. They also signed agreements on co-operation in the field of defence, co-operation in the field of geology and mineral resources, among others. This is expected to boost trade, particularly in uranium and diamonds, as well as heighten investment activities between the two countries

Russia has also become an increasingly important economic partner of Namibia. In May 2010, Namibia and Russia signed a memorandum on co-operation for exploration and development of Namibian uranium deposits. Currently, Russia is actively involved in the natural gas fields, where the Russian state owned gas and oil company, Gazprom, is heading a consortium to develop Namibia's large gas resources.

On 6 July 2011, mining and energy minister, Isak Katali announced that an estimated 11 billion barrels of oil had been found offshore in Namibian waters, with initial production scheduled for 2015.

Emerging partners are becoming increasingly important compared to traditional partners. However, for historical reasons and geographical reasons, South Africa still dominates Namibia's FDI and overall trade.

Poverty and unemployment

Poverty and inequality remain high in Namibia. The upper 20 per cent of the population lives on 78.7 per cent of the country's total annual income, while the bottom 20 per cent lives on a mere 1.4 per cent. About 35–40 per cent of the population depends on subsistence agriculture for its livelihood.

Some progress has been made towards the achievement of the Millennium Development Goals (MDGs). The goal of achieving gender parity in secondary education was met in 2008. The gender parity goal is likely to be met in primary and tertiary education before 2015. However, more needs to be done in other areas. The government considers education as the most important long-term investment if Namibia is to achieve sustained economic growth. Accordingly, it continues to allocate the largest share of the budget, 23 per cent, to this sector followed by health with 12 per cent in 2010. In spite of free and compulsory basic education until grade 10 or age of 16, the quality of education is low as measured by the generally low performance of students in Namibian schools, particularly in mathematics and English. Moreover, secondary schools fail to produce leaving students with the requisite skills needed by the economy.

The global economic downturn exacerbated unemployment in the country, which reached 51.2 per cent in 2010. The total number of the employed workforce was 331,000 in 2008. The National Labour Force Survey (NLFS) 2008 found that the agriculture sector was the largest employer (15.9 per cent), followed by the wholesale and retail sector (15.1 per cent). Unemployment is geographical, as well as gender- and age-based. Rural unemployment was 64.9 per cent and unemployment among rural women was 72.1 per cent, while unemployment among all women was 58.4 per cent. Youth unemployment was 68 per cent.

There is significant job-creation potential in rural areas. Farming, agro-processing, service industries and small- to medium-sized enterprises are crucial to realise both rural development and job-creation objectives. However, challenges remain due to limited access to land because of the slow pace of land reform.

Risk assessment

Economy	Fair
Politics	Fair
Regional stability	Good

COUNTRY PROFILE

Historical profile

1884 Declared a German territory (except Walvis Bay, which was occupied in 1878 by the British).

1920 Mandated to South Africa by the League of Nations.

1946 There was stalemate when the United Nations (UN) refused to allow South Africa to annex South West Africa (SWA) and South Africa refused to place SWA under UN trusteeship.

1958 The Ovamboland People's Congress, which later became the South West Africa People's Organisation (Swapo), was created by Herman Toivo Ya Toivo and others in the anti-contract labour movement.

1960 The Ovamboland People's Congress becomes Swapo.

1968 South West Africa officially renamed Namibia by UN General Assembly.

1966 South Africa introduced apartheid laws, the UN terminated its mandate and Swapo launched an armed struggle for independence.

1972 The UN General Assembly recognised Swapo as the 'sole legitimate representative of Namibian people'.

1977 The UN declared South Africa's decision to annex Walvis Bay as 'illegal, null and void and an act of colonial expansion'.

1985 South Africa established the Transitional Government (TG), an un-elected black majority government consisting of members of six different tribal parties, instructing it to draw up a constitution.

1988 South Africa turned down the TG's constitutional draft but eventually agreed, along with Angola, Cuba, (the then) USSR and USA, Namibian independence in exchange for removal of Cuban troops from Angola.

1989 Free and fair elections were held under the auspices of the UN. South Africa withdrew its forces. The Swapo leader, Sam Nujoma, formed a transitional ministerial team.

1990 Independence was granted and Nujoma became Namibia's first president.

1994 Walvis Bay and 12 offshore Penguin Islands were formally transferred from South African to Namibian sovereignty. In Namibia's first post independence presidential and National Assembly elections in December, Swapo and Nujoma defeated the Democratic Turnhalle Alliance party of Mishake Muyongo.

1998 Namibia, Angola and Zimbabwe sent troops to the Democratic Republic of Congo to support President Laurent Kabila against rebels.

1999 President Sam Nujoma and the ruling Swapo won the presidential and legislative elections.

2001 President Nujoma said he would not stand in the 2004 presidential election although he would remain as leader of Swapo until at least 2007.
2002 President Sam Nujoma dismissed his prime minister, Hage Geingob and replaced him with Theo-Ben Gurirab, the former foreign minister
2003 Flood waters from the Zambezi River affected 10,000 villagers in the eastern Caprivi.
2004 Germany expressed regret for the colonial-era killing of tens of thousands of ethnic Hereros. Hifikepunye Lucas Pohamba was chosen by Swapo to run in the presidential election and won with 76.4 per cent of the vote. In National Assembly elections, Swapo won 76.1 per cent of the vote (55 out of 72 seats).
2005 President Hifikepunye Pohamba appointed Nahas Angula as prime minister. The ministry of lands and resettlement announced that it would cost N$3.7 billion (US$555 million) over 15 years to implement the land reforms proposed by the government. While 33 million hectares of communal land will be converted to small-scale farming, controversially one aspect of the reforms is the expropriation of white farmer-owned lands.
2007 A rich deposit of uranium was found in the Erongo region. Sam Nujoma resigned as president of Swapo; he had led the party for 47 years. A joint dam and hydroelectric power station project was agreed between Angola and Namibia. A new political party, the Rally for Democracy and Progress (RDP), was formed.
2008 The location of a 500-year-old sunken treasure ship off the coast of Namibia was announced by the diamond company Namdeb during exploration operations. The finds included gold coins and tonnes of elephant tusks.
2009 In presidential and parliamentary elections, incumbents Hifikepunye Pohamba won 76.4 per cent of the vote and Swapo 75.3 per cent (54 seats out of 72).
2010 A landmark court case began in June, concerning the forced sterilisation of HIV positive women since the mid-1990s (the case involving as many as 230 women litigants, lasted into 2011). On 8 July, travel restrictions on people living with HIV/Aids and other contagious diseases were lifted. On 14 September nine members of parliament ended their boycott of parliament, imposed since January, after the Supreme Court struck down the case brought by opposition parties contesting the last parliamentary elections on a technicality.
2011 On 8 March, China's state-owned Guangdong Nuclear Power Holding Corporation (CGNPC) (nuclear energy producer) offered US$1.2 billion for the mining company, Kalahari Minerals, which has rights to mine uranium in Namibia. The deal fell through after the Japanese earthquake and *tsunami*, but talks were on again in November. On 31 March, a state of emergency was declared in the north of the country around the town of Oshakati after serious flooding following heavy seasonal rains. Over 20 people were drowned and around 10,000 people displaced, as well as damage to crops and livestock and roads washed away. On 6 July, mining and energy minister, Isak Katali announced that an estimated 11 billion barrels of oil had been found offshore in Namibian waters, with initial production scheduled for 2015.

Political structure

Constitution
In 1999 the constitution was altered to allow President Nujoma to serve a third term.
Independence date
1990
Form of state
Multi-party republic
The executive
Executive power rests with the president, who is head of state, elected by universal suffrage for a five-year term, with the assistance of a cabinet headed by a prime minister appointed by the president.
National legislature
Legislative power is vested in a bicameral parliament comprising a directly elected, 72-member National Assembly with a five-year term, and an indirectly elected National Council (26 members, two members from each of Namibia's 13 regions), with a six-year term.
Last elections
27–28 November 2009 (presidential and parliamentary)
Results: Presidential: Hifikepunye Pohamba (Swapo) won 76.4 per cent of the vote, Hidipo Hamutenya (Rally for Democracy and Progress (RDP)) 11.1 per cent; 10 other candidates won less than 3 per cent each.
Parliamentary: Swapo won 75.3 per cent of the vote (54 seats out of 72), RDP 11.3 per cent (8); seven other political parties shared the remaining 10 seats with none wining more than two, five other parties failed to win any seats.
Next elections
November 2015 (presidential and parliamentary)

Political parties

Ruling party
South West African People's Organisation (Swapo) (re-elected 16 Nov 2004)
Main opposition party
Rally for Democracy and Progress (RDP)

Population

2.14 million (2010)*
Last census: August 2001: 1,830,330
Population density: Two inhabitants per square km. Urban population: 31 per cent (1995–2001).
Annual growth rate: 2.3 per cent 1994–2004 (WHO 2006)
Ethnic make-up
87.5 per cent black, 6.5 per cent mixed race (coloured) and 6.0 per cent white.
Religions
Christianity (approximately 80 per cent), traditional beliefs (20 per cent).

Education

Primary schooling is compulsory and lasts for seven years. Secondary education is divided into two stages, junior secondary between the ages of 12 and 15 and senior secondary level lasting for another two years. A final two-year school course may be undertaken for the pre-university certificate, until aged 19.
The country has a serious lack of secondary school teachers and because of the remoteness of villages many older children are unable to complete high school. Public expenditure on education amounts to approximately 4 per cent of annual GDP.
Literacy rate: 83 per cent adult rate; 92 per cent youth rate (15–24) (Unesco 2005).
Compulsory years: Five to 21
Enrolment rate: 131 per cent gross primary enrolment, 62 per cent gross secondary enrolment; of relevant age group (including repeaters) (World Bank).

Health

As a result of HIV/Aids, the annual cost of public healthcare has risen steadily.
Over 68 per cent of infants aged less than one year are immunised against measles. Access to clean drinking water is available to over 77 per cent of the population.
HIV/Aids
Namibia has one of the highest rates of HIV infection in the world. If the trend continues, the number of individuals living with the disease will rise to 400,000 by 2006. Aids is the main single cause of death for all age groups. UNAIDS estimates that the annual loss to GDP per capita growth will be 1.5 per cent by 2010.
Life expectancy: 54 years, 2004 (WHO 2006)
Fertility rate/Maternal mortality rate: 3.8 births per woman, 2004 (WHO 2006); maternal mortality 230 per 100,000 live births (World Bank).
Child (under 5 years) mortality rate (per 1,000): 48 per 1,000 live births (World Bank)
Head of population per physician: 0.3 physicians per 1,000 people, 2004 (WHO 2006)

Welfare
The social pension scheme (from 1949) has massive anti-poverty objectives. Surveys in Namibia have shown that pension-dependent households are better off than small farmers. The scheme offers a non-contributory social pension for its elderly citizens. Namibia's 85,000 social pensioners receive a much lower amount each month compared to South Africa and Botswana. The social pension also supports unemployed adults, young grandchildren and other relatives. Increasingly, the pension is providing vital support to relatives of those suffering from HIV/Aids, with many elderly people fostering Aids orphans. The social pension costs the Namibian government an average of 4.8 per cent of total government expenditure.
Rape constitutes a massive problem in society. It is estimated that as many as 15,000 people a year could be victims of rape or attempted rape with only one in every 20 rapes being reported to the police.

Main cities
Windhoek (capital, estimated population 252,721 in 2005), Oshakati (53,736), Walvis Bay (49,656), Swakopmund (28,791), Otjiwarongo (26,334), Grootfontein (25,773), Rehoboth (21,899), Rundu (19,676).

Languages spoken
English is the first language of only 7 per cent of the population. All documents, notices and directional signs are in English. German and Afrikaans are widely used throughout the country.
There are six main African languages: Oshiwambo, Herero, Nama-Damara, Kwangali (Okavango region), Lozi (Caprivi region) and Tswana.

Official language/s
English

Media
The constitution guarantees freedom of the press, which is respected by the authorities.

Press
Dailies: In English and Oshiwambo, *The Namibia* (www.namibian.com.na) has the highest circulation; *New Era* (www.newera.com.na) is government owned; in Africaans *Die Republikein* (www.republikein.com.na) and in German *Allgemeine Zeitung* (www.az.com.na) all cover general news and current affairs.
Weeklies: In English, *Namibia Plus* (www.namibiaplus.com), *Windhoek Observer* and *The Southern Times* (www.southerntimesafrica.com) is published on Sunday.
Business: In English, the weekly *Namibia Economist* (www.economist.com.na) covers financial and economic news.
Periodicals: In English, *Insight Namibia* (www.insight.com.na) covers current affairs.

Broadcasting
The national public broadcaster is the Namibian Broadcasting Corporation (NBC) (www.nbc.com.na).
Radio: NBC (www.nbc.com.na) operates nine services over FM, medium wave and short wave in English, Afrikaans, German and seven local languages. There are many private, radio stations providing national networks including Radiowave (www.radiowave.com.na) and Omulunga Radio (www.omulunga.com) and Kanal 7 (www.k7.com.na).
Television: NBC (www.nbc.com.na) operates one channel, broadcasting locally produced and imported programmes in English. The private station Desert TV is located in Windhoek.

News agencies
National news agency: Nampa (Namibia Press Agency)
APA (African Press Agency): www.apanews.net

Economy
The economy is dominated by primary industry, in particular mining of diamonds and uranium, as well as farming and fishing. For historic and trade reasons, the economy is heavily integrated with neighbouring South Africa; the Namibian dollar is pegged at one-to-one with the South African rand, which is legal tender in Namibia, and the majority of imports and exports are generated by South Africa.
There is a pool of skilled workers and professional and managers that are employed in capital-intensive industries.
Tourism has become a major industry since the mid-1990s, with the fastest growth of all sectors and which unlike other sectors has registered continued growth over the past five years. In 2009, the service sector constituted 59.9 per cent of GDP, industry 32.7 per cent, of which manufacturing amounted to 14.7 per cent and agriculture 9.4 per cent.
GDP growth was 4.3 per cent in 2008, having fallen steadily from 7.1 per cent in 2006, but in 2009 as the global economic crisis cut world trade, especially in exports of minerals, the economy fell into recession of -0.7 per cent. As world trade picked up in 2010 GDP growth bounced back to 4.8 per cent.
The mining sector has experienced a decline, not only in investment since 2008, but also in exports, which were a record US$1.08 billion in 2006 and have since fallen annually to an estimated US$980.5 million in 2009. There is a projected resurgence in exports of US$1,411.7 million in 2010.
Revenue from the Southern African Customs Union (Sacu) tariff pool was some US$1.01 billion in 2009, the largest single contribution to government income. However, as a result of the global financial crisis, in 2010 Namibia's share of the pool was significantly lower at US$853 million. Namibia is also required to repay excess Sacu transfers of N$5.2 billion (US$710 million). Finance minister Saara Kuukongelwa-Amadhila was reported as saying she would not raise taxes, which may have lead to a cut in social spending, but the government continued to stimulate the economy by spending money on infrastructure and other projects designed to attract investment and generate employment.
The government is attempting to diversify economic activities. Namibia offers relatively low labour costs, and, at Walvis Bay, a strategic location for sea exports from the southern African region. The government is targeting manufacturing, trans-shipment and energy as the prime sectors for new business.
Unemployment continues to be a major problem with a rate of 51 per cent in 2009, together with under-employment at 15 per cent. The government is attempting to address this issue by, among other actions, a land re-allocation programme. Much will depend on the training opportunities for local farmers who are typically engaged in subsistence farming and herding.
Income inequality in Namibia is one of the largest in the world. In 2011, the UN Human Development Index (HDI) ranked Namibia 120 (out of 187) for development in health, education and income. In 2010, 47.2 per cent of the population experienced deprivation in at least one of the indicators. The government had introduced measures to alleviate high prices for food and fuel for the most vulnerable in the 2008/09 budget, while increasing payments to the elderly, orphans, vulnerable children and war veterans' allowances.
Under Namibia's millennium goal initiatives, the high rates of HIV/Aids had been reduced to 13.1 per cent of the adult population in 2009; in 2008 around 80 per cent of HIV positive Namibians were receiving antiretroviral (ARV) treatment.

External trade
Namibia is a member of the Southern African Customs Union (Sacu), with South Africa, Lesotho, Swaziland and Botswana. Sacu sets customs duties for commodities passing between member states and members share the common pool of customs and excise revenue on all external

trade. It is also a member of the Southern African Development Community (SADC), the objectives of which include reducing trade barriers, achieving regional development and economic growth and evolving common systems and institutions. The bulk of imports originate in South Africa.

Imports

Principal imports are foodstuffs, petroleum products and fuel, manufactured goods, machinery, equipment, chemicals and construction materials.

Main sources: South Africa (typically 68 per cent of total), UK (8 per cent), India (4 per cent).

Exports

Principal exports are diamonds (typically 35 per cent), copper, gold, zinc, lead, uranium and agricultural produce including cattle, processed fish and sheep (karakul) skins and wool.

Main destinations: South Africa (typically 32 per cent of total), UK (15 per cent), Angola (9 per cent).

Agriculture

Farming

The agricultural sector contributes around 11 per cent to GDP and employs 39 per cent of the workforce. Only half the country is suitable for farming. In the north, yields remain low on average, due to overgrazing.

Farming supports directly or indirectly some 70 per cent of the population.

There is wide disparity in land access between the 12,000, mainly white-owned, commercial farms and subsistence farmers, who number some 60 per cent of the population.

Commercial farming is dominated by livestock ranching – cattle in the north-central districts, sheep (karakul and mutton) and ostriches in the south – and accounts for 80 per cent of total agricultural output.

Namibia normally produces some 40 per cent of its maize requirements from commercial farms and is generally self-sufficient in millet, the main food crop grown in the north by communal farmers. Beef is the most high-value product and exports go to the EU with an annual quota of 60,000 tonnes.

Fishing

The south-east Atlantic is a rich fishing ground, with sardines, hake and mackerel being the main species.

The government declared a 370km exclusive economic zone and banned unlicensed foreign trawlers after independence. A new fishing policy designed to maximise shore-based processing, and long-term concessions to 159 operators (including 54 new ones) were granted.

Namibia has a 300-strong fishing fleet and foreign trawlers operate under charter. 60,000 tonnes of fish are caught annually, 90 per cent of which is exported. The industry employs 40,000 people and accounts for eight per cent of GDP.

In a meeting of African ministers in Namibia, held in 2009, members discussed illegal and unregulated fishing, which is estimated to cost Africa US$1 billion per annum in lost revenue and the threat to stocks and local artisan fishing.

Industry and manufacturing

The industrial sector contributes around 25 per cent of GDP and employs 8 per cent of the workforce.

There is a small and highly specialised manufacturing sector, concentrated in Windhoek and Walvis Bay, with food processing (meat, agronomic products, fish) and beverages (beer and soft drinks) predominant. Other activities include structural metal products, non-metal mineral products, wood furniture, leather goods.

An export processing zone (EPZ) regime was established in 1995; it provides incentives to investors in manufacturing plants producing goods mainly for export, including a zero income tax liability for an unlimited period.

Mining

The mining sector is the traditional backbone of the economy, contributing around 20 per cent to GDP.

Around 7 per cent of government revenues and a third of the country's foreign exchange earnings come from diamonds.

Namdeb Diamond Corporation (50 per cent owned by De Beers and 50 per cent owned by the Namibian government) mines the world's richest source of high quality gem diamonds onshore north of Oranjemund, while offshore diamond recoveries by De Beers Marine have expanded significantly since commercial mining began in 1991.

The Skorpion zinc mining complex is one of the largest zinc producers in the world. Costs of extraction at Skorpion are low at around US$0.40 per kg, compared to the industry average of around US$0.70 per kg. This puts it in a good position to compete in tough markets.

Primary gold production started in 1989 and significant quantities of copper, lead, pyrite, salt and zinc are also produced while there are large unexploited deposits of base, precious and industrial minerals. Marble, granite and semi-precious stones such as rose quartz, tourmaline, amethyst and blue-lace agate are also mined; the government is seeking to promote local value by adding processing. Larger mines are mainly owned by foreign multinationals from South Africa and the UK.

Namibia is also a major uranium producer.

Hydrocarbons

There are no known oil reserves in Namibia but exploration is ongoing; prospects are considered good in the offshore Lüderitz Basin. Namibia and Angola have agreed to explore blocks in the Namibe Basin, adjoining Angola's deepwater oil fields.

There is no refinery capacity and Namibia relies on imported petroleum products, which amounted to 21,000 barrels per day in 2008. Dependence on South Africa for oil products has been reduced with supplies also coming from Angola and other overseas refineries.

Natural gas reserves totalled around 62.3 billion cubic metres in 2008. The Kudu offshore gas field, in the south, contained some 36.8 billion cubic metres of natural gas.

Coal is not produced and only a small amount is imported from neighbouring countries to meet energy demands.

Energy

Total installed generating capacity was 264MW in 2007, production 1.64 billion kilowatt hours. Namibia and Angola have had plans to build a hydroelectric dam, to be located at Baynes, on the Kunene River, along the border with Angola since 2007. Another plan, for the 400MW Epupa hydroelectric plant, was given the go-ahead in April 2009. The US$7 billion project is scheduled to be completed by 2017. All new dam projects have attracted international pressure not to be built, especially across the Kunene River, one of only six perennial rivers in Africa, at a time of increased droughts. However Namibia's energy shortage is just as pressing and despite the potential for electricity generated from domestically produced natural gas and solar power projects, the dam is still favoured by government policy makers.

NamPower is the national electricity company responsible for generation, transmission and supply of electricity. It is a member of the Southern African Power Pool (Sapp); set up to provide reliable and economical energy supplies to all 12-member countries.

A power line from Victoria Falls in Zambia to Katima Mulilo in Namibia was commissioned by Presidents Mwanawasa and Pohamba in 2008. The 231km line will allow Zambia to supply 220 kilovolts of power to Namibia; it will form part of the Zimbabwe-Zambia-Botswana-Namibia (Zizabona) agreement, which will link the four country's power grids.

Financial markets

Stock exchange

Namibian Stock Exchange (NSE)

Banking and insurance
The banking sector is small, with four private commercial banks. The ratio of non-performing loans is relatively low, making the sector stable and financially sound.
Central bank
Bank of Namibia
Main financial centre
Windhoek

Time
GMT plus two hours

Geography
Namibia lies in south-western Africa, with South Africa to the south and south-east, Botswana to the east and Angola to the north. The country has a long coastline on the Atlantic Ocean. The narrow Caprivi Strip, between Angola and Botswana in the north-east, extends Namibia to the Zambezi river, giving it a border with Zambia. The arid Namib Desert stretches along the west coast, while the eastern-most area is part of the Kalahari Desert.
Hemisphere
Southern

Climate
Namibia has one of the driest climates in the world. Sub-tropical, the hottest months are January–February (20–29 degrees Celsius (C)) and the coldest are June–July (6–18 degrees C).

Entry requirements
Passports
Required by all and must be valid for six months after intended departure date.
Visa
Required by all, except tourist visitors, for up to 90 days, from North America, Australasia, most of Europe, and some Asian countries, for a full list of exceptions see www.mfa.gov.na. Business visas require a letter of invitation or a full list and addresses of business contacts to be visited in Namibia. A certified copy of the return ticket should also be submitted. For a multiple entry visa, application should be made to the Ministry of Home Affairs on arrival in Windhoek.
Currency advice/regulations
The import and export of local currency is limited to N$50,000. The import of foreign currency is unrestricted but must be declared on arrival, and export is allowed up to declared amount.
Customs
Personal items are duty-free. Hunting rifles require a permit that can be issued by customs on arrival; handguns are prohibited.

Health (for visitors)
Mandatory precautions
Yellow fever vaccination certificate required if arriving from an infected area.
Advisable precautions
Visitors should take precautions against all tropical diseases. Vaccinations for diphtheria, tetanus, hepatitis A and typhoid and polio are recommended. Hepatitis B vaccinations may be recommended. Malaria risk exists in most areas in the north. Water in all main towns is purified and safe to drink. There is a risk of rabies. To avoid the risk of bilharzia, only use well maintained, chlorinated swimming pools.
Tap water must be treated as unsafe unless boiled and filtered (bottled water is available in the main cities). Eat only well cooked meals, preferably served hot; vegetables should be cooked and fruit peeled. Dairy products are unpasteurised and should be avoided
A first aid kit that includes disposable syringes, is a reasonable precaution. Medical insurance is essential, including emergency evacuation, and an adequate supply of personal medicines is necessary.

Hotels
Classified from one to four stars. Accommodation in towns outside Windhoek is limited apart from Swakopmund so should always be booked well in advance.

Public holidays (national)
Fixed dates
1 Jan (New Year's Day), 21 Mar (Independence Day), 1 May (Workers' Day), 4 May (Cassinga Day), 25 May (Africa Day), 26 Aug (Heroes' Day), 10 Dec (International Human Rights Day), 25 Dec (Christmas Day), 26 Dec (Family Day).
Variable dates
Good Friday, Easter Holiday (Mar/Apr), Ascension Day (Apr/May).

Working hours
Banking
Mon–Fri: 0900–1530; Sat: 0830–1100.
Business
Mon–Fri: 0800–1700.
Government
Mon–Fri: 0800–1700.
Shops
Mon–Sat 0800–1800.

Telecommunications
Mobile/cell phones
There are GSM 900/1800 networks that cover most populated areas.

Electricity supply
220 V AC

Getting there
Air
National airline: Air Namibia
International airport/s: Windhoek Airport (WDH), 40km from city. Facilities include restaurant, bars, duty-free shops, post office, *bureau de change* and car hire. Taxis, minivans and buses are available to the city.
Airport tax: None
Surface
Road: Tarred highways link the South African border via Keetmanshoop to Windhoek then Oshakati and the northern border with Angola, and between Windhoek and Swakopmund-Walvis Bay. The new Trans-Kalahari highway from Botswana via Ghanzi, along with the Trans-Caprivi tarred highway, provide direct road links between Walvis Bay and central Africa.
Rail: Main line runs from South African border via Keetmanshoop and Windhoek to Swakopmund, Walvis Bay, and via Otavi to Tsumeb and Grootfontein, the northern railheads.
Main port/s: Walvis Bay is a modern, deep-water harbour, Lüderitz is older and smaller.

Getting about
National transport
Air: Flying is the most efficient way of connecting with all main towns, either using the extensive scheduled services or charter flights.
Road: Roads are generally well maintained. There are 64,799km of road, of which 7,841km are tarred, while the rest are gravel and earth. The former Owambo region in the north of the country is inhabited by about 44 per cent of the population, yet is served by only 5 per cent of the total road network.
The Trans-Kalahari and Trans-Caprivi highway provide the backbone of a network serving rural areas as well as connecting landlocked countries with the coast.
Buses: A luxury bus service exists between Windhoek and all major towns.
Rail: The main rail routes in Namibia are Windhoek-Keetmanshoop-De Aar, Walvis Bay-Swakopmund-Windhoek-Tsumeb and Lüderitz-Keetmanshoop. First- and second-class carriages are available on these routes. Light refreshments are offered on some services. On overnight services, seats in first-class compartments convert to four couchettes and those in second-class to six couchettes.
City transport
Taxis: Available in main towns; 10 per cent tip is usual.
Buses, trams & metro: Bus services are not well developed and there is generally no transport except taxis.
Car hire
Available in Windhoek city centre, international airport, Walvis Bay.
Although roads between major towns are generally of a good standard, the distances involved can be prohibitive; four-wheel drive is advisable if going off the main routes.
International driving licence is required.

Traffic drives on the left. The general speed limit is 60kph in built-up areas and 120kph on open roads. Safety belts must be used at all times.

BUSINESS DIRECTORY

Telephone area codes

The international dialling code (IDD) for Namibia is +264 followed by the area code and subscriber's number:

Keetmanshoop	631	Swakopmund	641
Luderitz	6331	Tsumeb	671
Mariental	661	Windhoek	61

Chambers of Commerce

Namibia Chamber of Commerce and Industry, 2 Jenner Street, PO Box 9355, Windhoek (tel/fax: 228-009; e-mail: nccihq@iwwn.com.na).

Windhoek Chamber of Commerce and Industries, 315 Swa Building, 7 Post Street Mall, PO Box 191, Windhoek (tel: 222-000; fax: 233-690; e-mail: whkchamber@namib.com).

Banking

Bank of Windhoek, 262 Independence Avenue, PO Box 15, Windhoek (tel: 299-1229; fax: 299-1285).

City Savings and Investment Bank, PO Box 63, FGI Building, Post St Mall, Windhoek (tel: 221-262; fax: 221-555).

Commercial Bank of Namibia, 12-20 Bulow Street, PO Box 1, Windhoek (tel: 295-9111, 295-2014; fax: 295-2046; e-mail: cbon@iwwn.com.na).

First National Bank Namibia, 209 Independence Avenue, PO Box 195, Windhoek (tel: 229-610; fax: 225-994).

Standard Bank Namibia, Mutual Platz Building, Post Street Mall, PO Box 3327, Windhoek (tel: 294-2283; fax: 294-2583).

Central bank

Bank of Namibia, PO Box 2882, 71 Robert Mugabe Avenue, Windhoek (tel: 283-5111; fax: 283-5067; e-mail: general.inquiries@bon.com.na).

Stock exchange

Namibian Stock Exchange (NSE): www.nsx.com.na

Travel information

Air Namibia, PO Box 731, Transnamib Building, Bahnhofstreet, Windhoek 9000; (tel: 299-6000; fax: 299-6168); Town Office (tel: 229-6444; fax: 299-6168); internet: www.airnamibia.com.na).

Automobile Association, PO Box 61, Windhoek (tel: 224-201).

Etosha Northern Tourism and Publicity Association, PO Box 779, Tsumeb (tel: 220-728; fax: 220-916).

Lodge and Guest Farm Reservations, PO Box 21783, Windhoek (tel: 226-979; fax: 226-999).

Namibia Resorts International, PO Box 2862, Windhoek (tel: 233-145; fax: 234-512).

Southern Tourism Forum, Private Bag 2125, Keetmanshoop (tel: 2095; fax: 3818).

Tour and Safari Association of Namibia, PO Box 5144, Windhoek (tel: 232-748; fax: 228-461).

National tourist organisation offices

Namibia Tourism Board, Independence Avenue, Private Bag 13346, Windhoek (tel: 290-6000; fax: 254-848; email: tourism@mweb.com.na; internet: www.namibiatourism.com.na).

Ministries

Ministry of Agriculture, Water and Rural Development, Private Bag 13184, Windhoek (tel: 202-9111; fax: 229-961).

Ministry of Basic Education and Culture, Private Bag 13186, Windhoek (tel: 293-9411; fax: 224-277).

Ministry of the Environment and Tourism, Private Bag 13346, Swabour Building, Independence Avenue, Windhoek (tel: 284-2111; fax: 229-936).

Ministry of Finance, Private Bag 13295, Windhoek (tel: 209-9111; fax: 236-454).

Ministry of Fisheries and Marine Resources, Private Bag 13355, Windhoek (tel: 205-3911; fax: 233-286).

Ministry of Foreign Affairs, Private Bag 13347, Windhoek (tel: 282-9111; fax: 223-937).

Ministry of Higher Education, Vocational Training, Science & Technology, Private Bag 13391, Windhoek (tel: 253-670; fax: 253-671).

Ministry of Information and Broadcasting, Private Bag 13344, Windhoek (tel: 283-911; fax: 222-343).

Ministry of Mines and Energy, 1 Aviation Road, Private Bag 13297, Windhoek (tel: 284-8111; fax: 283-643; email: info@mme.gov.na).

Ministry of Trade and Industry, Private Bag 13340, Windhoek (tel: 283-7111; fax: 220-148).

Ministry of Works Transport and Communication, Private Bag 13341, Windhoek (tel: 208-9111; fax: 228-560).

President's Office, State House, Private Bag 13339, Windhoek (tel: 220-010; fax: 221-770).

Prime Minister's Office, Private Bag 13338, Windhoek (tel: 287-9111; fax: 226-189; internet: http://opm.gov.na).

Other useful addresses

British High Commission, PO Box 22202, 116 Robert Mugabe Avenue, Windhoek (tel: 223-022; fax: 228-895; e-mail: bhc@iwwn.com.na).

Investment Centre, Private Bag 13340, Windhoek (tel: 283-7335; fax: 22-0278).

Meat Board of Namibia, PO Box 38, Windhoek (tel: 233-280; fax: 228-310).

Namibia Crafts Centre, 40 Talstreet, Windhoek (tel: 222-236).

Namibia Development Corporation, Private Bag 13252, Windhoek (tel: 206-9111; fax: 23-3943).

Namibia Power Corporation, PO Box 2864, Windhoek (tel: 205-4111; fax: 23-2805).

Namibian Embassy (USA), 1605 New Hampshire Avenue, NW, Washington DC 2009 (tel: (+1-202) 986-0540; fax: (+1-202) 986-0443; e-mail: embnamibia@aol.com).

Namibian Ports Authority, PO Box 361, Walvis Bay (tel: 20-8201; fax: 20-8242).

National Planning Commission (NPC), Office of the President, Private Bag 13356, Windhoek (tel: 222-549; fax: 226-501).

Offshore Development Company, Private Bag 13397, Windhoek (tel: 239-032; fax: 231-001).

Ombudsman's Office, Private Bag 13211, Windhoek (tel: 225-998; fax: 226-838).

Telecom Namibia, PO Box 297, Windhoek (tel: 201-2221; fax: 223-323).

TransNamib Ltd, Private Bag 13204, Windhoek (tel: 298-1111; fax: 298-2053).

UK High Commission, 116A Leutwein Street, PO Box 22202, Windhoek (tel: 223-022; fax: 228-895).

US Embassy, Private Bag 12029, 14 Lossen Street, Ausspannplatz, Windhoek (tel: 221-601; fax: 229-792).

Windhoek Show Society, PO Box 1733, Windhoek (tel: 224-748; fax: 227-707).

National news agency: Nampa (Namibia Press Agency), PO Box 26185, Windhoek (tel: 374-000; fax: 221-713; internet: www.nampa.org).

Internet sites

Africa Business Network: www.ifc.org/abn

AllAfrica.com: http://allafrica.com

African Development Bank: www.afdb.org

Africa Online: www.africaonline.com

Mbendi AfroPaedia (information on companies, countries, industries and stock exchanges in Africa): http://mbendi.co.za

Nauru

KEY FACTS

Official name: Republic of Nauru

Head of State: President Marcus Stephen (Dec 2007; re-elected 18 Apr 2008)

Head of government: President Marcus Stephens (re-elected 2008; re-elected Oct 2010)

Ruling party: There is no formal party system; parliament is traditionally dominated by independents that form factions.

Area: 21 square km

Population: 10,000 (2010)

Capital: Owing to its small size and absence of urban development, Nauru has no capital. Yaren is the main town.

Official language: Nauruan

Currency: Australian dollar (A$) = 100 cents

Exchange rate: A$1.03 per US$ (Oct 2011)

GDP per capita: US$5,632 (2009)

GDP real growth: -18.20% (2009)

GDP: US$55.00 million (2009)

Inflation: -0.50% (2010)

NOTA

10 November 2011, President Marcus Stephen resigned. He was initially replaced by Fredrick Pitcher, but on 15 November parliament changed its mind and voted Sprent Dabwido into the post instead.

Storm damage to the island's main port, and a weak demand for phosphate, combined to keep gross domestic product (GDP) growth flat in 2010. Ironically, repairs to the port, funded by the Russian Federation, are likely to contribute to growth of around 4 per cent in 2011 and 2012.

Increases in food and fuel prices and imports in 2011 are likely to be reflected in a rise in inflation to 2.5 per cent, while poor decisions by previous governments have left Nauru with an enormous debt problem – external debt in 2010 was estimated at A$265 million (US$257 million). This debt means that Nauru will be heavily dependent on donors in the medium-term, although revitalising the mining and quarrying industry, including coral aggregate used in construction, lead to growth in 2012. Tourism and fisheries offer scope for development.

COUNTRY PROFILE

Historical profile

1798 Sighted by the British and named Pleasant Island.
1887 Nauru became a German protectorate.
1888 Became part of the (German) Marshall Islands.
1900 Phosphate was discovered.
1906 Mining began under an agreement signed by the Australian Pacific Phosphate Company and the German government.
1914 Nauru was captured by Australian forces.
1919 After Germany's defeat, the island was placed under the joint administration of the UK, Australia and New Zealand. The three countries formed the British Phosphate Commission in order to share phosphate-mining revenues.
1942 Nauru was invaded by the Japanese.
1945 At the end of the Second World War, Nauru was made a UN Trust Territory under Australian Administration.
1968 The adoption of the Nauru constitution established it as the world's smallest republic with a parliamentary system of government. Hammer DeRoburt was Nauru's first head of state.
1970 Nauru took control of its phosphate industry. Nauru's per capita income became one the world's highest.
1976 Parliament unseated DeRoburt after objections to his autocratic style.
1978 DeRoburt was re-elected.
1989 Bernard Dowiyogo was elected president, defeating DeRoburt by 10 votes.
1995 Lagumot Harris defeated Dowiyogo.
1996 Harris resigned and Dowiyogo returned to power. Dowiyogo was ousted in parliament and Kennan Adeang became president; he in turn was replaced by Reuben Kun.
1997 Kinza Clodumar won the presidential election, backed by Bernard Dowiyogo.
1998 Dowiyogo replaced Clodumar as president.
1999 Dowiyogo was defeated in parliament and René Harris, a former president of the Nauru Phosphate Corporation, was elected president.
2000 René Harris resigned and Dowiyogo was re-elected president.
2001 Nauru agreed to Australia's proposal to house its asylum-seekers, refugees and illegal immigrants in Nauru for a fee. Parliament ousted Dowiyogo and re-elected former president, Lagumot Harris. The Financial Action Task Force (FATF) (established by the G-7 Summit of 1989) on money laundering blacklisted Nauru for not implementing appropriate legislation to curb money laundering, especially by the Russian mafia.
2002 Over 400 asylum-seekers bound for Australia were rescued from a sinking ship in the Indian Ocean and 293 were sent to Nauru which housed around 1,000 in detention.
2003 Bernard Dowiyogo ousted René Harris and became president. When Dowiyogo died of a heart attack Derog Gioura was appointed acting president. The US threatened to impose sanctions if Nauru did not halt the sale of passports and close down its banking sector, both allegedly used by the terrorist group al Qaeda. Ludwig Scotty won presidential elections. Scotty lost a no-confidence vote and was replaced by René Harris.
2004 Nauru defaulted on loan payments to Australia and had its assets seized when foreign debts were over US$165 million. Although René Harris organised a restructured loan he lost a vote of no confidence in parliament and Scotty was

re-appointed president. Australia installed officials in Nauru to handle state finances. Scotty declared a state of emergency and dissolved parliament after it failed to pass a reform budget. In parliamentary elections supporters of Scotty won.

2005 Ties were severed with China and links re-established with Taiwan. Nauru was removed from the FATF blacklist of countries lacking restrictions on international money laundering; the US also lifted its 2003 sanctions.

2007 In parliamentary elections, supporters of Ludwig Scotty won 14 seats out of 18. Scotty was re-elected president beating Marcus Stephen. President Scotty lost a vote of no confidence in parliament and Marcus Stephen was appointed in his place.

2008 The Australian offshore processing centre for asylum seekers was closed when the remaining 21 Sri Lankans, who had been granted refugee status, were flown to Australia. This brought to an end the controversial 'Pacific Solution' that Australia had instituted in 2002. The centre is said to have contributed around 20 per cent of Nauru's GDP, and employed about 100 people. President Stephen called a snap election after declaring a state of emergency, following political stalemate since he took office. President Stephen won most support with 12 members (out of 18) of his grouping elected; the remainder were either opposition or independent members. Former president, René Harris died.

2009 The Organisation for Economic Co-operation and Development (OECD) published a list of countries that had not implemented international tax information exchange standards, of which Nauru was one, despite signing a co-operation agreement in 2003.

2010 In a constitutional referendum in February, 66.96 per cent of voters rejected changes that included a directly elected president and a distribution of power and a strengthening human rights legislation. The President dissolved parliament in March and scheduled elections, one year earlier than planned, as a series of no-confidence motions in parliament had undermined his position and the budget was stalled. The April elections had no clear majority for or opposed to President Marcus Stephen. In another round in June, 17 of the previous candidates were re-elected, however nine were pro-Stephen, eight opposed and one independent. A state of emergency was imposed and government business carried on under presidential decree. In October, the Supreme Court rejected the oppositions' challenge to the president's imposition of a state of emergency and a deal was forged whereby Ludwig Scotty became Speaker of the House and, following an indirect presidential ballot, Marcus Stephen was re-elected president, beating Milton Dube by 11 votes to six.

2011 Nauru signed the UN Refugee Convention on 17 June, which precludes refugees being forcibly returned to their country of origin. The action will prevent re-opening of the Australian immigration detention centre on Nauru.

Political structure

Constitution

Republic

Voting is compulsory for all over the age of 20.

Independence date

31 January (anniversary of independence from Australia in 1968).

The executive

The president is head of state and head of government. The president, elected by parliament, governs for a three-year term, with the assistance of a cabinet of four or five ministers appointed from within parliament.

National legislature

Legislative power is vested in an 18-member unicameral parliament, elected for a three-year term in multi-seat constituencies.

Last elections

24 April and 19 June 2010 (parliamentary)

Results: Parliamentary: in both elections, nine non-partisan supporters of President Marcus Stephen and nine non-partisan opponents of the President were elected.

Next elections

2013 (parliamentary and presidential).

Political parties

Informal alliances and personal links rather than formal, strong party discipline.

Ruling party

There is no formal party system; parliament is traditionally dominated by independents that form factions.

Political situation

Government business became fraught in 2010 as parliament ground to a halt following the political stand-off between President Marcus Stephen and the opposition. President Stephen survived a series of no-confidence motions in parliament, while the opposition held up the budget, until in April when Stephen called a snap election to break the deadlock. However, the electorate did not look favourably on either camp and returned the same members of parliament; this happened twice. The Speaker was sacked by the president and in June and President Stephen declared a state of emergency. The opposition retaliated by challenging the legitimacy of the caretaker government in the Supreme Court in October 2010. However, the Supreme Court threw out the motion saying the president had every right to call a state of emergency, under the circumstances.

Parliament now has to find some consensus and bipartisan support for constitutional changes that will stop such deadlock in the future.

Population

10,000 (2010)

Last census: April 1992: 9,919

Population density: 475 inhabitants per square km (2010)

Annual growth rate: 2.5 per cent 1994–2004 (WHO 2006)

Ethnic make-up

Nauruan (58 per cent), other Pacific islanders (26 per cent), Chinese (8 per cent), European (8 per cent). The indigenous population is of Micronesian descent.

Religions

Protestant (66 per cent), Roman Catholic (33 per cent).

Education

Schooling is provided free and is compulsory from aged 4–16. 10 per cent of schoolchildren are expected to complete secondary education. The government has backed the 'one laptop per child' programme (OLPC).

Scholarships are available for higher education overseas.

Health

The population's general health is not good; Nauru has a high rate of type two diabetes, with one-third of adults suffering from the disease due to the consumption of large amounts of processed food. In 2004, a report ranked Nauruans as the most obese people in the world. A new diabetes centre has been set up as a focal point to provide multi-faceted treatment and education.

The World Health Organisation (WHO) released statistics in January 2011 that ranked Nauru's population with the world's highest level of obesity, with 97 per cent of men and 93 per cent of women overweight or obese. Associated chronic diseases, such as diabetes, heart disease and cancer are responsible for around 75 per cent of all deaths. A diet of processed foods, which are high in sugar and fat, have replaced the traditional diet of fish, coconuts and root vegetables and is held responsible for the condition of most people. Cultural values, which equate size with prosperity, also contribute to the condition.

Life expectancy: 61 years, 2004 (WHO 2006)

Fertility rate/Maternal mortality rate: 3.8 births per woman, 2004 (WHO 2006)

Birth rate/Death rate: 26 births per 1,000 population; seven deaths per 1,000 population (2003).
Child (under 5 years) mortality rate (per 1,000): 10.3 per 1,000 live births (2003)

Main cities
Owing to its small size and absence of urban development, Nauru has no capital. Yaren is the main town (estimated population 4,900 in 2003).

Languages spoken
Nauruan and English, which is widely spoken and used for most government and commercial purposes.
Official language/s
Nauruan

Media
Press
The government-owned, weekly *Nauru Bulletin*, publishes in Nauruan and English. Other newspapers include the fortnightly *Central Star News* published on Saturdays and *Nauru Chronicle*.
Broadcasting
The Nauru Broadcasting Service operates public radio and TV.
Radio: Radio Nauru operated two services on AM and FM, in English and Nauruan, with imported material from Radio Australia and the BBC.
Television: Nauru Television (NTV) moved its operation to New Zealand in 1991 and broadcasts via satellite and on video-tapes.
News agencies
ABC Pacific Beat:
www.radioaustralia.net.au/pacbeat
Pacific Magazine:
www.pacificmagazine.net

Economy
The economy, which once relied almost solely on phosphate mining to give the islanders in the 1960s the highest per capita income in the world, has virtually collapsed so that in 2009 the island was dependent on fishing rights and international grants and development funding and aid (particularly from Australia) to survive. The resumption of limited phosphate mining and its export by the Australian company Incitec Pivot, which invested A$6 million (US$7.9 million) in a government backed revitalisation of the industry, has shown small profits but can only provide limited respite. Reserves are expected to last until 2011. At the same time the government made commitments to refurbish the associated infrastructure.
With the help of the Pacific Island Forum the government is undertaking a strategic development programme to create a new sustainable economic framework for the future.
GDP growth plunged from 6.3 per cent in 2006 to -27.3 per cent in 2007, but rallied to 1 per cent in 2008 and is forecast to be 1.5 per cent in 2009. Inflation typically runs at around 3–4 per cent and the government often has difficulty in balancing the budget with poor agricultural productivity and little prospect for industrial expansion. Around 90 per cent of the workforce is unemployed and of the remaining 10 per cent the government employs 95 per cent of these.

External trade
Nauru is a member of the South Pacific Regional Trade and Economic Co-operation Agreement (Sparteca) along with 12 other regional nations, which allows products duty free access by Pacific Island Forum members to Australian and New Zealand markets (subject to the country of origin restrictions).
Imports
Imports include food, fuel, consumer goods, building materials, vehicles and machinery.
Main sources: Australia (typically over 60 per cent of total), South Korea, US, New Zealand.
Exports
Phosphates, besides financial services, are the sole export.
Main destinations: US (typically over 30 per cent of total), Australia, New Zealand, Japan.

Agriculture
Arable land is confined to a strip 150–300 metres between the beach and the cliff, surrounding a vast crater caused by the phosphate mine.
Artisanal vessels (canoes and aluminium dinghies) supply fish for local consumption. Most food is imported.
There are long-term plans to rehabilitate former mining land into agricultural land with funds from the Australian government.
Fishing
The total fish catch is typically 400 tonnes per annum.
In April 2010 the Parties to the Nauru Agreement (PNA) (eight island states including Nauru) collectively agreed to close to *purse seine* fishing in 4.55 million square kilometres of high seas in their area, from 1 January 2011, to vessels licensed to fish in their waters. The area involved stretches from Palau and Papua New Guinea in the west to Kiribati in the east, from the Marshall Islands in the north to Tuvalu in the south; it holds an estimated 25 per cent of the world's tuna supply.
On 12 April 2011, a summit of the Parties to the Nauru Agreement (PNA) concluded its strategy for a policy of sustainable fishing in the Pacific. The PNA treaty, which was established in 1989 and expires in 2012, is seen as in need of an overhaul. As a collective region (FSM, Kiribati, Marshall Islands, Nauru, Palau, PNG, Solomon Islands and Tuvalu) control around 25–30 per cent of world stocks of tuna. Only 5 per cent of sales revenue is returned to the PNA and ministers called for specific changes, including an increased share of profits, PNA crews on-board *purse seine* vessels (minimum 10 per cent), conservation and management measures including a limit to fish trapping (fish aggregating devices (FADs)), net mesh rules and the establishment of an observer agency and fisheries information management system.

Industry and manufacturing
Phosphate processing is the only industry.

Tourism
Nauru is not a tourist destination, but with the decline of phosphate reserves attempts have been made to develop it. There is a national tourism office. As well as being remote, the island's attractions are limited, diving and fishing being the main attractions. Infrastructure is weak. There are at present two hotels, both relatively expensive. The island is linked to Australia by Air Nauru.

Environment
Rehabilitation of the island is necessary after decades of phosphate mining. Nauru was one of the first countries to sign the Framework Convention on Climate Change. Rising sea levels related to global warming mean that in the future habitable low-lying land areas will be at risk from tidal surges and flooding.

Mining
Nauru's phosphate reserves, the legacy of millennia of fossilised bird excreta, represented the highest-grade phosphate ore in the world. It is estimated that reserves will be exhausted by around 2008. There are plans to reach deeper sources via boring coral, in a more involved secondary mining process.

Hydrocarbons
There are no known hydrocarbon reserves. Consumption of oil was 1,000 barrels per day (bpd) in 2008, all of which was imported.

Energy
Total installed generating capacity was 10MW in 2007, producing 3 million kilowatt hours. The Nauru Utilities Authority (NUA) is responsible for electricity generation. It is participating in the Pacific Islands review of renewable energies, specifically wind power, sponsored by the European Union.

Banking and insurance
There are no reliable commercial banking services in Nauru. Setting up a viable domestic banking system will be a major task to be addressed in the government's economic reform programme.
Central bank
The Bank of Nauru is insolvent and operates on a very limited basis.
Offshore facilities
Nauru is in the process of closing down its offshore banking sector, and thereby closing off access of criminal money laundering. The 2004/05 budget set aside funds for the establishment of a financial investigations unit to support the implementation process. The Organisation for Economic Co-operation and Development (OECD) published a list on 2 April 2009 of countries that had not implemented international tax information exchange standards, of which Nauru was one, despite signing a co-operation agreement in 2003.

Time
GMT plus 12 hours

Geography
Nauru is a small island in the central Pacific Ocean, lying about 40km (25 miles) south of the Equator and about 4,000km (2,500 miles) north-east of Sydney, Australia. Banaba (Ocean Island), in Kiribati, is about 300km (185 miles) to the east.
It is oval-shaped and was one of the Pacific's largest phosphate-rock islands (the phosphate has since been depleted), ringed by a wide coral reef that gives no natural harbour or anchorage. Sandy beaches fringe a fertile belt between the shore and a coral cliff that rises to a central plateau up to 60 metres above sea level. There are no rivers or large lakes and the populations' main source of fresh water is either the often brackish water of the 300 acre Buada lagoon, or rainwater; there is an underground lake in the south-east in the Moqua Cave.
Hemisphere
Southern

Climate
Tropical, tempered by sea breezes, but humid (80 per cent) with variable rainfall. Temperatures range from 24–34 degrees Celsius in the shade. Monsoon season from November–February; average annual rainfall is 2,060mm. Between May–October is the best time to visit.

Entry requirements
Passports
Required by all.
Visa
Required by all, except nationals of New Zealand for visits up to three months and South Korea for 14 days. Tourist visas, for up to 30 days, may be obtained on arrival by nationals of US, Canada, UK and Caribbean Commonwealth countries with proof of sufficient funds, accommodation and return/onward passage.
Business and visitors' visas from all other countries must be obtained in advance directly from the Department of Foreign Affairs in Nauru (details in Ministry Addresses).
Currency advice/regulations
The import of local and foreign currencies is unlimited but must be declared on arrival. Export of local currency is limited to the equivalent of A$2,500; amounts greater then this must be authorised by the Bank of Nauru. The export of foreign currency is unlimited.
Travellers cheques are readily accepted.
Customs
Personal property is duty-free.
Traditional artifacts of Nauru require an export licence.
Prohibited imports
Firearms, ammunition, pornography and illegal drugs.

Health (for visitors)
Mandatory precautions
Cholera vaccination certificate if arriving from or via an infected area within five days. Yellow fever vaccination certificate if arriving from an infected area.
Advisable precautions
Vaccination for diphtheria, tuberculosis, hepatitis A and B, polio, tetanus, typhoid. There is a rabies risk. Main water is chlorinated but may cause mild stomach upset. Local water may be contaminated. There are no medical specialists, and serious cases are sent to Australia so medical insurance, including emergency evacuation, is necessary.

Hotels
There are two hotels on the island the Menen and the Od-N-Aiwo.

Credit cards
All major credit and charge cards are accepted. ATMs are not available.

Public holidays (national)
Fixed dates
1 Jan (New Year's Day), 31 Jan (Independence Day), 17 May (Constitution Day), 25 Sep (Youth Day), 26 Oct (Angam Day), 25–26 Dec (Christmas).
Variable dates
Good Friday, Easter Monday and Tuesday.

Working hours
Banking
Mon–Thu: 0900–1600; Fri: 0900–1630.
Business
Mon–Fri: 0800–1200, 1330–1630.
Government
Mon–Fri: 0900–1700.
Shops
Mon–Fri 0800–1800. Some food shops are open for longer hours and at the weekend.

Telecommunications
There is an automatic island and international radio communications system in operation.

Electricity supply
110/240V AC, 50Hz

Weights and measures
Metric system

Social customs/useful tips
In business an informal attitude prevails, shirts and smart trousers or skirts are acceptable and only on very special occasions is more formal wear advisable. It is customary to shake hands on meeting and taking leave.
Gratuities are not customary. The minimum drinking age is 21 years.

Getting there
Air
National airline: Our Airline (formerly Air Nauru), with limited services to Brisbane (Australia), Kiribati and the Marshall Islands.
International airport/s: Nauru Island International (INU), there are few facilities; buses run to Yaren after each arriving plane and there is a courtesy bus provided by the Menen Hotel.
Airport tax: Departures tax: A$25.
Surface
Water: The main sealinks are with Australia, New Zealand and Japan. Without a natural harbour most commercial vessels moor offshore, in what are reputedly some of the world's deepest permanent anchorages, and passengers and cargo have to be ferried ashore.

Getting about
National transport
Road: A main road (19.3km) circles the island, and all residential areas are linked by surfaced roads. A regular local bus service operates around the island. Buada and the former phosphate areas are linked by an inland road.
Car hire
Car hire can be arranged locally. Traffic drives on the left. A national driving licence should suffice.

BUSINESS DIRECTORY
The addresses listed below are a selection only. While World of Information makes every endeavour to check these addresses, we cannot guarantee that changes have not been made, especially to telephone numbers and area codes. We would welcome any corrections.

Telephone area codes
The international direct dialling (IDD) code for Nauru is +674 followed by subscriber's number.

Useful telephone numbers
Police: 110
Fire: 119
Ambulance: 118 or 117

Banking
Central bank
Bank of Nauru, PO Box 289, Civic Centre, Aiwo District (tel: 444-3238/3267; fax: 444-3203; e-mail:bon@cenpac.net.nr).

Travel information
Air Nauru, Government Building, Yaren District (tel: 444-3141, 444-3418; fax: 444-3170).

Nauru International Airport, PO Box 40, Nauru Air Corporation (tel: 444-3754/3141; fax: 444-3282-3705).

Pacific Island Travel, Herengracht 495, 1017 BT Amsterdam, The Netherlands (tel: (+31) 020-626-1325; fax (+31) 020-623-0008; internet: www.pacificislandtravel.com).

National tourist organisation offices

National Tourist Office, c/o Special Project Officer (Culture and Tourism), Department of Island Development and Industry, Government Offices, Aiwo District (tel: 444-3191; fax: 444-3791).

Ministries
Address for all Government Offices: Government Offices, Yaren District.

Chief Secretary, Secretary to Cabinet, Public Service Commissioner and Registrar of Births, Deaths and Marriages (tel: 444-3133; fax: 444-3110).

Department of Foreign Affairs (tel: 444-3133; fax: 444-3105).

Secretary for Education (tel: 444-3130; fax: 444-3718).

Secretary for External Affairs (tel: 444-3191, 444-3701; fax: 444-3105).

Secretary for Finance (tel: 444-3285, 444-3287; fax: 444-3125).

Secretary for Health (tel: 444-3702; fax: 444-3106).

Secretary for Island Development and Industry (tel: 444-3281; fax: 444-3705) (economic development and privatisation and foreign investment).

Secretary for Justice (tel: 444-3747, 444-3160; fax: 444-3108).

Secretary for Works and Community Services (tel: 444-3703; fax: 444-3718).

Other useful addresses
Directorate of Telecommunications, Private Bag, Yaren (tel: 444-3132; fax: 444-3111).

Nauru Finance Corporation, PO Box 306, Yaren (tel: 3390; fax: 3345) (responsible for promoting economic diversification, including offshore banking).

Nauru Permanent Mission to the UN, 800 Second Ave, Suite 400D, New York, NY-10017 (tel: (+1-212) 937-0074; internet: www.un.int/nauru).

Internet sites
Nauru International Airport: www.airnauru.com.au

Nauru website: www.nauruwire.org

Nepal

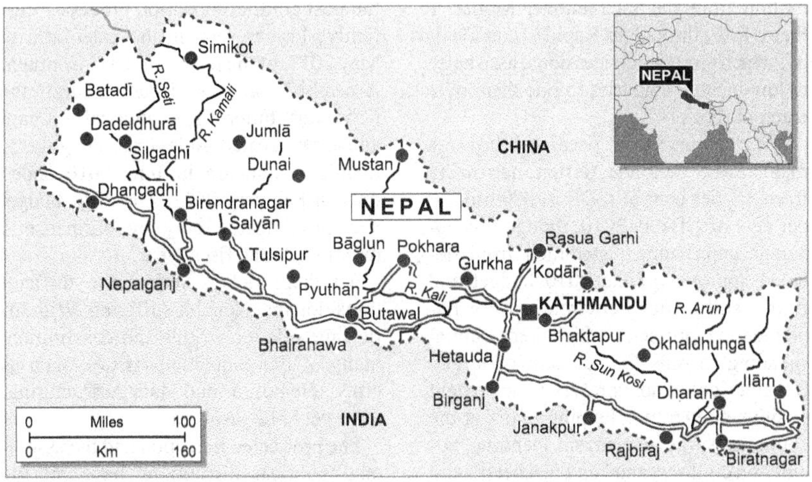

Nepal is one of the world's poorest countries, struggling to overcome the legacy of a 10-year Maoist insurrection. Until Nepal became a republic in May 2008, it had been ruled by monarchs or a ruling family for most of its modern history. A brief experiment with multi-party politics in 1959 ended with King Mahendra suspending parliament and taking sole charge in 1962.

The political problem

Prime Minister Baburam Bhattarai of the Maoist party took office at the end of August 2011 with the support of an alliance of Madhesi (Terai-based) parties. The Head of State is President Ram Baran Yadav who assumed office in July 2008. Nepal is in the process of drafting a new constitution in an elected body, the Nepalese Constituent Assembly (NCA). Due to divisions between the major political parties, the deadline for the new constitution has been extended several times, with the current deadline due to expire in May 2012. The new constitution is supposed to lead to a major restructuring of the state as Nepal will adopt federalism as a fundamental principal of governance. Elections at both national and local levels are supposed to be held after the constitution is promulgated.

Nepal is passing through a momentous and prolonged political transition. In the past five years, Nepal has seen the abolition of its monarchy, the signing of a peace agreement between the Maoists and the state, a new Interim Constitution, the election of the NCA (which declared Nepal a federal republic), five governments and the rise of a strong ethnic identity movement. In 2011 Nepal was still emerging from the after-effects of a violent 10-year conflict. Major milestones of the peace process are yet to be met, including the integration and rehabilitation of the former Maoist army. Progress in constitution writing has been slow due to divisions on key issues between the major political parties. One of the as yet unresolved issues for the new constitution is the nature, form and degree of de-centralisation of the state. Poor law and order is a growing concern, particularly in certain geographic areas. The conflict raised awareness that the Nepali state had been associated with exclusionary political, social and economic institutions that did not reflect the country's diversity. This has led to the rise of identity politics with an increasing demand for state recognition and greater accommodation of diverse social, cultural and ethnic identities.

The economy

Nepal's economic growth has been adversely (and seriously) affected by the political uncertainty. The focus on political

KEY FACTS

Official name: Nepal Adhirajya (Kingdom of Nepal)

Head of State: President Ram Baran Yadav (Nepali Congress) (from 23 Jul 2008)

Head of government: Prime Minister Baburam Bhattarai (Maoist) (from 28 Aug 2011)

Ruling party: Coalition of Nepali Congress and Communist Party of Nepal-Unified Marxist-Leninist (CPN-UML) (from 25 May 2009)

Area: 147,181 square km

Population: 29.96 million (2010)*

Capital: Kathmandu

Official language: Nepali (Devnagari script)

Currency: Rupee (NRs) = 100 paisa (the NRs is pegged to the Indian rupee – NRs 160 = Rs100) (Notes with the King's image became illegal tender on 17 March 2011)

Exchange rate: NRs78.36 per US$ (Oct 2011)

GDP per capita: US$562 (2010)

GDP real growth: 4.60% (2010)

GDP: US$15.80 billion (2010)

Labour force: 18.00 million (2009)*

Unemployment: 46.00% (2008)*

Inflation: 9.30% (2010)

Balance of trade: -US$4.11 billion (2010)

* estimated figure

transition and attainment of peace has meant that inadequate attention has been given to economic and other reforms that could improve the investment climate, stimulate growth and create more private sector jobs. Economic growth and increased private investment is dependent upon a political settlement that promotes greater law and order.

According to the Asian Development Bank (ADB) gross domestic product (GDP) growth inched up to 4.0 per cent in the fiscal year (FY) 2010 (which ended on 15 July 2010) from 3.8 per cent in the FY2009. The marginal improvement was made possible by a turnaround in growth in the relatively small industry sector (helped by fewer political strikes) and sustained expansion of services. A deceleration in remittance inflows due to the lagged impact of the global financial crisis weighed on economic activity, as did slowing agricultural output (for the second year running) due to a sparse monsoon.

The deceleration in remittance growth, alongside commercial banks' excessive lending to real estate and reduced liquidity in banking, drove interbank borrowing rates to a record high. Inflation stayed close to double digits owing to high food prices in the first half of 2010, which in turn originated in a low domestic crop and India's high food-inflation.

Exports as a share of GDP have been dwindling in the last few years, because low productivity and infrastructure bottlenecks have undermined competitiveness. Conversely, imports as a share of GDP have been increasing steadily over several years, with growth more pronounced in 2010, as gold imports swelled. (Gold has been the investment of choice, given the paucity of attractive alternatives in a correcting real estate market.) The widening trade deficit, coupled with slowing remittances, took the current account deficit to 2.7 per cent of GDP in 2010 from a surplus of 4.2 per cent of GDP the year before. This led to a US$113 million decline in official reserves. The authorities accessed US$42 million from the International Monetary Fund (IMF) through its Rapid Credit Facility, which provides concessional assistance to low-income countries to tide them over external shocks.

The previous years' fiscal stability was maintained, with the deficit narrowing from 3.3 per cent of GDP in 2009 to 2.0 per cent of GDP in 2010, though this apparent improvement stemmed from delayed approval of the 2010 budget and from a still difficult environment for implementing projects, which kept capital spending to only 70 per cent of target. Revenue collection preserved its recent positive momentum, helping to offset the continued surge in recurrent spending, notably on civil servants' and teachers' salaries. Small fiscal deficits and large grants by multilateral agencies have helped to improve the public debt position in recent years.

Despite a challenging political environment, the share of the population living below the national poverty line of about US$160 a year is estimated to have declined to 25 per cent in 2010 from 31 per cent in 2004, largely owing to robust remittance inflows, rapid urban growth, a decline in fertility and rising agricultural wages.

Strides have also been made in other Millennium Development Goals, such as child and maternal mortality, although greater efforts are needed to achieve similar progress in areas such as productive employment and child malnutrition. Efforts are also needed to reduce inequality – currently the highest in South Asia, with a Gini coefficient of 0.47.

Nepal's economic performance in 2011 and 2012 will rest primarily on progress in the post conflict transition process – currently slow as seen in the extension, to May 2012, of the tenure of the Constituent Assembly that was elected to draft the new constitution. The political vacuum and drift created following the government's resignation in June 2010 ended only in February 2011. The 2011 budget was promulgated only by ordinance 4 months into the fiscal year.

All these delays reflect the difficult transition that Nepal is suffering. With little time left for writing the constitution, many of the contentious issues, such as army integration and state restructuring, have yet to be resolved.

The protracted transition and the associated political disruptions have hit the economy. The delay in announcing the 2011 budget, for example, has undermined solid progress made in revenue mobilisation, which achieved 25 per cent average annual growth in the last 4 years. More important, it has deprived the population of a much hoped-for peace dividend, including greater capital spending and development benefits.

GDP growth was forecast to weaken slightly to 3.8 per cent in 2011. Agriculture was expected to grow by 4.0 per cent in 2011 (up from 1.3 per cent in 2010), largely due to a weather-induced recovery in the output of key summer crops. This improvement will not, however, be enough to offset the deceleration in non-farm activities. Political uncertainty, as well as power cuts (lasting as much as 14 hours a day since mid-February 2011) will continue to take a toll on non-farm activities.

GDP growth is expected to improve modestly to 4.0 per cent in 2012 (assuming continued normal weather conditions). A pickup in tourism related activities driven by the Nepal Tourism Year 2011 campaign should show a rise in services growth to 5.5 per cent when published

A modest upturn in construction activity, as the Nepal Rastra Bank's (NRB) (central bank) policy is absorbed, should lift industry's growth to 1.5 per cent. Year-on-year inflation reached 11.3 per cent in January 2011, largely reflecting

KEY INDICATORS — Nepal

	Unit	2006	2007	2008	2009	2010
Population	m	*27.11	*27.38	*27.64	*27.91	*29.96
Gross domestic product (GDP)	US$bn	8.87	10.30	12.30	12.60	15.80
GDP per capita	US$	333	377	444	452	562
GDP real growth	%	2.8	3.2	4.7	4.7	4.6
Inflation	%	8.0	6.4	7.7	13.2	9.3
Industrial output	% change	3.5	3.9	1.9	1.8	–
Agricultural output	% change	1.7	1.9	4.7	2.2	–
Exports (fob) (goods)	US$m	865.0	924.9	986.6	840.2	901.9
Imports (fob) (goods)	US$m	2,011.0	2,935.6	3,519.3	4,301.3	5,016.4
Balance of trade	US$m	-1,146.0	-2,007.6	-2,523.8	-3,461.1	-4,114.5
Current account	US$m	197.0	49.0	344.0	-256.1	-438.0
Exchange rate	per US$	71.08	62.95	69.76	77.54	73.16

* estimated figure

food and fuel price increases. A revision of the consumer price index – lowering the weight for food in line with the Fourth Household Budget Survey 2005/06 – has pulled inflation down by about one percentage point relative to the previous method.

Average inflation for 2011 is expected to be 10.0 per cent. High food and oil prices and the domestic distortions such as power cuts will continue to exert upward pressure, only part of which will be offset by the good harvest. With likely moderation in Indian prices 8.0 per cent average inflation is expected in 2012.

Risk assessment

Economy	Fair
Politics	Poor
Regional stability	Good

COUNTRY PROFILE

Historical profile

Modern Nepal began its formation in the second half of the eighteenth century, when the kingdom of Gorkha, led by Prithivi Narayan Shah, began to expand.
1769 Shah conquered Kathmandu and completed the unification of what is today's Nepal, laying the foundation of a dynasty that was to last until 2008 when parliament voted on 28 December 2007 to abolish the monarchy.
1792 Nepal's expansion was halted by Chinese armies in Tibet.
1816 Nepal became a British protectorate after the Anglo-Nepalese war. The treaty also established the boundaries as they are today.
1846 Jang Bahadur Rana extracted a decree from the monarch that transferred sovereign powers to the family of Ranas, who ruled as hereditary prime ministers for 104 years.
1923 Nepal's independence was recognised by Britain, although it retained control of the country's foreign affairs.
1950–59 King Tribhuvan fled to India, intensifying the revolt led by the Nepali Congress party (NC) against the Ranas. It ended with an agreement brokered by India which recognised the role of the monarch, legalised political parties and established a constitutional monarchy. In the eight years that followed, the King ruled the country while political parties took shape.
1953 Edmund Hillary of New Zealand and Nepal's Sherpa Tenzing Norgay were the first climbers to reach the summit of Mount Everest (known as Sagarmatha in Nepal).
1955 Nepal became a member of the United Nations. King Tribhuwan died and King Mahendra ascended the throne.
1959 The first, multi-party, election under a new constitution was won by the NC. B P Koirala became prime minister.
1960 King Mahendra seized control and suspended parliament and politics.
1962 He introduced a new constitution establishing a party-less Panchayat system which banned political competition and parties. The King retained absolute powers.
1972 King Mahendra died in 1972 and was succeeded by his son, King Birendra, who continued his father's policies.
1979 After a series of protests against the Panchayat system, the King ordered a national referendum: the choice was between a 'reformed' Panchayat, or a multi-party democracy. A narrow majority voted in favour of the Panchayat, with reforms allowing direct elections – but still on a non-party basis.
1985 The NC began a campaign of civil disobedience for the restoration of the multi-party system.
1986 Elections were boycotted by the NC.
1990 Pro-democracy protests were staged by the NC and leftist groups which resulted in killings and mass arrests by the police. The King bowed to pressure and agreed a new democratic constitution.
1991 The NC won the elections and Girija Prasad Koirala became prime minister.
1994 Koirala's government was toppled due to party infighting. The Communist Party of Nepal-United Marxist-Leninist (CPN-UML) emerged as the largest single party in the elections and formed a minority government.
1995 The CPN-UML government was toppled, making way for a number of coalition and minority governments, until another round of elections was held in 1999.
1996 While the mainstream parties jostled for power in the centre, the Maoists launched their 'people's war'.
1998 The CPN-UML suffered a major blow when a faction of the party broke away.
1999 The NC won the general elections; Krishna Prasad Bhattarai became prime minister.
2000 Bhattarai was forced to step down due to party infighting. Koirala became prime minister again. The NC remained effectively divided between the supporters of Koirala and Bhattarai.
2001 Crown Prince Dipendra killed his closest family members, including King Birendra and Queen Aishwarya, in a drunken shooting spree, before committing suicide. Gyanendra Bir Bikram Shah Deva became king. The Maoists increased their violent campaign of opposition. Koirala resigned and Sher Bahadur Deuba (NC) became prime minister. A truce was agreed between the rebels and the government but when peace talks failed the insurgency resumed.
2002 Maoists rebels successfully staged a five-day general strike after more than 500 people were killed in clashes with government forces. King Gyanendra dissolved parliament and called for fresh general elections; the ruling NC suspended Deuba from the party for advising the King to do so. King Gyanendra dismissed Deuba, abolished the Council of Ministers and assumed executive powers. The King appointed Lokendra Bahadur Chand as prime minister.
2003 Maoist rebels and the government agreed to a cease-fire. King Gyanendra appointed Surya Bahadur Thapa of the Rastriya Prajatantra Party (RPP) as prime minister. Maoists ended the truce. Violence and political stalemate marked the end of the year.
2004 Nepal became the 147th member of the World Trade Organisation (WTO). Prime Minister Thapa resigned after weeks of civil protest. Former prime minister, Sher Bahadur Deuba, was re-appointed. The government banned Nepalis from working in Iraq after 12 Nepalis were murdered while working there.
2005 King Gyanendra dismissed Deuba and assumed absolute power, citing the need to defeat the Maoists. A royal anti-graft commission sentenced former prime minister Deuba to two years imprisonment for corruption. The rebels declared a unilateral cease-fire. Maoists and opposition parties agreed a strategy to restore democracy.
2006 Nepal, Bhutan, Bangladesh, India, Maldives, Pakistan and Sri Lanka signed the South Asia Free Trade Agreement (SAFTA). A seven-party alliance led by former prime minister Girija Prasad Koirala (leader of NC), in opposition to the King, called mass pro-democracy demonstrations. Riots broke out in the capital, leaving several police and demonstrators dead. International calls urged the King to negotiate with his opponents and in the face of so much opposition the King reinstated parliament and was removed as head of the armed forces. Parliament restricted the powers of the King as executive rule was passed to the Council of Ministers. A peace agreement was signed between the government and Maoist insurgents, formally ending 10 years of internal conflict. Maoists rebels disarmed, monitored by the United Nations.
2007 The two chambers of parliament were replaced by a unicameral interim legislature, with Maoists holding 83 out of 330 seats, under the terms of the temporary constitution. An interim multi-party cabinet, including Maoists, was formed to prepare the way for legislative elections.

The special assembly was charged with writing a new constitution, including deciding on the future of the monarchy. Three bombs exploded in Kathmandu, the first terrorist attacks since the peace agreement in 2006. Maoist members of the interim government resigned in protest at the continued existence of the monarchy. Rebel Maoists were accused of attacking a UN Food Programme convoy, which was providing humanitarian aid to southern Nepal. Deadlock between Maoist and ruling parties over the abolition of the monarchy and the adoption of proportional representation led to the postponing of general elections. Parliament voted to abolish the monarchy, thereby resolving the crisis and five Maoists joined the cabinet in a number of key positions, including communication and information, which gave the Maoists control over the state-run media.

2008 In parliamentary elections the Communist Party of Nepal (Maoists), won 220 seats (out of 601), the Nepali Congress party 110 seats, the CPN-UML 103 seats, the Madhesi Jana Adhikar Forum 52 seats, the Tarai-Madhesh Loktantrik Party 20 seats; 20 other parties shared the remaining seats with none holding more than eight. The Constituent Assembly voted by 560–4 to declare the country a republic and depose King Gyanendra. Ex-King Gyanendra and his wife, Komal, took up temporary residence outside Kathmandu, becoming known as Mr Shah. Within days his former palace was turned into a museum; among the treasures are the royal throne and the priceless crown and sceptre. Interim Prime Minister Koirala announced he would resign if the candidate he supported for president, Ram Raja Prasad Singh, was defeated. In the presidential election no candidate won the necessary 298 votes for victory and a second round had to be scheduled, in which Ram Baran Yadav (NC) won 308 votes, beating Ram Raja Prasad Singh (nominated by the Maoists). Baran was sworn in as the first president of Nepal. Koirala tendered his resignation immediately after Baran took office. The Maoist leader, Prachandra (also known as Pushpa Kamal Dahal) was elected prime minister by parliament, with 80 per cent of votes, beating Sher Bahadur Deuba, the only other candidate. The collapse of the Koshi dam, in the south-east of Nepal, lead to severe flooding which forced over 50,000 people to flee their homes.

2009 The prime minister ordered the General Chief of Staff, Rookmangud Katawal, to integrate ex-Maoist rebel fighters into the army. When he refused he was dismissed and a political crisis followed when the president revoked the dismissal. Prime Minister Prachanda resigned in protest. A 22-party coalition, led by the NC and the CPN-UML formed the government. Madhav Kumar Nepal (CPN-UML) was sworn in as prime minister. In May, following years of campaigning, the UK granted full residency in Britain to Gurkha veterans with at least four years' service. Chairman of Nepal Constituent Assembly (NCA), Subash Nemwang, announced that the draft of the new constitution would be ready by the deadline of May 2010. A series of demonstrations and blockades in Kathmandu turned violent as Maoist activists protested against the governing coalition and called for a parliamentary debate over the power of the president.

2010 Nepal and China agreed the height of Mount Everest to be 8,848m, the snow height. China had previously argued that it should be 4m lower, at the rock height. In May the ruling coalition proposed extending the mandate of the NCA for one year, in an effort to complete work on the new constitution. However the majority Maoist party refused to extend it without Prime Minister Kumar stepping down from his post. In June, in an effort to break the deadlock Kumar resigned. However, by 7 September, parliament had failed seven times to elect his replacement and Kumar remained in office as acting-prime minister. The government lifted its 2004 ban on Nepalis working in Iraq. The ban had been widely flouted by Nepalis, but a recent US law which required all US companies with employees in Iraq to record them, risked not only the jobs of up to 30,000 Nepalis (and the remittances they provided) but also an imposition of legal penalties on them.

2011 On 12 January, the only prime ministerial candidate, Ram Chandra Poudel, withdrew and the 17th attempt to elect a prime minister was cancelled. The mandate for the UN peacekeeping mission, established in 2007, expired on 15 January. The government and Maoists agreed to continue arms monitoring arrangements. After seven months of deadlock and 16 attempted votes, Jhala Nath Khanal (CPN-UML) was elected prime minister on 3 February, following the Maoist's withdrawal of their own candidate and their support given to Khanal. Bank notes carrying an image of the King of Nepal ceased to be legal tender on 15 March; the central bank estimated that as much as Rp10 billion (US$135 million) was left un-exchanged. Mount Everest replaced the King's image. At the end of May members of parliament announced that parliament would be extended by three months so that details of the new constitution could be finalised. On 14 June, in a ceremony to mark the occasion, Prime Minister Khanal detonated the explosion that destroyed the last landmine, to finally clear all unexploded ordnance (UXO) from Nepal. In July, Nepal said it had commissioned a new survey to determine the exact height of Mount Everest in an effort to lay to rest the 'confusion' with China which, despite a 2010 agreement, continued to use the rock (rather than the snow) height during border talks. The generally accepted height of 8,848 metres had been recorded by an Indian survey in 1955; a US GPS survey recorded 8,850 metres in 1999, although this figure has not been accepted by either Nepal or China. On 14 August Prime Minister Khanal resigned, saying he was unable to forge a political consensus with other parties in order to form a government. On 28 August, parliament elected Baburam Bhattarai (Maoist) as prime minister, with 340 votes against Ram Chandra Poudel (CPN) with 235. An earthquake of magnitude 6.9 struck on 18 September in the Himalayan regions of India, Nepal and Tibet. The epicentre was the Indian state of Sikkim, where at least 50 people were killed and 150 injured.

Political structure

Constitution

An interim constitution came into effect on 15 January 2007, the constitution for the State of Nepal replaced the previous constitution of the Kingdom of Nepal.

An amendment passed in March 2007 changed the country to a federal state from a unitary one. It also increased the number of constituencies in the south to 50 per cent of the seats in parliament.

Form of state

Federal democratic republic

The executive

The president is the Head of State. Under an amendment to the interim constitution (January 2007) the president, vice president, prime minister and constituent assembly chairman and vice chairman would be elected based on a 'political understanding' or failing that by a simple majority vote.

Members of the Nepalese Constituent Assembly (NCA) provide the executive which makes up the government. The 26 seats of the NCA are divided among nine political parties, proportional to the popular vote received.

National legislature

The Nepal Constituent Assembly has 601 members, of which 240 are directly elected, 335 are elected by proportional representation and 26 members are nominated. The assembly will re-write the constitution and govern the country until an elected government can be decided. The assembly has a mandate until 2010. In August 2009 Nepal Constituent Assembly chairman Subash Nemwang expressed confidence that the draft of the new constitution would be ready by the deadline of May 2010.

Legal system

Independent judiciary

Last elections

10 April 2008 (parliamentary); 19 and 21 July 2008 (presidential, first and second round).

Results: Parliamentary: the Communist Party of Nepal (Maoists), won 220 seats (out of 601), the Nepali Congress Party 110 seats, the Communist Party of Nepal-Unified Marxist-Leninist (CPN-UML) 103 seats, the Madhesi Jana Adhikar Forum (MJF) (Madhesi People's Rights Forum) 52 seats, the Tarai-Madhesh Loktantrik Party (TMLP) 20 seats; 20 other parties shared the remaining seats –none with more than eight seats.

Presidential: (first round) Ram Baran Yadav (Nepali Congress) won 283 votes, Ram Raja Prasad Singh (Maoist) 270. (Second round): Yadav won 308 votes beating Singh. Paramananda Jha (Madhesi Jana Adhikar Forum (MJF) (Madhesi People's Rights Forum)) was elected vice president with 305 votes; Shanta Shrestha (Maoist) won 243.

Next elections

2010 (parliamentary) postponed.

Political parties

Ruling party

Coalition of Nepali Congress and Communist Party of Nepal-Unified Marxist-Leninist (CPN-UML) (from 25 May 2009)

Main opposition party

Communist Party of Nepal (Maoists)

Population

29.96 million (2010)*

Last census: June 2001: 23,151,423

Population density: 191 inhabitants per square km (2010)

Annual growth rate: 2.3 per cent 1994–2004 (WHO 2006)

Ethnic make-up

Nepal has a mixture of Indo-Caucasian and Tibeto-Mongoloid people and a number of Tibetan refugees. There are 61 different ethnic and caste groups and many have their own language and dialect.

Religions

Hinduism (90 per cent), Tibetan Buddhism (5.3 per cent), Islam (2.7 per cent). Nepal is a Hindu kingdom, but it allows other religions to practise their faiths. It is illegal to proselytise. The Kumari Devi is revered by both Hindus and Buddhists in Nepal as a 'living Goddess'.

Education

The education system is based on the Chinese model. A non-compulsory pre-school education can begin at aged three. Primary schooling lasts for five years at the end of which students are separated into academic and technical programmes.

The academic programme is divided into lower secondary, upper secondary and higher secondary schooling in a cycle of three, two and two years until the age of 18 when, if they have been successful, students may access higher education courses at university or other institutions. The three-year lower secondary schools are of two types: general and Sanskrit. Upon completing the second stage, exams undertaken by students allows advancement to the higher secondary school or graduation with a school leaving certificate.

The Tribhuvan University, Mahendra Sanskrit University, Kathmandu University and Purbanchal University and B P Korala Institute of Health Science mainly provide higher education.

The technical programme is divided into cycles of either four and two, or four and four, years and students graduate with either a craftsman's certificate at age 16 or a technical certificate at aged 18.

Literacy rate: 44 per cent adult rate; 63 per cent youth rate (15–24) (Unesco 2005).

Compulsory years: Six to 16.

Enrolment rate: 113 per cent gross primary enrolment of the relevant age group (including repeaters); 42 per cent gross secondary enrolment (World Bank).

Pupils per teacher: 39 in primary schools.

Health

National morbidity patterns show ailments related to inadequate water and sanitation account for more than 70 per cent of all sickness reported. Furthermore, around 10,000 people die from cancer after a long-term exposure of arsenic compounds in drinking water.

There were cases of polio reported t the World Health Organisation – Global Polio Eradication Initiative in 2006; the country had previously been free of the disease and its re-emergence was due to infected travellers.

HIV prevalence: 0.5 per cent aged 15–49 in 2003 (World Bank)

Life expectancy: 61 years, 2004 (WHO 2006)

Fertility rate/Maternal mortality rate: 3.6 births per woman, 2004 (WHO 2006)

Child (under 5 years) mortality rate (per 1,000): 61.0 deaths per 1,000 live births; 48 per cent of children aged under five are malnourished (World Bank).

Head of population per physician: 0.21 physicians per 1,000 people, 2004 (WHO 2006)

Welfare

The government of Nepal and the Asian Development Bank (ADB) signed a partnership agreement aiming to reduce the incidence of poverty from over 40 per cent of the population to less than 10 per cent by 2017. The problems related to rural poverty are being tackled by improving access to impoverished areas. Several non-government organisations have stepped up their aid to tackle poverty and disease in the country.

It is estimated that more than 10 out of 100 people in Nepal suffer from one or the other form of disability. The government does not have concrete programmes to address the problems facing the disabled.

Main cities

Kathmandu (capital, estimated population 812,026 in 2005), Biratnagar (185,000); Lalitpur (185,380); Pokhara (194,469); Birgañj (133,463), Dharan (110,475).

Languages spoken

Maithili, Bhojpuri, Hindi, Bengali and Newari are some other languages spoken. English is spoken, mainly in urban centres.

Official language/s

Nepali (Devnagari script)

Media

Press freedom and journalists were under pressure from the former royal regime and from within Maoist-held territories. Since the change in government all anti-media laws were struck down and the interim constitution guaranteed the freedom of the press.

Press

Dailies: Most newspapers are published in either Nepalese or English. The government owned *Gorkhapatra* (in English, *The Rising Nepal*) (www.gorkhapatra.org.np) is the oldest published daily; private newspapers include *Kantipur* (www.kantipuronline.com) which also publishes *The Kathmandu Post*. Other independents include *Nepal Samacharpatra* (www.newsofnepal.com) and *Rajdhani*.

Weeklies: News magazines include, *Nepali Times* (www.nepalitimes.com.np), *Spotlight* (www.nepalnews.com.np) and from the same publisher *The Weekly Telegraph* and the *People's Review* (www.peoplesreview.com.np).

Business: The monthly magazines *New Business Age* (www.nepalnews.com/new_businessage.php) is published by Mercantile Communications, which owns over a dozen other publications in Nepal.

Periodicals: Monthly magazines, in English, include *ECS* (www.ecs.com.np) on culture, *Wave* (www.wavemag.com.np), a gossip magazine and *Himal Southasian* (www.himalmag.com) has regional reviews. In Nepalese, *Himal Khabarpatrika* (www.himalkhabar.com) is a fortnightly news magazine.

Broadcasting

Radio: The state-run Radio Nepal (www.radionepal.org) reaches all areas and is listen to by up to 80 per cent of the population. Its national and regional programmes cover a wide range of shows in information, education and entertainment. There are many, private, commercial stations located regionally, which include Maitri FM (http://maitrifm.org), Annapurna FM (www.annapurnafm.com.np), Kantipur FM (www.kfm961.com) and Janakpur FM (www.janakifm.org.np).

Television: The state-run, commercial, Nepal Television (NTV) (www.nepaltelevision.com.np) broadcasts nationally and internationally via satellite. Other private TV stations include Avenues TV, a news channel, Channel Nepal (www.channelnepal.com), Image Channel TV (www.imagechannels.com) and Kantipur TV (www.kantipuronline.com).

News agencies

National news agency: Rastriya Samachar Samiti (RSS)

Nepalnews: www.nepalnews.com

Economy

Nepal is a largely underdeveloped country with a subsistence agricultural economy, which produces a surplus of rice and wheat, used for export to India. However, it is subject to adverse external factors, such as variable monsoon rains, that can influence economic growth. Remittances from Nepalese workers abroad have grown into a major source of foreign exchange, so that by 2008 it accounted for 20 per cent of GDP.

The structure of the economy is dominated by services, particularly transport and government services, which accounted for 49.6 per cent of GDP in 2008, with industry accounting for 16.7 per cent, of which manufacturing was 7.4 per cent (around 70 per cent of which is made up of export-destined carpets and garments), and agriculture 33.7 per cent of the economy.

GDP growth in 2007 was 3.2 per cent, which rose to 4.7 per cent in 2008 as the political situation stabilised once the country was declared a republic in 2008 and King Gyanendra was forced to abdicate. Nepal was not subject to many of the pressures of the global economic crisis, although inflation has remained high at 6.4 per cent in 2007, rising to 7.7 in 2008 and a revised forecast (by the Asian Development Bank) of 12.8 per cent in 2009; it is expected to fall to around 9.0 per cent in 2010.

As a young democracy, the uneasy peace between the largest party in parliament, the Communist Party of Nepal (Maoists), and an alliance of the Nepali Congress and Communist Party of Nepal-Unified Marxist-Leninist (CPN-UML) which holds office has been maintained. As such, it has encouraged external assistance from India, the UK, the US, Japan, Germany, the Scandinavian countries and several multilateral organisations. Such aid accounts for over 50 per cent of the country's development budget.

The poverty rate fell from 42 per cent in 1996 to 31 per cent by 2008. Nepal has abundant prospects for hydroelectricity production and plans to export surplus power. Its prospects depend largely on a stable government and improved infrastructure. Although tourism figures suffered during the earlier insurgency, there is scope for the sector's growth, based on the country's mountainous terrain offering climbing and trekking holidays, to become a healthy foreign exchange earner as well as employment provider.

External trade

Nepal is a member of South Asia Association for Regional Co-operation, which operates a preferential trading arrangement (Sapta) that covers 6,000 products. In 2004 the South Asia Free Trade Area was agreed by Sapta, to be implemented between the member states (India, Pakistan, Bhutan, Nepal, Bangladesh, Sri Lanka and Maldives) by 2012.

Remittances represent 20 per cent of GDP and are a major source of foreign exchange.

Hand woven carpets and valuable cashmere pashmina fabric (for couture clothing) are manufactured for exported.

Imports

The principal imports petroleum, vehicles and manufactured goods.

Main sources: India (typically 60 per cent of total), China (13 per cent), Singapore (2 per cent).

Exports

The principal exports are hand-made carpets, pashmina fabric and garments, wheat and rice.

Main destinations: India (typically 68 per cent of total), US (7 per cent), Bangladesh (6 per cent).

Agriculture

Farming

Agriculture accounts for around 40 per cent of GDP, providing most foreign exchange earnings and 80 per cent of employment. Only about 25 per cent of the total land area is cultivable; another 33 per cent is forested and most of the rest is mountainous. The lowland Terai region produces an agricultural surplus, part of which supplies the food-deficient hill areas.

Major food crops are rice, maize, wheat, barley and millet. The principal cash crops are sugar cane, soya beans, oilseeds, tobacco, potato and jute. Cattle, buffaloes, goats, sheep, pigs, yaks and poultry are also raised. River fish are an important source of protein.

Much of the agriculture is rain-fed and is carried out in the narrow strip of plains in the south along the border with India. Agricultural land is highly fragmented. Production is extremely vulnerable to adverse weather conditions, with little irrigation. Deforested plains and lower hilltops are terraced for rice production. Severe soil erosion is becoming a problem.

Nepal has removed all subsidies on fertilisers, which makes it difficult for Nepali produce to compete with highly subsidised Indian agro-products. There are some transport subsidies for taking fertilisers to remote districts.

Failure of two large-scale maize crops in 2009–10 called into question the quality of the maize-seed sold to the country by several multinational seed merchants. Tests by government agronomists could not determine whether the lost crops were killed off by unusually cold weather during the growing season or whether the original seeds were a hybrid unsuitable for Nepal, rather than the required genetically modified (GM) seed. GM seed is typically expensive and there are few obstructions to smuggled counterfeit seed from India.

Forestry

Forests occupy around 33 per cent of Nepal's land area. The canopy cover in the mid-hills is growing thicker as a result of the government's successful policy of handing over forests to local communities. Deforestation is still high in the government-managed forests of the plains, coupled with timber that is smuggled into India.

In June 2010 the government announced a two-month logging ban throughout the country, following indications that limits on logging had been exceeded and risked deforestation leading to flooding and landslides during the monsoon season.

Industry and manufacturing

Industry accounts for around 21.7 per cent of GDP. The sector consists mainly of manufacturing low-end consumer goods – principally carpets, garments and handicrafts. The development of this sector is constrained by poor infrastructure, a small local market, high industrial factor costs and lack of access to the sea.

Nepal offers duty concessions on raw material imports and start-up tax holidays for new industry, but foreign direct investment flows have remained slow.

Tourism
Tourism is an important element in the economy, although infrastructure is limited. Mount Everest is Nepal's greatest attraction.

Environment
The Sagarmatha (Mount Everest) Pollution Control Committee (SPCC), set up in 1991, spends US$15,000 cleaning up the Sagarmatha National Park every year. The government charges a minimum of US$50,000 for each expedition to Mount Everest, and ploughs back 30–40 per cent of this and other tourist fees to support the SPCC's work. Since the old trekking routes pose serious problems to the indigenous communities already, there are many opposing voices among the environmentalists in Kathmandu.

Mining
Mining and quarrying accounts for around 0.5 per cent of GDP.
Among the major known mineral reserves only limestone has been extracted for commercial use in considerable volumes. Nepal also has deposits of lead, zinc, marble, iron ore and magnesite.

Hydrocarbons
There are no known oil or natural gas reserves, although exploration is ongoing. Consumption of oil was 18,000 barrels per day in 2008, all of which was imported. Any use of natural gas is commercially insignificant.
Nepal has a small coal industry with reserves of around two million tonnes. Annual output meets less than 5 per cent of domestic demand and about 531,000 tonnes of coal are imported

Energy
Total installed generating capacity was 630MW in 2008, mostly supplied by hydropower, but with around 10 per cent from thermal plants. Electricity supplies only 1 per cent of Nepal's energy mix; wood fuel accounts for around 75 per cent, with agricultural waste providing most of the rest.
Hydropower offers the greatest potential, not only for sustainable energy with an estimated economically viable capacity of 43,000MW, but also a valuable component of GDP and foreign earnings in the export of surplus electricity. Early plans have foundered though, with local opposition to the new 750MW West Seti Hydro project in the remote Bajhang district, which was halted before construction was due to begin in 2008. Local people objected to the proposed terms of contract with an international consortium, whereby the project would provide Nepal with 10 per cent of the hydro plant's energy output and the remainder would be sold to northern India. Nevertheless, the government is seeking investment in more hydropower plants to increase total generating capacity to 10,000MW by 2020.

Financial markets
Stock exchange
Nepal Stock Exchange (Nepse)

Banking and insurance
Central bank
Nepal Rastra Bank
Main financial centre
Kathmandu

Time
GMT plus five hours and forty-five minutes

Geography
Nepal is a landlocked, roughly rectangular country located south of the Himalayan mountain range. It is about 885km long (east to west) and an average non-uniform, north-south width of 193km. The country is divided into five development regions and 75 districts. Ecologically, Nepal is divided into three regions–mountain, hill and terai (plains). India borders Nepal in the east, south and west. China borders Nepal in the north. The topography is rugged and harsh and with a vertical distance of less than 200km, the altitude changes from sea level to the highest point on earth – the 8,848m Mount Everest.
Hemisphere
Northern

Climate
The climate is generally temperate but harsh and cold at high altitudes. The low-lying plains are hot in summer and warm during the winters. The high mountains are permanently covered with snow (above 4,800 metres). High temperatures range between 17–30 degrees Celsius (C) and lows are in the range of 0–17 C. May–September is the monsoon season; July is the wettest month and also the hottest.

Dress codes
If travelling outside Kathmandu, it is respectable and practical to wear casual trousers and full-sleeved shirts and jackets. Shorts may be acceptable only in urban centres.

Entry requirements
Passports
Required by all except nationals of India. Entry may be refused, and airlines may not carry passengers holding passports with less than six months validity.
Visa
Required by all, except nationals of India with a valid national ID card. Tourist visas are issued on arrival. Overnight visas are issued free of cost.
Business visas are only issued to those who have been officially recognised as either a) the official representative (of a commercial entity that has obtained a licence to invest in the Kingdom of Nepal in a business or industrial enterprise) or b) an individual who has obtained a licence to invest in Nepal in export trade. Applications for multiple-entry business visas (one or five years) need to be made in advance. Applications should be made to the Director General, Department of Immigration, Kathmandu (www.immi.gov.np). An authorisation from the relevant Nepalese ministry is needed, as are photocopies of the relevant pages of the visitor's passport. The applicant will be sent application forms which must be returned fully completed. If accepted, the visa will be stamped on the visitor's passport at Kathmandu airport.
The Nepal Tourism Board website (www.welcomenepal.com) provides updated information on changes in related policies and rules.
Currency advice/regulations
The import of local and Indian currency is prohibited. On arrival, all foreign currency must be declared, export is limited to the amount declared. Foreign currency exchange receipts must be retained as only 10 per cent of local currency will be reconverted on departure. Export of local currency is prohibited. Currency can be exchanged at banks or authorised foreign exchange dealers and at major hotels. Only Indian and Nepalese nationals may carry Indian currency; possession of Indian Rs500 bills is illegal in Nepal. Travellers cheques are accepted in banks and large hotels.
Customs
Personal effects may be imported duty-free. Items such as cameras, laptop computers, portable music systems and 15 reels of film are permitted as long as they are re-exported.
Exports of antiques and religious artefacts must be certified and cleared by the Department of Archaeology. It is illegal to export goods which are over 100 years old, or endangered wildlife.
Prohibited imports
Narcotics, beef and beef products. Firearms, ammunition and explosives, wireless radio transmitters and precious metals require special licences.

Health (for visitors)
Mandatory precautions
Vaccination certificate for yellow fever if travelling from an infected area.
Advisable precautions
Vaccinations that are necessary include: cholera, diphtheria, tetanus, hepatitis A, polio and typhoid. Vaccinations that may be advised include: hepatitis B, tuberculosis, Japanese B encephalitis and rabies. Anti-malarial precautions should be

taken; the use of mosquito nets and repellents and covering up the body after dark can help avoid malaria, hepatitis B and encephalitis.
Use only bottled or boiled water for drinks, washing teeth and making ice. Eat only well cooked meals, preferably served hot; vegetables should be cooked and fruit peeled; avoid dairy products. A first-aid kit, including disposable syringes, would be useful.
Full medical insurance including emergency repatriation is strongly recommended.

Hotels
Nepal has about 100 tourist-class hotels, ranging from up-market five-star deluxe to those with one-star ratings. Other accommodation includes over 750 non-star-rated, but affordable and safe, speciality establishments.
Hotels may be full during the tourist season and it is advisable to book in advance.
Payment is required in foreign currency.

Credit cards
All major credit and charge cards are accepted by banks, tourist hotels and shops. ATMs can be found in Kathmandu.

Public holidays (national)
Fixed dates
11 Jan (National Unity Day – cancelled in 2007), 29 Jan (Martyrs' Day), 19 Feb (National Democracy Day), 8 Mar (Women's Day), 14 Apr (Nepali New Year), 9 Nov (Constitution Day), 29 Dec (King Birendra's Birthday).
Variable dates
Vasant Panchami (Jan/Feb), Shivaratri (Feb/Mar), Ghode Jatra (Festival of Horses) (Mar), Holi (Mar), Chaite Dashain (Mar/Apr), Ram Nawami (Birthday of Lord Ram) (Mar/Apr), Lord Buddha's Birthday (Apr/May), Rakshya Bandhan (Janai Purnima) (Aug), Gai Jatra/Procession of Cows (Aug/Sep), Krishna Asthami (Birthday of Lord Krishna) (Aug/Sep), Teej (Festival of Women) (Sep), Dasain (Durga Puja Festival) (Oct), Diwali/Deepawali (Oct/Nov), Indra Jatra/Festival of Rain God (Oct/Nov).
In general, Hindu and Buddhist festivals are declared according to local astronomical observations.

Working hours
Banking
Sun–Thu: 1000–1500, Fri: 1000–1200; Kathmandu Valley, Mon–Fri: 0900–1530. Some banks open at weekends.
Business
Sun–Fri: 1000–1700; Kathmandu Valley, Mon–Fri: 0900–1700
Government
Mon–Fri: 0900–1700 (summer); Mon–Fri: 0900–1600 (winter, mid-Nov–mid-Feb).
Shops
Sun–Fri: 1000–1900 (some shops also open on Saturdays).

Telecommunications
Mobile/cell phones
GSM 900 and 1800 services are available in populated areas.

Weights and measures
Metric system (local measures are also used).

Social customs/useful tips
The traditional form of greeting is called *namaste* – performed by placing the palms together at chest height and bowing slightly; it means 'I celebrate the divinity in you'. Some Nepali women may prefer not to shake hands with a man. Always use the right hand to eat or pass anything on. Remove shoes before entering temples and homes.
Do not take photographs before asking permission.

Security
Internal terrorist activities have seen indiscriminate attacks in and around the capital as well as tourist areas, visitors are advised to exercise extra vigilance and also take care to respect any local curfews.

Getting there
Air
National airline: Royal Nepal Airlines (all flights must be paid for in hard currencies).
International airport/s: Kathmandu Tribhuwan International (KTM), 6km from the city. Facilities include bank, *bureau de change*, duty free, post office and tourist information.
Airport tax: Departure tax to regional neighbours (excluding China): NRs1,356; departure tax to all other destinations NRs1,695.
Surface
Road: There are many access routes from India and Tibet, however visitors must use official crossings, which are open 24 hours. Visitors driving their own vehicle must possess a *international carnet*.
Rail: There are two lines in India that run to the border of Nepal at Birgani/Sunauli and at Jaynagar, but neither cross the border.

Getting about
National transport
Air: The only way to reach many parts of Nepal is by air. Nepal has 44 domestic airports and 120 helicopter landing strips. Royal Nepal Airlines and private airline companies have flights to and from these airports. Special helicopter charters can also be arranged. Flights may be delayed during the rainy months; otherwise, they are an efficient means of getting around.
Road: There is a road network of over 13,000km. Kathmandu, Pokhara and Biratnagar are linked by surfaced road. Transport is difficult outside main centres. The Mahendra Highway makes west Nepal accessible throughout the year. The mountainous nature of the country means that many of its roads are unusable, especially during the winter and the monsoon.
Buses: Long distance day or night bus services operate from Kathmandu to all cities of Nepal.
Rail: The only line serves Jaynagar to Janakpur and Bizalpura.
City transport
Taxis: Metered taxis can be hailed in Kathmandu. Private taxis are also available at the hotels, but they may cost more.
Buses, trams & metro: The airport bus to the city centre takes 35 minutes.
Car hire
Driving is on the left. An international driving permit is required. Local authorities also issue a local permit upon presentation of a national licence.
Chauffeur-driven car hire is available.

BUSINESS DIRECTORY
The addresses listed below are a selection only. While World of Information makes every endeavour to check these addresses, we cannot guarantee that changes have not been made, especially to telephone numbers and area codes. We would welcome any corrections.

Telephone area codes
The international direct dialling (IDD) code for Nepal is +977, followed by area code and subscriber's number:

Bhairawa	71	Janakpur	41
Bhaktapur	1	Kathmandu	1
Birgunj	51	Nepalgunj	81
Biratnagar	21	Patan	1
Dhangadhi	91	Pokhara	61

Useful telephone numbers
Police: 100
Directory enquiries: 197

Chambers of Commerce
Federation of Nepalese Chambers of Commerce and Industry, Shahid Shukra FNCCI Milan Marg, Teku, Kathmandu (tel: 426-2061; fax: 426-2007; email: fncci@mos.com.np).

Nepal Britain Chamber of Commerce and Industry, British Embassy Premises, Lainchaur, PO Box 106, Kathmandu (tel: 441-0583; fax: 441-8137; email: info@nbcci.org).

Nepal Chamber of Commerce, Chamber Bhawan, Kantipath, PO Box 198,

Kathmandu (tel: 422-2890; fax: 422-9998; email: chamber@wlink.com.np).

Nepal-US Chamber of Commerce and Industry, TNT Building, Tinkune, Koteshwor, PO Box 2769, Kathmandu (tel: 447-8020; fax: 447-4508; email: nusacci@vishnu.ccsl.com.np).

Banking

Agricultural Development Bank, Ramshahpath, Kathmandu (tel: 421-1744, 421-1802/3; fax: 422-5329).

Himalayan Bank Ltd, PO Box 20590, Karmachari Sanchaya Kosh Building, Tridevi Marg, Thamel, Kathmandu (tel: 422-7749, 425-0201; fax: 422-2800).

Nepal Arab Bank Ltd (Nabil Bank), PO Box 3729, Kantipath, Kathmandu (tel: 421-1784/6; fax: 422-6905).

Nepal Bangladesh Bank Ltd, PO Box 9062, Bijuli Bazar, Naya Baneshwor, Kathmandu (tel: 490-767/70; fax: 490-824, 493-259) .

Nepal Bank Ltd, Dharmapath, Kathmandu (tel: 422-1185, 422-4337; fax: 422-6905).

Nepal Grindlays Bank Ltd, PO Box 3990, Naya Baneswor, Kathmandu (tel: 421-2683/6; fax: 422-6762).

Nepal Indosuez Bank Ltd, PO BOx 3412, Durbar Marg, Kathmandu (tel: 422-8229; fax: 422-6349).

Rastriya Banijya Bank, Singha Durbar Plaza, Kathmandu (tel: 425-2595, 426-8409, 425-1982; fax: 425-2931).

Citibank, PO Box 2826, c/o Hotel Yak & Yeti, Durbar Marg, Kathmandu (tel: 422-8884; fax: 422-7884).

Standard Chartered Bank, PO Box 1526, Durbar, PO Box 1526, Durbar, Marg, Kathmandu (tel/fax: 422-0129).

Central bank

Nepal Rastra Bank, PO Box 73, Baluwatar, Kathmandu (tel: 422-1763; fax: 425-4170; e-mail: nrb@mos.com.np).

Stock exchange

Nepal Stock Exchange (Nepse): www.nepalstock.com

Travel information

Automobile Association of Nepal, c/o Traffic Police Office, Kathmandu (tel: 421-1093).

Everest Air, Durbar Marg, Kathmandu (tel: 422-4188; fax: 422-6795).

Himalayan Helicopters PVT Ltd, Durbar Marg, Kathmandu (tel: 421-7236; fax: 422-5150).

Kathmandu Tribhuvan International Airport, Air Traffic Controller, Gauchar (tel: 472-258 or 473-985, ext 486; fax: 474-180; e-mail: tiao@mod.com.mp).

Nepal Mountaineering Association, 16/53 Ramshah Path, PO Box 1435, Kathmandu (tel: 421-1596).

Royal Nepal Airlines, PO Box 401, RNAC Building, Kantipath, Kathmandu 711000 (tel: 421-4511; fax: 422-5348).

Tourist Information Centre, Basantpur, Kathmandu; Tribhuwan International Airport, Kathmandu (tel: 470-537).

Ministry of tourism

Ministry of Culture, Tourism and Civil Aviation, Bhrikutimandap, Kathmandu (tel: 425-6231/2, 425-6228; fax; 422-7281; email: tourism@mail.com.np).

National tourist organisation offices

Nepal Tourism Board, Tourist Service Centre, Bhrikutimandap, PO Bix 11018, Kathmandu (tel: 425-6909, 425-6229; fax: 425-6910; email: info@ntb.org.np; internet: www.welcomenepal.com).

Ministries

Ministry of Commerce, Babar Mahal, Kathmandu (tel: 223-489, 224-805; fax: 225-594).

Ministry of Finance, Hari Bhawan, Kathmandu (tel: 224-527, 227-367; fax: 227-529).

Ministry of Industry, Tripureshwor, Kathmandu (tel: 213-880, 213-838; fax: 226-112).

Ministry of Interior, Dept of Immigration, Bhrikutimandap, Kathmandu (tel: 422-3590, 422-1996; fax: 422-3127; email: deptimi@net.np; internet: www.immi.gov.np).

Office of the Prime Minister, Singh Durbar, Kathmandu (tel: 421-000; email: info@opmcm.gov.np).

Other useful addresses

Asian Development Bank (ADB), Nepal Resident Mission, Srikunj Kamaladi Ward No 31, Block 2597, Ka.Na.Pa. Kathmandu; Postal address: PO Box 5017 K.D.P.O., Kathmandu (tel: 422-7779; fax: 422-5063; email: adbnrm@mail.asiandevbank.org; internet: www.adb.org/).

British Embassy, Laimchaur, PO Box 106, Kathmandu (tel: 414-588, 410-583, 411-590, 411-281; fax: 411-789).

Department of Commerce, Kathmandu (tel: 422-7364, 422-7404).

Director General, Department of Immigration, Kathmandu (tel: 422-3681).

National Planning Commission, PO Box 1284, Singha Dubar, Kathmandu (tel: 421-5000).

Nepal Economic and Commerce Research Centre, PO Box 285, 7/358 Kohity Bahal, Kathmandu (tel: 421-5336).

Nepal Industrial Development Corporation (NIDC), NIDC Building, PO Box 10, Durba Marg, Kathmandu (tel: 411-211, 411-225).

Royal Nepalese Embassy (USA), 2131 Leroy Place, NW, Washington DC 20008 (tel: (+1-202) 667-4550; fax: (+1-202) 667-5534; e-mail: info@nepalembassyusa.org).

Trade Promotion Centre, Kathmandu (tel: 524-771, 524-772; fax: 521-637).

United Nations Development Programme, United Nations Building, Pulchowk, PO Box 7, Kathmandu (tel: 523-200; fax: 523-991).

National news agency: Rastriya Samachar Samiti (RSS), PO Box 222; Central Office, Bhadrakali Plaza, Kathmandu (tel: 426-2912; fax: 426-2744; internet: www.rss.com.np)

Internet sites

Asian Sources Online: http://asiansources.com

Government of Nepal: www.nepalgov.np

Market information: www.feer.com

News portal: www.nepalnews.com

Nepalese tourism: www.visitnepal.com

The Netherlands

KEY FACTS

Official name: Koninkrijk der Nederlanden (The Kingdom of The Netherlands)

Head of State: Queen Beatrix (crowned 30 April 1980)

Head of government: Prime Minister Mark Rutte (VVD) (from 14 Oct 2010)

Ruling party: Minority coalition: led by Volkspartij voor Vrijheid en Democratie (VVD) (People's Party for Freedom and Democracy), with Christen Democratisch Appèl (CDA) (Christian Democratic Appeal), with support from Partij voor de Vrijheid (PvdV) (Party for Freedom) (from 14 Oct 2010)

Area: 41,473 square km

Population: 16.61 million (2010)*

Capital: The Hague (seat of government); Amsterdam (legal and cultural)

Official language: Dutch and Frisian

Currency: Euro (€) = 100 cents (from 1 Jan 2002; previous currency guilder, locked at f2.20 per euro)

Exchange rate: €0.75 per US$ (Oct 2011)

GDP per capita: US$47,172 (2010)

GDP real growth: 1.70% (2010)

GDP: US$783.30 billion (2010)

Labour force: 7.82 million (2010)

Unemployment: 5.50% (2010)

Inflation: 0.90% (2010)

Oil production: 420.37 million (2009)

Balance of trade: US$57.29 billion (2010)

* estimated figure

The 2011 Dutch provincial elections produced a confused situation in which the government found itself depending on small fringe parties. The provincial elections are important since the 566 members of the 12 Provinciale Staten (PS) (Provincial Councils) in their turn elect the 75 members of the Eerste Kamer (First Chamber or upper house). The results showed that the Christen Democratisch Appèl (CDA) (Christian Democratic Appeal) lost 10 of their seats in the upper house, leaving them with only 11. The Volkspartij voor Vrijheid en Democratie (VVD) (People's Party for Freedom and Democracy) increased its number of seats to 16 from 14. The Partij voor de Vrijheid (PvdV) (Party for Freedom), which did not contest the last provincial elections in 2007, took 10 seats. Mr Rutte's ruling bloc had 37 seats, one short of a majority. Among Mr Rutte's possible coalition allies, the (protestant) Staatkundig Gereformeerde Partij (SGP) (Reformed Political Party) lost one of its two seats, while the recently formed (2009) 50PLUS (50+) got one seat. These results mean that the Cabinet will inevitably have to adjust its policies as Prime Minister Mark Rutte was obliged to negotiate with minority groupings that, rather improbably, drew their support from Protestants and the elderly.

The economy

By a long chalk, the Netherlands' most important trading partner is Germany. The Dutch economy was one of the few obvious beneficiaries of German unification (on 3 October 1990) as Dutch exports to Germany increased dramatically. Until 2008, the Netherlands' closeness to Germany and the importance of the German market had protected the Netherlands from the recessions which from time to time have beset the Anglo- Saxon economies.

In 2011 the concern was to emerge safely from the euro-zone crisis. Unlike the response of most European governments to the effects of the global financial crisis, the government that came to power in 2010 decided not to embark on programmes of structural economic reform. Mark Rutte, leader of the VVD had campaigned on ambitious promises to revitalise the Dutch economy. But there were no plans to reform the labour market or the inefficient subsidised housing market. The Netherlands' generous pension system will remain intact and the pension age will creep up by only a year, from 65 to 66 and not until 2020.

According to the International Monetary Fund (IMF) the Netherlands emerged from its deep recession in mid-2009, but in the first half of 2011 the recovery was still frail. The slump was caused by adverse trade and financial spillovers from the global crisis, which also forced large public intervention in the financial sector. Conversely, the subsequent upturn has been stimulated by strong exports. Despite a somewhat slower pace of recovery in the second half of the year, gross domestic product (GDP) grew 1.75 per cent in 2010. Unemployment has risen only modestly, in part because of labour hoarding and, according to the IMF, has been slightly declining since mid-2010. With output still well below its previous potential, inflation has remained subdued, though by mid-2011 it was picking up, largely because of rising oil prices.

The banking system's soundness has, in the view of the IMF, improved significantly, though weaknesses persist in the financial sector. Non-performing loans remained manageable at less than 3 per cent of total loans. Bank profitability, however, is still weak, although by mid-2011 it had recovered slightly. Pension funds faced the problems of extended longevity and persistent low interest rates. The insurance industry was also under strain. The Netherlands' housing and mortgage markets were relatively stable, although vulnerabilities existed. House prices steadied from mid-2009 to mid-2010, but seemed to have resumed a slow downward drift since then. IMF econometric models did not indicate that house prices were out of kilter. However, household debt has grown substantially in relation to disposable income, to an alarming 270 per cent in 2010, among the highest in advanced economies. The loan-to-value ratio of new mortgages has continued to rise from its already unusually elevated levels and exceeded 120 per cent in 2010 according to some measures.

The Netherlands' fiscal position inevitably deteriorated in 2009, but by 2011 was improving. The general government balance had weakened considerably in 2009, reaching a deficit of 5.5 per cent of GDP, on account of substantial stimulus measures and the free operation of automatic stabilisers to help stem the impact of the global crisis. However, unexpectedly strong tax receipts in 2010 helped reduce the deficit slightly to 5.25 per cent of GDP. Public debt rose to almost 64 per cent of GDP at end-2010, owing also to financial sector assistance not reflected in the deficit. Together with the impact of long-run aging pressures, the fiscal sustainability gap is estimated at about 7.5 per cent of GDP. Strong consolidation plans are being implemented with a view to reducing the deficit by 2015.

The IMF welcomed the Netherlands' export-led recovery and noted that remaining slack is dampening inflationary pressures from international commodity prices. Notwithstanding encouraging near-term prospects, the IMF considered that the risks to the economic outlook remain skewed to the downside. Over the longer term, fiscal risks could also mount as supply-side dislocations created by the global financial crisis and population aging weigh on potential growth.

Right turn

Popular reactions and concerns over the Netherlands' policies towards, and levels of, immigration suggest that ethnic strife may be bubbling away just below the surface. The complex accord that created the new Dutch centre-right minority government, consisting of the liberal VVD and the Christian Democrats, with the support of the far-right Party for Freedom, will need to demonstrate that it is practically workable. The government had the slenderest of majorities of just one in the 150-seat parliament.

Reflecting the Party for Freedom leader, Geert Wilders', controversial support, the government poposed to ban the Islamic veil and forbid police and workers in judicial institutions from wearing the headscarf. Immigration via marriage will be restricted. State subsidies for newcomers' language courses will be turned into loans and a failure to pass immigration tests could result in the refusal of residence permits. The coalition accord makes some play on heavy-handed police tactics in ethnically mixed neighbourhoods, but fails to mention inadequate infrastructure, school drop-out rates and depressingly low social mobility in deprived areas.

And despite the radical liberalism of both the VVD and Mr Wilders, there are hints of

KEY INDICATORS — The Netherlands

	Unit	2006	2007	2008	2009	2010
Population	m	16.35	*16.42	*16.50	*16.57	*16.61
Gross domestic product (GDP)	US$bn	670.92	779.40	877.00	794.80	783.30
GDP per capita	US$	41,046	46,906	52,500	48,223	47,172
GDP real growth	%	3.0	3.6	2.0	-4.0	1.7
Inflation	%	1.6	1.6	2.2	1.0	0.9
Unemployment	%	3.9	3.2	2.8	4.8	5.5
Natural gas output	bn cum	61.9	64.5	66.6	62.7	70.5
Exports (fob) (goods)	US$m	386,923.0	458,368.0	534,129.0	424,804.0	486,239.0
Imports (fob) (goods)	US$m	341,728.0	405,707.0	476,897.0	373,738.0	428,949.0
Balance of trade	US$m	45,195.0	52,679.0	57,231.0	51,066.0	57,290.0
Current account	US$m	55,874.0	47,376.0	41,978.0	38,892.0	56,212.0
Total reserves minus gold	US$m	10,802.0	10,270.0	11,476.0	17,871.0	18,471.0
Foreign exchange	US$m	9,327.0	8,749.0	9,369.0	8,613.0	8,902.0
Exchange rate	per US$	0.75	0.69	0.68	0.78	0.76

* estimated figure

conservatism about their plans. One strange measure was the proposal that the coffee shops of Amsterdam will become members-only clubs closed to foreigners. This may run counter to European legislation, however. Disappointingly for many, the Netherlands, a traditionally open society, looked set to adopt a more critical attitude towards the European Union (EU). The government is likely to oppose Turkey's EU membership bid and spending on foreign aid will be cut.

Risk assessment

Economy	Fair
Politics	Fair
Regional stability	Good

COUNTRY PROFILE

Historical profile

1579 The Protestant majority in the Netherlands rebelled against the Catholic Habsburg Empire and declared independence, with William of Orange crowned Prince William I of Holland and Zeeland. In the seventeenth century, the Netherlands became a powerful trading nation with an empire in the East Indies (modern day Indonesia) and the Caribbean. In the 1650s, the Dutch fought several wars against the English, mainly due to colonial rivalry.
1688 William of Orange (the grandson of William I) acceded to the English throne as William III, ending conflict between the two countries.
1704–06 The English army under John Churchill helped to defeat attempts by the combined armies of Austria and France to invade the Netherlands.
1804 The Netherlands was occupied by the French under Napoleon.
1812 The Netherlands was liberated by British and Prussian armies.
1815 A renewed invasion attempt by Napoleon was defeated at the Battle of Waterloo. Attempts to unify Catholic Belgium with the Netherlands at the Vienna Conference failed, and the two countries remained separate.
1914–18 The country remained neutral in the First World War.
1922 Women were given the vote.
1940–45 The Netherlands declared its neutrality but was occupied by Nazi Germany during the Second World War. The royal family was exiled in the UK.
1945 The Netherlands became a charter member of the United Nations.
1949 The policy of neutrality was abandoned and the Netherlands became a founder member of NATO. The Dutch East Indies became independent.
1958 The Netherlands was a founding member of the European Economic Community (EEC).
1980 Queen Juliana abdicated in favour of her eldest daughter Princess Beatrix. Prince Willem-Alexander became heir apparent.
1989 The Christen Democratisch Appèl (CDA) (Christian Democratic Appeal) and Volkspartij voor Vrijheid en Democratie (VVD) (People's Party for Freedom and Democracy) government fell when VVD refused to support proposals for a 20-year environmental protection programme. A centre-left cabinet was formed by CDA and the Partij van de Arbeid (PvdA) (Labour Party), with Ruud Lubbers as prime minister
1992–93 Ruud Lubbers' government was discredited by a serious economic recession.
1994 A three-party coalition, headed by Wim Kok (PvdA), and including VVD and Democraten 66 (D66) (Democrats 66) won elections. The CDA was frozen out of power for the first time since the First World War.
1999 The Netherlands was a founder member of European Economic and Monetary Union (Emu).
2000 Ruud Lubbers was chosen to head the UN High Commission on Refugees (UNHCR). After 25 years of debating, a bill to legalise euthanasia was approved.
2002 The euro currency replaced the guilder. Wim Kok resigned following a report that criticised Dutch troops in (former) Yugoslavia who had failed to stop the massacre of as many as 8,000 Muslims by Bosnian Serbs in Srebrenica in 1995. Pim Fortuyn, leader of the far-right, anti-immigration, Lijst Pim Fortuyn (LPF) (List Pim Fortuyn) party, was shot dead during election campaigning. CDA won elections and Jan Peter Balkenende became prime minister of a fragile coalition, which later collapsed and Balkenende resigned. Prince Claus von Amsberg, husband of Queen Beatrix, died.
2003 After early parliamentary elections, Jan Peter Balkenende was reinstated as prime minister to head a coalition government, led by the CDA, and including the VVD and the D66.
2004 Former Queen (1948–80) Juliana died. Prominent filmmaker Theo van Gogh was murdered by an Islamist radical; tit-for-tat attacks on Dutch mosques and churches ensued.
2005 The Netherlands rejected the proposed constitution of the EU. Parliament introduced a test of the Dutch language and culture for would-be immigrants.
2006 Prime Minister Balkenende resigned, following a row with D66 about immigration policies. Balkenende reformed the coalition government without the D66. In parliamentary elections, the ruling CDA won 41 seats (out of 150). The Socialistische Partij, (SP) (Socialist Party) increased its seat numbers to 25. The new right-wing Partij voor de Vrijheid (PvdV) (Party for Freedom) won nine seats, while the LPF failed to win any.
2007 Negotiations began between The Netherlands and Caribbean islands of Bonaire, Saba and St Eustatius (three of the five islands of the Netherlands Antilles) due to become city-states within the Kingdom of The Netherlands as the Netherlands Antilles ceases to exist as an entity. A coalition government was formed with the CDA, PvdV and Christen Unie (CU) (Christian Union), with Jan Peter Balkenende as prime minister. Relatives of victims of the Srebrenica massacre in Bosnia in 1995 filed a case against the UN and the Netherlands state, claiming negligence in allowing the massacre to take place.
2008 A ban on tobacco smoking in public places was introduced; no ban was introduced for smoking marijuana in designated coffee shops.
2010 The coalition government collapsed in February, following a disagreement over extending troop deployment to Afghanistan as part of NATO's forces. In new parliamentary elections on 9 June for the Tweede Kamer (second chamber), the centre-right VVD won 20.4 per cent of the vote and the right to form a coalition government. Dutch troops, who had been in Afghanistan since 2006, withdrew on 1 August; although there had been less than 2,000 troops, they were praised for their effectiveness in Uruzgan province. On 14 October a coalition government of VVD with CDA, and including the PvdV, was formed, led by Mark Rutte (VVD) as prime minister.
2011 On 9 June, The Netherlands announced that it would veto the EU decision (taken on 8 June), to admit Bulgaria and Romania into the Schengen area for passport-free travel of citizens and goods, and impose a one-year delay in view of the turmoil in the Middle East and its potential for Arab migration to the EU in 2011–12. Geert Wilders, of the far-right PvdV, who had been arrested in 2009 for inciting hatred against Muslims by making a film that linked radical Islamist actions to the Quran, was acquitted of all charges on 23 June. On 28 June parliament voted to ban the killing of animals for halal meat.

Political structure

Constitution

Under the constitution of 1983, The Netherlands is divided into 12 administrative provinces. Each province is run by a royal commissioner and an elected Provinciale Staten (regional parliamentary assembly). Each regional assembly elects its own governing executive (Gedeputeerde Staten) from among its members. Both council and executive are presided over by a royal commissioner, who is appointed by the crown.

The 672 municipalities, including the major cities, each have an elected council which in turn elects aldermen to sit on the municipal executive along with a mayor, who is appointed by the crown.

The constitution guarantees equality and freedom from discrimination on the grounds of religion, political opinion, race, or sex. The constitution is unique in placing upon the government a duty to promote environmental protection both domestically and internationally.

Where there is no adult successor to the throne or the serving monarch is unable to exercise royal prerogative, the national legislature has the power to appoint a temporary regent.

On 10 October 2010, the Caribbean islands of Curaçao and St Maarten joined Aruba (1986) as semi-autonomous countries within the Kingdom of the Netherlands; at the same time the Caribbean islands of Bonaire, St Eustatius and Saba became Bijzondere Gemeenten (special municipalities) of the Netherlands.

Form of state

Parliamentary democratic monarchy

The executive

The monarch is the head of state but has few executive powers. However it does become actively involved in resolving political crises (for example, at times when no agreement could be reached on the formation of a cabinet). The monarch has the power to appoint the prime minister (on the recommendation of the national assembly), to dissolve the national assembly and call new elections.

The principle executive functions are carried out by the prime minister, who is selected by the national assembly and appoints a council of ministers from both inside and outside the assembly. State ministers are not allowed to continue to sit as members of parliament.

National legislature

Legislative power is vested in the Staten Generaal (States General), a bicameral national assembly.

The 150-member Tweede Kamer (Second Chamber or lower house), is directly elected by the *d'Hondt* system of proportional representation (a system invented in The Netherlands which takes account of the country's provincial units) for a four-year term. It is empowered to review the actions of the cabinet, debate bills and pass approved measures to the Eerste Kamer (First Chamber or upper house), for enactment.

The First Chamber has 75 members who are indirectly elected by the 12 provincial councils, for a period of four years. The First Chamber does not initiate legislation, but is responsible for approving or rejecting bills presented by the Second Chamber. The First Chamber cannot amend legislation directly, but acts which it rejects are likely to be amended in the Second Chamber and represented for approval.

Legal system

The Supreme Court is the highest legal body in the country and it hears appeals arising from cases previously heard in the lower courts. It also has the power of cassation over legislation deemed to conflict with the constitution.

There are five Appeal Courts at lower levels. Most cases are heard either at the 19 Provincial Courts of Justice or at the 62 Municipal Courts. Judges are nominated by the crown and serve for life.

Last elections

9 June 2010 (parliamentary)

Results: Parliamentary (Tweede Kamer): Volkspartij voor Vrijheid en Democratie (VVD) (People's Party for Freedom and Democracy) won 20.4 per cent of the vote (31 seats out of 150), Partij van de Arbeid (PvdA) (Labour Party) 19.6 per cent (30), Partij voor de Vrijheid (PvdV) (Party for Freedom) 15.5 per cent (24), Christen-Democratisch Appèl (CDA) (Christian Democratic Appeal) 13.7 per cent (21), Socialistische Partij (SP) (Socialist Party) 9.9 per cent (15); Democraten 66 (D66) (Democrats 66) 6.9 per cent (10), Groen Links (GL) (Green Left) 6.6 per cent (10), Christen Unie (CU) (Christian Union) 3.3 per cent (five); 10 other political parties won less than 2 per cent each and only two shared the remaining four seats. Turnout was 74.6 per cent.

First Chamber (membership is by appointment only): CDA (23 seats); PvdA (19 seats); VVD (15 seats); SP (four seats); LPF (one seat); GL (five seats); D66 (three seats); CU (two seats); SGP (two seats); Onafhankelijke Senaatsfractie-Fryske Nasjonale Partij (FNP) (Frisian National Party) (one seat).

Next elections

2014 (parliamentary)

Political parties

Ruling party

Minority coalition: led by Volkspartij voor Vrijheid en Democratie (VVD) (People's Party for Freedom and Democracy), with Christen Democratisch Appèl (CDA) (Christian Democratic Appeal), with support from Partij voor de Vrijheid (PvdV) (Party for Freedom) (from 14 Oct 2010)

Main opposition party

With multiply parties in parliament no one party forms an official opposition.

Population

16.61 million (2010)*

Last census: January 2002: 16,105,285

Population density: 469 inhabitants per square kilometre. Urban population: 90 per cent.

Annual growth rate: 0.5 per cent 1994–2004 (WHO 2006)

Ethnic make-up

Dutch (96 per cent); others, predominantly Afro-Caribbean (Surinamese), Indonesian, Moroccan and Turkish (4 per cent).

Religions

Catholic (34 per cent), Protestant (28 per cent), Muslim (3 per cent), Jewish (1 per cent).

Education

Primary schooling may begin at aged four, and continue until aged 12. At aged 12, pupils are channelled into secondary schools with courses designed for their aptitude. The length of time in these schools varies dependent on the courses undertaken; mixed general and vocational courses last for four years and pre-university courses last six years.

Schools are either publicly maintained by government, state or municipal authorities, (attended by 28 per cent of children), or private schools, mostly denominational (attended by 72 per cent of children).

Total public expenditure on education is equivalent to approximately 5 per cent of annual GNP.

Compulsory years: 5 to 16.

Enrolment rate: 109 per cent and 106 per cent, male and female gross enrolment rates respectively, of relevant age groups for primary schools, (including repeaters); 126 per cent and 122 per cent, male and female gross enrolment rates respectively, of relevant age groups for secondary schools, (including repeaters), 1997–2000 (Unicef 2004).

Pupils per teacher: 14 in primary schools.

Health

The private sector is important in the supply of healthcare in the Netherlands and private health insurance is compulsory for most wage earners.

HIV/Aids

HIV prevalence: 0.2 per cent aged 15–49 in 2003 (World Bank)

Life expectancy: 79 years, 2004 (WHO 2006)

Fertility rate/Maternal mortality rate: 1.7 births per woman, 2004 (WHO 2006); maternal mortality 7 per 100,000 live births (World Bank).

Child (under 5 years) mortality rate (per 1,000): 4.8 deaths per 1,000 live births (World Bank)

Head of population per physician: 3.15 physicians per 1,000 people, 2003 (WHO 2006)

Welfare
The Netherlands provides generous income support linked to the minimum wage. However, following a government drive to limit the growth of social security spending, the criteria for eligibility for benefits has been narrowed and earnings-related benefits have been reduced from 80 to 70 per cent of previous income.
As in many EU countries, the ageing population is threatening to make the funding of state pensions an unsustainable burden on public finances over the next 30 years. In 2000, expenditure on pensions was some 5.7 per cent of GDP, but this is projected to rise to the equivalent of 8.4 per cent by 2020 and 11.2 per cent by 2030.

Main cities
Amsterdam (cultural capital, estimated population 740,094 in 2005), Rotterdam (603,139), The Hague (seat of government, 471,677), Utrecht (269,853), Eindhoven (208,706), Tilburg (201,573), Groningen (179,048), Almere (185,622), Breda (167,354), Nijmegen (158,347).

Languages spoken
English, German and French are widely spoken. About 2.9 per cent of the population speak Frisian, mostly in the province of Friesland in the north-east. Turkish and Arabic are also spoken.
Official language/s
Dutch and Frisian

Media
Press
A free press is guaranteed under the constitution
Dailies: There are around 50 daily newspapers. Leading national dailies include *De Telegraaf* (www.telegraaf.nl), *NRC Handelsblad* (www.nrc.nl), *Metro* (www.metronieuws.nl) (tabloid), *Nederlands Dagblad*, *Trouw* (www.trouw.nl), *Algemeen Dagblad* (www.ad.nl), *De Volkskrant* (www.volkskrant.nl), *Het Parool* (www.parool.nl) (tabloid).
Weeklies: A number of daily newspapers publish weekend editions including *De Telegraaf Weekeinde*, *NRC Handelsblad* and *De Volkskrant*. Magazines include *Vrij Nederland* (www.vn.nl) for general news; in English a newsletter Dutch News (www.dutchnews.nl) is published online, with political and general news.
Business: In Dutch, (with some online English translations), publications include the daily *Het Financieele Dagblad* (www.fd.nl), periodicals include *Intermediair* (www.intermediair.nl), with the biggest circulation figure *Management Team* (www.mt.nl), (fortnightly) is a major publication, *Elseviers Weekblad* (www.elsevier.nl) (weekly), *Bizz* (www.bizz.nl) (monthly) and *De Zaak* (www.dezaak.nl) (fortnightly); *Ondernemen* (www.mkb.nl) (monthly) for entrepreneurs and *Beleggers Belangen* (www.beleggersbelangen.nl) for investors.
Periodicals: Official government publications are provided by Overheid (www.overheid.nl) the state-owned press.
Broadcasting
Domestic, public broadcasting allocates broadcasting time by proportional representation. Programmes can be made by any group, political, religious or civil and airtime is allocated based on the number of member they have.
The Netherlands has the largest take-up of cable television and consequently viewers have access to an ample range of domestic and foreign channels. The Netherlands Public Broadcasting (Omroep) operates three national TV channels and seven radio stations plus a website (http://portal.omroep.nl) with video access.
Radio: In addition to the seven national channels including an external service (Radio Netherlands, in several languages, www.radionetherlands.nl), and special interest radio, there are 10 regional stations and approximately 180 local channels. There are over 3,000 local and regional commercial radio stations catering for all styles of music and information, some of the largest include Sky Radio (www.skyradio.nl) with continuous music, Radio 538 (www.radio538.nl). BNR Nieuwsradio (www.bnr.nl) is a business radio station (in Dutch).
Television: All analogue TV broadcasting was discontinued in December 2006; broadcasts are now digital and by 2008 between 80–85 per cent of all transmissions will be in high definition (HD). Omroep operates channels Netherlands 1, 2 and 3 (Ned 1, 2, 3) and the children's channel ZapTV; each province has at least one local channel. BVN (www.bvn.nl) broadcasts an external service worldwide.
TV programmes are broadcast in their original languages – often English – with Dutch subtitles.
Advertising
The Ministry of Education, Culture and Science oversees all compliance with the Advertising Code. The Media Authority supervises compliance in the broadcast medium. Information and advice for advertisers are given online (www.aeforum.org).
Advertising is accepted in all forms of media, although TV and radio advertising is restricted to 12 minutes per hour.

Economy
Not only does the Netherlands have a mature history of hydrocarbon sales, particularly natural gas sold to the European Union, it is also a major European transport hub, with Rotterdam as the world's fourth largest port and Europe's largest port, handling over twice as much as Europe's next largest port (Antwerp, Belgium); in 2009 it processed 387 million tonnes of freight, 34,000 sea-going vessels and 133,000 inland vessels. Manufacturing of machinery and equipment, chemicals and foodstuffs all contribute to strong foreign trade, which is the backbone of the Dutch economy, accounting for 30 per cent of gross national product (GNP) in 2009.
GDP growth in 2007 was 3.6 per cent, however the economy was hit hard by the global economic crisis and in the fourth quarter of 2008 the economy fell into recession, although the average growth rate for the year registered 2.0 per cent. By 2009 the growth rate was -4.0 per cent, which prompted the government to launch three economic stimulation packages over 2008–10, totalling over US$34.5 billion. The packages were needed to shore up the financial sector, including nationalising ABN Amro/Fortis Bank and aiding the ING insurance company, both of which carried significant US mortgage-backed securities (toxic debt) as recorded assets. Reaction to the crisis caused private consumption to slow, along with foreign trade. According to Organisation for Economic Co-operation and Development (OECD) statistics, exports of goods in 2009 fell to US$41.36 billion, down from US$52.84 billion in 2008. However year-on-year exports reported an increase of US$46.15 billion in the first quarter of 2010, up from US$38.14 for the same period in 2009, as a modest recovery got underway.
The Netherlands may only produce a small quantity of crude oil, but is a relatively large producer and supplier of natural gas. It is the European Union's largest natural gas producer (taking over from the UK in 2009), with production of 62.7 billion cubic metres.

External trade
As a member of the European Union, The Netherlands operates within a community-wide free trade area, with tariffs set as a whole. Internationally, the EU has free trade agreements with a number of nations and trading blocs worldwide.
The economy is open to foreign trade with 60 per cent of agricultural produce exported, and the majority of foreign earnings provided by services including international transport and distribution, banking and insurance. Industrial production includes processed foods, petrochemicals and plastics, machinery and vehicle assembly.

Imports
Main imports include machinery and vehicles, chemicals, fuels, consumer goods, foodstuffs and clothing.
Main sources: Germany (typically 16 per cent of total), Belgium (9 per cent), US (8 per cent).
Exports
Major exports include petroleum and natural gas, organic chemicals, agricultural products and foodstuffs, machinery, electronics and vehicles.
Main destinations: Germany (typically 21 per cent of total), Belgium (11 per cent), UK (8 per cent).

Agriculture
Farming
The agricultural sector employs 4 per cent of the workforce and contributes 3 per cent to annual GDP, accounting for 25 per cent of total exports.
Despite high population density in the Netherlands, approximately 70 per cent of all land area is under cultivation. Population growth and wider commercial land use, combined with rising water levels, are placing considerable pressure on land resources.
Overall, Dutch farms tend to be larger than those in other EU member states, with only 25 per cent of farms smaller than five hectares, compared to an EU norm of 50 per cent. Productivity rates are consequently higher than the EU average, and the Netherlands is a net contributor to the EU's Common Agricultural Policy (CAP) budget.
Fundamental reform to the CAP was introduced throughout most of the EU in 2005. The subsidies paid on farm output, which tended to benefit large farms and encourage overproduction, were replaced by single farm payments not conditional on production. This is expected to reward farms that provide and maintain a healthy environment, food safety and animal welfare standards. The changes are also intended to encourage market conscious production and cut the cost of CAP to the EU taxpayer.
Dutch farmers are one of the world's most prolific consumers of pesticides, using 19,000 tonnes of active chemical ingredients per annum (an average 10 kilograms per hectare), with potatoes and flower bulbs the most intensively sprayed crops.
Given the Netherlands' small surface area and high population density, farming is generally highly concentrated, specialised and efficient. Dairy farming is the most substantial activity, involving over a third of the country's farmers.
Traditional Dutch horticulture, in particular the production of flowers and bulbs, is the highest value-added sector. The Netherlands typically has over 24,000 hectares (ha) of land dedicated to open floriculture, and a further 7,000ha of floriculture under glass.
Fishing
The typical Dutch fish catch is over 500,000 tonnes per annum, of which approximately 450,000mt is seafood.
Around 20 per cent of the fish catch is exported, generating annual revenues of approximately US$250 million.
Forestry
Total forest area is 339,000 hectares (ha) or approximately 10 per cent of total land area. Almost all timber needs are imported, but The Netherlands is a major re-exporter of forest products.

Industry and manufacturing
The Netherlands has a broad industrial base. Due to the small home market, Dutch industry is heavily dependent on foreign trade. It is also reliant upon imports of raw materials as industrial inputs. As in most Western European countries, the industrial sector is increasingly focussed on high value-added manufacturing, where technological and skills advantages counteract the lower labour and production costs in emerging industrial economies. The Netherlands' lack of natural resources has increased its dependency on its manufacturing sector and imported materials.
Owing to rapid growth and the need for efficient land use, the construction industry is also significant and often pioneering in the field of space-saving design work.
Manufacturing accounts for 15.1 per cent of GDP and construction for a further 5.2 per cent.

Hydrocarbons
Proven oil reserves were 100 million barrels in 2007. Onshore deposits of oil were first discovered in the late 1930s near The Hague, but attention shifted in the 1940s to better deposits in the Schoonebeek region. Offshore oil, by comparison, is a relatively recent discovery. Average oil production in has fallen over recent years as a result of diminishing reserves in a number of oil fields in the Dutch sector of the North Sea.
The hydrocarbons sector accounts for approximately 9 per cent of GDP and employs 4 per cent of the workforce.
Proven natural gas reserves were 1.25 trillion cubic metres (cum), with production of 64.5 billion cum in 2007. The largest onshore gas field is at Groningen, first discovered in the 1960s. This was the main source of gas until the discovery of offshore deposits. Although it is expected that gas reserves will be depleted by 2030, the rate of new discoveries is sufficiently high that Dutch gas production is expected to continue beyond that time.
The Netherlands is a substantial net exporter of gas, importing only 8 per cent of total supplies and exporting approximately 48 per cent of domestic production. The first liquefied natural gas (LNG) terminal, Gas Access to Europe (Gate), began operations in the port of Rotterdam in September 2011. Gate cost €800 million (US$1.1 billion) and when fully operational will process 8.8 million tonnes of LNG per year. Plans for expansion, to be finalised in 2012, include a terminal for 16 billion cum LNG.
With proven low quality coal reserves of 500 million tonnes coupled with high labour costs and falling demand the last coal pit was closed in 1970. Approximately 320 million tonnes of coal were imported in 2007, of which over 90 per cent was consumed by domestic thermal power stations.

Energy
The Netherlands had an electricity capacity of 22.6GW in 2008, producing 97.3 billion kilowatts hours (kWh). Natural gas provides around 50 per cent of all electricity generation, the remainder is supplied by coal, then oil. Nuclear power and renewable energy sources supply less than 10 per cent. The government has made a commitment to increase to 20 per cent by 2020 the share of renewables to the country's energy mix, through research and development of energy technologies.
Essent is the Netherlands' market leader in provision of electricity and natural gas. It operates internationally through the integration of the Netherlands' national electricity grid with neighbouring countries.
There is one nuclear power station in operation which provides 3 per cent of generating capacity. Development of nuclear power has been slow owing to popular opposition. The attempt to force the reactor to close early was abandoned in 2006 following an agreement that the life of the plant would be limited to 2033.

Financial markets
Stock exchange
Euronext NV Amsterdam (AEX)
Commodity exchange
Liffe Connect

Banking and insurance
Banking supervision remains the responsibility of De Nederlandsche Bank (DNB). The oversight of currency transactions was in the hands of DNB until 2002, when it was assumed by the European Central Bank (ECB). Foreign banks operating in the Netherlands face no special restrictions.
The Dutch banking sector is dominated by three banking conglomerates, ABN Amro, ING Bank and Rabobank Nederland, which together control approximately 75 per cent of total domestic lending. Including Bank Nederlandse Gemeeten and the joint Belgian/Dutch banking group Fortis, these banks are estimated to hold almost

90 per cent of domestic banking assets, loans and deposits.
In 1995, ING bought Britain's Baring Bank for £1 when Baring was on the verge of collapse after the activities of employee and 'rogue trader' Nick Leeson. ING sold at a profit its remaining Baring division in 2004.

Central bank
De Nederlandsche Bank (DNB); European Central Bank (ECB).

Main financial centre
Amsterdam

Time
GMT plus one hour (daylight saving, late March to late October, GMT plus two hours)

Geography
The Netherlands is situated in Western Europe, bordered to the east by Germany and to the south by Belgium. The North Sea lies to the north and west, giving the country a coastline of over 450km.
Except for small areas in the east of the country, the Netherlands' topography is dominated by river plains and flatlands which provide excellent growing conditions for agriculture. The major rivers are the Neder-Rijn and the Waal.
More than a third of the country is below sea level and made up of *polder*, land reclaimed from the sea by the construction of successive sea-walls over the years, but especially since the 1930s.
In the south-west of the country, the major cities of Amsterdam, Rotterdam, The Hague and Utrecht form a heavily urbanised area known as the Randstad or ring city. The flat character of the land, population density and intensive land use have heightened awareness of environmental issues such as air, soil and water pollution and the threat of rising sea levels caused by global warming.

Hemisphere
Northern

Climate
The country has an equitable north European climate, with warm though often damp summers and occasionally severe winters. Average temperatures peak in July and August at around 17 degrees Celsius (C), but manage barely 2 degrees C in January and February before picking up sharply in April and May. Rainfall is heaviest in March and April, when on average 76mm and 81mm respectively are recorded. July and August, by comparison, are the driest months with 41mm and 43mm of rainfall respectively.

Dress codes
Formal dress is usual for business; otherwise, no special restrictions apply. Warm clothing is recommended in winter, especially in coastal regions.

Entry requirements
Passports
Required by all, except nationals of countries which are signatories of the Schengen Accords, which includes most EU/EEA member states, who may visit on national IDs.

Visa
Required by all, except nationals of EU and Schengen Accord signatory countries; North America, Australasia and Japan. For further exceptions contact the nearest consulate. Schengen visas cover all entry needs; for business trips, an original invitation from a business contact in The Netherlands is necessary when applying. A Schengen visa application (offered in several languages) can be downloaded from http://europa.eu/abc/travel/ see 'documents you will need'.

Currency advice/regulations
There are no restrictions on the import or export of local and foreign currencies. Travellers' cheques are widely accepted.

Customs
Personal items are duty-free. There are no duties levied on alcohol and tobacco between EU member states, providing amounts imported are for personal consumption.

Prohibited imports
Illegal drugs and firearms

Health (for visitors)
Nationals of the European Economic Area (EEA) countries and Switzerland can access reduced cost and sometimes free medical treatment using a European Health Insurance Card (EHIC) while visiting the EEA. Exceptions include nationals of the 10 countries, which joined the EU in 2004, whose EHIC is not valid in Switzerland. Applications for the EHIC should be made before travelling.

Hotels
Classified from one- to five-star by Netherlands Board of Tourism, the Royal Dutch Touring Club and the Royal Netherlands Automobile Club. Accommodation may be booked through the Netherlands Reservation Centre in Leidschendam (tel: (070) 202-500). It is advisable to book well in advance during spring and summer. Foreign nationals must present passports before booking in, and are automatically registered with local police.

Credit cards
All major credit cards are accepted.

Public holidays (national)
Fixed dates
1 Jan (New Year's Day), 30 Apr (Queen's Day), 4 May (Remembrance Day), 5 May (Liberation Day), 25–26 Dec (Christmas). Holidays that fall on the weekend are not taken *in lieu*.

Variable dates
Easter Monday (Mar/Apr), Whitsun (May/Jun), Ascension Day (Aug).

Working hours
Banking
Mon–Fri: 0900–1600, some open Sat and on late shopping evenings.

Business
Mon–Fri: 0830–1730.

Government
Mon–Fri: 0830–1700.

Shops
0830/0900–1730/1800 (half-day closing usually Mon or Wed). Main shops open Sat and Thu/Fri evening.

Telecommunications
Mobile/cell phones
There is comprehensive GSM coverage throughout the country.

Electricity supply
220V AC.

Social customs/useful tips
Appointments are necessary and business cards are exchanged, although the business climate is less formal than in some Western European countries and cordiality and consensus at business meetings are highly valued. The best months for business visits are considered to be March to May and September to November. When invited to a meal in a Dutch home it is usual to bring flowers or a small gift.

Security
There are no special problems with security in the Netherlands, although increased caution against petty theft is advised in the heavily populated areas of Rotterdam and Amsterdam.

Getting there
Air
National airline: KLM (Koninklijke Luchtvaart Maatschappij – Royal Dutch Airlines)
Air France acquired KLM in 2004.
International airport/s: Amsterdam Schiphol (AMS), 15km south-west of city; facilities include restaurants, duty-free shops, banks, showers, a business centre, conference rooms and car hire. There are regular, scheduled train and bus routes into the city, travel time 15–30 minutes. Taxis are numerous.
A direct, express train connects Schiphol with main cities in Holland, and some cities in Belgium.
A limited range of international flight destinations also originate from Eindhoven (EIN), 8km north of city; Maastricht (MST), 7km from city; Rotterdam (RTM), 8km north-west of city.
Airport tax: None

Surface
Road: Major routes from the rest of Europe are by a good network of

motorways, well signposted with green 'E' symbols, indicating international highways.
Water: There are good connections between all major European ports. Boat trains operate to the Hook of Holland from many European countries.
The Netherlands is a leading international maritime shipper with extensive port facilities.
Main port/s: Ferries berth at Vlissingen, Rotterdam and Hook of Holland (Hoek van Holland).

Getting about

National transport

Air: Groningen (GRQ) in the north has connecting flights to the international airports. Den Helder (DHR), in the west is one of the largest heliports in Europe providing access to offshore oil and gas fields; charter planes are also available. Other internal services link Amsterdam, Eindhoven, Rotterdam and Maastricht.
Road: Roadways include high speed expressways, limited access motorways, dual highways and secondary roads. All roads are well signposted with red 'A's indicating national highways, and smaller routes indicated by yellow 'N's.
Buses: Most bus services run between 0600–2330. The Interliner is a service used for longer distances and has very few stops. The Connexxion bus company serves the major part of Holland including the provinces of Noord and Zuid Holland, Gelderland, Overijssel and Zeeland.
Rail: There is an hourly service, running 24 hours, between Utrecht, Amsterdam, Schiphol, The Hague and Rotterdam. The Netherlands Railways operate an Intercity (IC) network connecting large cities. IC trains only stop at the major stations. Local trains provide transportation to smaller cities. Tickets can be purchased from railway stations prior to travelling.
Water: There is an extensive network of inland waterways. Scheduled boat services operate from Enkhuizen to Urk and Staveren and between the mainland and the islands in the north.

City transport

The country is divided into zones with set tariffs. A *strippenkaart*, containing 15 strip tickets, is valid throughout the country for travel on buses, trams and subways, including trips within cities. To travel within one zone costs two strips. An extra strip is charged for each subsequent zone. A time limit, notated on the back of the card, allows interchange with other transport systems within the same zone.
Taxis: Taxis have blue licence plates with black letters and figures. Taxis can be booked in advance or, in some larger cities, hailed on the street. Prices may vary between regions and are sometimes open to negotiation.
A *treintaxi* (train-taxi) is a publicly shared taxi, offering shared costs.
Buses, trams & metro: Amsterdam has an intergrated public transport service that runs between 0600–0030 daily throughout the city; night buses run between 0030– 0730. Tickets (*strippenkaart*) can be purchased from a tobacconist, post office or railway station. They should be franked when boarding, for each trip. Elsewhere, city buses run within the boundaries of larger towns. A metro runs in Rotterdam, as well as trams, which also run in The Hague. They typically run between 0600–0000. The metro and trams are usually faster than city buses.
Trains: The train to the city centre from Schiphol is an efficient mode of transport. Inter-city train tickets are not interchangeable with local passenger services.
Ferry: There are ferries running on the canals of Amsterdam and Rotterdam, although these services are more for tourist purposes than for convenience.

Car hire

Car hire is widely available, the minimum age is dependent on insurance usually 21 years. An international driving license is necessary for all non-EU drivers. Traffic drives on the right. Speed limits: urban areas 50kph, normal roads 80kph, motorways 120kph. The wearing of seat belts is compulsory. It is illegal to use a handheld mobile phone while driving (including times when vehicle is stationary in traffic). Do not ignore parking fees as failure can result in a fine and if not paid within 24 hours, the car will be towed away when the cost of retrieval becomes very high.

BUSINESS DIRECTORY

Telephone area codes

The international direct dialling (IDD) code for The Netherlands is +31, followed by area code and subscriber's number:

Amersfoort	33	The Hague	70
Amsterdam	20	Leiden	71
Breda	76	Rotterdam	10
Eindhoven	40	Tiel	344
Haarlem	23	Utrecht	30

Useful telephone numbers

Directory enquiries: 068-008 (national), 060-418 (international)
Operator: 060-410
Police/fire: 0611
National public transport information service: 0900-9292

Chambers of Commerce

American Chamber of Commerce in The Netherlands, 58 Scheveningseweg, 2517 KW The Hague (tel: 365-9808; fax: 364-6992; email: office@amcham.nl).

Amsterdam Chamber of Commerce, 5 De Ruyterkade, 1013AA Amsterdam (tel: 531-4000; fax: 531-4799; email: post@amsterdam.kvk.nl).

Arnhem Chamber of Commerce, 525 Kronenburginsel, 6800 KZ Arnhem (tel: 353-8888; fax: 353-8999; email: info@arnhem.kvk.nl).

British-Netherlands Chamber of Commerce, Oxford House, 328L Nieuwezijds Voorburgwal, 1012 RW Amsterdam (tel: 421-7040; fax: 421-7003; email: info@nbcc.co.uk).

Maastricht Chamber of Commerce, 5 Pierre de Coubertinweg, 6225 XT Maastricht (tel: 350-6666; fax; 350-6660; email: info@maastricht.kvk.nl).

Netherlands Federation of Chambers of Commerce, 1 Watermolenlaan, 3440 AG Woerden (tel: 426-911; fax: 426-216; email: site@vvk.kvk.nl).

Rotterdam Chamber of Commerce, 40 Blaak, 3000 AL Rotterdam (tel: 402-7777; fax: 414-5754; email: dvergeer@rotterdam.kvk.nl).

The Hague Chamber of Commerce, 30 Koningskade, 2502 LS The Hague (tel: 328-7100; fax: 326-2010; email: info@denhaag.kvk.nl).

Tilburg Chamber of Commerce, 1 Reitseplein, 5000 LG Tilburg, (tel: 594-4122; fax: 468-6215; email: info@tilburg.kvk.nl).

Utrecht Chamber of Commerce, 50 Kroonstraat, 3500 AA Utrecht (tel: 326-3211; fax: 231-2804; email: servicecenter@utrecht.kvk.nl).

Zwolle Chamber of Commerce, 1 Govert Flinckstrasse, 8021 ET Zwolle (tel: 455-3800; fax: 453-7424; email: info@zwolle.kvk.nl).

Banking

ABN-Amro, 10 Gustav Mahlerlaan, 1082 PP Amsterdam (tel: 628-9393; fax: 628-7637; e-mail: postbox@abnamro.com).

ASN Bank, 28 Alexanderstraat, 2514 JM The Hague (tel: 0800-0380; fax: 361-7948; e-mail: informatie@asnbank.nl).

NIB Capital Bank, 4 Carnegieplein, 2517 KJ The Hague (tel: 342-5425; fax: 363-5425).

ING Bank, De Amsterdamse Poort, 1102 MG Amsterdam (tel: 563-9111; fax: 563-5700; e-mail: info@ingbank.com).

Postbank NV, 506 Haarlemmerweg , 1014 BL Amsterdam (tel: 584-9111; fax: 584-6600; e-mail: postbank@postbank.nl).

Rabobank Nederland, 18 Croeselaan, 3521 CB Utrecht (tel: 216-0000; fax: 216-2672; e-mail: info@rabobank.nl).

Central bank
De Nederlandsche Bank, Head office, Postbus 98 1000 AB Amsterdam; 1 Westeinde, 1017 ZN Amsterdam (tel: 524-9111; fax: 524-2500; email: info@dnb.nl).

European Central Bank (ECB), Kaiserstrasse 29, D-60311 Frankfurt am Main, Germany (tel: (+49-69) 13-440; fax: (+49-69) 1344-6000; email: info@ecb.int).

Stock exchange
Euronext NV Amsterdam (AEX): www.euronext.com

Stock exchange 2
Chi-X: www.chi-x.com

Commodity exchange
Liffe Connect: www.nyse.com/nyseeuronext

Commodity exchange 2
Climex: www.climex.com

Travel information
Algemene Nederlandse Vereniging van VVVs (ANVV) (association of tourist information offices), 25 Hogeweg, 3814 CC Amersfoort (tel: 33-756-060; fax: 33-723-146; e-mail: anvv@euronet.nl).

Amsterdam Schiphol Airport, 202 Evert van der Beekstraat, Schiphol-Centrum, Haarlemmermeer (tel: 601-9111; fax: 604-1475; e-mail: info@schiphol.nl).

Amsterdam Tourist Office (VVV), 10 Stationplein, 1012 AB Amsterdam (tel: 551-2512; fax: 625-2869; e-mail: info@amsterdamtourist.nl).

KLM Royal Dutch Airlines, 55 Amsterdamseweg, Schiphol Airport, 1182 GP Amstelveen (tel: 20-649-9123; fax: 20-649-300; e-mail: info@klm.nl).

Netherlands Reservation Centre, 1 Nieuwe Gouw, 1442 LE Purmerend (tel: 299-689-144; fax: 299-689-154; e-mail: info@hotelres.nl).

National tourist organisation offices
Netherlands Board of Tourism and Conventions, (head office) Postbus 458; Vlietweg 15, Leidschendam (tel: 370-5705; fax: 320-1654; email: info@holland.com; internet: www.nbtc.nl and www.holland.com).

Ministries
Ministry of Agriculture, Nature Management and Fisheries, 73 Bezuidenhoutseweg, 2594 AC The Hague (tel: 378-6868; fax: 378-6100; email: info@minlnv.nl).

Ministry of Defence, 38 Kalvermarkt, 2511 CB The Hague (tel: 318-8802; fax: 318-8320; email: defensie.voorlichting@co.dnet.mindef.nl).

Ministry of Economic Affairs, 30 Bezuidenhoutseweg, 2594 AV The Hague (tel: 308-1986; fax: 347-4081; email: ezinfo@postbus51.nl).

Ministry of Education, Culture and Science, 4 Europaweg, 2711 AH Zoetermeer (tel: 323-2323; fax: 323-2320; email: info@minocw.nl).

Ministry of Finance, 7 Korte Voorhout, 2511 CW The Hague (tel: 342-7540; fax: 342-7900; internet: www.minfin.nl).

Ministry of Foreign Affairs, 67 Bezuidenhoutseweg, 2594 AC The Hague (tel: 348-6486; fax: 348-4848; email: dvl-info@minbuza.nl).

Ministry of General Affairs, 20 Binnenhof, 2513 AA The Hague (tel: 356-4100; fax: 356-4683).

Ministry of Health, Welfare and Sport, 5 Parnassusplein, 2511 VX The Hague (tel: 340-7911; fax: 340-7890; email: info@minvws.nl).

Ministry of Housing, Spatial Planning and the Environment, Rijnstraat 8, 2515 XP The Hague (tel: 339-3939; fax: 339-1352; email: info@minvrom.nl).

Ministry of the Interior and Kingdom Relations, Schedeldoekshaven 200, 2511 EZ The Hague (tel: 426-6426; fax: 363-9153; email: info@minbzk.nl).

Ministry of Justice, Schedeldoekshaven 100, 2511 EX The Hague 9 (tel: 370-6850; fax: 370-7594; email: voorlichting@minjus.nl).

Ministry of Social Affairs and Employment, 4 Anna van Hannoverstraat, 2595 BJ The Hague (tel: 333-4444; fax: 333-4033; email: info@minszw.nl).

Ministry of Transport, Public Works and Water Management, 1-6 Plesmanweg, 2597 JG The Hague (tel: 351-6171; fax: 351-7895; email: info@minvenw.nl).

Other useful addresses
Algemeen Nederlands Persbureau (national news agency), 49 Handelskade, 2288 BA Rijswick (tel: 70-414-1414; fax: 70-414-1401; e-mail: nieuwsdienst@anp.nl).

American Embassy, 102 Lange Voorhout, 2514 EJ The Hague (tel: 310-9209; fax: 361-4688; email: usemb@usemb.nl).

British Embassy, 10 Lange Voorhout, 2514 ED The Hague (tel: 427-0427; fax: 427-0345).

Congrestolken (conference interpreters), 11 Jan van Goyenkade, 1075 HP Amsterdam (tel: 625-2535; fax: 626-5642; e-mail: interpreters@conferenceinterpreters.com).

Euronext Amsterdam (stock exchange), Beursplein 5, 1012 JW Amsterdam (tel: 550-4444; fax: 550-4900; email: info@euronext.nl).

Federation for Dutch Export (Fenedex), 14 Raamweg 2596 HL The Hague (tel: 330-5600; fax: 330-5656; email: info@fenedex.nl).

Netherlands Convention Bureau, 166 Amsteldijk, 1079 LH Amsterdam (tel: 646-2580; fax: 644-5935; email: info@nlcongress.nl).

Netherlands Council for Trade Promotions (NCH), 181 Bezuidenhoutseweg, 2594 AH The Hague (tel: 344-1544; fax: 385-3531; e-mail: info@nchnl.nl).

Netherlands Development Finance Company, Anna van Saksenlaan 71, 2593 HW The Hague (tel: 314-9696; fax: 324-6187).

Netherlands Embassy (USA), 4200 Linnean Avenue, NW, Washington DC (tel: (+1-202) 244-5300; fax: (+1-202) 362-3430; email: webmaster@netherlands-embassy.org).

Netherlands Foreign Investment Agency (CBIN), 2 Bezuidenhoutseweg, 2594 AV The Hague (tel: 379-8818; fax: 379-6322; email: info@nfia.nl; internet: www.nfia.com).

Netherlands Foreign Trade Agency (EVD), 181 Bezuidenhoutseweg, 2594 AG The Hague (tel: 778-8888; fax: 778-8889; email: eic@info.evd.nl; internet: www2.holland.com/trade/).

Statistics Netherlands (CBS), 428 Prinses Beatrixlaan, 2273 XZ Voorburg (tel: 70-337-3800; fax: 70-387-7429; email: infoserve@cbs.nl; internet: (in Dutch): www.cbs.nl/enindex.htm).

Other news agencies: ANP (Netherlands National News Agency): www.anp.nl

Internet sites
Dutch Tourist Board: www.visitholland.com

Dutch yellow pages www.markt.nl./dyp/index-en.html

Netherlands web directory: www:nl-menu.nl

Tourist information: www:holland.com

Tourist information: www: nbt.nl

Hotel information: www:hotelsinholland.com

Statistics: www: cbs.nl:

Netherlands Embassy in the USA: www: netherlands-embassy.org

Dutch Railways: www: ns.nl

Ministry of Foreign Affairs: www: minbuza.nl

Dutch Parliament: www:parlement.nl

Ministry of Finance: www:minfin.nl

New Caledonia

COUNTRY PROFILE

Historical profile

1766 First sighted by Europeans.
1774 Captain James Cook named the island after the Latin name for Scotland.
1853 New Caledonia became a French colony.
1863 Nickel deposits were discovered. The displacement of villages which stood on new mine sites and the encroachment of settlers' cattle on Kanak (indigenous Melanesians) land provoked several rebellions, all of which were suppressed by the French authorities.
1864–97 The island grew as a penal colony.
1878 A Kanak revolt lead to over a 1,000 deaths.
1942 New Caledonia was transformed into a US military base during the Second World War.
1946 The colony became a French territory.
1980s Tensions increased between the Kanaks and European settlers, principally over land.
1988 Jean-Marie Tijbaou, leader of the Front de Libération Nationale Kanak et Socialiste (FLNKS) (Kanak and Socialist National Liberation Front), signed the Martignon Accord which divided New Caledonia into three distinct regions. It also proposed an end to rule from Paris and agreed a vote on independence in 1998.
1989 Tijbaou was assassinated.
1998 The referendum agreed in 1988 was postponed after the signing, between the government of France and FLNKS and Rassemblement pour la Calédonie dans la République (RPCR), of the Nouméa Accord on 5 May, giving increased autonomy and a referendum on independence to be held sometime between 1914–20.
1999 The French Loi Organique of 19 March agreed changes to the constitution, changing the national assembly into a more autonomous congress and restricting voting rights to those who have been resident for a minimum of five years.
2001 The territory's president, Jean Lèques, (RPCR), resigned. Pierre Frogier (RPCR) replaced him.
2002 Negotiations started on the future adoption of the euro. Land disputes caused ethnic clashes between native Kanaks and Wallisian immigrants.
2004 Parliamentary elections resulted in a four-party coalition government. Marie-Noëlle Thémereau (Avénir Ensemble (AE) (Future Together)) was elected president.
2005 Michel Mathieu was appointed High Commissioner.
2006 The French parliament voted on constitutional amendments to restrict the voting rights of settlers, who must be resident for 10 years before eligibility to vote.
2007 Marie-Noëlle Thémereau resigned and Harold Martin was elected President of the Congress. High Commissioner Mathieu resigned and was replaced by Yves Dassonville.
2008 Despite scientific claims that the rich coral lagoon in Goro would not be damaged by the release of liquid mining effluent, residents remained unconvinced and warned the authorities that they would keep a watch on the surrounding environment.
2009 A five-month epidemic of dengue fever, which intensified during the summer heat wave, killed two and infected over 3,000. Around 100,000 litres of toxic sulphuric acid spilled into North Bay Creek, killing thousands of fish and crustaceans in Prony Bay in the Southern Province. The Worldwide Fund for Nature called for the licence of the Vale-Inco Nickel plant to be suspended pending plant monitoring and emergency measures being brought up to specification. In Territorial Congress elections, anti-independence parties won 36 seats out of 54 and nationalists 10. Philippe Gomès was elected by parliament as president of the Congress.
2010 In June, President Philippe Gomes was indicted on suspicion of bribery, that his company had won a US$1.3 million contract to supply electrical units to Vale-Inco to the Brazilian mining company, which in turn had been granted an operating licence when Gomes was president of the South Province in 2005–06. On 6 October, Albert Dupuy was appointed as high commissioner.
2011 The government of President Gomés collapsed after ministers belonging to Union Calédonienne (UC) (Caledonian Union) resigned from the cabinet on 17 February. On 3 March, parliament elected a new government and Harold Martin was chosen as president. However,

KEY FACTS

Official name: Nouvelle Calédonie (New Caledonia)

Head of State: President of France President of France (Nicolas Sarkozy), represented by High Commissioner Yves Dassonville (from 9 Nov 2007)

Head of government: President of the Congress of New Caledonia, Harold Martin (from 10 Jun 2011)

Ruling party: Grand Coalition (government post are allocated in proportion to electoral victory and support of head of government) Le Rassemblement-UMP (The Rally-UMP) (from 2007; re-elected 10 May 2009)

Area: 18,575 square km – Grande Terre island: 16,600 square km

Population: 245,580 (2010)*

Capital: Nouméa (on Grande Terre)

Official language: French

Currency: Comptoirs Français du Pacifique franc (CFPf) = 100 centimes

Exchange rate: CFPf84.51 per US$ (Jan 2009); (pegged CFPf119.25 per euro)*

GDP per capita: US$36,311 (2009)

GDP real growth: 1.50% (2010)

GDP: US$8.90 billion (2010)

Labour force: 84,400 (2007)*

Inflation: 2.70% (2010)

Visitor numbers: 103,363 (2007)

* estimated figure

Martin's government collapsed on the same day following the resignation of one of its members. Harold Martin was elected as president on 17 March but again his government collapsed within the day after the resignations of some of his cabinet. Parliament re-elected Harold Martin as President of Congress on 10 June.

Political structure

Constitution

Under the Nouméa Accord of 1998, New Caledonia has a special status within the French constitution. The local government, elected by universal suffrage, has wider degrees of autonomy regarding legislative issues. Up until 2010, France will retain power only over justice, public order, currency, defence and foreign affairs outside the South Pacific region.

France is also obliged to conduct up to three referenda on independence between 2013–18. Until then, the High Commissioner has overall responsibility for the territory while the president of the Territorial Congress is the head of local government.

New Caledonia is represented in the French parliament by two deputies and two senators

The territory is divided into three provinces, each with its own assembly and local executive. There is an economic and social committee, which has an advisory role, and a Custom Senate, which advises the government on matters affecting the indigenous Kanak community.

Form of state

Self-governing territory of France

The executive

Executive power is exercised by the High Commissioner, with delegated power, for local administration, from France. The president of Congress advises the High Commissioner on matters of local jurisdiction.

The Congress elects the president who represents the congress and directs administrative services aided by an 11-member executive council drawn from Congress members (with at least one member from all political parties represented).

National legislature

Under the Loi Organique (Organic Act, 1999) the Congrès de la Nouvelle-Calédonie (Congress of New Caledonia) has enhanced powers to elect the government and enact legislation, separately from France. It has 54-members elected by proportional representation from the provinces of New Caledonia (32 from the South Province, 15 from the Northern Province and 7 from the Province des Iles Loyauté). All members serve for five-year terms.

To be eligible to vote for congress members, voters must have been resident for 10 years and resident for 20 years to vote in referenda scheduled in 2015–20.

Last elections

10 May 2009 (parliamentary)

Results: Parliamentary: Rassemblement pour une Calédonie dans la République (Le Rassemblement-UMP) (The Rally-UMP) won 13 seats (out of 54), Calédonie Ensemble (CE) (Caledonia Together) 12, Union Calédonienne (UC) (Caledonian Union) 8, Union Nationale pour l'Indépendance (UNI) (National Union for Independence) 8, Avenir Ensemble (Future Together) 6, Front de Libération Nationale Kanak et Socialiste (FLNKS) (Kanak and Socialist National Liberation Front) 3, Parti Travailliste (Labour Party) 3, Rassemblement pour la Calédonie 2, and Libération Kanak Socialiste (RPCR) (Rally for Caledonia in the Republic) 1. Turnout was 76.44 per cent.

Next elections

2014 (parliamentary)

Political parties

Ruling party

Grand Coalition (government post are allocated in proportion to electoral victory and support of head of government) Le Rassemblement-UMP (The Rally-UMP) (from 2007; re-elected 10 May 2009)

Main opposition party

Front de Libération Nationale Kanak et Socialiste (FLNKS) (Kanak and Socialist National Liberation Front) alliance

Political situation

With one of the world's largest reserves of nickel, the community in New Caledonia has been trying to balance the need for foreign direct investment to boost the economy and the damage mining can do to tribal lands and the environment. The indigenous Kanak people are opposed to the Goro-Nickel mining operation and since a court in 2006 rejected its legal bid to halt the biggest industrial project in the South Pacific have taken direct actions in their attempt to halt production. An estimated US$10 million in damage was caused to heavy machinery and vehicles in the US$1.88 billion Goro-Nickel plant when a riot, inspired by the Rheebu Nuu Committee, broke out in 2006. However, after police imposed rule, such action did not stop the project although the owner (Brazilian mining company CVRD) did review its investment and called for talks covering all aspects of local opposition, to reach a consensus. The plant was 70 per cent completed by 2008, after US$2.8 billion had been invested the expectation is that 4,500 tonnes per annum of cobalt will be produced by 2012. While mining output rose by 20 per cent in 2007, nickel production fell by 7 per cent, nevertheless world prices for commodities have given windfall bonuses.

In 2007, for the first time in its history, the National Assembly in France had to amend the French Constitution specifically to allow New Caledonia to impose voting restrictions in local elections, in accordance with the 1998 Nouméa Accord. Only residents who have lived in New Caledonia for 20 years may vote in local elections and referenda, including those due to be held between 2015–2020 concerning New Caledonia's independence from France.

Population

245,580 (2010)*

Last census: August 2004: 230,789

Population density: 11 inhabitants per square km.

Annual growth rate: 1.8 per cent (2003)

Ethnic make-up

Of the total population, 45 per cent are Melanesian Kanaks, 34 per cent Europeans (mainly French), 20 per cent are Wallisians and the remainder are mainly Tahitian, Indonesian and Vietnamese.

The wealthy southern province is mainly inhabited by Europeans and the remainder of the country is mostly populated by the poorer ethnic Kanak community.

Education

Education is provided free for the compulsory years. Primary education covers ages six to 11 years and secondary education from aged 12 to a maximum of 18 years. There is a major shortage in the supply of trained secondary school teachers.

Public expenditure on education is typically 7 per cent of GNP. Nearly US$30 million was allocated, up to 2005, to implement the government's policy of equity funding for the early childhood education sector. The government also doubled funding for adult literacy, setting aside US$18 million to fund the Adult Literacy Strategy. More emphasis has been given to Mäori and Pacific children with special educational needs.

In 2005 the government introduced a new primary school curriculum which places more emphasis on local culture and history and allows lessons to by taught in Kanak. The changes will come into force in early 2006.

Compulsory years: Six to 15

Enrolment rate: 101 per cent gross primary enrolment of the relevant age group (including repeaters) (World Bank 2003).

Pupils per teacher: 18 in primary schools.

Health

Life expectancy: 74 years (estimate 2003)

Fertility rate/Maternal mortality rate: 2.5 births per woman (World Bank)
Child (under 5 years) mortality rate (per 1,000): Seven deaths per 1,000 live births.

Main cities
Nouméa (capital, on Grande Terre, estimated population 89,207 in 2005) Le Mont Dore (26,180), Dumbea (26,290).

Languages spoken
Thirty Canaque languages are spoken. English is often understood.
Official language/s
French

Media
Press
In French, the only dailies newspaper is *Les Nouvelles Calédoniennes* (www.info.lnc.nc), weeklies include *Télé 7 Jours, Les Nouvelles Hebdo, L'Echo Calédonien, Dimanche Patinane* and *Femmes*, which is a women's magazine.
Broadcasting
The French overseas broadcaster RFO (www.rfo.fr) provides locally produced radio and television news and imported French programmes, as well as internet TV services.
Radio: RFO operates Radio France Internationale (http://www.rfi.fr). Private local radio services operate 24 hours a day; stations include NRJ (www.nrj.nc) and Radio Djiido (www.radiodjiido.nc).
Television: From France, RFO Nouvelle-Calédonie (http://nouvellecaledonie.rfo.fr) offers a fully range of programmes. Pay-to-view TV is also available.
Advertising
Advertising is available in the local press, on radio and TV and in cinemas.
News agencies
ABC Pacific Beat: www.radioaustralia.net.au/pacbeat
Pacific Magazine: www.pacificmagazine.net

Economy
There is a lack of economic diversity; however as New Caledonia has large deposits of nickel ore, around 25 per cent of world deposits, its economy is largely buoyed by sales of ore (which account for around 12 per cent of global nickel production) and from smelting enterprises, such as the development of the Koniambo deposit. The new and improved infrastructure made necessary by building the nickel plants will also benefit other sectors of the economy, such as tourism, education and health. Other activities include manufacturing of consumer goods and intermediate products such as electrical components and capital goods such as mechanical and electrical automotive parts. Other components of the economy include financial transfers from France and foreign aid. Agriculture includes production of premium coffee, meat and other food processing, and aquaculture includes fish processing and packaging.
The territory's other big source of foreign exchange is its tourist sector, which had been rising steadily since the 1990s, with cruise arrivals increasing. However by 2009 tourist numbers had slumped to a 15-year low with just 99,379 arrivals.
Citizens of New Caledonia have one of the highest per capita incomes in the Pacific region (after Australia and New Zealand) at US$36,132 in 2007, but which fell to US$35,679 in 2008. GDP growth in 2007 was 5.6 per cent but tumbled to 0.2 per cent in 2008 due to the global economic crisis which reduced exports of nickel, down from US$23.8 million in 2007 to US$15 million in 2008.
Although the French military presence in New Caledonia has been a source of internal tensions, it also makes a significant contribution to the local economy. France contributes around 25 per cent of GDP, 80 per cent of which covers healthcare, education and public sector wages.
New Caledonia uses the euro-pegged Comptoirs Français du Pacifique franc (CFPf) as its currency. The government began negotiations in 2002 over the adoption of the euro, which would boost the territory's chances of attracting investment and tourism, but has been unsuccessful in overcoming the objections of pro-independence groups.

External trade
As a *collectivité sui generic* of France, New Caledonia is a Special Territories of the European Union and apply its rulings and trade agreements.
Imports
Main imports are machinery and equipment, fuels, chemicals and foodstuffs.
Main sources: France (typically 26 per cent of total), Singapore (17 per cent), Australia (10 per cent).
Exports
Main exports are processed nickel ore and processed nickel, mechanical and electrical components and fish
Main destinations: France (typically 33 per cent of total), Japan (17 per cent), Spain (7 per cent).

Agriculture
Farming
The agricultural sector typically accounts for as little as 2 per cent of GDP. Although the soil is fertile, only 10 per cent of the land area is cultivated. There is a ratio of around 50-50 for locally grown to imported foods. The number of farmers has fallen by almost 50 per cent since the early 1990s, with the greatest percentage loss in the northern province.
About one-third of the main island's land area is devoted to cattle raising, chiefly on the central and north-west coasts. Exports of coffee and copra crops have increased since the 1990s.
Fishing
Tropical shrimp farming has been developed, although the farms are fragile as there is always the risk of disease. Fishing is both for local consumption and for export, mainly to Japan.
Annual fish production typically includes 2,800t marine fish, 1,900t other seafood and 343,000 units of pearls and shells.
Forestry
Domestic forests supply about 35 per cent of timber demand, with some reforestation undertaken.

Industry and manufacturing
The industrial sector typically contributes 20 per cent to GDP. Main industries include nickel processing, domestic equipment, clothing, foodstuffs and beer.
There are three major nickel processing projects in the pipeline. New Caledonia's only existing nickel processing plant, owned by the Société le Nickel (SLN), is undergoing renovations to increase production from 60,000 tonnes to 75,000 tonnes annually. SLN will increase activity at one of its mines to supply enough ore for the plant's increased capacity.
Construction of a US$1.50 billion Koniambo nickel processing plant in the north, with production starting in 2008 is projected to output 60,000 tonnes of nickel a year.

Mining
New Caledonia holds between 25–40 per cent of known world nickel deposits and is one of the world's largest producers.
There are several mines in New Caledonia, the principal ones are located at Koniambo, Tiebaghi, Thio, Kouaoua, Nepoui-Kopeto and Etoile du Nord.
The potential production capacity of the seven main nickel mining operators making up Société Le Nickel (SLN) has been estimated at 830,000 tonnes a year, with reserves expected to last until 2012. SLN is 60 per cent owned by France's Eramet and 30 per cent by the Société Minière de Sud Pacific (SMSP), which is owned by ethnic Kanak groups.
Nickel and ferronickel production accounts for up to 10 per cent of GDP and contributes 80 per cent of foreign earnings.
Chrome extraction is undertaken. There are also deposits of iron ore, copper, manganese, lead and zinc.
SLN is expanding its smelting plant in Nouméa, and in order to supply enough ore for the plant's increased capacity, it is increasing production at one of its mines from 250,000 tonnes to one million

tonnes a year, creating around 200 new jobs.
In 2004, a public enquiry on the future of the US$1.8 billion Goro nickel mining project in the Southern Province recommended the project go ahead, but precautions should be taken against environmental pollution.

Tourism
New Caledonia combines a traditional Melanesian culture overlaid with a French flavour. As such, it attracts many French visitors, fleeing a bleak Northern Hemisphere winter. The lagoons around New Caledonia, which include mangroves and the barrier reef, are listed as World Heritage Sites by Unesco.
In 2009 tourist numbers had slumped to a 15-year low with just 99,379 arrivals, which had been relatively constant at above this until 2009. The government has instigated measures to offer value-added holidays, including festivals held on different islands each year and a proposal for tourists to stay with local people and experience the culture first hand by fishing, working in 'gardens' (smallholder plots) and exploring the islands. There is a range of accommodation, from hotels to bungalows to traditional huts.

Hydrocarbons
There are no known natural gas or oil reserves. Consumption of oil was 13,000 barrels per day (bpd) in 2008, all of which was imported.
Imported coal was 336,000 tonnes in 2008, used in power generation.

Energy
Total installed generating capacity was 350MW in 2007, producing over 1.6 million kilowatt hours. Électricité et Eau de Caledonie and Enercal are responsible for electricity generation and supply. Around 80 per cent of electricity generation is produced by thermal generators. Renewable sources of energy, including hydroelectricity and wind generation, are growing in importance. The nickel extraction and smelting sectors consume around 75 per cent of electricity output.

Banking and insurance
Central bank
The Paris-based Institut d'Emission d'Outre-Mer (IEOM) provides all central banking services except foreign exchange reserves.
Main financial centre
Nouméa

Time
GMT plus 10 hours

Geography
New Caledonia comprises one large island and several smaller ones, situated in the south Pacific Ocean, about 1,500km (930 miles) east of Queensland, Australia. The main island is La Grand-Terre, it is long and narrow. Rugged mountains divide the west of the island from the east, and there is little flat land. The nearby Loyalty Islands and a third group of islands, the uninhabited Chesterfield Islands, lie about 400km north-west of the main island.
Hemisphere
Southern

Climate
Hot (average temperature 26 degrees Celsius (C)), with occasional tropical depressions and cyclones, from mid-November to mid-April; and cool (average temperature 23 degrees C), with moderate rains, from mid-May to mid-September. Rainfall is quite irregular and can be extremely heavy. The east coast (at about two metres per annum) has twice the rainfall of the west; the wettest months are January, February and March.

Entry requirements
Passports
Required by all, except certain French nationals; all passports must have at least six months validity from the date of visit.
Visa
Required by all, except citizens of EU, North America, Australasia and Japan, for stays up to one month; this includes business trips by representatives of foreign entities with an invitation from a local company or organisation. Proof of adequate funds for stay, an itinerary, a guarantee of repatriation if necessary and return/onward ticket are also required. For further exceptions, full details and a copy of the application form visit www.diplomatie.gouv.fr/thema/dossier.gb.asp and follow the path (going to France) to the database.
Currency advice/regulations
The import and export of local and foreign currencies are unristricted but amounts over CFPf 900,000 must be declared.
Customs
Personal effects are allowed entry duty-free. Duty is not payable on goods of EU origin, although all imported goods are subject to a general tax, and an increasing number of goods require import licences. Expensive items, such as laptop computers, may require proof of ownership when departing.
Prohibited imports
Parrots, parakeets, pigeons, turtle-doves and non-domestic mammals; plants and seeds require a health certificate.
Export of birds of paradise and objects of ethnographic interest are prohibited.

Health (for visitors)
Mandatory precautions
Vaccination certificate required for yellow fever if travelling from infected area.
Advisable precautions
Vaccination for diphtheria, tuberculosis, hepatitis A and B, polio, TB, tetanus, typhoid. There is a rabies risk.
There has been an increased risk of dengue fever, visitors are advised to use mosquito repellent, a mosquito net at night, and wear protective clothing at dawn and dusk, to reduce the risk.

Hotels
Tourist hotels are classified by category and size on the five-star system. Hotel tax is levied, the amount varying according to classification. Details of rural or tribal lodgings in some Melanesian villages and areas are available from tourist information offices. Upper-end bungalow accommodation is growing.

Credit cards
Most major credit cards are accepted.

Public holidays (national)
Fixed dates
1 Jan (New Year), 1 May (Labour Day), 8 May (1945 Victory Day), 14 Jul (Bastille Day), 15 Aug (Assumption Day), 24 Sep (New Caledonia Day), 1 Nov (All Saints' Day), 11 Nov (Armistice Day), 25 Dec (Christmas Day).
Variable dates
Easter Monday (Mar–Apr), Ascension Day (Apr–May).

Working hours
Banking
Mon–Fri: 0730–1545.
Business
Mon–Fri: 0730–1130, 1330–1730. Sat: 0730–1130.
Government
Mon–Fri: 0730–1130, 1215–1600.
Shops
Mon–Fri: 0730–1100, 1400–1800. Half-day Sat and Sun.

Telecommunications
Mobile/cell phones
There is a GSM 900 service that covers the coastal regions of Grand Terre and surrounding islands.

Electricity supply
220V AC, with two-pin plug fittings.

Weights and measures
Metric system

Social customs/useful tips
Tipping is not customary. Islanders find it offensive when women sunbathe topless.

Getting there
Air
National airline: Aircalin

International airport/s: Nouméa La Tontouta International (NOU), 48km from Nouméa; duty-free shop, bar, restaurant, bank, shops, car hire.
Airport tax: None
Surface
There are regular shipping services from Australasia, Europe, Japan and South East Asia.

Getting about
National transport
Air: Air Calédonie operates regular flights from Nouméa's domestic airport, Magenta, to the east and west coasts of Grande-Terre island and daily flights to the Ile des Pins, Maré, Tiga, Lifou and Ouvea. Charter and tour airplanes and helicopters are available.
Road: Grande-Terre, the main island, has a total road network of approximately 5,000km, about 71 per cent sealed in municipal areas and a considerable length of track suitable for four-wheel drive and similar vehicles. Exercise care driving along the west and east coasts, as some roads are not sealed. The Canala-Thio main road is one-way only, with direction of traffic changing at scheduled times.
Buses: Regular bus services operate on Grande-Terre.
Water: There is a high-speed catamaran link between Grande-Terre and Ile des Pins, and Loyalty Islands. Small trading vessels also sail to nearby islands.
City transport
Taxis: Taxis are available in the central square (Place des Cocotiers), with some operating 24 hours. Charges are for time and distance. There is a surcharge after 1900 and on Sundays.
Buses, trams & metro: Buses from the airport to city centre usually take about 60 minutes.
Car hire
Self-drive car hire is available in Nouméa. A current valid driving licence is required. Driving is on the right-hand side of the road.

BUSINESS DIRECTORY

The addresses listed below are a selection only. While World of Information makes every endeavour to check these addresses, we cannot guarantee that changes have not been made, especially to telephone numbers and area codes. We would welcome any corrections.

Telephone area codes
The international dialling code (IDD) for New Caledonia is +687 followed by subscriber's number.

Useful telephone numbers
Fire station: 18
Police: 17
Ambulance (Nouméa): 252-100

Banking
Bank of Hawaii-Nouvelle Calédonie, BP L3, 25 Avenue de la Victoire, Avenue Henri Lafleur, 98849 Nouméa Cedex (tel: 257-400; fax: 274-147).

Banque Calédonienne d'Investissement, BP K5, 50 Avenue de la Victore, 98849 Nouméa (tel: 256-565; fax: 274-035).

Banque Nationale de Paris Nouvelle Calédonie, BP K3, 37 Ave Henri Lafleur, 98800 Nouméa (tel: 258-400; fax: 258-459) .

Société Générale Calédonienne de Banque; 44 rue de l'Alma, Siége et Agence Principale, 98848 Nouméa (tel: 256-300; fax: 276-245).

Central bank
Institut d'Emission d'Outre-Mer (IEOM), 5 rue Roland Barthes, 75598 Paris Cedex 12, France (tel : (+33-1) 5344-4141; fax : (+33-1) 4347-5134; email: contact@ieom.fr).

European Central Bank, Kaiserstrasse 29, D-60311 Frankfurt am Main, Germany (tel: (+49-69) 13-440; fax: (+49-69) 1344-6000; e-mail: info@ecb.int).

Travel information
Air Caledonia, BP 98845 Nouméa (tel: 252-339; (bookings tel: 252-177); internet: www.air-caledonie.nc).

Aircalin, 8 rue Frederic Surleau, BP 3736, Nouméa (tel: 265-500; fax: 265-651; internet: www.aircalin.nc).

Destination Nouvelle Calédonie, 39-41 rue de Verdun, PO Box 688, Nouméa (tel: 272-632; fax: 274-623).

Nouméa La Tontouta International Airport, BP2, Tontouta 98840 (tel: 352-500; fax: 352-535; e-mail: ccita@cci.nc).

Nouméa Tourist Office, 24 rue Anotole France, BP 2828, Nouméa 98.800 (tel: 287-580; fax: 287-585).

National tourist organisation offices
New Caledonian Tourism Promotion Board (internet: www.nouvelle-caledonie-tourisme.nc).

Other useful addresses
Institut Territorial de la Statistique et des Etudes Economiques, PO Box 823, 5 rue Gallieni, Nouméa (tel: 275-481, 283-156; fax: 288-148).

South Pacific Commission, PO Box D5 Cedex, Nouméa (tel: 262-000; fax: 261-844).

Internet sites
South Pacific Tourism Organisation: www.tcsp.com/new_caledonia/index.html

New Caledonia tourism: www.nctps.com/home.cfm

New Caledonia tourism: www.newcaledonia.com.au

New Caledonia website (in French): www.yahoue.com

Travel information: http://perso.wanadoo.fr/caledonie/indexe.htm

New Zealand

KEY FACTS

Official name: The Dominion of New Zealand

Head of State: Queen Elizabeth II, represented by Governor General Sir Jeremiah (Jerry) Mateparae (from 31 Aug 2011)

Head of government: Prime Minister John Key (Nationals) (from 2008; re-elected 26 Nov 2011)

Ruling party: Coalition led by the National Party, with ACT New Zealand (ACT) and United Future (UF) (from 2008; re-elected 26 Nov 2011)

Area: 268,676 square km: North Island (115,690 square km); South Island (152,356 square km)

Population: 4.37 million (2010)*

Capital: Wellington

Official language: English, Māori

Currency: New Zealand dollar (NZ$) = 100 cents

Exchange rate: NZ$1.31 per US$ (Oct 2011)

GDP per capita: US$32,145 (2010)

GDP real growth: 1.50% (2010)

GDP: US$140.40 billion (2010)

Labour force: 2.35 million (2010)

Unemployment: 6.70% (2010)

Inflation: 2.30% (2010)

Balance of trade: US$2.37 billion (2010)

Foreign debt: US$59.08 billion (2008)

Annual FDI: US$602.21 million (2010)

* estimated figure

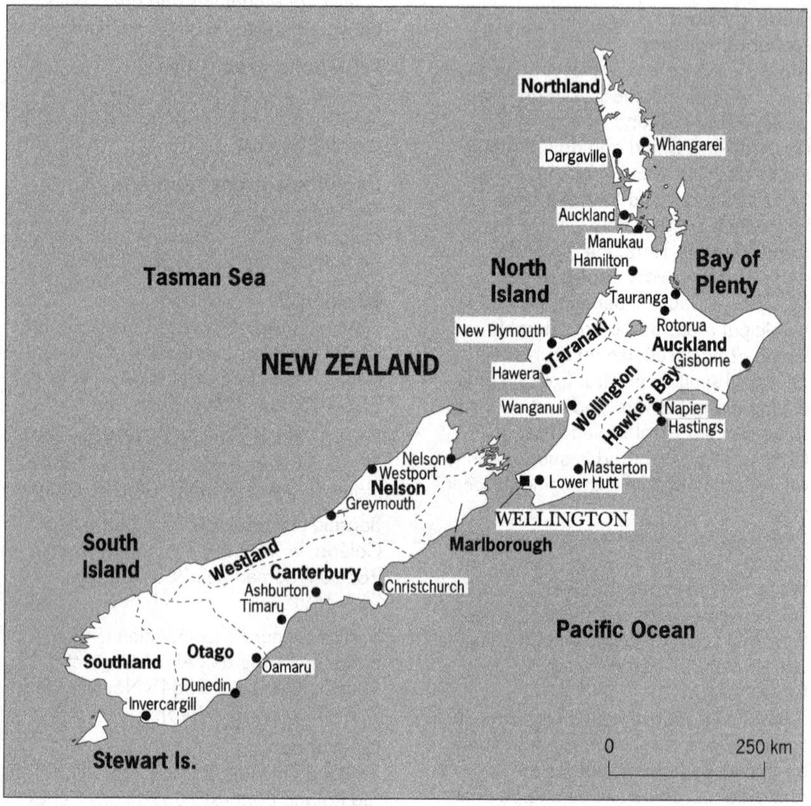

A shallow magnitude 6.3 earthquake occurred 10km south-east of Christchurch (South Island) on 22 February 2011. This had followed a deeper 7.1 magnitude earthquake that had occurred in the region on 4 September 2010. Christchurch continued to be affected by aftershocks, including a succession of strong aftershocks in June 2011. This included two aftershocks measuring 5.7 and 6.3 which caused minor injuries and further damage to buildings and infrastructure. The February earthquake killed 181 people and the combined earthquakes generated a total of 344,364 claims from New Zealand's Earthquake Commission. Damage to Christchurch was significant, particularly in the eastern suburbs. Before the 13 June aftershocks, the New Zealand Ministry of Civil Defence had approved the demolition or partial demolition of 323 buildings in Christchurch, a large number of which were classified as heritage buildings. Power has been restored, but Orion Energy cautioned at the time that power cuts were expected during winter. The waste water system remained severely damaged, and residents were asked to reduce water use.

Elections

In November 2011 New Zealand's ruling National Party claimed victory in the country's general election. 'For another three years there will be a National-led government in New Zealand,' incumbent Prime Minister John Key announced to his supporters in Auckland. The opposition Labour party, led by Phil Goff, conceded defeat, as its vote slumped.

Approval for Key

With all the results in, the ruling National Party had won 60 of the 121 seats in Parliament. This meant that the National Party would be able to continue governing with the help of the ACT New Zealand (ACT) and United Future (UF) parties, each of which won one seat. Mr Key was also thought to be planning talks with the Maori Party, which won three seats. However, the Maori Party had expressed its opposition to Mr Key's plans to sell off state assets. New Zealand's Green Party enjoyed its best performance to date in a parliamentary election, with some 11 per cent of the vote (13 seats). The populist New Zealand First party surprised many observers, with 6.8 per cent of the vote (eight seats). The economy had dominated the election campaign, with Mr Key's National Party promising to tackle national debt by selling stakes in state companies.

Voters appeared to approve of Mr Key's handling of both the Christchurch earthquakes and the deadly blast at the Pike River mine in November 2010. The All Blacks' win in the Rugby World Cup, played in New Zealand in 2011, certainly did Mr Key and his party no harm in the view of most analysts. The November 2011 election also invited New Zealanders to vote on whether to keep proportional representation for the country's elections. The results seemed to indicate most voters (54 per cent) had voted not to change the system they were familiar with.

The National Party's vote went up nationally by 6.5 per cent as that of the Labour Party fell nationally. The election result seemed to be an endorsement of the work done by the government; Labour MPs had spent months complaining about various issues, setting others up to complain, and even offering home owners affected by the earthquake more compensation than that proposed by the National Party. The fact that the Labour vote dropped by over ten per cent in the South Island's biggest city, Christchurch, suggested that Labour needed to re-think its strategy. Christchurch used to be called 'The People's Republic of Christchurch', the home of New Zealand's only 'wizard', but in 2011 it voted more strongly for the National Party than even Auckland. Some analysts suggested that the Labour Party might have a more widespread problem in the South Island.

And the economy?

New Zealand went into recession in mid-2008, a state of affairs that was prolonged by the onset of the global economic crisis. According to NZ Treasury analysis, the NZ economy contracted by 2.1 per cent overall in 2009 but by 2010 was in modest recovery, after experiencing three consecutive quarters of economic growth. Positive export performances have greatly assisted emergence from recession, with Asian demand for key exports such as forestry, dairy and meat rallying.

However, the expected recovery of the New Zealand economy during the second half of 2010 failed to materialise due to lacklustre consumer spending and the September 2010 Christchurch earthquake. Rebuilding Christchurch was a major objective of the New Zealand government's 19 May 2011 budget. NZ Treasury estimated the overall cost of the earthquakes at NZ$15 billion (US$11.45 billion) (eight per cent of GDP), with direct costs to the government of around NZ$8.8 billion (US$6.7 billion). The budget established a separate Canterbury Earthquake Recovery Fund appropriation of NZ$5.5 billion (US$4.2 billion) over six years to cover infrastructure, policy and emergency response costs.

The budget has trimmed funding for social and savings programmes inherited from the previous Labour-led government and 'reprioritised' existing funding in government agencies, with NZ$5.2 billion (US$3.6 billion) of savings to existing expenditure identified over the next five years. NZ$4 billion (US$3.1 billion) of those savings will be redirected to new spending in health; education; and national infrastructure projects such as Ultra-Fast Broadband, rail, schools and highway and electricity networks. The remaining NZ$1.2 billion (US$0.76 billion) will be used to reduce the government deficit over the next four years. Changes were made to government social programmes such as KiwiSaver, Working for Families and interest-free student loans. The government's estimates for economic growth over the next four years are positive, based on the boosts to the economy by the Rugby World Cup, rebuilding in Christchurch and continuing high commodity prices. They forecast growth at 1 per cent of GDP in 2011, 1.8 per cent in 2012, soaring to 4 per cent in 2013 before dropping to 3 per cent and 2.7 per cent in 2014 and 2015 respectively.

In its mid-2011 report on the New Zealand economy the International Monetary Fund (IMF) noted that recovery had stalled since mid-2010, reflecting soft domestic demand and the adverse impact of the two large earthquakes. Domestic demand has remained soft, as cautious households and businesses strengthened their balance sheets by slowing debt accumulation amid a weak housing market and an uncertain outlook. Moreover, the earthquakes had caused substantial damage and hurt confidence. Spare capacity helped contain inflation. The unemployment rate had hovered between 6–7 per cent in 2010, limiting labour cost growth. Following signs of recovery, the Reserve Bank of New Zealand (RBNZ) lifted its interest rate from a record low of 2.5 per cent to 3 per cent in mid-2010. As the recovery softened, the rate was kept on hold in late 2010 and early 2011. In mid-March 2011, the RBNZ reduced the interest rate

KEY INDICATORS — New Zealand

	Unit	2006	2007	2008	2009	2010
Population	m	4.14	4.24	4.28	*4.32	*4.37
Gross domestic product (GDP)	US$bn	105.34	131.00	131.10	117.80	140.40
GDP per capita	US$	25,129	31,063	30,777	27,293	32,130
GDP real growth	%	1.5	2.7	-0.1	-2.0	1.5
Inflation	%	3.4	2.4	4.0	2.1	2.3
Unemployment	%	3.8	3.6	4.2	6.4	6.7
Natural gas output	bn cum	3.9	4.0	3.8	4.0	*3.9
Coal output	mtoe	3.6	1.7	3.1	2.8	3.3
Exports (fob) (goods)	US$m	22,574.0	27,350.0	31,168.0	25,352.0	31,885.0
Imports (fob) (goods)	US$m	24,573.0	29,057.0	32,459.0	23,954.0	29,518.0
Balance of trade	US$m	-1,999.0	-1,708.0	-1,591.0	1,398.0	2,367.0
Current account	US$m	-9,082.0	-10,565.0	-11,322.0	-3,694.0	-5,903.0
Total reserves minus gold	US$m	14,068.0	17,247.0	11,153.0	15,594.0	16,723.0
Foreign exchange	US$m	13,916.0	17,124.0	10,955.0	13,982.0	15,133.0
Exchange rate	per US$	1.54	1.39	1.42	1.60	1.39

* estimated figure

by 50 basis points to limit downside risks as a result of the February earthquake.

The IMF noted that permanent income tax cuts and spending increases that were announced before the global crisis and introduced in late 2008 had provided a stimulus, but had also worsened the fiscal outlook. The fiscal deficit was projected to increase sharply to about 8 per cent of GDP in 2010/11, reflecting the impact of the earthquakes and slower-than-expected economic recovery.

New Zealand's banks remained profitable and capital adequacy improved. Non-performing loans increased to 2 per cent of total loans, still low by advanced country standards, and sound regulation and supervision helped maintain stability. Prudential measures and market pressures led to a reduction in the banks' sizable short-term wholesale borrowing.

The current account deficit narrowed to 2.25 per cent of GDP in 2010, well below the levels of about 8 per cent of GDP in 2005–08. This reflects weak domestic demand, terms of trade gains, and reinsurance inflows following the first earthquake. Net foreign liabilities have declined since 2008 but remained high at 82 per cent of GDP at end-2010. The trade-weighted exchange rate appreciated by about 30 per cent from the trough in early 2009 to April 2011, driven by higher commodity prices.

In the view of the IMF some uncertainty surrounded the economic outlook, particularly related to the size and timing of reconstruction from the earthquakes. In the near term, the earthquakes were expected to slow activity, with GDP growth projected at one per cent in 2011. For 2012, growth will be led by reconstruction.

Risk assessment

Economy	Fair
Politics	Good
Regional stability	Good

COUNTRY PROFILE

Historical profile

Migrants from Polynesia arrived in New Zealand and colonised it between 800–1000AD.

1642 Dutch explorer Abel Tasman was the first European to sight New Zealand.

1769 and 1779 British explorer James Cook charted the islands of New Zealand. After his second voyage, British and other European settlers began to arrive.

1815 The first British missionaries arrived in New Zealand.

1840 European settlers and the Mäori tribes signed the *Treaty of Waitangi*, under which European settlers agreed to respect Mäori land rights in return for recognition of British rule. The Treaty is generally considered to be the founding document of the nation.

1845–47 Mäoris revolted against land loss.

1852 New Zealand became a self-governing British colony.

1858 A series of major Mäori revolts began in response to encroachments by Europeans on to Mäori land.

1860–72 Mäoris revolted again. The conflict was resolved after the Europeans promised to abide by the *Treaty of Waitangi*.

1893 New Zealand became the first country to give women the right to vote.

1898 The government introduced old age pensions.

1907 New Zealand became an independent dominion within the British Empire.

1914–18 New Zealand fought alongside the UK during the First World War and suffered heavy casualties in the Gallipoli campaign in Turkey in 1915.

1931 The Westminster Declaration established the concept of a Commonwealth between the UK, New Zealand and several other former British colonies.

1939–45 New Zealand fought alongside the UK during the Second World War.

1947 Dominion status began to be phased out and replaced by the Commonwealth.

1951 New Zealand formed the ANZUS military pact with Australia and the US.

1963 New Zealand agreed to provide a military presence in Vietnam – initially with military advisors.

1965 Under increasing US pressure for the commitment of troops in Vietnam, a non-combative engineering force was augmented by a field artillery battery of around 120 men.

1972 The last New Zealand troops were withdrawn from Vietnam.

1975 A legal tribunal ruled that there should be an investigation into whether Mäori land rights under the *Treaty of Waitangi* had been systematically ignored. This led to a vast number of lawsuits under which Mäori tribes demanded financial reparations for the illegal confiscation of their lands.

1984 Prime Minister David Lange declared New Zealand a 'nuclear free zone' and forbade nuclear-powered vessels to dock at New Zealand ports.

1985 French secret agents bombed and destroyed the Greenpeace ship *Rainbow Warrior* in Auckland Harbour, killing one person.

1986 US suspended ANZUS obligations towards New Zealand.

1989 Lange resigned and was replaced by Geoffrey Palmer.

1990 The National Party (Nationals) won its first election victory for 10 years, with Jim Bolger becoming prime minister.

1993 The Nationals won the general elections. A referendum on electoral reform showed a majority in favour of proportional representation.

1996 New Zealand adopted a new parliamentary electoral system called Mixed Member Proportional (MMP) representation, which was designed to give better representation for smaller parties and the Mäori community.

1997 Bolger resigned rather than face a leadership challenge from cabinet minister Jenny Shipley, who went on to become New Zealand's first woman prime minister.

1998 The NP-led coalition collapsed, leaving the NP as a minority government reliant on support from independent MPs.

1999 New Zealand sent troops to join UN peace-keeping forces in East Timor. The opposition New Zealand Labour Party (NZLP) won general elections.

2001 The government re-nationalised Air New Zealand 12 years after it had been privatised.

2004 Official contact with Israel was suspended after two Israelis were jailed for attempting to obtain New Zealand passports for Mossad agents. A law was passed making all of the coastline public property; Mäori opposition claimed the law infringed the *Treaty of Waitangi*.

2005 Former prime minister David Lange died. Prime Minister Helen Clark formed a coalition government following an indecisive general election.

2006 Anand Satyanand became governor general. Te Arikinui Dame Te Atairangikaahu, the Great Chief of the Mäori population died, her eldest son Tuheitia Paki, became her successor.

2008 In parliamentary elections the opposition Nationals won 45.5 per cent of the vote (59 seats out of 122), the NZLP 33.8 per cent (43). John Key (Nationals) became prime minister.

2009 The economy recorded its worst official figures since the early 1990s as a recession was declared after growth fell for five consecutive quarter. Unemployment rose to 6 per cent in the second quarter (from a low of 3.5 per cent in the fourth quarter of 2007).

2010 in January, Fiji and New Zealand re-established diplomatic relations which had been broken in 2008. A settlement was reached in June between the government and Mäori negotiators, which allowed Mäoris the rights of 'customary title' to coastlines they have occupied since the *Treaty of Waitangi* (1840).

2011 On 22 February an earthquake struck Christchurch, New Zealand's second city, around mid-day, flattening some and damaging many buildings, including the spire of the iconic Christchurch Cathedral. By 28 February, following all hope that anyone else could be rescued alive, 163 people had been killed and over 300 people were still missing. The 23 February national census was postponed and re-scheduled for March 2013, due to the disruption caused by Christchurch earthquake. The estimate of damage was US$15 billion (NZ$20 billion); the government provided an initial support package of NZ$120 million to pay people unable to work due to the loss of business and workplaces. Engineers declared that over 30 per cent of all buildings in the centre of the city would have to be demolished and that hundreds of suburban homes may also need to be razed. The estimated cost of the damage caused by the earthquake had doubled by 31 August, to US$5.759 billion. Lieutenant-General Sir Jerry Mataparae was appointed as governor general, taking up his post on 31 August; he is the first Māori to be appointed to the position. During the Commonwealth Heads of Government summit, on 28 October, the 16 countries in which the British monarch is Head of State unanimously agreed to change the royal line of succession from that of first born son to the first born child (regardless of its gender). The change will be enacted after the succession of Prince William (currently second in line to the throne, after his father Prince Charles). Parliamentary elections were held on 26 November, in which the ruling Nationals won 48 per cent of the vote and increased its seats to 60 (up from 59 in 2008) out of 121, the opposition Labour Party won 27.1 per cent, winning 34 seats, losing nine from the last election. Prime Minister Key's coalition government has the strength and backing to control parliamentary business with the aid of one other parliamentarian. A referendum was also held on 26 November with the proposition should New Zealand keep the mixed member proportional (MMP) voting system; 53.74 per cent voted yes and 42.62 per cent voted no. The NP formed a coalition government with ACT and the UF on 5 December.

Political structure

Constitution

New Zealand has no written constitution. Its constitutional history dates back to the signing of the *Treaty of Waitangi* in 1840, when the indigenous Māori people ceded sovereignty over New Zealand to the British monarch. The Constitution Act 1986 brought together the most important constitutional provisions.

New Zealand is an independent parliamentary democracy and member of the Commonwealth. Government is based on the Westminster (United Kingdom) model.

Form of state

Constitutional monarchy

The executive

The head of state is the British sovereign, represented by a governor general who acts on the advice of the cabinet. The governor general is appointed by the sovereign on the advice of the New Zealand government.

The prime minister and cabinet are responsible to the legislature and are appointed by the governor general acting upon its advice. The prime minister and cabinet must be chosen from among elected members of parliament.

The Executive Council is a formal body made up of the cabinet and the governor general, who acts on the cabinet's advice. The cabinet consists of the prime minister and ministers, who must be chosen from among elected members of parliament.

National legislature

The unicameral parliament (the House of Representatives) typically has 120 members. Of which 70 are directly elected in 70 electorates (constituencies) with roughly the same number of voters. However as the South Island has a smaller population it has 16 guaranteed seats; elsewhere the voter numbers are divided by 16 to determine electorate boundaries, which may lead to a fluctuation in the total number of representatives elected. Seven seats are reserved for Māori representatives. There are an additional 50 members elected in national seats determined by proportional representation from party lists to reflect the overall share of votes cast. All members serve for up to three years.

Authority for raising revenue by taxation and for public expenditure must be granted by parliament. It also controls the government through its power to pass a resolution of no confidence.

Legal system

The law consists of common law, New Zealand statutes and some British statutes. The judiciary is independent from the executive. High Court judges, who also sit on the Court of Appeal, are appointed by the governor general and cannot be removed from office except by the sovereign or the governor general.

Last elections

26 November 2011 (parliamentary and referendum)

Results: Parliamentary: National Party (Nationals) 48 per cent of the vote (60 seats of 121), the Labour Party 27.1 per cent (34), the Green Party 10.6 per cent (13), New Zealand First 6.8 per cent (8), the Maori Party 1.4 per cent (3), ACT New Zealand 1.7 per cent (one), Mana 1 per cent (one), United Future 0.61 per cent (one); five other political parties polled too few votes and failed to win any seats. Turnout was 73.8 per cent.

Referendum: the proposition was, should New Zealand keep the mixed member proportional (MMP) voting system; 53.74 per cent voted yes and 42.62 per cent voted no.

Next elections

November 2011 (parliamentary)

Political parties

Ruling party

Coalition led by the National Party, with ACT New Zealand (ACT) and United Future (UF) (from 2008; re-elected 26 Nov 2011)

Main opposition party

The Labour Party

Population

4.37 million (2010)*

Last census: 7 March 2006: 4,143,282

Population density: 14 inhabitants per square km. Urban population: 86 per cent (1995–2001).

Annual growth rate: 1.0 per cent 1994–2004 (WHO 2006)

Ethnic make-up

Approximately 77.3 per cent of the population is of European origin, with Māoris representing another 14.5 per cent, Pacific Islanders 5.6 per cent and others 2.6 per cent. Pacific Islanders are attracted by job opportunities and a higher standard of living. However, socio-economic problems plague the Māoris and Pacific Islanders.

Religions

Anglican (25 per cent), Presbyterian (18 per cent), Roman Catholic (15 per cent), Methodist (5 per cent), Baptist (2 per cent) and other Christian religions (34 per cent).

Education

Education is free and secondary admission is non-selective. Primary education covers ages five to 12 years and secondary education ages 13 to 16 years. A one-year sixth form follows and leads to a one-year pre-university course.

Public expenditure on education is typically 7 per cent of GNP. Nearly NZ$30 million (US$14.5 million) was allocated to implement the government's policy of equity funding for the early childhood education sector and funding for adult literacy was doubled, to NZ$18 million (US$8.7 million) as part of the Adult Literacy Strategy.

A campaign was launched that targets the Māori community called *Te Mana*, with a specific objective of providing education

from a Mäori perspective to youths, parents, life-long learners and teachers. It uses television, IT and a magazine, which has expanded to include study guides and a website, with relevent, current and contemporary tutoring.
Literacy rate: 99 per cent, adult rate
Compulsory years: Six to 17
Enrolment rate: 101 per cent gross primary enrolment of the relevant age group (including repeaters); 113 per cent gross secondary enrolment (World Bank).
Pupils per teacher: 18 in primary schools

Health
The health system is made up of the public, private and voluntary sectors. The public sector provides free treatment at hospitals for immediate and major medical problems as well as chronic complaints, some continuing care and maternity and geriatric care. It also provides health benefits and subsidises pharmaceutical benefits and laboratory tests. The provision of mental health services is largely the responsibility of the public sector (with a small voluntary sector contribution) caring for both acute and chronic cases. It also provides free dental health treatment for school-age children. The public sector meets more than three-quarters of the total cost of healthcare and subsidises healthcare provided by general practitioners and specialists in private practice.
Private healthcare includes services provided by general practitioners, dentists, pharmacists and therapists in both public and private hospitals. The state subsidises many of these services although the main feature of this sector is the steady and rapid growth of private health and medical insurance.
HIV/Aids
HIV prevalence: 0.1 per cent aged 15–49 in 2003 (World Bank)
Life expectancy: 80 years, 2004 (WHO 2006)
Fertility rate/Maternal mortality rate: 2.0 births per woman, 2004 (WHO 2006); maternal mortality 15 per 100,000 live births (World Bank)
Birth rate/Death rate: 15 births and Seven deaths per 1,000 people (World Bank)
Child (under 5 years) mortality rate (per 1,000): 5.0 per 1,000 live births (World Bank)
Head of population per physician: 2.37 physicians per 1,000 people, 2001 (WHO 2006)

Welfare
New Zealand Superannuation (NZS), which is a universal, publicly provided pension, is at the core of its retirement income system provided to everyone over the age of 64 years and who meet certain residential qualifications. It is estimated that more than 92 per cent of older people receive NZS.
The government has tried to develop the welfare system, which actively works with beneficiaries to boost their skills. In 2002/03, a NZ$3 million (US$1.4 million) pilot programme was initiated to encourage sickness and invalids benefit recipients to participate in paid work and community-based activities.

Main cities
North Island: Wellington (capital, estimated population 184,257 in 2005); Auckland (426,457), Hamilton (155,698); Tauranga (108,756).
South Island: Christchurch (367,663), Dunedin (115,233), Nelson (59,587), Invercargill (48,371).

Languages spoken
Some Polynesian dialects are spoken and a variety of other languages, reflecting the diverse origins of New Zealand's immigrant population.
Official language/s
English, Mäori

Media
There is a free press although media content is subject to libel and contempt of court rulings. Media groups are privately owned by mostly international corporations.
Press
Ownership of the print media is dominated by Fairfax New Zealand and APN News and Media.
Dailies: There is no genuinely nationally circulated daily although, from Auckland, *The New Zealand Herald* (www.nzherald.co.nz) which has the largest circulation and from Wellington the *Dominion Post* (www.stuff.co.nz/dominionpost), can be purchased outside their core regions. Other city based newspapers include, from Christchurch *The Press* (www.thepress.co.nz) with the largest circulation in the South Island and *Otago Daily Times* (www.odt.co.nz) from Dunedin. There are a number of regional, daily newspapers which delivers up to date news covering local issues.
Weeklies: There are numerous magazines which cater for all interests. Many local newspapers are published once a week, including *Sunday Star Times* (www.sstlive.co.nz) and *Sunday News* (www.sundaynews.co.nz) is a tabloid along with *New Zealand Truth* (http://truth.co.nz). The *New Zealand Listener* (www.listener.co.nz) is a respected current affairs magazine. A publications for young women is *Indigo* (www.indigomag.co.nz), and *New Zealand Women's Weekly* (www.nzww.co.nz) for older women.
Business: There are several publications on offer including the daily *Businessday* (www.businessday.co.nz), the weekly *National Business Review* (www.nbr.co.nz) and the monthly *NZ Business* (www.nzbusiness.co.nz) and *Business to Business* (www.btob.co.nz). The monthly *University of Auckland Business Review* (www.uabr.auckland.ac.nz) and *Unlimited* (www.unlimited.co.nz) are journals reporting on emerging business issues, while *Her Business Magazine* (www.herbusinessmagazine.com) targets businesswomen.
Periodicals: The majority of local magazines and community newsletters are published monthly, including those which provide news in the Maori-language, such as the bi-monthly *Mana* covering Maori current affairs, and other languages of the Pacific communities such as Niuean, Tongan and Samoan. In English, popular monthly magazines include *Investigate* (www.investigatemagazine.com) on current affairs, *Metro* (www.metrolive.co.nz) on lifestyle and the annual *Jet Magazine* (www.jetmag.co.nz) a free-issue publication aimed at a youth market with articles on careers, education and training.
Broadcasting
Radio: Radio New Zealand (RNZ) (www.radionz.co.nz), it the national, public station with three networks: National Radio, Concert FM and AM Network. RNZ also operates an international service broadcasting mostly to the South Pacific via shortwave. There are numerous, private, commercial stations throughout the islands including Newstalk ZB (www.newstalkzb.co.nz) from Auckland, The Rock (www.therock.net.nz) from Wellington, Radio Live (www.radiolive.co.nz) from Christchurch and More FM (http://dunedin.morefm.co.nz) from Dunedin.
There are several government-funded and privately-owned radio stations broadcasting in the Maori-language.
Television: Analogue signals are expected to be replaced by digital services by no later than 2013. There are almost a dozen free-to-air channels, including those provided through digital signals. Pay-to-view TV is available via satellite and cable distribution.
The state-owned Television New Zealand (TVNZ) is funded by advertising revenue and is in competition for ratings with commercial TV networks, including TV3 (www.tv3.co.nz) and Prime TV (www.primetv.co.nz). There are local TV stations located in major towns and cities with minority interests such as the Chinese-language CTV8 (www.wtv.co.nz) or

horse and dog racing TAB Trackside (www.trackside.co.nz) or music and live performance such as C4 (www.c4tv.co.nz). Maori Television (www.maoritelevision.com) is a public channel.

Advertising

The Advertising Standard Authority (www.asa.co.nz) sets out the official principles and guidelines for all advertising. Newspapers earn the most from adspend at over NZ$800 million (US$586 million) in 2007, followed by television at over NZ$650 million (US$476 million). Radio and magazine advertising revenue amounts to around NZ$300 million (US$569 million) each and all other adspend, of less than NZ$20 million (US$14.6 million), is distributed between, among others, outdoor, direct mail, cinema and modern interactive advertising. The trend for advertising turnover 2002–07 shows a fall in all mediums, with the exception of interactive which grew steadily (albeit from a low baseline).

News agencies

New Zealand Press Association: www.nzpa-online.co.nz
Scoop: www.scoop.co.nz

Economy

New Zealand, a once agrarian economy with more head of sheep than people, has since moved to become a fully industrialised nation with a market economy that trades freely with its international partners. It has a historical tie to Australia, its largest single trading partner – merchandise trade totalled A$15,077 million (US$15,734 million) in 2010–11; Australian foreign direct investment (FDI) was A$38,947 million (US$40,645 million) in 2010. There is an agreement between the two countries whereby goods and services are traded freely, forming a single market. Agricultural produce, of meat (particularly lamb) and live animals, dairy, wool, wine, fruit and vegetables, is still the primary export, and totalled NZ$26,501 million (US$16,832 million) in 2009, while merchandise exports in total accounted for NZ$41,408 million (US$26,301 million). Other important industries include financial services, tourism, education and information technology and telecommunications.
GDP growth was 2.8 per cent in 2007, but as the global economic crisis struck in 2008 the economy slipped into recession with GDP growth of -0.1 per cent, which deepened to -2.0 per cent in 2009 and became the longest recession in New Zealand's history. GDP growth was 0.2 per cent in the last quarter of 2010, which boosted the annual rate of growth to 1.5 per cent. However, as the earthquake in Christchurch on 22 February 2011 will have an adverse impact on production and government spending, GDP growth was expected to decline in 2011, even though the Rugby World Cup, which was held in September and October 2011, was forecast to boost the economy by some US$1.2 billion.
Inflation which had been 2.4 per cent in 2007 jumped to 4.0 per cent in 2008, but fell back again in 2009 to 2.1 per cent due to weak economic activity and a drop in global oil prices. Unemployment grew steadily from 4.5 per cent in 2008 to 6.4 per cent in 2009 and remaining steady at 6.7 per cent in 2010. As a result, GDP per capita income fell from US$31,063 in 2007 to US$30,777 in 2008 and further still to US$27,293 in 2009; it rebounded to US$32,130 in 2010.

External trade

New Zealand (NZ) is a member of the South Pacific Regional Trade and Economic Co-operation Agreement (Sparteca) along with 13 regional nations, which allows products duty free access by Pacific Island Forum members to Australian and NZ markets (subject to the country of origin restrictions). Australia and NZ have formed a single market under their Closer Economic Relations (CER) agreement, which allows free trade in goods and many services. NZ is a member of the Trans-Pacific Strategic Economic Partnership (TPP) to liberalise trade in goods and services between Chile, Brunei and, if negotiations begun in 2008 are successful, the US. NZ has a number of bilateral free trade agreements (BFTA), notably with Thailand, China and Malaysia. Negotiations are underway for BFTAs with Japan and South Korea.
Exports contribute over 60 per cent of GDP, of which around 50 per cent is provided by agriculture produce. NZ supplies almost 40 per cent of mutton and lamb exports worldwide.

Imports

Main imports include vehicles, machinery and equipment, vehicles and aircraft, petroleum, electronics, textiles and plastics.
Main sources: Australia (typically 18 per cent of total), China (13 per cent), US (10 per cent).

Exports

Main exports include mutton and lamb, dairy products, timber and fish and light manufacturing including machinery.
Main destinations: Australia (typically 23 per cent of total), US (10 per cent), Japan (8 per cent).

Agriculture

Farming

The New Zealand (NZ) agricultural sector is almost unique among its developed nation competitors in being virtually free of subsidies, with farming produce being forced to compete against that produced in countries that do provide subsidies and incentives to their farmers. With a level of producer support estimate of 1 per cent (the OECD average is around 31 per cent) the agricultural industry still provides around 70 per cent of export earnings. The removal of subsidies was both a burden and a boon to the NZ industry. Farmers contended with a fluctuating international market, which was dependent on the state of the general economy and specifically the value of the NZ dollar, while reorganising and diversifying. To compete, the industry shed obsolete equipment and old practices in favour of reinvestment and embracing market economies. The industry also adopted the latest research and development findings, applying biotechnology and information technology to improve productivity.
Beef and sheep farming have been the mainstay of the country's agricultural sector for over a century. Since subsidies were withdrawn in 1982, these sectors have been rationalised and have seen a fall in the number of farms and animals. Productivity in meat and wool has increased since 1994 with 14 per cent more lambs born to 32 per cent fewer ewes. Weight gain of the average lamb at slaughter and lamb meat production have increased.
Production of sheep suffered during the winter of 2010 when freak snow and hailstorms, the worst recorded, killed up to one million lambs across New Zealand.
Dairy farming, particularly in the South Island, has increased with the addition of 1,650 new farms since 1994; the number of dairy cows rose by 52 per cent to 5.24 million.
The agriculture, fishing and forestry sectors together account for approximately 7–8 per cent of GDP and provide employment for over 11 per cent of the workforce. Of the total land area, grazing accounts for almost 12 million hectares (ha), horticulture over 100,000ha and planted forests 1.9 million ha.
Deer farming has led to a rapid growth in venison exports, and goats are reared for mohair. Wheat production is sufficient to meet national demand, as do crops including barley, maize and fresh vegetables. Other products include apples, pears, stone and berry fruits, citrus and sub-tropical fruits.

Fishing

The seafood industry is one of New Zealand's top five export earners. The total fish catch is typically around 700,000 tonnes per annum, of which 80 per cent is produced through marine fishing.
Following the annual meeting of the Commission for the Conservation of

Southern Bluefin Tuna (CCSBT), held on Cheju Island, South Korea, all members agreed to a 20 per cut in the roughly 17,000 tonnes in 2009 bluefin tuna catches from 2010. Scientists had warned that without a cut fish stocks could crash as numbers had become dangerously low.

Forestry

Forests cover about 27 per cent (eight million ha) of New Zealand's land area. Of this, around 6.2 million ha are indigenous forest and 1.9 million ha are plantations. The majority of plantations, cultivating exotic species, are in the central region of North Island. Some 95 per cent of plantations grow exotic softwoods, of which 80 per cent are *Pinus Radiata*, 10 per cent Douglas Fir and 10 per cent other species. The state owns 55 per cent of the exotic resource, with forestry companies, Māori incorporates, local authorities and individuals owning the remainder. Chile is New Zealand's major competitor in the market for *Pinus Radiata*. The planting of exotic species began on a large scale in 1923; there was a second major planting in the 1960s and these trees are now reaching maturity, which will boost the supply of mature trees over the medium-term. In the long term a vibrant log processing industry, comparable to that of the southern US, could be developed.

Industry and manufacturing

The industrial sector typically accounts for under a fifth of GDP, employs just over a fifth of the workforce, and accounts for a similar proportion of export earnings.
The industrialisation that took place from the mid-1980s helped increase the added value of New Zealand's traditional sectors. Meat, dairy and fruit produce are processed in New Zealand for markets in Asia and Europe. Biotechnology, communications and information technology are also sectors growing in importance.

Tourism

Tourism is one of the principal earner of foreign exchange. The sector, which provides employment for around 10 per cent of the workforce, typically contributes over 7 per cent to GDP. Visitor numbers continue to rise, drawn by the magnificent landscapes and layed back lifestyle of New Zealand.

Mining

The mining sector typically accounts for 2 per cent of GDP and employs 1.5 per cent of the workforce. Gold, silver, ironsand, clays, sand and aggregates are the main minerals mined. Ironsand is used to produce steel and is exported to Japan. Other metals include tungsten, manganese, copper, lead, zinc, tin, mercury (as cinnabar), platinum, titanium and aluminium (as bauxite). Non-metallic minerals include aggregates for roads; clays for ceramics and fillers; bentonite for bonding and drilling; limestone for agriculture and cement; and dolomite, serpentine, silica sand, sulphur, diatomite, mica, pumice and feldspar.

Hydrocarbons

Proven oil reserves were 148 million barrels (plus 69 million barrels in non-productive fields) in 2008, with production at 59,990 barrels per day (bpd). However, consumption is around 153,940bpd and New Zealand has to import petroleum products to meet its domestic demand. Refinery capacity is 107,000bpd.
Hydrocarbon fields are located onshore in the Taranaki Basin, yielding oil and gas-condensates and offshore in the Maui natural gas-condensate field as well as the Kupe and Pohokura gas discoveries.
Proven natural gas reserves were 25.5 billion cubic metres (cum) in 2008, with production at 4.6 billion cum and consumption of 3.7 billion cum. There is a 3,100km network of transmission pipelines and a 7,900km network of natural gas pipelines throughout North Island, allowing a deregulated market with a number of competing energy companies ready to supply gas to customers, using the network. Natural gas supplies are not available in South Island.
Proven coal reserves were 571 million tonnes in 2007, of which most, 538 million tonnes, was brown coal or lignite typically used for power generation.
Production was 2.8 million tonnes of oil equivalent (mtoe) a fall of 20.9 per cent on the 2006 figure of 3.5mtoe. Coal exports to Japan, India, South Africa, South America, Europe and China accounted for 2.2 million tonnes of output, with the remainder used in domestic power generation.

Energy

Total installed generating capacity was 8.86 gigawatts in 2007, producing 42.4 billion kilowatt hours. Around 70 per cent of generated electricity is produced from renewable sources, in particular hydropower and geothermal power.
The Huntly Power Station, situated close to Auckland, is the largest thermal power station in the country, producing up to 17 per cent of primary energy. Despite two upgrades, with the addition of new gas-fired turbine plants allowing production of 1,485MW, the station is destined to be closed by 2015, due to New Zealand's agreement on reducing its carbon dioxide emissions. However, decommissioning may be delayed if an alternative energy provider is not found to accommodate the annual growth in energy consumption, particularly in the Auckland area.

Financial markets

Stock exchange

New Zealand Stock Exchange (NZX)

Banking and insurance

Banking has been opened up to international competition, but domestic demand for credit remains weak. All but one of New Zealand's 18 banks are foreign-owned.

Central bank

The Reserve Bank of New Zealand (RBNZ) formulates and implements monetary policy and is the supervisory authority for New Zealand's registered banks.

Main financial centre

Wellington

Time

GMT plus 13 hours October–March;
GMT plus 12 hours March–October.

Geography

New Zealand is in the south-west Pacific, 1,600km south-east of Australia, separated from it by the Tasman Sea, and has no continental neighbours to the east before South America. Its combined length is over 1,600km and it is about 450km across at its widest point. Mount Cook in the Southern Alps is its highest point at 3,764 metres – one of more than 230 named peaks above 2,300 metres.
It consists of two main islands (North Island and South Island – usually referred to by locals as the mainland, as it is the larger of the two islands) and other outlying islands, the Stewart Island, off the southern tip of South Island and the Chatham Islands, 800km east of the South Island.
Geologically speaking, New Zealand is one of the youngest countries in the world, with a topography that is still being shaped by earthquakes, active volcanoes and glaciers.
The North Island has low-lying, rolling hills that rise to around 1,700 metres and form the heart of the area, with rich farmland on all sides. Lake Taupo, the largest in the North Island, is almost in the centre of the range, which is dominated by a volcanic plateau at Rotorua.
The South Island is much more rugged, with the Southern Alps that rise to over 3,000 metres running the length of the island. West of the Alps are rainforests and to the east farmland and the alluvial plains formed by rivers flowing down from the mountains. The Southern Alps contain glaciers, the largest of which is the Tasman glacier.
Stewart Island is largely low rolling hills which, unlike the two main islands, retains almost all of its native vegetation.

Hemisphere
Southern

Climate
New Zealand is a temperate country with a variable and unpredictable climate, generally drier and warmer on North Island than on South Island, particularly in winter. Rainfall averages 600–1,500mm annually and strong winds are common. On North Island, January temperatures average 18 degrees Celsius (C) and in winter 4 degrees C. It is 3 to 5 degrees C colder on South Island.

Dress codes
Visitors should take warm clothing during the winter months, from May to October. Even in the summer, from December to early March, a light sweater is an essential travelling item. Suits are worn for business meetings. For leisure, smart casual clothes are acceptable.

Entry requirements
Passports
Passports are required by all and must be valid for three months beyond the intended length of stay.
Visa
Required by all, except visitors from visa free countries. For a full list see www.immigration.govt.nz. Business visas may not be required for company representatives, a visitors visa is sufficient for stays up to three months. However proof of onward/return tickets and sufficient funds are required.
Currency advice/regulations
There are no restrictions on the import and export of local or foreign currencies.
Customs
Equipment used with animals, camping equipment, golf clubs and used bicycles must be declared.
Personal effects are allowed duty-free: 200 cigarettes, 4.5 litres of wine/beer, or goods up to the value of NZ$700 (or equivalent) are permitted.
Visitors arriving from countries suffering from certain diseases affecting livestock and plants may have items of clothing and produce disinfected.
Prohibited imports
Illegal drugs, plants or plant material, animals or by-products (these include any fruit, vegetables or meat – cooked or raw), biological specimens, artifacts made from endangered wildlife and weapons, such as flick knives, are prohibited. Firearms and ammunition require a permit.

Health (for visitors)
A reciprocal health agreement for urgent medical treatment exists with the United Kingdom. Some proof of UK residence will be required.
Mandatory precautions
There are no compulsory vaccinations.
Advisable precautions
Travellers are advised to have up-to-date tetanus and polio immunisations.

Hotels
Motel, serviced-unit accommodation is widespread. Neither a service charge nor tipping is customary. Advance booking is advisable for major hotels in urban centres.

Credit cards
All major credit cards are accepted.

Public holidays (national)
Fixed dates
1–2 Jan (New Year), 6 Feb (Waitangi Day), 25 Apr (Anzac Day), 25–26 Dec (Christmas).
Variable dates
Easter Holiday, Queen's Official Birthday (first Mon in Jun), Labour Day (Oct).

Working hours
Mid-December to mid-February is the summer holiday season during which the majority of New Zealanders take most of their annual leave.
Banking
Mon–Fri: 0900–1630.
Business
Mon–Fri: 0900–1700.
Government
Mon–Fri: 0800–1630.
Shops
Mon–Thu: 0900–1730; Fri: 0900–2100; Sat: 0900–1230. Some shops open on Sundays.

Telecommunications
Mobile/cell phones
GSM 900, 1800 and 3G services are available throughout most of the country.

Electricity supply
230/240V AC, 50 hertz, with three-pin flat plug fittings, most hotels supply 110V AC sockets for razors.

Weights and measures
Metric system

Social customs/useful tips
In general, be polite and patient. New Zealanders appreciate frankness and like prompt timekeeping for business meetings. Business can also be discussed over lunch and dinner. Late night life can be sparse. People tend to go to bed early and start work early.
Should a visitor be invited to a formal Mäori occasion the *hongi* (pressing of noses) is common.
Tipping is acceptable but is not particularly sought after and there is sometimes a built-in service charge at hotels and restaurants. There is a smoking ban in restaurants and pubs.

Security
The cities are safe, even at night.

Getting there
Air
National airline: Air New Zealand
International airport/s: Auckland International, Mangere (AKL), 22km south of Auckland; Christchurch International (CHC), 10km of the city; Wellington International (WLG), 8km south-east of the city; all with duty-free shop, bar, restaurant, bank, hotel reservations, post office, shops, car hire and office facilities. Taxi journeys from Auckland International Airport to the city centre take 35 minutes; from Christchurch Airport to city centre 15 minutes; from Wellington Airport to city centre 20 minutes.
Airport tax: Departures and security tax: up to NZ$30, depending on the airport; transit passengers up to 24 hours are exempt.
Surface
Water: Apart from cruise ships there are no regular passenger ships sailing to New Zealand. International shipping lines that maintain contacts with New Zealand may provide passenger services on cargo ships.
Main port/s: Auckland (containers), Dunedin, Lyttelton (containers), Tauranga, Wellington (containers), Port Chalmers (containers), Picton, Opua.

Getting about
National transport
Air: There are good regular air services between the four major cities (Wellington, Auckland, Christchurch and Dunedin) with links to smaller, regional towns and tourist centres. Internal air services serve around 30 airports.
Road: The road network includes over 11,000km of state highways. The main routes are surfaced, and roads are generally well-maintained.
On 1 August 2011, the minimum aged of a driver was raised from 15 to 16 years.
Buses: Luxury coach services link the main centres. Advance booking for these is advisable, especially during the main holiday periods (December–February and Easter).
Rail: The rail network operates over 4,300km of track linking cities and main towns with express services that have buffet cars.
Water: Interisland Lines operates a regular ferry service between Wellington and Picton several times a day. Advance booking is advisable, especially during the main holiday periods.
City transport
Taxis: Taxis may be hired from ranks or by telephone 24 hours a day, although there is an extra charge for telephone booking. Fares are generally charged per km, but rates vary throughout the country

and are generally higher at night and on weekends. Tipping is not customary.

Buses, trams & metro: Auckland's integrated transport system, in the city centre, is connected by the Britomart rail network that handles suburban and intercity trains, to buses and ferries. Wellington has a rail-metro with five lines terminating in the city centre. Christchurch has a comprehensive bus-metro.

There are good, privately operated, local buses in all urban areas.

Car hire

Car hire is available throughout the country; drivers must be over 21 years with either a national licence or international driving permit. It is advisable to book ahead at motels when touring. Driving is on the left-hand side of the road. Parking can be a problem in larger cities. Outside the major centres there is little traffic as country areas are sparsely populated.

BUSINESS DIRECTORY

The addresses listed below are a selection only. While World of Information makes every endeavour to check these addresses, we cannot guarantee that changes have not been made, especially to telephone numbers and area codes. We would welcome any corrections.

Telephone area codes

The international direct dialling code (IDD) for New Zealand is +64, followed by area code and subscriber's number:

Auckland	9	Nelson	3
Bay of Plenty	7	New Plymouth	6
Christchurch	3	Palmerston North	6
Dunedin	3	Rotorua	7
Gisborne	6	Tauranga	7
Hamilton	7	The South Island	3
Hastings	6	Timaru	3
Invercargil	3	Wanganui	6
Manawatu	6	Wellington	4
Napier	6	Whangarei	9

Useful telephone numbers

Emergency (all services): 111

Chambers of Commerce

American Chamber of Commerce in New Zealand, Affco House, 12-26 Swanson Street, PO Box 106002, Auckland Central 1001 (tel: 309-9140; fax: 309-1090; e-mail: amcham@amcham.co.nz).

Auckland Chamber of Commerce, 100 Mayoral Drive, PO Box 47, Auckland (tel: 309-6100; fax: 309-0081; e-mail: akl@chamber.co.nz).

British New Zealand Trade Council, PO Box 37162, Parnell, Auckland (tel/fax: 522-0526; e-mail: info@bnztc.co.nz).

Canterbury Employers Chamber of Commerce, 57 Kilmore Street, PO Box 359, Christchurch (tel: 366-5096; fax: 379-5454; e-mail: info@cecc.org.nz).

New Zealand Chambers of Commerce & Industry, 109 Featherston Street, PO Box 11043, Wellington (tel: 472-3376; fax: 471-1767).

Otago Chamber of Commerce & Industry, WestpacTrust Building, 106 George Street, Dunedin (tel: 479-0181; fax: 477-0341; e-mail: office@otagochamber.co.nz).

Wellington Regional Chamber of Commerce, 109 Featherston Street, PO Box 1590, Wellington 6015 (tel: 914-6500; fax: 914-6524; e-mail: info@wgtn-chamber.co.nz).

Banking

ANZ Banking Group (New Zealand) Limited, PO Box 1492, ANZ Tower, Level 9, 215-229 Lambton Quay, Wellington (tel: 496-6938; fax: 496-6934).

ASB Bank Ltd, 198-204 Lambton Quay, Wellington (tel: 499-0864; fax: 495-2102).

Bank of New Zealand, PO Box 2392, State Insurance Centre, 1 Willis Street, Wellington (tel: 474-6999; fax: 474-6861).

BNZ Finance Ltd; PO Box 401, Level 24, BNZ Centre, 1 Willis Street, Wellington (tel: 495-3630; fax: 495-3632).

National Bank of New Zealand Ltd, PO Box 1791, 1 Victoria Street, Wellington 6000 (tel: 498-6020; fax: 494-4023).

Reserve Bank of New Zealand, PO Box 2498, 2 The Terrace, Wellington (tel: 472-2029; fax: 473-8554).

Westpac Banking Corporation, PO Box 691, 157 Lambton Quay, Wellington (tel: 381-1430; fax: 470-8202).

Central bank

Reserve Bank of New Zealand, 2 The Terrace, PO Box 2498, Wellington (tel: 472-2029; fax: 473-8554; e-mail: rbnz-info@rbnz.govt.nz).

Stock exchange

New Zealand Stock Exchange (NZX): www.nzx.com

Travel information

Air New Zealand, Customer Support, Private Bag 92007, Auckland 1020 (tel: 255-8758; fax: 256-3531; internet site: www.airnz.co.nz/).

Intercity Coachlines (InterCity Group (NZ)), PO Box 26 601, Epsom, Auckland (tel: 623-1503; email: info@intercitygroup.co.nz; internet site: www.intercitycoach.co.nz).

Interislander (ferry service) (Ticket Office) PO Box 2085, Wellington (tel: 498-3302; fax: 498-3090; email: info@interislander.co.nz; internet site: www.interislander.co.nz).

Trains: tel (outside NZ): (+64-4) 495-0775; fax: (+64-4) 4728903; tel inside NZ: 0800-872-467; email: bookings@tranzscenic.co.nz; internet: www.transcenic.co.nz).

National tourist organisation offices

New Zealand Tourism Board, level 16, 80 The Terrace, PO Box 95, Wellington (tel: 917-5400; fax: 915-3817; internet: www.purenz.com).

Ministries

Ministry of Agriculture and Fisheries, PO Box 2526, Wellington (tel: 474-4100; fax: 474-4111).

Ministry of Civil Defence, PO Box 5010, Wellington (tel: 473-7363; fax: 473-7369).

Ministry of Commerce, PO Box 1473, Wellington (tel: 472-0030; fax: 473-4638).

Ministry of Consumer Affairs, PO Box 1473, Wellington (tel: 474-2750; fax: 473-9400).

Ministry of Defence, PO Box 5347, Wellington (tel: 496-0999; fax: 496-0859).

Ministry of Education, Private Bag 1666, Wellington (tel: 473-5544; fax: 499-1327).

Ministry for the Environment, PO Box 10362, Wellington (tel: 473-4090; fax: 471-0195).

Ministry of Foreign Affairs and Trade, Private Bag 18-901, Parliament Bldgs, Wellington (tel: 472-8877; fax: 472-9596).

Ministry of Forestry, PO Box 1610, Wellington (tel: 472-1569; fax: 472-2314).

Ministry of Health, PO Box 5013, Wellington (tel: 496-2000; fax: 496-2340).

Ministry of Māori Development, PO Box 3943, Wellington (tel: 494-7100; fax: 494-7010).

Ministry of Pacific Island Affairs, PO Box 833, Wellington (tel: 473-4493; fax: 473-4301).

Ministry of Research, Science and Technology, PO Box 5336, Wellington (tel: 472-6400; fax: 471-1284).

Ministry of Transport, PO Box 3175, Wellington (tel: 472-1253; fax: 473-3697).

Ministry of Women's Affairs, PO Box 10049, Wellington (tel: 473-4112; fax: 472-0961).

Ministry of Youth Affairs, PO Box 10300, Wellington (tel: 471-2158; fax: 471-2233).

Prime Minister and Cabinet Department, Executive Wing, Parliament Bldgs, Wellington (tel: 471-9700; fax: 473-2508).

Other useful addresses

Airways Corporation of New Zealand, 44-48 Willis Street, PO Box 294, Wellington (tel: 471-1888; fax: 471-0395; internet: www.airways.co.nz/).

British High Commission, PO Box 1812, 44 Hill Street, Wellington 1 (tel: 472-6049; fax: 471-1974).

British/New Zealand Trade Council Inc, 22 Newton Road, Newton, Auckland (tel: 378-9066; fax: 378-0539).

Central Region Health Authority, PO Box 10097, 155 The Terrace, Wellington (tel: 472-7633; fax: 472-7639).

Coal Corporation of New Zealand Ltd, PO Box 439, Wellington (tel: 474-3600; fax: 474-3601).

Commerce Commission, PO Box 2351, Wellington (tel: 471-0180; fax: 471-0771).

Conservation Department, PO Box 10420, Wellington (tel: 471-0726; fax: 471-1082).

Customs Department, PO Box 2218, Whitmore Street, Wellington (tel: 473-6099; fax: 473-7370).

Earthquake Commission, PO Box 311, Wellington (tel: 499-0045; fax: 499-0046).

Electricity Corporation of New Zealand, PO Box 930, Wellington (tel: 472-3550; fax: 473-7091).

Hillary Commission for Sport, Fitness and Leisure, PO Box 2251, Wellington (tel: 472-8058; fax: 471-0813).

Housing Corporation of New Zealand, PO Box 5009, Wellington (tel: 495-1045; fax: 472-3152).

Human Rights Commission, PO Box 6751, Wellesley Street, Auckland (tel: 309-0874; fax: 377-3593).

Inland Revenue Department, PO Box 2198, Wellington (tel: 472-1032; fax: 499-0806).

Internal Affairs Department, PO Box 805, Wellington (tel: 495-7200; fax: 495-7222).

Justice Department, PO Box 180, Wellington (tel: 472-5980; fax: 499-2295).

Labour Department, PO Box 3705, Wellington (tel: 473-7800; fax: 495-4009).

Land Corporation Ltd, PO Box 5349, Wellington (tel: 471-0400; fax: 473-4966).

New Zealand Embassy (USA), 37 Observatory Circle, NW, Washington DC 20008 (tel: (+1-202) 328-4800; fax: (+1-202) 667-5227; e-mail: nz@nzemb.org).

New Zealand Manufacturers' Federation, 3–9 Church Street, PO Box 11543, Wellington (tel: 473-3000; fax: 473-3004).

New Zealand Minerals Industry Association, Druids Building, 188 Lambton Quay, PO Box 5039, Wellington (tel: 499-9871; fax: 499-9873; email: nzmia@xtra.co.nz).

New Zealand Stock Exchange, Caltex Tower, 286-292 Lambton Quay, PO Box 2959, Wellington (tel: 472-7599; fax: 473-1470).

New Zealand Trade Development Board (TRADENZ), Pastoral House, 25 The Terrace, PO Box 10341, Wellington (tel: 499-2244; fax: 473-3193).

Overseas Investment Commission, 2 The Terrace, PO Box 2498, Wellington (tel: 471-3838; fax: 471-3655).

Race Relations Office, PO Box 12411, Thorndon, Wellington (tel: 499-5885; fax: 499-5998).

Radio New Zealand, PO Box 2092, Wellington (tel: 474-1555; fax: 474-1712).

Statistics Department, 85 Molesworth Street, PO Box 2922, Wellington (tel: 495-4600; fax: 472-9135).

Survey and Land Information Department, Private Box 170, Charles Ferguson Building, Wellington (tel: 473-5022; fax: 472-2244).

Telecom New Zealand, PO Box 1473, Christchurch (tel: 374-0253; internet: www.telecom.co.nz).

Television New Zealand Ltd, PO Box 3819, Auckland (tel: 377-0630; fax: 375-0828).

Tranz Rail Ltd, Private Bag, Wellington (tel: 498-3095; fax: 498-3322).

Treasury Department, PO Box 3724, Wellington (tel: 472-2733; fax: 473-0982).

Works and Development Services Corporation Ltd, PO Box 12041, Wellington (tel: 496-1300; fax: 471-0224).

Internet sites

AA Travel: www.aatravel.co.nz

Air New Zealand: www:airnz.com

Asia Pacific Economic Co-operation (APEC): www.apecsec.org.sg

Auckland Airport: www:auckland-airport.co.nz

Destination New Zealand (gateway site): www.destinationnz.co.nz

Economic & Trade Development Agency: www:nzte.govt.nz

General Information: www:nz.com

Immigration: www:immigration.govt.nz

Ministry of Foreign Affairs and Trade: www:mft.govt.nz

New Zealand Government: www.govt.nz

New Zealand Herald newspaper: www:nzherald.co.nz

Parliament: www:parliament.govt.nz

Reserve Bank: www:rbnz.govt.nz

Statistics: www:stats.govt.nz

Treasury: www:treasury.govt.nz

WebNZ Platinum Business Directory: http://nz.com/webnz/YellowPages

White Pages: www:whitepages.co.nz

Yellowpages: www:yellowpages.co.nz

Nicaragua

KEY FACTS

Official name: República de Nicaragua (Republic of Nicaragua)

Head of State: President Enrique Daniel Ortega Saavedra (from 2007; re-elected 6 Nov 2011)

Head of government: President Daniel Ortega (FSLN) (from 2007; re-elected 6 Nov 2011)

Ruling party: Frente Sandinista de Liberación Nacional (FSLN) (Sandinista National Liberation Front) (from 10 Jan 2007)

Area: 147,950 square km

Population: 6.82 million (2010)*

Capital: Managua

Official language: Spanish

Currency: Córdoba de oro (gold córdoba) (C) = 100 centavos

Exchange rate: C22.70 per US$ (Oct 2011)

GDP per capita: US$972 (2009)*

GDP real growth: 4.50% (2010)

GDP: US$6.15 billion (2009)

Inflation: 9.20% (2010)

Balance of trade: -US$1.64 billion (2010)

* estimated figure

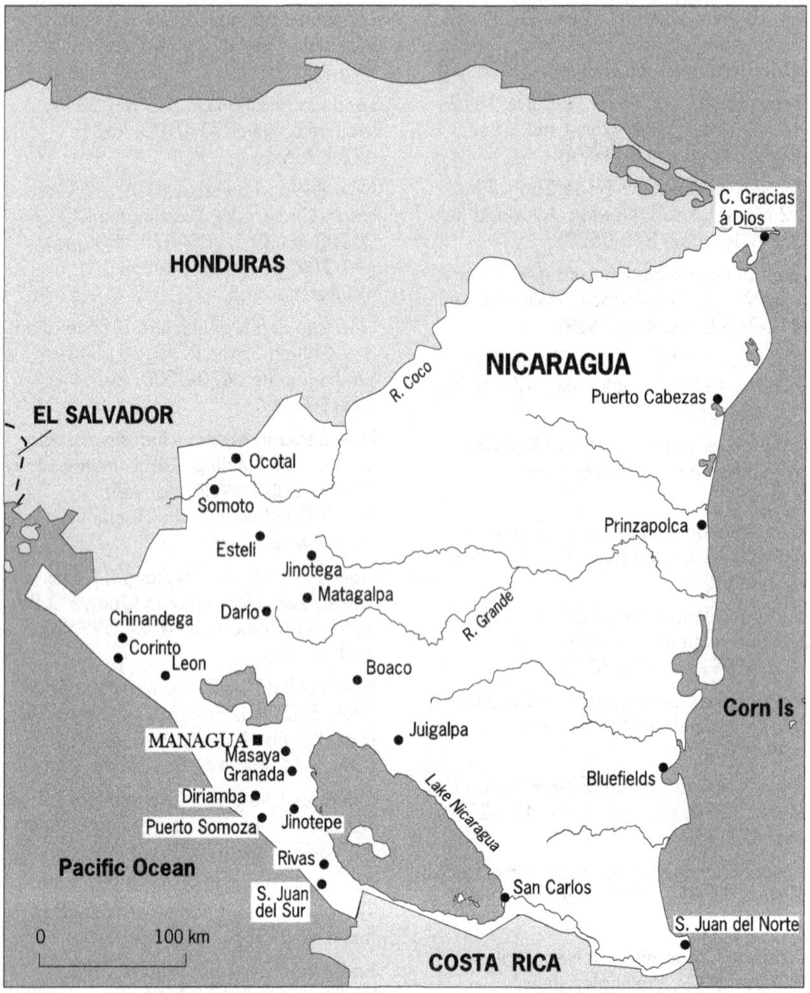

As Nicaragua's presidential election – due on November 6th 2011 – approached, a large proportion of the electorate had regarded it as no more than a plebiscite on the re-election of the incumbent Daniel Ortega for a further five year term, his third. Ortega and most of the Nicaraguan electorate did not appear overly concerned by the fact that if – as seemed likely – Ortega were to win, his election would be unconstitutional; illegal, in fact.

Populism

The election was also seen as something of a referendum on the sort of politics Nicaragua wished to opt for. The choice was between re-electing a populist *caudillo* (political leader) or preferring an institutional regime. Managua's more cynical observers welcomed the fact that the choice facing the electorate was no longer between a stereotyped left-wing party and an equally predictable party of right-wing conservatives. In this election campaign, the front runners were each Sandinista parties, the Frente Sandinista de Liberación Nacional (FSLN) (Sandinista National Liberation Front), led by a slightly more rotund Daniel Ortega and the Partido Liberal

Independiente (PLI) (Independent Liberal Party), led by the octogenarian Fabio Gadea. Mr Gadea could also count on the support of the Movimiento Renovador Sandinista (MRS) (Sandinista Renewal Movement). The third hat in the ring was that of former President Arnaldo Alemán.

According to the regional poll, *Latinobarómetro* Daniel Ortega is the second least popular leader in the Americas (after Fidel Castro). Given some of the other candidates for the title, this is no mean achievement. His unpopularity can largely be attributed to the corruption that has eroded Nicaragua's institutions on his watch. The 2008 elections were generally considered to have been fraudulent, illegally awarding some 40 local administrations to the FSLN. So obvious was the fraud that Nicaragua was denied some US$100 million in foreign aid. The run-up to the 2011 elections had revealed similar goings on. Allegedly voting cards were not delivered in a number of constituencies and very view foreign observers were to be admitted to monitor events.

The political polarisation between the FSLN and the PLI was recognisable through their supporters. The FSLN had widened its support away from what was its grassroots base. Ortega had strong support in Managua and among the poorer elements of Nicaragua's population. Fabio Gadea, owner of a well known radio station, was very popular in rural areas. At the beginning of November 2011, the opinion polls showed FSLN to be well in front, with 48 per cent of the popular vote. Trailing in third place, with only 11 per cent of the expected vote came Mr Alemán. The PLI blamed Alemán for splitting the opposition vote; Mr Alemán and his supporters normally supported President Ortega when it came to voting.

Ortega was also accused by his opponents of adopting the political position of Nicaragua's former dictator, Anastasio Somoza. One former FSLN guerrilla observed that: 'Daniel has done what all right-wing populist *caudillos* have done – liquidate the institutions and turn their family members into a close circle of loyal supporters.'

As it turned out the result in the presidential election was a 62.45 per cent win for Daniel Ortega, followed by Fabio Gadea with 31.06 per cent. The parliamentary elections followed the same format with 60.93 per cent of the vote for the FSLN, 31.53 per cent for the PLI and 6.43 per cent for the PLC.

It's the economy – Claro que sí!

Although some of the government's economic failures stem from its own corruption and incompetence, many of the problems are rooted in the chronically ailing health of the economy, which has been blighted by a series of natural disasters and poor prices for its main commodity exports, particularly coffee. Agriculture plays a very significant role in the economy of Nicaragua, contributing about a quarter of the country's total gross domestic product (GDP). The sector also employs up to 30 per cent of the total workforce. The principal export crop is coffee, which represents approximately a fifth of total export earnings. The Nicaraguan government is actively engaged in the agricultural sector although it is estimated that upwards of 60 per cent of cultivated land is in the hands of private smallholders. Despite continuous agrarian reform, food production has not kept up with demand owing mainly to poor weather, war damage and shortages of vital inputs.

During the 1980s, the national government of Nicaragua launched an unsuccessful policy of industrial development, premised on the promotion of joint public and private enterprises, in a bid to provide basic consumer goods at prices accessible to most people.

Unfortunately, one unforeseen consequence of this policy was the lowering of economic efficiency as a result of subsidies on state-produced goods. By the end of the decade, many private producers had been forced to close their factories, sell out to the state or just scale down activities

Viva Venezuela!

The FSLN declares itself to be socialist in creed. Certainly its revolutionary credentials are acceptable. But reality has crept up in the shape of a hard-headed approach to doing business. Foreign investors are wooed, the International Monetary Fund (IMF) has praised Nicaragua's 'courageous' efforts to develop macro-economic stability and the World Bank considers Nicaragua the easiest Central American country in which to do business – after Panama. Nicaragua also comes top in the regional foreign investment league. But as an August 2011 article in the London *Economist* pointed out, the investment figure is distorted by the presence of Venezuela in the equation. Nicaragua imports all its oil from Venezuela; in any normal market arrangement, the value of the oil would be US$1 billion. But Nicaragua only gets charged US$500 million, the balance being made up by 'soft' loans granted to an enterprise called Albanisa, which is jointly owned by the two countries' governments. Half the loans are 'invested' in well meaning programmes ranging from agricultural investments in livestock to transport schemes for subsidised bus travel. Venezuela is slowly becoming a major importer of Nicaraguan goods – the value of these imports have risen from a paltry 0.5 per cent of the total to 13 per cent in 2010, worth US$249 million. The balance available is invested in

KEY INDICATORS **Nicaragua**

	Unit	2006	2007	2008	2009	2010
Population	m	*5.91	*6.05	*6.19	*6.33	*5.82
Gross domestic product (GDP)	US$bn	5.29	5.72	6.37	6.15	–
GDP per capita	US$	959	1,017	1,123	1,082	–
GDP real growth	%	3.9	3.7	2.8	-1.5	4.5
Inflation	%	9.1	11.8	13.8	0.9	9.2
Industrial output	% change	–	–	1.4	-4.7	–
Agricultural output	% change	–	–	1.1	0.3	–
Exports (fob) (goods)	US$m	1,027.0	2,313.2	2,674.6	2,386.8	3,156.6
Imports (fob) (goods)	US$m	2,988.0	4,078.0	4,847.5	3,927.2	4,792.2
Balance of trade	US$m	-1,961.0	-1,764.8	-2,172.9	-1,540.0	-1,635.6
Current account	US$m	-700.0	-1,000.6	-1,512.9	-841.1	-963.4
Total reserves minus gold	US$m	921.9	1,103.3	1,140.8	1,573.1	1,799.0
Foreign exchange	US$m	921.5	1,103.2	1,140.7	1,408.6	1,637.5
Exchange rate	per US$	18.03	18.86	19.37	20.34	21.36

* estimated figure

more commercial projects such as businesses and property.

While welcoming what has been a life-saving initiative by the Chávez government, Nicaragua's newly elected government will need to be concerned about the future. President Chávez is known to be suffering from cancer and his successors may not share his revolutionary ardour. Nicaraguan ministers have already been making overtures to other sources of investment. Existing investors and manufacturers include blue-chip names such as BMW (Germany) and Levi-Strauss (US). The presence of household names such as these is in a number of ways quite surprising. According to the World Economic Forum, Nicaragua ranks very near the bottom in the global league table of independent judiciaries – 132nd out of 139. Importantly, under the North American Free-Trade Agreement Nicaragua benefits from tariff-free access to the US.

In its annual assessment of the Nicaraguan economy, the United Nations Economic Commission for Latin America and the Caribbean (ECLAC) notes that the Nicaraguan economy grew in 2010, with GDP expanding by just over 3.0 per cent compared with a 1.5 per cent contraction in 2009. This recovery was driven by rallying exports, which were up nearly 25 per cent on the strength of sales to new destinations such as Venezuela and Canada. The export products posting the largest gains were coffee, bovine meat, gold and sugar. Domestic consumption rose slightly (2.4 per cent) thanks to a 2.1 per cent increase in private consumption. Fuelled by the upswing in economic activity and rising oil and basic grain prices, inflation will be in the area of 8.5 per cent after closing 2009 at 0.9 per cent. Consumer and capital goods imports are expected to be higher, too, driving the current account deficit up to 16.5 per cent of GDP at year-end 2010. According to ECLAC estimates, economic activity will slacken slightly in 2011 and GDP will grow by some 3 per cent depending on the strength of the economic recovery in the United States, where a slowdown would decrease external demand. GDP growth by sector in 2010 was marked by a steady rise in manufacturing activity – the 8.9 per cent average annual increase to September stood in sharp contrast to the 2.9 per cent drop as of September 2009. The food and garment sectors contributed the most to this performance, growing by an average 40.3 per cent and 12.1 per cent respectively. The crop sector posted average growth of 3.8 per cent to September and the livestock industry recorded an average gain of 10.3 per cent. Commercial activity continued to rise, expanding by an annual average of 5.4 per cent. The financial sector contracted by an average 8.4 per cent, due above all to a decline in the issue of credits. The nominal wage at the national level posted year-on-year growth of 3.7 per cent to August, while the real wage recorded a slight year-on-year decline of 1.6 per cent for the same period. According to social security figures, the number of employees rose by 4.3 per cent in 2010.

The central government's fiscal account balance continued to improve thanks to higher-than-expected revenues under the amended Fiscal Equity Act that took effect in late 2009. The 1.1 per cent rise in fiscal revenues was a major factor in paring the central government deficit, including grants, which is expected to end 2010 at 1.1 per cent (2.8 per cent in 2009). The reduction in expenditure (from 24.3 per cent of GDP in 2009 to 23.7 per cent in 2010) was also key in narrowing the deficit and was achieved by holding the wage bill steady and cutting back subsidies for electricity consumption, thus improving macro- economic expectations and ensuring the continuation of the Extended Credit Facility Arrangement from the IMF, which was extended to 4 December 2011. This arrangement provides key guidance, especially in view of the risk of rising expenditure during the 2011 electoral period. Extending the IMF arrangement also ensured the flow of international co-operation resources, especially from multilateral sources.

Worthy of note is the contribution of Venezuela, which accounted for US$351.0 million (60.2 per cent) of the total US$582.9 million in resources received from official bilateral and multilateral sources as of June 2010; most of that contribution came under the PetroCaribe energy co-operation agreement. As part of the programme to strengthen the fiscal and quasi-fiscal accounts, the administration launched a programme to reform the power sector, clamping down on illegal connections and trimming the subsidy. The social security contribution rate was increased by one percentage point. These measures

helped reduce the impact of public sector operations on total aggregate demand by bringing the consolidated public sector debt down to no more than 2.3 per cent of GDP at year-end 2010.

Risk assessment

Economy	Fair
Politics	Poor
Regional stability	Good

COUNTRY PROFILE

Historical profile

1821 The Central American provinces (Costa Rica, Guatemala, Honduras, Nicaragua and El Salvador) declared independence from Spain.

1822 Central American provinces annexed themselves to the Mexican Empire, under General Agustín de Iturbde, later Emporer Agustín I.

1823 Agustín I was overthrown and Mexico became a republic. The Central American states formed the United Provinces of Central America.

1825 Costa Rica, Guatemala, Honduras, Nicaragua and El Salvador formed the Central American Federation (CAF).

1838 The CAF was dissolved and Nicaragua became a fully independent republic.

1856–57 Nicaragua was ruled by a US buccaneer, William Walker, who proclaimed himself president and was overthrown in 1857 following intervention by a Central American coalition.

1860 British ceded control over the Caribbean coast to Nicaragua.

1893 General José Santos Zelaya, a liberal, seized power and established a dictatorship.

1909 Zelaya was driven from office following a US-backed coup. Nicaragua allowed the US to run its customs and excise (raising money to pay the foreign debt), the national bank and the railway.

1912–25 The US established a number of military bases.

1929–33 Guerrillas led by Augusto César Sandino campaigned against the US military presence.

1934 Sandino was assassinated on the orders of the National Guard commander, General Anastasio 'Tacho' Somoza García. The US marines left with Somoza in power as a puppet dictator.

1956 General Somoza was assassinated; his son, Luis Somoza Debayle became president

1961 The Frente Sandinista de Liberación Nacional (FSLN) (Sandinista National Liberation Front) was founded. The Central American Common Market (CACM) was formed, comprising Nicaragua, Costa Rica, El Salvador, Honduras and Guatemala.

1967 Anastasio Somoza Debayle was officially elected president, succeeding his brother Luis.

1969 CACM collapsed following the 'soccer war' between El Salvador and Honduras.

1978 Prominent opposition leader and editor of *La Prensa* newspaper, Pedro Joaquín Chamorro was assassinated, leading to a general strike and consolidation within the opposition.
1979 The Somoza dynasty was overthrown by a cross-party junta led by the FSLN. The new government seized land and private businesses owned by Somoza and his allies, who had fled the country.
1981 The US broke off diplomatic links with Nicaragua claiming it was part of a communist 'evil empire'. A number of opposition leaders fled to Costa Rica and Honduras where they established guerrilla groups known as counter-revolutionaries or Contras.
1982 The US began the Contra war against Nicaragua, arming Contra supporters of the former Somoza regime and using bases in Honduras.
1984 Daniel Ortega, leader of the nine ruling *comandantes*, was elected president (the only opposition candidate withdrew). The US mined Nicaragua's harbours. Nicaragua began legal action against the US in the World Court for violating international law.
1986 The Nicaraguan government closed *La Prensa* after it began receiving funds from the CIA. The US was found to have given aid to the Contras, funded by arms sales from the US to Iran in what became known as the Iran-Contra Affair. The World Court found the US guilty of violating international law and ordered reparations. The US ignored the judgement.
1988 The government and the Contras agreed a cease-fire.
1990 The US-backed Unión Nacional Opositora (UNO) assumed office after elections in which it defeated the FSLN. The presidential opposition candidate, Violeta Chamorro, wife of the founding publisher of *La Prensa*, won presidential elections.
1994 Following defections from the UNO coalition, the *de facto* ruling coalition became a centrist block in alliance with the FSLN.
1997 President Alemán's right-wing Alianza Liberal Nicaragüense (ALN) (Nicaraguan Liberal Alliance), dominated by the Partido Liberal Constitucionalista (PLC) (Constitutionalist Liberal Party), became the largest single group in the National Assembly.
1998 Hurricane Mitch devastated large parts of Nicaragua.
1999 The FSLN and the AL entered into a pact in order to force through controversial laws that worked against the emergence of a 'third force' in Nicaraguan politics.
2000 The FSLN made significant gains in the municipal elections, winning the major cities including the capital, Managua.
2001 PLC and Enrique Bolaños (PLC) won office.
2003 The FSLN re-elected Daniel Ortega as party leader.
2004 Over 70 per cent of Nicaragua's debt to the World Bank was waived. An agreement was reached with Russia to cancel Nicaragua's huge debt with the former Soviet Union.
2005 Violent street protests erupted following fuel price rises. The government and an alliance of opposition parties in Congress began a power struggle over constitutional reforms but later agreed to delay reforms. The eighth national census recorded a population of 4,357,099.
2006 Daniel Ortega was elected president and the FSLN won 38 of the 90 seats in parliamentary elections. Tough laws that banned legal abortions, including those for women whose lives were at risk, were approved.
2007 Ortega was inaugurated as president. After eight years of conflict, the International Court of Justice (ICJ) ruled on a new maritime boundary between Honduras and Nicaragua which resulted in both countries having equal access to the rich fishing grounds and oil and gas exploration waters in the area.
2008 Nicaragua recognised the independence of Abkhazia and South Ossetia and agreed with Russia's position of support, while criticising Georgia for its attempts to regain control of its breakaway regions.
2009 Ousted president of Honduras, Manuel Zelaya, was forced to land in Managua following an abortive attempt to return home. Japan donated US$7.5 million for projects including road improvements. The Supreme Court amended the constitution to allow consecutive presidential terms in office.
2010 Daniel Ortega's way to a third term in office was cleared when a ruling by magistrates that over-turned the ban on re-elections was upheld by the Supreme Court. This was despite the fact that he had failed to persuade the national assembly to repeal the constitutional limit of two non-consecutive terms.
2011 A border dispute that had flared in November 2010 when Costa Rica complained to the ICJ that Nicaragua had sent troops and engineers illegally into its territory to dredge part of the San Juan River, was dampened in March following a court ruling on 8 March that each country must remove their troops from the disputed river border. Both sides welcomed the ruling. In parliamentary and presidential elections held on 6 November, the ruling party FSLN won 60.93 per cent of the vote and its leader Daniel Ortega won 62.45 per cent.

Political structure

In addition to their unicameral national parliaments, El Salvador, Guatemala, Honduras, Nicaragua, Panama and Dominican Republic also return directly-elected deputies to the supranational Central American Parliament.

Constitution

The National Assembly approved constitutional reforms in 2000 which provide outgoing presidents and vice presidents with a lifelong seat in the legislature. Other constitutional reforms included a reduction of the percentage of votes required to elect a president without the need for a run-off election, from 45 per cent to 35 per cent of the total, and the restructuring of the judiciary, the electoral authorities and the comptroller general's office, giving the two main parties a bigger share of the posts.
The country comprises 16 departments which are divided into two zones: the Pacific zone and the Atlantic zone.
The minimum voting age is 16 years.

Form of state

Presidential democratic republic

The executive

Power is vested in the president who is head of state and commander-in-chief of the armed forces, elected for a period of five years by universal adult suffrage. The president appoints a cabinet of ministers.

National legislature

The unicameral Asamblea Nacional (National Assembly) has 92 deputies in total, of which 90 members are elected by popular vote, by proportional representation from party lists, to serve for five-year terms. The former president of the republic holding office immediately before the incumbent president and the runner up in the last presidential election are also entitled to sit as deputies.

Legal system

The Nicaraguan legal system comprises civil and military courts. The highest court is the Supreme Court, which administers the judicial system and nominates all appellate and lower court judges. The Supreme Court consists of 12 magistrates elected for seven-year terms by the National Assembly.

Last elections

6 November 2011 (presidential and parliamentary)
Results: Parliamentary: Frente Sandinista de Liberación Nacional (FSLN) (Sandinista National Liberation Front) won 60.93 per cent of the vote, Partido Liberal Independiente (PLI) (Independent Liberal Party) 31.53 per cent, Partido Liberal Constitucionalista (PLC) (Constitutionalist Liberal Party) 6.43 per cent; two other parties each won less that 1 per cent of the vote.

Presidential (results as of 9 November 2011): Daniel Ortega (FSLN) won 62.45 per cent, Fabio Gadea (PLI) 31.06 per cent, Arnoldo Alemán (PLC) 5.91 per cent.

Next elections

November 2015 (presidential and parliamentary)

Political parties

Ruling party

Frente Sandinista de Liberación Nacional (FSLN) (Sandinista National Liberation Front) (from 10 Jan 2007)

Main opposition party

Partido Liberal Independiente (PLI) (Independent Liberal Party)

Population

6.82 million (2010)*

Last census: 25 April 2005: 4,357,099

Population density: 41 inhabitants per square km. Urban population: 57 per cent (1995—2001).

Annual growth rate: 2.1 per cent 1994–2004 (WHO 2006)

Ethnic make-up

Mestizo (mixed indigenous-European) (69 per cent), European (17 per cent), black (9 per cent) and indigenous people (5 per cent).

Creole and Indian peoples live in the eastern region of the country on the Atlantic coast. The Creoles number some 26,000, the Miskitos 182,000 and the Sumus 9,000. There are also two very small indigenous groups – the Ramas and the Garifunos.

Religions

The majority of the population is Catholic, although mainstream Protestant and evangelical groups make up 20 per cent of the population. The majority of the Atlantic coast population is Moravian. There is no official religion.

Education

Primary education is free for six years although a report issued by the Nicaraguan Office of the Advocate for Children and Youth revealed that 80 per cent of children in primary and secondary state schools were required to pay a minimum fee per month, including voluntary contributions to teachers' salaries and payments for examinations, in violation of the constitutional right to free education for children.

Secondary education runs in two cycles of three and two years and leads to higher education, or in a cycle of two and three years leading to a technical qualification. There are both state universities and private universities. The Consejo Nacional de Universidades is responsible for all higher education planning. Nicaragua's major institutions of higher education are the Jesuit-run Central American University, Managua (UCA), the public National Autonomous Universities in Managua and León (Unan) and the private, Harvard-affiliated Central American Institute of Business Administration (Incae) outside Managua.

Spending on primary education amounts to less than US$10 per capita.

Literacy rate: 77 per cent adult rate; 86 per cent youth rate (15–24) (Unesco 2005).

Compulsory years: 6 to 12.

Enrolment rate: 102 per cent gross primary enrolment of the relevant age group (including repeaters); 55 per cent gross secondary enrolment (World Bank).

Pupils per teacher: 36 in primary schools.

Health

Although public health improved during the 1990s, access to medical facilities continues to be uneven and many of the country's poor, particularly in rural areas and on the Atlantic coast, are experiencing inadequate healthcare due to government cutbacks in 2002/03. A growing market of private services exists, but the ministry of health continues to be the main provider of services for the Nicaraguan population as a whole.

Government spending emphasises primary healthcare with priority given to improving local healthcare systems, through national, departmental, regional and municipal co-ordination. The World Bank's International Development Association (IDA) funded the rehabilitation of healthcare centres, nutrition centres for children, and schools for training nurses and other healthcare workers, and the provision of social services.

HIV/Aids

HIV prevalence: 0.2 per cent aged 15–49 in 2003 (World Bank)

Life expectancy: 69 years, 2004 (WHO 2006)

Fertility rate/Maternal mortality rate: 3.3 births per woman, 2004 (WHO 2006); maternal mortality 150 per 100,000 live births (World Bank).

Child (under 5 years) mortality rate (per 1,000): 30 per 1,000 live births; 12.2 per cent of children under aged five are malnourished (World Bank).

Head of population per physician: 0.37 physicians per 1,000 people, 2003 (WHO 2006)

Welfare

Under the presidency of Arnoldo Alemán (1997—2001), welfare expenditure was squeezed as a result of the government's IMF-dictated austerity measures and high levels of debt servicing. Funds for social protection remain decentralised and the responsibility for resource management lies with local authorities. There are no clear regulations about the amount of money that can be allocated or is necessary for the municipalities. An increasing number of self-employed people do not have access to social protection mechanisms.

Nicaragua's welfare programme combines a traditional cash transfer programme with financial incentives for families to obtain preventive healthcare and education and to participate in other government-sponsored welfare-related programmes.

In 2001, the government initiated a welfare reform programme under the auspices of a three-year Poverty Reduction and Growth Facility (PRGF) arrangement with the IMF. Pension reform is central to the structural adjustment programme. A pension system of privately managed individual accounts was introduced in the last quarter of 2001. Under the pension reform, the country changed from a pay-as-you-go pension system to a defined contribution system in which contributions are safeguarded. The reform was designed to contain the fiscal deficit created by the previous system, broaden the base of contributors and contribute to the development of domestic financial markets.

The Nicaraguan Institute for Social Security and Welfare (INSSBI) operates nursing homes for the elderly and rehabilitation centres for the physically and mentally handicapped, for prostitutes, drug addicts and alcoholics.

Main cities

Managua (capital, estimated population 926,883 in 2005), León (168,122), Chinandega (121,929), Masaya (123,164), Granada (101,229).

Languages spoken

Some business people speak English. In the Bluefields (Atlantic) region, English is particularly widely spoken.

Many names of towns, medicines, foods, flora and fauna are in the Nahuate language.

On the Atlantic Coast, Indian towns and ethnic communities still preserve their language and cultural traditions. Autonomous law guarantees bilingual education in the Miskito, Creole, English, Sumus, Ramas and Garifuna dialects.

Official language/s

Spanish

Media

The constitution guarantees freedom of speech and there is no censorship.

Press

Dailies: In Spanish, the handful of newspapers include *La Prensa* (www-usa.laprensa.com.ni), which is conservative in tone, *El Nuevo Diario* (www.elnuevodiario.com.ni) a left-wing pro-Sandinista publication, *Bolsa de Noticias* (www.grupoese.com.ni) *Trinchera de la Noticia* (www.trinchera.com.ni) and the independent *Semanario Hoy* (www.semanahoydigital.com)

Weeklies: In Spanish, *Confidencial* (www.confidencial.com.ni) gives political analysis, *Semana Cómica* is a left-wing satirical magazine, *7 Días* (www.7dias.com.ni) is a family publication. In English, the bi-weekly *The Nicaraguan Post* (www.nicaraguanpost.com) covers general interest and news.

Business: The monthly *El Observador Economico* (www.elobservadoreconomico.com) is a magazine with a comprehensive review of national and international financial news.

Periodicals: In Spanish, the quarterly *El Pez y la Serviente* (www.elpezylaserpiente.com.ni) reviews culture, monthly magazines include *Envio*, the left-wing *Pensamiento Propio*, and the bi-monthly, *Crítica* and *La Avispa* are pro-Sandinista publications.

Broadcasting

Television and particularly radio are popular source of news and information.

Radio: Radio is an important source of news and information and has been the target of opposing forces at times of unrest.

There are over 100 radio stations, most of which are located around the capital. The government-owned Radio Nicaragua (www.radionicaragua.com.ni) is a national service. Other, private, commercial stations include Radio La Primerisima (www.radiolaprimerisima.com), Radio Corporación (www.radio-corporacion.com) and Radio Sandino (www.lasandino.net) a news channel.

Television: There are over 10 national television stations and about the same number of local stations, most of which are private and commercial. Larger stations include Televicentro (www.canal2tv.com), Canal 10 (www.canal10nicaragua.com) Nicavisión and CDNN 23.

News agencies

Other news agencies: Prensa Latina: www.plenglish.com

Economy

The Nicaraguan economy is one of the weakest and least competitive in the Americas (second only to Haiti), but has the potential for improvement based on its natural resources of geothermal power, gold, timber and other agricultural products. However, it is in need of foreign direct investment (FDI), which has not to date been forthcoming, due in large part to a history of military dictatorships replaced by a Communist government and followed by a civil war, plus a series of natural disasters and poor prices for its main commodity exports, particularly coffee. The country is stable but underdeveloped and Nicaragua remains plagued by poverty.

FDI was US$626 million in 2008, of which US$123 million was in telecommunications infrastructure and US$120 million in energy generation. In 2008 Iran began investing in Nicaragua, funding among other projects the US$230 million Bodoke hydroelectric dam in Jinotega Province, and a farm equipment assembly plant and two piers in the Pacific port of Corinto. In exchange Nicaragua exports coffee, meat and bananas to Iran. In 2009 FDI had fallen to US$434 million as global trade slowed. In March 2010 the construction of the US$697 million, 220MW, Tumarin hydroelectric power plant was begun, to be completed by the end of 2014.

GDP growth was 3.7 per cent in 2007, falling to 2.8 per cent in 2008, before slipping into recession in 2009 at -1.5 per cent. However, in 2010 it rebounded with a growth rate of 4.5 per cent. Inflation is a long-term problem – since 2005 it had remained at just over 9 per cent, but in 2008 it jumped to 13.8 per cent, but in response to the recession inflation fell to 0.9 per cent in 2009 before resuming a high rate of 9.2 per cent in 2010.

Around 20 per cent of the population live and work abroad sending home remittances, valued at US$818.1 million in 2008 (12.4 per cent of GDP) in 2008. However in 2009 remittances fell to US$768 (10.3 per cent of GDP) and rose to an estimated US$803 million in 2010 as the economy in host countries improved. Although the government is considering a plan to tax the money coming into the country, it has not moved forward with any definite proposals.

In 2004, the World Bank and the IMF wiped out 80 per cent of Nicaragua's debt by supporting US$4.5 billion of debt service relief, alleviating the pressure of a rising national debt. By 2009 international loans and grants amounted to US$656.9 million, less than the amount derived from remittances. However some European donors and the World Bank suspended US$120 million in aid to Nicaragua in 2009 due to concerns about electoral fraud and transparency in the 2008 mayoral elections. The loss caused a severe budget shortfall.

In 2011, the UN Human Development Index (HDI) ranked Nicaragua 129 (out of 187) for development in health, education and income. In 2010, 45.7 per cent of the population experienced deprivation in at least one of the indicators for poverty and 15.8 per cent were living on the equivalent of US$1.25 per day.

External trade

Nicaragua is a member of the Central America Free Trade Agreement (Cafta-DR), which includes the Dominican Republic, Costa Rica, El Salvador, Guatemala and the US; it is working to remove all tariffs and barriers between members by 2024. It is also a member of the Central American Common Market (CACM), along with El Salvador, Guatemala and Honduras, which has removed duties on most products between members and unified external tariffs.

The US is Nicaragua's largest trading partner, accounting for a fifth of the country's imports and receiving some 60 per cent of its exports. As Nicaragua has developed its manufacturing base, imports of services, intermediate goods and capital goods have all risen, while imports of consumer goods have slowed.

Imports

Principal imports include petroleum, consumer goods, machinery and equipment and raw materials.

Main sources: US (typically 20 per cent of total), Mexico (10 per cent), Venezuela (10 per cent).

Exports

Principal exports include coffee, tobacco, sugar and peanuts, beef, shrimp and lobster and gold, textiles and clothing.

Main destinations: US (typically 60 per cent total), Mexico (9 per cent), El Salvador (6 per cent).

Agriculture

Farming

Agriculture plays a very significant role in the economy of Nicaragua, contributing about a quarter of the country's total GDP. The sector also employs up to 30 per cent of the total workforce.

The principal export crop is coffee which represents around a fifth of total export earnings. Meat, cotton, bananas and sugar are the other main agricultural exports. Maize, rice, beans and sorghum are also grown. Timber, tobacco, sugar cane and rubber are geared towards Nicaragua's agro-industrial sector.

The Nicaraguan government is actively engaged in the agricultural sector although it is estimated that upwards of 60 per cent of cultivated land is in the hands of private smallholders. Despite continuous agrarian reform, food production has not kept up with demand owing mainly to poor weather, war damage and shortages of vital inputs.

Fishing

Nicaragua's typical annual fish catch is over 28,000mt, 16,500mt of which is shellfish. The main seafood exports are shellfish, particularly shrimp and lobster. Offshore fishing consists mainly of tuna, bass and mackerel. The government follows an export subsidy policy, providing tax rebates on every kilogramme of trawled shrimp and farmed shrimp exported.

Forestry

Some 3.2 million hectares (ha) of Nicaragua is covered by forests and woodlands, amounting to 60 per cent of the country's total landmass. Nicaragua has some of the largest humid tropical rainforests concentrated in the north and east, in the Caribbean lowlands. Forest lands lie principally in the southern Atlantic coastal region. Species include pine, cedar and other hardwoods covering four million hectares. The government is keen to develop plans for self-sustaining exploitation of the forests. The Food and Agriculture Organisation (FAO) has estimated timber reserves at 33 million cubic metres.

The forestry industry thrives on sawnwood production, most of which is exported. Nicaragua imports moderate quantities of paper and wood-based panels. Most of the forest wood is used for fuel consumption.

Industry and manufacturing

Since the 1990s, there has been significant growth in the non-traditional *maquiladora* (in bond) sector, which has made use of the country's free trade zones (FTZs). Concentrated mainly on textiles, particularly clothing, for the US market, the *maquiladora* sector has rapidly become a major sub-sector in Nicaraguan industry. Low labour costs and minimal labour regulation have made it both an attractive opportunity for foreign investors and a target for trade unions and labour rights activists.

The most important projects undertaken since the mid-1990s have reflected a renewed priority placed on large-scale agro-industrial production, which had been neglected by the government in the early 1990s. The two biggest have been the Timal sugar refinery and the Sebaco food processing complex.

Investment in Nicaragua's fledgling manufacturing sector is crucial and reliant on structural reforms to make the sector more competitive and efficient. In the past, investment resources were often diverted to the defence sector, while factories closed as a result of non-availability of replacement parts and basic inputs.

Tourism

Nicaragua's tourism sector expanded significantly throughout 2005. The sector now accounts for 6.9 per cent of total GDP and 5.6 per cent of total employment. Visitor numbers grew until 2001, when the 11 September terrorist attacks in the US damaged the sector. 483,000 arrivals were recorded in 2001, a decline of 0.6 per cent on the previous year. A further fall to 472,000 visitors occurred in 2002, but 2003 showed a recovery of 7.65 per cent. Visitor numbers, as at end 2004, were 521,800. Capital investment in the sector has increased accordingly and now constitutes 7.1 per cent of total capital investment in the economy.

The development of Nicaragua's tourism sector, which has considerable potential, especially ecotourism, has been obstructed by residual negative perceptions about its stability and inadequate infrastructure. These difficulties are gradually being overcome. A generous incentive law was introduced in 1999 to encourage tourist-related investment, but, while improving, infrastructure is still patchy. Despite the disadvantages under which it has operated, tourism has become Nicaragua's main source of foreign exchange, earning around US$110 million per annum. The majority of visitors come from the other Central American countries, but about a fifth are from the USA.

Environment

The deforestation and cultivation of marginal lands in Nicaragua contributed to the mudslides after Hurricane Mitch hit the country in late 1998, while flooding was made worse due to a lack of watershed management.

Mining

Nicaragua is endowed with deposits of both gold and silver. The country also has mineral deposits, including copper, zinc, platinum, iron, magnesium, chrome, titanium, tungsten, lead, cadmium, bismuth, bentonite, marble, clay, masonry stone, limestone and gypsum.

Gold and silver are mined intensively in Siuna and Bonanza, inland from the northern Atlantic coast region. More modest mining activity takes place in Chontales and Nueva Segovia. Geological studies of the region identify the existence of a reserve of gold in the area of La Libertad, which could have a productive lifetime of 70 years. The reserves are estimated at 3.8 million ounces of gold and 4.9 million ounces of silver.

All natural resources are state property and exploitation rights are leased on a long-term basis. Since huge portions of the central areas of Nicaragua's mineral reserves have already been leased, the scope for investment remains limited. The decline in global gold prices has affected the fortunes of foreign companies and the value of exports diminished.

The Toronto-based Black Hawk international mining and exploration company owns the El Limon mine through its 95 per cent-owned subsidiary Triton Minera SA. The mine, located 140km north of Managua, has been in continuous production for more than 50 years, gaining from both open pit and underground operations. Mill capacity is 1,000 tonnes per day and gold recoveries exceed 80 per cent.

Hydrocarbons

Industry experts in 2009 were confident that oil will be found offshore in Nicaraguan territorial waters. In March 2009 the state-owned oil company Petróleos de Nicaragua (Petronic) signed a deal with Vietnam's Vietnam Oil and Gas Group (Petrovietnam) to undertake joint exploration for oil and gas.

Oil consumption in 2008 was 29,000 barrels per day (bpd), all of which was imported, primarily from Mexico and Venezuela under the San José pact. Refinery capacity was 20,000bpd. Under a previous administration, Petronic contracted all rights to downstream facilities to the Swiss oil company Glencore in exchange for annual royalties. In 2007, under President Ortega's government, Petronic began importing oil from Venezuela and bypassing Glencore's chain of supply and selling up to 60 per cent of the country's oil directly to the public. In 2008 Petronic became the largest importer of oil into Nicaragua.

There are no proven natural gas reserves and use of gas is negligible. An existing gas pipeline from Mexico to Guatemala could be extended to Nicaragua as part of a wider Central American gas pipeline network. There is also the possibility of a pipeline from Colombia's northern offshore fields to Panama with connections to Nicaragua, but no plans have been formally agreed.

Coal is not produced and any amounts imported and consumed are commercially negligible.

Energy

Total installed generating capacity was 648MW in 2007, producing over 3.0 billion kilowatt hours (kWh). Consumption was 2.41 billion kWh and the excess generation was exported.

A major objective of the government remains the electrification of rural areas. A World Bank loan helped to fund the National Rural Electrification Program, which aims at bringing electric power to 90 per cent of rural areas by 2012.

The energy mix includes two hydroelectric plants, one geothermal plant, two diesel plants and five thermoelectric plants. The country will need to increase generating capacity to satisfy its 6 per cent annual growth and a new US$350 million, 180MW Tumarín hydroelectric power station was awaiting approval by the national assembly in June 2009.

The Empresa Nicaragüense de Electricidad (Enel) (Nicaraguan Electricity Company) is responsible for generation and distribution of electricity, while the Empresa Nacional de Transmisión

Eléctrica (Entresa) (National Electric Transmission Company) is responsible for transmission.

Financial markets
Stock exchange
Bolsa de Valores de Nicaragua (BVDN) (Stock Exchange of Nicaragua)

Banking and insurance
In recent years the banking and financial services sector of Nicaragua has undergone a degree of stabilisation, which in turn has resulted in increasing deposit levels. However, the sector still remains fragile and vocal critics have accused the regulatory authorities of failing to tackle the state banking system's overdue debt which has contributed to a feeling of pessimism in some quarters.
Moreover, the government's bail-out of the country's third largest bank – Interbank – in 2000 amid reports of widespread corruption did nothing to reassure foreign investors and donors of the legitimacy of the country's banking system. The failure of the Banco Nicaraguense de Industria y Comercio (Banic) to resolve its debt led to another government intervention in the banking sector in August 2001. Banic's assets and liabilities were subsequently auctioned off to Banpro, which had already absorbed Interbank in October 2000.
The chaos in the banking sector led to a shake-up of the regulatory system. In 2003, the government introduced a new, rigorous framework to bring the legal framework in line with the Basel Core Principles.
Although foreign banks were permitted to remain in Nicaragua when the banking system was nationalised in 1979, they were no longer permitted to accept local deposits. The branches of US, British and Canadian commercial banks continue to operate non-deposit business.
Central bank
Banco Central de Nicaragua (BCN)
Main financial centre
Managua

Time
GMT minus six hours

Geography
Nicaragua is in the central American isthmus, with the Pacific Ocean to the west and the Caribbean Sea to the east. Honduras is to the north and Costa Rica to the south. The Pacific plateau is noted for its rich lands, and is where the larger farms which grow crops for export are to be found, particularly in the northern area of Chinandega. The Atlantic plateau, occupying fully half of the national territory, is largely pasture savannah; small gold and silver mines are also found in this area. The lands along the Rio Coco (forming the border with Honduras) are a rich banana-growing area, and are worked largely by the Miskito Indians. Tropical rainforest predominates in the southern Atlantic coast adjacent to Costa Rica. Corn Island, in the Caribbean Sea, is home to a fishing community.
Hemisphere
Northern

Climate
Nicaragua has a semi-tropical climate; the hottest month is May (27–32 degrees Celsius (C) in Managua) and the coldest is January (23–30 degrees C in Managua). Temperatures may be up to 10 degrees C lower in the mountain range that runs the length of the country. The rainy season (May–December) is referred to as 'winter'; and the dry season (December–April) as 'summer'.

Dress codes
On the most formal of occasions Nicaraguan men traditionally wear the Caribbean-style *guayabera*, in white, although an increasing number of men today prefer to wear a suit and tie.

Entry requirements
Passports
Required by all and must be valid for at least six months from the date of entry, with onward/return tickets and proof of sufficient funds for length of stay.
Passports and entry cards must be carried at all times.
Visa
Most visitors may not need a visa; contact the nearest Nicaraguan consulate for details of requirements. Many visitors may visit with a tourist card that is issued on arrival, for a fee of US$10, paid in US dollars for either up to 30 or 90 days. A valid entry stamp is necessary to exit the country, therefore any extension must be applied for locally; failure to do so will result in a fine.
Visitors who are admitted using a tourist card for business trips must provide a letter of introduction from their employer or an invitation from a Nicaraguan company.
Currency advice/regulations
The import and export of local and foreign currency is unlimited, but amounts over the equivalent of US$10,000 must be declared.
Customs
Personal items, including cameras, personal music players and laptop computers to the value of US$500 are duty-free.
Prohibited imports
Fresh and canned meat and diary products. Firearms require a licence.
The export of archaeological artefacts and gold are prohibited.

Health (for visitors)
Mandatory precautions
Yellow fever vaccination certificate if arriving within six months from an infected area.
Advisable precautions
Inoculations and booster should be current for tetanus, hepatitis A and typhoid. There may be a need for vaccinations for diphtheria, tuberculosis, hepatitis B. Use malaria prophylaxis if travelling outside urban areas. Malaria, hepatitis B and dengue fever are caused by mosquitoes, precautions including mosquito repellents, nets and clothing covering the body after dark should be used. There is a risk of rabies in rural areas.
There is a shortage of routine medications and visitors should take all necessary medicines with them. A first aid kit that includes disposable syringes, is a reasonable precaution. Outside the main hoteld use only bottled or boiled water for drinks, washing teeth and making ice. Eat only well cooked meals, preferably served hot; vegetables should be cooked and fruit peeled. Dairy products are unpasteurised and should be avoided, unless cooked. Healthcare is not to Western standards and medical insurance, including emergency evacuation, is necessary.

Hotels
Availability is limited but there are a few good hotels in Managua, the main coastal towns and along the Pan-American Highway. Bills are subject to 15 per cent sales tax, and must usually be paid in dollars. A 10 per cent tip is usual.

Credit cards
International credit and debit cards are accepted in banks in large towns.

Public holidays (national)
Fixed dates
1 Jan (New Year's Day), 1 May (Labour Day), 19 Jul (Liberation Day), 14 Sep (Battle of Jacinto), 15 Sep (Independence Day), 25 Dec (Christmas Day).
Variable dates
Maundy Thursday, Good Friday.

Working hours
Banking
Mon–Fri: 0830–1830; Sat: 0830–1230. Some banks close may close for an hour at lunch time.
Business
Mon–Fri: 0800–1700; Sat: 0800–1300.
Government
Mon–Fri: 0800–1700.

Telecommunications
Mobile/cell phones
There are GSM 1900 services available in most west-coast cities and a few east coast urban areas. A GSM 850 service is planned.

Electricity supply
110V AC, 60 cycles

Social customs/useful tips
It is helpful to know something of the political background and affiliations of those you are meeting.
Men and women shake hands in Nicaragua and social kisses on one cheek are also exchanged. The use of titles, such as Doctor, Arquitecto, Licenciado, Profesora, is widespread and it is courteous to learn and use the correct titles for both men and women.
Do not immediately launch into a business conversation. It is considered polite to first get to know the person to whom you are talking.
A small gift for the host or hostess is always appreciated.
Late-night parties, with dinner served at 2200 or 2300, are common. Guests need not plan to arrive on time for a large social gathering as being up to two hours late is acceptable. For smaller gatherings, arrival about 30 minutes later than the specified time is considered appropriate.

Security
Nicaragua had a low rate of violent crime compared to other Central American countries and armed groups involved in the civil war were demobilised however street crime is rising and visitors are advised not to walk alone at night.

Getting there
Air
National airline: Nicaragüenses de Aviación (Nica Airlines)
International airport/s:
Managua-Augusto César Sandino (MGA), 9km from city; duty-free shop, bar, restaurant, post office, shops (restricted hours in some instances), banks.
Airport tax: Departure tax: US$35 (may be included in the price of a ticket); excluding transit passengers.
Surface
Road: The Pan-American Highway is well maintained and runs from Honduras, through Managua, to Costa Rica.
Water: Shipping lines from North and South America and Europe regularly visit Nicaragua.
Main port/s: Bluefields, Corinto, Puerto Cabezas, Puerto Sandino, San Juan de Sur, Puerto Arlen Siu.

Getting about
National transport
Air: Nicaragüenses de Aviación (Nica Airlines) runs regional, passenger and cargo services.
Road: The western region is provided with most sealed roads connecting the more populated areas of the country. There is only one major road to the Caribbean side and this stops, before the coast, at Rama.
Buses: Services are regular and connect main towns served by the road system (eg Managua-Rama, Managua-León, Chinandega, Corinto), however they are not advised for foreign travellers.
Water: A boat service links Rama and Bluefields port on the Caribbean coast.
City transport
Taxis: Taxis are the best way to get around most cities; fares should be negotiated in advance of journeys and tipping is not necessary.
Buses, trams & metro: City buses are cheap but crowded.
Car hire
Foreign licences are acceptable for short stays (up to 30 days). Due to poor public transport, hired cars may often be the best way to get around in Managua. However roads are often in poor repair and need a skilled driver to avoid mishap. Drivers in accidents are always arrested even if they are insured and appear to be blameless. Licensed drivers can be hired, through local car rentals, who are familiar with local roads and conditions and, in the case of a traffic accident, will be taken into custody, in accordance with the law.

BUSINESS DIRECTORY

The addresses listed below are a selection only. While World of Information makes every endeavour to check these addresses, we cannot guarantee that changes have not been made, especially to telephone numbers and area codes. We would welcome any corrections.

Telephone area codes
The international dialling code (IDD) for Nicaragua is +505, followed by area code and subscriber's number:

León	311	Managua	2

Chambers of Commerce
American Chamber of Commerce of Nicaragua, Centro Finarca, PO Box 2720, Managua (tel: 67-3098; fax: 67-3099; e-mail: amcham@amchamnic.org.ni).

Nicaraguan Cámara de Comercio, Rotonda Gueguense, PO Box 135, Managua (tel: 68-3505; fax: 68-3600; e-mail: comercio@ibw.com.ni).

Banking
Banco de América Central (BAC), Apdo 2304 Managua (tel: 670-220; fax: 670-224).

Banco de Crédito Centroamericano (Bancentro), Edificio Bancentro, KM. 4-1/2 Carretera Masaya (tel: 782-777; fax: 786-001).

Banco de Exportación (Banexpo), Centro Comercial Metrocentro, Managua.

Banco de la Producción (Banpro), Plaza Libertad, Contiguo a Metrocentro, Apdo 2309, Managua (tel: 782-508/783-278/784-188; fax: 784-113).

Banco de Préstamos (Banpres), Esquina Opuesta Hotel Intercontinental, Managua (tel: 23-046/223-048; fax: 23-057).

Banco Europeo de Centro América SA (BECA), Apdo 188, Managua (fax: 783-827).

Banco Mercantil, Gerente General Oscar Martín Aguado A., Plaza Banco Mercantil, Managua (tel 668-228/668-231; fax: 668-024).

Banco Nacional de Desarrollo (Banades), Apdo 328-1447, Managua (tel: 671-334; fax: 670-869).

Central bank
Banco Central de Nicaragua, Km 7 carretera sur, PO Box 2252, Managua (tel: 65-0500; fax: 65-0561; e-mail: bcn@bcn.gob.ni).

Stock exchange
Bolsa de Valores de Nicaragua (BVDN) (Stock Exchange of Nicaragua): www.bolsanic.com

Travel information
Aerolíneas Nicaragüenses (AERONICA), Contiguo Aeropuerto Internacional August C Sandino, Apdo 3688, Managua, JR (tel: 31-801).

Instituto Nicaragüense de Turismo, Avenida Bolivar Sur, Apdo 122, Managua (tel: 25-436; fax: 25-314).

Ministry of tourism
Ministry of Tourism, Residencial Bolonia, Hotel Intercontinental, 1c. al Oeste 1c. al Sur, Managua (tel: 226-610, 222-6617; fax: 226-618).

Ministries
Ministry of Agriculture and Livestock, Km 8 1/2, Carretera a Masaya, Managua (tel: 76-0200; fax: 76-0256).

Ministry of Construction and Transport, Frente Al Estadio Nacional, Managua (tel: 22-5111; fax: 22-6429).

Ministry of Economy and Development, Carretera a Masaya, Km 6 1/2 Frente a Centro Comercial Camino de Oriente, Managua (tel: 67-0161; fax: 78-4590).

Ministry of Education, Centro Cívico Camilo Ortega, Managua (tel: 65-0046; fax: 65-0715).

Ministry of the Environment and Natural Resources, Carretera Norte, Km 12 1/2, Managua (tel: 63-1343; fax: 63-2833).

Ministry of External Co-operation, Casa Ricardo Morales Aviles, Managua (tel: 28-5002; fax: 28-2026).

Ministry of Finance, Frente a la Asamblea Nacional, Managua (tel: 22-7231; fax: 78-5984).

Ministry of Foreign Affairs, Barrío Altagracia, Frente a Restaurante Los Ranchos, Managua (tel: 66-6222; fax: 66-2572).

Ministry of Health, Complejo Concepción Palacios, Managua (tel: 89-7554; fax: 89-7997).

Ministry of Industry and Commerce, Km 6, Carretera Masaya, Apdo 2412, Managua.

Ministry of the Interior, Barrio 19 de Julio, Edif Silvio Mayorga, Managua (tel: 85-005; fax: 627-910).

Ministry of Labour, Estadio Nacional, 300 vs. al Norte, Managua (tel: 28-1168; fax: 28-2028).

Ministry of the Presidency, Avenida Bolivar, Detrás de la Asamblea Nacional, Managua (tel: 78-5299; fax: 22-3448).

Ministry of Social Action, Pista de Resistencia ENEL Central, 150vs. al Sur, Managua (tel: 67-2907; fax: 67-0768).

Ministry of Tourism, Residencial Bolonia, Hotel Intercontinental, 1c. al Oeste 1c. al Sur, Managua (tel: 22-6610, 22-6617; fax: 22-6618).

Ministry of Transport and Construction, Frente al Estadio Nacional, Managua (tel: 283-698, 282-061, 225-954; fax: 282-161).

Ministry of Works, Estadio Nacional, 400 Metros Al Norte, Managua (tel: 226-002, 222-115, 226-677; fax: 622-103).

Other useful addresses

Association of Nicaraguan Producers and Exporters of Non-Traditional Products (APENN), Del Restaurante Terraza 1/2 C Al Norte (tel: 668-276, 668-279).

Bank of Central American Economic Intergration (BCIE), Edificio BCIE, 2do, piso, Plaza España, Managua (tel: 66-4120; fax: 66-4125).

British Embassy, El Reparto Los Robles 1, entrada principal de la Primera Etapa, Los Robles, Managua (tel: 780-014, 780-887, 674-050; fax: 784-085).

Central American Institute of Business Administration (INCAE), Carretera Sur Km 15 1/2, Managua.

Centre of Export and Investments, Hotel Intercontinental, 1c, abajo 3 1/2c al Sur, Managua (tel: 68-1063; fax: 66-4476; e-mail: cei@cei.lbw.com.ni).

Development Bank (BID), Carretera a Masaya, Km 4 1/2, Managua (tel: 67-0831; fax: 67-3469).

Dirección General de Promoción de Exportaciones, Km 6, Carretera a Masaya, Apdo 2412, Managua, JR.

Empresa Nicaragüense de Promoción de Exportaciones, Apdo 1449, Managua.

Exports of the Handicraft Industry, S.A., Centro de Feria la Pinata (tel: 670-358; fax: 670-192).

Institute of Local Governments, Los Arcos, Entrada principal, 20 varas al Sur, Managua (tel: 66-6050; fax: 44-4567).

Institute of National Technology, Centro Cívico, Managua (tel: 65-0049; fax: 65-1976).

Institute of Nicaraguan Insurance and Reinsurance, Carretera Sur, Km 4 1/2, Managua (tel: 68-0239; fax: 68-0265).

Institute of Nicaraguan Social Security (NSS), Semáforos del Hotel Intercontinental, 2c abajo, 1c al lago, Contiguo a Policlínica Central, Managua (tel: 22-7445; fax: 22-7454).

Institute of Statistics and Censors, Frente Hospital Lenin Fonséca, Managua (tel: 66-7663; fax: 66-7872).

International Development Agency (AID), Semáforos Centroamérica, 400 mts al Oeste, Managua (tel: 67-3909; fax: 77-0210).

Nicaraguan Electricity, Frente Entrada a Colegio Rigoberto López, Pérez, Managua (tel: 77-4159; fax: 67-1700).

Nicaraguan Centre of Technological Information (CENIT), Sandy's 11/2 C. Arriba (tel: 675-325).

Nicaraguan Canals and Irrigation Authority, Carretera Sur Km 5, Managua (tel: 66-7863; fax: 66-7872).

Nicaraguan Development Fund, AP 2598, Managua (tel: 666-077, 666-066).

Nicaraguan Embassy (USA), 1627 New Hampshire Avenue, NW, Washington DC 20009 (tel: (+1-202) 939-6531; fax: (+1-202) 939-6532; ofemb@embanic.org).

Nicaraguan Institute for Economic and Social Investigations (INIES), del Hospital Alejandro Davila Bolanas, 3 c. al Lago, Managua.

Nicaraguan Investment Fund (of Central Bank), Shell de Colonia Centroamericana, Media al Lago, Managua.

Nicaraguan Telephone Company, Residencial Villa Fontana, Edificio Ville Fontana, Managua (tel: 28-5280; fax: 28-4628).

Port Authority, Residencial Bolonia, Optica Nicaragüense, 1c al Lago, 1c abajo, Managua (tel: 66-3274; fax: 66-4622).

Superior Council of Private Enterprise (COSEP), del Restaurante Terraza, Media cuadra al lago, Managua.

UN High Commission for Relief (ACNUR), Residencial Bolonia, Contiguo a Viajes Atlantida, Managua (tel/fax: 68-0476).

US Embassy, Apdo 327, Managua (tel: 666-010).

World Bank, Plaza España, Edificio Málaga, Modulos No A 1/A 22, Managua (tel: 26-0562; fax: 661-000).

Internet sites

Banco Central de Nicaragua: www.bcn.gob.ni

Nicaraguan Centre for Exports and Investments (CEI): www.cei.org.ni

Organisation of American States: www.oas.org

Ministry of Foreign Affairs: www.cancilleria.gob.ni

Nicaraguan stock exchange: http://bolsanic.com

Nicaraguan Solidarity Campaign: www.nicaraguasc.org.uk

Nicaragua Network: www.nicanet.org

La Prensa: www.laprensa.com.ni

El Nuevo Diario: www.elnuevodiario.com.ni

La Noticia: www.lanoticia.com.ni

Niger

KEY FACTS

Official name: République du Niger (Republic of Niger)

Head of State: President Mahamadou Issoufou (from 7 Apr 2011)

Head of government: Prime Minister Brigi Rafini (from 7 Apr 2011)

Ruling party: Coalition led by Parti Nigerien pour la Démocratie et le Socialisme (PNDS) (Niger Party for Democracy and Socialism) and independents (from 7 April 2011)

Area: 1,267,000 square km

Population: 15.20 million (2010)*

Capital: Niamey

Official language: French; Hausa is the major *lingua franca* especially for trade

Currency: CFA franc (CFAf) = 100 centimes (Communauté Financière Africaine (African Financial Community) franc). New notes have been issued; old notes cease to be legal tender from Jan 2005.

Exchange rate: CFAf488.90 per US$ (Oct 2011); CFAf655.95 per euro (pegged from Jan 1999)

GDP per capita: US$371 (2009)*

GDP real growth: 5.50% (2010)*

GDP: US$5.26 billion (2009)*

Inflation: 4.30% (2009)

Balance of trade: -US$437.40 million (2008)

* estimated figure

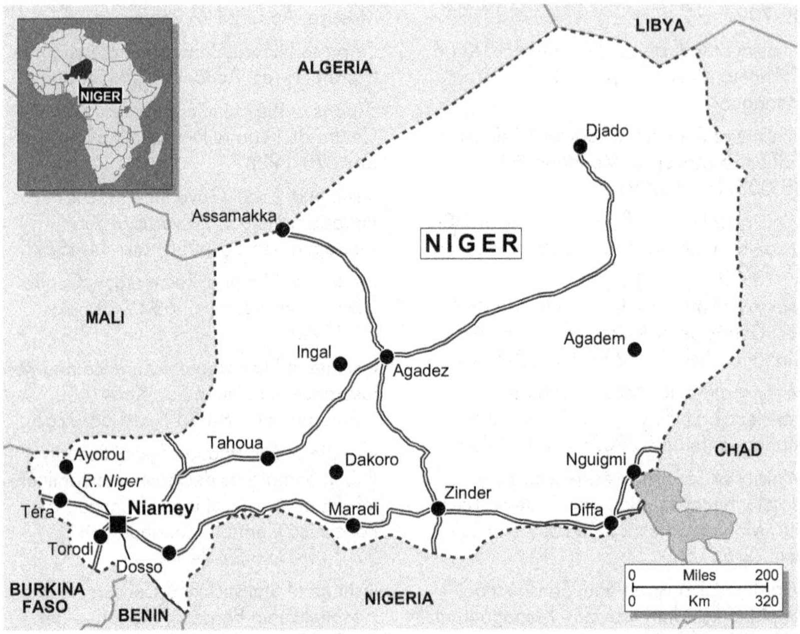

Niger in 2010 had its moments. First there was the on-going drought and famine, then a coup in February which bought Colonel Salou Djibo to power, floods overtook the drought, and a referendum in October giving immunity to the February coup leaders lead to presidential and parliamentary elections in January 2011. The Conseil Suprême pour la Restauration de la Démocratie (CSRD) (Supreme Council for the Restoration of Democracy) which had been set up after the coup had appointed a civilian prime minister – Mahamadou Danda – to oversee the transition to civilian rule. The CSRD also established the National Consultative Council, charged with drawing up a new constitution to restore democracy, sound management of public finances and national reconciliation.

The second round of the presidential election, held on 12 March 2011, was won by Mahamadou Issoufou (of the Parti pour le Socialisme et la Démocratie au Niger (PSDN) (Party for Socialism and Democracy in Niger)). He appointed Brigi Rafini as prime minister, to lead a coalition government with most members drawn from the PSDN and others independent members of parliament. Issoufou was sworn in on 7 April, ending the military transition that began in February 2010 with the overthrow of president Mamadou Tandja, who had been seeking to stay in office beyond his legal two terms.

The economy

The *African Economic Outlook 2011* (AEO), published jointly by the African Development Bank and the Organisation for Economic Co-operation and Development, reported that real gross domestic product (GDP) growth in 2010, estimated at 5.5 per cent, was essentially the result of the dynamism of the agricultural sector. After a disastrous 2009, when GDP shrank by 1.2 per cent after exceptional 9.5 per cent growth in 2008, the winter season was productive and harvests were abundant throughout the country.

The industrial sector is dominated by mining, in particular of uranium, coal, gold and silver. Uranium production, which amounted to 3,241 tonnes in 2009, totalled 812 and 1,118 tonnes respectively in the first two quarters of 2010. Coal production, which amounted to 225,072 tonnes in 2009, totalled 80,222 tonnes in the first quarter of 2010 and 59,232 tonnes in the second, which, on a full year basis, would represent an increase of 24 per cent. Gold production, which amounted to 2,067 kilos in 2009, totalled 549 and 630 kilos in the first two quarters of 2010. The increase in gold production seen in 2010 should continue and even accelerate in 2011–12.

International trade and development

Niger's political upheavals in 2009 and 2010, together with the drought which necessitated extra food imports, meant that the trade deficit increased in 2010 to -15.3 per cent of GDP. This negative performance was the result of a 20 per cent increase in imports compared to 2009, principally in the form of energy products (hydrocarbons and electricity) which rose 42 per cent, and cereals, which increased 89.7 per cent. Exports rose nearly 13 per cent compared to 2009, boosted by a 33 per cent increase in exports from the uranium sector, thanks above all to higher uranium production by the Société des Mines de l'Aïr (Somaïr). This positive export result was also helped by gold production, which increased by virtually 50 per cent in relation to 2009.

Political tensions following the establishment of the 6th Republic in August 2009 resulted in wariness among virtually all the country's economic partners, the European Union (EU) and the United States first among them. Numerous technical and economic co-operation agreements were suspended. However, Niger, like other West African Economic and Monetary Union (Waemu) countries, has yet to ratify an economic partnership agreement with the EU. So for the time being, Niger is still benefiting from the Everything But Arms initiative, which gives it free access to EU markets.

The private sector in Niger is one of the engines of economic growth. The modern private sector is of modest size. According to estimates, about 600 companies employ a little more than 8,000 people and pay a combined wage bill of about CFAf15.3 billion (US$31.3 million), which is about one third that of the public service sector. Formal industrial and manufacturing activities employ about 2,000 people and are extremely limited in number. They account for about one in 10 companies and are not very productive. These companies are particularly affected by competition from smuggled and illegal imports and reductions in tariff and non-tariff barriers in the context of sub-regional integration. They are also heavily dependent on imported inputs and suffer from an absence of integration in the local economy.

The informal private sector, excluding agriculture, is estimated to account for 30 per cent of the economy. If the rural sector is included, the informal economy represents close to 75 per cent of Niger's production. Since 1998 the informal sector has progressed by 4 per cent per year, driven mainly by cross-border commercial activity.

Despite the economic crisis and political disruption, foreign direct investment (FDI) in Niger showed a very appreciable increase in 2010, rising from CFAf345.6 billion (US$706 million) in 2009 to CFAf495.3 billion (US$1.1 billion). This is probably due to the fact that France's AREVA and China National Petroleum Corporation and China Nuclear International Uranium Corporation respected their commitments to invest in the mining and oil sectors. Projections for 2011 indicate that there will nevertheless be a small 5.6 per cent reduction.

Apart from the opprobrium cast on Niger as a result of the 2010 coup, mostly by the West, Niger has long maintained diplomatic relations with the emerging powers and in particular with China, Iran and Pakistan. China has been developing its position for some years and it now rivals France as Niger's leading economic and trading partner.

In 2011 the Arab Spring brought more trouble to Niger, first in the form of some 54,000 people fleeing the conflict in Libya, according to the International Organisation for Migration. Then on 14 September officials confirmed that Saadi Gadafi, one of former Libyan leader Col Muammar Qadafi's sons, had arrived in Niamey and had been granted refuge. This had been an awkward decision for the government to make – Saadi's father had, after all, been generous to Niger while he was alive.

Risk assessment

Politics	Improving
Economy	Improving
Regional stability	Fair

COUNTRY PROFILE

Historical profile

1800s The British were the first Europeans to explore the area.

1891–1911 France colonised the region, although it did not gain full control until much later and even then resistance movements continued.

1960 Niger gained independence from France under the presidency of Hamani Diori.

1974 Diori was overthrown and replaced by Lieutenant Colonel Seyni Kountche.

1987 Kountche died and was replaced by Brigadier Ali Saibou.

1989 Civilian rule was re-introduced with a new constitution, under a one-party system. Ali Saibou was re-elected president.

1990 The Tuareg people in the north began a rebellion.

1991 Saibou lost power to a transitional government led by Andre Salifou.

1992 A referendum overwhelmingly approved a new multi-party constitution

1993 Multi-party elections resulted in Mahamane Ousmane being elected president; his coalition, the Alliance of the Forces of Change (AFC), won most seats in parliament.

1995 A peace accord was signed between the government and the Tuareg.

KEY INDICATORS — Niger

	Unit	2006	2007	2008	2009	2010
Population	m	*12.95	*13.35	*13.77	*14.19	*15.20
Gross domestic product (GDP)	US$bn	3.58	*4.17	5.39	*5.26	–
GDP per capita	US$	*276	*313	*392	*340	–
GDP real growth	%	5.1	*3.2	*9.3	*1.0	*5.2
Inflation	%	1.4	3.3	7.6	4.3	–
Exports (fob) (goods)	US$m	508.0	663.3	912.3	–	–
Imports (fob) (goods)	US$m	748.3	914.6	1,349.7	–	–
Balance of trade	US$m	-240.3	-251.3	-437.4	–	–
Current account	US$m	-313.7	-351.3	-651.4	*-1,172.0	–
Total reserves minus gold	US$m	370.9	593.0	702.1	655.5	760.3
Foreign exchange	US$m	357.8	579.3	687.4	556.9	663.4
Exchange rate	per US$	496.60	454.40	447.81	514.03	495.28

* estimated figure

1996 Ousmane was toppled in a coup and replaced by Ibrahim Maïnassara Baré. A military-backed civilian government was formed. Maïnassara won the presidential election.
1997 A peace accord with the last Tuareg rebel group was signed.
1999 President Maïnassara was assassinated and Major Daouda Mallam Wanké assumed power. A new constitution was approved, which balanced the power between the president, prime minister and the National Assembly. Mamadou Tandja won the presidential election.
2000 Droughts caused widespread food shortages.
2001 After another poor harvest, food prices escalated and famine ensued.
2002 The EU granted US$319.5 million for Niger's poverty reduction effort.
2003 The US claimed Iraq had attempted to purchase uranium from Niger, in violation of UN sanctions. The claim was rejected by the government.
2004 The World Bank and the IMF supported a US$1.20 billion debt relief programme. Incumbent Tandja was re-elected president and the ruling Mouvement National pour la Société du Développement (MNSD) (National Movement for the Society of Development) won the parliamentary elections.
2005 Hama Amadou became prime minister. Taxes were increased by 20 per cent and sparked widespread protests. The UN warned that three million faced starvation due to a severe drought after locusts had damaged crops.
2006 The government began repatriating Mahamid Arab settlers to Chad.
2007 Niger assumed control of the island of Lete and other islands in the river Niger in accordance with an International Court of Justice ruling settling a border dispute with Benin. Opponents accused the government of embezzling US$9 million from foreign donor funds for education, between 2002–06. Prime Minister Hama Amadou lost four votes of no confidence in parliament and the president appointed Seyni Oumarou as prime minister.
2008 New satellite images released showed that extensive tree planting has transformed once deforested areas.
2009 The constitutional court ruled that President Tandja's plan to hold a referendum to extend his time in office by a third term was illegal. Opposition parties and civil society groups formed a coalition, La Coordination des Forces Démocratiques pour la République (CFDR) (Co-ordination of Democratic Forces for the Republic) to resist his proposal. However, President Tandja dissolved parliament and suspended the constitution, and assumed power by presidential decree. Opposition leaders described the action as a *coup d'état*. Despite a call by the opposition to boycott the referendum on extending Presidential Tandja's term in office, according to official statistics, 92.5 per cent voted in favour of the proposition, with a turnout of 68.26 per cent. CFDR claimed the turnout was less than 7 per cent. An opposition leader, Marou Amadou, was abducted by uniformed men (thought to be from the Republican Guard), shortly after being released by a court on charges of breaching state security – he had called for protests against the referendum result. President Tandja appointed Ali Badjo Gamatié as prime minister. In parliamentary elections, which were boycotted by the opposition, the ruling MNSD won a majority with 76 seats (out of 113). The Economic Community of West African States (Ecowas) announced that it did not recognise the legitimacy of Mamadou Tandja's presidency.
2010 Colonel Salou Djibo mounted a *coup d'état* that toppled President Tandja on 18 February and installed a military junta, the Conseil Suprême pour la Restauration de la Démocratie (CSRD) (Supreme Council for the Restoration of Democracy) on 19 February, by which Colonel Djibo was proclaimed president. Both the AU and France condemned the actions. The CSRD appointed Mahamadou Danda as caretaker prime minister on 23 February. The military government announced in May that a constitutional referendum would be held in October followed by a presidential election on 26 December, with a run-off in January 2011, if no clear winner was chosen. In August, the UN's World Food Programme (UN-WFP) declared that Niger was facing its worst ever food crisis, with around 7.3 million people (almost half the population) in desperate need of food, following crop failures after a drought in 2009. Heavy rains broke the prolonged drought but were too late to save harvests and bought flooding that damaged homes and stored grain instead. A constitutional referendum was held on 31 October; 90.18 per cent voted in favour of changes to give immunity to the February coup leaders and requiring a transition of power by 6 April 2011.
2011 In parliamentary elections that had been postponed from December 2010 and held on 31 January, Parti Nigerien pour la Democratie et le Socialisme-Tarayya (PNDS) (Nigerien Party for Democracy and Socialism-Tarayya) won 39 seats out of 113 and the MNSD 26 seats. In the first round of presidential elections held at the same time, of the four candidates standing Mahamadou Issoufou (PNDS) won 36.1 per cent, Seyni Oumarou (MNSD) 23.2 per cent of the vote. In the run-off, held on 12 March, Issoufou won 57.95 per cent and Oumarou 42.05 per cent; turnout was 48.2 per cent. Oumarou conceded defeat on 17 March. The president and government took office on 7 April, when Mahamadou Issoufou immediately appointed Brigi Rafini (an ethnic Tuareg) as prime minister, plus forming a coalition government with most members drawn from the PNDS and other posts given to independent members of parliament (MP). In April, the International Organisation for Migration stated that Niger was providing emergency relief and accommodation to over 54,000 people fleeing the conflict in Libya. Ten people were arrested on 2 August accused of a coup attempt in July, while a further suspect was reported to be on the run. Officials confirmed on 14 September that Saadi Qadafi, one of fugitive Libyan leader Col Muammar Qadafi's sons had arrived in Niamey and had been granted refuge.

Political structure

Constitution

A referendum was held on 4 August 2009 to agree a new constitution which includes: an extension to President Tanja's mandate until 2012, during which time a new constitution will be drafted and proposed; the system of government will change from semi-presidential to full presidential; no limit to the term in office for a president; a new bicameral parliament would include a senate.
The constitution was amended in November 2010 to give immunity to the February 2010 *coup d'état* leaders and require that a transition of power be made by 6 April 2011.

Form of state

Presidential, unitary, multiparty republic.

The executive

The directly elected president is the Head of State, elected for a five-year term, renewable only once.
The president, shares power with the prime minister but has final responsibility for co-ordinating the actions of the executive branch of government. The president names the prime minister, from a list of three candidates, who become head of government and is accountable to parliament.

National legislature

The unicameral Assemblée Nationale (National Assembly) has 113 members elected for a maximum five-year term.

Legal system

Based on French civil law system and customary law.

Last elections

4 August 2009 (constitutional amendment); 31 January 2011 (parliament), 31 January and 12 March 2011 (presidential, first round and runoff)

Results: Referendum: 90.18 per cent voted in favour of changes.
Parliamentary: Parti Nigerien pour la Démocratie et le Socialisme (PNDS) (Niger Party for Democracy and Socialism) won 39 seats (out of 113), Mouvement National de la Société de Développement (MNSD) (National Movement for a Developing Society) 26, Mouvement Démocratique Nigérien pour une Fédération Africaine (Moden-FA) (Nigerien Democratic Movement for an African Federation) 24, Alliance Nigérienne pour la Démocratie et le Progrès (ANDP) (Nigerien Alliance for Democracy and Progress) eight, Rassemblement pour la Démocratie et le Progrès (RDP) (Party for Democracy and Progress) seven, Union pour la République (UPR) (Union for the Republic) six, Convention Démocratique et Sociale (CDS) (Democratic and Social Convention) two; one seat undeclared. Turnout was 52.8 per cent.
Presidential, first round: Mahamadou Issoufou (PNDS) won 36.1 per cent of the vote, Seyni Oumarou MNSD 23.2 per cent, Hama Amadou (Moden-FA) 19.8 per cent, Mahamane Ousmane (CDS) 8.4 per cent. Runoff: Issoufou won 57.95 per cent of the vote, Oumarou 42.05 per cent; turnout was 48.2 per cent.

Next elections

2015 (parliamentary and presidential).

Political parties

Ruling party

Coalition led by Parti Nigerien pour la Démocratie et le Socialisme (PNDS) (Niger Party for Democracy and Socialism) and independents (from 7 April 2011)

Main opposition party

Parti Nigerien pour la Démocratie et le Socialisme (PNDS) (Niger Party for Democracy and Socialism)

Population

15.20 million (2010)*
Last census: May 2001: 10,790,352 (provisional)
Population density: Eight inhabitants per square km. Urban population: 21 per cent (1995–2001).
Annual growth rate: 3.3 per cent 2007 (INS)

Ethnic make-up

Hausa (56 per cent), Djerma (22 per cent), Tuareg (8 per cent).

Religions

Islam (85 per cent), traditional beliefs (14.5 per cent), Christianity (0.5 per cent).

Education

Public expenditure on education is around 2 per cent of GDP.
Primary education is free and compulsory and lasts until aged 12. Secondary schooling is divided, beginning with the first cycle secondary school from aged 12 to 16, then second cycle secondary school from aged 16 to 19, when students are expected to graduate with a Baccalauréat. Alternatively, at aged 16 students may elect to undertake a three year technical course. All education is conducted in French.
Literacy rate: 17 per cent adult rate; 25 per cent youth rate (15–24) (Unesco 2005).
Compulsory years: 6 to 12
Enrolment rate: 29 per cent gross primary enrolment, 7 per cent gross secondary enrolment; of relevant age groups (including repeaters) (World Bank).
Pupils per teacher: 41 in primary schools

Health

Improved water sources are available to 59 per cent of the population.
There were cases of polio reported to the World Health Organisation – Global Polio Eradication Initiative in 2006; the country had previously been free of the disease and its re-emergence was due to infected visitors from Nigeria.

HIV/Aids

There are an estimated 64,000 people living with HIV/Aids, of which 36,000 are women. In addition there are 5,900 children (0–17) HIV positive and 24,000 orphans. In 2003 there were 4,800 deaths due to Aids, although Niger has so far escaped much of the African pandemic. However, with 25–35 per cent of sex workers testing positive, there is a chance that increased population mobility and a lack of condom use could make Niger vulnerable.
HIV prevalence: 1.2 per cent aged 15–49 in 2003 (World Bank)
Life expectancy: 41 years, 2004 (WHO 2006)
Fertility rate/Maternal mortality rate: 7.8 births per woman, 2004 (WHO 2006); maternal mortality 590 per 100,000 live births (World Bank).
Child (under 5 years) mortality rate (per 1,000): 154 per 1,000 live births; 40 per cent of children aged under five are malnourished (World Bank).
Head of population per physician: 0.03 physicians per 1,000 people, 2004 (WHO 2006)

Welfare

Around 61.4 per cent of the population live on less than US$1 per day and 85.3 per cent live on less than US$2 per day. The distribution of wealth is highly unequal with a Gini index of 50.5 and the richest 20 per cent of the population owning 53.3 per cent of the total wealth.

Main cities

Niamey (capital, estimated population 794,814 in 2005), Zinder (205,520), Maradi (179,040), Agadez (95,083), Tahoua (82,636), Arlit (90,669) (built for the uranium industry).

Languages spoken

The distribution of languages is dependent on the ethnic groups within Niger. The Hausa are the largest group and their language is recognised as a national language, as is Songhai-Zarma (Djerma) the next largest language group. Tamashek, which is spoken by the Tuareg, is related to Berber. Others languages in daily use include Fulani, Arabic, Kanauri, Courmantché and Toubou.

Official language/s

French; Hausa is the major *lingua franca* especially for trade

Media

Despite laws which provide for freedom of the press there are government restrictions and journalists are subject to intimidation so that self-censorship is practiced.

Press

With low literacy levels there are few publications on offer. In French, *Le Sahel* is the government daily; weeklies include the weekend *Sahel Dimanche* and *Le Républicain Niger* (www.republicain-niger.com), which is an independent magazine. Tam Tam (www.tamtaminfo.com) is an online publication in French.

Broadcasting

The national, state-run broadcaster is the Office de Radiodiffusion Télévision du Niger (ORTN) (www.ortn.ne).
Radio: Due to the low literacy rate radio services are the main medium of mass communication and sources of news and information.
ORTN (www.ortn.ne) operates the only national radio station called La Voix du Sahel (www.ortn.ne) with programmes in French, Arabic, Hausa and local languages. There are several private radio stations which target specific audiences with programmes of social development, health, education and the interests of women, such as Anfani FM and Tambara FM. Entertainment radio includes Radio et Musique, Horizon FM and Tenere FM.
Television: ORTN (www.ortn.ne) operates two channels. TV Sahel is the national network using satellite technology and Tal TV is a digital service for the capital and its environs. A private stations Tenere TV and the pay-to-view Telestar are based in the capital.

News agencies

APA (African Press Agency): www.apanews.net
Reuters Africa: http://africa.reuters.com

Economy

As one of the least developed countries in the world, Niger's economy is dominated by agriculture and the export of uranium from the world's largest deposits situated in the north of the country. In 2011, the UN Human Development Index (HDI) ranked Niger at 186 out of 187 for its development in health, education and income. In 2010 69.4 per cent of the population experienced deprivation in at least one of the indicators and 43.1 per cent were living on an equivalent of US$1.25 per day. Per capita income was estimated at US$340 in 2009 with most of the population sustained by subsistence agriculture, which is the main source of income for most households; livestock production is mostly exported to neighbouring countries, particularly Nigeria.

GDP growth was 3.3 per cent in 2007 and grew to 9.5 per cent in 2008, due to an excellent harvest that increased agricultural production by 25 per cent, however by 2009 growth had slowed to an estimated 1 per cent as global trade was cut. GDP growth was forecast to rise to 5.2 per cent in 2010 as trade picked up.

The industrial sector also grew through the increase in electricity production, telecommunications and transport which reflected the expansion in public and private investment, particularly in mining and infrastructure construction. In 2009 the French mining company, Areva, signed a US$1.7 billion deal with the government to develop the Imouraren uranium field, which when in full production (scheduled for 2012, although in late 2011 there were rumours of a delay) will double Niger's uranium output.

Uranium exports provide the largest proportion of foreign exchange. Government revenue is around 17.5 per of GDP, of which mining receipts accounted for over 60 per cent. Uranium exports require special licences which are only granted to registered buyers, particularly in France and Japan. In the long-term, Niger hopes to move away from its dependence on uranium through the exploitation of other mineral resources, such as gold and oil. The Samira Hill gold mine, operated by a Moroccan-Canadian consortium, with a 20 per cent Niger stake, has been in production since 2004. Two new gold seams were found in 2008, close to the current operation.

External trade

It is a member of the Economic Community of West African States (Ecowas), which was set up to promote economic integration among members. Niger is also a member of the West African Economic and Monetary Union (WAEMU) using the common currency, the CFA franc.

Along with uranium exports, live animal exports, primarily to Nigeria, are also very important to the economy.

A weak industrial and manufacturing sector typically requires domestic needs to be met by imports.

Imports

Principal imports are foodstuffs, consumer goods, machinery, vehicles and parts, petroleum and cereals.

Main sources: France (typically 16 per cent of total), China (13 per cent), US (7 per cent).

Exports

Principal exports are uranium ore, gold, livestock, cow-peas and onions.

Main destinations: France (typically 35 per cent of total), Nigeria (17 per cent), Japan (13 per cent).

Agriculture

Farming

Subsistence farming and stock rearing contribute around 40 per cent to GDP and employ 70 per cent of the workforce. Less than 3 per cent of the total land area is cultivated.

Hides and skins and cotton account for around 20 per cent of export earnings.

The government is encouraging market gardening – galmi onions are an important cash crop.

Production of the two principal food crops, millet and sorghum, is generally insufficient to satisfy domestic needs, even in times of good rains, and is supplemented by food aid. Other food crops include rice, cowpeas and green beans.

Recurrent drought and desertification have had a serious impact on livestock rearing and have led to significant food shortages with disastrous consequences. The government is investing heavily in anti-desertification schemes and is encouraging animal husbandry.

Industry and manufacturing

The industrial sector is small-scale, contributing around 7 per cent to GDP and employing 5 per cent of the workforce.

Manufacturing is concentrated on the processing of agricultural commodities such as sugar refining, brewing, cotton ginning, tanning and flour/rice milling.

Other activities include small-scale production of cement and metals, textiles, plastics, soft drinks and construction materials.

Industrial development is handicapped by the shortage of capital and skilled labour and by the country's weak infrastructure.

Tourism

The tourist sector is expected to contribute 1.7 per cent of GDP and provide employment for 3.5 per cent of the workforce. There is much room for expansion and travel and tourism is estimated to attract 9.1 per cent of all capital investment.

Environment

In June 2010 the African Union backed a proposal to build the 'Great Green Wall' project, of a 15km wide, 7,775km long, continuous belt of trees from Senegal in the west to Djibouti in the east (traversing 11 countries) in an effort to halt the advance of the Sahara Desert. The trees to be used would be drought-adapted, preferably native to the area from a list of 37 possible species, and should help to slow soil erosion and filter rain water.

Mining

The mining sector accounts for around 11 per cent of GDP and employs 5 per cent of the workforce.

Niger is the third-largest exporter of uranium and has been the country's principal export since early 1970s. Proven reserves total 280,000 tonnes with extraction undertaken mainly at two opencast mines, at Arlit and Akouta. Production stagnated at 3,000–3,200 tonnes due to a world slump in the demand for uranium. Production has increased in recent years, but depressed prices on the world market have seen the value of uranium exports fall. The major export markets are France, Japan, Spain, Germany and Egypt. On 6 January 2009, Niger licensed the French nuclear energy group Areva to operate the Imouraren mine. The mine will become the largest in Africa and the second largest in the world, it is expected to begin production of uranium in 2012, producing 5,000 tonnes per year. Areva will invest US$1.51 billion, over 60 per cent of the initial investment and will take a two-thirds stake in the mine, with the government owning the remainder.

Other minerals exploited are the tin-bearing ore cassiterite, phosphates, molybdenum, salt and coal. There are also known reserves of iron ore.

The Samira gold mine in Niamey, in the Koma Bangou concession in west Niger, produces around 5,000 ounces of gold annually and, before 2011, is expected to produce three tonnes and earn US$28 billion. The government owns 20 per cent and two Canadian mining companies the other 80 per cent of the mine. Gold prospecting agreements have been reached with three other Canadian companies for further research in the region.

Imperial Metals is drilling for diamonds on the M'Banga concession.

Hydrocarbons

There are proven (amounts have not been disclosed) oil reserves in the Agadem block in the Termit Basin in the south-west. Since 2003 the China National Petroleum Corporation (CNPC) (a

state oil company) increased its presence in Niger so that by June 2008 CNPC was given oil exploration rights in a deal local mining unions described as secretive and contemptuous of regulations and which was condemned by civil rights groups, who want the spending of investment funds to be scrutinised by parliament. A security warning that prevented drilling of the 68,800 square kilometre Tenere oil field, imposed in 2007, was lifted in December 2009. Concern is centred on the benefit to the country from oil profits being either squandered or corruptly embezzled. Investment of US$5 billion is allocated to oil production, a 2,000km pipeline and the building of a 20,000 barrels per day (bpd) oil refinery.
All domestic oil consumption is provided by imports, which were 6,000bpd in 2008.
In July 2009, Algeria, Niger and Nigeria signed an agreement to build a 2,580km trans-Sahara gas pipeline (TSGP) traversing all three countries, which is estimated will cost US$13 billion and transport up to 30 billion cum of natural gas, destined for Europe. Three foreign energy companies also expressed an interest in investing in the project, Russia's Gazprom, France's Total and the Anglo-Dutch Shell.
There are small coal reserves at Tchirozerine (1,000km north of the capital). These reserves stand at around 780,000 tonnes. Annual production is typically 200,000 tonnes of bituminous (brown coal) used in power generation. There is negligible domestic demand, although this may be set to rise. There has been a further discovery of coal reserves in Takanamat, in central Niger.
Natural gas is neither produced nor consumed.

Energy
Total installed generating capacity was 105MW in 2007, producing around 200 million kilowatt hours; only 12 per cent of the population has access to mains electricity. Niger has an estimated hydroelectric potential of 250MW, but an agreement with Nigeria whereby 45MW of electricity is guaranteed from Nigeria in return for the uninterrupted flow of water along the Niger River inhibits Niger's ability to dam the river in its territory. There are small-scale, isolated diesel generators providing the majority of the country's community needs. The majority of the population relies on non-commercial biomass, mostly fuel wood, for cooking, lighting and power.
It may be possible to use the 1.3 million tonnes of agricultural waste to produce biogas, but no plans exist for its exploitation. Solar panels are being introduced by private individuals.

Financial markets
Stock exchange
Afribourse (Bourse Régionale des Valeurs Moblières) (BRVM)

Banking and insurance
Central bank
Banque Centrale des Etats de l'Afrique de l'Ouest
Main financial centre
Niamey

Time
GMT plus one hour

Geography
Niger is a landlocked country in western Africa, with Algeria and Libya to the north, Nigeria and Benin to the south, Mali and Burkina Faso to the west and Chad to the east. It is 80 per cent desert, in the north, and 20 per cent savannah in the south. In the central north there is a volcanic mountain range, Aïr Massif, which includes Mount Gréboun, the tallest peak at a height of 1,944 metres. The Niger river flows from Mali to Nigeria through Niger in the south west for about 563km and a small portion of Lake Chad occupies the south-eastern corner of Niger.
Hemisphere
Northern

Climate
Niger is very hot with temperatures ranging from 28–44 degrees Celsius. There is rain mainly in the south from June–September. Frequent Sahara dust storms occur from November–January. The dry season is from October–May.

Entry requirements
Passports
Required by all and must have at least six month validity left; nationals of certain African countries may visit with national ID cards.
At each overnight stay passports must be presented to the police. As passports are stamped each time, they will require enough blank pages for the visit. Travel by any other route than that stamped in the passport by the police is forbidden.
Visa
Required by all, except citizens of some African countries close to Niger. Contact the nearest Niger embassy for further details and an application form. Visitors are required to supply proof of return/onward passage and funds, for living expenses of US$500. All documents require a French translation.
An exit permit will be required for all visitors that required an entry visa, from the Immigration Department in Niamey, before departure.
Currency advice/regulations
The import of local currency is unlimited; export is limited to CFAf25,000. Import and export of foreign currency is unlimited.
Travellers cheques are accepted in hotels and banks; to avoid extra exchange charges cheques in euros are recommended.

Health (for visitors)
Mandatory precautions
A yellow fever and cholera vaccination certificate is required if arriving from an infected area.
Advisable precautions
Inoculations and booster should be current for tetanus, hepatitis A, diphtheria, typhoid and yellow fever. There may be a need for vaccinations for tuberculosis, hepatitis B and meningitis and cholera.
Anti-mosquito measures including mosquito repellents, nets and clothing covering the body should be used for protection against hepatitis B and yellow fever. There is a risk of rabies.
There is a shortage of routine medications and visitors should take all necessary medicines with them. A first aid kit that includes disposable syringes is a reasonable precaution. Use only bottled or boiled water for drinks, washing teeth and making ice. Eat only well cooked meals, preferably served hot; vegetables should be cooked and fruit peeled. Dairy products are unpasteurised and should be avoided, unless cooked.
Medical insurance is essential, including emergency evacuation, and an adequate supply of personal medicines is necessary.

Hotels
There are good hotels in Niamey. A 5 per cent service charge is usually added to bills.

Credit cards
International credit and debit cards are accepted in a limited number of places.

Public holidays (national)
Fixed dates
1 Jan (New Year's Day), 24 Apr (National Concord Day), 1 May (Labour Day), 3 Aug (Independence Day), 18 Dec (Republic Day), 25 Dec (Christmas Day).
Variable dates
Islamic New Year (two days), Easter Monday (Mar/Apr), Eid al Adha (two days), Birth of the Prophet (two days), Eid al Fitr (four days).
Islamic year 1433 (26 Nov 2011–14 Nov 2012): The Islamic year contains 354 or 355 days, with the result that Muslim feasts advance by 10–12 days against the Gregorian calendar. Dates of feasts vary according to the sighting of the new moon, so cannot be forecast exactly.

Working hours
Banking
Mon–Fri: 0800–1100 and 1600–1700.

Business
Winter: Mon–Fri: 0730–1230, 1500–1800; Sat: 0730–1230.
Summer: Mon–Fri: 0730–1230, 1530–1830; Sat: 0730–1230.
Government
Oct–Feb: Mon–Fri: 0730–1230 and 1500–1800; Mar–Sep: Mon–Fri: 0730–1230 and 1530–1830.
Shops
Mon–Fri: 0800–1200, 1600–1900; Sat: 0800–1200.

Telecommunications
Mobile/cell phones
There are 900 GSM services available in larger town in the south.

Electricity supply
220/380V AC, 50 cycles

Getting there
Air
International airport/s: Niamey International (NIM), 12km south-east of city; bar, currency exchange, post office, shops, car hire, hotel courtesy coaches.
Airport tax: None
Surface
Road: There are road connections and border crossings with all neighbouring countries. Access from Algeria and Mali is difficult, but a surfaced road connects Benin with Niamey. Access from Chad may be restricted.
Water: Ferries on the Niger River coming from Mali are dependent on the water level.

Getting about
National transport
Air: Charter flights are available in Niamey.
Road: Main highways link Tillabery with N'guigmi, Tahoua and Arlit, however not all roads are open to visitors without a permit. Petrol is not always available. Best months for road travel December–March. Visitors must report to police on arrival at main centres.
Buses: Services operate from Niamey to Zinder, Agadez, and other towns.
City transport
Taxis: Fixed rates apply for long-distance and urban services. Taxis in Niamey are cheap and widely available. Tipping is optional.
Journey time from airport to city centre 10 minutes.
Car hire
Self-drive or chauffeur-driven cars are available in Niamey. Chauffeurs are compulsory outside the capital. International driving licence required. Petrol and spares are in short supply and there are no recovery services.

BUSINESS DIRECTORY
The addresses listed below are a selection only. While World of Information makes every endeavour to check these addresses, we cannot guarantee that changes have not been made, especially to telephone numbers and area codes. We would welcome any corrections.

Telephone area codes
The international direct dialling code (IDD) for Niger is +227, followed by subscriber's number.

Useful telephone numbers
Police: 17
Fire: 18

Chambers of Commerce
Maradi Chamber of Commerce and Agriculture, PO Box 79, Maradi (tel: 410-366; fax: 410-451).

Niger Chamber of Commerce, Agriculture, Industriy and Handicrafts, Place de la Concertation, PO Box 209, Niamey (tel: 732-210; fax: 734-668; e-mail: cham209n@intnet.ne).

Zinder Chambre of Commerce and Agriculture, PO Box 83, Zinder (tel: 510-087; fax: 510-217).

Banking
Bank of Africa (Niger, Head Office); BP 10 973, Immeuble Sonara II, Niamey (tel: 733-620, 733-621; fax: 733-818).

Banque Centrale des Etats de l'Afrique de l'Ouest (Agency); BP 487, Rond Point de la Poste, Niamey (tel: 722-491/92; fax: 734-743).

Banque Commerciale du Niger (Head Office); BP 11 363, Rond Point Maourey, Niamey (tel: 733-915, 733-331; fax: 732-163).

Banque Internationale pour l'Afrique au Niger (Head Office); BP 10350, Avenue de la Mairie, Niamey (tel: 733-101; fax: 733-595; e-mail: bia@intnet.ne).

Banque Islamique du Niger pour le Commerce et l'industrie (BINCI), BP 12754, Immeuble El-Nasr, Niamey (tel: 732-730, 732-740; fax: 734-735).

Caisse de Prêts aux Collectivités Territoriale, BP 730, Route Torodi, Rive droite, Niamey (tel: 723-412, 723-080).

Caisse Nationale d'Epargne, Avenue du Niger, BP 11778 Niamey (tel: 732-498, 732-499; fax: 735-812)

Crédit du Niger, BP 213, Blvd de la République, Niamey (tel: 722-701, 722-702; fax: 722-390).

Ecobank-Niger, BP 13804, Niamey (tel: 737-181, 901-052; fax: 737-204, 737-203).

Société Nigérienne de Banque, BP 891, Ave de la Mairie, Niamey (tel: 734-569, 734-643; fax: 734-693).

Central bank
Banque Centrale des Etats de l'Afrique de l'Ouest, Direction Nationale, Rue de l'Uranium, PO Box 487, Niamey (tel: 722-491; fax: 734-743).

Stock exchange
Afribourse (Bourse Régionale des Valeurs Moblières) (BRVM): www.brvm.org

Travel information
Niamey International Airport, ASECNA, BP 1096, Niamey (tel: 732-517/518/519, 732-381/382; fax: 735-512).

Ministry of tourism
Ministère du Tourisme et d'Artisanat BP 12710, Niamey, Niger (tel: 736 522; fax: 732 387).

National tourist organisation offices
Office du Tourisme du Niger, BP 612, Niamey.

Other useful addresses
Centre for Investment Promotion, BP 12129, Niamey (tel: 736-836; fax: 736-772).

Conseil National de Développement, c/o Ministry of Planning, Niamey (tel: 722-233).

Direction des Statistiques, c/o Ministry of Planning, Niamey (tel: 722-799).

Embassy of the Republic of Niger, 154 rue du Longchamp, 75116 Paris, France (tel: (+33-1) 4504 8060; fax: (+33-1) 4504 7973).

Niger Embassy (US), 2204 R Street, NW, Washington DC 20008 (tel: (+1-202) 483-4224; fax: (+1-202) 483-3169; e-mail: ambassadeniger@hotmail.com).

Office Nationale des Ressources Minières (Onarem), BP 210, Niamey (tel: 723-935).

Société Nationale de Commerce et de Production du Niger, BP 615, Niamey.

Société Nigérienne de Produits Pétroliers (Sonidep), BP 2735, Niamey (tel: 733-335).

Sonhotel (Société Nigerienne de Gestion des Hôtels de l'Etat) (tel: 732-387).

Syndicat des Commerçants, Importateurs et Exportateurs du Niger, BP 535, Niamey.

Internet sites
Africa Business Network: www.ifc.org/abn

AllAfrica.com: http://allafrica.com

African Development Bank: www.afdb.org

Africa Online: www.africaonline.com

Nigeria

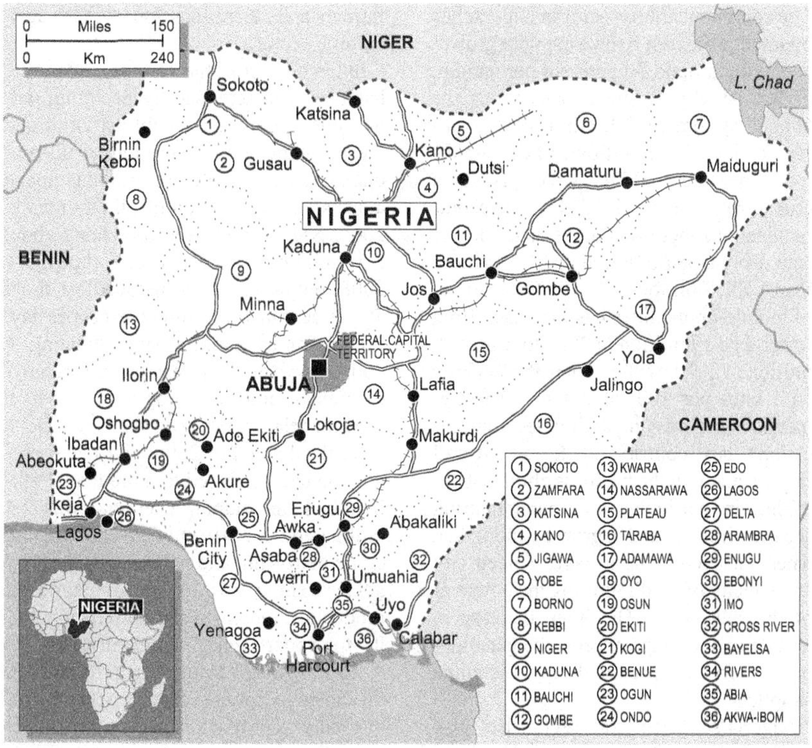

Nigeria at the end of 2011 could be said to be in the throes of the worst disruptions since the Biafran war of the late 1960s. The Boko Haram Islamic militant group from the north, although comparatively few in number, had committed several attacks on Churches, resulting in revenge attacks on Mosques, and government buildings. The government is hard pressed as to how to handle the group, whose urban guerrilla tactics have represented a new challenge with which they have been struggling to cope. Abubakar Kari, a political scientist from the University of Abuja, was reported by the British Broadcasting Corporation (BBC) as saying he believed the destruction of Boko Haram's headquarters in Borno state capital Maiduguri in 2009, when their founder and leader, Muhammad Yusuf, was captured and then killed in custody, is when the problem escalated. Hundreds of members of the group died and ever since it has been attacking government targets in retaliation. 'The rise of Boko Haram is largely as a result of incompetence, lack of foresight and insensitivity from the Nigerian state,' Mr Kari said.

Still no results

President Goodluck Jonathan was re-elected in the April 2011 presidential elections with a convincing majority of 58.89 per cent of the vote. However, final results of the parliamentary elections were still not available eight months later in December. The provisional results showed a win for the People's Democratic Party (PDP) with 147 seats (out of 360), and the Action Congress of Nigeria (ACN) with 57 seats in second place. According to the Nigerian Independent National Electoral Commission there were still 92 results unannounced at the end of the year.

The economy

The Nigerian government's current economic policies are focused on addressing

KEY FACTS

Official name: Federal Republic of Nigeria

Head of State: President Goodluck Jonathan (from 2010; re-elected 16 Apr 2011)

Head of government: President Goodluck Jonathan (from 2010; re-elected 16 Apr 2011)

Ruling party: People's Democratic Party (PDP) (since 1999; re-elected May 2007)

Area: 923,768 square km

Population: 158.30 million (2010)*

Capital: Abuja – federal capital since 1991; Lagos – commercial capital.

Official language: English

Currency: Naira (N) = 100 kobo

Exchange rate: N159.65 per US$ (Oct 2011)

GDP per capita: US$1,389 (2010)

GDP real growth: 8.40% (2010)

GNP per capita: US$216.80 billion (2010)

Inflation: 13.70% (2010)

Oil production: 2.40 million bpd (2010)

Balance of trade: US$20.24 billion (2010)

Annual FDI: US$6.05 billion (2010)

* estimated figure

key infrastructural shortcomings as a crucial element in setting the stage for longer-term stable growth in an effort to break the past 30 years of uncontrolled boom-and-bust cycles. The *African Economic Outlook 2011* (AEO), published jointly by the African Development Bank and the Organisation for Economic Co-operation and Development, notes that in recent years, the performance of the economy has responded positively to efficiency gains from economic reforms and, with the benefit of high oil prices, has generated strong growth. Economic growth at 7.0 per cent in 2009, and at an even stronger estimated 8.1 per cent in 2010 in the aftermath of the global economic crisis, underscored the resilience of the economy and reflected the prudence of economic policies.

In 2009, the government had eased the credit crunch by lowering interest rates. It had also recapitalised struggling banks. These policies maintained the confidence of lenders and borrowers in the financial market and stimulated the economy. With the unfolding global economic recovery supporting high oil prices, Nigeria can expect to maintain strong growth in 2011 and 2012. Improved access to credit from the reformed banking sector and enhanced provision of domestic energy supplies are also expected to support continued improved performance of the non-oil sector. Real GDP growth is thus projected to remain robust at 6.9 per cent in 2011 and at 6.7 per cent in 2012.

The AEO noted that strong growth in output recorded in 2010 was supported by the expansion in oil production following relative peace in the Niger Delta region, but the key driver of growth remained the non-oil sector. Non-oil growth averaged 8.3 per cent in 2010 and accounted for 84.8 per cent of total GDP. The main growth drivers in the non-oil sector were telecommunications, general commerce, manufacturing, agriculture and services. The communications sector in Nigeria has boomed in the past five years, with growth averaging around 30 per cent per annum, driven largely by the expansion of the Global System for Mobile (GSM) communications. Large inflows of foreign direct investment (FDI) have played a crucial role. The stock of FDI in telecommunications increased more than 200 per cent, from US$7.5 billion in 2005 to more than US$18 billion in 2010. The number of mobile-phone lines has increased from fewer than 19 million in 2005 to nearly 80 million in 2010, with teledensity reaching 54.2 lines per 100 inhabitants. The tremendous progress made in telecommunications has contributed to an overall improvement in the business climate, benefiting in particular the manufacturing sector, which, in 2010, grew by more than 6 per cent even with shortage of electricity and paucity of credit limiting the potential of the sub-sector. The huge increase in mobile phone usage reflects the generally poor service provided by landline suppliers.

Nigeria's agricultural sector has also performed remarkably well, with an estimated growth rate in 2010 exceeding 6.0 per cent, reflecting the good weather conditions that boosted crop production. The government's effort to address protracted issues of inadequate credit and high interest rates in agricultural lending through the Commercial Agricultural Credit Scheme (CACS) has also benefited agricultural expansion: in 2009/10 the government made N200 billion (US$1.25 billion) available at low interest rates to farmers and other practitioners in the agricultural sector.

In the oil sector, the previous five years has been characterised by declining output, due largely to militant activities and the accompanying disruption of oil-producing activities. Before militants began attacks and destruction of oil facilities in 2005, Nigeria had been producing about 2.5 million barrels per day (bpd). By 2008, output had been reduced by about 40 per cent to 1.5 million barrels per day. Production appeared to stop declining in 2009, however, following the federal government's amnesty programme, which brought relative peace to the Niger Delta area. By the end of 2009, petroleum production had increased to more than 2 million bpd, an output level that was 2.4 million bpd in 2010. Oil GDP, comprising crude petroleum and natural gas, grew by 3.9 per cent in 2010. At the same time, oil production remained the dominant activity for export and government revenues. According to government records, in 2010 oil and gas accounted for about 96 per cent of total export receipts and nearly 66 per cent of total government revenues. Oil reserves at the end of 2010 stood at 37.2 thousand million barrels, according to *BP Statistical Review of World Energy 2011*.

Although Nigeria's reserves of gas at the end of 2010 were, at 5.3 trillion cubic metres (cum) the highest in Africa, annual production of 33.6 billion cum was third highest in Africa, behind Algeria (80.4 billion cum) and Egypt (61.3 billion cum). The chief reason for this is the difficulty of moving the gas to market. Much of what is produced is flared.

In line with the high infusion of funds into the telecommunication and oil industries, total investment in the economy has remained high. In 2010, a 4.5 per cent increase in the volume of investment represented about 1.7 per cent of real GDP growth. The contribution of investment to GDP growth is expected to increase to about 2.5 per cent in 2011, but to fall slightly to 2.3 per cent in 2012 as investor confidence in the economy wanes in the wake of the political process. Indeed, Nigeria's prospects of enhancing investment contribution to growth will be better

KEY INDICATORS — Nigeria

	Unit	2006	2007	2008	2009	2010
Population	m	*140.00	*143.85	*147.81	*151.87	*158.30
Gross domestic product (GDP)	US$bn	146.89	207.10	173.40	168.00	216.80
GDP per capita	US$	1,153	1,401	1,142	1,112	1,298
GDP real growth	%	6.2	6.0	5.6	7.0	8.7
Inflation	%	8.3	11.6	12.4	12.5	13.7
Oil output	'000 bpd	2,460.0	2,356.0	2,170.0	2,061.0	2,402.0
Natural gas output	bn cum	28.2	35.0	35.0	24.9	33.6
Exports (fob) (goods)	US$m	61,600.0	66,040.0	83,587.0	59,318.0	73,698.0
Imports (fob) (goods)	US$m	34,096.0	28,291.0	36,867.0	29,047.0	53,461.0
Balance of trade	US$m	27,504.0	37,748.0	472,171.0	30,271.0	20,237.0
Current account	US$m	13,891.0	30,829.0	31,624.0	22,889.0	2,476.0
Total reserves minus gold	US$m	42,299.0	51,334.0	53,002.0	44,763.0	34,919.0
Foreign exchange	US$m	42,298.0	51,333.0	53,000.0	42,382.0	32,339.0
Exchange rate	per US$	128.16	118.04	118.54	148.90	150.30

* estimated figure

served if official policy, which establishes a series of incentives to attract foreign capital, is reconciled with what appears to be popular opposition to the presence of foreign investors in certain sectors of the economy. In 2009, for example, the overturn of several licences and contracts by the government, which it alleged had been improperly awarded by the previous government, dented the country's image amongst international investors.

Several measures were pursued in 2010 to block revenue leakages. These included a forensic audit of the Nigerian National Petroleum Corporation (NNPC) and process audits of internally generated remittances from ministries, departments and agencies (MDAs). The government also required MDAs and parastatals to submit their revenue and expenditure estimates. It has enhanced these measures in 2011 by issuing a directive to more than 32 parastatals – including the NNPC, the Central Bank of Nigeria (CBN), the Federal Inland Revenue Service and other revenue-generating agencies – to submit their budgets to the National Assembly, in line with the provision of the Constitution and the Fiscal Responsibility Act.

These policy measures have contributed to improving domestic-revenue mobilisation. In 2009, tax revenue rose to 6.9 per cent of GDP and is estimated to have remained stable at about 6.4 per cent of GDP in 2010.

The private sector

Corruption within public agencies continues to be a major obstacle for foreign investors. Nigeria had been making progress in the Transparency International Corruption Perception Index since 2002, culminating in its best score of 2.7 in 2009. In 2010, however, Nigeria's rating fell to 2.4. Although the country's legal, accounting and regulatory systems meet international standards, enforcement is inconsistent and often appears arbitrary.

Nigeria's progress in the structural transformation of its economy has been slow and uneven. The economy remains structurally unbalanced with lack of diversification – the economy depending largely on crude oil – constituting a major impediment to the flourishing of the domestic economy. Years of reforms have not succeeded in improving the investment environment. The World Bank's *Doing Business* ranking in 2011 shows Nigeria's general rank to have deteriorated to 137 out of 183 countries, from 134 in the 2010 ranking. Deterioration is also recorded in this latest ranking for most of the key indicators, including Starting a Business (110), Dealing with Construction Permits (167), Registering Property (179), Getting Credit (89), Protecting Investors (59), Paying Taxes (134) and Closing a Business (99). Nigeria's performance remained unchanged for only two indicators – Trading Across Borders (146) and Enforcing Contracts (97) – and there was no improvement in any of them. Ongoing reform to diversify the economy clearly needs to be fast-tracked. In the banking sector, an adequate flow of credit to the real sector needs to be ensured. In addition, reforms in the power and other economic-infrastructure sectors need to be stepped up to promote private-sector/foreign investment and employment-generating growth.

International trade and development

Nigeria's external position is heavily influenced by developments in the international oil market. The country is both a major exporter of crude oil and a major importer of petroleum products. Nigeria is the world's eighth largest exporter of crude oil but imports almost 90 per cent of domestically consumed petroleum products.

Total exports rose in 2010 as a result of higher oil prices and increased output. At the same time, a fall in infrastructure outlays brought about a decline in imports, leading to a sharp rise in the trade account.

Over the past decade, the makeup of Nigeria's donors and investors has changed significantly, with new entrants from the emerging economies playing an increasingly important role. China, India, Brazil and other developing countries are providing Nigeria with new sources of financing, enabling Nigeria to lessen its dependence on traditional donors from countries largely in the West.

China-Nigeria relations date back to 1972, when diplomatic relations were established between the two countries, and, according to *Time Magazine*, one of the best Chinese restaurants in the world could be found down an alleyway off Broad Street in Lagos. Today, China-Nigeria relations span a wide spectrum of areas including politics, trade, investment, aid, technology, science, culture, education, health and military. China is now one of Nigeria's top-ten trading partners. In addition, China has shown interest in investing in all sectors of the Nigerian economy. The growing economic ties between China and Nigeria are such that, today, Nigeria has become China's third biggest trading partner in Africa after South Africa and Egypt. The value of bilateral trade between China and Nigeria accounts for more than 14 per cent of the total trade between China and Africa.

By the end of 2010, China had set up more than 30 solely funded companies and joint ventures in Nigeria. The notable projects executed by China in Nigeria include the Abuja All-Africa Games village and the rehabilitation of the Nigerian railway system. The 2009 fifth Session of the Nigeria-China Joint Commission for Economic and Technical Co-operation set out the roadmap for future co-operations between the two countries. In the main these include Chinese banks being encouraged to establish their presence in Nigeria; Chinese investors encouraged to participate in the development of the Nigerian gas sub-sector and to increase crude-oil imports from Nigeria; China to speed up the development and completion of free trade zones, such as the Lekki and Ogun/Guangdong Free Trade Zones; and China to co-operate with Nigeria in the area of capacity building.

India's relations with Nigeria were originally built upon historical and political considerations. Economic links between the two countries are now stronger, with Nigeria being India's biggest trading partner in Africa. Bilateral trade between the two countries was estimated at about US$8.7 billion in March 2010, with Nigeria's exports to India at around US$7.3 billion. In 2010, Nigeria was the largest African crude-oil supplier to India, at about 400,000bpd.

Indian investments in Nigeria cover areas such as manufacturing, pharmaceuticals, plastics, engineering, information technology and communications. Indian companies have invested in the Ajaokuta Iron and Steel Industry, as well as the Aladja Steel complex in the Delta state. Nigeria has actively encouraged Indian companies to invest and expand Nigeria's mining and development of coal, gold, iron, ore, chrome, lead and other mineral resources.

Employment

Unemployment continues to be a major problem despite recent strong economic growth. According to the finance ministry, unemployment in Nigeria stands at about 19.7 per cent, but according to analysts, the real unemployment figure is probably higher if rural and urban joblessness amongst Nigerian youths are factored into the equation. Under-employment is also a serious problem in Nigeria. Total under-employment in 2009 was estimated at 21.3 per cent; the figures for the rural areas and the southern region being 20.5 per cent and 26.2 per cent, respectively.

The government aims to undertake some direct action to generate employment. A Public Works Programme was scheduled to commence across the 36 states and the federal capital territory in 2011. This programme will engage private-sector contractors to implement simple, labour-intensive public works in areas such as the renovation and maintenance of buildings such as schools, hospitals, road rehabilitation etc.

Health and education

In order to meet its health goals, Nigeria needs to tackle such socio-cultural factors as poverty, ignorance, harmful religious practices and biases. To achieve the desired results, there is a need for proper sensitisation of the population on health issues and for the involvement of traditional institutions. For example, the 2009 resistance of parents to the government's polio-immunisation efforts, especially in the northern part of the country, was finally tackled with the involvement of traditional institutions.

In the education sector, the government is addressing some of the problems that have bedevilled the education system by increasing spending on education, especially through Universal Basic Education (UBE), aimed at providing free education for all pupils at the primary and junior secondary school levels. The UBE has been successful in increasing the primary-school enrolment rate from 84 per cent in 2000 to 90 per cent in 2009. The total secondary-school enrolment rate has also risen, from 34 to 38 per cent during the same period.

Risk assessment

Economy	Fair
Politics	Fair
Regional stability	Fair

COUNTRY PROFILE

Historical profile

Between the eleventh and fourteenth centuries, a number of Islamic Hausa kingdoms flourished in the area of modern-day Nigeria, while in the fourteenth and fifteenth centuries the Yoruba Empire developed into a regional power in the south. The Ibo (Igbo), with a diffuse political structure, lived in the east. The Yoruba first made contact with Europeans (Portuguese) in the fifteenth century, who, along with other European nations, began trading in slaves from West Africa.

Mid-1800s There were several civil wars in Yorubaland and in the 1850s the British established themselves in Lagos.

1914 The Colony and Protectorate of Nigeria, the territory that is now Nigeria, was governed by the British through local leaders.

1919 A post-war League of Nations mandate gave some four-fifths of what was then Kamerun to France, and the remainder, bordering Nigeria, to Britain. It became part of Nigeria.

1922 A legislative council was set up. Much local power was left in the hands of traditional chiefs.

1947 A constitution established a federal system of government which attempted to take into account the interests of the three main regions of the colony – the northern and mainly Muslim Hausa and Fulanis, the predominantly Catholic Ibo in the south-east and the mixed Anglican and Muslim Yoruba in the south and west.

1960 Nigeria became independent. Sir Abubakar Tafawa Balewa became prime minister of a coalition government.

1963 The Federal Republic of Nigeria was proclaimed.

1966 In January Sir Abubakar Tafawa Balewa was killed in a coup lead by Major General Johnson Aguiyi-Ironsi. In July Ironsi was killed in a counter-coup lead by Lieutenant-Colonel Yakubu Gowon.

1967 Three eastern, Ibo, states attempted to secede, starting the Biafran Civil War, which was to become one of Africa's most bloody eras. Estimates for the death toll during the war range between 500,000 and two million.

1970 The Civil War ended with the surrender of the Biafran leaders, lead by Colonel Emeka Ojukwu, who went into exile in Côte d'Ivoire.

1970s The Opec-led doubling of the price of oil in October 1973 and again in 1974, led to Nigeria becoming one of Africa's wealthiest states. Nigeria experienced a construction and consumer boom until the price of oil plummeted in the early 1980s.

1975 Yakubu Gowon was overthrown by Brigadier Murtala Ramat Mohammed.

1976 In an attempted coup Murtala Mohammed was assassinated and replaced by Lieutenant-General Olusegun Obasanjo, who had been his deputy. Obasanjo was instrumental in introducing an American-style presidential constitution, which called for elections for the hand over of by the military.

1979 The first elections under the new constitution saw Alhaji Shehu Shagari, a northerner, become president.

1983 Shagari was re-elected in the August elections, which were widely held to be unfair. In December Major-General Muhammad Buhari seized power in bloodless coup.

1985 General Ibrahim Babangida seized power in another bloodless coup. He was widely supported by intellectuals, the press, some former politicians and the business community. The General pledged to return Nigeria to civilian rule, but the hand-over date was repeatedly postponed.

1993 Elections were held, but were later annulled when it appeared that Chief Moshood Abiola was about to win. Babangida stepped down from office. General Sani Abacha seized power in a *coup d'état*. He began to suppress all opposition.

1994 Abiola declared himself president, but was promptly arrested.

1995 Ken Saro-Wiwa, Nigerian writer and advocate of the Ogoni people in eastern Nigeria, and eight other minority rights activists, were executed. There was international outrage against both the government and Shell Oil Company, which had allegedly polluted Ogoni land. Nigeria was suspended from the Commonwealth and the EU imposed sanctions.

1998 Abacha died and General Abdulsalami Abubaker became Head of State. Chief Abiola died while still in custody.

1999 State legislative, National Assembly and presidential elections were held. Olusegun Obasanjo was declared president.

2000 *Sharia* (Islamic law) was adopted in several northern states despite opposition by the Christian minority. Religious and ethnic tensions grew and hundreds of deaths resulted from clashes between Muslims and Christians. Equatorial Guinea and Nigeria signed a treaty agreeing the demarcation of their maritime border.

2001 The heads of Nigeria's army, navy and air force were asked to retire. President Obasanjo set up a National Security Commission in an attempt to halt the communal violence, sparked mainly by religious differences, which had resulted in thousands of deaths.

2002 Nigeria rejected the International Court of Justice (ICJ) ruling that gave sovereignty of the oil-rich Bakassi peninsula to Cameroon. Clashes in Lagos between northern Hausas and southern Yorubas lead to some 100 deaths.

2003 The People's Democratic Party (PDP) won the 12 April legislative elections with large majorities in the Lower House and the Senate. Olusegun Obasanjo (PDP) won the 19 April presidential election with over 60 per cent of the vote. EU observers said the elections were marred by 'serious irregularities'.

2004 The UN brokered talks between Nigeria and Cameroon concerning their disputed border and both countries agreed to start joint security patrols. Religious clashes in the central Plateau State resulted in a local state of emergency; clashes between gangs in the oil city of Port Harcourt lead to as many as 500 deaths, according to Amnesty International. Swiss authorities said that they would unfreeze most of the US$500 million deposited in Switzerland by the ex-dictator Sani Abacha.
2005 Two-thirds of Nigeria's US$30 billion foreign debt was written off by Paris Club lenders.
2006 The Central Bank of Nigeria (CBN) announced that 13 banks faced liquidation for failing to meet the N25 billion capitalisation targets. Nigeria ceded the Bakassi Peninsula to Cameroon in accordance with the 2002 ICJ ruling. Foreign workers were kidnapped in the Niger Delta area, and pipelines damaged, by militants demanding more control of the oil revenues. Nigeria was able to pay off the remainder of its Paris Club debt after record oil prices.
2007 Umaru Yar'Adua (PDP) was elected president. The Movement for the Emancipation of the Niger Delta (Mend) threatened to resume attacks on oil facilities and to abduct foreign workers in pursuit of their aims to gain more oil revenue for their region. The agreement to hand over parts of the Bakassi Peninsula to Cameroon was rejected by the Senate.
2008 Two leaders of Mend were extradited from Angola. Yar'Adua was confirmed as president following challenges to the elections which were dismissed by a tribunal. Nigeria finally handed over to Cameroon the disputed maritime territory off the Bakassi Peninsula.
2009 Eleven opposition parties united to challenge the PDP in the 2011 parliamentary elections. The previous attempt at a grand coalition in the 1980s was thwarted by the electoral commission. Islamist extremist groups, known as Boko Haram, attacked and killed over 140 people across four states in northern Nigeria. The violence was ended after the army shelled the compound in Maiduguri in which many militants were entrenched. The leader of Boko Haram, Mohammed Yusuf, later died in police custody. Hundreds of combatants of Mend surrendered their weapons to the government in an amnesty ceremony. A small faction of Mend said it would continue to resist the oil industry in the Delta region. President Yar'Adua flew to Saudi Arabia for treatment for a heart condition on 23 November. He left under 'mysterious' circumstances and without informing parliament.
2010 President Yar'Adua died on 5 May, aged 58 years. He had been having medical care for heart and kidney problems in Saudi Arabia for three months and returned to Nigeria in February. Acting-President Goodluck Jonathan (since 10 February), was sworn in as president on 6 May. He removed the chairman of the election commission, Maurice Iwu, in April, following wide criticism that Iwu had failed to control the 2007 elections. Namadi Sambo, governor of Kaduna State, was confirmed as vice president by both houses of parliament on 18 May. In June, the CBN extended loans of US$3.3 billion to Nigerian Eagle Airlines, which had been at risk of bankruptcy. The bank had already loaned five other Nigerian airlines amounts totalling over US$2 billion. Under an agreement signed in May, the China State Construction Engineering Corporation (CSCEC) will build a US$8 billion oil refinery in the Lekki free trade zone in Lagos, with three refineries in total; the refineries should go some way to relieving Nigeria's shortage of refined fuel. In July a junior finance minister asserted that the state-controlled Nigerian National Petroleum Corporation (NNPC) was unable to pay its debts of over US$5 billion and that it was technically insolvent. He maintained that it owed the Federation Account around US$3 billion for distribution to various levels of federal government. NNPC claimed that government subsidies of US$7 billion, for providing refined petroleum products at less than market prices to the public, were unpaid. In August in an effort to clean up the Nigerian Stock Exchange, the Securities and Exchange Commission sacked its director general, Ndi Okereke-Onyuike, and suspended its chairman. In September President Jonathan announced he would stand in the 2011 presidential elections, breaking an unwritten agreement within his party that presidential candidates would rotate between the north (typically Muslim) and the south (typically Christian). Aliyu Gusau resigned as national security advisor to run against President Jonathan in the October PDP primaries. A car bomb exploded in Abuja on 1 October as Nigeria celebrated 50 years of independence. At least 12 people were killed by the explosion. In November Atiku Abubakar emerged as a consensus candidate from the north to challenge President Jonathan in the ruling party primaries.
2011 President Jonathan won party primaries held in Abuja on 13 January. Parliamentary elections were postponed first from 2 April to 4 April and were finally held on 9 April; 360 members of the House of Representatives and 109 senatorial seats were in contention, 74 million registered voters chose between 54 political parties. In presidential elections that had been postponed until 16 April, incumbent Goodluck Jonathan won a convincing majority with 58.89 per cent of the vote, his closest rival, Muhammadu Buhari (CPC), won 31.98 per cent. Riots broke out in northern states after the results were announced and the Red Cross reported that 'tens of thousands' of people had fled their homes as over 200 people were killed and hundreds arrested. Results of the parliamentary elections held on 9 April were not announced for several weeks. By the end of June preliminary results were that the ruling PDP had won 123 seats and ACN 47 in the house of representatives (HR) and 45 and 13 seats in the Senate respectively. Logistical problems in 15 senatorial and 48 HR constituencies postponed elections until 26 April. On 4 July, the Independent National Electoral Commission (INEC) said it was postponing its announcement of a definitive account of parliamentary elections and requested continued patience from all parties. In July, President Jonathan announced that he would ask parliament to amend the constitution so that a presidential term in office would be extended, but limited to one term only. On 3 August, the Dutch-owned oil company Shell admitted full liability for environmental damage done to the Niger Delta from two massive oil spills originating from its oil wells. The UN estimated an initial US$1 billion for the cost of the clean-up, which could take up to 30 years. The terrorist Islamic group, Boko Haram was held responsible for an attack on a Christian church close to Abuja, on Christmas day, killing 40 people.
2012 As of 1 January, definitive elections results for the outstanding 126 parliamentary seats were still unpublished.

Political structure

Constitution

The 1979 constitution was amended in 1999, when significant powers were devolved to the 36 states.
The political system is divided into three tiers: the federal or central level, the state level and local government.
Under a presidential system, the president, who is also the commander-in-chief of the armed forces, is vested with executive powers under the constitution of the federal republic. The president and his ministers form the federal executive council with the president as the chairman.
A similar structure exists in the states where the governor and his commissioners form the state executive councils. Each state has a legislature, executive and judiciary, although their legislative arm is unicameral.

Form of state
Federal republic comprising 36 states and the Federal Capital Territory (FCT, Abuja).
The executive
The Federal Executive Council is headed by an elected president who serves no more than two four-year terms.
The president is both Head of State and head of government, initiating the policies and programmes of the government and ensuring that they are implemented after they have been passed into law by the legislature. The success or failure of any government depends largely on the incumbent president who combines the roles of the chief executive with those of the ceremonial Head of State.
Despite his wide-ranging power, the president has restrictions, which include ratification of all his major appointments by the National Assembly. The president is excluded from membership of both houses of the National Assembly.
Although he is empowered to conduct foreign affairs, all treaties require the ratification of the Senate. Only the National Assembly can declare war and peace.
While he appoints members of the judiciary, he cannot remove them.
National legislature
The federal, bicameral National Assembly consists of the House of Representatives (lower house), with 360 members elected by majority vote in single-seat constituencies, and the Senate (upper house) with 109 members; three elected from each of the 36 states and one from the federal capital territory (FCT). All members of the National Assembly serve for four-year terms.
Each of the states of the federation has a unicameral legislature.
Legal system
Nigeria's legal system is based on English common law, Nigerian customs and tradition, and *Sharia* (Islamic law). *Sharia* predominates in the northern Islamic states.
Last elections
16 April 2011 (presidential); 9 April 2011 (parliamentary).
Results: Presidential: Goodluck Jonathon (PDP) won 58.89 per cent of the vote, Muhammadu Buhari (CPC) 31.98 per cent, Nuhu Ribadu (ACN) 5.41 per cent, Ibrahim Shekarau (ANPP) 2.4 per cent; 16 other candidates each won less than 1 per cent of the vote.
Parliamentary (house of representatives) (preliminary results): People's Democratic Party (PDP) won 123 seats (out of 360), Action Congress of Nigeria (ACN) 47, All Nigeria People's Party (ANPP) 25, Congress for Progressive Change (CPC) 30, other parties nine. By end-June 2011, 126 results were unannounced.
Senate (74 seats in contention), PDP 45, CAN 13, ANPP seven, CPC five, other parties four.
Next elections
2015 (presidential and parliamentary)

Political parties

Ruling party
People's Democratic Party (PDP) (since 1999; re-elected May 2007)
Main opposition party
Action Congress of Nigeria (ACN)

Population

158.30 million (2010)*
Last census: 21 March 2006: 140,003,542 (provisional)
Population density: 128 inhabitants per square km. Urban population: 45 per cent (1995—2001).
Annual growth rate: 2.4 per cent 1994–2004 (WHO 2006)
Internally Displaced Persons (IDP)
250,000 (UNHCR 2004)
Ethnic make-up
Hausas (21 per cent), Yorubas (20 per cent), Ibos (17 per cent) and Fulani (9 per cent) comprise the four major tribes.
Religions
Islam (about 50 per cent), Christianity (about 40 per cent), traditional beliefs (about 10 per cent).

Education

Primary schooling lasts for six years. Admittance to secondary schooling is through examination. Junior secondary school lasts for three years until age 15 with progress on to senior secondary school until age 18. Some students may undertake technical, vocational schooling from age 12 and can undertake academic and specialised subjects and graduate at age 18.
Around 7 per cent of the government's budget is allocated to education.
Literacy rate: 67 per cent adult rate; 89 per cent youth rate (15–24) (Unesco 2005).
Compulsory years: Six to 15
Enrolment rate: 98 per cent gross primary enrolment of relevant age group (including repeaters); 33 per cent gross secondary enrolment (World Bank).
Pupils per teacher: 34 in primary schools

Health

The Federal Ministry of Health (FMOH) provides policy and technical guidance to the 36 states and the federal capital territory (Abuja), co-ordinating state efforts towards the goals set by the national health policy. Annual health expenditure stands at around 3–4 per cent of GDP, of which government spending is approximately 23 per cent and foreign spending about 7 per cent.
The primary healthcare network has seriously declined with low level coverage of services such as immunisation and supply of essential drugs. The Health System Fund is a major project implemented by the state and federal ministries of health aimed at institutional development, training and an essential drug programme.
Nigeria has a growing problem of HIV/Aids as well as a significant rise of other non-communicable diseases, however, with 65 per cent of the population living below the poverty line, health measures can provide only short-term solutions to systemic problems.
Nigeria is one of only two countries that exports polio (the other is India), according to the World Health Organisation – Global Polio Eradication Initiative (WHO – Polio Eradication). In November 2011, the UN announced that an outbreak of polio had recurred in Northern Nigeria with 53 cases reported so far in 2011, compared to 11 in 2010. There has been a history of mistrust by local people to immunisation and the WHO plans to target the population with more health benefits by combining the polio vaccinations with anti-malaria treatments and integrated healthcare. Some 30 million children were vaccinated against polio during 2009, sponsored by the UN Children's fund, the World Health Organisation and the Nigerian health ministry.
Improved water sources are available to 39 per cent of the population.
HIV/Aids
An estimated 3.5 million adults and children are living with HIV/Aids and there are over one million orphans due to Aids.
HIV prevalence: 5.4 per cent aged 15–49 in 2003 (World Bank)
Life expectancy: 46 years, 2004 (WHO 2006)
Fertility rate/Maternal mortality rate: 5.7 births per woman, 2004 (WHO 2006); maternal mortality 800 per 100,000 live births (World Bank).
Birth rate/Death rate: 39.6 births and 13.9 deaths per 1,000 people
Child (under 5 years) mortality rate (per 1,000): 98 per 1,000 live births; 28.7 per cent of children aged under five-years suffer malnutrition (World Bank).
Head of population per physician: 0.28 physicians per 1,000 people, 2003 (WHO 2006)

Welfare

The Nigerian public service schemes, the private sector self-administered and insured scheme, the National Provident Fund (NPF) and the Nigeria Social Insurance Trust Fund (NSITF) schemes, provide for old age, survivorship, invalidity and industrial injury benefits, gratuity and

pension. The Workmen's Compensation Act provides for industrial injury benefits. Despite the existence of these bodies, the social security system is virtually non-existent in Nigeria.
The pensions fund management is divided into two categories: government schemes and occupational schemes. The government scheme provides basic social benefits that are not earnings-related, and earnings-related pension provisions. Such schemes are funded mainly through contributions from the government, with minimal contributions from the scheme members. The government policy allows individuals in self-employment to claim premiums paid to any insurance company, provided such premiums do not exceed 10 per cent of the individuals total income. This is in addition to any relief claimed in respect of life assurance policies. The occupational pension schemes consists of private companies' schemes, which are employment related and financed jointly by the employers and employees.

Main cities
Abuja (Federal Capital Territory in central Nigeria – estimated population 147,996 in 2005). Lagos (former capital – estimated population 8.7 million).
Capitals of the 36 states are: Kaduna (state of Kaduna) (1.4 million (m)), Kano (Kano) (3.0m), Jos (Plateau) (705,360), Sokoto (Sokoto) (455,642), Maiduguri (Borno) (854,613), Ilorin (Kogi – formerly Kwara) (735,478), Ibadan (Oyo) (2.5m), Port Harcourt (Rivers) (972,301), Calabar (Cross River) (439,656), Bauchi (Bauchi), Minna (Niger), Makurdi (Benue), Abeokuta (Ogun) (542,900), Akure (Ondo), Ikeja (Lagos), Owerri (Imo), Katsina (Katsina), Uyo (Akwa Ibom), Benin City (Edo) (1.0m), Enugu (Enugu) (563,619), Yola (Adamawa), Umuahia (Abia), Awka (Anambra), Asaba (Delta), Birnin Kebbi (Kebbi), Lokoja (Kogi), Yenogou (Bayelsa), Abakaliki (Eboniyi), Ado-Ekiti (Ekiti), Gombe (Gombe), Lafia (Nassarawa), Gusau (Zamfara), Osogbo (Osun), Jalingo (Taraba), Dutse (Jigawa), Damaturu (Yobe).

Languages spoken
English is used in business and public life. Hausa, Yoruba and Ibo are widely spoken.
Official language/s
English

Media
The constitution guarantees freedom of the press. However the intimidate of journalists and editors by security forces has resulted in beatings and detentions. State authorities have also charged editors and owners with sedition or security implications for articles with which they have take exception.
Libel is a criminal offence, with the onus of truth of opinion or valued judgement placed on the defendant, so that self-censorship is not unknown.
Press
Dailies: There are over a dozen newspapers published in both the morning and evening, although not all are nationally distributed. Three evening papers are published in Lagos and one in Ibadan.
In English, government-owned newspapers include *Daily Times of Nigeria* (www.dailytimes-nigeria.com), *New Nigerian* (www.newnigeriannews.com) and *Daily Independent* (www.independentng.com). Independent newspapers include *The Guardian* (www.ngrguardiannews.com), *Daily Vanguard* (www.vanguardngr.com), *Punch* (www.punchng.com) and the *Daily Sun* (www.sunnewsonline.com), which is a tabloid.
Weeklies: There are several news magazines published including *Newswatch* (www.newswatchngr.com) and *Tell* (www.tellng.com).
Business: In English, several publications are available, *Business Day* (www.businessdayonline.com) and *Financial Standard* (www.financialstandardnews.com) are dailies, other journals include *Business Eye* (www.businesseyeng.com), and *Business Life* (www.thenigeriabusiness.com).
Periodicals: Monthly magazines include *The President* for current affairs, *Ovation* (www.ovationinternational.com) for society and lifestyles and *Genevieve* for young women.
Broadcasting
Both federal and state governments operate radio stations and most operate television services, in English and local languages.
Radio: Due to the low literacy rate radio services are the main medium of mass communication and sources of news and information. Radio station must be licensed to operate.
The Federal Radio Corporation of Nigeria (FRCN) operates Radio Nigeria (www.radionigeriaonline.com) a national network which includes regional programming and the external service Voice of Nigeria (www.voiceofnigeria.org) broadcasting in English, French and Arabic as well as five local languages. There are many other, private stations including Brilla FM (http://brila-fm.the11sow.com) from Lagos, Aso Radio from Abuja and Cosmo FM (www.cosmofm.com) from Enugu.
Television: Licensing rules require locally made content to amount to around 60 per cent which places additional costs on private broadcasters, plus insufficient advertising revenues limits the potential for free-to-air services; pay-to-view TV is growing in popularity.
The national, state-owned broadcaster is the Nigerian Television Authority (NTA) (www.ntaplus.com) operates a number of regional stations to make up a comprehensive network. Other private, regional TV stations include AIT (www.daarnews.com) from Lagos and Abuja, Silverbird TV (www.silverbirdgroup.com) from Lagos and Port Harcourt and Channels TV (www.channelstv.com).
News agencies
National news agency: NAN (News Agency of Nigeria)
APA (African Press Agency): www.apanews.net
Reuters Africa: http://africa.reuters.com

Economy
Nigeria has vast wealth in petroleum reserves, however as the most populous country in Africa with 158.3 million inhabitants its per capita income in 2010 was just US$1,298. It has Africa's second largest oil reserves (after Libya) at 37.2 billion barrels, with production at 2.40 million barrels per day, at the end of 2010; it is one of Africa's biggest petroleum exporters. There were natural gas reserves of 5.3 trillion cubic metres (cum) at the end of 2010, with production of 33.6 billion cum (an increase of 35.7 per cent on the 2009 production figure), of which, 12 million cum was exported via the new West African Gas Pipeline (WAGP) to Ghana and the remainer converted to liquefied natural gas (LNG) and exported to Asia, Europe and North America.
The exploitation of Nigeria's oil reserves has created political and economic turmoil and has not benefited the majority of its population in tangible ways, with the loss of huge sums of oil revenues due to fraud and embezzlement by the ruling elite. High levels of inflation and a lack of investment in non-oil sectors have also contributed to Nigeria's economic woes. Foreign debt was a serious problem until the Nigerian democratic political system was re-introduced and international donors agreed to write-off US$18 billion in Nigerian debt in 2006.
The structure of the economy reflects the influence of the hydrocarbon sector, with industry accounting for over 40 per cent of GDP, agriculture over 30 per cent and services over 25 per cent. GDP growth was 6.0 per cent in 2008, increasing to 7 per cent in 2009 and higher still to 8.7 per cent in 2010, reflecting the marked increase in exports of natural gas. High inflation is a long-term problem,

averaging 15 per cent between 2000–05 but falling to 8.2 per cent in 2006 and further still to 5.4 per cent in 2007; it sprang back to 11.6 per cent in 2008 due to higher food and local fuel prices and continued to grow, to 12.5 per cent, in 2009 and as world trade weakened further to 13.7 per cent in 2010.
The International Monetary Fund (IMF) considered that Nigeria had weathered the global economic crisis better than other oil-based economies in 2008, due in large part to economic reforms undertaken before 2008.
In July 2010 a new bank was founded, the Asset Management Corporation of Nigeria (Amcon), specifically to siphon off toxic debts owned by domestic banks. This followed a US$4 billion bailout of nine of the biggest banks in Nigeria in 2009. The bad debts were replaced with government-guaranteed bonds to re-invigorate the banking sector as a whole and make it attractive to new investors. The high global prices for oil in 2008 boosted Nigeria's current account, which rose from US$31.2 billion in 2007 to US$42.3 billion in 2008, and gave it the cushion necessary for the external shock of capital outflows of foreign investor's equities.
Diversification of the economy is a major objective. In 2008, the government announced a new strategy for structural reforms and a national development plan called *Vision 2020*. Not only are there proposals to reform the petroleum industry to produce a single omnibus of laws to provide a framework for the industry, other sectors will be given specific consideration. Among these are agriculture and food security, business, tourism, education, manufacturing, health and housing (with consideration for 20 other sectors).
In 2011, the UN Human Development Index (HDI) ranked Nigeria as 156 (out of 187) for development in health, education and income and in 2010, 57.3 per cent of the population was experiencing deprivation in a least one indicator. The inequality and poverty that has caused ethnic tensions and resulted in violence and death between residents, newcomers and migrant workers, as seen in 2009–10, may continue until the economy can generate and maintain an income for the majority of the population.

External trade

Nigeria is a member of the Economic Community of West African States (Ecowas), which was set up to promote economic integration among members. It is a member of the Anglophone, West African Monetary Zone (WAMZ), which plans to introduce a common currency. WAMZ will eventually be merged with the Francophone-members' currency to produce a single currency (the eco) for the region.
The oil sector is vital to the economy as it provides over 20 per cent of GDP, 90 per cent of foreign earnings and around 65 per cent of budget revenue.
As Africa's most populous nation, Nigeria is required to import food and goods.

Imports

Principal imports include fuel (Nigeria does not operate oil refineries), industrial raw materials, machinery, chemicals, vehicles, manufactured goods, food and live animals.
Main sources: China (typically 15 per cent of total), US (8 per cent), Belize (7 per cent).

Exports

Principal exports are crude oil and petroleum products (typically 95 per cent of total), cocoa, rubber, timber and manufactured goods.
Main destinations: US (typically 43 per cent of total), India (10 per cent), Brazil (7 per cent).

Agriculture

Farming

The sector has suffered a relative decline because of the dominance of oil in the economy, but it is still the main area of employment, employing around half the workforce.
Land suitable for arable production has been put at 25 per cent of the total area, of which about 12 per cent is currently cultivated. The country suffers from soil degradation, deforestation and water pollution.
Key government policies include food self-sufficiency and boosting non-food crops to meet demand from the agri-processing sector. The sector is still dominated by unproductive smallholders raising subsistence crops such as sorghum, maize, cassava, yams, millet, rice and increasing quantities of wheat – up to 70 per cent of which is for private consumption. Nigeria is a leading world producer of cassava and the second largest producer of ginger.
Plantations, sometimes owned by, or in partnership with, multinational corporations, are gaining ground in producing raw materials for commercial use, for example grain for breweries. Irrigation schemes, higher producer prices, the expansion of credit and improvements in the rural infrastructure are beginning to show positive results.
Cash crops include cocoa, rubber (nearly all exported), coffee, cotton and palm kernels. Cocoa is Nigeria's largest foreign exchange earner after oil. The palm oil sector is being redeveloped. Livestock farming is important, while poultry farming is rapidly increasing.

Fishing

Over N30 billion (US$238 million) is spent annually on fish imports despite the country's large fishing potential.
There is extensive fishing in the Niger River network and along the south coast.

Forestry

Nigeria has 15 per cent forest cover and an additional 54 per cent of other wooded land comprising mainly savannah. There are growing forestry operations in the tropical zones in southern Nigeria and north of Port Harcourt. The extensive network of national parks and reserves protect around 5 per cent of its forests.
Nigeria is one of the largest wood producers in Africa showing an annual harvest of more than 100 million cubic metres, most of which is used for fuel consumption. The large-scale industrial forestry sector produces sawn timber, plywood, particleboard and paper mostly to meet local demands.
Northern Nigeria is most threatened by deforestation and government concerns over desertification led to urgent action plans including a US$44.5 million National Tree Nursery Programme. However in 2008 the National Forest Conservation Council of Nigeria (NFCCN) reported that of the 50 million seedlings planted each year in the 11 northern states, 37.5 million died within two months. The remaining 12.5 million seedlings are insufficient to create a deforestation-reforestation equilibrium. An estimated 40.5 million tonnes is used as firewood in the north annually.

Industry and manufacturing

Production costs in industry are considerably increased by a lack of basic infrastructure, which compels every factory to have its own standby electricity plant and sometimes a water borehole. Companies also find it difficult to source vital components from abroad with uncertain supplies of foreign exchange, although this situation is gradually improving thanks to the liberalisation of the economy.
The textile industry used to be one of Nigeria's more productive sectors. However, the Kano Textile Traders Association claims that imports of finished textile materials from China, Pakistan and India have resulted in the collapse of the textile industry. WTO agreements blocking advantageous exports to the US, and Ecowas tariff reductions allowing cheaper imports from neighbouring countries, have reduced the number of textile firms from a high of 250,000 to a current 50,000 with only 65 textile mills remaining. The number of job loses amounts to around 200,000.

Tourism

Nigeria has many diverse environments and attractions to offer the intrepid traveller, as well as marketing the country as a destination for eco-tourists it also emphasises it peoples and local customs.

Environment

Drilling operations in the Niger Delta region have created huge pollution problems from oil spills and explosions. Oil exploitation has been a fact of life for many people living in the Delta, particularly the Ogoni people.

Nigeria's pollution problems are exacerbated by the fact that the country does not have a pollution control policy. Analysts have reported that during oil production, Nigeria flares more natural gas than any other country in the world, contributing to global warming. The government hopes to end gas flaring by 2008.

In June 2010 the African Union backed a proposal to build the 'Great Green Wall' project, of a 15km wide, 7,775km long, continuous belt of trees from Senegal in the west to Djibouti in the east (traversing 11 countries) in an effort to halt the advance of the Sahara Desert. The trees to be used would be drought-adapted, preferably native to the area from a list of 37 possible species, and should help to slow soil erosion and filter rain water.

Mining

Nigeria used to be one of the world's largest producers of tin, with production based around the highland district of Jos. It is now the smallest of the Association of Tin Producing Countries (ATPC). The country's only tin smelter is at Makeri. Tin reserves are estimated at 16,000 tonnes. Independent estimates place iron ore reserves at 800 million tonnes, averaging 37 per cent metal content.

Deposits of uranium, lead, zinc, tungsten and gold have not yet been exploited. There are 65 sites in Nigeria where gold has been located. The Iperindo gold project in Oshun State has a resource of some 400,000 ounces of gold.

Nigeria Mining Corp has taken up a number of projects including gold, tantalum and tin with the aim of attracting more capital in anticipation of increased private sector involvement.

Work on a new mine was begun in May 2009, which will be become the world's second-largest uranium mine, producing 5,000 tonnes per annum. The French-based Areva will provide the majority of the investment of US$1.5 billion and will take a majority share in its profits. The mine is located in the north in the traditional region of the Tuareg people.

Hydrocarbons

Proven oil reserves were 37.2 billion barrels in 2010, with production at 2.4 billion barrels per day (bpd); Nigeria is the world's twelfth and Africa's largest producer of crude oil. The economy is heavily dependent on the petroleum sector, which accounts for over 95 per cent of export earnings and around 85 per cent of government revenue. The Nigerian National Petroleum Corporation (NNPC) is the commercial entity through which the government Department of Petroleum Resources (DPR) participates in the oil industry. The NNPC is responsible for all upstream and downstream developments, including exploration, production and distribution activities within the sector. It also regulates and supervises the oil industry.

Under the constitution, all hydrocarbon reserves are the legal property of the federal government, therefore all oil companies in production have a portion of their revenue, appropriated by the government; typically this amounts to almost 60 per cent of all revenue generated by the industry.

The industry has been traditionally located in the south-eastern Niger River Delta, which has become a battleground for indigenous peoples, with militants of the Movement for the Emancipation of the Niger Delta (Mend) demanding more control and redistribution of profits from oil production. Supplies of oil and gas have been targeted with pipeline vandalism and oil siphoning – which has resulted in a number of major explosions with hundreds of deaths each year. The government estimates that around 300,000bpd of oil is sold illegally on to the black market – with militant take-overs of facilities and foreign workers kidnapped. Such attacks have hampered production, down as low as 1.8 billion bpd in 2008, and forced some oil companies to shut-in (suspend) production.

Corruption has been blamed for much of the squandering of the billions of US dollars in oil revenue earned since the 1960s, so much so that of the 20 million people in 3,000 communities living in the Niger River Delta, 70 per cent are reckoned to live on less than US$1 per day.

In May 2010, a US$23 billion contract was signed between the NNPC and the China State Construction Engineering Corporation (CSCEC). Under the agreement three oil refineries and a storage complex will be built, adding 750,000 barrels per day to refining capacity. The refineries will be built in Bayelsa, Kogi and Lagos states. China will receive future oil and gas contracts in exchange. Later in July it was announced that the first refinery would be built in the Lekki free trade zone in Lagos.

Offshore oil fields are located in the Gulf of Guinea and the Bights of Benin and Bonny. The Shell Company halted production of 225,000bpd at its Bonga deepwater oilfield, 120km off the coast, when it was attacked by militants of the Mend; it resumed production in 2008, following more security provided by government forces. The shutdown had cut Nigeria's total output by 10 per cent.

Ongoing exploration is focussed on deep and ultra-deep locations in the Chad basin.

Nigeria has four refineries with a total capacity of 500,000bpd, however only one was operational in 2008 due to poor maintenance, corruption, fire and theft, plus interrupted flows of crude oil from oilfields. Around 85 per cent of Nigeria's refined oil must be imported.

Proven gas reserves were 5.3 trillion cubic metres (cum) in 2010, with production at 33.6 billion cum. Although this constitutes a 35.7 per cent increase on the 2009 production of 24.8 billion cum, it is down on the highs of 35 billion cum in 2007–08. Nigeria is the world's eleventh largest and Africa's second largest source (after Algeria) of natural gas. Nigeria would like to use gas as its principle source of domestic energy, however capital investment has not been forthcoming for the necessary infrastructure projects to collect, process and distribute natural gas. Much of the associated natural gas is flared at source (at oil-heads), losing an estimated US$1.46 billion per annum in revenue for NNPC, as well as meaning that less is available domestically for energy purposes. The majority of natural gas production is used in exports of liquefied natural gas (LNG), 23.9 billion cum in 2010 and Spain was the single largest recipient with 7.8 billion cum.

The West African Gas Pipeline (WAGP), funded by US oil company Chevron Texaco and the governments of Nigeria, Ghana, Togo and Benin, began pumping natural gas to Ghana in 2008, providing 120 million cum in 2010. Togo and Benin are supplied with substantially smaller amounts. Chevron Texaco will manage the pipeline, for a fixed fee, until 2016.

In 2009, Algeria, Niger and Nigeria signed an agreement to build a 2,580km trans-Sahara gas pipeline (TSGP) traversing all three countries. It is estimated it will cost US$13 billion and transport up to 30 billion cum of natural gas, destined for Europe. Three foreign energy companies also expressed an interest in investing in the project, Russia's Gazprom, France's Total and the Anglo-Dutch Shell. Days before the TSGP agreement Gasprom formed a joint venture with NNPC to invest US$2.5 billion in Nigerian natural gas production infrastructure, including pipelines, refineries and gas-fired power stations.

Coal reserves are plentiful, although production only supplies a tiny percentage of domestic energy requirements. Coal exports are negligible, due to obsolete equipment and a lack of investment following years when the coal sector was a government monopoly.

Energy

Total installed generating capacity was 5,960MW in 2006, producing over 22.1 billon kilowatt hours, of which 53 per cent was produced by oil, 39 per cent by natural gas and 7 per cent by hydroelectric power.

The state-owned Power Holding Company of Nigeria (PHCN) is responsible for generating, transmission, distribution and sale of electricity in Nigeria. However it is a poorly functioning company and lack of capacity and outages are commonplace. The government is in the process of privatising it, by unbundling aspects of the business.

In 2007 it was estimated, by one government department, that Nigeria must invest US$20 billion to bring its power infrastructure up to a level for a efficiently functioning economy. In 2008 the Lagos *Independent* newspaper quoted the sum as US$100 billion, which included the cost of support and ancillary work and workers. The World Bank estimated that Nigeria loses US$600 million in lost production each year through inadequate supplies of electricity.

Over 50 per cent of the population is not connected to electricity supplies and the population, mainly rural, relies on biomass (wood fuel, kerosene and charcoal) for energy, which has led to considerable deforestation. The Egbin thermal power station, outside Lagos, is the country's largest electricity plant, fuelled by oil. In 2008, of its six installed generators, only four were working and only two worked during peak periods. Other thermal and hydroelectric stations have also been neglected. It is common for international companies setting up in business in Nigeria to provide their own power, as do many individuals who generate electricity for their own domestic and commercial use. In 2005, the Rural Electrification Agency (REA) was established to improve access to electricity, however corruption by REA officials caused the agency to be abolished in 2009.

Nigeria is a member of the West African Power Pool and has been considering the feasibility of constructing power lines between Nigeria and Niger, Benin and Burkina Faso since 2007.

Financial markets

Stock exchange

Nigerian Stock Exchange (NSE). Plans to de-mutalise the NSE were at an early stage in August 2010.

Banking and insurance

Nigeria's banking sector is the second-largest in Africa behind South Africa, but it has experienced difficulties in recent years. Since the late 1990s, the Central Bank of Nigeria (CBN) has worked towards cleaning up the banking sector.

The end of military rule in 1999 saw international banks return to Nigeria, although they concentrate their operations in Lagos and Abuja supplying services for big businesses and Nigerian expatriates. The CBN does not differentiate between licensing of commercial and merchant banks, which enables merchant banks to issue cheques and allows them to access the CBN's clearing house.

In 2005 the CBN began restructuring the banking sector by setting a minimum capital requirement that has forced banks into consolidation. The IMF is advising the CBN on the banking reform programme.

A persistent obstacle to the banking sector's development is Nigeria's culture of fraud; the CBN has been keen to address, the advance fee fraud scams, run by criminal gangs. A Financial Intelligence Unit monitors the banking environment to strengthen the anti-money laundering framework that is under way.

Other problems include the federal and state governments' borrowing from domestic banks, which has severely restricted liquidity in the banking sector.

It was announced in March 2005 that the introduction of the shared currency, the Eco, in Nigeria, Ghana, Guinea, Sierra Leone and The Gambia, which was due in July 2005, would be postponed. The currency was proposed to facilitate trade and growth with an ultimate plan to merge it with the CFA franc.

On 1 January 2006 the CBN announced that 13 banks faced liquidation for failing to meet its N25 billion capitalisation target.

Central bank

Central Bank of Nigeria (CBN)

Main financial centre

Lagos

Offshore facilities

Nigeria is on the Organisation for Economic Co-operation and Development (OECD) Financial Action Task Force (FATF) list of non-co-operative countries on money laundering.

Time

GMT plus one hour

Geography

Nigeria is bordered to the west by Benin, to the north by Niger, to the north-east by Chad, to the east by Cameroon and to the south by the Bight of Benin (Atlantic Ocean). The main rivers, the Niger and Benue, merge in the centre of the country, dividing it into three main regions of north, south and east. The north consists of dry savannah, the south of jungle, with mangrove swamps nearer the coast, and the east of a plateau leading into the country's only major mountain range along the Cameroon border.

Hemisphere

Northern

Climate

The climate varies from tropical on the coast to sub-tropical in the north. There are two main seasons, the rainy season from April to October and the dry season from November to March, which is characterised by a cool dust haze from the Sahara known as the *harmattan*.

Average temperatures remain fairly constant throughout the year at 29 degrees Celsius (C) in the south. The average daytime temperature in the north is 42 degrees C, but the temperature can drop to as low as 6 degrees C at night.

Humidity is high in the south, with a maximum varying from 100 per cent to 80 per cent. Rainfall is heavy on the coast, ranging from about 180cm a year in the south-west to 430cm in the south-east.

Near-temperate conditions are common on the central plateau and along the hilly north-eastern border with Cameroon.

Dress codes

Suits or traditional dress are worn for business meetings, but otherwise dress is informal. Women are advised to dress modestly, especially in the Islamic north. For social occasions, dress as for a business meeting.

Entry requirements

Passports

Required by all and must be valid for six months beyond the date of departure.

Visa

Required by all; some exceptions are made for citizens of countries located close to Nigeria. Visas should be obtained before arrival, contact the nearest consular office, or see www.nigeriabusinessinfo.com/visas.htm for details.

Business visitors will require a letter of invitation, from an organisation or individual, addressed to the Visa Section of the High Commission or Embassy. A declaration of full compliance of all entry requirements or proof of sufficient funds for expenses (such as traveller's cheques to be cashed in Nigeria), must be lodged. Any individual inviting a visitor must attach photocopies of the first five pages of his/her own passport, while a resident must enclose a copy of his/her residence permit.

Currency advice/regulations

The import and export of local currency is limited to N20. The import of foreign

currency is unlimited but must be declared, its export is limited to N100. Visitors are advised not to use unauthorised currency exchange methods, which are illegal.
Travellers cheques have limited use in cities and larger towns.

Customs
Laws against exporting Nigerian antiquities are strictly enforced.

Prohibited imports
Sparkling wines and beer, fruits and vegetables, eggs and cereals, precious metals and textiles including mosquito netting.

Health (for visitors)

Mandatory precautions
Yellow fever vaccination certificate required if coming from an infected area.

Advisable precautions
Inoculations and booster should be current for tetanus, polio, hepatitis A, diphtheria, typhoid and yellow fever. There may be a need for vaccinations for tuberculosis, hepatitis B and meningitis and cholera. Use malaria prophylaxis (which will also provide protection for hepatitis B and yellow fever) including mosquito repellents, nets and clothing that fully cover the body after dark. There is a risk of rabies.
Other diseases that require preventative measures are HIV/Aids, hepatitis C and E; to avoid bilharzia, use only well-maintained and chlorinated swimming pools. Use only bottled or boiled water for drinks, washing teeth and making ice. Eat only well cooked meals, preferably served hot; vegetables should be cooked and fruit peeled. Dairy products are unpasteurised and should be avoided, unless cooked.
Walking in bare feet, or even open sandals, can attract parasites, notably jikkers. Visitors should seek advice before accepting treatment involving hypodermic needles or blood transfusions. Medical insurance is essential, including emergency evacuation, and an adequate supply of personal medicines is necessary.

Hotels
There is a wide range of hotels available, though rooms are difficult to obtain and expensive in Lagos. Bills must be paid for in foreign currency and a high deposit in advance is required to cover the estimated length of stay. Most major hotels are air-conditioned.

Credit cards
Credit cards are not widely used.

Public holidays (national)

Fixed dates
1 Jan (New Year's Day), 1 May (Workers' Day), 29 May (Democracy Day), 1 Oct (National Day), 25–26 Dec (Christmas).

Variable dates
Easter (Mar/Apr), Eid al Adha, Birth of the Prophet, National Day (first Mon in Oct), Eid al Fitr.
Holidays that fall at the weekend may be taken on Monday.

Islamic year 1433 (26 Nov 2011–14 Nov 2012): The Islamic year contains 354 or 355 days, with the result that Muslim feasts advance by 10–12 days against the Gregorian calendar. Dates of feasts vary according to the sighting of the new moon, so cannot be forecast exactly.

Working hours

Banking
Mon: 0800–1500; Tue–Fri: 0800–1330 (some banks work until 1600 or 1700); Sat, some banks only: 1000–1500.

Business
Mon–Fri: 0800–1230 and 1400–1630. Some offices also Sat: 0800–1200.

Government
Mon–Fri: 0730–1530, some states also Sat: 0800–1300.

Shops
Mon–Fri: 0800–1200 and 1430–1800; Sat: 0800–1300.

Telecommunications

Mobile/cell phones
There are GSM roaming facilities available, with coverage throughout most of the country.

Electricity supply
230V AC, 50 cycles

Social customs/useful tips
Because of the prodigious traffic jams, called 'go-slows', which often grip Lagos, it is hard to be punctual, so both Nigerians and expatriates are generally tolerant of latecomers.
Appointments with government officials should be made in advance. With business executives, a more informal attitude prevails. Business cards are exchanged after introduction and business is mostly conducted in English. Meetings can be long and they are less formal than in Europe. It is customary to shake hands on meeting and taking leave.
Confirm the business organisation's status with the Chamber of Commerce, Corporate Affairs Commission, Abuja and the Federal Ministry of Commerce and Tourism, Abuja, before entering into a firm contract.
Local customs and conventions should be adhered to, particularly in Muslim areas in the northern states. Women should not wear trousers.
Gifts are welcomed but not essential, unless hospitality extends to accommodation and/or meals, in which case gifts are expected on departure.
Gratuities are around 10 per cent. A service charge is usually added to restaurant and hotel bills. Tips are not expected by taxi drivers. Giving *dash* or gratuities for other commercial services is widespread, although officially discouraged .

Security
Security remains a serious problem in several Nigerian cities, but chiefly in Lagos. The biggest threat comes from armed robbers. They either attack houses at night or, more frequently, stop cars at gunpoint on urban or country expressways and order the driver to hand over the keys. Petty theft is also common; moneybelts are advisable.
During outbreaks of violence, the capital is likely to be dotted with checkpoints manned by armed police, where visitors should remain calm and courteous. It is not necessary to offer a bribe at these roadblocks.

Getting there

Air
International airport/s: Abuja Nnamdi Azikiwe (ABV), 35km from city; Kano-Mallam-Aminu Kano (KAN), 8km from city; Lagos-Murtala Muhammed (LOS), 22km from city. All airport facilities include duty-free shop, restaurant, bar, bank, post office, car hire.
It is advisable to be met at Lagos airport by someone you know, or someone who can prove their identity. Also make sure you do not give your passport to anyone but the immigration officer. Check in early for flights as overbooking is common.
Airport tax: None

Surface
Road: There are good roads linking Niger (Maradi, Zinder, Agadez, Niamey) to Kano, and from Benin; there are all-weather roads from Cameroon (Maroua, Mokolo) and Chad (N'Djamna). The southern road from Cameroon (Mamfe) to Enugu is not generally recommended.
Water: Nigeria has the biggest port facilities and international sailings in the region.
Main port/s: Apapa (Lagos), Port Harcourt, Calabar and the Delta Port complex including Warri, Sapele and Koko.

Getting about

National transport
Air: There is a number of local airlines providing intercity services. Routes and airlines frequently change.
Road: A national road network system of 113,000km links all main centres. Principal main roads connect Lagos and Port Harcourt in the south with Kano and Katsina in the north. The motorway running from Lagos-Ibadan is often congested. There are often long delays in major towns.

Some secondary roads can become impassable during rainy season.
Buses: Scheduled coach services include: Kaduna-Jos; Lagos-Umuahia.
Rail: There are some 3,500km of railway, mostly single track.
Rail travel is cheap, but slow. There are two classes. Some trains have restaurant cars and buffet facilities and some have air-conditioning.
There are two main rail lines: Lagos-Kano Express (via Ibadan and Minna) with branches to Baro, Kaura Namoda and Nguru, Plateau Express (Lagos-Jos); and Port Harcourt-Kano with branch to Jos and Maiduguri.
Water: There are over 8,575 km of waterways including the Niger and Benue rivers, with ferry services on these and along the southern coast.

City transport

Taxis: Taxis are widely available in Lagos and other main towns. The traditional taxis are usually yellow Peugeots in Lagos (these charge by distance), other colours elsewhere. Also numerous cars belonging to car hire companies. Taxi ranks are mainly found at the big hotels. Fare and tip should be agreed before starting journey. All drivers should have an Identity Card.
Journey time from Lagos Murtala Mohammed Airport to city centre is around 40 minutes, but can take several hours if the traffic is heavy.

Car hire

Available in most of the large towns through the main hotels. International driving licence and two passport-sized photographs required; chauffeur-driven services generally recommended.
Be aware that in Lagos the Lagos State Traffic Management Authority (Lastma) has wide powers and frequently stops and seizes vehicles for minor, alleged, offences. On the spot 'fines' are frequently suggested. Owners of vehicles that are impounded have to pay a daily charge to recover them.

BUSINESS DIRECTORY

The addresses listed below are a selection only. While World of Information makes every endeavour to check these addresses, we cannot guarantee that changes have not been made, especially to telephone numbers and area codes. We would welcome any corrections.

Telephone area codes

The international direct dialling code (IDD) for Nigeria is +234, followed by area code and subscriber's number:

Abuja	9	Katsina	65
Akure	34	Lagos	1
Bauchi	77	Maiduguri	76
Calabar	87	Makurdi	44
Enugu	42	Minna	66
Ibadan	22	Owerri	83
Ikeja	1	Oyo	38
Ilorin	31	Port Harcourt	84
Jos	73	Sokoto	60
Kaduna	62	Yola	75
Kano	64	Zaria	69

Useful telephone numbers

Police	199
Fire and ambulance	999

Chambers of Commerce

Abuja Chamber of Commerce and Industry, International Trade Fair Centre, Airport Road, PO Box 86, Abuja (tel: 523-0453; fax: 523-6231; e-mail: anmgbemere@hotmail.com).

British-Nigerian Chamber of Commerce, Ebani House, 149 Broad Street, Lagos (tel: 264-1266; fax: 266-0298; e-mail: hq@n-bcc.org).

Enugu Chamber of Commerce, Industry, Mines and Agriculture, International Trade Fair Complex, Abakaliki Road, PO Box 734, Enugu (tel: 250-575; fax: 252-186; e-mail: eccima@infoweb.abs.net).

Ibadan Chamber of Commerce and Industry, Commerce House, Ring Road, PO Box 5168, Ibadan (tel: 317-223; fax: 311-647; e-mail: icci@infoweb.abs.net).

Kaduna Chamber of Commerce, Industry, Mines and Agriculture, Kaduna-Zaria Road, Rigachikun, PO Box 728, Kaduna (tel: 318-794; fax: 318-795; e-mail: kadccima@inet-global.com).

Kano Chamber of Commerce and Industry, Trade Fair Complex, Zoo Road, PO Box 10, Kano (tel: 666-936; fax: 667-138; e-mail: kaccima@hotmail.com).

Lagos Chamber of Commerce and Industry, 1 Idowu Taylor Street, Victoria Island, PO Box 109, Lagos (tel: 774-6617; fax: 262-3665; e-mail: inform@lagoschamber.com).

National Association of Chambers of Commerce, Industry and Agriculture, 15A Ikorodu Road, Maryland, PO Box 12816, Lagos (tel: 496-4727, 496-4737; e-mail: naccima@pinet.com.ng).

Port Harcourt Chamber of Commerce, Industry, Mines and Agriculture, 169 Aba Road, PO Box 71, Port Harcourt (tel: 330-394; fax: 243-307; e-mail: phccima@hotmail.com).

Banking

Nigerian Industrial Development Bank Ltd (NIMB), PMB 205, 1st Floor, NIMB Building, 4th Avenue, Plot 207, Cadastral Zone AO, Off Herbert Macaulay Way, Central Business District, Abuja (tel: 234-6579; fax: 234-6578).

Commercial Bank (Crédit Lyonnais Nigeria) Ltd, PMB 12829, Plot 146B Ligali Ayorinde, Victoria Island Annex, Lagos (tel: 262-5700; fax: 262-5699).

Ecobank Nigeria plc, 2 Ajose Adeogun St, Victoria Island, Lagos (tel: 262-0910/4; fax: 261-6568, 262-0920).

Investment Banking & Trust Co Ltd (IBTC), PMB 71707, IBTC Place, Walter Carrington Crescent, Victoria Island, Lagos (tel: 262-6520/40; fax: 262-6541/2; e-mail: IBTC@IBTCLagos.com; internet site: http://www.IBTCLagos.com).

Lion Bank of Nigeria plc, PMB 12852, 121/125 Broad St, Lagos (tel: 266-914, 266-7735).

Nigerian Industrial Development Bank Ltd (NIDB), PMB 2357, NIDB House, 63/71 Broad St, Lagos (tel: 266-3495, 266-1545; fax: 266-7074, 266-6733).

Central bank

Central Bank of Nigeria, Central Business District, Cadastral Zone, PO Box 0187, Garki, Abuja (tel: 234-3191; fax: 234-3137; email: info@cenbank.org).

Stock exchange

Nigerian Stock Exchange (NSE): www.nigerianstockexchange.com

Travel information

ADC Airlines (tel: 271-4020; reservations: 496-1942; internet: www.adcairlines.com).

Virgin Nigeria, Head Office, 3rd Floor, Ark Towers, Plot 17, Ligali Ayorinde Street, Victoria Island Extension, Lagos (tel: 460-0505, 271-1111; internet: www.virginnigeria.com).

Ministry of tourism

Federal Ministry of Culture and Tourism, Area 1 Secretariat Complex, Garki, Abuja (tel: 234-2727).

National tourist organisation offices

Nigerian Tourism Developemnt Corporation, Old Secretariat, Area 1, Garki, PMB 167, Abuja (tel: 234-2764; fax: 234-2775; e-mail: information@nigeriatourism.net).

Ministries

Federal Ministry of Agriculture and Rural Development, Area 1 Secretariat Complex, Garki, Abuja (tel: 314-1185).

Federal Ministry of Aviation, New Federal Secretariat Complex, Shehu Shagari Way, Abuja (tel: 523-2112).

Federal Ministry of Commerce, Area 1 Secretariat Complex, Garki, Abuja (tel: 234-1884).

Federal Ministry of Communications, New Federal Secretariat Complex, Shehu Shagari Way, Abuja (tel: 523-7183).

Federal Ministry of Culture and Tourism, Area 1 Secretariat Complex, Garki, Abuja (tel: 234-2727).

Federal Ministry of Defence, Ship House, Central Area, Abuja (tel: 234-0534).

Federal Ministry of Education, New Federal Secretariat Complex, Shehu Shagari Way, Abuja (tel: 523-2800).

Federal Ministry for Federal Capital Territory, Area 11, Garki, Abuja (tel: 523-4014).

Federal Ministry of Finance, Garki, Abuja (tel: 234-4686).

Federal Ministry of Foreign Affairs, Maputo Street, Zone 3 Wuse District, Abuja (tel: 523-0576).

Federal Ministry of Health, New Federal Secretariat Complex, Shehu Shagari Way, Abuja, (tel: 523-0576).

Federal Ministry of Industries, Area 1 Secretariat Complex, Garki, Abuja (tel: 523-0576).

Federal Ministry of Information, Radio House, Herbert Macaulay Way, Garki, Abuja (tel: 234-6350).

Federal Ministry of Internal Affairs, Area 1 Secretariat Complex, Garki, Abuja (tel: 234-6884).

Federal Ministry of Justice, New Federal Secretariat Complex, Shehu Shagari Way, Abuja (tel: 523-5194).

Federal Ministry of Labour and Productivity, New Federal Secretariat Complex, Shehu Shagari Way, Abuja (tel: 523-5980).

Federal Ministry of Police Affairs, New Federal Secretariat Complex, Shehu Shagari Way, Abuja (tel: 523-0549).

Federal Ministry of Power and Steel, New Federal Secretariat Complex, Shehu Shagari Way, Abuja (tel: 523-7064).

Federal Ministry of Science and Technology, New Federal Secretariat Complex, Shehu Shagari Way, Abuja (tel: 523-3397).

Federal Ministry of Solid Minerals Development, New Federal Secretariat Complex, Shehu Shagari Way, Abuja (tel: 523-5830; fax: 523,6518; e-mail: minsolmindev@linkserve.com).

Federal Ministry of Sports and Social Development, New Federal Secretariat Complex, Shehu Shagari Way, Abuja (tel: 523-5905).

Federal Ministry of Transport, National Maritime Agency Building, Central Area, Abuja (tel: 523-7053).

Federal Ministry of Water Resources, Area 1 Secretariat Complex, Garki, Abuja (tel: 234-2376).

Federal Ministry of Women's Affairs and Youth Development, New Federal Secretariat Complex, Shehu Shegari Way, Abuja (tel: 523-7051).

Federal Ministry of Works and Housing, Mabushi Districti, Abuja (tel: 521-1622).

Other useful addresses

African Petroleum plc, AP House, 54-56 Broad Street, PO Box 512, Lagos (tel: 260-0050/9, 260-0145/9; fax: 263-5290).

Bureau of Public Enterprises, 1 Osun Crescent, Off Ibrahim Babangida Way, Maitama, Abuja (tel: 413-4673; fax: 413-4674; internet: www.bpeng.org).

British High Commission, Dangote House, Aguyi Ironsi Street, Maitama District, Abuja (tel 413-4559–64 (6 lines); fax: 413-4565, 413-3888; email: visa.enquiries.abuja@fco.gov.uk).

Britain Nigeria Business Council, 2 Vincent Street, London, SW1P 4LD (tel: (+44-20) 7828-9661; fax: (+44-20) 7828-9779; email: bnbc-uk@btconnect.com)

Chevron Nigeria Ltd, 2 Chevron Drive, Lekki Peninsular, PMB 12825, Lagos.

Economic Community of West African States (Ecowas), 6 King George V Road, Lagos (tel: 260-0720/5).

Manufacturers' Association of Nigeria, 12th Floor, Unity House, 37 Marina, PO Box 3835, Lagos.

National Council on Privatisation, Secretariat, Bureau of Public Enterprises, 1 Osun Crescent, Off Ibrahim Babangida Way, Maitama District, PMB 442, Garki, Abuja (tel: 413-4660/4670/4673; fax: 413-4671/4672/4674; e-mail: bpegen@micro.com.ng).

National Maritime Authority, 4 Burma Road, Apapa, Lagos.

National Planning Commission, Federal Secretariat, Shehu Shagari Way, Abuja (tel: 523-6628; fax: 523-6625).

National Science & Technology Development Agency, PO Box 12695, Lagos.

Nigerian Communications Commission, 72 Ahmadu Bello Way, Benue Plaza, Abuja (tel: 234-2327, 234-4590/2; fax: 234-4593; email: ncc@cyberspace.net.ng; internet site: www.ncc.gov.ng).

Nigeria Export Processing Zone Authority, 4th Floor, Radio House, Herbert Macauley Way (South), PMB 037, Garki Abuja (tel: 234-3060; fax: 234-3061).

Nigerian Embassy (USA), 1333 16th Street, NW, Washington DC 20036 (tel: (+1-202) 986-8400; fax: (+1-202) 462-7124).

Nigeria-São Tomé and Príncipe Joint Development Authority, Plot 1101 Aminu Kano Crescent, Wuse II, Abuja (tel: 524-1069; fax: 524-1052; e-mail: enquiries@nigeriasaotomejda.com; internet: www.nigeriasaotomejda.com).

Ports Sector Reforms, Bureau of Public Enterprises, 1 Osun Crescent, Off Ibrahim Babangida Way, Maitama, PMB 442, Garki, Abuja (tel: 413-4634/46; fax: 413-4671/2/4; email: husmanbpeng.org).

National news agency: NAN (News Agency of Nigeria)

Internet sites

Portal site: www.nigerianation.com

Africa Business Network: http://www.ifc.org/abn

AllAfrica.com: http://allafrica.com

African Development Bank: http://www.afdb.org

Africa News Online: http://www.allafrica.com

Africa Online: http://www.africaonline.com

Mbendi AfroPaedia (information on companies, countries, industries and stock exchanges in Africa): http://mbendi.co.za

Movement for the Survival of the Ogoni People (MOSOP): www.mosopcanada.org/ index1.html

Niue

KEY FACTS

Official name: Republic of Niue

Head of State: Queen Elizabeth II, represented by the Governor General of New Zealand and High Commissioner Mark Herbert Blumsky (from Oct 2010)

Head of government: Prime Minister Toke Talagi (elected by parliament 2008; re-elected 7 May 2011)

Ruling party: There are no political parties; parliamentarians sit as independents

Area: 256 square km

Population: 1,000 (2010)*; over 20,000 Niueans reside in New Zealand.

Capital: Alofi is the main town.

Official language: English, Niuean

Currency: New Zealand dollar (NZ$) = 100 cents

Exchange rate: NZ$1.30 per US$ (Oct 2011)

GDP per capita: US$10,277 (2009)

GDP real growth: 0.10% (2009)

GDP: US$15.80 million (2009)

Inflation: 11.70% (2009)

Aid flow: US$2.60 million (annually)

* estimated figure

COUNTRY PROFILE

Historical profile

The first inhabitants arrived from Tonga, Samoa and Fiji between AD600 and AD1000.

1774 Visited by Captain James Cook and given the name, Savage Island

1846 Conversion to Christianity commenced by the London Missionary Society.

1900 Niue became a British protectorate.

1901 Niue was formally annexed to New Zealand, as part of the Cook Islands.

1960 The first Niue Assembly was established.

1974 Niue was granted 'self-government in free association with New Zealand'. It became the smallest self-governing state with that status.

1982 Robert Rex was elected prime minister.

1992 Robert Rex died. He was succeeded by Young Vivian.

1993 Frank Lui won the election and became prime minister.

1996 Lui was re-elected.

1999 Sani Elia Lakatani of the Niue People's Party (NPP) was elected prime minister.

2001 The US imposed trading sanctions on Niue due its tax haven status. A census recorded 1,799 people.

2002 All 20 members of the Niue Assembly were re-elected and Young Vivian (NPP) was elected prime minister.

2003 The NPP was dissolved, despite which the coalition government continued.

2004 A 300km per hour cyclone, Heta, devastated Niue.

2005 A census recorded that the population figure was 1,600, a drop of almost 200 people, with the village of North Alofi losing 113 of its 256 residents. There are some 20,000 Niueans living abroad, mostly in New Zealand; the government is trying to encourage them to return. Young Vivian retained his parliamentary seat unopposed and was re-elected prime minister.

2006 Niue had been suffering from frequent power failures when one of its generators was damaged causing further problems in pumping water from the reservoir. The island's electricity network was over 30 years old and due for upgrading; a new replacement, five tonne generator was flown in from New Zealand at short notice.

2008 In parliamentary elections 20 independent members were elected (nine unopposed). Toke Talagi was elected prime minister. 500 educational laptops were distributed among all school children, allowing them to web-surf via existing wireless internet services.

2009 The Organisation for Economic Co-operation and Development (OECD) published a list of countries that had not implemented international tax information exchange standards, of which Niue was one despite signing a co-operation agreement in 2002.

2010 Air New Zealand began a direct weekly flight between Auckland and Niue. New Zealand appointed Mark Blumsky as high commissioner in October.

2011 In parliamentary elections were held on 7 May 20 non-partisan candidates were elected. Toke Talagi was re-elected as prime minister (with 12 votes). On 19 July, the New Zealand government announced it would committed US$12.65 million (NZ$15 million) to help Niue develop into a 'boutique tourism destination', building on Niue's natural beauty and environment as the main attraction for adventure holidays.

Political structure

Constitution

Under the 1974 constitution, New Zealand remains responsible for defence and foreign affairs and is ready to provide necessary economic and administrative assistance. Niueans are New Zealand citizens.

The head of state, the British monarch, is represented in Niue by the Governor General of New Zealand.

Village affairs are handled by 14 village councils of three to five members, elected to three-year terms in conjunction with the Community Affairs Office.

Form of state

Self-governing state, in free association with New Zealand.

The executive

The four-member executive cabinet is headed by a prime minister elected by the Legislative Assembly, who in turn appoints three ministers.

National legislature

The island is governed by the 20-member Niue Assembly – 14 elected from village constituencies and six from the common roll – elected by popular vote for a three-year term.

Last elections

7 May 2011 (parliamentary)

Results: Parliamentary: 20 non-partisan candidates were elected.

Next elections

2011 (parliamentary)

Political parties

The Niue political system is not based on formal political organisations. Until 2003, two loose groupings existed: the Niue People's Party (NPP) and the Alliance of Independents. The NPP was dissolved in July 2003 and all candidates since then have run as independents.

Ruling party

There are no political parties; parliamentarians sit as independents

Population

1,000 (2010)*; over 20,000 Niueans reside in New Zealand.

Last census: 9 September 2006: 1,625

Population density: 8 inhabitants per square km (2001).

Annual growth rate: -2.1 per cent 1994–2004 (WHO 2006)

Ethnic make-up

The population is mainly of Polynesian (Tongan) descent, with some New Zealand elements.

Religions

Predominantly Christian.

Education

The education system is modelled on New Zealand's with services provided free until aged 14. For the first four years teaching may be in either Niuean or English. In 2004, the schools increased the content of Niuean language in the curriculum. The government has backed the 'one laptop per child' programme (OLPC).

Compulsory years: Five to 14

Health

Life expectancy: 71 years, 2004 (WHO 2006)

Fertility rate/Maternal mortality rate: 2.8 births per woman, 2004 (WHO 2006)

Main cities

Alofi (estimated population 404 in 2004).

Languages spoken

English is widely understood. The people who live in the north speak a Polynesian dialect which differs from the dialect of the people living on the rest of the island who speak a language closer to Tongan.

Official language/s

English, Niuean

Media

There is limited media availability.

Press

The weekly *Niue Star* is a private newspaper published in English and Niue. A fortnightly newspaper *Niuean* (www.niuean.com) is published in Australia. An online news round-up is *Niue Business News* (www.webpost.net/nb/nbn).

Broadcasting

The Broadcasting Corporation of Niue operates the only radio (Radio Sunshine) and television station, which broadcasts in English and Niue in the evenings only.

Radio: Radio Sunshine broadcasts are transmitted on AM594/FM91 six days/week during limited hours.

Television: Television Niue broadcasts in English and Niue in the evenings only, usually 1730–2200.

News agencies

ABC Pacific Beat:
www.radioaustralia.net.au/pacbeat
Pacific Magazine:
www.pacificmagazine.net

Economy

Niue's economy is wholly dependent on financial assistance from New Zealand, which contributes around 40 per cent of GDP. Per capita income at over US$8,200 is one of the highest of the Pacific islands and kept artificially high by New Zealand's aid.

The local economy is based on government employment and subsistence farming, raising vegetables, fruit, pigs and poultry for family consumption. Industry is limited to agricultural production, although some small building and joinery operations have been started. Sales of postage stamps and remittances from Niuean workers overseas are important sources of revenue.

New Zealand began the process of accustoming Niue to fiscal responsibility in 2004 by providing capital investment (NZ$30 million (US$44 million) up to 2009) to fund infrastructure projects to boost tourism, a sector thought likely to become Niue's major source of foreign exchange.

In order to boost Niue's meagre income, the government leases international telephone codes for use by foreign companies and has built a quarantine station for alpaca – a wool-bearing llama-like South American mammal – *en route* to Australia. Marketing of the '.nu' Internet domain name has been a controversial income source. The government is also hoping to gain revenue from investment partnerships in fishing and organic products and is seeking interest in developing tourism.

External trade

Niue is a member of the South Pacific Regional Trade and Economic Co-operation Agreement (Sparteca) along with 12 other regional nations, which allows products duty free access by Pacific Island Forum members to Australian and New Zealand markets (subject to the country of origin restrictions).

Imports

Main imports are food, live animals, construction materials, manufactured goods, vehicles, fuels and medicines.

Main sources: Principally from New Zealand, Fiji, Japan, Samoa, Australia, US.

Exports

Agricultural products – fish, taro, copra, honey, vanilla, passion fruit, paw paws, root crops and limes, financial and telecommunication services.

Main destinations: Principally to New Zealand, Fiji, Cook Islands, Australia

Agriculture

Development of agriculture has been hindered by the limited amount of fertile or cultivable land, lack of surface water and susceptibility to drought conditions. Only 20 per cent of land can be used for agriculture. Cyclones are a major problem. Alienation of land is forbidden, but leases may be granted for a maximum term of 66 years.

Limes and passion fruit are grown for export. Goats have been introduced on a trial basis.

Annual fishing production typically includes 200t marine fish. A new fish plant employs 30 people.

About 20 per cent of the land area is forest with millable timber, and logging serves local demand.

Malaysian logging companies have approached the government to harvest timber from the small hardwood forests. Not everyone is in agreement with such production that could leave the island deforested and the terrain at more risk from cyclones.

Industry and manufacturing

The Office of Economic Affairs is responsible for planning and financing productive ventures relating to agriculture, tourism and industry. Niue Handicrafts handles production and marketing of objects plaited from pandanus and coconut palm leaves.

Small-scale industries include honey extraction and bottling, saw milling, joinery, furniture and handicrafts.

Investment has been made in the vanilla and forestry industries.

Tourism

Development of tourism is a priority, with emphasis on eco-tourism, but has been impeded by poor planning, uncertain air connections with New Zealand and nature in the form of seasonal cyclones. Visitor numbers have been small but rising prompting additional flights by Polynesian Airlines.

Hydrocarbons
There are no known hydrocarbon reserves. Consumption of oil was around 30 barrels per day (bpd) in 2007, all of which was imported.

Energy
Total installed generating capacity was 1MW in 2007. The Niue Power Corporation is responsible for electricity generation and supply. The majority of the population relies on non-commercial biomass, mostly fuel wood for cooking, lighting and power.

Banking and insurance
Central bank
Reserve Bank of New Zealand
Offshore facilities
In 2002, the introduction of US sanctions on banking activities was a major blow to Niue. The US accused Niue of having connections to Latin American tax haven operations.
Niue licensed six offshore banks operating in Australia, which the Organisation for Economic Co-operation and Development (OECD) wanted to close down. In 2002, the Niue Legislative Assembly repealed the legislation which authorised the issuing of banking licences and Niue was removed from the OECD Financial Action Task Force (FATF) blacklist of places associated with money laundering. The OECD published a list on 2 April 2009 of countries that had not implemented international tax information exchange standards, of which Nuie was one, despite signing the co-operation agreement in 2002.

Time
GMT minus eleven hours

Geography
Niue is a coral island in the Pacific Ocean about 480km (300 miles) east of Tonga and 930km (580 miles) west of the southern Cook Islands. It rises to only 65 metres, as an outcrop, from the sea, with a steep and jagged coastline. The land has many caves and fissures and although is has no rivers there are plenty of wells to keep the topsoil fertile.
Hemisphere
Southern

Climate
Subtropical and humid, with temperature 25–30 degrees Celsius and average rainfall of nearly 200cm per annum.

Entry requirements
Passports
Required by all.
Visa
Not required by tourist visitors staying less than 30 days. Visitors are required to have return/onward tickets and all necessary entry documentation for the next destination, as well as sufficient funds for length of stay and suitable accommodation. Visitors may extend their stay by applying to the Immigration officials upon arrival, an extension permit of three months (cost of NZ$30) is usually granted.
Visas are required by all visitors for stays of over 30 days. Further information may be obtained from the Immigration Department, PO Box 69, Alofi, Niue Island (email: immigrationniue@mail.gov.nu).
Currency advice/regulations
The import of local currency is unlimited; export is limited to NZ$10,000. The import of foreign currency must be declared; export is limited to the amount declared.
Customs
Personal items are duty free, only one personal electronic item, camera or binoculars are allowed.
The export of native artifacts, coral and rare shells is prohibited.
Prohibited imports
Firearms and ammunition require a permit from the Chief of Police in Alofi.

Health (for visitors)
Mandatory precautions
Vaccination certificates for yellow fever are required if travelling from infected area.
Advisable precautions
Vaccinations for diphtheria, TB, hepatitis A and B, polio, tetanus and typhoid are all recommended. There is a rabies risk. It is advisable to take water precautions.

Public holidays (national)
Fixed dates
1 Jan (New Year's Day), 4 Jan (Takai Commission Holiday), 6 Feb (Waitangi Day), 25 Apr (Anzac Day), 16–19 Oct (Constitution Celebrations), 17 Oct (Peniamina's Day), 25–26 Dec (Christmas).
Holidays that fall on the weekend are taken *in lieu* on the following Monday/Tuesday.
Variable dates
Good Friday (Mar/Apr), Easter Monday (Mar/Apr), Queen's Official Birthday (first Mon in Jun).

Working hours
Banking
Mon–Thur: 0900–1500; Fri: 0830–1500.
Business
Mon–Fri: 0730–1530.
Shops
Mon–Fri: 0830–1600; Sat: 0830–1500.

Telecommunications
Mobile/cell phones
The Harris Cellular Network provides fixed and mobile coverage.

Social customs/useful tips
It is customary to shake hands on meeting and taking leave. Gratuities are not encouraged.

Getting there
Air
There are limited connections from Auckland, New Zealand; Sydney, Australia; Samoa; Fiji and Los Angeles, US.
International airport/s: Hanan (IUE), 7km north of Alofi.
Airport tax: Departure tax: NZ$25
Surface
There are no port facilities. Ships anchor off Alofi and barges transfer cargo.

Getting about
National transport
Road: There are approximately 130km of all-weather road and 96km bush track negotiable by heavy trucks and four-wheel drive vehicles. A 60km road circles the island and roads link main centres.
Car hire
Visitors with an foreign driver's licence must obtain a local licence from the Niue police department before driving a hired vehicle. It is advisable to reserve hire vehicles before arrival.
Driving is on the left.

BUSINESS DIRECTORY
The addresses listed below are a selection only. While World of Information makes every endeavour to check these addresses, we cannot guarantee that changes have not been made, especially to telephone numbers and area codes. We would welcome any corrections.

Telephone area codes
The international direct dialling code (IDD) for Niue is +683 followed by subscriber's number.

Useful telephone numbers
Police, fire and ambulance:	999/4000
Hospital:	998

Chambers of Commerce
Niue Chamber of Commerce and Industry, PO Box 160, Alofi (tel: 43-99; fax: 40-17; e-mail: chamber@sin.net.nu).

Banking
Westpac Banking Corporation, PO Box 76, Alofi (tel: 4221; fax: 4043).
Central bank
The Reserve Bank of New Zealand, PO Box 2498, Wellington, New Zealand (tel: (+64-4) 472-2029; fax: (+64-4) 473-8554).

Travel information
Air Nauru, Government Building, Yaren District, Republic of Nauru (tel: (+674) 3141, 3418; fax: (+674) 3170).

Matavai Resort (hotel), PO Box 133, Alofi (tel: 4360, email: matavai@niue.nu).

Niue International Airport (Hanan), PO Box 83, Alofi (tel: 4020, 4133, 4096; fax: 4010).

National tourist organisation offices
Niue Tourism Office, PO Box 42, Alofi (tel: 4224; fax: 4225; internet site: http://www.niueisland.com).

Other useful addresses
Broadcasting Corporation of Niue, PO Box 26, Alofi (tel: 4026; fax: 4217).

Business Advisory Service, Alofi (tel: 4228).

Department of Immigration, PO Box, Alofi (tel: 4349, 4333; fax: 4336; email: immigrationniue@mail.gov.nu).

Office of Economic Affairs, PO Box 42, Alofi (tel: 4126).

Office of the Prime Minister. PO Box 40, Alofi (tel: 4200; fax: 4206, 4232).

Office of the Secretary to Government, PO Box 67, Alofi (tel: 4017; fax: 4232).

Internet sites
Niue government website: http://www.gov.nu

Niue website: http://www.niueisland.nu

South Pacific Tourism Organisation: http://www.tcsp.com/niue/index.html

Norfolk Island

KEY FACTS

Official name: Norfolk Island

Head of State: Queen Elizabeth II of Australia; represented by Administrator (appointed by Governor General of Australia) Owen Edward John Walsh (from Oct 2008)

Head of government: Chief Minister André Nobbs (from Mar 2007)

Ruling party: None, legislative assembly members sit as independents

Area: 35 square km

Population: 2,085 (2009)*

Capital: Kingston

Official language: English

Currency: Australian dollar (A$) = 100 cents

Exchange rate: A$1.03 per US$ (Oct 2011)

Visitor numbers: 40,000 (annually)

* estimated figure

COUNTRY PROFILE

Historical profile

1774 First European sighting of Norfolk Island by Captain James Cook. He named the island in honour of the Ninth Duchess of Norfolk.
1788 Norfolk Island was occupied by the British.
1790 A settlement was established to supply the New South Wales penal colony.
1814 The settlement was abandoned.
1825 The island was re-settled as a penal colony.
1856 The British authorities moved the 193 descendants of the *Bounty* mutineers from Pitcairn Island to Norfolk Island.
1858 16 Pitcairners returned to Pitcairn Island after a dispute with the British about land ownership. Other Pitcairners followed.
1897 Norfolk Island became a dependency of New South Wales.
1914 Norfolk Island became a Territory under the authority of the Commonwealth of Australia.
1979 The Norfolk Island Act conferred a measure of self-government.
1992 Norfolk Islanders became entitled to vote in elections for the Australian parliament.
2000 Norfolk Islanders signed a deal with genetic researchers to study the population for genes that predispose people to high blood pressure or migraines.
2001 A census recorded a total population of 2,601 including 564 tourists and visitors.
2002 The killing of an Australian tourist, Janelle Patton, was the first murder to take place on the island since the 1850s.
2004 Deputy Chief Minister Ivens Buffett was shot dead; his son was later acquitted of his murder.
2006 A census recorded a total population of 2,523 including 660 tourists and visitors. The Australian government published its Commonwealth Grants Commission report on the financial capacity of Norfolk Island.
2007 A branch of the Australian Labor Party (ALP) was established to work to reform the political system. A New Zealander, Glenn McNeill was convicted of the murder of Janelle Patton. In legislative assembly elections André Nobbs won most votes and was elected chief minister.
2010 Island council elections were held in March in which the nine candidates (out of 28 in total) that won most votes were elected. Legislation under consideration in May by the Australian parliament to impose more accountability and good governance on Norfolk Island public spending had the effect of warning the island's government that new proposals by Australia would restrict its power to operate independently. In November, Norfolk Island was chosen to be the first country worldwide to pilot a personal carbon-trading programme. The inhabitants were encouraged to sign up for the scheme whereby they receive carbon credits to be exchanged for energy or petrol, when they take actions against obesity and climate change.
2011 On 2 March the Australian government published the *Norfolk Island Road Map*, outlining its plans for changes to its funding for the territory. It identified the need for change to the status of the island as a semi-autonomous, self-governing territory to one under more direct control from Canberra. The Australian Regional Development and Local government body will undertake a 'community survey' of the population and economic conditions of Norfolk Island to determine the long-term needs of both. The Australian government agreed to provided A$14.1 million (US$14,778 million) in emergency financial assistance in September, through a funding agreement for 2011/12.

Political structure

Constitution

The Norfolk Island Act of 1979 provides for an administrator (appointed by the Governor General of Australia and responsible to the Australian government), a Legislative Assembly and Executive Council. The Act provides that proposed laws passed by the legislative assembly must be presented to the administrator for assent. Both the legislative assembly and Executive Council are presided over by the president of the legislative assembly. Since 1992, Norfolk Islanders are entitled to vote in elections for the Australian parliament.

Form of state

Self-governing Territory of Australia

The executive
The Executive Council is made up of five members of the legislative assembly; each member holds the position of minister, with one or more portfolios. The Executive Council passes laws and devises governmental policy, which is agreed or not by the administrator.
National legislature
The unicameral, Norfolk Legislative Assembly has nine members, elected from a list of candidates, to serve for a three-year term.
Legal system
The judicial system consists of a Supreme Court and a Court of Petty Sessions.
Last elections
21 March 2007 (parliamentary)
Results: Parliamentary: nine non-partisan candidates were elected; André Nobbs received most votes. Turnout was 91.2 per cent.
Next elections
2013 (parliamentary)

Political parties
There are no political parties in the legislative assembly; all members sit as independents.
Ruling party
None, legislative assembly members sit as independents
Political situation
The Norfolk Islanders are an independent people who consider their state to predate that of the Commonwealth of Australia, the country to which they were tied by a British administration in 1897.
The Australian government published its *Norfolk Island Road Map* on 2 March 2011, outlining its plans for change to its funding for the territory. It identified three pillars that were fundamental in underpinning the changes: providing economic diversity for sustained growth; providing social cohesion; and resilience and protecting the island's unique heritage and environment. Visitor numbers have been declining since 2000 and the economy has become unsustainable in its current form, so much so that the island's government is unable to operate without cash injections from the commonwealth government. The Road Map said that reforms in governance and economic development must be undertaken or the prospects for Norfolk Island will remain unchanged and that the infrastructure had declined and there is little prospect of improvement without change.
Seven, specific proposals were submitted for discussion, the most controversial of which for the islanders were the imposition of Australian management, which would include paying all national and state taxes in operation in Australia, an opening up the economy to foreign investment and allowing immigration from the mainland. The Road Map was quick to unite any negative proposal with its corresponding benefit and emphasised that the changes would be undertaken in partnership with the people's wishes. Nevertheless, the opening remarks that the status quo could not be maintained requires the population to find accommodation for these changes in someway, before any implicit threat or sanctions were used to force the issue.

Population
2,085 (2009)*
Last census: 8 August 2006: 2,523, including 660 tourists and visitors.
Population density: 50.2 inhabitants per sq km.
Annual growth rate: 1.3 per cent (2003)
Ethnic make-up
Approximately 37 per cent of the permanent population were born on Norfolk Island (of which 47 per cent are of Pitcairn descent), 31 per cent were born on the Australian mainland and 23 per cent were born in New Zealand.
Religions
Anglicans (40 per cent), Roman Catholics (12 per cent), Uniting Church of Australia (16 per cent) and Seventh-Day Adventist (5 per cent).

Education
Infant, primary and secondary schooling is provided by the Norfolk Island Government. Education is free until the age of 15.
Compulsory years: six to 15

Main cities
Burnt Pine, Kingston.

Languages spoken
English is spoken in business circles. Norfolk, a dialect derived from the language evolved by the *Bounty* mutineers and their Tahitian wives (a mixture of mainly English and Tahitian) and brought by settlers from Pitcairn Island in the nineteenth century, is also in use.
Official language/s
English

Media
Press
There are two local weekly newspapers *The Norfolk Islander* and the *Norfolk Window*. National newspapers from Australia and New Zealand are available.
Broadcasting
Radio: The Norfolk Island Government Broadcasting Services operates the radio station. Radio Norfolk broadcasts on AM and FM for 10 hours per day during the week and for six to seven hours during the weekend.
Television: The privately owned TVN station broadcasts local material. Satellite services relay TV programmes from Australian.
News agencies
Norfolk Online: www.norfolkonline.nlk.nf

Economy
Norfolk Island's economy is based largely on its tourist industry, catering mainly to visitors from Australia (around 80 per cent of total) and New Zealand. It receives indirect funding from Australia through Australian federal agencies (of between A$3–4 million (US$3.8–5 million) per year) and grants provided to offshore Australian communities; Australia has also restored a number of historic buildings and provides certain technical services for public works on the island.
In addition to importing most of its requirements, Norfolk Island has developed a re-export industry geared to its tourist industry.
Sales of Norfolk Island postage stamps contribute to the island's revenue. Australian income tax and other federal taxes, such as goods and services tax (GST), property tax or stamp duty, do not apply in Norfolk Island, although locally raised taxes do.
The Australian government agreed to provided A$14.1 million (US$14,778 million) in emergency financial assistance in September 2011, through a funding agreement for 2011/12.

External trade
As a self-governing territory of Australia, Norfolk Island maintains strong links with the mainland but not an open market; taxes are levied on imports to provide government revenue. Exports to Australia are duty free, subject to the country of origin restrictions.
Imports
Main imports are petroleum, food, consumer goods, alcohol, building materials, footwear and clothing.
Main sources: Australia, New Zealand, neighbouring Pacific islands, Asia and EU
Exports
Main commodity exports are seeds from the Norfolk Island pine, gerbera and kentia palm, avocados and small quantities of timber, ceramics and local crafts and postage stamps.
Main destinations: Australia, neighbouring Pacific islands, New Zealand and the European Union.

Agriculture
Only 12 per cent of land is cultivatable so production is constrained by poor terrain, porous soil, a low water table and fragmented holdings. Many farms are run on a part-time basis. Crops tend to be seasonal, and provide cereals, vegetables

and fruit. There is a successful commercial hydroponic vegetable garden. Livestock is limited to cattle and poultry and the island is self-sufficient in beef, poultry and eggs.
The lack of a harbour restricts fisheries development, and catches serve local consumption only.
The Norfolk Island pine and kentia palm seeds are an important export and some hardwood afforestation is being undertaken.

Industry and manufacturing
The island produces its own handicrafts, chocolates, beers, liqueurs (including an 'aromatised whiskey' called *Convict's Curse*) and arabica coffee. Grapes are being planted for a wine industry.

Tourism
Since the mid-1960s, tourism has been the mainstay of the island's economy. The Norfolk Island Government Tourist Bureau promotes Norfolk Island in Australia and New Zealand, the island's primary markets. Approximately 30,000 tourists visit Norfolk Island each year.
It is a sub-tropical island with world-class scuba diving and fishing. There are areas of sub-tropical rainforest, much of it protected in national parks, with a network of tracks which is ideal for walking, birdwatching, cycling or horse riding.

Hydrocarbons
There are unexploited offshore oil and gas fields. All petroleum products are imported from Singapore refineries via New Caledonia and Fiji, around 33 per cent of the price of oil is transport, handling and insurance costs.

Energy
The Norfolk Island Administration operates six 1MW 16-cylinder diesel engines, producing 7 million kilowatt hours per annum. Anywhere between 10–20 per cent of total energy generated is used in refrigeration plants. A past study has determined that any move to use renewable energy will likely be a wind/diesel combination system.

Banking and insurance
There are branches of the Commonwealth Bank of Australia (which has an ATM) and Westpac Banking Corporation on the island.

Time
GMT plus eleven and a half hours.

Geography
Norfolk Island lies off the eastern coast of Australia about 1,400km east of Brisbane, to the south of New Caledonia and 640km north of New Zealand. Norfolk Island is hilly and fertile, with a coastline of cliffs. It is about 8km long and 4.8km wide. The territory also includes uninhabited Phillip Island 7km south of the main island.

Hemisphere
Southern

Climate
The island has a sub-tropical climate. Temperatures can range from 11–27 degrees Celsius, with an average rainfall of 1,346mm per year. November tends to be the driest month and the wetter months are May to August. Most rain falls at night. Average morning humidity is around 80 per cent.

Dress codes
Clothing should be comfortable and casual to suit the subtropical climate. A sweater is advisable on winter nights. A hat and sunscreen are necessary in summer.

Entry requirements
Passports
Required for all.

Visa
Required by all, except Australian and New Zealand citizens.
Any visitor who is in possession of an Australian visa may stay for up to 30 days, with travel insurance and confirmed accommodation obtained prior to arrival.
Most citizens of EU and North America can apply for an Australian Electronic Travel Authority (ETA), issued by a travel agent or airline, or online. See www.eta.immi.gov.au for details of those eligible, and follow links to the application site. ETA-eligible business visitors may stay for up to three months without additional documentation.
Those not eligible for an ETA must apply using form 456, through the nearest embassy or mission. Business visas will require a letter of invitation from a local company or organisation, a business letter from an employer stating purpose of trip and details of employee's function, proof of sufficient funds, and a full itinerary.
Further details and application form can be obtained at www.immi.gov.au/allforms.

Currency advice/regulations
There are no restrictions on import and export of local and foreign currency.

Customs
Some medications may be restricted and visitors should declare all prescription drugs.

Prohibited imports
Illicit drugs, dangerous weapons, fruit, vegetables, flowers and seeds; pork and poultry from New Zealand are also prohibited. Firearms require a permit.

Health (for visitors)
Mandatory precautions
Vaccination certificates required for yellow fever if travelling from an infected area.

Advisable precautions
Vaccination for diphtheria, TB, hepatitis A and B, polio, tetanus, typhoid. Rabies is a risk.

Public holidays (national)
Fixed dates
1 Jan (New Year's Day), 26 Jan (Australia Day), 6 Mar (Foundation Day), 25 Apr (Anzac Day), 8 Jun (Bounty Day), 25–26 Dec (Christmas).
If Christmas Day or New Year's Day falls on a Saturday, the next Monday is given as a holiday.

Variable dates
Good Friday and Easter Monday (Mar/Apr), Queen's Official Birthday (second Mon in Jun), Show Day, Thanksgiving Day (last Wed in Nov).

Working hours
Banking
Mon–Thu: 0930–1600; Fri: 0930–1700.

Business
Mon, Tue and Thu, Fri: 0900–1700; Wed and Sat: 0900–1200.

Government
Mon–Fri: 0800–1630.

Shops
Mon–Tues, Thu–Fri: 0900–1700; Wed/Sat: 0900–1230. Some shops open on Sun.
Supermarket, Mon–Sat: 0800–1800; Sun: 0900–1800.

Telecommunications
Mobile/cell phones
In 2002, the Norfolk Island residents voted against allowing a mobile phone service on the Island.

Electricity supply
Diesel generated 240V 50 cycles.

Social customs/useful tips
Tipping is not expected. It is customary to shake hands on meeting and taking leave. Punctuality on social occasions is appreciated.

Getting there
Air
The only air connections are provided by OzJet and Air New Zealand which fly from the east coast of Australia and New Zealand.
International airport/s: Norfolk (NLK).
Airport tax: A$30 for international departures, payable at the airport when leaving or at the Visitor Information Centre prior to departure.

Surface
Water: Ships anchor offshore.

Getting about

National transport

Road: The entire road network amounts to 200km.

Buses: There is no public transport system on the island, but tour buses are available for tourists.

City transport

Taxis: There is a limited taxi service.

Car hire

Arrangements may be made locally for hiring cars, motorcycles and bicycles.

BUSINESS DIRECTORY

The addresses listed below are a selection only. While World of Information makes every endeavour to check these addresses, we cannot guarantee that changes have not been made, especially to telephone numbers and area codes. We would welcome any corrections.

Telephone area codes

The international direct dialling (IDD) code for Norfolk Island is +672, followed by area code 3 and subscriber's number.

Useful telephone numbers

Police: 922
Fire: 955
Ambulance: 911
Telephone exchange: 22-244

Banking

Commonwealth Bank of Australia, Burnt Pine (tel: 22-144).

Westpac Banking Corporation, Burnt Pine (tel: 22-120).

Travel information

Norfolk Island Airport, P.O.Box 149, Norfolk Island (tel: 22-445; fax: 23-201; email (manager): grobinson@airport.gov.nf).

The Travel Centre, PO Box 172, Norfolk Island (tel: 22-502; fax: 23-205; email: travel@travelcentre.nf).

National tourist organisation offices

Norfolk Island Government Tourist Bureau, PO Box 211, Norfolk Island (tel: 22-147; fax: 23-109; email: info@norfolkisland.com.au).

Other useful addresses

Postal services for Norfolk Island have an Australian postal code – NSW 2899, Australia – to be added to the end of an address.

Customs House, Taylors Road, Norfolk Island (tel: 22-899; fax: 23-260; email customs@admin.gov.nf; internet: www.customs.gov.nf).

Legislative Assembly, Old Military Barracks, Quality Row, Kingston, Norfolk Island (tel:22-003; fax: 22-624; email: clerk@assembly.gov.nf).

Internet sites

Australian Government (see territories of Australia): www.ag.gov.au

Northern Marianas

KEY FACTS

Official name: Commonwealth of the Northern Mariana Islands

Head of State: President of the United States of America Barack Obama (from 20 Jan 2009)

Head of government: Governor Benigno R Fitial (Covenant) (from 2006; re-elected 23 Nov 2009)

Ruling party: Republican Party (since 2007; re-elected 7 Nov 2009)

Area: 471 square km (14 islands) – Saipan (122 square km); Tinian (101 square km)

Population: 61,000 (2010)*

Capital: Garapan (Saipan)

Official language: English

Currency: US dollar (US$) = 100 cents

* estimated figure

COUNTRY PROFILE

Historical profile

Ancestors of the native Chamorros settled on the islands in about 2000 BC.
1521 Magellan claimed the islands for Spain.
1698 The native population was transferred to Guam.
1899 The Germans bought the islands from the Spaniards.
1914 The Japanese seized the islands from the Germans.
1947 Northern Marianas was the first Japanese territory in the Western Pacific to be invaded by the US; it became a part of the Trust Territory of the Pacific Islands (TTPI), administered by the US, under a mandate granted by the UN.
1975 In a referendum islanders voted to become an unincorporated territory of the United States under a covenant.
1977 A new local constitution was adopted.
1978 The Commonwealth of Northern Mariana Islands (CNMI) was created, as the TTPI was dissolved.
1980s Tourism and clothing manufacture became major industries, leading to foreign contract workers outnumbering local residents.
1984 Many US civil and political rights were made available to the islands' residents.
1986 Following the end of the UN mandate, the islands, under the *Covenant to Establish a Commonwealth of the Northern Mariana Islands (CNMI) in Political Union with the United States*, acquired US Commonwealth status and residents were granted US citizenship
1990 The UN Security Council formally terminated its Trusteeship. Under the covenant, the US has responsibility for foreign affairs and defence but CNMI is exempt from customs and labour laws.
2001 The Republican Party was re-elected and Juan Babauta (Rep) was elected governor.
2003 The Covenant Party won the parliamentary elections.
2004 Anatahan's active volcano had a small eruption. Northern Marianas and Guam were struck by super-typhoon Chaba.
2005 Numerous (over 500) small earthquakes were recorded on three uninhabited islands. Anatahan volcano continued erupting, with the largest eruption sending ash up to a height of 15,000 metres. In gubernatorial elections, Benigno Fitial won 28.1 per cent and unseated the incumbent, Juan Babouta.
2006 The CNMI revised its agreement with the US for increased environmental protection on the US missile testing range on Kwajalein Atoll. Two extra seats were added to the House of Representatives.
2007 In parliamentary elections the Covenant party lost much of its support as the Republicans won 12 seats (out of 20), the Covenant Party four, independents three and the Democrats one, in the House of Representatives. In the Senate, of the three seats in contention, independents won two and the Covenant Party one.
2008 The Northern Mariana Islands Delegate Act (immigration, security and labour act) was passed by the US Congress.
2009 The US announced the establishment of a protective marine zone around the Pacific islands it was responsible for, totalling 500,000 square km of sea and sea floor. Mining and commercial fishing, out to 50 nautical miles (54.26km) from shore, was banned. Lieutenant Governor Timothy Villagomez resigned, following his conviction on corruption charges including conspiracy, theft of US government funds, bribery and wire fraud; Eloy S Inos replaced him. Responsibility for immigration was taken out of the hands of CNMI officials and given to a US federal government agency, which now applies the same visa regulations as the mainland US. Tourism was the first industry to be hit by the changed rules, as the process of visiting became more difficult and time consuming. However, the handover does curb illegal activity of multinational criminal gangs from China and Japan, while controlling access to the vital US naval base. In the gubernatorial election neither of the leading candidates won sufficient votes for an outright win; the runoff was won by incumbent Governor Fitial. In parliamentary elections, the Republican Party won the single largest number of seats (nine out of 20) and won four seats out of nine in the Senate.
2010 From March–September, the island of Tinian lost its only ferry service (providing a link to Saipan) while its commercial owners removed the vessel for essential maintenance. The resident population

took part in the United States census on 1 April, which, after personal details, included questions on race, housing and internet and mobile phone access. The Northern Marianas College (NMC) was given notice by the US-based Western Association of Schools and Colleges to show 10 specific improvements in administration by 15 October or risk losing accreditation. Over 700 students at the only college in CNMI receive a total of US$2.6 million from the Pell Scholarship fund, which would be withdrawn without a college to attend. Gregorio Sablan (independent) won re-election as Delegate to the US Congress on 2 November.
2011 Acting Governor Inos declared a state of emergency on 22 July, due to 'an imminent threat of disruption of the delivery of critical healthcare services... due to a severe cash shortage'. The health care system is operating with a US$3 million debt and with a lack of vital medical laboratory supplies. There was a shortage of funds for re-supply, putting patients lives at risk.

Political structure

Constitution

The 1978 constitution was fully effective until 1986. It provides for an executive governor and a bicameral legislature. It also obligates the people of the Northern Mariana Islands to adopt a Commonwealth Constitution providing for a republican form of government which contains a bill of rights.
CNMI citizens have US citizenship and have a degree of autonomy and are exempt from some US federal laws concerning employment and immigration. CNMI defers to the US for foreign policy and defence and CNMI citizens do not vote in US presidential elections. There is one resident representative present in the US Congress and federal government.

Form of state

Democratic, self-governing commonwealth

The executive

An executive governor and lieutenant governor are elected every four years by universal suffrage.

National legislature

A bicameral legislature consisting of a 20-member House of Representatives and a nine-member Senate (with staggered terms); all elected in single-seat constituencies for two-year terms.

Legal system

The system is based on US jurisprudence but is exempt from US laws for customs, wages, immigration and taxation.

Last elections

7 November 2009 (parliamentary); 7/23 November 2009 (gubernatorial and runoff)

Results: Parliamentary: (House of Representatives) Republican Party won nine seats (out of 20), Covenant Party seven, independents four. Senate: (six seats up for election) Republican Party won four seats (out of nine), independents two (Covenant Party lost two seats).
Gubernatorial (first round): Benigno Fitial (Covenant Party) won 36.21 per cent of the vote, Heinz Hofschneider (Republican) 36.27 per cent, Juan 'Pan' Guerrero (independent) 19.34 per cent, Ramon Deleon Guerrero (independent) 7.96 per cent. Runoff: Fitial won 51.4 per cent, Hofschneider 48.6 per cent; turnout was 76 per cent.

Next elections

November 2013 (parliamentary and gubernatorial)

Political parties

Ruling party

Republican Party (since 2007; re-elected 7 Nov 2009)

Main opposition party

Covenant Party

Political situation

In 2007 the US Senate took a long hard look at the state of the CNMI Covenant Implementation Act, and its exemption from immigration and employment laws. The US federal government proposed a federalisation bill to bring the immigration system under its control. It was seen that CNMI authorities were unable to provide a fully comprehensive screening process for all visitors and migrant workers to the islands. US concerns regarding this did not only cover security – the CNMI was seen as a backdoor route to the US – but also problems of human trafficking, particularly of girls for the sex-trade and inappropriate migrant workers' visas. A federal minimum wage bill was also included in the federalisation bill.
Further study questioned why there were so many migrant workers, and concluded there was a historical legacy following the collapse of the garment manufacturing industry and the general downturn in tourism.
The CNMI federalisation bill came into force in November 2009.
In March 2011, the Republican controlled US-Congress voted to rescind the voting rites of representations of CNMI, effectively disenfranchising their electorate in policies that directly affect them.

Population

61,000 (2010)*
Last census: April 2000: 69,221
Population density: 143 inhabitants per square km.
Annual growth rate: 3.3 per cent (2003)

Ethnic make-up

There are tensions between the resident population and people from other countries – Philippines, Republic of Korea, Thailand and China. Approximately 75 per cent of the native population is Chamorro, the rest are Carolinian.

Religions

Roman Catholic and indigenous beliefs.

Education

Education is based on the US system. There are several private schools available to cater for the international community.
Literacy rate: 97 per cent, adult rate.
Compulsory years: Six to 16

Health

The major medical needs of the population are met by the Commonwealth Health Centre (CHC). The CHC operates inpatient and outpatient services. There is 24-hour emergency care available provided by a team of emergency nurses, emergency physicians and support staff. In addition to the CHC, there are several private health clinics. All medical services are required to meet US standards, although the cost of medical care is much cheaper than in the US.

Main cities

Garapan/Susupe (Saipan) (capital, population 4,105 in 2005), Kagman (8,012), San Antonio (6,001).

Main islands

Six islands, including the three largest (Saipan, Tinian and Rota) are inhabited.

Languages spoken

Chamorro and Carolinian are the native tongues and are widely spoken. Japanese and Korean are also spoken.

Official language/s

English

Media

Press

The daily newspaper *Saipan Tribune* (www.saipantribune.com) has the largest circulation, while *Marianas Variety* (www.mvariety.com) has news covering from other Micronesian islands.

Broadcasting

Radio: There are several radio stations including the public KRNM (www.krnm.org), commercial KRSI (www.pacificnewscenter.com), KPXP (www.radiopacific.com/p99) and KWAW (www.magic100radio.com). Religious stations include KFBS (www.febc.org) and KYOI.
Television: The TV station WSZE 10 transmits via cable and satellite.

News agencies

ABC Pacific Beat: www.radioaustralia.net.au/pacbeat

Pacific Magazine:
www.pacificmagazine.net

Economy

The economy of the islands is small and has few natural resources. Bilateral aid from the US remains an important source of income, particularly aid directed towards improving the inadequate infrastructure. In 2006 an unfunded government liability of US$500 million in the Defined Pension Plan was identified and prompted new legislation in 2007, for the introduction of a new pension system designed to be self-sustaining through employee's contributions. However, by September 2009 the government had suspended pension payments as the national pension fund was in imminent danger of bankruptcy. A US court had ruled in June that full restitution of lost investment payments should be paid by the CNMI government to the CNMI employees' pension fund.

An election to choose the CNMI Delegate to the US Congress took place on 2 November 2010, despite a cash-strapped administration being short of the US$128,000 necessary to hold it. From 1 October government departments were partially closed down as the wrangle in both houses of parliament failed to break the deadlock over the CNMI budget. Several years of overspending has left the country with a deficit of US$170 million, in violation of the constitution. But neither political parties could agree which public services should be cut to bring down spending, so Governor Fitial signed an executive order which temporarily laid off over 1,400 workers. Ten days later the budget was finally passed and the emergency measure saved US$750,000 in government salaries – enough to pay for the elections – while austerity measures began to be felt by all the citizens of the islands.

Tourism is the mainstay of the economy. In 2009 the former chief justice said that restrictive land laws as enshrined in the constitution made foreign investors reluctant to do business in CNMI as leased land could only be held by non-CNMI people for up to 40 years and 55 years for public and private land respectively. The constitution regarding land ownership may be reconsidered in 2011.

The textile sector, which has been in decline since the US halted its Multi-Fibre Agreement (MFA), lost US$518.4 million in export revenue between 2004–07; nevertheless garment manufacturing is still the largest export, with the bulk of production going to the US.

A Seattle-based fishing company secured a 30-year contract to begin long-line fishing for swordfish, tuna and other species in CNMI waters in 2008.

Despite millions of US dollars being available through development and capital improvement funds, by 2009 much of the money had gone unspent due to the lack of an auditing entity in place to allow funds to be transferred from the US and for it to be fully documented and accounted for.

External trade

As a self-governing territory of the US, CNMI has an open market with the US. Tourism is the main provider of foreign exchange, with Japanese visitors accounting for 51.4 per cent of total numbers in 2007. The textile sector, which is in decline due to the US halting its Multi-Fibre Agreement (MFA), lost US$518.4 million in export revenue between 2004–07; nevertheless garment manufacturing still provides the highest export revenue, with the bulk of production going to the US.

Imports

Principal imports are food, construction equipment and materials, petroleum products and consumer goods.

Main sources: US, Japan

Exports

The principal export is garments; minor exports include livestock, tuna fish, fruit and vegetables.

Main destinations: Mainly to US

Agriculture

Farming

The agricultural sector contributes approximately 14 per cent to annual GDP. Cultivable land is rich and volcanic.

Vegetables such as coconuts, breadfruit, tomatoes, melons and cucumbers are widely grown on smallholdings. Livestock is reared for export. The copra industry is also important.

Fishing

The fishing sector has revived following a blanket ban in some areas, introduced in 2000, due to over-fishing. Stocks include black-tip sharks, tuna, emperor ship and bonito. Tuna is transshipped en route to the US via the canneries at Pago Pago (Fagatogo) in American Samoa.

Industry and manufacturing

The industrial sector contributed approximately 19 per cent to annual GDP while the garment industry flourished under the Multi-Fibre Agreement (MFA). However, when this ended in 2004 exports to the US were threatened by even cheaper exports from China and a number of factories closed, putting some 2,000 workers out of their jobs.

Other industrial activity consists of construction, small-scale fish processing and handicrafts manufacture.

Tourism

Tourism is an important sector of the economy, though not as dominant as it was during the 1990s. Japan continues to provide the vast majority of visitors, followed by Korea and, to a lesser extent, the US.

In 2008 as the cost of oil rose worldwide, many Pacific island tourism industries suffered a fall in tourist arrivals as Japan-based airlines charged passengers up to an additional US$150 per trip to their destinations on top of the regular airfare.

Hydrocarbons

There are no known hydrocarbon reserves and all petroleum needs are met by imports.

Energy

With the rise in global oil prices, which has impacted on the price of energy production, there has been an expansion in the use of renewable energy, such as solar-photovoltaic panels for water heaters and lighting and wind turbines.

Banking and insurance

Central bank

US Federal Reserve (Washington DC)

Time

GMT plus 10 hours

Geography

The Northern Marianas Islands comprises 16 islands across 640km of the western Pacific Ocean, about 5,300km (3,300 miles) west of Hawaii. The islands are part of the chain of Mariana Islands. The ones in the south are formed of limestone terraces, and those in the north are volcanic, several of which are still active. The largest volcano, Agrihan, is also the tallest peak in the islands at 965 metres. Saipan is a fertile island with lagoons and rolling hills. Rota has dense rain forests and is largely undeveloped.

Climate

The climate is tropical marine.

Entry requirements

Passports

Passports required by all except US citizens with proof of citizenship; (all US nationals require a passport for re-entry to the US from January 2007).

Visa

Required by all. There are a few exceptions for visits up to 30 days. See www.cnmiago.gov.mp or www.mymarianas.com for a full list and details or contact the Division of Immigration for further information. All applications must be made at least four weeks before intended departure.

Prohibited entry
See www.mymarianas.com for a full list and details, contact the Division of Immigration for further information.
Currency advice/regulations
The US dollar is the official currency. There are no restrictions on import and export of local and foreign currency, however all amounts over US$10,000 (or foreign equivalent) must be declared.
Prohibited imports
Fruits, vegetables, plants and soils, meat and meat products, live animals and animal products.
Firearms and ammunition require a permit, obtained in advance. For more information see: www.cnmiago.gov.mp.

Health (for visitors)
Mandatory precautions
Vaccination certificate required for yellow fever if travelling from an infected area.
Advisable precautions
Vaccination for diphtheria, TB, hepatitis A and B, polio, tetanus, typhoid. Rabies risk. Water from the mains is usually chlorinated and although safe to drink, may cause mild abdominal upsets. Drinking water outside the main cities and towns may be contaminated. Sterilisation by boiling is thus advisable.
Full medical facilities are available, although they are not free of charge. Health insurance is advisable.

Hotels
There is a 10 per cent hotel tax. A tip of 10–15 per cent is usual.

Credit cards
Major credit cards are accepted on Saipan and at car rental agencies on Rota.

Working hours
Banking
Mon–Thu: 0900–1500, Fri: 1000–1800.
Business
Mon–Fri: 0800–1200, 1300–1700.
Government
Mon–Fri: 0730–1130, 1230–1630.
Shops
Mon–Sat: 0800–2000, Sun: 0800–1800.

Telecommunications
Mobile/cell phones
A 1900 GSM service is available.

Electricity supply
220/240V, 50Hz

Weights and measures
Imperial

Getting there
Air
International airport/s: Saipan International (SPN), 13km south-east of Garapan, with duty-free shops, bar, restaurant, currency exchange, shops and car hire. Taxis are available to the centre of town.
Airport tax: None
Surface
Main port/s: Saipan, Tinian, Rota.

Getting about
National transport
Air: There are several daily flights between Saipan and Tinian and between Rota and Saipan.
Road: Roads are good on the main islands, particularly around the main centres. Driving is on the right-hand side.
Buses: There is no public bus system on Saipan, although shuttle buses run between the major towns.
Water: There are sea links between the islands.
City transport
Taxis: A taxi service is available on Saipan. Taxis are metered and privately owned.
Buses, trams & metro: Tour bus from airport to city centre, journey time is about 15 minutes.

BUSINESS DIRECTORY

The addresses listed below are a selection only. While World of Information makes every endeavour to check these addresses, we cannot guarantee that changes have not been made, especially to telephone numbers and area codes. We would welcome any corrections.

Telephone area codes
The international direct dialling (IDD) code for Northern Marianas is +1 670, followed by the subscriber's number.

Useful telephone numbers
Police, fire, ambulance: 911

Chambers of Commerce
Saipan Chamber of Commerce, PO Box 500806, Saipan MP 96950 (tel: 233-7150; fax: 233-7151; e-mail: saipanchamber@saipan.com).

Banking
Central bank
Bank of Saipan, PO Box 500690, Saipan MP 96950 (tel: 235-6260; fax: 235-1802; email: bankofsaipan@saipan.com).

Federal Reserve System, 20th Street and Constitution Avenue, NW, Washington DC 20551 (tel: (202) 452-3000; fax: (202) 452-3819).

Travel information
Continental Micronesia, PO Box 138CK, Saipan (tel: 234-8223; fax: 234-8358).

Pacific Island Travel, Herengracht 495, 1017 BT Amsterdam, The Netherlands (tel: (+31-20) 626-1325; fax (+31-20) 623-0008; internet: www.pacificislandtravel.com).

Saipan International Airport, PO Box 1055, Saipan (tel: 664-3500/01; fax: 234-5962; e-mail: cpa.admin@saipan.com).

Travel Bureau, PO Box 503 Rota (tel: 532-3561; fax: 532-3562).

National tourist organisation offices
Marianas Visitors Authority, P O Box 500861, Saipan, (tel: 664-3200/3201; fax: 664-3237; internet: www.mymarianas.com).

Other useful addresses
All Northern Marianas postal addresses have the US zip code: MP 96950, USA

Commonwealth of the Northern Mariana Islands, Caller Box 10,007, Saipan, (tel: 664-2200; internet: www.gov.mp).

Division of Immigration, Office of the Attorney General, Afetna Square Bld, San Antonio Village, PO Box 10007, Saipan (tel: 236-0922, 236-0923; fax: 664-3190; internet: www.cnmiago.gov.mp).

Internet sites
Commonwealth of the Northern Marianas General Information: www.gov.mp

Marianas Variety, newspaper: www.mvariety.com

Saipan Tribune: www.saipantribune.com

US Office of Insular affairs: www.doi.gov/oia

Norway

KEY FACTS

Official name: Kongeriket Norge (Kingdom of Norway)

Head of State: King Harald V (since 17 Jan 1991)

Head of government: Prime Minister Jens Stoltenberg (DNA) (elected 2005; re-elected 14 Sep 2009)

Ruling party: Coalition led by Det Norske Arbeiderparti (DNA) (Norwegian Labour Party) with Sosialistisk Venstreparti (SV) (Socialist Left Party) and Senterpartiet (SP) (Centre Party) (elected 2005; re-elected 14 Sep 2009)

Area: 323,985 square km

Population: 4.89 million (2010)*

Capital: Oslo

Official language: Norwegian

Currency: Norwegian krone (Nkr) = 100 ore

Exchange rate: Nkr5.87 per US$ (Oct 2011)

GDP per capita: US$84,444 (2010)

GDP real growth: 0.40% (2010)

GDP: US$414.50 billion (2010)

Labour force: 2.59 million (2010)

Unemployment: 3.50% (2010)

Inflation: 2.40% (2010)

Oil production: 2.14 million bpd (2010)

Balance of trade: US$58.39 billion (2010)

Annual FDI: US$11.75 billion (2010)

* estimated figure

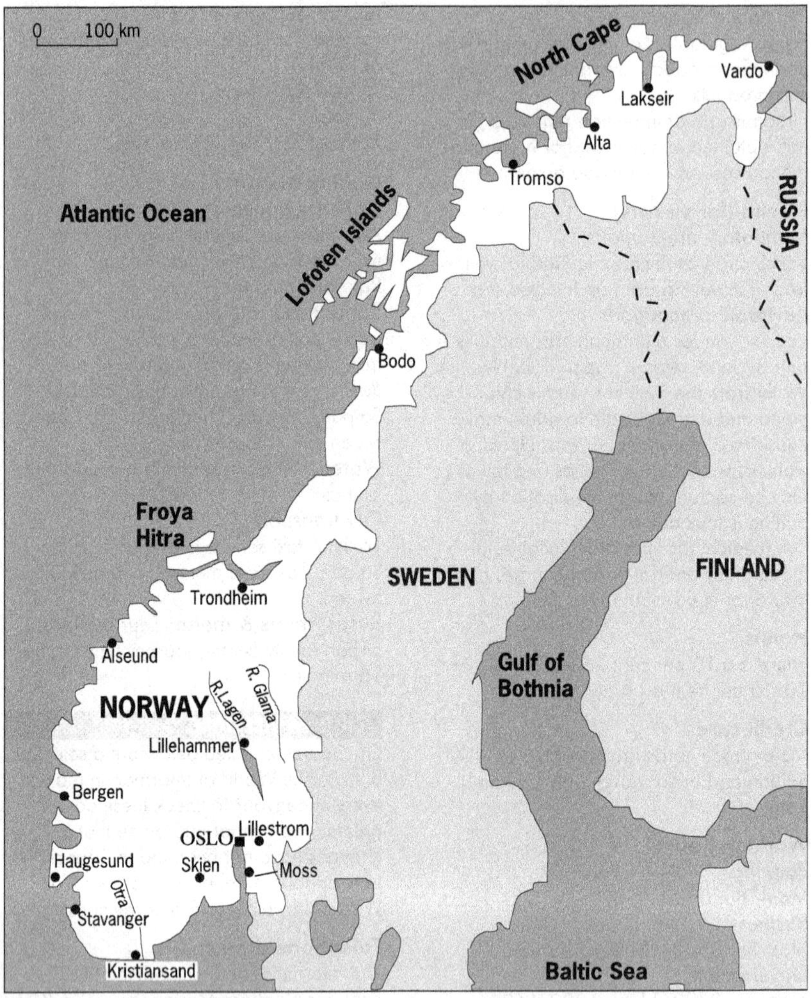

The archetypal stable European state, Norway is a constitutional monarchy complete with a parliamentary system of government. The King of Norway's power is almost exclusively ceremonial, with the majority of power in the hands of the office of the prime minister.

Norway's normal peace and tranquility was rudely shattered when, in July 2011 the worst criminal massacre in Norway's post-war history took place on the small island of Utoeya near Oslo, in which 85 young people attending a youth Labour Party meeting were gunned down, not long after the gunman had killed a further seven in a car bomb explosion in the capital. Initial suspicions of a terrorist attack were swept away by the realisation that Mr Breivik was a sad psychopath.

Elections

Still in a state of shock from the Breivik attacks, in September 2011 Norwegians went to the polls in local government elections. Although these do not necessarily determine shifts in national policy, they give politicians and analysts a reasonable indication of any major political mood swings. The conservative Høyre (H) (Right) was the biggest winner, while Det

Norske Arbeiderparti (DNA) (Norwegian Labour Party) managed to hang on as the biggest single party. The smaller parties on both the far right and far left suffered the biggest losses, with voters deserting both the Fremskrittspartiet (FrP) (Progress Party) and the Sosialistisk Venstreparti (SV) (Socialist Left Party). The election results provided another signal that Norwegian politics was moving towards a system dominated by the two big parties, each influenced by centrist forces. Leaders of both the Høyre and DNA parties said they would seek co-operation with the small parties at the centre, not least the Venstre (Liberal Party), which ended up with a bigger share of the vote than the FrP in a number of cities, including Oslo. Analysts saw the election results confirming a need for voters to take comfort within the larger, more moderate parties, not least after the July massacre.

With virtually all of the results in, the Høyre were able to claim a gain of some 8.8 percentage points from the last local elections in 2007, with 28 per cent of the vote. It appeared that Norway's relatively right-wing FrP lost many of its voters to the Høyre, with the FrP logging the biggest single loss of six full points, to claim only 11.5 per cent of the vote on a national basis. In Oslo, its numbers were even worse, at only 7.2 per cent of the vote while the Høyre soared nearly 11 points to claim 36.1 per cent of the vote and retain the mayor's seat.

The DNA, which had consistently led in the opinion polls leading up to the election, remained Norway's biggest party with 31.7 per cent of the vote on a national basis, up two points from the local elections four years ago. It failed, however, to score the victory it wanted in the capital and lost in a few key cities like Tromsø and Drammen. While DNA leader and Prime Minister Jens Stoltenberg called the results 'impressive' because parties in national government often lose at the local level, analysts claimed the DNA didn't do as well as expected. The biggest government loser was the socialist left (SV), which fell two points to land at only 4 per cent of the vote on a nationwide basis. It was the worst election for SV in years, leaving it the smallest of the major parties.

The economy motors on.

According to the International Monetary Fund (IMF), since 2008 Norway's gross domestic product (GDP) has grown steadily at an annual pace of 2–3 per cent, supported by robust growth in consumer spending and favourable terms of trade. By the end of 2010 output had surpassed pre-recession levels and unemployment remained low. This solid recovery has been aided by supportive policies, including low interest rates and a temporary fiscal stimulus employed during the recession.

Growth in GDP is expected to be around 2.5 per cent both in 2011 and 2012. Expansion will be driven mainly by domestic demand, given strong wage growth, continued momentum in the housing market and sluggish growth amongst major trading partners. The closing of the output gap, along with strong wage pressures, should result in a gradual rise in inflation from its current low rates toward a 2.5 per cent target. Over the medium term, growth is expected to rebalance away from domestic demand as macro-economic policies tighten, the housing market gradually cools and external demand slowly improves. Under this central scenario, mainland growth over the medium term is projected to be close to its trend rate of 2.75 per cent.

In the view of the IMF, however, there are significant risks pertaining to this scenario, including the euro-zone economic turmoil. Norway's economy is better placed than many in Europe to weather an intensification of euro-zone stress, given its low sovereign risk and the limited direct exposure of Norway's banks to the most vulnerable euro-zone countries. Nonetheless, severe stress would undoubtedly affect Norway via shaken consumer confidence, lower exports to Europe, lower oil prices and strains in international interbank markets, which are a key funding source for Norway's largest banks. Next comes the risk of elevated house prices and high household debt. Norwegian house prices have soared over the last decade and continue to climb at a rapid pace. Although this may partly reflect supply constraints and solid population growth, standard metrics suggest a risk of overvaluation: Norway has the highest house price-to-rent ratio relative to its historical average amongst all Organisation for Economic Co-operation and Development (OECD) economies and the house price-to-income ratio exceeds levels reached prior to the late 1980s house price crash. Any fall in house prices could pose a major risk, as it would dampen consumption and reduce residential investment. Moreover, Norway has one of the highest ratios of household debt to disposable income amongst OECD economies. Very high household debt levels imply that a house price drop could also push up default rates and stress banks' balance sheets.

The broadly neutral fiscal stance for 2012 envisaged in the budget is, in the view of the IMF, appropriate, given heightened global risks. Norway has been well served by its fiscal guidelines, which call for a gradual phasing in of petroleum revenues. Within these guidelines and given the closing output gap, fiscal

KEY INDICATORS — Norway

	Unit	2006	2007	2008	2009	2010
Population	m	4.64	4.67	4.80	4.84	*4.89
Gross domestic product (GDP)	US$bn	337.43	391.50	450.90	383.00	414.50
GDP per capita	US$	72,768	82,077	94,196	79,085	84,144
GDP real growth	%	2.5	2.7	0.7	-1.7	0.3
Inflation	%	2.3	0.8	3.8	2.2	2.4
Unemployment	%	3.4	2.5	2.6	3.2	3.5
Oil output	'000 bpd	2,778.0	2,556.0	2,455.0	2,342.0	2,137.0
Natural gas output	bn cum	87.6	89.7	99.2	103.5	106.4
Exports (fob) (goods)	US$m	122,789.0	140,273.0	168,816.0	121,986.0	132,691.0
Imports (fob) (goods)	US$m	62,933.0	77,237.0	85,985.0	66,674.0	74,300.0
Balance of trade	US$m	59,856.0	63,036.0	82,831.0	55,312.0	58,391.0
Current account	US$m	58,278.0	63,657.0	83,825.0	53,531.0	51,444.0
Total reserves minus gold	US$m	56,841.6	60,839.6	50,949.8	48,859.3	52,797.9
Foreign exchange	US$m	56,181.4	60,294.1	50,214.1	45,718.6	49,740.2
Exchange rate	per US$	6.18	5.53	5.64	6.28	6.04

* estimated figure

adjustment will be needed over the medium term to rebuild fiscal buffers. The contractionary effects of fiscal tightening can be offset by keeping monetary policy looser than it would be otherwise, thereby ensuring that inflation rises to the target by the end of the policy horizon and that the output gap stays closed. Such a mix of relatively tight fiscal and loose monetary policy would also contain any risks of excessive exchange rate appreciation and associated competitiveness problems.

Norway faces large long-run fiscal challenges. Oil revenue, as well as non-oil revenue that is indirectly dependent on oil production, is projected to decline over time as a per cent of GDP. At the same time, spending on healthcare and age and disability pensions will steadily increase – even after the cost-saving effects of recent pension reforms – due to population aging and an increase in demand for healthcare services as a percentage of income. In addition, the large drop in real long-term interest rates in major economies over the last decade suggests that the real return on the Petroleum Fund of Norway (more commonly referred to as the Oil Fund) may well fall short of the assumed 4 per cent for an extended period. To help smooth out the required adjustment, the IMF recommends that consideration should be given to spending less than 4 per cent of the Oil Fqwund's capital. Options for further reform include requiring employers to contribute to longer-term sick leave benefits (currently they contribute only for the first 16 days), increasing the use of social security physicians in assessing eligibility for disability benefits, reforming public sector pensions in line with recent reforms of the National Insurance Scheme and changing the annual increase in pensions from wage growth minus 0.75 per cent to the more internationally common practice of CPI inflation..

Tax reforms could also bolster financial stability, economic efficiency and equity. The very large subsidies for owner-occupied housing in Norway's tax code encourage households to accumulate excessive mortgage debt while disproportionately benefiting high-income households. Reducing these subsidies would strengthen financial stability while increasing progressively and economic efficiency. Tax reforms could also promote financial stability by reducing incentives for excessive leverage in both the financial and non-financial corporate sectors.

Energy

Norway, the largest holder of natural gas and oil reserves in Europe, provides much of the oil and gas consumed on the continent. In 2010, Norway was the second largest exporter of natural gas in the world, second only to Russia. In 2010, crude oil, natural gas and pipeline transport services accounted for almost 50 per cent of Norway's exports by value, 21 per cent of GDP and 25 per cent of government revenues, according to the Norwegian Petroleum Directorate. Although Norway's oil production peaked in 2001 at 3.42 million barrels per day (bpd) and declined to 2.13 million bpd in 2010, according to the US Energy Information Administration (EIA), natural gas production has been steadily increasing since 1993, reaching 3.76 trillion cubic feet (tcf) in 2010.

The agreement between Norway and Russia, which defined their maritime boundaries in the Barents and Arctic Seas and resolved their 40-year old dispute, was finally ratified by both governments in early 2011 and went into effect in July 2011. The agreement requires the two countries to develop jointly cross-border oil and gas deposits. This refers to a 176,000 square kilometre maritime area which straddles the Barents and Arctic Seas.

According to The *Oil and Gas Journal* (OGJ), Norway had 5.67 billion barrels of proven oil reserves in January 2011, the largest oil reserves in western Europe. All of Norway's oil reserves are located offshore on the Norwegian Continental Shelf (NCS), which is divided into three sections: the North Sea, the Norwegian Sea and the Barents Sea. The bulk of Norway's oil production occurs in the North Sea, with smaller amounts in the Norwegian Sea and new exploration and production activity occurring in the Barents Sea. Statoil ASA was created by the merger of Statoil and Norsk Hydro in October 2007. It is 67 per cent-owned by the Norwegian government and is the largest operator in Norway, controlling 80 per cent of Norway's oil and gas production. It also has interests in more than 30 other countries. State-owned Petoro manages the commercial aspects of the government's financial interests in petroleum operations and associated activities. It acts as the licensee for production licences and companies.

Norway's state subsidy of oil and gas exploration, introduced in 2005, refunds 78 per cent of the exploration costs to the companies. In addition, taxes from oil activities have been reduced, which has attracted additional international investment in Norway's oil and gas sectors. In 2010, Norway produced 2.13 million bpd of oil liquids, of which about 88 per cent was crude oil. Norway's petroleum production has been gradually declining since 2001 as oil fields have matured. However, Norway's National Petroleum Directorate (NPD) expects that production will rise marginally in 2011 over 2010 and remain fairly steady over the next few years. But in the longer term the number and size of new discoveries will be a critical factor in maintaining production levels. The Norwegian government is focusing on increasing recovery in producing fields, further exploring areas that are already open for the petroleum industry and opening new areas to exploration. In 2010, 45 exploration wells were drilled, 16 discoveries were made and 4 new fields came on-stream. Norway's national statistics bureau reported that it estimates record total investments in oil and gas activity of US$21 billion in 2011.

According to the International Energy Agency (IEA), Norway exported an estimated 1.6 million bpd of crude oil in 2010. The 5 top importers of Norwegian oil in 2010 were the United Kingdom (43 per cent), the Netherlands (18 per cent), France (7 per cent), Germany (5 per cent) and the United States (5 per cent).

Natural gas

According to the OGJ, Norway had 72 trillion cubic feet (tcf) of proven natural gas reserves as of January 2011. Despite the maturation of its major natural gas fields in the North Sea, Norway has been able to sustain annual increases in total natural gas production by continuing to develop new fields.

Norway produced 3.76tcf in 2010, up from 3.65tcf in 2009 and has been increasing its natural gas production every year since 1994. Norway's NPD forecasts production of 3.85tcf in 2011, reaching 3.96tcf in 2015. Norway exported about 3.6tcf of natural gas in 2010, 94 per cent of its production. Most of it was transported to Europe via its extensive export pipeline infrastructure and a smaller amount via liquefied natural gas (LNG) tanker. The country is the second-largest supplier of natural gas to the European Union, behind Russia, supplying about 18 per cent of Europe's total gas demand in 2010. The largest outlets for Norway's natural gas pipeline exports in 2010 were Germany, the United Kingdom and France. In 2010, shipments of Norwegian LNG totaled 138bcf, up from 112bcf in 2009. OECD European countries received about 74 per cent of the total, with Spain importing almost half of that. The United

States imported about 5 per cent or 26.8bcf. Norway has long-term contracts with Spain's Iberderola and the US company El Paso.

Risk assessment

Economy	Good
Politics	Good
Regional stability	Good

COUNTRY PROFILE

Historical profile

1397 Under the Kalmar Union, the Kingdom of Norway ceased to exist as a separate nation and was ruled by Danish governors.
1720 Norway, a dominion of Denmark, was lost to Sweden following the Great Nordic War.
1814 An *Act of Union* with Sweden recognised Norway as an independent Kingdom with its own constitution and parliament.
1905 The Norwegian parliament dissolved the *Act of Union* with Sweden. A plebiscite voted for full independence and a return to a monarchy. Denmark's Prince Frederick VIII became Norway's King Haakon VII.
1911 Norwegian Roald Amundsen was the first person to reach the South Pole, 35 days before Englishman Robert Scott.
1914–18 Norway adopted a policy of neutrality in the First World War.
1920 An international agreement on the Svalbard Arctic archipelago gave full sovereignty to Norway.
1940 Despite its neutrality, Norway was invaded and occupied by the Germans in the Second World War. There was active resistance to the Nazi puppet government of Vidkun Quisling.
1945 Norway abandoned its policy of neutrality and lent troops to take part in the Allied war effort.
1949 Norway became a member of NATO.
1935–65 With the exception of the years of German occupation Det Norske Arbeiderparti (DNA) (Norwegian Labour Party) held continuous office.
1952 Norway joined the Nordic Council, set up to promote co-operation between Nordic parliaments.
1959 Norway was a founding member of the European Free Trade Association (Efta).
1957 King Olav V came to the throne.
1965 Centre-right coalition unseated the DNA government.
1960–80s From the late 1960s to early 1980s oil and gas were discovered in the Norwegian sector of the North Sea and within a decade their exploitation accounted for one-third of Norway's GDP.
1972 Norwegians rejected a proposal for membership of the European Community (EC).
1973–1981 Minority DNA government held power.
1981–86 The first majority conservative government since 1928 came to power. Following labour disputes, the government was defeated on its austerity programme.
1986 Minority DNA government was elected with Harlem Brundtland as Norway's first female prime minister.
1989 The election was won by a coalition of conservative, Christian democrat and centre parties.
1991 King Olav V died; he was succeeded by his son Harald V.
1992 Norway withdrew from the International Whaling Treaty, provoking international controversy.
1994 In a referendum, membership of the European Union (EU) was rejected by 52.2 per cent of voters (turnout was 88.6 per cent).
1993 Norway brokered secret negotiations for a peace deal between Israel and the Palestinian Liberation Organisation that led to the *Oslo Accords*.
1997 Kjell Magne Bondevik led a minority centrist coalition government.
2000 The government fell after Bondevik was defeated in a vote of no-confidence over controversial plans to build new gas-fired power plants. Jens Stoltenberg led a DNA government.
2001 Norway and Australia became embroiled in a diplomatic row following the attempt by a Norwegian-registered cargo ship to land Afghan refugees it had rescued at sea ashore in Australia. Parliamentary elections were inconclusive and Bondevik returned as prime minister, leading a centre-right coalition.
2003 Norway took the lead in trying to broker a peace deal in Sri Lanka.
2004 The government intervened to end a strike by oil workers seeking better pension rights and job security.
2005 In Parliamentary elections a coalition of socialist parties led by DNA won 87 out of 169 parliament seats. Stoltenberg became prime minister for the second time. Norway became embroiled in two diplomatic rows, one with Russia, the other with Spain, over fishing rights off the Norwegian island of Svalbard.
2006 A law came into effect making it mandatory for all private companies to allocate 40 per cent of all board of director positions to women. The Statoil and Norsk Hydro companies announced the merger of their offshore operations.
2007 A referendum was passed which amended the constitution, abolishing the bicameral division of Storting (parliament) after the next elections.
2008 State income from the petroleum sector was a record high of net Nk356 billion (US$61.19 billion), representing around 32 per cent of total government income and equating to some Nk80,000 (US$13,750) for each citizen),
2009 Norway's trade balance was at its lowest since 2005, at US$3.4 billion (Nk22.2 billion), due mainly to a decrease in exports, notably the lower value of crude oil. Voting in municipal elections in 2011 can now take place from resident's homes, following plans announced by the ministry of local government to test an online voting system. In parliamentary elections the ruling DNA-led coalition won 86 seats (out of 169); Prime Minister Jens Stoltenberg remained in office. The bicameral division of the Storting was abolished following the general elections, as agreed in the constitutional changes of 2007.
2010 In April, an agreement on the Arctic border between Norway and Russia in the Barents Sea, which cuts across an oil and natural gas rich region, was finally resolved after several decades of discussions. It was considered 'good and balanced' by Russian President Medvedev. The maritime agreement was formally signed on 15 September.
2011 Anders Behring Breivik confessed to the mass-murder of at least 76 people in two atrocities carried out on 22 July. Breivik gunned down around 70 people on Utoeya Island in Lake Tyrifjorden (40km west of Oslo), where a youth summer-camp for members of the ruling DNA was underway, having earlier exploded a car-bomb in the government district of Oslo. Breivik was identified with extreme, nationalist ideologies following a 1,500 page manifesto posted on the internet just hours before the outrages. On 1 August, Norway withdrew from the air attacks on Libya by a NATO-led coalition. The Norwegian air force took part in 583 missions, out of a total 6,498 missions flown by NATO since a no-fly-zone was imposed over Libya in March. On 29 November, two psychiatrists declared that Anders Behring Breivik was suffering from paranoid schizophrenia and in a psychotic state when he killed 77 people and injured 151. He is unlikely to stand trial and will be admitted to a secure psychiatric hospital instead.

Political structure

Constitution

Norway has the oldest constitution in Europe and the second oldest worldwide (after the US) still in operation. The constitution dates from 17 May 1814 and is grouped into five areas of interest, the form of government, executive power, rights of the citizen and legislative power, judicial power and general provisions. Any amendment to the constitution requires majority support in both the Storting and approval in a referendum.

Form of state

Parliamentary democratic monarchy

The executive

Executive power (nominally held by the monarch) is exercised by the Statsråd (Council of State), which is led by the prime minister, who is responsible to the Storting (parliament).

The Council of State is appointed by the monarch, with the approval of parliament. Following parliamentary elections, the leader of the majority party or the leader of the majority coalition is usually appointed as prime minister by the monarch, with the approval of the parliament.

National legislature

A referendum held in 2007 approved changes to the constitution whereby the previous bicameral parliament became unicameral.

Legislative power is vested in a unicameral Storting (parliament) comprising 169 members elected by proportional representation in 19 multi-seat constituencies for four-year terms. There is no constitutional mechanism for dissolving the Storting between elections.

Legal system

The legal system is a mixture of customary law, civil law, and common law traditions. The Hoyesterett (Supreme Court) renders advisory opinions to the legislature, when asked. Justices are appointed by the monarch. Norway accepts compulsory International Court of Justice (ICJ) jurisdiction, although with reservations.

Last elections

14 September 2009 (parliamentary)

Results: Det Norske Arbeiderparti (DNA) (Norwegian Labour Party), won 35.4 per cent of the vote (64 of 169 seats), Fremskrittspartiet (FrP) (Progress Party) 22.9 per cent (41), Høyre (Right) 17.2 per cent (30), Sosialistisk Venstreparti (SV) (Socialist Left Party) 6.2 per cent (11), Senterpartiet (SP) (Centre Party) 6.2 per cent (11), Kristelig Folkeparti (KrF) (Christian Democrats) 5.5 per cent (10), Venstre (V) (Liberal Party) 3.9 per cent (2). Turnout was 75.7 per cent.

Next elections

September 2013 (parliamentary)

Political parties

Ruling party

Coalition led by Det Norske Arbeiderparti (DNA) (Norwegian Labour Party) with Sosialistisk Venstreparti (SV) (Socialist Left Party) and Senterpartiet (SP) (Centre Party) (elected 2005; re-elected 14 Sep 2009)

Main opposition party

Fremskrittspartiet (FrP) (Progress Party)

Population

4.89 million (2010)*

Last census: November 2001: 4,520,947

Population density: 15 inhabitants per square km. Urban population: 75 per cent (1995—2001).

Annual growth rate: 0.6 per cent 1994–2004 (WHO 2006)

Ethnic make-up

Predominantly Norwegian. In addition, there are about 60,000 Sami (Lapps), mainly in the north of the country, although there are substantial Sami communities in larger cities.

Religions

More than 90 per cent of all Norwegians belong to the Church of Norway, an Evangelical Lutheran denomination. There are also small Roman Catholic, Jewish and Muslim communities.

Education

All public education in Norway is free. Primary education lasts for seven years; lower secondary education and upper secondary education, which is not compulsory, last for three years, from 13 to 16 and 16 to 19 respectively. On completion of a three-year course at an upper secondary school, students can apply to university. Alternatively, students may, at aged 16, undertake either technical training at vocational schools or practical training at apprenticeship schools; for three years.

Primary and lower secondary education is founded on the principle of every individual having a statutory right to primary, lower secondary and upper secondary education in a unified school system that provides equal education for all on the basis of a single national curriculum.

The right to upper secondary education has been in force since 2000, while the right to primary and lower secondary education was implemented from 2002.

Higher education in Norway is mainly offered at state institutions, notably four universities, six university colleges, 26 state colleges and two art colleges. A degree candidate may combine studies from universities and colleges, as the courses offered are at the same academic level. The 26 colleges primarily offer shorter courses of a more vocational nature than those offered by the universities.

Compulsory years: Six to 16

Enrolment rate: 100 per cent gross primary enrolment of the relevant age group (including repeaters); 119 gross secondary enrolment (World Bank).

Pupils per teacher: Seven in primary schools

Health

A national health insurance scheme covers medical treatment in hospitals and the reimbursement of costs for medical attention and medicines for certain chronic diseases. Sickness benefit is paid for short-term illness, while chronic or long-term illness is covered by a disability allowance. A small sum is charged for medicine and primary care. The majority of hospitals are state-run.

HIV/Aids

HIV prevalence: 0.1 per cent aged 15–49 in 2003 (World Bank)

Life expectancy: 80 years, 2004 (WHO 2006)

Fertility rate/Maternal mortality rate: 1.8 births per woman, 2004 (WHO 2006); maternal mortality 6 per 100,000 live births (World Bank).

Birth rate/Death rate: 13 births and 10 deaths per 1,000 population (World Bank).

Child (under 5 years) mortality rate (per 1,000): 3.4 per 1,000 live births (World Bank)

Head of population per physician: 3.13 physicians per 1,000 people, 2003 (WHO 2006)

Welfare

The extensive welfare system has greatly reduced the gap between rich and poor. Social security legislation stipulates that everyone has the right to employment, housing, education, welfare and healthcare. The main general social insurance schemes are the National Insurance Scheme (NIS) and the Family Allowance Scheme. The NIS is a compulsory insurance and pension system and covers pensions, unemployment pay and healthcare for all Norwegians.

A basic retirement pension, adjusted annually, is guaranteed for all Norwegians of 67 years and older regardless of assets or previous income.

Non-pensioners whose income falls below a certain minimum qualify for supplementary benefits. These may include loans or other financial assistance from the local municipality. All families with children under 16 receive a family allowance according to the number of children.

The government subsidises low-cost housing through loans with low rates of interest and easy repayment terms. Families living in housing financed by a state bank can receive an allowance for housing costs should they have difficulties meeting their living expenses.

Main cities

Oslo (capital, estimated population 526,090 in 2005), Bergen (239,329), Stavanger (112,983), Trondheim (155,248), Bærum (104,220), Fredrikstad (70,053), Kristiansand (76,167), Tromsø (62,200).

Languages spoken
Norwegian has two main dialects: Bokmål and Nynorsk. Finnish and Sámi are also spoken. English is widely understood and spoken, especially in urban areas.
Official language/s
Norwegian

Media
Press
Freedom of the press is guaranteed by the constitution. The majority of the press is privately-owned and explicitly partisan. Since the early 1990s only three media owners have accounted for 55–60 per cent of the total sales of newspapers – Schibsted, Orkla and A-Pressen, all of which are Norwegian companies.
There are over 200 newspaper titles, Norway has the world's highest level of newspaper readership. Activity is concentrated in south-eastern Norway, especially around Oslo where the majority of papers are published, while local papers tend to dominate each particular region.
Dailies: In Norwegian, two newspapers dominate the national press, *VG* (www.vg.no) and *Dagbladet* (www.dagbladet.no). Other newspapers include *Aftenposten* (www.aftenposten.no), which stopped its online English publication in 2008; *Dagsavisen* (www.dagsavisen.no) and *Nordlys* (www.nordlys.no). Some regional newspapers publish daily such as *Stavanger Aftenblad* (www.aftenbladet.no) and *Bergens Tidende* (www.bt.no). In English, *The Norway Post* (www.norwaypost.no) provides general and international news.
Weeklies: A number of daily newspapers publish weekend editions. In Norwegian, *Se og Hør* and *Her og Hå* vie with one another for readership, with popular articles on celebrities and royal news. Others magazines include *Allers*, for the older woman, *Norsk Ukeblad* for younger women and *Vi Menn* for young men.
Business: A large number of business publications cover various aspects of trade and industry. In Norwegian, the leading daily financial newspaper, in tabloid form is *Dagens Naeringsliv* (DN) (www.dn.no), it is owned by Norge Handels og Sjøfartstidende (www.nhst.no) media conglomerate, which also publishes other trade papers. Hegnar Media (www.hegnar.no) publishes several business publications including *Kapital*, a comprehensive financial magazine and *Finansavisen*. Other, weekly publications include *Handelsbladet FK* (www.handelsbladetfk.no) a retail trade magazine, *Fiskeribladet Fiskaren* (www.fiskeribladetfiskaren.no), a magazine for the fishing industry and *Bondebladet* (www.bondebladet.no), an agricultural newspaper.
Periodicals: A large number of general and special interest magazines exist. Those aimed at women of all ages have the largest circulations, including, in Norwegian, the monthly magazines *Eva* for women, the bi-monthly *Tigue* (www.tique.no) is aimed at young women and *Henne* (www.henne.no) for women's fashion and style. The popular magazine *Mann* is aimed at young men. The quarterly *Vinduet* (www.vinduet.no) is a literary publication.
Broadcasting
The Norwegian Broadcasting Corporation's (NRK) (www.nrk.no) is the national, public broadcaster providing domestically produced programmes for radio, television and digital services, which is funded by a licence fee.
Radio: There are many radio stations broadcasting, with a wide variety of programming. NRK Radio (www.nrk.no) operates three national networks P1, P2 and P3 (Petre), along with several regional and local stations. It also runs an overseas, shortwave service, Radio Norway International. Other, private, commercial stations that comprise networks are NRJ (www.nrj.no), Radio Modum (www.radiomodum.no) and Radio 1 (www.radio1.no).
Television: The switch over from analogue television to digital services is expected to be completed by December 2009.
NRK (www.nrk.no) operates two TV channels. The main, commercial channel is TV2 (www.tv2.no), which broadcasts a combination of local and imported programmes. TV Norge (www.tvnorge.no) provides commercial TV via satellite. There are other, interest-led TV stations such as Rikstoto Direkte (www.rikstoto.no), a horse-racing channel or Visjon Norge (www.visjonnorge.no) a Christian content channel.
There are over a dozen different European channels broadcasting via satellite or cable, including several pan-Scandinavian channels.
Advertising
All usual media sources are available, including new outlets such as the internet and mobile/cell advertising. However, traditional print media has the biggest share of total annual adspend, typically over US$1.5 billion, of around 55 per cent followed by television advertising at around 30 per cent. There are restrictions on the advertising of tobacco and alcohol which are both banned, while pharmaceutical drugs, products aimed at children and political content material are banned on television.
News agencies
National news agency: NTB (Norsk Telegrambyrå)

Economy
The population of Norway has the second highest per capita income in the world (after Luxembourg) at US$84,144 in 2010. The economy is unique among Western European countries for its large and dominant offshore oil sector. It also has one of the world's largest and most modern maritime fleets, which supports its metalworking and shipbuilding skills. Other industrial sectors include timber, pulp and paper products, chemicals and fishing.
Norway had proven oil reserves of 6.7 billion barrels and 2.0 trillion cubic metres of natural gas at the end of 2010. Oil and gas extraction accounted about 15 per cent of GDP in 2009, but was projected to fall to around 11 per cent in 2010. Since the 1980s the economy has experienced a major structural change, becoming increasingly focussed on service industries, which account for about 37 per cent of GDP. The manufacturing sector is important, particularly in metals and chemicals. Traditional primary sectors, like agriculture, forestry and fishing, have declined; forestry and forest products account for around 0.6 per cent of GDP, farming accounts for 0.5 per cent and fishing 0.4 per cent of GDP; an increasing amount of foodstuffs have to be imported. However, Norway has a thriving aquaculture industry, farming salmon, cod, halibut and shellfish, of which salmon accounts for 85 per cent of total farmed and sold, and typically accounts for around 5 per cent of total export revenue.
A buoyant energy sector, with a revenue surge during the peak global oil prices of 2008 to US$110 billion (up from US$82 billion in 2007), provided the country with strong fundamentals which off-set the effects of the global economic crisis. Income from oil exports is invested in the Government Pension Fund (formerly the Petroleum Fund) – assets stood at over Nkr2.5 trillion (around US$40 billion) in 2009.
GDP growth was 2.7 per cent in 2007, falling to 0.7 per cent in 2008 before falling into recession with growth of -1.7 per cent in 2009, as the global economic crisis cut exports of oil and forced the banking sector to impose a credit squeeze. Domestic credit grew by 14 per cent in 2007 but had fallen to around 5 per cent by 2009. All growth in credit began to decline sharply in the last half of 2008, commercial credit growth (excluding financial enterprises) peaked at around 22 per cent in 2007 before plunging to

around -2 per cent by 2009. GDP growth in 2010 was a very modest 0.3 per cent, with a forecast of 1.7 per cent for 2011. A key challenge for the government is the tight nature of its labour market, especially in the construction and health sectors. Norwegian firms have had to look abroad to fill vacancies, as the unemployment rate is relatively low at around 3.1 per cent in 2009 and 3.5 per cent in 2010. A shortage in the labour market in the recent past has caused high wage growth, leading to a loss of competitiveness in Norwegian exports.

External trade

Norway is a member of the European Economic Area (EEA) which maintains an internal market with, although not joining, the EU. The EU consults EEA members before making its decisions on community legislation. The EEA agreement allows freedom of movement of goods (excluding, to a significant degree, agriculture and fisheries), persons, services and capital.

Norway is the third largest exporter of oil and gas worldwide that, along with shipping, provides the county's principal foreign exchange earnings.

Norway has a thriving aquaculture industry, farming salmon, cod, halibut and shellfish, of which salmon accounts for 85 per cent of total farmed and which is sold mostly to the EU, accounting for 4.5 per cent of total export revenue.

Imports

Main imports include machinery, vehicles and equipment, consumer goods, chemicals, metals and foodstuffs.

Main sources: Sweden (typically 15 per cent of total), Germany (13 per cent), Denmark (7 per cent).

Exports

Principal exports are crude oil and petroleum products, natural gas, machinery and equipment, metals, chemicals, ships, manufactured items, primary goods such as timber, ore, fish and foodstuffs.

Main destinations: UK (typically 30 per cent total), Germany (13 per cent), The Netherlands (10 per cent).

Agriculture

Farming

The agricultural sector typically accounts for 2 per cent of GDP and employs around 6 per cent of the workforce. Grain and fodder are main lowland crops; mountain farms mainly raise livestock and grow fodder. Grain production is increasing, especially barley and oats, although wheat and rye are increasing in importance. The main grain-growing districts are in southern and central Norway. Coarse fodder, mostly hay and silage, can be cultivated at high altitudes and in the far north. Other crops include potatoes, other roots, berries and fruits. Crop yields per hectare have risen consistently over the last three decades. Some dairy produce is exported and there is self-sufficiency in meat, milk, cheese, butter, fish and potatoes.

Norway's agricultural policy has two main aims. The first is to promote a high degree of self-sufficiency in animal products and secondly to ensure an adequate livelihood for the country's 120,000 farmers and smallholders. In many regions, agriculture and related activities are the main source of income. Farm prices are set annually by agreement between the government and agricultural organisations.

Almost all farmland is privately owned and farms tend to be small. Produce is bought and distributed by large co-operative purchasing and sales organisations.

The total cultivated area is just over 868,500 hectares (ha), only 3 per cent of the mainland area. Agricultural production is hampered by difficult topographical conditions and an unfavourable climate. However, Norwegian agriculture is generally efficient, with a high degree of mechanisation and emphasis on training and research.

Fishing

Fishing is a significant industry in the northern and western regions. Fish, including farmed fish, is Norway's second largest export group, accounting for 20 per cent of all exports. Mackerel, cod and capelin are the main species caught, but catches have been falling because of overfishing. The typical annual export value of fish is between Nkr 25–30 billion (US$3.3– 4 billion) and as a whole the fishing industry provides work for 23,000 people.

Fish farms produce mainly salmon and trout, although some are experimenting with other fish, such as halibut. Norway has the world's largest farmed salmon industry, producing about half the total supplies of Atlantic salmon. Demand for farmed salmon has increased by 20–30 per cent annually, but production normally exceeds demand. The emerging new markets in southern Europe are seen as a useful outlet for the surplus, even though salmon exports are in competition with EU production and the EU sets a minimum price requirement for sales from Norway. Salmon comprises 31 per cent of Norway's fish exports.

In October 2008, Norway was forced to undertake the decontamination of infected rivers by culling fish to kill off a deadly parasite (*Gyrodactylus Salaris* (Gs)). After the rivers were purged of fish, fry of replacement stocks, particularly Atlantic salmon, were re-introduced.

Forestry

Forest cover is estimated at 8.8 million hectares (ha). In 1990–2000, forest cover increased by an annual average of 31,000ha. Some 22 per cent of the total land area is productive woodland. Most forests are situated in southern and central Norway. Spruce, used for making pulp and paper, makes up about 50 per cent of the forest. Pines account for about 30 per cent and broad-leafed trees for around 15 per cent. Mechanisation and automation have allowed logging in previously inaccessible forest land.

About 85 per cent of forest land is privately owned by farmers. The forestry sector has a well-developed co-operative sales apparatus. Forest-owner organisations have become more active in processing.

The forestry and the forest-products industry, contributes heavily to local economies. Norway exports nearly 90 per cent of the paper and paperboard production and nearly a quarter of the pulp production. Imports of roundwood and sawnwood, mainly from Sweden, have increased considerably. Per capita consumption of forest products is among the highest in Europe.

Industry and manufacturing

The industrial sector typically accounts for around 32 per cent of GDP and employs 19 per cent of the workforce. Manufacturing accounts for barely 13 per cent of both GDP and employment (compared with around 22 per cent in 1970) and has developed more slowly than in most other industrial countries. The main industries include chemicals, fish processing, metals, timber and pulp and paper production.

The goals of industrial policy have traditionally been to maximise employment and the quality of production, maintain the rural population, promote a just and equitable distribution of wealth and income, and keep control over natural resources. Secondary goals have been to control inflation, protect the environment and achieve a balance between imports and exports.

The state channels financial resources to industry on concessionary terms through its Industry Fund and via state banks. Enterprises in depressed or uncompetitive markets are also given soft loans through the state-run District Development Fund.

The government aims for around 2 per cent of GDP to be invested in research and development (R&D). Priorities for R&D spending are biotechnology, communications, electronics, metallurgical technology and aquaculture.

Tourism

Discount airlines and direct flights were credited with providing the strong growth in tourism. Booking for cruise liners visiting Norway have passed 300,000 and the growth in cruising has risen fourfold in 20 years.

Environment
With the highest environmental standards in the world, sulphur emissions have plummeted by over 80 per cent since 1980. Pollution is kept low by the country's extensive hydroelectric production, although per capita nitrogen oxide emissions are among the highest in the world.

Mining
Norway has a highly skilled workforce, experienced in mining, quarrying and processing.
Activity is confined to small-scale mining of iron ore, copper, titanium, coal (on Spitsbergen), zinc, lead and pyrites. Most of these ores and concentrates are exported. Mining continues to contract, causing many problems in areas where there is no alternative employment. However, the country's mining potential has yet to be fully explored and it is believed that Norway has the capacity to develop super-quarries.
On the south coast, near Lillesand, feldspars and quartz are found. Graphite, with differing carbon content and quality, is produced on the island of Senja and research is being carried out to upgrade the quality. Large dimension stones like granite, marbles and quartzites, are available in large quantities. Larvikite is one of the most predominant stones, there are also exclusive marbles, including Norwegian Rose, to be found in the north. From the quarries in northern and central Norway high quality quartzite and phullite-slate are processed. Rock aggregate is found along the coast, in both large sizes and quantities, making transportation very easy.

Hydrocarbons
Proven oil reserves were 6.7 billion barrels in 2010, with production at 2.1 million barrels per day (bpd), a reduction of 9.4 per cent on the 2009 figure of 2.4 million bpd. Domestic consumption was only 239,000bpd and the remainder is exported. Norway is the world's third largest net oil exporter after Saudi Arabia and Russia and is also a major non-Opec (Organisation of Petroleum Exporting Countries) member and is not bound by cartel export limits. All of its reserves are located offshore in three sites, the North Sea (where most production takes place), the Norwegian Sea (where production is smaller) and the Barents Sea (where no production takes place but reserves are considered to be extensive).
Statoil (71 per cent owned by the government) controls 60 per cent of all oil and gas production and administers subsidiaries in concomitant industries.
Pipelines link offshore platforms with onshore terminals through an extensive sub-sea network. One pipeline links the Ekofisk system in the North Sea to the north-east of England, supplying 900,000bpd of oil.
Proven natural gas reserves were 2.0 trillion cubic metres (cum) in 2010, with production of 106.4 billion cum. This marks a steady increase in not only production from 46 billion cum in 1998 but also an increase in reserves from 1.48 trillion cum as new fields came online.
Norway was the sixth-largest gas producer in the world in 2010 and is a major supplier of natural gas to Western Europe, exporting 100 billion cum, principally to the UK, Germany and France.
The only coal reserves in production comes from Spitsbergen, on the Svalbard Islands, off the country's northern coast, which provides for the only coal-fired power plant in operation.

Energy
Total installed generating capacity was 28 gigawatts (GW) in 2007, producing over 135 billion kilowatt hours, which typically exceeds domestic demand; all surplus is exported to Sweden and Denmark.
The electricity industry is deregulated, but state-owned entities remain active within the sector, particularly in generation and distribution. Statkraft, the largest publicly owned utility, controls over 30 per cent of total generating capacity and is increasing its market share by acquiring interests in regional power companies.
Hydroelectric plants supply 99 per cent of total output, but seasonal weather conditions may impact on output, requiring imports to meet needs at such times; Norway is connected to the Scandinavian power grid.
The government has encouraged diversification in the energy market and licences have been issued for gas-fired power plants and wind farms.

Financial markets
Stock exchange
Oslo Børs (Oslo Stock Exchange)

Banking and insurance
Central bank
Norges Bank (Bank of Norway)
Main financial centre
Oslo

Time
GMT plus one hour (daylight saving, late March to late October, GMT plus two hours)

Geography
Norway lies on the west side of the Scandinavian peninsula, in north-west Europe. Its extended coastline faces the North Sea and the North Atlantic Ocean. It is the fifth-largest country in Europe and it has the third-lowest population density in Europe after Greenland and Iceland. The coastline measures 28,000km if fjords and inlets are included, 2,650km if they are not.
The capital, Oslo, in the south, lies on the same latitude as Greenland and Alaska, while Hammerfest on the northern tip of the Norwegian mainland, is the most northerly town in the world. The Svalbard Arctic archipelago is part of Norway, and sovereignty is also exercised over Jan Mayen island and the uninhabited island dependencies of Bouvet and Peter I. In Antartica, Queen Maud Land is a Norwegian dependency.
Norway shares a 1,619km land border with Sweden, and within the Arctic Circle, a 716km frontier with Finland and a 196km border with Russia.
The terrain mostly consists of high plateaux, deep fjords and mountains. More than 70 per cent of the mainland consists of mountains, glaciers, lakes, forest and moorland. The highest peak is Galdhoepiggen in the south which reaches 2,469 metres above sea level.
Only 2.8 per cent of the land area is cultivable soil, while another 20 per cent is productive forest.
Hemisphere
Northern

Climate
Influenced by the Atlantic Gulf Stream and westerly winds, the climate is much warmer than that of other countries on the same latitude. The temperature varies little from north to south, but there is a big contrast between the inland and coastal regions. In winter, while the interior freezes hard, most fjords and harbours remain ice-free. The average annual temperature is 8 degrees Celsius (C) along the west coast, and minus 2 degrees C in the northernmost county, Finnmark. January and February are the coldest months, while July and August are the warmest. The average annual rainfall is 1,960mm in Bergen and 740mm in Oslo. Northern Norway is popularly known as the 'Land of the Midnight Sun'. In Finnmark the midnight sun is visible from mid-May to late-July, and the period of darkness lasts from mid-November to late-January.

Dress codes
Clothing to suit the climate is vital because of the extremes in weather; heavy coats, warm boots, gloves and ear protection are required in winter and light clothing in summer. Normal European business attire, otherwise dress is generally casual.

Entry requirements

Passports

Passports are required by all and must be valid for three months beyond the date of stay. Nationals of countries which are signatories of the Schengen Agreement may visit on national IDs.

Visa

Visas are not required by nationals of most European countries, US, Canada, Australasia, Japan or transit passengers. For further exceptions, contact the nearest embassy. AA Schengen visa application (offered in several languages) can be downloaded from http://europa.eu/abc/travel/ see 'documents you will need'. Business visitors require a letter of invitation from a Norwegian entity, giving the nature and duration of the stay, with proof of accommodation.

Currency advice/regulations

The import and export of local currency is limited to Nkr25,000. The export of foreign currency is unlimited if proof of import or conversion from another currency can be produced.

Travellers cheque are widely accepted.

Customs

Personal effects duty-free, plus duty-free allowance. Imported products from certain countries such as Japan, South Korea and some East European countries require a licence. Imported cars are heavily taxed.

Prohibited imports

Illegal drugs, firearms.

Health (for visitors)

Nationals of the European Economic Area (EEA) countries and Switzerland can access reduced cost and sometimes free medical treatment using a European Health Insurance Card (EHIC) while visiting the EEA. Exceptions include nationals of the 10 countries which joined the EU in 2004 whose EHIC is not valid in Switzerland. Applications for the EHIC should be made before travelling.

Mandatory precautions

None

Hotels

There is a wide range of hotels available in most towns. There is no official rating system in operation. Private accommodation can be obtained through local tourist offices or accommodation offices in central railway stations. There is a service charge of 15 per cent included in the bill, but tipping is also expected.

Credit cards

Major credit and charge cards are accepted. ATMs are widely accepted.

Public holidays (national)

Fixed dates

31 Dec–1 Jan (New Year, from midday 31 Dec), 1 May (Labour Day), 17 May (Constitution Day), 24 Dec (Christmas Eve, afternoon only), 25–26 Dec (Christmas).

Variable dates

Maundy Thursday, Good Friday, Easter Monday, Ascension Day, Whit Monday.

Working hours

Banking

Mon–Thu: 0900–1600; Fri: 0900–1700; Sat: 0900–1200.

Business

Mon–Fri: 0900–1600.

Government

Mon–Fri: 0830–1600.

Shops

Mon–Wed: 0900–1700; Thu: 0900–1900; Sat: 0830–1300.

Many shops are increasingly introducing longer opening hours, and some are open on Sundays.

Telecommunications

Mobile/cell phones

GSM 3G, 900 and 1800 services are available in inhabited areas.

Electricity supply

220V AC

Social customs/useful tips

Punctuality is expected. Shake hands on meeting. Business lunches are rare. The main meal of the day is generally taken at home at 1700 hours, though people will expect to eat later if invited out.

Security

Serious crime is not a big problem. It is usually safe to walk at night in major cities, such as Oslo and Bergen, although some neighbourhoods are less safe than others. Car theft, on the other hand, is fairly common, especially in the major cities.

Getting there

Air

National airline: SAS Braathens

International airport/s: Oslo International Airport (OSL) (Gardermoen) 47km north of city. Facilities include duty-free shops, banks/*bureaux de change*, restaurants, car hire and dry cleaning. Business lounge including Internet facilities.

Other airport/s: Bergen (BGO), 19km from city; Stavanger (SVG), 14.5km south-west of city.

Airport tax: None

Surface

Road: The are several routes across the border from Sweden in the east and Finland in the north. These roads may be closed in winter.

Rail: There are daily train connections between Stockholm-Oslo-Trondheim. There are also train connections between Oslo-Gothenburg-Copenhagen-Helsingborg.

Water: There are frequent ferry services to Denmark, UK and Germany.

Main port/s: Oslo, Kristiansand, Bergen and Larvik.

Getting about

National transport

Air: Efficient services, operated by various carriers, link all major and many smaller towns. Charter sea and land planes are widely available.

Road: The road network is extensive; main highways are kept open although certain roads in the mountainous areas could be closed in winter and spring.

Buses: There is an extensive bus network. The main bus company is the Nor-Way Bussekspress with routes connecting every main city. Tickets can be purchased on the buses.

Rail: Norway has a good, though somewhat limited, national rail system. All railway lines are operated by the Norwegian State Railways (Norges Statsbaner or NSB). From Oslo, the main lines go to Stavanger, Bergen, Åndalsnes, Bodø and Sweden.

Water: There are regular and efficient motor ship services visiting all the major ports. There are also numerous local ferry, hydrofoil and catamaran services.

City transport

Taxis: Taxis are available in most cities. They can be obtained at ranks or by telephone (Oslo 388-090, Bergen 900-990, Stavanger 526-040). Telephone numbers of taxi stands are listed in the directory under *Drosjer*. Meters are compulsory. It is not expected that the tip will be more than small change.

In addition to regular taxis, there are airport taxis, cheaper taxis which must be ordered in advance by groups of up to three people, and wheelchair taxis.

Buses, trams & metro: There are eight tram lines and five metro lines in Oslo, plus numerous bus services. Public transport runs from 0530–2400 everyday. Tickets are best pre-purchased and self-cancelled, there is one hour's free transfer between any of the modes. (www.trafikanten.no can offer more information). Buses serving the airport take about 45 minutes and there is also a new regional bus station for services further afield.

Trains: A high-speed airport express train leaves every 10 minutes to and from Oslo's central station (20 minutes).

Ferry: Ferries from Oslo to Bygdøy leave from Rådhusbrygge, while ferries to the island in Oslofjord leave from Vippetangen.

Car hire

Available from airports and major towns. For travel between towns public transport tends to be quicker and much cheaper. Studded or winter tyres are recommended during winter. There are strict laws against drinking and driving and wearing seatbelts is compulsory. The speed limit in built-up areas is 50kph and 80kph on highways.

BUSINESS DIRECTORY

The addresses listed below are a selection only. While World of Information makes every endeavour to check these addresses, we cannot guarantee that changes have not been made, especially to telephone numbers and area codes. We would welcome any corrections.

Telephone area codes

The international direct dialling (IDD) code for Norway is +47, followed by subscriber's number.

Chambers of Commerce

American Chamber of Commerce in Norway, 20C Drammesveien, PO Box 2604 Solli, 0203 Oslo (tel: 2254-6040; fax: 2254-6720; fax: amcham@amcham.no).

Bergen Chamber of Commerce and Industry, 11 Olav Kyrresgt, 5014 Bergen (tel: 5555-3900; fax: 5555-3901; email: firmapost@bergen-chamber.no).

British-Norwegian Chamber of Commerce, 1 Dronning Maudsgate, 0250 Oslo (tel: 2311-1790; fax: 2283-4120; email: bncc@c21.net).

Kristiansand Chamber of Commerce, PO Box 269, 4663 Kristiansand (tel: 3812-3970; fax: 3812-3979; email: post@kristiansand-chamber.no).

Oslo Chamber of Commerce, 30 Drammensveien, PO Box 2874 Solli, 0230 Oslo (tel: 2212-9400; fax: 2212-9401; email: mail@chamber.no).

Stavanger Chamber of Commerce, 1 Rosenkildetorget, PO Box 182, 4001 Stavanger (tel: 5151-0880; fax: 5151-0881; email: post@stavanger-chamber.no).

Trondheim Chamber of Commerce, PO Box 778 Sentrum, 7408 Trondheim (tel: 7388-3110; fax: 7388-3111; email: firmapost@trondheim-chamber.no).

Tromsø Chamber of Commerce and Industry, 83 Grønnegata, PO Box 464, 9255 Tromsø (tel: 7766-5230; fax: 7766-5253; email: firmapost@tromso-chamber.no).

Banking

Christiania Bank og Kreditkasse, PO Box 1166, N-0107 Oslo (tel: 2248-5000; fax: 2248-4749).

Den norske Bank, Stranden 21, Aker Brygge, N-0021 Oslo (tel.: 2248-1050; fax: 2248-1870; internet: www.dnb.no; email: dnb@dnb.no).

Fokus Bank A/S, Vestre Rosten 77, PO Box 6090, N-7466 Trondheim (tel: 7288-2011; fax: 7288-2061).

Postbanken, Akersgata 68, N-0180 Oslo (tel: 2297-6000; fax: 2297-7665; internet: www.postbanken.no).

Central bank

Norges Bank, Bankplassen 2, PO Box 1179, Sentrum, 0107 Oslo (tel: 2231-6000; fax: 2241-3105; email: central.bank@norges-bank.no).

Stock exchange

Oslo Børs (Oslo Stock Exchange): www.oslobors.no

Travel information

Noges Automobilforbund (NAF), Storgata 2, N-0155 Oslo (tel: 2234-1400).

Nor-Way Bussekspress, Karl Johans gate 2; NO-0154 Oslo (tel: 8154-4444; fax: 2200-1631; email: administrasjon@nor-way.no; internet: www.nbe.no).

Road User Information Centre (tel: 2265-4040).

SAS Braathens, Oksenøyveien 3, Fornebu; PO Box 0080, Oslo (tel: 9150-54000; internet: www.sasbraathens.no).

National tourist organisation offices

Norwegian Tourist Board, Stortorvet 10, N-0155 Oslo; PO Box 722 Sentrum, N-0105 Oslo (tel: 2414-4600; fax: 2414-4601; e-mail: norway@ntr.no; internet: www.visitnorway.com).

Ministries

Department of Transport and Communications, Akersgaten 59, PO Box 8010 Dep, N-0030 Oslo (tel: 2224-9090; fax: 2224-9571).

Ministry of Agriculture, PO Box 8007 Dep, N-0032 Oslo (tel: 2224-9090; fax: 2224- 9555).

Ministry of Finance (Finansdepartementet), Akersgaten 40 (Blokk G), PO Box 8008 Dep, N-0030 Oslo (tel: 2224- 9090; fax: 2224-9510; internet: www.finans.dep.no).

Ministry of Foreign Affairs, 7 Juni-Plassen/Victoria Terrasse, PO Box 8114 Dep, N-0032 Oslo (tel: 2224-3600; fax: 2224-9580/81).

Ministry of Industry and Trade, Grubbegt 8, PO Box 8148 Dep, N-0033 Oslo (tel: 2224-9090; fax: 2224-9565).

Ministry of Petroleum and Energy, Einar Gerhardsens Plass 1, PO Box 8148 Dep, N-0033 Oslo (tel: 2224-6107; fax: 2224-9525).

Other useful addresses

Directorate of Immigration, PO Box 8108 Dep, N-0032 Oslo (tel: 2335-1500; fax: 2335-1504).

Næringslivets Hovedorganisasjon (Confederation of Norwegian Business and Industry), Middelthuns Gate 27, Pb 5250 Majorstua, N-0303 Oslo (tel: 2296-5000; fax: 2296-5593).

Norges Eksportrad (Export Council of Norway), Drammensveien 40, N-0243 Oslo (tel: 2292-6300: fax: 2292-6400).

Norges Varemesse (the Norwegian Trade Fair Foundation), PO Box 75, NO-2001 Lillestrøm (tel: 6693-9100: fax: 6693-9101; internet: www.messe.no).

Norinform, Norwegian Information Service, PO Box 241 Sentrum, N-0103 Oslo (tel: 2211-4685; fax: 2242-4887).

Norwegian Trade Council, N-0243 Oslo (tel: 2292-6300; fax: 2292-6400).

Oslo Bors (stock exchange), Tollbugaten 2, Box 460, Sentrum, 0105 Oslo (tel: 2234-1700; fax: 2234-1925; email: info@ose.no; internet: www.oslobors.no).

Royal Norwegian Embassy (US), 2729 34th Street, NW, Washington DC 20008 (tel: (+1-202) 333-6000; fax: (+1-202) 337-0870; email: emb.washington@mfa.no).

Statistics Norway, PO Box 8131 Dep, N-0033 Oslo 1 (tel: 2109-0000; fax: 2109-4973; internet: (English section) www.ssb.no//www-open/english/).

National news agency: NTB (Norsk Telegrambyrå), PO Box 6817, St Olavs Plass, N-0130 Oslo (tel: 2203-4400; email: marked@ntb.no).

Other news agencies: NW (Nyhetsbyrået Newswire): www.newswire.no

Internet sites

National bus company: www.nbe.no

National railway company: www.nsb.no

Nordic Pages: www.markovits.com/nordic

Yellow Pages: www.gulesider.no

Oman

KEY FACTS

Official name: Sultanatu Oman (Saltanat Uman) (Sultanate of Oman)

Head of State: Sultan Qaboos bin Said (from 1970)

Head of government: Sultan Qaboos bin Said (from 1970)

Ruling party: Political parties are not permitted.

Area: 320,000 square km (including Kuria Muria Islands)

Population: 2.69 million (2010; census figure)

Capital: Muscat (Masqat)

Official language: Arabic

Currency: Omani rial (RO) = 1,000 baiza

Exchange rate: RO0.38 per US$ (Oct 2011)

GDP per capita: US$18,657 (2010)

GDP real growth: 4.20% (2010)

GDP: US$55.60 billion (2010)

Inflation: 3.30% (2010)

Oil production: 865,000 bpd (2010)

Balance of trade: US$18.73 billion (2010)

Annual FDI: US$2.33 billion (2010)

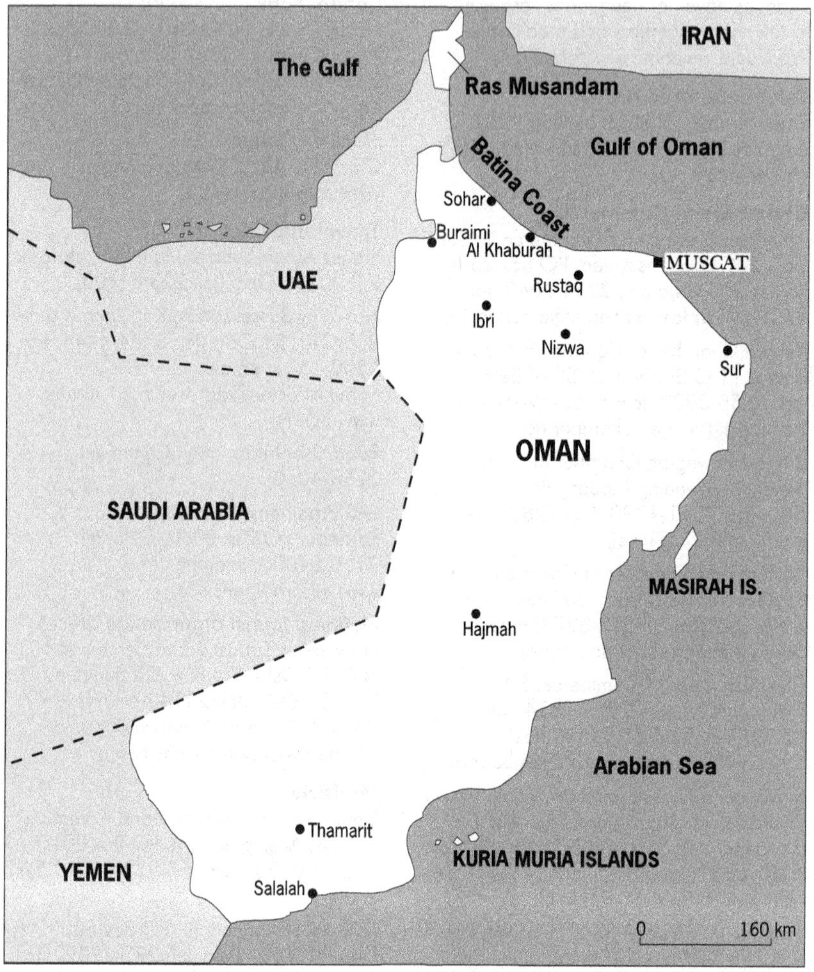

The year started badly for Oman with the killing in January 2011 of two people in clashes between security forces and protesters in the town of Sohar. The protestors, probably inspired by events in Tunisia and Egypt, were calling for political reforms. Despite the fatalities, which were a rude shock for the Sultanate, the protests were a relatively subdued affair when compared to events in Tunisia, Egypt and even Bahrain. In addition to those killed, a further five people were said to have been wounded when police fired tear gas and rubber bullets at protesters. Demonstrations were also reported to have taken place in the southern town of Salalah, in Dhofar. Protests in the capital, Muscat, were even more subdued, with a small crowd of some 300 people calling for greater democracy and jobs. Until the protests, Oman had largely been spared the unrest which has affected other Arab states in recent months. The state-controlled Oman News Agency said a number of demonstrators were involved in 'riots' that resulted in public and private property being destroyed. According to official sources, vandal groups had imperiled the safety of citizens and their properties, resulting in some injuries. On the back foot, Sultan Qaboos bin Said, the ruler of Oman, changed six ministers in his cabinet in what he termed 'the public's interest' and announced that social benefits for students would be boosted.

The 2011 protests, however muted, represented the biggest challenge to Qaboos' authority since the Dhofar insurgency movement of the 1970s when Oman found itself virtually at war with the neighbouring People's Democratic Republic of the Yemen (PDRY) – which was later subsumed into the single state of Yemen. With the help of foreign (largely from the UK) advisers and a sizeable mercenary force, the PDRY forces (themselves largely from Cuba and the former East Germany) were eventually defeated in the late 1970s.

The oldest independent state in the Arab world, Oman has been ruled by Sultan Qaboos since he seized power from his father, Sultan Said bin Taimur, in 1970. There is an elected Consultative Assembly but not all Omani adults are eligible to vote in elections for the Assembly and it is purely advisory, with no legislative powers. Oman's dynasty of sultans can be traced back to 1741, which is when the Ottoman invaders were expelled. The right to vote was instituted in 2003 although democratisation has been limited: Sultan Qaboos bin Said is an absolute ruler and female participation in politics is marginal. Although in the 15 October elections for the consultative assembly in which 1,300 candidates took part, 77 were women.

The economy

In its end-2011 report on the Omani economy, the International Monetary Fund (IMF) reported that economic activity was accelerating. Driven by new oil extraction technologies and increasing government spending, overall gross domestic product (GDP) growth is projected to reach 5.5 per cent in 2011 with 6.4 per cent growth in the non-hydrocarbon sector. Price pressures have remained contained and average annual inflation was projected at 4.1 per cent in 2011. Despite strong economic growth, unemployment among Omani nationals is high and a major social concern. In response, the government raised the minimum wage for Omani workers in the private sector, established an unemployment benefit, increased the number of government jobs, and raised enrollment in higher education.

Fiscal and external balances have strengthened in line with higher oil prices. Due to rapid growth in oil revenue and despite an expected 17 per cent increase in government expenditure, the overall fiscal and external surpluses are projected to reach 8.2 and 12.7 per cent of GDP in 2011, respectively. The rise in expenditure has mainly been driven by increased hiring in response to high unemployment.

According to the IMF, the Omani economy was largely unaffected by recent turmoil in international financial markets. While regional unrest has created some additional uncertainty, Omani banks had little exposure to the euro-zone. Credit to the private sector continued to pick up and was projected to grow by over 11 per cent in 2011. With about 80 per cent of Oman's oil-dominated exports going to Asia, the impact of the European crisis will be limited as long as it does not translate into significantly lower oil prices. Oman's domestic banking system appeared sound. The system is well capitalised, with a capital adequacy ratio of 14.3 per cent at the end of September 2011 (against the regulatory limit of 12 per cent). Stress testing conducted by the Central Bank of Oman (CBO) indicated that most banks were in a position to cope with significant macro-economic shocks.

In the view of the IMF, the economy looked set for continued expansion in 2012. Given a projected 10 per cent increase in government expenditure and with some slowdown in hydrocarbon output, overall GDP growth is projected to edge down to 5 per cent in 2012. Inflation is expected to remain moderate at an annual rate of about 3.5 per cent, and the fiscal and external surpluses are projected to stay high at about 8 per cent and 10 per cent of GDP, respectively.

The large public investment programme that is already underway will help sustain growth over the medium term. Major projects in progress include a rail network and new air and sea ports. Government plans also reflect a strong emphasis on education and social infrastructure. With civil investment by the central government projected to average about 16 per cent of non-hydrocarbon GDP over 2012–16, annual non-hydrocarbon GDP growth is expected to stay at about 5.5 per cent over the medium term. Oil production is expected to plateau and then slightly decline, leading to a small contraction in real hydrocarbon GDP. The IMF considered the main risk to the medium term outlook to be a prolonged drop in oil prices. Higher government spending meant that a higher oil price would be needed to balance the budget. The IMF projects a breakeven price of US$81 per barrel in 2012, rising to US$105 by 2016. A drop in oil prices from the prevailing historically high levels could quickly lead to large fiscal deficits. If sustained, lower oil prices could force a pull back in spending and lead to sharply reduced growth in the non-oil economy.

Oman's hydrocarbon reserves are relatively modest and cannot continue to support economic growth in the long-run. The IMF noted that there had been progress towards diversification, with non-hydrocarbon exports – mainly petrochemicals, fertilisers, and metals – now accounting for over 20 per cent of total exports. The non-hydrocarbon export industries, however, are highly energy intensive, do not generate many jobs, nor contribute much to government revenue.

KEY INDICATORS **Oman**

	Unit	2006	2007	2008	2009	2010
Population	m	2.58	2.74	2.87	*2.96	2.69
Gross domestic product (GDP)	US$bn	35.73	41.60	5.99	53.40	55.60
GDP per capita	US$	14,032	15,180	21,646	18,013	18,657
GDP real growth	%	6.7	6.7	12.9	1.1	4.1
Inflation	%	3.2	5.9	12.6	3.5	3.3
Oil output	'000 bpd	743.0	718.0	728.0	810.0	865.0
Natural gas output	bn cum	25.1	24.1	24.1	24.8	27.1
Exports (fob) (goods)	US$m	21,586.0	24,692.0	37,719.0	27,651.0	36,601.0
Imports (fob) (goods)	US$m	9,896.0	14,343.0	20,707.0	16,052.0	17,874.0
Balance of trade	US$m	11,691.0	10,349.0	17,012.0	11,600.0	18,726.0
Current account	US$m	4,328.0	2,463.0	5,469.0	-287.0	5,096.0
Total reserves minus gold	US$m	5,014.0	9,523.5	11,581.9	12,202.9	13,024.4
Foreign exchange	US$m	4,970.2	9,485.1	11,541.1	11,856.3	12,671.3
Exchange rate	per US$	0.39	0.38	0.38	0.38	0.38

* estimated figure

Energy

Like most of its neighbours, Oman is dependent upon its oil sector for the majority of its export revenues and budgetary requirements. Oman possesses the largest oil reserves of any non-Organisation of the Petroleum Exporting Countries (Opec) country in the Middle East and significant reserves of natural gas, of which it is a leading exporter regionally. Exports of natural gas have diversified the economy away from oil, but Oman will remain highly dependent on its hydrocarbon sectors for the foreseeable future. Oman is pursuing economic diversification, however its industrialisation programme is itself reliant upon increased volumes of petroleum and natural gas as feedstock. This leaves Oman's efforts to expand its economy largely dependent on the sectors from which it is attempting to diversify.

According to the *Oil & Gas Journal* (OGJ), Oman had total proven reserves at the end of 2010 of 5.5 billion barrels of oil. Oman's reserves are found mainly in the north and central onshore areas, comprised of disparate clusters of smaller fields. This geological composition makes production costs some of the highest in the region. The transition into secondary and tertiary extraction techniques will only increase these costs even further. Oman has thus far implemented a successful programme to reverse the decline in production experienced for most of the past decade, deploying some of the most sophisticated methods of oil extraction

Oman's ministry of oil and gas co-ordinates the state's role in the country's hydrocarbon sectors. Final approval on policy and investment, however, rests with the Sultan, who also holds the office of prime minister. The implementation of oil policy is done through an integrated company in which the Sultanate of Oman owns a majority stake. Petroleum Development Oman (PDO) holds more than 90 per cent of Oman's oil reserves and is responsible for 80 per cent of its production. Aside from the government's 60 per cent share, Shell (34 per cent), Total (4 per cent), and Portugal's Partex (2 per cent) all own stakes in PDO.

Given the technical difficulties involved in production, the contract terms for international oil companies (IOCs) have become more favorable than elsewhere in the region, some allowing significant equity stakes in certain projects. Occidental Petroleum has the largest presence of any foreign firm and is the second largest oil-producer in Oman. Other major players with interests in Oman include: Shell, Total, Partex, BP, China National Petroleum Corporation, KoGas (South Korea), and Repsol (Spain). In 2010, BG (British Gas that was) abandoned Oman because of inadequate findings in exploration at its concession areas.

Oman produced some 868,000 barrels per day (bpd) of total petroleum liquids in 2010, 865,000bpd of which was crude oil. Average oil production in Oman has increased by over 20 per cent for the past three years, from a low of 714,000bpd in 2007. PDO owns a concession which previously encompassed most of the country, Block-6, which has since been broken up and parceled out in successive bidding rounds. Much of the production growth has come from the success of international firms in developing former portions of Block-6. Tethys Oil of Sweden in particular has received encouraging results, hitting oil at various wells in two of its onshore blocks in 2010, which could indicate a higher potential for sustained production levels.

As long ago as 2002, PDO initiated a review of its mature oil fields to determine the feasibility of enhanced oil recovery (EOR) techniques which would help boost production yet again. A massive EOR programme was implemented, using varied techniques on a field-by-field basis, according to the geology. The future of Oman's oil sector is now dependent upon these EOR techniques.

Oman's EOR programme consists of three different general methods of extracting oil, some of which have never been used on a commercial scale previously. Miscible gas injection, steam (thermal) injection, and polymer flooding are the cornerstone of Oman's efforts to step up production. In 2009, Oman consumed approximately 115,000bpd of petroleum products. Consumption has increased over the last decade, more than doubling from a level of 52,000bpd in 2000. This has largely been attributable to Oman's industrialisation and expanding petrochemical sector, along with better roadways and an expanding vehicle fleet. Although Oman is a significant net exporter of petroleum, it is not a member of OPEC. As is the case with other exports from the Gulf, Asia provides the main consumer markets for Omani crude, led by China and Japan.

Oman's pipeline system is mostly focused on delivering crude oil to the country's only oil export terminal at Mina al-Fahal. Located near the capital, Muscat, both the export terminal at Mina al-Fahal and the main oil line feeding the facilities are run by PDO. Pipelines also feed industrial complexes and petrochemical plants, which form an integral part of economic diversification and Oman's expansion into downstream activities. PDO operates about 1,000 miles of oil pipelines which run throughout the country.

Oman continues to pursue the building of a large refinery and petrochemical complex at al-Duqm in southern Oman, which would be geared toward export markets. Under a memorandum of understanding (MoU) signed in July 2009, a joint venture between the Omani government and international investors would build a 200,000–300,000bpd refinery, a crude oil export terminal, and several large petrochemical facilities.

Oman had proven reserves of natural gas amounting to 30 trillion cubic feet (Tcf) as of 1 January 2011, according to the OGJ. Due to increased domestic consumption, gas re-injection use, and export obligations, Oman requires increasing volumes of natural gas. The ministry of oil and gas has announced plans to reassess natural gas reserves, seeking to increase reserves by a trillion cubic feet per year for the next 20 years, through programmes akin to the EOR techniques being implemented in the oil sector.

Given domestic consumption and the long-term liquefied natural gas (LNG) export contracts, the country has too little feedstock for electricity generation at seasonal peak times. This shortfall has resulted in service interruptions that have slowed industrialisation and economic diversification programmes, as well as economic growth generally. A regional power grid is being constructed between all Gulf Co-operation Council (GCC) members, of which Oman is one. This will create the possibility to import electricity, especially from neighboring UAE and its planned nuclear plants, and lessen the strain on domestic natural gas supplies used as feedstock. This prospect will only emerge in the medium-term however, largely after 2017 when UAE's nuclear plants begin to come on-line.

PDO has an even greater presence in the natural gas sector than in the oil sector. The government enlists foreign companies in new exploration and production projects, requiring the sophisticated technology and expertise of the private sector. Developing gas projects with foreign firms such as Occidental, BP, and Petronas will determine Oman's future production. The Oman Gas Company (OGC) directs the country's natural gas transmission and distribution systems. The OGC is a joint venture between the Omani ministry of oil and gas (80 per cent) and Oman Oil Company (20 per cent). The Oman Liquefied Natural Gas Company (OLNGC), owned by a consortium including the government and Shell, operates all LNG activities in the sultanate.

Risk assessment

Economy	Good
Politics	Poor
Regional stability	Good

COUNTRY PROFILE

Historical profile

Ibadite imams of the Ibadiyah Islamic sect, both hereditary and elected, first began to rule the area in the 800s.
1507–1650 The Portuguese occupied Muscat and established a garrison there until they were expelled by Imam Sultan bin Saif.
1737–49 The Persians invaded and after they were driven out, the Al bin Said dynasty came to power, which still rules the country today.
1798 The first treaty of friendship was signed between Oman and Britain.
1800s The Omani empire expanded to include Zanzibar and Mombasa and parts of the Indian subcontinent. When Sultan Said bin Sultan (known as Said the Great) died in 1856, his empire was divided: one son became Sultan of Zanzibar and the other the Sultan of Muscat and Oman.
1913 After an uprising against the Sultan, control of Oman split, with the interior being ruled by Ibadit imams and the coast by the Sultan.
1932 Said bin Taimur became Sultan.
1959 The Sultan regained control of the interior from the Ibadit imams.
1965–75 A rebellion in the southern region of Dhofar, led by the Popular Front for the Liberation of Oman (PFLO), was put down with the help of soldiers from India, Iran, Jordan, Pakistan, Saudi Arabia, the Trucial States and Britain.
1964 Oil was discovered.
1967 Oil extraction began.
1970 Qaboos bin Said, aged 30, overthrew his father, Said bin Taimur. Sultan Qaboos started to open up the country and, using money from oil, built roads, schools and hospitals and gave homes to people and boats to fishermen. He set in place strict environmental laws.
1971 Oman joined the Arab League.
1978 Sultan Qaboos was active in helping implement the Camp David Accords, signed by Israel and Egypt.
1981 The political and economic union, Co-operation Council for the Arab States of the Gulf (CCASG) (known as Gulf Co-operation Council (GCC)) was formed by Bahrain, Kuwait, Oman, Qatar, Saudi Arabia and the United Arab Emirates (UAE).
1985 Oman established full diplomatic relations with the Soviet Union for the first time.
1991 During the Gulf War, Oman was used as a base for forces fighting Iraq. Sultan Qaboos established the Majlis al Shura (Consultative Council).
1996 Sultan Qaboos promulgated the Basic Statute of the State, or Basic Law, the Gulf's first written constitution. A new bicameral parliament was inaugurated, consisting of an upper chamber or Majlis al Dawla (Council of State) (41 members appointed by the monarch) and a transformed lower chamber (Majlis al Shura) (Consultative Assembly), with 83 members elected by limited suffrage. The Assembly and the Council of Ministers meet once a year at which Cabinet members present their departments' plans. Majlis al Shura power is limited to proposing and reviewing legislation and, although it can affect policy on minor issues, it remains relatively powerless as executive power remains with the Sultan.
1997 The Sultan issued a decree allowing women to stand for election to, and vote for, the Majlis al Shura; two women were elected.
1999 Oman and the UAE signed a border agreement, defining their common frontier.
2000 Majlis al Shura elections took place, involving just 25 per cent of the adult population; no political parties were allowed and all candidates were hand-picked by the Sultan. Oman joined the World Trade Organisation (WTO).
2001 Oman became an important base for international military operations against the Taliban government in Afghanistan.
2002 Voting rights were extended to all citizens over the age of 21.
2003 The 83-seat Majlis al Shura was freely elected for the first time.
2004 Sultan Qaboos appointed Oman's first female minister with a portfolio (in higher education).
2005 A state security court convicted 31 people of plotting to overthrow the Sultan and install an Islamist government.
2006 Oman signed a free trade agreement with the US.
2007 The Arabian Oryx sanctuary became the first site to be removed from Unesco's World Heritage list, as Oryx numbers dwindled and the park was reduced in size by 90 per cent.
2008 A common market was created by the GCC. Citizens of these countries are now allowed to travel between and live in any of the six states, where they may find employment, buy properties and businesses and use the educational and health facilities freely.
2009 The Information Technology Authority was re-branded as e.oman (www.ita.gov.om). The website, in English and Arabic, provides information on all government departments and services.
2010 Investment of US$1.3 billion in new power plants was contracted out to a consortium of South Korean and German companies in September. Two thermal electricity generating plants producing up to 750MW will be built to the north-west of Muscat by April 2013.
2011 Demonstrations in the second city of Sohar, in which one person is said to have been shot by police, led to a number of concessions, including promises of jobs and benefits being made by the Sultan. On 10 August plans were announced to build a factory to make electric cars. The cars were designed by Sultan al Amri, and a prototype is scheduled for completion by June 2012. On 13 October Sultan Qaboos decreed that the parliament would be granted oversight powers. In elections for the consultative assembly, held on 15 October, 1,300 candidates took part (77 of whom were women); 84 candidates were elected as independent members of the assembly.

Political structure

Constitution

In November 1996, Sultan Qaboos bin Said promulgated the 'Basic Statute of the State', or Basic Law, the Gulf's first written constitution, that clarified the royal succession, provided for a legislature and guaranteed basic civil liberties for Omani citizens within a framework of Islamic and traditional law.
The country is divided into 59 *wilayat* (regions), each under the authority of a wali (governor). There are special governates for the cities of Muscat and Salalah, with Muscat consisting of six separate *wilayat*.

Independence date

18 November 1970.

Form of state

Absolute monarchy

The executive

Executive and legislative power lies with Sultan Qaboos bin Said, who appoints the Council of Ministers and other officials and promulgates laws by decree.

National legislature

The bicameral parliament consists of the Majlis al Shura (Consultative Assembly) (lower house) with 83 members elected by majority vote, to serve for four-year terms in an entirely consultative capacity and the Majlis al Dawla (Council of State) (upper house) with 59 members appointed by the Sultan; this house enacts not only laws it recommends but also those submitted by the lower house, with the exception of specific laws that must be referred to the Sultan. It also administers other state councils and committees.

Legal system

The legal system is mainly the preserve of Sharia courts, which apply Islamic law. The local courts are administered by *qadis* (Islamic judges) appointed by the minister of justice. Appeals from local courts are heard at the Court of Appeal in Muscat.

Last elections

15 October 2011 (consultative assembly)

Results: Consultative assembly: of the 1,300 candidates taking part (77 of whom were women); 84 candidates were elected as independent members of the assembly.

Next elections

2015 (consultative council)

Political parties

Ruling party

Political parties are not permitted.

Main opposition party

There is no legal opposition.

Population

2.69 million (2010; census figure)

Last census: December 2003: 2,340,815

Population density: 11 people per square km. Urban population: 76 per cent (1995–2001).

Annual growth rate: 1.8 per cent 1994–2004 (WHO 2006)

Ethnic make-up

Predominantly Arab, with non-Arab pockets in long-established Baluchi, Iranian and Gujarati communities. Many Omanis are of Zanzibari descendancy (prior to 1964, Zanzibar had been part of the Sultanate of Oman).

Religions

Islam is the official religion. The majority are Ibadi Muslims with about one-quarter being Sunnis. There is a small concentration of Shi'ite Muslims in Muscat.

Education

The government sponsors literacy centres in an attempt to improve the literacy rate. Primary education lasts from aged six to 12. Secondary education consists of two stages: first the preparatory school for three years then the secondary school for a further three years. Islamic Institute secondary schools accept students who have completed their preparatory study in a mosque. It teaches the same subjects as secondary schools but with an emphasis on Islam and the Arabic language.

Literacy rate: 74 per cent adult rate; 99 per cent youth rate (15–24) (Unesco 2005).

Compulsory years: None.

Enrolment rate: 76 per cent gross primary enrolment of relevant age group (including repeaters); 67 per cent gross secondary enrolment (World Bank).

Pupils per teacher: 26 in primary schools.

Health

Free medical care is available throughout the Sultanate for all Omani citizens.

HIV/Aids

HIV prevalence: 0.1 per cent aged 15–49 in 2003 (World Bank)

Life expectancy: 74 years, 2004 (WHO 2006)

Fertility rate/Maternal mortality rate: 3.6 births per woman, 2004 (WHO 2006); maternal mortality 19 per 100,000 live births (World Bank).

Birth rate/Death rate: 28 births and 3 deaths per 1,000 people respectively (World Bank).

Child (under 5 years) mortality rate (per 1,000): 10 per 1,000 live births (World Bank)

Head of population per physician: 1.32 physicians per 1,000 people, 2004 (WHO 2006)

Welfare

Most Omanis depend on the extended family for financial support. Since 1984 the Ministry of Social Affairs has run a scheme of monthly welfare payments for eight categories of Omani citizens, provided that they can prove indigence. The categories are: orphans, divorcees, people unable to work, refugees, widows, spinsters, people over 60 years of age and the families of prisoners.

The Sultanate of Oman has extended social security benefits for workers in the private sector. Since the issue of the Social Insurance law in 1992, the Public Authority for Social Insurance (PASI) has registered companies and establishments in the private sector including workers and their families, who are entitled to receive sickness, injury and disability benefits, pension and death compensation.

The Association for the Welfare of Handicapped Children, a charitable organisation, supplements the work of the ministry of social affairs, labour and vocational training with centres at Al-Khoudh, Quriyat and Bilad Banu Bu Hassan. The government has made donations towards women's training centres and nurseries for childcare. Special attention is given to the needs of the disabled, particularly young people who are encouraged to join the training centre at Al-Khoudh. The centre also cares for severely disabled children between 3—14 years of age. The ministry has developed sport facilities as part of the disabled welfare programme. The Oman Charitable Organisation (OCO), a non-governmental body, has co-operated with the ministry to build 45 shelters at a cost of RO58,500 (US$152,161) for the Bedu living in remote areas of the country and assisted with programmes for the disabled.

Main cities

Muscat (Masqat) (capital, estimated population 23,479 in 2005), Salalah (159,491), Sohar (105,585), Bawshar (154,878), Matrah (152,350), Ibri (99,142).

Media

Press

Government censorship is applied to political and cultural items and due to the law that requires all publications and journalists be licensed by the Ministry of Information, with stiff penalties for transgressions, has resulted in widespread journalistic self-censorship.

Dailies: In English, the *Oman Daily Observer* (www.omanobserver.com) is government-owned, while the Times of Oman (www.timesofoman.com) and *Oman Tribune* (www.omantribune.com), *and Week* (www.freetheweek.com) are independent. In Arabic, *Oman Daily* (www.omandaily.com), *Al Shabiba* (www.shabiba.com), *Alquds Newspaper* and the independent daily *Al-Watan* (www.alwatan.com).

Business: In English, *Business Today*, *Zawya* a business directory; multiply publications (by www.apexstuff.com) include *Oman 2day* and the free publication *The Week*.

Periodicals: In English, the monthly *Oman Today* (www.apexstuff.com) is a lifestyle publication.

Broadcasting

Radio: Radio Oman (www.oman-radio.gov.om/rdeng) is government-run, while Hala FM (www.ohigroup.com/ohigroup/news2.asp), which opened in May 2007, is privately owned. Presentations are in both English and Arabic.

Television: Oman has two government-run television channels (www.oman-tv.gov.om/tveng) and domestic satellite dishes allow programmes from Saudi Arabia, Yemen and the UAE to be received.

Advertising

With the rise of English-language media, in particular through satellite television, western advertisers are rapidly developing the industry in Oman. Apex Press has several English titles which take international advertising.

News agencies

National news agency: Oman News Agency (ONA), PO Box 3659, 112, Ruwi, Oman (tel: 2460-5659; email: editorarabic@omannews.com; internet: www.omannews.com).

Economy

With a population of less than three million and a relatively high per capita income, Oman is classed as a high income country by the World Bank, and relies on the export of its hydrocarbon natural resources for its income. At the end of 2010 Oman had reserves of 5.5 billion barrels of oil, with production of 865,000 barrels per day. Oman also has reserves of 700 billion cubic metres of natural gas, with production at 27.1 billion cum per day, of which 11.49 billion cum were exported in liquefied natural gas form and shipped to South Korea and Japan. In 2009 the Omani budget stated that oil and gas revenues contributed 75 per cent of total government revenue.

With an economy so highly skewed the non-hydrocarbon sectors are weak and under-developed. The government introduced policies in 2006 to spend more on other industrial activities and tourism and to encourage private sector investment to counter the dominance of hydrocarbons in the economy. However, with the high price of oil in 2008 its measures have been less effective.

GDP growth was 6.7 per cent in 2007, rising to 12.9 in 2008, before dropping to 1.1 per cent in 2009 as world trade almost stopped. However as the global economy picked up in 2010 so did GDP growth, which registered 4.1 per cent. Inflation, which had been relatively low until 2005 at 1.9 per cent, jumped to 5.9 by 2007. It hit a high of 12.6 in 2008, caused by the weak US dollar which is used to buy higher costing imports, before falling back to 3.5 per cent in 2009 as weaker domestic spending cut imports. In 2010 inflation returned to the 2006 level of 3.3 per cent. A reduction in exports in 2009 resulted in a current account deficit of around 2 per cent of GDP.

Oman did not suffer unduly during the global economic crisis as its banks remain tightly controlled and well capitalised. The banking sector continued to be profitable, albeit at a lower level than previous years.

External trade

In 2005 the Greater Arab Free Trade Area (Gafta) was ratified by 17 members, including Oman, creating an Arab economic bloc. A customs union was established whereby tariffs within Gafta will be reduced by a percentage each year, until none remain. In 2009, Oman was considering the viability of introducing value added tax (VAT) if it joined the Gafta customs union.

A US-Oman free trade agreement (OFTA) became operational in 2009.

Imports

Principal imports are machinery and transport equipment, manufactured goods, food, livestock and lubricants.

Main sources: UAE (typically 27 per cent of total), Japan (16 per cent), US (6 per cent).

Exports

Crude oil (typically 70 per cent of total exports), liquefied natural gas (LNG), fish, processed copper, textiles and dates.

Main destinations: China (typically 30 per cent of total), UAE (11 per cent), Japan (11 per cent).

Agriculture

Farming

Agriculture accounts for around 3 per cent of GDP and employs around 200,000 people. Agriculture and fisheries account for an average 35 per cent per annum of Oman's main non-oil exports. Main crops include dates, alfalfa, lucerne, wheat, mangoes, limes and bananas, with market gardening of tomatoes, cabbages, aubergines, okra and cucumbers.

The shortage of water and pasture and the salinity of the soil are the main constraints on agricultural development. The emphasis of government investment in this sector has been on digging wells, repairing old irrigation systems and building dams to trap rainwater which previously ran off into the sea. Irrigation studies show potential arable land to be twice that under cultivation, but agriculture already uses over 90 per cent of the available water. Apart from a narrow coastal strip (the Batinah coastline), most of Oman is either mountain or desert.

A network of collection and distribution centres is run by the Public Authority for Marketing Agricultural Produce (Pamap). Pamap exports fruit and vegetables, particularly bananas, and operates a banana ripening and packing factory at Salalah and a handling centre at al Suwaiq.

Fishing

The fishing industry is well developed and has helped to diversify the economy. Stocks include between 15,000 and 27,000 tonnes of kingfish, 50,000 tonnes of tuna and 2,000 tonnes of shellfish. The total fish catch typically varies between 118,000 to 160,000 tonnes per annum. Fish and shellfish exports totaled $104.7 million in 2006.

Oman Fisheries Co SAOG is the largest fishing company in the country. It undertakes processing and marketing of fish and fishery products, which are approved for export to European countries. Exports include fresh fish, frozen fish and seafood (prawns, crabs and lobsters). The Gulf Co-operation Council (GCC) states are the destination for almost half of Omani fish exports.

Forestry

There is very little forest or woodland in Oman with forest cover estimated at 1,000 hectares, mainly composed of scattered areas of Juniperus forest in the Hajar Mountains. About 10 million date palms are grown along the northern Batinah coastal strip. Although some wood is used for domestic consumption, there is no significant commercial exploitation. Much of the demand for wood and paper products is met through imports.

Industry and manufacturing

The government is acutely aware that oil reserves are low and the population is growing significantly with a high proportion of young people. As a result, government policy aims to promote growth and employment through encouraging private sector investment in industry. This has been done by offering incentives such as tax exemptions, customs protection, soft or interest-free loans and by providing infrastructure, usually in the form of industrial estates. It favours small- to medium-sized industries which are import-substituting, use local raw materials, have a relative advantage in export markets or employ a high ratio of Omanis.

A series of five-year development plans, started in 1976, outline the government's main objectives of self-sufficiency, import substitution and the diversification of the economy to reduce reliance on oil. The five-year plans call for the manufacturing, trade and financial services sectors to contribute 80 per cent to annual GDP by 2020.

Tourism

As part of its programme of diversification, the government has introduced measures designed to promote private sector participation in the tourist industry. Tourism is believed to be capable of generating more foreign earnings and employment opportunities than heavy industry. The government wants tourism to account for 5 per cent of GDP by 2020. The sector, following World Trade Organisation advice, has targeted upmarket visitors, but more recently the example of Dubai has stimulated interest in the mass market. In 2005, the construction of a huge, privately-financed resort called 'Blue City', costing US$15 billion, was announced. The project, covering 35 square kilometres along the al-Sawardi sea-front, will take 15 years to complete.

Mining

Mining typically contributes around 1 per cent to annual GDP and employs around 3 per cent of the workforce.

Oman has large resources of industrial rocks and minerals, some of which are already being exploited. They include silica sand, dolomite, limestone, gypsum, ornamental stone, clays, rockwool, iron oxides, heavy sands, wollastonite, celestite, asbestos, aggregate, laterite and barite.

Mineral deposits of copper, manganese, lead, iron, zinc, chrome, phosphates, gold, silver and nickel exist, many of them in inaccessible areas.
Government policy is to exploit raw materials wherever commercially feasible and diversify the development of its mineral resources. As in other sectors of the economy, the government aims for self-sufficiency and the mineral-based industry is expected to contribute significantly to the growth of GDP in coming years. The indigenous mineral-based industries include cement, limestone, ceramics and construction and the production of processed marble, gold ore, chromite, industrial and edible salt and clays. The government has encouraged the processing of ores within Oman rather than exporting them untreated.
In the late 1990s, the Japan International Corporation discovered new gold and copper deposits at Ghuzayn and Daris, which led to the development of potential areas for copper and gold mineralisation. Copper and chromite are mined near Sohar by thegovernment-owned Oman Mining Company (OMCO). Saudi Arabia is the main market for cathode copper production. There are probable copper ore reserves of 15.2 million tonnes at Rakah and Hayl al Safil in the Willayat of Yanqul, about 275km from the smelter. Chromite reserves are put at two million tonnes and annual production is around 6,000 tonnes. Chromite is exported to Japan and China. Gold and silver are produced from the copper oxide deposits by the OMCO processing plant.

Hydrocarbons
Proven oil reserves were 5.6 billion barrels in 2007, with production at 718,000 barrels per day (bpd), a reduction of 4.6 per cent on the previous year. Although Oman is an oil exporter , it is not a member of the Organisation of Petroleum Exporting Countries (Opec). The oil sector is a major provider of revenue for the economy, at around 75 per cent of all export earnings and 40 per cent to GDP.
Oman's oil reserves are declining and production falling, however the government has invested in enhanced oil recovery projects and production techniques on existing oil fields and new exploration, while at the same time continuing to diversify the economy away from the oil sector.
Proven natural gas reserves were 1.73 trillion cubic metres (cum) in 2007, with production at 59.8 billion cum. Domestic consumption has grown steadily and the export of liquefied natural gas (LNG) has become a significant element in Oman's export revenue with 12.17 billion cum, going mostly to the Far East, in 2007.
Coal deposits with reserves of over 22 million tonnes have been discovered in the Wadi Muswa and Wadi Fisaw areas of Sharqiya region near Sur. Coal from the Al Kamil field is of good quality, and could be used to provide the energy for a 300MW generator over a period of some 40 years, using 600,000 tonnes annually.

Energy
Total installed electricity generating capacity was around 3.3GW in 2007, all of which was provided by conventional thermal power stations. Demand is growing rapidly at 5 per cent per annum. The government plans to have liberalised the energy market by 2009 and international investors have been invited to finance new independent power projects (IPPs) to help increase generating capacity.
The 280MW Al Kamil power plant, built by International Power plc, the 430MW Barka power plant, owned by AES, the 240MW integrated power plant, owned by PSEG and supplying the Dhofar region, and the 140MW plant at Qarn Alam, owned by Bharat Heavy Electricals, are all run on natural gas.
A Gulf Co-operation Council (GCC) project to link the six member states (Saudi Arabia, Qatar, Bahrain, Kuwait, Oman and the United Arab Emirates) to an integrated power-grid began in 2005. The first phase of the GCC power grid was completed in July 2009 at a cost of US$1,095 million, linking Saudi Arabia, Bahrain, Kuwait and Qatar through 800km of transmission lines. Kuwait and Saudi Arabia will each receive an extra 1,200MW of power capacity and later, the UAE will receive 900MW, Qatar 750MW, Bahrain 600MW and Oman 400MW. In the first phase, a 400kV overhead line links Kuwait's Al Zour power station with Doha, and a 400kV submarine line to Saudi Arabia with Bahrain. The second phase will link the UAE with Oman. The resulting two mega-grids will be joined in the final phase.

Financial markets
Stock exchange
Muscat Securities Market (MSM)

Banking and insurance
Oman has a robust banking sector both foreign and domestic with two specialised banks subsidised by the government – the Oman Housing Bank and the Oman Bank for Industrial Development. However, experts believe the sector is over-banked and have called for mergers to consolidate the sector.
A royal decree was issued in May 2011 allowing for a new, stand-alone Islamic bank based in Oman, called the Bank Nizwa. Operations may not begin until 2012 or until the Central Bank of Oman develops and adopts the regulatory and supervisory regime to enable Islamic banking. In July, further details were released. The CBO had overseen the set-up of a panel to organise the Islamic-compliance of the new bank and organisers were planning on opening Bank Nizwa either at the end of 2011 or the beginning of 2012 in Muscat. With assets of RO150 million (US$390 million), of which 40 per cent will be raised through an initial offer of public shares, the bank will be the first to offer Sharia-compliant financial products to the local market, using exclusive accounts.
Central bank
Central Bank of Oman
Main financial centre
Muttrah Business District

Time
GMT plus four hours

Geography
Oman lies at the south-eastern tip of the Arabian peninsula, bordering Yemen, Saudi Arabia and the United Arab Emirates (UAE). The Musandam Peninsula in the far north is separated from the rest of Oman by UAE territory. The coastline is 1,700km long.
There are two distinct areas of population, centred on the Hajar mountains, with a narrow, fertile strip along the coast, in the north and the Batinah plain and its hinterland in the south. Between them lies 800km of virtually uninhabited gravel plain.
Hemisphere
Northern

Climate
Most of the country is hot and arid, with noon temperatures in summer exceeding 40 degrees Celsius (C) and annual rainfall of around 100mm. There is a higher rainfall over the mountains. The southern region, however, has a tropical climate, with noon temperatures between 27 and 33 degrees C all year round and a rainy season from June to August.

Dress codes
Formal clothing is recommended for public places and in general the body should be fully covered. Businessmen should wear suits and ties to appointments, but the jacket can be carried. Shorts are not allowed, except for sports. Women are advised to dress modestly. Swimwear should be worn only at hotel pools and on the beach.

Entry requirements
Passports
Required by all, except citizens of some neighbouring countries. Passports must be valid for six months beyond the date of visit.

Visa
Required by all. Details for tourist or business visitors listed at www.destinationoman.com, follow link to *Plan your trip*, then *Getting there*. Visas may be obtained at a point of entry (all land and sea ports, but only at Seeb International airport if arriving by air).
Those who do not appear on the list of eligibility should contact the nearest Omani Embassy and apply for a visa as required. Oman has a joint visa agreement with the Emirate of Dubai – visitors with a visa for either country may cross to the other without a further visa, however the term of visit is a maximum of three weeks.
Prohibited entry
Holders of Israeli passports
Currency advice/regulations
The import and export of local and foreign currency is unlimited; Israeli currency is prohibited.
Travellers cheques are widely available.
Customs
Personal effects and one bottle of alcohol per non-muslim adult are duty-free.
Prohibited imports
Firearms, ammunition, narcotics and pornography. Certain food items and plant materials may be quarantined. Clothing bearing Koranic inscriptions is banned. Although goods of Israeli origin and imports from Israel are no longer illegal in Oman, goods produced by companies boycotted by the Arab League are prohibited.

Health (for visitors)
Mandatory precautions
Vaccination certificate against yellow fever if travelling from infected area.
Advisable precautions
Health facilities in the city are good but expensive for foreigners; health insurance is therefore recommended for visitors. All visitors should carry a list of their generic medication and if necessary their own hypodermic needles.
Inoculations and boosters should be current for tetanus, hepatitis A, and typhoid. There may be a need for vaccinations for tuberculosis, diphtheria, polio hepatitis B. Use malaria prophylaxis for visits to the far north of the country, including Musandam province, which will also provide protection for hepatitis B, these include mosquito repellents, nets and clothing that covers the body after dark. There is a risk of rabies. Avoid bathing in freshwater, use only well-maintained and chlorinated swimming pools.
Milk is unpasteurised and should be boiled or avoided. Meat, fish and vegetables should be served cooked and fruit peeled before consumption.
Between April and October the sun is very strong and sunscreens, protective clothing, sunglasses and hats are necessary.

Hotels
There are several five-star hotels in Muscat/Muttrah/Ruwi Capital Area. There is a lack of hotels in provincial towns, although a programme of expansion is underway.
A service charge of 10 per cent is included in all bills.
Dhofar coast beaches are the main tourist area.

Credit cards
Major credit cards are widely accepted. ATMs are available in largerly bank branches.

Public holidays (national)
Fixed dates
1 Jan (New Year's Day), 18 Nov (National Day), 19 Nov (Sultan's Birthday), 31 Dec (Bank Holiday).
Variable dates
Islamic New Year, Eid al Adha (four days), Eid Milad Nnabi (birth of prophet), Ascension of Mohammed, Eid al Fitr (three days), Birth of the Prophet (two days).
Islamic year 1433 (26 Nov 2011–14 Nov 2012): The Islamic year has 354 or 355 days, with the result that Muslim feasts advance by 10–12 days against the Gregorian calendar each year. Dates of the Muslim feasts vary according to sightings of the new moon, so cannot be forecast exactly.

Working hours
Work hours are affected by Ramadan, the Muslim holy month of fasting during daylight hours.
Banking
Sat–Wed: 0800–1200.
Business
Sat–Wed: 0800–1300, 1400–1900; Thu: 0800–1300.
Government
Sat–Wed: 0730–1430.
Shops
Sat–Thu: 0900–1300, 1400–2100. Supermarkets and shopping malls: 0900–2200, with short lunch breaks.

Telecommunications
Mobile/cell phones
GSM 900 services are available in inhabited areas.

Electricity supply
220/240V AC, with two or three-pin round, or three-pin flat types, plug fittings.

Weights and measures
Metric.

Social customs/useful tips
Handshaking is the normal form of greeting and business cards are exchanged at business meetings. Appointments are required for business meetings.
It is discourteous to eat, drink or smoke in front of Muslims in daylight hours during Ramadan. It is polite to accept the refreshments customarily offered to visitors. Alcohol is available in hotel bars and restaurants. Non-Muslims with liquor permits from the Omani police can buy alcoholic drinks at special stores for consumption at home.
The government regularly issues strong-worded ordinances designed to keep the country clean and tidy. It is an offence, for example, to drive a dirty car or hang out washing in view of main roads. Foreigners should take care to observe these regulations, although the police rarely enforce them.

Security
Visitors should keep in touch with developments in the Middle East as any increase in regional tension might affect travel advice. Oman is the most stable country in the Arabian peninsula. Even levels of petty crime are minimal.

Getting there
Air
National airline: Oman Air (regional airline); Oman is a shareholder of Gulf Air (international airline).
International airport/s: Seeb International Airport (MCT), 40km from Muscat, with duty-free shops and a restaurant; Salalah International Airport, near the southern city of Salalah.
Airport tax: None
Surface
Road: The Yemen border is not open to travellers, but there are road links with the United Arab Emirates, including regular bus services between Muscat and Dubai.
Water: There are some ferry services into Muscat from other Gulf States.

Getting about
National transport
Air: There are six civil airports. Oman Air operates scheduled flights to Salalah Airport, Fahud and Marmul. There are also flights to the Musandam Peninsula, Buraimi, Sur and the island of Masirah. All flights should be booked well in advance and confirmed on the day before travelling.
Road: An excellent asphalt road system links all the main centres. A 780km highway links Dhofar with the north and the national network.
There are over 9,000km of paved roads (550km of dual carriageway) and over 22,000km of unpaved track roads. Improvements and the widening of existing highways is on-going, as are linking roads between towns and villages of the interior.

Buses: The Oman National Transport Company (ONTC) operates national bus services and local services in the capital area.
Taxis: There is an excellent network of minibuses which operate as service taxis linking up the major centres of population.
Water: There are regular ferry services from Muscat to Khasab on the Musandam Peninsular.

City transport

Taxis: Taxis are expensive by Gulf standards; they should have a scale of charges, but it is advisable to negotiate fares in advance (there are no meters). Tipping is not usual. Some hotels offer a courtesy pick-up service; others offer the service but charge.
Buses, trams & metro: An urban bus service operates in Muscat, but is not recommended for visitors.

Car hire

It is necessary to hold an international driving licence when hiring a car in Oman. Check licence rules in advance. Speed limits are 120kph and driving is on the right-hand side of the road. Most hotels have self-drive car hire facilities.

BUSINESS DIRECTORY

The addresses listed below are a selection only. While World of Information makes every endeavour to check these addresses, we cannot guarantee that changes have not been made, especially to telephone numbers and area codes. We would welcome any corrections.

Telephone area codes

The international direct dialling (IDD) code for Oman is +968, followed by subscriber's number.

Useful telephone numbers

Capital area
Police: 560-099
Fire: 999
International operator: 195
International enquiries: 197
Directory enquiries: 198
Operator: 190

Chambers of Commerce

Oman Chamber of Commerce and Industry, PO Box 1400, Ruwi 112 (tel: 2470-7674; fax: 2470-8497; email: occi@chamberoman.com).

Banking

Bank Dhofar, PO Box 1507, Ruwi 112 (tel: 2479-0466; fax: 2479-7246; email: info@bankdhofar.com).

BankMuscat, PO Box 1708, 112 Ruwi (tel: 2445-6365; fax: 2445-6077; email: info@bankmuscat.com).

Industrial Bank of Oman, PO Box 2613, Ruwi 112 (tel: 2470-6786; fax: 2470-6986; email: indlbank@omantel.net.om).

Majan International Bank, PO Box 2717, Ruwi 112 (tel: 2478-0388; fax: 2478-0643; email: majanbk@omantel.net.om).

National Bank of Oman, PO Box 2613, 112 Ruwi (tel: 2470-6786 fax: 2470-6986; email: ask@nbo.om).

Oman Arab Bank, PO Box 2010, Ruwi 112 (tel: 2470-6265; fax: 2479-7736; email: mktoab@omantel.net.om).

Oman Development Bank, PO Box 309, Muscat 113 (tel: 2473-8021; fax: 2473-8026; email: odebe@omantel.net.om).

Oman Housing Bank, PO Box 2555, Muscat 112 (tel: 24704-444; email: i-ohb@i-ohb.com.om).

Oman International Bank, PO Box 1216, P C 112 Ruwi (tel: 2457-6039, 2457-6618; fax: 2457-6040; email: omintbnk@omantel.net.om).

Central bank

Central Bank of Oman, PO Box 1161, Ruwi 112 (tel: 2470-6175; fax: 2470-5961; email: markazi@omantel.net.com).

Stock exchange

Muscat Securities Market (MSM): www.msm.gov.om

Travel information

Seeb International Airport, PO Box 58, Muscat 111 (tel: 2451-9285; fax: 2451-0805).

Gulf Air, PO Box 1444, Ruwi 112 (tel: 2470-3222; fax: 2479-3381).

Oman Air, PO Box 58, Seeb International Airport, Muscat 111 (tel: 2451-9953; fax: 2452-1075).

Oman Automobile Association, PO Box 2874, Muscat 111 (tel: 2451-0239; fax: 2451-0276; email: omanauto@omantel.net.om).

Oman Aviation Services, PO Box 58, Muscat 111 (tel: 2451-9237; fax: 2451-0805).

Oman National Transport Company, PO Box 620, Muscat 113 (tel: 2459-0046, 2459-0603; email: ontc01@omantel.net.om).

Ministry of tourism

Directorate General of Tourism, Ministry of Commerce and Industry, PO Box 550, Muscat 113 (tel: 2477-16527; fax: 2477-14213; e-mail: dgt@mocioman.org; internet: omantourism.gov.om).

Ministries

Ministry of Agriculture and Fisheries, PO Box 467, Muscat 113 (tel: 2469-6300; fax: 2460-5304).

Ministry of Awqaf and Religious Affairs, PO Box 3232, Ruwi 112 (tel: 2469-6870; fax: 2460-1109).

Ministry of Civil Service, PO Box 3994, Ruwi 112 (tel: 2469-6000; fax: 2460-1771).

Ministry of Commerce and Industry, PO Box 550, Muscat 113 (tel: 2477-13500; fax: 2477-17239).

Ministry of Defence, PO Box 113, Muscat 113 (tel: 2431-2605; fax: 2470-2521).

Ministry of Education, PO Box 3, Muscat 113 (tel: 2477-5209; fax: 2470-8485).

Ministry of Foreign Affairs, PO Box 252, Muscat 113 (tel: 2469-9500; fax: 2469-6641).

Ministry of Health, PO Box 393, Muscat 113 (tel: 2460-2177; fax: 2460-2647).

Ministry of Higher Education, PO Box 82, Ruwi 112 (tel: 24695330; fax: 2469-4481)

Ministry of Housing, Electricity & Water, PO Box 1491, Ruwi 112 (tel: 2460-3800; fax: 2469-9180).

Ministry of Information, PO Box 600, Muscat 113 (tel: 2460-3222; fax: 2460-1638; internet: www.omanet.com).

Ministry of Interior, PO Box 127, Ruwi 112 (tel: 2460-2244; fax: 2466-0644).

Ministry of Justice, PO Box 354, Ruwi 112 (tel: 2469-7699; fax: 2460-2725).

Ministry of Legal Affairs, PO Box 578, Ruwi 112 (tel: 2460-5802; fax: 2460-5697).

Ministry of National Economy, PO Box 506, Muscat 113 (tel: 2473-8201; fax: 2473-7068).

Ministry of National Heritage & Culture, PO Box 668, Muscat 113 (tel: 2460-2555; fax: 2469-7060).

Ministry of Oil and Gas, PO Box 551, Muscat 113 (tel: 2460-3333; fax: 2469-6972).

Ministry of Regional Municipalities, Environment and Water Resources, PO Box 323, Muscat 113 (tel: 2469-2550; fax: 2469-3995).

Ministry of Social Development, [PO Box 560, Muscat 113 (tel: 2460-2444; fax: 2469-9357).

Ministry of Transport and Telecommunications, PO Box 338, Ruwi 112 (tel: 2469-7888; fax: 24696817).

Other useful addresses

British Embassy, PO Box 300, 185 Mina al Fahral, Muscat 113 (tel: 2469-3086; fax: 2469-3088; email: becomu@omantel.net).

Capital Market Authority, PO Box 3265, Ruwi 112 (tel: 2482 3600; fax: 2481 6260).

Development Council, PO Box 881, Muscat 113 (tel: 2469-8900; fax: 2469-6285).

High Commitee for Conferences, PO Box 891, Muscat 113 (tel: 2469-8221; fax: 2460-7497).

Muscat Securities Market, PO Box 3265, Ruwi 112 (tel: 2482-3600; fax: 2481 5776).

Oman International Trade and Exhibitions (OITE), PO Box 112, Ruwi 112 (tel: 2456-4303; fax: 2456-5165; email: oitex@omantel.net.om).

Oman Oil Company, PO Box 261, Qurm 118 (tel: 2456-7392; fax: 2456-7386; email: oman-oil@omantel.net.om).

Omani Centre for Investment Promotion and Export Development, PO Box 25, Wadi Kabir 117 (tel: 2481-2344; fax: 2481-0890; email: info@ociped.com).

Omani Embassy (USA), 2535 Belmont Road NW, Washington DC 20008 (tel: (+1-202) 387-1980; fax: (+1-202) 745-4933; email: emboman@erols.com).

Petroleum Development Oman (PDO), PO Box 81, Muscat 113 (tel: 2467-8111; fax: 2467-7106).

Salalah Port Services Company, PO Box 105, Muscat 118 (tel: 2456-7188; fax: 2456-7166).

US Embassy, PO Box 202, Medinat Al Sultan Qaboos, Muscat 115 (tel: 2469-8989; fax: 2469-9189; email: aemctcns@gto.net).

National news agency: Oman News Agency (ONA), PO Box 3659, 112, Ruwi, Oman (tel: 2460-5659; email: editorarabic@omannews.com; internet: www.omannews.com).

Internet sites

Arab net: www.arab.net

Arabia on-line: www.arabia.com

Gulf business explorer: www.igulf.com

Official tourist site: www.destinationoman.com

Oman online archives of political, economic and business news: www.newsbriefsoman.info

Times of Oman: http://omantimes.com/

KEY FACTS

Official name: Islami Jamhuriya e Pakistan (Islamic Republic of Pakistan)

Head of State: President Asif Ali Zardari (from Sep 2008)

Head of government: Prime Minister Makhdoom Syed Yousaf Raza Gilani (PPP) (from 25 Mar 2008)

Ruling party: Coalition led by the Pakistan People's Party (PPP) with Pakistan Muslim League-Nawaz (PML-N), Pakistan Muslim League-Qaid e Azam (PML-QA), Awami National Party (ANP), Jamiat Ulema e Islam (JUI) (Assembly of Islamic Clergy) and Muttahida Qaumi Movement (MQM) (from 9 Mar 2008)

Area: 803,943 square km

Population: 165.15 million (2010)*

Capital: Islamabad

Official language: Urdu (national language) and English

Currency: Rupee (Rp) = 100 paisa

Exchange rate: Rp87.42 per US$ (Oct 2011)

GDP per capita: US$1,050 (2010)

GDP real growth: 4.80% (2010)

GDP: US$174.90 billion (2010)

Labour force: 53.78 million (2009)

Unemployment: 14.00% (2009)* (plus additional underemployment)

Inflation: 11.70% (2010)

Balance of trade: -US$11.42 billion (2010)

Annual FDI: US$2.02 billion (2010)

* estimated figure

Pakistan

Pakistan in 2011 could hardly be described as a happy country. Its increasing international isolation was amply symbolised by the US led capture and killing of Osama bin Laden, the leader of the terrorist orgnisation al Qaeda, in late April 2011, an operation in Pakistan's heartland which, it later transpired, was carried out without prior consultation or co-ordination with the Pakistani authorities.

Bin Laden

Curiously, the killing of bin Laden revealed the importance of the fault line that lay between Pakistan and its biggest ally, the United States. That bin Laden's location in the small inland town of Abbottabad was identified without the involvement or assistance of the Pakistan government spoke volumes. It confirmed that the US regarded Pakistan's military and intelligence services as unreliable allies, not to be trusted with confidential information. In the final analysis it was not the ability to deploy sophisticated technology that won the day. Rather, it was what the CIA would have called 'humint' (human intelligence). Bin Laden's most trusted courier, on whom the al Qaeda chief appeared to rely, had not been properly trained. Used to maintain contacts with the outside world, he had become a creature of habit. Thus, when detainees at the US military prison at Guantánamo Bay, a 'leased' facility in Cuba, gave the courier's pseudonym to American interrogators and said that the man was a protégé of Khalid Sheikh Mohammed, one of the organisers of the attacks on the World Trade Center in New York, the follow up had more in common with Sherlock Holmes or Hercules Poirot than computer technology. American intelligence officials had learned the courier's real name in 2007, but it took another two years for them to work out where he was based.

In August 2009 the courier was tracked to the Abbottabad compound only an hour's drive north of Islamabad. By

September 2009 the CIA had come to the conclusion that bin Laden might be hiding there. Thus, it turned out that the world's most wanted man was not holed up in the mountains of Pakistan or Afghanistan as had long been thought, but in a slightly tacky house (surprisingly valued at some US$1 million) surrounded by a four metre wall topped by barbed wire on Abbottabad's outskirts. Amazingly, the house had neither telephone nor Internet connections. American officials believed that the compound, built in 2005, was designed for the specific purpose of hiding bin Laden.

After some months the US authorities decided that the intelligence justified taking action against the al Qaeda leader. Even after the mission had been signed off by the President, Mr Obama chose to keep Pakistan's government in the dark about the operation. This was hardly surprising: the US government had never accepted Pakistan's insistence that bin Laden was not within their jurisdiction. Leaked US diplomatic cables revealed constant US pressure on Pakistan to help locate and capture bin Laden. Embarrassingly, when asked about bin Laden's whereabouts during a Congressional visit to Islamabad in September 2009, Pakistan's interior minister, Rehman Malik, had replied that he 'had no clue', but added that he did not believe that bin Laden was in the area.

Where did we begin?

The history of foreign military involvement in Pakistan has been less than successful. The UK managed to keep some sort of grip on the sub-continent while under colonial rule, but was less that successful in controlling Afghanistan. The end of the Indian Empire in 1947 and the division of what had been known as India into a broadly Muslim Pakistan and a Hindu India was catastrophic, verging on civil war between the two communities. Since the start of the US led campaign against the Taliban, Islamic extremists (and formerly the country's rulers) in Afghanistan in 2001, sectarian violence has risen sharply in Pakistan, accounting for an estimated 2,500 deaths. Much of this violence was attributed to links between militants in Pakistan and extemist groupings like al Qaeda, a number of which had arrived from Afghanistan. At the same time it suited Pakistan's military to use real and perceived threats from India to keep its seat at the top table of Pakistani decision-making, particularly on foreign policy. Civilian political parties, whether it be the secular Pakistan People's Party (PPP) or the center-right Pakistan Muslim League-Nawaz (PML-N) of Nawaz Sharif, have not been slow to exploit Islamic causes for short-term political gains.

The central irony has been that Pakistan's army and its intelligence service, the Inter-Services Intelligence Agency (ISI) have been extensively funded by the United States and Saudi Arabia, initially and supposedly, to wage a military campaign against the Soviets in Afghanistan in the 1980s. Ahmed Rashid, in his excellent study *Descent into Chaos* estimated that 'Between 1982 and 1990, the CIA, working with the ISI and Saudi Arabia's intelligence service, funded the training, arrival and arming of some thirty-five thousand Islamic militants from forty-three Muslim countries in Pakistani madrassas.' This, he perspicaciously warned, 'will sow the seeds of al Qaeda and turn Pakistan into the world center of jihadism for the next two decades.'

Theories also exist that Pakistan government agencies have found it useful to deploy militant Islam groups to wage war against India in Kashmir. Encouraged by what was seen as a victory, many militant groupings turned against Pakistan's alliance with the United States and this lead to attacks on the Pakistani state apparatus. With often split loyalties, Pakistan's army has seen fit to support some militant groups as strategic assets in India and Afghanistan. A parallel theory is that Islamic radicalisation in Pakistan is a result of the Pakistani army's decades-long policy to export militancy abroad. The objective was not to cause Pakistani politics to become extremist. The best laid plans, however... Pakistan's army failed to take on board the risk that these militant groups would undermine large swathes of Pakistani society. Religious political parties may have fared badly in the polls, but with some success, they have attempted to shape Pakistani public opinion.

Assassinations

Being a politician in Pakistan is a dangerous business. In early 2011, Punjab Governor Salman Taseer and Pakistan Minorities Minister Shahbaz Bhatti were both assassinated for the crime of calling for the reform of the country's blasphemy laws, which allow offenders to be punished by death. The laws have been criticised by international human rights groups for persecuting minorities.

The military rules, or does it?

Pakistan remains a praetorian state structured and geared to service, above all, the needs of a military that remains every bit as convinced as ever that Pakistan's national interest is synonymous with its institutional priorities and the preservation of its position as the final arbiter of political power and patronage. Indeed,

KEY INDICATORS **Pakistan**

	Unit	2006	2007	2008	2009	2010
Population	m	155.40	158.17	160.97	*163.77	*165.15
Gross domestic product (GDP)	US$bn	127.00	143.20	164.60	166.50	174.90
GDP per capita	US$	817	905	1,022	1,017	1,050
GDP real growth	%	6.9	6.8	3.7	2.0	3.8
Inflation	%	7.9	7.7	12.0	20.8	11.7
Unemployment	%	6.2	5.3	5.2	*14.0	–
Industrial output	% change	5.0	8.8	1.7	-1.9	–
Agricultural output	% change	1.6	4.1	1.1	4.0	–
Natural gas output	bn cum	30.7	30.8	37.5	30.9	39.5
Coal output	mtoe	1.9	4.6	1.9	1.6	1.5
Exports (fob) (goods)	US$m	16,764.0	18,121.0	21,094.0	18,329.0	2,146.3
Imports (fob) (goods)	US$m	23,967.0	28,761.0	38,185.0	28,526.0	32,879.0
Balance of trade	US$m	-7,203.0	-10,640.0	-17,092.0	-10,197.0	-11,416.0
Current account	US$m	-5,015.0	-6,878.0	-13,874.0	-3,583.0	-1,490.0
Total reserves minus gold	US$m	11,543.0	14,044.0	7,194.0	11,318.0	14,346.0
Foreign exchange	US$m	11,328.0	13,829.0	7,011.0	9,938.0	13,115.0
Exchange rate	per US$	61.02	61.14	70.41	81.71	85.19

* estimated figure

Pakistan's foreign and national security policies are primarily controlled by the military. In the absence of civilian oversight and given the military's history, greater abuses will ensue unless Pakistan's elected institutions assert themselves.

To complicate an already fraught situation, in late 2011 it was hardly a secret that the government and the military were engaged in both a legal and political confrontation over the so-called 'Memogate' affair. The case arose after a Pakistani-American businessman claimed that in May 2011, Husain Haqqani, former Pakistani ambassador to the US, had asked him to deliver a memo to the then US joint chiefs-of-staff chairman Mike Mullen. The unsigned memo, which the businessman intermediary Mansoor Ijaz insisted came from the highest Pakistani government authority, appealed for US help to quell a suspected Pakistan military coup following the killing of Osama bin Laden. Predictably, Mr Haqqani has denied any knowledge of the memo, as did Pakistan's President Asif Ali Zardari. Mr Haqqani was barred from leaving Pakistan while the commission completed its enquiry into whether criminal proceedings should proceed. Pakistan's military leadership claimed the memo constituted a conspiracy to damage it. In November 2011 Pakistan's more cynical observers interpreted Mr Zardari's trip to Dubai, reportedly for medical treatment, as a precaution against similar travel restrictions.

Pakistan's military has long defended its right to intervene in politics, even if it is seen as too weak to do so following the US raid on the bin Laden compound and its own failure to stem violent militancy. But its support for the judicial inquiry offers a legitimate means of destabilising, perhaps even unseating, a civilian administration that has sought to curtail its powers. Were the enquiry commission to find grounds on which Mr Haqqani had a criminal case to answer, the decision would almost certainly involve Mr Zardari in complicated proceedings and could even result in his resignation.

The (anti-) American factor

Anti-Americanism, especially in the wake of the Afghan war has caused growing intolerance in Pakistani society. Since 2001, Pakistan has co-operated with the United States in targeting terrorist sanctuaries in its tribal areas. Cynics consider the Pakistani army to be selective in the terrorist groups it targets. The army's perceived action against groups such as al Qaeda and its affiliates has led to an unexpected response within Pakistan. Militants, in particular the Pakistani Taliban, now target the Pakistani state and its agencies. Almost all the country's religious parties hold the United States responsible for the increasing violence and suicide bombings inside Pakistan. Those who demand a more secular government and society are considered simply to be supporting the US position. One US-based Pakistani analyst, Dr Hasan Askari Rizvi, seems to have put his finger on a nerve, noting that 'Over time, Pakistani society has drifted towards religious extremism. Religious sentiment has seeped deep into government circles and into the army and police at lower levels.' Other analysts say the Pakistani army and intelligence services use religious groups to manipulate their relationship with the United States. Mr Rashid writes that Pakistan's security agencies unleash these groups on the streets as 'part of a wider cat and mouse escalation between the US and the Pakistani military.'

For Pakistan to resolve the tensions between liberals and Islamists and to emerge as a modern, democratic state, the army will have to give up support for militant groups and rethink its foreign policy on Afghanistan and India. Writing in the *Crisis Guide* Hassan Abbas a fellow of the Asia Society, claimed that 'Without a friendly, peaceful, relationship with India, Pakistan cannot even dream about such a scenario.'

Nuclear deals?

In mid-2011 Pakistan's military establishment faced another embarrassment when revelations surfaced claiming to provide proof of a deal between senior Pakistani army officers and representatives of the North Korean government for the sale of nuclear arms technology.

An article in the *Washington Post* suggested that the former director of Pakistan's nuclear weapons programme, Abdul Qadeer Khan, had released documents from his house arrest endorsing his claims that senior Pakistani military officials had received bribes of US$3 million in cash, as well as expensive jewellery. The army officers in question were General Jehangir Karamat, a former Chief of Army Staff, and Lieutenant General Zulfiqar Khan. The two Generals issued denials of the claims, but the US newspaper claimed that the article had the support of US officials. Reports in 2010 had confirmed that North Korea had an active uranium enrichment programme designed to make fissile material for nuclear weapons. Pakistan's government fears that leaks of this sort could result in the US requesting the de-commissioning of its nuclear programme, placing it at a disadvantage with neighbouring India.

The economy

According to the Asian Development Bank (ADB) Pakistan's economic performance in the financial year 2010 (which ended June 2010) and into 2011 reflected largely the same structural weaknesses that contributed to its 2008 macro-economic crisis. Energy shortages and security issues held the economic rebound for 2010 to 4.1 per cent and slowed growth in the period 2008–10 to an average of only 3 per cent, well below the 8 per cent needed just to create jobs for its young population.

Little recent progress has been made in raising per capita incomes or reducing poverty. Delays in implementing policy measures and fiscal management practices necessary for macro-stability have undermined investment in infrastructure and production capacity. The modest expansion in 2010 benefited from fiscal and monetary policies in 2009 that eased macro-economic imbalances by year-end and from a decline in inflation that improved consumer confidence. Higher remittances provided additional support to an expansion of private consumption, as did improvements in rural income from increases in administered commodity prices. Heightened security concerns lifted public consumption, pushing total consumption's contribution to growth to nearly 80 per cent.

On the supply side, transitory improvements in large-scale manufacturing partly reversed two years of decline and supported a recovery in services, led by wholesale and retail trade. Agriculture expanded by a modest 2 per cent, due to weak performance by major crops. According to the ADB, the fragility of the recovery was underlined by continued investment contractions. Infrastructure shortages and security issues contributed to a 5.1 per cent decline of gross private capital formation. Gross fixed capital formation contracted by 2.0 per cent in 2010, coming on the heels of an 11.3 per cent decline the previous year. 2010 also saw a third consecutive year of decline in investment in large-scale manufacturing (down 15.4 per cent) and electricity and gas (by 11.0 per cent). Overall, the steady decline in total gross fixed investment as a share of gross domestic product (GDP) from 20.5 per cent in 2006 to 15.0 per cent in

2010 will hinder future growth prospects. Private savings have similarly declined, owing in part to the failure of key asset rates to keep pace with inflation, leading to either negligible or negative real returns.

Pakistan's fiscal balance deteriorated in 2010, reflecting delays in putting through planned policy measures to improve revenue performance and limit the burden on the deficit of losses at state-owned enterprises (SOEs) and of energy-related subsidies. The fiscal deficit widened from 5.3 per cent of GDP in 2009 to 6.3 per cent in 2010, well in excess of the revised target of 5.1 per cent. Revenue targets in the 2010 budget, too, were missed and Federal Board of Revenue (FBR) tax receipts continued to decline as a share of GDP, reaching a 30-year low of 9.0 per cent in 2010.

Pakistan's budget expenditure is relatively rigid and it is difficult to offset over-runs in one category with reductions in another. Inflexible current expenditure (such as security, interest and pensions) alone absorbed revenue of 7.4 per cent of GDP in 2010, or about 82 per cent of tax receipts. Subsidies amounted to another 1.7 per cent of GDP. The government curtailed the federal public sector development programme (PSDP) to 3.5 per cent of GDP to ease deficit pressure.

The ADB noted that Pakistan's inflation fell to 11.7 per cent in 2010 from 20.8 per cent in 2009. As it moderated, the State Bank of Pakistan (SBP) (central bank) lowered the interest rate in steps from 14 per cent to 12.5 per cent. Financing the current account deficit became more difficult over the year: the capital and financial accounts fell by almost 13.4 per cent, after a 26.2 per cent decrease in the previous year. Foreign direct investment (FDI) flows continued to fall in response to infrastructure and security concerns, with communications, transport and power accounting for much of the decline.

Pakistan's gross reserves improved, benefiting from International Monetary Fund (IMF) releases under a stand-by arrangement, rising to US$16.8 billion by end 2010. The nominal exchange rate depreciated by 6.3 per cent, but Pakistan's inflation, high relative to that of its trading partners, lifted the real exchange rate by 1.0 per cent.

Public debt (excluding guarantees) as a share of GDP continued to climb in 2010. Government domestic debt amounted to 37.0 per cent of GDP, including commodity debt and liabilities of SOEs. External debt rose to 31.9 per cent of GDP, including 0.6 per cent of GDP in external liabilities of SOEs. Interest payments due on domestic debt represent a heavy burden, accounting for 3.9 per cent of GDP in 2010, or 43 per cent of revenue. External debt amortisation payments, excluding amounts owed to the IMF, were relatively stable for 2010–13 at about US$3.3 billion. Amounts due for 2012 and beyond will be raised substantially by repayment obligations to the IMF.

The severe floods in July–August 2010 affected 2011's prospects. Damage was less severe than initially feared, but agriculture and communications were hit hard. Total damage was put at more than US$10 billion, half in agriculture. For other areas, notably power and transport, damage was mild but widespread.

Information for the first 6 months of 2011 points to a 1.7 per cent contraction of large-scale manufacturing centered on textiles, food processing and petroleum products, bringing the large-scale manufacturing index for September 2010 to its lowest since July 2007. With growth prospects reduced to 2.5 per cent for 2011, average growth for 2008–11 is expected to fall to 2.9 per cent. Persistent energy shortages and security issues were expected to hold growth to 3.7 per cent for 2012, providing scant improvement on recent trends.

Inflation accelerated after the floods, to 15.7 per cent in September 2010, reflecting actual and expected shortages. It remained above 15 per cent through December 2010, falling to 14.2 per cent in January 2011, owing to a government-freeze on oil and electricity prices. It was expected to remain high through 2011, for an average annual 16.0 per cent and was then expected to recede in 2012 to 13.0 per cent.

Pakistan began 2011 with a budget that was based on policy measures that proved difficult to carry out. Revenue targets called for an improbable 26 per cent growth of tax receipts, well over the 5-year average of 14 per cent. Meeting them would have been hard even if a reformed General Sales Tax had come into effect. A reformed tax was initially scheduled for July 2010, but the process remained politically contentious and any changes to the tax looked set to have a limited effect on 2011 receipts.

This tardiness, combined with the impact of the floods and wide tax exemptions for those in flood-affected areas, held tax revenue growth to 10.9 per cent in the first 7 months of 2011, making a further decline in the tax-to-GDP ratio likely.

Current expenditure was under pressure due to a 50 per cent wage increase for government workers, exacerbated by government failure to budget adequately for subsidies needed to cover the gap between notified and cost-recovery electricity tariffs. An annual budget allocation of Rp30 billion (US$0.34 billion) to cover the tariff differential turned out well short of expected cost and because of lack of policy measures total energy-related subsidies are expected to reach Rp200 billion (US$2.29 billion). Part of this gap was to be covered by 2 per cent monthly increases in electricity tariffs to bring them into line with cost recovery.

With a fiscal deficit at 2.9 per cent of GDP in the first half of 2011, the annual fiscal target was also revised to 5.5 per cent reflecting higher international food and energy prices, escalating subsidies and subdued revenue performance. With lower foreign funding, deficit financing is expected to rely heavily on the domestic banking system. After easing in 2010, government borrowing from that source has surged in 2011, reaching Rp379 billion (US$4.34 billion) by 12 February, compared with Rp330.4 billion (US$3.78 billion) for 2010 as a whole. Pakistan's banks expressed a preference for low-risk lending to government to offset flood-related increases in non-performing loans, while weak post-flood economic activity and rising borrowing costs held back demand for borrowing.

Pakistan's fiscal prospects for 2012 looked likely to improve as long as the political environment eases sufficiently to implement the revenue-enhancing and fiscal-management initiatives. Progress is expected in implementing reforms for the energy sector consistent with a move toward financial viability with a phased elimination of subsidy requirements, leaving enhanced fiscal space for development programmes.

Risk assessment

Economy	Fair
Politics	Poor
Regional stability	Poor

COUNTRY PROFILE

Historical profile

1906 The Muslim League was founded to promote Indian Muslim separatism.

1940 The Muslim League endorsed the idea of a separate nation for Indian Muslims.

1947 Pakistan (including East Pakistan or what is now Bangladesh) was granted independence as a British Dominion

following the partition of the British Indian Empire. The partition of the sub-continent into mainly Hindu India and the Muslim-majority state of Pakistan led to the death of hundreds of thousands as up to 15 million people moved from across the new border. The ruler of the Muslim-majority states of Jammu and Kashmir joined secular India rather than Islamic Pakistan. India and Pakistan have disputed Kashmir ever since.
1948 Muhammed Ali Jinnah, the first governor general of Pakistan, died. Pakistan and India fought over the disputed territory of Kashmir.
1951 Liaquat Ali Khan, Jinnah's successor, was assassinated.
1956 The Islamic Republic of Pakistan was proclaimed.
1958 Martial law was declared and General Ayub Khan took power.
1960 Ayub Khan became president.
1965 Pakistan and India fought over Kashmir.
1969 General Yahya Khan took control when Ayub Khan resigned.
1970 Tensions between East and West Pakistan escalated following the separatist Awami League's success in the general elections.
1971 A civil war broke out when East Pakistan attempted to secede. India intervened in support of East Pakistan, which broke away to become Bangladesh.
1972 The Simla peace agreement set a new line of control (LoC) in Kashmir; India and Pakistan agreed to settle the dispute through peaceful and mutual means.
1973 Zulfiqar Ali Bhutto became prime minister.
1977 Allegations that Bhutto's party, the Pakistan People's Party (PPP), had won the general elections due to vote-rigging sparked widespread civil disturbances. General Zia ul Haq led a military *coup d'état* and deposed Bhutto.
1978 General Zia became president.
1979 The deposed prime minister Zulfiqar Ali Bhutto was hanged, having been convicted of murdering a political rival. His trial was widely condemned as unfair.
1980 The US pledged military assistance to Pakistan in order to strengthen the Islamist opposition to the Soviet occupation in Afghanistan.
1985 After nearly eight years of martial law, parliamentary democracy with a civilian prime minister was reintroduced.
1986 Benazir Bhutto, (the daughter of former prime minister Bhutto), returned from exile to lead the PPP.
1988 Former military dictator and president, Zia ul Haq, remained pre-eminent until he died with the US ambassador and top Pakistani army officers in a mysterious air crash. General elections on a party basis were finally allowed and were won by the PPP; Benazir Bhutto became Pakistan's first woman prime minister.
1990 President Ghulam Ishaq Khan dismissed Bhutto on charges of incompetence and corruption; Nawaz Sharif (Pakistan Muslim League (PML)) was elected prime minister.
1991 Sharif began a programme of economic liberalisation and incorporated *Sharia* (Islamic law) into the legal code.
1993 President Khan dismissed Prime Minister Sharif (for corruption); the supreme court quashed the presidential order and Sharif was reinstated. However, both president and prime minister were forced to resign later. In the elections that followed, Farooq Ahmad Khan Leghari was elected president and Benazir Bhutto returned to power and formed a government by allying with a number of smaller parties.
1996 President Leghari dismissed Bhutto's government for corruption.
1997 The Pakistan Muslim League (PML) won the elections and Nawaz Sharif returned to power as prime minister.
1998 Muhammad Rafiq Tarar became president. Both India and Pakistan conducted underground nuclear tests, leading to widespread international condemnation and US sanctions.
1999 Benazir Bhutto and her husband were convicted of corruption and given jail sentences *in absentia*; they remained in exile. Over 1,000 people died in clashes between Pakistani and Indian forces around Kargil in Kashmir. General Pervez Musharraf led a military coup that deposed Sharif. Pakistan was expelled from the Commonwealth.
2000 US President Bill Clinton visited and urged a return to democracy. Sharif was sentenced to life imprisonment on hijacking and terrorism charges, but was later pardoned and sent into exile in Saudi Arabia.
2001 General Musharraf assumed the presidency (dismissing the incumbent President Tarar) and dissolved parliament. Musharraf backed the US war on terrorism in Afghanistan, which led to the US lifting some of the sanctions imposed after the 1998 nuclear testing.
2002 A referendum approved Musharraf's presidency for a further five years. Mir Zafarullah Khan Jamali was elected prime minister. Tension between India and Pakistan increased and only intense diplomatic efforts prevented war.
2003 A cease-fire began across the LoC – the first formal cease-fire since the insurgency began in 1989. After a two-year ban, Pakistan and India agreed to resume direct air links and allow over-flights. President Musharraf survived an assassination attempt.
2004 Prime Minister Vajpayee of India visited Pakistan for a summit meeting. Pakistan was re-admitted to the Commonwealth. Prime Minister Jamali resigned; Shaukat Aziz replaced him.
2005 The first bus-link for 57 years between divided India- and Pakistan-held Kashmir commenced. Pakistan, Bhutan, Bangladesh, India, Maldives, Nepal and Sri Lanka signed the South Asia Free Trade Agreement (Safta). In October an earthquake with its epicentre in Kashmir kills tens of thousands of people.
2006 A third bus link between Pakistan and India was launched – the service (Lahore-Amritsar) became the first direct link across divided Punjab since partition in 1947. Pakistan test-fired several nuclear-capable short-range ballistic missiles.
2007 The US reported the Al Qaeda leadership was hiding in Pakistan; the government denied this. President Musharraf suspended chief justice Iftikhar Chaudhary; the move lead to protests across the country. He was reinstated by the Supreme Court in July. The leader of the Muttahida Majlis e Amal (MMA), Pakistan's biggest Islamic party, resigned in protest against moves to allow President Musharraf to stand for a second term in office. The Supreme Court revoked the exile order of former president Nawaz Sharif but he was initially denied entry when he attempted to return to stand for president. Musharraf won the October presidential election in parliament although the supreme court refused to declare him winner until after it ruled whether he had been eligible to stand while still army chief. Musharraf declared a state of emergency in November, allowing him to purge the supreme court. He resigned from the army and was declared president. Mohammad Mian Soomro was sworn in as interim prime minister of a care-taker government. Commonwealth leaders suspended Pakistan's membership, declaring that the state of emergency was 'unreasonable and unjustified'. The state of emergency was lifted. Former prime minister Benazir Bhutto returned from exile in October, but did not stand for president; she was assassinated on 27 December while campaigning in Rawalpindi. Following the reading of her will, her son Bilawal Bhutto Zardari was appointed as leader of the PPP, with day-to-day control held by her widower, Asif Ali Zardari. Al Qaeda was accused of her murder. Parliamentary elections were postponed by one month to allow for another leader of PPP to be chosen.
2008 In parliamentary elections the opposition parties PPP and PML-N together gained more seats (171 seats out of 342) than PML-QA (51 seats), which backed

the president. The PPP and PML-N agreed to form a coalition along with other political parties including the Awami National Party (ANP). Parliament elected Makhdoom Syed Yousaf Raza Gilani (PPP) as prime minister. President Musharraf resigned, following parliamentary threats of impeachment and Mohammad Mian Soomro became interim president. The government banned the Taliban militant group, Tehreek e Taliban Pakistan (TPP). The ruling coalition collapsed when the PML-N split over a dispute about reinstating the judges previously dismissed by Musharraf. Parliament elected Asif Ali Zardari as president.

2009 The government agreed to the enforcement of *Sharia* (Islamic law) in the Swat valley in the north-east in return for a cease-fire by the Taliban. The move was criticised as an abrogation of responsibility by the government. The Taliban attacked a police academy in Lahore, killing 18 and injuring 95 in an eight-hour battle, which prompted army retaliation and a full-scale assault on Taliban strongholds. The presidents of Afghanistan and Pakistan agreed to increase military co-operation against Islamic extremists operating from strongholds in their shared border areas. Around two million people fled fighting in the north-east and sought refuge in camps elsewhere in Pakistan. After weeks of fighting, the Swat valley was declared safe for civilians and thousands of displaced peoples began to return home. The Supreme Court in July acquitted opposition leader, Nawaz Sharif, on hijacking charges, allowing him to stand for public office. A UN inquiry team began work into the assassination of Benazir Bhutto. In a ruling the Supreme Court abolished the amnesty that protected senior politicians, including President Zardari, from prosecution. Ahmed Mukhtar, the defence minister, became the first politician to face charges of corruption.

2010 A UN report, published in April, into the assassination of Benazir Bhutto in 2008 concluded that her death could have been prevented. The report criticised the Pakistani criminal investigation that followed, which had not pursued those who had organised the killing and that the country's politicised intelligence agencies had hampered the UN's investigation. Landmark legislation was enacted in April to limit the powers of the president so that the office became a titular position and the executive could no longer dismiss an elected government. The Northwest Frontier Province (NWFP) was renamed the Khyber Pakhtunkhwa; the proposal had sparked violence and a general strike among the ethnic Hazara in the region before the legislation was ratified; the majority Pashtun supported the name change. Monsoon rains, which began in July, were so severe that by the beginning of August an estimated 14 million people were affected by flood waters, which were registered as the worst flooding in Pakistan's recorded history. Over 1,600 people died as violent waters washed away whole villages, as well as a substantial amount of the country's infrastructure. Water borne infections quickly became a public health issue as hundreds of thousands of people were left homeless and without food and drinking water. The estimated cost of rebuilding roads was US$59 million with a further US$30 million for the power infrastructure. Some 557,000 hectares of cropland were flooded. By the end of the year, round 20 million people had been affected and the homes of seven million people destroyed, mostly along the Indus Valley.

2011 Unicef reported in January that in the southern province of Sindh 23 per cent of the population were malnourished following the flood of 2010. Agricultural land was damaged from sand deposited on top of fertile soil during the flood, hampering annual crop planting. The cabinet resigned on 9 February. Prime Minister Gilani announced the move live on television, as part of a plan to reduce the number of ministers by a third and to cut government spending. The government's only Christian cabinet member, Shahbaz Bhatti, was murdered on 2 March, reportedly by the Taliban, over his stance against blasphemy laws which he considered were used exclusively against minority groups. On 30 March India's cricket team beat Pakistan in a World Cup semi-final played in the Indian city of Mohali. Indian Prime Minister Manmohan Singh and Prime Minister Yousuf Raza Gilani watched the match together. In discussions the two premiers pledged to 'normalise relations'. Osama Bin Laden, the leader of al Qaeda, was shot dead by US military Special Forces in his fortified hideout, on the outskirts of Abbottabad in north-west Pakistan on 2 May. The body of Bin Laden was flown first to Afghanistan and then buried at sea. On 11 July, the US announced a cut in its military aid for Pakistan of US$800 million. The US Joint Chief of Staff, Admiral Mullens stated to a US Senate inquiry, on 22 September, that the militant Islamist 'Haqqani network (allied to the Taliban), for one, acts as a veritable arm of Pakistan's Inter-Services Intelligence Agency' (ISIA). He referred to two terrorist attacks, one on coalition troops and the other on the US embassy, both in Kabul and in September, of which, he said the Haqqani network had support from the ISIA.

Political structure

Constitution

The federal constitution comprises four semi-autonomous provinces – Punjab, Sindh, Khyber Paktoonkhwa (previously North West Frontier Province) and Baluchistan – as well as federally administered tribal areas (FATAs) and the federal capital area (FCA) of Islamabad. The constitution is an amended version of one promulgated in 1973.

In October 2002, parliament and regional assemblies were elected for the first time since they were suspended following the military take-over led by General Pervez Musharraf in October 1999. Everyone over the age of 18 years and who is not deemed insane is allowed to vote. The president is chosen by the four provinces and the two chambers of parliament.

In April 2010 the National Assembly (lower house) unanimously approved constitutional changes limiting the powers of the president. The changes will come into law once the Senate (upper house) has signed the bill. These will be the first amendments to the constitution since 1973. The measures will reduce the powers of the president, making the prime minister the most powerful person in the country. The amendments include: removing the president's power to dismiss elected governments, appoint the chief election commissioner and impose emergency rule in the provinces; judges will be appointed by a judicial commission; elections of the prime minister and chief ministers of the provinces will no longer be by secret ballot; and prime ministers may stand for more than two terms. The North West Frontier Province becomes Khyber Paktoonkhwa ('Khyber side of the land of the Pjakhtuns').

Independence date

14 August 1947

Form of state

Federal Islamic republic

The executive

The president is elected by an electoral college, consisting of members of the senate and national assembly, as well as members of provincial assemblies. The presidential term of office is five years, for a maximum two-terms. The president must be a Muslim, as per the state religion, Islam.

Legislation, enacted in April 2010, limited the powers of the president to that of a titular Head of State, with ceremonial duties only.

National legislature

The bicameral Majlis i Shura (parliament) comprises the National Assembly (lower house) and Senate (upper house). National Assembly has 342 members in total, of which 272 are directly elected in

single-seat constituencies. An additional 10 seats are reserved for religious minorities and 60 seats for female members, filled by proportional representation among parties that win over 5 per cent of the vote. All members are elected for five-year terms. The lower house has the responsibility to review the budget.
The Senate has 100 members elected by the provincial assemblies and allocated according to the four provinces and Federal Capital Area (FCA). The president may not dissolve the senate.

Legal system

The Supreme Court is the highest court of justice. Each of the four provinces has a High Court. The Federal *Sharia* (Islamic) Court hears appeals against the decisions of lower courts under Islamic laws in force concurrently with ordinary laws, and its decisions can be appealed before a *Sharia* Appellate Bench of the Supreme Court.
Each province is divided into a number of districts, each of which is under the judicial jurisdiction, both civil and criminal, of a principal court presided over by a district or sessions judge. Subordinate civil judges and magistrates dispense justice at lower levels of the judicial hierarchy.
Following the coup of 12 October 1999, the army declined to adopt martial law. Therefore, the judicial system continues to operate.

Last elections

18 February 2008 (parliamentary); 6 September 2008 (presidential vote in parliamentary).
Results: Parliamentary: the PPP won 124 seats (out of 342) PML-N 91, PML-QA 54 and Muttahida Qaumi Movement (MQM) 25, Awami National Party 13, Muttahida Majlis e Amal Pakistan alliance 7, Pakistan Muslim League 5, independents 18, three other parties won one seat each.
Presidential referendum: Asif Ali Zardari won with 481 votes (out of 699), Saeed uz Zaman Siddiqui won 153 and Mushahid Hussain won 44.

Next elections

February 2013 (parliamentary)

Political parties

Ruling party

Coalition led by the Pakistan People's Party (PPP) with Pakistan Muslim League-Nawaz (PML-N), Pakistan Muslim League-Qaid e Azam (PML-QA), Awami National Party (ANP), Jamiat Ulema e Islam (JUI) (Assembly of Islamic Clergy) and Muttahida Qaumi Movement (MQM) (from 9 Mar 2008)

Population

165.15 million (2010)*
Last census: March 1998: 130,579,571
Population density: 209 inhabitants per square km (2010)
Annual growth rate: 2.3 per cent 1994–2004 (WHO 2006)

Ethnic make-up

Punjabi, Sindhi, Pashtun, Baluchi and others including Mohajirs (Muslim emigrés from India). The populations are relatively homogeneous in Punjab, Baluchistan and North Western Frontier Province (NWFP) (predominantly Pashtun), but Sindh is more diverse, with many non-Sindhi communities in the cities of Karachi and Hyderbad. Precise ethnicity statistics are unobtainable, but a regional population breakdown can be used as an approximate estimate of ethnic proportions in the country as a whole. The most recent figures are as follows: Punjab (56 per cent), Sindh (23 per cent), NWFP (13 per cent) and Baluchistan (5 per cent).
Pakistan is home to millions of Afghan refugees and to one million illegal immigrants from Bangladesh, Sri Lanka, Iran, Iraq and India.

Religions

Islam 97 per cent, Christianity 1.5 per cent, Hinduism 1.5 per cent.

Education

More than 200,000 extra teachers have been recruited since 2001, most under US donor funding estimated at US$10 million.
The government proposes to establish an international centre of computer science in collaboration with the European Centre of Nuclear Physics. Free internet connections have been extended to public sector universities. A nationwide network of schools called the National Centres for the Rehabilitation of Child Labour (NCRCL) has been set up with 33 schools in areas where child labour is rampant.
Literacy rate: 42 per cent adult rate; 54 per cent youth rate (15–24) (Unesco 2005).
Compulsory years: Five to 15
Enrolment rate: 40 per cent in secondary schools.
Pupils per teacher: 40 in primary schools.

Health

Many in poorer rural areas have limited access to healthcare facilities. Although there have been improvements in provision, facilities remain relatively poor, and there are still fewer than 800 hospitals for the entire country, providing less than one hospital bed for every 1,000 people.
Pakistani authorities have made some efforts to provide increased preventive health care. Particular attention has been given to the provision of safe drinking water supplies, and the government claims that about 88 per cent of the Pakistani population have access to safe drinking water. The World Bank estimates that this is accurate for urban areas only, and the figure among the rural population is thought to be lower, with only about 50 per cent having access to proper sanitation.
Some areas of the country's health services improved over the previous decade, including better access to immunisation and family planning services. Low government expenditure and the poor quality of private health care continue to be a problem. One quarter of the national budget is spent on the military, compared with less than 7 per cent on health.
Polio is endemic. The World Health Organisation – Global Polio Eradication Initiative (WHO – Polio Eradication) said that improvements in vaccination programmes could only be successful when the central government and the Federally Administered Tribal Areas (FATA) region of North West Frontier Province (NWFP) in particular were fully engaged with the problem. Pakistan liaises with Afghanistan concerning the shared corridor of transmission in the NWFP and southern Afghanistan. In August 2011, Unicef reported there had been an increased number of polio cases since the beginning of the year, with the majority of cases from the western, and largest, state of Baluchistan. The UN said Pakistan was the 'last polio reservoir worldwide', which was standing in the way of total eradication of the disease. A new vaccination campaign for 16.5 million children in districts of highest risk was held on 19–21 September 2011.

HIV/Aids

HIV prevalence: 0.1 per cent aged 15–49 in 2003 (World Bank)
Life expectancy: 62 years, 2004 (WHO 2006)
Fertility rate/Maternal mortality rate: 4.1 births per woman, 2004 (WHO 2006)
Birth rate/Death rate: 9.51 deaths to 32.11 births per 1,000 people (World Bank).
Child (under 5 years) mortality rate (per 1,000): 74 per 1,000 live births (2003); 38 per cent of children aged under five are malnourished (World Bank).
Head of population per physician: 0.74 physician per 1,000 people, 2004 (WHO 2006)

Welfare

A Poverty Alleviation Programme includes pension, death and marriage grants, and a policy formulated for the elimination of bonded and child labour. An estimated 40 per cent of the urban population lives in slums or other poor housing areas.

Main cities

Islamabad (capital, estimated population 955,629 in 2005), Karachi (12.2 million (m)), Lahore (6.4m), Lyallpur (2.5m),

Faisalabad (2.5m), Rawalpindi (1.7m), Gujranwala (1.6m), Multan (1.5m), Hyderabad (1.3m), Peshawar (1.5m).

Languages spoken

There are 69 other languages, including Punjabi, Sindhi, Pashtu, Baluchi, Seraiki.

Official language/s

Urdu (national language) and English

Media

Press

Legislation gives the government powers to close media and Internet outlets. Foreign correspondents are allowed to move freely in Pakistan, but are barred from some border areas.

Dailies: There are over 100 national and regional daily newspapers representing all local languages with around 25 published either in English or as an English version of a local language.

In English, *Dawn* (www.dawn.com) is the leading newspaper; others include *Daily Times* (www.dailytimes.com.pk), *Nation* (www.nation.com.pk), *Post* (www.thepost.com.pk), *Karachi News* (www.kashmirnews.com), *Daily Mail* (http://dailymailnews.com), *Statesman* (www.statesman.com.pk) and *Pakistan Observer* (www.pakobserver.net).

In Urdu, the leading newspaper is *Daily Jang* (www.jang.com.pk), others include *Daily Khabrain* (www.khabrain.com), *Daily Nawa i Waqt* (www.nawaiwaqt.com.pk), *Daily Al Akbar* (www.alakhbar.com.pk), *Daily Ausaf* (www.dailyausaf.com), *Daily Millat* (www.millat.com) and *Daily Asas* (www.dailyasas.com.pk). In Sindh, the largest circulation is *Daily Kawish* (www.dailykawish.com) and the *Daily Ibrat* (www.dailyibrat.com).

Weeklies: In English, *The Friday Times* (www.thefridaytimes.com) is an independent newspaper; magazines include the *Herald* (www.dawn.com/herald), *Newline* (www.newsline.com.pk) and *Weekly Cutting Edge* (www.weeklycuttingedge.com). In Urdo, *Akhbar e Jehan* (www.akhbar-e-jehan.com).

Business: In English, two publications, based in Karachi, include *Pakistan and Gulf Economist* (www.pakistaneconomist.com), (international magazine) and *Business Recorder* (www.brecorder.com), with industry specific news.

Periodicals: Almost all major foreign magazines are available in Pakistan, although specific issues may be banned from time to time if they carry material deemed offensive to Islam or critical of Pakistan.

Broadcasting

The Pakistan Electronic Regulatory Authority (Pemra) (www.pemra.gov.pk) is the official organisation that regulates broadcast operations. There are state controlled and privately operated radio and television stations.

Only a Pakistani national or permanent resident may own and operate a broadcast company.

Radio: The state-run Pakistan Broadcasting Corporation (PBC) (www.radio.gov.pk) operates a nationwide service as well as regional and local services. It also operates a range of external services in 15 languages.

Television: The Pakistan Television Corporation (PTV) (www.ptv.com.pk) provides national as well as regional services. In 2002 the first private satellite TV station licenses were issued, by 2007, 20 had been granted and were operational. DawnNews is an English language news channel. ATV (terrestrial); Aaj TV, Indus TV and Ary Digital are satellite stations. Films shown on television are censored to meet conservative Islamic standards of morality.

In June 2008 the authorities in UAE, asked Geo TV news channel to suspend transmission of two talk shows that were critical of President Musharraf. It is assumed that Pakistan put pressure on the UAE. Geo TV announced that rather than stop transmissions of 'objective and unbiased' information to millions of Urdu-speaking people worldwide it might move its operations to either the UK or Hong Kong.

Advertising

Advertising is available in the press, in cinemas and on commercial radio and television.

News agencies

National news agency: Associated Press of Pakistan (APP)

The News Network International (NNI) www.nni-news.com.pk

Pahel www.pehel.com

Economy

Pakistan is characterised as an emerging economy, it has a service sector that constituted 54.2 per cent of GDP in 2009 while industry made up 24.3 per cent, of which manufacturing was 17.1 per cent, and agriculture was still an important constituent at 21.6 per cent of GDP. Agriculture provides 45 per cent of all employment. Over 10 million bales of cotton are produced per annum, which are either channelled into Pakistan's textile industries which export 60 per cent of their production, or exported raw. Pakistan is the world's second largest producer of chickpeas and a major producer and exporter of other agricultural products such as fruit, sugar cane, rice and wheat. Heavy industry includes mining, hydrocarbon extraction, petroleum refining and chemical production. With such a mixed economy the country should be able to maintain a steady increase in economic growth, however it is subject to internal and external pressures, natural and manmade shocks. Pakistan has suffered from increasing internal insurgency, as well as fighting along its border with Afghanistan. This has led to the breakdown of civil order in several provinces. The economy in such regions cannot be productive and may have an effect on long-term development. The military requires a higher proportion of GDP than would be expected during a period of peace. Although the US provides funds for military aid, money that could be used for development is allocated elsewhere.

In 2007 GDP growth was 6.8 per cent, which fell to 3.7 per cent in 2008 as the global economic crisis impacted on the economy and as output in manufacturing slowed and exports fell. However a bumper crop of wheat in 2008 and a fall in imports as well as increased remittances (which contribute around 4 per cent of GDP) from the seven million overseas workers, plus international aid (much through military spending by the US) maintained the growth. Pakistan did not experience a recession and GDP growth in 2009 although low at 1.7 per cent, remained positive. Remittances in 2009 amounted to US$8.72 billion, rising to an estimated US$9.4 billion in 2010. The growth rate for 2010 was forecast to be 3.8 per cent before widespread destruction from severe flooding in 2010, which displaced millions of residents along the Indus valley, caused a humanitarian disaster and overwhelmed the civil administration. The loss of crops was estimated at US$5 billion and livestock of US$106 million, while 20 per cent of the cotton crop was lost. In 2011 hundreds of thousands were still homeless and production in much of the flooded areas had not returned to pre-2010 levels.

Inflation has been a long-term problem, although typically remaining below 10 per cent. However when bank credit in the private sector was severely curtailed in 2008 the year-on-year inflation in October leapt to 25 per cent, although the annual rate was 12 per cent. In 2009, inflation soared to 20.8 per cent before falling back to 11.7 per cent in 2010.

In 2011, the UN Human Development Index (HDI) ranked Pakistan 145 (out of 187) for development in health, education and income and in 2010, 53.4 per cent of the population experienced deprivation in at least one indicator for poverty, while 22.6 per cent lived on the equivalent of US$1.25 per day.

External trade

Pakistan is a member of South Asia Association for Regional Co-operation, which operates a preferential trading arrangement that covers 6,000 products. The South Asia Free Trade Area (Safta) is due to be implemented between the seven member states (Bangladesh, Bhutan, India, Maldives, Nepal, Pakistan and Sri Lanka) in 2012.

Foreign exchange revenue comes from textiles and garment production, remittances and thirdly cotton (Pakistan is the fourth largest producer, worldwide), combined with shipping and industrial manufacturing foreign trade accounts for about 35 per cent of GDP.

Imports

Main imports include petroleum and derivatives, capital machinery, plastics, vehicles, edible oils, paper products, iron, steel and tea.

Main sources: Saudi Arabia (typically 14 per cent of total), China (11 per cent), UAE (9 per cent).

Exports

Main exports include textiles (garments, bed linen, cotton cloth, and yarn), cotton, rice, leather goods, sports goods, chemicals, carpets and rugs, oil, natural gas and fertilisers.

Main destinations: US (typically 18 per cent of total), UAE (10 per cent), Afghanistan (7 per cent).

Agriculture

Farming

Agriculture represents around a quarter of GDP and is the driver of the economy, supplying food and raw materials for the manufacturing sector. Sustainable economic development requires long-term growth in agriculture. Main food crops include wheat, rice, maize, barley, millet, sorghum, sugar cane, tobacco, groundnuts, pulses, potatoes, onions, mangoes and citrus fruit. Cotton is the main cash crop and the largest foreign exchange earner, with productivity rising as greater use is made of insecticides. Rice is also an important export. Livestock production includes goats, sheep, cattle, buffaloes, pigs, donkeys, horses, mules, camels and poultry, and accounts for around 7.5 per cent of GDP, providing meat, eggs, dairy products, leather and wool, as well as draught power and fertiliser for cultivation. There are around 27 million hectares available for agriculture. Typically 26 per cent of agricultural land is given over to arable crops, while 6.25 per cent is permanent pasture. There are grazing difficulties in border regions, where Afghan refugees have brought about three million head of cattle with them.

The agricultural policies pursued by successive governments have traditionally been geared towards attaining self-sufficiency in the production of foodstuffs, increasing cash crop production and maximising foreign exchange earnings from the export of agricultural commodities such as cotton and rice. There was a record cotton crop harvested in 2004, which was attributed to an increase in area cultivated and productivity through the use of fertilisers.

In 2005, the government removed the 25 per cent import duty on imported raw and refined sugar. The removal was prompted by an expected shortfall of about a half a million tonnes in sugar. The sugar cane harvest was lower than expected as some farmers switched some land use over to cotton growing in expectation of higher profits, which resulted in local sugar prices rising sharply. Cane growers are critical of the poor condition of canals that provide an inadequate irrigation system, which currently hampers production. They are pressing for long-term investment to provide new dams and improve the canal network.

Owing to a shortage of unused cultivatable land, planners have concentratied on increased yields per hectare rather than an expansion of planted acreage. The government announced support for procurement prices for all major crops before sowing, and has encouraged farmers to adopt modern cultivation practices by providing them with subsidised inputs such as chemical fertilisers, pesticides and improved seed varieties. As the use of these inputs has become more popular and the government's budgetary constraints have become more pressing, these subsidies are gradually being phased out, but farmers are being compensated through rising crop prices.

The extended use of pesticides and fertilisers has been accompanied by a selective mechanisation of farm operations, facilitated by a liberal import policy for farm machinery and an expansion of domestic manufacturing capacity for the production of agricultural equipment. Mechanisation has become a routine operation for small farmers, who hire harvester's from richer farmers, and gain a higher yield in return. Farmers have called on the government to address the problems constraining the agricultural sector by allowing them a three-year remission period on their debts, deregulation, improving irrigation and water use and waiving tax and loan recovery in the areas worst hit by drought. Special attention is being given to the problems of small farmers who suffer mainly from a lack of finance. To alleviate this problem, the government has traditionally adopted a liberal stance towards the provision of rural credit, which is disbursed by the state-run Agricultural Development Bank of Pakistan (ADBP), commercial banks and co-operatives.

Fishing

Pakistan is largely self-sufficient in freshwater fish and seafood, with an active fishing fleet operating out of Karachi and on the Indus river. The typical annual fish catch is around 600,000 tonnes, of which 380,000 tonnes is through marine fishing. Around 87,000 tonnes of fish is exported, almost all of which is freshwater fish.

Forestry

Forests cover only 17,000 square kilometres, equivalent to 3 per cent of the country. A higher level of forestation is needed to improve the quality of the environment, reducing the severity of flooding and the impact of strong winds and sandstorms. The authorities have encouraged a growth in forests, with forest cover increasing by an average of 1.84 per cent per annum.

Industry and manufacturing

Industry contributes around 25 per cent to annual GDP, employing an estimated 17 per cent of the labour force.

Manufactured and semi-manufactured goods, mainly cotton textiles and garments, account for around 60 per cent of Pakistan's exports. The manufacturing sector depends on the agricultural sector for most of its raw materials: cotton for weaving, spinning and processing industries, leather and wool for handicrafts and carpet weaving. There is a growing emphasis on private sector development, with around 85 per cent of manufacturing output in private hands.

Tourism

Tourism has been slow to develop, hampered by lack of facilities and infrastructure as well as fears of terrorist attacks, hijackings and kidnappings which are endemic in some areas of the country. A large proportion of visitors tend to be overseas Pakistanis and their families. The improvement of relations with India resulted in the opening of borders and easing of movement between the two countries and there was an increase in the number of visitors from other Asian countries.

Environment

In its efforts to improve living standards for its citizens Pakistan has compromised environmental standards in favour of economic development. Hazardous chemicals, including agricultural run-off, industrial activity and vehicle emissions all add to pollution in general and water contamination in particular.

Mining

Pakistan has deposits of a wide range of minerals, including uranium, rock phosphate, gypsum, iron ore, copper, gold, silver, magnesium, chromite, antimony, barite, rock salt, sulphur, porcelain, china clays and gemstones.

The government is seeking to enhance the role of the mining sector, which has historically played a negligible role in the Pakistan economy. In the past, priority has been given to the further development of rock phosphate mining at Kakul in the North West Frontier Province and the establishment of copper and iron ore mines at Saindak and Nokundi in Baluchistan. These projects have been delayed by insufficient investment, economic inviability and the poor quality of reserves.

Pakistan typically produces nine million tonnes of limestone, 800,000 tonnes of rock salt, 300,000 tonnes of argonite and marble, 30,000 tonnes of barytes, 30,000 tonnes of soap stone, 15,000 tonnes of sulphur, 2–3,000 tonnes of bauxite and 23 tonnes of uranium per annum.

The militant Islamist Taliban, which took over control of the Swat Region and a centre of emerald mining in February 2009, reopened mines to all who agreed to abide by its rules. The projected yield of gemstones was 13.2 million carats. Concern is growing that profits from mining will be channelled into weapons purchases and jihad terrorism.

Hydrocarbons

Proven oil reserves were 289 million barrels per day (bpd) of oil in 2007, with production at 68.4 million bpd. Punjab and Sindh provinces provide all of Pakistan's oil output. However consumption was 390 million bpd in 2007 with the shortfall made up of imports. The government wants to reduce dependency on imports and has encouraged foreign investment to boost production and raise domestic capacity. Exploration is taking place both onshore and offshore. Pakistan has a total refinery capacity of 269,000bpd

The majority state-owned Pakistan Petroleum is the largest oil and gas exploration and production company.

Proven natural gas reserves were 0.85 trillion cubic metres (cum) at the end of 2008, with production at 37.5 billion cum, all of which is consumed domestically. Natural gas accounts for around half of Pakistan's energy requirements. A 2,700km pipeline from Iran to India via Pakistan has been under negotiation for several years but by 2009 Pakistan was unhappy about the gas pricing offered by Iran and was considering withdrawing from the project and was looking to import liquefied natural gas (LNG) from Qatar instead. The Ministry of Petroleum estimated that LNG would save on the US$7.4 billion cost of construction and maintenance of the pipeline.

The government has set up the Gas Regulatory Authority (GRA) and Petroleum Regulatory Board (PRB) to separate out government functions from state-owned entities that are in the process of being privatised.

Proven coal reserves were 1.9 billion tonnes in 2007, of which only one million is the commercially valuable anthracite, while the majority is brown coal, typically used in thermal power stations. Substantial new deposits, of higher quality coal, have been located in the Thar Desert region. In March 2009, the South Korean Pan Energy Development Company (Pedco) and the UAE's Bin Din Group signed agreements for a stake in coal blocks with an estimated 2.56 billion tonnes of coal reserves.

Energy

Total installed generating capacity was 19.4 gigawatts (GW) in 2006. In 2007, hydropower was 33 per cent of production with thermal power plants providing almost all of the remainder. There are plans to increase the share of alternative energy sources, such as solar and wind, to 10 per cent of the energy mix. The two nuclear power stations produce less than 1 per cent, with another coming online in 2010. Less than half the population is connected to the national grid and significant growth in demand is expected in the long-term. An extra 3,504MW is expected to be added to the national grid by the end of 2009, due to investment by the federal government as a commitment to reduce load shedding. Power will be generated principally from two new power plants Malakand III, 81MW, and Attock General Power plant, 165MW, plus efficiency gains at existing plants and 19 other smaller projects brought forward operationally.

Crippling power shortages that had sparked riots across Pakistan in 2009–10 resulted in government measures to reduce demand. As from April 2010 the weekend has been extended from one to two days and street markets are to close earlier, while government offices had their power cut by 50 per cent. The energy shortfall is estimated to be 3,668MW per day and the measures announced should save 1,500MW per day; businesses and domestic power will continue to be cut as the ailing power infrastructure fails to meet demand.

Much of the energy sector is owned by the state and dominated by two parastatal utility companies: the Water and Power Development Authority (Wapda) and the Karachi Electricity Supply Company (KESC), plus a number of small, independent power producers. KESC was sold to foreign investors in 2005, but with the government retaining a 26 per cent share in the company. Plans to privatise Wapda will follow its division into three generating and eight distribution companies and one transmission entity.

In July 2011 Iran agreed to sell 1,700MW of electricity to Pakistan at reduced rates, in an effort to overcome Pakistan's energy crisis. The Makran region already receives 35MW from Iran, but demand has increased sufficiently for an additional 70MW; the Gawadar Port will receive 100MW

Financial markets

Stock exchange

Karachi Stock Exchange (KSE)

Commodity exchange

National Commodities Exchange Limited (NCEL)

Banking and insurance

The banking sector is dominated by state-owned banks: the United Bank Ltd (UBL), Habib Bank Ltd (HBL) and the National Bank of Pakistan (NBP).

In June 2002, the Islamic bench of Pakistan's Supreme Court reversed a decision made in 1999 to outlaw charging interest on bank transactions as un-Islamic. The move came less than a week ahead of a deadline by which all financial institutions had to conform to an Islamic system of banking, which prohibits fixed rates of interest. If the measures had gone ahead, Pakistan would have become the first country to adopt a pure Islamic system. Banks had argued that full Islamicisation of the banking system would create chaos, leading to a possible collapse of the financial sector. Foreign banks were prepared to quit Pakistan if interest charging was abolished. International lenders were also wary of the changes, jeopardising Pakistan's ability to secure foreign loans.

Instead of converting to a fully Islamic financial system, Pakistan has effectively had to accept, at least in the medium-term, a dual system which allows Islamic and conventional banks to coexist. The problem facing Pakistan is the high level of non-performing loans (NPLs) in the banking system caused mainly by economic mismanagement in the past.

In September 2010 Moody's credit rating agency warned that there was a danger of a sharp increase in the number of non-performing loans after the flood crisis. Rural areas were initially hit, but with so many businesses affected it was felt that the formal economy could be undermined and impact onto the banking sector.

Central bank

State Bank of Pakistan

Main financial centre

Karachi

Time
GMT plus five hours

Geography
Pakistan is a wedge-shaped country bordering India to the east, China to the north-east, Afghanistan to the north and Iran to the west. Its southern boundary is the shore of the Arabian Sea.
Pakistan has some of the hottest deserts and highest mountains in the world. The areas north of the capital Islamabad are mountainous, with a temperate climate. The world's second-highest mountain, K-2 (8,611 metres), also known as Mount Godwin Austen, is located in the Karakoram Range, where the Himalayas meet the Hindu Kush.
The plains of the Punjab and Sindh, irrigated by the Indus river and its tributaries, are the main agricultural areas. Apart from its temperate Makran coast on the Arabian Sea, Baluchistan is a vast and mostly empty area of deserts and low bare hills.

Hemisphere
Northern

Climate
The terrain ranges from mountainous to desert, and the climate varies accordingly. It is cool in the mountains and foothills, with rain in summer and snow in winter, and hot in summer and cool in winter in plateau regions, with some rain in winter. The Indus valley experiences year-round heat, with extreme heat and dry winds in summer. Temperatures vary from an average of 15 degrees Celsius (C) in January to an average of 37 degrees C in May–July. Summer temperatures can rise as high as 50 degrees C in northern Sindh and eastern Baluchistan. The monsoon season lasts from mid-July–September when the average monthly rainfall amounts to 16cm. The best time for tourists to visit is between October and April.

Dress codes
Pakistan is an Islamic country where modesty in dress is the rule. The widely worn national dress is the *salwaar kameez*, a unisex combination of baggy shirt and trousers completely covering the arms and legs. Western-style suits are seen only in big cities. Tourists are advised to dress modestly, especially when outside cities like Karachi, Lahore and Islamabad. Women are expected to dress soberly and act discreetly and a headscarf is essential when visiting holy places.

Entry requirements

Passports
Required by all and must be valid for six months beyond date of visit.

Visa
Required by all. Business travellers must provide, an invitation or sponsorship from a local company or organisation; a business letter of intention from an employer; a full itinerary; proof of financial guarantee of maintenance and emergency repatriation and proof of return/onward passage, with their application form. See www.mofa.gov.pk and follow link to consular services for full details and embassy locations worldwide.
Visitors staying over 30 days must register with the District Foreigners Registration Office within 30 days of arrival; over-staying the visa allowance can be treated as a criminal offence. Indian and Afghan visitors must register within 24 hours of arrival.

Prohibited entry
Israeli passport holders.

Currency advice/regulations
The import and export of local currency is limited to Rp100, in denominations up to Rp10 only. The import and export of foreign currency is unlimited; on departure, only amounts up to Rp500 may be reconverted into foreign currency and only with official exchange receipts.
Travellers cheques, in US dollars or pound sterling, are accepted in banks and major shops and hotels (all other currencies may attract higher exchange rates.

Customs
Personal effects are allowed duty-free. Visitors are not permitted to import alcohol. Motor vehicles may be imported duty-free for a period of up to three months. Export of certain antiques may require a permit.

Prohibited imports
Firearms and ammunition (without a permit), obscene and subversive publications. Fruit and plants may be destroyed to prevent agricultural diseases entering the country.

Health (for visitors)

Mandatory precautions
A vaccination certificate is required for yellow fever and cholera, if travelling from an infected area.

Advisable precautions
Inoculations and booster shots should be current for cholera, tetanus, hepatitis A, diphtheria, and typhoid. There may be a need for vaccinations for polio, tuberculosis, hepatitis B, Japanese B encephalitis and meningitis.
Use malaria prophylaxis (which will also provide protection for hepatitis B and encephalitis) including mosquito repellents, sleeping nets and clothing that cover the body after dark. There is a risk of rabies. Use only bottled or boiled water for drinks, washing teeth and making ice. Eat only well cooked meals, preferably served hot; vegetables should be cooked and fruit peeled. Avoid uncooked dairy products and salad, and food from street vendors. Healthcare facilities outside Islamabad and Karachi are limited, medical insurance is essential including emergency evacuation. A supply of any regular medicines required should be taken, with their prescription details and a full first-aid kit would be useful.

Hotels
There are modern hotels in major centres; price and quality can vary substantially and advanced booking is advised and a check of reservation before departure.
A 17.5 per cent room tax is added to bills; further tipping optional.

Credit cards
Major credit cards are accepted in limited outlets. ATMs are found in city centres and at airports.

Public holidays (national)

Fixed dates
23 Mar (Pakistan Day), 1 May (May Day), 14 Aug (Independence Day), 9 Nov (Iqbal Day), 25 Dec (Birthday of Qaid-i-Azam/Christmas).

Variable dates
Eid al Adha (two days), Eid al Fitr (three days), Islamic New Year, Ashura (two days), Birth of the Prophet.

Islamic year 1433 (26 Nov 2011–14 Nov 2012): The Islamic year contains 354 or 355 days, with the result that Muslim feasts advance by 10–12 days against the Gregorian calendar. Dates of feasts vary according to the sightings of the new moon, so cannot be forecast exactly.

Working hours
As from April 2010 the weekend was extended from one to two days and street markets closed earlier.

Banking
Mon–Thu and Sat: 0900–1330; Fri: 0900–1230.

Business
Mon–Thu and Sat: 0900–1700; Fri: 0900–1230, 1430–1700.

Government
Mon–Thu and Sat: 0900–1700; Fri: 0900–1230.

Shops
Sat–Thu: 0800/0900–1800/1900.

Electricity supply
220–240V AC, with two or three-pin round plug fittings.

Weights and measures
Metric system (local units are also in use).

Social customs/useful tips
It is customary to shake hands on meeting and taking leave; business cards are exchanged after introductions. Business appointments should be made in advance. The attitude to punctuality is variable. Visits during Ramadan should be avoided. Visitors should make themselves familiar with local customs and care should be

taken to respect Muslim conventions. For instance, only use the right hand when shaking hands and passing or receiving anything.

Security

Visitors should keep in touch with regional conditions as any increase in political tensions might affect travel advice. Personal security arrangements should be thoroughly considered throughout a visit.

There is a risk from indiscriminate attacks and sectarian violence, including tribal killings, armed car-jacking, robbery, kidnap, murder and bombings in public places such as markets, offices and public transport. Although these may not be aimed at foreigners, there is always a risk of being caught up in such attacks.

Large-scale demonstrations that become violent can occur, throughout Pakistan, at short notice. Visitors should monitor local media and avoid any demonstrations announced or gatherings encountered.

There is also a threat of criminal violence, including theft, burglary and the kidnapping of businessmen, especially in Karachi. Visitors of visibly western origin should not linger in public places. In major towns, especially Karachi, visitors should confine themselves to business areas, and avoid the back streets and bazaars.

Avoid long road journeys (except between major cities), cross-country journeys, and non-essential travel to the border areas of Afghanistan and India (Kashmir province). If visitors must travel to these regions, contact with Pakistani authorities should be made in advance. Police protection may be arranged, as necessary; advice about a No Objection Certificate (issued by the Pakistani Ministry of Foreign Affairs) can also be obtained.

Getting there

Air

National airline: Pakistan International Airlines (PIA)

International airport/s: Karachi International (Jinnah International) Airport (KHI), 12km north-east of Karachi; duty-free and tax-free shops, bar, restaurant, buffet, bank, hotel reservations, post office, shops.

Other airport/s: Lahore (LHE), 3km south-east of Lahore; restaurant, bank, post office, shops, car hire; Peshawar (PEW), 4km from Peshawar; Islamabad International (ISB), 8km from Islamabad; restaurant, car hire, banks, post office.

Airport tax: Departure tax: Rp400–800 (cash only), amount depends on airport; transit passengers are exempt.

Surface

Road: Generally in poor condition. There is access via India (Amritsar-Lahore) and China (the 805km Karakoram Highway serving Sinkiang Province-Islamabad and Rawalpindi via the Khunjerab Pass), plus road connections to Iran. The route from China is open to foreigners, but not to most Pakistanis.

Routes from Afghanistan (via Qandhar-Chaman-Quetta or Kabul-Peshawar), are closed following the fighting in that country.

Rail: A line runs from Iran (Zahedan-Naukundi-Quetta).

The train service between Pakistan and India was restored in 2004 – one train a week between Lahore in Pakistan and Attari in India.

Water: There are some ferry services from Bombay, although these are not widely used.

Main port/s: Karachi and Bin Qasim (south-east of Karachi).

Getting about

National transport

Air: Four carriers operate daily flights to 37 cities, providing better access than other forms of travel.

Road: The 800km Karakoram Highway permits entry to northern areas. The only multi-lane road is a two-lane highway linking Karachi and Peshawar. Although a new network of highways has greatly facilitated inter-city road travel, it can still be long, hot and harrowing. Avoid travelling at night on mountain roads in northern areas.

Buses: The air-conditioned Flying Coach national buses running between main centres (hourly between Lahore and Rawalpindi) are recommended over the local buses, which are colourful but not very reliable. Seats should be booked in advance.

Rail: There is an extensive rail network with over 8,775km of track, but it is slow and somewhat dilapidated. It is not suited to the business traveller working to a tight timetable. The main route runs Karachi-Lahore-Rawalpindi-Peshawar, with three classes. Certain services include air-conditioning, restaurant cars, sleeping cars, ice containers and women only accommodation. Advance booking is generally advisable, and is essential for some services.

Water: Although the Indus is unnavigable in many places, there are some passenger boats operating on certain stretches, which are recommended more for tourism than commercial travel.

City transport

Business travellers are advised to avoid arriving in Karachi at night and to ensure they are met at the airport.

Taxis: Taxis can be hired at all big hotels, and provide the most practical way for visitors to travel in cities. It is advisable to keep the taxi for the return trip as taxis do not usually cruise looking for passengers and there are not many taxi stands. Waiting costs are low, especially when compared to the time and trouble the traveller would face in looking for another taxi. Hotel taxi drivers are more likely to speak at least some English than those from taxi stands. Metered taxis are painted black and yellow, although the meter may not be used. Tipping normally 10 per cent.

Car hire

Self-drive and chauffeur-driven car hire is available, and minibuses may be hired. Driving is on the left-hand side of the road. National licence and international driving permit required.

BUSINESS DIRECTORY

The addresses listed below are a selection only. While World of Information makes every endeavour to check these addresses, we cannot guarantee that changes have not been made, especially to telephone numbers and area codes. We would welcome any corrections.

Telephone area codes

The international direct dialling (IDD) code for Pakistan is +92 followed by area code and subscriber's number:

Faisalabad	41	Multan	61
Gujranwala	431	Peshawar	91
Hyderabad	221	Quetta	81
Islamabad	51	Rawalpindi	51
Karachi	21	Sialkot	432
Lahore	42	Sukkur	71

Useful telephone numbers

Karachi

Police: 222-222/224-400
Fire: 74-891
Ambulance: 73-259/70-600
International calls: 0102
Calls to India, Bangladesh, China: 102
To check on booked call: 0104

Islamabad

Police: 23-333
Fire: 27-222
International call: 109
To check on booked call: 103

All places

Directory enquiries: 17

Chambers of Commerce

American Business Council of Pakistan, NIC Building, PO Box 1322, Abbasi Shaheed Road, Karachi 74400 (tel: 567-6436; fax: 566-0135; email: abcpak@cyber.net.pk).

Federation of Pakistan Chambers of Commerce and Industries, Federation House, Sharea Firdousi, Main Clifton Road, Karachi 75600 (tel: 587-3691; fax: 587-4332; email: info@fpcci.com.pk).

Hyderabad Chamber of Commerce and Industry, PO Box 99, Aiwan-e-Tijarat,

Saddar, Hyderabad (email: hcci@paknet3.ptc.pk).

Islamabad Chamber of Commerce and Industry, Aiwan-e-Sanat-o-Tijarat, Islamabad (tel: 225-0526; fax: 225-2950; email: icci@brain.net.pk).

Karachi Chamber of Commerce and Industry, PO Box 4158, Aiwan-e-Tijarat, Karachi 74000 (tel: 241-6091; fax: 241-6095; email: info@karachichamber.com).

Lahore Chamber of Commerce and Industry, 11 Sharah-e-Aiwan-eTijarat, Lahore (tel: 630-5538; fax: 636-8854; email: sect@lcci.org.pk).

Quetta Chamber of Commerce and Industry, PO Box 117, Zarghoon Road, Quetta (tel: 824-857; fax: 821-948; email: qcci@hotmail.com).

Rawalpindi Chamber of Commerce and Industry, Chamber House, 108 Adamjee Road, Rawalpindi (tel: 556-6238; fax: 558-6849; email: chamber@rcci.org.pk).

Overseas Investors Chamber of Commerce and Industry, Chamber of Commerce Building, Talpur Rd, Karachi (tel: 241-0814; fax: 242-7313; email: oicci@global.net.pk).

Banking

Allied Bank of Pakistan, Khayaban-e-Iqbal, Main Clifton Road, Bath Island, Karachi (tel: 567-8155; fax: 568-3312, 568-0134).

Federal Bank for Co-operative, 85-W, Rizwan Centre, Blue Area, PO Box 1218, Islamabad (tel: 81-2469).

Faysal Bank, PO Box 472, 11/13 Trade Centre, I. I. Chundrigar Road, Karachi (tel: 263-8011-20; fax: 263-7975).

Habib Bank, Habib Bank Plaza, 1.1 Chundrigar Road, Karachi (tel: 241-8000/8034; fax: 241-4191).

Industrial Development Bank of Pakistan, State Life Building 2, Off 1.1. Chundrigar Road, Wallace Road, Karachi (tel: 241-9160/9168; fax: 241-1990).

Metropolitan Bank, PO Box 1289, Spencer's Building, I.I. Chundrigar Road, Karachi (tel: 263-6740; fax: 263-0404/5).

Muslim Commercial Bank, Adamjee House, 1.1 Chundrigar Road, Karachi 74000 (tel: 241-4090/9, 241-4110/9; fax: 241-3116).

National Bank of Pakistan, 1.1 Chundrigar Rd, Karachi (tel: 241-6789; fax: 241-6769).

United Bank, 1.1 Chundrigar Road, PO Box 4306, Karachi (tel: 2417100; fax: 243-7068).

Central bank

State Bank of Pakistan, PO Box 4456, I.I Chundrigar Road, Karachi 74000 (tel: 111-727-111; fax: 921-2440; email: info@sbp.org.pk).

Stock exchange

Karachi Stock Exchange (KSE): www.kse.com.pk

Stock exchange 2

Lahore Stock Exchange: www.lahorestock.com

Commodity exchange

National Commodities Exchange Limited (NCEL): www.ncel.com.pk

Travel information

Aero Asia, Karachi (tel: 778-3476, 778-3033).

Automobile Association of West Pakistan, 8 Multan Rd, PO Box 76, Lahore.

Karachi Automobile Association (KAA), Standard Insurance House, 1 Chundrigar Rd, Karachi 0226 (tel: 232-173).

Pakistan International Airlines (PIA), PIA Bldg, Quaid-e-Azam International Airport, Karachi 75200 (tel: 412-011; fax: 772-7727, 457-0419).

Ministry of tourism

Ministry of Culture and Tourism, 13-T/U, Comm Area, F-7/2, Islamabad (tel: 27-023).

National tourist organisation offices

Pakistan Tourism Development Corporation, House 2, St 61, F-7/4, PO Box 1465, Islamabad 44000 (tel: 811-001/2/3/4; fax: 824-173).

Ministries

Ministry of Commerce, Industry and Production, Block A, Pakistan Secretariat, Islamabad (tel: 921-0277; fax: 920-5241; email: mincom@meganet.com.pk).

Ministry of Communications and Railways, Block D, Pakistan Secretariat, Islamabad (tel: 920-1252; fax: 920-6171).

Ministry of Culture, Sports, Minority Affairs and Youth, College Road, Shalimar 7/2, Islamabad (tel: 921-3121; fax: 922-1863).

Ministry of Defence, Pakistan Secretariat No II, Rawalpindi 46000 (tel: 927-1114; fax: 927-1115).

Ministry of Education, Block D, Pakistan Secretariat, Islamabad (tel: 920-1401; fax: 920-2851; email: pak@yahoo.com).

Ministry of the Environment, Local Government, Rural Development, Labour, Manpower and Overseas Pakistanis, Islamabad (tel: 922-4579; fax: 920-2211; email: envir@isb.compol.com).

Ministry of Finance, Revenues, Economic Affairs, Planning and Development, and Statistics,Block Q, Pakistan Secretariat, Islamabad (tel:920-3687; fax: 921-3780; email: finance@isb.paknet.com.pk).

Ministry of Food, Agriculture & Livestock, Block B, Pakistan Secretariat, Islamabad (tel: 920-3307; fax: 922-1246).

Ministry of Foreign Affairs, Constitution Avenue, Islamabad (tel: 921-0335; fax: 920-4205; email: pak.fm@usa.net).

Ministry of Health, Block C, Pakistan Secretariat, Islamabad (tel: 921-1622; fax: 920-5481; email: sehat@apollo.net.pk).

Ministry of Information and Ministry Development, Cabinet Block, Pakistan Secretariat, Islamabad (tel: 920-7314; fax: 920-2448; email: dgep@isb.comsats.net.pk)

Ministry of the Interior, Block R, Pakistan Secretariat, Islamabad (tel: 921-0086; fax: 920-1472).

Ministry of Kashmir Affairs, Northern Affairs, States and Frontier Region, Housing and Works, Block R, Pakistan Secretariat, Islamabad (tel: 920-3032; fax: 920-2494; email: safron@isb.perd.net.pk).

Ministry of Law, Justice, Human Rights and Parliamentary Affairs, Islamabad (tel: 921-0062; fax: 920-2628; email: molaw@comsats.net.pk).

Ministry of Petroleum and Natural Resources, Block A, Pakistan Secretariat, Islamabad (tel: 921-1220; fax: 920-1770; email: info@mpnr.gov.pk).

Ministry of Religious Affairs, Zakat and Usher, Plot 20, Ramna-6, Islamabad (tel: 920-1909; fax: 920-1646; email: mara@paknet.ptc.pk).

Ministry of Science and Technology, Shaheed-e-Millat Secretariat, Islamabad (tel: 920-8026; fax: 920-2603; email: minister@most.gov.pk).

Office of the President, Constitution Avenue, Islamabad (tel: 922-0136; fax: 920-3938; email: psecyp@isb.paknet.com.pk).

Office of the Chief Executive, Islamabad (tel: 922-2666; fax: 920-4632).

Other useful addresses

All-Pakistan Textile Mills Association, 44-A Lalazar, Off MT Khan Rd, PO Box 5446, Karachi (tel: 552-296).

Asian Development Bank, Pakistan Resident Mission, Overseas Pakistani Foundation (OPF) Building, Sharah-e-Jamhuriyat, G-52, Islamabad (tel: 825-011; fax: 823-324; email: adbpim@mail.asiandevbank.org).

Board of Investment, Saudi Pak Tower, 61-A Jinnah Ave, PO BOx 3100, Islamabad (tel: 817-165/2, 218-267/6; fax: 217-665, 215-554, 263-9580).

British High Commission, Diplomatic Enclave, Ramna 5, PO Box 1122, Islamabad (tel: 822-131/5; fax: 826-217).

British Deputy High Commission, York Place, Clifton, Karachi 6 (tel: 532-041/6; fax: 587-4014).

British Trade Office, 65 Mozang Road, PO Box 1679, Lahore (tel: 631-6589/90; fax: 631-6591).

Export Promotion Bureau, Government of Pakistan, Block A, Finance & Trade Centre, Sharea Faisal, Karachi (tel: 566-0305/9; fax: 566-0300, 568-0422/4010).

Institute of Marketing Management, 68-B Block 2, PECHS, Karachi (tel: 455-8365).

Islamabad Stock Exchange (tel: 215-047/50).

Karachi Cotton Association, Cotton Exchange Bldg, 1.1 Chundrigar Rd, Karachi (tel: 241-0336/2570).

Karachi Stock Exchange (Guarantee) Ltd, Stock Exchange Bldg, Stock Exchange Rd, Karachi 2 (tel: 242-5501/2/3/4/5; fax: 241-0825).

Lahore Stock Exchange (tel: 636-8000, 636-8333).

Oil Companies Advisory Committee, 5th Floor, Karim Chambers, Mereweather Rd, Karachi (tel: 568-2246/8).

Pakistan Art Silk Fabrics & Garments Exporters Association, 204 Amber Estate, Shahrah-e-Faisal, Karachi (tel: 360-919, 368-488).

Pakistan Cotton Association, 5 Amber Court, Shaheed-e-Millat Rd, Karachi (tel: 438-461).

Pakistan Embassy (USA), 2315 Massachusetts Avenue, NW, Washington DC 20008 (tel: (+1-202) 939-6200; fax: (+1-202) 387-0484; email: parepwashington@erols.com).

Pakistan Fruit & Vegetables Exporters, Importers & Manufacturers Association, 8 New Onion & Potato Market, University Rd, Karachi (tel: 493-7126, 493-125).

Pakistan Handicrafts Manufacturers & Exporters Association, MA Jinnah Rd, Karachi (tel: 772-8121).

Pakistan Shipowners Association, Ralli Brothers Bldg, Talpur Rd, Karachi (tel: 242-7154).

Privatisation Commission, Government of Pakistan, 5A Constitution Avenue, EAC Building, Islamabad (tel: 920-5146; fax: 920-3076, 921-1692; email: info@privatisation.gov.pk).

Sindh Coal Authority, F-158/A-I, Block 5, Clifton, Karachi (tel: 583-3549, 583-3550; fax: 587-4708).

National news agency: Associated Press of Pakistan (APP), 18 Mauve Area, G-7/1, Islamabad (Tel: 220-3064–67; email: news@app.com.pk; internet: www.app.com.pk) (state run).

Internet sites

Gateway site for official and media information: www.islamabad.net

Karachi Airport: www.karachiairport.com

Pakistan argricultural information: www.pakissan.com

Pakistan Government Homepage: www.pak.gov.pk

Pakistan Yellow pages: www.jamal.com

Trade index of Pakistan: www.PakistanBiz.com

UK trade export site: www.tradepartners.gov.uk

Palau

KEY FACTS

Official name: Belu'u era Belau (Republic of Palau)

Head of State: President Johnson Toribiong (from 15 Jan 2009)

Head of government: President Johnson Toribiong (from 15 Jan 2009)

Ruling party: Members of the national congress sit as independents

Area: 380 square km

Population: 20,000 (2010)*

Capital: Melekeok, on Ngerekebesand Island, since 2006 (Koror: commercial centre)

Official language: English on all islands; there are four officially recognised dialects (Palauan, Sonsoralese, Tobi, Angaur – on Angaur, Japanese is also included as official)

Currency: US dollar (US$) = 100 cents

GDP per capita: US$8,911 (2008)

GDP real growth: 0.50% (2010)

GDP: US$197.60 million (2009)

Inflation: 3.80% (2010)

* estimated figure

Tourism accounts for about half of Palau's gross domestic product (GDP). In 2010, after four years of contraction, there was growth of about 2.0 per cent following on improved advertising and promotion. The combination of a new airline and charter connections led to an increase in arrivals of 11.7 per cent as the global economy recovered. Growth in visitor numbers from Japan and Taiwan was particularly strong.

Palau's grants from the US under the Compact of Free Association will cease in 2024 – it is therefore important to gradually reduce current expenditure to more sustainable levels. The original budget for 2010 seemed to mark a start in this process by reducing public expenditure by some 10 per cent, however, according to the Asian Development Bank, a supplementary budget later reversed the spending cuts, restoring current expenditure to the 2009 level. In the coming years the government will have to bite the bullet and make cuts in particular to wage bills in the public service and purchases of goods and services. An increase in utility charges will also be unpopular, but necessary.

Maintaining growth in the tourism sector is vital for the island's survival. Visitor arrivals performed well in the first quarter of 2011 and are projected to increase by around 7.0 per cent for the whole year. This will feed through to GDP growth of 2.0 per cent in 2011 and 1.5 per cent in 2012.

COUNTRY PROFILE

Historical profile

1686 Spain claimed the Caroline Islands, including Palau.
1783 A British landing on Palau inaugurated a century of trading links.
1885 The Spanish claim to the Caroline Islands was upheld by the Pope.
1899 Spain sold the islands to Germany.
1914 Japan occupied the islands.
1947 Palau became part of the Trust Territory of the Pacific Islands, administered by the US under an UN trusteeship mandate.
1978 Palau voted against becoming a part of the Federated States of Micronesia.
1980 Palau adopted its own constitution in July.
1981 Palau became the Republic of Palau with Haruo Remeliik as its first president.
1982 A Compact of Free Association with the US (CFA) was signed.
1985 President Remeliik was assassinated in June. Lazarus Salii was elected president in September.
1987 Palau voted to amend its constitution to allow approval of the CFA by a simple majority.
1988 The Palau Supreme Court ruled the constitutional change invalid on procedural grounds. President Salii committed suicide in August. Ngiratkel Etpiison elected president in November.
1989 Agreements with the US provided aid for paying off foreign debt and funds for new development.
1992 Kuniwo Nakamura became president.
1993 Palau voted in a referendum to adopt the CFA.
1994 Palau became an independent republic under the CFA.
1996 President Kuniwo Nakamura was re-elected.
2000 Tommy Remengesau became president.
2003 A new airport terminal, costing US$16 million, was completed.
2004 Incumbent Tommy Remengesau was re-elected president.
2006 The government began relocation to the new capital of Melekeok, on Babeldaob Island. Some departments such as the police, immigration and customs remained on Koror, still the largest settlement. The Pacific Savings Bank (PSB) collapsed. Following an independent investigation criminal charges were brought against all of the PSB's board of directors and senior managers. US$1.5 million was lost from pension deposits in the uninsured PSB.
2007 Convictions were achieved in Palau's first case of human trafficking.
2008 In parliamentary elections all candidates stood as independents. In presidential elections Johnson Toribiong was elected as incumbent Tommy Remengesau was required to stand down.
2009 An agreement between the US and Palau resulted in 17 ethnic Uighurs, originally from China and held in the

US-detention prison in Guantanamo Military Base as suspected Islamist terrorists, were resettled in Palau.
2010 A new airline, Pacific Flier, began operations in April with a direct air link between Palau and Brisbane, Australia. Other destinations include The Philippines and Guam. On 21 July, the first resident ambassador to Palau, Helen Reed-Rowe, presented her credentials to the US Senate Foreign Relations Committee (in Washington) for approval. On 30 July negotiations between the US and Palau over the amount to be given by the US under the CFA was in contention as Palauan officials objected to the aspect of micro-managing the US proposed would impose before paying US$250 million in assistance for the period 2010–25. However the US remained firm in its proposals.
2011 By 11 March, Palau had received a total of US$12.6 million in grants from the US, UN, South Korea and Taiwan, to be used in road and civic projects, health services and programmes, a tourist rest centre and the Palau Congress Project. A state of emergency was declared at the end of September due to the lack of fresh water for its residents. The New Zealand Red Cross and Australian authorities responded by delivering personnel and supplies.

Political structure

Constitution
The constitution was promulgated in January 1981.
Each state has a governor.
A council of chiefs advises the government on matters of traditional law and custom.
Voting: universal suffrage over 18 years.
Form of state
Republic, in free association with the US.
The executive
The president is head of state and head of government, elected for a four-year term by popular vote. Presidents may stand for only two terms.
National legislature
The bicameral Olbiil Era Kelulau (OEK) (National Congress) comprises a nine-seat Senate (upper chamber) and a 16-member House of Delegates (lower chamber); both elected by popular vote for four-year terms.
Legal system
The legal system is based on Trust Territory laws, acts of the legislature, municipal, common and customary laws.
Last elections
4 November 2008 (presidential and parliamentary)
Results: Presidential: Johnson Toribiong won 51 per cent of the vote, Elias Camsek Chin won 49 per cent.
Parliamentary: non-partisans were elected – no political parties exist.
Next elections
2012 (presidential and parliamentary)

Political parties

There are no political parties.
Ruling party
Members of the National Congress sit as independents
Political situation
Palau's largest foreign earnings come from tourism, remittances and revenue from the Compact of Free Association (commonly referred to as the Compact) which Palau has with the US. And while the Compact brings in a regular income each year, it is capped and extra income from the other two are subject to the mercy of external pressures and vagaries. Added to which frequent disasters caused by hurricanes snap up any reserves that may be around. No matter how detailed Palau's economic plans are, they are always prone to external disruption and as such the government has poor a track record for steady fiscal management.
In 2010, former president, Tommy Remengesau, declared the Palau was over governed, with one national and 16 state governments for 20,000 people. Perhaps this is why the aid package of US$250 million offered by the US for 2010–25 was rejected by Palau in July 2010. In exchange for the aid, the US insisted in more input in Palauan economic matters. This was rejected by Palau negotiators, saying the US wanted to micromanage Palauan affairs and didn't acknowledge the Palau was a sovereign nation.
Palau is divided between those that call for complete independence and accepting the country's debt liabilities, and those content to stay with the *status quo*, even if that means losing a little more independence to the US.

Population

20,000 (2010)*
Last census: 1 April 2006: 19,907
Population density: 45 inhabitants per square km (2010)
Annual growth rate: 1.6 per cent 1994–2004 (WHO 2006)
Ethnic make-up
Palauan (Micronesian with Malayan and Melanesian mixtures) 70 per cent; Asian (Filipinos, Chinese, Taiwanese and Vietnamese) 28 per cent; white 2 per cent.
Religions
Predominantly Christian, although one third of the population practise an indigenous religion known as Modekngei.

Education

The school system of Palau follows that of the US. Education is compulsory until the age of 14. Palauian and English are taught in schools, but English has gradually become the main instruction medium. There were 22 elementary schools, one high school, seven private schools and one community college. Around 94 per cent of school-aged children attend school and 97 per cent complete elementary school. The completion rate for high school students is 78 per cent.

Health

Only around 75 per cent of the population have access to medical facilities.
Life expectancy: 68 years, 2004 (WHO 2006)
Fertility rate/Maternal mortality rate: 1.4 births per woman, 2004 (WHO 2006)
Child (under 5 years) mortality rate (per 1,000): 23 per 1,000 live births (World Bank)

Welfare

There is no social welfare system.

Main cities

Koror (capital, population 13,027 in 2005), Meyuns (1,210).

Languages spoken

Local languages and Japanese spoken in some states.
Official language/s
English on all islands; there are four officially recognised dialects (Palauan, Sonsoralese, Tobi, Angaur – on Angaur, Japanese is also included as official)

Media

Press
The Government Media Office publishes the *Palau Gazette* monthly.
Dailies: In English *Marianas Variety* and the *Independent* published abroad but read in Palau. Regional online newspaper *Pacific Magazine* (www.pacificmagazine.net).
Weeklies: In English *Tia Belau*, *Palau Horizon*; in Palau *Roureur Belau*. These are independent local publications. Regional, online *Inside Oceania* (www.insideoceania.com)
Broadcasting
Radio: In Palau and English, Eco Paradise FM, is government-operated; T8AA radio station, WWFM and KRFM, and a Christian religious broadcaster (High Adventure Ministries), are independent.
Television: Over 90 per cent of households have cable television, there are no local or regional TV broadcasts. Island Cable Television ((www.palaunet.com/CableTV.asp) is the only cable provider.
News agencies
Palau National Communications Corporation (PNCC), PO Box 99, Koror, Palau 96940 (tel: 587-9900; email:

edcarter@palaunet.com; internet: www.palaunet.com)
ABC Pacific Beat: www.radioaustralia.net.au/pacbeat
Pacific Magazine: www.pacificmagazine.net

Economy
Palau has one of the highest standards of living in the Pacific and is classified as a middle-income country.
Since the end of Japanese occupation in 1945, the US has retained control over defence and foreign policy matters in return for several hundred million dollars in aid over 15 years (1994–2009). Of the US$630 million guaranteed under the Compact of Free Association with the US, US$70 million was placed in an investment fund, to provide a US$5 million boost to the annual budget.
The economy is based on agriculture and fishing, with a growing tourism sector based on sailing, scuba diving and sports-fishing.
Foreign fishing vessels (mainly from Japan and Taiwan) pay royalties to fish in Palau's Exclusive Economic Zone. The government is investigating alleged use of the territory for money laundering activities.
A two-lane highway, Compact Road, around the main island, Babeldaob, is an important addition to Palau's infrastructure and basis for economic growth. With the road's completion, all Palau's major public infrastructure projects that started after the signing of the Compact in 1994 were concluded.

External trade
Palau is a member of the South Pacific Regional Trade and Economic Co-operation Agreement (Sparteca) along with 12 other regional nations, which allows products duty free access by Pacific Island Forum members to Australian and New Zealand markets (subject to country of origin restrictions). Palau has become a major investment destination for Chinese entrepreneurs wishing to benefit from its unlimited access to US markets.
Commercial fishing licences for foreign trawlers have become an important source of foreign earnings.

Imports
Principal imports are machinery and equipment, manufactured goods, fuels, metals, live animals and foodstuffs.
Main sources: US (Guam), Japan, Singapore, Taiwan.

Exports
Main exports include shellfish, tuna, copra and garments, which have become a major export following investment by Chinese firms, eager to take advantage of Palau's access to the US market.
Main destinations: US, Japan, Singapore

Agriculture
Farming
Agriculture accounts for around 1 per cent of GDP, with farming accounting for around 0.5 per cent. Subsistence farming of taro, bananas, sweet potatoes, tapioca and vegetables, with pig and poultry raising, is the main occupation. Commercial farming is practised where climate and soils are favourable. Land is parcelled into an estimated 20,000 holdings; a Land Commission maintains a register to provide security of land tenure for Palauan citizens.

Fishing
Fishing supplies the principal source of protein and export revenues. Fishing revenue is valuable because of the sale of fishing licences to large foreign fleets, permitting them to fish within Palau's Exclusive Economic Zone.
In April 2010 the Parties to the Nauru Agreement (PNA) (eight island states including Palau) collectively agreed to close to *purse seine* fishing in 4.55 million square kilometres of high seas in their area, from 1 January 2011, to vessels licensed to fish in their waters. The area involved stretches from Palau and Papua New Guinea in the west to Kiribati in the east, from the Marshall Islands in the north to Tuvalu in the south; it holds an estimated 25 per cent of the world's tuna supply.
On 12 April 2011, a summit of the Parties to the Nauru Agreement (PNA) concluded its strategy for a policy of sustainable fishing in the Pacific. The PNA treaty, which was established in 1989 and expires in 2012, is seen as in need of an overhaul. As a collective region (FSM, Kiribati, Marshall Islands, Nauru, Palau, PNG, Solomon Islands and Tuvalu) control around 25–30 per cent of world stocks of tuna. Only 5 per cent of sales revenue is returned to the PNA and ministers called for specific changes, including an increased share of profits, PNA crews on-board *purse seine* vessels (minimum 10 per cent), conservation and management measures including a limit to fish trapping (fish aggregating devices (FADs)), net mesh rules and the establishment of an observer agency and fisheries information management system.

Industry and manufacturing
Small-scale industries include handicrafts, garments, fish processing, bottling, bakeries and boat building. Industry typically represents around 7–9 per cent of GDP, but has been boosted by on-going activity in the construction industry to around 15 per cent.

Tourism
Tourism is Palau's principal economic activity. It caters largely to the Asian market, most visitors coming from Taiwan and Japan. Arrivals, which had shown healthy growth in the mid-1990s, peaking at 73,719 in 1997, fell sharply from 1998 as a result of the economic recession, followed by the depreciation of the Japanese yen against the US dollar in 2000–02 and the 11 September 2001 terrorist attacks in the US. Despite the outbreaks of SARS in 2003 and dengue fever in 2004, the sector has recovered, recording 83,041 tourist arrivals in 2004.

Hydrocarbons
Fossil fuel makes up for around 85 per cent of Palau's energy requirements. Currently, Palau relies on the import of hydrocarbons from the US to meet its requirements.
A round of oil exploration licensing began in May 2009, with the assistance of the World Bank.

Energy
Installed generating capacity of 10MW is produced from hydropower, providing 30 million kilowatt hours per year. Diesel-fired generators also provide electricity. The Palau Utilities Corporation (PUC) is responsible for generation and supply of electricity
In 2008, as the implementation of national electrification, based on solar-photovoltaic systems, was about to begin PUC participated in technical training workshops run by Pacific Power Association (PPA) and E8 (utility companies from G8 countries offering help and sponsorship in renewable energies).
Long term considerations include ocean thermal energy conversion (otec) exchanges, proposed by the World Energy Council, to produce around 3,000kW of electricity, rising to 30,000kW as the project expands. However overseas sponsorship, necessary to develop the exchange plant, remains unavailable.

Banking and insurance
Palau has a well-developed banking sector with 12 commercial banks in operation and one development bank, several of which are representative offices of US or Asian corporations. US banks are dominant, holding around 80 per cent of deposits. The main banks are the Bank of Guam and the Bank of Hawaii.

Time
GMT plus ten hours

Geography
Palau consists of more than 200 islands in a chain about 650km (400 miles) long, lying about 7,150km (4,450 miles) south-west of Hawaii and about 1,160km

(720 miles) south of Guam. Together with the Federated States of Micronesia, Palau forms the archipelago of the Caroline Islands.

Babeldaob is the largest island in Palau, and in the centre of its east coast is the new site for the capital, Melekeok, (relocation began on 7 October 2006) and is home to Lake Ngardok, the largest body of freshwater (5 square km) in Palau; Meyuns, the second largest settlement, is also located on the northern shore, and the international airport is in the south. Koror Island (still with the largest settlement, Koror) is connected to Malakal Island (location of Koror's port) by two land bridges and a man-made bridge to Babeldaob Island.

The islands are composed largely of volcanic and limestone rock with coral reefs encircling the inhabited islands. The tallest peaks are on Babeldaob and Koror, with elevations of 217 metres (m) and 628m, respectively.

Hemisphere

Northern

Climate

Warm and humid, with temperatures between 23–30 degrees Celsius and humidity around 80 per cent. Rainfall (variable, minimum 250 mm/year), can occur in downpours. Typhoons are possible.

Entry requirements

Passports

Required by all. US citizens may visit with photo ID, however all US nationals require a passport for re-entry to the US from January 2007).

Visa

Required by all and issued by travel agent or airline for visits up to 30 days with proof of return/onward passage and adequate funds for maintenance. Extended entry permits are issued on application to Chief of Immigration, Bureau of Legal Affairs, Ministry of Justice, PO Box 100, Koror, Palau 96940.

Special regulations may apply to some non-tourist destinations within the islands.

Currency advice/regulations

No restrictions on import and export of local and foreign currency. Foreign currency over US$5,000 must be declared.

Prohibited imports

Illegal drugs and weapons

Health (for visitors)

Mandatory precautions

Cholera and yellow fever immunisations are required for those arriving from infected areas.

Advisable precautions

Vaccination for diphtheria, TB, hepatitis A and B, polio, tetanus and typhoid are recommended. There is a rabies risk.

Hospitals often expect immediate cash payment for medical treatment.

Hotels

There are hotels and guest-houses in Melekeok, Koror, Peliliu and Angaur.

Credit cards

Major credit cards are widely accepted at main visitor facilities.

Public holidays (national)

Fixed dates

1 Jan (New Year's Day), 15 Mar (Youth Day), 5 May (Senior Citizens' Day), 1 Jun (President's Day), 9 Jul (Constitution Day), 1 Oct (Independence Day), 24 Oct (United Nations Day), 25 Dec (Christmas Day).

Variable dates

Labour Day (first Mon in Sep), Thanksgiving Day (last Thu in Nov).

Working hours

Banking

Mon–Thu: 1000–1500, Fri: 1000–1800.

Business

Mon–Fri: 0900–1700.

Government

Mon–Fri: 0900–1700.

Shops

Mon–Sat: 0800–2000; Sun 0800–1800.

Telecommunications

Mobile/cell phones

There are 900/1800 GSM services available.

Electricity supply

115V AC 60Hz, with flat, two or three pin plugs.

Social customs/useful tips

An informal attitude prevails in business. Business cards are sometimes exchanged. Business is usually conducted in English. Visitors should familiarise themselves with local customs. Permission should be sought before photographing people. Gratuities are optional.

Getting there

Air

National airline: A new carrier, Pacific Flier, began operations with a direct air link between Palau and Brisbane, Australia in April 2010. Other destinations include The Philippines and Guam.

International airport/s: Koror Babeldaob (ROR), 19km north-east of Airai, on Babeldaob. Unmetered taxis, with fixed fares, are available, travel time to Koror 30 minutes. Hotel shuttle buses are available if requested when making bookings.

Airport tax: US$20

Surface

Water: Malakal Harbour is the main commercial port facility in Palau. Cargo ships that carry passengers visit occasionally.

Getting about

National transport

Road: Outside administrative areas, the road network may consist of tracks not passable to ordinary vehicles. Ngiwal, Melekeok and Ngaremlengui each have road systems which link up with the main hamlets.

Driving is on the right with 40km per hour as the maximum allowable speed. Passing is prohibited anywhere in Palau.

In July 2005, Japan awarded almost US$20 million in grants to improve Palau's roads.

Water: The islands of Peleliu and Anguar are served by municipal boats. Other inter-island services rely on privately operated boats.

City transport

Taxis: Although taxis are not metered all fares are fixed, enquire before travelling.

BUSINESS DIRECTORY

The addresses listed below are a selection only. While World of Information makes every endeavour to check these addresses, we cannot guarantee that changes have not been made, especially to telephone numbers and area codes. We would welcome any corrections.

Telephone area codes

The international direct dialling code (IDD) for Palau is +680, followed by subscriber's number.

Useful telephone numbers

Ambulance: 488-1411

Police: 911

Chambers of Commerce

Palau Chamber of Commerce, PO Box 1742, Koror 96940 (tel: 488-3400; fax: 488-3401; e-mail: pcoc@palaunet.com).

Banking

Bank of Guam, PO Box 338, Koror 96940 (tel: 488-1648/2696/2697; fax: 488-1384).

Bank of Hawaii, PO Box 340, Koror 96940 (tel: 488-2602/2428; fax: 488-2427).

Bank Pacific, PO Box 1000, Koror 96940 (tel: 488-5635; fax: 488-4752).

Pacific Savings Bank, PO Box 399, Koror 96940 (tel: 488-1859/1860; fax: 488-1858; email: bank@palaunet.com).

First Commercial Banking, PDC Building; PO Box 1605, Koror 96940 (tel: 488-6297/8/9; fax: 488-6295).

Central bank

National Bank of Palau, PO Box 816, Koror 96940 (tel: 488-2578; fax: 488-2579; internet: ndbp.com).

Travel information

Continental Micronesia, PO Box 138CK, Saipan MP 96950, Northern Mariana

Islands (tel: (+1-670) 234-8223; fax: (+1-670) 234-8358).

National tourist organisation offices

Palau Visitors' Authority, PO Box 256, Koror, ROP 96940 (tel: 488-2793/1930; fax: 488-1453; internet site: http://www.visit-palau.com).

Ministries

Bureau of Commercial Development, PO Box 1471, Koror, 96940 (tel: 488-2502).

Bureau of Education, PO Box 189, Koror 96940 (tel: 488-1464; fax: 488-1465; email: moe@palaugov.net).

Bureau of National Treasure (tel: 488-2501; email: bnt@palaugov.net).

Other useful addresses

British High Commissioner (for information on Palau), Victoria House, 47 Gladstone Rd; PO Box 1355, Suva, Fiji (tel: (+679) 322-9100).

Office of the President, PO Box 100, Koror, ROP 96940 (tel: 488-2403/2828; fax: 488-2424/1662).

Palau Embassy (USA), Suite 400, 1700 Pennsylvania Ave, NW Washington, DC 20006 (tel (+1-202) 452-6814; fax (+1-202) 452-6281; internet: www.palauembassy.com).

Palau Liaison Office (Hawaii), 1441 Kapiolani Blvd, Suite 1120, Honolulu, Hawaii 96814 (tel: (+1-808) 941-0988/89; fax: (+1-808) 943-1689).

Palau Liaison Office (Guam) ITC Bldg, Suite 615, PO Box 9457, Tamuning, Guam 96911 (tel: (+1-671) 646-9281/81).

Internet sites

Government of Palau: www.palaugov.net

Destination Micronesia, Palau: www.destmic.com/palau.html

US Office of Insular affairs: www.doi.gov/oia

Yellow Pages: http://directory.palaunet.com/yellowpages

Palestine

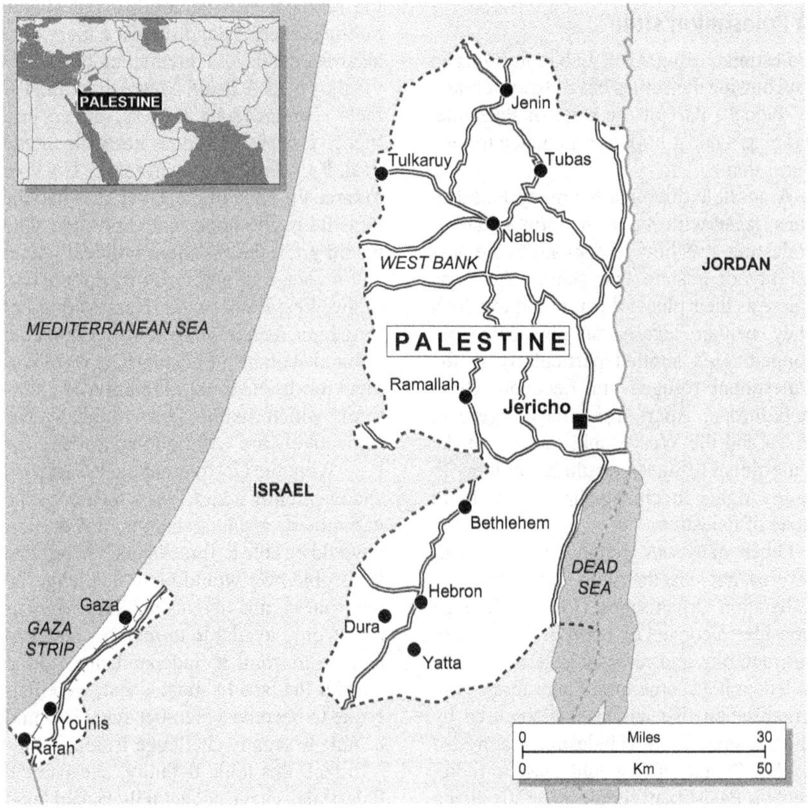

In a manner that no analyst could possibly have foreseen, the so-called Arab Spring cast the question of Palestinian independence and its relationship with Israel in a completely different light. A tentative rapprochement between traditionally opposed Palestinian factions, signed in Cairo in May 2011, was directly attributed to the spectacular demise of Egypt's President Hosni Mubarak. The view among the youth of the Mahgreb was that the days in which authoritarian Arab rulers could use the Palestinian question to disguise their own shortcomings were over.

The United Nations

The proposed United Nations' (UN) September 2011 debate on the admission of a Palestinian state took on a new importance. Polls conducted in the newly liberated North African states certainly confirmed the view that the Palestinian question was the biggest single obstacle to peace in the Middle East. American interference in the region came a close second. Whether this view was shared by Israel's belligerent Prime Minister Benjamin Netanyahu was doubtful; however, what gave the Palestinian people increased optimism was the perceived certainty that the tide of international opinion was now in their favour. Mid-2011 saw the US and Israel using every tool in the diplomatic bag to prevent the Palestinian Authority (PA) from calling on the UN Security Council and its General Assembly from recognising the existence of a Palestinian state. Not that recognition, by itself, would change that much. But – at least in the view of the PA – it would be a serious propaganda blow to Israel.

KEY FACTS

Official name: Palestine

Head of State: President of the Palestinian Council Mahmoud Abbas (Fatah) (since 15 Jan 2005)

Head of government: Prime Minister Salam Fayyad (Fatah) (since 17 Jun 2007)

Ruling party: Coalition: Harakat al Muqawama al Islamia (Hamas) (Islamic Resistance Movement); Harakat al Tahir al Watani al Falistin (Fatah) (Movement for the National Liberation of Palestine); and independents (since 17 Mar 2007)

Area: 6,257 square km (West Bank 5,879 square km; Gaza Strip 378 square km)

Population: 4.00 million (2010)* (2.5 million (2007)* West Bank only) (Around three million Palestinians live in Jordan)

Official language: Arabic

Currency: Israeli new shekel and Jordanian dinar (NIS)

Exchange rate: NIS3.75 per US$ (Oct 2011) and JD0.71 per US$ (Oct 2011)

GDP per capita: US$1,258 (2007)*

GDP real growth: -8.00% (2007)*

Labour force: 774,000 (2004)

Unemployment: 28.80% (2007) Gaza Strip (18.0% West Bank only)

Inflation: 6.90% (2007) (11.0% Sep 2007–Mar 2008)

Balance of trade: -US$1.30 billion (2003)

* estimated figure

The UN is not the place where this will get sorted out, but there is a more subtle truth too. Thanks to the huge mountain of UN resolutions denouncing the occupation and demanding a just resolution, from 242 and 338 onwards, the impression has been created that it is here that the Palestinians will find justice and perhaps progress to liberation. This is something of an illusion. Many observers feel that Palestinians would be better off forgetting the UN and instead starting a non-violent uprising. The lessons of the Arab Spring could not be clearer: this was now the way to create political change, not by pettifogging negotiation over the words, commas and procedures of 'Resolutions' that were never likely to see the light of day in the corridors of the UN.

UNESCO

The US had lobbied hard to try and force the Palestinians to back down before the vote, but at the end of October 2011 the UN Educational, Scientific and Cultural Organisation (Unesco), voted in favour of membership for the Palestinians – a move opposed by Israel and the United States. Of the 173 countries voting, 107 were in favour, 14 opposed and 52 abstained. In response, Washington announced it is cutting funding to Unesco. Its membership dues provide around a fifth of the organisation's budget, amounting to some US$70 million a year, or 22 per cent of its annual budget. 'We were to have made a US$60 million payment to Unesco in November and we will not be making that payment,' state department sources confirmed. A US law passed in the 1990s allows Washington to cut funding to any UN body that admits Palestine as a full member. Many Unesco members had appeared to put politics before money when voting in favour of the Palestinian bid. A number of these have, between them, pockets deep enough to make up the US budget shortfall. Arab states had been instrumental in getting the vote passed despite the intense opposition from the US. The Unesco victory was a boost for the Palestinian President Mahmoud Abbas. He had lost ground to his rival Harakat al Muqawama al Islamia (Hamas) (Islamic Resistance Movement) when the Islamist movement secured the release of hundreds of Palestinian prisoners in exchange for captured Israeli soldier Gilad Shalit just weeks earlier.

Unesco membership may seem a strange and short step to Palestinian statehood. But Palestinian leaders see it as part of a broader push to get international recognition and pressure Israel.

Unesco was the first UN agency the Palestinians have sought to join since submitting their bid for recognition to the Security Council in September 2011. In the emotional session, China, Russia, India, Brazil and South Africa voted in favour of Palestinian membership, while the US, Canada and Germany voted against and the UK abstained.

A Palestinian state?

Palestinian refugees in Lebanon living in and outside the camps have always dreamt of being a part of the state of Palestine. Hoping against hope for a chance to visit Jerusalem.

A possible dilemma for many Palestinians, faced with moves to form a state of Palestine, was how to respond to the possibility of a state that shared the same name as their place of origin but to which they neither legally or physically belonged. This applied particularly to the Palestinian refugees in Lebanon, Syria and Jordan. Apart from the refugees in Gaza and the West Bank, the rest of the Palestinian refugees would be unlikely to enjoy rights to citizenship in the future state of Palestine.

Other questions remained to be answered, not least the future of the Palestine Liberation Organisation (PLO). Although considered corrupt by many and in need of restructuring and re-organisation the PLO still does hold some sort of legitimacy as an organisation that has been recognised by the UN since 1974. If Palestine is admitted to the UN, the PLO would cease to represent the Palestinian people at the UN, being replaced by the PA. Palestinians were initially taken aback by Barack Obama's refusal to recognise Palestine as a mini-state with a disfigured geography and no sovereignty and his urging the world community not to recognise it. But the Arab Spring saw the US wrong-footed and less relevant to the future of the Middle East. Sadly, it is important to stress at the outset that whether the UN grants the PA, the government of a state under occupation, observer status as a state, or refuses to do so, either outcome will be in the interest of Israel. For the Palestinian perception is that US policy has largely been determined by Israel's interests and it is clear that whatever strategy garners international support, with or without US and Israeli approval, to be approved it must guarantee Israeli interests. The UN vote is a case in point.

Possible outcomes

The 2011 Arab uprisings have raised Palestinian expectations and have challenged the *modus vivendi* the PA has with Israel. Furthermore, with the increase in Palestinian grass-roots activism to resist the Israeli occupation, the PA has decided to shift the Palestinian struggle from a popular mobilisation it will not be able to control and which it fears could topple it, to the international legal arena. The PA hopes that this shift from the popular to the juridical will demobilise Palestinian political energies and displace them onto an arena that is less threatening to the survival of the PA itself. Meanwhile, the PA feels abandoned by the US, frozen in a 'peace process' that does not seek an end goal. PA politicians opted for the UN vote to force the hand of the Americans and the Israelis, in the hope that a positive vote would grant the PA more political power and leverage to maximise its domination of the West Bank (under Hamas) (but not East Jerusalem or Gaza (under Harakat al Tahir al Watani al Falistin (Fatah) (Movement for the National Liberation of Palestine), which neither Israel nor Hamas respectively are willing to concede to the PA). Were the UN to grant the PA its wish and eventually admit it as a member state with observer status, then, the PA argues, it would be able to force Israel's hand. The PA's objective would be to challenge Israel internationally using legal instruments only available to member states to force it to grant it 'independence'. What worries the Israelis most is that, were Palestine to become a member state, it would be able to legally challenge Israel.

In fact, this logic is faulty, because the Palestinians have not actually lacked legal instruments to challenge Israel. On the contrary, international instruments have been activated against Israel since 1948 by the UN's numerous resolutions in the General Assembly as well as in the Security Council, not to mention the more recent use of the International Court of Justice in the case of the Wall. The problem has never been the Palestinians' ability or inability to marshal international law or legal instruments to their side. Instead, the problem is that the US blocks international law's jurisdiction from being applied to Israel through its veto power. The US simply uses its veto power in the UN Security Council. Quite how this would change if the PA became a UN member state with observer status is unclear.

For many Palestinians, the question on the table before the UN was not whether the UN should recognise the rights of the Palestinian people to a state, in accordance with the 1947 UN Partition Plan, which would grant them 45 per cent of historic Palestine, or even of a Palestinian state within the 5 June1967 borders along the Green Line, which would grant them 22 per cent of historic Palestine. For them, UN recognition ultimately means the negation of the rights of the majority of the Palestinian people in Israel, in the diaspora, in East Jerusalem and in Gaza.

The Gaza conundrum

In 2005 Israel, under the premiership of Ariel Sharon, withdrew its 9,000 settlers from Gaza and ended its military presence. There followed over five years of steady economic decline; under Israeli occupation, farming had been the main economic activity in Gaza providing around ten per cent of Israel's total agricultural output and generating US$25 million of horticultural produce annually. After years of neglect, during which time most of the agricultural infrastructure had been pillaged, 2009 saw a re-birth. The farms on the strip of land known as al Muharrat (literal translation 'Liberated Lands') are beginning to provide not only employment (in 2011 there was a 500 strong work-force) but also produce for the 1.6 million Palestinians crammed into the tiny strip of land. This is Palestinian Gaza's first tentative step towards food security.

The economy

The Israeli-Palestinian conflict has been one of the most intractable and damaging conflicts in recent world history. Its resolution has long been one of the most sought-after objectives of the international community. The Oslo Accords signed between the Israelis and Palestinians in 1993–95 offered the first real hope for its peaceful resolution. Under these accords, the PA was established with the task of building new institutions from scratch and developing a policy and legal framework for the West Bank and Gaza (the IMF uses the abbreviation WBG) that could provide the basis for a future Palestinian state. Considerable progress was made toward these objectives, until the outbreak of the second *Intifada* in 2000. Despite efforts to put the peace process back on track (the road map), the situation continued to deteriorate, culminating with the election of the Hamas-led government in 2006, the subsequent Israeli blockade and the effective division of WBG into separate political blocs for Gaza and the West Bank. The PA persisted with reforms, implemented since 2007 by Prime Minister Fayyad's government with assistance of the international community. The latest move is the reconciliation agreement signed in Cairo in May 2011 between the PA and Hamas and which calls for the formation of an interim unity government and national elections within a year.

The common perception that Palestine is little more than a failed state is wide of the mark. The IMF was mandated to engage with the PA under the Oslo Accords. The IMF cannot provide financial support to WBG (because it is not a member state), but it is able to provide policy advice in the macro-economic, fiscal and financial areas and it has been doing this since 1994. It has also been providing technical assistance with a focus on tax administration, public expenditure management, banking supervision and regulation and macro-economic statistics. IMF staff also worked with the PA to develop the Palestinian Reform and Development Plan presented at the Paris Donors' Conference in 2007 and, more recently, its successor Palestinian National Development Plan, published in 2011. IMF staff reports reviewing progress in implementing the plans, with a focus on the macro-economic and fiscal areas, has been taken into account by donors in their disbursement decisions. The IMF notes that gross domestic product (GDP) per capita in WBG has fluctuated widely since 1994. From 1994 to 1999, the early years following the Oslo agreement, rising GDP per capita reflected increased private sector confidence and institution-building as the PA took over key administrative responsibilities from the government of Israel, with open borders between Palestinian areas and Israel. From 2000 to 2002, per capita GDP declined sharply with the unfolding of the second *Intifada* and sharp intensification of trade restrictions. From 2003 to 2005, it recovered to the 1994 level, in response to the limited relaxation of restrictions. GDP per capita then dipped again reflecting the onset of Gaza's blockade, before recovering in 2007 following the advent of Prime Minister Fayyad's government. Only by 2009, GDP per capita in WBG had fully recovered to its 1994 level. The movement of overall GDP per capita reflects a wide divergence in regional output paths. The West Bank's GDP per capita has grown steadily since 2007 and is projected to be about 70 per cent above its 1994 level by 2014. In contrast, Gaza's GDP per capita has been on a downward trend since the blockade in 2006, with its recovery starting only in 2009. In Gaza, GDP per capita is still 35 per cent below its 1994 level.

The improvement in macro-economic conditions in the West Bank since 2007 and especially in 2009 and 2010, has reflected solid economic management by the PA, a relaxation of Israeli restrictions on movement and access as well as improved business confidence and substantial donor aid inflows. However, Gaza's situation remains difficult despite the lifting in mid-2010 of restrictions on imports of consumer goods and investment inputs for donor-supervised projects. Severe restrictions remain in place in Gaza on exports, on the movement of people across Gaza's external borders and on private sector imports of raw materials and capital goods. The rate of unemployment remains very high (15 per cent in the West Bank and 26 per cent in Gaza), especially among young Palestinians (29 per cent in WBG).

Despite these difficult conditions, steady reforms in the public finance management system have enabled the PA to tightly control expenditures, apply budget preparation and execution practices and establish fiscal transparency and accountability in line with international standards. These reforms, along with a prudent fiscal policy, have contributed to a rise in the quality of spending and a sharp reduction in donor aid for recurrent spending, from US$1.8 billion in 2008 to US$1.1 billion in 2010 (from 28 to 14 per cent of GDP), with a view to a further reduction to less than US$1 billion in 2011. However, this good fiscal performance has been marred by accumulation of payment arrears and domestic debt mostly owing to repeated shortfalls in aid disbursements.

The Palestine Monetary Authority (PMA)'s institutional reforms have enabled it to fulfill core functions of a central bank. These functions include the application of a rigorous banking supervision and regulatory framework, providing a strong credit and payment infrastructure and monitoring compliance with a governance code and an anti-money laundering law. The PA has also made major strides since 2008 in raising the quality, transparency and timeliness of the WBG's economic and financial statistics. The Palestinian Central Bureau of Statistics (PCBS) is expected to meet all the requirements of the IMF's Special Data Dissemination Standard (SDDS) in 2011, reflecting the best practices applied by the PCBS as well as by the ministries and agencies that provide the source data. Based on the track record of reforms and institution-building in the public finance and financial areas, IMF staff consider that the PA is now able to conduct the sound economic policies expected of a future well-functioning Palestinian state.

The WBG economy has not been significantly affected by the recent global crisis, due to the lack of strong trade and financial links with the rest of the world and conservative banking practices. So far, the spillovers from the regional events in 2010–11 have also been limited. The Palestinian economy, however, is facing increased risks and growth in the West Bank and has slowed down. This slowdown is due to continued fiscal retrenchment, declining aid, a consequent liquidity crisis, as well as slower easing of Israeli restrictions since mid-2010. Concerted actions by the PA, the government of Israel and donors are essential to stem the risks. The PA should maintain its solid record of accomplishment by accelerating key structural reforms. These reforms include implementing civil service reform, restoring the viability of the public pension system, continued improvement of the social safety net, full phasing out of electricity subsidies and improving the legal and regulatory framework for businesses. In the view of the IMF, the Israeli government must phase out remaining restrictions as soon as possible, to maintain the growth momentum, rebalance the composition of output and reduce regional disparities. The donors should disburse the pledged aid in a timely and predictable manner, to prevent liquidity problems and expenditure arrears.

Risk assessment

Politics	Fair
Economy	Fair
Regional stability	Poor

COUNTRY PROFILE

Historical profile

1922 The Ottoman Arab territory of Palestine was mandated to Britain; it was divided into Palestine and Transjordan.
1929 Riots in Jerusalem between Arab Palestinians and Jews were sparked by a dispute over the use of the western wall of the Al Aqsa Mosque (the site is sacred to Muslims, and Jews claim it as part of their temple).
1936–39 The Arab Higher Committee opposed Jewish immigration to Palestine and the Peel Commission concluded that the mandate was unworkable. Legislation limiting the number of Jewish immigrants was introduced by the British government.
1945 Many of the Jews who had survived the Nazi German Holocaust arrived and Jewish extremists began to oppose Britain's immigration legislation.
1946 Transjordan became independent and was later re-named Jordan.
1947 Britain decided to leave. The UN adopted Resolution 181, which called for the establishment of both Jewish and Arab states within Palestine and a partition plan was drawn up, based solely on population, with Jerusalem as an international zone under UN jurisdiction. The Jews agreed to the partition; the Arabs did not.
1948 Conflict ensued between Arabs and Jews. Jewish leaders announced the formation of the State of Israel, open to the immigration of Jews from all countries. Egypt, Iraq, Lebanon, Syria and Jordan joined Palestinian and other Arab guerrillas and invaded Israel. The armistice agreements extended the territory under Israel's control beyond the UN partition boundaries. Many Arabs became refugees in surrounding Arab countries, ending the Arab majority in the new Jewish state. Palestinians refer to this period as *al Nakkba*, the catastrophe.
1957 Harakat al Tahir al Watani al Falistin (Al Fatah) (Movement for the National Liberation of Palestine) was formed by Arab students, including Yasser Arafat – an Egyptian Palestinian, who grew up in the Gaza Strip.
1964 The Palestine Liberation Organisation (PLO) was founded in Egypt as a Palestinian nationalist umbrella organisation dedicated to the establishment of an independent Palestinian state; later, it operated from Lebanon.
1967 Israel launched and won the Six Day War against Egypt, Jordan and Syria, taking control of the Sinai peninsular and the Gaza Strip, which had been Egyptian territory, together with the Golan Heights, formerly claimed by Syria. Around 300,000 Palestinian Arabs fled to Jordan. After the Six-Day War, control of the PLO devolved to the leadership of the various fedayeen militia groups, the most dominant of which was Yasser Arafat's Al Fatah. Israel's settlement policy started; it occupied the Sinai peninsular (returned to Egypt in 1982), the Golan Heights, the Gaza Strip and the West Bank, including East Jerusalem; the Jews transferred to these areas became known as settlers.
1969 Arafat was appointed chairman of the PLO's Executive Committee.
1970 Civil war (Black September) between the Jordanian army and Palestinians followed airplane hijackings by a Palestinian resistance group. The PLO was forcefully expelled from its bases in Jordan and moved to Lebanon.
1973 Lebanon was used by the Palestinians as a base for activities against Israel. In retaliation, Israeli commandos raided Beirut, killing three associates of Yasser Arafat. Arab states officially recognised the PLO as the representative of the Palestinians.
1981 Israel annexed East Jerusalem.
1982–85 Israel invaded Lebanon to prevent the PLO from carrying out armed resistance to its rule in the occupied territories of the Gaza Strip and the West Bank. A Western multinational force monitored the evacuation of the PLO; it relocated to Tunis, where it stayed until it moved to the Palestinian autonomous areas (Gaza and Jericho) in 1994.
1987 The Palestinians launched an *intifida* (uprising) against the Israelis. The Harakat al Muqawama al Islamia (Hamas) (Islamic Resistance Movement) was formed in the Gaza Strip, with two objectives: armed resistance to Israeli rule in the West Bank and the Gaza Strip and the establishment of a sovereign, independent state located in historic Palestine (present-day Israel, the West Bank, and the Gaza Strip). There was an upsurge in violence as large numbers of Jews from the Soviet Union began to settle in the West Bank and the Gaza Strip.
1988 The State of Palestine was declared, as outlined in the UN partition plan 181, the new state being recognised only by states that did not recognise Israel.
1993–95 The Oslo Peace Accords laid the basis for transfer of authority from the Israeli military administration to the PLO in the Gaza Strip and an undefined area around the town of Jericho in the West Bank. A follow-up treaty, Oslo II, was signed, which envisaged Palestinian autonomy with Israeli troop units withdrawing from the West Bank.
1996 Yasser Arafat was elected president of the Palestinian Legislative Council (PLC), the assembly of the Palestinian Authority (PA).
1998 The Wye peace agreement between the Israelis and the Palestinians, brokered by the US, ended 19 months of deadlock in the peace process.
2000 Israel agreed to allow the PA to control 39.8 per cent of the West Bank. However, after Israel's right-wing opposition leader, Ariel Sharon, visited the Temple Mount in Jerusalem and reiterated Israel's claims to Muslim holy places in the city, a second *intifada* was launched and a total blockade was imposed by Israel on the West Bank and Gaza.
2001 Israel declared the PA to be a terrorist-supporting organisation and launched Operation 'Defensive Shield', invading the PA-controlled West Bank and Gaza, attacking its institutions and besieging Arafat's headquarters. Deaths in Israel by Palestinian suicide bombers increased.
2002 Saudi Arabia proposed a peace initiative and a UN Security Council resolution endorsed a Palestinian state and called for the cessation of hostilities. Israel

besieged Arafat's compound in Ramallah and reoccupied most of the West Bank. For five weeks the Israeli army surrounded militants and civilians taking sanctuary in the Church of the Nativity in Bethlehem; it ended when 13 militants were sent into exile. Israel began building a wall as a barrier between it and Gaza claiming it was the only way to control infiltration of militant terrorists.
2003 The US proposed a *Road Map to Peace*, with a cease-fire and end to Jewish settlements in the occupied territories and the creation of an independent Palestinian state by 2005. Ahmed Qureia became prime minister.
2004 Israel's Sharon, declared he would remove all Jewish settlements in Gaza. President Yasser Arafat became ill and died in Paris.
2005 Mahmoud Abbas was elected president of the Palestinian Authority by an overwhelming majority. He persuaded Hamas and Islamic Jihad to agree an unofficial cease-fire. At the Sharm el Sheikh summit in Egypt, a truce was signed by Sharon and Abbas, ending four years of violence between Israel and Palestine. President Abbas and the Israeli cabinet approved the removal of Jewish settlers from Gaza and parts of the West Bank.
2006 Mahmoud Abbas announced that he would only remain as president until 2009. Parliamentary elections were won convincingly by Hamas with a majority of 74 seats. Ismail Haniya was appointed prime minister and the new Hamas-dominated parliament revoked legislation passed by the previous Fatah-dominated parliament, which had given increased powers to the president, including the right to allocate key administrative posts to Fatah members. Hamas refused to recognise Israel, renounce violence or accept previous agreements made by Fatah. International sanctions were imposed, which caused financial hardship as government benefits and wages went unpaid and supplies to hospitals ran out. The president undertook negotiations with Israel and Hamas in an attempt to broker an accommodation and allow financial aid to resume.
2007 Rival Hamas and Fatah gunmen began a deadly power struggle in the Gaza Strip, killing over 20 people. A new government of unity was announced by President Abbas and Prime Minister Haniya. A new cabinet was approved by the legislative council (83:3). The US and EU continued to withhold recognition of the unity government until it recognised the state of Israel and renounced violence. Violence erupted again and a power struggle resulted in Hamas gaining control of Gaza while local Hamas leaders fled to Egypt. The president, based in the West Bank, dismissed Prime Minister Haniya and appointed Salam Fayyad while announcing that he would rule by presidential decrees; Hamas officials rejected this decision. The president swore in his new cabinet in Ramallah and outlawed a Hamas paramilitary force (the Executive Force) and other allied militia. However presidential rule was not enforced in Gaza. The US signed an agreement to give the PA US$80 million towards reforming their security services. Israel imposed an economic embargo on Gaza after Hamas gained control of the territory and restricted Gaza Strip entry and exit. The number of humanitarian convoys for Gaza halved from 3,000 to 1,500. Israel imposed further Gaza sanctions on fuel and energy supplies in retaliation for rockets fired into Israel. Palestinian leaders claimed this amounted to collective punishment (a war crime under the Geneva Convention). The Israeli Supreme Court agreed that cutbacks in fuel were legal but that a cut-back in electricity supplies had to be delayed. A US$7 billion foreign aid package was agreed by donor countries, to help underpin a viable Palestinian state and avoid bankruptcy. Hamas, which did not attend the conference, rejected the measures and although money was designated for Gaza the territory did not benefit from the aid. The World Bank warned that unless Israel lifted its system of restrictions on the movement of goods, finance and Palestinian people the measures could not rebuild the economy.
2008 Following an Israeli army operation against Hamas forces in Gaza, 200 rockets were fired into Israel and in response, Israel imposed power cuts on Gaza. Petrol for vehicles and fuel for the Hamas-run power plant in the Gaza Strip were reduced. Within days the UNHCR called the situation in Gaza desperate; adding that electricity provided by generators in hospitals was only able to power equipment and could not provide the heating necessary during winter. Following international disquiet Israel eased the blockade of energy supplies while Palestinian militants exploded holes in the border wall near the Rafah crossing between Gaza and Egypt allowing thousands of people to cross and stock up on essential supplies. Israel demanded that the border be closed to prevent the restocking of militant's armouries. Egypt rejected the demand, allowing access on humanitarian grounds. George Habbash, founder of the radical Popular Front for the Liberation of Palestine (PFLP), died. Egypt closed the Rafah border, but other openings elsewhere were made and hundreds more Palestinians continued to cross into Egypt. Hamas and Egyptian officials reached an agreement, whereby all Palestinians would return to Gaza, except those seeking medical treatment in Egypt and those travelling to a third country. Following a speech by US President Bush, President Abbas accused the US of bias towards Israel, as Bush said that the Arab world had to reform and the US was Israel's closest ally. Mahmoud Darwish, Palestine's respected poet and author of its 1988 declaration of independence, died. President Abbas extended his term in office until 2010. Israel began a bombardment of and then an offensive on the Gaza Strip.
2009 Over 1,000 Palestinians were killed and 4,700 wounded in Israel's offensive, with an estimated 35,000 people displaced. UN and EU representatives called for a halt to the military action and for the supply of humanitarian aid to be allowed. Israel agreed to a daily aid convoy during a three-hour cease-fire. After Israel declared a cease-fire, Hamas announced that it would stop launching missiles into Israel. The UN estimated that rebuilding in the Gaza Strip would cost around US$1.9 billion. A large stockpile of 7,000kg of unexploded ordnance (UXO), gathered up and held under the supervision of Gaza-Hamas officials, was stolen. Included in the stockpile were white phosphorus shells and 2,000 pound and 500 pound bombs. The US announced that it would donate US$900 million in aid towards the recovery of the Gaza Strip; the money would not be given to Hamas, but rather to non-governmental organisations (NGOs) and the PA. By the time of a cease-fire, 90 per cent of Gaza's residents had only intermittent electricity and 50,000 people were without mains water. The border with Israel was closed to all but essential supplies while peace negotiations continued. At an international donor conference held to support the rebuilding of the Gaza Strip, US$4.5 billion was pledged. The money was offered to the PA and not Hamas. Prime Minister Salam Fayyad resigned in a move to allow a power-sharing government of national unity, to include members of the Gaza Strip's Hamas leadership. Following an investigation by the UN Human Rights Council, the legality of Israel's three-week offensive in Gaza was questioned. The Council determined that there had been a disproportionate use of force by Israel – the overall ratio of deaths was 1,434 in Gaza (the Palestinian authorities broke the numbers down as 960 civilians, 239 uniformed police and 235 'fighters') to 13 in Israel. Israel accused the Council of seeking to 'demonise' it and later challenged the number of dead as 1,166, of which 709 were 'terror operatives'. The UN appointed Richard Goldstone, a South African judge and former war crimes

prosecutor, as its investigator into alleged violations of international law during Israel's conflict in the Gaza Strip. The UN inquiry into attacks on UN property during the Israeli Gaza offensive accused the Israeli army of six incidents of taking 'inadequate' precautions to protect the premises and causing deaths and injuries of people sheltering inside. Hamas was accused of one attack. President Abbas re-appointed Salam Fayyad as prime minister (of Fatah controlled West Bank territories). The exiled leader of the Palestinian Hamas in Gaza, Khaled Meshaal, rejected the terms for a Palestinian state as proposed by Israeli Prime Minister Netanyahu. Conditions for the state included demilitarisation and recognition of Israel as a Jewish state. Meshaal said this was 'merely self-governance under the name of a country'. The International Red Cross reported that 1.5 million people living in Gaza were unable to rebuild their lives as they have no access to building materials and the water supply and sanitation system are near to collapse. Poverty was described as at an 'alarming' level and medical treatment was limited. President Abbas announced that presidential and parliamentary elections in all Palestinian territories were scheduled for 24 January 2010. Hamas rejected this saying that any ruling by what it saw as an unconstitutionally sitting president could not be legitimate. The elections were postponed.

2010 After Israel added the Tomb of the Patriarchs in Hebron to their list of national heritage sites in March the Palestinian cabinet met in Hebron as a sign of protest. The first commercial and privately-organised convoy of goods (clothes and shoes) since 2005 was allowed into the Gaza Strip in April, following pressure on the Israeli government by both the UN and EU to lift its blockade. Nine activists were killed by Israeli security forces when they stormed a ship in international waters; it had been attempting to break the blockade of Gaza. The attack led to UN condemnation in May. Israel announced in June that it would ease the Gaza Strip blockade and allow more civilian items into the territory. In August Palestine and Israel agreed to resume peace talks after a two year gap, which began between Israeli Prime Minister Netanyahu and President Mohmoud Abbas in Washington on 2 September, hosted by President Obama and chaired by US Secretary of State, Hillary Clinton. The negotiations began with a dinner at the White House, which President Mubarak of Egypt and King Abdullah of Jordan also attended.

2011 On 15 March, thousands joined matching demonstrations of unity in Gaza City and Ramallah (West Bank), calling for an end to the political deadlock between Hamas and Fatah. A group of 21 prominent Israelis signed an open letter in May calling on the international community to recognise a Palestinian state in Jerusalem, the West Bank and Gaza. From 28 May the Egyptian government relaxed restrictions at the Rafah border crossing with the Gaza Strip, allowing women, children and men over 40 to pass freely. Men aged between 18 and 40 still require a permit, and trade is prohibited. An agreement was reached between Fatah and Hamas on 4 May, aimed at ending their division. The settlement will result in a joint interim government for Palestine before parliamentary elections are held in 2012. A UN report, published in June, put unemployment in Gaza at 45.2 per cent, one of the world's highest rates. On 13 August, President Abbas announced that on 20 September the Palestinian territories would submit an application to the UN for international recognition of statehood. The recognition would be for an independent, sovereign state within the West Bank, Gaza Strip and East Jerusalem. Despite pressure from other members, including US President Obama, on 23 September, President Abbas formally applied for membership of the UN and that Palestine be recognised as a sovereign state. On 5 October the board of the cultural agency Unesco agreed to put forward to its member states Palestine's bid for full membership. A prisoner swap deal between the Hamas and the Israeli government involving the young Israeli soldier, Gilad Shalit, and 'hundreds' of Palestinian prisoners was agreed in the Israeli parliament by 26–3 votes on 11 October. Sargeant Shalit had been held for five years. On 24 November, Hamas and Fatah agreed to parliamentary elections, to be held in May 2012, following power-sharing talks held in Egypt. Members of opposing factions will be released by either side before preparations for the elections are undertaken.

Political structure

Constitution

A provisional framework for the Palestinian state was approved by the Palestinian Legislative Council in a 1996 Draft Basic Law. This law will be fully endorsed when a permanent settlement is achieved.

Independence date

13 September 1993

Form of state

Parliamentary Democracy

The executive

Executive power is vested in the head of the Palestinian National Authority (PNA – also known as the Palestinian Authority (PA)), who is president, elected by direct universal suffrage for up to two four-year terms, and Head of State.

The president is head of armed and security forces, is responsible for initiating and proposing laws and foreign policy. The president appoints a prime minister, who forms a cabinet.

National legislature

The schism between the Hamas-led Gaza Strip and the Fatah-led West Bank has resulted in two independently operating administrations, with Hamas operating without a Fatah elected executive and Fatah rejecting the authority of the Hamas dominated legislative council.

The unicameral Palestinian Legislative Council (PLC) was established in 1994 and is composed of 132 members plus the president as an *ex officio* member. The PLC's members are elected in 16 multi-seat constituencies for 5-year terms.

Legal system

The Basic Law provides for an independent judiciary.

The High Judicial Council oversees the administration of a hierarchy of courts beginning with the magistrate courts, Courts of first Instance, Courts of Appeal and The Supreme Court.

Last elections

25 January 2006 (parliamentary); 9 January 2005 (presidential).

Results: Presidential: Mahmoud Abbas, also known as Abu Mazen, candidate of the mainstream Fatah, was elected president of the Palestinian council with 62.3 per cent of the vote against independent candidate, Mustafa Barghouti, 19.8 per cent. Turnout was 70 per cent.

Parliamentary: Hamas won 74 seats (out of 132); Fatah won 45 seats. The Popular Front for the Liberation of Palestine (PFLP) won 3 seats. Three groupings (The Alternative, Independent Palestine and Third Way) won 2 seats each. Independents won the 4 remaining seats. Turnout was 78.2 per cent.

Next elections

24 January 2010 (presidential and parliamentary) postponed.

Political parties

Ruling party

Coalition: Harakat al Muqawama al Islamia (Hamas) (Islamic Resistance Movement); Harakat al Tahir al Watani al Falistin (Fatah) (Movement for the National Liberation of Palestine); and independents (since 17 Mar 2007)

Population

4.00 million (2010)* (2.5 million (2007)* West Bank only) (Around three million Palestinians live in Jordan)

Last census: 1 December 2007: 3,761,646

Population density: 489 inhabitants per square km. Urban population: 54 per cent (1994–2000).
Annual growth rate: 2.3 per cent (2003)
Ethnic make-up
Gaza: Palestinians and other Arabs (99.4 per cent), Israelis (0.6 per cent).
West Bank: Palestinians and other Arabs (83 per cent), Israelis (17 per cent).
Religions
The majority of the population is Muslim (mainly Sunni); also Jewish and Christian minorities.

Education
Formal basic education is provided to the majority of those who are of primary school age (94.7 per cent), although the quality of education does not correspond to the rising demand.
The education sector has suffered tremendous decline since the Israeli occupation. Most of the schools in the Gaza Strip are overcrowded and run two to three shifts per day. It is estimated that there are 1,175 schools of which 995 are in the West Bank and 180 in the Gaza Strip. The education ministry in its five-year reform project (2000–05) is keen on developing a Palestinian curriculum emphasising studies in Palestinian identity and has invested in providing textbooks and improving the teaching methods in schools. It will also encourage the private sector to invest in vocational training, which otherwise concentrates on building and running cultural centres.
There are six universities in the West Bank and two in the Gaza Strip. West Bank Universities include Birzeit, Al Najah, Bethlehem, Al Quds University, Hebron University and Al Quds Open University.
The UN began distributing laptop computers to thousands of children attending school in the Gaza Strip in April 2010, in a measure to improve education in the region's disrupted school system. The laptops include textbooks used in primary school curriculum and teaching aids.

Health
The Israeli occupation has almost paralysed the provision of healthcare to the civilian population. Most hospitals and clinics are unable to operate and as a result 73 per cent of Palestinians in rural areas are deprived of medical treatment. Vaccinations among children have been largely hindered spreading the fear of epidemics. Moreover, elderly people with chronic diseases suffer from acute shortages of medicine.
A hospital in Gaza, funded by the EU, is largely unworkable as staff, patients and supplies are denied access by Israeli authorities during times of trouble.
Life expectancy: 73 years (estimate 2003)
Fertility rate/Maternal mortality rate: 4.9 births per woman (2003)
Birth rate/Death rate: 37.5 births per 1,000 population; 4.1 deaths per 1,000 population (2003).
Child (under 5 years) mortality rate (per 1,000): 22 per 1,000 live births (2003)

Welfare
The UN World Food Programme (WFP) aims to provide basic food support to 500,000 non-refugee Palestinians, in the West Bank and Gaza Strip. It targets those who have been classified as 'social hardship cases' (360,000 people according to latest estimates) and are eligible for welfare assistance from the PNA. In Jerusalem, an Emergency Food Crisis Group, chaired by WFP, has been established with the help of other UN agencies, non-governmental organisations and donors.
The Israeli occupation has forced the poverty level higher than ever before. While unemployment stands at 30 per cent, an estimated 40 per cent of Palestinian households have a monthly income that is less than US$200 per month. The percentage is 45 per cent in Gaza and 37 per cent in the West Bank.
Estimates show that 38 per cent of refugees live in the Palestinian territories; 15.8 per cent in the West Bank and 21.9 per cent in the Gaza Strip. The PNA along with other international non-government organisations have been struggling to rehabilitate the housing conditions of people in the refugee camps such as Jenin and Nablus. The Palestinian Housing Council has been active in providing low cost housing. More than 400,000 Palestinians are deprived of electricity and running water.

Main cities
Gaza Strip: Gaza (also called Gaza City) (estimated population 495,207 in 2005); Deir al Balah (61,581), became the first town to come under Palestinian self-rule in 1994, Rafah (130,621).
West Bank: East Jerusalem (261,043), Jericho (20,544), Ramallah (25,479), Nablus (135,253), Hebron (165,968).

Media
Press
A number of Palestinian newspapers are based in Nazareth, outside the PNA.
Dailies: In Arabic *Al Quds*, *Al Hayat al Jadedah*, Al Ayyam Daily Newspaper. In English, *Palestine Times* and *Bethlehem News*.
Weeklies: Weeklies include *Kul-Alarab*, *Assabeel Weekly*, *Filsteen Almoslima* and *Akhbar Alnaqab*.
Periodicals: In Arabic, *Al Ayyam*.
Broadcasting
The Palestinian Broadcasting Corporation broadcasts from Ramallah.
Radio: In Arabic, the Voice of Palestine, run by Hamas, and Gaza FM.
Television: The official Palestinian Broadcasting Corporation broadcasts televisions programmes from Ramallah as well as a satellite channel.
News agencies
In English, Arabic, WAFA Palestine News Agency (http://english.wafa.ps), Ma'an News Agency (www.maannews.net/en), Ramattan (www.ramattan.com/default-en.asp).

Economy
Although the West Bank and Gaza Strip make up the combined territory of Palestine, each region has worked autonomously since 2007 following the Hamas victory in parliamentary elections. After violent clashes with Fatah, Hamas took over the Gaza Strip and a political and economic schism occurred between the two territories. Hamas, based in the Gaza Strip, refused to acknowledge Israel as a legitimate state and renounce violence as a means of opposition to Israel and was subsequently shunned by most foreign governments. The West Bank, home of the rival, Fatah-led president, began negotiations to work with the international community and has since been rewarded with international aid and relations. The Gaza Strip is under blockade by Israel which refuses to allow any commercial supplies into the territory and restricts energy supplies and humanitarian aid to a minimum. The UN complained, in January 2010, that Israel was blocking 26 of its building projects including homes, schools and health clinics by denying permission for materials to pass through their border controls. Economic activity in the Gaza Strip is almost non-existent. The UN estimated that the economic cost following the 2008–09 Israeli incursion, for rebuilding in the Gaza Strip, would be around US$1.9 billion, as over 50,000 people were homeless and around 400,000 people were without running water.
At an international donor conference held in March 2009, to support the rebuilding of the Gaza Strip, US$4.5 billion was pledged by international governments and organisations. However the money was offered to the Palestinian Authority based in the West Bank and not Hamas.
The International Monetary Fund (IMF) estimated that the GDP growth of Palestine shrank to 0.5 per cent in 2007 and would only reach 0.8 per cent in 2008, figures much lower than the estimated 3.5 per cent that it could have achieved if the

Israeli blockade had been lifted from the Gaza Strip. The economy of the West Bank has improved as tourists have returned to Bethlehem and freight transport has grown, leading to an increased average daily wage and a fall in unemployment.
The Palestinian economy is characterised as aid-dependent, severely affected by land shortages and other deficiencies that have resulted in few opportunities for new private investment. Of the US$500 million set aside for development in the territories, the IMF stated that only US$300 million would be spent in 2008 due to the 'economic and security restrictions'.
A report issued by the World Bank in April 2011 said that the high rate of growth was too dependent on donor money. It felt that the 9.3 per cent growth in 2010 was 'unsustainable' while Israeli restrictions on the private sector continued. It also said that both territories suffered from high unemployment and poverty.

External trade
Palestine has no operational ports or airports to ship goods directly to markets other than Israel. Since Hamas took control of the Gaza Strip and Israel closed the border, manufacturing has all but collapsed, as 80 per cent of businesses have closed in this region. On the other side of the border raw materials and goods destined for Gaza began to pile up, stranded in Israel's Ashod port. The land border with Egypt, at Rafah in southern Gaza, was also closed by Israel.
All import and export information refers to the West Bank territory only.
Imports
Food, consumer goods and construction materials.
Main sources: Israel and Egypt
Exports
Citrus fruit, flowers, olives, fruit, vegetables, furniture and limestone.
Main destinations: Israel, Egypt, Jordan

Agriculture
The sector has been badly damaged by the Israeli-Palestinian conflict since 2000 when agriculture contributed 7 per cent to GDP and employed about 25 per cent of the workforce.
Before the second *intifida* and the Israeli invasion of the West Bank and Gaza, about a quarter of the land area was cultivated and smallholdings of five hectares (ha) or less dominated. Crops, including olives, grapes and almonds, took up 60 per cent of cultivated rain-fed areas and field crops (mainly cereals) about 30 per cent. Olive growing accounted for more than 50 per cent of cultivated land.
The Separation Barrier has led to confiscation and levelling of Palestinian lands and by mid-2004 around 260 square kilometres, or 15 per cent of agricultural land had been lost to production.

Industry and manufacturing
There are proposals by a US-Led syndicate to invest US$500 million in industry and manufacturing after the withdrawal of Israeli troops from Gaza, but only if Israel allows free access of goods through its territory to overseas markets.
A UN report, published in June 2011, put unemployment in Gaza at 45.2 per cent, one of the world's highest rates.

Tourism
Foreign investment has been sought to help develop tourism facilities throughout the West Bank; however, the fledging tourism sector has been devastated by the conflict with Israel.

Hydrocarbons
Extensive gas reserves were located off the Gaza Strip coastline in 2000. However the ongoing hostilities between Palestine and Israel has hampered any exploitation. A proposal by Israel to pump natural gas from the only two wells in the Gaza Strip's gas field (which contain 33 billion cubic metres of natural gas), to the Israeli terminal at Ashkelon was put on hold when the major UK operator withdrew from negotiations in 2007. However further talks began in June 2008.
All hydrocarbons must be delivered to the Gaza Strip through Israeli borders and are subject to embargo.

Energy
The Gaza Strip has one power station. During the Israeli military action in December–January 2008/09, a number of small diesel generators were destroyed and the embargo left the territory dangerously low on fuel.

Financial markets
The second mobile (cell) operator, Wataniya Palestine Mobile Telecommunications Company began trading on 9 January 2011 on the Palestine Stock Exchange
Stock exchange
Palestine Stock Exchange (PEX)
Commodity exchange
Palestine Securities Exchange (PSE)

Banking and insurance
Central bank
The Palestine Monetary Authority (PMA), was established in 1995, with responsibilty for licensing, supervising and inspecting banks; determining the liquidity requirements on all deposits held by banks operating in the self-rule areas; managing foreign exchange reserves and foreign currency transactions. The PMA also has the power to regulate and supervise capital activities in the self-rule areas including the licensing of capital market institutions, finance companies and investment funds.
Main financial centre
Ramallah

Time
GMT plus two hours (daylight saving GMT plus three hours)

Geography
Palestine consists of the Gaza Strip and the West Bank, which together measure 6,020 square km. The Gaza Strip is level, fertile, coastal land of only 5–12km wide and 45km long to the south-west of Israel and on the Mediterranean sea. It is almost entirely surrounded by Israel but has a short border with Egypt in the south.
The West Bank is 5,655 square km within the demarcation line set up in 1949. It is an area west of the Jordan River, including much of Jerusalem and areas north and south of the city, the borders of which have been in dispute since the 1967 *Six Day War*. Jordan lies to the east and in the south-east the border runs through the Dead Sea, the lowest lying land on earth at 399 metres below sea level.
The land is generally fertile, although arid.
Hemisphere
Northern

Climate
Summer (Apr–Oct): temperatures range from 23 degrees Celsius (C) to 31 degrees C; humidity 70–75 per cent. Winter (Nov–Mar): temperatures range from 15–20 degrees C. Rainfall: Nov–Mar in periodic downpours.

Entry requirements
Passports
Required by all. The only routes to the Palestinian territories are through Israel and visitors must comply with Israeli requirements before access is allowed to the West Bank or Gaza Strip. Israel imposes tight restrictions and passport holders are advised to contact Israeli authorities for written permission to cross into the Gaza Strip in advance of travelling. At the border crossing it can take at least five working days for the documentation to be verified.
The Israeli Ministry of the Interior insists that Palestinian citizens holding dual nationality must enter and leave Israel on a Palestinian passport; they are required to obtain travel documents to depart.
NB An Israeli stamp, or exit stamp from any of the neighbouring countries, will mean entry is barred to almost any other Arab country. It is possible to request that the passport should not be stamped and a separate form is stamped instead and attached to the passport; the form can be removed when exiting the country.

Visa
Egypt and Jordan have open borders with Palestine, access was via the Allenby bridge (West Bank-Jordan) or the border crossing at Rafah (Gaza-Egypt). However, since Israel commands these access points and limits admission, practical entry can only be gained through Israel. Israel has agreements with 65 countries for visa-free travel, including most citizens from Europe, the Americas, Australasia and some Asian countries (visa applications can be downloaded from: www.mfa.gov.il/mfa and follow link from *About the ministry* to *Consular affairs*, then *Services for foreign nationals only*). Travel within the West Bank and Gaza usually involves passing through multiple Israeli military checkpoints.
Currency advice/regulations
Most places accept US dollars, Israeli shekels and Jordanian dinars.
Customs
Video cameras and other electronic items must be declared to customs at Israeli points of entry.
Prohibited imports
Fresh meat and fruit and vegetables from Africa are prohibited by Israel.

Hotels
There is a lack of good hotels in the West Bank and Gaza.

Public holidays (national)
Fixed dates
14 Nov (National Day)
Variable dates
Eid al Adha, Islamic New Year, Birth of the Prophet, Ascent of the Prophet, Eid al Fitr.
Islamic year 1433 (26 Nov 2011–14 Nov 2012): The Islamic year contains 354 or 355 days, with the result that Muslim feasts advance by 10–12 days against the Gregorian calendar. Dates of feasts vary according to the sighting of the new moon, so cannot be forecast exactly.

Working hours
The official weekend is Friday, and the working week varies, to accommodate Muslim, Christian or Jewish religious schedules.
Banking
Sat–Thu: 0800–1230. Some larger bank branches re-open Mon–Thu: 1500–1700.
Business
Sat–Thu: 0800–1430.
Government
Sat–Thu: 0800–1430.
Shops
Sat–Thu: 0800–1900. Christian owned shops open on Friday and close on Sunday.

Telecommunications
Mobile/cell phones
There is a 900 GSM service available throughout the territories.

Security
Foreign nationals are warned not to travel to the West Bank and Gaza Strip, which are subject to terrorist and military activity.

Getting there
Air
International airport/s: Dahaniya Gaza International Airport is not in operation. It is located south of Gaza City near the Egyptian border.
Surface
Gaza is accessible from the Rafah border with Egypt in the south; only women, children and men over 40 to pass freely. Men aged between 18 and 40 require a permit, and trade is prohibited. The Allenby Bridge crossing from the West Bank into Jordan is controlled by Israel.
Road: Private vehicles cannot cross from Israel into the Gaza Strip and may be stopped at checkpoints entering or leaving the West Bank.
The border crossing from Egypt, at Rafah, for foot-traffic, opens from 0900–2100, Saturday–Thursday (excluding public holidays).
Main port/s: An internationally funded port was opened in the late 1990s, with the aim of reducing the need for Palestinian trade to go through Israel before reaching the outside world. However, access to and from the port has become restricted due to the Israeli occupation of the West Bank and Gaza Strip in early 2002. All access to Gaza is via the port of Haifa.

Getting about
National transport
Road: Gaza Strip has a small, poorly developed road network.
West Bank has 4,500km of roads, of which 2,700km are paved; Israel developed many highways to service their settlements.
Buses: Buses run from East Jerusalem to Nablus and between Tel Aviv and Ramallah.
Taxis: Collective taxis regularly commute between Gaza and Ramallah, Jerusalem or Hebron.
City transport
Taxis: Taxis operate in the main cities.
Car hire
Palestinian licence plates are either green or blue, whereas Israeli number plates are yellow. Visitors are advised not to drive vehicles with yellow licence plates in the West Bank or Gaza Strip.

BUSINESS DIRECTORY
The addresses listed below are a selection only. While World of Information makes every endeavour to check these addresses, we cannot guarantee that changes have not been made, especially to telephone numbers and area codes. We would welcome any corrections.

Telephone area codes
The international direct dialling code (IDD) for Palestine is +970, followed by area code and subscriber's number:

Bethlehem	2	Jericho	2
Gaza	7	Jerusalem	2
Hebron	2	Nablus	9
Jenin	6	Ramallah	2

Chambers of Commerce
Bethlehem Chamber of Commerce and Industry, PO Box 59, Bethlehem (tel: 274-2742; fax: 276-4402; e-mail: bcham@palnet.com).

European Palestinian Chamber of Commerce, 19 Nablus Road, PO Box 20185, Jerusalem (tel: 626-4883; fax: 626-4975; e-mail: epcc@palnet.com).

Federation of Palestinian Chambers of Commerce, Industry and Agriculture, Al-Rashid Street, PO Box 54107, Jerusalem (tel: 628-0727; fax: 628-0644; email: fpccia@palnet.com).

Gaza Palestinian Chamber of Commerce, PO Box 33, Gaza (tel: 282-1172; fax: 286-4588; e-mail: gazacham@palnet.com).

Hebron Chamber of Commerce and Industry, King Faisal Street, PO Box 272, Hebron, West Bank (tel: 222-8218; fax: 222-7490; e-mail: hebcham@hebronet.com).

Jenin Chamber of Commerce, Industry and Agriculture, City Centre, Jenin (tel: 250-1107; fax: 250-3388; e-mail: jencham@hally.net).

Jericho Commercial, Industrial and Agricultural Arab Chamber, PO Box 91, Jericho (tel: 232-3313; fax: 232-2394; e-mail: jercom@palnet.com).

Jerusalem Arab Chamber of Commerce, Al-Rashid Street, PO Box 19151, Jerusalem 91191 (tel: 628-2351; fax: 627-2615; e-mail: chamber@alqudsnet.com).

Nablus Chamber of Commerce and Industry, PO Box 35, Nablus (tel: 238-0335; fax: 237-7605; e-mail: nablus@palnet.com).

Qalqilya Chamber of Commerce, Industry and Agriculture, PO Box 13, Qalqilya (tel: 294-1473; fax: 294-0164; e-mail: chamberq@hally.net).

Ramallah and Albeireh Chamber of Commerce and Industry, PO Box 256, Ramallah (tel: 295-6043; fax: 298-4691; e-mail: ramcom@palnet.com).

Tulkarm Chamber of Commerce and Industry, PO Box 51, Tulkarm (tel: 267-1010; fax: 267-5623; e-mail: tulkarm@palnet.com).

Banking

Al-Ahli Jordan Bank, Al-Quds Street, PO Box 550, Ramallah (tel: 998-6370; fax: 998-6372).

Al-Ittihad Bank for Saving and Investment, Commercial Centre, Al-Barid Street, PO Box 1557, Ramallah (tel: 298-6412/5; fax: 298-6416).

ANZ Grindlays, PO Box 19390, East Jerusalem (tel: 626-3444; fax: 626-3311).

Arab Bank, Al-Harajeh, PO Box 1476, Ramallah (tel: 298-2456; fax: 298-2444).

Arab Land Bank, PO Box 565, Jerusalem/Ramallah Road, Ramallah (tel: 298-5958; fax: 295-8426/5).

Arab Palestinian Investment Bank, Regional Headquarters, Al-Harajeh Building, PO Box 1268, Ramallah (tel: 298-7126; fax: 298-7125).

Bank of Jordan, Al-Quds Street, PO Box 1328, Ramallah (tel: 295-2696; fax: 295-2705).

Bank of Palestine, Al-Rimal Quarter, Omar El-Mukhtar Street, PO Box 50, Gaza (tel: 286-5676; fax: 282-8974).

British Bank of the Middle East, PO Box 2067, Al-Quds Street, Ramallah (tel: 298-7802, 298-1551; fax: 298-7804).

Cairo Amman Bank, Wadi El-Tuffah Street, PO Box 665, Hebron (tel: 993-6768; fax: 993-6770).

Cairo Amman Bank, El-Hussein Circle, Nablus (tel: 238-1301; fax: 238-0188).

Commercial Bank of Palestine, Al-Awdah Street, PO Box 1799, Ramallah (tel: 295-4102; fax: 295-3888).

Jordan Gulf Bank, Al-Sa'ah Circle, Ramallah (tel: 998-7680; fax: 998-7682).

Jordan Housing Bank, Rukab Street, PO Box 1473, Ramallah (tel: 998-6255; fax: 998-6275).

Jordan Kuwait Bank, Commercial Centre, Sufian Street, PO Box 33, Nablus (tel: 237-7223; fax: 237-7181).

Palestinian Construction Bank, Al-Bireh, Al-Silwadi Building, Ramallah (tel: 995-4796; fax: 995-4797).

Palestinian International Bank, PO Box 1244, Gaza (tel: 282-7360; fax: 282-5269).

Palestinian Investment Bank, Midan Al-Nahda, Al-Hilal Street, PO Box 3675, Ramallah (tel: 998-7880; fax: 998-7881).

Palestinian Islamic Bank, PO Box 1244, Al-Rimal Quarter, Omar El-Mukhtar Street, Gaza (tel: 282-7360; fax: 282-5269).

Central bank

Palestine Monetary Authority, Nablus Road; PO Box 452,, Ramallah (tel: 240-9920/1; fax: 240-9922/24; e-mail: info@pma.gov.ps).

Stock exchange

Palestine Stock Exchange (PEX)

Stock exchange 2

Palestine Securities Exchange (PSE): www.p-s-e.com

Travel information

The Higher Council for the Arab Tourist Industry, PO Box 19850, East Jerusalem (tel: 628-1805; fax: 628-7981).

Ministry of tourism

Ministry of Tourism and Antiquities, Manger Street; PO Box 534, Bethlehem (tel: 274-1581/2/3; fax: 274-3753; email: mota@pl.org; internet site: www.visit-palestine.com).

Ministries

Ministry of Agriculture, Abu Khadrah Building, Gaza (tel: 286-5990; fax: 286-3926).

Ministry of Economy and Trade, PO Box 1629, Ramallah, West Bank (tel: 298-1214/5; fax: 298-4011).

Ministry of Finance, Omer El-Mokhtar Street, Government Departments Complex, Gaza (tel: 282-4368; fax: 282-3356).

Ministry of Housing, PO Box 4034, Omer El-Mokhtar Street, Government Departments Complex, Gaza (tel: 282-2233/4; fax: 282-2235).

Ministry of Industry, PO Box 1629, Ramallah, West Bank (tel: 298-7641/2; fax: 298-7440).

Ministry of Planning and International Co-operation, PO Box 4017, Omer El-Mokhtar Street, Government Departments Complex, Gaza (tel: 282-9260; fax: 282-4090).

Ministry of Telecommunications, Gaza (tel: 282-5612; fax: 282-4555).

Other useful addresses

Arab Medical Professions College, Al-Bireh (tel: 995-5611).

Birzeit University, Ramallah (tel: 995-7650; fax: 995-7656).

College of Islamic Studies, PO Box 21402, Beit Hanina (tel: 585-3918).

Fine Arts Institute, Ramallah (tel: 995-5974).

Girls' Arts College, PO Box 19377, Jerusalem (tel: 627-3477; fax: 627-3477).

Hebron Polytechnic College, Hebron (tel: 992-8912; fax: 993-8912).

Hebron University, Hebron (tel: 992-0995).

Higher Council for the Arab Tourist Industry, PO Box 19850, East Jerusalem (tel: 628-1805; fax: 628-3981, 628-7981).

Ibrahimieh Community College PO Box 19014, Jerusalem (tel: 626-4216; fax: 628-2925).

Jerusalem Open University, PO Box 51800, Jerusalem (tel: 581-7237; fax: 581-6734).

Khaduri College, PO Box 7, Tulkarem (tel: 671-026; fax: 672-7733).

Palestine Agricultural Relief Committee (PARC), PO Box 25128, Jerusalem (tel: 583-1897, 583-3818; fax: 582-1898).

Palestinian Economic Council for Development and Reconstruction (PECDAR), PO Box 1629, Dahyet El-Bareed, West Bank (tel: 574-7040; fax: 574-9032).

Palestine Securities Exchange, PO Box 128, Nablus, West Bank (tel: 237-5946; fax: 237-5945).

Palestinian Standards Institute, PO Box 1648, Nablus, West Bank (tel: 238-5721; fax: 237-5745).

Palestine Telecommunications Company Ltd (Patel), PO Box 1570, Al-Adel Street, Nablus (tel: 237-6225; fax: 237-6227; e-mail: paltel@palnet.com).

Internet sites

Palestine and Holy Land Tourism Guide: www.palguide.com

Palestinian National Authority (links to other sites): www.palestine-net.com

Palestinian News Agency: http://english.wafa.ps

The Electronic Intifada: http://electronicintifada.net

Panama

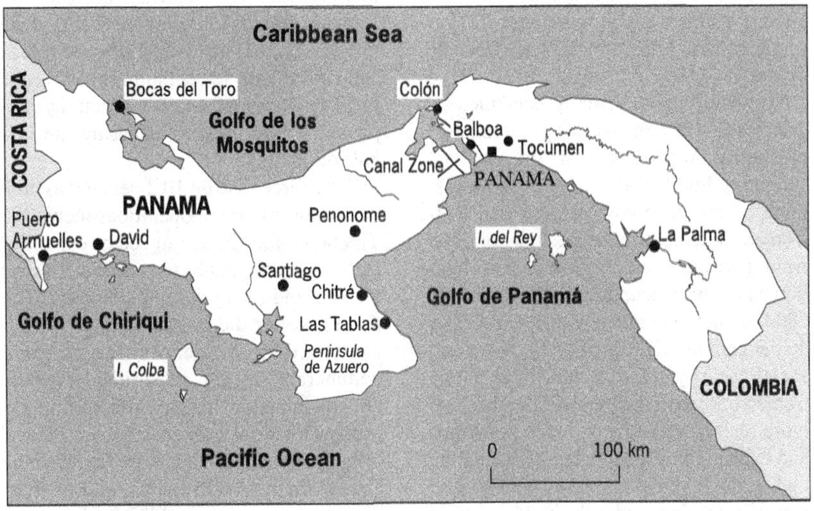

In the five years to 2010, Panama's economy registered the fastest rate of growth – around 8 per cent – in its gross domestic product (GDP) in the American continent. In terms of pure purchasing power, Panama in 2011 was one of the five 'richest' countries on mainland Latin America. The Panama Canal, something of a barometer on world trade levels, showed increased traffic which, combined with higher tolls, in 2011 generated attractive levels of revenue some 20 per cent higher than 2010. In 2010, the Canal's Pacific entrance port of Balboa had been the busiest in Latin America. On an official visit to Singapore in 2010 Panama's President Martinelli was reported in the London *Economist* as saying 'We copy a lot from Singapore and we need to copy more.'

The canal

Shortly after casting his vote in the presidential elections in 2009, Ricardo Martinelli announced that if elected he would 'initiate a process of transparency that does not exist in Panama' and put into jail those who were found guilty of corruption. Mr Martinelli, a 59-year-old business tycoon took office at the beginning of July 2009 when the term of the incumbent President Martín Torrijos expired. It was the second time Martinelli had run in a presidential race. In the 2004 election, he had finished last out of four candidates with only 5.3 per cent of the vote.

The money laundering issue

Panama's embarrassing inclusion on the Organisation for Economic Co-operation and Development (OECD) grey list of countries demonstrating inadequate financial transparency in October 2009 appeared not to take into account its highly regulated banking sector. It also overlooked the fact that on the Group of Seven (G7) ranking of its members' anti-money laundering measure, Panama came a very respectable fourth among 30 countries. Part of the problem probably lay in Panama's history, long seen as little more than a US colony, sharing even its currency with the neighbour to the north. Hard-wired into modern Panamanian politics is a desire to demonstrate that it is now paddling its own governmental canoe. The OECD criteria require the establishment of 12 active tax information exchange agreements; Panama considers that its system of checks and balances, combined with the effects of a lingering Hispanic bureaucracy, is more than enough to comply with international expectations. The G7 survey certainly seemed to bear this out. The other part of the problem was that Panama's taxation

KEY FACTS

Official name: República de Panamá (Republic of Panama)

Head of State: President Ricardo Alberto Martinelli Berrocal (CD) (took office 1 Jul 2009)

Head of government: President Ricardo Martinelli (CD)

Ruling party: Coalition led by Cambio Democrático (CD) (Democratic Change), supported by Partido Unión Patriotica (PUP) (Patriotic Union Party), Partido Panameñista (PP) (Panameñista Party), Movimiento Liberal Republicano Nacionalista (Molirena) (Nationalist Republican Liberal Movement) (from May 2009)

Area: 77,082 square km

Population: 3.41 million (2010; census figure)

Capital: Panama City

Official language: Spanish

Currency: Balboa (B and US$) and US dollar = 100 cents

Exchange rate: B and US$1.00 per US$ (fixed peg)

GDP per capita: US$7,593 (2010)

GDP real growth: 7.50% (2010)

GDP: US$26.80 billion (2010)

Labour force: 1.33 million

Inflation: 3.50% (2010)

Balance of trade: -US$4.62 billion (2010)

regime, however strict, only applies to domestic income. Panama has been less than enthusiastic in entering into double taxation, preferring instead to actually abolish double taxation agreements. Panamanian efforts to strike deals with particular countries were also under way – talks had reportedly been held with a number of European countries, as well as with Mexico. However, little had actually emerged from these negotiations, suggesting that the countries involved were conscious of the OECD requirements.

Canal roots

The Panama Canal has never loomed larger in Panama's economic aspirations. The Canal is not only central to the country's future, but is a traditionally sensitive subject. The key event in Panamanian politics in 2006 was the approval given, in a plebiscite, for the expansion of the Canal. Overall, the expansion project will involve the construction of a third set of locks permitting much larger vessels to transit the Canal from 2014. The estimated cost of the related works is US$5.3 billion.

Another aspect of Panama's relations with the US is a combination of location and surprisingly lax corporate laws. The writer remembers the group of English speaking lawyers, mostly trained in the US and the UK who as long ago as 1967 would meet at a well known airport hotel on Friday evenings to compare notes. Known as *la Siesta Lounge Lisards*, between them they accounted for the bulk of overseas business in Panama. In 2009 an article in the London *Economist* reported that companies could be established in a matter of minutes with no obligations to pay foreign taxes. Its location mid-way between drug producers and their major customers made it an obvious haven for drug revenues. The same report observed that the construction boom that had been seen since 2008 was thought to be drug fuelled. Panama's growing number of skyscrapers were known locally as 'Cocaine Towers'.

Not that Panama actually depended on drug revenues for its long established prosperity. According to the International Monetary Fund (IMF) in its 2010 assessment of the economy Panama had confronted the global financial crisis of 2008 from a strong position. Fiscal consolidation and rapid economic growth during 2004–08 helped reduce public debt below 40 per cent of GDP. Supported by tax and social security reforms, the fiscal policy framework was strengthened and became more resilient. The banks' loan portfolios had expanded only moderately during the high-growth years and the system was on a strong footing and subject to a sound regulatory framework. In addition, when the global crisis struck, the ambitious seven-year Panama Canal expansion project was already well-underway, providing timely support to economic activity.

Up, up and away

In 2011 Panama's economy was expected to grow by 7.5 per cent, in the view of the United Nations Economic Commission for Latin America (ECLAC), boosted by both public and private projects under way. These included the widening of the Panama Canal, building Panama's first subway system, upgrading the transport system, building a copper mine in the Donoso District and continued work on hydropower and other infrastructure projects.

These projects were expected to translate into high rates of GDP growth. Preliminary figures indicated that most of the growth in 2010 had been in three sectors. Transport and telecommunications, the primary sector of economic activity, expanded by 14.0 per cent during the first half of 2010.

Commerce rose by 10.2 per cent as both wholesale and retail operations increased. The hotel and restaurant sector expanded by 9.6 per cent thanks to increasing visitor arrivals and rising domestic demand. The fishing sector did not perform as well; it contracted by 18.1 per cent as captures of commercial species and shrimp larvae declined. Industrial fishery and shrimp exports were also down sharply.

Panama's import tariffs are known to be among the lowest in Latin America. Foreign direct investment (FDI) is high, averaging some 9 per cent of GDP. The fiscal balance of the non-financial public sector posted a deficit of 0.3 per cent of GDP for the first half of 2010,

in line with the fiscal responsibility act that went into effect in January 2009. Excluding 'exceptional circumstances' the act capped the fiscal deficit at 2 per cent of GDP in 2010.

Panama's fiscal accounts for December 2010 were expected to show a slight surplus in the area of 1.0 per cent of GDP. These projections were based on measures that led to an increase of approximately 12.7 per cent in central government nominal current revenue in 2010 – outpacing the 4.0 per cent rise forecast for total spending during the same period.

Increased tax revenues were expected to help fund the many public projects planned for the next few years. Along with the expected high rates of growth, this was anticipated to push Panama's debt down to below 40 per cent of GDP in 2011 compared with 42.4 per cent in 2010.

Inflation measured by the consumer price index was 4.1 per cent higher in October 2010 than in October 2009, driven by food and fuel prices. The largest increases were in transport, tobacco, recreation, health and clothing. The rate of inflation was expected to hold both at year-end 2010 and over the next two years as oil and international food prices rise.

KEY INDICATORS **Panama**

	Unit	2006	2007	2008	2009	2010
Population	m	*3.28	*3.34	*3.40	*3.46	3.41
Gross domestic product (GDP)	US$bn	17.13	19.74	23.10	24.70	26.80
GDP per capita	US$	5,217	5,904	6,784	7,133	7,593
GDP real growth	%	8.6	11.1	10.1	2.4	7.5
Inflation	%	2.5	4.1	8.8	2.4	3.5
Industrial output	% change	8.8	11.7	14.2	3.1	–
Agricultural output	% change	2.3	1.7	6.0	-6.5	–
Exports (fob) (goods)	US$m	8,509.0	9,311.6	10,289.4	10,904.3	11,330.4
Imports (fob) (goods)	US$m	11,649.0	12,624.9	15,003.0	12,930.6	15,945.8
Balance of trade	US$m	-3,140.0	-3,313.3	-4,713.6	-2,026.3	-4,615.4
Current account	US$m	-552.0	-1,579.0	-2,863.0	-43.5	-2,953.2
Total reserves minus gold	US$m	1,335.0	1,935.1	2,423.8	3,028.3	2,714.5
Foreign exchange	US$m	1,315.9	1,915.4	2,404.7	2,741.5	2,432.9
Exchange rate	per US$	1.00	1.00	1.00	1.00	1.00

* estimated figure

Unemployment, at 7.7 per cent for 2010, was little changed to the 7.9 per cent recorded in 2009. Many of the factors that will fuel economic growth in Panama from 2011 are linked to investment and capital-intensive activities (like infrastructure and widening the Panama Canal), so the underemployment and unemployment rates will lag behind the pick-up in economic growth. These indicators are not expected to improve in 2011.

The national banking system rallied in 2010 and is expected to perform even better in 2011. The current account ended the first half of 2010 with a deficit of US$1.336 billion (5.0 per cent of GDP). This was approximately twice the deficit recorded for the same period in 2009. The reason is two-fold. The balance of goods deficit of US$2.077 billion (7.8 per cent of GDP) was some US$446 million higher than for the first half of 2009 as total imports of goods rose by 11.4 per cent and total exports increased by only 6.1 per cent owing, above all, to an 8.2 per cent drop in domestic exports. And the income balance deficit rose by some US$183 million. Both effects were offset by an increase in the financial account surplus, due mainly to a US$236.4 million rise in foreign direct investment for a total of US$1.144 billion as of June 2010.

Risk assessment

Economy	Good
Politics	Improving
Regional stability	Good

COUNTRY PROFILE

Historical profile

1502 European explorers first visited Panama.
1519 Panama became part of the Vice-royalty of New Andalucia.
1821 Following independence from Spanish rule Panama joined the union of Central American provinces and became part of the confederacy of Gran Colombia (Gran Colombia collapsed in 1830 and Panama became part of Colombia).
1846 The US signed a treaty with Colombia to build a railway across the isthmus.
1880 A canal, to link the Atlantic and Pacific oceans, was begun by Ferdinand de Lesseps, (who had previously built the Suez Canal), with French backing. Tropical disease killed thousands of workers; financial difficulties halted the project.
1903 After Colombian parliamentarians refused to endorse a treaty with the US to build a canal the US encouraged the Panamanians to rebel and declare independence. The new rulers signed a treaty with the US that gave rights for the building and independent operation of a canal and surrounding area called the Canal Zone. The treaty was granted in perpetuity.
1914 The Panama Canal was completed.
1939 Panama ceased to be a US protectorate.
1941–68 Panama was mostly ruled by presidents representing the landowners, traders and building companies. Arnulfo Arias, although ousted in 1941, was an unpredictable populist orator, much loved by the crowds. He was in and out of office between 1949–68.
1968 Omar Torrijos became president.
1977 President Omar Torrijos and US president Jimmy Carter signed a treaty under which the US would hand back control of the canal to Panama and withdraw its troops by the end of 1999.
1981 Torrijos, president since 1968, died in a plane crash.
1983 General Manuel Antonio Noriega became commander of the National Guard. He increased his own power and that of the guard, which he renamed the Panama Defence Forces and assumed *de facto* rule of Panama.
1988 The US accused Noriega of drug trafficking. Noriega declared a state of emergency.
1989 The opposition, Alianza Democrática de Oposición Civilista (Civil Democratic Opposition Alliance) and its presidential candidate Guillermo Endara, won the elections. Noriega declared the results invalid. The US increased diplomatic pressure and threats until Noriega declared a 'state of war'. The US invaded and removed Noriega from power. He was taken to the US to stand trial on charges of drug smuggling. Endara became president.
1991 Constitutional changes adopted included the abolition of a standing army.
1992 Noriega was found guilty of drug offences and sentenced to 30 years in a US prison.
1994 Ernest Pérez Balladares won the presidential election.
1999 Mireya Elisa Moscoso Rodríguez of the Partido Arnulfista (PA) (Arnulfista Party) won the presidential elections, becoming Panama's first female president.
2000 Under the Torrijos-Carter treaty ownership and control of the Panama Zone was handed back to Panama on 1 January. President Moscoso set up a tribunal to investigate crimes and human rights abuses during the military rule of 1968–89. The PA lost control of the National Assembly and an alliance led by the Partido Revolucionario Democrático (PRD) (Democratic Revolutionary Party) formed a majority.
2002 Panama signed a framework trade agreement with its five Central American neighbours to boost trade in the region. The PA gained from the defections of three members of the opposition PRD when they voted to approve Moscoso's appointees for the Supreme Court. The three deputies were accused by the PRD of accepting US$1 million in bribes. President Moscoso set up a commission to investigate corruption.
2003 Panama's first free trade agreement (FTA) was established with El Salvador.
2004 Martín Torrijos won the presidential election. The PRD won parliamentary elections and formed a coalition government. The Panama Canal made record profits of US$1 billion during the financial year.
2006 Parliament approved a US$5.25 billion programme to widen the Panama Canal. A referendum approved the project, beginning in 2008, scheduled to be completed by 2014.
2007 Work began to widen the Panama Canal with an additional series of locks.
2009 The US agreed to extradite former president Noriega to France on money-laundering charges, following his early release from jail (for good behaviour) in 2007. In parliamentary elections the political bloc which supported the president, including Cambio Democrático (CD) (Democratic Change), supported by Partido Unión Patriotica (PUP) (Patriotic Union Party), Partido Panameñista (PP) (Panameñista Party) and Movimiento Liberal Republicano Nacionalista (Molirena) (Nationalist Republican Liberal Movement) won 42 seats in the national assembly, the PRD won 26 seats. In the presidential election, also held in May, Ricardo Martinelli (CD) won 61 per cent, Balbina Herrera, supported by the incumbent PRD, won 37 per cent.
2010 From January–May there were 288 deaths attributed to firearms; a new draft legislation to regulate the possession and carrying of weapons (particularly firearms) was introduced to provide some measure of gun control. On 7 July, former dictator, Manuel Noriega was convicted of laundering US$7 million in drug money and sentenced to seven years in prison by a French court.
2010 In July, Manuel Noriega was informed by French authorities that he would be extradited to Panama before the end of the year. On 11–12 August, a bilateral conference of ministers of El Salvador and Panama began, discussing mutual concerns and possible co-operation in health, education, finance, investment and trade. The minister of tourism forecast that by December Panama would have reached its goal of hosting two million visitors in one year.

Political structure
In addition to their unicameral national parliaments, El Salvador, Guatemala, Honduras, Nicaragua, Panama and Dominican Republic also return directly-elected deputies to the supranational Central American Parliament.
Constitution
Panama's constitution dates from 1972 and was reformed in 1983 and 1994.
Form of state
Presidential democratic republic
The executive
The president is both head of state and head of government, elected for a period of five years by universal adult suffrage. The Cabinet is appointed by the president.
National legislature
The unicameral Asamblea Legislativa (National Assembly) has 71 members directly elected in single (typically rural) constituencies and multi-seat (typically urban) constituencies, by proportional representation from party lists, to serve for five-year terms.
Legal system
The Corte Suprema de Justicia (Supreme Court of Justice) has nine judges appointed for 10-year terms. There are five superior courts and three courts of appeal.
Last elections
3 May 2009 (presidential and parliamentary)
Results: Presidential: Ricardo Martinelli (Cambio Democratico (CD) (Democratic Exchange) won over 60 per cent of the vote, Balbina Herrera (PRD) 36 per cent. Parliamentary: Partido Revolucionario Democrático (PRD) (Democratic Revolutionary Party) won 26 seats (out of 71), Partido Panameñista (PP) (Panameñista Party) 21, Cambio Democrático (CD) (Democratic Change) 15, Partido Unión Patriotica (PUP) (Patriotic Union Party) 4, Independents 2, Movimiento Liberal Republicano Nacionalista (Molirena) (Nationalist Republican Liberal Movement) 2, Partido Popular (People's Party) 1; turnout was 70.05 per cent.
Next elections
May 2014 (presidential and parliamentary)

Political parties
Ruling party
Coalition led by Cambio Democrático (CD) (Democratic Change), supported by Partido Unión Patriotica (PUP) (Patriotic Union Party), Partido Panameñista (PP) (Panameñista Party), Movimiento Liberal Republicano Nacionalista (Molirena) (Nationalist Republican Liberal Movement) (from May 2009)
Main opposition party
Partido Revolucionario Democrático (PRD) (Democratic Revolutionary Party)

Population
3.41 million (2010; census figure)
Last census: May 2000: 2,83177
Population density: 36 inhabitants per square km. Urban population: 56 per cent of the total (1994–2000).
Annual growth rate: 2.0 per cent 1994–2004 (WHO 2006)
Ethnic make-up
The population is predominantly mestizo, a mingling of indigenous Indian groups, Spanish and African (65 per cent), and Afro-Caribbean (14 per cent). Indians make up approximately 6 per cent of the total population. There are also descendants of North Americans, Chinese, French, Italians, Greeks and Asians (15 per cent).
The most numerous of Panama's indigenous groups are the Guaymi Indians who live primarily in the western provinces of Chiriqui, Bocas del Toro and Veraguas. The next most populous indigenous group is the Cuna, who live mainly in the San Blas Islands and along the nearby coast. The Choco is another indigenous group.
Religions
Traditionally the population is about 90 per cent Roman Catholic, with Protestants, Muslims, Baha'i and Hindus accounting for 5 per cent.

Education
Schooling lasts for 12 years, six years each in an elementary and a secondary school. Education is free up to university level. University education lasts for six years. There are three universities and nearly one in three of the relevant age group attends them.
Higher education is mainly provided by universities, schools and institutes. There are both public and private universities. State universities are autonomous. The University of Panama is responsible for establishing the guidelines relating to the universities in the country.
Literacy rate: 92 per cent adult rate; 97 per cent youth rate (15–24) (Unesco 2005).
Compulsory years: Six to 15
Enrolment rate: 106 per cent gross primary enrolment of relevant age group (including repeaters); 69 per cent gross secondary enrolment (World Bank).

Health
Panama has both a free public health care system and a private system that are generally served by the same professionals. Panama's hospitals, clinics and insurance plans are scrambling to meet the healthcare needs of wealthier Panamanians, many of whom are retired US civil servants. The cost of healthcare in Panama is lower than in the US and is often of better quality. This is fuelling 'healthcare tourism', with US citizens visiting Panama for medical and surgical treatment.
HIV/Aids
HIV prevalence: 0.9 per cent aged 15–49 in 2003 (World Bank)
Life expectancy: 76 years, 2004 (WHO 2006)
Fertility rate/Maternal mortality rate: 2.7 births per woman, 2004 (WHO 2006)
Child (under 5 years) mortality rate (per 1,000): 18 per 1,000 live births (World Bank)

Welfare
There is a large difference between welfare levels in the cities and in the countryside in Panama. While the percentage of the population below the poverty line is 15 per cent in urban areas, it rises to 65 per cent in rural areas. The national average is 37 per cent.
Panama's social security system is financed through a 6.75 per cent contribution from individual incomes and a 2.75 per cent contribution from company payrolls. Retirement ages are 62 for men and 57 for women. Medical services are provided through the Social Insurance Fund. Sick workers can claim 70 per cent of their average earnings from the last two months for a maximum period of 52 weeks.

Main cities
Panama City (capital, estimated population 490,347 in 2005), San Miguelito (339,803), Tocumen (112,217), Arraiján (97,530), David (85,164), Colón (51,801).

Languages spoken
English is widely used, so much so that Panama should be considered bilingual. English is particularly spoken along the Caribbean coast and in the capital. Three distinct indigenous groups, the Cuna, Guaymi and Choco, also speak either Cuna, Movere or Embera.
Official language/s
Spanish

Media
Press
Dailies: In Spanish, *La Prensa* (www.prensa.com), *El Heraldo* (www.elheraldo.com.co), *La Crítica Libre* (www.critica.com.pa), *La Estrella de Panamá* (www.estrelladepanama.com) and *El Siglo* (www.elsiglo.com), and *La República* (evening). Online newspapers *El Panama America* (www.pa-digital.com.pa).
Weeklies: In English, *The Panama News* (www.thepanamanews.com) and *The*

News Herald (www.newsherald.com) in Panama City.
Business: In Spanish, *Revista Centro Financiero* (www.asociacionbancaria.com) published by the central bank, *FOB Zona Libre De Colón* (www.colonfreezone.com) (trade directory) and *Capital Financiero* (www.capitalfinanciero.com).
Periodicals: There are some periodicals featuring travel and holiday news.
Broadcasting
The vast majority of television and radio broadcasting is in Spanish. There are 82 AM and 31 FM radio stations and six television stations.
Radio: In English, Panama FM (http://panamafm.com) regional station. In Spanish, RPC Radio (www.rpcradio.com), Meto 103.5 (www.meto103-5.com), Super Q (www.superqpanama.com), Omega Stereo (www.omegastereo.com) and KW Continente (http://kwcontinente.net). There are a number of local, commercial radio stations.
Television: Commercial stations, in Spanish, RPC TV (www.rpctv.com), Telemetro (www.telemetro.com) and Televisora Nacional (TVN) (www.tvn-2.com). FETV (www.fetv.org) is an educational channel.

Economy

Panama has few primary resources; it relies instead on the ownership and management of the Panama Canal, which links the Pacific and Atlantic Oceans, and is a strategic component of world trade. Opened in 1914 it was under the control of the United States, then a joint US-Panama administration from 1979 until 31 December 1999 when the Panama Canal Authority took command. Work began in 2007 to widen the Canal to allow passage of larger super tankers; the work is scheduled for completion in 2014.
The country has developed a strong service sector, not only to international trade but also insurance and banking, which contributes around 75 per cent of GDP. The banking sector has been judged by the International Monetary Fund (IMF), as being 'well-capitalised, liquid, subject to effective supervision and have strong financial soundness indicators'. While the sector was not immune from the adverse effects of the global economic crisis in 2008, it remained stable. The canal, container ports and the Cólon Free Zone, which offers duty-free storage and redistribution to over 1,000 foreign companies, contribute around 20 per cent of GDP alone. Other service industries include tourism and flagship registration.
Unlike other Central American countries, Panama does not have to rely on primary industries for GDP growth as its services sector helps protect it from the consequences of adverse weather conditions on the agricultural sector and of low global commodity prices, which have affected neighbouring economies.
GDP growth in 2007 was a record 12.1 per cent based on construction, it fell to 10.1 per cent in 2008, before dropping sharply to 3.2 per cent in 2009 as the global economic crisis cut world trade, and revenues from the Canal. In 2010 growth rebounded to 7.5 per cent as international trade picked up. Inflation jumped from 4.2 per cent in 2007 to 8.8 per cent in 2008, before falling back to 2.4 per cent in 2009 and only increasing by 3.5 per cent in 2010. The official unemployment rate recorded a downward trend, from 9.1 per cent in 2006, to 4.7 per cent in 2007 and then 4.2 per cent in 2008; however the under-employment rates for the last half of 2000 years are thought to be much higher.
Despite its economic strength, Panama has an unequal income distribution, and since the mid-1990s it has been addressing the issues of poverty. In 2011, the UN Human Development Index (HDI) ranked Panama at 58 (out of 187) in the High Human Development category for development in health, education and income. The HDI ranking showed Panama's development trend was higher than the average for other countries within Latin America and the Caribbean. The poverty rate has been reduced from 37.3 per cent in 1997 to 32.4 per cent in 2008 and extreme poverty reduced from 18.8 per cent in 1997 to 14.2 per cent in 2008.

External trade

Panama does not belong to any regional trade or economic bloc but it does have bilateral free trade agreements with Chile, El Salvador, Singapore, Taiwan and all Central American countries, excluding Mexico.
Panama has on of the world's largest merchant fleet due to flagship registration, of around 7,000 ships. In 2009 the Panama Canal provided passage for 14,342 ships between the Pacific Ocean and the Caribbean Sea.
The Colón Free Zone (CFZ) provides the focus for foreign investment in a duty-free manufacturing zone, which is dominated by electronics, watches, pharmaceuticals, toiletries, clothing and jewellery, food processing, sugar refining and garment manufacturing.
Imports
Principal imports are capital goods, foodstuffs, consumer goods, intermediate goods and chemicals.
Main sources: US (typically 30 per cent of total), Costa Rica (5 per cent), Japan (5 per cent).
Main suppliers to the Colón Free Zone are Japan, (typically 20 per cent of total value), US (15 per cent), Taiwan (10 per cent) and Hong Kong (10 per cent).
Exports
Principal commodities are garments, bananas, shrimp, sugar and coffee.
Main destinations: US (typically 40 per cent of total), The Netherlands (10 per cent), Costa Rica (6 per cent).
Re-exports
Petroleum (to the US).

Agriculture

Farming
Panama's principal cash crops include bananas, sugar cane and coffee. Approximately 60 per cent of the country's total landmass is in agricultural use. About 16 per cent is cultivated while the remainder is natural pasture and forest. Food production does not meet domestic demand and consequently food imports are supplied by the US in order to meet the shortfall.
Panama's trading regime has been liberalised to reduce the average tariff level to 15 per cent for agricultural goods, regarded as one of the lowest in Latin America.
The agricultural sector is ailing and has experienced difficulties resulting both from metereological factors and poor demand for products. The strengthening of the agricultural sector is a government priority and includes upgrading irrigation systems and equipment. Problems include the decline in the price of coffee on international markets, which threatens to deepen rural poverty.
Fishing
The vast majority of Panama's annual fish catch is exported to the US- approximately 80 per cent- with the EU being the second biggest buyer of Panamanian fish.
Deep-sea shrimp fishing is the major activity in the sector and this type of fishing increased in increased in importance after the improvement to the port and fishing terminal at Vacamonte was completed in 1994.
Freshwater fishing and marine products have increased in production steadily since the 1990s. Lobster exports rose by 39 per cent and there were also increases in the sales of fresh and frozen fish. The exception was shrimp exports, which dropped by 50 per cent.
Forestry
The majority of Panama's forested area has semi-deciduous tropical moist vegetation, while plantation forest comprises mainly pine. Approximately 40 per cent of the country's total landmass is covered by forests.
Panama has a large network of protected forest areas. However, large-scale

deforestation has led to an annual average loss of 1.65 per cent, the equivalent of 52,000ha of forest cover.
The forest industry produces modest quantity of industrial roundwood, which is used for manufacturing sawnwood and panels. Some amount of forest products particularly paper is imported.

Industry and manufacturing
Panama's industrial sector remains relatively small scale, contributing around 12 per cent to total GDP and employing 16 per cent of the total workforce. The sector is predominantly geared toward domestic consumption.
The main industrial centres are Panama City and Colón, inclusive of food processing (about a third of the gross value of manufacturing output), textiles and clothing, footwear and leather goods, chemicals, plastics, paper, beverages, cigarettes, construction materials and petroleum products from the Las Minas refinery near Colón (capacity 100,000bpd).
The emphasis is on encouraging foreign investment in labour-intensive, light assembly, export-based industries.

Tourism
Tourism is now a very important industry in Panama. The sector has been actively developed by the national government as a key economic sector and accounts for approximately 13.5 per cent of total GDP and 12.9 per cent of total employment in the country.
Still at an early stage of development, tourism offers considerable potential for growth. In addition to the Canal, there is a variety of inland and coastal destinations, particularly conducive to ecotourism, and heritage attractions.
The target for tourist arrivals in 2011 was two million. Cruise ship visits are being encouraged and account for a growing proportion of arrivals.

Environment
Deforestation continues at an alarming rate, even in National parks and the Canal watershed. About 80 per cent of Panama's coral reefs have been destroyed.
Soil erosion is becoming a serious problem in many areas, and Panama's desert in the province of Los Santos (the legacy of slash and burn ranching activities) is expanding.
Illegal gold mining by Colombian immigrants is also contaminating rivers and local water supplies in the Darien and Portobello National parks.
There is serious pollution in the Bay of Panama.

Mining
At present, the mining sector of the Panamanian economy contributes very little to GDP and accounts for a small section of the total labour force. Approximately 0.1 per cent of GDP is generated by the sector and 0.2 per cent of total employment is accounted for by it. However, the mining sector in Panama is, at present, severely underdeveloped. It is estimated that, if properly developed, the sector could grow to contribute as much as 15 per cent of total GDP and directly employ up to 4,000 people.
The government is keen on promoting exploration of gold and copper deposits. Tax concessions and other benefits are available to foreign companies interested in developing the resources. However, proposals for new mines often face strong local opposition.
Copper reserves in Panama are considered to be relatively large with significant deposits in Cerro Colorado and Petaquilla, although the development of the mines has been slow. It is estimated that copper reserves at Cerro Colorado are one billion tonnes, making it one of the world's largest deposits. The Petaquilla studies show copper reserves of 1.1 billion tonnes and significant quantities of gold and molybdenum. The Cerro Quema mine has estimated gold reserves in the region of 300,000 ounces of microscopic gold.
There are also known reserves of manganese, and limited extraction of limestone, clays, gravel and sea salt. Cement is produced by Empresa Estatal de Cemento Bayano at a plant with a capacity of 300,000 tonnes per year (tpy).

Hydrocarbons
There are no hydrocarbon reserves; all energy needs must be met by imports. Consumption of oil was 92,000 barrels per day (bpd) in 2007. There were two separate proposals in 2007, by multinational consortiums, for oil refineries producing two million bpd in one case and processing 350,000bpd of crude oil in the other and which would have turned Panama into a petrochemical hub. But by 2008 the first had been shelved as the global economic crisis worsened and the latter was still subject to determining it's viability.
The Panama Canal is a major transit centre and Panama is very important to the hydrocarbon industry. Petroleum, at 15 per cent of total canal shipments, is the largest single commodity (by tonnage) to pass through the canal, around two-thirds from the Atlantic to the Pacific. A US$100 million contract for construction of the second phase of the Trans-Panama Pipeline, including expansion of terminal facilities (for 5.4 billion barrels of oil) and the oil pipeline from Chiriqui Grande on the Atlantic coast to Puerto Armuelles on the Pacific coast, was signed on 15 October 2009. The pipeline will be used to transport African and Atlantic region oil speedily to the Pacific coast for onward shipment to the US West Coast.
Although there have been some discoveries of oil and gas deposits these have not been in commercially viable quantities.
In 2006 a natural gas pipeline from Venezuela to Colombia, Panama and Ecuador was inaugurated. The first section (225km) to Colombia, was completed in 15 months.
There are coal deposits in the provinces of Colón and Chiriquí but are not used.

Energy
Total installed generating capacity was 1.49GW in 2006. Around 80 per cent of electricity is generated by hydropower. The remaining 20 per cent of capacity is provided by conventional thermal power by the Panama Canal Authority. Consumption is growing at 4 per cent per annum and growth in capacity is expected to increase by 1,000MW between 2009–12, as hydroelectric plants come online at Los Algarrobos and Los Planetas in 2009 and Dos Mares in 2010 and the largest, Changuinola in 2012; other smaller plants will also become operational.

Financial markets
Stock exchange
Bolsa de Valores de Panamá (Panama Stock Exchange)

Banking and insurance
The banking and financial services sector is regulated by the Comisión Bancaria Nacional. The central bank carries out retail and commercial transactions and development banking, it is government-owned and operates as a depository of public funds. Only coins are minted locally, the notes in circulation being US dollars. Interest rates follow US dollar rates.
Panama banking was rated as top for tier one capital, among banks in Central America, as recently as 2004. The Panamanian banking sector is expected to benefit from growth in Central America rather than trying to compete against Brazil, Mexico or Argentina. Before the overall liberalisation of the banking sector in Latin America, banks had used Panama as a base to target markets in the rest of the region; those same banks can now target other Latin American markets directly.
Although it does not have the same size of assets in its banking sector, Panama has always seen its main competitors as the Cayman Islands and the Bahamas. Panama requests all banks to have a physical presence in the country.
Central bank
Banco Nacional de Panamá

Main financial centre
Panama City

Time
GMT minus five hours

Geography
Panama is a narrow country situated at the southern end of the isthmus separating North and South America. To the west is Costa Rica and to the east is Colombia in South America. The Caribbean Sea lies to the north and the Pacific Ocean to the south.
The eastern section of the country, adjoining Colombia, is thinly populated. The western section of the country, near the Costa Rican border, is the richest agricultural area.
Hemisphere
Northern

Climate
For its relatively small area, the geography of Panama's 'S'-shaped isthmus is quite varied and consists of three distinct areas.
The largest, which accounts for approximately 85 per cent of the land area, is lowland coastal areas, with a tropical rainy climate. Here the temperature ranges from 21 degrees Centigrade (C) to 31 degrees C. The rainy season is approximately April–December, with the heaviest rains falling in November (about 570mm). Rainfall is significantly heavier on the Pacific coast than on the Caribbean. The driest season is January—April. About 10 per cent of the land area lies between 700 metres and 1,490 metres and has a temperate climate.
The remaining 5 per cent of the land is at an altitude of about 1,520 metres and is cold.

Dress codes
Like most of Central America, Panama remains fairly conservative and formal in respect of dress. Although Panama City is cosmopolitan, it is not considered proper for adults to wear shorts in the city, regardless of the heat. It is also considered inappropriate for women to wear shorts in public, either in the city or countryside. A certain amount of leniency is allowed to foreigners, who are thought not to know any better.
For business appointments, men should wear suits and women should wear dresses. A man may wear a *panabrisa*, a loose fitting, short sleeved shirt, which is not tucked into the trousers. However, these are not generally worn by top officials or businessmen during formal business meetings.

Entry requirements
Passports
Required by all, valid for six months.
Visa
Required by all, except nationals of EU/EEA and most Latin American countries, Israel, Singapore and North and South Korea. For latest information, see http://panama.embassy.uk.com.
Currency advice/regulations
There are no restrictions on the import and export of local or foreign currencies. Local currency exists only as coins and is interchangeable with US currency of the same denomination.

Health (for visitors)
Mandatory precautions
Cholera vaccination certificate if arriving from an infected area. Yellow fever vaccination certificate may be required for visits to certain regions.
Advisable precautions
A yellow fever vaccination certificate is required only for those who are going to visit the provinces of Bocas del Toro and Darien. Typhoid and polio vaccinations are advisable. Malaria risk exists in rural areas – prophylaxis recommended (in some places malaria is reported to be resistant to chloroquine). Water precautions should be taken, especially outside cities. Rabies is endemic.
Medical insurance is necessary as medical charges are high.

Hotels
There is a wide variety of hotels available. It is advisable to book in advance, particularly between December and May. There is a 10 per cent government surcharge on bills.

Credit cards
Major credit cards are accepted.

Public holidays (national)
Fixed dates
1 Jan (New Year), 9 Jan (Martyrs' Day), 1 May (Labour Day), 15 Aug (Panama City Day/Assumption Day), 3 Nov (Independence from Colombia Day), 4 Nov (Flag Day), 5 Nov (Colón City Independence Day, Colón City only), 10 Nov (First Call for Independence from Spain), 28 Nov (Independence from Spain Day,), 24 Dec (Christmas Eve), 25 Dec (Christmas Day), 31 Dec (New Year's Eve).
For public holidays falling on a Sunday, the following Monday is observed as a holiday.
Variable dates
Carnival (two days, Feb), Ash Wednesday, Maundy Thursday, Good Friday.

Working hours
Banking
Mon–Sat: 0800–1300.
Business
Mon–Fri: 0800–1200, 1400–1700; Sat: 0800–1200.
Government
Mon–Fri: 0900–1700.
Shops
Mon–Sat: 0800–1200, 1400–1800/1900.

Electricity supply
110V AC, 60 cycles (domestic), 220V AC (industrial).

Social customs/useful tips
The use of titles, such as Doctor, Arquitecto, Licenciado, Profesora, is widespread, and it is courteous to learn and use the correct titles for both men and women. Do not immediately launch into a business conversation. It is considered polite to first get to know the person to whom you are talking.
Men and women shake hands in Panama and social kisses on one cheek are also exchanged. At a large social gathering do not expect your host or hostess to introduce you to every individual. Feel free to circulate and introduce yourself. A small gift for the host or hostess is always appreciated.
Late night parties with dinner served at 2200 or 2300 are common. It is accepted to be up to two hours late for a large social gathering, 30 minutes for smaller gatherings.
Panama is an eclectic country, with a ready acceptance of immigrants from all over the world. Public celebrations therefore express the hybrid nature of its diverse cultures. Although once part of Colombia, Panamanian culture and traditions are uniquely its own and show Caribbean rather than South American influence. However, there is little interchange between different social and ethnic groups.
Do not take photos without permission, especially of Indians. Be prepared to pay for them if permission is given.

Security
Common street crime has always been prevalent in Panama City and Colón, but poverty as a result of the disrupted economy has worsened the situation. Visitors are warned specifically to avoid the San Miguelito squatter section of Panama City.
The Judicial Technical Police (PTJ) is responsible for the struggle against the still prevalent narcotics traffic. The PTJ, which is supposed to work jointly with the Customs Service, is composed of former Panamanian Defence Force members and is widely reported to be corrupt.

Getting there
Air
National airline: Copa Airlines (Compañía Panameña de Aviación)
International airport/s: Panama City-Tocumen (PTY), 27km from city;

duty-free shop, restaurant, buffet, bank, post office, car hire.
Airport tax: US$20.
Surface
Road: The Pan-American Highway is the main route into Panama from Costa Rica. The border with Colombia is forested and unsafe.
Rail: Panama has no rail connections with neighbouring countries.
Water: Cruise ships call at the ports of Colon on the Atlantic coast and Panama city on the Pacific coast.
Main port/s: Balboa (Pacific), Cristóbal (Atlantic).

Getting about

National transport
Air: Several domestic airlines link Panama City with all parts of the country.
Road: The road system is generally good, but sections can be unpassable in the rainy season (Apr–Dec). The Panama section of Pan-American Highway connects Chepo and Panama City with the Costa Rican border. The Trans-Isthmian Highway links Panama City and Colón.
Buses: Regional buses link most towns. Ticabus run modern air-conditioned service to main centres; it is advisable to book in advance.
Rail: The Panama Canal Railway Company operates trains daily (Mon–Fri) between Panama City and Colón.
City transport
Taxis: Travel by taxi is inexpensive. Taxis are readily available and can be ordered by telephone. Taxis are not metered, fares being regulated and fixed according to the number of zones traversed. The drivers carry a map of the zones for consultation. Fares should be agreed beforehand.
Car hire
Available in main towns and at the airport. International licence required. After 90 days a local permit is required.

BUSINESS DIRECTORY

The addresses listed below are a selection only. While World of Information makes every endeavour to check these addresses, we cannot guarantee that changes have not been made, especially to telephone numbers and area codes. We would welcome any corrections.

Telephone area codes

The international direct dialling (IDD) code for Panama is +507, followed by the customer's number.

Chambers of Commerce

American Chamber of Commerce and Industry of Panama, PO Box 168, Balboa Ancon, Panama (tel: 269-3881; fax: 223-3508; e-mail: amcham@panamcham.com).

Colón Cámara de Comercio, Agricutura e Industrias, Calle 6, Avenida Amador Guerrero 322, Colón (tel: 441-7223; fax: 441-7281; e-mail: camcolon@pananet.com).

Panama Cámara de Comercio, Industria y Agricultura, Avenidas Cuba y Ecuador 33A, PO Box 74, Zona 1, Panama (tel: 225-1233; fax: 227-4186; e-mail: infocciap@panacamara.com).

Panama Federacion de Cámaras de Comercio e Industria, Avenida Cuba, Zona 1, Panama (tel: 225-4615; fax: 227-4186).

Banking

Asociación Bancaria de Panamá, Apartado 4554, zona 5, Panama (tel: 263-7044).

Banco Comercial de Panamá SA (BANCOMER), PO Box 7659, Panama (tel: 263-6800; fax: 263-8033).

Banco Continental de Panamá SA, PO Box 135, Via España, Panama 9A (tel: 263-5955; fax: 263-7646).

Banco Disa, PO Box 7201, Panama 5 (tel: 263-5933; fax: 264-1084).

Banco de Latinoamérica SA (BANCOLAT), PO Box 4401, Panama 5 (tel: 264-0466; fax: 263-7368).

Banco del Istmo SA, PO Box 6-3823, El Dorado, Panama (tel: 269-5555; fax: 269-5168).

Banco del Pacífico SA, PO Box 6-3100, El Dorado, Panama (tel: 263-5833; fax: 263-7481).

Banco General SA, PO Box 4592, Panama 5 (tel: 227-3200; fax: 227-3427).

Banco Internacional de Costa Rica SA (BICSA), PO Box 600, Panama 1 (tel: 263-6822; fax: 263-6393).

Banco Internacional de Panamá SA (BIPAN), PO Box 11181, Panama 6 (tel: 263-9000; fax: 263-9514).

Banco Latinoamericano de Exportaciones SA (BLADEX), PO Box 6-1497, El Dorado, Panama (tel: 263-6766; fax: 269-6333).

Banco Nacional de Panamá, International Operations Department, PO Box 5220, Panama 5 (tel: 263-8292).

Banco Panamericano SA (PANABANK), PO Box 1828, Panama 1 (tel: 262-0881; fax: 269-1537).

Comisión Bancaria Nacional, Piso 12, Edificio de Boston, Viá Espana, Panama (tel: 223-2855; fax: 223-2864).

Central bank
Banco Nacional de Panamá, Via Espana 120, Torre Banco Nacional, PO Box 5220, Panama 5 (tel: 205-2000; fax: 205-2150; e-mail:mercador@banconal.com.pa).

Stock exchange
Bolsa de Valores de Panamá (Panama Stock Exchange): www.panabolsa.com

Travel information

Copa Airlines, Avenida Justo Arosemena y Calle 39, Apartado 1572, Panama (tel: 227-5232; fax: 227-1952).

National tourist organisation offices
Instituto Panameño de Turismo, Centro de Convenciones Atlapa, PO Box 4421, Zona 5, Panama (tel: 226-7000; fax: 226-4002; e-mail: infotur@ns.ipat.gob.pa).

Ministries

Ministry of the Canal (tel: 263-4545; fax: 263-4355).

Ministry of Commerce and Industry, Edificio de la Loteria, Piso 21, Ave Cuba, Apartado 9658, Zona 4, Panama (tel: 227-4177; fax: 227-3927).

Ministry of Development and Agriculture, Edificio 576, Altos de Curundu, Avenida Frangipany, Panama (tel: 232-5041; fax: 232-5044).

Ministry of Education, Apartado 2440, Zona 3, Panama (tel: 262-2000; fax: 262-9087).

Ministry of Employment and Social Welfare, Apartado 2441, Zona 3, Panama (tel: 225-7503; fax: 225-4529).

Ministry of Finance and Treasury, Calle 35 y 36 entre Ave, Perú y Cuba, Apdo 5245, Zona 5, Panama (tel: 227-4879; fax: 227-2357).

Ministry of Foreign Affairs, Amador, Edificio, Panama 4 (tel: 228-2815; fax: 227-2716).

Ministry of Government and Justice, Calle 1 a, San Felipe, Apartado 1628, Zona 1, Panama (tel: 212-0287; fax: 212-0372).

Ministry of Health, Calle 36 y Ave Cuba, Apartado 2048, Zona 1, Panama (tel: 225-6080; fax: 227-5276).

Ministry of Housing, Ave Mexico y calle 12 de octubre, Apartado 5228, Zona 5, Panama (tel: 262-4358; fax: 262-9250).

Ministry of Labour and Social Welfare, Avenida Balboa, Edif de Diego, 7 Piso, Apdo 2441, Zona 3 (tel: 225-7503; fax: 225-4529).

Ministry of Planning and Economic Policy, Via Espana, Edif OGAWA, Apartado 2694, Zona 3, Panama (tel: 269-2810; fax: 264-7755).

Ministry of the President, Palacio Presidencial, San Felipe, Panama (tel: 227-9662; fax: 227-4119).

Ministry of Property and Finance, Calle 35 y 36, entre Ave Perú Ave Cuba, Pamana (tel: 227-3992; fax: 227-2357).

Ministry of Public Works, Curundu Edif 1019, Apartado 1632, Zona 1, Panama (tel: 232-5333; fax: 232-5776).

Other useful addresses

ARI Promotion and Marketing Department, PO Box 2097, Balboa Ancón, Panama (tel: 228-8037/5668; fax: 228-1698/7488; e-mail: ari@sinfo.net).

Asociación Panameña de Radiodifusión SA, Avenida 11 y Calle 28, Apdo 1795, Panama City (tel: 225-0160).

British Embassy, Commercial Section, Torre Swiss Bank, 4, Urb Marbella, Calle 53, Apdo 889, Panama 1 (tel: 269-0866; fax: 223-0730).

Central Post Office, Plaza Catedral, Calle 6, Panama City.

Colón Free Zone, Avenida Roosevelt, Apdo 1118, Colón (tel: 441-5794, 441-5114, 445-1033, 445-1559; fax: 445-2165).

Consejo Nacional de Inversiones (CNI), Edif Banco Nacional de Panamá, Apdo 2350, Panama (tel: 647-211).

Consular and Maritime Affairs, PO Box 5245, 50th Street and 69th Street, Plaza Guadalupe, San Francisco, Panama 5 (tel: 270-0166, 277-0326; fax: 270-0716).

Corporación Azucarera La Victoria, Apartado 1228,, zona 1, Panama (tel: 229-4797; fax: 229-4806).

Dirección Nacional de Medios de Comunicación Social (Panamanian Media Authority), Ministerio de Gobierno y Justicia, Apartado 1628, zona 1, Panama (tel: 262-3197/3166; fax: 262-1490).

Empleos y Servicios de Oficina SA (translator Service), Avenida 4, Panama City (tel: 225-0527).

Instituto de Recursos Hidráulicos y Electrificación (IRHE), Edif Poli, Avenida Justo Arosemanay 26 Este, Apdo 5285, Panama 5 (tel: 262-6272).

Instituto Panameño de Comercio Exterior, Avenida Manuel Icaza, Apdo 1897, El Dorado 6, Panama.

Panama Stock Exchange, Calle Elvira Mendez y Calle 52, Edificio Vallarino, Panama (tel: 269-1966; fax: 269-2457).

Panamanian Embassy (USA), 2862 McGill Terrace, NW, Washington DC 20008 (tel: (+1-202)-483-1407; fax: (+1-202)-483-8413: e-mail: panaemb@erols.com).

ProPrivat, Ave Perú y Calle 35, Apartado Postal 1464-Paitilla, Panama (tel: 225-0123/6172/4387/0630; fax: 227-4620).

Sindicato de Industriales de Panamá, Apdo 952, Panama City (tel: 230-0619).

US Embassy, Avenida Balboa entre Calle 37 y 38, Apdo 6959, Panama 5 (tel: 227-1777; fax: 203-9470).

Internet sites

Daily internet newspaper: *El Siglo*: http://www.elsiglo.com

General information on doing business in Panama:
www.infonetsa.com/infonetsa/incorp/buss1.htm

Papua New Guinea

KEY FACTS

Official name: The Independent State of Papua New Guinea (PNG)

Head of State: Queen Elizabeth II; represented by Governor General Sir Michael Ogio (from 25 Feb 2011); Governor General Paulias Matane (from 12 Dec 2011) *The occupancy of the office is in dispute.*

Head of government: Prime Minister Peter O'Neill (PNCP) (from 2 Aug 2011); Prime Minister Michael Somare (NAP) (re-appointed 14 Dec 2011). *The occupancy of the office is in dispute.*

Ruling party: Coalition led by the National Alliance Party (NAP), with People's National Congress Party (PNCP) (from 2002; re-elected Jul 2007)

Area: 462,840 square km

Population: 6.86 million (2010)*

Capital: Port Moresby

Official language: English, Tok Pisin, Motu

Currency: Kina (K) = 100 toea

Exchange rate: K2.72 per US$ (Oct 2011)

GDP per capita: US$1,488 (2010)

GDP real growth: 7.00% (2010)

GDP: US$9.70 billion (2010)

Inflation: 6.60% (2010)

Balance of trade: US$1.52 billion (2009)

* estimated figure

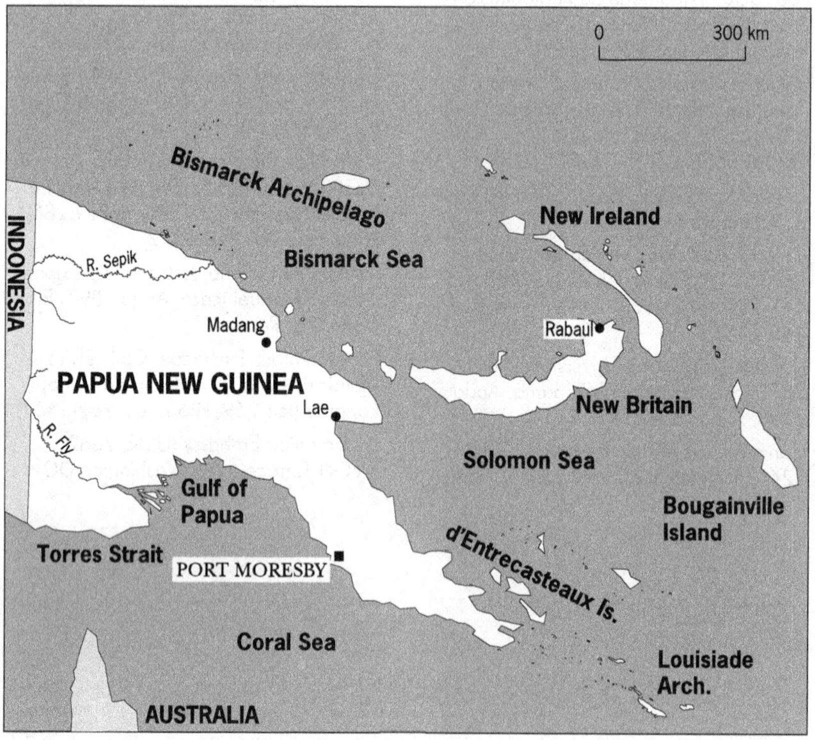

Linguistically, Papua New Guinea (PNG) is certainly the world's most diverse country, an anthropologists's paradise with an estimated 700 plus native tongues. Roughly 80 per cent of PNG's people live in rural areas with few or no modern facilities. Such is the mountainous terrain that most tribes in the isolated interior have little contact with one another, let alone with the outside world and still live within a non-monetarised economy dependent on subsistence agriculture. At the end of the Second World War, PNG was just emerging from traditional modes of life and educational facilities – whether supplied by government funds, aid or missionary donations. The indigenous population lived (and many still do) in small villages, clans and tribes, separate from one another geographically and socially. This division has evolved into strong local and regional sentiments; consequently, the central government has found it difficult to impose national cohesion.

Resource rich

PNG is rich in gold, oil, gas, copper, silver, timber and is home to abundant fisheries. Its population of less than 7 million is strikingly diverse, organised in small, fragmented social groups and speaking over 800 distinct languages. The economy is highly dualistic, consisting of an enclave based formal sector that focuses mainly on large-scale export of natural resources and an informal sector dominated by the subsistence and semi-subsistence activities of the majority rural population, although a local non-mineral small- and medium-sized (SME) sector is now emerging. The PNG economy has weathered recent years of global economic volatility well. Stronger macro-economic management has turned a series of positive external income shocks and large new investments into the longest uninterrupted period of economic growth since the country's independence in 1975. Despite a significant shock to its export prices, the

economy slowed only modestly in 2009, to expand by 5.5 per cent, before recovering to around 7 per cent growth in 2010 and an expected 9 per cent expansion in 2011.

Prudent macro-economic management helped to transform the commodity price booms into resiliency to the crises in the global economy. During the first mineral price boom, the government prudently capped growth of public spending; saved temporary windfall mineral revenue; and paired down its most expensive external debt – the non-mineral budget deficit. This key indicator of fiscal stance in a resource rich economy remained largely steady at around 5–6 per cent of gross domestic product (GDP), close to the estimated long-term sustainable level. With the decline of prices of copper and oil, two of PNG's main export commodities, in 2008-09, these prudent policies provided the space for a significant fiscal impulse to the external shock. The expansion in the 2009 and 2010 budgets constituted slippages from the government's medium-term fiscal framework, but the 2011 budget reconfirms the government's recommitment to cautious fiscal policies. Going forward, the government plans to compliment a stronger fiscal rule with a framework of offshore sovereign wealth funds (SWF). These will serve fiscal stabilisation, savings and public investment goals into the long-term and will be formalised through an organic law.

The turn-around from the economic crises of the late 1990s has been broadly based. While the US$15 billion PNG-liquefied natural gas (LNG) project investment has been the most notable, other investments, in communications, construction and real estate, for example, have given significant impetus and created spillovers into other sectors. These investments have supported growth in formal employment but created shortages of skilled labour. Indeed by 2012 the economy was characterised by various bottlenecks, as investments in new supply lagged the growth in demand, allowing suppliers to charge sharply higher prices. In addition to the scarcity of skilled labour, most notable have been shortages of land in the main urban centers, inadequate infrastructure such as port handling capacity and electricity supply and transportation services. Together these factors, plus the resurgence in global energy prices, have lifted official CPI inflation to the high-single digits in 2011 and the true rate is likely to be higher given weakness in the coverage and measurement of the official CPI. Monetary policy has responded by allowing the exchange rate to appreciate, tightening the policy interest rate and increasing banks' reserves requirements (so reducing the amount of liquidity in the banking system).

The economy

The snappily named 'PNG LNG Project' at Kokopo, is already a significant force in the economy. Implemented by a consortium of international and domestic investors led by ExxonMobil, the expected investment of around US$15 billion is nearly double PNG's current annual GDP. The project received the final investment decision approval in December 2009 and sales and purchase agreements were completed in February 2010. Major construction work soon commenced and is expected to peak in 2012. The first gas shipments are scheduled in late 2014.

There has also been important progress in key areas of structural reform in recent years; in particular, opening markets in telecommunications and air transport has produced major welfare gains for the population. To diversify the economy and increase employment, attention is needed to challenges such as maintaining law and order; improving the business climate; commercialising state-owned enterprises; reducing the regulatory and licensing burden; and equitably accessing resources (including land) for development. Improving infrastructure – electricity, telecommunications, road and other transport – continues to be a critical precondition for accelerated private sector-led growth. Translating strong macro-economic performance and extractive industry revenues into a broad improvement in living standards remains the key challenge for PNG.

In its 2011 resumé of PNG economic prospects, the Asian Development Bank (ADB) notes that plans have also been disclosed for a second LNG project, to cost US$4 billion; construction could start in 2012. Given uncertainty about the construction timetable, the outlook does not factor in any direct impact from this proposal.

Construction of the first LNG plant will accelerate this year (it faced some delays in 2010 owing to land access and compensation issues), thereby increasing activity in the construction and transport industries in particular. The PNG government estimates that only 4.5 per cent of project investment will be retained in the domestic economy because most of the outlays are for imported goods and services. The US$1.4 billion Ramu nickel/cobalt mine, delayed in 2010 over environmental concerns, was expected to start production in 2011. Output from some operating mines is projected to rise, too. However, crude oil extraction rates will continue to fall as fields mature.

The high global prices pertaining for agricultural commodities were likely to stimulate production in 2011. Cocoa output was expected to rebound after crops suffered from disease in 2010 and coffee production should rise, weather permitting. On the balance of these factors, GDP growth was forecast to step up to 7 per cent by the end of 2011, then ease to about 6.5 per cent in 2012 when construction of the first LNG plant starts to taper off.

Price pressures intensified in 2011 in view of the demands on labour and

KEY INDICATORS **Papua New Guinea**

	Unit	2006	2007	2008	2009	2010
Population	m	*6.13	*6.32	*6.20	*6.30	*6.86
Gross domestic product (GDP)	US$bn	5.58	6.40	8.10	8.10	9.70
GDP per capita	US$	947	1,055	1,306	1,272	1,488
GDP real growth	%	3.7	6.5	6.6	5.5	7.0
Inflation	%	3.5	0.9	10.7	6.9	6.6
Exports (fob) (goods)	US$m	4,453.0	4,822.0	5,823.0	4,391.0	–
Imports (fob) (goods)	US$m	2,970.0	2,629.0	3,148.0	2,870.0	–
Balance of trade	US$m	1,483.0	2,193.0	2,675.0	1,521.2	–
Current account	US$m	128.0	208.0	805.0	-671.6	-2,293.0
Total reserves minus gold	US$m	1,400.7	2,053.7	1,953.4	2,560.6	3,033.7
Foreign exchange	US$m	1,400.0	2,052.9	1,952.6	2,377.7	3,017.6
Exchange rate	per US$	2.96	2.75	2.70	2.75	2.72

* estimated figure

resources from the first LNG plant. Supply-side constraints were apparent in construction and transport, particularly in the property markets in Port Moresby and Lae and in skilled labour.

Higher global food and oil prices, coupled with the depreciation seen in 2010 of the kina (against the Australian dollar especially) fuelled inflation, which was projected to accelerate to average about 8.0 per cent in 2011 and remain near this rate in 2012. The Bank of Papua New Guinea (central bank) is expected to tighten monetary policy as inflation pressure builds.

The 2011 budget targets a balanced position, excluding trust fund expenditure. Nevertheless, there may be pressures on the government to spend more from trust funds ahead of the elections expected in 2012. Further, a large portion of previous years' trust fund withdrawals may yet be spent. Such expenditure would result in a fiscal deficit and add to inflation pressures.

A buildup in net foreign assets has partially offset the impact of a reduction in net domestic assets on growth in money supply. This could add to inflation if the trend continues in 2011.

In the external accounts, higher levels of imports for resource projects will continue to widen the current account deficit, to around 35 per cent of GDP in 2011 and 2012. This gap will be largely financed by foreign direct investment (FDI). Foreign reserves are expected to remain adequate in terms of import cover.

The forecasts could prove pessimistic due to an early start to work on the second LNG plant or from higher than expected prices for export commodities. The main downside risk is seen in further delays to large resource projects from disputes over land and compensation for landowners. In the medium term, production from the first LNG plant will underpin growth in GDP, but the likelihood of more such plants is uncertain. There are also uncertainties over mineral production: several large mines are forecast to close sometime in 2012–15. It will be important that the authorities are cautious about committing to any substantial increases in expenditure, given that they will not receive significant revenue from the first LNG plant until 2018 and that receipts from mining depend on global prices and the life of the mines.

Political musical chairs

On 10 December 2010, the Supreme Court ruled that the re-election by parliament of Governor General Sir Paulias Matane was unconstitutional and removed him from office; Jeffery Nape became acting governor general. However, on 20 December, Jeffery Nape resigned without explanation and on 14 January 2011, parliament elected Michael Ogio as governor general.

Prime Minister Somare voluntarily stepped down from office on 14 December 2010, in order to clear his name following accusations of failing to submit full annual financial statements in the 1990s and foreign minister Sam Abal stood in as prime minister. But, after five weeks out of office on leave-of-absence while awaiting an investigation and following legal advice that a prime minister could not step aside temporarily, Prime Minister Somare resumed his premiership on 17 January. As parliament had already adjourned until 10 May it was unable to question his behaviour. On 21 March, a leadership tribunal found Prime Minister Somare guilty on 13 counts of not filing, or late filing or incomplete filing of financial annual returns to the country's Ombudsman Commission. The public prosecutor called for Somare's dismissal from office. However, the leadership tribunal decided to suspend Somare from office for two weeks and Sam Abal became acting prime minister.

Somare did not return to office and on 18 April announcing instead that he was taking indefinite medical leave; he was later admitted to hospital for heart surgery in Singapore. By 2 August, disgruntled members of Somare's National Alliance Party (NAP), seeing no end to Somare's absence (he remained in intensive care in hospital) joined with opposition members and voted to declare the office of prime minister vacant and together voted into office Peter O'Neill (People's National Congress (PNC)) as prime minister. On 4 August, the courts rejected an appeal that O'Neill's election was unconstitutional.

In a *volte face* of an earlier decision, on 12 December 2011, the Supreme Court ruled that the removal of Michael Somare as prime minister had been unconstitutional, despite retrospective legislation passed by parliament earlier in the day to legalise his unseating. Governor General Michael Ogio supported the legal ruling and swore Somare – now recovered – back into office. However, Peter O'Neill refused to step down as prime minister and caused a political deadlock.

Parliament voted to suspend Ogio and appointed Jeffery Nape as Acting Governor General; he then swore in Peter O'Neill and his government and PNG had two prime ministers and two governor generals and both sides were adamant that the constitutions supported each of their positions.

Bemused outsiders look on; the military refused to take sides and on 19 December, the chief of the public service in PNG said that the administration recognised O'Neal as prime minister, because he had control of the cabinet and parliament. On 18 January 2012, Michael Somare was ejected by the deputy speaker of the house of parliament as he attempted to take his seat.

Bougainville

Nowhere is PNG's lack of cohesion more evident than in the autonomous island of Bougainville. A colonial accident allocated the island to PNG despite the islanders' tribal allegiances to the more distant Solomon Islands. PNG had, in colonial days been administered by Australia, the Solomon Islands by the United Kingdom. A decade of civil war on Bougainville ended in 1997 with agreement on a peace formula that granted the breakaway island autonomous status. This was the first step in a process meant to lead to a vote on independence from PNG to be held between 2015 and 2020. Complete, genuine independence for Bougainville seemed something of a tall order. Hopes for the island's future prosperity were pinned on revenues from the vast Panguna copper mine. It is estimated that some one billion tonnes of copper and gold lie beneath the abandoned mine. It was a disagreement over the distribution of income from the mine that triggered the secession movement in 1989.

Expatriates

The larger part of PNG's expatriate community are Australian. But as expatriates have been replaced by young Papua New Guineans, strains have been felt in the economy and politically. Often, relatively young locals – with a good general education but lacking specific training – have been called upon to take over responsible positions from well-trained and experienced expatriates. At one stage, a lack of trained accountants meant that budgets were being drawn up irresponsibly and controls, checks and balances not being monitored. A further problem was that while young Papua New Guineans had attended universities in PNG and overseas, in their homes and often in their offices, they were still junior family members, obliged to defer to their elders.

Risk assessment

Politics	chaotic
Economy	Good
Regional stability	Good

COUNTRY PROFILE

Historical profile

1526 Islanders first traded with ships from China and the Malay Empire. Portuguese sailor Jorge de Meneses is the first European visitor. He names one of the islands 'ilhas dos Papuas' ('land of fuzzy-haired people)'.
1546 The Spanish explorer Inigo Ortiz de Retes named the other main island New Guinea because the islanders looked like the people of Guinea in Africa.
1768 French explorer Louis-Antoine de Bougainville landed on the islands during his circumnavigation of the world.
1873 Port Moresby was named after one of several English explorers to lay claim to the island for Great Britain.
1942–45 Parts of both territories were occupied by Japanese forces during the Second World War.
1949 A joint administration for the two territories was established by Australia. The union was named the Territory of Papua and New Guinea.
1971 The territory was renamed Papua and New Guinea.
1975 Became independent as Papua New Guinea.
1988 Conflict on Bougainville Island began when a number of locals, unhappy with the level of royalties they were receiving from the Panguna copper mine and concerned about its environmental impact, began to protest. The islanders' opposition organised itself into the Bougainville Revolutionary Army (BRA) and full-scale war began.
1989 Panguna mine was closed down by protesters.
1997 Prime Minister Julius Chan attempted to hire UK-based mercenaries to quell the nine-year Bougainville uprising, prompting intervention by the Australian navy and the resignation of Chan. Bill Skate, a reformist, was elected prime minister of a government largely dominated by politicians from the previously ousted government.
1998 The government signed a truce with the secessionist group, the Bougainville Reconciliation Government (BRG), seeking to end the nine-year rebellion on the island of Bougainville, in which up to 20,000 are believed to have been killed. The People's Progress Party (PPP) left the ruling coalition, joining opposition parties and groups in an attempt to oust Skate's government. The prime minister announced the suspension of parliament.
1999 The interim BRG held its first sitting. Skate resigned from the PNG premiership and was replaced by Mekere Morauta of the People's Democratic Movement (PDM).
2000 Morauta was forced to adjourn parliament after a bid to limit inter-party defections threatened to trigger a vote of no confidence in his government. Local landowners brought a suit against Rio Tinto in the US courts, for environmental and social damage at Panguna.
2001 The government signed the Bougainville Peace Agreement with the BRG. PNG accepted Australian aid in return for taking asylum-seekers who sought to settle in Australia.
2002 The National Alliance Party (NAP) won parliamentary elections. Michael Somare became prime minister.
2003 A new heads of agreement was signed for the proposed US$6 billion PNG gas pipeline to Queensland, Australia. The Supreme Court ruled that the election of Albert Kipalan as governor general was invalid. Pato Kakaraya was elected governor general. PNG signed an agreement to introduce more Australian involvement in areas of law and order and public administration PNG.
2004 The Supreme Court ruled the election of Pato Kakaraya as governor general null and void and ordered a new election. Prime Minister Somare dismissed the People's National Congress (PNC) ministers from the cabinet. Talks began to finalise the constitution for the autonomous government of Bougainville province. Paulias Matane was sworn in as governor general of PNG.
2005 Joseph Kabui (Bougainville People's Congress) won presidential elections of the Bougainville Autonomous Government. Rebel leader of the Bougainville secessionists, Francis Ona, died.
2006 Continuous, heavy rains early in the year caused destruction and food shortages in several provinces.
2007 A new system of voting was introduced; majority voting was replaced by limited preferential voting (of three most preferred candidates). Prime Minister Michael Somare was re-elected by parliament with 86 votes to 21 for Julius Chan.
2008 The president of Bougainville, Joseph Kabui, died; vice president John Tabinaman became acting president. A national disaster was declared after a huge king tidal wave flooded villages and towns along 500km of the northern coastline around Wewak, affecting over 50,000 people and making over 500 people homeless.
2009 James Tanis took office as president of Bougainville. Over 200 police officers were sent to the region of the Porgera gold mine in the central highlands, following a breakdown of law and order which had disrupted day-to-day life for villagers in Enga Province. Two new highlands region provinces were approved by parliament. Hela and Jiwaka will be formed from the existing Southern and Western Highlands provinces.
2010 In the Bougainville presidential elections John Momis beat six other candidates including incumbent James Tanis, with 52.35 per cent of the vote; he was sworn into office on 10 June; James Tanis was appointed as vice president. Parliament reappointed Paulias Matane as governor general on 25 June. In August the developers of a multi-billion dollar liquefied natural gas (LNG) project voiced concerns at the series of obstructions that halted work on the construction of a gas condensation plant in the highlands, due to landowners' obstructions. The landowners claimed compensation had not been paid for the work underway and that contract work had not been delegated to their companies. On 10 December, the Supreme Court ruled as unconstitutional the re-election by parliament of Governor General Sir Paulias Matane and removed him from office. Jeffery Nape became Acting Governor General on 13 December. On 14 December Prime Minister Somare voluntarily stepped down in order to clear his name, following accusations of failing to submit full annual financial statements in the 1990s. Foreign minister Sam Abal stood in as prime minister. On 20 December, Nape resigned without explanation.
2011 On 14 January, parliament elected Michael Ogio (NA) as Governor General, beating the opposition candidate Sir Pato Kakaraya (by 65 votes to 23). After five weeks out of office on leave-of-absence while awaiting an investigation into the non-submission of financial records, and following legal advice that a prime minister could not step aside temporarily, Prime Minister Somare resumed his premiership on 17 January. As parliament had already adjourned until 10 May it was unable to question his behaviour. Sir Michael Ogio was sworn in on 25 February. On 21 March, Prime Minister Somare was found guilty of 13 counts of not filing, or late filing or incomplete filing of financial annual returns to the country's Ombudsman Commission, by a leadership tribunal. On 22 March, the public prosecutor called for Somare's dismissal from office. On 24 March the leadership tribunal decided to suspend Somare from office for two weeks. He was suspended on 4 April and Sam Abal became acting prime minister. Somare did not return to office and on 18 April announced that he was taking indefinite medical leave; he was later admitted to hospital for heart surgery in Singapore. Disgruntled NAP members of parliament, seeing no end to Somare's absence, as he remained in intensive care in hospital, joined with opposition members and voted to declare the office of prime minister vacant and together voted in (70-24) Peter O'Neill (PNC) as prime minister on 2 August. Arthur Somare (son of the former

prime minister), who had been charged with the same offence as his father (of misconduct in office by failure to submit financial statements over several years), lost his appeal in court on 2 August to delay his trial until leadership of the NAP was concluded. On 4 August, the courts rejected an appeal that O'Neill's election was unconstitutional. On 12 August, Prime Minister O'Neill announced an investigation would begin into allegations of corruption by a government department and the loss of US$883.9 million in public funds. Nineteen MPs, of the NAP were expelled from the party on 7 September for supporting the opposition in deposing Michael Somare and electing Peter O'Neill as prime minister. They also supported disqualification of Somare from parliament due to his continued absenteeism. During the Commonwealth Heads of Government summit, on 28 October, the 16 countries in which the British monarch is Head of State unanimously agreed to change the royal line of succession from that of first born son to the first born child (regardless of its gender). The change will be enacted after the succession of Prince William (currently second in line to the throne, after his father Prince Charles). On 24 November, a proposal to amend the constitution was agreed to create 22 parliamentary seats, one for each province, set aside exclusively for female representatives. However, to amend the constitution and enact the proposal would require more members of parliament to participate than voted in favour of the original proposal. On 12 December, the Supreme Court ruled that the removal of Michael Somare as prime minister in August was unconstitutional, despite retrospective legislation passed by parliament earlier in the day to legalise his unseating. Governor General Paulias Matane supported the legal ruling and swore Somare back into office; Peter O'Neill refused to step down as prime minister. On 14 December the Governor General swore in Somare's government. However parliament voted to suspend Ogio and appointed Jeffery Nape as Acting Governor General; he then swore in Peter O'Neill and his government. The military refused to take sides. On 15 December, the rival attorney generals agreed to discuss a possible solution to the political crisis of two prime ministers vying for power. On 19 December, the chief of the public service in PNG said that the administration recognised O'Neal as prime minister, because he had control of the Cabinet and parliament.

Political structure

Constitution

The political structure is that of a unicameral parliamentary democracy. The present constitution came into effect in 1975 when the country became independent within the Commonwealth.
The 1975 constitution provided for the decentralisation of power to 20 provincial governments. Since then, Papua New Guinea (PNG) has been developing a system of local government.
An amendment to the constitution in 1977 led to the formation of 20 elected provincial governments which enjoy limited legislative and administrative powers and are funded mainly by central government.
Administrative divisions:
Bougainville became an autonomous region in 2005, with PNG's federal government retaining control over defence and the economy.

Independence date

16 September 1975

Form of state

Sovereign independent state; it is a member of the Commonwealth.

The executive

The British monarch is the head of state and is represented by the governor general whose normal term of office is six years. Effective power resides with the prime minister and his cabinet, the National Executive Council. The governor general is appointed on the recommendation of the National Executive Council and on the basis of a simple majority vote in parliament. The prime minister is appointed by the head of state on the proposal of parliament.

National legislature

The unicameral National Parliament has 109 members, of which 89 are elected by limited preferential voting in open electorates and 20 from provincial electorates (two new provinces were inaugurated in 2009 but no new constituencies were announced). All members are elected for five-year terms. Parliament votes for the prime minister (typically the leader of the largest party), the speaker and deputy speaker (the latter may not hold ministerial posts).

Legal system

The legal system is based on English common law. The national judicial system comprises the Supreme Court, the national court and subsidiary courts. The Supreme Court is responsible for all matters concerning the interpretation of the constitution and is the final court of appeal. The Chief Justice is appointed by the head of state and the judiciary is formally independent of other branches of government.

Last elections

30 June–14 July 2007 (parliamentary); 21 May 2010 (Bougainville presidential).
Results: Parliamentary: National Alliance Party (NAP won 30 seats (out of 109); of the other 19 political parties none won more than eight seats (63 seats in total), plus 16 independents.
Bougainville presidential: John Momis beat six other candidates with 52.35 per cent of the vote.

Next elections

June 2012 (parliamentary)

Political parties

Papua New Guinea has no real party system and most members of parliament function as independents, although they have various party labels.

Ruling party

Coalition led by the National Alliance Party (NAP), with People's National Congress Party (PNCP) (from 2002; re-elected Jul 2007)

Main opposition party

People's Democratic Movement (PDM)

Population

6.86 million (2010)*
Last census: July 2000: 5,190,786
Population density: 15 inhabitants per square km (2010)
Annual growth rate: 2.4 per cent 1994–2004 (WHO 2006)

Ethnic make-up

Most of the population is Melanesian. There are numerous other ethnic groups in Papua New Guinea's 20 provinces, including those of Papuan, Polynesian and Micronesian descent. There is a sizeable minority of Australians, some Europeans and a small Chinese community in the country's limited commercial centre.

Religions

The indigenous population is mainly pantheistic, although a significant proportion has adopted Christianity. There are more than 10 different Christian religious groups in the country, including a substantial Roman Catholic congregation (22 per cent of the population) and various Protestant congregations (44 per cent). Indigenous beliefs account for 34 per cent of the population.

Education

Education standards before independence were poor, reflected in low literacy levels in the workforce. School fees have to be paid although these are subsidised by the government. Staff shortages remain an acute problem at secondary level. Lack of materials and up to date curricula are further burdens for the education system.
The government has backed the 'one laptop per child' programme (OLPC).
Despite these disadvantages, there has been some development, made possible by help from the Australian government, through AusAid. AusAid has improved the condition of student housing and provided science laboratories in several schools.
In March 2009 the European Union warned the government that a grant of

US$53 million, to improve teacher training and to purchase school text and library books would be withdrawn following the government's failure to provide detailed plans for the money's allocation.
Literacy rate: 66 per cent, adult rates (2003).
Enrolment rate: 80 per cent gross primary enrolment of relevant age group (including repeaters); 47 per cent gross secondary enrolment (World Bank).
Pupils per teacher: 38 in primary schools.

Health
The death toll from a three-fold disease of cholera, flu and dysentery killed over 400 people, prompting the WHO to issue a warning to the government, which declared a state of emergency in 2009 and provided medical aid to Morobe Province, as the disease was spreading into the Eastern Highlands and Gulf Province. By April 2010 the disease had spread along the north coast and reached Port Moresby, initially killing three people. Fears grew that the poor living conditions in the city's squatter settlements would provide ample victims for an epidemic. The population suffers from poor health. The government provides hospitals and other health care facilities, but while hospital treatment is available in all major centres, they have varying levels of service and efficiency. A charge on the basis of ability to pay is levied for health services, although most people are treated free or make only a small contribution.
In 2004, health authorities stated that the maternal death rate in PNG was greater than in any other Pacific island; over 1,000 women per annum, die of complications. In 2010, due to worryingly high maternal mortality figures (one in seven chance of death) in remote communities, prompted the government to train village health volunteers to provide basic medical treatment. An Australian charity will issue birthing kits, which include some of the basic equipment needed during a delivery.
PNG is to receive US$20 million to fight malaria from the Global Fund, set up to fight malaria, Aids and tuberculosis. Insecticide impregnated anti-malaria nets have been provided by the World Health Organistion and Australian aid to increased numbers of children and reduced the incidence of the desease, acknowledged as the number one killer of children in PNG.
An agreement of employment between the governments of PNG and Cuba in 2006, allowed 20 Cuban doctors to work in rural areas of PNG to overcome an acute shortage.

HIV/Aids
There is a serious AIDS epidemic in PNG, which has the largest number of HIV positive citizens in the Pacific region. While the prevalence rate is only 2 per cent, for those at most risk the rate is 16 per cent. In 2002, 15,000 people had the disease, by 2005 the reported number was over 40,000, however screening of 3,000 A&E patients at the Port Moresby General Hospital found 18 per cent were HIV positive; other evidence indicates the current prevalence rate is doubling each year. In 2004 a survey found that 1 per cent of expectant mothers were testing positive for HIV and fears are that PNG has reached the trigger point for a widespread epidemic of Aids.
In 2005 220 new HIV/Aids cases were being reported monthly, the overall number of HIV/Aids cases was 60,000. In 2006, the health minister reported that the infection rate in some remote parts of the country was over 10 per cent and nationwide the rate was rising by 30 per cent per annum.
HIV prevalence: 2 per cent aged 15–49 in 2005
Life expectancy: 60 years, 2004 (WHO 2006)
Fertility rate/Maternal mortality rate: 3.9 births per woman, 2004 (WHO 2006)
Birth rate/Death rate: 31 births per 1,000 population; 7.6 deaths per 1,000 population (2003).
Child (under 5 years) mortality rate (per 1,000): 69 per 1,000 live births (2003)

Welfare
A number of defined-contribution provident funds provide limited social benefits. A National Provident Fund (NPF) provides social benefits for employees of private-sector companies with 20 or more personnel, while the Public Officers' Superannuation Fund (POSF) provides a similar facility for public servants.

Main cities
Port Moresby (capital, estimated population 299,396 in 2005), Lae (82,527), Kokopo (33,805), Arawa (40,266), Madang (29,015), Goroka (18,639).

Languages spoken
Tok Pisin or Pidgin is the lingua franca of the islands. It is derived from Melanesian Pidgin and includes German and English words. English is spoken by only 1–2 per cent of the population but is the language of government and business, however in parliamentary sessions, Pidgin is used. Motu is spoken by Motuan villagers and has been modified into Police Motu which is spoken widely in the southern region. There are 715 indigenous languages.

Official language/s
English, Tok Pisin, Motu

Media
Press
There are numerous newspapers and magazines published in English, Tok Pisin and vernacular languages.
Dailies: In English, the two main daily newspapers are *The National* (www.thenational.com.pg) and *Papua New Guinea Post-Courier* (www.postcourier.com.pg) published Monday to Friday.
Weeklies: *Times of Papua New Guinea* is a well-regarded weekly publication in English.
Broadcasting
Radio: The government-owned National Broadcasting Commission (NBC-PNG) (www.nbc.com.pg) operates two AM networks and a FM commercial station broadcasting in English, Tok Pisin and various other local languages. Two other independent, national commercial radio stations are in operation, Nau FM and Yumi FM; plus broadcasts are received from Australia.
Television: Fiji Television Limited owns PNG's only television station EMTV, which has an estimated 2.5 million audience and about 38 per cent of the advertising market. The Media council monitors the output for local content and community initiatives in broadcasting.

Economy
Papua New Guinea (PNG) has a variety of natural resources, including gold, timber, hydrocarbons, fish and copper. Its mining sector provided record revenue in 2008 as global prices for minerals surged. However the industry has to contend with poor communications, the lack of infrastructure and tough terrain that means extraction and transport is laborious and expensive. Mineral extractions, including oil and gas, are exploited mainly by foreign interests and account for nearly three-quarters of all exports and around 50 per cent of GDP. A project to supply liquefied national gas (LNG) was agreed in 2009 with initial investment of US$100 million. When fully in production it is expected that the LNG project (with a maximum capacity of 60 million barrels of oil equivalent and with a 30-year life) will increase the estimated GDP by 15–20 per cent. The construction of infrastructure and plant for the LNG project is expected to increase annual gross national income (GNI) by 9 per cent during its five years of building (2008–13). A 20-year agreement for 36.3 million tonnes of PNG LNG to be sold to China was signed in November 2009.
Industry dominates the economy and constituted some 44 per cent in 2009, with

agricultural as the second most important sector at 36 per cent of GDP; services provided 20 per cent of GDP.
GDP growth in 2008 was 6.6 per cent with strong growth in the non-mineral sector (construction and communications in particular). Growth had been expected to be better that this but high energy costs and imports depressed the economy, so that in 2009 growth fell to 5.5 per cent as world trade weakened. Growth rebounded in 2010 to 7 per cent and was forecast to climb higher to 9 per cent as the hydrocarbons industry expands.
In 2011, the UN Human Development Index (HDI) ranked PNG 153 (out of 187) for development in health, education and income. The majority of the population live outside the narrow organised economic activity – 85 per cent of the population depend on subsistence farming for their livelihood. Around 40 per cent of the population survive on less than US$1.25 per day. Only around 2 per cent of the land is suitable for agriculture, mainly in coastal areas and upland plateaux. Some cash crops, such as coffee, palm oil and tea, are nevertheless grown and exported. The World Bank ranked PNG as a lower middle income country, with a GNI per capita of US$976, which allows loans by international investment banks to be granted with concessions and low interests.

External trade

Papua New Guinea is a member of the South Pacific Regional Trade and Economic Co-operation Agreement (Sparteca) along with 12 other regional nations, which allows products duty free access by Pacific Island Forum members to Australian and New Zealand markets (subject to the country of origin restrictions). It is also a member of the Melanesian Spearhead Group (with Fiji, Solomon Islands and Vanuatu) as a sub-regional trade group, whereby customs tariffs have been harmonised under the Melanesian free trade agreement (MFTA).

Imports

Principal imports are machinery and transport equipment, manufactured goods, food, fuels and chemicals.
Main sources: Australia (typically 43 per cent of total), Singapore (16 per cent), China (10 per cent).

Exports

Principal exports are oil, gold, copper ore, timber, palm oil, coffee, cocoa and shellfish.
Main destinations: Australia (typically 30 per cent of total), Japan (10 per cent), China (6 per cent).

Agriculture

Farming

Agriculture accounts for around 27 per cent of GDP. More than 80 per cent of the population depend on agriculture for their livelihoods. Approximately 5 per cent of land area is cultivated arable, which is restricted by dense rain forests and mountainous terrain.
Coconuts, coffee, cocoa, palm oil, rubber and tea are grown as cash crops on plantations, emloying around one-third of those engaged in agriculture.
Processing, quality control and pricing for main crops are the concern of the Coffee Marketing Board and the Copra Marketing Board, which operate stabilisation funds for these products and for cocoa. Smallholdings produce 70 per cent of all coffee for export, in addition to subsistence crops of yams, sago, cassava, bananas, pineapples, vegetables, sweet potatoes, tea, natural rubber, groundnuts, sorghum and rice, with some raising of pigs, goats and poultry. Food production has kept pace with the population growth.

Fishing

One considerable resource Papua New Guinea has yet to exploit is its fishing grounds, probably the world's richest. The total annual fish catch is over 300,000 tonnes, but the country's waters have been estimated to be capable of supplying up to one million tonnes of fish a year. PNG's waters are home to more than 1,800 different species of fish. Activity in the sector is largely centred on domestic fleets tapping the country's 2.3 million square kilometres exclusive fishing zone. Foreign fleets have been excluded from the zone. PNG has become one of the biggest players in the Western tuna fish industry. The growth of the industry has been encouraged by favourable government policies such as the removal of export duties on fisheries products.
Investment in a marine park was announced by the government in 2007. The park of 860 acres at Vidar, outside Madang, with an estimated cost of US$36.3 million, will include a jetty for small boats and a wharf for large purse seiners, a fish market, cold rooms, ice-making and processing plants and other facilities including a township. PNG provides 10 per cent of the world's supply of tuna but its status as a primary industry does not return value-added revenue. The European Union, the biggest consumer of Pacific tuna, has negotiated with PNG to provide more favourable terms for importing its tuna.
In April 2010 the Parties to the Nauru Agreement (PNA) (eight island states including PNG) collectively agreed to close to *purse seine* fishing in 4.55 million square kilometres of high seas in their area, from 1 January 2011, to vessels licensed to fish in their waters. The area involved stretches from Palau and Papua New Guinea in the west to Kiribati in the east, from the Marshall Islands in the north to Tuvalu in the south; it holds an estimated 25 per cent of the world's tuna supply.
On 12 April 2011, a summit of the Parties to the Nauru Agreement (PNA) concluded its strategy for a policy of sustainable fishing in the Pacific. The PNA treaty, which was established in 1989 and expires in 2012, is seen as in need of an overhaul. As a collective region (FSM, Kiribati, Marshall Islands, Nauru, Palau, PNG, Solomon Islands and Tuvalu) control around 25–30 per cent of world stocks of tuna. Only 5 per cent of sales revenue is returned to the PNA and ministers called for specific changes, including an increased share of profits, PNA crews on-board *purse seine* vessels (minimum 10 per cent), conservation and management measures including a limit to fish trapping (fish aggregating devices (FADs)), net mesh rules and the establishment of an observer agency and fisheries information management system.

Forestry

The economy benefits from huge exports of tropical logs, while the sawn timber industry caters to domestic demands. Forests and woodlands cover around 93 per cent of land area, but are subject to deforestation for tropical timber exports and to pollution from mining projects. The government is seeking to regain control of an industry which seems to have operated outside existing regulations and in which political corruption has played an important part. There has been little monitoring of commercial operations and reforestation is inadequate.PNG has a relatively small plantation estate.
PNG has an established presence in the Asian log market and exports around one million cubic metres of logs annually to South Korea, as well as around 400,000 cubic metres to Japan.
In July 2011, landowners in the Western Province won a landmark legal case against the Malaysian logging company, Concord Pacific Limited, which was ordered to pay US$97 million for environmental damage due to its illegal logging.

Industry and manufacturing

The industrial sector, including mining, accounts for around 40 per cent of GDP and employs 10 per cent of the workforce. Manufacturing accounts for around 9 per cent of GDP.
Industry is focussed on mining (gold, silver, copper), crude oil and processing agricultural products. Copra crushing, palm and coconut oil processing, sugar

processing, brewing, meat production, plywood production and wood chip production are prominent. Government policy, through the Industrial Centres Development Corporation, aims to promote non-mining sectors, particularly import substitution and export-oriented industries such as manufacturing and downstream processing. Main activities include boat-building, steel fabrication and manufacture of cement, paper products, soap, matches, chemicals, paint, sawn timber, furniture, plywood, bottles and cigarettes.

Tourism

Tourism is at an early stage of development, but, with over 90 per cent of the land area still forested, there is enormous potential especially for adventure and eco-tourism. The authorities recognise the economic value of tourism and have stepped up promotion and infrastructure development. Australia is the largest market, followed by Japan and other Asian countries. Around two-thirds of visits are for business purposes, but leisure tourism is an increasing proportion of the total, enhanced by cruise ship visits.

Unesco added the Kuk Early Agricultural Site to its World Heritage List in July 2008.

Environment

Papua New Guinea, Philippines, Indonesia, Australia and Solomon Islands are the countries with the most coral reef fish species.

Mining

Mining contributes around 8 per cent of GDP. Copper and gold are the most important export minerals. Most mineral resources are difficult and costly to extract. PNG, the Federated States of Micronesia and the Solomon Islands will submit a joint proposal to the United Nations in 2009 to develop the Ontong Java Plateau, which is part of their extended continental shelf, for mineral prospecting.

In 2009 the Simberi mine announced an increase of its proven reserves of gold by 4.7 million ounces and of silver by 10 million ounces.

The world's first commercial mining of high-grade ores from the sea floor will begin in PNG waters in 2010, following successful exploration programmes in 2009.

In 2010, sediment from the gold mine that washed down the Watut River destroyed the river system and surrounding area, taking the livelihood of thousands of villagers. The Australian-based Newcrest Mining accepted responsibility and paid compensation.

The government granted a 20-year mining lease in January 2011 to the Canadian company, Nautilus Minerals to mine, among other ores, gold and copper from the seabed in the Bismarck Sea, which is in PNG territorial waters. This will be the world's first commercial seabed mining operation and is expected to produce in total around 1.3 million tonnes of ore annually (80,000 tonnes of copper, 150,000–200,000 ounces of gold), with the operation fully underway by June 2013. 2014. The PNG government negotiated to invested up to 30 per cent of the operations, (US$103 million) over 2011–14.

Hydrocarbons

Proven oil reserves were negligible at 240 million barrels in 2007.

The government created Petromin (PNG) Holdings in 2007, to manage state interests in the energy and mining commodities sectors. It works with foreign partners to explore, develop and produce oil, gas and mining ores. Under legislation, the state could acquire up to 22.5 per cent interest in all petroleum development projects. There is active exploration for oil both onshore and offshore.

PNG may have substantial untapped reserves of oil and gas, but the rugged terrain and the problems of inaccessibility are major obstacles to exploration with recovery costs very high. There can also be problems in gaining permission to exploit tribal lands.

InterOil Corporation completed the construction of PNG's first oil refinery at Napa Napa in 2004. The refinery can process 32,500bpd at full capacity and supply the PNG domestic market, leaving 35 per cent of its output for foreign export.

Drilling of the Panakawa oil prospect is scheduled to begin in 2009, by the Australian-based New Guinea Energy Limited. The prospect is estimated to contain 187 million barrels and will be used in export sales.

Proven natural gas reserves were 400 billion cubic metres (cum) in 2010, domestic consumption is negligible and any production is due for use in liquefied natural gas (LNG) projects. In 2009, InterOil Corp reported that, in total, it had discovered a further 280 billion cum of natural gas onshore. The field will be used to supply natural gas to the proposed US$11 billion Liquid Niugini Gas project, near Port Moresby, where it will be turned into LNG, at an estimated rate of nine million tonnes per annum. Landowners of the LNG site claimed, in 2009, that they had not been compensated for its use, just as the royalties from the project were being allocated. The National Court ordered that any agreement regarding the proposed LNG project could not be legally binding unless proper procedures stipulated by PNG laws were reached. Landowners who had taken legal action for compensation must be included in any later agreements. The construction of a second LNG plant was agreed in December 2009, with the Canadian oil and gas company, InterOil.

Two gas pipelines linking PNG to Queensland, Australia, were proposed but have been halted due to environmental concerns and access through native lands.

A 20-year agreement for 36.3 million tonnes of PNG LNG to be sold to China was signed in November 2009.

Coal is neither produced nor imported.

Energy

Total installed generating capacity was 500MW in 2006. Hydropower produces 220MW, with another 513MW under construction and 11MW planned. The major hydroelectric schemes are located at Port Moresby, Ramu River and the Gazelle Peninsula. The energy mix also includes oil-turbines with natural gas-turbines in the region of Kutubu supplying 42MW to the local Porgera gold mine. Geothermal power is in operation on the island of Lihir supplying 56MW of electricity to the local gold mine.

Plans for a new hydroelectric power plant in PNG to supply electricity to northern Queensland were announced in September 2010. The Australian power company Origin Energy and PNG's Energy Developments will build the power plant, with the first phase generating 1800MW to be supplied via an undersea cable to Townsville by about 2020. Environmentalists have condemned the proposals.

In November 2011, a joint project between the government and the Asian Development Bank to fund a rural electrification programme was completed and began supplying hydroelectricity to Bougainville and the provinces of Central and Oro from January 2012.

Financial markets

Stock exchange

Port Moresby Stock Exchange (PoMSOX)

Banking and insurance

Central bank

Bank of Papua New Guinea

Main financial centre

Port Moresby

Time

GMT plus 10 hours

Geography

Papua New Guinea (PNG) has only one land border with Indonesia, which lies at the west end of the island of New Guinea. PNG lies across the Torres Stait, north of the north-eastern extremity of Australia. Although the bulk of the country's land area is formed by the mainland, PNG includes many smaller islands, principally the Bismark Archipelago, which largely comprises New Britain, New Ireland and Manus, and the North Solomon Islands of which Bougainville and Buka are the largest. PNG has coastlines extending for a total of 5,152km; its highest point is Mount Wilhelm, at 4,509 metres.

The country is a land of great geographic diversity. The coast is low-lying swamp, the central core has a massive system of mountain ranges but there is also an extensive range of foothills as well as volcanoes (PNG forms a constituent part of the Pacific 'Rim of Fire' – a line of tectonic activity, which produces many volcanoes in a string that stretches from New Zealand in the south-east and circles the Pacific up to the Aleutian Islands and down along the US west coast). The country has substantial mineral wealth and good agricultural potential with fertile soil and abundant rainfall. There are large expanses of tropical forest and good fishery stocks.

Hemisphere

Southern

Climate

Papua New Guinea has a tropical climate with an average maximum temperature of 33 degrees Celsius (C) and an average minimum of 22 degrees C. Temperature and humidity are fairly constant throughout the year. The Highlands region has a more temperate climate than the rest of the country. Papua New Guinea also has seasonal monsoons, varying considerably between regions. Rainfall totals up to 4,600mm per year in some areas.

Dress codes

As Papua New Guinea is in the tropics, light clothes are worn at all times, although travellers to the Highlands may require sweaters for the evening. Business wear is usually lightweight trousers and a short sleeved shirt. The Australian sartorial influence can be seen in the wearing of shorts and long socks by males even in administrative positions. Jackets are not normally required but safari suits are often worn. Formal evening wear is seldom required but sometimes tropical formal wear is stipulated on invitations and this would mean a long sleeved shirt and tie for men and a cocktail dress for women.

Entry requirements

Passports

Required by all. Passports must be valid for 12 months from the date of entry.

Visa

Required by all. Contact the nearest PNG Consulate for visa details and application form.

All travellers should be in possession of sufficient funds for onward or return flight before the expiry date of their visa.

Visa conditions are liable to change and should be checked before travelling.

Currency advice/regulations

The import of local and foreign currency is unlimited. Export of local currency is limited to K200; foreign currency is limited to K10,000 (equivalent), amounts greater require approval from the Central Bank.

Travellers cheques are readily accepted; to avoid additional exchange charges cheques should be in Australian or US dollars or pound sterling.

Customs

The export of items of ethnographic interest is banned.

Health (for visitors)

Mandatory precautions

Vaccination certificates for yellow fever if travelling from an infected area.

Advisable precautions

Vaccinations that are necessary include typhoid, tetanus, and hepatitis A. Vaccinations that may be advised include diphtheria, hepatitis B, tuberculosis, Japanese B encephalitis and rabies. Anti-malarial precautions must be taken when visiting all but the central highlands; the use of mosquito nets and repellents and covering up the body after dark can help avoid malaria, hepatitis B, dengue fever and encephalitis (which is a risk in remote regions only). There is a very high prevalence of HIV/Aids.

Use only bottled or boiled water for drinks, washing teeth and making ice. Eat only well cooked meals, preferably served hot; vegetables should be cooked and fruit peeled. Eating grouper, snapper, amberjack, and barracuda reef fish can frequently result in ciguatera poisoning; the toxin remains active even when the fish is well cooked.

A full, first-aid kit would be useful. Visitors should seek advice before accepting treatment involving hypodermic needles or blood transfusions. Medical insurance is essential, including emergency evacuation, and an adequate supply of personal medicines is necessary.

Hotels

In addition to Western-style hotels, the Tourist Board operates a scheme of village-style guest-houses run by nationals. Tipping is not usual.

Public holidays (national)

Fixed dates

1 Jan (New Year's Day), 13 Jun (Queen's Birthday), 16 Sep (Independence Day), 25–26 Dec (Christmas).

Days *in lieu* are given for holidays that occur at the weekend, usually at the beginning of the following week.

Variable dates

Good Friday and Easter Monday (Mar/Apr), Anzac Remembrance Day.

Working hours

Banking

Mon–Thu: 0845–1500; Fri: 0845–1600.

Business

Mon–Fri: 0800–1630.

Government

Mon–Fri: 0800–1600.

Shops

Mon–Fri: 0900–1630/1700; Sat: 0900–1200. Markets open all daylight hours.

Telecommunications

Mobile/cell phones

There is a 900 GSM service available in the capital and six of the larger towns.

Electricity supply

240/415V AC, 50 cycles; plugs are three-pin Australian type.

Weights and measures

Metric system

Social customs/useful tips

The use of first names is common in business, reflecting the tendency (of Australian origin) towards informality. The Papua New Guineans have a relaxed attitude to punctuality and this can make it difficult for the foreign visitor to keep to a schedule of appointments or to make business arrangements.

The belief in magic and sorcery is still widespread. There is little interest in national issues but local group and tribal sympathies are strong. Pressure from the provinces has resulted in the formation of a separate and tribal level of provincial government.

The traditional (custom) land tenure system promotes social stability and equal access to land within clans. Land disputes are endemic.

Tipping is not practised or encouraged.

Security

It has been advised that visitors to Papua New Guinea (PNG) should take care and ensure their personal safety at all times. PNG is characterised by regionalism and tribalism, with widespread corruption and prevalent violent crime bordering on anarchy. Law and order remain very weak in Port Moresby and Lae, reflecting the rising level of unemployment in the urban areas and a breakdown in the customary lines of authority. Criminal gangs of so-called 'rascals' have become a serious problem, and particularly worrying is a growing tendency in some areas in the use of firearms. Robbery, vehicle hijacks, assaults and random shootings are all common.

Violent incidents can occur without warning and while foreigners are not necessarily the target they are visible and can be engulfed by them. Outside urban areas the situation is better, although sporadic tribal fighting is common and areas where it is reported, such as the Southern Highlands Province, is a particularly dangerous area and should be avoided.

Getting there

Air

National airline: Air Niugini

International airport/s: Port Moresby Jacksons International (POM), 11km south of the city; duty-free shop, bar, bank, hotel reservations and car hire. Buses and taxis are available to the city, journey time 20–60 minutes.

Airport tax: Departure tax K30; transit passengers are exempt.

Surface

Water: Cruise ships call, and passenger accommodation is sometimes available on cargo ships from Australia, the Far East, Europe and the west coast of the US.

Main port/s: Port Moresby, Lae and Madang; Rabaul (on New Britain).

Getting about

National transport

Air: Domestic air services provide the only realistically efficient and speedy way of accessing all areas in PNG. Air Niugini, AirLink and Islands Nationair, operate scheduled and charter flights. Some flights may use light aircraft or helicopters to the hundreds of smaller air strips in remote locations.

Road: There are over 19,000km of roads; only around 5,000km are paved. The highland interior is still underdeveloped; most of the road systems form coastal networks with little connection between individual provinces.

Water: Inland waterways total 10,940km but there are no public transport systems using them. Ferries to other PNG islands and river transport may be available on an *ad hoc* basis.

City transport

Taxis: Metered taxi services are available in main centres, but are scarce and expensive. Negotiate fares wherever possible.

Buses, trams & metro: PMVs (public motor vehicles), usually light buses or covered trucks, operate within and between main centres from bus shelters in towns (or they can be hailed elsewhere).

Car hire

It is not recommended that visitors drive into the interior where the roads are rugged, unpredictable and without rescue service. A number of international car hire companies operate in the cities. A national driving licence is required.

BUSINESS DIRECTORY

The addresses listed below are a selection only. While World of Information makes every endeavour to check these addresses, we cannot guarantee that changes have not been made, especially to telephone numbers and area codes. We would welcome any corrections.

Telephone area codes

The international direct dialling (IDD) code for Papua New Guinea is +675 followed by subscriber's number.

Useful telephone numbers

Police, fire and ambulance: 000

Chambers of Commerce

Lae Chamber of Commerce and Industry, PO Box 265, Lae, Morobe Province (tel: 472-2340; fax: 472-6038; e-mail: lcci@global.net.pg.

Papua New Guinea Chamber of Commerce and Industry, PO Box 1621, Trukai Building, Lawes Road, Konebadu, Port Moresby, NCD (tel: 321-3057; fax: 321-0566; e-mail: pngcci@global.net.pg).

Port Moresby Chamber of Commerce and Industry, PO Box 1764, Monian Tower, Douglas Street, Port Moresby (tel: 321-3077; fax: 321-4203; e-mail: info@pomcci.org.pg).

Banking

ANZ Banking Group (PNG), 3rd Floor, Defens Haus, Cnr Champion Parade and Hunter St, Port Moresby (tel: 322-3333; fax: 322-3306).

Bank South Pacific Limited (BSP), PO Box 173, Douglas Street, Port Moresby 121 NCD (tel: 321-2444; fax: 321-7302).

Indosuez Niugini Bank Limited, PO Box 1390, Burns Haus, Champion Parade, Port Moresby (tel: 321-3533; fax: 321-3115).

Maybank (PNG) Limited, PO Box 882, Waigani Drive, Waigani (tel: 325-0101; fax: 325-6128).

Central bank

Bank of Papua New Guinea, PO Box 121, ToRobert Haus; Crn Douglas Street, Port Moresby 111 (tel: 322-7200; fax: 321-1617; e-mail: webmaster@bankpng.gov.pg).

Stock exchange

Port Moresby Stock Exchange (PoMSOX): www.pomsox.com.pg

Travel information

Airlink Ltd, PO Box 1208, Madang Province, 511 (tel: 852-2933; fax: 852-2725; email: info@airlink.com.pg).

Air Niugini, PO Box 7186, Boroko 111 (tel: 325-9000; fax: 327-3482).

East New Britain Tourist Bureau, PO Box 385, Rabaul 611 (tel: 982-8697; fax: 982-8634).

Islands Nationair, PO Box 488, Boroko 111 (tel: 325-4055; fax: 325-5059).

Melanesian Tourist Services, PO Box 707, Madang 511 (tel: 854-1300; fax: 852-3543; internet: www.meltours.com).

Port Moresby Jacksons International Airport, PO Box 684, Boroko, Port Moresby (tel: 324-4400, 324-4755; fax: 325-0833).

National tourist organisation offices

PNG Tourism Promotion Authority, 2nd Floor, Pacific MMI Building, Champion Parade; PO Box 1291, Port Moresby 121 (tel: 320-0211; fax: 320-0223; internet: www.pngtourism.org.pg).

Ministries

Ministry of Agriculture and Livestock, PO Box 417, Konedobu NCD (tel: 325-9544; fax: 325-9722).

Ministry of Bougainville Affairs, House Tisa (2nd Floor), PO Box 343, Waigani NCD (tel: 325-2977; fax: 325-8038).

Ministry of Churches, Family Affairs, & NGO's, National Parliament, PO Parliament, Port Moresby NCD (tel: 327-7350; fax: 320-0903).

Ministry of Civil Aviation, PO Box 684, Boroko NCD (tel: 323-6185; fax: 325-1919).

Ministry of Commerce and Industry, PO Box 375, Waigani NCD (tel: 327-6621; fax: 323-3050).

Ministry of Defence, Murray Barracks, Free Mail Bag Service, Boroko NCD (tel: 327-346; fax: 327-7480).

Ministry of Education, Culture and Science, PSA Haus, PO Box 446, Waigani NCD (tel: 323-3944; fax: 327-7480).

Ministry of Employment and Youth, PO Box 5644, Boroko NCD (tel: 327-7578; fax: 327-7480).

Ministry of Environment, PO Box 6601, Boroko NCD (tel: 325-0174; fax: 325-0182).

Ministry of Finance and Internal Revenue, PO Box 777, Port Moresby NCD (tel: 322-6613; fax: 322-6856).

Ministry of Fisheries, Investment Haus (8th Floor), PO Box 2016, Port Moresby NCD (tel: 321-3443; fax: 320-3024).

Ministry of Foreign Affairs and Trade, PO Box 422, Waigani NCD (tel: 327-7545; fax: 325-4467).

Ministry of Forests, PO Box 1550, Boroko NCD (tel: 327-7591; fax: 327-7589).

Ministry of Health, Aopi Centre (5th Floor), PO Box 807, Boroko NCD (tel: 301-3605; fax: 301-3604).

Ministry of Justice, Po Box 591, Waigani NCD (tel: 323-0138; fax: 323-0241).

Ministry of Lands, Aopi Centre (4th Floor), PO Box 5665, Boroko NCD (tel: 301-3102; fax: 301-3205).

Ministry of Mining and Energy, NIC Building (1st Floor), Private Mail Bag, Port Moresby NCD (tel: 327-7350; fax: 320-0903).

Ministry of Petroleum and Gas, Parliament House, Waigani NCD (tel: 327-7752; fax: 327-7753).

Ministry of Police and Correctional Institution Services, PO Box 5097, Boroko NCD (tel: 327-7519; fax: 327-7528).

Ministry of Provincial and Local level Government Affairs, PO Box 1287, Boroko NCD (tel: 301-1000; fax: 325-0553).

Ministry of Public Enterprises, Communications and Assisting Prime Minister on Infrastructure and Public Investment Program Matters, PO Parliament, Waigani NCD (tel: 327-7366; fax: 327-7387).

Ministry of Public Service, Morauta House, (2nd Floor, PO Box 519, Waigani NCD (tel: 327-6440; fax: 323-3050).

Ministry of Rural Development, PO Box 639, Waigani NCD (tel: 327-6767; fax: 327-6349).

Ministry of Transport, PO Box 1489, Port moresby NCD (tel: 321-1866; fax: 320-0556).

Ministry of Treasury and Corporate Affairs, Vulupindi Haus (4th Floor), PO Box 710, Waigani NCD (tel: 328-8460; fax: 328-8433).

Office of the Prime Minister, Parliament House (4th Floor), National Parliament, Waigan NCD (tel: 327-7489; fax: 327-7497).

Other useful addresses

British High Commission, Kiroki Street, Waigani, PO Box 4778, Boroko, Port Moresby (tel: 321-1677; fax: 325-3547).

Bureau of Customs, PO Box 932, Port Moresby NCD (tel: 321-2488; fax: 321-3004).

Department of Industrial Development, PO Box 5644, Goroko (tel: 327-2286).

Electricity Commission of PNG, PO Box 1105, Boroko NCD (tel: 324-3200; fax: 325-0072).

Forest Research Institute, PO Box 314, LAE, Morobe Province (tel: 342-4188; fax: 432-4357).

Investment Promotion Authority, PO Box 5053, Boroko NCD (tel: 321-7311; fax: 321-2819).

National Curltural Commission, PO Box 7144, Boroko NCD (tel: 325-3288; fax: 325-9119).

National Housing Corporation, PO Box 1550, Boroko NCD (tel: 324-7200; fax: 325-9918).

National Institute of Standards and Industrial Technology, PO Box 3042, Boroko NCD (tel: 327-2102; fax: 325-2403).

National Statistical Office, PO Wardstrip, Waigani NCD (tel: 327-1499; fax: 325-1869).

Papua New Guinea Embassy (US), Suite 805, 1779 Massachusetts Avenue, NW, Washington DC 20036 (tel: (+1-202) 745-3680; fax: (+1-202) 745-3679; e-mail: kunduwash@aol.com).

Papua New Guinea Investment Corporation, PO Box 155, Port Moresby (tel: 321-2855; fax: 321-1240).

Post and Telecommunication Corporation, PO Box 1349, Boroko NCD (tel: 300-4000; fax: 300-4098).

Small Business Development Corporation, PO Box 481, Port Moresby NCD (tel: 325-0100; fax: 325-3725).

US Embassy, PO Box 1492, Port Moresby (tel: 321-1455; fax: 321-3423).

Internet sites

Asian Development Bank: www.adb.org

Government departments: www.pngonline.gov.pg

Investment promotion authority: www.ipa.gov.pg

PNG Business listings: www.pngbd.com

Tourism Council of the South Pacific: www.tcsp.com

Paraguay

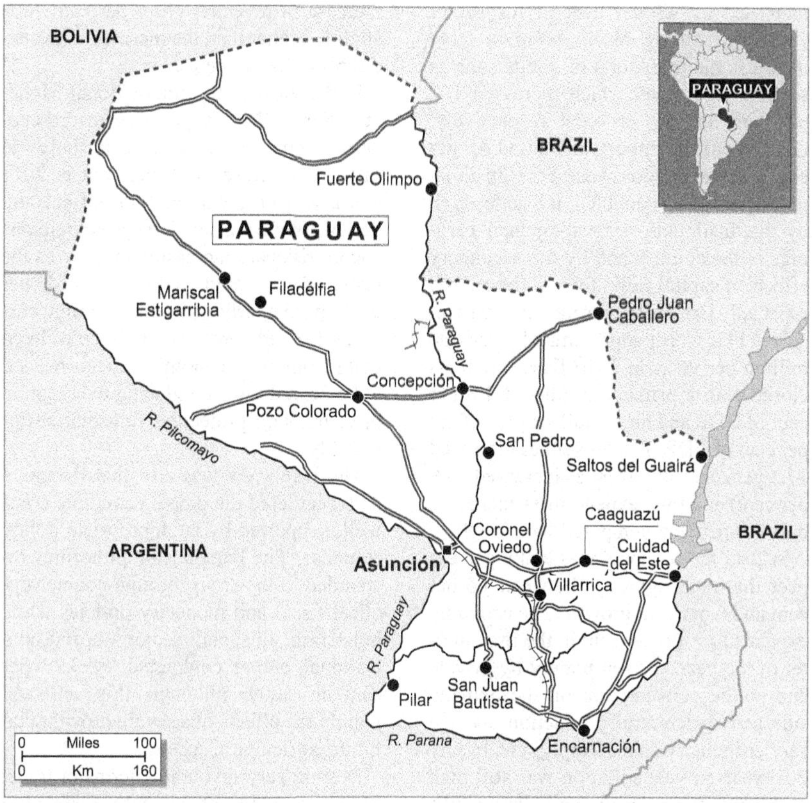

KEY FACTS

Official name: República del Paraguay (Republic of Paraguay)

Head of State: President Fernando Armindo Lugo Méndez (APC) (since 15 Aug 2008)

Head of government: President Fernando Lugo

Ruling party: Alianza Patriótica por el Cambio (APC) (Patriotic Alliance for Change) political alliance of eight parties led by the Partido Liberal Radical Auténtico (PLRA) (Authentic Radical Liberal Party) (from 15 Aug 2008)

Area: 406,752 square km

Population: 6.45 million (2010)*

Capital: Asunción

Official language: Spanish and Guaraní

Currency: Guaraní (G) = 100 pesos

Exchange rate: G4,180.00 per US$ (Oct 2011)

GDP per capita: US$2,886 (2010)

GDP real growth: 15.30% (2010)

GDP: US$18.50 billion (2010)

Inflation: 4.70% (2010)

Balance of trade: -US$1.53 billion (2010)

Annual FDI: US$426.70 million (2010)

* estimated figure

In the first few years of the twenty-first century, a series of provocative attacks by the tiny Ejército Paraguayo Popular (EPP) (Paraguayan People's Army) placed Paraguay's President Fernando Lugo on the back foot, in a similar position to the region's right-wing leaders of the 1970s and 1980s. In Paraguayan politics this was something of a new, if unpleasant, experience. Despite having a right wing dictatorship and a rubber-stamping parliament in the Alfredo Stroessner era (1954–89), Paraguay had not generated guerrilla movements. Founded in 2001, the EPP is thought to have no more than 20 armed members and has been behind only a few crimes. But these have left their mark and been shocking: in 2004 it kidnapped and murdered Cecilia Cubas, the daughter of a former president. Officials say it has ties to Colombia's Fuerzas Armadas Revolucionarias de Colombia-Ejército del Pueblo (Farc) (Revolutionary Armed Forces of Colombia-Peoples' Army). It is reportedly sheltered by peasant groups, drug traffickers and corrupt police.

EPP

A maverick EPP has been a nightmare for poor Mr Lugo, an ordained Catholic clergyman who had risen rapidly though the ranks of the Catholic Church. In 2009 the EPP kidnapped Fidel Zavala, a well-known rancher, held him for 94 days and released him only once a ransom was paid. In April 2011 an EPP member killed a police officer and three ranch workers. The opposition has criticised the president for being soft on the guerrillas, going as far as claiming that he once knew some of their leaders through the church.

In response to these attacks, the president asked Congress to grant him emergency powers, which it did in late April (after the kidnapping of Mr Zavala). The law, valid in five departments for 30 days, authorised arrests without a warrant and allowed the army to join the police in security operations. Mr Lugo sent 1,000 extra troops to the region, bringing the total to 3,000. Mr Lugo's crackdown produced indifferent results. The government claimed the arrest of Jesús Ortiz, allegedly an EPP technician, in May. Mr Ortiz was actually apprehended in a different area than that covered by the new measure. If the results were indifferent it was hardly surprising. According to one report, the military deployment turned out to be a farce. Despite these setbacks, Mr Lugo wanted Paraguay's Congress to make permanent the provision allowing the army to accompany police. However, the campaign against the EPP was generally popular, both with wealthy farmers and with peasants. The eradication of the EPP will require the state's presence in the countryside to be increased, as well as better co-ordination between the police and the army.

A strong economy

The Paraguayan economy, the World Bank notes, experienced an extraordinary growth of 15 per cent in 2010 placing it in second place in terms of gross domestic product (GDP) growth. The Bank notes that this success was the result of the combination of several factors: external conditions favorable to primary production; sound and predictable macro-economic bases; a solid financial system; a successful fiscal stimulation policy in 2009; transfers of the Executive Branch (to sub-national governments and in conditional cash transfers); investment in public works; housing construction; poverty reduction; response and important placement of credit of the private and public financial sectors; increase in domestic consumption and private investment.

Strong exports

In 2010 Paraguay's total recorded exports increased by 43 per cent in respect of 2009. The strong results were in large measure due to exports of goods such as soybean and meat, which increased 102 per cent and 59 per cent respectively. Other recorded imports increased 45 per cent over the previous year. Foreign direct investment (FDI) doubled; it was fostered by multinationals reinvesting their earnings in the country and by the secondary effects of capital flows toward the region, especially Brazil. At present, Paraguay receives FDI worth approximately US$400 million per year. In 2010 fiscal accounts closed with a primary surplus of 1.8 per cent of GDP and an overall surplus of 1.4 per cent of GDP. Total revenues increased 17.1 per cent (tax revenues increased 23.9 per cent) and total expenditures increased only 8.9 per cent compared with 2009.

In 2011 the economy was looking at expected growth figures of between 4.5 per cent and 6 per cent growth. The economy expanded by 4.6 per cent in the first quarter of the year –driven mainly by private and public consumption on the demand side and agricultural production and the service industry on the supply side. In July 2011year-on-year inflation was still high at just below 9 per cent, while Paraguay's currency, the guaraní, experienced an appreciation of 15 per cent in the first half of the year contributing to a trade deficit as imports continued to exceed exports. The position of Paraguay's international reserves continued to rise and has reached a historically high level of US$5 billion. The surplus of fiscal accounts continued in the second half of the year (2011) as the increase in revenues (17.6 per cent) was slightly higher than the increase in expenditures (17.3 per cent).

In the view of the International Monetary Fund (IMF) supportive macro-economic conditions will contribute to inflation of close to 10 per cent in 2011 and a widening external current account deficit. While the banking system remains sound, risks are increasing, mainly as the result of very rapid credit growth (40 per cent), particularly of credit in foreign currency (58 per cent). The IMF considered that Paraguay's economic policies needed to be geared toward reducing overheating pressures and protecting financial sector stability.

The IMF view was also that Paraguay had weathered the global economic crisis well, supported by an appropriate policy response. The Paraguayan authorities responded to the crisis through counter-cyclical fiscal and monetary policies while bolstering financial sector supervision. National output contracted by 3.75 per cent in 2009, although this reflected mainly the effects of a severe drought that hit the agricultural sector.

Despite very favourable terms of trade, the external current account weakened in 2010, driven mainly by rapid domestic demand growth. The current account deficit rose to 2.75 per cent of GDP (from near balance in 2009), reflecting very rapid import growth and a drop in remittances. However, with strong private capital inflows, notably FDI, the Banco Central del Paraguay (BCP) (central bank) continued accumulating international reserves, which rose to US$4.2 billion (23 per cent of GDP) at end-2010. The real effective exchange rate appreciated slightly during the year, driven by the strengthening of the guarani against the US dollar. The central bank raised interest rates by 775 basis points in the year from mid-2010 (375 basis points in 2011), starting from a level close to zero. Real interest rates, however, remained in negative territory.

At the end of May 2011, the guarani had risen by about 10 per cent vis-à-vis the US dollar compared to end-2010. The appreciation of the guarani reflected mainly improved terms of trade, seasonal

KEY INDICATORS — **Paraguay**

	Unit	2006	2007	2008	2009	2010
Population	m	*5.92	*6.03	*6.15	*6.30	*6.45
Gross domestic product (GDP)	US$bn	9.80	12.20	16.90	14.70	18.50
GDP per capita	US$	1,568	2,026	2,747	2,337	2,886
GDP real growth	%	4.3	6.8	5.8	-3.8	15.3
Inflation	%	9.6	8.1	10.2	2.6	4.7
Industrial output	% change	3.5	1.0	4.0	0.3	–
Agricultural output	% change	3.5	14.3	9.0	-45.8	–
Exports (fob) (goods)	US$m	4,026.0	5,652.1	7,768.8	5,783.8	8,312.2
Imports (fob) (goods)	US$m	5,383.0	6,185.0	8,809.0	6,917.3	9,839.3
Balance of trade	US$m	-1,357.0	-532.9	-1,040.2	-1,133.5	-1,527.1
Current account	US$m	128.0	184.0	-412.0	-149.1	-596.2
Total reserves minus gold	US$m	1,701.7	2,463.0	2,844.6	3,838.6	4,136.8
Foreign exchange	US$m	1,531.5	2,385.4	2,767.3	3,632.0	3,933.7
Exchange rate	per US$	2,635.50	5,032.70	4,363.20	4,965.40	4,735.50

* estimated figure

liquidation of export proceeds and increased private capital inflows, especially FDI .

Risk assessment

Economy	Good
Politics	Fair
Regional stability	Good

COUNTRY PROFILE

Historical profile

1537 The Spanish began colonising the plains of Paraguay.
1811 Paraguay gained independence from Spain.
1864–70 A disastrous war against Argentina, Brazil and Uruguay was lost. It halved Paraguay's population and stripped it of 155,400 square km of land.
1870 Occupation forces set up a provisional government with a liberal-democratic constitution, although the constitution was never put into practice.
1874 The Partido Colorado (PC) (Colorado Party) (also known as the Red Party), representing the land-owning elite, was formed.
1887 The Liberal party, who advocated a minimal state and representative government, was formed.
1883 A Colorado government began driving peasants off the land and selling it to foreign investors.
1904 After a revolution the Liberal party seized power and introduced political and economic changes.
1932–35 The Chaco War with Bolivia over disputed territory.
1936 The army, which held the government responsible for loosing the Chaco War, overthrew the government of President Eusobio Ayala (Liberal) in February and installed war hero Rafael Franco as president, an act that virtually destroyed the Liberals as a political force. The Partido Revolucionario Febrerista (PRF) (*Febrerista* Revolutionary Party) government was a mix of political ideologies, including Communists and Fascists. It implemented land re-distribution and workers rights. Franco's government had popular support but its policies were hastily devised and led to protests when Decree Law 152, promising a 'totalitarian transformation', was announced. The divergent political opinions within the government finally pulled it apart, although Franco continued to hold power with a new party, the Unión Nacional Revolucionaria (Revolutionary National Union). He was unable to provide more land to his peasant supporters and was undermined by Liberal party supporters in the army.
1937 Franco lost support of the army when he withdrew troops from the territories won in Chaco in 1935. The army revolted and returned the Liberal party to power.
1938 A treaty was signed between Bolivia and Paraguay following an international peace conference. It returned most of the disputed land to Bolivia.
1940 The military regime installed Higinio Morínigo, a follower of Nazi Germany's Adolf Hitler, as president.
1946 Following the defeat of Germany and Japan, Paraguay's chief trading partners, Morínigo legalised liberal, communist and *Febrerista* parties.
1947 Paraguay descended into civil war, following the emergence of political divisions within the army.
1948 The PC deposed Morínigo, leading to a series of coups and short-lived regimes.
1949 Federico Chaves became president.
1954 General Alfredo Stroessner led a *coup d'état* that deposed Chaves. Stroessner was re-elected seven times under the constitutional 'state-of-siege' provision. His dictatorship was ruthless against all opposition.
1967 A new constitution endorsed Stroessner's dictatorship. Paraguay was isolated within the world community.
1989 Stroessner was deposed in a bloodless coup by General Antonio Rodríguez who later won the presidential election. However the military-backed National Republican Association-PC won the parliamentary elections.
1993 Juan Carlos Wasmosy was elected president and the PC won a majority of parliamentary seats in the first free presidential and multi-party elections.
1998 Raúl Cubas Grau (PC) won the presidential election, despite allegations of fraud.
1999 Cubas resigned, following the assassination of his vice president, Luís Argaña. Luis González Macchi was appointed as interim president.
2000 Supporters of dissident Colorado leader, General Lino Oviedo, staged an unsuccessful coup. Oviedo fled and was found by Brazilian police at a Brazilian border hideout.
2001 Paraguay asked for, but was denied, Oviedo's extradition.
2002 President Macchi was accused of corruption. Violent street protestors demanded his resignation. He was impeached by congress.
2003 President Macchi survived his impeachment trial; the Senate voted 25–18 against him, short of the two-thirds majority (30 votes) necessary to remove him from power. Nicanor Duarte Frutos won presidential elections. Macchi was again charged with corruption and put on trial.
2004 Former military commander, General Oviedo, was arrested after returning from exile in Brazil. An estimated 464 shoppers were killed in a fire in a three storey supermarket, it was the worst fire in Latin American history. The daughter of former president, Raúl Cubas, was kidnapped.
2005 The body of Cecilia Cubas was found in a shallow grave. President Nicanor ordered a crackdown on organised crime, blamed for widespread kidnapping and murder. Paraguay hosted the world's first conference of landlocked nations, which was attended by 30 states.
2006 A new socialist movement, Tekojoja (Equality), was launched to contest the 2008 presidential elections with the former Bishop Fernando Lugo as candidate.
2008 In presidential elections, Fernando Armindo Lugo Méndez (Partido Demócrata Cristiano) (PDC) (Christian Democratic Party) won 41 per cent of the vote, ending the rule (since 1948) of the PC, whose candidate Blanca Ovelar won 31 per cent, Lino Oviedo (Unión Nacional de Ciudadanos Éticos) (National Union of Ethical Citizens) (Unace) won 22 per cent. In elections for the Chamber of Deputies the ruling Colorado Party won 29 seats and the opposition Partido Liberal Radical Auténtico (PLRA) (Authentic Radical Liberal Party) won 26 seats, the Unión Nacional de Ciudadanos Éticos (UNCE) (National Union of Ethical Citizens) won 16 seats; all other political parties won less than five seats.
2009 An agreement was signed by the presidents of Bolivia and Paraguay settling a border dispute which had led to the Chaco Wars in the 1930s. The accord leads the way to more development of oil and gas fields in the Chaco region. Brazil agreed to triple its payment to Paraguay for the operation of the Itaipú hydroelectric power station on their shared border. Paraguay also gained permission to sell excess electricity to a third-party from 2023.
2010 In April the security forces mounted a large operation against left-wing insurgents in the north, blamed for a series of violent incidents.
2011 An experimental titanium oxide extraction plant was opened on 5 August in Minga Pora, east of Asunción. According to the operators of the plant the titanium deposits could be the largest in the world. A referendum was held on 9 October, in which 80 per cent voted in favour of giving voting rights to expatriate nationals. However turnout was only 12.5 per cent and the decision must be endorsed by the congress to be enacted.

Political structure

Constitution

Paraguay became an independent republic in 1811. Under the dictatorship of

Alfredo Stroessner (1954–89) a new constitution was introduced in 1967 which granted strong powers to the executive, entrenching political control in the hands of the ruling Partido Colorado (PC) (Colorado Party). In 1992, a new constitution was enacted.
There are 19 departments and 213 municipalities each with their own directly elected administration.
In 1990, a new electoral law was passed. Among its provisions were the introduction of proportional representation, provision for a second round in the event that no candidate secures an absolute majority in presidential elections, the prohibition of compulsory deductions from salaries of public-sector workers for political parties, the selection of party authorities by the direct vote of all members, a ban on party affiliation by members of the armed forces and the police and the lifting of a previous ban on electoral alliances by political parties.

Form of state

Presidential democratic republic

The executive

Under the constitution executive power is exercised by the president of the republic, who must be a Roman Catholic. The president is elected directly by popular vote for five years and formulates and enacts legislation. Executive power rests with the president who appoints a council of 11 ministers. The president has powers to rule by decree when congress is in recess. The president cannot be re-elected.

National legislature

The bicameral Congreso Nacional (National Congress), consists of the Cámara de Diputados (Chamber of Deputies) (lower house) with 80 members and the Cámara de Senadores (Chamber of Senators) (upper house) with 45 members. Members of both houses are elected by proportional representation to serve for five-year terms.

Legal system

At the apex of the judiciary is the Supreme Court which has the power to declare legislation unconstitutional. The five members of the Supreme Court are appointed by the president and their tenure of office coincides with that of the presidency. There are appeal courts and lower level criminal and civil courts.

Last elections

20 April 2008 (presidential and parliamentary)

Results: Presidential: Fernando Lugo (PDC) won 41 per cent, Blanca Ovelar (PC) won 31 per cent, Lino Oviedo (Unace) won 22 per cent.
Parliament (Chamber of Deputies): the Asociación Nacional Republicana-Partido Colorado (National Republican Association-Colorado Party) (Colorado Party) won 29 seats (out of 80), the Partido Liberal Radical Auténtico (PLRA) (Authentic Radical Liberal Party) won 26 seats, the Unión Nacional de Ciudadanos Éticos (UNCE) (National Union of Ethical Citizens) won 16 seats; all other political parties won less than five seats. (Senate) the Colorado Party won 15 seats (out of 45), the PLRA won 14 seats, the UNCE won 9 seats and the Movimiento Patria Querida (MPQ) (Beloved Fatherland Movement) won 4.

Next elections

2013 (parliamentary and presidential)

Political parties

Ruling party

Alianza Patriótica por el Cambio (APC) (Patriotic Alliance for Change) political alliance of eight parties led by the Partido Liberal Radical Auténtico (PLRA) (Authentic Radical Liberal Party) (from 15 Aug 2008)

Main opposition party

Asociación Nacional Republicana-Partido Colorado (National Republican Association-Colorado Party) (Colorado Party)

Population

6.45 million (2010)*

Last census: August 2002: 5,163,198

Population density: 12 inhabitants per square km. Urban population: 56 per cent (1994–2000).

Annual growth rate: 2.5 per cent 1994–2004 (WHO 2006)

Ethnic make-up

Over 95 per cent of the population is of Spanish-Guaraní origin. There are approximately 40,000 indigenous people in the country, most of whom live in the Chaco region.
In addition, there are large Korean, German and Japanese immigrant communities, along with small Italian and Polish communities, and some communities of people originating from Lebanon, Taiwan and Hong Kong.

Religions

Roman Catholicism is the state religion and is practised by 90 per cent of the population, the remainder are mostly Protestants.

Education

There are just over 4,300 primary schools and an estimated 92 per cent of the relevant age group attends primary school. Secondary education begins aged 13 years and comprises two cycles of three years each.
Paraguay has two universities – the National and the Catholic. The state-run Universidad Nacional de Asunción has a student enrolment of around 20,000. It comprises 11 faculties, law and social sciences, medicine, economics, chemistry, dentistry, philosophy, agriculture, veterinary science, fine arts, architecture and engineering. It also has six Institutes and six Higher Schools.

Literacy rate: 92 per cent adult rate; 96 per cent youth rate (15–24) (Unesco 2005).

Compulsory years: Seven to 13

Enrolment rate: 111 per cent gross primary enrolment of relevant age group (including repeaters); 47 per cent gross secondary enrolment (World Bank).

Pupils per teacher: 21 in primary schools

Health

HIV/Aids

HIV prevalence: 0.5 per cent aged 15–49 in 2003 (World Bank)

Life expectancy: 72 years, 2004 (WHO 2006)

Fertility rate/Maternal mortality rate: 3.8 births per woman, 2004 (WHO 2006); maternal mortality 190 per 100,000 live births (World Bank).

Child (under 5 years) mortality rate (per 1,000): 25 per 1,000 live births (World Bank)

Head of population per physician: 1.11 physicians per 1,000 people, 2002 (WHO 2006)

Welfare

The Social Security Institute was formed by Decree Law 17071 in 1948, and is regulated by Decree Law 1860 of 1950. The laws refer to health, medical care and sickness benefits. Workers, their wives and children up to 16 have the right to receive medical, surgical and dental attention, medicine and hospitalisation, as well as cash subsidies for temporary illnesses, maternity and death. Old age pensions are paid to those who have made the necessary contributions. The social security system is in disarray and in 2001 the IMF urged the government to stop lending money to the system.
Women must not work for three weeks before or six weeks after childbirth. During these periods a woman receives a cash subsidy from the Social Security Institute. The worker has the right to receive an allowance equal to 5 per cent of the legal minimum wage for each child under 17 for whose maintenance and education he is responsible. This allowance is wholly the employer's expense and is discontinued once the worker's wage reaches 200 per cent more than the legal minimum.

Main cities

Asunción (capital, estimated population 520,722 in 2005), Cuidad del Este (266,366) (on the Brazilian border), Capiatá (236,725), Luque (212,359), Ñemby (105,492), Limpio (103,018), Fernando de la Mora (121,768), Encarnación (77,278) (on the Argentine border), Pedro Juan Caballero (68,349).

Languages spoken
Guaraní, the aboriginal Indian tongue is widely spoken. In some rural districts, the less educated speak little or no Spanish.
Official language/s
Spanish and Guaraní

Media
Press
Dailies: In Spanish, the main national dailies and Sunday newspapers are *ABC Color* (www.abc.com.py), *Diario Popular* (www.diariopopular.com.py), *Ultima Hora* (www.ultimahora.com), *La Nacion* (www.lanacion.com.py), and *Viva Paraguay* (www.vivaparaguay.com).
Weeklies: In Spanish, *Paraguay Ahora* (www.paraquayahora.com), La Síntesis Económic (http://kaavo.pol.com.py).
Periodicals: Itacom (www.itacom.com.py), Neike (www.neike.com.py), PPN (Portal Paraguayo de Noticias) (www.ppn.com.py), Paraguay Aldia (www.paraguayaldia.com), Paraguay News (www.paraguaynews.com.py), Zeta Revista (www.revistazeta.com.py), regional publications, International Action (www.accion.org), UnMundo Améruca Latina (www.un-mundo.org, in English: http://amlat.oneworld.net).
Broadcasting
Radio: The government-owned Radio Nacional del Paraguay (www.rnpy.com), broadcasts on AM and FM; there are several private radio stations. Radio Cardinal (www.cardinal.com.py), Radio Nanduti (www.nanduti.com.py), Radio Venus (www.venus.com.py), Radio Venus (www.fmradiocity.com), Radio Canal 100 (www.canal100.com.py).
Television: There are several television channels, all privately owned with broadcasts in Spanish – Sistema Nacional de Televisión (SNT, Canal 9) (www.snt.com.py), RED Guarani (Canal 2) (www.redguarani.com.py), Telefuturo (Canal 4) (www.telefuturo.com.py), Red Privada de Televisión (El Trece, Canal 13) (www.rpc.com.py), Paravision (Canal 5) (www.canal5paravision.com). These broadcasters syndicate their programmes around the country and on cable TV.
News agencies
None are based in Paraguay but Mercopress (www.mercopress.com) specialises in news from Latin America countries within Mercosur and the Falkland Islands.

Economy
Paraguay has evolved into a modern service sector driven economy, with services constituting 59.5 per cent of GDP in 2009. Agriculture is still important, comprising 19.3 of GDP, with industry 21.3 per cent, of which manufacturing was 13 per cent. Agricultural products account for the majority of export items, especially soya beans, cotton, cattle, timber and sugar. International trade is an important aspect of the economy with goods purchased from Japan and the US and re-exported (around 50 per cent of all imported goods are re-exported at a profit with little or no changes made to them). Although there are few mineral resources and little heavy industry, Paraguay operates the world's largest, single, hydroelectric power station, Itaipú on the River Paraná, which generates up to US$360 million per year from the sale of electricity to Brazil.
GDP growth in 2008 was 5.8 per cent but fell into recession in 2009 at -3.8 per cent, due to the global economic crisis that cut trade, in the case of Paraguay in meat and soya beans. On top of this a drought in the latter part of 2008 reduced harvests. However, when world trade picked up in 2010 GDP growth surged back to 15.3 per cent. Inflation rose from to 8.1 per cent in 2007 to 10.2 per cent in 2008, before dropping to 2.6 per cent in 2009; it rose again in 2010 to 4.7 per cent.
In 2011, the UN Human Development Index (HDI) ranked Paraguay 107 (out of 187) for development in health, education and income. In 2010, 48.5 per cent of the population experienced deprivation in at least one indicator of poverty and 5.1 per cent of the population were living on the equivalent of US$1.25 per day.
Paraguay is subject to a widespread informal economy with smuggling to and from neighbouring countries a problem for government revenue collection.
Remittances in 2008 were a record high of US$579 million, which fell to US$555 million in 2009 (3.7 per cent of GDP) as the economies of host countries weakened; remittances bounced back with an estimated US$573 million in 2010. Fifty per cent of all remittances come from workers in Europe.

External trade
As a member of Mercosur, the world's fourth largest free-trade zone, Paraguay (along with Argentina, Brazil and Uruguay), has access to a market of over 200 million consumers. Paraguay is also an associate member of the Andean Community (AC), since Mercosur negotiated a free trade area with AC.
Paraguay's economy is predominately agricultural which constitutes over 25 per cent of GDP and exports represent a large portion of this. The world's largest single hydroelectric generating facility at the Itaipú Dam, is jointly owned and operated by Paraguay and Brazil; US$360 million per year of electricity is exported to Brazil.
Imports
Main imports include road vehicles, consumer goods, tobacco, petroleum products and electrical machinery.
Main sources: China (typically 28 per cent of total), Brazil (27 per cent), Argentina (14 per cent).
Exports
Main exports include cattle, cotton, grains, soya beans, sugar and timber, animal feed, cotton, meat, edible oils, leather and electricity.
Main destinations: Uruguay (typically 18 per cent of total), Argentina (16 per cent), Brazil (14 per cent).
Re-exports
The country re-exports significant amounts of US products to regional neighbours. Around 50 per cent of all imported goods are re-exported at a profit with little or no changes made to them. There is evidence of trade through informal channels such as smuggling.

Agriculture
Farming
The agricultural sector remains important to the country's economy. The sector employs approximately 40 per cent of the labour force and contributes 29 per cent to total GDP.
Agricultural products account for more than 90 per cent of exports, of which cotton and soya beans together account for more than two-thirds of export earnings. Sawn timber, meat products and, to a lesser extent, fruit, vegetables and hides are also exported. Sugar cane, wheat, tobacco and various new specialist crops for industrial use are expanding as more land comes under cultivation. Paraguay has nearly achieved self-sufficiency in basic foodstuffs (rice, maize, wheat, beans). Approximately 5 per cent of total land area is arable land or under permanent crops, pasture constitutes 35 per cent of the land and 50 per cent is woodland/forest. While the fertile eastern region is ideal for arable farming and cattle grazing the rich soil has been subject to erosion since the 1970s. There are extensive forests with a variety of timbers. The potential of the Chaco region to the west is still to be realised, dependent as it is upon the exploitation of its known groundwater resources for irrigated farming.
Agricultural production fluctuates from year to year owing to climatic conditions (both flooding and drought) and widespread smuggling (particularly livestock and soya beans).
Fishing
Despite its landlocked geographical status, Paraguay's annual fish catch amounts to approximately 10,000 tonnes. The illegal trade of fishery products remains a

problem despite attempts by the authorities to bring it under control.

Forestry

Paraguay has a significant area of forested land, accounting for approximately 30 per cent of the country's total landmass. The majority of the forested areas are to the east of the Paraguay river. Historically, deforestation has been a problem in Paraguay. The country lost, on average 0.51 per cent of forest cover each year during the 1990-2000 period. This amounted to a decrease of 123,000 hectares year on year.

Local forest resources produce moderate volumes of sawn timber and panels, most of which is usually exported. Domestic demand for paper is usually met by imports. Consumption of wood fuel is significant.

Industry and manufacturing

In a typical year for the economy of Paraguay the industrial sector accounts for approximately a quarter of total GDP.

Though Paraguay is South America's least industrialised country, the sector does account for just under 20 per cent of the total workforce.

Manufacturing is small-scale and geared to the processing of primary products with agro-industry representing about 70 per cent of total industrial production. Construction contributes approximately 6 per cent of GDP. Manufacturing is centred on the processing of agricultural products, particularly textiles, cotton yarn, wood products, beef products, and industrial and edible oils. The country is self-sufficient in cement and there is an oil refinery (capacity 10,000 barrels per day (bpd)) and steel works (150,000 tonnes per year).

Contrasting with other Latin American countries, which have undergone a process of industrialisation based on import-substitution, development strategy in Paraguay has emphasised export-led growth. This involved minimal protection for domestic industry, whose growth problems have been compounded by the small size of the home market, high freight costs for imported products and the effects of extensive smuggling of a wide range of consumer goods from neighbouring countries.

Tourism

The tourism industry of Paraguay remains underdeveloped, with potential for greater economic productivity. The sector's contribution to total GDP has increased to 7.3 per cent and now accounts for 6.4 per cent of total employment.

In a typical year 211,400 people visit the country, with most arriving from Argentina and Brazil, often on day trips in search of bargains and duty-free goods.

Environment

In 2004, USAID reported that indiscriminate exploitation threatened the country's natural resources. In the eastern border region, which had been largely uncultivated until the 1970s, the rich topsoil was severely eroded and unmanaged use of land was jeopardising the largest underground water aquifer on the continent.

Mining

Paraguay's mining sector is negligible, contributing just 0.5 per cent to GDP in a typical year. The national government has attempted to introduce a programme of financial incentives in order to promote exploration for petroleum, lead and uranium. It has also encouraged mineral prospecting by granting tax concessions. However, few commercial reserves have been discovered and the sector employs just 0.3 per cent of the country's total workforce.

Studies commissioned by the Dirección General de Recursos Minerales (DGRM), with the support of the United Nations Development Programme (UNDP), have revealed that opportunities exist for the commercial extraction of marble, pyrophyllite, granite, slate, talc, gypsum and lignite.

Paraguay has limited proven mineral reserves and at present mining is concentrated on the extraction of salt, gypsum, limestone, kaolin and other clays. Prospecting has revealed the existence of uranium and bauxite, manganese, iron ore and copper. From the 1990s, none have been found in large enough quantities to overcome the high extraction costs involved.

According to CIC Resources mining company, the deposits at an experimental titanium oxide extraction plant that it operates in Minga Pora, east of Asunción, could be the largest in the world. The plant opened on 5 August 2011.

Hydrocarbons

There are no proven oil reserves in Paraguay; consumption of imported oil (refined oil, lubricants and aviation fuel) was 30,000 barrels per day (bpd) in 2008.

Oil exploration continues but has failed to find reserves of commercial value. Oil deposits in the border regions of Formosa (Argentina) and Chaco (Bolivia) exist and the prospects of finding oil in Paraguay are thought to be promising. The state-owned Petropar refinery near Asunción can produce 7,500bpd of refined oil.

There are no reserves of natural gas and consumption is negligible, although were there to be discoveries of commercially viable natural gas in the north-western Chaco region, it is anticipated that gas use would grow. There are discussions about constructing an 850km pipeline to the capital Asunción from southern Bolivia, which would also mean demand for natural gas in Paraguay would increase, along with the country becoming an important transit centre for Bolivian natural gas.

Coal is neither produced nor imported.

Energy

Total installed generating capacity was 10.1 gigawatts (GW) in 2008, producing around 92 billion kilowatt hours (kWh).

Paraguay's electricity needs are almost entirely met by hydropower and it is a net exporter of electricity, mostly to Brazil and Argentina.

The bulk of electricity supplies come mainly from the world's largest hydroelectric plant, Itaipú on the River Paraná, which produces 13.3GW and is jointly run by Brazil and Paraguay. Brazil financed the Itaipú construction using Paraguay's resources; all excess electricity produced by Itaipú is sold to Brazil. In May 2009 a review of the contractual agreement was discussed at ministerial level as Paraguay maintained that the price paid by Brazil for its electricity had not increased since Itaipú became operational in 1973; Brazil considered Paraguay must take into account the investment Brazil originally made. Other hydroelectric plants include the 3.1GW Yacyretá plant and 2.8GW Corpus Christi on the Paraná, co-owned with Argentina, and the wholly owned Acaray of 210MW.

The government has plans to increase the use of biofuels and the production of ethanol from sugar cane. Although rural communities still use wood fuel, solar energy sources are being introduced.

Financial markets

Stock exchange

Bolsa de Valores y Productos de Asunción (BVPASA) (Asunción Stock Exchange)

Banking and insurance

Paraguay's banking and financial services sector has suffered from numerous crises and bad loans. The sector has undergone slow reform and the government has persisted in its policy of propping up ailing banking houses over recent years.

A new Bank of the South, with a headquarters in Venezuela, will be launched in 2008 to provide an alternative source of development funding for the participating countries. Assets of US$7 billion will underpin its operations.

Central bank

Banco Central del Paraguay.

Time

GMT minus four hours (daylight saving, Otober–March, GMT minus three hours)

Geography

Paraguay is a landlocked country in central South America. Bolivia lies to the north, Brazil to the east, and Argentina to the south and west. The River Paraguay effectively splits the country in two, with an area known as the Chaco to the west, which comprises 61 per cent (246,950 square km) of the country's land area, but only 3 per cent of the national population. In contrast, the eastern region is a much richer area in which most of the population is concentrated. This region is divided into two by a high ridge of hills. East of the hills lies the Paraná Plateau which is 300–600 metres high, and in the west lies a fertile, treeless pampas that floods once a year and stretches to the River Paraguay.

The Chaco is scrub forest used mostly for cattle. Much of the area is a national park, with jaguars, tapirs, puma and wild hog found here.

Hemisphere

Southern

Climate

The climate is subtropical with an average annual temperature of 23 degrees Celsius (C). The hot season is October–March and the average temperature rises to 32 degrees C. The temperate season is from April to September when the average temperature is 15 degrees C. The heaviest rains take place during this period, and the average annual rainfall is 1,500mm. In spring and autumn the arrival of cold fronts from the south can cause temperatures to fall suddenly by 10–20 degrees C within a few hours.

Dress codes

In the cities, businessmen wear European-style clothing; shorts are normally worn only for recreation.

Entry requirements

Passports

Required by all, except tourists from the Mercado Común del Sur (Mercosur) (Common Market of the South).

Visa

Required by all except citizens, visiting as tourists, from countries included on the list found at www.paraguayembassy.co.uk/exemptlist.htm. All visits must commence within 90 days of visa issue. Business travellers should either contact the nearest consular section to request an application form. An invitation from a local company or organisation, provision of adequate funds for stay and proof of return/onward passage are necessary.

Currency advice/regulations

There are no restrictions on the import and export of foreign or local currency. Travellers cheques have limited acceptance.

Health (for visitors)

Mandatory precautions

Yellow fever vaccination certificates are required if arriving from an infected area.

Advisable precautions

Inoculations and booster should be current for tetanus, hepatitis A and typhoid. There may be a need for vaccinations for tuberculosis, diphtheria, yellow fever and hepatitis B. The use of malaria prophylaxis (including mosquito repellents, nets and clothing that cover the body after dark) will also provide protection for hepatitis B and yellow fever. There is a risk of rabies. Mains water is usually safe to drink in Asunción and other major towns. Elsewhere precautions should be taken. Bottled water is advisable for the first few weeks of any stay. Milk is unpasteurised and should be boiled. Dairy products likely to have been made from local milk should be avoided, and meat and fish should be well cooked.

Medical insurance is essential, including emergency evacuation; an adequate supply of personal medicines is necessary.

Credit cards

International credit cards are widely accepted. ATMs are found in most towns.

Public holidays (national)

Fixed dates

1 Jan (New Year's Day), 1 Mar (Heroes' Day), 1 May (Labour Day), 15 May (Independence Day), 12 Jun (Peace of Chaco), 15 Aug (Foundation of Asunción), 29 Sep (Battle of Boquerón), 8 Dec (Immaculate Conception), 25 Dec (Christmas Day).

Variable dates

Maundy Thursday, Good Friday.

Working hours

Banking

Mon–Fri: 0845–1500.

Business

Mon–Fri: 0800–1200 and 1430–1900; Sat: 0800–1200.

Government

Mon–Fri: 0700–1300.

Shops

Mon–Sat: 0900–2100. Some shops open 0730–2000.

Telecommunications

Mobile/cell phones

There are limited 850/1900 GSM services located in the capital and towns close by.

Electricity supply

220V AC, 50 cycles

Social customs/useful tips

Business people are punctual and expect appointments to be kept. Business cards are exchanged on visits and it is usual to shake hands when arriving or leaving an office or home. The best time to visit is between May and September

While most businessmen may speak English, it is advantageous to have some knowledge of Spanish. It is important to use the correct mode of address in writing or in speech.

Most businessmen do not wear a jacket and tie during office hours, but visitors, including businesswomen, are advised to wear lightweight business suits.

A 10–15 per cent tip is usually included on hotel and bar bills.

Security

Normal precautions apply. The level of street crime is much lower than other countries in Latin America.

Getting there

Air

National airline: Transportes Aéreo del Mercosur (TAM Mercusor).

International airport/s: Asunción-Silvio Pettirossi International Airport (ASU), 16km from city; *bureau de change*, duty-free shops, restaurants and car hire. Travel time to city centre by taxi or bus is 20 minutes.

Airport tax: International departures US$25; 24-hour transit passengers exempt.

Domestic departures from Asunción Pettirossi International Airport (ASU) US$4.

Surface

Road: There are paved roads from Brazil (Rio de Janeiro-Asunción; length 1,700km) and from Argentina (Buenos Aires-Asunción, length 1,450km) which are considered good, less so the access from Bolivia.

Rail: A regular service by means of a train-ferry runs from Concepión to Posadas (Argentina), where a connection can be made to Buenos Aires. Services are slow.

Water: There are ferry links with Argentina, Bolivia and Brazil. For journeys to Buenos Aires check the route chosen is the most direct. From Brazil, boats connect Corumba with Asunción.

Main port/s: Asunción (on River Paraguay) is approximately 1,500km from the sea; Concepción, in suitable conditions, is accessible by ocean-going ships.

Getting about

National transport

Air: There are six carriers operating scheduled services to most parts of the country. Planes can be chartered and seats booked on air taxis for many destinations. Flights are frequently affected by weather.

Road: Around 10 per cent of the total network is surfaced, those serving main centres are in good condition. The main route is triangular, linking Asunción, Encarnación and Ciudad del Este. The Trans-Chaco Highway runs to the Bolivian border, but is paved for only half the distance. Some unsurfaced roads are closed in bad weather; service stations etc may be widely spaced.

Buses: There are frequent express services linking major towns; for longer distances it is advisable to make advance bookings (eg Asunción-Encarnación; Asunción-Ciudad del Este).

Rail: The main route is Asunción-Villarrica-Encarnación but the service is slow.

Water: The river Paraná is a major access route from the Atlantic coast. Asunción-Concepción service is not frequent and takes 24 hours, Asunción-Pilar 20 hours, and Asunción-Encarnación nine hours.

City transport

Taxis: In Asunción metered taxis operate with a minimum fare system; they can be hired on a time basis; a 10 per cent tip is optional.

Buses, trams & metro: Private companies operate bus and minibus services in the capital. Two tram routes also operate.

Car hire

Foreign or international licences are acceptable. Chauffeur and self-drive cars are available at reasonable rates.

BUSINESS DIRECTORY

The addresses listed below are a selection only. While World of Information makes every endeavour to check these addresses, we cannot guarantee that changes have not been made, especially to telephone numbers and area codes. We would welcome any corrections.

Telephone area codes

The internatioanl direct dialling (IDD) code for Paraguay is +595, followed by area code:

Asunción	21	Encarnación	71
Ciudad Del Este	61	Pilar	86
Concepción	31	Villarrica	541
Coronel Oviedo	521		

Chambers of Commerce

American-Paraguayan Chamber of Commerce, General Diaz 521, Edificio El Faro Internacional, Piso 4, Asunción (tel: 442-136; fax: 442-135; e-mail: pamchamb@conexion.com.py).

British–Paraguayan Chamber of Commerce, Gral Diaz 521, Edificio Internacional Faro, Piso 2, Asunción (tel/fax: 498-274; e-mail:britcham@infonet.com.py).

Paraguay Cámara Nacional de Comercio y Servicios, Estrella 540-550, Asunción (tel: 493-321; fax: 440-817; e-mail: info@ccparaguay.com.py).

Banking

Private Banking Association (ABP), Juan O'Leary y Estrella, 30 Piso Asunción (tel: 491-450; fax: 491-450).

Banco Alemán Paraguayo, Estrella No 505 y 14 de mayo, Zona Postal 1428, Asunción (tel: 490-166/9, 444-714/6; fax: 447-645).

Banco Comercial Paraguayo, Av Mariscal López 780, Zona Postal 2350, Asunción (tel: 207-251/7, 440-504; fax: 207-259).

Banco Continental, Estrella No 621, Apartado postal 2260, Asunción (tel: 446-915/18; fax: 442-001, 441-377).

Banco de Asunción, Palma Esquina 14 de mayo, Asunción Central (tel: 493-191/8; fax: 493-190).

Banco de Inversiones del Paraguay, Palma No 202, Esquina Nuestra Señora de la Asunción, Apartado postal 702, Asunción (tel: 449-550, 498-593/94; fax: 443-749).

Banco de la Nación Argentina, Chile y Palma, Apartado postal 064, Asunción (tel: 447-433, 449-463; fax: 444-365).

Banco del Paraná, Yegros y 25 de mayo, Apartado postal 2298, Asunción (tel: 446-827, 446-691/5; fax: 498-909).

Banco do Brasil, Oliva y Nuestra Señora de la Asunción, Apartado postal 667, Asunción (tel: 90-121, 90-126; fax: 448-761).

Banco do Estado de Sâo Paulo, Ind Nacional, Esquina Fulgencio R Moreno, Apartado postal 2211, Asunción (tel: 494-981/3; fax: 494-985).

Banco Exterior, Yegros y 25 de mayo, Apartado postal 824, Asunción (tel: 492-072/9; fax: 448-103).

Banco Finamerica, Chile y Oliva, Apartado postal 824, Asunción (tel: 491-021/025; fax: 445-159, 445-604).

Banco General, Chile y Haedo, Apartado postal 3202, Asunción (tel: 496-815/9; fax: 496-822).

Banco Holandés Unido, E V Haedo 103, Esquina Independencia Nacional, Apartado postal 1180, Asunción (tel: 490-001; fax: 491-734).

Banco Nacional de Fomento, Independencia Nacional y Cerro Cora, Asunción (tel: 444-440/1/2/3; fax: 446-053).

Banco Paraguayo Oriental de Inversión y Fomento, Azara 197 Esquina Yegros, Apartado postal 1496, Asunción (tel: 444-212 al 16; fax: 446-820).

Banco Real del Paraguay, Calle Estrella y Alberdi, Apartado postal 1442, Asunción (tel: 493-171/80; fax: 443-664).

Banco Sudameris Paraguay, Independencia Nacional y Cerro Cora, Apartado postal 1433, Asunción (tel: 494-542/8, 444-172/3).

Citibank, Chile, Esquina Estrella, Apartado postal 1174, Asunción (tel: 494-951/9; fax: 444-820).

Inter-American Development Bank (IDB), Edif. Aurora 1-3 pisos, Caballero esq Eligio Ayala, Casilla 1209, Asunción (tel: 492-061; fax: 446-537).

Interbanco, 14 de mayo 339, Apartado postal 392, Asunción (tel: 494-992/5; fax: 448-587).

ING Bank (Internationale Nederlanden Bank), Av España y San Rafael, Apartado postal, 10007 Asunción (tel: 606-423; fax: 606-437).

Lloyds Bank, Palma Esq Juan E O'Leary, Casilla Postal 696, Asunción (tel: 443-580; fax: 443-569).

Central bank

Banco Central del Paraguay, Federación Rusa y Sargento Marecos, Asunción (tel: 619-2061; fax: 610-088; e-mail: ccs@bcp.gov.py).

Stock exchange

Bolsa de Valores y Productos de Asunción (BVPASA) (Asunción Stock Exchange): www.bvpasa.com.py

Travel information

Dirección Nacional de Turismo, Palma 468, Alberdi/Oliva, Asunción (tel: 441-530; fax: 491-230).

Transportes Aéreo Marilia (TAM), Oliva 467, Asunción (tel: 91-041; fax: 96-484).

National tourist organisation offices

Secretaría Nacional de Turismo, Palma 468, Casi 14 de Mayo, Edificio Central, Asunción (tel: 494-110; internet: www.senatur.gov.py).

Ministries

Ministry of Agriculture and Livestock, Presidente Franco 479, Asunción (tel: 443-791, 449-614; fax: 441-036).

Ministry of Defence, Avenids Mcal López y Vice Pte Sánchez, Asunción (tel: 204-771; fax: 211-583).

Ministry of Education and Culture, Chile 898 c/ Humaitá, Asunción (tel: 443-078; fax: 443-919).

Ministry of Exterior Relations, Presidente Franco c/ O'Leary, Asunción (tel: 493-872; fax: 493-910).

Ministry of Finance, Chile 128 esq Palmas, Asunción (tel: 440-010; fax: 448-283).

Ministry of Foreign Affairs, Juan E O'Leary y Pte, Franco, Asunción (tel: 494-593, 493-872; fax: 493-910).

Ministry of Health and Public Welfare, Av Petirrossi y Brasil, Asunción (tel: 207-328; fax: 206-700).

Ministry of Housing, Chile 128 c/ Palma, Asunción (tel: 440-010; fax: 448-283).

Ministry of Industry and Commerce, Avenida España 323, Asunción (tel: 204-638; fax: 213-529; internet site: www.mic.gov.py).

Ministry of the Interior, Chile c/ Manduvirá, Asunción (tel: 493-661; fax: 448-446).

Ministry of Justice and Labour, Avda Dr Gaspar Rodriguez de Francia c/ EE UU, Asunción (tel: 447-196, 491-555; fax: 440-066).

Ministry of Public Health and Social Welfare, Av Pettirossi c/Brasil, Asunción (tel: 207-328; fax: 206-700).

Ministry of Public Works and Communications, Olivia c/ Alberdi, Asunción (tel: 444-411, 496-666; fax: 443-625).

Other useful addresses

Administración Nacional de Electricidad (ANDE) (National Electricity Board), España el Padre Caroloto 360, Asunción (tel: 22-713/719).

Administración Nacional de Telecom (Antelco – Telecommunications Authority), Alberdi, esq General Diaz, Asunción (tel: 44-001).

Agencia Publicitaria Visión, 25 de Mayo, 966, Asunción (tel: 24-796).

Asociación Paraguaya de Cias de Seguros, 15 de Agosto esq Lugano, Casilla 1435, Asunción (tel: 446-474; fax: 444-343).

British Airways, Azara 192, Asunción (tel: 490-020).

British Embassy, Av. Boggiani 5848, C/R16 Boquerón, Casilla 404, Asunción (tel: 595-21 612 611; fax: 595-21 605 007).

Association of Cotton Ginners, CADELPA, Av Boggiani 4744, Asunción (tel: 595 21 609-272; fax: 595 21 600-739).

Customs Office, Colón c/ Plaza Isabel La Católica, Asunción (tel: 492-202, 495-086; fax: 445-085).

Dirección General de Estadísticas y Censos (National Statistics Office), Dr Miguel Torres, Asunción (tel: 610-331, 663-489).

Federation of Agroindustrial Exporters (FEDEXA), Brasilia 840 c/Sgto Gauto, Asunción (tel: 208-855, 205-749; fax: 213-971).

Federation of Industrial and Commercial Production (FEPRINCO), Palma 751 c/ Ayolas, Edif Unión Club, Piso 3, Asunción (tel: 444-963; fax: 446-638).

Importens Association (Centro de Importadores), Montevideo 671, Montevideo 671 c/ E V Haedo, Asunción (tel: 441-295, 490-291; fax: 441-295).

Industrial Union of Paraguay (UIP), Cerro Corá 1038 Casilla 782, Asunción (tel: 212-556; fax: 312-260).

Municipality of Asunción, Mariscal López y Cap. Villamayor Bloque A, 1er Piso Asunción (tel: 610-576, 610-577; fax: 610-578).

Paraguayan Embassy (USA), 2400 Massachusetts Avenue, NW, Washington DC 20008 (tel: (+1-202) 483-6960; fax: (+1-202) 234-4508; e-mail: embapar@erols.com).

Petróleos Paraguayos (Petropar), Oliva 299, 4er Piso, Casilla 571, Asunción (tel: 95-117).

Planning Office, Pdte Franco c/ Ayolas, Edif Ayfra, Piso 3, Asunción (tel: 491-159, 448-366; fax: 496-510).

Private Construction Association (CAPACO), Victor Hugo casi Cervantes, Asunción (tel: 295-424).

Pro Paraguay (Promotion of Exporters and Importers), Padre Cardozo 469 c/ España, Asunción (tel: 208-276, 208-641; fax: 200-425).

Rural Association of Paraguay (ARP), Ruta Transchaco Km 14, Mariano Roque Alonso (tel: 291-036, 291-061; fax: 291-061).

Siderurgia Paraguaya (Sidepar), Azara 197, 6er Piso, esq Yegros, Casilla 2441, Asunción (tel: 95-963).

Soybean Exporters Association (CAPECO), Av Brasilia 840, Asunción (tel: 208-855; fax: 595 21 213 971).

US Embassy, Avenida Mcal Lopez 1776, Casilla 402, Asunción (tel: 213-715; fax: 213-728).

Water Authority (Corporación de Obras Sanitarias Corposana), JoséBerges: e/Brasil y San José, Asunción (tel: 25-001/003).

Internet sites

ABC Color (newspaper): www.diarioabc.com.py

Noticias (newspaper): www.diarionoticias.com.py

Office of the President: www.presidencia.gov.py

The Congress of Paraguay: www.camdip.gov.py

Peru

KEY FACTS

Official name: República Peruana (Peruvian Republic)

Head of State: President Ollanta Moisés Humala Tasso (from 28 Jul 2011)

Head of government: Prime Minister Óscar Valdés (from 10 Dec 2011)

Ruling party: Coalition led by (Gana Perú) (Win Peru) (from 28 Jul 2011)

Area: 1,285,216 square km

Population: 29.46 million (2010)*

Capital: Lima

Official language: Spanish, Quechua and Aymara

Currency: Nuevo sol (S/) = 100 centimos

Exchange rate: S/2.77 per US$ (Oct 2011)

GDP per capita: US$5,172 (2010)

GDP real growth: 8.80% (2010)

GDP: US$152.80 billion (2010)

Labour force: 4.70 billion (2010)

Unemployment: 7.90% (2010) (plus additional underemployment)

Inflation: 1.50% (2010)

Oil production: 157,000 bpd (2010)

Balance of trade: US$6.75 billion (2010)

Annual FDI: US$7.33 billion (2010)

* estimated figure

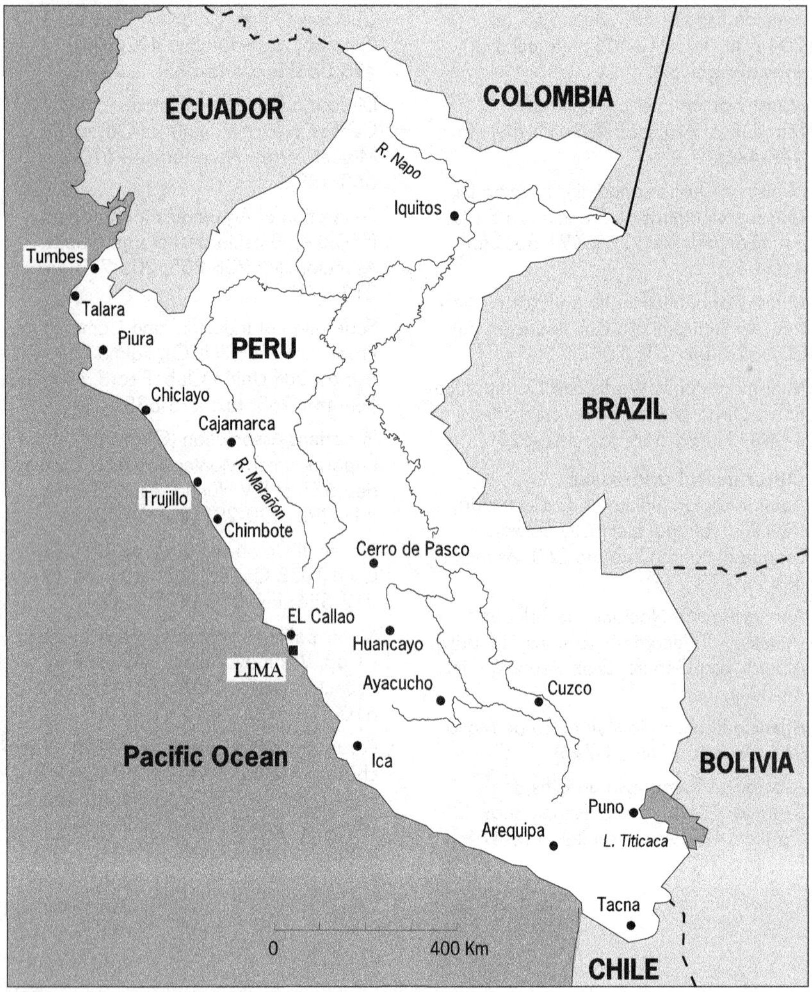

Ollanta Humala surprised many of his critics on assuming power at the end of July 2011 by appointing a centre-left, almost politically neutral cabinet that included a number of technocrat appointees. News of Mr Humala's first two economic appointments, Luis Castillo and Julio Velarde, cetainly calmed the markets. If Humala's critics were surprised, the international financial markets certainly weren't, taking the change of government in their stride. Concerns that Peru would become a Pacific outpost for the anti-American policies of Venezuela's Hugo Chávez proved unfounded, possibly due to the ill-health of the Venezuelan President, who was reportedly suffering from cancer and undergoing repeated treatments in Cuba. Following Mr Humala's inaugural address, the opinion polls showed that almost 70 per cent of Peruvians were optimistic about Mr Humala's plans for the economy and for social reforms.

Ojalá, Humala

Humala, a populist Peruvian politician who promised reforms in education and services to the poor, was sworn in as the nation's president at the end of July 2011.The election had been a close run affair, won by Mr Humala with 52 per cent against his rival, Keiko Fujimori with 48 per cent. In his first address as president, the newly elected Mr Humala predictably stressed the equality of Peruvians, stating that he wanted Peru to be 'a place where everyone enjoys the same rights to abundance and happiness. Economic growth and social inclusion must march together,' he said, outlining this as his governing philosophy. Mr Humala succeeded Alan García, who had overseen a period of strong economic growth as president. Despite this, García (who had previously been president in the 1980s) had remained unpopular, often criticised for promoting business at the expense of indigenous groups and the environment.

The Ollanta Humala who won the election appeared to be a different politician than that of the early campaigning. His red sweater was changed for a suit and (probably at the suggestion of his campaign managers) he began to wear a tie. He also announced that he was a committed Catholic, a move that the radicsl presidents of Venezuela and Ecuador, Messrs Chávez and Correa, had found to give an election advantage.

More than a decade earlier, a younger Lieutenant Colonel Humala had headed a military insurrecton against former President Alberto Fujimori (father of rival presidential candidate Keiko Fujimori) and currently in prison serving a 25-year sentence for human rights abuses. The military uprising placed Humala in the national spotlight. He also took on the Shining Path, a brutal populist insurgency that had terrorised Peru in the late 1980s and 1990s. Remnants of that group still operate and sporadic violence linked to the drug trade is often blamed on them.

Economy doing well?

According to the World Bank and other forecasters, Peru could look forward to growth of 7 per cent in 2011, making it one of the fastest-growing economies in Latin America. Although under President García Peru had been something of a Latin American economic *wunderkind* for most of the twenty-first century, impoverishment levels had remained obstinately high, bracketing some 30 per cent of the population as living in poverty in 2011. Peruvian social expenditure in 2010 was only 8 per cent of GDP, compared to 19 per cent in Chile and 20 per cent in Brazil. In 2010, 20 per cent of Peruvian families lacked drinking water. Peru's income tax level, at 9 per cent, was also the lowest in the region.

An early announcement by the Humala administration was the proposed introduction of a rise in the minimum wage to 750 soles (US$273) per month in 2012, an increase of 36 per cent over the 2010 figure. If market reaction was subdued, it was probably because analysts had already factored in the fact that a relatively high proportion – possibly as high as between 60–75 per cent of the population – are in the informal, *gris* sector of the economy. Thus, the increase in the minimum wage and the other social improvement measures had the advantage of a diluted impact, costing the Peruvian exchequer a modest US$275 million in its first year.

Like a number of Latin American economies, Peru came through the global financial crisis relatively unharmed, managing to maintain GDP growth, employment creation and poverty reduction. This meant that Peruvians had high expectations, seeking more immediate, tangible rewards from their country's impressive economic progress. Peruvians' disappointment was that while the economy as a whole has done well, salaries have remained depressed during the same period.

Nadine – the new Evita? Or just the power behind the throne?

She may be 14 years younger than her husband, but Nadine Heredia Alarcón (aka Mrs Humala) is considered by many Peruvian politicians and analysts to be the power behind the throne. Mr Humala's charismatic wife was constantly at his side during the presidential campaign. If Humala represents the more visible, more acceptable face of the new Peruvian administration, his wife is more than an attractive companion. In the view of many, it is Nadine who runs the Presidential Show.

US State Department cables released by *Wikileaks* report former US ambassador to Peru, Peter Michael McKinley as describing Nadine as the 'political brain of Humala'. Ambassador McKinley was also reported as observing that in meetings where Nadine was not present Humala appeared to be much more relaxed and able to speak freely on a number of topics. It was also reported that a number of key appointments within the administration were made at Nadine's insistence. The right-wing Fujimorista party have not minced their words in criticising Nadine. In April 2011 Irma Monte, Director of the Fuerza 2011 (Force 2011) movement weighed in 'Definitely, Ollanta is dominated by Nadine Heredia. She is the political force in his government's plan. She is more dangerous than him and thinks radically. She comes across as problematic, looking for opportunities for insurgency and a revolution in popular thinking.' Nadine has rebutted the accusations, saying '... they have made me the advisor, even the general. But all I am is as person of confidence; naturally, I am

KEY INDICATORS **Peru**

	Unit	2006	2007	2008	2009	2010
Population	m	27.64	27.41	28.70	29.10	*29.46
Gross domestic product (GDP)	US$bn	93.03	109.07	127.40	126.80	152.80
GDP per capita	US$	3,366	3,797	4,446	4,356	5,172
GDP real growth	%	7.6	9.0	9.8	0.9	8.8
Inflation	%	2.0	1.8	5.8	2.9	1.5
Unemployment	%	8.5	8.4	8.4	8.3	7.9
Industrial output	% change	9.5	10.1	10.1	-2.4	–
Agricultural output	% change	3.3	7.2	7.2	1.7	–
Oil output	'000 bpd	116.0	114.0	120.0	145.0	157.0
Natural gas output	bn cum	1.8	2.7	3.4	3.5	7.2
Exports (fob) (goods)	US$m	21,754.0	27,956.0	31,529.0	26,885.0	35,565.0
Imports (fob) (goods)	US$m	14,197.0	19,599.0	28,439.0	21,011.0	28,815.0
Balance of trade	US$m	7,557.0	8,356.0	3,090.0	5,873.0	6,750.0
Current account	US$m	2,589.0	1,220.0	-4,722.0	248.0	-2,315.0
Total reserves minus gold	US$m	16,733.3	26,856.5	30,271.5	32,012.6	42,647.9
Foreign exchange	US$m	16,732.4	26,852.7	30,262.5	30,999.8	41,652.8
Exchange rate	per US$	3.27	3.13	2.92	3.01	2.83

* estimated figure

his wife.' Nadine's background is straightforward enough: she studied communications in the University of Lima, followed by a masters degree in sociology at Lima's Catholic University of Peru. In her student days she appears to have held left-wing views. Interestingly, as is the case with her husband, in her schooldays she and her schoolmates were obliged to render homage to the Inca Empire.

Mrs Humala's left wing views may have been suppressed or put on hold following her husband's success. But reports published in 2009 suggested that she enjoyed close links with Hugo Chávez's government in Venezuela. Venezuelan internet blogs had reported in 2009 that Nadine Humala was paid US$4,000 per month as the 'Lima correspondent' of the *Caracas Daily Journal*. For any foreign correspondent to be paid as much as US$4,000 was surprising; all the more-so in the case of the pro-Chávez *Daily Journal* which lacked as much as a paid circulation. It also appeared that not a single article had appeared carrying the by-line of Nadine Humala or Nadine Heredia. The Venezuelan leader had, it was thought, seen Mr Humala joining the ranks of Chávez sympathisers alongside Bolivia's Evo Morales and Christina Kirchner. In the event, the role model of preference was not that of Venezuela but rather of Brazil.

The unorthodox political antecedents of Ollanta Humala are also worthy of consideration. His father, Isaac Humala, funded a creed called *emocacerism*, named after one Avelino Caceres a hero of Peru's war against Chile in the late nineteenth century. The slogan of the creed, or movement, was 'America for the Americans', which meant, in the usage of the day, the native Americans. Bolivia's leader Evo Morales has inadvertently picked up on some of the themes of Humala pére. Mr Humala's brother Antauro is currently serving a 25 year prison sentence for his part in an uprising in 2005 known a the *Andahuaylazo* after the town where troops commanded by Humala frére attacked a police station. In early 2011, immediately after Mr Humala's election victory, another brother, Alexis, turned up in Moscow claiming to be authorised to sign governmental agreements, a claim quickly denied by his president elect brother.

A number of the social programmes introduced or planned by the Humala government are closely modelled on those of Brazil. In addition to the increase in the minimum wage, the government also planned to introduce a non-contributory basic pension of some US$90.00 per month for the elderly, a state run child-care programme and more scholarships for Peruvian students wishing to study abroad. A gradual introduction of all these programmes meant that the cost to the Peruvian exchequer in the first year would be contained at a modest US$275 million.

Hydrocarbons

If Peru still has a major role to play on the world's energy stage, it is not due to a lack of natural resources. The country's gas reserves are the sixth largest in South America, some 12.2 trillion cubic feet according to the US based *Oil and Gas Journal* (OGJ). Gas production in 2010 was a modest 255.6 billion cubic feet (bcf), the bulk of which was exported. In June 2010 Peru began exporting gas from its liquefied natural gas (LNG) plant at Pampa Melchorita, capable alone of producing 215bcf annually. The major gas reserve is the Camisea project in the south-east, which since the inception of production in 2004 has grown at the staggering annual rate of 37 per cent. In 2011 a further gas field at Madre de Dios was being developed, with some estimates forecasting production to be as large as that at Camisea.

Although natural gas and, to a lesser extent, hydroelectricity, will dominate Peru's energy make-up for the foreseeable future, Peru had confirmed oil reserves of 533 million barrels in January 2011. Peruvian government estimates of oil reserves reach as high as 6 billion barrels. Oil production in 2010 was estimated at 158,328 barrels per day (bpd) by the OGJ. A lack of refining capacity means that the bulk of crude oil production is exported. Oil consumption is significantly higher than production, resulting in net annual imports of almost 100,000bpd in 2009. Half of the imported oil is supplied by Ecuador. Increased domestic use of natural gas has meant that annual rises in domestic oil consumption have been contained at around two per cent.

Some 50 international oil companies are involved in oil production in Peru in one way or another, although four – Occidental, Pluspetrol, Petrobras and Petrotech predominate. The 2010 bidding round for new exploration saw an additional 14 licences awarded. Half of the Peruvian Amazon is covered by oil exploration blocks, although concerns over oil spills and excessive drilling construction obliged Peru's supreme court to call a temporary halt to oil exploration in the Amazon region in 2009.

Roughly half of Peru's oil reserves are located offshore. In December 2010 the US based BPZ Energy began production at the offshore Corvina field in the north-west of Peru. The same company holds two licences for the neighbouring Tumbes basin. Colombia's Ecopetrol won exploration rights for five blocks in the Huallaga and Maranon river basins. The same company also formed a consortium with the Spanish oil company, Repsol, for Peruvian projects.

Risk assessment

Economy	Good
Politics	Good
Regional stability	Good

COUNTRY PROFILE

Historical profile

1500s The Inca empire stretched from the Pacific Ocean east to the sources of the Paraguay and Amazon rivers and from the region of modern Quito in Ecuador south to the Maule River in Chile.

1532 Francisco Pizarro of Spain led an armed expedition into the region. Weakened by a civil war over succession to the throne, the Inca Empire was easily overturned by the Spanish.

1542 The vice-royalty of Peru was established with Lima as its capital.

1569 Francisco de Toledo was appointed by the Spanish crown to administer the colony. He established a harsh, repressive system of government that ensured political stability by co-opting indigenous people as low-level officials. The system of government lasted for almost 200 years.

1820 José de San Martín led an invasion army into Peru with the support of rebel Chilean troops in a regional war against Spanish imperial rule.

1821 Peru became independent from Spain after San Martín's forces captured Lima.

1824 Simón Bolívar (who later led Bolivia to independence) became head of state of a centralised state, which included a unicameral legislature.

1826 Bolívar left Peru, which was subsequently ruled by a series of military commanders.

1845 Ramón Castilla became president, ensuring a period of stability and economic development.

1860 Peru adopted a liberal constitution for the first time.

1864 Peru went to war with Spain over control of the guano-rich Chincha Islands. Aided by Ecuador, Bolivia and Chile, Peru defeated the Spanish.

1879–84 Peru backed Bolivia in the War of the Pacific with Chile, but Chile invaded Peru and occupied Lima.
1884 The Treaty of Ancón was signed with Chile. Peru's nitrate-rich province of Tarapacá was handed over to Chile, which also occupied the provinces of Tacna and Arica. The poor state of the nation's economy, weakened by war and the loss of resource-rich regions, undermined governments for the next 30 years.
1895 Civilian rule began, although it was tainted by corruption and economic mismanagement.
1919 President Augusto Leguía launched an *autogolpe* (self-coup), against his own government in order to abolish democratic rule and establish a dictatorship.
1924 The Alianza Popular Revolucionaria Americana (APRA) (American Revolutionary People's Alliance), the country's first mass-based political party, was formed and led by Haya de la Torre.
1930 Leguía was overthrown by a group, including the military, the ruling oligarchy and APRA. A tripartite system of government was formed between the three groups; APRA soon left the alliance to lead a series of popular uprisings. In the early 1930s, APRA was banned.
1933 Luis Miguel Sánchez Cerro, president since 1931, was assassinated. The Congress appointed General Benavides as president.
1939 Manuel Prado y Ugarteche (a moderate) was elected president; he relaxed the government's attitude to APRA.
1945 Free elections took place and José Luís Bustamente y Rivero won the presidency.
1948 General Manuel Odría, staged a *coup d'état*. His military *junta* banned the APRA.
1962 The APRA became the largest party in congress, but fell short of the one-third required to form a government. It entered into a coalition with former military leader Manuel Odría and his supporters. The military seized power and called new elections.
1963 The election of Fernando Belaúnde Terry as president marked the beginning of a brief period of genuine democracy in Peru.
1968 Belaúnde nationalised Standard Oil's Peruvian subsidiary, the International Petroleum Company (IPC). General Juan Velasco Alvarado led a palace coup that removed Belaúnde from office. The military *docenio* (12-year rule) began.
1970s The Maoist *Sendero Luminoso* (Shining Path) terrorist group was formed by Abimael Guzman.
1975 Velasco was removed from office by General Franscisco Morales Bermúdez.
1978 A Constituent Assembly was elected, with leftist parties winning an unprecedented 36 per cent of the vote, although APRA won most of the seats.
1979 A new constitution was promulgated, which provided for free elections to be held every five years.
1981 Belaúnde returned to power after fresh elections enabled by the new constitution. The Peruvian economy was in a weak state, aggravated by the guerrilla group, Shining Path, which attacked rural areas and imposed its rule on villages. Military efforts to eliminate Shining Path were ineffectual. It is estimated that over 70,000 people were killed during the insurgency led by Shining Path. Debt repayment was suspended and Peru was denied further international loans.
1985 Alan García Pérez (APRA) won the presidential election. He campaigned to remove the military and police 'old guard'.
1987 Peru faced bankruptcy; writer Mario Vargas Llosa and his New Libertad movement blocked plans to nationalise banks.
1990 Alberto Fujimori won the presidential election. Under international pressure he introduced a programme of sweeping economic reforms by removing state subsidies, privatising state-owned assets and reducing state involvement in virtually all aspects of the economy. These measures reduced inflation and increased growth.
1992 Guzman, the leader of the Shining Path, was captured. Fujimori instigated an *autogolpe*. He suspended the constitution, dismissed the National Assembly and assumed wide emergency powers, appointing ministers to a new, smaller, unicameral chamber. The economy had begun to recover but regional disparity had increased.
1993 The constitution was reinstated with some amendments.
1995 President Fujimori was elected for a second term. Several setbacks undermined his position including the collapse of foreign direct investment due to the worldwide effects of the Asian financial crisis, and the damage to agriculture from *El Niño*.
2000 Fujimori was sworn in for a third presidential term – after much-criticised elections – without a controlling majority in the National Congress. Fraud tainted his presidency and a bribery scandal prompted him to flee to Japan, from where he resigned. Valentin Paniagua became caretaker president.
2001 Alejandro Toledo won the presidential election and his party, Perú Posible (PP), won the congressional elections.
2002 Power was devolved with the election of 25 regional presidents. The centre-left APRA, led by former president Alan García Pérez, took 12 of the 25 regional presidencies.
2003 Toledo's presidency lost its popular support. He dismissed Beatriz Merino as prime minister and appointed Carlos Ferrero Costa.
2004 President Toledo reshuffled his cabinet for the fifth time since coming to power.
2005 Prime Minister Carlos Ferrero resigned after the president appointed his close friend Fernando Olivera Vega as foreign minister. Pedro Pablo Kucznski became prime minister. Former President Fujimori was arrested in Chile. Peru and the US signed a trade agreement.
2006 Alan García Pérez (APRA) won a second (not-consecutive) presidential election. An APRA-led coalition government was formed. Abimael Guzman, leader of the Shining Path, was retried for terrorism and sentenced to life imprisonment. An earthquake struck south of Lima, killing hundreds and demolishing many buildings along the coast near the epicentre.
2008 Controversial land laws designed to open up the Amazon to development, which had been approved by decree by President García, were repealed by congress. The entire cabinet resigned following an oil scandal, when audio tapes implicated ministers in bribe taking. President García appointed Yehude Simon Munaro, a popular left-wing regional governor, as prime minister.
2009 A free trade agreement (FTA) with the US was signed. Negotiations for the FTA had been completed in 2006 but ratification was held up over US concerns about labour-rights and Peruvian government environmental policies regarding risks to the Amazon rain forest. Following protests and a month-long blockade of roads, rivers and fuel pipelines, which culminated in violence between indigenous Amazonians and police in which 34 people were killed, the national congress repealed land laws that had allowed logging, oil and natural gas exploration and other developments in the Amazon rainforests. Prime Minister Yehude Simon resigned and the President appointed Ángel Javier Velásquez Quesquén as prime minister.
2010 A new political party, to represent the interests of the indigenous Amazon Indians, was launched in August. The objectives of the Alianza para una Alternativa para la Humanidad (APHU) (Alliance for an Alternative for Humanity) is to campaign to protect both the rights of the aboriginal inhabitants and their rainforest home in the Andes Mountains and Amazon region. In a cabinet reshuffle President García appointed José Antonio Chang as prime minister on 14 September. Coca farmers overran the power plant in the regional capital, Pucallpa, for

several hours on 20 September, in protest at plans to destroy their coca crops. The UN estimates that cultivation of Peruvian coca rivals that of Colombia, the farmers (*cocaleros*) claim the leaves of the coca plant have been chewed by indigenous people for many centuries.
2011 On 18 March, Prime Minister José Chang resigned and on 19 March, Rosario Fernández was sworn in as prime minister. The conservative, Partido Nacionalista Peruano (PNP) (Peruvian Nationalist Party) formed a coalition to contest the elections, under the name Gana Perú (Peru Wins). In parliamentary elections held on 10 April, Gana Perú won 25.27 per cent of the vote (47 seats out of 130). Ten candidates contested the 10 April presidential election, in which former army officer, Ollanta Humala faced Keiko Fujimori, daughter of disgraced ex-leader Alberto Fujimori. Ollanta Humala Tasso (Gana Perú) won 31.7 per cent of the vote and his closest rival Keiko Fujimori Higuchi (Fuerza 2011) (Force 2011) 23.5 per cent. However, as no candidate won the minimum 50 per cent of votes a run-off took place on 5 June, in which Humala won 51.49 per cent and Fujimori 48.51 per cent. Humala was sworn in on 28 July; he appointed Salomón Lerner (independent) as prime minister. By 8 August, Brazilian authorities feared that a remote indigenous tribe, photographed for the first time in the Amazon in 2008, had had their land and village 'invaded and looted' by 'Peruvian drug traffickers' and many killed. Prime Minister Salomon Lerner resigned on 10 December, following a week of street protests objecting to a huge, open-cast gold and copper mine in the northern, Cajamarca region. The violence resulted in the declaration of a state of emergency as the demonstrations hindered Peru's biggest project that had attracted US$4.8 billion alone in foreign direct investment (FDI). President Humala appointed Óscar Valdés as prime minister.

Political structure

Constitution

Peru's constitution dates from 29 December 1993. The country is divided into 25 regions which each elect a president once every five years. Regions are divided into provinces, which in turn are divided into districts governed by mayors elected by direct popular vote every three years. The voting age is 18 years.

Form of state

Presidential democratic republic

The executive

Executive power is vested in the president, who is elected for a five-year term by universal adult suffrage. The president governs with the assistance of a prime minister and an appointed Council of Ministers. The prime minister is president of the Council of Ministers.

National legislature

The unicameral Congreso de la República (Congress of the Republic) has 120 members, directly elected by proportional representation, for five-year terms. Voting is compulsory for those aged 18–70.

Legal system

The judiciary consists of a 16-member Supreme Court, the ministry of justice and the nine-member Constitutional Court. By constitutional right the judiciary is entitled to at least 2 per cent of the central government budget. Members of the Supreme Court are appointed by the president. The posts are permanent, but members of the court must be aged over 50 and retire at 70.

Last elections

10 April 2011 (parliamentary); 10 April and 5 June 2011 presidential, first round and runoff)

Results: Parliamentary: (Gana Perú) (Win Peru) won 25.27 per cent of the vote (47 seats out of 130), Fuerza 2011 (Force 2011) 22.96 per cent (37) Alianza Electoral Perú Posible (Possible Peru Electoral Alliance) (coalition of three political parties) 14.83 per cent (21), Alianza por el Gran Cambio (Alliance for Great Change) (coalition of four political parties) 14.41 per cent (12), Alianza Solidaridad Nacional (National Solidarity Alliance) (coalition of four political parties) 10.21 per cent (nine), Alianza Popular Revolucionaria Americana (APRA) (American Revolutionary Popular Alliance) 6.42 per cent (four); seven other political parties each won less than 3 per cent and failed to win any seats.
Presidential, first round: Ollanta Humala Tasso (Gana Perú) won 31.7 per cent of the vote, Keiko Fujimori (Fuerza 2001) 23.5 per cent of the vote, Pedro Pablo Kuczynski (PPK) 18.5 per cent, Alejandro Toledo (Perú Posible) 15.6 per cent, and Luis Castañeda (Solidaridad Nacional) 9.8 per cent; five other candidates each won less than 1 per cent. Second round: Humala won 51.49 per cent, Fujimori 48.51 per cent.

Next elections

2016 (presidential and parliamentary)

Political parties

Ruling party

Coalition led by (Gana Perú) (Win Peru) (from 28 Jul 2011)

Main opposition party

Unión por el Perú (UP) (Union for Peru)

Population

29.46 million (2010)*

Last census: 21 October 2007: 27,412,640

Population density: 20 inhabitants per square km. Urban population: 73 per cent (1995–2001).

Annual growth rate: 1.6 per cent 1994–2004 (WHO 2006)

Ethnic make-up

45 per cent indigenous, 37 per cent *mestizo*, 15 per cent white, 3 per cent black, Asian or other.

Religions

Catholic (95 per cent), others (5 per cent).

Education

Adult literacy is relatively high in Peru. The 9 per cent difference in male and female litracy reflects the gender division in education provision.
The government provides free education for children up to the age of 15. Primary education lasts for six years, with secondary education divided into two stages of three and two years each. In rural areas, 40 per cent of the children traditionally help in the fields, with all but a few abandoning their schooling.

Literacy rate: 85 per cent adult rate; 97 per cent youth rate (15–24) (Unesco 2005).

Compulsory years: Six to 15

Enrolment rate: 123 per cent gross primary enrolment of the relevant age group (including repeaters); 73 per cent gross secondary enrolment (World Bank).

Pupils per teacher: 27 in primary schools

Health

About three million people are in the pension and health schemes administered by the state-owned Peruvian Institute of Social Security (IPSS). Salaried workers are obliged to contribute to the scheme, which provides free health care.
The health ministry budget covers health care for those outside the IPSS system. A small charge is made for treatment under this service.

HIV/Aids

HIV prevalence: 0.5 per cent aged 15–49 in 2003 (World Bank)

Life expectancy: 71 years, 2004 (WHO 2006)

Fertility rate/Maternal mortality rate: 2.8 births per woman, 2004 (WHO 2006)

Child (under 5 years) mortality rate (per 1,000): 26 per 1,000 live births; 8 per cent of children aged under five are malnourished (World Bank).

Welfare

Peru reformed its pension system in 1993, allowing the investment of individual accounts in real assets and introducing private pension funds to replace state pensions. In addition, the system provides disability and survivors' benefits

administered by insurance companies, and old-age pensions.
Employees are required to pay social security taxes equivalent to 13 per cent of their gross income into the public Oficina de Normalización Provisional (ONP) pension fund. Alternatively, employees may opt to pay 11.4 per cent of their salary into a private pension scheme. Workers are allowed to continue joining the old pay-as-you-go system, although the new system urges employers to pay more per worker into the private system than they were paying under the old system. One major challenge for the pension system in Peru is that as much as 51 per cent of the workforce is in the informal economy, covered by neither the old nor the new system.

Main cities

Lima (capital, estimated population 8.7 million in 2005), Arequipa (848,333), Trujillo (744,314), Chiclayo (567,675), Iquitos (426,464), Piura (356,637), Pucallpa (310,269), Sullana (200,661), Tacna (284,929).

Languages spoken

English is spoken in the main tourist regions.

Official language/s

Spanish, Quechua and Aymara

Media

Press

Dailies: Most national dailies and Sunday newspapers are published in Lima, in Spanish, including *El Comercio* (www.elcomercio.com.pe) *El Mundo*, *Expreso* (http://www.expreso.com.pe), *La Tribuna* (www.le-tribuna.org), *Ojo* (www.ojo.com.pe) – the largest selling newpaper, *El Peruano* (www.elperuano.com.pe) – the official State Gazette, *Horas Libre* (www.24horaslibre.com), *La República* (www.larepublica.com.pe) and *Correo* (www.correoperu.com.pe). There are also local publications for regional cities.
Weeklies: In Spanish *Caretas* (www.caretas.com.pe), *Gatopardo* (www.gatopardo.com), *Sí* (www.rcp.net.pe), *Crónica Viva* (www.cronicaviva.com.pe). In English, *Peru Finance*.
Online, in English, Lima Post (www.limapost.com) and Inside America-Peru (www.insideperu.com).
Business: In Spanish, *Business* (www.businessperu.com.pe), and *Punto de Equilibrio* (www.puntodeequilibrio.com.pe), *Gestión* (www.diariogestion.com.pe) and *Nuevo Oiga* (www.peru.com/revistas/oiga/index.asp).

Broadcasting

Radio: In Spanish, Radio Programas de Peru (RPP) (www.rpp.com.pe), Panamericana Radio (www.radiopanamericana.com), CPN Radio (www.cpnradio.com.pe), Radio Nacional (www.radionacional.com.pe) (government operated). Other regional and local radio stations, mainly commercial, broadcast in AM and FM throughout Peru.
Television: In Spanish, Panamericana Televisión (www.pantel.com.pe), Frecuencia Latina (www.frecuencialatina.com.pe), Andina de Radiodifusión (ATV) (www.atv.com.pe), América TV (www.americatv.com.pe), Uranio 15 (www.uranio15.com) and the state-owned Televisión Nacional de Pere, TVPeru (www.tvperu.gob.pe).

News agencies

Andina (Agencia Peruana de Noticias), Ave Alfonso Ugarte 873, Lima 1 (tel: 315-0400; email: andina@editoraperu.com.pe; internet: www.andina.com.pe).

Economy

Peru has large deposits of gold, silver, copper and other metals and its mineral resources, at a time when world prices for minerals have been high, have been a boon to the economy. As a result Peru has had one of the world's highest GDP growth rates of over 6 per cent since 2005 and did not experience recession during the global economic crisis. In 2007 GDP growth was 8.9 per cent and in 2008 it reached an estimated 9.8 per cent, it was, however, predicted to fall to 5–5.5 per cent in 2009 as exports fell.
The government increased domestic spending by 13.1 per cent (US$28.34 billion) in its 2010 budget to encourage economic growth and GDP growth was expected to slow to just 1 per cent.
Peru was given an investment grade credit rating in 2008 of BB by Standard and Poor's, which was reflected by other major international credit ratings agencies. It was upgraded to BB+ in March 2009.
Peru is classed as a upper middle income country by the World Bank, and according to national statistics the poverty rate was 36.2 per cent in 2009 (down from 54.8 per cent in 2001), of which 12.6 per cent of the population were living in extreme poverty. However both the poverty rate and unemployment rate (9.4 per cent in 2004 to 8.6 in 2008) have steadily fallen as Peru has addressed articles of the Millennium Development Goals.
The structure of the economy is dominated by the service sector at over 58 per cent of GDP, industry (including mining) at 35 per cent, of which manufacturing is 15 per cent, and agriculture as the remainder. Remittances in 2009 amounted to US$2.3 billion, of which 50 per cent is sent from expatriate workers in the US.

External trade

Peru is a member of the Asia-Pacific Economic Co-operation (Apec) forum and the Andean Community, which with Mercado Común del Sur (Mercorsur) (Southern Common Market) formed the South American free trade area (Safta).
Principal manufacturing includes textiles, consumer goods, processed food and fish products, and cement. Mining production includes silver (Peru is the world's second-largest producer), gold (it is the world's sixth-largest producer) and copper, with zinc and lead.

Imports

Principal imports are petroleum and petroleum products, plastics, machinery, vehicles, iron and steel, wheat, foodstuffs and processed food.
Main sources: US (typically 35 per cent of total), China (10 per cent), Spain (9 per cent).

Exports

Main exports include minerals (typically 40 per cent of total), crude oil and petroleum products, and coffee, agricultural products and foodstuffs.
Main destinations: US (typically 19 per cent of total), China (12 per cent), Switzerland (10 per cent).

Agriculture

Farming

The agricultural sector employs approximately 33 per cent of the population and contributes 9 per cent to GDP. Less than 3 per cent of Peru's land area is devoted to arable production and permanent crops. Subsistence farming predominates and productivity is low due to drainage and salinity problems, although productivity increased during the 1990s.
The government has given priority to farming as part of its programme to channel resources to the poorer regions and increase self-sufficiency. The highest priority sectors include rice, corn and wheat. By reviving traditional irrigation and terracing methods the government hopes to extend cultivation through the use of marginal land, while also promoting modern farming techniques.
Production has increasingly begun to focus on the winter export markets of the EU and the US. It is along the northern coast of Peru where export crops such as oranges, mangoes, asparagus, passion fruit and limes are grown, together with cotton, rice and sugar for the domestic market.
Animal husbandry (sheep, poultry and cattle) is important in southern regions.
Coffee production is receiving considerable support from the US Agency for

International Development (USAID), the United Nations Development Programme (UNDP) and GTZ, the German technical co-operation agency.

Fishing

One of the world's largest suppliers of fishmeal, Peru is also a major producer of canned, frozen and salted fish.

The shrimp industry has traditionally been a source of local employment, mainly in the northern coastal departments of Tumbes and Piura. Large quantities of shrimp are exported to the US, Canada, Spain and Taiwan. The shrimp industry is investing in improving the water quality of ponds and is also importing genetically treated baby shrimps to prevent white spot virus attacks in the future, which had caused production to decline.

Forestry

A little over half of the country's total landmass is covered by forests, most of which are located in the montaña region. The northern Pacific coast has areas of dry forests and savannas. The state owns all natural forests. There are significant numbers of privately-owned plantations, primarily consisting of eucalyptus. Estimates in 2002 showed that forest cover was about 65 million ha.

Peru produces a variety of woods including cedar, mahogany, dyewoods and other products, such as rubber and raw quinine from the Amazon Basin. Most production is geared towards sawn timber and panels with some quantities of bagasse pulp and solid wood products.

Industry and manufacturing

The industrial sector of the Peruvian economy makes a significant contribution of approximately 37 per cent to total GDP. About 15 per cent of the country's total workforce is employed in industry.

Manufacturing activity, centred in Lima and Callao, includes food processing, beverages, fishmeal, chemicals, petrochemicals, rubber, plastics, basic metallurgy, metal products, cement, textiles, footwear, paper products, machinery and motor vehicle assembly. Large firms dominate the sector.

Traditionally, Peruvian governments have taken an interventionist and protectionist approach in order to support local industries and promote employment. By 2003, the Toledo administration had overseen the privatisation of all but a few of the state-owned industries not already sold by the previous Fujimori administration.

Tourism

The development of the tourist industry continued throughout 2005. Travel and tourism now accounts for 8.2 per cent of total GDP and employs 7.6 per cent of the country's workforce.

With its rich variety of environments and archaeological sites, Peru has much to offer and tourism is becoming an important contributor to the country's economic revival. More then a million visitors were recorded in 2000. Although numbers fell in late 2001, as a consequence of the earthquake in June and the 11 September terrorist attacks in the US, they picked up again during 2002, a trend which continued in 2003. An important agreement was reached with the US in 2002, allowing unlimited air traffic between the two countries. Some 927,400 people visited Peru in 2004.

Mining

Peru's mining sector contributes approximately 15 per cent to total GDP. The country remains one of the world's largest producers of silver, copper, zinc and lead. The mining sector as a whole accounts for around 8 per cent of total employment in Peru.

Copper dominates the economy, not only as the main export earner, but also as a major source of employment. Export revenue is set to rise as new investments come on stream. Southern Peru Copper Corporation, controlled by US-based Asarco, remains the largest copper producer with an annual output of around 340,000 tonnes of fine copper content from its mining operations at Toquepala and the open pit Cuajone mine. Minera Yanacocha gold mine is the largest private gold producer in Peru, producing 40 per cent of the country's gold production. Other important minerals include tin, iron and steel.

By 2002, the state's role in the sector was limited to supervising the commitments made by companies and administering new concessions. International companies such as Asarco, Avocet Ventures, Barrick Gold, BHP, Cyprus and Arequipa Resources generate much of Peru's mineral production.

Barrick Gold's Lagunas Norte gold deposit exploration during 2002 resulted in an increase in its estimated resource from 3.5 million to 7.3 million ounces of gold.

In 2004, after the President had promulgated a law to levy royalties of 1–3 per cent of sales on some mining companies, Anglo American pulled out of an auction to develop a large copper deposit. Violence directed against foreign mining interests in Peru has led the national government to attempt to clamp down on activists.

Hydrocarbons

Proven oil reserves were 1.2 billion barrels in 2010; production was 157,000 barrels per day (bpd), an increase of 8.2 per cent on the 2009 figure of 145,000bpd. With oil consumption at nearly 184,000bpd, Peru needs to import oil, mainly from Colombia, Ecuador and Venezuela. Peru awarded 13 contracts to international oil companies on 20 April 2009, valued at US$650 million; these contracts brought the total number of exploration licences to 92.

Proven natural gas reserves were 360 billion cubic metres (cum) in 2007. The largest gas reserves are located in Camisea in the Amazon basin. Construction of the first liquefied natural gas (LNG) plant in South America began in June 2010. The US$3.8 billion, Melchorita plant will have a capacity of 4 million tonnes per year and will process 17 billion metres of natural gas per day. A consortium of four companies (one Peruvian and three foreign) will build and operate the plant, while the gas pipeline company, Transportadora de Gas del Perú, will provide the gas to be supplied to the domestic market.

Peru produces a small amount of coal, although it is almost entirely reliant on imports to meet domestic consumption levels. In a typical year, it produces 20,750 tonnes, and imports 1,230,000 tonnes, of coal.

Energy

Total installed generating capacity was 6,100MW in 2007, of which around 50 per cent is provided by hydropower and the remainder by conventional thermal power. However around 80 per cent of electricity is derived from hydroelectric stations while thermal power plants only operated during peak periods or when lack of rain suppresses hydroelectric output.

Following the partial privatisation of the energy market, begun in the 1990s, investment in gas-fired power stations has grown. Around 80 per cent of the population had access to electricity in 2007, although rural areas are typically still without electricity.

By 2008 there were 38 generation, 6 transmission and 22 distribution companies operating in Peru, all of which were created out of publicly owned entities and are overseen by government agencies responsible for national strategy, policy, environment and renewable energies.

The SNMPE (Sociedad Nacional de Minería, Petróleo y Energía) (National Society for Mining, Petroleum and Energy), whose members contribute 95 per cent of all power generated, announced in 2008 that there were plans to develop a number of new power stations. These included a hydroelectric power station in El Platanal that will generate 220MW, an additional gas-turbine at the Chilca I thermoelectric power station to generate a further 193.5MW, a gas-turbine to generate 192MW at the Kallpa power station and another gas-turbine to be installed at the

Edegel project to produce 164.5 MW. Together these will increase Peru's electricity generating capacity by 770MW. All gas will be supplied from the Camisea gas field.

Financial markets

Stock exchange

Bolsa de Valores de Lima (BVL) (Lima Stock Exchange)

Banking and insurance

Peru's banking and financial services sector has suffered a series of external shocks in recent years, with the Asian crisis, *El Niño* and turmoil in Brazil and Russia affecting confidence in emerging markets. Restoring confidence in Peru is widely considered to be just a matter of time, with the country's regulatory system among the most effective in the region. Moreover, the presence of foreign competition (foreign banks account for four of the country's top five banks), a tough provisioning system and a federal programme to facilitate commercial debt restructuring, meant that in 2002 the Peruvian banking sector was less affected by external crises than many in the region. Peru's banking sector includes over 25 commercial banks and a number of local savings banks, with the four largest groups accounting for over 60 per cent of the systems assets, loans and deposits.

Central bank

Banco Central de Reserva del Perú

Main financial centre

Lima

Time

GMT minus five hours

Geography

The geography of Peru, the third-largest country in South America, ranges from Andean peaks almost 7,000 metres high to tropical Amazonian rain forests and burning coastal deserts.

Peru is bordered by Ecuador and Colombia to the north, Brazil and Bolivia to the east, Chile to the south and the Pacific Ocean to the west.

Almost half the population lives in a narrow coastal strip which covers about 10 per cent of the country's total area. The coastal zone, running 3,079km from Ecuador to Chile, is a desert cut by rivers and oases which are fed by melting snow from the Andes.

The Andes cover around 30 per cent of Peru and form a plateau averaging 3,000 metres high studded with towering peaks. The highest summit is Huascaran at 6,768 metres. In the Andes there are many fertile valleys, such as those of Cuzco and Cajamarca. Lake Titicaca in the south, at an altitude of 3,815 metres, is the highest navigable lake in the world. East of the Andes, around 60 per cent of Peru's area is covered by the jungle of the Amazon basin. Ecuador claims a large section of the northern Amazonian territory. The area is flat and very low. Iquitos, the main town in the area, is about 4,000km from the mouth of the Amazon but only 106 metres above sea level.

Hemisphere

Southern

Climate

Although Peru lies between the equator and the tropic of Capricorn, only the Amazonian jungle has a typically tropical climate, with high rainfall and humidity and little seasonal change in temperatures.

The effects of altitude in the Andes and the cold Humboldt current flowing up from the south moderates the climate in the central and coastal sections.

Temperatures in the capital, Lima, vary only slightly throughout the year due to the cold Humboldt current. They rarely rise above 28 degrees Celsius (C) in summer or dip below 12C in winter. Although Lima is set in a coastal desert, with annual rainfall around 48mm, the sky is overcast with a thick sea mist from June to September. This can be so dense as to resemble light drizzle and requires the use of a raincoat. In the Andes, the rainy season lasts from December to March and makes some road travel hazardous. About three-quarters of Cuzco's average annual rainfall of 80cm falls in this period.

Dress codes

Peruvians dress relatively informally, especially in the summer months from January to March when many government officials and other professionals go to work in casual loose-fitting clothes. In winter, jackets and ties for men and skirts for women are more common.

Entry requirements

Passports

Required by all.

Visa

Tourist visas are not required by nationals of EU/EEA countries, the Americas, Australasia and the Pacific, Asia and South Africa, for visits of up to 90 days. Business visas, valid for 90 days, are required by nationals of all countries. Applications must include a letter of introduction from the employer or, where self-employed, the local chamber of commerce, detailing the purpose of the visit and length of stay, together with proof of adequate funds and return/onward passage.

For further information see http://peru.embassyhomepage.com.

Currency advice/regulations

There are no restrictions on the import and export of local currency or on the import of foreign currency, the export of which is restricted to the amount imported.

Health (for visitors)

Mandatory precautions

A yellow fever vaccination certificate is required if arriving from an infected area.

Advisable precautions

Yellow fever vaccination is recommended (essential for visits to some rural areas). Diphtheria, TB, typhoid, polio, tetanus and hepatitis A and B vaccinations are also advisable.

Malaria risk exists in some rural areas – prophylaxis is recommended.

Water precautions should be taken – it is advisable to drink only bottled water.

Hotels

In main centres hotels are classified by stars (maximum five) according to available facilities. In smaller towns, the best accommodation is often the government-run *Hoteles Turistas*. Hotel bills include a 10 per cent service charge; for stays of less than 60 days, foreign visitors are exempted from the 19 per cent government sales tax on presentation of travel documents.

Visitors arriving in Lima are well advised to inform their hotel of their arrival flight number and time. Most major hotels operate a free courtesy coach service to Jorge Chávez airport and will meet arriving guests.

Public holidays (national)

Fixed dates

1 Jan (New Year's Day), 1 May (Labour Day), 24 Jun (Inti Raymi), 29 Jun (St Peter and St Paul's Day), 28–29 Jul (Independence Day Celebrations), 30 Aug (St Rose of Lima Day), 8 Oct (Battle of Angamos Day), 1 Nov (All Saints' Day), 8 Dec (Immaculate Conception), 24–25 Dec (Christmas).

Variable dates

Maundy Thursday, Good Friday.

Working hours

Banking

Mon–Fri, Jan–Mar: 0815–1130.
Mon—Fri, Apr–Dec: 0915–1245. Some banks may open afternooons.

Business

Mon–Fri: 0900–1300 and 1430–1630.

Government

Mon–Fri: 0900–1300 and 1430–1630.

Shops

Mon–Sat: 1000–1300 and 1600–1900.

Telecommunications

Mobile/cell phones

GSM 1900 service available around the largest cities and towns.

Electricity supply

Generally 220V AC, 60 cycles. Exceptions include Arequipa (220V AC, 50 cycles) and Iquitos (110V AC, 60 cycles).

Social customs/useful tips

It is customary to shake hands on meeting and taking leave. Professional titles should be used and although most people have two family names, only the first is used.
The style of business is generally relaxed and the informal *tu* form is commonly used with younger Spanish-speaking business visitors. Meetings should be arranged in advance and reconfirmed.
Visiting cards are used. While Peruvians are sometimes inclined to be late for appointments, visitors are expected to be punctual.
Never point the soles of your feet at anyone; it is considered highly insulting.

Security

Internal terrorist groups no longer pose a threat to security in most regions, but *Sendero Luminoso* (Shining Path) terrorists are still active in the remoter areas of central Peru Apurimac. There is a risk of armed robbery and hijacking of buses and cars on the road between Lima and Cuzco.
It is not considered safe to walk around the centre of Lima at night. There is a high level of street crime particularly in the city centre. Extreme caution should be taken on all streets, especially in pedestrian precincts. Visitors should be careful not to display valuables – especially at bus stations, railways and airports. Travellers should never journey outside the principal cities after dark and as a general rule are advised to use air travel wherever possible.
If you are robbed, report immediately to the nearest police station and ensure you receive a certified copy of the official statement.

Getting there

Air
National airline: LAN Perú.
International airport/s: Lima, Jorge Chávez International (LIM), 16km west of city; duty-free shop, bar, restaurant, bank, post office, shops, car hire.
Airport tax: US$30.25.
Surface
Road: There is road access and bus services from neighbouring countries. The Pan-American Highway passes through Peru, from Ecuador in the north to Chile in the south.
In January 2011 a road from Nazca on the Peruvian coast, across the Andes cordillera to Cusco and on to Inapari on the border with Brazil was officially opened by some 30 racing drivers. The road is expected to increase trade between the two countries, especially Brazilian exports to Asia. There are, however, fears for the ecology of region as the road opens up the area to miners with heavy equipment to replace the old panners. Migration too is having an effect as miners move from the Andes to the Amazon. The 2,589km road took five years to build.
Main port/s: Callao, San Martin, Matarani.

Getting about

National transport
Visitors are advised to contact the tourist police or the South American Explorers' Club in Lima for up-to-date information on travel to the interior of the country.
Air: There are regular services between Lima and all main towns, provided by several operators, including Aerocóndor Perú, LAN Perú, Star Perú and Taca Perú. There are 19 airports which receive domestic flights; another 22 airports operate charter and support services.
Due to weather conditions flights may be delayed or cancelled. It is essential to reconfirm bookings as flights are often overbooked.
Road: The Pan-American Highway, paved over most of the distance, runs north to south along the coast from the Ecuador border to the Chilean border (with a north-east arm into the Sierra, through Arequipa and on to the Bolivian frontier). The Trans-Andean Highway runs from Lima to Pucallpa, via La Oroya and Huanuco. The Central Highway connects Lima with La Oroya, Huancayo, Huancavelica, Ayacucho, Cuzco and Puno (linking with the Pan-American Highway spur from Arequipa).
In the rainy season (Dec–Apr) landslides are frequent, causing blockages and delays.
Buses: Cheap but fairly uncomfortable services are available on the Pan-American Highway north to Ecuador, south to Chile and on the highway to Callejon de Huaylas in northern Andes. Yellow city buses and mini-buses connect Lima with Callao and the residential suburbs.
Rail: There are regular rail services between Lima and La Oroya with branches to Cerro de Pasco, Huancayo and Huancavelica. The Southern Railway of Peru operates between Arequipa and Puno (on Lake Titicaca) with one weekly connection (Wed) by steamer across the lake to Bolivia. Also regular rail connections from Puno to Cuzco. A short line runs from Tacna to Arica in Chile. Railways have separate summer and winter schedules.
City transport
Taxis: Taxis are the best means of travel in the main cities. For safety reasons, radio-controlled taxis and, in Lima, yellow registered taxis should be used rather than unlicensed or cruising taxis. The passenger should avoid taxis containing anyone other than the driver and always lock the rear doors and close the rear windows if possible.
Recognised taxi ranks (*estaciones*) are found at hotels and airports. Taxis are not metered and fares should be agreed in advance.
Car hire
Major international companies operate in Lima and other main centres. Chauffeur and self-drive cars available. International licence preferred and credit cards essential. Cost includes basic insurance cover.
Traffic is congested in Lima.

BUSINESS DIRECTORY

The addresses listed below are a selection only. While World of Information makes every endeavour to check these addresses, we cannot guarantee that changes have not been made, especially to telephone numbers and area codes. We would welcome any corrections.

Telephone area codes

The international dialling code (IDD) for Peru is +51 followed by area code and subscriber's number:

Amazonas	41	Junin	64
Ayacucho	66	Lima	1
Cajamarca	76	Loreto	65
Cuzco	84	San Martin	42

Useful telephone numbers

Police: 105
Fire: 116
Ambulance: 117

Chambers of Commerce

American Chamber of Commerce of Peru, Avenida Ricardo Palma 836, Lima 18 (tel: 241-0708; fax: 241-0709; e-mail: amcham@amcham.org.pe).

British-Peruvian Chamber of Commerce, Avenida José Larco 1301, Lima 18 (tel: 617-3090; fax: 617-3095; e-mail: bpcc@bpcc.org.pe).

Lima Cámara de Comercio, Avenida Gregorio Escobedo 398, Lima 11 (tel: 463-8080; fax: 463-2837; e-mail: presidencia@camaralima.org.pe).

Trujillo Cámara de Comercio y Producción de la Libertad, Jirón Junín 454, PO Box 729m Trujillo (tel: 231-114; fax 242-888; e-mail: camara@camaratru.org.pe).

Banking

Banco Banex, Av República de Panamá 3680, San Isidro, Lima 27 (tel: 210-0071; fax: 440-3298).

Banco do Brasil SA, Avenue Camino Real 348, Torre el Pilar Piso 9, San Isidro, Lima 27 (tel: 221-2258; fax: 442-4208).

Banco Continental, Av República de Panamá 3073, 27 Lima (tel: 421-7272; fax: 441-8922).

Banco de Comercio, Jr Lampa 560, Piso 2, Lima 1 (tel: 428-9400; fax: 426-8454).

Banco de Crédito del Perú, Av Huarochiri y Calle Centenario, 156 URB Las Ladera de Melgarejo, Lima 12 (tel: 349-0304; fax: 349-0548).

Banco de Desarrollo, Jr Camaná 700, Lima 1 (tel: 428-6360; fax: 427-7665).

Banco Exterior de Los Andes y de España, Extebandes, Av Canaval Y Moreyra 454, Lima 27 (tel: 442-2121; fax: 440-4572).

Banco Financiero Del Perú, Avenue Ricardo Palma 229, Lima 18 (tel: 241-0324; fax: 447-8766).

Banco Interamericano de Desarrollo, Paseo de la República 3245, 14th Floor, PO Box 270154, San Isidro, Lima 27 (tel: 442-3400).

Banco Interamericano de Finanzas (BIF), Ricardo Rivera Navarrete 543, Lima 27 (tel: 221-2888; fax: 221-2489).

Banco Interandino Saema, Augusto Tamayo 120, Lima 27 (tel: 471-7777; fax: 441-1404).

Banco Internacional Del Perú (Interbanc), Jr De La Unión 600, Lima 1 (tel: 427-2000; fax: 426-2630).

Banco Latino, Av Paseo de la República 3505, Lima 27 (tel: 422-1290; fax: 442-6200).

Banco del Libertador, Av P De la República 3245, San Isidro, Lima 27 (tel: 442-1661; fax: 441-4908).

Banco de Lima, Esquina Puno y Carabaya 698, Lima 1 (tel: 426-8676; fax: 426-2356).

Banco Mercantil del Peru SA, Av Rivera Navarrete 641, Lima 27 (tel: 442-1290; fax: 442-5277).

Banco de la Nación (national bank), Av Nicolas de Piérola, Lima 1 (tel: 426-2000; fax: 426-1133).

Banco del Nuevo Mundo, Av Paseo de la República 3033, 27 Lima (tel: 472-5121; fax: 440-2940).

Banco del Progreso - Probank, Av Javier Prado Este 595, 27 Lima (tel: 421-2800; fax: 441-1058).

Banco Regional del Norte (Norbank), Av Emancipación 199, Lima 1 (tel: 422-3589; fax: 442-2703).

Banco República, Jr Camaná 700, Lima 1 (tel: 444-3214; fax: 444-3774).

Banco Santander, A Tamayo 120, San Isidro, Lima 27 (tel: 221-5000; fax: 221-5001).

Banco Solventa, Av Aviación 2401, Piso 11, San Borja (tel: 225-0505; fax: 225-0505).

Banco Sudamericano SA, Av Camino Real 815, Lima 27 (tel: 221-1111; fax: 442-3392).

Banco del Sur del Perú (Bancosur), Chinchón 986, San Isidro, Lima 27 (tel: 442-1170; fax: 442-1178).

Banco del Trabajo, Av Paseo de La República 3587, San Isidro, Lima 27 (tel: 421-9000; fax: 421-2521).

Banco Wiese Ltdo, Jr Cuzco 245, Lima 1 (tel: 428-6000; fax: 426-3977).

Citibank NA, Av Camino Real 456, Torre Real, Piso 5TO, Lima 27 (tel: 421-400; fax: 440-9044).

Central bank

Banco Central de Reserva del Perú, Miroquesada 441, Lima (tel: 613-2000; fax: 427-5880; e-mail: webmaster@bcrp.gob.pe).

Stock exchange

Bolsa de Valores de Lima (BVL) (Lima Stock Exchange): www.bvl.com.pe

Travel information

South American Explorers Club, Cale Piura 135, Miraflores, Lima (tel: 445-3306; e-mail: limaclub@saexplorers.org).

Tourist Bureau of Complaints, PO Box 1596, Lima (tel: 224-7888; e-mail: postmaster@indecopi.gob.pe).

Tourist Police (speak several languages; wear white belts over their green dress uniforms), Lima (tel: 225-8698; fax: 476-7708); toll-free number for tourists outside Lima: 0800-42579).

Ministry of tourism

Ministry of International Trade and Tourism, Calle 1 Oeste No 50, Urbani Córpac, Edificio Mincetur, San Isidro, Lima (tel: 224-3347; fax: 224-3264; e-mail: informa@mincetur.gob.pe).

National tourist organisation offices

PromPeru, Calle 1 Oeste No 50, Urbanización Córpac, Edificio Mincetur, San Isidro, Lima (tel: 224-3131; Fax: 224-7134; e-mail: postmaster@promperu.gob.pe).

Ministries

Ministry of Agriculture, Avenida Salaverry s/n, Jesús Maria, Lima (tel: 433-3034; fax: 432-9098).

Ministry of Defence, Avenida Arequipa 291, Lince, Lima (tel: 435-9567; fax: 433-5150).

Ministry of Economy and Finance, Jr Junín 339, Lima (tel: 427-3930; fax: 431-7836).

Ministry of Education, Avenida San Develde 160, San Borja, Lima (tel: 436-1240; fax: 433-0230).

Ministry of Energy and Mines, Avenida Las Artes s/n, San Borja, Lima (tel: 475-0206; fax: 475-0689).

Ministry of Fisheries, Calle Uno Oeste s/n, Urbanización Corpac, San Isidro, Lima (tel: 224-3336; fax: 224-3233).

Ministry of Foreign Affairs, Palacio de Torre Tagle, Jr. Ucayali 363, Lima (tel: 427-3860; fax: 426-3266).

Ministry of Health, Avenida Salaverry Cdra 8, Jesús María, Lima (tel: 432-3535; fax: 431-3671).

Ministry of the Interior, Plaza 30 de Agosto 150, San Isidro, Lima (tel: 475-2995; fax: 441-5128).

Ministry of Justice, Scipión e Llona 350, Miraflores, Lima (tel: 441-7320; fax: 440-4407).

Ministry of Labour and Social Promotion, Avenida Salaverry 655, Jesús Maria, Lima (tel: 433-2512; fax: 433-8126).

Ministry of the Presidency, Avenida Paseo de la República 4297, Lima (tel: 446-5886; fax: 447-0379).

Ministry of Transport, Communications, Housing and Construction, Avenida 28 de Julio 800, Lima 1 (tel: 433-1212; fax: 433-9378).

Ministry for Women's Promotion and Human Development, Avenida Emancipación 235 o Esquina Jr Camaná 616, Lima 1 (tel: 426-4336).

Other useful addresses

Adex (export association), Javier Prado Este No 2875, San Borja, Lima (tel: 346-2530; fax: 346-1879; e-mail: postmast@adex.org.pe).

Andean Group, Avda Paseo de la República, Casilla Postal 3237, Lima.

Asociación de Bancos del Perú (Bank Association), Av Antonio Miro Quesada 247 of 409, Lima 1 (tel: 428-8850, 427-6378, 428-5136).

British Embassy, Edif El Pacífico Washington, Piso 12, Plaza Washington, Esq Avda Arequipa, Casilla 854, Lima 100 (tel: 334-738, 839, 334-932; fax: 334-735); for genuine emergency outside hours, leave message on answerphone (tel: 433-4738, 433-4839, 433-4932).

Centromin (Empresa Minera del Centro del Perú SA), Avda Javier Prado Este 2175, San Borja, Apdo 2412, Lima 34 (tel: 365-924; fax: 358-782).

Cepri (Electroperú Privatisation), Avda Pedro Miotta s/n, Lima 29 (tel: 661-844; fax: 661-899).

Cofide (Corporación Financiera de Desarrollo), Camino Real 390, San Isidro, Lima 27 (tel: 422-550; fax: 423-384).

Conaco (Confederación Nacional de Comerciantes) (National Federation of Commerce), Avenida Abancay 210, Lima (tel: 273-528, 286-026).

Conite (National Commission for Investments and Foreign Technology), Avenida Abancay 500, Piso 6 (MEF), Lima 1.

Copri (Private Investment Promotion Committee), Comité Especial de Minero Perú SA, Bernardo Monteagudo No 222, Piso 12, Lima 17 (tel: 461-4300; fax: 462-7049).

Corpac (Corporación Peruana de Aeropuertos y Aviación Comercial), Aeropuerto Internacional Jorge Chávez, Avenida Faucett s/n, Callao (tel: 529-570).

DHL Worldwide Courier, Avenida La Marina 2469, San Miguel (tel: 525-559).

Electroperú, Centro Cívico, Paseo de la República 144, Lima 1 (tel: 310-664).

Empresa Nacional de Ferrocarriles del Perú, Ancash 207, Apdo 1379, Lima (tel: 289-440).

Enapu SA (National Port Company), Avenida Guardia Chalaca s/n, Callao (tel: 299-210).

Hierroperú(State Iron Company of Peru), Avenida Paseo de la República 3587, Lima (tel: 410-636).

International Translation Service, Avenida Arequipa 3200, San Isidro, PO Box 6046, Lima (tel: 411-396).

Lima Stock Exchange, Pasaje Acuna 191, Lima (tel: 286-280; fax: 337-650).

Mineroperú (State Mining Company of Peru), Avenida Bernardo Monteagudo Orrantia 222, Magdalena del Mar, Lima (tel: 620-740; fax: 627-049).

Peruvian Embassy (USA), 1700 Massachusetts Avenue, NW, Washington DC (tel: (+1-202) 833-9860; fax: (+1-202) 659-8124; e-mail: peru@peruemb.org).

PetroPerú (State Petroleum Company), Paseo de la República 3361, San Isidro, Lima 27 (tel: 411-919).

PromPerú, Comisión de Promoción del Perú (investment promotion), Edificio Mitinci, Piso 13, calle 1 Oeste S/N, Lima 27 (tel: 224-3125/3271/3279; fax: 224-3323; e-mail: perunet@promperu.gob.pe).

Skyway SA (international courier), Centro Com. Camino Real, 1103, PO Box 2552, Lima 100 (tel: 402-353, 229-225, 416-725).

Sociedad de Industrias (Society of Industries), Los Laureles 365, San Isidro, Lima 27 (tel: 408-700).

US Embassy, Avda Garcilaso de la Vega 1400, Apdo 1995, Lima 100 (tel: 338-000; fax: 316-682).

Internet sites

PromPerú, Comisión de Promoción del Perú (for general information on Peru and daily updates): http://www.rcp.net.pe/perunet

ADEX, Asociacion de Exportadores: http://www.adexperu.org.pe

Philippines

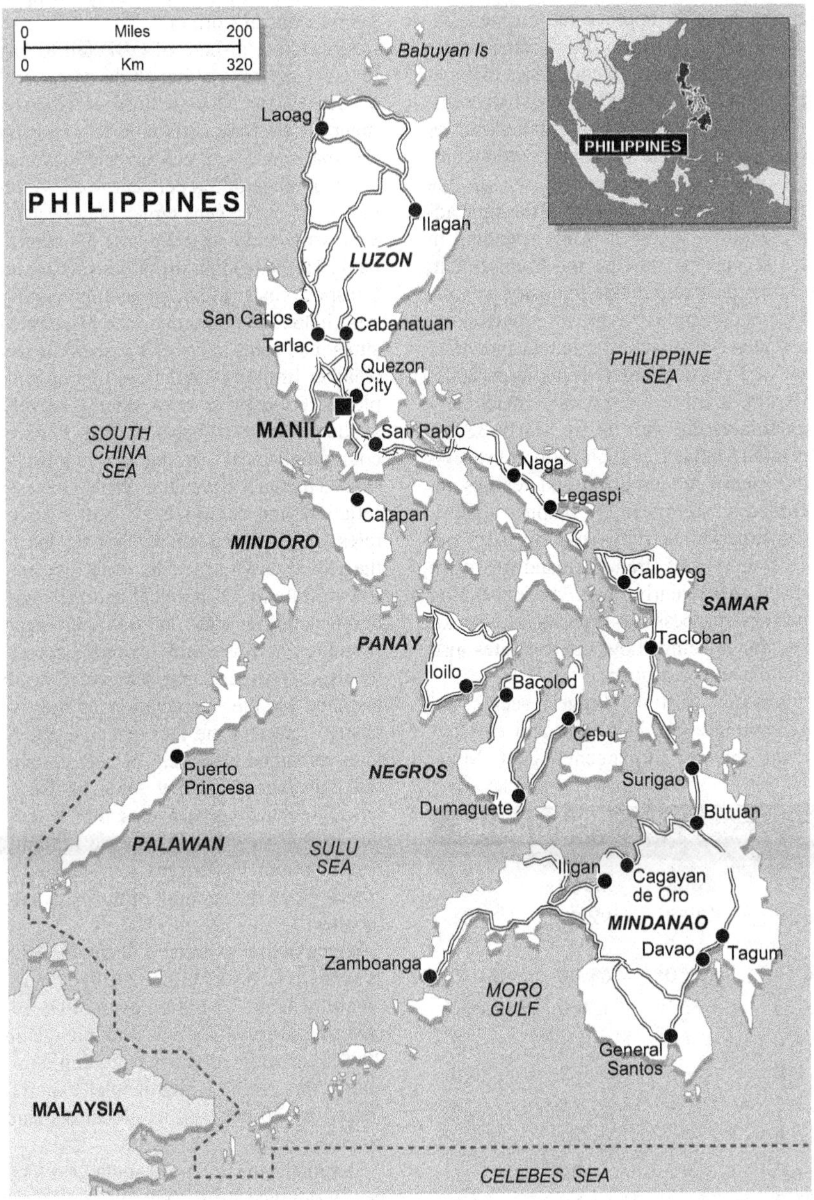

KEY FACTS

Official name: Republika ng Pilipinas (Republic of the Philippines)

Head of State: Benigno Aquino III (LP) (from 29 Jun 2010)

Head of government: Benigno Aquino III (LP)

Ruling party: Partido Liberal (Liberal Party) (coalition with Kalapian ng mga Kaibigan sa Kaunlaran (KKK) (Friends Of Development – City of Hagonoy) (from 29 Jun 2010)

Area: 300,439 square km (7,107 islands)

Population: 94.01 million (2010)*

Capital: Manila (on Luzon)

Official language: Filipino (based on Tagalog)

Currency: Peso (P) = 100 centavos

Exchange rate: P43.73 per US$ (Oct 2011)

GDP per capita: US$2,007 (2010)

GDP real growth: 7.30% (2010)

GDP: US$188.70 billion (2010)

Labour force: 38.91 million (2010)

Unemployment: 7.30% (2010)

Inflation: 2.80% (2010)

Balance of trade: -US$10.38 billion (2010)

Annual FDI: US$1.71 billion (2010)

* estimated figure

Political compacency, bolstered by a system that almost inevitably results in the perpetuation of family dynasties and readily corruptible public officials, has ill-served the Philippines. This oligarchic political system inevitably overwhelms any good intentioned and reformist president, but also permits free-for-all campaigning and promises based on money rather than principles, where the best and the brightest, but poor, have no realistic chance of being elected.

High hopes

When all is said and done, President Benigno (NoyNoy) Aquino III, (son of the late, almost legendary, Corazón Aquino and her asassinated husband) whatever his noble intentions, rhetorics, catch phrases and promises will find it hard to transform Philippines' society without first embarking on serious constitutional revision. Secondly he will also need to ensure some sort of continuity of administration, policies and projects and finally he will need to undertake drastic electoral reforms. A discredited electoral system and surfeit of money have inevitably resulted in the perpetuation of family dynasties, corruptible public officials and docile police officers. Whistle blowers have no credibility.

President Aquino was certainly helped by a strong recovery in 2010 that lifted gross domestic product (GDP) by 7.3 per cent, as private consumption accelerated and exports and investment rebounded from the slump of 2009. Nearly 60 per cent of total growth came from private consumption, which rose by 5.3 per cent. Remittances from overseas workers remained a key support to consumption, growing by 8.2 per cent to US$18.8 billion (currency appreciation meant that the increase in peso terms was 2.4 per cent).

Investment contributed about 40 per cent of total growth, the highest proportion in 10 years. Fixed capital outlays climbed by 17.1 per cent, with equipment investment surging by 25.7 per cent. Double-digit growth was recorded for investment in a broad range of equipment, including that for agriculture, construction, mining, metalworking, transport and telecommunications. Fixed investment as a ratio to GDP edged up to 15.7 per cent, the strongest rate in 6 years. A recovery in exports and robust consumption underpinned this strong investment, with support from higher corporate earnings and low interest rates. After the presidential and legislative elections in May 2010 had gone smoothly, businesses generally were optimistic about the new government's commitment to improve the business climate. Surveys on business expectations showed steady gains in confidence throughout the year. Net exports, which had been a drag on GDP growth during the global recession, also made a positive contribution.

Government expenditure rose in the first half of the year, before the new administration reined in some spending in the second half to curb the fiscal deficit. On the production side, industry was the main contributor to growth, overtaking services. Manufacturing output increased by 12.3 per cent, after shrinking in 2009. Export-oriented electrical machinery manufacturing shot up by nearly 33 per cent and industries such as food processing, petroleum products and textiles recorded significant output gains. Construction activity rose by 10.5 per cent, driven by strong demand for office space, particularly from the expanding business process out-sourcing sub-sector and for housing. Low interest rates also stimulated construction.

Services, still the biggest sector and generating about half GDP and employment, grew by 7.1 per cent in 2010. Much of the growth came from retailing, which was boosted by remittance inflows. Other high-growth components were business process outsourcing, finance and real estate. Dry weather caused by an El Niño weather pattern cut agricultural output, however, by 0.5 per cent, a second consecutive year of weak performance (production was flat in 2009 mainly owing to severe tropical storms).

Agriculture's share of GDP fell to just under17 per cent, although the sector still accounted for about a third of employment. The strong economic rebound did not spark inflation, consumer prices rose by an average of 3.8 per cent, well within the 3.5–5.5 per cent target range set by Bangko Sentral ng Pilipinas, the central bank. Higher global oil prices pushed up transport costs (although an appreciating peso helped to damp imported price pressures) and electricity costs rose as the dry weather limited output from hydropower plants. Food price rises were relatively subdued, in part because rice imports countered local production shortfalls caused by the bad weather. With moderate inflation, the central bank kept interest rates in 2010 at the low levels it set during the global downturn – the overnight borrowing rate at 4.0 per cent and the overnight lending rate at 6.0 per cent. Pressures to raise rates to more normal levels as the economy rebounded were lessened by the appreciation of the exchange rate and the fact that real policy rates remained positive. The central bank did, however, withdraw some of the liquidity-enhancing measures that it took during the recession. Domestic liquidity rose by about 11 per cent, a moderate increase given the strength of the economic recovery.

Merchandise exports shot up by 34.8 per cent to US$50.7 billion in 2010 (an increase of US$13.1 billion over 2009), recovering from a 22 per cent plunge in 2009. Electronic products including semiconductors (three fifths of total exports) surged by 40 per cent as global demand bounced back.

Shipments to China and south-east Asia nearly doubled from 2009, on healthy recoveries there. China accounted for 11.1 per cent of total exports, well up from 7.6 per cent in 2009, while south-east Asia's share went up to 22.5 per cent from about 15 per cent. The share of exports going to the United States fell to 14.7 per cent from 17.7 per cent. Imports rose by 31.5 per cent or by US$14.6 billion, reflecting strong demand for capital equipment, consumer goods, imported inputs for

KEY INDICATORS Philippines

	Unit	2006	2007	2008	2009	2010
Population	m	86.97	88.57	90.34	92.20	*94.01
Gross domestic product (GDP)	US$bn	117.56	144.13	167.50	161.00	188.70
GDP per capita	US$	1,352	1,625	1,851	1,746	2,007
GDP real growth	%	5.4	6.6	4.2	1.1	7.6
Inflation	%	6.2	2.8	9.3	3.2	3.8
Unemployment	%	8.0	7.3	7.4	7.5	7.3
Industrial output	% change	4.5	6.8	5.0	-0.9	–
Agricultural output	% change	3.8	4.8	3.2	0.0	–
Exports (fob) (goods)	US$m	46,158.0	49,321.0	48,202.0	37,510.0	50,684.0
Imports (fob) (goods)	US$m	53,113.0	57,557.0	60,748.0	46,388.0	61,068.0
Balance of trade	US$m	-6,955.0	-8,236.0	-12,582.0	8,878.0	-10,384.0
Current account	US$m	5,347.0	6,351.0	3,633.0	8,552.0	8,465.0
Total reserves minus gold	US$m	20,025.0	30,211.0	33,193.0	38,783.0	55,363.0
Foreign exchange	US$m	19,891.0	30,071.0	33,047.0	37,504.0	53,991.0
Exchange rate	per US$	51.31	46.15	44.32	47.68	45.11

* estimated figure

export-oriented manufacturing and dearer oil. The deficit in merchandise trade widened by 17 per cent to US$10.4 billion, reflecting the higher growth in imports than in exports. Coupled with the turnaround to net inflows in the capital and financial account in 2010, the overall balance-of-payments surplus rose to 7.6 per cent of GDP. Net portfolio investment amounted to US$4.0 billion, driven by renewed global appetite for emerging markets. Net foreign direct investment remained low by regional standards, at US$1.2 billion in 2010.

Successful issuance of sovereign bonds eased concerns about financing the fiscal deficit. The government sold its first issue of peso-denominated global bonds in September 2010 and followed up with another large issue (equivalent to US$1.25 billion of 25-year bonds priced to yield 6.25 per cent) in January 2011. These issues, sold at a time of relatively low global interest rates, helped to reduce the government's foreign exchange risk and lengthen its debt profile.

The outlook for 2011 and 2012 assumes that the government follows through on its commitments to improve the fiscal position, governance and the business environment and that some of its planned public/private partnership projects start in the forecast period.

On fiscal policy, the government pulled back the deficit in 2010 to 3.7 per cent of GDP from 3.9 per cent in 2009. It trimmed non-interest expenditure in the second half by 0.4 per cent year on year, after 15.8 per cent growth in the first half. It also showed some progress in strengthening the tax target. Fiscal policy will likely be less stimulative to the economy in 2011, given that the authorities aim to reduce the deficit to 3.2 per cent of GDP.

Sustained business optimism points to further growth in private investment. The outlook for business confidence for the second quarter of 2011 rose to the highest level since surveys started in 2001.

Taking into account these factors and the base effect of the strong recovery in 2010, the ADB forecast GDP growth at 5.0 per cent in 2011, quickening to 5.3 per cent in 2012. This projection reflected, besides higher prices for imported oil, rises in utility charges and public transport fares. Higher global food prices will also put upward pressure on inflation. On the basis of a deceleration in global commodity prices, inflation in 2012 is forecast to ease to 4.3 per cent. Growth in merchandise exports is seen pulling back from last year's levels to about 11 per cent in the forecast period. Imports will likely grow slightly faster than that on the back of the projected growth in consumer demand and investment, as well as higher oil and commodity prices. The trade deficit is set to widen, but the services account will remain in surplus, largely because of growth in business process outsourcing. Remittances will remain a significant contributor to current account surpluses, which are forecast at about 4 per cent of GDP during the period.

The government has committed to reduce the budget deficit to 2.0 per cent of GDP by 2013 and the debt to 47 per cent of GDP by 2016. On the revenue side of the budget, the government is to raise the tax-to-GDP ratio from 12.8 per cent in 2010 to 16–18 per cent over a number of years. Risks to the growth and inflation forecasts are global economic growth that is weaker than expected, interruptions to remittance inflows and higher than forecast increases in global oil and food prices. There is a risk that the disruption to supply chains after the Japanese earthquake could dent manufacturing production and exports in 2011. Electronics and semiconductors, major export industries in the Philippines, depend heavily on components from Japan. Lack of progress in the public/private partnership programme or in efforts to improve governance and public finances would likely undermine business confidence. A severe La Niña could delay agriculture's recovery.

Risk assessment

Economy	Good
Politics	Good
Regional stability	Good

COUNTRY PROFILE

Historical profile

1898 During the Spanish-American War, the independence of the Philippines was declared by General Emilio Aguinaldo, leader of the revolutionary movement, with the support of the US. Spain ceded the islands to the US under the Treaty of Paris.

1935 A constitution was ratified by plebiscite, giving the Philippines internal self-government and providing independence after 10 years.

1946 The islands were occupied by Japanese forces from 1942–45. US rule was restored at the end of the Second World War, and the Philippines became an independent republic with Manuel Roxas as its first president.

1965 After a succession of presidents, under the control of US economic interests and the Filipino land-owning class, Ferdinand Marcos won elections.

1972 Martial law was imposed by the President, in order to deal with subversive activity and to introduce drastic reforms.

1973 A new constitution was ratified by President Marcos. Transitional provisions gave the president the combined authority of the presidency and the premiership without any fixed term of office.

1981 Martial law was lifted.

1986 Ferdinand Marcos claimed to have defeated his challenger, Corazon Aquino, in the general election. However, it was so blatantly rigged that the result triggered a popular revolt. Marcos and associates fled the country and Aquino took over.

1987 A plebiscite ratified a new constitution with Aquino as president. Congressional elections confirmed her popular support.

1992 In the presidential and legislative elections, Aquino's chosen successor, Fidel Ramos, succeeded her as president, although his supporters failed to achieve an overall majority in the legislature.

1994 President Ramos' Lakas ng Edsa (Lakas-NUCD) (National Union of Christian Democrats) party formed an electoral pact with the Laban ng Makabayang Masang Pilipino (LaMMP) (Struggle of the Nationalist Filipino Masses).

1995 Candidates representing the Lakas-NUCD/LDP alliance secured the bulk of the seats contested in the mid-term elections.

1996 A peace agreement was reached with Mindanao's Muslim rebels, the Moro Islamic Liberation Front (MILF).

1998 Joseph Estrada easily won the presidential elections. Estrada replaced Ramos, who during his six years in power had built up a reputation for ensuring the political stability and economic growth urgently required after the Marcos era.

2000 President Estrada was impeached by the lower house of the legislature after allegations that he had accepted bribes and diverted taxes for personal use.

2001 Estrada was stripped of his powers by a Supreme Court ruling, paving the way for the inauguration of Vice President Gloria Macapagal Arroyo as president. Supporters of President Arroyo won control of the Senate in the legislative elections. The government's offer of enhanced autonomy to Mindanao, instead of independence, was turned down by the MILF.

2002 Filipino and US military forces launched joint exercises near to the stronghold of Abu Sayyaf, the high-profile Islamist rebel group, believed to have links with the al Qaeda terrorist group. Tensions in southern Philippines increased following a declaration made by exiled Filipino Muslim leader Nur Misuari for an independent Muslim state. Indonesia,

Malaysia and the Philippines signed a pact to counter terrorism and to stop a network that is believed to be bent on turning all three into a single Islamic state.
2004 Gloria Arroyo was elected president, defeating her nearest rival, actor Fernando Poe. A typhoon and powerful storms caused major floods and mudslides that killed hundreds of people.
2005 The two-year cease-fire with the MILF was broken when heavy fighting broke out between government troops and the MILF.
2006 The death penalty was abolished
2007 The body of Khaddafy Janjalani, the leader of Abu Sayyaf was found; the army stated he had been killed during fighting in 2006. Former president, Joseph Estada, was found guilty of corruption and embezzlement of an estimated US$84 million; he was sentenced to life imprisonment. An agreement was reached between the government and the MILF, the main separatist group, on a boundary for a Muslim homeland in the southern region of Mindanao.
2008 In a negotiated settlement the government and the MILF agreed to an enlarged autonomous region in the south of the country for the Muslim rebel separatist group. Critics said the deal effectively established an independent state within the Philippines, contrary to the constitution. The Supreme Court blocked the territorial aspect of the agreement, forcing the government to break the deal. Fierce fighting broke out as militants, led by the MILF, attacked towns and villages in the previously designated border area. The government estimated 100,000 people had been killed and hundreds of thousands had been displaced since the insurrection began in the 1970s.
2009 The Philippines was removed from an OECD blacklist of secretive tax havens and placed on a grey list of countries that have agreed to adhere to tax disclosure standards, although without legislation enacting it. Former president Corazon Aquino died.
2010 The ruling Lakas-Kampi-CMD coalition won 38.1 per cent (105 seats out of 228) in parliamentary elections held in May. Nine candidates took part in presidential elections held at the same time. Benigno Aquino III (LP) was elected with 42.1 per cent of the vote, while his closest rival, former president Joseph Estrada (Pwersa ng Masang Pilipino) (Force of the Filipino Masses) (FFM) won 26.3 per cent. President Aquino was sworn into office on 29 June. GDP growth of 7.9 per cent for the first two quarters was the strongest growth recorded since the late 1980s. A super-typhoon (called a *Megi* with the highest rating of force four) hit the Philippines in October, bringing 200km-an-hour winds and heavy rainfall; it was the worst typhoon for over a decade.
2011 The Philippines suffered a series of floods and mudslides through January, caused by severe rains, which killed 51 and affected 1.6 million people in total. Four years after losing the vote and a long legal battle to achieve a recount, Aquilino Pimentel was finally declared a winner and took his seat as a senator in August. Extensive and severe flooding in northern Philippines caused widespread destruction in the central Luson region north of Manila, following typhoons on 27 September and 1 October. Hundreds of thousands of people had to be evacuated, with an initial death toll of 60 people and 30 missing. On 18 November, former president, Gloria Arroyo, was arrested for electoral fraud during the 2007 presidential elections. Devastating flash floods and landslides killed over 650 people, with another 900 missing, on the southern island of Mindanao following tropical storm Washi.

Political structure

Constitution

Between January 1987 and February 1988, the Philippines adopted a new constitution, elected a newly created two-tier congress, and voted in provincial governors, and town and city councils around the country. The written constitution provides for a presidential system of government with separation of powers and was ratified by national referendum in February 1987. The drafting of the constitution was designed to prevent the emergence of another dictator.

Its principal provisions are that sovereignty resides in the people, and all government authority emanates from them; war is renounced as an instrument of national policy; and civilian authority is supreme over military authority. It has wide powers to check the presidency, including presidential impeachment, the right to lift any imposition of martial law, veto of presidential appointments and human rights protection. These steps completed the rebuilding of democratic structures after two decades of martial law and dictatorial rule by Ferdinand Marcos, whose presidency was ended in the near-bloodless revolution of February 1986.

Suffrage is granted to all citizens over 18 years of age who have resided for at least one year previously in the Philippines, and for at least six months in their voting district. Voting is by secret ballot.

Local government is vested in 13 regions, with provincial, city and municipal councils.

Independence date

12 June 1898

Form of state

Republic

The executive

Executive power is vested in the directly elected president and an appointed cabinet.

The constitution allows the president a single six-year term and prevents any vice president from serving for more than two successive terms.

The president is head of state, chief executive of the republic and commander-in-chief of the armed forces. The vice president is elected on a separate ticket and may represent a different political party.

National legislature

The bicameral legislative congress consists of the Kapulungán ng mgá Kinatawán (House of Representatives, commonly referred to as the Congress) and the Senado (Senate). Congress has no more than 250 representatives directly elected for three-year terms, of which 212 are district representatives of geographical areas with populations of around 250,000 and the remainder in number are sector representatives elected through party lists up to 20 per cent of the total number of representatives. The Senate has 24 members, elected nationally (across electoral boundaries) to serve for six years. All senators must be aged over 35 years and have been born in the Philippines. An alternate 50 per cent of the senate are elected every three years.

All financial legislation and powers to check the presidency, including impeachment, the right to lift any imposition of martial law, veto of presidential appointments and human rights protection is exclusively the responsible of Congress, while the senate is exclusively responsible for ratifying treaties.

Legal system

Based on Spanish and Anglo-American law.

There is a formal separation of powers between legislative, executive and judiciary. There are also the following courts: the Supreme Court, the court of appeals (formerly the intermediate apellate court), regional trial courts, metropolitan trial courts, municipal trial courts and municipal circuit trial courts. Other laws have created special courts such as the Sandiganbayan (with an anti-corruption brief), and the Sharia courts (for matters involving Muslims). The Supreme Court comprises a chief justice and 14 associate judges, 10 of whom are required to declare on constitutional matters.

Last elections

10 May 2010 (house of representatives and 50 per cent of senate and presidential)

Results: Parliamentary (House of Representatives): Lakas ng Edsa (Lakas),

Kabalikat ng Mamamayang Pilipino (Kampi) Christian Muslim Democrats Party CMD (coalition of five political parties) won 38.1 per cent (106 seats out of 228), Partido Liberal (Liberal Party) (coalition of three political parties), 20.3 per cent (45), Nacionalista Party (NP) (National Party) (coalition of four political parties) 11.4 per cent (31), seven independent candidates won a total of 2.43 per cent (seven) (Pwersa ng Masang Pilipino (PMP) (Force of the Filipino Masses) (coalition of two political parties and seven independents) 2.8 per cent (six). The remaining seats were won between 16 political parties that each won less than 1 per cent of the vote; the remaining 57 seats were determined by proportional representative votes by party lists. Turnout was 78.95 per cent.
Presidential: Benigno Aquino III (LP) won 42.1 per cent of the vote, Joseph Estrada (PMP) 26.3 per cent, Manuel Villar (NP) 15.4 per cent, and Gilberto Teodoro (Lakas) 11.3 per cent; five other candidates each won less than 4 per cent.

Next elections

2013 (presidential and House of Representatives and half of Senate)

Political parties

Ruling party

Partido Liberal (Liberal Party) (coalition with Kalapian ng mga Kaibigan sa Kaunlaran (KKK) (Friends Of Development – City of Hagonoy) (from 29 Jun 2010)

Main opposition party

Lakas ng Edsa (Lakas), Kabalikat ng Mamamayang Pilipino (Kampi) Christian Muslim Democrats Party CMD (coalition of five political parties)

Population

94.01 million (2010)*

Last census: 1 August 2007: 88,574,614

Population density: 313 inhabitants per square km (2010)

Annual growth rate: 2.0 per cent 1994–2004 (WHO 2006)

Ethnic make-up

Filipinos are of Malayan descent with Chinese and Spanish ancestries. There are around six million tribal Filipinos – 60 ethnological groups – comprising approximately 8 per cent of the total population, mainly around North Luzon, central Luzon and western Mindanao and the Sulu Islands.

Religions

The Philippines is the only country in Asia with a Christian majority. About 85 per cent of the population are baptised Roman Catholics; a sect, the Philippine Independent Church which, since 1902, has not recognised the authority of the Holy See, (4 per cent). There is a strong Muslim presence (5 per cent) especially on Mindanao and a Protestant minority (4 per cent). Buddhism and other beliefs (2 per cent) account for the remainder.

Education

Primary education lasts for four years followed by two years of intermediate and four years of secondary education. Instruction is in both English and Filipino at elementary level, while English is the usual language at secondary level and beyond. However, a curriculum for secondary schools, introduced in 1989, made Filipino (Tagalog) the language of instruction for all subjects except mathematics and the sciences.
Both public and private universities offer higher education. Estimates in 2001 showed that 72 per cent of all students were enrolled in private higher education institutions. Public expenditure on education typically amounted to 3.4 per cent of annual gross national income between 1994–1997.

Literacy rate: 93 per cent adult rate; 95 per cent youth rate (15–24) (Unesco 2005).

Compulsory years: 6 to 12

Enrolment rate: 117 per cent gross primary enrolment of relevant age group (including repeaters); 78 per cent gross secondary enrolment (World Bank).

Pupils per teacher: 35 in primary schools

Health

HIV/Aids

HIV prevalence: 0.1 per cent aged 15–49 in 2003 (World Bank)

Life expectancy: 68 years, 2004 (WHO 2006)

Fertility rate/Maternal mortality rate: 3.1 births per woman, 2004 (WHO 2006); maternal mortality 170 per 100,000 live births (World Bank).

Child (under 5 years) mortality rate (per 1,000): 27 per 1,000 live births; 32 per cent of children aged under five are malnourished (World Bank).

Welfare

The government runs a comprehensive social security scheme, providing a retirement fund, hospital coverage, funeral grants, sickness and disability leave and maternity benefits. Three separate and complementary social security programmes are operated by the state. The first is the basic scheme, providing a pension plan and illness, disability and maternity leave. The second is employee compensation covering disability or work related death and the third is medical care, providing for hospital coverage. Despite government intentions, only a small proportion of the population benefit from these schemes. Income disparities are extreme, with approximately one out of every four residents in Manila a squatter. Two-thirds of the population live below the national poverty line, with the richest 20 per cent typically receiving more than half of the country's income. At least five million families are estimated to be in extreme poverty or severely malnourished.

Main cities

Manila (on Luzon) (capital, estimated population – excluding urban areas – 1.6 million (m) in 2005). Quezon City (2.6m), Caloocan (1.4m), Cebu, on Visayas (776,140), is competing with Manila as the country's business capital; Davao, on Mindanao (804,074); Tagig (605,875), Las Piñas (584,813), Pasig (563,498), Parañaque (535,833), Iloilo, on Panay (395,809).

Languages spoken

English is widely understood and generally used in government and commerce.
There are altogether 11 long-established cultural and racial groups, each with their own language. The major linguistic groups are Tagalog, Ilocano, Cebuano, Hiligaynon, Bicolana, Waray, Pampanago and Pangasinense. Other languages include Leytenhon-Samarnon, Maranao, Tausog and highland ethnic languages. Based on a survey by the national census and statistics office, a representative population of 8.6 million Filipinos showed that 2.5 million speak Tagalog as a mother language and 2.1 million speak Cebuano. The rest of the surveyed population speak one of the more than 80 other dialects in the country. Arabic and Chinese dialects are spoken by a minority of the population.

Official language/s

Filipino (based on Tagalog)

Media

Press

Dailies: Others are *The Daily Tribune* (www.tribune.net.ph), *Malaya* (www.malaya.com.ph), *Manila Standard* (online: www.manilastandardtoday.com) *The Manila Times* (www.manilatimes.net) and the *Manila Bulletin* (www.mb.com.ph) with a large circulation, *Philippines Daily Inquirer* (www.inquirer.net). Major regional dailies, in English, include *Sun Star Sebu* (www.sunstar.com.ph/cebu), *Mindanao Times* (www.mindanaotimes.com.ph), Davao Today (www.davaotoday.com) and *Minda News* (www.mindanews.com). In Tagalog, *Abante* (www.abante.com.ph), *Ang Pilipino Star Ngayon* (www.philstar.com) and *Taliba* (www.journal.com.ph).
English language newspapers with Online editions updated regularly include the *Philippine Star* (www.philstar.com) and

Philippine Daily Inquirer and *Philippines News.Net* (www.philippinesnews.net). English language newspapers with Online editions updated regularly include the *Philippine Star* (www.philstar.com) and *Philippine Daily Inquirer* and *Philippines News.Net* (www.philippinesnews.net)

Weeklies: The leading magazines, in English, are *Cosmopolitan Philippines* (www.cosmomagazine.com.ph) for women, *Candy* (www.candymag.com) for teenagers, *FHM Philippines* (www.fhm.com.ph) for men and *Bayani Magazine* (http://bayanimagazine.com) on general interest. In Tagalog, *Pinoy Weekly* (www.pinoyweekly.org).

Business: In English, national and Manila based *Business World* (www.bworldonline.com), *Business Mirror* (www.businessmirror.com.ph). Agricultural and agribusiness publications are issued by the Philippine Council for Agriculture, Forestry and Natural Resources Research and Development.

Periodicals: Periodicals include the women's quarterly *Attitude*.

Broadcasting

Radio: There are 350 local radio stations, of which around 10 per cent are either government-owned, non-commercial religious or educational stations, the remaining 90 per cent are commercial broadcasters. National radio networks include Bombo Radyo (www.bomboradyo.com), FEBC (Far East Broadcasting Company) (www.febc.org), MBC Radio (www.mbcradio.net), Radio Philippines (www.radiophilippines.com). and the state-owned PBS (Philippine Broadcasting Service). In Tagalog, RMN Networks (www.rmn.com.ph).

Television: In English, ABS-CBN (www.abs-cbnnews.com), GMA Network (www.gmanews.tv). Online television services in English and Tagalog, iGMA TV (www.igma.tv) and Filamvision TV (www.filamvision.tv).

There are over 50 originating television stations around the country, five of them in Manila, and about 30 relay stations.

Advertising

Advertising is available in the press, radio, television, cinemas and via direct mail.

News agencies

Philippines News Agency (PNA), 2nd Floor, National Media Center, Visayas Ave, Diliman, Quezon City, Metro Manila (tel: 920-6551–65; internet: www.pna.gov.ph).

Economy

The Philippines has a variety of thriving sectors. Agriculture is an important component of the economy, employing 34 per cent of the workforce, of which some 16 per cent were farmers, forestry workers and fishermen in 2009, accounting for around 15 per cent of GDP. The Philippines' other important primary industry, mining, is becoming a leading source of export revenue. There are reserves of gold, copper, chromite and nickel ore, as well as oil, natural gas and coal; but the largest components of the Philippines' mining sector are stone quarrying and salt farms (around 40 per cent and 20 per cent of total respectively). There is a successful high-tech industry of manufactured electronic components and automotive parts and well as service industries including call centre facilities – the Philippines is second after India in Asia.

GDP growth in 2007 was a high of 6.6 per cent, which fell during the global economic crisis to 4.2 per cent in 2008 and further still to 1.1 per cent in 2009 as world trade was severely weakened. However, in 2010 as the world economy picked up GDP growth reached 7.6 per cent. Inflation, which had been 2.8 per cent in 2007 rose sharply to 9.3 per cent in 2008, before falling back to 3.2 per cent in 2009 and only inching up to 3.8 per cent in 2010.

Unemployment remains a long-term problem although the percentage fell from 11.4 per cent in 2005 to 8.0 per cent in 2006, which continued within 1.0 per cent 2007–10. There was an estimated increase in underemployment from over 18 per cent to over 19 per cent in 2009.

Around eight million Filipinos work overseas – remittances in 2009 were US$19.76 billion (11.7 per cent of GDP), and are estimated to have grown to US$21.3 billion in 2010. Against the benefits of this source of revenue must be offset the structural consequences of the continuing loss of professional, skilled and unskilled workers to the economy. The growth rate in remittances in 2009 was 5.61 per cent, of which sea-based remittances rose by 12.06 per cent – Philippine seamen are considered skilled operatives, with years of crewing experience. The global recession had an impact on the number of migrant workers overseas as factories closed or reduced their workforces and foreign workers were the first to be laid off; thousands of Philippine migrant workers have been forced to return home.

In 2011, the UN Human Development Index (HDI) ranked the Philippines 112 (out of 187) for national development in health, education and income. In 2010, 47.4 per cent of the population experienced deprivation in at least one indicator for poverty, while 22.6 per cent lived on the equivalent of US$1.25 per day.

External trade

The Philippines is a member of the Association of Southeast Asian Nations (Asean) Free Trade Area (Afta) and maintains a list of goods that have preferential import duties between members and a programme of tariff reductions due to be introduced in the next few years.

The country has some of the world's highest levels of mineral reserves, including copper, gold and zinc; most deposits have yet to be exploited. There is an extensive heavy industrial sector as well as a manufacturing sector with commodities dominated by electronic goods which represent around 60 per cent of exports. Foreign trade accounts for 95 per cent of GDP and remittances are an important source of foreign revenue.

Imports

Principal imports are petroleum and oil products, transport equipment, capital machinery, plastics, ores and scrap metal, telecommunication equipment, consumer goods and food.

Main sources: US (typically 13 per cent of the total), Japan (12 per cent), Singapore (11 per cent).

Exports

Principal exports are semiconductors, electrical and electronic equipment, vehicles, garments, optical and medical instruments, petroleum products, gold, copper concentrates and chemicals, processed foods, fruits and nuts, garments and textiles.

Main destinations: US (typically 17 per cent of total), Japan (16 per cent), Chine (12 per cent).

Agriculture

Farming

Agriculture, once the main contributor to GDP, has lost its position to the services sector. It accounts for around 14 per cent of GDP and employs about 41 per cent of the labour force.

Some 35 per cent of the total land area is used to cultivate food crops, mostly on smallholdings.

About one-third of the population depends on coconuts, the major export crop. Other commercial crops include sugar cane, hemp, bananas, coffee, tobacco, peanuts and various fruits. Rice and maize production is sufficient to meet domestic demand and other crops include sweet potatoes, cassava, plantains, pineapples, mangoes and cocoa.

The Asian Development Bank has highlighted the need for further reforms to stimulate rural development, to improve irrigation systems, which cover only 42 per cent of irrigatable areas, and to improve the yield and production of paddy rice.

Livestock reared for local consumption include cattle, goats, pigs and poultry.

A record rice harvest of 7.57 million tonnes was recorded in the first half of 2011, a 14.4 per cent year-on-year increase over 2010. The wheat harvest was also up by 37 per cent year-on-year at 3.3 million tonnes. The Department of Agriculture put the increase down to irrigated farmland and sufficient rainwater for all farming.

Fishing

The fishing industry is a big export earner for the Philippines. During the mid-1990s, the annual net trade surplus in fish products amounted to almost US$100 million. In recent years, thousands of hectares, estimated at 40 per cent of former sugar lands, have been converted into shrimp aquaculture ponds. The southern Philippines have traditionally been bountiful for tuna fishermen, but the tuna catch decreased during the 1990s. There is massive overcapacity at Philippine canneries and fishing companies blame years of unrestrained plunder, rising imports and the destruction of the habitat for the slump in the annual catch.

Since the government initiated a reef development plan to create artificial fish spawning grounds, production of fish has increased dramatically, and the Philippines now boasts the largest area of developed estuarine fishponds in south-east Asia.

Following the annual meeting of the Commission for the Conservation of Southern Bluefin Tuna (CCSBT), held on Cheju Island, South Korea, all members agreed to a 20 per cut in the roughly 17,000 tonnes in 2009 bluefin tuna catches from 2010. Scientists had warned that without a cut fish stocks could crash as numbers had become dangerously low.

Forestry

Woodland and forests cover 51 per cent of the land area and contain an estimated 1.45 billion cubic metres of hardwood. Exports of logs were phased out to assist the local timber processing industries. The reafforestation programme is markedly behind schedule, but is being accelerated.

Industry and manufacturing

The industrial sector accounts for around a third of GDP and employs 16 per cent of the workforce.

Food and beverage processing is the main manufacturing activity, including sugar, meat, fruit and vegetables, fish and shrimp processing, soft drinks and alcoholic beverages. Electronics (semiconductors, circuit boards etc) has been the fastest growing sector of the economy. Production of computers and computer parts is principally carried out by Japanese, US, South Korean and Taiwanese companies. Other major industries include petroleum and coal products, chemicals and chemical products. Main light industrial products, which are often produced from imported materials or components, are cotton and textiles, vehicles, chemicals, machine tools and electrical and consumer goods such as refrigerators, radios, TVs, freezers, air-conditioning equipment, sewing machines and watches.

Tourism

Tourism is under-developed, despite recognition of its economic potential and the attractiveness of the Philppines as a destination. Although visitor numbers are rising, at around two million visitors a year, the Philippines compares badly with its regional rivals. The Philippines lacks adequate tourist infrastructure and accommodation away from the resort areas. There are few international airports outside Manila to allow growth in tourism from North America and Europe and terrorism fears are a deterrent. The US remains the largest market with around 20 per cent of all visitors. The government is seeking to promote the Philippines as a tourist destination, although not with the vigour of even its smallestr rivals.

Environment

Tree felling in the 1980s caused erosion and soil degradation, and in 1989 deforestation was prohibited by law.

New mining regulations introduced after copper leakages into river systems in the mid-1990s, stipulate that companies must allocate 10 per cent of initial costs for environmental improvements, and set aside a further 3–5 per cent of mining and milling costs for an environmental protection programme, to be audited annually.

Fishing methods using dynamite and cyanide to stun tropical fish in the coral reefs have poisoned the reef and killed other sea creatures living there.

Philippines, Indonesia, Australia, Papua New Guinea and Solomon Islands are the countries with the most coral reef fish species.

Mining

The mining sector accounts for 2 per cent of GDP and a similar proportion of the workforce.

The Philippines is the second largest gold producer in Asia (after Indonesia) and one of the top 20 producers in the world. It also produces large quantities of silver. There are copper reserves estimated at 3.6 billion tonnes.

Nickel (fourth-largest reserves in the world after Cuba, New Caledonia and Indonesia), chromium, manganese, zinc, mercury, sand, gravel and rock asphalt are also mined. Other metal and mineral resources include iron ore (reserves, mainly laterite, 1.3 billion tonnes), molybdenum, lead, platinum, palladium, cadmium, cobalt, uranium, phosphate, guano, sulphur, pyrites, limestone, shale, gypsum, clay, kaolin, feldspar and silica sand. Large mineral resources, scattered throughout the archipelago, remain unmeasured and untouched.

Hydrocarbons

Proven oil reserves were 139 billion barrels and production was 23,000 barrels per day (bpd) in 2007. The Philippines is still heavily reliant on imports of crude oil and petroleum products, although the high cost of oil has made investment in exploration appear reasonable and a number of major oil companies had started either exploring or drilling for oil in 2008. The offshore, Galoc oilfield began production in 2008 and holds an estimated 23.5 million barrels oil and the Calauit field, with an exstimated 40 million barrels oil is expected to go into production in 2009.

The Philippines, along with China, Taiwan, Brunei, Malaysia and Vietnam, claims the potentially oil-rich Spratly Islands.

Proven natural gas reserves were 98.6 billion cubic metres (cum) in 2008. Natural gas is being used to replace oil for electricity generation. The US$4.5 billion development of the Malampaya offshore field, containing up to 73.2 billion cum of gas, is one of the country's largest investments ever seen. The field is being developed by an international consortium, including operator Shell Philippines Exploration (SPEX) (45 per cent), Texaco (45 per cent) and the Philippine National Oil Company (PNOC) (10 per cent).

The Philippines has around 264 million tonnes of recoverable coal reserves and produces around two million tonnes per year (tpy), which satisfies around 25 per cent of annual domestic consumption. The remaining 75 per cent is imported, primarily from Indonesia, China and Australia. The sector has been affected by the increasing use of natural gas.

Energy

Total installed generating capacity is 15.5 gigawatts (GW), of which 68 per cent is thermal (gas, oil, coal and solid fuel), 15 per cent hydroelectric and 17 per cent other, mostly geothermal. The country is spearheading the development of environmentally friendly electricity generation. The Philippines has the potential for self-sufficiency in electricity generation thanks to its vast geothermal energy reserves. The first merchant power plant of 49.37MW became operational in 2007 and there are plans for two more such power plants to come online by 2011.

The government has proposed plans for a further 70 hydropower plants with a potential capacity of 2.6GW.

The government also plans to complete the restructuring process that involves privatisation of the energy market and full electrification of the archipelago.

Financial markets

Stock exchange

Pamilihang Sapi ng Pilipinas (Philippines Stock Exchange) (PSE)

Banking and insurance

The government made its first step to liberalise the banking sector in 2000 when it introduced a general banking law, allowing foreign banks to gradually take over domestic banks. However, the government continues to intervene in the sector, bailing out banks that experience difficulties.

Philippines was removed from the OECD Financial Action Task Force (FATF) list of non-co-operative countries on money laundering in 2005.

Central bank

Bangko Sentral ng Pilipinas (Central Bank of the Philippines).

Main financial centre

Manila, Makati

Offshore facilities

Time

GMT plus eight hours

Geography

The Philippines is an archipelago of 7,107 islands, some large and some only islets, stretching more than 1,700km north to south. Fewer than 5,000 of the islands have names, and less than 2,000 are inhabited. The nearest neighbours are Indonesia and parts of Malaysia to the south and Taiwan to the north. To the west, across the South China Sea, are Vietnam and peninsular Malaysia. The Pacific Ocean is to the east. The Philippines is situated in the centre of the Asia Pacific region – Japan, South Korea, Hong Kong, Thailand, Malaysia, Singapore and Indonesia can all be reached within two to four hours flying time.

Nearly 95 per cent of the population live on the 11 largest islands. These are mostly mountainous, except for coastal areas and the central plain on Luzon, the largest island (104,683 square km). The second largest island is Mindanao (94,596 square km) in the south, followed by Palawan (14,896 square km), Panay (12,327 square km) and Mindoro (10,245 square km).

There are some 40 active volcanoes (including Balusan and Mayon, both of which erupted in 2006) scattered across the country, and 21 less active ones.

Hemisphere

Northern

Climate

The climate is tropical, with an average temperature of 27 degrees Celsius.

Tropical storms and typhoons are common between July–October and they can hit any part of the country. The Philippines is vulnerable to the *El Niño* phenomenon, which has severely affected agricultural output. The climate is drier and more comfortable between October–February, and can be very pleasant at the higher elevations.

Dress codes

National dress, often worn by men in the office or at any formal occasion, is the *barong* or embroidered native shirt worn outside the trousers. Reflecting US influence, business suits are almost as prevalent. National dress for women, a scoop-necked dress with ballooning short sleeves, is worn at formal social occasions, not for work. Leisure wear tends to be 'smart casual'.

Entry requirements

Passports

Required by all, valid for six months beyond date of departure.

Visa

Visas are not required by nationals of most countries, including business travellers, for visits of up to 21 days, with valid passports and proof of return/onward passage. For details see www.gov.ph/faqs/visa.asp.

Currency advice/regulations

Import and export of local currency up to P10,000 is allowed; amounts exceeding this figure require authorisation from the Central Bank of the Philippines. There are no restrictions on the import and export of foreign currency, subject to declaration of amounts over P10,000.

Travellers cheques and major foreign currencies may be cashed in large commercial banks and by central bank dealers in Manila, and they are also accepted in most hotels, restaurants and shops. Always use authorised money changers or banks. Outside the capital, it is advisable to carry a sufficient amount of local currency when travelling to provinces, as there is a shortage of exchange facilities.

Customs

Personal effects are allowed duty-free. Visitors may import motorcycles and boats duty-free for stays of up to one month; longer stays require a bond guaranteeing re-export.

Health (for visitors)

Mandatory precautions

Vaccination certificate required for yellow fever if travelling from an infected area.

Advisable precautions

Vaccinations for diphtheria, tuberculosis, hepatitis A and B, Japanese B encephalitis, polio, tetanus and typhoid are advisable. Anti-malaria precautions should be taken if travelling outside urban areas.

There is a rabies risk. Tap water is generally clean and safe to drink in the towns.

Hotels

A service charge of 13 per cent and a government tax of 10 per cent are usually added to hotel bills, and gratuities are not necessary, although it is customary to leave small change.

Credit cards

International credit cards are widely accepted in major establishments throughout big cities.

Public holidays (national)

Fixed dates

1 Jan (New Year), 9 Apr (Bataan and Corregidor Heroes Day), 1 May (Labour Day), 12 Jun (Independence Day), 1 Nov (All Saints' Day), 30 Nov (Bonifacio Day), 25 Dec (Christmas Day), 30 Dec (Rizal Day), 31 Dec (New Year's Eve).

Variable dates

Easter, National Heroes Day (last Sun in Aug), Eid al Fitr.

Easter is a major holiday in the Philippines and travel may be disrupted.

Working hours

Working hours vary. Some banks and offices open for a half day on Saturday and, in the Manila area, many shops open for a half day on Sunday.

Banking

Mon–Fri: 0900–1600. Automated banking systems exist (24 hours).

Business

Mon–Fri: 0800–1200/1300, 1300/1400–1700; Sat: 0830–1200.

Government

Mon–Fri: 0730–1130, 1230–1630 or 0800–1200, 1300–1700.

Shops

Mon–Sat: 0930–2030. Most tourist shops open on Sundays.

Telecommunications

Mobile/cell phones

Electricity supply

220 or 110V AC, 60 cycles with flat and round two-pin plug fittings.

Weights and measures

Metric system, with some local units still in use.

Social customs/useful tips

It is customary to shake hands on meeting and taking leave. If people have an academic or professional title (eg doctor, director) they should be addressed by their title. Senior citizens should be treated with particular respect. Shoes should be removed before entering someone's home. Central to Filipino values is the concept of maintaining 'face'. Anything which appears to constitute a slight to a Filipino can have serious consequences. Criticism, however mild, of anyone present is to be avoided. New ideas need to be carefully introduced. A strong personal element to relationships, including those of business and state, makes refusal of frequently proffered hospitality offensive. It can be common to receive a positive answer to a question when the appropriate answer is negative. Reciprocity of hospitality is also required. Despite the appearance of extensive westernisation, conservative values usually apply.

Religious matters are taken seriously, but so is superstition to the extent that no building displays a thirteenth floor. Belief in witches happily co-exists alongside more mainstream religions.

Punctuality is aimed at, but not always achieved. Tips of about 10 per cent for most services are considered standard. Gift-giving, on the smallest pretext, is widely practised, although the gift itself may be inexpensive.

Old-style chivalry towards women reigns supreme, disguising the extent to which women's dominance at home translates into effective control of the Filipino male. Male visitors will be offered companions as a matter of course, but should not extend this apparent availability into loose behaviour with women outside the bounds of the sex industry.

The most important tradition is that of *utang na loob*, or a lifelong debt of gratitude. This is not just a matter of mutual back-scratching. It is a deeply felt belief that even small favours can never be fully repaid, so that complex networks of loyalties develop, providing a hidden structure to relationships.

Another important tradition is that of *pakikisama*, or co-operating with the team view. Group identification is all-important, reaching back to one's class at school, or to one's village of origin. Approval of the group is often needed before any serious decision is reached. In this context, the supreme importance of family links can be seen, and the paramount significance of family honour understood.

Security

Widespread poverty makes robbery the most common crime. Changing money at a black-market operator will probably deliver you into the hands of pickpockets outside. Foreigners are rarely targetted for more violent crimes.

Getting there

Air

National airline: Philippine Airlines (PAL)
International airport/s: Ninoy Aquino International Airport (MNL) is 12km south of Manila; facilities include bank, duty-free shop, restaraunts, post office and car hire. Mactan-Cebu International Airport (CEB), on Mactan Island, is 9km from Cebu City and 45km from Manila.
Airport tax: P550.

Surface

Water: It may be possible to find a freight ship which will carry passengers from nearby Malaysian or Indonesian ports, but schedules are unreliable. Cruise ships stop in Manila Bay. There is danger from smugglers and pirates operating between Borneo and Mindanao.
Main port/s: Manila, Batangas City, Cebu, Davao, Iloilo, Zamboanga, Cagayan de Oro, Subic Bay Freeport.

Getting about

National transport

Air: Philippine Airlines (PAL), Cebu Pacific Air, and Air Philippines are the main operators of relatively inexpensive domestic flights.
Road: The network of highways is mainly confined to coastal areas. The Maharlika Highway runs from Luzon to Mindanao, with connecting ferry services.
Buses: There are bus services between Manila and the rest of the country. Air-conditioned buses are available. There is no central bus terminal in Manila, each company having its own terminal.
Rail: The only railway line is on Luzon island, running south from Manila to Legazpi. A line from Manila to San Fernando and San Jose in the north is not open. Both lines are single track and narrow gauge. Train services are slow; some have restaurant cars and air-conditioning.
Water: Inter-island services are operated by several companies, some with air-conditioned cabins and dining rooms. There are numerous public and private ports, many serving coastal shipping traffic.

City transport

If travelling by road, allow extra travel time between appointments – there are many traffic jams. Tricycles (motorbikes with sidecars) and trishaws are a cheap alternative for shorter distances around towns.
Taxis: Taxis are plentiful and cheap, but not easy to hail. Because traffic is heavy, drivers will often refuse to go beyond the local district. It may be worthwhile retaining a driver for the day. Taxis are metered, but passengers need to ensure that the drivers switch them on; if they make excuses, they should not be engaged. Tipping taxi drivers is not customary.
Buses, trams & metro: Numerous inexpensive bus services operate in and around main centres, but they can be crowded, and knowledge of the area is recommended before travelling by bus. *Jeepneys* are shared taxis, which ply regular routes and are cheap.
The Metrorail Light Rail Transit (LRT) is an overhead railway which runs from north to south Manila.

Car hire

Self-drive and chauffeur-driven car hire is available. It is advisable to hire a car and driver. Local driving habits make traffic conditions extremely difficult. International driving licences are acceptable. Driving is on the right-hand side of the road.

BUSINESS DIRECTORY

The addresses listed below are a selection only. While World of Information makes every endeavour to check these addresses, we cannot guarantee that changes have not been made, especially to telephone numbers and area codes. We would welcome any corrections.

Telephone area codes

The international dialling code (IDD) for the Philippines is +63, followed by the area code and subscriber's number:

Bacolod	34	Iloilo	33
Cebu	32	Manila	2
Dagupan	75	San Pablo	49
Davao	82		

Useful telephone numbers

Manila

Police:	599-011
Fire:	581-176

Chambers of Commerce

American Chamber of Commerce of the Philippines, Corinthian Plaza, Paseo de Roxas, Legazpi Village, PO Box 2562, Makati, Manila (tel: 818-7911; fax: 811-3081; e-mail: info@amchamphilippines.com).

British Chamber of Commerce of the Philippines, c/o British Embassy, 6752 Ayala Avenue corner Makati Avenue, Makati, Manila (tel: 580-8359; fax: 893-9073; e-mail: administrator@bccphil.com).

Cebu Chamber of Commerce and Industry, CCCI Center, Corner 11th and 13th Avenues, North Reclamation Area, Cebu City (tel: 232-1421; fax: 232-1422; e-mail: ccci@gsilink.com).

Davao City Chamber of Commerce and Industry, DCCII Building, JP Laurel Avenue, Davao City (tel: 221-4148; fax: 226-4433; e-mail: dccii@skynet.net).

European Chamber of Commerce of the Philippines, Axa Life Center, Sen Gil Puyat Avenue corner Tindalo Street, Makati, Manila (tel: 845-1324; fax: 845-1395; e-mail: info@eccp.com).

Philippine Chamber of Commerce and Industry, Salcedo Towers, 169 HV dela Costa Street, Salcedo Village, Makati, Manila (tel: 844-5713; fax: 843-4102; e-mail: pcci@philcham.com).

Banking

Allied Banking Corp, Allied Bank Centre, 6754 Ayala Avenue corner Legaspi Street,

Makati, Manila (tel: 816-331; fax: 816-0921).

Bank of the Philippine Islands, PO Box 1827 MCC, BPI Bldg, Ayala Avenue, corner Paseo de Roxas, Makati City (tel: 818-5541; fax: 815-9434).

Development Bank of the Philippines, DBP Building, Makati Avenue corner Sen Gil Puyat Avenue, Makati, Manila (tel: 818-9511; fax: 818-6699).

Equitable PCI Bank, Equitable PCI Bank Tower 1, Makati Avenue corner HV Dela Costa Street, Makati, Manila (tel: 817-7330; fax: 817-6984).

Land Bank of the Philippines, 319 Sen Gil Puyat Avenue, Makati, Manila (tel/fax: 814-0179).

Metrobank, Metrobank Plaza Building, Sen Gil Puyat Avenue, Makati, Manila (tel: 810-3311; fax: 817-6248; e-mail: metrobank@metrobank.com.ph).

Philippine National Bank, Cacho-Gonzales Bldg, cor Aguirre & Transierra Sts, Legaspi Village, Makati City 1229 (tel: 892-8780; fax: 840-3039).

Rizal Commercial Banking Corporation, RCBC Building, 333 Sen Gil Puyat Avenue, Makati, Manila (tel: 819-3061; fax: 891-0775).

Security Bank Corporation, SBTC Building, 6776 Ayala Avenue, Makati, Manila (tel: 888-7340; fax: 893-2563; e-mail: inquiry@securitybank.com.ph).

Union Bank of the Philippines, SSS (Makati) Building, Ayala Avenue corner Herrera Street, Makati, Manila (tel: 892-0011; fax: 840-0168).

Central bank

Bangko Sentral ng Pilipinas, A Mabini Street, Corner Pablo Ocampo Street, Malate, Manila 1004 (tel: 524-7011; fax: 523-6210; e-mail: bspmail@bsp.gov.ph).

Stock exchange

Pamilihang Sapi ng Pilipinas (Philippines Stock Exchange) (PSE): www.pse.org.ph

Stock exchange 2

Philippine Dealing Exchange (PDEx): www.pdex.com.ph

Travel information

Automobile Association Philippines, PO Box 999, 683 Aurora Boulevard, Quezon, Manila (tel: 723-0808; fax: 726-5878; e-mail: aaphils@greendot.com.ph).

Cebu Pacific Air, Robinsons Equitable Building, Ortigas Centre, Pasig, Manila (tel: 702-0888; fax: 637-9170; e-mail: feedback@cebupacificair.com).

Hotel and Restaurant Association of the Philippines, Regina Building, Legazpi Village, Makati, Manila (tel: 815-4659; fax: 815-4663; e-mail: hrap@mnl.sequelnet).

Manila Ninoy Aquino International Airport, NAIA Complex, Pascay, Manila (tel: 877-1109; fax: 833-1180; e-mail: info@miaa.gov.ph).

Philippine Airlines (PAL), PO Box 954, Philippine Airlines Centre, Legazpi Street, Makati, Manila (tel: 818-0111; fax: 818-3298; e-mail: webmgr@pal.com.ph).

Philippine Travel and Tourism Council, 1102 City and Land Mega Plaza, Ortigas Centre, Pasig, Manila (tel: 687-4812; fax: 931-8307; e-mail: info@philippinetourism.org).

Ministry of tourism

Department of Tourism, Kalaw Street, Rizal Park, Manila (tel:525-2000; fax: 521-7374; e-mail: webmaster@tourism.gov.ph).

National tourist organisation offices

Philippine Tourism Authority, Kalaw Street, Ermita, PO Box 1813, Manila (tel: 524-7141; fax: 521-8113; e-mail: info@philtourism.gov.ph).

Ministries

Office of the President, Malacanang Palace , JP Laurel Street, San Miguel, Manila (tel: 564-1451; fax: 742-1641).

Department of Agrarian Reform, Elliptical Road, Diliman, Quezon City (tel: 928-3979; fax: 929-3088).

Department of Agriculture, Elliptical Road, Diliman, Quezon City (tel: 920-4358; fax: 920-3986).

Department of Budget and Mangement, General Solano Street, San Miguel, Manila (tel: 735-4929; fax: 735-4927).

Department of Defence, Camp Aguinaldo, Quezon City (tel: 911-6193; fax: 911-6213).

Department of Education, Culture and Sports, Meralco Avenue, Pasig, Manila (tel: 634-2925; fax: 636-4876).

Department of Energy, PNCP Complex, Meritt Road, Fort Bonifacio, Makati, Manila (tel: 844-2850; fax: 817-8603).

Department of Environment and Natural Resources, Visayas Avenue, Diliman, Quezon City (tel: 929-6633; fax: 920-4352).

Department of Finance, Vito Cruz corner Mabini Street, Malate, Manila (tel: 523-4255; fax: 521-9495).

Department of Foreign Affairs, 2330 Roxas Boulevard, Pasay, Manila (tel: 831-8955; fax: 832-1597).

Department of Health, Rizal Avenue, Santa Cruz, Manila (tel: 743-8301; fax: 711-6055).

Department of the Interior and Local Government, EDSA corner Reliance Street, Mandaluyong, Manila (tel: 631-8777; fax: 631-8831).

Department of Justice, Padre Faura Street, Ermita, Manila (tel: 521-8344; fax: 521-1614).

Department of Labour and Employment, San Jose Street, Intramuros, Manila (tel: 527-2118; fax: 527-3499).

Department of Public Works and Highways, Bonifacio Drive, Port Area, Manila (tel: 527-4111; fax: 527-5635).

Department of Science and Technology, General Santos Avenue, Bicutan, Taguig, Manila (tel: 837-2939; fax: 837-2937).

Department of Social Welfare and Development, Constitution Hills, Quezon City, Manila (tel: 931-8101; fax: 931-8191).

Department of Tourism, Kalaw Street, Rizal Park, Manila (tel:524-1751; fax: 521-7374).

Department of Trade and Industry, 385 Sen Gil Puyat Avenue, Makati, Manila (tel: 895-3515; fax: 896-1166).

Department of Transportation and Communications, Ortigas Avenue, Pasig, Manila (tel: 726-7106; fax: 632-9985).

National Economic and Development Authority, Amber Avenue, Pasig, Manila (tel: 631-3716; fax: 631-3747).

Other useful addresses

ASEAN Investment Promotion Agency, Board of Investments (BOI), Industry and Investments Building, 385 Sen Gil J Puyat Avenue, Makati, Manila (tel: 890-1332; fax: 895-3512).

ASEAN Secretariat, 70 Jl Sisingamangaraja, Jakarta 12110, Indonesia (tel: 62 (21) 726-2991; fax: 739-8234; e-mail: termsak@asean.or.id).

Asian Development Bank, 6 ADB Avenue, Mandaluyong, Manila (tel: 632-4444; fax: 636-2444; e-mail: information@adb.org).

Board of Investments, Industry and Investments Building, 385 Sen Gil Puyat Avenue, Makati, Manila (tel: 897-6682; fax: 895-3521; e-mail: mis@boi.gov.ph).

British Embassy, L V Locsin Building, 6752 Ayala Avenue corner Makati Avenue, Makati, Manila (tel: 816-7116; fax: 819-7206).

Bureau of Export Trade Promotion, New Solid Building, 357 Sen Gil Puyat Avenue, Makati, Manila (tel: 899-0133; fax: 890-4707; e-mail: betpod@dti.gov.ph).

National Economic Development Authority, NEDA Building, Blessed Joseph Maria Escriva Drive, Pasig, Manila (tel:

631-0945; fax: 633-6011; internet site: http://www.neda.gov.ph).

Petroleum Association of the Philippines, c/o 7/F Basic Petroleum Building, C. Palanca Jr Street, Legaspi Village, Makati, Manila (tel: 817-3329; fax: 817-0191).

Philippine Convention and Visitors Corporation, Legazpi Towers, 300 Roxas Boulevard, Pasay City, Manila (tel: 525-9318; fax: 521-6165; e-mail: pcvcnet@info.com.ph).

Philippine Electronics & Telecommunications Federation, 7/F PS Bank Building, Tindalo Street corner Sen.Gil Puyat Avenue, Makati, Manila (tel/fax: 813-6397).

Philippine Exporters Confederation, Roxas Boulevard corner Sen Gil Puyat Avenue, Pasay City, Manila (tel: 833-2531; fax: 831-2132; e-mail: philxprt@l-next.net; internet : www.philexport.org/launch/index.htm).

Philippines Embassy (US), 1600 Massachusetts Avenue, NW, Washington DC 20036 (tel: (+1-202)-467-9300; fax: (+1-202)-467-9417; e-mail: uswashpe@aol.com).

Philippines Food Processors and Exporters Organisation, Suite 304, JS Contractor Building, 423 Magallanes Street, Intramuros, Manila (tel: 527-5540; fax: 527-5539).

Philippine Information Agency, PIA Building, 1100 Visayas Avenue, Quezon City, Manila (tel: 921-7941; fax: 920-4394; e-mail: odg@pia.gov.ph).

Philippine Iron and Steel Traders Association, 700 Aurora Boulevard, Quezon City, Manila (tel: 722-0536; fax: 721-3599).

Philippine International Trading Corporation, Philippines International Centre, 46 Sen Gil Puyat Avenue, Makati, Manila (tel: 845-4376; fax: 845-4363; e-mail: pitc@info.com.ph).

Philippine Stock Exchange, Exchange Road, Ortigas Centre, Pasig, Manila (tel: 636-0122; fax: 634-5920; e-mail: write@pse.org.ph).

Subic Bay Metropolitan Authority, Building 229, Waterfront Road, Subic Bay Freeport Zone, Olongapo City (tel: 252-4365; fax: 252-3014; e-mail: bgroup@sbma.com).

Textile Producers Association of the Philippines, Room 513, Downtown Center Building, 516 Quintin Paredes Street, Binondo, Manila (tel: 241-1144; fax: 241-1162).

US Embassy, 1201 Roxas Boulevard, Ermita, Manila (tel: 523-1001; fax: 522-4361).

Internet sites

Philippine Consulate General Toronto (gateway site): www.philcongen-toronto.com/links.htm

Philippine National Statistics Offices: http://www.census.gov.ph/

Tanikalang Ginto (small gateway site): www.filipinolinks.com/business/businformation.html

Pitcairn Island

KEY FACTS

Official name: Pitcairn, Henderson, Ducie and Oeno Islands (Pitcairn Island)

Head of State: Queen Elizabeth II, represented by UK High Commissioner to New Zealand and Governor (non-resident) of the Pitcairn Islands George Fergusson (since 2 May 2006)

Head of government: Commissioner of Pitcairn (based in New Zealand), Leslie Jaques

Area: 27 square km (four islands)

Population: 46 (2008) (all on Pitcairn Island)

Capital: Adamstown

Official language: English

Currency: Pound sterling (£) (£=100 pence); New Zealand dollar (NZ$=100 cents)

Exchange rate: £0.64 per US$ (Oct 2011); NZ$1.30 per US$ (Oct 2011)

COUNTRY PROFILE

Historical profile

1767 Pitcairn's island (as it was originally called, after the young seaman on the *Swallow* who first spotted it) was sighted and its position recorded, although the longitude was incorrect. The island was uninhabited.

1790 Pitcairn's inaccessibility made it a perfect hideaway for the survivors of the mutinous crew of the British *HMS Bounty*, led by the Master's Mate, Fletcher Christian, and their Tahitian consorts when they arrived in January. Because the island's longitude had been incorrectly recorded in 1767 (it was in fact some 200 miles from its recorded position), it was 18 years before an American whaler, the *Topaz* next found the island.

1808 The community of descendants of Christian's original 27-strong group of settlers was discovered by a group of American whalers.

1838 Pitcairn Island was constituted a British colony when Captain R Elliot of *HMS Fly* gave the Pitcairners formal authority to elect 'a magistrate or elder to be periodically chosen among themselves and answerable for their proceedings to Her Majesty's government'.

1855 The prison on Norfolk Island was decreed to be shut down, but because of increased whaling activity and other traffic in the South Pacific it was considered by the British government to be prudent to colonise the island on a permanent basis. As the resources of Pitcairn Island were by now deemed to be insufficient for the islanders it was suggested that the Pitcairners might relocate to Norfolk Island, a similarly isolated island.

1856 The British offer of Norfolk Island was accepted and all 193 islanders were moved on the *Morayshire*, with their material possessions, including animals, tools, relics and documents, arriving on 8 June.

1858 16 of the original Pitcairners left Norfolk Island and returned to Pitcairn Island after a land ownership dispute; the second Pitcairn settlement was established. They were followed by other disenchanted groups over the next decade.

1998 Pitcairn became a member of the Secretariat of the Pacific Community.

1999 British economic aid to the island was withdrawn, including subsidised electricity and the cost of bringing in goods.

2000 British police began investigating allegations of child molestation by islanders.

2003 A scientific diving expedition began studying marine life surrounding the islands. Thirteen men went on trial accused of sex crimes. Islanders warned that if the men were jailed their society would collapse through lack of manpower. The UK dismissed Pitcairn Island commissioner, Leon Salt, amid claims that he had obstructed the pursuit of the alleged child rapists. The first child since 1986 was born.

2004 The Supreme Court of Pitcairn Island (sitting in New Zealand) found six men, including the mayor Steve Christian, guilty of sex crimes; four were sentenced to between two and six years in prison and two to community service. Jay Warren, who had been cleared of indecent assault, was elected mayor. Leslie Jacques was appointed Commissioner of Pitcairn by the British government. A UK fund of US$15.3 million was set up to aid development on the island.

2005 The Supreme Court rejected the appeal of the men convicted of sexual assault, and confirmed Britain's sovereignty and jurisdiction over the islands.

2006 The UK Privy Council turned down the last appeal by the defendants convicted of sex offences. The first full-time policeman was appointed.

2007 A new silver enamelled coin was issued, with an engraving of a rat to coincide with the Chinese year of the rat. Although the face value has NZ$2 the coins retail for NZ$79 (US$70). The second child since 1986 was born on the island.

2009 Mike Warren was elected mayor for a three-year term. The 200-year-plus ban on alcohol was lifted, although the ban remains operative for crew members of the two longboats which transfer supplies from passing ships to the island.

2010 Governor George Fergusson visited the island in March to officially proclaim and sign the new Pitcairn Island constitution. Consultation with the islanders had resulted in a document that enshrined basic human rights and education up to the age of 15, as well as reasserting the

constitutional arrangements for the island in respect to the UK.
2011 The British, Royal Society of Protection of Birds (RSPB) launched a programme to eradicate rodents on Henderson Island (a the World Heritage-listed site), in a bid to protect the Henderson petrel. The rodents had been introduced by settlers.

Political structure

Constitution

The Pitcairn Order of 1970 and the Pitcairn Royal Instructions provide for the constitution. It established the office of governor, who is appointed by the British monarch.
The governor has full legislative authority and has the power to create laws, subject to approval by the monarch. The UK government has the power to legislate directly for Pitcairn Island.
A new constitution was declared in March 2010, following consultation with the islanders. It enshrines basic human rights and the provision of education up to the age of 15, as well as reasserting the constitutional arrangements for the island in respect to the UK.

Form of state

British dependent territory

The executive

The UK High Commissioner to New Zealand is also the governor of Pitcairn Island. He is represented on the island by the governor's representative.
The non-resident commissioner of Pitcairn serves as liaison between the governor and the Island Council.

National legislature

The unicameral Island Council has 10 members plus two *ex officio* posts of mayor and Chairmanship of the Council. Four popularly elected council members with the council chairman co-opts a sixth member. The Queen's representative appoints two members, one of which is the Island Secretary and the tenth council member is a commissioner who liaises between the governor and council. The council deals with internal matters and decisions made are implemented by an internal committee. The chairman and councillors are elected on 24 December each year.

Legal system

The Island Court is presided over by the Island Magistrate elected every three years.

Last elections

December 2004

Results: Jay Warren was elected mayor for a three-year term. Mike Warren was elected to the Chairmanship of the Council. The chairman and councillors are elected in December each year.

Political parties

There are no political parties.

Political situation

The community has begun to rebuild both physically and metaphorically since the convictions of six men for sex offences in 2004. With the celebration of Bounty Day on 20 January 2008, which included families re-united and the women verses men tug-of-war (the women won), plus the UK government funded development to give the islanders more contact with the outside world with the construction of a slipway to allow boats to land, for which a scheduled boat services is planned, running from Mangareva in French Polynesia, six time per year, it is intended that the island's unhealthy isolation will be ended.

Population

46 (2008) (all on Pitcairn Island)

Last census: December 1991: 66

Annual growth rate: Declined by 1.32 per cent in 2002.

Ethnic make-up

The inhabitants are mostly descendants of mutineers from the *Bounty*, and Tahitian women, who settled in Pitcairn in 1790.

Religions

Christian (Seventh-day Adventist).

Education

Island children go to school in New Zealand when they are 16 and few return.

Languages spoken

Pitkern (Pitcairn dialect – a mixture of English and Polynesian) uses many eighteenth century expressions.

Official language/s

English

Media

Press

The Pitcairn Islands Study Centre (PISC) publishes *Pitcairn Log* and the Online *Pitcairn News Page* (http://library.puc.edu/pitcairn/index.shtml), covering key news stories. The Pitcairn Islands Study Group (PISG) publishes a *UK Log* newsletter. With an English edition, the German *Mare* magazine publishes regular columns including items about Pitcairn.

Periodicals: The *Pitcairn Miscellany* (www.miscellany.pn), started in 1959, publishes monthly, with a circulation of over 3,000 sent to subscribers worldwide. The *Pitcairn Postcard Magazine* is an occasional publication illustrating Pitcairn Island postcards, for collectors and people interested in Pitcairn.

Economy

The major sources of public revenue are the sale of postage stamps, which were first introduced in 1940, to collectors, however following the global economic crisis there was a downturn in the market, which led to financial reserves being exhausted. Other possible sources of revenue include the sale of handicrafts to passing ships and the lease of the internet suffix '.pn'. A limited amount of honey is exported and, while Pitcairn's isolation means that the honey produced is pure and disease free its distance from most markets limit its potential. The islanders have set up the Pitcairn Island Producer's Co-operative (PIPCO) to promote honey production.
Except for minor licences, there is no formal taxation – every person between the ages of 15–65 is required to perform public work each month, in lieu of taxation. Allowances and wages are paid to members of the community who participate in local government activities and who perform communal services. Local expenditure is estimated and controlled by the Island Council. The financial administration for Pitcairn Island is vested in the governor.
There is no price index maintained on the island and there are no statistics relating to external trade, GDP, trade balance etc. There is no retail trading except for a small co-operative store which was established on the island in 1967. Bartering is an important part of the economy. Modest and simple banking facilities are proposed, to allow islanders access to funds through the treasurer's office and made available for purchases in New Zealand.
A US$6 million upgrade of the island's infrastructure began in 2005, with the start of upgrades for roads and slipway, and construction of the new jetty. By improving facilities and offering jobs in tourism, agriculture and fisheries, the British government is hoping that the population can be doubled to a more sustainable level.

External trade

Sales of postage stamps no longer have pre-eminence since a turndown in the market. All export goods are marketed by mail order through the Internet.

Imports

The principal imports are fuel oil, machinery, building materials, textiles, flour, sugar and other foodstuffs.

Exports

The main exports are handicrafts, woodcarvings, basketry and honey. Fruit and vegetables are sold to visiting ships.

Agriculture

Farming

The island has highly fertile volcanic soil and rainfall is adequate. Main crops include a wide variety of fruits and vegetables, including citrus, sugar cane, watermelons, bananas, yams, beans and honey. Taro and coconuts are also grown. There is some goat and poultry rearing.

In 2005 the development of a new, US$14,000, nursery began. The potential for exporting Pitcairn plants will be investigated.

Fishing

Fish is caught for the islanders' own consumption.

Industry and manufacturing

Production is limited to handcrafted miro-wood carvings, basketry, Pitcairn Island flags and postage stamps.

Tourism

There are no beaches on Pitcairn and landing on Pitcairn is tricky. The construction of a new jetty began in February 2005.

The UK government has made US$6.6 million available to improve roads, a slipway and the jetty, in anticipartion of attracting tourists.

There will be no more than 30 visitors at any one time and the emphasis will be on ecotourism. The improvements began in February 2005.

Environment

Deforestation is a problem, caused by historic slash-and-burn agriculture and settlement.

Mining

Manganese, iron, copper, gold, silver, and zinc have been discovered offshore.

Hydrocarbons

There are no known hydrocarbon reserves and all petroleum needs are met by imports.

Energy

Electricity is produced by diesel generators, allowing 10 hours of electricity per day. Two small wind turbines will be built to provide 24-hour electricity.

Time

GMT minus nine hours

Geography

The islands consist of Pitcairn Island and three uninhabited islands, Henderson, Ducie and Oeno. Pitcairn is situated about midway between Peru and New Zealand. The island is volcanic in formation and has a rocky coastline with cliffs. Pawala Valley Ridge, 347 metres, is the highest point.

Hemisphere

Southern

Climate

Subtropical and humid, with temperatures ranging from 13–30 degrees Celsius (C), averaging 18 degrees C in August and 24 degrees C in February. There are south-east trade winds. The rainy season runs from November to March with a possibility of typhoons. Rainfall varies, but can exceed 2,000mm per year.

Entry requirements

Passports

Required by all, valid for six months beyond the intended length of stay.

Visa

Required by all; referred to as a Licence to Land and Reside. This should be applied for, from the governor (Pitcairn Island Administration Office in Auckland), for visits up to six months. The application must include a certificate of good health, proof of return/onward passage, US$300 per week for maintenance and health insurance (including emergency repatriation). See http://www.government.pn/noticapp.htm for the full list of requirements.

Health (for visitors)

Mandatory precautions

Vaccination certificates are required for yellow fever if travelling from an infected area.

Advisable precautions

Vaccination is recommended for diphtheria, tuberculosis, hepatitis A and B, polio, tetanus and typhoid. There is a risk of rabies.

Public holidays (national)

Fixed dates

New Year's Day (1 Jan), Bounty Day (28 Apr), Christmas Day (25 Dec), Family Day (26 Dec).

Variable dates

Good Friday, Easter Monday, Early May Bank Holiday, Queen's Birthday (second Sat in Jun).

Telecommunications

External contacts used to be by SSB, wireless telegraphy, radio telephone and one satellite phone; some islanders are amateur radio enthusiasts. Since 2006 however, every home on the island has a telephone with broadband internet access, and live television broadcasts.

Getting there

Air

Pitcairn Island is not accessible by air. The nearest airstrip is on Mangareva, in French Polynesia, which is served weekly by Air Tahiti. Boats may be chartered to sail to Pitcairn.

Surface

Water: Cruise ships make brief stopovers and yachts may be chartered from Mangareva and Tahiti. Otherwise, the only shipping services are occasional supply and mail ships from New Zealand, which will accept passengers for Pitcairn. As there are no port facilities for large vessels, longboats are used to pick up mail, passengers, etc, and, consequently, contact and therefore landing may be prevented by adverse weather conditions.

Getting about

National transport

Road: There is only one paved road. The Hill of Difficulty from the Botany Bay jetty to Adamstown was formerly a dirt track, which became impassable in bad weather. It was surfaced in 2005. Other routes are still dirt tracks. Walking and all-terrain bikes are the principal means of getting about.

Water: In Bounty Bay, on the north side of the island, there is a slip for launching the islanders' longboats.

BUSINESS DIRECTORY

The addresses listed below are a selection only. While World of Information makes every endeavour to check these addresses, we cannot guarantee that changes have not been made, especially to telephone numbers and area codes. We would welcome any corrections.

Telephone area codes

The international direct dialling (IDD) code for Pitcairn Island is +124 followed by the subscriber's number.

Ministries

Pitcairn Islands Administration, PO Box 105-696, Auckland, New Zealand (tel: (+64-9)-366-0186; fax: (+64-9)-366-0187; e-mail: admin@pitcairn.gov.pn).

Other useful addresses

Pitcairn Islands Philatelic Bureau, PO Box 17184, Karori, Wellington, New Zealand (tel: (+64-4) 476-9507; fax: (+64-4) 476-9506; e-mail: stamps@pitcairn.gov.pn).

Pitcairn Island Producers Co-operative (PIPCO), PO Box 69, Adamstown, Pitcairn Island (Fax: (+872) 7612-24116).

Pitcairn Island Study Center, Pacific Union College, 1 Angwin Avenue, Angwin, CA 94508, USA (tel: (+1-202) 707-965-6625; fax: (+1-202) 707-965-6504; e-mail: hford@puc.edu).

Pitcairn Log, Editor Dr Everett L Parker, 719 Moosehead Lake Road, Greenville, ME 04441 9727, USA (e-mail: eparker@midmaine.com).

Internet sites

Pitcairn Island Study Centre: http://library.puc.edu/pitcairn/index.shtml

Pitcairn Island Web Site: http://www.lareau.org/pitc.html

Pitcairn Islands Office: http://www.pitcairn.pn

Pitcairn Islands Study Group: http://www.pisg.org

Pitcairn Miscellany: http://www.miscellany.pn

Pitcairn News: http://www.pitcairnnews.co.nz

Poland

In October 2011 Prime Minister Donald Tusk achieved the impressive feat of being the first Polish Prime Minister to be re-elected since the end of Soviet rule in 1989. The election results gave Mr Tusk's Platforma Obywatelska (PO) (Civic Platform) party enough seats to continue in a ruling coalition. The centre-right Civic Platform took 39 per cent of the vote, against 32 per cent for the Prawo i Sprawiedliwosc (PiS) (Law and Justice) party. The leader of the PiS, Jaroslaw Kaczynski, had no choice but to admit defeat.

According to Poland's electoral commission the Civic Platform's 39 per cent translated into 206 seats in the 460-member lower chamber. Mr Tusk's coalition ally, the Polskie Stronnictwo Ludowe (PSL) (Polish Peasant Party), won 8.6 per cent of the vote, or 28 seats. PiS won 158 seats; a new liberal pro-secular party, Ruch Palikota (RP) (Palikot's Movement), came third with 10 per cent, giving it 40 seats; the Sojusz Lewicy Demokratyczne (SLD) (Democratic Left Alliance) was the fifth party to make it into parliament, taking 8.2 per cent and 27 seats. The Mniejszosc Niemiecka (MN) (German Minority) had 0.2 per cent of the vote, securing one seat.

Thanks for avoiding recession

Having steered Poland to four years of economic growth against a backdrop of global financial crisis Mr Tusk's victory was to be expected. Quite remarkably, Poland had been the only European Union (EU) member state to avoid recession.

KEY FACTS

Official name: Rzeczpospolita Polska (Republic of Poland)

Head of State: President Bronislaw Komorowski (took office 6 Aug 2010)

Head of government: Prime Minister Donald Tusk (PO) (from 2007: re-elected 9 Oct 2011)

Ruling party: Coalition government led by Platforma Obywatelska (PO) (Civic Platform) (since 2007; re-elected 9 Oct 2011)

Area: 312,683 square km

Population: 38.18 million (2010)*

Capital: Warsaw

Official language: Polish

Currency: Zloty (Zl) = 100 groszy

Exchange rate: Zl3.29 per US$ (Oct 2011)

GDP per capita: US$12,300 (2010)

GDP real growth: 3.80% (2010)

GDP: US$468.50 billion (2010)

Labour force: 17.66 million (2010)

Unemployment: 12.10% (2010)

Inflation: 2.60% (2010)

Balance of trade: -US$11.41 billion (2010)

Annual FDI: US$9.06 billion (2010)

* estimated figure

Mr Tusk renewed his alliance with the agrarian based PSL, which said it was willing to team up with the Civic Platform again once the offer was made. Mr Tusk had campaigned on his economic success and also vowed to pursue a steady rapprochement with Russia, despite rows over missile defence and gas pipelines as well as the conduct of an inquiry into a plane crash that killed Poland's president last year. The leader of the opposition Law and Justice Party, Jaroslaw Kaczynski, is known for his mistrust of the two countries which invaded Poland during World War II – Germany and the USSR. He also attracts support from Polish Eurosceptics.

The economy

According to the International Monetary Fund (IMF) Poland's robust and well-balanced economic growth in 2011 reflects its sound fundamentals and strong policies. In the first three quarters of the year, gross domestic product (GDP) grew by 4.25 per cent, led by fixed investment and exports. Private sector employment grew by 2.25 per cent. Annual inflation in October 2011 was 4.25 per cent and core inflation (which excludes food and energy prices) was 2.75 per cent. The current account deficit widened slightly to about 5 per cent of GDP in the four quarters to mid-2011 and was mostly financed by capital transfers from the EU (2 per cent of GDP) and foreign direct investment (FDI) inflows.

GDP growth, however, is expected to slow and risks are increasing, reflecting a deteriorating external outlook. Financial strains in the rest of Europe have already led to an easing of capital inflows and downward pressure on the exchange rate. Weakening external demand will dampen export growth and reduce demand for investment projects, which in turn should lower import growth. While Poland may be less affected by the worsening external environment than some other countries, given its lower share of exports to GDP and well-capitalised and profitable banking system, the IMF expected GDP growth to slow to 2.5 per cent in 2012, albeit with large uncertainties around this forecast. Given the possibility of escalating financial and sovereign stress in the rest of Europe, risks to Poland were also firmly on the downside.

The IMF also welcomed Poland's fiscal consolidation and the government's ambitious plans for structural reforms. In 2011, the fiscal deficit was projected to fall to 5.5 per cent of GDP. For 2012, the IMF's preliminary assessment was that the additional fiscal measures in the draft budget would help reduce the deficit to 3.25 per cent of GDP. This would represent significant progress towards Poland's medium-term objective of a deficit of one per cent of GDP, which is necessary to put debt firmly on a downward path. Given an expected slowdown in economic growth, Poland's monetary policy needed to respond to signs of easing inflationary pressures. Over the past six months, with inflation above the 2.5 per cent target but without evidence of second-round effects and the economic outlook dimming, the central bank has appropriately kept the interest rate unchanged. The IMF expects inflation to fall gradually, initially reflecting lower food and energy price inflation. In the view of the IMF inflation in 18–24 months time (i e late 2013–14) is more likely to undershoot than overshoot the target.

Poland's banking sector has continued to perform strongly, but – given the large external risks – it remained important to further strengthen the sector's resilience. The IMF welcomed the proposal of the financial supervisor to encourage banks with riskier profiles to retain profits, so as to build further capital buffers. Given Polish banks' large foreign liabilities and the associated risk of liquidity shortages, the authorities' close monitoring of liquidity and the central bank's readiness to provide liquidity support seemed to the IMF to be appropriate.

World Bank endorsement

The World Bank took a similarly encouraging view to the IMF of Poland's economy, noting that Poland had shown remarkable resilience to the global financial crisis. In the decade leading up to the crisis, Poland's increasing integration with Europe had brought about strong economic expansion and rapid convergence to EU income levels. However, as the crisis broke out, this integration made Poland vulnerable to the collapse in regional capital, trade and labour flows. Poland's companies, workers and households have, never-the-less, weathered well the impact of the global financial crisis. In 2009, Poland became a high-income country with per capita gross national income (GNI) of US$12,260.

As noted by the IMF, in 2009, Poland was the only country in the EU to avoid a decline in economic activity. Poland's economy actually grew by 1.7 per cent, while the EU declined by 4.2 per cent and the EU10 region by 3.5 per cent. In the World Bank's view, Poland's economic slowdown was muted for four main reasons: the relatively large domestic economy and limited exposure to the decline in world trade; the flexible exchange rate regime; limited vulnerabilities in Poland's banking system due to slower credit growth than in other countries of Central and Eastern Europe; and the government's appropriate policy responses during the crisis.

In 2010 Poland was one of the fastest growing EU countries; GDP expanded by 3.8 per cent, the fourth highest rate in the

KEY INDICATORS **Poland**

	Unit	2006	2007	2008	2009	2010
Population	m	*38.12	*38.14	*38.10	*38.10	*38.18
Gross domestic product (GDP)	US$bn	341.72	420.28	528.30	430.20	468.50
GDP per capita	US$	8,959	11,157	13,858	11,288	12,300
GDP real growth	%	5.8	6.8	5.1	1.6	3.8
Inflation	%	1.0	2.5	4.2	3.5	2.6
Unemployment	%	13.9	12.7	9.8	11.0	12.1
Natural gas output	bn cum	4.3	4.3	4.1	4.1	4.1
Coal output	mtoe	67.0	57.1	60.5	56.4	55.5
Exports (fob) (goods)	US$m	110,330.0	144,609.0	177,278.0	139,956.0	162,267.0
Imports (fob) (goods)	US$m	126,013.0	160,162.0	201,655.0	144,432.0	173,681.0
Balance of trade	US$m	-15,683.0	-15,553.0	-24,377.0	-4,476.0	-11,414.0
Current account	US$m	-11,084.0	-15,479.0	-26,909.0	-7,207.0	-259,829.0
Total reserves minus gold	US$m	46,371.1	62,966.8	59,305.6	75,923.3	88,821.8
Foreign exchange	US$m	46,107.0	62,720.3	58,931.0	73,393.6	86,317.4
Exchange rate	per US$	3.10	2.76	2.41	3.12	3.02

* estimated figure

EU. While growth in 2009 had been mainly due to the positive contribution from net exports, growth in 2010 was driven by domestic factors. Growing domestic demand was fuelled by rebuilding of stocks and private consumption and supported by the overall resilience of the labour market and reviving bank credit expansion to households.

Private investment remained weak, reflecting low capacity utilisation, uncertainty about economic developments in the euro area and a severe and snowy winter followed by floods and heat waves in the summer. The decline in private investment was largely compensated by a double-digit expansion in public investment, which constituted about 30 per cent of total investment. Public investment was stimulated largely by European Union funds, including preparations for the forthcoming European Football Championships (being held in Poland and the Ukraine) in 2012, in addition to the reconstruction in areas affected by the severe floods in the spring.

Inflation exceeded the upper limit of the Narodowy Bank Polski (NBP) (National Bank of Poland) (central bank)'s tolerance band of 1.5–3.5 per cent by 0.1 percentage points in January and February 2011 for the first time since September 2009. In May 2011, the inflation rate reached 5 per cent. The increase resulted from the rise in international commodity prices and the rise in the VAT rate by one percentage point. The NBP expected inflation to drop below the 3.5 per cent upper threshold towards the middle of 2012.

Risk assessment

Economy	Good
Politics	Good
Regional stability	Good

COUNTRY PROFILE

Historical profile

Poland's geographical position between east and west Europe has put it at the mercy of the great European powers.

1918 An independent republic was declared at the end of the First World War.

1919–21 The Polish-Russian War broke out in February 1919. After the Poles defeated the Russians during the Battle of Warsaw in August 1920, a peace treaty was eventually signed in April 1921.

1939 The Second World War began as Germany, with military assistance from the Soviet Union, invaded Poland. German forces occupied Poland until 1945, when the Soviet Union, now on the side of the Allies, liberated the country.

1945 After the end of the Second World War, Poland came under the Soviet Union's sphere of influence and it annexed Poland's eastern provinces. The Soviet Union established a puppet government in Poland, comprised mostly of communists of the Polskiej Partii Robotniczej (PPR) (Polish Workers' Party) and Polskiej Partii Socjalistycznej (PPS) (Polish Socialist Party). Communist rule did not end until 1989.

1948 The PPR and PPS merged to form the Polska Zjednoczona Partia Robotnicza (PZPR) (Polish United Workers' Party) to cement Poland's one-party political system.

1956 Riots due to food shortages resulted in the reinstatement of Wladyslaw Gomulka as the first secretary of the PZRP. Gomulka had been distrusted as too liberal in 1948. Liberalisation and some economic reform ensued.

1970 Food price strikes brought about the resignation of Gomulka, who was succeeded by Edward Gierek.

1980–82 The rise of the trade union, *Solidarnosc* (Solidarity), under Lech Walesa, followed strikes at the Gdansk, Gdynia and Szczecin shipyards. The right to form independent unions was recognised by the government. General Wojcieck Jaruzelski succeeded Gierek as PZPR leader. Serious unrest continued during the 1980s, including a period of martial law, the imprisonment of *Solidarnosc* leaders and the abolition of independent unions.

1987 Government plans for rapid economic reform necessitating further hardship were rejected in a referendum, but political reform was approved.

1988 A series of politically motivated strikes kept up pressure on the government for change.

1989 As the rule of communism ebbed semi-free elections for the national assembly were held. Seats for the Sejm were allocated one-third to communists, one-third to existing communist coalition partners and one-third were free-to-vote, the majority of which were won by supporters of *Solidarnosc*. Poland's Third Republic was declared on 19 July.

1990 Lech Walesa became Poland's first democratically elected president.

1991 The first completely free parliamentary elections were held, resulting in the election of a new centre-right government under Prime Minister Jan Olszewski. He was succeeded by Waldemar Pawlak, who was unable to form a government.

1992 Hanna Suchocka became prime minister (Poland's fifth prime minister since the end of communist rule in 1989).

1993 Suchocka resigned and elections, under the new 5 per cent threshold rule (parties not reaching this level of the vote are not eligible for parliamentary representation), reduced the number of parties in parliament. Voters opted for a slowdown in the pace of market-led economic reforms by bringing back the former communists – the Sojusz Lewicy Demokratycznej (SLD) (Democratic Left Alliance). A coalition government of the SLD and the Polskie Stronnictwo Ludowe (PSL) (Polish People's Party) was formed. Waldemar Pawlak of the PSL became prime minister.

1995 Aleksander Kwasniewski (SLD) was elected president.

1996 Poland became a member of the Organisation for Economic Co-operation and Development (OECD). A political wing of *Solidarnosc* was founded as the Akcja Wyborcza Solidarnosc (AWS) (Solidarity Electoral Action)

1997 A new constitution strengthened the powers of parliament. The AWS formed a centre-right coalition government with Unia Wolnosci (UW) (Freedom Union) after the election.

1999 Poland joined NATO.

2000 UW withdrew from the coalition government in order to slow pace of reform. Kwasniewski was re-elected president.

2001 After parliamentary elections, Leszek Miller, leader of the centre-left SLD, formed a left-wing coalition government with the Unia Pracy (UP) (Labour Union) and the PSL.

2003 The coalition split when the PSL was ejected from government after it refused to vote in favour of government legalisation. The SLD and UP carried on as a minority government.

2004 Poland joined the EU.

2005 The referendum on the EU constitution was postponed indefinitely. The Prawo i Sprawiedliwosc (PiS) (Law and Justice) party won 28 per cent of the vote. Lech Kaczynski was elected president and a new PiS minority government was formed with eight non-partisan members of parliament providing support; Kazimierz Marcinkiewicz became prime minister.

2006 The PiS party established a new ruling coalition with Samoobrona Rzeczypospolitej Polskiej (SRP) (Self-Defence of the Polish Republic) and Liga Polskich Rodzin (LPR) (League of Polish Families). Kazimierz Marcinkiewicz resigned as prime minister and was replaced by the president's twin brother, Jaroslaw Kaczynski. A new lustration law was introduced designed to purge ex-communist and communist collaborators from current positions of power.

2007 The Bishop of Warsaw resigned as Archbishop just hours after being appointed, following revelations that he had collaborated with the Polish communist

secret police. The coalition government broke down, but a minority government remained in power. In snap parliamentary elections the opposition Platforma Obywatelska (PO) (Civic Platform) won. It immediately began talks to form a coalition and Donald Tusk became prime minister. Poland became a member of the European Union Schengen area whereby all travellers may cross borders without a passport or visa.
2008 Prime Minister Donald Tusk announced that Poland aimed to join the euro-zone by 2011. Former Communist leader General Jaruzelski was put on trial for the imposition of martial law in 1981.
2009 Poland marked the anniversary of the doomed Warsaw uprising in 1944 when an estimated 250,000 civilians, 18,000 Polish fighters, and 17,000 Nazi troops were killed during two months of fighting. The city was virtually destroyed and around 500,000 residents were expelled by the occupying Nazi force.
2010 President Lech Kaczynski was killed in an aeroplane crash in Smolensk (Russia) on 10 April, along with all other passengers. He had been on his was to attend a memorial service for the Polish victims of the Katyn massacre in 1940. Bronislaw Komorowski was appointed acting president on 10 April. In the first round of presidential elections, held on 20 June, 10 candidates were nominated; Acting President, Bronislaw Komorowski (PO) won 41.22 per cent of the vote and the former prime minister, Jaroslaw Kaczynski (PiS) won 36.74 per cent, Grzegorz Napieralski (Sojusz Lewicy Demokratycznej (SLD) (Democratic Left Alliance)) 13.68 per cent. With no candidate winning over 50 per cent of the vote a run-off was held on 4 July. Komorowski won 52.63 per cent of the vote, Kaczynski 47.37 per cent. Bronislaw Komorowski was sworn into office on 6 August. In September, the European Commission reported that Poland had been the largest recipient of EU funds in 2009, receiving 6.5 billion (US$9.1 billion). On 26 November the Russian Duma passed a resolution confirming that Josef Stalin had, according to papers kept in a secret archive, given the direct order for the massacre of 22,000 Polish officers at Katyn in 1940.
2011 An official report released on 29 July, into the death of former president Lech Kaczynski, in the April 2010 plane crash in Russia, concluded that incorrect and confusing Russian instructions were as much to blame for the accident as Polish officials who applied undue pressure on the Polish pilots, even though they had insufficient experience in flying the Tupolev 154 airplane. In parliamentary elections, held on 9 October, all 460 Sejm seats and all 100 Senate seats were in contention and for the first time the Senate was chosen by the first-past-the-post electoral system. The PO was returned to power with 39.18 per cent of the vote (206 seats out of 460) and the opposition Prawo i Sprawiedliwosc (PiS) (Law and Justice) won 32.11 per cent (158). Prime Minister Tusk remained in office.

Political structure

Constitution

The 1952 constitution was amended in 1989 and 1990. Poland is divided into 49 regional *vovoids* (administrations).

Independence date

11 November 1918

Form of state

Parliamentary democratic republic

The executive

The president is head of state, directly elected by universal suffrage for a five-year term. The president has the power to dissolve parliament and nominates the prime minister. Supreme executive power is vested in the Council of Ministers, headed by the prime minister, responsible to the Sejm.

National legislature

The bicameral Zgromadzenie Narodowe (National Assembly) consists of the Sejm (lower house) with 460 members elected by proportional representation in multi-seat constituencies, and the Senat (Senate) with 100 members elected in 40, multi-seats constituencies. Members of both houses serve for four-year terms.

Legal system

The apex of the legal structure is the Supreme Court, whose judges are elected by the State Council for five years. The Council also appoints a prosecutor general. Below the Supreme Court are district and special courts. Family courts deal with cases involving divorce and domestic relations.

Last elections

9 October 2011 (parliamentary); 20 June and 4 July 2010 (presidential: first round and runoff)

Results: Parliamentary (Sejm): Platforma Obywatelska (PO) (Civic Platform) won 39.18 per cent of the vote (206 seats out of 460), Prawo i Sprawiedliwosc (PiS) (Law and Justice) 32.11 per cent (158), Ruch Palikota (RP) (Palikot's Movement) 10.02 per cent (40), Polskie Stronnictwo Ludowe (PSL) (Polish Peasant Party) 8.36 per cent (28), Sojusz Lewicy Demokratyczne (SLD) (Democratic Left Alliance) 8.24 per cent (27), Mniejszosc Niemiecka (MN) (German Minority) 0.2 per cent (one). Senate: PO won 62 seats (out of 100), PiS 32, PSL two, independents four.
Presidential (first round): Bronislaw Komorowski (PO) won 41.22 per cent of the vote, Jaroslaw Kaczynski (PiS) 36.74 per cent, Grzegorz Napieralski (SLD) 13.68 per cent; seven other candidates each won less than 3 per cent of the vote. Turnout was 54.94per cent. Second round: Komorowski won 53.01 per cent of the vote, Kaczynski 46.99 per cent. Turnout was 55.31per cent.

Next elections

October 2011 (parliamentary); June 2014 (presidential)

Political parties

Ruling party

Coalition government led by Platforma Obywatelska (PO) (Civic Platform) (since 2007; re-elected 9 Oct 2011)

Main opposition party

Prawo i Sprawiedliwosc (PiS) (Law and Justice)

Population

38.18 million (2010)*

Last census: May 2002: 38,230,080

Population density: 127 inhabitants per square km. Urban population: 62 per cent (1995–2001).

Annual growth rate: 0.0 per cent 1994–2004 (WHO 2006)

Ethnic make-up

Poland is one of the most ethnically uniform countries in Europe. The non-Polish population, including Ukrainians, Germans and Russians, accounts for only 1.3 per cent of the total population.

Religions

The population is predominantly Roman Catholic. There are small communities of Protestants, Orthodox Christians and Jews.

Education

Public expenditure on education is typically equivalent to 7.5 per cent of annual GNP, including subsidies to private education at the primary, secondary and tertiary levels.
Education is provided free of charge; primary schooling lasts for eight years followed by secondary, academic and technical or vocational qualifications.
Under the former communist state, technical education was biased towards heavy industries and the decline of these industries has left large sections of the mature workforce in need of retraining. Current government aims are to improve education and information technology skills as part of its long-term growth programme.
Students attending Poland's most prestigious universities must pass a tough entrance exam. Since 1990, over 280 private universities have opened, providing an extra 50,000 graduates for the employment market. Typical fees for private universities can vary from US$530 (the average monthly wage), up to

US$1,855 per annum, for high cost subjects like medicine.
Compulsory years: 7 to 14
Enrolment rate: 96 per cent gross primary enrolment,98 per cent gross secondary enrolment, of relevant age groups (including repeaters) (World Bank).
Pupils per teacher: 15 in primary schools.

Health

Primary healthcare is provided by a network of healthcare centres and specialist physicians. Initial reforms during the 1990s started with the decentralisation of healthcare (mostly primary care) and the introduction of new payment mechanisms to doctors. This led to a range of publicly subsidised private providers.
The concept of primary healthcare is now based on family medicine. Clinics are run by family practitioners who provide a wide range of healthcare services, or make referals to contracted specialists. Development according to this model has signalled movement towards the privatisation of state-owned primary healthcare. Private healthcare services are provided to eligible individuals via contracts with sickness funds.
A common form of mobile healthcare delivery is the non-public clinic (*npzoz*), which typically employs two or more doctors. The high investment cost has limited the number of private hospitals to gynaecological and surgical clinics.

HIV/Aids

HIV prevalence: 0.1 per cent aged 15–49 in 2003 (World Bank)
Life expectancy: 75 years, 2004 (WHO 2006)
Fertility rate/Maternal mortality rate: 1.2 births per woman, 2004 (WHO 2006); maternal mortality 8 per 100,000 live births (World Bank).
Child (under 5 years) mortality rate (per 1,000): 6.0 per 1,000 live births (World Bank)
Head of population per physician: 2.47 physicians per 1,000 people, 2003 (WHO 2006)

Welfare

Poland has operated a dual state-run social insurance system and a mandatory private insurance system since 1999. The system, for those under the age of 30, who are obliged to join, consists of a modified social insurance and individual accounts.
Social insurance covers employees, members of co-operatives, self-employed artisans, homeworkers, lawyers and clergy. Special systems exist for independent farmers.
Poland is unique among the former Soviet bloc countries in creating Kasa Rolniczego Ubezpiecznia Spolecznego (KRUS) (Office of Rural Social Insurance), a farmers' social security system, distinct and separate from the workers' system.

Main cities

Warsaw (capital, estimated population 1.7 million in 2005), Lodz (783,022), Krakow (763,826), Wroclaw (642,889), Poznan (581,698), Gdansk (461,818), Szczecin (418,401), Bydgoszcz (376,407), Lublin (363,607)

Languages spoken

There is a small German-speaking community and German is widely understood and spoken. Kashubian, Ukrainian and Belarusian are also spoken. English and French are used in business circles.

Official language/s

Polish

Media

Press

Dailies: In Polish, the leading newspapers are *Rzeczpospolita* (www.rzeczpospolita.pl), *Gazetta Wyborcza* (www.gazetawyborcza.pl), with English online version and *Trybuna Slaska* (www.trybuna.com.pl). Other, mainly tabloids, include *Super Express*, (www.se.com.pl), *Dziennik* (www.dziennik.pl), *Fakt* (http://efakt.pl) and regional newspapers including *Gazeta Krakowie* (www.gk.pl) Krokaw, *Glos Wielkopolski* (www.glos.com) Pozan, *Kurier Szczecinski* (www.kurier.szczecin.pl) Szczecin, *Dziennik Baltycki* (www.dziennikbaltycki.pl) Gdansk, and *Zycie Warszawy* (*Life*) (www.zw.com.pl) Warsaw.
Weeklies: In Polish, the most influential weeklies are *Polityka* (polityka.onet.pl), *Wprost* (*News*) (www.wprost.pl), *Gazeta Polska* (www.gazetapolska.pl) and *Newsweek Polska* (www.newsweek.pl). Others include *Nie* (satirical), *Przyjaciolka* (womens' magazine), *Poradnik Domowy* (home ideas). Sports magazines, TV/radio guides and youth magazines are also widely available.
Business: In Polish, newspapers include *Parkiet* (www.parkiet.com) and *Puls Biznesu* (www.pb.pl). The most influential periodicals are *Gazeta Bankowa* (*Bankers' Weekly*) (www.gazetabankowa.pl), *Zycie Gospodarcze* (www.nzq.pl) (economic weekly), *Rynki Zagraniczne* (www.rynkizagraniczne.pl) (three per week; foreign trade), *Gazeta Prawna* (*Legal Gazette*) and *Handel Zagraniczny* (*Foreign Trade*). In English, *The Warsaw Voice* (www.warsawvoice.pl), *Polish Market* (http://polishmarket.com.pl) and *Warsaw Business Journal* (www.wbj.pl).

Broadcasting

Radio: There are many public and commercial radio stations. The public broadcaster, Polskie Radio, operates six nationally channels including an external service broadcasting in several languages including English (www.polskieradio.pl/zagranica/gb). There are around six commercial radio networks broadcasting locally and nationally in FM and AM.
Television: The national broadcasting corporation is Telewizja Polska Spólka Akcyjna (TVP SA, known as PTV), with three commercial channels, broadcasting general programmes with an additional four speciality channels. International, satellite and pay-for-TV networks are also available.

Advertising

Print advertising is on the increase, due mainly to many new titles plus improved availability of raw materials. A number of privately owned or co-operative advertising and business consultancies have appeared. TV and radio are popular advertising media.

News agencies

Polska Agencja Prasowa (PAP), ul. Bracka 6/8, 00502 Warsaw, (tel: 628-001, 628-0710; internet: www.pap.pl).

Economy

Poland has a long tradition of heavy industry in coal, iron and steel, which now includes shipbuilding, petrochemicals and car-making as well as textiles. Its service industries include information technologies and accounting centres for international companies. It also exports meat, dairy produce, fruit, vegetables and processed foods, including confectioneries.
The Polish economy was the sixth largest in the EU in 2009 and maintained economic growth throughout the global economic crisis and avoided going into recession, although GDP growth fell progressively, from 6.8 per cent in 2007 to 5.1 per cent in 2008, before dropping sharply to 1.6 per cent in 2009 as world trade slowed down. However in 2010, GDP growth picked up, as the world economy grew, and registered 3.8 per cent.
The structure of the economy is dominated by the service sector at over 65 per cent of GDP, with industry providing 30 per cent, of which manufacturing is 18 per cent, and agriculture the remainder. Economic reforms, begun in the 1990s, have resulted in a comprehensive move from the previously communist centrally-planned economy to a market orientated economy, with the sale of small- and medium-sized state entities. The government did, however, keep control of what it considered strategic industries or those unattractive to a potential buyer through privatisation, such as energy and the railways. Investment and restructuring, encouraged by foreign direct investment

(FDI) (a record US$23.6 trillion in 2007, down to US$9 trillion in 2010), has improved the steel and energy sectors, but problems still remain in turning around other sectors.

Poland improved its rating for starting a business in 2010, from 145th in 2009 to 117th, although its overall rating for doing business remained 72 out of 183 and it became more difficult to hire and fire employees and obtain construction permits. Poland has access to US$68 billion in structural adjustment and cohesion funds from the EU (2007–13) for development and integration.

Agriculture employs around 15 per cent of the workforce but as it only provides less than 5 per cent of GDP it is relatively – compared to other EU member states – unproductive, due to the earlier lack of, or restricted, investment opportunities. Nevertheless, Poland is Europe's leading producer of potatoes and the world's leading producer of sugar beets triticale.

External trade

As a member of the European Union, Poland operates within a community-wide free trade area, with tariffs set as a whole. Internationally, the EU has free trade agreements with a number of nations and trading blocs worldwide.

Manufacturing represents around 20 per cent of GDP, of which almost 75 per cent is foreign trade. Imports recently have been predominately capital goods for industrial retooling. Poland's industrial sector produces vehicles, machinery, telecommunications, building supplies and processed food.

Imports

Main imports include machinery and transport equipment (over 35 per cent), petroleum and lubricants, intermediate manufactured goods and raw materials, chemicals, minerals and related materials.

Main sources: Germany (typically 24 per cent of total), Russia (9 per cent), China (7 per cent).

Exports

Principal exports are semiconductors and electronic equipment (over 35 per cent), machinery and transport intermediate manufactured goods, miscellaneous manufactured goods, processed food and live animals.

Main destinations: Germany (typically 25 per cent of total), Italy (7 per cent), France (6 per cent).

Agriculture

Farming

Poland's large agricultural sector remains handicapped by structural problems, surplus labour, small farms and a lack of investment. There are about 2 million small private farms averaging eight hectares in size. Production is concentrated in livestock farming (dairy and pigs), cereals, potatoes, sugar beet and oilseed. Pork and poultry output has increased considerably. The agricultural sector contributes around 3 per cent to GDP and employs around a quarter of the workforce.

The agricultural sector is subject to the reformed Common Agricultural Policy (CAP), whereby subsidies are no longer paid on farm output, which tended to benefit large farms and encourage overproduction, but rather on single farm payments not conditional on production. Full implementation of CAP will be completed by 2013.

Poland is a major exporter of meat, dairy produce, fruit, vegetables and processed foods, including confectioneries.

Fishing

Poland has no immediate access to oceanic fishing grounds, but it has its own deep-sea fleet, which has been granted an EU export licence. It has about 44 fish processing plants regulated by EU requirements.

While annual fish consumption has remained stable – at around 215,000 tonnes – Poland's fishing industry is in decline, with the local catch representing an estimated 41.7 per cent of domestic consumption.

Forestry

Forests account for less than 33 per cent of Poland's land area. Over 90 per cent of forested land is available for wood supply and the most common species are coniferous, mostly Scots pine. Pollution and insect infestation have degraded much of the forestry resources, although the government has attempted to repair the damage by placing most of the forests under protection. Only the Bialowieza primeval forest is excluded from harvesting.

Industry and manufacturing

The industrial and manufacturing sectors form the mainstay of the economy, accounting for around a third of GDP. Heavy export-based industries, such as shipbuilding, metallurgy (particularly steel), chemicals, motor vehicles and cement, dominate. The 1990s saw growth in sectors such as electronics and light industries, while food processing, glass, beverages, textile and forestry industries are also significant. The Polish car market is the sixth largest in Europe behind Germany, Italy, France, UK and Spain. The best investment opportunities are considered to be in food, textiles, timber, paper, mechanical engineering and furniture.

The steel sector was the focus of early restructuring plans in preparation for entry into the EU. Progress has been slow due to opposition from trade unions.

Tourism

Poland is a popular destination, which is recovering from the effects of the general slump in world tourism from 2008–09. The sector, employs around 8 per cent of the workforce. Most visitors are from neighbouring countries, in particular Germany.

The sector is dominated by the formerly state-owned Orbis SA company, a holding company for Orbis Travel, Orbis Transport and Orbis Hotels.

Poland is seen as having the potential for much greater development since accession to the EU. It is thought that Poland could have over US$23 billion in tourism receipts and 1.5 million jobs if the focus on travel and tourism were fully met.

Environment

Cutting pollution was a condition for Poland's entry into the EU. While industry has tackled its pollution domestic consumers burn coal in boilers and fires, and more people are buying cars to add to the growing traffic jams on Poland's roads (motor vehicle population is expanding at 30 per cent a year).

Mining

Rich mineral resources include the largest deposits of copper ore in Europe and substantial deposits of coal, zinc-lead ores, sulphur and salt. Lesser deposits include nickel and precious metals such as silver.

Hydrocarbons

Proven oil reserves were 96 million barrels in 2007, while production was 37,150 barrels per day (bpd). However, as consumption was 523,980bpd imports were necessary to make up the shortfall. Poland relies on crude oil imports, mostly from Russia, its refinery capacity is 497,000bpd and any surplus is exported.

Proven natural gas reserves were 167 billion cubic metres (cum) in 2007, with production meeting around 50 per cent of local needs and the rest supplied from Russia. In October 2010 agreement was reached with Russua's Gazprom for the supply of 10 billion cum of gas a year from 2012–22. There are concerns that this will make Poland over-dependent on Russia.

The state-owned Polskie Górnictwo Naftowe i Gazownictwo (PGNiG), is responsible for all aspects of hydrocarbons including exploration, production, import and storage. It owns around 16,400km of transmission pipelines. It has plans to build a liquefied natural gas (LNG) regasification terminal at Swinoujscie by the end of 2011, with a capacity of 2.5 billion cubic metres of LNG per annum.

Proven coal reserves were 7.5 billion tonnes in 2007; production was 88.3 million tonnes. Poland is the EU's foremost producer of coal, with production greater than the combined amount produced by the four other EU coal-mining countries. Kompania Weglowa is one of the largest coal mining companies in Europe, operating 23 mines. The majority of Poland's coal is the commercially valuable anthracite and exports, mostly to Europe, are a major source of foreign exchange. At 97 per cent of the country's primary energy production and 65 per cent of electricity generation, coal dominates Poland's energy mix.

Energy
Total installed electricity capacity is 33 gigawatts (GW), with peak-demand at around 24GW. Coal-fired power pants are located at mine heads, where the country's entire lignite (brown coal) production is used to generate electricity.
In 2007 the government undertook a programme of consolidation of state-owned companies to produce a national company to oversee strategic energy resources, a fuel and generation group, and other regional entities that provide sales of electricity.
Poland exports over 16 billion kilowatt hours (kWh) to neighbouring countries. In 2010 the government was planning to sell Energa, a state owned power generator, to PGE the largest state controlled utility.

Financial markets
Stock exchange
Gielda Papierów Wartosciowych w Warszawie (Warsaw Stock Exchange) (WSE)
Commodity exchange
Warszawska Gielda Towarown (WGT) (Warsaw Commodity Exchange)

Banking and insurance
Banks are moving into new areas, such as investment banking, retail banking and asset management. Foreign banks have increased their involvement in the sector – over 70 per cent of Polish banking assets are administered by foreign companies.
In the period 2000–05 the banking sector expanded by 14 per cent per annum as foreign competition increased and banking services attracted more customers.
Central bank
Narodowy Bank Polski (NBP) (National Bank of Poland)
Main financial centre
Warsaw

Time
GMT plus one hour (daylight saving, late March to late October, GMT plus two hours)

Geography
Poland is situated to the north of Central Europe, with Germany to the west, the Czech Republic to the south-west, Slovakia to the south and the Russian Federation enclave around Kaliningrad on the Baltic coast to the north. There is a short border with Lithuania to the north-east and Belarus lies beyond the northern part of the eastern border and Ukraine the southern. Poland has a 520km coastline along the Baltic Sea to the north-west. The country's borders are marked by the Odra and Neisse rivers in the west, the River Bug in the east, the Sudetic Mountains in the south-west and the Carpathian range of mountains in the south-east.
The highest point in the country is 2,499 metres at Rysy on the border with Slovakia. The two major rivers are the Odra and the Vistula which rise in the Sudetic and Carpathian mountains respectively, along the southern borders, and flow into the Baltic Sea.
Hemisphere
Northern

Climate
Poland has a continental climate with cold winters and warm summers. The mountainous regions of the south have a long, cold winter and a relatively short summer. Areas around the Baltic are warmer, with an average temperature of minus one degree Celsius (C) in January and 18 degrees C in July. Southern Poland has annual rainfall of more than 1,500mm, while the rest of the country experiences moderate rainfall of 500–650mm per year. The Vistula and Odra rivers are usually frozen for about two months each year.

Dress codes
Dress codes are generally similar to western European. Lightweight clothing is required from June to August, medium to heavyweight for the rest of year, plus a heavy topcoat in winter.

Entry requirements
Visitors are required to possess sufficient funds for stay, Zl100 per day (or foreign equivalent) and Zl300 per day for medical expenses (or valid insurance).
Passports
Required by all, except members of the EU, EEA and Switzerland who may use a valid national ID card. Passports must be valid for at least three months from date of arrival.
Visa
Required by all, except nationals of EU and Schengen area signatory countries, North America, Australasia and Japan. For further exceptions contact the nearest embassy. A Schengen visa application (offered in several languages) can be downloaded from http://europa.eu/abc/travel/ see 'documents you will need'. For details of those who must apply for a visa see www.polandembassy.org and follow link from *consular services* to *visas for Poland*. Contact the nearest embassy consular section for further information and application form.
Those business people who require a visa should have a formal invitation from a local company or organisation giving specific details regarding the purpose and duration of the intended trip. Also required are a company letter from the applicant's employer regarding his/her status, proof of financial means and receipt of payment for full board accommodation, and return/onward passage.
Currency advice/regulations
The import or export of local currency is limited to the equivalent of eur10,000.
The import and export of foreign currency is unlimited, although all amounts must be declared on entry.
Travellers cheques are accepted in larger bank branches only.
Customs
Personal items, including one example of electronic items, are duty-free. There are no duties levied on alcohol and tobacco between EU member states, providing amounts imported are for personal consumption.
Artistic items dated before 1945 should have customs clearance before export.
Prohibited imports
Illegal drugs, poisons and explosives. Plants and animals are restricted. Firearms and ammunition require a permit.

Health (for visitors)
Nationals of the European Economic Area (EEA) countries and Switzerland can access reduced cost and sometimes free medical treatment using a European Health Insurance Card (EHIC) while visiting the EEA. Exceptions include nationals of the 10 countries, which joined the EU in 2004, whose EHIC is not valid in Switzerland. Applications for the EHIC should be made before travelling.
Mandatory precautions
None.
Advisable precautions
Hepatitis A, tetanus and polio immunisations. Rabies is a health risk.

Hotels
Most locally run hotels belong to the Orbis hotel chain and are classified one- to four-star. Internationally run chains include the Intercontinental, Holiday Inn and Novotel. Accommodation can be scarce in all main towns, so it is advisable to book well in advance. In an emergency a large travel agency or airline may be able to provide a hotel room. Bills include a 10 per cent service charge; tipping around 10 per cent is customary.

Credit cards
International credit cards are accepted where displayed signs are shown.

Public holidays (national)
Fixed dates
1 Jan (New Year's Day), 1 May (Labour Day), 3 May (National Day), 15 Aug (Assumption Day), 1 Nov (All Saints' Day), 11 Nov (Independence Day), 25–26 Dec (Christmas).
Variable dates
Easter Monday (Mar/Apr), Corpus Christi (May/Jun).

Working hours
Banking
Mon–Fri: 0800–1800.
Polski Bank Kredytowy, Warsaw Okecie airport Mon–Fri: 0730–1700, Sat: 0730–1130. Banks at Katowice Pyrzowice airport Mon–Fri: 0830–1500.
Business
Mon–Fri: 0800–1600.
Government
Mon–Fri: 0800/0900–1500/1600.
Post Offices, Mon–Fri: 0800–2000.
Shops
Mon–Fri: 1100–1900; Sat: 1000–1500, general shops.
Mon–Fri: 0600/0700–1800/1900, food shops.
Commercial companies and shops, other than food shops, close on 'Free Saturdays' which vary between businesses, but usually three per month (one for shops).

Telecommunications
Mobile/cell phones
There are GSM 900/1800 and a 3G services available throughout country with more 3G services planned.

Electricity supply
Domestic 220V AC, 50 cycles; adaptor need for continental-type, round two-pin sockets.

Weights and measures
Metric system

Social customs/useful tips
Organisations do not stop for lunch in the middle of the day. The main meal *obiad* is taken from 1500. Formal address in the Polish language is expected. Polite small talk is appreciated as a prelude to talking business.

Security
Poland has no particular problem with security and street crime, although since the collapse of communism, street crime has increased. Normal precautions should be followed.

Getting there
Air
National airline: LOT Airlines (Polskie Linie Lotnicze)
International airport/s: Warsaw-Okecie (WAW), 10km south-west of the city (20–40 minutes by bus; 20–30 minutes by taxi); duty-free shops, post office, banks and *bureaux de change*, bars and restaurants, left-luggage, tourist information and car hire.
Other airport/s: Kraków-Balice (John Paul II International) (KRK), 11km from the city. Wroclaw-Strachowice (WRO), 10 km from the city. Katowice International (KTW), 34km from the city. Gdansk-Trojmaaaiasto (GDN), 10km from the city.
Airport tax: None
Surface
Road: Access is best through Germany and the Czech Republic. All vehicle documentation should include car registration, driver's national driving licence and valid Green Card motor insurance. An International Driving Permit is also required.
Rail: EuroCity rail services from Western Europe pass through Germany (from Berlin, travelling time is approximately 80 minutes), the Czech Republic or the Slovia Republic. Main lines also link Warsaw with Cologne, Vienna, Budapest and Prague. There are car-sleeper services from the Hook of Holland to Poznan/Warsaw.
Water: Pol Ferries operates between Poland and Sweden, Denmark and Finland.

Getting about
National transport
Air: LOT operates regular services connecting all major cities.
Road: Approximately 154,000km surfaced roads, of which 80 per cent are main roads.
The motorways include a north-south expressway, the Polish section of the Helsinki-Warsaw highway, known as the Via Baltica, and an expressway from Golonice to Opole.
Buses: Extensive bus and coach services are operated by Polish Motor Communications (PKS) and Polski Express.
Rail: There are approximately 30,000km of track. Some lines are narrow-gauge, and some are steam-hauled. Diesel is typical with only 33 per cent of the lines electrified. Regular services are operated by Polskie Koleje Panstwowe (PKP) (Polish State Railways), connecting major towns. Intercity express trains are inexpensive and reliable.
Polrailpass tickets valid for between 8–30 days are available from travel agents and railway offices, both locally and internationally. For an additional sum tickets for sleeping berths are available.
Water: About 4,000km of navigable inland waterways, including about 400km of canals. Ferries and hydrofoils link Baltic resorts in summer.

City transport
Taxis: Metered taxis are available in all main towns; they can be hired from ranks or ordered by phone. Payment in hard currency may be required; tipping is usual. A surcharge is imposed for journies between 2300–0500, out of town, and at weekends.
Buses, trams & metro: Regular public transport operates 0530–2300. Good bus services in all towns, also trams in some. Tickets for Warsaw can be bought at RUCH kiosks and used indiscriminately. In Warsaw seven-day tram tourist tickets can be bought at 37 Senatorska Street (entrance E) (Mon–Wed: 0730–1700, Thu–Fri: 0730–1400).
A metro is in operation in Warsaw.
Car hire
A hirer must be over 21 and have held a full licence for a year. Rental firms are available in all main towns through Orbis. International driving licence and insurance cover recommended. Minimum renting period is 24 hours. Payment is by cash or credit card. Speed limits: built-up areas 60kph, normal roads 90kph, motorways 100kph.

BUSINESS DIRECTORY

The addresses listed below are a selection only. While World of Information makes every endeavour to check these addresses, we cannot guarantee that changes have not been made, especially to telephone numbers and area codes. We would welcome any corrections.

Telephone area codes
The international direct dialling code (IDD) for Poland is +48, followed by area code and subscriber's number:

Bialystok	85	Lódz	42
Bydgoszcz	52	Lublin	81
Gdansk	58	Poznan	61
Katowice	32	Szczecin	91
Kraków	12	Warsaw	22
Leszno	65	Wroclaw	71

Useful telephone numbers
Ambulance: 999
Police emergency service: 997
Fire Brigade: 998
Customs information: 694-5596
Central Tourist Information Office: 270-000
Intercity directory assistance: 912
Local directory assistance: 911/913
Radiotaxi: 919 (complaints 224-444)

Chambers of Commerce
American Chamber of Commerce in Poland, Warsaw Financial Centre, 53 ulica Emilii Plater, 00-113 Warsaw (tel: 520-5999; fax: 520-5998; e-mail: office@amcham.com.pl).

British-Polish Chamber of Commerce, 2 ulica Zimna, 100-138 Warsaw (tel:

654-5971; fax: 621-1937; e-mail: bpcc@bpcc.org.pl).

Banking

AmerBank, Marszalkowska 115, 00-102 Warsaw.

American Express Bank, ul Krakowskie Przedmiescie 11, 00-068 Warsaw.

Bank Gospodarki Zywnosciowej (commercial bank), ul Grzybowska 4, 00-131 Warsaw.

Bank Polska Kasa Opieki SA (Grupa Pekao), Grzybowska 53/57, PO Box 1008, 00-950 Warsaw (tel: 656-0000; fax: 656-0004; e-mail: info@pekao.com.pl).

Bank Przemyslowo-Handlowy (Bank BPH), ul Na Zjezdzie 11, 30-527 Krakow.

Bank Rozwoju Eksportu SA (export development bank), PO Box 728, Bankowy 2, 00-950 Warsaw (tel: 829-0000; fax: 829-0081).

Bank Zachodni we Wroclawiu (Western Bank in Wroclaw), 41–43 Ofiar Oswiecimskich St, 50-850 Wroclaw.

Bre Bank SA, ul Senatorska 18, PO Box 728, PL 00-950 Warsaw (tel: 829-0000; fax: 829-0033).

Citibank, ul. Senatorska 12, 00-082 Warsaw (tel: 657-7200).

Creditanstalt, ul Prosta 69, 00-838 Warsaw (tel: 637-9000; fax: 637-9099).

ING Bank, ul. Emilii Plater 28 pietro 7, 00-950 Warsaw (tel: 630-5695).

Lodzi Bank Rozwoju SA, PO Box 465, ul Piotrkowska 173, 90-950 Lodz.

National Credit Bank, Nowy Swiat 6–12, 00-950 Warsaw (tel: 210-321; fax: 296-988).

Polski Bank Rozwoju SA (Polish development bank), ul Zurawia 47–49, 00-680 Warsaw (tel: 628-0490, 628-0790; fax: 628-6164; (Saturday 2120-828); satellite phone and fax: (39) 120-828, 120-844).

Powszechny Bank Gospodarczy w Lodzi, Pilsudskieo 12, 90-950 Lodz (tel: 361-470, 362-886; fax: 362-870).

Powszechna Kasa Oszczednosci Bank Panstwowy (state savings bank), ul Swietokrzyska 11–21, 00-950 Warsaw (tel: 220-0321, 226-3839; fax: 226-3863).

WBK (Wielkopolski Bank Kredytowy SA), 60-967 Posnan Place, Wolnosci 16 (tel: 56-4900; fax: 52-1113).

Central bank

Narodowy Bank Polski, ul Swietokrzyska 11/21; PO Box 1011, 00-919 Warsaw (tel: 653-1000; fax: 620-8518; e-mail: nbp@nbp.pl).

Stock exchange

Gielda Papierów Wartosciowych w Warszawie (Warsaw Stock Exchange) (WSE): www.gpw.pl

Commodity exchange

Warszawska Gielda Towarown (WGT) (Warsaw Commodity Exchange): www.wgt.com.pl

Travel information

Central Bus Station, Warszawa Zachnodnia Aleje Jerozolimskie 144 (tel: 236-394/6).

Central Railway Station, Warszawa Centralna 54 Aleje Jerozolimskie (tel: 255-001, 255-000).

Foundation for Tourism Development, Ul Mazowiecka 7, 00059 Warsaw (tel: 269-238; fax: 269-695).

International train connections – information (tel: 204512); local train connections – information (tel: 200-361).

LOT, Aleje Jerozolmskie 6579, 00-697 Warsaw (reservations in Poland, tel: 0801-703-703; fax: 630-5229); airport information in Warsaw (tel: 650-4220); internet: www.lot.com).

Lufthansa Warsaw Airport Office (tel: 650-4510); town office, Al Jerozolimskie 56c, Warsaw (tel: 630-2555; fax: 630-2535); Katowice Airport Office (tel: 184-5045); town office Al Korfantego 51, Katowice (tel: 106-2443; fax: 106-2444).

Orbis, 16 Bracka Street, 00-028 Warsaw (tel: 829-3939; fax: 827-3301).

State Sports and Tourism Administration, Swietokrzyska 12, 00916 Warsaw (fax: 694-5176).

Warsavawfie Centrum Informacji Gurwstycznej (Warsaw Tourist Information Centre), Zankowy Square 1/13, 00-262 Warsaw (tel: 635-1881).

Ministry of tourism

National Administration of Tourism and Physical Culture, ul. Swietokrzyska 12, 00-916 Warsaw (tel: 694-5555; fax: 826-2172).

Ministries

Ministry of Agriculture and Rural Development, ul Wspólna 30, 00-930 Warsaw (tel: 623-1000; fax: 623-2750; e-mail: kancelaria@minrol.gov.pl).

Ministry of Culture and National Heritage, Ul Krakowskie Przedmiescie 15/17, 00-071 Warsaw (tel: 620-0231; fax: 826-7533).

Ministry of Defence, ul Klonowa 1, 00-909 Warsaw (tel: 845-0441; e-mail: bpimon@wp.mil.pl).

Ministry of Education, Al Szucha 25, 00-918 Warsaw (tel: 628-0461; fax: 628-0461; e-mail: minister@men.waw.pl).

Ministry of the Environment, ul Wawelska 52/54, 02-922 Warsaw (tel: 825-0001; fax: 253-332; e-mail: info@mos.gov.pl).

Ministry of Foreign Affairs, Al Szucha 23, 00-580 Warsaw (tel: 523-9000; fax: 629-0287; e-mail: poland@mfa.gov.pl; internet: www.msz.gov.pl).

Ministry of Health, ul Miodowa 15, 00-923 Warsaw (tel: 831-3441; fax: 831-1553; e-mail: rzecznik@mzios.gov.pl).

Ministry of Internal Affairs and Administration, ul Batorego 5, 02-514 Warsaw (tel: 621-0251; fax: 628-9983; e-mail: wp@mswia.gov.pl).

Ministry of Justice, Al Ujazdowskie 11, 00-950 Warsaw (tel: 521-2808; fax: 628-1692; nagorska@ms.gov.pl).

Ministry of Labour and Social Policy, ul Nowogrodzka 1/3/5, 00-513 Warsaw (tel: 661-0100; fax: 628-4048; e-mail: bip@mpips.gov.pl).

Ministry of Post and Telecommunications, pl Malachowskiego 2, 00-940 Warsaw (tel: 656-5000; fax: 826-4840; e-mail: rzecznik@ml.gov.pl).

Ministry of Transport and Maritime Economy, ul Chalubinskiego 4/6, 00-928 Warsaw (tel: 624-4000; fax: 628-5365).

Ministry of the Treasury, ul Krucza 36, 00-522 Warsaw (tel: 695-9000; fax: 625-1114; e-mail: minister@mst.gov.pl).

President's Office, ul Wiejska 10, 00-902 Warsaw (tel: 695-2900; fax: 695-3819; e-mail: listy@prezydent.pl).

Prime Minister's Office, Al Ujazdowskie 1/3, 00-583 Warsaw (tel: 694-66983; fax: 625-2637; e-mail: cirinfo@kprm.gov.pol).

Other useful addresses

British Consul (Szczecin), Ul Starego Wiarusa 32, 71-206 Szczecin (tel: 487-0302; fax: 487-3697).

British Embassy, Corporate Centre, 2nd Floor, Emilii Plater 28, Warsaw 00-688 (tel: 625-3030; fax: 625-3472); Aleja Roz 1, 00-556 Warsaw (tel: 628-1001/5; fax: 621-7161).

Central Board of Customs, Swietokrzyska 12, 00-916 Warsaw (tel: 694-5555). Press Office (tel: 694-5882; fax: 827-3427).

Central Statistical Office, International Co-operation Division, Al Niepodleglosci 208, 00-925 Warsaw (tel: 608-3113; fax: 608-3870; e-mail: j.szczerbinska@gus.stsp.gov.pl).

Co-operation Fund, Ul Zurawia 4a, 00-503 Warsaw (tel: 693-5165/827/868; fax: 693-5815/365).

Energy Restructuring Group, Ministry of Industry and Trade, 2 Mysia Street, 00926 Warsaw 63 (tel: 625-6280; fax: 625-6305, 628-0970).

Euro Information Centre Network/Correspondence Centre, Ul Zurawia 6/12, 00-503 Warsaw (tel: 625-1319; fax: 625-1290).

European Integration Committee, Aleje Ujazdowskie 9, 00-583 Warsaw (tel: 694-7354; fax: 629-4888).

Foreign Trade Research Institute Market Information Center of Foreign Trade, Krucza 38/42, 00-512 Warsaw (tel: 629-1222; fax: 628-8680).

Foundation for Privatisation, 36 Ul Krucza, 00525 Warsaw (tel: 628-2198/99; fax: 625-1114); external department (tel: 693-5419, 693-5818; fax: 693-5300).

Government Centre for Strategic Studies, Wspolna 4, 00-926 Warsaw (tel: 661-8111); Press Office (tel: 661-8664; fax: 629-1619).

Government Information Department, Ul. Wiejska 4/6, 00-902 Warsaw (tel: 694-2500; fax: 694-1911).

Housing and Urban Development Office, ul. Wspolna 2, 00-926 Warsaw (tel: 661-8111; fax: 628-5887).

Industrial Development Agency, ul Wspolna 4, 00-930 Warsaw (tel: 628-7954, 628-0934; fax: 628-2363).

Main Post Office (open 24 hours), 31–33 Swietokrzyska Street, Warsaw.

National Administration of Tourism and Physical Culture, ul. Swietokrzyska 12, 00-916 Warsaw (tel: 694-5555; fax: 826-2172).

Parliament, Sajm RP, ul. Wiejska 4/6/8, 00-902 Warsaw (tel: 694-2500; fax: 694-2215).

Polcargo (cargo experts and supervisors), Zeromskiego 32, Box 223, 81963 Gdynia (tel: 213-921/957).

Polish Agency for Foreign Investment (PAIZ), Al Roz 2, 00-556 Warsaw (tel: 621-6261; fax: 621-8427).

Polish Chartering Agents (Polfracht), Ul Pulaskiego 8, Box 206, 81368 Gdynia (tel: 214-991).

Polish Corporation of Trade Fairs and Economic Exhibition Organisers, Ul Glogowska 26, 60-734 Poznan (tel: 661-532, 692-245; fax: 661-053; e-mail: korptarg@soho-online.com).

Polish Embassy (USA), 2640 16th Street, NW, Washington DC 20009 (tel: (+1-202) 234-3800; fax: (+1-202) 328-6271; e-mail: information@ioip.com).

Polish Foundation for Promotion and Development of SMEs, Ul Zurawia 4a, 00-503 Warsaw (tel: 693-5868/18/27; fax: 693-5815/365).

Polish State Railways (PKP), Ul Chalubinskiego 4/6, 00-928 Warsaw (tel: 628-4909, 293-596; fax: 244-039, 621-9557, 244-870).

Polska Agencja Interpress (Polish information agency), Ul Bagatela 12, 00-585 Warsaw (tel: 628-2221; fax: 628-4651).

Polska Agencja Prasowa (Polish press agency), Ul Jerozolimskie 7, 00-950 Warsaw (tel: 628-0001).

Polskie Linie Oceaniczne (Polish Ocean Lines), Ul 10 Lutego 24, 81-364 Gdynia (tel: 201-901).

Poznan International Fair Co Ltd, Ul Glogowska 14, 60-734 Poznan (tel: 869-2000; fax: 866-5827; e-mail: info@mtp.com.pl); Department of Services (tel: 668-320, 692-547; fax: 660-642); Department of Employment (contracts out exhibition stall personnel) (tel: 666-721, 692-250; fax: 665-827).

State Committee of Science and Technology, ul, Wspolna 1/3, 00-529 Warsaw (tel: 628-4071; fax: 628-0922).

Technology Agency, Krucza 38/42, 00-512 Warsaw (tel: 661-8610; fax: 628-3611).

Telekomunikacja Polska SA, Special Projects Department, Ul Obrzezna 7, 02-691 Warsaw (tel: 275-037; fax: 276-789); External Department, Telephony Polskie Fundacja (Polish Telephone Foundation), Al Stanow Zjednoczonych 24, 03-964 Warsaw (tel/fax: 136-833; fax: 120-544).

Universal SA (foreign trading company), Al Jerozolimskie 44, 00-950 Warsaw (tel: 8144-3135, 693-6091/92; fax: 278-312).

Internet sites

Official Website of Poland: http://poland.pl

Business Directory: www.polish-bus.com/anghome.html

Business Polska: www.polska.net

Polish company directory: www.teleadreson.com.pl

Polish Embassy, London: http://home.btclick.com/polishembassy

Polish Tourism: www.poland-tourism.pl

Warsaw Business Journal: www.wbj.pl

Portugal

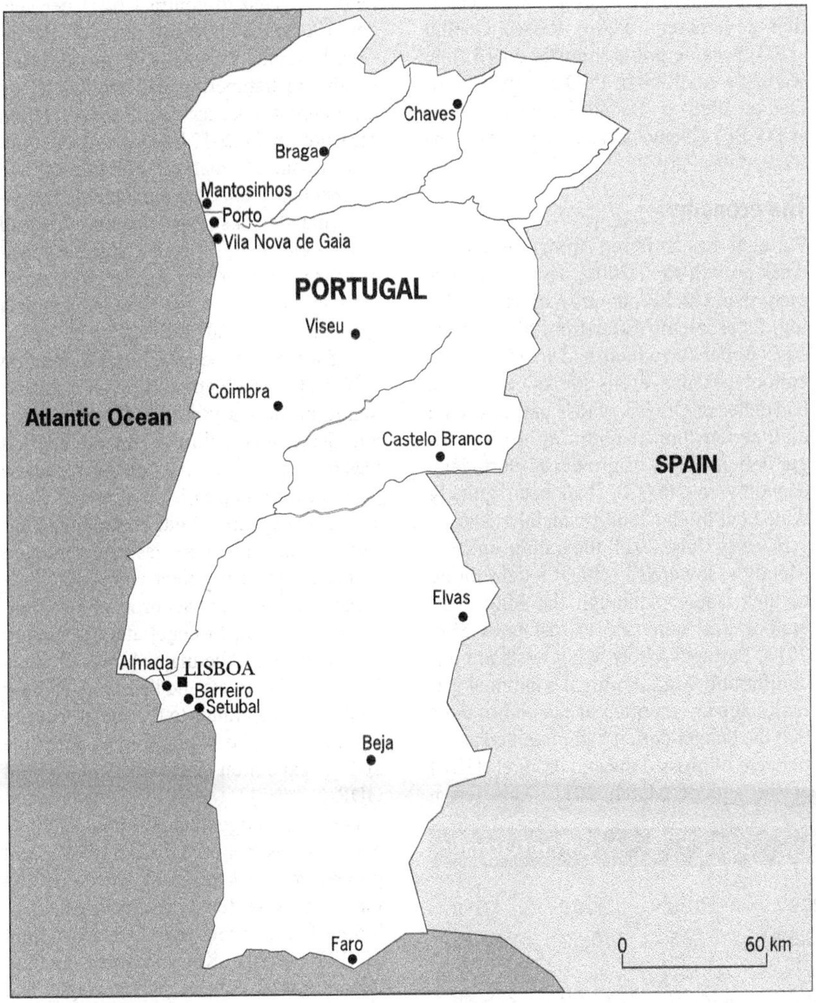

KEY FACTS

Official name: República Portuguesa (Portuguese Republic)

Head of State: President Aníbal Cavaco Silva (PSD) (from 2006; re-elected 23 Jan 2011)

Head of government: Prime Minister, Pedro Passos Coelho (PSD) (from 21 Jun 2011)

Ruling party: Coalition led by Partido Social Democrata (PSD) (Social Democratic Party), with the Centro Democrático e Social-Partido Popular (CDS-PP) (Democratic and Social Centre-Popular Party) (from 21 Jun 2011)

Area: 92,072 square km

Population: 10.64 million (2010)*

Capital: Lisbon

Official language: Portuguese

Currency: Euro (€) = 100 cents (from 1 Jan 2002; previous currency escudo, locked at esc200.48 per euro)

Exchange rate: €0.75 per US$ (Oct 2011)

GDP per capita: US$21,559 (2010)

GDP real growth: 1.40% (2010)

GDP: US$229.30 billion (2010)

Labour force: 5.58 million (2010)

Unemployment: 11.00% (2010)

Inflation: 1.40% (2010)

Balance of trade: -US$23.75 billion (2010)

Annual FDI: US$1.48 billion (2010)

* estimated figure

In August 2011, only three months after granting the Lisbon government a US$111 billion bailout, officials from the International Monetary Fund (IMF), the European Commission and the European Central Bank were back in town to see how things were going. To be reviewed were progress with budget cuts and the economic reforms designed to stimulate growth. In June 2011 Portugal found itself not only with a new government, but with a new kind of government.

Socrates goes

For the first half of 2011, Portugal's politicians had been divided over a new round of public sector cuts. Their differences only served to make the need for a euro-zone rescue look more likely. When the Partido Socialista (PS) (Socialist Party) government fell in March 2011, it was largely through a lack of any significant political support. As is so often the case with Portuguese politics, short-term political interest and a background of chronic economic austerity brought about the collapse of Prime Minister José Socrates'government. Mr Socrates had endeavoured to maintain Portugal's already battered international credibility in the face of market doubts about its solvency, hoping against hope that conditions for Portugal's borrowing would somehow become more favourable. His government tendered its resignation after the entire parliamentary opposition rejected its latest austerity package. Bowing to the inevitable, this had in deed been pretty severe, including cuts of up to 10 per cent in all state pensions above ?1,500 (US$2,010) a month, further tax rises, cuts in spending on infrastructure and healthcare and measures to liberalise the labour market and rented housing sector. Political divisions were not mended by the fact that the austerity measures were announced by the finance minister at a press conference in Brussels, without any negotiations with parliamentary parties or even prior notice to the head of state. Such was the unpopularity of the measures that parliamentary support for them evaporated, leaving Mr Socrates with a minority government and no consensus of support to get the austerity measures adopted.

The denouement of the proposed austerity measures showed Portuguese politics in a bad light. Party politics had seemed to come before economic priorities. The prime minister, for whatever reason, had outstripped the brief of his minority government, while the Partido Social Democrata (PSD) (Social Democratic Party) seemed concerned that its support for the government would hurt its electoral chances in future. Even the President chose to abandon his previous institutional co-operation with the government.

Election results

Parliamentary elections were held on 5 June, and the incumbent PS lost, wining only 28.05 per cent of the vote. The opposition PSD won 38.63 per cent (105 seats out of 230) and the right to form a coalition government. Pedro Passos Coelho (PSD) became prime minister on 15 June leading a coalition of PSD and the Centro Democrático e Social-Partido Popular (CDS-PP) (Democratic and Social Centre-Popular Party).

The economy

Portugal has suffered from chronically weak growth since 2001, with unemployment rising and economic activity declining. Its problems differ from those of the Irish Republic, which had to resort to a bailout because of its banks' excessive bad debts, or Greece, whose bail-out came after serious 'under-reporting' of its budget deficit. Signs of growth in Portugal's economy in 2006–07 had been quickly wiped out by the 2008 financial crisis.

In early July 2011 the rating agency, Moody's, lowered Portugal's debt rating to junk status. Although the May 2011 bailout was supposed to last until May 2013, Portugal's borrowing costs are uncomfortably high. Portugal's national statistics agency reported at the end of June that the budget deficit had remained at 8.7 per cent of gross domestic product (GDP) at the end of March 2011. This left a shortfall of three per cent to be cut by the end of the year.

The independent finance minister, Vitor Gaspar, published forecasts that Portugal's economy would contract by 2.3 per cent in 2011 and by 1.7 per cent in 2012. According to the IMF, however, growth in 2011 is likely to be somewhat better than expected, but the recession in 2012 is now projected to be more pronounced, with GDP expected to contract by 3 per cent and risks to the outlook tilted to the downside. From the external side, global headwinds are hampering exports, while, on the internal side, the fiscal consolidation measures in the 2012 budget, tighter credit and financial market conditions and weaker confidence are dampening domestic demand. Consumer price inflation will remain elevated, reflecting significant indirect tax and tariff increases. The economy is expected to recover, albeit at a gradual pace, in 2013.

In the view of the IMF, implementation of the 2011 budget has proved difficult. While preliminary data indicate that the end-September ceiling on the cash deficit was met, spending overruns for the whole year could add up to 1.5 per cent of GDP. These unexpected budget pressures reflect in large part slippages in expenditure controls and insufficient corrective measures. Against this backdrop, the government is seeking to negotiate a voluntary agreement with the major banks to transfer part of the assets and liabilities of these banks' pension funds to the social security system, to make it possible to meet the 2011 fiscal deficit target of 5.9 per cent of GDP.

The 2012 budget includes bold and welcome measures to bring the fiscal programme back on track. In the IMF's view, it is consistent with meeting the ambitious fiscal target of a 4.5 per cent deficit of GDP in 2012. Key measures, particularly nominal cuts in public wages and pensions and increases in indirect taxes, are also appropriate in view of the need to switch from a consumption-based to a more export-led growth model. But implementation of the 2012 budget will need to be accompanied by supportive measures to address still rising spending arrears and to reduce other fiscal risks, particularly at the level of local and regional governments and state-owned enterprises. In this context, the envisaged adjustment programme for Portugal's troubled autonomous region of Madeira will provide an opportunity to signal that errant fiscal behavior at the regional and local levels will no longer be tolerated.

KEY INDICATORS — **Portugal**

	Unit	2006	2007	2008	2009	2010
Population	m	10.59	10.62	*10.63	*10.63	*10.64
Gross domestic product (GDP)	US$bn	194.97	223.30	244.90	227.90	229.30
GDP per capita	US$	18,418	21,019	23,070	21,408	21,559
GDP real growth	%	1.3	1.9	0.0	-2.7	1.4
Inflation	%	3.0	2.4	2.7	-0.9	1.4
Unemployment	%	7.7	7.7	7.6	9.5	11.0
Exports (fob) (goods)	US$m	43,259.0	52,801.0	57,871.0	44,494.0	48,913.0
Imports (fob) (goods)	US$m	64,451.0	79,251.0	91,659.0	68,904.0	72,665.0
Balance of trade	US$m	-20,872.0	-26,450.0	-33,787.0	-24,417.0	-23,751.0
Current account	US$m	-18,283.0	-23,516.0	-31,852.0	-23,952.0	-22,605.0
Total reserves minus gold	US$m	2,064.0	1,258.0	1,309.0	2,455.0	3,652.0
Foreign exchange	US$m	1,835.0	1,044.0	1,022.0	811.0	2,013.0
Exchange rate	per US$	0.75	0.69	0.68	0.78	0.76

* estimated figure

Portugal's major banks are facing fresh challenges to strengthen their capital positions. The authorities are putting in place rules that will regulate the temporary use of public funds for recapitalising banks. These rules will need to respect the interests of taxpayers, preserve the stability of the banking system and comply with European Union state aid rules. A balanced and orderly deleveraging of the banking sector over the medium term will allow banks to address their funding imbalances, while safeguarding adequate credit to the more productive sectors of the economy.

Overall, in the view of the IMF, the Portuguese government's economic programme is off to a good start. However, its success crucially depends on the continued implementation of a wide range of structural reforms that will remove the rigidities and bottlenecks behind Portugal's decade-long growth stagnation. In order to improve labour cost competitiveness, wages in the private sector should follow the lead taken by the public sector in implementing sustained pay cuts. Measures to reduce dismissal costs and increase wage flexibility at the company-level are on the table. As for tackling entrenched practices that distort competition, a strengthening of the competition framework is underway. Progress has also been made on liberalising the telecommunication markets. Nevertheless, more progress on curbing price rises in sheltered sectors, particularly energy and regulated professions, is needed.

Risk assessment

Economy	Poor
Politics	Fair
Regional stability	Good

COUNTRY PROFILE

Historical profile

1383 The seventh Portuguese King, Fernando I, died. The Spanish Castillians invaded Portugal in an attempt to claim the country's throne.
1385 João I of Avis defeated the Castillians and became King.
1400s Portugal expanded its trading routes by colonising parts of Africa, Asia and the Americas.
1558 Portugal tried to colonise Morocco. After Portugal was defeated, the country went into economic and imperial decline.
1580 King Phillip II of Spain invaded Portugal. It remained under Spanish rule until a revolt in 1640.
1600s Portugal colonised Brazil and became a major gold exporter. Portugal became a major trading partner to Britain.
1793–1801 Portuguese and Spanish troops invaded France, but were defeated. Portugal was forced to temporarily break relations with Britain as part of a peace settlement with France.
1807–10 Portugal re-established relations with Britain and declared its neutrality. France and Spain invaded Portugal three times after it had refused to break relations with Britain. A joint Anglo-Portuguese Army eventually expelled the occupation forces.
1822–24 Brazil declared its independence in 1822. An attempt to introduce a new constitution in Portugal failed. Royalists refused to accept the constitution, which would have separated the powers of the monarchy, government and judiciary, and launched uprisings against the government. Power remained in the hands of the monarchy.
1828–51 Liberals rebelled against the Royalist government. Despite splitting into moderate and radical elements, the Liberals eventually gained control of the government.
1907–08 The Republicans, who were gaining support among the population, failed in an attempt to overthrow the government of João Franco.
1908 Republican extremists assassinated King Carlos I. His son, Manuel II succeeded him, becoming Portugal's last king.
1910 The army overthrew the monarchy forcing the King to abdicate. A Republican government was installed and Portugal was declared a republic. Teófilo Braga was appointed as Portugal's first president.
1911 A new constitution was introduced confirming Portugal's republican status and introducing a bicameral legislature.
1914–18 Portugal fought alongside Britain and France in the First World War.
1926 A military *coup d'état* overthrew the government and replaced it with a *junta*. The coup leader, General Gomes da Costa, was temporarily appointed head of the *junta* before General Óscar Fragoso Carmona replaced him.
1928 General Carmona was appointed president and Colonel José Vicente de Freitas became prime minister.
1932 A civilian academic, António de Oliveira Salazar, was appointed prime minister. Salazar introduced a new constitution consolidating authoritarian government.
1939–45 Portugal was neutral during the Second World War, but allowed the Allies to establish military bases in the Azores.
1955 After initially being blocked by the Soviet Union, Portugal was allowed to join the UN.
1968 Marcello José das Neves Caetano succeeded Salazar who had suffered a stroke and was in a coma.
1970 António de Oliveira Salazar died.
1974 A group of army officers of the Movimento das Forças Armadasa (MFA) (Armed Forces Movement), and led by General António de Spínola staged a *coup d'état* and overthrew Caetano's government. A provisional coalition government restored civil liberties and freedom of the press, abolished the secret police and freed political prisoners.
1975 Portugal granted independence to its African territories, where wars against nationalist forces had long been a drain on the economy; military spending had absorbed about 40 per cent of GDP per annum. Portugal also withdrew from East Timor. Many expatriates returned from former colonies. In the first free parliamentary elections victory went to the Partido Socialista (PS) (Socialist Party). Mário Lopes Soares became prime minister and General Antonio Ramalho Eanes won the presidency. Banks and many industries were nationalised.
1976 A new constitution was introduced, officially establishing Portugal as a parliamentary democracy. The constitution was later amended in 1982, 1989, 1992 and 1997.
1977–86 A period of political instability with 17 left-wing coalition governments in power.
1986 Portugal joined the forerunner of the EU, the European Community (EC). Former prime minister Mário Soares became the first civilian president for 60 years.
1987 In the general election, Partido Social Democrata (PSD) (Social Democratic Party) became the first majority party in parliament since the 1974 revolution. Anibal Cavaco Silva was elected prime minister.
1991 Mário Soares was re-elected president and PSD won re-election. Portugal took Australia to the International Court of Justice (ICJ), on behalf of then Timor-Leste, a former colony, alleging Australia had failed to observe the rights of the Timorese to national self-determination, when it recognised Indonesia's occupation of Timor-Leste in 1975.
1995 PSD lost to the PS in the general election. António Guterres became prime minister. The ICJ ruled it did not have jurisdiction in the matter of Australia actions concerning Timor-Leste.
1996 The presidential election was won by the PS's Jorge Sampaio.
1998 Portuguese voters narrowly rejected in a referendum a proposal to legalise abortion.
1999 António Guterres and the PS were re-elected. Macau, Portugal's last colonial territory was returned to China. Portugal joined the EU single currency unit.

2001 Jorge Sampaio was re-elected as president for a second five-year term. Guterres resigned, as prime minister after the PS was defeated in local elections.
2002 Euro currency replaced the escudos. José Manuel Durão Barroso (PSD) formed a coalition government comprising PSD and Partido Popular (PP) (Popular Party).
2003 The last extension on the Via Infante motorway Lisbon-Algarve-Spain (known as the A22) was opened.
2004 Prime Minister Barroso resigned; he assumed the presidency of the European Commission.
2005 The opposition PS won parliamentary elections and José Sócrates (PS) became prime minister. Portugal's constitutional court ruled against the government's decision to hold a referendum on relaxing the country's abortion laws. The country's economic rating was downgraded, by Standard and Poor's, from AA to -AA, as a result of the deterioration in public finances and the lack of fiscal reforms necessary to boost fiscal dynamics. The government introduced a radical budget designed to cut public spending in an attempt to revive the economy and cut a deficit that was twice the level permitted under EU monetary rules.
2006 Aníbal Cavaco Silva won the presidency.
2007 Mass demonstrations protested the government's austerity measures. A new law permitting abortion within the first ten-weeks of pregnancy was introduced in alignment with most other EU countries.
2008 Official approval of Portuguese spelling in line with Brazilian practice was given by parliament.
2009 Portugal signed a loan agreement with São Tomé and Príncipe, to allow its former colony's currency, the dobra, to be anchored to the euro. In parliamentary elections, the ruling PS won 37.7 per cent of the vote (96 seats of 230) and the opposition PSD 30 per cent (78); Prime Minister José Sócrates (PS) remained in office.
2010 Torrential rain caused severe flooding on the island of Madeira in February, resulting in the death of 42 people; the flooding later caused landslides, further endangering islanders. In May value added tax (VAT) was increased to 21 per cent and income tax raised, along with higher corporation taxes, as part of the government's latest austerity measures to cut the budget deficit. A heat wave in July resulted in massive forest fires across northern Portugal in August.
2011 Presidential elections were held on 23 January, in which three candidates took part. Incumbent Aníbal Cavaco Silva (PDS) won 52.9 per cent and his closest rival, Manuel Alegre (PS), won 19.8 per cent. The turnout was low at 46.6 per cent. The government resigned on 23 March following parliament's rejection of its third austerity budget. Socrates remained in office as caretaker prime minister until an early general election was called. Portugal became the third euro-zone state to request financial aid. The European Central Bank (ECB) and the International Monetary Fund (IMF) agreed on 3 May to offer Portugal €78 billion (US$116 billion) in financial assistance. Caretaker Prime Minister Socrates, assured both parties that the deficit would be cut by 5.9 per cent in 2011/12, by 4.5 per cent in 2012/13 and 3 per cent in 2013/14. In parliamentary elections held on 5 June, the ruling PS lost power, wining only 28.05 per cent of the vote. The opposition Partido Social Democrata (PSD) (Social Democratic Party) won 38.63 per cent (105 seats out of 230). The PSD won the right to form a coalition government. Pedro Passos Coelho (PSD) became prime minister on 21 June leading a coalition of PSD and the Centro Democrático e Social-Partido Popular (CDS-PP) (Democratic and Social Centre-Popular Party). On 5 July Portugal's debt was downgraded to junk status by credit ratings agency Moody's.

Political structure

Constitution

The constitution was promulgated in 1976 and amended in 1982, 1989, 1992 and 1999. Voting is by direct universal suffrage. Voting age: 18 years.

Form of state

Parliamentary democratic republic

The executive

The president, who is directly elected for a maximum of two consecutive terms of five years, appoints a prime minister, and, on his recommendation, the rest of the government. The president can dissolve parliament, call elections and is supreme commander of the armed forces.The president can dissolve parliament, call elections and is supreme commander of the armed forces.
The principal organ of executive power within the government is the Council of Ministers which is responsible to parliament.

National legislature

The unicameral Assembléia da República (Assembly of the Republic) has 230 members elected for four-year terms by proportional representation. There is a fixed number of representatives, two, for each autonomous region of the Azores and Madeira, Portuguese nationals living in Europe and Portuguese nationals living elsewhere in the world. The size of the electorate determines the number of representatives for all other mainland Portuguese constituencies.

Legal system

The legal system is based on the 1976 constitution.

Last elections

23 January 2011 (presidential); 5 June 2011 (parliamentary)

Results: Presidential: Aníbal Cavaco Silva (PSD) won 52.9 per cent, Manuel Alegre (PS) 19.8 per cent, Fernando Nobre (independent) 14.1 per cent, Francisco Lopes (Partido Comunista Português (PCP) (Portuguese Communist Party)) 7.1 per cent; turnout was 46.63 per cent.
Parliamentary: Partido Social Democrata (PSD) (Social Democratic Party) won 40.3 per cent of the vote (108 seats out of 230), Partido Socialista (PS) (Socialist Party) 29.3 per cent (74), Centro Democrático e Social-Partido Popular (CDS-PP) (Democratic and Social Centre-Popular Party), 12.2 per cent (24), Coligação Democrática Unitária (CDU) (Democratic Unity Coalition (alliance of the Partido Comunista dos Trabalhadores (Communist Party) and Partido Ecologista (Os Verdes) (Ecologist Party (The Greens)) 8.2 per cent (16), Bloco de Esquerda (BE) (Left Block) 5.4 per cent (eight); 12 other political parties each won less than 2 per cent of the vote and failed to win any seats. Turnout was 58.1 per cent.

Next elections

2016 (presidential); 2013 (parliamentary)

Political parties

Ruling party

Coalition led by Partido Social Democrata (PSD) (Social Democratic Party), with the Centro Democrático e Social-Partido Popular (CDS-PP) (Democratic and Social Centre-Popular Party) (from 21 Jun 2011)

Main opposition party

Partido Socialista (PS) (Socialist Party)

Population

10.64 million (2010)*

Last census: March 2001: 10,148,259 (provisional; includes the Azores and Medeira Islands)

Population density: 109 inhabitants per square km. Urban population: 66 per cent of the total (1995–2001).

Annual growth rate: 0.4 per cent 1994–2004 (WHO 2006)

Ethnic make-up

Predominantly Portuguese. There are immigrant groups from former African colonies – Cape Verde, Mozambique, Angola, Guinea-Bissau and São Tomé. Also from East Timor and Chinese from Macao. There were 200,000 members of ethnic minorities in Portugal in 2000 (1.8 per cent of the total population).

Religions

Roman Catholic (97 per cent), Protestant denominations (1 per cent).

Education

Basic education is undertaken between the ages of six and 15. Secondary education is optional and is undertaken over three years. Higher education is divided into two sub-systems: university education and non-university higher education and it is provided in autonomous public universities, private universities, polytechnic institutions and private higher education institutions of other types. The two systems of higher education are linked and it is possible to transfer from one to the other. It is also possible to transfer from a public institution to a private one and vice versa.

Literacy rate: 94 per cent male, 89 per cent female; adult rates (World Bank).

Enrolment rate: 128 per cent gross primary enrolment of the relevant age group (including repeaters); 98 per cent gross secondary enrolment (World Bank).

Pupils per teacher: 12 in primary schools.

Health

Health care is delivered under a national health service, which is accessible to all Portuguese citizens and to citizens of member states of the EU.

HIV/Aids

HIV prevalence: 0.4 per cent aged 15–49 in 2003 (World Bank)

Life expectancy: 78 years, 2004 (WHO 2006)

Fertility rate/Maternal mortality rate: 1.5 births per woman, 2004 (WHO 2006); maternal mortality 8.0 per 100,000 live births (World Bank).

Birth rate/Death rate: 11 deaths to 12 births per 1,000 people (World Bank).

Child (under 5 years) mortality rate (per 1,000): 4.0 per 1,000 live births (World Bank).

Head of population per physician: 3.42 physicians per 1,000 people, 2003 (WHO 2006)

Welfare

Portugal's social security system is characterised by a general contributory scheme covering all workers and their families, with special arrangements for self-employed persons and a non-contributory protection scheme for people facing social or economic problems. Benefits available under the general scheme include sickness (cash benefits), birth/adoption, accidents at work and occupational diseases, invalidity, old age and death, unemployment and dependants.

Self-employed persons are entitled to a compulsory insurance scheme and there is an opt-in extended benefits scheme relating to sickness, occupational diseases and dependants. Membership of the general scheme is compulsory. In addition, there is a voluntary social security scheme for those not in work or who are in work but are not covered by the general scheme. As a rule, the employer pays the contributions and deducts the employee's social security contribution from his or her pay. Employers are also responsible for full financing of the protection of employees against accidents at work and occupational diseases.

Main cities

Lisbon (capital, estimated population 530,321 in 2005), Oporto (249,260), Amadora (163,335), Braga (121,487), Coimbra (107,490).

Languages spoken

Business languages include English, Spanish and French.

Official language/s

Portuguese

Media

Press

Dailies: In Portugese, *Jornal de Noticias* (http://dn.sapo.pt) is the largest daily.. Others include *Diario de Noticias* (http://dn.sapo.pt), *Record*, *Correio da Manha* and *Público* (ww2.publico.clix.pt), *Destak* (www.destak.pt), government announcements and politics in *Diário da República* (www.dre.pt), and *Correio da Manha* (www.correiomanha.pt). On Madeira *Diário de Notícias* (www.dnoticias.pt), the *Tribuna da Madeira* (www.tribunadamadeira.pt) and *Jornal da Madeira (www.jornaldamadeira.pt); in English, The Madeira Times* (www.themadeiratimes.com), In the Azores, *O Açoriano Oriental* (http://acorianooriental.sapo.pt) and Diario Insular (www.diarioinsular.com).

Weeklies: Major weeklies are published in Lisbon. The most widely circulated is *Expresso* (http://expresso.clix.pt), others include *O Independente* (www.oindependente.pt) and *Sol* (http://sol.sapo.pt/). Political and news publications include *Courrier Internacional* (http://clix.courrierinternacional.com.pt), *Focus* (http://html.impala.pt) and *Sábado* (www.sabado.xl.pt). Women's magazines include *Mulher Moderna* (www.mulhermoderna.com), *Exame* and *Activa* are both imprints of (www.edipresse.com).*Máxima* (www.maxima.xl.pt), *Guia*, *Maria* and *Marie Claire* are also popular. *Sojornal* is a general interest weekly. *The News* is Portugal's national weekend newspaper. *Visão* (http://aeiou.visao.pt). In English, with news and current affairs are *The Portugal News* (www.the-news.net), *The Resident* (www.portugalresident.com) and *Euro Weekly News* (www.euroweeklynews.com).

Business: In Portuguese, the most influential business newspapers are *Diário Económico* (http://diarioeconomico.sapo.pt), *Jornal de Negócios* (www.jornaldenegocios.pt), *Oje* (www.oje.pt), and *Vida Económica* (weekly) (www.centroatl.pt). Many newspapers have economic sections.

Broadcasting

The national public broadcaster is Radio e Televisão de Portugal (RTP) (www.rtp.pt), which runs television, radio, teletext and online, transmits national and regional programmes including services to the Madeira Islands and the Azores.

Radio: There are over 280 radio stations, almost all of which are commercial, RTP runs Antena 1–3, and an external service broadcasting to Africa. The Roman Catholic Church operates Radio Renascença, the only private national radio station. The major commercial stations are Radio Comercial (radiocomercial.clix.pt), TSF (http://tsf.sapo.pt) and Radio Clube Portugues (http://radioclube.clix.pt)

Television: RTP operates two channels on the mainline and regional services to the Azores and Madeira and the external services RTP Africa and RTP Internacional. SIC (http://sic.sapo.pt) and TVI (www.tvi.iol.pt), which has close ties with the Roman Catholic church in Portugal, are private stations. There are satellite TV broadcasts from several international sources.

Advertising

Television is the most popular medium, taking about 45 per cent of total advertising, followed by radio, newspaper and magazine advertisements. Other methods used are cinema shorts, posters, direct mail and door-to-door canvassing. There are about 50 advertising agencies, mainly specialising in radio and TV work and newspapers

News agencies

National news agency: Lusa News Press Agency

Economy

Portugal has a small mixed economy with a heavy dependence on foreign trade and few natural resources. The service sector, which comprises, tourism, government services, retail and recreation is the largest component of GDP at 66 per cent, and employs over 50 per cent of all workers. The industrial sector and an export-oriented manufacturing sector accounts for almost 30 per cent of GDP, and includes a globally recognised die and mould making industry for automobile assembly and one of Europe's largest electricity operators, EDP (Energias de Portugal), as well as textiles, clothing and footwear, cork and wood products, wine and port, porcelain and glass. Agriculture and fishing accounts for only 4 per cent of GDP.

The global economic crisis caused a deep recession in Portugal in 2008 as GDP growth fell from 1.9 per cent in 2007 to -0.8 per cent in 2008 and was predicted to fall further in 2009, to either -1.4 per cent according to government figures, or -2.1 per cent according to the Banco de Portugal, which then predicted that GDP growth would reach 0.3 per cent in 2010 due to moderate rates of consumption.

While the national unemployment rate was typically 7–9 per cent (2007–09), regionally it can be as high as 15 per cent, such as in the Vale do Ave. In December 2009 the national unemployment rate was over 10 per cent.

The economy is classed as underperforming, having one of the lowest GDP per capita (US$22,997) in Western Europe. In December 2009 the international ratings agency Standard and Poor's lowered Portugal's long-term credit rating from 'stable' to 'negative', with a pessimistic outlook concerning the country's structural weaknesses, with its poor competitiveness that could hamper growth and Portugal's capacity to strengthen its public finances and reduce debt.

A 2010 austerity budget was announced in March, designed to cut the public deficit to 8.3 per cent of GDP (down from 9.3 per cent in 2009) and return the country's spending to the EU mandated 3 per cent by 2013. The measures planned included public workers' pay freeze and cuts in pensions. Portugal's 10-year cost of borrowing reached a peak of almost 8 per cent on 2 March 2011 when it was required to borrow US$1.38 billion (€1 billion), through a Treasury bill sale. On 16 March the international ratings agency Moody's downgraded Portugal's sovereign debt rating from A1 to A3 and warned that it may be downgraded further due to the country's poor economic outlook. The EU Central Bank and the International Monetary Fund (IMF) agreed on 3 May 2011 to offer Portugal €78 billion (US$116 billion) in financial assistance. The three-year loan agreement should allow Portugal to reach its budget deficit targets without a run on its economy. Caretaker Prime Minister Socrates, assured both parties that the deficit would be cut by 5.9 per cent in 2011/12, by 4.5 per cent in 2012/13 and 3 per cent in 2013/14.

Portugal's debt was downgraded to junk status by credit ratings agency Moody's on 5 July. Moody's considered the risk of Portugal needing further assistance was increasing.

External trade

As a member of the European Union, Portugal operates within a community-wide free trade area, with tariffs sets as a whole. Internationally, the EU has free trade agreements with a number of nations and trading blocs worldwide.

Around 70 per cent of GDP is provided through foreign trade, of which 80 per cent is with other EU members. The modern manufacturing sector provides a major input of mould-making items for Europe's automotive industry. Important export products include marble, wine, especially port, and cork as well as mineral ores.

Imports

Main imports are machinery and transport equipment, chemicals, petroleum, textiles and agricultural products.

Main sources: Spain (typically 29 per cent of total), Germany (12 per cent), France (8 per cent).

Exports

Main exports include clothing and footwear, machinery, chemicals, cork and paper products and hides, port and sherry.

Main destinations: Spain (typically 25 per cent of total), Germany (12 per cent), France (11 per cent).

Agriculture

Farming

About 34 per cent of the land area is arable, 9 per cent is under pasture and 32 per cent is used for forestry or is woodland. Farming is the most backward sector of the economy and crop yields and animal productivity are well below the EU average due to a legacy of low agricultural investment, minimal machinery, little use of fertiliser, poor soil quality and a fragmented land tenure system.

The agricultural sector is subject to the reformed Common Agricultural Policy (CAP), whereby subsidies are no longer paid on farm output, which tended to benefit large farms and encourage overproduction, but rather on single farm payments not conditional on production.

Portugal is the world's largest exporter of tomato paste and a leading exporter of wine. Its principal agricultural imports are wheat and meat.

The main crops grown in Portugal are cereals (wheat, barley, corn and rice), potatoes, grapes, olives and tomatoes.

Fishing

The waters around Portugal are rich fishing grounds. Sardines, anchovies and tuna are caught near the coast and species such as cod are caught by deep sea trawlers in the North Atlantic.

Portugal's territorial waters were ceded to the EU on its accession. This stimulated investment of the fishing sector and helped modernise the industry.

Forestry

Portugal's forests are a major natural resource. More than one-third of the country's total continental territory (3.1 million hectares out of a total of 8.9 million hectares) is forested, notably with pine, cork oak and eucalyptus. More than 90 per cent of forested land is privately owned, the highest proportion in the EU. Portugal's cork production supplies around 52 per cent of the world market. Cork forests are declining and being replaced by eucalyptus plantations as plastic corks become more popular in wine bottles. Eucalyptus trees are contributing to desertification as they require large amounts of water to grow.

The summers of 2003 and 2005 saw large-scale devastation of Portugal's forests through fire, particularly in the north and centre of the country. In 2003 alone, 215,000 hectares, an area approximately the size of Luxembourg, were destroyed.

Industry and manufacturing

Although it contributes around 38 per cent to GDP and employs 32 per cent of the workforce, industry remains relatively underdeveloped and dependent on imported energy and materials.

Portugal faces a difficult transition from traditional industries – clothing, textiles and footwear – afflicted by low value-added products, inefficient management and outmoded technology, to a diversified industrial base.

Important industries include processed cork, paper, cement, fertilisers, steel and glassware. High-growth sectors include vehicle manufacture, semiconductors, electronics, plastics, food processing and franchising.

Tourism

Portugal is said to have an Atlantic front and Mediterranean heart. Its history is interwoven with world events, as its pioneering explorers opened up sea routes to start an empire spanning three continents. Portugal has 13 sites on the UN World Heritage list, including prehistoric rock art, the historic centre of Oporto, the landscape of Sintra and the largest surviving laurel forest (on the island of Medeira). Its lush northern lands produce the grapes necessary for its famous ports (fortified wines) and its sun-bathed southern regions attract many tourism from Northern Europe in particular.

Travel and tourism is an important component of the economy and typically accounts for 13–14 per cent of GDP and employs 16–17 per cent of workers annually. The global economic crisis impacted on the sector with visitor revenue falling from a high of US$14 billion in 2008 to US$12.3 billion in 2009; in 2010 spending increased marginally to US$12.9 billion and further still to an anticipated US$13.3 billion in 2011.

Capital investment in travel and tourism has included the increased use of broadband internet connections to boost bookings. In 2011 such investment was estimated to be over 10 per cent of total capital investment.

Mining

The mining sector contributes around 1 per cent of GDP and employs a similar fraction of the workforce. Although there is considerable mineral wealth, deposits are scattered and not easily exploitable on a large scale. The most important mineral resources include non-metallic ores such as rock salt, pyrites (the reserves in the Alentejo region make up nearly 23 per cent of total worldwide reserves) and excellent quality marble. Large reserves of uranium are also available. Small-scale mining of tin, copper, tungsten concentrates, marble, stone and iron pyrites takes place.

Hydrocarbons

There are no known oil reserves so Portugal is investing over US$35 million (2006–11) in renewable energies in a concerted effort to reduce its hydrocarbon imports.

The state-owned Galp Energia (Petróleos e Gás de Portugal) is responsible for oil and gas businesses. It controls the only refining company Petrogal, which operates two oil refineries with a total capacity of 304,174 barrels per day (bpd) and its distribution operation, plus GDP which is responsible for natural gas imports, transport and distributions. It also has foreign energy interests, including exploration and production and energy generation.

Consumption of natural gas has grown considerably from 116 million cubic metres (cum) in 1997 to 4.4 billion cum by 2005. In 2009 the Algerian state-owned Sonatrach which had been supplying 2.5 billion cum, was given a licence to sell its natural gas directly to Portuguese consumers, to be supplied via the Maghreb-Europe gas pipeline, and assuring Portugal's long-term energy supply.

A liquid natural gas (LNG) re-gasification terminal has been built at the port of Setubal, south of Lisbon, connected by a pipeline extended along the Atlantic coast to the northern town of Braga. The pipeline is linked to the European natural gas network via Spain, providing an alternative source of supply for Europe. LNG is imported from Algeria and Nigeria.

Reserves of coal are scarce and of poor quality, production ceased in 1994. Any use of coal is commercially insignificant.

Energy

Total installed generating capacity was 12.2 gigawatts (GW) in 2005.

Portugal has invested heavily in renewable energies and in 2008 had the world's largest photovoltaic (Serpa solar power plant) energy project, with an 11MW power plant, covering 61 hectares, producing 3,000MW hours (at maximum output), located in the south of the country. Another, larger solar plant is under construction nearby. In the north, the world's first commercial wave farm, offshore near Póvoa de Varzim, was opened in 2008. Wind farms provide 2,124MW in 2008, with an additional 908MW under construction.

Energias de Portugal (EdP) is the national power utility and one of the largest energy companies in Europe. Portugal and Spain's electricity grids are integrated.

Financial markets

Stock exchange

Euronext NV Lisbon

Commodity exchange

Liffe Connect

Banking and insurance

In 2008 the government announced it was going to nationalise Banco Portugues de Negócios after the bank ran up losses of almost US$900 million.

Central bank

Banco de Portugal (Bank of Portugal); European Central Bank (ECB).

Main financial centre

Lisbon

Time

GMT (daylight saving, late March to late October, GMT plus one hour)

Geography

Mainland Portugal lies on the west side of the Iberian peninsula with the furthermost point of western Europe jutting into the Atlantic Ocean. The 837km coastline runs down along the west and south coast. Spain borders Portugal in the north and east. There are two archipelagos in the Atlantic Ocean – the Azores and the Madeira Islands.

All inclusive, Portugal is 92,080 square km in size. There are six major rivers, three of which rise in Spain and flow into the Atlantic Ocean. The Duoro in the mountainous north runs east-west across the country and used to provide an important shipping route. It flows through the city of Oporto. The longest river, the Tagus, has a large estuary, on which the capital, Lisbon, sits and is navigable for over 100km by seagoing ships. The Guadiana in the south, forms part of the border with Spain. The tallest peaks at 1,991 meters (m) are in the Serra da Estrela, in central Portugal. In the south the land is rolling hills and plains.

Lying south-west of the European mainland, the Azores consist of three scattered groups of nine inhabited islands and several uninhabitable ones, and include 12 active volcanoes. The Madeira archipelago is west of North Africa and has only two inhabited islands. The Azores and Madeira are volcanic in origin with steep topographies, the tallest – and youngest due to the continued lava flows that add to its mass – is located on Pico (Azores), at 2,321m high.

Hemisphere

Northern

Climate

Situated in the middle of the northern hemisphere, Portugal has a mild welcoming climate. However, the difference between the north/south and coast/inland weather is marked. Inland areas have more variable weather than coastal regions. To the south of the Tagus river the Mediterranean influences are clear. Long, hot, humid summers and dry, short, relatively mild winters. May–October dry and warm, November–April cool with rain in north, mild in south (though often wet and windy January–March). Temperatures vary between 8–28 Celsius.

Dress codes

Business people dress conservatively in dark blue or grey suits and ties.

Entry requirements

Passports

Required by all, except members of the EU, EEA and Switzerland who may use a valid national ID card. Passports must be valid for at least three months from date of arrival.

Visa

Required by all, except nationals of EU and Schengen Accord signatory countries, North America, Australasia and Japan. For further exceptions contact the nearest Portuguese consulate or a travel agent. Schengen visas cover all entry needs..For business trips, an original invitation from a business contact in Portugal is necessary, plus proof of accommodation booking and a letter from an employer giving the purpose and duration of the visit, when applying. A Schengen visa application (offered in several languages) can be downloaded from http://europa.eu/abc/travel/ see 'documents you will need'.

Currency advice/regulations

The import of local and foreign currency is unlimited but amounts over eur5,000 should be declared on entry. Export of local currency is limited to eur5,000 and an equivalent amount in foreign currency may require currency exchange receipts to be produced.

Travellers cheques are readily accepted.

Customs

Personal items are duty-free. There are no duties levied on alcohol and tobacco between EU member states, providing amounts imported are for personal consumption only. The export of luxury goods, such as gold, silver and jewellery, is limited to the value of eur150, without special permission.

Health (for visitors)
Nationals of the European Economic Area (EEA) countries and Switzerland can access reduced cost and sometimes free medical treatment using a European Health Insurance Card (EHIC) while visiting the EEA. Exceptions include nationals of the 10 countries, which joined the EU in 2004, whose EHIC is not valid in Switzerland. Applications for the EHIC should be made before travelling.

Mandatory precautions
Yellow fever vaccination certificate required for Azores and Madeira only if arriving from infected areas.

Advisable precautions
Immunisations that may be recommended is for hepatitis A and tuberculosis (although not for a short duration stay).

Hotels
A full range of hotels are available throughout the country, and are classified from one- to five-star. There is a 10 per cent service charge but a tip is also expected.

Credit cards
All usual credit cards are widely accepted. ATMs are readily available.

Public holidays (national)

Fixed dates
1 Jan (New Year's Day), 25 Apr (Liberty Day), 1 May (Labour Day), 10 Jun (Portugal Day), 15 Aug (Assumption Day), 5 Oct (Republic Day), 1 Nov (All Saints' Day), 1 Dec (Restoration of Independence Day), 8 Dec (Immaculate Conception), 25 Dec (Christmas).

Variable dates
Carnival (Feb), Good Friday (Mar/Apr), Corpus Christi (May/Jun).

Working hours

Banking
Mon–Fri: 0830–1500. Some banks in Lisbon open until 1800.

Business
Mon–Fri: 0900–1300 and 1500–1900.

Government
Mon–Fri: 0930–1200 and 1430–1800, closed 1730 on Mon and Tue.

Shops
Mon–Fri: 0900–1300, 1500–1900; Sat: 0900/1000–1300 general shops.
Mon–Sun: 1000–2300/2400 shopping centres/malls.

Telecommunications

Mobile/cell phones
There are 900/1800 and 3G GSM services available throughout the country.

Electricity supply
220V AC, with two round-pin plugs.

Social customs/useful tips
The Portuguese like to entertain. Lunch usually takes place between 1200 and 1400, dinner between 1900 and 2200. The Portuguese are extremely courteous, helpful and open to foreigners. Men always shake hands when they meet strangers or male friends. Women often kiss each other or their male friends once on each cheek.
It is impolite to refuse an offer of coffee. Tips should be given to anyone who carries out a service for you. There is no set rule on how much to tip.

Getting there

Air
National airline: TAP-Air Portugal.
International airport/s: Lisbon (LIS), 7km north of capital. Facilities include 24-hour *bureau de change*, banks, tourist information, post office, duty-free shops and car hire.
A special *aerobus* departs for the city centre every 20 minutes. Other express buses run to the railway station and other destinations around the country. Taxis are available, with a surcharge after 2200hrs.
Other airport/s: Oporto (OPO), 11km from city, Faro (FAO), 4km from city; Funchal (FNC) on Maderia; and Santa Maria (SMA) in the Azores, 3.2km from Vila do Porto.
Airport tax: None

Surface
Road: There are only road connections with Spain, of which the principle are motorways (with tolls), these in turn connect to the trans-European road network. Smaller cross-border roads maintain traditional routes.
Rail: There are four cross-border railway lines from Spain via either Salamanca, Santiago de Compostela, Badajoz or Madrid, which is the hub for lines to France.
Water: There are car ferry services from Plymouth or Portsmouth (UK) to Santander or Bilbao (northern Spain) respectively, from March–December.
The islands of Madeira and Azores have regular ferry services to the mainland of Spain and Portugal as well as to Grand Canary and Cape Verde.
Main port/s: The three most important ports are Lisbon, Leixes (Oporto) and Sines (south of Lisbon).

Getting about

National transport
Air: TAP and domestic charter airlines operate scheduled flights between most major cities, Madeira and the Azores.
Road: The Lisbon-Oporto, Lisbon-Algarve and Lisbon-Badajoz roads are national highway, toll roads. The road network has been upgraded in recent years and while local roads can often be narrow they link all rural communities with provincial roads.
Buses: Regular coach services, *Expresso* are inter-city and *Rápidas* link major regional towns, they can provide a quicker alternative service than by rail, although with a relatively higher priced ticket.
Rail: Caminhos de Ferro Portugueses (CP) operates about 3,600km of track, of which 500km are electrified. The *Alfa Pendular* provides a high-speed service between Oporto-Faro via Lisbon (journey time around six hours) reservations must be made and bookings can be made online. Regional services are available between cities and main towns.
Water: The 800km of inland waterways are only rarely used. Some coastal shipping operates, including services to Madeira and the Azores.

City transport
Taxis: Lisbon taxis are green and black. They are relatively cheap and offer an efficient service. A tip of 15 per cent is expected. Taxis may be scarce during rush-hours.
Buses, trams & metro: Lisbon has some steep climbs and there are three *elevadors* (funiculars – cable cars) from Baixa to the Bairro Alto neighbourhood and the Santa Justa. Buses run throughout the city.
The metro (from 0630–0100) provides four lines within the city and links to five suburban lines. the remaining services for the city.
Other cities and towns have public bus services.
Ferry: There are two ferry companies operating in Lisbon on the river Tagus. CP provides links from the city centre to Barreiro, on the south shore, which connects with the railway line to the Algarve. Transtejo provides services to Montijo, Seixal and Cacilhas.

Car hire
Self-drive and chauffeur-driven cars are available throughout the country.
An international driving licence or full national licence is required, as well as an international insurance Green Card. The wearing of seat belts is compulsory and all vehicles must carry a warning red triangle and warning waistcoats (fluorescent jackets) when leaving a vehicle during a breakdown or emergency.
Detailed motoring information is available from Automovel Clube de Portugal in Lisbon.
Driving in Portugal can be hazardous. In proportion to the number of vehicles, the country has one of the highest death and accident rates in Europe.

BUSINESS DIRECTORY

The addresses listed below are a selection only. While World of Information makes every endeavour to check these addresses, we cannot guarantee that changes have not been made, especially to telephone numbers and area codes. We would welcome any corrections.

Telephone area codes

The international dialling code (IDD) for Portugal is +351, followed by area code and subscriber's number:

Beja	284	Faro	289
Braga	253	Lisbon	21
Braganca	273	Madeira	291
Coimbra	239	Oporto	22
Covilha	275	Ponta Delgado	296

Chambers of Commerce

American Chamber of Commerce in Portugal, 155 Rua D Estefânia, 1000-154 Lisbon (tel: 357-2561; fax: 357-2580; e-mail: nop37676@mail.telepac.pt).

British-Portuguese Chamber of Commerce, 8 Rua da Estrela, 1200-669 Lisbon (tel: 394-2020; fax: 394-2029; e-mail: info@bpcc.pt).

Coimbra Chamber of Commerce and Industry, Rua Coronel Júlio Veiga Simão, Edificio Novotecna, 3020-260 Coimbra (tel: 497-160; fax: 494-066; e-mail: geral@cec.org.pt).

Madeira Chamber of Commerce and Industry, 41 Avenida Arriaga, 9004-507 Funchal (tel: 206-800; fax: 206-868; e-mail: geral@acif-ccim.pt).

Oporto Chamber of Commerce and Industry, Rua Ferreira Borges, Palácio da Bolsa, 4050-253 Oporto (tel: 399-000; fax: 399-090; e-mail: cciporto@mail.telepac.pt).

Ponta Delgada Chamber of Commerce and Industry, 13 Rua Ernsto do Canto, 9504-531 Ponta Delgada, Azores (tel: 305-000; fax: 305-050; e-mail: ccipd@ccipd.pt).

Portuguese Chamber of Commerce and Industry, 89 Rua das Portas de Santo Antão, 1169-022 Lisbon (tel: 322-4050; fax: 322-4051; e-mail: geral@port-chambers.com).

Banking

Associação Portuguesa de Bancos (Portuguese Bankers' Association), 35 Avenida da República, Lisbon (tel: 357-9804; fax: 357-9533, 352-9682).

Banco BPI SA, Rua do Comércio 132, Lisbon (tel: 887-4801, 887-3161, 311-1000; fax: 346-7308).

Banco Comercial Português SA, International Division, Rua Augusta 62—74, Lisbon (tel: 321-1780, 312-5936; fax: 321-1789; e-mail: dint@bcp.pt); Investor Relations Division (tel: 321-1080; e-mail: investors@bcp.pt).

Banco Espírito Santo e Com de Lisbon, Avenida da Liberdade 195, Lisbon (tel: 315-8331; fax: 353-2931, 350-8977).

Banco Internacional de Crédito, Avenida Fontes Pereira de Melo 27, Lisbon (tel/fax: 315-7135).

Banco Mello, Av José Malhoa, Lote 1682, Lisbon (tel: 720-1500; fax: 720-1766, 720-1599; e-mail: investor@bancomello.pt).

Banco Nacional Ultramarino (commercial bank), Av 5 de Outubro 175, Lisbon (tel: 793-3223, 793-0112; fax: (International Department) 793-8952).

Banco Pinto e Sotto Mayor (commercial bank), Rua do Ouro 28, Lisbon (tel: 340-3000, 347-6261; fax: (International Department) 357-3973).

Banco Português do Atlântico SA, Tagus Park, Edif Serv 1, Piso 2, Oeiras (tel: 422-4000; fax: 422-4489).

Banco Santander Portugal SA, Praça Marquês de Pombal 2, Lisbon (tel: 310-7000; fax: 315-4963).

Banco Totta & Açores SA (commercial bank), Rua do Ouro 88, Lisbon (tel: 321-3000; fax: 321-1582).

Caixa Geral de Depósitos (savings bank), International Department, Largo do Calhariz, Lisbon (tel: 790-5018; fax: 790-5068).

Central Banco de Investimento SA, Rua Castilho 233-4, Lisbon (tel: 386-4097; fax: 387-3208).

Credito Predial Português, Rua Augusta 237, Lisbon (tel: 321-4200; fax: (International Department) 313-7438).

Finibanco, Av de Berna, 10-1064, Lisbon (tel: 790-2800; fax: 790-2801).

Central bank

Banco de Portugal, 27 Rua do Ouro 1100-150 Lisbon (tel: 321-3200; fax: 346-4843; email: info@bportugal.pt).

European Central Bank (ECB), Kaiserstrasse 29, D-60311 Frankfurt am Main, Germany (tel: (+49-69) 13-440; fax: (+49-69) 1344-6000; email: info@ecb.int).

Stock exchange

Euronext NV Lisbon: www.euronext.com

Stock exchange 2

Chi-X: www.chi-x.com:

Commodity exchange

Liffe Connect: www.nyse.com/nyseeuronext

Travel information

Comissão Municipal de Turismo de Lisboa, Pavilhao Carlos Lopes, Parque Eduardo VII, 1070 Lisbon (tel: 315-1915/6/7/8; fax: 352-1472).

Comissão Municipal de Turismo do Oporto, Rua Clube dos Fenianos 25, 4000 Oporto (tel: 323-303, 312-543; fax: 208-4548).

Costa Verde Tourism Office, Praça D Joao I 43, 4000 Oporto (tel: 317-514).

Lisbon Airport Tourism Office, 1700 Lisbon (tel: 849-4323/3689; fax: 848-5974).

Lisbon Tourist Office, Palácio Foz, Praça dos Restauradores, 1200 Lisbon (tel: 346-3314/3643; fax: 346-8772).

Madeira Tourism Office, Avenida Arriaga 18, 9000 Funchal (tel: (+091) 229-057, 225-658; fax: (+091) 232-151; internet: www.madeiraguide.com).

Pousadas of Portugal, Rua Soares de Passos, 3 Alto de Santo Amaro, 1300-314 Lisbon (tel: 844-2001; fax: 844-2085; internet: www.pousadas.pt).

Regiao de Turismo da Planicie Dourada, Praca da Republica 12, 7800 Beja (tel: 321-369; fax: 326-332).

National tourist organisation offices

Portuguese Tourism Board (ITP), Rua Ivone Silva, Lote 6, 1050-124 Lisbon (tel: 781-0000; fax: 793-7537; email: info@iturismo.pt; internet: www.iturismo.pt).

Ministries

Ministry of Agriculture, Food and Fisheries, Praça do Comércio, 1149-010 Lisbon (tel: 346-3151; fax: 347-7890).

Ministry of Culture, Palácio Nacional da Ajuda, 1349-003 Lisbon (tel: 361-4500; fax: 364-9999).

Ministry of Defence, Avenida Ilha da Madeira, 1400-204 Lisbon (tel: 303-4500; fax: 303-4525).

Ministry of Economy, Rua da Horta Seca 15, 1200-221 Lisbon (tel: 322-8600; fax: 322-8741).

Ministry of Education, Avenida 5 de Outubro 107-13, 1069-018 Lisbon (tel: 795-0330; fax: 793-3618).

Ministry for Employment, Praça de Londres 2-14, 1049-056 Lisbon (tel: 844-1700; fax: 847-0027).

Ministry of the Environment, Rua do Século 51-2, 1200-433 Lisbon (tel: 3223-2500; fax: 323-2531).

Ministry of Finance, Avenida Infante D Henriques 5, 1149-009 Lisbon (tel: 888-4675; fax: 886-0032).

Ministry of Foreign Affairs, Largo do Rilvas, 11399-030 Lisbon (tel: 394-6000; fax: 390-9708).

Ministry of Health, Avenida João Crisóstomo 9-6, 1049-062 Lisbon (tel: 354-4560; fax: 354-0302).

Ministry of Home Affairs, Praça do Comércio, 1149-015 Lisbon (tel: 323-3000; fax: 342-7372).

Ministry of Industry and Energy, Rua da Horta Seca 15, 1200 Lisbon (tel: 346-3091/6091; fax: 347-5901).

Ministry of Justice, Praça do Comércio, 1149-019 Lisbon (322-2300; fax: 347-9208).

Ministry of Planning, Public Works and Territorial Administration, Palacio Penafiel, Rua de S Mamede ao Caldas 21, 1149-050 Lisbon (tel: 886-1119; fax: 886-3827).

Ministry of Science and Technology, Praça do Comércio - Ala Oriental, 1149-003 Lisbon (tel: 881-2000; fax: 888-2434).

Ministry of Social Security, Rua Rosa Araújo 43, 1250-194 Lisbon (tel: 353-0049; fax: 353-0074).

Prime Minister's Office, Rua da Imprensa a Estrela 2, 1200 Lisbon (tel: 397-4091; fax: 395-1616).

Other useful addresses

Agencia de Informação LUSA (news agency), Rua Dr João Couto, Lote C, Lisbon (tel: 714-4099).

Associação Industrial Portuguesa, Apt 5200, Praça das Indústrias, 1301 Lisbon (tel: 360-1500).

Associação Industrial Portuense, Avenida da Boavista 2671, Oporto (tel: 615-8500; fax: 617-6840).

Bolsa de Valores de Lisboa (Lisbon Stock Exchange), Edificio da Bolsa, Rua Soeiro Pereira Gomes, Lisbon (tel: 790-0000; fax: 795-2021; e-mail: Infomktg@bvl.pt; internet site: www.bvl.pt/).

Comissão Co-ordenação Regiao (CCR) Norte, Rua Rainha D Estefania 251, Oporto (tel: 695-236/7/8/9/0; fax: 600-2040).

CCR Algarve, Praça da Liberdade 2, Faro (tel: 802-401; fax: 803-591).

CCR Lisboa e Vale do Tejo, Rua Artilharia Um 33, Lisbon (tel: 387-5541; fax: 691-292).

Instituto de Apoio às Pequenas e Médias Empresas Industriais (IAPMEI), Rua Rodrigo da Fonseca 73, Lisbon (tel: 562-211).

Instituto Nacional de Estatistica (INE), Av António José de Almeida 2, Lisbon (tel: 847-0050; fax: 848-9480; internet site: www.ine.pt).

Investimentos Comércio e Turismo de Portugal (ICEP), (e-mail: icepdiesnar@mail.telepac.pt; internet: www.icep.pt).

Portugal Telecom (PT), Investor Relations, Lisbon (tel: 500-1701, 500-8739; e-mail: manuel.j.castela@telecom.pt).

Portuguese Embassy (USA), 2125 Kalorama Road, NW, Washington DC 20008 (tel: (+1-202) 328-8610; fax: (+1-202) 462-3726; e-mail: embportwash@mindspring.com).

Privatisation Office, c/o Ministério das Finanças – Commissão de Acompanhamento das Privatizacões (c/o Ministry of Finance – Commission for the Accompaniment of Privatisations), Av Infante D Henrique 5, Lisbon (tel: 618-0057).

Radiotelevisão Portuguesa – RTP (Portugal's radio/television broadcaster), 197 Avenida 5 de Outubro, Lisbon (tel: 793-1774; fax: 796-6227).

Sociedade de Desenvolvimento da Madeira SA (SDM), 1st Floor, 9 Rua da Mouraria; PO Box 4164, Funchal, Madeira (tel: (351-291) 201-333; fax: (351-291) 201-399; email: sdm@sdm.pt; internet site: www.sdmadeira.pt).

Sociedade Independente de Comunicação – SIC (independent broadcasting company), 119 Estrada da Outurela, Carnaxide, Linda a Velha (tel: 417-3138; fax: 417-3118).

Televisão Independente – TVI (independent television broadcasting), Pt16-s 603-B Rua 3, Matinha, Lisbon (tel: 858-7968; fax: 858-2319).

National news agency: Lusa News Press Agency, Rua Dr Joao Couto, Lote C P 1503-809 Lisbon (tel: 711-6500; email: agencialusa@lusa.pt; internet:www.lusa.pt).

Other news agencies: Photonews (Agência Noticiosa) (www.photonews.com.pt)

Internet sites

Guide to business: www.portugaloffer.pt

Icep Portugal (business promotion): www.portugalinbusiness.com

Portugal portal: www.portugal.org

Lisbon Airport: www.ana-aeroportos.pt

Tourist portal: www.portugalvisitor.com

Yellow Pages: www.paginasamarelas.pt

Puerto Rico

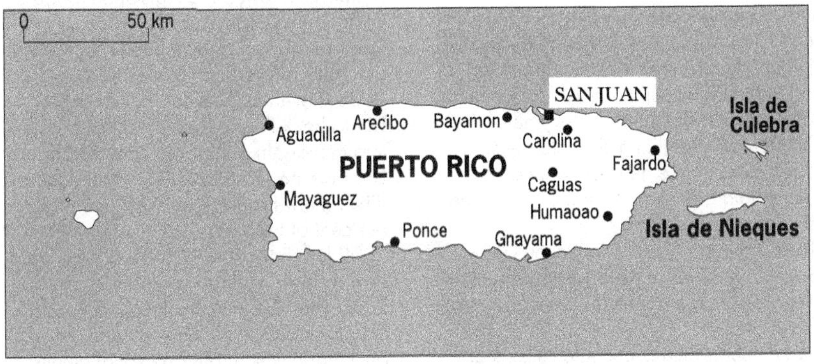

In June 2011, President Barack Obama made the first official US presidential visit to Puerto Rico since 1962. This was not out of a desire to sample the island's 'tropical breezes', nor of concern for the incidence of 'tropic diseases'. He was directly appealing to a powerful bloc of voters, some of whom were thousands of miles away - the 4.6 million Puerto Ricans in the mainland United States.

Citizens of Puerto Rico cannot vote in the US House of Representatives (Congress), Senate or presidential elections (although they can vote for candidates to become presidential candidates). But their relatives living in the US can vote at all levels of political representation, hence President Obama's visit.

Puerto Ricans in US

Nearly one in five of US-based Puerto Ricans - more than 847,000 - live in Florida, up by 75 per cent since 2000, according to census figures. The growth rate was even more rapid in central Florida, where 300,000 now live. Puerto Ricans, inspired by their Cuban cousins, are seeking to establish themselves as the next political force in Florida, very much as the Cuban-American community did two decades ago.

Despite these ethnic concentrations, the influx of Puerto Ricans to the mainland US hasn't been reflected in elected offices. There is only one Puerto Rican in the Florida State Legislature. None represents Florida in Congress and only a few hold local office. Puerto Rican activists were trying to get districts that are being redrawn by local governments and the US Legislature to favour the election of Hispanics. Puerto Ricans make up 13 per cent of the population of Orange County, 27 per cent of Osceola County and 8 per cent of Seminole, far and away the highest concentrations in the state. It is anticipated these changes will lead to Puerto Rican success in the 2012 elections, including Puerto Rican county commissioners, legislators and members of Congress.

Companies from the US mainland once flocked to Puerto Rico to set up factories in the island's tax-free environment. Towns like Barceloneta, population 20,000, found themselves hosting dozens of pharmaceutical companies. Called 'Viagra town' by some due to the amount of the drug produced there, Barceloneta was almost totally dependent upon pharmaceutical companies for employment and revenue needs. However, lower production costs elsewhere in Latin America and Asia have forced companies to either relocate of close.

Cuban support

In June 2011, at a UN decolonisation committee meeting, Cuba's permanent representative to the condemned US inertia in progressing a process of decolonisation for Puerto Rico, saying that Puerto Ricans were unable to exercise their legitimate right to genuine self-determination,

Constitutional status - same again

In 2011, a special US presidential taskforce for the third time advocated holding a referendum on whether or not

KEY FACTS

Official name: Estado Libre Asociado de Puerto Rico (Commonwealth of Puerto Rico)

Head of State: US President Barack Obama

Head of government: Governor Luis Fortuño (PNP) (from 2 Jan 2009)

Ruling party: Partido Nuevo Progresista (PNP) (New Progressive Party) (from 2 Jan 2009)

Area: 8,897 square km (Puerto Rico comprises the main island plus two smaller islands (Vieques and Culebra) and numerous smaller islets.)

Population: 3.73 million (2010; census figure)

Capital: San Juan

Official language: Spanish, English

Currency: US dollar (US$) = 100 cents

Exchange rate: US$1.00 per US$ (fixed rate)

GDP per capita: US$15,690 (2009)

GDP real growth: -3.80% (2010)

GDP: US$63.80 billion (2010)

Inflation: -3.80% (2010)

Balance of trade: US$20.16 billion (2009)*

* estimated figure

Puerto Ricans wanted a change in the status of their island. In the case of a 'yes' vote, a second referendum on whether the island's people wanted outright independence or to become the 51st state of the USA would be held. Although support for independence in Puerto Rico rarely shows over 3 per cent support in opinion polls, many Puerto Ricans still regarded it as a possible option.

Puerto Rico has one resident commissioner in the Congress of United States, but as of January 2011 the commissioner no longer had the right to vote in committees. The political situation within the island commonwealth is more varied than that in mainland US. The major political parties are the opposition Partido Popular Democrático (PPD) (Popular Democratic Party), which supports an enhanced commonwealth status, the ruling Partido Nuevo Progresista (PNP) (New Progressive Party), which supports full US statehood for the island and Partido Independentista Puertorriqueño (PIP) (Puerto Rican Independence Party), which supports the independence from the US. PPD followers are known as *los populares* and identified by the colour red. PNP followers are known as *los penepes* and identified by the colour blue. PIP followers are known as *los pipiolos* and identified by the colour green.

Other fringe political groups include the Fuerzas Armadas de Liberación Nacional (FALN) (Armed Forces for National Liberation), Voluntarios por la Revolución Puertorriqueña (VRP) (Volunteers of the Puerto Rican Revolution), Fuerzas Armadas de la Resistencia Popular (FARP) (Armed Forces of Popular Resistance). There is little evidence of armed insurrections being planed or even considered by any of the above.considered by any of the above.

Risk assessment

Economy	Fair (heavily subsidised)
Politics	Fair (underrepresented in US)
Regional stability	Good

COUNTRY PROFILE

Historical profile

1493 The island was inhabited by some 100,000 Taíno Indians (an Arawak culture that also occupied most of Hispaniola and part of Cuba) at the time of the first European sighting by Columbus.
1508 Juan Ponce de Léon landed from Hispaniola and took control of the island. He named it San Juan.
1898 The island was ceded to the US by Spain at the end of the Spanish-American war. The US ruled it as an unincorporated territory.
1917 Puerto Ricans became citizens of the US.
1948 Puerto Rico elected Luis Muñoz Marín as its first governor.
1952 A new constitution designated Puerto Rico a self-governing commonwealth within the US.
1967 A plebiscite rejected the option of becoming a state of the US.
1993 The statehood option was rejected for a second time in a national referendum.
1998 The option of statehood was narrowly rejected in favour of maintaining the constitutional *status quo*.
2000 Sila Maria Calderón Serra became the first female governor. Partido Popular Democrático (PPD) (Popular Democratic Party) won the parliamentary elections.
2001 The Blue Riband Commission was empanelled to review large transactions made by the previous (Rosselló) administration.
2003 Closure of the US navy base on Vieques lost Puerto Rico an estimated US$300 million per year in revenues.
2004 Aníbal Acevedo Vilá won gubernatorial elections.
2005 Although a referendum approved the proposal that the Senate and House of Representatives be replaced by a unicameral legislature, the House of Representatives allowed the legislation to lapse.
2006 The US Supreme Court turned down an appeal to give Puerto Ricans voting rights in presidential elections.
2008 Governor Acevedo called on the UN to back Puerto Rico's right of self-determination. In gubernatorial elections, Luis Fortuño (Partido Nuevo Progresista (PNP) (New Progressive Party)) won 52.8 per cent of the vote.
2009 Luis Fortuño (PNP) was inaugurated as governor in January.
2010 The resident population of Puerto Rico took part in the United States census on 1 April, which, after personal details, included questions on race, housing and internet and mobile phone access. The government announced in June that existing birth certificates would be declared invalid and that all citizens would be issued with new ones by September in an effort to combat identity theft. Criminal organisations have targeted Puerto Rico as birth certificates of nationals give rights to US passports; the US State Department had discovered that around 40 per cent of fraudulent US passport applications were using birth certificates from Puerto Rico. In the first step in the process, on 30 April, the US House of Representatives voted to allow a referendum in Puerto Rico on statehood and possible independence; the measure must also be passed by the US Senate. On 30 April US banking regulators shut down three Puerto Rican banks and sold their deposits to other financial institutions. The move cost the Federal Deposit Insurance Corporation (FDIC) US$5.3 billion as the banks were insolvent and unable to trade due to large numbers of unsustainable loans. In May, the US pharmaceutical company, Pfizer, closed its chemical plant in Puerto Rico with the loss of 6,000 jobs at a time of high unemployment.
2011 In March, the Republican controlled Congress voted to rescind the voting rites of representations of American Samoa, Guam, CNMI, Puerto Rico and the US Virgin Islands, effectively disenfranchising their electorate in policies that directly affect them.

Political structure

Constitution

The local government consists of executive, legislative and judicial branches.

KEY INDICATORS — Puerto Rico

	Unit	2006	2007	2008	2009	2010
Population	m	3.93	*3.96	*4.00	*4.00	3.73
Gross domestic product (GDP)	US$bn	56.70	58.60	60.80	62.80	63.80
GDP per capita	US$	14,427	14,873	15,392	15,690	–
GNP real growth	%	0.5	-1.2	-2.9	-4.0	-3.8
Inflation	%	15.1	3.0	9.6	0.3	2.5
Unemployment	%	10.4	10.9	11.6	–	–
Exports (fob) (goods)	US$m	60,119.0	61,321.0	*63,954.0	*60,808.0	–
Imports (fob) (goods)	US$m	42,630.0	46,041.0	*44,929.0	*40,652.0	–
Balance of trade	US$m	17,489.0	15,280.0	*19,025.0	*20,156.0	–
Exchange rate	per US$	1.00	1.00	1.00	1.00	1.00

* estimated figure

Puerto Rico has 78 municipal governments.
Detailed laws governing the status and relationship of the Commonwealth of Puerto Rico with the US cover, among other aspects: military conscription, tax and trade, social security, citizenship, constitutional changes and internal autonomy.
There is universal suffrage from aged 18 years.

Form of state

Puerto Rico is an overseas commonwealth territory and freely associated state of the US.
Both the constitution of Puerto Rico and the US constitution are applicable. Puerto Rican nationals are US citizens but do not vote in US presidential elections.

The executive

The Head of State is the president of the US.
Executive power is exercised by the governor, elected by popular vote every four years, who leads a cabinet of 15 ministers.

National legislature

The bicameral Asamblea Legislativa (Legislative Assembly) includes the Cámara de Representantes (Chamber of Representatives), with 51 members, elected for four-year terms, 40 elected in single-seat constituencies and 11 by proportional representation from a national list. Up to an additional three seats can be allocated to allow the opposition to have one-third of the seats.
The Senado (Senate) has 28 members, elected for four-year terms – 16 members elected in two-seat constituencies and 11 by proportional representation from a national list and one additional seat to allow the opposition to have one-third of the seats.

Legal system

The civil and commercial codes; penal, procedural, public (including constitutional) laws are fashioned after US models.

Last elections

4 November 2008 (gubernatorial and parliamentary)
Results: Gubernatorial: Luis Fortuño (PNP) won 52.8 per cent, Aníbal Acevedo Vilá (PDP) 41.3 per cent, three other candidates did not gain more than 3 per cent. Turnout was 78 per cent.
Senate: PNG won 17 seats (out of 27); PPD won nine seats; and Partido Independentista Puertorriqueño (PIP) (Puerto Rican Independence Party) one seat.
House of Representatives: PNG won 32 seats (out of 51); PPD won 18 seats; and PIP one seat.

Next elections

November 2012 (gubernatorial and parliamentary)

Political parties

Ruling party

Partido Nuevo Progresista (PNP) (New Progressive Party) (from 2 Jan 2009)

Main opposition party

Partido Popular Democrático (PPD) (Popular Democratic Party)

Population

3.73 million (2010; census figure)
Last census: April 2000: 3,808,610
Population density: 436 inhabitants per square km. Urban population: 76 per cent (World Bank 2002).
Annual growth rate: 0.9 per cent (2003); projected 0.7 per cent 2002–15.

Ethnic make-up

There is a fusion of three main cultures: native Indian, European and African.
The Spanish *conquistadores* initially came to the New World without wives or family and married into the native population, producing the *mestizo* (Spanish and Taío) and the *mulatto* (Spanish and African) groups.
The Spanish settlers brought in African slaves to work in the sugar cane plantations. When migration restrictions were relaxed, more Spanish came, together with a large contingent of Corsicans and a small number of Irish.
Thousands of mainland Americans have established themselves in Puerto Rico and migrants have also come from the Dominican Republic, Canada, Europe, Asia, Cuba and South and Central America.

Religions

99 per cent of the population are Christians (85 per cent Roman Catholic). Religion has traditionally played an important role in the island's history. The religious groups have been instrumental in fostering community co-operation and providing health and educational services.

Education

Six years of elementary (primary) school are followed by three years of junior high school and three years of senior high school. All teaching is conducted in Spanish, although English is a compulsory subject at all levels. There are 34 post-school educational institutions, both government and private. The State University has three main campuses and six colleges. Special training programmes are provided in technical and vocational schools, as well as on-the-job training for labour skills for which a workforce does not exist.
Literacy rate: 93.7 per cent male, 94 per cent female; adult rates (World Bank).
Compulsory years: Six to 16

Health

HIV/Aids

It is estimated that there are 7,397 people living with HIV/Aids.
Life expectancy: 79 (estimate 2005)
Fertility rate/Maternal mortality rate: 1.75 per woman (2005)
Birth rate/Death rate: 12.88 births and 7.54 deaths per 1,000 population (2005)
Child (under 5 years) mortality rate (per 1,000): 9.28 per 1,000 live births (2005)

Welfare

The US social security system is in operation, together with Puerto Rico's own health, unemployment, and workers' compensation schemes. Employer contributions to the unemployment and social security funds are compulsory. Despite a high per capita national income, about 60 per cent of the population were recorded as living below the official US poverty line, and 45 per cent of the population received federal food stamps. Federal medical aid is also provided. These provide an important cushion against the effects of unemployment, to which a further safety valve is supplied by emigration. There are more Puerto Ricans living in New York than in San Juan.

Main cities

San Juan (capital, population estimated at 421,356 in 2005), Bayamón (208,138), Ponce (153,496), Carolina (173,386).

Languages spoken

Spanish is the primary language of the vast majority of Puerto Ricans. English as an important second language is taught in public and private schools from first grade through to tertiary institutions. Government affairs are conducted in Spanish while English is the language of commerce.

Official language/s

Spanish, English

Media

Press

Dailies: The three main dailies widely circulated include *El Vocero de Puerto Rico* (www.vocero.com), *El Nuevo Día* (www.elnuevodia.com) and *Primera Hora* (www.primerahora.com). Other regional dailies and those published from San Juan are *El Impacto* (www.elimpacto.com) and *El Vocero* (www.vocero.com).
In English *San Juan Star* (www.thesanjuanstar.com) *Puerto Rico Herald* (www.puertorico-herald.org) (published by the statehood campaign) and *Caribbean Business* (http://pal.prwow.com).
Weeklies: *Caribbean Business*.
Business: A multilingual, regional publication *América Economía* (www.americaeconomia.com) is the leading magazine.
Periodicals: In Spanish *La Estrella de Puerto Rico* (www.periodicolaestrella.com), *El Expresso* (www.elexpresso.com), *La*

Esquina (www.laesquina.com), *El Periódico* (www.elperiodico.com), Bilingual (Spanish and English) publications include *El Boricua* (www.elboricua.com) featuring people and culture, *An(with a wavy line ontop)il* (www.plazaboricua.com).

Broadcasting

Radio: There are over 20 public and commercial radio stations, broadcasting news, music and special interest programmes. Spanish is the typical broadcast language including Radio Puerto Rico (www.radiopr740.com) and Sistema102 (www.sistema102.com); there is one local radio station broadcasting in English, WOSO (www.woso.com).

Television: The public broadcast service TUTV (www.tutv.puertorico.pr) transmits educational and international material. Other, commercial stations, Telemundo (http://tv.telemundo.yahoo.com), Televincento (www.wapa.tv) and Univision (http://univision.centennialpr.net) broadcast a wide variety of programmes in Spanish.

Around 115 national commercial radio stations and nine television stations broadcast. There are satellite TV broadcasts from several international sources.

Economy

The economy of Puerto Rico is influenced and affected by the US economy, from which it derives much of its commercial investment and federal aid. Over 45 per cent of GDP is generated by the manufacturing sector, much of which is hi-tech industries, including capital-intensive industries and knowledge intensive industries, such as pharmaceuticals, electronics and biotechnology. The service sector, which generates over 50 per cent of GDP is dominated by financial services (15 per cent of GDP alone) and includes construction, transport, communications, utilities and public services. Over five million visitors arrive each year – in 2008 tourism generated a record US$6.32 billion, which fell in 2009 to US$5.88 billion, before recovering in 2010 with a contribution to GDP of US$6.01 billion. Tourism employs 5.5–6.0 per cent of the work force. Agriculture accounts for less than 1 per cent of GDP.

Major improvements to Puerto Rico's business environment include the slashing of capital gains taxes and lowering operating costs for manufacturing plants. Puerto Ricans do not pay federal income taxes, and the local authorities have discretion to design tax incentives to attract foreign direct investment (FDI). The government has lobbied for permanent tax exemption status, saying this would be the best way to secure the Commonwealth's fiscal autonomy from the US federal government. With approximately 50 per cent of the economy supported by special exemptions for foreign firms, the repeal of tax incentives would severely undermine Puerto Rico's ability to compete with its Caribbean neighbours, prompting concern that the economy could collapse. Regional agreements such as the North American Free Trade Agreement (Nafta) made countries such as Mexico attractive low wage, tariff free alternatives to Puerto Rico.

Always susceptible to external shocks due to the reliance on imports, particularly petroleum products, the economy suffered with negative GDP growth from 2007 when it was -1.2 per cent (down from 0.5 per cent in 2006). Growth fell further to -2.9 per cent in 2008 as the global economic crisis cut visitor numbers while energy and food imports rose in price; by 2009 the economy was in deep recession with growth of -4 per cent, which remained negative in 2010 at -3.8 per cent. Inflation yo-yoed from 15.1 per cent in 2006 to 3.0 per cent in 2007, 9.6 per cent in 2008, 0.3 per cent in 2009 and climbing to 2.5 per cent in 2010. High unemployment, which is categorised as a long-term problem, reached 16.5 per cent in 2009.

External trade

As an overseas commonwealth territory of the United States, the US has authority over interstate trade, commerce and customs administration. Puerto Rico is part of the North American Free Trade Agreement (Nafta).

Since Nafta was signed, the level of exported manufactured goods has fallen as Mexico, with its lower unit costs, has become a major supplier to the US and Canada. However, while low paid jobs were lost to Mexico there was an increase in pharmaceutical and hi-tech manufacturing in Puerto Rico.

The US accounts for over 75 per cent of imports and exports. Most trade is intra-company shipments, as parts from US companies are imported and finished goods are exported in return. This flow of materials and products creates profits for private companies and jobs for workers in Puerto Rico and the US.

With few natural resources the balance of payments is still reliant on US federal aid and tax incentives.

Imports

Principal imports include petroleum and derivatives, chemicals, capital machinery and electronic components, textiles and yarns, raw and processed foodstuff, building materials and manufacturing raw materials.

Main sources: US (typically 50 per cent of total), Ireland (20 per cent), Nigeria (5 per cent).

Exports

Principal exports include chemicals, pharmaceuticals, medical products and equipment, finished goods, electronics, clothing, tuna and other fish products, beverages, tropical fruit, dairy and meat.

Main destinations: US (typically 76 per cent of total), Germany (5 per cent), The Netherlands (3 per cent).

Agriculture

Farming

The agricultural sector is small-scale and only contributes 0.3 per cent to GDP while employing 2 per cent of the workforce. Only 10 per cent of land is suitable for agriculture. An additional 25 per cent of the island is composed of uplands, partially suited for agricultural purposes. Dairy and livestock farming is of increasing importance.

Farming on the island has changed considerably since the 1940s and 1950s, when traditional small-scale farming methods prevailed and sugar cane, coffee and tobacco were the dominant crops. Of these, only coffee has survived, but it lags behind milk and poultry production. Milk production accounts for 34 per cent of total gross farm income. Changes in consumer preferences are slowly taking place as the population ages.

Around 90 per cent of food requirements are met by imports. Almost all of Puerto Rico's farm output is consumed locally, although small quantities of coffee are exported to Europe and Japan. Some fruit and vegetables, mangoes, tomatoes and onions also go to Europe.

Agriculture has been traditionally based on sugar, coffee, pineapples, plantains, bananas, livestock products and poultry. Sugar production declined during the 1980s, partly due to the closure of the Central Cambalache sugar mill in 1982. Coffee production meets only three-quarters of local demand but half of production is exported. Livestock production has not displayed the same rate of decline as arable agriculture, but is still insufficient to meet local demand. The cost of imported feed represents a major constraint on development.

Fishing

Although fishing is conducted on a relatively small scale, it is nevertheless important. Puerto Rico used to be a major tuna supplier to the USA but in recent times has faced a number of problems such as increased competition from south-east Asia. The annual production of processed fish is around 4,000 tonnes.

Industry and manufacturing

The industrial sector forms the mainstay of the economy, contributing approximately 42 per cent to GDP and employing 11 per cent of the workforce. Financial services produce 17 per cent of GDP and trade accounts for 11.6 per cent, other industries produce less than 10 per cent of GDP. Most of the island's manufacturing output is shipped to mainland US.

Industrialisation has been the focus of government economic policy since the late 1940s when a programme known as 'Operation Bootstrap' was launched. In 1950, there were 82 industrial plants in Puerto Rico, but by 1965 there were around 1,000. Since then industrial development has tended to be more capital intensive and dependent upon highly skilled labour.

Production is centred on food processing, textiles, petrochemicals, rum distilling, pharmaceuticals, metal fabrication and assembly of electrical/electronic components.

Most of the assembly industries are US-owned and are heavily dependent on the US market. Manufacturers exporting goods to the US benefit from being within the US Customs zone, with the US dollar as the local currency, and US legal protection of intellectual property – particularly useful for IT industries.

The US Commerce Department's Foreign Trade Zones Board has approved the conversion of all the island's industrial parks into free trade zones (FTZs). This, together with Puerto Rico's generous incentives package and skilled workforce has in the past made the island a prime destination for companies looking to expand or relocate. However, competition, from Mexico in particular, has had an adverse effect.

The island's agricultural industry makes an important contribution to the economy through the food industry services of prepared food and retail sales.

The pharmaceutical industry is crucial to Puerto Rico; 16 of the top 20 pharmaceutical drugs in the US are manufactured in Puerto Rico and all the leading US manufacturers are represented, some with major investments. In May 2010, the US pharmaceutical company, Pfizer, closed its chemical plant in Puerto Rico with the loss of 6,000 jobs at a time of high unemployment. There is heavy investment by US computer and electronics companies, footwear and rubber goods manufacturers. The K-Mart Corporation, the US retailing group, is well represented in Puerto Rico.

Tourism

Tourism is an important source of revenue and Puerto Rico benefits from its connection with the US, from where 80 per cent of visitors come. Although it is a major player in the region, the sector accounts for only around 7 per cent of GDP, a much lower share than other major destinations in the Caribbean.

To meet the growing pressure of competition from its neighbours, Puerto Rico has embarked on a vigorous programme of promotion and infrastructure development, with particular attention on the US and European markets. The new, self-contained, all-inclusive resort – Paradisus Puerto Rico, owned by Spain's Sol-Melia – comprises a 500 room hotel and individual accommodation, with sports, entertainment and convention centre. In 113 acres of the Puerto Rico Convention District, on the peninsula of Isla Grande, the US$415 million Convention Centre has over 175,000 square metres, it was the largest such facility in the Caribbean. Previously unexploited parts of the island are being marketed.

Mining

Activity in this area is extremely small – production is centred on non-metals such as stone, sand, salt and clay.

There are small unquantified reserves of copper, nickel, cobalt, iron, chromium, lead, gold and silver.

Hydrocarbons

There are no known hydrocarbon reserves and all needs are met by imports. Oil imports were 189,980 barrels per day (bpd) in 2008.

An oil refinery, operated by Caribbean Petroleum (GulfPR), sited in Bayamón and able to process 48,000bpd, is not currently operational.

Liquefied natural gas (LNG) imports were 708 million cubic metres (cum) in 2007, mainly from Trinidad and Tobago. A re-gasification terminal and power plant in Punta Guayanilla, Peñuelas, are owned and operated by the independent energy company EcoEléctrica.

All coal imports are used in the coal-fired power plant in Guayama.

Energy

Total installed generating capacity was 5.4 gigawatts in 2006. The Puerto Rico Electric Power Authority (Prepa) is responsible for generating, transmitting and distributing practically all electricity used. It is the second-largest municipally-owned US utility. Over 90 per cent of all energy is produced from petroleum sources. The independent energy company EcoEléctrica provides electricity from its liquefied natural gas (LNG) fired power plant to the power grid. Over 85MW is provided by hydropower. Many companies still maintain their own generators as essential back-up.

Banking and insurance

The Puerto Rican commercial banking system had comprised about 17 banks with around 300 branches in 2009. On 30 April 2010, US banking regulators shut down three Puerto Rican banks and sold their deposits to other financial institutions. The move cost the Federal Deposit Insurance Corporation (FDIC) US$5.3 billion as the banks were insolvent and unable to trade due to large numbers of unsustainable loans.

Major US banks include Citibank, Chase Manhattan and First National Bank of Boston. Foreign banks include Royal Bank of Canada, Bank of Nova Scotia, Banco Central de Madrid, Banco Bilbao Vizcaya and Banco de Santander.

Banco Popular de Puerto Rico, Puerto Rico's largest bank, continues to expand into US Hispanic markets.

Central bank

There is no central bank.

Such functions as fiscal agent for the Commonwealth of Puerto Rico and its public entities, and the provision of development loans to the public as well as the private sector, are undertaken by the Government Development Bank for Puerto Rico (GDB).

Time

GMT minus four hours

Geography

Puerto Rico comprises the main island, together with the small offshore islands of Vieques and Culebra and many other smaller islets, lying about 80km (50 miles) east of Hispaniola (Haiti and the Dominican Republic) in the Caribbean Sea. Roughly 160km long by 48km wide, Puerto Rico is the smallest and most westerly of the Greater Antilles. The centre of the island is composed of dead volcanoes, the highest of which, the Cordillera Central, has an elevation of 1,325 metres. To the north of the mountains lies a belt of broken limestone country, and then a fertile coastal plain. The whole island is well supplied with rivers. Only about 1 per cent of the country remains forested and is largely reserved.

Hemisphere

Northern

Climate

Tropical with extremes of heat tempered by constant sea winds. Temperatures are 28–30 degrees Celsius (C) in summer, and 21–26 degrees C in winter. Rainfall is heaviest in the second half of the year, especially June–October. Puerto Rico lies in the 'hurricane belt'.

Dress codes

Suits and ties are customary for businessmen since almost all offices are air conditioned. A jacket and tie may be required in first class restaurants. The Hispanic Caribbean *guayabera*, a long decorated shirt, is worn increasingly commonly.

Entry requirements

US entry requirements apply.

Passports

Required by all, valid for six months from date of entry.

Visa

Required by all, except nationals of Canada and Visa Waiver Scheme countries in possession of machine-readable passports; otherwise, visas must be applied for. Visits, for both tourism and business, and visas are valid for up to 90 days. A return/onward ticket is also required. Further information can be found at http://travel.state.gov.

Currency advice/regulations

There are no restrictions on the import or export of local and foreign currencies, subject to declaration of amounts in excess of US$10,000.

Health (for visitors)

The standard of health care in both government and private hospitals is high, but expensive.

Mandatory precautions

None

Advisable precautions

Hepatitis A occurrs in the northern Caribbean. There is also a risk of rabies. Travellers should consider vaccination before travelling. Dengue fever, transmitted by mosquitoes, is endemic in rural areas. Its initial symptoms may be similar to influenza. Bilharzia parasites may be present in rivers.

No special precautions are necessary for food and drink.

Hotels

There are several modern business hotels in San Juan. There are also *paradores*, government-owned inns, that are of a reasonable standard. Fifteen per cent tip usual.

Public holidays (national)

Fixed dates

1 Jan (New Year's Day), 6 Jan (Epiphany), 10 Jan (Eugenio Maria De Hostos' Birthday), 22 Mar (Emancipation Day), 4 Jul (US Independence Day), 25 Jul (Constitution Day), 26 Jul (José Celso Barbosa's Birthday), 11 Nov (Veterans' Day), 19 Nov (Discovery of Puerty Rico Day), 25 Dec (Christmas Day).

Each town celebrates a festival or fiesta in honour of a local patron saint. These can last up to 10 days.

Variable dates

Eugenio Maria de Hostos' Birthday (second Mon in Jan), Martin Luther King's Birthday (third Mon in Jan), Washington's Birthday (third Mon in Feb), Good Friday, José de Diego Day (Apr), Memorial Day (last Mon in May), Luis Muñoz Rivera's Day (Jul), Labour Day (first Mon in Sep), Columbus Day (second Mon in Oct), Thanksgiving Day (fourth Thu in Nov).

Working hours

Banking

Mon–Fri: 0830–1430. (Some banks 0830–1700; some banks open Sat.)

Business

Mon–Fri: 0800–1700.

Government

Mon–Fri: 0800–1630.

Telecommunications

Puerto Rico's telecommunications system is fully integrated with that of the US.

Mobile/cell phones

The main providers of mobile phone services are Centennial, Cingular, MoviStar, Suncom, Verizon and Sprint PCS.

Electricity supply

120V AC

Social customs/useful tips

Despite links with the US and the almost universal ability in the business community to understand English, the use of Spanish by the visitor is appreciated.

Hotel and restaurant staff, and taxi drivers, may expect tips of 15–20 per cent. Service charges are rarely included in restaurant bills.

Puerto Rico combines the lifestyle and social customs of the modern US and the traditional Spanish-speaking Caribbean.

Security

Poverty and unemployment have helped to contribute to a growing crime rate, particularly in San Juan. As in all cities, it is unwise to leave articles unattended in parked cars or hotel rooms.

Getting there

Air

There are direct flights from Europe. Latin American countries are connected via Miami. There are also numerous other connections via New York. Other US cities are also well connected to Puerto Rico.

International airport/s: Luis Muñoz Marín (SJU), 14km east of San Juan; duty-free shop, restaurants, bank, post office, shops, car hire.

Airport tax: None

Surface

Main port/s: San Juan, Ponce and Mayagüez.

Getting about

National transport

Air: Several local airlines operate flights within Puerto Rico, as well as island-hopping trips. Charter services are available.

Road: An extensive network of modern roads and highways link all main centres.

Buses: Regular bus (*guagua*) services operates in San Juan from central terminal at Plaza Colón.

Buses are scarce after 2100.

Taxis: Officially regulated, independently owned *públicos* (publicly shared) taxis have 'P' or 'PD' at the of end a licence plate and run regular routes from established points, picking up and dropping off passengers along the way. They are an inexpensive way of reaching urban areas and provincial towns less accessible by public transport.

Water: There is a ferry service linking the islands of Culebra and Vieques to the port of Fajardo, on the east coast of Puerto Rico.

City transport

Taxis: Special tourist taxis (*Taxi Turístico*) operate between the airport and main tourist areas around San Juan. They operate on a zonal basis and charge set fares. Commercial taxis are metered and can be hired by the hour.

Buses, trams & metro: There are good bus services (*guaguas*) in San Juan. Services outside the capital are less reliable. A metro system *Tren Urbano* (Urban Train) provides regular services running through the San Juan metropolitan area.

Car hire

The major car hire companies are represented. Parking is in short supply.

BUSINESS DIRECTORY

The addresses listed below are a selection only. While World of Information makes every endeavour to check these addresses, we cannot guarantee that changes have not been made, especially to telephone numbers and area codes. We would welcome any corrections.

Telephone area codes

The international dialling code (IDD) for Puerto Rico is +1, followed by area code (787) and subscriber's number.

Chambers of Commerce

Puerto Rico Chamber of Commerce, PO Box 9024033, San Juan 00902 (tel: 721-6060; fax: 723-1891; e-mail: camarapr@camarapr.net).

West of Puerto Rico Chamber of Commerce, PO Box 9, Mayagüez 00681 (tel: 832-3749; fax: 832-4287).

Banking

Banco Comercial de Mayagüez, Mayagüez 00708 (tel: 834-3717).

Banco de Ponce, Plaza Degetau, Ponce 00731 (tel: 842-8000).

Banco Popular, M. Rivera Avenue and Bolivia Street, Hato Rey, San Juan (tel: 765-9800; fax: 764-1706).

Banco Santander de Puerto Rico, 207 Ponce de León Avenue, Hato Rey, San Juan (tel: 759-7070; fax: 751-3639).

Government Development Bank for Puerto Rico, PO Box 42001, San Juan 00940-2001 (tel: 726-2525).

Central bank

Government Development Bank for Puerto Rico, PO Box 42001, San Juan 00940-2001 (tel: 722-2525; fax: 721-5496; e-mail: gdbcomm@bgf.gobierno.pr).

Federal Reserve System, 20th Street and Constitution Avenue, NW, Washington DC 20551 (tel: (+1-202) 452-3000; fax: (+1-202) 452-3819).

Travel information

National tourist organisation offices

Puerto Rico Tourism Company, La Princesa Building, 2 Paseo La Princesa, PO Box 902-3060, Old San Juan 00902 (tel: 721-2400; fax: 725-4417).

Ministries

Department of Agriculture, PO Box 10163, San Juan (tel: 721-2120; fax: 723-9747).

Department of Economic Development and Commerce, F.D. Roosevelt Ave 355, 4th Floor, Hato Rey, 00918 (tel: 764-1175 fax: 765-7709).

Department of Education, PO Box 190759, 00919 (tel: 758-4949; fax: 250-0275).

Department of Justice, PO Box 191, 00912 (tel: 721-2900; fax: 724-4770).

Department of Labour and Human Resources, 505 Munoz Rivera Avenue, 00918 (tel: 754-5353; fax: 753-9550).

Department of Natural and Environmental Resources, PO Box 5887, 00906 (tel: 724-8774; fax: 723-4255).

Department of the State, PO Box 3271, 00902 (tel: 722-2121; fax: 725-7303).

Department of the Treasury, PO Box 4515, 00902 (tel: 721-2020; fax: 723-6213).

Department of Transportation and Public works, PO Box 41269, 00940 (tel: 722-2929; fax: 728-8963).

Government of Puerto Rico Economic Development Administration, PO Box 362350, San Juan 00936 (tel: 758-4747; fax: 764-1415).

Office of the Governor, La Fortaleza, 00901 (tel: 721-7000; fax: 721-7483).

Other useful addresses

Caribbean Development Programme, Puerto Rico Department of State, PO Box 3271, San Juan, 00912 (tel: 721-1751; fax: 723-3304).

Legislative Assembly, Capitol Building, 00901 (tel: 724-5200; fax: 724-2428).

Puerto Rico Bankers' Association, 820 Banco Popular Center, San Juan, 00918 (tel: 753-8630; fax: 754-6077).

Puerto Rico Industrial Development Company (FOMENTO), FD Roosevelt Ave, Hato Rey, San Juan, 00918; PO Box 362350, San Juan, PR 00936-2350 (tel: 758-4747; fax: 754-9640; internet site: http://www.pridco.com).

Puerto Rico Manufacturers' Association, PO Box 192410, San Juan, 00919 (tel: 759-9445; fax: 756-7670).

Puerto Rico Ports Authority, PO Box 362829, San Juan (tel: 723-2260; fax: 724-6444).

San Juan Convention Bureau, Ashford Avenue 1110, San Turce, 00907 (tel: 725-2110).

Supreme Court, Supreme Court Building, 00901 (tel: 723-6033; fax: 725-4910).

Internet sites

Puerto Rico Tourism Company: http://www.gotopuertorico.com

Urban transit: http://www.urbanrail.net

Welcome to Puerto Rico: http://www.topuertorico.com

Yellow and White Pages: www.escapetopuertorico.com/ypages

KEY FACTS

Official name: Dawlat Qatar (State of Qatar)

Head of State: Emir Sheikh Hamad bin Khalifa al Thani (since Jun 1995)

Head of government: Prime Minister Sheikh Hamad bin Jassem bin Jaber al Thani (appointed Apr 2007)

Area: 11,437 square km

Population: 1.70 million (2010; census figure)

Capital: Doha

Official language: Arabic

Currency: Rial (QR) = 100 dirhams

Exchange rate: QR3.64 per US$ (fixed)

GDP per capita: US$76,168 (2010)

GDP real growth: 16.30% (2010)

GDP: US$129.50 billion (2010)

Inflation: -2.40% (2010)

Oil production: 1.57 million bpd (2010)

Balance of trade: US$30.73 billion (2010)

Annual FDI: US$5.53 billion (2010)

Qatar

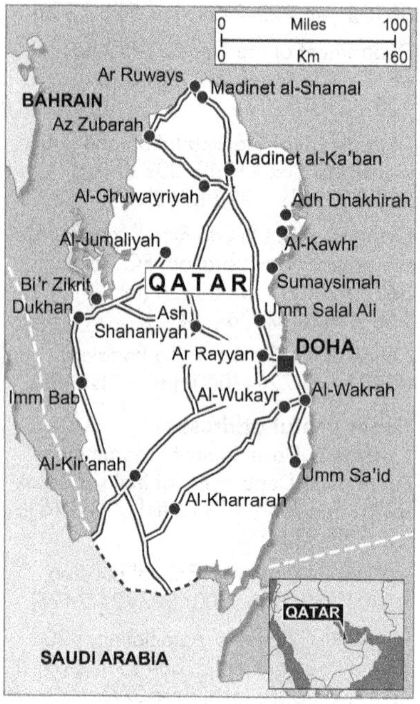

Readers prepared to cast an eye over the Qatar Chapter of the 1975 edition of the *Middle East Review* can be excused for wondering if this is indeed the same country that bears its name in 2011. Then as now, the emirate was ruled by the al Thani family (with the odd palace coup changing the hierarchy in between), in 2011 the Emir – Sheikh Hamad bin Khalifa al Thani – is as likely to be seen in Paris (accompanied by his glamorous wife, Sheikha Moza), London or New York as in Doha. In 1975 Qatar still had close ties with Dubai (the two emirates had once shared a currency (as had Bahrain and Abu Dhabi), but in the intervening decades Dubai had embraced 'bling' (tourism, horse-racing and even artificial ski-slopes) whereas Wahhabi Qatar had chosen a more measured developmental path, buttressed by its massive gas revenues.

In 2011, two defining moments in Qatar's recent history occurred. One was the emirate's high profile participation in the North Atlantic Treaty Organisation (NATO) lead military action to depose Libya's renegade dictator, Colonel Qadafi. The Doha government reportedly gave the rebel government as much as US$400 million, provided military aircraft and crews and secured (it held the Presidency at the time) the support of the Arab League for NATO intervention. To NATO's concern, it was rumoured that much of Qatar's generous monetary aid ended up in the hands of Islamists. The other, less publicised, but as important, moment was the supply of 'reconnaissance officers and observers' to Bahrain under the aegis of the Gulf Co-operation Council (GCC). The bulk of the troops sent into Bahrain were from Saudi Arabia. The *Middle East Spectator* noted that the issue here was not so much one of quelling popular protests, rather that Saudi Arabia and the Gulf States (including Qatar) were 'protecting their interests'. These interests do not lie only in protecting their governments and borders, but also in protecting their responsibilities – critically the contracts according to which they provide other countries with oil, contracts that they must act to protect. These are strategic obligations, including commitments to China, a nuclear state and a United Nations Security Council member; to India, a giant nuclear state; to Japan, the world's second biggest economy, and to Pakistan. A GCC spokesman stated that 'When the Gulf States sign contracts and the situation changes and instability prevails in the region, the value of insurance policies increases.' In the case of Qatar, its participation in the GCC action, however minimal, sat uncomfortably with what the London *Economist* described as 'Cheerleading the Arab Spring'. Inevitably, the Qatari intervention in Bahrain received little press or media comment or coverage within Qatar.

Preying on the minds of Qataris is the menacing presence of Iran across the Gulf. On the Arab side of the Gulf, Iran is seen as a subversive Shi'a power. One theory is that Iran has been targeting Bahrain as the soft underbelly of the Gulf. Bahrain's rulers may be Sunni, but the bulk of its population is Shi'a.

Democracy?

The principal catalyst for change in Qatar's recent history has been the overthrow of his father by Qatar's current ruler, Sheikh Hamad bin Khalifa al Thani, in 1995. Despite the ruling family's efforts to modernise Qatar's social and political infrastructure, to achieve anything corresponding to North American or European democratic 'normalcy' Qatar still has a long way to go. Elections first promised in 2005 have been placed on the back burner. Qatar's clearly identifiable policy of seeking the international high ground through initiatives such as the Qatar Foundation, al Jazeera, its support for the Libyan rebels and occasional lip service to increased democracy, are seen by many as no more than a means by which the ruling family can maintain its well paid, unaccountable, status. In late 2011 Sheikh Hamad announced that Qatar's first parliamentary elections would be held in 2013.

Perhaps ironically for a hereditary state, in May 2011 Qatar hosted in Doha a conference on democracy in the region. Planned long in advance of the Arab Spring, it would have been difficult for the conference's timing to have been more sensitive. Many of its neighbours feel that Qatar, host to the al Jazeera radio and television network (established following the closure of the BBC's Arabic television service in 1996), has played a provocative role (often perceived by many neighbouring countries as unnecessarily provocative) in supporting Arab uprisings. Al Jazeera also set up – presumably funded by Qatar – a rebel Libyan television station broadcasting from Qatar, all of 2,000 miles distant. Secular Arab liberals regard with suspicion al Jazeera's generous coverage of Islamists, which appeared to reflect the Qatari government's apparent support for both Hamas in Palestine and Hezbollah in Lebanon. Qatar is, of course, able to fund this maverick stance out of petty cash resources.

Qatar's current system of government is a far cry from anything resembling democracy. Decisions are taken by an inner circle consisting of only three people: the Emir, Sheikh Hamad bin Khalifa al Thani; his cousin Sheikh Hamad bin Jassim al Thani who in addition to being prime minister, also holds the foreign affairs brief; and the third member, Sandhurst educated Crown Prince Tamim, who is in charge of Qatar's armed forces. Although Qatar has been seen to flaunt its wealth and ability to exercise its will over large parts of the Middle East, at heart – despite its substantial wealth – the country's leadership still seems modest both in outlook and ambition.

According to CIA reports (see 'Energy' below) Qatar's energy resources give it the highest income per capita in the world, estimated by some analysts at an annual US$179,000, by others at 'only' US$80,000. The description 'Qatari citizen' applies only to some 250,000 residents out of a total population estimated at 1.7 million. In addition to the material benefits of citizenship, true Qataris enjoy a pretty cushy existence with lifelong welfare.

Energy

In recent years the Qatari government has devoted most resources to the development of natural gas, particularly for export as liquefied natural gas (LNG). Though only producing LNG since 1997, Qatar is now the world's largest supplier. Qatar is also a member and host country for the Gas Exporting Countries Forum (GECF), an organisation formed in 2001 to promote the interest of the world's major gas producers. In 2010, preliminary estimates from Qatar National Bank indicated that the oil and gas sectors accounted for over half of Qatar's 2010 gross domestic product (GDP). Qatar is wholly dependent on oil and natural gas for all of its primary energy consumption. Although the transportation sector continues to contribute significantly to growth, all electricity capacity in Qatar is gas-fired. Qatar's total primary energy consumption in 2008 surpassed one quadrillion Btu for the first time, having almost doubled since 2001.

According to the *Oil & Gas Journal* (OGJ), in January 2011, Qatar had 25.4 billion barrels of proven oil reserves. Qatar was the sixteenth largest crude oil exporter in the world in 2009 and of the 12 Organisation for Petroleum Exporting Countries (OPEC) members, ranked eleventh in crude oil exports (its production exceeding only that of Ecuador). The onshore Dukhan field, located along the west coast of the peninsula, is the country's oldest producing oil field, though it has been surpassed in production volumes by the offshore Al Shaheen field, which averaged about 300,000 barrels per day (bpd) in 2009.

State-owned Qatar Petroleum (QP) controls all aspects of Qatar's upstream and downstream oil sector. While QP owns and operates the onshore Dukhan field and the offshore Maydan Mahzam and Bul Hanine fields, the remaining offshore fields are operated by international oil companies via production sharing agreements (PSAs). In an effort to increase production and reserves, QP has offered more favorable terms for PSAs in recent years, thereby also increasing oil revenues and mitigating gas-related capital expenditures.

In 2009, Qatar produced approximately 1.2 million bpd of total liquids: 830,000bpd of crude and 380,000bpd of non-crude liquids. Preliminary estimates for production in 2010 indicate total production of liquids to be about 1.4 million bpd: 850,000bpd of crude and 590bpd of non-crude liquids. The country's crude oil production capacity was estimated to be just over 1 million bpd in 2010, falling just below its condensate and natural gas

KEY INDICATORS — Qatar

	Unit	2006	2007	2008	2009	2010
Population	m	0.84	*0.93	*1.00	*1.20	*1.70
Gross domestic product (GDP)	US$bn	52.72	71.00	102.30	83.90	129.50
GDP per capita	US$	62,914	76,374	79,409	59,545	74,901
GDP real growth	%	15.0	18.0	17.7	12.0	16.6
Inflation	%	11.8	13.8	15.0	-4.9	-2.4
Oil output	'000 bpd	1,133.0	1,197.0	1,378.0	1,345.0	1,569.0
Natural gas output	bn cum	49.5	59.8	76.6	89.3	116.7
Exports (goods)	US$m	39,276.0	51,482.0	71,193.0	52,171.0	76,415.0
Imports (goods)	US$m	21,767.0	27,172.0	34,848.0	34,260.0	45,687.0
Balance of trade	US$m	17,509.0	24,310.0	36,345.0	17,911.0	30,728.0
Current account	US$m	16,113.0	21,828.0	33,138.0	12,997.0	24,728.0
Total reserves minus gold	US$m	5,382.7	9,416.4	9,649.5	18,369.7	30,620.8
Foreign exchange	US$m	5,307.1	9,345.0	9,553.0	17,868.9	30,111.6
Exchange rate	per US$	3.64	3.64	3.64	3.63	3.64

* estimated figure

liquids (NGL) production capacity for the same year.

As an OPEC member, Qatar is allocated a specific crude production target by the Organisation (currently 731,000bpd), but condensate and NGLs are not included in the target. Condensate and NGLs have therefore risen as a proportion of Qatar's total petroleum production. The US government Energy Information Administration (EIA) estimates that condensate and NGL production almost doubled from 2007 to 2010, from 287,000bpd to 567,000bpd.

Although Qatar's petroleum production has grown steadily since 2002, Qatar's fields are maturing and output at Dukhan – formerly the largest producing field – is in decline. To offset anticipated declines, enhanced oil recovery (EOR) techniques are being considered for several fields including Al Shaheen, Dukhan, Bul Hanine and Maydan Marjam. Danish company Maersk's offshore field Al Shaheen is an important source for future production growth. Though it averaged just under 300,000bpd of production in 2009, Maersk completed an expansion project in 2010 that increased its production capacity to 525,000bpd.

According to the OGJ, Qatar's proven natural gas reserves stood at approximately 896 trillion cubic feet (tcf) as of 1 January 2011. Qatar holds almost 14 per cent of total world natural gas reserves and is the third-largest in the world behind Russia and Iran. The majority of Qatar's natural gas is located in the offshore North Field, which spans an area roughly equivalent to Qatar itself. Part of the world's largest non-associated natural gas field, the North Field is a geological extension of Iran's South Pars field, which holds an additional 450tcf of recoverable natural gas reserves.

To an even greater extent than in the oil sector, QP plays a dominant role in Qatar's natural gas sector, leading upstream and downstream projects. Qatar's focus on natural gas development tends to be integrated large-scale projects linked to LNG exports or downstream industries that utilise natural gas as a feedstock. Therefore, foreign company involvement has favoured international oil companies with the technology and expertise in integrated mega-projects, including ExxonMobil, Shell and Total. However, QP has maintained a majority share in most of its gas projects – in particular Qatargas Operating Company Limited (Qatargas) and Ras Laffan Company Limited (RasGas). The LNG companies handle all upstream to downstream natural gas transportation themselves, while the Qatar Gas Transport Company (known as Nakilat, which means 'carriers' in Arabic, is responsible for shipping Qatari LNG.

Qatar continues to expand natural gas production. In 2009, Qatar produced 3,154 billion cubic feet (bcf) of natural gas, three times the amount produced in 2000. Although the increase in natural gas production fuels the growing natural gas requirements of domestic industry and its gas-to-liquids (GTL) projects, the bulk of this increase is going towards LNG exports. During 2009, Qatar exported over 2,400bcf of natural gas, of which about 70 per cent was LNG. Qatar currently exports about 2bcf per day of natural gas to the UAE and Oman through the Dolphin pipeline.

Qatar is the world's leading LNG exporter. In 2009, it exported nearly 1,800bcf of LNG. Japan, South Korea and India were the primary destinations for Qatar's LNG exports, accounting for about 57 per cent in 2009. European markets including Belgium, the United Kingdom and Spain were also significant buyers of Qatari LNG, accounting for an additional 33 per cent. Although Qatar began exporting LNG only in 1997, heavy government emphasis on this sector – both in terms of making investments and attracting foreign investors – contributed to the rapid development of Qatar's LNG capacity. Qatar's LNG sector is dominated by Qatargas, which operates four major LNG ventures (Qatargas I-IV) and Ras Laffan Company Limited (RasGas), which operates three major LNG ventures (RasGas I-III). RasGas is 70 per cent-owned by QP and 30 per cent-owned by ExxonMobil, while the Qatargas consortium includes QP, Total, ExxonMobil, Mitsui, Marubeni, ConocoPhillips and Shell. Each venture has an individual ownership structure, though QP owns at least 65 per cent of all of them.

Risk assessment

Economy	Good
Politics	Poor
Regional stability	Fair

COUNTRY PROFILE

Historical profile

632 Advent of Islam.
1700s Mining and pearl fishing settlements were established along the coast.
1868 Qatar's first Al Thani Emir, Sheikh Mohammed bin Thani, signed a treaty with Britain.
1871–1916 A treaty with the Turks allowed them to place a garrison in Doha. After Turkey entered the First World War on the side of Germany, the Turkish forces were expelled by the British.
1916 Qatar became a British protectorate with Sheikh Abdullah bin Jassim al Thani as ruler.
1930 The collapse of the pearl trade devastated the economy.
1939 Oil was discovered, but the Second World War delayed exploitation.
1949 Qatar began exporting oil.
1950s Qatar's infrastructure was modernised and extended, using oil revenues.
1968 Britain announced its intention to withdraw from the Gulf by 1971.
1971 Qatar became independent. Land disputes with Bahrain ensued.
1972 Sheikh Khalifa bin Hamad al Thani became Emir after deposing his uncle.
1980s and 1990s Qatar had territorial disputes with Bahrain and Saudi Arabia.
1981 The political and economic union, the Co-operation Council for the Arab States of the Gulf (CCASG) (known as Gulf Co-operation Council (GCC)) was formed by Bahrain, Kuwait, Oman, Qatar, Saudi Arabia and the United Arab Emirates (UAE).
1990 After Iraq invaded Kuwait, Qatar allowed foreign forces into the country and Qatari troops took part in the liberation of Kuwait.
1995 In a bloodless coup, Sheikh Hamad bin Khalifa al Thani, replaced his father Sheikh Khalifa.
1996 Qatar began exporting liquefied natural gas. Based in Qatar and funded by the Emir, the pan-Arab Al Jazeera satellite TV station was launched.
1999 A democratisation programme began when male citizens over the age of 18 were allowed to vote in municipal council elections. Only half the 40,000 eligible to vote actually registered.
2000 The Emir's cousin and 32 others were jailed for life for planning a coup, in 1996, which was foiled.
2001 The International Court of Justice settled a land dispute between Qatar and Bahrain, awarding Zubarah town and the shallows surrounding the islet of Fasht el Dibal to Qatar. A border dispute with Saudi Arabia was also settled. WTO trade talks, held in Doha, called for the US, EU and Japan to open their markets and remove agricultural export subsidies.
2002 The Al Udeid air base was redeveloped in preparation for the Iraq War when it became the HQ for the US Central Command.
2003 A referendum approved a new constitution, which guarantees equal rights and a 45-member parliament. The Emir named his younger son, Prince Tamim, as

crown prince, replacing his elder son Prince Jassim.
2004 The exiled former Chechen president, Zelimkhan Yanderbiyev, was assassinated in Doha; two Russian agents were convicted of the murder. Around six thousand members of the Al Ghfran clan, a sub-set of one of Qatar's largest tribes, had their citizenship revoked on the grounds that they held dual nationality with Saudi Arabia.
2005 A suicide bombing in Doha injured 12 and killed one Briton; it was the first major terrorist attack in Qatar. The new constitution was implemented. Work began on building the world's largest liquefied natural gas plant, with joint US-Qatar investment of US$14 billion.
2007 Sheikh Abdullah bin Khalifa resigned as prime minister and was replaced by Sheikh Hamad bin Jassem.
2008 A common market was created by Bahrain, Kuwait, Oman, Qatar, Saudi Arabia and UAE, the six wealthiest Gulf states. Citizens of these countries are now allowed to travel between and live in any of the six states, where they may find employment, buy properties and businesses and use the educational and health facilities freely. Qatar, Iran and Russia formed a technical committee to lead an Opec-style, international exporting organisation for natural gas.
2009 Qatar (the only Arab Gulf state with trade agreements) cut trade ties with Israel following Israel's offensive in Palestine.
2010 Elections for the legislative assembly due to be held in June were postponed, when the Emir extended its term in office until 2013. The Gulf's second largest stock exchange, by market value, in Qatar, set up a new trading system on 5 September, in a bid to become the primary bourse among Gulf states. Electronic trading went live using the NYSE Euronext's universal trading platform (UTP) technology.
2011 The Qatar Red Crescent (QRC) was one of the first humanitarian organisations to provide food aid to Somalia in February. As part of the *National Development strategy 2011–2016*, expatriates may be offered permanent residency if they meet 'pre-determined criteria'. The policy is aimed at attracting and retaining Qatar's high skilled workforce. The policy will also review and revise the sponsorship system in operation in 2011, in which employers have full control over residence and the work undertaken as well as permission of entry and exit. According to the US-magazine *Global Finance* Qatar became the world's richest nation in 2010. A comparison of countries' gross domestic product (GDP) and GDP per capita (using purchasing power parity (PPP)) was used to determine the rankings. Luxembourg came second on the list and Kuwait third. Qatar played a leading role in providing support for Libya's rebels, with both funds and projects such as Libya TV, set up to counter pro-Gadafi propaganda. It has also helped market Libya's oil and is well placed to assist in further development of Libya's natural gas reserves.

Political structure

Constitution

A new, written constitution came into effect on 8 June 2005. It provides for the hereditary rule of the al Thani family. A new unicamal, legislative authority was inaugurated.

Independence date

3 September 1971

Form of state

Constitutional Emirate

The executive

Executive power is vested in the Emir, who is the Head of State. He appoints a prime minister and ministers. He also appoints 15 members of the Majlis al Shura. The Emir is the supreme commander of the armed and security forces.

National legislature

In 2009, the unicameral Majlis al Shura (Consultative Assembly) had 35 appointed members who, as an Advisory Council, was consulted by the Emir.
From 2010, 30 members of the Consultative Assembly will be directly elected by universal suffrage (aged over 18 years); 15 members will be appointed by the Emir. The Assembly will be responsible for approving the budget (but not drafting it), reviewing the performance of ministers and drafting and voting on proposed legislation; all legislation must by endorsed by the executive authority.

Legal system

Two former court systems – civil and *Sharia* (Islamic law) – were merged under a higher court, the Court of Cassation, established for appeals, under a new judiciary law issued in 2003.

Last elections

None

Next elections

The first legislative elections was scheduled for 2013.

Political parties

Ruling party

Political parties are not permitted.

Population

1.70 million (2010; census figure)
Last census: March 2004: 744,029
Annual growth rate: 4.2 per cent 1994–2004 (WHO 2006)

Ethnic make-up

Arab (40 per cent), Pakistani (18 per cent), Indian (18 per cent), Iranian (10 per cent), others (14 per cent).
Expatriates comprise about 80 per cent of the total population. Some foreign nationals have been resident in Qatar for many years and come largely from the Indian sub-continent, other Arab countries and south-east Asia. The number of non-national children is high, indicating a trend among non-nationals to settle in the country.

Religions

Islam is the state religion. Most Qataris (95 per cent) are Sunni Muslims of the strict Wahhabi sect, known as *muwahhidun* (unitarians); they shun the veneration of saints and shrines. The small Hindu and Christian communities do not have formal places of worship.

Education

Primary education begins at aged six and lasts until aged 12. From aged 12 to 15 students attend a preparatory school and if they pass their promotional examination go forward to secondary school. There are three different types of secondary schools: academic, commercial and technical, and each offer three-year courses. However, girls are only allowed to attend the academic secondary schools.
In 2004, Qatar announced that it would spend US$900 million on a huge new medical teaching hospital to be built on the outskirts of Doha; it is expected to be completed by 2008. An endowment of US$8 billion will also be provided to carry out research. The hospital's teaching programme will be run in partnership with the US Cornell University, and have US$200 million per annum to spend on research, initially concentrating on women's health and paediatric medicine. The emphasis on research is a new direction for medical facilities in the region.
Literacy rate: 83 per cent, adult rate (2003)
Compulsory years: None.

Health

All residents have access to free medical services.
Life expectancy: 76 years, 2004 (WHO 2006)
Fertility rate/Maternal mortality rate: 2.9 births per woman, 2004 (WHO 2006)
Birth rate/Death rate: 16 births per 1,000 population; 4.4 deaths per 1,000 population (2003).
Child (under 5 years) mortality rate (per 1,000): 11 per 1,000 live births (2003)
Head of population per physician: 2.22 physicians per 1,000 people, 2001 (WHO 2006)

Welfare

The state provides generous welfare services for indigenous Qataris.

Main cities
Doha (capital, estimated population 339,847 in 2004), ar Rayyan (251,437), al Wakrah (27,462).

Media
Press
The government formally lifted censorship of the media in 1995 and since then government interference has remained limited although censorship is implicit and self-censorship by editors common.
Dailies: The main daily newspapers in Arabic are *al Sharq (The East)* (www.al-sharq.com), *al Raya (The Banner)* (www.raya.com), *al Watan (The Homeland)* (www.al-watan.com) and the regional publication *al Arab* (www.alarabonline.org) of political matters.
In English, *Qatar Post* (www.qatarpost.com), *Qatar Journal* (www.qatarjournal.com) and *The Peninsula* (www.thepeninsulaqatar.com) is the leading English newspaper. A regional publication is *The Gulf Times* (www.gulf-times.com).
Weeklies: The *Gulf Times* is published in English.
Periodicals: In Arabic, the monthly *al Sehah Magazine* publishes items on health. In English, *This is Qatar* is a tourist magazine, *Qatar Falcon* (http://www.qatar-falcon.com) is a lifestyle publication aimed at male readers, while *Zawya* (www.zawya.com) is an online business magazine, with news and features.
Broadcasting
Isreal began a boycott of al Jazeera on 12 March 2008 in reaction to what it claimed was al Jazeera's bias when it reported on the conflict in Gaza – Israeli action in bombing the territory was not matched by reports of missiles fired on the city of Ashkelon.
Radio: Radio broadcasts are in Arabic, with other services in English, French and Urdu also available. The government run, Qatar Broadcasting Service broadcasts nationally. A few local radio stations also broadcast in FM and AM.
Television: Although privately funded, al Jazeera (www.aljazeera.com) has grown in size and reputation from a regional TV Channel, to an international broadcaster with an English language service that was launched in 2006 and video streaming supplied over the Internet. The state television runs three channels, including one for the Koran channel and two others in Arabic and English channel. Cable satellite TV is also available throughout Qatar and offers some 20 channels.
Advertising
Advertising is available in the press, on commercial TV and in cinemas.

News agencies
National news agency: Qatar News Agency

Economy
The economy is dominated by the production of, and revenue from, Qatar's hydrocarbon sector. Oil and gas reserves were 25.9 billion barrels of oil and 25.3 trillion cubic metres (cum) of natural gas at the end of 2010. Between them they provide over 60 per cent of GDP. Production of oil was 1.57 million barrels per day (bpd) in 2010; production of natural gas was 116.7 billion cum per annum (a 30.7 per cent increase on the 2009 production level). Qatar has the world's third largest deposits of natural gas and is the world's largest exporter of liquefied natural gas (LNG) totalling 75.75 billion cum in 2010 (up from 39.68 billion cum in 2008). South Korea, Japan and India each imported over 10 billion cum of Qatar LNG in 2010; Qatar also exported 17.41 billion cum by gas pipeline to the UAE.
Qatar was not affected by the global economic crisis in 2008 as its banks are tightly regulated and well capitalised.
Since 2004, GDP growth has remained in the mid-teens, with only one dip below 10 per cent, in 2005, due to a fall in global oil prices. GDP growth in 2007 was 18.0 per cent, which fell to 17.7 per cent in 2008, despite the expansion of hydrocarbon production and a strong performance in manufacturing, construction and financial services. As global trade slumped GDP growth also fell, to 12.0 per cent in 2009 before rebounding to 16.6 per cent in 2010.
Inflation remained high, peaking at 15.0 per cent in 2008 due to high prices for imported food and housing rents. Per capita income reached a record US$79,409, making Qatar one of the world's wealthiest populations in 2008, before falling to US$59,545 in 2009 and recovering in 2010 to US$74,901.
Hydrocarbons account for over 50 per cent of the economy, financial services around 10 per cent, construction 8 per cent, trade, restaurants and hotels 7 per cent, transport and communications 5 per cent and manufacturing 5 per cent. As the demand for hydrocarbons was at an all-time high in 2008 nominal GDP was US$110.7 billion, which fell to US$98.3 billion in 2009 as global trade slowed down, before rebounding to a projected US$126.9 billion in 2010 as worldwide growth picked up.
To improve the country's long-term prospects, the government has introduced incentives to encourage diversification towards the non-oil sector, in particular light industry. It has also relaxed its restrictive policies on foreign investment and encouraged stronger private investment. Although key personnel involved in all projects must be Qatari, the foreign investment law allows 100 per cent foreign equity in most commercial sectors, including agriculture, manufacturing, healthcare, education, tourism, power and water plants and mining.
Contracts to build the US$11 billion New Doha International Airport (NDIA) were signed in 2004 and phases one and two of the airport construction are due for completion in 2011, with final completion in 2012. This large investment has been an impetus for growth and will assist the country's diversification strategy by encouraging tourism.
As part of the *National Development strategy 2011–2016*, expatriates may be offered permanent residency if they meet 'pre-determined criteria'. The policy is aimed at attracting and retaining Qatar's skilled workforce. The policy will also review and revise the sponsorship system in operation in 2011, in which employers have full control over residence and the work undertaken as well as permission for entry and exit.

External trade
In 2005 the Greater Arab Free Trade Area (Gafta) was ratified by 17 members, including Qatar, creating an Arab economic bloc. A customs union was established whereby tariffs within Gafta will be reduced by a percentage each year, until none remain.
Qatar is the world's largest exporter of liquefied natural gas (LNG) and operates the biggest processing facility, which can process over 30 billion cubic metres (cum) of natural gas. It has other heavy industrial processing sites producing fertilisers and petrochemicals and a steel plant.
Imports
Principal imports are machinery and vehicles, manufactured goods and building materials, foodstuffs and live animals, (virtually everything – except concrete and steel bars – has to be imported).
Main sources: Japan (typically 10 per cent total of), US (9 per cent), Germany (8 per cent).
Exports
Exports are dominated by LNG, crude oil, petroleum products, fertilisers and steel.
Main destinations: Japan (typically 34 per cent of total), South Korea (22 per cent), Singapore (12 per cent).

Agriculture
Farming
The agricultural sector only contributed 0.2 per cent to GDP; it employs 1 per cent of the workforce, nevertheless the country is 70 per cent self-sufficient in summer vegetables and 40 per cent in winter vegetables; 25 per cent in dairy

produce and 10 per cent in cereals.
Other crops include fruit, dates, fodder crops and cereals.
All agricultural land in Qatar is owned by the government, which is keen to support and encourage agricultural production. However, this is limited by the scarcity of water and the unfavourable terrain. A new industrial project began in Ras Laffan, providing desalinated water as part of a plan for further irrigation. Only about 8,000 hectares of the estimated 65,000 hectares of cultivable land (5.7 per cent of the total land area) is farmed.
Major emphasis is placed on educating the population in agricultural techniques, experimenting with new methods of cultivation and developing better marketing structures.
One project considered vital to long-term productivity is experimental cultivation of crops on sand using solar energy and sea water.

Fishing

Fish catches meet 70 per cent of demand. Fish stocks have declined as a result of water pollution.

Industry and manufacturing

The industrial sector contributes 7.6 per cent of GDP; it employs around 25 per cent of the working population.
Non-oil, heavy industry, often developed as state-owned joint ventures, received the bulk of government investment in industry and now contributes about 9 per cent of national revenues. The government offers incentives to encourage private sector development of light industry. Industries include the production of intermediate building materials (cement, concrete, moulded aluminium, marble tiles and paving stone), food processing, freezing and packaging, paper products, batteries, paint, plastics, detergents, lubricants, household utensils and furniture. The government has pledged to spend US$110 million in industrial plant development, most of which is concentrated in the industrial city of Messaieed.

Tourism

Tourism is a growth industry and is being developed as part of the government's programme of economic diversification. Qatar is promoted as an up-market destination, with the emphasis on resorts, festivals, shopping, conferencing, culture and sport. Government backing is given for massive investment into the creation of the facilities and infrastructure, with the aim of increasing visitor numbers by three times the 400,000 (in 2005) by 2011. Several luxury hotels have been marketed to Europeans and neighbouring GCC visitors. A new international airport at Doha, scheduled for completion by 2015, is envisaged as a regional gateway.
The sector is estimated to attracted 10 per cent of total capital investment per annum and tourism generates around 18 per cent of total export revenue.

Environment

Among the proposals to meet the country's water shortage are the construction of a 700km pipeline from the Karun River in northern Iran to Qatar, as well as the development of more desalination plants.

Hydrocarbons

Proven oil reserves were 25.9 billion barrels in 2010 with production at 1.569 million barrels per day (bpd) in 2010. The hydrocarbons sector contributes around 60 per cent to GDP. The largest oil field is onshore at Dukhan, along the west coast, which produces around half of Qatar's total oil output. There are six other oil fields and if the country's production levels remained constant reserves would last until 2070. The state-run Qatar Petroleum (QP) has overall control of all aspects of the industry, not only holding the rights to all petroleum resources but also including operational exploration, production, refining, transport and storage of hydrocarbons. QP entered into a number of production sharing agreements (PSAs) with companies such as ExxonMobil, Chevron, Total and BP Amoco after the oil sector was opened up to foreign investment. However no onshore discoveries of oil have been made since the 1990s and only the offshore Al Shaheen field, operated by the Danish-based Maersk Oil and Gas, is being developed. The largest percentage of crude oil is exported to Japan. On 26 May 2011, PetroChina received its first LNG train of 145,000cum from Qatar at its new terminal at Rudong in Jiangsu Province.
There are three export terminals; two primarily for the export of oil and the other, at the Ras Laffan Industrial City, is mainly for the export of liquefied natural gas (LNG).
Proven natural gas reserves were 25.3 trillion cubic metres in 2010, with production at 116.7 billion cubic metres (cum). Qatar has the third largest reserves of natural gas (behind Russia and Iran), possessing around 15 per cent of the world's reserves, concentrated largely in the massive North Field, off the north-east coast, which is the largest known non-associated gas field in the world. There is a natural gas pipeline to the United Arab Emirates and Oman as part of the Dolphin Project to connect to these countries natural gas networks.
Qatar is the world's largest exporter of LNG with exports of 94.9 billion cum in 2010. The world's largest plant converting natural gas to liquid (GTL) began production in Ras Laffan Industrial City, in June 2011; at full production (in 2012) it will process 45.3 million cum of natural gas into 120,000 barrels of condensate LPG and ethane per day and 140,000 barrels of GTL products.
Any coal imported is commercially insignificant.

Energy

Total installed generation capacity was 3,500MW in 2007. Natural gas is the source of energy for all public power plants and provides 79 per cent of all electricity generation, the remainder is provided by oil.
As a result of steadily rising demand, the government has embarked on a process of restructuring the electricity sector with an emphasis on attracting foreign investment through independent power projects (IPPs). Nevertheless, the partially state-owned General Electricity and Water Corporation (QEWC, known as Kahramaa) keeps control of transmission and distribution activities, while retaining a monopoly as sole purchaser of all generated electricity.
The Ras Abu Fontas power station has been re-furbished with an increased generating capacity of 1,030MW. An additional 2,567MW generating capacity will be added by 2010 with the completion of two new power stations. A Gulf Co-operation Council (GCC) project to link the six member states (Saudi Arabia, Qatar, Bahrain, Kuwait, Oman and the United Arab Emirates) to an integrated power-grid began in 2005. The first phase of the GCC power grid was completed in July 2009 at a cost of US$1,095 million, linking Saudi Arabia, Bahrain, Kuwait and Qatar through 800km of transmission lines. Kuwait and Saudi Arabia will each receive an extra 1,200MW of power capacity and later, the UAE will receive 900MW, Qatar 750MW, Bahrain 600MW and Oman 400MW. In the first phase, a 400kV overhead line links Kuwait's Al Zour power station with Doha, and a 400kV submarine line to Saudi Arabia with Bahrain. The second phase will link the UAE with Oman. The resulting two mega-grids will be joined in the final phase.

Financial markets

In 2005 government plans to develop a regional financial services centre were agreed. Initially the centre will provide Qatar-based project financing, bond insurance and asset management to financial institutions and allow them to enter the liquefied natural gas markets. A regulator was appointed to the post of head of the financial services centre in March 2005.

Stock exchange

Doha Securities Market (DSM)

Banking and insurance

The banking sector consists of 15 commercial banks, including seven locally owned banks. There are 12 insurance companies, the majority of which are foreign-owned; the largest is the locally-owned Qatar Insurance Company.

An agreement was reached between Saudi Arabia, Kuwait, Bahrain and Qatar to establish the Gulf Co-operation Council (GCC) Monetary Council to be established (originally in 2009), marking plans to set up a regional central bank, to be based in Riyadh (Saudi Arabia). The GCC Monetary Council will oversee the introduction of a monetary union, due to be in operation by 2013.

In February 2011, the Central Bank of Qatar ordered all non-Islamic lenders to stop offering Islamic banking services or to restructure them into conventional loans or sell them to Islamic financial operators by the end of 2011. The move was seen to benefit purely Islamic operators in Qatar, at the expense of foreign (non-Islamic) banks and financial institutions. However, within a week, the chief executive of the Doha Bank declared that while no Islamic accounts would be closed no new business would be undertaken and indicated a relaxation in the original direction.

Central bank

The Qatar Central Bank (QCB)

Main financial centre

Doha

Time

GMT plus three hours

Geography

Qatar occupies a peninsula, projecting northwards from the Arabian mainland, on the west coast of the Gulf. It is bordered, to the south by Saudi Arabia and the United Arab Emirates. The archipelago of Bahrain lies to the north-west. On the opposite side of the Gulf lies Iran.

The terrain consists primarily of sand dunes laid over flat rocky areas or salt flats, with some limestone outcrops, particularly in the west around Dukhan and in the north around Fuwairit.

Hemisphere

Northern

Climate

Desert climate with extremely hot and humid summers, when temperatures can reach 44 degrees Celsius from July–September, and mild winters with occasional rainfall.

Entry requirements

Passports

Required by all.

Visa

Required by all; except nationals of neighbouring countries.

For all others, requirements are subject to change and it is advisable to contact an embassy of Qatar for up-to-date information. Business and tourist visas (valid for 21 days) may be obtained on arrival. However, obtaining a visa in advance will save time.

Prohibited entry

Holders of passports issued by Israel.

Currency advice/regulations

There are no exchange restrictions. Israeli currency is prohibited.

Customs

Personal effects are duty-free. Certain goods (firearms, ammunition, drugs and alcohol) may only be imported under licence.

Import of pork and pork products, cultured pearls, and obscene or seditious literature is forbidden.

Importers must register with the Controller of Companies and appear on the Chamber of Commerce's register of importers.

All foodstuffs must be labelled in Arabic.

Prohibited imports

Alcohol, even for personal consumption.

Health (for visitors)

Mandatory precautions

Vaccination certificate against yellow fever if travelling from infected area.

Advisable precautions

Inoculations and boosters should be current for tetanus, polio, typhoid and hepatitis A. There may be a need for vaccinations for tuberculosis, diphtheria and hepatitis B. In border areas with Saudi Arabia rabies is considered high risk and therefore any animal or bat bites should be assessed carefully.

A supply of any regular medicines required should be taken, with their prescription details; medical insurance, which includes emergency evacuation, is recommended.

Hotels

There is a large selection of first-class hotels. Tax of 15 per cent is added to the bill.

Credit cards

Major credit cards are accepted.

Public holidays (national)

Fixed dates

27 Jun (Accession of the Emir), 3 Sep (Independence Day), 31 Dec (banks only).

Variable dates

Eid al Adha (five days), Islamic New Year, Eid al Fitr (four days),

Islamic year 1433 (26 Nov 2011–14 Nov 2012): The Islamic year has 354 or 355 days, with the result that Muslim feasts advance by 10–12 days against the Gregorian calendar each year. Dates of the Muslim feasts vary according to sightings of the new moon, so cannot be forecast exactly.

Working hours

Friday is the official weekend holiday.

During Ramadan, the Muslim holy month of fasting during daylight hours, most officials work 0900–1300.

Banking

Sat–Wed: 0730–1330.

Business

Sat–Thu: 0800–1200, 1600–1900.

Government

Sat–Thu: 0700–1400.

Shops

Sat–Thu: 0830–1230, 1630–2030; Fri: most shops are closed, although some supermarkets are open.

Telecommunications

Mobile/cell phones

There is a 900/1800 GSM service available throughout the country.

Electricity supply

220/240V AC, with three-pin flat plug fittings most common.

Weights and measures

Metric system; other weights are still in use, however.

Social customs/useful tips

Correspondence and technical literature is acceptable in English.

At business meetings it is not uncommon for several people to be present. While in negotiations be careful about committing yourself orally. In a traditional Muslim Sharia Court, oral evidence carries far more weight than written. You should also be aware that you will be held to the letter of any agreement.

Keep contracts as simple as possible; the main part should be couched in easily translated terms with detailed ramifications of the deal relegated to annexes. Amendments should be avoided as they are considered dishonourable. Increasingly, be prepared to consider contracts under local law – with the provision of neutral (ie Swiss, Dutch) arbitration.

In public places, women should dress modestly.

Refrain from taking photographs without permission.

Pork should not be eaten in the presence of Muslims. It is polite to avoid eating, drinking or smoking in front of Muslims, during daylight hours in the month of Ramadan (when such consumption in public is illegal).

The purchase of alcohol is restricted to expatriate residents with a special liquor permit (not available to Muslims) and its consumption is confined to their private homes. Alcohol is a particularly sensitive subject in Qatar and the utmost discretion must be shown at all times by those permitted to consume it.

Getting there

Air

National airline: Qatar Airways

International airport/s: Doha International (DOH), 8km from city, with restaurant, bank, hotel reservations, shops, car hire.

A taxi from the airport to the city centre takes about 15 minutes. The larger hotels will send transport to the airport to collect their guests.

Airport tax: None

Surface

Road: Tarmac roads link all towns and villages in Qatar with Saudi Arabia. It is also possible to enter by good roads from the UAE.

Main port/s: Passenger services through Mina Salman, Mina Manama and Mina Muharroq, with ferries to Iran and Bahrain.

Getting about

National transport

Road: There are more than 1,000km of good roads (some dual carriageway), with a ring road system around Doha.

The Trans-Arabian Highway which links Doha with Saudi Arabia provides a continuous land connection between Qatar and Europe. Another highway which was build in conjunction with the UAE, links Qatar with the Gulf countries' network.

Buses: Doha's public bus service provides transport to and from the neighbouring towns. There is no public transport within the city.

City transport

Taxis: Taxis are orange and white and have black-on-yellow number plates, with metered fares.

Two-tier (day and night) fare system applies within the Doha city limits. They can be hired on a time basis, with a set hourly rate.

Some hotels offer a courtesy pick-up service; others offer the service but charge. A limousine can be booked through the hotel.

Car hire

If hiring for more than seven days, it is necessary to obtain a 30-day local licence – international or foreign licences are not acceptable. For this, a foreign or international licence, a letter from a local sponsor and passport must be produced within a week of arrival, and a test on road signs may be required. Third-party insurance is compulsory.

Speed limits are 60kph in cities and 100kph on highways. Traffic drives on the right.

Air-conditioned cars are available for hire, with a driver, and can be delivered to the airport or hotel.

BUSINESS DIRECTORY

The addresses listed below are a selection only. While World of Information makes every endeavour to check these addresses, we cannot guarantee that changes have not been made, especially to telephone numbers and area codes. We would welcome any corrections.

Telephone area codes

The international dialling code (IDD) for Qatar is +974, followed by subscriber's number.

Useful telephone numbers

Emergency (all services):	999
International operator:	150
Directory enquiries:	180
International enquiries:	190
Telegram service:	130
Speaking clock (English):	140
Ship to shore:	864-444

Chambers of Commerce

Qatar Chamber of Commerce and Industry, PO Box 402, Doha, (tel: 455-9111; fax: 466-1693; email: infor@qcci.org; internet: www.qcci.org).

Banking

Al Ahli Bank of Qatar, PO Box 2309, Doha (tel: 4326-611; fax: 4444-652).

Al Mashriq, PO Box 173, Doha (tel: 4413-213; fax: 4413-880).

Arab Bank Ltd., PO Box 172, Doha (tel: 4437-979; fax: 4410-774).

Bank Saderat Iran, PO Box 2256, Doha (tel: 4414-646; fax: 4428-077).

Banque Paribas, PO Box 2636, Doha (tel: 4433-844; fax: 4410-861).

Bank Sederat Iran, PO Box 2256, Doha (tel: 4414-646; fax: 4430-121).

Bank of Oman Ltd., PO Box 173, Doha (tel: 4413-213; fax: 4413-800).

Commercial Bank of Qatar Ltd, PO Box 3232, Doha (tel: 4490-222; fax: 4438-182).

Doha Bank, PO Box 3818, Doha (tel: 4456-660; fax: 4416-631).

Grindlays Qatar Bank, PO Box 2001, Doha (tel: 4425-466; fax: 4428-077).

HSBC Bank of the Middle East, PO Box 57, 810 Abdulla bin Jassim Street, Doha (tel: 4438-2100; fax: 4416-353).

Qatar Industrial Development Bank, PO Box 22789, Doha (tel: 4421-600; fax: 4416-631).

Qatar International Islamic Bank, PO Box 664, Doha (tel: 4409-409; fax: 4444-101).

Qatar Islamic Bank, PO Box 559, Doha (tel: 4438-000; fax: 4412-700).

Qatar National Bank, PO Box 1000, Doha (tel: 4407-407; fax: 4413-753; e-mail: webmaster@qatarbank.com).

Standard Chartered Bank, PO Box 29, Doha (tel: 4414-252; fax: 4413-739).

United Bank Ltd, PO Box 242, Doha (tel: 4438-666; fax: 4424-600).

Central bank

Qatar Central Bank, Corniche Street; PO Box 1234, Doha (tel: 445-6456; email: webmaster@qcb.gov.qa; internet: www.qcb.gov.qa).

Stock exchange

Doha Securities Market (DSM): www2.dsm.com.qa

Travel information

Doha International Airport information (tel: 4438-111).

Gulf Air, PO Box 138, Manama, Bahrain (tel: (+973) 322-200; fax: (+973) 440-466).

Qatar Airways, Almana Tower, PO Box 22550, Doha (tel: 4430-707; fax: 4352-433).

Qatar National Hotels Co, PO Box 2977, Doha (tel: 4426-414; fax: 4431-223).

National tourist organisation offices

Qatar Tourism Authority, P.O. Box 24624, Doha (tel: 441-1555; fax: 437-2993; email: info@experienceqatar.com; internet: http://experienceqatar.com)

Ministries

Ministry of Amiri Diwan Affairs, PO Box 923, Doha (tel: 4468-333; fax: 4412-617).

Ministry of Communications and Transport, PO Box 3416, Doha (tel: 4464-000; fax: 4413-886).

Ministry of Defence, PO Box 37, Doha (tel: 4604-111; fax: 4608-366).

Ministry of Education, PO Box 80, Doha (tel: 4333-444; fax: 4413-954).

Ministry of Electricity and Water, Department of Electricity, PO Box 41, Doha (tel: 4326-622; fax: 4426-608).

Ministry of Endowments and Islamic Affairs, PO Box 232, Doha (tel: 4452-222).

Ministry of Finance, PO Box 83, Doha (tel: 446-1444; fax: 441-3617).

Ministry of Foreign Affairs, PO Box 250, Doha (tel: 4334-334; fax: 4442-777).

Ministry of Information and Culture, PO Box 1836, Doha (tel: 4831-333; fax: 4831-518).

Ministry of Interior, PO Box 920, Doha (tel: 4430-000; fax: 44330-168); Passport and Immigration Division, PO Box 122, Doha (tel: 4443-300); Police Headquarters, PO Box 920, Doha (tel:

4330-000); Police Traffic Division, PO Box 8989, Doha (tel: 4868-000; fax: 4872-624); Residence Permits, PO Box 122, Doha (tel: 4325-588); Visa Section, PO Box 122, Doha (tel: 4328-129).

Ministry of Justice, PO Box 2377, Doha (tel: 4435-777; fax: 4832-868).

Ministry of Labour, Social Affairs and Housing, PO Box 201, Doha (tel: 4321-955; fax: 4432-929).

Ministry of Municipal and Agricultural Affairs, PO Box 2727, Doha (tel: 4336-336; fax: 4430-239).

Ministry of Public Health, PO Box 42, Doha (tel: 4441-555; fax: 4429-565).

National Oil Distribution Company (NODCO), PO Box 50033, Mesaieed (tel: 4776-555; fax: 4771-232).

Other useful addresses

Broadcasting and Television Corporation, PO Box 1836, Doha (tel: 4831-333; fax: 4831-518).

Central Tenders Committee, PO Box 1968, Doha (tel: 4413-089; fax: 4439-360).

Department of Civil Aviation, PO Box 3000, Doha (tel: 4426-262; fax: 4429-070).

Department of Commercial Affairs, PO Box 22355, Doha (tel: 4432-103; fax: 4431-412).

Department of Customs, PO Box 81, Doha (tel: 4457-457; fax: 4414-959).

Department of Economic Affairs, PO Box 1968, Doha (tel: 4416-234; fax: 4415-731).

Department of Environmental Affairs, PO Box 7634, Doha (tel: 4320-825; fax: 4415-246).

Department of Financial Affairs, PO Box 83, Doha (tel: 4461-444; fax: 4413-617).

Department of Industrial Development, PO Box 2599, Doha (tel: 4832-121; fax: 4832-024).

Department of Museum and Antiquities, PO Box 2777, Doha (tel: 4438-123).

Department of Post, PO Box 713, Doha (tel: 4835-555; fax: 4837-777).

Department of Safety, Quality and Environment, PO Box 47, Doha (tel: 4402-538; fax: 4402-207).

Department of Water, PO Box 162, Doha (tel: 4494-444).

Doha Securities Market, PO Box 22114, Doha (tel: 4328-025; fax: 4326-497).

Exhibitions Department, PO Box 1968, Doha (tel: 4834-450; fax: 4834-480).

Exploration and Development of New Ventures Department, PO Box 3212, Doha (tel: 4491-288; fax: 4831-850).

Government House, jPO Box 83, Doha (tel: 4461-444).

HH the Emir's Doha Palace, PO Box 923 (tel: 4415-888).

Information and Computer Services Department, PO Box 47, Doha (tel: 4402-240; fax: 4413-629).

Al Jazeera Satellite Channel, PO Box 23123, Doha (tel: 4890-890; fax: 4885-333).

Legal Affairs and Contracts Department, PO Box 3212, Doha (tel: 4491-467; fax: 4831-752).

Materials Department, PO Box 47, Doha (tel: 4332-222; fax: 4343-458).

Petroleum Engineering Department, PO Box 47, Doha (tel: 4402-440; fax: 4402-215).

Pharmaceuticals and Medicines Control Department, PO Box 1919, Doha (tel: 4447-828; fax: 4425-399).

Qatar Broadcasting Services, PO Box 3939, Doha (tel: 4894-4444; fax: 4894-202).

Qatari Business Association, PO Box 24475, Doha (435-3120; fax:435-3834).

Qatar Clean Energy Company (QACENCO), PO Box 22074, Doha (tel: 4415-556; fax: 4415-640).

Qatar Embassy (USA), 4200 Wisconsin Avenue, NW, Washington DC 20016 (tel: (+1-202) 274-1603; fax: (+1-202) 237-0061; email: washington@mofa.gov.qa).

Qatar Fertiliser Company (QAFCO), PO Box 50001, Doha (tel: 4770-252; fax: 4771-655).

Qatar Fuel Additives Company (QAFAC), PO Box 22700, Doha (tel: 4433-700; fax: 4433-766).

Qatar General Petroleum Corporation, Headquarters: PO Box 3212, Doha (tel: 4491-491; fax: 4836-999; internet: www.qgpc.com.qa); Oil and Gas Operations: PO Box 47, Doha (tel: 4402-000).

Qatar Liquefied Gas Company (QATARGAS), PO Box 22666, Doha (tel: 4739-400; fax: 4739-423).

Qatar National Cement Company, PO Box 1333, Doha (tel: 4350-800).

Qatar Petrochemical Company (QAPCO), PO Box 756, Doha (tel: 4321-105; fax: 4324-700).

Qatar Public Telecommunications Corp, PO Box 217, Doha (tel: 4400-333; fax: 4413-904).

Qatar Steel Company Ltd, PO Box 50090, Doha (tel: 4770-011; fax: 4771-424).

Qatar Television, PO Box 1944, Doha (tel: 4894-444; fax: 4438-316).

Ras Laffan Liquefied Natural Gas Company, PO Box 2400, Doha (tel: 4859-400; fax: 4833-855).

State Audit Bureau, PO Box 2466, Doha (tel: 4441-000; fax: 4412-101).

Qatar Financial Centre, PO Box 23245, Doha (tel: 4945-508; fax: 4830-928; email: info@qfc.com.qa, website: www.qfc.com.qa).

Qatar Financial Centre Regulatory Authority, PO Box 22989, Doha (tel: 4945-433; fax: 4835-031; email: info@qfcra.com.qa, website: www.qfcra.com.qa).

National news agency: Qatar News Agency

Internet sites

Arab net: www.arab.net/welcome.html

Arabia on line: www.arabia.com

Gulf business explorer: www.igulf.com/main.htm

Qatar Investment Promotion Department: www.investinqatar.com.qa

Qatar website: www.dib-qatar.com

Qatar yellow pages: www.qatar-yellowpages.com

Réunion

COUNTRY PROFILE

Historical profile

The island was uninhabited until the beginning of the seventeenth century when Arab explorers called it Diva Margabin. The Portuguese renamed it Ilha Santa Apolonia and the French settlers called it l'Île Bourbon. After the French Revolution it was given its current name, La Réunion.

1642 The island was first occupied by France and was ruled as a colony.

1946 La Réunion became a French Département d'Outre-Mer (DOM) (Overseas Department).

1973 The headquarters of French military forces in the Indian Ocean was established on the island.

1974 La Réunion was further incorporated into the French political system and granted the status of region of France.

1983 France granted autonomy in the administration of La Réunion through devolution, establishing a Regional Council.

1992 A contentious newcomer to local politics, Camille Sudre, the owner of a pirate television station, created the Free-DOM party, which won the largest block of seats in the Regional Council. The result was annulled when Sudre's TV broadcasts for his party were deemed to have been political propaganda.

1993 The Free-DOM party led by Camille Sudre's wife, Marguerite, won the elections with a reduced majority.

1996 Unemployment reached 40 per cent.

1998 Paul Vergés was elected head of the regional council.

2001 Gonthier Friederici became *préfet*.

2002 La Réunion adopted the euro as its official currency.

2004 Dominique Vian took office as *préfet*.

2005 Laurent Cayrel was appointed *préfet*.

2006 Pierre-Henry Maccioni was appointed *préfet*. An estimated one-third of the population were afflicted by the mosquito-borne chikungunya disease which killed several hundred; the tourist industry suffered a sharp downturn and French army sanitisation crews were drafted in to spray insecticide.

2008 In local elections Nassimah Dindar was re-elected Conseil Général. She organised a broad spectrum political coalition including the Mouvement Démocrate (MoDem) (Democratic Movement) with Parti Socialiste (PS) (Socialist Party), Parti Communiste de Réunion (PCR) (Réunion Communist Party), Union pour un Mouvement Populaire (UMP) (Popular Movement Union) and other various small, right-wing groupings.

2009 A new metalled road, Route 17, connecting the north and south of the island, was opened by François Fillon (Etats Généraux (Overseas Estates General)).

2010 Growth in tourist numbers from the EU, in the first half of the year, was up 23 per cent. Didier Robert was elected president of the Regional Council in March. Three areas of outstanding natural beauty and biodiversity, pitons, cirques and remparts, in the central region of the Réunion National Park were added to the Unesco World Heritage list on 1 August.

Political structure

Constitution

28 September 1958 (French Fifth Republic)

Under the 1946 constitution of the French Fourth Republic, La Réunion became a Département d'Outre-Mer (DOM) (Overseas Department) of France. In 1974, it was granted additional status as a region of France.

La Réunion is represented in the French National Assembly in Paris by five directly elected deputies and in the Senate by three indirectly elected senators.

Since 1983, following the French government's policy of decentralisation, regional councils have been elected with powers similar to those of the regions.

Administration is by a préfét appointed by the government in Paris.

The local government comprises a Conseil Général (General Council) of 44 members and a 45-member Conseil Régional (Regional Council), both directly elected for six-year terms.

There are five *arrondisements*.

Form of state

Democratic, presidential republic

Département d'Outre-Mer (DOM) (Overseas Department) of France, with additional status as a région (region) of France.

The executive

A préfet, appointed from Paris, governs the locally elected Conseil Général (General Council).

KEY FACTS

Official name: La Réunion

Head of State: President of France Nicolas Sarkozy represented by *Préfet* Pierre-Henry Maccioni (from Aug 2006)

Head of government: President of the Conseil Général Nassimah Dindar (since 2004; re-elected March 2008); President of the Conseil Régional Didier Robert (from 26 Mar 2010)

Ruling party: Coalition led by Mouvement Démocrate (MoDem) (Democratic Movement), with Parti Socialiste (PS) (Socialist Party), Parti Communiste de Réunion (PCR) (Réunion Communist Party), Union pour un Mouvement Populaire (UMP) (Popular Movement Union) (from 24 Mar 2008)

Area: 2,512 square km

Population: 765,000 (2010)*

Capital: Saint Denis

Official language: French

Currency: Euro (eur) = 100 cents

Exchange rate: eur0.75 per US$ (Oct 2011)

* estimated figure

National legislature
La Réunion is represented in the French National Assembly by five directly elected deputies, for five-year terms and in the Senate by three indirectly elected senators for three-year terms.
The Conseil Général (General Council) has powers similar to those of mainland regions of France.
The local government comprises a *Conseil Régional* (regional council) with 45 members, elected for four-year terms by proportional representation.
Legal system
French legal system
Last elections
March 2004 (Conseil Général and Conseil Régional)
Next elections
2010 (Conseil Général and Conseil Régional)

Political parties
Free-DOM (right-wing group); Parti Communiste de Réunion (PCR) (Réunion Communist Party); Rassemblement pour la République (RPR) (Gaullist Rally for the Republic); two factions of the Parti Socialiste (PS) (Socialist Party); Union pour la France (UPF) (Union for France); Union pour la Démocratie Française-Centre Démocratique Sociale (UDF-CDS) (Union for French Democracy-Social Democratic Centre).
Ruling party
Coalition led by Mouvement Démocrate (MoDem) (Democratic Movement), with Parti Socialiste (PS) (Socialist Party), Parti Communiste de Réunion (PCR) (Réunion Communist Party), Union pour un Mouvement Populaire (UMP) (Popular Movement Union) (from 24 Mar 2008)

Population
765,000 (2010)*
Last census: 1 January 2006: 781,962
Population density: 262 inhabitants per square km. Urban population: 69 per cent.
Annual growth rate: 1.8 per cent (2003)
Ethnic make-up
African (64 per cent), Indian (28 per cent), European (2.2 per cent) and Chinese (2.2 per cent) descent.
Religions
The majority of the population is Roman Catholic (86 per cent); there are also groups of Hindus, Muslims and Buddhists.

Education
Literacy rate: 89 per cent, adult rate (2003)

Health
Health services comply with French standards, there are some 1,270 doctors, 275 pharmacies and 17 hospitals, including clinics.
Life expectancy: 73.4 years (estimate 2003)
Fertility rate/Maternal mortality rate: 2.5 births per woman (2003)
Birth rate/Death rate: 20 births per 1,000 population; 5.5 deaths per 1,000 population (2003).
Child (under 5 years) mortality rate (per 1,000): Eight per 1,000 live births (2003)

Main cities
Saint Denis (capital, estimated population 140,415 in 2005), Saint Paul (100,849), Saint Pierre (76,900), Le Tampon (69,043), Saint Louis, Le Port, Saint André.

Languages spoken
As well as French, Creole is commonly spoken.
Official language/s
French

Media
Press
In French, *Le Journal de L'Ile* (www.clicanoo.com) and *Temoignages* (www.temoignages.re) are published daily in St Denis. Regional publications, in English, include *APA* (www.apanews.net) and *Panapress* (www.panapress.com).
Broadcasting
RFO Réunion (http://reunion.rfo.fr) is the pubic broadcasting network providing radio and television programmes originating from France. The private TV station Antenne Réunion Télévision (www.antennereunion.fr) provides a range of local news and international programmes. All broadcasts are in French.
News agencies
Imaz Press Réunion, (tel: 200-656; email: fax: 200-549; email: ipr@ipreunion.com; internet: www.ipreunion.com).

Economy
La Réunion is dependent on France for 75 per cent of its GNP.
The service sector accounts for 75 per cent of GDP, with tourism providing around 80 per cent of foreign exchange. Agriculture, particularly sugar cane production provides around 10 per cent of GDP. Although social indicators are good, unemployment is a pressing problem affecting almost 40 per cent of the labour force. There is a large income and social divide between the majority of the population, which is impoverished and black, and the rich minority, which is white or Indian.

External trade
As a département d'outre-mer (DOM) of France, Réunion is integrated as an outermost region of the European Union and adopts all EU trade agreements.
Imports
The main imports are manufactured goods, food, beverages, tobacco, machinery and transportation equipment, raw materials, and petroleum products.
Main sources: France (typically over 60 per cent), Bahrain (3.0 per cent), Germany (3.0 per cent), Italy (3.0 per cent).
Exports
The main export is sugar (over 60 per cent), rum and molasses, perfume essences and lobster.
Main destinations: France (typically over 70 per cent), Japan (6.0 per cent), Comoros (4.0 per cent).

Agriculture
Farming
Sugar cane, the main crop, is grown on 30,900 hectares. Cash crops include tea and tobacco. Ylang-ylang, vetiver and geraniums are used as components of aromatic essences.
The agriculture sector contributes about 8 per cent to GDP and employs approximately 13 per cent of the workforce.
Around 22 per cent of the land is cultivated. Much of the island's food supply is imported.
Fishing
Typical annual fish catches are over 4,000mt and crustacea catches are over 15mt.

Industry and manufacturing
The industrial sector contributes about 19 per cent to GDP and employs some 12 per cent of the workforce.
The production of processed sugar and rum accounts for most industrial activity.
The Ecopipe steel pipe mill (funded by the French government and South African private capital) started operations in 1997 at Le Port, on the west coast of Réunion. It has the capacity to produce 15,000 tonnes a year and employs 80 people.

Tourism
Tourism is now the principal economic activity. As a *département* of France, the majority of visitors tend to be French. Numbers fell as a consequence of the 11 September 2001 terrorist attacks in the US, when worldwide travel dropped. In 2003 recovery was under way with 432,000 tourist arrivals recorded. La Réunion's link with France gives its tourism sector an edge, in the European market, over its local rivals.
Air Austral is able to offer the cheapest flights from Europe to the region, while the island's currency is the euro.

Mining
There are no significant mineral resources.

Hydrocarbons
There are no hydrocarbon reserves. Réunion relies entirely on imported petroleum products, provided through France, although fuel distribution and marketing is carried out by commercial oil companies. Natural gas is neither produced nor consumed.

Energy
Total installed generating capacity was 44MW, approximately 60 per cent of which is provided by hydropower. Réunion has one thermal power plant that runs on imported coal. This produces around 39 per cent of Réunion's electricity needs.

Banking and insurance
Central bank
Banque de France; European Central Bank (ECB).

Time
GMT plus four hours

Geography
Réunion is an island in the Indian Ocean, lying about 800km (500 miles) east of Madagascar. It is a volcanic, mountainous island.
Hemisphere
Southern

Climate
The climate varies greatly according to altitude: at sea-level, it is tropical, with average temperatures between 20 and 28 degrees Celsius (C); in the uplands, it is much cooler, with average temperatures between 8 and 19 degrees C. From July to November, the temperature in high altitude places can drop to 10 degrees C during the day and to 6 degrees C at night.
Rainfall is abundant; the cyclone season lasts from December to April.
Summer runs from November to April with an average temperature of 27 degrees C. Winter stretches from May to October with an average temperature of 23 degrees C.

Dress codes
Generally light summer clothes are required, with some woollen garments for chilly evenings.

Entry requirements
Passports
Required by all, except nationals of EU/EEA countries, Monaco, Switzerland with national identity cards; passports must be valid for three months beyond date of departure,
Visa
Required by all, except nationals of EU/EEA countries, North America, Australasia, Japan, Israel and some other countries for stays up to three months. Nationals of the US, Canada and several other countries need a visa if they receive a salary. Nationals of EU/EEA countries, the Vatican, Liechtenstein and Monaco do not require long-term visas issued for stays in excess of three months. Proof of adequate funds for stay, an itinerary, a guarantee of repatriation if necessary, return/onward ticket and, for business travellers, an invitation from a local company or organisation are also required. .
Currency advice/regulations
There are no restrictions on the import or export of local and foreign currenc, subject to declaration of amounts over eur7,600.

Health (for visitors)
There are no compulsory vaccinations. Passengers from endemic countries should be inoculated against yellow fever.
Advisable precautions
Vaccinations for diphtheria, tetanus, typhoid fever, hepatitis A and tuberculosis are advisable, and precautions should be taken against malaria. Malaria and chikungunya are caused by mosquitoes, precautions including mosquito repellents, nets and clothing covering the body should be used.

Credit cards
Major credit cards are accepted.

Public holidays (national)
Fixed dates
1 Jan (New Year's Day), 1 May (Labour Day), 8 May (1945 Victory Day), 14 Jul (Bastille Day), 15 Aug (Assumption Day), 1 Nov (All Saints' Day), 11 Nov (Armistice Day), 20 Dec (Abolition of Slavery Day), 25 Dec (Christmas Day).
Variable dates
Good Friday, Easter Monday, Ascension Day, Whit Monday.

Working hours
Banking
Mon–Fri: 0800–1600.
Business
Mon–Fri: 0800–1200; 1400–1800.
Government
Mon–Fri: 0800–1900; Sat: 0900–1400.
Shops
Mon–Sat: 0830–1200; 1430–1800.
Some food stores are open on Sunday.

Telecommunications
Mobile/cell phones
There are GSM 900 and 1800 services available.

Electricity supply
220V

Weights and measures
The metric system is in use.

Getting there
Air
National airline: Air Austral.
International airport/s: Roland-Garros Airport (RUN), 8km from Saint Denis; post office, restaraunts, duty free shop, car hire.
Other airport/s: Pierrefonds Airport (ZSE), 5km from Saint Pierre.
Airport tax: None.
Surface
Water: There are limited passenger services to Réunion. A cruise liner from Mauritius visits regularly.
Main port/s: Port Réunion.

Getting about
National transport
Road: A *route nationale* circles the island, following the coast and linking all the main towns, and another crosses the island from south-west to north-east linking Saint Pierre and Saint Benoît. There are 370km of main roads, 754km of secondary roads and nearly 1,600km of smaller secondary roads, all in good condition.
Buses: A comfortable bus service (*cars jaunes*), links most towns.
Car hire
A French or international driver's licence is required. The highway code is the same as for France. Driving is on the right.

BUSINESS DIRECTORY
The addresses listed below are a selection only. While World of Information makes every endeavour to check these addresses, we cannot guarantee that changes have not been made, especially to telephone numbers and area codes. We would welcome any corrections.

Telephone area codes
The international dialling code (IDD) for Réunion is +262; this is followed by another 262 and then the subscriber's number.

Useful telephone numbers
Available services for visiting cell phone users:

Emergency calls: (free)	112
Telephone enquiries: (call SFR for information)	222
Suberscriber services: (local rate)	900

Chambers of Commerce
Réunion Chamber of Commerce Industry, 13 Rue Pasteur, PO Box 120, 97463 Saint-Denis cedex (tel: 942-100; fax: 942-290; e-mail: sg.dir@reunion.cci.fr).

Banking
Banque de la Réunion, 27 rue Jean Chatel, 97711 Saint Denis, Cedex 9 (tel: 400-157; fax: 400-060).

Banque Nationale de Paris Intercontinentale (BNPI), 67 rue Juliette-Dodu, Saint Denis (tel: 403-030).

Banque Régionale d'Escompte et de Depot (BRED), 33 rue Victor-Mac-Auliffe, Saint Denis (tel: 901-560).

Caisse d'Epargne Ecureuil, 55 rue de Paris, Saint Denis (tel: 948-000).

Crédit Agricole, 18 rue Félix-Guyon, Saint Denis (tel: 909-100).

Banque Française Commerciale (BFC'OI'), 60 rue Alexis-de-Villeneuve, Saint Denis (tel: 405-555).

Central bank

Banque de France, 1 rue la Vrillière, 75001 Paris, Dept 75, France (tel: (+33-1) 4292-4292; fax: (+33-1) 4292-4500)

European Central Bank (ECB), Kaiserstrasse 29, D-60311 Frankfurt am Main, Germany (tel: (+49-69) 13-440; fax: (+49-69) 1344-6000).

Travel information

Air Austral, PO Box 611, 4 Rue de Nice, 97473 Saint Denis Cedex (tel: 909-090; fax: 909-09; e-mail: reservation@air-austral.com).

Air France, PO Box 845, 7 Avenue de la Victoire, 97477 Saint Denis Cedex (tel: 403-800; fax: 403-840; e-mail: mail.runsh@airfrance.fr).

Fédération Réunionnaise du Tourisme, Résidence Sainte Anne, 18 rue Sainte Anne, 97400 Saint Denis (tel : 413-967; fax : 943-180; e-mail: fr-pat@wanadoo.fr).

Maison de la Montagne, 5 rue Rontaunay, 97400 Saint-Denis (tel: 907-878; fax : 418-429; e-mail : resa@reunion-nature.com).

Ministry of tourism

Delegation Régionale au Commerce, à l'Artisanat et Tourisme, Préfecture de la Réunion, 31 rue de Paris, 97400 Saint-Denis (tel: 319-999; fax: 316-666; e-mail: DRT974@tourisme.gouv.fr).

National tourist organisation offices

Comité du Tourisme de la Réunion, PO Box 615, Place du 20 Décembre 1848, 97472 Saint Denis Cedex (tel: 210-041; fax: 210-021; e-mail: ctr@la-reunion-tourisme.com).

Ministries

Direction Départementale des Affaires Sanitaires et Sociales, Rue Georges Brassens, BP 199, 97490 Sainte-Clothilde (tel: 486-060; fax: 486-008).

Direction Départementale du Travail et de l'Emploi, 24 Rue Maréchal Leclerc, 97488 Saint Denis Cedex (tel: 486-600; fax: 486-666).

Direction Régionale des Affaires Culturelles, 31 Rue Amiral Lacaze 97400 Saint Denis (tel: 219-171; fax: 416-193).

Direction Régionale de la Jeunesse et des Sports, 14 Allée des Saphirs, BP 297, 97487 Saint Denis Cedex (tel: 901-616; fax: 213-864).

Other useful addresses

Agence Nationale pour l'Emploi 10 Rue Champ Fleury, 97490 Sainte Clothilde (tel: 219-236; fax: 417-383).

Association pour le Développement Industriel de la Réunion, 18 Rue Milius, 97468 Saint Denis Cedex (tel: 214-269; fax: 203-757).

British Consul, 94b Avenue Leconte Delisle, 97490 Sainte Clotilde (tel: 291-491; fax: 293-991).

Civil Aviation Management, 11 Avenue de la Victoire, 97489 Saint Denis Cedex (tel: 930-000; fax: 211-331).

Compagnie Générale Maritime (CGM), 2 Rue de l'Est, BP 2010, 97822 Le Port Cedex (tel: 420-088; fax: 432-304).

Conseil Economique et Social de la Réunion, PO Box 7191, 10 Rue du Béarn, 97719 Saint Denis (tel: 979-630; fax: 979-631; e-mail: webmaster@cesr-reunion.fr).

Conseil Général, Hôtel du Département, 2 Rue Source, 97400 Saint Denis (tel: 903-030; fax: 903-999).

Conseil Régional, Hôtel de la Région, Avenue René Cassin, Le Moufia, 97494 Sainte Clothilde Cedex (tel: 487-000; fax: 487-071).

Institut National de la Statistique et des Etudes Economiques, Service Régional de la Réunion, 15 Rue de l'Ecole, 97490 Sainte Clotilde (tel: 295-157).

Palais du Justice, 166 Rue Juliette Dodu, 97488 Saint Denis (tel: 405-858; fax: 219-532).

Rectorat de la Réunion, 24 Avenue Georges, Brassens, 97702 Saint Denis, Messagerie Cedex 9 (tel: 481-010; fax: 481-366).

Société de Développement Economique de la Réunion (SODERE), 26 Rue Labourdonnais, 97469 Saint Denis (tel: 200-168; fax: 200-507).

Internet sites

Africa Business Network: http://www.ifc.org/abn

African Development Bank: http://www.afdb.org

Mbendi AfroPaedia (information on companies, countries, industries and stock exchanges in Africa): http://mbendi.co.za

Romania

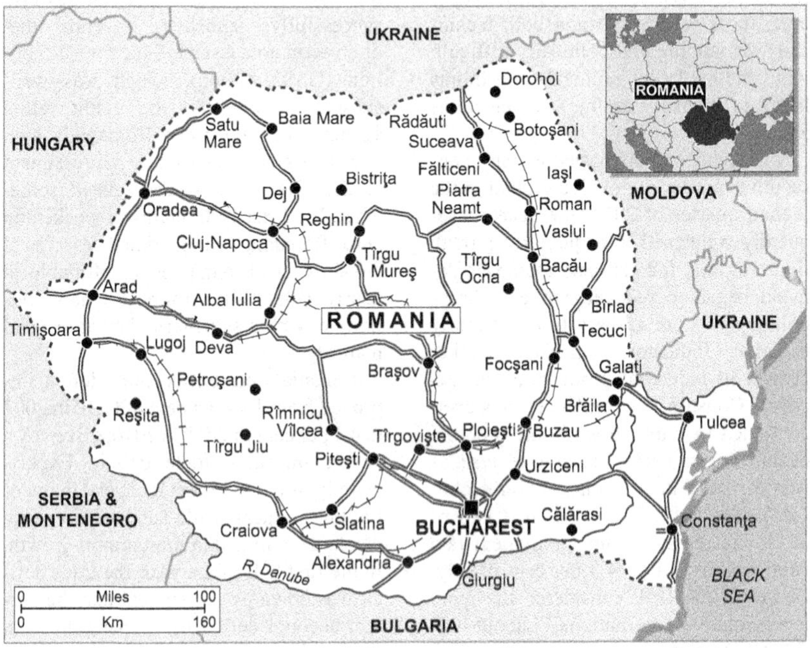

In mid-2010 the Romanian government had received a sharp warning shot fired across its bows when, taking their cue from the late Vaclav Havel's iconic *The Power of the Powerless*, tens of thousands of public sector workers took to the streets of Bucharest, the Romanian capital, to protest against the government's plans to cut wages and pensions. The government had proposed draconian wage cuts of 25 per cent and pension cuts of 15 per cent in order to reduce the budget deficit. International markets were beginning to doubt the resolve of the Romanian government to address its structural problems. An auction of government debt in early 2010 had failed to attract sufficient interest. Romania's economy shrank more than 7 per cent in 2010, forcing recourse to an International Monetary Fund (IMF) bail-out in order to meet its wage bill. The public sector in Romania accounts for some thirty per cent of national employment. By European standards this is a relatively commendable proportion. The comparable figure for France is no less than 55 per cent. The new austerity measures were designed to enable Romania to qualify for the next installment of a US$25 billion IMF loan. The protest was without doubt one of the largest since the Romanian Revolution that eventually secured the installation of democracy and the end of the Ceaucescu régime. The protestors' criticism was directed at the government of Prime Minister Emil Boc and President Traian Basescu.

The economy

In the view of the IMF, Romania's gross domestic product (GDP) growth weakened in The second quarter of 2011, but a good harvest was expected to contribute to a rise of 1.5 per cent for 2011 as a whole. In 2012, growth was expected to accelerate to 3.5–4 per cent. However, recent developments in Europe, in particular the euro-zone crisis, had boosted downside risks. As a consequence, Romania's currency, the leu had lost the gains made earlier in the year. Banking sector risks have also heightened. Over 30 per cent of Romania's banking sector is in Austrian hands, 22 per cent is Greek-owned with Portuguese, Italian and French banks also present in the country. Attending a

KEY FACTS

Official name: Romania

Head of State: Head of State: President Traian Basescu (from 2004; re-elected 6 Dec 2009)

Head of government: Prime Minister Emil Boc (PD-L) (since 2008; re-appointed 23 Dec 2009)

Ruling party: Coalition (known as Da PNL-PD): Alianta Dreptate si Adevar (DA) (Justice and Truth Alliance) led by Partidul National Liberal (PNL) (National Liberal Party), Partidul Democrat (PD) (Democratic Party), Uniunea Democratica Maghiara din Romania (UDMR) (Hungarian Democratic Alliance of Romania), Partidul Conservator (PC) (Conservative Party) (since 2004)

Area: 237,500 square km

Population: 21.44 million (2010)*

Capital: Bucharest

Official language: Romanian

Currency: New leu (plural lei) (Nleu) = 100 ban

Exchange rate: Nleu3.25 per US$ (Oct 2011)

GDP per capita: US$7,542 (2010)

GDP real growth: -1.30% (2010)

GDP: US$161.60 billion (2010)

Labour force: 4.24 billion (2010)

Unemployment: 7.60% (2010)

Inflation: 6.10% (2010)

Oil production: 89,000 bpd (2010)

Balance of trade: -US$7.80 billion (2010)

Annual FDI: US$3.45 billion (2010)

* estimated figure

conference organised by the London *Economist* magazine, Romania's bankers pointed out that the country's banking system was still solid and that the risk that the subsidiaries of foreign banks might become bankrupt and need renationalisation was zero. Even if parent banks were restricting capital flows, Romania remained attractive compared to other countries in the region, according to a vice governor of Romania's Banca Nationala a Romaniei (BNR) (National Bank of Romania) (central bank).

Romania's inflation dropped sharply in June–July 2011, but was still expected by the IMF to remain above the central bank's inflation target of around the 3 per cent mark in 2011 before returning to the target range in 2012. Romania's continued strong export performance was expected to stabilise the current account deficit below 5 per cent in 2011–12. The IMF noted that implementing the ambitious structural reform agenda and achieving the fiscal goals for 2012 would be challenging. Romania's fiscal performance appeared to be on track to meet the 2011 deficit target and the authorities' plans for 2012 could well deliver a deficit of under 3 per cent of GDP in cash terms. However, reaching the authorities commitment to the European Union (EU) of under 3 per cent of GDP in accrual (ESA) terms will require additional adjustment of at least 0.5 per cent of GDP to cover the inclusion by Eurostat of additional entities into the general government account, as well as the traditional gap between cash and accrual totals.

The government is proceeding with plans to improve the governance and regulation of the state-owned enterprises (SOE) in the energy and transport sectors, as well as plans for the restructuring and/or privatisation of key firms. However, these reforms remain both technically demanding and politically difficult, with the volatile political constraints likely to intensify as the 2012 elections approach.

Although Romania posted its third consecutive quarter of positive growth in the second quarter of 2011, the pace subsequently weakened to a quarterly growth figure of only 0.2 per cent. Domestic demand began to recover, while – disappointingly – net exports turned slightly negative. Indicators suggested weaker growth in industrial production and exports. Consumer confidence, however, continued to improve while the monthly decline in retail sales began to reverse, as was the case in the construction sector. Job losses had halted in the first half of 2011, the registered unemployment rate continued to fall, to 4.8 per cent in July. However, the IMF considered the more representative International Labour Office (ILO) measure to show a rate of 7.3 per cent in July 2011.

Inflation dropped to 4.9 per cent in July from its peak of 8.5 per cent in May 2011, reflecting a large decline in food prices and the elimination of the 2010 VAT increase from the 12-month index. As the labour market gradually stabilised, wages were starting to rise in nominal terms, but real wages and unit labour costs were still declining.

Between January and May 2011, portfolio inflows rose and the authorities also successfully launched a euro medium-term note issue in June for €1.5 billion (US$2 billion), which was well-subscribed. In July, the credit rating agency Fitch upgraded Romania's long term foreign currency rating to investment grade. The leu also appreciated somewhat, by 3 per cent against a weakening euro. Romania's international reserves at end-July 2011 remained comfortable at nearly €35 billion (almost US$47 billion), covering short-term debt at residual maturity.

Romania's current account deficit improved from 13.4 per cent of GDP in 2007 to 4.1 per cent of GDP in 2010, driven by a strong shrinking trade deficit. Exports were booming with the recovery in major trading partners while subdued domestic demand continued to limit import growth. In the first half of the year, the trade deficit was down by 22 per cent and the current account deficit by 29 per cent from the previous year. The trade balance continued to improve fuelled by strong exports, particularly in the machinery and automotive sectors. With the help of the current transfers to the public sector, mainly due to disbursements from EU funds approved in 2010, the current account dropped to around 3 per cent of GDP on a 12-month rolling basis through June.

Romania's GDP growth was expected to reach 1.5 per cent in 2011, initially led by exports, with domestic demand recovering gradually in the second half of the year, reflecting good agricultural output and a recovery in the labour market. In 2012, growth was expected to accelerate to 3.5–4 per cent, with the recovery shifting from external to domestic demand as consumption recovered and investment increased with rising EU funds absorption. Increased investor confidence, coupled with planned privatisation under the programme, are expected to bring renewed FDI and capital inflows.

KEY INDICATORS — Romania

	Unit	2006	2007	2008	2009	2010
Population	m	21.64	21.56	21.49	21.40	*21.44
Gross domestic product (GDP)	US$bn	122.65	169.30	200.10	161.50	161.60
GDP per capita	US$	5,668	7,850	9,310	7,542	7,542
GDP real growth	%	7.9	6.2	7.1	-7.1	-1.3
Inflation	%	6.5	4.8	7.8	5.6	6.1
Unemployment	%	5.5	4.1	4.0	6.3	7.6
Oil output	'000 bpd	105.0	105.0	99.0	93.0	89.0
Natural gas output	bn cum	12.1	11.6	11.5	10.9	10.9
Coal output	mtoe	7.4	9.0	6.5	5.7	5.8
Exports (fob) (goods)	US$m	30,206.0	40,349.0	49,626.0	40,713.0	49,411.0
Imports (fob) (goods)	US$m	35,859.0	64,689.0	76,721.0	50,482.0	57,216.0
Balance of trade	US$m	-5,653.0	-24,340.0	-27,095.0	-9,482.0	-7,805.0
Current account	US$m	-12,748.0	-22,899.0	-24,885.0	-7,482.0	-6,480.0
Total reserves minus gold	US$m	28,066.0	37,194.0	36,868.0	40,757.0	43,361.0
Foreign exchange	US$m	28,066.0	37,194.0	36,747.0	39,344.0	42,303.0
Exchange rate	per US$	2.81	2.43	2.52	3.05	3.18

* estimated figure

Risk assessment

Economy	Fair
Politics	Fair
Regional stability	Fair

COUNTRY PROFILE

Historical profile

1881 After surviving numerous invasions and regional upheavals, Romania became an independent country headed by a monarchy.
1918 Romania supported the Allies during the First World War and gained territory close to its borders.
1919 Hungary attacked Romania in retaliation for lost territory. The Romanians quickly defeated Hungary and briefly occupied parts of the country.
1920 Romania gained further parts of Hungarian territory through the Treaty of Trianon.
1929–34 Romania's agricultural sector was severely affected by a collapse in international grain prices. With the country in recession, the fascist and German-funded Iron Guard movement increased in popularity. In 1933, the organisation assassinated the prime minister, Ion Duca.
1938 King Carol, the head of state, declared Romania a royalist dictatorship and appointed a right-wing government. Carol ordered the arrest and execution of members of the Iron Guard.
1940 Military officers, helped by the Iron Guard, seized power. General Ion Antonescu forced Carol to abdicate. Carol's son, Michel V, replaced him as King. German troops were deployed in Romania and the country joined the Axis powers.
1941 The Iron Guard attempted to rebel against the Romanian government after they were ordered to disarm. A joint Romanian and German operation crushed the Iron Guard's rebellion.
1943 The Soviet Union invaded Romania.
1944 Antonescu's government was overthrown and replaced by a Communist coalition government.
1947–48 The monarchy was deposed and the Communist government declared the Romanian People's Republic.
1965 Nicolae Ceausescu took the position of first secretary of the Partidul Comunist Roman (RCP) (Romanian Communist Party).
1974 Ceausescu became president.
1985–86 An austerity programme lead to food shortages and widespread power cuts.
1987 The army occupied power plants and crushed workers' demonstrations in Brasov.
1989 Riots in the city of Timisoara ignited a nationwide revolt. Parts of the army joined the revolutionaries, forming the Frontul Salvarii Nationale (FSN) (National Salvation Front). Ceausescu and his wife, Elena, were summarily executed by a military tribunal and nearly 45 years of Communist dictatorship came to an abrupt and bloody end.
1990 Ion Iliescu was elected president, winning 85 per cent of the vote as the FSN candidate. Petre Roman formed a new government.
1991 Roman resigned as prime minister and was replaced by Teodro Stolojan after his reform programme led to civil unrest. Stolojan successfully guided Romania's new constitution through a referendum and parliamentary vote.
1992 Presidential elections were again won by Iliescu, who had formed his own political party, the Frontul Democrat al Salvarii Nationale (FDSN) (Democratic National Salvation Front), following a split within the FSN.
1996 Iliescu stood again for the presidency and was defeated by Emil Constantinescu of the Conventia Democrata Romana (CDR) (Romanian Democratic Convention) coalition. Victor Ciorbea (of the ruling CDR coalition). The FSN re-named itself the Partidul Democratiei Sociale din Romania (PDSR) (Democratic Social Party of Romania).
1998 Ciorbea resigned and was replaced by Radu Vasile.
1999 After relations with his cabinet collapsed, Vasile was replaced as prime minister by Mugur Isarescu.
2000 Cyanide leaked from a mine in northern Romania and polluted rivers in Hungary and Yugoslavia. Ion Iliescu won the presidency in the second round of voting. After parliamentary elections Adrian Nastase became prime minister, heading a coalition government, comprising the PDSR, Partidul Social Democrat Romania (PSDR) (Romanian Social Democratic Party) and the Partidul Umanist din Romania (PUR) (Humanist Party of Romania).
2001 Iliescu's PDSR merged with the PSDR to become the Partidul Social Democrat (PSD) (Social Democratic Party).
2003 In a referendum, 90 per cent of voters approved constitutional amendments to bring Romanian law in line with EU law.
2004 Romania joined NATO. Bucharest mayor (he later resigned as required by the constitution), Traian Basescu of the Partidul Democrat-Liberal (PD-L) (Democratic Liberal Party), won the runoff presidential election. Basescu appointed Calin Popescu Tariceanu (PNL) as prime minister.
2005 Romania approved the EU accession treaty. The currency was re-valued at the rate of 10,000 old lei to one new leu. Prime Minister Tariceanu resigned, but after severe flooding killed 20 people, he retracted his resignation in order to focus on the reconstruction of the country.
2006 The EU officially agreed Romania's membership providing strong curbs were imposed on organised crime and corruption.
2007 Romania joined the EU. Parliament impeached President Basescu on charges of unconstitutional conduct during months of dispute between the president and prime minister. A later referendum on impeachment failed. The Constitutional Court reinstated Basescu's presidency.
2008 In new elections the Partidul Social Democrat-Partidul Conservator (Alianta PSD+PC) (Social Democratic Party-Conservative Party) alliance won by a tiny majority, 33.09 per cent (114 seats) in the vote in the Chamber of Deputies; the PD-L with 32.4 per cent (115), won most seats for a single party. The PSD and PD-L formed a ruling coalition and President Basescu appointed Emil Boc (PD-L) as prime minister,
2009 The International Court of Justice ruled on a maritime boundary dispute between Romania and Ukraine. A new border settled a 40-year disagreement (over an area of the Black Sea) by extending a line offshore from the land border, giving Romania and Ukraine both a segment of what is thought to contain rich fields of hydrocarbons. Both countries agreed to the court ruling. The PSD withdrew from the coalition government in protest at the sacking of the PSD interior minister, who had implied potential fraud in the upcoming presidential elections. The ruling PD-L continued as a minority government. However it later lost a vote of no-confidence in parliament and was forced to resign. President Basescu nominated firstly Lucian Croitoru and later Liviu Negoita as prime minister, but the PSD majority in parliament insisted that Klaus Iohannis should by prime minister; a stalemate followed as neither side backed down. A referendum agreed to abolish the senate and reduce the number of parliamentarians to a maximum of 300. In a runoff presidential election, incumbent Traian Basescu won 50.33 per cent of the vote, Mircea Geoana (PSD) 49.66 per cent. Breaking the deadlock, parliament agreed to President Basescu's nomination of Emil Boc as prime minister.
2010 In August, French authorities began repatriating to Romania foreign-born Roma people living without permits in camps around France; the move sparked condemnation from the EU and human rights groups'.
2010 In May the government announced a package of austerity measures, including large-scale cuts to public sector wages and pensions. There were protests in Bucharest. In June the constitutional court ruled that the proposed 15 per cent cut in state pensions was unconstitutional. Boc said the alternative was to increase VAT to 24 per cent in order to cut the deficit. In

July further austerity measures, including a 25 per cent cut in public sector wages, lead to more protests. Romania's high level of corruption became an issue when the EU called on Romania to take urgent action to tackle crime and corruption, and France and Germany blocked Romania's membership of the Schengen passport-free zone, saying it still needed to make 'irreversible progress' against corruption and organised crime.
2011 On 9 June, The Netherlands announced that it would veto the EU decision (taken on 8 June), to admit Bulgaria and Romania into the Schengen area for passport-free travel of citizens and goods, and impose a one-year delay in view of the turmoil in the Middle East and its potential for Arab migration to the EU in 2011–12.

Political structure

Constitution

The 1991 constitution proclaimed a democratic, pluralist system of government in which citizens' freedom and rights are guaranteed, although there are no specific measures protecting minority rights. It also stipulated the separation of the three public authorities – legislative, executive and judicial.

In 2003, the constitution was changed to bring it in line with EU law, in which private property is guaranteed, the police is demilitarised and the justice system is independent; ethnic minorities may use their mother tongue when dealing with the state and foreigners are permitted to buy land in Romania.

Both parliament and the president are elected by universal vote every four years. The president may not remain a member of any political party, and is limited to a maximum two terms in office. The minimum voting age is 18 years.

Romania is divided into 40 administrative counties, with Bucharest divided into administrative sectors. Each county, town and village has its own local authority headed by an elected, executive mayor and an elected council. Local government is based on the principle of local autonomy and decentralisation of public services, with locally elected mayors, city and county councils. A prefect for each county is appointed by central government as the ultimate authority for that region.

Form of state

Parliamentary democratic republic

The executive

The president nominates the prime minister and the government on the basis of a vote of confidence from parliament and is the commander-in-chief of the armed forces. The president's term of office is four years, renewable once only.

National legislature

The unicameral, Parlamentul Romaniei (Romanian Parliament) consists of the Camera Deputatilor (Chamber of Deputies) with 300 deputies, directly elected by mixed member proportional representation, members are required to be of a minimum age of 23 years and to serve for four-year terms.

Legal system

The legal system is based on the Napolenic Code and the 1991 constitution. There is an independent judiciary, although judges are appointed by the president and parliament. The Supreme Court comprises judges appointed by the president for a term of six years. It administers law, but cannot undertake judicial review. This is undertaken by the Constitutional Court, which comprises nine judges appointed by the president and parliament for a period of nine years.

Last elections

30 November 2008 (parliamentary); 22 November / 6 December 2009 (presidential and runoff).

Results: Parliamentary: chamber of deputies, the Partidul Social Democrat-Partidul Conservator (Alianta PSD+PC) (Social Democratic Party-Conservative Party alliance) won 33.1 per cent of the vote for the (114 seats out of 334), the Partidul Democrat-Liberal (PD-L) (Democratic Liberal Party) 32.4 per cent (115), the Partidul National Liberal (PNL) (National Liberal Party) 18.6 per cent (65) the Uniunea Democrata Maghiara din România (UDMR) (Democratic Union of Hungarians in Romania) 6.2 per cent (22) and the Partidul România Mare (PRM) (Greater Romania Party) 3.2 per cent (0). Senate: the Alianta PSD+PC won 34.2 per cent (49 seats out of 137), PD-L 33.6 per cent (51), PNL 18.7 per cent (28), UDMR 6.4 per cent (9) and the PRM 3.6 per cent (0). Turnout was 39.2 per cent.

Presidential (first round): Traian Basescu (PD-L) won 32.4 per cent of the vote, Mircea Geoana (PSD) 31.2 per cent, Crin Antonescu (PNL) 20.02 per cent; of the nine other candidates all won less than 6.0 per cent. Turnout was 54.4 per cent. (Runoff): Basescu won 50.33 per cent, Geoana 49.66 per cent.

Next elections

2012 (parliamentary); 2013 (presidential).

Political parties

Ruling party

Coalition (known as Da PNL-PD): Alianta Dreptate si Adevar (DA) (Justice and Truth Alliance) led by Partidul National Liberal (PNL) (National Liberal Party), Partidul Democrat (PD) (Democratic Party), Uniunea Democratica Maghiara din Romania (UDMR) (Hungarian Democratic Alliance of Romania), Partidul Conservator (PC) (Conservative Party) (since 2004)

Main opposition party

Partidul Social Democrat-Partidul Conservator (Alianta PSD+PC) (Social Democratic Party-Conservative Party alliance)

Population

21.44 million (2010)*

Last census: March 2002: 21,680,974

Population density: 98 inhabitants per square km. Urban population: 55 per cent (1995–2001).

Annual growth rate: -0.5 per cent 1994–2004 (WHO 2006)

Ethnic make-up

Romanian (89 per cent), Hungarian (9 per cent), German (0.4 per cent), Ukrainian, Serb, Croat, Russian Turk and Gypsy (1.6 per cent). The Hungarian minority live principally in the Transylvania region. Around half of the then resident ethnic Germans returned to Germany in 1990 and many of the remainder have followed in recent years. Other small ethnic groups include Jews and a number of Greeks and Armenians.

Religions

Romanian Orthodox (70 per cent), Roman Catholic (6 per cent, of which 3 per cent are Uniate), Protestant (6 per cent), and unaffiliated (18 per cent). Since the revolution of 1989 there has been complete religious freedom. The dominant religion is Romanian Orthodox, with over 18 million believers, headed by a Patriarch based in Bucharest. The Roman Catholic Church has approximately 1.35 million members, and includes adherents of the Armenian, Latin and Romanian (Byzantine) rites. The Hungarian and German minorities are predominantly Protestant, and there are communities of the Old-Rite Christian Church (an Orthodox sect) and the Armenian-Gregorian Church. Despite emigration there is still a small Jewish community.

Education

Romania's transition to a market economy made a comprehensive reform of the education sector necessary. The World Bank has supported three reform projects with loan contributions amounting to US$170 million. The centralised education system, with a standard curriculum and ineffective student evaluation system, has been replaced by a flexible curriculum framework, alternative textbooks and a modern evaluation system. Improvements in teacher training, financing and management are under way.

Primary education begins at age seven and lasts until age 11. Lower secondary education lasts for four years until age 15. Upper secondary courses take another four years to complete. Romania's five types of secondary schools specialise in

different areas of education, including general secondary schools, vocational and art schools, those specialising in physical education and teacher training.
Minority language schooling is available, mainly in Hungarian and German. Higher education is offered in both public and private institutions.
Public expenditure on education typically amounts to 3.6 per cent of annual gross national income.
Literacy rate: 97 per cent adult rate; 98 per cent youth rate (15–24) (Unesco 2005).
Compulsory years: Seven to 15.
Enrolment rate: 104 per cent gross primary enrolment of relevant age group (including repeaters); 78 per cent gross secondary enrolment (World Bank).
Pupils per teacher: 20 in primary schools.

Health
As primary healthcare units suffer due to financial shortage, there is over-concentration of already scarce resources on hospitals. Outbreaks of infectious diseases, often contracted in hospitals, are common.
HIV/Aids
HIV prevalence: 0.1 per cent aged 15–49 in 2003 (World Bank)
Life expectancy: 72 years, 2004 (WHO 2006)
Fertility rate/Maternal mortality rate: 1.3 births per woman, 2004 (WHO 2006)
Birth rate/Death rate: 10.8 births per 1,000 population; 12.3 deaths per 1,000 population (2003).
Child (under 5 years) mortality rate (per 1,000): 18 per 1,000 live births (2003)
Head of population per physician: 1.9 physicians per 1,000 people, 2003 (WHO 2006)

Welfare
The comprehensive state insurance scheme, with premiums paid by enterprises and institutions on behalf of employees, provides free health care and benefits for all Romanian citizens. An unemployment allowance was created in 1991 and there are also funds allocated to sickness benefits, children's allowance and pensions. Employers make social security contributions of 28—38 per cent, unemployment fund contributions of 5 per cent and disabled fund contributions of 1 per cent on gross salaries. Employees pay 3 per cent of gross salaries to the supplementary pension fund and 1 per cent to the unemployment insurance fund.
There is high unemployment in Romania and there has been a 40 per cent fall in real wages since 1989. Survival is partly due to the fact that most Romanians do not pay rent or have a mortgage, since over 90 per cent were able to buy their homes for the equivalent of a few months rent after the revolution. Many also have small plots of farm land for subsistence farming. It is expected that there will be a housing crisis for future generations, with many houses too small to be occupied by more than one family. Mortgages to buy houses are very expensive and are almost impossible to obtain. The government's housing programme aims to complete the tower blocks and apartments that were left unfinished after the revolution, and then allocate funds to social housing.
There is wide variation between urban and rural infrastructure, with less than 10 per cent of country dwellers living in houses with running water and sewerage.

Main cities
Bucharest (capital, estimated population 1.9 million in 2005), Iasi (326,502), Constanta (314,490), Cluj-Napoca (316,400), Timisoara (321,930), Ploiesti (234,920),

Languages spoken
The most significant minority language is Hungarian. German and English are spoken in tourist regions. Romanian, although a Romance language developed from Latin, has influences from Slavic languages as well as Hungarian, French and Turkish.
Official language/s
Romanian

Media
Press
The press is highly regionalised and includes publications in minority languages such as Hungarian, German and Serbian. Over 60 per cent of the population read one or more newspapers a day. There are around 10 national dailies, as well as dailies and weeklies published in the main cities. Newspapers tend to be independent, governmental or published by a political party.
Dailies: The most important independent national dailies in Romanian are *Evenimentul Zilei* (www.evz.ro) is a mass-market newspaper, *Adevarul* (www.adevarul.ro), *Cronica Romana* (www.cronicaromana.ro), *Curierul National* (www.curierulnational.ro), *Libertatea* (www.libertatea.ro) and *Romania Libera* (www.romanialibera.ro).
In English, *Nine O'Clock* (www.nineoclock.ro), *Jurnalul National* (www.jurnalul.ro) and *Evenimentul* (www.evenimentul.ro) have English online editions. In German, *Allgemeine Zeitung für Rumanien* is published five times a week and *Hermannstadter Zeitung* (www.hermannstaedter.ro); in Turkish *Zaman* (www.zaman.ro) and in Hungarian, *Uj Magyar Szo* (www.maszol.ro) *Háromszék* (www.3szek.ro) and *Krónika* (www.kronika.ro).
Regional dailies include *Azi* (www.azi.ro/) *Gardianul* (www.gardianul.ro), *Ieseanul* (www.ieseanul.ro) and *Observator de Constanta* (www.observator.ro).
Weeklies: The Sunday newspapers include *Adevarul, Cronica Romana, Curierul National, Nine O'Clock* (English) and *Azi*.
Business: In Romanian, *Bursa* (www.bursa.ro) reports on the stock exchange, *Capital* (www.capital.ro), *Sàptàmàna Financiarà* (www.sfin.ro) and *Ziarul Financiar* (www.zf.ro) deal with financial news. In English, *Bucharest Business Week* (www.bbw.ro) and *The Diplomat* (www.thediplomat.ro) is publish weekly.
Periodicals: Many special interest and business publications are published, mostly by independent companies.
Broadcasting
Radio: There are several domestic stations with the state-owned Radio Romania (www.srr.ro) providing four nationwide networks, featuring news, music and cultural shows, plus an international channel in English and 11 other languages. Commercial radio stations include Europa FM (www.europafm.ro), Kiss FM (www.mykiss.ro), Pro FM (www.profm.ro) and Radio 21 (www.radio21.ro).
Television: The state-owned television, Televiziunea Romana (TVR) (www.tvr.ro) operates two channels – Romania 1 and TVR2. Commercial networks include Antena 1 (www.antena1.ro), Prima TV (www.primatv.ro), Acasa TV (www.acasatv.ro) and Realitatea TV (www.realitatea.net) showing domestic and international programmes.
Advertising
Advertising agencies, some in joint ventures with Western firms (UK-based Saatchi & Saatchi and Lintas Worldwide) operate throughout the country. As well as advertising through television and radio, cinema advertising is increasingly popular with billboard locations growing and advertising on public transport vehicles common.
News agencies
National news agency: Rompres

Economy
The economy is diverse with a wide range of productive sectors. Romania has a substantial industrial base which accounts for over 25 per cent of GDP, primarily in mining of iron ore; around 20 per cent of industrial production includes a wide range of manufacturing enterprises, such as construction materials, chemicals, food processing, textiles and clothing. The service sector accounts for over 65 per cent of GDP; agriculture accounts for less than

10 per cent of GDP but employs around 30 per cent of the workforce in 2009. The country has a broad range of energy resources; including oil, natural gas and coal, as well as electricity produced from hydro and nuclear power stations, the output of which can be utilised locally and the excess exported.
The economy was hit by the global economic crisis, but not until 2009. GDP growth in 2007 was 6.2 per cent, and remained high at 7.1 per cent in 2008, but fell into recession with growth of -7.1 per cent in 2009. Although the economy improved in 2010 GDP remained at a recessionary -1.3 per cent.
Unemployment rose from 4 per cent in 2008, 6.3 in 2009, to 7.6 per cent in 2010, while the nominal rate of wage growth fell from 23.6 per cent per annum in 2008 to 5.9 per cent in 2009. Inflation remained above 5 per cent from 2004–06, and then spiked at 7.8 per cent in 2008, a figure markedly higher than the 4.8 per cent in 2007 as well the 5.6 per cent in 2009.
The government increased the rate of value added tax (VAT) by 5 per cent to 24 per cent in July 2010. The move was part of austerity measures designed to cut the budget deficit and meet conditions set by the International Monetary Fund (IMF) in order to qualify for a loan of US$20 billion.
A significant factor in Romania's success is the number of foreign investors, attracted by a favourable corporate tax regime, low wages and a stable and strengthening currency. Membership of the EU, bringing with it funds as well as more investment, has further strengthened the economy, although the EU is still urging Romania to fight corruption
An important source of consumer revenue is the remittances sent by migrant workers living abroad. In 2008, a record US$9.38 billion was sent to families in Romania, which fell to US$4.93 billion in 2009 (4.4 per cent of GDP) and was estimated to have fallen further to US$4.52 in 2010.
The down side of this departure of large numbers of workers to countries offering higher wages, which was accelerated with entry into the EU, is that it is leaving Romania with a labour shortage, which could impede economic expansion. It has also been forecast by the Demographic Research Centre of the National Institute for Economic Research (INCE) of the Romanian Academy that by 2050 the population could decrease by almost 23 per cent (from 21 million in 2008 to 17 million in 2050) if the falling birth and rising death rates continue and citizens are lost through emigration).

External trade
As a member of the European Union, Romania operates within a communitywide free trade area, with tariffs set as a whole. Internationally, the EU has free trade agreements with a number of nations and trading blocs worldwide.
Foreign trade represented 85 per cent of GDP and is expected to rise further since entry to the EU. Over 30 per cent of trade is with the EU while Russia supplies the majority of Romania's energy imports.

Imports
Main imports include machinery and equipment, fuels and minerals, chemicals, textile and products, basic metals and agricultural products.
Main sources: Germany (typically 16 per cent of total), Italy (11 per cent), Hungary (5 per cent).

Exports
Main exports include clothing and footwear, metals and metal products, machinery and equipment, minerals and fuels, chemicals and agricultural products.
Main destinations: Germany (typically 17 per cent of total), Italy (16 per cent), France (7 per cent).

Agriculture

Farming
The agricultural sector accounts for 12.8 per cent of GDP and employs 25 per cent of the workforce. The total agricultural area is 147,900 square km, of which 94,100 square km is arable. Arable land, pastures and hayfields cover 59.5 per cent of Romania, forests 26.7 per cent and vineyards 2.5 per cent.
Romania is Central Europe's most important agricultural producer, after Poland. Important agricultural produce includes grapes (the leading European producer), corn, wheat, maize, rye, sugar beet, oilseed, potatoes, plums, apples and meat. Although there has been progress in restructuring the sector, it has been slower than international financial institutions would like. Moreover, concerns have also been expressed at the re-introduction of import barriers and subsidies to protect the sector from Hungarian wheat and flour exports.
The restitution and privatisation of land has – in comparison with enterprise privatisation – advanced at a rapid pace, with over 85 per cent of agricultural land in private ownership. Land restitution was highly politicised, with arguments surrounding the amount of land that was returned to claimants. Claims exceeded by a third the amount of land held in state hands, and delays in the process held up investment in the sector. Although land restitution was a major step forward, problems facing the sector include the small size of farms, no functioning land market, very few rural credit and investment schemes, and an extremely limited distribution and marketing infrastructure.
The agricultural sector is subject to the reformed Common Agricultural Policy (CAP), whereby subsidies are no longer paid on farm output, which tended to benefit large farms and encourage overproduction, but rather on single farm payments not conditional on production. Full implementation of CAP will be completed by 2013.

Fishing
Romania's fishing sector has declined in the past decade, making little contribution to GDP. National consumption is falling too. Fisheries in the Black Sea have been spoilt by eutrophication and overfishing. Carp, mackerel and sardines are the principal catches. European spratt and anchovy are also plentiful. There are an estimated 10,000 persons working in the fishing industry.
Fish farming, including primary processing, packaging and trade will be improved through major investment projects.

Forestry
Forest and other wooded land accounts for less than one-third of the land area, with forest cover estimated at 6.4 million hectares (ha). Most of the forest area is located in the Carpathian mountainous region in the centre and west of the country. About nine-tenths of the forest is available for wood supply and is largely semi-natural. The growing stock consists of Norway spruce as the principal coniferous species, with beech and oak the main deciduous varieties. Although most of the forest is owned by the state, claims for restitution have increased private ownership.
Forests provide sufficient raw materials for the domestic industry to meet internal demands and also product for exports. Romania has a well developed timber and wood processing industry, concentrated in the northern regions of Moldavia and Transylvania. Substantial investments have been made to modernise older mills so as to improve its existing export base. Over half of the sawnwood production is exported, while more value-added products such as parquet, solid wood panels and furniture are obtained from hardwoods. Most of the paper demand is met by imports.

Industry and manufacturing

The industrial sector accounts for 36.3 per cent of GDP with manufacturing accounting for 27 per cent of GDP.
The main industries are textiles and footwear, light machinery and auto assembly. Mining, timber, construction materials, chemicals, food processing and

petroleum refining are all also significant sectors.

Tourism
The tourism sector declined following the collapse of Communism, despite the wealth of attractions. Poor infrastructure, including existing but deteriorating facilities, and inadequate marketing, as well as competition from neighbouring destinations, have contributed to the malaise. The sector contributes only 1.3 per cent to GDP. The industry supplies 115,000 jobs, which amounts to 1.2 per cent of the workforce.

Mining
Taken together, the mining and hydrocarbons sectors account for around 13 per cent of GDP and employ 8 per cent of the workforce. Output dramatically declined in the 1990s, reflecting prolonged restructuring. Romania's mining industry is well developed, although it suffers from outdated technology and a lack of investment.
Mineral deposits include salt, lignite, iron ore, bauxite, manganese and small quantities of gold, zinc, uranium, tin and copper.
Romania aims to exploit domestic resources instead of relying on imports, even if the initial cost is high. Annual zinc output is around 28,000 tonnes, aluminium output around 150,000 tonnes and copper output around 30,000 tonnes. Minvest, privatised in 1999, accounts for 60 per cent of Romania's copper production.
The government opened the gold mining sector to foreign exploration in 1999. Gabriel Resources, a Canadian company, are behind a US $400 million project to create Europe's largest open-pit gold mine in the Rosia Montana valley. The International Finance Corporation (IFC) have refused financial backing to the proposal, which would displace 2,000 residents and produce high levels of hazardous cyanide.

Hydrocarbons
Proven oil reserves were 600 million barrels in 2007. Consumption was 219,000 barrels per day (bpd) and Romania imported 105,000bpd in 2007. Although production covers just over half of total consumption, Romania has the potential to become self-sufficient in oil and could become an important oil producer. Idle oil wells are being re-opened following the liberalisation of state prices and rising world prices.
The industry is independent with government owning shares in oil companies. Petrom is the largest oil and gas group, involved in exploration and production; public ownership is just 20.64 per cent of shares. Rompetrol is the second largest and an important multinational oil company in the EU. Russia's Lukoil is a major player in the downstream sector, owning the third-largest, and modernised, refinery in Romania. Other refinery owners have also sought external links, although the Romanian government is in general wary of Russian interests expanding into the domestic industry. Romania was instrumental in launching the Pan-European Oil Pipeline (PEOP) project, which will transport Caspian oil through Romania, Serbia, Croatia, and Slovenia to the Italian port of Trieste.
Proven natural gas reserves were at 101 billion cubic metres (cum) in 2007. Even though Romania is Central and Eastern Europe's largest natural gas producer, production has fallen from 17.4 billion cum in 1997 to 12 billion cum in 2006. Production in 2008 was 11.3 billion cum while consumption was around 18 billion cum; the shortfall was made up solely of Russian gas imported by pipeline through Ukraine. Romania is looking for not just alternative sources of natural gas but a security in its sources. Russian gas supplies have been disrupted in two consecutive winters (2008/09) by disputes between Russia and Ukraine, when supplies were suspended. Bulgaria, Italy and Russia are building a southern European gas pipeline (South Stream) that avoids traversing Ukraine and in February 2009 Russia invited Romania to join the project. However the prospects of diversification are better with natural gas from Central Asia, delivered by the Nabucco pipeline which will cross Romania and terminate in Austria. Construction of this pipeline began in 2009 and is scheduled to be completed by 2012; Romania has declared the South Stream to be costly and only in its nascent state.
Romgaz operates the national gas distribution system and is entirely owned by the state.
Proven coal reserves were 554 million tonnes in 2007, of which the majority is brown coal, typically used in power plants. Production was 39 million tonnes in 2006, a figure that has grown steadily since a low of 25 million tonnes in 1999 when industrial action by miners, antiquated equipment and lack of investment had stifled production. The government has backed plans to restructure and reinvest in the industry since 2000, and while the number of mines and miners has fallen coal is planned as a part of the energy mix until 2020.

Energy
Total installed generating capacity was 20.3 gigawatts (GW) in 2006. Romania has an energy mix that included coal (41.5 per cent), natural gas (16.7 per cent), oil and derivatives (0.7 per cent), hydro (32.0 per cent) and nuclear (9.2 per cent) in 2006. By 2008, nuclear energy was contributing around 20 per cent of electricity following the opening of the Cernavoda-1 nuclear power plant, which became operational in 2007. The potential for renewable energy is great but by 2009 any contribution to national electricity production was negligible.

Financial markets
Stock exchange
Bursa de Valori Bucuresti (Bucharest Stock Exchange)
Commodity exchange
Bursa Monetar Financiară si de Mărfuri Sibiu (BMFMS) (Sibiu Monetary Financial and Commodities Exchange)

Banking and insurance
Since the early 1990s, the banking sector has undergone major restructuring and privatisation, although some areas of the banking, insurance, legal and financial sectors require upgrading. About 55 per cent of the banking system is foreign owned. Privatisation of Romania's largest bank, Banca Comerciala Romana (BCR), is scheduled for completion in 2006. When both BCR and Casa de Economii si Consemnatiuni (CEC) are privatised, the banking sector will be 90 per cent foreign owned and highly competitive.
Central bank
Banca Nationala a Romaniei (BNR) (National Bank of Romania)
Main financial centre
Bucharest

Time
GMT plus two hours (daylight saving, late March to late October, GMT plus three hours)

Geography
Romania is situated in south-eastern Europe in the lower Danube basin bordering the Black Sea to the south-west (250km of coastline). Much of the country forms part of the Balkan Peninsula. Romania is the largest of the Balkan states. Ukraine is to the north, Moldova to the north-east, Hungary to the north-west, Serbia and Montenegro and Macedonia to the south-west and Bulgaria to the south. Romania is divided into four geographical areas. Moldavia and Transylvania (forest and mountains) make up the northern half, which is divided by the Carpathian Mountains. South of the Carpathians is the Danube plain of Walachia (including Bucharest), with the lower Danube marking the border with Bulgaria. Romania's Black Sea coastline incorporates the Danube delta and the port of Constanta.
Hemisphere
Northern

Climate
Romania has a moderate, continental temperate climate with long hot summers and cold winters. Snow falls throughout the country, although winters are coldest in the Carpathian mountains with snow between December and April, and mildest on the Black Sea coast. Mean temperatures in Bucharest are minus 2 degrees Celsius (C) in January and 23 degrees C in July. The coldest month is January with a mean temperature of minus 7 degrees C, rising to a peak of 30 degrees C in July. Temperatures can differ by 5–10 degrees C from the plains to the mountains. The wettest month is June with approximately 85mm of rain; the driest September with 30mm. The Black Sea water temperatures are 20-28 degrees C in July and August.

Dress codes
The business dress code is usually informal, with ties, sports jackets or blazers acceptable for meetings.
Clothing should be medium-weight, plus a heavy topcoat and overshoes for winter. Lightweight clothing and a light raincoat are advisable for summer.

Entry requirements
Passports
Required by all, valid for six months from date of arrival.
Visa
Required by all, except nationals of EU/EEA countries, USA, Canada, Japan, Israel and some other countries. Transit visas are required by nationals of some countries. For full details of countries affected by all visa requirements, see www.roembus.org. An application form can also be downloaded. Business visitors, when required to apply for visas, should provide an employer's letter certifying purpose of visit, an invitation from a local company, proof of sufficient funds, travel insurance and return/onward passage.
Currency advice/regulations
The import and export of local currency is prohibited. There are no restrictions on the import of foreign currency, subject to declaration over €10,000 (or foreign equivalent); export of foreign currency is limited to the unused amount, subject to presentation of exchange receipts.
Changing money at private exchange offices is often better than at banks. Kiosks are required to advertise an official rate, but ask if they can offer a better deal.
Romania is largely a cash-only economy. In Bucharest and main centres, major credit cards may be accepted at large hotels, car hire firms and stores; travellers cheques can be changed at banks and hotels. US dollars are the preferred hard currency.
Customs
Personal effects, 200 cigarettes and two litres of alcoholic beverages and small gifts are permitted duty-free. Banned imports include ammunition, explosives, narcotics and pornography.

Health (for visitors)
Hospital emergency rooms provide free first aid, but charge for all other medical services.
Mandatory precautions
There are no special requirements.
Advisable precautions
Typhoid, diphtheria and both hepatitis A and B inoculations are recommended, as well as inoculation against tick-borne encephalitis. It is advisable to boil water or drink bottled water where possible, although water in mountainous regions is supplied from local springs and is safe. Rabies is a health risk.
Basic medical supplies are limited, especially outside major cities, so always travel with sufficient medication.

Hotels
Classified as de luxe, A and B. Accommodation outside Bucharest is generally cheaper. Advisable to purchase pre-paid vouchers for accommodation through travel agents, as a confirmed reservation, if not pre-paid, is not a guarantee of accommodation.

Credit cards
Credit cards are not widely used but are accepted in most major hotels. American Express, Visa and Eurocard are preferred. Credit card transactions are charged at a worse rate than that offered by exchange bureaux

Public holidays (national)
Fixed dates
1–2 Jan (New Year's Day), 1 May (Labour Day), 1 Dec (National Day), 25–26 Dec (Christmas).
Variable dates
Orthodox Easter Sunday, Orthodox Easter Monday

Working hours
Banking
Mon–Fri: 0900–1200 and 1300–1500. Creditbank, Bucharest Otopeni airport, open 1000–1800 daily.
Business
Mon–Fri: 0800–1700, lunch usually 1230–1300. Business hours can be haphazard with many offices closing on Friday afternoons.
Government
Mon–Fri: 0800–1700, lunch usually 1230–1300.
Shops
Mon–Fri: 0900–1800; Sat: 0900–1400.

Telecommunications
Mobile/cell phones
There is widespread coverage, particularly in the major cities.

Social customs/useful tips
Traditional Central European courtesies with a measure of Latin informality are expected. Punctuality is observed to a degree. Shaking hands is the traditional form of greeting. Accepting hospitality from and giving social invitations to officials is normal, usually taking place in restaurants or hotels.
Smoking is prohibited on public transport and in cinemas and theatres, although many Romanians smoke and Western cigarettes are greatly appreciated.
Tips are expected by porters, chambermaids and taxi drivers.
Anyone photographing demonstrations risks arrest.
It is advisable to avoid the many stray dogs in and around Bucharest.

Security
Crimes against tourists are a growing problem in Romania. Money exchange schemes targetting travellers are becoming increasingly common. Bogus policemen are an increasing hazard for the unwary business traveller. Their technique is to demand to see proof of identification, and then make off with a visitor's wallet. Keep passports separate from other valuables.
Extreme caution must be taken with unofficial change vendors: they are illegal and often fraudulent.

Getting there
Air
National airline: Tarom (Transporturile Aeriene Romane) (Romanian Air Transport)
International airport/s: Henry Coanda International Airport (OTP), 16km north of Bucharest; bank, post office, duty-free shop, car hire
Airport tax: None
Surface
Road: International roads connect Romania with Hungary. The E64 from Budapest goes through Arad, Brasov, Campina and Ploiesti to Bucharest. From Germany, the E60 goes via northern Hungary before going through Oradea. The route from Bucharest to Ukraine goes north through Bacau and to Chernovtsy in southern Ukraine. From Moldova, take the road from the border to the town of Husi. The better road links are via Germany, Austria and Hungary.
Rail: There are good rail connections with all neighbouring countries.
Water: Ships provide regular passenger services and cruises on the Danube, starting at Passau in Germany, through

Austria, Slovakia, Hungary, Serbia, to Giurgiu (48km from Bucharest), and finally Constanta on the Black Sea.
Main port/s: Black Sea ports: Constanta, Mangalia and Sulina.
Danube ports: Orsova, Drobeta-Turnu Severin, Turnu Magurele, Giurgiu, Oltenita, Calaras, Cernavoda. Braila, Galati and Tulcea are both river and sea ports. The Danube is used heavily for freight transport since the opening of the canal link with the Black Sea.

Getting about

National transport

Air: Tarom and Carpatair operate regular internal services to main centres in Romania.
Road: Romania has around 78,000km of roads, of which 14,500km are national roads; 4,680km of the national roads are included within the European Road Network ('E' roads).
Buses: There are regular inter-city connections and local services to most towns and villages.
Rail: There is an extensive rail network. Efficient and cheap services operate between all main cities and towns. In addition to slower local services, there are express and inter-city services with dining and sleeping cars. Bucharest's principal station is the *Gara de Nord*.
Water: The principal navigable waterway is the Danube, on which cruises are available.

City transport

Taxis: Taxis are readily available in main centres and are inexpensive. Authorised taxis are identified by a 'Taxi' sign on the roof. Metered taxis should be used, although drivers may need to be reminded to switch them on. While a taxi may be hailed in the street, it is advisable to arrange a taxi by telephone, preferably from a company. A 10 per cent tip is normal. Informal operators at the main hotels and the airport overcharge and should be avoided.
Buses, trams & metro: It is easy to get around by bus, both within towns and cities and cross-country, but they are often slow, over-crowded and uncomfortable. Trams and trollies also run in many centres. Tickets are purchased from booths and in some hotels; they should be punched immediately upon entering the vehicle. There is a metro system in Bucharest.

Car hire

Self-drive and chauffeur-driven cars are available from international and local companies in the main cities and airports. International or national driving licences are required. Traffic drives on the right, although Romanian driving can be very unpredictable. Speed limits are 120km per hour on highways, 90km per hour on other roads and 50km per hour in built-up areas.

BUSINESS DIRECTORY

The addresses listed below are a selection only. While World of Information makes every endeavour to check these addresses, we cannot guarantee that changes have not been made, especially to telephone numbers and area codes. We would welcome any corrections.

Telephone area codes

The international dialling code (IDD) for Romania is +40, followed by area code and subscriber's number:

Braila	239	Gaesti	245
Brasov	268	Oradea	259
Bucharest	21	Ploiesti	244
Cluj-Napoca	264	Sibiu	269
Constanta	241	Timisoara	256

Useful telephone numbers

Fire brigade: 981
Police: 955
Ambulance: 961
Special ambulance service (pregnant women or women with small children): 969
Emergency hospital: 679-4310
Special information: 951
Time: 958
Railway information: 952
Weather report: 959
Enquiries: 930, 931, 932

Chambers of Commerce

American Chamber of Commerce in Romania, Union International Centre, 11 Ion Cimpineanu Street, Sector 1, 78664 Bucharest (tel: 315-8694; fax: 312-4851; e-mail: amcham@amcham.ro).

Brasov Chamber of Commerce and Industry, 18-20 M Kogalniceanu Street, 2200 Brasov (tel: 412-357; fax: 477-333; e-mail: ccibv@ccibv.ro).

Constanta Chamber of Commerce, Industry, Shipping and Agriculture, 84 Mircea cel Batran Street, bl MF1, Constanta tel: 619-854; fax: 619-454; e-mail: office@ccina.ro)

Prahova Chamber of Commerce and Industry, 8 Cuza Voda Street, Ploiesti (tel: 513-122; fax: 516-666; e-mail: office@cciph.ro).

Romania and Bucharest Chamber of Commerce and Industry, 2 Octavian Goga Boulevard, Sector 3, Bucharest (tel: 322-9535; fax: 322-9542; e-mail: ccir@ccir.ro).

Sibiu Chamber of Commerce, Industry and Agriculture, 1 Telefoanelor Street, 2400 Sibliu (tel: 210-503; fax: 211-831; e-mail: cciasb@cciasb.ro).

Timisoara Chamber of Commerce, Industry and Agriculture, 3 Piata Victoriei, 300030 Timisoara (tel: 490-766; fax: 490-311; e-mail: cciat@cciat.ro).

Banking

Banca Agricola, B-dul Voda, Sector 3, Bucharest (tel/fax: 323-6027).

Banco Comerciala Romana, B-dul Regina Elisabeta 5, Sector 3, Bucharest (tel: 312-6185; fax: 312-0056).

Bankco-op, 13 Ion Ghica St, Bucharest (614-3900; fax: 312-0037).

Romanian Bank for Development, 4 Doamnei St, Bucharest (tel: 613-3200, 615-9600; fax: 615-7603).

Romanian Commercial Bank, 14 Republicii Ave, Bucharest (tel: 614-5680, 615-7560; fax: 614-3213).

Central bank

National Bank of Romania, 25 Lipscani Street, Bucharest (tel: 313-0410; fax: 312-3831; e-mail: bnr@bnro.ro).

Stock exchange

Bursa de Valori Bucuresti (Bucharest Stock Exchange): www.bvb.ro

Stock exchange 2

Sibex (Bursa Monetar Financiara Si De Marfuri Sibiu): www.sibex.ro

Commodity exchange

Bursa Monetar Financiară si de Mărfuri Sibiu (BMFMS) (Sibiu Monetary Financial and Commodities Exchange): www.bmfms.ro

Travel information

Association of Ecotourism in Romania, Gabroveni Street 2, Sector 3, Bucharest (tel: 319-742; fax: 828-721; e-mail: roving@deltanet.ro).

Henri Coanda International Airport, 224E Bucharest Road, Otopeni (tel: 204-1200; fax:201-4990; e-mail: otp@otp-airport.ro).

Romanian Automobile Club (Automobil Clubul Roman), 27 Tache Ionescu Street, 010353 Bucharest (tel: 317-8253; fax: 317-3964; e-mail: acr@acr.ro).

Tarom (Airline), Victoria Sq., 59 Buzesti Street, Bucharest (tel: 204-6464; fax: 204-6427; e-mail: agvictoria@tarom.ro).

Ministry of tourism

Ministry of Transport, Construction and Tourism, Bulevardul Dinicu Golescu 38, 010873 Bucharest 1 (tel: 319-6112; fax: 319-6204; e-mail: relpub@mt.ro).

National tourist organisation offices

Autoritatea Nationala Pentru Turism, Bulevardul Dinicu Golescu 38, 010873 Bucharest 1 (tel: 314-9957 fax: 314-9964; ie-mail: promovare@mturism.ro).

Ministries

Ministry of Agriculture, Blvd Carol I 24, 70312 Bucharest (tel: 614-4020; fax: 312-4410).

Ministry of Communications and Information Technology, 14 Libertatii Blvd, 76106 Bucharest 5 (tel: 400-1100, 312-0017; fax: 400-1329; internet site: http://www.mcti.ro).

Ministry of Culture, Piata Presei 1, Bucharest 71341 (tel: 223-1516; fax: 223-4951).

Ministry of Defence, Str Izvor 1-3, 70642 Bucharest (tel: 410-4040; fax: 312-0863).

Ministry of Foreign Affairs, Aleea Modrogan 14, 71274 Bucharest (tel: 212-2160; fax: 230-7489).

Ministry of Health, Str Ministerului 1-3, 70109 Bucharest (tel: 222-3850; fax: 312-4916).

Ministry of the Interior, Str Mihai Voda 3-5, 070622 Bucharest (tel: 311-2021; fax: 614-0909).

Ministry of Justice, Bd Mihail Kogalniceanu 33, 70602 Bucharest (tel: 614-4400; fax: 323-6179).

Ministry of Labour and Social Protection, Str Dem I Dobrescu 2, 70119 Bucharest (tel: 222-3850; fax: 312-2768).

Ministry of National Education, Str Gen Berthelot 28-30, 70749 Bucharest (tel: 614-4588; fax: 312-4719).

Ministry of Privatisation, Str Ministerului 2-4, 70109 Bucharest (tel: 222-3850; fax: 312-0809).

Ministry of Public Finance, Str Apolodor 17, 70663 Bucharest (tel: 410-3400; fax: 312-2077).

Ministry of Public Works and Land Use Planning, Str Apollodor 15-17, Sector 6, 70663 Bucharest (tel: 410-1933; fax: 411-1138).

Ministry of Youth and Sports, Str Vasile Conta 16, 70139 Bucharest (tel: 211-5550; fax: 211-1710).

Office of the Prime Minister, Piata Victoriei 1, 71201 Bucharest (tel: 212-1660; fax: 222-5814).

Presidency of Republic, Building Geniului 1 Cotroceni Palace, Bucharest 76238 (tel: 410-0581; fax: 312-1247).

Other useful addresses

Administration of Sulina Free Trade Zone, Dr Marcovici Str 2, Ground Floor, Bucharest (tel: 613-8733).

Agency for Restructuring, 152 Calea Victoriei, Sector 1, Bucharest (tel: 212-2424; fax: 212-1176).

Asigurara Romaneasca SA (Asirom), Str Smirdan 5, 70406 Bucharest (tel: 312-5020; fax: 312-4819).

British Embassy, Str Jules Michelot 24, 70154 Bucharest (tel: 312-0303; fax: 312-9741).

Centrul Roman pentru Dezvoltarea Intreprinderilor Mici si Mijlocii (Crimm)-PMU, 20 Ion Campineanu Str, Sector 1, 70709 Bucharest (tel: 311-1995/6/7; fax: 312-6966).

Chamber of Deputies, 1 Parlamentului Str, Bucharest (tel: 335-0111; fax: 312-0827).

Constanta South Free Zone Administration, Ferry Boat Terminal Building Agigea, code 8711, Jud Constanta (tel: 741-378, 618-718, 619-100 (ext 2118, 2162); fax: 639-000, 619-729, 693-913).

Council for Reform, Piata Victoriei 1, 71201 Bucharest (tel: 222-3687; fax: 222-4686).

Council for Economic Co-ordination, Strategy and Reform, Piaja Victorei 1, 71201 Bucharest (tel: 222-3687, 312-4767; fax: 222-4686).

Department for European Integration (tel: 312-6928; fax: 312-6929).

Department of Public Information (tel: 222-3619; fax: 222-6088).

Department for Selective Restructuring of the State Ownership Fund, 6-10, Callea Grivitei, Sector 1, Bucharest (tel: 650-4822; 659-7693).

Economic Reform and Strategy and Co-ordination Council, 1 Victoriei Sq, Bucharest (tel: 617-7977; fax: 312-4686).

Fiman Fund PMU, 6-8 Povernei Str, Bucharest (tel: 212-2912; fax: 211-1937).

Insurance and Reinsurance Company SA (Aatra), Str Smirdan 5, 79118 Bucharest (tel: 150-986; fax: 139-306).

Land Reclamation Agriculture Department, Sos Oltenitei 35-37, 75501 Bucharest (tel: 634-5020; fax: 312-3712).

Lignite Public Authority, Str Tudor Vladimirescu 2, 1400 Târgu-Jiu (tel: 321-2513; fax: 321-664).

National Administration of Roads, Blvd Dinicu Golescu 38, 77113 Bucharest (tel: 312-8496).

National Agency for Privatisation, Str Ministerulei 2-4, 4th Floor, Bucharest sector 1 (tel: 615-8558, 614-9495, 312-3030, 614-7854; fax: 312-0809/3030, 613-6136).

National Committee for Statistics, 16 Libertatii Str, Sector 5, Bucharest (tel: 312-4875; fax: 312-4873).

National Council for Environmental Protection, Piata Victorei 1, Bucharest (tel: 143-400).

Navrom (Romanian Shipping Company), 8700 Constanta (tel: 615-821; fax: 618-413).

Nord-Est Press (Independent news agency), Str Smirdan 5, 6600 Iasi (tel/fax: 144-776).

Petrotel SA, Str Mihai Bravu 235, Jud Prahova, 2000 Ploiesti (tel: 146-671; fax: 142-408).

Project Implementation Unit within the Authority for Privatisation and Management of the State Ownership, Bucharest (tel: 303-6417; fax: 303-6416).

Radiodifuziuna Romana, Str Gral Berthelot 61-62, PO Box 63-1200, Bucharest (tel: 633-4710; fax: 312-3640).

Radioteleviziuna Romana (Romanian Radio and Television), Calea Dorobantilor 191, PO Box 63-1200, Bucharest (tel: 334-710; fax: 337-544).

Radio Nord-Est, Str Smirdan 5, 6600 Iasi (tel: 145-530; fax: 146-363).

Rafo SA, Str Cauciucului 2, Jud Bacau, Onesti (tel: 324-786; fax: 323-267).

Research Institute for Foreign Trade, Str Apollodor 17, 5 Bucharest (tel: 312-3652, 631-1293; fax: 312-5652).

Romanian Agency for Energy Conservation, Splaiul Independentei 202A, 77208 Bucharest (tel: 650-6470; fax: 312-3197).

Romanian Commodity Exchange, 71341 Bucharest 1, Presei Libere Sq, Bucharest (tel: 01-617-2231; fax: 01-312-2167).

Romanian Development Agency (RDA), Boulevard Magheru 7, Bucharest 1 (tel: 615-6686, 312-3311; fax: 613-2415).

Romanian Embassy (USA), 1607 23rd Street, Washington DC 20008 (tel: (+1-202)-332-4846; fax: (+1-202)-232-4748; e-mail: info@roembus.org).

Romanian Government, 1 Victoriei Sq, Bucharest (tel: 222-3677; fax: 222-6088).

Romanian National Commission for Unesco, Str Anton Cehov 8, 71292 Bucharest (tel: 633-3223; fax: 312-763).

Romanian Parliament, Calea 13, Septembrie 1, 76117 Bucharest (tel: 335-0111).

Romanian Post Office, 14 Libertatii Avenue, 70106 Bucharest 5 (tel: 400-1102; fax: 400-1515).

Romanian State Railways (SNCFR), Blvd 38 Dinicu Golescu, Sector 1-Cod 78123 Bucharest (tel: 617-0148).

Romexpo SA (Trade fairs and exhibitions). Bd Marasti 65-67, 71331 Bucharest (tel: 618-1160; fax: 618 3725).

Rompres (Romanian News Agency), Piata Presei Libere I, 71341 Bucharest (tel: 618-2878; fax: 617-0487).

Secretariat for the Privatisation and Restructuring Programmes within the Council for Co-ordination, Strategy and Economic Reform, 1 Piata Victoriei, Sector 1, Bucharest (tel: 312-8445, 222-8335; fax: 312-6932).

Senate of Romania, 1 Revolutiei Sq, Bucharest (tel: 615-0200, 617-0160; fax: 312-1752).

Societatea Nationala a Cailor Ferate, State Ownership Fund, CA Rosetti Str 21, Bucharest (tel: 611-4943).

State Ownership Fund, RDA Business Centre, World Trade Plaza, 2 Expozitiei Avenue, Ground Floor, Bucharest (tel: 230-0760).

Supreme Court of Justice, 4 Rahovei Str, Bucharest (312-0920; fax: 613-0882).

Prosecutor General's under the Supreme Court of Justice, 2-4 Unirii Ave, Bucharest (tel: 631-1750, 781-3065; fax: 781-6210).

Televiziuna Romana – Telecentrul Bucuresti, Calea Dorobantilor 191, PO Box 63-1200, Bucharest (tel: 633-4710; fax: 633-7544).

USA Embassy, Str Tudor Arghezi 7-9, Bucharest (tel: 312-4042; fax: 312-0395).

National news agency: Rompres' Piata Presei Libere 1, Sector 1, Bucharest 013701 (tel: 207-6110; fax: 317-0707; email: rompers@rompres.ro; internet: www.rompres.ro).

Other news agencies: Mediafax (www.mediafax.ro)

Internet sites

Association of Ecotourism in Romania: http://www.eco-romania.ro

Yellow Pages: /www.romanianyellowpages.com/~mozaic

Romanian Home Page: http://www.ici.ro/romania

Romanian National Tourist Office: http://www.romaniantourism.com

Russia

KEY FACTS

Official name: Rossiiskaya Federatsiya (Russian Federation)

Head of State: President Dmitry Medvedev (from 7 May 2008)

Head of government: Prime Minister Vladimir Putin (appointed 8 May 2008)

Ruling party: Yedinaya Rossiya (YR) (United Russia) (elected 2003; re-elected 4 Dec 2011)

Area: 17,075,000 square km

Population: 142.94 million (2010)*

Capital: Moscow

Official language: Russian

Currency: Rouble (R) = 100 kopeks

Exchange rate: R32.24 per US$ (Oct 2011)

GDP per capita: US$10,437 (2010)

GDP real growth: 4.00% (2010)

GDP: US$1,465.10 billion (2010)

Labour force: 75.44 million (2010)

Unemployment: 7.50% (2010) (with additional underemployment)

Inflation: 6.90% (2010)

Oil production: 10.27 million bpd (2010)

Balance of trade: US$151.68 billion (2010)

Annual FDI: US$42.87 billion (2010)

* estimated figure

In September 2011 Russians learned, with little surprise, that their prime minister and former president, Vladimir Putin, was most likely to be their next President, swapping jobs with President Medvedev in the March 2012 elections. Looking strangely distant, Mr Putin was rumoured to have undergone plastic surgery to remove the bags under his eyes. One commentator described him as looking like a short-sighted Daniel Craig (i e James Bond). Whether it was Botox, or blepharoplasty, it confirmed Mr Putin's anxiety to be seen as a man's man (and by extension, a woman's man), fighting bears, riding topless on a motorcycle or showing off his fishing skills (or lack of them). In his speech to the congress of the Yedinaya Rossiya (YR) (United Russia) party Mr Putin told the delegates that 'the task before us is not only to pour honey, but sometimes to administer bitter medicine.'

Job swap

Although a number of 'straw' candidates would probably be put up to run against him, Mr Putin's 'election' as president looks to be a shoe-in. It appeared likely that Mr Putin would be president until 2024 when he would be 70. If he did run the full term, he would become Russia's longest-serving president since Josef Stalin. If the days of Stalinism were over, the new 'ism' was Putinism and it was beginning to acquire some of the characteristics of the Stalin era. Amazingly, Mr Putin advised the YR delegates that the swap arrangement had been agreed 'years before', thereby confirming that Mr Medvedev had been little more than a puppet.

Party delegates, as well as most Russians, seemed prepared to turn a blind eye to Mr Putin's democratic deficiencies, preferring to see him as their country's saviour. But the deficiencies were there for all to see. Free speech was stifled, often violently; many democratic processes had simply been hijacked – not least the presidential elections. Some of the victims of this process – such as the former president of Yukos, Mikhail Khodorkovsky – had acquired symbolic status. At the beginning of 2011, Mr Khodorkovsky, who was already serving an eight-year term for tax evasion, was sentenced to a further six years in jail, this time for fraud. Former president and reformer, Mikhail Gorbachev, has warned Russians that the democratic rights they had struggled for in the early 1990s had been lost. Under Putin, Russia faced a period of economic and political stagnation. Greater uncertainty was caused by the fact that the 'Putin' majority appeared to be shrinking, borne out by the slide in the poll ratings of both Putin and Medvedev. In the late summer of 2011 both men endeavoured to reverse the trend: Mr Putin by being filmed scuba diving off the Taman Peninsula, Mr Medvedev, somewhat less dramatically, by recounting on live television the glories of the 2008 invasion of Georgia.

The first high-profile casualty of Mr Putin's announcement that he would seek re-election as president was Russia's respected finance minister, Alexei Kudrin, who tendered his resignation saying that he 'unconditionally refused' to serve under Mr Medvedev. 'The differences I have will not allow me to be in the government.' Mr Medvedev attacked Kudrin's remarks as 'improper' and demanded that he retract them or resign. Mr Kudrin's disenchantment was shared by a number of politicians. Mr Medvedev's chief economic aide tweeted 'There is no cause for joy. It's a good time to switch over to a sports channel.' Boris Nemtsov, the leader of the Partiya narodnoi svobodi (Parnas) (People's Freedom Party) declared it a 'catastrophic scenario'. Even Mikhail Prokhorov, the billionaire leader of the recently created Pravoe Delo (PD) (Right Cause) party (and owner of the US-New Jersey Nets basket ball team) resigned expressing his distaste for the sham political process.

Paranoia?

Mr Putin's announcement certainly shattered any US illusions that the wind of change was blowing through Russian foreign policy. It had been rumoured that during the May 2011 meeting of the G8 countries, the US and Russia were close to signing a missile defence agreement. The

agreement did not get signed as each side hedged with conditions described as 'reminiscent of Cold War days'. Russia is, effectively, the only body politic capable of mounting a nuclear attack on the US. Despite the chilled relations that are likely to follow the election paralysis Russia's response even to new NATO radar sites is one of paranoia, a paranoia generated from the top levels of government. Russia's reaction to the US senate resolution on Georgia caused further ripples of paranoia. Exception was taken to the resolution's use of the word 'occupation' to refer to Russia's military presence in Abkhazia and South Ossetia. The cease-fire agreement between Georgia and Russia required Russian troops to withdraw to their pre-war positions. Russia argued that its formal recognition of the two break-away states changed all that. Thus, the US insistence that Abkhazia and South Ossetia were 'occupied by the Russian Federation' caused sensitive Russian hackles to rise.

The behaviour of Russia in 2011 rather resembled that of a 1930s Chicago gangster. The importance given to the detail of correct appearance and behaviour was directly proportional to the failure to meet even basic international standards. Thus, this member of the G8 managed to rank 154th (out of the178 states rated) alongside such luminary bastions of freedom and fair play as Guinea Bissau and the Central African Republic in the respected Transparency International 2010 rankings. In between glad-handing fellow heads of state at international gatherings, President Dimitry Medvedev quietly acknowledged that some thirty-three billion dollars – three per cent of Russia's annual GDP – is illegally spirited away each year.

Now for Navalny...

Perhaps the saddest aspect of this all-engulfing corruption is not so much its existence, but the fact that not only the government, but also the judiciary are involved up to their eyes. Thus, those seriously enough aggrieved to take their case to court often find that they themselves are accused of some arcane, backdated offence such as tax avoidance or allegedly illegal corporate activities. An almost lone exception in exposing and challenging cases of manifest corruption is the website: www.rospil.info and its founder, Alexei Navalny. By 2010 Mr Navalny had become the Russian *Don Quixote de nos jours* (today's Don Quixote). By tilting at the windmills of corruption and at those responsible for and benefiting from it, he had acquired an almost legendary reputation among the Russian middle classes, at the same time becoming a seriously irritating thorn in the side of the Kremlin. A May 2011 profile of Mr Navalny published in the London *Financial Times* reflected that Mr Navalny's website 'had gained notoriety throughout Russia, publishing documents which purport to show the pervasive corruption at the heart of the decade old regime of former President, now Prime Minister, Vladimir Putin'. Quoted in an article in the *New Yorker* by Julia Joffe, when asked on live radio what he thought of Mr Putin's ruling YR party, Mr Navalny replied: 'I think very poorly of United Russia. United Russia is the party of corruption, the party of crooks and thieves. And it is the duty of every citizen to make sure that this party is destroyed.'

Responding to a blog posted on www.rospil.info which asked readers whether they agreed with his claims about United Russia, according to Ms Joffe's article, a whopping 96.6 per cent of some 40,000 respondents agreed. The Kremlin's response was predictable; in May 2011 Mr Navalny was accused of defrauding a state-owned timber company of over one million roubles (roughly US$32,000) for, rather improbably, encouraging it to enter a deal, which in the end turned out to be unprofitable. In Anglo Saxon legal terms this would be comparable to suing an editor at Bloomberg for publishing a 'buy' recommendation that failed to deliver.

... and Nemtsov.

If Mr Navalny represented a new breed of Russian political critics, Boris Nemtsov could probably be described as belonging to the old school. What they held in common was a form of running guerrilla warfare with the Kremlin. Mr Nemtsov is probably the highest profile opposition leader in Russia; he was deputy prime minister under President Yeltsin in the 1990s and has vigorously joined in criticism both of corruption and of the Kremlin's constant limitation of political freedoms. In February 2011 Mr Nemtsov and his number two, Vladimir Milov (co-chairmen of Parnas) were ordered to pay 100,000 roubles each to Russian oil magnate Gennady Timchenko for slandering him in a booklet they co-authored, entitled *Putin. Results. 10 Years*. The court also ordered the two politicians to publish a retraction of a statement in the publication that Mr Timchenko had been a 'nobody' until Mr Putin's rise to power. The booklet had alleged (reflecting widespread popular belief) that Mr Putin had amassed substantial riches as the beneficial owner of Swiss-based company Guvnor, co-owned by Mr Timchenko, a company that oversees the export of around thirty per cent of Russian hydrocarbon exports. The Kremlin was clearly concerned about the threat posed by Mr Nemtsov's Parnas which, in addition to his experience also counted former prime minister Mikhail Kasyanov, former Duma (parliament) deputy, Vladimir Ryzkhov and Vladimir Milov a former deputy energy minister, as members. In mid-June 2011, however, the Parnas was refused registration on a technicality.

Not that this would have come as a surprise for Mr Nemtsov, who had already found himself in jail for a couple of weeks on spurious charges in January 2011. Mr Nemtsov's treatment bore the hallmarks of the administration's treatment of oil tycoon Mikhail Khodorkovsky. In a television phone-in appearance in December 2010 Mr Putin had happily anticipated court judgements on Mr Khodorkovsky, an assumption of guilt that few dared to challenge – not even the judges. Mr Khodorkovsky was sentenced to a further 14 years in jail. The most interesting aspect of the trial was the allegation by the presiding judge's press secretary, Natalia Vasilyeva, that he had been forced to implement the judgement. Miss Vasilyeva did not mince her words 'Everyone in the judicial community understands perfectly that this is a rigged case, a fixed trial.' Theories abounded as to why a young assistant, who had only been in the job for a matter of months, chose to make her statement. All the theories shared a common undercurrent, that of political intervention in the judicial process.

In mid-2011 Mr Nemtsov, while appearing to be the most experienced opposition politician, was not the only likely contender. Metals billionaire Mikhail Prokhorov, the leader of the new pro-business party, Right Cause, also put himself forward. The new party claimed to champion liberal economics and sought to appeal to Russia's middle class. Right Cause had not a single seat in Russia's Duma, but none the less sought to push the Communist Party into third place. The fact that Mr Prokhorov was reported to be the third richest man in Russia - with a personal fortune estimated at US$18 billion - would normally have prevented him from seeking election. Political eyebrows were raised when he also announced that Right Cause was not running as an opposition party, but as an 'alternative'. Mr Prokhorov had at one time gone so far as to state his opposition to Mr Putin's YR, but had significantly refrained from any overt criticism. Many observers saw the emergence of Right Cause, which had promised to support Mr Medvedev's candidacy for president, as no more than a Kremlin inspired ruse to legitimise the elections. What appeared clear was that in 2011 Mr Putin's gloved hand was beginning to show itself in an increasingly unsubtle, occasionally sinister fashion in the run up to the elections.

KEY INDICATORS — Russia

	Unit	2006	2007	2008	2009	2010
Population	m	142.80	142.10	142.00	141.90	*142.94
Gross domestic product (GDP)	US$bn	988.67	1,289.58	1,660.00	1,229.20	1,465.10
GDP per capita	US$	6,923	9,100	11,690	8,694	10,437
GDP real growth	%	7.4	8.2	8.5	-7.8	4.0
Inflation	%	9.7	9.0	14.1	11.7	6.9
Unemployment	%	7.2	6.1	6.2	8.4	7.5
Industrial output	% change	5.3	5.4	3.1	-10.8	–
Agricultural output	% change	1.7	2.6	8.5	0.2	–
Oil output	'000 bpd	9,769.0	9,978.0	9,886.0	10,032.0	10,270.0
Natural gas output	bn cum	6,121.0	607.4	601.7	527.5	588.9
Coal output	mtoe	144.5	94.5	152.8	140.7	148.8
Exports (fob) (goods)	US$m	303,926.0	355,465.0	471,603.0	303,388.0	400,419.0
Imports (fob) (goods)	US$m	159,838.0	223,421.0	291,861.0	191,803.0	248,738.0
Balance of trade	US$m	144,088.0	132,043.0	179,742.0	111,585.0	151,681.0
Current account	US$m	94,257.0	76,600.0	102,400.0	49,518.0	70,599.0
Foreign debt	US$bn	257.2	310.0	402.5	–	–
Total reserves minus gold	US$m	295,567.6	464,379.0	412,548.0	416,648.9	443,585.8
Foreign exchange	US$m	295,277.1	464,004.3	411,494.0	405,824.9	432,948.5
Exchange rate	per US$	27.19	25.58	24.85	31.74	30.37

* estimated figure

The economy falters

Russia's economy bears many of the characteristics of the underdeveloped economies of Africa rather than the industrialised economies of Europe and North America. The largest single determinant of economic prosperity is the price of its hydrocarbon exports and the level of demand for those exports. The global economic uncertainty of mid-2011 saw Russia begin to take protective measures by selling its gold in international markets. The attraction for Russia was that gold was at a record price at a time when the country was beginning to feel the economic pinch. Despite its massive hydrocarbon reserves the prospect of running a chronic trade deficit began to appear likely.

As the twenty-first century advanced, Russia's hydrocarbons were beginning to look like something of a poisoned chalice. While they had earned massive mounts of foreign currency, they had done so at the cost of developing other aspects of the economy, aspects which might have generated more jobs, more investment and permitted higher levels of technology transfer. Oil and gas exports may account for around 50 per cent of budget revenues and a disproportionately large 25 per cent of gross domestic product (GDP), but as a rule the oil industry only generates significant levels of employment if its revenues are channelled back into the economy. This has certainly not been the case in Russia, where widespread corruption has meant that revenues are siphoned off into foreign bank accounts rather than invested productively.

Russia's GDP grew by an estimated 4 per cent in 2010, having contracted by 7.9 per cent in 2009. The 2010 growth figure would have been higher had it not been for the worst summer drought on record that lead to a ban on exports of wheat and other grains. Higher prices for food products meant that the consumer price index rose, pushing the annual inflation rate for 2010 to nearly 9 per cent. Forecast figures for 2011 were for inflation to fall back to 6.5 per cent and for annual GDP growth to be roughly the same as 2010, at 4.2 per cent. Figures for both inflation and exports will also be affected by oil and gas prices.

Other factors likely to affect the economy include the level of state social spending. This has traditionally risen in pre-election periods and most analysts expected the same to occur in late 2011 and early 2010. In 2011 social spending was expected to account for 28 per cent of the federal budget, reaching the rouble equivalent of US$97 billion. While this would be twice the level of defence spending and would inevitably be geared to increase the government's popularity, it was unlikely to have any beneficial effect on the economy as a whole.

The Russian stock market presents an intriguing picture. According to a report in the *International Herald Tribunal*, in the twenty years since the end of the Soviet Union, the Russian stock market has been either in the top five best-performing markets in the world, or in the bottom five (with one exception). The report noted that Russia is highly vulnerable to the price of oil. The Russian government estimates that it will need to collect taxes on oil at prices above US$120 per barrel to balance the budget. In 2011, as the price struggled to reach that level, the Russian finance ministry has needed to borrow from both domestic and foreign lenders.

Modernisation

Given the limited amount of freedom of expression and discussion that is allowed in Russia, it is hardly surprising that there has been little amounting to public debate on the future of the economy. The most significant discussion there has been has taken place in the meetings of a so-called 'commission on modernisation' headed by Mr Medvedev. The commission has been more of a catalyst than a legislative office, with some ministries responding more readily than others. The speed and extent of response has generally been a function of the loyalty (and of the extent to which they are beholden) of individual ministers to former president Putin. In 2011 all moves within government ministries and agencies had to be seen in the context of the 2012 elections. Favours needed to be returned, obligations met. Few of the decisions taken had much to do with improved governance or with greater efficiency. Underlying them, yet again, was the common theme of corruption, this time at the highest levels of government.

After years of talks, in late 2010 Russia and the European Union (EU) reached agreement on terms for Russia's entry into the World Trade Organisation (WTO). The agreement in principle meant that Russia's entry could be completed by the end of 2011. Agreement on the terms had been reached with the US in late September 2010. The EU has been seeking Russia's WTO membership for some time, essentially so that there would exist a legal framework within which issues of disagreement could be addressed and resolved. The only obvious immediate impact would be on the export tariffs on timber introduced by Russia in 2007. This had been particularly damaging to EU member Finland. In the longer term, most analysts doubted that WTO membership would be particularly advantageous to Russia, since there are no tariffs applicable to its largest exports to the EU – oil and gas. But the supposition was that Moscow believes WTO membership would be necessary to attract the levels of investment needed to modernise the economy. Serious concerns remained among both investors and entrepreneurs over the extent to which the rule of law applied in Russia. Whatever WTO membership might do to improve perceptions, they would almost certainly be overruled by the negative perceptions resulting from Mr Putin's announcement that he was seeking the presidency again.

Gold

Fortuitously, Russia is the world's fourth largest gold producer, after China, Australia and the United States. As reported in the Paris based *International Herald Tribunal*, a non-committal official statement announced that 'The Bank of Russia is not committed to buying any particular amount of gold. Nor is there any official target amount of gold purchases. The bank buys gold at a market price and its buying intentions completely depend on the market conditions.' In sharp contrast to the tight government control exercised on hydrocarbon exports, Russia's gold markets are relatively free, allowing traders to take advantage of the characteristically high prices experienced during economic crises.

Oil and gas

According to the *BP Statistical Review of World Energy, 2011* (BP Statistics) Russia had reserves of 77.4 billion barrels of oil at the end of 2010; with production at 10.27 million barrels per day (bpd) and consumption of 3.20 million bpd, there is 7.07 million bpd available for export, including roughly 4.0 million bpd of crude oil and the remainder in refined products. Russia's oil exports fall under the jurisdiction of the state-owned pipeline monopoly, Transneft. Most of Russia's resources are located in Western Siberia, between the Ural Mountains and the Central Siberian Plateau. Eastern Siberia holds some reserves, but the region has had little exploration.

Most of Russia's oil production comes from the Western Siberian oilfields, Priobskoye, Prirazlomnoye, Mamontovskoye, Malobalykskoye and Surgut. The Sakhalin group of fields, offshore in the Okhotsk Sea, in the Far East is expected to contribute to most of Russia's oil production in the near term. In the longer-term, untapped oil reserves in Eastern Siberia, the Caspian Sea and Sakhalin are expected to play a larger role and several international oil companies, including ExxonMobil, Shell and BP are actively working in this area.

Most of Russia's production remains dominated by domestic firms. Following the collapse of the Soviet Union, Russia undertook privatisation of the oil industry, however the consolidation that followed transformed the sector into one dominated by a few privately-owned companies that drove the growth in the sector starting in the late 1990s. In 2003, the oil company, BP invested in TNK (formerly Tyumen Oil Company), forming TNK-BP, one of country's major oil producers. This was followed by the entrance of ConocoPhillips into the Russian oil exploration and production. Subsequent attempts by foreign firms to increase their investment in Russia were unsuccessful. The state-run Rosneft acquired most or the Yukos assets (which had previously been controlled by Mikhail Khodorkovsky until it went bankrupt and Mr Khodorkovsky was imprisoned) and became the largest oil producer in Russia. While foreign companies can invest in Russia, this is generally done with a Russian company, usually Rosneft.

Russia has a significant refining capacity, comprising 40 oil refineries with a total crude oil processing capacity of 5.555 million bpd, according the BP statistics. Rosneft, the largest refinery operator controls 1.3 million bpd and operates Russia's largest refinery, the 385,176bpd Angarsk facility. Other companies with sizeable refining capacity in Russia include Lukoil (975,860bpd) and TNK-BP (690,000bpd).

The majority of Russian exports (80 per cent) are destined for European markets, particularly Germany and The Netherlands. Around 12 per cent of Russia's oil exports go to Asia, while 6 per cent are exported to North and South America, with the majority of those exports going to the United States (5 per cent of total exports).

In 2009, Russia exported an average of 306,000bpd to China via rail. However Russia plans on increasing exports to China significantly in the future. The planned Eastern Siberia–Pacific Ocean oil (ESPO) pipeline, for exports of crude oil to Japan and South Korea has a spur, completed in September 2010, allowing significant increase in export volumes to China – 300,000bpd until 2030, under a US$25 billion loan-for-oil deal agreed in 2009.

... and the gas

According to the BP Statistics, in 2010, Russia held the world's largest natural gas reserves, with 44.8 trillion cubic metres (cum), representing 23.9 per cent of the world's total reserves. Russian natural gas production was 588.9 billion cum in 2010, an increase of 11.6 per cent on its 2009 level of production and representing 18.4 per cent of total world production. The majority of these reserves are located in Siberia, with the Yamburg, Urengoy and Medvezh'ye fields alone accounting for about 45 per cent of Russia's total reserves. More than half of all reserves are located in Siberia. Significant reserves are also located in northern Russia.

In 2010 Russia was the world's second-largest natural gas producer (372.7 million cum), second only to the United States (621.0 million cum), however it was the world's largest exporter with199.85 million cum. Increased production was due to increased sales as Europe – Russia's main market for natural gas – experienced a harsh winter. Also, production in 2009 had experienced a decreased of 17 per cent year over the year due to a downturn in global trade and demand so that production reached the lowest level since 1992. The largest concentration of natural gas is located in Siberia, where about 95 per cent of production is concentrated. Some of the most prolific fields in this area include Yamburg, Urengoy, and Medvezh'ye, and all of the supplies are licensed to Gazprom, Russia's state-run natural gas exploration and production company. Russia exports significant amounts of natural gas (through its Gazprom's subsidiary Gazexport) to customers in the Commonwealth of Independent States (CIS), but its most lucrative market is the European Union, followed by Turkey, Japan, South Korea and Taiwan.

Terror

In late January 2011 a suicide bomber killed 35 people and injured a further 100 or so at Moscow's Domodedovo airport. This followed an earlier suicide bombing on the Moscow metro, in March 2010, which killed 40 people. As in so many aspects of Russian society, the institutions charged with the protection of civilians proved not to be up to the job. Some reports suggested that officers of the Federal'naya Sluzhba Bezopasnosti (FSB) (Federal Security Service) were more interested in conducting private business than in doing their job. But criticism and allegations of corruption within the FSB came perilously close to touching a raw nerve; Mr Putin is a former KGB (the forerunner of the FSB) officer and enjoys a cosily close relationship with the FSB. Violent attacks of the sort seen at Domodedovo airport and in the metro left the FSB simply guessing at the identity of the perpetrators. But no heads rolled, no apologies were made.

Risk assessment

Economy	Fair
Politics	Poor
Regional stability	Fair

COUNTRY PROFILE

Historical profile

The first monarchic dynasty ruled from the ninth century and built Kiev as its capital. It was overthrown by the Mongol invasion in the thirteenth century.

In the fifteenth century, the Grand Prince of Moscow, Ivan III, annexed the rival principalities of Russia and became its first national sovereign.

Ivan IV (Ivan the Terrible) further expanded Russia's frontiers and became the first holder of the title of Tsar.

1613 Michael Romanov was elected tsar, establishing the Romanov dynasty, which ruled Russia until the 1917 revolution.

Peter the Great (1682–1725) and Catherine the Great (1762–96) consolidated the regime.

1772 Russia started expanding its territory. It acquired the Crimea and over the next 40 years parts of Poland, Ukraine, Belarus, Moldova and Georgia.

1812 The French invasion of Russia ended when France was driven out.

In the mid-nineteenth century, most of Siberia was annexed and expansion to the south and east continued until 1905.

1914–16 After initial success in the First Would War against Germany and Austria, military defeats weakened the position of the Tsar as personal head of the army and increased political and economy tensions.

1917 In February Tsar Nicholas II was forced to abdicate. The liberal government was overthrown in a Bolshevik coup, under the leadership of Lenin.

1918–20 A civil war raged between the communist Bolsheviks and anti-Bolsheviks, the right-wing white army. The Tsar and his family, captives of the Bolsheviks, were executed by their jailers on 17 July 1918, to prevent them from being liberated by Tsarist forces. The civil war ended in defeat for the white army, despite assistance from Britain, France, Japan and the US.

1922 The Union of Soviet Socialist Republics (USSR) was formed by Russia, Ukraine, Belarus and the Transcaucasus region.

1924 Following Lenin's death, Josef Stalin took over the leadership of the USSR as the general secretary of the Communist Party of the Soviet Union (CPSU) and a period of industrialisation, collectivisation of agriculture and purges of Stalin's opponents began. Key leadership rival Leon Trotsky was exiled in 1927 and assassinated in 1940.

1939 The USSR signed a non-aggression pact, the *Molotov-Ribbentrop Treaty*, with Nazi Germany. Soviet forces assisted the German invasion of Poland. The USSR also invaded Finland but was forced to respect Finnish independence in a 1940 peace agreement.

1940 Stalin ordered the execution of up to 22,000 captured Polish army officers at Katyn, near Smolensk in Russia.

1941 After the USSR was invaded by Germany, it joined the Allies and declared war on the Axis powers.

1944–45 The USSR liberated parts of Eastern Europe and Eastern Germany, these being pulled into its sphere of influence after the Second World War. Western Europe, meanwhile, fell under the sphere of influence of the US, marking the start of the Cold War.

1949 The USSR became the world's second nuclear power (after the US), when it exploded its first atomic bomb.

1953 Following Stalin's death, Nikita Krushchev took over the leadership of the USSR.

1955 The Warsaw Pact was established by the USSR and its satellite Eastern European states as a security apparatus to defend the region against NATO.

1962 The USSR's deployment of nuclear missiles in Cuba, within striking distance of the US, led to the 14-day missile crisis between the US and the USSR.

1964 After Krushchev's fall from power the USSR was led by Leonid Brezhnev.
1979 Soviet forces invaded Afghanistan to prop up the communist Afghan government.
1982 After Brezhnev's death, Yuri Andropov became leader of the USSR.
1984 Konstantin Chernenko replaced Andropov, following his death.
1985 Chernenko died. His successor, Mikhail Gorbachev, instigated a programme of social, political and economic reforms, centred on *perestroika* (restructuring) and *glasnost* (openness).
1989 The USSR withdrew from Afghanistan. Communist rule ended in most of Eastern and Central Europe.
1991 Gorbachev survived a coup attempt by communist hard-liners, but lost power; he dissolved the CPSU, the communist central committee. In the ensuing power vacuum Boris Yeltsin emerged as a leader when he prevented a military takeover in Moscow. He was elected Russia's president. The USSR ceased to exist on 31 December and the Commonwealth of Independent States (CIS) was formed by 11 of the former USSR republics, including Russia. Dzhokhar Dudayev won presidential elections in Chechnya and proclaimed independence from Russia. The remains of the last Tsar and his family, found in 1989, were identified after two years of forensic and DNA tests.
1992 Yeltsin appointed Yegor Gaidar acting prime minister. Yeltsin appointed Viktor Chernomyrdin prime minister.
1993 Yeltsin ordered the army to crush an anti-government uprising in Moscow and end a parliamentary sit-in. The Federal Assembly, comprising the State Duma and the Federation Council replaced the Supreme Soviet. A referendum approved a new constitution that gave the president sweeping powers.
1994 Russian troops invaded Chechnya, which is *de facto* independent, but *de jure* part of Russia. Uzbekistan and Russia signed an economic integration treaty.
1995 In Duma elections, the reformed Kommunisticheskaya Partiya Rossiiskoi Federatsii (KPRF) (Communist Party of the Russian Federation) won the largest vote. Chechen rebels seized hundreds of hostages during a raid on the southern Russian town of Budennovsk. More than 100 are killed in the ensuing violence.
1996 Yeltsin was re-elected president. Russia joined in G7 discussions on nuclear security. Chechen rebels seized thousands of hostages in the Russian town of Kizlyar. Chechen President Dudayev was killed by the Russian air force; he was succeeded by Zelimkhan Yandarbiyev. A peace treaty was signed between Russia and Chechen separatists, temporarily ending the conflict. Chechen forces drove the Russian army out of the capital, Grozny.
1997 Yeltsin and the Belarusian president, Aleksander Lukashenko, signed the Treaty on the Union of Belarus and Russia. The treaty aimed at increasing political and economic co-operation between the two states. Yeltsin and the new Chechen president, Aslan Maskhadov, signed a formal peace agreement.
1998 The Russian rouble collapsed, sending Russia into temporary economic crisis as it defaulted on foreign debts. The bodies of the last Russian Tsar and his family were interred in the Cathedral of Saints Peter and Paul in St Petersburg.
1999 An Islamist separatist group declared the Russian republic of Dagestan to be independent. Chechen fighters under the command of the former prime minister of Chechnya, Shamil Basayev, invaded Dagestan in support of the separatists. Yeltsin appointed Vladimir Putin as prime minister. A series of bomb explosions in Russian cities were blamed on Chechen separatists and Russia launched a second invasion of Chechnya. Yeltsin resigned before the official end of his term. Putin became acting president.
2000 Vladimir Putin was elected president. The presidents of Belarus, Kazakhstan, Kyrgyzstan, Russia and Tajikistan (formerly the Customs Five) established the Eurasian Economic Community (EEC). Mikhail Kasyanov became prime minister.
2001 The Russian army started a gradual withdrawal of troops from Chechnya. The main pro-Putin parties created the Yedinaya Rossiya (YR) (United Russia) party by merging the ruling Mezhregional'noye Dvishenie Yedinstvo (Medved) (Inter-Regional Movement Unity) and the Otechestvo-Vsya Rossiya (OVR) (Fatherland-All Russia). Tajikistan, China, Russia, Kazakhstan, Kyrgyzstan and Uzbekistan formed the Shanghai Co-operation Organisation (SCO) and agreed to fight ethnic and religious militancy, while promoting investment and trade.
2002 The US and Russia agreed to cut 70 per cent of their nuclear arsenals. Chechen Prime Minister Ilyasov resigned and was appointed by President Putin as Russia's federal minister of Chechnya affairs. Akhmed Kadyrov, appointed Mikhail Babich as prime minister of Chechnya. Chechnya's leading rebel warlord, Shamil Basayev, claimed responsibility for the Moscow theatre siege, during which 119 hostages died.
2003 Kadyrov appointed Anatoly Popov as Chechen prime minister. Russia, Ukraine, Kazakhstan and Belarus signed an economic union treaty. The YR won parliamentary elections.
2004 President Putin dismissed Prime Minister Kasyanov and appointed Mikhail Fradkov, in his place. Putin was re-elected president.
In Chechnya, Sergei Abramov was confirmed as prime minister of a pro-Moscow government. The president, Akhmad Kadyrov, was killed in an explosion and Abramov won the presidential elections. At least 330 people died in the Beslan school massacre when Russian troops stormed the school held by Chechen terrorists, in an attempt to free the hostage schoolchildren and teachers.
2005 Russian special forces killed the Chechen rebel leader, Maskhadov. Russia gave asylum to exiled President Askar Akayev of Tajikistan. State control was tightened through media and electoral laws. A diplomatic row developed when Ukraine refused to pay a four-fold increase in the price of gas and Gazprom cut off supplies. The row escalated and antagonised the EU when supplies to some of its member states were also cut by default. Germany and Russia signed an agreement to build a gas pipeline beneath the Baltic Sea and secure Russian natural gas for Western Europe.
2006 The rouble was made fully convertible against foreign currencies. President Abdul-Khalim Sadulayev of Chechnya was killed by Russian forces. Russia denied it was responsible for the death in the UK of outspoken critic of Putin's regime and former security service officer, Aleksandr Litvinenko, by radioactive poison. Belarus became the latest former Soviet-satellite country to be given an ultimatum to pay the market price for Russian gas or be denied supplies.
2007 The transit oil pipeline through Belarus was shut-down after Belarus attempted to impose a transit tax on the oil; Russia accused Belarus of siphoning off oil. President Putin dismissed Chechen president, Alu Alkhanov and appointed Ramzan Kadyrov in his place. The Russians planted their flag below the North Pole using two mini-submarines in an action laying claim to the potential oil and minerals below the seabed. The US and Canada both criticised the claim and launched competing claims. The North Pole (administered by the International Seabed Authority) was regarded as being not subject to any one country's claim. The remains of the last two missing children of Tsar Nicholas II, including his son Alexei, were found near Ekaterinburg. In parliamentary elections YR won over 64.3 per cent of the vote (315 seats out of 450); the KPRF party 11.6 per cent (57). The OSCE declared the election to be 'not fair and failed to meet many… commitments and standards for democratic elections'.

2008 The number of members of the Federal Assembly was reduced to 168. In the presidential elections, Dmitry Medvedev won with 70.3 per cent of the vote. International observers criticised the election campaign for not allowing candidates equal access to the media. After President Medvedev was sworn into office he appointed Vladimir Putin, who had accepted the offer of chairmanship of the ruling YR party, as prime minister. Russia backed South Ossetia when Georgia attacked separatist forces in its break-away territory. Russian forces ejected Georgian troops and later recognised the independence of the Russian enclaves, South Ossetia and Abkhazia. Winner of the Nobel Prize for Literature in 1970, Alexander Solzhenitsyn, died. The international global financial crisis caused the Moscow stock exchange to fall sharply; the government instituted a US$68 billion package to stabilise its banking system. Parliament voted to increase a president's term in office from four years to six, from 2012.
2009 A three-week international row between Russia and Ukraine, in which several European countries lost their gas supply as Gazprom shut-down its supplies, was resolved, but only after EU officials advised national gas suppliers to sue Russia and Ukraine for the break in supplies. President Medvedev welcomed US President Obama to Moscow; there were talks about limiting nuclear weapons. The Russian rights activist Nataliya Estemirova was murdered in Chechnya and her body dumped in Ingushetia.
2010 The new Severo-Kavkazsky federalny okrug (North Caucasian federal district) was created by presidential decree on 19 January; it was formed by a split in the South Caucasian federal district, in the extreme south-west of Russia. It has an area of 170,700 square kilometres, with a population of over 10 million; its administrative capital is Pyatigorsk. The Verkhny Lars-Kazbegi border checkpoint between Georgia and Russia, which had been closed in 2006, was reopened in March. The US and Russia signed another nuclear disarmament treaty in Prague (Czech Republic) on 8 April. The treaty limits the number of warheads and launchers each country may possess. The signing took place only after the US scrapped previous plans for a 'missile shield' based in Eastern Europe which Russia considered provocative. In April, an agreement on the Arctic border between Norway and Russia in the Barents Sea, which cuts across an oil and natural gas rich region, was finally resolved after several decades in dispute and considered 'good and balanced' by President Medvedev. On 6 June a customs union between Russia, Belarus and Kazakhstan became fully operational. In July the government announced plans to sell its stake in 11 state-owned companies. It is hoped the sale will raise some US$29 billion over the next three years in what will be Russia's biggest privatisation since the 1990s. After a prolonged drought a temporary ban on the export of wheat was imposed in August. Wild fires, caused by a severe heat wave in July and August, covered over 170,000 hectares in the south and west of the country; over 40 people were killed, around 2,000 homes were engulfed within the many individual fires and about one-third of the grain harvest was destroyed. President Medvedev sacked the mayor of Moscow, Yuri Luzhkov, in September. It was rumoured that he would form a political party, although he would not run for president nor stand in parliamentary elections. On 26 November the Duma passed a resolution confirming that Josef Stalin had, according to papers kept in a secret archive, given the direct order for the massacre of 22,000 Polish officers at Katyn in 1940. President Medvedev said, in his videoblog in November, that 'if a political opposition doesn't stand the slightest chance of winning a fair election, then it degrades and becomes marginalised' and 'if the ruling party never has to worry about losing an election anywhere, then it too degrades' the process and ultimately leads to stagnation.
2011 The upper house of the Duma approved the nuclear disarmament agreement with the US, signed in 2010, on 26 January. The New Start (Strategic Arms Reduction Treaty), replaces the 1991 disarmament treaty, which had lapsed in 2009. New Start will cut warheads by 30 per cent from the previous limit and allow verifiable inspection of each other's capabilities. On 22 June the Central Election Commission announced it had refused to register Partiya Narodnoi Svobodi (Parnas) (People's Freedom Party) a new, liberal, political party. The party leaders included four prominent opposition figures. The justice ministry said the party failed to meet several legal requirements and all members will be barred from standing in the next general elections. The Nord Stream pipeline carrying Russian gas direct to Germany and the rest of Europe was opened on 6 September. The pipeline is the first to by-pass Ukraine and other central European countries. Vatentina Matviyenko, former governor of St Petersburg, was elected Speaker of the upper house on 21 September. She is a supporter of Putin and replaces Sergei Mironov of the Spravedlivaya Rossiya (SR) (A Just Russia) who was ousted in May. Prime Minister Putin announced on 24 September that he would stand in 2012 presidential elections. On 18 November, the presidents of Russia, Belarus and Kazakhstan signed an agreement to set targets for setting up an internal market, the Eurasian Union, by 2015. A Eurasian Commission will begin an overseeing role for integration on 1 January 2012. On 25 November, the date of the next presidential election was set by parliament for 4 March 2012. Elections for the lower house of parliament were held on 4 December, in which the four political parties that had been present in the last session in parliament, plus seven other political parties that had been granted registration, took part. As expected YR won a majority with 49.29 per cent (238 seats, out of 450), but its result was down from the 315 seats in the 2007 elections. The KPRF won 92 seats and the new party SR, won 64 and LDPR won 56 seats; turnout was 60.2 per cent. Thousands of protestors took to the streets of Moscow and other cities on 5-7 December, defying a ban on rallies. Hundreds were arrested. On 7 December former president Mikhail Gorbachev (of the USSR), declared 'the authorities must admit that numerous instances of vote-rigging and fraud have taken place, and the announced results do not reflect the voters' wishes', and 'the current authorities should make only one decision - annul the election results, and hold a new poll.' The Central Election Commission stated that 'recorded violations were insignificant...' On 8 December, Prime Minister Putin accused US authorities of inciting opposition protests to the election results. The official US response to the results had been of 'serious concerns', with US Secretary of State Hillary Clinton saying that they were neither free not fair.

Political structure

Constitution

The constitution was adopted in December 1993. The Russian Federation consists of 89 republics and regions, including the federal cities of Moscow and St Petersburg.

If the ruling party has over two thirds of the Duma seats it has enough power to amend the constitution unchallenged.

Electoral system: universal direct suffrage over the age of 18.

Parliament voted in 2008 to increase a president's term in office from four years to six, from 2012.

Form of state

Federal state with a republican form of government

The executive

Executive power is held by the president, who has the right to veto parliamentary legislation, while issuing decrees on which the Federal Assembly may advise but not

veto. The president is elected for a four-year term.
The cabinet is appointed by the prime minister, who is appointed by the president.
The State Council of the Russian Federation, which has consultative functions only, was formed in 2000. It advises the president on issues concerning the relationship between the central administration and the regions.
In 2008 parliament voted to increase a president's term in office from four years to six, from 2012.

National legislature
The 1993 constitution created a bicameral Federal'noye Sobraniye (Federal Assembly), comprising the Gosudarstvennaya Duma (State Duma, commonly called Gosduma, lower house) with 450 seats elected by proportional representative from party lists, and the Sovet Federatsii (Federation Council, upper house) with 168 seats of two deputies from each of Russia's 84 republics and regions, appointed by regional legislatures; all serve for four year terms.

Legal system
The legal system is based on civil law. There is judicial review of legislative acts. The top levels of the judicial branch consist of: the Constitutional Court, which reviews the constitutionality of federal legislation; the Supreme Court, which is the highest civil and criminal judiciary body; and the Supreme Arbitration Court, which resolves economic disputes between subjects of the Federation. The Supreme Court and Supreme Arbitration Court preside over a federal system of lower criminal and civil courts.

Last elections
2 March 2008 (presidential); 4 December 2011 (parliamentary)
Results: Presidential: Dmitry Medvedev won 70.3 per cent of the vote, Gennady Zyuganov won 17.7 per cent, Vladimir Zhirinovsky won 9.3 per cent; turnout was 69.8 per cent.
Parliamentary: Yedinaya Rossiya (YR) (United Russia) 49.29 per cent (238 seats, out of 450 (down from 315 in the 2007 elections), Kommunisticheskaya Partiya Rossiiskoi Federatsii (KPRF) (Communist Party of the Russian Federation) 19.2 per cent (92), Spravedlivaya Rossiya (SR) (A Just Russia) 13.25 per cent (64), Liberal'no-Demokraticheskaya Partiya Rossii (LDPR) (Russia's Liberal Democratic Party) 11.68 per cent (56); no other political party won enough votes to win seats. Turnout was 60.2 per cent.

Next elections
2016 (parliamentary); March 2012 (presidential).

Political parties

Ruling party
Yedinaya Rossiya (YR) (United Russia) (elected 2003; re-elected 4 Dec 2011)

Main opposition party
With such an overwhelming majority in parliament for the ruling YR, to achieve the semblance of parliamentary debate an opposition had to be appointed by the government, which has come to be called a 'systemic opposition' by opponents of the process.

Population
142.94 million (2010)*
Last census: March 2002: 145,537,200 (provisional)
Population density: Nine inhabitants per square km. Urban population: 73 per cent (1995—2001).
Annual growth rate: -0.3 per cent 1994–2004 (WHO 2006)

Internally Displaced Persons (IDP)
330,000 (UNHCR 2004)

Ethnic make-up
Russian (82 per cent), Tatars (4 per cent) and Ukrainians (3 per cent).

Religions
The majority of the population is Christian, mainly Russian Orthodox. Religion, while not actually forbidden under communism, was officially discouraged. Religious observance and interest is growing steeply with the relaxation of state restrictions. Russian Orthodox Christmas was made an official holiday for the first time in 1991.
Russia also has sizeable Muslim (12 million) and Jewish (700,000) minorities.

Education
After compulsory education at age 15, secondary (complete) general education begins. Students may also enter vocational schools or non-university level higher education institutions. Initial vocational schools offer one-and-a-half to two years of vocational education. Secondary (complete) general education continues for two years and ends when students are aged 17–18 years.
Higher education is provided by 553 public and 260 non-public accredited higher education institutions. Education in public higher education is free of charge. There are three levels of higher educational institutions including those lasting between two to four years and an advanced level lasting between five and six years. The government aims to diversify higher education courses and boost the private sector. In addition to universities in the public and private sector, there are 3,000 non-university institutions in Russia.
Literacy rate: 100 per cent adult rate; 100 per cent youth rate (15–24) (Unesco 2005).
Compulsory years: Six to 15 years.
Enrolment rate: 107 per cent total primary enrolment of the relevant age group (including repeaters) (World Bank).
Pupils per teacher: 20 in primary schools.

Health
In 2006 President Putin announced government sponsored health measures to reduce the falling birth rate, low life expectancy and unusually high male mortality rate. Russia is investing US$7 billion in four 'national projects', one of which is healthcare. Child benefits are being increased and one-off payments made to mothers to encourage fertility. Nevertheless, Russia has one of the highest rates of abortion in the world, with 66 terminations for every 100 pregnancies. Fertility rates fell from 2.19 births per woman in 1986–87 to 1.34 in 2003 and is still below the 2.1 births necessary to sustain population growth.
In every hour they is only one birth for 77 deaths and Russia has been warned that its population could crash by 2050 if the trend is not reversed. Mortality rates have ballooned for a wide number of reasons including poor diet, disease, alcoholism and risky activities – Russia has twice as many road accident fatalities as any other G8 country.

HIV/Aids
HIV/Aids has spread in Russia at a time when infection rates have been steady and declining for a number of years in Europe and North America. Few Russians can afford the expensive new treatments that have been discovered in the past few years. HIV/Aids cases have more than trebled since 2000. Russian health officials blame the high number of HIV/Aids cases on intravenous drug use rather than sexual activity.
HIV prevalence: 1.1 per cent aged 15–49 in 2003 (World Bank)
Life expectancy: 65 years, 2004 (WHO 2006)
Fertility rate/Maternal mortality rate: 1.3 births per woman, 2004 (WHO 2006)
Birth rate/Death rate: 10 births per 1,000 population; 14 deaths per 1,000 population (2003).
Child (under 5 years) mortality rate (per 1,000): 16 per 1,000 live births (World Bank)
Head of population per physician: 4.25 physicians per 1,000 people, 2003 (WHO 2006)

Welfare
In 2005, widespread demonstrations forced Vladimir Putin to amend newly instigated reforms to the benefits system after they were introduced. The plan to offer cash payments in exchange for what had been free services such as medicines,

transport and subsidised housing continued but the amounts were increased and pension payments brought by a month. About 34 million pensioners, infirm and war veterans are estimated to be affected by the changes, with the lowest payments at just US$7.5 per month. Critics said that the implimentation of the change was mishandled and the calculations sloppy, whereas the government believes that 'monetising' benefits was the only option to streamline social benefits and generate considerable cost savings. This set-back is thought, by some, to risk Putin's reform agenda.
Given budgetary constraints, reforms are targetted at increasing the transparency and efficiency of Russia's main social funds and eliminating unproductive social programmes. There have been massive increases in health service funding, especially to reduce infant mortality rates and bring healthcare up to world standards. Maternity benefits are being enhanced in order to induce women to stay at home for two or three years.
The tax code has been used to unify and reduce the different social security contributions but, despite recent tax cuts, average real incomes remain low.
Unemployment benefits based on past earnings remain very low due to high inflation. Income inequality levels have consequently been increasing and it is estimated that about 20.4 per cent of the population live below the minimum subsistence level laid down by the state.

Main cities

Moscow (capital of the Russian Federation, estimated population 10.4 million (m) in 2005); St Petersburg (formerly Leningrad) (4.2m); Novosibirsk (1.4m); Nizhny Novgorod (formerly Gorki, 1.3m); Yekaterinburg (formerly Sverdlovsk) (1.3m); Samara (formerly Kuybyshev) (1.2m); Rostov-on-Don (1.0m); Omsk (1.1m); Kazan (capital of the sovereign republic Tatarstan) (1.1m); Cheljabinsk (1.1m); Volgograd (1.0m), Ufa (1.1m); Vladivostok (601,161); Irkutsk (599,718); Krasnodar (655,736).

Languages spoken

There are as many as 100 local ethnic languages, some of the larger groupings include Baskin, Chuvash Tatar and Yakut. Russian is spoken throughout the country. Russian and most local languages are written in variants of the Cyrillic alphabet, which was devised by the ninth century saints, Cyril and Methodius. In September 2000, the Tatarstan republic (population four million, a large minority of whom are Russian) began a 10-year transition period for the switch in schools from Cyrillic to the Latin alphabet for the local Turkic language. Russian is the second language spoken in Tatarstan. However, Russian MPs voted in June 2002 to make the use of the Cyrillic alphabet mandatory throughout the country.
In 2003, the State Duma passed a law making Russian the official state language, prohibiting the use in public documents of foreign words or expressions that have Russian-language equivalents).
Ukrainian, Mordvin and Chechen are also spoken.

Official language/s

Russian

Media

In February 2008 the worldwide human right's campaigning organisation, Amnesty International, stated that freedom of speech was 'shrinking alarmingly' with intimidation and arbitrary laws to curb outspoken media outlets and NGOs, while others alleged the extrajudicial killing of journalists.

Press

Dailies: There are many national and regional newspapers, most of which publish in Russian with a few in minority languages, as well as English. Some regional news is published over the Internet only while others are published (see www.wps.ru, monitoring – regional press). Major nationals in Russian are *Izvestia* (www.izvestia.ru) owned by Gazprom and *Rossiyskaya Gazeta* (www.rg.ru) is government owned. The *Komsomolskaya Pravda* (www.kp.ru) is a mass-circulation paper while *Nezavisimaya Gazeta* is an influential privately owned daily. *Kommersant* (www.kommersant.ru) is business orientated while *Trud* (www.trud.ru), is a socialist minded paper. In English, *The Moscow Times* (www.themoscowtimes.com) and its companion newspaper the *St Petersburg Times* (ww.sptimes.ru) report, among other things, on politics and business.
Weeklies: In Russian, the most popular publication is *Argumenty i Facty (Arguments & Facts)* (www.aif.ru) containing in-depth analysis of political and economic events. Others include *Itogi* (www.itogi.ru), *Ogonyok* (www.ogoniok.com) and *Profil* (www.profile.ru) and the *Moskovskie Novosti* (www.mn.ru) is a weekly international socio-political newspaper. In English, *Russia Profile* (www.russiaprofile.org) is published 10 times per year, the *Moscow News Weekly* (www.mnweekly.ru) and *The Russia Journal* (www.russiajournal.com) contain weekly news, analysis, and political opinion.
Business: *Moscow Times* is an English-language business publication.
Periodicals: In English, *Russia Profile* (www.russiaprofile.org) is published 10 times per year, and *Vladivostok News* (http://vn.vladnews.ru) both cover political and business information.

Broadcasting

Russian authorities pressured all radio stations to stopped broadcasting the BBC's Russian services in 2007.
Radio: There are two national state-run radio networks, Radio Russia (www.radiorus.ru) and Radio Mayak (www.radiomayak.ru). There are many commercial radio stations broadcasting in regional markets, Russkoye Radio (www.rusradio.ru) and Moscow Echo (www.echo.msk.ru) are the two most important.
The Voice of Russia (http://ruvr.ru) broadcasts programmes in 33 languages to 160 countries worldwide.
Television: Since 2001 the independence of Russian television has been circumscribed by government regulations that restricted majority foreign ownership and banned some stations, particularly those critical of the government.
The state-run Russia TV Channel (www.rutv.ru) network, the state part-owned Channel One (www.1tv.ru) and the Gazprom-owned NTV (www.ntv.ru), broadcast nationally. Fully commercial stations include Centre TV (www.tvc.ru) and Ren TV (www.ren-tv.com). Russia Today (www.russiatoday.ru) with news programming is state-funded and broadcasts in English, by satellite and cable.

Advertising

Commercial advertising is widely available. Limited television and radio advertising is available to Western companies; billboards and illuminated signs can be bought in most major cities.

News agencies

National news agency: Itar-Tass News Agency

Economy

With a vast territory that spans 11 time zones it isn't surprising that the Russian Federation has a diverse economy that ranges from its high-tech space programme, which can provide tourist jaunts into space for the (immensely) rich, to primary industries such as agriculture - with over 50 per cent of all farms and garden plots privately owned - and all technological and service industries in between. However, dominating all of its many productive sectors the production and supply of hydrocarbons has become Russia's foremost wealth creating industry, so much so that exports and access to further supplies has become an instrument of state policy. Russia has large reserves of oil – 77.4 billion barrels at the end of 2010 (5.6 per cent of the world's total), and even larger reserves of natural gas – 44.8 trillion cubic metres (cum) (23.9 per cent of the world's total). Over 75 per cent of oil exports are delivered to Europe, and 93 per cent of natural gas. Russia has been able to use its dominance as a supplier of hydrocarbons to energy-hungry Europe as a bargaining tool to assert its influence in international affairs. In 2009, Russia loaned its traditional ally, Serbia, US$1.5 billion to help cover its budget deficit and rebuild its infrastructure, while Russia pushed for the Southern Stream natural gas pipeline to traverse the Balkans through Serbia. On 8 November 2011, the prime ministers of Germany, France and The Netherlands and President Medvedev were at the ceremony in Lubmin to begin the flow of natural gas via the US$10.2 billion, 1,200km, Nord Stream, underwater pipeline from Russia to Germany. It has an initial annual capacity of 27.5 billion cum (for domestic use and forward distribution); a dual pipeline is under construction and due for completion in 2012.

GDP has been strong for a number of years with highs of 8.2 per cent in 2007 and 8.5 per cent in 2008 as world prices for oil reached record levels. However, the global economic crisis adversely affected the Russian economy, mainly through the falling sales and reduced prices of hydrocarbons and the loss of capital inflows, so that in 2009 GDP growth contracted sharply to -7.8 per cent, due to falling domestic demand and lower imports. Profits for the state-owned energy company, Gazprom, dropped by 50 per cent in the first half of 2009 as it paid more for natural gas it purchased from Central Asia and there was a fall in demand for energy from Europe. In 2010 as world trade picked up, GDP growth returned to a positive 4.0 per cent. Other pressures on the economy include rising inflation, which jumped from 9.0 per cent in 2007 to 14.1 per cent in 2008, and remained in double digits at 11.7 in 2009, before dropping sharply to 6.9 per cent in 2010

Russia fell from its ranking as one of only two world superpowers in 1991 and is currently regarded as an 'upper middle-income' economy, with per capita income peaking in 2008 at US$11,704, before falling to US$8,545 in 2009 as the economy contracted. For Russia to regain its former glory it will have to develop a more diverse economy. Its industrial base is in places still old, outmoded and unproductive; its people, while generally well educated, are unused to the capitalist ethos of work smart and earn more, embrace change and survive.

In 2009 the service sector constituted 62.5 per cent of GDP, industry 32.8 per cent, of which manufacturing was 15 per cent, and agriculture 4.7 per cent.

Russia's strategy has been to bring a value-added price to its supplies of oil and natural gas, so that when its hydrocarbon reserves are finally depleted, it will have diversified into enough external markets for the shock to be minimal.

Gazprom has a monopoly on the 'right to export natural gas' which was reinforced through a statute in 2006, in the face of European opposition and the *Energy Charter Treaty* (signed in 1991) which should give open access to pipelines and investment in new markets. Gazprom began by buying into foreign exploration and drilling technologies through partnerships with overseas companies and then demanding that oil and natural gas pipelines become jointly owned in foreign territories. Any opposition to these strategies risked bans on developing Russian energy fields by foreign companies and the halt in supplies through territories of unwilling partners. The option for new gas and oil pipelines under construction is now only considered through joint partnerships.

The old adversary, the US, used Gazprom's aggressive and expansionist policies, which had precluded foreign ownership, as evidence that Russia was not ready to join the World Trade Organisation (WTO). However, in December 2011, after 18 years of negotiation, Russia finally joined the organisation.

In July 2011, the government announced plans to sell its stake in 11 companies. It is hoped the sale will raise some US$29 billion over the next three years in what will be Russia's biggest privatisation since the 1990s.

External trade

The Russian Federation leads the Commonwealth of Independent States (CIS), of former republics of the defunct Soviet Union, which promotes trade, cultural and legal ties among members, however it does not operate a free trade zone due to differences in economic objectives, degrees of reforms and economic development. Russia has observer status membership of the World Trade Organisation (WTO) and at the beginning of 2010 was still in negotiation for full membership.

A bilateral trade agreement with the EU was signed on 7 December 2010. The agreement paved the way for Russia's membership of the WTO in 2011; Russia is the last major economy to become a member of the WTO.

On 19 October 2011, a free trade agreement (FTA) was signed by Russia with seven of its former Soviet republics: Armenia, Belarus, Kazakhstan, Kyrgyzstan, Moldova and Tajikistan. The FTA must be ratified by all relevant parliaments before its instigation in 2012.

Russia has immense mineral deposits of diamonds, precious metals and coal as well as timber and is a leading world supplier of oil and natural gas, which represents around 80 per cent of its exports. Foreign trade amounts to over 55 per cent of GDP. Investment in industry, manufacturing and infrastructure has been low and hampers progress.

Russia inherited the majority of the Soviet Union's military industrial base and weapons are the largest manufactured items exported.

Imports

Principal imports include vehicles, consumer goods, medicines, meat, sugar, machinery and equipment, and semi-finished metal products.

Main sources: China (typically 13 per cent of total), Germany (13 per cent), Japan (7 per cent).

Exports

Principal exports include petroleum and derivatives, natural gas, timber, metals, chemicals, and a wide variety of civilian and military manufactures.

Main destinations: The Netherlands (typically 12 per cent of total), Italy (7 per cent), Belarus (5 per cent).

Agriculture

Farming

Production in the agricultural sector in Russia has fallen since reforms began in 1992, following the substantial reduction in large state subsidies. The livestock sector contracted by about half. Progress has been particularly slow in land reform, and Russia still lacks a free market in agricultural land. Agricultural production contributes only 7 per cent of GDP, with 133 million hectares (ha) of arable land, and a large agrarian workforce constituting nearly 14 per cent of the total.

The sector has suffered due to incomplete agriculture-specific and economy-wide institutional reform, such as price and trade reform, as well as privatisation. Russia has the potential to increase grain exports significantly if such reforms are implemented and the situation seems to be improving. Wheat and barley are the most significant crops produced in Russia that are widely traded on world markets.

Severe drought in 2010 forced Russia to impose a grain export ban from August until 2011; drought and wildfires destroyed around one-third of all grain harvests.

Fishing

There has been a very noticeable drop in recorded fish production in Russia, since the end of the Soviet era. Production shortfalls have resulted in rising prices and steadily increasing imports of fish and fishery products.

Russia's lucrative caviar industry, based on the Caspian Sea and long stymied by dwindling stocks, was effectively shut down in 2001–02 by an international ban on the export of caviar products, imposed by the Convention on International Trade in Endangered Species (Cites).

In addition to the consequences of major economic and political changes, aquaculture and inland capture fisheries continue to face problems from environmental impacts on water resources affecting living aquatic resources. The environmental degradation of inland waters through industrial, urban and agrochemical pollution, and the damming of major rivers has had significant local impacts on fish stocks. As a result of the large-scale uptake of water for irrigation, the original fish fauna of Russia has been significantly modified.

Production from subsistence and recreational fisheries is seldom accurately reflected in the official statistics, and it is likely that production from these sectors plays an important role for food supply in the country. However, capture fisheries in many inland waters of the region, including, in particular, reservoirs and lakes, continue to depend heavily on stocking of fry and fingerlings produced in hatcheries, lake farms and artificial spawning grounds, or by other types of enhancement measures.

Improved stocking and fisheries management measures provide the potential for significant increases in fish production from reservoirs and lakes in Russia. It is estimated that fisheries production from reservoirs could be increased between four and six-fold by improved stocking; inland fish production could realistically be doubled by 2010. It is expected that recreational fisheries, often contributing significantly to household food supply, will gain increasing importance.

The annual total fish catch is approximately five million tonnes (t). Russia imports some 6,000t of sea products while it exports around 117,000t annually.

Forestry

Russia has by far the largest forested area of any country in the world with forest and other wooded land constituting more than half of its land area estimated at 851.3 million hectares (ha) or almost 55 per cent of the total land area. Russia accounts for more than 20 per cent of global forest resources, more than 35 per cent of temperate/boreal forests in terms of area and 45 per cent in terms of growing stock. The area of forest is fairly stable, showing a marginal average annual increase of 0.02 per cent, or the equivalent of 135,000ha of forest cover. The importance of Russia's forests as a regulator of the global carbon balance, and mitigation of climate change, is difficult to overestimate.

The predominant coniferous species are larch and spruce. The deciduous species are represented mainly by birch, aspen and oaks (either European or Mongolian), and hornbeam, ash, maple and elm to a lesser degree. Mature and over-mature stands, situated mainly in the Asian part of Russia, prevail and about two-thirds of the forest is available for wood supply.

Russia is one of the largest producers and exporters of industrial roundwood in the world market. Significant volumes of sawn wood, plywood and pulp and paper are exported. The forest industry is almost completely privatised, although the forests and the roundwood production remain under state control.

Industry and manufacturing

The industrial sector accounts for 30 per cent of GDP and provides employment for a third of the working population.

Factors that continue to dog efficiency include wasteful consumption of fuel and raw materials, antiquated machinery, poor technology and management and overstaffing. Early on in the reform process emphasis was placed on individual enterprise and factory production decisions, resulting in anarchic management practices.

Major production bottlenecks in the 1990s included steel, construction inputs (such as cement) and consumer and light industry products (such as television sets, robots and computers).

Emphasis during the 1990s was on light industry, modernisation and computerisation. Towards the end of the 1990s, there were attempts by major industrial and manufacturing companies to consolidate their activities, with many mergers. The sector remains reliant on large- and medium-sized firms to increase production and stimulate growth, particularly in engineering and metallurgy working.

Tourism

Russia is a vast land that can offer visitors a range of holidays to suit any requirement. Its tourist infrastructure is centred on traditional resorts and facilities that cater for the large domestic market, and a newer market for foreign travellers. Some 80 per cent of foreign visitors specifically visit the imperial sites of St Petersburg and Moscow. Domestic travel and tourism represents over three times the amount to the economy than foreign visitors. In 2010, domestic consumption, including expenditure on preparation for travel and tourism, was US$61.775 billion; direct spending for travel and tourism was US$47.040 billion.

Travel and tourism typically constitutes around 6 per cent of GDP, with 5.5 per cent of employment related to the industry.

Russian tourists leaving for foreign destinations outnumber visitors arriving and may explain why capital investment has risen from US$2.780 billion in 2005 to US$6.970 billion in 2010. Real growth in investment has fallen steadily from 34.6 per cent of total capital investment in 2005 to -8.2 per cent in 2010.

Mining

Russia is the world's largest producer of iron ore, asbestos, manganese ore, nickel, chromite, platinum group metals and potassium salts, and the second-largest producer of gold, lead and phosphate ores. There are vast reserves, but extraction has been held back due to rising production costs, labour shortages and a shortage of technology.

Major foreign exchange earners include gold and diamonds. Estimated annual production of diamonds is 12,000 tonnes.

Russia is estimated to have 30 per cent of world iron ore reserves and 20 per cent of many other minerals. Significant quantities of iron ore, chromium, nickel, asbestos and fertiliser materials are exported.

There are large deposits of antimony, beryllium, cadmium, mercury, molybdenum, tin and vanadium plus workable deposits of all rare earth metals.

Large-scale investment in the sector is improving extraction and processing techniques, while reducing wastage and controlling production costs. Gold production in 2005 totalled 157.6 tonnes, much of which originates in Russia's Sakha Republic (formerly Yakutia). This represents a decline in production of nearly 7 per cent since 2004.

Hydrocarbons

Russia is a major exporter of hydrocarbons. Proven oil reserves were 77.4 billion barrels 2010, mostly located in Siberia. Production was 10.2 billion barrels per day (bpd). In 2009 Russia became the world's largest oil exporter, superseding Saudi Arabia as Opec members had cut back on oil production, however Russia maintained its lead into 2010. Russia has 41 refineries with a total capacity of 5.55 million bpd, which require further development and investment to increase production, due to their inefficiency and ageing. Most exports of Russian oil are in the form of fuel oil and diesel and as domestic refineries concentrate on production for export there is a shortfall of around 50 per cent in high-octane petroleum which must be imported. The oil pipeline network bringing oil to markets in Europe and the Far East has grown significantly. The network began under the Soviet regime, running to CIS states and former Soviet states, but new markets have required an expansion and modernisation. Before the global financial crisis Russia was the principal shareholder in all pipeline projects but by 2008 when oil prices had fallen and money markets were not investing it was forced to barter oil for investment in new pipelines. In 2009 China agreed to invest in completing the East Siberian-Pacific Ocean (ESPO) pipeline, which will be routed via the Russian terminal in Yakutia south into China. On Sakhalin Island, an all-year-round new oil and liquefied natural gas export terminal began operations in 2008.

Proven natural gas reserves were 44.8 trillion cubic metres (cum) in 2010. Russia has the world's largest deposits of natural gas and is the leading gas exporter. Production was 588.9 billion cum in 2010, which was a rise of 11.6 per cent on the 2009 figure and provided 18.4 per cent of the world's total production.

Russia exported 186.5 billion cum of natural gas via pipelines to Europe in 2010, the majority of which was transported via the Ukraine. The first phase of the new East Siberia-Pacific Ocean (ESPO) oil pipeline was completed in January 2010, operated by Transneft. The 2,757km pipeline from Taishet (in the Irkutsk region) to Skovorodino (near the Chinese border), will be added to with a further 2,100km by 2012, from Skovorodino to Kozmino, replacing the current shipment of Russian oil by train between these locations. The 1,213km Blue Stream pipeline, between Russia and Turkey transports 5 billion cum of natural gas annually. Construction of the North European Gas Pipe-line (NEGP), linking Vyborg in Russia to Greifswald in Germany began with onshore pumping facilities in 2005 and when the project is completed in 2011 it will have a capacity of 27.5 billion cum annually. Gazprom holds a 51 per cent stake in the NEGP venture, with former German chancellor Gerhard Schröder chairman of the project. In 2007 Gazprom and the Italian energy company ENI agreed to build the South Stream Gas Pipeline under the Black Sea and through Bulgaria, bringing gas directly to West European countries. The NEGP and SSGP are tangible measures built to avoid suspension of gas supplies due to political actions by either Russia or an existing pipeline's host country.

Russian company, Rosneft, signed a joint venture with the Sharjah-based Crescent Petroleum company to invest US$630 million in a 70 billion cubic metre natural gas and 16 million tonne gas condensate, concession. The gas field is planned to be operational by 2013. This is the first upstream project undertaken by an UAE-Russian partnership.

Proven coal reserves totalled 157.0 billion tonnes in 2010, of which 108 billion tonnes is brown coal typically used in power stations. Russian coal reserves are second only to those in the US, the world's largest. Production has risen by around 30 per cent since 1997 and government policy is to increase the number of coal-fired power stations.

Russia considers its hydrocarbon reserves as a strategic state asset and while oil and gas companies are publicly listed they are all headed by strong supporters of the current political regime, consolidated by Vladimir Putin since 1999. The hydrocarbon sector is dominated by state-owned enterprises, foremost of which are Gazprom (gas) and Rosneft (oil). Russian oligarchs, who were the first to assume control of the hydrocarbon sector after the fall of the Soviet Union, have either been co-opted into a close partnership with the government, and thereby following its lead which may be contrary to the company's commercial interests, or have been forced out of power and company assets seized by the state. Government policy appears to be to use hydrocarbon supplies as a tool to reassert Russian influence in the world.

A US$25 billion deal was signed in 2009, whereby China will be supplied with Siberian oil in exchange for Chinese. The Chinese Development Bank will loan Rosneft and Transneft, the Russian state oil company and pipeline company, US$15 billion and US$10 billion respectively; in return 300,000 barrels a day of oil annually will be supplied to China until 2029.

Energy

Russia is the second-largest generator of electricity in the world, with total installed capacity of 217GW and an output of about 904 billion kWh (2006), of which about 63 per cent is produced thermally, 21 per cent by hydropower and 16 per cent nuclear generation. Government policy is to expand nuclear generation and hydropower to allow greater exports of hydrocarbons.

As part of the liberalisation of the energy market, the former state-owned RAO Unified Energy System utility holding company was merged with the Federal Grid Company in July 2008 to form the RAO UESR, responsible for electricity generation, power stations, distribution and sales.

By 2010, 10 nuclear reactors will be due for closure. However, the government intends to extend their working lives. Russia announced it will build 40 nuclear reactors by 2020 to prevent an energy crisis and, by March 2009, five new nuclear power plants were under construction. Russia exports electricity to CIS states as well as China, Poland, Turkey and Finland.

Financial markets

Stock exchange

Moscow Interbank Currency Exchange (Micex)

Banking and insurance

Most major banks are located in Moscow. The majority of Russian banks suffer from being undercapitalised and the high rate of inflation has constantly eroded their reserves. This is not surprising given the high degree of fragmentation in the sector. The system has been criticised for having too many owner-operators; this is a situation with potential for abuse. The retail banking sector is still in its infancy and branch networking is not particularly common.

Foreign banks are not permitted to open their own branches in Russia and instead must rely upon subsidiaries, which drives up their costs. President Putin reiterated his opposition to direct foreign entry in December 2005. The US has protested this decision and has pointed out that Russia's desire to join the WTO will require banking liberalisation.

In June 2003, Russia was removed from the Organisation for Economic Co-operation and Development (OECD) black list of havens for money laundering.

Beginning 29 July 2004, the Central Bank revoked the licences for operations of three Moscow banks: the Commercial Bank of Savings, the Industrial Export-Import Bank and the Investment and Commercial Moscow Housing Construction Bank.

Central bank

Central Bank of the Russian Federation

Main financial centre

Moscow

Time

The Russian Federation covers nine time zones, from GMT plus three hours to GMT plus 12 hours. The previous 11 time zones were reduced to nine in March 2010. Daylight saving was abolished from March 2011 (ie the last use of daylight saving was in March 2010). Domestically, Russia refers to Moscow standard time (MST).

Kaliningrad Oblast: GMT plus three hours (MST minus one).

Moscow and Samara: GMT plus four hours (MST)

Yekaterinburg: GMT plus six hours (MST plus two).

Tomsk and Novosibirsk: GMT plus seven hours (MST plus three).

Krasnoyarsk: GMT plus eight hours (MST plus four).
Irkutsk: GMT plus nine hours (MST plus five).
Yakutsk: GMT plus 10 hours (MST plus six).
Valdivostok and Sakhalin: GMT plus 11 hours (MST plus seven).
Magadan and Kamchatka Peninsula: GMT plus 12 hours (MST plus eight).

Geography

The Russian Federation is the largest country in the world at 17.07 million square km. Even European Russia (west of the Ural Mountains), which is only a quarter of the total landmass, dwarfs all other European countries. Major cities and towns are concentrated in western Russia, with the population thinning out to the far north and east.

Norway lies to the far north-west of Russia, with Finland, Estonia, and Latvia to the north. Belarus and Ukraine lie to the south-west of European Russia, the southern borders of which are with the Trans-Caucasian states of Georgia and Azerbaijan, and with Kazakhstan. In the north-west, near St Petersburg, there is a short coastline where there is access to the Baltic Sea via the gulf of Finland. Towards the south, European Russia has a coastline on the Black Sea in the south-west, with the Caspian Sea to the east. Beyond the Ural Mountains, the Siberian and Far Eastern regions have southern frontiers with the People's Republic of China, Mongolia, and in the south-east, North Korea. The eastern coastline is on the Sea of Japan, the Sea of Okhotsk, the Pacific Ocean and the Barents Sea. The northern coastline is on the Arctic Ocean. The region around Kaliningrad on the Baltic Sea is separated from the rest of the Russian Federation by Lithuania to the north and east, and has a coastline on the Baltic Sea.

The territory includes a wide variety of physical features. European Russia and western Siberia form a vast plain. Between the Black and Caspian Seas in the south, the land is more undulating, until it reaches the foothills of the Caucasus mountain range in the far south. The northern regions of both Asian and European Russia are inhospitable areas, much of the territory being covered by permafrost.

Europe's highest mountain, Elbrus (at 5,642 metres), is just on the Russian side of the Georgian border. Russia has Europe's longest river, the 3,690km Volga which rises north-west of Moscow and flows east before turning south to the Caspian Sea. The two largest lakes in Europe are also in Russia. Lake Ladoga (18,390 square km) and Lake Onega (9,600 square km) are both north-east of St Petersburg. Lake Baikal, located in the south-east in Siberia, at over 31,000 square km is the world's deepest and largest (by volume) freshwater lake, containing 20 per cent of the planet's liquid freshwater.

Hemisphere

Northern

Climate

The climate in Russia is extremely varied. The north is arctic, with an extensive zone of permafrost, but there are a few sub-tropical zones in the southern region of the country. The majority of the land mass is continental or moderate continental. The Russian winter is deservedly famous: winter snow cover lasts as long as 160 days in St Petersburg.

Moscow has a warm spring with an average temperature of 18 degrees Celsius (C) in the period April to May. It is often hot in summer (June to August 20–30 degrees C), mild in autumn (September to October 10–15 degrees C) and freezing (down to minus 30 degrees C) for the rest of the year. Average annual rainfall is 575mm.

Average temperatures in the southern Siberian town of Irkutsk range from minus 21 degrees C in January to 18 degrees C in July. Average annual rainfall is 458mm, most of which falls in the summer. In the far north of Siberia, the average January temperature is minus 47 degrees C.

The far eastern region combines the extreme temperatures of Siberia with monsoon-type conditions common elsewhere in Asia. The mean temperature in January in the eastern port of Vladivostok is minus 14 degrees C; in August the average is 21 degrees C.

In the more moderate western portion of Russia, the average January temperature is slightly below zero. Summer is very hot in some areas. The snow in European Russia begins to melt in March and the muddy transition period demands waterproof footwear.

Dress codes

Dress well as business people are judged by their attire. Warm outer clothes, hats, gloves and footwear are essential in winter, although interiors are well heated. The most important factor is neatness. Shoes should be polished and clothes pressed. Russians themselves do not always wear a suit and tie at business meetings, but it is wise to err on the safe side. Dark suits, white shirts and conservative ties are the norm, with business suits for women. Formal evening wear is not normally necessary. Summer dress is modest.

Entry requirements

Passports

Required by all.

Visa

Required by all. See www.rusemblon.org/ and follow link to application forms to download a visa form. US citizens should see www.russianembassy.org for further information. All travellers should check the general information links to see if the additional requirements affect them. All applications should be submitted to the closest Russian consulate.

Visitors must register their visas within three working days of arrival in Russia with the local branch of the ministry of the interior. Most major hotels will do this for their guests automatically. All visas are issued with an exit visa included.

Business travellers must include, with their application, a letter of invitation from the Russian foreign ministry or its regional representatives or ministry of the interior or its local offices. The letter must contain the official seal and legal address of the agency, a document registration number, date of registration, the signature and name of official authorised to issue invitations, and a travel itinerary with dates of stay and names of persons involved. A letter from an employer (or own letter if self-employed) giving personal details, a full itinerary, purpose of visit and a guarantee accepting full responsibility for any expenses incurred must also to be included. The right to request the submission of all original documents is reserved by the embassy, and multiple entry visas require original letters of invitation in all cases.

Currency advice/regulations

The import and export of local currency is prohibited. The import of foreign currency is unlimited up to US$10,000 (or equivalent), but amounts over US$3,000 must be declared. Export of foreign currency is limited to the amount declared on arrival. It is illegal to exchange money anywhere except official exchange facilities; shops, hotels and restaurants may advertise dollar prices, but bills must be paid in roubles. It is advisable to retain all exchange receipts.

Travellers cheques have limited acceptance. Unmarked US dollar bills in good condition should be used for travel to more remote regions.

Customs

The customs declaration made on entry must be retained for exit, this allows for personal items, such as jewellery, cameras, computers and musical instruments to remain duty-free.

Retain all shop receipts and certificates of money exchange for customs formalities on exit.

In 2006, 250g caviar per person was allowed for export, with proof of purchase from licensed purveyors.

Prohibited imports

Firearms, ammunition, illegal drugs, precious metals and furs, radio, electrical items, fruit and vegetables, sturgeon and sturgeon products and photographic and printed material that vilifies the Russian Federation.

Live animals, antiques and works of art require permits.

Health (for visitors)

Advisable precautions

Inoculations and boosters should be current for tetanus, hepatitis A and diphtheria. There may be a need for vaccinations for typhoid, tuberculosis, hepatitis B and meningitis (Moscow only). Visitors to Asian and far-eastern provinces may need vaccinations for Japanese B encephalitis and cholera. There is a risk of rabies.

Water precautions outside main cities are recommended (purification tablets may be useful or use bottled or boiled water for drinks, washing teeth and making ice – especially in St Petersburg, where the water supply may be infected by giardia).

Mosquito repellents and long clothing will help avoid hepatitis B and Japanese B encephalitis; there is a risk of HIV/Aids.

Russian medical care is not up to Western standards and medical insurance, including emergency evacuation, is necessary. A travel kit including a disposable syringe is a reasonable precaution. A supply of any regular medicines required should be taken, with their prescription details and it could be wise to have precautionary antibiotics if going outside major urban centres.

Hotels

Moscow has an increasing number of Western-run hotels. Accommodation is difficult to obtain in Moscow at short notice. It is crucial to make bookings in advance as hotels refuse to check in a guest without a reservation. First-class and tourist class are available, with all prices fixed by Intourist. Main hotels have foreign currency restaurants and bars. Tipping is increasingly common, typically 10 per cent.

Credit cards

Credit cards are not widely accepted outside Moscow and St Petersburg. ATMs are widely available.

Public holidays (national)

Fixed dates

1–10 Jan (New Year Holidays), 23 Feb (Defender's Day), 8 Mar (Women's Day), 1 May (Labour Day), 9 May (Victory Day), 12 Jun (Russia Day), 4 Nov (National Unity Day).

Days *in lieu* are given for holidays that occur at the weekend, usually at the beginning of the following week.

Variable dates

Russian Orthodox Christmas

Working hours

Banking

Mon–Fri: 0930–1730.

Business

Mon–Fri: 0900–1800 (appointments best between 0900–1000).

Shops

Mon–Sat: 0900–1900.

Telecommunications

Mobile/cell phones

There are limited 900, 1800, 900/1800 GSM services available in Moscow, St Petersburg and other major cities.

Electricity supply

220V AC

Social customs/useful tips

A firm handshake is important as is negotiating an agenda at the beginning of the meeting. Smoking in meetings is very common. Ask permission before lighting a cigarette and offer cigarettes generously. Written communications are particularly important with large bureaucracies. Address the recipient formally and keep a copy of everything.

It is customary to take a small gift on a business or social visit. Offering basic food is considered insulting. Offer little luxuries.

It is impolite to take along people who are not invited to a social function. If you are offered a second helping of caviar, resist the temptation and refuse. The offer will be made again, but it is polite to refuse the first time.

Many Russians take certain superstitions somewhat seriously. Do not give an even number of flowers, for example, as this is for funerals only; do not greet people in a doorway – it is considered unlucky.

Security

The normal precautions should be taken when visiting Russia – avoid showing large amounts of cash or expensive personal belongings. Avoid travelling alone at night in Moscow and St Petersburg, particularly on the metro.

Getting there

Air

National airline: Aeroflot – Russian Airlines

International airport/s: Moscow-Sheremetyevo International (SVO), 29km north-west of city centre; St Petersburg-Pulkovo (LED), 17km from city. Both airports have duty-free shops, banks, *bureau de change*, restaurants.

Taxis, to Moscow city centre (journey time 30–40 minutes) and fixed route and buses are available. There are scheduled express coaches and trains to other destinations.

There are taxis to St Petersburg (journey time 10 minutes) as well as buses.

Airport tax: None

Surface

Road: Major European highways connect Moscow via Kiev (Ukraine), Minsk (Belarus), Riga (Latvia), Warsaw (Poland) and Scandinavia to St Petersburg via Helsinki (Finland). The Verkhny Lars-Kazbegi border checkpoint between Georgia and Russia, which had been closed in July 2006, was reopened in March 2010.

Rail: The Russian/CIS rail network (around 87,079km) extends to all Russian Federation countries. The main European rail services are through Germany including a sleeper service from Cologne to Moscow and the *Mockva Express* via Berlin-Warsaw-Moscow.

Through-trains are also available from other Western and Eastern European cities and from Turkey, Iran, and the *Trans-Siberian Express* from Mongolia and China.

Water: There are sea links from Finland, Norway, Sweden and Germany and from the Ukraine in the west. In the east, a weekly ferry runs between Vladivostok and Niigata-Fushiki in Japan.

Main port/s: Vladivostok, Magadan, Nakhodka, St Petersburg and Kaliningrad. Links to the Atlantic are provided by the Murmansk (Arctic Ocean) and Archangelisk ports (during summer months only).

Getting about

National transport

Air: There is an extensive internal air service which provides the only viable option for travelling between cities. Domestic services are operated by Aeroflot and Transaero (due to a small fleet, flights are more often delayed than those of Aeroflot). Sky Express, a budget airline, began operations in early 2007. It will initially fly between Moscow and Sochi on the Black Sea, charging US$19, compared to Aeroflot's rate of US$120.

The internal air network centres around Moscow. Domestic airports include Vnukovo (VKO), 29km south-west of city; Domodedovo (DME), 40km south-east of city and Irkutsk (IRK), 7km from city.

Road: Distances between major cities are extensive: Moscow to St Petersburg 692km (432 miles); Moscow to Odessa 1,347km (837 miles). Approximately 60 per cent of the road network needs to be rehabilitated or upgraded. In general the few roads connecting with Siberia are impassable during winter. Secondary roads are often untarred.

Buses: Long-distance coach services operate.

Rail: Rail is the major means of transport. There is a cheap and efficient service to all major towns. There is an extensive network of commuter and inter-city services, most offering first and second class seats or accommodation.

The rolling stock needs modernising and trains are typically over-crowded and over-booked. Food is often available on inter-city services but, because of the generally poor quality, most passengers bring their own. Many carriages have a samovar which produces hot water for drinks. Security can be a problem, especially on overnight services. The famous Trans-Siberian railway stretches from Moscow to Vladivostok.

The railways are wide gauge. Almost all the rail network is electrified. Sleepers should be booked well in advance.

Water: Rivers play an important role in transport; in summer it is possible to travel great distances either by cruises or river passenger boats. Routes include: St Petersberg-Astrakhan on the Caspian sea, and St Petersberg-Rostov-on-Don on the Black Sea. These routes may include detours via Moscow.

The largest inland waterway is the River Volga. There are a number of inland ports and canals.

City transport

Taxis: Use only officially marked taxis and do not share them with strangers. Taxis are yellow with a checkerboard stripe and a green light at the top right hand corner of the windscreen indicating availability; they can be hired at taxi ranks or by booking in advance. Beware of illegal taxi touts operating at both the airport and city centre.

Tariffs for foreigners are often subject to negotiation and may be charged in hard currency.

It is possible to find a reliable taxi firm in the airport arrivals section at Moscow airport. Payment is by credit card though fares may have to be negotiated with the driver as the fare shown on the meter may not correspond with the fare asked. Arrangements to be met at the airport in advance can be made by contacting Intourist, or telephoning Moscow Taxi (tel: 238-1001).

Buses, trams & metro: Cheap and reliable, though often crowded, available from 0600–0100. Bus services 5817 and 551 from Moscow airport to the city centre operate between 0500–2359 every 10 minutes, with a journey time of 30–45 minutes. Long distance coach services operate.

Trains: An express train service from Moscow airport to the city centre operates every 30 minutes.

Car hire

Available in major towns. International driving licence required with Russian translation of details. Notification of route to be taken should be given if travelling outside main cities.

Visitors travelling in private cars should be in possession of their passport and visa, and an itinerary card complete with visitor's name and citizenship and car registration number.

Traffic drives on the right. Speeds are limited to 60kph (37mph) in built-up areas and 90kph (55mph) elsewhere. Cars are required to display registration plates and stickers denoting the country of registration.

BUSINESS DIRECTORY

The addresses listed below are a selection only. While World of Information makes every endeavour to check these addresses, we cannot guarantee that changes have not been made, especially to telephone numbers and area codes. We would welcome any corrections.

Telephone area codes

The international direct dialling code (IDD) for Russia is +7, followed by the area code and subscriber's number:

Chelyabinsk	3512	St Petersburg	812
Ekaterinberg	3432	Smolensk	481
Kaliningrad	401	Tula	487
Moscow	495	Vladivostok	4232
Nizhny Novgorod	8312	Yakutsk	41122

Useful telephone numbers

International operator: (English-speaking operator): 8196

General enquiries (Moscow area): 09

Police: 02

Fire: 01

Ambulance: 03

Chambers of Commerce

American Chamber of Commerce in Russia, 7 Dolgorukovskaya Street, Moscow 127006 (tel: 961-2141; fax: 961-2142; e-mail: info@amcham.ru).

Moscow Chamber of Commerce and Industry, 22 Akademika Pilyugina Street, Moscow 117393 (tel: 132-7510; fax: 132-0547; e-mail: mtpp@mtpp.org).

Nizhny Novgorod Region Chamber of Commerce and Industry, 1 Oktyabrskaya Square, Nizhny Novgorod 603005 (tel: 194-210; fax:194-009; e-mail: tpp@rda.nnov.ru).

Russian Federation Chamber of Commerce and Industry, 6 Ilyinka Street, Moscow 109012 (tel: 929-0009; fax: 929-0360; e-mail: tpprf@tpprf.ru).

St Petersburg Chamber of Commerce and Industry, 46-48 Chaikovsky Street, St Petersburg 191194 (tel: 279-2833; fax: 272-6406; e-mail: spbcci@spbcci.ru).

South Ural Chamber of Commerce and Industrym 63 Vasenko Street, Chelyabinsk 454080 (tel: 661-816; fax: 665-223; e-mail: mail@tpp.chelreg.ru).

Smolensk Chamber of Commerce and Industry, 12 Karl Marx Street, Smolensk 214000 (tel: 554-142; fax: 237-450; e-mail: smolcci@keytown.com).

Tula Chamber of Commerce and Industry, 25 Krasnoarmeisky Prospekt, Tula 300600 (tel: 364-517; fax: 360-216; e-mail: tulacci@tula.net).

Banking

Agropromstraybank, Krasina Per, 123056 Moscow (tel: 254-4263; fax: 254-7081).

Gazprombank, Nametkina Str 16B, 117420 Moscow (tel: 719-1697/17; fax; 719-1763).

ING Bank Eurasia, ul Krasnaya Presnya 31, 125178 Moscow (tel: 755-5400; fax: 755-5459; fax: 755-5499).

Sberbank (savings bank), Vavilova Str 18, 117817 Moscow (tel: 971-4981, 957-5690, 957-5862; fax: 957-5731; internet site: http://www.sbrf.ru).

SDM Bank, 73 Volokolamskoe Shosse, 123424 Moscow (tel: 490-1545, 491-7572, 490-0703; fax: 490-6509).

United Export Import Bank (UNEXIM), 11 Masha Paryvaeva Street, PO Box 207, 107078 Moscow (tel: 232-3727; fax: 975-2205; e-mail: mailbox@mail.unexim.ru).

Vnesheconombank (Bank for Foreign Economic Affairs), Akademika Sakharova Prospekt 9, 107996 Moscow (tel: 207-1037).

Vneshtorgbank (Bank for Foreign Trade), Kuznetskiy Most Str 16, 103031 Moscow (tel: 929-8900; fax: 956-3727).

Central bank

Central Bank of the Russian Federation, 12 Neglinnaya Sreet, 107016 Moscow (tel: 771-9100; fax: 921-6465; e-mail: webmaster@www.cbr.ru).

Stock exchange

Moscow Interbank Currency Exchange (Micex): www.micex.com

Stock exchange 2

Russian Trading System: www.rts.ru

Travel information

Aeroflot, 37/9 Leningradsky Prospect, Moscow 125836 (tickets and enquiries, tel: 223-5555; fax: 186-2092; internet: www.aeroflot.ru/eng/).

Intourist, 150, Prospect Mira, Moscow 129366 (tel: 956-4207; fax: 730-1957; email: info@intourist.ru; internet: www.intourist.com/ENG/).

Russian National Group, Suite 214, 5/10 Chistoprudni Blvd, Moscow (tel: 980-8440; 980-8441; internet: www.russia-travel.com).

JSC Russian Railways (JSCo RZD), Novaya Basmannaya 2, 107174 Moscow (tel: 262-9901; email: info@rzd.ru; internet: www.eng.rzd.ru).

Ministries

Ministry of Agriculture and Food, 1-11 Orlikov Lane, Moscow 107139 (tel: 207-8000; fax: 207-8362, 288-9580).

Ministry of Atomic Energy, 24-26 Bolshaya Ordynka Str, Moscow 101100 (tel: 239-4753; fax: 233-4679).

Ministry for Civil Defence, Emergencies and Disaster Resources, 3 Teatralniy Pr-D, Moscow 103012 (tel: 926-3901; fax: 924-5683).

Ministry for Communications, 7 Tverskaya Str, Moscow 119332 (tel: 229-6966, 292-7070; fax: 292-7128).

Ministry of Construction, Comp 2, 8 Stroitelei Str, Moscow 117987 (tel: 930-1755; fax: 938-2202).

Ministry for Co-operation Between CIS Member Countries, 7 Varvarka Str, Moscow 103073 (tel: 206-1365; fax: 206-1084).

Ministry of Culture, 7 Kitaiskiy Pr-D, Moscow 103693 (tel: 925-1195; fax: 928-1791).

Ministry of Economics, 19 Noviy Arbat Str, Moscow 103025 (tel: 203-7534; fax: 203-7482).

Ministry of Education, 6 Chistoprudniy B-R, Moscow 101856 (tel: 927-0568; fax: 924-6989).

Ministry for Environmental Protection and Natural Resources, 4-6 B Gruzinskaya Str, Moscow 123812 (tel: 254-7683; fax: 254-8283).

Ministry of Finance, 9 Ilyinka str, Moscow 103097 (tel: 298-9101, 923-0967; fax: 925-0889).

Ministry of Foreign Affairs, 32-34 Smolenskaya-Sennaya Sq, Moscow 121200 (tel: 244-1606; fax: 230-2130).

Ministry for Foreign Economic Relations, 32-34 Smolenskaya-Sennaya Sq, Moscow 121200 (tel: 244-2450; fax: 244-3068/3981).

Ministry for Fuel and Power Development, 7 Kitaiskiy Pr, Moscow 103074 (tel: 220-5500; fax: 220-4818).

Ministry of the Interior, 16 Zhitnaya Str, Moscow 117049 (tel: 237-7585, 924-6572, 222-6669; fax: 925-2098).

Ministry of Justice, 4 Vorontsovo Pole Str, Moscow 109830 (tel: 209-6009/98; fax: 916-2903).

Ministry of Labour, 1 Birzhevaya Sq, Moscow 103706 (tel: 261-2030, 928-8208; fax: 230-2407).

Ministry for Nationalities and Regional Policy, 19 Trubnikovskiy Lane, Moscow 121819 (tel: 248-8635; fax: 202-4490).

Ministry of Public Health, 3 Rakhmanovskiy Lane, Moscow 103051 (tel: 928-4478; fax: 921-0128).

Ministry for Railways, 2 Novo-Basmannaya Str, Moscow 107174 (tel: 262-9901; fax: 262-9095).

Ministry for Science and Technology, 11 Tverskaya Str, Moscow 103905 (tel: 229-1192; fax: 230-2823).

Ministry for Social Protection, Bld 1, 4 Slavianskaya Sq, Moscow 103715 (tel: 220-9511/9384; fax: 924-3690).

Ministry of Transport, 10 Sadovo-Samotyochnaya Str, Moscow 101433 (tel: 200-0809; fax: 200-3356).

Other useful addresses

British Consulate, Sfoskaya Nberezhnaya 14, Moscow (tel: 956-7420; fax: 956-7420).

British Consulate, St Petersburg, Pl Proletarsky, Dikatury 5, 193124 St Petersburg (tel: 325-6036; fax: 325-6037; e-mail: uk.stpet@vmail.sprint.com).

British Consulate for Southern Russia, Petrak, 3a Fabrichnaya Street, Novorossisk (tel: 93-319; fax: 34-959).

British Embassy, Kutuzovsky Prospekt 7/4, Moscow 121248 (tel: 956-7200, 956-7477; fax: 956-7480, 956-7420; e-mail: uk.moscw@vmail.sprint.com).

British Trade Office, 4th Floor, 15a Gogol Street, Ekaterinburg 620151 (tel: 564-931; fax: 592-901; e-mail: uk.ekate@vmail.sprint.com).

BSCC British-Russian Business Centre, 42 Southwark Street, London SE1 1UN (tel: (+44-(0)171) 403-1706; fax: (+44-(0)171) 403-1245); 22/25 Bolshoi Strochenovskiy Pereulok, Moscow 113054 (tel: 230-6120; fax: 230-6124).

Delegation of the European Union (Office of), 2/10 Astakhovsky Pereulok, Moscow 109208 (tel: 956-3600; fax: 956-3615).

Expocentr, 1a Sokolnicheskiy val, Moscow 107113 (tel: 268-7083) (responsibility for organising, on a commercial basis, international and foreign exhibitions and symposia).

Foreign Investment Promotion Centre (FIPC), Ul Novy Arbat 19, 119898 Moscow (tel: 203-4863; internet site: www.fipc.ru/fipc/).

Foreign Trade Arbitration Commission, Moscow (tel: 205-6855).

Government of St. Petersburg, Smolny, 193060 St Petersburg (tel 576-4501; fax: 576-7827; internet: http://eng.gov.spb.ru).

Interstate Statistical Committee of the Commonwealth of Independent States, 39 Myasnitskaya Str, Moscow 103450 (tel: 207-4237/4802/4567; fax: 207-4592; e-mail: Statpro@Sovam.com).

Russian Federation Embassy (USA), 2650 Wisconsin Avenue, NW, Washington DC 2007 (tel: (+1-202) 298-5700; fax: (+1-202) 298-5735; e-mail: russ-amb@cerfnet.com).

Russian Federation Foreign Trade Organisation, Barrikabnaya Str Bld 8-5, 123242 Moscow (tel: 254-8090; fax: 253-9675).

Russian Information Telegraph Agency (ITAR-TASS) (news agency), Tverskoy bul 10, Moscow (tel: 3229-8053).

Russian Television and Radio, Corolov St 12, Moscow (tel: 217-7898; fax: 288-9508).

State Committee for Statistics, 39 Myasnitskaya Street, Moscow 103450 (tel: 207-4902; fax: 207-4640).

TACIS Technical Assistance Centre, 165 Nemirovicha-Danchenko, Novosibirsk 630087 (tel: 465-395, 464-836; fax: 464-426; e-mail: centre@tac.sib.ru).

US Consulate, St Petersburg (tel: 275-1701).

National news agency: Itar-Tass News Agency: 10–12 Tvershoy Blvd, Moscow 125993 (email: info@itar-tass.com; internet: www.tass-online.ru).

Other news agencies: RIA Novosti, 4 Zubovsky Blvd, Moscow 119031 (tel: 637-2424; internet: http://en.rian.ru).

Interfax, 2 Pervaya Tverskaya-Yamskaya Ul, Building 1, Moscow 127006 (tel: 250-9840; fax: 250-9727; internet: www.interfax.ru).

Internet sites

Moscow Guide: www.moscow-guide.ru

Rusline (government information, company directories): www.rusline.com

Russian tourism: www.visitrussia.com

Russian travel: www.realrussia.com

Russian web portal: www.ru

Rwanda

KEY FACTS

Official name: Republika y'u Rwanda (Republic of Rwanda)

Head of State: President Paul Kagame (FPR) (elected 2000; re-elected Aug 2010)

Head of government: Prime Minister Pierre Damien Habumuremyi (from 7 Oct 2011)

Ruling party: Coalition led by Front Patriotique Rwandais (FPR) (Rwandan Patriotic Front) (Tutsi-dominated) with six other political parties (elected 2003; re-elected Sep 2008)

Area: 26,338 square km

Population: 10.41 million (2010)*

Capital: Kigali

Official language: Kinyarwanda, French and English.

Currency: Rwanda franc (Rwf)

Exchange rate: Rwf599.99 per US$ (Oct 2011)

GDP per capita: US$562 (2010)

GDP real growth: 6.50% (2010)

GDP: US$5.60 billion (2010)

Inflation: 2.30% (2010)

Balance of trade: -US$768.00 million (2009)

Annual FDI: US$42.33 million (2010)

* estimated figure

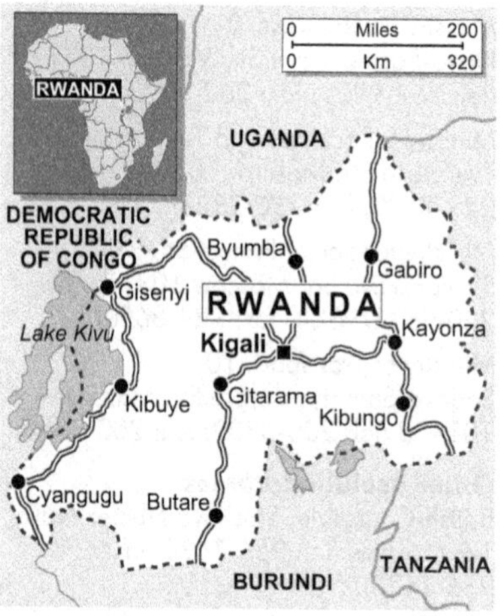

In less than 20 years, Rwanda has transformed itself from a by-word for lethal inhumanity to one of Africa's most promising democracies. The government of President Paul Kagame has implemented a raft of reforms and strategies to improve the quality of life for Rwandans and support neighbouring countries in their efforts to rid themselves of rebel militias. Rwanda became the first sub-Saharan African country to be ranked as highly as 58 out of 183 in 2011 in the World Bank's *Doing Business* report. Within Africa, Rwanda's ranking rose from 37 in 2006 to five in 2011, equalling its neighbour Burundi.

Medium-term strategy

In 2008 the government published its *Economic Development and Poverty Reduction Strategy* (EDPRS), which runs from 2008–12 in which it identified 384 policy actions necessary to guide the allocation of budgetary resources. These policies are clustered around three overarching themes of economic, social and governance. According to the *African Economic Outlook 2011* (AEO), published jointly by the African Development Bank and the Organisation for Economic Co-operation and Development, by mid-2010, 374 of the 384 policy actions had been implemented and government spending on key priority areas of the EDPRS had already exceeded 94 per cent by early in 2010. Commitment has led to a decline in the expenditure share of wages and salaries, and of goods and services, and a rise in the share of public investment in total government expenditure.

Reforms of the Rwandan Revenue Authority (RRA) paid off in higher collections of direct taxes and some indirect taxes. This increased revenue offset shortfalls in international trade taxes that originate mainly from shifts in imports from the East African Community (EAC) and the Common Market for Eastern and Southern Africa (Comesa), a decline that led to corresponding reductions in government revenues.

Partnership with China

Rwanda has formed partnerships with China, which are not wholly trade related. Chinese companies which operate in Rwanda and are expected to grow significantly by 2015, have contributed foreign direct investment (FDI), which saw a record high of US$118.7 million in 2009, before falling to US$42.3 million in 2010, according to the World Bank. The Chinese company Star Media, a digital pay-to-view television operator, began operations in 2009 and has plans to diversify as a wireless internet service provider. China is engaged in a project to rehabilitate roads in urban areas, particularly in the capital, Kigali. It has expressed interest in collaborating in the government's effort to build enough power plants to double capacity in the next few years. The importance of Chinese investment, which has helped create jobs and led to a transfer of skills and technology, cannot be overstated. India is also an important partner, with agreements for technical co-operation in both countries and trade in Indian and pharmaceutical products, transport equipment and machinery in Rwanda, while Rwandan students attend Indian educational institutions.

Education

Rwanda has a large population with little suitable land for agriculture, which leaves the rural workforce in need of employment.

It may have just been pique at France's continued investigation into the Rwandan genocide and President Kagame's role in it, but in 2008 the government decided that all education would be taught in English, the *lingua franca* of the modern world. Since 2005, Rwanda has raised the level of school enrolment in both secondary and tertiary education. In 2010 all candidates wrote their national examinations in English and in January 2012, 4,000 newly recruited teachers of English are being introduced into schools throughout the country.

Social development

The government acknowledges the high level of economic inequality amongst the population, which could hamper progress. The major factors in income disparities are the level of education attained by heads of households and regional inequalities. In 2011, the UN Human Development Index (HDI) ranked Rwanda 166 (out of 187) for national development in health, education and income. In 2010, 53.2 per cent of the population experienced at least one indicator of poverty and 76.8 per cent were living on the equivalent of US$1.25 per day. However, since the depths of the genocide of the mid-1990s Rwanda has made continued improvement so that by 2011, it was just below the regional HDI average. The EDPRS policy on health is for preventive measures before the need for curatives. The target for reducing infant and maternal mortality, has resulted in a cut of one-third by 2009–10. Other goals, set by UN World Health Organisation, are also progressing.

Auld Lang Syne

President Paul Kagame returned the state visit of President Nicolas Sarkozy, in September 2011, five years after diplomatic relations had been broken. The visit was to attend a gathering of Rwanda's diaspora in Europe and to mend fences with France.

In January 2012, a French court declared that President Kagame was cleared of the murder of former president Habyarimana, whose plane crash was the incident that sparked the start of the Rwandan genocide.

Risk assessment

Politics	Fair
Economy	Fair
Regional stability	Fair

COUNTRY PROFILE

Historical profile

1899 Rwanda, which for a long time had been an independent monarchy, was absorbed into German East Africa.
1916 It was taken over by Belgium, along with what is now Burundi.
1918 After the First World War ended, the two became Ruanda-Urundi, a Belgian-administered trust territory of the League of Nations (and later, the UN).
1950s Belgium had generally favoured the minority Tutsis as their Rwandan auxiliaries. They flourished and became more educated and prosperous than the majority Hutus. However, it was the Tutsis who agitated for independence after the Second World War and the Belgians switched their allegiance, promoting the Hutus, thereby laying the seeds of the genocide to follow. Belgian missionaries also encouraged the formation of a modern Hutu identity.
1959–63 Vengeful Hutus killed some 15,000 people, mainly Tutsis. Some 100,000 Tutsis fled, mainly to Uganda and Burundi.
1961 Rwanda's monarchy was abolished and a republic was proclaimed.
1962 Independence was granted. Belgium pulled out of the region.
1973 President Gregoire Kayibanda, was overthrown by Major General Juvenal Habyarimana. Habyarimana began a regime that stripped the Tutsis of their wealth and status; an estimated one million fled the country. The Front Patriotique Rwandais (Rwandan Patriotic Front) (RPF) was formed from this group, aiming to invade Rwanda and overthrow Habyarimana.
1990 Some 10,000 rebel Tutsi guerrillas the (RPF) invaded Rwanda from Uganda and occupied several towns.
1993 President Habyarimana signed a power-sharing agreement with the Tutsis (the Arusha Accord). A UN mission was sent to monitor the agreement.
1994 The death of Habyarimana in a plane crash (which also killed the president of Burundi), triggered the breakdown of civil society. Extremist Hutu militia began the systematic murder of Tutsis. Within four months an estimated 800,000 Tutsis and moderate Hutus were killed. The Tutsis RPF forced the militia to flee, taking with them around two million Hutu refugees, who fled in fear of reprisal for the genocide, into neighbouring Democratic Republic of Congo (DRC), Tanzania and Burundi.
1995 The militia responsible for the genocide were able to take control of the refugee camps and deter people from returning to Rwanda on pain of death. Mass repatriation efforts were complicated by screening operations, which were needed to identify genocide rebels from genuine refugees. President Pasteur Bizimungu and a transitional coalition government were sworn in. Rwanda applied to become a member of the Commonwealth.
1999 An extension of the transitional government's term of office was approved.
2000 Pasteur Bizimungu resigned and Paul Kagame was officially elected president (the first Tutsi to hold presidential office since Rwanda's independence in 1961) in a joint vote of the Rwandan legislature and cabinet. Ethnic Hutu, Bernard Makuza, was appointed prime minister.
2001 A peace agreement was signed between Rwanda and Uganda. A new national flag, emblem and anthem were unveiled.
2002 Rwanda and DRC signed a peace agreement.
2003 In a referendum, voters approved a new, more democratic constitution. Incumbent Paul Kagame won the

KEY INDICATORS — Rwanda

	Unit	2006	2007	2008	2009	2010
Population	m	9.20	*9.39	*9.68	*9.80	*10.41
Gross domestic product (GDP)	US$bn	2.87	3.40	4.50	5.20	5.60
GDP per capita	US$	312	363	465	533	562
GDP real growth	%	5.5	7.9	11.2	4.1	7.5
Inflation	%	8.8	9.1	15.4	10.3	2.3
Exports (fob) (goods)	US$m	142.0	184.0	257.0	193.0	–
Imports (fob) (goods)	US$m	438.0	637.0	880.0	961.0	–
Balance of trade	US$m	-296.0	-452.0	-623.0	-768.0	–
Current account	US$m	-134.0	-83.0	-252.0	-379.0	-381.0
Total reserves minus gold	US$m	439.7	552.8	596.3	742.7	812.8
Foreign exchange	US$m	416.8	528.7	564.9	611.8	684.2
Exchange rate	per US$	551.71	546.96	546.85	568.28	583.13

* estimated figure

presidential elections and the ruling party, FPR, won the parliamentary elections.
2004 Kagame denied he ordered the attack on the president's plane in 1994 which had sparked the genocide. Former president Bizimungu was sentenced to 15 years imprisonment for embezzlement and inciting violence.
2005 The Forces Democratiques de Liberation du Rwanda (FDLR) (Democratic Liberation Forces of Rwanda) declared a cease-fire. A mass release of 36,000 prisoners took place as part of the process of reconciliation; many had confessed to acts of genocide.
2006 The country's 12 administrative provinces were replaced by a larger number of ethnically-diverse districts. Roman Catholic priest, Fr Athanase Seromba, was convicted of involvement in the genocide by the International Criminal Tribunal for Rwanda (ICTR), and sentenced to 15 years imprisonment. Relations with France deteriorated as a French judge investigating the shooting down of President Juvénal Habyarimana's plane in 1994 and the killing of its French crew, accused President Kagame and nine top officials with involvement in the assassination. The president has immunity from prosecution as head of state and he strenuously denied the RPF were responsible for the death of the former president. A counter claim by Rwandan officials accused French authorities of attempting to divert international attention away from French collaboration in the Hutu regime responsible for the genocide. The Mouvement Démocratique Républicain (MDR) (Democratic Republican Movement) was banned following allegations that it promoted genocide ideology.
2007 The Communaute Economique des Pays des Grands Lacs (CEPGL) (Great Lakes Countries Economic Community) was re-launched by Burundi, DRC and Rwanda. CEPGL is intended to promote regional economic co-operation and integration. President Kagame pardoned former president Pasteur Bizimungu. The death penalty was repealed. The traditional *Gacaca* courts trying genocide suspects, had their mandate extended into 2007. Rwanda became a full member of the East African Community (EAC).
2008 Accusations and counter-accusations of who was responsible for the 1994 genocide broke out between Rwanda and France following the acquittal by a French Appeals court of two men said to have played crucial roles in the slaughter – one a former priest and the other a former provincial governor. At the same time arrest warrants were issued in France for senior aides to President Kagame, accused of responsibility for the aeroplane crash of former president Habyarimana. In parliamentary elections the ruling FPR (predominately ethnic Tutsi) won 78.8 per cent (42 seats out of 53 directly elected seats), the opposition (predominately ethnic Hutu) Parti Social Démocrate (Social Democratic Party) (SDP) won 13.1 per cent (7 seats); turnout was 96.5 per cent. The ICTR, convicted former army general Theoneste Bagosora of inciting the 1994 genocide and sentenced him to life in prison. (Bagosora and two co-defendants had led a Hutu committee that organised the massacre of ethnic Tutsis. He had also set up the *Interahamwe* (gangs of Hutu extremists), which carried out much of the killings.)
2009 Rwandan government troops crossed into DRC in a joint military operation to eliminate Rwandan Hutu militia, exiled in DRC since 1994 and causing widespread mayhem in DRC's eastern province, and generally destabilising the region. Former general and rebel leader Laurent Nkunda was arrested in Rwanda, having fled his stronghold in Bunagana (DRC). The Tanzanian-based ICTR, found Callixte Kalimanzira guilty of genocide and sentenced him to 30 years in jail. He had been interior minister and a close ally of then president, Bizimungu. The defence ministry announced that Rwanda was free of unexploded ordnance (UXO), after it completed a de-mining campaign ahead of the 2010 deadline set by the Ottawa Convention. Rwanda was admitted as a member of the Commonwealth of Nations.
2010 French President Nicolas Sarkozy made an historic visit to Rwanda in February and acknowledged that France had made 'serious errors of judgement' during the 1994 genocide; but he did not voice an apology. Transparency International, the Berlin-based anti-corruption watch-dog, included Rwanda in its East African bribery survey for the first time, where it scored best in East Africa with a prevalence of 6.6 per cent, compared to Burundi, the worst, with 36.7 per cent. Critics said this was because Rwanda was a police state, although in Kenya and Burundi the police were considered to be high on the list of corrupt institutions. Four candidates took part in presidential elections held on 9 August. Incumbent Paul Kagame (FPR) won with 93.1 per cent of the vote while his closest rival, Jean Ntawukuriryayo (SDP), won 5.1 per cent; turnout was 97.5 per cent.
2011 Joseph Habineza, minister for youth and sport, resigned on 16 February following allegations of improper behaviour after photographs taken in 2008 appeared on the internet. In May the ICTR, in Arusha found former army chief Augustin Bizimungu guilty of genocide and sentenced him to 30 years in prison. Augustin Ndindiliyimana was found guilty at the same time, but while Bizimungu was said to have been in 'complete' control of the men he commanded, Ndindiliyimana had only 'limited control' and was given a lesser goal sentence of 12 years. President Kagame appointed Bernard Makuza as a senator and replaced him as prime minister with Pierre Habumuremyi, who took office on 7 October.

Political structure

Constitution

A new 2003 constitution prevents a one-party dominance of the political system and bans incitement to racial hatred. It stipulates that no party can hold more than 50 per cent of the seats in cabinet, even if it secures an absolute majority in parliamentary elections.
The president, prime minister and president of the lower house cannot belong to the same party.

Form of state

Republic

The executive

The president is eligible for election for a maximum of two seven-year terms. Candidates must be Rwandan and over 35 years of age. Election is by universal suffrage with a simple majority of votes cast.

National legislature

The bicameral Inteko Ishinga Amategeko (Parlement) (parliament) consists of a lower and upper chambers. The Umutwe w'Abadepite (Chambre des Députés) (Chamber of Deputies) has 80 members, of which 53 are elected by proportional representation, 24 are female members elected by provincial councils, two are elected by the National Youth Council and one by the Federation of Associations of Disabled Persons. All deputies serve five-year terms.
The Umutwe wa Sena (Sénat) (senate) has 26 members, 12 of whom are elected, eight are appointed by the president, four are designated by the Forum of Political Organisations and two are appointed by the universities or institutions of higher learning. All serve eight-year terms. In addition, former heads of state may become members, providing they completed their terms in office or resigned voluntarily.

Last elections

15 September 2008 (parliamentary); 9 August 2010 (presidential).
Results: Parliamentary: Front Patriotique Rwandais (FPR) (Rwandan Patriotic Front) coalition of seven political parties won 78.8 per cent (42 seats out of 53 directly elected seats), the Parti Social Démocrate (Social Democratic Party) (SDP) 13.1 per cent (seven), the Parti Liberal (Liberal Party) 10.6 per cent (four). Turnout was 96.5 per cent.

Presidential: Paul Kagame won 93.1 per cent of the vote, Jean Ntawukuriryayo 5.1 per cent; turnout was 97.5 per cent.

Next elections

2013 (chamber of deputies); 2017 (presidential).

Political parties

Ruling party

Coalition led by Front Patriotique Rwandais (FPR) (Rwandan Patriotic Front) (Tutsi-dominated) with six other political parties (elected 2003; re-elected Sep 2008)

Main opposition party

Social Democratic Party (SDP)

Population

10.41 million (2010)*

Last census: 16 August 2002: 8,128,553

Population density: 300 per square km. Urban population: 10 per cent.

Annual growth rate: 4.9 per cent 1994–2004 (WHO 2006)

Ethnic make-up

There are three ethnic groups: the Hutu (90 per cent), the Tutsi (9 per cent) and the Twa (1 per cent).

Religions

Roman Catholic (56 per cent), Protestant (26 per cent), Adventist (11.1 per cent), Islam (4.6 per cent), indigenous beliefs (0.1 per cent).

Education

On completion of primary education, a competitive entrance examination allows students to progress to the first cycle secondary school for general education, from age 13 to 16. The second cycle secondary school covers either modern or classical humanities, from age 16 to 19. Technical education is provided for students who have completed two to three years general secondary education, although some may begin straight from primary education joining four-year courses. In October 2008 the government decided that all teaching classes would be undertaken using English instead of French. The decision will include every educational institution from nursery schools to universities. The decision was officially based on Rwanda joining the English-speaking East African Community (EAC) and the increasing use of English in business circles. However the political tension with France since 1994, when France was accused of supporting the Hutu Militia in genocide, has also added to the government's commitment to change.

Literacy rate: 69 per cent adult rate; 85 per cent youth rate (15–24) (Unesco 2005).

Compulsory years: Seven to 13.

Enrolment rate: 95.5 per cent net primary (World Bank).

Health

HIV/Aids

The average life expectancy of Rwandan citizens has reduced to under 40 due to the Aids epidemic. In 2003 there were 230,000 people HIV positive, of which 130,000 were women. There were also 22,000 children (0–17 years) with HIV/Aids and 160,000 orphans created by Aids. There has been evidence that national adult prevalence has fallen in Rwanda since reaching a peak in the mid-1990s (UNAID 2003).

HIV prevalence: 5.1 per cent aged 15–49 in 2003 (World Bank)

Life expectancy: 46 years, 2004 (WHO 2006)

Fertility rate/Maternal mortality rate: 5.6 births per woman, 2004 (WHO 2006)

Birth rate/Death rate: 40 births per 1,000 population; 21.7 deaths per 1000 population (2003).

Child (under 5 years) mortality rate (per 1,000): 118.0 per 1,000 live births (World Bank)

Head of population per physician: 0.05 physicians per 1,000 people, 2004 (WHO 2006)

Welfare

More than half the population live below the national poverty line. According to the 2002 UN Development Report, 84.6 per cent of the population exist on less than US$2 per day and 35.7 per cent on less than US$1 per day.

Main cities

Kigali (capital, estimated population 718,414 in 2005),Gitarama (108,760), Ruhengeri (81,960), Butare (88,585), Byumba (70,781), Gisenyi (79,959), Cyangugu (75,085).

Languages spoken

KiSwahili is also used among traders.

Official language/s

Kinyarwanda, French and English.

Media

Press

There are only two domestically published newspapers, *La Nouvelle Relève* (www.orinfor.gov.rw), is government owned and printed in French, *The New Times* (www.newtimes.co.rw) is privately owned and printed in English.

A magazine, published regionally in French *Jeune Afrique* (www.jeuneafrique.com) covers news and interviews. Internet outlets in English include Inside Rwanda (www.insideworld.com/rwanda), and Rwanda Information Exchange (www.rwanda.net), and in French, Observatoire de l'Afrique Centrale (www.obsac.com).

Broadcasting

Radio: Most residents of Rwanda receive their news from radio broadcasts and the most listened to radio station is the government-owned, commercial Radio Rwanda (www.orinfor.gov.rw) broadcasting in KiSwahili, Kinyarwanda, French and English. There are six other private radio stations, including Radio Maria with religious programmes.

BBC radio broadcasts in the Kinyarwanda language were suspended in April 2009 due to a bias concerning the 1994 genocide as detected by the government. The BBC reports were considered to deny the genocide, a claim the BBC rejected saying its reports only differed from the interpretation the government had of the genocide.

Television: Television Rwandaise (TVR) is the only television broadcasting company in the country.

News agencies

This is no national news agency but the African Press Agency (APA) (www.africanewsagency.org) and Panapress (www.panapress.com) report on news from Rwanda.

Economy

Rwanda has few natural resources. The country's economy is still largely based on agriculture, dominated by small family-run farms. In 2009, the service sector was 51.3 per cent of GDP, agriculture 34.2 per cent and industry 14.5 per cent, of which, manufacturing was 6.4 per cent. Rwanda is the most heavily populated country in Africa and suffers from land shortages with the average farm size at half a hectare, enough for subsistence farming only. The land, with its steep mountain slopes, is not practical for most agribusiness purposes. Government land ownership has also increased pressure and reduced opportunities for development. Government aid and land reforms have been underway to give secure tenure and user rights since the 1990s.

Agricultural production is led by exports of tea and coffee, plus pyrethrum (used in insect repellent), which together account for around 40 per cent of export earnings. GDP growth since 2006 has fluctuated from a low of 5.5 per cent in 2007 before doubling to 11.2 per cent in 2008. The slump in world trade lead to a sharp fall in exports causing a five-year low in GDP growth of 4.1 per cent in 2009, which picked up in 2010 to 7.5 per cent as global trade strengthened. The positive GDP growth was attributed to a robust expansion in agriculture facilitated by the government's crop-intensification programme (including providing seed and fertiliser to farmers and expanding harvest storage facilities) and good harvests.

Industrial production, including manufacturing, construction and mining, all registered growth, largely due to private sector investment. According to the World Bank, total foreign direct investment was a record high of US$118.7 million in 2009, but fell to a five-year low of US$42.3 million in 2010. Tourism, centred on the rare mountain gorillas and other upscale tourist venues, have grown in importance but still require investment to take full advantage of resources.
In 2011, the UN Human Development Index (HDI) ranked Rwanda 166 (out of 187) for national development in health, education and income. In 2010, 53.2 per cent of the population experienced at least one indicator of poverty and 76.8 per cent were living on the equivalent of US$1.25 per day. However, since the depths of the genocide of the mid-1990s Rwanda has made continued improvement so that it by 2011, it was just below the regional average.

External trade
Rwanda is a member of the Common Market for Eastern and Southern Africa (Comesa), and operates within a free trade zone with 13 of the 19 member states. Around 35 per cent of all imports originate in Africa
Rwanda is a member of the East African Community (EAC) (with Burundi, Kenya, Tanzania and Uganda). The East African Community Common Market Protocol (EACMP) was launched on 1 July 2010, which will lead to the free movement of labour, capital, goods and services between member states as well as employment opportunities and easier flow of investment capital. The signed protocol now requires that legislation in all states must be harmonised to conform to its jurisdiction.
As a landlocked country, the infrastructure must be maintained to move any imports and exports from neighbouring countries, which increases shipping costs; there is no railway linking Rwanda to the Tanzanian rail system. Rwanda has few natural resources and imports its energy (beyond bio-fuels) as well as capital goods. Exports are limited to cash crops – tea represents 60 per cent – and pyrethrum, the extract of which is used in insect repellent.

Imports
Principal imports include foodstuffs, machinery and equipment, steel, petroleum products, cement and construction materials.
Main sources: Kenya (typically 15 per cent of total), Uganda (15 per cent), UAE (8 per cent).

Exports
Principal exports are tea, coffee, pyrethrum, animal hides and tin ore.
Main destinations: China (typically 30 per cent of total), Belgium (16 per cent), Democratic Republic of Congo (13 per cent).

Agriculture
Farming
The agricultural sector contributes about 40 per cent to GDP and employs 90 per cent of the labour force. Approximately 30 per cent of the land area is cultivated arable land, 31 per cent pasture and 9 per cent forest; tree planting programmes are under way to combat deforestation.
The main food crops are beans (17 per cent of cultivated land), sweet potatoes (14 per cent), sorghum (7 per cent), plantains, bananas, potatoes, cassava and maize. Crop yields fluctuate due to drought, soil erosion and underinvestment.
The coffee industry is scheduled for privatisation although little progress has been made. Coffee production fell so the government is encouraging the growth of speciality coffees that receive higher prices on the international market. If this move is successful, export revenues could be boosted, but if not, it is unlikely the failing coffee industry will recover swiftly. Tea overtook coffee as the country's main export.
Food production was boosted in early 2008 when high-yielding seed varieties provided by under the Crop Intensification Project proved successful.

Industry and manufacturing
Industries include brewing, food processing, cigarette production, soaps, plastics, tin smelting and textiles. Growth of the sector is limited by the small domestic market, transport difficulties and irregular supply of imported fuels and raw materials which comprise 77 per cent of inputs.

Tourism
Rwanda receives around 16,000 tourists annually and is aiming to become Africa's newest eco-tourism destination. It plans to raise the number of visitors to 70,000 by 2010 and boost tourism income to US$99 million a year.
In 2008 the governments of Democratic Republic of Congo, Rwanda and Uganda agreed to joint measures to protect the mountain gorillas found within their shared border regions. Tourists visiting the area to view the endangered great apes raise a combined US$5 million for the countries concerned.

Environment
In 2008 the governments of Democratic Republic of Congo, Rwanda and Uganda agreed to joint measures to protect the mountain gorillas found within their shared border regions. Tourists visiting the area to view the endangered great apes raise a combined US$5 million for the countries concerned. However, poaching and civil strife have dropped the numbers of gorillas to critically endangered levels, so that a 10-year conservation project which focuses of security and encouraging local people to preserve the animals and habitat is seen as the only hope for the gorilla's survival

Mining
The mining sector contributes 7 per cent to GDP and employs 1 per cent of the workforce.
Extraction of cassiterite (known reserves 90,000 tonnes) has been carried out since 1985, on an artisanal scale only.

Hydrocarbons
No significant reserves of hydrocarbons have been found in Rwanda, but oil exploration licences were issued in February 2009. All petroleum products must be imported, via Kenya/Uganda and Tanzania. Rwanda signed an agreement with Uganda in April 2008 to extend the proposed 320km Eldoret-Kampala (Kenya-Uganda) oil pipeline, construction of which began in April 2009, to be completed by 2012. The proposed oil pipeline will benefit Rwanda through the lower costs of transportation of imported oil.
There are around 70 billion cubic metres of methane gas in Lake Kivu, with a regenerative capacity of around 250 million cubic metres per annum. In 2009 Rwanda signed an agreement with the US company, Contour Global, to produce 100MW of energy from methane gas.
Natural gas and coal are neither produced nor imported.

Energy
Total installed generating capacity was 72.4MW in 2009, using hydropower, conventional thermal power and solar. Over 15MW of electricity is imported from the Ruzizi hydropower station located in Democratic Republic of Congo (DRC).
The World Bank has assisted Rwanda with funding for an urgent electricity rehabilitation project (2005–09), to improve generation and the power system to alleviate the numerous power cuts, including funds for a new thermal power station, which became operational in January 2009, producing an additional 20MW and designed to replace in part the country's extensive rented diesel generators. It also provided technical and administrative assistance as well as support in plans for future generation using renewable energies.
The potential for geothermal generation was estimated at 170–300MW and a preliminary assessment confirmed the prospects for development. An investigation, sponsored by the Belgium government,

into the development of wind farms will be undertaken shortly.
The US company Contour Global will produce 100MW of energy from methane gas by 2034, according to a 2009 agreement with the government. The gas will be extracted from Lake Kivu, in the western province, for electricity generation. A pilot project undertaken produced 2MW, 25MW will be produced by 2010 and 75MW by the end of 2012, all destined for the energy grid.
The Ministry of Infrastructure is responsible for energy policy and the state-owned company, Electrogaz, which is responsible for generation, transmission and distribution of energy. Only 6 per cent of the population has access to electricity, with an increase to 16 per cent by 2012. The remainder of the population and the subsistence-farming sector in particular currently relies on wood and charcoal.
The Ministry of Infrastructure is responsible for energy policy and the state-owned company, Electrogaz is responsible for generation, transmission and distribution of energy. Only 6 per cent of the population has access to electricity, with an increase to 16 per cent by 2012. The remainder of the population and the subsistence-farming sector in particular currently relies on wood and charcoal.

Financial markets
Stock exchange
A new securities exchange, the Rwanda Capital Market, was set up by the Central Bank of Rwanda in Kigali in January 2008. To begin with it will deal in domestic corporate and treasury bonds, although other products such as shares will be included as the operation develops. The exchange is seen as an alternative market for cheaper financing than that offered by commercial banks.

Banking and insurance
Central bank
Banque Nationale du Rwanda
Main financial centre
Kigali

Time
GMT plus two hours

Geography
Rwanda is a landlocked country in central Africa, just south of the Equator, bounded by the Democratic Republic of Congo to the west, where Lake Kivu (one of the Great Lakes) provides the border; Uganda is to the north, Tanzania to the east and Burundi in the south.
Rwanda has rolling hill terrain for most of its eastern region. However, a chain of rugged, volcanic mountains runs from the north-west south to the border with Burundi in the south-west. The highest peak is Mount Karisimbi (4,532 metres). To the west of the mountain range Lake Kivu flows into the Congo River basin through the Ruzizi River valley, a section of Africa's Great Rift Valley. The south is swamp and savannah, which, in the south-east, peters out into desert.
Hemisphere
Southern

Climate
Warm, tempered by altitude. Rainfall is low and is concentrated in two seasons from mid-January to mid-May, and mid-October to mid-December. Temperatures in Kigali range from 12–14 degrees Celsius (C) at night to 28–32 degrees C during the day. Cooler in the highland areas.

Entry requirements
Passports
Required by all. Passports must be valid for six months from date of visit.
Visa
Are required by all, except nationals of US, Germany, Canada, Uganda, Tanzania, Kenya, Burundi and the DRC for visits up to 90 days; entry permits are issued on arrival, when visitors must provide evidence of sufficient funds for stay and return/onward passage.
Business travellers or tourists staying for longer must apply for a visa. A business visa requires a letter of introduction by an employer stating purpose of visit. Contact the nearest Rwanda Consulate for further details.
Currency advice/regulations
Import and export of local currency is limited to a maximum Rwf5,000. Import of foreign currency is unlimited, but amounts should be declared; export is only allowed up to the amount declared.
Travellers cheques are not readily accepted.
Customs
Personal possessions are duty-free. Export of game trophies require agreement from the relevant authority.

Health (for visitors)
Mandatory precautions
Yellow fever vaccination certificate is required by all.
Advisable precautions
Hepatitis A, tetanus, typhoid and polio vaccinations. Malaria prophylaxis is recommended. Water precautions should be taken. Aids is prevalent. There is a rabies risk.

Hotels
Tend to be expensive in Kigali; cheaper in Butare, Gisenyi and Ruhengeri. Advisable to book in advance.

Public holidays (national)
Fixed dates
1 Jan (New Year's Day), 28 Jan (Democracy Day), 7 Apr (Genocide Memorial Day), 1 May (Labour Day), 1 Jul (Independence Day), 4 Jul (Liberation Day), 15 Aug (Assumption Day), 25 Sep (Republic Day), 1 Nov (All Saints Day), 25–26 Dec (Christmas).
Variable dates
Good Friday and Easter Monday (Mar/Apr).

Working hours
Banking
Mon–Fri: 0800–1200, 1400–1800; Sat: 0800–1300.
Business
Mon–Fri: 0800–1230, 1330–1700.
Government
Mon–Fri: 0800–1230, 1330–1700.
Shops
Dawn to dusk.

Telecommunications
Mobile/cell phones
A GSM900 coverage exists.

Electricity supply
220V AC

Security
The threat of attack from rebel groups continues and despite the cease-fire and elections in neighbouring DRC, the border regions are volatile. Local advice should be sought by those proposing to visit such areas; a military escort may be necessary. Kigali and major towns in the east, such as Butare and Gitarma, can be visited, but precautions need to be taken. Cars should not be left unattended in the centre of town and walking after dark or carrying large amounts of money or valuables is ill-advised.

Getting there
Air
National airline: Rwandair Express
International airport/s: Kigali-Kanombe (KGL), 12km east of city; duty-free shop, bar, currency exchange, post office, shops, coach, taxi service.
Airport tax: None
Surface
Road: Roads from Uganda,Tanzania and Burundi are well-surfaced.
Water: Although landlocked there is a link on Lake Kivu, between the north and south.
Main port/s: Gisenyi, Cyangugu.

Getting about
National transport
Air: Rwandair Express operates a limited internal service.
Road: All cities are linked to Kigali by paved roads, and the roads Ruhengeri-Cyanika and Kayonza-Kagitumba are paved. Other

roads are poor with many being impassable in bad weather.

Buses: Reliable regular bus services are available from Kigali to the main cities and between some cities themselves. Private minibuses (belonging to an association called ATRACO) also operate between Kigali and other cities.

Water: Services run between Gisenyi and Cyangugu, on Lake Kivu.

City transport

Taxis: They can be found in large towns; fares should be agreed at the start of journey and tipping is not necessary.

Car hire

Limited service is available in Kigali. International driving licence is required. All-weather roads are sparse and in poor condition.

BUSINESS DIRECTORY

The addresses listed below are a selection only. While World of Information makes every endeavour to check these addresses, we cannot guarantee that changes have not been made, especially to telephone numbers and area codes. We would welcome any corrections.

Telephone area codes

The international dialling code (IDD) for Rwanda is +250, followed by subscriber's number.

Chambers of Commerce

Fédération Rwandaise du Secteur Privé, PO Box 319, Kigali (tel: 583-538/41; fax: 583-532; e-mail: frsp@rwanda1.com).

Banking

Banque à la Confiance d'Or, BP 2059, Kigali (tel: 575-780, 75-763; fax: 575-761).

Banque Commerciale du Rwanda, BP 354, Boulevard de la Revolution, Kigali (tel: 575-591, 576-117; fax: 573-395).

Banque Continentale Africaine (Rwanda) SA, BP 331, 20 Kigali, Boulevard de la Revolution, Kigali (tel: 574-456/7/8; fax: 573-486).

Banque de Commerce, de Developpement et d'Industrie, BP 3268, Kigali (tel: 574-143, 574-132, 74-427; fax: 573-790, 74-479).

Banque de Kigali, BP 175, 63 Avenue du Commerce, Kigali (tel: 576-931/2/3/4; fax: 573-461, 75-504).

Banque Nationale du Rwanda, BP 531, Kigali (tel: 574-282, 575-249; fax: 572-551).

Banque Rwandaise de Developpment, BP 1341, Kigali (tel: 575-079, 575-080; fax: 573-569).

Campagne Generale de Banque, BP 5230, Kigali (tel: 586-875; fax: 586-876).

Union des Banques Populaires du Rwanda, BP 1348, Kigali (tel: 573-564; fax: 573-579).

Central bank

Banque Nationale du Rwanda, Avenue Paul VI, BP 531, Kigali (tel: 574-282; fax: 572-551; e-mail: webmaster@bnr.rw).

Travel information

Air France, BP 411, Kigali (tel: 575-566).

Rwandair Express, Ground & 2nd floor, Centenary House, Av de Revolution; BP 7275 Kigali (575-757, 503-687; fax: 503-686; internet: www.rwanda.com).

Office Rwandais du Tourisme et des Parcs Nationaux, BP 905, Kigali (tel: 576-514/5, 573-396; fax: 576-512; e-mail: Ortpn@rwandatel1.rwanda1.com).

Rwanda Travel Service, BP 140, Kigali (tel: 572-210).

Rwanda Explorations, BP 1514, Kigali (tel: 573-284).

Ministries

Ministry of Agriculture and Animal Resources, PO Box 621, Kigali (tel: 586-104; fax: 587-038; internet: www.minagri.gov.rw).

Ministry of Comerce, Industry, Investment, Promotion, Tourism and Co-operatives (tel: 574-725, 574-734; fax: 575-465; email: jnsengiyumva@minicom.gov.rw: internet: www.minicom.gov.rw).

Ministry of Education, Science, Technology and Scientific Research, BP 622 Kigali (tel: 583-051; fax: 582-161; email: info@mineduc.gov.rw).

Office of the Prime Minister, Kigali (tel: 585-444/5, 584-648; fax: 583-714; internet: www.primature.gov.rw).

Other useful addresses

Agence Rwandaise de Presse (ARP), 27 avenue du Commerce, BP 83, Kigali (tel: 575-665).

Economat Général (tobacco exports), BP 45, Ruhengeri.

L'Institut des Sciences Agronomiques du Rwanda, BP 138, Butare.

Office des Cafés, BP 104, Kigali (tel: 575-277).

Office du Pyrèthre au Rwanda, BP 79, Ruhengeri.

Office du Thé, BP 1344, Kigali (tel: 572-416).

Rwandan Embassy (USA), 1714 New Hampshire Avenue, NW, Washington DC 20009 (tel: (+1-202) 232-2882; fax: (+1-202) 232-4544; email: rwandemb@rwandemb.org).

Internet sites

General information: www.rwanda.net

Africa Business Network: www.ifc.org/abn

African Development Bank: www.afdb.org

Africa Online: www.africaonline.com

AllAfrica.com: http://allafrica.com

Mbendi AfroPaedia (information on companies, countries, industries and stock exchanges in Africa): http://mbendi.co.za

Official website of government of Rwanda: www.gov.rw

St Helena

KEY FACTS

Official name: St Helena Colony with Dependencies

Head of State: Queen Elizabeth II, represented by Governor and Commander-in-Chief Mark Andrew Capes (from 29 Oct 2011)

Ruling party: All members of the legislative council stand as independents

Area: 122 square km

Population: 4,250 (2010)*

Capital: Jamestown

Official language: English

Currency: St Helena pound (StH£) = 100 pence

Exchange rate: StH£0.64 per US$ (Oct 2011); (pegged to pound sterling)

GDP per capita: US$2,500 (2003)

Labour force: 3,500 (2003)

Unemployment: 14.00% (2003)

Inflation: 3.20% (2003)

Balance of trade: -US$14.43 million (2003)

* estimated figure

COUNTRY PROFILE

Historical profile

1502 St Helena was sighted by Portuguese mariners on 21 May (St Helena's Day).

1513 The island was first settled.

1633 The Dutch claimed possession.

1659 The East India Company took possession of the uninhabited island.

1673 The island was briefly captured by the Dutch, before being regained by the East India Company.

1815 Napoleon Bonaparte was exiled to the island, where he died in 1821; his body was returned to France in 1840.

1834 The island passed under British control.

1981 The Nationality Act ended the islanders' British citizenship and right of abode, which they had held since 1673.

1992 The islanders established a Citizenship Commission, which began its case to regain full British citizenship.

2002 Full British citizenship was restored to the islanders.

2004 Michael Clancy became Governor and Commander-in-Chief.

2005 An environmental team from the UK conducted the first stage of investigations required to carry out an Environmental Impact Assessment (EIA) for the proposed new airport on Prosperous Bay Plain.

2007 Andrew Gurr took office as governor.

2008 The UK government's plans to sponsor construction of the airport were halted.

2009 The proposed new constitution was debated in the Executive Council (Exco), but failed to be passed. Governor Gurr, in an article printed in the *St Helena Herald*, said that it was 'inarguable that our progress as an island will be held back if we remain stuck in the time warp of the existing 1988 constitution'. He also said that the UK Parliamentary under secretary of state at the foreign and commonwealth office would continue to consult with the elected members of the Exco, to ensure he had the most complete advice available before making a decision. Tristan da Cunha and Ascension Island have already voted in favour of the proposed changes. Elections for the Exco were held and the six candidates who won the most votes from both the East and West constituencies were elected.

2010 A Memorandum of Understanding (MoU) was signed between the UK's Department for International Development (DfID) and St Helena on 20 December. The signing indicated that both parties agreed on what St Helena intended to do to implement the reforms needed in preparation for the new airport. It was a wide ranging document and included a series of undertakings to see through substantial improvements in organisation, legislation and performance to stimulate local and inward investment related to the airport and tourism.

2011 At the end of June the Exco signed a MoU with the UK 'to implement the reforms necessary to open the island's economy to inward investment and increased tourism'. The act will simplify the requirements for non-St Helenians to enter, settle and work on the island and acquire land. On 23 September, Governor Gurr's term in office ended and Attorney General Ken Baddon was sworn in as acting governor on 24 September, until Mark Andrew Capes takes up the post in 29 October.

Political structure

St Helena has an appointed governor assisted by an Executive Council (the chief secretary, the financial secretary, attorney general and committee chairmen) and also by a Legislative Council (made up of the same ex-officio members and 12 elected members). Restoration for the islanders of full British citizenship was granted in May 2002.

The creation of a new overseas territories minister within the Foreign and Commonwealth Office (FCO) and the establishment of an Overseas Territories Consultative Council were both implemented in 1999, but responsibility for the British Overseas Territories, including St Helena, remains divided between the FCO and the Department for International Development.

Constitution

The 1988 St Helena Constitution Order came into force in February 1989. It sets out the separation of powers and the responsibilities of the executive, legislature and judiciary.

The proposed new constitution was debated in the Legislative Council (Legco) on 29 June 2009. The vote was four Elected Members in favour and four against; the Speaker voted against and the motion for change failed. Governor Gurr, in an article printed in the *St Helena Herald*, said that it was 'inargurable that our progress as an island will be held back if we remain stuck in the time warp of the existing 1988 constitution'. He also said that the UK Parliamentary under secretary of state at the foreign and commonwealth office would continue to consult with the Elected Members of the Legco, including the 4 members not present at the vote, to ensure he had the most complete advice available before making a decision. Tristan da Cunha and Ascension Island have already voted in favour of the proposed changes.

Form of state

As a British Overseas Territory, St Helena is a dependency of St Helena.

The executive

As a British Overseas Territory, St Helena has an appointed governor assisted by an Executive Council with three *ex-officio* appointments (the chief secretary, the financial secretary, attorney general and committee chairmen) and five elected members of the Legislative Council.

The creation of a new overseas territories minister within the Foreign and Commonwealth Office (FCO) and the establishment of an Overseas Territories Consultative Council were both implemented in 1999, but responsibility for the British Overseas Territories, including St Helena, remains divided between the FCO and the Department for International Development.

National legislature

The unicameral legislative assembly has 12 members elected for four-year terms. There are also three *ex-officio* appointments including the chief secretary, the financial secretary and the attorney general.

Last elections

4 November 2009 (Legislative Council)

Results: Legislative Council: the six candidates who won the most votes in both the East and West constituencies (12 in total) were elected, with a turnout of 58 per cent

Next elections

2013 (Legislative Council)

Political parties

No parties exist.

Ruling party

All members of the legislative council stand as independents

Political situation

St Helena, suffers from depopulation and dependency. As experienced by so many small communities, St Helena is losing too many of its young and potentially most valuable members to the outside world, even though families welcome the immediate value of remittances.

The goal the UK government towards its dependency is self-sufficiency. In its 2008 *Sustainable Development Plan* (SDP) it outlined six objectives necessary for future sustainability: improved access – there is no air access and sea connections are slow and costly; improved standard of education; development of a sustainable and vibrant economy; and promote and develop a sustainable workforce; develop a healthy community in a safe environment and establish the democratic and human rights and self-determination of the people of St Helena.

However even as it published its SDP the UK government halted plans to build an airport on St Helena, closing off one avenue of economic growth. Better education is a long-term objective but in the meantime newly qualified students and possible entrepreneurs are leaving and depriving the island of most of its talent.

Whether St Helena can reverse the stance by the new UK administration remains to be seen.

Population

4,250 (2010)*

Last census: 10 Febuary 2008: 4,255 (provisional)

Population density: 43.8 inhabitants per square km.

Annual growth rate: 0.5 per cent (2003)

Ethnic make-up

Black African (50 per cent), white (25 per cent), Chinese (25 per cent).

Religions

Anglican (majority), Baptist, Seventh-Day Adventist, Roman Catholic.

Main cities

Jamestown (capital, estimated population 1,500 in 2003).

Languages spoken

Official language/s

English

Media

Press

Weeklies: The *St Helena Herald* (www.news.co.sh) is government funded while *The St Helena Independent* (www.saint.fm/Independent/) is independent.

Business: A publication, giving sailing, details of the Royal Mail Service (RMS) ship *St Helena* (www.albionshipping.co.uk), which has a regular service to the island from UK and Cape Town. The Gulf and South Atlantic Fisheries Foundation publishes a newsletter concerning fishery matters (www.gulfsouthfoundation.org/newsletters).

Periodicals: The St Helena News Bureau publishes the periodical *St Helena and South Atlantic News Review* and the monthly *The St Helena Catalogue*.

Broadcasting

Radio: The government-funded Radio St Helena (www.news.co.sh) operates on short wave (AM) daily, with relays of a number of BBC World Service programmes. Saint FM (www.saint.fm) features music, local events and information.

Television: There is no locally made television service. Cable & Wireless provides a two channel television service relaying selected programmes from BBC World, CNN, Supersport, Discovery Channel and MNET, a South African commercial service.

Economy

St Helena depends on aid from the UK for between 20–25 per cent of its recurrent public sector budget. In 2010 the Department for International Development (DfID) provided over £20 million (US$31 million) in budgetary aid, educational support and development programmes among others. The St Helena Development Agency (SHDA) is a government sponsored agency set up to attract inward investment, help local business development, support start up schemes and encourage youth entrepreneurship.

Other means of income include fishing licence sales, local fishing catches, philatelic sales, coffee, livestock and timber, together with remittances from the estimated 1,700 offshore workers.

Andrew Weir Shipping Ltd manages the Royal Mail ship *RMS St Helena* which provides a regular re-supply service. Plans to build an airstrip were approved in a referendum held in 2002, but due to the rising cost planning was halted in 2008.

St Helena was originally developed as a re-victualling post for East India Company ships returning from the east. With the decline of sail from the 1870s, the island has struggled to find a basis for its economy. The production of New Zealand flax was started in 1874 and had some success during times of high world prices. However, St Helena's terrain is not suited to plantation cropping and the industry, heavily subsidised for most of its history, finally collapsed in 1966.

External trade

As a UK Overseas Territory St Helena is a part of the European Union's Association of Overseas Countries and Territories (OCT Association), and some EU laws apply.

The small quantity of coffee exported, three tonnes per year, produces one of the world's most expensive beverages.

Fishing licences and frozen and canned tuna provide most foreign earnings.

Imports

Principal imports are foodstuffs, tobacco, petroleum, animal feed, building materials, vehicles and parts, machinery and parts.

Main sources: UK (typically over 50 per cent of total), South Africa (10 per cent), Spain (10 per cent).

Exports

Principal exports are fish (frozen, canned, and salt-dried skipjack, tuna), coffee and handicrafts.

Main destinations: Tanzania (typically over 35 per cent of total), US 15 per cent, Japan 15 per cent.

Agriculture

Farming

St Helena's volcanic origins, hills and deep valleys dominate the landscape. Semi-desert gives way to upland grasslands and lush valleys over a very short distance.

Arable and garden land is about 3 per cent of the total area, forest and woodland 5 per cent, pasture 11 per cent, barren and badland 53 per cent. New Zealand flax (hemp) was grown until the 1960s, but much of this land is now planted with trees. Principal crops include potatoes, coffee, bananas, vegetables, sweet potatoes.

Livestock raising is a main activity but there is no dairy production and all dairy products are imported.

Agricultural production does not meet demand. Seed potatoes, onions and eggs are all imported in quantity.

Fishing

In the past, the government of St Helena earned StH£1.0 million (US$1.4 million) per annum from fishing licence revenue, but fish stocks have declined.

There is a local fishery run by the St Helena Fisheries Corporation, which buys the fish from the local fishermen.

The fishing boats range from eight to 13 metres in size and fish on a daily basis. They meet EU standards and carry ice with them. All of the catch is landed within 12 hours.

St Helena has satellite surveillance, but no patrol boat to stop unlicensed boats fishing the waters.

Industry and manufacturing

Local fishermen sell their catch to the St Helena Fisheries Corporation (a government parastatal). St Helena Fisheries Corporation sells its product in frozen and smoked form primarily to the UK and South Africa and supplies the domestic market.

Working in partnership with the St Helena Fisheries Corporation, Argos Helena Ltd, a joint UK-Spanish owned company, runs a blast freezer and fish processing/canning facility. Locally caught high-quality tuna is processed for export to the European Union and the Far East. The Corporation's fish products have organic certification from the Soil Association in the UK.

Tourism

St Helena has few resources and a declining population. Tourism is seen as a means of rescuing the island's economy and future. However, until the new airport is ready, access is restricted. Heavy seas make yachting anchorage unsafe.

The only means of reaching the island at the moment is by the RMS *St Helena*, which carries only 128 passengers on a round trip from UK (Portland) twice a year, and monthly from Cape Town to Walvis Bay (Namibia), St Helena and Ascension Island.

Although the rugged nature of the island has precluded air access, the possibility of constructing an airstrip is being investigated.

Tourism is a key target area in developing St Helena's economy. In June 2010 a Provisional Tourism Commission was appointed to oversee the future development of the tourist industry; in July a new Tourism Development Executive was appointed, as well as a Sales and Marketing Executive, who will be based in the UK and liaise closely with Andrew Weir Shipping Ltd to increase traffic on the *St Helena*.

Hydrocarbons

St Helena does not have any hydrocarbon reserves and relies entirely on the import of petroleum products to meet energy needs. St Helena does not import natural gas or coal.

Energy

The installation of a wind turbine in 2007, by the UK government, provided 240kW for the 1MW power grid, reducing the island's dependence on diesel fuel.

Time

GMT

Geography

St Helena is situated in the South Atlantic Ocean and is 1,950km (1,200 miles) due west from the south-west coast of Africa and 2,900km (1,800 miles) east of South America. The nearest land is one of its dependencies, Ascension Island, 1,130km (700 miles) to the north-west.

The island is of volcanic in origin. It is mountainous, presenting an almost continuous line of high, sheer cliffs, cut only by a few narrow and steep-sided valleys around its coastline. It is criss-crossed by deep valleys and slopes steeply from the central ridges to the sea. The highest point is Diana's Peak (820 metres above sea-level).

Hemisphere

Southern

Climate

Summer temperatures range from 21–29 degrees Celsius (C); winter 18–24 degrees C on coasts; inland temperatures may be five degrees lower; annual average rainfall in Jamestown is around 200mm, inland up to 950mm.

Entry requirements

Passports

Required by all.

Visa

All visiters must have the Administrator's written permission to land, before travelling. An *Ascension Island Entry Permit* form (valid for St Helena), to be completed, can be downloaded from www.ascension-island.gov.ac/visitors.htm. Entry is only granted with evidence of visitors full medical insurance policy, covering medical evacuation by air, when necessary.

Currency advice/regulations

Travllers cheques are accepted in the bank.

Customs

Prohibited imports

Obscene or pornographic materials are prohibited.

Firearms, ammunition, fruit, vegetables and plant materials require an import permit.

Health (for visitors)

There is one general hospital based in Jamestown and six health clinics on the island. The health service is not free and all St Helenians have to pay fees for medical treatment. UK Passport holders visiting the island pay local rates for medical treatment, while non-UK residents have to pay higher fees.

Mandatory precautions

None.

Hotels

There are three hotels on the island, reservations are necessary from December–March.

Credit cards

Major credit cards are accepted in a few locations.

Public holidays (national)

Fixed dates

1 Jan (New Year's Day), 21 May (St Helena Day), 25–26 Dec (Christmas).

Variable dates

Good Friday and Easter Monday (Mar/Apr), Pentecost (May/Jun), August Bank Holiday (last Mon in Aug).

Working hours

Banking

Mon–Sat: 0845/0900–1500/1600; except Thu: 0845–1200. Opening hours may be varied when a cruise ship is visiting.

Business

Mon–Fri: 0830–1230 and 1300–1600.

Government

Mon–Fri: 0830–1230, 1300–1600.

Shops

Mon–Sat: generally 0900–1700.

Getting there

Air

St Helena has no airport and can only be reached by sea. Wideawake Airfield on Ascension Island is the nearest airfield. It is a US military base, and will allow private air-charter access to Wakefield in 2007–08. Passengers for St Helena will need to transfer to a boat to reach the island.

Surface

Water: The *RMS St Helena* operates twice a year from the UK (Portland) and monthly from Cape Town to Walvis Bay (Namibia), St Helena and Ascension Island. The ship is operated under contract by Passenger Services Department, Andrew Weir Shipping Ltd (see travel information addresses).

Air connections can be made with the ship either through Cape Town, via commercial flights, or via military flights from Royal Air Force Brize Norton in Oxfordshire, UK to Ascension Island.

Main port/s: Jamestown

Getting about

National transport

Road: Road network of 80–85km classified as all-weather; at least further 60km surfaced and 25–30km suitable for dry-weather travel only. Roads are best described as steep and tortuous. Because most roads are single lane, motoring etiquette requires the driver coming down to make way for upcoming traffic.

BUSINESS DIRECTORY

The addresses listed below are a selection only. While World of Information makes every endeavour to check these addresses, we cannot guarantee that changes have not been made, especially to telephone numbers and area codes. We would welcome any corrections.

Telephone area codes

The international dialling code (IDD) for St Helena is +290 followed by subscriber's number.

Chambers of Commerce

St Helena Chamber of Commerce, c/o The Castle, Jamestown. (fax: tel: 22-58; fax: 25-98).

Banking

Bank of St. Helena, Post Office Building, Main Street, Jamestown STHL 1ZZ (tel: 2390; fax: 2553; internet: www.SaintHelenaBank.com).

Travel information

For air travel and bookings on the RMS St Helena:

Passenger Services Department, Andrew Weir Shipping Ltd, Dexter House, 2 Royal Mint Court, London EC N4XX, UK (tel: (+44-20) 575-6480; fax: (+44-20) 575-6200; e-mail: reservations@aws.co.uk).

St Helena Line, Andrew Weir Shipping (SA) Pty Ltd, 3rd Floor, BP Centre, Thibault Square, Cape Town, South Africa (tel: (+27-21) 425-1165; fax: (+27-21) 421-7485; e-mail: sthelenaline@mweb.co.za; internet site: www.aws.co.uk).

Miss Kerry Yon, Solomon and Co plc, Jamestown (tel: 2523; fax: 2423; e-mail: solco.shipping@helanta.sh).

National tourist organisation offices

St Helena Tourism, Jamestown (tel: 2158; fax: 2159; email: StHelena.Tourism @helanta.sh; internet: www.sthelenatourism.com).

Ministries

Governor's Office, The Castle, Jamestown (tel: 2555; fax: 2598; e-mail: OCS@helanta.sh).

Other useful addresses

Argos Atlantic Cold Stores, PO Box 151, Jamestown (tel: 2333; fax: 2334; e-mail: argos@argonaut.co.sh).

Cable & Wireless Fax Bureau, The Briars, Jamestown.

Director of Inward Investment, Office of the Chief Secretary, Government of St Helena, Jamestown (tel: 2470; fax: 2598; e-mail: DEPD@atlantis.co.ac).

Information Office, Broadway House, Jamestown (tel: 2612; fax: 2159; email: StHelena.Tourism@atlantis.co.ac).

Miles Apart (books, maps, videos on South Atlantic Islands), 5 Harraton House, Exning, Newmarket, Suffolk CB8 7HF, UK (tel: (+44-1638) 577-627: fax: (+44-1638) 577-874); 5929 Avon Drive, Bethesda, Maryland 20814, USA (tel/fax: (+1-301) 571-8942; e-mail: familycarter@msn.com).

The Postmistress, The Philatelic Bureau, The Post Office, Jamestown (fax: 2242).

St Helena Commercial Representative, Mr Wes Huxtable, 1 The Stables, Great Hyde Hall, Sawbridgeworth, Herts CM21 9JA, UK (tel: (+44-1279) 725-833; fax: (+44-1279) 724-894; e-mail: weston@huxtable.freeserve.co.uk).

St Helena Desk Officer, Foreign and Commonwealth Office, King Charles Street, London SW1A 2AH, UK (tel: (+44-20) 270-2695).

St Helena Development Agency, No 2 Main St, Jamestown (tel: 2920, fax: 2166, e-mail: shda@atlantis.co.uk).

The St Helena Link (cultural information), Trevor Hearl, 49 Noverton Lane, Prestbury, Cheltenham, Glos GL52 5DD, UK (tel/fax: +44 (0)1242-244-430).

Internet sites

East India Company (coffee): www.theeastindiacompany.com

St Helena Development Agency: www.shda.helanta.sh/

St Helena government: www.sainthelena.gov.sh

St Helena News: www.news.co.sh

St Helena web portal: www.sthelenaonline.com

St Kitts and Nevis

COUNTRY PROFILE

Historical profile

1623 Britain settled St Christopher (known as St Kitts), which became the first British colony in the West Indies.
1628 Nevis was settled by the British.
1816 Anguilla was joined to the territory.
1932 The St Kitts and Nevis Labour Party (SKNLP) was formed and campaigned for independence for the islands.
1958 St Christopher-Nevis-Anguilla became a member of the attempted West Indies Federation.
1962 The West Indies Federation was dissolved after the departure of Jamaica.
1967 St Christopher-Nevis-Anguilla, became a self-governing state in association with the UK. A House of Assembly replaced the Legislative Council, the administrator became governor and the chief minister became the state's first premier. The pro-independence SKNLP, became the ruling political party. The UK retained responsibility for defence and foreign relations.
1971 Anguilla reverted to being a British Dependent Territory after renouncing the rule of St Kitts.
1980 The SKNLP lost power to a coalition of the People's Action Movement (PAM) and the Nevis Reformation Party (NRP).
1983 Independence from Britain was attained.
1995 The SKNLP returned to power.
1997 The Nevis Island Assembly (NIA) elections were won by the Concerned Citizens' Movement (CCM).
1998 A referendum on independence for Nevis failed to achieve the two-thirds majority required for approval.
2000 The ruling SKNLP was re-elected and Denzil Douglas began a second term as prime minister.
2003 The largest hotel complex in the eastern Caribbean region opened at Frigate Bay.
2004 The NaturalSweet Corporation invested US$90 million for the cultivation and commercial development of stevia, a natural herbal plant. The ruling SKNLP won the parliamentary elections.
2005 The last harvest of sugar cane was delivered to the only remaining refinery, which ceased operations after the last run was made, and ended a centuries' old industry.
2006 The Nevis Reform Party (NRP) won NIA elections; Joseph Parry became prime minister of Nevis.
2008 Cotton lint from the first crop of Sea Island cotton since 2004 was ginned on Nevis. The total of 10,000kg was exported.
2009 An inquiry began into the governance of Nevis, particularly the financial instructions under which it was governed by the CCM party before 2006. A representative of the Japanese development fund visited Nevis and proposed financial assistance for an irrigation system in cotton production. Scheduled parliamentary elections were postponed until 2010. Basseterre was announced as the proposed headquarters of the Libyan Development Bank of the Eastern Caribbean.
2010 With only two week's official notice, a general election was held in January. The incumbent SKNLP won six seats out of 11 and continued in power; Prime Minister Douglas remained in office. Of the four new electricity generators delivered in August, two were in operation by November, producing an additional 15.6MW of power for St Kitts. The US-based airline, American Eagle, began daily flights between Puerto Rico and Nevis on 16 December.
2011 The NRP won NIA elections held on 11 July; Joseph Parry remained in post as premier of Nevis. On 1 August citizens of the Organisation of Eastern Caribbean States (OECS) – Antigua and Barbuda, Dominica, Grenada, St Kitts and Nevis, St Lucia and St Vincent and the Grenadines – were granted freedom of movement, allowing them to reside, work, establish businesses and provide services throughout the organisation.

Political structure

Constitution
The constitution of 1983 gives the island of Nevis considerable autonomy within a federal framework.

Form of state
Independent parliamentary democratic state; it is a member of the Commonwealth with the British monarch as head of state, represented by a governor general, who exercises executive power.
Nevis has limited self-government.

National legislature
The legislature is the National Assembly comprising 11 members elected for a

KEY FACTS

Official name: Federation of St Christopher and Nevis

Head of State: Queen Elizabeth II; represented by Governor General Sir Cuthbert Montroville-Sebastian (since 1996)

Head of government: Prime Minister Denzil Douglas (SKNLP) (since 1995; re-elected 25 Jan 2010)

Ruling party: St Kitts and Nevis Labour Party (SKNLP) (since 1995; re-elected 25 Jan 2010)

Area: 269 square km

Population: 54,841 (2010; census figure)

Capital: Basseterre (St Kitts)

Official language: English

Currency: East Caribbean dollar (EC$) = 100 cents

Exchange rate: EC$2.70 per US$ (fixed)

GDP per capita: US$9,636 (2010)

GDP real growth: -1.50% (2010)

GDP: US$531.00 million (2010)

Inflation: 2.50% (2010)

Balance of trade: -US$142.74 million (2010)

five-year term (eight from St Kitts, three from Nevis) plus three appointed members.
The cabinet headed by a prime minister is collectively responsible to the National Assembly.

Legal system

The legal system is based upon English common law. Appeals go to the Eastern Caribbean Supreme Court based on Saint Lucia. The final court of appeal is the Privy Council in the UK.

Last elections

25 January 2010 (National Assembly); 11 July 2011 (Nevis Island Assembly (NIA)

Results: National Assembly: the Labour Party won 46.96 per cent of the vote (six seats out of 11), the People's Action Movement 32.24 per cent (two), Concerned Citizen's Movement 10.99 per cent (two), Nevis Reformation Party 9.75 per cent (one); turnout was 81.24 per cent.
NIA: Nevis Reformation Party (NRF) won 50.2 per cent of the vote (three seats out of five), Concerned Citizen Movement 49.8 per cent (two); turnout was 81.2 per cent.

Next elections

2015 (National Assembly); 2016 (NIA)

Political parties

Ruling party

St Kitts and Nevis Labour Party (SKNLP) (since 1995; re-elected 25 Jan 2010)

Political situation

St Kitts and Nevis has not avoided the economic pressures following the global economic downturn and despite record export sales to the US in the first half of 2010 – US$25.7 million, up from US$48.4 million in 2009 – it still has to contend with the introduction of several new taxes, including value added tax (VAT) of 17 per cent from 1 November 2010.
In May 2010 trade negotiators of the Organisation of Eastern Caribbean States (OECS), including those of St Kitts and Nevis, had to discuss how the organisation was going to prepare for the removal of government subsidies for export, typically used to attract foreign direct investment, which will be removed by 2015, in accordance with World Trade Organisation (WTO) requirements.

Population

54,841 (2010; census figure)

Last census: May 2001: 45,841

Population density: 114 inhabitants per square km. Urban population: 34 per cent (1995–2001).

Annual growth rate: 0.5 per cent 1994–2004 (WHO 2006)

Ethnic make-up

Black African (91 per cent), mixed race (5 per cent), Asian (3 per cent), British, Portuguese and Lebanese descent (1 per cent).

Religions

Anglican (25 per cent), Methodist (25 per cent), Pentecostal (8 per cent), Moravian (7 per cent), other Protestant (12 per cent), Roman Catholic (7 per cent), Hindu (1 per cent).

Education

As part of an educational initiative, 2,400 laptops were delivered from Taiwan in August 2011, to be distributed to high school students (aged 14–16 years). Another batch of 2,400 is due in October–November for students aged 11–13 years.

Compulsory years: Five to 17

Enrolment rate: 101 per cent boys, 94 per cent girls gross primary enrolment of relevant age group (including repeaters) (Unicef 2004).

Health

Life expectancy: 71 years, 2004 (WHO 2006)

Fertility rate/Maternal mortality rate: 2.4 births per woman, 2004 (WHO 2006)

Birth rate/Death rate: 18.5 births per 1,000 population; nine deaths per 1,000 population (2003).

Child (under 5 years) mortality rate (per 1,000): 19 per 1,000 live births (World Bank)

Main cities

Basseterre (capital of St Kitts, estimated population 13,043 in 2005), Charlestown (capital of Nevis, 1,944).

Languages spoken

Official language/s

English

Media

Press

There are no daily newspapers. Weekly publications include *The Democrat* (www.pamdemocrat.org), *The Leewards Times* (www.leewardstimes.com), Sun St Kitts Nevis (http://sunstkitts.com), *The St Kitts and Nevis Observer* and the bi-weekly *Labour Spokesman* (www.labourworksforme.com).
A regional online publication Caribbean Net News (www.caribbeannetnews.com) covers news from St Kitts and Nevis.

Broadcasting

The government-owned commercial radio and television station is ZIZ (www.zizonline.com).

Radio: There are ten radio stations, including two government-owned ZIZ and Big Wave. Commercial stations on St Kitts include Sugar City Rock (www.sugarcityrock.com) Kyss FM (kyssonline.com) and on Nevis, Voice of Nevis (VON) (www.vonradio.com), Choice FM (http://choicefm1053.com) and Radio Paradise in Nevis.

Television: There is ZIZ Television which airs on two free cable channels and Winn FM (www.winnfm.com).

Economy

The economy of the islands is largely based on tourism, manufacturing and agriculture. The tourism sector is a major source of foreign exchange. Tourist numbers in 2009 increased, despite the depression in visitor numbers due to the global economic crisis, with cruise liner passenger numbers rising from 2,842 in 2008 to 12,516 in 2009. A new scheduled flight to St Kitts by British Airways also kept visitor numbers higher than could have been expected given the downturn in the tourist sector worldwide. Growth in

KEY INDICATORS — St Kitts and Nevis

	Unit	2006	2007	2008	2009	2010
Population	m	0.05	*0.05	*0.05	*0.05	0.05
Gross domestic product (GDP)	US$bn	0.50	0.51	0.57	0.56	0.53
GDP per capita	US$	9,569	9,883	10,764	10,315	9,636
GDP real growth	%	6.4	2.0	4.6	-5.5	-1.5
Inflation	%	8.5	4.5	5.4	2.0	2.5
Exports (fob) (goods)	US$m	58.3	57.7	69.0	57.6	57.9
Imports (fob) (goods)	US$m	219.6	239.5	285.8	266.0	200.7
Balance of trade	US$m	-161.3	-181.8	-216.9	-208.5	-142.7
Current account	US$m	-85.1	-111.3	-180.8	-184.8	-96.0
Total reserves minus gold	US$m	88.7	95.8	110.4	136.4	168.9
Foreign exchange	US$m	88.6	95.7	100.3	122.9	155.7
Exchange rate	per US$	2.70	2.70	2.70	2.70	2.70

* estimated figure

light manufacturing is constrained by shipping costs which at a time of high fuel costs has added up to 11 per cent to manufacturing costs since 2008. Traditional sugar cane cultivation ceased in 2005, with plantations being cleared for land development. As the agricultural sector is unable to feed the population imported food is a major drain on foreign reserves. Commercial agricultural production is led by tropical fruit and coconuts. The cultivation of cotton was re-introduced in 2008, after a gap of four years, when a valuable contract for over 3,200kg of cotton lint for export to Japan was agreed.
St Kitts belongs to the East Caribbean Currency Union, under the supervision of the Eastern Caribbean Central Bank (which is based in Basseterre), with a common currency (the EC$) and shared resources and reserves pooled for economic stability. It offers offshore banking and financial services.
GDP growth was 0.9 per cent in 2007, which rose to 2.4 per cent in 2008, before falling to a predicted -2.0 per cent in 2009 as the worldwide recession depressed the tourist sector and domestic demand was dampened. Inflation was 4.5 per cent in 2007, rising to 5.4 per cent in 2008 as the prices of imported petroleum and food rose, before falling back to a predicted 3.4 per cent as world prices dropped.

External trade

As a member of the Caribbean Community and Common Market (Caricom), St Kitts and Nevis operates within the single market (Caribbean Single Market and Economy (CSME)), which became operational in 2006. Goods, services, businesses and money are free to move within the CSME without barriers and tariffs. It is also a member of the Eastern Caribbean Currency Union (ECCU) using the East Caribbean Dollar (EC$).
Since the closure of the sugar industry exports have fallen sharply so that light manufacturing and tourism provides foreign earnings. The cultivation of cotton was re-introduced in 2008, after a gap of four years, when a valuable contract for over 3,200kg of cotton lint for export to Japan was agreed.

Imports

Main imports are food, machinery, manufactured goods, petroleum and derivatives.
Main sources: US (typically 59 per cent of total), Trinidad and Tobago (11 per cent), Japan (4 per cent).

Exports

Main exports are electrical appliances, electronic items and instrumentation, plastics, food and beverages and cotton.
Main destinations: US (typically 87 per cent of total), UK (2 per cent), Antigua and Barbuda (2 per cent).

Agriculture

Farming

The agricultural sector contributes around 3 per cent to GDP.
Historically, the most important crop had been sugar, however the sugar industry was closed down by the government and land re-deployed, although not necessarily for agricultural purposes.
Diversification into food crops has been encouraged to reduce dependence on imports.
The manufacture of cotton lint was re-introduced in 2008, after a gap of four years, when a valuable contracts for over 3,200kg of cotton lint for export to Japan were agreed. Old, retired ginnery equipment was renovated with new parts before the work could begin; when the operation is fully functional the machinery will be able to gin 900kg per day. Processing raw cotton began in 2008, however the only supply available came from government owned farms, after the first year of cotton cultivation, but supplies from private sources are expected to maintain the volume of production in future.

Fishing

Inshore fishing is a traditional occupation and a significant source of protein.
The fisheries management unit introduced new fishing methods resulting in a fish catch that increased over 40 per cent during the first year. Other improvements include a new fisheries complex, housing commercial storage and a fish market, constructed in Basseterre on St Kitts, while on Nevis the largest fishing facility includes a fish processing plant, walk-in freezers and market, is sited in Charlestown.

Industry and manufacturing

The industrial sector contributes around 24 per cent to GDP, with manufacturing contributing around 10 per cent.
Manufacturing activities have declined, with contraction in electrical and electronic components, due to poor US demand. The recession also led to a decline in domestic demand for locally produced manufactured goods.
In March 2004, the government approved a US$90 million investment plan by NaturalSweet Corporation to proceed with the cultivation and commercial development of stevia, a natural herbal plant, and construction of a plant to produce a dietary supplement.

Tourism

The two-island federation offers tourists a range of beach resorts that are not densely populated, but with leisure activities and quality dining. The industry is aimed at visitors from the US and Europe. However, in a move to open up its market base, it advertises regionally and in Asia and Australasia too.
The tourism sector was disrupted by external shocks beginning in 2007, at the beginning of the global economic crisis, when visitors from the US and Europe failed to arrive. As the crisis deepened so did the drop in tourism's contribution to GDP. In 2005, the tourism industry directly contributed 12.3 per cent of GDP, by 2009, at the lowest level during the crisis this figure had fallen to 7.1 per cent of GDP. Not only were visitor numbers down but their spending fell from US$121 million in 2005 to US$80 million in 2009.
In August 2011, St Kitts and Nevis was voted as the best Caribbean vacation destination and ranked sixth for affordable vacations. Visitors arriving by cruise liners make up around 80 per cent of all visitors, although air passengers stay for longer and use a greater variety of services and facilities.

Hydrocarbons

There are no known hydrocarbon reserves. Consumption was 1,000 barrels per day of oil in 2008, all of which was imported. In 2005, St Kitts and Nevis, plus a number of other Caribbean states, signed an agreement with Venezuela to establish PetroCaribe, a multi-national oil company, owned by the participating states. PetroCaribe buys low-priced Venezuelan crude oil under long-term payment plans.
The planned natural gas pipeline from Trinidad and Tobago linking the Caribbean islands could mean St Kitts and Nevis will be able to import natural gas in the future.

Energy

Total installed generating capacity was 20MW in 2007, producing over 130 million kilowatt hours.. The Nevis Electricity Company (Nevlec) provides energy for both islands. Plans for the commercial development of a geothermal-fuelled power plant, developed by the Eastern Caribbean Geothermal Development Project (ECGDP) (or Geo-Caraïbes) which is estimated will provide 60–120MW overall, will be operated by the West Indies Power Limited (WIPL), which is owned by ECGDP countries. The government invested US$22 million in infrastructure and the purchase of four new 4MW electricity generators, delivered in 2010. Two were operational in Basseterre in November 2010 producing an additional 15.6MW of power for St Kitts and the remaining two became operational in 2011.

Energy from biomass is being considered. The sugar cane industry was closed down as uneconomical, but with the rise in hydrocarbon prices ethanol from sugar cane is seen as an alternative and a study to determine the viability of a limited revival of the sugar cane industry is underway.

Financial markets
Stock exchange
Eastern Caribbean Securities Exchange (ECSE)

Banking and insurance
The state-owned Development Bank provides credit to finance agriculture, industry, education and mortgages.
The seven members of the Organisation of Eastern Caribbean States (OECS), Antigua and Barbuda, Dominica, Grenada, Montserrat, St Kitts and Nevis, St Lucia and St Vincent and the Grenadines, share a common currency and central bank. The British Virgin Islands and Anguilla are associate members.
Central bank
East Caribbean Central Bank (ECCB)
Main financial centre
Bassetterre
Offshore facilities
After St Kitts and Nevis was listed by the OECD as a tax haven which was unco-operative in fighting money laundering, the government passed the Money Laundering (Prevention) Bill, the Financial Services Intelligence Unit Bill and the Financial Services Commission Bill. The latter Bill established the Financial Services Commission as the main regulatory body for the offshore sector.

Time
GMT minus four hours

Geography
St Kitts and Nevis is situated at the northern end of the Leeward Islands chain of the West Indies, with Saba and St Eustatius (both in the Netherlands Antilles) to the north-west, Barbuda to the north-east and Antigua to the south-east. Nevis lies about 3km (2 miles) to the south-east of St Kitts, separated by a narrow strait.
They are rugged volcanic islands covered with either original rich tropical rainforests or cultivated sugar cane plantations. St Kitts has a large crater, Mount Liamuiga, of 1,200 metres (m) high. In the south-east a peninsula stretches into the Caribbean Sea. Nevis is a circular island with a range of mountains. The highest peak, Mount Nevis, is 985m high.
Hemisphere
Northern

Climate
Tropical, tempered by trade winds, with an annual mean temperature of 27 degrees Celsius. December–April are the driest months. Rain can occur throughout the year, although generally wetter from May–October.

Entry requirements
Passports
Required by all except Canadian or US nationals with proof of identity (all US and Canadian nationals require a passport for re-entry to their country from January 2007). Passports must be valid for at least six months after date of entry.
Visa
Required by all with some exceptions; see www.gov.kn and follow link to *Information for non-citizens*, to view a list of those who require a visa and to download an application form. From May 2009 EU citizens may make a short-stay visit, for up to three months, without a visa.
Further information should be obtained from the nearest consulate.
Currency advice/regulations
The import of local and foreign currency is unlimited but must be declared; export of either is limited to the amount declared on arrival.
Travellers cheques in major currencies are widely accepted.

Health (for visitors)
Mandatory precautions
Vaccination certificates for yellow fever and cholera required when travelling from infected areas.
Advisable precautions
Typhoid, polio vaccinations. Water precautions.

Hotels
Advisable to book in advance. A 9 per cent room tax is added to bills and 10 per cent service charge usual.

Credit cards
Major credit and charge cards are widely accepted. ATMs are widely available.

Public holidays (national)
Fixed dates
1 Jan (New Year's Day), 2 Jan (Carnival Day), 1 May (Labour Day), 12 Jun (Queen's Birthday), 19 Sep (Independence Day), 25–26 Dec (Christmas).
Variable dates
Good Friday and Easter Monday (Mar/Apr), Whit Monday (May/June), Queen's Official Birthday (second Sat in Jun), August Monday (first Mon in Aug).

Working hours
Banking
Mon–Thu: 0800–1400; Fri: 0800–1600; Sat: 0830–1100.
Business
Mon–Fri: 0800–1200, 1300–1600/1630. Businesses generally close Thu afternoons and open Sat: 0800–1600.
Government
Mon–Fri: 0800–1200, 1300–1600/1630.

Telecommunications
Mobile/cell phones
There are 850/1900 and 900/1800 GSM services in operation.

Electricity supply
220V AC, 60 cycles. (Some hotel supplies are at 110V AC.)
Electricity is supplied from diesel engine generators and is available island-wide.

Getting there
Air
There are no direct intercontinental flights, only flights from regional hubs land in St Kitts or Nevis.
International airport/s: Robert Llewellyn Bradshaw International Airport (RLB), 3.2km from Basseterre, duty-free shop, restaurant, hotel reservations.
Taxis from the airport have regulated fares.
Other airport/s: Newcastle Airfield (NEV), 11km from Charlestown on Nevis.
Airport tax: Departure tax: EC$60
Surface
Water: There are regular ferry services between St Maarten and St Kitts. Cruise ships visit.
Main port/s: Basseterre (St Kitts) has a deep-water harbour, Charlestown (Nevis).

Getting about
National transport
Road: There is a 300km road network. Main routes cover perimeters of both islands.
In 2006 a new by-pass to reduce traffic congestion in Basseterre was opened. It was funded through a loan of US$7.56 million by the Caribbean Development Bank (CDB).
Buses: Privately operated buses provide a regular but unscheduled service.
Water: There are regular daily ferry services between the islands of St Kitts and Nevis.
City transport
Taxis: Serve both islands with set fare systems; 10 per cent tip usual.
Car hire
It is advisable to reserve a hire car well in advance. National licence required in order to obtain visitor's temporary licence. Traffic drives on the left.

BUSINESS DIRECTORY

The addresses listed below are a selection only. While World of Information makes every endeavour to check these addresses, we cannot guarantee that changes have not been made, especially to telephone numbers and area codes. We would welcome any corrections.

Telephone area codes
The international direct dialling code (IDD) for St Kitts and Nevis is +1 869, followed by subscriber's number.

Useful telephone numbers
Emergency: 911
Fire: 333
Air Ambulance: 465-2801
JNF General Hospital: 465-2551

Chambers of Commerce
St Kitts/Nevis Chamber of Industry and Commerce, South Independence Square, PO Box 332, Basseterre (tel: 465-2980; fax: 465-4490; e-mail: skchamber@caribsurf.com).

Banking
Bank of Nevis, The Main Street, Box 450, Charlestown, Nevis (tel: 469-5564/5796; fax: 469-5798).

Bank of Nova Scotia, Fort Street, Box 433, Basseterre, St Kitts (tel: 465-4141; fax: 465-8600).

Barclays Bank, The Circus, Box 42, Basseterre, St Kitts (tel: 465-2519/10/2449/1081/2264; fax: 465-1041).

Development Bank of St. Kitts & Nevis, Church Street, Box 249, Basseterre, St. Kitts (tel: 465-2288/2964/4041; fax: 465-4016).

National Bank, Central Street, Box 343, Basseterre, St Kitts (tel: 465-2204; fax: 465-1050).

Nevis Co-Op Banking Company, Chapel Street, Box 60, Charlestown, Nevis (tel: 469-5277/0113/4; fax: 469-1493).

Royal Bank of Canada, Cnr Bay Road & Fort Street, Box 91, Basseterre, St Kitts (tel: 465-2259/2409/2389/4374; fax: 465-1040).

Central bank
Eastern Caribbean Central Bank, Bird Rock Road, PO Box 89, Basseterre (tel: 465-2537; fax: 465-5615; email: info@eccb-centralbank.org).

Stock exchange
Eastern Caribbean Securities Exchange (ECSE): www.ecseonline.com

Travel information
Nevis Tourism Bureau, Charlestown, Nevis (tel: 469-1042; fax: 469-1066).

St Kitts-Nevis Hotel and Tourism Association, PO Box 438, Basseterre, St Kitts (tel: 465-5304; fax: 465-7746).

Ministry of tourism
Ministry of Trade, Industry and Tourism (National Development Corporation), Government Headquarters, Basseterre (tel: 465-2521, 465-4106; fax: 465-5202, 465-1778).

National tourist organisation offices
St Kitts-Nevis Department of Tourism, Pelican Mall, PO Box 132, Basseterre, St Kitts (tel: 465-2620; fax: 465-4040).

Ministries
Ministry of Agriculture, Lands, Housing and Development, Education, Youth and Community Affairs, Government Headquarters, PO Box 186, Basseterre (tel: 465-2521; fax: 465-9069).

Ministry of Finance, Marketing and Development Department, Rams Building, Liverpool Row, Basseterre, St Kitts (tel: 465-1153; fax: 465-1154).

Ministry of Health, Labour and Women's Affairs, Government Headquarters, Basseterre (tel: 465-2521; fax: 456-1316).

Office of The Prime Minister, Government Headquarters, PO Box 186, Basseterre (tel: 465-2103; fax: 465-1001).

Other useful addresses
Attorney General's Office, Government Headquarters, Basseterre (tel: 465-2521; fax: 465-5202).

Eastern Caribbean Securities Exchange, PO Box 94, Bird Rock, Basseterre (tel: 466-7192; fax: 465-3798; email: Info@ECSEonline.com).

Financial Services Department, PO Box 186, Basseterre (tel: 466-5048; fax: 466-5317; internet: www.fsd.gov.kn).

Government Offices, Administration Building, Charlestown (465-5521; fax: 465-5202).

Investment Promotion Agency, Bay Road, Basseterre (tel: 465-4106).

Embassy of St Kitts and Nevis (USA), OECS Bldg, 3216 New Mexico Ave, NW Washington DC 20016 (tel: (+1-202) 686-2636; fax: (+1-202) 686-5740).

St Kitts-Nevis Information Service, Government Headquarters, Church Street, Basseterre (tel: 465-2521; fax: 466-4504; email: skninfo@caribsurf.com; internet: www.gov.kn).

St Kitts-Nevis Manufacturers' Association, PO Box 392, Basseterre (tel: 465-6226).

Internet sites
Caribbean Export Development Agency: www.cartis.com/

Government website: www.gov.kn

Organisation of American States: www.oas.org

St Lucia

KEY FACTS

Official name: St Lucia

Head of State: Queen Elizabeth II; Governor General Dame Calliopa Pearlette Louisy (since 1997)

Head of government: Prime Minister Prime Minister Stephenson King (UWP) (from Sep 2007)

Ruling party: United Workers Party (UWP) (elected Dec 2006)

Area: 616 square km

Population: 173,720 (2010; census figure)

Capital: Castries

Official language: English

Currency: East Caribbean dollar (EC$) = 100 cents

Exchange rate: EC$2.70 per US$ (fixed)

GDP per capita: US$5,668 (2010)

GDP real growth: 0.80% (2010)

GDP: US$985.00 million (2010)

Inflation: 1.80% (2010)

Balance of trade: -US$315.16 million (2010)

COUNTRY PROFILE

Historical profile

1605 Britain made an unsuccessful attempt to colonise the islands which were populated by a Carib people.
1642 France claimed sovereignty.
1814 After changing hands 14 times during the seventeenth and eighteenth centuries, St Lucia became a British colony. It formed part of the Windward Islands.
1924 A representative government was introduced.
1936 A constitution was provided with a legislative council of elected representatives.
1951 The first elections, under universal adult suffrage, were won by the St Lucia Labour Party (SLP).
1958 St Lucia joined the UK-sponsored West Indies Federation.
1962 The West Indies Federation was dissolved.
1964 Sugar cane production was abandoned.
1967 St Lucia became a self-governing associated state, with full autonomy over internal affairs. The UK retained control of foreign affairs and defence.
1979 St Lucia gained independence within the Commonwealth.
2002 Hurricane Lili destroyed around half of the annual banana crop.
2003 An amended constitution replaced the oath of allegiance to the British monarch with a pledge of loyalty to St Lucia. Julian Hunte, St Lucia's foreign minister, was elected president of the UN General Assembly's June session, the smallest country ever to lead the 191-member world body.
2004 The Caribbean Development Bank (CDB) approved a loan to help St Lucia build infrastructure against flooding in coastal cities.
2006 Air Jamaica introduced non-stop flights from New York. The opposition United Workers Party (UWP) won 11 seats (out of 17) in parliamentary elections, the incumbent SLP won six. Sir John Compton became prime minister.
2007 Diplomatic relations with Taiwan were re-established, after a 10-year break. Prime Minister Sir John Compton died and Stephenson King was elected prime minister by the ruling UWP.
2009 The EU signed an agreement with the government to provide financial assistance to fund a US$100 million general hospital, with a 122-bed facility. The first national forest inventory since the 1980s began, aimed at providing a current comprehensive survey of forest resources, including trees, animals and birds.
2011 On 20 June, the World Bank agreed to a zero interest loan of US$5.6 million to fund an improved electricity distribution system and to diversify energy production (including renewable energy sources). On 1 August citizens of the Organisation of Eastern Caribbean States (OECS) – Antigua and Barbuda, Dominica, Grenada, St Kitts and Nevis, St Lucia and St Vincent and the Grenadines – were granted freedom of movement, allowing them to reside, work, establish businesses and provide services throughout the organisation.

Political structure

Independence date
22 February 1979

Form of state
Parliamentary democracy

The executive
The British monarch is Head of State and represented by the governor general. The prime minister exercises executive power.

National legislature
The bicameral parliament has a House of Assembly with 17 members directly elected in single-member constituencies, for five-year terms. The Senate has 11 nominated members, six appointed by the prime minister, three by the leader of the opposition and two chosen by the governor general.
Universal age of suffrage 18.

Legal system
The legal system is a hybrid of English common law with a strong influence of French civil law.
Appeals are heard by the Eastern Caribbean Supreme Court. The final court of appeal is the Judicial Council of the Privy Council in the UK.

Last elections
December 2006 (parliamentary)
Results: Parliamentary: the United Workers Party (UWP) won 11 out of the 17 seats total, and the St Lucia Labour Party (SLP) won six.

Next elections
December 2011 (parliamentary)

Political parties
Ruling party
United Workers Party (UWP) (elected Dec 2006)
Main opposition party
St Lucia Labour Party (SLP)

Population
173,720 (2010; census figure)
Last census: May 2000: 157,164
Population density: 253 inhabitants per square km. Urban population: 38 per cent (1995—2001).
Annual growth rate: 0.9 per cent 1994–2004 (WHO 2006)
Ethnic make-up
Black African (90 per cent), mixed race (6 per cent), East Indian (3 per cent).
Religions
Roman Catholic (90 per cent), Anglican (3 per cent) other Protestant (7 per cent).

Education
The education system is in great need of reform. Hampering the development of the island's education is the instructor-led method of learning but there has been little attempt to progress to a more learner-orientated approach.
The secondary education system will benefit from the construction of two new schools, with allocated funds of US$23 million, in 2005/06. The new facilities, one geared to the arts and the other towards agriculture and science will provide places for over 700 students. The government is aiming to achieve universal secondary education and has been aided by the World Bank Education Development Plan.
Compulsory years: 4 to 16.
Enrolment rate: 101 per cent primary and 85 per cent secondary enrolment; 111 per cent and 104 per cent enrolment respectively of boys and girls of relevant age group (including repeaters) (Unicef 2004).

Health
The provision of healthcare will be changed within 2005/06 when the environment levy will be replaced with a fixed tax on consumer goods of between 3.5–4 per cent and will be called the health and environment levy. It is expected to raise US$11 million to fund services for most of the population.
The government is concerned about the loss of medical personnel. Nurse migration, due to low pay, lack of opportunities and poor working conditions, has left Victoria Hospital the principal hospital facility chronically understaffed.
The European Commission has granted US$23 million in 2005 for a new hospital to replace Victoria Hospital, to be built on a new site. Construction is scheduled to begin in early 2006.

HIV/Aids
The Caribbean has the second highest rate of HIV/aids infection, after sub-Saharan Africa and the impact on the economy is already being felt with St Lucia losing around US$74 million since the mid-1980s. In 2005 the Global Fund to Fight Aids approved a grant of US$10.1 million, over 2005–10, to help St Lucia fight the epidemic. The programme is targetting a 50 per cent reduction in HIV patients and HIV/Aids deaths as well as mother-to-infant transmission reduced from 30 per cent to less than 10 per cent.
Life expectancy: 74 years, 2004 (WHO 2006)
Fertility rate/Maternal mortality rate: 2.2 births per woman, 2004 (WHO 2006)
Child (under 5 years) mortality rate (per 1,000): 16 per 1,000 live births (World Bank)

Welfare
The social welfare system in St Lucia has been described as unfair, partial and out of touch with social realities and legislation is out of date. The Catholic Church run homes for the elderly and assistance is provided to the needy. There is no law protecting children born outside of marriage with regard to their property rights and no laws against sexual harassment.

Main cities
Castries (capital, estimated population 12,196 in 2005).

Languages spoken
English and French patois.
Official language/s
English

Media
Press
Weeklies: There are no daily newspapers, weeklies include *The Vanguard*, *The Voice of St Lucia* published on Wednesday and *The Crusader* and *The Star* (www.stluciastar.com), appear on Saturday. Online publications *Saint Lucia One Stop* (www.sluonestop.com) a local news service covering local news and business and *St Lucia Mirror* (www.stluciamirroronline.com) and *One Caribbean* (www.onecaribbeanmedia.net), based in Trinidad. Another regional online publication is Caribbean Net News (www.caribbeannetnews.com), which reports news from St Lucia.
The *Saint Lucia Nationwide*(www.stlucia.gov.lc – follow link from NTN) is published weekly by the Department of Information Services concerning government news and notices.
Broadcasting
Radio: In 2004 a radio service – Radio Caricom, the Voice of the Caribbean Community – was launched with St Lucia being one of the 'pilot states' in the project, which eventually will be available to all Caricom member states.
Commercial radio stations includes Radio Saint Lucia (RSL) (www.rslonline.com) is government-owned, Radio 100 (www.htsstlucia.com), affiliated to HTS, and Hot FM (www.caribbeanhotfm.com)
Television: The three networks are private, Daher Broadcasting service (DBS), Catholic Broadcasting (CBTN) and the commercial Helen Television Systems (HTS) (www.htsstlucia.com), which also runs a radio station. For a fee, there is cable television providing 40 channels of international and local viewing.

KEY INDICATORS — **St Lucia**

	Unit	2006	2007	2008	2009	2010
Population	m	0.17	0.17	0.17	*0.17	0.17
Gross domestic product (GDP)	US$bn	0.93	0.96	1.00	0.97	0.98
GDP per capita	US$	5,546	5,700	5,863	5,671	5,668
GDP real growth	%	5.0	1.5	0.7	-5.2	0.8
Inflation	%	3.6	1.9	7.2	0.6	1.8
Exports (fob) (goods)	US$m	116.0	101.2	165.7	183.0	206.4
Imports (fob) (goods)	US$m	524.0	541.7	604.8	474.8	521.5
Balance of trade	US$m	-408.0	-440.5	-439.1	-291.7	-315.2
Current account	US$m	-298.0	-344.7	-346.6	-187.1	-150.5
Total reserves minus gold	US$m	134.5	153.7	142.8	174.8	206.3
Foreign exchange	US$m	132.2	151.2	140.3	150.6	182.3
Exchange rate	per US$	2.70	2.70	2.70	2.70	2.70

* estimated figure

Economy

With an economy that is largely governed by the vagaries of the tourist industry St Lucia is vulnerable to external shocks. The spending capacity of foreign visitors, which may be limited by their domestic economy, plus internal problems such as hurricane damage or rising world commodity prices, can combine to make directing the economy more a reactive than a proactive process.

Banana production is the other main contributor to GDP. Under an agreement with the European Union bananas were exported to the EU under preferential access measures. However, after 15 years of dispute with the World Trade Organisation (WTO), in December 2009 the EU agreed to end the preferential treatment of former colonial countries and cut (REMOVE? OR REDUCE?) quotas to Latin American countries. Nevertheless, financial support continues to be offered to banana growers to help them adjust to the new trading regime. By 2008 St Lucia supplied less than 50,000 tonnes of bananas to the EU, down by around 10,000 tonnes since 1999. Other cash crops include mangoes and avocados; a lucrative deal was signed in 2005 to supply over 25 tonnes of cocoa beans to a leading US chocolate manufacturer. Other development projects focus on computer-driven information technology.

GDP growth had been 5.0 per cent in 2006, boosted by the Cricket World Cup which saw increased construction of sporting and tourist facilities. Foreign direct investment (FDI) was 25.1 per cent in 2006 and 26.4 per cent of GDP in 2007. However, GDP growth fell to 1.7 per cent in 2007, due to the contraction in banana exports following damage during the hurricane season. FDI fell to 10.6 per cent of GDP in 2008 as GDP growth slowed further to 0.7 per cent and the global economic crisis cut the number of tourists visiting the island. The economy fell into recession in 2009 with growth of -2.5 per cent. Inflation peaked at 7.2 per cent in 2008, but fell to 3.2 per cent by the end of March 2009, with the annual inflation rate falling to 0.6 per cent, as domestic demand fell sharply and world commodity prices stabilised.

As public expenditure rose in 2009 the government introduced revenue enhancing measures such as increased petrol prices and a value added tax (VAT); although VAT had still not been instigated as of May 2010.

External trade

As a member of the Caribbean Community and Common Market (Caricom), St Lucia operates within the single market (Caribbean Single Market and Economy (CSME)), which became operational in 2006. Goods, services, businesses and money are free to move within the CSME without barriers and tariffs. It is also a member of the Eastern Caribbean Currency Union (ECCU) using the East Caribbean Dollar (EC$).

Foreign earnings are principally generated by tourism, as Saint Lucia is a prime yachting centre and cruise destination, and remittances. The small manufacturing sector is diverse producing clothing, processed coconuts, electronic components and beverages.

Imports

Main imports are food, manufactured goods, machinery and transport equipment, chemicals and fuels.

Main sources: US (typically 43 per cent of total), Trinidad and Tobago (24 per cent), Japan (4 per cent).

Exports

Main exports are bananas, clothing, cocoa, vegetables, fruits and coconut oil.

Main destinations: US (typically 34 per cent of total), Trinidad and Tobago (23 per cent), UK (15 per cent).

Agriculture

Farming

The agricultural sector used to be the mainstay of the economy, but has been overtaken by tourism. Over 50 per cent of the total area is cultivated arable land. The main export crop is bananas and St Lucia continues to be the leading Windward Island banana producer. However, the EU no longer offers preferential treatment for St Lucia exports and St Lucia will have to work hard to maintain export levels in the face of stiff competition from larger Central and South American plantations.

Diversification into other cash crops has been encouraged. A multimillion-dollar deal was signed between St Lucia and the World's Finest Chocolate Inc to supply 256,800 kilograms of cocoa beans a year. There has been an increase in non-banana agriculture production, in particular in copra cultivation, which has resulted in increased exports of coconut oil to Jamaica. Also grown are traditional fruits and vegetables for the domestic and regional markets, and tree crops, such as mangoes and avocados.

Fishing

The typical total annual fish catch is over 2,000t, shellfish, molluscs and cephalopods account for another 77t per annum.

Industry and manufacturing

The manufacturing sector is negligible and manufacturing activity is dominated by food and drinks production, electrical products and corrigated paper production.

Tourism

Tourism has become the most important sector generating most activity in St Lucia's economy. Travel and tourism represents over 40 per cent of the country's economy.

The Cricket World Cup will be held on the island in 2007, and several projects are designed to be completed to accommodate sports fans. Three new developments will add greatly to St Lucia's capacity for tourism. Eco-tourism will benefit from a new aerial tram project that provides a raised, suspended ride through the rain-forest canopy in the Babonneau forest.

Hydrocarbons

There are no known hydrocarbons reserves; all petroleum products must be imported, which in 2008 were 3,000 barrels per day of oil. In 2005, St Lucia, plus a number of other Caribbean states, signed an agreement with Venezuela to establish PetroCaribe, a multi-national oil company, owned by the participating states. PetroCaribe buys low-priced Venezuelan crude oil under long-term payment plans.

Energy

Total installed generating capacity was 80MW in 2007. St Lucia is committed to investment in renewable energy sources including a 4.25MW wind farm, 400KW biomass (methane), geothermal, solar and hybrid projects of any combination. Hydropower offers the greatest potential for energy with conventional technology and new ocean thermal energy conversion (otec).

The government-owned utility company, Lucelec, is responsible for generation, transmission and distribution of electricity. The main power station is Cul de Sac, south of Castries with a hydroelectric dam in Roseau and a geothermal project in Soufrière.

Plans for the commercial development of a geothermal-fuelled power plant, developed by the Eastern Caribbean Geothermal Development Project (ECGDP) (or Geo-Caraïbes) which is estimated will provide 60–120MW overall, will be operated by the West Indies Power Limited (WIPL), which is owned by ECGDP countries.

On 20 June 2011, the World Band agreed to a zero interest loan of US$5.6 million to fund an improved electricity distribution system and diversity of energy production (including renewable energy sources).

Financial markets

Stock exchange

Eastern Caribbean Securities Exchange (ECSE)

Banking and insurance
The seven members of the Organisation of Eastern Caribbean States (OECS), Antigua and Barbuda, Dominica, Grenada, Montserrat, St Kitts and Nevis, St Lucia and St Vincent and the Grenadines, share a common currency and central bank. The British Virgin Islands and Anguilla are associate members.
Central bank
Eastern Caribbean Central Bank, St Kitts and Nevis
Offshore facilities
St Lucia is a relatively new entrant to the offshore financial sector. The Organisation for Economic Co-operation and Development (OECD) removed St Lucia from its blacklist of non-complainant government implementing anti-money laundering legislation after St Lucia introduced measures consistent with the OECD's call for transparency in the banking sector.

Time
GMT minus four hours

Geography
St Lucia is in the Windward Islands group of the West Indies, 40km (25 miles) to the south of Martinique and 32km (20 miles) to the north-east of St Vincent, in the Caribbean Sea. The island is volcanic, with spectacular mountain scenery.
Hemisphere
Northern

Climate
The mean annual temperature is 26 degrees Celsius. The island is cooled by the north-east trade winds. The weather is driest from January–April. The rainy season is from July–October.

Entry requirements
Passports
Required by all, except US, Canadian, French and UK citizens who possess valid identification, return tickets and are staying for less than eight days (all US and Canadian nationals require a passport for re-entry to their country from January 2007).
Visa
Requirements vary for citizens, country by country. See www.stlucia.gov.lc under *FAQ*, see *Do I need a Visa?* for a full list and procedures, plus an application form to be downloaded.
Currency advice/regulations
The import and export of local and foreign currency is unrestricted.
Travellers cheques, in US dollars, are widely accepted.

Health (for visitors)
Mandatory precautions
Yellow fever vaccination certificate required if arriving from an infected area.
Advisable precautions
Typhoid, polio vaccination. Medical services are limited. Travel insurance is essential, including cover for repatriation. Hospitalisation is costly and doctors often expect immediate cash payment before treatment begins.

Hotels
Bills include 8 per cent tax and usually a 10 per cent service charge.

Credit cards
Major credit and charge cards are accepted in large shopping areas. ATMs are widely available.

Public holidays (national)
Fixed dates
1–2 Jan (New Year), 22 Feb (Independence Day), 1 May (Labour Day), 1 Aug (Emancipation Day), 13 Dec (St Lucia Day), 25–26 Dec (Christmas).
Variable dates
Good Friday, Easter Monday, Whit Monday, Corpus Christi (May/Jun), Thanksgiving Day (first Mon in Oct).

Working hours
Banking
Mon–Thu: 0800–1400, Fri: 0800–1700. Banks are closed on weekends and public holidays. The Bank of Saint Lucia and First National Bank open Sat 0800–1200 at sub-branches in and around Rodney Bay.
Business
Mon–Fri: 0800–1230, 1330–1630.
Government
Mon–Fri: 0800–1230, 1330–1630.
Shops
In Castries (some shops may vary), Mon–Fri: 0830–1630, Sat: 0800–1230. In Sunny Acres, Mon–Sat: 0900–1900. In Rodney Bay, Mon–Thu: 0900–1900, Fri–Sat: 0900–2000. All shops, except supermarkets, close Sunday.

Telecommunications
Mobile/cell phones
There are 850/900/1800/1900 GSM services operating throughout most of the territory.

Electricity supply
220V AC, 50 cycles; UK standard 3-pin plugs.

Weights and measures
The metric system was introduced in 2005 however the imperial system is still used unofficially.

Getting there
Air
National airline: LIAT (St Lucia is a major shareholder in this regional airline).
International airport/s: Hewanorra International Airport (UVF), 67km south of Castries, duty-free shop, bar, restaurant, shops, car hire, VIP business lounges. Caters for intercontinental flights. Transport from the airport includes taxis, buses and helicopter (by reservation).
Vigie (SLU), 3km from Castries, bar, restaurant, car hire. Caters for regional flights only.
Airport tax: Departure tax: EC$54
Surface
Main port/s: Castries, Vieux Fort, Soufrière.

Getting about
National transport
Road: All centres are served by a well maintained road network. Main roads constitute over half of 800km network.
Buses: Unscheduled local basic services are offered by independent drivers.
Water: Boats ply to various destinations.
City transport
Taxis: Taxis are relatively cheap and widely available. A fixed rate system operates but it is advisable to negotiate fares in advance, especially for long journeys. Tips are not expected.
Car hire
Available in Castries, Vieux Fort and Soufrière and through hotels. A national or international licence is acceptable. Traffic drives on the left.

BUSINESS DIRECTORY

The addresses listed below are a selection only. While World of Information makes every endeavour to check these addresses, we cannot guarantee that changes have not been made, especially to telephone numbers and area codes. We would welcome any corrections.

Telephone area codes
The international direct dialling code (IDD) for St Lucia is +1 758, followed by subscriber's number.

Useful telephone numbers
Emergencies: 911
Tourist Board: 452-5968, 453-0053

Chambers of Commerce
St Lucia Chamber of Commerce, Industry and Agriculture, Vide Bouteille, PO Box 482, Castries (tel: 452-3165; fax: 453-6907; e-mail: info@stluciachamber.org).

Banking
Bank of Nova Scotia, 6 Wm Peter Blvd, Box 301, Castries (tel: 452-2292, fax: 453-1051; e-mail: bns@candw.lc).

Barclays Bank, Bridge Street, Box 335, Castries (tel: 452-3306; fax: 452-6860).

CIBC Caribbean, Wm Peter Blvd, Box 350, Castries (tel: 452-3751; fax: 452-3735).

Caribbean Banking Corporation, Micoud Street, Box 1531, Castries (tel: 452-2265; fax: 452-1668, 451-7484).

First National Bank of St Lucia Ltd, 21 Bridge Street, Box 168, Castries (tel: 450-7000; fax: 453-1630).

National Commercial Bank of St Lucia, Waterfront Branch, Box 1031, Castries (tel: 452-2103/3562; fax: 453-1604, 451-7106; e-mail: ncbslu@candw.lc).

Royal Bank of Canada, Wm Peter Blvd, Box 280, Castries (tel: 452-2245, 451-6537; fax: 452-7855).

St Lucia Development Bank, National Insurance Bldg Block A, Waterfront, Box 368, Castries (tel: 452-3561/1493, 453-0236; fax: 453-6720).

Central bank

Eastern Caribbean Central Bank, Agency Office, PO Box 295; Ground Floor, Michael Chastnet's Colony House, John Compton Highway Castries (tel: 452-7449; fax: 453-6022; email: eccbslu@candw.lc).

Stock exchange

Eastern Caribbean Securities Exchange (ECSE): www.ecseonline.com

Travel information

St Lucia Helicopters, PO Box 2047, Gros Islet (tel: 453-6950; fax: 425-1553; internet: www.stluciahelicopters.com).

St Lucia Hotel and Tourism Association, Pointe Seraphine, PO Box 545, Castries (tel: 452-5978).

Ministry of tourism

Ministry of Commerce, Tourism, Investment and Consumer Affairs, 4th Floor, Heraldine Rock Building, Waterfront, Castries (tel: 468-4202, 468-4204; fax: 451-6986; email: mitandt@candw.lc).

National tourist organisation offices

St Lucia Tourist Board, PO Box 221; Sureline Building, Vide Boutielle, Castries (tel: 452-4094; fax: 453-1121; email: slutour@candw.lc; internet: www.stlucia.org).

Ministries

Ministry of Agriculture, Fisheries and Forestry, Stanislaus James Building, Waterfront, Castries (tel: 468-4210; fax: 453-6314; internet: www.slumaffe.org).

Ministry of Commerce, Tourism, Investment and Consumer Affairs, 4th Floor, Heraldine Rock Building, Waterfront, Castries (tel: 468-4202, 468-4204; fax: 451-6986; email: mitandt@candw.lc).

Ministry of Communications, works, Transport and Public Utilities, Union, Castries (tel: 468-4300; email: min_com@candw.lc).

Ministry of Education, Human Resources Development, Youth and Sorts, Francis Compton Building Waterfront, Castries (tel: 486-5203; fax: 453-2299; internet: www.education.gov.lc).

Ministry of External Affairs, International Trade and Civil Aviation, Conway Business Centre, Waterfront, Castries (tel: 468-4501/2; fax: 452-7427; email: foreign@candw.lc).

Ministry of Finance, International Financial Services and Economic Affairs, 2nd Floor, Bridge Street, Castries (tel: 468-5520; fax: 451-9231; email: minfin@gosl.gov.lc).

Ministry of Health, Human Services, Family Affairs and Gender Relations, Chaussee Road, Castries (tel: 452-2859; fax: 452-5655; email: health@candw.lc).

Ministry of Home Affairs and Internal Security, Erdistron's Place, Manoel Street, Castries (tel: 452-3772; fax: 453-6315).

Ministry of Labour, Public Service and Co-operatives, 2nd Floor, Greaham Louisy Administrative Building, Waterfront, Castries (tel: 468-2202, 468-2205; fax: 453-1305; email: minpet@candw.lc).

Ministry of Physical Development, Housing and Environment, 3rd Floor, Greaham Louisy Administrative Building, Waterfront, Castries (tel: 568-4402; fax: 452-2506; email: econdept@candw.lc).

Ministry of Social Transformation, Culture and Local Government, 4th Floor, Greaham Louisy Administrative Building, Waterfront, Castries (tel: 468-5101, 468-5108; fax: 453-7921).

Other useful addresses

British High Commission, 24 Micoud St, Castries (tel: 452-2484; email: britishhc@candw.lc).

Cable & Wireless Public Telex Booth, Bridge Street, Castries (tel: 452-3301; fax: 452-2363).

Embassy of St Lucia 3216 New Mexico Avenue, NW, Washington, DC 20016, USA (tel: (+1-202) 364-6792, fax: (+1-202) 364-6723; email: eofsaintlu@aol.com; internet: www.sluonestop.com).

Financial Centre Corporation, NIS Building, Ground Floor, The Waterfront, Castries (tel: 455-7700; fax: 455-7701; email: fcc@stluciaoffshore.com; internet: www.pinnaclestlucia.com).

National Development Corporation (NDC), PO Box 495, Monplaisir Building, Brazil Street, Castries (tel: 452-3614; fax: 452-1814; email: devcorp@candw.lc; internet: www.stluciandc.com).

National Research & Development Foundation (NTDF), PO Box 3067, La Clergy, Castries (tel: 452-4253; fax: 453-6389; email: ntdf@candw.lc).

Organisation of Eastern Caribbean States Natural Resources Management Unit (OECS NRMU), PO Box 1383, Morne Fortune, Castries.

Police Headquarters, Bridge Street, Castries (tel: 452-3854/5).

St Lucia Air and Sea Ports Authority, Micoud St, PO Box 651, Castries (tel: 452-2893; fax: 452-2062).

St Lucia Yacht Services Ltd, PO Box 188, Castries (tel: 452-5057).

Windward Islands Banana Growers' Association (WINBAN), Box 115, Compton Building, William Peter Boulevard, Castries (tel: 452-3975).

Internet sites

Government of St Lucia: www.stlucia.gov.lc

The Star Newspaper: www.stluciaStar.com

St Lucia Search Engine: www.stlucia.com

St Vincent and the Grenadines

KEY FACTS

Official name: Commonwealth of St Vincent and the Grenadines

Head of State: Queen Elizabeth II; Governor General Sir Frederick Ballantyne (from 2002)

Head of government: Prime Minister Ralph Gonsalves (ULP) (since 2001; re-elected 2010)

Ruling party: Unity Labour party (ULP) (from 2001; re-elected 2010)

Area: 388 square km

Population: 109,000 (2010)*

Capital: Kingstown

Official language: English

Currency: East Caribbean dollar (EC$) = 100 cents

Exchange rate: EC$2.70 per US$ (fixed)

GDP per capita: US$5,229 (2010)

GDP real growth: -2.30% (2010)

GDP: US$561.00 million (2010)

Inflation: 1.50% (2010)

Balance of trade: -US$254.10 million (2010)

* estimated figure

COUNTRY PROFILE

Historical profile

The country's first known inhabitants were Arawak Indians, who were later driven out by Carib Indians.

1498 The principal island was sighted by Columbus. No immediate European immigration followed this discovery.

1779 France occupied the island.

1783 Possession of the islands, as part of the Windward Islands, was passed from France to Britain under the Treaty of Versailles.

1795 Thousands of Carib Indians were deported to Belize, following an uprising.

1812 The volcano, La Soufrière, erupted and destroyed most of the island of St Vincent.

1834 After the emancipation of slaves by Britain, indentured labour from the East Indies and Portugal was brought in to remedy the labour shortage.

1958 St Vincent and the Grenadines became part of the UK-sponsored West Indies Federation.

1962 The West Indies Federation was dissolved.

1969 The territory gained internal self-government, the UK retained responsibility for foreign affairs and defence.

1979 St Vincent and the Grenadines gained independence within the Commonwealth.

1998 The New Democratic Party (NDP), led by Prime Minister James Mitchell, was re-elected.

2000 Prime Minister Mitchell stepped down and Arnhim Eustace became prime minister. Anti-government demonstrations forced the government to hold early elections.

2001 The Unity Labour Party (ULP) won early elections and Ralph Gonsalves became prime minister.

2002 Sir Charles James Antrobus, governor general since 1996, died; Sir Frederick Ballantyne became governor general.

2003 The leaders of the Organisation of the Eastern Caribbean States (OECS) agreed to an economic union and introduced a common passport for nationals of the member countries.

2005 Parliamentary elections were won by the ULP.

2006 Taiwan gave a grant of US$15 million and provided a loan of US$10 million, to assist in the construction of an international airport on St Vincent. Taiwan and St Vincent celebrated 25 years of diplomatic relations.

2009 The Millennium Bank, based in St Vincent, was accused by the US regulators of fraudulently selling certificates of deposit and of making 'blatant misrepresentations and glaring omissions' when selling products to US customers. The government put the Millennium Bank into receivership, with loses of US$68 million. A constitutional referendum was held to decide whether to abolish the monarchy (removing Queen Elizabeth II). However, the vote in favour was 43.13 per cent, short of the two-thirds in favour necessary for the proposal to succeed.

2010 In parliamentary elections held on 13 December, the ruling ULP won eight seats (out of 15), the New Democratic Party (NDP) won the remaining seven. Prime Minister Gonsalves remained in office.

2011 On 1 August citizens of the Organisation of Eastern Caribbean States (OECS) – Antigua and Barbuda, Dominica, Grenada, St Kitts and Nevis, St Lucia and St Vincent and the Grenadines – were granted freedom of movement, allowing them to reside, work, establish businesses and provide services throughout the organisation. A memorandum of understanding (MOU), was signed on 16 August, with Armajaro Trading Limited to reintroduce cocoa cultivation.

Political structure

Constitution

The 1979 constitution is being reviewed by the Constitutional Review Commission (CRC); the first interim report was made in 2004.

Independence date

27 October 1979

Form of state

Parliamentary democracy, within the Commonwealth.

The executive

The British monarch is Head of State and represented by a governor general, but both are largely ceremonial functions. Executive power is exercise by the prime minister and the cabinet.

The governor general appoints senators for the House of Assembly, four on the advice of the prime minister and two on the advice on the leader of the opposition.

National legislature
The unicameral, House of Assembly, has 21 members, six of which are appointed by the governor general and 15 directly elected. The parliamentary term of office is five years, although the prime minister may call elections earlier.
Legal system
The legal system is based on English common law with variations. Magisterial district courts exercise both civil and criminal jurisdiction up to a certain limit. The primary court of first instance is the High Court of Justice, from which appeal is made to the Eastern Caribbean Court of Appeal. Final appeals go to the Privy Council in the UK.
Last elections
13 December 2010 (parliamentary)
Results: Parliamentary: Unity Labour Party (ULP) won eight seats (out of 15), the New Democratic Party (NDP) seven.
Next elections
2015 (parliamentary)

Political parties
Ruling party
Unity Labour party (ULP) (from 2001; re-elected 2010)
Main opposition party
New Democratic Party (NDP)
Political situation
Prime Minister Ralph Gonsalves called into question the leadership, in particular the political directorate, of the 15-member, regional grouping of the Caribbean Community (Caricom). After years of discussion it had not, by June 2010, achieved the level of progress he thought was possible and still had to introduce a fully functional Caricom single market and economy (CSME) by 2015, but which had suffered several setbacks in the progress towards the CSME.

Population
109,000 (2010)*
Last census: May 2001:109,202 (provisional)
Population density: 293 inhabitants per square km. Urban population: 56 per cent (1995—2001).
Annual growth rate: 0.5 per cent 1994–2004 (WHO 2006)
Ethnic make-up
Most of the population are the descendants of African slaves brought to the island to work on plantations. There are also a few white descendants of English colonists, as well as some East Indians, Carib Indians and a minority of mixed race.
Religions
Anglican (32 per cent), Methodist (18 per cent), Roman Catholic (10 per cent), Seventh-Day Adventist, Hindu, other Protestant (40 per cent).

Education
Education is not compulsory, but children are expected to attend school between the ages of five and 15. Public schooling is provided free of charge up to age 15, although books and equipment have to be supplied by parents. An estimated 95 per cent of the population attend school, but attendance may drop when family needs are pressing. There are 65 primary schools and 23 secondary schools. Around 10 per cent of the population have no formal education and are illiterate.
The emphasis on academic subjects in secondary schools has shifted to include more practical courses like carpentry and agricultural studies.

Health
Health care is free until the age of 17. There are six public hospitals in Kingstown and five other hospitals in rural areas. There is also a mental health institution and an old people's residence.
A national family planning policy has been in place since 1974 and as a result the fertility rate has dropped considerably.
Life expectancy: 69 years, 2004 (WHO 2006)
Fertility rate/Maternal mortality rate: 2.2 births per woman, 2004 (WHO 2006)
Birth rate/Death rate: 17 births per 1,000 population; six deaths per 1,000 population (2003).
Child (under 5 years) mortality rate (per 1,000): 23 per 1,000 live births (World Bank)

Welfare
The social welfare system is weak. There is no national health insurance, nor any pension allowance for the elderly. The infant mortality rate is high.
There is a limited framework for the protection of children and the number of child abuse cases that are reported is high.
The situation is generally difficult for disabled people, who seldom leave their homes. There is one institution that offers care and support to the elderly.

Main cities
Kingstown (capital, estimated population 16,031 in 2005), Barrouallie (1,318), Layou (1,164), George Town (1,117).

Languages spoken
English, Vincentian Creole
Official language/s
English

Media
Press
Dailies: *The Daily Herald* was the first international daily newspaper published from Kingstown. A regional online publication Caribbean Net News (www.caribbeannetnews.com) covers news from the islands.
Weeklies: Publications include *The News*, *The Vincentian* (www.thevincentian.com) and *Searchlight* (www.searchlight.vc).
Broadcasting
Radio: There are five radio stations; the National Broadcasting Corporation (NBC) (www.nbcsvg.com) is the oldest and part government-owned network. Hitz FM (www.svgbc.com) is affiliated to SVGTV, We-FM (www.999wefm.com) is a private commercial service; Praise FM (www.praisefmsvg.com) is a Christian station; First FM and Hot 97 are local stations without internet access.
Television: The government-owned free-to-air SVGTV (www.svgbc.com) has six channels covering news, entertainment and sport. Cable TV provides US programmes for paying customers.

KEY INDICATORS — St Vincent and the Grenadines

	Unit	2006	2007	2008	2009	2010
Population	m	0.11	*0.11	*0.11	*0.11	*0.11
Gross domestic product (GDP)	US$bn	0.50	0.55	0.58	0.57	0.56
GDP per capita	US$	4,695	51,859	5,437	5,291	5,229
GDP real growth	%	6.9	8.0	-0.6	-2.5	-2.3
Inflation	%	3.0	6.9	10.1	0.6	1.5
Exports (fob) (goods)	US$m	41.2	51.4	57.2	54.8	43.6
Imports (fob) (goods)	US$m	237.7	287.9	328.7	293.9	297.7
Balance of trade	US$m	-196.5	-236.6	-271.5	-239.2	-254.1
Current account	US$m	-117.9	-190.9	-227.9	-198.1	-206.0
Total reserves minus gold	US$m	78.7	87.0	83.7	87.8	112.7
Foreign exchange	US$m	77.9	86.2	82.9	75.2	110.8
Exchange rate	per US$	2.70	2.70	2.70	2.70	2.70

* estimated figure

Economy
Tourism and agriculture are the principal sectors of the economy. Bananas dominate export commodities, while the Grenadines are a centre of high-end tourism, specialising in luxury hotels and Caribbean yachting.
GDP growth was 7.6 per cent in 2006 and 7.0 per cent in 2007, buoyed by construction and the tourist sector. However growth plummeted to 0.9 per cent in 2008 due to a drop in tourist numbers, completion of major phases of construction projects and a disease that blighted the banana sector. As growth slackened, domestic spending dropped in line with a fall in disposable incomes. Value added tax (VAT) was introduced in 2007, with a rate of 15 per cent on goods and services and 10 per cent on tourist accommodation; inflation rose from 3.0 per cent in 2006 to 6.9 per cent in 2007, but coupled with world high prices for food and petroleum, it peaked at 11.6 per cent in September 2008, although the average was 8.7 per cent for the year.
The impact of the global economic recession in the US and UK cut tourist arrivals and has put in abeyance foreign direct investment (FDI) projects as investors became more cautious and credit tighter. Remittances from overseas workers also slowed in 2008 as wages remained static and jobs became scarce.
The banking sector, which is dominated by subsidiaries of Canadian banks, is well capitalised and had limited exposure to the distress experienced by other financial institutions worldwide. The Millennium Bank, based in St Vincent, was accused by the US regulators in March, of fraudulently selling certificates of deposit and that is made 'blatant misrepresentations and glaring omissions' when selling products to US customers. The government put the Millennium Bank into receivership, with loses of US$68 million.
St Vincent and the Grenadines is a member of the Caribbean Single Market and Economy (CSME), and the Eastern Caribbean Currency Union (ECCU) using the East Caribbean Dollar, both organisations impose measures on the economy that may not allow the government to take its own decisions, but rather within a collective decision making process achieves regional stability.

External trade
As a member of the Caribbean Community and Common Market (Caricom), St Vincent and the Grenadines operates within the single market (Caribbean Single Market and Economy (CSME)), which became operational on 1 January 2006. Goods, services, businesses and money are free to move within CSME without barriers and tariffs. It is also a member of the Eastern Caribbean Currency Union (ECCU) using the East Caribbean Dollar. Although the export of bananas produces around 50 per cent of all commodity sales, tourism is the principal foreign exchange earner as the Grenadines is a popular high-end tourist destination.

Imports
Main imports are machinery and telecommunication equipment and manufactured goods, foodstuffs, fertilisers and fuels.
Main sources: US (typically 37 per cent of total), Trinidad and Tobago (21 per cent), UK (6 per cent).

Exports
Main exports are bananas, taro and arrowroot starch.
Main destinations: Grenada (typically 18 per cent of total), Trinidad and Tobago (17 per cent), St Lucia (15 per cent).

Agriculture
Farming
The agricultural sector is traditionally the mainstay of the economy, but its contribution to GDP, which stood at 40 per cent in 1960, has fallen to around nine per cent. Half of the total land area is arable with only a small proportion unused. St Vincent is the world's leading producer of arrowroot and an exporter of coconut oil. Carrots and plantains are also cash crops. The main food crops are sweet potatoes, tannias, yams, vegetables, and various fruits.
Bananas (grown mainly on small farms under the auspices of St Vincent Banana Growers Association) are the main export crop. The production of bananas, and earnings from their export, have declined in recent years. Unfavourable weather conditions, a sharp fall in the average domestic currency price received for fruit, and a reduction in the average green wholesale price of fruit have weakened the industry.
The EU phased out preferential treatment for banana producers from former colonies and the liberalisation of the banana trade has made it difficult for family-run businesses in St Vincent to compete on the world market.
A memorandum of understanding (MOU), was signed on 16 August 2011, with Armajaro Trading Limited to reintroduce cocoa cultivation. Armajaro Trading undertook to provide the seedlings and commercial loans for investment in tools and equipment and fertilizers, while the government will provide exclusivity in the sales and marketing of chocolate products to Armajaro Trading.

Fishing
The typical total annual fish catch is over 45,800t. Shellfish, molluscs and cephalopods account for another 1,800t per annum.

Industry and manufacturing
The industrial sector employs around 8 per cent of the workforce and contributes 10 per cent to GDP.
Activity is primarily based on agricultural processing. Units in operation include those producing cigarettes, tobacco products, coconut oil, textiles and clothing, soft drinks, fruit juices, milk, beer, rum, furniture, arrowroot starch, tyre retreading, concrete blocks and quarry products. A flour mill, serving all the Windward Islands, a box factory and a yacht building yard are the main export industries.
The sector has continued to contract since 1999, although in 2004 the brewery, the second largest manufacturer, reported its best year since then.

Tourism
Tourism is a vital part of the islands' economy. The percentage of GDP in 2005 was 10.3 per cent (and 10 per cent of GDP growth for the year) while the sector employs 9.6 per cent of the work force.
St Vincent is a volcanic island and has only one white sand beach; the industry is thus limited, and there is only minimal scope for further expansion. The Grenadines have more white sand beaches, and the government has stepped up promotional work in the sector's main markets of the US, the UK, Canada and the Caribbean. Infrastructure is being gradually upgraded. Particular attention has been paid to encouraging the cruise ship market. Visitor numbers increased in the first half of 2006 by 31 per cent to 176,122, compared to a fall of 12.4 per cent in the corresponding period for 2005. The turnaround was largely attributable to growth of 84 per cent in cruise ship passengers.

Hydrocarbons
There are no known hydrocarbon resources. Consumption was 2,000 barrels per day (bpd) in 2008, all of which was imported. In 2005, St Vincent and the Grenadines, plus a number of other Caribbean states, signed an agreement with Venezuela to establish PetroCaribe, a multi-national oil company, owned by the participating states. PetroCaribe buys low-priced Venezuelan crude oil under long-term payment plans.
Any natural gas or coal used is commercially insignificant.

Energy
Total installed generating capacity was 35MW in 2006, of which 44 per cent is produced by hydropower. The government is exploring ways to tap the active (but dormant) volcano, La Sourière, for

geothermal energy. Many people have private generators.

Financial markets
Stock exchange
Eastern Caribbean Securities Exchange (ECSE)

Banking and insurance
The banking sector contributes around 6 per cent of GDP.
The seven members of the Organisation of Eastern Caribbean States (OECS) (Antigua and Barbuda, Dominica, Grenada, Montserrat, St Kitts and Nevis, St Lucia and St Vincent and the Grenadines), share a common currency and central bank. The British Virgin Islands and Anguilla are associate members.
Central bank
Eastern Caribbean Central Bank, St Kitts and Nevis.
Offshore facilities
The offshore financial centre is an important element of the economy.

Time
GMT minus four hours

Geography
St Vincent and the Grenadines is an archipelago of islands and cays (low-lying coral islets) in the Caribbean located in the Windward Islands group, approximately 160km west of Barbados in the West Indies. St Lucia is 34km to the north-east and Grenada is to the south. St Vincent, is a volcanic island, is 29km long and 18km wide and the most northerly of the chain. Of the Grenadines there are 32 islands and cays (not all inhabited) of which the principal islands of the group are Bequia, Canouan, Mustique, Mayreau, Isle D'Quatre and Union Island. St. Vincent has a mountainous centre with an inactive (since 1979) volcano, La Soufrière (1,220 metres (m)) at the north end of the island. The mountains are covered in rich rainforests with a 21m waterfall at Baleine.
Hemisphere
Northern

Climate
Tropical, tempered by trade winds, with temperature range 18–32 degrees Celsius. High levels of rainfall from May–November, especially in the north.

Entry requirements
Passports
Required by all. All visitors must have proof of a return/onward passage and enough funds for their stay.
Visa
Not required, except for nationals of the Dominican Republic, Jordan, Syria, Iran, Iraq, Lebanon and Nigeria who must apply to the Ministry of National Security in Kingstown (details in *Addresses* following).
Currency advice/regulations
The import of local and foreign currency is unlimited; export is limited to the amount declared on arrival.
Travellers cheques (in US dollars) are widely accepted.

Health (for visitors)
Mandatory precautions
Yellow fever vaccination certificate required if arriving from an infected area.
Advisable precautions
Typhoid, polio vaccination.

Hotels
Wide range of good hotels available at reasonable prices, except on the privately owned islands of Palm, Mustique and Petit St Vincent, where rates are higher. Seven per cent tax is added to room rates; 10 per cent tip is usual if service charge not included on bill.

Public holidays (national)
Fixed dates
1 Jan (New Year's Day), 14 Mar (National Heroes' Day), 1 May (Labour Day), 1 Aug (Emancipation Day), 27 Oct (Independence Day), 25–26 Dec (Christmas). If a holiday falls on a Sunday, the following Monday is taken as a public holiday.
Variable dates
Good Friday, Easter Monday, Whit Monday, Carnival Monday (first Mon in Jul), Carnival Tuesday (first Tue in Jul).

Working hours
Banking
Mon–Fri: 0800–1300; also Fri: 1500–1700.
Business
Mon–Fri: 0800–1200, 1300–1600; Sat: 0800–1200.
Government
Mon–Fri: 0800–1615.
Shops
Mon–Fri: 0800–1200, 1300–1600; Sat: 0800–1200.

Telecommunications
Mobile/cell phones
There are 850, 900/1800, 900/1900 GSM services available throughout most of the territories.

Electricity supply
220/240V AC, 50 cycles with flat three-pin plugs.

Getting there
Air
National airline: LIAT (Leeward Islands Air Transport)
International airport/s: ET Joshua Airport (SVD) on St Vincent, 3km from Kingstown. Flights arrive from surrounding Caribbean islands only. Facilities include duty-free shops, restaurant and car hire.
Airport tax: Departure tax: EC$40.
Surface
Water: Cruise ships make regular stops. International shipping lines that maintain contacts with St Vincent may provide passenger services on cargo ships.
Main port/s: Kingstown (only deep-water harbour in country).

Getting about
National transport
Air: There are four local airports on Bequia, Mustique, Canouan and Union Island suitable for light aircraft only. LIAT, SVG Air, Mustique Airways provide scheduled services between Kingstown and most domestic islands.
Road: There is almost 600km of paved roads with the Leeward and Windward highways circling St Vincent. Interior roads are narrow with steep inclines.
Buses: Buses are fairly widespread. Stopping is on demand rather than at pre-specified points.
Water: There are regular, scheduled inter-island ferry services providing round trips between the large inhabited islands.
City transport
Taxis: The rate of fares are set by the government but taxis are unmetered and fares should be agreed at the start of a journey. Prices increase from late at night to early morning. Tipping is up to 10 per cent.
Car hire
Either an International Driving Permit must be stamped at the central police station, or a temporary driving licence can be obtained (for a fee) from the police station on Bay Street, or the Licensing Authority on Halifax Street (Kingstown, St Vincent), with the presentation of a valid overseas driving licence, is necessary.
Driving is on the left, road signs are limited and it is recommended drives should use the horn on sharp curves and turns.

BUSINESS DIRECTORY
The addresses listed below are a selection only. While World of Information makes every endeavour to check these addresses, we cannot guarantee that changes have not been made, especially to telephone numbers and area codes. We would welcome any corrections.

Telephone area codes
The international direct dialling code (IDD) for St Vincent is +1-784, followed by subscriber's number.

Useful telephone numbers
Local information: 118.
International information: 115.
Police: 457-1211.
Kingstown General Hospital: 456-1185.

Chambers of Commerce
St Vincent Chamber of Commerce and Industry, Corea's Building, Halifax Street, PO Box 134, Kingstown (tel: 457-1464;

fax: 456-2994; e-mail: svgcic@caribsurf.com).

Banking

Bank of Nova Scotia, 76 Halifax Street, Box 237, Kingstown (tel: 457-1601; fax: 457-2623).

Barclays Bank, Halifax Street, PO Box 604, Kingstown (tel: 456-1706; fax: 457-2985).

CIBC Caribbean, Halifax Street, Box 212, Kingstown (tel: 457-1587; fax: 457-2873).

Canadian Imperial Bank of Commerce, Halifax Street, Box 212, Kingstown (tel: 457-1587/2873; fax: 457-2873).

Caribbean Banking Corporation, 81 South River Road, Box 118, Kingstown (tel: 456-1501; fax: 456-2141).

Development Corporation, Sharpe Street, Box 841, Kingstown (tel: 457-1358; 457-2838).

First St Vincent Bank, Lot 112 Granby Street, Box 154, Kingstown (tel: 456-1873; fax: 457-2675).

National Commercial Bank, Bedford Street, Box 880, Kingstown (tel: 457-1844; fax: 457-2612).

New Bank, Blue Caribbean Bldg Bay Street, Box 1628, Kingstown (tel: 457-1411, 456-2453; fax: 457-1357).

Owens Bank, Box 1045, Kingstown (tel: 457-1230; fax: 457-2610).

St. Vincent Co-operative Bank, Corner Long Lane Upper & South River Road, Box 886, Kingstown (tel: 456-1894).

Central bank

Eastern Caribbean Central Bank, Agency Office, PO Box 839, Granby Street, Kingstown (tel: 456-1413; fax: 456-1412).

Stock exchange

Eastern Caribbean Securities Exchange (ECSE): www.ecseonline.com

Travel information

Air Martinique (tel: 458-4528; fax: 458-4187).

LIAT Ltd, VC Bird International Airport, PO Box 819; Coolidge, Antigua (tel: (+1-268) 480-5634; fax: (+1-268) 480-5635; email: customerrelations@liatairline.com).

Mustique Airways, PO Box 1232, Arnos Vale (tel: 458-4380; fax: 456-4586).

St Vincent and The Grenadines Hotel and Tourism Association, PO Box 834, E T Joshua Int'l Airport, Kingstown, St Vincent (tel: 458-4379; fax: 456-4456; email: svghotels@caribsurf.com or office@svghotels.com; internet: www.svghotels.com).

SVG (airline), Arnos Vale (tel: 457-5124; fax: 457-5077; internet: www.svgair.com).

Ministry of tourism

Ministry of Tourism, Youth and Sports, Cruise Ship Terminal, Harbour Quay, St. Vincent (tel: 457-1502; fax: 451-2425).

National tourist organisation offices

Department of Tourism, Bay Street, PO Box 834, Kingstown (tel: 457-1502; fax: 451-2425; email: tourism@caribsurf.com; internet: www.svgtourism.com).

Ministries

Ministry of Agriculture and Labour, Administrative Building, Kingstown (tel: 456-1410; fax: 457-1688).

Ministry of Communications and Works, Administrative Building, Kingstown (tel: 456-1111; fax: 456-2168).

Ministry of Education, Youth and Women's Affairs, Administrative Building, Kingstown (tel: 457-2282; fax: 457-1114).

Ministry of Foreign Affairs and Tourism, Administrative Building, Kingstown (tel: 456-1111; fax: 456-2610).

Ministry of Health and the Environment, Administrative Building, Kingstown (tel: 457-1729; fax: 456-2610).

Ministry of Housing, Local Government and Community Development and Sports, Administrative Building, Kingstown (tel: 456-1111; fax: 456-2610).

Ministry of Legal Affairs and Information, Administrative Building, Kingstown (tel: 456-1111; fax: 457-2898).

Ministry of National Security, Halifax Street, Kingstown, St Vincent (tel: 451-2707; fax: 451-2820; email: office.natsec@mail.gov.vc).

Ministry of Trade, Industry and Consumer Affairs, Administrative Building, Kingstown (tel: 457-1223; fax: 457-2880).

Office of The Prime Minister, Administrative Building, Kingstown (tel: 456-1703; fax: 457-2152).

Other useful addresses

British High Commission PO Box 132, Granby Street, Kingstown (tel: 457 1701; fax: 456 2750; email: bhcsvg@caribsurf.com).

National Broadcasting Corporation, PO Box 705, Kingstown (tel: 457-1111).

Offshore Finance Authority, Kingstown (tel: 456-2577; fax: 457-2568; email: info@stvincentoffshore.com; internet: www.stvincentoffshore.com).

Radio St Vincent and the Grenadines, PO Box 705, Kingstown (tel: 456-1516).

Statistical Office, Central Planning Division, Ministry of Finance and Planning, Kingstown (fax: 457-2943).

St Vincent and the Grenadines Embassy (US), Suite 102, 1717 Massachusetts Avenue, Washington DC 20036 (tel: (+1-202) 462-7806).

St Vincent Development Corporation (DEVCO), PO Box 841, Granby Street, Kingstown (tel: 457-1358; fax: 457-2838).

Internet sites

Caribbean newspaper online: http://caribbeannetnews.com

Official government website: www.gov.vc

Samoa

KEY FACTS

Official name: Malotuto'atasi o Samoa (Independent State of Samoa) (dropped 'Western' 1997)

Head of State: O le Ao o le Malo, Tupuola Efi (from 11 June 2007)

Head of government: Prime Minister Tuila'epa Sailele Malielegaoi (HRPP) (since 1998; re-elected Mar 2011)

Ruling party: Human Rights Protection Party (HRPP) (since 1982; re-elected Mar 2011)

Area: 2,840 square km (nine islands): Savai'i (1,708); Upolu (1,118)

Population: 183,000 (2010)*

Capital: Apia (on Upolu)

Official language: Samoan

Currency: Tala or Samoan dollar (S$) = 100 senes, or cents

Exchange rate: S$2.38 per US$ (Oct 2011)

GDP per capita: US$2,788 (2010)

GDP: US$556.00 million (2010)

Inflation: -0.02% (2010)

Balance of trade: -US$244.92 million (2010)

* estimated figure

There were declines in tourism receipts, agriculture and remittances in 2010, matched by increases in transport and telecommunications, construction and manufacturing, leaving gross domestic product (GDP) flat for the year. Visitor numbers rose by 3.5 per cent to 131,300, but earnings fell by 6.0 per cent to US$130 million; remittances were also down, by 5.3 per cent, to US$148.8 million. The Asian Development Bank estimates growth for 2011 at 2.1 per cent, on the back of a rise in government spending and private consumption. The government expenditure allocated for the ongoing post-*tsunami* reconstruction will continue to provide employment.

The elections in March 2011 passed off relatively smoothly. The ruling Human Rights Protection Party (HRPP) won 29 seats (out of 49) and is supported by seven independent members. Tuila'epa Sailele Malielegaoi continued as prime minister.

Is it yesterday or tomorrow?

In 1884 the International Meridian Conference agreed on a 24-hour clock and set the International Dateline at longitude 180o, with a few zigs and zags. It put the islands of (then Western) Samoa and American Samoa to the west of the dateline, that is, they were one of the first peoples to greet a new day. Then in 1892 an American businessman persuaded them to switch to the east, making trading with the US, the islands' then largest trading partner, easier.

By 2011 Western Samoa was Samoa, there were almost as many Samoans living in New Zealand and Australia as in Samoa itself, and Samoa was trading more with its western neighbours than across the Pacific to North and South America. But being to the east of the dateline, and 23 hours behind Sydney, meant that in reality they had only three trading days a week.

So in May 2011 the government decided that on 29 December 2011 Samoa would slip from one side of the Dateline to the other. It will lose its unique selling point for tourists of being the last place on earth to see the sunset, to becoming one of the first. But with American Samoa just one hour's flying time away, and still to the east of the Dateline, it will become possible to have two birthdays (or none) every year.

Samoans have already had to cope with switching from driving on the right to driving on the left (in 2009, and also to fit in with life in Australasia), so moving straight from 29 December to 31 December 2011 should not be a problem. Just so long as someone remembers to change the date on all the computers... (Remember that millennium bug?)

The last country to shift the dateline was the fellow Pacific island group of Kiribati, which used to straddle the dateline. In that case the shift meant that the nine, largely unpopulated, islands on the eastern side joined the 24 islands on the west. And as an unintended consequence, when the millennium came, the i-Kiribati became the first to see the sun and television crews from around the world were there to record it.

COUNTRY PROFILE

Historical profile

The first Polynesians settled in the islands around 600BC. A former German protectorate, Samoa was governed by New Zealand from 1914 until its citizens voted for independence in 1961. The Independent State of Samoa was known as Western Samoa until 1997.

1722 The Dutch navigator, Jacob Roggeveen, was the first European to sight the islands.

1831 The London Missionary Society arrived in Samoa to convert native Samoans, establishing a British presence.

1889 The *Treaty of Berlin* between Britain, the US and Germany promised an independent Samoan government.

1899 The Berlin treaty was annulled by the *Tripartite Treaty*, which granted the US rights to all eastern islands of the Samoan group and gave Germany the remainder. In exchange for withdrawing its claim to Samoa, Britain gained control of Germany's rights in Tonga, Niue and the Solomon Islands (excluding Bougainville).

1914 New Zealand occupied Western Samoa during the First World War and continued to administer it after the War under a League of Nations' mandate.

1929 Eleven members of the Mau independence movement were killed by New Zealand authorities.

1946 After the Second World War, Western Samoa was administered as a UN Trust Territory by New Zealand.

1961 A UN-supervised plebiscite voted for independence.
1962 Western Samoa became the first Pacific island to declare independence.
1970 Western Samoa became a member of the Commonwealth.
1990 Voters approved universal suffrage and increased the legislature's term from three to five years.
1991 The general election employed universal suffrage for all those over 21.
1997 The constitution was amended and Western Samoa was re-named Samoa.
1998 The government imposed restrictions on the media.
2000 Samoa was one of the first to sign the Pacific Island Countries (free) Trade Agreement. Two former cabinet ministers, sentenced to death for a murder attempt on a fellow politician who could have exposed them for corruption, had their death sentences commuted to life imprisonment.
2001 Incumbent prime minister, Tuiaepa Sailele Malielegaoi (Human Rights' Protection Party (HRPP)) won a closely run election and retained control with the support of independent members.
2002 New Zealand formally apologised for its poor treatment of Samoan citizens in colonial times.
2004 The death penalty, which had not been used since the 1930s, was abolished.
2006 HRPP was re-elected, winning 36 of the 49 parliamentary seats.
2007 Susuga Malietoa Tanumafili II died aged 94. Tupua Tamasese Tupuola Tufuga Efi (known as Tuiatua Tupua Tamasese Efi) was appointed by parliament as O le Ao o le Malo (traditional head of state) Tupuola Efi.
2009 Following a Supreme Court ruling that Tautua Samoa (TS) had not been registered to participate in the general elections all nine members (forming the opposition) chose to sit in parliament as independents. However the speaker of parliament disqualified them, as the constitution required that they stand for re-election if they remained as a political party. The road code changed to introduce right-hand driving. An earthquake, of 8.3 magnitude, struck offshore in the Pacific Ocean and caused a devastating *tsunami* that swept over several Samoan islands, killing more than 140 people, including 25 in American Samoa. International aid was provided including emergency supplies.
2010 Daylight saving was introduced on 26 September, moving its times from GMT minus 11 hours to GMT minus 10 hours.
2011 In parliamentary elections held on 4 March, the ruling HRPP won 29 seats out of 49. Seven independent members also support the HRPP. The opposition TS won 13 seats. Samoa's first period of daylight saving ended on 3 April. On 9 May the Samoan government approved the International Date Line Act 2011 to change Samoa from being on the east of the International Dateline to being on the west, so that Samoa will be one of the first countries to begin the daily cycle and not the last to see the sun set; in effect it moves a day ahead in time and comes into line with its trading partners in Oceania and Australasia. On Thursday 29 December at 11.59.59 Samoa will lose one day and move forward to Saturday 31 December at 00.00.

Political structure

Constitution

The O le Ao O le Malo (Head of State) acts as a constitutional monarch with the power to dissolve the Fono (legislative assembly) and to appoint a prime minister with its recommendation.

Independence date

1962

The executive

Executive power rests with the prime minister who selects a 12-member cabinet. The Head of State (O le Ao o le Malo) does not play an active role in government. He appoints the prime minister on the Fono's recommendation and approves the laws passed by the Fono. The Head of State is elected for a five-year term.

National legislature

The unicameral Fono has 49-members, of which 47 are *matais* (traditional clan leaders) elected in six two-seat and 35 single constituencies. The remaining two members are elected by and represent non-ethnic Samoans. All members are elected for five-year terms.

Last elections

4 March 2011 (parliamentary)

Results: Parliamentary: the Human Rights Protection Party (HRPP) won 29 seats (out of 49), Tautau Samoa (TS) 13, independents (supporting HRPP) seven; turnout was 90 per cent.

Next elections

2011 (parliamentary)

Political parties

Ruling party

Human Rights Protection Party (HRPP) (since 1982; re-elected Mar 2011)

Main opposition party

Tautua Samoa (TS)

Political situation

The devastating tsunami that killed more than 140 people, in 2009, left several islands in need of widespread reconstruction. In October 2010, the opposition Samoan Democratic United Party (SDUP) queried where the tsunami relief funds had been spent? A New Zealand TV3 documentary claimed that an amount of the aid monies had been misappropriated. The government strenuously denied the accusations saying that the money was budgeted to be spent over a four-year recovery period as pledges were paid. Despite opposition by the National Council of Churches and the Tautua Somoa Party (TSP) a new casino legalisation bill was passed in October 2010. Prime Minister Tuila'epa expected the first casino to be in operation in mid-2011, although in the meantime, the Totalisator Agency Board would undertake research into what type of casino was best.

Population

183,000 (2010)*

Last census: 5 November 2006: 179,186 (provisional)

KEY INDICATORS — Samoa

	Unit	2006	2007	2008	2009	2010
Population	m	*0.19	*0.19	*0.19	*0.19	*0.18
Gross domestic product (GDP)	US$bn	0.49	0.51	570.00	557.00	0.56
GDP per capita	US$	2,537	2,902	2,802	3,078	2,780
GDP real growth	%	5.5	2.0	4.6	-5.5	0.0
Inflation	%	8.5	4.5	5.4	2.0	-0.2
Exports (fob) (goods)	US$m	11.0	12.2	11.2	10.2	35.1
Imports (fob) (goods)	US$m	199.0	241.1	204.3	227.6	280.0
Balance of trade	US$m	-188.0	-228.9	-193.2	-217.4	-244.9
Current account	US$m	-100.0	-123.0	-195.0	-152.0	-58.9
Total reserves minus gold	US$m	80.7	95.3	87.1	165.8	208.4
Foreign exchange	US$m	75.9	90.2	81.9	145.0	189.0
Exchange rate	per US$	2.77	2.62	2.64	2.73	2.48

* estimated figure

Population density: 64 inhabitants per square km (2010)
Annual growth rate: 1.0 per cent 1994–2004 (WHO 2006)
Ethnic make-up
Samoan (92.6 per cent); European and Polynesian mixed race (7 per cent); Europeans (0.4 per cent).
Religions
Christian

Education
The introduction of the bilingual, single curriculum in primary and secondary schools has increased the number of students successfully completing schooling. Teaching methods and teacher's tools, including dictionaries, grammars and workbooks for teachers, were re-oriented so that the focus became localised and seen as more relevant to the student's lives. The dual streaming of academic and non-academic students in secondary schools was discontinued and has improved the educational outcome of more students.
Literacy rate: 98.9 per cent, adult male rate; 98.4 per cent adult female rate (World Bank).
Compulsory years: Five to 13
Enrolment rate: 91.9 per cent net primary enrolment; 67.4 per cent net seconday enrolment (World Bank).

Health
Life expectancy: 68 years, 2004 (WHO 2006)
Fertility rate/Maternal mortality rate: 4.3 births per woman, 2004 (WHO 2006)
Birth rate/Death rate: 15 births per 1,000 population; six deaths per 1,000 population (2003).
Child (under 5 years) mortality rate (per 1,000): 19 per 1,000 live births (World Bank)

Main cities
Apia, on Upolu (capital, estimated population 39,813 in 2005).

Languages spoken
English is widely spoken. The Samoan language has an equal status with English in schools.
Official language/s
Samoan

Media
Press
Publications are typically printed in both English and Samoan. Locally published newspapers include the *Samoa Observer*, a leading daily and *Samoa News* (www.samoalive.com) publishes every weekday. *Samoa Weekly* and *Talamua Magazine* are privately owned and *Savali* is a government-owned periodical. Online news networks include Pacific Islands Report (www.eastwestcenter.org) and Samoa Live (www.samoalive.com). Several Samoan (and English) language publications are printed in New Zealand, including *Samoana Samoa Star* and *Samoa Sun*.
The monthly *Women's Times* became a weekly edition from July 2011.
Dailies: The *Samoa Observer* is a leading daily. *Samoa Live* (www.samoalive.com/samoanews.htm) is the leading local on-line network with regional Asia Pacific and international news links. Other regular publications include the *Samoa Times* and *South Seas Star*.
Weeklies: Local weekly publications include *Newsline*, *Le Samoa*, *Samoa Post* and *Samoa Weekly*.
Business: *Talanei News* (www.samoana.org/talanei) covers business news.
Periodicals: Periodicals include *Savali* and *Samoa Sports Monthly*.
Broadcasting
It is possible to pick up television and radio broadcasts from American Samoa.
Radio: There are three commercial FM stations and the Samoa Broadcasting Corporation operates commercial AM and FM radio stations.
Television: There are four TV stations the state-run SBC, and the private O Lau TV broadcasting 24 hours, TV3 broadcasting for 12 hours, and CCTV relays programmes from the Chinese state-run broadcaster.
Advertising
All radio stations and most weekly newspapers accept advertising and there are a few opportunities for billboards however cinemas do not offer advertising.
News agencies
ABC Pacific Beat:
www.radioaustralia.net.au/pacbeat
Pacific Magazine:
www.pacificmagazine.net
Pacific Islands New Association (Pina):
www.pina.com.fj

Economy
There are four main sources of income for the Samoan economy: development aid, tourism, agricultural exports and remittances. Agricultural exports provide over 90 per cent of export revenue. The structure of the economy in 2008 was 60 per cent services, 29.3 per cent by industry, of which manufacture comprised 11.7 per cent, and 10.8 per cent agriculture. The agricultural sector employs around 60 per cent of the labour force in subsistence farming, while export products are centred on the coconut, with sales of copra and coconut oil and cream. The manufacturing sector is largely geared to fabricating vehicle parts for use in car assembly in Australia, under a market-access concession arrangement.
GDP growth was 2.2 per cent in 2007, which rose to 4.8 per cent in 2008 but which plummeted in 2009 to a projected -5.5 per cent as growth in all sectors except services contracted. Inflation rose from 4.5 per cent in 2007 to 6.2 per cent in 2008 and was expected to rise further to 14.2 per cent by 2009.
The tourism sector is strong, providing around 20 per cent of GDP; however it is subject to damage from weather and natural disasters in the Samoan Pacific region. A *tsunami*, caused by an offshore earthquake, swept over much of the southern coast of Upolu in October 2009, devastating not only much of the tourist infrastructure, but also deterring many from visiting; eighteen resorts and family-run properties were destroyed and pristine beaches scarred and littered with debris. The *tsunami* also destroyed a huge portion of Samoa's staple food crop, taro. Visitor numbers in 2008 were 122,163 which grew to 128,804 in 2009, as 17 cruise liners stopped off, bringing 16,633 passengers to visit; two more liners than in 2008.
Remittances were 25.5 per cent of GDP in 2005 (last published statistics by the International Monetary Fund (IMF)), but due to the global economic crisis work and wages have been subject to external pressures and remittances are expected to show a fall.
Samoa is a stable democratic country that has taken measures to liberalise its economy in an attempt to attract foreign direct investment (FDI).

External trade
Samoa is a member of the South Pacific Regional Trade and Economic Co-operation Agreement (Sparteca) along with 12 other regional nations, which allows products duty free access by Pacific Island Forum members to Australian and New Zealand markets (subject to the country of origin restrictions).
Foreign trade underpins the economy in three major fields, agricultural produce, manufacturing and capital flows. Tourism, particularly by expatriates, and remittances (over 25 per cent of GDP) has covered Samoa's persistently large trade deficit for a number of years. Manufacturing is largely based on automotive components that are shipped to Australia. Agricultural products are mostly exported for processing except coconuts and their derivates. Around 15 per cent of all exports are bound for European markets.
On 16 December 2011, Samoa was given approval to join the World Trade Organisation (WTO), the 153rd nation to do so. Ratification of the membership

agreement should take place by 15 June 2012.

Imports

Principal imports are machinery and equipment, industrial supplies and foodstuffs.

Main sources: Australia (typically 25 per cent of total), New Zealand (23 per cent), US (13 per cent).

Exports

Although automotive parts (manufactured in Samoa's Foreign Trade Zone) are the major export items they are not included in government statistics on exports commodities as they are part of the market-access concession arrangement with Australia and are considered outside the domestic economy, only providing employment and peripheral trade. Agricultural produce constitutes 90 per cent of Samoan commodity exports, including (by volume) coconut oil, fresh fish, coconut cream, nonu fruit, spring water, beer, copra and taro.

Main destinations: Australia (typically 80 per cent of total), New Zealand (10 per cent), American Samoa (4 per cent).

Agriculture

Farming

Agriculture, including fishing, typically accounts for 17 per cent of GDP and employs over 60 per cent of the workforce with smallholdings producing surpluses in Samoa's fertile volcanic soil, enough for healthy export sales. Production of subsistence crops include cassava, breadfruit maize and taro.

Export of nonu juice has in the past replaced fresh fish as Samoa's principal foreign exchange earner. Other produce under development includes macadamia nuts, annatto (dye), timber and cattle.

A shipment of sheep arrived from Fiji where they had been specially bred to have a high meat content and to be suitable for tropical climates.

Fishing

Fishing is one of Samoa's major export earners. The typical annual fish catch is around 11,000t (an increase from 7,500t in 1998); there are concerns that overfishing is depleting fish stocks. The Chicken of the Sea Samoa Packing plant was closed in September 2009 with the loss of around 2,000 jobs.

Forestry

Typical annual production includes 131,000 cubic metres (cum) roundwood, 61,000cum industrial roundwood, 21,000cum sawnwood, 58,000cum sawlogs & veneer logs, 70,000cum wood fuel.

Industry and manufacturing

The industrial sector typically accounts for over 25 per cent of GDP and employs approximately 6 per cent of the workforce.

Small-scale manufacturing and industry has expanded. The government's industrial area of Vaitele (on Upolu) houses a brewery, a cigarette factory and a match factory.

Other industries include copra processing, food processing, light engineering, woodworking and manufacture of coconut oil, paint, concrete and construction materials, bottled gases, plastic bags, corned beef and garments. US food processors have expressed interest in investing in fish-processing capacity.

Output of automotive wiring harnesses for export increased following the extension of the Yazaki Samoa plant, the largest employer. However production fell in 2004. Garment exports also declined when production was interupted by a move to new premises.

Industrial production grew in 2004 by 2.6 per cent, led by construction both private and public. The construction sector, following the damage from Cyclone Heta in January 2004, sparked a boom and coupled with major building projects in offices, schools, the National University of Samoa and the facilities for the South pacific Games, have more than bolstered the declines seen in other areas of the economy.

Tourism

Tourism is the main economic activity and the largest foreign exchange earner. The number of visitors continues to rise by about 20 per cent. The main markets are American Samoa and New Zealand.

There is still competition between tourists and business travellers for limited accommodation; however this should ease when the new hotels and resorts are finally completed by 2007.

Hydrocarbons

As there are no hydrocarbon reserves, Samoa relies entirely on the import of petroleum products, of which refined oil makes up around 58 per cent of Samoa's energy consumption. Imports come from New Zealand, Australia, Fiji and the US, averaging 1,000 barrels per day. Samoa does not import natural gas or coal.

Energy

Total installed generating capacity was 31MW in 2006. The autonomous government-owned, Electric Power Corporation (EPC) has sole responsibility to generate, transmit, distribute and sell electricity in Samoa with 95 per cent penetration. Hydropower provides 50 per cent of all electricity from five hydro, several diesel- and a solar-powered plants operated by EPC. Plans are underway to develop renewable energy based on wind, solar, hydro and bio-fuels.

Growth in demand is rising; as a result of low rainfall and lack of maintenance of old plants, output from several power stations was suspended in 2008 and rationing was introduced during daylight hours. In January 2010 the government commissioned feasibility studies to determine the potential for the EPC to build five new hydroelectric plants, with two sites on Savaii and three on Upolu. Funds for an initial three plants will be forthcoming and the remaining two will be scheduled for implementation at a later date.

Banking and insurance

The government has increased its deposits in the banking system over the last few years, enabling commercial banks to lend and boosting private sector credit growth. Banks are strongly capitalised and earn good profits.

Central bank

Central Bank of Samoa

Time

GMT plus 13 hours; daylight saving, GMT plus 14 hours.

On 9 May 2011, the Samoan government decided that, from 29 December, the International Date Line would be shifted from west to east, so that Somoa will be one of the first countries to begin the daily cycle and not one that completes the cycle; in effect it moves a day ahead in time and comes into line with its trading partners in Oceania and Australasia. On Thursday 29 December at 11.59.59 Samoa will lose one day and move forward to Saturday 31 December at 00.00.

Geography

Samoa lies in the southern Pacific Ocean about 2,400km north-east of New Zealand and about 450km west of American Samoa. Samoa comprises two large islands – Savii and Upolu, separated by a 13km ocean channel – and seven small, mostly uninhabited islands. The total land area is 2,934 square km. Savii and Upolu are coral fringed, rugged volcanic mountains rising to 1,856 metres (m) and 1,115m respectively.

Hemisphere

Southern

Climate

Temperatures 24–30 degrees Celsius (hottest in March) and high humidity. Rainy season November–April, rainfall at least 5,000 mm/year, heaviest in January.

Entry requirements

Passports

Required by all and valid for six months beyond the date of departure. Proof of onward/return passage and visa documentation for following destination, booked accommodation and sufficient funds for stay are required.

Visa
Not required by tourists for a period not exceeding 60 days. American Samoan and US citizens resident in American Samoa may visit with a 14–30 days visitor permit.
Business visitors should apply for a temporary resident permit from the Samoan Immigrations Department. Requirements and application form can be found at www.samoaimmigration.gov.ws under *Permit Services*.
Currency advice/regulations
The import of local and foreign currency is unlimited. Export of local currency is prohibited and foreign currency is limited to the amount imported.
Travellers cheques are accepted in banks and larger hotels.
Customs
Personal effects allowed duty-free.
Prohibited imports
Firearms, ammunition, explosives, illegal drugs and pornography. Plants, seeds, soil and animals may be imported subject to approval from the Department of Agriculture.

Health (for visitors)
Mandatory precautions
Vaccination certificate for yellow fever if travelling from an infected area.
Advisable precautions
Vaccinations for diphtheria, tuberculosis, hepatitis A and B, polio, tetanus, typhoid. There is a rabies risk.

Hotels
Most hotels are located close to the capital. There are five standards available from deluxe and superior to budget.

Credit cards
Major credit cards are accepted; ATMs are available.

Public holidays (national)
Fixed dates
1–2 Jan (New Year), 25 Apr (Anzac Day), 10 May (Mothers-of-Samoa Day), 1 Jun (Independence Day), 3 Nov (Arbor Day), 25–26 Dec (Christmas).
Variable dates
Good Friday, Easter Monday, Labour Day (first Mon in Aug), *Lotu-a-Tamaiti* (second Mon in Oct, the day after White Sunday).

Working hours
Banking
Mon–Fri: 0900–1500. Larger branches are open Sat: 0900–1200.
Business
Mon–Fri: 0800–1200, 1300–1630.
Government
Mon–Fri: 0800–1200, 1300–1630.
Shops
Mon–Fri: 0800–1200, 1330–1630; Sat: 0800–1230.

Telecommunications
Telephone/fax
Samoa uses satellite communications and some domestic transmissions are conducted over microwave, generally in less densely populated areas, and between the islands of Upolu and Savaii. All can be adversely affected by bad weather.
Mobile/cell phones
A GSM 900 service is in operation.

Electricity supply
240V AC, with flat, three-pin plugs (Australian style).

Weights and measures
Imperial system, with metric systems in use.

Social customs/useful tips
Appointments should be made in advance. Ties need only be worn for formal meetings. English is used for business and commerce. Care should be taken to respect local customs and practices. Samoans do not like to disagree with someone in authority, or not give the anticipated reply, which can lead to misunderstandings by foreign visitors (a 'yes' can mean 'no'). Gratuities are optional and gifts for excellent service are appreciated. The minimum drinking age is 18 years.

Getting there
Air
National airline: Polynesian Airlines
International airport/s: Faleolo International (APW), 34km west of Apia, with banks, post office, duty-free and car hire. There are taxis and buses to the city.
Airport tax: Departures tax: S$40
Surface
Water: Ferry services operate from American Samoa; cargo ships also carry passengers from New Zealand, Australia, Japan and other Pacific islands, as well as Europe and the US.
Main port/s: Apia and Asau

Getting about
National transport
Air: Polynesian Airlines operates regular services between Faleolo (Upolu) and Maota (south-east Savii).
Buses: Scheduled bus services operate in and around Apia and Salelologa (Savai'i).
Water: Daily ferry services operate between Salelologa (Savai'i) and Mulianua (Upolu).
City transport
Taxis: Taxi service is available in Apia.
Car hire
International or national driving licence required. Traffic drives on the righ (from 6 September 2009).

BUSINESS DIRECTORY

The addresses listed below are a selection only. While World of Information makes every endeavour to check these addresses, we cannot guarantee that changes have not been made, especially to telephone numbers and area codes. We would welcome any corrections.

Telephone area codes
The international direct dialling (IDD) code for Samoa is +685 followed by subscriber's number.

Useful telephone numbers
Police, fire and ambulance: 999.

Chambers of Commerce
Samoa Chamber of Commerce and Industry, PO Box 2014, Lotemau Centre, Vaea Street, Apia (tel: 21-237; fax: 21-578; email: info@samoachamber.com).

Banking
ANZ Bank (Samoa) Ltd, PO Box L1855, Beach Road, Apia (tel: 22-422; fax: 24-595, 23-807).

Australia and New Zealand Banking Group Ltd, PO Box L1855, Apia (tel: 22-422; fax: 24-595).

Development Bank of Samoa, PO Box 1232, Apia (tel: 22-861; fax: 23-888).

International Business Bank Corp Ltd; Level 2, Chandra Hse, Convent St, Apia (tel: 22-393; fax: 23-253).

National Bank of Samoa Limited; PO Box L3047, Apia (tel: 23-077; fax: 23-085).

Pacific Commercial Bank Ltd, PO Box 1860, Beach Road, Apia (tel: 20-000; fax: 22-848).

Central bank
Central Bank of Samoa, Central Bank Building, Private Bag, Apia (tel: 34-100; fax: 20-293; e-mail: cbs@samoa.net; internet: www.cbs.gov.ws).

Travel information
Faleolo International Airport, Private Bag, Apia (tel: 23-201, 23-202, 42-050; fax; 24-281; e-mail: etuale@samoa.net).

Mulifanua Ferry Terminal Pier, PO Box 3267, Apia.

Polynesian Airlines, PO Box 599, Beech Road, Apia (tel: 21-261; fax: 20-023).

Samoa Shipping Corp, Shipping House, Matautu-tai; PO Bag, Apia (tel: 20-935/6; fax: 22-352; email: info@samoashipping.com).

Ministry of tourism
Samoa Tourism Authority, PO Box 2272, Apia (tel: 63-500; fax:20-886; email: info@visitsamoa.ws).

National tourist organisation offices
Samoa Visitors' Bureau, PO Box 862, Apia (tel: 20-878; fax: 20-886; e-mail: samoawsvb@pactok.peg.apc.org; internet site: www.visitsamoa.ws).

Ministries

Ministry of Agriculture, Quarantine Division, P O Box 1874, Apia (tel: 22-561; fax: 24-576; internet: www.samoaquarantine.gov.ws).

Ministry of Commerce, Industry and Labour, Level 4, ACB Building, Apia (tel: 20-441/2; internet: www.mcilsamoa.ws).

Ministry of Finance, Central Bank Bld, Matafele; Private Bag, Government of Samoa, Apia (tel: 34-333; fax: 21-321; internet: www.mof.gov.ws).

Ministry of Prime Minister and Cabinet, Samoa Immigration, Lever 2, Lober Bld; PO Box L1861, Apia (tel: 20-291/2; fax: 22-243; internet: www.samoaimmigration.gov.ws).

Other useful addresses

Asian Development Bank (ADB), South Pacific Regional Mission, La Casa di Andrea, Fr. Dr. W. H. Lini Highway; PO Box 127, Port Vila, Vanuatu (tel: (+678-2) 23-300; fax: (+678-2) 23-183; email: adbsprm@adb.org; internet: www.adb.org/SPRM).

Department of Statistics, PO Box 1151, Apia.

Department of Trade, Commerce and Industry, Chandra House, Trade Information Centre, PO Box 862, Apia (tel: 20-471; fax: 21-504; email: IPU@tci.gov.ws; internet: www.tradeinvestsamoa.ws).

Government of Samoa, PO Box L 1864, Apia (tel: 24-799, 63-115; fax: 21-742, 26-396; e-mail: contact@govt.ws).

Samoa Mission to the United Nations, 800 Second Avenue, Suite 400J, New York, NY 10017 (tel: (+1-212) 599 6196; fax: (+1-212) 599 0797).

Internet sites

Government of Samoa: www.govt.ws

Ministry of Commerce, Industry and Labour: www.mcil.gov.ws

Ministry of Finance: www.mof.gov.ws

Samoa Head of State: www.head-of-state-samoa.ws

Samoa Immigration: www.samoaimmigration.gov.ws

Samoa Industry of Manufacturers and Exporters: www.same.org.ws

Samoa International Finance Authority: www.sifa.ws

Samoa Live: www.samoalive.com

South Pacific Tourism Organisation: www.tcsp.com

San Marino

KEY FACTS

Official name: Serenissima Repubblica di San Marino (Most Serene Republic of San Marino)

Head of State: Two Capitani-Reggenti (Captains-Regent), elected for six month terms: Gabriele Gatti (PDCS), Matteo Fiorini (Alleanza Popolare (AP) (from 1 Oct 2011)

Head of government: Secretary of State for Foreign and Political Affairs, Antonella Mularoni (from 3 Dec 2008)

Ruling party: The Patto per San Marion (Pact for San Marino) coalition (comprising Partito Democratico Cristiano Sammarinese (PDCS) (Sammarinese Christian Democratic Party), Europopolari per San Marino (EPS) (Euro-Enthusiasts for San Marino) and Arengo e Libertà (AL) (Arengo and Freedom) alliance, with Alleanza Popolare (AP) (Popular Alliance), Lista della Libertà (LdL) (Freedom List) and Unione Sammarinese dei Moderati (USdM) (Sammarinese Union of Moderates) (from 9 Nov 2008)

Area: 61 square km

Population: 33,163 (2010)*

Capital: San Marino

Official language: Italian

Currency: Euro (eur) = 100 cents

Exchange rate: eur0.75 per US$ (Oct 2011)

Labour force: 22,600 (2008)

Unemployment: 3.10% (2008); 4.71 per cent (May 2011)

* estimated figure

COUNTRY PROFILE

Historical profile

San Marino is completely surrounded by Italy. It is the oldest surviving republic in the world, having been an independent republic since the year 301AD.
1600 The constitution was ratified.
1926 An additional electoral law was passed, which serves some of the functions of a constitution.
1988 San Marino joined the Council of Europe.
1990–92 A coalition of Partito Democratico Progressista (PDP) (Progressive Democratic Party) (ex-communists) and Partito Democratico Cristiano Sammarinese (PDCS) (San Marino Christian Democratic Party) took office.
1992 PDCS formed a coalition with the Partito Socialista Sammarinese (PSS) (San Marino Socialist Party). San Marino became a member of the UN.
1993 In the general election, the PDCS won 26 seats and the PSS 14 seats; the coalition continued.
1998 After general elections, the PDCS/PSS coalition continued.
2001 Differences within the PDCS/PSS coalition led to early parliamentary elections (originally scheduled for 2003), but resulted in a continuation of the coalition.
2002 San Marino, in line with Italy, replaced the lira with the euro currency.
2005 The Partito dei Socialisti e dei Democratici (PSD) (Party of Socialists and Democrats) was formed from the amalgamation of PSS and the Partito dei Democratici (PD) (Democratic Party).
2006 The PDCS won elections, but the PSD formed a coalition government with two other parties.
2008 In parliamentary elections the opposition, four-party centre-right Patto per San Marion (Pact for San Marino) coalition won 54.2 per cent of the vote (35 seats out of 60). Antonella Mularoni was appointed Secretary of State for Foreign and Political Affairs.
2009 Massimo Cenci (NPS) and Oscar Mina (PDCS) took office as captains-regent; six months later, Stefano Palmieri (AP) and Francesco Mussoni (PDCS) took over. An emergency census was conducted in response to the number of bogus residency claims filed by foreign residents in an effort to avoid paying tax in their own countries.
2010 Marco Conti (PDCS) and Glauco Sansovini (Alleanza Nazionale (AL) (National Alliance)) were elected as captains-regent in April. In May the Italian finance minister declared that San Marino was on Italy's blacklist for not agreeing to full transparency and to disclose details of bank deposits of Italian residents. In June, the San Marino justice minister rejected the criticism saying that depositing money was not a crime and that rather than this being a matter of transparency it was one of San Marino's sovereignty.
2011 On 1 April, Maria Luisa Berti (Noi Sammarinesi (NS) (We Sammarinese)) and Filippo Tamagnini (PDCS) took office as captains-regent; both are members of the Pact for San Marino ruling coalition. On 1 October Gabriele Gatti (PDCS), Matteo Fiorini (Alleanza Popolare (AP) took office as captains-regent.

Political structure

Constitution

The constitution was ratified on 8 October 1600. An additional electoral law was passed in 1926, which serves some of the functions of a constitution.
The country is divided into nine *castelli* (municipalities), each governed by a Captain.

The executive

The Consiglio Grande e Generale (CGeG) (the Great and General Council) elects two members every six months to act as captains-regent, who functions jointly as heads of state and, together with a 10-member Congress of State (cabinet), exercise executive power. The secretary of state for foreign affairs has come to assume many of the prerogatives of a prime minister.
The Congress of State is elected by the CGeG for a five-year term.

National legislature

Legislative power is vested in the unicameral Consiglio Grande e Generale (CGeG) (Great and General Council), with 60 members elected by universal adult suffrage for five-year terms. It has the responsibility of electing the 10-member congress of state.

Legal system

Last elections

9 November 2008 (parliamentary)
Results: Parliamentary: the Patto per San Marion (Pact for San Marino) coalition (comprising Partito Democratico Cristiano

Sammarinese (PDCS) (Sammarinese Christian Democratic Party), Europopolari per San Marino (EPS) (Euro-Enthusiasts for San Marino) and Arengo e Libertà (AL) (Arengo and Freedom) alliance, with Alleanza Popolare (AP) (Popular Alliance), Lista della Libertà (LdL) (Freedom List) and Unione Sammarinese dei Moderati (USdM) (Sammarinese Union of Moderates)) won 54.2 per cent of the vote (35 seats out of 60). The Riforme e Libertà (Reforms and Freedom) coalition (comprising Partito dei Socialisti e dei Democratici (PSD) (Party of Socialists and Democrats) with the Sinistra Unita (SU) (United Left) and Democratici di Centro (DdC) (Centre Democrats)) 45.8 per cent (25). Turnout was 68.5 per cent.

Next elections

2013 (parliamentary)

Political parties

Ruling party

The Patto per San Marion (Pact for San Marino) coalition (comprising Partito Democratico Cristiano Sammarinese (PDCS) (Sammarinese Christian Democratic Party), Europopolari per San Marino (EPS) (Euro-Enthusiasts for San Marino) and Arengo e Libertà (AL) (Arengo and Freedom) alliance, with Alleanza Popolare (AP) (Popular Alliance), Lista della Libertà (LdL) (Freedom List) and Unione Sammarinese dei Moderati (USdM) (Sammarinese Union of Moderates) (from 9 Nov 2008)

Main opposition party

Riforme e Libertà (Reforms and Freedom) coalition comprising Partito dei Socialisti e dei Democratici (PSD) (Party of Socialists and Democrats), Sinistra Unita (SU) (United Left) and Democratici di Centro (DdC) (Centre Democrats).

Political situation

An emergency census got underway in September 2009, in response to the number of bogus residency claims filed by foreign residents in an effort to avoid paying tax in their own countries.

In May 2010 the Italian finance minister declared that San Marino was on Italy's blacklist for not agreeing to full transparency and disclosing details of bank deposits of Italian residents. So it was somewhat obtuse that the San Marino justice minister to rejected the criticism saying that depositing money was not a crime and that rather than this being a matter of transparency it was one of San Marino's sovereignty.

Population

33,163 (2010)*

Last census: July 2000: 26,941

Population density: 433 inhabitants per sq km.

Annual growth rate: 0.9 per cent 1994–2004 (WHO 2006)

Ethnic make-up

The population includes Sammarinese and Italians.

Religions

Roman Catholic

Education

Schooling is free of charge and until aged 16. Primary schooling lasts until aged 11, then on to lower secondary education for three years, from ages 11 to 14, of general education, then the last two years of either technical or specialised academic study.

Higher secondary schools, from aged 16 to 19, provide two-year courses in preparation for higher education.

Higher education is provided by the Università degli Studi della Repùbblica di San Marino, and its Istituto di Cibernetica.

Compulsory years: 6 to 15.

Health

The age of the population has risen, reflecting a general trend in Western Europe.

Life expectancy: 82 years, 2004 (WHO 2006)

Fertility rate/Maternal mortality rate: 1.2 births per woman, 2004 (WHO 2006)

Birth rate/Death rate: 10.5 births per 1,000 population; eight deaths per 1,000 population (2003).

Child (under 5 years) mortality rate (per 1,000): 4.0 per 1,000 live births (World Bank)

Main cities

San Marino (capital, estimated population 2,276 in 2005); Serravalle/Dogano (4,813); Borgo Maggiore (2,442), Murata (1,580).

Languages spoken

Italian

Official language/s

Italian

Media

Press

In Italian, the two dailies published are *La Tribuna Sammarinese* (www.latribunasammarinese.net) and *San Marino Oggi*, with periodicals *San Marino* and *La Sportivo*. In Italian, L'Informazione di San Marino (www.libertas.sm) and San Marino Notizie (www.sanmarinonotizie.com) are online news outlets, while *Italica* (www.italica.sm) is in English.

Broadcasting

Radio: The government-controlled San Marino RTV (www.sanmarinortv.sm) broadcasts over several wavebands in FM. Some regional Italian stations can also be received.

Television: RTV operates the television station while some regional Italian broadcasts can also be received.

Economy

The economy is closely linked with that of Italy, which surrounds it geographically. The economy is diverse, with tourism being the main source of revenue, providing around 50 per cent of GDP, including duty-free sales of goods to tourists. Traditional industries include quarrying for building stone, ceramics, leather goods, textiles, wine and food production and lately, electronics manufacturing. Sales of postage stamps and coins to collectors provide 10 per cent of the government's income. Italy compensates San Marino, in the form of an annual subsidy, for relinquishing certain rights.

GDP growth was 3.5 per cent in 2007, which fell to -1.1 per cent in 2008 and was projected to fall again to -5.0 per cent in 2009. Unemployment and inflation rose from 3.0 per cent and 2.5 per cent respectively in 2007 to 3.1 per cent and 4.3 per cent in 2008. However, only unemployment was projected to rise in 2009, to 5.1 per cent, as business activity declined, while inflation was projected to fall to 2.4 per cent as oil and food prices declined in price and imports (much of which comes from Italy) fell.

While San Marino adopted the euro as its currency, it is not formally part of the eurozone and is not a member of the European Central Bank. As such it did not have access to Euro-system liquidity when the global economic crisis struck in 2009 and its banking system came under stress as it only had indirect access to the EU payment system via Italian banks. Consequently, local banks were under greater credit risk and additional cost through cross-border transactions. Nevertheless, the banking system has contributed to high growth, despite the largest bank in San Marino facing financial difficulties in 2008/09 and the accusations of money-laundering levelled at senior bank officials.

External trade

San Marino does not belong to the European Union but as it maintains a customs and currency union with Italy and uses the euro it has *de facto* ties with the EU. Italy accounts for 87 per cent of all external trade.

Imports

Imports predominantly consist of food and manufactured goods.

Exports

Important exports include financial services, building stone, lime, timber, hides and ceramics; foodstuffs, live animals, chestnuts, wheat, wine and baked goods,

Agriculture
Farming
The republic was formerly dependent on agriculture and forestry. The agricultural sector employs around 1 per cent of the workforce. Approximately 17 per cent of the land is arable. Principal crops include olives, grapes, wheat and corn.

Industry and manufacturing
Quarrying for building stone is a traditional industry.
Manufacturing employs 41 per cent of the workforce, construction 11 per cent, and services, transport and communications 19 per cent.

Banking and insurance
The banking sector is of strategic importance to San Marino's economy, making a sizeable contribution to the state revenue; its banks are profitable, well-provisioned and cost efficient. The Istituto di Credito Sammarinese (ICS) operates as a central bank, although it does not have an independent monetary policy.
San Marino is a signatory of a new EU tax agreement with non-EU countries. San Marino will impose a withholding tax, up to 35 per cent, to be passed to the tax department of an EU citizen's country, but retaining the anonymity of the saver.
San Marino has also agreed to supply information on tax fraud, for criminal or civil trials, and notify EU member states about additional malpractices.
Central bank
Banca Centrale della Repubblica di San Marino (Central Bank of the Republic of San Marino); European Central Bank (ECB).

Time
GMT plus one hour (daylight saving, late March to late October, GMT plus two hours)

Geography
San Marino is a landlocked country of 61.2 square kilometres, entirely surrounded by and located in central Italy. The Italian region of Emilia-Romagna borders to the north and east and the Marche to the south and west. The capital, also called San Marino has eight satellite villages. The geography is mountainous dominated by Mount Titano, the highest peak.
Hemisphere
Northern

Climate
San Marino enjoys a Mediterranean climate with warm summers and dry, cold winters. Temperatures can range between 0–30 degrees Celsius.

Dress codes
Lightweight clothing for summer, medium-weight and topcoat for winter.

Entry requirements
As per Italy
Passports
Required by all and passports must be valid for three months from arrival. Nationals of countries which are signatories of the Schengen Accords, which includes most EU/EEA member states, San Marino and Croatia, may visit on national IDs.
Visa
No visa requirements for citizens of most of Europe, the Americas, Australasia and some Asian countries, visiting for up to 90 days. For a full list, and further information for those citizens not included on the list of visa-free travel, visit www.ambwashingtondc.esteri.it and see *consular services*. A Schengen visa application (offered in several languages) can be downloaded from www.eurovisa.info/ApplicationForm.htm.
Business travellers who do not have visa-free arrangements must provide a letter from their employer guaranteeing travel expenses, including full itinerary and purpose of the trip. Letters of invitation from all Italian companies to be visited, and a current (not over 90 days) *Visura Camerale* issued by the Italian Chamber of Commerce should be attached; a return/onward ticket must be produced before collection of the passport and visa from the issuing consulate, which may request any additional documents at its discretion.
Within eight days of arrival in San Marion the visa traveller must appear before local police authorities to receive a Residency Permit and will also need to show proof of health insurance.
Prohibited entry
Visitors may be refused entry for public security or health reasons, or if not holding visible means of support and onward/return tickets and documents for their next destination.
Currency advice/regulations
The import and export of local or foreign currency up to eur10,300 is allowed. Any amount over this must be declared on Form V2 at customs on arrival.

Health (for visitors)
Mandatory precautions
None
Advisable precautions
Up-to-date tetanus and polio immunisations are recommended. Long-term visitors should consider hepatitis A immunisation.

Hotels
There are approximately 30 hotels of various standards.

Credit cards
Credit cards are widely accepted.

Public holidays (national)
Fixed dates
31 Dec–1 Jan (New Year), 6 Jan (Epiphany), 5 Feb (Liberation Day), 25 Mar (Arengo Day), 1 Apr (Captains Regent Investiture Day), 1 May (Labour Day), 28 Jul (Fall of Fascism Anniversary), 15 Aug (Assumption Day), 3 Sep (Republic Day), 1 Oct (Captains Regent Investiture Day), 1 Nov (All Saints' Day), 2 Nov (All Souls' Day), 8 Dec (Immaculate Conception), 24–26 Dec (Christmas).
Holidays which falls on a Sunday are observed on Monday.
Variable dates
Good Friday, Easter Monday, Corpus Christi (May/Jun).

Working hours
Banking
Mon–Fri: 0830–1330, 1530–1630.
Shops
Mon–Sat: 0830–1300, 1530–1930.

Telecommunications
Mobile/cell phones
Networks 900/1800 GSM are in operation.

Electricity supply
220V AC 50Hz

Getting there
Air
Closest international airports: Rimini (RMI) (Italy) 27km, or Bologna (BLQ) (Italy) 135km.
Surface
There are regular bus services, by highways, from Rimini or Bologna, Italy. The nearest railhead is at Rimini.

Getting about
National transport
The roads are good. A funicular (cable car) operates between Borgo Maggiore and the capital.

BUSINESS DIRECTORY

The addresses listed below are a selection only. While World of Information makes every endeavour to check these addresses, we cannot guarantee that changes have not been made, especially to telephone numbers and area codes. We would welcome any corrections.

Telephone area codes
The international direct dialling (IDD) code for San Marino is +378 followed by 0549 and subscriber's number.

Chambers of Commerce
Agency for Promotion and Development of the Economy, 33 Via G Giacomini, 47890 San Marino (tel: 914-001; fax: 913-473; e-mail: info@apse.sm).

Banking
Central bank
Banca Centrale della Repubblica di San Marino (Central Bank of the Republic of San Marino), 120 Via del Voltone, 47890 San Marino (tel: (+378) (0)549 882-325; fax: (+378) (0)549 882-328).

European Central Bank (ECB), Kaiserstrasse 29, D-60311 Frankfurt am Main, Germany (tel: (+49-69) 13-440; fax: (+49-69) 1344-6000).

Travel information
National tourist organisation offices
Ufficio di Stato per il Turismo (state tourist office), Contrada Omagnano 20, 47031, San Marino (tel: 882-998).

Other useful addresses
Azienda Autonoma di Stato Filatelica e Numismatica (AASFN) (stamps and coins), 5 Piazza Garibaldi, 47031 San Marino (tel: 882-370; fax: 882-363; e-mail: aasfn@omniway.sm).

British Consulate, 2 Lungarno Corsini, 1-50123 Florence, Italy (tel: (+39-055) 212-594; fax: (+39-055) 219-112).

Direzione Generale PPTT (post and tele-communications),17 Contrada Omerelli, San Marino (tel: 882-555; fax: 992-760).

Notizie de San Marino, Radiotelevisione Italiana, 14 Viale Mazzini, 1-00195 Rome, Italy (fax: (+39-06) 372-5680).

Office for Industry, Handicrafts and Trade, Palazzo Mercuri, San Marino (tel: 992-745, 991-385).

Secretariat of State for Finance and the Budget, Palazzo Begni, San Marino (tel: 992-345).

Internet sites
San Marino tourism authority: www.visitsanmarino.com

Web portal for trade: www.tradecenter.sm/index_e.htm

São Tomé and Príncipe

KEY FACTS

Official name: República Democrática de São Tomé e Príncipe (Democratic Republic of São Tomé and Príncipe)

Head of State: President Manuel Pinto Costa (from 3 Sep 2011)

Head of government: Prime Minister Patrice Trovoada (ADI) (from 2008; re-elected 14 Aug 2010)

Ruling party: Coalition led by Acção Democrática Independente (ADI) (Independent Democratic Action) (from Aug 2010)

Area: 964 square km

Population: 165,000 (2010)*

Capital: São Tomé

Official language: Portuguese

Currency: Dobra (Db) = 100 centavos

Exchange rate: Db18,175.00 per US$ (Oct 2011)

GDP per capita: US$1,174 (2009)*

GDP real growth: 4.30% (2009)*

GDP: US$191.20 million (2009)*

Inflation: 16.90% (2009)

* estimated figure

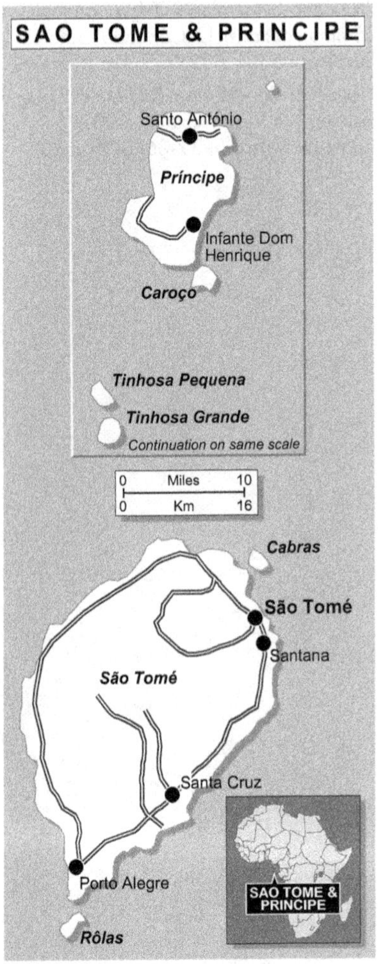

Ten candidates took part in the first round of presidential elections, held on 17 July 2011, but none won the required 51 per cent of the vote for outright victory. Manuel Pinto da Costa (independent), who had been leader of the Movimiento de Libertaçao de São Tomé e Príncipe (MLSTP) (Movement for the Liberation of São Tomé and Príncipe), when São Tomé and Príncipe (STP) became independent in 1975 – and was the country's first president – won the first round with 35.8 per cent of the votes. A runoff was held on 7 August, when Pinto da Costa won 52.88 per cent of the vote; his opponent, Evaristo Carvalho of the ruling Acção Democrática Independente (ADI) (Independent Democratic Action) and speaker of parliament, won 47.12 per cent. President Pinto da Costa took office on 3 September.

President Pinto da Costa, who had a reputation for authoritarian rule during his first terms in office as president (1975–1991), had promised during his campaign in 2011 not to repeat his old style. Instead, he focussed on the need for political stability and the tackling of widespread corruption.

Government role

Prime Minister Patrice Trovoada (ADI) had been re-elected in August 2010 to carry out the government's programme seeking to transform the country and diversify its economy, through policies to promote good governance; economic growth and development; national and social cohesion; and the rule of law. Since then, the new government has pledged to continue the reforms in public finance management undertaken by the previous administration. The main government change in 2010 was the transfer of the department of co-operation from the ministry of foreign affairs to the ministry of planning and finance (MPF), in order to highlight the importance of official development assistance (ODA) to the budget. Monetary policy is geared towards maintaining the euro currency peg, introduced in January 2010.

The World Bank's *Doing Business* 2011 report ranked STP 178 out of 183 countries, due to its lax regulatory enforcement, inadequate infrastructure and past political unrest. The report considered the investment laws and regulations were onerous, and bureaucracy could be cumbersome and prone to corruption. Other deterrents to investment include foreign exchange controls, some restrictions to capital transactions, land ownership issues and the influence the government maintains on everyday business. The judicial system is currently the weakest link in the STP's administration, as legal enforcement of contracts is close to non-existent. However, foreign and domestic firms are treated equally under the law.

Partnerships

The International Monetary Fund (IMF) forecast that the economy would expand by 7.0 per cent in 2011 and 7.5 per cent in 2012. The authorities are keen to broaden the long-standing relationship with STP's former colonial power, Portugal. European Union partners still dominate trade flows, although oil imports from Angola now account for approximately 20 per cent of STP's total imports. STP's strategy is to encourage foreign direct investment (FDI) from emerging economic partners to develop oil exploration, tourism and other economic activities.

In a time of increased competition for scarce resources, STP is pragmatically seeking to engage with various emerging partners while nurturing collaboration with traditional partners. Prime Minister Trovoada has expressed his interest in diversifying trade and diplomatic ties with emerging partners in order to spur STP's development. Economic growth in 2011–12 will be driven by FDI in oil exploration and the construction of a new deepwater seaport – a project the prime minister remains committed to, in order to transform STP's economy into a regional hub for transhipment activity.

Partners from emerging economies have long played a crucial role in STP's economic and social development. Taiwan has the longest track record, but India and Brazil are intensifying their bilateral co-operation. Nigeria, Angola and increasingly other neighbouring countries are also engaging more pro-actively with STP.

Slow progress

According to the *African Economic Outlook 2011* (AEO), published jointly by the African Development Bank and the Organisation for Economic Co-operation and Development, poverty was estimated at 54 per cent in 2009, and was widespread in rural and peri-urban areas. Despite economic growth the government has not managed to overcome social and developmental challenges, and only three Millennium Development Goals (MDGs) may be achieved by the country by 2015: universal primary education, the reduction of infant mortality and improved maternal health.

STP was the 47th African nation to join the Indian government's Pan-African e-Network Project. This project will link STP to the other countries of the African Union via video-conference, focusing on health services and linking the main hospital on the island of São Tomé with more than 10 Indian hospitals.

In 2011, the UN Human Development Index (HDI) ranked STP 144 (out of 187) for national development in health, education and income. Of its population 44.7 per cent experience multiple deprivations in the same household.

Risk assessment

Economy	Fair
Politics	Fair
Regional stability	Fair

COUNTRY PROFILE

Historical profile

1469–72 The islands were first sighted by Portuguese sailors.
1485 The town of São Tomé was founded; Príncipe was not settled until 15 years later. The islands quickly became the largest sugar producing area in the world, using slave labour.
1700–1800 Coffee and cocoa plantations were also set up using slave labour.
1875 Slavery was abolished, only to be replaced by a system of forced labour. The labour force consisted mainly of workers brought by the Portuguese from Angola, Mozambique and Cape Verde. On several occasions they launched rebellions against their colonial rulers which were brutally suppressed.
1951 The islands became an overseas province of Portugal.
1974 The end of fascist rule in Portugal marked the beginning of independence for its overseas colonies. A transitional government was established.
1975 The Democratic Republic of São Tomé and Príncipe gained independence from Portugal. The only legal party, the Movimiento de Libertação de São Tomé e Principe (MLSTP) (Movement for the Liberation of São Tomé), made a clean sweep in the general elections and its leader, Manuel Pinto da Costa, became the first president. The economy was hard-hit when Portugal withdrew support. Most plantations were quickly nationalised and foreign investors and workers left; the islands developed strong links with Cuba. Under colonial administration there had been little investment in education or healthcare systems for the local population; at independence the literacy rate was 10 per cent and there was only one doctor in the entire country.
1980s A severe drought and a drop in world prices for cocoa crippled the economy. Pinto da Costa began a process of dropping economic ties with the Eastern Bloc in favour of a capitalist, market economy.
1989 Changes within MLSTP began; multi-party democracy was introduced as an objective.
1990 The MLSTP changed its name and adopted MLSTP-PSD (Social Democratic Party) to fight the next election. A multi-party constitution was approved by referendum, allowing direct and free elections for the presidency and legislature.
1991 The ruling MLSTP-PSD lost the country's first election, defeated by the Partido da Convergencia Democrática-Grupo de Reflexão (PCD-GR) (Democratic Convergence Party-Reflection Group). Miguel Trovoada, an independent candidate supported by the PCD-GR, was elected president. The currency was devalued by 40 per cent as part of stringent austerity measures, imposed by the International Monetary Fund (IMF) and the World Bank in exchange for economic assistance.
1994 The MLSTP-PSD won most seats in the National Assembly but fell short of an overall majority.

KEY INDICATORS — São Tomé and Príncipe

	Unit	2006	2007	2008	2009	2010
Population	m	0.16	0.16	0.16	*0.16	*0.17
Gross domestic product (GDP)	US$bn	0.12	0.14	0.17	*0.19	*0.20
GDP per capita	US$	769	*880	*1,108	*1,174	–
GDP real growth	%	6.7	6.0	5.8	5.5	6.5
Inflation	%	23.1	18.6	26.1	16.9	*12.3
Exports (fob) (goods)	US$m	3.0	6.8	7.8	9.2	–
Imports (fob) (goods)	US$m	59.0	64.9	92.2	83.8	–
Balance of trade	US$m	-56.0	-58.1	84.3	-74.6	–
Current account	US$m	-49.0	-55.4	-93.5	-78.8	*-78.0
Total reserves minus gold	US$m	34.2	39.3	–	–	–
Foreign exchange	US$m	34.1	39.3	–	–	–
Exchange rate	per US$	6,780.00	14,101.00	15,450.00	16,208.00	18,499.00

* estimated figure

1995 Príncipe was granted autonomy; the MLSTP-PSD won most seats in its assembly. Strikes by public employees for promised pay rises destabilised the president and government. An abortive coup resulted in the formation of a coalition government which included members of the Ação Democrática Independente (ADI) (Independent Democratic Action), the Coligação Democrático da Oposição (CDO) (Democratic Opposition Coalition) and the Frente Democrática Crista (FDC) (Christian Democratic Front).
1996 Trovoada was re-elected president. Prime Minister Armindo Vaz d'Almeida was removed from office and his position was taken by Raw Wagner da Conceiçao Bragança Neto (MLSTP-PSD).
1998 Elections to the National Assembly resulted in a victory for the centre-left MLSTP-PSD.
2001 Fradique de Menezes won the presidential election.
2002 National Assembly elections were won by the MLSTP; Gabriel Costa became prime minister. He was dismissed by de Menezes in September and replaced in October by Maria das Neves, the country's first female prime minister.
2002 MLSTP won parliamentary elections; Maria das Neves, the country's first female prime minister replaced Gabriel Costa.
2003 The constitution was revised. A military coup staged by Major Fernando Pereira toppled the government while President de Menezes was out of the country. President de Menezes signed an accord with the coup leaders, which restored democratic rule and included an amnesty for the insurgents. Prime Minister das Neves resigned but was reappointed several days later. Bidding began for offshore oil blocs controlled by São Tomé and Príncipe and Nigeria.
2004 The president and prime minister clashed over control of oil deals. Maria das Neves was dismissed after a series of corruption scandals and Damião Vaz d'Almeida became prime minister.
2005 Maria do Carmo Silveira was nominated prime minister after Vaz d'Almeida's resigned.
2006 MLSTP was defeated in parliamentary elections, by a coalition led by the president's Movimento de Libertação de São Tomé e Príncipe-Partido Social Democrata (MLSTP/PSD) (Movement for the Liberation of São Tomé and Príncipe/Social Democratic Party). Tomé Vera Cruz became prime minister. Fradique de Menezes was re-elected president.
2008 Prime Minister Tomé Vera Cruz resigned, having failed in parliament to get the 2008 budget passed; Patrice Trovoada (ADI) was appointed as prime minister, but he lost a censure motion (30–23). The president appointed Joaquim Rafael Branco (MLSTP/PSD) as prime minister.
2009 A coup attempt was foiled; 36 of its perpetrators were arrested and a cache of arms were discovered in the home of opposition politician, Arlecio Costa. The requirement that European visitors must have a vaccination certificate for yellow fever was withdrawn, with the hope this would boost tourism. A government agreement was signed with the Spanish Aresa Group to provide a regular ferry service between the islands of São Tomé and Príncipe. Portugal signed a loan agreement with the government, to allow the dobra currency to be anchored to the euro.
2010 A memorandum of understanding (MOU) was signed in April to set up a joint São Tomé and Cape Verde company to run a high-speed ferry service between the two countries; however by July 2011 the service was still not operating. Parliamentary elections that had been postponed in February were held on 1 August. The Acção Democrática Independente (ADI) (Independent Democratic Action) won 26 seats (out of 55) and the ruling MLSTP-PSD won 21, with a turnout of 88 per cent.
2011 In the first round of presidential elections, held on 17 July, 10 candidates took part but none won the required 51 per cent of the vote for outright victory. Manuel Pinto da Costa (independent), who had been leader of the MLSTP when São Tomé and Príncipe became independent in 1975 and was the country's first president, won most votes with 35.8 per cent. He duly won the run-off on 7 August with 52.88 per cent of the vote to 47.12 per cent for Evaristo Carvalho (Acção Democrática Independente) (ADI) (Independent Democratic Action), the speaker of parliament. President Costa took office on 3 September.

Political structure

Constitution

The 5 November 1975 constitution was revised in September 1990, following a national referendum, which approved a multi-party constitution, allowing direct and free elections for the presidency and legislature. The constitution was revised again in January 2003.
The island of Príncipe was granted political and administrative autonomy in April 1995.

Form of state

Sovereign, unitary and democratic state.

The executive

The president is elected for a maximum of two five-year terms of office.

National legislature

The unicameral Assembleia Popular Nacional (National People's Assembly) 55 members elected by proportional representation in seven multi-seat constituencies (districts), to serve for four-year terms. There are six district assemblies on Sao Tomé and a seven-member regional assembly on the island of Príncipe.

Legal system

Portuguese legal system. The Supreme Court is appointed by the National Assembly.

Last elections

1 August 2010 (parliamentary); 17 July and 7 August 2011 (presidential first round and runoff)

Results: Parliamentary: Acção Democrática Independente (ADI) (Independent Democratic Action) won 26 seats (out of 55), Movimento de Libertação de São Tomé e Príncipe-Partido Social Democrata (MLSTP-PSD) (Movement for the Liberation of São Tomé and Príncipe-Social Democratic Party) won 21, Partido de Convergência Democrática-Grupa de Reflexão (PCD-GR) (Democratic Convergence Party-Reflection Group) won seven, Movimento Democrático das Forças da Mudança-Partido Liberal (MDFM-PL) (Force for Democratic Change Movement-Liberal Party) won one. Turnout was 88 per cent.
Presidential (first round): Manuel Pinto da Costa won (independent) 35.8 per cent of the vote, Evaristo Carvalho (ADI) 21.8 per cent, Maria das Neves (independent) 14 per cent, and Delfim Neves (four-party coalition of PCD-GR, MDFM-PL) 13.9 per cent; six other candidates each won less that 5 per cent. Turnout was 68.4 per cent. Runoff: Costa 52.88 per cent, Carvalho 47.12 per cent; turnout was 74.0 per cent.

Next elections

2014 (parliamentary); 2016 (presidential)

Political parties

Ruling party

Coalition led by Acção Democrática Independente (ADI) (Independent Democratic Action) (from Aug 2010)

Main opposition party

Movimento Democrático das Forças da Mudança-Partido Liberal (MDFM-PL) (Force for Change Democratic Movement-Liberal Party)

Population

165,000 (2010)*

Last census: August 2001: 137,599

Population density: 151 inhabitants per square km. Urban population: 48 per cent.

Annual growth rate: 2.0 per cent 1994–2004 (WHO 2006)

Ethnic make-up
There are five groups among the islands' inhabitants: the Filhos da Terra are the descendants of imported slaves and Europeans (mostly Portuguese); the Angolares are descendants of former castaway slaves from Angola, now primarily fishermen; the Forros are descendants of slaves freed when slavery was abolished in 1875; the Servicais are migrant labourers from Angola, Mozambique and Cape Verde, and the Tongas are their children, born on the islands.
Religions
Eighty per cent of the population are Roman Catholic, Evangelical Protestant or Seventh-Day Adventist.

Education
The literacy rate for the period 1995–2001 was estimated at 63 per cent.

Health
Life expectancy: 59 years, 2004 (WHO 2006)
Fertility rate/Maternal mortality rate: 3.9 births per woman, 2004 (WHO 2006)
Birth rate/Death rate: 42 births per 1,000 population; seven deaths per 1,000 population (2003).
Child (under 5 years) mortality rate (per 1,000): 75 per 1,000 live births (World Bank)
Head of population per physician: 0.49 physicians per 1,000 people, 2004 (WHO 2006)

Main cities
São Tomé (capital, estimated population 56,166 in 2005) Trinidade (6,636), Santo Amaro (8,411).

Languages spoken
Portuguese is spoken by 95 per cent of the population; Lungwa Santomé is the main national dialect and Fôrro and Crioulo are also spoken.
Official language/s
Portuguese

Media
Press
In Portuguese, there are two weekly newspapers, *Diário da República* (www.cstome.net) and the official organ of Ministry of Information *Revolução*. The weekend newspaper and magazine is *Povo* and the sole independent periodical is *O Parvo*.
Jornal de São Tomé and Príncipe (www.jornal.st) is an online news outlet, in Portuguese.
Broadcasting
Radio: Radio Nacional de São Tomé e Príncipe broadcasts two FM services in Portuguese from Lisbon, Portugal. The French radio station RFI (www.rfi.fr), from neighbouring Cameroon, can also be picked up along with Voice of America (VoA).
Television: The state-run television service is Televisao Saotomense (TVS).

Economy
Agriculture is the mainstay of the economy, with cocoa being the major cash crop, representing around 80 per cent of total commodity exports. Foreign aid, most particularly from Portugal, is also an important factor, along with revenue from oil exploration companies prospecting for oil offshore in São Tomé and Príncipe's territorial waters in the Gulf of Guinea. Nigeria and São Tomé have a contract whereby joint development will result in 60 per cent of proceeds going to Nigeria and the remainder to São Tomé.
Although the dominant crop on São Tomé is cocoa, other export crops include copra, palm kernels, and coffee. Domestically, fishing and a small industrial sector processing local agricultural products and producing a few basic consumer goods provide an inadequate employment environment. However, the islands have potential for tourism, and the government is attempting to improve the undeveloped tourism infrastructure.
GDP growth in 2008 was 5.8 per cent, which fell marginally to 5.5 per cent in 2009 as the global financial crisis forced a decline in foreign investment, before rising to 6.5 per cent in 2010. Inflation, a long-term problem, was 26.1 per cent in 2008 as imports were at a record high. It fell to 16.9 per cent in 2009, as the government imposed tightening fiscal and monetary policies, coupled with falling world food and oil prices, and further still, to 12.3 per cent in 2010 and is expected to average 7 per cent over 2011.
In 2009, Portugal signed a loan agreement with the government, to allow the dobra currency to be anchored to the euro.
Oil production is unlikely to come on-stream until late-2011, when the enormous impact of oil receipts will be managed by an oil revenue management law, with a percentage of the profits channelled into a trust fund for future generations. Revenue from oil is expected to pay debts and provide more government spending, particularly on poverty reduction schemes. There are already some benefits as construction and other activities increase to cater to the industry.
In 2011, the UN Human Development Index (HDI) ranked São Tomé e Príncipe 144 (out of 187) for national development in health, education and income.

External trade
São Tomé and Príncipe is a member of the Common Market for Eastern and Southern Africa (Comesa), and operates within a free trade zone with 13 of the 19 member states.
It is a mono-exporter with around 80 per cent of all commodity exports being cocoa that is shipped mainly to Europe.
New found oil deposits are not expected to be in production until 2010, when it will radically increase foreign earnings.
Imports
Principal imports are machinery and electrical equipment, food products and petroleum products.
Main sources: Portugal (typically 56 per cent of total), Belgium (10 per cent), Japan (9 per cent).
Exports
Principal exports are cocoa, copra, coffee, palm oil.
Main destinations: Japan (typically 77 per cent of total), Belgium (8 per cent), The Netherlands (6 per cent).

Agriculture
Farming
Plantation agriculture forms the basis of the economy, but growth is slowing. Cocoa is the main crop, accounting for around 90 per cent of exports. Cocoa production, once the biggest in the world, has fallen over the years and now totals about 4,000 tonnes a year. The plantations were nationalised after independence to their detriment, but have since been privatised.
The second-largest export crop is coffee; other cash crops are copra, palm kernels, cinnamon, pepper and breadfruit. Priority is being given to the diversification of food crops in an effort to reduce the large food import bill.
Fishing
Fishing remains small-scale, but is being encouraged for local consumption and possible future export.

Industry and manufacturing
The industrial sector is limited to small-scale manufacturing concerns such as soap, soft drinks, timber processing, palm oil, bricks and textiles. The development of oil fields in the Gulf of Guinea is likely to increase industrial activity associated with the sector, particularly construction. In 2002, the government announced it was developing a number of export processing zones (EPZs) in order to exploit the country's position as a regional trading platform. These will give incentives to investors, with tax breaks and free movement of goods.

Tourism
Tourism is under-developed. It has tended towards the luxury market, catering mainly to Portuguese and French visitors. The sector has potential and infrastructure is being expanded.

Mining
São Tomé and Príncipe has no mineral resources.

Hydrocarbons
There are no known hydrocarbon reserves. São Tomé and Príncipe is dependent on imported refined oil products, which was 1,000 barrels per day in 2007. Oil-derived products supply 96 per cent of commercial energy requirements. The World Bank estimated that oil imports consume 20–25 per cent of total export revenue. Distribution and marketing of fuels is carried out by the state-owned oil company, Empresa Nacional de Combustiveis e Oleos (Enco).
São Tomé and Príncipe has established a joint authority with Nigeria to manage offshore oil exploration in the oil-rich Gulf of Guinea. Under the accord, Nigeria will receive 60 per cent of revenues and São Tomé and Príncipe 40 per cent. Preliminary indications suggest that there may be substantial commercial reserves of oil in the area. Exploratory drilling for oil will begin in the fourth quarter of 2009, offshore in the Nigeria-São Tomé Joint Development Zone.

Energy
Installed electricity generating capacity is around 12MW, of which over 50 per cent is provided by hydro plants and the remainder by diesel generators. The national power grid is only operational in the densely populated area of northeast São Tomé. There is great need to increase capacity, by at least 3MW, just to meet demand; blackouts are frequent.
The state-owned monopoly, Empresa Nacional de Água e Electricidade (EMAE) (National Water and Electricity Enterprise) is responsible for generation, transmission and distribution of electricity. But the government is considering privatising the utility in an attempt to find investment and instil commercial principles. EMAE owed Angola US$5 million for fuel in December 2008.
The World Bank has stated that São Tomé and Príncipe has the potential to increase capacity, estimated up to a potential of 6,000MW, through development of major and minor hydroelectric power plants. However it also questioned São Tomé and Príncipe's ability to service the loan.

Banking and insurance
Main financial centre
São Tomé.

Time
GMT.

Geography
The islands of the Republic of São Tomé and Príncipe, are located in the equatorial Atlantic Ocean, about 300–250km off the coast of Gabon, in the Gulf of Guinea. Both islands are remnants of an extinct volcanic mountain range. The tallest mountain is São Tomé Peak (2,024 metres) on the island of São Tomé. Príncipe's mountains have lush forests with swift streams flowing down to the sea. The country also includes the rocky islets of Caroço, Pedras and Tinhosas, off Príncipe, and Rôlas, off São Tomé.
Hemisphere
Northern

Climate
Equatorial with high temperatures and humidity. Average temperatures remain fairly constant throughout the year with a daily range from 20–32 degrees Celsius (C). Driest month July, wettest March.

Entry requirements
Passports
Required by all.
Visa
Required by all; apply well in advance. European visitors should contact the São Tomé e Príncipe consulate in Brussels; US visitors should contact the consulate in either New York or Atlanta; visitors from Canada and Australia should contact the Canadian embassy in Libreville in Gabon (See: Other useful addresses, for further information).
Currency advice/regulations
There are no restrictions on the import of local or foreign currency. Export is allowed up to the amount declared on entry.
Travellers cheques are not widely accepted. US dollars and euro are easily converted, other currencies may attract higher exchange fees.

Health (for visitors)
Mandatory precautions
Yellow fever vaccination certificate is required by all, except visitors from Europe (from April 2009).
Advisable precautions
Inoculations and boosters should be current for cholera, tetanus, yellow fever, hepatitis A, diphtheria, typhoid and polio. There may be a need for vaccinations for tuberculosis, hepatitis B and meningitis. Use malaria prophylaxis (which will also provide protection against yellow fever, dengue fever, hepatitis B and encephalitis) including mosquito repellents, sleeping nets and clothing that cover the body after dark. To avoid bilharzia, avoid exposure to fresh water and use only well-maintained, chlorinated swimming pools.
There is a risk of rabies.
Use only bottled or boiled water for drinks, washing teeth and making ice. Eat only well cooked meals, preferably served hot; vegetables should be cooked and fruit peeled. Dairy products are unpasteurised and should be avoided, unless cooked. There is a shortage of routine medications, including sun-screens, and visitors should take all necessary medicines with them. A first aid kit that includes disposable syringes, is a reasonable precaution.
Healthcare is not to Western standards and medical insurance, including emergency evacuation, is necessary.

Hotels
There is a limited number of reasonable hotels.

Public holidays (national)
Fixed dates
1 Jan (New Year's Day), 3 Feb (Heroes' Day), 1 May (Labour Day), 12 Jul (Independence Day), 6 Sep (Armed Forces Day), 30 Sep (Agricultural Reform Day), 26 Nov (Argel Accord Day), 21 Dec (São Tomé Day, Catholic), 25 Dec (Christmas Day).
Variable dates
Ash Wednesday, Good Friday.

Working hours
Banking
Mon–Fri: 0730–1130, 1430–1630.
Business
Mon–Fri: 0730–1200, 1430–1800.
Government
Mon–Fri: 0800–1200, 1500–1800; Sat: 0800–1300.
Shops
Mon–Sat: 0800–1200, 1500–1900.

Telecommunications
Mobile/cell phones
A 900 GSM service is available over most of the islands of São Tomé and Príncipe.

Electricity supply
220V AC

Weights and measures
Metric

Social customs/useful tips
Business is conducted in Portuguese. Many executives speak French, and some speak English.

Getting there
Air
The national airlines of Portugal (TAP) and Angola (TAAG), fly services to São Tomé.
National airline: Air São Tomé e Príncipe (KY), flies to Gabon only.
International airport/s: São Tomé (TMS), 5.5km from town. A minibus, taxi and buses provide transport to the centre of town.
Airport tax: Departure tax: US$21 or €24, in cash.
Surface
Water: A high-speed ferry service between São Tomé and Cape Verde is planned by the ferry company Expresso LDA with a one-way journey taking five

days. The ferry will have 400 berths and a capacity of 800 passengers. Although planning began in 2010, the service was still not operational in July 2011.

Main port/s: São Tomé, this is not a deep-water harbour so few international ships visit.

Getting about

National transport

Air: Restricted services link the two islands. Travellers should book their seats well in advance, to avoid being stranded.

Road: There are only about 300km of roads, of which about two-thirds are asphalted, but the network is being improved.

Buses: Frequent, efficient service on São Tomé. Limited bus service on Príncipe.

City transport

Taxis: On São Tomé a minivan or *collectivo* shared taxi can be taken to anywhere on the island. There are no fixed schedules and they leave only when they are full; this is no other public transport available.

BUSINESS DIRECTORY

The addresses listed below are a selection only. While World of Information makes every endeavour to check these addresses, we cannot guarantee that changes have not been made, especially to telephone numbers and area codes. We would welcome any corrections.

Telephone area codes

The international dialling code (IDD) for São Tomé and Príncipe is +239, followed by subscriber's number.

Chambers of Commerce

Camara de Comircio, Industria, Agricultura e Servicios, Avenida Marginal 12 de Julho, PO Box 527, Saõ Tomé (tel: 22-2723; fax: 22-1409; e-mail: ccias@cstome.net).

Banking

Banco Comercial do Equador, CP 361, Rua de Moçambique, São Tomé (tel: 22-3829; fax: 22-1989).

Banco Internacional de S Tomé e Príncipe, CP 536, Praça da Independência 3, São Tomé (tel: 22-1445; 22-5821; fax: 22-2427, 22-3462).

Central bank

Banco Central de São Tomé e Príncipe, CP 13, Praça da Independencia, São Tomé (tel: 22-1269, 22-1300; fax: 22-501, 22-2777; email: bcentral@cstome.net; internet: www.bcstp.st).

Travel information

TAP (Air Portugal), CP 414; Avenida Marginal 12 de Julho, São Tomé (tel: 22-2307, 22-1528).

National tourist organisation offices

Tourism Office, CP40, Avenue Marginal, 12 de Julho, São Tomé (tel: 221-542).

Ministries

Ministry of Commerce, Industry and Tourism, Largo das Alfândegas São Tomé; CP 201, São Tomé e Príncipe (tel: 22-4657, 22-4872, 22-4975).

Ministry of Foreign Affairs, Avenida 12 de Julho, São Tomé (tel: 22-2309; fax: 22-3237; email: popgender@sctome.net).

Ministry of Planning and Finance, Largo das Alfândegas São Tomé (tel: 22-4172/3; fax: 22-2182; email: fpublica@cstome.net).

Office of the President, Avenida da Independência, São Tomé (tel: 22-1143; fax: 22-1226).

Office of the Prime Minister, Rua do Município, São Tomé (tel: 22-3596, 22-4189; fax: 22-1670).

National Assembly, Palácio dos Congressos, São Tomé (tel: 22-1899, 22-2986; fax: 22-2835).

Other useful addresses

Canadian embassy, PO Box 4037 Libreville, Gabon (tel: (+241) 737-354; fax: 737-388; email: ibrve@dfait-maeci.gc.ca).

Directorate of Finance, Praça da Independência, São Tomé; CP 168, São Tomé and Príncipe (tel: 22-2372, 22-1484; fax: 22-1182; email: financas@cstome.net).

Nigeria-São Tomé and Príncipe Joint Development Authority, Plot 1101 Aminu Kano Crescent, Wuse II, Abuja, Nigeria (tel: (+234-9) 524-1069; fax: (234-9) 524-1052; e-mail: enquiries@nigeriasaotomejda.com; internet: www.nigeriasaotomejda.com).

São Tomé and Príncipe Embassy (USA), 7th Floor, 400 Park Avenue, New York 10044 (tel: (+1-212) 317-0533; fax 317-0580; email: stp1@attglobal.net; internet: www.saotome.org).

São Tomé and Príncipe Consulate (USA), Suite 305, 512 Means Street, Atlanta GA 30318, USA (tel: (+1-404) 221-0203; fax: (+1-404) 221-1006; e-mail: consul@saotome.org; internet: www.saotome.org).

São Tomé and Príncipe Embassy, Square Montgomery, 175 Avenue de Tervuren, 1150 Brussels, Belgium (tel: (+32-2) 734-9966; fax: (+32-2) 734-8815).

STP-Press, c/o Rádio Nacional de São Tomé e Príncipe, Avenida Marginal de 12 de Julho, CP 44, São Tomé (tel: 22-217).

São Tomé and Príncipe Telecom (CST), Av Marginal 12 de Julho, São Tomé; CP 141, São Tomé and Príncipe (tel: 22-2273; internt: www.cst.st).

Internet sites

AllAfrica information: http://allafrica.com/saotomeandprincipe

National Assembly (in Portuguese): www.parlamento.st

São Toméand Príncipe tourist site: www.saotome.st

São Tomé and Príncipe website: www.sao-tome.com

KEY FACTS

Official name: Mamlaka al Arabiya as Sa'udiya (The Kingdom of Saudi Arabia)

Head of State: Custodian of the Two Mosques King Abdullah bin Abdul Aziz al Sa'ud (from 1 Aug 2005)

Head of government: King Abdullah bin Abdul Aziz al Sa'ud

Ruling party: None

Area: 2,149,690 square km (approximately)

Population: 27.14 million (Census: April 2010)

Capital: Riyadh

Official language: Arabic

Currency: Saudi riyal (SR) = 100 halalas

Exchange rate: SR3.75 per US$ (fixed)

GDP per capita: US$16,996 (2010)

GDP real growth: 3.70% (2010)

GDP: US$443.70 billion (2010)

Inflation: 5.40% (2010)

Oil production: 10.01 million bpd (2010)

Balance of trade: US$153.72 million (2010)

Annual FDI: US$21.56 billion (2010)

Saudi Arabia

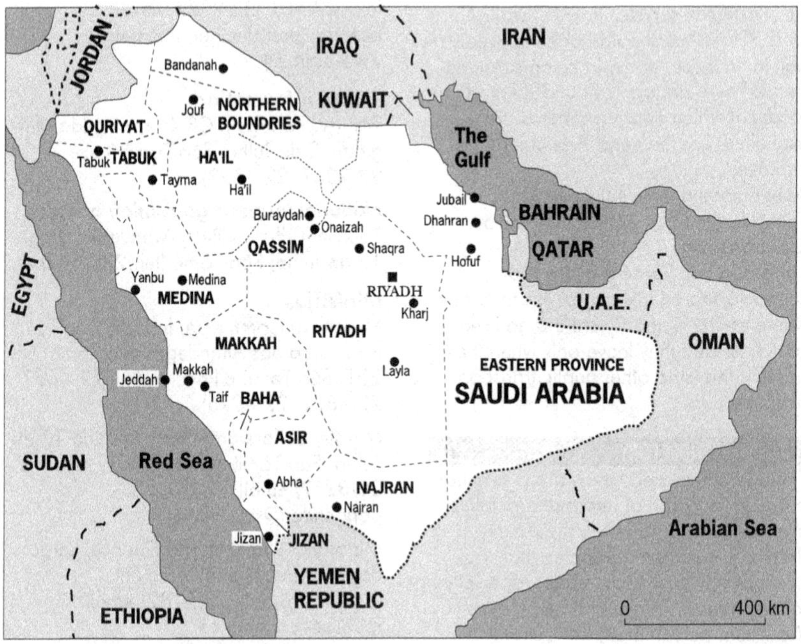

In 2011 Saudi Arabia managed to maintain a relatively low international profile. For one of the world's almost medieval monarchies, this could be termed something of a success. Significantly, the headlines with which the Kingdom closed the year related not so much to progress, but quite the opposite. In mid-December 2011 the British Broadcasting Corporation's (BBC) correspondent reported that a Saudi woman had been beheaded in the Northern Province of Jawf for practising 'witchcraft and sorcery' according to the interior ministry. According to the BBC, Amina bint Abdul Halim bin Salem Nasser was, it seemed, the second person to be executed for witchcraft in Saudi Arabia in 2011. A Sudanese man was executed in September 2011 also on sorcery charges and in 2007, an Egyptian national was beheaded for allegedly casting spells to try to separate a married couple. Last year, a Lebanese man facing the death penalty on charges of sorcery, relating to a fortune-telling television programme he presented, was freed after the Saudi Supreme Court decreed that his actions had not harmed anyone.

Ms Nasser's case was not a matter of rough justice being meted out by a local court. The interior ministry apparently also confirmed that the verdict against Ms Nasser had been upheld by Saudi Arabia's highest courts. *al-Hayat*, an Arabic language daily newspaper quoted an officer of the Saudi religious police as saying that she was in her 60s and had tricked people into giving her money, claiming that she could cure their illnesses. The respected human rights group Amnesty International, which had campaigned for Saudis previously sentenced to death on sorcery charges, said it had never heard of her case until now. Amnesty says that Saudi Arabia does not actually define sorcery as a capital offence. However, some of the country's more conservative Wahhabist clerics have urged the strongest possible punishments against fortune-tellers and faith healers as a threat to Islam.

The Arab Spring

That the Saudi response to the Arab Spring should be highlighted by a crackdown on sorcery somehow suggested that the country's rulers were rather missing the point. But in Saudi Arabia the government has rarely managed to respond with subtlety to the numerous challenges confronting it. Of all the Middle East's non-democratic countries few could be more exposed to the winds of change blowing through the region than Saudi Arabia. Thus, as soon as signs of an uprising showed themselves in neighbouring, if tiny, Bahrain, Saudi Arabia used the cover of the Gulf Co-operation Council (GCC) to dispatch troops to Manama to shore up a fellow, Sunni, monarch who looked to be endangered. Similarly, the Saudi response to the protracted uprising in Yemen was to shelter President Ali Abdullah Saleh while he prepared for an attempted return to power. Saudi links with Egypt's Military Council were also reported to be close, as were – perhaps understandably – those with the kingdoms of Jordan and Morocco. In the case of Syria, Saudi Arabia has preferred to stand back from moves by the Arab League to intervene. However unacceptable Syria's President Bashar al Assad might be, from a Saudi Arabian perspective the alternative might well prove to be even worse. In the early stages of what was to become the Syrian civil war, King Abdullah had unhesitatingly declared his support for President Assad.

Quoted in the *New York Times*, Prince Waleed bin Talal al Saud, billionaire businessman and nephew of King Abdullah, summed up the Saudi stance thus: 'We are not trying to get our way by force, but to safeguard our interests.' However, the three concerns that Saudi Arabia, rather ironically, shared with Israel looked to be in play: its relationship with the US, its interest in maintaining the *status quo* and its paranoiac obsession with Shi'a Iran. US support for the Arab Spring and its identification with the views of the Arab Street certainly run counter to Saudi interests making the US, in the view of one Saudi commentator, 'an unreliable partner'.

Of the three, the overriding preoccupation is with Iran and the fear that Iran would be able to take advantage of any perceived lack of Arab unity to interfere in the affairs of Arab countries. In the build-up to the US departure from Iraq, there were signs of rifts between Iraq's Sunni and Shi'a communities and between their elected representatives. The swift intervention in Bahrain arose from Saudi fears that the rout of the minority Sunni monarchy might pave the way to an elected Shi'a state just 25 kilometres away across the King Fahd causeway. The speed with which Saudi armoured cars were able to cross over to Bahrain underlined the possibility of the reverse happening.

Saudi nervousness over the rise of Middle Eastern populist leaders dates back to the 1950s, when Egypt's King Farouk was deposed by a military coup, leading to years of hot and cold confrontation between the two Middle East majors. In 2011, Saudi Arabia lost little time in offering refuge to deposed Tunisian President Zine al Abidine Ben Ali and his family. In Libya, Saudi Arabia seemed to offer lip-service to the Arab League and United Nations resolutions, but left other Arab countries, particularly Qatar and the United Arab Emirates (UAE) to do the heavy lifting in terms of military and logistical support.

Reform – 'looser reign, uncertain gain'

The Saudi regime has relied on a delicate balance between the strictures of its Wahhabist interpretation of Islam, popular disenchantment with a manifestly primitive form of government, immense wealth and tight policing. Under the rule of King Abdullah, it is certainly the case that there has been some relaxation. But to a neutral observer, much of this 'relaxation' can hardly be classed as 'progress'. Religious tolerance is virtually non existent. In its 2010 assessment of the human rights situation in the Kingdom (prepared before the onset of the Arab Spring), the US-based organisation Human Rights Watch (HRW) notes that since assuming power in 2005, King Abdullah 'has loosened the reins stifling Saudi society, but has instituted few lasting changes.' HRW fears that should the 86-year old King's enthusiasm for reform fade, or his successors begin to tread more conservative paths, his legacy 'would be one of a brief respite of fresh air, but not one of institutional reform.' Central to King Abdullah's proposed reforms have been four areas directly linked to the supposed advancement of the human rights of Saudi citizens: women's rights, freedom of expression, judicial fairness and religious tolerance.

In 2010, according to HRW, Saudis are freer than they were five years ago: Saudi women are less subject to rigid sex segregation in public places, citizens have greater latitude to criticise their government, and reform in the justice system may bring more transparency and fairness in judicial procedures. However, HRW singles out the fourth area of reform, religious tolerance, where King Abdullah's promotion of global interfaith dialogue has not borne fruit at home. 'Relations between Shi'a and Sunni Saudis remain as bad as ever and the government continues to systematically discriminate against Shi'a.' The elephant in the room, that few Saudis dare even mention, is the widespread existence of corruption. Saudi Arabia ranks a lowly 57th out of the 183 countries surveyed in the 2011 Transparency International Corruption Perceptions Index. HRW suggests that the responsibility lies with King Abdullah himself, 'a monarch, in his mid-80s, who has shied away from adopting the often-simple measures needed to entrench rights, build capacity to enforce them and generate the

KEY INDICATORS — Saudi Arabia

	Unit	2006	2007	2008	2009	2010
Population	m	23.70	*24.29	*24.90	*25.50	27.14
Gross domestic product (GDP)	US$bn	349.14	384.43	469.40	379.50	443.70
GDP per capita	US$	15,050	15,825	18,855	14,871	16,996
GDP real growth	%	4.3	3.3	4.2	0.1	3.7
Inflation	%	2.3	4.1	9.9	5.1	5.4
Oil output	'000 bpd	10,859.0	10,413.0	10,846.0	9,713.0	10,007.0
Natural gas output	bn cum	73.5	74.4	80.4	78.5	83.9
Exports (fob) (goods)	US$m	211,305.0	233,311.0	313,481.0	192,307.0	251,149.0
Imports (fob) (goods)	US$m	63,914.0	82,595.0	101,454.0	89,101.0	97,432.0
Balance of trade	US$m	147,391.0	150,716.0	212,027.0	105,206.0	153,717.0
Current account	US$m	99,066.0	93,379.0	132,322.0	22,765.0	66,751.0
Total reserves minus gold	US$m	27,523.0	33,760.0	30,342.0	409,694.0	444,722.0
Foreign exchange	US$m	25,971.0	32,308.0	28,223.0	396,748.0	432,094.0
Exchange rate	per US$	3.75	3.74	3.75	3.75	3.75

* estimated figure

political will to hold rights violators accountable.' As a result, any newly gained freedoms are, for the most part, neither extensive nor firmly grounded. Systematic discrimination against women persists; freedom of expression and judicial fairness are limited. King Abdullah's reforms have tended to put the religious establishment on the defensive, but 'the limited degree of reform that has taken place suggests the elite is still floating trial balloons, undecided about the type of government and society it wants to steer towards.'

The economy

In the view of the International Monetary Fund (IMF) Saudi Arabia has been able to translate its oil wealth into advances in social outcomes. Most indicators are close to the average for both the G-20 countries and other emerging market commodity exporters (Chile and Mexico), but remain below those of the advanced economy commodity exporters (Australia and Norway). Nonetheless, important social issues remain. In particular, pressure on housing resources and unemployment are longstanding concerns – which have been highlighted in previous development plans – that have yet to be resolved and could intensify in the face of still high rates of population growth.

The confluence of high oil prices, increased oil export volumes, substantial international reserves and the absence of debt, provides a significant opportunity to address these social priorities. The challenge then is how government can best respond, while fostering the emergence of a private sector capable of creating sufficient new jobs but without heightening near or medium-term fiscal sustainability risks and vulnerabilities.

Following the global financial crisis, the Saudi economy strengthened as oil prices increased with the rebound in global economic activity and fiscal spending stimulated an acceleration in non-oil gross domestic product (GDP) growth. Fiscal and external balances improved with higher oil revenues. The knock-on effects on financial markets from unrest elsewhere in the region appear to have been limited.

Following the decline in growth in 2009, the economy recovered in 2010 and early 2011 along with the general recovery in global demand. Overall real GDP growth rose from 0.1 per cent in 2009 to 4.1 per cent in 2010, driven by a rebound in oil sector GDP growth as well as an acceleration in non-oil GDP growth from 3.5 per cent to 4.9 per cent with strong support from public spending.

The profitability of private companies listed on the stock exchange also improved significantly in 2010 – net profits were 56 per cent higher than in 2009. Available leading indicators – point of sale transactions, real credit and business confidence surveys – all suggest a further strengthening of activity in 2011, with oil production now also increasing to compensate for lower output from Libya. Inflation increased in 2010 driven by food prices as underlying inflation was stable, before slowing in early 2011. Inflation rose from 4.2 per cent in 2009 to 5.4 per cent in 2010 before easing to 4.6 per cent in May 2011. Food prices contributed 1.7 percentage points to headline inflation during 2010, reflecting increases in world commodity prices. Rental prices continue to be the other major contributor to inflation.

The IMF notes that Saudi Arabia's fiscal accounts moved back into surplus in 2010 as increased oil revenues more than offset rising fiscal spending. Fiscal spending continued to grow in 2010 – although at a slower pace than in the past five years – exceeding the approved budget by a wide margin as the wage bill and capital spending surpassed their respective targets. Overall revenue increased in line with global oil prices, while non-oil revenue declined marginally compared to 2009, due to below average growth in the private sector and lower investment income, reflecting the low yields in international financial markets.

The external current account surplus strengthened in 2010 reflecting stronger global demand and higher oil prices. The increase in oil export revenue – about 85 per cent of overall export revenue – more than compensated for a rise in imports and net factor income outflows, with the current account surplus increasing from US$20.9 billion in 2009 (5.6 per cent of GDP) to US$66.8 billion in 2010 (15.4 per cent of GDP). This resulted in an overall balance of US$35.1 billion in 2010 and an increase in the Saudi Arabian Monetary Authority's (SAMA) gross foreign assets to US$444 billion (representing just over two years of import cover).

Interest rates remained low, in line with domestic monetary indicators and monetary conditions in the US.

The large Saudi labour market attracts workers from all over the world and remittances from Saudi Arabia – US$194 billion during 2000–10 – constitute a significant income source for several countries in the Middle East as well as South and East Asia. Further, increased fiscal spending by Saudi Arabia, including at the height of the global financial crisis, has an important positive knock-on for demand from regional and global trading partners.

Energy

Saudi Arabia accounts for more than two-thirds of spare capacity in global oil supply. As unrest erupted in several countries in the region, Saudi Arabia announced that it would increase its supply in order to offset any shortfall in the market.

According to the US government's Energy Information Administration (EIA) Saudi Arabia was the world's largest producer and exporter of total petroleum liquids in 2010 and the world's second largest crude oil producer behind Russia. Saudi Arabia's economy remains heavily dependent on crude oil. Oil export revenues have accounted for 80–90 per cent of total Saudi revenues and above 40 per cent of the country's GDP.

Saudi Arabia has been shifting its focus beyond increasing its upstream oil production since Saudi Arabian Oil Company (Saudi Aramco) said that it had reached its target production capacity of 12 million barrels per day. In addition, its spare oil production capacity is well above Saudi Arabia's stated target of 1.5–2 million barrels per day. Subsequently, Saudi Arabia is moving to diversify its economy by expanding its refining, petrochemicals and mineral products industries (such as high-value fertilisers).

Saudi Arabia's hydrocarbon sector operations are dominated by the state-owned oil company, Saudi Aramco. Saudi Aramco is the world's largest oil company in terms of proven reserves and production of hydrocarbons. Saudi Arabia's ministry of petroleum and mineral resources and the Supreme Council for Petroleum and Minerals have oversight of the sector and Saudi Aramco directly. The Supreme Council, which is comprised of members of the royal family, industry leaders and government ministers, is responsible for petroleum and natural gas policy-making, including contract review, as well as Saudi Aramco's strategic planning. The ministry is responsible for national planning in the area of energy and minerals, including petrochemicals.

In addition to being the largest producer, Saudi Arabia is also the largest consumer of petroleum in the Middle East, particularly in the area of transportation fuels and direct burn for power generation. Domestic consumption growth has been spurred by the economic boom due to historically high oil prices and large fuel subsidies. In 2008, Saudi Arabia was the 15th largest consumer of total primary energy, of which almost 60 per cent was petroleum-based and the rest natural gas. Saudi Arabia is moving forward with plans to produce power from nuclear reactors by 2020 in order to meet domestic power needs and to free up oil and natural gas for export and higher-end uses than direct burn for power generation. In the interim, Saudi Arabia is participating in the GCC's efforts to link the power grids of member countries in order to reduce shortages during peak power periods.

According to the *Oil and Gas Journal* (OGJ), at the end of 2010 Saudi Arabia contained approximately 260 billion barrels of proven oil reserves (plus 2.5 billion barrels in the Saudi-Kuwaiti shared Neutral Zone), amounting to around one-fifth of proven, conventional world oil reserves. Although Saudi Arabia has around 100 major oil and gas fields (and more than 1,500 wells), over half of its oil reserves are contained in only eight fields, including the giant 1,260 square mile Ghawar field (the world's largest oil field, with estimated remaining reserves of 70 billion barrels). The Ghawar field alone has more proven oil reserves than all but six other countries.

Saudi Arabia maintains the world's largest crude oil production capacity, estimated by the US EIA at over 12 million bpd at end-2010. Over 2 million bpd of capacity was added in 2009 with the addition of increments at Khurais, AFK (Abu Hadriya, Fadhili and Khursaniyah), Shaybah and Nu'ayyim.

For 2010, the EIA estimates that Saudi Arabia produced on average 10.2 million bpd of total oil, comprising crude oil, lease condensate, natural gas liquids and other liquids (including half of the Saudi-Kuwaiti Neutral Zone's 600,000bpd). In addition to 8.4 million bpd of crude oil, Saudi Arabia produced around 1.8 million bpd of natural gas liquids (NGLs) and other liquids, which are not subject to Opec quotas. Saudi Arabia, a leading world producer of NGLs, has experienced a rise in demand for NGLs from developing countries, including India (the leading export destination), where it is used for cooking and transportation.

Saudi Arabia exported an estimated 7.5 million bpd in 2010, the majority of which was crude oil. Asia now receives an estimated 55 per cent of Saudi Arabia's crude oil exports, as well as the majority of its refined petroleum product and NGL exports.

In 2009, Saudi Arabia exported an average of 1 million bpd of petroleum liquids to the United States (down from (1.5 million bpd in 2008), accounting for 9 per cent of total US petroleum imports. For this time period, Saudi Arabia ranked fourth after Canada, Mexico and Venezuela as a petroleum exporter to the United States. Other major Saudi customers included Japan (1.2 million bpd), South Korea (850,000bpd) and China (839,000bpd).

Natural gas

According to the OGJ, Saudi Arabia has proven natural gas reserves estimated at 275 trillion cubic feet (tcf), fourth largest in the world behind Russia, Iran and Qatar. Over 12tcf was added in 2010. However, about 50–60 per cent of the natural gas in Saudi Arabia is associated with petroleum deposits, or found in the same fields as crude oil; plans to increase production of this type of gas remain linked to an increase in oil production. About 57 per cent of Saudi Arabia's proven natural gas reserves consist of associated gas at the giant onshore Ghawar field and the offshore Safaniya and Zuluf fields. Of the remaining 100tcf of free (non-associated) natural gas, 75 per cent is sour (high sulfur) or in tight formations, leaving only 25tcf of conventional natural gas deposits that are easy to develop.

Rapid reserve development is necessary for Saudi Arabia's plans to fuel the growth of the petrochemical sector, as well as for power generation and for water desalination. Saudi Arabia had set a goal of meeting 10 per cent of global petrochemical demand by 2015, with natural gas a primary feedstock. According to Saudi Aramco forecasts, natural gas demand in the kingdom is expected to more than double to 14.5 billion cubic feet per day (bcf/d) by 2030, up from an estimated 7.1 bcf/d in 2007. In order to free up petroleum for export, all current and future gas supplies (except natural gas liquids) reportedly remain earmarked for use in domestic industrial consumption and desalination.

According to the June 2011 issue of the *BP Statistical Review of World Energy*, gas production was 2.9 trillion cubic feet (tcf) in 2010. However, in the view of the EIA natural gas production remains limited, as soaring costs of production, exploration, processing and distribution of gas have squeezed supply, while an estimated 13 to 14 per cent of total production is lost to venting, flaring, reinjection and natural processes according to Opec and other sources. Saudi Arabia has no net imports or exports of natural gas. According to Saudi Aramco, only 15 per cent of Saudi Arabia has been 'adequately explored for gas'.

Because most of its natural gas reserves are from associated gas, Saudi Arabia is constrained from boosting its gas production from these reserves because of Opec crude oil production restraints. To meet growing domestic needs, the petroleum ministry and Saudi Aramco announced a US$9 billion strategy to add 50tcf of non-associated reserves by 2016 through new discoveries (and potentially another 50tcf of associated reserves). According to Saudi Aramco, exploration and development will also commence in non-producing areas such as the Red Sea, northern and western Saudi Arabia and the Nafud basin, north of Riyadh.

Risk assessment

Economy	Good
Politics	Poor
Regional stability	Fair

COUNTRY PROFILE

Historical profile

1871 The Ottomans took the province of Al Ahsa.

1891 The Rashidi family seized control of Riyadh from the Sa'ud family, which was exiled to Kuwait.

1902 Abd al Aziz and other members of the deposed Sa'ud family regained control of Riyadh, expelling the Rashidis.

1913 Al Ahsa was taken back from the Ottomans by Abd al Aziz. The Anglo-Ottoman Convention established the 'Blue Line' as the eastern Arabian boundary between the Ottoman and British empires.

1914 Abd al Aziz signed a treaty with the Ottomans.

1915 The first Anglo-Saudi treaty provided recognition of Abd al Aziz.

1919–26 Between 1919 and 1925, Abd al Aziz defeated the four Arabian states of Hejaz, Asir, Ha'il and Jauf and incorporated them. Abd al Aziz took Makkah (Mecca) from King Ali of al Hejaz. In 1925, Medina, Yanbu and Jeddah surrendered to Abd al Aziz, and in 1926, Abd al Aziz was proclaimed King of Al Hejaz and Sultan of Najd and its dependencies.

1927 In the second Anglo-Saudi treaty, the British recognised the full independence of Abd al Aziz, while the Saudi leader acknowledged the British treaty

relationships with the sheikhdoms of the Gulf.
1932 The Kingdom of Saudi Arabia was established when the two monarchies of Najd and Al Hejaz merged, with Abd al Aziz as King.
1933 Abd al Aziz's eldest son, Sa'ud, was named crown prince.
1938 Oil was discovered and production started under California Arabian Standard Oil Company (CASOC).
1944 CASOC changed its name to Arabian American Oil Company (Aramco).
1945 Oil exploration and exploitation increased after the Second World War and the country's infrastructure was modernised and developed with the growing oil revenues.
1953 King Abd al Aziz died and was succeeded by Crown Prince Sa'ud ibn Abdul Aziz al Sa'ud.
1960 Saudi Arabia was a founding member of the Organisation of Petroleum Exporting Countries (OPEC).
1964 King Sa'ud was deposed by his brother, Faisal ibn Abdul Aziz al Sa'ud, previously the crown prince and prime minister.
1972 Saudi Arabia gained control of 20 per cent of Aramco.
1973 Saudi Arabia lead an oil boycott against Western countries that had supported Israel in the 6 October War against Egypt and Syria. Oil prices subsequently quadrupled and the world economy went into depression.
1975 King Faisal was assassinated by one of his nephews and was succeeded by Khalid ibn Abdul Aziz al Sa'ud.
1979 Saudi Arabia cut off diplomatic relations with Egypt after the Egyptian-Israeli Peace Treaty was signed. The Grand Mosque of Makkah was seized by extemists; the government regained control and executed those captured.
1980 Saudi Arabia took over full control of Aramco.
1981 The political and economic union, Co-operation Council for the Arab States of the Gulf (CCASG) (known as the Gulf Co-operation Council (GCC)) was formed by Bahrain, Kuwait, Oman, Qatar, Saudi Arabia and the United Arab Emirates (UAE).
1982 King Khalid died and Fahd ibn Abdul Aziz al Sa'ud, his brother, became King.
1986 The King Fahd Causeway between Bahrain and Saudi Arabia was opened.
1987 Diplomatic relations with Egypt were resumed.
1991 Saudi Arabia was the launch pad for a US-led military operation to eject Iraqi forces that had occupied Kuwait in 1990.
1992 King Fahd announced that the country's Basic Law, which stipulated that the Quran was the country's constitution, and that he proposed setting up a *Majlis al Shura* (Consultative Council).
1993 King Fahd decreed the division of Saudi Arabia into thirteen administrative divisions. The *Majlis al Shura* was inaugurated in December, with 60 members nominated by the King, and a chairman.
1994 Osama bin Laden, who was later to become notorious as the leader of al Qaeda, a terrorist organisation, reportedly responsible for flying two aircraft into the World Trade Centre in New York in September 2001, was stripped of his Saudi nationality.
1995 King Fahd suffered a debilitating stroke and handed over *de facto* power to Crown Prince Abdullah.
1996 A bomb exploded at the US military complex near Dhahran.
1997 The *Majlis al Shura* membership was increased from 60 to 90.
1999 Women were allowed to attend a session of the *Majlis al Shura* for the first time.
2000 Yemen and Saudi Arabia signed a treaty resolving 65 years of dispute over land and sea boundaries.
2001 Saudi Arabia and Iran signed a security accord to combat terrorism, drug trafficking and organised crime. Out of 19 hijackers involved in the 11 September attacks in the US, 15 were Saudi nationals. King Fahd said that terrorism should be eradicated and that it is prohibited by Islam. Identity cards were issued to women for the first time.
2002 New criminal rights came into force banning torture and giving suspects legal representation. Crown Prince Abdullah proposed a peace initiative for Israel and Palestine, at the Beirut Summit of the Arab League. He suggested a settlement between Israel and the whole Arab world if Israel withdrew from all Palestinian territories it had occupied since 1967.
2003 Saudi Arabia denied US air bases and troops access to Iraq through its territory during the second invasion of Iraq. More than 300 Saudi intellectuals, including women, signed a petition calling for far-reaching political reforms and around 270 people were arrested when attending a rally in Riyadh, also calling for political reform. King Fahd granted wider powers to the *Majlis al Shura*, enabling it to initiate legislation without first seeking his permission.
2004 There was a stampede at the Haj pilgrimage in February, in which 251 people died. Security forces killed local al Qaeda leader, Abdul Aziz al Muqrin.
2005 Male Saudis voted in the first-ever nationwide municipal elections. King Fahd died and was succeeded by his half-brother, Crown Prince Abdullah bin Abdul Aziz. Saudi Arabia became a member of the World Trade Organisation.
2006 A committee of princes was created, under the Allegiance Institution Law, to ensure the orderly succession to the throne.
2008 A common market was created by Bahrain, Kuwait, Oman, Qatar, Saudi Arabia and the UAE, the six wealthiest Gulf States. Citizens of these countries are now allowed to travel between and live in any of the six states, where they may find employment, buy properties and businesses and use the educational and health facilities freely.
2009 Saudi Arabia awarded a key contract to build a new railway system between the major religious sites of Mecca, Mina, Arafat and Muzdalifah to the China Railway Company. The US$1.8 billion contract is expected to be completed by 2011. In a major re-organisation of his government, King Abdullah sacked two powerful religious officials – a senior judge, who said killing owners of satellite television stations that broadcast immoral programmes was permitted, and the head of the Commission for the Promotion of Virtue and the Prevention of Vice. The Commission was accused of using brutality to enforce Wahhabism, the conservative form of Islam practised in Saudi Arabia. The first female cabinet minister was appointed – for women's affairs – by King Abdullah. Hundreds of people were evacuated from 240 villages as security forces began enforcing a 10km buffer zone along the border with Yemen. The move was intended to prevent Yemeni rebels from taking shelter along the Saudi Arabian border while carrying on their insurgency in northern Yemen.
2010 In February, BAE (British Aerospace Engineering) Systems was fined £285 million (US$452.9 million) for corruption and false accounting during the record al Yamamah arms deals begun in 1985. Use of the roaming internet receiver and email facilities in BlackBerry were temporarily blocked from 6 August, due to the authority's inability to regulate the device's stored electronic data and instant messaging. On 13 September, a deal with the US worth US$60 billion was the largest arms contract either country had ever negotiated.
2011 Ex-president Zine al Abidine Ben Ali of Tunisia and his family found sanctuary in Saudi Arabia when they fled on 15 January. After months of protests in Yemen, President Saleh was injured on 3 June, during an attack on his Sana'a palace compound. Saleh left Yemen on 6 June to receive medical treatment in Saudi Arabia. On 7 August he left hospital but chose to remain in Saudi Arabia. On 7 August King Abdullah condemned the

escalating bloodshed in Syria and called on its leadership to 'stop the killing machine'. On 15 August, the Islamic Development Bank allocated US$2.2 million for food aid to famine victims in Somalia. On 25 September King Abdullah announced that women will be given the right to vote and run in future municipal elections, as well as be appointed to the Shura Council. There were clashes between security forces and protesters in the eastern province of Qatif on 4 October; 14 people were reported to be injured. The Saudi Press Association said there had been 'incitement from a foreign country that aims to undermine the nation's security and stability'. Crown Prince Sultan bin Abdulaziz al Saud died on 22 October, after a long illness. On 28 October, Nayef bin Abdulaziz al Saud was named crown prince of Saudi Arabia. Fourteen people are reported to have been injured in clashes in eastern Saudi Arabia, home to many Shia and the scene of protests earlier this year.

Political structure

Constitution

Saudi Arabia is an absolute monarchy. The country's 1992 Basic Law declares that the Quran is the country's constitution.

A system of provincial government was introduced in 1993. Thirteen regional authorities, subdivided into 103 governorates, provide provincial services alongside district councils and tribal and village councils. The 13 provinces are governed by princes or close relatives of the royal family and governors are appointed by the King.

Independence date

1927

Form of state

Absolute monarchy

The executive

The King (Custodian of the Two Holy Mosques), exercises absolute power as Head of State, head of government and general commander of the armed forces. The 25-member Council of Ministers, an executive body appointed for a four-year term by the King, serves as an instrument of royal authority, passing legislation that becomes law once ratified by royal decree. The majority of the Council is comprised of members of the royal family, with the King as Council leader.

National legislature

There is no elected legislature. A Majlis al Shura (Consultative Council) was formed in 1993; it provides a forum for debate. There are 90 members, all appointed by the King, serving four-year terms. In 2003, wider powers were granted to the Majlis al Shura, enabling it to initiate legislation without first seeking the King's permission.

Legal system

Saudi Arabia has judicial-Islamic courts of first instance and appeals based on *Sharia* (Islamic law) and the *Sunna* (practices or mode of life) of the Prophet Mohammed. Judges are appointed by the King on the recommendation of the Supreme Judicial Council, comprised of 12 senior jurists. Royal decrees and ministerial resolutions have been used to complement *Sharia* in modern Saudi Arabia and a dual system has developed. *Sharia* judgements generally override the judgements of non-*Sharia* tribunals. The King is the final court of appeal and has the power of sentencing or pardoning those found guilty of breaking the law.

In 2002, a new criminal justice system came into force, which included a ban on torture and the right of suspects to legal representation.

Next elections

There are no Consultative Council elections. Elections at municipal level were held for the first time in 2005. The next municipal elections are due on 29 September 2011.

Political parties

Ruling party

None

Population

27.14 million (Census: April 2010)

Last census: April 2010: 27,136,977

Population density: Urban population: 85 per cent (1995–2001).

Annual growth rate: 2.8 per cent 1994–2004 (WHO 2006)

Ethnic make-up

The majority of Saudis originate in the peninsula and are of Arab extraction, but there is a sizeable minority of the population which has migrated mainly from central Asia and China. One-third of the population is non-Saudi. Most of these are from Yemen, Pakistan, Thailand and the Philippines as well as a significant number from Western Europe and North America.

Religions

The majority of the population is Wahhabi (Sunni) Muslim, with around 8 per cent Shi'a Muslim, the latter being mainly located in the Hasa (Eastern) Province. Sufism is practised throughout the Hejaz, and there is a Sunni Salafi opposition movement which, in particular, opposes the authoritarian rule of the clergy.

Islam's two holiest cities of Makkah (Mecca) and Medina are both in Saudi Arabia.

Despite Islam's recognition of Christians and Jews as People of the Book, public adherence to other faiths is forbidden in the Kingdom.

Education

Although education at all levels is free, it is not compulsory. Both primary and secondary education last for six years and begin at the ages of six and 12 years respectively. On average, boys receive an extra year of schooling (nine years) compared to girls and their education is completely segregated.

The educational system is geared to a future of high technology with computer science taught as a basic subject in secondary schools. However, the education system is widely recognised as being outdated and inefficient. There are over 22,700 schools and colleges, which are attended by about five million students. In 2010–11, around 120,000 students had their overseas graduate education and training funded by the state at a cost of US$6 billion. The funding was part of a larger spending programme, to increase the number of trained engineers, lawyers, medical personnel and information technologists in Saudi Arabia.

Literacy rate: 78 per cent adult rate; 97 per cent youth rate (15–24) (Unesco 2005).

Enrolment rate: 77 per cent boys; 75 per cent girls, total primary enrolment (including repetition rates) of the relevant age group between 1994–2000 (World Bank).

Pupils per teacher: 13 in primary schools.

Health

All medical care, including the cost of medicines, is provided free for Saudi citizens.

Saudi Arabia provides a two-tier health service plan. The first tier comprises a network of over 3,500 primary healthcare centres and clinics established throughout the country. These centres are supplemented by a fleet of mobile clinics that routinely visit the more remote villages and provide basic medical services. A network of over 300 advanced hospitals and specialised clinics spanning the urban areas constitute the second tier of health services with a capacity of almost 45,000 beds. The King Fahd Medical City in Riyadh is probably the largest medical facility in the Middle East.

Life expectancy: 71 years, 2004 (WHO 2006)

Fertility rate/Maternal mortality rate: 3.9 births per woman, 2004 (WHO 2006)

Birth rate/Death rate: 37 births per 1,000 population; six deaths per 1,000 population (2003).

Child (under 5 years) mortality rate (per 1,000): 46 deaths per 1,000 live births (2004)

Head of population per physician: 1.37 physicians per 1,000 people, 2004 (WHO 2006)

Welfare

The General Organisation for Social Insurance (GOSI) administers programmes that support workers or their families in cases of disability, retirement and death and also covers occupational hazards for employees. Another major programme provides social security pensions, benefits and relief assistance to the disabled, the elderly, orphans and widows without income.

Out of the 60 centres around the country that care for those with social, economic and physical problems, six specialise in rehabilitation of juvenile delinquents, nine in assisting the elderly and 14 in caring for orphans. A particularly important government policy has been to provide interest-free, easy-term loans towards low cost home construction for students and low-income employees.

Main cities

Riyadh (capital, estimated population 5.2 million (m) in 2010), Jeddah (3.5m), Mecca (Makkah) (1.5m), Dammam (1.1m), Medina (al Madinah) (1.1m).

Media

Press

The press is closely monitored and subject to legal restrictions affecting freedom of expression, censorship is strict and criticism of the government is rare. Most newspapers are privately owned. There was a slight increase in press freedom after the accession of King Abdullah in 2005 although in August 2007 *al Hayat* was banned for a number of days after it had 'crossed a red line' by criticising the ministry of agriculture's handling of the death of over 2,000 camels from poisoning. In May 2010 Jamal Khashoggi, editor-in-chief of *al Watan*, resigned after the paper published an opinion piece on Salafism, a form of Islam at the heart of the Saudi state.

Dailies: Leading newspapers are regionally based. In Arabic, from Dammam *al Yaum Newspaper* (www.alyaum.com), from Riyadh *al Watan* (www.alwatan.com.sa), *al Jazirah* (www.al-jazirah.com), *al Sharq al Awsat* (www.asharqalawsat.com) and *al Riyadh* (www.alriyadh.com). From Jeddah, *Okaz* (www.okaz.com.sa) and *al Hayat* (www.daralhayat.com), also published in English as well as *Arab News* (www.arabnews.com) and *The Saudi Gazette* (www.saudigazette.com.sa). Many foreign publications can be found in the Kingdom.

Weeklies: There are a number of magazines and periodicals, including *al Yamama* and *Igraa*. *Um al Qura* is the official weekly newspaper issued by the Saudi government.

Business: The leading business journal is the *Saudi Economic Survey* (weekly in English).

Periodicals: *Alnafetha*

Broadcasting

The Broadcasting Service of the Kingdom of Saudi Arabia (BSKSA) is responsible for all transmissions and no private radio or television networks are allowed to broadcast in Saudi Arabia but may operate from neighbouring countries.

Radio: Saudi Radio (www.saudiradio.net) is state-run, with regional programming and broadcasts in Arabic and English. It runs overseas services in Urdu, Indonesian, Persian, French, Somali and Swahili. Aramco Radio is a private amateur radio station from Dhahran broadcasting in English. Voice of America (VoA) can be received.

Television: BSKSA operates four TV networks including al Ikhbariya a news channel. The private and independent satellite broadcaster Arab Radio and Television Network (known as ART) (www.art-tv.net), based in Jeddah, operates 10 domestic and five international channels, by subscription. There are many satellite and cable TV stations operating from outside Saudi Arabia.

A new 24-hour international news channel, Alarab, is due to launch on 12 December 2012. The channel will be aimed at an Arabic-speaking audience worldwide.

Advertising

Saudi Arabia is the largest advertising market in the Gulf, with total advertising expenditure typically reaching US$300 million per annum. Newspaper advertising is the most popular form, representing over 60 per cent of total spending. All advertising is subject to review of content and image.

News agencies

National news agency: Saudi Press Agency (SPA)

Economy

With the world's largest reserves of oil and as a leading member of the Organisation of the Petroleum Exporting Countries (Opec), Saudi Arabia's economy is dominated by oil and gas. Reserves at the end of 2010 stood at 264.5 billion barrels of oil and 8.0 trillion cubic metres (cum) of natural gas. Oil production was 10 million barrels per day (bpd) and natural gas production was 83.9 billion cum per annum in 2010 and provided 85.3 per cent of government revenue in 2009, rising to 90.3 per cent in 2010.

After ten years of steadily increasing oil prices on the international markets, the sharp increase in 2008, managed to push GDP growth up to 4.2 per cent, before falling sharply to 0.1 per cent in 2009 as the global economic crisis cut trade and production and the price of oil fell by 63 per cent within one year. The record high global oil prices in 2008 had contributed to a trade balance of US$212.3 billion. As global markets fell sharply in 2009 and year-on-year oil sales slumped by -7.8 per cent, so that the trade balance fell to US$105.4. It picked up in 2010 with a preliminary return to US$153.9 billion.

Inflation jumped from 4.1 per cent in 2007 to 9.9 per cent in 2008 as imported food prices were at a record high, before falling to 5.1 per cent in 2009 which kept steady at 5.4 per cent in 2010.

Saudi Arabia's other industrial sectors include mining of gold, silver, copper and zinc, phosphates, uranium, bauxite, tungsten, zinc, coal and iron. The amount of arable land is comparatively small and agricultural production is limited; exported produce includes dates, grains, livestock and vegetables. Imported items include manufactured goods, vehicles and spare parts, clothing and textiles, livestock, foodstuffs and processed foods.

Structural reforms and an expansion of the non-oil economy have increased employment rates; the government's target is to create 800,000 new jobs a year for Saudi nationals. Further investment in private sector growth through increased spending, in places where social and private returns are judged to be best, are underway, including infrastructure development. Plans by the government to invest US$400 billion in upgrading infrastructure by 2013 were announced in October 2010. Priority will be given to power and water supplies, transport, education, retail, real estate and hydrocarbon installations. Foreign direct investment (FDI) remained steady at around US$23 billion during the global economic crisis.

Ultimately, the economy is underpinned by Saudi Arabia's vast oil reserves, which will last another century at current rates of production. Diversification is needed to strengthen the economy, but the economy's reliance on oil will continue.

External trade

In 2005 the Greater Arab Free Trade Area (Gafta) was ratified by 17 members, including Saudi Arabia, creating an Arab economic bloc. Gafta includes a customs union in which tariffs are reduced by a percentage each year, until none remain. Saudi Arabia was a founder member of the Organisation of the Petroleum Exporting Countries (Opec) which organises oil production policies of 13 member countries.

As a member of the WTO, Saudi Arabia has undertaken to liberalise its trade regime and accelerate its integration into the world economy.
Possessing one-quarter of the world total reserves of oil, crude oil, refined petroleum products and natural gas account for 90 per cent of total exports and 75 per cent of government revenues.

Imports

Main imports are vehicles, machinery and equipment, industrial raw materials and, clothing, textiles, livestock and foodstuffs.
Main sources: US (typically 14 per cent of total), China (10 per cent), Germany (9 per cent).

Exports

Petroleum and its refined products dominate exports, with minor trade in agricultural products, minerals and ores, petrochemicals and construction.
Main destinations: Japan (typically 27 per cent of total), US (18 per cent), United Arab Emirates (4 per cent).

Agriculture

Farming

The sector contributes around 5 per cent to GDP and employs 4 per cent of the labour force. Agricultural produce accounts for only around 5 per cent of non-oil exports.
Agricultural development projects have helped Saudi Arabia achieve self-sufficiency in wheat, eggs, some dairy products and vegetables. The development of water desalination plants is crucial to future development.
The role of agriculture in the overall economy is being re-evaluated. Subsidies have created large surpluses of wheat, while agricultural production has depleted scarce water supplies.
The agricultural sector is heavily subsidised and accounts for 90 per cent of Saudi Arabia's 14–16 billion cubic metres of annual water consumption. The policy of agricultural expansion has come under heavy criticism, as some 3,000 tonnes of water is required to produce one tonne of wheat, most of which is then exported. At present rates of depletion, fossil water sources are not expected to last more than 20 years. The importance of conservation and subsidy reduction to slow water demand is clear, but this needs to be balanced against the need to expand Saudi Arabia's agricultural output.
In September 2011, the government decided that by 2016 it will have ceased to buy locally produced wheat. The move is in order to conserve fresh water which is currently being used to irrigate the wheat.
Most agricultural activity is north of Riyadh in Qasim, Hail and Al-Jauf areas and on a smaller scale in Wadi Dawasir and Abha. Despite significant growth in agricultural production, Saudi Arabia increasingly relies on imports to meet the demands of a rapidly growing population.

Fishing

Saudi Arabia has a small and developing fishing industry. The Saudi Fisheries Company (SFC) operates the fishing fleet, comprising 49 vessels. SFC operates four processing plants in Dammam, Jazan, Jeddah and Riyadh. Annual catch includes bream, barracuda, mackerel, sardine and tuna.

Forestry

Forest and wooded land accounts only for 1 per cent of Saudi Arabia's total land area. Most wood products are imported,

Industry and manufacturing

Saudi Arabia's economy is dominated by the oil industry, with the majority of manufactured goods imported and the services sector largely supporting the hydrocarbon sector. The industrial sector accounts for around 55 per cent of GDP, while manufacturing accounts for only 10 per cent.
The government has played a major role in the economy since an industrialisation programme was launched in the 1960s. Despite attempts to develop the private sector and withdraw the state from the economy, such attempts have not progressed very far. The main sector, oil, is dominated by the largest domestic oil company – the 100 per cent state-owned Saudi Arabian Oil Company (Saudi Aramco). Upstream oil exploration and development, the country's most lucrative industry, is closed to foreign investment, with all activities undertaken by Saudi Aramco.
The state also intervenes in the price of domestic goods, with significant subsidies provided on a wide range of agricultural, utility and industrial products. As a result, the domestic economy rarely reflects international market prices.
In June 2010 a wholly Saudi Arabian designed and produced car, the *Ghazal 1*, went into production. The car was designed by students of the King Saud University in Riyadh to be able to cope with the climate of the Middle East; 20,000 cars will be produced annually when the full capacity is achieved.
A new, *Nitaqat* system was introduced in 2011 whereby all companies operating in Saudi Arabia are rated into three categories, red, yellow and green, for their percentage of Saudi employees. Those rated as green have achieved the percentage target as set by the government. Those rated as yellow have not, but have enough Saudi employees that they have a grace period until the third quarter of 2012 to achieve the percentage target, while the foreign employees' work visas of these companies will not be renewed beyond 2017. Those companies rated red do not have enough Saudi employees and must employ more by the end of 2011 or face punitive measures; they also will not be able to renew the work visas of their foreign employees at all. This system has led to companies rated red to quickly employ unqualified Saudi personnel, who are only required to sign-in for work, to avoid the sanctions threatened by the government.

Tourism

Little effort has been made to attract non-Arab tourists. The annual pilgrimage (*haj*) brings some two million Muslim visitors each year to the holy cities, Makkah and Medina. Other principal destinations are the capital, Riyadh, and the commercial centre, Jeddah.
The government has established a commission for tourism to develop the sector as part of its diversification policy. Facilities are being expanded to encourage the domestic population to spend their holidays in the country (an estimated US$6 billion is spent on overseas vacations each year) and pilgrims on haj to extend their visits. With the basic infrastructure already developed, resources are going into accommodation and recreational facilities, including resort cities and amusement parks.
The commission has also been charged with developing plans to promote the country to non-Muslim visitors. Around 6,000 such tourists visit each year, mainly in groups organised by Saudi Arabian Airlines. The development of Saudi holiday destinations for western tourists may prove to be difficult to achieve, as local conditions clash with tourist expectations. Not all historic sites are open to non-Muslims, while hotel resorts must conform to Islamic traditions of modest dress, temperance and the social separation of men and single women.

Mining

The exploitation of mineral resources other than oil is the responsibility of the petroleum and minerals resources ministry.
The principal minerals are gold, silver, copper, zinc, lead, iron, magnesite, bauxite, phosphates, beryl, fluorite, magnesium, salt and sulphur and certain radioactive minerals. Other sought-after minerals are those used for making cement and plaster such as granite, sandstone, coral stone and marble. Saudi Arabia is self-sufficient in these materials.
Industrial minerals produced include limestone, gypsum, sulphur, marble, clay and salt. Much of the mineral deposits can be extracted by surface mining or quarrying.
A new mining code passed in 2005 sought to attract more foreign companies,

mainly by giving them greater freedom to invest as they see fit. Gold exploration has been opened up to foreign companies for the first time.

Hydrocarbons

At of 264.5 billion barrels of proven oil reserves at the end of 2010 (with a further 2.6 billion barrels in the border neutral zone shared with Kuwait), Saudi Arabia provides over 20 per cent of the entire world's oil supplies and had maintained for many years the largest crude oil production, but due to Opec members cutting back oil production in 2009, its supremacy was overtaken by Russia, with production of 10 billion barrels per day (bpd) in 2010. The state-owned Saudi Aramco is the world's largest oil corporation, with responsibility for exploration, production, marketing and shipping of the country's hydrocarbons. Saudi Arabia is a key player in the Organisation of Petroleum Exporting Countries (Opec) and manages its oil production inline with Opec quotas and world prices.

There are five major oil fields both on- and offshore, the largest of which is the Ghawar field in the eastern province, producing around 50 per cent of all production.

Saudi Arabia had a total refinery capacity of 2.1 million bpd in 2010. The new and refurbished Petro Rabigh petro-chemical refinery on the Red Sea produces hundreds of thousands of polyethylene, polypropylene, monoethylene glycol and propylene oxide, has been enhanced following Saudi Aramco's signed agreement with Japan's Sumitomo Chemical Company to develop phase two of the Petro Rabigh refinery.

There are around 14,500km of oil pipelines, including the major East-West Crude Oil Pipeline (Petroline) supplying oil to the Red Sea terminals for shipment to Europe. Running parallel to this is the natural gas liquids (NGLs) pipeline.

Saudi Arabia is also a leading exporter of NGLs (propane and butane among others), which are not subject to Opec quotas. In 2007, 1.5 billion bpd of NGLs were produced, the single largest importer of which was India.

Proven natural gas reserves were 8.0 trillion cubic metres in 2010, with production at 83.9 billion cum, an increase of 7.0 per cent over the previous year. There has been a steady increase in production from the 45.6 billion cum recorded in 1997, all of which has been consumed domestically; This market is, however, limited, despite high subsidises and a growth in energy use. The role of gas production has been overshadowed by oil production, which because it provides Saudi Arabia with the bulk of the country's revenue has seen the opportunity of natural gas production relegated to a peripheral role. Following a policy decision to free up more oil for export further exploration and development of natural gas fields will be undertake. Almost all natural gas in production is associated with oil production; an estimated 13–14 per cent of total production is lost through venting, re-injection and natural waste due to the initially high cost of packaging the supply.

Energy

Total installed generating capacity was 33.53GW in 2006, all of which is produced by conventional thermal power stations. The sector was a monopoly-controlled by the Saudi Electricity Company (SEC), which is a joint-stock company 50 per cent owned by the Saudi government. However independent water and power projects (IWPP) have been introduced with schemes that allow private investment up to 60 per cent equity in IWPPs, with the remainder shared between the SEC and the Public Investment Fund (PIF). The first phase of the GCC power grid was completed in July 2009 at a cost of US$1,095 million, linking Saudi Arabia, Bahrain, Kuwait and Qatar through 800km of transmission lines.

By 2016 a planned 10 IWPPs will be launched, at a total cost of US$16 billion. Four of these projects alone will provide an addition 7,000MW. By 2020 the country plans to have a total installed generating capacity of 66GW.

Financial markets

Stock exchange

Tadawul (Saudi Stock Exchange)

Banking and insurance

Islamic banking rules are in force. The sector comprises 10 domestically-owned banks. Foreigners cannot own more than 49 per cent of domestic banks and foreign participation is mostly in the form of joint-ventures.

An agreement was reached between Saudi Arabia, Kuwait, Bahrain and Qatar to establish the Gulf Co-operation Council (GCC) Monetary Council to be established (originally in 2009), marking plans to set up a regional central bank, to be based in Riyadh (Saudi Arabia). The GCC Monetary Council will oversee the introduction of a monetary union, due to be in operation by 2013.

Central bank

Saudi Arabian Monetary Agency (SAMA)

Main financial centre

Riyadh

Time

GMT plus three hours

Geography

Saudi Arabia is bordered to the north by Egypt (the Sinai Peninsula), Jordan, Iraq and Kuwait; to the south by Yemen, Oman, the United Arab Emirates, Qatar and Bahrain (connected by a causeway); to the west by the Red Sea; and to the east by the Persian Gulf.

Saudi Arabia is a mainly barren land covering an area of 2.24 million square km. On the western coast is the Tihama plain, a hot region almost devoid of rainfall but with a humid coast. Inland from the Tihama rises a steep escarpment. In the centre of the Kingdom lies the Najd region and the Rub al-Khali (Empty Quarter) lies in the south-east. The eastern province, containing the oil fields, has an undulating topography with rocky outcrops.

Hemisphere

Northern

Climate

Average maximum temperatures are 38 degrees Celsius (C) in summer and the winter minimum is 13 degrees C. The summers are generally hot and dry (although humidity in some areas may reach 90 per cent) and the winters are cold. The coastal towns tend to be hot and humid all year. Rainfall in the Kingdom rarely exceeds 250mm a year, except in the extreme south-west.

Dress codes

A lightweight suit or jacket and trousers are advised. A tie and a long sleeved shirt should be worn at business meetings, but a jacket is not essential. Women should dress modestly, covering their arms and knees. Expatriate women often find it convenient to wear an *abaya*, a wrap-around shoulder cloak.

Entry requirements

Passports

Required by all, valid for six months from date of entry, except pilgrims with passes.

Visa

Required by all. Pilgrims should apply for visas through a visa agency accredited to an embassy of Saudi Arabia. During Haj and Umrah, pilgrims and visitors must have a valid certificate of vaccination against the ACWY strains of meningitis.

For business visas a letter of invitation from a Saudi company, endorsed by a Saudi Chamber of Commerce and Industry, must be faxed directly by the sponsor company to the Consulate to which the application is submitted. The original or copy of this invitation, together with an introductory letter from the employee's company addressed to the Embassy, should be submitted with the application form.

Women visitors are required to be met by their sponsor upon arrival. Women travelling alone, who are not met by sponsors, may experience delays before being allowed to enter or, if in transit, to continue their journey.

Prohibited entry

Travellers who arrive obviously inebriated are liable to arrest or deportation. Israeli nationals are barred from entering the Kingdom and an Israeli visa or stamp in a visitor's passport is likely to result in a ban on entry. Consultation with Saudi officials prior to departure is strongly recommended.

Currency advice/regulations

There are no restrictions on the import or export of local and foreign, except Israeli, currencies.

Customs

Personal effects are allowed duty-free. Duty is chargeable on many imported items, starting at 12 per cent but rising to 20 per cent for goods normally manufactured in the Kingdom; no duty on samples of low value.

Prohibited imports

The penalty for smuggling, promoting or circulating illegal drugs is capital punishment.

Other prohibitions include anything with an alcoholic content, certain foodstuffs (such as pork), pornography and censored literature. Prescription drugs should be carried only in small quantities in original containers. Dogs are banned, with the exception of guard dogs, hunting dogs and guide dogs.

Health (for visitors)

Mandatory precautions

A certificate of vaccination against yellow fever is required if travelling from an infected area.

During Haj and Umrah, pilgrims and visitors must have a valid certificate of vaccination against the ACWY strains of meningitis.

Advisable precautions

Vaccinations against cholera, typhoid and polio are recommended. Medical facilities in the Kingdom are excellent and there are few obvious health hazards.

Saudi Arabia is considered a high risk area for rabies, any animal or bat bites should be assessed carefully.

Hotels

There are many good hotels in the Kingdom. Alcoholic drinks are strictly prohibited.

Credit cards

All major credit cards are accepted.

Public holidays (national)

The Islamic year contains 354 or 355 days, with the result that Muslim feasts advance by 10–12 days against the Gregorian calendar. Dates of feasts vary according to the sighting of the new moon, so cannot be forecast exactly.

During the Haj, which immediately precedes Eid al Adha, government offices and some businesses close for 10 days. Work schedules may be seriously disrupted during the month of Ramadan, and businesses may take time off for other Islamic holidays.

Fixed dates

23 Sep (Saudi National Day)

For civil purposes, Saudi Arabia uses the Umm-ul-Qura calendar.

Variable dates

Eid al Adha (five days), Eid al Fitr (three days).

Islamic year 1433 (26 Nov 2011–14 Nov 2012): The Islamic year contains 354 or 355 days, with the result that Muslim feasts advance by 10–12 days against the Gregorian calendar. Dates of feasts vary according to the sighting of the new moon, so cannot be forecast exactly.

Working hours

Banking

Sat–Wed: 0830–1200 and 1700–1900; Thu: 0830–1130; 1000–1330 during Ramadan.

Business

Sat–Wed: 0800–1200, 1630–2000 in Riyadh; 0900—1330, 1630–2000 in Jeddah; 0730–1200, 1430–1730 in Eastern Province (closed Thu afternoon and Fri).

Private business offices in other areas: 0800–1200; 1500–1800.

Government

0730–1430 (Sat–Wed); 1000–1430 during Ramadan.

Shops

0800/0830–1200 and 1600–2100/2200; closed Thursday and Friday and four times a day for prayer for up to half an hour.

Telecommunications

Mobile/cell phones

Some Blackberry functions (such as instant messaging service) have been banned since August 2010.

Electricity supply

127V or 220V AC, 60 cycles, with two-pin European-type plugs and both bayonet and screw light fittings in use. 380V AC, 60 cycles is used by industry.

Social customs/useful tips

Punctuality is not always a Saudi virtue. While the foreign businessman will be expected to arrive at a meeting punctually, his Saudi counterpart may think nothing of being late or even of not showing up at all. Always shake hands (with your right hand) on meeting and leaving.

Take account of business hours and prayer times when making appointments; Saturday to Thursday is working week in Saudi Arabia.

Hospitality to the stranger lies at the heart of Arabian life. It is polite to accept at least one cup of tea or coffee when it is offered: oscillate the coffee cup when you do not want any more, otherwise the server will continue to fill it. Do not eat or drink with the left hand, as it is considered unclean; do not point the sole of your shoe at a Saudi at any time. You may ask after a man's children but not after his wife.

Saudi women are generally barred from public life. They do not drive and schools and universities are segregated.

The possession of alcohol is illegal. Although it is discreetly available it should not, in general, be offered to Saudis.

Some Blackberry functions (such as instant messaging service) were scheduled to be banned in August 2010.

Security

Visitors should keep in touch with developments in the Middle East as any increase in regional tension might affect travel advice.

The level of street crime has traditionally been far lower than in the west however, the influx of immigrant workers since the early 1970s has encouraged incidents of theft, although murder and violent crimes such as mugging and rape remain relatively rare.

Getting there

Air

National airline: Saudi Arabian Airlines (Saudia).

International airport/s: Jeddah-King Abdul Aziz International (JED), 18km north of city;, restaurant, bank, post office, shops, car hire and special pilgrimage facilities (during the annual pilgimages, the number of passengers using Jeddah airport can swell by 1.5m adding considerable delays to passport and visa controls); Riyadh-King Khaled International (RUH), 35km from the city; mosque, post office, bank, restaurant, shops, car hire.

Airport tax: SR50; not applicable to pilgrims.

Surface

Road: There are links to all countries sharing a common border with Saudi Arabia, as well as Bahrain via the causeway.

Main port/s: Dammam, Jeddah, Jizan, Jubail, Ras Tanura and Yanbu.

Getting about

National transport

Non-Muslims may not travel to the holy cities of Medina and Makkah (Makkah).

Air: Air travel is the most convenient way of getting around Saudi Arabia; there are numerous airports. Saudi Arabian Airlines operates a comprehensive schedule of domestic flights between Jeddah and Riyadh and other major centres. Always confirm flight bookings 24-hours before take-off, especially during the annual pilgrimage (Haj).

Road: The total length of the Saudi road network is over 156,000km, of which around 50,000km is asphalted and the remainder earth-surfaced. The main centres are linked by the Trans-Arabian Highway. Much of the network is of a high standard and undergoes regular maintenance and improvement.

Buses: Saudi Arabian Public Transport Company (SAPTCO) operates frequent bus services throughout the country on numerous local and national routes. Travel by bus is comparatively cheap and an increasingly favoured means of seeing the country.

Rail: Daily rail service links Riyadh and Damman, with refreshments and air-conditioning available.

City transport

Taxis: Taxis are yellow and should have a visible meter and taxi number in addition to normal registration. If using a taxi, it is adviable to agree the fare in advance. Taxi drivers do not expect a tip.

White limousines are operated by a number of companies within the cities and especially to and from airports. Fixed fares for specific journeys are prominently displayed at airports and available from drivers.

Car hire

Available at airports and main hotels. Driving licence required. Valid licences from most countries will be accepted by car hire companies. Women are not allowed to drive (although in 2008 two Saudi Scholars said that there is nothing in Islamic law that forbids women drivers). Driving is on the right-hand side of road at maximum 110kph on motorways and 40kph in cities. Insurance claims are not legally enforceable unless a police certification of the damage is obtained. Chauffeur-driven service is usually recommended.

BUSINESS DIRECTORY

Telephone area codes

The international direct dialling (IDD) code for Saudi Arabia is +966, followed by area code and subscriber's number:

Jeddah	2	Medina	4
Hofuf	3	Qatif	3
Makkah	2	Riyadh	1

Useful telephone numbers

Emergency police:	999
Ambulance:	997
Traffic accidents:	993
Fire:	998
Directory enquiries:	905

Chambers of Commerce

Abha Chamber of Commerce & Industry, PO Box 722, Abha (tel: 227-1818; fax: 227-1919).

Al-Baha Chamber of Commerce & Industry, PO Box 311, Al-Baha (tel: 725-0476; fax: 727-0146).

American Business Association - Eastern Province, PO Box 1868, Al-Khobar 31952 (tel: 882-5288 ext 1253; fax: 882-5288 ext 1497; e-mail: abaep@al-bustinet.com).

American Businessmen's Group of Riyadh, PO Box 8273, 11482 Riyadh (tel: 478-2738; fax: 476-4363).

British Businessmen's Group - Jeddah, PO Box 393, Jeddah (tel: 622-5550; fax: 622-6249; e-mail: bbj@tri.net,sa).

Eastern Province Chamber of Commerce and Industry, PO Box 719, Dammam 31421 (tel: 857-1111; fax: 857-0607).

Jeddah Chamber of Commerce and Industry, PO Box 1264, Jeddah 21431 (tel: 651-5111; fax: 651-7373; e-mail: info@jcci.org.sa; website: www.jcci.org.sa).

Jizan Chamber of Commerce & Industry, PO Box 201, Jizan (tel: 322-5155; fax: 322-3635).

Makkah Chamber of Commerce and Industry, PO Box 1086, Makkah (tel: 534-3838; fax: 534-2904).

Medina Chamber of Commerce and Industry, PO Box 443, Medina (tel: 826-8961; fax: 826-8965).

Najran Chamber of Commerce & Industry, PO Box 1138, Najran (tel: 522-2216; fax: 522-3926).

Riyadh Chamber of Commerce and Industry, PO Box 596, Riyadh 11421 (tel: 404-0044; fax: 402-1103; website: www.riyadhchamber.com).

Tabuk Chamber of Commerce & Industry, PO Box 567, Tabuk (tel: 422-0464; fax: 422-7387).

Taif Chamber of Commerce and Industry, PO Box 1005, Taif (tel: 736-6800; Fax: 738-0040).

Yanbu Chamber of Commerce & Industry, PO Box 58, Yanbu (tel: 322-7722; fax: 322-6800).

Banking

Arab National Bank, PO Box 56921, Riyadh 11411 (tel: 402-9000; fax: 403-0052).

Al Bank al Saudi al Fransi, PO Box 56006, Riyadh 11421 (tel: 477-4770; fax: 404-2311).

Al Rajhi Banking & Investment Corporation, PO Box 28, Riyadh 11411 (tel: 405-4244; fax: 403-2969).

Bank al Jazira, PO Box 6277, Jeddah 21442 (tel: 660-8820; fax: 661-3044).

National Commercial Bank, PO Box 3555, Jeddah 21421 (tel: 644-6644; fax: 643-7670; internet site: http://www.alahli.com/islamic_banking).

Riyad Bank, PO Box 22622, Riyadh 11411 (tel: 401-0908; fax: 404-0090).

Saudi American Bank, PO Box 833, Riyadh 11421 (tel: 477-4770).

Saudi British Bank, PO Box 9084, Riyadh 11413 (tel: 405-0677; fax: 405-0660).

Saudi Hollandi Bank, PO Box 1467, Riyadh (tel: 406-7888; fax: 401-0968).

Saudi Investment Bank, PO Box 3533, Riyadh (tel: 477-8433; fax: 478-1557).

Central bank

Saudi Arabian Monetary Agency, PO Box 2992, Riyadh 11169 (tel: 463-3000; fax: 466-2936; e-mail: info@sama.gov.sa).

Stock exchange

Tadawul (Saudi Stock Exchange): www.tadawul.com.sa

Stock exchange 2

Capital Market Authority (CMA): www.cma.org.sa

Travel information

Saudi Arabian Airlines, PO Box 620, Jeddah 21231 (tel: 684-2000; fax: 686-4552; e-mail: webmaster@saudiairlines.com.sa).

National tourist organisation offices

Supreme Commission for Tourism, Kindi Center, PO Box 66680, Riyadh 11586 (tel: 480-8855; fax: 480-8844; e-mail: info@sctsaudi.com).

Ministries

Ministry of Agriculture & Water, PO Box 2639, Airport Road, Riyadh 11195 (tel: 401-6666; fax: 403-1415).

Ministry of Communication, PO Box 3813, Airport Road, Riyadh 11178 (tel: 404-3000; fax: 403-1401).

Ministry of Defence and Aviation, Airport Road, Riyadh 11165 (tel: 478-5900; fax: 401-1336).

Ministry of Education, Airport Road, Riyadh 11148 (tel: 404-2888; fax: 401-2365).

Ministry of Foreign Affairs, Nesseriya St. Riyadh 11124 (tel: 406-7777; fax: 403-0159; internet: www.mofa.gov.sa).

Ministry of Health, PO Box 21217, Airport Road, Riyadh 11176 (tel: 401-2220; fax 402-9876).

Ministry of Higher Education, PO Box 1683, Riyadh 11153 (tel: 464-4444; fax: 441-9004).

Ministry of Information, PO Box 843, Nasseriya Street, Riyadh 11161 (tel: 401-4440; fax: 402-3570).

Ministry of Interior, PO Box 2933, Airport Road, Riyadh 11134 (tel: 401-1944; fax: 403-1185).

Ministry of Islamic Affairs, Endowments, Call and Guidance, Riyadh 11232 (tel: 473-0401).

Ministry of Labour & Social Affairs, PO Box 1182, Omar Ibn Al-Khatab Street, Riyadh 11157 (tel: 477-1480; fax: 477-7336).

Ministry of Justice, University Street, Riyadh 11137 (tel: 405-7777).

Ministry of Municipal and Rural Affairs, PO Box 5736, Nasseriya Street, Riyadh 11136 (tel: 441-5434; fax: 456-3196).

Ministry of Petroleum/Mineral Resources, PO Box 757, Airport Road, Riyadh 11189 (tel: 478-1661; fax: 479-3596).

Ministry of Pilgrimage, Omar Ibn Al-Khatab Street, Riyadh 11183 (tel:402-2200; fax: 402-2555).

Ministry of Post, Telegraphs & Telephones, Intercontinental Road, Riyadh 11112 (tel: 463-7225; fax: 405-2310).

Ministry of Public Works & Housing, Weshem Street, PO Box 56059, Riyadh 11151 (tel: 402-2268; fax: 402-2723 (public works), 406-7376 (housing)).

Other useful addresses

Arabian Oil Company, PO Box 256, Khafji 31971 (tel: 766-0555; fax: 766-2001).

Arab Petroleum Investments Corporation, PO Box 448, Dhahran Airport 31932 (tel: 864-7400; fax: 894-5076).

Arab Satellite Communiction Organisation, PO Box 1038, Riyadh 11431 (tel: 464-6666; fax: 465-6983).

Central Department of Statistics, PO Box 3735, Off Airport Road, Riyadh 11187 (tel:405-9638; fax: 405-9493).

Central Planning Organisation, Ministry of Planning, Riyadh.

Civil Defence, Airport Road, Riyadh 11174 (tel: 479-2828; fax: 478-0846).

Customs Department, PO Box 3483, Riyadh 11471 (tel: 401-3334; fax: 404-3412).

Dammam Seaport (King Abdul Aziz Sea Port) PO Box 28062, Dammam 31188 (tel: 833-2500; fax: 857-9223).

Dhahran International Expo, PO Box 7519, Dammam 31742 (tel: 833-7900; fax: 833-8010).

Director-General of Mineral Resources, PO Box 2880, Jeddah 21461 (tel: 631-0355; fax: 631-0357).

Directorate General of Zakat and Income Tax, Off Airport Road, Riyadh 11187 (tel: 404-1537; fax: 404-1495).

Federation of GCC Chambers, PO Box 2198, Dammam 31451 (tel: 826-5943; fax: 826-6794).

General Electricity Corp. (ELECTRICO), PO Box 1185, Riyadh 11431 (tel: 477-2772; fax: 477-5322).

General Organisation for Petroleum & Minerals (PETROMIN), PO Box 757, Riyadh 11189 (tel: 498-0995).

General Organisation for Social Insurance (GOSI), PO Box 2963, Riyadh 11461 (tel: 477-7735; fax: 477-9958).

General Organistion for Technical Education and Vocational Training, PO Box 7823, Riyadh 11472 (tel: 405-2770; fax: 406-5876).

General Ports Authority, PO Box 5162, Riyadh 11422 (tel: 476-0600).

General Presidency for Girls' Education, Television Street, Riyadh 11192 (tel: 402-9877; fax: 403-9570).

Grievances Court (Diwan-Al-Mazalem) Morabba-Nasseria Street, Riyadh 11138 (tel: 402-1724; fax: 403-4296).

Institute of Public Administration (IPA), PO Box 205, Riyadh 11411 (tel: 476-1600; fax: 479-2136).

International Airports Projects, PO Box 6326, Jeddah 21174 (tel: 685-4200).

Irish Embassy, Diplomatic Quarter, PO Box 94349, Riyadh 11693 (tel: 488-2300; fax: 488-0927; e-mail: irishembassy@awalnet,net.sa).

Jeddah Broadcasting Service, Broadcasting Station, Jeddah.

Jeddah Seaport, (Jeddah Islamic Port) PO Box 9285, Jeddah 21188 (tel: 643-2552).

Meteorology and Environment Protection Agency, PO Box 1358, Jeddah 21431 (tel: 651-8887).

National Guard, PO Box 9799, Riyadh 11423 (tel: 491-2400; fax: 491-2824).

Presidency of Civil Aviation, Off Palestine Road East, PO Box 887, Jeddah 21421 (tel: 667-9000).

Real Estate Development Fund, PO Box 5591, Riyadh 11433 (tel: 477-5120; fax: 479-0148).

Royal Commission for Jubail and Yanbu, PO Box 5864, Riyadh 11432 (tel: 479-4444; fax: 477-5404).

Saline Water Conversion Corporation (SWCC), PO Box 5968, Riyadh 11432 (tel: 463-0501; fax: 463-1952).

Saudi Arabian Airlines Corporation, PO Box 620, Jeddah 21421 (tel: 684-2000; fax: 686-4552).

Saudi Arabian Embassy (USA), 601 New Hampshire Avenue, NW, Washington DC 20037 (tel: (+1-202 -342-3800; fax: (+1-202) 944-3140; e-mail: info@saudiembessy.net).

Saudi Arabian Oil Company (Saudi Aramco), PO Box 5000, Dhahran Airport 31311 (tel: 875-5229; fax: 876-6520).

Saudi Arabian Standards Organisation, PO Box 3437, Riyadh 11471 (tel: 479-3332; fax: 479-3063).

Saudi Aramco (Saudi Arabian Oil Company), PO Box 5000, Dhahran 31311 (tel: 875-4915; fax: 873-8490).

Saudi Basic Industries Corporation (SABIC), PO Box 5105, Riyadh 11422 (tel: 401-2033; fax: 401-2045).

Saudi Export Development Centre, PO Box 16683, Riyadh 11474 (tel: 405-3200; fax: 402-4747).

Saudi Fund for Development, PO Box 50483, Riyadh 11523 (tel: 464-0292; fax: 464-7450; e-mail: info@sfd.gov.sa; website: www.sfd.gov.sa).

Saudi National Shipping Company, Po Box 8931, Riyadh 11492 (tel: 478-5454; fax: 477-8036).

Saudi Ports Authority, Riyadh 11188 (tel: 405-0005; fax: 405-9974).

Saudi Public Transport Co, PO box 10667, Riyadh 11443 (tel: 454-5000; fax: 454-2100).

Saudi Railroad Organisation, PO Box 92, Dammam 31411 (tel: 871-2222; fax: 827-1130).

Saudi Red Crescent Association, al Dhabab Road, Riyadh 11129 (tel: 406-9072; fax: 405-1566).

Youth Welfare Organisation, PO Box 965, Riyadh 11421 (tel: 401-4576; fax: 401-0376).

National news agency: Saudi Press Agency (SPA)

Internet sites

Arab net: www.arab.net/welcome.html

Arabia on line: www.arabia.com

Saudi Arabia Information Resourse (in London): wwwsaudinf.com

Saudi Embassy, UK, with web links to other Saudi enterprises: www.saudiembassy.org.uk/index2.htm

Senegal

KEY FACTS

Official name: République du Sénégal (Republic of Senegal)

Head of State: President Abdoulaye Wade (PDS) (since 2000; re-elected 25 Feb 2007)

Head of government: Prime Minister Souleymane Ndéné Ndiaye (from 30 Apr 2009)

Ruling party: Coalition: Sopi (Change) alliance led by Parti Démocratique Sénégalais (PDS) (Senegalese Democratic Party) and Ligue Démocratique-Mouvement pour le Parti du Travial (LD-MPT) (Democratic League - Movement for the Labour Party) (since 2001; re-elected 3 Jun 2007)

Area: 196,192 square km

Population: 12.51 million (2010)*

Capital: Dakar

Official language: French

Currency: CFA franc (CFAf) = 100 centimes (Communauté Financière Africaine (African Financial Community) franc).

Exchange rate: CFAf488.90 per US$ (Oct 2011); CFAf655.95 per euro (pegged from Jan 1999)

GDP per capita: US$981 (2010)

GDP real growth: 4.20% (2010)

GDP: US$12.90 billion (2010)

Inflation: 1.20% (2010)

Balance of trade: -US$3.40 million (2008)

Annual FDI: US$237.19 million (2010)

*estimated figure

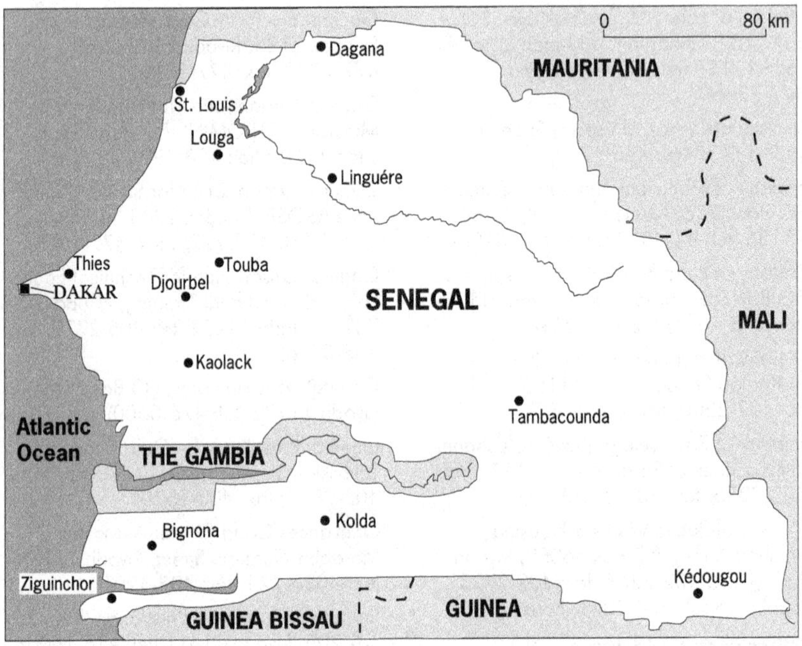

In an announcement on his Television Futurs Medias (TFM), one of Africa's greatest musical stars, Youssou N'Dour, said he would run against incumbent President Abdoulaye Wade in the February 2012 elections. The 85-year old Wade is on shaky ground by running for a third term since a constitutional amendment agreed in a referendum held on 7 January 2001 and promulgated later the same month states that a president may stand for only two terms. Mr Wade's argument is that the referendum was agreed only after he had started his second term in 2000, and it should therefore be regarded as his first term. Those of a suspicious turn of mind believe this manoeuvring is to give more time for Wade's son, Kirim Wade, to prepare to succeed his father.

N'Dour's move has rather distracted the other parties, including the main opposition, Parti Socialiste Sénégalais (PS) (Socialist Party), which boycotted the 2007 elections, from deciding on a single opposition candidate to Mr Wade. Should Youssour N'Dour win he will be the second musician, after Michel 'Sweet Micky' Martelly in Haiti, to come to power in 12 months.

The economy

After two years marked by the effects of the global financial crisis, the Senegalese economy began to recover in 2010 thanks to the global economic recovery and the measures taken by the authorities to boost national economic activity. According to the *African Economic Outlook 2011* (AEO), published jointly by the African Development Bank and the Organisation for Economic Co-operation and Development, gross domestic product (GDP) was estimated to have grown from 2.2 per cent in 2009 to 4.2 per cent in 2010, and is projected to reach 4.5 per cent in 2011.

Analysis of the basic macroeconomic indicators in 2010 reveals the start of a recovery in the Senegalese economy. The average annual rate of inflation (1.0 per cent in 2009) was 1.2 per cent in 2010. In 2011 inflation measured by the GDP deflator is forecast at 3 per cent largely as a result of higher energy prices. The expected change in the investment rate measured by the Gross Fixed Capital Formation (GFCF) is positive at 23.9 per cent of GDP in 2010 and 24.1 per cent in

2011. The tax-burden rate of 18.9 per cent in 2010 also complies with the requirements of the sub-regional convergence criteria (greater than or equal to 17 per cent).

Senegal's good rate of revenue collection, up by 11 per cent compared to 2009, and control of the increase in public expenditure (7.1 per cent) characterised Senegal's fiscal policy in 2010. The overall budget deficit, including grants, improved 0.4 percentage points, from 4.9 per cent of GDP in 2009 to 4.5 per cent in 2010. It was estimated at 5.8 per cent in 2011.

Agriculture

Groundnut production increased from 731,000 tonnes in 2009 to 1.032 million tonnes during the 2009/10 season and is expected to reach 1.064 million tonnes in 2010/11, representing a 3 per cent increase. Nevertheless, the groundnut sector is going through a difficult period because of the low prices paid to producers. On the ground, production is harvested and delivered to the oil manufacturers by the licensed private marketing agents, known as *opérateurs privés stockeurs*, who are responsible for obtaining financing from banks. The producer price of groundnuts is set following consultation between the oil manufacturers and *Comité national interprofessionnel de l'arachide* (CNIA) (National Committee for Stakeholders in the Groundnut Industry). For the 2009/10 season, the CNIA set a price of CFAf165 (US$0.34) per kilo. This included a state subsidy of CFAf45 (US$0.09).

The low producer price was underlined by a recent study undertaken by agronomists, which found that the farm-gate price for the 2009/10 season should have been CFAf192 (US$0.39), meaning a loss of CFAf27 (US$0.06) per kilo for producers. For the 2010/11 season, the price set by the CNIA remains at CFAf165 (US$0.34), with the state subsidy reduced to CFAf15 (US$0.03) per kilo. In addition to the low price, the season started late.

Dysfunctional marketing compounds the farmers' problems, which sometimes lead farmers to sell their harvest at much lower prices than the set price of CFAf165 (US$0.34) (a kilo of groundnuts at local markets costs CFAf90 (US$18)). Cotton production fell in the 2009/10 season to 18,500 tonnes, down from 26,256 tonnes in 2008/09. The 2008/09 season also saw falls in the production of cassava (71 per cent), cowpeas (-31 per cent) and sesame (38 per cent). During the 2010/11 campaign the decline in production of cassava, cowpeas and sesame has continued (respectively, -18.1 per cent, -17.5 per cent and -91 per cent). However, cotton production has recorded a turnaround, with an increase of 26 per cent over the 2009/10 season.

International trade and development

Senegal's external position was marked by an improvement of its current account due to the reduction of its trade deficit. The current account deficit was estimated at 5.9 per cent of GDP in 2010, down from 6.7 per cent in 2009. The trade balance deficit decreased from CFAf957.7 billion (US$1.96 billion) in 2009 to CFAf941.5 billion (US$1.93 billion) in 2010, having improved by CFAf16.2 billion (US$33.1 million). As a share of GDP, it decreased from 15.9 per cent in 2009 to 14.8 per cent in 2010, and is projected to reach 14.4 per cent in 2011. The deficit diminished because Senegal's imports (CFAf40.5 billion (US$828 million)) increased less than its exports (CFAf56.8 billion (US$116 million)) in 2010. On a year-on-year basis, exports grew by 5.7 per cent in 2010, thanks mainly to increased sales of groundnut products (+40.7 per cent), cotton (+70.5 per cent), phosphoric acid (+64.1 per cent), fish (+4.9 per cent) and petroleum products (+6.5 per cent).

The growth in exports in 2010 was thanks to the good 2009/10 agricultural season, which saw groundnut production break the million tonne mark and an upturn and recovery in Industries Chimiques du Senega (ICS) (Chemical Industries of Senegal) activities following the recapitalisation in 2008. Imports also grew, from CFAf1.948 trillion (US$3.98 billion) to CFAf1.988 trillion (US$4.06 billion) in 2010. Much of this 2.1 per cent growth came from increased imports of petroleum products (+12.9 per cent) and capital equipment (+6.1 per cent). Petroleum products were the main imports in 2010, accounting for 28.1 per cent of the total, followed by capital equipment (25.5 per cent). Food products, which were the main imports in the early 2000s, were only the third largest type of import in 2010, accounting for 21.4 per cent of the total.

Since 2000, Senegal has initiated new partnerships with emerging countries, particularly China, India and Iran. The main achievements are to be found in the areas of training, infrastructure and transport.

Doing business

In the World Bank's *Doing Business* ranking for 2011, Senegal was placed 152nd out of 183 countries, one place lower than in 2010. The country has been asked to make efforts to reduce the high cost of transactions. Nevertheless, the 2011 report highlights progress in various areas.

Senegal was placed 25th for improvements to the business climate and for the ease of obtaining construction permits. It is also one of the few non-OECD countries to have successfully set up a one-stop shop to facilitate business start-up. Other positive points were also highlighted in the area of cross-border trade. Senegal is praised for the various institutions that exist to create good governance and is also an active member of

KEY INDICATORS **Senegal**

	Unit	2006	2007	2008	2009	2010
Population	m	11.94	12.23	12.52	12.80	*12.51
Gross domestic product (GDP)	US$bn	9.16	11.12	13.40	12.80	12.90
GDP per capita	US$	768	910	1,066	984	981
GDP real growth	%	2.1	5.0	3.2	2.2	4.2
Inflation	%	2.1	5.9	5.8	-1.7	1.2
Industrial output	% change	3.8	5.6	-3.2	4.6	–
Agricultural output	% change	-2.9	-6.0	19.6	7.2	–
Exports (fob) (goods)	US$m	1,519.0	1,673.8	–	–	–
Imports (fob) (goods)	US$m	3,437.0	-4,163.8	–	–	–
Balance of trade	US$m	-1,918.0	-1,310.8	–	–	–
Current account	US$m	-895.0	-906.0	-1,645.0	-1,474.0	-1,067.0
Total reserves minus gold	US$m	1,334.2	1,660.0	1,601.3	2,123.2	2,047.5
Foreign exchange	US$m	1,331.8	1,657.3	1,598.6	1,916.1	1,844.0
Exchange rate	per US$	496.60	454.40	447.81	514.03	495.28

* estimated figure

the Inter-Governmental Action Group against Money-Laundering in West Africa

Health care

In terms of the Millennium Development Goals (MDGs), Senegal is somewhat behind schedule in the area of healthcare, mainly because of difficult access to care and vaccine stock-outs in certain rural areas. The infant-child mortality rate is approximately 21 per cent, with 25 per cent of those deaths occurring during the prenatal period. Another poor statistic is the high maternal mortality rate, with 401 deaths per 100,000 live births in 2010.

Progress has been made, however, in controlling the prevalence of HIV/Aids, which remains at 0.7 per cent (0.9 per cent of women and 0.4 per cent for men). The authorities have reduced the cost of antiretroviral treatment by 90 per cent. Further, as part of the social measures related to healthcare taken in 2010, on 1 May 2010 the government made artemisinin combination therapies (ACTs) for malaria free. In addition to free anti-malarial drugs, the cost of treatment for haemodialysis was reduced by 80 per cent as of 7 April 2010. In terms of budgetary policy, substantial efforts were made to try to achieve the MDGs. Nevertheless, the share of the budget allocated to healthcare in 2010 was 10 per cent, still below the 15 per cent threshold set by the World Health Organisation (WHO).

Risk assessment

Economy	Fair
Politics	Poor
Regional stability	Fair

COUNTRY PROFILE

Historical profile

1960 Senegal gained independence from France as part of the Federation of Mali, which almost immediately collapsed due to conflicts between the political leaders of the two territories (former French Soudan and Senegal). An independent Senegal was proclaimed under President Léopold Senghor.

1978 The first multi-party elections were held.

1980 President Senghor resigned.

1981 Abdou Diouf became president.

1982 Fighting began in Casamance between the Movement des Forces Démocratiques de Casamance (MFDC) (Democratic Forces of Casamance Movement), a separatist movement, and Senegalese government troops.

1983 The ruling Parti Socialiste Sénégalais (PS) (Senegal Socialist Party) returned to power with an overwhelming majority.

1993 Diouf was re-elected.

1998 Parliamentary elections were won by the PS. The constitution was amended to include a second legislative chamber, the Senate, with the president appointing 20 per cent of the delegates and most of the rest chosen by an electoral college. The opposition boycotted the Senate elections and the PS won all the seats, later winning a majority in the elections for the expanded National Assembly.

1999 The government entered into a peace initiative with the secessionist MFDC, which resulted in a cease-fire later in the year.

2000 Presidential elections were won by Abdoulaye Wade, of the Parti Démocratique Sénégalais (PDS) (Democratic Party of Senegal). President Wade dissolved the Senate which removed the Senate leader who, under the constitution, would assume the presidency in the event the incumbent was incapacitated.

2001 A 90 per cent vote favoured the proposed new constitution that limited presidential power. President Wade's coalition won the parliamentary elections.

2002 The EU paid Senegal US$63 million for fishing rights to exploit Senegalese waters until 2006.

2003 The MFDC declared the Casamance secessionist war was over. President Wade and King Mohammed VI of Morocco agreed a mutual political and economic accord.

2004 The president and Father Diamacoune Senghor, leader of the MFDC, signed a peace deal.

2005 Travel between Senegal and The Gambia was blockaded in a dispute, which broke out over border ferry tariffs.

2006 Agreement was reached with Spain to promote a legal migration policy. Salif Sadio, leader of a breakaway faction of the MFDC refused to accept the 2004 peace agreement.

2007 Parliamentary elections were postponed following a legal challenge of gerrymandering. Abdoulaye Wade won the presidential election beating four other candidates. Later, in general elections the ruling Sopi alliance won 69.2 per cent of the vote (131 seats, out of 150). The opposition had boycotted the election. Cheikh Hadjibou Soumaré became prime minister. The Senate was reinstated, with elections for one-third of its members, while the president appointed the remaining two-thirds.

2009 Chinese President Hu Jintao agreed US$90 million in aid for Senegal. Prime Minister Cheikh Hadjibou Soumaré resigned and Souleymane Ndéné Ndiaye became prime minister. Parliament agreed to the creation of a new post of vice president, to be a presidential appointee. Observers considered the post had been created for Kirim Wade, the president's son, to be groomed as next president.

2010 In April, the 50 years anniversary of independence celebrations began as Senegal closed all French military bases in the country. Eight days of national mourning in July was observed following the death of the Grand Marabout, El Hadji Serigne Mouhamadou Lamine Bara Mbacké, hereditary religious leader of the Islamic Mourides movement. The unusually high summer heat damaged the mango crop, with production falling by 70–80 per cent in Casamance. Insect infestation and groundwater salinity also contributed to a reduced harvest. Senegal's ambassador in Tehran was recalled on 15 December after Iran's failure to give a 'satisfactory' explanation for an arms shipment that was seized in Nigeria and which was said to be destined for The Gambia. There was speculation that the arms were to be sent to the Casamance independence movement.

2011 A proposed constitutional change to reduce the proportion of votes needed to elect the president from 50 per cent to 25 per cent and avoid a run-off election was dropped in June after protests outside Dakar's parliament. President Wade had also wanted to create an elected post of vice president. Foreign Minister Madicke Niang announced on 10 July that Senegal was suspending the repatriation of Chad's former president, Hissène Habré, on the grounds that he might be tortured. Habre had been sentenced *in absentia* for killing and torturing opponents 1982–90. On 9 August the Islamic Development Bank (IDB) agreed to loan Senegal US$95 million to fund a 70MW electricity generator.

Political structure

Constitution

The 2001 constitution allows for the formation of opposition parties, gives enhanced status to the prime minister and sets the length of the president's term of office at five years. It also gives the president power to dissolve the National Assembly after it has served for two years and call fresh parliamentary elections.

Form of state

Unitary republic

The executive

Executive power is vested in the president who is head of state and commander-in-chief of the armed forces. The president is directly elected by universal adult suffrage, for a five-year term, renewable once.

In the event of the presidency falling vacant, the president of the National Assembly automatically becomes head of state.

National legislature
The bicameral Parlement du Sénégal (Parliament of Senegal) is comprised of the Assemblée Nationale (National Assembly) with 120 directly elected members for five-year terms and the Sénat (Senate) with 100 members, of which 65 are appointed by the president and 35 elected by local and regional councillors. The president appoints a prime minister who in turn appoints a Council of Ministers in consultation with the president.
Legal system
The members of the Supreme Court of Justice are appointed by the president, on the advice of the Superior Court of Magistrates, which determines the constitutionality of laws. The High Court of Justice is appointed by the National Assembly from its members; it has the power to impeach the president or members of the government.
Last elections
25 February 2007 (presidential); 3 June 2007 (parliamentary).
Results: Presidential: Abdoulaye Wade won 55.9 per cent of the vote, the next candidate, Idrissa Seck, won 14.9 per cent. Turnout was 70.5 per cent.
Parliamentary: Sopi alliance won 69.2 per cent of the vote (131 seats out of 150); Takku Defaraat Sénégal (TDS) 5 per cent (three); Defar Senegal 4.9 per cent (three); Waar Wi coalition 4.4 per cent (three); ten other political parties won one seat each. Turnout was 34.75 per cent.
Next elections
2014 (presidential); 2012 (parliamentary).

Political parties
Ruling party
Coalition: Sopi (Change) alliance led by Parti Démocratique Sénégalais (PDS) (Senegalese Democratic Party) and Ligue Démocratique-Mouvement pour le Parti du Travial (LD-MPT) (Democratic League - Movement for the Labour Party) (since 2001; re-elected 3 Jun 2007)
Main opposition party
Parti Socialiste Sénégalais (PS) (Socialist Party) (boycotted 2007 elections).

Population
12.51 million (2010)
Last census: December 2002: 9,956,202 (provisional)
Population density: 45 inhabitants per square km. Urban population: 48 per cent (1995–2001).
Annual growth rate: 2.5 per cent 1994–2004 (WHO 2006)
Internally Displaced Persons (IDP)
5,000 (UNHCR 2004)
Ethnic make-up
Wolof (43 per cent), Pular (24 per cent), Serer (15 per cent), Jola (4 per cent), Mandinka (3 per cent), Soninke 1 per cent), European and Lebanese (1 per cent).

Religions
Islam (94 per cent), Christian (mainly Roman Catholic) (5 per cent), indigenous beliefs (1 per cent).

Education
The investment in education amounts to 3.2 per cent of GDP. The government is pursuing a broad based programme to eliminate illiteracy by 2010.
Primary education is provided free of charge and is officially compulsory. However, attendance is low and on average approximately half the relevant age groups do not attend. School attendance rates in urban areas can be as high as 80 per cent, while those of rural areas can be as low as 30 per cent.
Secondary school lasts for seven years and is divided into two cycles of four- and three-years. The first cycle is middle school when all students undertake general education. At the age of 16, all those that pass an exam can choose between a general; short or long term technical; vocational or professional, upper secondary school. Only the general and professional schools culminate in a baccalauréat (at age 18) and students can continue to Dakar University or the smaller university at Sanar near Saint Louis. Vocational and technical secondary schools concentrate on applied subjects, particularly agriculture.
Literacy rate: 39 per cent adult rate; 53 per cent youth rate (15–24) (Unesco 2005).
Compulsory years: Six to 12.
Enrolment rate: 71 per cent gross primary enrolment of relevant age group (including repeaters); 16 per cent gross secondary enrolment (World Bank).
Pupils per teacher: 58 in primary schools.

Health
In 2008 pharmacists in a nationwide general strike protested at the illegal sale of fake drugs, worth an estimated US$23.7 million per year and centred openly in a compound in the capital, Dakar. There has been a rise in 'unknown' and 'inexplicable' medical cases which are being linked to the use of medicines brought from street vendors.
HIV/Aids
HIV prevalence: 0.8 per cent aged 15–49 in 2003 (World Bank)
Life expectancy: 55 years, 2004 (WHO 2006)
Fertility rate/Maternal mortality rate: 4.9 births per woman, 2004 (WHO 2006)
Birth rate/Death rate: 36 births per 1,000 population; 11 deaths per 1,000 population (2003).

Child (under 5 years) mortality rate (per 1,000): 78 per 1,000 live births (World Bank)
Head of population per physician: 0.06 physicians per 1,000 people, 2004 (WHO 2006)

Welfare
Most Senegalese are heavily indebted and poverty stricken. According to the World Bank, around 26 per cent of the population live below US$1 a day and around 68 per cent live on less than US$2 a day. There is a state medical service and workers receive some maternity and family benefits, but the welfare system is unable to provide sufficient economic security for Senegal's poor.

Main cities
Dakar (capital, estimated population 2.0 million in 2005), Touba (428,059), Thiès (240,152), Rufisque (187,203), Kaolack (173,782), Mbour (170,699), Ziguinchor (162,436), St Louis (130,750).

Languages spoken
The main national languages are Jola-Fogny, Malinke, Mandinka, Pulaar, Serere-Sine, Soninke and Wolof. There are 36 spoken living languages. In business, it is essential to speak French. Very few executives speak English.
Official language/s
French

Media
Press
The press is subject to a *Code de la Presse*, adopted in March 1979, which stipulates that owners of national newspapers and magazines must be Senegalese. The same *Code de la Presse* provides for regulation and authorisation of journalists working in the national press, although there are no restrictions on the publication and distribution of the papers and magazines themselves.
Dailies: In French national newspaper include *Le Soleil* (www.lesoleil.sn) is government-controlled, privately owned are *Sud quotidien* (www.sudonline.sn), *Le Quotidien* (www.lequotidien.sn) *Wal Fadjri L'Aurore* (www.walf.sn) and *L'Actuel* (www.lactuel.info), *Il est Midi* (www.ilestmidi.net), *Le Messager* (www.lemessager.sn), *L'Observateur* (www.lobservateur.sn), *L'Office* (www.loffice.sn) and *L'AS* (www.las.sn).
Periodicals: Various political parties and independent owners publish journals, mostly available in French. There are several satirical journals including *Le Cafard Libéré* and *Vive la République* (weeklies) and *Le Politicien* (fortnightly). Other monthly publications include *Afrique Tribune, Démocratie* and *Le Tournant; Le Journal de l'Economie* is a business magazine.

Broadcasting
Radiodiffusion-Télévision du Sénégal (ORTS) is the state-run broadcaster.
Radio: For most people radio is the main medium for news and information. ORTS operates regional, national, and international networks and an FM station in Dakar, broadcasting in French, Portuguese, Arabic, English and six African languages.
There are four private radio stations located mainly in Dakar, Sud FM (www.sudonline.sn) operated by the telecommunications company Groupe Sud, Sept FM, Walf FM (www.walf.sn) operated by Groupe Wal Fadjri, Radio Dunyaa and Radio Future Medias. The online portal www.seneweb.com provides access to several radio broadcasts and newspaper publications.
Television: ORTS has two television channel. Commercial satellite and cable TV are also available. There are many production companies operating out of Senegal for the West African market.
News agencies
National news agency: Agence de Presse Senegalaise (APS)

Economy
In 2009, the service sector constituted 61.7 per cent of GDP, with tourism an important sector; industry was 21.7 per cent, of which manufacturing comprised 12.7 per cent; agriculture was 16.6 per cent, of which fishing was a major component.
There is a relatively advanced industrial sector that employs over 17 per cent of the population in energy production, phosphoric acid (used in fertilisers) and the manufacturing of construction materials. However, with a semi-arid terrain Senegal's population is largely rural and most of the workforce is employed (although not necessarily paid) in the production of groundnuts (peanuts).
Agriculture is subject to a number of external pressures such as pest infestations and poor weather, which can adversely affect harvests.
GDP growth was 5.0 per cent in 2007, falling to 3.2 per cent in 2008 as the global economic crisis cut exports; the economy weakened further in 2009 with GDP growth falling to 2.2 per cent. However Senegal avoided recession and as world trade picked up, GDP growth registered an increase to 4.2 per cent in 2010. Inflation reacted to the slowdown and registered a jump from 2.1 per cent in 2006 to 5.9 per cent in 2007, which remained constant until deflation of -1.7 per cent hit in 2009; in 2010 inflation returned but by only 1.2 per cent.
Around 500,000 Senegalese work abroad (mainly in West Africa, France and Italy) and provided remittances of US$1.28 billion in 2008, which fell to US$1.19 billion in 2009 (9.1 per cent of GDP) and an estimated US$1.16 billion in 2010.
Unemployment remains one of Senegal's most prominent problems with only just over half the population in waged jobs; the majority of unemployed are the urban young. High unemployment rates hinder the reduction of poverty. In 2011, the UN Human Development Index (HDI) ranked Senegal 155 (out of 187) for national development in health, education and income. In 2010, 57.4 per cent of the population experienced at least one indicator of poverty, while 33.5 per cent lived on the equivalent of US$1.25 per day.
The International Monetary Fund (IMF) stated that positive GDP growth in 2010 was possible as the world economy recovered and remittances stabilised. However without strong growth the outcome of poverty-alleviation measures was likely to be limited. Senegal was not directly hit be the global banking crisis, due to its relatively limited international integration, but non-performing loans increased in 2009 and several banks did not meet their targets for financial soundness.

External trade
Senegal is a member of the Economic Community of West African States (Ecowas), which was set up to promote economic integration among members, and is also a member of the West African Economic and Monetary Union (WAEMU) using the common currency, the CFA franc.
Foreign trade provides around 70 per cent of GDP. Industrial production includes mining, energy production and construction materials. Manufacturing includes foreign-owned assembly production of vehicles and other consumer goods and food processing of domestic agricultural products.
Imports
Principal imports are food and beverages, petroleum, capital goods, fuels, semi-manufactured goods and vehicles.
Main sources: France (typically 17 per cent of total), Nigeria (12 per cent), Thailand (7 per cent).
Exports
Principal exports are processed fish and groundnuts (peanuts), petroleum products, limestone, iron ore, gold and phosphates, cotton and textiles.
Main destinations: Mali (typically 23 per cent of total), India (12 per cent), France (8 per cent).

Agriculture
Farming
Agriculture contributes around 17 per cent to GDP and employs 70 per cent of the working population. Farming is carried out almost exclusively on smallholdings and is relatively inefficient. Agricultural development has been hindered by poor transport infrastructure. The main subsistence crops are sorghum and millet, although production of rice is increasing. Agricultural output is rising, supplying the domestic market and providing exports of out-of-season fruit and vegetables to European markets. Cash crops include groundnuts, cotton and sugar. Groundnut farming is crucial to the economy and employs a large percentage of the rural population.
Both groundnut and cotton output have been affected by the lack of farm credit and high levels of debt. The government established an agricultural development bank, the Caisse Nationale de Crédit Agricole and village co-operatives, which enjoyed greater autonomy. It also privatised the Société National de Commercialisation des Oléagineux de Sénégal (Sonacos), the national groundnut company. Sugar cane is the only sector with large plantations, which are operated by Compagnie Sucrière du Sénégal (CSS).
Cattle, sheep and goats are widely kept for domestic use. Poultry numbers are showing a long-term increase and there has been a marked increase in the sheep population since the mid-1980s.
Fishing
Fishing is important for the export revenues from the fish processing and canning industries, as well as licence revenues from foreign ships operating in Senegalese waters. Fish and fish products are typically the largest single item in export earnings. The fisheries sector is targetted for expansion, with assistance being given to artisan fishermen, and the development of producer groups. Finance for this programme is partly derived from the foreign fishing licence revenues. The Senegalese government is supporting the development of marine fish farming (tuna, oysters, prawns and lobsters).
In 2002, Senegal refused to extend a fishing rights accord which had allowed EU vessels to fish in Senegalese waters since 1997. The EU and Senegal clashed over which areas should be fished and the length of the rest periods, which are essential for fish stock recovery. The Senegalese authorities raised the problem of overfishing and illegal methods employed by EU trawlers, which is causing fish stocks to plummet and has put Senegalese fishermen's livelihoods at risk; around 500,000 people in Senegal depend on the fishing industry for an income.
Forestry
Forest resources in Senegal are modest, although the country is well forested with 38 per cent forest cover estimated at 6.2 million hectares (ha) and an additional 30

per cent of other wooded land. Deforestation occurs at an average rate of 0.7 per cent per year. Desertification continues to be a major environmental problem in northern Senegal. The country has established significant areas of plantation forest to meet fuel and fodder needs. A programme of reforestation now under way aims to include the revival of gum arabic production.
Wood is mostly used for fuel consumption, while production of sawn timber and industrial roundwood caters to the domestic market. Some amount of wood and paper is also imported.

Industry and manufacturing
The industrial sector contributes around 25 per cent to GDP, with the manufacturing sector contributing 17 per cent of GDP. Most industry is located inside the Dakar area of the Cap Vert peninsula. The only heavy export industries are an oil refinery at Dakar-Mbao, a sulphuric/phosphoric acid plant at Darou Khoudou and a fertiliser complex at Mbao.
The main industrial activity is light industry, processing locally-produced primary commodities for export and manufacturing import substitution goods to meet local demand. The government's industrial policy aims to make the economy more market-responsive and less centrally controlled. This entails a reduction in government participation in industry, price liberalisation and the encouragement of foreign investment (through a more favourable tax regime) and small businesses (through special incentives). It gives priority to high-value and export industries, especially chemicals, textiles, food processing and leather goods. The food-processing sector and, to a lesser extent, textile manufacturing, are influenced heavily by agricultural performance, as they rely mainly on locally produced inputs. Therefore, industrial performance is affected by climatic conditions in a similar way to the agricultural sector.
Light industry is mostly privately-owned and relies heavily on foreign capital and management skills. Lack of adequate infrastructure has curtailed industrial development outside the capital.

Tourism
The state tourism agency is involved both in promoting the country in Europe (particularly in Italy and the UK), and in encouraging foreign investment in the development of further tourist facilities. The government sees tourism as a key foreign currency earner.

Environment
In June 2010 the African Union backed a proposal to build the 'Great Green Wall' project, of a 15km wide, 7,775km long, continuous belt of trees from Senegal in the west to Djibouti in the east (traversing 11 countries) in an effort to halt the advance of the Sahara Desert. The trees to be used would be drought-adapted, preferably native to the area from a list of 37 possible species, and should help to slow soil erosion and filter rain water.

Mining
The mining sector contributes around 7 per cent to GDP and employs 3 per cent of the workforce.
Extraction of calcium and phosphates from open mines near Thiès are the most important mining activities. Workable deposits are estimated at around 130 million tonnes. Production (around 1.5 million tonnes per annum) is mainly for export, although it is also an important source of supply for the fertiliser complex at Mbao. Phosphates represent around 17 per cent of export earnings, although production declined by 30 per cent over the 1990s. The phosphate mine in the Matam area holds deposits of around 40.5 million tonnes.
Titanium, zircon and rutile are mined along the south coast of Cap Vert. The total available iron ore reserves at the Faleme iron ore project near the Mali border are estimated at 391 million tonnes, enough to sustain mining activities for over 30 years at the planned production rate of 12 million tonnes of marketable products per year. The Farangalia and Goto deposits hold estimated reserves of 250 million tonnes.

Hydrocarbons
There are no known oil reserves although exploration offshore and along the coast has been ongoing since the early 2000s.
All of Senegal's oil requirements are met by imports. Downstream, the Société Africaine de Raffinage (SAR) refinery has a nominal capacity of 17,000 barrels per day (bpd). Consumption is typically over 20,000bpd.
Natural gas reserves are estimated at 11 billion cubic metres (cum), primarily located offshore; consumption is 275,000 cum per day. All natural gas is pumped directly to a gas-powered electricity generating plant.
Any use of coal is commercially insignificant.

Energy
Total installed electricity generating capacity was 422MW in 2006, producing 256 gigawatt hours (gWh). Electricity is supplied from six thermal stations. Virtually all commercial energy requirements are imported.
Only one in three people in Senegal has access to electricity. In rural areas, wood fuel provides for most, with consequently serious deforestation. A programme of re-forestation is under way.
The government's 10-year energy plan aims to substitute 50 per cent of imported oil by local products, including oil/gas from the Dome Flore offshore field, peat deposits from Niayés and the expansion of hydropower from the Senegal and Gambia Rivers. It has been estimated that Senegal could produce 11 terrawatt hours (tWh) a year, given full exploitation of its hydro capacity.
The government has failed to divest the Société Nationale d'Electricité (Senelec), the state-owned electricity company, despite two attempts at privatisation. In 2008 the World Bank agreed a loan of US$80 million to Senegal to rationalise the energy sector and sustain long-term development.

Financial markets
Stock exchange
Afribourse (Bourse Régionale des Valeurs Moblières) (BRVM)

Banking and insurance
Eight commercial banks operate in Senegal, with the three largest banks holding approximately two-thirds of total deposits.
The largest bank in Senegal is the Société Générale de Banques au Sénégal (SGBS). The SGBS faces strong competition from its main rival, the Banque International pour le Commerce et l'Industrie du Sénégal (BICIS).
The banking sector is overseen by the Banque Centrale des Etas de l'Afrique de l'Ouest (BCEAO), which sets policy throughout the Union Economique et Monetaire Ouest Africaine (UEMOA) (West African Economic and Monetary Union).
Central bank
Banque Centrale des Etats de l'Afrique de l'Ouest (BCEAO)
Main financial centre
Dakar

Time
GMT

Geography
Senegal lies on the west coast of Africa, bordered to the north by Mauritania, to the east by Mali, and to the south by Guinea and Guinea-Bissau. Senegal surrounds the small state of The Gambia, which straddles the River Gambia in the south-west of Senegal, and forms a narrow enclave extending some 320 kilometres (200 miles) inland.
The country is low-lying and flat, and is situated in the savannah grasslands. Apart from the River Gambia and the Senegal River, which forms the northern boundary, most rivers are seasonal and dry up in the arid winter months.

Hemisphere
Northern

Climate
The climate is tropical in the south (Casamance) and more temperate in the north.
The best time to visit is October—June, when it is cool and dry. The safest time to avoid the rain is mid November—April, but it is hot and humid during the day (cooler at night). During the rainy season, July—September, the humidity gets very high and the days very hot. In the southern part of the country, the rainy season can extend through October.

Dress codes
There is no restriction on clothing, although women are advised to dress modestly. In the dry season lightweight European clothing is suitable, and many government ministers wear lounge suits. Businessmen and other officials wear local dress – the *boubou*. Tropical clothing (not white) is necessary in the wet season.

Entry requirements
Passports
Required by all.
Visa
Required by all; except nationals of the EU, North America, Japan and many countries in the region for visits up to 90 days (for a full list of exceptions see www.senegalembassy.co.uk). Visitors should contact the nearest consulate to obtain an application form. Proof of return/onward passage is necessary.
Business travellers should include a letter of invitation, from a local company or organisation, and a business letter of intent, with their application form.
Currency advice/regulations
The import of local and foreign currency is unlimited. Export of local currency is only allowed to other African Financial Community countries and only up to CFAf20,000; export of foreign currency is limited to the equivalent of CFAf50,000. All foreign currency must be declared on arrival and departure.
Travellers cheques should be euro or US dollars to avoid additional exchange fees.
Customs
Alcoholic spirits are not duty-free.

Health (for visitors)
Mandatory precautions
A yellow fever certificate is required if arriving from an endemic area.
Advisable precautions
Inoculations and boosters should be current for tetanus, hepatitis A, diphtheria, typhoid and yellow fever. There may be a need for vaccinations for tuberculosis, hepatitis B and meningitis and cholera.
Anti-mosquito measures including mosquito repellents, nets and clothing covering the body should be used for protection against hepatitis B and yellow fever. Rabies is a risk. Bilharzia is present, visitors should avoid wadding in fresh water, only use well maintained, chlorinated swimming pools.
There is a shortage of routine medications and visitors should take all necessary medicines with them. A first aid kit that includes disposable syringes is a reasonable precaution. Use only bottled or boiled water for drinks, washing teeth and making ice. Eat only well cooked meals, preferably served hot; vegetables should be cooked and fruit peeled. Dairy products are unpasteurised and should be avoided, unless cooked.
Healthcare is not to Western standards and medical insurance, including emergency evacuation, is necessary.

Hotels
Air-conditioned hotels are available in Dakar, although they can be expensive. Hotel bills usually include service charges and local tax. Tipping is therefore optional.

Credit cards
Major credit cards are accepted; charge cards are not accepted. There are ATMs in Dakar.

Public holidays (national)
Fixed dates
1 Jan (New Year's Day), 4 Apr (Independence Day), 1 May (Labour Day), 15 Aug (Assumption Day), 1 Nov (All Saints' Day), 25 Dec (Christmas Day).
Variable dates
Eid al Adha, Islamic New Year, Birth of the Prophet, Easter Monday (Mar/Apr), Ascension Day, Whit Monday, Eid al Fitr.
Islamic year 1433 (26 Nov 2011–14 Nov 2012): The Islamic year contains 354 or 355 days, with the result that Muslim feasts advance by 10–12 days against the Gregorian calendar. Dates of feasts vary according to the sighting of the new moon, so cannot be forecast exactly.

Working hours
Banking
Mon–Thu: 0730–1300, 1400–1630; Fri: 0730–1300, 1530–1730.
Business
Mon–Fri: 0800–1230, 1300–1600.
Government
Mon–Fri: 0800/ 0900–1200, 1500–1800; Sat: 0800/0900–1200.
Shops
Mon–Sat: 0800–1200, 1430–1800.

Telecommunications
Mobile/cell phones
There are GSM 900 services available over half of the country.

Electricity supply
127/220V AC, 50 cycles, with mainly round two-pin plugs.

Social customs/useful tips
Visitors should be punctual for appointments and visiting cards should be presented at business meetings. French-style formalities are observed. These include shaking hands when greeting and before departing.
Use the right hand when shaking hands and passing or receiving anything.
A service charge is normally added to the bill. Gratuities are not customary for taxis.
The minimum drinking age is 20 years.
Smoking is banned in some public places, including mosques.

Security
Purse snatching and pickpocketing is on the increase, particularly in the downtown area of Dakar. Avoid political gatherings and street demonstrations and maintain security awareness at all times.
The permission of the Senegalese authorities is required for travel to certain areas of the Casamance region where attacks from armed separatist rebels and bandits occur.

Getting there
Air
National airline: Air Sénégal
International airport/s: Dakar-Léopold Sédar Senghor (DKR), 17km north west of city; duty-free shop, bar, restaurant, bank, post office, car hire and taxis.
In 2006 the ministry of tourism announced plans for a new international airport at Diass, 45km from Dakar. It will replace the existing Dakar airport and be named Aéroport International Blaise Diagne. The plans are for an initial capacity of three million passengers; it is anticipated it will relieve congestion around Dakar and encourage the creation of an economic development zone.
Airport tax: None
Surface
Road: Principal road routes are from the Gambia, Mali, Mauritania – those from Guinea are not generally recommended.
A 720 metre bridge over the Mansoa river has improved the traffic flow on the trans-African coastal road between Bissau, Guinea-Bissau, and Senegal.
Rail: A rail service operates between Dakar and Bamako (Mali) via Kaolack and Tambacounda.
Water: Cargo ships carrying passengers have services from Spain, France, Morocco and the Canary Islands.
Main port/s: Dakar is the second-largest port in West Africa and serves Senegal, Mauritania and the Gambia. The port has extensive facilities for fishing vessels and fish processing.

Getting about

National transport

Air: Air Sénégal links Dakar with all the main towns. Small aircraft can be chartered from Amana Air Charters.

Road: Tarred roads are mainly near the coast; inland areas are served by roads of variable quality. Main highways: Dakar to St Louis, Rosso, Djourbel, Joal, Kaolack and Ziguinchor.

Buses: Coach services Dakar-Ziguinchor; Tambacounda-Ziguinchor; Tambacounda-Gaoual are operated subject to demand.

Rail: The railway links Dakar with Tambacounda to the east, and with St Louis and Linguère to the north-east.

Water: The Senegal river in the north is only navigable for parts of the year: for three months as far as Kayes (Mali); for six months as far as Kaedi (Mauritania); and all year as far as Rosso and Podor. Other rivers include the Saloun and the Casamance.

City transport

Taxis: Taxis are plentiful in Dakar, all are fitted with meters. Rates are greater after midnight. Tipping is not customary.

Buses, trams & metro: Large green and yellow public buses operate a regular flat-fare service.

Car hire

An international or national driving licence, insurance and car registration document (*Carte Grise*) are required. Vehicles coming from the right always have right of way.

BUSINESS DIRECTORY

The addresses listed below are a selection only. While World of Information makes every endeavour to check these addresses, we cannot guarantee that changes have not been made, especially to telephone numbers and area codes. We would welcome any corrections.

Telephone area codes

The international dialling code (IDD) for Senegal is +221, followed by subscriber's number.

Useful telephone numbers

Police: 823-7149, 823-2529, 823-8383.

Chambers of Commerce

Union des Chambres de Commerce, d'Industrie et d'Agriculture de Senegal, 1 Place de l'Independence, PO Box 118, Dakar (tel: 823-7189; fax: 823-9363; e-mail: cciad@telecomplus-sn).

Dakar Chambre de Commerce, d'Industrie et d'Agriculture, 1 Place de l'Indépendance, PO Box 118, Dakar (tel: 823-7189; fax: 823-9363; e-mail: ccaid@telecomplus.sn).

Diourbel Chambre de Commerce, d'Industrie et d'Agriculture, PO Box 7, Diourbel (tel/fax: 971-1203; e-mail: ccdiour@cyg.sn).

Fatick Chambre de Commerce, d'Industrie et d'Agriculture, PO Box 66, Fatick (tel/fax: 949-1425).

Kaolack Chambre de Commerce, d'Industrie et d'Agriculture, Rue Noirot, PO Box 203, Kaolack (tel: 941-2050; fax: 941-2291; e-mail: cciak@visto.com).

Kolda Chambre de Commerce, d'Industrie et d'Agriculture, Quartier Escale, PO Box 23, Kolda (tel: 996-1230; fax: 996-1068; e-mail: cciakd@sentoo.sn).

Louga Chambre de Commerce, d'Industrie et d'Agriculture, 2 Rue Glozel, Quartier Thiokhma, PO Box 26 Louga (tel: 967-1114; fax: 967-4658; e-mail: ccial@sentoo.sn).

Saint Louis Chambre de Commerce, d'Industrie et d'Agriculture, 10 Rue Blanchot, PO Box 19, Saint Louis (tel: 961-1088; fax: 961-2980; e-mail: cciasl@tpsnet.sn).

Tambacounda Chambre de Commerce, d'Industrie et d'Agriculture, PO Box 27, Tambacounda (tel: 981-1014; fax: 981-2995).

Thies Chambre de Commerce, d'Industrie et d'Agriculture, 96 Avenue Lamine Gueye, PO Box 3020 Thies (tel: 951-1002; fax: 951-1397; e-mail: cciath@tpsnet.sn).

Ziguinchor Chambre de Commerce, d'Industrie et d'Agriculture, Rue de Général de Gaulle, PO Box 26, Ziguinchor (tel: 991-1310; fax: 991-2163).

Banking

Banque de l'Habitat du Sénégal, PO Box 229, 69 Boulevard Général de Gaulle, Dakar (tel: 8231-004; fax: 8238-043).

Banque Internationale pour le Commerce et l'Industrie du Sénégal SA, PO Box 392, 2 Avenue du Président L Senghor, Dakar (tel: 8390-390; fax: 8233-707).

Banque Islamique du Sénégal, PO Box 3381, Immeuble Abdallah Fayçal, Dakar (tel: 8496-262; fax: 8224-948) .

Banque Senegalo-Tunisienne (BST), PO Box 4111, Immeuble Kebe, 97 Avenue André Peytavin, Dakar (tel: 8237-576; fax: 8238-238).

Caisse Nationale de Crédit Agricole du Sénégal, PO Box 3890, 45 Avenue Albert Sarraut, Dakar (tel: 8222-300; fax: 8212-606).

Compagnie Bancaire de l'Afrique Occidentale, PO Box 129, 2 Place de l'Indépendance, Dakar (tel: 8231-000; fax: 8232-005).

Crédit Lyonnais Sénégal, PO Box 56, Boulevard El Hadji Djily Mbaye, Angle Rue Huart, Dakar (tel: 8231-008; fax: 8238-430).

Société Générale de Banques au Sénégal SA, PO Box 323, 19 Avenue du Président L Senghor, Dakar (tel: 8395-500; fax: 8219-119).

Central bank

Banque Centrale des Etats de l'Afrique de l'Ouest, Boulevard du Général de Gaulle, Angle Rue 11; PO Box 3159, Dakar (tel: 889-4545; fax: 823-5757).

Stock exchange

Afribourse (Bourse Régionale des Valeurs Moblières) (BRVM): www.brvm.org

Travel information

Air Sénégal International, 45 Albert Sarraut Ave, Dakar (tel: 842-4100, 823-4970; internet: www.air-senegal-international.com).

Amana Air Charters, 2 Rue Galandou Diouf, Dakar (tel: 842-2911/2933

Ministry of tourism

Ministry of Tourism and Air Transport, 23 Rue Calmette, BP 4049, Dakar (tel: 8229-226; fax: 8229-413; email: mtta@primature.sn; internet: www.tourisme.gouv.sn).

National tourist organisation offices

National Tourist Office, 23 Rue Calmette, PO Box 4049, Dakar (tel: 8229-226; fax: 8229-413).

Ministries

Ministry of Armed Forces, Batîment Administratif, Avenue Roume, Dakar (tel: 8231-216; fax: 8236-338).

Ministry of Commerce, Batîment Administratif, Avenue Roume, Dakar (tel: 8229-542; fax: 8219-132).

Ministry of the Habitat, Ex-Camp Lat-Dior, Dakar (tel: 8233-278; fax: 8236-245).

Ministry of the Interior, Place Washington, Dakar (tel: 8234-151; fax: 8210-542).

Ministry of Justice, Batîment Administratif, Avenue Roume, Dakar (tel: 8238-042; fax: 8232-727).

Ministry of Modernisation of the State, Rue Emile Zola, Dakar (tel: 8232-922; fax: 8229-764).

Ministry of National Education, Rue Calmette, Dakar (tel: 8224-123; fax: 8218-930).

Ministry of Tourism and Environment, 23 Rue Calmette, BP 4049, Dakar (tel: 8211-126; fax: 8229-413).

Ministry of Women, Children and the Family, Rue Beranger Ferraud, Dakar (tel: 8236-919; fax: 8236-673).

Prime Minister's Office, Batîment Administratif, Avenue Roume, Dakar (tel: 8224-917; fax: 8225-578).

Other useful addresses
British Embassy, 20 rue du Docteur Guillet, PO Box 6025, Dakar (tel: 8237-392, 8239-971; fax: 8232-766).

Direction de la Statistique, BP 116, Dakar (tel: 8230-881).

Foire Internationale de Dakar, route de l'Aéroport, BP 3329, Dakar (tel: 8231-011).

Port Autonome de Dakar, 35 boulevard de la Libération, Dakar (tel: 8224-545, 8227-421).

Senegalese Embassy (UK) 39 Marloes Road, London W8 6LA (tel: (+44-(0)20) 7937-7237, 7938-4048; fax: (+44-(0)20) 7938-2546; internet: www.senegalembassy.co.uk).

Senegalese Embassy (US), 2112 Wyoming Avenue, NW, Washington DC 20008 (tel: (+1-202) 234-0540; fax: (+1-202) 352-6315).

Société de Développement Agricole et Industriel du Sénégal, 23 avenue Roume, PO Box 222, Dakar (tel: 8251-818).

Société Nationale d'Etudes et de Promotion Industrielle, BP 100, derrière Residence Seydou Nourou Tall, Dakar (tel: 8252-130).

Société Nationale des Télécommunications du Sénégal (SONATEL), 6 rue Wagane Diouf, BP 62, Dakar (tel: 8231-023, 8214-242).

Société Nouvelle des Etudes de Développement en Afrique, 36 rue Calmette, PO Box 2084, Dakar (tel: 8234-231).

Syndicat des Commerçants, Importateurs et Exportateurs de l'Ouest Africaine (Scimpex), angle rue Parent et avenue Abdoulaye Fadiga, PO Box 806, Dakar (tel: 8213-662).

US Embassy, avenue Jean XXIII, PO Box 49, Dakar (tel: 8234-296; fax: 8222-991).

National news agency: Agence de Presse Senegalaise (APS), 58 Bld de la République; BP 117, Dakar (tel: 821-1427; fax: 822-0767; email: aps@aps.sn; internet: www.aps.sn).

Internet sites
Africa Business Network: www.ifc.org/abn

AllAfrica.com: http://allafrica.com

African Development Bank: www.afdb.org

Press agency (in French): www.aps.sn/

Web portal: www.au-senegal.com/

Serbia

For most of 2011 Serbian politics has been dominated by its aspiration to become a member of the European Union (EU). Although membership of the European club elsewhere may have become less than universally popular, in Serbia it still mattered. Croatia's progress in joining the EU only stiffened Serbian sinews. For some time Serbia has felt rebuffed by Brussels, sensing a loss of interest in further expansion. One Belgrade commentator writing on the *Transconflict* website described his country's position as one of 'insular sullenness and lack of leadership' that had 'left it with nowhere else to go.'

The EU question

For most of 2011 the Serbian government was pinning its hopes on the EU summit of heads of government in early December. The meeting, Belgrade hoped, would rubber stamp Serbia's official candidature for membership. However, as Winston Churchill would have had it, 'Events' in the form of the euro-zone crisis and a disagreement between the EU and the UK, got in the way. EU enlargement was a casualty; Serbia was politely informed that it would have to wait until March for a decision. March 2012 is two months before the

KEY FACTS

Official name: Republika Srbije (Republic of Serbia) (ROS)

Head of State: President Boris Tadic (since Jul 2004, re-elected 3 Feb 2008)

Head of government: Prime Minister Mirko Cvetkovic (took office 7 Jul 2008)

Ruling party: Coalition: led by Za Evropsku Srbiju (ZES) (For a European Serbia) (five political parties, led by Demokratska stranka (DS) (Democratic Party)), with Ujedinjeni Regioni Srbije (URS) (United Regions of Serbia) (three parties led by G17 Plus) and SPS-JS (three parties led by Socijalisticka Partija Srbije (SPS) (Socialist Party of Serbia)), plus a number of other minority parties (from Jun 2008)

Area: 77,474 square km

Population: 7.43 million (2010)*

Capital: Belgrade

Official language: Serbian

Currency: Dinar (D) = 100 paras

Exchange rate: D75.83 per US$ (Oct 2011)

GDP per capita: US$5,233 (2010)

GDP real growth: 1.80% (2010)

GDP: US$38.70 billion (2010)

Unemployment: 17.20% (2010)*

Inflation: 6.20% (2010)

Balance of trade: -US$6.34 billion (2010)

* estimated figure

possible date of Serbia's next elections, in May 2012. So a positive decision from Brussels a matter of weeks before the election could only help the incumbent Demokratska Stranka (DS) (Democratic Party) of President Boris Tadic.

Reportedly, the EU decision hinged on Serbia's recognition – or the lack of it – of Kosovo's independence. Serbian sources were quick to point out that five of the EU's 27 countries still do not recognise Kosovo. Other sources claimed that the decision was due to the fact that recently German and Austrian peacekeepers had been injured by Serbs during unrest in northern Kosovo. It was rumoured that some of the Serbs involved in the unrest were in fact paid agents of Serbia. It seemed that the Serbian government had realised that it had shot itself in the foot. No sooner had Prime Minister Tadic suggested that it was clearly in Serbia's interest that the barricades were dismantled, then they were.

The EU's decision created some political casualties in Belgrade, notably the resignation of Deputy Prime Minister Bozidar Djelic, who had been in charge of the Brussels negotiations. The Brussels setback also placed foreign minister Vuk Jeremic under a very visible cosh. At the end of 2011 uncertainty surrounded the extent to which the delayed approval might begin to reshape Belgrade politics. Serbia's next EU-sponsored talks with Kosovo had been due to take place at the end of September 2011. However, the unrest in northern Kosovo resulted in their postponement.

Serbia and Kosovan officials had already met on a number of occasions in 2011 under the auspices of the EU-facilitated dialogue, reaching outline agreements on a number of relatively minor technical issues. Further progress was marred by Serbia's rejection of a customs stamp agreement in July, which in a tit-for-tat response resulted in the imposition by Kosovo of an embargo on trade with Serbia. After a rise in tensions over the summer, during which Kosovo deployed its police to the two northern border crossings with Serbia, agreement on a customs stamp was reached at a meeting in early September 2011. The agreement stipulated that both countries would begin to lift their mutual trade embargoes. Quite apart from the question of Kosovo's recognition, the Serbs had also been asked by Brussels to dismantle, as a precondition of candidacy, what were described as 'parallel structures' set up by Serbian local government administrations in Kosovo. However, in late 2011 most other EU countries had other fish to fry. In many Serbian eyes the relatively cosy relationship betweeen Germany and Croatia did not work in their favour. Were German foreign policy to prevail, Croatian EU membership in 2013 may usher in a period where Brussels considers the *status quo*, at least as far as enlargement of the EU is concerned, may be the more attractive option. The prospect of admitting a country with Serbia's troubled recent history, not to mention its relationship with Russia, may be a bridge too far. In some German eyes, Serbia and its closeness to Russia represented something of a European startegic fault line.

The economy

In the view of the International Monetary Fund (IMF), substantial progress has been made by Serbia in the last ten years. In 2001, Serbia was recovering from the ravages of war, international sanctions and economic mismanagement: output had collapsed, inflation was rampant and the external position was non-viable. In a report on the Serbian economy, the IMF considered that macro-economic stabilisation had for the most part been achieved over the past decade, debt was manageable and there was a modern banking system in place. IMF support had helped Serbia navigate the global crisis and safeguard financial stability and recovery was in train. But despite these successes, significant vulnerabilities and a large structural reform agenda remained.

The IMF concluded that a new IMF-supported programme could help Serbia complete and entrench the transition to a more balanced growth model and tackle its remaining structural reform challenges. In particular, a new arrangement could play a useful role as a co-ordination device for the government and serve as an anchor for polices in a pre-election year, send a positive signal to investors and co-ordinate the contribution of other international financial institutions (such as the World Bank and the EU).

The IMF also noted that Serbia's progress on the structural reform agenda had lagged. To transition to a more balanced growth model, Serbia still needed to address significant challenges and vulnerabilities and implement far-reaching reforms. In the view of the IMF, while there was progress in several areas, macro-economic performance fell short of expectations. Robust but unbalanced growth amid large capital inflows and lagging structural reforms had contributed to rising external imbalances and vulnerabilities in the run-up to the global crisis. The IMF's 2009 Stand-By Arrangement, subsequently extended and augmented, had certainly facilitated an orderly rebalancing of the economy amid the global crisis and helped safeguard financial sector stability. The IMF programme's focus on three main elements – fiscal adjustment, bailout of foreign banks and exceptional financing – had seemed to be appropriate.

Risk assessment

Economy	Fair
Politics	Fair
Regional stability	Fair

KEY INDICATORS **Serbia**

	Unit	2006	2007	2008	2009	2010
Population	m	*7.45	*7.45	*7.38	*7.38	*7.43
Gross domestic product (GDP)	US$bn	31.78	41.68	50.10	42.90	38.70
GDP per capita	US$	3,994	5,477	6,782	5,809	5,233
GDP real growth	%	5.7	5.4	3.8	-3.5	1.0
Inflation	%	12.7	6.5	12.4	8.1	6.2
Unemployment	%	20.8	18.1	13.6	–	–
Exports (fob) (goods)	US$m	6,487.0	8,776.5	20,039.9	8,367.8	9,818.8
Imports (fob) (goods)	US$m	13,119.0	17,916.1	40,542.7	15,031.1	16,163.1
Balance of trade	US$m	-6,632.0	-9,139.6	-20,502.8	-6,663.3	-6,344.3
Current account	US$m	-3,966.0	-6,346.2	-8,648.0	-2,412.3	-3,115.0
Total reserves minus gold	US$m	11,647.7	13,892.6	11,122.8	14,769.2	12,714.6
Foreign exchange	US$m	11,638.9	13,891.8	11,120.7	14,749.9	12,711.7
Exchange rate	per US$	61.46	54.20	55.72	67.58	77.73

* estimated figure

COUNTRY PROFILE

Historical profile

The Serbs are believed to be an ethnic Slavic clan that had settled in the Balkans by the eleventh century. A Serbian state was established in the twelfth century.
1389 The Turks defeated the Serbs at the Battle of Kosovo, and Serbia became an Ottoman subject state.
1860 Turkish troops left. Serbia signed a series of alliances with Montenegro, Romania and Greece. The Serbia-Greece pact assigned ownership of Bosnia and Hercegovina (BiH) to Serbia, with Thessaly and Epirus going to the Greeks.
1876 Serbia was again defeated by Turkey, although Austrian protection prevented the Serbs from falling under Turkish rule.
1878 Austria invaded Serbia. The Treaty of Berlin settled Serbian independence. Montenegro was also recognised as an independent state and doubled in size.
1913 The London Conference reduced the territory claimed by Albania after recognising its independence. Kosovo was granted to Serbia and Cameria (Chamouria) to Greece.
1914 Growing hostility in relations between the Serbs and the Habsburgs of Austro-Hungary came to a head with the assassination of the Austrian Archduke Frans Ferdinand by a Serbian nationalist, Gavrilo Princip. Austria and Germany declared war on Serbia, resulting in the First World War.
1918 The defeat of the Austro-Hungarian empire during the World War One saw the creation of the Kingdom of the Serbs, Croats and Slovenes, encompassing Bosnia and Hercegovina (BiH), Croatia, parts of Dalmatia and Macedonia, Montenegro, Serbia, Slavonia and Slovenia.
1921 Prince Alexander, Regent of Serbia, became King.
1929 Following disputes between Serbs and Croats, King Alexander assumed dictatorial powers and the country was renamed Yugoslavia.
1934 King Alexander was assassinated in Marseilles while on a state visit to France.
1941 Parts of Yugoslavia were occupied by the Germans, Italians, Hungarians and Bulgarians.
1945–46 Following the end of the Second World War, Serbia and Montenegro became two of the constituent republics of the Federal People's Republic of Yugoslavia.
1948 Yugoslavia was expelled from the Communist Information Bureau (Cominform), responsible for co-ordinating Communist activities throughout the world.
1953 Tito was elected president in January. Constitutions adopted in 1953, 1963 and 1974 increased the autonomy extended to the country's constituent republics.
1955 After building a relationship with the West, Yugoslavia restored relations with the Soviet Union.
1960–70s To keep Yugoslavia out of the Cold War, President Tito pursued a policy of non-alignment and the country became one of the founder members of the Non-Alignment Movement (NAM). In 1963 the official name was changed to the Socialist Federal Republic of Yugoslavia.
1980 Tito died. A system of a collective (rotating) presidency was adopted.
1989 Differences and friction between the wealthier republics, Slovenia and Croatia, and the different ethnic groups intensified. Serbian and Montenegrin constitutions were inaugurated.
1990 Multi-party elections brought into power a government in Croatia which supported outright independence.
1991–92 The secession of Croatia, Slovenia and BiH led to invasions of these republics by the Jugoslovenska Narodna Armija (JNA) (Yugoslav National Army). In Slovenia, the JNA was promptly defeated. JNA units were eventually incorporated into the ethnic Serb armies in BiH and the Krajina region in Croatia. The reduced Yugoslav state, renamed the Federal Republic of Yugoslavia (FRY), comprised Serbia, Montenegro, Vojvodina and Kosovo; it was not internationally recognised and was deprived of its UN seat.
1993 Zoran Lilic was elected FRY president, replacing Dobrica Cosic, who had criticised the president of Serbia, Slobodan Milosevic.
1995 Milosevic was one of the signatories of the Dayton Peace Agreement, which ended the civil war in BiH.
1996 FRY and Croatia signed an agreement of mutual recognition, formally ending five years of hostility.
1997 Milosevic, for 10 years the president of Serbia, took over as the FRY president. A coalition government, led by Milosevic's Socialisticka Partija Srbije (SPS) (Socialist Party of Serbia), remained in power in Serbia, despite losing its parliamentary majority in elections. The first election for the presidency of Serbia was invalidated because less than half the electorate voted; Milan Milutinovic was elected president of Serbia at the end of the year.
1998 Since the 1980s, the Milosevic regime had been gradually reducing the civil rights of the ethnic Albanians in Kosovo. Opposition to this gathered momentum during the 1990s as the Ushtria Çlirimtare e Kosovës (UÇK) (Kosovo Liberation Army) began to carry out armed offensives and bombings against the Yugoslav authorities. By the beginning of the year, the UÇK controlled approximately half of the province of Kosovo. FRY security forces launched a counter-offensive against the UÇK, destroying villages and displacing many thousands of Kosovans. Mirko Marjanovic (Montenegrin prime minister since 1994) was re-appointed in Montenegro.
1999 Vuk Draskovic resigned from the FRY government and took his party out of the coalition. After unsuccessful mediation and increased violence in Kosovo, NATO launched air strikes in March against FRY targets, centred primarily on Belgrade. In June, FRY forces withdrew entirely from Kosovo. NATO deployed peace-keeping troops in Kosovo, which became an international protectorate under UN control.
2000 Milosevic called early elections for the FRY presidency. Vojislav Kostunica of the Demokratska Opozicija Srbije (DOS) (Democratic Opposition of Serbia, a coalition formed to challenge Milosevic's rule) won the election but Milosevic remained in power (officially his term in office was to end in 2001). Street protests and workers strikes ensued until 5 October when the Radio Televizije Srbije (RTS) (Radio Television Serbia) broadcast offices were stormed and Milosevic was toppled. Kostunica became president of FRY. The DOS won FRY parliamentary elections, held in December. Local elections, held in Kosovo, were won by the Lidhja Demokratike e Kosovës (LDK) (Democratic League of Kosovo), led by Ibrahim Rugova. The Federal Republic of Yugoslavia (FRY) was allowed back into the UN after eight years of exclusion.
2001 Milo Djukanovic's Pobjeda je Crne Goru (PjCG) (Victory for Montenegro) coalition won the Montenegrin parliamentary elections. Slobodan Milosevic was extradited to stand trial at the International Criminal Tribunal for the former Yugoslavia (ICTY) in The Hague. The UN mission in Kosovo set up the Provisional Institutions of Self-Government (PISG), and included an assembly, mandated to elect a president and prime minister of the territory. The LDK won 46 per cent of the vote in the Assembly of Kosovo elections, but failed to get a majority.
2002 The Kosovo assembly elected Ibrahim Rugova as president; Bajram Rexhapi of the Partia Demokratike e Kosovës (PDK) (Democratic Party of Kosovo) was elected as prime minister of a power-sharing 10-member cabinet. Montenegrin President Milo Djukanovic's Demokratska Lista za Evropsku Crnu Goru (DLECG) (Democratic List for a European Montenegro) alliance won the Montenegro parliamentary elections. Parliamentary Speaker Natasa Micic was appointed Serbia's acting president after the

results of three separate presidential elections were declared invalid due to insufficient voter turnout.
2003 The FRY state was reconstituted and renamed the State Union of Serbia and Montenegro; a looser federation of its two member states, Serbia and Montenegro and two autonomous provinces of Vojvodina (within Serbia) and Kosovo and Metohia (under UN administration). FRY President Kostunica stepped down and was replaced as head of state of Serbia and Montenegro by Svetozar Marovic, a Montenegrin. Serbian prime minister, Zoran Djindjic, was assassinated. In parliamentary elections an alliance of three political blocs headed by the Demokratska Stranka Srbije (DSS) (Democratic Party of Serbia), led by Zoran Zivkovic won. Later, the Srbije Demokratska Stranka (SDS) (Serbian Democratic Party) and the Narodna Demokratska Stranka (NDS) (People's Democratic Party) merged with the DSS.
2004 Boris Tadic, a pro-West liberal, was elected president of Serbia. Vojislav Kostunica replaced Zivkovic as leader of the DSS and became prime minister. In Kosovo, parliamentary and presidential elections took place; the LDK won the parliamentary elections and Ramush Haradinaj became prime minister. Incumbent President Ibrahim Rugova was re-elected
2005 The Kosovo prime minister Haradinaj resigned and Adem Salihaj replaced him. The US resumed aid to Serbia as a reward for improved co-operation with the ICTY. The European Union (EU) agreed to open talks with Serbia and Montenegro on a stabilisation and association agreement that could lead to EU membership. Five former Serbian policemen accused of taking part in the 1995 Srebrenica massacre went on trial in Belgrade.
2006 Kosovo president, Ibrahim Rugova, died; he had been considered a moderate Kosovo-Albanian leader and his death just as negotiations on the future of Kosovo were about to start, was considered a setback. He was succeeded by Fatmir Sejdiu. Agim Çeku became prime minister of Kosovo. Slobodan Milosevic was found dead of a heart attack in his cell in The Hague. The EU broke off membership talks with Serbia and Montenegro, citing failure by the authorities to arrest war crimes suspect Ratko Mladic. Montenegro formally declared independence from Serbia; Serbia declared itself the union's legal successor. Joachim Rucker took office as the head of the UN Interim Administration Mission in Kosovo. A referendum agreed by 51.5 per cent of the electorate (excluding ethnic Albanians from Kosovo) to constitutional changes. Among the articles promulgated was a ban on capital punishment and human cloning, guaranteed human rights and a degree of autonomy for the province of Vojvodina. Controversially, however, other articles claimed sovereignty over the UN-administered province of Kosovo and enshrined the Cyrillic alphabet (unused by ethnic minorities) as the official script.
2007 A coalition of the Demokratska Stranka (DS) (Democratic Party) – led by President Tadic – and the DSS won Serbian parliamentary elections with 112 seats (65 and 47 seats respectively). The far-right Srpska Radikalna Stranka (SRS) (Serbian Radical Party) was the largest single bloc with 81 seats. Such a large proportion of the electorate supporting the SRS, with a staunch nationalist agenda, was seen as an impediment to Serbia's EU membership aspirations. Serbia rejected the UN plan of self-rule, although not independence, for Kosovo. No agreement was reached during the first round of talks on the future of Kosovo: Serbian authorities offered broad autonomy but the province's ethnic Albanians demanded full independence. Kosovo parliamentary elections were won by the Democratic Party, led by Hashim Thaçi, the pro-independence candidate and former leader of the Kosovo Liberation Army (KLA). The UN proposed a multinational tribunal to include representatives from the EU, US, Russia and Serbian and Albanian Kosovas. Two camps developed with the US and Albanian Kosovas advocating a fully independent Kosovo, while Serbia and Russia staunchly opposed it. Albanian Kosovas threatened to declare a unilateral declaration of independence (UDI) if talks failed to find a negotiated peace. Hashim Thaçi became prime minister of the Assembly of Kosovo, as leader of a coalition led by the PDK) and LDK.
2008 In Serbian presidential elections, Boris Tadic won 51.61 per cent of the vote. Thaçi became prime minister of Kosovo, which shortly after declared its independence. A riot broke out in Belgrade as many countries immediately recognised the newly independent Kosovo. Russia pledged its support for Serbia, while some EU countries with unresolved independence situations or historic sensibilities (Cyprus, Romania and Slovakia) also said they would not recognise the new state. Mobs attacked foreign embassies, targeting the US embassy in particular, until the EU threatened to suspend entry negotiation talks if the violence did not stop. Prime Minister Kostunica resigned following his inability to get his cabinet to reject closer ties to the EU, in protest at the EU's backing of Kosovo's independence. President Tadic called a snap general election. In parliamentary elections the coalition Za Evropsku Srbiju (ZES) (For a European Serbia) (five political parties, led by DS), led by Kostunica, won 78 seats out of 250, the Serbian Radical Party won 56. ZES won the right to form a government. a ruling coalition was formed with Ujedinjeni Regioni Srbije (URS) (United Regions of Serbia) (three parties led by G17 Plus) and SPS-JS (three parties led by Socijalisticka Partija Srbije (SPS) (Socialist Party of Serbia)), plus a number of other minority parties. As a last act of the outgoing government in Serbia the Serbian minister for Kosovo set up a new parliament in the divided city of Mitrovica (in Kosovo) for minority Serbs. Ethnic Serbs insisted that the new Kosovan constitution did not apply to them. The new Kosovan Serb Assembly in Mitrovica challenged the legitimacy of the Kosovan Assembly and the *de facto* partition of Kosovo. Parliament approved President Tadic's nomination of Mirko Cvetkovic as prime minister. The former Bosnian Serb leader Radovan Karadzic was arrested in Belgrade and extradited to stand at the UN War Crimes Tribunal in The Hague on charges of genocide. After months of obstruction, parliament ratified the pre-accession Stabilisation and Association Agreement with the EU. The agreement is subject to the arrest of the remaining two Serb war crimes suspects. The Montenegro ambassador was expelled following formal recognition of Kosovo by Montenegro.
2009 Kosovo's unilateral declaration of independence (UDI) came before the International Court of Justice (ICJ) as Serbia attempted to prevent further international recognition. Serbia maintained that the declaration was a 'flagrant violation' of international law while Kosovo contended that Serbia's brutality meant they had no right to rule. Serbia wanted to force Kosovo back into negotiations. The rail link between Belgrade and Sarajevo (Bosnia and Hercegovina), closed since the conflict in the 1990s, was re-opened.
2010. In March, the Serbian parliament voted to offer an apology for the Srebrenica massacre in 1995 of 8,000 Bosniaks, perpetrated by Serb forces in Bosnia. However, the resolution failed to acknowledge the incident as an 'act of genocide' as recognised by the UN war crimes tribunal in The Hague. The ICJ ruled in July that Kosovo's UDI from Serbia did not violate international law. The ruling allows more countries to recognise Kosovo as a sovereign state. Croatia extradited Sretko Kalinic to Serbia on 25 August; he had been convicted *in absentia* in 2003 for the assassination of Prime Minister Djindic. Serbia signed a protocol in September to jointly establish a new company, called Cargo 10, with Macedonia, Croatia and Slovenia, to incorporate their railway companies. On 25 October EU foreign ministers agreed to pass Serbia's request for membership to the European Commission. This was a major step forward, only hampered by the outstanding arrest warrant on Ratko Mladic; to which end the government increased the reward for his arrest from US$1.4 million to US$14 million.

2011 Thousands congregated in front of parliament on 6 February in protest at the poor condition of the economy. The opposition leader, Tomislav Nikolic (SRS), called on the government to hold early national elections or face further civil unrest. The first high-level talks between Serbia and Kosovo began in Brussels (Belgium) on 8 March, sponsored by the EU. The focus of the meeting was daily, co-operative issues such as telecommunications and airspace. Progressive Party leader, Tomislav Nikolic, said that he would go on hunger strike until the government agreed to elections. He made the announcement at an anti-government protest in Belgrade on 16 April. Ratko Mladic was arrested in a village north of Belgrade on 26 May; despite an appeal against extradition he was flown to The Hague on 31 May to await trial at the ICTY on charges including genocide. He appeared before the court on 3 June, declining to plead against what he called 'obnoxious' charges. He then boycotted his next hearing on 4 July when he was due to enter his pleas. Goran Hadzic, the last remaining fugitive war crimes suspect sought by the ICTY, was arrested in the Fruska Gora region north of Belgrade on 20 July; his extradition to The Hague to stand trial was quickly approved by a Serbian court. on 12 October the EC recommended Serbia for EU candidate status, but said talks could only start after it normalised ties with Kosovo. On 2 December, an EU-mediated agreement was reached between Serbia and Kosovo to jointly manage and to 'gradually set up the joint, integrated, single and secure posts at all their common crossing points.'

Political structure

Constitution

The constitution was promulgated in 1990 and has articles that covers the soveignty of state, the legal system and executive. A referendum on constitutional amendments was held in 2006 with over 100 new or amended articles agreed.

Independence date

Form of state

Democratic republic

The executive

The president is the head of state, directly elected for a term of five years; for two-terms only. The president nominates a prime minister, after conferring with the largest political party in the national assembly. Other powers include dissolving parliament, calling elections and vetoing legislature until it has been reconsidered. The government is comprised of the prime minister and cabinet ministers approved by the national assembly.

Kosovo has its own president and government which are responsible for the economy, education, health, agriculture and tourism, but requires UN approval to introduce or change any new legislation in these areas. The UNMIK representive also has the power to dissolve the Kosovo assembly and call new elections. The president is appointed by the Kosovan assembly for a period of three years.

National legislature

The national assembly (narodna skupstina) is unicameral, with 250 members, elected for four-year terms, by general election. It is the highest law making body in the country with the power to elect and dismiss the president, vice president, prime minister and any other person in a constitutionally mandated post.

Serbia has *de jure* sovereignty of Kosovo, however *de facto* government of the province is under the auspices of the UN Mission in Kosovo (UNMIK) and local Provisional Institutions of Self-Government (PISG).

Legal system

The legal system is based on the written constitution which states basic provisions and guarantees for a range of individual and collective rights, including civil laws. The court system is governed by the Supreme Court, the highest civil and criminal court in Serbia. The constitutional charter of Serbia was ratified in 2003. The Constitutional Court, which deals with the law and the constitution, comprises judges elected for a period of six years by the national assembly upon the recommendation of the Council of Ministers.

Last elections

11 May 2008 (parliamentary); 20 January and 3 February 2008 (presidential, two rounds).

Results: Parliament: Za Evropsku Srbiju (ZES) (For a European Serbia) coalition won 38.7 per cent of the vote (102 seats of 250), Srpska Radikalna Stranka (SRS) (Serbian Progressive Party) 29.1 per cent (78), Demokratska Stranka (DS) (Democratic Party of Serbia) - Nova Srbija (New Serbia) coalition 11.3 per cent (30), Socijalisticka Partija Srbije (SPS) (Socialist Party of Serbia) coalition 7.9 per cent (20), and Liberalno-Demokratska Partija (LDP) Liberal Democratic Party 5.2 per cent (13). Turnout was 60.7 per cent. Presidential: first round Boris Tadic (DSS) won 35.39 per cent of the vote, Tomislav Nikolic (SRS) won 39.99 per cent; no other candidate won more than 8 per cent. Second round, Boris Tadic won 51.61 per cent of the vote, Tomislav Nikolic won 47.69 per cent.

Next elections

2012 (presidential and parliamentary)

Political parties

Ruling party

TCoalition: led by Za Evropsku Srbiju (ZES) (For a European Serbia) (five political parties, led by Demokratska stranka (DS) (Democratic Party)), with Ujedinjeni Regioni Srbije (URS) (United Regions of Serbia) (three parties led by G17 Plus) and SPS-JS (three parties led by Socijalisticka Partija Srbije (SPS) (Socialist Party of Serbia)), plus a number of other minority parties (from Jun 2008)

Main opposition party

Srpska Radikalna Stranka (SRS) (Serbian Radical Party) (far right)

Population

7.43 million (2010)*

Last census: March 2002: 7,445,531 (exludes Kosovo and Metohia).

Population density: 104 inhabitants per square km. Urban population: 52 per cent (1995–2001).

Annual growth rate: 0.0 per cent 1994–2004 (WHO 2006)

Ethnic make-up

Serbian (63 per cent), Albanian (14 per cent), Montenegrin (6 per cent) and Hungarian (4 per cent).

Religions

Serbian Orthodox (65 per cent), Islam, Roman Catholic and Protestant

Education

With less developed education systems than Slovenia and Croatia during the Tito period, Serbia had an adult illiteracy rate of 10 per cent in 1990 (in Kosovo, the figure was then 17 per cent).

Primary education lasts for eight years from aged seven. Secondary education is provided in grammar, vocational and art schools with courses lasting up to four years. Higher education is provided in universities and colleges.

There are four universities in Serbia (Belgrade, Novi Sad, Nis and Kragujevac) and one in Kosovo (Pristina). However, graduate unemployment is high.

There was a major exodus of younger and more educated people abroad during the 1990s. In 1994 alone, around 100,000 people, or around 1 per cent of the population, may have emigrated.

During the lead-up to the conflict in Kosovo, education was a very controversial issue, with the majority Albanian population refusing to be taught in the Serbian language. Alternative or Albanian language education thus emerged in Kosovo.

Literacy rate: 99 per cent total; 97 per cent female; adult rates (Unicef 2004).

Compulsory years: 7 to 15

Enrolment rate: 66 per cent gross primary enrolment, 59 per cent gross secondary enrolment; of relevant age group (including repeaters) (Unesco).

Pupils per teacher: 20 primary; 14 secondary, (Unesco 2002)

Health

Since 1992, the extent and quality of healthcare provision has sharply deteriorated. However, a well-developed private healthcare system has emerged for the better-off. Largely free at the point of delivery and funded by a universal social insurance tax levied on all employees and employers, public healthcare provision now require all kinds of charges, most notably for imported medications.

Life expectancy: 73 years, 2004 (WHO 2006)

Fertility rate/Maternal mortality rate: 1.6 births per woman, 2004 (WHO 2006)

Birth rate/Death rate: 12.7 births and 10.6 deaths per 1,000 population (2003)

Child (under 5 years) mortality rate (per 1,000): 12 per 1,000 live births (World Bank)

Head of population per physician: 2.06 physicians per 1,000 people, 2002 (WHO 2006)

Welfare

Welfare provision in Serbia was relatively generous during the Tito period, when retirement pensions were around 80 per cent of average monthly incomes. Since 2000, the World Bank has helped fund pensions and social benefits. A three-year Country Assistance Stratergy (CAS) includes reducing poverty levels through improved social protection.

Main cities

Belgrade (capital, estimated population 1.1 million in 2005), Novi Sad (194,374), Niš (175,477), Kragujevac (157,166); Priština (capital of Kosovo) (169,354), Prizren (110,482).

Languages spoken

Croatian, Bosnian, Hungarian, Slovak, Albanian (principally in Kosovo), Macedonian and Slovenian are all spoken. English is the most commonly used foreign business language. Other languages include German, Russian and Italian.

Official language/s

Serbian

Media

Press

Dailies: National publications in Serbian, include *Danas* (www.danas.co.yu), *Vecernje Novosti* (www.novosti.co.yu), *Politika* (www.politika.co.yu), *Glas Javnosti* (www.glas-javnosti.co.yu) and *Borba* (www.borba.co.yu). Regional papers in Serbian include *Dnevnik* (www.dnevnik.co.yu) from Novi Sad, *24 Sata* (www.24sata.co.yu) and *Kurir* (www.kurir-info.co.yu) are tabloids from Belgrade. In English *Blic* (www.blic.co.yu), *Balkan Web* (www.balkanweb.com/maineng.htm), *Kosovo Daily* (www.kosovodaily.com) and Belgrade News*www.belgradenews.com*.

Weeklies: In Serbian, *Nedeljne Telegraf* (www.nedeljnitelegraf.co.yu) is the largest weekly tabloid newspaper. *Vojvodina* (www.vojvodina.com) is an independent, open weekly newspaper about cultural, political, economic, agriculture and sports. Other significant weeklies are *NIN* (www.nin.co.yu), *Standard* (www.standardmagazin.com) and *Vreme* (www.vreme.com).

Business: The main magazine, in English, is *Ekonomist* (www.ekonomist.co.yu/eng).

Broadcasting

The Broadcasting Agency Council (BAC) oversees radio and television output and licenses operators.

Radio Televizije Srbije (RTS) (Radio Television Serbia) (www.rts.co.yu) is the national, public, state broadcaster, with two television channels and three radio stations with internet access and podcasts.

Radio: There are many private radio stations. B92 (www.b92.net) has a youthful audience; Medunarodni Radio Serbija (www.radioyu.org); Radio Index (www.indexradio.com) and Radio Pink (www.rtvpink.com). International radio stations from US, UK, France and Germany can be received.

Television: Independent networks include TV Pink (www.rtvpink.com) and TV-Avala (www.tv-avala.com) showing popular international programmes and local content shows.

Advertising

All principal media are available through advertising agencies or directly. There are Western agencies operating in Belgrade. Tobacco and alcohol advertising is banned on television.

News agencies

National news agency: Tanjug

Economy

Despite an economy largely dominated by the service industry, 69.4 per cent in 2009, Serbia also has an old, established industrial sector that constitutes 27.7 per cent of GDP, with large deposits of lead, zinc and coal (lignite) for energy generation making the extraction industry an important element of the economy. The manufacturing sector includes furniture, clothes, pharmaceuticals and machinery.

Agriculture represents 12.9 per cent of GDP, with the main crops being cereals such as corn (maize), which is also the leading agricultural export product (1.6 million tonnes in 2009, a record for Serbia), wheat, fruit, livestock and dairy products and alcohol.

Serbia's economy has been adversely affected by its recent history. Its GDP growth in 1999 was -17.7 per cent due to the fighting between ethnic groupings and international sanctions. But from 2000 when it began to rebuild its infrastructure and introduce reforms, working towards a free-market economy, Serbia has enjoyed consistently high GDP growth, until 2007 when it was 5.4 per cent; GDP growth then fell to 3.8 in 2008. In 2009, the economy fell into recession with GDP growth of -3.5 per cent before recovering with a modest 1 per cent growth in 2010.

Inflation has been persistent and long term. It had fallen to a single digit figure of 6.5 per cent in 2007, after years of over 10 per cent but jumped back to 12.4 per cent in 2008. During the global recession, in 2009, inflation was 8.1 per cent, falling to 6.2 per cent in 2010.

The unemployment rate in 2010 was estimated at 17.2 per cent, although when under-employment and those engaged in the informal economy the rate is added then the estimated rate is at over 30 per cent. Remittances in 2009 were US$5.41 billion (12.6 per cent of GDP), a reduction on the US$5.54 billion in 2008; however in 2010 remittances recovered to an estimated US$5.58 billion.

Emergency loans of US$530 million and US$2.6 billion had been approved by the International Monetary Fund (IMF) for Serbia in 2009. The loans were designated to be used to strengthen Serbia's hard currency and stabilise its local currency. A condition of the loans was a restrictive budget that cut public spending. Russia also loaned US$1.5 billion in 2009 to cover Serbia's budget deficit which had risen to 3 per cent of GDP.

EU foreign ministers agreed to ratify the Stabilisation and Association Agreement, which Serbia signed in 2008, and which progresses Serbia's application to join the European Union, which will ultimately offer wide-ranging benefits. However, in December 2011 the European Council postponed giving official candidate status to Serbia. The government had been hopeful, especially since the border agreement with Kosovo that had recently been signed, but under German pressure the decision on membership was put back to 2012.

External trade

Serbia is a member of the Central European free trade agreement (Cefra) which, by 2007, following the loss of those countries that had joined the European Union, had eight countries all located in the Balkans (apart from Moldova). It has duty-free access for agricultural products to the EU under the autonomous trade measures (ATMs) until 2010, but with exceptions, including sugar, wine and young cattle for which quotas apply.

Foreign trade is underdeveloped and imports sustain a distorted balance of payments. Serbia has large deposits of minerals (coal, lead, zinc, copper and gold) but lack of investment has hampered development, which in turn hinders

growth in the economy. Manufacturing includes foodstuffs, furniture and base metals.
In 2010, Serbia was in negotiations to become a member of the World Trade Organisation.

Imports
Main imports include machinery and vehicles, fuels and lubricants, consumer goods, chemicals, food and live animals and raw materials.
Main sources: Russian Federation (typically 15 per cent of total), Germany (12 per cent), Italy (10 per cent).

Exports
Principal exports include manufactured goods such as electrical machinery and appliances; wheat and corn (maize), fruit, wine, live animals, minerals and energy.
Main destinations: Bosnia and Hercegovina (typically 12 per cent of total), Montenegro (12 per cent), Germany (10 per cent).

Agriculture

Farming
Agriculture is the mainstay of the economy, accounting for up to 70 per cent of GDP. The main crops are wheat, maize, sugar beet and tobacco. There are extensive orchards and livestock is reared. Agricultural exports and imports are important for the whole economy. Animal husbandry is still developing and is of minor importance.
About 80 per cent of the total agricultural area, which is the equivalent of 4.96 million hectares, is under mixed farming systems with elements of ecological farming. Most of the highly productive soil, located in the lowlands, receives small quantities of rainfall.
The agricultural sector in Serbia is hampered by shortages of industrial goods such as fertiliser, with an estimated US$44 million investment needed to ensure sufficient supplies of agri-chemicals annually. The country also suffers periodically from droughts which reduce agriculture production and economic growth.

Forestry
Forestry has experienced only slight falls in output, mainly because at times shortages of other fuels increase the demand for firewood locally.

Industry and manufacturing

Prior to the 1999 Kosovo War, Serbia and Montenegro had a diversified industrial base with major industries including metal processing, food production, textile and other manufacturing. The industrial sector accounted for almost US$1 billion of former Yugoslavia's exports. Much of the energy-dependent industry, including chemicals and iron and steel, collapsed because of shortages of energy and raw materials following the imposition of UN sanctions in 1999.
The damage done by the Nato bombing campaign to manufacturing was second only to the destruction to hydrocarbons and energy production. Total industrial production is thought to have fallen by 60 per cent, with whole sectors being wiped out. The sector's share of GDP dropped from 45 per cent to 15–20 per cent. Previously, over 40 per cent of the labour force were employed in industry, but more than 100,000 jobs were lost immediately as a result of industrial destruction. Financial aid and FDI have been crucial to rebuilding Serbia industrial base.

Tourism

The revival of the tourist sector is seen as central to the reconstruction of the economy of Serbia after the upheavals of recent years. It had serious war-damage, but has gradually recovered. Considerable investment in renovation and expansion of infrastructure is required to sustain continued growth.

Mining

Serbia has a significant mining sector. Lead and zinc are produced in substantial quantities. There is a large gold and silver mine at Bor in eastern Serbia. The fact that many of the most valuable non-ferrous metal mineral deposits are in Kosovo makes the area of great economic importance. In the longer-term, there is likely to be considerable foreign investor interest in Serbia's non-ferrous metal mineral ore resources, particularly copper and gold.

Hydrocarbons

Serbia has oil reserves of around 78 million barrels. Most oil production is undertaken in the autonomous province of Vojvodina. Production is insufficient to meet domestic consumption, which at over 90,000 barrels per day (bpd), must be supplemented by imports.
In 2008 a trade and co-operation agreement was signed between Serbia and Russia, whereby Russia would underwrite the construction of a 400km section of the South Stream gas pipeline traversing Serbia, which will integrate Serbia into the large European infrastructure project and will give Serbia sustainable gas supplies in winter. An underground gas storage facility will also be constructed at Banatski Dvor to store excess Russian gas production. A controlling interest in the state-owned Nafta Industrija Srbije (NIS) was sold to the Russian Gazprom Neft, for □400 million (US$520 million), with a guaranteed investment of □500 million (US$651.2 million) to refurbish and modernise industrial facilities. NIS produces hydrocarbons in Serbia and Angola with production at one million tonnes per year. It owns oil refineries and a liquefied natural gas plant and downstream distribution outlets.
Proven natural gas reserves were 481 billion cubic metres (cum) in 2006. However, with production of 254 million and consumption of 2.4 billion cum, Serbia has to import supplies of over 2.0 million cum from Russia to meet demand.
Small deposits of coal are extracted from mines in the Kolubara and Kostolac basins in central Serbia.

Energy

Total installed generating capacity was 9.3 gigawatts in 2006, before the break-up of Serbia, Montenegro and Kosovo; figures for an independent Serbia are not yet available. The energy market is state-owned and centralised under the Electric Power Industry of Serbia (EPS), which has a monopoly on generation and provision of electricity, and has a net capacity of 8,355MW which comprises 5,171MW coal-fired thermal plants, 2,831MW hydro plants and 353MW oil and natural gas-fired plants. There is also 89MW of installed capacity generated by geothermal power. Elektromreza Srbije (EMS) is responsible for transmission.

Financial markets

Stock exchange
Beogradska Berza (Belgrade Stock Exchange) (BSE)

Banking and insurance

Begradska Banka, Jugobanka, Investbanka and Beobanka, four of the country's old banking giants, were closed down in 2002. By 2006 Beobanka was merged with the Greek, Alpha Bank and the Hungarian OTP Bank bought almost 90 per cent of the provincial Niska Bank.

Central bank
Narodna Banka Srbije (NBS) (National Bank of Serbia).

Main financial centre
Belgrade

Time

GMT plus one hour (daylight saving, late March to late October, GMT plus two hours)

Geography

Landlocked and situated in the central Balkan Peninsula in south-eastern Europe, Serbia consists of two parts: the Great Danubian Plains of Vojvodina to the north, where the two main rivers are the Sava and the Danube, which meet at Belgrade; and the hilly and forested areas of inner (central) and southern Serbia, where the main rivers are the Drina, Morava and Vardar.
Serbia is bordered by Hungary to the north; Croatia, Bosnia and Hercegovina (BiH) and Montenegro to the west and

south-west; Albania and Macedonia to the south and south-east; and Bulgaria and Romania to the east. Serbia has borders with Croatia and Romania along the River Danube. The River Drina marks the border between Serbia and BiH.

Hemisphere

Northern

Climate

The climate is largely continental. The summers are very hot and the winters bitterly cold. The average summer temperature in Belgrade is 22 degrees Celsius (C) and in winter the average temperature is zero degrees C. Precipitation is generally constant, with average annual rainfall in Belgrade of around 635mm. Snowfall is extensive in winter.

Entry requirements

Passports

Required by all.

Visa

Required by all, with the exception of nationals of most European countries, North America, Australasia and a number of other countries. A full list of exceptions and lengths of stay permitted will be found at www.mfa.gov.yu/Visas/f_without_visa.htm.

Currency advice/regulations

There are no restrictions on the import of local or foreign currencies. Local currency in excess of D120,000 must be declared and shown to have been acquired abroad. Foreign currency may be declared against a receipt which will allow re-export.

Customs

Various personal articles and goods are allowed duty-free.

Health (for visitors)

Mandatory precautions

None required

Advisable precautions

Hepatitis A and B, diphtheria, polio, TB, typhoid, tetanus vaccinations are recommended. There is a rabies risk.

Hotels

Hotels are classified into five categories: L (extra), A, B, C and D; boarding houses into three, I, II and III. There is a 10–20 per cent service charge. Visitors must also pay a residential tax, which varies between regions.

Credit cards

International credit cards are accepted in large hotels and businesses in Serbia.

Public holidays (national)

Fixed dates

1 Jan (New Year's Day), 7 Jan (Orthodox Christmas Day), 15 Feb (Serbia National day), 1–2 May (Labour Days), 9 May (Victory Day).

Variable dates

Orthodox Good Friday, Orthodox Easter Monday.

Working hours

Banking

Mon–Fri: 0700–1500; Sat: 0800–1400. Belgrade airport 0800–2000.

Business

Mon–Fri: 0800–1500.

Government

Mon–Fri: 0730–1530.

Shops

Mon–Fri: generally in larger towns: 0800–2000 (some shops closing between 1200 and 1700); Sat: 0800–1500.

Telecommunications

Mobile/cell phones

There are GSM 900/1800 services available throughout most of the country.

Electricity supply

220V, 50Hz with European flat and round, two-pin plugs.

Social customs/useful tips

Punctuality depends on the ethnic region: it is important in some, more casual in others. As elsewhere, it is customary to shake hands on meeting and taking leave.

Do carry some form of identity at all times. Appointments must be made in advance. Business cards should indicate academic/professional titles and are exchanged after introduction. Many executives speak a second language, including German, English, Italian or Russian. There are some restrictions on photography.

Security

Visitors are advised to avoid Kosovo unless absolutely necessary and should remain vigil if required. Armed conflict continues in parts of Kosovo, and the crime rate (including violent crime) is high. Any travel into these areas should only take place in organised groups after seeking advice from the local authorities before the journey is made.

Getting there

Air

National airline: JAT Airways

International airport/s: Belgrade Nikola Tesla Airport (LYBE), 18km west of Belgrade.

Airport tax: Around D1,200, but may be included in ticket price.

Surface

Road: There are border crossings from Hungary, Romania, Bulgaria, and Albania, Bosnia and Hercegovina, Croatia, Macedonia and Montenegro.

The E5 highway, part of the pan-European 'Corridor 10' road and rail project linking Germany to Greece, will traverse Serbia from the Hungarian to the Macedonian borders when completed. Construction of the southern part of the Serbian section of the highway has been held up due to lack of funding.

Rail: There are rail links with neighbouring countries. The newly reopened Belgrade and Sarajevo line takes six hours by train.

Water: Ships provide regular passenger services and cruises on the Danube from Germany, passing through Serbia. There are also links with the rivers Rhine and Main and the Black Sea.

Getting about

National transport

Air: JAT Airways flies several domestic routes and provides a charter service.

Road: There are some 48,423km of roads, including 374km of motorways. The main route links Belgrade with Subotica (via Novi Sad), Kragujevac and Nis. Road maintenance is often inadequate.

Buses: An extensive network of express buses links Serbia's cities, although fuel shortages can often restrict services. Multi-journey tickets are available and sold through tobacconists. In general, fares paid to the driver are usually double the price of pre-purchase tickets.

Rail: There are around 4,000km of track, of which over a quarter is electrified. Maintenance of track and stock has deteriorated in recent years. The services are often overcrowded, unpunctual and slow. International express trains link Belgrade with Subotica, Novi Sad, Kragujevac, Nis and Pristina.

Water: There is a well established inland waterways system, based on the Danube, Sava, Tizsa and Begej rivers.

City transport

Taxis: Good services operate in most large cities and towns. All taxis are metered. There are taxi stands in central locations, but they can also be hailed in the street. Taxis are cheaper in Belgrade if arranged by telephone.

Buses, trams & metro: All cities and towns are served by buses; trams only in the centre of Belgrade and in Subotica. The service is generally regular.

Car hire

Cars can be hired in most main towns through travel agencies. There is a speed limit of 120kph on motorways and 60kph in built-up areas. Drive on the right and give way to traffic from the right unless clearly marked otherwise. Seat belts are compulsory in front seats.

To be on the safe side, carry an international driver's licence as well as a national licence.

BUSINESS DIRECTORY

Telephone area codes

The international direct dialling (IDD) code is +381, followed by area code and subscriber's number:

Belgrade	11	Pec	39
Kragujevac	34	Podgorica	81
Krusevac	37	Pristina	38
Leskovac	16	Uzice	31
Novi Sad	21		

Useful telephone numbers
Police: 92
Fire: 93
Ambulance: 94

Chambers of Commerce
American Chamber of Commerce in Serbia, 30 Vlajkoviceva, 11000 Belgrade (tel: 334-5961; fax: 324-7771; e-mail: info@amcham.yu).

Belgrade Chamber of Economy , 12 Kneza Milosa, 11001 Belgrade (tel:264-1355; fax: 264-2029; e-mail: mmj@komberg.org.yu).

Kragujevac Chamber of Commerce and Industry, 10 Mose Pijade, 34000 Kragujevac (tel: 335-805; fax: 334-049; e-mail: rpkkg@eunet.yu).

Serbian Chamber of Commerce and Industry, 13-15 Resavska, 11000 Belgrade (tel: 324-0611; fax: 323-0949; e-mail: centar@pks.co.yu).

Uzice Regional Chamber of Commerce, 52 Dimirija Tucovica, 31000 Uzice (tel: 513-483; fax: 514-184; e-mail: office@rpk-uzice.co.yu).

Banking
Association of Serbian Banks (Udruzenje Banaka Srbije), Bulevar Kralja Aleksandra 86, 11000 Belgrade (tel: 302-0760; fax: 337-0179).

JIK Banka, Knez Mihailova 42, Belgrade (tel: 632-822; fax: 183-198).

JUBMES Banka, Bulevar Avnoja 121, 11070 Belgrade (tel: 220-5500; fax: 311-0217; e-mail: jubmes@jubmes.co.yu).

Kreditna Banka Beograd, Lenjinov Bulevar 111, Belgrade (tel: 222-4428; fax: 144-923).

Panonska Banka, Bulevar Oslobodenja 76, Novi Sad (tel: 488-7100; e-mail: office@panban.co.yu).

PKB Banka, 29 Novembra 68a, Belgrade (tel: 753-366; fax: 750-932).

Privredna Banka, Brace Jugovica 17, Belgrade (tel: 623-272; fax: 627-247).

Vojvodjanska Banka, Trg Slobode 7, 21000 Novi Sad (tel: 621-277; fax: 021-624-940).

Central bank
Narodna Banka Srbije (NBS) (National Bank of Serbia), 12 Kralja Petra Street, 11000 Belgrade, (tel: 302-7100; fax: 302-7381; e-mail: gen.sec@nbs.yu).

Stock exchange
Beogradska Berza (Belgrade Stock Exchange) (BSE): www.belex.co.yu

Travel information
AutomobileAssociation of Serbia (AMSS), Kneginje Zorke 58, Belgrade (tel: 333-1100; fax: 245-1078; e-mail: info@amss.org.yu).

JAT Airways, Bulevar Umetnosti 16, 11070 Belgrade (tel: 311-4222; fax: 311-1082; e-mail: jatairways@jat.com).

Ministry of tourism
Ministry of Trade, Tourism and Services, Nemanjina Street 22-26, Belgrade (tel: 361-0579; fax: 361-0258; e-mail: kabinet@minttu.sr.gov.yu).

National tourist organisation offices
National Tourism Organization of Serbia, Decanska 8, 11000 Belgrade (tel: 323-0566; fax: 322-1068; e-mail: ntos@yubc.net).

Ministries
Ministry of Agriculture, Forestry and Water Management, 22-26 Nemanjina Street, Belgrade (tel: 306-5038; fax: 361-6272; e-mail: office@minpolj.sr.gov.yu).

Ministry of Capital Investment, 22-26 Nemanjina Street, Belgrade (tel: 361-6426; fax: 361-7486; e-mail: cabinet@mki.sr.gov.yu).

Ministry of Culture, 3 Vlajkoviceva Street, Belgrade (tel: 339-8404; fax: 339-8936; e-mail: kabinet@min-cul.sr.gov.yu).

Ministry of Diaspora, 42 Svetozara Markovica, Belgrade (tel: 263-8033; fax: 263-7624; e-mail: info@mzd.sr.gov.yu).

Ministry of Economy, 16 Kralja Milana Street, Belgrade (tel: 361-7599; fax: 361-7640; e-mail: officempriv@mpriv.sr.gov.yu).

Ministry of Education and Sport, 22-26 Nemanjina Street, Belgrade (tel: 361-6357; fax: 361-6491; e-mail: webmaster@mps.sr.gov.yu).

Ministry of Energy and Mining, 22-26 Nemanjina Street, Belgrade (tel: 334-6755; fax: 361- 6603; e-mail: kabinet@mem.sr.gov.yu).

Ministry of Finance, 20 Kneza Milosa Street, Belgrade (tel: 361-4972; fax: 361-8914; e-mail: informacije@mfin.sr.gov.yu).

Ministry of Foreign Affairs, 24-26 Kneza Milosa Street, Belgrade (tel: 361-6333; fax: 361-8366; e-mail: mfa@smip.sv.gov.yu).

Ministry of Health, 22-26 Nemanjina Street, Belgrade (tel: 361-6251; fax: 656-548; e-mail: kabinet.zdravlje@zdravlje.sr.gov.yu).

Ministry of the Interior, 101 Kneza Milosa Street, Belgrade (tel: 306-2000; fax: 361-7814; e-mail: muprs@mup.sr.gov.yu).

Ministry of International Economic Relations, 10 Vlajkoviceva Street, Belgrade (tel: 361-7583; fax: 363-3142; e-mail: cabinet@mier.sr.gov.yu).

Ministry of Justice, 22-26 Nimanjina Street, Belgrade (tel: 361-6548; fax: 361-6419; e-mail: kabinet@mpravde.sr.gov.yu).

Ministry of Labour, Employment and Social Affairs, 22-26 Nemanjina Street, Belgrade (tel: 361-3734; fax: 363-1792; e-mail: kabinet@minrzs.sr.gov.yu).

Ministry of Public Administration and Local Self-Government, 6 Bircaninova Street, Belgrade (tel: 268-5387; fax: 268-5315; e-mail: info.mpalsg@mpalsg.sr.gov.yu).

Ministry of Religion, 11 Nemanjina Street, Belgrade (tel: 306-5960; fax: 363-3446; e-mail: kabinet.mv@mv.sr.gov.yu).

Ministry of Science and Environmental Protection, 22-26 Nemajina Street, Belgrade (tel: 268-8047; fax: 361-6516; e-mail: info@mntr.sr.gov.yu).

Ministry of Trade, Tourism and Services, Nemanjina Street 22-26, Belgrade (tel: 361-0579; fax: 361-0258; e-mail: kabinet@minttu.sr.gov.yu).

Other useful addresses
British Embassy, Resavska 46, 11000 Belgrade (tel: 264-5055; fax:265-9651; e-mail: belgrade.man@fco.gov.uk).

Kosovo Trust Agency, Ilir Konushevi 8, Pristina, Kosovo (tel: 500-400; fax: 248-076; e-mail: kta@eumik.org).

Novinska Agencija Tanjug (news agency), Obilicev Venac 2, Box 439, Belgrade 11001 (tel: 332-221).

Roads Directorate of the Republic of Serbia, Ljube Cupe 5, 11000 Belgrade (tel: 454-779; fax: 444-5557; e-mail: dzpnapl@eunet.yu).

Statistical Office of the Republic of Serbia, Milana Rakica 5, 11000 Belgrade (tel: 241-2922; fax: 240-1284; e-mail: stat@statserb.sr.gov.yu).

US Embassy, Kneza Milosa 50, 11000 Belgrade (tel: 361-9344; fax: 361-5489; e-mail: belgradeacs@state.gov).

National news agency: Tanjug, Obilicev Venac 2, Belgrade 11000 (tel: 328-8285; fax: 263-3550; email: direkcija@tanjug.co.yu; internet: www.tanjug.co.yu).

Other news agencies: Beta News Agency (www2.beta.co.yu); FoNet (www.fonet.co.yu), Tiker (www.tiker.co.yu).

Internet sites
Belgrade News: www.belgradenews.com

European Commission/World Bank, Balkans reconstruction web site: www.seerecon.org

Seebiz (business portal): www.seebiz.eu

Seychelles

KEY FACTS

Official name: Republic of Seychelles

Head of State: President James Michel (from 2004; re-elected 19–21 May 2011)

Head of government: President James Michel

Ruling party: Parti Lepep (People's Party) (PP) (from 1993; re-elected 1 Oct 2011)

Area: 453 square km

Population: 87,000 (2010)*

Capital: Victoria

Official language: Creole, French and English

Currency: Seychelle rupee (SR) = 100 cents

Exchange rate: SR12.43 per US$ (Oct 2011)

GDP per capita: US$10,682 (2010)

GDP real growth: 6.20% (2010)

GDP: US$936.00 million (2010)

Inflation: -2.40% (2010)

Balance of trade: -US$508.34 million (2010)

Visitor numbers: 174,529 (2010)

* estimated figure

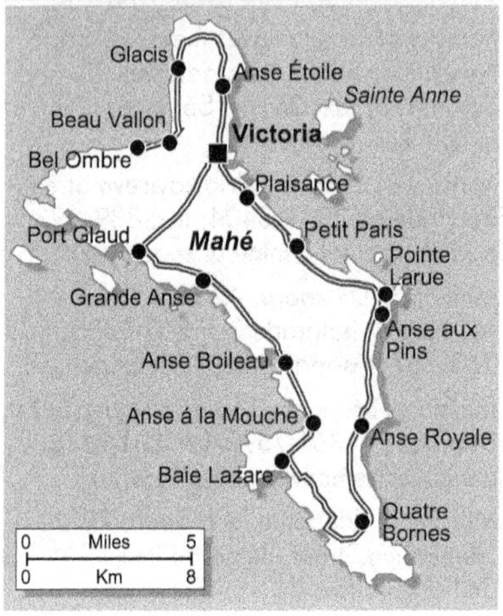

Presidential elections were held on 19–21 May 2011 in which four candidates took part. Incumbent James Michel of the Front Progressiste du Peuple Seychellois (FPPS) (Seychelles People's Progressive Front) won with 55.46 per cent; the opposition leader Wavel Ramkalawan (Seychelles National Party (SNP)) won 41.43 per cent. It was almost an exact repeat of the 2007 election results, including the third placing of independent Philippe Boullé with 1.66 per cent; Ralph Volcere (New Democratic Party (NDP)) achieved 1.45 per cent.

Early parliamentary elections were held on 29 September–1 October 2011, which the two main opposition parties – Mouvement Populaire Démocratique (Popular Democratic Movement) (PDM) and Seychelles National Party (SNP) – boycotted. This left the contest between the Parti Lepep (People's Party) (PP) which won 88.6 per cent of the vote (all of the 31 seats available) and the Mouvement Populaire Démocratique (Popular Democratic Movement) (PDM) which won 10.89 per cent (but no seats). The turnout was 74.3 per cent, but 31.9 per cent of votes cast were spoiled.

Still the best

The Seychelles has the highest standard of living in Africa, with a per capita income of US$10,617 in 2010. The government allocated about 43 per cent of the country's budget, or 5 per cent of GDP, to healthcare and education, reflecting that poverty and social welfare programmes rank high on the government's priorities. It maintains free access to education and health for all citizens. Primary and secondary levels of education are free and compulsory (10 years), while 80 per cent of secondary school graduates proceed to tertiary education.

Royal patronage

The choice of Seychelles by the UK royal couple Prince William and Kate Middleton (Duke and Duchess of Cambridge) for their honeymoon provided a fillip to the tourist industry.

According to the *African Economic Outlook 2011* (AEO), published jointly by the African Development Bank and the Organisation for Economic Co-operation and Development, the service sector is dominated by tourism, which is the principal source of foreign exchange. Tourism accounts for 25.5 per cent of GDP. Tourist numbers fell from a record 161,273 visitors in 2007 to 159,416 in 2009; before recovering with another record, of 174,529 visitors, in 2010. The majority visit from France, Germany and the UK.

In 2010, the Seychelles economy recovered after important fiscal measures were taken to address the 2008 debt crisis. The country also weathered the recent global financial and economic crisis relatively well. Nevertheless, the Seychelles remains highly exposed to external shocks from piracy threats in the Indian Ocean, the European economic situation and further depreciation of the euro. A further depreciation of the euro could affect the country's still fragile external position.

United we stand

The Seychelles consists of some 115 islands, spread across 1.3 million square miles – ideal pirate territory. So much so that the government signed Status of Forces Agreements (SOFAs) with the US, France and the EU in late 2009. The EU Atalanta naval mission was expanded in response to increased piracy in the Indian Ocean with the EU using manned aircraft and the US unmanned drones to improve surveillance. The Seychelles regularly sends troops to potentially vulnerable outer islands to check activity in its 320km maritime exclusive economic zone (EEZ). In February 2011, the government negotiated a four-party agreement with the Somali Transitional Federal Government and the breakaway governments of Somaliland and Puntland (Somalia) on the repatriation of convicted Somali pirates.

Partnerships

The trend towards forging partnerships with countries of emerging economies has grown to include China, the United Arab Emirates (UAE), India, Saudi Arabia and Brazil. Others, although to a lesser extent, include Malaysia, Indonesia, Singapore and Turkey. Most relationships with these countries involve trade, investment and aid. China, UAE and India have become the most important partners since 2006. India is the oldest of these partnerships and has the most comprehensive partnership packages including telecommunications, healthcare provisions, education, military aid and a US$10 million soft loan to the Development Bank of Seychelles. China has provided soft loans for the infrastructure of water and sewage provision and energy. The UAE provides military and coast guard support, as well as various equipment, and provision of laptop computers for school children.

Traditional partners have provided assistance in economic growth, governance and increasing human capital.

Doing business

A number of constraints still affect the business environment despite the measures that the government has recently put in place. The World Bank 2011 *Doing Business* report shows that the Seychelles slipped to a rank of 95 out of 183 countries in 2010 in the ease of doing business index, compared to a ranking of 92 in 2009.

Jaws attacks twice

The Seychelles' good publicity as a honeymoon destination suffered a severe setback when a British groom was killed by a shark on 17 August 2011, just two weeks after a French visitor was killed on the same beach. The director of the Seychelles Tourism Board, Alain St Ange said the second attack was caused by a 'foreign shark' and was a 'freak accident'; sharks are not known to inhabit the shores of Seychelles and the last recorded shark attack was in 1963. Shark experts from South Africa were called on for to help in removing the shark

Risk assessment

Economy	Fair
Politics	Good
Regional stability	Fair

COUNTRY PROFILE

Historical profile

1794 The islands were taken over by the British and administered from Mauritius.
1903 Seychelles became a separate colony.
1948 The first elections to the legislative assembly took place.
1964 The Seychelles' first political organisations were established – the Seychelles Democratic Party (SDP) led by James Mancham and the Front Progressiste du Peuple Seychellois (FPPS) (Seychelles People's Progressive Front) (formerly the SPUP) of France-Albert René.
1975 The Seychelles was granted internal self-government; the SDP and the FPPS formed a coalition government under the premiership of Mancham.
1976 Became an independent republic. James Mancham became president and René became prime minister.
1977 René seized power in an armed coup
1978 A new constitution established a one-party state with the FPPS as the sole legal party.
1981 A group of mercenaries from South Africa attempted to overthrow René and return Mancham to power.
1982 A mutiny in the army was put down by pro-government troops.
1991 René re-established a multi-party democracy.
1993 Multi-party presidential and legislative elections resulted in a landslide victory for President René and the FPPS.
1998 Presidential and legislative elections were again won by President René and the FPPS.
2001 Presidential elections resulted in a victory for President René (54.2 per cent of the vote).
2002 The FPPS won the parliamentary elections.
2004 President René, who had came to power in a bloodless coup in 1977, retired and Vice President James Michel was sworn in as president.
2006 In presidential elections, incumbent James Michel (FPPS) was re-elected. There was a record annual number of 140,627 visitors. To avoid environmental degradation through mass-tourism a cap of 200,000 visitors will be encouraged. The tourist industry intends to promote its attractions to visitors from the high-end of the market.
2007 The FPPS won 56.16 per cent of the vote in parliamentary elections; the Seychelles National Party (SNP) won 43.84 per cent. Seychelles was re-admitted to

KEY INDICATORS — **Seychelles**

	Unit	2006	2007	2008	2009	2010
Population	m	*0.08	*0.08	*0.08	*0.08	*0.09
Gross domestic product (GDP)	US$bn	0.78	0.91	0.82	767.00	0.94
GDP per capita	US$	9,366	10,728	9,640	8,973	10,682
GDP real growth	%	5.3	7.3	-1.9	-7.6	6.2
Inflation	%	-1.4	5.3	37.0	31.8	-2.4
Exports (fob) (goods)	US$m	427.0	391.7	496.8	432.5	407.3
Imports (fob) (goods)	US$m	579.0	804.0	1,004.9	759.1	915.6
Balance of trade	US$m	-152.0	-412.3	-508.1	-326.6	-508.3
Current account	US$m	-175.5	-213.0	-406.9	-284.2	-483.5
Total reserves minus gold	US$m	112.9	40.8	63.8	190.6	235.6
Foreign exchange	US$m	112.9	40.8	63.8	178.3	223.8
Exchange rate	per US$	5.49	6.70	9.46	13.61	12.07

* estimated figure

the Southern African Development Community (SADC).

2008 The global economic crisis had an adverse effect on the tourist industry; the International Monetary Fund agreed to extend a two-year US$26 million loan to the country. It also suggested moves to restructure the economy, including floating the Seychelles rupee, allowing citizens to hold foreign currencies and setting a minimum salary among other measures.

2009 The president called on international creditors to cancel around US$400 million in foreign debt. The ruling FPPS changed its name to the Parti Lepep (People's Party) (PP).

2010 Around 85 per cent of Seychelles' public debt was successfully reduced and rescheduled by February; external debt stock fell from 92 per cent of GDP in 2009 to 54 per cent in March. On 13 July, the government estimated that the Seychelles was losing 4 per cent of GDP due to Somali piracy. A record number of tourists (174,529) visited the island, with most arriving from France, Italy, Germany and the UK.

2011 In February, the government negotiated with the Somali Transitional Federal Government and the breakaway governments of Somaliland and Puntland (Somalia) to form a four-party agreement on repatriation of convicted Somali pirates. Four candidates took part in presidential elections held on 19–21 May. Incumbent James Michel (FPPS) won with 55.46 per cent, opposition leader, Wavel Ramkalawan (SNP) won 41.43 per cent. It was almost an exact repeat of the 2006 election results, including the third placing of independent Philippe Boullé with 1.66 per cent; Ralph Volcere (New Democratic Party (NDP)) achieved 1.45 per cent. The September parliamentary elections were boycotted by the main opposition party, the SNP, in protest at the failure by the government to revise electoral laws and the amount of spending political parties were allowed for election campaigning. Voting began in outlying islands on 29–30 September and the rest of the country on 1 October. The PP won 88.6 per cent of the vote and all of the 31 seats available; 31.9 per cent of votes cast were spoiled.

Political structure

Constitution

In a June 1993 referendum, a new constitution was approved, institutionalising multi-party politics and providing for the establishment of a National Assembly.

Form of state

Republic

The executive

Executive power rests with the president, elected for a five-year term; renewable three times.

National legislature

The unicameral Assemblée Nationale (National Assembly) has 34 members, of which 25 are directly elected by majority vote in single-seat constituencies, the remaining nine are elected by proportional representation. All members serve for five-year terms.

Last elections

19–21 May 2011 (presidential); 29 September–1 October 2011 (parliamentary)

Results: Presidential: James Michel (FPPS) won 55 per cent of the vote, Wavel Ramkalawan (SNP) 41 per cent, Philippe Boullé (independent) 1.66 per cent, Ralph Volcere (New Democratic Party (NDP)) 1.45 per cent.

Parliamentary: the Parti Lepep (People's Party) (PP) won 88.6 per cent of the vote (all of the 31 seats available) the Mouvement Populaire Démocratique (Popular Democratic Movement) (PDM) 10.89 per cent (0). Turnout was 74.3 per cent, but 31.9 per cent of votes cast were spoiled. The two main opposition parties (Mouvement Populaire Démocratique (Popular Democratic Movement) (PDM) and Seychelles National Party (SNP)) boycotted the elections.

Next elections

2016 (parliamentary and presidential)

Political parties

Ruling party

The People's Party (PP) (formerly the Front Progressiste du Peuple Seychellois (FPPS) (Seychelles People's Progressive Front)) (since 1993; re-elected May 2007)

Main opposition party

Mouvement Populaire Démocratique (Popular Democratic Movement) (PDM), but without any seats in parliament.

Population

87,000 (20110*

Last census: August 2002: 81,755

Population density: 178 inhabitants per square km. Urban population: 65 per cent (1995–2001).

Annual growth rate: 0.7 per cent 1994–2004 (WHO 2006)

Ethnic make-up

The islanders have a variety of ethnic origins – African, French, Indian, Chinese and Arab.

Religions

Practically the whole population is Christian, with 87 per cent belonging to the Roman Catholic faith.

Education

The government provides free education. The school-going age population is largely concentrated on Mahe, the main island where most of the economic activities are concentrated. There are only two private schools as well as public schools. Total expenditure in public education has grown in real terms. The pupil per capita cost in (public) primary schools is typically US$910.

Literacy rate: 90 per cent (plus)

Compulsory years: 6 to 15

Pupils per teacher: 15 in primary schools (Unesco)

Health

The Victoria Hospital has about 445 beds and there are 56 in-patient admissions per bed per year. Health care is provided free of charge.

Life expectancy: 72 years, 2004 (WHO 2006)

Fertility rate/Maternal mortality rate: 2.1 births per woman, 2004 (WHO 2006)

Birth rate/Death rate: 17 births per 1,000 population; 6.5 deaths per 1,000 population (2003).

Child (under 5 years) mortality rate (per 1,000): 11 per 1,000 live births (World Bank)

Head of population per physician: 1.15 physicians per 1,000 people, 2004 (WHO 2006)

Welfare

The social security law requires employers and employees to contribute to a national pension programme that gives retirees a modest pension. Self-employed persons contribute by paying 15 per cent of gross earnings. The government also provides low-cost housing and housing loans. There is welfare provision for children and the disabled.

Main cities

Victoria, on Mahé island (capital, estimated population 29,298 in 2007).

Languages spoken

Creole is the local language, but English is used in business and government circles. French is also widely spoken.

Official language/s

Creole, French and English

Media

Freedom of speech has been improved since 1993 however tough libel laws are used by the government to contain opposition opinion.

Press

Dailies: The government-owned newspaper *Seychelles Nation* (www.nation.sc) is published from Monday to Saturday.

Weeklies: *The People* (www.thepeople.sc) is published by the FPPS political party, while *Le Nouveau Seychelles Weekly* (www.seychellesweekly.com), and *Regar* are FPPS-opposition.

Periodicals: *The People* is a monthly publication. A few periodicals are also published in English, French and Creole.

Broadcasting

The state-run, Seychelles Broadcasting Corporation (www.sbc.sc) (formerly known as Radio Television Seychelles) operates the only television network along with its radio services in Creole, English and French. Both mediums carry advertising. Reception is good on Mahé and the other main islands.

Radio: Along with Paradise FM, the SBC service, international broadcast from, RFI, BBC and VOA may be picked up on shortwave radios.

News agencies

The African Press Agency (ww.apanews.net) and Panapress (www.panapress.com) provide information from the Seychelles.

Economy

The service sector, dominated by tourism (over 75 per cent), constituted over 45.3 per cent of GDP in 2009, with industry comprising 19.7 per cent, of which manufacturing was 11.8 per cent and agriculture 2 per cent.

GDP growth was 9.6 per cent in 2007, as a record 161,273 tourists visited the islands, but growth rapidly fell to -1.3 per cent in 2008 as the global economic crisis struck; tourist numbers fell by 19 per cent in 2009 and GDP growth was 0.7 per cent. As global trade picked up, so growth returned to a pre-2007 level of 6.2 per cent. After two years of low inflation, when in 2006 it was a deflationary -1.9 per cent, inflation began to rise in 2007, to 5.3 per cent, soaring sharply in 2008 to 37.0 per cent as the global prices of imported food and fuel climbed and remaining high at 31.9 per cent in 2009 before plunging back into deflation of -2.4 per cent in 2010. Despite the swings in the economy, the Seychelles still has the highest standard of living in Africa, with a per capita income of US$10,617 in 2010.

Although tourism provides vitally needed foreign exchange, the government has acknowledged that tourism also has inherent drawbacks such as damage to the environment, major foreign currency spending on food, goods and services and fuel imports. The risk to the Seychelles is in becoming an economic monoculture, which would be at the mercy of external shocks and forces. The government is intent on developing other means of income such as the fishing industry, which is currently a major foreign currency earner, telecommunications, financial services, light industry and international conferences. However, this will require considerable foreign investment and the government will need to institute policies and adopt attitudes more compliant to investors. Foreign direct investment has grown steadily from US$85.8 million in 2005 to US$368.9 million in 2010.

External trade

The Seychelles is a member of the Common Market for Eastern and Southern Africa (Comesa), and operates within a free trade zone with 13 of the 19 member states.

The visible trade deficit is partially offset by earnings from tourism which is the main foreign exchange earner, plus foreign aid and investment, rental from a US satellite tracking station and a BBC relay station.

Preferential import tariffs are granted to goods from Indian Ocean Commission (IOC) member countries – Mauritius, Comoros, Madagascar, Réunion. In return, Seychelles receives preferential import tariffs from IOC countries.

Imports

Principal imports are machinery and equipment, foodstuffs, petroleum products and chemicals.

Main sources: United Arab Emirates (typically 17 per cent of total), Saudi Arabia (14 per cent), Singapore (8 per cent).

Exports

Principal exports are canned tuna, fresh/frozen fish, copra and various herbs and spices including vanilla, cinnamon, nutmeg and mace.

Main destinations: Saudi Arabia (typically 36 per cent of total), France (23 per cent), UK (18 per cent).

Re-exports

Petroleum products.

Agriculture

Farming

With the expansion of the tourist industry, the overall importance of agriculture to the economy has declined, although it is still important as a source of foreign exchange and employment. There is a shortage of cultivable land and fertile soil. Approximately 4 per cent of the total land area is agricultural, much of which is given over to copra and cinnamon, which are the major export crops. Farming is traditionally organic and eco-friendly. Small quantities of coconuts, vanilla, tea and limes are exported. Crops grown for local consumption include tropical fruits, cassava, sweet potatoes, yams, sugar cane, bananas, tea and vegetables; rice, the staple food crop, has to be imported. Seychelles is self-sufficient in pork, chicken, fish and some vegetables.

There are a number of large farms, 650 small farms and thousands of smallholdings, which the government hopes will reduce dependence on imported foods.

Government reforms include privatisation of state farms, while setting up smaller co-operatives, new marketing structures, upgrading infrastructure and irrigation facilities for farms. An animal feed factory has been established by the Seychelles Marketing Board (SMB) to support production of meat and eggs. About 98 per cent of milk is imported. The government is encouraging the production of bananas and mangoes.

Fishing

The fishing industry is an important source of income and foreign exchange, accounting for around 85 per cent of domestically-produces exports. It is being expanded as part of the government policy of economic diversification, with foreign companies being encouraged to become involved. HJ Heinz acquired a 60 per cent majority stake in the government-owned Indian Ocean Tuna processing factory. Heinz has invested nearly US$8 million in the plant, which operates in the country's International Trade Zone. France and Italy are the main importers of Seychelles tuna.

The Seychelles sells fishing licences in its exclusive 1.3 million square km economic zone. Despite the desire for a growth in capacity and productivity through the development of commercial fishing operations, small-scale artisanal fishing still represents about one-third of fishing exports.

In a meeting of African ministers in Namibia, held on 2 July 2009, members discussed illegal and unregulated fishing, which is estimated to cost Africa US$1 billion per annum in lost revenue and the threat to stocks and local artisan fishing.

Industry and manufacturing

The industrial sector, includes production in mining, manufacturing, construction and power.

There is a small-scale manufacturing sector. The main activities include the production of canned tuna, soft drinks, juices, jams, beer, cigarettes, paints, assembling of television sets and processing of cinnamon and coconuts.

Emphasis is on private-sector investment. The government aims to expand light industry in other areas such as artisanal products, packaging, assembly and services.

Tourism

The numerous islands that make up the Seychelles offer the many tourists a relaxing, tropical experience. Attractions include coral beaches, water sports and local wildlife. The tourist industry has become the most important sector in the economy, constituting 55.1 per cent of GDP in 2010. This was, however, the lowest recorded share of GDP since

2005; in 2007 the sector's share was a record high of 64.3 per cent of GDP, with earnings of US$590 million, of which visitor spending was US$323 million. The global economic crisis has had a deep impact on tourism as visitors from Europe and other Western nations fell. In 2009–10, employment and capital investment in the industry was cut and visitor spending was correspondingly down. The prospects for 2011 were encouraging with all aspects of tourism showing growth.
The Seychelles National Assessment Report (2004–2009) outlining government and industry planning has been steadily introduced. The Report included providing value for money and value added holidays, improved training for tourism staff, improved access by air and sea, diverse attractions and activities and protection of the environment. In 2009, the Seychelles Tourism Board was privatised, to make it more responsive to the industry. Several large hotels were refurbished to attract a higher level of clientele.
In May 2011, the UK-royal couple chose the Seychelles for their honeymoon giving the islands an instant cache. However a few months later, Seychelles suffered some bad publicity, following rare shark attacks on two tourists, who were killed in individual attacks, off the Anse Lazio beach. The beach was later closed and a search was made of the predator.

Mining
Some granite is quarried. Offshore surveys have indicated the presence of certain metals on the seabed.

Hydrocarbons
The Seychelles has some known hydrocarbon deposits but due to their size and inaccessibility they have not yet been exploited. However in December 2008 licences were issued to two relatively small oil companies to begin exploration of offshore oil deposits. Some gas reserves have been found offshore, but they have not been exploited.
The parastatal Seychelles Petroleum Company (Sepec) is responsible for purchasing, supplying, transhipment and trading in petroleum. It operates ports and storage terminals, including a 880 tonne liquefied petroleum gas (LPG) storage and cylinder filling plant.
The parastatal Seychelles National Oil Company (Snoc) implements state policy on hydrocarbon exploration.
Any use of natural gas or coal is commercial insignificant.

Energy
Total installed generating capacity was 95MW in 2006, generating 210 million kilowatt hours per year. Electricity is provided from liquefied petroleum gas (LPG) and diesel-fired turbines.

Banking and insurance
Central bank
Central Bank of Seychelles

Time
GMT plus four hours

Geography
There are around 115 islands and islets comprising the Seychelles, which cover more than 1.3 million square km in the Indian Ocean, North of Madagascar and over 1,500km from the coast of Kenya. The major islands are a compact group of 41 granite islands, the largest of which includes Mahé, Praslin and La Digue. These islands have high central granite ridges, the highest of which is Morne Seychellois (905 metres) on Mahé. Other islands are composed of coral and are low-lying; many are sparcely populated and four are uninhabited bird sanctuaries. All major islands are lush with vegetation dependent on the surface composition – forests cover the granite islands and coconut palms the coral islands.
Hemisphere
Southern

Climate
Tropical and humid. Average daily temperature are 24–32 degrees Celsius throughout the year. Hottest months are December–May; the wettest are from December–March and cooler from June–November. The islands lie outside the cyclone belt.

Entry requirements
Passports
Required by all and must be valid for at least six months beyond length of stay.
Visa
A Visitor's Permit is issued on arrival, valid for four weeks (extensions are possible for three-month periods). From May 2009 EU citizens may make a short-stay visit, for up to three months, without a visa. All visitors must have confirmed accommodation and sufficient funds for the intended length of stay and hold onward/return tickets or pay a deposit equivalent to the value of a return ticket to the country of origin.
Currency advice/regulations
Unlimited import/export of foreign currency is permitted. Only legal to exchange foreign currencies for Seychelles Rupees through a bank.
Travellers may take or send out of Seychelles up to SR100 of domestic currency.
Customs
Personal items, including one video and one single frame camera, a musical instrument, an item of portable electronic equipment and personal music player. Video tapes must be declared. Animals and agricultural products require an entry permit.
Prohibited imports
Firearms, illegal drugs and spear-fishing equipment.

Health (for visitors)
Mandatory precautions
Yellow fever certificate if arriving from infected area.
Advisable precautions
Inoculations and boosters should be current for tetanus, hepatitis A and diphtheria. There may be a need for vaccinations for typhoid, tuberculosis, hepatitis B and cholera. Anti-mosquito measures including mosquito repellents, nets and clothing covering the body should be used for protection against dengue fever, hepatitis B and chikungunya fever, which include mosquito repellents and nets and clothing that covers the body after dark. There is a risk of rabies.
There is a shortage of routine medications and visitors should take all necessary medicines with them. A first aid kit that includes disposable syringe, is a reasonable precaution. Use only bottled or boiled water for drinks, washing teeth and making ice. Eat only well cooked meals, preferably served hot; vegetables should be cooked and fruit peeled. Dairy products are unpasteurised and should be avoided, unless cooked.
Healthcare is not to Western standards and medical insurance, including emergency evacuation, is necessary.

Hotels
Good standard and widely available. All the large hotels in Mahé are on the beach. Advisable to book and confirm reservation in advance, particularly at Christmas and during August. Government trades tax of 5 per cent is added to bill, and usually also a service charge. Tipping optional.

Credit cards
Major credit cards widely accepted.

Public holidays (national)
Fixed dates
1–2 Jan (New Year), 1 May (Labour Day), 5 Jun (Liberation Day), 18 Jun (National Day), 15 Aug (Assumption Day/La Digue Festival), 1 Nov (All Saints' Day), 8 Dec (Immaculate Conception), 25 Dec (Christmas Day).
Variable dates
Good Friday (Mar/Apr), Corpus Christi (May/Jun).

Working hours
Banking
Mon–Fri: 0830–1300; Sat: 0800–1200.
Business
Mon–Fri: 0800–1200, 1300–1600.

Government
Mon–Fri: 0800–1200, 1300–1600.
Shops
Mon–Fri: 0800–1200, 1330–1700; Sat: 0800–1200; some open Sun morning.

Telecommunications
Mobile/cell phones
There are 900 and 1800 GSM services available throughout Mahé and surrounding islands.

Electricity supply
240V AC, 50 cycles. Plugs are three-pin bayonet.

Getting there
Air
National airline: Air Seychelles
International airport/s: Seychelles International (SEZ), on Mahé Island, 10km from Victoria; duty-free shop, bar, restaurant, bank and car hire.
Airport tax: Included in ticket price
Surface
Water: International shipping lines that maintain contacts with Seychelles may provide passenger services on cargo ships.
Main port/s: Victoria, on Mahé island.

Getting about
National transport
Air: Air Seychelles operates regular services from Mahé to Praslin, Desroches, Fregate, Bird and Dennis islands. Aircraft charters are available to Assumption, Farquhar and Poivre. Helicopter Seychelles provides services and charters from Mahé.
Road: Only three islands have metalled road, Mahé, La Digue and Praslin; all other roads are unpaved tracks.
Buses: The Seychelles Public Transport Corporation (SPTC) operate regular services on Mahé from Victoria and Praslin, between 0520–2130.
Water: There are regular ferry services; a catamaran, Cat Cocos, links Mahé-Praslin, traditional schooners link Praslin-La Digue and La Digue-Mahé.
City transport
Taxis: Taxis are available on Mahé and Praslin, they are privately operated, but with government controlled rates. On Praslin a surcharge is levied between 2200–0600.
Car hire
There are a limited number of hire cars available on Mahé and Praslin; reservations during peak seasons should be made well in advance. A foreign or international driving licence is required. Driving is on the left, the speed limit outside urban areas is 65kph and 40kph in towns.

BUSINESS DIRECTORY

The addresses listed below are a selection only. While World of Information makes every endeavour to check these addresses, we cannot guarantee that changes have not been made, especially to telephone numbers and area codes. We would welcome any corrections.

Telephone area codes
The international dialling code (IDD) for Seychelles is +248, followed by subscriber's number.

Chambers of Commerce
Seychelles Chamber of Commerce & Industry, Ebrahim Building, PO Box 1399, Victoria, Mahé (tel: 323-812; fax: 321-422; e-mail: scci@seychelles.net).

Banking
Barclays Bank (Seychelles), PO Box 167, Victoria (tel: 383-838; email: barclays@seychelles.net).

Bank of Baroda, PO Box 124, Victoria, (tel: 323-037/8; email: baroda@seychelles.net).

Habib Bank, PO Box 702, Victoria (tel: 224-371/2; email: habibsez@seychelles.net).

Mauritius Commercial Bank (Seychelles), PO Box 122, Victoria (tel: 284-555; email: contact@mcbseychelles.com).

Nouvobanq (Seychelles International Mercantile Banking Corporation), PO Box 241, Ground Floor, Victoria House, State House Avenue, Victoria (tel: 293-000; fax: 224-670; email: nvb@nouvobanqu.sc).

Seychelles Savings Bank Limited; PO Box 531, Independence Ave, Victoria (tel: 293-000; fax: 224-713; email: ssb.savingsbank.sc).

Central bank
Central Bank of Seychelles, Independence Avenue, PO Box 701, Victoria, Mahé (tel: 225-200; fax: 224-958; e-mail: cbs@seychelles.sc).

Travel information
Air Seychelles, Victoria House, PO Box 386, Victoria (tel: 225-300; fax: 225-159; internet: www.airseychelles.com).

Helicopter Seychelles, Providence Industrial Estate; PO Box 595, Victoria (tel: 385-858; fax: 373-055; internet: www.helicopterseychelles.com).

Island Development Co (charter flights), New Port; PO Box 638, Mahé (tel: 224-640; fax: 224-467; email: idc@seychelles.sc).

National Travel Agency, Kingsgate House, PO Box 611, Victoria (tel: 224-900; fax: 225-111).

Seychelles Tourist Office–La Digue, La Passes, La Digue (tel/fax: 234-393; email: stbladigue@seychelles.sc).

Seychelles Tourist Office–Praslin, Iles des Palmes Airport, Grand Anse, Praslin (tel: 233-346; fax: 233-571; email: praslin@seychelles.sc).

Travel Services (Seychelles) Ltd., Victoria House, PO Box 356, Victoria (tel: 322-414; fax: 325-010).

Ministry of tourism
Ministry of Tourism and Transport, Independence House, PO Box 92, Victoria (tel: 225-313; fax: 225-131).

National tourist organisation offices
Seychelles Tourist Board, Bel Ombre; PO Box 1262, Victoria, Mahé (tel: 671-300, fax: 620-620; internet: www.seychelles.com).

Ministries
Investment Development Advisory Services (IDEAS), c/o Ministry of Finance and Communication, 3rd Floor, Central Bank Building, Box 313, Victoria (tel: 225-252; fax: 225-265).

Ministry of Administration and Manpower, National House, PO Box 56, Victoria (tel: 383-000; fax: 224-936).

Ministry of Agriculture and Marine Resources, Independence House, PO Box 166, Victoria (tel: 224-030; fax: 225-245).

Ministry of Community Development, Independence House, PO Box 199, Victoria (tel: 224-030; fax: 225-287).

Ministry of Education and Culture, Mont Fleuri (tel: 224-777; fax: 224-859).

Ministry of Finance and Communication, 3rd Floor, Central Bank Building, PO Box 313, Victoria (tel: 225-252; fax: 225-265).

Ministry of Foreign Affairs, Planning and Environment, Mont Fleuri (tel: 224-688; fax: 224-845).

Ministry of Health, PO Box 52, Mont Fleuri (tel: 388-000; fax: 224-792).

Ministry of Industry, Maison du People, Victoria (tel: 224-030; fax: 225-086).

Ministry of Local Government Youth and Sports, Oceangate House, Victoria (tel: 225-477; fax: 225-262).

Other useful addresses
Island Development Company (IDC), PO Box 638, New Port, Victoria (tel: 224-640; fax: 224-467).

Public Utilities Corporation (PUC) (Electricity), PO Box 174, Victoria (tel: 322-444; fax: 321-020). (Water) Unity House, PO Box 34, Victoria (tel: 322-444; fax: 322-127).

RTS Radio, PO Box 321, Union Vale, Victoria (tel: 224-161).

RTS TV, PO Box 321, Hermitage, Mahé (tel: 224-161).

Seychelles Agricultural Development Company Ltd., PO Box 172, Victoria (tel: 276-618).

Seychelles Broadcasting Corporation, Hermitage, PO Box 321, Victoria (tel: 224-161; fax: 224-641).

Seychelles Embassy (USA), Suite 400C, 800 Second Avenue, New York, NW, 10017 (tel: (+1-202) 972-1785; fax: (+1-202) 972-1786; e-mail: seychelles@un.int).

Seychelles Fishing Authority (SFA), PO Box 449, Victoria (tel: 224-521; fax: 224-508).

Seychelles Industrial Development Corporation (SIDEC), PO Box 537, Victoria (tel: 224-941; fax: 225-121).

Seychelles International Business Authority (SIBA), PO Box 991, Central Bank Building, Victoria (tel: 225-402; fax: 225-851).

Seychelles Licensing Authority, PO Box 3, Francis Rachel Street, Victoria (tel: 224-314; fax: 224-256).

Seychelles Marketing Board, PO Box 516, Victoria (tel: 224-444).

Seychelles National Statistics Bureau, PO Box 206, Victoria, (internet: www.seychelles.net/misdstat).

Seychelles Timber Company, Grand Anse, Mahe (tel: 278-343).

State Assurance Corporation ofSeychelles, Pirate's Arms Building, PO Box 636, Victoria (tel: 225-000; fax: 224-495).

Internet sites

Africa Business Network: www.ifc.org/abn

AllAfrica.com: http://allafrica.com

African Development Bank: www.afdb.org

Africa Online: www.africaonline.com

Mbendi AfroPaedia (information on companies, countries, industries and stock exchanges in Africa): http://mbendi.co.za

Seychelles Nation online: www.nation.sc

Sierra Leone

Sierra Leone is one of the poorest countries in the world with GDP per capita of just US$326.

In 2011 the UN Human Development Index (HDI) ranked Sierra Leone 180 out of 187 countries for national development in health, education and income. In 2010, 57 per cent of the population experienced at least one indicator of poverty, while 62.8 per cent lived on the equivalent of US$1.25 per day.

The civil war, which was officially declared as ended in 2002, had blighted the education of a generation and in 2010, 59.1 per cent of the adult population were illiterate. Although Sierra Leone's status as a poor country remains, it has a better record than other poor countries for education, despite its chronic shortage of trained teachers. In 2001 primary school enrolment ratio was 39 per cent boys; 34 per cent girls (Unicef 2004); between 2005–09 primary school net enrolment/attendance was 69 per cent (Unicef 2010).

The life expectancy of a Sierra Leonean born in 2011 is 47.8 years, which is 16.4 years less than its near neighbour Ghana, ranked eighth in sub-Saharan Africa's HDI. In 2011, the Kissy United Methodist Church Eye Hospital (known as Sarolla) treated 11,888 patients and performed over 1,800 eye surgeries, including 840 for cataract, 81 for glaucoma (Sarolla is one of just two hospitals in Sierra Leone to undertake such operations).

The economy

The *African Economic Outlook 2011* (AEO) report, published jointly by the African Development Bank and the Organisation for Economic Co-operation and Development, notes that having recorded 4.5 per cent in 2010, growth is projected to rise to 5.1 for 2011 and to gradually recover to 6.0 per cent in 2012. The medium-term outlook for the Sierra Leonean economy is positive, but even more could be done on the structural reform side to help bring the country on a path of high growth and the job creation needed for significant improvements in people's living standards. Growth is being driven by exports of minerals and cash crops due to the global recovery, the expansion of the service sector, increased agricultural productivity, and continued investment in infrastructure. The recent completion of the Bumbuna power station has already started to yield benefits. The government has undertaken key reforms (for instance, in the financial sector, tax reforms) that will bring benefits only later, but which bode well for the country's future.

Even though Sierra Leone weathered the economic crisis well, the 6 per cent growth forecast for 2012 will still be below pre-crisis growth rates. This points to the need for further growth acceleration if the country is to overcome its economic fragility and reduce the income gap with more advanced economies. Macro-economic policies can help in this regard by gradually moving towards a rule-based, counter-cyclical framework; and making achievement of high growth a key policy priority.

Inflation started to decline in 2011 after rising to 18 per cent in September 2010 due to fiscal expansion and the one-off effect from the introduction of goods and service tax (GST). On the supply side, expanded domestic food production is expected to offset rising food prices. Supported by appropriate monetary and fiscal policies and a stabilised nominal exchange rate, average inflation is expected to decline to upper single digits in 2011

KEY FACTS

Official name: Republic of Sierra Leone

Head of State: President Ernest Bai Koroma (APC) (elected 8 Sep 2007)

Head of government: President Ernest Bai Koroma

Ruling party: All People's Congress (APC) (elected 11 Aug 2007)

Area: 72,325 square km

Population: 5.75 million (2010)*

Capital: Freetown

Official language: English

Currency: Leone (Le) = 100 cents

Exchange rate: Le4,406.02 per US$ (Oct 2011)

GDP per capita: US$326 (2010)

GDP real growth: 5.00% (2010)

GDP: US$1.91 billion (2010)

Inflation: 17.80% (2010)

Balance of trade: -US$373.00 million (2010)

* estimated figure

and ease further by the end of 2012. Additional pressures to raise public sector wages, a weakening of the exchange rate, and higher than expected increases in food and fuel prices constitute the main risks to the inflation outlook.

Rich pickings

Many foreign interests look at Sierra Leone as a potential source of (mutual) benefit and it isn't too surprising to find evidence of illegal mining and diamond smuggling and outright corruption. In 2011, the forestry ministry said that if illegal logging, which is denuding forests and is the major source of environmental degradation, was not stopped all forests could be lost by 2018. President Koroma banned exports of timber and increased the powers of the Anti-corruption Commission-Sierra Leone (ACC-SL) to include arrest and prosecution of suspects.

Legitimate mining has benefits, with around a quarter of taxes levied on diamond production reinvested in mining communities to provide social assets such as schools and roads, as well as co-operatives to help miners market their finds. In 2010 mining constituted over 90 per cent of exports, mostly comprising artesian diamonds. Rutile, bauxite and kimberlite mines have resumed operations since the end of the civil war and other mines are expected to start again before 2013.

The International Monetary Fund (IMF) has noted that legal mining of iron ore could give Sierra Leone an estimated GDP growth rate of 51.4 per cent in 2012, the highest in the world.

In 2009 oil was discovered offshore, in the deep waters of Sierra Leone-Liberian basin, with up to two billion barrels of oil possible – however, commercial production is still several years off. Sierra Leone also has other natural resources such as timber, fresh water and offshore fishing grounds.

Conservation model

The Gola Forest National Park, in the south-east of Sierra Leone, was established in 2010 and was opened by President Koroma on 3 December 2011 as part of the cross-border 'Trans-boundary Peace Park' with Liberia. The park, of 74,800 hectares, is the last intact rainforest in the Upper Guinea Area and the project was inaugurated to create unity between the two countries.

The park is also recognised as a potentially valuable source of funds for conservation projects. It is intended to be a model for achieving a sustainable habitat for all living within its boundary. However, within weeks of the park's opening one of the seven communities living within it announced they plan to sue their hereditary chief for leasing their traditional land, in April 2011, to the UK-owned mining company Sable Mining. A spokesperson for the park said it was a case of a local man duping a foreign company, while the government issued a statement saying all sale of land and mining in the state forest is illegal.

Civil society

Presidential and parliamentary elections are scheduled for 1 August 2012 and politicians were already canvassing though most of 2011. Former junta leader (in 1996), Julius Maada Bio (Sierra Leone People's Party (SLPP)) declared his candidacy for president. Incumbent, Ernest Bai Koroma (All People's Congress (APC)) will be the man to beat.

The on-going devolution of state functions to local government will enhance the role of the mayor and councillors and make them more clearly defined, with educational qualifications required to undertake the role. Local councils were re-introduced in 2004, but after so long out of use (they were abolished in 1972) the role of councillors became misunderstood, so that by 2010 most people looked on them as patrons of a community, to be used as a sponsor for largess. While the process was supposed to be undertaken from 2004 progress has been slow, focussing on primary health, education and agriculture.

Risk assessment

Economy	Developing
Politics	Fair
Regional stability	Fair

KEY INDICATORS — Sierra Leone

	Unit	2006	2007	2008	2009	2010
Population	m	*5.59	*5.74	*5.80	*5.89	*5.75
Gross domestic product (GDP)	US$bn	1.42	1.66	1.95	1.88	1.91
GDP per capita	US$	254	290	332	311	326
GDP real growth	%	7.4	6.4	5.5	3.2	5.0
Inflation	%	9.5	11.7	14.8	9.2	17.8
Industrial output	% change	–	–	2.0	-2.0	–
Agricultural output	% change	–	–	6.1	6.6	–
Exports (fob) (goods)	US$m	244.0	292.9	270.3	270.4	362.9
Imports (fob) (goods)	US$m	363.0	395.4	511.9	511.9	735.9
Balance of trade	US$m	-119.0	-102.6	-241.5	-241.5	-373.0
Current account	US$m	-51.0	-57.0	-290.1	291.0	-482.9
Total reserves minus gold	US$m	183.9	216.6	220.2	405.0	409.0
Foreign exchange	US$m	154.7	185.8	189.7	215.3	224.8
Exchange rate	per US$	2,970.11	2,989.20	3,330.71	3,946.00	3,978.10

* estimated figure

COUNTRY PROFILE

Historical profile

1787 The state was founded by the British as a homeland for freed slaves.

1808 Freetown became a British colony. Over the following 60 years around 70,000 ex-slaves arrived in the country, mainly in the Freetown area. The colonial authorities appointed non-indigenous Africans to the civil service and senior administrative positions, thus laying the foundation for future civil strife.

1954 Sierra Leone was allowed some degree of self-rule through a new local administration. Sir Milton Margai of the Sierra Leone People's Party (SLPP) was appointed the head of the newly-established administration.

1961 Sierra Leone gained independence from Britain in April, but remained part of the Commonwealth. Sir Milton Margai became the country's first prime minister.

1964 Following Sir Milton's death, his half-brother, Sir Albert Margai, was appointed prime minister.

1967 The All Peoples Congress (APC) won the parliamentary election, its leader, Siaka Stevens, was appointed prime minister. Sierra Leonean military officers staged a coup.

1968 After an army revolt, Stevens and the APC returned to government.

1971 Sierra Leone became a republic. Stevens was appointed as the country's first president.

1978 A new constitution established one-party rule with the APC as the only legal party.
1985 Stevens retired, Major General Joseph Momoh became president.
1991 Rebels opposed to the Momoh government – principally the Revolutionary United Front (RUF) led by Foday Sankoh – launched a series of attacks, which took much of the eastern part of the country. They were backed by Liberia.
1992 A coup brought Captain Valentine Strasser to power. He presided over a military government, which suspended the constitution and ruled by decree.
1996 Strasser was deposed by Brigadier Julius Bio. Multi-party elections ended four years of military rule. Ahmed Tejan Kabbah (SLPP) became president.
1997 Major Johnny-Paul Koroma led a coup and ousted Kabbah, who went into exile. The Armed Forces Revolutionary Council (ARFC) was installed, backed by the RUF. International sanctions were imposed. The Economic Community of West African States (Ecowas) dispatched a peace-keeping force – Ecowas Monitoring Group (Ecomog) – in order to reinstate the government of President Kabbah. A peace accord was reached in October.
1998 Ecomog launched a military offensive against the AFRC after Koroma showed no sign of implementing the 1997 agreement and stepping down from power. Ecomog ejected the AFRC from Freetown and Kabbah returned to Sierra Leone. The RUF remained in control of large areas outside the capital. The civilian population in rebel held territories were subjected to brutal treatment, with limb amputations meted out to victims of all ages.
1999 RUF rebels counter-attacked the capital and were finally driven off after weeks of fierce fighting. Liberia was accused of supporting the rebels and trading weapons for diamonds, mined in rebel territories. The government and the RUF signed a peace agreement, allowing for the deployment of UN peace-keeping forces.
2000 Foday Sankoh condemned the presence of UN forces in the country. The UN reported that civilians continued to be mutilated, raped and abducted in rebel held areas. RUF rebels clashed with UN troops when they were required to disarm. Over 13,000 UN troops held a limited peace in the south while British paratroopers trained government forces. Under a UK plan, several thousand British troops arrived to stabilise President Kabbah's regime. Sankoh was captured in Freetown where he had been hiding for weeks. Within two months, Britain withdrew most of its forces leaving a contingent to continue training local government forces.
2001 Military operations continued to push into lawless regions of the country and restore civil society. Legislative and presidential elections were postponed due to the unstable security situation.
2002 The 11-year civil war was officially declared ended and state of emergency measures were lifted. Ahmad Tejan Kabbah (SLPP) won a landslide victory as president. The SLPP won the parliamentary elections.
2003 Agriculture production recovered to pre-war levels, as many people displaced during the civil war returned to their homes. Rebel leader Foday Sankoh died of natural causes while awaiting trial for war crimes.
2004 The first local elections in more than three decades were held. A war crimes court, staffed by senior US legal personnel, began taking evidence for a court mandated for three years and empowered to 'arrest, try and convict' those accused of war crimes.
2005 The UN agreed that Charles Taylor should be handed over to Sierra Leone to stand trial for war crimes perpetrated by Sierra Leone insurgents he had supported while he was Liberian president. The last UN-troops withdrew.
2006 Former Liberian president Charles Taylor was flown from his exile in Nigeria to Freetown, where he was wanted for war crimes and his alleged role in Sierra Leone's civil war. Taylor was transferred to stand trial in the International Court of Justice (ICJ) in The Hague (The Netherlands). The transfer was made possible after the UK agreed to provide detention facilities if Taylor was convicted. In a deal with creditors, around 90 per cent of Sierra Leone's debt, worth about US$1.64 billion, was written off following measures undertaken to stabilise the economy, tackle poverty and improve governance, with reforms in the economy, health, education and government administration. External debt was reduced to around US$110 million.
2007 The Paris Club of creditors forgave a further US$218 million of Sierra Leone's debt. The World Bank advised that the money which would have been spent on debt servicing should be spent on 'legitimate things for the people'. The vital Mano River Bridge, connecting Sierra Leone with Liberia, was officially re-opened. In general elections the opposition APC won 59 seats (out of 112), the SLPP 43. After two rounds in the presidential election, Ernest Bai Koroma (APC) won 54.6 per cent and Solomon Berewa (SLPP) won 45.5 per cent.
2009 A special international court (modelled on the Second World War Nuremberg tribunal) convicted three men of the RUF – 'Interim Leader' Issa Hassan Sesay, former commander Morris Kallon and Chief of Security Augustine Gbao – of war crimes including murder, rape, enforced recruiting of child soldiers, sexual slavery and the mutilating of limbs, which took place under their leadership during the civil war.
2010 In March, two senior officers of the defence ministry were indicted for corruption in the country's first major criminal case against corrupt officials. They were convicted, fined and imprisoned. On 12 August, the Sierra Leonean Human Rights Commission called for the uncut diamonds that Charles Taylor had given to fashion model Naomi Campbell at a party in South Africa and which she had given to aid the Nelson Mandela Children's Fund, to be returned to benefit the people of Sierra Leone. UN sanctions, including a ban on diamond exports and an arms embargo, imposed in 1998 were lifted in September. On 15 November a new offshore oil field discovery was announced by the Spanish oil company, Repsol.
2011 Former junta leader (1996), Julius Maada Bio (Sierra Leone People's Party (SLPP)) declared his candidacy for the 2012 presidential elections to be held on 1 August.

Political structure

Constitution

The 1991 referendum, adopting a multi-party parliamentary system, based on the US model, was amended in 2002, and introduced the District Block System (DBS) for voting.

Independence date

27 April 1961

Form of state

Unitary republic

The executive

Executive power is vested in the president, who is both Head of State and head of government. The president is directly elected for up to two, five-year terms. The president appoints ministers, approved by parliament. The cabinet is composed of ministers who are answerable to the president.

National legislature

The unicameral Parliament (sometimes referred to as the House of Representatives) has 124 members, of which 112 are elected in multi-seat constituencies by proportional representation from party lists – with a threshold of 12.5 per cent necessary for any constituency. The remaining 12 members are indirectly elected paramount chiefs. All members serve for five-year terms.

Legal system

It is based on English law and is composed of a Supreme Court, Appeals Court and a High Court.

A special war crimes court, operating under Sierra Leonean law, was set up in 2004 to try those accused of heinous war crimes.

Last elections

11 August 2007 (parliamentary); 11 August/8 September 2007 (presidential)

Results: Presidential: (first round) Ernest Bai Koroma (APC) won 44.3 per cent of the vote; Solomon E Berewa (SLPP) 38.3 per cent; Charles F Margai (People's Movement for Democratic Change (PMDC)) 13.9 per cent. In second round, Koroma won 54.6 per cent of the vote, Berewa won 45.5 per cent. Turnout 68.1 per cent.

Parliamentary: the APC won 59 seats (out of 112), the SLPP 43, the People's Movement for Democratic Change (PMDC) 10.

Next elections

2012 (presidential and legislative)

Political parties

Ruling party

All People's Congress (APC) (elected 11 Aug 2007)

Main opposition party

Sierra Leone People's Party (SLPP)

Population

5.75 million (2010)*

Last census: December 2004: 4,963,298 (provisional)

Population density: 66 inhabitants per square km. Urban population: 37 per cent (1995–2001).

Annual growth rate: 2.6 per cent 1994–2004 (WHO 2006)

Ethnic make-up

African groups: Temne (30 per cent), Mende (30 per cent), others (20 per cent)); Creole (Krio) (descendants of freed Jamaican slaves settled in the Freetown area in the late-18th century) (10 per cent); refugees from Liberia's civil war and small numbers of Europeans, Lebanese, Pakistanis and Indians.

Religions

Islam (60 per cent), indigenous beliefs (30 per cent), Christian (10 per cent).

Education

Government plans to increase primary school enrolment and to reduce the gender gap in education has only been under way since 2001 and while enrolment levels are rising the gender gap has also widened. The civil conflict has left about 50 per cent of primary schools functioning in inadequate accommodation. Unicef is assisting in the provision of teaching and learning materials and teacher training, it is also funding the Complementary Rapid Education for Primary Schools (CREPS) programme, designed to enable over-aged children to complete the primary school programme.

Primary education begins at aged six and lasts for six years. Junior secondary school lasts for three years. Students who are successfully may progress to the senior secondary school for a further three years and then onto university.

The University of Sierra Leone is the only institute of higher learning.

Literacy rate: 36 per cent (2004)

Compulsory years: Six to 12.

Enrolment rate: Primary school net enrolment/attendance was 69 per cent; 2005–09 (Unicef 2010).

Health

UN programmes aid the healthcare system to improve the country's ranking in the Human Development Index which is only one higher than Niger which, in 2005, is the lowest ranking. Around 70 per cent of the population lives below the poverty line.

Technical aid, rehabilitation and funding will be provided through a four-year programme (2004–07), including measures to improve water sources and sanitation and HIV/Aids education and prevention.

Donor support will have to be sustained over the long-term to cope with the ongoing rehabilitating of civil war amputees.

In April 2010, a new healthcare programme was launched providing treatment free of charge for pregnant women, breast-feeding mothers and children under the age of five years.

HIV/Aids

Aids has killed between two to three times more people than during the civil war, yet has received relatively little attention.

Around 68,000 people are infected with HIV/Aids, 3,300 of them are under 15-years-old. Since the beginning of the epidemic, over 56,000 children have lost their mother or both parents. The spread of the disease is due to a low prevelance of condom use.

HIV prevalence: 0.9 per cent adult population (government statistic)

The Global Fund to Fight HIV/Aids, Tuberculosis and Malaria states government statistic significantly underestimates the prevalence rate and puts the figure closer to 3.4 per cent generally, and 5 per cent in Freetown. An international medical charity that undertook a study in Freetown in 2004 found a prevalence rate of 4.6 per cent among prenatal women, a typically non-risk group, which suggests the prevalence rate could be higher even than the Global Funds' estimation.

In 2005 the government announced that it would undertake a nationwide survey to provide 'baseline information' about HIV/Aids in Sierra Leone.

Life expectancy: 39 years, 2004 (WHO 2006)

Fertility rate/Maternal mortality rate: 6.5 births per woman, 2004 (WHO 2006); maternal mortality, 1,800 per 100,000 live births (Unicef 2004).

Birth rate/Death rate: 44 births per 1,000 population; 20.7 deaths per 1,000 population (2003).

Child (under 5 years) mortality rate (per 1,000): 166 per 1,000 live births (World Bank)

Head of population per physician: 0.03 physicians per 1,000 people, 2004 (WHO 2006)

Main cities

Freetown (capital, estimated population 1.1 million in 2004), Koidu (113,700), Makeni (110,700), Bo (82,400).

Languages spoken

English is the main medium for business. Mende is spoken principally in the south, Temne in the north and Krio (English-based Creole) is spoken by 10 per cent of the population and understood by 95 per cent.

Official language/s

English

Media

Press

Dailies: In English, main newspapers are *Concord Times* (www.concordtimessl.com), *Standard Times Press* (http://standardtimespress.net) and *Awoko* (www.awoko.org), *Awareness Times* (http://awarenesstimes.com) and Christian Monitor (www.christian-monitor.org).

Weeklies: Weeklies include *New Sierra Leonean*, *Vision* and *Weekend Spark*.

Business: The Ministry of Information and Broadcasting publishes the quarterly *Sierra Leone Trade Journal*.

Broadcasting

Radio: The government-owned Sierra Leone Broadcasting Service (SLBS) broadcasts in English, French and local languages. There are several private stations operating in the Freetown area, including Sky FM, Kiss Fm, Radio Democracy (run by the UN) and Voice of the Handicapped (set up for the disabled, injured during the civil war, but attracting a wider audience). International broadcast from RFI and BBC can be received.

Television: There are two commercial TV stations (mainly received in Freetown area) operated by SLBS and ABC TV.

News agencies

The African Press Agency (ww.apanews.net) and Panapress (www.panapress.com) provide information from Sierra Leone.

Economy

The economy is still dependent on its agricultural base, which although primarily subsistence farming, constituted 51.4 per

cent of GDP in 2009; the services sector comprised 26.6 per cent and industry 22.1 per cent. The extraction industry consists of mining large quantities of alluvial diamonds, plus deposits of other valuable minerals such as rutile, bauxite, gold and iron ore. Sierra Leone's mining sector is of vital importance to bringing in foreign exchange. Before 1995 and the beginning of a series of civil wars, when its rutile (titanium ore) and bauxite operations closed down, the sector used to contribute around 20 per cent of GDP. In 2010 mining constituted over 90 per cent of exports, mostly artesian diamonds. Rutile, bauxite and kimberlite mines have resumed operations and other mines are expected to start again before 2013.
Sierra Leone also has other natural resources such as timber, fresh water and offshore fishing grounds; its agricultural products include coffee, palm oil, cassava and rice and livestock
Since 2002, when the civil war ended, the economy has recovered, albeit from a low base, with GDP growth peaking at 9.7 per cent in 2004, but which fell steadily after this. In 2007, GDP growth was 6.4 per cent, falling to 5.5 per cent in 2008, and further still to 3.2 per cent in 2009 at the depth of the global economic slump, as monetary inflows were curtailed. Inflation has been historically high and long-term, but it dropped briefly below double digits to 9.5 per cent in 2006, but rising again in 2007 to 11.7 per cent and then 14.8 per cent in 2008, when energy and food prices were at a record highs; in 2009 inflation dropped to 9.2 per cent as prices stabilised, returning to a high of 17.8 per cent in 2010.
In 2011, the UN Human Development Index (HDI) ranked Sierra Leone180 (out of 187) for national development in health, education and income. In 2010, 57 per cent of the population experienced at least one indicator of poverty, while 62.79 per cent lived on the equivalent of US$1.25 per day. To promote growth and reduce poverty the government has focused on six key areas: state security, a sustainable fiscal position, raising domestic savings and investment, increasing infrastructure, agricultural and rural development and promoting the private sector.
Diamond exports are the largest foreign exchange earner, with annual production estimated at between US$250–300 million, despite losses through illegal smuggling activities. Around a quarter of taxes levied on diamond production is reinvested in mining communities to provide social assets such as schools and roads, as well as co-operatives to help miners market their finds.
The economy is broadly open and the government is attempting to attract direct foreign investment (FDI) through the sale of state-owned financial, utility, commercial and transport entities. FDI was US$86.6 million in 2010, down from a high of US$96.6 million in 2007. Because outright sale of national assets might be unpalatable to the majority of Sierra Leoneans, the government proposed incremental privatisation, with management contracts offered along with public/private partnerships. Sierra Leone has one of the worst rates of gross domestic savings in Africa and much remains to be done to encourage a reversal in this pattern.
In 2009, oil was discovered offshore in Sierra Leone waters, possibly up to two billion barrels of oil. However, commercial production is several years off.

External trade

Sierra Leone is a member of the Economic Community of West African States (Ecowas), which was set up to promote economic integration among members. It has a customs union with Liberia and Guinea.
Mining natural resources provides the majority of export earnings with gem-quality diamonds being paramount. Diamond exports, up to 2007, were officially reported to be a record breaking 449,988 carats, worth US$102 million, with an estimated US$175 million due for the year. Exports of rutile (titanium ore) and bauxite resumed in 2005. Cash crops, coffee, cocoa and palm oil, are exported to Europe.

Imports

Principal imports are foodstuffs (typically over 30 per cent of total value), machinery and vehicles, manufactured goods, fuels and lubricants, building materials, cloths and textiles.
Main sources: China (typically 10 per cent of total), Côte d'Ivoire (9 per cent), US (8.0 per cent).

Exports

Commodity exports include diamonds, rutile, bauxite, coffee, cocoa, fish and live animals.
Main destinations: Belgium (typically 40 per cent of total), US (23 per cent), France (6 per cent).

Agriculture

The civil war seriously disrupted agricultural activity, destroying the homes and livelihood of many farming families. This will impact on food security for a number of years to come.
The agricultural sector contributes around 50 per cent to GDP and employs 65–75 per cent of labour force. Many young people have left rural areas since 2002 to find work in the cities.
Area under cultivation is approximately 25 per cent of the total land area. It is limited by a traditional land tenure system and is mostly in the hands of smallholders engaged in subsistence farming.
Major cash export crops are cocoa, coffee, palm kernels and ginger. Despite government efforts towards self-sufficiency, rice imports have risen. Other food crops include maize, cassava, sweet potatoes and sorghum.
Production has been hampered by poor infrastructure, a lack of incentives and a poor marketing and distribution system.

Fishing

The fishing sector has two distinct patterns. Coastal fishing, undertaken by men, is commercially driven with catches either sold fresh or preserved for transport inland. Inland fishing is performed by women and largely for private consumption.
While coastal fishing fleets have contracted over the 2000s production has risen.
The majority of vessels harvest shrimps.

Forestry

The majority of timber production is used as domestic fuel.
The Gola Forest Reserve, on the eastern border with Liberia, was designated as a national park. In 2008, the government re-imposed an export ban on timber. It accused foreign companies, in particular Chinese loggers, of plundering the country's timber assets and causing serious soil erosion. The ban will be lifted when a policy that benefits local communities and re-planting has been achieved.

Industry and manufacturing

The industrial sector accounts for around 30 per cent of GDP and employs 5 per cent of the workforce.
The sector is mainly limited to food processing and light manufacturing of consumer goods such as cigarettes, alcoholic beverages, plastic footwear, nails, paint and confectionery. Emphasis is placed on import substitution industries, but attempts to establish heavy industry have met with only limited success and have been undermined by political instability.
Expansion is limited by weak local demand, power shortages, foreign exchange shortages and low investment.

Tourism

The country has much to offer with a diverse landscape and friendly people although continued peace is paramount.
The main foreign investors in Sierra Leone's tourist sector are Chinese companies who see the opportunities for refurbished and new tourist attractions as sound investments. A US$266 million ocean-front tourism complex with holiday homes, golf course and five-star hotel,

was signed in 2004. Another US$270 million invested in various hotels developments is expected to help set off a tourism boom.

Mining

The mining sector contributes around 35 per cent to GDP and employs 10 per cent of the workforce.

Diamonds play an essential part in the economy. The government, in an effort to bring artisanal mining into legal and regulated operation and minimise smuggling, has introduced a certification system for exporting diamonds and created a mining community development fund to return a percentage of the taxes back to the local population.

Sierra Leone has one of the world's largest deposits of rutile (a titanium ore). The Sierra Rutile mining operation was closed and damaged during the civil war.

Bauxite mining is also an important sector with large reserves at Sieromco and Port Loko. Production was suspended due to the civil war. Foreign investment is necessary to begin a re-start operation.

Hydrocarbons

All hydrocarbon needs are met by imports.

There are large deposits of oil and natural gas offshore within the West African region, which are not economically viable to extract currently. In November 2010, the US energy company Anadarko Petroleum announced that it had discovered oil offshore in Sierra Leone's territorial waters.

Energy

Total installed electricity generating capacity was 118MW in 2006, mostly from conventional oil-fired thermal power stations.

Around 5 per cent of the population has access to electricity and blackouts are frequent due to the unstable power supply. The Sierra Leone Electricity Company (SLEC) oversees electricity generation and supply.

A 50MW Bumbuna hydroelectric project began construction on the Seli River in 1980s but was halted in the 1990s during the civil war. However, international loans of US$91.8 million, funnelled through the World Bank, allowed building to continue, so that by April 2009 water was being captured, prior to release for production. A stable supply of electricity and a reduction in the unit price of electricity will be the initial benefits of the project.

The government, in an effort to find renewable sources of energy, is considering biomass, of which 656,000 tonnes of crop waste is produced annually, which could produce 2,700 gigawatt hours (gWh); solar photovoltaic for lighting and water pumping; wind power to suit intermittent use and an increase in hydropower. It has been estimated that Senegal could produce 11 terrawatt hours (tWh) a year, given full exploitation of its hydro capacity. There is an extra 50MW capacity by hydropower under construction with another 85MW planned.

The serious energy shortage has forced many citizens to buy personal diesel generators; the majority of the population uses biomass (wood fuel, kerosene and charcoal) for energy.

Banking and insurance

The banking sector has been weakened by war. However, the government has given the central bank power to tighten fiscal controls and prepare some for sale.

The IMF is wary of donor funds that are distributed through local banks, bypassing the close scutiny and anti-corruption measures instituted by the central bank.

It was announced in 2005 that the introduction of the shared currency, the eco, in Sierra Leone, Ghana, Guinea, Nigeria and The Gambia, would be postponed. The currency was proposed to facilitate trade and growth with an ultimate plan to merge it with the CFA franc.

Central bank

Bank of Sierra Leone

Main financial centre

Freetown

Time

GMT

Geography

Sierra Leone – lion mountains, as named by an early Portuguese explorer – lies on the west coast of Africa; Guinea encircles it from the north-west around to the east and Liberia borders it to the south. There is a 400km Atlantic coastline in the west. The Guinea highlands cross the country from the south-east to the north. The tallest peak is Bintimani (1,948 metres) in the Loma Mountains of central Sierra Leone. There are a number of rivers, two of which have estuaries navigable by ocean-going ships, the Jong and the Rokel. The Freetown peninsular is heavily forested, mangrove swamps line the coast with savannah stretching to the once thickly forested central inland that has been largely cleared for agriculture.

Hemisphere

Northern

Climate

Is tropical, with high humidity and rainfall; the dry season is November–April. It is wet for the rest of year. The daily temperature range is 21–32 degrees Celsius, which remains fairly constant throughout the year.

Entry requirements

Passports

Required by all and must be valid for six months beyond date of entry.

Requirements may be subject to change at short notice; contact an embassy or consulate before departure.

Visa

Required by all, and must be obtained in advance. Citizens of Ecowas countries are exempt. Contact the nearest embassy for an application form. All visas require evidence of return/onward passage; tourists must provide evidence of hotel reservations.

Business visitors should include a letter of invitation from a local contact and a letter of introductory from their employer outlining the purpose of the trip, the nature of business and contacts in Sierra Leone. For new business, an applicant must provide evidence of commercial veracity and financial standing.

Currency advice/regulations

The import and export of local currency is limited to Le50,000. Import of foreign currency is unlimited however it must be declared and cash must not exceed US$5,000 (or equivalent); export is limited to the amount declared on arrival.

It is illegal to exchange money anywhere except official exchange facilities at banks and *bureau de change*.

Travellers cheques have very limited use.

Customs

All visitors must complete a customs declaration form on entering the country.

All gem stones require an export licence.

Prohibited imports

Illegal drugs, firearms and explosives, pornography and live animals.

It is illegal to export gold and historical artefacts, live animals, firearms and explosives.

Health (for visitors)

Mandatory precautions

Yellow fever, malaria and cholera vaccination certificates are required.

Advisable precautions

Hepatitis A, tetanus, polio, and typhoid vaccinations. Malaria prophylaxis should be taken. HIV/Aids is prevalent. Water precautions should be taken. There is a rabies risk. Use only well maintained, chlorinated swimming pools to avoid bilharzia. Lassa fever can be contracted in Kenema and the east; seek urgent medical advice for any fever not positively identified as malaria.

Visitors should carry basic medical supplies and any prescription medication necessary. Medical and emergency insurance (to include repatriation) is strongly recommended.

Hotels

Available in Freetown, especially at Lumley Beach, within easy taxi access of the centre of Freetown. Limited availability outside capital. Credit cards accepted only in major hotels and payment required in US dollars. A service charge is usually included in bill.

Credit cards
Not accepted. The government tourist organisation operates an international hotel reservation service that allows pre-payment of hotel accommodation by credit card (see: www.visitsierraleone.org/hotel-reservation.asp).

Public holidays (national)
Fixed dates
1 Jan (New Year's Day), 27 Apr (Independence Day), 25–26 Dec (Christmas).
Variable dates
Eid al Adha (Tabaski), Birth of the Prophet, Good Friday and Easter Monday (Mar/Apr), Eid al Fitr (Korité).
Islamic year 1433 (26 Nov 2011–14 Nov 2012): The Islamic year contains 354 or 355 days, with the result that Muslim feasts advance by 10–12 days against the Gregorian calendar. Dates of feasts vary according to the sighting of the new moon, so cannot be forecast exactly.

Working hours
Banking
Mon–Thu: 0800–1330; Fri: 0800–1400.
Business
Mon–Fri: 0800–1200, 1400–1630.
Government
Mon–Fri: 0800–1230, 1330–1645; close 1500 on Fri.
Shops
Mon–Fri: 0800–1200, 1400–1630; shops open Sat.

Telecommunications
Mobile/cell phones
There are several GSM 900 and 900/1800 services available throughout most of the country.

Electricity supply
230/240V AC, 50 cycles. Voltage fluctuation and power cuts occur.

Social customs/useful tips
Carry some form of identification at all times.
Punctually and business cards are expected.

Security
Sierra Leone has begun to emerge from a brutal civil war and the security situation is improving. Visitors should take care travelling outside the capital at night, as much for the poor state of the roads as any criminal intent.

Getting there
Air
International airport/s: Freetown-Lungi International (FNA), 20km north of city; bar, currency exchange, post office, shops. The airport is on the opposite bank of the Sierra Leone River from Freetown which must be crossed either by helicopter, hovercraft or ferry.
Airport tax: Departure tax US$20, payable in hard currency; transit passengers are exempt.
Surface
Road: There are routes from Conaky (Guinea Republic). Access to Liberia requires a special permit to transit the border region in a private vehicle. The vital Mano River bridge connecting Sierre Leone with Liberia was officially reopened in June.
Water: Regional services run from Guinea and Liberia. International shipping lines that maintain contacts with Sierra Leone may provide passenger services on cargo ships.
Main port/s: Freetown

Getting about
National transport
Public transport is neither reliable nor safe. The heavy rainy season, which lasts for several months between May and November makes travel to outlying areas both difficult and hazardous.
Air: Internal air services were begun in 2006 by Eagle Air, which operates a 17 seat aircraft to Bo, Kenema and Yengema. Information is limited and visitors should contact local travel agents for further details.
Road: Most main roads in Freetown are paved but have potholes; unpaved side streets are generally poor. A major road resurfacing and repair programme in Freetown is slowly improving the quality of roads in the city. Most roads outside Freetown are unpaved. All roads are unlit and many in need of repair.
Buses: Buses in Freetown tend to be overcrowded and unreliable. Regular service Freetown-Kambia, Freetown-Pendembu, Freetown-Makeni-Kabala.
City transport
Public transport, when it exists, is unreliable.
Taxis: Available at the airport and in main towns; fares by negotiation; tipping is not usual. It is considered safer to use taxis that work in conjunction with an hotel.
Buses, trams & metro: There are buses from the airport to the city centre, but the services can be erratic.
Helicopter: Services operate between Freetown and Lungi airport – flight time five minutes.
Ferry: Links Lungi Airport with central Freetown and Lumley Beach area.
Car hire
Car hire is available at relatively high rates. International driving licence required.

BUSINESS DIRECTORY

The addresses listed below are a selection only. While World of Information makes every endeavour to check these addresses, we cannot guarantee that changes have not been made, especially to telephone numbers and area codes. We would welcome any corrections.

Telephone area codes
The international direct dialling code (IDD) for Sierra Leone is +232, followed by area code and subscriber's number:

Freetown	22	Kenema	32

Chambers of Commerce
Sierra Leone Chamber of Commerce, Guma Building, Lamina Sankoh Street, (tel: 226-305; fax: 220-696; e-mail: cocsl@sierratel.sl).

Banking
Bank of Sierra Leone, PO Box 30, Siaka Stevens Street, Freetown (tel: 226-501; fax: 224-764).

First Merchant Bank of Sierra Leone Ltd, Sparta Building, 12 Wilberforce Street, Freetown (tel: 228-493; fax: 228-318).

National Development Bank Ltd, 21/23 Siaka Stevens Street, Freetown (tel: 226-791/2; fax: 224-468).

Rokel Commercial Bank (Sierra Leone) Ltd, PO Box 12, 25-27 Stevens Street, Freetown (tel: 222-501; fax: 222-563).

Sierra Leone Commerical Bank Ltd, 29-31 Siaka Stevens Street, Freetown (tel: 225-264; fax: 225-292).

Standard Chartered Bank Sierra Leone Ltd, PO Box 1155, 9 -11 Lightfoot Boston Street, Freetown (tel: 226-220, 225-021; fax: 225-760).

Union Trust Bank Ltd, 2 Howe Street, Freetown (tel: 222-792, 226-954; fax: 226-214).

Central bank
Bank of Sierra Leone, Siaka Stevens Street, Freetown (tel: 226-501; fax: 224-764; e-mail: info@bankofsierraleone.org).

Travel information
Astraeus (charter flights) Astraeus House, Faraday Court, Faraday Road, Crawley, West Sussex, RH10 9PU (tel:

(+44) 1293-819800; fax: (+4 4) 1293-819832; internet: www.flyastraeus.com).

BMED (airline), Hetherington House, Bedfont Road, Heathrow Airport, Middlesex TW19 7NL (tel: (+44-20) 8630-4212; fax: (+44-20) 8630-4007; internet: www.flybmed.com).

Freetown International Airport, 15 Rawdon Street, Freetown (tel: 223-881; fax: 224-653; internet: www.freetownairport.org).

Ministry of tourism
Ministry of Tourism and Culture, Stadium Hostel, Syke Street, Freetown (tel: 241-256).

National tourist organisation offices
National Tourist Board of Sierra Leone, Room 100, Cape Sierra Hotel, Aberdeen; PO Box 1435, Freetown (tel: 236-620; fax: 236-621; email: info@welcometosierraleone.org or mailto:ntbslinfo@yahoo.com; internet: www.welcometosierraleone.org).

Ministries

Department of Finance, Secretariat Building, George Street, Freetown (tel: 26-911, 22-211; fax: 28-355).

Ministry of Information and Broadcasting, Youyi Building, Brookfields, Freetown.

Ministry of Tourism and Culture, Wallace Johnson Street, Freetown (tel: 26-345, 24-776).

Ministry of Trade and Industry, Ministerial Building, George Street, Freetown (tel: 26-045, 22-755, 22-706; fax: 28-373).

Other useful addresses

Central Statistics Office, Tower Hill, Freetown (tel: 223-897, 224-267).

National Trading Co, Howe Street, Freetown (tel: 223-986, 226-179).

Sierra Leone Embassy (USA), 1701 19th Street, NW, Washington DC 20009 (tel: (+1-202) 939-9261; fax: (+1-202) 483-1793; e-mail: fsec@embassyofsierraleone.org; internet: www.sierra-leone.org).

Sierra Leone Export Debelopment and Investment Corp, 18/20 Walpole Street; Private Mail Bag 6, Freetown (tel: 229-760, 227-604; fax: 229-097; email: info@sledic-sl.org; internet: sledic-sl.org).

SierraTel, Wallace Johnson Street, Freetown (tel: 222-801, 224-591).

Sierra Leone High Commission (UK), 245 Oxford Street, London W1D 2LX (tel: (+44-20) 7287-9884; fax: (+44-20) 7734-3822; e-mail: info@slhc-uk.org.uk; internet: www.slhc-uk.org.uk).

Sierra Leone Ports Authority, PO Box 386, Freetown.

The Chief Immigration Officer, Rawdon Street, Freetown (tel 227-174; fax: 224-761).

Internet sites

Africa Business Network: www.ifc.org/abn

African Development Bank: www.afdb.org

AllAfrica.com: http://allafrica.com

Africa Online: www.africaonline.com

Mbendi AfroPaedia (information on companies, countries, industries and stock exchanges in Africa): http://mbendi.co.za

Sierra Leone: www.sierra-leone.org

Sierra Leone government: www.sierraleone.gov.sl

Singapore

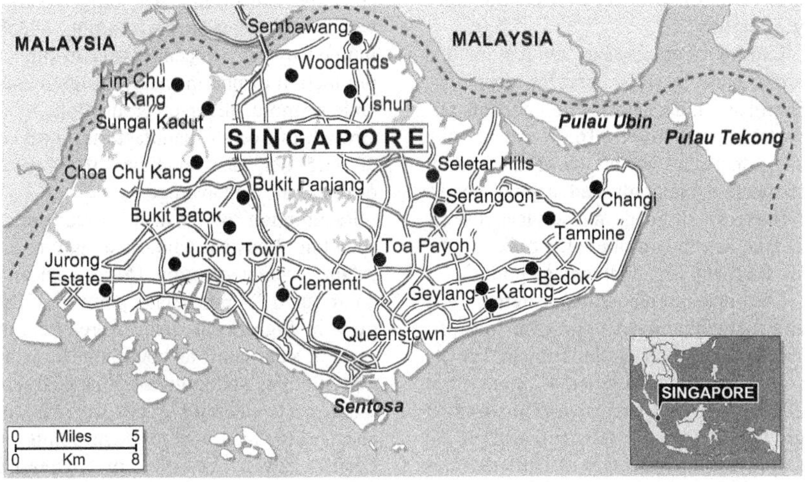

After Monaco (Monte Carlo) Singapore is the most densely populated country on earth, with 7,315 inhabitants per square mile. Traditionally, Singaporeans had as much physical space within which to operate as they did political as the People's Action Party (PAP) kept the island's inhabitants to its rather strait-laced interpretation of the true path.

PAP fatigue

August 2011 saw the end of over 40 years of obedient acceptance by Singapore's electorate of the PAP hegemony. The presidential election saw voters give the PAP a sharp kick in the backside. Tony Tan, the PAP candidate safely counting on the support of Prime Minister Lee Hsien Loong just managed to scrape home with a margin of less than 8,000 votes over his principal rival, Tan Cheng Bock. In little more than three months, the PAP, which has governed the island state since 1959, had seen its so-called popularity plummet. In the May 2011 parliamentary elections the PAP had secured just over 60 per cent of the vote, its lowest return since Singapore split with Malaysia in 1965. Worryingly for the PAP, the three non-PAP candidates in the presidential election collectively polled more votes than the PAP.

Confirmed as president for a period of six years, Mr Tan – who had been the favourite to win the election – could reflect on Singapore's clear entry into a new, multi-party era. Singapore's Presidency is a non-executive position, but with the power of veto over how the country's foreign reserves are managed and over budgetary dispositions. The president also has some say in the appointment of high level public officials. The writing that the two 2011 elections placed firmly on the wall was that Singapore could no longer be governed in the same authoritarian way as the past, even though the rigid governments of the past had turned Singapore into one of the world's wealthiest and most developed countries.

The election results suggested that previous governments, in their obsession with creating and investing their citizens' wealth, had overlooked the social problems that these policies were generating. Singapore's citizenry were faced with continually rising prices, unaffordable property prices alongside an increasing immigrant population and growing gap between the country's wealthiest and its growing middle class.

The Obedient Wives Club

One event that provided an interesting insight into current gender and social perceptions in Singapore was the 2011 establishment of the so-called 'Obedient Wives Club' (OWC), which had already

KEY FACTS

Official name: Repablik Singapura, Xinjiapo Gongheguo, Singapur Kutiyarasu, Republic of Singapore

Head of State: President Tony Tan Keng Yam (from 1 Sep 2011)

Head of government: Prime Minister Lee Hsien Loong (appointed 12 Aug 2004; re-elected 7 May 2011)

Ruling party: People's Action Party (PAP) (since 1965; re-elected 7 May 2011)

Area: 636 square km

Population: 3.77 million (2010)*

Official language: English, Mandarin Chinese, Malay, Tamil.

Currency: Singapore dollar (S$) = 100 cents

Exchange rate: S$1.30 per US$ (Oct 2011)

GDP per capita: US$43,117 (2010)

GDP real growth: 14.50% (2010)

GDP: US$222.70 billion (2010)

Labour force: 1.99 million (2009)

Unemployment: 4.30% (2009)

Inflation: 2.80% (2010)

Balance of trade: US$46.76 billion (2010)

Annual FDI: US$38.64 billion (2010)

* estimated figure

caused controversy when it set up in Malaysia and Indonesia. Singapore's complex racial make-up, comprising ethnic Chinese, Malay and Indian groupings did not respond positively to the arrival of the OWC. The Islamic religious Council of Singapore attacked the OWC as 'myopic' and the Association of Women for Action and Research (Aware) countered that 'What the club (the OWC) signifies is a regression, a moving backwards in what women and other progressive men – Muslim and non-Muslim – are trying to do for gender equality here in Singapore.' Despite the Singaporean democracy's generally authoritarian posture, in mid-2011 a gay and lesbian friendly event entitled Pink Dot attracted an estimated 10,000 supporters including gay Muslim men and women wearing pink hijabs. The event underlined the surprisingly progressive demands and nature of much of Singaporean society.

The economy

Singapore's 2008-09 recession turned out less deep than feared, replaced by a broad-based expansion. Output losses have been recouped and medium term issues are again at the top of Singapore's policy agenda.

The International Monetary Fund (IMF) notes that economic activity started to shrink in the second quarter of 2008. At its low mark a year later, GDP was 9 per cent lower than pre-crisis. The output recovery has been as swift as the contraction. Growth has been double-digit for three of the last four quarters, reaching nearly 39 per cent (quarter-on-quarter, seasonally adjusted annualised rate) in the first quarter of 2011. Price dynamics have mirrored those of output.

This open economy rebounded to the scorching pace of 14.5 per cent in 2010. Export-oriented manufacturing and financial services rode the global recovery in trade and investment. Growth was particularly strong in the first half of 2010, given the low base set by the contraction a year earlier.

Exports of goods and services in real terms grew by 19.2 per cent, driven by chemicals and electronic components and parts. Imports rose by 16.6 per cent, with sharp increases in imports of raw and intermediate materials and capital goods. Net exports of goods and services rose by 38 per cent to contribute the bulk of total GDP growth (10.5 percentage points).

The impact of rebounding external trade and manufacturing spilled over into private consumption and investment. Private consumption increased by 4.2 per cent in 2010, adding 1.6 percentage points to total growth. A stronger labour market lifted employment and wages. Visitor arrivals jumped by 20.2 per cent, helping to fuel a 7.1 per cent rise in retail sales in real terms.

Fixed investment increased by 5.1 per cent, adding 1.4 percentage points to GDP growth. That reflected public and private sector investment in buildings as well as business investment in machinery, equipment, and software. Government consumption rose by 11.0 per cent, accounting for 1.2 percentage points of the GDP growth, largely on increased social spending in education, health and public housing.

KEY INDICATORS — Singapore

	Unit	2006	2007	2008	2009	2010
Population	m	4.40	*4.59	*4.66	*4.66	*3.77
Gross domestic product (GDP)	US$bn	136.57	167.00	181.90	183.30	222.70
GDP per capita	US$	31,028	36,384	38,972	36,112	43,117
GDP real growth	%	8.1	8.8	1.5	-0.8	14.5
Inflation	%	0.9	2.1	6.6	0.6	2.8
Unemployment	%	3.6	3.0	3.2	4.3	3.1
Exports (fob) (goods)	US$m	274,980.0	303,136.0	342,776.0	273,411.0	358,485.0
Imports (fob) (goods)	US$m	230,233.0	254,036.0	316,161.0	243,180.0	311,727.0
Balance of trade	US$m	44,747.0	49,099.0	26,615.0	30,231.0	46,758.0
Current account	US$m	29,765.0	39,209.0	36,011.0	32,628.0	49,558.0
Total reserves minus gold	US$m	136,260.0	162,957.0	174,193.0	187,803.0	225,715.0
Foreign exchange	US$m	135,814.0	162,517.0	173,649.0	186,005.0	223,890.0
Exchange rate	per US$	1.54	1.45	1.41	1.36	1.36

* estimated figure

On the production side, the more export-oriented sectors saw the fastest growth. Manufacturing accounted for nearly half the GDP growth, after contracting in 2008–09. Precision engineering and electronics posted gains of 40 per cent and 35 per cent, respectively, on the back of revitalised export demand for semiconductor-related equipment and consumer electronics. The biggest surge was in biomedical manufacturing, which jumped by 50 per cent owing to higher production of pharmaceutical ingredients and a more diverse production mix. Growth in overall manufacturing peaked at 41.5 per cent in June 2010, on a 6-month moving average basis.

Resumption of growth in consumer spending boosted wholesale and retail trading, which grew by 15 per cent and contributed 2.4 percentage points to GDP growth. Significant gains were seen in sales of such items as household furnishings, clothing and footwear. Financial services accelerated by 12.2 per cent in 2010, accounting for 1.5 percentage points of GDP growth, because of increased non-bank and business lending and expansion by investment banks.

Growth in construction moderated to 6.1 per cent in 2010 from 17.0 per cent in the previous year, as some major public projects were completed. Private construction picked up for housing (due to rising house prices) and for commercial and industrial buildings (benefiting from the economic recovery). Construction contracts awarded to private-sector firms doubled in value in 2010, to US$14 billion.

Services, accounting for 70 per cent of total employment, generated nearly all the new jobs in 2010. The number of people employed rose by 112,500 to 3.1 million. The overall unemployment rate, including foreign workers, declined to 2.2 per cent (3.1 per cent for citizens and permanent residents). The rapidly expanding domestic and external demand was accompanied by a rise in inflation to 4.6 per cent by year-end; inflation averaged 2.8 per cent in 2010. Major causes were an increase in the cost of automobile certificates of entitlement and rising prices for housing, which contributed to higher accommodation costs. Food prices also started to pick up from about April 2010 and by year-end contributed about one-tenth of overall inflation.

The Monetary Authority of Singapore (MAS) tightened its policy stance as recovery took hold and inflation picked up. The MAS sets policy by managing the

Singapore dollar in a band against a basket of currencies by changing the midpoint, slope, or width of the band. In April 2010 it recentered the band, providing more room for the Singapore dollar to appreciate. Later in the year, as the labour market tightened and capacity utilisation rose, the MAS steepened and widened the band, allowing for still further appreciation. During 2010, the currency appreciated by 6.8 per cent against the US dollar. Liquidity in the economy remained high and broad money grew by 8.6 per cent.

In the external accounts, a 31.1 per cent rise in merchandise exports in 2010 outpaced a 27.6 per cent increase in merchandise imports, and the trade surplus rose to US$46.6 billion. Together with the external balances for services and income, the current account surplus climbed to the equivalent of 22.2 per cent of GDP. International reserves rose by about 20 per cent to US$225.7 billion (cover for 6.6 months of goods and services imports).

Economic prospects

Global economic growth, in particular, projected strong expansion in much of Asia, lays the ground for solid growth in Singapore 2011 and next. However, growth in net exports will moderate substantially in 2011 due to base effects and higher imports to support investment. Expected growth of manufacturing suggests that industries, including electronics and biomedical, will need to invest in capacity expansion. Investment will remain strong in construction, given solid demand for residential and commercial buildings and extension of the mass transit rail system.

The low rate of unemployment, however, coupled with a government commitment to restrict the use of low-skilled foreign labour (in moves to raise productivity) will put upward pressure on costs and could act as a drag on some industries.

Retail sales, excluding automobiles, rose by 13.5 per cent in real terms in January 2011. Further growth in incomes and the upward trend in visitor arrivals will continue to stimulate growth in retail sales this year. Monetary policy is expected to tighten further. Strong recovery in 2010 put the economy back on, if not above, its potential output, so that further growth in 2011 is likely to exert pressure on inflation. The monetary authorities will likely consider steepening the slope of the currency's trading band, giving more room for it to appreciate.

Fiscal policy, in contrast, is likely to have a neutral impact on the economy. Operating expenditure in FY2011 (ending 31 March 2012) has been increased to support social spending in education, health and public housing. Growth in development expenditure is budgeted to decelerate, since some transport projects have been completed. The government is making a cash transfer to citizens this year, but the amount is relatively small.

Once these strands are woven, the economy is forecast to grow by 5.5 per cent in 2011, with the potential to surprise on the upside (if a better than expected performance by industrial economies and Asian trading partners materialises). In 2012, growth is forecast to moderate further to 4.8 per cent as the economy returns to its long-run trajectory. Inflation quickened to 5.5 per cent in January 2011, driven by rising costs of transport and housing. It is seen staying relatively high through the first half of 2011 before moderating. Year-average inflation is put at 3.2 per cent, easing in 2012 as the rate of cost increases and imported food and fuel decelerates.

Risks are both on the down- and up-side. As well as the tight domestic labour market that could retard expansion in some industries this year, higher than assumed global commodity prices would hurt manufacturing industry, as would weaker than projected global trade. The impact on supply chains from the March earthquake in Japan is unclear, but Singapore's direct trade with that country is now low (as a proportion of total trade, exports to Japan averaged 5.8 per cent in the past decade, down from 7.4 per cent in the 1990s, while imports declined to an average of 10.5 per cent from 18.0 per cent).

On the upside, a better performance by industrial economies and Singapore's Asian trading partners would likely have a significant impact on this open economy.

Although tested, Singapore's financial system withstood the world recession well. As global market volatility subsided, financial activities staged a rapid recovery beginning in early 2009. Banking and insurance led the way, while brokerage and wealth management were slower in posting gains.

From a historical perspective, Singapore's exit from recession has been more vigorous than those following the 2001 dotcom crash and the 1997-98 Asian crisis. Improved global demand and sentiment as well as strong domestic policies and resilient labour markets have limited the severity of the downturn and set the stage for the expansion underway.

Macroeconomic management started to transition out of crisis relief mode late last year. Policy normalisation has by now been achieved. Monetary, fiscal and macro-prudential policies are appropriately calibrated to sustain the expansion and curb risks in the goods and asset markets. Medium-term issues are again at the top of the policy agenda.

The economy is projected to expand nearly 10 per cent in 2010. Both external and domestic demand should continue to support growth, although the exceptional momentum of the first quarter is bound to wane. As the output gap turns positive, inflation will be trending up, in part because of one off factors.

Risk assessment

Politics	Good
Economy	Good
Regional stability	Good

COUNTRY PROFILE

Historical profile

The Republic of Singapore consists of Singapore Island, where Singapore City is located, and 57 smaller islands. One of these, Pedra Branca (Batu Putih), is claimed by Malaysia.

1819 Sir Stamford Raffles established a trading station in Singapore for the British East India Company. Singapore's free trade policy with no taxation attracted merchants from the entire region. The port captured much of the *entrepôt* trade of the East Indies. During the nineteenth century thousands of immigrant Chinese, Indians, Indonesians and Malays emigrated there.

1824 The Sultan of Johore allowed the British East India Company full control of the territory.

1826 Singapore, Malacca and Penang were incorporated into the Straits Settlements, part of the British East India Company.

1867 The Straits Settlements became a crown colony.

1942 During the Second World War, the island was captured and controlled by the Japanese.

1945 The British regained control of Singapore.

1946 The Straits Settlement dissolved. Penang and Malacca became part of Malaya while Singapore was made into a British Crown Colony.

1954 Lee Kuan Yew founded the People's Action Party (PAP). It attracted a strong following among the poor and the non-English speaking population.

1959 Singapore achieved internal self-government. The PAP won the election and Lee Kuan Yew became the first prime minister. Under his leadership, government opposition was suppressed and

he attracted much international criticism for his authoritarian approach. Nevertheless, Singapore became a financial and industrial powerhouse.
1963 Singapore became a state of the Federation of Malaysia.
1965 The Republic of Singapore was legally declared an independent, sovereign state.
1967 Singapore was a founder member of the Association of Southeast Asian Nations (Asean).
1971 The last British troops were withdrawn from Singapore.
1984 For the first time in Singapore's political history, two opposition MPs were elected to parliament.
1990 Goh Chok Tong took over from Lee Kuan Yew as prime minister.
1993 In the first direct presidential election, Ong Teng Cheong (PAP), secured the post.
1999 Sellapan Ramanathan (S R Nathan) was elected president.
2001 A political rally by parliamentarian J B Jeyaretnam of the Workers' Party of Singapore (WPS) was allowed to take place – the first permitted outside an election period.
2003 The Sars virus infected 206 people and killed 31. A free trade agreement with the US came into effect.
2004 Lee Hsien Loong became prime minister following Goh Chok Tong's retirement.
2005 President S R Nathan was appointed to a second term after all other rivals were disqualified.
2006 The PAP was re-elected. The IMF and World Bank held their annual meeting in Singapore, which earned an unprecedented rebuke for seeking to prevent accredited activists from attending the meeting; Singapore was obliged to abide by its obligations as host nation.
2009 The economy contracted by 19.7 per cent in the first quarter, its highest since records began. New laws were enacted requiring all outdoor gatherings to have a police permit and banning the filming of police officers. The recession eased as the economy expanded at a 20.4 per cent annualised rate.
2010 The constitution was amended in April. A change to the electoral system increased the allowed number of Non-Constituency Members of Parliament (NCMP) from six to nine and gave admittance to parliament of the best-performing, losing parliamentary candidates. In July Nominated MPs (NMP) became a permanent component of parliament, to provide alternative, non-partisan views during debates. In July, Tamasek, the government's sovereign wealth fund, showed an increase in value of 42 per cent as the economy improved following recovery from the global economic crisis; GDP growth was 15 per cent year-on-year for the second quarter of the year. The government announced that investment in research and development would be increased by 20 per cent until 2015, by spending US$12 billion (1 per cent of GDP). Private industry is expected to match and double the amount.
2011 In parliamentary elections held on 7 May the PAP won with 60.1 per cent of the vote (81 seats out of 87). The Workers' Party won 12.8 per cent (six) and although the number was low, it still marked a weakening of the supremacy of PAP in parliament. Rancour within PAP at the discordant election campaign, led to former prime ministers, Lee Kuan Yew and Goh Chok Tong, retiring from active politics and giving up all government posts on 16 May. In a joint statement they said it was time for 'a younger generation to carry Singapore forward in a more difficult and complex situation'. Both had won seats in the 7 May elections. In August, the government decided to change employment regulations for expatriate workers in Singapore. From January 2012 expat workers (not permanently resident) must earn US$2,500 per month in their home country before they will be eligible for an employment pass in Singapore. In a closely run presidential election held on 27 August, Tony Tan Keng Yam won with 35.19 per cent of the vote against Tan Cheng Bock with 34.85 per cent (turnout was 94.65 per cent). Tony Tan took office on 1 September.

Political structure

Constitution

The 1959 constitution was amended in 1965, 1988, 1991 and 1996. Consequently, there are now 15 Group Representation Constituencies (GRCs) which elect teams of up to six members of parliament. At least one member of each team has to be of minority (non-Chinese) ethnic origin. The number of single member constituencies has been reduced from 21 to eight.

In the 1991 amendment, the position of president was modified to become a directly elected post with a six-year term. The responsibilities of the office were extended to include the safeguarding of Singapore's financial reserves, and the right to veto senior civil service and judicial appointments. Only those who have served as cabinet ministers, chief justice, senior civil servants or have headed a large company are eligible as presidential candidates.

The constitutional was amended in April 2010. A change to the electoral system increased the allowed number of Non-Constituency Members of Parliament (NCMP) from six to nine and was intended to give admittance to parliament of the best-performing, losing parliamentary candidates. In July Nominated MPs (NMP) became a permanent component of parliament, to provide alternative, non-partisan views during debates.

Elections must be held within three months of the dissolution of parliament.

There is full adult suffrage; voting is compulsory for all citizens aged 21 years and over.

Independence date

9 August 1965

Form of state

Republic

The executive

Executive power is vested in the cabinet, which is presided over by the prime minister and responsible to the unicameral parliament. The political hegemony of the People's Action Party (PAP) is absolute and parliamentary oversight of executive power is virtually non-existent. In 1995, a three-judge tribunal ruled that the president had no power to veto any bill that sought to restrict his existing powers.

National legislature

The unicameral Parliament of Singapore has elected and non-constituency (nominated) members (MPs) in single or group representation constituencies (GRCs). Following the 2006 elections, there are a total 94 MPs, including 84 directly elected, nine nominated and one GRC member. All serve for a five-year term.

Political parties field a team of 3–6 candidates (of which one must belong to a minority race) to contest GRCs.

There is a provision in the constitution for up to nine nominated MPs, appointed by the president for terms of 2.5 years to contribute non-partisan and independent views in parliament.

Legal system

Singaporean law is based on English common law.

The independence of the judiciary is safeguarded by the constitution. Judicial power is vested in Singapore's Supreme Court and in the Subordinate Courts. The Supreme Court consists of the High Court, the Court of Appeal and the Court of Criminal Appeal. The chief justice is appointed by the president, acting on the advice of the prime minister.

The Subordinate Courts consist of District Courts, Magistrates' Courts, Juvenile Courts, Coroners' Courts and Small Claims Tribunals. District judges, magistrates and coroners are appointed on the recommendation of the chief justice.

Although the constitution stipulates that the judiciary should act independently of government, it rarely does so in practice. Judges and judicial officials are appointed and dismissed by the president and

judicial redress against abuses of executive power is therefore limited.
Sharia is the religious court with jurisdiction over Muslim law and domestic proceedings between Muslim parties.

Last elections
7 May 2011 (parliamentary); 27 August 2011 (presidential)
Results: Parliamentary: Parliamentary: the People's Action Party won 60.1 per cent of the vote (81 seats out of 87), the Workers' Party (WP) 12.8 per cent (six), the National Solidarity Party (NSP) 12 per cent (none).
Presidential: Tony Tan Keng Yam won 35.19 per cent of the vote, Tan Cheng Bock 34.85 per cent, Tan Jee Say 25.04 per cent, Tan Kin Lian 4.91 per cent; turnout was 94.65 per cent.

Next elections
May 2016 (presidential and parliamentary)

Political parties

Ruling party
People's Action Party (PAP) (since 1965; re-elected 7 May 2011)

Main opposition party
Workers' Party (WP)

Population

3.77 million (2010)*
Last census: June 2000: 4,017,700
Population density: 7,126 inhabitants per square km (2010), one of the world's highest population densities.
Annual growth rate: 2.4 per cent 1994–2004 (WHO 2006)

Ethnic make-up
Singapore is a multi-racial society. There are approximately 950,000 non-nationals. Chinese make up the majority of the population (77 per cent), and Malays (14 per cent), Indians (8 per cent), and other ethnic groups (1 per cent) make up the remainder.

Religions
Buddhism (32 per cent), Taoism (22 per cent), Islam (Sunni) (15 per cent), Christianity (13 per cent) and Hinduism (3 per cent) are the main religions. Other religions include Zoroastrianism (0.6 per cent) and Judaism. The constitution provides for freedom of worship.

Education

Primary school lasts for six years between the ages six and 12. Lower secondary education last for four years and students must attain good exam results to progress on to higher secondary school for a further three years, before advancing to higher education. There are three kinds of tertiary institutions: universities, polytechnics, and other centres of public and private training. The government almost wholly finances the National University of Singapore and the Nanyang Technological University. Many Singaporean students go abroad for their university education, increasingly to the US.
Singapore has the campuses of many US universities – the University of Chicago, the Johns Hopkins University, the University of California and the Cornell and Stanford universities to name a few. In 2005 the prestigious Indian Institute of Management-Bangalore (IIM-B) opened a campus in the country.
Literacy rate: 93 per cent adult rate; 100 per cent youth rate (15–24) (Unesco 2005).
Compulsory years: 6 to 12
Enrolment rate: 94 per cent gross primary enrolment of relevant age group (including repeaters); 74 per cent gross secondary enrolment (World Bank).
Pupils per teacher: 25 in primary schools

Health

Singapore has managed to create a developed country healthcare system at relatively little cost. The health care system has a mixture of private and public provision and shows radically improved healthcare indices.
The private sector provides over 60 per cent of primary healthcare through doctors in private practice. Hospital healthcare is mostly public sector, with only 20 per cent of beds in the private sector. The government provides public subsidies through a ward system in public hospitals. Basic healthcare is financed through Central Provident Fund (CPF) Medisave accounts. Between 6 and 8 per cent of a worker's monthly contribution to the CPF, depending on age, is set aside for Medisave, a mandatory national health programme which encourages individuals to pay for their own healthcare. An additional endowment fund, Medifund, is targetted at poor and indigent Singaporeans.
Government officials have warned that if Singapore's predominantly Chinese population age too quickly, this could lead to expensive healthcare problems. Official statistics show that the number of Singaporeans aged 64 and above will rise fourfold to make up 20 per cent of the total population by the year 2030, when the population is projected to decline after it has reached a 7.9 million peak.

HIV/Aids
HIV prevalence: 0.2 per cent aged 15–49 in 2003 (World Bank)
Life expectancy: 80 years, 2004 (WHO 2006)
Fertility rate/Maternal mortality rate: 1.3 births per woman, 2004 (WHO 2006)
Birth rate/Death rate: 12.8 births per 1,000 population; 4.3 deaths per 1,000 population (2003).
Child (under 5 years) mortality rate (per 1,000): 3.6 per 1,000 live births (2003)
Head of population per physician: 1.4 physicians per 1,000 people, 2001 (WHO 2006)

Welfare

The government discourages dependence on the state for social security; rather, all workers and employers contribute to the compulsory savings scheme, the CPF. The CPF has developed into a wide-ranging social security scheme covering retirement, home ownership and health needs. Members can withdraw their savings upon reaching 55 but must set aside a minimum amount to ensure they have enough money for their retirement. The minimum amount to be saved every year was capped at S$80,000 (US$43,618) in 2003. Employment assistance is provided free of charge by the Ministry of Manpower.
Some 85 per cent of the population is housed in accommodation built and developed by the Housing and Development Board (HDB), set up in 1960 as a statutory board of the Ministry of National Development to provide low-cost public housing.

Main cities

Singapore is a city-state (estimated population 4.4 million in 2005).

Languages spoken

English is the main administrative language and is almost universally understood. In parliamentary debates, members may speak in English, Malay, Mandarin Chinese or Tamil, and simultaneous translations are provided. Other dialects of Chinese, mostly Hokkien (Fukienese) and Cantonese, are also spoken.
Most Singaporeans are bi- or tri-lingual.

Official language/s
English, Mandarin Chinese, Malay, Tamil.

Media

Press
Newspapers and magazines are published only under government licence in a highly regulated market. The government has a reputation of litigation for defamation, which has led to widespread self-censorship.
Singapore Press Holdings (SPH) is one of the largest companies listed on the Singapore Exchange, controlling 15 newspapers, a number of regional magazines and a book distribution network.
Dailies: The two main Chinese-language dailies are *Lian He Zao Bao* (United Morning News) and *Lian He Wan Bao* (United Evening News). The major

English-language dailes are *The Straits Times* and *Business Times*. *Berita Harian* (in Malay) and *Tamil Murasu* (in Tamil) have smaller circulations. International editions of foreign newspapers are also available.
Weeklies: Most daily newspapers have a Sunday edition with extended features.
Business: In Chinese, the highest circulation papers are *Lianhe Zaobao* (United Morning News) (www.zaobao.com) a major regional and international news gathering organ and *Lianhe Wanbao* (United Evening News). In English, *The Straits Times* (www.straitstimes.com), *Business Times* (www.businesstimes.com.sg), *The New Paper* (http://newpaper.asia1.com.sg) a tabloid and *Today* is a free issue. In Malay *Berita Harian* (http://cyberita.asia1.com.sg) and in Tamil, *Tamil Murasu* (http://tamilmurasu.tamil.sg) is a broadsheet.
Periodicals: In English, *The Executive* (www.executive.sg) is published monthly. The Singapore International Chamber of Commerce publishes a quarterly, *Business Minds* (www.sicc.com.sg) with business, corporate and personnel news. There are also numerous interest and trade publications, including *Singapore Business Federation* (www.sbf.org.sg).

Broadcasting
The government-owned MediaCorp operates the national television and radio stations.
Radio: MediaCorp operates 14 radio stations broadcasting in English, Mandarin, Malay and Tamil. There are a number of private, commercial stations.
Television: MediaCorp has a monopoly with six free-to-air TV channels, broadcasting in the four official languages. Private satellite dishes are banned however foreign broadcasts are available through cable TV.

Advertising
Advertising is available in the press, on commercial radio, television, cinemas and via direct mail and house-to-house distribution of samples. Outdoor advertising, especially posters used for short-term advertising campaigns are widely used. Expenditure on advertising is typically around 1 per cent of GDP. There are also numerous trade magazines and trade fairs for business-to-business marketing.

News agencies
Singapore Press Releases on the Internet (Sprinter) (www.sprinter.gov.sg), operated by Ministry of Information, Communications and the Arts, Singapore (tel: 6270-7988; internet: www.mica.gov.sg).

Economy
The economy is highly developed and integrated into global trade. The structure of the economy is dominated by the service sector, which accounts for almost 70 per cent of GDP, with financial services providing a major source of foreign exchange. Manufacturing, particularly of electronic components, pharmaceuticals and telecommunications equipment, and produced by many multinational corporations sited in Singapore, accounts for 26 per cent of GDP. Industrial production includes oil refining and storage, shipbuilding and aircraft repairs and maintenance. Singapore is less than 640 square kilometres in area and agriculture represents less than 0.5 per cent of GDP; it lacks any natural resources, but has capitalised upon its human resources and strategic location on the Straits of Malacca, where it has become a leading entrepôt and major shipping hub. Singapore is one of the world's leading destinations for FDI.
As Singapore has an economy that is dependent on foreign trade it was one of the first countries in Asia to go into recession at the start of the global economic recession and to suffer a prolonged setback in its GDP growth which dropped from 8.8 per cent in 2007 to 1.5 per cent in 2008, before falling into recession of -0.8 per cent in 2009 as world trade was at its weakest and exports fell and imports rose. In the 2009 financial year, the government introduced one of the largest stimulus packages among advanced economies of S$20.5 billion (US$29.3 billion), around 8 per cent of GDP. To strengthen Singapore's long-term prospects the package focussed on employment, supporting companies, enhancing competitiveness, stimulating bank lending and supporting families. As a result, and when global trade picked up, GDP growth resurged in 2010 to 14.5 per cent. Inflation, which had been a low 2.1 per cent rose sharply to 6.6 per cent in 2008, before dropping to 0.6 per cent in 2009; it returned to 2.8 per cent in 2010. The Singapore dollar was allowed to rise against the US dollar in April 2010, in a measure to tackle inflation, increasing in value by 1.25 per cent.

External trade
Singapore belongs to the Association of Southeast Asian Nations (Asean) Free Trade Area (Afta) and maintains a list of goods that have preferential import duties between members and a programme of tariff reductions due to be introduced in the next few years. It is also a member of the Asia-Pacific Economic Co-operation (Apec) forum, which is a group of 21 countries that border the Pacific. The objective of Apec is to facilitate trade, economic growth and investment in the region.
Foreign trade is a major function of the economy equalling over 300 per cent of GDP. Many multinational corporations have manufacturing bases (accounting for around 65 per cent of total output) and direct export sales operations in Singapore. Of the major economic sectors, electronics represents 40 per cent of industrial production with petrochemicals 20 per cent. Singapore and Hong Kong vie for leading position as the world's busiest container port and entrepôt. Almost 50 per cent of exports are re-exports and, due to the lack of land for agricultural purposes, the majority of foodstuffs and fuel have to be imported.

Imports
Principal imports are machinery and equipment, mineral fuels, chemicals and food, live animals and foodstuffs.
Main sources: Malaysia (typically 12 per cent of total), US (12 per cent), China (11 per cent).

Exports
Principal exports are machinery and equipment (including electronics), consumer goods, chemicals and fuels.
Main destinations: Malaysia (typically 12 per cent of total), Indonesia (11 per cent), Hong Kong (10 per cent).

Agriculture
Farming
Only 3 per cent of Singapore's land area is used for agriculture. Singapore has some 2,000 licensed farms producing poultry, eggs, vegetables, fruit, orchids (both for domestic demand and export) and ornamental plants. Less than 6 per cent of fresh vegetables is produced locally, with the rest imported from Malaysia, Indonesia, China and Australia. Although agriculture plays only a minor role in Singapore's economy, the Primary Production Department promotes intensive farming methods. Agri-technology parks have been developed on 554 hectares of land in Murai, Sungai Tengah, Nee Soon and Loyang.

Fishing
With limited agricultural and water resources, there is little scope for the development of Singapore's fisheries, although fish is an important component of the Singaporean diet. Singapore relies mainly on imports for domestic consumption. The government's priority is to increase imports through trade relations. The quality of Singapore's own catch is often decsribed as poor. Rapid urbanisation and development have damaged natural habitats and caused the quality of inshore fish to deteriorate.
Forests constitute only 7 per cent of the total land area of Singapore. There are three major forest reserves – Bukit Timah , Palau Ubin and Sungei Buloh. Singapore

produces plywood and veneer and imports pulp and paper.

Industry and manufacturing

The industrial sector accounts for around 35 per cent of GDP. Manufacturing employs around 19 per cent of the workforce and construction employs a further seven per cent. Electronics is the largest industry and typically contributes about 14 per cent to GDP, accounting for 70 per cent of non-oil exports. The second largest industry group encompasses life sciences, chemicals and petroleum refining. Other major industries include transport equipment, especially shipbuilding, and related repair and conversion activities.

Tourism

Tourism contributes around three per cent of GDP. Government policy is to build on the sector's success and increase its role in the economy as a means of diversification. To this end, two huge casino resorts are being planned.

Singapore's major markets are Indonesia, China, Malaysia, Japan, Australia, UK, India, US, South Korea and Thailand.

Environment

The Singapore Green Plan (SGP), released in 1992, called for 5 per cent of the country's land to be classified as protected areas. Around S$3 billion (US$1.7 billion) was allocated towards the upgrade of sewage treatment, a refuse incineration plant and improvements to water sources in 2002.

Mining

Hydrocarbons

Singapore does not have any oil or natural gas reserves and is entirely reliant on imports. However, Singapore is one of Asia's principal oil refining centres, with 11 refineries and total oil refining capacity of around 1.3 million barrels per day (bpd). Along with Singapore's large refining industry there has been rapid growth of the petrochemical industry.

Demand for natural gas in Singapore is rising, due to the government's policy of cutting carbon emissions in power generation and the growing petrochemical industry. Singapore depends on Malaysia and Indonesia for a steady supply of natural gas for power generation. This includes 4.3 million cubic metres (cum) per day from Malaysia through the first Asian trans-national gas pipeline, and 9.9 million cum of gas per day via another pipeline from Indonesia.

Any use of coal is commercially insignificant.

Energy

Total installed electricity-generating capacity was 9.5 gigawatts (GW) in 2006. The electricity is supplied by four thermal power stations, fuelled primarily by natural gas.

Financial markets

Stock exchange

Singapore Exchange (SGX)

Commodity exchange

Singapore Commodity Exchange (Sicom)

Banking and insurance

A bill amending income tax laws to comply with Organisation for Economic Co-operation and Development (OECD) standards was passed by parliament in October 2009. The bill, which allows the government to ask banks for client information, will move Singapore closer to being taken off the OECD's 'grey list' of countries considered to be unco-operative over tax. The banks hope this will make Singapore more attractive to clients from the Middle East and Europe.

Central bank

Monetary Authority of Singapore

Main financial centre

Singapore

Time

GMT plus eight hours

Geography

Singapore consists of the main island of Singapore and 58 smaller islands, more than 20 of them inhabited. Lying 137km north of the equator, it is linked to peninsular Malaysia in the north by a causeway carrying a road, railway and water pipeline across the narrow Straits of Johor, and separated from Indonesia to the south by the Straits of Singapore.

The island of Singapore itself is 42km long and 23km wide, with a coastline measuring 138km. It can be divided into three broad regions: a central hilly region, an area of hills and valleys in the west, and a relatively flat eastern region.

Hemisphere

Northern

Climate

The climate is equatorial, with uniformly high temperatures, high humidity and mean annual rainfall of 2,463mm with no defined wet or dry season. Mean daily temperatures range from a minimum 24 degrees Celsius (C) to a maximum 31 degrees C. The hottest month is May. The driest month is July, with an average rainfall of 70mm. November to January are generally the cooler and wetter months. Sometimes it rains for several days continuously and there may be serious flooding. Between monsoons, from April to November, there are regular pre-dawn thunderstorms, known as *Sumatras*. Singapore has an average of 180 lightning days a year.

Dress codes

Dress is generally informal, with light summer clothing the norm. A shirt and tie, or a safari suit, is the usual office dress for men, although jackets may be required in some restaurants for dinner; women should also dress smartly for business. Singapore's predominantly Chinese population follows Western fashion; a small section among the minority Indian and Malay communities wear traditional dress.

Entry requirements

Passports

Required by all, valid for six months beyond date of departure.

Visa

Visas are not required by nationals of most countries; a list of the countries whose nationals require visas is given on app.ica.gov.sg/travellers/entry/visa_requirements.asp. Social visit passes are issued on arrival to all other visitors by Immigration Officers, who determine the length of visit and grant social visit passes on the basis of sufficient funds for maintenance during the expected stay and confirmed return/onwards passage (including relevant visas for further destinations).

Prohibited entry

Singapore has tough laws against drug trafficking. The death penalty is mandatory for trafficking above certain prescribed levels.

Currency advice/regulations

There are no restrictions on the import or export of local or foreign currencies. Credit cards and travellers cheques are widely accepted.

Customs

One litre each of spirits, wine and beer. Tobacco products are not duty-free and must be declared.

Prohibited imports

Include chewing gum, chewing tobacco and imitation tobacco products, cigarette lighters of pistol or revolver shape, controlled drugs and psychotropic substances, endangered species and by-products, firecrackers, obscene articles, publications, video tapes and software, reproduction of copyright publications, video tapes or disks, records or cassettes, or seditious and treasonable materials.

Health (for visitors)

Mandatory precautions

Yellow fever vaccination certificates for anyone who, within the preceding six days, has been to an infected area.

Advisable precautions

Vaccinations for diphtheria, tuberculosis, hepatitis A and B, polio, tetanus and typhoid are advisable. Tap water is safe.

All necessary medicines (especially sleeping pills, depressants, stimulants, etc) must have a physician's certification declaring their prescribed use.

The Singapore Medical Centre, on the sixth floor of Tanglin shopping centre, houses a large community of specialist doctors.

Hotels
There are numerous five-star international-class hotels with shopping arcades, bars and swimming pools. Tipping is discouraged. A 4 per cent tax and a 10 per cent service charge are generally added to the hotel bill.

Credit cards
All major credit cards are widely accepted.

Public holidays (national)
Owing to its multi-ethnic composition, Singapore celebrates a wide range of religious festivals and holidays in addition to those listed. Many festivals are based on a lunar calendar, while the dates of some are only finalised at the last minute.
Check with the Singapore Tourist Promotion Board for exact dates and locations affected.

Fixed dates
1 Jan (New Year's Day), 1 May (Labour Day), 9 Aug (National Day), 25 Dec (Christmas Day).

Variable dates
Chinese New Year (Jan/Feb), Good Friday, Vesak Day, Diwali (Oct/Nov), Eid al Adha, Eid al Fitr.

Working hours
During the Lunar New Year, many Chinese firms close for the whole week.

Banking
Mon–Fri: 1930–1500; Sat: 0930–1200; 0900–1500 (selected banks only).

Business
Mon–Fri: 0900–1300, 1400–1700.

Government
Mon–Fri: 0800–1300, 1400–1700.

Shops
Mon–Sat: 1930–2100. Some shops, particularly in tourist areas, open on Sundays.

Electricity supply
220—240V, 50 Hz, with three-pin (square) plug fittings.

Weights and measures
Metric system, with local variations.

Social customs/useful tips
Singaporeans are highly 'face' conscious and try to avoid self-embarrassment at all time.
Observe local etiquette – suit jackets remain off only as a concession to the climate, otherwise Western-style business formalities are in place.
Visiting cards are essential (although government officials do not use them). The cards should be presented with both hands. As a courtesy, it is a good idea to have cards printed in both Chinese and English. Cards should never be written on, put away before the meeting is over, or left behind.
When addressing Chinese persons, family or surname is mentioned first. When addressing Malay persons, the first of their two family names is used. Singaporean Indians use many different conventions.
Men and women should not touch each other. The heads of children should not be patted.
Tipping is not customary; it is not illegal, but is officially discouraged. In hotels and restaurants a 10 per cent service charge is included in the bill.
On-the-spot fines can be imposed for some offences. Smoking is not permitted in public buildings and restaurants, and is restricted in other public places.
Singapore celebrates the religious and cultural festivals of its four major communities, and therefore the year is punctuated by a series of colourful festivals.
Celebration of the Chinese New Year, the main event in the Chinese calendar, centres on traditional reunion dinners and visits to friends and relations. Business people should avoid visiting at Christmas, Easter, Chinese New Year, Islamic and Hindu religious holiday periods.

Security
Tourists can walk the streets without fear of being robbed or attacked.

Getting there
Air
National airline: Singapore Airlines.
International airport/s: Singapore-Changi International Airport (SIN), 20km north-east of city; bank, bureau de change, duty-free shop, post office, restaurants, shops, car rental. A third terminal is scheduled to open in 2008.
Airport tax: The departure tax of S$21 is usually included in the price of the air ticket.

Surface
Road: Road transport arrives via two causeways from Malaysia, with express bus services from Kuala Lumpur and Johor Bahru.
Rail: There are rail services to Kuala Lumpur and Bangkok.
Water: There are excellent sea links with other countries.

Getting about
National transport
Road: The road network comprises some 2,900km of roads, including about 100km of expressways. Vehicular access to the Central Business District (CBD) is restricted and there are charges for vehicles entering the area at certain times.
Buses: Timetables for the extensive and inexpensive bus network are widely available at news-stands. Fares to various destinations are displayed on a signboard on the front of the bus stop.
Rail: The light overland railway network reaches all districts of Singapore Island.
Water: Regular ferry services from the World Trade Centre operate to some of the islands; others may be reached by charter boats.

City transport
Taxis: Metered, air-conditioned taxis are widely available from taxi pick-up points and can be hailed in the street. Taxi companies are allowed to set their own fares. The basic meter fare is displayed on the window of the rear door and details of surcharges are displayed on the fare card in all taxis.Taxis can also be hired by the hour.
Buses, trams & metro: The easy-to-use bus service is extensive.
The Mass Rapid Transit system (MRT) is fast, clean and efficient. It comprises three lines running north/south, east/west and north/east with around 70 underground and elevated stations.

Car hire
An international driving licence is required for car hire. Driving is on the left. Coupons for use of the public car parks managed by the Urban Redevelopment Authority (URA) or Housing & Development Board (HBD) can be purchased at post offices, URA parking kiosks and some gas/petrol stations. Car hire companies are listed in the Yellow Pages of the telephone directory.

BUSINESS DIRECTORY
The addresses listed below are a selection only. While World of Information makes every endeavour to check these addresses, we cannot guarantee that changes have not been made, especially to telephone numbers and area codes. We would welcome any corrections.

Telephone area codes
The international direct dialling (IDD) code for Singapore is +65, followed by subscriber's number.

Useful telephone numbers
Police: 999
Fire/ambulance: 995
Directory enquiries: 103
International calls: 104
International enquiries: 162
Trunk calls to Malaysia: 109
Time of Day: 1711
Flight information: 6542-1234
Bus information: 6287-2727
AA road service (24 hrs): 6748-9911
Post Office information: 6533-0234, 6532-4536
Immigration Department: 6532-2877
Telecoms Customer Services Centres: 6734-3344, 6534-3111

Chambers of Commerce

American Chamber of Commerce in Singapore, Shaw Centre, 1 Scotts Road, Singapore 228208 (tel: 6235-0077; fax: 6732-5917; e-mail: info@amcham.org.sg).

British Chamber of Commerce Singapore, Cecil Court, 138 Cecil Street, Singapore 069538 (tel: 6222-3552; fax: 6222-3556; e-mail: info@britcham.org.sg).

Singapore Chinese Chamber of Commerce & Industry, SCCCI Building, 47 Hill Street, Singapore 179365 (tel: 6337-8381; fax: 6339-0605; e-mail: corporate@sccci.org.sg).

Singapore Indian Chamber of Commerce and Industry, Tong Eng Building, 101 Cecil Street, Singapore069533 (tel: 6222-2855; fax: 6223-1707; e-mail: sicci@sicci.com).

Singapore International Chamber of Commerce, John Hancock Tower, 6 Raffles Quay, Singapore 048580 (tel: 6224-1255; fax: 6224-2785; e-mail: general@sicc.com.sg).

Singapore Malay Chamber of Commerce, 72A Bussorah Street, Singapore 199485 (tel: 6297-9296; fax: 6392-4527; e-mail: smcci@singnet.com.sg).

Banking

ABN Amro Bank NV, 63 Chulia Street (tel: 6231-8888; fax: 6532-3108).

ABSA Bank Ltd, 7 Temasek Boulevard, Suntec Tower One (tel: 6333-1033; fax: 6333-1066).

Agricultural Bank of China, 80 Raffles Place, UOB Plaza 2 (tel: 6535-5255; fax: 6538-7960).

American Express Bank Ltd, 16 Collyer Quay, Hitachi Tower (tel: 6538-4833; fax: 6534-3022).

Arab Bank plc, 80 Raffles Place, UOB Plaza 2 (tel: 6533-0055; fax: 6532-2150).

Arab Banking Corporation (BSC), 35-01 Republic Plaza Singapore, 9 Raffles Place, 048619 (tel: 6535-9339; fax: 6532-6288).

Bangkok Bank plc, 180 Cecil Street (tel: 6221-9400; fax: 6225-5852).

Bank of America, National Association, 9 Raffles Place, Republic Plaza Tower 1 (tel: 6239-3888; fax: 6239-3068).

Bank of China, 4 Battery Road, Bank of China Building (tel: 6535-2411; fax: 6534-3401).

Bank of East Asia Ltd, 137 Market Street, Bank of East Asia Building (tel: 6224-1334; fax: 6225-1805).

Bank of India, 138 Robinson Road, Hong Leong Centre (tel: 6222-0011; fax: 6225-4407).

Bank of Montreal, 150 Beach Road, Gateway West (tel: 6296-3233; fax: 6296-5044).

Bank of New York, 1 Temasek Avenue, Millenia Tower (tel: 6432-0222; fax: 6337-4302).

Bank of Nova Scotia, 10 Collyer Quay, Ocean Building (tel: 6535-8688; fax: 6532-2440).

Bank of Singapore, Tong Eng Building, 101 Cecil Street 01-02, 0106 (tel: 6223-9266).

Bank of Tokyo-Mitsubishi Ltd, 9 Raffles Place, Republic Plaza (tel: 6538-3388; fax: 6538-8083).

Chase Manhattan Bank, Shell Tower, 50 Raffles Place, 048623 (tel: 6530-4135, 6224-2888; fax: 6530-4331).

Far Eastern Bank, 156 Cecil Street, Far Eastern Bank Building, PO Box 2950, 0106 (tel: 6221-9055).

Hongkong & Shanghai Banking Corp Ltd, 21 Collyer Quay, 19-00 Hongkong Bank Building (tel: 6530-5412; fax: 6225-0663).

Indian Overseas Bank, 64 Cecil Street, IOB Building (tel: 6225-1100; fax: 6224-4490).

Industrial and Commercial Bank, ICB Building, 2 Shenton Way, 0106 (tel: 6221-1711).

Overseas Chinese Banking Corporation, OCBC Centre, 65 Chulia Street, 0104 (tel: 6535-7222; fax: 6533-7891).

Overseas Union Bank, OUB Centre, 1 Raffles Place, 0104 (tel: 6533-8686; fax: 6533-2293).

Standard Chartered Bank, 6 Battery Road (tel: 6225-8888; fax: 6225-9136).

United Overseas Bank, UOB Plaza, 80 Raffles Place, 048624 (tel: 6533-9898; fax: 6534-2334).

Central bank

Monetary Authority of Singapore, MAS Building, 10 Shenton Way, Singapore 079117 (tel: 6225-5577; fax: 6229-9229; e-mail: webmaster@mas.gov.sg).

Stock exchange

Singapore Exchange (SGX): www.sgx.com

Commodity exchange

Singapore Commodity Exchange (Sicom): www.sicom.com.sg

Travel information

Automobile Association of Singapore, 336 River Valley Road, AA Centre, Singapore (tel: 6333-8811; fax: 6733-50944; e-mail: aasmail@aas.com.sg).

Singapore Airlines, Airline House, 25 Airline Road, Singapore 819829 (tel: 6541-4855; fax: 6542-3002).

Ministry of tourism

Ministry of Trade and Industry, 100 High Street, 09-01 The Treasury, Singapore 179434 (tel: 6225-9911; fax: 6332-7260; e-mail: mti_email@mti.gov.sg).

National tourist organisation offices

Singapore Tourism Board, Tourism Court, 1 Orchard Spring Lane, Singapore 247729 (tel: 6736-6622; fax: 6736-9423; e-mail: ms@stb.com.sg).

Ministries

Ministry of Communications, 39th Storey PSA Building, 460 Alexandra Road, Singapore 119963 (tel: 6270-7988; fax: 6279-9734).

Ministry of Defence, Gombak Drive (off Upper Bukit Timah Road), Mindef Building, Singapore 2366 (tel: 6760-8188; fax: 6762-0112).

Ministry of Development, c/o Meeting Planners Pte Ltd, 2nd Floor, Pico Centre, 20 Kallang Avenue, Singapore 1233 (tel: 6297-2822; fax: 6296-2670, 6292-7577).

Ministry of Environment, Sewerage Department, 14-00 Environmental Building, 40 Scotts Road, Singapore 228231 (tel: 6732-7733; fax: 6731-9699 (sewerage dept), 6731-9456 (general).

Ministry of Finance, 8 Shenton Way, 43rd, 45th, 46th and 50th Storey, Treasury Building, Singapore 0106 (tel: 6225-9911; fax: 6320-9435 (budget), 6320-9932 (PSD), 6224-6847 (revenue)).

Ministry of Foreign Affairs, 250 North Bridge Road, 07-00 Raffles City Tower, Singapore 0617 (tel: 6336-1177, 6330-5795 (after hours); fax: 6339-4330).

Ministry of Information, Communications and the Arts, Public Relations Department, 460 Alexandra Road 36-00, PSA Building, Singapore 0511 (tel: 6270-7988; fax: 6279-9765); Media Division, MITA Building, 140 Hill Street, 2nd Storey, Singapore 179369 (tel: 6837-9666).

Ministry of Manpower, 18 Havelock Road, Singapore 059764 (tel: 6438-5122; fax: 6534-4840; internet: www.mom.gov.sg).

Ministry of National Development, National Development Building, Maxwell Road, Singapore 0106 (tel: 6222-1211; fax: 6322-6254).

Ministry of Trade and Industry, 100 High Street, 09-01 The Treasury, Singapore 179434 (tel: 6225-9911; fax:

6332-7260; e-mail: mti_email@mti.gov.sg).

Other useful addresses

American Business Council, 10-12 Shaw House, 354 Orchard Road, Singapore 0923 (tel: 6235-00770).

ASEAN Investment Promotion Agency, Economic Development Board, 250 North Bridge Road, 24-00 Raffles City Tower, Singapore 0617 (tel: 6336-2288; 6338-8265).

ASEAN Secretariat, 70 A J1 Sisingamangaraja, Jakarta 12110, Indonesia (tel: (+62-21) 726-2991,) (+62-21) 724-3372; fax: (+62-21) 724-3504, (+62-21) 739-8234; e-mail: asean.or.id).

The Association of Banks in Singapore, 12-08 MAS Building, 10 Shenton Way, Singapore 0207 (tel: 6224-4300; fax: 6224-1785).

The Association of Small & Medium Enterprises, Blk 139 Kim Tain Road, Singapore 0316 (tel: 6271-2566; fax: 6271-1257).

British Business Association, 41 Duxton Road, Singapore 0208 (tel: 6227-7861; fax: 6227-7021).

British Businessmen's Association, 3rd Floor, Inchcape House, 450-452 Alexandra Road, Singapore 0511 (tel: 6475-4192).

British Council, 30 Napier Road, Singapore 1025 (tel: 6473-1111; fax: 6472-1010).

British High Commission, Tanglin Road, Singapore 912401 (tel: 6474-0461; fax; 6475-2320).

Civil Aviation Authority of Singapore, Singapore Airtropolis, Changi Airport (tel: 6542-1122; fax: 6545-6222).

Construction Industry Development Board, Annexe A, 3rd Storey, National Development Building, 9 Maxwell Road, Singapore 0106 (tel: 6225-6711; fax: 6225-7307).

Controller of Immigration, 95 South Bridge Road, Pidemco Centre, Singapore (tel: 6532-2877; fax: 6530-1840).

Customs & Excise Department, 03-01 & 10-01 World Trade Centre, 1 Maritime Square, Singapore 099253 (tel: 6272-8222; fax: 6375-2090).

Economic Development Board, 24-00 Raffles City Tower, 250 North Bridge Road, Singapore 0617 (tel: 6336-2288; fax: 6339-6077).

Export Credit Insurance Corporation of Singapore Ltd, 10 Shenton Way, 17-03 MAS Building, Singapore 0207 (tel: 6220-8344; fax: 6224-2887).

Housing and Development Board, 3451 Jalan Bukit Merah, HDB Centre, Singapore 0315 (tel: 6273-9090).

Immigration Department, 7th & 8th Storey, 08-26 Pidemco Centre, 95 South Bridge Road, Singapore 0105 (tel: 6532-2877; fax: 6530-1840).

Inland Revenue Authority of Singapore, Fullerton Building, B1-00 Fullerton Square, Singapore 049178 (tel: 6535-4244; fax: 6535-5393).

International Merchandise Mart PTE Ltd (IMM), Unit 04-01, 2 Jurong East Street 21, Singapore 609601 (tel: 6568-2000; fax: 6568-2500).

Jurong Town Corporation, Jurong Town Hall, 301 Jurong Town Hall Road, Singapore 609431 (tel: 6560-0056; fax: 6565-5301).

National Arts Council, Arts Division, MCD Building, 512 Thomson Road, Singapore 1129 (tel: 6258-9595; fax: 6350-6118).

National Productivity Board, 2 Bukit Merah, Central NPB Building, Singapore 0315 (tel: 6734-5534).

Port of Singapore Authority (PSA), PSA Building, 460 Alexandra Road, Singapore 119963 (tel: 6274-7111; fax: 6274-4677).

Public Utilities Board, PUB Building, 111 Somerset Way, Singapore 0207 (tel: 6235-8888; fax: 6731-3020).

Registry of Trade and Businesses, 05-01/15 International Plaza, 10 Anson Road, Singapore 0207 (tel: 6227-8551; fax: 6225-1676).

Singapore Confederation of Industries (formerly Singapore Manufacturers' Association), SMA House, 20 Orchard Road, Singapore 238830 (tel: 6338-8787; fax: 6339-3340).

Singapore Embassy (US), 3501 International Place, NW, Washington DC 20008 (tel: (+1-202)-537-3100; fax: (1-202)-537-0876; e-mail: singemb.dc@verizon.net).

Singapore Hotel Association, 11 Mount Sophia, Singapore 228461 (tel: 6339-9918; fax: 6339-3795).

Singapore Importers and Exporters Association, 2nd Floor, 76-C Robinson Road, Singapore 0106 (tel: 6222-3451).

Singapore Institute of Standards and Industrial Research (SISIR), 1 Science Park Drive, Singapore 0511 (tel: 6778-7777; fax: 6778-0086).

Singapore International Monetary Exchange (SIMEX), Square, 07-00 OUB Centre, Singapore 0104 (tel: 6535-7282; fax: 6535-7382).

Stock Exchange of Singapore, 26-01/08 The Exchange, 20 Cecil Street, Singapore 049705 (tel: 6535-3788; fax: 6535-0775).

Telecommunication Authority of Singapore, TAS Building, 35 Robinson Road, Singapore 068876 (tel: 6738-7788; fax: 6733-0073).

Trade Development Board, 07-00 Bugis Junction Office Tower, 230 Victoria Street, Singapore 188024 (tel: 6271-9388; fax: 6274-0770).

US Embassy, 30 Hill Street, Singapore 0617 (tel: 6338-0251; fax: 6338-8472).

Work Permit and Employment Department, Ministry of Labour, 18 Havelock Road, Singapore 059764 (tel: 6534-1511; fax: 6539-5344/5).

Internet sites

Singapore Connect: http://sgconnect.asia1.com.sg

Singapore Government: http://www.gov.sg

Singapore Statistical Office: http://www.singstat.gov.sg

Singapore Yellow Pages: http://www.yellowpages.com.sg

Sint Maarten

KEY FACTS

Official name: Sint Maarten (St Maarten)

Head of State: Queen Beatrix of The Netherlands, represented by Governor Eugene Holiday (from 10 Oct 2010)

Head of government: Prime Minister Sarah Westcot-Williams (from 10 Oct 2010)

Ruling party: Coalition government led by Democratische Partij Sint Maarten (DPSM) (Democratic Party of St Maarten) (from 10 Oct 2010)

Area: 34 square kilometres

Population: 37,249 (2010; census figure)

Capital: Philipsburg

Official language: Dutch and English (official)

Currency: Netherlands Antilles guilder (Naf) = 100 cents

Exchange rate: Naf1.79 per US$ (Oct 2011); (official rate pegged to US$ since Jan 2000)

COUNTRY PROFILE

Historical profile

The islands of the Netherlands Antilles were first inhabited by Carib and Arawak Indians.

1493 Christopher Columbus was the first European to sight the islands.

1499 The Spanish explorer, Alonso de Ojedo, visited Curaçao but left without establishing a settlement.

1527 The islands were settled, mainly by Spanish and Portuguese Jews escaping persecution.

1634 The Dutch East India Company took over the islands, 'persuading' the settlers to depart, first from St Maarten and later from Aruba.

1642–46 Peter Stuyvesant was governor.

1816 After a number of changes in possession, the islands – Curaçao, Aruba and Bonaire (part of the Leeward Islands), St Eustatius, Saba and Sint Maarten (half of which is the French territory of St Martin) (which are part of the Windward Islands) – were confirmed as Dutch territory.

1863 Slavery was abolished.

1916 The first oil refinery was opened in Curaçao.

1954 Internal autonomy was granted as associated states within a federacy.

1986 Aruba separated from the other islands and became a self-governing member of the Kingdom of The Netherlands. The remaining islands became the Antilles of Five.

1998 A general election resulted in a six-party coalition government under Prime Minister Suzanne Camelia-Römer.

1999 The Partido Laboral Krusado Popular (PLKP) (Labour Party People's Crusade) left the coalition, to be replaced by the Partido Antiá Restrukturá (PAR) (Party for the Restructured Antilles), with Miguel Pourier becoming prime minister.

2000 In a referendum, St Maarten voted in favour of separate status within the Kingdom of The Netherlands and no longer to be a part of The Netherlands Antilles government.

2002 The ruling coalition was returned to power in the elections.

2004 The coalition government avoided collapse, caused by a corruption crisis, when support was offered by the Democratische Partij (DP) (Democratic Party) of Bonaire. However the collapse finally arrived when the National People's Party (PNP) withdrew citing its unwillingness to work with Justice Minster Ben Komproe. Prime Minister Louisa-Godett resigned and Etienne Ys became prime minister.

2005 The islanders of Curaçao voted to become an autonomous state within the Kingdom of The Netherlands and break with The Netherlands Antilles. The tiny neighbouring island, Sint Eustatius, decided to remain within the Antilles.

2006 Emily de Jongh-Elhage became prime minister, following parliamentary elections. The islands of Curaçao and St Maarten signed an agreement of independence with The Netherlands to become autonomous territories within the Kingdom of the Netherlands. At the same time Bonaire, Saba and St Eustatius will become city-states of the Kingdom of the Netherlands. When these changes are enacted the Netherlands Antilles will cease to exist. A new terminal at Curaçao International Airport was opened, designed to accommodate around 1.6 million passengers per year. The growth in tourism on the island and in the region is seen as a major industry and a phase two expansion is planned for when arrivals are expected to reach 2.5 million in 2031.

2007 Negotiations for a change in their status began between Bonaire, Saba and St Eustatius and The Netherlands.

2010 In January, in the last general election to be held before The Netherlands Antilles ceases to exist as a country, the Partido Antiá Restrukturá (PAR) (Party for the Restructured Antilles) won six seats out of 22 and the right to form a coalition government. In island council elections held in September, the Democratische Partij Sint Eustatius (DPSE) (Democratic Party of Sint Eustatius) won 17 per cent of the vote (two seats out of 15), National Alliance (alliance of two parties) 46 per cent (seven), United People 36 per cent (six). A national census was undertaken in July, that recorded a number of 37,249 people. Following coalition talks Sarah Westcot-Williams (DPSE) became prime minister of the independent St Maarten on 10 October. On 10 October the Netherlands Antilles ceased to exist and Curacao and St Maarten became autonomous countries within the kingdom of The Netherlands. Bonaire, St Eustatius and Saba

became Bijzondere Gemeenten (special municipalities).
2011 On 15 April, Puerto Rico's JetBlue Airways announced plans to launch a daily, nonstop service from San Juan to St Maarten starting from mid-November.

Political structure
Constitution
A new constitution was formed in 2010.
Independence date
Form of state
Parliamentary democratic monarchy.
On 10 October 2010, the Caribbean islands of Curaçao and St Maarten joined Aruba (1986) as semi-autonomous countries within the Kingdom of the Netherlands; at the same time the Caribbean islands of Bonaire, St Eustatius and Saba became Bijzondere Gemeenten (special municipalities) of the Netherlands.
Legal system
The legal system is based on Dutch civil law, with some English common law. Judges are appointed by the monarch. Rights of appeal exist from The Netherlands Antilles Court of Appeals to the Supreme Court of The Netherlands, in The Hague.
Last elections
September 2010 (island council)
Results: Island council: Democratische Partij Sint Eustatius (DPSE) (Democratic Party of Sint Eustatius) 17 per cent of the vote (tow seats out of 15), National Alliance (alliance of two parties) 46 per cent (seven), United People 36 per cent (six).

Political parties
Ruling party
Coalition government led by Democratische Partij Sint Maarten (DPSM) (Democratic Party of St Maarten) (from 10 Oct 2010)

Population
37,249 (2010; census figure)
Last census: July 2010: 37,249
Ethnic make-up
African and mixed race (85 per cent), Carib Amerindian, white, East Asian.
Religions
Baptist, Roman Catholic, Protestant, Jewish, Seventh-Day Adventist and others.

Health
Curaçao has two general hospitals and one surgical hospital and receives patients from the other islands of the former Netherlands Antilles. Most health professionals receive training in The Netherlands.
It is estimated that around 30 per cent of the population of the former Netherlands Antilles suffer from hypertension; psychological problems are also highly prevalent among adults. The general standard of health among the Antilleans is poor, with poor nutrition and little or no exercise undertaken by the adult population. The Dutch government has assigned priority to encouraging the population to develop healthier lifestyles.
HIV/Aids
There is a national strategic action plan to halt the rapid spread of the disease. The drugs problem on the islands could prove to be a potent source of transmission.
Life expectancy: 76.3 years (estimate 2003)
Fertility rate/Maternal mortality rate: 2.1 births per woman (World Bank)
Birth rate/Death rate: 16 births per 1,000 population; 6.4 deaths per 1,000 population (2003).
Child (under 5 years) mortality rate (per 1,000): 11 per 1,000 live births (2003)

Welfare
A public insurance programme covers 100 per cent of health care costs for blue-collar workers. There is also an insurance fund for retired workers. Private companies also provide insurance plans for their employees. A social security fund covers employees of small private establishments.

Languages spoken
English is the most widely spoken, although with a strong local dialect. Dutch is typically used in official documents, particularly in the legal field. Spanish and French are also spoken.
Official language/s
Dutch and English (official)

Media
Press
Dailies: The only regional daily newspaper is *Amigoe* (www.amigoe.com), and the local *Daily Herald* (www.thedailyherald.com).
Broadcasting
There are several radio stations broadcasting, including Island 92 (www.island92.com), SXM radio (www.sxmradio.com), which offers a number of genres. The Leeward Broadcasting Corporation broadcasts in Sint Maarten. Channel 15 is the television station broadcasting, which belongs to the SXM network (www.sxmtv.15.com).

Economy
The former Netherlands Antilles economy, virtually devoid of natural resources, was heavily service-oriented, 84 per cent of GDP, and based largely on tourism with offshore financial services.
St Maarten's economy is dominated by toursim. Agriculture only accounts for 1 per cent of GDP, producing aloes, sorghum, vegetables and tropical fruit. Dutch aid remains important to the economy. The unemployment rate remains high at over 15 per cent. The island have a higher per capita income and a well-developed infrastructure, compared with other countries in the region.

External trade
There is trade in high-quality jewelry, sold to tourist.
Imports
Foodstuff, gold and other precious metals, gem stones, consumer goods, vehicles, household goods, petroleum products and energy.

Agriculture
The agricultural sector contributes 1 per cent to GDP and employs 5 per cent of the workforce.
About 8 per cent of total area is cultivated arable land. Soil is generally poor and rainfall inadequate for most crops.
Small amounts of fruit and vegetables are grown for local consumption

Tourism
Tourism is the major industry and the majority of visitors are from the US (around 40 per cent of stay-over arrivals), followed by South America, the Netherlands, Canada and the Caribbean.

Banking and insurance
Under an EU tax directive introduced in 2005 in a number of associate and dependent EU countries, impose a withholding tax to be passed to the relevant EU country but typically retains the anonymity of the saver. Withholding taxes began at 15 per cent and will rise to 35 per cent by 2011.
The Netherlands Antillies has also agreed to supply information on tax fraud, for criminal or civil trials, and notify EU member states about additional malpractice.

Time
GMT minus five hours (minus six hours during summer daylignt saving).

Geography
Sint Maarten is the southern 34 square kilometres of the island it shares with the French territory of Saint Martin (37square km), in the Windward islands located 250km north of the coast of Guadeloupe, in the Caribbean Sea.
The terrain is dry and volcanic, with little fresh water available and scant rainfall. There are several mountains, of which Pic Paradis is the largest (424 metres). There are two saltwater pans within Sint Maarten and a large one shared with St Martin. Tourists are drawn to the extensive white beaches and azure waters around the coasts on which its towns are built – the interior of the island is largely uninhabited.
Hemisphere
Northern

Climate
The average annual temperature is 27 degrees centegrade, the total average rainfall is 995mm. Along with all Caribbean islands St Maarten is subject to hurricans, typically between June–Septermber.

Entry requirements
Passports
Required by all and must be valid for at least three months from date of departure.
Visa
Not required by nationals of countries which are signatories of the Schengen Accords, which includes most EU/EEA member states; North America and Australasia for visits up to three months.
Work permits must be obtained before arrival. See www.stmaarten-info.com (information page) for details.
All visitors must provide evidence of sufficient funds for their stay and a return/onward ticket.
Currency advice/regulations
There are no restrictions regarding the import and export of local or foreign currencies.
The US dollar is freely used and travellers cheques are widely accepted. ATM machines often accept international bank cards.
Customs
Prohibited imports
Include illegal drugs, weapons, ammunition, explosives and incendiary items, live animals and fresh foolstuffs, without permits.
It is illegal to export coral and marine shells from Sint Maarten.

Hotels
There are numerous hotels and of a range of qualities, all located near beaches. A government tax of 5 per cent and 10–15 per cent is added to the bill.

Credit cards
All major cards are accepted.

Public holidays (national)
Fixed dates
1 Jan (New Year's Day), 30 Apr (Queen's Birthday), 1 May (Labour Day), 11 Nov (St Maarten Day), 25–26 Dec (Christmas).
Variable dates
Good Friday and Easter Monday (Mar/Apr) Publis Day and Carnival (two day in Apr) Ascension Day (Aug), Kingdom Day (Dec).

Working hours
Banking
Mon–Fri: 0830–1200, 1330–1630.
Business
Mon–Fri: 0830–1200, 1330–1630.
Government
Mon–Fri: 0830–1200, 1330–1630.
Shops
Mon–Sat: 0800–1200, 1400–1800.
Tourist shops open on Sundays and public holidays and when cruise ships call.

Telecommunications
Mobile/cell phones
There are several 900, 900/1800 GSM services covering the island.

Electricity supply
110V with US style plugs and sockets.

Getting there
Air
National airline: Windward Islands Airways and AirStMaarten are both commercial organisations.
International airport/s: Princess Juliana International Airport (SXM); located 15km northwest of Philipsburg, with shops and restaurants. Intercontinental flights arrive during the main holiday seasons and inter-regional flights, particularly to other small Caribbean islands, throughout the year. Taxis, car hire and limousines, with chauffeur, are available.
Airport tax: All fees are included in the price of ticktes.
Surface
There are no road borders between the French north and Sint Maarten.
Water: There are ferries operating between Sint Maarten, Saint-Martin, St Eustatius and Saba.

Getting about
Car hire
Car and motorcycle hire is widely available. An international licence is required. Chauffeured limousines are also available, with daily rates.

BUSINESS DIRECTORY
The addresses listed below are a selection only. While World of Information makes every endeavour to check these addresses, we cannot guarantee that changes have not been made, especially to telephone numbers and area codes. We would welcome any corrections.

Telephone area codes
The international dialling code (IDD) for St Maarten is + 599, followed by area code and subscriber's number.

Useful telephone numbers
Police emergency	911
Ambulance emergency Fire	919
Police and immigration department	542-2222
Lt. Governor's Office	542-6085
Tourism office	557-7966

Banking
Algemene Bank Nederland, Frontstraat, PO Box 295, Philipsburg, St Maarten (tel: 9542-7520).

Windward Islands Bank Ltd, Pondfill, Philipsburg, PO Box 220, St Maarten (tel: 542-2313; fax: 542-4761; internet: wib-bank.net).

Scotiabank, Backstreet 61, Philipsburg, PO Box 303, St Maarten (tel: 542-3317; fax: 542-2435; email: bns@stmaarten@scotiabank.com).

Ministries
The Lieutenant Governor, Government Administration Bld, Clem Labega Sq, Philipsburg (tel: 542-6085; fax: 952-4884).

Office of the Minister Plenipotentiary of the Netherlands Antilles, Badhuisweg 175, 2597 JP The Hague, The Netherlands (tel: (+31-70) 351-2811; fax: (+31-70) 351-2722).

Other useful addresses
St. Maarten Medical Centre, Cay Hill, (tel: 543-1111).

Internet sites
Government of St Maarten: www.stmaarten-info.com

Princess Juliana International Airport: www.pjiae.com

St Maarten tourist information portal: www.st-maarten.com

KEY FACTS

Official name: Slovenská Republika (Slovak Republic)

Head of State: President Ivan Gasparovic (formerly HZD) (from 2004, re-elected Apr 2009)

Head of government: Caretaker Prime Minister Iveta Radicová (SDKÚ) (elected 9 Jul 2010; re-appointed 25 Oct 2011)

Ruling party: Coalition led by Slovenská Demokratická a Krestanská Únia-Demokratická Strana (SDKÚ-DS) (Slovak Democratic and Christian Union-Democratic Party), with Sloboda a Solidarita (SaS) (Freedom and Solidarity Party), Krest'ansko-Demokratické Hnutie (KDH) (Christian Democratic Movement) and Most-Híd (Bridge) (from 9 Jul 2010); re-appointed 25 Oct 2011)

Area: 49,035 square km

Population: 5.43 million (2010)*

Capital: Bratislava

Official language: Slovak

Currency: Euro (€) = 100 cents (from 1 Jan 2009; previous currency Slovak koruna, locked at Sk30.126 per euro)

Exchange rate: €0.75 per US$ (Oct 2011)

GDP per capita: US$16,104 (2010)

GDP real growth: 4.00% (2010)

GDP: US$87.50 billion (2010)

Labour force: 2.70 million (2010)

Unemployment: 12.55% (2010)

Inflation: 0.70% (2010)

Balance of trade: US$182.00 million (2010)

Annual FDI: US$553.14 million (2010)

* estimated figure

Slovakia

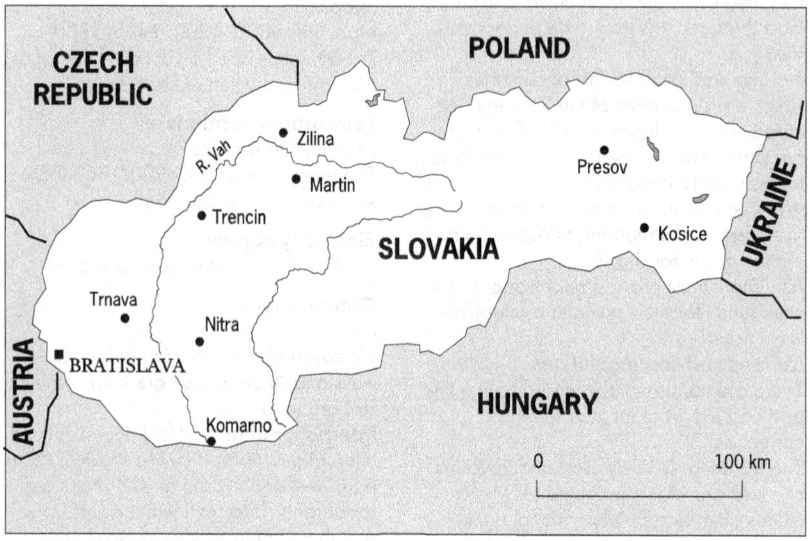

The decision of the Slovakian parliament in May 2011, albeit by a slender majority, to reject the euro-zone proposals to bail out Greece had two dramatic consequences. The first was to prevent the euro-zone from going ahead with the bail-out, which required a majority vote. The second was to cause the fall of the coalition led by the photogenic Iveta Radicová of the Christian Democrats, nicknamed the 'Tatra Tigress'. Mrs Radicová's Slovenská Demokratická a Krestanská Únia-Demokratická Strana (SDKÚ-DS) (Slovak Democratic and Christian Union-Democratic Party) party held only 28 of the 150 parliamentary seats. But she had eventually been able to form a government commanding 79 seats. Slovakians were well aware that sooner or later they would inevitably fork out to cover the holes appearing in other peoples' economies. But the vote did at least make sure that in Brussels officials began to pay them some attention.

The politics

The British Broadcasting Service (BBC) reported that Brussels' fear was that the Slovaks had fallen out of love with the euro, less than three years after they became only the second former communist country (after Slovenia) to adopt it. Slovakia was not deaf to the calls of Messrs Merkel and Sarkozy that the bail-out fund needed to be bolstered to protect the euro-zone from succumbing to Greek contagion. But the enthusiasm of the Slovakians for the EU, and more particularly euro, membership had certainly been dampened; it had not, however, totally disappeared. Slovaks were well informed as to the pros and cons of playing the European game, but if anything had been overlooked, it was the possible need for Slovakians to put their hands in their pockets to come to the rescue of fellow euro-zone members.

There are 150 members in the Slovak Parliament, known as the National Council. In fact the majority of them – government and opposition – were in favour of beefing up the European Financial Stability Facility Fund (EFSF). But many of those in Prime Minister Iveta Radicová's four-party centre-right governing coalition expressed deep misgivings when the euro-zone agreed in July to increase the EFSF to ?440 billion (US$580 billion) and give it new powers, including the ability to buy sovereign debt on secondary markets.

As other euro-zone countries ratified the proposals and the debt crisis deepened, most of the Slovak coalition fell into line –

except for Richard Sulik, leader of the neo-liberal Sloboda a Solidarita (SaS) (Freedom and Solidarity Party) and his 21 MPs. 'There's a lot of talk at the moment about solidarity, that Slovakia must show solidarity with other countries,' Mr Sulik told journalists. 'The average pension in Slovakia is less than 400 euros (US$536). The average pension in Greece is ?1,400 (US$2,600).' Mr Sulik said, going on to say: 'It's impossible to explain to a Slovak pensioner that he or she has to contribute – in the form of higher value added tax (VAT) for example – towards Greek pensions. Or towards Italian MPs' salaries, the highest MPs' salaries in Europe,' he added.

That, in a nutshell, is the argument of those like Richard Sulik who oppose bolstering the bailout fund. Better to let Greece go bankrupt, he said, expressing a sentiment that some, but not most, Slovaks share. Observers assumed and Brussels hoped, that Mr Sulik would crumble under the weight of European pressure. He did not. Compromises – from both sides – were offered and rejected, although few were realistic. Mr Sulik stood his ground: no bailout.

Prime minister Iveta Radicová had stuck her neck out for the euro when she linked a parliamentary vote on legislation to boost the powers of the EFSF, the euro-zone's main bail-out fund, to a motion of confidence in her government. She lost on both counts, deserted by the SaS, a zealously *laisser-faire* junior partner in her four-party coalition. Some Slovakians placed their hopes in Robert Fico, former prime minister and leader of the leftist opposition, who is known to support the EFSF. But Mr Fico sensed an opportunity to wound and perhaps bring down the government, hastening early elections he is likely to win. His party, Smer-Sociálna Demokracia (Smer) (Direction party-Social Democracy), was to abstain from the vote. Eventually a deal was done. It included calling an early general for March 2012. The vote against the bailout was lost and Slovakia became the last euro-zone country to ratify the bailout fund and – *en passant* – the first one to lose a government over it. Having lost the vote of confidence, Mrs Radicová became caretaker prime minister until the elections.

The economy

In its May 2011 report the International Monetary Fund (IMF) noted that the Slovak economy continued its robust recovery. The upturn has been stronger than in most of Slovakia's neighbours, reflecting strong fundamentals and a surge in the export-oriented manufacturing sector, which benefited from a revival in global demand. In tandem, the financial sector has regained strength, profits in the corporate sector are recovering, real estate prices have stabilised and the fiscal position is improving.

The growth outlook for 2011 and beyond is, according to the IMF, favourable. While growth will still be driven mainly by the export sector, a gradual rebound in domestic demand would provide some boost and broadly offset the withdrawal of fiscal support. Overall, the IMF projects real GDP growth of about 3.75 per cent in 2011 and of about 4.25 per cent in 2012–15, among the strongest performances in the European Union, but still significantly below the pre-crisis rate of expansion.

The economic recovery has had little positive effect on employment. The unemployment rate has climbed to over 14 per cent and is even higher among low-skilled workers and in less prosperous regions. With the turnaround in economic activity, employment started to recover in late 2010, but the gains, so far, have been small and insufficient to prevent an increase in long-term unemployment.

Inflation dropped to among the lowest in the euro-zone in 2010, but accelerated in early 2011. Reflecting the global increase in the price of oil and other commodities and in part because of indirect tax hikes at the beginning of 2011, CPI inflation jumped to 3.8 per cent (year-on-year) in March 2011. However, as core inflation remains well-anchored, the projected tightening of monetary conditions will help reduce CPI inflation to below 3 per cent in 2012 and beyond.

The 2011 budget includes a significant fiscal consolidation package that is projected to reduce the general government deficit to about 5 per cent of GDP. A structural drop in revenue and continued strong expenditure growth kept the fiscal deficit in 2010 at around 8 per cent of GDP for a second year in a row. The high deficits contributed to a rapid increase in the general government debt to around 41 per cent of GDP. Yet, this ratio is still relatively low and market confidence has remained intact – reflected in a relatively low risk premium over corresponding euro-zone benchmark bonds.

Financial conditions and the situation of the financial sector have, according to the IMF, improved. Credit growth is recovering gradually and monetary conditions are supportive with a low interest rate. Banks have enhanced their balance sheets and improved capital and liquidity ratios. Their profits rebounded in 2010, reflecting cost cutting measures, higher interest rate spreads and lower provisions, notwithstanding a still high level of non-performing loans.

Risk assessment

Politics	Good
Economy	Good
Regional stability	Good

COUNTRY PROFILE

Historical profile

Slovakia, called Oberungarn (Upper Hungary) in some older maps, had politically

KEY INDICATORS — Slovakia

	Unit	2006	2007	2008	2009	2010
Population	m	5.41	5.40	5.41	*5.42	*5.43
Gross domestic product (GDP)	US$bn	56.05	74.99	95.20	88.20	87.50
GDP per capita	US$	10,357	13,857	16,282	16,282	16,104
GDP real growth	%	8.5	10.5	5.8	-4.8	4.0
Inflation	%	4.4	2.8	3.9	0.9	0.7
Unemployment	%	10.4	8.4	7.7	11.4	12.5
Exports (fob) (goods)	US$m	41,735.0	57,806.0	70,271.0	55,515.0	64,665.0
Imports (fob) (goods)	US$m	44,283.0	58,715.0	71,170.0	53,799.0	64,484.0
Balance of trade	US$m	-2,549.0	-909.0	-899.0	1,715.0	182.0
Current account	US$m	-3,937.0	-3,998.0	-6,185.0	-2,810.0	-3,009.0
Total reserves minus gold	US$m	12,647.0	18,032.0	17,854.0	692.0	719.0
Foreign exchange	US$m	12,645.0	18,026.0	17,805.0	50.0	52.0
Exchange rate	per US$	26.45	23.23	21.36	0.78	0.76

* estimated figure

been a part of the Hungarian kingdom for centuries, ever since the Moravian Kingdom had been destroyed in 902.
1536–1783 Bratislava, formerly Pressburg, was the capital of Hungary.
1867–1917 The Habsburg domains in central Europe were reconstituted as the dual monarchy of Austria-Hungary. Slovakia's struggle for independence suffered a setback when Hungary's parliament gained a large degree of political autonomy from the Austrian administration in Vienna. The policy of Magyarisation that the Hungarian administration strove to achieve – Hungarian was to be the exclusive language of administration, jurisdiction and education – was most disturbing to Slovakia.
1918 At the end of the First World War, Slovakia announced its independence from the Austro-Hungarian empire and incorporation into the new Republic of Czechoslovakia with Thomas Masaryk as the country's first president.
1938 Czechoslovakia ceded its German-speaking areas of Sudetenland to Germany.
1939–45 The country fell under German control until the end of the Second World War.
1946 The Czechoslovak Communist Party (CPCz) formed a power-sharing government following national elections.
1948 After mass protests and strikes orchestrated by the Communists, a government crisis left the CPCz with a majority in government.
1949–67 Stalinist-style rule, complete with party purges.
1968 Alexander Dubcek, the CPCz leader, introduced the policy of 'socialism with a human face', which ended with the crushing of the reformist movement by the Soviet army.
1969–88 There were on-going protests at occupation by the Soviet troops. Václav Havel and a group of dissidents called for the restoration of civil and political rights. Mass demonstrations in 1988 marked the anniversary of the 1968 invasion.
1989 The new spirit of *glasnost* was met with scepticism as the government initially resisted political and economic change. However, large public demonstrations in the major cities, the 'Velvet Revolution', led to the resignation of the Communist Party leadership. Václav Havel was elected president and a pluralistic political system and market economy were introduced.
1990 The country was renamed the Czech and Slovak Federative Republic. The first free elections since 1946 led to the establishment of a coalition government involving all major parties, with the exception of the CPCz, and Havel was re-elected president.
1991 The Soviet forces completed their withdrawal.
1992 In elections, the Czech voters backed the centre-right, while the Slovaks supported Slovak separatists and left-wing parties. Vladimir Meciar (a supporter of Slovak separatism) became Slovak prime minister. He opposed the rapid privatisation of the public sector proposed by the Czech prime minister, Václav Klaus. Neither was prepared to compromise and so agreed to the separation of Slovakia, despite President Havel's objections.
1993 Czechoslovakia divided into two independent countries, the Czech Republic (comprising the regions of Bohemia and Moravia) and the Slovak Republic (Slovakia). Michal Kovac became president of the Slovak Republic, with Vladimir Meciar continuing as prime minister.
1994 Meciar was voted out of office and was replaced by Jozef Moravcik. But following National Council elections Meciar was returned to power.
1998 Kovac's presidential term expired and Prime Minister Meciar assumed some presidential powers. Mikulas Dzurinda became prime minister as opposition parties refused to co-operate with Meciar, despite his party, Hnutie Za Demokratické Slovensko (HZDS) (Movement for Democratic Slovakia), gaining most seats in the general elections.
1999 Rudolf Schuster was elected president.
2000 The Slovenská Demokratická a Krestanská Únia-Demokratická Strana (SDKÚ-DS) (Slovak Democratic and Christian Union-Democratic Party) backed Mikulas Dzurinda in the next elections.
2002 The parliamentary elections were won by the SDKÚ-DS, which formed a coalition with the Hungarian Coalition Party (SMK), the Christian Democratic Movement (KDH) and the New Citizen Alliance (ANO). Nato invited Slovakia to join its alliance.
2003 Referendum voters approved European Union (EU) membership.
2004 Ivan Gasparovic won the presidency. Slovakia became an EU member.
2005 Slovakia entered the European Exchange Rate Mechanism (ERM II).
2006 The left-leaning Smer-Sociálna Demokracia (Smer) (Direction party-Social Democracy) won the general elections. Agreement between Smer, the Ludová Strana-Hnutie Za Demokratické Slovensko (LS-HZDS) (People's Party-Movement for a Democratic Slovakia), and the Slovenská Národná Strana (SNS) (Slovak National Party), created a coalition government. Robert Fico (Smer) became prime minister.
2007 Slovakia became a member of the EU Schengen area; all citizens may cross borders without a passport or visa.
2008 An agreement for visa-free visits of citizens to the US was signed.
2009 The national currency, Koruna, was replaced by the euro on 1 January, set at the official exchange rate of Sk30.1260 per euro. In presidential elections held in parliament, no candidate won over 50 per cent in the first round; in the runoff incumbent Ivan Gasparovic (candidate of the ruling coalition) won 55.5 per cent of the vote, Iveta Radicová (joint candidate of opposition parties) won 44.5 per cent. A new language law was introduced, making the use of minority languages (mainly Hungarian) in official government business a finable offence. The law was condemned by Hungary, which asked for EU support in condemning the law.
2010 In parliamentary elections held in June the ruling Smer won 34.8 per cent of the vote (62 seats out of 150), the largest vote for a single party; a centre-right grouping won 79 seats. The president invited Prime Minister Fico (Smer) to form a new government. When Fico failed, the president asked Iveta Radicová to form a government. She became Slovakia's first woman prime minister on 9 July, at the head of a centre-right, four-party coalition of SDKÚ-DS, SaS, KDH and Bridge. A referendum to reduce the number of deputies in parliament from 150 to 100, implement internet voting and eliminate fees for state broadcasting, as well as measures to boost public transparency and reduce fiscal burdens, was set for 18 September; it failed through lack of voter turnout.
2011 Slovakia voiced opposition to the second fiscal bailout of Greece by Euro-partners in July. As the second poorest nation (after Estonia) in the euro-zone it objected to its funds being used on a 'richer' country's debts. Along with Finland, Germany and The Netherlands it wanted more austerity and reforms from Greece as well as Greek state property used as collateral, plus private creditors to accept at least a US$43 billion share as their own liability. Parliament voted against the government's motion to support the EU-EMU bailout of weaker economies on 11 October. On 13 October an agreement was reached with the opposition whereby the EU ratification bill would be passed in exchange for early general elections. On 25 October, the government was reinstated in a caretaker function, but with reduced powers. Vaclav Havel, the first post-Communist president of Czechoslovakia (1989–1993; 1993–2003 Czech Republic only) died on 18 December. He oversaw the transition to democracy of Czechoslovakia and its division when the Czech Republic and Slovakia were created.

Political structure

Constitution

The constitution was ratified in 1992. No new government can be formed until the president has accepted the resignation of

the former one. Further amendments in January and February 2001 created an independent council, increasing the powers of the constitutional court, and paved the way for reform of the public administration.
With reference to accession to EU and NATO, an amendment to the constitution was approved on 1 July 2001, which reclassified the relationship between national and international law, introduced judicial regulations and allowed for the creation of a second tier of self-administrative government in the regions.
Electoral system: Universal direct suffrage for party lists. All electoral coalitions have to win 5 per cent of the vote for every party they contain.

Independence date
1 January 1993

Form of state
Parliamentary democratic republic

The executive
Executive power lies with the prime minister and ministers, the former being appointed by the president.
The head of state is the president, elected by the National Council of the Slovak Republic by secret ballot for a period of five years. A majority of three-fifths of all deputies' votes is required for the president to be elected.

National legislature
The unicameral Národná Rada (National Council) has 150 members, directly elected by proportional representation from party lists, to serve for four-year terms.

Legal system
Slovakia's legal system is partly based on the Czechslovakian system introduced before independence in 1993. The judiciary is independent of the government, although the president appoints judges to both the Constitutional Court and Supreme Court. The Constitutional Court is responsible for ensuring that legislation adheres to the constitution and 13 judges are appointed for a period of 12 years. Judges of the Supreme Court are appointed for an unlimited time period.
As part of the process toward accession to the EU, Slovakia has been attempting to harmonise its existing and new legislation with that of the organisation.

Last elections
12 June 2010 (parliamentary); 21 March / 4 April 2009 (presidential and runoff)
Results: Parliamentary: Strana Smer-Tretia Cesta (Smer) (Direction Party) won 34.8 per cent of the vote (62 seats out of 150), Slovenská Demokratická a Krestanská Únia (SDKÚ) (Slovak Democratic and Christian Union) 15.2 per cent (28), Sloboda a Solidarita (SaS) (Freedom and Solidarity Party) 12.1 per cent (22), Krest'ansko-Demokratické Hnutie (KDH) (Christian Democratic Movement) 8.5 per cent (15), Most-Híd (Bridge) 8.1 per cent (14), Slovenská Národná Strana (SNS) (Slovak National Party) 5.1 per cent (9), the Ludová Strana - Hnutie za Demokratické Slovensko (LS-HZDS) (People's Party-Movement for a Democratic Slovakia) 4.3 per cent (0), Strana madarskej koalície-Magyar Koalíció Pártja (SMK-MKP) (Party of the Hungarian Coalition) 4.3 per cent (0). Turnout was 58.8 per cent.
Presidential: (first round) Ivan Gasparovic won 46.7 per cent, Iveta Radicová 38.1 per cent, Frantisek Miklosko 5.4 per cent, Zuzana Martináková 5.1 per cent; turnout was 43.6 per cent. (Runoff) Gasparovic won 55.5 per cent; Radicová 44.5 per cent. Turnout was 51.6 per cent.
European parliament (June 2009): turn out was the lowest of the 27 countries at 19 per cent, compared to 17 per cent in 2004.

Next elections
10 March 2012 (parliamentary); 2014 (presidential)

Political parties

Ruling party
Coalition led by Slovenská Demokratická a Krestanská Únia-Demokratická Strana (SDKÚ-DS) (Slovak Democratic and Christian Union-Democratic Party), with Sloboda a Solidarita (SaS) (Freedom and Solidarity Party),
Krest'ansko-Demokratické Hnutie (KDH) (Christian Democratic Movement) and Most-Híd (Bridge) (from 9 Jul 2010); re-appointed 25 Oct 2011)

Main opposition party
Smer-Sociálna Demokracia (Smer) (Direction party-Social Democracy)

Population

5.43 million (2010)*
Last census: May 2001: 5,379,455
Population density: 110.4 inhabitants per square km. Urban population: 58 per cent (1995–2001).
Annual growth rate: 0.1 per cent 1994–2004 (WHO 2006)

Ethnic make-up
The chief non-Roma minorities are Hungarians (10.8 per cent of the population), Czechs (3 per cent), Ruthenians, Ukrainians, Germans and Poles. Roma, although making up only 1.5 per cent of the overall population, make up a significant minority in some areas, and are growing faster than the national average.

Religions
Roman Catholic (60.3 per cent), Protestant (8.4 per cent), Orthodox (4.1 per cent).

Education

Slovakia has universal literacy and offers free education to all. Enrolment at all levels is high and there is no noticeable gender disparity. Languages of instruction are English and Slovak, although Hungarians may be taught in their own language.
Literacy rate: 100 per cent adult rate; 100 per cent youth rate (15–24) (Unesco 2005).
Compulsory years: 6 to 15
Enrolment rate: 102 per cent total primary enrolment, 94 per cent gross secondary enrolment; of the relevant age groups (including repeaters); (World Bank).
Pupils per teacher: 20 in primary schools

Health

There is a significant disparity between male and female life expectancy (9 years), partly due to the unbalanced diet and high cigarette and beer consumption by men, which the government is attempting to reduce.

HIV/Aids
HIV prevalence: 0.1 per cent aged 15–49 in 2003 (World Bank)
Life expectancy: 74 years, 2004 (WHO 2006)
Fertility rate/Maternal mortality rate: 1.2 births per woman, 2004 (WHO 2006)
Birth rate/Death rate: 10 births per and nine deaths per 1,000 population (2003).
Child (under 5 years) mortality rate (per 1,000): 7.0 per 1,000 live births (World Bank)
Head of population per physician: 3.18 physicians per 1,000 people, 2003 (WHO 2006)

Welfare

Slovakia has a 42.5 hour working week with a minimum wage set by the government. It has a well-developed social security system, including health, unemployment and pension benefits. Employees contribute 12 per cent of their wages to social security schemes and employers an additional 38 per cent.

Main cities

Bratislava (capital, estimated population 424,207 in 2005), Košice (236,519), Presov (94,639), Nitra (86,407), Zilina (85,956).

Languages spoken

The Czech and Slovak languages are mutually comprehensible. Hungarian is widely spoken, especially in the south and east.
A large proportion of the population, particularly those engaged in industry and foreign trade, speaks German. Russian is also spoken by some executives. English is increasing, especially among the younger generation.

Official language/s
Slovak

Media

Press

Dailies: There are national and regional dailies, most published in Slovakian, including *Pravda* (www.pravda.sk), *Praca* (www.praca.sk), *Novy CAS* (www.bleskovky.sk),*SME* (www.sme.sk). In Hungarian, *Új Szó* (www.ujszo.com) and in English *Slovak Spectator* (www.slovakspectator.sk).
Regional publications in Slovakian includes, *Korzár* (www.cassovia.sk/korzar) from Kosice, *Presovsky Vecernik* (www.slovanet.sk/vecernik/pv) from Presov and *Nitrianske Noviny* (www.mynoviny.sk) from Nitra.
Weeklies: Magazines in Slovakian include *Plus 7 Dni* (www.plus7dni.sk), *Tyzden* (www.tyzden.sk) and in Hungarian *Vasárnap* (www.vasarnap.com).
Business: Magazines, in Slovakian, include *Profit* (http://profit.etrend.sk) and in English *Trend* (http://english.etrend.sk). Newspapers in Slovakian *Hospodarske Noviny* (www.hnonline.sk) and *Profini* (www.profini.sk).
Many dailies include sections on business news.
Periodicals: *Slovak Spectator*, an English-language newspaper, is published every second Wednesday.

Broadcasting

Radio: There are over 20 private, commercial radio stations. The public Slovensky Rozhlas (Slovak Radio) broadcasts nationwide as well as international programmes. Other major radio stations includes Radio Expres (www.expres.sk), Radio Viva (www.radioviva.sk), Radio Okey (www.okey.sk) and Fun Radio (www.funradio.sk).
Other European radio stations are available.
Television: There are several networks available including, TV Markiza (www.markiza.sk) which has the largest audience, Slovenská televízia (Slovak TV) (www.stv.sk) is the public channel, Joj TV (www.joj.sk) and the news channel TA3 (www.ta3.com), which broadcasts regional programmes via cable.
Reception of broadcasts from neighbouring countries allows greater variety.

Advertising

There are a number of foreign and domestic advertising agencies. The most commonly used media include newspapers, radio and television. Billboards and posters are widely used.

News agencies

TASR, Pribinova 23, 81928 Bratislava 111 (tel: 5921-0152; fax: 5296-3405; email: export@tasr.sk; internet: www.tasr.sk).
Sita (Slovak news agency) (www.sita.sk).

Economy

Since joining the European Union (EU) in 2004 Slovenia's economy experienced a period of rapid growth, based on a vibrant export sector. GDP growth averaged 7.4 per cent over 2004–08 as the unemployment rate fell from around 19 per cent in 2001 to 12.5 per cent in 2010. Heavy industries include steel, aluminium and petroleum production and vehicle manufacturing; Slovakia had the highest global per capita car production in 2009. Lighter industries include electronic component manufacturing, paper and household machines goods. There are rich farmlands in the south of Slovakia and wine is an important export commodity, along with grains, live animals and fruits and vegetables.
GDP growth in 2007 was a record 10.5 per cent, which fell to 5.8 per cent in 2008 as energy and food prices soared and the global economic crisis weakened exports. The government introduced stimulus packages in late 2008 and early 2009, including tax reductions and subsidies and measures to increase liquidity in the corporate sector and incentives to speed up the use of EU funds. Despite this, in 2009 the economy fell into recession with GDP growth of -4.8 per cent. However, a recovery was achieved in 2010 with growth of 4 per cent. The trade balance that had been -US$2.55 billion as imports outstripped exports in 2006 was reversed by 2009 and was US$1.72 billion as imports were cut by over 11 per cent.
Slovakia was ranked 43 (out of 183 countries) in the World Bank's annual *Ease of doing business* index in 2011, with a skilled workforce, flat rate corporate and personal tax of 19 per cent and a generally liberal labour code, all of which encouraged much of the foreign direct investment (FDI) of US$553.1 million in 2010. Other member states of the EU account for the greater proportion of FDI.

External trade

As a member of the European Union, Slovakia operates within a community-wide free trade area, with tariffs set as a whole. Internationally, the EU has free trade agreements with a number of nations and trading blocs worldwide.
Foreign trade represents over 160 per cent of GDP, of which the greater part is automobile assembly – in 2006 Slovakia produced more cars per head than any other country worldwide. Traditional heavy industry is being replaced in importance by manufacturing of consumer goods, electronics and engineering and the petrochemical industry.
Natural resources, geared to exports, include mineral extraction (high-grade iron ore, copper, lead, and zinc) and forestry products.

Imports

Principal imports include capital machinery and transport equipment (over 40 per cent), electrical equipment, intermediate and other manufactured goods, fuels and chemicals.
Main sources: Germany (typically 20 per cent of total), Czech Republic (11 per cent), Russia (11 per cent).

Exports

Principal exports include vehicles (around 30 per cent), machinery and energy and electrical equipment, base metals, minerals, chemicals, plastics and timber.
Main destinations: Germany (typically 20 per cent of total), Czech Republic (13 per cent), France (7 per cent).

Agriculture

Farming

The agricultural sector suffered from under-investment during the communist era. In an attempt to increase productivity, a land restitution act was adopted in 1990, under which all agricultural land taken by the state between 1948–55 was returned to its original owners.
Agriculture contributes around 3.5 per cent to GDP. Wheat, maize and barley are exported. Only 10 per cent of potato requirements are imported and about 20 per cent of raw sugar requirements. Slovakia is a net importer of oil crops, although the margin is very small, with equal amounts of rape and mustard seed imported and exported. Slovakia is mostly self sufficient in meat, eggs and milk.
The agricultural sector is subject to the reformed Common Agricultural Policy (CAP), whereby subsidies are no longer paid on farm output, which tended to benefit large farms and encourage overproduction, but rather on single farm payments not conditional on production.

Fishing

The fishing sector, based on inland fisheries and imported sea-fish, is not significant, producing around 2,500 tonnes a year.

Forestry

Forest and other wooded land accounts for over two-fifths of the land area, with forest cover estimated at 2.1 million hectares (ha). More than 80 per cent of the forest is available for wood supply and the rest is preserved. The ownership structure of forest areas has changed considerably since 1990 as a result of privatisation and restitution. Half of the forested area is state-owned.
Consumption of forest products per capita is below the European average. Nearly all of the roundwood is processed in the country, using much of the hardwood and softwood species. Slovakia is a net

exporter of forestry products and although the industry is in need of modernisation, it is a significant earner of foreign exchange. Over three-quarters of sawnwood produced is exported, mostly to Hungary. The pulp industry utilises half of the hardwood production, recovered paper and some non-wood fibre pulp. The bulk of exports also constitute paper and pulpboard.

Industry and manufacturing
Industry accounts for around 30 per cent of GDP and 30 per cent of employment. Industrial production fell by approximately 20 per cent after the end of the Communist regime and privatisation has been unable to inject the necessary cash required for investment. Compared to neighbouring Hungary and Czech Republic, Slovak industry is marked by inefficiency, hidden bankruptcies and government subsidies.
The principal industries are the manufacture of machinery, chemicals and rubber, food and beverages, and iron metallurgy. Slovakian industry remains more vulnerable to the instability of Eastern European markets than its Czech neighbour. The long-term prospects for the sector depend on how successfully the country can recover from the dislocation of its traditional markets and find new ones for such key industries as steel. Half of all foreign direct investment (FDI) in Slovakia goes to the manufacturing sector.

Tourism
Tourism has been slow to develop, the government providing little incentive. EU accession boosts the number of visitors to Slovakia by over one million each year, but many visits were for short periods of a few days. The government is seeking to encourage more domestic tourism.

Mining
Slovakia has workable deposits of antimony ore, mercury, iron ore, copper, lead, zinc, precious metals, limestone, dolomite, gravel, brick loam, ceramic materials and stone salt. In each case, except iron ores, only small quantities are actually mined.

Hydrocarbons
Oil reserves have been virtually exhausted and Slovakia must rely on imports to meet its consumption level of 83,000 barrels per day (bpd) of oil. Oil imports come from Russia through two pipelines to the Slovnaft refinery in Bratislava and the rest to the Czech Republic.
Natural gas reserves of 15 billion cubic metres are almost exhausted and Slovakia relies on the imports to meet its demands for 6.5 billion per annum. Almost all natural gas is imported from Russia. Slovakia is also an important transit route for Russian gas exports, as around 25 per cent of gas consumed in Western Europe travels across its territory.
Coal is mined on a large scale. Reserves could last more than 40 years. Most is low quality brown coal (lignite) and looks likely to diminish as a key energy source due to the amount of pollution it causes.

Energy
Total installed electricity generating capacity was 7.36GW. Slovakia had five Chernobyl-style nuclear reactors in operation but an agreement with the EU saw the closure of three in 2008 and an upgrade in two. Before their shutdown nuclear energy supplied 57 per cent of electricity.
The state-owned Slovenske Elektrarne (Slovak Electric) was partially sold off with 66 per cent purchased by the Italian Enel energy company. As a condition of the sale Enel agreed to invest €1.8 billion (US$2 billion) to increase generating capacity. Slovak Electric also operates thermal and hydroelectric plants.

Financial markets
Stock exchange
Burza Cennych Papierov v Bratislave (BSSE) (Bratislava Stock Exchange)

Banking and insurance
Slovakia's banking system has been reformed, although the sector has been plagued by bad debts coupled with massive losses affecting a third of banks. As a result, economic structuring has been essential to both macroeconomic stability and the integrity of the banking sector.
Many of the country's larger banks have been privatised. In early 2002, a 66.7 stake in Slovenska Poistovna (Slovak Insurance Bank) was sold to Germany's Allianz AG for US$142 million. Smaller banks have closed as the central bank has imposed a tough regulatory framework on commerce, with greater power given to creditors.
Central bank
Narodna Banka Slovenska (NBS) (National Bank of Slovakia)
Main financial centre
Bratislava

Time
GMT plus one hour (daylight saving, late March to late October, GMT plus two hours)

Geography
Slovakia is a landlocked, hilly country in the heart of Europe. Around 80 per cent of the country has an altitude of over 750 metres above sea level. The High Tatra Mountains in the north give way to large lowlands, broad valleys and meadows in the south.
Slovakia is bordered by the Czech Republic to the west (the border is 215km long), by Poland to the north (444km), Ukraine to the east (90km), Hungary to the south (515km) and Austria to the south-west (the border with Austria is only 15km from the capital, Bratislava).
The High Tatra Mountains are on the northern Polish border and the Low Tatras are in the centre and east of the country. The highest peak is Gerlach in the High Tatras (2,655 metres), with the lowest point the Bodrog river near Streda and Bodrogom (95 metres).
There are numerous rivers flowing south to the lowland areas, including the Váh, Nitra, Hron and Hornád. The River Danube marks part of the southern border. The lowland areas are in the south-west and south-east of the country.
Hemisphere
Northern

Climate
Slovakia has a continental climate (warm summers and cold winters). Summer maximum temperatures are 32 degrees Celsius (C) to 35 degrees C; July is the hottest month (average 30 degrees C). Minimum temperatures are minus 12 degrees C to minus 20 degrees C. January is the coldest month (average minus 8 degrees C). Long-term average rainfall is approximately 490mm.

Dress codes
Most people dress in standard casual wear. For winter, mediumweight clothing is required with a heavy coat. For summer, lightweight clothing is suitable. For business meetings, men should wear a suit and tie.

Entry requirements
Passports
Required by all. Passport must be valid for eight months from the date of issue of the visa.
Visa
Required by all, except nationals of EU and Schengen area signatory countries, North America, Australasia and Japan. For further exceptions contact the nearest embassy or see www.foreign.gov.sk (or www.slovakia.org and follow link through tourism to visa information). A Schengen visa application (offered in several languages) can be downloaded from http://europa.eu/abc/travel/ see 'documents you will need'.
Visitors are required to have onward/return passage.
Currency advice/regulations
Import of local currency is prohibited. There are no restrictions on import of foreign currency, but it must be declared on arrival.
Local currency up to Sk100 can be exported, and foreign currency up to the amount declared on entry.

Customs
Personal items are duty-free. There are no duties levied on alcohol and tobacco between EU member states, providing amounts imported are for personal consumption.
Items of value, such as cameras, should be declared.

Health (for visitors)
Nationals of the European Economic Area (EEA) countries and Switzerland can access reduced cost and sometimes free medical treatment using a European Health Insurance Card (EHIC) while visiting the EEA. Exceptions include nationals of the 10 countries, which joined the EU in 2004, whose EHIC is not valid in Switzerland. Applications for the EHIC should be made before travelling.
Mandatory precautions
Full medical insurance, covering the whole territory of the Slovak Republic, is required. Random checks at Slovak points of entry are carried out and entry can be refused if no medical insurance for the whole country can be produced.

Credit cards
Credit cards are generally accepted by major hotels and restaurants.

Public holidays (national)
Fixed dates
1 Jan (New Year's Day/Independence Day), 6 Jan (Epiphany), 1 May (Labour Day), 8 May (Liberation of the Republic), 5 Jul (Ss Cyril and Methodius Day), 29 Aug (Slovak National Uprising Day), 1 Sep (Constitution Day), 15 Sep (Our Lady of the Seven Sorrows Day), 1 Nov (All Saints' Day), 17 Nov (Freedom and Democracy Day), 24–26 Dec (Christmas).
Variable dates
Good Friday, Easter Monday.

Working hours
Banking
Mon–Fri: 0800–1700. There are also exchange offices in the main city centres, which operate seven days a week until 1900.
Business
Mon–Fri: 0800–1600.
Government
Mon–Fri: 0900–1700.
Shops
Mon–Fri: 0900–1800; Sat: 0900–1200; some shops remain open late on Thursday evenings.

Electricity supply
220V, 50 cycles AC

Weights and measures
Metric system. In addition, the following measures are used: quintal or metric hundredweight = 100 kg. Food is usually purchased by the decagramme and kilogram.

Social customs/useful tips
Appointments should be made in advance and punctuality is important. Shaking hands is customary when meeting people and on parting. Business is conducted in Slovak; many executives speak a second language – German, Russian or English. When drinks are served, it is considered polite to wait for everyone to be served and then wish each person *Nazdravi* ('to your health'). At meals it is usual to wait for everyone to be served before starting and to wish everyone *bon appetit* or *dobrou chut* just before eating. The terms *Pan* (Mr), *Pani* (Mrs) and *Slecna* (Miss) are used. *Slecna* is used for single women under 30 only; single women over 30 will usually be addressed as *Pani*.
Gratuities are between 5 and 10 per cent. The minimum drinking age is 18 years. When visiting private homes it is customary to take flowers for the hosts. Visitors also generally leave their shoes in the hallway, partly as a mark of respect and partly because of pollution in the streets. Men always take off their hats indoors. Illegally parked cars tend to be towed away by the police and it is advisable to park at attended car parks where the cost is relatively low.

Security
Street crime, especially in the towns, has become a problem since the 1989 revolution because the police tend to keep a low profile. Although the situation has improved, it is still advisable to carry as little in the way of valuables and cash as possible. Car vandalism and theft are also problems.

Getting there
Air
National airline: Slovak Airlines
International airport/s: MR Stefanik Airport (BTS), 9km from Bratislava; post office, bank, bureau de change, restaurants, duty free shop, car hire.
Airport tax: None
Surface
Slovakia is included in the Pan-European Corridor 5 scheme. The project has some 3,270km of railways, linking Kiev in the Ukraine with western Europe via Italy, and 2,850 of new and upgraded roads.
Road: There is ample road access from Czech Republic, Poland, Ukraine, Hungary and Austria. There is a motorway from Bratislava to Prague.
Rail: Slovakia has rail connections with Vienna, Hamburg, Berlin, Warsaw, Budapest, Moscow and St Petersburg.
Water: Ships provide regular passenger service and cruises on the Danube, from Passau and Regensburg (Germany) via Vienna (Austria). There are also links with the Rhine and Main rivers and the Black Sea.

Getting about
National transport
Air: There are internal connections provided by Slovak Airlines, SkyEurope Airlines and Air Slovakia.
Road: The road network is extensive and in good condition. The major route is from Bratislava to Presov and Kosice.
Buses: There is an extensive coach network.
Rail: Slovakia has a rail network of 3,665km, of which around 1,590km are electrified. There are frequent express services between Bratislava and the main centres and tourist destinations.
Water: The principal navigable waterway is the Danube, on which cruises are available.
City transport
Taxis: Taxis are available in all main towns and are relatively cheap. They are metered, but passengers should ensure that the driver switches them on before starting off.
Buses, trams & metro: Bratislava and other cities are well served by trams, trolley-buses and buses. Tickets can be purchased at news-stands or from dispensers at the queues.
Car hire
Car hire is available in major towns. Traffic drives on the right. There is an extensive network of roadside restaurants and petrol stations. Emergency telephones are located at half mile intervals on motorways and the emergency system is generally quick and reliable.

BUSINESS DIRECTORY

The addresses listed below are a selection only. While World of Information makes every endeavour to check these addresses, we cannot guarantee that changes have not been made, especially to telephone numbers and area codes. We would welcome any corrections.

Telephone area codes
The international direct dialling code (IDD) for Slovakia is +421, followed by area code and subscriber's number:

Banska Bystricá	48	Nitra	37
Bratislava	2	Presov	51
Kosice	55	Zilina	41
Liptoský Mikuláš	44		

Useful telephone numbers
Police: 158
Ambulance: 155
Fire: 150
Directory enquiries: 154

Chambers of Commerce
American Chamber of Commerce in the Slovak Republic, Hotel Danube, 1 Rybne namestie, 81338 Bratislava (tel: 5934-0508; fax: 5934-0556; e-mail: director@amcham.sk).

Banska Bystrica Regional Chamber of Commerce and Industry, 4 namestie S Moysesa, 97401 Banska Bystrica (tel: 412-5643; fax: 412-5636; e-mail: sopkrkbb@sopk.sk).

Bratislava Regional Chamber of Commerce and Industry, 6 Jasikova, 82673 Bratislava (tel: 4829-1257; fax: 4829-1260; e-mail: sopkrkbl@scci.sk).

British Chamber of Commerce in the Slovak Republic, 14 Cukrova, 81339 Bratislava (tel/fax: 5292-0371; e-mail: director@britcham.sk).

Kosice Regional Chamber of Commerce and Industry, 48/A Trieda SNP, 04011 Kosice (tel: 641-9477; fax: 641-9470; e-mail: sopkrkke@scci.sk).

Lucenec Regional Chamber of Commerce and Industry, 2 Vajanskeho, 98401 Lucenec (tel: 433-3939; fax: 433-3937; e-mail: sopkrklc@scci.sk).

Nitra Regional Chamber of Commerce and Industry, 4 Akademicka, 94901 Nitra (tel: 653-5466; fax: 733-6739; e-mail: sopkrknr@scci.sk).

Presov Regional Chamber of Commerce and Industry, 22 Masarykova, 08001 Presov (tel: 773-2818; fax: 773-2413; e-mail: sopkrkpo@scci.sk).

Slovak Chamber of Commerce and Industry, 9 Gorkeho, 81603 Bratislava (tel: 5443-3291; fax: 5413-1159; e-mail: sopkurad@sopk.sk).

Trencin Regional Chamber of Commerce and Industry, 2 Jilemnickeho, 91101 Trencin (tel: 652-3834; fax: 652-1023; e-mail: sopkrktn@scci.sk).

Trnava Regional Chamber of Commerce and Industry, 2 Trhova, 91701 Trnava (tel: 551-2588; fax: 551-2603; e-mail: sopkrktt@sopk.sk).

Zilina Regional Chamber of Commerce and Industry, 31 Halkova, 01001 Zilina (tel: 723-5101; fax: 723-5102; e-mail: sekrza@za.scci.sk).

Banking

Citibank (Slovakia),Mlynské nivy 43, 82501 Bratislava (tel: 5823-0224; fax: 5823-0211).

Consolidation Bank SFI, Cintorisíka 21, 81499 Bratislava (tel: 368-011; fax: 321-353).

Crédit Lyonnais Bank Slovakia, Medena 22, 811 02 Bratislava (tel: 325-320).

Deíl n Banka as, Frantiskánske nám 8, 81310 Bratislava (tel: 333-376; fax: 330-376).

General Credit Bank, Námestie SNP 19, 81856 Bratislava (tel: 531-7283; fax: 531-7020/05).

ING Bank, Kolarska 6, 811 06 Bratislava PO Box 123 (tel: 5346-111).

Investment and Development Bank, Stúrova 5, 81855 Bratislava (tel: 326-121; fax: 321-433).

Istrobanka as, Laurinská 1, 81101 Bratislava (tel: 539-7524; fax: 533-1744).

Konsolidacna Banka Bratislava, Cintorinska 21, 814 99 Bratislava (tel: 321-387; fax: 321-353).

Polnobanka as, Vajnorská 21, 83265 Bratislava (tel: 273-964; fax: 259-024).

Post Bank, PO Box 149, Gorkého 3, 81499 Bratislava (tel: 329-253; fax: 211-204).

Slovak Savings Bank, Námestie SNP 18, 81607 Bratislava (tel: 560-6580; fax: 560-6220).

TATRA Bank, Vajanského nábrezie 5, 81006 Bratislava (tel: 210-3519; fax: 324-760).

Volksbank, Námestie SNP 15, 81000 Bratislava (tel: 381-1140; fax: 364-847).

Central bank

Narodna banka Slovenska (National Bank of Slovakia), Imricha Karvasa 1, 81325 Bratislava (tel: 5787-1111; fax: 5787-1100; e-mail: webmaster@nbs.sk).

Stock exchange

Burza Cennych Papierov v Bratislave (BSSE) (Bratislava Stock Exchange): www.bsse.sk

Travel information

Air Slovakia BWJ, Pestovatelská ul c 2, 821 04 Bratislava (tel: 4342 2744; fax: 4342 2742; e-mail:

Association of Slovak Information Centres, Námestie Mieru 1, 03101 Liptoský Mikuláš (tel: 551-4541; fax: 551-4448; e-mail: info@airslovakia.sk)

Slovak Airlines, Ivanka Airport, Bratislava (tel: 4857-5170/1).

Slovak Association of Travel Agents, Bajkalská 2, 821 01 Bratislava 2, (tel: 5823-3385; fax: 5341-9058; email:sacka@ba.sknet.sk).

Slovak Republik Automobile Association (Autoklub SR), Údernicka 14, 85101 Bratislava (tel: 6383-4567; fax: 6383-4678; e-mail: autoklub@autoklubsr.sk).

Slovak Tourist Board (Bratislava branch), PO Box 97, Záhradnícka 153, 82005 Bratislava 25, (tel: 5070-0801; fax: 5557-1649; email: sacrba@sacr.sk).

Ministry of tourism

Ministry of Economy, Tourism Department, Mierova 19, 82715 Bratislava (tel: 4854-2315; fax: 4854-3321; e-mail: info@economy.gov.sk).

National tourist organisation offices

Slovak Tourist Board, Námestie L Štúra 1, PO Box 35, 974 05 Banská Bystrica, (tel: 413-6146-8; fax: 413-6149; email: sacr@sacr.sk).

Ministries

Ministry of Administration and Privatisation of National Property, Drienova 24, 82009 Bratislava (tel: 230-678; fax: 233-335).

Ministry of Agriculture, Dobrovicova 12, 81266 Bratislava (tel: 368-561, 456-111; fax: 3066-294).

Ministry of Construction and Public Works, Spitalska 8, 81644 Bratislava (tel: 536-1111; fax; 536-1203).

Ministry of Culture of the Slovak Republic, Dobrovicova 12, 81331 Bratislava (tel: 323-295; fax: 368-140).

Ministry of Defence, Kutuzovova 7, 83247 Bratislava (tel: 250-320; fax: 258-907).

Ministry of Economy of the Slovak Republic, Mierová 19, 82715 Bratislava (tel: 574-1407; fax: 237-827).

Ministry of Education and Sciences, Stromova 1, 81330 Bratislava (tel: 370-4111; fax: 370-4333).

Ministry of the Environment of the Slovak Republic, Namestie L Stura 1,, 81235 Bratislava (tel: 516-2458; fax: 516-2457).

Ministry of Finance of the Slovak Republic, Stefanovicova 5, 81308 Bratislava (tel: 518-2562; fax: 396-146).

Ministry of Foreign Affairs, Hlboka Cesta 3, 83336 Bratislava (tel: 438-1111; fax: 438-2005; internet: http://www.foreign.gov.sk).

Ministry of Health, Limbova 2, 83105 Bratislava (tel: 377-940; fax: 377-659).

Ministry of the Interior, Pribinova 2, 81272 Bratislava (tel: 546-1111; fax: 368-835).

Ministry of Justice, Zupné námestie 13, 81311 Bratislava (tel: 535-3111; fax: 531-5952).

Ministry of Labour, Social Welfare and Family of the Slovak Republic, Spitálska 4, 81643 Bratislava (tel: 338-2414; fax: 362-150).

Ministry of Transport and Communications, Nam Slobody 6, 81005 Bratislava (tel: 395-251; fax: 256-414).

Office of the Government, Nam Slobody 1, 84218 Bratislava (tel: 359-5111; fax: 397-595).

Office of the President, Stefanikova ul 1, 81104 Bratislava (tel: 531-7567; fax: 531-7065).

Other useful addresses

Bratislava International Commodity Exchange, Ruzinovská 1, 82102 Bratislava (tel: 522-6311; fax: 522-6318).

Bratislava Stock Exchange, Vysoká 17, 81499 Bratislava (tel: 386-121; fax: 386-103).

British Embassy, Panskà 16, 81101 Bratislava (tel: 5441-9632; fax: 5441-0002; e-mail: bebra@internet.sk).

Federation of Employers' Unions and Associations of Slovak Republic, Information and Consulting Centre, Drienová 24, 82603 Bratislava (tel: 235-024; fax: 233-542).

National Agency for Development of Small and Medium Enterprises, Nevädzová 5, 82101 Bratislava (tel: 237-472/563, 231-873; fax: 522-2434); External Advisors (tel: 237-472; fax: 522-2434); BIC (Business Innovation Centre) (tel: 290-7417; fax: 522-2434, 290-7217).

National Property Fund PARP PMU, Drienova 27, 82656 Bratislava (tel: 561-1258, 561-1230, 561-1447, 235-280, 231-300, 231-531; fax: 561-1446, 235-280); external department (tel: 250-248; fax: 259-208).

Slovak National Agency for Foreign Investment and Development (SNAFID), Sládkovicova 7, 81106 Bratislava (tel: 533-5175; fax: 533-5022); Slovenska polnohospodarska a potravinarska komora, Krizna 52, 82108 Bratislava (tel: 566-2657, 526-1778; fax: 526-7336, 211-251).

Slovak Republic Embassy (USA), 3523 International Court, NW, Washington DC 20008 (tel: (+1-202) 237-1054; fax: (+1-202) 237-6438; e-mail: info@slovakembassy-us.org).

Statistical Office of the Slovak Republic, Mileticova 3, 82467 Bratislava (tel: 215-802; fax: 214-587).

Transport Department, Dept of European Integration, Namestie Slobody 6, 81370 Bratislava (tel: 499-766, 498-156 Ext. 331, 498-841, 495-251; fax: 499-761).

Internet sites

Slovakia Daily Surveyor: http://www.slovensko.com

Slovaks and Slovakia: http://www.slovak.com

Slovak Republic Government: http://www.government.gov.sk

Slovak Tourist Board: http://www.slovakiatourism.sk

Slovenia

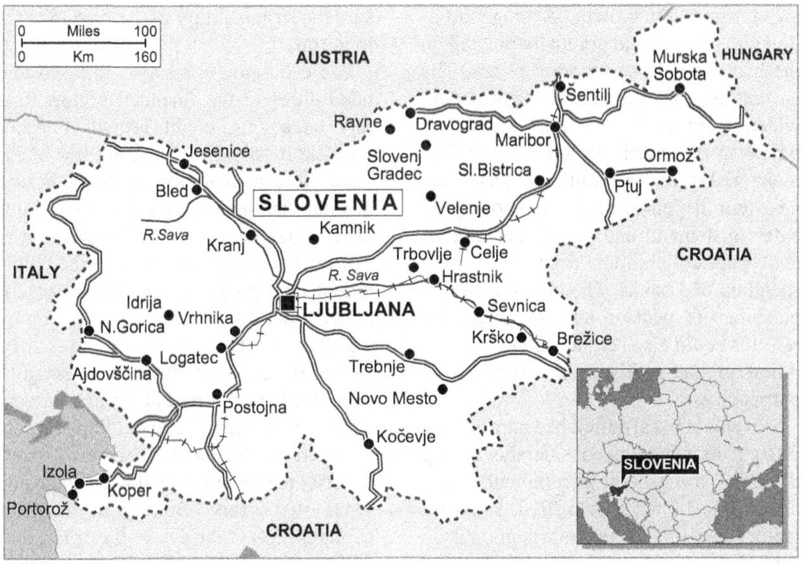

During and following the disintegration of the Yugoslav Federation, Slovenia – which for a ten day period in 1991 had actually found itself at war with the Yugoslav army – looked to Western Europe as its mentor and example. Neighbouring Austria became the role model, a country that Slovenia emulated in adopting a rather superior attitude not only to 'rump' Yugoslavia, but also towards much of Eastern Europe.

Coalition crisis

Twenty years on, in September 2011 Slovenia found itself facing challenges rather different from those of 1991. The fall of the coalition government risked plunging Slovenia into deep crisis; it could hardly have happened at a worse time – Slovenia's economy was hardly in good shape and the euro-zone, which Slovenia had so proudly joined in 2007, was looking a less than viable project. When the government of Prime Minister Borut Pahor lost a no-confidence vote by 51 votes to 36 on 20 September, it rendered Mr Pahor something of a lame duck. Under the constitution unless the opposition managed to organise an alternative government by October 20, President Danilo Turk would need to call an election to take place by the end of the year.

The no-confidence vote had been about changes to the Slovenian pension system, but it had an unfortunate knock-on affect for the European Union (EU), which needs the unanimous backing of all 17 euro-zone members to upgrade the ?440 billion (US$590 billion) European Financial Stability Facility. Slovenians don't see why they should help bail-out other less financially prudent (or transparent) countries than themselves and are unhappy about agreeing to the upgrade. Mr Pahor's set back could delay, or worse, the ratification process. Both the European Commission and the Slovenian ministry of finance expressed their confidence in Slovenia's continuing support for the bail-out plan. Opinion polls suggested that less than 13 per cent of Slovenians considered the outgoing government to have been successful, which promised little support for Mr Pahor in an election contest. In the event, the parliamentary elections were held on 4 December, and the new (founded on 22 October by Zoran Jankovic) centre-left party, Lista Zorana Jankovica-Pozitivna Slovenija (LZJ-PS) (Zorana Jankovica's Party-Positive Slovenia) won 28.5 per cent (29 seats out of 90) and the right to form a coalition government. No coalition had been

KEY FACTS

Official name: Republika Slovenija (Republic of Slovenia)

Head of State: President Danilo Türk (from 22 Dec 2007)

Head of government: Caretaker-Prime Minister Borut Pahor (SD); Prime Minister-elect Zorana Jankovica (LZJ-PS) (from 4 Dec 2011)

Ruling party: Outgoing party: Socialni Demokrati (SD) (Social Democrats). Coalition to be led by Lista Zorana Jankovica-Pozitivna Slovenija (LZJ-PS) (Zorana Jankovica's Party-Positive Slovenia) (from 4 Dec 2011); as of 1 January 2012 other coalition partners are still to be announced.

Area: 20,251 square km

Population: 2.05 million (2010)*

Capital: Ljubljana

Official language: Slovene

Currency: Euro (€) = 100 cents (from 1 Jan 2007; previous currency tolar, locked at T239.64 per euro)

Exchange rate: €0.75 per US$ (Oct 2011)

GDP per capita: US$23,706 (2010)

GDP real growth: 1.20% (2010)

GDP: US$47.80 billion (2010)

Labour force: 936,000 (2010)

Unemployment: 10.70% (2010)

Inflation: 1.80% (2010)

Balance of trade: -US$1.60 billion (2010)

Annual FDI: US$366.16 million (2010)

* estimated figure

NOTA

4 December 2011, in early parliamentary elections the new party Lista Zorana Jankoviæa-Pozitivna Slovenija (LZJ-PS) (Zorana Jankovica's Party-Positive Slovenia) won 28.5 per cent (29 seats out of 90) and the right to form a coalition government. Zorana Jankoviæa (LZJ-PS) became prime minister-elect.

formed as of 1 January 2012 and Mr Pahor continued as a caretaker prime minister.

The Economy – recovering?

The political uncertainty that Slovenia found itself in in late 2011 did little to assist in the task of restoring confidence in the economy. The government had to revise downwards its economic growth forecast for 2011 from 2.2 per cent to 1.5 per cent, partly due to the economic woes of its major economic partners, namely Germany. The government also had to cut government expenditure by ?365 million (US$490 million) to cope with a drop of revenues and to meet the initially planned public deficit of 5.5 per cent of gross domestic product (GDP) for this year. Slovenia's economy is gradually recovering following one of the sharpest GDP declines in the euro-zone during the crisis. GDP declined over 10 per cent from peak to trough owing to a sharp decline in external demand; a significant tightening in external credit conditions forcing banks to curtail domestic credit supply; and an abrupt end of a construction and housing price boom. GDP growth reached 1.2 per cent in 2010, led by rising exports. Weak domestic demand led to negative core inflation and greatly reduced the current account deficit. The current account deficit shrank from 6.7 per cent of GDP in 2008 to 1.2 per cent in 2010, reflecting mainly the end of the construction boom. Average CPI inflation was 1.8 per cent in 2010, mainly because of rising fuel and energy prices. The average unemployment rate increased to 7.2 per cent in 2010 up from 4.8 per cent at end 2008.

The International Monetary Fund (IMF) had expected Slovenia's GDP to grow by 2 per cent in 2011. According to the IMF, the pick-up in growth reflected mainly a recovery in the manufacturing sector and inventory rebuilding. However, investment looked likely to be low due to asset disposal in Slovenia's highly indebted corporate sector. High unemployment and fiscal retrenchment had a negative effect on consumption growth. Average inflation was projected to gradually pick up on the back of high commodity prices. The current account deficit was expected to widen again as the economy recovered, but not as much as in pre-crisis times. The main risks to the outlook were the near-term dependence of the recovery on external demand and significant contingent public liabilities from entitlement spending and banks. The continued postponement of pension and labour market reforms could also lead to further deterioration in competitiveness and potential output growth.

Slovenia's fiscal deficit had narrowed in 2010. After widening considerably during the crisis, the general government deficit declined to 5.2 per cent in 2010. The main factors were one-off revenue gains, cuts in capital transfers and the containment of the wage bill. The deficit was expected to continue narrowing in 2011 primarily through further wage bill rationalisations, reduced indexation of pensions and other entitlements and capital expenditure and capital transfer cuts. The Slovenian authorities aimed to reduce the fiscal deficit to below 3 per cent by 2013. In the long term, according to the IMF, pension expenditure posed a challenge to fiscal sustainability. Somewhat surprisingly, Slovenia was forecast to have one of the largest pension expenditures in the EU by 2050 if no reforms were implemented. The authorities started addressing the challenge with the pension reform that will increase the effective retirement age and lower the replacement rate. But additional reforms would be necessary to ensure the sustainability of the system in the long run.

The economic crisis also exposed vulnerabilities in the financial sector. Rapidly expanding credit growth financed with short-term external bank borrowing came to a sudden stop in 2008. Banks' profitability and asset quality deteriorated with aggregate profits turning negative in 2010 due to high loan losses to the highly indebted corporate sector. Total assets declined and corporate credit growth remained, in the words of the IMF, 'anaemic'. Slovenian banks are among the most thinly capitalised in the EU, particularly the domestic banks. Publicly announced recapitalisations were sufficient to offset the accumulated losses of the previous two years. But, given the thin capitalisation at the eve of the crisis, they will not be sufficient to create new lending capacity.

In summary, the IMF noted that, despite the authorities' commendable policy response, Slovenia had experienced one of the largest drops in output in the euro area. The domestic boom, fuelled by easy external financing conditions and an expansionary fiscal policy, came abruptly to an end with the global financial crisis. While a gradual recovery was underway, important challenges remained. The current reforms were, in the view of the IMF, a step in the right direction, but looked likely to fall short of generating the required savings in the long run. The IMF recommended a more rapid increase in the retirement age and eventual indexation. Perhaps worryingly, the IMF also recommended the Slovenian authorities to prepare contingency measures should unpopular pension reform measures be rejected.

The IMF also pointed out that structural reforms in the labour and product markets would play a crucial role. It viewed the loosening of labour market restrictions, phasing-out of wage indexation schemes and elimination of pay increases unrelated to productivity gains as critical in reducing unemployment. Improved competition in product and financial markets would also foster FDI inflows.

KEY INDICATORS — Slovenia

	Unit	2006	2007	2008	2009	2010
Population	m	2.01	2.03	2.05	*2.05	*2.05
Gross domestic product (GDP)	US$bn	38.24	47.20	54.60	49.20	47.80
GDP per capita	US$	19,021	23,511	27,149	24,390	23,706
GDP real growth	%	5.7	6.8	3.7	-8.1	1.2
Inflation	%	2.5	3.6	5.7	0.9	1.8
Unemployment	%	5.9	7.7	6.7	7.3	10.7
Exports (fob) (goods)	US$m	21,397.0	27,123.0	29,562.0	22,532.0	24,359.0
Imports (fob) (goods)	US$m	22,856.0	29,432.0	33,404.0	23,524.0	25,961.0
Balance of trade	US$m	-1,458.0	-2,310.0	-3,842.0	-991.0	-1,602.0
Current account	US$m	-1,076.0	-2,222.0	-302.4	-720.0	-388.0
Total reserves minus gold	US$m	7,036.1	979.8	868.1	966.1	962.8
Foreign exchange	US$m	6,987.1	942.0	809.9	589.5	543.2
Exchange rate	per US$	190.61	0.69	0.68	0.78	0.76

* estimated figure

Risk assessment

Economy	Fair/poor
Politics	Fair
Regional stability	Good

COUNTRY PROFILE

Historical profile

In the thirteenth century, Slovenia became a hereditary possession of the House of Habsburg.
1867 The Slovenes fell under the jurisdiction of the Austrian Crown.
1918 After the downfall of the Austro-Hungarian Empire, Slovenia became a part of the new Kingdom of Serbs, Croats and Slovenes, encompassing Bosnia and Hercegovina (BiH), Croatia, parts of Dalmatia and Macedonia, Montenegro, Serbia, Slavonia and Slovenia.
1921 Prince Alexander, Regent of Serbia, became King.
1929 Following disputes between Serbs and Croats, King Alexander assumed dictatorial powers and the country was renamed Yugoslavia.
1934 King Alexander was assassinated in Marseilles while on a state visit to France.
1941 Yugoslavia was divided between Germany, Italy, Hungary and Bulgaria.
1945 Following the end of the Second World War, Slovenia became a constituent republic of the Yugoslav Federation. Josip Broz Tito assumed power, and a Soviet-style constitution was adopted. The other republics were: Bosnia and Hercegovina (BiH), Croatia, Macedonia, Montenegro and Serbia, and the two autonomous regions of Vojvodina and Kosovo.
1950-80s Constitutions adopted in 1953, 1963 and 1974 increased the autonomy of the constituent republics. The ruling Slovene Communists supported the Croats' demand for a confederate Yugoslavia during the 1960s and 1970s, although never to the point of provoking repression.
1980 Tito died. A system of a collective (rotating) presidency was adopted.
1986 Milan Kucan became the leader of the Slovene Communists.
1990 Kucan guided Slovenia towards independence following multi-party general elections, resulting in a six-party centre-right coalition, the Demokratska Opozicija Slovenije (DeMOS) (Democratic Opposition of Slovenia), under the leadership of Lozle Peterle.
1991 After a 10-day war against the Yugoslav army, Slovenia won independence. A border dispute began following the collapse of Yugoslavia between Croatia and as Slovenia. With such a small coastline (46km) Slovenia was intent on using the small Bay of Piran, on the Adriatic Sea, to give it access to international waters; Croatia also claimed the bay.
1992 Slovenia was admitted to the UN. Following the collapse of the DeMOS government, Janez Drnovšek took over as interim prime minister. In the parliamentary elections, the Liberal Democrats emerged as the largest party and Janez Drnovšek became prime minister at the head of a five-party coalition. Milan Kucan was elected president.
1994 The Liberal Democrats merged with the Democratic Party and the Ecologists to create the Liberalna Demokracija Slovenije (LDS) (Liberal Democracy of Slovenia).
1996 After the general elections, the LDS and its former opponent, Slovenska Ljudska Stranka (SLS) (Slovenian People's Party) formed a coalition with the Demokratièna Stranka Upokojencev Slovenije (DeSUS) (Democratic Party of Slovenian Pensioners). Drnovšek was re-elected prime minister.
1997 Kucan was re-elected president for a second and last consecutive five-year term.
2000 Withdrawal of the SLS from the government coalition prompted its collapse. A centre-right government, composed of the SLS and Slovenski Krsèanski Demokrati (SKD) (Slovenian Christian Democratic Party), together with the Socialdemokratska Stranka Slovenije (SDSS) (Social Democratic Party of Slovenia) was formed. The general election was won by the LDS, led by the former prime minister, Janez Drnovšek, who formed a coalition government.
2002 NATO invited Slovenia to join the alliance and the EU confirmed Slovenia's accession. Prime Minister Janez Drnovšek won the presidential run-off. Anton Rop of the LDS, the senior coalition party, was elected prime minister with 63 votes for and 24 votes against (to be elected, Rop needed a minimum of 46 votes from the members of parliament).
2003 In a referendum, 89.6 per cent of Slovenes voted to join the EU and 66 per cent voted to join NATO.
2004 Slovenia joined NATO and the EU. Slovenska Demokratska Stranka (SDS) (Slovenian Democratic Party) won the parliamentary elections and Janez Jansa was elected prime minister by parliament.
2005 Parliament ratified the EU constitution.
2006 EU finance ministers gave final approval to Slovenia's application to adopt the euro currency.
2007 Slovenia joined the European Economic and Monetary Union (EMU) and introduced the euro as its official currency. Danilo Türk won presidential elections after two rounds. Slovenia became a member of the European Union Schengen area within which all travellers may cross borders without a passport or visa.
2008 Former president and prime minister, Janez Drnovšek died. In parliamentary elections the Socialni Demokrati (SD) (Social Democrats) won 30.5 per cent of the vote (29 seats, out of 90) and the ruling SDS 29.3 per cent (28); turnout was 62.3 per cent. A coalition was formed by SD, Zares-Nova Politika (Z-NP) (For Real-New Politics) and LDS. Later SD, LDS and DeSUS formed a government. Borut Pahor (SD) became prime minister.
2009 Slovenia vetoed Croatia's accession attempt, citing an on-going territorial dispute as the obstacle for agreement – Croatia wanted its border with Slovenia to be halfway through the Bay of Piran and submitted maps and documents to EU negotiators showing this.
2010 In May, the Organisation for Economic Co-operation and Development (OECD) voted unanimously to admit Slovenia as a member. In a referendum held in June, just 51.49 per cent of the vote was in favour of allowing international arbitration to resolve the border dispute concerning the Bay of Piran. A five-person panel, including one Slovene and one Croat, will settle the matter. Slovenia signed a protocol in September to jointly found a new company, Cargo 10, with Macedonia, Serbia and Croatia to incorporate their railway companies.
2011 On 25 May, the panel to settle the Bay of Piran dispute submitted their arbitrated agreement to the UN for registration. A decision, binding on both parties, is expected to be given by the UN in 2014. A referendum was held on 5 June, in which voters overwhelmingly rejected changes to counter the black economy. They also voted against opening up state security archives, and against amendments to the state pension system, which would have raised the age of retirement to 65. The failure of the proposals runs against government legislation introduced into parliament in December 2010. On 20 September the government lost a vote of no-confidence in parliament. According to the constitution, a new prime minister must be appointed within 30 days or a general election must be held. Early parliamentary elections were held on 4 December, in which the new party, Lista Zorana Jankovica-Pozitivna Slovenija (LZJ-PS) (Zorana Jankovica's Party-Positive Slovenia) won 28.5 per cent (29 seats out of 90) and the right to form a coalition government.

Political structure

Constitution

The Slovenian constitution was adopted in December 1991 and amended in 1997 and 2000.

Form of state

Parliamentary democratic republic

The executive

The president, who is elected for a five-year term, by universal adult suffrage, is head of state and commander-in-chief of the armed forces.

The president proposes a candidate for prime minister to the Skupšcina Slovenije (Assembly of Slovenia) after consultation with parliamentary groups. The assembly has the final power of appointment of the prime minister and the government.

National legislature

The bicameral Parlament Slovenije (Slovenian Parliament), consists of the Drzavni Zbor (National Assembly) (lower house) with 88 members elected by proportional representation in multi-seat constituencies and two representatives of Italian and Hungarian ethnic minorities (with an absolute veto in matters concerning their communities), serving for four-year terms, and the Drzavni Svet (National Council) (upper house) with 40 members nominated from interest groups; 22 represent local district interests, six represent non-commercial activities, four are employer representatives, four employee representatives and four represent artisans and professionals. The government is made up of members of the National Assembly, and is answerable to that body. National Council members have a mainly advisory role, but may veto decisions of the National Assembly and must approve the composition of any government; members serve for five-year terms.

Legal system

The legal system is based on the 1991 constitution.

The judiciary is structurally independent from the government, with the Constitutional Court empowered to determine the conformity of national legislation with the constitution. All civil and criminal cases are dealt with by eight basic and four higher courts, and the Supreme Court is the final court of appeal. Prosecutions are the responsibility of the Public Prosecutor and to safeguard defendants rights there is also a Public Attorney. The Justice Ministry is the administrative authority of the Slovenian judiciary.

Last elections

4 December 2011 (parliamentary); 21 October/11 November 2007 (presidential).

Results: Parliamentary: Lista Zorana Jankovica-Pozitivna Slovenija (LZJ-PS) (Zorana Jankovica's Party-Positive Slovenia) (Positive Slovenia) won 28.5 per cent (29 seats out of 90), Slovenská Demokratska Stranka (SDS) (Slovenian Democratic Party) 26.2 per cent (26), Socialni Demokrati (SD) (Social Democrats) 10.5 per cent (10), Državljanska lista Gregorja Viranta (DLGV) (Gregor Virant's Civic Party) 8.4 per cent (eight), Demokraticna Stranka Upokojencev Slovenije (DeSUS) (Democratic Party of Pensioners of Slovenia) 7.0 per cent (six), Slovenska Ljudska Stranka (SLS) (Slovenian People's Party) 6.9 per cent (six), Nova Slovenija-Kršcanska ljudska stranka (Nova Slovenija) (New Slovenia-Christian People's Party) 4.8 per cent (four) (representatives of Hungarian and Italian communities two); turnout was 65 per cent.

Presidential: (first round) Lojze Peterle won 28.5 per cent of the vote, Danilo Türk 24.5 per cent, Mitja Gaspari 24.1 per cent, and Zmago Jelincic 19.3 per cent.

Next elections

2015 (parliamentary); 2012 (presidential)

Political parties

Ruling party

Outgoing party: Socialni Demokrati (SD) (Social Democrats). Coalition to be led by Lista Zorana Jankovica-Pozitivna Slovenija (LZJ-PS) (Zorana Jankovica's Party-Positive Slovenia) (from 4 Dec 2011); as of 1 January 2012 other coalition partners are still to be announced.

Main opposition party

As of 1 January, to be determined

Population

2.05 million (2010)*

Last census: March 2002: 1,964,036 (provisional)

Population density: 99 inhabitants per square km. Urban population: 51 per cent (1995–2001).

Annual growth rate: 0.0 per cent 1994–2004 (WHO 2006)

Ethnic make-up

Around 88 per cent of the population are Slovenes, with small numbers of ethnic Serbs, Croats, Muslims, Albanians, Hungarians, Italians and Germans. Only the Italian and Hungarian communities are officially recognised minorities.

Religions

Roman Catholic (71 per cent), Lutheran (1 per cent), Islam (1 per cent).

Education

Unlike other parts of the former Yugoslavia, where adult illiteracy remains a major socioeconomic problem, Slovenia has always had a relatively highly educated society. Adult illiteracy is therefore virtually non-existent.

Primary and initial secondary schooling are combined in one school for nine-years. At aged 15 students are channelled onto one of three paths, general, technical or vocational. General and technical education lasts for four years, while vocational courses last for either two or three years.

As a critical determinant of future socio-economic development, higher education experienced significant growth during the 1990s. Unesco estimates total gross enrolment rates for tertiary education at over 60 per cent. Law, business and economics remain popular courses, while further education institutions find it difficult to attract students to technical courses, resulting in a lack of skills in certain sectors of the workforce.

Literacy rate: 100 per cent adult rate; 100 per cent youth rate (15–24) (Unesco 2005).

Compulsory years: 6 to 15

Enrolment rate: 98 per cent gross primary enrolment, 92 per cent gross secondary enrolment; of relevant age groups (including repeaters) (World Bank).

Pupils per teacher: 12 in primary schools.

Health

Formerly entirely state controlled and funded, healthcare is now a growing private sector activity so that Slovenia is comparable with the EU for healthcare provision. In the long-term though, more funds will have to be directed towards it due to its ageing population. Healthcare provisions also includes a well-developed network of medicinal spas for all types of ailments. Lower healthcare charges attract paying customers from neighbouring countries.

Private health insurance is increasing rapidly and the government has encouraged additional forms of health insurance, and the preparation of national preventative programmes, that should reduce dependency on the state and bolster private sector provision.

HIV/Aids

HIV prevalence: 0.1 per cent aged 15–49 in 2003 (World Bank)

Life expectancy: 77 years, 2004 (WHO 2006)

Fertility rate/Maternal mortality rate: 1.2 births per woman, 2004 (WHO 2006)

Birth rate/Death rate: Nine births per 1,000 population; 10 deaths per 1,000 population (2003).

Child (under 5 years) mortality rate (per 1,000): 4.0 per 1,000 live births (World Bank)

Head of population per physician: 2.25 physicians per 1,000 people, 2002 (WHO 2006)

Welfare

The Pension and Disability Act, which significantly reformed the pension system, became effective from 2000 and consists of a reformed pay-as-you-go scheme, with a supplementary fund as part of waged contracts. The minimum age of retirement for women has gradually risen

and the amount of full pensions reduced relative to the wage rate.
The government ensured better legal protection for workers by defining their rights at the minimum level, and strengthened investment in the area of labour, family and social welfare.

Main cities

Ljubljana (capital, estimated population 264,265 in 2005), Maribor (92,443), Celje (38,601), Kranj (35,907).

Languages spoken

The main minority languages are Albanian, Hungarian and Italian, but Hungarian and Italian are officially recognised. Serbian, Croatian, German, English and French are also spoken.
Regional identities and dialects remain very strong.

Official language/s

Slovene

Media

Press

Dailies: A major publishing organisation *Delo* (www.delo.si) (with an English online edition) produces two dailies (including *Slovenske Novice* and *Ne Delo*), four magazines (including a free monthly magazine, *Delnicar*, with the highest circulation) and has three internet portals. Other national publications include *Dnevnik* (www.dnevnik.si), *Vecer* (www.vecer.si) and *Zurnal* (www.zurnal24.si). Major regional newspapers include *Direkt* (www.direkt.si) and *Ekipa-sport.so* both tabloids, from Ljubljana as does the *Slovenia Time* (www.sloveniatimes.com) published in English. From Celje *Novi Tednik* (www.novitednik.com) in Slovene, *Nepujsag* (www.nepujsag.net) is published in Hungarian in Lendava.
Weeklies: In Solvene, the variety includes *Demokracija* (www.demokracija.si) and *Dolenjski List* (www.dol-list.si), *Gorenjski Glas* (www.g-glas.si), *Jana*, *Kmecki Glas* (www.czd-kmeckiglas.si), *Mariborcan* (www.revijakapital.com/mariborcan), *Mladina* (www.mladina.si), *Primorske Novice* (www.primorske.si), and *Vestnik Murska Sobota* (www.p-inf.si) provide general information and local news. *Druzina* (www.druzina.si) is a Roman Catholic publication,
Based abroad, *TOL* reports on central European issues. The government publication *Sinfo* covering politics, business, culture can be accessed online (www.ukom.gov.si).
Business: In Slovene, the national publication *Podjetnik* (www.podjetnik.com) and the regional *Kapital* (www.revijakapital.com) are magazines, *Finance* (www.finance.si) is a regional newspaper. In English, *Slovenian Business Report* (www.sbr.si).
Periodicals: The free monthly newspaper, *Delnicar*, has the highest circulation.

Broadcasting

Radio: There are many commercial radio stations. RTV Slovenija (www.rtvslo.si) is the state-owned radio station which is the market leader with three national channels, of which one broadcasts in Italian, one in Hungarian and one in Slovene. During the tourist season, there are broadcasts in German and English each day covering: news, traffic news, local weather and tourist directions. Other major radio stations include Radio Hit (www.r-hit.si) and Radio City (www.radiocity.si).
Television: The state-owned Radio Televizija Slovenija (RTV) (www.rtvslo.si), broadcast in Slovene, Italian and Hungarian. The privately owned commerical TV stations Pop Tv (http://24ur.com) broadcasts foreign programmes. Both TV stations offer programmes online. Satellite and cable TV is also available, including TV Si21 (http://tv.si21.com).

Advertising

Advertising outlets are available on TV, radio, billboards and in newsprint.

News agencies

STA (Slovenska Tiskovna Agencija), Cankarjeva 5, PO Box 145, 1101 Ljubljana, (tel: 241-0100; fax: 426-6050; email: desk@sta.si; internet: www.sta.si).
In Slovene, Morel (www.kabi.si).

Economy

Slovenia was one of the most prosperous regions of former Yugoslavia, and continued to be so after its independence. It has natural resources of coal, mercury and timber, which supply raw materials for the country's manufacturing sector, producing metal work, chemicals, paper, construction materials and furniture, household goods and electronic equipment, clothing and foodstuffs.
The service sector constitutes over 60 per cent GDP. Agriculture contributes only around 1 per cent of GDP, with the cultivation of crops and livestock.
The economy improved quickly following its adoption of the euro in 2007 with GDP growth of 6.8 per cent in 2007, falling to 3.7 per cent in 2008 as energy and food costs rose to a record high. The global economic crisis caused a dramatic contraction in 2009 when the economy fell into recession with growth of -8.1 per cent. In 2010, the economy recorded a modest recovery with growth of 1.2 per cent, although the economic outlook is still tied to Germany's economic growth, as Slovenia's single largest trading partner.
Unemployment rose from 9.2 per cent in 2009 to 10.7 per cent in 2010, as thousands of workers were laid off; the minimum wage was cut and public sector worker's salaries were reduced.
Foreign direct investment (FDI) had reached a record US$1.94 billion in 2008, but had fallen to US$366.2 million in 2010; it is predicted that FDI will pick up as more state-owned entities are put up for sale.

External trade

As a member of the European Union, Slovenia operates within a community-wide free trade union, with tariffs sets as a whole. Internationally, the EU has free trade agreements with a number of nations and trading blocs worldwide.
Foreign trade represents over 130 per cent of GDP, of which over 60 per cent is with the EU. The manufacturing sector is diversified with food processing, electrical equipment and electronics, textiles and timber products. Wine and animal husbandry are important agricultural exports, while industrial and mineral extraction represents around 30 per cent of GDP.

Imports

Main imports are vehicles, machinery, manufactured goods, chemicals, petroleum and derivatives and foodstuffs.
Main sources: Germany (typically 19 per cent of total), Italy (12 per cent), Croatia (9 per cent).

Exports

The principal exports are manufactured goods, machinery and transport equipment, chemicals and food.
Main destinations: Germany (typically 19 per cent of total), Italy (18 per cent), Austria (12 per cent).

Agriculture

Farming

Agriculture accounts for around 2.5 per cent of GDP and employs six per cent of the workforce. Farming is generally carried out on smallholdings of less than 25 hectares (ha). There are also a number of large farms and co-operatives which produce most food exports as well as food consumed domestically. Agricultural production fell substantially after independence, but recovered quickly and is above pre-independence levels.
The restoration of farming land and forests to claimants continues, although agricultural development is still being held up. Several issues pertaining to rural development, including aid to underdeveloped regions and environmental programmes, are on the political agenda.
The agricultural sector is subject to the reformed Common Agricultural Policy (CAP), whereby subsidies are no longer paid on farm output, which tended to benefit large farms and encourage overproduction, but rather on single farm payments not conditional on production.

Fishing
The annual commercial catch of fish amounts to between 1,815 and 2,270 tonnes. This excludes the catches of private fishermen estimated between 182 and 272 tonnes. Another 136 tonnes of fish is obtained by mariculture. About 454 tonnes of freshwater fish is bred on fish farms. Slovenia imports about 7,258 tonnes of fish annually.
Slovenia's legislation on fisheries is largely oriented towards Europe, although more resources will be necessary to meet the requirements of the EU's Common Fisheries Policy (CFP). Slovenia has a fisheries agreement with Croatia and is also a member of the General Fisheries Commission for the Mediterranean.

Forestry
Slovenia has a significant forestry sector. Forest cover is estimated at 1.1 million hectares (ha). The sector has a long tradition of sustainable management and less than a third of the forest area is publicly owned. Only a small area of forest is available for wood supply. Forestry forms the basis of a number of key industrial sectors, notably furniture making, paper, pulp and construction materials. The industry includes both large and small saw mills, which rely on the domestic supply of raw materials. Paper is mainly exported to European countries. Per capita consumption of forest products remains around the European average.

Industry and manufacturing
Manufacturing accounts for 24 per cent of GDP and industry overall for 32 per cent.
The manufacture of capital goods has traditionally been the mainstay of Slovenia's industry, with iron and steel, metal working and machine-building accounting for a third of total manufactured added value. With intermediate goods accounting for 15 per cent and consumer goods for 55 per cent of manufactured added value, Slovenia has all the characteristics of an advanced industrial economy.
Slovenia is anxious to boost its exports to the EU. This strategic redirection of its industrial exports will require a complete restructuring of its entire industrial sector.
The major structural problems are low levels of new investment, over-manning, technological backwardness and too many industrial enterprises for what is now a small domestic market with limited export potential. The newer and rising consumer goods industries, such as electrical products, are expected to become more capital intensive in order to compete internationally. High-technology industries based on computing and high added-value have yet to make a significant appearance.

Tourism
Tourism is a major industry, offering coastal holidays, skiing, golf and other sports, spa treatment and river trips. It employs some 16,000 people. Slovenia can provide around 80,000 beds in various accommodation facilities (hotels, motels, tourist villages, health-resorts, boarding-houses) all over the country.

Hydrocarbons
Oil reserves have been exhausted and Slovenia relies entirely on imports of petroleum products. Consumption was 60,000 barrels per day (bpd) of oil in 2007. Nafta Lendava is the only refinery in the country, with a capacity of 14,000bpd.
Proven natural gas reserves are negligible and Slovenia relies entirely on Algerian and Russian gas imports of over 1.1 billion cubic metres per annum. The state-owned natural gas company, Geoplin, is responsible for transit, supply and sale of natural gas in Slovenia
Slovenia has proven coal reserves, mainly lignite found in the Saleška Valley near Velenje, and sub-bituminous coal in several other parts of the country. Exploitable reserves at Velenje amount to 227 million tonnes; production could be sustained for 60 years. The sub-bituminous reserves are of low quality with high ash and sulphur content. Coal provides for one-quarter of the country's energy needs.

Energy
Slovenia has installed electricity capacity of 3GW, generated by thermal, hydropower and nuclear stations. The sole nuclear plant, sited at Krško, is jointly owned with Croatia. Slovenia is a net exporter of electricity.

Financial markets
Stock exchange
Ljubljanska Borza (Ljubljana Stock Exchange)

Banking and insurance
Slovenia has a well-developed banking sector. The central bank and the finance ministry are responsible for implementing EU banking directives.
Nova Ljubljanska Banka (NLB) and Nova Kreditna Banka Maribor, both state-owned, dominate the sector, together holding some 40 per cent of banking assets. The merger of the Abanka and Banka Vipa in December 2002 created a new bank, Abanka Vipa, which now has a major slice of the Slovenian banking sector.
Foreign banks own around 30 per cent of the banking sector. Approximately 96 per cent of SKB Banka was sold to France's Société Générale and a 34 per cent stake in NLB was sold to Belgium's KBC Bank.

Central bank
Banka Slovenije (BSI) (Bank of Slovenia)
Main financial centre
Ljubljana

Time
GMT plus one hour (daylight saving, late March to late October, GMT plus two hours)

Geography
Slovenia is bordered by Italy to the west, Austria to the north, Hungary to the east and Croatia to the south. There is a 46km coastal strip on the Gulf of Trieste in the Adriatic Sea, around the Istrian port of Koper.
An Alpine terrain covers over half Slovenia's area, stretching down from the north. This region is dominated by the Julian Alps in the north-west, where Mount Triglav (2,864 metres), the tallest peak, is located. The Slovene Alps are covered in forests, including some remnants of primeval forests, particularly around Kocevje in the south, and producing scores of rivers. The river Sava rises from two headstreams in the Julian Alps and flows down for 933km to the river Danube in Serbia.
The other half of the country is Mediterranean, one part of which, around the region of Karst, has a limestone landscape. A geological phenomenon where water has eaten into the rock has produced numerous sinkholes and cave networks and has given its name to a branch of science – karstology. The large Pannonian plain, in the east (around 20 per cent of the country) is fertile farmland and the source of thermal and mineral water springs.
Hemisphere
Northern

Climate
Ljubljana has an average summer temperature of 25 degrees Celsius (C) and in winter –3 degrees C. Precipitation is heavy, with an annual average rainfall of 1,407mm. Air pollution has had an adverse effect on the weather, notably in the Ljubljana Basin.
The north has an alpine climate with warm summers and cold winters, the west has Mediterranean weather with hot summers and mild winters and the east has a continental climate with hot summers and cold winters.

Dress codes
Formal dress is the norm for business and social meetings in Slovenia. Business visitors should be smartly dressed.

Entry requirements
Passports
Required by all except nationals of countries which are signatories of the Schengen Accords, which includes most

EU/EEA member states, who may visit on national IDs. Passports must be valid for three months beyond the visit.

Visa

Required by all, except nationals of EU and Schengen area signatory countries, North America, Australasia and Japan. See www.mzz.gov.si and follow path to *Embassies, Diplomatic Missions and Consulates* for a list of Slovene consulates and further information for other visitors regarding necessary documentation. A Schengen visa application (offered in several languages) can be downloaded from http://europa.eu/abc/travel/ see 'documents you will need'.

Currency advice/regulations

The import and export of local currency is unlimited, however amounts over T3 million (or foreign equivalent) must be declared. Slovenia will join the European Monetary Union on 1 January 2007 when the euro will become legal tender along side the tolar, which will be withdrawn after 14 days.

Travellers cheques are widely accepted.

Customs

Personal items are duty-free. There are no duties levied on alcohol and tobacco between EU member states, providing amounts imported are for personal consumption.

All items of cultural value, including artistic, archaeological, ethnographic, scientific and antiques over 100 years are prohibited from being exported.

Health (for visitors)

Nationals of the European Economic Area (EEA) countries and Switzerland can access reduced cost and sometimes free medical treatment using a European Health Insurance Card (EHIC) while visiting the EEA. Exceptions include nationals of the 10 countries which joined the EU in 2004 whose EHIC is not valid in Switzerland. Applications for the EHIC should be made before travelling.

Credit cards

International credit and charge cards are widely accepted. Credit cards can be used to get cash advances from banks.

Public holidays (national)

Fixed dates

1–2 Jan (New Year), 8 Feb (Preseren/Culture Day), 27 Apr (Resistance Day), 1–2 May (Labour Day), 25 Jun (National Day), 15 Aug (Assumption Day), 31 Oct (Reformation Day), 1 Nov (All Saints' Day), 25 Dec (Christmas Day), 26 Dec (Independence Day).

Holidays that fall at the weekend are not replaced.

Variable dates

Easter Monday

Working hours

Banking

Mon–Fri: 0730–1800; Sat: 0730–1200.

Business

Mon—Fri: 0800—1600.

Government

Mon–Fri: 0800–1600.

Shops

Mon–Fri: 0700–1900 or 0800–2000; some shops also open Sat: 0800–1300/1500, Sun: 0800–1200.

Telecommunications

Mobile/cell phones

GSM 900 and 1800 services available throughout most of the country.

Electricity supply

220V AC, with round two-pin plugs.

Weights and measures

Metric system

Social customs/useful tips

For business meetings, when appointments are made, visitors should be punctual. Business cards are essential.

Slovenia has a reputation for being efficient and reliable. Executives will generally have a good knowledge of German, English and sometimes Italian. There is a well-developed network of local agents, advisers, consultants and lawyers willing to act for foreign companies.

Slovenians are a rather reserved people with a tendency towards formality. As in Austria and Germany, titles are widely used. Informality on the part of a foreigner is not considered acceptable. It is not unusual for Slovenians to prefer to hold business discussions over lunch.

Athough smoking is generally accepted, it is restricted in many public places and buildings.

Visitors should carry some form of identity at all times.

Security

Slovenia has a low crime rate. Sometimes tourists are the targets of pickpockets and purse-snatchers, especially on the trains.

Getting there

Air

National airline: Adria Airways

International airport/s: Ljubljana (LJU), 27km from city centre, facilities include duty-free shops, bank, post office, restaurant, internet access and car hire. Buses provide access to Ljubljana (travel time 45 minutes). Taxis are available.

Other airport/s: Maribor (MBX) and Portoroz (POW) have European connections. They are open only during daylight hours.

Airport tax: None

Surface

Slovenia is included in the Pan-European Corridor 5 scheme. The project has some 3,270km of railways, linking Kiev in the Ukraine with western Europe via Italy, and 2,850km of new and upgraded roads.

Road: Most frontier posts are open for road traffic from Italy, Austria, Hungary and Croatia; almost all border crossings are open 24 hours.

Rail: Connections are available from major European cities. The Eurocity Mimara train connects Zagreb, Ljubljana, Munich and Leipzig. Direct trains to Slovenia are available from Italy (Rome, Milan, Venice and Trieste), Austria (Vienna and Villach) and Hungary (Budapest). Transport for cars may be available on some routes.

Water: A catamaran runs regular scheduled trips between Venice-Portoroz and Piran, between March–October.

Main port/s: Koper, Izola, Piran and Portoroz.

Getting about

National transport

Air: Domestic airports are situated at Maribor (MBX) in eastern Slovenia, with Potoroz (POW) on the Adriatic coast. There are regular services from the capital, Ljubljana.

Road: There is an extensive network of roads in Slovenia, many of which are in good condition. The main arterial road running south-west to north-east is a stretch of the Pan-European Corridor 5. The roads can be congested particularly during peak periods but have clear signposts, with rest and food facilities.

The following are toll motorways: Ljubljana-Razdrto, Arja vas-Hoce and Ljubljana-Kranj.

Buses: Good nationwide services operated by a number of companies.

Rail: There are good rail connections and rail travel is inexpensive. A high-speed train links Ljubljana-Maribor throughout the year and Ljubljana-Koper during the summer only. Intercity and Urban trains run to most regions

City transport

Taxis: Metered taxis are available in Ljubljana and other major towns. A tip of 10 per cent is expected.

Buses, trams & metro: Most city centres are served by trams, and the suburbs by buses. Service is inexpensive and regular, but radically reduced at night. Exact fares are required on the bus or tram, or tokens can be purchased from kiosks, post offices and in supermarkets beforehand.

Car hire

Many major car hire companies operate from the airport and capital. A full national driving licence and third party insurance for foreigners is compulsory. Speed limits are 130kph on motorways, 100kph on open highways, 90kph on urban roads outside residential areas and 50kph in cities and towns. Safety belts are compulsory and school buses must not be overtaken.

The AMZS (Automobile Association of Slovenia) provides a good emergency roadside service.

Much of the centre of Ljubljana has been pedestrianised and traffic is very congested. Finding parking spaces can be very difficult; use of a car in the city on weekdays is not advisable.

BUSINESS DIRECTORY

The addresses listed below are a selection only. While World of Information makes every endeavour to check these addresses, we cannot guarantee that changes have not been made, especially to telephone numbers and area codes. We would welcome any corrections.

Telephone area codes

The international direct dialling code (IDD) for Slovenia is +386, followed by area code and subscriber's number:

Celje	3	Murska Sobota	02
Koper	5	Nova Gorica	5
Kranj	4	Novo Mesto	7
Krsko	7	Postojna	5
Ljubljana	1	Ravne	2
Maribor	2	Trbovlje	3

Useful telephone numbers

Emergency 112

Chambers of Commerce

American Chamber of Commerce in Slovenia, 55 Pod Hribom, 1000 Ljubljana (tel: 581-6285; fax: 581-6111; e-mail: office@am-cham.si).

Koper Chamber of Commerce and Industry, 2 Ferrarska, 6000 Koper (tel: 639-5311; fax: 639-5316; e-mail: kozlovic@hg.gzs.si).

Ljubljana Chamber of Commerce and Industry, 9 Dimiceva, 1504 Ljubljana (tel: 230-1133; fax: 431-3040; e-mail: samardzija@hg.gzs.si).

Maribor Chamber of Commerce and Industry, 24 Talcev, 2000 Maribor (tel: 220-8700; fax: 252-2283; e-mail: breznik@hg.gzs.si).

Northern Primorska Chamber of Commerce and Industry, 3 Trg Edvarda Kardelja, 5000 Nova Gorica (tel: 330-6030; fax: 330-6031; e-mail: velikonja@hg.gzs.si).

Novo Mesto Chamber of Commerce and Industry, 5 Novi Trg, 8000 Novo Mesto (tel: 332-2182; fax: 332-2187; e-mail: goles@hg.gzs.si).

Postojna Chamber of Commerce and Industry, Cankarjeva 6, 6230 Postojna (tel: 720-0111; fax: 726-5344; e-mail: tiselj@hg.gzs.si).

Slovenia Chamber of Commerce and Industry, 13 Dimiceva, 1504 Ljubljana (tel: 589-8000; fax: 589-8100; e-mail: infolink@gzs.si).

Banking

Abanka Vipa dd, Slovenska 58, 1517 Ljubljana (tel: 471-8100; fax: 432-5165; email: info@abanka.si; internet site: www.abanka.si).

Bank Austria dd, Smartinska 140, 1000 Ljubljana (tel: 587-6600; fax: 587-6684; email: info@si.bacai.com).

Banka Celje dd, Vodnikova 2, 3000 Celje (tel: 543-1000 fax: 548-3511; email: info@banka-celje.si).

Banka Koper, Pristaniska 14, 6502 Koper (tel: 665-1100; fax: 639-7842; email: infor@banka-koper.si; internet site: www.banka-koper.si).

Factor Banka dd, Tivolska 48, 1000 Ljubljana (tel: 230-6600; fax: 230-7760; email: info@factorb.si).

Gorenjska Banka dd, Bleiweisova 1, 4000 Kranj (tel: 208-4000; fax: 202-1503; email: info@gbkr.si).

Hypo-Alpe-Adria Bank dd, Trv Osvobodine fronte 12, 1000 Ljubljana (tel: 300-4400; fax: 300-4401; email: hypo-banka@hypo.si).

Koroska Banka dd, Glavni trg 30, 2380 Slovenj Gradec (tel: 884-9111; fax: 884-2382).

Krekova Banka, Slomskov trg 18, 2000 Maribor (tel: 229-3100; fax: 252-2261; email: info@krekova-banka.si).

Nova Kreditna Banka Maribor, Vita Kraigherja 4, 2505 Maribor (tel: 229-2290; fax: 252-4333, 252-4371; email: info@nkbm.si).

Nova Ljubljanska Banka dd, Trg Republike 2, 1520 Ljubljana (tel: 425-0155; fax: 252-2422; email: info@nlb.si).

Postna Banka Slovenije dd, Vita Kraigherja 5, 2000 Maribor (tel: 228-8200; fax: 228-8210; email: info@pbs.si).

Probanka dd, Gosposka Ulica 23, 2000 Maribor (tel: 252-0500; fax: 252-5882; email: info@probanka.si).

SKB Banka dd, Ajdovscina 4, 1513 Ljubljana (tel: 433-213; fax: 231-4549: email: info@skb.si).

Slovenska Investicijska Banka dd, Copova 38, 1000 Ljubljana (tel: 242-0300; fax: 242-0521; email: sib@si-banka.si).

Slovenska Zadruzna Kmetijska Banka dd, Kolodvorska 9, 1000 Ljubljana (tel: 472-7100; fax: 472-7405); email: info@szkbanka.si).

Volksbank-Ljudska Banka dd, Dunajska 128a, 1101 Ljubljana (tel: 530-7400; fax: 520-7555; email: banka@volksbank.si).

Central bank

Banka Slovenije, Slovenska 35, 1505 Ljubljana (tel: 471-9000; fax: 251-5516; email: bsl@bsi.si; internet: www.bsi.si/en).

Stock exchange

Ljubljanska Borza (Ljubljana Stock Exchange): www.ljse.si

Travel information

Adria Airways, Kuzmiceva 7, 1000 Ljubljana (tel: 369-1000; fax: 230-1325; internet: www.adria.si).

Automobile Association of Slovenia, Dunajska 128a, SI-1000 Ljubljana (breakdown assistance tel: 530-5353; internet: www.amzs.si).

Ljubljana Airport, Zg Brnik 130a, 4210 Brnik (tel: 4-206-1981; fax: 4-202-1220; email: info@lju-airport.si; internet: www.lju-airport.si).

Slovenian Tourist Information Centre, Krekov trg 10, 1000 Ljubljana (tel: 306-4575/6; fax: 306-4580; email: stic@ljubljana-tourism.si; internet: www.ljubljana-tourism.si).

National tourist organisation offices

Slovenska Turisticna Organizacija (Slovenian Tourist Organisation), WTC, Dunajska 156, 1001 Ljubljana (tel: 589-1840; fax: 589-1841; e-mail: info@slovenia-tourism.si; internet: www.slovenia-tourism.si).

Ministries

Ministry of Agriculture, Forestry and Food, Dunajska 52, 1000 Ljubljana (tel: 478-9000; fax: 478-9021; email: janez.vertacnik@gov.si).

Ministry of Culture, Cankarjeva 5, 1000 Ljubljana (tel: 478-5900; fax: 478-5901; email: mkinfo@gov.si).

Ministry of Defence, Kardeljeva ploscad 25, 1000 Ljubljana (tel:471-2211; fax: 131-8164; email: darko.lubi@pub.mo-rs.si).

Ministry of the Economy, Kotnikova 5, 1000 Ljubljana (tel: 478-3600; fax: 478-3522; email: tatjana.zabasu@gov.si).

Ministry of Education, Science and Sport, Zupanèièeva 6, 1000 Ljubljana (tel: 478-5437; fax: 478-5669; email: info@mss.edus.si).

Ministry of Environment and Spatial Planning, Dunajska 48, 1000 Ljubljana (tel: 478-7400; fax: 478-7422; email: info.mop@gov.si).

Ministry of Finance, Zupanèièeva 3, 1502 Ljubljana (tel: 478-5211; fax: 478-5655; email: tilen.majnardi@mf-rs.si).

Ministry of Foreign Affairs, Presernova 25, 1000 Ljubljana (tel: 478-2000; fax: 478-2340; email: info.mzz@gov.si).

Ministry of Health, Stefanova 5, 1000 Ljubljana (tel: 478-6001; fax: 478-6058; email: ministrstvo.zdravsto@gov.si).

Ministry of the Information Society, Langusova 4, 1000 Ljubljana (tel: 478-8223; fax: 478-8142; email: mid@gov.si).

Ministry of the Interior, Stefanova 2, 1000 Ljubljana (tel: 472-5111; fax: 251-4330;email: jelka.smreka@mnz.si).

Ministry of Justice, Zupanèièeva 3, 1000 Ljubljana (tel: 478-5211; fax: 251-0200; email: stojan.klancar@gov.si).

Ministry of Labour, Family and Social Affairs, Kotnikova 5, 1000 Ljubljana (tel: 478-3450; fax: 478-3456; email: zmaga.grah@gov.si).

Ministry of Transport, Langusova 4, 1000 Ljubljana (tel: 478-8000; fax: 478-8139; email: mpz.info@gov.si).

Office for European Affairs, Subièeva 11, 1000 Ljublijana (tel: 478-24-47; fax: 478-2310; email: svez@gov.si).

President's Office, Erjavceva 17, 1000 Ljubljana (tel: 478-1205; fax: 478-1357).

Prime Minister's Office, Gregorèièeva 20, 1000 Ljubljana (tel: 478-1000; fax: 478-1607).

Other useful addresses

Agency of the Republic of Slovenia for Restructuring and Privatisation, Kotnikova Ulica 28, 1000 Ljubljana (tel: 131-2122; fax: 131-6011).

British Embassy, Fourth Floor, Trg Republike 3, 1000 Ljubljana (tel: 200-3910; fax: 425-0174; email: info@british-embassy.si).

Government Office for European Affairs, Subiceva 11, 1000 Ljubljana (tel: 478-2228; fax: 478-2310).

Government of the Republic of Slovenia, Gregorciceva 20, 1000 Ljubljana (tel: 478-1100; fax: 478-1607).

Government PR and Media Office, Slovenska 29, 1000 Ljubljana (tel: 478-2629; fax: 251-2312; internet: www.uvi.gov.si/eng).

Institute for Macroeconomic Analysis and Development, Gregorciceva 25, 1000 Ljubljana (tel: 478-2112; fax: 478-2070).

Ljubljana Stock Exchange, Trg Republike 3, 1000 Ljubljana (tel: 477-5500; fax: 477-5507, 477-5508).

Slovenian Embassy (USA), 1525 New Hampshire Avenue, NW, Washington DC 20036 (tel: (+1-202) 667-5363; fax: (+1-202) 667-4563; email: slovenia@embassy.org).

Small Business Development Centre, Dunajska 156, 1001 Ljubljana (tel: 189-1870; fax: 188-1178).

Statistical Office of the Republic of Slovenia, Vozarski Pot 12, 1000 Ljubljana (tel: 241-5300; fax: 241-5344).

Trade and Investment Promotion Office (TIPO), Kotnikova 28, 1000 Ljubljana (tel: 478-3557; fax: 478-3599; email: tipo@gov.si; internet site: www.investslovenia.org).

Internet sites

Republic of Slovenia website: www.sigov.si

Slovenske Zeleznice (Slovenian Railways): www.slo-zeleznice.si/en/home

Solomon Islands

KEY FACTS

Official name: Solomon Islands

Head of State: Queen Elizabeth II, represented by Governor General Frank Kabui (from 7 July 2009)

Head of government: Prime Minister Danny Philip (RDP) (from 25 Aug 2010)

Ruling party: Coalition led by Reform Democratic Party (RDP) (from 25 Aug 2010)

Area: 27,556 square km – Guadalcanal: 5,302 square km

Population: 538,000 (2010)*

Capital: Honiara (on Guadalcanal)

Official language: English

Currency: Solomon Islands dollar (SI$) = 100 cents

Exchange rate: SI$7.40 per US$ (Oct 2011)

GDP per capita: US$1,340 (2010)

GDP real growth: 5.60% (2010)

GDP: US$712.00 million (2010)

Inflation: 1.00% (2010)

Balance of trade: -US$75.78 million (2009)

* estimated figure

NOTA

10 November 2011, Prime Minister Danny Philip resigned and on 16 November parliament elected Gordon Darcy Lilo as prime minister.

The economy of the Solomon Islands did pretty well in 2010. Gross domestic product (GDP) was 4.0 per cent, after a fall of 1.2 per cent in 2009. Growth was led principally by logging, exports of which rose by about 30 per cent as demand in Asia helped to lift international prices. Palm oil and cocoa production also rose, although copra production declined; the fish catch was up. Growth in 2011 is expected to be even better at 7.5 per cent, reports the Asian Development Bank. The Gold Ridge mine in Guadalcanal is due to start production in 2011 while there is expected to be a rise in foreign investment in mining. Overall, growth is forecast at 4.0 per cent for 2012.

Coalition government

Twelve new political parties took part in the August 2010 elections with 509 candidates (including 25 women) standing for the 50 elected members of parliament. The Solomon Islands Democratic Party (SIDP) won 14 seats in total, independents 16, the Reform Democratic Party (RDP) and Party for Rural Advancement (PRA) three each. With no party winning a clear cut majority a coalition government was agreed, led by the newly formed Reform Democratic Party (RDP). The RDP leader, Danny Philip, was elected as prime minister, having gained support from 26 out of 50 elected members of parliament. The government's parliamentary majority was cut following the death of a sitting member and, on 30 November 2010, the jailing of a cabinet minister, Jimmy Lusibaea, for unlawful wounding while a member of theMalaita Eagles Force (MEF) militia which had seized control of the capital, Honiara, during ethnic violence in 2000. However, he was released on 20 January 2011, successfully arguing that under the *The Townsville Peace Agreement* (which had ended the violence) he should not have been prosecuted. His release led to political turmoil. The governor general was asked to call an emergency sitting of parliament, but Prime Minister Philip insisted that only he had the constitutional power to convene parliament and that he had enough support for his government to continue in office. Five ministers resigned and the opposition claimed two had joined the opposition. After much bickering, by 21 April, Prime Minister Philip had regained control of parliament.

COUNTRY PROFILE

Historical profile

The Solomon Islands were settled between 2,000–3,000BC by Austronesians, Neolithic people from south-east Asia.

1568 The Spanish explorer, Álvaro de Mendaña, first visited the islands. The islands were named after King Solomon as Mendana hoped that the islands were rich with gold.

The islands were left alone until the mid-nineteenth century when whaling ships stopped off for supplies.

1893 The central islands became a British protectorate.

1899 In the *Tripartite Treaty*, Britain gained control of the whole of the Solomon Islands in exchange for withdrawing its claim to Samoa.

1942–45 During the Second World War, Japanese occupied the islands and US troops fought one of the fiercest battles on Guadalcanal.

1945 Britain resumed the administration of the islands.

1946 An independence movement was founded to resist British rule.

1976 Self-government was granted.

1978 The Solomon Islands became fully independent.

1997 In the general election Bartholomew Ulufa'alu (Liberal Party) (a Mataita) won.

1999 Ethnic violence broke out on Guadalcanal as a native militia, the Isatabu Freedom Movement (IFM), tried to evict thousands of immigrant Malaitan. The Malaita Eagles Force (MEF) militia seized control of the capital, Honiara, claiming it was protecting Malaitan interests.

2000 Fighting broke out between the IFM and MEF. The MEF seized the parliament and forced Prime Minister Ulufa'alu to resign. The violence resulted in the breakdown in civil order with security and police forces often siding with one faction or another. The IFM and MEF signed *The Townsville Peace Agreement* in Australia. Unarmed peace-keepers were deployed.

2001 The IFM rebel leader, Selwyn Sake, was murdered. Sir Allan Kemakeza,

(People's Alliance Party (PAP)), was elected prime minister by the new 50-member parliament.
2002 The economy began to collapse, as the government was unable to pay wages and fund services. Law and order began to disintegrate.
2003 A formal request to regional neighbours for international assistance to avert a spiral of anarchy led to the deployment of the Regional Assistance Mission of the Solomon Islands (Ramsi), including 300 police officers, which began to restore order and disarm militant groups. Infamous rebel leader, Harold Keke, viewed by many as a bandit warlord, particularly after he ordered the razing of two villages, surrendered to Ramsi forces. With peace restored Ramsi was scaled down.
2004 Nathaniel Waena became governor general. A constitution for a new federal system of government was drafted.
2005 The EU signed an agreement to provide US$13 million in aid. Keke was sentenced to life imprisonment for murder. The political party Solomon Islands Social Credit Party (Socreds) was founded. It advocated domestic control of the economy and full monetary and financial reform along social credit lines.
2006 Snyder Rini (an ethnic Chinese) (Association of Independent Members (AIM)) was elected prime minister, but rioting broke out following the announcement, with extensive damage caused to the commercial centre of Honiara, particularly to Chinese businesses, and he was forced to stand down within eight days. Manasseh Sogavare (Socreds) was elected prime minister. Julian Moti fled from Papua New Guinea, wanted by the Australian Federal Police on charges of sex tourism crimes.
2007 Prime Minister Sogavare appointed Julian Moti as the attorney general. Australian soldiers raided the prime minister's office in a search of Moti. The Sogavare government was defeated in a parliamentary vote of no confidence. Derek Sikua was elected prime minister by 32 to 15 votes for Patterson Oti. Moti was extradited to Australia.
2009 The SkyAirWorld carrier collapsed owing tens of million of US dollars. Scheduled flights from Honiara to Brisbane (Australia) were cancelled. The final report on the Commission of Inquiry into the 2006 Honiara riots said the riots had been orchestrated by criminals and that compensation to Chinese businesses that took the brunt of the violence would cause further anger against the Chinese community. The Inquiry also said that the Royal Solomon Islands Police (RSIP) force failed in its duty to protect persons and property and further that it was still unable to do its duty. A five-member panel to lead the nation's Truth and Reconciliation Commission (TRC) was announced. The TRC will consider the cause and effect of the ethnic tensions and violence that struck the islands between 1998–2003. Frank Kabui was elected governor general by parliament.
2010 The Ownership, Unity and Responsibility Party (OUR) was created in January, led by former prime minister Manasseh Sogavare. In April, six opposition political parties agreed to form an alliance to fight the 24 April general elections and, if they won, to form a coalition government. However any leadership would be determined after the elections. Parliamentary elections were held on 4 August and 509 candidates (including 25 women) and 12 new political parties took part. No political party achieved outright power and a coalition government was formed with Danny Philip (of the newly formed Reform Democratic Party (RDP)) was elected as prime minister, having gained support from 26 out of 50 elected members of parliament. The government's parliamentary majority was cut following the death of a sitting member and, on 30 November, the jailing of a cabinet minister, Jimmy Lusibaea, for unlawful wounding while a member of the MEF during ethnic violence in 2000.
2011 On 20 January, Lusibaea was released having successfully argued that under the *The Townsville Peace Agreement* he should not have been prosecuted. On 24 January, four cabinet ministers resigned. The opposition first called on the prime minister to recall parliament, before asking the governor general to convene an emergency sitting of parliament to discuss the situation. Prime Minister Philip insisted that only he had the constitutional power to convene parliament and that he had enough support for his government to continue in office. By 27 January five ministers had resigned and the opposition claimed two had joined the opposition. The government re-valued the currency with an increase of 5 per cent on 16 June, following advice from the central bank. The action intended to reduce the cost of living as imported goods fall in price. In July, approval was granted for three new overseas diplomatic missions for the Solomon Islands, to Cuba, New Zealand and Switzerland. By 21 April, Prime Minister Philip had regained control of parliament and remained in post. On 28 July, the remote community of Ontong Java Atoll banned all government officials and the community's member of parliament from visiting their island, in protest at the lack of attention given by officials to the needs of the people concerning services, transport and traditional sources of food and income.

Political structure

Constitution

The constitution of May 1978 delegates authority from the British monarch, through the governor general appointed on the recommendation of parliament. There are nine administrative areas each governed by elected provincial assemblies, and the tenth, Honiara, is administered by a town council.
A draft constitution for a new federal system of government is expected to be ready by July 2009.

Independence date

1978

Form of state

Independent democracy, with British monarch as Head of State

KEY INDICATORS — Solomon Islands

	Unit	2006	2007	2008	2009	2010
Population	m	0.50	*0.51	*0.52	*0.54	*0.52
Gross domestic product (GDP)	US$bn	0.33	0.59	0.65	0.66	0.71
GDP per capita	US$	923	1,153	1,236	1,223	1,340
GDP real growth	%	6.1	10.7	7.3	-2.2	5.6
Inflation	%	8.1	7.7	17.4	7.1	1.0
Exports (fob) (goods)	US$m	114.0	164.5	210.5	163.4	–
Imports (fob) (goods)	US$m	195.7	262.0	292.9	239.2	–
Balance of trade	US$m	-81.7	-97.5	-82.4	-75.8	–
Current account	US$m	-92.4	-151.9	-216.4	-139.0	-182.0
Total reserves minus gold	US$m	104.4	119.1	89.6	146.0	265.8
Foreign exchange	US$m	103.6	118.2	88.7	130.6	250.7
Exchange rate	per US$	7.42	7.11	7.74	7.84	8.06

* estimated figure

The executive
The Head of State is the British Monarch, who is represented by the Governor General, who is chosen by the National Parliament, for a term of five years.
Executive power rests with the prime minister as head of government.
National legislature
The unicameral, National Parliament has 50 members, elected in single-seat constituencies for four-year terms. A parliament may be dissolved by a majority of its members before the term expires. Parliament elects the prime minister from its membership; the prime minister appoints a cabinet of 18 ministers.
Every five years parliament votes in a governor general, a post that is largely ceremonial with few daily political functions.
Last elections
4 August 2010 (parliamentary); 15 June 2009 (governor general)
Results: Parliamentary: the Solomon Islands Democratic Party (SIDP) won 14 seats in total (out of 50), independents won 16, Reform Democratic Party (RDP) three, Party for Rural Advancement (PRA) three; no other political party won more than three seats.
Governor general: in the fourth and final round, Frank Kabui (30 votes), Edmund Andresen (8) and Sir Nathaniel Waena (7).
Next elections
2014 (governor general – chosen by parliament); 2014 (parliament)
Political parties
Ruling party
Coalition led by Reform Democratic Party (RDP) (from 25 Aug 2010)
Main opposition party
None specifically
Political situation
The state premier, Stephen Panga revealed plans to build the capital island, Guadalcanal's own provincial centre and local government headquarters, in October 2010. Of the nine provinces of the Solomon Islands, Guadalcanal is the only one without a provincial centre and Mr Panga stated that Honiara need one separate from the national capital. The estimated cost of the Dorma Development Project was US$105 million.
However the Isatabuan population may look on these plans as a way of asserting their dominance on the island of Guadalcanal rather than as a practical way of governing their province and it will be up to central government to provide the support and funds to take the plans to fruition.
As the political situation stabilised following the intervention of the Regional Assistance Mission of the Solomon Islands (Ramsi), lead by Australia, in 2003, the Solomon Islands has been reasserting not only its internal authority but also its sovereign rights. Inter-ethnic violence, as thousands of outer-islanders relocated to central island looking for work, caused much death, destruction and mayhem. The economy was left in tatters and it took the concerted efforts of regional powers to bring the failing state back into viability.
In March 2009 the Solomon Star newspaper conducted a poll of readers asking how they rated Ramsi's work compared to when it first arrived; 44.4 per cent thought it was excellent, 27.7 per cent worse, 10.5 per cent good, 9.8 per cent very good, 4.8 per cent poor and 2.9 per cent not good. Based on these figures 64.7 per cent of votes were positive about Ramsi and 35.4 per cent were negative.

Population
538,000 (2010)*
Last census: November 1999: 409,042
Population density: 18 inhabitants per square km (2010)
Annual growth rate: 2.8 per cent 1994–2004 (WHO 2006)
Ethnic make-up
About 93 per cent Melanesian, 4 per cent Polynesian, 1.5 per cent Micronesian, European, Chinese and others. Many of the inhabitants of Western and Choiseul Provinces in Malaita are from Papua New Guinea. Ethnic disputes have simmered since the end of the Second World War, as Malaitans have migrated to Guadalcanal for work.
Religions
Anglican (45 per cent), Roman Catholic (18 per cent), other Protestants (33 per cent). There are some native religions, especially on Malaita.

Education
Primary education last for six years. Lower secondary schooling lasts for three years and finishes at aged 15. Upper secondary school lasts for two years and is completed in a one-year sixth form. Students who have completed these years may attend a one-year's foundation programme to enter the University of the South Pacific; or enrol in a college of higher education. The Solomon Islands has one of the lowest literacy rates in the world and the government intends to tackle this with the aid that has been forthcoming since 2003 so that by 2005 free education was offered to all primary school aged children. The government has backed the 'one laptop per child' programme (OLPC).
Compulsory years: Six to 15
Enrolment rate: 104 per cent boys, 90 per cent girls: gross primary enrolment (including repeaters); 21 per cent boys, 1 per cent girls: gross secondary enrolment (Unicef 2004).

Health
The Solomon Islands suffer from one of the highest malaria incidence rates in the world. It varies across the country with Honiara, Western Province and Choiseul Province the worst affected. Population growth and the mortality of mothers and children are one of the highest in the South Pacific due to endemic infectious diseases and low quality of rural health care.
Hospitals and pharmacies are limited, there are eight hospitals, the largest is the Central Hospital in Honiara. Church missions provide medical facilities on outlying islands. Serious health conditions usually require immediate medical evacuation to the nearest reliable medical facilities which are in Australia or New Zealand.
Government statistics on infant mortality in 2010 showed that despite 20 years of sustained investment in healthcare the rate of child deaths had not fallen.
Life expectancy: 68 years, 2004 (WHO 2006)
Fertility rate/Maternal mortality rate: 4.2 births per woman, 2004 (WHO 2006)
Birth rate/Death rate: 32.5 births per 1,000 population; four deaths per 1,000 population (2003).
Child (under 5 years) mortality rate (per 1,000): 19 per 1,000 live births (World Bank)

Welfare
Political instability and fighting have caused extensive damage requiring emergency rehabilitation of critical infrastructure. The Post-Conflict Emergency Rehabilitation Project entails restoration of government offices, roads, bridges, water supply and sanitation facilities, schools, and health facilities. The cost of restoration work on Guadalcanal and nearby provinces has been estimated at between US$30–35 million.

Main cities
Honiara, on Guadalcanal (capital, estimated population 59,288 in 2005), Gizo (on Gizo Island) (3,408), Auki (on Malaita) (1,745), Noro (3,720), Tulagi (1,234)

Languages spoken
There is no main native language although nearly all the languages are distantly related to the Oceanic Austronesian language group. There are at least 12 different language groups containing 87 various languages and dialects. Melanesian pidgin is the *lingua franca*. It has evolved since the time of the first traders, whalers, missionaries and labour recruiters. The vocabulary is derived from English with Melanesian syntax and uses different intonations. English, as a first

language, is spoken by 1–2 per cent of the population.

Official language/s

English

Media

Press

Dailies: In English, *Solomon Star* (www.solomonstarnews.com) is the only domestic newspaper. Online news is published by *Solomon Times Online* (www.solomontimes.com) and *People First* (www.peoplefirst.net.sb). Published abroad, other internet news outlets report on the Solomon Islands *Event Polynesia* (www.eventpolynesia.com), *Pacific Islands Report* (http://pidp.eastwestcenter.org) and *Pacific Beat* (www.radioaustralia.net.au/pacbeat) from Australia.

Periodicals: There are a number of publications, *Link* and *Solomon Nius* are government-owned, private monthlies include *Agrikalsa Nius* and *Citizen's Press; Mere Save* is a women's magazine.

Broadcasting

Radio: The public service broadcaster is SIBC (the Solomon Islands Broadcasting Corporation) (www.sibconline.com.sb), which produces radio programmes in English and Pidgin, transmitting on medium and short waves, plus FM, to local and overseas populations from Honiara, Gizo (in Western Province) and Lata.

Television: Terrestrial television services are not available, although satellite transmissions can be received.

Advertising

Newspapers, radio and cinemas accept advertising.

News agencies

ABC Pacific Beat:
www.radioaustralia.net.au/pacbeat
Pacific Magazine:
www.pacificmagazine.net
Pacific Islands New Association (Pina):
www.pina.com.fj

Economy

After the end of the ethnic struggles of 1999–2003, the country was bankrupt and had to rely on international aid and foreign investment to lead to a slow recovery, before national production could again contribute. Primary products are mainly fish and timber (despite seriously denuded forests), although the growth of palm oil production is likely to outstrip both within the next decade. Most of the population live in rural areas and survive through subsistence farming.

The Guadalcanal Plains Palm Oil Limited (GPPOL), the Solomon Island's largest private employer, announced in April 2010 that it planned to double in size by 2020 as its investments in plantations of palm oil grow. The Gold Ridge gold mine on Central Guadalcanal reopened in March 2010. The rich seas around the islands offer the potential for foreign exchange and the domestic economy negotiations must be completed to resume tuna fishing and canning for export markets.

GDP growth in 2007 was 10.7 per cent, which fell to 6.9 per cent in 2008 and was predicted to fall further to 0.4 per cent in 2010. However, the Asian Development Bank published a revised prediction of GDP growth of 2.6 per cent for 2010. As the economy was growing so was the current account balance, which in 2007 was –US$67 million, rising to –US$120 million in 2008 when world food and fuel prices were at an all-time high; inflation in the Solomon Islands was also at a record 16.5 per cent in 2008, but fell back to 8.3 per cent in 2009. As the economy shrank domestic demand fell and by 2009 the current account balance was predicted to have fallen to –US$74 million.

The prospects for the Solomon Islands are considered to be challenging. Although it avoided much of the banking crisis in 2008 it is still subject to external shocks and coupled with a lower logging output could see slower short-term growth.

The government re-valued the currency with an increase of 5 per cent on 16 June 2011, following advice from the central bank. The action should reduce the cost of living as imported goods fall in price.

External trade

The Solomon Islands is a member of the South Pacific Regional Trade and Economic Co-operation Agreement (Sparteca) along with 12 other regional nations, which allows products duty free access by Pacific Island Forum members to Australian and New Zealand markets (subject to the country of origin restrictions). It is also a member of the Melanesian Spearhead Group (with Fiji, Papua New Guinea and Vanuatu), which is a sub-regional trade group, whereby customs tariffs have been harmonised under the Melanesian free trade agreement (MFTA).

There are industries in timber, fishing, copra and palm oil and gold extraction.

A new, regular, once a month, cargo shipping service came into operation in September 2010, calling at Sikaiana; links to the six other remote islands will begin at a later date, planned for 2011. The service is supported by the government and the Asian Development Bank (ADB).

Imports

Principal imports are food, plant and equipment, manufactured goods, fuels and chemicals.

Main sources: Singapore (typically 28 per cent of total), Australia (25 per cent), Japan (5 per cent).

Exports

Principal exports are timber, fish, copra, palm oil and cocoa.

Main destinations: China (typically 50 per cent of total), South Korea (7 per cent), Thailand (7 per cent).

Agriculture

Farming

Agriculture typically accounts for over 60 per cent of GDP and almost three-quarters of the workforce. About 25–30 per cent of total land area is suitable for intensive, non-traditional agriculture, mainly on Guadalcanal. Over 85 per cent of land is communally owned, which deters investment.

The islands are self-sufficient in beef and vegetables. Copra and cocoa are produced for market on smallholdings and private plantations.

The Government Shareholding Agency, in association with major plantations, has been encouraging new coconut and cocoa planting and extension of the palm oil plantations.

Fishing

Commercial fishing and fish processing around the islands is mainly of skipjack tuna. Fish exports account for about one-third of total export earnings. Domestic seafood demand is served by small, local operations.

The first black cultured pearls, produced over a seven-year period at a demonstration farm near Gizo, were auctioned in 2004.

In April 2010 the Parties to the Nauru Agreement (PNA) (eight island states including the Solomon Islands) collectively agreed to close to *purse seine* fishing in 4.55 million square kilometres of high seas in their area, from 1 January 2011, to vessels licensed to fish in their waters. The area involved stretches from Palau and Papua New Guinea in the west to Kiribati in the east, from the Marshall Islands in the north to Tuvalu in the south; it holds an estimated 25 per cent of the world's tuna supply.

On 12 April 2011, a summit of the Parties to the Nauru Agreement (PNA) concluded its strategy for a policy of sustainable fishing in the Pacific. The PNA treaty, which was established in 1989 and expires in 2012, is seen as in need of an overhaul. As a collective region (FSM, Kiribati, Marshall Islands, Nauru, Palau, PNG, Solomon Islands and Tuvalu) control around 25–30 per cent of world stocks of tuna. Only 5 per cent of sales revenue is returned to the PNA and ministers called for specific changes, including an increased share of profits, PNA crews on-board *purse seine* vessels (minimum 10 per cent), conservation and management measures including a limit to fish trapping (fish aggregating devices (FADs)), net mesh rules and the establishment of an observer agency and fisheries information management system.

Forestry

Logging is one of the country's main economic lifelines, contributing around 18 per cent of GDP. The forests contain some 170,000 hectares of exploitable land having 13 million cubic metres of commercial timber. However, instead of the 250,000cum recommended by environmentalists as sustainable felling, felling described as 'unsustainable' by the Asian Development Bank, accelerated as logging companies increased production ahead of new legislation aimed at curbing exploitation of the natural forests.

In June 2011, a successful export order from India was granted to local landowning farmers of plantation teak trees (grown since the late-1990s) ready for harvesting.

Industry and manufacturing

The industrial sector accounts for around 5 per cent of GDP and employs some 5 per cent of the workforce.

Manufacturing activities include palm oil, rice milling, fish smoking, canning and freezing, saw milling, copra drying, food processing, tobacco, soft drinks, production of nails, detergents and soaps, wood and rattan furniture, fibreglass articles, boats, clothing, handicrafts, shell jewellery, buttons.

Most timber is exported as logs, but an increasing proportion is being sawn; the government hopes to develop wood processing to enable profitable marketing of sawn timber and veneers.

Tourism

Tourism in normal circumstances constitutes an important element of the economy, with diving and fishing being popular attractions. Visitors arrive, especially from Australia and New Zealand, although poor air services remain an impediment. There has also been a revival of hotel construction and refurbishment.

Environment

The Solomon Islands was ranked second, after Indonesia, for coral reef fish species and the range and variety of its corals.

The main environmental problems are deforestation, soil erosion and major, possibly irreversible, destruction to coral reefs There is a lack of resources to control the activities of the logging companies.

Mining

The mining sector typically accounts for 1 per cent of GDP, and employs 1 per cent of the workforce.

Panning of alluvial gold produces some 50–100kg per annum.

Undeveloped mineral resources include small deposits of copper, lead, zinc, silver, nickel, cobalt, bauxite, phosphates and asbestos.

Bugotu Nickel Ltd is working on a feasibility study of the latteritic nickel deposits on Takata and San Jorge, Isabel Province. The nickel resource is estimated at 45 million tonnes. Sumitomo Metal Mining report a 'promising deposit on Choiseul Island while in March 2010 the government announced it was putting to tender the Nickel Mine in Isabel Province.

Ross Mining of Australia opened the Gold Ridge gold mine, 45km from Majuro, with reserves of about three million ounces which will last over 10 years. Violence of the civil unrest initially caused the operations at the mine to be suspended. Then the world economic crisis delayed the 2009 opening of the mine due to the inability of the Australian owners to find debt funding. The Gold Ridge Mine will pour its first gold in March 2011, and is set to be a major foreign exchange earner for the Solomon Islands.

The Solomon Islands, the Federated States of Micronesia and Papua New Guinea will submit a joint proposal to the United Nations in 2009 to develop the Ontong Java Plateau, which is part of their extended continental shelf, for mineral prospecting.

Hydrocarbons

There are no hydrocarbon reserves and imported petroleum products are required to meet all domestic demand, which was 2,000 barrels per day in 2008.

Energy

Total installed generating capacity is 12MW. The state-owned Solomon Islands Electricity Authority (SIEA) is responsible for generation, transmission, distribution and sale of electricity.

Although hydropower provided negligible electricity in 2006, it offers the Solomon Islands its best plans for viable and sustainable energy supplies in the future. Plans include 20MW of electricity from hydropower. In the future, the World Energy Council considers the Solomon Islands has good prospects for using ocean thermal energy conversion (otec) exchanges to produce electricity.

A feasibility study for a new hydroelectric power plant on the Tina River, 30km south-east of Honiara, was completed in September 2010. Solomon Islands' electricity charges are among the most expensive in the world and the new power plant would reduce them and slash Honiara's carbon emissions by up to 70 per cent.

Locally grown and produced bio-fuel (coconut oil) is replacing motor oil in outboard motors on boats and small fishing craft.

Banking and insurance

The ADB considers the banking sector to employ limited competition with strong participation by Australian financial institutions.

Central bank

Central Bank of Solomon Islands

Main financial centre

Honiara, on Guadalcanal Island

Time

GMT plus 11 hours

Geography

The Solomon Islands lie in the south-western Pacific Ocean, to the north-east of Australia and Papua New Guinea, its closest neighbour, and north of Vanuatu. The country comprises hundreds of mainly small islands, extending over an area of around 28,500sq kilometres. There are six main islands: Guadalcanal, where the capital, Honiara, is located, Choiseul, San Cristobal, Makira, New Georgia and Malaita. The islands are mountainous and forested, with active as well as dormant volcanoes.

Hemisphere

Southern

Climate

Warm and humid, equatorial with average temperatures from 22 degrees Celsius (C) (mountainous areas inland) to 28 degrees C (coastal areas). Rainfall averages about 3,500mm per annum, but varies greatly according to location and mostly falls Nov–Apr, when cyclones may occur as well.

Entry requirements

Passports

Required by all, valid for at least six months.

Visa

Visas required by all except nationals of most EU countries, North America, Australasia and some other countries. (For a list of countries for which prior approval is required, see www.commerce.gov.sb/Divisions/Immigration/Immigration_Requirements.htm.) Travellers with onward passage and adequate funds are issued on arrival with a visitor's permit for up to three months.

Currency advice/regulations

There are no restrictions on the import of local currency, but export is limited to SI$250, or on the import of foreign currencies, subject to declaration; re-export is limited to the amount imported.

Customs

Personal effects (including an allowance of alcoholic beverages and tobacco) are allowed duty-free up to SI$500. Import licences are required for most goods and specific licences are required for fruit, vegetables and animal products.

Prohibited imports

Weapons without a police permit, narcotics and pornography.

Health (for visitors)

Mandatory precautions

Vaccination certificate required for yellow fever if travelling from an infected zone.

Advisable precautions

Vaccination for diphtheria, tuberculosis, hepatitis A and B, polio, tetanus, typhoid. Malaria is a problem, especially in Honiara, and prophylaxis should be taken. Hookworm is endemic and any itchy rash should be checked by a physician. There is a rabies risk.

Hotels

There are over 60 hotels. Visitors are advised to book well in advance. Hotel tax of 10 per cent is added to bill. In addition to Honiara's three hotels, there are resorts, guesthouses and government resthouses of varying standards and quality scattered throughout the islands. Tipping is not customary or encouraged.

Public holidays (national)

Fixed dates

1 Jan (New Year's Day), 7 Jul (Independence Day), 25 Dec (Christmas Day), 26 Dec (National Day of Thanksgiving). Each province celebrates their own public national holiday: 25 Feb (Choiseul), 2 Jun (Isable), 8 Jun (Temotu), 29 Jun (Central Island), 20 Jul (Rennell), 1 Aug (Guadalcanal), 3 Aug (Makira/Ulawa), 15 Aug (Malaita), 7 Dec (Western Province).

Variable dates

Good Friday, Easter Monday, Queen's Official Birthday (second Fri in Jun).

Working hours

Banking

Mon–Fri: 0830–1500.

Business

Mon–Fri: 0730/0800–1200, 1300–1630/1700; Sat: 0730/0800–1200.

Government

Mon–Fri: 0800–1200, 1300–1630.

Shops

Mon–Fri: 0800–1700; 0800–1200; Sat: 0800–1200. Many shops open Sat afternoon and Sun; Chinese stores often open at other times. There are several 24-hour stores in Honiara.

Telecommunications

Postal services

There is no local delivery system.

Mobile/cell phones

A second mobile/cell network, Bemobile, came into operation in the urban area of Honiara in August 2010, with SMS services, interconnect and data services.

Electricity supply

240/220V AC with flat three-pin plug fittings and bayonet-type sockets, typical of Australia.

Weights and measures

Officially, the metric system is in use.

Social customs/useful tips

Tipping is not customary, and visitors are strongly advised to refrain from the practice. Women should avoid wearing shorts and make sure their legs are adequately covered to avoid giving offence. The social structure of the Solomon Islands is extremely complex, with traditions, culture and even language varying from island to island and among villages on the same island.

Security

The security situation has improved since 2003, however resources are still limited and response times to calls for assistance may be slow. Attacks on foreign nationals are rare however personal security precausions should be taken if visiting the island of Malaita and rural Guadalcanal. Swearing is a crime and can lead to large civil fines and even jail.

Getting there

Air

National airline: Solomon Airlines.

International airport/s: Henderson International (HIR), 13km from Honiara; bank, duty free shop and car hire.

Airport tax: SI$40.

Surface

Water: Regular shipping links with Australia, New Zealand, Hong Kong, Japan, UK and Europe.

Getting about

National transport

Air: Solomon Airlines fly regular services from Henderson Airport to main islands and towns. Charter flights are available.

Road: Surfaced roads are concentrated on Guadalcanal and Malaita and few are properly maintained. Other roads, mostly in the rural areas, are coral or gravel surfaced, supplemented by dirt tracks. Terrain can be difficult.

Buses: Bus services operate in and around Honiara.

Water: Inter-island shipping services are operated by the government and also by private companies and missionaries. There are large passenger boats, and cargo vessels also carry passengers in varying degrees of comfort.

City transport

Taxis: Taxis are available in Honiara and Auki and can be booked in advance or hailed in the street. As they are not metered, it is advisable to agree the fare before the journey starts.

Car hire

Car hire is available in Honiara. Driving is on the left.

BUSINESS DIRECTORY

The addresses listed below are a selection only. While World of Information makes every endeavour to check these addresses, we cannot guarantee that changes have not been made, especially to telephone numbers and area codes. We would welcome any corrections.

Telephone area codes

Dialling code for Solomon Islands, IDD access code +677 followed by subscriber's number.

Useful telephone numbers

Police and fire: 23-666
Fire: 999
Ambulance: 25-566
Marine emergency: 21-535
Emergencies outside Honiara: 111
Directory enquiries: 101
Overseas operator: 102
Shipping and time: 107
Operator assistance: 100
Customs: 22-301
Immigration: 22-243

Chambers of Commerce

Solomon Islands Chamber of Commerce and Employers, PO Box 70, Honiara (tel: 23-342; fax: 21-851; e-mail: chamberc@solomon.com.sb).

Banking

Australia and New Zealand Banking Group Ltd (ANZ), PO Box 10, Honiara (tel: 21-111; fax: 26-937; e-mail: solomons@anz.com).

Development Bank of Solomon Islands, PO Box 911, Honiara (tel: 21-595; fax: 23-715; e-mail: dbsi@welkam.solomon.com.sb).

National Bank of Solomon Islands, PO Box 37, Honiara (tel: 21-874; fax: 23-478; e-mail: nbsi@welkam.solomon.com.sb).

Westpac Banking Corporation, 721 Mendana Avenue, PO Box 466, Honiara (tel: 21-222; fax: 24-957).

Central bank

Central Bank of Solomon Islands, PO Box 634, Honiara (tel: 21-791 fax: 23-513; e-mail: info@cbsi.com.sb).

Travel information

Guadalcanal Travel Service, Mendana Avenue, PO Box 114, Honiara (tel: 22-586; fax: 26-184; e-mail: gts@welkem.solomon.com.sb).

Henderson International Airport, PO Box G8, Honiara (tel: 36-720; fax: 36-775; e-mail: civilair@welkam.solomon.com.sb).

Solomon Islands Airlines, PO Box 23, Mendana Avenue, Honiara (tel: 20-031; fax: 20-232; e-mail: solair@welkam.solomon.com.sb).

Western Province Tourism Association, PO Box 56, Gizo (tel: 30-254; fax: 39-240)

Ministry of tourism

Ministry of Culture and Tourism, PO Box G26, Honiara (tel: 28-603; fax: 27-587; e-mail: commerce@commerce.gov.sb).

National tourist organisation offices

Solomon Islands Visitors Bureau, P.O.Box 321, Medana Avenue, Honiara (tel: 22-442; fax: 23-986; e-mail: info@sivb.com.sb).

Ministries

Ministry of Agriculture and Fisheries, PO Box G13, Honiara (tel: 21-327; fax: 21-955).

Ministry of Commerce, Industries and Employment, PO Box G26, Honiara (tel: 21-849; fax: 25-084).

Ministry of Education and Human Resources Development, PO Box G28, Honiara (tel: 23-900; fax: 20-485).

Ministry of Finance, PO Box 26, Honiara (tel: 23-700; fax: 20-392).

Ministry of Foreign Affairs, PO Box G10, Honiara (tel: 21-250; fax: 20-351).

Ministry of Forest Environment and Conservation, PO Box G24, Honiara (tel: 25-848; fax: 21-245).

Ministry of Health and Medical Services, PO Box 349, Honiara (tel: 20-830; fax: 20-085).

Ministry of Home Affairs, PO Box G11, Honiara (tel: 21-621; fax: 22-606).

Ministry of Justice and Legal Affairs, PO Box 404, Honiara (tel: 21-181; fax: 25-610).

Ministry of Lands and Housing, PO Box G38, Honiara (tel: 21-430; fax: 20-094).

Ministry of Mines and Energy, PO Box G37, Honiara (tel: 21-521; fax: 25-811).

Ministry of National Planning and Development, PO Box G30, Honiara (tel: 25-063; fax: 25-138).

Ministry of Police and National Security, PO Box G4, Honiara (tel: 22-208; fax: 25-949).

Ministry of Post and Telecommunication, PO Box G25, Honiara (tel: 21-821; fax: 21-472).

Ministry of Provincial Government and Rural Development, PO Box G35, Honiara (tel: 21-140; fax: 21-289).

Ministry of Transport, Works and Utilities, PO Box G8, Honara (tel: 26-560; fax: 26-458; e-mail: sidapp@pipolfastaem.gov.sb).

Ministry of Youth, Women, Sports and Recreation, PO Box G39, Honiara (tel: 25-490; fax: 25-686).

Office of the Prime Minister, PO Box G1, Honiara (tel: 22-202, 21-863; fax: 21-608, 25-470).

Other useful addresses

Controller of Customs and Excise, Customs and Excise Division, Ministry of National Planning and Development, PO Box G30, Honiara.

Foreign Investment Board, Ministry of Commerce, Industries and Employment, PO Box G26, Honiara (tel: 21-849; fax: 25-084).

Governor General, PO Box 252, Honiara (tel: 22-222, 21-777; fax: 23-335).

Investment Corporation of Solomon Islands Ltd, PO Box 570, Honiara (tel: 22-511; fax: 21-263).

Solomon Islands Ports Authority, PO Box 307, Honiara (tel: 22-646; fax: 23-994).

Solomon Islands Statistics Office, PO Box G6, Honiara (tel: 23-700).

Telekom Office, Mendana Avenue, Honiara (tel: 21-576; fax: 23-110).

Trading Co (Solomons) Ltd, Mendana Avenue, PO Box 114, Honiara (tel: 22-588).

Internet sites

Asia Business Connection (gateway site): http://asiabiz.com

Somalia

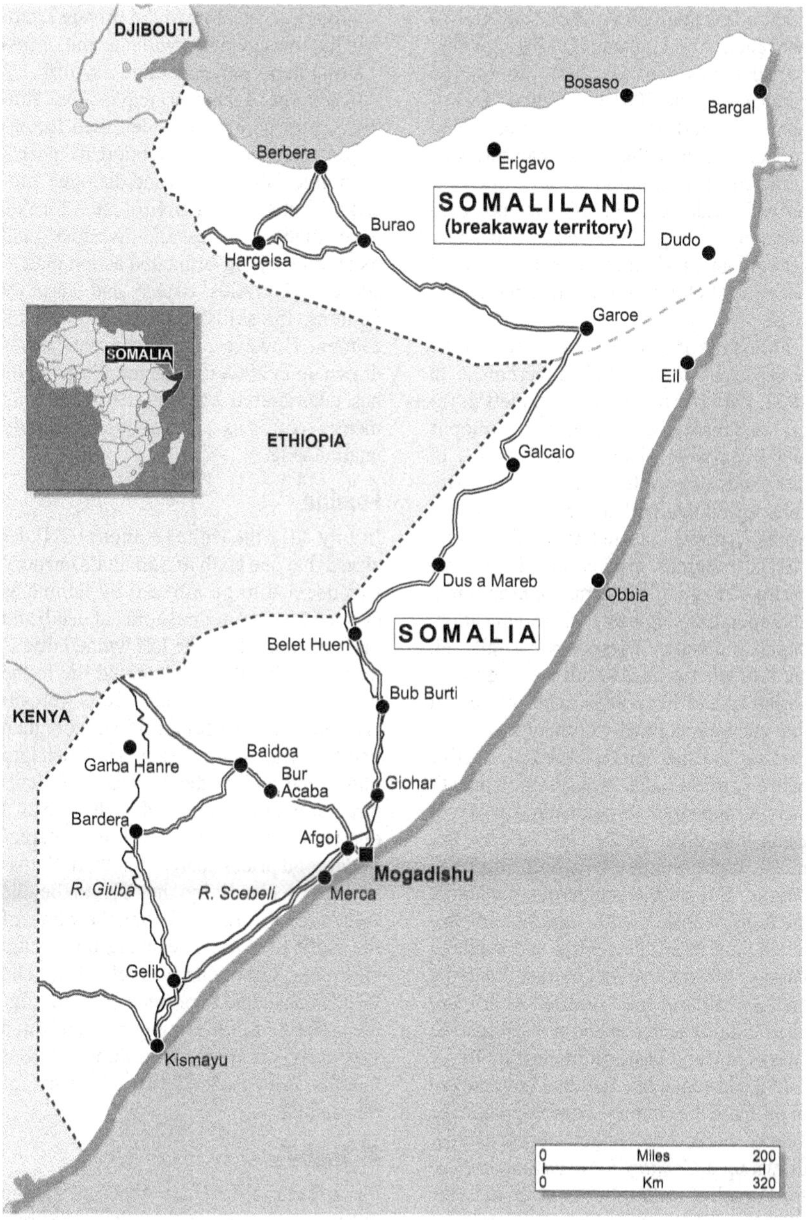

KEY FACTS

Official name: Jamhuriyadda ee Soomaaliya (Republic of Somalia)

Head of State: President Sharif Ahmed (from 31 Jan 2009)

Head of government: Prime Minister Abdiweli Mohamed Ali (from 28 Jun 2011)

Ruling party: None

Area: 738,000 square km

Population: 9.40 million (2010)*

Capital: Mogadishu

Official language: Somali

Currency: Somali shilling (SoSh) = 100 centesimi

Exchange rate: SoSh1,570.00 per US$ (Oct 2011)

GDP per capita: US$600 (2009, PPP)*

GDP real growth: 2.60% (2009)*

GDP: US$2.73 billion (2009)*

Labour force: 3.45 million (2007)

Inflation: 30.00% (2007)

Balance of trade: -US$335.00 million (2004)*

Foreign debt: US$2.60 billion (2003)

* estimated figure

NOTA

Somalia is experiencing profound political crisis and instability. Travel to the country should be avoided unless absolutely necessary. Visitors should seek advice prior to departure, and register their presence with the diplomatic representatives of their own country on arrival.

In 2011 Somalia continued to be torn apart by a nightmare combination of Islamist Groups – notably the highly organised al Shabab – clam militia, regional administrations and an ineffective central government supported by the African Union, Kenya and Ethiopia.

Failed state

The civil conflict, continuing insecurity in many parts of the country and poor or even non-existent access to services and infrastructure, have made conditions in Somalia worse than in virtually any other

Somaliland

Head of State: President Ahmed Mohamed Mohamoud (from10 Jul 2010)

Area : 137,600 square kilometres

Population : 3.5 million

Capital: Hargeisa

Official languages: Principally Somali; Arabic and English are also official languages

Currency: Somaliland shilling (SlSh)

Main exports: Livestock

Somaliland announced its unilateral declaration of independence (UDI) in May 1991. Although Somaliland has its own currency and an established and functioning democracy, no foreign government has recognised it as a legitimate entity.

Puntland

Head of government: Abdirahman Muhammad Mahmud Farole (from 8 Jan 2009)

Area : 212,510 square kilometres

Population : 2.4 million

Capital: Garowe (administrative); Bosasso (commercial)

Official languages: Somali, Arabic

Currency: Somali shilling (SoSh)

Main exports: Livestock

Although a self-governing autonomous state since 1998, Puntland has no plans for independence from Somalia.

country on the planet. Sporadic warfare, drought, famine and negative developments in income poverty, continuing declines in education and health simply serve to underline the seriousness of a desperate situation.

In a rather bleak 2008 assessment of the situation in Somalia, the World Bank noted that some 43 per cent of Somalis live on less than US$1.00 per day and 73 per cent live on less than US$2.00 per day. Somalia was ranked 161st out of 163 countries on the 2001 UN Human Development Report (it has not been possible to collect data since then, but it can safely be assumed that conditions have not improved and have probably worsened considerably). Only 22 per cent of primary school-age children are in school and 22 per cent of children die before the age of five.

Following the brutal civil war and the collapse of the central government in 1991, public infrastructure was left in ruins, social services collapsed, livelihoods and lives were shattered and scores of thousands of people were displaced. Despite this, the remarkable resilience of the Somali people has led to civil society, NGOs, religious groups and the private sector struggling on to maintain minimal and sporadic services such as education, health and water. These services fall well short of what is needed but the overall situation would have been even worse – if that can be imagined – without them. The resolve and the demonstrated productive capacity of Somalis, locally and in the Diaspora, appeared to persuade the World Bank that, given peace and security, Somalia might one day be whole and prosperous. But despite numerous mediation attempts, conflict with intermittent violence persists in the central and southern parts of the country. In contrast, Puntland and Somaliland (see Profile) have managed to limit violence and re-establish the rule of law and basic public institutions.

In the absence of a national government to promote the country's development, the World Bank has, rather optimistically, drawn up a *Country Re-engagement Note* for Somalia, seeking to 'contribute to the provision of basic public goods, accelerate socio-economic recovery and create an enabling environment for long-term institutional and policy change.' The Bank's strategy for Somalia has been articulated around three pivotal principles:

- the provision of public goods in the absence of a fully functional national government in Somalia. It also embodies a strong regional public goods dimension, with potentially positive spillover effects for neighboring countries in all the proposed areas of intervention.
- a focus on interventions which are not likely to be reversed in the event of instability. Such interventions include knowledge-intensive investments aimed at capacity and institution-building.
- a strong income-generation emphasis through its support to the private sector in the livestock area with the aim of fostering important economic pay-offs.

In support of these principles, four strategic entry points were identified for engagement in Somalia: support to macro-economic data analysis and dialogue; creation of an enabling environment for the, once highly successful, livestock and meat industry; co-ordinated action plan to address HIV/Aids issues; and capacity building for skills development/training centres. However, since the report was drawn up in 2008 the situation in Somalia has deteriorated even further, rendering many of its objectives simply unattainable.

Famine

In July 2011 the United Nations (UN) declared that one sixth of Somalia's territory was deemed to be affected by famine as defined by certain thresholds of death and malnutrition rates. The UN warned that as many as 750,000 people could die in the very near future unless aid efforts were increased. A further four million, more than half the official population, had fallen into nutritional and medical crisis as agricultural production slumped to less than a quarter of its average level and international food prices soared. Southern Somalia was declared by the UN to be the epicentre of a crisis affecting the whole of the Horn of Africa, reaching the capital city (or at least what was left of it). The UN had hesitated to provide mortality figures relating to the famine, but confirmed that over the preceding three or four months they added up to tens of thousands.

Al Shabab

Part of the problem facing the UN and the aid agencies active in Somalia is the presence of the militant Islamist group al Shabab. Faced with the presence of militant Islam many aid agencies have simply retreated. The International Committee of the Red Cross and a number of Muslim charities have continued to deliver food aid to Shabab-controlled areas, but much of the supplies fail to reach their destination, intercepted by al Shabab gunmen or simply sold on – allegedly on a massive scale – by contractors hired by the UN. A report commissioned by the UN alleged that up to 50 per cent of aid supplies was being either diverted or sold. The report – according to the *New York Times* – said that the problem was so serious that aid supplies should be suspended altogether. To make matters worse, it was also alleged that regional Somali administrations were co-operating with the Somali pirates infesting the seas off the Horn of Africa, not only supplying them with food but also selling them visas and diplomatic passports. It emerged that a number of those responsible for preparing the UN report had received death threats, forcing their re-location from UN offices in Kenya to UN headquarters in New York.

In the second half of 2011, al Shabab's fortunes appeared to be waning. Although the organisation could still count on thousands of foot soldiers, spurred on by differing motivations, several of its leaders, including the high profile Fazul Abdullah Mohammed, have been killed. Ironically, its self serving policy of hijacking and selling UN food supplies also appeared to have backfired. As large swathes of Somali territory fell prey to famine, so whole areas were left uninhabited, rendering al Shabab's recruitment drives pointless.

Economic decline

Gross domestic product (GDP) per capita is estimated to have declined from US$280 in 1989 to US$226 in 2002 after which no reliable figures exist. Extreme poverty is estimated at 43 per cent, but is 10 percentage points higher for rural and nomadic populations. General poverty afflicts 73 per cent of households, but reaches 80 per cent in rural and nomadic populations. Income inequality is significant with the poorest 10 per cent of the population receiving only 1.5 per cent of total income. Households in the top 20 per cent of income distribution receive more than half of the total income.

There have been modest gains in education indicators in recent years, but all are still extremely low. Gross primary school enrolment of 22 per cent remains the lowest in the world. One in five Somalis is illiterate. Twice as many girls as boys attend primary and secondary school. Twice as many men as women are literate. Somalia's health indicators are also among the worst in Africa. Life expectancy is 47 years and under-five and maternal mortality rates are a staggering 224 and 11 per 1,000 live births, respectively. A majority of the population (71 per cent) does not receive minimum dietary energy.

Economic data on Somalia are non-existent. Somalia's review of overdue financial obligations and co-operation with the International Monetary Fund continue to be postponed due to the absence of a recognised government and the lack of official information on economic and financial developments.

Somalia has been without an effective central government since President Siad Barre was overthrown in 1991. However unattractive the Siad Barre dictatorship might have been, the alternative has – for most Somalis – proved far worse. However, the Barré regime relied to a considerable degree on Soviet fundng, which dried up at the beginning of the 1990s. There followed years of fighting between rival warlords and an inability to deal with famine and disease have led to the deaths of up to one million people. A two-year United Nations' humanitarian effort primarily in the south was able to alleviate famine conditions, but having suffered significant casualties, the UN withdrew in 1995. Order had not then been restored. Prime ministers come and go, and the 'cabinet', if it can be called such, sits in Nairobi or not at all.

Risk assessment

Economy	Poor
Politics	Non-existent
Regional stability	Poor

Somaliland

Economy	Fair
Politics	Fair

COUNTRY PROFILE

Historical profile

1900 Somalia was controlled by the British in the north (British Somaliland Protectorate), and Italy in the south (Italian Somaliland).

1950–60 Italian Somaliland was a UN Trust Territory, under Italian administration.

1960 The northern and southern regions were united when granted independence from the UK and Italy. Aden Abdullah Osman Daar was elected president.

1967 Abdi Rashid Ali Shermarke won the presidential election.

1969 President Shermarke was assassinated in a *coup d'état* and the military leader, Mohammed Siad Barre, became president. The country was renamed the Somali Democratic Republic, political parties were banned and the National Assembly dissolved.

1970 Barre declared Somalia a socialist and one-party state under the Somali Revolutionary Socialist Party.

1974–75 Major droughts affected thousands and caused widespread starvation.

1977 Ethnic Somalis in the Ogaden rebelled against Ethiopian control and war began when Somali troops invaded the territory.

1978 Abdullahi Yusuf Ahmed led a failed military coup against Barre.

1980s There were devastating droughts which caused widespread starvation throughout most of the decade.

1981 The president appointed members of his own Marehan clan to government posts, at the expense of other, Mijertyn and Isaq, clans.

1982 Disaffected clans, with Ethiopian military support, attacked government positions. Although the government repulsed the rebels, clashes continued throughout the 1980s.

1988 A peace agreement with Ethiopia ended the Ogaden war but civil tensions increased.

1989 As the security situation worsened, Barre offered to resign and hold free elections in 1990.

1991 President Barre fled after rebels entered Mogadishu and the state of Somalia collapsed. Numerous international efforts were made to resolve the situation but effective central government was lacking for almost a decade. Warlords controlled territories through violence and clan allegiances as civil society degenerate into fiefdoms of factional fighting. The self-styled Republic of Somaliland (in the north), headed by Mohammed Ibrahim Egal, broke away from war-torn Somalia.

1992 After a period of intense conflict between the numerous clans, the US sent a force to protect the UN humanitarian aid effort and help restore order.

1993 The Addis Ababa Accords were signed. The UN began peace-keeping operations, taking over from US Marines. US Task Force Rangers launched a military offensive (later known as the Battle of Mogadishu) against General Aideed and the Somali National Alliance (SNA). Eighteen US troops, and up to 1,000 Somalis, were killed.

1994 The US withdrew all of its forces from Somalia.

1995 The remainder of the UN peacekeeping force withdrew.

1996 General Aideed died from gunshot wounds. His son, Hussein Aideed, replaced him as head of the clan-based gang.

1997 Twenty-six of Somalia's 28 factions signed the Cairo Declaration peace accord.

1998 The leaders of the northeastern region of Puntland, including Abdullahi Yusuf Ahmed, declared the region autonomous.

1999 Inter-clan violence continued in central and southern Somalia. President Guelleh of Djibouti announced an international peace plan based on the participation of Islamic and civil groups rather than warlords.
2000 A four-month reconciliation conference in Djibouti ended when the transitional national government (TNG) elected a civilian as the country's first president since 1990 – Abd al Qasim Salad Hassan. Hussein Aideed, and other warlords, in Somalia, and Abdullahi Yusuf, president of Puntland, opposed the TNG.
2001 Militia loyal to Aideed attacked TNG forces. Jama Ali Jama deposed Abdullahi Yusuf as president of Puntland but was later overthrown by Abdullahi Yusuf who recaptured the presidency, with the help of Ethiopian forces. The president of Somaliland, Muhammad Haji Ibrahim Egal, died and was succeeded by Dahir Riyale Kahin.
2002 A cease-fire was agreed between 21 warring factions and the TNG.
2003 Dahir Riyale Kahin of the ruling United People's Party (UDUB) (Somaliland), won presidential and parliamentary elections. A peace conference, the Somali National Reconciliation Conference, was set up in Kenya
2004 At peace talks, warlords and politicians signed a deal to set up a new parliament; the Transitional National Assembly (TNA) was inaugurated and for security reasons continued to be held in Kenya. Abdullahi Yusuf, (president of Puntland), won the TNA presidential elections held. Abdullahi appointed Mohammed Ali Ghedi as prime minister. Hundreds of deaths were caused by the south-Asian *tsunami* that hit the coastline of Puntland.
2005 Authority within the country was maintained by rival warlords who controlled various tribal lands.
2006 Fighting broke out between forces of the Islamic Courts Union (ICU), which had restored some order to parts of the capital through the use of *Sharia* (Islamic law), and warlord militias. The ICU gained full control in the capital and most of central and southern Somalia. Sheikh Hassan Dihir Aweys was appointed head of the ICU, which was renamed Midowga Maxkamadaha Islaamiga (Supreme Islamic Courts Council) (SICC). Mogadishu's international airport and seaport were reopened. Peace talks failed between the transitional government and the SICC and fighting resumed. Ethiopian ground and air forces entered Somalia in support of the transitional government. The SICC was routed and the transitional government took control of Mogadishu.
2007 Fighting in the capital erupted as factions supporting the president and prime minister clashed over interests in oil exploration contracts. The head of the World Food Programme UN humanitarian agency was kidnapped in Mogadishu. The main market in Mogadishu, which provided trade of essential goods for around 85 per cent of residents and traders throughout the country, was destroyed by fire. The UN reported that 400,000 people had fled from Mogadishu. Mohammed Ali Ghedi resigned as prime minister and Nur 'Adde' Hassan Hussein was appointed in his place. The prime minister announced that he would be replacing the 30-member cabinet with a much smaller cabinet.
2008 The UN Security Council extended the AU-led mission to Somalia by six months from February and again from August. Representatives of the Transitional Federal Government (TFG) and the Alliance for the Re-liberation of Somalia (The Alliance) signed an agreement in August, to cease hostilities, the result of several months of talks in Djibouti. By the end of the year Islamist forces not only controlled northern regions, but also took over much of the south. Ethiopia announced its troops would leave in December and would not be replaced by African Union peacekeepers as had been expected. The government of Somalia was left without military support. By December over 80 per cent of the country's army and police force had deserted, in some cases taking weapons, uniforms and vehicles with them. On 14 December the president sacked Prime Minister Hussein and his government for failing to bring security to the country. However, the prime minister denied the president had the power to replace him. The president appointed Muhammad Mahmud Guled Gamadhere as prime minister on 14 December. Moves to impeach the president reached the required one-third vote by 17 December. Charges against him included nepotism, illegally printing money, being autocratic and failing to foster the peace process. The UN decided that UN peacekeeping troops could not be sent to Somalia, as neither side of the conflict could agree their role. On 22 December the AU agreed to extend its military mission until February 2009. President Abdullahi Yusuf Ahmed lost a vote of confidence in parliament and resigned on 29 December, when Adan Mohamed Nuur (also known as Adan Madobe) became acting president.
2009 Ethiopia began withdrawing its troops on 2 January. Abdirahman Mohamed Farole was elected, by parliament, as president of Puntland on 8 January. Islamist insurgents seized the government's capital city of Baidoa on 26 January, (just hours after Ethiopian troops had withdrawn) and imposed *Sharia* (Islamic law). Sheikh Sharif Ahmed, a moderate Islamist, was elected president by parliament on 31 January. Omar Abdirashid Ali Sharmarke, nominated by the president, was approved by parliament and was sworn into office as prime minister on 13 February. On 2 March, the president announced the introduction of *Sharia* nationwide, in an agreement with religious leaders and rival political factions; it was endorsed by the government on 10 March. Islamist forces attacked Mogadishu in May and in June the president declared a state of emergency following the killing of the security minister and over 20 others in a suicide bombing, as violence intensified. An appeal was made for troops from neighbouring countries to intervene during battles between government and Islamist troops. Ethiopia decided that it would only intervene if the fighting threatened its national security. Hundreds of politicians fled the country, leaving the national assembly membership dangerously close to the 250 needed to make up a quorum. On 25 September in the secessionist Republic of Somaliland the upper house of parliament extended the term of office for President Dahir Riyale Kahin.
2010 The WFP pulled out of southern Somalia in January after threats from Islamist groups. Following a two-year delay due to security worries, a presidential election was held in Somaliland on 26 June, in which three candidates took part. Ahmed Silanyo won 49.59 per cent of the vote, incumbent Dahir Kahin won 33.23 per cent. President elect Ahmed Mahamoud Silanyo will be sworn in on 27 July. In August the UN Food and Agriculture Organisation reported that some two million Somalis still needed emergency food supplies. This was despite a good harvest of sorghum and maize after better than average rains. On 18 September Horn Afrik and GBC radio stations were raided by militants from al-Shabab and Hizbul Islam. In September Somaliland and Puntland, once-warring territories in northern Somalia, rather surprisingly agreed in principle to work together to tackle common security threats. The US banned all cargo from Somalia from 8 November. Omar Sharmarke resigned as prime minister in September 2010. He was criticised for failing to defeat the Shabab. Once again feuding within the transitional government left the country without a functioning government. The president appointed Mohamed Abdullahi Mohamed as prime minister on 14 October, the appointment was confirmed by parliament on 31 October.
2011 On 3 February, parliament extended its mandate until 2014, following

approval by the AU, despite failing to enact a new constitution and organising national elections by August 2011. On 24 March, the General Service Union of the Kenyan police force crossed into Somalia at the border town of Liboi, to confront the militant forces of the al Shabab. It was the first time that Kenyan forces had directly fought al Shabab, which was accused of raids into Kenya. On 28 March the government itself extended its mandate by another year, despite criticism from donors and attacks by Islamist extremists. On 6 June, the UN announced that it would undertake an investigation into the breakdown in order in South Kordofan between Sudan and South Sudan in May. In June, rival leaders within government agreed to postpone parliamentary elections until 20 August 2012; the president and speaker of parliament retain their posts. Prime Minister Mohamed Abdullahi Mohamed announced his resignation on 19 June. The aid agency Save the Children reported in June that some 1,300 people, including at least 800 children, are arriving daily at the Dadaab refugee camp in Kenya. They are driven to make the arduous journey by a combination of severe drought, the on-going conflict and rising food prices. The Dadaab refugee camp had a population of over 350,000 in mid-2011. Prime Minister Mohamed Abdullahi Mohamed announced his resignation on 19 June, and Abdiweli Mohamed Ali was appointed as his replacement on 23 June, and was sworn into office as prime minister on 28 June. A crisis in malnutrition that developed over months as a two-year drought caused widespread failure in crop and animal production caused tens of thousands of vulnerable people not only to seek food in neighbouring Kenya but also flee the internal conflict. The UN estimated that 10 million people in the Horn of Africa were affected by drought and food insecurity. The Islamist group al Shabab announced on 6 July that it had lifted its ban (imposed in 2009) on foreign aid agencies providing relief in the territories under its control. On 20 July, the UN officially declared a famine in Bakool and Lower Shabelle in southern Somalia, while other areas were considered at extreme risk. The area experienced the worst drought for over 50 years. The southern areas are largely controlled by al Shabab and despite its promise of safe passage for aid workers and aid supplies the UN and US have demanded further safety guarantees from armed groups before they allow their staff to enter the areas in need. It was estimated that US$300 million was needed to provide aid for 8–10 weeks from the middle of July. Prime Minister Ali announced the creation of a special force to protect convoys delivering famine aid. Al Shabab militants withdrew from Mogadishu on 6 August. On 9 August, as the first shipment of food aid reached the city, the AU called for another 1,000 troops to protect the food aid and to secure and consolidate military gains in Mogadishu. Turkey's Prime Minister Erdogan and his family visited Mogadishu on 19 August. Another state (the Bay region) was declared a famine zone by the UN on 5 September, with around 750,000 people at risk of starvation. On 9 September, Mohamed Ibrahim was appointed as deputy prime minister. Two major telecommunications companies and a major money transfer firm were temporarily banned at the end of September after al Shabab demanded the companies pay *zikat*, a form of charity paid by Muslims. Aid agencies say that if al Shabab persist in their demands there will be a severe knock on effect for the poor of Somalia who rely in remittances from abroad during a time of famine in particular. The UN's Secretary General Ban Ki-moon visited Mogadishu on 9 December and met the prime minister. Mr Ban was visiting at a time when UN-backed AU forces were in deadly battle with al Shabab, in and around the city. Nevertheless he still intended to discuss not only the famine in the south of Somalia, but also the UN's impatience at the situation concerning corruption and divided political leadership. A deadline was issued that unless serious progress towards a new constitution and a reformed parliament was accomplished by August 2012, then funding from the UN would be curtailed.

Political structure

The self-styled republics of Somaliland and Puntland have their own elected governments (but are unrecognised internationally). In April 2002, a new state was declared in south-western Somalia.

Constitution

The Somali National Reconciliation Conference, held in Mbagathi, Nairobi, Kenya, began in 2003 and the Leaders Committee agreed that Somalia should adopt a federal system of government, with selection of the MPs being carried out by the signatories (political leaders) to the Declaration of Cessation of Hostilities signed in Eldoret, Kenya, in 2002, and by certain politicians, who were officially invited.

If the government fails to complete the process of federalism throughout Somalia within a period of two-and-a-half years, parliament should withdraw its vote of confidence, necessitating the formation of a new transitional government to complete the process of federalism within one year.

Form of state

Federal republic

The executive

The president is elected by parliament. The prime minister is appointed by the president.

National legislature

In November 2008, in UN-backed reconciliation negotiations, parliament agreed to increase the number of members of parliament from 275 to 550. Apart from the existing arrangement of 61 seats each allocated to four main tribal groupings and 31 seats divided between the remaining small tribal groupings, 200 more seats will be allocated to opposition representatives and 75 reserved for civil society groups. However, Islamist groups that control much of Somalia were not party to the agreement.

Legal system

At independence in 1960, Somalia had four legal systems: English common law, Italian law, Islamic Sharia and Somali customary law. In 1973, the Siad Barre regime introduced a unified civil code. There is no national judicial system.

Last elections

10 October 2004 (presidential election by the Transitional National Assembly in Kenya)

26 June (Somaliland, presidential)

Results: Presidential: Abdullahi Yusuf Ahmed won 189 votes (out of 275); Abdullahi Ahmed Addou won 79 votes. Somaliland, presidential: Ahmed Mahamoud Silanyo (Kulmiye Nabad, Midnimo iyo horumar iyo (Peace, Unity and Development Party) (PUDP)) won 49.59 per cent of the vote, Dahir Riyale Kahin (Ururka Dimuqraadiga Ummadda Bahawday (United People's Democratic Party) (UPDP)) 33.23 per cent, Faysal Cali Warabe (Ururka Caddaalada iyo Daryeelka (For Justice and Development) (FJD)) 17.18 per cent.

Next elections

20 August 2012 (parliamentary); senior political posts are elected by the Transitional Federal Parliament (TFP)

Political parties

There are no formal political parties. Warlords and their supporters wield most of the power. Political organisation largely reflects membership of clans and sub-clans.

Ruling party

None

Population

9.40 million (2010)*

Last census: February 1987: 7,114,431

Population density: 15 inhabitants per square km. Urban population: 28 per cent (1995–2001).

Annual growth rate: 2.3 per cent 1994–2004 (WHO 2006)

Internally Displaced Persons (IDP)
375,000 (UNHCR 2004)
Ethnic make-up
Somali (85 per cent), Bantu, Arabs and others (15 per cent).
Religions
Islam is the state religion (majority Sunni Muslims) (98 per cent), Christian minority (2 per cent).

Education
The UN Children's Fund (Unicef) supports 352 primary schools in central and southern Somalia, out of 418 that are operational. Additionally, Unicef has rehabilitated 35 schools, trained 2,300 teachers and initiated a school improvement programme. Several non-government organisations have concentrated on adult literacy programmes and civic education. Private education has recently been re-established in Somali, although school fees are proving to be out of reach of the ordinary Somali family.
Somaliland expatriates residing in the United Arab Emirates (UAE) have initiated efforts to raise funds for the Amoud University. The University, established in 1997 in Boroma, is essentially a community project. In June 2003, Somalia opened its first medical college, the Benadir University Medical College (BUMC), since 1991. BUMC will be funded by donations from Somali physicians and by tuition fees.
The education sector received only 12 per cent funding in the Consolidated Appeals Process (CAP), 2003. About 40 per cent of all teachers are unqualified and many have not completed their primary school education.
Literacy rate: 17.1 per cent, adult rate: 35 per cent, adult rate for the urban population; 10 per cent for rural and nomadic populations (2003).
Female adult literacy is estimated to be 52 per cent of the male rate.
Compulsory years: Six to 14.
Enrolment rate: Primary school enrolment increased by 29 per cent in 2002, compared to 2001, and there were 30 per cent more teachers. In 2003, one out of six children received formal primary education. Female primary school enrolment was 53 per cent of the male rate.

Health
The country's health services collapsed during the war and access to healthcare depends mostly on external assistance. Unicef remains the key provider of essential medical services and supplies to 123 maternal and child health centres, 174 health posts, and 16 hospitals.
Surveys in areas with high concentrations of displaced families show malnutrition rates as high as 40 per cent. Only 1.5 per cent of one to two years old are vaccinated. In addition, Somalia has the highest incidence of tuberculosis in the world, while cholera is endemic in most areas. In 2004, Somalia was removed from the UN list of countries with endemic polio.
It is estimated that 31 per cent of the population have access to improved water facilities.
Life expectancy: 44 years, 2004 (WHO 2006)
Fertility rate/Maternal mortality rate: 6.3 births per woman, 2004 (WHO 2006)
Birth rate/Death rate: 46.4 births per 1,000 population; 17.6 deaths per 1,000 population (2003).
Child (under 5 years) mortality rate (per 1,000): 133 per 1,000 live births (World Bank)

Welfare
Insecurity continues to be the greatest threat to the lives and welfare of the population, who are highly dependent on external assistance. International aid is jeopardised by widespread factional fighting, the kidnapping of aid workers and also by the mining of all major roads in Northern Gedo, the area most in need of food aid. An estimated 400,000 Somalis are internally displaced.
Although the World Food Programme (WFP) supports the repatriation of refugees with a nine-month food supply or cash equivalent, more than 10 per cent of the population require emergency food assistance. In May 2003, the WFP distributed 1,355 tonnes of food around Somalia.

Main cities
Somalia: Mogadishu (capital, estimated population 1.2 million in 2004), Kismayu (209,300), Merca (179,700).
Somaliland: Hargeisa (241,200), Berbera (222,700), Burao (55,900), Erigavo (19,100).
Puntland: Bosaso (33,200), Garowe (22,800), Galkayo (20,100), Lasanod (16,000).

Languages spoken
Somali is one of the major languages of Africa and belongs to a set of languages called lowland Eastern Cushitic. It did not have a written form until the Latin script was adopted in 1972. Arabic, Italian and English (mainly for business) are also in use.
Arabic and English are to be the second official languages of the Transitional Federal Government of Somalia, as agreed on 5 July 2003 at the Somali National Reconciliation Conference.
Official language/s
Somali

Media
Press
Dailies: In Somalia, newspapers include *Xog-Ogaal Qaran News* (www.qarannews.com), *Codka xoriyadda* and *Ayaamaha*.
Dhambaal News (www.dhambaalnews.com) and *Jamhuuriya* (www.jamhuuriya.info) are based in Somaliland. In English, *Somaliland Times* (www.somalilandtimes.net) and the Awdal New Network (www.awdalnews.com) gives online news from Somaliland.
There are a number of internet news outlets aimed at the Somali diaspora including www.luuliyo.com, www.waagacusub.com, www.hiiraan.com, www.hormoodnews.com and www.banadir.com (with articles in English).
Weeklies: Publications include *Dadka*, *Panorama*, *Republican* (Hargeisa), *Sanca* and *Xurmo*.
Periodicals: Monthly publications include *Ayaamaha* and *Himilo*.
Broadcasting
Radio: In June 2007 the government ordered the closure of the three main radio stations in the capital (Shabelle Media Network, Horn Afrik and IQK). The order was rescinded four days later, reportedly after pressure from the US ambassador to Kenya.
The governments in the breakaway provinces of Somaliland and Puntland maintain a tight control on broadcasting in their areas. The Transitional Federal Government closed the Shabelle Media Network, Banadir Radio and Radio Simba on 12/13 November 2007, without explanation. The information minister said the stations had been 'carrying false reports and misrepresenting the activities of the security forces'. Critics claimed the government was closing down independent news outlets that did not report pro-government news.
There is no national, domestic broadcaster however the many independent radio stations provide the principal source of news for the population. Radio Magadishu is government-run with coverage limited to the capital. The FM stations Radio HornAfrk (www.hornafrik.com), Radio Shabelle (www.shabelle.net) and Radio Banaadir (www.radiobanadir.com) all broadcast in the capital. Radio Hargeisa (www.radiohargeysa.net) is Somaliland government-owned; the privately owned Radio Galkayo (www.radiogaalkacyo.com) and Voice of Peace broadcast in Puntland.
Television: Two private TV networks exist, Somali Telemedia Network (STN) and HornAfrk TV (www.hornafrik.com),

broadcast international produced programmes. Somaliland National TV (SLNTV) is government-owned. Somali Broadcasting Corporation (SBC) is a private station in Puntland.

News agencies

There is no official agency but APA and Panapress report on Somali matters.

Economy

The state of Somalia is not blessed with natural resources and the greater proportion of the population relies on subsistence faming, although there are commercial banana plantations in the south, and remittances from abroad.

There has been no effective government since the 1980s, with internal conflict disrupting any progress towards a productive civil society. Somalia's Transitional Federal Government lacks international recognition and its administration does not have sufficient authority to gather statistics for even superficial analyses.

The informal economy has been a mainstay for the population, based mainly on ownership of livestock and land. The traditional trade in exports of livestock to Arab Gulf states has been periodically suspended due to animal health concerns. International economic agencies are reluctant to invest in the country until it can achieve a measure of peace and the rule of law. Even so, a Coca-Cola bottling plant opened in 2004, becoming the largest investment the country had received since 1991.

The situation is complicated by the break-away Republic of Somaliland, which has become an autonomous zone with its own currency and government. Somaliland represents the strongest local economy and has undergone something of a boom since it declared independence in 1991. The autonomous region has undergone a modest transformation with infrastructural improvements and an emergent business elite. Without international recognition, however, Somaliland cannot access funds from the IMF or World Bank or develop trade relations. Around 70 per cent of the population receive help in the form of remittances.

Another autonomous region, the Puntland State of Somalia, has its own chaotic economic policy, where many Somalis wish to remain part of Somalia. Puntland faces many of the problems faced by Somalia proper, including factional fighting and almost complete economic collapse.

Somali pirates have become the scourge of the Somalia coast and further into the Indian Ocean. Ships are routinely hijacked and held for ransom for millions of dollars, paid by ship owners and insurance companies. In 2008 there were 111 acts of piracy (out of a total 293 worldwide) undertaken by Somali pirates; double the number in 2007. In 2009 214 attacks took place. The piracy has become a business in which wealthy Somalis (including some members of the Diaspora) purchase, finance and outfit skiffs, mother-ships and crews, enabling gangs to select targets and intercept laden cargo ships, oil tankers and private yachts. International maritime opposition includes military naval vessels on patrol but the vast region limit their effectiveness. It is estimated that around US$30 million per year of illegal money is funding the northern port towns of Harardhere, Eyl and Bossaso and their thriving economies.

External trade

While Somalia belongs to the African, Caribbean and Pacific Group of States (ACP Group) which has a trade agreement with the European Union, it does not have a central government authority that can provide evidence of conformity of international and official regulations. Nevertheless, less formal trade is undertaken with regional neighbours, while remittances provide the majority of foreign earnings.

The continuing need for the large-scale import of fuels and food results in an ongoing poor balance of trade. There is a tradition of livestock exports to the Arab Gulf states.

There is an illegal trade in *qat* (called *jaad* in Somalia, an additive, mild hallucinogen) between Somalia, Ethiopia and Yemen.

Imports

Principal imports are manufactures, petroleum products, foodstuffs and construction materials.

Main sources: Djibouti (typically 31 per cent of total), India (8 per cent), Kenya (8 per cent).

Exports

Principal exports are livestock, bananas, hides, fish, charcoal and scrap metal.

Main destinations: UAE (typically 54 per cent of total), Yemen (20 per cent), Oman (6.0 per cent).

Agriculture

Farming

Agriculture is the most important sector in the economy. It contributes about 65 per cent to GDP and employs 65 per cent of the working population. It is often badly affected by drought, as well as by the chaos of recent years.

Livestock, particularly camels, is the principal foreign exchange earner, accounting for 40 per cent of GDP. Exports are mainly to Arabian Gulf states and formerly to Saudi Arabia. A Saudi ban on the import of allegedly diseased Somali livestock has damaged the trade.

Much of the land is desert or semi-desert and only 13 per cent is cultivated, making food security a constant concern. Some crops are grown on the fertile land in the Juba and Scebali valleys, but the farmers have been displaced by nomads.

Subsistence farmers grow maize and sorghum. Wheat and rice are imported.

The most important cash crops are bananas, cotton and frankincense.

In 2006, the Supreme Islamic Courts Council (SICC) issued a directive to halt the production of charcoal. Somalia lost 1.2 million hectares, or 14 per cent of its forest cover between 1990–2005 and has had a serious detrimental effect on the environment. The principal export of charcoal is to Gulf states, where wood from mango trees is highly favoured and a bag of charcoal can cost as much as US$15 each.

Industry and manufacturing

The industrial sector is small, contributing about 5 per cent to GDP and employing 8 per cent of the working population.

The principal industries are meat and fish processing, sugar refining, fruit and vegetable canning, textiles and leather goods. Many factories are idle, because foreign exchange shortages have cut off foreign inputs.

Tourism

There are no tourism facilities.

Mining

There are significant mineral resources, but they have not yet been commercially exploited. The most important regions include an area extending from the Ethiopian border to beyond Berbera in Somaliland and west of the River Scebali near Mogadishu. The former contains reserves of copper, gold, molybdenum and bismuth, while the latter contains iron, gold and apatite.

The country also contains reserves of uranium, marble, manganese, tin, beryl and columbite. Salt and gypsum were extracted commercially before the civil war began.

Hydrocarbons

Although there are no proven oil reserves, although the potential for oil and gas is high. Major Western oil companies ceased exploration after the outbreak of the civil war in 1991. In 2007 a Kuwait and Indonesian consortium was created to undertake further exploration under a preliminary agreement of partnership with a newly formed state company, Somalia Petroleum Corporation. Downstream, Somalia has a single oil refinery with a capacity of 10,000 barrels per day (bpd), although it has not been in use for some years and is in a state of disrepair.

The breakaway region of Somaliland (also called Puntland), in the north, undertook oil exploration under its own offices, sparking clan warfare in March 2009 over ownership of land being investigated. The Nogal and Dharoor basins are considered to have a high probability of oil and gas.
Somalia relies heavily on imports of oil for its fuel needs.
Total proved natural gas reserves are around 5.6 billion cubic metres located in one gas field, although political and economic chaos has prevented exploitation. Currently, there is no production or import of natural gas.
Coal is neither produced nor imported.
Puntland: The Canadian company Africa Oil announced that it would begin drilling for oil in its leased sites in the Nugaal and Dharoor Valley in Puntland from mid-2010.

Energy
Total installed generating capacity is 80MW, all of which is provided by diesel-fired generators. The state-owned Ente Nazionale Energia Elettrica (ENEE) has a monopoly of generation, transmission and distribution and supply. Much of the energy infrastructure has been damaged or destroyed and the unstable state of the country hinders re-development.
Somalia has been identified as a prime location for wind farms but until the country has some degree of stability no development is likely.

Banking and insurance
The first commercial bank to be established since 1990, the Universal Bank of Somalia (UBSOM), was launched on 22 January 2002. The bank is 51 per cent owned by Somalis and 49 per cent by overseas investors. UBSOM has links with 62 overseas banks in 72 countries.
Central bank
Central Bank of Somalia
Main financial centre
Mogadishu

Time
GMT plus three hours

Geography
Somalia lies on the east coast of Africa, with Ethiopia to the north-west and Kenya to the west. There is a short frontier with Djibouti in the north-east. Somalia has a long coastline of 3,200km on the Indian Ocean and the Gulf of Aden, forming the Horn of Africa.
The country is shaped like the number 7 with the northern top stretching west along the coast of the Gulf of Aden. Here the land is a desert plain that rises to the Ogo and Migiurtinia mountains fringing the coastline, – of which the highest peak is Surud Ad at 2,408 metres (m).
Southwards, the land becomes more fertile savannah which eventually runs into an arid and extensive region of sand dunes and rugged plateau. There are few rivers, the largest are in the central and southern regions, the Webi Guiba and Webi Scebeli rise in Ethiopia and flow into the Indian Ocean. The north has no permanently flowing rivers, the Daror and the Nugaaleed are intermittent streams.
Hemisphere
Northern

Climate
Tropical. Humid on coast, drier in north. Average temperatures 27–32 degrees Celsius (C) throughout year, but can reach 42 degrees C on coast. Dry seasons from January–February and August–September. Rainy seasons from March–June and October–December.

Dress codes
Lightweight clothes are required. Women should dress modestly.

Entry requirements
Passports
Required by all.
Visa
The civil war has disrupted consular services worldwide. Visas are required by the break-away territories of Somiland and Puntland and can be obtained at the port of entry. Travellers should contact their own ministry of foreign affairs for advice about local conditions and travelling to Somalia and breakaway provinces.
Currency advice/regulations
Import/export of only small amounts of local currency is allowed. Import of foreign currency is unlimited, but it must be declared on a form for which a small charge may be made. Currency transactions should be recorded at each exchange. Export of foreign currency is limited to the amount declared on arrival.
The Somali shilling is the unit of currency, except in Somaliland, which uses the Somaliland shilling. US dollars are accepted everywhere.

Health (for visitors)
Mandatory precautions
Yellow fever and cholera certificates if arriving from an infected area.
Advisable precautions
Hepatitis A and E are widespread and hepatitis B is hyper-endemic. Vacinations for meningococcal meningitis, yellow fever, cholera, typhoid and polio vaccinations are advisable. Malaria prophylaxis should be taken as risk exists throughout the country (two types of prophylaxis are recommended); anti-mosquito measures include mosquito repellents, nets and clothing covering the body, these offer protection against hepatitis B. Tap water must be treated as unsafe unless boiled and filtered. Eat only well cooked meals, preferably served hot; vegetables should be cooked and fruit peeled. Dairy products are unpasteurised and should be avoided.
A comprehensive medical pack and all medication is essential for the traveller as there is little to be found in the country. Medical insurance is essential, including emergency evacuation.

Hotels
Available in principal towns. Service charge of 10 per cent added to bills.

Credit cards
Credit cards are not accepted in Somalia.

Public holidays (national)
Fixed dates
1 Jan (New Year's Day), 1 May (Labour Day), 26 Jun (Independence Day), 1 Jul (Foundation Day).
Variable dates
Eid al Adha, Ashura, Birth of the Prophet, Eid al Fitr (three days).
Islamic year 1433 (26 Nov 2011–14 Nov 2012): The Islamic year contains 354 or 355 days, with the result that Muslim feasts advance by 10–12 days against the Gregorian calendar. Dates of feasts vary according to the sighting of the new moon, so cannot be forecast exactly.

Working hours
Banking
Sat–Thu: 0800–1130.
Business
Sat–Thu: 0800–1230, 1630–1900.
Government
Sat–Thu: 0800–1400.
Shops
Sat–Thu: 0900–1300, 1600–2000.

Telecommunications
Mobile/cell phones
There are several GSM 900 and 900/1800 services available.

Electricity supply
220V AC, 50 cycles. The electricity system is poor.

Social customs/useful tips
Islamic customs should be respected. It is the convention to use the right hand when shaking hands and passing or receiving anything. Muslims are not permitted to drink alcohol or eat pork. Do not smoke or drink in public during Ramadan. Refusal of offered refreshment is considered discourteous. Shoes should be removed on entry to mosques.
Khat was banned by the Islamists in November 2006. It is a stimulant and commonly chewed by men, inducing a state of calm and sometimes causing aggressive behavior. It is grown in much of the Horn of Africa, including Kenya, and exported to Yemen.

In January 2011 hand-shaking between men and women who are not related was banned by al Shabab in the town of Jowhar, which they control. They are also barred from chatting or walking together in public; punishment will be according to Sharia.

Security

Any visit to Somalia should be undertaken only after a risk assessment has been carefully weighed; terrorism is a constant threat. Armed robbery and kidnapping by numerous bands of militia is endemic. Hargeisa, capital of the self-declared Republic of Somaliland is the only place that may offer a relatively secure environment in the country. Foreign nationals should register their presence with their respective diplomatic representatives.

Getting there

Air

National airline: Damal Airlines (based in the UAE) operates scheduled regional flights from eight airports in Somalia.
International airport/s: Mogadishu International (MGQ), 6.4km from city. This airport was re-opened on 15 July 2006.

Surface

Road: There are road links with Kenya in the south and Djibouti in the north. Four-wheel drive vehicles are recommended.
Main port/s: El Ma'an, Bassasso, Kismayu, Merca, Mogadishu.
Berbera is the economic lifeline for the self-declared Somaliland Republic.

Getting about

National transport

Air: Damal Airlines flies to nine towns throughout the country, including Mogadishu.
Road: Travel may be restricted and local enquiries should be made. There were good roads from Mogadishu to Kismayu (via Merca) and Baidoa in the southern part of the country, and to Hargeisa and Berbera in the north. However, since the civil strife began conditions have deteriorated. Most other routes are mainly tracks and gravel roads. Driving is on the right.
Water: Coastal shipping of both freight and passengers is extensive. The number of incidents of piracy off the Somali coast has increased sharply in the last few years.

City transport

Taxis: Fares are by negotiation and tipping is not usual. Taxis can be hired on a time basis.

Car hire

Car hire is available in Mogadishu although foreign visitor should avoid driving alone until the politicial situation in Somalia improves.
There are no traffic lights in the country except in Hargeisa in Somaliland. The condition of the roads makes driving difficult and night driving is dangerous due to the absence of lighting.

BUSINESS DIRECTORY

The addresses listed below are a selection only. While World of Information makes every endeavour to check these addresses, we cannot guarantee that changes have not been made, especially to telephone numbers and area codes. We would welcome any corrections.

Telephone area codes

It is unlikely that all landlines quoted are working.
The international direct dialling (IDD) code for Somalia is +252, followed by area code and subscriber's number:

Mogadishu	1	Hargeisa	2

Chambers of Commerce

Somalia Chamber of Commerce, Industry and Agriculture, PO Box 27, Via Asha, Mogadishu (tel: 281-866).

Somaliland Chamber of Commerce, Hargeisa (tel: 523-143; email: hargcham@yahoo.com; internet: www.somalilandchamberofcommerce.com).

Banking

Commercial and Savings Bank of Somalia, PO Box 203, Juley Street 1st, Mogadishu (tel: 22-861, 22-959).

Central bank

Central Bank of Somalia, PO Box 11, Corso Somalia 55, Mogadishu, Somalia (tel: 215-241).

Travel information

Daallo Airlines, # 30 Street, Baraka Market, Mogadishu (tel: 215-301; fax: 216-248; email: daallo@globalsom.com; internet: www.daallo.com).

Damalair, PO Box 27449, Dubai UAE (tel :+ (+971-4) 271-5005; fax: (+971-4) 272-0890; email: airdamal@emirates.net.ae; internet: www.damalair.co.ae).

Somali Airlines (operations suspended), PO Box 726, Via Medina, Mogadishu.

Other useful addresses

Agricultural Development Corporation, PO Box 930, Mogadishu.

Livestock Development Agency of Somalia, PO Box 1759, Mogadishu.

National Petroleum Agency of Somalia, PO Box 573, Mogadishu.

Somali Broadcasting Service, Ministry of Information and National Guidance, Private Bag, Mogadishu (tel: 2455).

Statistical Department, PO Box 1742, Mogadishu (tel: 80-385).

Internet sites

Africa Business Network: www.ifc.org/abn

African Development Bank: www.afdb.org

Africa Online: www.africaonline.com

AllAfrica.com: http://allafrica.com

Puntland State of Somalia: http://members.tripod.com/~Puntland/

Somalia News: www.somalianews.com

Somaliland official website: www.somalilandgov.com

United Nations Somalia: www.unsomalia.org

Wakiil Business Centre: www.wakiil.com

South Africa

KEY FACTS

Official name: Republic of South Africa

Head of State: President Jacob Gedleyihlekisa Zuma (ANZ) (from 9 May 2009)

Head of government: President Jacob Zuma (ANZ) (from 7 May 2009)

Ruling party: African National Congress (ANC) (since 1994; re-elected 22 Apr 2009)

Area: 1,127,200 square km

Population: 49.99 million (2010)*

Capital: Cape Town (legislative); Johannesburg (financial); Pretoria (to be renamed Tshwane) (administrative); Bloemfontein (judicial)

Official language: Afrikaans, English, Ndebele, Sesotho, Northern Sotho, SiSwati, Tsonga, Tswana, Venda, Xhosa, Zulu.

Currency: Rand (R) = 100 cents

Exchange rate: R8.04 per US$ (Oct 2011)

GDP per capita: US$7,158 (2010)

GDP real growth: 2.80% (2010)

GDP: US$257.30 billion (2010)

Labour force: 17.39 million (2010)

Unemployment: 24.90% (2010)

Inflation: 4.30% (2010)

Balance of trade: US$3.84 billion (2010)

Annual FDI: US$1.57 billion (2010)

* estimated figure

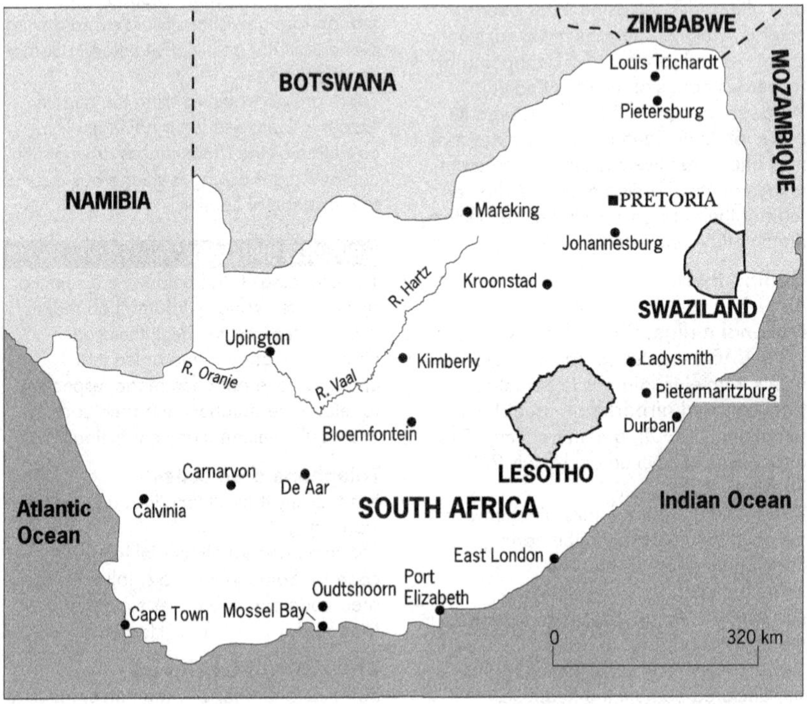

After the excitement of the Vuvuzela and the FIFA World Cup in 2010, 2011 was enlivened more by politics that sport. And in April South Africa became the 'S' in Brics – the group of so-called 'emerging' economies of Brazil, Russia, India, China and now South Africa. Domestically, Julius Malema hit the headlines when he was accused of bringing the reputation of the ANC into disrepute by proposing the overthrow of the sovereign government of Botswana. As a result he was suspended from the African National Congress (ANC) until 2016. Despite this he is seen as a rival and possible successor to President Jacob Zuma.

The economy

The diplomatic weight of South Africa is more than proportional to its economic and demographic size. The *African Economic Outlook 2011* (AEO), published jointly by the African Development Bank and the Organisation for Economic Co-operation and Development, reports that real GDP grew year-on-year by 2.8 per cent in 2010, recovering from the low base of a 1.7 per cent contraction in 2009. GDP growth was primarily driven by steady recovery in consumer spending. It is expected to increase to 3.6 per cent by 2011, still held back by sluggish domestic investment and tighter fiscal spending. In 2012, real GDP growth is expected to increase to 4.3 per cent. The main risk to the outlook for 2011 and 2012 is the outlook for the global economy.

The mining sector's real value-added recovered in 2010, registering a 4.2 per cent increase. However, output recovery was uneven across sectors owing to diminishing gold reserves, infrastructure constraints and an uneven recovery in global demand. Strikes by the National Union of Metalworkers (NUM) and mine workers in September 2010 affected production in coal and platinum mines. Overall, high commodity prices drove growth in mining revenues in 2010, in spite of revenues being negatively affected by an appreciation of the rand. The mining and quarrying sector expanded by 17 per cent during the fourth quarter of 2010 contributing significantly to the improvement in GDP growth.

Real value added grew by 5.1 per cent in the manufacturing sector in 2010, recovering from a 10.4 per cent contraction in 2009. This was due to recovering industry confidence and strong demand for iron and steel, non-ferrous metals, machinery, and electrical equipment – much of it driven by the FIFA World Cup. However, the recovery was not as strong as expected due in part to liquidations and to the prolonged industrial action in the automotive industry. Export-oriented manufacturing was negatively affected by the rand's appreciation against major currencies. The 2011 outlook for growth in manufacturing output remains modest because of structural constraints.

The agricultural sector rebounded and increased by 0.9 per cent in real value added in 2010 primarily as a result of a bumper harvest in maize. The maize harvest, the biggest in nearly three decades, was due to unexpectedly good rains, an increase in maize plantings, and greater use of genetically modified seed. This reduced food price inflation to 1.2 per cent in 2010. Consumer price inflation also slowed to reach a 3-year low of 4.3 per cent.

On the expenditure side, real private consumption was up by an estimated 4 per cent in 2010, after a 2.0 per cent contraction in 2009. Again, growth was attributed to FIFA World Cup related consumption, increased household real disposable incomes, and lower interest rates that encouraged household borrowing. Real disposable income, for example, increased by an estimated 4.6 per cent. Private consumption thus became a driver of recovery in the South African economy in 2010. Continued, though modest, recovery is expected in 2011 with a projected 3.4 per cent growth in private consumption. However, it is not expected to match the one-off surge produced by the World Cup.

Households deleveraged less than expected during the crisis, and indebtedness remained high at 78.5 per cent of disposable income in 2010. Household borrowing gained momentum driven in part by mortgage borrowing which had recovered by October 2010 to a year-on-year growth rate of 4.7 per cent as interest rates and the lending criteria of banks eased.

Private investment did not recover to the expected levels, growing only at 0.5 per cent in 2010. Robust growth in private investment is not expected before 2012, with its growth rate projected to pick up to 7.5 per cent and 10.5 per cent in 2011 and 2012. In some sub-sectors, the observed trend is explained in part by a return to trend growth. The contraction in the construction industry, for example, came after years of double digit growth prior to the economic recession. It was mostly fuelled by excess demand on the local market, but also got a boost from World Cup related construction such as football stadia. The moderation in housing prices in 2010, despite improvements in mortgage borrowing, was a sign of increased supply.

Other key determinants of private investments in 2010 were firm liquidations, which remained high. Total loan advances to companies started off at a year-on-year growth rate of -5.7 per cent in January 2010 and only recovered to positive growth of 1.4 per cent in September 2010. Industrial imports did not recover until the third quarter of 2010. Private investment is expected to pick up – from 0.5 per cent in 2010 to 7.5 per cent in 2011 and 10.5 per cent in 2012 – as capital flows to emerging markets begin to accelerate and as the recovery begins to take hold in Organisation for Economic Co-operation and Development (OECD) countries.

Infrastructure bottlenecks and labour market constraints are likely to prevent a return to the pre-crisis growth rates in 2011 and 2012. However, growth in the medium term (post-2012) is expected to be stronger as the massive infrastructure development projects being undertaken by state-owned enterprises, such as ESKOM and Transnet, start to bear fruit. South Africa's close economic ties to the global economy also imply that growth will be affected by the evolution of the European Union (EU), US and Chinese economies, and the trend of capital flows to emerging markets.

Government spending supported the economy throughout the recession as it responded by expanding public spending on social assistance. According to the Treasury, the structural fiscal deficit widened from 2.25 per cent to 4.1 per cent of GDP between fiscal year 2008/09 and fiscal year 2010/11 partially due to increased coverage of social transfer programmes.

The average Consumer Price Index (CPI) inflation for 2010 was 4.3 per cent, down from 7.1 per cent in 2009, due to a decline in the price of imported manufactured goods (a result of the strong local currency) and very low inflation in food and petrol prices. The inflation projections depend on what happens with administered prices, i e prices set by the government, and also with wages, commodity prices, oil and food items in particular, and with the exchange rate. Inflation is expected to increase to 5.3 per cent in 2011 on the back of rising commodity prices. A weakening rand is expected to contribute to rising prices. CPI inflation is expected to reach 5.6 per cent in 2012.

KEY INDICATORS — South Africa

	Unit	2006	2007	2008	2009	2010
Population	m	47.48	47.85	48.68	*49.32	*49.99
Gross domestic product (GDP)	US$bn	257.28	282.63	276.80	287.20	357.30
GDP per capita	US$	5,418	5,906	5,685	5,824	7,158
GDP real growth	%	5.4	5.6	3.6	-1.8	2.8
Inflation	%	4.7	7.1	11.5	7.1	4.3
Unemployment	%	25.6	24.3	22.9	23.9	24.9
Industrial output	% change	4.3	4.8	1.0	-7.2	–
Agricultural output	% change	-13.1	2.9	18.8	-3.2	–
Coal output	mtoe	144.8	139.6	141.1	140.9	143.0
Exports (fob) (goods)	US$m	75,171.0	76,184.0	86,118.0	66,542.0	85,700.0
Imports (fob) (goods)	US$m	71,243.0	81,890.0	90,566.0	66,009.0	81,862.0
Balance of trade	US$m	3,928.0	-5,705.0	-4,448.0	534.0	3,838.0
Current account	US$m	-16,602.0	-20,556.0	-19,593.0	-11,295.0	-10,117.0
Total reserves minus gold	US$m	23,057.0	29,589.0	30,584.0	35,237.0	38,175.0
Foreign exchange	US$m	22,720.0	29,234.0	30,238.0	32,432.0	35,419.0
Exchange rate	per US$	6.77	7.04	8.26	8.47	7.32

* estimated figure

International trade and relations

In 2010, the current account deficit shrank to 2.8 per cent of GDP from 4.1 per cent in 2009. The deficit is forecast at 3.4 per cent of GDP in 2011 and 4.3 per cent in 2012. The trade deficit decreased as imports contracted by more than exports in value terms, despite the continued appreciation of the rand. Some observers have concluded that the export recovery was sustained because of an improvement in manufacturing production while the sluggish recovery of consumer spending kept a lid on import demand. In fact, the rebound in import volumes has been considerably greater than that of export volumes but the price of exports has increased more relative to the price of imports.

Export growth was particularly significant in the intermediate goods and raw materials classifications, driven by activity in emerging economies and by the strong recovery in commodity prices. Exports of mining products increased in 2010 while the agriculture, forestry and fishing sector recorded a contraction in exports, with cereal exports particularly hard hit. The recovery led total imports of goods and services to increase, mainly driven by consumer goods and by intermediate goods. Although imports of capital goods recovered, imports of raw materials came under pressure as a reflection of relatively weak levels of domestic production and investment.

In terms of the regional distribution of trade, export demand from emerging economies, particularly in Asia, gained further ground. Asia again claimed the largest share of exports in the first quarter of 2010, with China the leading destination. The leading product categories to Asia included iron ores, platinum, coal and ferro-alloys. South Africa's trade balance with the rest of the African continent continued in surplus. The value of exports to the rest of Africa declined in 2010, although as a percentage of imports, South Africa's share of imports in the rest of Africa increased. Imports from the rest of Southern African Development Community (SADC) have been recovering gradually. Subsequent to the implementation of the SADC Free Trade Agreement (FTA) in 2008, delays in laying the groundwork for a customs union have prevented such the union from coming into effect by 2010, as had been planned.

China became the topmost destination for South Africa's exports in mid-2009 and is also South Africa's leading source of imports. India currently ranks eighth as a source of imports. As a destination for exports, India ranked sixth in 2010. China, and to a lesser extent India, have become dominant trading partners not only compared to other emerging partners but also compared to traditional partners as well. China's 14 per cent share of imports in the first three quarters of 2010 overshadowed Germany's 11.6 per cent and the US's 7 per cent. Similarly, China's 9.3 per cent share of South Africa's exports surpassed the 8.8 per cent and 8.1 per cent claimed by the US and Japan, respectively.

South Africa exports a narrow range of mineral and resource-intensive products to China: metals, minerals and other commodities. By contrast, South Africa imports a widening range of higher value-added products from China, including clothing, data processing machines, printing machinery, bulldozers and motor vehicles. Indian exports to South Africa are dominated by petroleum products (other than crude), electrical and electronic equipment, as well as pharmaceutical products. Its imports from South Africa consist largely of inorganic chemicals, coal and coal products.

China is the dominant investment partner amongst emerging partners having reached fifth in terms of the value of its stock of foreign direct investment (FDI) in early 2010, with R33 billion (US$4.1 billion). The figure is considered to understate reality. This status was reached notably fast since China's stock of FDI back at the beginning of 2008 was only R480 million (US$59.7 million). The subsequent acquisition of a 20 per cent stake in Standard Bank by the Industrial Commercial Bank of China (ICBC) was central to this rise. Yet, South Africa ranks second (behind the Democratic Republic of Congo) in China's mining investment in Africa with five projects in total, mainly focused on chrome. Other investments have been in metals followed by chemicals, food and tobacco, consumer electronics, automotives and communications. In late 2010, a US$877 million Chinese investment from Jinchuan and the China-Africa Development Fund into the Johannesburg Stock Exchange (JSE)-listed junior platinum firm Wesizwe Platinum was announced.

South Africa has put a lot of political effort into engaging diplomatically both industrial and fellow southern countries since the country's democratic transformation. The South African Development Agency (SADPA) was launched in 2011 to inform and direct the country's development assistance. Almost all development assistance has been directed at the African continent so far, with a strong focus on member countries of the Southern African Development Community (SADC). This focus is not expected to change. The government argues that the SADPA will boost the country's status as an emerging economic power and champion of the African continent, and improve accountability about the way funds are being disbursed.

Doing business

South Africa is second behind Mauritius in the World Bank's *Doing Business* rankings. Progress has been made in crime prevention: national crime statistics for 2009/10 show that street robberies declined by 10.4 per cent, bank robberies by 8.8 per cent, and truck and car hijackings by 6.8 per cent. Violent crime also declined, with murder down by 8.6 per cent. Reliability of police services also marginally improved in 2010 relative to 2009, according to the global competiveness index (GCI). Improvements are also due to the tightening of security during the FIFA World Cup.

On the other hand, according to Transparency International, the Corruption Perceptions Index (CPI) has deteriorated further, from 4.7 in 2009 to 4.5 in 2010. The Broad-based Black Economic Empowerment Programme is also perceived as being vulnerable to political influence, as is the issuing of mining rights. The Directorate for Priority Crime Investigation (also known as the Hawks) established in mid-2009 to fight corruption, organised crime, and economic crime had made several thousand arrests against organised crime and commercial crime by mid-2010, with conviction rates of 15 per cent and 60 per cent respectively. Despite a large number of incidents of corruption being investigated, fewer convictions were made.

Public trust in politicians, judicial independence, and decisions of government officials also deteriorated in 2010, according to the GCI. While the political environment remains stable, slow delivery on key social goals – youth unemployment and inequality in particular – remains a major risk.

Employment

Just over a million jobs were lost between late-2008 and mid-2010. Losses were concentrated in the manufacturing, trade and construction sectors. Of the unemployed, youth were hardest hit as there were not enough jobs to absorb the number of new entrants to the labour market.

In the first three months of 2010, 40 per cent of youth aged 16 to 30 were unemployed, compared with 16 per cent for those aged 30 to 65. Although total employment increased by 56,000 over 2010 and unemployment had declined marginally to 24 per cent by the fourth quarter, the labour market remains very weak – the share of employed to the population decreased from 41.1 per cent in the first quarter to 40.8 per cent in the fourth quarter of 2010.

The New Growth Path, released in November 2010, sets a target of creating 5.5 million jobs over the next decade. If government succeeds in achieving this goal, the unemployment rate would drop by 10 percentage points from 25.3 per cent to around 15 per cent. The government plans to reform rural development policy and to promote educational and skills development. For example, the government will re-prioritise the co-ops that enable small producers to enter formal value chains. To enhance education and skills development, the government plans to provide targeted programmes to increase the number of individuals with skills that are vital and/or scarce by 2014. It calls for 30,000 engineers and 50,000 artisans with skills in construction, mining, manufacturing and new industries such as in the green economy.

Risk assessment

Economy	Fair
Politics	Fair
Regional stability	Good

COUNTRY PROFILE

Historical profile

1652 The Dutch East India Company set up a supply station which became Cape Town, supplying sailing ships to and from the Dutch East Indies (Indonesia).
1795 Britain took control of the Cape.
1806 The Cape Colony became British and settlement began in 1820.
1835 Mass treks by Afrikaners (Boers) moved inland, fighting the Ndebele and Zulus.
1899–1902 After many battles, the Boer War was eventually won by the British. With the signing of the Treaty of Vereeniging on 31 May 1902, all Boers became British subjects.
1910 The Union of South Africa was established from the former British colonies of Cape and Natal and the Boer republics of Transvaal and Orange Free State. South Africa became a self-governing dominion led by former Boer generals.
1912 The Native National Congress, the precursor to the African National Congress (ANC), was founded.
1913 The Land Act was introduced to prevent blacks, except those in Cape Province, from buying land outside reserves.
1914 The National Party was founded.
1919 South West Africa (Namibia), formerly a German colony, came under South African administration.
1948 Apartheid (separateness) laws, excluding non-whites from political and economic influence, were applied by successive National Party governments.
1950 The population was classified by race. The Group Areas Act was passed to segregate blacks and whites. The South African Communist Party (SACP) was banned. The ANC responded with a campaign of civil disobedience led by Nelson Mandela.
1960 Apartheid laws were brutally enforced; the most notorious incident was the Sharpeville massacre. The ANC became the main black political organisation opposing the government and consequently was banned.
1961 South Africa was declared a republic and left the Commonwealth. Mandela launched the ANC's military wing which began a campaign of disruption and sabotage.
1964 Nelson Mandela, leader of the ANC, was jailed for life. The UN imposed sanctions against South Africa.
1976 More than 600 people were killed in the Soweto uprising.
1983 An interim constitution established power-sharing of three population groups (whites, Asians and mixed race (coloured)), effectively excluding participation of blacks.
1989 P W Botha (prime minister from 1978–83 and president from 1983–89) was replaced by F W de Klerk; he began a reform programme that started the dismantling of apartheid.
1990 Nelson Mandela was released from prison on 11 February. The ban on the ANC was lifted. Namibia was granted independence.
1991 The last apartheid laws were repealed. Fighting broke out between the ANC and the Zulu Inkatha movement.
1993 A non-racial constitution was formulated through a multi-racial negotiating forum. A transitional Government of National Unity (GNU) was established replacing the three-chamber, racially-based, parliament. Oliver Tambo, long-time anti-apartheid campaigner and former leader of the ANC died.
1994 In the first non-racial, fully democratic elections, the ANC won a majority of seats in parliament and Nelson Mandela became president. South Africa successfully reapplied for Commonwealth membership and took up its seat in the UN General Assembly for the first time in 20 years. South Africa's new flag was unveiled in April.
1996 The new constitution was adopted. A Truth and Reconciliation Commission (TRC) was set up. Those that perpetrated and suffered human rights abuse were allowed to record their experiences for mutual recognition.
1997 Nelson Mandela resigned as president of the ANC.
1998 The TRC branded apartheid a crime against humanity and held the ANC accountable for numerous human rights abuses. South Africa intervened militarily in Lesotho to prevent civil war breaking out in the kingdom.
1999 Nelson Mandela resigned as president and Thabo Mbeki was elected as his successor by the National Assembly. The ANC increased its share of the election vote and formed a coalition government with the mainly Zulu Inkatha Freedom Party (IFP).
2000 The Democratic Party, the New National Party (NNP) and the Federal Alliance merged to form the Democratic Alliance (DA), which won a quarter of the vote in local elections.
2001 South Africa began importing generic HIV/Aids drugs after 39 multi-national pharmaceutical companies stopped legal action. The High Court ruled that pregnant women must be given anti-retroviral drugs to prevent HIV transmission to their infants.
2002 The name of Northern Province was changed to Limpopo Province. The Organisation of African Unity (OAU) became the African Union (AU) with President Mbeki as the first chairman. 2003 Walter Sisulu, a key veteran figure in the anti-apartheid struggle, died.
2004 The ruling ANC won a landslide victory and Thabo Mbeki was elected unopposed for a second term as president. Black economic empowerment (BEE) legislation was enacted; its objectives are to address economic inequalities such as the imbalance in ethnic ownership and lack of black opportunity and aspirations, caused by decades of apartheid. The legislation is binding on all public companies and government entities.
2005 Mbeki dismissed his deputy, Jacob Zuma, who was charged with corruption. Phumzile Mlambo-Ngcuka was named as his successor.
2006 Zuma was acquitted of rape charges and reinstated as ANC deputy president. The corruption charges against him were dismissed. Johannesburg International Airport's name was changed to OR Tambo International Airport.
2007 Jacob Zuma was elected leader of the ANC.
2008 The High Court ruled that Chinese South Africans would be re-classified as

'black' people so that they could benefit from government policies to help those previously disadvantaged under the old apartheid system. The controversial land reform bill was postponed. Following the statement by the judge in the failed trial of Jacob Zuma for corruption in 2005 that the prosecution had been politically motivated parliament forced President Mbeki to resign. Several senior cabinet members also resigned. Parliament voted for Kgalema Motlanthe (ANC) as president; Motlanthe served the remainder of Mbeki's presidential term. South Africa declared a state of emergency along its border with Zimbabwe due to the number of fleeing Zimbabweans who were suffering from cholera and needing treatment.
2009 The High Court ruled in February that South African citizens living abroad should be allowed to vote in general elections, allowing around two million expatriates to participate in the country's political life. In parliamentary elections, the ANC won 65.9 per cent of the vote, a fall of 33 seats and less than the two-thirds majority needed to change the constitution without parliamentary support. The DA won 16.7 per cent and gained control of the Western Cape Province. The newly created Congress of the People (Cope), led by former president Mbeki won 7.4 per cent. ANC leader, Jacob Zuma, was elected as president.
2010 The unemployment rate was recorded at over 24 per cent in February. Eugene Terre Blanche, the ultra-right-wing supremacist, was killed in April, by two of his employees, aged 15 and 21 years old. In July, in a landmark trial, South Africa's former chief of police, Jackie Selebi, was found guilty of corruption and sentenced to 15 years in jail. Nobel peace laureate Archbishop Desmond Tutu announced that he was to retire from public life. In a move that President Zuma said would 'correct the wrongs of the past' the government announced in July that it planned to abolish six of the 13 traditional rulers' offices, as the incumbents died. A number of traditional leaders had been created during the apartheid era, at the expense of the original monarchs; this was seen as a move to divide the people. They had little real power, but were semi-important cultural figures. The Zulu and Xhosa kings will remain. The Independent Democrats (ID) party announced it would merge with the DA in August, in preparation of fighting the next general elections (due in 2014). The national census was undertaken on the night of 9–10 October; final results will be published in March 2013. President Zuma reshuffled his cabinet in November, firing eight ministers. This was the first change for 17 months.
2011 The special dispensation that allowed Zimbabweans to cross into South Africa during the political disturbances in 2009 to stay in South Africa was due to end in mid-2011. On 9 February, President Zuma attended the summit of the Bric (Brazil, Russia, India, China) group of emerging economies by invitation, to strengthen the African ties to the economic organisation. South Africa became a member of the re-named Brics in April. President Zuma announced the setting up a commission to investigate a 1990s multi-billion US$ arms deal. There had long been allegations against members of the ANC, including against himself in 2009, before he became President. On 10 November, Julius Malema (seen by many as a future leader of the ANC), accused of bringing the reputation of the ANC into disrepute when he proposed the overthrow of the sovereign government of Botswana, was suspended from the ANC until 2016.

Political structure

Constitution

The constitution was implemented in February 1997.
South Africa consists of a central government and nine provincial governments. The head of a province is called a premier.
The right to regional autonomy is enshrined in the constitution, subject to the principles of the national constitution.
Electoral system: list-system proportional representation based on universal adult suffrage, aged over 18.
The High Court ruled in February 2009 that South African citizens living abroad should be allowed to vote in general elections. The decision was referred to the Constitutional Court for confirmation, which if passed would allow around two million expatriates to participate in the country's political life.

Independence date

31 May 1961

Form of state

Federal republic

The executive

Executive powers are vested in the president, who is both Head of State and head of government, and is elected by the National Assembly for no more than two, five-year terms.
The president, must appoint all but two cabinet members from National Assembly members.

National legislature

The bicameral legislature consists of the National Assembly with 400 members, elected by proportional representation with seats apportioned according to the share of the vote.
The National Council of Provinces (NCOP) reviews and aligns national legislation that affects the provinces. Each of the nine provinces has a delegation of 10 members (six permanent and four special) headed by the premier of the province. Permanent delegates are members of parliament (MPs); special delegates are provincial legates, who may be recalled by their provinces at any time. Ten representatives of organised local governments also serve but may not vote.
Both institutions serve for five-year terms.

Legal system

Based on Roman-Dutch law and the constitution.
An anti-prejudice law was passed in 2000.

Last elections

6 May 2009 (presidential); 22 April 2009 (parliamentary)
Results: Presidential: Jacob Zuma (ANC) was elected by the National Assembly unopposed.
Parliamentary: ANC won 69.69 per cent (264 seats, out of up to 400), Democratic Alliance (DA) 16.7 per cent (67), Congress of the People (Cope) 7.42 per cent (30), Inkatha Freedom Party (IFP) 4.55 per cent (18); nine other political parties each won less than 1 per cent of the vote and the remaining seats. Turnout was 77.3 per cent.

Next elections

2014 (presidential and parliamentary)

Political parties

Ruling party

African National Congress (ANC) (since 1994; re-elected 22 Apr 2009)

Main opposition party

Democratic Alliance (DA). In August 2010 the DA announced it would unite with the Independent Democrats (ID). ID municipal officials will join the DA after the 2011 local elections; provincial and national legislators will join after the 2014 general election.

Population

49.99 million (2010)*
Last census: October 2001: 44,819,778 (provisional)
Population density: 35 inhabitants per square km (2000). Urban population: 58 per cent of the total population (1995–2001).
Annual growth rate: 1.4 per cent 1994–2004 (WHO 2006)

Ethnic make-up

Black (75 per cent), white (13 per cent), coloured (9 per cent), Asian (3 per cent).

Religions

Christian (68 per cent), Islam (2 per cent), Hindu 1.5 per cent, indigenous beliefs and animist 28.5 per cent.

Education

Public expenditure on education amounts to 5.5 per cent of GDP.

Primary education begins at age six and lasts for six years. Junior secondary school lasts until age 15 when students may choose between an academic programme lasting a further three years at a senior secondary school or a vocational, technical course lasting two years in technical schools.

Government strategy for national schooling includes higher qualified teachers appointed to poorer schools and equalising school expenditure for all racial groups.

Literacy rate: 86 per cent adult rate; 92 per cent youth rate (15–24) (Unesco 2005).

Compulsory years: Six to 15

Enrolment rate: 133 per cent gross primary enrolment of relevant age group (including repeaters); 95 per cent gross secondary enrolment (World Bank).

Pupils per teacher: 45 in primary schools.

Health

There are major national programmes in operation including the Integrated Nutrition Programme, the Polio and Measles Immunisation Campaign and Telemedicine (an interactive medical exchange based on information technology).

A R40 million (US$4.6 million) protocol signed between South Africa, Swaziland and Mozambique to control the spread of malaria lays the basis for a common programme of action in these countries.

HIV/Aids

South Africa has one of the highest HIV/Aids infection rates in the world, an estimated 5.6 million people are HIV positive, which has the largest number of individuals living with the virus in a single country. A study of HIV/Aids infection rates, published in 2009, revealed that the rate had levelled off at 10.9 per cent for those aged two-years and older. Typically, those worst effected are women between the ages of 20–34 at 33 per cent HIV-positive. This trend suggests there will be noticeably fewer mid-adult women than men by 2020. By 2009 deaths by Aids-related illness were expected to exceed all other causes of death. The use of condoms has increased sharply. Government policy was changed from April 2010, following an announcement by President Zuma in 2009 in which he said that all babies less than one year old, if tested HIV positive, would be treated with anti-retroviral (ARV) drugs. Around 59,000 infants are born with HIV each year in South Africa. The level of infection in 2009 did not increase although the level of deaths from Aids is expect to rise up to 2014 as long-term patients succumb to the disease.

With a change in government policy since 2008, the number of people receiving ARV medication has doubled to 1.5 million by 2011; another one million will receive ARVs by 2014. In 2011, 10.6 per cent of the population were living with HIV (5.38 million) and there were 2.1 million Aids orphans. Around one-third of all children, an estimated 5.7 million, may lose one or both parents to Aids by 2015. The treatment to prevent mother-to-child transmission had expanded so that in 2011, 95 per cent of infected pregnant women received ARVs, up from 30 per cent in 2007. Free circumcision, which reduces the risk of transmission by up to 60 per cent, according to state health facilities, coupled with a decrease since 2009 in the number of new infections, may indicate that young people are changing their sexual behaviour.

Former president Nelson Mandela publicly announced that his son had died of Aids, in 2005, saying, 'Let us give publicity to HIV/Aids and not hide it, because the only way of making it appear to be a normal illness, just like TB, like cancer, is always to come out and say somebody has died because of HIV.' In 2004, Inkatha opposition leader, Mangosuthu Buthelezi, had announced that his son had also died of Aids.

South Africa is still in the process of addressing the deprivation wrought on black communities during the apartheid era including, poverty, poor primary healthcare, minimal education and families fractured by migratory work. The South African pharmaceutical company, Aspen, was granted approval by US regulators to manufacture and supply ARV drugs for domestic patients.

HIV prevalence: 21.5 per cent, aged 15–49 years

5.3 million adults and children living with HIV

27.9 per cent pregnant women (attending antenatal services) HIV positive

2.9 million women living with HIV

370,000 Aids deaths (adults and children) in 2003

(UNAids estimates, end 2003)

Life expectancy: 48 years, 2004 (WHO 2006)

Fertility rate/Maternal mortality rate: 2.8 births per woman, 2004 (WHO 2006)

Birth rate/Death rate: 18.9 births per 1,000 population; 18.4 deaths per 1,000 population (2003).

Population data issued by South Africa's Medical Research Council in March 2004 recorded a 44 per cent increase in adult deaths between 1998–2003, after population growth and improved registration had been factored in; deaths of women 20–49 increased by 168 per cent. It was concluded that this growth was due to Aids.

Child (under 5 years) mortality rate (per 1,000): 53 per 1,000 live births (World Bank)

Head of population per physician: 0.77 physicians per 1,000 people, 2004 (WHO 2006)

Welfare

The social assistance programme of the Department of Social Development provides benefits to approximately three million people comprising the elderly, persons with disabilities and children under the age of seven years. The government has emphasised the need to transform expensive institutional services into a more self-reliant approach towards individual and community care. Access to welfare grants is, however, limited. The State Maintenance Grants have been phased out and the availability of services for victims of violence across the country remains equally limited. Lack of an integrated approach towards allocations, capacity to spend and monitor the funds are some of the key problems relating to the distribution of poverty relief funds.

Main cities

Pretoria (Tswane Municipal Municipality is the central area) (capital, estimated population, 1.0 million (m) in 2005), Cape Town (Kaapstad (in Afrikaans) and iKapa (in Xhosa)) (legislative capital, 2.4m), Durban (eThekwini) (2.1m), Johannesburg (financial capital 1.5m), Soweto (1.0m), Port Elizabeth (848,400), East London (208,851), Benoni (359,491), Vereeniging (341,109), Bloemfontein (judicial capital, 328,311).

Languages spoken

Official language/s

Afrikaans, English, Ndebele, Sesotho, Northern Sotho, SiSwati, Tsonga, Tswana, Venda, Xhosa, Zulu.

Media

Two moves in late 2010, a Media Appeals Tribunal being considered by the ANC and a protection of information bill going through parliament, have alarmed the local media. A statement by 37 editors in August 2010 say that the moves will restrict freedom of speech and expression as set out in the constitution. The tribunal will have the power to judge complaints made against print media while the bill would give ministers and officials powers to classify information as secret if they consider it to be 'in the national interest'.

Press

Press freedom is guaranteed by the constitution. The Freedom of Commercial Speech Trust plays an important role in industry self-regulation, forestalling government intervention.

Dailies: Newspapers published in major cities may be available throughout the country as reflect national and local news. News 24 (www.news24.com) is a media organisation that has a number of Afrikaans titles: *Die Burger*, *Volksblad*, *Rapport*, *Jou Geldsaka*, *Sondag*, and *NetAfrikaans* among others.

From Cape Town, in English, *Cape Argus* (www.capeargus.co.za), the *Cape Times* (www.capetimes.co.za), and in Afrikaans *Die Burger* (www.dieburger.com).

From Johannesburg, in English, *The Times* (www.thetimes.co.za), which includes a business section and *Sunday Times*, *Citizen* (www.citizen.co.za), *The Star* (www.thestar.co.za) and *Sowetan* (www.sowetan.co.za). In Chinese *China Express* (www.sa-cnet.com) and *China News* (www.chinanews.co.za).

From Pretoria, in English, *Pretoria News* (www.pretorianews.co.za), *Society News* (www.societynews.co.za) and in Afrikaans *Rekord* (www.rekord.co.za).

From Durban, in English, *Daily News* (www.dailynews.co.za) and *Post* (www.thepost.co.za) (with Indian sections), in Zulu *Isolezwe* (www.isolezwe.co.za) and *Ilanga* (www.ilanganews.co.za).

Weeklies: In English, *Daily Mail & Guardian* (www.mg.co.za), is the leading independent newspaper, *The Sunday Tribune* (ww.sundaytribune.co.za), *Sunday Independent* (www.sunday.co.za), *Sunday World* (www.sundayworld.co.za) and *Weekend Post* (www.weekendpost.co.za). In Afrikaans *Landbou Weekblad* (www.landbou.com).

Business: Publications, in English, include *Business Day* (www.businessday.co.za) *Financial Mail* (http://free.financialmail.co.za), *Cape Business News* (www.cbn.co.za), *Business Report* (www.busrep.co.za), *Guateng Business* www.news24.com/Gauteng_Business/Home) and in Afrikaans *Sake* (www.news24.com/Sake/Home). *Personal Finance* (www.persfin.co.za) covers financial and investment issues. *Destiny* (www.mydestinymag.com) is a business magazine aimed at women

Broadcasting

The South African Broadcasting Corporation (SABC) is the state-owned national broadcaster.

Radio: There are numerous commercial radio stations particularly located around cities and large towns. Services are broadcast in various languages particular to local language spoken in the locale. SABC operates 20 regional and national services in 11 languages and an external radio service broadcasting in short wave to the African continent.

Other major commercial stations include SA FM (www.safm.co.za), East Coast Radio (www.ecr.co.za), Jacaranda FM (www.jacarandafm.com), Cape Talk (www.capetalk.co.za) and Radio Algoa (www.radioalgoa.com).

Television: SABC operates three national channels and two pay-to-view channels. Commercial stations with free-to-air television includes e.tv (www.etv.co.za) and pay-to-view M-Net (www.mnet.co.za) showing many internationally made programmes.

During an election period the media is monitored by the Independent Media Commission.

News agencies

SAPA (South African Press Association)

National news agency: PO Box 7766, Cotswold House, Greenacres Office Park, Cnr Victory & Rustenburg Roads, Victory Park, Johannesburg, 2000 (tel: 782-1600; fax: 782-1587/8; email: comms@sapa.org.za; internet: www.sapa.org.za).

Economy

The South African economy is modern, diverse and open, with well-developed sectors in mining, agriculture, manufacturing and services. However, there is an imbalance in society where the top 20 per cent hold 62.7 per cent of the country's wealth, and an underclass of poor, often unemployed people who live in townships, where the bottom 20 per cent hold 3.1 per cent of the country's wealth. In 2011, the UN Human Development Index (HDI) ranked South Africa 123 (out of 187) for national development in health, education and income. In 2010, 42.3 per cent of the population experienced at least one indicator of poverty, while 17.4 per cent lived on the equivalent of US$1.25 per day. The uneven distribution of wealth in South Africa is a result of its historically segregated society and although there has been a concerted effort to produce a more equitable structure the economy is still split largely between the affluent white minority and the poorer black majority. Whites still own large tracts of fertile land and direct most of the industry and service sectors, which the ANC-led government has tried to address through the Black Economic Empowerment (BEE) law that requires not only black employment but also their fostering and promotion within companies and organisations. The lack of training during the apartheid period led to a lack of black managers and executives. Many major employers now have courses or back scholarships to redress the situation. Another aspect of BEE is black ownership of shares in companies, which has led to some criticism that only cronies of the ruling ANC are benefiting.

The economy is largely based on the country's abundant mineral and energy resources. Manufacturing is underpinned by the mining sector while gold and diamonds dominate exports. Foreign investors are attracted by the country's robust infrastructure, with developed transport, water and electricity networks. Dams have been built on the rivers and provide water for irrigation, industrial and household use. There are also developed professional services while the stock exchange is ranked world class.

GDP growth was 5.6 per cent in 2007, falling to 3.6 per cent in 2008 during the global economic crisis and in 2009 the economy entered recession with growth of -1.7 per cent, following a strong slowdown in the manufacturing and mining sectors. The economy picked up in 2010 with GDP growth of 2.8 per cent as global trade recovered.

Inflation had been rising since 2004 from a low 1.4 per cent to 7.1 per cent in 2007 and peaking at 11.5 per cent in 2008 due to high global oil prices and higher food prices. As demand slowed, the inflation rate fell back to 7.2 per cent in 2009 and further down to 4.3 per cent in 2010. Unemployment, at a time of rising participation was falling in 2007 at 22.3 per cent (down from 22.6 per cent in 2006), but as the global economic crisis caused a credit squeeze and failing businesses, the unemployment rose to reached 23.9 per cent in 2009, and 24.9 per cent in 2010, of which the unemployment rate was 25.3 per cent in the last half of the year. In the fourth quarter of 2010, 4,396,000 people were registered unemployed.

The service sector in 2009 accounted for 65.8 per cent of GDP, agriculture 3.0 per cent and industry 31.1 per cent, of which manufacturing was 15.1 per cent. While industry and manufacturing registered only 1–1.2 per cent growth in 2008 all sectors contracted in 2009. South Africa's tourism sector has expanded considerably since the end of the apartheid era but it still has a way to go before reaching its full potential.

The government with its many social problems to tackle has increased spending on public services including a commitment to provide antiretroviral (ARV) treatment to all that require it. In 2011, 10.6 per cent of the population were living with HIV (5.38 million) and there were 2.1 million Aids orphans. By 2011, 1.5 million HIV-positive people and 95 per cent of infected pregnant women were receiving ARVs.

External trade

South Africa is a member of the Southern African Development Community (SADC),

the objectives of which include reducing trade barriers, achieving regional development and economic growth and evolving common systems and institutions. Its currency, the rand, is also legal tender throughout the Common Monetary Area (CMA) (Swaziland, Lesotho and Namibia).
With its immense mineral wealth, South Africa is the world's leading exporter of gold and platinum. It is also one of the leading world producers of diamonds, wine, railroad rolling stock, mining equipment and synthetic fuels. Exports provide almost 50 per cent of GDP and world commodity prices strongly affect the balance of trade.
In 2009 international donors pledged US$1 billion to upgrade transport links across eastern and southern Africa, in an initiative to carry goods to market cheaper and faster. Not only will roads and rail links be improved, but also time-consuming official procedures will be streamlined for efficiency.

Imports

Principal imports are machinery and equipment, vehicles, petroleum and natural gas, chemicals, scientific instruments and foodstuffs.

Main sources: Germany (typically 11 per cent of total), China (11 per cent), US (8 per cent).

Exports

Principal exports are gold (around 20 per cent of total), diamonds, metals and metal products, minerals, machinery and equipment. Other major exports are granite, asbestos, iron, manganese, chrome and titanium ore.

Main destinations: Japan (typically 11 per cent of total), US (11 per cent), Germany (8 per cent).

Agriculture

Farming

South African agricultural is open to market forces and farmers take responsibility for production decisions, and pricing and distribution. The country has achieved self-sufficiency in staple grains, such as maize and wheat, and basic foodstuffs such as fresh milk and other dairy products, meat, vegetables and fruit. The sector employs over 10 per cent of the workforce.
LandCare is a key community support programme in the National Department of Agriculture which aims to promote sustainable land management practices and prevent land degradation in rural areas. The government policy of forging partnerships to stimulate black empowerment is growing within the agricultural sector. Nevertheless land reforms to enable black farmers access to quality land has been slow. The controversial land reform bill was postponed in 2008. Government says that it still wants to redistribute around a third of white owned farmland by 2014. South Africa has about 33 per cent of the southern hemisphere's deciduous fruit market in Europe. After minerals and metals, deciduous fruit is the country's largest export industry. The wine industry yields significant indirect benefits for the economy as a major employer and exporter. However, growth and competitiveness in the wine and tobacco industries is likely to be hampered by higher excise duty. Oilseed production for bio-diesel offers a unique opportunity to facilitate such partnerships.

Fishing

The general policy towards fisheries has been the protection of marine ecology and the promotion and sustained utilisation of the sea and its resources.
South Africa is largely self-sufficient in white fish and has a substantial export surplus and is self-sufficient in canned fish. Some 10 per cent of the abalone yield and 25 per cent of rock lobster is marketed locally and the rest is exported, mainly to the Far East. Cultivation of oysters and mussels is growing steadily and the possibility of cultivating abalone is being researched.
Of domestic fishmeal demand of 260,000 tonnes per year (tpy), 60,000tpy is locally produced and the rest is imported.
Fishing quotas for foreign vessels are issued in terms of formal bilateral fisheries agreements. Of all the quota fish caught in South Africa's exclusive fishing zone (200 nautical miles offshore), foreign catches make up only 2.4 per cent. The figure does not include non-quota species such as tuna. Foreign boats are allocated quotas for hake, hose mackerel and squid.
In a meeting of African ministers in Namibia, held on 2 July 2009, members discussed illegal and unregulated fishing, which is estimated to cost Africa US$1 billion per annum in lost revenue and the threat to stocks and local artisan fishing.
Following the annual meeting of the Commission for the Conservation of Southern Bluefin Tuna (CCSBT), held on Cheju Island, South Korea, all members agreed to a 20 per cut in the roughly 17,000 tonnes in 2009 bluefin tuna catches from 2010. Scientists had warned that without a cut fish stocks could crash as numbers had become dangerously low.

Forestry

About 7 per cent of the total land area is forested, with forest cover estimated at 8.9 million hectares (ha). About 27 per cent of the total land area is wooded. The country has extensive forest plantations and a large network of more than 200 protected areas covering nearly 5 per cent of the forest areas, including around 20 national parks. Deforestation accounts for around 1 per cent per annum or the equivalent of 8,000ha of forest cover. Government policy has focussed on making South Africa self-sufficient in wood and wood products, taking into account the country's limited water supply and scarcity of suitable habitats. Industrial roundwood is produced in large quantities. The forestry industry is dependent on resources available from plantations and produces a wide range of wood and paper products. Although it produces and exports pulp and paper, significant volumes of paper are also imported.

Industry and manufacturing

South Africa is one of Africa's most industrialised countries and enjoys a strong resource base. Most of the raw materials and semi-manufactured goods required by industry are available from local sources. Only clothing and textiles, furniture (hardwoods), chemicals and transport equipment (components) still rely to a lesser extent on imports of raw materials or intermediate goods. Output is dominated by engineering and metal products, especially steel, and it has become a world leader in manufacturing railway rolling stock, mining equipment and other machinery. Major steel companies include Iscor and Highveld Steel.
Other major growth areas are automobile production and the chemical industry. Although food and tobacco processing remain of great importance, their share of total output has fallen significantly. Food products, iron and steel and transport equipment together account for about a third of total gross manufacturing output. Other manufactures include paper and paper products, fabricated metal products, electrical and non-electrical machinery.

Tourism

The tourism sector typically contributes up to 5 per cent of GDP and is an important source of foreign exchange. Europe constitutes the greater part of the overseas market (typically 65 per cent), followed by Asia (15 per cent), North America (12 per cent), Australasia (5 per cent), the Middle East (2 per cent) and the Indian Ocean Islands (1 per cent).
South Africa's tourism sector has expanded considerably since the end of the apartheid era but it still has a very long way to go before reaching its full potential. The country, which receives 52 per cent of the 13.4 million visitors to southern Africa each year, is positioning itself as the hub of a region-wide 'tourism park' wherein visitors will be able to move from one southern African country to another

without going through formal borders. By pooling their resources and attractions together, southern African countries hope to emulate the islands of the Caribbean and increase tourist numbers. In the meantime, South Africa is steadily moving towards becoming the most popular conference destination in Africa.

Environment
In 2008 South Africa announced that for the first time in 13 years it would begin a cull of elephants in a measure to control their numbers and reduce the impact that large herds have on the natural environment, other wildlife and human crops and habitation.

Mining
South Africa is the world's foremost producer and exporter of gold and platinum, and a significant exporter of diamonds, iron ore, asbestos, manganese ore, vanadium, ferro-chromium, chrome ore and granite.
International commodities traded in US dollars have all been affected by the rise in the rand since 2003 and most mining companies have experienced a drop in profits due to the disparity of expenses incurred in other currencies
A leading aluminium manufacturer, Alcan, has plans to build a smelter at Coega, near Port Elizabeth. Originally production would have reached 600,000 tonnes annually, however, in September 2005 plans were halted while a feasibility study was undertaken to facilitate a 900,000 tonnes processing plant. A smelter is expected to be operational by 2008.
The government has begun plans to introduce a state diamond trader company and producers such as UK-based, diamond company De Beers (founded in South Africa and the world's leading diamond trading company) would be required to forward a percentage of rough diamonds intended for export to the new Diamond Exchange and Export Centre (DEEC) for cutting and polishing by local craftsmen.
At least 40 per cent of the world's total recoverable gold reserves are in South Africa. Precious metals' producers will also be required to refine more of their output locally to provide more metals for South African design and manufacturing.
The mining sector only accounts for 6 per cent of GDP and South Africa sees value added diamond and gold processing as a source of added revenue and employment. The mining sector employs 6 per cent of the country's labour force and contributes up to one-third of the export revenue.

Hydrocarbons
Proven oil reserves were 15 million barrels in 2007, while consumption was 555,000 barrels per day (bpd) which was almost entirely supplied by imports. Most comes from the Middle East, chiefly Iran and Saudi Arabia. To reduce a dependency on this region South Africa has agreements with Angola, Equatorial Guinea and Nigeria for oil supplies, which will either be consumed locally or refined for export to regional southern Africa, East Africa and the Indian sub-continent.
The Petroleum, Oil and Gas Corporation of South Africa (PetroSA) is responsible for managing the country's petroleum industry's commercial assets. South Africa has Africa's second largest refinery system (after Egypt), with a capacity of over 500,000bpd, producing high-octane petroleum, distillates, kerosene and alcohols. In April 2009 a contract was signed for 19 electric motor-driven pumps and pumping stations along a 525km pipeline to transport diesel, petrol and jet fuel from Durban to the inland Guateng region with construction to begin in 2010.
There has been much investment in synthetic fuels and South Africa is the world's largest producer of oil from coal. Around 36 per cent of South Africa's liquid fuels are synthetic produced by the Sasol company from a mix of low-grade coal and small quantities of natural gas, sourced either locally or from Mozambique.
Proven natural gas reserves were 9 billion cubic metres in 2008. Production is estimated at around 1.4 billion cubic metres per annum, all of which is consumed locally in synthetic fuel production.
There were proven reserves of 30.2 billion tonnes of coal in 2010, and is South Africa's primary fuel. This is 3.8 per cent of the world's total and South Africa is a major exporter globally. Coal provides a significant source of foreign exchange. Most of South Africa's reserves are bituminous, with 45 per cent ash content and only one per cent sulphur content. Around 70 per cent of the recoverable reserves are located in three fields – Waterberg, Witbank and Highveld. Production levels were around 134.6 million tonnes of oil equivalent (toe) with 88.7 million toe consumed domestically.

Energy
Total installed generating capacity was 40.4 gigawatts (GW) in 2007, almost 60 per cent of the total electricity generated on the continent of Africa. Energy provides around 15 per cent of GDP. South Africa exports electricity to Botswana, Lesotho, Mozambique, Namibia, Swaziland and Zimbabwe.
The self-financing state energy company, Eskom, has an installed generating capacity of about 38.4GW and produces around 95 per cent of the country's total electricity with the balance made up by mines, industry and municipalities with their own small stations. It is responsible for generation, distribution and sales of electricity. However only a third of the population has access to the national grid; this has grown since 1990 as 3.5 million homes have been electrified with the aim of 100 per cent access for 2012. It operates 17 coal-fired power stations, two hydroelectric, two pumped storage schemes, two gas turbine stations and the country's only nuclear power plant, at Koeberg. The largest generating stations are in Mpumalanga province, adjacent to vast coal reserves. Eskom is the fourth-largest power company in the world by capacity and is being restructured with a view to eventual privatisation.
In early 2008 South Africa experienced severe shortages of electricity as demand outstripped supply. Not only were domestic customers left without energy but neighbouring countries were also cut off from their supply. The government implemented a rapid programme of expansion of the electricity infrastructure by independent power producers, including two new coal-fired power stations due to come on-stream in 2013. The 2,000MW nuclear power station is likely to remain the only nuclear facility for some time, but proposals for a new one are under consideration. Three obsolete power stations will be upgraded and re-opened at a cost of US$1.96 billion. In 2009 two projects will be completed, the Drakensberg hydro scheme and two open-cycle gas turbines will be built. Renewable energy sources account for around 5 per cent of primary energy needs.
In 2009 the African Development Bank loaned the energy company Eskom US$2.77 billion to finance construction of the Medupi power plant. The 4,800MW facility located in Limpopo Province will be the first new power station built by Eskom since the 1980s. The plant is scheduled to be completed by February 2012.

Financial markets
Stock exchange
JSE Securities Exchange (JSE)

Banking and insurance
The financial services sector has changed rapidly since South Africa re-entered the global economy in the 1990s. Domestic banks have restructured and foreign banks compete fiercely in the commercial sector.
The South African Reserve Bank (SARB) (central bank) supervises the domestic and international activities of banks, discount houses and building societies. It issues the country's currency and is the custodian of South Africa's gold and foreign exchange reserves. It is responsible for the implementation of monetary policy which it formulates in conjunction with the finance ministry.
Central bank
South African Reserve Bank (SARB)

Main financial centre
Johannesburg

Time
GMT plus two hours

Geography
South Africa occupies the southern extremity of the African continent. It is bordered by Namibia to the north-west, by Botswana and Zimbabwe to the north, by Mozambique to the north-east, and by Swaziland to the east; Lesotho is a 30,000 square km country isolated within South Africa's territory.
South Africa's coastline stretches over 2,500km from the Namibian border on the Atlantic coast in the west, around the Cape of Good Hope to the Mozambique border on the Indian Ocean coast in the east. The land along the coast is low-lying but quickly rises to mountainous escarpments that separate it from the high plateau of the interior. The highest region in South Africa is the Drakensberg Mountains in the east, which also straddle the border with Lesotho. Njesuthi is South Africa's tallest peak at 3,408 metres (m), although the Drakensberg's highest mountain is Thabana Ntlenyana (3,482m) in Lesotho.
The Kalahari desert in the north-east border region with Namibia and Botswana stretches for 900,000 square km. Much of the central plane is grassland and *veld* (savannah) that stretches to the coast in the east and is flanked in the west by highlands.
Hemisphere
Southern

Climate
There are regional variations due to relative elevations. The Cape coastal area is warm and temperate throughout the year with temperature ranges in Cape Town between 13–20 degrees Celsius (C); inland Pretoria and other high *veld* areas have temperature ranges of 13–22 degrees C and Johannesburg, slightly lower 11–19 degrees C. On the Natal coast humidity can be high during the summer, while the winters are drier with temperatures in Durban 17–24 degrees C. The highest temperatures are recorded in the Kalahari desert and the coldest are recorded in the remote Roggeveld Mountains in the west; the Drakensberg Mountains have snow on their peaks in winter.

Entry requirements
Passports
Required by all and must be valid for 30 days beyond date of departure.
Visa
Are not required by nationals listed at www.southafricahouse.com under *Home Affairs* then *Visa exempt countries* then *foreign citizens* then *Visas*, lastly see *Who needs a visa*. All other nationals must apply to the nearest South African consulate, see www.home-affairs.gov.za/forms.asp for a visa application form; visas must be applied for before arrival.
Business travellers should contact a South African consulate for further information.
All visitors must have proof of return/onward passage, and may have to show evidence of sufficient funds for the intended stay.
Currency advice/regulations
Import of local currency is limited to R5,000 and export to R500 per person.
Import of foreign currency is unlimited but must be declared; export is limited to the amount declared.
Travellers cheques (in major currencies) are widely accepted.
Customs
Personal items are duty-free.
Prohibited imports
Illegal drugs, pornography, firearms, ammunition, flick-knives and explosives. Meat, dairy products and processed cheeses. Plants and plant materials, honey, margarine and vetegable oils require an import permit.

Health (for visitors)
Mandatory precautions
Yellow fever vaccination certificate required if travelling from infected areas, (certificates are not valid until 10 days after immunisation).
Advisable precautions
Vaccinations are necessary for typhoid and hepatitis A and B; vaccination for hepatitis A is advisable. To avoid the risk of bilharzia, only use well-maintained, chlorinated swimming pools. Malaria exists throughout the year in certain areas of northern Transvaal, eastern low veld and northern Natal; prophylaxis should be taken for visits to these areas. Water precautions should be taken in rural areas. HIV/Aids is prevalent.

Hotels
A wide choice is available in main commercial centres. It is advisable to make reservations well in advance, especially during December and January, March and April.

Credit cards
Major credit and charge cards are widely accepted. ATMs are widely available.

Public holidays (national)
Fixed dates
1 Jan (New Year's Day), 21 Mar (Human Rights Day), 27 Apr (Freedom Day), 1 May (Worker's Day), 16 Jun (Youth Day), 9 Aug (National Women's Day), 24 Sep (Heritage Day), 16 Dec (Reconciliation Day), 25 Dec (Christmas Day), 26 Dec (Day of Goodwill).
Holidays that fall on Sunday are taken on Monday.
Variable dates
Good Friday, Family Day (on Easter Monday) (Mar/Apr)

Working hours
Banking
Mon–Fri: 0830–1530; Sat: 0830–1100. Some banks have extended hours.
Business
Mon–Fri: 0730/0830–1600/1700. Some businesses have extended hours.
Government
Mon–Fri: 0730/0830–1600/1700.
Shops
Mon–Fri: 0830–1700; Sat: 0830–1300. Certain shops are open on Sundays.

Telecommunications
Mobile/cell phones
There are GSM roaming facilities available, with coverage throughout most of the country.

Electricity supply
Usually 220/230V AC, but 220/250V in Port Elizabeth and 250V in Pretoria.

Social customs/useful tips
There are no particular taboos, but visitors should be mindful that in certain parts of the country strong racist attitudes still prevail. It is best not to get involved in political discussions.
Visitors should not photograph security institutions.

Security
Visitors should avoid visiting black townships without guidance from reliable local residents and without a trustworthy companion. Certain townships in the Pretoria-Witwatersrand-Vereeniging region and around the Cape Town, Durban and Pietermaritzburg regions should be avoided unless a visit is absolutely necessary – notably Thokoza, Sebokeng, Alexandra, Boipatong, Katlehong, Langa, Mitchell's Plain, Gugulethu, Khayelitsha, Crossroads, KwaMashu and Mpumulanga.
Periodic attacks on visitors to townships have occurred and the crime rate has soared as unemployment and politically-related violence have increased.
Street crime is less of a problem in major urban areas, though care must be taken in central Johannesburg at night. Care must also be taken when visiting extreme right-wing strongholds such as Ventersdorp in the Western Transvaal. It is advisable not to carry unnecessary valuables, expensive jewellery and large amounts of money.
Crime in Johannesburg continues to escalate. Do not resist if confronted. Avoid walking in the streets alone after shopping. Use taxis at night and only those booked through a reputable hotel or among those listed in the official Johannesburg guide. Keep car doors locked

while you are in the vehicle or when it is parked. If you are driving after dark, keep car doors locked and avoid slowing down.

Getting there

Air

National airline: South African Airways

International airport/s: OR Tambo International Airport (name changed from Johannesburg Intenational (JNB) in October 2006), serves as a hub for flights to other countries in the region. It is 24km from city, duty-free shop, bar, restaurant, bank, post office, shops, car hire; Cape Town International (CPT), 22km east of city, duty-free shop, car hire, bank, bar and restaurant; Durban International (DUR), 16km from city, duty-free shop, car hire, bank, bar and restaurant. Taxis and buses serve all airports.

Other airport/s: Bloemfontein (BFN), 10km east of the city; Port Elizabeth (PLZ), 25km from the city.

Airport tax: None

Surface

Road: Possible from Botswana, Lesotho, Namibia, Swaziland, Zimbabwe and Mozambique. Travellers are generally advised to check regulations and conditions regarding entry by road with the Automobile Association of South Africa.

The Maputo Corridor project includes a link from the Atlantic coast at Namibia's Walvis Bay across the Kalahari desert to join the South African road network, linking the western side of southern Africa with the Indian Ocean at Maputo, Mozambique. There is a toll road between Witbank in South Africa and Maputo.

Rail: There are services from Mozambique, Botswana, Zimbabwe and Namibia.

Water: Cruise ships call at some Indian Ocean islands.

Main port/s: Cape Town, Durban, Port Elizabeth and East London.

Getting about

National transport

Air: All major cities and towns are linked with regular, scheduled services. South African Airways, InterAir and Airlink fly domestic routes.

Road: Extensive network of tarred roads, including 51,000km linking main centres. There is a further 130,000km of untarred roads – some of the remoter sections can become impassable in wet weather.

Buses: Inter-city services are operated by Greyhound, Citiliner and other private companies. Vehicles are a good standard.

Rail: Network of some 24,000km with good services throughout the country. Reservations for express trains should be made well in advance. Two classes available, but visitors are advised to travel first class. Most long distance mainline trains have restaurant cars and all have sleeping accommodation (*couchettes* operated in both first- and second-class).

Named services include: Blue Train, a luxury service, running three times a week (Pretoria-Johannesburg-Cape Town; with sleeping accommodation, restaurant cars, air-conditioning, suites, staterooms available); Trans Orange, once a week (Durban-Cape Town); Trans Natal, daily (Durban-Johannesburg). The O R Tembo International Airport to central Johannesburg section of the Guatrain was opened on 10 June 2010, just in time for the start of the World Cup. The remaining 50km to Pretoria is scheduled for completion in 2011.

City transport

Taxis: Widely available in all towns. Taxis cannot be hailed in the street but must be booked or called from a rank. Fares within a city depend on distance and time, while longer distance fares are lower and should be agreed in advance. A 10 per cent tip is usual.

Buses, trams & metro: There are exstensive bus networks in all main towns. Fares in Cape Town and Johannesburg are zonal, with payment in cash or with ten-ride pre-purchase 'clipcards' from kiosks. In Pretoria there are various pre-purchase ticket systems. In Durban conventional buses vie for passengers with minibuses and combi-taxis (both legal and illegal); also found in other South African towns. Although cheap and very fast, they should be used with care.

Trains: There are frequent local trains in the Cape Town and Pretoria and Johannesburg urban areas. All trains have first- and second-class accommodation.

Car hire

Self-drive and chauffeur-driven cars are widely available. An international driving licence is required unless visitor's national licence carries the photograph and signature of the holder.

Driving is on the left. Speed limits: built-up areas 60kph; country roads 100kph; declared freeways and some main roads 120kph. Heavy fines for speeding.

BUSINESS DIRECTORY

Telephone area codes

The international dialling code (IDD) for South Africa is +27, followed by area code and subscriber's number:

Bloemfontein	51	Ladysmith	361
Cape Town	21	Pietermaritzburg	331
Durban	31	Port Elizabeth	41
Johannesburg	11	Pretoria	12

Chambers of Commerce

American Chamber of Commerce, 60 Fifth Street, PO Box 1132, Houghton 2041, Johannesburg (tel: 788-0265; fax: 880-1632; e-mail: administrator@amcham.co.za).

Bloemfontein Chamber of Business, 37 Kellner Street, PO Box 87, Bloemfontein 9300 (tel: 447-3368; fax: 447-5064; e-mail:bcci@intekom.co.za).

Cape Town Regional Chamber of Commerce and Industry, 19 Louis Gradner Street, PO Box 204, Cape Town 8000 (tel: 402-4300; fax: 402-4302; e-mail: info@capechamber.co.za).

Durban Chamber of Commerce & Industry, 190 Stanger Street, PO Box 1506, Durban 4000 (tel: 335-1000; fax: 332-1288; e-mail: chamber@durbanchamber.co.za).

Johannesburg Chamber of Commerce and Industry, Private Bag 34, Corner Empire Road and Owl Street, Auckland Park 2006, Johannesburg (tel: 726-5300; fax: 782-2000; e-mail: info@jcci.co.za).

Ladysmith Chamber of Commerce and Industry, PO Box 7, Ladysmith 3370 (tel: 631-0541; fax: 637-4407; e-mail: lcci@futurenet.co.za).

Pietermaritzburg Chamber of Business, Royal Show Grounds, Commercial Road, PO Box 11734, Dorpspruit 3206, Pietermaritzburg (tel: 345-2747; fax: 394-4151; e-mail: pcb@futurenet.co.za).

Port Elizabeth Regional Chamber of Commerce and Industry, 22 Grahamstown Road, PO Box 2221, North End 6056, Port Elizabeth (tel: 484-4430; fax: 487-1851; e-mail: info@pechamber.org.za).

Pretoria Chamber of Commerce and Industry, 852 Park Street, PO Box 40653, Arcadia 0007, Pretoria (tel: 342-3236; fax: 342-1486; e-mail: pcci@mweb.co.za).

South African Chamber of Business, 24 Sturdee Avenue, PO Box 213, Saxonwold 2132, Johannesburg (tel: 446-3800; fax: 446-3847; e-mail: info@sacob.co.za).

Banking

Absa Bank Ltd, 2nd Floor, ABSA Towers North, 180 Commissioner Street, Johannesburg 2001 (tel: 350-4000; fax: 350-3768).

International Bank of Southern Africa Ltd, 3rd Floor, Sunnyside Ridge Bldg, 32 Princess of Wales Terrace, Parktown, Johannesburg 2193 (tel: 644-3300, 643-6740, 643-6743; fax: 643-1122).

Nedcor Bank Ltd, 135 Rivonia Rd, Sandown, Sandton, Johannesburg 2001 (tel: 294-4444; fax: 295-5555).

South African Bank of Athens Ltd, Bank of Athens Building, 116 Marshall Street, Johannesburg 2001 (tel: 832-1211; fax: 838-1001, 833-7976).

Standard Bank of South Africa Ltd, 5 Simmonds Street, Johannesburg 2001 (tel: 636-9111; fax: 636-3544).

Central bank
South African Reserve Bank, 370 Church Street; PO Box 427, Pretoria 0001 (tel: 313-3911; fax: 313-3197; email: www.reservebank.co.za).

Stock exchange
JSE Securities Exchange (JSE): www.jse.co.za

Stock exchange 2
Bond Exchange of South Africa (BESA): www.bondexchange.co.za

Travel information
Airlink, Bonaero Park, Johannesburg (tel: 961-1700; fax: 395-1076; internet: www.flyairlink.com)

Automobile Association of South Africa, Denis Paxton House, Alladale Road, Kyalami Midrand 1685; PO Box 596, Johannesburg 2000 (tel: 799-1000; fax: 799-1960; e-mail: aasa@aasa.co.za).

Blue Train Reservations, PO Box 2671, Joubert Park 2044 (tel: 334-8459; fax: 334-8464; e-mail: bluetrain@transnet.co.za).

Coach Services: Translux Express, PO Box 2383, Johannesburg 2000 (tel: 774-3333; fax: 774-3318); Greyhound Coach Lines, PO Box11229, Johannesburg 2000 (tel: 830-1301; fax: 830-1528); Intercape Mainliner, PO Box 618, Bellville 7535 (tel: 386-4400; fax: 386-2488).

Eastern Cape Tourism Board, PO Box 186, Bisho 5605 (tel: 635-2115; fax: 636-4019; e-mail: info@ectourism.co.za).

Free State Department of Environmental Affairs and Tourism, PO Box 264, Bloemfontein 9300 (tel: 403-3435; fax: 448-8361).

Gauteng Tourism Authority, The Rosebank Mall, Rosebank 2196 (tel: 327-2000; fax: 327-7000; e-mail: tourism@gauteng.net).

Interair South Africa, Private Bag 8, PO JHB Int'nl Airport 1627, Johannesburg (tel: 616-0636; fax: 616-0930; email: info@interair.co.za).

KwaZulu-Natal Tourism Authority, PO Box 2516, Durban 4000 (tel: 304-7144; fax: 305-6693; e-mail: info@tourism-kzn.org).

Mpumalanga TourismAuthority, PO Box 679, Nelspruit 1200 (tel: 752-7001; fax: 759-5441; e-mail: mtanlpsa@cis.co.za).

Northern Cape Tourism Board, Private Bag X5017, Kimberley 8300 (tel: 832-2657; fax: 831-2937; e-mail: tourism@northerncape.org.za).

Northern Province Tourism Board, PO Box 1309, Pietersburg 0700 (tel: 288-0099; fax: 288-0094; e-mail: ceo@greatnorth.co.za).

North-West Parks and Tourism Council, PO Box 4488, Mmabatho 2735 (tel: 386-1225; fax: 386-1158; e-mail: nwptb@iafrica.com).

Rovos Rail Reservations, Victoria Hotel, PO Box 2837, Pretoria 0001 (tel: 323-6052; fax: 323-0843).

South African Airways, Private Bag X13, JHB Int'nl Airport, 1627; Airways Park, 32 Jones Road, Kempton Park, Johannesburg International Airport (tel: 978-1000; fax: 978-3507; internet: www.flysaa.com).

South African National Parks, 643 Leyds Street, Muckleneuk, Pretoria; PO Box 787, Pretoria 0001 (tel: 343-1991; fax: 343-0905; e-mail: reservations@parks-sa.co.za).

Western Cape Tourism Board, Private Bag X9108, Cape Town 8000 (tel: 426-5639; fax: 426-5640; e-mail: info@capetourism.org).

Ministry of tourism
Ministry of Environmental Affairs and Tourism, Fedsure Forum Building, 315 Pretorius Street, Pretoria; Private Bag X447, Pretoria 0001 (tel: 310-3611; fax: 322-0082).

National tourist organisation offices
South African Tourism, Bojanala House, 12 Rivonia Road, Illovo 2196 (tel: 778-8000; fax: 778-8001; e-mail: info@southafrica.net; internet site: http://www.southafrica.net).

Ministries
NB For the following Ministry addresses: Pretoria (administrative), Cape Town (legislative).

Ministry of Agriculture and Land Affairs, Private Bag X250, Pretoria 0001 (tel: 319-6886; fax: 321-8558); Private Bag X9087, Cape Town 8000 (tel: 465-7690; fax: 465-6550).

Ministry of Arts, Culture, Science and Technology, Private Bag X727, Pretoria 0001 (tel: 337-8378; fax: 324-2687); Private Bag X9156, Cape Town 8000; (tel: 465-4850; fax: 461-1425).

Ministry of Communications, Private Bag X882, Pretoria 0001 (tel: 427-8111; fax: 362-6915); Private Bag X9151, Cape Town 8000 (tel: 462-1632; fax: 462-1646).

Ministry of Correctional Services, Private Bag X853, Pretoria 0001 (tel: 323-8803; fax: 323-4111); Private Bag X9131, Cape Town 8000 (tel: 462-2314; fax: 465-4375).

Ministry of Defence, Private Bag X427, Pretoria 0001 (tel: 355-6119; fax: 347-0118); PO Box 47, Cape Town 8000 (tel: 469-6070; fax: 465-5870).

Ministry of Education, Private Bag X603, Pretoria 0001 (tel: 312-5501; fax: 323-5989); Private Bag X9034, Cape Town 8000 (tel: 465-7350; fax: 461-4788).

Ministry of Environmental Affairs and Tourism, Private Bag X447, Pretoria 0001 (tel: 310-3611; fax: 322-0082); Private Bag X9154, Capetown 8000 (tel: 465-7240; fax: 465-3216).

Ministry of Finance, Private Bag X115, Pretoria 0001 (tel: 323-8911; fax: 323-3262); PO Box 29, Cape Town 8000 (tel: 464-6100; fax: 461-2934).

Ministry of Foreign Affairs, Private Bag X152, Pretoria 0001 (tel: 351-0005; fax: 351-0253); 120 Plein St, Cape Town 8001 (tel: 464-3700; fax: 465-6548).

Ministry of Health, Private Bag X399, Pretoria 0001 (tel: 328-4773; fax: 325-5526); Private Bag X9070, Cape Town 8000 (tel: 465-7407; fax: 465-1575).

Ministry of Home Affairs, Private Bag X741, Pretoria 0001 (tel: 326-8081; fax: 321-6491); Private Bag X9102, Cape Town 8000 (tel: 461-5818; fax: 461-2359).

Ministry of Housing, Private Bag X645, Pretoria 0001 (tel: 421-1311; fax: 341-8513); Private Bag X9029, Cape Town 8000 (tel: 465-7295; fax: 465-3610).

Ministry of Intelligence Services, PO Box 56450, Arcadia 0007(tel: 338-1800; fax: 323-0718); PO Box 51278, Waterfront 8002 (tel: 401-1800; fax: 461-4644).

Ministry of Justice and Constitutional Development, Private Bag X276, Pretoria 0001 (tel: 323-8581; fax: 321-1708); Private Bag X256, Cape Town 8000 (tel: 465-7506; fax: 465-2783).

Ministry of Labour, Private Bag X499, Pretoria 0001 (tel: 322-6523; fax: 320-1942); Private Bag X9090, Cape Town 8000 (tel: 461-6030; fax: 462-2832).

Ministry of Minerals and Energy, Private Bag X646, Pretoria 0001 (tel: 322-8695; fax: 322-8699); Private Bag X9111, Cape Town 8000 (tel: 462-2310; fax: 461-0859).

Ministry of Provincial and Local Government, Private Bag X802, Pretoria 0001 (tel: 334-0705; fax: 326-4478); Private Bag X9123, Cape Town 8000 (tel: 462-1441; fax: 461-0851).

Ministry of Public Enterprises, Private Bag X15, Hatfield 0028 (tel: 431-1000; fax: 342-7224); Private Bag X9079, Cape Town 8000 (tel: 461-6376; fax: 465-2381).

Ministry of Public Service and Administration, Private Bag X884, Pretoria 0001 (tel: 314-7911; fax: 328-6529); Private Bag X9148, Cape Town 8000 (tel: 465-5491; fax: 465-5484).

Ministry of Public Works, Private Bag X890, Pretoria 0001 (tel: 324-1510; fax: 325-6380); Private Bag X9155, Cape Town 8000 (tel: 462-4184; fax: 461-6962).

Ministry of Safety and Security, Private Bag X463, Pretoria 0001 (tel: 339-2800; fax: 339-2819); Private Bag X9080, Cape Town 8000 (tel: 465-7400; fax: 461-2073).

Ministry of Social Development, Private Bag X885, Pretoria 0001 (tel: 312-7637; fax: 321-2658); Private Bag X9153, Cape Town 8000 (tel: 465-4011; fax: 465-4469).

Ministry of Sport and Recreation, Private Bag X869, Pretoria 0001 (tel: 334-3100; fax: 321-8493); Private Bag X9149, Cape Town 8000 (tel: 465-5506; fax: 465-4402).

Ministry of Trade and Industry, Private Bag X274, Pretoria 0001 (tel: 322-7677; fax: 322-7851); Private Bag X9047, Cape Town 8000 (tel: 461-7191; fax: 465-1291).

Ministry of Transport, Private Bag X193, Pretoria 0001 (tel: 309-3131; fax: 328-3194); Private Bag X9129, Cape Town 8000 (tel: 465-7260; fax: 461-6845).

Ministry of Water Affairs and Forestry, Private Bag X313, Pretoria 0001 (tel: 36-8733; fax: 328-4254); Private Bag X9052, Cape Town 8000 (tel: 464-1500; fax: 465-3362).

Office of the President, Private Bag X1000, Pretoria 0001 (tel: 337-5100; fax: 321-8870); Private Bag X1000, Cape Town 8000 (tel: 464-2100; fax: 464-2123).

Other useful addresses

Association of Advertising Agencies (AAA), PO Box 2289, Parklands 2121 (tel: 781-2772; fax: 781-2796; e-mail: aaa@gem.co.za).

Afrikaanse Handelsinstituut (AHI) (Afrikaans Trade Institute), Lynnwood Galleries, 354 Rosemary Street, Lynnwood 0081; PO Box 35100, Menlopark 00101 (tel: 348-5440; fax: 348-8771; e-mail: pta@ahi.co.za).

Association of Marketers (ASOM), 8 Sloane Street, Bryanston, Sandton; PO Box 98859, Sloane Park 2152, Bryanston (tel: 706-1633; fax: 706-4151; e-mail: asom@pixie.co.za).

Board on Tariffs and Trade, Fedlife Forum, Cnr Van der Walt and Pretorius Streets, Private Bag X753, Pretoria 0001 (tel: 322-8244; fax: 322-0149).

British High Commission, 255 Hill Street, Arcadia, Pretoria 0002 (tel: 483-1200; fax: 483-1302); 91 Parliament Street, Cape Town 8001 (tel: 461-7220; fax: 461-0017).

Chamber of Mines of South Africa, PO Box 61809, Marshalltown 2107 (tel: 498-7100; fax: 834-4251).

Chemical & Allied Industries Association, 15th Floor, Metal Box Centre, 25 Owl Street, Auckland Park 2006 (tel: 482-1671; fax: 726-8310).

Clothing Federation of South Africa, 42 van der Linde Street, Bedfordview 2008 (tel: 622-8125; fax: 622-8316).

COEGA Development Corporation, Libra Chambers, Cnr Oakworth Road and Carnarvon Place, Humerail, Port Elizabeth; Private Bag X13130, Humewood, Port Elizabeth 6013 (tel: 507-9111; fax: 585-5445; e-mail: info@coega.co.zu).

Government Communications and Information System (GCIS), 356 Vermeulen Street, Pretoria; Private Bag X745, Pretoria 0001 (tel: 314-2127; 325-2030; e-mail: govcom@gcis.pwv.gov.za; internet site: http://www.gcis.gov.za).

ICC Durban (international convention centre), 45 Ordnance Road, Durban 4001; PO Box 155, Durban 4000 (tel: 360-1000; fax: 360-1005; e-mail: mktg@icc.co.za).

Industrial Development Corporation of South Africa, 19 Fredman Drive, Sandton 2146; PO Box 784055, Sandton 2146 (tel: 269-3000; fax: 269-3116; e-mail: callcentre@idc.co.za).

Iscor Limited, Roger Dyason Road, Pretoria West; PO Box 450, Pretoria 0001 (tel: 307-3000; fax: 307-4721; e-mail: webmaster@iscor.com).

JSE Securities Exchange (stock exchange), 1 Exchange Square, 2 Gwen Lane, Sandown, Sandton 2196; Private Bag X991174, Sandton 2146 (tel: 520-7000; fax: 520-8584; e-mail: miscellaneous@jse.co.za).

South African Association for the Conference Industry (SAACI), PO Box, Kloof 3640 (tel 764-6977; fax: 764-6974; e-mail: sec@saaci.co.za).

South African Business Initiative for Reconstruction and Development, 17th Floor, Metal Box Centre, 25 Owl Street, Auckland Park 2092 (tel: 482-5100; fax: 482-5507).

South African Diamond Board, 5th Floor, SA Diamond Centre, 240 Commissioner Street, Johannesburg 2001 (tel: 334-8980/6; fax: 334-8898; e-mail: mabombol@sadb.co.za).

South African Embassy (USA), 3051 Massachusetts Avenue, NW Washington, DC (tel: (+1-202) 232-4400; fax: (+1-202) 265-1607; e-mail: safrica@southafrica.net).

South African Foreign Trade Organisation (SAFTO), Export House, 71 Maud Street, Sandton; PO Box 782706, Sandton 2146 (tel: 883-3737; fax: 883-6569; e-mail: safto@apollo.is.co.za).

South African Petroleum Industry Association, Trust Bank Centre, Adderley Street, Cape Town 8001; PO Box 7082, Roggebaai 8012 (tel: 419-8054; fax: 419-8058).

Statistics South Africa, Steyn's Building, 274 Schoeman Street, Pretoria 0002; Private Bag X44, Pretoria 0001 (tel: 310-8911; fax: 322-3374; e-mail: info@statssa.pwv.gov.za; internet site: www.statssa.gov.za/).

Trade and Investment South Africa, Rex Welsh House, Maud Street, Sandown, Sandton 2196; PO Box 782084, Sandton 2146 (tel: 884-2206; fax: 884-3236; e-mail: isa@isa.org.za).

US Embassy, 877 Pretorius Street, Pretoria; PO Box 9536, Pretoria 0001(tel: 342-1048; fax: 342-2244).

National news agency: Sapa PO Box 7766, Cotswold House, Greenacres Office Park, Cnr Victory & Rustenburg Roads, Victory Park, Johannesburg, 2000 (tel: 782-1600; fax: 782-1587/8; email: comms@sapa.org.za; internet: www.sapa.org.za).

Internet sites

African Development Bank: www.afdb.org

Africa Online: www.africaonline.com

AllAfrica.com: http://allafrica.com

International Finance Corporation: www.ifc.org/abn

Johannesburg Stock Exchange: www.jse.co.za/

Development Bank of South Africa: www.dbsa.org

Mbendi AfroPaedia (information on companies, countries, industries and stock exchanges in Africa): http://mbendi.co.za

Province of the North West Tourist Board: www.tourismnorthwest.co.za/

South African Development Community (SADC): www.sadcreview.com

South African Futures Exchange: www.safex.co.za/

South African yellow pages: www.ipages.co.za/

Trade Web: www.trade.co.za/

South Georgia

KEY FACTS

Official name: South Georgia and the South Sandwich Islands (SGSSI)

Head of State: Queen Elizabeth II; represented by Commissioner Alan Edden Huckle (resides in Falkland Islands) (from July 2006)

Area: 3,755 square km

Population: 20 (2004) (British Antarctic Survey (BAS) scientists)

Capital: King Edward Point (administrative centre)

Official language: English

Currency: Falkland Islands pound or pound sterling (FI£ or £) = 100 pence

Exchange rate: FI£ or £0.64 per US$ (Oct 2011); (pegged to pound sterling)

COUNTRY PROFILE

Historical profile

1775 Captain Cook landed and took formal possession of South Georgia and the South Sandwich Islands (SGSSI).
1904 A whaling station was established by the Norwegian C A Larsen.
1908 The UK government annexed SGSSI by Letters Patent as part of the Falkland Islands Dependencies and the islands came under UK administration.
1965 Leith Harbour, the last shore-based whaling station in South Georgia, was closed.
1982 Argentine military forces occupied South Georgia for 22 days. South Georgia and the South Sandwich Islands became overseas territories of the UK.
2001 The UK military garrison closed and was replaced by a British Antarctic Survey (BAS) base at King Edward Point. There is a science station for biological study on Bird Island.
2005 A revised version of the 2000 environment management plan was made available on the British Antarctic Survey's website. The new plan was published in 2006 and sets out environmental policies for the next five years.
2006 Alan Huckle became Commissioner.
2009 Doctor Martin Collins was appointed as the new Senior Executive; he is a member of the UK delegation to the scientific committee of the Convention on the Conservation of Antarctic Marine Living Resources (CCAMLR – pronounced 'Kammelar'), which manages marine resources in the Southern Antarctic Ocean.
2010 In the Falkland Islands *Economic Development Strategy* released in July, part of the plans, the bilateral fisheries agreement with South Georgia, will be re-negotiated so that the Falkland Islands fishing interests are better promoted and receive priority in the allocation of fishing rights.
2011 In May, a rodent eradication programme was initiated targeted at rats and rabbits (which had been accidentally introduced over the years) that have had a detrimental impact on seabirds and penguin colonies and the habitat in general. In July it was announced that the ashes of Frank Wild were to be disinterred from a chapel in South Africa and buried in Grytviken cemetery on South Georgia in November. Wild had been Earnest Shackleton's second-in-command on the *Endurance* expedition and charged with leading the men left on Elephant Island when Shackleton went for help.

Political structure

South Georgia and the South Sandwich Islands (SGSSI) are British overseas territories, legally distinct from the Falkland Islands but, for convenience, they are administered from the Falkland Islands. With no indigenous or permanent inhabitants, there is no need for representative government, but a separate constitution for the territory was promulgated in 1985. The governor of the Falkland Islands is also the commissioner for the SGSSI; in this capacity he consults the Falklands Executive Council on those matters relating to the territory which might affect the Falkland Islands.
Other administrative posts based in Stanley, Falkland Islands, include the assistant commissioner who is also director of the SGSSI Fisheries, a financial secretary and attorney general. The marine officer, based at King Edward Point, is responsible for customs, immigration, posts and fisheries liaison.

Population

20 (2004) (British Antarctic Survey (BAS) scientists)

Main cities

King Edward Point (administrative centre); Grytviken, formerly a whaling station on South Georgia, was the garrison town.

Languages spoken

Official language/s
English

Media

Press
Weeklies: The South Atlantic Remote Territories Media Association publishes an online newsletter which includes articles on South Georgia (www.sartma.com).

Economy

Income is derived from fishing licences, fees for trans-shipping fish catches, tourist landing charges and the sale of postage stamps.
The South Georgia Environmental Management Plan covering the period from 2006 to 2010, has the British government committed to providing a sustainable policy

framework which conserves, manages and protects the rich natural environment, at the same time allowing for human activities and the generation of revenue.

Agriculture

Fishing

Large-scale fishing began in 1969/70 by Soviet bloc countries. In 1993, the UK extended its territorial waters around the SGSSI from 19.3km (12 miles) to 321.8km (200 miles) and created the SGSSI Maritime Zone. In 1996, new laws opened fishing grounds with a licensing scheme. Approximately 100–200,000 tonnes of krill are caught around South Georgia each year. The SGSSI government applies conservation measures to the maritime zone, but has the right to impose additional measures if appropriate. There is satellite imagery surveillance of the fishing zone.

The toothfish total allowable catch (TAC) for the 2006/07 season was increased by 15 per cent by the SGSSI and approved by the Convention for the Conservation of Antarctic Marine Resources

Tourism

Visitors arrive mainly by tour ships, although an international airport is planned. The largest number come from the US (32 per cent) , followed by the UK (25 per cent) and Germany (15 per cent). Extended walks, ie more than one kilometre from the landing site, are growing in popularity, as are visits to the nesting sites of the wandering albatross, especially Prion Island, which is carefully managed.

Environment

South Georgia is the breeding ground for some 85 per cent of the world's southern fur seal population, as well as significant populations of elephant seals, albatrosses, petrels and penguins. In 1910, reindeer were introduced by Norwegian whaling companies.

The South Sandwich Islands represent a maritime ecosystem.

Time

GMT minus two hours

Geography

South Georgia is an isolated, mountainous sub-Antarctic island, which lies in the South Atlantic Ocean, 2,150km east of Tierra del Fuego and about 1,390km east-south-east of the Falkland Islands. Surrounded by cold waters originating from the Antarctic, South Georgia has a harsher climate than expected from its latitude. More than 50 per cent of the island is covered by permanent ice with many large glaciers reaching the sea at the head of fjords. The main mountain range is the Allardyce Range, which has its highest point at Mount Paget (2,960m).

The South Sandwich Islands, which comprise a chain of active volcanic islands around 240km long, lie about 750km south-east of South Georgia. The climate is wholly Antarctic and in the late winter, the islands may be surrounded by pack ice.

Hemisphere

Southern

Climate

South Georgia and the South Sandwich Islands are prone to very sudden and unexpected changes of weather brought on by the Antarctic Convergence, where cold waters flowing up from Antarctica meet warm water from the north. The average temperature in summer is -2 degrees Centigrade.

Entry requirements

Only a limited number of visitors are allowed to land each year. All visitors must apply to the Office of the Commissioner, South Georgia and South Sandwich Islands, Government House, Stanley, Falkland Islands (tel: (+500) 27-433, fax: (+500) 27-434; e-mail: gov.house@horizon.co.fk) at least 60 days in advance of their journey for permission to land. Application forms can be obtained from the Commissioner's office or on-line from the official South Georgia government website (www.sgisland.org). Details of all places to be visited must be provided and there is a landing fee. There are no search-and-rescue facilities.

Passports

Passports must be valid for a minimum of six months.

Visa

Not required, but visitors must report to the Marine Officer at King Edward Point, Cumberland Bay East.

Health (for visitors)

Advisable precautions

There are no medical facilities available. Comprehensive medical emergency insurance is necessary as well as sufficient stocks of prescribed medication. Sunburn is a problem in this sub-polar region, sunblock should be applied regularly.

All of the historic buildings in the territory present a safety risk; they are storm damaged and flimsy, causing wind blown asbestos particles. Visitors should not approach within 200 metres of them without permission of the Marine Officer at King Edward Point.

Credit cards

The museum shop accepts VISA and Mastercard, but not American Express.

Working hours

Government

Mon–Fri (winter): 0900–1315, 1430–1730; Mon–Fri (summer): 1100–1315, 1630–1930.

Telecommunications

Postal services

A new post code for the islands has been issued through the Universal Postal Union: SIQQ 1ZZ.

Getting there

Air

There is currently no routine air access, but there are plans for an international airport.

Surface

The only access is by yacht or cruise ships.

Getting about

National transport

Road: There are no roads.

BUSINESS DIRECTORY

Telephone area codes

There are no land lines on South Georgia. All communications are by either radio or mobile/cell phones

Other useful addresses

British Antarctic Survey, High Cross, Madingley Rd, Cambridge CB3 OET, UK (tel: (+44-1223) 221-400; fax: (+44-1223) 362-616; e-mail: information@bas.ac.uk).

Licensing Officer SGSSI, Fisheries Department, Stanley, Falkland Islands (tel: (+500) 27-260; fax: (+500) 27-265; e-mail: fish.fig@horizon.co.fk).

Office of the Commissioner, South Georgia and South Sandwich Islands, Government House, Stanley, Falkland Islands (tel: (+500) 27-433, fax: (+500) 27-434; e-mail:gov.house@horizon.co.fk).

Project Atlantis (Environmental and educational resource) Dundee University, 23 Springfield, Dundee, Scotland DD1 4JE (tel: (+44) (0)1382 388-159; internet: www.atlantishome.org).

Internet sites

British Antarctic survey: www.antartic.ac.uk

British Geographical Survey: www.bgs.ac.uk

Government website: www.sgisland.org

Information for Yachts visiting South Georgia: www.rccpf.org.uk/ anc click on *Index MAPS showing PUBLICATIONS*.

South Atlantic Remote Territories Media Association: www.sartma.com

South Georgia Heritage Trust: www.sght.org

University of Dundee educational resource: www.atlantishome.org

South Sudan

On 9 July, after decades of civil war, South Sudan became an independent state, having officially seceded from Sudan. A number of issues, most notably surrounding borders, oil revenue-sharing and currencies, have yet to be resolved. But the participation of Sudan's president, side-by-side with his Southern counterpart at the new nation's inauguration, was an encouraging indication of positive prospects for good co-operation and, ultimately, sustainable peace between the two countries. Quite a lot had been stacked against the prospect of a peaceful resolution to years of strife, including history, oil, tribal loyalties and tribal militia, currency claims and widespread corruption.

Peace at last?

The conflicts between the largely Arab North and the mostly Christian South lasted almost 50 years, since 1956 when the British handed over control to Khartoum. During the ensuing period an estimated 2 million people lost their lives. Millions more became refugees.

The longest of the two civil wars was that between the Northern Sudanese government in Khartoum and the government of the South (1956–72 and 1983–2005). The North/South war ended with the signing of the Comprehensive Peace Agreement (CPA) that was in place from 2005 through 2011. As part of the CPA, a referendum took place in January 2011 during which the people of South Sudan voted to secede from the North and in July 2011, Sudan became two countries: Sudan and the Republic of South Sudan. Abyei, a significant oil producing region on the North/South border was also expected to carry out a referendum in January to determine which side it would join, but this did not take place and uncertainties regarding the status of Abyei remain. Other territorial disputes along the North/South border continue, specifically in the areas of South Kordofan and Blue Nile where clashes have taken place.

The economy

The World Bank notes that South Sudan still shows the signs of a long civil war and, despite its oil wealth, ranks among the least developed countries in the world. On almost all Millennium Development Goal indicators, the South scores lower than both the North as well as the average for sub-Saharan Africa – in some instances by a large margin. About half of the country's children enrol in primary school, yet only 10 per cent complete it. Infrastructure is alarmingly poor: paved roads cover just about 100 kilometres in a country close to the size of France, no airports meet international civil aviation standards and river channels have not yet been made navigable.

South Sudan is described by the World bank as 'at an early stage of economic development', but has great potential. According to the World Bank, 85 per cent of Southern Sudan's population lives in poverty, almost double the proportion in the North, where the figure is just over 45 per cent. A majority of the population eke out a living on little more than US$0.75 a day. The UK based charity Oxfam reports that in the South, a teenage girl has a higher chance of dying in childbirth than finishing elementary education. It is estimated that as few as 500 girls a year actually finish primary education.

On the plus side, aside from oil, the new country has untapped potential. There are large livestock, fishery and forestry resources, which, assuming adequate rainfall and fertile land, could hold promise for labour-intensive agricultural exports. Importantly, developing agriculture in South Sudan could reduce the dependence on oil. Making the most of these assets to generate sustained and inclusive growth calls for transparent and effective budget processes, a robust legal framework and strengthened financial sector. Expertise from abroad would help in this regard – also to build much-needed capacity to put into operation basic government institutions, including a central bank to introduce and manage a new currency.

For both Sudan and South Sudan, future prosperity – which will help to cement peace – will depend to a large part on increased economic co-operation and trade between the two countries.

KEY FACTS

Official name: South Sudan (Janub as Sudan)

Head of State: President Salva Kiir Mayardit (SPLA/M) (from 9 Jul 2011)

Head of government: Vice President Riek Machar (SPLA/M) (from 9 Jul 2011)

Ruling party: Sudan People's Liberation Army/Movement (from 9 Jul 2011)

Area: 644,329 square kilometres

Population: 8.26 million (2008 census, disputed)

Capital: Juba

Official language: English

Currency: South Sudan Pound (SS£)

GDP per capita: US$448 2010*

* estimated figure

Outstanding issues

Three key issues are at the heart of the negotiations taking place under the auspices of the African Union. The first is oil sharing. The 50/50 split of oil revenues was scheduled to end at independence, but how future oil revenues will be divided remains open. South Sudan is expected to pay Sudan a transit fee for the use of its pipeline, but the amount of the fee has not yet been established, nor is it clear how much revenue sharing will take place. South Sudan has claimed that the North wants US$32.00 per barrel, roughly corresponding to one third of the total value, which the South finds exorbitant.

Secondly, debt: there exists a tentative agreement that Sudan would take over all debt on the condition that creditors commit to debt relief within two years and that South Sudan help lobby in support of Sudan. Should this fail, debt would be apportioned based on a formula that has yet to be determined.

Finally, currency. North and South Sudan had agreed that the South would continue to use the Sudanese pound for a transitional period. However, almost immediately after July 2011 both North and South had issued new currencies. The result of this was that the South ended up with a reported US$700 million of bank notes that can only be used in the North. The parties therefore need to agree on what will happen with the Sudanese pounds that are currently circulating in the South.

One possible area of disagreement was sorted out sooner than expected: the 2,000km border between the two countries. Tentative agreement on the line and on the nature of the UN Mission to monitor it was reached in July 2011.

Beyond these issues for short-term resolution, South Sudan faces other, more long-term problems. Human capital levels are extraordinarily low. At 37 per cent, the youth literacy rate is half the sub-Saharan Africa average. With one-third of South Sudan's population under the age of 10, boosting educational levels is vital to the country's development.

Another difficulty is the lack of basic infrastructure. In addition to the dearth of paved roads outside Juba, the capital, there is no airport that meets international civil aviation standards and river channels are still unnavigable. Progress is being made on increasing electricity generation capacity, but blackouts are frequent and businesses make much use of generators.

South Sudan has approached the International Monetary Fund (IMF) for technical assistance in building the capacity and institutions to manage its nascent economy. This is particularly important for assisting the Bank of South Sudan to become a full-fledged central bank. The IMF stands ready to provide technical assistance in its areas of core expertise to enable the design, implementation and monitoring of sound macro-economic policies, including by developing a fiscal framework, establishing the central bank and its core activities, building statistical capacity and putting in place the legislative framework required for effective economic and financial management. To fund this assistance, the IMF intends to seek donor contributions to a special trust fund for IMF capacity building in South Sudan. The trust fund would total US$10.6 million for a period of just under four years.

Many South Sudanese hopes are pinned on the country's extensive diaspora. An estimated 100,000 refugees returned to the South in the period October 2010–February 2011, placing unforeseen demands on the South's inadequate social services. Other refugees make remittances from overseas and, most valuable of all, some US and European educated Sudanese have returned home to invest their capital and skills in the country's future.

Oil, key to the immediate future

Several factors complicate Sudan's split, but the most contentious is the division of oil resources. In a nutshell, while the majority of the oil fields are found in the south (about 75 per cent, depending on specific field allocations), conversely, the entire pipeline, refining and export infrastructure is in the North. Co-operation between the two countries will be essential.

Oil plays a major role in the economy of both the Sudans. According to the IMF, in South Sudan oil represents an overwhelming 98 per cent of total revenue. Under the CPA, South Sudan was given some degree of autonomy from the North but revenues from oil produced in South Sudan were shared equally. In the view of the US government's Energy Information Administration (EIA) the loss of oil revenues will have a serious impact on the economy of North Sudan at a time when it is still facing international sanctions.

Historical statistics relating solely to South Sudan were barely available in 2011. Overall (North and South Sudan) oil production began in the late 1990s and grew rapidly starting in July 1999 with the completion of an export pipeline that runs from central Sudan to Port Sudan on the Red Sea. In 2010, EIA estimates that crude oil production averaged just over 470,000 barrels per day (bpd). First half 2011 data indicate a slight decline, averaging about 460,000bpd. As a result of uncertainties regarding security and boundary issues, there has been limited additional investment in the oil industry.

The volume of oil produced in South Sudan's oil fields appeared to be peaking in mid-2011, which makes it probable that this key source of export revenue will decline over time. With technology improvements, oil extraction in the existing fields could be made more efficient and new sources of oil might be discovered. But these are both long-term propositions, making it essential the government identify other ways of developing new, non-oil sources of revenue.

Nilepet is South Sudan's national oil company but its role has yet to be fully determined. Foreign companies involved in Sudan's oil sector are primarily from Asia. They are led by the China National Petroleum Corporation (CNPC), India's Oil and Natural Gas Corporation (ONGC) and Malaysia's Petronas.

The exploration and development of Sudan's oil resources and infrastructure, both North and South, have been controversial from the beginning. International human rights organisations accused the Sudanese government of financing human rights abuses with oil revenues, including the mass displacement of civilians near the oil fields. Factional fighting and rebel attacks on oil infrastructure have kept oil production and exploration from reaching full potential. CNPC, the largest investor in Sudan, has had workers and facilities attacked while at the same time, China has faced international condemnation for its investments in Sudan. The United States prohibits US nationals from engaging in any transactions or activities related to the petroleum or petrochemical industries in the entire territory of Sudan, for the time being including Southern Sudan, as a result of the conflict in Darfur.

Transit fees

In late 2011, the two countries had yet to come to an agreement regarding the transit fees to be paid by South Sudan for the use of the oil pipeline to the Red Sea. The North was seeking fees that would offset the looming loss of its 50 per cent share of the South's oil revenue and was most recently reported to be charging about US$23–33 per barrel, while the South was seeking terms that were more in line with international standards (below US$1.00 per barrel) and offering to sell the North discounted oil. South Sudan has also been in talks with interested companies to create a possible 2,200 mile (3,600km) export pipeline from the South to Kenya's port in Lamu. But this would take 2–3 years to build and its development will depend on the terms of any agreement between the governments of South Sudan and Kenya, as well as interested companies.

Outlook

Perhaps unsurprisingly, violence was not long in showing itself in South Sudan after the July division. The lack of a competent police force and of paved roads meant that the militia gunmen who had once defended their countrymen against attacks from the North now swung round to defend local, tribal interests in the South. Nowhere was this worse than in the eastern state of Jonglei, where in September 2011 there were tit-for-tat clashes between the Dinka and Murle tribes as they went to war over cattle. It was reported that some 600 Loo Nuer had been killed and as many as 200 children abducted. Much of these tribal tensions can be directly attributed to poverty, fuelled by a lack of jobs and the easy availability of weapons. The UN peacekeeping mission drafted in to sort out the problem was small enough to make it a token rather than substantive force. The extent to which outbreaks of this sort become the norm will determine the type of society that South Sudan can hope to be.

Meanwhile revenue from oil will provide an opportunity to invest in social and infrastructure development. A portion of this revenue also needs to be set aside for the future, given that production is already starting to decline.

Risk assessment

Economy	Poor
Politics	Poor
Regional stability	Poor

COUNTRY PROFILE

Historical profile

The history before the nineteenth century is largely based on oral traditions, which traditionally say that the Nilotic people arrived in South Sudan before the tenth century. The non-Nilotic, Azande people came to South Sudan, from the Congo River area, in the sixteenth century. In the seventeenth century, the Avungara people arrived and quickly established dominance over the resident Azande and ruled as an ambitious and combative elite. The geography of southern Sudan limited the advance of Islam into the region from the north and allowed the traditional social and cultural heritage to continue, while political and religious institutions grew. The Azande maintained their independence from the France and Belgium, who had successfully colonised neighbouring territories.

1821 The vast swamps (Sudd) of southern Sudan kept many ousiders away and left it undisturbed by the Arab-controlled northern regions until the Turkish Ottoman Empire defeated Egypt and conquered northern Sudan. The Ottoman's set up Egypt as its proxy ruler of Sudan.

1839 A slave trade was developed with black male Africans seized for the Egyptian army and black women and children from the south traded in Arab markets.

1869 After the opening of the Suez Canal, the British became involved in Sudan's affairs, through its association with Egyptian governance of Sudan.

1870s Egypt colonised southern Sudan.

1878 Egypt established the province of Equatoria (much of modern-day Darfur, Western Equatoria, Eastern Equatoria, Central Equatoria and part of Somalia), in the southern Sudan and banned slavery, at the behest of Britain.

1881 In northern Sudan, Mohammed Ahmed, who proclaimed himself the long-looked-for Mahdi (the guided one), led his followers, the Muslim Sudanese, in a rebellion against Egyptian rule.

1885 The Mahdi's army massacred the British army, under General Gordon, sent to quash the rebellion. The Mahdi united the tribes in a modern Islamic state and undermined the basis of the province of Equatoria.

1889 The nascent, Egyptian province of Equatoria ceased to exist and became inconsequential regions of Sudan.

1898 The Mahdi was defeated by the British and Anglo-Egyptian army.

1899 Sudan was ruled as an Anglo-Egyptian condominium, although north and south Sudan were governed as separate administrative regions.

1947 At the end of the Second World War the Conference of Juba, under the auspices of Great Britain and Egypt, it was agreed to unify politically, northern Sudan and colonial southern Sudan.

1948 A legislative assembly for the unified Sudan was established.

1953 Great Britain and Egypt agreed to grant Sudan independence.

1955 Troops of the Sudan Defence Force (of southern Sudan) mutinied as a southern member of the national assembly was put on trial. The mutiny was suppressed, but some troops fled into the countryside and became the core of a poorly armed and ill-organised rebel fighting force (later founding the Anya-Nya guerrilla army).

1956 Sudan gained independence. With the rejection of southern calls for, if not secession or even a federation, then more regional autonomy and greater development in the south, a secessionist movement developed led by the surviving mutineers and students from the south, who formed the Anya-Nya guerrilla army. The political and sometimes violent conflict became polarised between the largely Muslim north and the largely Christian/Animist south.

1958 A military coup in the north, led by General Ibrahim Abboud overthrew the civilian government of Prime Minister Abd Allah Khalil. Martial law was declared and Abboud proclaimed himself prime minister of Sudan.

1962 Civil war began in the south, led by the Anya-Nya movement.

1964 The October Revolution overthrew Abboud and a national government for Sudan was established.

1969 Colonel Jaafar Mohammed al Nimieri led the May Revolution military coup, installing a revolutionary council in Sudan.

1971 The Southern Sudan Liberation Movement (SSLM) was founded by former lieutenant Joseph Lagu; it encompassed all southern rebel forces, with a unified command structure and objectives for independence. It assumed the right to represent the interests of the people of the south.

1972 Nimieri became the country's first elected president of Sudan and negotiated with Joseph Lagu (SSLM) at the conference on peace in Ethiopia. An estimated 500,000 people had been killed since 1955. The Addis Ababa Agreement ended the first Sudanese civil war, through the creation of the Southern Sudan Autonomous Region (SSAR).

1978 Oil was discovered in southern Sudan.

1983 President Nimieri officially declared Sudan an Islamic State, introduced *Sharia* (Islamic law) and revoked the SSAR agreement. The Sudan People's Liberation Movement (SPLM) was established under the leadership of Colonel John Garang (who was head of the armed, Sudan People's Liberation Army (SPLA)) and gained control of much of the south; it campaigned for a united Sudan and blamed the central government for policies leading to Sudan's disintegration.

1985–86 Nimieri was ousted in a bloodless coup and after a brief period of military rule, Sadiq al Mahdi, the great-grandson of the Great Mahdi, became prime minister of Sudan after elections in 1986.

1986 Peace talks began between John Garang (SPLM) and Sadiq al Mahdi in Ethiopia, which culminated in the Koka

Dam declaration. It was agreed to abolish *Sharia* in the south and a constitutional conference was proposed. The divided political situation in the north militated against a peaceful solution and insurgent fighting continued.

1988 A new agreement was reached, negotiated by a government coalition political party and the SPLM and called the November Accords, but Prime Minister Sadiq al Mahdi was political weak and was unable to ratify the accords.

1989 Sadiq al Mahdi was replaced following another bloodless coup by the National Salvation Revolution, backed by the fundamentalist Islamic political party, National Islamic Front (NIF) (Al Jabhah al Islamiyah al Qawmiyah); Omar Hassan Ahmad al Bashir became chairman of the Revolutionary Command Council for National Salvation (RCCNS). An informal ceasefire broke down.

1992 The Sudanese pound was replaced as the currency by the Sudanese dinar. The central government mounted a military operation to take all rebel towns in the south, and captured the SPLA's headquarters in Torit. Riek Machar and Lam Akol attempted to overthrow the leadership of John Garang by forming the Nasir Faction. William Nyuon Bany formed a second rebel faction.

1993 Kerubino Kwanyin Bol formed a third rebel faction in the south. The three dissident rebel factions formed a coalition called SPLA-United. However clashes between these rebel factions caused Western powers to overlook their importance. The RCCNS was abolished after Omar al Bashir was appointed president; Sudan returned to civilian rule, although with one political party (Al Muttamar al Watani (National Congress Party) (NCP)) exercising dominance, and the country was not strictly a democracy. Non-Muslim judges from the south were transferred to the north and were replaced with Muslim judges. Non-Muslim citizens were subject to arrest and punishment under Islamic religious laws (*Sharia*).

1994 The *Declaration of Principles* (DoP), an initiative sponsored by Eritrea, Ethiopia, Uganda and Kenya, set out objectives for a just and comprehensive peace settlement, was promulgated. Signatories to the DoP included the government of Sudan and the SPLM and SPLA (later reformed into SPLM/A)

1995 Political parties of the north and south formed the National Democratic Alliance. Eritrea, Ethiopia and Uganda increased their military support of SPLA.

1996 Omar al Bashir won the presidential election.

1997 The Khartoum Peace Agreement between the central government and seven southern groups, led by John Garang, was ratified by the National Assembly.

1998–99 Voters in a referendum endorsed a new Sudanese constitution. Sudan began to export oil from southern Sudan. After a power struggle within the ruling NCP, between President Bashir and Hassan al Turabi (a hardline Islamist and ideologue), the President imposed a state of emergency and dissolved the National Assembly.

2000 Omar al Bashir and the NCP were re-elected. Most opposition parties boycotted the elections.

2002 After peace talks in Kenya, the government and the SPLA signed the Machakos Protocol: the government accepted the right of the south to seek self-determination after a six-year interim period.

2003 China and the Sudan announced a US$1 billion investment plan to enhance Sudan's oil infrastructure including the construction of a 750-kilometre-long pipeline between Sudan's largest oil deposits in the Kordofan oilfield and the coast.

2004 President Bashir agreed to grant autonomy to the south for six years, split the country's oil revenues with the southern provinces and allow the southerners to vote in a referendum on independence at the end of the six-year period.

2005 The government and the Sudan People's Liberation Army (SPLA) signed the Comprehensive Peace Agreement (CPA), ending the 22-year civil war. Among other things the agreement began a period of transition until 2009, when parliamentary and state legislative elections were scheduled to take place and provided for an equal sharing of oil revenues between the north and south, with special administrative status given to the oil producing province of Abyei. SPLA leader, John Garang, was appointed vice president of Sudan for the six-year period of reconciliation; MORE INFO the new constitution gave a large degree of autonomy to the south. John Garang was killed in a helicopter crash; riots broke out in Khartoum, between black southern Sudanese and northern Arabs. Garang's deputy, Salva Kiir, was named his successor as vice president of national Sudan and president of southern Sudan.

2006 The UN envoy, Jan Pronk, was expelled for claiming that government troops had suffered defeats in southern Sudan. The Kordofan oilfield was attacked by the SPLA.

2007 The currency was changed from the dinar (in use since 1992), back to the pound; the exchange rate was set at S£1 to 100 old dinar. Vice President Kiir accused the national government of supporting militia operating in the south, claiming that they had not been disarmed, and the central government had failed to share the wealth of resources found in the south. The oil producing province of Abyei had been subject to continued armed attacks by the SPLA, so finally the governments in agreement with the SPLM asked the Permanent Court of Arbitration (PCA) (based in The Hague) to rule on the disputed border between the north and south.

2008 The PCA gave its ruling in July and concluded that Sudan's argument that Abyei only constituted a small sliver of land south of the Kiir/Bahr el Arab River was erroneous and awarded 10,460 square kilometres to South Sudan. It also rejected South Sudan's argument that its demarcation in the eastern and western boundaries was legitimate and awarded those areas, including much of the oil reserves in the area, to Sudan. It also affirmed the right of traditional pastoral herdsmen to continue to use both sides of the border areas in the province of Kordofan for their flocks (over 18,500 square km).

2009 Lam Akol created his own political party SPLM-Democratic Change and split from the SPLM, claiming it had failed to fully govern southern Sudan. Both political parties nominated candidates to challenge President Bashir in the next Sudanese presidential election. A delay in completing a census forced the postponement of presidential and parliamentary elections throughout Sudan. The census was criticised by political leaders in the south who said that the southern Sudanese population had been under-recorded.

2010 Almost all of the political parties based in southern Sudan had withdrawn from the presidential elections by 1 April due to concerns over fraud and security during voting and that the electoral process had been rigged to favour the ruling NCP. President Bashir threatened to cancel a referendum on independence in the south in face of the boycotts. Over 11–15 April, general elections took place (they were extended by two days due to organisational problems and high voter turnout), the NCP won 68.2 per cent of the vote, the SPLM won 22 per cent, Popular Congress 4 per cent. President Bashir was re-elected with 68.24 per cent of the vote. Two election monitoring organisations declared that the elections failed to meet full international standards due to intimidation and harassment, although neither called for a re-election. The announcement of the results was delayed until the end of April as counting took longer than anticipated. At the same time a presidential election was undertaken in Southern Sudan; Salva Kiir (SPLM) won 92.99 per cent of the vote, Lam Akol (SPLM-Democratic Change) 7.01 per cent. On 14 May, Sudan signed an agreement with Egypt, Ethiopia, Uganda, Tanzania and Rwanda to redistribute their relative share of Nile waters; negotiations had been ongoing since 1977. On 21 May, Salva Kiir was sworn in as the first elected president of southern Sudan. The referendum on independence for southern Sudan was set for 9 January 2011. The UN estimated that some 51,000 people travelled south in time to register their vote (14 November–4 December). By October, a referendum in Abyei region on whether it should join north or south Sudan and due to be held on the same day as southern Sudan's referendum on independence, was still in doubt. President Bashir announced on 19 December that if the South broke away the north would adopt an Islamic constitution.

2011 The referendum in southern Sudan began on 9 January, to determine its future as either a province of Sudan or as an independent country; the vote, over nine days, was overwhelmingly in favour of independence. The result was 98.83 per cent of the vote in favour, 1.17 per cent against independence. On 16 February, it was decided by the ruling committee of the SPLM that South Sudan would be the official name of the country when it came into existence on 9 July. On 12 March, militia supporting rebel leader General George Athor attacked the town of Malakal, in oil-rich state of Upper Nile. Official talks with Sudan representatives were suspended following southern Sudan's accusations that President Bashir was plotting to overthrow the southern Sudan government, orchestrated by the Sudanese military intelligence agency. It was claimed that Sudan was 'creating, training, supplying and arming militia groups' in southern Sudan, overseen by President Bashir. Fighting between the SPLA and those loyal to rebel-leader, George Athor, killed 70 people in three states on 17–18 March. A UN resolution extending its peacekeeping mission in the region until 9 July was unanimously adopted on 27 April. It also announced that it intended to establish a successor mission after independence. The finance minister announced that a new currency, the South Sudan Pound, will be issued on 9 July initially valued on par with the Sudan pound.

Political structure

Constitution

The interim constitution for southern Sudan was inaugurated in 2005, as agreed under the Comprehensive Peace Agreement (CPA) with Sudan. It established an autonomous government, headed by a president, who is head of government and commander-in-chief of the Sudan People's Liberation Army (SPLA). A presidential term in office is five-years, with a limit of two terms.

A new, draft constitution was finalised in March 2011. However national discussion and a final constitution will be voted on and ratified after independence in July 2011.

Form of state

Presidential democracy

The executive

The president is elected by popular vote and is head of government and appoints a cabinet, approved by parliament. The presidential office is limited to two, five-year terms.

National legislature

The unicameral, South Sudan Legislative Assembly (SSLA). The membership was previously constituted on the basis of the power-sharing formulas in the 2005 Comprehensive Peace Agreement (CPA) and members in post on 9 July 2011 were elected in the April 2010 Sudan general elections.

Legal system

The interim constitution mandated a decentralised institution that is independent of the executive and legislature and with its own budget, so as not to be dependent on the government. Judicial power is derived from the people and exercised in courts in accordance with customs, values, norms and in conformity with the constitution and legislation.

The structure of the judiciary is modelled on the UK judiciary and is headed by a Supreme Court (based in Juba), which is the highest legal institution. Below this court are the Courts of Appeal (based in three state capitals), High Courts (based in all state capitals), County Courts and other courts deemed necessary to establish. The president of the Supreme Court is answerable to the president and parliament for the administration of the judiciary.

Last elections

11–15 April 2010 (presidential first and second rounds); 20 January 2011 (independence referendum)

Results: Presidential: Salva Kiir (SPLM) won 92.99 per cent of the vote, Lam Akol (SPLM-(Democratic Congress) DC) 7.01 per cent.

Referendum: 98.83 per cent of the vote in favour, 1.17 per cent against.

Next elections

Not known

Population

8 million (2010 estimate)

Last census: 2008: 8,260,490 million (disputed figure)

Internally Displaced Persons (IDP)

The UN Office for the Co-ordination of Humanitarian Affairs (OCHA) estimated that there were 213,832 returnees to South Sudan (October–February 2010–11) and more people were expected to return from Uganda and Sudan, which would strain food security throughout the country in 2011.

Ethnic make-up

There are over 200 ethnic groups, but the people are socially, culturally and historically related to the peoples of east Africa. The largest group are the Dinka.

Religions

Mainly Christian, animist and traditional beliefs

Education

Only 37 per cent of the population above aged six has attended school.

The Juba National University is based in Khartoum and provides instruction in English for South Sudan students. In 2011 it was in the process of being relocated to South Sudan.

In October 2010, the Dr John Garang International School opened, and in January 2011 it moved to a permanent location in Juba, where it operates a first school, on the UK system. When its intake is complete it will provide education for 350 children, with classes of 25–30 per teacher. It is divided into four stages, kindergarten, pre-school, Key Stage 1 (Years 1 and 2) for children aged five and six and Key Stage 2 (Years 3, 4, 5 and 6) children aged seven–10. The educational year begins in September and finishes in July. Plans for the construction of a high school in 2012 are advancing.

The Southern Sudan Interactive Radio Instruction (SSIRI) provides at-a-distance educational programmes for children (called The Learning Village) and adults (including English), as well as training for teachers, including classroom management. It is funded by US Agency for International Development and administered by the Education Development Centre (EDC). The Association for the Development of Education in Africa (ADEA) in conjunction with educationalists and ministers in Juba, identified the needs of South Sudan to develop educational services for the population.

All statistics on South Sudan were gathered from the National Education Statistical Booklet, Ministry of Education (South Sudan 2009).

Literacy rate: 27 per cent of the population aged above 15 years are literate. Literacy in males is 40 per cent, 16 per cent in females. Urban adult literacy rate: 53 per cent, 22 per cent rural rate. Literacy rate of population aged 15–24 years 40

per cent, of which male rate 55 per cent, 28 per cent female.
Enrolment rate: 72 per cent gross enrolment. Net enrolment in primary school 72 per cent.
Pupils per teacher: 52 students per teacher (average class size 129 students)

Health
In January 2011 there were only 130 doctors in South Sudan and as well as a chronic lack of other medical staff.
All statistics gathered from Southern Sudan Centre for Census, Statistics and Evaluation (SSCCSE)
HIV/Aids
HIV prevalence: 1.6 per cent (SSCCSE 2010)
Life expectancy: 42 years (SSCCSE 2010)
Fertility rate/Maternal mortality rate: 2,054 maternal deaths per 100,000 live births
Child (under 5 years) mortality rate (per 1,000): 102 deaths per 1,000 live births (SSCCSE 2006)
Head of population per physician: 80,000 per doctor (2011)

Main cities
Juba (capital), Aweil, Bentiu, Bor, Kwajok, Malakal, Rumbek, Torit, Wau, Yambio, Yei.

Languages spoken
Colloquial Arabic is widely spoken and Juba Arabic (a pidgin) is spoken in the capital. Native languages include Dinka, Nuer and Ubangian.
Official language/s
Dinka

Media
Press
There are a number of online news outlets, although most are published from abroad.
Weeklies: In English, the *Juba Post* (http://jubapost.org) reports on news, politics, business and other domestic issues. It accepts advertising for both its hardcopy and online editions.
Broadcasting
Radio: Internews operates a community service for the region including South Sudan (www.internews.org), although it is based in the US. The BBC also has services operating (www.bbc.co.uk/worldservice)
The Southern Sudan Interactive Radio Instruction (SSIRI) provides at-a-distance educational programmes for children (called The Learning Village) and adults (including English), as well as training for teachers, including classroom management.
News agencies
National news agency: South Sudan News Agency (www.southsudannewsagency.com)

Economy
South Sudan has fertile soil suitable for subsistence farmers growing a variety of crops including plantains, sorghum, cassava, millet, groundnuts, maize, okra, millet, rice, sweet potatoes, wheat, sesame and beans. The Ngok Dinka and Misseryia people have traditional use of land for grazing cattle in Abyei (check spelling elsewhere), straddling the new border between Sudan and South Sudan. Other livestock includes chickens and goats as well as cattle (dairy and beef) in drier, less fertile areas. Mineral deposits include uranium, gold and copper, among others.
There are large petroleum deposits that were developed by the central government of Sudan, in partnership with foreign, principally Chinese, oil companies. At the end of 2009, Sudan had proved reserves of 6.7 billion barrels of oil, with production of 4.9 million barrels per day (bpd) of oil. Since the referendum on independence that confirmed South Sudan's future as a sovereign nation the division of oil production and revenue has become a source of contention. Sudan could lose as much as 75 per cent of the oil revenue, which will be vital for South Sudan's future development. The two governments are in negotiation for a royalty on previous investment, development and infrastructure costs on the exploitation of the oil fields.
The World Bank administers the Multi-Donor Trust Fund-South Sudan (MDTF-SS), which has a total of US$232.5 million to invest in capacity building support to the newly formed government of South Sudan. The World Bank advised the new government that anti-corruption measures to ensure good governance when disbursing national revenue derived from petroleum sales should be enacted before the country comes into being on 9 July 2011.
In early 2011 there were less than 50km of metalled roads in South Sudan, around 80 per cent of the population lived in traditional timber round houses (*tukul*) without electricity or running water, and 90 per cent were living on less than US$1 per day. The UN Food and Agriculture Organisation (FAO) stated that almost 50 per cent of the population were in need of food assistance.
The Bank of South Sudan (BoSS) announced in May 2011 that bank notes for the new currency (the South Sudan Pound (SS£)) had been ordered for delivery and distribution by 9 July; it was expected that it would take around four months to complete a full exchange. All Sudanese pounds in circulation in South Sudan will be exchanged for the new money at S£1=SS£1. It was estimated that S£2 billion (US$750 million) was in circulation in early 2011. The first bank notes issued will be to the value of SS£50.
On 20 April 2011 South Sudan formally applied for membership of the International Monetary Fund (IMF), which will allow it draw on financial technical assistance and loan arrangements in the future.

External trade
South Sudan's future trading will be with traditional partners including all of its neighbours, however in the short term it will need to develop a modern infrastructure to sustain anything but the current, improvised, transportation of goods from anywhere in the region.
Oil flows north to the Mediterranean ports in Sudan. In early 2011 there were less than 50km of metalled roads, severely hampering private business expansion.
Exports
Petroleum piped through Sudan (for onward delivery to China and other destinations).

Agriculture
Farming
The soil is fertile and crops under cultivation include plantains, sorghum, cassava, millet, groundnuts, maize, okra, millet, rice, sweet potatoes, wheat, sesame and beans. Livestock includes cattle (dairy and beef), chickens and goats.
Fishing
Artisan fishermen catch freshwater fish for domestic consumption.
Forestry
Teak wood is a valuable export.
In 2007, a report by the UN Environment Programme, stated that South Sudan had lost 40 per cent of its forests since 1960s and that desertification was progressing south due to land degradation. It recommended measures to impede the growth of the Sahara, including a reduction in slash-and-burn for agricultural purposes. The need for charcoal was also noted as a potential source of conflict between Sudan and South Sudan, with sufficient supplies for Sudan only being manufactured in South Sudan by 2017.

Industry and manufacturing
In 2008, 53 per cent of the working population were unpaid family members and only 12 per cent of the working population were paid employees. Of the 7,333 formal businesses in the ten state capitals, 84 per cent were retail or restaurants.

Tourism
While the potential for eco-tourism is high, there is little infrastructure to attract any but the most intrepid traveller. South Sudan is the location of the world's largest freshwater swamp (the Sudd) which can increase in size to 130,000sq km during the rainy season and is Africa's

largest wetland, and an important habitat for fish, birds and mammals.

Environment

In June 2010 the African Union backed a proposal to build the 'Great Green Wall' project – a 15km wide, 7,775km long, continuous belt of trees from Senegal in the west to Djibouti in the east (traversing 11 countries, including South Sudan) in an effort to halt the advance of the Sahara Desert. The trees to be used would be drought-adapted, preferably native to the area from a list of 37 possible species, and should help to slow soil erosion and filter rain water.

Mining

There are under-exploited deposits of uranium, iron ore, chromium, zinc, tungsten, mica, gold and copper. However these are becoming globally more sought after commodities and development is expected in the medium-term.

At the end of 2009, Sudan had proved reserves of 6.7 billion barrels of oil, with production of 4.9 million barrels of oil per day. An expected 85 per cent of total production and 75 per cent of total Sudanese revenue reverted to South Sudan on independence on 9 July 2011. However Sudan is in negotiation for a royalty on its investment on development and infrastructure costs in the exploitation of this oil.

Energy

South Sudan has very poor energy infrastructure. The majority of the population uses bio-fuel to light their homes and cook their food. South Sudan has the potential to produce a large quantity of hydroelectricity and in 2010 the authorities identified eleven likely sites for hydroelectric power plants.

In February 2011 the second electricity generation and distribution system was launched in the town of Kapoeta (Eastern Equatoria), with an initial capacity of 894kW and 700 service connections. The US funded the project (US$4 million), to include personnel training along with the infrastructure. The first electricity project was established in Yei (Central Equatoria), in 2008 and the third projects with a similar generation and distribution system was launched later in February 2011 in Maridi (Western Equatoria).

Banking and insurance

The Bank of South Sudan (BoSS) was launched in 2006 to provide a financial and banking structure for the newly formed interim government under the Wealth Sharing Agreement with Sudan in 2004.

There were three commercial banks operating in South Sudan in 2010, the Nile Commercial Bank (NCB), the Kenya Commercial Bank (KCB) and the Ivory Bank. The government has called on other foreign banks to increase their quality of operations in South Sudan for business, NGOs and foreign consulates and international organisations.

In 2010, only 1 per cent of the population had access to, or made use of, a bank account.

Central bank

Bank of South Sudan (BoSS)

Main financial centre

Juba

Time

GMT plus three hours (South Sudan does not use daylight saving).

Geography

South Sudan is bounded by Ethiopia in the east, Kenya, Uganda and the Democratic Republic of Congo in the south and the Central African Republic in the west, with Sudan in the north. It has a rainforest environment that includes the 30,000 square kilometres (sq km) Sudd swamp formed by the White Nile. The Sudd is the world's largest freshwater swamp, which can increase in size to 130,000sq km during the rainy season.

The river Kirr (Gurf) (Bahr el Arab) became the border between Sudan and South Sudan, it flows through the province of Kordofan and is a tributary of the Upper (White) Nile. Mount Kinyeti Imatong is the highest peak, situated in the Jebel Marra range located along the border with Uganda. The Nuba Hills, in the centre of north South Sudan, are rugged granite peaks that rise sharply out of the plains with fertile slopes and clay pits between hills.

Southern Sudan is composed of ten states: Western Bahr el Ghazal, Northern Bahr el Ghazal, Unity, Warab, Lakes, Western Equatoria, Eastern Equatoria, Central Equatoria, Jonglei and Upper Nile.

Hemisphere

Northern

Climate

South Sudan has a tropical climate that varies from over 35 degrees Celsius (C) (centigrade) in summer to around 20 degrees C in winter. The rainy season is May–October and the humidity only falls between November–March.

Dress codes

Western business clothing is acceptable.

Entry requirements

Passports

Required by all. Passports must be valid for six months from date of entry.

Currency advice/regulations

Banks exchange the local currency for foreign currency at a fix rate and the US dollars is accepted in all money exchange establishments. Currency exchange bureaus use a flexible rate which may offer a better market rate, however they may not be able to re-convert local currency when a visitor departs. On arrival it is advisable to have plenty of lower denomination bank notes for use in exchange.

Health (for visitors)

Mandatory precautions

Valid yellow fever and cholera certificates are required if travellers are arriving from infected areas, or travellers are intending to visit the south of Sudan.

SUE: I picked this up from our Sudan entry and have now confused myself! Does this now mean all travellers to South Sudan must have a cert or just those moving from South to north?

Advisable precautions

Vaccinations for yellow fever, diphtheria, tetanus, polio, hepatitis A and typhoid are recommended. Other vaccinations that may be recommended are cholera, tuberculosis, hepatitis B and meningitis. There is a risk of rabies. Malaria is prevalent throughout the country. Anti-mosquito measures including repellents, nets and clothing that cover the body should be used (these will also provide protection against hepatitis B and yellow fever). Tap water must be treated as unsafe unless boiled and filtered (bottled water is available in the main cities). Eat only well cooked meals, preferably served hot; vegetables should be cooked and fruit peeled. Dairy products are unpasteurised and should be avoided. Use only well maintained, chlorinated, swimming pools as bilharzia can be contracted from streams and rivers.

Hotels

There are several hotels of differing quality in and around Juba.

Credit cards

Not readily accepted.

Working hours

Shops

In 2011, there were three supermarkets in Juba, plus outdoor traditional markets.

Telecommunications

Mobile/cell phones

The local operator, Vivacell, extended operations to include more rural areas in 2011.

Sudanese mobile phone operators provide 900/1800 and 3G 2100 services that may operate around urban areas of South Sudan.

Security

There are armed attacks on oil fields and trips outside the capital should be arranged through local contacts. Landmines remain a major hazard in South Sudan, especially south of Juba. Visitors should remain on main roads only. Armed militia loyal to local interests in Upper Nile, Blue Nile and Bahr al Ghazal pose a threat. Crimes against person and property are frequent in South Sudan and while the police force is fledgling all care should be taken to minimise risk.

Conflict in neighbouring countries occasionally spills over into South Sudan. The armed and lawless militia, the Lord's Resistance Army poses a threat to all along the southern border with Uganda. Banditry is prevalent in South Sudan.

Getting there

Air

National airline: South Sudan does not have a national airline but a number of international carriers land in Juba.

International airport/s: The Juba Airport (JUB), is an airfield located north of Juba. It accepts international flights but has few amenities for travellers.

Surface

Road: A project to pave the 192 kilometres, Juba-Nimule highway to Kampala (Uganda) began in February 2011. When completed (early 2012) an extension to Mombasa (Kenya) will be undertaken. Until the road is metalled, the bus journey between Juba and Kampala is around eight hours.

Water: Rivers provide transport but no scheduled services exist.

Getting about

National transport

There are no paved roads in any directions except north from Juba to Sudan.

BUSINESS DIRECTORY

The addresses listed below are a selection only. While World of Information makes every endeavour to check these addresses, we cannot guarantee that changes have not been made, especially to telephone numbers and area codes. We would welcome any corrections.

Telephone area codes

The international direct dialling code (IDD) for South Sudan is +249, followed by area code:

Aweil	844	Malakal	831
Bentiu	861	Torit	322
Juba	811	Wau	841
Kwajok	569	Yei	249

Banking

Central bank

Bank of Southern Sudan (BoSS), PO Box, Juba South Sudan; Juba Town Centre, Between the Ministry of Telecommunications and Postal Services (GOSS) Building and the Central Equatoria Taxation Department (tel: 811-820218, 911-820211; fax 811-820211, 811-823939; internet: www.bankofsouthernsudan.org; email: info@bankofsouthernsudan.org).

Other useful addresses

Southern Sudan Centre for Census, Statistics and Evaluation, PO Box 137, Juda (email: SSCCSE@gmail.com or info@SSCCSE.org).

National news agency: South Sudan News Agency (www.southsudannewsagency.com)

Internet sites

Government of Southern Sudan (GOSS): www.goss-online.org

Southern Sudan Centre for Census, Statistics and Evaluation (SSCCSE): www.SSCCSE.org

Spain

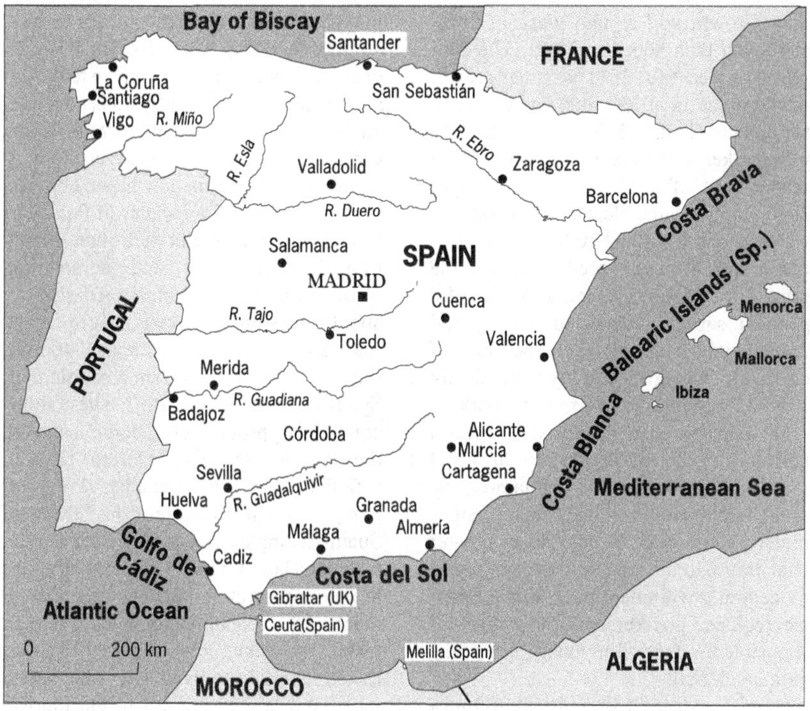

Spain's faltering economic recovery began to run out of steam again after the second quarter of 2011. The government's austerity drive had resulted in diminished national and regional government expenditure. Putting on a brave front, the secretary of state for the economy, José Manuel Campa, observed that the global slow-down, particularly in the euro-zone, had made it exceptionally difficult for the economy to grow at the forecast annual rate of 1.3 per cent.

Lack of confidence

The figures suggested a general lack of confidence in Spain's economic prospects as household spending fell 0.2 per cent from a year earlier; in the previous quarter household expenditure had fallen by 0.1 per cent, although in the quarterly comparison stressed by the government, it had actually risen by 0.6 per cent. Of greater significance was the fact that public spending had fallen by an annual 1.0 per cent in the second quarter, way down on the 2.6 per cent rise in the first three months of 2011. The important economic motor of exports also suffered a setback, as export growth slipped to an annual 8.4 per cent, down from the 12.1 per cent growth recorded in the first quarter. The quarterly fall in exports was a worrying 1.9 per cent, offset to a degree by the growth in exports services – principally tourism – which rose by 5.4 per cent.

Up to the first half of 2011, Spanish exports totalled eur106,363 million (US$140 million), representing an increase of 18.5 per cent over the previous year. The European Union (EU) accounted for 66.5 per cent of exports. Exports to neighbouring France, Spain's largest market (with 18.1 per cent), rose by 11.3 per cent, while exports to Germany (10.4 per cent) rose by 14.7 per cent in the same period. In mid-2011 a large question mark hovered over the ability of these and other countries to maintain the rate of increase. A spokesman for Spain's national Institute of External Commerce (ICE) observed that '... Spain has survived previous economic crises thanks to exports. We will have to be

KEY FACTS

Official name: Reino de España (Kingdom of Spain)

Head of State: King Juan Carlos I (since 1975)

Head of government: Prime Minister José Luis Rodríguez Zapatero (PSOE) (since 2004; re-elected 12 Apr 2008)

Ruling party: Partido Socialista Obrero Español (PSOE) (Spanish Socialist Workers' Party) (since 2004; re-elected 9 Mar 2008)

Area: 504,782 square km, including the Balearic and Canary Islands, and the Ceuta and Melilla enclaves in North Africa

Population: 46.07 million (2010)*

Capital: Madrid

Official language: Castilian Spanish, Catalan (in Catalonia including the Balearics), Basque (in the Basque provinces), Valencian (Province of Valencia), Galician (Galicia).

Currency: Euro (€) = 100 cents

Exchange rate: €0.75 per US$ (Oct 2011)

GDP per capita: US$30,639 (2010)

GDP real growth: -0.10% (2010)

GDP: US$1,409.90 billion (2010)

Labour force: 23.09 million (2010)

Unemployment: 20.10% (2010)

Inflation: 2.00% (2010)

Balance of trade: -US$62.35 billion (2010)

Foreign debt: US$2,166.00 billion (Aug 2010)

* estimated figure

NOTA

20 November 2011, early parliamentary elections were won by the Partido Popular (PP) (Popular Party) with 44.6 per cent of the vote (186 seats out of 350), the outgoing Partido Socialista Obrero Español (PSOE) (Spanish Socialist Workers' Party) won 28.7 per cent (110 seats). Mariano Rajoy Brey (PP) became prime minister, taking office on 20 December.

attentive to what happens this time round, especially as some of our neighbouring economies seem to be slowing down.' According to the Institute, 28.4 per cent of Spanish companies expect their export orders to increase, while 46.2 per cent expect them to hold up. ICE also expected the value of Spanish exports to hold up, unlike in previous crises when devaluation was the order of the day. The 2008–11 economic crisis also differed from earlier cases in that a larger proportion of Spanish trade was in the services sector. In the twenty-first century, Spanish companies such as Telefónica, Repsol, BBVA and Santander operated on a global scale. A negative factor in the development of Spanish trade was the fact that the government still needed to resolve the problems facing the banking sector; as long as Spanish companies were denied access to credit facilities, then exports would inevitably suffer. Spanish companies also needed to develop sales to emerging markets such as those of Asia (notably India and China), Oceania and Africa, where growth remained strong.

In fact, even before the bond-markets had begun to focus their sights on the weaknesses of the Spanish economy, official data published at the beginning of August 2011 had already undermined the government's forecasts for growth. The figures that showed GDP growth between April and June 2011 were 0.5 per cent down on the previous year, 0.2 as against 0.7 per cent. For the government's optimistic forecast of 1.3 per cent to be met, Spain's growth for the second half of 2011 would have to come in at three times that registered for the first half of the year. The Florus de Lemus Institute of Madrid's Carlos III University observed that 'The Spanish economy is completely stagnant, and there is not enough growth to prevent further deterioration of the labour market.' To add to the gloom, a report published by the BBVA banking group added that 'Growth will remain weak in 2011, and lower than hoped in 2012.' The consensus forecast for 2011 was that growth would come in at less than one per cent. Mr Zapatero had, in 2009, forecast that the jobs market would begin recovering in the second half of 2010. In the summer of 2010, as it became clear that his forecast was way out, Mr Zapatero had simply carried things forward, predicting that the growth would now be seen in 2011. Independent surveys suggested that around 230,000 jobs had been lost in the first half of 2011, fixing unemployment firmly around the symbolic five million mark.

Mr Zapatero had promised to reform pensions by the end of January 2011 and to restructure collective bargaining by mid-March. He had also, rather ambitiously, promised to introduce greater bank transparency, not only to be imposed by central government but also the Spanish regional governments, now also responsible for controlling their share of the national deficit.

Spanish industrial and agricultural productivity continues to lag behind its competitors. A survey conducted by FEDEA-Mckinsey estimated that Spanish competitiveness had deteriorated against that of Germany by 33 per cent over the ten year period to 2009. An overall employment rate of 66 per cent had once been forecast for 2010 and per capita GDP had originally (before the international financial crisis) been targeted to reach the EU average by 2010. These ambitions turned out to be optimistic as an increasing number of manufacturing jobs and facilities were moved to more competitive Asian centres. Alongside the global crisis, Spanish industry has been slow to wake up to the uncomfortable reality that Spain is no longer an obviously attractive manufacturing centre for more developed economies. Within the EU, Spain now has to compete not only with the low wages of Poland or Slovakia, but also with their more highly trained workforces. And competition from within the EU is no longer what it's about – jobs are also being lost to China, India and Vietnam. An estimated 40 multinationals have shut up shop or sold their Spanish facilities since 2002. These shortcomings in productivity, combined with the Partido Socialista Obrero Español (PSOE) (Spanish Socialist Workers' Party)'s failure to address the reform of Spain's complex and outdated tax and labour legislation have meant that although to date job creation has remained strong, much of the economy continues to rely on labour-intensive, low wage jobs. Spain risked reverting to its pre-EU role, where jobs were largely created in the tourism and agricultural sectors, or by state subsidised industries. Patent applications are low, as are the levels of exports classified as hi-tech.

KEY INDICATORS — Spain

	Unit	2006	2007	2008	2009	2010
Population	m	44.07	44.87	*45.62	*45.83	*46.07
Gross domestic product (GDP)	US$bn	1,231.73	1,438.96	1,602.00	1,464.00	1,409.90
GDP per capita	US$	27,950	32,067	35,377	31,946	30,639
GDP real growth	%	3.9	3.8	0.9	-3.6	-0.1
Inflation	%	3.6	2.8	4.1	-0.3	2.0
Unemployment	%	8.5	8.3	11.3	18.0	20.1
Coal output	mtoe	6.1	20.1	5.5	4.1	3.3
Exports (fob) (goods)	US$m	220,774.0	256,682.0	285,896.0	223,981.0	252,974.0
Imports (fob) (goods)	US$m	325,444.0	380,198.0	415,532.0	286,813.0	315,323.0
Balance of trade	US$m	-104,670.0	-123,516.0	-129,636.0	-62,833.0	-62,350.0
Current account	US$m	-106,399.0	-145,275.0	-153,665.0	-80,375.0	-64,342.0
Total reserves minus gold	US$m	10,822.0	11,480.0	12,414.0	18,205.0	19,146.0
Foreign exchange	US$m	10,088.0	10,792.0	11,540.0	12,787.0	13,306.0
Exchange rate	per US$	0.75	0.69	0.68	0.78	0.76

* estimated figure

Deficit agreement?

As rumours abounded about the health of the Spanish economy and government finances, the leaders of Spain's ruling PSOE and the opposition (conservative) Partido Popular (PP) (Popular Party) agreed in late August 2011 to amend the Constitution to set a cap on the public deficit based on a commitment to limit spending. The new legislation, to be adopted by the end of June 2012 requires central government budgetary deficits to be contained at 0.26 per cent of GDP, and regional budget deficits to be limited to 0.14 per cent, resulting in a notional limit of 0.40 per cent deficit limit agreement. Both Brussels and the Bank of Spain had warned of the specific risk which the state of regional and local finances posed to the Spanish economy. The threat came not just from the size of potential debts, but also from the opacity that had traditionally surrounded the question. These deficit limits can be revised at three-yearly intervals with effect from 2015. A key factor in announcing the reform was the support of the PP. The possibility of a joint announcement was expected to help Spain manoeuvre the difficult period between the end of the summer holiday period and the elections, which had been brought forward from 2012 to November 2011.

The word 'notional' was used advisedly. Opposition to the proposed legislation had come from many quarters. In pole position were the Catalan and Basque nationalist parties, members of which expressed serious reservations, not to mention open opposition to the plan to include budgetary limits in the Constitution. The amendment, if approved, will be the biggest constitutional change in the document's history. The ruling Socialist party was divided over the issue, but it was thought that the party's candidate in the November 2011 elections was less than enthusiastic. With little more than two months to go before voting day, it seemed that the outgoing prime minister, José Luis Rodríguez Zapatero, had not secured the backing of his party's elders, not to mention his successor.

The government's hope was that the proposed constitutional amendment would send a signal to the international financial markets that the government was serious in its efforts to address the deficit problem. Anything that suggested the government was in fact divided over the issue was likely to have the opposite effect. In late August 2011 it seemed that the Spanish government and the opposition urgently needed to explain their thinking to the electorate as well as to their national and regional political supporters. Press reports following the initial announcement of the Constitutional reforms suggested that Prime Minister Zapatero was having second thoughts on the scope of the changes, and considering instead the introduction of a clause on budget stability but leaving the actual amount proscribed until after the November elections. It seemed, however, that the need to impress and contain the international financial markets prevailed.

There goes summer

Following the summer of 2011, Spain's ministers also needed to do a bit of explaining. In the second quarter of 2011 1,771 Spanish companies were forced to call creditors' meetings – over 20 per working day. The figure represented a 16.5 per cent increase over the previous year according to the National Statistics Institute (INE). Not that the previous quarter's figures had been much better: in those three months 1,803 companies had declared themselves bankrupt. Many of these companies were active in the construction industry, but they also generated subsidiary business – plumbing, electrical installations and real estate agents. The first seven years of the century had been a boom period for the construction sector, but after 2008 debt replaced prosperity, decline replaced growth, bankruptcy replaced payments. In many cases delayed payments were almost as much a problem as non-payments; this was especially the case with payments from government departments and agencies. The president of the Federation of the Self-Employed Workers' Associations estimated that its membership was owed as much as €13.3 billion (US$17.5 billion). The crisis has lead to a culture of austerity, forced upon many small businesses and traders by the obligation to pay their quarterly value added tax bills on time, even if they have not yet collected on those invoices. One tax accountant estimated that this meant that small businesses had advanced some €1.8 billion (US$2.4 billion) to an 'unappreciative' government. But any hopes that the summer would see the economy boosted by increased tourist arrivals were dashed by indications that the economic decline had in fact accelerated in August 2011. Opinion polls showed that business leaders were less confident than had been the case in July.

If Spanish ministers needed to do some explaining, so did some of its politicians. Revelations made on the parliamentary website (causing it to crash) showed that one deputy owned no less than 22 properties, and that a further eight were euro-millionaires before any property holdings were taken into account. One of the wealthiest members of parliament was the PP Javier Gómez Darmedaril, the owner of the 22 apartments and houses according to his 2010 tax return. Another Senator, José Luis Barreiro, owned 17 properties including a hotel in the Canary Islands. Mr Zapatero came out of the exposé rather well, having a joint bank account with his wife of €34,925 (US$45,950) and pension savings totalling €3,463 (US$4,560). In contrast, the leader of the PP, Mariano Rajoy, had bank and share deposits of almost €600,000 (US$789,500) as well as properties in Madrid, Galicia and the Canary Islands. Both these leaders were outclassed by the leader designate of the PSOE, Alfredo Pérez Rubalcaba, who reported having €1 million (US$1.3 million) in the bank, a Madrid apartment and – no debts. The wealthiest politician was the ex-minister, Mercedes Cabrera with more than €6 million (US$7.9 million) in investments held jointly with her husband – a financial analyst.

Elections

At the end of July 2011 Prime Minister Zapatero decided that enough was enough. His popularity ratings were lower than ever and the economy teetered on the brink of default. Mr Zapatero opted out by calling a general election to take place on 20 November 2011. If the game was up for Mr Zapatero as prime minister, the same was the case for his anointed successor, Alfredo Pérez Rubalcaba, who opinion polls suggested had no chance of keeping the discredited PSOE in power. Barring an unprecedented political surprise, the opposition PP lead by the uncharismatic Mariano Rajoy looked certain to win. The uncertainty lay in the size of the victory – at the beginning of August 2011 the PSOE seemed to be cutting back the PP's poll lead. This suggested that although the PP looked set to win, it might not secure an outright victory. The prospect of a minority government, forced to seek accommodations with its prospective coalition partners sent shivers down the backs, not only of the PP, but more critically down the backs of the international financial markets. Mr Rajoy had taken over the leadership of his party from former prime minister José María Aznar, whose inept handling of the 2004 Madrid terrorist attacks had cost his party what had looked to be a certain election victory.

The end of the Zapatero era was disappointing for many Spaniards, not least those who had once welcomed his arrival on the political scene. The August 2011 proposal for constitutional reform was seen by many as a public relations ploy, lacking substance and legitimacy. Mr Zapatero had become a Micawberish figure, hoping that things will turn out for the best when reality dictates otherwise. The constitutional reform itself was seen as bereft of teeth. The new legislation would set a limit to Spain's deficit, but not to its spending. The exact figure would be set by a new 'organic' law, which may be modified from time to time. The law's objective – the reduction of the deficit to manageable proportions – might not be reached until 2020, and now sanctions existed to thwart those who chose not to obey it. Critics – from both government and opposition – considered that the legislation was likely to increase the malaise of Spanish citizens, adversely affect the PSOE's electoral expectations as well as depicting the PSOE in a subservient role in government and – critically – open up new budget battles with Spain's regional governments. Worryingly, the swift adoption of the constitutional reforms had taken place without any public consultation or the involvement of Spain's minority parties.

Mr Rajoy's big promise was that of economic reform. But quite how his vaunted 'austerity without pain' was to be achieved without inflicting further pain on an already battered electorate, remained a mystery.

Following the local and regional elections of May 2011, when the PP trounced the PSOE, the PP controlled 11 of Spain's 17 autonomous governments. The structure of Spanish government, with extensive economic decision-making devolved to regional governments lies at the heart of many of the central government's economic problems. The outgoing finance minister, Elena Salgado, sought to limit regional budget deficits to 1.3 per cent of GDP in 2011. Ms Salgado's efforts to persuade local authorities to return funds advanced on false premises – or at least based on false forecasts – failed miserably. In their place, the finance minister came up with a muddled scheme whereby the Madrid government would lend (on soft terms) local governments half the money due to be repaid.

Some local governments simply chose to ignore Ms Salgado's interdictions. This was the case in Catalonia, where flouting the Madrid dictat is something of a national sport. Catalonia's minority nationalist government had established a budget deficit of 2.7 per cent of GDP, double the Salgado limit. If a PP government is to achieve the planned deficit reduction from the 6.00 per cent of GDP forecast for 2011 to 4.4 per cent in 2012, controlling Spain's wayward regions will be an essential component.

Convivencia

Following the 2004 Madrid bombings, the Zapatero government has found itself in something of a muddle as to what to do about its Muslim population, which is estimated to number around one million. Since the *reconquista* of 1492 when Spain's Muslim and Jewish populations were summarily deported, Spaniards have not had to worry much about co-habiting with 'foreign' religious groupings. Although Spain's Muslim community is small in comparison to those of some other west European countries, the proximity of Morocco and other predominantly Muslim countries makes it a very real issue. The realisation that Spain's Muslims constitute a real religious grouping is not easy for all Spaniards to accept. Least of all in those areas where unemployment is high. Under the aegis of the 1992 Foundation for Co-existence, which brought together Islamic, Jewish and Protestant groupings, the Zapatero administration has struggled to find a way of reconciling the ambitions and aspirations of its Muslim population with the distrust and religious opposition felt by a large part of the population. Mr Zapatero has referred to Spain's 'alliance of civilisations', but many suspect that this is part of a growing desire among the Socialist government to be all things to all men.

Risk assessment

Economy	Poor
Politics	Fair
Regional stability	Good

COUNTRY PROFILE

Historical profile

1492 Spain began colonising much of the Americas, beginning with Hispaniola (Haiti and the Dominican Republic), following Christopher Columbus' landings in the region.
1556 Spain took control of Melilla in Morocco.
1560s Spain colonised the Philippines.
1668 Spain took control of Ceuta in Morocco.
1702–14 The major European powers fought to install a new monarchy in Spain in the War of the Spanish Succession, following the death of Charles II in 1700. France eventually installed the grandson of Louis XIV, Philip of Anjou, as the King of Spain.
1778 Spain took control of Fernando Pó (Bioko, now part of Equatorial Guinea).
1808–13 The Spanish fought against French rule in the War of Independence.
1868 The army revolted against the Spanish monarchy. A military government, led by General Juan Prim, took power. Prim offered the Spanish crown to the son of Italian king Victor Emmanuel II, Amadeo of Savoy.
1873 Prim was assassinated. Amadeo of Savoy left Spain after failing to get installed as the new king. The remnants of the government announced the creation of the First Spanish Republic.
1874 Attempts to introduce constitutional and political reforms to the Republic failed and the monarchy was restored.
1884 Spain took control of the Spanish Sahara (now Western Sahara); it became a province of Spain in 1934.
1885 Spain established the colony of Spanish Guinea in Central Africa, comprising Río Muni and Fernando Pó.
1898 Spain lost control of Cuba, Guam, the Philippines and Puerto Rico, after being defeated in Cuba by the US.
1912 Spain and France partitioned Morocco into protectorates. Spain established the Spanish Morocco protectorate.
1923 The war in Morocco and an economic recession resulted to an authoritarian government in Spain, led by General Miguel Primo de Rivera.
1926 The Spanish and French defeated the Moroccans, bringing the war to an end.
1930 After failing with economic and political reforms, Primo de Rivera resigned from government
1931 Republican parties won the municipal elections, which led the Spanish King, Alfonso XIII, to abdicate. The Second Republic was declared.
1936–39 Civil war broke out when the democratically elected Republican government was attacked in an attempted *coup d'état*. The Nationalist alliance composed of monarchists, right-wing parties and the army, led by Francisco Franco y Bahamonde, fought to take control of Spain. Fascist Germany and Italy, ignoring arms embargoes, supported Franco's forces with men and materials. The government, denied legitimate arms from other European sources, gained the backing of the Soviet Union and welcomed over 56,000 overseas volunteers to fight in the International Brigades.
1939 Nationalist forces won the Civil War. General Franco became Head of State, established a dictatorship, restricted individual liberties and severely repressed all challenges to his power.
1955 An isolated Spain was allowed to join the UN.
1956 Spain granted Morocco independence, but retained control of the Ceuta and Melilla enclaves in northern Morocco.
1958 Spain handed the Tarfaya enclave in West Africa over to Morocco.
1959 The Euskadi ta Azkatasuna (ETA) (Homeland and Freedom) group was formed with the aim of creating an independent Basque region.
1968 Spanish Guinea in West Africa gained independence and was renamed Equatorial Guinea.
1969 Spain withdrew from the Sidi Ifni enclave in West Africa, handing it over to Morocco.
1973 Prime Minister Admiral Luis Carrero Blanco was assassinated by the terriorist group, Euskadi Ta Askatasuna (ETA)

(Basque Homeland and Freedom), after the government had executed a number of Basque militants.
1975 General Franco died. Juan Carlos, grandson of the last King, Alfonso XIII, was crowned King Juan Carlos I and became Head of State. Spain withdrew from Western Sahara.
1977 Restrictions on political activity were lifted and free parliamentary elections were held. The Union de Centro Democrático (UCD) (Union of the Democratic Centre) coalition, led by Adolfo Sáurez González, won.
1978 A new constitution confirmed Spain as a parliamentary monarchy with freedom for political parties and enshrined the 'indissoluble unity of the Spanish nation'. It also recognised the right to autonomy of its 'nationalities and regions'.
1980s Referenda on regional autonomy in the Basque region and Catalonia began the process of devolution. Spain was divided into 17 provinces, each with a president and parliament, plus the two self-governing enclaves on the north African coast – Ceuta and Melilla.
1981 The paramilitary *Guardia Civil* (Civil Guard) attempted a *coup d'état*, holding members of the cabinet and parliament hostage. The coup was aborted when King Carlos demanded that the military must remain loyal to the crown and the constitution.
1982 The Partido Socialista Obrero Español (PSOE) (Spanish Socialist Workers' Party), under Felipe González, won the general election. Morocco laid claim to Ceuta, Melilla and the Canary Islands.
1983 A secret death squad known as the Grupo Antiterrorista de Liberacion (GAL) (Anti-Terrorist Group) was set up funded by the Interior Ministry in order to combat ETA. Between 1983 and 1987, 28 people were murdered by the GAL in what became known as Spain's 'dirty war'. Several of those killed later turned out to have no connection with ETA and revelations surrounding the death squads' activities later contributed to the downfall of the PSOE government.
1986 Spain joined the EU.
1986–96 The PSOE won the 1986, 1990 and 1993 parliamentary elections and Felipe González served four terms as prime minister.
1995 José María Aznar, leader of the opposition Partido Popular (PP) (Popular Party) survived an assassination attempt by ETA.
1996 Aznar became prime minister of a PP minority government.
1998 ETA announced a unilateral ceasefire. It was blamed for more than 800 deaths since its campaign of terror began in 1968.
2000 ETA called off its ceasefire. The PP won parliamentary elections.
2001 A new round of talks began between Britain and Spain on the future of Gibraltar.
2002 Euro currency replaced the peseta. An international incident occurred when 12 Moroccan soldiers landed on the disputed tiny uninhabited *Isla del Perejil* (Parsley Island), close to the Spanish-controlled Ceuta enclave in Morocco. Spain re-occupied the island, to which Morocco lays claim and calls *Leila*.
2003 The Batasuna (Unity) party (previously the Herribatasuna party), believed to be the political organisation representing ETA, was banned. Government support for the US-lead coalition invasion of Iraq was opposed by an estimated 85 per cent of the population, causing a further deterioration in support for the PP.
2004 ETA announced a cease-fire. Ten co-ordinated bombs exploded on four commuter trains in Madrid, during the morning rush hour, killing 191 people and injuring over 1,800. ETA denied responsibility; a gang of extremist Islamists, who later committed suicide in a bomb blast during a police raid, were identified as the culprits. The Madrid atrocity had an immediate effect on the electorate, who gave a victory to the opposition party, PSOE, in the general elections. José Luis Rodríguez Zapatero (PSOE) was sworn in as prime minister.
2005 In Basque regional elections the moderate nationalist ruling party lost ground to the Socialists but retained office. At least 250,000 people marched in Madrid to protest against the government's intention to negotiate with ETA. Spain reinforced fences protecting Ceuta and Melilla, its enclaves in North Africa, after hundreds of would-be immigrants attempted to storm the territories. Spain launched an investigation into allegations that CIA planes made secret stopovers on Spanish territory for purposes of extraordinary rendition, whereby foreign suspects were sent to another country for interrogation under less humane conditions.
2006 Spain agreed to write off most of the debt owed to it by Bolivia. ETA announced a complete cease-fire. In a local referendum residents of Catalonia voted by 73.9 per cent in favour of greater regional autonomy and self-government; plans are expected to include the right to spend tax revenues and to have more control over airports and immigration. The outcome prompted other regions, such as Galicia, Valancia, the Balearic Islands and Andalusia to push for greater autonomy. ETA exploded a car bomb in a Madrid airport car park, killing two people and ending a nine-month cease-fire. However ETA also claimed that its cease-fire was still in effect. Over 31,000 African migrants (six times the numbers arriving in 2005), lacking work permits, made the hazardous ocean journey to the Canary Islands in an attempt to enter the EU for work and a better life.
2007 ETA called off its 15-month cease-fire. Spanish police arrested 23 senior members of Batasuna. Of the 28 defendants on trial for the 2004 Madrid train bombings three were found guilty and sentenced to thousands of years in prison, while seven were acquitted, including the alleged mastermind.
2008 In the general election the ruling PSOE won 169 seats, short of the 176 needed for an outright parliamentary majority. The opposition PP won 154 seats. The re-election of José Zapatero as prime minister was not a foregone conclusion. In the first round of voting in the Congress of Deputies, with a majority of 176 votes required, he won only 168 with 158 against and 23 abstentions. In the second round, when only a simple majority was required, he won with 169 votes. Zapatero took office and named a new cabinet with a majority of women members. The senate voted overwhelmingly to adopt the European Union's Lisbon Treaty. Once King Juan Carlos signed the treaty, Spain became the 23rd EU state to ratify it.
2009 The economy officially entered recession; the unemployment rate reached 17.4 per cent.
2010 After six quarters of falling growth the economy grew by 0.1 per cent for the first three months of 2010; in the same week it was announced that the unemployment rate had reached 20 per cent. The Catalonia parliament voted by 68 to 55 to become the first mainland region in Spain to ban bullfighting, from January 2012. ETA announced a cease-fire on 5 September, but the Basque and Spanish central government dismissed the declaration as 'meaningless' as ETA had not renounced violence or its dissolution.
2011 A smoking ban in bars and restaurants came into effect on 2 January. In February Spain's number of unemployed was 4.7 million, some 20.5 per cent of the population. On 2 April, Prime Minister Zapatero announced that he would not seek a third term in parliamentary elections due in 2012. An earthquake, of magnitude 5.2 struck Lorca in south eastern Spain on 11 May, killing nine people and leaving over 3,000 people homeless. On 21 May, thousands of young unemployed, including many graduates, protested in Puerta del Sol in Madrid, angry at the government's economic policies that left so many of them unemployed (44.6 per cent of under 25-year olds). By July the protests had grown into a movement of disaffected called *El Indignado*

(The Indignant), which on 27 July began a 1,500km march to Brussels (headquarters of the EU) to complain about how the EU's financial markets had had a detrimental effect on Spain's economic stability and their future. On 29 July the prime minister called for elections on 20 November, four months earlier than expected, to 'project political and economic certainty'. A visit by the Pope in August to celebrate mass at the end of World Youth Day was marred by protests against the cost of the visit, and by a violent rain squall that blew off the Pope's skull cap. The last bullfight in Catalonia was held on 25 September.

Political structure

Constitution

The constitution dates from the advent of democracy in 1978. Most laws are debated and passed in Congress first, and then in the Senate, the upper house, which can send back amended bills. In case of emergency, the government may issue decrees. They are called Decree Laws if they require ratification by parliament. All laws require the king's ratification and come into force when published in the Official Bulletin.

There are 17 *comunidades autónomas* (autonomous regions): Andalucia, Aragón, Asturias, Baleares (Balearic Islands), Canarias (Canary Islands), Cantabria, Castilla-La Mancha, Castilla y León, Cataluñya, Comunidad Valencian, Extremadura, Galicia, La Rioja, Madrid, Murcia, Navarra, País Vasco (Basque country). Spain also has sovereignty of five communities on and off the coast of Morocco: the coastal ports of Ceuta and Melilla are administered as autonomous regions; the islands of Chafarinas, Peñon de Alhucemas and Peñon de Velez de la Gomera are under direct Spanish administration.

Autonomous regions have regional parliaments and governments with varying degrees of powers on local affairs. Three regions with a tradition of autonomy and their own language – the Basque country (Euskadi), Cataluñya and Galicia – have these wider powers. The Basque government, for example, raises its own taxes. There is universal suffrage from age 18.

Form of state

Federal parliamentary democratic monarchy

The executive

The president of the government (prime minister) appoints the cabinet and has executive power. He is appointed by the head of state and his appointment must be ratified by the national legislature.

National legislature

The bicameral Las Cortes Generales (The General Courts) is composed of the Congreso de los Diputados (Congress of Deputies) (lower house) with 350 members, elected by popular vote on block lists by proportional representation in provincial constituencies, who serve for four-year terms.

In the Senado de España (Senate of Spain) (upper house) has 259-members in total, of which 208 are directly elected and 51 are appointed by regional legislatures. Members serve for four-year terms; appointed members may be recalled by their respective legislatures at any time. Parties need to gain at least 3 per cent of the vote to gain representation in either house.

Legal system

The Spanish legal system is based on civil law. The Supreme Court is at the summit of the judiciary. There are also 16 Division High Courts, 50 Provincial High Courts and, below these, Courts of First Instance, District Courts, Municipal and Peace Courts. Spain does not accept compulsory jurisdiction by the International Court of Justice (ICJ).

Last elections

9 March 2008 (parliamentary)

Results: Parliamentary: PSOE won 43.64 per cent of the vote (169 seats out of 350); PP, 39.94 per cent (154); Izquierda Unida (UL) (United Left) 3.8 per cent (two), Convergència i Unió (CiU) (Convergence and Union) (coalition of two Catalán parties) 3.3 per cent (10), Esquerra Republicana de Cataluyna (ERC) (Catalan Republican Left) 1.17 per cent (three), Eusko Alberdi Jeltzalea-Partido Nacionalista Vasco (EAJ-PNV) (Basque Nationalist Party) 1.2 per cent (six); Coalición Canaria (CC) (Canary Island Coalition) 0.65 per cent (two); Bloque Nacionalista Galego (BNG) 0.82 per cent (two); Unión, Progreso y Democracia (UPD) (Union, Progress and Democracy) 1.2 per cent (one); Nafarroa Bai (NaBai) (Navarre Yes) 0.25 per cent (one). Senate: PP won 101 seats (out of 208) plus 23 appointed, PSOE 89 plus 19, Entesa Catalana de Progrés (coalition of four parties from Catalonia) 12 plus four, CiU four, plus three, EAJ-PNV two, plus two.

Next elections

20 November 2011 (parliamentary)

Political parties

Ruling party

Partido Socialista Obrero Español (PSOE) (Spanish Socialist Workers' Party) (since 2004; re-elected 9 Mar 2008)

Main opposition party

Partido Popular (PP) (Popular Party)

Population

46.07 million (2010)*

Last census: November 2001: 40,847,371 (including offshore territories)

Population density: 79 inhabitants per square km. Urban population: 78 per cent (1995–2001).

Annual growth rate: 0.7 per cent 1994–2004 (WHO 2006)

Ethnic make-up

In addition to Spaniards, there are several minor groups, including Gypsies, Portuguese, Latin Americans and North Africans.

Religions

Roman Catholic (94 per cent), Islam, Protestant and Jewish.

Education

Primary schooling begins at the age of six and lasts for six years. Secondary schooling lasts until aged 16 (both of which are provided free). Final exams allow progression to higher secondary schools which teach either academic or vocational programmes. Teaching may be carried out in Spanish, Catalan, Basque, or Galician.

Private schools are responsible for the education of more than 30 per cent of children.

Higher education is only possible after successfully sitting an entrance exam. There are some 20 state universities, four polytechnics, two independent universities and eight technical universities. The development of alternative forms of higher education have made access to established universities more selective. It has also been proposed that the present five-year university degree courses be reduced to three years.

Public expenditure on education typically amounts to 5 per cent of annual gross national income.

Literacy rate: 97.9 per cent, adult rates (2003)

Compulsory years: Six to 16

Enrolment rate: 109 per cent, gross primary enrolment of relevant age group (including repeaters); 120 per cent, gross secondary enrolment (World Bank).

Pupils per teacher: 15 in primary schools

Health

As Spain's economy has grown, spending on healthcare has risen, reaching 7.5 per cent of GDP, spending just below the Organisation for Economic Co-operation and Development (OECD) average of 7.7 per cent on medical goods and services. Most of this expenditure is in the form of state funding at 71.4 per cent. Efforts are under way to cut the state's pharmaceutical bill, representing 20 per cent of total public health spending. Pre-paid healthcare plans amount to 14.1 per cent of the 28.6 per cent of GDP spent privately on health costs.

The health sector, under the authority of INSALUD, the National Institute of Health, includes hospitals, community health centres and emergency services. The social security health scheme covers all insured persons and their dependants.

HIV/Aids

HIV prevalence: 0.7 per cent aged 15–49 in 2003 (World Bank)

Life expectancy: 80 years, 2004 (WHO 2006)

Fertility rate/Maternal mortality rate: 1.3 births per woman, 2004 (WHO 2006)

Birth rate/Death rate: 10 births per 1,000 population; 9.5 deaths per 1,000 population (2003).

Child (under 5 years) mortality rate (per 1,000): 4.0 per 1,000 live births (World Bank)

Head of population per physician: 3.30 physicians per 1,000 people, 2003 (WHO 2006)

Welfare

The National Institute of Social Security oversees a national insurance scheme, which is compulsory for all employed and self-employed workers. It provides a range of benefits including those for sickness, maternity, accident insurance, retirement pensions and unemployment benefits. Contributions are paid by employees, employers and the state. The employed are classified in a series of professional and labour categories for the purpose of determining social security taxes. Each category has maximum and minimum contribution bases which are revised annually. The state pays retirement pensions from the age of 65 for men and women. Spain offers a special system of unemployment protection for casual workers in agriculture. The Rural Employment Plan combines employment policy measures and social welfare benefits. The benefit is granted to workers who have paid contributions under the Agricultural Social Security Scheme and is equivalent to 75 per cent of the national minimum wage payable for a maximum period of 180 days.

Main cities

Madrid (capital, estimated population 2.9 million in 2005), Barcelona (capital of Catalonia) (1.5 million), Valencia (741,100), Seville (685,393), Zaragoza (621,164), Málaga (525,662), Bilbao (344,236), Murcia (384,429), Córdoba (309,882), Las Palmas (Majorca) (354,863), Las Palmas (Grand Canary) (354,863).

Languages spoken

Castilian Spanish is the principal language; Catalán, Galician, Euskera (Basque), Aragonese and Asturian are also spoken. English and French are spoken in most business circles.

Official language/s

Castilian Spanish, Catalan (in Catalonia including the Balearics), Basque (in the Basque provinces), Valencian (Province of Valencia), Galician (Galicia).

Media

The constitution enshrines the right to free expression of thoughts, ideas and opinions.

Press

The printed media market is mature with a wide variety of respected titles backed up by a plethora of specialist publications.

The media is largely free, although the government has closed down two Basque newspapers, *Egin*, in 1998 and *Euskaldunon Egunkari* in 2003, accusing them of being linked with the terrorist organisation ETA.

Concerns have been raised that media outlets has been unduly influenced by political pressure.

Ownership is largely concentrated in the control of a few large media groups; foreign investment has been redirected to focus on periodicals.

Dailies: There are over 100 newspapers published daily, although most have circulations of less than 100,000. The major dailies are published in Madrid but other cities have their own dailies, particularly in Catalonia and the Basque region. Most publish in Spanish or in regional languages; some are bilingual. Free-issue newspapers account for around 51 per cent of the market.

In Spanish, with the largest circulation *El País* (www.elpais.com) is socialist in character in a tabloid format and has regional and international editions, *ABC* (www.abc.es) is a centre-right paper, *El Mundo* (www.elmundo.es) is a conservative publication. Other newspapers with smaller circulations, from Barcelona *La Vanguardia* (www.lavanguardia.es) and *El Periodico de Catalunya* (www.elperiodico.com) with articles in Catalan; from Bilbao *El Correo* (www.elcorreodigital.com) and *El Diario Montanes* (www.eldiariomontanes.es); from Andalucia *Diario de Cadiz* (www.diariodecadiz.es),*Cordoba* (www.diariocordoba.com) and *Metro* (www.diariometro.es) Seville; from the Balearic Islands *Diario de Ibiza* (www.diariodeibiza.es) and *Mallorca Confidencial* (www.mallorcaconfidencial.com); from Canary Islands *La Provincia* (www.laprovincia.es) and *El Dia* (www.eldia.es); from La Coruna *Xornal* (www.xornal.com) with articles in Galacian; from Andoain *Berria* (www.berria.info) in Basque.

English, French and Germany newspapers are published in areas with large expatriate communities and tourist areas.

Weeklies: There are several general and special interest magazines and news magazines such as *Cambio 16*, *Sábado Gráfico* and *El Tiempo* (www.tiempodehoy.com). *El Mundo* has a Sunday edition called *La Revista*. In the Canary Islands *Canarias 7* reports news items, *Metropolitan* from Barcelona. *Ragazza* (www.ragazza.orange.es) *Inerviú* (www.interviu.es) and *Diez Minutos* (www.diezminutos.orange.es) are tabloid magazines.

Business: In Spanish, *Cinco Días* (www.cincodias.com), *Expansión* (www.expansion.com), *La Gaceta de los Negocios* (www.negocios.com/gaceta), *Agenda de la Empresa Andaluza* (www.agendaempresa.com), *Vigo Empresa* (www.puertodevigo.com), *El Economista* (www.eleconomista.es), *El Mundo Financiero* (www.elmundofinanciero.com) and *Negocio* (www.neg-ocio.com). Weekly financial publications in Spanish include *Su Dinero*, *Levamte-El Mercantil Valencia* (www.levante-emv.com) from Valencia and *Actualidad Económic* (www.actualidad-economica.com) from Madrid.

Periodicals: A number of specialist magazine exist including *Planeta Humano* and *Qué*, bi-monthly covering people and current affairs.

Broadcasting

National public radio and television services are provided by Radiotelevisión Española (RTVE) (www.rne.es), which is funded by state subsidies and advertising.

Radio: The public broadcaster Radio Nacional de España (RNE) (www.rne.es), provides four national services. There are several commercial networks, the largest of which is Cadena SER (www.cadenaser.com) with over 50 regional stations.

There are over 100 radio stations, which have a presence in every region, including overseas territories, providing services over the internet.

Television: Televisión Española (TVE) (www.rtve.es) broadcasts several channels, from popular local programmes such as long-running dramas to international imported shows and special interest programmes. There are another three private terrestrial channels and six regional public broadcasters with 10 channels between them, some in Catalan and Basque. Digital and satellite TV networks have expanded rapidly and the government has plans to discontinue free-to-air analogue signals by 2010. National commercial channels include Tele Cinco (www.telecinco.es), Antena 3 (www.antena3tv.com) and Cuatro (www.cuatro.com).

Advertising

All usual media are available although TV and public hoardings tend to be most popular method, although radio, newspaper and cinema advertising is also widespread.

News agencies

EFE (government-owned), Espronceda, 32. 28003 Madrid (tel: 346-7519; fax: 346-7173; internet: www.efe.com).
Colpisa (private) (www.colpisa.com).
Europa Press (private) (www.europapress.es with specific sections on regional news).

Economy

Spain has a mixed economy with large agricultural and industrial sectors, as well as important tourism and banking sectors. It is the world's largest olive oil producer, from 2.4 million hectares of olive groves producing almost one million tonnes in 2008–09, and a major contributor to the European Union's agricultural production of fruit, vegetables and wine; it also has Europe's largest fishing fleet, which operates in all oceans. It has become an important automotive manufacturer and its tourism industry is one of the most highly developed in Europe.

GDP growth in 2007 was 3.6 per cent which fell to 0.9 per cent in 2008. The economic situation worsened as the global economic crisis struck Spain hard and the International Monetary Fund (IMF), predicted that Spain would slipped into recession in 2009 with growth at -3.6 per cent, later revised downward to -4.0 per cent by July 2009. The fundamental problem for the economy was a huge trade deficit of about US$48 billion in 2008, caused in large part by Spain's requirement to import petroleum products (at a time of record high prices), which caused the inflation rate to rise sharply to 5 per cent. The second problem was a property market that had been fuelled by unsustainable loans and that collapsed so that by January 2009 deflation became a reality at -0.8 per cent and Spain slipped into recession in February. The number of registered unemployed in January 2009 jumped to a record 3.3 million, with a national monthly rate of 6.0 per cent.

Spain's economy crept out of recession in the first quarter of 2010, when GDP grew by 0.1 per cent, ending six consecutive quarters of contraction. However, 20 per cent of workers were unemployed in April, the highest figure since 1997.

The banking sector during the global economic crisis did not experience the trauma suffered in other developed countries as longstanding financial rules required high levels of capitalisation, rules less in force elsewhere. Spain's largest institution, Banco Santander, took the opportunity to expand by buying up weaker banks in the Europe and South America.

In April 2010 the economy of Greece faced international scrutiny and censure, as it was unable to service its debts so that a rescue package had to be provided by the Central European Bank and the IMF. Speculation followed as to whether Spain was also in a weakened state due to its widening budget deficit. Despite denials that its public debt was only 55 per cent of GDP and 20 points below the European average, the bond markets suffered a big fall as investors adopted a less tolerant attitude. Two international credit rating agencies, Standard and Poor's and Fitch, cut Spain's rating from AAA to AA+ in April and May 2010, due to the country's weaker GDP growth prospects and resulted in an increase the cost of Spain's foreign borrowing.

External trade

As a member of the European Union, Spain operates within a community-wide free trade area, with tariffs set as a whole. Internationally, the EU has free trade agreements with a number of nations and trading blocs worldwide.

While agriculture provides less than 4 per cent of GDP, Spain never-the-less produces Europe's largest supply of citrus and strawberries and is the world's leading olive oil produce, the third largest wine producer and has Europe's largest fishing fleet. Manufacturing includes textiles, food processing, naval engineering, vehicle assembly and machinery; new technology includes information technology and telecommunications.

Exports account for around 55 per cent of GDP, while tourism (Spain is a worldwide top tourist destination) had provided most foreign earnings, despite the strength of the euro which reduced tourist visitor numbers.

Imports

Main imports include machinery and equipment, petroleum and natural gas, chemicals, semi-finished goods, foodstuffs, consumer goods, and medical instruments.

Main sources: Germany (typically 15 per cent of total), France (12 per cent), Italy (9 per cent).

Exports

Commodity exports include machinery, vehicles, pharmaceuticals, medicines, consumer goods and agricultural products: olive oil and wine.

Main destinations: France (typically 19 per cent of total), Germany (15 per cent), Italy (10 per cent).

Agriculture

Farming

Fundamental reform to the Common Agricultural Policy (CAP) was introduced throughout most of the EU in 2005. The subsidies paid on farm output, which tended to benefit large farms and encourage overproduction, were replaced by single farm payments not conditional on production. This is expected to reward farms that maintain a healthy environment, food safety and animal welfare standards. The changes are also intended to encourage market conscious production and cut the cost of CAP to the EU taxpayer.

Spain is the world's largest producer of olive oil: the industry has been modernising, although olive groves, mainly located in Andalucia, typically suffer periodic drought and work is usually undertaken by low paid migrant workers. The revised CAP should benefit the region by limiting unsustainable growth.

Spain is now the third-largest wine producer in Europe after France and Italy, with a growing tendency towards the quality end of the wine market. EU restrictions limit the amount of land available for vineyards and, with domestic consumers developing a taste for wines of increased quality, the price of grapes and available vineyards has increased enormously. Newer regions are producing quality wines to rival those of the long established Rioja and *Penedes denominaciones*. Cava, the Spanish wine made using the champagne method, is gaining a global reputation for quality and value. Notable among these are Ribera de Duero in Castilla y Leon, where the legendary Vega Sicilia wines are produced, and the *Priorat denominaciones* in Catalonia.

Fishing

As the owner of the largest fishing fleet in the EU, Spain is also the largest consumer of seafood and seafood products in the EU. Spain's total fish catch continues to decline as a result of depleted stocks and lower limits on catches in both EU and non-EU waters. Spain's seafood trade is mainly conducted with other EU countries, Argentina, Morocco and Namibia.

Forestry

Forest and other wooded land accounts for about half the land area, with forest cover estimated at 14.3 million hectares (ha). Most of the forest is available for wood supply. The area of forest has been expanding strongly, at an annual average increase of 0.62 per cent per year. About 80 per cent of forest is privately owned, while the remaining area is mostly owned by municipalities. Forest and other wooded land accounts for 50 per cent of total land area. About 45 per cent of the forest is available for wood supply. The

main species are Scots and Aleppo pine, oak, beech, chestnut, poplars and eucalyptus.
Imported raw materials including eucalyptus pulpwood and hardwood logs are used for all primary forest products. Spain is a net importer of paper and sawnwood, although part of the pulp production is exported.

Industry and manufacturing
The industrial sector contributes approximately 34 per cent to GDP and employs over 29 per cent of the labour force. Since joining the EU, Spain's industry and manufacturing sectors have undergone modernisation and restructuring, assisted by large levels of foreign direct investment (FDI). The automotive, telecommunications and chemical industries dominate the sector.
Industrial production grew by 3.3 per cent year-on-year in August 2005 but fell to 0.5 per cent growth in September.

Tourism
The tourist industry has had a long and vital influence on Spain's GDP growth, beginning in the 1970s as mass tourism developed, offering cheap packaged beach holidays with virtually guaranteed sun.
The sector contributed around 18 per cent of GDP in the 1980s, but this fell as low as 14.5 per cent in 1993 as other sectors within the economy grew and new foreign markets began offering stiff competition. By 2003–05 travel and tourism constituted between 15–16.5 per cent of GDP, but as the global economic crisis struck and visitors from Europe, Spain's prime market, failed to travel the industry went into recession in 2007. In 2008 all sectors of the industry recorded a fall, including hotel occupation, flights and sea and rail passengers, the only exception was day-trip arrivals which showed a modest growth of 0.6 per cent. The industry fared even worse in 2009 as the recession deepened and all sections recorded negative growth. In the first quarter of 2009, 5.6 million foreign tourists visited Spain, which was a 16.3 per cent fall for the same period in 2008.
Spain's economic decline also affected domestic tourism, which added to the industry's malaise so that unemployment for the country in general included a sizable portion of jobs in travel and tourism.
The industry picked up in 2010, with total number of foreign visitors at 52.68 million; however this was only marginally better than the 52.5 million in 2009. Indications are that 2011 had positive growth as total visitor numbers picked up by 6.6 per cent. Nevertheless, the effect of years in decline has resulted in over capacity of hotel rooms, domestic airports and car rentals. The sector will have to streamline and reorganise its base to compete for business in a contracted market.

Mining
The mining sector contributes 1 per cent to GDP. Spain is the world's second-largest producer of natural stone, which accounts for 15 per cent of the total value of Spanish mining. Marble has become a particularly important source of foreign exchange earnings. Gold, silver and copper mining take place on a small scale. Spain also extracts lignite, iron ore, mercury, pyrites, zinc, lead, copper and tungsten. The traditional production of uranium ore in Spain ceased with the closure of Mina Fé in Salamanca.

Hydrocarbons
Total proven oil reserves were 150 million barrels in 2007; production is negligible The largest domestic production comes from the Casablanca complex, in the Mediterranean, which provides 5,600 barrels per day (bpd). Consumption was 1.6 million barrels per day (bpd) making Spain heavily dependent on imported oil, mainly from Mexico and Russia. Spain's multinational conglomerate, Repsol YPF, is a major international oil company, with operations in 29 countries, concerned in both upstream and downstream oil sectors, including exploration, production, transporting and refining oil, which is then traded on the global market. Repsol YPF also owns networks of petrol stations. Spain's total crude oil refining capacity stood at 1.27 million bpd in 2007. Oil consumption relative to that of natural gas has fallen steadily since the 1980s. Repsol YPF has five refineries which, in 2009, were about to be upgraded to meet EU-set standards for refined fuel.
Natural gas production ceased in 2007. Consumption was 35.1 billion cubic metres in 2007, all of which was supplied by imports, mainly through pipelines. Enagás was a former parastatal which was privatised in the 1990s, but still retains responsibility for the entire gas pipeline network; it also owns regasification plants and storage facilities. There are international natural gas pipelines; the first connection was from Larrau (France) to Calahorra in 1993 and later the Maghreb-Europe pipeline bringing Algeria gas, via Morocco, through Cadiz became operational in 1996. The Medgas, a parallel pipeline to the Maghreb-Europe, will increase supplies to European customers. Construction was completed in December 2008 and flows should begin at the end of 2009. Spain is the world's third largest consumer of liquefied natural gas (LNG), which is processed at five sites, which between them receive 11.1 per cent of the gas transported worldwide.
Coal production has fallen steadily, from 35.3 million tonnes per annum in 1997 to 24.8 million tonnes in 2007; consumption was 47.4 million tonnes in 2006. In 2002, the EU ordered Spain to lower its coal production by 65 per cent by 2010 and cease government subsidies by 2008. Environmental restrictions on Spain's largest indigenous energy source may leave its coal uncompetitive in the open market.

Energy
Total installed generating capacity was 71,270MW in 2006, producing 283 billion kilowatt hours. Around 20 per cent was provided by renewable energy, mostly wind generation. In January 2009 electricity by renewable sources had reached 34.8 per cent. In some regions of Spain 70 per cent of electricity needs are provided by renewables. Spain has a sophisticated energy mix including thermal (oil and natural gas), hydro, nuclear, solar (including the 11MW, 40 storey, 600 mirror solar tower in Andalusia), wind and biomass.
There are four major electricity companies operating as regional suppliers, although they have been allowed to market their products freely elsewhere from 2003. Endesa, is the largest energy company in Spain and is a subsidiary of the Italian energy company Enel, with over 10 million customers at home and the same number abroad. Red Eléctrica de España (REE) is responsible for most of the Spanish national grid and management and co-ordination of the international electricity flows. In 2004, Spain signed an agreement with Portugal to work towards integrating their respective electricity markets.

Financial markets
Stock exchange
Bolsas y Mercados Españoles (BME)

Banking and insurance
In June 2009 the government set up a US$12.7 billion bank fund, which any failing bank in Spain could call on for support through capital injections, mergers or restructuring. The new fund could eventually be subsidised by public finance up to US$103 billion.
Central bank
Banco de España; European Central Bank (ECB).
Main financial centre
Madrid

Time
Mainland – GMT plus one hour (daylight saving: late March–October, GMT plus two hours) = mainland
Canaries – GMT (daylight saving, GMT plus one hour)

Geography

Spain is situated in south-western Europe. It occupies most of the Iberian peninsula, sharing it with Portugal to the west. The country includes the Balearic Islands in the Mediterranean Sea (200km south-east of Barcelona), the Canary Islands in the Atlantic Ocean and two small enclaves in Morocco. Mainland Spain is bounded to the north by the Cantabrian Sea, the Pyrenees and France, to the east by the Mediterranean, and to the south by the Straits of Gibraltar and Morocco.

Mountains ranges, including the Pyrenees, run from the Atlantic in the north to the Mediterranean coast. Another band runs down the east to the Sierra Nevada in the south, which includes the largest mainland mountain Mulhacén at 3,482 metres (m). Land in the south is dry with many traditional olive groves. The flat central plateau (*meseta*) occupies much of the land around the capital, Madrid. The longest river, the Ebro, is 940km, beginning in the Cantabrian mountains of the north-east and flowing into the Mediterranean. The River Tagus runs for 716km through central Spain and 322km in Portugal.

The Canary Islands are rugged volcanic Atlantic Ocean outcrops. Of the 13 islands six are uninhabited. Pico de Teide, on Tenerife, at 3,718 metres is Spain's tallest mountain.

Hemisphere

Northern

Climate

Most of Spain has a Mediterranean climate with mild winters and hot summers, although the mountainous north is colder and wetter. Temperatures range from 40 degrees centigrade Celsius (C) to minus 15 degrees C.

Dress codes

Particular attention is paid to dress, although dress codes are not rigid. Most businessmen and male officials wear suits and ties during business hours.

Entry requirements

Passports

Are required by all non-EU visitors and must be valid for at least six months beyond the planned stay. EU visitors and nationals of Andorra, Liechtenstein, Malta, Monaco and Switzerland may use valid national ID cards.

Visa

Required by all; except nationals of EU and Schengen Accord signatory countries. Tourists from North America and Australasia may visit, visa-free, for up to 90 days. All other nationals, visiting for business purposes, should contact the nearest Spanish embassy for a visa application form. A Schengen visa application (offered in several languages) can be downloaded from http://europa.eu/abc/travel/ see 'documents you will need'.

Currency advice/regulations

The import of foreign and local currency is unlimited. Export of local currency is unlimited but amounts over €6,000 must be declared. Export of foreign currencies over the equivalent of €3,050 in bank notes and travellers cheques must be declared.

Travellers cheques are widely accepted.

Customs

Personal items are duty-free. There are no duties levied on alcohol and tobacco between EU member states, providing amounts imported are for personal consumption. The Canary Islands are not a member of the EU.

Health (for visitors)

Nationals of the European Economic Area (EEA) countries and Switzerland can access reduced cost and sometimes free medical treatment using a European Health Insurance Card (EHIC) while visiting the EEA. Exceptions include nationals of the 10 countries which joined the EU in 2004 whose EHIC is not valid in Switzerland. Applications for the EHIC should be made before travelling.

Mandatory precautions

None

Advisable precautions

Up-to-date tetanus and polio immunisations are recommended. Long-term visitors should consider hepatitis A immunisation. Tap water may not be safe to drink outside the major cities and visitors are advised to drink bottled mineral water.

Hotels

Hotels are classified from one- to five-star, plus a 'Grand De Luxe' category (pensions/hostels classified from one- to three-star). *Paradores* (national tourist inns) are also increasingly popular. Accommodation should be booked well in advance, especially during holiday season. NB: *Term Residencia* denotes establishments without dining-room facilities.

Credit cards

All major credit and charge cards are accepted. ATMs are widely available.

Public holidays (national)

Fixed dates

1 Jan (New Year's Day), 6 Jan (Epiphany), 1 May (Labour Day), 15 Aug (Assumption Day), 12 Oct (National Day), 1 Nov (All Saints' Day), 6 Dec (Constitution Day), 8 Dec (Immaculate Conception), 25 Dec (Christmas Day).

Variable dates

Good Friday (Mar/Apr).

Working hours

Executives rarely arrive in their offices before 0900. Many then go out for coffee, and again for a snack at 1200 to keep them going until a late lunch. Lunches, no earlier than 1400, and often preceded by a visit to a bar for an aperitivo, are abundant and lengthy. A business lunch, always accompanied by wine, coffee, brandy and cigars, can last from three to five hours. It is considered impolite to get down to business until after dessert. Although many go home for lunch and a brief siesta, an increasing number of companies in big cities are abolishing the long lunch break. In December 2005 the government officially abolished the *siesta* when a law was published decreeing that lunch breaks would be one hour only, thereby allowing civil servants to finish work at 6pm.

In the hot summer months, most ministries and many companies close down for the day at 1400 or 1500. In August, many businesses close down completely.

Banking

Mon–Fri: 0830–1400. In some autonomous regions larger bank branches may open later in the afternoon and on Saturday morning, between Apr–Sep.

Business

Usually open Mon–Fri: 0900–1400 and 1630–1930.

Government

Vary considerably from region to region and according to time of year. In Madrid: Mon–Fri: generally 0900–1330 and 1500–1800; except Jul and Aug, 0830–1430 (1400 on Fri) with only skeleton staff remaining during afternoon.

Shops

Mon–Sat: 0930–1330, 1700–2030; Department stores and malls Mon–Sat: 1000–2200.

Telecommunications

Mobile/cell phones

There are 3G and 900/1800 GSM services.

Electricity supply

220V AC with round, two-pin plugs.

Social customs/useful tips

A ban on smoking in public places was introduced on the 1 January 2006. It was extended to bars and restaurants from 2 January 2011.

Handshaking is the customary form of greeting. Although English is widely spoken, an effort to speak Spanish is appreciated. Business cards are frequently exchanged as a matter of courtesy.

Meals are taken later in Spain than in other European countries which means that people go to bed later and also generally go to work later. Dinner is after 2200 and people rarely go to bed before

2400. Leaving someone's home before 0100 can be taken as a sign of boredom. It is acceptable to telephone someone at home until 2400.
Spaniards generally use two surnames, the last being their mother's surname. When addressing someone, either personally or in correspondence, only the first of the surname is used. *Don* is a widely used title of respect, and is used in conversation with the christian name only.
The *tu* (more intimate second person singular) form is today used widely, even on first acquaintance.
Entry into the EU in 1986 has slowly changed customs as Spaniards are keen to be seen as Europeans. However, they remain very attached to an informal and relaxed way of life and enjoyment is an important part of life. Many cities and villages have their annual festivals which would not be complete without dance, songs, wine and a bullfight. Bullfighting remains popular despite a budding animal protection movement, and soccer remains by far the most popular sport.
Family and friendship ties are of major importance and often a source of mutual favours. Regional origins also command loyalties. Spaniards, even children of migrants to big cities, constantly refer to their home province. In Catalonia Catalan is very much, and very proudly, the *lingua franca*, and it helps at least to be able to greet people in Catalan. This is less the case in the Basque country, where fewer people speak Basque, and is not an issue either in Valencia or in Galicia, both of which have their own languages, but where Castilain Spanish is the *lingua franca* for day-to-day purposes.
A ban on clothing that might make identification difficult, such as the burqa, niqab, balaclavas, motorbike helmets and ski masks, is scheduled to come into effect in Barcelona's public installations in the second half of 2010.

Security
A chronic drug problem, coupled with persistent unemployment and frequent amnesties for petty criminals, has caused an increase in petty crime in big cities. Mugging has become frequent, and often violent, in tourist areas. Many insurance companies no longer cover the theft of car radios.

Getting there
Air
National airline: Iberia.
International airport/s: Madrid Barajas (MAD), 13km north-east of Madrid. Facilities include banks, restaurants, duty-free and car hire. There are buses, taxis and a railway service to the city centre.
Continental and regional fights arrive at Alicante (ALC), 12km south-west of city; Barcelona (BCN) 10km south-west of city; Bilbao (BIO), 9km from city; Málaga (AGP) 8km south-west of city; Santiago de Compostela (SCQ), 10km north-east of city; Seville (SVQ), 12km east of city, Valencia (VLC), 10km west of city. Also on Balearic Islands: Palma de Mallorca (PMI), 9km south-east of Palma; on Canary Islands: Gran Canaria (LPA), 19km south of Las Palmas; Tenerife TCI Sur Reina Sofia (TFS), 61km south-west of Santa Cruz de Tenerife.
Airport tax: None
Surface
Road: There are several good quality toll motorways connecting Spain to France and Portugal.
Rail: Services radiate from the Madrid hub and express services connect to the pan-European network, through France. There are several services connecting Portugal.
Water: The are regular ferry and shipping services from UK (Plymouth-Santander), France (Marseilles-Alicante) and Algeria (Algiers-Alicante).
Main port/s: Barcelona, Valencia, Alicante, Málaga, Algeciras, Cádiz, La Coruña, Bilbao, Vigo.

Getting about
National transport
Air: Frequent services from Madrid to all major urban centres are operated by Iberia.
Road: Roads are based on radial routes centred on Madrid. They are often very busy during the holiday season. Good roads connect all main towns. There is a network of over 150,000km, including 2,000km of motorways (usually toll) mostly confined to coastal regions. As an energy-saving measure, deduction in the motorway speed limit from 120kph to 110kph from 7 March 2011 was announced on 25 February by Deputy Prime Minister Alfredo Pérez Rubalcaba. The measure was reversed in late June 2011 after 'circumstances changed', reported Mr Pérez, and the country had saved Spain eur450 million (US$320 million). Spain imported some 9 per cent of Libya's oil before the revolt there began; Repsol, the Spanish oil company, was forced to shut down production.
Buses: There are regular bus and coach services between main towns.
Rail: There are approximately 14,410km of track, of which about 11,500km is operated by Red Nacional de Ferrocarriles Españoles (RENFE) (National Network of Spanish Railroads) and the rest (narrow gauge) by Ferrocarriles Españoles de Via Estrecha (FEVE). A high-speed link between Madrid and Barcelona, operated by RENFE, opened in February. The train will take just over two and a half hours over the 550Km (342 miles).
Water: Regular steamer and hydrofoil services operated by Compañía Transmediterránea connect Balearic Islands with Barcelona, Valencia and Alicante. Also weekly ferry service to Las Palmas (Canary Islands) from Barcelona.
City transport
Taxis: Available in most major cities; all metered. Tend to have a distinct colour in each city. Tipping between 5–10 per cent.
Car hire
Available at competitive rates in most large towns. A national driving licence is normally all that is required. Drive on the right. Speed limits are 60kph in towns, 100kph on national highways, 120kph on motorways and 90kph on other roads. Traffic coming from right generally has priority. Seat belts must be worn in front seats. Spanish drivers tend to drive faster than their northern counterparts.

BUSINESS DIRECTORY
The addresses listed below are a selection only. While World of Information makes every endeavour to check these addresses, we cannot guarantee that changes have not been made, especially to telephone numbers and area codes. We would welcome any corrections.

Telephone area codes
The international direct dialling (IDD) code for Spain is +34 followed by area code and subscriber's number:

Alicante	96	León	987
Avilés	98	Madrid	91
Barcelona	93	Málaga	95
Bilbao	94	Salamanca	923
Cádiz	956	Santander	942
Cartagena	968	Seville	95
Castellón de la Plana	964	Tarragona	977
Ceuta	952	Valencia	96
Granada	958	Valladolid	983
Huelva	959	Vigo	986
La Coruña	981	Zaragoza	976

Chambers of Commerce
American Chamber of Commerce in Spain, 8 Tuset, 08006 Barcelona (tel: 415-9963; fax: 415-1198; e-mail: info@amchamspain.com).

Barcelona Cámara de Comercio, 452 Avenguda Diagonal, 08006 Barcelona (tel: 416-9300; fax: 416-9301).

Bilbao Cámara Oficial de Comercio, Industria y Navegación, 50 Almeda Recalde, 48008 Bilbao (tel: 470-6500; fax: 443-6171; e-mail: info@camarabilbao.com).

British Chamber of Commerce in Spain, 21 Calle Bruc, 08010 Barcelona (tel: 317-3220; fax: 302-4896; e-mail: britchamber@britchamber.com).

Cádiz Cámara Oficial de Comercio, Industria y Navegación, 4 Antonio López, 11004 Cádiz (tel: 010-000; fax: 250-710; e-mail: ccincadiz@camerdata.es).

Consejo Superior de Cámaras de Comercio, Industria y Navegación de España, Calle Velazquez 157, 28002 Madrid (tel: 590-6900; fax: 590-6908; e-mail: csc@cscamaras.es).

Córdoba Cámara Oficial de Comercio e Industria, Pérez de Castro 1, 14003 Córdoba (tel: 296-199; fax: 202-106; e-mail: info@camaracordoba.com).

Franco-Spanish Chamber of Commerce and Industry, Calle Ruiz de Alarcon 7, 28014 Madrid (tel: 522-6742; fax: 523-3642; e-mail: lachambre@lachambre.es).

French Chamber of Commerce and Industry in Barcelona, Passeig de Gràcia 2, 08007 Barcelona (tel: 270-2450;fax: 270-2451; e-mail: ccfbcn@ccfbcn,es).

Granada Cámara Oficial de Comercio, Industria y Navegación, Paz 18, 18002 Granada (tel: 536-276; fax: 536-292; e-mail: ccigranada@camaras.org).

Las Palmas de Gran Canaria Cámara Oficial de Comercio, Industria y Navegación , León y Castillo 24, 35003 Las Palmas de Gran Canaria (tel: 391-045; fax: 362-350; e-mail: webmaster@cameraalp.es).

Madrid Cámara Oficial de Comercio e Industria, Calle Huertas 13, 28012 Madrid (tel: 538-3500; fax: 538-3677; e-mail: camaramadrid@camaramadrid.es).

Málaga Cámara Oficial de Comercio, Industria y Navegación, Cortina del Muelle 23, 29015 Málaga (tel: 221-1673; fax: 222-9894; e-mail: info@camaramalaga.com).

Mallorca, Ibiza y Formentera Cámara de Comercio, Estudio General 7, 07001 Palma de Mallorca (tel: 710-188; fax: 726-302; e-mail: ccinmallorca@camaras.org).

Sevilla Cámara Oficial de Comercio, Industria y Navegación, Plaza de la Contratación 8, 41004 Sevilla (tel: 211-005; fax: 225-619; e-mail: ccinsevilla@camaradesevilla.com).

Valencia Cámara de Comercio, Industria y Navegación, Poeta Querol 15, 46002 Valencia (tel: 103-900; fax: 531-742; e-mail: info@camaravalencia.com).

Zaragoza Cámara Oficial de Comercio e Industria, Calle Isabel La Catolica 2, 50071 Zaragoza (tel: 306-161; fax: 357-945; e-mail: cci@camarazaragoza.com).

Banking

Banco Atlántico SA, Diagonal 407 bis, Barcelona (tel: 237-1240).

Banco Bilbao Vizcaya Argentaria, Plaza de San Nicolás 4, 48005 Bilbao (tel: 424-4620).

Banco de la Exportación SA, Barcas 10, Valencia 2 (tel: 351-7862).

Banco de Sabadell, Plaza Sant Roc 20, 08201 Sabadell (tel: 726-2100).

Banco Español de Crédito (Banesto), Paseo de la Castellana 7, Madrid (tel: 338-1000).

Banco Internacional de Comercio, José Ortega y Gasset 56, 28006 Madrid (tel: 402-8362).

Banco Popular Español, Velázquez 34, 28001 Madrid (tel: 435-3620).

Banco Santander Central Hispano (BSCH) (established April 1999), Apartado de Correos 00045, Santander (tel: 221-200).

La Caixa de Catalunya, Avinguda Diagonal 621, Barcelona 08028 (tel 934-045000).

Confederación Española de Cajas de Ahorros (confederation of Spanish savings banks), Alcalá 27 Madrid 14 (tel: 232-7810).

Consejo Superior Bancario (central committee of Spanish banking), José Abascal 57, Madrid 9 (tel: 441-0611).

La Caixa de Barcelona (savings bank), Avinguda Diagonal 530, 08006 Barcelona (tel: 201-6666).

Central bank

Banco de España, Alcalá 48, 28014 Madrid (tel: 338-5000).

European Central Bank (ECB), Kaiserstrasse 29, D-60311 Frankfurt am Main, Germany (tel: (+49-69) 13-440; fax: (+49-69) 1344-6000; email: info@ecb.int).

Stock exchange

Bolsas y Mercados Españoles (BME): www.bolsasymercados.es

Travel information

Federación Española de Hoteles, Orense 32, 28020 Madrid (tel: 556-7112; fax: 556-7361; e-mail: federahoteles@ipf.es).

Iberia, 130 Velazquez Madrid, (tel: 902-400-500 (bookings); www.iberia.com).

Instituto De Turismo De España (Turespaña) 6 Jose Lázaro Galdiano, 28071 Madrid (tel: 343-3500; internet: www.tourspain.es/en).

Ministry of tourism

Ministerio de Industria, Turismo y Comercio, José González de Galdiano 6, Madrid (tel: 343-3621; email: turespaña@turespaña.es

Ministries

Ministry for Development, P de la Castellana 67, 28071 Madrid (tel: 597-7000; fax: 597-8502).

Ministry of Economy, Finance and Trade, Alcalá 9, Madrid 28071 (tel: 595-8000).

Ministry of Education and Culture, Alcalá 34, 28071 Madrid (tel: 532-5089; fax: 532-5873).

Ministry of the Environment, Pza San Juan de la Cruz, 28071 Madrid (tel: 597-7000; fax: 597-6349).

Ministry of Foreign Affairs, Pza de la Provincia 1, 28071 Madrid (tel: 379-9549).

Ministry of Health and Consumer Affairs, P del Prado 18-20, 28071 Madrid (tel: 596-1000; fax: 429-3525).

Ministry of Industry and Energy, Paseo de la Castellana 160, Madrid 16 (tel: 349-4806).

Ministry of the Interior, P de la Castellana 5, 28071 Madrid (tel: 537-1000; fax: 537-1177).

Ministry of Justice, San Bernardo 45, 28071 Madrid (tel: 930-2000).

Ministry of Labour and Social Affairs, Agustín de Bethencourt 4, 28071 Madrid (tel: 553-6000; fax: 554-7528).

Ministry of Public Administrations, P de la Castellana 3, 28071 Madrid (tel: 586-1000; fax: 319-2448).

President's Office, Complejo de la Moncloa, 28071 Madrid (tel: 335-3535).

Other useful addresses

Agencia EFE, SA (news agency), Espronceda 32, Apartado 1112, 28003 Madrid (tel: 441-5599).

Agencia para el Desarrollo, Consejeria de Economia e Innocacion Tecnologica, Comunidad de Madrid (fax: 420-6456, 399-7451; e-mail: agencia.desarrollo@madrid.org).

Bolsa de Comercio de Valencia (stock exchange), Pascual y Genis 19, 46001 Valencia (tel: 352-1487).

Bolsa de Madrid (stock exchange), Palacio de la Bolsa, Plaza de la Lealtad 1 (tel: 232-8484).

Central de Reservas de los Paradores de España, Calle Velázquez 25, 28001 Madrid (tel: 435-9700/9744/9768/9814).

Confederación Española de Organizaciones Empresariales (Spanish confederation of employers' organisations), Diego de León 50, 28006 Madrid (tel: 262-4410).

Fira de Barcelona, Avenida Reina Maria Cristina s/n, 08004 Barcelona (tel: 423-3101; fax: 423-8651).

IFEMA (Feria de Madrid), Parque Ferial Juan Carlos 1, 28042 Madrid (tel: 722-5180/5000; fax: 722-5801; e-mail: infoifema@ifema.es).

Instituto Nacional de Estadística, Paseo de la Castellana 183, E-28071 Madrid (tel: 583-9100; fax: 573-2713).

Instituto Nacional de la Seguridad Social, Subdirección General de Relaciones Internacionales, Padre Damián 4, 28036 Madrid (tel: 450-1900).

Spanish Embassy (USA), 2375 Pennsylvania Avenue, NW, Washington DC 20037 (tel: (+1-202) 452-0100; fax: (tel: (+1-202) 833-5670; e-mail: spain@spainemb.org).

Internet sites

Andalucia: www.andalucia.com

Balearics: www.caib.es

Bank of Spain: www.bde.es

Barcelona: www.bcn.es

Basque Country: www.euskadi.net

Bilbao: www.bilbao.net

Canary Islands: www.gobcan.es

Current affairs: www.sispain.com

El Pais newspaper: www.elpais.es

Galicia: wwwxunta.es

Government spokesman: www.la-moncloa.es

Hotel reservations: www.red2000.com

Iberia: www.iberia.com

Madrid: www.munimadrid.es

Ministry of Tourism: www.tourspain.es

Paradores (hotels): www.parador.es

Renfe (national railways): www.renfe.es

Spain statistics: www.ine.es/welcoing.htm

Spanish Rail Service: www.spanish-rail.co.uk

Spanish Tourism: www.spain.info

Spanish yellow pages (in Spanish): www.paginasamarillas.es

Stock Exchange: www.bolsamadrid.es

Train information: www.renfe.es

Valencia: www.gva.es

Sri Lanka

KEY FACTS

Official name: Sri Lanka Prajathanthrika Samajavadi Janarajaya / Llankais Sananayaka socialisak kutiyarasa / Democratic Socialist Republic of Sri Lanka

Head of State: President Mahinda Rajapaksa (UPFA) (since 2005; re-elected 26 Jan 2010)

Head of government: Prime Minister Disanayaka Mudiyanselage Jayaratne (from 21 Apr 2010)

Ruling party: Coalition government led by United People's Freedom Alliance (UPFA) (elected 2004; re-elected 21 Apr 2010)

Area: 65,610 square km

Population: 20.65 million (2010)*

Capital: Colombo (official capital); many governmental functions are centred in Sri Jayawardenepura, a suburb of Colombo.

Official language: Sinhala, Tamil, English

Currency: Rupee (Rs) = 100 cents

Exchange rate: Rs110.20 per US$ (Oct 2011)

GDP per capita: US$2,435 (2010)

GDP real growth: 9.10% (2010)

GNP per capita: US$49.70 billion (2010)

Labour force: 7.57 million (2009)

Unemployment: 5.70% (2009)

Inflation: 5.90% (2010)

Balance of trade: -US$12.16 billion (2010)

Annual FDI: US$478.21 million (2010)

* estimated figure

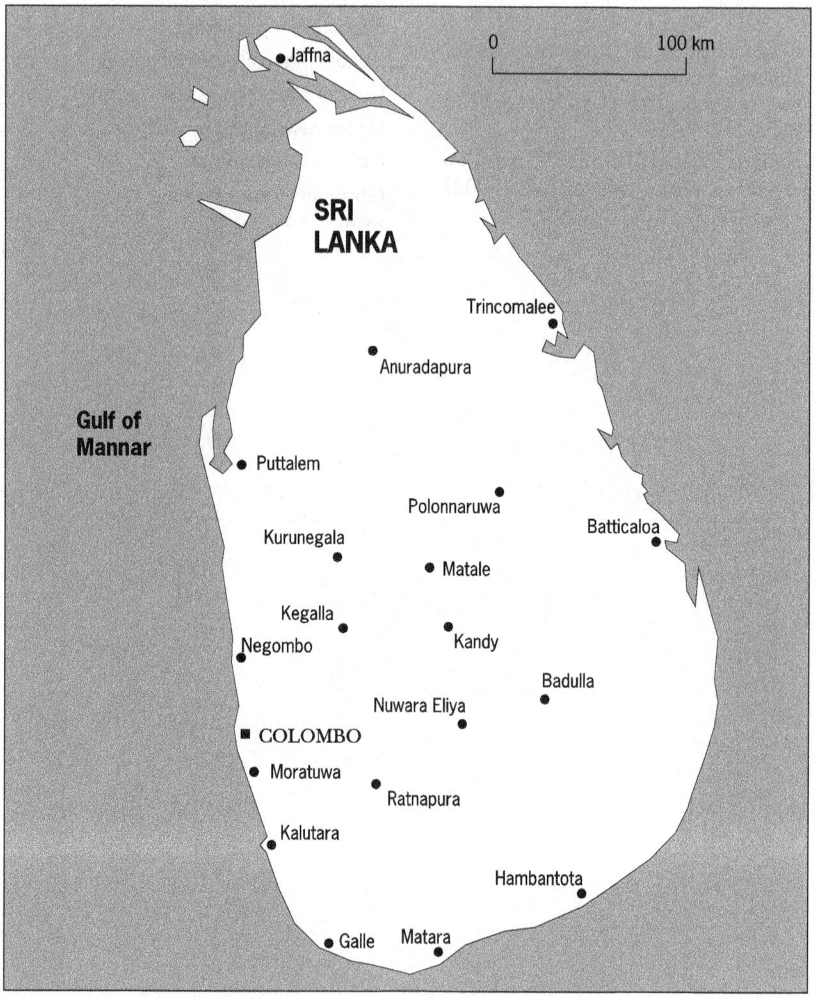

Although Sri Lanka's civil war between the Tamil and Sinhalese communities is officially over, in 2011 the after effects certainly lingered on. In March 2009 the United Nations Secretary General Ban Ki-moon insisted that the Sri Lankan government investigate alleged human rights abuses, particularly during the government's final push against the Liberation Tigers of Tamil Eelam (LTTE) (Tamil Tigers). Having appeared to agree to the investigation, President Mahinda Rajapaksa later backtracked, saying that he had never accepted the proposal. In 2010 the UN Secretary General instigated his own enquiry setting up his own independent Panel of Experts on Accountability in Sri Lanka. The report was published in March 2011 and reported that tens of thousands of people lost their lives in a three month period in early 2009. Most of these deaths were, according to the UN report, the result of government shelling in what had been officially declared 'no fire' zones. The report also claimed that the government had shelled UN food distribution lines, as well as 'systematically' shelling hospitals on what had been the frontlines.

Not all the apparent war crimes were committed by the government, according to the UN report. The Tamil Tigers had refused civilians permission to leave the conflict zones, apparently using them as hostages and shooting those who tried to escape. In its resumé, the UN considered that both sides had committed crimes against humanity and war crimes. The report also criticised the Sri Lankan government's own Lessons Learnt and Reconciliation Commission for a lack of impartiality and a failure to meet the standards agreed upon by President Rajapaksa and the UN Secretary General. Sadly, the UN's own report looked likely to be consigned to a filing cabinet, as not only the Sri Lankan government, but the international community failed to respond. A war crimes enquiry looked less than likely.

President Rajapaksa and his family hail from the area around Hambantota. Coincidentally, that is where Sri Lanka's new airport and deep sea port are being built. The airport is to be built with a US$209 million soft loan from China. The sea port, which will be the biggest in South Asia, is also being built with China reportedly underwriting some three quarters of the US$1.25 billion cost. China has established itself as the biggest lender to Sri Lanka. Some reports put the number of Chinese workers in Sri Lanka at an astounding 25,000.

Mahinda Rajapaksa first became President in the 2005 presidential elections when Ratnasiri Wickremanayake was appointed prime minister. President Rajapaksa stood for re-election two years before the end of his term, in January 2010, and was re-elected by a margin of 18 per cent over the opposition candidate, retired Army General Sarath Fonseka. The presidential elections were soon followed by a large victory for Rajapaksa's United People's Freedom Alliance (UPFA) coalition in the April 2010 parliamentary elections, where it captured 144 out of 225 seats possible, just short of a two-thirds majority. The remaining parliamentary seats were secured by the United National Front, a coalition of three opposition Sinhalese parties led by Ekshat Jathika Pakshaya (EJP) (United National Party) (60), the Illankai Tamil Arasu Kachchi (Tamil National Alliance) (TNA (14) and the Democratic National Alliance (DNA) (7). President Rajapaksa appointed D M Jayaratne as prime minister on 21 April.

The economy

According to the Asian Development Bank (ADB) the economy rebounded in 2010, with gross domestic product (GDP) growth estimated at 7.6 per cent, after 3.5 per cent in 2009. Continued benefits from the end of the long-running civil conflict in 2009, such as improved business and tourist confidence plus more land available for agriculture, as well as the global return to growth, underpinned the strong performance. The overall optimism was reflected in the stock market's doubling. With the revival of paddy and fisheries production in the former conflict areas of Northern and Eastern provinces, agriculture grew at 6.5 per cent in 2010. Good weather and fertiliser support by the government helped.

With the improved domestic business climate, the upturn in domestic and external demand and gradually improving infrastructure, industry grew by 8.0 per cent. Services, which account for nearly 60 per cent of GDP, recorded growth of 7.6 per cent. This was mainly due to the expansion of wholesale and retail trade, the revival in tourism – which contributed to robust performance in hotels and restaurants – and the impressive performance of the banking, insurance and real estate sub-sector. Tourist arrivals increased by 46 per cent to 654,477 in 2010, the highest number on record.

Annual average inflation as measured by the Colombo Consumer Price Index reached 5.9 per cent in 2010, up from a 25-year low of 3.4 per cent in 2009. Import duty reductions and subsidies that maintained stable fuel prices partly compensated for the rising global commodity prices' impact on domestic inflation. Nevertheless, overall inflation increased steadily from mid-year to reach 7.8 per cent in February 2011, with the rise due to escalating food prices that were 13 per cent higher than a year earlier. Core inflation was on a downward trend throughout 2010, continuing in the first two months of 2011.

Commercial banks' average lending rate continued to decline gradually in 2010 to 9.3 per cent by year-end. The Central Bank of Sri Lanka reduced the reverse repurchase rate, the main policy rate, twice (and again in January 2011 to 8.5 per cent). As interest rates edged down, growth in credit to the private sector came back strongly after 2009's shrinkage, reflecting commercial banks' improved lending appetites.

The government tightened the budget deficit to 8.0 per cent in 2010 from 9.9 per cent in 2009. The ADB reported that the deficit narrowed through current expenditure being cut by 1.5 percentage points as a share of GDP. The ratio of government debt to GDP fell to an estimated 84 per cent at end-2010 from 86 per cent a year earlier but the total stock of government debt increased by 11 per cent.

After a 12.7 per cent fall in 2009, exports recovered to expand by 17.3 per cent in 2010. Industrial exports accounted for 74 per cent of export earnings (of which more than half came from textiles and clothing) and agricultural exports 25 per cent. Exports to major regions increased even though the European Union (EU) withdrew concessions under its

KEY INDICATORS **Sri Lanka**

	Unit	2006	2007	2008	2009	2010
Population	m	19.77	*19.93	*20.08	*20.24	*20.65
Gross domestic product (GDP)	US$bn	26.96	32.30	39.60	41.30	49.70
GDP per capita	US$	1,364	1,623	1,972	2,041	2,435
GDP real growth	%	7.3	6.8	6.0	3.5	8.0
Inflation	%	9.5	15.8	22.6	3.4	5.9
Unemployment	%	6.5	6.0	5.2	5.7	–
Industrial output	% change	7.2	7.6	5.9	4.2	–
Agricultural output	% change	4.7	3.4	7.5	3.2	–
Exports (fob) (goods)	US$m	6,883.0	7,640.0	8,137.0	7,085.0	8,307.0
Imports (fob) (goods)	US$m	10,253.0	10,167.0	12,607.0	9,186.0	12,161.0
Balance of trade	US$m	-3,370.0	-2,527.0	-4,470.0	-2,101.0	-3,853.0
Current account	US$m	-1,434.0	-1,498.0	-3,719.0	-292.0	-1,471.0
Total reserves minus gold	US$m	2,837.0	3,515.0	2,563.0	4,616.0	6,710.0
Foreign exchange	US$m	2,762.0	3,433.0	2,487.0	4,521.0	6,634.0
Exchange rate	per US$	107.82	108.90	108.33	114.94	113.06

* estimated figure

Generalised System of Preferences Plus in August 2010.

As the economy recovered in 2010 there was a marked increase in imports (about 32 per cent), though this upsurge in large part reflected higher global prices, especially of oil. The steeper rise in imports than exports pushed out the trade deficit to 10.5 per cent of GDP, from 7.5 per cent a year earlier.

The strong resurgence in tourism as well as freight- and port-related activities brought an upturn in the services sector surplus. Growth momentum in remittances continued, reaching 24 per cent. These items helped to counterbalance the large trade deficit to hold the current account deficit to 3.8 per cent of GDP. Supported by healthy capital flows, the balance of payments recorded an estimated overall surplus of about 1.8 per cent of GDP in 2010. Foreign direct investment (FDI) strengthened sharply, to an estimated US$500 million from US$384 million in 2009, although in the view of the ADB, at only about one per cent of GDP it is very low for an economy of Sri Lanka's size and development level.

Investor sentiment was strengthened by the simultaneous approval of the third and fourth tranches of the International Monetary Fund (IMF) stand-by arrangement in June and the fifth tranche in September, 2010. Both Standard and Poor's and Moody's raised the country's outlook to stable and Fitch to positive. Supported by the success of the bond issue and the release of IMF funding tranches, gross official reserves reached US$6.6 billion, covering 5.9 months of imports. The Sri Lanka rupee climbed gradually against the US dollar by about three per cent to reach SLRs111.1 by end-2010.

After the rebound of 2010, in the view of the ADB, the economy was expected to show continued high growth of 8.0 per cent in 2011, supported by some strengthening in external demand, and to maintain growth at that level in 2012. The ADB also considered that the services and industry sectors will lead growth in 2011; agriculture is likely to have been hampered by heavy rains and consequent flooding that affected several provinces in January–February 2011. Rising global food and oil prices and a shortfall in domestic supply of agricultural produce due to the flooding looked likely to stoke inflation, but, according to the ADB, by only up to around 8 per cent. With the economy now on a higher growth trajectory and inflation pressures rising, however, monetary tightening may well be needed later in the year.

The ADB expects the 2011 budget deficit to come down to 6.8 per cent of GDP from 8.0 per cent in 2010, split equally between a 0.6 per cent increase in revenue and a 0.6 per cent cut in expenditure. Government expenditure is forecast to rise moderately in nominal terms as the government is looking to cap public investments at around the 2010 level of 6–7 per cent of GDP. A sharp one-third increase in private investment is seen driving growth higher.

Risk assessment

Economy	Good
Politics	Fair
Regional stability	Fair

COUNTRY PROFILE

Historical profile

1815 The British became the first colonial power to win control of the island, which became known as Ceylon. Tamils from India were brought over to work on the plantations.
1931 The right to vote was introduced by the colonial authorities, who also established a system of power-sharing with the people of Ceylon.
1948 Ceylon gained full independence from British rule.
1949 The right to vote was taken away from Indian Tamils.
1951 Solomon Bandaranaike left the ruling Ekshat Jathika Pakshaya (EJP) (United National Party) to form the Sri Lanka Nidahas Pakshaya (Sri Lanka Freedom Party) (SLFP).
1953 A decision by the EJP government to cut the rice ration in the slump following the Korean War saw riots assume insurrectionary proportions.
1956 Bandaranaike became prime minister. Sinhala was made the state language by Bandaranaike's SLFP government, sparking anti-Tamil pogroms.
1959–60 Bandaranaike was assassinated by a Buddhist monk in 1959. His widow, Sirimavo Bandaranaike, was elected SLFP leader and prime minister the following year. She stepped up the nationalisation programme.
1964 A pact with India forced half a million Indian Tamil plantation workers to return to India.
1965 The EJP won elections and began attempts to reverse the nationalisation programme.
1970 Sirimavo Bandaranaike began what would be her second term as prime minister, which would last until 1977.
1971 A rural uprising led by the Marxist Janatha Vimukthi Peramuna (JVP) (People's United Liberation Front) was crushed.
1972 The country changed its name from Ceylon to Sri Lanka and Buddhism became the country's official religion.
1976 The main Tamil party, the Federal Party, and other Tamil groups, formed the Tamil United Liberation Front (TULF), calling for a separate Tamil state in the northern and eastern parts of the country. The Liberation Tigers of Tamil Eelam (LTTE, also known as the Tamil Tigers) was formed.
1977 A constitutional amendment was passed which established a presidential system of government from the end of the year. In elections, the TULF won all the seats in Tamil areas.
1978 J R Jayewardene became the country's first executive president. Continued violence and pressure from the Tamils led the government to recognise the Tamil language in the new constitution.
1983–84 Tamil terrorist activity and anti-Tamil pogroms broke out. The latter constituted the worst outbreak of violence for many years, sparking a state of emergency. India began training Tamil guerrillas. Conflicts developed in the north of the island between the army and the Tamil Tigers.
1985 The first attempts at peace talks with the LTTE failed.
1986 Violence continued to convulse the northern and eastern provinces. Sri Lanka's relations with India were severely strained by the violence. India mediated informally between TULF legislators, Tamil leaders and the Sri Lankan government.
1987 Following an accord with India, more than 7,000 Indian troops were sent to Sri Lanka to try to implement a peace accord. The government agreed and signed accords that created new councils for Tamil areas in the north and east.
1989 Ranasinghe Premadasa was sworn in as president. The state of emergency which had been in force since May 1983 was repealed.
1990 Indian troops went home after losing more than 1,000 soldiers and failing to achieve their objectives. The LTTE controlled large parts of northern Sri Lanka.
1991 The LTTE was implicated in the assassination of Indian prime minister Rajiv Gandhi.
1993 President Premadasa was killed in an LTTE bomb attack.
1994 The Bahejana Nidasa Pakhsaya (People's Alliance) (PA), a left-wing nine-party coalition centred on the SLFP, won the legislative elections. The prime minister, Chandrika Bandaranaike Kumaratunga (SLFP), was elected president. She appointed her mother, Sirimavo Bandaranaike, as prime minister.
1996 The LTTE bombed the capital, Colombo, leading to a nationwide state of emergency.

1998 Sri Lanka's fiftieth anniversary celebrations were marred by renewed fighting between the army and separatist LTTE in the north of the country. The Tamil Tigers bombed Sri Lanka's holiest Buddhist site and captured key northern towns in a large offensive.
1999 President Kumaratunga won her second and final term in office; she had been partially blinded in one eye in a terrorist bombing at an election rally.
2000 Government forces lost control of a key military base in the north to Tamil Tiger separatists. Norway began mediation talks between the government and the LTTE. The general elections resulted in a hung parliament, with the PA dependent on two moderate Tamil-linked parties for support. Former prime minister (the world's first female head of government) Sirimavo Bandaranaike died soon after casting her vote.
2001 The LTTE was declared a terrorist organisation by Britain and Canada. The LTTE destroyed half Air Lanka's fleet of airplanes at Colombo's airport. President Kumaratunga announced a snap general election, which were won by the opposition EJP.
2002 It was estimated that 64,000 people had been killed since the LTTE's armed struggle for independence began. A cease-fire, negotiated by Norway, came into effect, ending the civil war. The ruling EJP won local elections, which were also billed as a referendum on peace plans. The ban on the LTTE was lifted as a prelude to peace talks at which the LTTE dropped its demand for independence in favour of regional autonomy with self-government.
2003 The LTTE withdrew from peace talks, as it demanded interim executive powers over the north and east, where the Tamil population is concentrated. Peace talks stalled and fearing the break-up of Sri Lanka, the president suspended parliament and deployed troops in Colombo as a state of emergency was declared.
2004 President Kumaratunga called snap elections, which were won by the United People's Freedom Alliance (UPFA) and Mahinda Rajapaksa became prime minister. An earthquake off the Indonesian island of Sumatra caused a *tsunami* that devastated coastal areas of north and eastern Sri Lanka; the final estimate in Sri Lanka was 35,322 dead or missing and 516,150 people displaced.
2005 Reconstruction of the coastal regions under *de facto* control of the LTTE devastated by the *tsunami* was necessary in many areas. The government planned to give the LTTE separatists a key role in the distribution of international aid that had been received and encourage peace talks in the process. However only reduced aid was provided and anger mounted in the stricken areas. The nationalist JVP pulled out of the government coalition in protest and reduced the government's working majority. The foreign minister, Lakshman Kadirgaamar, was assassinated. Mahinda Rajapaksa (UPFA) won presidential elections; Ratnasiri Wickremanayake was appointed prime minister.
2006 The South Asia Free Trade Agreement (SAFTA) came into effect between Sri Lanka, Bhutan, Bangladesh, India, Maldives, Nepal and Pakistan. The EU added the LTTE to its list of terrorist organisations (a move that followed the US and India), and froze all LTTE financial assets held within the EU. The United Nations Children's Fund (Unicef) accused the LTTE of abducting and recruiting children as soldiers. The number of dead attributed to the conflict since 1972 was estimated at 60,000.
2007 S P Thamilselvan, a leading political member of the LTTE, was killed in a government air raid.
2008 The prime minister announced a formal ending to the 2002 cease-fire with the LTTE.
2009 Government forces over-ran the LTTE's *de facto* capital of Kilinochchi in the north, after more than a decade of being held by the rebels. There was also heavy fighting as government forces took control of the strategic causeway linking the Jaffna Peninsula and strongholds of the LTTE with the mainland, along with the last rebel region of Mullaitivu in the north-east. In the 25-year conflict for a Tamil homeland an estimated 70,000 people had been killed. The LTTE agreed to international calls for a cease-fire but refused to lay down its arms, a prerequisite of the government, which in turn rejected any consideration of a conditional truce. The UN requested another cease-fire, to allow trapped civilians, estimated at 50,000–100,000, in the area to flee; this was rejected. Victory, after 26 years, was declared by President Rajapaksa as government troops over-ran the last enclave of the LTTE and the deaths of its leaders were announced, including its founder Velupillai Prabhakaran. Provincial elections were held for the Jaffna Municipal Council; the governing UPFA won 13 seats (out of 23) and the Illankai Tamil Arasu Kadchi (Tamil National Alliance) eight; of the four other candidates running for office two won seats. The government finally allowed refugees who had been held in camps since the end of the fighting to leave at will. They had previously been prevented from leaving before they had been screened for links with the Tamil Tigers. It was announced that there would be 22 candidates in the forthcoming presidential election, including the incumbent and Sarath Fonseka, the former army commander.
2010 The EU withdrew trade benefits in February because of human rights concerns. As a result exports to the EU faced higher tariffs. In presidential elections held in January, incumbent Mahinda Rajapaksa was re-elected with 57.88 per cent of the vote; his closest rival, Sarath Fonseka (New Democratic Front (NDF)) 40.15 per cent. The Supreme Court decided that as the presidential election had been called two years early, President Rajapaksa's new term in office would begin in November and he could remain in power until 2016. The state of emergency, in place since 1983, was extended by parliament on 9 March until after the legislative elections in April. Over 7,000 candidates competed for 225 seats in the unicameral parliament. The ruling UPFA won 144 seats, gaining 39 seats over the 2004 elections. The United National Front, a coalition of three opposition Sinhalese parties led by Ekshat Jathika Pakshaya (EJP) (United National Party) won 60 seats, the Illankai Tamil Arasu Kachchi (Tamil National Alliance) (TNA) won 14, the Democratic National Alliance (DNA) won seven; turnout was 61.3 per cent. President Rajapaksa appointed D M Jayaratne as prime minister on 21 April. Restrictions (introduced in 2006) on the right to hold public meetings were lifted on 5 May; other powers, such as detaining terror suspects indefinitely and without charge remained. In July the cabinet, chaired by the President, held a special symbolic meeting in Kilinochchi, the former capital of the Tamil Tigers. It reviewed the progress of reconstruction, which is hampered by deposits of unexploded ordinance (UXO). The cabinet agreed, among other changes, to reduce the price of diesel in the Northern Province. In August a commission set up to examine the conduct of the civil war held its first public meeting. A new seaport, funded by Chinese loans, in southern Hambantota, including four terminals (two for cargo and two for fuel bunkering), was opened in August; another equally large phase is under construction. Mahinda Rajapaksa's 30 month sentence for violating military procurement procedures was confirmed by the president in September. Former presidential candidate and army chief, Sarath Fonseka was convicted in a military court in September, on charges of making irregular purchases for the military while in charge; he was sentenced to 30 months in prison. He will face further charges in a civilian court for allegedly employing army deserters and revealing

state secrets, which could carry a sentence of 20 years in prison.
2011 The UN report into the official conduct of the Sri Lankan civil war was published on 25 April. It concluded that there was evidence of the government and military being responsible for war crimes and crimes against humanity. The report dealt with the period from September 2008 to May 2009 and the military assault on the north-eastern coast, the heartland of the LTTE. Although the government had refused all UN interviews with its military personnel the Expert Panel, appointed by the UN Secretary General, had considerable information given to them by credible outside agencies, media and individuals from which to draw their conclusions. The government claimed the findings were 'baseless, biased and unilateral'. President Rajapaksa received a summons, issued by a US federal court on 19 June, linked to three civil cases filed under the Hague Convention, by relatives of Tamil victims of alleged extra-judicial killings during the civil war.

Political structure

Constitution

The constitution dates from 1978, when a presidential system of government was established. Local authority is represented by 24 district councils in nine provinces and the Pradesiya Sabas (councils based on local administrative divisions). The devolution of power is limited, partly due to non-implementation, and partly due to the fact that Article 2 of the constitution stipulates a unitary state. Also politically significant is Article 9, which guarantees the 'foremost place' to Buddhism among faiths and stipulates the duty of the state to protect and sustain the religion. Both are obstacles to any scheme for devolution. Article 76 further stipulates that parliament may not 'abdicate or in any manner alienate its legislative power', complicating the creation of an autonomous Tamil entity.
The constitutional situation reflects events in 1987, when a peace accord was signed with India, which had intervened to protect the Tamil population. The Indo-Sri Lankan accord introduced a tier of government at provincial level, with elected provincial councils and certain powers delegated from the central government. Traditionally there are nine provinces, but the accord provided for the temporary merger of the Northern and Eastern Provinces (those regarded by Sri Lankan Tamils as their traditional homelands), pending a referendum for which the political conditions have not yet materialised.
The constitution provides the executive and security forces with sweeping powers on the declaration of a state of war. The Public Security Ordinance grants the armed forces wide powers of arrest and confiscation and allows home entry without a warrant once a war footing is declared. A two-thirds parliamentary majority is required for the removal of the president or amendment of the constitution.

Independence date

4 February 1948

Form of state

Socialist democratic republic

The executive

The president is directly elected for a six-year term and is head of state, head of the executive, head of government and head of the armed forces. No presidential incumbent may serve more than two terms. The president has the power to appoint or dismiss the prime minister (whose powers are relatively limited) and the cabinet and to dissolve parliament. After the election victory of the EJP in December 2001, President Kumaratunga agreed to delegate some of her extensive powers to the cabinet.

National legislature

The unicameral Parliament of Sri Lanka has 225 members elected by proportional representation, off which 196 are elected in 22 multi-seat electoral districts and the remainder by party lists nationally dependent on the share of the vote. All serve for six-year terms.

Legal system

The judiciary is formally independent of the executive. The Supreme Court has sole jurisdiction over interpretation of the constitution. It is also the final arbiter in settling charges against the president. The legal code reflects the system of English law inherited in 1948, with subsequent amendments in line with legal changes in the UK.

Last elections

8 April 2010 (parliamentary); 26 January 2010 (presidential).
Results: Parliamentary: Eksath Janatha Nidahas Sandhanaya (United People's Freedom Alliance (UPFA) coalition of over 11 political parties) won 60.33 per cent of the vote (144 seats out of 225); Eksath Jathika Pakshaya (United National Front (four Sinhalese parties led by Ekshat Jathika Pakshaya (EJP) (United National Party)) 29.34 per cent (60); Illankai Tamil Arasu Kachchi (Tamil National Alliance) (TNA) 3.94 per cent (14), Democratic National Alliance (DNA) 5.5 per cent (seven). Turnout was 61.3 per cent.
Presidential: Mahinda Rajapaksa (United People's Freedom Alliance) 57.88 per cent of the vote, Sarath Fonseka (New Democratic Front) 40.15 per cent; 20 other candidates won less than 1 per cent each. Turnout was 74.5 per cent.

Next elections

2015 (parliamentary); 2016 (presidential)

Political parties

Ruling party

Coalition government led by United People's Freedom Alliance (UPFA) (elected 2004;re-elected 21 Apr 2010)

Main opposition party

United National Alliance (three Sinhalese parties led by Ekshat Jathika Pakshaya (EJP) (United National Party)

Population

20.65 million (2010)*
Last census: July 2001: 16,864,544 (provisional)
Population density: 315 inhabitants per square km (2010)
Annual growth rate: 1.0 per cent 1994–2004 (WHO 2006)

Ethnic make-up

Sinhalese (74 per cent), Tamils (18 per cent), Moors (7 per cent), others (1 per cent).
Sri Lankan Tamils form the overwhelming majority in the Northern Province. The Eastern Province is ethnically mixed with three groups in sizeable numbers – Sri Lankan Tamils, mainly Tamil-speaking Moors (Muslims) and Sinhalese. Indian Tamils, descendants of those brought over by the British to work the tea plantations, are concentrated in the plantation districts of the Central Highlands. Elsewhere the Sinhalese are in the majority and make up about three-quarters of the total population.

Religions

Buddhism (69 per cent), Hinduism (16 per cent), Christian (8 per cent), Muslim (7 per cent). Sinhalese are predominantly Theravada Buddhists and Tamils are Hindus, while Arab and Malay descendants are mainly Muslims.

Education

Public investment in education amounts to 1.3 per cent of GDP. Universal primary education and gender parity, at this level, have been achieved.
Primary and junior secondary school are compulsory, lasting until aged 14. Senior secondary and collegiate schools are discretional and last until aged 18. All schooling until this age is provided free.
Teaching is provided in English, Sinhala, Tamil and GCE exams at aged 16 must include a language subject in the student's mother tongue of Sinhalese or Tamil.
The education sector faces problems such as declining efficiency and quality of educational institutions and a shortage of teachers, nevertheless, standards are high and the importance allocated to education is evident in the high literacy rates.

Sri Lanka has received assistance from the World Bank, via the International Development Association (IDA). The ongoing Second General Education Project contributed a US$70.3 million for programmes based on improving enrolment, curriculum development and textbook provision. The Asian Development Bank has provided concessional loans to aid the North and East Community Restoration Development project to fund, among other programmes, educational facilities damaged during the internal conflict.

Literacy rate: 92 per cent adult rate; 97 per cent youth rate (15–24) (Unesco 2005).

Compulsory years: Five to 14

Enrolment rate: 110 per cent, gross primary enrolment of relevant age group (including repeaters); 74 per cent, gross secondary enrolment (World Bank).

Pupils per teacher: 28 in primary schools.

Health

World Bank estimates show that the average life expectancy is higher than in most developing countries and the infant mortality rate is relatively low. Sri Lanka's social indicators showed steady improvement during the 1990s including a decline in the maternal mortality rate. There is increased access by the rural population to safe water (from 29 per cent to over 83 per cent) and sanitation (from 39 per cent to over 60 per cent). However, relevant sources indicate increased incidences of malaria and a high malnutrition rate for children under the age of five. The government's *Samurdhi* (Prosperity) Programme is assisting, particularly the most vulnerable groups, to reduce child malnutrition. Adolescent health services, nutrition and geriatric services and institutions are under strain. The use of traditional medicine (*ayurveda*) to supplement public healthcare is widespread.

HIV/Aids

HIV prevalence: 0.1 per cent aged 15–49 in 2003 (World Bank)

Life expectancy: 71 years, 2004 (WHO 2006)

Fertility rate/Maternal mortality rate: 1.9 births per woman, 2004 (WHO 2006); maternal mortality 30 per 100,000 live births (World Bank).

Birth rate/Death rate: 16 births and 6.5 deaths per 1,000 population (2003)

Child (under 5 years) mortality rate (per 1,000): 13 per 1,000 live births (World Bank)

Head of population per physician: 0.55 physicians per 1,000 people, 2004 (WHO 2006)

Welfare

Despite sustained government efforts to introduce various poverty reduction programmes such as direct income transfers and subsidies, about 21 per cent of the country's population are poor. However, estimates on the poverty level exclude the conflict-centered north-east, which has about 2.8 million people, 15 per cent of the total population.

For a number of years poor families have been able to benefit from a food stamps project which provides vouchers for food. A much more ambitious poverty alleviation scheme, the *Janasaviya* programme, begun in the mid-1990s, entitled families to a monthly payment for the purchase of specific consumer goods. The Prosperity Programme is another government sponsored poverty reduction scheme, introduced in 1994, which aims to provide social services and a social safety net to very poor households. Two projects, funded by the Asian Development Bank, are the Emergency Assistance for the Rehabilitation of North and East Sri Lanka, and the Eastern Province Coastal Community Development Project.

Old age, disability and death have been covered since 1958 by a social insurance programme funded from the Employees' Provident Fund (EPF). Employers pay 12 per cent of salaries to the EPF, the country's main social insurance fund, with a further 8 per cent taken from employees. A social assistance programme for the unemployed – arguably the hallmark of a comprehensive welfare system – saw legislation introduced in 1995 in advance of a three-stage phasing in of the programme, aimed at families earning less than Rs1,000 (US$10.41) per month.

Main cities

Colombo (capital, estimated population 651,889 in 2005); many of the governmental functions are centered in Sri Jayawardenepura, a suburb of Colombo, 118,556), Dehiwala-Mount Lavinia (216,695), Moratuwa (185,581), Kandy (112,256), Jaffna (144,650).

Languages spoken

The national languages, Sinhala and Tamil, are widely spoken. English is commonly used in government and is spoken by about 10 per cent of the population.

Official language/s

Sinhala, Tamil, English

Media

The human rights watchdog, Amnesty International said that between 2006 and Februray 2008 at least 10 media workers had been killed and others abducted, detained or 'disappeared'. Tamil journalists working in the conflict areas of the north and east of the country were most at risk, while Sinhalese journalists in the south faced official intimidation, especially if they reported on corruption.

Press

The government assumed wide powers to censor the press under a Public Security Ordinance in 2000. Media outlets are divided along language and ethnic lines and offer services in major languages only.

The government reinstated the Press Council in June 2009, in the face of strong opposition from media outlets that claimed self-censorship, introduced in 2003, had been working satisfactorily. The Press Council has the power to charge, fine and imprison journalists who transgress the press code. Campaigner for press freedom claim that Sri Lanka is 'one of the most dangerous places for journalist to operate in'.

Dailies: In Singhala, *Dinamina* is government-owned, *Lankadeepa* (www.lankadeepa.lk) and *Lakbima* (www.lakbima.lk) are private.

In Tamil, *Uthayan* (www.uthayan.com), *Virakesari* (www. Virakesari.lk) and *Thinakkural* (www.thinakural.com) are privately owned.

In English, *Daily News* (www.newslk.com) is government-owned, *The Island* (www.island.lk), and *Daily Mirror* (www.dailymirror.lk) are private. There are a number of English online news outlets including (*http://123srilanka.com*), (*www.lankatruth.com*), (*http://news.onlanka.com*) and (*www.srilankanewsfirst.com*).

Weeklies: The *Sunday Observer The Sunday Leader* (www.thesundayleader.lk), *Sunday Island* and *Sunday Times* (www.sundaytimes.lk), are published weekly, together with Sinhalese and Tamil weeklies such as *Virakesari Illustrated Weekly*.

Business: Several newsletters of specific interest are published by various representative groups including *Ceylon Commerce* by the Ceylon Chamber of Commerce (www.chamber.lk), *Industrial Ceylon* by the Ceylon National Chamber of Industries, *Business Lanka* and *Expo News* by the Ministry of Trade and Shipping Information Service, *Sri Lanka Ports News* by the Sri Lanka Ports Authority, *Clothing* magazine by the Clothing Industry Training Institute and the *Sri Lanka Investment News* by the Greater Colombo Economic Commission. An Indian publication *Business Today* (www.business-today.com) is also widely read.

Periodicals: Some of the popular and useful periodicals include *Explore Srilanka*, *Lanka Monthly Digest* (www.lmd.lk) and the fashion magazine *Satyn*.

Broadcasting

Radio: The state-owned Sri Lanka Broadcasting Corporation (www.slbc.lk) transmits six services with commercial programmes in Sinhala, Tamil and English. ABC Radio is the largest commercial network with five national stations, MBC (www.maharaja.lk) has four radio channels. There are dozens of local, privately operated radio stations, mostly broadcasting in FM including TNL Rocks (www.tnlrocks.com) and Yes FM (www.yesfmonline.com). External services are broadcast, on short wave, by Colombo International Radio in over six languages to central Asia.

Television: The state controlled Sri Lanka Rupavahini Corporation (SLBC) (www.rupavahini.lk), which operates two channels and Independent Television Network (ITN) (www.itn.lk) one. Other private operators include Sirasa TV (www.sirasa.com), MTV (www.capitalmaharaja.com), Swanavahini (www.swarnavahini.lk) in Sinhala and Shakthi TV (www.webtv.lk) in Tamil.

Advertising

Press, cinema, commercial television and radio all accept advertising. Outdoor advertising is widespread; direct mail advertising must conform to a code of practice.

News agencies

The Sinhalaya News Agency (www.news.sinhalaya.com).

Economy

In 2009, the composition of the economy was dominated by the service sector with 57.7 per cent, industry at 29.7 per cent, of which manufacturing was 18.1 per cent, and agriculture at 12.6 per cent.

The tourist sector, which provides vital foreign exchange, fell by -1.1 per cent in 2009, but by January 2010, visitor numbers had increased by 31.9 per cent so that the annual rate of tourism grew by 10.7 per cent.

New industries, such as information technology (IT), software development and communications (call centres) are contributing an increasingly larger share of overall GDP. Traditional industries include garment and leather goods manufacturing, rubber products and food processing. Natural resources include mined sapphires and rubies, which are processed domestically for the tourist trade, limestone and graphite, mineral sands and phosphate. Agricultural products are led by tea leaf production, rice, coconuts and spices. Agriculture and industry are located particularly in the southern and western parts of the country.

Since the civil war with the separatist Liberation Tigers of Tamil Eelan (LTTE, known as the Tamil Tigers), was resolved in 2009, Sri Lanka has begun to reintegrate its economy with the world market. However, this was at the worst period for international trade. GDP growth in 2007 was 6.8 per cent, falling to 6 per cent in 2008 and down to 3.5 per cent in 2009, before a resurgence of 8 per cent in 2010.

Despite not falling into recession during the global recession, Sri Lanka has underlying problems that need addressing, such as improving the infrastructure and investing in people by increasing skills and education. Foreign exchange reserves fell to dangerously low levels in 2009 as the balance of payments gap widened. The International Monetary Fund (IMF) assisted with a US$2.6 billion loan to support the government deficit. Sri Lanka had one of the highest public debt-to-GDP ratios among emerging market countries in 2011, but the IMF expects this to fall steadily as the economy rebounds.

Following the defeat of the LTTE, an initial hard-line stance by the government forced the captured civilian population in the Northern Province to live in camps, causing the EU to withdraw trade benefits in February 2010 because of human rights concerns. However, post-war reconstruction of both the physical infrastructure and the economy is being aided by international assistance which began by addressing the needs of the estimated 300,000 internally displaced persons (IDPs). The strategy for returning the country to lasting peace is a combination of demilitarisation, development, democratisation and devolution.

In 2011, the UN Human Development Index (HDI) ranked Sri Lanka 97 (out of 187) for national development in health, education and income. In 2010, 38.7 per cent of the population experienced at least one indicator of poverty, while 7 per cent lived on the equivalent of US$1.25 per day.

External trade

Sri Lanka is a member of South Asia Association for Regional Co-operation, which operates a preferential trading arrangement that covers 6,000 products. In 2004 the South Asia Free Trade Area (Safta) was ratified, to be implemented between the seven member states (Bangladesh, Bhutan, India, Maldives, Nepal, Pakistan and Sri Lanka) by 2012.

Traditional plantation produce (tea, rubber and coconuts) continue to have a significant influence on export earnings, however clothing and leather product manufacturing is now the largest sector accounting for 39 per cent of total output followed by the production of food, beverages and tobacco at 22 per cent. The industrial sector also includes petrochemicals, plastics and processed rubber. There is a growing trade in information technology and software development. The export of precious gems is a modest but important export addition to foreign earnings.

Imports

Major imports are textile fabrics, mineral products, petroleum, foodstuffs, machinery and transport equipment.

Main sources: India (typically 21 per cent of total), Singapore (12 per cent) Iran (9 per cent).

Exports

Major exports are textiles and apparel, tea and spices, diamonds, emeralds, rubies, coconut products, rubber manufactures and fish.

Main destinations: US (typically 23 per cent of total), UK (13 per cent), Germany (6 per cent).

Agriculture

Farming

Sri Lanka's economy is becoming more service-oriented and less dependent on agriculture. The sector includes mostly large state-owned tea, rubber and coconut plantations and smaller holdings where rice, sugar cane, cassava, sweet potatoes, soya beans, other vegetables, cashew nuts, cocoa, castor, spices, chillies, onions and other crops are produced, sometimes at virtually subsistence level. Other agricultural products include cinnamon and coffee. Sri Lanka is self-sufficient in rice, the main food crop. Livestock raised include buffaloes, goats, pigs, sheep and poultry.

Agricultural productivity on the small farms is low. The sector as a whole is struggling against declining terms of trade, with a general decline in the price of commodities like coconut and rubber coupled with rising costs, particularly transport.

Plantation crops provide export earnings, although output has declined in recent years. Sri Lanka exports 44 per cent of its rubber output, with production increasingly shifting to crepe rubber and latex. Tea is the most important agricultural export, although there is a lot of room for productivity gains. Smallholdings account for around 58 per cent of total output. The sector is showing signs of improvement. Private tea plantations owned by foreign investors are increasingly common and a number of new tea-blending units have become operational, helping to increase the added value of tea.

Production has matched the steady increase in world demand for spices. Sri Lanka produces over 85 per cent of the world's demand for cinnamon. Spice production accounts for over 95,000 hectares of land.

Poor weather in 2011 lead to the tea harvest at medium altitudes declining by up to 20 per cent, although the harvest at the lowest level maintained its crop. Overall the harvest was down by 8 per cent in August year-on-year compared with 2010.
Cottage industries such as poultry farming, home gardening and bee-keeping are becoming increasingly popular among returnees in Sri Lanka's former northern conflict zone as alternatives to regular jobs.

Fishing

The government undertook to re-invest in boats and harbour infrastructure following destruction due to the 2004 tsunami. Those unwilling to go back to sea were retrained for onshore work, particularly in the building trade.
Fishing typically accounts for 2 per cent of GDP. Production includes prawns, shrimps, lobsters, crabs and sea cucumbers, for export and local consumption. The fisheries produce in the region of 200,000 tonnes of marine fish per year, 30,000 tonnes of freshwater fish and 10,000 tonnes of crustaceans.
New companies engaged in marine fishing qualify for a five-year tax holiday. Fishing activity has been affected both by higher petroleum prices and by the poor security situation.

Forestry

About 38 per cent of the land area (1.94 million hectares) is forested, and forestry accounts for 2 per cent of GDP, providing timber for local demand. Around 15 per cent of land area is subject to national protection. Forests of broadleaved, deciduous and evergreen are adapted to dry and monsoon seasons. Savannah and thorn woodland are found beside coastal areas populated by mangroves. Plantations account for around 316,000 hectares (ha) of forest cover and are established at a rate of 3,100ha per year. In the 1990s, Sri Lanka lost almost 20 per cent of its natural forest, at an average of 35,000ha per annum, so that only small fragments of tropical rainforest remain, each less than 10,000 hectares in area. Illegal logging has removed timber from unprotected forests, adding to the reduction. Some tropical timber plantations provide teak, eucalyptus, pine and mahogany, which are commercially farmed, with exports of timber and forestry products totalling US$33.7 million, and imports amounting to US$204.7 million, in 2004. Most paper is imported. Non-wood forest products harvested include bamboo, rattan, gums, resins and medicinal plants, cinnamon, cloves, nutmeg and cardamom.

Industry and manufacturing

Industry contributes around 27 per cent of GDP. One-third of manufacturing output, which accounts for around 15 per cent of GDP, is based on raw materials from the agricultural sector. There are 10 dedicated Export Processing Zones, mainly employing female labour.
A master plan for industrial development, co-ordinated with the Japanese International Co-operation Agency (JICA) and the United Nations Industrial Development Organisation (Unido), identifies electronics, information technology, rubber and plastics, machinery, footwear, textiles and apparel and agro-based industries as target sectors, with policy development responsibilities for these sectors shared between JICA and Unido.

Tourism

Since 2003, benefiting from the truce with the Tamil Tigers, the tourism sector staged a recovery with visitor numbers passing the half million mark, and continuing to grow. The main markets are Europe and the US, but there has been a growth in the numbers of arrivals from other Asian countries and Australia.

Mining

Mining and quarrying account for around 2 per cent of GDP and employ 1 per cent of the workforce. Sri Lanka is rich in minerals such as ilmenite, plumbago, graphite, dolomite, kaolin, rutile, feldspar, quartz, mica, monazite, apatite, industrial clays and limestone. Precious and semi-precious stones, such as sapphires, rubies, catseyes, alexandrites, aquamarines, garnets, tourmalines, zircons, topaz, spinels, amethysts and moonstones provide increasing export income.

Hydrocarbons

Although Sri Lanka has no proven hydrocarbon reserves, there are indications of deposits offshore of around a billion barrels, and exploration is continuing. Sri Lanka consumes in excess of 85,000 barrels per day (bpd) of oil, all of which is imported. It is used for power generation and transport.
In 2008, Sri Lanka granted oil exploration rights to its offshore, north-western Mannar Basin, to three foreign oil companies; drilling began in August. Cairn Lanka (a subsidiary of UK-based Cairn Energy) announced on 3 October 2011 that it had discovered natural gas deposits in the Mannar Basin offshore of Sri Lanka; this was the first natural gas find for Sri Lanka.
Any use of coal is commercially insignificant.

Energy

Total installed generating capacity was 2.98 gigawatts (GW) in 2006. The energy mix was 41 per cent petroleum, 49 per cent biomass and traditional fuels and 10 per cent hydro. Almost 50 per cent of oil is used in transport and 25 per cent in electricity generation. Around 60 per cent of the population has access to mains electricity.
Electricity consumption is expected to increase by 3 per cent per annum. The government acknowledges that generation in the long-term cannot rely on hydropower or biomass-based energy supplies, due to the limitation of further hydroelectric development and an increasing standard of living for the population. In the medium term, reliance on imported hydrocarbons must suffice until indigenous oil and natural supplies are available.

Financial markets

Stock exchange

Colombo Stock Exchange (CSE)

Banking and insurance

In November 2009 HSBC became the first bank to announce it would open a branch in Jaffna, planned for January 2010. The opening will demonstrate the bank's confidence in the economy's emergence after the civil war which ended in May 2009.
There are 26 commercial banks, but the sector is dominated by two state banks – Bank of Ceylon and People's Bank — which hold 55 per cent of market share. The government's deficit financing crowds out the private sector, meaning that banks have traditionally focussed on the public sector and reap high spreads from soaring interest rates. Meanwhile, deposit rates are low thanks to Sri Lanka's closed capital account and lack of competition among banks. This has created a perverse situation, where, although government security yields are higher than those from risky bank deposits, money keeps flowing into the banks.
The dominance of the two state banks is holding back development of the sector. Government-mandated lending policies mean that the two are effectively the industry's interest rate setters. Monopoly yields insulate the public banks from competitive problems that would otherwise be caused by managerial slack, poor asset bases and high costs. Organised resistance from unions and a desire to keep the banks' huge funds within the public sector have so far ruled out privatisation, although there are signs the government is amenable to gradual privatisation and an eventual stock market listing.

Central bank

Central Bank of Sri Lanka

Main financial centre

Colombo

Time

GMT plus 5 hours 30 minutes

Geography

Sri Lanka lies on the same continental shelf as India, from which it is separated by the shallow Palk Strait. The relief is dominated by the central highland massif, with an average elevation of over 1,500 metres, situated in the south central part of the island. This is surrounded by upland ridges and valleys which in the south-west of the island continue to the coast. The eastern region is an undulating plain with isolated hills and the north has flat, low and fertile plains intersected by ridges.

Hemisphere

Southern

Climate

Colombo and the south-west experience monsoon rains May–September; the likely temperature range is 22–31 degrees Celsius (C) with average annual rainfall of 2,240mm. The north-east experiences monsoon rains November–February; lower temperatures (down to 10 degrees C) occur inland at higher altitudes, with average rainfall of 1,000–1,500mm a year.

Dress codes

Men usually wear a lightweight or tropical suit and tie for business meetings, and women mostly dress conventionally. On social occasions, dress as for business meetings unless stipulated otherwise. Rainwear is needed, as are warmer clothes for the hilly areas, especially between November and February. Discreet dress in public places is appreciated.

Entry requirements

Passports

Passports are required by all, and must be valid for at least three months from the date of issue of visa.

Visa

From 1 January 2011 tourists or business travellers will need to apply for their visas in advance, usually online via a new site, www.eta.gov.lk and pay a processing fee of US$50 for tourists, US$60 for business travellers or US$25 for transit passengers. Only those from Singapore or The Maldives will be exempt.

Currency advice/regulations

The import of local currency is limited to Rs1,000; export is limited to Rs250. The import of Indian and Pakistani foreign currency is prohibited, all other foreign currency is unlimited but amounts over US$5,000 (or equivalent) must be declared; export of foreign currency is limited to the amount declared on arrival. Travellers cheques are accepted in banks.

Customs

Personal effects are allowed duty-free, however, valuable items (including jewellery) must be declared and must be re-exported on departure. Tobacco imports are not duty-free.

Prohibited imports

The import of firearms, ammunition, explosives, dangerous weapons, illegal drugs and pornography is strictly prohibited.
The export of antiques, rare books, palm leaf manuscripts, rare anthropological material and any wild animal (including ivory), bird or reptile, tea or rubber is prohibited.

Health (for visitors)

Medical facilities are adequate if limited. Immediate cash payment is often required by doctors and hospitals.

Mandatory precautions

A vaccination certificate for yellow fever is required if travelling from an infected area. Infants under one year are exempt.

Advisable precautions

Vaccinations for diphtheria, tuberculosis, hepatitis A and B, Japanese B encephalitis, polio, tetanus and typhoid are recommended. Malaria, dengue fever and chikungunya fever are caused by mosquitoes; precautions including mosquito repellents, nets and clothing covering the body should be used. There is a rabies risk. Water should be boiled and filtered before drinking. Fruit must be washed in such water and peeled.
Medical insurance, including emergency evacuation, is necessary.

Hotels

A 10 per cent service charge is added to hotel bills.

Credit cards

Major credit cards are widely accepted; charge cards have limited acceptance.

Public holidays (national)

Fixed dates

1 Jan (New Year's Day), 4 Feb (Independence Day), 13–14 Apr (Sinhala and Tamil New Year), 1 May (Labour Day), 17 Dec (Ramazan), 25 Dec (Christmas Day).

Variable dates

Good Friday, Tamil Thai Pongal Day (Jan), Mahasivarathri (Feb), Vesak (Buddha Purnima) (May), Diwali (Hindu, Oct/Nov), Eid al Adha, Birth of the Prophet Mohammed, Eid al Fitr.
Although not official public holidays, Poya holidays are observed on the day of each full moon.
Hindu, Muslim and Buddhist festivals are timed according to local sightings of various phases of the moon.

Working hours

Banking

Mon–Fri: 0900–1500.

Business

Mon–Fri: 0900–1700.

Government

Mon–Fri: 0830–1615.

Shops

Mon–Fri: 0900–1730; Sat: 0900–1300.

Telecommunications

Mobile/cell phones

GSM 900 and 1800 services cover much of the island, particularly in the east and populated areas.

Electricity supply

230–240V AC, 50 cycles

Weights and measures

Metric system (local units also in use)

Social customs/useful tips

Alcoholic drinks are not served in hotels or restaurants on *Poya* (full moon) days. Footwear and headgear should be removed before entering Buddhist shrines; photographing statues of the Buddha is acceptable but not posing beside them; a yellow-robed Buddhist *bhikku* should not be asked to pose for photographs nor should visitors attempt to shake hands with him.
Filming with a video camera and other photography near military and government installations is prohibited.
Appointments should be made in advance. Punctuality is appreciated. Men shake hands on meeting and taking leave. Some people may prefer not to shake hands with those of the opposite sex.
The form of address is Mr or Mrs followed by family or surname, and people with an academic or professional title should be addressed by their full title.
Visitors should take note of local customs and take care to respect religious conventions. It is the convention to use the right and not the left hand when shaking hands and passing or receiving anything.
Restaurants usually add a service charge but further gratuities are optional.

Security

Visitors should avoid areas north of Puttalam, Anuradhapura and Nilaveli as well as the eastern side of the island south of Trincomalee including Batticaloa.
The areas once under conflict were heavily mined and travelling off main roads can be hazardous; warning notices are posted. Visitors must comply with any instruction issued at road blocks and security checks.
Registration with the relevant national embassy on arrival is highly advisable.

Getting there

Air

National airline: SriLankan Airlines
International airport/s: Colombo Bandaranaike International (CMB) in Katunayake, 29km north of Colombo, with duty-free shops, bar, restaurant, bank, post office and car hire. There are taxis, bus and rail links.

Airport tax: Departure tax: Rs1,000

Surface

Water: Ferry services between Colombo and Tuticorin in Tamil Nadu state of India were resumed on 14 June after almost 30 years of having been suspended due to the security situation. There will be two round trips per week initially.

Main port/s: Colombo, Trincomalee, Galle, Kandasanturai.

Getting about

National transport

Air: There are airports in Batticaloa, Gal Oya, Palali and Trincomalee; the airport at Jaffna is currently closed.

Road: The extensive road network has 27,000km of road, 19,000km of which is surfaced. Over 90 per cent of all haulage is transported by roads.

Buses: Express services are available to all main destinations and should be booked in advance. Some services have air-conditioning.

Rail: An intercity express train runs between Colombo and Kandy. There are regular services linking Colombo to other main centres. Some services offer air-conditioning, dining cars and first-class accommodation. The service to Jaffna has been discontinued.

City transport

Taxis: Metered taxis are usually found in large towns, they may have yellow tops and red numbers on a white plate.
Air-conditioned taxis cost 10 per cent more. A 10 per cent tip is usual.

Car hire

Self-drive and chauffeur-driven car hire are available although chauffeur-driven cars are generally recommended. If driving, do not ignore 'no parking' signs (in Colombo vehicles parked illegally are destroyed by security forces suspecting a terrorist bomb). It is highly advisable to be aware of all traffic laws and parking restrictions. Driving is on the left.

Traffic is generally congested and the average rate of progress on roads nationwide is 30kph. Many roads are one-way only.

A national or international driving licence must be presented for local endorsement (on weekdays only) at the Automobile Association offices in Colombo.

BUSINESS DIRECTORY

The addresses listed below are a selection only. While World of Information makes every endeavour to check these addresses, we cannot guarantee that changes have not been made, especially to telephone numbers and area codes. We would welcome any corrections.

Telephone area codes

The international direct dialling code (IDD) for Sri Lanka is +94, followed by area code and subscriber's number:

Colombo Central	11	Moratuwa	11
Dehiwela	11	Negombo	31
Galle	91	Nuwara Eliya	52
Jaffna	21	Panadura	34
Kandy	81	Trincomalee	26
Kurunegala	37		

Useful telephone numbers

Police, fire and ambulance	90
Emergency	433-333
Accident service	693-184/185
Directory enquiries	161
International calls	100
Speaking clock	104

Chambers of Commerce

American Chamber of Commerce in Sri Lanka, Colombo Hilton Hotel, Lotus Road, Colombo 1 (tel: 233-6073; fax: 233-6072; e-mail: amcham@itmin.com).

Ceylon Chamber of Commerce, 50 Navam Mawatha, PO Box 274, Colombo 2 (tel: 245-2183; fax: 243-7477; e-mail: info@chamberlk).

Federation of Chambers of Commerce and Industry of Sri Lanka, 29 Gregory's Road, PO Box 2015, Colombo 7 (tel: 698-225; fax: 699-530; e-mail: info@fccisl.org).

National Chamber of Commerce of Sri Lanka, 450 DR Wijewardene Mawatha Street, PO Box 1375, Colombo 10 (tel: 268-9600; fax: 268-9596; e-mail: sg@nccsl.lk).

Banking

Bank of Ceylon, 4 Bank of Ceylon Mawatha, Colombo 1 (tel: 244-8348; fax: 244-8606).

Commercial Bank of Ceylon, 21 Bristol St, Colombo 1 (tel: 244-5010; fax: 244-9889; email: email@combank.net).

DFCC Bank, 73/5 Galle Road, Colombo 3 (tel: 244-0366; fax: 244-0376; email: dfcc@sri.lanka.net).

Hatton National Bank, 10 RA de Mel Mawatha, Colombo 3 (tel: 234-3473; fax: 244-0658).

National Development Bank, 40 Navam Mawatha, Colombo 2 (tel: 243-7701; fax: 244-0262).

Pan Asia Bank, 450 Galle Road, Colombo 3 (tel: 256-5564; fax: 256-5576; email: panasia@pabnk.lk).

People's Bank, 110 Sir James Peiris Mawatha, Colombo 2 (tel: 232-4188; fax: 244-7671).

Sampath Bank, PO Box 997, Sampath Centre Building, 110 Sir James Peiris Mawatha, Colombo 2 (tel: 230-0260; fax: 230-0143).

Seylan Bank, Ceylinco Seylan Towers, 90 Galle Road, Colombo 3 (tel: 243-7901; fax: 243-3072).

Union Bank of Colombo, World Trade Centre, Echelon Square, Colombo 1 (tel: 234-6346; fax: 234-6356).

Central bank

Central Bank of Sri Lanka, PO Box 590, 30 Janadhipathi Mawatha, Colombo 1 (tel: 247-7000; fax: 247-7712; e-mail: cbslgen@sri.lanka.net).

Stock exchange

Colombo Stock Exchange (CSE): www.cse.lk

Travel information

Atlas Lanka (Pvt) Ltd, 86/1. Chatham Street, Colombo 1 (tel: 233-4255/6; fax 243-5292; email: atlaslka@sltnet.com).

Automobile Association of Ceylon, 40 Sir Macan Markar Mawatha, Galle Face, Colombo 3 (tel: 242-1528; fax: 244-6074).

Bandaranayake International Airport, Katunayake (tel: 225-2861; fax: 225-3187).

SriLankan Airlines, Level 22, East Tower, World Trade Centre, Echelon Square, Colombo 1 (tel: 733-5555; fax: 733-5122; internet: www.srilankan.aero).

Ministry of tourism

Ministry of Tourism, 64 Galle road, Colombo 03 (tel: 238-5241; fax: 239-9274; internet: www.slmts.slt.lk).

National tourist organisation offices

Sri Lanka Tourist Board, 80 Galle road, Colombo 03 (tel: 243-7059/60; fax: 244-0001; internet: www.srilankatourism.org).

Ministries

Ministry of Agriculture, Sampathapay, 82 Rajamalwatte Road, Battaramulla (tel: 288-6623).

Ministry of Aviation and Airports Developments, 64 Galle Road, Colombo 3.

Ministry of Buddha Sasana and Religious Affairs, 135 Anagarika Dharmapala Mawatha, Colombo 7 (tel: 232-9064; fax: 243-7992).

Ministry of Constitutional Affairs and Industrial Development, 73/1 Galle Road, Colombo 3 (tel: 232-7553; fax: 244-9402).

Ministry of Co-operative Development, 349 Galle Road, Colombo 3.

Ministry of Cultural Affairs, Sethsiripaya, Battaramulla.

Ministry of Defence, 155 Baladaksha Mawatha, Colombo 3 (tel: 243-0860; fax: 254-1529).

Ministry of Development, Rehabilitation & Reconstruction of the East and Rural

Housing Development, 43/89 Bristol Building, York Street, Colombo 1.

Ministry of Development, Rehabilitation & Reconstruction of the North and Tamil Affairs, North and East: 121 Park Road, Colombo 5.

Ministry of Education, Isurupaya, Sri Jayewardenepura Kotte, Battaramulla (tel: 286-5141; fax: 286-5162).

Ministry of Ethnic Affairs and National Integration, 152 Galle Road, Colombo 3.

Ministry of Finance and Planning, Secretariat Building, Colombo 1 (tel: 243-3937; fax: 244-9823; email: minfi@boisrilanka.org).

Ministry of Fisheries and Aquatic Resources Development, Maligawatte, Colombo 10 (tel: 244-6183; fax: 254-1184).

Ministry of Foreign Affairs, Republic Building, Colombo 1 (tel: 232-5371; fax: 244-6091; email: for_min@sri.lanka.net).

Ministry of Forestry and Environment, Unity Plaza Building, Colombo 4 (tel: 258-8274; fax: 258-3290).

Ministry of Health, Suwasiripaya, 385 Wimalawasa Mawatha, Colombo 10 (tel/fax: 269-2694).

Ministry of Higher Education and IT Development, 18 Ward Place, Colombo 8.

Ministry of Highways, Sethsiripaya, Battaramulla.

Ministry of Information and Media, World Trade Centre, Echelon Square, Colombo 1.

Ministry of Internal & International Commerce, Muslim Religious Affairs, and Shipping Development, Insurance Building, Vauxhall Street, Colombo 2.

Ministry of Irrigation and Water Resources Management, 500 TB Jayah Mawatha, Colombo 10 (tel: 268-7491; fax: 269-4968).

Ministry of Justice, Superior Courts Complex Colombo 12 (tel: 232-9044; fax: 232-0785).

Ministry of Labour, Labour Secretariat, Kirula Road, Colombo 5 (tel: 258-8078; fax: 258-2938).

Ministry of Land Development and Minor Export Agriculture, Govijana Mandiraya, Rajamalwatte Road, Battaramulla.

Ministry of Estate Infrastructure and Livestock Developemnt, 45 St Michaels Road, Colombo 3.

Ministry of Mahaweli Development, 500 TB Jayah Mawatha, Colombo 10 (tel: 268-7491; fax: 268-7386).

Ministry of Plan Implementation, Sethsiripaya, Battaramulla (tel: 286-2721; fax: 286-2478).

Ministry of Ports Development and Development of the South, 45 Laden Bastian Road, Colombo 1 (tel: 242-1231; fax: 242-3485).

Ministry of Post and Telecommunications, Sethsiripaya, Battaramulla.

Ministry of Power and Energy, 80 Flower Road, Colombo 7.

Ministry of Provincial Councils and Local Government, 330 Union Place, Colombo 2 (tel: 242-1211; fax: 234-7529).

Ministry of Public Administration, Home Affairs and Plantation Industries, Independence Square, Colombo 7 (tel: 269-6211; fax: 269-5279).

Ministry of Rural Industrial Development, Janakala Kendraya, Pelawatte, Battaramulla.

Ministry of Samurdhi, Rural Development, Parliamentary Affairs and Up-Country Development, 7A Reed Avenue, Colombo 7 (tel: 268-9589; fax: 268-8945).

Ministry of Science and Technology, 320 TB Jaya Mawatha, Colombo 10.

Ministry of Social Services and Housing Development for Fishing Community, Sethsiripaya, Battaramulla.

Ministry of Transport, 1 DR Wijewardana Mawatha, Colombo 10 (tel: 268-7105; fax: 269-4547).

Ministry of Urban Development, Construction and Public Utilities, Sethsiripaya, Battaramulla (tel: 286-2721; fax: 286-4765).

Ministry of Vocational Training, 475/32 Kotta Ropad, Rajagiriya.

Ministry of Womens Affairs, 177 Nawala Road, Colombo 5.

Ministry of Youth Affairs, 7A Reed Avenue, Colombo 7.

Other useful addresses

Board of Investment of Sri Lanka (BOI), World Trade Centre, Echelon Square, Colombo 1 (tel: 243-6639; fax: 244-7994; internet: www.boisrilanka.com/boihome/boi.htm).

British High Commission, 190 Galle Road, Colombo 3 (tel: 243-7336; fax: 243-0308; email: bhc@eureka.lk).

Colombo Plan, 28 St Michael's Road, Colombo 3 (tel: 256-4448; fax: 256-4531; email: cplan@slt.lk).

Colombo Stock Exchange, World Trade Centre, Echelon Square, Colombo 1 (tel: 244-6581; fax: 244-5279; internet: www.lanka.net/cse).

Sri Lanka Embassy (USA), 2148 Wyoming Avenue, NW, Washington DC 20008 (tel: (+1-202) 483-4025; fax: (+1-202) 232-7181; email: slembassy@starpower.net).

Sri Lanka Export Credit Insurance Corporation, Export Guarantee House, Colombo 2 (tel: 271-9410; fax: 271-9400; email: slecic@tradenetsl.lk).

Sri Lanka Export Development Board, 42 Navam Mawatha, Colombo 2 (tel: 230-0675; fax: 230-0715; email: serve@edbtradenetsl.lk).

Sri Lanka Importers', Exporters' and Manufacturers' Association, PO Box 12, Colombo 10 (tel: 269-6321; fax: 252-2524; email: sliema@isplanka).

Sri Lanka Tea Board, 574 Galle Road, Colombo 3 (tel: 258-2236; fax: 258-9132; email: tboard@sri.lanka.net).

US Embassy, 210 Galle Road, Colombo 3 (tel: 244-8007; fax: 243-7345; email: cdscmb@usia.gov).

Internet sites

InfoLanka (gateway site): www.infolanka.com

Sri Lanka Telecom directory: www.slt.lk

Sri Lanka, virtual library: www.lankalibrary.com

Tamilnet: www.tamilnet.com

Sudan

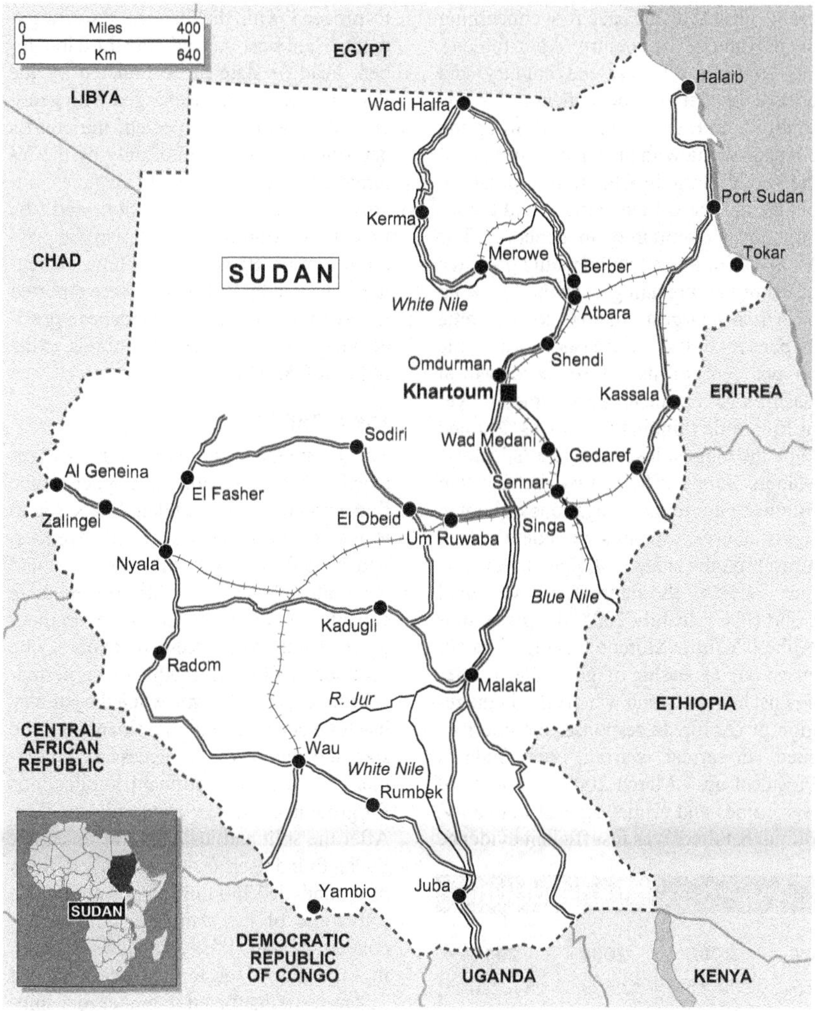

The biggest event in Sudan's post independence history occurred on 9 July 2011 with the division of the troubled country into two. Sudan's breakaway southern half was to be known simply as 'South Sudan' with the north, or as it was called by the *Economist* magazine, 'Rump' Sudan retaining the title of 'Sudan'. Sudan has seen a number of protracted conflicts since its independence in 1956 that have severely hindered economic development, particularly of natural resources. The most recent of these, in the western province of Darfur (2003–11), has brought with it international condemnation, internally displaced populations and sanctions affecting the country as a whole.

Darfur and the tradition of warfare

Warfare of one sort or another is very much hard-wired into the system in Sudan. Tensions abound and arms are the widespread norm. In early 2011 two of the three rebel groups operating in Darfur, the Justice and Equality Movement (JEM) and the Liberty and Justice Movement (LJM), agreed to accept concessions on wealth and power sharing and enter talks with the government. The third group on

KEY FACTS

Official name: Jamhuryat es Sudan (Republic of Sudan)

Head of State: President Omar Hassan Ahmad al Bashir (from1993; re-elected Apr 2010)

Head of government: President Omar Hassan Ahmad al Bashir

Ruling party: Al Muttamar al Watani (National Congress Party) (NCP) (from 1998; re-elected Apr 2010)

Area: 1,861,484 square km

Population: 43.20 million (2010)

Capital: Khartoum

Official language: Arabic

Currency: Sudanese pound (S£) = 100 piastre (The pound was adopted in 2007; S£1 = 100 old Dinar)

Exchange rate: S£2.68 per US$ (Oct 2011)

GDP per capita: US$1,705 (2010)

GDP real growth: 5.10% (2010)

GDP: US$68.40 billion (2010)

Inflation: 13.00% (2010)

Oil production: 486,000 bpd (2010)

Balance of trade: US$2.56 billion (2010)

Foreign debt: US$37.98 billion (Dec 2010)

Annual FDI: US$2.89 billion (2010)

the rebel map, the Sudan Liberation Army (SLA) simply failed to turn up in the Gulf State of Qatar where the talks were held. Despite the presence of a 22,000 strong joint UN-African Union Mission in Dafur (UNAMID) peacekeeping force, in early 2011 the situation in Darfur was reported to be deteriorating. President al Bashir fears another humiliating loss of territory.

The longest of the two wars was between the northern Sudanese government in Khartoum and the government of the South in Juba (1956–72 and 1983–2005). The North-South civil war ended with the signing of the Comprehensive Peace Agreement (CPA) that was in place from 2005 to 2011. As part of the CPA, a referendum took place in January of 2011 during which the people of South Sudan voted to secede from the North and on 9 July 2011, Sudan became two countries: Sudan and the Republic of South Sudan. Abyei, a significant oil producing region on the North-South border was also expected to carry out a referendum in January to determine which side it would join, but this did not take place and uncertainties regarding the status of the oil-rich Abyei region remain; Abyei straddles the border between the two Sudans, with both sides laying claim to it. Other territorial disputes along the North/South border continue, specifically in the areas of South Kordofan and Blue Nile where clashes have taken place between government troops and rebels who previously fought alongside the forces of South Sudan. Fighting has also flared up in the border region of the (so far) inappropriately named state of Unity.

Sudan's government had naively expected to receive some sort of blessing and welcome into the club of internationally acceptable administrations by agreeing to the country's division. This did not happen for the obvious reason that Sudan was dragging its feet in meeting its obligations under the CPA. For some years, Sudan's leader, Omar Hassan al Bashir had found himself on the back foot concerning the division of the country. After fomenting conflicts all over the country and openly opposing independence for the south Mr al Bashir finally had no option but to go along with the wishes not only of the south's largely Christian population, but also of the United Nations and the international community in general. Thus Mr al Bashir knew that he would go down in history as presiding over the break-up of Africa's largest country, losing some 30 per cent of its land area as well as some 80 per cent of its oil reserves. Mr al Bashir's government had assumed power in 1989 little thinking that it was destined to be the biggest loser in Sudan's history. Matters were not helped by the fact that following numerous allegations of human rights abuses, Sudan's president found himself on the sharp end of an arrest warrant issued by the International Criminal Court (ICC). In July 2008, the prosecutor of the ICC Luis Moreno Ocampo had accused Mr al Bashir of genocide, crimes against humanity and war crimes in the region of Darfur. In response, the court issued an arrest warrant for Sudan's President on 4 March 2009 on counts of war crimes and crimes against humanity, ruling that there was insufficient evidence to prosecute him for genocide. However, after an appeal by the prosecution, the Court ruled that in fact there was adequate evidence for charges of genocide to be brought and issued a second warrant on three separate counts. All the arrest warrants, were transmitted via the Sudanese government which, since it is itself governed by the President, was not disposed to proceed with the President's arraignment. Mr al Bashir is only the third incumbent head of state to be indicted by the ICC and the first to be charged with genocide. As was to be expected, the court's decision was opposed not only by the international governmental agencies involved – the African Union and the League of Arab States, but also the governments of Russia and China. Documents leaked by WikiLeaks were reported to have revealed that the Sudanese president had also embezzled state funds, to the order of US$9 billion.

The economy

The independence of South Sudan will inevitably have a significant impact on the Sudanese economy. Sudan looks set to lose some 75 per cent of its oil revenues, which could translate into domestic and external imbalances. With oil revenue constituting more than half of government revenue and 90 per cent of exports, the economy will need to adjust to a permanent shock, this at a time when the country has little access to external financing. The size and nature of the necessary adjustment could have significant implications for growth and macro-economic stability. After the split and losing its oil revenues, Sudan found itself facing monthly deficits of around US$350 million per month unless some of the shortfall could be recouped via transit fees. To make its point, in August 2011 customs officers in Port Sudan were instructed to embargo a shipment of 600,000 barrels of oil from the South Sudan until the fees were paid in full. Sudan will likely have to exercise fiscal restraint by streamlining non-priority spending, reducing fuel subsidies, reducing tax exemptions and enhancing revenue administration. Continuing to allow greater exchange rate flexibility, tightening monetary policy and implementing structural reforms in a timely manner will also be crucial.

According to the International Monetary Fund (IMF) a large part of the fiscal adjustment was expected to fall on the expenditure side. Ministry of finance estimates suggested that the long-term fiscal adjustment may need to accommodate a

KEY INDICATORS — Sudan

	Unit	2006	2007	2008	2009	2010
Population	m	*36.22	*37.16	*39.15	*39.74	*43.20
Gross domestic product (GDP)	US$bn	36.40	46.50	58.00	52.70	68.40
GDP per capita	US$	1,005	1,252	1,522	1,346	1,705
GDP real growth	%	11.3	10.5	6.8	4.6	5.1
Inflation	%	7.2	8.0	14.3	11.3	13.0
Oil output	'000 bpd	397.0	457.0	480.0	490.0	486.0
Exports (fob) (goods)	US$m	5,813.0	8,879.2	11,670.5	8,473.2	11,404.3
Imports (fob) (goods)	US$m	7,105.0	7,722.4	8,229.4	8,528.0	8,839.4
Balance of trade	US$m	-1,292.0	1,156.8	3,441.1	-54.8	2,564.9
Current account	US$m	-5,489.0	-3,447.1	-1,313.6	-4,232.3	-1,164.8
Total reserves minus gold	US$m	1,659.9	1,377.9	1,399.0	1,094.2	–
Foreign exchange	US$m	1,659.9	1,377.9	1,399.0	897.0	–
Exchange rate	per US$	2.17	2.01	2.09	2.30	2.50

* estimated figure

revenue loss as high as 36.5 per cent of total revenues. Sudan faced the daunting challenge of balancing fiscal consolidation against the pressing needs for its planned development agenda. The extent of the shock to the economy in the short-run was unclear. Agreement on transition transfers between the two Sudans, however unlikely, could provide a gradual shift to the long-term revenue loss. During the first half of the year, it became apparent that a revised budget for the second half of 2011 would be needed. The government announced that the amended budget would be based on several options pending the outcome of negotiations with South Sudan on arrangements affecting the oil sector. The worst case assumption for the fiscal plan was the estimated revenue loss of 36.5 per cent referred to earlier, although this figure might be adjusted if the outcome of final negotiations allowed. Other elements included a 3-year emergency plan (the so called 'salvation programme') and a longer term 5-year strategic plan covering the period 2012–16. For Sudan the 3-year plan was the key element to smooth the transition into the new post-secession era as it developed a macro framework to re-orient the economy from an oil-led to an agriculture sector-led model with the inclusion of appropriate social safety measures.

Inflation

Sudan's inflation rate in April and May 2011 remained in double figures, albeit lower than the March level. The 12-month inflation rate was 16.8 per cent in May 2011, lower than the 17.1 per cent in March and the 16.9 per cent registered in February. The decline was largely due to the slight ease in food price inflation (cereals, rice, vegetables and fruits), which decreased to 18.8 per cent compared to 20.4 per cent in March 2011. As reported by the Central Bank of Sudan, imported inflation increased to 12.4 per cent in April 2011 compared to 9.1 per cent in December 2010. This is largely attributed to the knock-on effect of the exchange rate impact on imported consumer goods as well as the cost of locally produced goods through higher cost of imported raw materials.

Energy

Oil plays a major role in the economy of Sudan both north and South. According to the International Monetary Fund (IMF), oil represented over half of government revenue and 90 per cent of export earnings for north Sudan in 2010. Under the CPA (which ended on 9 July), South Sudan had been given some degree of autonomy from the north, but revenues from oil produced in what was to became South Sudan were shared equally. This arrangement ceased after South Sudan's independence. Most of Sudan's oil is produced in what is now the South (about 75 per cent, depending on specific field allocations), but the entire pipeline, refining and export infrastructure is in the north.

In the near-term, both countries will remain co-dependent in terms of the oil industry. The loss of oil revenues will have a serious impact on the economy of north Sudan at a time when it is still facing international sanctions – while land-locked South Sudan is dependent on the north to export its crude. At the time of writing, the two countries had yet to come to an agreement regarding transit fees. The north was seeking fees that would offset the loss of its 50 per cent share of the South's revenue and was most recently reported to be charging about US$23–33 per barrel, while the South was seeking terms that were more in line with international standards (below US$1.00 per barrel) and offering to sell the north discounted oil..

Historical statistics relating solely to South Sudan were barely available in 2011. According to *Oil and Gas Journal* (OGJ), Sudan had five billion barrels of proved oil reserves in January 2011, up from an estimated 563 million barrels in 2006. Other analysts put reserve estimates as low as 4.2 (Wood Mackenzie) or as high as 6.7 billion barrels (*BP Statistical Review of World Energy 2011*). The majority of reserves are located in the Muglad and Melut basins. Due to civil conflict, oil exploration has mostly been limited to the central and south-central regions of the country. Natural gas associated with oil production is mostly flared or re-injected. In 2009, there were announcements of natural gas discoveries in Sudan but these have yet to be determined as commercially viable.

Exploration and development of Sudan's oil resources has been controversial. International human rights organisations have accused the Sudanese government of financing human rights abuses with oil revenues, including the mass displacement of civilians near the oil fields. Factional fighting and rebel attacks on oil infrastructure have kept oil production and exploration from reaching full potential. China National Petroleum Corporation (CNPC), the largest investor in Sudan, has had workers and facilities attacked while at the same time, China has faced international condemnation for its investments in Sudan.

The United States prohibits its nationals from engaging in any transactions or activities related to the petroleum or petrochemical industries in the entire territory of Sudan (including South Sudan) as a result of the conflict in Darfur. Sudan also faces sanctions from the United Nations (UN) and the European Union (EU) which include arms embargos, travel bans and restrictions on financial activities that may impede the peace process – without specifically addressing the petroleum sector.

The Sudan National Petroleum Corporation (Sudapet), north Sudan's national oil company, is active in the country's oil exploration and production. However, due to its limited technical and financial resources, Sudapet often develops joint ventures with foreign companies in oil projects but remains a minority shareholder. North Sudan is planning to carry out a licensing round for blocks in the northern and western (Darfur) part of the country.

Oil production had began in the late 1990s and grew rapidly starting in July 1999 with the completion of an export pipeline that runs from central Sudan to Port Sudan. In 2010, the US government's Energy Information Administration (EIA) estimated that crude oil production averaged just over 470,000 barrels per day (bpd). First half 2011 data indicate a slight decline, averaging about 460,000bpd. As a result of uncertainties regarding security and boundary issues, there has been limited additional investment in the oil industry. Overall, Sudan's production is sourced from two groups of blocks in addition to output from smaller, newer areas that have recently come on-stream.

In 2010, Sudan consumed around 98,000bpd. The remaining crude was exported almost exclusively to Asian markets. According to international trade data, in 2010 China imported around 250,000bpd (just over 65 per cent of total Sudanese exports and 5 per cent of Chinese imports) followed by Malaysia (45,000bpd) and Japan (40,000bpd). Sudan also exports some processed fuels to neighbouring countries. Ethiopia imports most of its fuel from Sudan but official data on trade volumes is not available.

Sudan has three refineries located in Khartoum, Port Sudan and El-Obeid. The Khartoum refinery was expanded in 2006 from a capacity of 50,000bpd to 100,000bpd. The expansion allowed for the processing of both Nile and Fula blends of crude for domestic consumption as well as product exports. The Port Sudan facility is located near the Red Sea and has a refining capacity of 21,700bpd. In September 2005, a contract was awarded to Petronas (of Malaysia) to build a new refinery at Port Sudan. The refinery was to be designed to process the highly acidic Dar blend but this project has been postponed several times and the status is currently unknown. The El-Obeid refinery is the smallest with an estimated capacity of 10,000bpd.

Risk assessment

Economy	Fair
Politics	Poor
Regional stability	Fair

COUNTRY PROFILE

Historical profile

1821 The swamps of southern Sudan were unaffected by the Arab-controlled northern regions until the Turks defeated Egypt, conquered northern Sudan and opened the south to trade.
1869 After the opening of the Suez Canal, the British became involved in Sudan.
1881–85 Mohammed Ahmed, who proclaimed himself the long-looked-for Mahdi (the guided one), led his followers, the Muslim Sudanese, in a rebellion against Egyptian misrule; General Gordon was sent by Britain to quash the rebellion. In 1885, Gordon and the British army were massacred by the Mahdi's army at Khartoum. Sudan was ruled by the Mahdi for the next 17 years. The Mahdi united the tribes in a modern Islamic state.
1898 The Mahdi was defeated by the British and Anglo-Egyptian army.
1899 Sudan was ruled as an Anglo-Egyptian condominium until it achieved independence as a parliamentary republic in 1956.
1945 At the end of the Second World War, political parties emerged. The Umma Party was created by supporters of the Mahdi while the Ashiqqa Party was established by rivals of the Mahdi and eventually became the National Union Party (NUP).
1956 Sudan gained independence. With southern calls for a federation or even secession rejected, a civil war broke out between the largely Muslim north and the largely Christian/Animist south.
1958 A military coup led by General Ibrahim Abboud overthrew the civilian government of Prime Minister Abd Allah Khalil. Martial law was declared and Abboud proclaimed himself prime minister.
1962 Civil war began in the south, led by the Anya Nya movement.
1964 The 'October Revolution' overthrew Abboud and a national government was established.
1969 Colonel Jaafar Mohammed al Nimieri led the 'May Revolution' military coup, installing a revolutionary council.
1972 Nimieri became the country's first elected president and gave the southern provinces a degree of autonomy under the Addis Ababa agreement between the government and the Anya Nya, reducing the level of fighting.
1978 Oil was discovered in southern Sudan.
1983 The President increased the Islamisation campaign when the autonomy agreement was revoked and *Sharia* (Islamic law) was introduced. In the south the Sudan People's Liberation Movement (SPLM) was established; its armed wing, the Sudan People's Liberation Army (SPLA) gained control of much of the south.
1985–86 Nimieri was ousted in a bloodless coup and after a brief period of military rule, Sadiq al Mahdi, the great-grandson of the Great Mahdi, became prime minister after elections in 1986.
1989 Sadiq al Mahdi was replaced following another bloodless coup by the National Salvation Revolution; Omar Hassan Ahmad al Bashir became chairman of the Revolutionary Command Council for National Salvation (RCCNS).
1992 The Sudanese pound was replaced as the currency by the Sudanese dinar.
1993 The RCCNS was abolished after Omar al Bashir was appointed president; Sudan returned to civilian rule, although with one political party exercising dominance – Al Muttamar al Watani (National Congress Party) (NCP), the country was not strictly a democracy.
1995 Egyptian President Mubarak accused Sudan of being involved in an attempt to assassinate him in Addis Ababa.
1996 The first presidential and legislative elections since the coup in 1989 were held; Omar al Bashir was elected president for a five-year term. Sanctions were imposed against Sudan by the UN for the country's failure to extradite three men suspected of involvement in the 1995 attempted assassination of Mubarak.
1997 The Khartoum Peace Agreement was ratified by the National Assembly. Peace talks between the SPLA and the government resumed in Nairobi.
1998–99 Voters in a referendum endorsed a new constitution. Sudan began to export oil. After a power struggle within the ruling NCP, between Bashir and Hassan al Turabi (a hardline Islamist and ideologue), the President imposed a state of emergency and dissolved the National Assembly.
2000 Omar al Bashir and the NCP were re-elected. Most opposition parties boycotted the elections.
2001 Hassan al Turabi, was arrested and his party, the National Islamic Front (NIF), was banned. The UN Security Council approved the lifting of sanctions imposed in 1996. The UN's World Food Programme estimated that three million people were facing famine.
2002 After peace talks in Kenya, the government and the SPLA signed the Machakos Protocol: the government accepted the right of the south to seek self-determination after a six-year interim period.
2003 Rebels in the western region of Darfur started an uprising by attacking government targets, claiming the region was being neglected by Khartoum. Hassan al Turabi was released and the ban on the NIF was lifted. China and the Sudan announced a US$1 billion investment plan to enhance Sudan's oil infrastructure, including increased capacity at the Khartoum refinery and construction of a 750-kilometre-long pipeline between the Kordofan oilfield and the coast.
2004 A campaign to quell the insurrection in Darfur began; thousands of people were displaced by the fighting. Army officers and opposition politicians, including al Turabi, were arrested over an alleged coup plot. Bashir agreed to grant autonomy to the south for six years, split the country's oil revenues with the southern provinces and allow the southerners to vote in a referendum on independence at the end of the six-year period. The conflict in the western region of Darfur between nomad Arab militia and black African villagers gained world attention. The government denied that it supported the *Janjaweed* militias, accused of systematic killings of African villagers, and said that there was no evidence of any atrocities.
2005 The government and the Sudan People's Liberation Army (SPLA) signed a peace agreement which ended the 22-year civil war. The agreement began a period of transition to run until 2009, when parliamentary and state legislative elections would take place. SPLA leader, John Garang, was appointed vice president for the six-year period of reconciliation, and a new constitution gave a large degree of autonomy to the south. Security forces arrested many members and top officials of the main opposition Umma Party (UP), because of planned celebrations marking an anti-government uprising in 1986. Sudan said it had found quantities of oil in its western region of Darfur. John Garang was killed in a helicopter crash; riots broke out in Khartoum,

between black southern Sudanese and northern Arabs. Garang's deputy, Salva Kiir, was named his successor as vice president of national Sudan and president of southern Sudan. Chad declared 'a state of belligerence' with Sudan. In an effort to ease tensions between the two countries, President Obasanjo of Nigeria, as head of the African Union, attempted mediation between a Sudanese envoy and Chad's President Déby, but with little success.

2006 The AU extended the mandate for its peacekeeping force by a further 10 months. Chad broke-off diplomatic relations with Sudan, following attacks on Chadian towns by Sudanese backed Chad rebels based in the Darfur region. A UN resolution was passed calling for a 20,000 international force of soldiers and police to be admitted to the Darfur region as peace-keepers. President Bashir remained uncompromising in its opposition to intervention. The UN envoy, Jan Pronk, was expelled for claiming that government troops had suffered defeats in southern Sudan.

2007 The currency was changed from the dinar (in use since 1992), back to the Sudanese pound (S£); the exchange rate was set at S£1 to 100 old dinars. Vice President Kiir accused the national government of supporting militia operating in the south, who had not been disarmed, and failing to share the wealth of resources found in the south. An agreement was signed between Sudan, Chad and the Central African Republic whereby no shelter would be given to rebel movements from another country. The minister of humanitarian affairs, Ahmed Haroun and a Janjaweed leader, Ali Mohammed Ali Abd al Rahman (known as Ali Kushayb) were indited by the International Criminal Court for crimes against humanity, committed during attacks on the civilian population of Darfur. The UN voted for a UN peacekeeping force to be sent to Sudan to bolster African Union (AU) troops already deployed in Darfur to protect civilians. An AU base, staffed by mostly Nigerian troops acting as military observers, was attacked by heavily armed rebels; 10 soldiers were killed and the incident sparked international condemnation. Dissident members of the SLA, the Justice and Equality Movement (JEM), were blamed for the attack. Rebels burned down the AU-base town of Haskanita. The UN Mission (Unmis) reported the town was under the control of government troops. The government announced a unilateral ceasefire in Darfur in advance of peace talks, despite two rebel groups boycotting the talks, which were being held in Libya. The SLA-Unity and the JEM groups decided not to attend the talks as other, smaller, rebel groups had also been invited. Representatives approached SLA-Unity and JEM to reconsider their decision. Meanwhile, the northern National Congress Party and southern Sudan People's Liberation Movement finally agreed to implement all provisions of the 2005 peace agreement. The UN–AU Mission in Darfur (Unamid) began operations, replacing the AU forces. The oil producing province of Abyei was subject to continued armed attacks by the SPLA, so finally the government, in agreement with the SPLM asked the Permanent Court of Arbitration (PCA) (based in The Hague) to rule on the disputed border between the north and south.

2008 The International Criminal Court (ICC) accused President al Bashir of genocide in Darfur and formally requested a warrant for his arrest. Sudan does not recognise the ICC and claimed the move was a 'foreign conspiracy'. The AU called on the UN to suspend the war crimes accusation against President Bashir, saying it would jeopardise the on-going peace process. The PCA ruling concluded that the government in Khartoum's argument that Abyei only constituted a small sliver of land south of the Kiir/Bahr el Arab River was erroneous and awarded 10,460 square kilometres to southern Sudan. It also rejected southern Sudan's argument that its demarcation in the eastern and western boundary areas was legitimate and awarded those areas, including much of the oil reserves in the area, to Khartoum. It also affirmed the right of traditional pastoral herdsmen to continue to use both sides of the border areas in the province of Kordofan for their flocks (over 18,500 square km).

2009 The ICC issued a warrant for the arrest of President Bashir on two counts of war crimes and five counts of crimes against humanity. Sudan dismissed the charges and re-affirmed its position of non-co-operation with the ICC. Sudan expelled 10 foreign aid agencies within hours of the issue of the arrest warrant. General elections to be held in 2009 were postponed until 2010; when undertaken, there would be six elections, including national presidential and parliamentary, the south Sudanese presidency and parliament and state gubernatorial and assemblies. The government reversed its earlier decision and invited new aid-NGOs into the country and allowed those already in operation to expand their activities. The ruling SPLM of the autonomous southern region split when Lam Akol created his own political party SPLM-Democratic Change, claiming the SPLM had failed to govern South Sudan. Both parties will nominate a candidate to challenge President Bashir in the next presidential elections. A delay in completing a census forced the postponement of presidential elections. The census was criticised by political leaders in the south who said that the southern Sudanese population had been under-recorded.

2010 The government agreed a ceasefire with the JEM rebels in Dafur in February. Almost all of the political parties based in southern Sudan threatened to withdraw from the presidential elections by 1 April, due to fears concerning fraud and security during the voting. They maintained that the electoral process had been rigged to favour the ruling NCP. President Bashir threatened to cancel a referendum on independence in the south in the face of the boycotts; the elections were duly held. The presidential and parliamentary elections scheduled to be held between 11–13 April were extended by two days due to organisational problems and high voter turnout. Two election monitoring organisations declared that the elections failed to meet full international standards due to intimidation and harassment, although neither called for a re-election. The announcement of the results was delayed until the end of April as counting took longer than anticipated. President Bashir (NCP) won 68.24 per cent of the northern presidential vote and his political party NCP won 68.2 per cent. Salva Kiir (SPLM) was sworn in as the first elected president of southern Sudan on 21 May. On 14 May, Sudan signed an agreement with Egypt, Ethiopia, Uganda, Tanzania and Rwanda to redistribute their relative share of Nile water; negotiations had been taking place since 1977. Opposition leader, Hassan al Turabi, who had been imprisoned by the government in May, was released on 30 June. In July the ICC added a second arrest warrant for President Bashir, for genocide. The referendum on independence for the South was scheduled for 9 January 2011, although a referendum in Abyei region, to be held on the same day on whether it should join the north or the south was still in doubt in October. Voter registration for the referendum started on 14 November and was due to end on 4 December but was extended for four days. The UN reckoned that some 51,000 people travelled south to register in time. President Bashir announced on 19 December that if the south broke away, the north would adopt an Islamic constitution.

2011 A seven-day referendum in southern Sudan, which begun on 9 January, to determine its future as either a province of Sudan or as an independent country, was overwhelmingly in favour of independence. The result was 98.83 per cent of the vote in favour, 1.17 per cent against independence. On 16 February, it was decided by the ruling committee of the SPLM that South Sudan would be the official name of the country when it comes into existence on 9 July. On 19 May a group of army personnel of Sudan were ambushed while being escorted out of Abyei by UN peacekeepers and 22 men were killed in what the UN called 'a criminal attack', while the US called on South Sudan to 'account' for the attack. In retaliation, on 22 May northern military 'repelled enemy forces' according to Sudanese state news and occupied Abyei. The UN condemned the escalation in violence and called on Sudan to withdraw its military from the disputed town and region of Abyei, as a UN peacekeeping force was caught in the middle of what South Sudan called an 'invasion'. Around 20,000 people fled from Abyei to South Sudan. On 24 May armed men looted and burned buildings in Abyei as the UN warned Sudan that it was 'responsible for maintaining law and order' and that it should 'intervene to stop criminal acts'. On 25 May, President Bashir refused to withdraw troops from Abyei saying the area belonged to Sudan. In a deal mediated by the AU on 31 May, Sudan and South Sudan agreed to set up a demilitarised zone along their 2,100km border, including Abyei. The zone is to be jointly patrolled. However, on 27 July, the UN Security Council authorised the deployment of a 4,200-strong Ethiopian force (UN Interim Security Force for Abyei – UNISFA) as the violence continued. In the meantime President Bashir arrived in China, a day late after his plane turned back to Tehran (where he had been attending an anti-terrorism conference) on 26 June. China is not a member of the ICC and does not recognise the arrest warrant for Mr Bashir, issued in 2009. Sudan introduced a new set of bank notes on 24 July and only issued them in the north, thus rendering worthless all stocks of Sudanese pounds kept in the south. South Sudan's minister of peace, Pagan Amum, accused Sudan of starting an 'economic war'. China's foreign minister, Yang Jiechi, arrived in Khartoum on 7 August where he had talks before travelling to South Sudan for talks with President Kiir. China was concerned to maintain its supply of oil which now comes from both Sudan and South Sudan. On 3 September, the government closed the Khartoum offices of the largest opposition political party, SPLM-North, on the grounds that it was not a legally represented political party. There was violence in Blue Nile State, between the army and ex-rebel militia loyal to Governor Malik Agar (chairman of SPLM-North). On 14 September the President named Adam Youssef, a politician from Darfur, to replace Salva Kiir (who became president of South Sudan in July) as one of two vice presidents. An agreement on border crossings between Sudan and South Sudan was signed in Khartoum on 19 September; 10 border crossings will be opened to ease communications. The agreement was brokered by the AU and is hoped to demonstrate the willingness of the two countries to co-operate.

Political structure

Constitution

A multi-party parliamentary system was introduced in 1986, comprising a five-member Supreme Council and a 360-member Majlis Watani (National Assembly).

In 1994, the government increased the number of states to 26. Each state has a wali (governor), legislative council and council of ministers. In March 2002, the government indicated that it would replace elections for the wali with a system of electoral colleges which would submit six possible candidates, giving the president the final decision on appointments.

A new constitution was promulgated on 1 January 1999, allowing opposition political associations to register prior to the elections. Eligibility for voting was reduced from 18 to 17 years on 3 January 1999.

Independence date

1 January 1956

Form of state

Federal republic

The executive

The president has inherited most of the powers of the now disbanded Revolutionary Command Council of National Salvation (RCCNS), which assumed unified powers in the 1989 military coup. These include the right to override constitutional elections to the 26 state governorships. Executive power at the operational level resides with the cabinet, which includes both civilian and military representatives. In 2002, the government scrapped the two-term limitation to the presidency. The president is directly elected by universal suffrage.

National legislature

The national assembly elected in 2000, was suspended by presidential decree a year later. It was superseded by a new, bicameral parliament, established in 2005 following agreement between the Sudanese government and the southern-based Sudan People's Liberation Army (SPLA). The new Majlis Watani (National Assembly) will have 450 members (from the 2010 elections), chosen to represent the government, SPLA and other political parties. The Majlis Welayat (Council of States) has 50 members who are indirectly elected by subordinate state legislatures. Members of both chambers serve for six-year terms.

Legal system

Sharia (Islamic law) with an admixture of English common law operates officially at the federal level, although individual states choose whether or not it should apply at state level. In practice the legal system is split along political lines, with *Sharia* imposed universally in the north, but ineffective in the rebel-held south. The judiciary is in theory politically independent under the constitution introduced at the beginning of 1999. However, military or paramilitary elements influence the judiciary or operate direct extra-judicial military rule throughout the country.

Last elections

11–15 April 2010 (parliamentary; presidential, first and second rounds); 11–15 April 2010 (South Sudan: presidential first and second rounds).

Results: Parliamentary: Al Mu'tamar al Watani (National Congress Party) (NCP) won 68.2 per cent of the vote, Al Harakat al Shaabia Le Tahreer al Sudan (Sudan People's Liberation Movement) (SPLM) won 22 per cent, Al Mu'tamar al Sha'bi (Popular Congress) 4 per cent.

Presidential: Omar Hassan Ahmad al Bashir (NCP) won 68.24 per cent of the vote, Yasir Arman (SPLM) 21.69 per cent; of the 10 other candidates none won more than 4 per cent and 8 won less than 1 per cent.

South Sudan presidential: Salva Kiir (SPLM) won 92.99 per cent of the vote, Lam Akol (SPLM-(Democratic Congress) DC) 7.01 per cent.

Next elections

October 2016 (presidential and parliamentary); 9 January 2011 (referendum on independence in the South).

Political parties

Ruling party

Al Muttamar al Watani (National Congress Party) (NCP) (from 1998; re-elected Apr 2010)

Main opposition party

Sudan People's Liberation Movement (SPLM)

Population

43.20 million (2010)

Last census: 22 April 2008: 39,154,490

Population density: Urban population: 37 per cent of the total population.

Annual growth rate: 2.2 per cent 1994–2004 (WHO 2006)

Internally Displaced Persons (IDP)

4.0 million (UNHCR 2004)

Ethnic make-up

Black (52 per cent), Arab (39 per cent), Beja (6 per cent). In the north and central regions the population consists mainly of Muslim Arabs and Nubians. In the south the people are socially, culturally and historically related to the peoples of east Africa.

Religions

Islam (Sunni Muslim) in the north (70 per cent); in the south traditional beliefs (25 per cent) and Christianity (5 per cent).

Education

Elementary education for those aged six to 12 years is free. Intermediate education starts at the age of 13 and lasts three years. Secondary education starts at 16 years and also lasts for three years. Students completing secondary education are eligible for university. There are five universities, two in Khartoum (one is a branch of Cairo University), an Islamic university at Omdurman and universities at Juba and Wad Medani.

Public expenditure on education typically amounts to 1 per cent of annual gross national income.

Unicef has voiced concerns at the low-level of public spending on education and at low enrolment and high dropout rates, calling for, among other things, significantly increased public spending, stronger teacher training and in particular the attention given to girls' education. Interventions to promote girls' education have resulted in an increase in the enrolment of girls by 5.7 per cent. The percentage of total girls' enrolment increased marginally from 45.3 per cent in 2000–01 to 45.6 per cent in 2001–02. Nationally, enrolment in primary schools increased by 5.8 per cent.

In 2002 Unicef undertook, with BRAC (an international NGO educational organisation specialising in providing schooling in poor rural areas), to provide 100 primary schools under the Village Girls Schools Project, in southern Sudan, within three years.

Literacy rate: 60 per cent adult rate; 79 per cent youth rate (15–24) (Unesco 2005).

Compulsory years: Six to 14.

Enrolment rate: 51 per cent gross primary enrolment of relevant age group (including repeaters); 21 per cent gross secondary enrolment (World Bank).

Pupils per teacher: 29 in primary schools.

Health

Public health services are organised by the ministry of health. Some health care is provided free of charge. Total expenditure on health is about 3.5 per cent of GDP, of which government spending is about 19 per cent.

In 2004 epidemiologists of the Global Polio Eradication Initiative announced that new cases of polio had been confirmed in the Darfur region of Sudan. The infection is believed to have spread from Northern Nigeria.

HIV/Aids

The conflict in southern Sudan has left many destitute; UN peacekeepers are expected to provide a buffer between the warring sides and when this happens UNAids will send in teams to ensure HIV/Aids is not an inevitable consequence of the peace-keepers' arrival and the sex-industry that usually develops in conflict zones.

HIV prevalence: 2.3 per cent aged 15–49 in 2003 (World Bank)

Life expectancy: 58 years, 2004 (WHO 2006)

Fertility rate/Maternal mortality rate: 4.3 births per woman, 2004 (WHO 2006)

Birth rate/Death rate: 36.5 births per 1,000 population; 9.6 deaths per 1,000 population (2003).

Child (under 5 years) mortality rate (per 1,000): 63 per 1,000 live births (World Bank)

Head of population per physician: 0.22 physicians per 1,000 people, 2004 (WHO 2006)

Welfare

Social insurance in Sudan is not provided through the government. There is no social security budget.

Main cities

Khartoum (capital, estimated population 1.7 million in 2005), Omdurman (3.0 million), Khartoum North (1.7 million), Port Sudan (504,868), Nyala (496,695), Kusti (306,721), Kassala (386,510), Wad Medani (315,105), Juba (198,527), Atbara (103,734).

Languages spoken

Arabic and English are used in business. African languages include Nilotic and Nilo-Hamitic. The government is considering eliminating the official teaching and use of English as part of its Islamisation programme.

Official language/s

Arabic

Media

The broadcast media is tightly constrained by censorship laws and statutory government ownership. There is a military censor permanently stationed in Sudan television to ensure the official line is always adopted. Print media enjoys a less restrictive regime but authorities have mechanism to control and influence items published, which had resulted in an unsurprising amount of self-censorship.

Press

Press restrictions have eased with increasing discussion of some domestic and foreign policy issues. Ownership of publications by individuals or political groups is banned. The board and chairman of a publication must be government-appointed, and 26 per cent of the publisher's equity goes to the government. The National Press and Publications Council (NPPC) has the power to suspend any publication. A wide variety of English and Arabic-language publications operate in the shadow of the government's information policy.

Dailies: Most newspapers are published in Khartoum. In Arabic, national publications include *Al Ayaam* (www.alayaam.net), *Al Rayaam* (www.rayaam.net), a mass circulation private newspaper; regional publications include *Al Sahafah* (www.alsahafa.info), *Akhbar Al Youn* (www.akhbaralyoumsd.net), *Al Mshaheer* (www.almshaheer.com), *Al Sudani* (www.alsudani.info). In English, leading independent include *Khartoum Monitor* and *Sudan Vision*. Online news is published by Sudan Tribune (www.sudantribune.com) and Sudan Online (www.sol-sd.com).

Weeklies: In Arabic, publications include *Al Sudan al Jadid* and *Al Fajr* (bi-weekly).

Periodicals: Periodicals include the Arabic political monthly magazine *Addaraweesh* (published in the UK) and the political newspaper *Mehairah* covering current affairs. *Sudanow* is government owned and *Al Midan* is the monthly organ of the Sudanese Communist party (www.midan.net).

Broadcasting

All broadcasting is controlled by the National Radio and Television Corporation based in Omdurman.

Radio: The government-owned The Sudan National Radio Corporation (www.sudanradio.info) broadcasts daily radio programmes in Amharic, Arabic, English, French, Somali and Tigrinya. The privately owned Mango 96 FM is a music station. The internationally funded Miraya radio station (www.mirayafm.org), is run by the UN, broadcasting in Arabic and English it is based in Juba.

Television: The government-owned Sudan National Broadcasting Corporation (SNBC) (www.srtc.gov.sd) has a monopoly for internal broadcasting. The government-owned Juba TV is based in the semi-autonomous south.

There are restrictions on satellite dish ownership, but satellite services are offered in tandem with domestic. A six-channel pan-Arab cable network offers CNN, Saudi Middle East Broadcasting Corporation (MEBC), Kuwait-TV and Dubai-TV.

Economy

Sudan's economy is a mix of agriculture, predominantly subsistence farming and cash crops such as gum Arabic, sesame and cotton, and industrial production concentrated in oil production and car and truck assembly.

Sudan's GDP growth had been the highest in its region over 2003–08, averaging 8 per cent, and had reached 11.3 per cent in 2006; but it fell to 10.2 per cent in 2007. It still maintained growth of 6.8 per cent in 2008, during the world economic crisis when oil prices were at a record high, bringing higher oil export receipts. However, world food prices in 2008 were also at a record high, which depressed imports so that the balance of trade in 2008 only varied by a drop of some US$600 million. In percentage terms the current account deficit was reduced to around 5 per cent of GDP, compared to the 11 per cent of GDP in 2007. There was a sharp fall in global oil prices at the end of 2008 so that by 2009 falling oil revenues put a significant pressure on public finances and reversed earlier revenue gains. GDP growth in 2009 was estimated at 4 per cent.

Non-oil GDP growth is predicted to average 4 per cent in 2009–10 and as global trade recovers is excepted to average 6 per cent over 2011–15.

The Sudanese pound fell in valued by about 7 per cent and 20 per cent against the US dollar and the European euro respectively from September 2008–December 2008.

Economic growth is principally fuelled by oil production, although it has resulted in little improvement to living standards for the majority of the population. Oil export revenue account for over 70 per cent of Sudan's total export earnings. Most oil fields are located in the south-west, which had been subject to armed conflict until political dialogue and accommodation allowed improved security in the area and a degree of expansion of oil production.

The expanding oil and gas reserves have been developed largely with the assistance of China. However oil reserves are finite and at current rates of extraction are predicted to be exhausted by 2030. Production is expected to peak in 2011–12.

An escalating humanitarian crisis in Dafur in the west is attracting international scrutiny and is likely to put pressure on the government and economy. Hundreds of thousands have been displaced and farms have been deserted.

Remittances, at US$1,769 million in 2007, is a major source of income for poor families, with per capita income falling from US$1,522 in 2008 to an estimated US$1,388 in 2009. According to the UN Development Programme (UNDP), over 34 per cent of the population are living in poverty and over 60.9 per cent of adults over aged 15 literacy rate (with 70 per cent female over aged 15 illitracy rate). Sudan has a strategy for poverty reduction based on macroeconomic development and private sector growth.

External trade

In 2005 the Greater Arab Free Trade Area (Gafta) was ratified by 17 members, including Sudan, creating an Arab economic bloc. A customs union was established whereby tariffs within Gafta will be reduced by a percentage each year, until none remain.

Around 70 per cent of total export revenue is generated by crude oil. In 2010, Sudan was in negotiation to join the Organisation of the Petroleum Exporting Countries (Opec).

Industrialisation is limited and although Sudan is considered a major source of minerals, exploration and commercialisation is underdeveloped.

Imports

Principal imports are foodstuffs, manufactured goods, refinery and transport equipment, medicines and chemicals, textiles and wheat.

Main sources: Saudi Arabia (typically 25 per cent of total), China (8 per cent), UK (7 per cent).

Exports

Principal exports are crude oil and petroleum products, cotton, sesame, livestock, groundnuts, gum Arabic and sugar.

Main destinations: China (typically 80 per cent of total), Japan (7 per cent), UAE (2 per cent).

Agriculture

Farming

Sudan is a semi-arid country and a large part is desert. Irrigated farmland constitutes about one-fifth of the total cultivated area, but produces about 50 per cent of total crop production. The traditional farming areas are semi-arid and used for livestock rearing, while export crops are grown in the irrigated areas, mostly in the Gezira area between the Blue and White Niles. The country is often racked by drought and famine.

The majority of the population work on the land. Principal export crops are cotton, oil seeds (mainly groundnuts and sesame) and gum arabic (used in soft drinks, baking, cosmetics, pharmaceuticals and other industrial applications), of which Sudan is the world's largest producer. Main food crops include sorghum (dura) and millet. Cotton is the main cash crop providing 45 per cent of agricultural export earnings, followed by gum arabic and sesame (21 per cent). Livestock-raising is of considerable importance, employing about 40 per cent of the population. Sudan is aiming to become self-sufficient in rice and tea production.

Sudan has attempted to tackle the problem of land usage. Government policy aims to increase the area of cultivable land (only about 10 per cent of the potential arable land is under cultivation) through the rehabilitation and expansion of existing irrigation schemes. A planting scheme has given precedence to food crops over land devoted to cotton production and export.

In 2009, Cadburys, the UK top selling chocolate manufacturer, will source around 15,000 tonnes of cocoa per annum from Ghana, in a Fairtrade deal that will invest £45 million (US$64 million) from 2009–19.

Despite the insurity and harrassing from bandits, a booming trade in livestock has thrived for more than two decades along the borders between Somalia, Ethiopia and Kenya.

Fishing

Sudan possesses vast freshwater and marine fishing potential. The freshwater sources comprise rivers and lakes. The Nile alone has an estimated potential output of 60,000 tonnes of fish a year, but the fisheries are barely exploited. Fishing on the Red Sea coastline is also under-exploited and is being encouraged with government assistance.

Over 95 per cent of the Sudanese catch of fish is obtained from inland fisheries on the Nile, its tributaries and associated swamp lands. Subsistence fishing is widespread, but the commercial sector is under-developed. Marine fishing is mainly carried out by artisanal fishermen in small boats.

Sudan exported around US$1 million of fish per annum before the war, but now exports only a small amount of dried and salted fish.

Forestry

Sudan has 17 per cent forest cover, most of which is located in the mountains and the wooded savannahs. In 1990—2000, forest cover diminished by an average of 1.44 per cent per annum or around 960,000 hectares (ha) per year. Rapid deforestation is a result of demand for fuelwood. Sudan produces a large amount of industrial roundwood, mainly for posts and poles, and also produces sawnwood, although not enough to ensure self-sufficiency. Sudan's most important non-wood forest product is gum arabic. Sudan is also one of the world's main producers of olibanum resin.

Industry and manufacturing

The industrial sector'S main activities are oil refining, agricultural products, textiles and leatherwares.

Environment

In June 2010 the African Union backed a proposal to build the 'Great Green Wall' project, of a 15km wide, 7,775km long, continuous belt of trees from Senegal in the west to Djibouti in the east (traversing 11 countries) in an effort to halt the advance of the Sahara Desert. The trees to be used would be drought-adapted, preferably native to the area from a list of 37 possible species, and should help to slow soil erosion and filter rain water.

Mining

The mining sector has played a relatively insignificant role in the country's economic development. Chromite, gypsum, gold, copper and iron ore are exploited on a commercial basis. Other mineral deposits include zinc, lead, talc, coal, nickel and tin, phosphate and uranium, but not in sufficient quantities to develop. If financial and infrastructural problems can be overcome, the sector could make a significant contribution to the economy.

Hydrocarbons

Proven oil reserves were 6.7 billion barrels in 2010, with production at 486,000 barrels per day (bpd). Sudan had the fifth largest proven oil reserves in Africa, located in south-west Sudan in the Muglad and Melut basins, but with the independence of South Sudan in 2011, where most reserves are held, Sudan no longer has significant reserves. It is thought that other reserves will be located in the Blue Nile basin and in the Red Sea area.

Western oil companies have been deterred from investing in the Sudanese oil sector by US sanctions and the country's continued instability, but Asian countries, principally China, India and Malaysia, have been very active, seeking to secure Sudanese oil for their own burgeoning requirements.

Sudan has four oil refineries, a total capacity of 142,000bpd. An agreement to build a new refinery in Port Sudan, which was signed in 2005 with the Malaysian company, Petronas, had, by 2008, been suspended due to rising costs. Sudan exports both crude and refined oil.

Total natural gas reserves were estimated at 113 billion cubic metres (2006), but gas production is negligible. Sudan does not consume natural gas and none is imported. This could change if gas fields are developed, but investor interest in this sector is low.

Coal is neither produced nor imported.

Energy

Total installed electricity generation capacity was 563MW in 2006. The state-owned National Electricity Corporation is responsible for generation, distribution and transmission of electricity. The energy mix is 60 per cent oil, and 40 per cent hydropower, which is subject to weather conditions.

The Roseires dam on the Blue Nile produces a large proportion of Sudan's electricity, with installed capacity of 274MW. Hydroelectric sources are being expanded and the gross theoretical capability is 48 terrawatt hours. New dams are under construction, including the Merowe dam, inaugurated in March 2009 and the Kajbar dam providing an extra 1,250MW. Both dams were controversial as the water catchment area displaced a number of communities and resulted in forced resettlements and in the case of the Kajbar dam the flooding and destruction of ancient Nubian archaeological sites.

Financial markets

Stock exchange

The first stock exchange opened in January 1995.

Banking and insurance

Central bank

Bank of Sudan

Main financial centre

Khartoum

Time

GMT plus two hours

Geography

Sudan lies in north-eastern Africa. It is the largest country in Africa and the ninth largest in the world. It lies entirely within the tropics and is bordered by Egypt and Libya in the north, Ethiopia, Eritrea and the Red Sea in the east, Kenya, Uganda and the Democratic Republic of Congo in the south and the Central African Republic and Chad in the west.

The River Nile and its tributaries, the White and Blue Niles, are the country's most important physical features. The Blue Nile, in particular, plays a vital economic role, supporting 40 per cent of the current irrigated area and with the potential to support 70 per cent of future irrigated land. The Blue Nile is prone to serious seasonal flooding.

The topographic features are a large, broad plain with mountains to the north-east along the coast of the Red Sea and in the south-eastern border region with Uganda and Kenya. This is the location of Mount Kinyeti (3,187 metres) the country's tallest peak.

Hemisphere

Northern

Climate

Tropical in the south, hot and dry in the north. In Khartoum, the hottest month is May (26–42 degrees Celsius (C)), the coldest is January (16–32 degrees C). The northern zone receives very little rainfall and is mainly desert. The south is mainly tropical while the central zone is semi-arid grassland.

From mid-April to the end of June the climate is extremely hot and dry. Sandstorms (*haboobs*) are frequent in desert areas between April and September. The rainy season extends from July to September. During this period road travel outside the cities is difficult. In Khartoum, the average temperature by day in the summer is 42 degrees C and 32 degrees C in the winter.

Dress codes

Formal clothing should be worn for business and social engagements. Lightweight clothing is essential at all times, although visitors should carry some warmer clothing if travelling to Sudan during the winter months (November to March). A light raincoat is needed during the months of July, August and September. Women should be aware of the fact that the north is predominantly Muslim and are advised to dress modestly.

Entry requirements

Passports

Required by all. Passports must be valid for six months from date of entry.

Visa

Required by all. For information see www.sudanembassy.org and follow the link to *visa/passport*.

Business visas require a letter of invitation from a sponsoring company giving purpose of visit, duration of stay, a commitment to financial responsibility and references, plus copies of commercial correspondence with entities in Sudan.

Visitors are required to register with the Aliens Department within three days of their arrival (hotels will do this). Once registered, they are not required to obtain an exit visa.

Contact the closest consulate for further information.

Prohibited entry

Nationals of Israel and holders of passports with Israeli travel stamps,

Currency advice/regulations

The import and export of local currency is prohibited. Import of foreign currency is unlimited but must be declared; export is limited to the amount declared.

Travellers cheques have limited acceptance.

Customs

Alcohol is strictly forbidden; products from Israel are prohibited.

Health (for visitors)

Mandatory precautions

Valid yellow fever and cholera certificates are required if travellers are arriving from infected areas, or travellers are intending to visit the south of Sudan.

Advisable precautions

Vaccinations for yellow fever, diphtheria, tetanus, polio, hepatitis A and typhoid are recommended. Other vaccinations that may be recommended are cholera, tuberculosis, hepatitis B and meningitis. There is a risk of rabies. Malaria is prevalent throughout the country. Anti-mosquito measures including repellents, nets and clothing that cover the body should be used (these will also provide protection against hepatitis B and yellow fever). Tap water must be treated as unsafe unless boiled and filtered (bottled water is available in the main cities). Eat only well cooked meals, preferably served hot; vegetables should be cooked and fruit peeled. Dairy products are unpasteurised and should be avoided. Use only well maintained, chlorinated, swimming pools as bilharzia can be contracted from streams and rivers.

Medical facilities are scarce outside Khartoum. A first aid kit that includes disposable syringes is a reasonable precaution. Medical insurance is essential, including emergency evacuation, and an adequate supply of personal medicines is necessary.

Hotels

Accommodation can be difficult to obtain outside Khartoum and Port Sudan. Advisable to book in advance. Service charge of 10 per cent is usual. Hotel bills are subject to 10 per cent sales tax.

Credit cards

Credit cards may be accepted but visitors should ensure that they have sufficient hard currency (preferably US dollars) to cover their expenses during their stay.

Public holidays (national)

Fixed dates

1 Jan (Independence Day), 30 Jun (Revolution Day), 25 Dec (Christmas Day).

Variable dates

Eid al Adha, Coptic Christmas (Jan), Islamic New Year, Birth of the Prophet, Coptic Easter (Mar/Apr, two days), Eid al Fitr (three days).

Islamic year 1433 (26 Nov 2011–14 Nov 2012): The Islamic year contains 354 or 355 days, with the result that Muslim feasts advance by 10–12 days against the Gregorian calendar. Dates of feasts vary according to the sighting of the new moon, so cannot be forecast exactly.

Working hours

Banking

Sat–Thu: 0830–1200.

Business

Sat–Thu: 0800–1430.

Government

Sat–Thu: 0800/0830–1330/1400.

Shops

Sat–Thu: 0800–1330, 1730–2000.

Telecommunications

Mobile/cell phones

There are 900 and 900/1800 GSM services available in large urban areas only.

Electricity supply

240V AC

Social customs/useful tips

Visitors should address Sudanese males using the form *Sayed* (meaning Mr) with the first name only. There are a large number of local traditions and most Muslim customs are observed. Politeness and patience are more important than punctuality. Women are often not present at business or social gatherings. There is a ban on alcohol and gambling in the north.

Some souvenirs, such as cheetah skins, although available in the *souks* (markets) are banned by the Government.

Military establishments should not be photographed, nor should bridges, dams, rail and air transport facilities. Visitors should not attempt to photograph Sudanese people without permission or if they appear reluctant. Photography permits issued by the Tourist Information Office in Khartoum are often ignored by the authorities, who may confiscate film and camera.

Most banks in Sudan are heavily fortified and resemble prisons as much as they do commercial institutions.

The Islamic legal and moral code, *Sharia*, is in operation in the north.

Security

Southern Sudan, the Nuba mountains, the Ethiopian and Eritrean borders and the Kassala area near the Eritrean border are all zones of military activity, (including the laying of anti-personnel landmines), and are insecure. There is banditry in Darfur state. Travel in these areas should be avoided unless work is absolutely essential. In general, no land borders into or out of Sudan can be crossed safely, with the exception of the Wadi Halfa crossing into Egypt. The political situation in Sudan is not stable and foreign nationals should contact their embassy, and keep in contact throughout their stay. Before embarking, visitors are advised to consult their embassy for an up-to-date appraisal of the situation, as well as brief themselves regarding developments in the wider region. Demonstrations should be avoided and British and US citizens may wish to keep a low profile.

Getting there

Air

National airline: Sudan Airways

International airport/s: Khartoum (KRT), 4km from city; duty-free shop and restaurant.

Airport tax: Departure tax: US$20, except transit passengers.

Surface

Road: There are road links, with varing degrees of accessibility, to all surrounding countries. Drivers wishing to enter Sudan by road must apply for permission in Khartoum or from overseas representatives. Applicants must list vehicle and passenger details, with supporting documents from a recognised motoring organisation, or a guarantee from a bank or registered business.

Most border crossings remain dangerous, with the exception of the relatively secure border with Egypt via Wadi Halfa.

Rail: A railway line runs from Cairo to the Aswan High Dam in Egypt; passengers can then take a river boat on to Wadi Halfa just inside the Sudanese border, and train to Khartoum.

Water: The only major harbour is Port Sudan on the Red Sea coast. International shipping lines that maintain contacts with Sudan may provide passenger services on cargo ships.

Sudan's River Transport Corporation (RTC) operates a Nile ferry from Aswan in Egypt to Wadi Halfa, the service can be is hindered by local conditions and circumstances.

Main port/s: Port Sudan.

Getting about

National transport

Travellers must obtain special permits to travel anywhere outside Khartoum. These are obtainable from the Passport and Immigration Office in Khartoum. Before travelling, it is advisable to check the security situation in the area. Visitors arriving in any town or city in Sudan must register with the police on arrival and show the necessary paperwork.

Permits are required to visit archaeological or historical sites. These can be obtained from the Department of Antiquities in Khartoum.

Air: Sudan Airways operates a regular service between Khartoum, Port Sudan and El Obeid and other larger towns. Small air taxi companies fly from Khartoum to main towns.

Road: Main tarred roads are the 1,186km route from Port Sudan to Khartoum, from Port Sudan to Kassala and on to Shavak, from Khartoum to Sennar and on to Malakal. Another 800km of tarred roads exist, but the rest of the country's 48,000km network is of very variable quality.

Buses: Scheduled coach services include Khartoum-Kosti, Khartoum-Omdurman, Khartoum-El Fasher, Juba-Nimule, Juba-Faradge.

Rail: A network links Khartoum with Port Sudan, Kassala, Wau, Nyala and Wadi Halfa, but not Juba. The condition of the network is very dilapidated and services can be very slow.

There are three-classes offered but only first class is suitable for business travel.

Water: There are ferries operating on the White and Blue Niles but may not offer a complete journey as underinvestment has left waterways in need of repair and redevelopment.

City transport

Taxis: Easily available in Khartoum and can be hailed, or taken from ranks. Fares are negotiatable and should be agreed before start of any journey.

Car hire

Available in main centres. A national or international driving licence is required.

BUSINESS DIRECTORY

The addresses listed below are a selection only. While World of Information makes every endeavour to check these addresses, we cannot guarantee that changes have not been made, especially to telephone numbers and area codes. We would welcome any corrections.

Telephone area codes

The international dialling code (IDD) for Sudan is +249, followed by area code and subscriber's number:

El Obeid	81	Khartoum North	85
Kassala	41	Port Sudan City	31
Khartoum	11		

Chambers of Commerce

Union of Sudanese Chambers of Commerce, Gamhoria Street, PO Box 81, Khartoum (email: chamber@sudanchamber.org).

Banking

Bank of Khartoum, PO Box 1008, Khartoum.

Farmers Commercial Bank, PO Box 1116, Kasr Avenue, Khartoum.

Tadamon Islamic Bank, PO Box 3154, Baladia Avenue, Khartoum.

Al-Baraka Bank, PO Box 3583, Al-Baraka Tower, Khartoum.

El Nilein Industrial Development Bank, PO Box 466, 1722 United Nations Square, Khartoum.

Central bank

Bank of Sudan, Al-Gamaa Avenue, PO Box 313, Khartoum, Sudan (email: sudanbank@sudanmail.net).

Travel information

River Transport Corporation, PO Box 284, Khartoum North.

Sudan Airways, SDC Building, Street 15, New Extension, PO Box 253, Khartoum.

Ministry of tourism

Ministry of Tourism and Wildlife, PO Box 22213, Khartoum (email: postmaster@sudan-tourism.gov.sd; internet: www.sudan-tourism.gov.sd).

Ministries

Ministry of Agriculture and Forests, Khartoum.

Ministry of Animal Welfare, Khartoum.

Ministry of Aviation, Khartoum.

Ministry of Culture and Information, Khartoum.

Ministry of Defence, Khartoum.

Ministry of Education, Khartoum.

Ministry of Energy and Mining, Khartoum.

Ministry of the Environment and Tourism.

Ministry of Finance & National Economy, Khartoum.

Ministry of Foreign Affairs, Khartoum.

Ministry of Health, Khartoum.

Ministry of Higher Education and Scientific Research, Khartoum.

Ministry of the Interior, Khartoum.

Ministry of National Industry, Khartoum.

Ministry of Public Services, Khartoum.

Ministry of Social Planning, Khartoum.

Ministry of Trade, Khartoum.

Ministry of Transport, Khartoum.

Other useful addresses

National Corporation for Antiquities and Museums, PO Box 178, Khartoum.

Sudanese Embassy (USA), 2210 Massachusetts Avenue, NW, Washington DC 20008 (tel: (+1-202) 338-8565; fax: (+1-202) 667-2406; email: info@sudanembassyus.org).

Internet sites

Africa Business Network: www.ifc.org/abn

AllAfrica.com: http://allafrica.com

African Development Bank: www.afdb.org

Africa Online: www.africaonline.com

Mbendi AfroPaedia (information on companies, countries, industries and stock exchanges in Africa): http://mbendi.co.za

The Sudan Page: www.sudan.net

KEY FACTS

Official name: Republiek Suriname (Republic of Suriname)

Head of State: President-elect Desiré (Desi) Delano Bouterse (from 12 Aug 2010)

Head of government: President Ronald Venetiaan (since 2000; re-elected 2005)

Ruling party: Coalition: De Mega Combinatie (Mega Combination, alliance of four political parties, led by Nationale Democratische Partij (National Democratic Party) (NDP) (from 2010)

Area: 163,265 square km

Population: 525,000 (2010)*

Capital: Paramaribo (Parbo)

Official language: Dutch

Currency: Suriname dollar (Su$) = 100 cents

Exchange rate: Su$3.30 per US$ (Oct 2011)

GDP per capita: US$6,975 (2010)

GDP real growth: 4.40% (2010)

GDP: US$3.70 billion (2010)

Inflation: 6.90% (2010)

Balance of trade: US$625.70 million (2010)

* estimated figure

Suriname

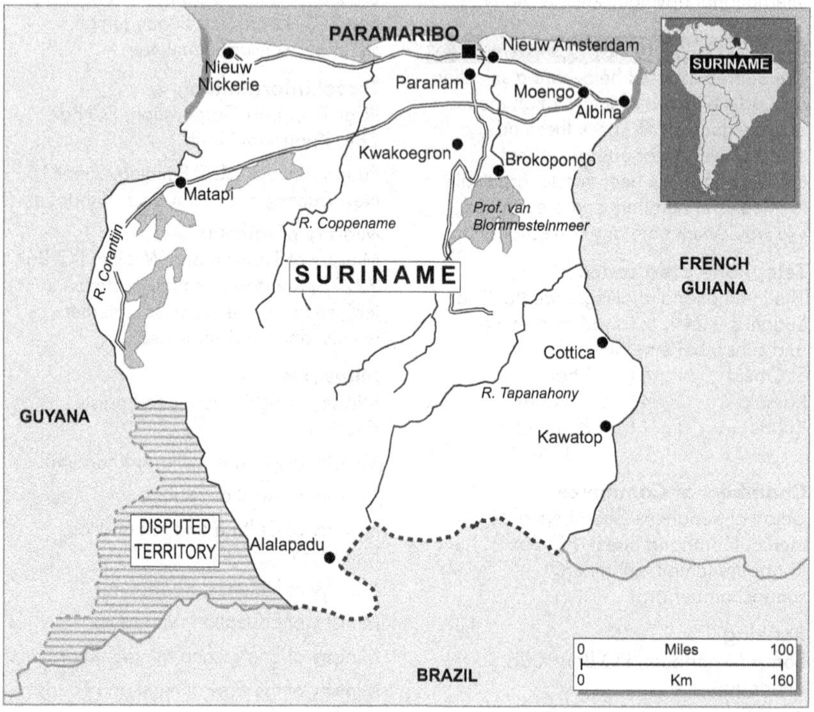

Suriname, together with Guyana, is the only non-insular member of a group of low-lying coastal countries that share similar sustainable development challenges, officially known as 'The Small Island Developing States' (SIDS) a recognised category of nation states with special environmental and other needs. Most SIDS will be and some already are, experiencing the most severe impacts of climate change; some of these islands and countries may even disappear as a result of sea-level rise; others, as is the case with Suriname, are likely to experience severe devastation and may even become uninhabitable. Suriname is particularly vulnerable to the negative impacts of climate change due to its low-lying coastal zone which contains most of Suriname's fertile land and a concentration of the main economic activities and the majority of the 522,000 population. Any significant sea-level rise may inundate large parts of this coastal zone. Suriname is one of the ten countries with the largest share of their population – in the case of Suriname 76 per cent – living within ten metres of sea level. In most other respects, Suriname's global profile errs on the low side. Thus, the South American republic's 2009 decision to establish diplomatic relations with the Republic the Maldives of could be claimed as the year's high spot.

Still growing

Faced with a sharp output decline in the alumina sector and lower alumina and oil prices, economic growth is estimated by the International Monetary Fund (IMF) to have slowed to 2.5 per cent in 2009, from 6 per cent in 2008. Potential output growth is estimated at about 5 per cent of GDP. Twelve-month inflation is estimated to have fallen from 14.5 per cent in 2008 to less than 1 per cent in 2009, reflecting lower international prices for food and fuel and softer domestic demand. Food, energy and transportation weigh heavily in the consumer price index (CPI) (55 per cent) and their domestic prices had fallen rapidly over the previous twelve months. Although an upturn had been registered in the price of these goods, core inflation continued to level off.

Suriname's external current account balance was estimated to have shifted from a surplus of 4 per cent of GDP in 2008 to a deficit of 2 per cent in 2009. The trade surplus narrowed significantly, despite an increase in gold and oil exports. Lower alumina exports allowed for some crude oil used in the refining process to be redirected for exports and, as a result, crude oil exports rose by around 35 per cent in volume terms. In the capital account, a drawdown from the Netherlands Treaty Fund was used in August 2009 to clear longstanding arrears with Brazil, totalling US$118 million. Suriname's international reserves were estimated by the IMF to be the equivalent of 5.25 months of imports at end-2009, up from 4.25 months in 2008.

The fiscal balance was estimated to have deteriorated by 4 per cent of GDP in 2009 the underlying balance, which excludes one-off transactions, was projected to deteriorate by close to 5 per cent of GDP.

In the period 2006–08, the public sector accounts registered large surpluses (about 2 per cent of GDP on average) thanks to rising revenues from robust economic growth, including from the buoyant mineral sectors. The drop in oil and mineral prices since late 2008 and a substantial reduction in alumina output depressed tax revenues in 2009. Indeed, the revenue situation would have been even worse, if not for exceptionally high dividend receipts from the state-owned oil company, Staatsolie, and from the Centrale Bank van Suriname (central bank). The cyclical deterioration in public finances in 2009 was amplified by a surge in non-interest current account spending arising from civil service wage increases starting in March 2009, higher spending on goods and services (2.5 per cent of GDP) and elevated pension and other transfer payments, including those for a mortgage subsidy scheme covering the 2009–10 period

In the view of the IMF, the medium-term economic outlook for Suriname is favourable. The government scenario included gradually phasing in the second stage of the wage reform programme, starting in 2011. After a further small deterioration in 2010, mainly reflecting carry-over effects from the counter-cyclical policies initiated in 2009, the fiscal accounts would progressively improve and revert back to a small surplus beginning in 2014, as economic output and commodity prices recover. Over the medium-to-long term, revenues would be expected to benefit from a permanent boost from a higher level of government participation in the alumina and gold sectors. The external current account balance looked likely to deteriorate in the near term before rebounding beginning in 2013, when large bauxite and gold mines come on stream. The expansion of Staatsolie's oil refining capacity would also help reduce the need for imported refined petroleum products beginning in 2013. Under this scenario, both the public and the external debt levels remain low and manageable over the medium term, at below 23 per cent of GDP and 11 per cent of GDP, respectively.

The IMF considered that the economic risks to the outlook were broadly balanced for the near term and tilted to the upside for the medium term. In the recent period, local gold production has surged in response to high prices, while the economic recovery in Asia has helped support alumina prices. In the short run, downside risks to the economic outlook are associated with the possibility of a slower global recovery than anticipated. There is also a risk that, in the run-up to the May 2010 elections, government spending on wages and goods and services increases excessively. Additional budgetary costs could also arise in connection with the need to recapitalise two state-owned banks and resolve the problems facing Clico Life Insurance Company Suriname. Over the medium term, large capital projects by the government and Staatsolie are expected to sustain growth through 2013, when a major increase in alumina and gold production is also expected There are some political risks and uncertainties associated with the 2010 general elections. The newly elected legislature, the National Assembly, will be charged with choosing the President of the Republic by a two-thirds majority. If it fails to do so after two attempts, the election of the president will be referred to the larger People's Assembly. The latter, which is empowered to elect the president by a simple majority, comprises Members of the National Assembly, as well as local and districts councilors. Given Suriname's indirect and complex process for electing the president, there is a risk that the new office holder may not be determined for an extended period following the parliamentary elections. There is also a risk of political stalemate if the president is elected by the People's Assembly and does not muster the support of the National Assembly.

Tentative politics

The results of the May 2010 elections in Suriname provoked predictable reactions from the interested parties. The outcome was that the political alliance – De Mega Combinatie (Mega Combination – led by the Nationale Democratische Partij (National Democratic Party) (NDP), of which former military dictator Désiré Delano Bouterse is chairman, captured 23 of the 51 seats in the National Assembly. Bouterse is still perceived as a charismatic and pragmatic man of action and his alliance appealed to the young and poor with promises of easy jobs and cheap housing.

Suriname's memories are short. The young have no recollection of Bouterse's blotchy record of governance. He had seized power in a coup d'etat in 1980 and

KEY INDICATORS — **Suriname**

	Unit	2006	2007	2008	2009	2010
Population	m	*0.50	*0.51	*0.52	*0.52	*0.53
Gross domestic product (GDP)	US$bn	2.14	2.40	3.10	3.00	3.70
GDP per capita	US$	4,225	4,752	5,927	5,676	6,975
GDP real growth	%	3.8	5.2	6.0	2.5	4.4
Inflation	%	11.3	6.4	14.6	0.7	6.9
Exports (fob) (goods)	US$m	1,174.4	1,359.0	1,708.1	1,404.3	2,068.5
Imports (fob) (goods)	US$m	1,013.4	1,185.3	1,349.7	1,295.5	1,442.8
Balance of trade	US$m	161.0	173.7	358.4	108.8	625.7
Current account	US$m	110.4	184.9	353.0	209.5	692.2
Total reserves minus gold	US$m	215.3	400.9	433.3	659.0	638.9
Foreign exchange	US$m	204.9	390.4	423.3	522.9	505.3
Exchange rate	per US$	2.75	2.74	2.74	2.75	2.75

* estimated figure

left office only under intense international pressure in 1987, seizing power again in another coup d'etat in 1990. He still faces criminal charges for his role in the 'extra-judicial' execution of political opponents in 1982. He was also convicted in a court in the Netherlands for trafficking cocaine from Suriname to the Netherlands in 1999, but avoided serving a sentence because both countries prohibit extradition of each others' citizens. Bouterse's party was also part of President Jules Wijdenbosch's 1996 coalition administration which practically bankrupted the country. Its foreign policy provoked aggression against Guyana and also defied the Caribbean Community.

It was not surprising, therefore, that the election results generated uneasiness and despondency. Outgoing President Ronald Venetiaan who lead the minority Nieuwe Front voor Democratie (NF) (New Front for Democracy and Development) alliance confirmed that his group would not work with the Combinatie as long as Mr Bouterse remained in control. Dutch foreign minister, Maxime Verhagen said that The Netherlands respected the will of the electorate but added that 'the past could not be forgotten.'...Mr Bouterse had been sentenced to an 11-year prison term in The Netherlands for drug dealing and, in Suriname, a case about the murders of December 1982 is still proceeding. Suriname's president has to be elected by a two-thirds vote in the National Assembly. But the 20 or so ethno-political parties jostle for power through a half-dozen shifting alliances in which no single party can claim an absolute majority.

Whatever the outcome, Guyanese will long remember that, 25 years ago, it was Bouterse's administration that launched Operation Schoon Schip (Clean Sweep) in which over 5,000 Guyanese and Haitian workers were expelled, some being physically molested and having their possessions confiscated. Guyanese will remember, also, that Wijdenbosch's administration inflicted humiliating conditions on Guyana over the Canawaima ferry project which now flies the Suriname national flag and is subject to the jurisdiction only of Suriname's courts.

Since 2005 Suriname's politics have been static. Then, in the national election held in May, the ruling NF coalition suffered a significant setback due to widespread dissatisfaction with the state of the economy and the public perception that the NF had produced few tangible gains. The NF won just 23 seats, falling short of a majority in the National Assembly and immediately entered into negotiations with the Maroon-based 'A' Combination and the A-1 Coalition to form a working majority. Desi Bouterse's NDP more than doubled its representation in the National Assembly, winning 15 seats. Bouterse, the NDP's declared presidential candidate, withdrew from the race days before the National Assembly convened to vote for the next president and tapped his running mate, Rabin Parmessar, to run as the NDP's candidate. In the National Assembly, the NF challenged Parmessar's Surinamese citizenship, displaying copies of a Dutch passport issued to Parmessar in 2004. Parmessar was eventually allowed to stand for election and parliament later confirmed his Surinamese citizenship. After two votes, no candidate received the required two-thirds majority, pushing the final decision in August 2005 to a special session of the United People's Assembly, where President Venetiaan was re-elected with a significant majority of votes from the local, district and national assembly members gathered. His running mate, Ramdien Sardjoe, was elected as vice president. While the Venetiaan administration has made progress in stabilising the economy, tensions within the coalition have impeded progress and stymied legislative action.

Risk assessment

Politics	Fair
Economy	air
Regional stability	Good

COUNTRY PROFILE

Historical profile

1602 Dutch traders arrived.
1651 British settlers and plantation owners arrived in the region and set up the first community and commercial estates using African slaves.
1652 Britain ceded territory to The Netherlands (later referred to as Dutch Guiana) and gained New Amsterdam (New York) in exchange.
1800s After slavery was abolished, indentured labourers from China, India and Java were brought in to work on plantations.
1916 The mining of bauxite began and gradually become the country's principal export.
1948 The country was renamed Suriname
1954 Suriname gained self-government from The Netherlands, which continued to control defence and foreign affairs.
1975 Full independence was granted. Johan Ferrier became president and Henck Arron of the Nationale Partij Suriname (NPS) (National Party of Suriname) became prime minister. Around 30 per cent of the population emigrated to The Netherlands, fearing an early collapse of the new country.
1980 A military coup, led by Sergeant-Major Desi Bouterse, ousted first Prime Minister Arron and then President Ferrier, who was ultimately replaced by Henk Chin A Sen. Bouterse ruled through the National Military Council, imposing martial law, censorship and banning political parties.
1982 Fiscal aid from The Netherlands and the US was halted following the murder of 15 members of the opposition by the army.
1985 The ban on opposition parties was lifted and a new constitution, which included a strong military role, was devised.
1987 A democratically elected president and a 51-seat National Assembly were re-established. Elections were won by an opposition coalition. A National State Council of politicians and military was established under the constitution, but with an ill-defined 'advisory' role it did not achieve satisfactory government.
1990 Bouterse staged another coup and resumed power.
1991 A civilian government was elected. International aid was resumed. Bouterse retired from the army and founded the Nationale Democratische Partij (NDP) (National Democratic Party). Ronald Venetiaan was elected president.
1996 The nationalistic NDP won a majority of seats in the general elections and joined a coalition government. President Jules Wijdenbosch, an ally of Bouterse, named him special advisor and gave him diplomatic immunity from foreign drug smuggling charges.
1999 A poor economy resulted in widespread strikes, which brought down the government.
2000 Early elections were won by a coalition, Nieuwe Front voor Democratie (NF) (New Front for Democracy); Ronald Venetiaan became president. International relations with Guyana deteriorated over a disputed maritime boundary, including an area rich in oil.
2004 The Suriname guilder (fl) was converted to the Suriname dollar (Su$), at a rate of Su$1.00 per fl1,000. The UN attempted to resolve the maritime dispute with Guyana.
2005 The ruling NF coalition narrowly won parliamentary elections. After two unsuccessful presidential elections, Ronald Venetiaan won in the third round.
2006 Major floods devastated homes of around 30,000 people in Upper Suriname. The country's long-term foreign currency, sovereign credit rating was raised from -B to B, as efforts to pay back loans were seen as largely successful. The

EU provided eur20 million (US$15.4 million) to upgrade the country's infrastructure and reconstruct the banana industry.
2007 The Japanese agreed to finance the construction of a new fishery centre, meeting international standards and capable of providing modern facilities for the enlarged fishing fleet. The UN ruled that both Suriname and Guyana should share the oil-rich offshore territory.
2008 Desi Bouterse, the former dictator went on trial for the murder of 15 political opponents in 1982. A three-month US humanitarian mission began providing medical treatment and engineering projects in rural areas. Suriname joined the International Criminal Court (ICC).
2009 High school teachers, customs officers, fire fighters and waste collectors went on strike in a dispute with the government over discrepancies within a newly introduced salary scheme for the public sector. The UK-based multinational BHP Billiton sold all of its interest in the bauxite mines it operated in Suriname to domestic mining companies.
2010 In parliamentary elections held in May, the newly established De Mega Combinatie (Mega Combination) coalition of four political parties, led by the NDP, won a total of 23 seats out of 51, enabling it to control the national legislature though a coalition. On 19 July Desi Bouterse was elected president by a more than two-thirds majority of parliament.
2011 In July, Suriname re-applied for membership of the Organisation of Islamic Conference (OIC). On 21 July, The Dubai (United Arab Emirates) ports' operators DP World, purchased controlling interests in two Paramaribo ports, Integra Ports Services (IPS) and Suriname Ports Services (SPS).

Political structure

Independence date
25 November 1975 (from The Netherlands)

Form of state
Parliamentary democratic republic

The executive
The presidency is decided by an electoral colleges based in parliament, for a term of five years. The president is Head of State, head of government and commander-in-chief of the armed forces. During a term in office, the president is accountable to the national assembly. The president has wide executive power to appoint and dismiss ministers, enact laws and declare war (with the assent of the national assembly).
The political system is multi-party and numerous parties must form coalitions to come to power. To win the presidency, a coalition needs a two-thirds majority in the national assembly. Failing three rounds, the vote goes to the United People's Congress, which contains assembly members and local and regional councillors, which elects a president by a simple majority.

National legislature
The unicameral De Nationale Assemblée (commonly referred to as DNA) (National Assembly) has 51 members, elected by proportional representation, for five-year terms.

Last elections
25 May 2010 (parliamentary); 19 July 2010 (presidential, indirect).
Results: Parliamentary: De Mega Combinatie (Mega Combination, coalition of four political parties, led by Nationale Democratische Partij (National Democratic Party) (NDP) won 40.22 per cent of the vote (23 seats out of 51), Nieuwe Front voor Democratie (NF) (New Front for Democracy and Development, coalition of four parties) 31.65 per cent of the vote (14), Volksalliantie Voor Vooruitgang (People's Alliance for Progress, coalition of three parties) 12.98 per cent (6), Partij voor Democratie en Ontwikkeling door Eenheid (Party for Democracy and Development through Unity) 5.09 per cent (1), A Combinatie (A-Com) (A Combination, coalition of three parties) 4.7 per cent (seven); four other political parties and coalition failed to win any seats. Turnout was 73.21 per cent.
Presidential: parliament voted for Dési Bouterse by 36 votes (out of 50), Chandrikapersad Santokhi 13.

Next elections
May 2010 (parliamentary)

Political parties

Ruling party
Coalition: De Mega Combinatie (Mega Combination, alliance of four political parties, led by Nationale Democratische Partij (National Democratic Party) (NDP) (from 2010)

Main opposition party
Nieuwe Front voor Democratie (NF) (New Front for Democracy and Development, coalition of four parties).

Population
525,000 (2010)*
Last census: August 2004: 492,829
Population density: Three inhabitants per square km. Urban population: 75 per cent (1995—2001). Urban population growth rate: 1.3 per cent (2000–05).
Annual growth rate: 0.8 per cent 1994–2004 (WHO 2006)

Ethnic make-up
East Indian (37 per cent), Creole (31 per cent), Javanese (15 per cent), Black (10 per cent), Indian (3 per cent), Chinese (2 per cent).

Religions
Hindu (25 per cent), Protestant (25 per cent), Roman Catholic (23 per cent), Islam (20 per cent), traditional beliefs (5 per cent).

Education
Primary schooling begins at age 6 and last until aged 12. An exam deteremines the route either to a general lower secondary, or technical school. Advancement at age 16, following further exams, leads to either an academic, pre-university senior, or upper vocational, school. Teaching may be delivered in either Dutch or English.
Higher education is provided through either a Univerisity, Institute, Academy, or Polytechnic College.
Literacy rate: 93 per cent adult rate.
Compulsory years: 7 to 12.
Enrolment rate: 92.18 per cent net primary; 2.93 per cent net secondary enrolments.
Pupils per teacher: 17 in primary schools.

Health

HIV/Aids
HIV prevalence: 1.7 per cent aged 15–49 in 2003 (World Bank)
Life expectancy: 67 years, 2004 (WHO 2006)
Fertility rate/Maternal mortality rate: 2.6 births per woman, 2004 (WHO 2006)
Birth rate/Death rate: 19.4 births per 1,000 population; 6.8 deaths per 1,000 population (2003).
Child (under 5 years) mortality rate (per 1,000): 30 per 1,000 live births (World Bank)

Main cities
Paramaribo (Parbo) (capital, estimated population 254,147 in 2005), Lelydorp (16,016), Nieuw Nickerie (11,396).

Languages spoken
Sranan Tongo (Creole) is the *lingua franca*. English, Sarnami (Hindi), Javanese and Chinese are also spoken.

Official language/s
Dutch

Media

Press
Daily newspapers include *De Ware Tijd* (www.dwtonline.com) and *De West* (www.dewestonline.cq-link.sr) and a periodical *Dagblad Suriname* (www.dbsuriname.com).

Broadcasting
Radio: All stations broadcast programmes in Dutch with other local languages. Stichting Radio Omroep Suriname (SRS) is government-owned; commercial stations include Radio Paramaribo, Radio Apintie (www.apintie.fm), Radio Nickerie (RANI),

Radio 10 (www.radio10.sr); ABC (www.abcsuriname.com) is a radio and TV broadcasting station.
Television: Government-owned commercial TV services include STVS (www.parbo.com/stvs) and ATV (http://www.atv.sr).
News agencies
Other news agencies: Caribbean Net News: www.caribbeannetnews.com

Economy

The major economic resource of Suriname is bauxite, which is either exported as aluminium oxide or refined and exported as aluminium. Other primary industries include gold mining, oil production, agriculture, with production of bananas, rice, citrus fruits, fish and shellfish and timber for exports.

GDP growth in 2007 was 5.4 per cent, which rose to 6.0 per cent in 2008 but although predicted to fall to 1.5 per cent in 2009, was later estimated to have grown by 2.5 per cent. Inflation, which had been fuelled by globally high prices for oil and food, had been at 15 per cent in 2008, but it dropped to less than 1.0 per cent in 2009 as food and fuel prices fell, along with domestic demand.

Although Suriname did not suffer firsthand from the global economic crisis as its banking sector is considered conservative, it did feel the effects as foreign direct investment (FDI) was cut and the mining sector lost an estimated US$1 billion in aluminium production and processing when the Australian-based, BHP Billiton closed down its mining operation in Suriname at the end of 2008; it had ceased all operations in Suriname by 2010. The US-based Alcoa's US$65 million expansion of its Paranam alumina refinery, opened in 2005, produces 250,000 tonnes per year and is the only remaining alumina refinery in operation.

The Netherlands government agreed to restart aid flows, allowing Suriname to not only access international development finance but also to re-pay outstanding loans, in 2009, of US$118 million to Brazil.

Migrant workers and the remittances they send home constitute an important resource for many families in Suriname. The emigration rate was 36 per cent in 2007, most of which were destined for Europe. Remittances in 2007 totalled US$140 million. However, as the global economic crisis worsened jobs and wages were cut leading to reduced prospects and benefits.

External trade

As a member of the Caribbean Community and Common Market (Caricom), Suriname operates within the single market (Caribbean Single Market and Economy (CSME)), which became operational in 2006. Goods, services, businesses and money are free to move within CSME without barriers and tariffs.

Natural resources include a major world source of bauxite, rainforest timbers, gold, iron ore, seafood and agricultural products.

Imports

Principal imports are capital equipment, petroleum, foodstuffs, cotton and consumer goods

Main sources: US (typically 24 per cent of total), Trinidad and Tobago (21 per cent), The Netherlands (20 per cent).

Exports

Principal exports are aluminium oxide, gold, crude oil, timber, shrimp and fish, rice and bananas.

Main destinations: Canada (typically 14 per cent of total), Belgium (12 per cent), Switzerland (9 per cent).

Agriculture

Just 0.5 per cent of Suriname's total landmass is accounted for by permanent crop and arable land, concentrated predominantly along the coastal plain. Despite the dearth of land devoted to agricultural activities, Suriname is self sufficient in most basic foodstuffs and the sector accounts for up to 10 per cent of total GDP. Some 20 per cent of the country's workforce is employed in the agricultural sector.

The staple food crop and most important agricultural export is rice, the farming of which is highly mechanised. Suriname exports 40,000 tonnes of rice annually to the EU. Other major crops include palm oil, coconuts, bananas, sugar, citrus fruits and coffee.

The commercial fishing industry accounts for about 7 per cent of Surinam's total export earnings; the sector has grown in importance in recent years. Fishing for shellfish, in particular, has increased. The typical total fish catch is over 19,000mt, plus over 7,700mt of other seafood, per annum.

A new fishery centre, providing mooring facilities, an ice factory, freezing stations, fuel stop and workshops for the enlarged fishing fleet was underconstruction in 2007, with finance provided by the Japanese government.

Suriname has vast forestry resources in relation to its size. Approximately 80 per cent of the country's total landmass is covered by forests and woodland, but just 2 per cent is exploited as access is limited.

Industry and manufacturing

Industrial activities in Suriname centre on the processing of agricultural produce (particularly timber), bauxite mining and timber processing. The sector contributes approximately 15 per cent to total GDP and employs one fifth of Suriname's labour force.

In 2003, Alcoa announced a US$65 million, 250,000 tonne expansion to its Paranam alumina refinery, which will increase capacity by approximately 12 per cent. The project was completed midway through 2005.

Tourism

The travel and tourism industry is growing in Suriname. Employment in the sector has risen to 4.9 per cent of the workforce and tourism now represents 5.4 per cent of the country's total GDP.

Ecotourism is growing in importance and has contributed to the permanent protection of 1.62 million ha of tropical forests.

Mining

In a typical year for the economy of Suriname the mining sector contributes approximately 12 per cent of total GDP. The sector also employs some 5 per cent of the country's total workforce.

One of the largest producers of bauxite in the world, Suriname's reserves stand at 600 million tonnes. The US imports 400,000 tonnes of alumina from Suriname each year and it contributes up to 60 per cent of exports and 10–15 per cent of government income.

The deposits in the major mining areas, Moengo and Paranam, are maturing and were expected to reach the end of their life in 2006. Another, new production site opened in 2006, at Kaaimangrasie and Klaverblad, and are expected to last until 2010. Other reserves in the east, west and north of Suriname are expected to last until 2025.

Annual gold production is valued at US$25 million per annum, although 80 per cent of this is in the informal sector and much of the country's gold output is smuggled away into French Guiana. In 2004 Cambior, the Canadian mining company, began shipment of gold bars from their Rosebel Gold mine. It is expected that 220,000 ounces of gold will be produced in the first year valued at US$157 per ounce; the government will receive 2.2 per cent royalties from the mine.

Other commercially viable minerals include iron ore, copper, nickel, platinum and kaolin.

In 2006, a new bauxite mine opened, with reserves of an estimated 13.5 million tonnes.

Hydrocarbons

Total proven oil reserves were 111 million barrels in 2007, with production at 5.4 million barrels from the Saramacca and Calcutta oil fields. Sustainable production is determined at 16,000 barrels per day (bpd). The state-owned Staatsolie has a

monopoly and is responsible for exploration, production and refining crude oil, alone or in conjunction with other oil companies.
While oil exploration was focussed onshore up to 2007, it moved offshore along Suriname's coastal area after a UN tribunal made a decision concerning the disputed oil-rich territory claimed by both Guyana and Suriname. The ruling declared that both countries were entitled to explore the region off the Atlantic coastline with Suriname being granted 17,871 square kilometres. An estimate of the recoverable oil in the area is 2 billion cubic metres (15 billion barrels) and 1.19 trillion cubic metres of gas.
The country's only oil refinery produces 7,000bpd of diesel, fuel oil and bitumen. Staatsolie has plans to increase this amount to 15,000bpd by 2012. In 2005, Suriname, plus a number of other Caribbean states, signed an agreement with Venezuela to establish PetroCaribe, a multi-national oil company, owned by the participating states. PetroCaribe buys low-priced Venezuelan crude oil under long-term payment plans.
Any use of natural gas or coal is commercially insignificant.

Energy
Total installed electricity generation capacity was 389MW in 2007, producing over 1.6 billion kilowatt hours. Around 75 per cent of all electricity was generated by hydropower. One of the world's largest man-made lakes, of around 1,560 square kilometres (depending on rainfall), the Brokopondo Reservoir, provides the water for the dam which generates the energy for the bauxite refinery in Paranam on the Suriname River. It typically allocates 25 per cent of its electricity output to power 75 per cent of the capital Paramaribo's needs.

Banking and insurance
Suriname's banking sector has traditionally been highly indebted and needs reform. The government has equity stakes in six of Suriname's eight banks, including a 10 per cent stake in the largest bank, De Surinaamse Bank. Domestic borrowing is mostly undertaken by the government.
Central bank
Centrale Bank van Suriname
Main financial centre
Paramaribo.

Time
GMT minus three hours

Geography
Suriname is located on the northern coast of South America, facing the Atlantic Ocean. It is bordered by French Guiana to the east, Guyana to the west and Brazil to the south.
The terrain is hilly and most of the country is covered by tropical rain forests, except along a narrow strip of low-lying coastal plain. This area, which is swampy, is 80km at its widest and is home to most of the population. There is a 3,000km network of rivers, most of which flow northwards into the Atlantic Ocean. River travel is the main means of access into the forested interior. The most important rivers are the Corantijn, Suriname, Mariwijne and Coppename. A huge man-made lake, the WJ van Blommestein Meer, one of the largest reservoirs in the world, lies astride the Suriname river in the north-east of the country.
Hemisphere
Northern

Climate
Tropical but cooled by trade winds. Rain throughout the year but heaviest from November–January and from April–July. Average daily temperature remains fairly constant throughout the year at 27 degrees Celsius (C); daily range from 22–35 degrees C from May–October; slightly lower temperatures from November–April.

Entry requirements
Passports
Required by all, valid for six months from date of arrival.
Visa
Required by nationals of most countries; for current list of exceptions, see www.surinameembassy.org. All visitors must have return/onward passage. Business visas require a letter from the employing company explaining the purpose of visit, and the details of all the contacts in Suriname plus an itinerary.
Currency advice/regulations
Import and export of local currency is limited to Su$150. There are no restrictions on the import and export of foreign currencies, subject to declaration of amounts over US$10,000

Health (for visitors)
Mandatory precautions
Yellow fever vaccination certificate required if arriving from an infected area.
Advisable precautions
Yellow fever, typhoid and polio vaccinations. Malaria prophylaxis recommended and water precautions should be taken.

Hotels
Paramaribo and Nieuw Nickerie have a number of modern hotels but beds are limited. Service charge of 10 per cent is usual.

Public holidays (national)
Fixed dates
1 Jan (New Year's Day), 1 May (Labour Day), 1 Jul (Abolition of Slavery Day), 25 Nov (Independence Day), 25–26 Dec (Christmas).
Variable dates
Holi (Hindu, Mar), Good Friday, Easter Monday, Eid al Fitr.
In addition, Chinese, Jewish and Indian businesses will be closed for their own religious holidays.

Working hours
Banking
Mon–Fri: 0800–1500.
Business
Mon–Fri: 0730–1630.
Government
Mon–Fri: 0700–1500.
Shops
Mon–Fri: 0700/0730–1630; Sat: 0730–1300.

Electricity supply
110/127V and/or 220V AC, 60 cycles

Getting there
Air
National airline: Surinam Airways (SLM).
International airport/s:
Paramaribo-Johan Adolf Pengel International Airport (PMB), 46km from city; duty-free shop, bank, cafeterias, car hire.
Airport tax: US$35, payable only in US dollars or euros.
Surface
Road: A coastal road links Paramaribo with Guyana (at Nieuw Nickerie) and French Guiana (at Albina).
Water: There are sea links with the US and Europe. Car ferry services run from French Guiana and Guyana.
Main port/s: Paramaribo.

Getting about
National transport
Most infrastructure has been on the country's narrow coastal plain, with links to the interior weak. Much of the sparsely-populated country is accessible only by air or river.
Air: Domestic flights to towns in the interior are operated from Zorg en Hoop airfield near Paramaribo by Surinam Airways and Gum Air. Charter services are available.
Road: There are over 4,000km of roads, of which around a quarter are paved. Coastal towns are linked by road from Nieuw Nickerie in the west, through Paramaribo, to Albina in the east. Roads in the interior are not surfaced and are poorly maintained.
Bridges over the Coppename and Suriname rivers link the east and west of the country.
Buses: Paramaribo and most towns have a local bus service. Bus routes link coastal towns but service is irregular and tends to be crowded.

Water: River transport is the main means of travel in the interior and in some coastal areas.

City transport

Taxis: Taxis are available, but scarce after 10 pm and on Sundays and holidays. They are not metered and fares should be agreed in advance of journey.

Car hire

Available in Paramaribo at the airport and through main hotels and the Tourist Information Office. International driving licences required.

BUSINESS DIRECTORY

The addresses listed below are a selection only. While World of Information makes every endeavour to check these addresses, we cannot guarantee that changes have not been made, especially to telephone numbers and area codes. We would welcome any corrections.

Telephone area codes

The international dialling code (IDD) for Suriname is +597 followed by subscriber's number.

Chambers of Commerce

Suriname Chamber of Commerce & Industry, PO Box 139, Mr JC de Miranda Straat, Paramaribo (tel: 473-527; fax: 470-802; e-mail: chamber@sr.net).

Banking

De Surinaamse Bank NV, Henck Arronstraat 26-30, Paramaribo (tel: 471-100; fax: 477-835).

Finabank NV, Dr. S. Redmondstraat 55-61, Paramaribo.

Hakrinbank NV, Dr S. Redmondstraat 11-13, Paramaribo (tel: 477-722; fax: 472-066).

Landbouwbank NV, Lim A Postraat 28-30, Paramaribo (tel: 475-945, 475-101; fax: 410-821).

Nationale Ontwikkelingsbank (NOB), Coppenamelaan 160-162, Paramaribo (tel: 465-000; fax: 497-192).

RBTT Bank (Suriname), Kerkplein 1 Paramaribo (tel: 471-555; fax: 411-325).

Surinaamse Postspaarbank (SPSB), Knuffelsgracht 11-13, Paramaribo (tel: 472-256; fax: 472-952).

Surinaamse Volkscrediet Bank (VCB), Steenbakkerijstraat 2, Paramaribo (tel: 472-616; fax: 472-616).

Central bank

Centrale Bank van Suriname, PO Box 1081, Waterkant 16-20, Paramaribo (tel: 473-741; fax: 476-444; e-mail: info@cbvs.sr).

Travel information

Surinam Airways, Jagernath Lachmonstraat 136, PO Box 2029, Paramaribo (tel: 465-700; fax: 491-213; e-mail: publicrelations@slm.firm.sr).

Tourist Information Centre, Waterkant 1, Fort Zeelandia Complex, Paramaribo (tel: 479-200; fax: 477-786; e-mail: stsmktg@sr.net).

Ministry of tourism

Ministry of Transport, Communication and Tourism, Prins Hendrikstraat 26-28, Paramaribo (tel: 420-422; fax: 420-425; e-mail: odc@minctc.sr).

National tourist organisation offices

Suriname Tourism Foundation, Dr JF Nassylaan 2, Paramaribo; PO Box 656, Paramaribo (tel: 410-357; fax: 477-786; email: info@suriname-tourism.org).

Ministries

Ministry of Agriculture, Animal Husbandry and Fisheries, Cultuurtuinlaan, Paramaribo (tel: 474-177; fax: 470-301).

Ministry of Defence, Kwattaweg 29, Paramaribo (tel: 474-244; fax: 420-055).

Ministry of Economic Affairs, Kleine Waterstraat 4, Paramaribo (tel: 75-080).

Ministry of Education, Dr. F. Kaffiludistraat 117-123, Paramaribo (tel: 498-383; fax: 495-083).

Ministry of Finance, Onafhandelijkheidsplein 3, Paramaribo (tel: 472-619; fax: 476-314).

Ministry of Foreign Affairs, Gravenstraat 6-8, Paramaribo (tel: 471-209; fax: 410-851).

Ministry of Justice and Police, Gravenstraat 1, Paramaribo (tel: 473-033; fax: 412-109).

Ministry of Internal Affairs, Onafhankelijkheidsplein 2, Paramaribo (tel: 476-461; fax: 421-170).

Ministry of Labour, Wagenwegstraat 22, Paramaribo (tel: 477-045; fax: 410-465).

Ministry of Natural Resources, Mr. Dr. J.C. de Mirandastraat 13-15, Paramaribo (tel: 473-420; fax: 472-911).

Ministry of Planning and International Co-operation, Dr. S Redmondstraat 118, Paramaribo (tel: 473-628; fax: 421-056).

Ministry of Public Health, Gravenstraat 64, Paramaribo (tel: 474-841; fax: 410-702).

Ministry of Public Works, Verlengde Coppenamestraat 167, Paramaribo (tel: 462-500; fax: 464-901).

Ministry of Regional Development, Van Rooseveltkade 2, Paramaribo (tel: 471-574).

Ministry of Social Affairs and Housing, Waterkant 30-32, Paramaribo (tel: 472-610; fax: 470-516).

Ministry of Trade and Industry, Nieuwe Haven, Paramaribo (tel: 479-886; fax: 477-602).

Ministry of Transportation, Communications and Tourism, Prins Hendrikstraat 26-28, Paramaribo (tel: 420-422; fax: 470-425).

President of the Republic of Suriname, Onafhankelijkheidsplein, Paramaribo (tel: 472-841; fax: 475-266).

Vice President and Council of Ministers, Dr. S. Redmondstraat, 1e Etage, Paramaribo (tel: 474-805; fax: 472-917).

Other useful addresses

Algemene Aannemers Vereniging (AAV), Gravenstraat 73, Paramaribo (tel: 478-419; fax: 474-531).

Associatie van Surinaarns Bedrijfsleven (V.S.B.), Domineestraat 33 boven, Paramaribo (tel: 476-585; fax: 421-160).

Orde van Raadgavende Ingenieursbureaus in Suriname (ORIS), P.O. Box 1864, van Roosmalenstraat no. 30, Paramaribo (tel: 472-275, 474-381; fax: 474-408).

Stichting Planbureau Suriname, PO Box 172, Dr S. Redmondstraat 110, Paramaribo (tel: 473-146).

Suriname Embassy (USA), Suite 108, 4301 Connecticut Avenue, NW, Washington DC 20008 (tel: (+1-202) 244-7488; fax: (+1-202) 244-5878; e-mail: embsur@erols.com).

Vereniging Surinaams Bedrijfsleven (Suriname Trade and Industry Association), Prins Hendrikstraat 18, PO Box 111, Paramaribo (tel: 475-286/7; fax: 472-287).

Internet sites

De Ware Tijd (English bulletin available): http://www.dwt.net

Economic Commission for Latin America and the Caribbean: http://www.eclac.cl

Inter-American Development Bank: http://www.iadb.org

Organisation of American States: http://www.oas.org

Latin World: http://www.latinworld.com

Latin Trade Online: http://www.latintrade.com

Republic of Suriname homepage: http://www.sr.net.srnet/InfoSurinam

Swaziland

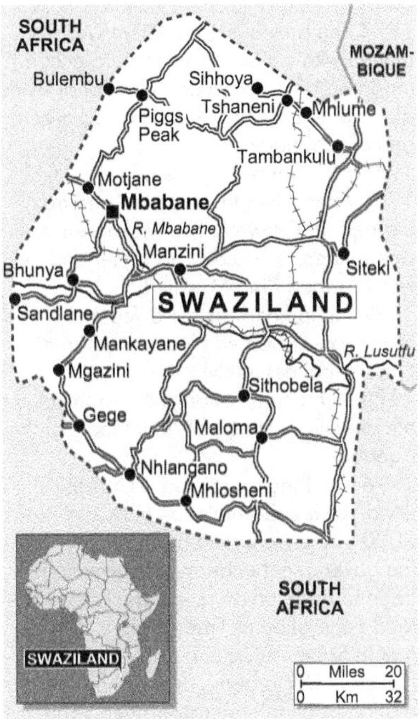

The global economic crisis in 2009 cut Swaziland's chief revenue source, that generated by the Southern African Customs Union (Sacu), from US$9.2 million in 2009/10 to US$3.4 million in 2010/11. This put the government under increasing financial pressure, causing an increase in the already seriously fractured political climate of sub-Saharan Africa's only absolute monarchy.

In October 2010, the International Monetary Fund (IMF) predicted that unless the government confronted this fall in revenue from Sacu, public debt would jump from 19 per cent of GDP to 31 per cent of GDP by 2011.

According to the *Southern Africa Report* (October 2011), the King is supported in his rampant spending through direct annual grants from the state, worth R230 million (US$29.4 million). This was added to in 2011 by R300 million (US$38.4 million) for upgrades to the network of royal palaces for the king and his 13 wives. The state also provides bloated salaries and perks for MPs, cabinet ministers and royals deployed in government. The rest is directed on lavish construction projects, notably the second international airport with its R2 billion (US$256 million) price-tag. In addition, the state supports a 36,000-strong civil service (for a population of 1.1 million) that imposes a public wage bill of 18 per cent of GDP.

Opposition and confrontation

There were a number of organised pro-democracy protests throughout 2010, which while the economy was relatively stable were dismissed as a citizen's freedom of expression. But as the economic crisis deepened, so the dissatisfaction increased. The Swaziland United Democratic Front (SUDF), a coalition of labour federations, political organisations, students and civil society organisations, called for a week-long series of mass protests, beginning on 18 March 2011, in protest at the cut in public sector pay. As announced, thousands of public sector workers marched through the capital, Mbabane, including an estimated 10,000 nurses, teachers and students, finishing up outside the office of the prime minister where a petition was delivered.

In April the response to growing protests became more hostile and while two activist leaders were arrested for a brief time during pro-democracy rallies of 6 April. Baton wielding police broke into the offices of the teacher's union on12 April, following the use of tear-gas and water cannons to break up a banned demonstration. Prime Minister Sibusiso Dlamini extolled his senators not to panic and said that the country would continue to be governable as per the wishes of the Swazi nation.

Who pays...?

According to the *African Economic Outlook 2011* (AEO), published jointly by the African Development Bank and the Organisation for Economic Co-operation and Development, a Fiscal Adjustment Roadmap (FAR) (for 2010/11–2014/15) was prepared as part of the negotiations with the IMF in late October 2010. The government was keen to unlock external donor support. Among other things, such as public wage freezes and job losses, the IMF

KEY FACTS

Official name: Umbuso weSwatini (Kingdom of Swaziland)

Head of State: King Mswati III

Head of government: Prime Minister Barnabas (Bheki) Sibusiso Dlamini (appointed by the King on 16 Oct 2008)

Ruling party: Political parties are *de facto* banned

Area: 17,363 square km

Population: 1.19 million (2010)*

Capital: Mbabane (administrative capital); Lobamba (legislative capital and the seat of the monarchy)

Official language: English and siSwati

Currency: Lilangeni – plural Emalangeni (E) = 100 cents; at par with the South African Rand

Exchange rate: E8.04 per US$ (Oct 2011)

GDP per capita: US$3,061 (2010)

GDP real growth: 2.00% (2010)

GDP: US$3.60 billion (2010)

Inflation: 4.50% (2010)

Balance of trade: -US$121.30 million (2009)

* estimated figure

recommended the speedy introduction of a value added tax (VAT) and reduction of the budget (16.4 per cent of GDP in 2010/11) by 5 per cent per annum beginning 2011/12 until 2013/2014. A revitalisation of the private sector through improving the business environment and using existing and emerging partnerships was also considered vital for a quick economic turnaround.

Help from the neighbours?

However by August 2011, following cuts in the public sector wages bill and the halt in capital projects and cancelling the lavish, public anniversary coronation celebrations (due on 25 April), and with the collapse in the economy imminent, King Mswati went cap in hand to South African President Jacob Zuma for help. An emergency loan of R2.4 billion (US$355 million) in soft loans was agreed, on the proviso that the IMF reforms were undertaken, along with political reforms. The loans were to be paid in three tranches, beginning in August, the second in October and a final amount in February 2012. The South African *Business Day* reported in October that King Mswati was reluctant to agree to the conditions of the loan, thereby preventing any of the loan funds from being transferred. The IMF refused to bail out the economy, citing the Swazi government's failure to reduce the budget deficit, amend the income tax demand and reduce the bloated bureaucracy.

King Mswati returned to South Africa in early October to renegotiate the terms of the loan, and to have the conditions on democratic change dropped. But following the outcry from many sides when the first announcement had been made, Pretoria refused the request. In November the Swazi government failed to pay over US$10 million of grant money to Aids-orphans, according to an IMF official. In December, a total of US$59 million was withheld by the government from its annual contribution to the Public Service Pension Fund (PSPF). The government was turning to all means possible to shore up its coffers, but with increasingly desperate methods, likely to have long-term and possibly unforeseen outcomes.

Judgement of Solomon

South Africa is placed in a tricky situation, because if it does not help Swaziland it risks a failed state on its doorstep and if it does help there is no guarantee that the administration of Swaziland will follow the suggested path of sustainable economic growth.

Risk assessment

Economy	Poor
Politics	Poor
Regional stability	Fair

COUNTRY PROFILE

Historical profile

1903 After a period of rivalry between the British and the Boers, Swaziland became a British protectorate.
1963 Swaziland's first constitution was introduced.
1964 The first elections resulted in victory for the Imbokodvo National Movement (INM).
1967 Swaziland was granted internal self-government as a protected state. Sobhuza II was recognised as King and head of state; Prince Makhosini Dlamini, leader of the INM, was appointed prime minister.
1968 Independence was granted.
1973 The King revoked the Westminster-based constitution and banned political parties.
1978 The previous constitution was replaced with a system designed to accommodate both western and traditional styles of government but still maintained a ban on Political parties.
1982 King Sobhuza II died.
1986 After a lengthy selection and training period, Crown Prince Makhosetive was chosen to succeed his father and he was crowned King Mswati III.
1992 Parliament was dissolved and Swaziland was governed by a *Liqoqo* (traditional tribal assembly).
1993 Democratic reforms led to the people directly electing some members of the *Liqoqo*.
1996 The King appointed a Constitutional Review Commission (CRC).
2000 The government put five critics of the government under house arrest and banned trade union meetings. The Swaziland Federation of Trade Unions (SFTU) met in South Africa and drew up the Nelspruit Declaration, demanding the formation of an interim government. The government amended the labour laws. Swaziland became eligible for US African Growth and Opportunities Act (AGOA) benefits.
2001 A number of political activists were forced into exile in South Africa. Decree 2 was issued by King Mswati, giving the monarch power to overrule court decisions. It was soon repealed after the US threatened to end the country's benefits under AGOA.
2002 The Internal Security Bill was enacted, which made it illegal to display support for any political party. The Libyan leader, Colonel Muammar al Qadafi, visited Swaziland to give his support to the monarchy.
2003 The October Parliamentary elections were considered by the opposition to be meaningless since political parties are outlawed.
2004 The UN declared Swaziland had the world's highest rate of HIV; 4 in 10 people were estimated to be HIV positive. King Mswati ordered new palaces to be built for each of his eleven wives, at a total cost of US$15 million.
2005 A two-day general strike by pro-democracy supporters protested against a new constitution that entrench the King's power further.

KEY INDICATORS — Swaziland

	Unit	2006	2007	2008	2009	2010
Population	m	1.01	1.02	1.02	*1.03	*1.19
Gross domestic product (GDP)	US$bn	2.79	2.94	2.80	3.00	*3.70
GDP per capita	US$	2,544	2,892	2,778	2,500	*3,133
GDP real growth	%	2.8	3.5	3.1	1.2	*2.0
Inflation	%	5.3	8.2	13.1	7.4	*4.5
Industrial output	% change	1.3	2.1	2.4	1.2	–
Agricultural output	% change	4.7	2.7	2.4	1.2	–
Exports (fob) (goods)	US$m	1,877.0	1,744.8	1,570.4	1,572.8	–
Imports (fob) (goods)	US$m	1,192.0	2,015.9	1,580.3	1,704.0	–
Balance of trade	US$m	685.0	-271.1	-909.0	-131.2	–
Current account	US$m	98.1	-65.5	-231.7	-425.9	-731.0
Total reserves minus gold	US$m	372.5	762.6	751.9	958.9	756.3
Foreign exchange	US$m	358.9	748.3	737.9	879.0	677.9
Exchange rate	per US$	6.77	7.04	8.26	8.47	7.32

* estimated figure

2006 A new constitution was promulgated in which the absolute power of the King remained inviolate; the King is above the law and not accountable to his people, with direct control of all security forces, governmental bodies and government posts. South African police shot at protestors blockading a border crossing into Swaziland; the protestors were demanding political reform.
2007 Six opposition members who took part in the border blockade were charged with sedition. Protests for democratic reforms were held.
2008 The opposition declared it would boycott upcoming elections in protest at the lack of multi-party elections. The King appointed Barnabas (Bheki) Sibusiso Dlamini as prime minister
2010 Swaziland remained the country with the highest prevalence of HIV in the world. In February the head of UNAids called for greater national response to the disease. Justice minister Ndumiso Mamba resigned in August after allegations that he was having an affair with King Mswati's 12th (of 13) wives.
2011 Following a pay-freeze of government workers, protesters took to the streets of the capital Mbabane, delivering a petition calling on the government to resign; some blamed it for corruption and were critical of the plans for lavish anniversary coronation celebrations, due on 25 April. Police used tear gas and water cannon to disperse protesters calling for elections. Swaziland has Africa's last absolute monarchy; political parties were banned 30 years ago. South Africa gave Swaziland an emergency loan of US$355 million on 3 August. The following week the University of Swaziland failed to open for the new academic year; officials gave the reason as non-payment of student fees by the government. An immediate national debate ensued as to whether the money should be spent on repaying loans that had been provided to the government by domestic companies that now needed the money back to ease their cash flow and continue in business, or whether public workers should be paid to continue the business of government. By mid-September, the head of the Swaziland Principals Association confirmed that most schools in Swaziland were shut because of the financial crisis. The emergency loan from South Africa had yet to arrive.

Political structure

Constitution

The constitution was promulgated in 1978. The country is run on a dual system. The traditional structure of Swaziland is headed by the Ingwenyama (the lion) (King), the Ndlovukazi (the she-elephant) (Queen Mother), and the more than 300 Chiefs who control the largely rural population. The other is the western-style central government, headed by the King, acting together with parliament, cabinet and civil service. Succession to the throne is governed by Swazi law and custom.
The draft of a proposed new constitution was written in 2003. However, it was available only in English and is also to be published in SiSwati during 2004, after which there is to be a further period of national consultation..
The Kingdom is divided into four regions.

Form of state

Absolute monarchy

The executive

Under the 1978 constitution, considerable executive power is vested in the monarch and exercised through a cabinet of ministers (all appointed by the monarch). Royal decrees carry the full force of law.

National legislature

There is a bi-cameral Libandla (legislature) consisting of the Senate (20 members appointed by the King; additional 10 members elected by the House of Assembly from among its own membership), and the Liqoqo (House of Assembly) (55 elective members, directly elected every five years (the first time in 1993), with voters electing one representative from each of the *tinkhundla* (traditional assemblies); 10 further members appointed by the King).

Legal system

The legal system is based on South African Roman-Dutch law in statutory courts and Swazi traditional law and custom in traditional courts. The Court of Appeal is the highest court in Swaziland. Court decisions are often overruled by the King.

Last elections

October 2003 (*Liqoqo*, traditional tribal assembly)
Results: *Liqoqo*: the elections were considered by the opposition to be meaningless since political parties are outlawed. Only one of the elected MPs has a political affiliation (former prime minister Obed Dlamini, a member of the Ngwane National Liberation Congress). Several other members of outlawed parties contested seats as independent candidates; turnout was low.

Political parties

Ruling party

Political parties are *de facto* banned

Population

1.19 million (2010)*
Last census: 11 May 2007: 953,524 (provisional)
Population density: 59 inhabitants per square km. Urban population: 27 per cent (1995–2001).
Annual growth rate: 1.0 per cent 1994–2004 (WHO 2006)

Ethnic make-up

Africans (97 per cent), Europeans (3 per cent).

Religions

Christianity (60 per cent), traditional beliefs (40 per cent).

Education

Although education is subsidised by government, free public education remains a distant goal. School drop-out rates for children of vulnerable households are increasing, with more than 10 per cent of school drop-outs in the first term due to families forced to use school fees to pay the rising costs of staple foods.
It is estimated that through the loss of parents, due to HIV/Aids, 10 per cent of households are headed by a child.
A survey in 2001 showed there were 728 schools in the country, of which 549 were primary and 179 were secondary/high schools. The University of Swaziland provides higher education. There is scope for vocational training, including nursing, although there are no training institutes for doctors and dentists.
Literacy rate: 82 per cent adult rate (2003)
Compulsory years: None.
Enrolment rate: 128 per cent boys, 121 per cent girls gross primary enrolment (including repeaters); 60 per cent gross secondary enrolment (Unicef 2004).
Pupils per teacher: 37 in primary schools; 20 in secondary schools.

Health

HIV/Aids

Swaziland has one of the highest HIV/Aids rate in the world. In a 2005 antenatal survey of pregnant women aged 25–29 the prevalence rate was 56.3 per cent. The number of orphans of Aids is estimated to be between 10–15 per cent of the population in 2010, with the gender imbalance stark as the disease strikes down a disproportionate number of females.
Food security in Swaziland is directly linked to the toll on its young, productive adults, during its longstanding HIV/Aids epidemic. UNAIDS estimates that the annual loss to GDP per capita due to Aids was around 1.2 per cent by 2010. Demographically, urban populations have fallen by 5 per cent as HIV sufferers return to their family farms to receive care.
About 230,000 people are HIV-positive, of whom 65,000 depend on state hospitals to give them free antiretroviral drugs.
HIV prevalence: 42.6 per cent in 2005 (UNAIDS)
Life expectancy: 37 years, 2004 (WHO 2006)
Fertility rate/Maternal mortality rate: 3.8 births per woman, 2004 (WHO 2006)

Birth rate/Death rate: 29 births and 21 deaths per 1,000 people (2003)
Child (under 5 years) mortality rate (per 1,000): 105 per 1,000 live births (2003); 10 per cent of children aged under five are malnourished (World Bank).
Head of population per physician: 0.16 physicians per 1,000 people, 2004 (WHO 2006)

Welfare
UN estimates show that 66 per cent of Swaziland's population live below the poverty line. The average unemployment rate is about 40 per cent, although this figure is higher in rural areas.
According to the UN World Food Programme in early 2002, some 144,000 people required food aid after a severe drop in agricultural production. The total food aid amounted to 17,720 tonnes.

Main cities
Mbabane (administrative capital, estimated population 81,594 in 2005), Lobamba (legislative capital and the seat of the monarchy), Manzini (36,594), Matsapha.

Languages spoken
Most Swazis are bi-lingual in English and SiSwati. In 2006 concern was expressed that teaching of SiSwati was less than English and that under 25 per cent of students who sat the 2005 Junior Certificate SiSwati examination passed; 92 per cent sitting the English language examination passed.
Official language/s
English and SiSwati

Media
Censorship extends to all radio and television output, excluding the Christian radio station. The print media is also restricted with the only privately owned newspaper reduced to commenting on news trivia while all adverse comments concerning the King are avoided.
Press
Dailies: In English, the privately owned *Times of Swaziland* (www.times.co.sz) is a tabloid style newspaper and *The Swazi Observer* (www.observer.org.sz) is an establishment newspaper.
Weeklies: Both dailies have weekend editions , *Times of Swaziland Sunday*, *The Weekend Observer* (www.observer.org.sz).
Periodicals: The *Dzadze Family Magazine* caters to women and consumer interests.
Broadcasting
Radio: The state-run Swaziland Broadcasting and Information Service operates three channels, the siSwati channel, the English channel and the Information service. The US-owned evangelical Trans World Radio (www.twr.org.za) has transmitters in Swaziland and broadcasts regionally.
Television: The state-run Swaziland Television Authority transmits most services in English with some in siSwati.
News agencies
There is no official agency but APA (www.apanews.net) and Panapress (www.panapress.com) report on Swaziland matters.

Economy
In 2009 the composition of the economy was evenly dominated by manufacturing and the service sector at 44.4 per cent and 43.3 per cent respectively, agriculture constituted 7.3 per cent of GDP and heavy industry 5 per cent. Manufacturing includes foodstuffs, soft drinks, canned fruit and confectionary, plus forestry products, wood pulp, paper and board products and furniture and others such as soaps and detergents.
Up to 60 per cent of government spending was funded by receipts from the Southern African Customs Union (SACU), but in 2010 these receipts were cut by 60 per cent, which plunging the economy into crisis. By 22 June 2011 the government was unable to pay its own employees and King Mswati personally engaged in talks with South African president, Jakob Zuma, for financial aid, needed to balance Swaziland's budget and more immediately to pay its civil servants. Capital projects, such as the Sikhuphe International Airport were stalled due to lack of funds and the King cancelled his silver jubilee celebrations for 2011. A R2.4 billion (US$355 million) in soft loans was agreed, to be paid in three tranches, beginning in August. In September, a South African treasury spokesman said that no money would be transferred (and had not been) until the paperwork was signed. Government bills went unpaid, the university was closed at the end of the 2010 academic year and the government reached its formal credit limit at the Central Bank of Swaziland. The International Monetary Fund refused to bail out the economy, citing the Swazi government's failure to reduce the budget deficit, amend the income tax demand and reduce the bloated bureaucracy.
GDP growth was 3.1 per cent in 2008, falling to 1.2 per cent in 2009 as the global economic crisis cut trade in general. As markets picked up, so did growth, to 2.0 per cent in 2010, however due to Swaziland's fiscal deficit of 14.3 per cent of GDP for 2010/11, growth for 2011 was forecast to fall into a recessionary -2.1 per cent.
Subsistence agriculture provides a livelihood for 75 per cent of the working population. The latest statistics, published in 2007, estimated that over 26 per cent of the population was HIV positive, the highest rate in the world, and that there were over 100,000 orphans. The economic burden of the disease has largely fallen on extended families and non-governmental agencies (NGOs). The UN Food and Agricultural Organisation (FAO) provides funds for Junior Field and Life Schools to offer secure communities for children to grow up in while learning the skills of farming, lost to them through the deaths of their parents.
According to the 2011 UN Human Development Index (HDI), Swaziland was ranked 104 (out of 187), for national development in health, education and income, which was marginally above the average for sub-Saharan Africa. In 2010, 44.5 per cent of the population experienced at least one indicator of poverty and 78.59 per cent were living on the equivalent of US$1.25 per day. In October 2010, the FAO reported that around 25 per cent of the population required food assistance.

External trade
Swaziland is a member of the Common Market for Eastern and Southern Africa (Comesa), and operates within a free trade zone with 13 of the 19 member states. It is a member of the Southern African Development Community (SADC), the objectives of which include reducing trade barriers, achieving regional development and economic growth and evolving common systems and institutions. It is also is a member of the Common Monetary Area (CMA) (South Africa, Lesotho and Namibia) where the South African rand is legal tender throughout.
Sugar and soft drinks concentrate are the leading export earners, with timber and derivative the next important exports. Coal and gold mining have declined and their share of exports is no longer significant. Likewise, garment manufacturing no longer plays a leading role in export sales.
Imports
Principal imports are vehicles, machinery, foodstuffs, petroleum and chemicals.
Main sources: South Africa (typically 93 per cent of total), Namibia (2 per cent), Lesotho (1 per cent)
Exports
Principal exports are soft drink and concentrates, sugar, wood pulp, citrus and canned fruit and garments.
Main destinations: South Africa (typically 45 per cent of total), Botswana (32 per cent), UK (14 per cent).

Agriculture
Farming
The agricultural sector contributes around 13 per cent to GDP and employs half of the working population.
Sugar cane is the principal crop. 38,000 hectares of land are given over to it. With

yields of 100 tonnes per hectare, Swaziland is one of the world's most efficient sugar producers. All sugar cane is grown under irrigation. The industry is regulated by the Swaziland Sugar Association (SSA). Sugar is Swaziland's highest export earner and accounts for 51 per cent of total agricultural production, 24 per cent of GDP, 13 per cent of total exports and 57 per cent of foreign exchange earnings.
Commercial farming, on the 40 per cent of the land owned by individual (mainly non-Swazi) freeholders, is centred on sugar, citrus, pineapples, tobacco and cotton.
Most maize and cotton is grown by small-scale farmers on Swazi Nation Land (SNL) (60 per cent of the land). Smallholders own 80 per cent of the livestock. The country's main food crops are maize, beans, groundnuts and sorghum. Food self-sufficiency declined in the 1990s and efforts to expand local fruit and vegetable production by the National Agricultural Marketing Board (Namboard) have had only a limited impact.

Forestry

Forests cover 8 per cent of total land area.

Industry and manufacturing

The industrial sector employs over a fifth of the workforce. It is traditionally centred on the agro-industries: sugar refining, fruit canning and woodpulp processing. The forest products sector is one of the world's main sources of unbleached pulp.
Starting with textile production, the modern industrial sector has grown rapidly, with the South African market its main outlet. The US's African Growth and Opportunities Act (AGOA) enabled Swazi textile producers to access lucrative US markets, although the US has threatened to withdraw these benefits unless the government undergoes democratic reform. The textile industry was affected in 2005 by increasing competition following the ending of the Agreement on Textiles and Clothing and by reduction of exports caused by the stronger rand.
Other activities include brick manufacture and shoe production.

Tourism

Tourism is in the early stages of developement. It is a growing sector which is being actively developed by the government. The main source of visitors is South Africa, reflecting the strong rand, followed by other neighbouring countries, Germany, the Netherlands, the UK and France.

Mining

Mining activity has declined due to the depletion of iron ore, diamonds, gold and tin and the closure of the Bulembu asbestos mine. Coal is mined for export to South Africa; around 600,000 tonnes of anthracite were produced in 2004. Mineral production accounts for around 2 per cent of GDP.

Hydrocarbons

There are no known oil or natural gas reserves; Swaziland is therefore entirely dependent on imported fuels, which amount to 4,000 barrels of oil per day.
There are substantial reserves of high-quality anthracite coal, which is extracted at the Maloma colliery for export to South Africa. Swaziland's domestic low-quality coal requirements, necessary for electricity generation, are met by imports from South Africa. Coal reserves at the dormant EmaSwati Colliery, Mpaka are estimated at 150 million tonnes.

Energy

Total installed generating capacity was 147MW in 2006, around 85 per cent of electricity is supplied by South Africa and the remainder from Mozambique. A feeder line connecting South Africa and Mozambique crosses Swaziland.
Hydropower supplies 62MW to the country's overall generating capacity. A hydroelectric station at Maguga Dam on the Komati River, has begun operations, contributing a maximum output of 20MW.
Swaziland belongs to the Southern African Development Community (Sadc), which has plans to expand hydropower to utilise the combined potential of 114,000MW available.
In 2008 the government called for tenders to build and operated a 1,000MW coal-fired power plant at the dormant EmaSwati Colliery, Mpaka, to utilise Swaziland's huge reserves. Initial construction should be completed by 2012 with full production by 2014.

Financial markets

Stock exchange

Swaziland Stock Exchange (SSE)

Banking and insurance

Central bank

Central Bank of Swaziland

Main financial centre

Mbabane

Time

GMT plus two hours

Geography

Swaziland is a landlocked country that is surrounded on three sides by South Africa and on its forth side by Mozambique. It is one of the smallest country in Africa and is located on the eastern flank of the Drakensberg mountains extending to the Lubombo escarpment in the east.
These volcanic mountains produce a landscape of high veld with altitudes of 1,800 meters (m) in the north, south and west dropping down to middle veld of between 400–600m to the lowlands or bush veld at around 300m. There are five major rivers and their tributaries running through the country with large lakes and waterfalls and is a major habitat for rare birds and invertebrates.

Hemisphere

Southern

Climate

Temperatures range from about 7–10 Celsius (C) (with occasional frost) during April–September, to 20–30 C during August–January. The wettest months are December and March.
The mountainous high veld region to the north-west has a temperate climate with hot, wet summers and dry winters when the temperature rises during the day but with cold nights. The adjacent middle veld has a warm temperate climate, while further to the east lies the sub-tropical low veld, including the Lubombo plain and escarpment.

Entry requirements

Passports

Required by all.

Visa

Required by all; except citizens of UK, North America, Australasia and others listed at www.gov.sz, see *Entry requirements* under *Tourism, Environment and Community*. To stay over 60 days requires a visa extension, to be obtained from the immigration department.

Currency advice/regulations

The import and export of local and foreign currency is unlimited. It is advisable to exchange local currency before leaving Swaziland as the lilangeni is not readily accepted elsewhere.
Travellers cheques are widely accepted.

Health (for visitors)

Mandatory precautions

A yellow fever certificate is required if arriving from an infected area.

Advisable precautions

Vaccinations for diphtheria, tetanus, hepatitis A and typhoid are recommended. Other vaccinations that may be advised include tuberculosis, cholera and hepatitis B. There is a risk of rabies.
Anti-malaria prophylaxes are needed in all but the high elevations. There is a very high prevalence of HIV/Aids.
Water precautions are essential. Eat only cooked food, served hot; avoid dairy, pork and salads; all fruits should be peeled. To avoid bilharzia, use only well maintained, chlorinated swimming pools.
Any medicines required by the traveller should be brought into the country and it would be wise to have precautionary antibiotics if going outside major urban centres. A travel kit including a disposable syringe is a reasonable precaution.

Medical insurance is essential, including emergency evacuation.

Hotels
There is no official rating system. Accommodation is fairly scarce, especially during national holidays, so rooms should be booked well in advance. Bills generally include the service charge, but a 10 per cent tip is also usual. A 10 per cent government tax is added to the room rates.

Credit cards
Major credit and charge card are accepted.

Public holidays (national)
Fixed dates
1 Jan (New Year's Day), 19 Apr (King's Birthday), 25 Apr (National Flag Day), 1 May (Labour Day), 22 Jul (Birthday of the late King), 6 Sep (Independence Day), 25–26 Dec (Christmas).
Variable dates
Good Friday, Easter Monday, Ascension, Umhlanga/Reed Dance Day^ (Aug/Sep).
^Dependent on local sightings of the moon.

Working hours
Banking
Mon–Fri: 0830–1300/1430; Sat: 0830–1100.
Business
Mon–Fri: 0800–1300, 1400–1700; Sat: 0815 or 0830–1230.
Government
Mon–Fri: 0800–1300, 1400–1700.

Telecommunications
Mobile/cell phones
There is a 900 GSM service throughout most of the country.

Electricity supply
230V AC, 50 Hz, with round, three-pin plugs.

Security
If you enter Swaziland from South Africa by road, on the N4, via the Oshoek border post, avoid travelling after dark as there is a risk of hijacking.

Getting there
Air
National airline: Royal Swazi National Airways
International airport/s: Matsapha (MTS), 9km south-west of Manzini, 40km from Mbabane; refreshments, currency exchange, car hire. There are no direct intercontinental flights, but regular services operate regionally, particularly from South Africa. Swazi Express provides a regional air service
Airport tax: Departures tax: E20
Surface
Road: There are tarred roads from Johannesburg and Durban and from Mozambique (Siteki-Lomahasha road). All Swazi border posts open daily throughout the year; hours of operation vary. Vehicles are subject to searches.
Rail: There is a rail service between Durban (South Africa) and Maputo (Mozambique) via Mpaka in the central eastern district of Lubombo.

Getting about
National transport
Road: The network is fairly well developed. An ongoing project improved the network with the provision of a dual carriageway and toll road between Manzini-Mbabane, which was opened in October 2003 and completed the Matspha-Mbabane-Ngwenya highway.
Buses: There is a good system that extends throughout the country.
Taxis: Minibus taxis run shorter routes than the buses, at slightly higher prices.
City transport
Taxis: Scarce. Best to order from hotel. A tip is usual.
Car hire
Self-drive cars are available at airport and city centre; a national driving licence is required. Driving is on the left and the maximum speed limit is 80kph.

BUSINESS DIRECTORY
The addresses listed below are a selection only. While World of Information makes every endeavour to check these addresses, we cannot guarantee that changes have not been made, especially to telephone numbers and area codes. We would welcome any corrections.

Telephone area codes
The international direct dialling code (IDD) for Swaziland is +268, followed by subscriber's number.

Chambers of Commerce
Swaziland Chamber of Commerce and Industry, PO Box 72, Mbabane (tel: 404-4408; fax: 404-5442; e-mail: chamber@dial.pipex.sz).

Banking
First National Bank of Swaziland Ltd, 2nd Floor, Sales House Building, Mbabane (tel: 404-5401/2/3; fax: 404-4735).

Nedbank (Swaziland) Limited, PO Box 68, Corner Plaza Mall Street and Bypass Road, Mbabane (tel: 404-3351/5; fax: 404-4060).

Standard Bank Swaziland Ltd, Standard House, Swazi Plaza, Mbabane (tel: 404-6930/1/2, 404-6599, 408-30/4; fax: 404-5899).

Swazibank, PO Box 336, Gwamile Street (tel: 404-2551; fax: 404-1241: email: vinahnkambule@swazibank.sz).

Central bank
Central Bank of Swaziland, PO Box 546, Warner Street, Mbabane (tel: 404-2000; fax: 404-0063; email: info@centralbank.org.sz).

Swaziland Stock Exchange (SSE): www.ssx.org.sz

Travel information
Hotels and Tourism Association of Swaziland, PO Box 462, Mbabane (tel: 404-2218; fax: 404-4516).

Royal Swazi National Airways, PO Box 939, Matsapa Airport, Manzini.

Swazi Express (charter airline), Matsapha (tel: 518-6840; fax: 518-7160; internet: www.swaziexpress.com).

Ministry of tourism
Ministry of Tourism, Environment and Communications, 2nd Floor, Income Tax Bld, Mhlambanyatsi Road; PO Box 2653, Mbabane (tel: 404-4556; fax: 404-5415).

National tourist organisation offices
Swaziland Tourism Authority, PO Box A1030, Mbabane (tel: 405-7510; internet: www.welcometoswaziland.com).

Ministries
Cabinet Office, PO Box 395, Mbabane (tel: 404-2251; fax: 404-3943).

Ministry of Agriculture and Co-operatives, PO Box 162, Mbabane (tel: 404-2731; fax: 404-4700).

Ministry of Broadcasting, Information and Tourism, PO Box 338, Mbabane (tel: 404-2761/9; fax: 404-2774).

Ministry of Defence, PO Box 1928, Mbabane (tel: 404-2809; fax: 404-2483).

Ministry of Economic Planning and Statistics, PO Box 602, Mbabane (tel: 404-3765; fax: 404-2157).

Ministry of Education, PO Box 39, Mbabane (tel: 404-2491; fax: 404-3880).

Ministry of Enterprise and Employment, PO Box 451, Mbabane (tel: 404-3201; fax: 404-4711); Trade Promotion Unit (tel: 404-5180).

Ministry of Finance, PO Box 443, Mbabane (tel: 404-8148; fax: 404-3187).

Ministry of Foreign Affairs and Trade, PO Box 518, Mbabane (tel: 404-2661; fax: 404-2669).

Ministry of Health and Social Welfare, PO Box 5, Mbabane (tel: 404-2431; fax: 404-2092).

Ministry of Home Affairs, PO Box 432, Mbabane (tel: 404-2941; fax: 404-4303).

Ministry of Housing and Urban Development, PO Box 1832, Mbabane (tel: 404-6035; fax: 404-4085).

Ministry of Justice and Constitutional Development, PO Box 924, Mbabane (tel: 404-3531; fax: 404-4796); Attorney General's Chambers, PO Box 578, Mbabane (tel: 404-2807).

Ministry of Natural Resources and Energy, PO Box 57, Mbabane (tel: 404-6244; fax: 404-2436); Geological Survey & Mines, PO Box 57, Mbabane (tel: 404-2411). Rural Water Supply, PO Box 961, Mbabane (tel: 404-1231).

Ministry of Public Service and Information, PO Box 338, Mbabane (tel: 404-2761; fax: 404-2774).

Ministry of Public Works and Transport, PO Box 58, Mbabane (tel: 404-2321; fax: 4042364); Civil Aviation (tel: 404-2420).

Prime Minister's Office, PO Box 395, Mbabane (tel: 404-2251; fax: 4043943). Deputy Prime Minister's Office, PO Box A33 Swazi Plaza (tel: 404-2723; fax: 404-4085).

Other useful addresses

Central Co-operative Union, PO Box 551, Manzini (tel: 505-2787; fax 505-5313; email: ccu.admin@africaonline.co.sz).

Central Statistics Office, PO Box 456, Mbabane (tel: 404-2151/4; fax: 404-2157).

Central Transport Administration, PO Box 378, Mbabane (tel: 404-2871; fax: 404-3002).

Civil Service Board, PO Box 158, Mbabane (tel: 404-2601).

Cotton Board, PO Box 230, Manzini (tel/fax: 505-2775).

Federation of Swaziland Employers, PO Box 777, Mbabane (tel: 404-0768; fax: 404-6107; email: fse@realnet.co.sz).

National Agricultural Marketing Board, PO Box 1713, Matsapha (tel: 518-5211; fax: 518-4088).

National Maize Corporation, PO Box 158, Manzini (tel: 518-7432; fax: 518-4461).

Parliament, King's Office (tel: 416-1080). Parliament Offices (tel: 416-1286).

Police Headquarters, PO Box 49, Mbabane (tel: 404-2051).

Posts and Telecommunications Corporation, PO Box 125, Mbabane (tel: 404-2341; fax: 404-3130).

Small Enterprise Development Co Ltd, Mbabane Industrial Sites, PO Box A186, Swazi Plaza (tel: 404-2811; fax: 404-0723).

Statistics Department, PO Box 456, Mbabane (tel: 404-2151; fax: 404-2157).

Swazi Business Growth Trust, PO Box 78, Eveni (tel: 404-4705; fax: 404-4783).

Swaziland Citrus Board, PO Box 343, Mbabane (tel: 404-3547).

Swaziland Commercial Board, PO Box 509, Mbabane (tel: 404-2930).

Swaziland Cotton Board, PO Box 230, Manzini (tel: 505-2775).

Swaziland Dairy Board, PO Box 2975, Manzini (tel: 505-8262).

Swaziland Electricity Board, PO Box 258, Mbabane (tel: 404-6668; fax: 404-2335).

Swaziland Embassy (USA), 1712 New Hampshire Ave, NW, Washington DC 20009 (tel: (1-202) 234-5002; fax: (1-202) 234-8059; e-mail: embassy@swaziland-usa.com).

Swaziland Industrial Development Company, PO Box 866, Mbabane (tel: 404-3391; fax: 404-5619).

Swaziland International Trade Fair, PO Box 877, Manzini (tel: 505-4242; fax: 505-2314).

Swaziland Investment Promotion Authority, PO Box 4194, Mbabane H100 (tel: 404-0470; fax: 404-3374; email: sipa@business-swaziland.com).

Swaziland National Housing Board, PO Box 798, Mbabane (tel: 404-5610; fax: 404-5224).

Swaziland Railway, PO Box 475, Mbabane (tel: 404-27211; fax: 404-7210).

Swaziland Sugar Association, PO Box 445, Mbabane (tel: 404-2646).

Swaziland Television Authority, PO Box A146, Swazi Plaza (tel: 404-3036; fax: 404-2093).

Tinkhundla Headquarters, PO Box A33, Swazi Plaza, Mbabane (tel: 404-2723; fax: 404-4058).

Water Services Corporation, PO Box 20 Mbabane (tel: 404-5584; fax: 404-5355).

Internet sites

Africa Business Network: www.ifc.org/abn

AllAfrica.com: http://allafrica.com

African Development Bank: www.afdb.org

Africa Online: www.africaonline.com

Mbendi AfroPaedia (information on companies, countries, industries and stock exchanges in Africa): http://mbendi.co.za

Simunye news service: www.swazis.org.uk/~news/

Swazi news: www.swazinews.co.sz/about.htm

Swazi Observer: www.swaziobserver.sz/

Swaziland Solidarity Campaign: www.swazis.org

Sweden

KEY FACTS

Official name: Konungariket Sverige (The Kingdom of Sweden)

Head of State: King Carl XVI Gustaf

Head of government: Prime Minister Fredrik Reinfeldt (Moderata) (since 2006; re-elected 19 Sep 2010)

Ruling party: Coalition Alliansen (Alliance), Moderata Samlingspartiet (Moderata) (Moderate Coalition Party), with Centerpartiet (Cp) (Centre Party), Folkpartiet Liberalerna (FpL) (Liberal People's Party) and Kristdemokraterna (KD) (Christian Democrats) (since 2006; re-elected 19 Sep 2010)

Area: 448,964 square km

Population: 9.38 million (2010)*

Capital: Stockholm

Official language: Swedish

Currency: Swedish krona (SKr) = 100 öre

Exchange rate: SKr6.87 per US$ (Oct 2011)

GDP per capita: US$48,875 (2010)

GDP real growth: 5.50% (2010)

GNP per capita: US$455.80 billion (2010)

Labour force: 4.96 million (2010)

Unemployment: 8.40% (2010)

Inflation: 1.90% (2010)

Balance of trade: US$10.88 billion (2010)

Foreign debt: US$553.30 billion (Jun 2010)

* estimated figure

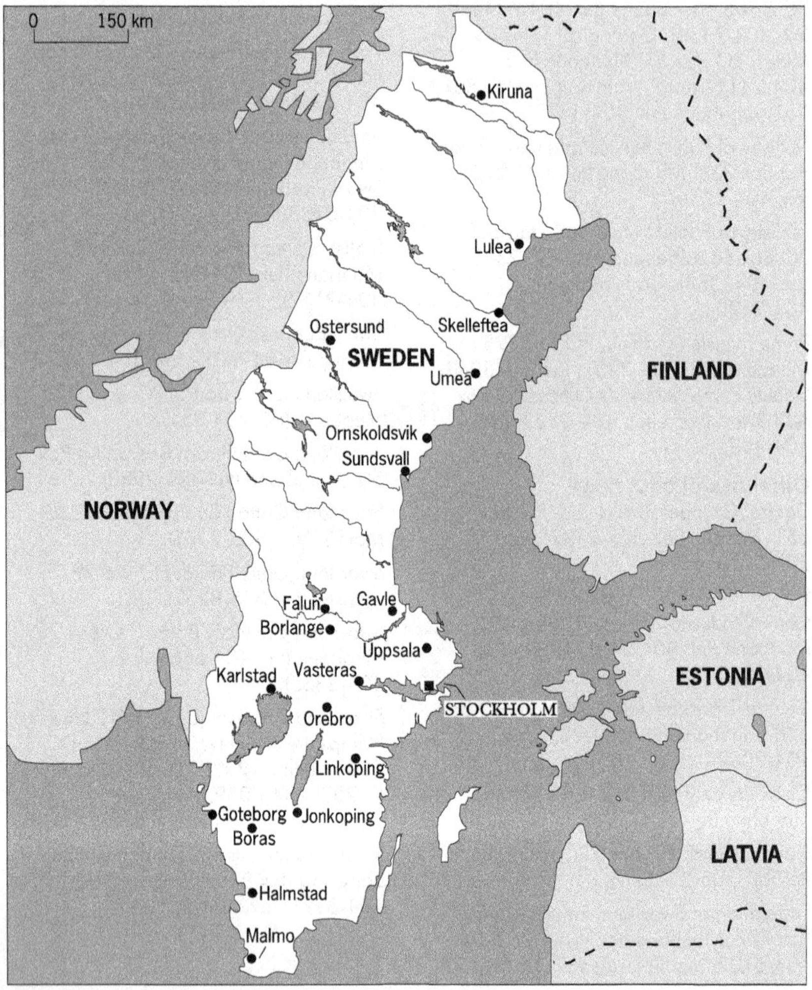

Sweden is different: or at last it likes to be considered different. For years it was seen as a Nordic utopia which managed to combine a contradictory cocktail of high taxes, an all embracing welfare state, and prosperity. Swedes happily drove their Saabs, called their friends on their Ericcson mobiles and took summer holidays in their remote summer cottages. The leaders of other European countries, particularly those of left wing leanings, could only look on in perplexed envy.

End of the dream

The idyll inadvertently projected in the films of Ingmar Bergman and many of his contemporaries continued until the 1990s. Then Sweden discovered the harsh truth that budgets eventually have to be balanced. As the number of benefit recipients steadily increased, so did the number of people employed in essentially unproductive jobs; according to an article by James Bartholomew in the London *Spectator*, more than one Swede in five of working age was receiving one benefit or another. The truth dawned, voters turned their backs on the Arbetarepartiet-Socialdemokraterna (Labour Party-Social Democrats, known as Socialdemokratiska (S) (Social Democrats) party, preferring the acceptance of reality promised by the opposition centre-right coalition government, of the Centerpartiet (Cp) (Centre Party) and Moderata Samlingspartiet (Moderata) (Moderate Party) which won the 1991 election. Benefits were reduced, as were their time limits. Sweden underwent not only social changes, but (for Sweden) far-reaching economic changes as well. A wide range of businesses were de-regulated; these included the railways, the postal service, electricity generation and agricultural production. Alongside these changes have been taxation reforms which have reduced the top rate of taxation from 80 per cent to 60 per cent. (In the 1960s it used to be jokingly claimed that the top rate of tax for someone whose partner also worked could exceed 100 per cent). Inheritance tax was found to be counter-productive and simply abolished. Sweden may have begun to abandon a state run economy in favour of one that is partially privatised, but by the standards of much of the US and certainly by most Republicans, its economy would still be seen as almost 'communist'.

Sweden's health service is also partly privatised; a first visit to the doctor is charged at the flat rate of (approximately) US$30.00; most general practitioners work in what are essentially private practices. Similarly, an increasing number of schools are private – receiving the same amount of money per pupil as is the case in state-run schools. A number of government hospitals are in fact contracted out to private companies to operate.

As is the case with many European economies, youth unemployment in Sweden is alarmingly high. But unlike many of its neighbours, in Sweden the local authorities responsible for administering unemployment benefits apply strict criteria for qualification, with the result that many young Swedes simply do not qualify.

How times change. In 2011, the internationally recognised automotive manufacturer Saab suspended production in April, when suppliers stopped delivering parts. The worker's union considered forcing Saab into bankruptcy so that the workers could access unemployment payments and compensation for lost earnings. The company owed a total of US$211 million and was seeking to negotiate repayment over a longer term. When the company sought protection from its creditors on 8 September to avoid immediate bankruptcy, it was rejected by the courts. On 22 September, Saab was given the right to voluntarily reorganise itself after it successfully appealed against a ruling of bankruptcy given on the previous day. The company will realign its cost structure as it concludes an investment agreement with two Chinese vehicle manufacturers, PangDa Automobile Trade and Zhejiang Youngman Lotus Automobile; completion is expected in November.

Risk assessment

Economy	Good
Politics	Good
Regional stability	Good

COUNTRY PROFILE

Historical profile

1397 Union of Kalmar united Denmark, Sweden and Norway under a single monarch with Denmark the dominant power.
1520 The Massacre of Stockholm occurred when the Danish King Kristian II, in an attempt to assert his supremacy, executed resisting Swedish noblemen, which led to a revolt, headed by Gustav Eriksson Vasa.
1523 King Kristian II was defeated by Vasa, who was crowned Gustav I. Sweden was separated from the Union. Vasa's victory heralded the start of Sweden's ascendancy in Europe.
1611 Gustav II Adolph (Gustavus Adolphus) became King. He engaged in expansionist policies and attempted to gain control of the Baltic trading routes; this brought him into conflict with neighbouring states.
1629 Sweden fought to possess Prussia and Pomerania (now part of Germany) in the Thirty Years War.
1632 Gustav II was killed at the battle of Lutzen (in Saxony, now part of Germany) and was succeeded by his daughter, Kristina.
1654 Kristina abdicated after converting to Catholicism – an act that was unacceptable in Lutheran Sweden.
1700 Start of the Great Nordic War when Russia, Denmark, Norway and Poland formed an alliance against Sweden and its 15-year old King Karl XII in an attempt to retrieve some of their lost lands.
1700–1720 A succession of battles resulted in the loss of all Swedish lands in Germany, the Baltic provinces of Russia and much of Finland. Success against the Danes in Norway allowed Sweden to consolidate into easily defended borders.
1718 The power of the monarchy diminished and was vested in the Council of Aristocrats who depended on parliament for its authority.
1772 King Gustav III began reforms that strengthened the power of the monarchy. These developments resulted in an almost absolute monarchy.
1792 King Gustav III was assassinated by members of the Swedish nobility. Gustav IV Adolf became King.
1808–09 Sweden was defeated by the Russians. Finland, which was then part of Sweden, was ceded to Russia. King Gustav IV Adolf was replaced by Karl XIII in 1809.
1814 Sweden entered a union with Norway.
1905 The emergence of Norwegian nationalism led Norway to declare independence. A parliamentary form of government emerged in Sweden.
1920s The Sveriges Socialdemokratiska Arbetarparti (Swedish Social Democratic Party) first came to power. It typically contested elections under the name Arbetarepartiet-Socialdemokraterna (Labour Party-Social Democrats) but was

KEY INDICATORS Sweden

	Unit	2006	2007	2008	2009	2010
Population	m	9.11	*9.17	*9.17	*9.22	*9.38
Gross domestic product (GDP)	US$bn	393.61	455.32	479.00	405.40	455.80
GDP per capita	US$	43,190	49,554	52,181	43,986	48,875
GDP real growth	%	4.0	5.6	-0.2	-4.4	5.5
Inflation	%	1.5	1.7	3.3	2.2	1.9
Unemployment	%	7.0	6.1	6.2	8.3	8.4
Exports (fob) (goods)	US$m	148,756.0	169,339.0	185,878.0	133,330.0	160,392.0
Imports (fob) (goods)	US$m	127,341.0	153,934.0	167,759.0	120,499.0	149,514.0
Balance of trade	US$m	21,415.0	15,405.0	18,119.0	12,831.0	10,879.0
Current account	US$m	33,303.0	38,886.0	37,279.0	30,232.0	28,744.0
Total reserves minus gold	US$m	24,778.0	27,044.0	25,896.0	42,860.0	42,565.0
Foreign exchange	US$m	24,074.0	26,382.0	25,127.0	38,543.0	37,919.0
Exchange rate	per US$	6.83	6.52	6.29	7.45	7.21

* estimated figure

commonly referred to as the Socialdemokraterna (Social Democrats). Except for a brief period during 1936, the Social Democrats stayed in power from 1932 to 1976.
1939–45 Sweden declared its neutrality during the Second World War, although German troops were transported through its territory to Norway. Sweden also supplied Nazi Germany with iron ore until 1943.
1952 Sweden became a founder member of the Nordic Council.
1959 Sweden became a founder member of the European Free Trade Area (EFTA) with Austria, Denmark, Norway, Portugal, Switzerland and the UK.
1969–71 Olof Palme (prime minister 1969–76 and 1982–86) introduced constitutional reforms. The bicameral legislature was replaced by a unicameral legislature, elected by proportional representation.
1975 A new constitution was promulgated; it reduced the power of the monarchy and limited its role to that of figurehead and ceremonial duties.
1976 A centre-right coalition government, the Centerpartiet (Cp) (Centre Party), and Moderata Samlingspartiet (Moderata) (Moderate Party) won the parliamentary election.
1978 The coalition government collapsed due to disagreement about economic problems and the building of a controversial nuclear power plant. The former coalition partner, Folkpartiet Liberalerna (FpL) (Liberal People's Party) formed a new government.
1979 The Cp won the parliamentary elections by a one seat majority.
1982 The Socialdemokraterna won the parliamentary elections. Olof Palme became prime minister again.
1986 Palme was assassinated in Stockholm by an unknown gunman.
1991 After parliamentary elections, Moderata formed the government with Carl Bildt as prime minister.
1994 The Socialdemokraterna won the general election. Sweden joined Nato's Partnership for Peace (PfP) military co-operation programme.
1995 Sweden joined the EU.
1996 Carlsson stepped down as the leader of the SSA and prime minister. Göran Persson replaced him.
1998 Following parliamentary elections the SSA formed a minority government. The reduced vote for the Socialdemokraterna was believed to be due to widespread anger at social expenditure cuts.
2002 The Socialdemokraterna won the parliamentary elections and continued to lead a minority government that relied on support from the Vänsterpartiet (V) (Left Party) and the Miljöpartiet de Gröna (MP) (Environmental Party the Greens).
2003 Foreign Minister Anna Lindh was stabbed to death in a Stockholm department store. In a referendum voters narrowly defeated the proposal to join the single European currency.
2004 The man who confessed to killing Anna Lindh was convicted of her murder and sentenced to life imprisonment, overturning a previous ruling which consigned him to a psychiatric hospital.
2006 In parliamentary elections the ruling Socialdemokraterna narrowly lost with 46.2 per cent against the opposition coalition, led by Moderata Samlingspartiet (Moderate) (Moderate Coalition Party), which won with 48.1 per cent of the vote (178 seats in the 349 legislative assembly); turnout was 80.4 per cent. Fredrik Reinfeldt (Moderate) became prime minister.
2008 Around 100 countries took part in a conference held outside Stockholm to discuss support and efforts to restore stability and rebuild a functioning economy in Iraq. De rödgröna (Red-Green) coalition was formed by three opposition policital parties to contest the general elections in 2010.
2009 After 17 years of sanctions imposed against Iraq by the UN, the Swedish airline, Nordic Leisure, flew the first commercial flight between Iraq and Europe, with around 150 passengers, mainly Iraqis. Scheduled flights are expected to arrive in Baghdad weekly.
2010 Crown Princess Victoria married Daniel Westling (becoming Prince Daniel, Duke of Västergötland) in June. In parliamentary elections held on 19 September, the ruling Social Democrats won 30.66 per cent of the vote (112 seats out of 349), closely followed by Moderata with 30.06 per cent (107). The right-wing nationalist Sverigedemokraterna (SD) (Sweden Democrats) won 5.7 per cent and its first seats in parliament (20). A coalition of four centre-right parties, formally called the Alliansen (Alliance), consisting of the Moderata, MP, Cp and KD, retained power although as a minority government; Fredrik Reinfeldt remained as prime minister.
2011 On 17 August, it was announced that Crown Princess Victoria was expecting her first child. The internationally recognised automotive manufacturer Saab sought protection from its creditors on 8 September to avoid immediate bankruptcy. However, the court rejected its application saying Saab didn't fulfil the legal grounds necessary to grant the company protection. The company had suspended production in April, when suppliers stopped delivering parts. The worker's union were considering forcing Saab into bankruptcy so that the workers could access unemployment payments and compensation for lost earnings. The company owed a total of US$211 million and was seeking to negotiate repayment over a longer term. Four people suspected of planning a terrorist attack on the city of Gothenburg were arrested on 11 September. On 22 September, Saab was given the right to voluntarily reorganise itself after it successfully appealed against a ruling of bankruptcy given on the previous day. The company will realign its cost structure as it concludes an investment agreement with two Chinese vehicle manufacturers, PangDa Automobile Trade and Zhejiang Youngman Lotus Automobile; completion is expected in November.

Political structure

Constitution

The constitution consists of four separate documents: the *Regeringsformen* (Instrument of Government) passed in 1974, *Successionsordningen* (Act of Succession) dating from 1810, the *Tryckfrihetsförordningen* (Freedom of the Press Act) of 1949 (originating from 1766), and the *Yttrandefrihetsgrundlagen* (Freedom of Expression Act) of 1991.
There are 288 municipalities throughout the country, each with a popularly elected council. Immigrants, resident for three years, have the right to vote and run for office in local elections.
Universal suffrage is at aged 18. Voter turnout is traditionally high, between 85–90 per cent.
Under proportional representation 310 parliamentary seats are allocated on a constituency basis, in 28 multi-member constituencies; the remaining seats are divided nationally. To win parliamentary representation, a party must poll either 4 per cent overall – to receive a seat from the national allocation – or 12 per cent in any one constituency for a seat from the national remainder.

Form of state

Parliamentary democratic monarchy

The executive

Executive power is exercised by the Regeringen (cabinet) which is led by the prime minister (elected by parliament) and is responsible to parliament. The prime minister appoints members of the cabinet.

National legislature

The unicameral Riksdag (parliament) has 349 members directly elected by proportional representation, for a four-year term. In the event of an early dissolution, the new parliament serves only the remainder of the previous parliament's term.

Legal system

The legal system is divided into the general courts and the general administrative courts. The general courts are composed of a Supreme Court (Högsta domstolen), six Courts of Appeal and 95 District Courts which are responsible for criminal cases involving individuals. The Supreme Court is the highest court in the land and is composed of 16 judges appointed by the government. The general administrative courts are responsible for cases involving public authorities and individuals.

Last elections

19 September 2010 (parliamentary).

Results: Parliamentary: the Arbetarepartiet-Socialdemokraterna (Labour Party-Social Democrats, known as Socialdemokratiska (S) (Social Democrats) won 30.66 per cent of the vote (112 seats out of 349), Moderata Samlingspartiet (Moderata) (Moderate Party) 30.06 per cent (107), Miljöpartiet de Gröna (MP) (Environmental Party the Greens) 7.34 per cent (25), Folkpartiet Liberalerna (FpL) (Liberal People's Party) 7.06 per cent (24), Centerpartiet (Cp) (Centre Party) 6.56 per cent (23), Sverigedemokraterna (SD) (Sweden Democrats) 5.7 per cent (20), Kristdemokraterna (KD) (Christian Democrats) 5.6 per cent (19), Vänsterpartiet (V) (Left Party) 5.6 per cent (19); turnout was 84.63 per cent.

Next elections

September 2014 (parliamentary)

Political parties

Ruling party

Coalition Alliansen (Alliance), Moderata Samlingspartiet (Moderata) (Moderate Coalition Party), with Centerpartiet (Cp) (Centre Party), Folkpartiet Liberalerna (FpL) (Liberal People's Party) and Kristdemokraterna (KD) (Christian Democrats) (since 2006; re-elected 19 Sep 2010)

Main opposition party

Arbetarepartiet-Socialdemokraterna (Labour Party-Social Democrats, known as Socialdemokratiska (S) (Social Democrats)

Population

9.38 million (2010)*

Last census: 31 December 2003: 8,975,670

Population density: 20 inhabitants per square km. Urban population: 83 per cent (1995–2001).

Annual growth rate: 0.2 per cent 1994–2004 (WHO 2006)

Ethnic make-up

Native Swedes account for 88 per cent of the population. Around 50 per cent of all foreign nationals are from other Nordic countries (Denmark, Finland, Iceland and Norway).

Sweden has two minority groups of native inhabitants in the north: the Finnish speaking people of the north-east and an estimated 17,000 Sámi (Lapp) people.

Religions

About 90 per cent of the population belong to the Church of Sweden (Lutheran); there are 8 per cent other Protestants and 1 per cent Roman Catholics.

Education

Pre-school classes are offered to any six year old enrolled, the first (and compulsory) school begins at aged seven; both are free of charge and the majority are run by municipalities. In 2001–02 over one million pupils were enrolled (within both); independent schools accounted for 1 per cent of enrolments. The average number of pupils per school was 209, with an average of 108 pupils in independent schools. Many schools are now working with integrated age levels where children of different ages are taught together in the same class. Around three-quarters of all compulsory schools are connected to the Internet. At aged 16 students who have successfully completed their compulsory schooling progress to upper secondary school. Nearly all pupils continue to the upper secondary school. Each municipality has the right to establish its own upper secondary schools and a national curriculum provides a basis for further studies and basic eligibility for higher education.

Higher education is offered in 13 state-run universities and 23 university colleges. There are also three private universities: Chalmers University of Technology, the University College of Jönköping and the Stockholm School of Economics. Further education for adults (aged 20 years and over) is offered within the public adult education system through municipal adult education.

Literacy rate: 99 per cent, adult rate (2003)

Compulsory years: 7 to 16

Enrolment rate: 107 per cent gross primary enrolment, 140 per cent gross secondary enrolment: of relevant age groups (including repeaters and training for unemployed within the age group) (World Bank 2001).

Pupils per teacher: 12 in primary schools

Health

Sweden has for many years actively worked with health promotion in line with the World Health Organisation's (WHO) European 'Health for All' policy. There is a close collaboration between the government and local and regional providers of public medical and healthcare services.

A governmental body, the National Public Health Committee, is responsible for providing many recommendations to the government, along with wide-ranging consultation, is being used as a basis for the future development of the healthcare system.

The public sector finances health services, through taxation, for the entire population although the Federation of Health Insurance Societies, (established in 1907), helps to promote a national compulsory system of health insurance.

HIV/Aids

HIV prevalence: 0.1 per cent aged 15–49 in 2003 (World Bank)

Life expectancy: 81 years, 2004 (WHO 2006)

Fertility rate/Maternal mortality rate: 1.7 births per woman, 2004 (WHO 2006)

Birth rate/Death rate: 9.7 births and 10.6 deaths per 1,000 people (2003)

Child (under 5 years) mortality rate (per 1,000): 2.8 per 1,000 live births (World Bank)

Head of population per physician: 3.28 physicians per 1,000 people, 2002 (WHO 2006)

Welfare

The Swedish social insurance system is managed by the state and is compulsory for everyone, providing means-tested and general benefits. The main goal of the social insurance is to provide protection against loss of income and is composed of sickness insurance, early retirement pensions, occupational injury insurance and old age pensions. The Social Services Act of 1982 regulates the welfare benefit system while the National Board of Health and Welfare (Socialstyrelsen) supervises the overall quality of social service provision.

A Social Insurance Act was introduced in 2001, dividing social insurance into two categories: a domicile-based insurance scheme, which provides guaranteed benefits, and a work-related insurance scheme, which safeguards against loss of income. These insurance systems are available to anyone living or working in Sweden. Social insurance is divided into 50 per cent going into pensions, 25 per cent to sickness and disability benefit and 15 per cent to families with children.

The pension system was reformed in 1998 and is composed of various components, including an income-related pension, a premium pension and a guaranteed pension. The premium pension allows a person to invest their own funds into part of the pension scheme. A state pension is guaranteed to all the population on a low income or without any income.

Main cities

Stockholm (capital, estimated population – excluding urban areas – 770,284 in 2005), Göteborg (480,461), Malmö (269,543), Uppsala (182,767).

Languages spoken
Finnish, Skäine and Sámi are spoken. English, and to a lesser extent German, are also widely spoken.
Official language/s
Swedish

Media
Press
Dailies: In Swedish, the most influential nationals are either owned or run by political parties and trade unions. These include *Aftonbladet* (www.aftonbladet.se) (Social Democratic), *Dagens Nyheter* (www.dn.se) (Liberal, independent), *Expressen*(www.expressen.se) (Liberal), *Göteborgs-Posten* (www.gp.se) (Liberal), *Svenska Dagbladet* (www.svd.se) (Conservative) *Sydsvenska Dagbladet* (www.sydsvenskan.se) and *Aktuellt I Politiken* (www.aip.nu). In Finnish *Ruotsin Suomalainen* (www.ruotsinsuomalainen.com). Regional publications in Swedish, include from Stockholm *Kristdemokraten* (www.kristdemokraten.com) *Metro* (www.metro.se), from *GT* (www.gt.se), from Malmo *Kvallsposten* (www.kvp.se) and *SVT Sydnytt* (www.svt.se/sydnytt) and from Uppsala *Upplands Nyheter* (www.upplandsnyheter.se) and *Uppsalanytt* (www.uppsalanytt.se).
Weeklies: Main Sunday newspapers and weekly publications include for men *Café* (www.cafe.se), *Se och Hör* (TV listings), *Aftonbladet* (www.aftonbladet.se) and *Dagens Nyheter* (www.dn.se).
Business: In Swedish, *Affärsvärlden* (www.affarsvarlden.se) is the oldest and most respected business magazine. Other publications include the weekly *Ekonominyheterna* (http://ekonominyheterna.se) an affiliate of *Veckans Affärer*, the daily *Dagens Industri* (http://di.se) and *Finanstidningen* (owned by the major media organisation Modern Times Group). *Fri Kopenskap* (www.fri-kopenskap.se) and *Privata Affarer* (www.privataaffarer.se) are published in Stockholm.
Periodicals: These include *Galago* (on culture), *Grönköpings Veckoblad* (www.gronkoping.nu) a literary magazine *Moderna*, *Slitz* (www.slitz.se) is a magazine for men. Two major women's magazine include *Amelia* (www.amelia.se), published fortnightly, which is Sweden's most popular and *Vecko Revyn* (www.veckorevyn.com) is a tabloid style publication.
Broadcasting
All broadcasting is overseen by Granskningsnamnden (Swedish Broadcasting Commission). State broadcasting is provided by Sveriges Television and Radio.
Radio: There are four national radio stations provided by Sveriges Radio (www.sr.se), with news broadcasts provided in 14 foreign languages. External services can by accessed via short wave, or on-demand through the internet, which also has archived and live transmissions. There are around commercial 100 radio stations some of which have drawn together to produce near-national networks. The largest stations and networks include Rix FM (www.rixfm.com), NRJ (www.nrj.se), Mix Megapol (www.mixmegapol.com) and Radio Match (www.radiomatch.com).
Television: All Swedish television will be provided by digital signals by 2008. Most homes have cable or satellite reception with dozens of channels on offer. Sveriges Television (svt.se) has 2 major networks and a 24 hour news channel, as well as special interest programmes via satellite TV. There are four commercial TV channels including TV3 (www.tv3.se), TV4 (www.tv4.se), Kanal 5 (http://kanal5.se) and ZTV (www.ztv.se).
Advertising
Sophisticated and of a high standard, but tends to be expensive. All media are available except state radio and state television. The promotion of alcohol consumption is not allowed (except for light beers) and toys and confectionary during children's television, while tobacco advertising is restricted to the print media only.

Economy
Sweden is an advanced economy that has many resources, from primary industries to sophisticated industrial processes to high-end service industries that rank its economy within the world's top 35 by GDP. Its main industries include agriculture, principally timber production of its 41 million hectares of mixed forests which are used in timber, panels, pulp and paper manufactured products. The service industries include tourism and financial services, with the Nordic Stock Exchange (OMX) centred in Stockholm.
GDP growth was 2.6 per cent in 2007, but in 2008 the economy fell into recession when GDP was -0.2 per cent as the global economic crisis struck and exports of Swedish consumer durables fell. As credit was severely limited and financial wholesale markets closed, investment dried up so that in 2009 the situation deteriorated further with GDP growth at -4.4 per cent. The government, in response and in tandem with other European Union economies, introduced economic expansionist measures by allowing its budget to move from a surplus of 2.5 per cent of GDP in 2008 to a deficit of 4 per cent in 2009.
To support its banking system the government introduced new rules that required greater capitalisation by banks while setting up credit facilities for banks to offer long-term security on loans; it also set up the National Debt Office that bought up bank's non-performing loans and issued treasury bills to boost the bond market. As Swedish exports are predominately capital goods and consumer durables its was highly vulnerable to international shocks and was one of the first economies to go into recession, it may not recover before countries that are the markets for its goods come out of recession. Income, unemployment and confidence in Sweden have been depressed, which has slowed private consumption, another inhibiting force weakening GDP growth.

External trade
As a member of the European Union, Sweden operates within a community-wide free trade area, with tariffs set as a whole, however it does not belong to the European Monetary Union and retains the krona as its currency. Internationally, the EU has free trade agreements with a number of nations and trading blocs worldwide. Over 50 per cent of all exports are traded with the EU.
Foreign trade accounts for 85 per cent of all trade and exports provide 45 per cent of GDP, of which over 35 per cent is electronic equipment, 14 per cent intermediate capital goods, 8 per cent consumable durables, 8 per cent chemical and fertilisers and 5 per cent food and agricultural products.
Imports
Main imports include machinery, petroleum and derivatives, chemicals, vehicles, iron and steel, foodstuffs, consumer goods and clothing.
Main sources: Germany (typically 18 per cent of total), Norway (9 per cent), Denmark (9 per cent).
Exports
Major exports include vehicles, automotive and engineering and electronic parts and products, pharmaceuticals, fertilisers, paper products, pulp and timber, iron, steel and electricity.
Main destinations: Norway (typically 11 per cent of total), Germany (10 per cent), UK (7 per cent).

Agriculture
Farming
Although Sweden is one of the biggest countries in Europe, its arable land amounts to only 2.8 million hectares (ha) constituting about 7 per cent of the total land area. Grain is harvested on 45 per cent of arable land. Agriculture contributes 2 per cent of GDP and employs less than 2 per cent of the total work force. Dairy products, grains, sugarbeets and

potatoes are produced. There are 1.7 million cows in the country. Over the past decade, cattle herd numbers have fallen while yields have risen.

Most farms are family concerns, in which the work is done by members of the family. Part-time farming, with income supplemented by other employment (eg forestry), has become a common feature. Restructuring and modernisation of equipment have resulted in fewer but larger farms. Farming is concentrated in the southern regions, where livestock farming predominates.

Sweden's adherence to the EU's Common Agricultural Policy (CAP) has brought some regulation of agriculture. Agricultural support policies have been adjusted to CAP, including production quotas and increased export subsidies. Import licences are required for certain agricultural commodities. Fundamental reform to the CAP was introduced in 2005. The subsidies paid on farm output, which tended to benefit large farms and encourage overproduction, were replaced by single farm payments not conditional on production. This is expected to reward farms that provide and maintain a healthy environment, food safety and animal welfare standards. The changes are also intended to encourage market conscious production and cut the cost of CAP to the EU taxpayer.

Fishing

The Swedish market for seafood is typically over 150,000 tonnes annually calculated on the basis of product weight. Estimated output from the domestic seafood processing sector amounts to around 85,000 tonnes per year. About 75 per cent of this amount is for the home market with marinated herring the most important product. Over half of the fishing industry is located in western Sweden. In addition to coastal and deep-sea fishing around the western coast, Sweden has an abundance of natural lakes, which can provide enough fish to meet domestic needs.

Most fish imports are from Norway and Denmark, which together typically account for 75 per cent of total Swedish imports, indicating the importance of the Scandinavian link in its seafood industry. As the EU presses for radical reform to its Common Fisheries Policy (CFP), Sweden is expected to support its principles based on the ecosystem approach.

Forestry

Forest and other wooded land accounts for nearly 75 per cent of the land area, with forest cover estimated at 27.1 million hectares (ha). Approximately 23 million ha of forest area is available for wood supply.

The forest industry and forestry account for more than 4 per cent of Sweden's GDP, 12 per cent of industrial employment and 15 per cent of Sweden's exports. Sweden's pulp and paper industry is the third-largest in Europe after Germany and Finland. About one-third of Sweden's wood pulp and over half its paper and board are exported. Sweden accounts for more than 13 per cent of paper demand in the EU.

Following large scale divestiture, 52 per cent of forest land is owned privately, 24 per cent is owned by the state (primarily through Sveaskog AB) and 24 per cent through commercial companies.

Industry and manufacturing

The powerful industrial sector contributes 29 per cent of GDP and accounts for 75 per cent of all exports. It is a key reason why the Swedish people have one of the highest standards of living in the world. Industrial strength was traditionally based on extensive reserves of iron, timber and the rivers and lakes that provided cheap energy, although in recent years hi-tech production has increased in significance. With such a small domestic market, industry has always had to look overseas for survival and it has profited from the development of a mature export culture.

The state is gradually decreasing its ownership in firms under its control. The government is committed to ending state subsidies for inefficient industries. As a result of this policy, traditional sectors, such as shipyards and the textile industry, have virtually ceased to exist. In other traditional industries, there has been drastic rationalisation and concentration on narrow segments of the market.

The industrial sector is based largely on indigenous resources (iron ore, timber and water-power). Major industries include motor vehicles, food processing, chemicals, iron and steel, transportation equipment, electrical and electronic equipment and forestry products. Sweden's industrial structure tends to be centred on large, capital-intensive companies, due to the nature of tax, social security and labour market regulations, which do not favour smaller firms.

Engineering is Sweden's main industrial sector, accounting for around a third of industrial output and for a similar proportion of exports. The country's main engineering companies include Ericsson, Electrolux, Volvo (owned by Ford), SKF, Saab, Scania and Sandvik. Manufacturing employs approximately 30 per cent of the workforce.

The Organisation for Economic Co-operation and Development (OECD) recently named Sweden as one of the leading countries in the Internet and other information technology (IT) markets, along with the US and Finland. In the same month, Sweden topped the International Data Corporation's (IDC) Information Society Index of 55 countries in the IT sector. IT remains an important contributor to the economy. Internet companies in Sweden are managing to survive the burst of the 'dotcom' bubble and the country is at the forefront of the development of mobile telephone Internet technology. Sweden is also beginning to lead the way in the biotechnology sector and has more biotech companies per capita than any other country.

Timber production accounts for just over a fifth of industrial output. Sweden has a large forestry sector supplying raw materials to industry and for export. With 57 per cent of the land area covered in forest, Sweden has the largest timber reserves in Western Europe.

Tourism

Tourism is an important part of the growing service sector in Sweden, with the industry accounting for 2.7 per cent of Sweden's GDP. Tourist arrivals typically numbered over 10 million, mainly from Norway and Germany. The sector employs around 00,000 people a comprising almost 3 per cent of the workforce.

Mining

The mining sector typically accounts for 9 per cent of GDP and employs 0.5 per cent of the industrial workforce.

Sweden is rich in mineral deposits, the most important of which are iron ore, zinc, lead, copper, silver and pyrites. There are also large deposits of uranium, exploitation of which has been held back by environmental and political objections. Swedish companies focus on making high quality speciality iron and steel.

Sweden's share of total world iron ore output comes to around 2 per cent, making Sweden one of the largest iron ore exporters in Europe. Sweden's shares of the Western world's production of copper, lead and zinc concentrates amount to 1 per cent, 3.7 per cent and 3.3 per cent, respectively.

Hydrocarbons

Sweden is poor in hydrocarbon resources and has limited reserves. As a result, oil represents a large proportion of total Swedish imports, 350,110 barrels per day (bpd) in 2007. Swedish refineries have an annual capacity of 434,000bpd. The largest, Scanraff, north of Göteborg, has a capacity of over 200,000bpd. Natural gas is imported in small quantities through a pipeline from Denmark across the Baltic Straits, for use in southern Sweden.

Energy

Total installed generating capacity is 33.9 gigawatts (GW), which has remained largely unchanged since 1997. However, consumption has been rising so that

Sweden imports electricity from other Nordic countries to make up its shortfall. In June 2010 parliament approved the replacement of the country's 10 existing nuclear reactors (located at three power plants), which supply half of Sweden's domestic electricity needs, with new nuclear reactors. Hydropower provides 44.5 per cent of energy needs and the remainder is provided by renewable energy sources such as biofuels, geothermal, wave and wind power. Manufacturing and district heating systems are replacing hydrocarbon for renewables.

The state utility is Vattenfall; other providers are majority foreign owned, E.ON Sweden (German) and Fortum Oy (Finnish).

Financial markets

Stock exchange

Stockholmsbörsen (Stockholm Stock Exchange)

Banking and insurance

Liberalisation and increased openness has boosted the competitiveness of the Swedish financial sector. There have been serveral mergers between banking and insurance firms. There is a predominance of large corporations in the sector. More than 70 per cent of people in this sector are employed by firms with a payroll of more than 200.

Central bank

Sveriges Riksbank

Main financial centre

Stockholm

Time

GMT plus one hour (daylight saving, late March to late October, GMT plus two hours)

Geography

Sweden is situated in northern Europe. It occupies about 66 per cent of the Scandinavian peninsula and is bordered by Finland to the north-east and Norway to the west. Sweden has a long coastline, with the Baltic Sea and the Gulf of Bothnia to the east and the Skagerrak and Kattegat to the south-west.

Approximately 15 per cent of Sweden lies north of the Arctic Circle. There are thousands of lakes and islands. Around 54 per cent of the country is covered in coniferous forests. Agricultural land is located in the southern plains, where the population is most concentrated. The central region comprises lowlands. The west bordering Norway is mountainous, from which numerous rivers drain into the Gulf of Bothnia; the highest point in Sweden at 2,111m is Mount Kebnekaise.

Hemisphere

Northern

Climate

Because of the Atlantic gulf stream, Sweden has a milder climate than some other regions in the same latitude. The average winter temperature in the north, where there is always snow from December to March, is minus 13 degrees Celsius (C), in central Sweden minus 3 degrees C and in the south minus 1 degree C. In summer average temperatures are 13 degrees C in the north, 18 degrees C in central Sweden and 17 degrees C in the south.

Dress codes

Clothing to suit the climate is vital because of the extremes. Heavy coats, warm boots, gloves and ear protection are required in winter and light clothing in summer.

Swedes can be informal in business attire, but suits are worn at business meetings and for social events in the evening.

Entry requirements

Passports

Required by all, except nationals of countries which are signatories of the Schengen Accords, which includes most EU/EEA member states, who may visit on national IDs.

Visa

Required by all, except nationals of EU countries, Iceland, Norway, North America, Australasia and Japan, for up to three months. For those requiring a visa, a Schengen visa covers all entry needs; for business trips, an invitation from a business contact in Sweden and proof of occupation and travel funds should be included when applying. A Schengen visa application (offered in several languages) can be downloaded from http://europa.eu/ abc/travel/ see 'documents you will need'.

Currency advice/regulations

There are no restrictions on the import and export of local or foreign currencies.

Customs

Personal items are duty-free.There are no duties levied on alcohol and tobacco between EU member states, providing amounts imported are for personal consumption.

Health (for visitors)

Nationals of the European Economic Area (EEA) countries and Switzerland can access reduced cost and sometimes free medical treatment using a European Health Insurance Card (EHIC) while visiting the EEA. Exceptions include nationals of the 10 countries which joined the EU in 2004, whose EHIC is not valid in Switzerland. Applications for the EHIC should be made before travelling.

Mandatory precautions

Vaccination certificates not required unless travelling from an infected area.

Advisable precautions

Up-to-date tetanus and polio immunisations are recommended.

Hotels

There is no official rating system in operation. There is a shortage of accommodation in major cities so reservations should be made well in advance.

Public holidays (national)

Fixed dates

1 Jan (New Year's Day), 6 Jan (Epiphany), 1 May (Labour Day), 6 June (National Day), 24–26 Dec (Christmas).

Variable dates

Good Friday, Easter Monday, Ascension Day, Whit Monday, Midsummer Holiday (fourth Sat in Jun), All Saints' Day (first Sat in Nov).

Working hours

Banking

Mon–Fri: 0930–1500 (larger branches open longer).

Business

Mon–Fri: 0830–1700 (often closed one hour earlier in summer).

Government

Mon–Fri 0900–1700.

Shops

Mon–Fri: 0900–1800 (closed 1400 or 1600 on Sat).

Telecommunications

Mobile/cell phones

Pay-as-you-go phones are extremely popular, and make up 44 per cent of all subscriptions. Telia accounts for 51 per cent of all mobile phone subscriptions, followed by Tele2 with 33 per cent and Europolitan with 16 per cent.

Electricity supply

220V AC

Social customs/useful tips

Swedes appreciate punctuality. A gift of flowers is usual when visiting a business partner's home for the first time. Guests should not start drinking before their hosts have proposed their health.

Think twice before refusing to go to a sauna with a host, since such an invitation is seen as a gesture of confidence and friendship by your host. Business meetings are sometimes conducted in saunas.

Security

Sweden has very low rates of violent crime, but some districts in the major cities should be avoided, particularly at night and particularly by women. Car burglaries and drugs-related crimes are increasing.

Getting there

Air

National airline: Scandinavian Airlines System (SAS).

International airport/s: Stockholm-Arlanda (ARN), 45km north of capital; Stockholm-Västerås (VST), 5km east of Västerås; Göteborg-Landvetter (GOT), 25km east of Göteborg; Malmö-Sturup (MMX), 30km east of Malmö.
Airport tax: None
Surface
Road: Sweden can be reached by road from Denmark via the Øresund tunnel and bridge link between Copenhagen and Malmö. There is also road access from Norway and Finland.
Rail: Statens Jarnvagar (SJ) (State Railways) is the major rail company in Sweden. It runs international high-speed trains between either Stockholm/Göteborg-Copenhagen (Denmark) – journey time five hours/3.30 hours; Stockholm-Oslo – journey time 4.45 hours. These services offer business class accommodation. Overnight trains with sleeping coaches are available between Berlin (Germany) and Malmö.
Water: There are ferry links with ports in northern and eastern Europe.

Getting about
National transport
Air: There are daily flights connecting all main towns, some by SAS and others by small local airlines.
Road: Sweden has a well-developed and maintained road network totalling about 420,000km, two-thirds of which are privately-managed, including unpaved forestry roads. Most private roads are open to the public. At least 95 per cent of traffic is carried by the national and municipal roads. There are around 20,000km of motorways.
Dipped headlights during the day are mandatory. The roads are snow-bound or icy during the winter months, when appropriate tyres are a requirement.
Buses: Efficient bus service, mainly controlled by the Statens Jarnvagar (SJ) (State Railways). Services integrated with rail service.
Rail: There are good, reliable rail links between most major cities and towns, especially in the south. Seats on express services must be booked in advance.
Water: There is an extensive ferry network in and around Sweden.
City transport
Taxis: Available in all major towns. If you order a taxi in advance there is an extra charge. Some taxi companies offer flat rates for travel within urban areas, and others have special fares for women travelling alone at night.
Gratuities for taxis are around 10 per cent.
Buses, trams & metro: All rail, bus and tram services have a unified ticketing system. Books of 20 travel coupons are available for purchase at Press Agency news-stands.
A city transfer service links Arland and Västerås airports with Stockholm city centre, with a journey time of about 40 minutes. The journey time from Västerås airport is around 75 minutes.
Trams run in the southern parts of Bromma and Lidingö.
Metro: The *Tunnelbana* serves many districts of Stockholm, with 100 stations marked by a blue T sign. The extended rail service includes outlying suburbs.
Car hire
Available at all airports and in most towns and cities.

BUSINESS DIRECTORY

The addresses listed below are a selection only. While World of Information makes every endeavour to check these addresses, we cannot guarantee that changes have not been made, especially to telephone numbers and area codes. We would welcome any corrections.

Telephone area codes
The international direct dialling code (IDD) for Sweden is +46, followed by area code and subscriber's number:

Gävle	26	Malmö	40
Göteborg	31	Norrköping	11
Helsingborg	42	Oxelösund	155
Jönköping	36	Stockholm	8
Karlskrona	455	Sundsvall	60
Karlstad	54	Umeå	90
Luleå	920	Uppsala	18

Useful telephone numbers
Police, fire and ambulance: 112

Chambers of Commerce
American Chamber of Commerce in Sweden, 3 Jakobs Torg, PO Box 16050, 10321 Stockholm (tel: 5061-2610; fax: 5061-2910; e-mail: amcham@chamber.se).

British Swedish Chamber of Commerce, 3 Jakobs Torg, PO Box 16050, 10321 Stockholm (tel: 5061-2617; fax: 5061-2915; e-mail: bscc@chamber.se).

Central Sweden Chamber of Commerce, 1 Linnévägen, PO Box 296, 80104 Gävle (tel: 662-080; fax: 662-099; e-mail: chamber@mhk.cci.se).

East Sweden Chamber of Commerce, 3 Nya Rådstugugatan, 60224 Norrköping (tel: 28-5030; fax: 13-7719; e-mail: info@east.cci.se).

Jönköping Chamber of Commerce, 11 Elmiavägen, 55454 Jönköping (tel: 301-430; fax: 129-579; e-mail: jncci@jn.wtc.se).

Mid Sweden Chambe of Commerce, 26 Kyrkogatan, 85232 Sundsvall (tel: 171-880; fax: 618-640; e-mail: sdl@mid-chamber.cci.se).

Southern Sweden Chamber of Commerce and Industry, 2 Skeppsbron, 21120 Malmö (tel: 690-2400; fax: 690-2490; e-mail: info@handelskammaaren.com).

Stockholm Chamber of Commerce, 9 Västra Trädsgårdsgatan, PO Box 16050, 10321 Stockholm (tel: 5551-0000; fax: 5663-1635; e-mail: info@chamber.se).

Swedish Chambers of Commerce, 9 Västra Trädsgårdsgatan, PO Box 16050, 10321 Stockholm (tel: 5551-0036; fax: 5663-1637; e-mail: info@chamber.se).

Uppsala Chamber of Commerce, Uppsala Science Park, 75183 Uppsala (tel: 502-950; fax: 554-458; e-mail: info@uppsala.chamber.se).

Wermland Chamber of Commerce, 6 Södra Kyrkogatan, 65224 Karlstad (tel: 221-480; fax: 221-490; e-mail: info@wermland.cci.se).

Western Sweden Chamber of Commerce and Industry, 18 Mässens Gata, PO Box 5253, 40225 Göteborg (tel: 835-900; fax: 835-936; e-mail: info@handelskammaren.net).

Banking
Götabanken, Sveavägen 14, 10377 Stockholm (tel: 790-4000) and Hamngatan 16, 40509 Gothenburg (tel: 625-000).

Handelsbanken, 20540 Malmö (tel: 245-000; fax: 236-134).

Nordea, Västra Trädgårdsgatan 17, 5 tr, 10571 Stockholm (tel: 614-8558; fax: 614-7530).

Skandinaviska Enskilda Banken, Kungsträdgårdsgatan 8, 10640 Stockholm (tel: 763-5000; fax: 242-394).

Svenska Bankforeningen (Swedish bankers' association), Regeringsgatan 42, Box 7603, 10394 Stockholm (tel: 243-300).

Svenska Handelsbanken, Kungsträdgårdog 2, 10670 Stockholm (tel: 701-1000; fax: 611-5071).

Svenska Sparbanksforeningen (Swedish savings banks' association), Drottninggatan 29, Box 16426, 10327 Stockholm (tel: 572-000).

SwedBank, Brunkebergstorg 8, 10534 Stockholm (tel: 790-1000).

Central bank
Sveriges Riksbank, Brunkebergstorg 11, SE-103 37 Stockholm (tel: 787-0000; fax: 210-531; e-mail: registratorn@riksbank.se).

Stock exchange
Stockholmsbörsen (Stockholm Stock Exchange): www.omxnordicexchange.com

Stock exchange 2
NGN-Borsen (Nordic Growth Market) (NGM): www.ngm.se

Travel information
Kungliga Automobil Klubben (KAK), Blasieholmshamnen 6, 11148 Stockholm (tel: 678-0055; fax: 678-0068; e-mail: info@kak.se).

SJ AB (State Railways), 105 50 Stockholm (tel: 762 20 00; fax: 762 24 24; website: www.sj.se); on-line booking at www.swedenbooking.com).

Svenska Turistföreningen (Swedish Tourist Association), Stureplan 4, PO Box 25, 10120 Stockholm (tel: 463-2100; fax: 678-1958; info@stfturist.se).

Svensk Turism AB, Kammakargatan 39, Box 1158, 11181 Stockholm (tel: 762-7400; e-mail: info@svenskturism.se).

Scandinavian Airlines System (SAS), Frösundaviks Allé 1, 19587 Stockholm (tel: 797-0000; fax: 797-1603).

National tourist organisation offices
VisitSweden (The Swedish Travel and Tourism Council), Sveavögen 21, Box 3030, 103 61 Stockholm (tel: 789-1000; fax: 789-1031; e-mail: reception@visitsweden.com).

Ministries
All ministries in Sweden have the same address: S-10333 Stockholm (tel: 405-1000; fax: 723-1171).

Invest in Sweden Agency, S-10338 Stockholm (tel: 676-8876/0; fax: 676-8888).

National Board of Forestry, S-55183 Jönköping (tel: 155-600; fax: 190-740).

National Board of Trade, Box 1209, S-11182 Stockholm (tel: 791-0500; fax: 200-324).

National Electrical Safety Board, Box 1371, S-11193 Stockholm (tel: 453-9700; fax: 453-9710).

National Maritime Administration, S-60178 Norrköping (tel: 191-000; fax: 101-949).

National Post and Telecom Agency, Box 5398, S-10249 Stockholm (tel: 678-5500; fax: 678-5505).

Statistics Sweden, Karlavägen 100, S-11581 Stockholm (tel: 783-4000; fax: 661-5261).

Swedish Board of Agriculture, S-55182 Jönköping (tel: 155-000; fax: 190-546).

Swedish Board of Customs, Box 2267, S-10317 Stockholm (tel: 789-7300; fax: 208-012).

Swedish Civil Aviation Administration, S-60179 Norrköping (tel: 192-000; fax: 192-575).

Swedish Board for Investment and Technical Support, BITS, Box 7837, S-10398 Stockholm (tel: 678-5000; fax: 678-5050).

Swedish National Board of Fisheries, Lilla Bommen 6, S-40126 Göteborg (tel: 630-300; fax: 156-577).

Swedish National Board for Industrial and Technical Development (NUTEK), S-11786 Stockholm (tel: 681-9100; fax: 196-826).

Swedish National Road Administration, S-78187 Borlänge (tel: 75-000; fax: 84-640).

Swedish Nuclear Power Inspectorate, S-10658 Stockholm (tel: 698-8400; fax: 661-9086).

Swedish Patent Office, Box 5055, S-10242 Stockholm (tel: 782-2500; fax: 666-0286).

Swedish Standards Institution, Box 3295, S-10366 Stockholm (tel: 613-5200; fax: 411-7035).

Swedish Trade Council, PO Box 5513, S-11485 Stockholm (tel: 783-8500; fax: 662-9093).

Other useful addresses
British Embassy, Skarpögatan 6-8, Box 27819, 11593 Stockholm (tel: 671-9000; fax: 662-9989 (commercial section).

Federation of Commercial Agents of Sweden, Hantverkargatan 46, 11221 Stockholm (tel: 540-975).

Federation of Commercial Agents of Sweden, Western Division, Box 36059, 40013 Göteborg (tel: 192-045).

Federation of Swedish Industries, Storgatan 19, 11485 Stockholm (tel: 783-8000; fax: 662-3595).

Federation of Swedish Wholesalers and Importers, Grevgatan 34, Box 5512, 11485 Stockholm (tel: 635-280).

Handels Arbetsgivareorg (HAO) (commercial employers' confederation), Box 1720, 11187 Stockholm (tel: 762-7700).

Kungl Automobil Klubben (KAK) (Royal Automobile Club), S. Blasieholmshamnen 6, S-11148 Stockholm (tel: 678-0055; fax: 678- 0068).

Motormännens Riksförbund (Automobile Association), Sturegatan 32, PO Box 5855, 10248 Stockholm 5 (tel: 782-3800; fax: 666-0371).

SACO/SR (confederation of professional associations), Box 2206, 10315 Stockholm (tel: 225-200).

Sollentunamassan (organisers of trade fairs), Box 174, 19123 Sollentuna (tel: 925-900; fax: 929-774).

Stockholmsbörsen, SE-10578 Stockholm (tel: 405-6000; fax: 405-6001).

Stockholm Technical Fair (Stockholmsmassan AB), Alvsjo, 12580 Stockholm (tel: 749-4100; fax: 992-044).

Svenska Arbetsgivareforeningen (employers' confederation), Sodra Blasieholmshammen 4A, 10-330 Stockholm (tel: 762-6000; fax: 762-6290).

Sveriges Exportrad (Swedish Trade Council), PO Box 5513, 11485 Stockholm (tel: 783-8500; fax: 663-6706).

Swedish Embassy (USA), Suite 900, 1501 M Street, NW, Washington DC 20005 (tel: (+1-202) 467-2600; fax: (+1-202) 467-2699; e-mail: ambassaden.washington@foreign.ministry.se).

Swedish Institute, Box 7434, 10391 Stockholm (tel: 789-2000).

Swedish Trade Fair Foundation (Svenska Massan), Skanegatan 26, Box 5222, 40224 Göteborg (tel: 109-100; fax: 160-330).

TCO (central organisation of salaried employees), Box 5252, 10245 Stockholm (tel: 782-9100).

Tidningarnas Telegrambyrå (news agency), Kungsholmstorg 5, 10512 Stockholm (tel: 132-600; fax: 515-377).

Other news agencies: TT (Tidnignarnas Telegrambyrå) 105 12 Stockholm, (tel: 692-2600; fax: 692-2855; email: redaktionen@tt.se). TT is a private independent agency.

Internet sites
Export directory: http://www.swedishtrade.se/sed

Government of Sweden: www.sweden.gov.se

Invest in Sweden Agency: http://www.isa.se/

Statistics Sweden: http://www.scb.se/eng/index.asp

Swedish Statistics network: www.svenskstatistik.net/eng/index.htm

Virtual Sweden: http://www.sweden.se

Visit Sweden: http://www.visit-sweden.com

Switzerland

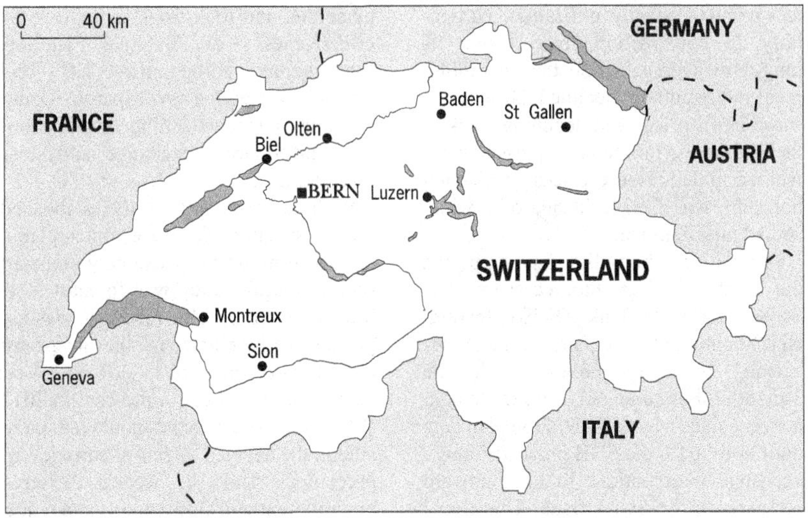

Unlike its banking system, the politics of Switzerland can hardly be said to be of international interest. A rotational system whereby the post of head of state is automatically changed between the Swiss Cantons at four yearly intervals makes an already predictable political scenario all the more so. The current (January 2012) Federal President is Eveline Widmer-Schlumpf, who holds the position until the 1 January 2013. Switzerland is unusual in having a collective head of state, and seven-member Federal Council, which doubles up as the country's cabinet.

Under the Swiss political system, voters are given a direct say in their own affairs through a uniquely Swiss form of direct democracy. Voters go to the polls several times a year to vote in national or regional referendums and people's initiatives. Constitutional proposals and major international treaties must be put to the vote and parliamentary decisions can be subjected to a vote by collecting 50,000 signatures.

Federal parliamentary elections were held on 23 October 2011, with modest gains for the centrist political parties and reversing the trend towards polarisation as seen in 1990s and 2000s. The Schweizerische Volkspartei (SVP) (Swiss People's Party) remained as the single largest political party in parliament, having won 26.6 per cent of the vote (54 seats out of 200) and will be the strong centre of a coalition government.

European relations

Switzerland has not found it easy to adapt to a rapidly changing Europe. Unable to isolate itself from developments on the continent, it can not ignore wider trends towards globalisation. The nature and form of its relations with the European Union (EU) remain unresolved. Switzerland's relations with the EU have not been all sweetness and light. The little matter of secret bank accounts still irks the tax authorities of the rest of Europe. The global financial crisis however, has brought the question of bank secrecy into sharper focus. A spokesman for the Swiss private bankers association once described the Organisation for Economic Co-operation and Development (OECD), the body charged with eliminating tax avoidance schemes as a 'tax cartel'. In 2009, evidence submitted to the US authorities suggested that the UBS (Union de Banques Suisses) bank alone had some 20,000 offshore US clients holding some US$20 billion in Switzerland.

As governments the world over sought to shore up their finances, tax avoidace was an obvious target and Switzerland found itself the flag carrier of often barely

KEY FACTS

Official name: Schweizerische Eidgenossenschaft (German); Confédération Suisse (French); Confederazione Svizzera (Italian) (Swiss Confederation)

Head of State: Federal President Micheline Calmy-Rey (from 1 Jan 2011): President-elect Eveline Widmer-Schlumpf (SVP) (from 1 Jan 2012)

Head of government: Federal President Hans-Rudolf Merz

Ruling party: Coalition led by the Schweizerische Volkspartei (SVP) (Swiss People's Party) (since 1999; re-elected 2011)

Area: 41,293 square km

Population: 7.83 million (2010)*

Capital: Bern (German)/Berne (French)

Official language: German, French, Italian and Romansch

Currency: Swiss franc (Swf) = 100 centimes

Exchange rate: Swf0.91 per US$ (Oct 2011)

GDP per capita: US$67,246 (2010)

GDP real growth: 2.60% (2010)

GDP: US$523.80 billion (2010)

Labour force: 4.59 million (2010)

Unemployment: 3.90% (2010)

Inflation: 0.70% (2010)

Balance of trade: US$15.87 billion (2010)

legal offshore banking arrangements. Worldwide the sums were thought to be enormous. Switzerland was thought to account for about one third of the world's US$11,000 billion clandestine wealth. Leading the charge against Swiss banks in Europe was the Swiss government's *bete noire*, Peer Steinbruck, onetime German finance minister, who had declared that the Swiss had to understand that the days of bank secrecy 'were over'. The Swiss are, reluctantly, moving towards compliance and the days of the totally secret bank account are numbered.

The Swiss franc had reached an all-time high against the euro on 31 August 2010 (Swf 1.02 per US$1) as money flowed in from investors worried about sovereign risk elsewhere in the world. The Swiss National Bank (SNB), lost Swf14 billion (US$12.9 billion) in the first half of the year while attempting to hold the currency down against the euro and maintain its global competitiveness. A year later, on 10 August, the SNB again took action to reduce the value of the Swiss franc by increasing the supply of francs and undertaking foreign exchange swaps. International investors had been buying Swiss francs as other major currencies came under threat. By 9 August the franc had almost reached parity with the euro and the high value against the US dollar was hurting exports.

Inevitably strong economy

According to the International Monetary Fund (IMF), the Swiss economy has experienced a strong, broad-based recovery. After falling by 1.9 per cent in 2009, output grew by 2.6 per cent in 2010. Domestic demand was underpinned by sound balance sheets, low interest rates and a rebound in employment and immigration. Exports increased more strongly than expected, on the back of robust external demand and in spite of a 10-per cent appreciation in the exchange rate. Trade and current account surpluses continued to expand. Capacity utilisation, particularly in construction, rose above its long-term average while the unemployment rate gradually declined. Despite the surge in oil prices and declining slack in the economy, inflationary pressures remained muted. House prices accelerated but there was little evidence of a widespread misalignment.

Swiss monetary policy has supported the swift exit from the recession. The Swiss National Bank (SNB) (central bank) continued to implement an expansionary monetary policy, with the 3-month Libor target range at zero to 0.75 per cent since March 2009. From that date until mid-2010, the SNB pursued foreign exchange interventions to limit upward pressure on the Swiss franc. The global market recovery and favourable financing conditions, together with financial sector measures contributed to improving banks' profitability and capital and liquidity positions in 2010. However, there was evidence of increased risk taking in mortgage lending, in the context of persistently low interest rates and high competition among banks.

Recommendations from the 'too big to fail' banking commission, now under discussion in Parliament, include supplementing minimum Basel common equity requirements with loss-absorbing buffers in the form of contingent convertible capital, which may be lowered depending on measures to reduce inter- connectedness and complexity. Switzerland's Financial Market Supervisory Authority (FINMA) developed a risk-based approach, increased on-site inspections, hired more personnel and took steps to improve the effectiveness of external auditors. Inter-agency co-operation has been strengthened with a new tripartite Memorandum of Understanding on collaboration, information exchange and crisis management.

With the recovery firmly established, the Swiss authorities were contemplating an exit from their expansionary monetary policy. Fiscal policy was forecast to be broadly neutral. The recovery was expected to moderate in the near-term. Growth was projected to slow to 2.4 per cent in 2011 and to 1.8 per cent in 2012. While domestic demand should remain resilient, the delayed effects of currency appreciation and a weaker external environment will slow exports and reduce the trade surplus. Headline and core inflation should remain muted at around 1 per cent in 2011–12. However, there remained large uncertainties related mainly to global developments.

The IMF noted that, while the normalisation of the monetary policy stance would contribute to reducing macro-financial concerns, it might not suffice to address loosening lending standards in the mortgage market. So called 'macro-prudential' measures were recommended, in the absence of any system-wide self-regulation. The IMF noted that the Swiss banks' performance had improved, but vulnerabilities remained. They commended the authorities for their efforts to promote legislation aimed at reducing the risks posed by Switzerland's two largest banks.

KEY INDICATORS — Switzerland

	Unit	2006	2007	2008	2009	2010
Population	m	7.29	*7.30	*7.31	*7.34	*7.83
Gross domestic product (GDP)	US$bn	387.98	423.94	550.30	494.60	523.80
GDP per capita	US$	53,245	59,473	67,560	67,560	67,246
GDP real growth	%	3.2	3.6	2.1	-1.9	2.7
Inflation	%	1.4	0.8	2.4	-0.4	0.7
Unemployment	%	3.4	2.5	2.6	3.7	3.9
Exports (fob) (goods)	US$m	167,251.0	200,109.0	214,332.0	206,119.0	258,388.0
Imports (fob) (goods)	US$m	162,213.0	187,076.0	227,380.0	204,728.0	242,518.0
Balance of trade	US$m	5,038.0	13,033.0	13,952.0	1,391.0	15,870.0
Current account	US$m	56,382.0	43,531.0	43,102.0	41,072.0	70,363.0
Total reserves minus gold	US$m	38,094.0	44,474.0	44,474.0	98,199.0	223,481.0
Foreign exchange	US$m	37,364.0	43,867.0	43,867.0	91,614.0	217,347.0
Exchange rate	per US$	1.20	1.15	1.08	1.08	1.04

* estimated figure

Risk assessment

Economy	Good
Politics	Good
Regional stability	Good

COUNTRY PROFILE

Historical profile

Switzerland was part of the Holy Roman Empire until 1499 when it gained independence. Switzerland's Roman connection remains strong. The Pope is still guarded by a some 135-strong Swiss Guard, drawn largely from the Catholic cantons of central Switzerland.

1515 Switzerland declared its neutrality after nearly being defeated by the French and Venetians.
1648 The Peace of Westphalia concluded the Thirty Years' War in Europe and recognised Swiss independence.
1815 The Congress of Vienna restored independence to Switzerland after it had been annexed by France as part of the Napoleonic Empire during 1798–1803. The Congress laid down the principle of the perpetual neutrality of Switzerland.
1874 The modern constitution was inaugurated.
1914–18 Switzerland was neutral during the First World War.
1919–20 The Treaty of Versailles again recognised Switzerland's neutrality. In 1920, the country joined the League of Nations, but did not join its successor, the UN, when it was formed in 1945.
1939–45 Switzerland pursued a policy of neutrality during the Second World War, but refused refuge to Jews trying to escape German-occupied Europe and traded gold with the Nazis. Swiss banks also provided interest free credits to the Axis powers, which enabled Germany to finance its war effort.
1959 Switzerland was a founder member of the European Free Trade Agreement (EFTA).
1971 Women were granted the right to vote.
1986 The Swiss population rejected UN membership in a referendum.
1988 Switzerland's first female minister, Elisabeth Kopp, resigned from her post following accusations that she had violated official secrecy laws by tipping off her husband about an inquiry into his business affairs.
1992 In a referendum on Swiss membership of the European Economic Area (EEA), a free trade agreement between the EU and EFTA, opponents of the pact won with 50.3 per cent of the vote. Switzerland joined the World Bank and IMF.
1998 Swiss banks agreed to a US$1.25 billion settlement with Jewish Holocaust survivors and families.
1999 Ruth Dreifuss became Switzerland's first female president. The Schweizerische Volkspartei (SVP) (Swiss People's Party) won the largest electoral victory for any party in Switzerland for over 80 years.
2001 The national airline, Swissair, went bankrupt.
2002 Switzerland joined the UN. An independent panel of historians concluded Swiss authorities knew of the fate of Jewish refugees turned away in 1942 and that Swiss banking bolstered the economy of Nazi Germany, although not enough to have prolonged the Second World War.
2003 The SVP won the biggest share of the vote in the parliamentary elections at the expense of the Christlich-Demokratische Volkspartei (CVP) (Christian Democratic People's Party).
2004 Swiss banks began to inform EU tax departments on personal accounts held by EU taxpayers. Stem cell research was agreed in a referendum.
2005 New compliance banking laws, introduced to curtail money laundering, and the EU-wide decline in personal tax rates led to a reduction in the flow of money into Switzerland's banks.
2006 Genetically modified crops were banned for five years. Tough new asylum laws were introduced.
2007 Violence erupted in Berne during the election campaign of the ruling, anti-immigration party, SVP, when left-wing protesters began hurling rocks and bottles. The SVP went on to win the highest number of votes (29 per cent) in general elections. however, as there was no clear winner a coalition of four parties was formed. One of the world's largest, and Switzerland's biggest, bank, UBS, was forced to write off US$10 billion in bad US sub-prime mortgage debts.
2008 UBS declared its losses were greater than originally announced, with a total of US$22 billion lost by the end of the first quarter. A referendum, whereby Swiss communes could vote to limit naturalisation of foreigners in individual cases, was rejected. Switzerland joined the Schengen Agreement group of countries allowing free movement for EU citizens and external visitors with a Schengen visa.
2009 Hans-Rudolf Merz (FDP) became federal president for the year. The government eased banking laws to allow the sharing of bank data to crack down on offshore tax evasion and avoid being listed as a non-co-operative tax haven by the Organisation of Economic Co-operation and Development (OECD). The economy officially slipped into recession for the first quarter as UBS reported a further loss of US$1.32 billion.
2010 Doris Leuthard (CVP) became federal president in January. Drawings and manuscripts of Franz Kafka, which had been secured in a Swiss vault since the 1940s, were finally seen by one academic on 23 August, after a long legal battle of ownership agreed on this compromise. Israel claims the documents as national treasure, while the daughters of Esther Hoffe, secretary to Kafka's friend Max Brod, who was entrusted with the work, claim they are part of their inheritance. The Swiss franc reached an all-time high against the euro on 31 August (Swf 1.02 per US$1) as money flowed in from investors worried about sovereign risk elsewhere in the world. The Swiss National Bank (SNB), lost Swf14 billion (US$12.9 billion) in the first half of the year while attempting to hold the currency down against the euro and maintain its global competitiveness.
2011 Micheline Calmy-Rey (SP) became federal president in January. On 10 August, the SNB took action to reduce the value of the Swiss franc by increasing the supply of francs and undertaking foreign exchange swaps. International investors had been buying Swiss francs as other major currencies came under threat. By 9 August the franc had almost reached parity with the euro and the high value against the US dollar was hurting exports. Federal parliamentary elections were held on 23 October, with modest gains for the centrist political parties and reversing the trend towards polarisation as seen in 1990s and 2000s. The SVP remained as the single largest political party in parliament, having won 26.6 per cent of the vote (54 seats out of 200) and will be the strong centre of a coalition government. On 14 December, Eveline Widmer-Schlumpf was elected as president for 2012 (174 out of 239 votes).

Political structure

Constitution

Switzerland's constitution dates back to 1874 and has been much amended over the years. It unites more than 3,000 communes and 26 cantons and half-cantons in a confederation which devolves considerable powers to local bodies.
Responsibility for determining and administering civil, penal and commercial law, foreign and trade issues, defence, communications, social insurance and energy is reserved for the federal government.
The cantons and half-cantons, each of which have their own constitution and government, are responsible for the administration of federal law as well as their own cantonal laws. The communes have local autonomy over roads, local public utilities and the granting of citizenship.
Major issues are frequently decided by referendum. The constitution, or any of the country's federal laws, may only be amended by the passage of a proposal by national referendum. A national referendum may be called if a petition is signed by 50,000 people (on a legislative matter) or 100,000 people (on a constitutional matter). In some cantons, referenda may be necessary to approve all changes in cantonal legislation. The federal government, or its political opponents, may also initiate a referendum on any issue. Voter turnout averages 40–50 per cent. Since the constitution's inception, voters have been asked to approve over 148 amendments.

Independence date

1 August 1291

Form of state
Federal parliamentary democratic republic
The executive
The chief executive organ in the country is the Federal Council, whose seven members each hold a ministerial portfolio, and whose president and vice president are appointed each calendar year on a rotating basis from among its members.
National legislature
The bicameral Federal Assembly consists of the National Council with 200 members directly elected by proportional representation in constituencies containing around 37,500 electorates. The Council of States has 46 members who represent cantons (local district administrations). All members of the Federal Assembly serve four-year terms.
The Federal Assembly supervises the army, the civil service and the administration of the law as well as electing the Federal Supreme Court, the Federal Tribunal of Insurance and the Federal Council.
Legal system
Customary law marginally influences the civil law system. Individual cantons elect and maintain their own magistracy. Each canton has justices of the peace, District Courts, Labour Courts, Courts for Tenancy, an Appeal Court, a Cassation Court and, for more important cases under penal law, a Jury Court. Apart from military courts, there are just two federal judicial authorities: the Federal Supreme Court and the Federal Tribunal of Insurance.
Last elections
23 October 2011 (federal assembly)
Results: National Council: the Schweizerische Volkspartei (SVP) (Swiss People's party) won 26.6 per cent of the vote (54 seats out of 200), the Sozialdemokratische Partei (SPS) (Social Democrat Party) 18.7 per cent (46), the Freisinnig-Demokratische Partei (FDP) (Freethinking-Democratic Party) 15.1 per cent (30), the Christlich-Demokratische Volkspartei (CVP) (Christian Democratic People's Party) 12.3 per cent (28), the Grüne Partei (GPS) (Green Party), 8.4 per cent (15), Grünliberale Partei (GLP) (Liberal Green Party) 5.4 per cent (12), Bürgerlich-Demokratische Partei (BDP) (Conservative Democratic Party) 5.4 per cent (nine); three other political parties and one independent each won no more than 2 per cent and shared six seats, four parties won no seats. Turnout was 49.1 per cent.
Next elections
October 2015 (parliament)

Political parties
Ruling party
Coalition led by the Schweizerische Volkspartei (SVP) (Swiss People's Party) (since 1999; re-elected 2011)
Main opposition party
Grüne Partei der Schweiz (GPS) (Green Party of Switzerland)

Population
7.83 million (2010)
Last census: December 2000: 7,204,055
Population density: 182 inhabitants per square km. Urban population: 67 per cent of the total population (1995–2001).
Annual growth rate: 0.4 per cent 1994–2004 (WHO 2006)
Ethnic make-up
Switzerland is dominated by Germans (65 per cent), French (18 per cent) and Italians (10 per cent). Foreigners comprise 19.7 per cent of the population. In a referendum held in September 2000, the Swiss voted against limiting the proportion of foreigners to 18 per cent.
Religions
Roman Catholic (46 per cent), Protestant (40 per cent).

Education
With no central ministry of education, each of the 26 Swiss cantons (semi-autonomous regions) have overall and exclusive responsibility for education. Private schools exist at the level of vocational secondary school but do not attract federate funding or canton control.
Most cantons set the number of compulsory years for primary schooling at six, some others set it at four or five; for lower secondary school most set the minimum years at three, and some at five or four; whichever cycle is used, overall, compulsory schooling lasts for nine years. Teaching is given in the language of the canton. At aged 16, students can go into upper level secondary schools (either private or state-run), which offer general or vocational programmes and last for between three and four years. General secondary education (*Matura*), offers academic study, preparing a student for university. Technical high schools provide a range of vocational and training programmes. Typically 85 per cent of students complete upper secondary school.
Switzerland has 12 universities and higher education colleges. There are also a number of science universities and more than 20 polytechnics (*Fachhochschulen*). In the 1990s, the cantons began a reform of the educational system to ensure that it provided the best means of maintaining a high degree of educated citizens.
Literacy rate: 99 per cent, adult rate (2003)
Compulsory years: Six to 15.
Enrolment rate: 97 per cent gross primary enrolment of relevant age group (including repeaters); 100 per cent gross secondary enrolment (World Bank).
Pupils per teacher: 19 in primary schools.

Health
Healthcare services are entirely private and individuals are expected and, in some areas, obliged, to cover themselves with private health insurance policies. Each canton has responsibility for the provision of healthcare. The type of hospital a patient may be admitted to will depend on the level of health insurance the person holds.
HIV/Aids
HIV prevalence: 0.4 per cent aged 15–49 in 2003 (World Bank)
Life expectancy: 81 years, 2004 (WHO 2006)
Fertility rate/Maternal mortality rate: 1.4 births per woman, 2004 (WHO 2006); maternal mortality five per 100,000 live births (World Bank).
Birth rate/Death rate: 9.6 births and 8.8 deaths per 1,000 people (2003)
Child (under 5 years) mortality rate (per 1,000): 4.3 per 1,000 live births (World Bank)
Head of population per physician: 3.61 physicians per 1,000 people, 2002 (WHO 2006)

Welfare
Switzerland's comprehensive social welfare system is funded by the state, by employer contributions and by employee national insurance contributions. It is a legal requirement that all citizens residing for three months or more in Switzerland must take out minimum healthcare insurance.
Unemployment insurance is compulsory and many employees are also insured against accidents at work. Old age, disability and widow(er)s' pensions are paid out of compulsory contributions. The precise arrangements may differ in each canton.
Over 20 per cent of the federal budget is spent on social welfare. Some social security schemes have their own separate budgets.

Main cities
Bern/Berne/Bienne (capital, estimated population 119,250 in 2005), Zürich (332,800), Geneva/Genève (178,034), Basel/Basle (163,186), Lausanne (112,136).

Languages spoken
The national languages are German in central and eastern areas (64 per cent), French in the west (19 per cent) and Italian in the south (8 per cent).
Raeto-Romansch is spoken in the south-east (1 per cent). English is widely spoken.
There are two forms of German spoken. High German, or Hochdeutsch is only

spoken in formal situations or used for written work; Swiss-German, or Schwyzertütsch is spoken by all in daily life in German-speaking Switzerland, using different dialects and is incomprehensible to all who speak High German.

Official language/s

German, French, Italian and Romansch

Media

Press

There is a decentralised press owing to regional variations in language and culture, producing a large number of publications with relatively small circulation. There are more than 600 newspapers in total and nearly 2,000 magazines.

Dailies: About 120 regional newspapers (75 per cent printed in German and 20 per cent in French). The most popular includes, *20 Minutten* (www.20min.ch), a free publication with a tabloid style; from Zurich, *Blick* (www.blick.ch) and *Tages Anzeiger* (www.tagesanzeiger.ch); from Genéva, *Le Temps* (www.letemps.ch) and *Tribune de Genéva* (www.tdg.ch); from Lugano *Corriere del Ticino* (www.cdt.ch); from Bern *Berner Zeitung* (www.bauernzeitung.ch); from Lausanne, *Le Matin* (www.lematin.ch) and from Basel *Basler Zeitung* (www.baz.ch).

Weeklies: Many dailies have weekend editions including *Sonntags Blick*, *Le Matin Dimanche* and *Sonntags Zeitung*. A Swiss edition of a French magazine is *l'Hebdo* (www.hebdo.ch) is available in French speaking cantons.

Business: Daily newspapers include *Neue Zürcher Zeitung* (www.nzz.ch) from Zürich and is of international repute; *Cash* (www.cash.ch) for finance and Handelzeitung (www.handelszeitung.ch), *Agefi* (www.agefi.com). Others periodicals include *Finanz und Wirtschaft* (www.fuw.ch) (twice weekly) *Swiss News* (www.swissnews.ch) and *Bilanz* (www.bilanz.ch) (monthlies).

Periodicals: In German, *The Panorama Journal* (www.panoramajournal.ch) reports on events, sport and life in the Bern area; *Der Schweizerische Beobachter* (www.beobachter.ch), is a consumer magazine; *Nebelspalter* (www.nebelspalter.ch), is a satirical magazine; *Pro* (www.pro-helvetia.ch) is a Swiss Arts Council publication,

Broadcasting

A fee for reception of any radio or television signal is levied by Billag AG (www.billag.ch). The Federal Office of Communications (www.bakom.ch) has overall responsibility for broadcast media. Digital Audio Broadcasting (DAB) was underway in 2007 and expected to be fully implemented nationally within a few years. The public broadcaster is SRG SSR Idée Suisse (www.srg-ssr.ch), which operates national radio and television stations, broadcasting in Swiss-German (www.drs.ch), French (www.rsr.ch), Italian (www.rtsi.ch) and Rumansch (www.rtr.ch).

Radio: Apart from the national networks provided by SRG SSR Idée Suisse, independent radio stations are typically exclusive to a city or region, including from Bern, Radio BE1 (www.radiobe1.ch), from Zürich, Energy Züri (www.energyzueri.ch) and Radio 24 (www.radio24.ch), and from Basel, Radio 105 (www.105.ch) and Radio X (www.radiox.ch).

SRG SSR Idée Suisse broadcasts an international service in nine languages.

Most radio stations provide services over the internet.

Television: There are over 80 local and regional TV stations providing services for all linguistic populations. Pay-for-view, satellite and cable television are available.

Advertising

The various languages adds to the expense of advertising, which on commercial TV is only allowed at specific times. Newspapers, cinemas and direct mail are widely used, but poster advertising is confined to selected sites. Information can be obtained from the Union Suisse d'Agences-Conseils en Publicité in Zürich. The main advertising media are newspapers and magazines.

Economy

Switzerland is world renowned for its financial services – which together with education, scientific research and tourism accounts for over 75 per cent of its GDP. It has international brand names in watch-making, pharmaceuticals, precision instruments, luxury jewellery and consumer durables. It is one of the wealthiest countries in the world, with a highly skilled labour force and ready access to the European Union (EU). Despite not being a member of the EU, the Swiss economy remains heavily dependent on the economic fortunes of the EU and the euro. Swiss exports are dominated by chemicals and machinery and electronic goods. The EU takes over 65 per cent of Swiss exports (19 per cent to Germany alone) and supplies 76 per cent of imports (over one-third from Germany).

GDP growth was 3.6 per cent in 2007, but with the economy adversely affected by the global economic crisis in 2008, growth slowed to 2.1 per cent and Switzerland slipped into recession as GDP for the first quarter of 2009 shrank to 0.8 per cent, with an annual rate of -1.9 per cent; deflation was also manifest, having fallen from an inflation rate of 2.4 per cent in 2008 to -0.5 per cent in 2009. However, as global trade picked up in 2010, so did growth, to 2.7 per cent.

Swiss banking was badly damaged by significant losses due to bad debts, as the banking system became embroiled in the worldwide credit squeeze and toxic debt scandal of 2008, created by the collapse of the sub-prime market in the US. Switzerland's UBS AG is one of the world's top-10 banks and coupled with Credit Suisse, the country's next largest bank, had combined assets in 2009 of US$900 billion, twice the size of the Swiss economy, and secured around 60 per cent of total Swiss banking assets and deposits. However, in 2008 UBS AG lost over US$39 billion and had to be rescued by the government. In 2010, the Swiss financial regulator called for greater powers to liquidate failing banks. UBS AG recovered and recorded pre-tax profits of at least US$2.36 billion for the first quarter of 2010; it was the second quarter in a row of recorded profit.

In 2009, the banking sector also had to deal with international pressure to accept concessions on bank secrecy. Swiss banking is well known for its 'numbered accounts' and secrecy laws. But in an effort to avoid joining the Organisation for Economic Co-operation and Development (OECD) blacklist of non-co-operative tax havens, Switzerland eased its banking laws to allow the sharing of bank data.

On 10 August 2011, the Swiss National Bank (SNB) took action to reduce the value of the Swiss franc by increasing the supply of francs and undertaking foreign exchange swaps. International investors had been buying Swiss francs as other major currencies came under threat. By 9 August the franc had almost reached parity with the euro and the high value against the US dollar was hurting exports.

External trade

Although Switzerland has consistently rejected EU membership, it is a member of the European Economic Area (EEA), which gives it access to the EU's single market. It has a trade agreement with the EU on a number of measures including trade in processed agricultural goods, customs fraud and taxation.

Foreign trade accounts for almost 80 per cent of all trade with exports providing 45 per cent of GDP, of which industry accounts for around 30 per cent. Over 60 per cent of exports are destined for the EU. Precision tools and equipment, pharmaceuticals and chemicals, electrical and electronic goods are important export items, while banking, insurance and tourism provide the greater part of foreign earnings.

Imports

Main imports are machinery, chemicals, vehicles, metals, agricultural produce and textiles.

Main sources: Germany (typically 33 per cent of total), Italy (11 per cent), France (10.0 per cent).

Exports

Principal exports include mechanical and electrical machinery, medical instruments, chemicals, pharmaceuticals, clocks and watches, textiles and clothing, metals, jewellery and foodstuffs.

Main destinations: Germany (typically 19 per cent of total), US (10 per cent), Italy (9 per cent).

Agriculture

Farming

The agricultural sector contributes around 2.9 per cent to GDP and employs four per cent of the workforce, with activity concentrated on dairy farming. Agriculture is a state subsidised sector – approximately 75 per cent of a farmer's income is financed by subsidies. There are around 80,000 peasant farms of less than 20 hectares (ha) remaining, and of these barely half provide full-time occupations for their owners. Holdings of over 20ha number around 13,000. The average farm is less than 16ha in size. Pasture land totals some 8,500 square km, equivalent to a fifth of the total land area. A further 11,700 square km is given over to arable land, orchards and vineyards.

Farming is highly mechanised, with one of the highest tractor densities in the world. Farmers have use of large and expensive equipment through machinery syndicates. Government fixing of minimum prices means that meat, sugar, vegetables and fruit are two or three times more expensive than in neighbouring countries, a situation which international agencies such as the World Trade Organisation are anxious to see rectified. There are protective customs barriers and other duties on imported goods as well as actual import restrictions, so that the domestic market remains highly protected, a significant factor in Switzerland's opposition to EU membership.

Fishing

Switzerland's fish industry, based on 123,000 hectares of lakes, is insignificant and declining. Untreated industrial and agricultural effluents are polluting fisheries, while canalisation, underground channelling of watercourses and the absence of suitable spawning grounds have contributed to the reduction of fish habitats.

There are more than 50 fish species found in Swiss waters, but only a few have been used by the fishing industry for food. Catches consist for the most part of lake herring and perch together with various other types of whitefish. Catches of whitefish and perch have steadily declined.

Only around 5 per cent of the fish and fish products consumed within the country are obtained from domestic sources.

Forestry

Forest and other wooded land accounts for nearly a third of the land area, with forest cover estimated at 1.19 million hectares. 90 per cent of the forest area is available for wood supply. 4.5 million cubic metres of wood is produced annually There has been a steady rise in growing stock with afforestation accounting for an annual average increase of 4,000ha of forest covers between 1990 and 2000. More than two-thirds of the forest area is under public ownership.

Domestic consumption is 6.4 million cubic metres. Sensitivity about preserving the scenic environment is high. In light of acid rain damage, particularly in the north-west, as well as increased competition in the sector, the prospects for further growth in production appear limited.

The forest industry has to cope with high labour costs. Although paper production is sufficient to meet domestic demands, the industry is partly dependent on pulp imports. Per capita consumption of forest products remains above the European average.

Industry and manufacturing

The industrial sector contributes approximately 30 per cent to GDP and employs about 33 per cent of the labour force. The well-developed export-oriented manufacturing sector is centred on the production of finished goods. Traditional industries include machines, tools, pharmaceuticals, textiles, watchmaking, food processing, chemicals and engineering. Among well-known Swiss companies are Nestlé and Novartis. There is an increasing emphasis on specialisation and the development of high technology products. Swiss companies spend 2.9 per cent of GDP on research and development, one of the highest figures in the world. Switzerland is home to the world's biggest clock and watch industry, which produces about 8 per cent of annual export revenues.

Tourism

Tourism has traditionally been one of Switzerland's most reliable sources of foreign exchange, especially during the winter when the country becomes a popular destination for skiers. Germany continues to be the main source of visitors, followed by the US and the UK.

China has designated Switzerland as an approved destination for its holidaying citizens. Chinese visitors could swell Switzerland's arrival numbers by millions.

Mining

Switzerland is not richly endowed with mineral deposits. Only rock salt and building materials are mined or quarried in significant quantities.

Hydrocarbons

Switzerland has no fossil energy resources apart from a small deposit of natural gas at Finsterwald, which is not under current production. All hydrocarbon needs are imported, including 241,670 barrels per day (bpd) of oil; domestic oil refinery capacity is 132,000bpd. Imported natural gas was 3.4 billion cubic metres in 2006. Coal consumption, which is around 100,000 tonnes of oil equivalent, has declined in recent years, largely for environmental reasons.

Energy

Total installed generating capacity was 17.5 gigawatts (GW) in 2006. Electricity consumption has been growing at 2 per cent since the 1980s and planners see 2020 as the year of shortage if measures are delayed to expand generation. Hydroelectricity is the only natural energy resource, although expansion has been deemed unfeasible; it supplies 12 per cent of total energy requirements. There are five nuclear reactors with total installed capacity of 3.2GW. In May 2011 the government announced it would be phasing out nuclear power, amid growing public hostility to the industry. The five ageing plants will not be replaced after they reach the end of their lifetimes between 2019 and 2034. They will not, however, be decommissioned early.

Switzerland imports and exports electricity to and from France, Germany and Italy. The energy market was liberalised in 2007, with local energy companies allowed to compete nationally while retaining close links to their cantons. The national electricity grid operator, Swissgrid, is responsible for distributing power generated by the power companies The Swiss Federal Office of Energy (SFOE) is responsible for national policy for the implementation of renewable energies.

Financial markets

Stock exchange

Borse (SWX) (Swiss Exchange)

Banking and insurance

Switzerland is the world's biggest offshore private banking centre, but banking secrecy laws and a favourable taxation regime are coming under increasing scrutiny in the light of the dormant accounts scandal and the possibility of EU membership. In an effort to avoid joining the global list of non-co-operative tax havens, held by the Organisation of Economic Co-operation and Development (OECD), Switzerland eased its banking laws to allow the sharing of bank data that cracks down on offshore tax evasion.

The Swiss proviso is that only 'concrete and justified' requests will be acted on. Switzerland is a signatory of a new EU tax agreement, introduced in 2005 in a number of non-EU countries. Switzerland will impose a withholding tax, up to 35 per cent, to be passed to the tax department of an EU citizen's country, but retaining the anonymity of the saver, instead of informing the relevant EU country about the amount of money in savings accounts and allowing tax to be levied from the home country.

Switzerland has also agreed to supply information on tax fraud, for criminal or civil trials, and notify EU member states about additional malpractices.

Were Switzerland to join the EU its competitive advantage in financial services would almost certainly be reduced. Banking remains the largest sector in the canton of Zürich, but the success of these operations lies increasingly with their non-Swiss business.

New banking rules were introduced in January 2003 requiring proof of identity, nationality and date of birth for the ultimate owners of bank accounts opened by financial intermediaries.

Central bank

Swiss National Bank (SNB)

Time

GMT plus one hour (daylight saving, late March to late October, GMT plus two hours)

Geography

Switzerland is a landlocked country bordered by Germany to the north, Austria to the east, Italy to the south and France to the west.

Located high in the Alpine region of western Europe, most of the country's land area is too mountainous to permit any great density of population, which means that most of the country's population reside in the low-lying urban areas. About half of the country's total land area is covered by rock, water or glaciers, or is forested, and a further quarter is either under grass or cultivation.

Hemisphere

Northern

Climate

Geographic factors mean, inevitably, that Switzerland experiences particularly marked variations in weather. While winters are generally severe, especially at higher altitudes, summers tend to be warmer than in the countries to the north. Low-lying areas are often wet. Zürich is prone to a heavy atmosphere in certain wind conditions. Temperatures range from about minus 1 degrees Celsius (C) to 18 degrees C.

Dress codes

Business attire is formal. Warm clothing is essential from September to May, especially in the higher altitudes.

Entry requirements

Passports

Required by all, valid for three months beyond date of departure.

Visa

Switzerland joined the Schengen Agreement group of countries on 12 December 2008, allowing free movement for EU citizens and external visitors with a Schengen visa. A Schengen visa application (offered in several languages) can be downloaded from http://europa.eu/abc/travel/ see 'documents you will need'.

Currency advice/regulations

There are no restrictions on the import or export of local and foreign currencies.

Customs

Personal effects and gifts up to value of Swf300 are duty-free.

Health (for visitors)

Nationals of the European Economic Area (EEA) countries and Switzerland can access reduced cost and sometimes free medical treatment using a European Health Insurance Card (EHIC) while visiting the EEA. Exceptions include nationals of the 10 countries which joined the EU in 2004 whose EHIC is not valid in Switzerland. Applications for the EHIC should be made before travelling.

Mandatory precautions

Vaccination certificates are not usually required.

Advisable precautions

Medical insurance is advisable as treatment is expensive.

Hotels

Hotels keep a high standard throughout the country, and are classified by the Swiss Hotel Association from one- to five-star. A 15 per cent service is included on bill. Reservations should be made well in advance during the winter holiday season.

Credit cards

All major credit cards are accepted.

Public holidays (national)

Fixed dates

1 Jan (New Year's Day), 1 Aug (National Day), 25 Dec (Christmas).

Variable dates

Good Friday, Easter Monday, Ascension Day, Whit Monday.

Working hours

Banking

Regional variations but generally Mon–Fri: 0830–1630. Money exchange at any airport and larger railway stations daily until 2200.

Business

Mon–Fri: 0800–1200, 1330–1700.

Government

Mon–Fri: 0730–1145, 1330–1800, or 0800–1230, 1315–1730.

Shops

Mon–Fri: 0800–1215, 1330–1830 (in larger cities also during lunch hours but Mon morning often closed); Sat: 0830–1600.

Telecommunications

Mobile/cell phones

There are 3G, 900/1800 GSM services available.

Electricity supply

220V AC, 50Hz

Social customs/useful tips

Appointments should always be made before making visits. If the appointment cannot be kept, this should be communicated.

Hand-shaking is frequent. When invited to dinner in a private house, flowers or chocolates for the hosts are the usual gifts. When drinks are served, it is customary to wait until all the party has been attended to, and then to raise the glass with a salute to each.

The Swiss are proud of their often colourful cultural traditions. Traditional costume is still worn daily in a few areas of the country, although in most areas, it is restricted to celebrations and tourist-related events.

Security

There are no special problems with security in Switzerland; normal precautions apply, especially in the cities.

Getting there

Air

There are regular flights by all major international airlines.

National airline: Swiss International Airlines (Swiss)

International airport/s: EuroAirport Basle-Mulhouse-Freiburg (BSL), 5km from Basle; Berne-Belp (BRN), 9km from city; Geneva International (GVA), 5km north of city; Zürich (ZRH), 9km north of city. Zürich and Geneva airports are directly linked to the national rail system.

Airport tax: None.

Surface

There are good road and rail links with all surrounding countries. It is advisable to book for rail travel beforehand.

Road: Major roads and tunnels link Switzerland to all neighbouring countries.

Water: There is limited access by water from France, Germany and Italy.

Getting about

National transport

Air: There are several daily flights linking Zürich, Geneva, Basle, Lugano and Berne.

Road: There is a road network of around 72,000km, including 17,000km of motorways. Roads are of good quality, but travel can be slow due to the terrain and the volume of traffic.

Rail: There are over 5,000km of track, practically all electrified. About 60 per cent is operated by Schweizerische Bundesbahnen (SBB) (Swiss Federal Railways) and the rest by about 120 small private companies. Rail journeys between major towns rarely exceed two or three hours.

In December 2007 the Lötschberg rail tunnel was opened between Bern and Valais cantons. It is estimated that the link will save up to an hour across the Alps. It will allow heavier trains, including 'piggy back' services for lorries.

Water: All the larger lakes are serviced by steamers operated by SBB.

City transport

A train from Zürich airport to the city centre takes about 12 minutes, while a taxi can take more than twice as long.

All local city transport is linked together on the same ticketing system. Tickets should be purchased before boarding from ticket dispensers by the stops.

Taxis: Widely available but they do not ply for hire. Zürich taxis have a higher tariff than elsewhere. A 15 per cent service charge is included; no tip required.

Buses, trams & metro: Good services in major towns. Tickets should be bought in advance from vending machines. Multi-journey tickets also available. Flat fare up to five stops.

Car hire

Self-drive and chauffeur-driven cars available in all main towns. A valid national or international driving licence is required, and insurance is compulsory. Speed limits are 50kph in built-up areas, 80kph on normal roads and 120kph on motorways. Further information can be obtained from the Touring Club Suisse (TCS) or the Automobil Club der Schweiz/Automobile Club Suisse (ACS).

BUSINESS DIRECTORY

The addresses listed below are a selection only. While World of Information makes every endeavour to check these addresses, we cannot guarantee that changes have not been made, especially to telephone numbers and area codes. We would welcome any corrections.

Telephone area codes

The international direct dialling (IDD) code for Switzerland is +41, followed by area code and subscriber's number:

Basel	61	Lucerne	41
Bern	31	Neuchâtel	32
Fribourg	26	St Gallen	71
Geneva	22	Winterthur	52
Lausanne	21	Zürich	1

Useful telephone numbers

Police: 117
Fire brigade: 118
Ambulance: 144
Motor breakdown service: 140
Swiss Air Rescue: 47-47-47
Emergency service of Touring Club of Switzerland: 35-80-00

Chambers of Commerce

American Swiss Chamber of Commerce,41 Talacker, 8001 Zurich (tel: 211-2454; fax: 211-9572; e-mail: info@amcham.ch).

Basel Chamber of Commerce, 67 Aeschenvorstadt, 4010 Basel (tel: 270-6060; fax: 270-6005; e-mail: hkbb@hkbb.ch).

Bern Chamber of Commerce and Industry, 1 Gutenbergstrasse, PO Box 5464, 3001 Bern (tel: 388-8787; fax: 382-8788; e-mail: info@bern-cci.ch).

British-Swiss Chamber of Commerce, 155 Freiestrasse, 8032 Zürich (tel: 422-3131; fax: 422-3244; e-mail: bscc@bscc.co.uk).

Fribourg Chamber of Commerce, Industry and Services, 37 Route du Jura, 1706 Fribourg (tel: 347-1220; fax: 347-1239; e-mail: cfcis@cci.ch).

Geneva Chamber of Commerce and Industry, 4 Boulevard du Théâtre, PO Box 5039, 1211 Genève 11 (tel: 819-9111; fax: 819-9100; e-mail: ccig@cci.ch).

St Gallen-Appenzell Chamber of Commerce and Industry, 16 Gallusstrasse, 9001 St Gallen (tel: 224-1010; fax: 224-1060; e-mail: sekretariat@ihk.ch).

Swiss Business Federation, 47 Hegibachstrasse, 8032 Zürich (tel: 421-3535; fax: 421-3434; e-mail: info@economiesuisse.ch).

Swiss Chambers of Commerce and Industry, 47 Avenue d'Ouchy, PO Box 315, 1001 Lausanne (tel: 613-3535; fax: 613-3505 e-mail: info@cci.ch).

Vaud Chamber of Commerce and Industry, 47 Avenue d'Ouchy, 1001 Lausanne (tel: 613-3535; fax: 613-3505; e-mail: cvci@cvci.ch).

Winterthur Chamber of Commerce, 15 Neumarkt, 8401 Winterthur (tel: 213-0763; fax: 213-0729; e-mail: info@haw.ch).

Zürich Chamber of Commerce, 5 BleicherwegPO Box 3058, 8022 Zürich (tel: 217-4050; fax: 217-4051; e-mail: direktion@zurichcci.ch).

Banking

Banque Cantonale de Genève, Quai de l'Ile 17, Case postale, 1211 Genéve 2 (tel: 317-2727; fax: 793-5960).

Banca della Svizzera Italiana, 2 Via Magatti, 6901 Lugano (tel: 587-111).

Bank Leu, Bahnhofstrasse 32, CH-8001 Zürich (tel: 219-1111).

Crédit Suisse, Paradeplatz 8, CH-8021 Zürich (tel: 215-1111).

Crédit Suisse, Pl Bel-Air 2, Case postale, 1211 Genève 70 (tel: 391-2111; fax: 391-2591).

Sociéte de Banque Suisse, rue de la Confédération 2, Case postale, 1211 Genève 2 (tel: 375-7575; fax: 376-5024).

Swiss Bank Corporation, Aeschenvorstadt 1/Gartenstrasse 9, Basel (tel: 202-020).

Swiss Bankers' Association, Aeschenplatz 4, Postfach 4182, CH-4002 Basel (tel: 235-888).

Swiss Volksbank, Weltpoststrasse 5, 3015 Bern (tel: 328-111).

Union de Banques Suisses, Rue Rhone 8, Case postale, 1211 Genève 2 (tel: 388-1111; fax: 388-9652).

Union Bank of Switzerland, Bahnhofstrasse 45, CH-8000 Zürich (tel: 234-1111).

United European Bank, 11 Quai des Bergues, CP 2280, 1211 Genève (tel: 907-2111; fax: 732-3002).

Zürcher Kantonalbank, Bahnhofstrasse, PO Box 4039, 8022 Zürich (fax: 211-1525).

Central bank

Schweizerische Nationalbank, Börsenstrasse 15, 8022 Zürich (tel: 631-3111; fax: 631-3911; e-mail: snb@snb.ch).

Stock exchange

Borse (SWX) (Swiss Exchange): www.swx.com

Stock exchange 2

Berner Börsenverein (BX Berne Exchange): www.berne-x.com

Travel information

Automobile Club de Suisse (ACS), Wasserwerkgasse 39, 3000 Bern (tel: 328-3111; fax: 311-0310; e-mail: acszv@acs.ch).

Swiss Travel Centre, Grubenstrasse 12, 8045 Zürich (tel: 210-5500; fax: 210-5501; e-mail: information@stc.ch).

Touring Club Suisse (TCS), Chemin de Blandonnet 4, 1214 Vernier, Geneva (tel: 417-2727; fax: 417-2020; e-mail: info@tcs.ch).

National tourist organisation offices

Switzerland Tourism, Tödistrasse 7, 8002 Zürich (tel: 288-1111; fax: 288-1205; email: info@myswitzerland.com).

Ministries

Bundesamt für Statistik (BFS) (central statistics office), Schwarzftorstrasse 96, CH-3003 Bern (tel: 323-6011; fax: 323-6061).

Federal Department of Finance, Bundesgasse 3, 3003 Bern (tel: 66-111).

Federal Department of Public Economy, Bundeshaus-Ost, 3003 Bern (tel: 612-111).

Federal Office for Industry, Crafts and Labour, Bundesgasse 8, CH-3003 Bern (tel: 612-944).

Swiss Federal Tax Administration, Eidgenössische Steuerverwaltung, Eigerstrasse 65, CH-3003 Bern (tel: 617-112).

Other useful addresses

British Embassy, Thunstrasse 50, CH-3005 Berne 15 (tel: 352-5021/6; fax: 352-0583).

Embassy of the United States of America, Jubilumstrasse 93, CH-3005 Berne (tel: 357-7011; fax: 357-7344).

Fédération Suisse des Agences de Voyages, Postfach, Hardstrasse 316, CH-8027 Zürich (tel: 426-442)

Swiss Embassy (USA), 2900 Cathedral Avenue, NW, Washington DC 20008 (tel: (+1-202) 745-7900; fax: (+1-202) 387-2564; e-mail: vertretung@was.rep.admin.ch).

Swiss Federation of Commerce and Industry, Börsenstrasse 26, CH-8022 Zürich (tel: 221-2707).

Swiss Lawyers' Federation, Lavaterstrasse 83, CH-8027 Zürich (tel: 202-5650).

Swiss News Agency, Langgasstrasse 7, CH-3012 Bern (tel: 244-461).

SWX Swiss Exchange, Selnaustrasse 30, Postfach, CH-8021 Zürich (tel: 229-2111).

Union Suisse d'Agences-Conseils en Publicité (advertising), Kurfürstenstr 80, CH-8002 Zürich (tel: 202-6540).

Other news agencies: SDA+ATS (in German) (www.sda.ch).

Swiss Infor (operated by SRG SSR Idée Suisse in nine languages) (www.swissinfo.org).

Internet sites

Details of government departments: www.admin.ch/ch/e/index.html

Index of Swiss business and tourism: www.swissdir.ch

Swiss Federal Statistical office: www.admin.ch/bfs/eindex.htm

Yellow pages Switzerland: www.pages-jaunes.ch/index.html

Syria

KEY FACTS

Official name: Jumhuriya al Arabya as Suriya (Syrian Arab Republic)

Head of State: President Bashar al Assad (since 2000)

Head of government: Prime Minister Adel Safar (appointed 3 Apr 2011)

Ruling party: Al Jabha al Wataniyyah at Wahdwamiyyah (National Progressive Front) (NPF), a coalition of 10 parties led by Hizb al Ba'ath al Arabi al Ishtiraki (Ba'ath Party) (Arab Socialist Rebirth Party) (re-elected Apr 2007)

Area: 185,180 square km (plus 1,295 square km Israeli-controlled Golan Heights)

Population: 20.13 million (2010)*

Capital: Damascus

Official language: Arabic

Currency: Syrian pound (Syr£) = 100 piastres

Exchange rate: Syr£48.85 per US$ (Oct 2011)

GDP per capita: US$2,877 (2010)

GDP real growth: 3.20% (2010)

GDP: US$59.30 billion (2010)

Unemployment: 9.00% (2008)* (Including a percentage of Iraqi refugees)

Inflation: 4.40% (2010)

Oil production: 385,000 bpd (2010)

Balance of trade: -US$3.05 billion (2009)

Annual FDI: US$1.38 billion (2010)

* estimated figure

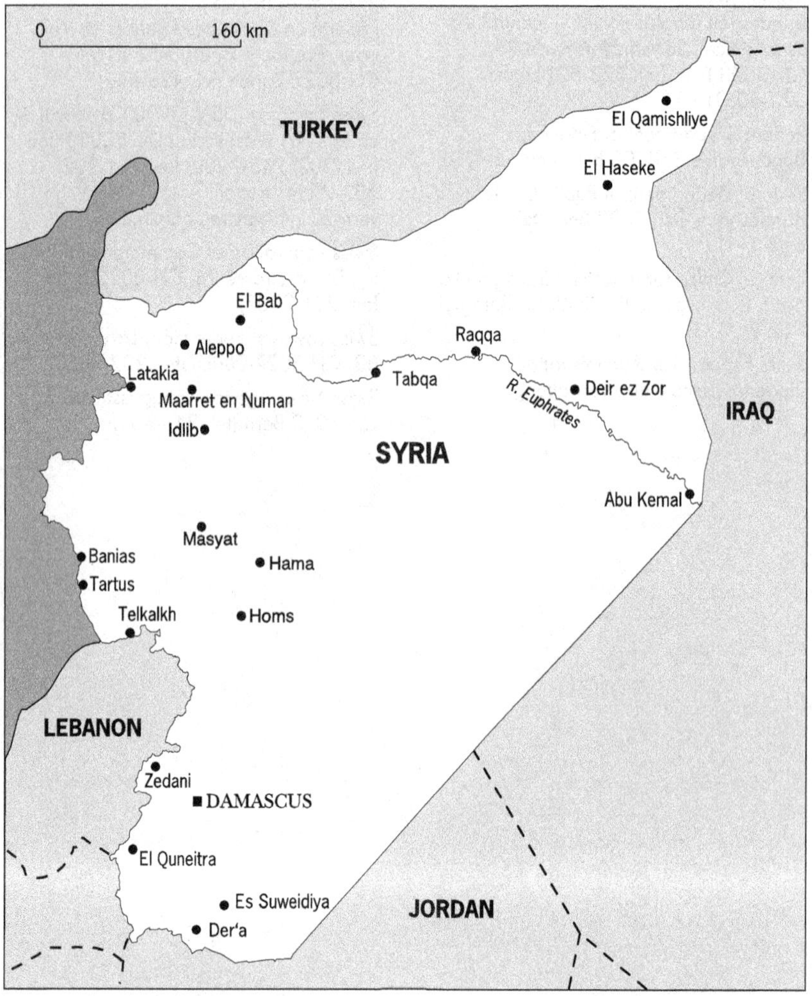

As 2011 ended, the Syrian uprising that had begun in March 2011 showed no signs of abating. Quite the contrary; estimates put the number of dead as high as 5,000. Bashar al Assad's government appeared indifferent to international criticism, wavering between a stance of dismissive impatience with what were described as 'terrorist' incursions to announcing luke-warm reforms that generally failed to see the light of day. China and Russia, probably for different reasons, demonstrated a more calculated indifference, steadfastly opposing United Nations (UN) initiatives to bring the Syrian government into line. Syria itself was deep in its most acute isolation and fast becoming a pariah state.

Those countries that – under the aegis of the North Atlantic Treaty Organisation (NATO) – had been willing to intervene in Libya baulked at a similar approach to Syria. In contrast to the ethnically and religious homogeneity of Libya, Syria is an altogether more complex mosaic of tribes, religions, sects and loyalties. By the end of 2011, the prospect of the uprising metamorphosing into civil war loomed nearer. In December the Arab League voted, rather half heartedly, to send a small number of observers to report on the situation. However, the mission's ability to report and observe was severely hindered by the constant presence of government 'minders', quick to intervene if it was felt that meetings or conversations might be detrimental to the interests of the regime.

Not only Syria, or even its immediate neighbours, but also the Arab League states, the US, the European Union (EU), neighbouring Turkey and Iran, not to mention Israel, all have a vested interest in the eventual outcome of the Syrian unrest. Syria's isolation had hardly happened overnight, but in August 2011 President Barack Obama of the US finally ran out of patience and called for Syria's President Bashar al Assad to step down and stop his troops from attacking his subjects. Mr Obama also ordered a new set of official US sanctions including the dramatic step of freezing all Syrian assets in the US and banning American individuals and companies from transacting any business with the Syrian government.

The prospect of a fully effective economic blockade is simply impossible without the co-operation of Iraq, Lebanon and Jordan. Turkey, a member of NATO, is the joker in the pack. By the end of 2011 Ankara seemed to have found itself, perhaps unwillingly and certainly surprisingly, to have assumed the role of Sunni leadership, in the face of Shi'ite heretics, mostly from Iran (but also Iraq, Alawis in Syria and Hezbollah). Under the NATO aegis, Ankara allows the deployment of missile defense systems in its territory, directed not only against Iran but also against Russia. Neither Russia (which has built its large, and only, Mediterranean naval base on Syria's coast, nor the Assad régime, was still able to pretend that all was normal at the end of 2011.

The Syrian opposition grouping – the Syrian National Council (SNC) – appears largely to consist of Muslim Brotherhood members, with a sprinkling of Kurds. The leader, Burhan Ghalioun, is described by many commentators as an opportunist Paris exile with minimal credibility. In an interview with the *Wall Street Journal* he seemed intent on calming the fears of the United States and, more particularly Israel, claiming that a new Syrian government would sever all Syria's links with Iran and cease support for Hezbollah in Lebanon and Hamas in Gaza.

The military grouping, the Free Syrian Army (FSA) claims to have as many as 15,000 army defectors. That figure probably includes mercenaries and what many Syrian civilians describe as 'armed gangs'. There is a clear fault line between the SNC and the FSA. The SNC is supposedly opposed to force, while the FSA is armed, increasingly well organised and carries out attacks on Syrian soldiers as well as Ba'ath party offices.

The SNC needs to persuade interested parties that Syria must at all costs avoid the nightmare of another massacre, which, in late 2011 looked quite likely to happen in Homs. Perhaps ironically, although both groupings are based in Istanbul, the SNC and the FSA seem unable to agree on a great deal. But if the Syrian opposition wasn't able to sort itself out, the same was the case with the Arab League. The Arab League working party on Syria consisted of the six Gulf Co-operation Council (GCC) monarchies plus Morocco and Jordan. The League's observers belatedly ventured in to Syria at the beginning of 2012, but generally found themselves on a hiding to nothing, dodging crossfire while trying to listen to a beseeching public on the one hand, their government minders on the other.

NATO's tactics regarding Syria have been less than clear cut. Probably because with all the will in the world, the Syrian situation takes some patience for even hardened Syria watchers to follow and understand. If in Libya Colonel Qadafi was playing chess with his opponents, Bashar al Assad was indulging in three dimensional chess with his opposition in Syria.

As the protests had worn on in 2011 and increased both in size and intensity, a number of Syrian cities, notably Homs (Syria's third largest city), Hama (its fourth) Deir ez Zor its fifth) and the southern town of Deraa (where the uprising started) began to emerge as the places putting up the most armed resistance to the regime. The government was able to reassert its control in the small town of Rastan only after five days of intense fighting. Reports of frequent armed clashes in Homs and Hama continued. July 2011 saw seventy protesters killed by government forces in just two days in Hama. The régime appeared to be largely successful in containing the protests in Damascus itself, where unrest was contained to one or two districts, Midan and Kafr Souseh, and in Syria's second city, Aleppo, where heavy policing seemed to keep matters under control. Most of the defecting soldiers who managed to leave Syria ended up in Turkey where they were reported to be joining the FSA. Meanwhile, Syria's Alawite led army (the ruling family are also Alawites) remained loyal to the lonely Mr Assad.

The factor unifying Syria's protestors was a desire to see the end of the Assad régime and the repressive security infrastructure it had built around it. However strong and purposeful this sense of unity was, what was equally certain was that the longer term objectives of the protestors differed as much as did their religions, sects, tribes and ancestry. The protestors were reported to be at pains to point out that there were no problems between them. But, from the very start of the

KEY INDICATORS — Syria

	Unit	2006	2007	2008	2009	2010
Population	m	18.94	*19.41	*19.88	*20.37	*20.13
Gross domestic product (GDP)	US$bn	33.50	40.60	54.50	52.50	59.30
GDP per capita	US$	1,769	2,090	2,740	2,579	2,877
GDP real growth	%	5.1	4.3	5.2	4.0	3.2
Inflation	%	10.6	4.7	15.2	2.5	4.4
Industrial output	% change	3.2	7.7	-2.3	-2.3	–
Agricultural output	% change	3.7	-3.2	6.0	6.0	–
Oil output	'000 bpd	417.0	394.0	398.0	376.0	385.0
Natural gas output	bn cum	5.5	5.3	5.5	5.8	7.8
Exports (fob) (goods)	US$m	7,205.0	11,756.0	15,334.0	10,883.0	–
Imports (fob) (goods)	US$m	10,325.0	12,277.0	16,107.0	13,933.0	–
Balance of trade	US$m	-3,120.0	-521.0	-773.0	-3,049.0	–
Current account	US$m	-614.0	459.0	66.0	-1,161.0	-2,593.0
Total reserves minus gold	US$m	–	17,013.0	17,062.0	17,398.0	19,465.0
Foreign exchange	US$m	–	16,955.0	17,006.0	16,960.0	19,035.0
Exchange rate	per US$	52.21	51.10	46.35	46.70	46.94

* estimated figure

anti-government protests in Syria in early 2011 there was an armed and violent element in the opposition. The question was to what extent that unruly element looked like taking control and if so, when that was likely to happen. Most of the protestors, it seemed, insisted that they wanted their revolution to remain a peaceful one. Despite occasional flare-ups, there is no real history of chronic sectarian strife in Syria. By September 2011, however, in spite of a considerable loss of life, there was no sign of an end to the stalemate between the forces of change and those clinging to continuity. Even the Muslim Brotherhood, membership of which carries the death penalty, adheres to a non-violent future for Syria. The majority of the Brotherhood in Syria seems to be against political Islam.

In September, Syrian officials claimed that over 800 police and soldiers had been killed 'by terrorists'. That figure compared with over 2,700 civilians killed, the number estimated by the United Nations and endorsed by independent bodies such as Amnesty International and the Red Cross. In August 2011 a report by the UN High Commissioner for Human Rights referred to violations of human rights that 'may amount to crimes against humanity'. In the largely Alawite port town of Latakia official forces were supported by *shabiha* casuals, thought to be commanded by the President's cousins, Munzer and Bashar al Assad. *shabiha* thugs had attacked Alawite and Sunni groups in Latakia reportedly posing as Sunnis. During the Syrian army's 15-year occupation of Lebanon, it had acquired a reputation for inefficiency, using obsolete equipment manned by reluctant conscripts. On its own turf, however, it proved to be a more professional, flexible force. In sharp contrast with its role in Lebanon, in Syria the army's principal role was the protection of the regime, not the suppression of a contrary populace.

Following the US initiative to impose sanctions, EU leaders followed suit by announcing that new sanctions were under consideration. However, two key UN Security Council members, China and Russia, were opposed to any such move, to the extent of even refusing to consider it, boycotting the meetings called to discuss it. The Russian UN ambassador Vitaly Churkin (who had once been the USSR Ambassador in Syria) had gone on record that this was not the time to sanction Syria. Some progress had been recorded by the UN when, at the beginning of August 2011 Russia and China had at least backed a statement by the Security Council that condemned the Syrian government's suppression of protest and called for an end to the violence. The sanctions sought by the EU and the US would impose a travel ban on 22 members of the Assad family and associates and an asset freeze on 23 Syrians, including President Assad himself. It seemed that President Assad had been excluded from the travel ban to provide him a with possible escape option. Also under consideration was a ban on imports of Syria oil. Although these were not large, their loss would represent a major setback on the Syrian scale of things.

Arab *Froideur*

Arab states that had formerly been sympathetic to Bashar al Assad began to distance themselves, some by breaking off diplomatic relations. Kuwait and Saudi Arabia withdrew their ambassadors, as did (perhaps surprisingly) Bahrain. Others not normally considered to be particularly concerned with developments – Brazil, India and South Africa – sought meetings with Syrian foreign minister Walid Mouallem to express their disapproval. In August 2011, Turkish foreign minister Ahmet Davutoglu arrived in Damascus following a statement by Turkish Prime Minister Recep Tayyip Erdogan that his country had run out of patience with the Syrian government. Syria's annual trade with Turkey in 2010 had amounted to US$2.5 billion. In the holy month of Ramadan, which began in August 2011, it was estimated that over 300 Syrians had been killed by government forces, 200 of them in the city of Hama. Hama, famous amongst other things for its water wheels, was the scene of a massacre by government forces in 1982 in which an estimated 20,000 citizens died in a matter of days as President Hafez Assad, father of the present incumbent, sought to quell an alleged uprising by the Muslim Brotherhood. One of the conundrums of the harsh treatment meted out to the protestors was that it seemed to be ordered by the President himself, despite his televised broadcasts offering an end to such brutality (which were to continue well into October). As spring advanced into summer Mr Assad's promises included the lifting of the emergency laws and other reforms. Another promise to legalise opposition parties was dismissed as simply unrealistic. This caused many observers to think that it was no longer President Bashar al Assad, an ophthalmologist by profession, who was calling the shots, but his younger brother Maher, who controls both the Presidential Guard and the élite Fourth Division of the army. Other members of the President's kitchen cabinet are his brother-in-law, Assef Shawqat the army's deputy chief of staff and Rami Makhlouf, the President's cousin and reputed to be Syria's richest businessman.

Iran

Mid-2011 saw Iran doing its best to prop up the failing regime of Syria's Bashar al Assad, while celebrating the fall of Egypt's Hosni Mubarak. Mubarak's fall was a tactical victory for Iran, inasmuch as any likely successor would be more favourably disposed towards Iran than the fallen despot. Iran could also derive some satisfaction from the fact that President Ahmedinejad's reputation and that of his country had, according to reports in the international press, improved immeasurably in the Gulf region following the end of the Gulf War 'proper'. In 2011, Bashar al Assad was Iran's closest ally. However, Arab regional powers, notably Saudi Arabia, are anxious to cut Iran down to size and would see the toppling of his closest regional supporter as a step in the right direction.

In the earlier part of 2011 Iran had called upon Syria to adopt a less brutal stance towards the Syrian protest movement. Distancing itself as far as it could from the Syrian leadership, Tehran had called on Damascus at least to talk to the protestors. President Ahmadinejad had gone so far as to suggest that Damascus should enter dialogue with the protestors, saying (without so much as a tongue in its cheek) that 'a military solution is never the right solution.' Such is the importance of its relationship with Damascus that for Iran any dilution would be perceived as a diminution of Iran's regional power and authority. Syria's ruling Alawi minority is Shi'a rather than Sunni, hence the strength of its links with Shi'a Iran. Elsewhere, Iran's client state by design, Bahrain, reflected similar Sunni-Shi'a imbalances as a Sunni monarchy endeavoured to bottle up the dissent spilling over from its Shi'a majority.

The energy card

The prolonged uprising of 2011 threw into sharp relief the importance of Syria's oil. Syria is the only oil producer in the Eastern Mediterranean. By Middle Easter standards production is not that high, averaging some 400,000 barrels per day (bpd) in 2010. Most of this is exported, via the Mediterranean to EU markets. Germany takes some 32 per cent of Syrian exports, followed by Italy with 31 per cent and France, with 11 per cent. This provided the EU with an obvious sanction possibility – that of banning oil and gas exports to the EU. The only problem with this move was that in all likelihood sympathetic neighbours such as Iran, or even Iraq, would step into the breach and purchase Syrian oil to re-sell it.

If oil was a bargaining card for Syria, it was one that had already past its sell-by date. In the first decade of the 21st century, Syria's oil trade went from a surplus of US$1.9 billion in 2006 to a deficit of US$100 million in 2008. The net picture was confused by the subsidies that the Syrian government allocated to petroleum products. Plans to phase out the subsidies have already been announced, but in the sensitive political climate of the uprisings, it was deemed not to be in the Syrian government's interest to allow pump prices to rise.

According to the US-based *Oil and Gas Journal* (OGJ), Syria had petroleum reserves of 2.5 billion barrels at the beginning of 2011. Most of these are found in the east of the country bordering the Euphrates, with one or two smaller fields found in the central area. Daily production had peaked at 582,000bpd in 1996, falling to sixty per cent of the peak figure by 2010, when it averaged a modest 387,000bpd. The most important fields are the Omar and Jbessa fields with, according to the OGJ, production capacities of 100,000bpd and 200,000bpd respectively. Both of these fields are operated by the Al Furat Petroleum Company, owned by a consortium comprising Shell Oil (29.7 per cent), China National Petroleum Corporation (20.3 per cent) and the Syrian Petroleum Company (SPC) (50.00 per cent). SPC has been seeking opportunities for increasing oil exploration with a view to reversing the decline in production. Efforts have been hampered, however, by the ban on US investment in Syria, which has obliged Syria to work with companies from the EU (also under threat) as well as from China and India. Bids from a 2010 bidding round were accepted from Total (France) and Petro Canada in May 2011.

Despite the uncertain, even violent, social and political climate, The Syrian Ministry of Petroleum and Mineral Resources , together with the SPC placed three offshore blocks up for bids in March 2011, with a deadline of early October 2011. Bids have also been invited for oil shale exploration in al Khanasir, some 100km south of Syria's second city, Aleppo. The closing date for these bids is November 2011; initial estimates put the tar-shale deposits at around 39 billion tons, corresponding to some 285 billion barrels.

In 2010 Syrian net petroleum exports according to the US government Energy Information Administration (EIA) were estimated at 109,000bpd, a slight drop over the 2009 figure of 117,000bpd. Most oil exports go through Baniyas and Tartous. Smaller amounts go through Latakia. All Syria's oil terminals are connected to Syria's refineries via the country's pipeline network. The backbone of this network is the 500km 250,000bpd Tel-Adas-Tartous crude pipeline which links the major fields to the Port of Tartous and the refinery at Homs.

Additionally two major pipelines were built across Syria to take oil from Saudi Arabia and Iraq to the Mediterranean terminals. In 2011, neither of these were in operation. The 500,000bpd Tapline was originally constructed in the 1940s to carry Saudi crude oil to Lebanese export terminals. It was closed in the 1970s as uneconomical; sporadic – but unrealistic – plans have been produced to reopen the pipeline. The second pipeline was constructed during the 1950s to transport oil from Kirkuk in Northern Iraq to the Syrian Banias terminal. In June 2011 Syria and Iraq signed a Memorandum of Understanding (MoU) to repair the existing pipeline system and to build a further two pipelines to carry heavy and light crude oil from Iraqi fields to the Mediterranean.

Syria's refineries were capable of handling 240,000bpd in January 2011 according to the OGJ. Syria desperately needs additional refining capacity, but the acutely uncertain political climate has made any serious foreign participation unlikely. This has obliged Syria to seek support from the also-rans of the international oil industry. In December 2010 Venezuela signed a MoU to construct the 144,000bpd Froklos refinery, a project stalled since March 2008. A refinery at Deir al Zor (the scene of violent anti-government projects in mid-2011) has been discussed with Chinese companies; this project was also to have begun construction in 2008.

All Syria's natural gas reserves are deployed domestically. A quarter of these are destined for oilfield re-injection, with the rest destined for power generation and other domestic purposes. While Syrian natural gas production is rising, estimated at 291 billion cubic feet annually, the rate of development is not enough to meet demand, which is expected to double by 2020. This means that Syria will have to import increased quantities of natural gas. The confirmed discovery of substantial deposits of offshore gas by Israel has increased optimism on the part of neighbouring Mediterranean countries, including Syria. Before the descent of large parts of Syria into chaos in 2011, the Syrian government had announced a long-term plan to become a transit state for gas supplies from Egypt, Iraq, Iran and Azerbaijan. The deterioration of Syria's relations with Turkey placed a question mark over the construction of a short pipeline in the north of the country. Similar agreement had been signed with Azerbaijan; this would permit 35 billion cubic feet to flow, doubling to 70 billion cubic feet per year by 2015.permit 35 billion cubic feet to flow, doubling to 70 billion cubic feet per year by 2015.

Risk assessment

Economy	Poor
Politics	Poor
Regional stability	Poor

COUNTRY PROFILE

Historical profile

The history of Syria has been moulded by three historical processes: the movement of tribes from the Arabian Peninsula and the mingling with peoples of earlier settlements to form a rural population whose languages and customs have been Semitic for thousands of years; the movement of armies and goods along the great trade routes and the establishment of alien governments in the towns and valleys; and the resistance of the mountain communities to the incursions of foreign peoples and ideas.

After forming successively part of the Egyptian, Babylonian, Hittite, Greek and Roman empires, Syria fell to the Muslim armies in AD 636. The majority of the people became Muslim and Arabic replaced the older Semitic tongue. After the capital of the Islamic Caliphate moved from Damascus to Baghdad in AD750, parts of Syria came under external, including Crusader, domination until the whole area became part of the Ottoman Empire in 1516 and remained so until 1918. In the great days of Ottoman rule Syria prospered, but by the nineteenth century it was socially and economically stagnant.

After the defeat and disintegration of the Ottoman Empire in 1918, Syria was occupied by allied (French and British) troops. Prince Faisal, military leader of the Arab revolt against the Ottomans established himself as King of Damascus, but at the same time, the allies allocated the mandate for the whole of Syria to France, which had long-standing ties with the Levant states and aimed to control them politically. In 1920, the French ousted Faisal and installed their own administration. In the 20 years of the French mandate there was some economic and social progress, but prolonged political unrest as the Sunni majority rejected French rule. In 1941 Syria was occupied by the British and Free French forces and at the end of the war, with British support, Syria secured independence and the withdrawal of French troops. There followed a period of political instability, a number of *coups d'état* and an abortive union with Egypt until, in 1966, a group of radical members of the Hizb al Ba'ath al Arabi al Ishtiraki (Ba'ath Party) (Arab Socialist Rebirth Party) seized power. Army Chief and defence minister General Hafez al Assad took power in 1970. Sunni Muslims, who had traditionally dominated Syrian political life found themselves replaced by the Ba'athist socialists, comprising Alawites (such as the Assad family) Druzes and other minorities.

Historical profile

636 Muslim armies conquered Syria

1516 Syria became part of the Ottoman Empire.

1831–39 Egypt occupied Syria.

1915 Jamal Pasha, determined to tighten the Ottoman Empire's control of the region, hanged 21 Arabs in the city squares of Damascus and Beirut. The Martyrs' Day national holiday in Syria and Lebanon commemorates this event.

1918 End of the Ottoman Empire in Syria. Prince Faisal entered Damascus and assumed control of all Syria except for the area along the Mediterranean coast where the French were garrisoned.

1919 Prince Faisal convened the General Syrian Congress, which declared Syria sovereign and free. Arabic was declared the official language.

1920 France and Britain refused to recognise Syrian independence and under the Sykes-Picot Agreement Syria became a French Mandate, ending Syrian independence.

1925–26 Insurgent action resulted in France bombarding Damascus.

1928 The French allowed the formation of the Al Kutlah al Wataniyah (National Bloc), composed of various nationalist groups centred in Damascus. A constituent assembly drafted a constitution that included the reunification of Syria and denied the authority of France; it was rejected by the French High Commissioner.

1930 A constitution was imposed by the French.

1936 France agreed to Syrian independence, subject to France remaining dominant in military and economic fields.

1941 Allied forces occupied Syria. General de Gaulle promised an end to the French mandate.

1943 The National Bloc Syria won new parliamentary elections. Parliament elected Shukri al Kuwatli as Syria's first president.

1945 Syria became a Charter member of the United Nations (UN) (an indication of its sovereign status) and signed the pact of the League of Arab States (Arab League).

1946 A UN resolution prompted France to relinquish control and the sovereign state of Syria came into being.

1947 The Hizb al Ba'ath al Arabi al Ishtiraki (Ba'ath Party) (Arab Socialist Rebirth Party) was founded by Michel Aflaq.

1948–49 Syria contributed to a pan-Arab military force that failed to occupy the newly-created state of Israel.

1949 President al Kuwatli was overthrown in a military coup.

1953 In a referendum, Syrians approved a new constitution making Syria a presidential republic.

1954 Civilian government was re-installed; Shukri al Kuwatli returned from exile and was elected president. Syria moved towards greater economic and political co-operation with Egypt.

1958–61 A United Arab Republic (UAR) was formed between Syria and Egypt, following a referendum in both countries. Egyptian president, Gamel Abdel Nasser, became president of both states, Cairo was chosen as the capital and a new federal constitution was adopted. Nasser dissolved all political parties.

1961 Discontent at Egyptian domination led to the overthrow of the UAR, by a military *coup*, which dissolved the partnership.

1963 The Ba'ath Party seized control.

1967 Israel launched and won the June Six Day War taking control of the strategic Golan Heights from Syria.

1970 Former air force commander and defence minister, Hafez al-Assad, seized power in a bloodless coup.

1971 Al Assad was elected president. He was re-elected for four successive seven-year terms in 1978, 1985, 1992 and 1999.

1973 A new constitution was adopted. In the 6 October War (also known as the Yom Kippur War), Egypt and Syria invaded Israel to reclaim some of the land lost in the Six Day War, but despite some early strategic gains for Egypt and Syria, Israel counter-attacked and repelled the invasion, re-conquering the Golan Heights.

1974 Diplomatic relations with the US were resumed.

1975 President al Assad offered peace with Israel if it agreed to withdraw from all occupied Arab land. The offer was rejected.

1976 The Syrian army intervened in the Lebanese civil war to ensure the *status quo*; the Maronite leadership remained in power.

1980 Syria backed Iran in the Iran-Iraq War.

1981 Israel formally annexed the Golan Heights.

1982–87 Israel invaded Lebanon and attacked the Syrian army based there. After hostilities ended, Syrian forces remained in Lebanon.

1990 Syria participated in the US-led allied military operations against Iraq.

2000 President Hafez al Assad died. The Ba'ath party amended the constitution, reducing the minimum age for a president from 40 to 34 years, thereby allowing former President Hafez al Assad's son, Bashar al Assad, to become president.

2001 The UN General Assembly voted Syria a two-year seat on the Security Council.

2002 Syria, along with Cuba and Libya, were added to the original list (Iran, Iraq and North Korea) of the US' so-called Axis of Evil states. Syria denied US allegations that it was acquiring weapons of mass destruction.

2003 Muhammed Naji al Otari was appointed prime minister.

2004 The US imposed economic sanctions, citing Syria's support for terrorism and failing to stop militants entering Iraq from Syria. A UN Security Council resolution called for Syrian forces to leave Lebanon; Syria re-deployed some of its troops stationed around Beirut.

2005 Syrian troops were withdrawn from Lebanon following mass anti-Syrian protests in Beirut, and after accusations that Syria was responsible for the car bomb attack that killed former Lebanese prime minister, Rafik Hariri. The ruling Ba'ath party relaxed a number of laws that sanctioned some independent political parties, granted more press freedom and relaxed the state of emergency (that had been in place since 1963). UN investigators were allowed to question Syrian officials about the assassination of Rafik Hariri. Interior minister, Ghazi Kanaan, accused of being involved in the murder of Hariri, was found dead, apparently of suicide. An official UN interim report implicated senior Syrian and Lebanese security officials in the killing of Hariri; Syria rejected the report. Following weeks of pressure, Syria agreed to allow five senior officials to be interviewed by the UN investigator, Detlev Mehlis.

2006 The Danish and Norwegian embassies in Damascus were attacked after worldwide Muslim condemnations of cartoons depicting the Prophet Mohammed were published in a Danish newspaper. Syria and Iraq restored diplomatic relations after a 25-year gap and became an increasingly safe haven for those fleeing the war in Iraq.

2007 The dominant Ba'ath Party-led Al Jabha al Wataniyyah at Wahdwamiyyah (National Progressive Front) (NPF) coalition won parliamentary elections. Bashar al Assad's presidency was endorsed by referendum. Tough visa requirements were imposed on Iraqis, as the influx of refugees grew. Israel bombed and

destroyed what it claimed was a secret nuclear reactor.
2008 The US published satellite images of what was called Syria's secret plutonium-producing nuclear reactor, claiming North Korea had helped build it. The site was cleared before UN inspectors from the International Atomic Energy Agency (IAEA) visited the site. The preliminary investigation declared the results inconclusive. An agreement to improve diplomatic relations was reached and a common border to be formally demarcated between Lebanon and Syria agreed. In a move to recognise Lebanon's sovereignty and independence, Syria established full diplomatic relations with Lebanon, and established a new embassy in Beirut.
2009 The first high-level talks since 2005 between the US and Syria took place in Damascus. The Damascus securities exchange began trading stocks for the first time.
2010 A ban on smoking in enclosed public places such as restaurants and cafés was imposed in April; the ban includes the traditional *nargile* (hubble-bubble). In May, the US renewed its sanctions on Syria, first imposed in 2004, after President Obama said Syria continued to support terrorism and was pursuing development of weapons of mass destruction. A ban on the *niqab* (full face veil worn by Muslim women) was introduced in all Universities, both public and private, in July. The *hijab* (headscarf) was deemed acceptable. Lebanese Prime Minister Hariri visited in July to discuss bilateral relations and closer ties. On 6 September, Hariri stated that his accusation that Syria was responsible for the murder of his father was an error and that it was a 'political accusation'.
2011 Demonstrations against the Assad regime in the southern city of Deraa and the northern port of Latakia in March lead to concerns that they undermined the government's authority. On 29 March, the government resigned as a response to widespread discontent with the political system. Muhammad Naji Otari remained in post as caretaker prime minister. On 3 April President Assad asked former agriculture minister Adel Safar to form a new cabinet. President Assad issued a decree granting citizenship to tens of thousands of Kurds. The Kurds make up as much as 15 per cent of the population and had long demanded citizenship. President Assad announced a new cabinet on 15 April. On Syria's Independence Day (17 April) there were a number of protests in Aleppo, Deraa and Suweida. The army killed 10 people and arrested 499 men in house-to-house raids in Deraa on 1 May. Civil rights groups claimed 560 people had been killed by security forces in Syria since protests began against the al Assad regime on 18 March. On 18 May, the US imposed economic and travel sanctions on President Bashar al Assad, for human rights abuses since the civil unrest began. The US had already imposed sanctions on the brother and cousin of President Assad in April. On 8 June, France and the UK sponsored a resolution in the UN Security Council condemning Syria's use of violence to suppress its protestors. However, the resolution did not include a proposal to use military action if the condemnation was ignored. On 12 June the army attacked the town of Jisr al Shughour to 'restore security' after 120 security personnel had allegedly been killed on 6 June. Citizens fled either into the surrounding countryside or across the border into Turkey, where refugee camps were hastily set up; by 13 June over 5,000 people had found sanctuary. China, Russia and Brazil expressed their concerns over the proposed UN resolution of condemnation. President Assad's television speech on 20 June gave nothing new in the way of reforms and was greeted with scepticism by protesters. On 1 July, the largest anti-government demonstration in the country so far was held in Hama. As a result, the governor was sacked and security forces sent to the city. In early July Amnesty International called for an international investigation into the violence committed by the security forces, including crimes against humanity. The National Salvation Council, a 25-member body, including Islamists, liberals and independents, elected from a group of around 300 opposition activists, met in Istanbul on 17 July. On 25 July state media reported that the government had adopted a draft law allowing the formation of political parties other than the ruling Ba'ath party, providing they were not based on religion, tribal or regional support. Large anti-government protests in Hama on 29 July, with barricades thrown up at road entrances to the city, lead to the army attacking the city on 31 July and 1 August. Hundreds of protestors were reported to have been killed, following the shelling of the city by tanks. The government crackdown continued and by 5 August an estimated 2,000 people had been killed by troops. The US, Russia and Turkey warned President Bashar al Assad of the consequences of continued violence towards the people of Syria. World leaders joined together on 18 August and called on President Assad to step down, as the UN said that the excessive force used to suppress protests 'may amount to crimes against humanity'. A smoking ban was introduced for enclosed public spaces on 18 August, with a fine of Syr£100,000 (around US$2,100) for individuals and Syr£1 million (around US$210,000) for businesses transgressing. In early September, the EU banned imports of oil. On 15 September, a national council was formed including Kurds, Islamists, secularists and members of grassroots committees. Its given aims were to 'convey the Syrian people's just problems on the international platform, to form a pluralist and democratic state'. During a meeting in Istanbul (Turkey) on 1–2 October the newly combined opposition, the Syrian National Council (SNC), agreed to its structure and aims. The SNC, led by Chairman Burhan Ghalioun, will challenge the regime of President Bashar al Assad to bring about democracy in Syria. On 7 October Mishaal al Tammo, a Kurdish member of the opposition national council, was assassinated. On 14 October, the UN estimated that since March the number of people killed had exceeded 3,000 and that the authorities had 'manifestly failed to protect its population'. On 16 November the newly created Free Syrian Army (FSA) (of defecting soldiers), attacked an air force intelligence base in the suburbs of Damascus, in its most daring assault on government forces and installations to date. On 17 November, the Arab League issued a deadline for the government to 'stop the bloody repression' and begin 'real dialogue toward real reform' by 20 November or risk sanctions. On 28 November the Arab League imposed sanctions against Syria, which included curbs on transactions with the Syrian Central Bank and halting the funding of projects by the Arab League. The sanctions followed the failure of Syria to meet the deadline for allowing Arab League observers into the country to monitor anti-government protests. Syria responded by calling the actions a betrayal of Arab solidarity. On 30 November, Turkey imposed a number of sanctions against Syria that included suspension of financial dealing with and a freeze of assets of the Syrian government and a travel ban on the Syrian leadership; an arms ban is already in place.

Political structure

Constitution

The 1973 constitution was based on five principles: Syrian Arab revolution to achieve unity, freedom and socialism; Arab unity against the threat of imperialism and Zionism; socialism as a fundamental necessity; economic freedom and social liberalisation; Arab revolution towards world liberalisation.
Constitutional articles include a definition of Syria as an Arab state, with a planned socialist economy; that the state religion is Islamic and the Ba'ath party is the leading political party.

Independence date

17 April 1946

Form of state

Socialist democratic republic that has been run by a military regime since 1963.

The executive

The president is Head of State, and has almost absolute power as the country is a

one-party state with a disproportionate share of power in the hands of the Hizb al Ba'ath al Arabiyah al Ishtiraki (Ba'ath Party) (Socialist Arab Rebirth Party) and minority Alawite community.
Presidential candidates are nominated by parliament and agreed by referendum, for a seven-year term.
The president appoints and dismisses the vice presidents, the prime minister and the Council of Ministers. He holds the posts of commander-in-chief of the armed forces and secretary general of the Ba'ath Party. The Council of Ministers is headed by the prime minister and its members are appointed from the ruling party.

National legislature

The unicameral Majlis al Shaab (People's Council) has 250 members, directly elected in 15 multi-seat constituencies (in which the NPF is guaranteed 167 seats), for four-your terms. The assembly proposes the presidential candidate but may not initiate laws; it may assess and may occasionally modify those proposed by the executive branch.

Legal system

The judiciary is guaranteed independence under the constitution, however in practice, the minister of justice has the power to appoint, promote and transfer members of the judiciary and has undue influence. The legal system has separate religious and secular courts using *Sharia* (Islamic law) and a civil law code respectively.
Syria has not accepted compulsory International Court of Justice (ICJ) jurisdiction.

Last elections

22 April 2007 (parliamentary); 27 May 2007 (presidential (referendum))
Results: Parliamentary: Al-Jabha al-Wataniyyah at-Wahdwamiyyah (National Progressive Front) (NPF), a coalition of 10 parties led by Hizb al Ba'ath al Arabi al Ishtiraki (Ba'ath Party) (Arab Socialist Rebirth Party), won 169 seats (out of 250); 81 seats were won by independents. Turnout was 56.12 per cent.
Presidential: Bashar al Assad received 97.62 per cent of the vote. He was nominated by the ruling Ba'ath Party and ran unopposed.

Next elections

May 2011 (presidential); 2011 (parliamentary)

Political parties

Ruling party

Al Jabha al Wataniyyah at Wahdwamiyyah (National Progressive Front) (NPF), a coalition of 10 parties led by Hizb al Ba'ath al Arabi al Ishtiraki (Ba'ath Party) (Arab Socialist Rebirth Party) (re-elected Apr 2007)

Main opposition party

Most political opposition is severely repressed and leading critics of the government are in exile.

Population

20.13 million (2010)*
Last census: September 2004: 17,921,000
Population density: 104 inhabitants per square km. Urban population: 51 per cent of the total in 2006 (WHO 2008).
Annual growth rate: 2.7 per cent 2006 (WHO 2008)

Ethnic make-up

Arabs (90 per cent); Kurds, Armenians and Assyrians (10 per cent).

Religions

About 90 per cent of the population are Muslim with those of the Sunni denomination outnumbering Alawi (Shi'a) Muslims by about six to one. The remainder are Christian (8 per cent), Druze and Jewish (2 per cent). Religious freedom is provided by the constitution.

Education

Primary schooling lasts for six years. Secondary education, which begins at the age of 12, also lasts for six years and is divided into two three-year cycles. Students may either enter the general or the technical branches, although entry is selective and is based on the Intermediate Level Diploma (*al Kafa'a*) examination. The first cycle is introductory. Technical secondary education is divided into industrial and commercial tracks. There are agricultural and technical schools and four universities, at Damascus, Aleppo, Tishreen and Homs. All higher education institutions are state-controlled and state-financed.
Literacy rate: 80.8 per cent adult rate; 95 per cent youth rate (15–24) (latest figures WHO 2008, Unesco 2005).
Compulsory years: Six to 12.
Enrolment rate: 101 per cent gross primary enrolment, of relevant age group (including repeaters); 43 per cent gross secondary enrolment (World Bank).
Pupils per teacher: 23 in primary schools.

Health

Per capita total expenditure on health (2005) was US$61; of which per capita government spending was US$31, at the international dollar rate, (WHO 2008).
Improved souces of water are available to 89 per cent of the population.
Medical services are relatively well developed in larger towns and cities, with 14 hospital beds per 10,000 head of population, but there is considerable variation in rural areas.

HIV/Aids

HIV prevalence: 0.1 per cent aged 15–49 in 2003 (World Bank)
Life expectancy: 72 years, 2006 (WHO 2008)
Fertility rate/Maternal mortality rate: 3.2 births per woman, 2006; maternal mortality 130 deaths per 100,000 live births (WHO 2008).
Child (under 5 years) mortality rate (per 1,000): 13 per 1,000 live births (2006); 8.5 per cent of children aged under five are malnourished (WHO 2008).
Head of population per physician: 5 physicians per 10,000 people, 2006 (WHO 2008)

Welfare

The government maintains a basic range of social welfare provisions, including free healthcare for low-income groups, and is officially committed to improving the quality of state welfare provision as economic conditions allow. The government claims that the expansion of the private sector has led to more young children working.
The labour and social affairs minister is responsible for enforcing minimum wage levels in the public and private sectors.
The law does not protect temporary workers who are not subject to regulations on minimum wages.

Main cities

Damascus (capital, estimated population over 4.0 million in 2008), Aleppo (Halab) (4.3 million), Homs (1.4 million).

Media

Press

Dailies: The state runs four national and many regional newspapers with news contained in them provided by the Syrian Arab News Agency (SANA). In Arabic, *Al Thawra* (www.althawranews.net), has the largest circulation; *Al Baath* (http://albaath.online.fr) (official publication of the Ba'ath Party); *Tishreen* (www.tishreen.info) and in English *Syria Times* (http://syriatimes.tishreen.info). The first private, political daily newspaper to open since 1963 was *Al Watan* (www.al-watan.com).
Weeklies: In Arabic, *Tishreen al Osboi* a political magazine and *Mawkef al Riyadhi* (http://riadi.alwehda.gov.sy) covering sports news are government-run. *Star Syria* (www.star-sy.com) is a youth magazine.
Business: In Arabic, *Al Iqtissad wal Nagl* (www.aliqtisad.com) is a monthly magazine; *Al-Iqtissadiya (www.iqtissadiya.com) for business and political news.*
Periodicals: There are over 140 private magazines and others produced by government departments, state organisations, trade unions, political, professional and religious associations. In Arabic, *Al*

Arabieh and *Ayam Al Osrah* (www.ayam-mag.com) are women's magazines; *Al Maaloumatieh* is a consumer magazine. In Arabic and English, *Al Nashra al Ektisadyeh* (www.dcc-sy.com) is published by the Chamber of Commerce. In Arabic and French, *Ougarit* (www.ougarit.org) (quarterly) and *Maaber* (www.maaber.org) for culture and literature. In English, *Syria Today* (www.syria-today.com) for current affairs.

Broadcasting

Radio: The state radio service, Radio Sout Al Sha'ab (www.rtv.gov.sy) broadcasts domestic and external programmes in Arabic, French, English, Russian, German, Spanish, Portuguese, Polish, Turkish and Bulgarian. Private radio stations, all broadcasting from Damascus, include Farah FM (www.farah.fm), Rotana Style FM (www.rotana.net) and Syria Al Ghad (www.syriaalghad.com).

Television: Syrian television (www.rtv.gov.sy) operates two terrestrial channels and a satellite station. Many households subscribe to satellite television providers and the only private station based in Syria, Al Sham, competes for audiences with pan-Arab and Western (generally for expatriate communities) TV satellite stations.

The minster of information plans to license up to a further 24 private satellite television channels.

Advertising

All advertising is controlled by the Arab Advertising Organisation (AAO). There are restrictions on advertising alcohol, cigarettes and the use of women in commercials. Advertising is available in the press, public cinemas, on commercial TV and outdoors public spaces in main centres but carry government and municipal taxes. Direct mail is also available.

News agencies

National news agency: SANA

Other news agencies: All4Syria (www.all4syria.org).

Economy

The main sectors of an economy which is struggling to emerge from decades of over-centralisation and stagnation are agriculture and hydrocarbons. While agriculture accounts for around 25 per cent of GDP, involves a quarter of the population and ensures self-sufficiency in food, Syria has been dependent on its oil and gas reserves to sustain the economy. Hydrocarbons, which typically contribute 20 per cent to GDP, have been responsible for 65 per cent of exports and 50 per cent of government revenue. Production and exports, however, are falling as the existing fields decline. It is forecast that, in the absence of the discovery of significant new deposits in the meantime, Syria will become a net importer of oil by 2012 and run out of oil by 2020. Unless other activities are developed and foreign direct investment (FDI) attracted quickly, Syria could find itself relegated to the status of a low-income country.

The government is attempting to diversify and modernise the economy, but there are obstacles to be overcome. The economy has for several decades been under tight state control and while the need to introduce market-based practices has been acknowledged since the nineties, restructuring has been slow, impeded by vested interests, corruption and bureaucratic inertia. A number of reforms have been introduced, but only in recent years has the process been pursued with any vigour and much remains to be done. Dismantling the centralised controls and rationalising the regulatory system are essential to increase FDI, levels of which have been low and mainly from the oil and gas industry. The political uncertainty occasioned by Syria's international and regional relations, particularly US antagonism and close ties to Iran, add to the caution of potential investors. Reforms have stimulated growing interest, nevertheless, and there has been a growth in FDI from the Gulf states and Lebanon, themselves wary of investing in the West in the current political climate.

As the pace of reform has increased, particularly in the banking sector, where private banking has been allowed, the economy has shown improvements. Exports of manufactured goods have increased, while the services sector has done well, due mainly to the expansion of tourism. Around three-quarters of visitors to Syria come from the Gulf states, but the government, recognising the contribution tourism makes to the economy, is seeking to expand the sector and to construct infrastructure more suitable to a wider market. Increased FDI is essential for further development, as is a more benign political environment. Tourism is already next only to agriculture and oil in importance to the economy.

The economy is not keeping pace with the growth in population. The official unemployment figure was 9 per cent in 2008, but was probably higher. Around 75 per cent of the population is below the age of 35, and 40 per cent are aged below 15. For those in work, pay is low. An important source of income is remittances from the huge number of Syrians working abroad; currency transfer by expatriates is also an important source of foreign exchange for the government. A third of the population is estimated to live in varying degrees of poverty.

External trade

In 2005 the Greater Arab Free Trade Area (Gafta) was ratified by 17 members, including Syria, creating an Arab economic bloc. A customs union was established whereby tariffs within Gafta will be reduced by a percentage each year, until none remain. It is also a signatory of the Euro-Mediterranean Partnership agreement, which provides for the introduction of free trade between the EU and 10 Mediterranean countries by 2012.

Foreign trade provides almost 70 per cent of GDP and over 65 per cent of all exports are oil and its derivatives, and natural gas. As manufacturing provides only around 25 per cent of GDP, its importance to exports is less than that of agriculture which exports livestock and cereals and the majority of the annual cotton lint harvest not used domestically for spinning and garment production.

Imports

Major imports are capital machinery and vehicles, food and livestock, appliances, chemicals, plastics, various yarns and paper.

Main sources: Russia (typically 10 per cent of the total), China (7 per cent), Ukraine (5 per cent).

Exports

Main exports are crude oil, petroleum products, cotton, clothing, fruits, vegetables, wheat, meat and live animals.

Main destinations: Italy (typically 20 per cent of total), France (9 per cent), Saudi Arabia (9 per cent).

Agriculture

Farming

Agriculture remains a leading sector of the economy, contributing approximately 25 per cent to GDP and employing around a quarter of the labour force. Agricultural land is mainly privately owned. Approximately 31 per cent of the total land is cultivated. Much of Syria is mountainous and part of the eastern part of the country is desert or semi-desert. The fertile areas include the coastal strip and the Euphrates and Khabur valleys. Intensification of farming in the rain-fed areas is ongoing; these areas account for more than 80 per cent of the total crop area. The al Thaura dam on the Euphrates, built with Russian technology, brings irrigation to a vast area.

Main crops are cotton, wheat and barley. Wheat and barley together account for two-thirds of the cultivated area. Extreme fluctuations in grain production from year to year caused by rainfall variability have traditionally caused much hardship for the rural population. Cotton is the main cash crop. Other leading crops include vegetables, citrus fruits, olives, tobacco and sugar beet. Sheep and goats are grazed in many areas. Wool is also an important product.

Annual population growth in Syria is estimated at 3 per cent, and to ensure food security for its growing population, the government is focussing on a food self-sufficiency strategy, improving crop production technology and crop diversification.

Fishing

Syria's small annual fish catch is mostly destined for the domestic market.

Forestry

Syria is lightly forested with less than 3 per cent of forest or woodland cover. In ancient times, Syria had extensive mountain forests but these have largely been cleared or degraded and only remnants of mixed coniferous forest remain. The predominant species include *Abies cilicica, Pinus halipensis* and *Pinus brutia*. Syria has established a moderately large area of plantations based on cypress, pine and eucalyptus species. The country has a modest network of protected areas – State Forest Protection Zones provide the most substantive forest conservation measures. Syria produces very modest volumes of sawn timber, veneer, plywood and particleboard. The majority of demand for wood and paper products is met by imports.

Industry and manufacturing

In the mid-1960s the government began a policy of rapid industrialisation, especially in the areas of iron and steel and other heavy industries. Factories turn out a wide range of products, including tractors and television sets. In 2007 the state-owned Handasieh, in partnership with the Iranian car manufacturer Khodro Iran, began production of Syria's first, domestically built automobile.

Many of Syria's industries are agrarian-based, such as food processing and textiles. Sugar processing, an important activity, is mainly conducted by state-owned enterprises. The textile industry is the oldest-established, contributing approximately 15 per cent of export earnings. Other industries include cement, soap, glass, footwear, leather goods and brassware.

Tourism

Tourism is increasingly important, with Syria's magnificent castles and other historical sites attracting over one million tourists a year. Aleppo in the north has been designated a World Heritage Site. A peace agreement between Israel and its Arab neighbours, including Syria, is required for Syria to fully develop its tourist potential which derives from its close proximity to Western Europe, its Mediterranean coastline and its rich history and historical sites.

Tourism is geared to the Middle East market and is heavily concentrated in Damascus. Tourists are mainly Lebanese and Jordanian, although Syria is also popular with the French and citizens from the former Soviet Union. Tourists from other Arab countries account for some 75 per cent of total visitors. Iranian pilgrims are a significant tourist category who visit religious sites around Syria. American- and Canadian-Syrian visitors are also increasing.

Syria joined the Euromed Heritage Programme, a computerisation project, sponsored by the EU, which focusses on cultural tourists of archaeology, arts and history, promoting sites through the internet.

Mining

The mining sector contributes up to 10 per cent to GDP and employs around 5 per cent of the working population. Syria has large phosphate deposits which are used in its growing fertiliser industry. Approximately 76 per cent of phosphate mined is exported, with 10 per cent used at the Homs fertiliser factory. Other mineral resources include gypsum.

Hydrocarbons

Proven oil reserves totalled 2.5 billion barrels at the end of 2007; production was 394,000 barrels per day (bpd). The government plans to increase domestic consumption of natural gas, allowing more oil to be exported, if it can develop local gas resources and secure gas imports from regional sources. However, with fixed and subsidised oil prices, persuading the population to switch to gas may prove to be a painful process.

The Syrian Petroleum Company (SPC) is responsible for all upstream production and development, often in partnership with small to medium sized foreign oil companies. Further oil production will be intensified through enhanced oil recovery measures.

There are two state-owned oil refineries, in Baniyas and Homs, with a total capacity of 239,865bpd. The construction of three new refineries, with an additional 380,000bpd has been planned since 2005, but without tangible results in 2008. In December 2010, Syria and Venezuela signed a memo of understanding (MOU), for the joint development of the Froklos oil refinery, in eastern Homs. The refinery was originally planned in 2008, to process 140,000 barrels per day (bpd), at an estimated cost of US$5 billion to build. The MOU covers the work on planning, construction and operating the plant.

Total gas reserves were estimated at 0.28 trillion cubic metres (cum) at the end of 2008, when output was 5.5 billion cum.

The Syrian Gas Company (SGC) owns around 75 per cent of all domestic gas fields and is responsible for industry strategy, including the adoption of investor-friendly policies. There are ongoing international agreements for exploration and joint production of natural gas fields. The first commercial flows of natural gas began in April 2010, from the US$1.2 billion Ebla gas development, which includes the Ash Shaer and Cherrife developments of over 1,251 square kilometres. The Ebla facility, which includes a gas gathering and compression station, around 80km of gas pipeline and a gas treatment plant, is designed to produce 2.3 million cum per day, plus liquefied petroleum gas (LPG)

Syria is beginning to convert oil-fired electrical generating plants to natural gas, as oil stocks decline, but will be dependant on imported gas from other Middle Eastern countries.

There are several pipelines either in operation, under construction or being planned. A 32km gas pipeline, Gasyle 1, connecting the Syrian Banias gas pipeline to the Deir al Ammar Beddawi power plant in northern Lebanon was built to export Syrian gas, but political and economic considerations have changed its role and it is expected to become a spur of the natural gas pipeline running from Egyptian gas fields in Sinai to Jordan and Syria – with a possible extension to Turkey and Europe.

Coal is not produced but around 2,000 tonnes of coke per annum is imported.

Energy

Total installed generating capacity was 7,502MW in 2007, producing over 35 billion kilowatt hours (kWh). The government is promoting the rapid development of gas production for electricity generation and converting oil-fired electrical generating plants to natural gas. The Tishreen Power Plant will be expanded, following a contract signed in October 2009 with the Bharat Heavy Electricals Limited (BHEL) of India, to increase generating capacity by 400MW, at a cost of €300 million (US444.6 million). Two new generators of 200MW are scheduled to be installed by August 2012.

The state-run Public Establishment for Electricity Generation and Transmission (PEEGT) is responsible for generation and transmission and the Public Establishment for Distribution and Exploitation of Electrical Energy (PEDEEE) deals with sales and distribution. Annual growth in consumption has been 7 per cent and generating capacity must have an additional 3,500MW by 2010 to meet domestic demand. However, lack of investment has hampered efforts.

Power failures have been experienced during summer when drought conditions have suspended operation of the three hydroelectric power stations on the Euphrates River. Despite shortcomings in its system, Syria is a net exporter of electricity, being part of an integrated power grid linked to Jordan, Lebanon and Turkey.

Financial markets

Syria's first stock exchange since the 1960s opened for business on 9 March 2009, under the supervision of the Syrian Commission on Financial Markets and Securities, in a crucial step by government to liberalise the state-controlled economy. The Damascus Securities Exchange initially trades in six companies, on the two days a week it operates.

Stock exchange

Damascus Securities Exchange

Banking and insurance

A series of reforms since 2000 has included official approval of private banking, in joint ventures, with foreign equity limited to 49 per cent, to be sited in 'free zones'. The role and status of the central bank was redefined with the establishment of the Conseil Monétaire et de Crédit (CMC) (Monetary and Credit Council) which was established to supervise monetary policy and co-ordinate the activities of private banks. Restrictions on the trading of foreign currency and the need for a majority local partner will be a disincentive to a wider pool of potential participants.

Three Lebanese banks – Fransabank, Banque Européenne pour le Moyen Orient and Société Générale Libano-Européenne de Banque – opened branches in the free zones. Five other non-Syrian banks, including the Jordanian Arab Bank and Housing Bank for Trade and Finance (HBTF) were later given approval to begin trading.

The government has eased the ban on domestic nationals opening foreign currency accounts. Nevertheless this reform has been of limited benefit as it is still technically illegal to hold hard currency and most Syrians continue to channel their funds through Lebanese banks. The lack of domestic credit and the poor quality of Syria's banking sector represent a major hindrance to the development of the country's economy.

Central bank

Central Bank of Syria

Main financial centre

Damascus

Time

GMT plus two hour (daylight saving, April to October, GMT plus three hours)

Geography

Syria is bordered by Turkey to the north; by the Mediterranean Sea and northern Lebanon to the west; by Israel and Jordan to the south; and by Iraq to the east. Western Syria contains a series of mountain ranges, lying parallel to the Mediterranean. The northern range is separated from Syria's coastline by a narrow plain. The highest peak is Jabal ash Shaykh (Mount Hermon) in the extreme south-west of the country. To the east of the mountains, the Euphrates River crosses partly cultivatable plains in the north, while the central and southern areas consist mainly of desert plains.

Hemisphere

Northern

Climate

Syria has a moderate Mediterranean climate, four distinct seasons, and cloudless blue skies for the greater part of the year. Temperatures in autumn and spring range between 20 and 25 degrees Celsius (C), 30–35 degrees C in summer (May–September) and 5 to 10 degrees C in winter. Winter is generally moderate but wet in the coastal region and cold inland; summer is hot and dry inland, hot and humid on the coast.

Dress codes

Lightweight clothing is needed during the hottest months (May–September). Both men and women should dress discreetly in public.

Entry requirements

Passports

Passports are required by all and must be valid for at least a month from the date of visit. Passports that carry an Israeli visa are prohibited.

Visa

Required by all except Arab nationals. All visas should be acquired before travelling. Business visas require a letter of introduction and full itinerary along with the application. Contact the nearest consulate for further details.

Visa extensions are needed for visits over 15 days and can only be obtained from the Syria Immigration and Passport Administration.

Prohibited entry

Nationals of Israel, holders of passports with evidence of travel in Israel.

Currency advice/regulations

The import and export of local and foreign currency is limited to US$5,000 (or equivalent).

Travellers cheques are not widely accepted outside the main cities.

Customs

Personal items are duty-free. Gold jewellery must be declared on arrival.

Prohibited imports

Firearms, ammunition; birds and bird products.

Health (for visitors)

Medical services are well developed and many doctors speak English.

Mandatory precautions

A certificate of vaccination against yellow fever is required if travelling from an infected area.

Advisable precautions

Typhoid, tetanus, hepatitis A and polio immunisations are recommended, and anti-malaria precautions should be taken. There is a risk of rabies.

Hotels

Rooms are in short supply, and it is essential to book in advance. At first-class and international hotels, it will be necessary to pay in foreign currency (Arab nationals and resident foreigners exempted).

Hotels in Damascus are located close to most tourist attractions.

Credit cards

Credit cards are accepted in main business areas – contact the card provider for more details. Charge cards are not accepted.

Public holidays (national)

Fixed dates

1 Jan (New Year's Day), 8 Mar (Revolution Day), 21 Mar (Mothers' Day), 17 Apr (Independence Day), 1 May (Labour Day), 6 May (Martyrs' Day), 6 Oct (Liberation War Day), 25 Dec (Christmas Day). Holidays that fall at the weekend are taken later *in lieu*.

Variable dates

Eid al Adha (three days), Islamic New Year, Birth of the Prophet, Eid al Fitr (three days).

Islamic year 1433 (26 Nov 2011–14 Nov 2012): The Islamic year contains 354 or 355 days, with the result that Muslim feasts advance by 10–12 days against the Gregorian calendar. Dates of feasts vary according to the sighting of the new moon, so cannot be forecast exactly.

Working hours

Friday is the weekend break.

Banking

Sat–Thu: 0800–1400; early closing Thu.

Business

Sat–Thu: 0830–1430.

Government

Sat–Thu: 0830/0900–1300/1400, 1600/1700–1900/2000.

Shops

Sat–Thu: 0930–1400, 1630–2100 (summer); Sat–Thu: 0930–1400, 1600–2000 (winter).

Telecommunications

Mobile/cell phones

Two networks exist: GSM 900 and 1800

Electricity supply
220V, 50Hz AC with European, two-pin plugs.

Weights and measures
Metric system (local units also in use).

Social customs/useful tips
Appointments should be made in advance. Punctuality is appreciated. It is conventional to shake hands on meeting and taking leave. Sometimes a conference visit is a way of doing business. The host may hold several conversations with guests at the same time. It is not customary to start talking business immediately. At meetings it is polite to drink coffee or tea, when offered. It is useful for business cards to have Arabic translations on the reverse side. A few words of Arabic will be appreciated.
Smoking in cafes, restaurants and other public places, including educational institutions, health centres, sports halls, cinemas, theatres and public transport, was banned by presidential decree in October 2009. There is a fine of Syr£2,000 (US$46). The ban includes the hubble-bubble pipe.
Do not drink in public during Ramadan. Islamic customs should be respected. Shoes should be removed on entry to mosques. Women should dress modestly. It is the convention to use the right and not the left hand when shaking hands and passing or receiving anything.
Alcohol is available to visitors.
Do not photograph anything remotely connected with the armed forces, including radio transmission aerials, and remember that some Syrians, particularly in rural areas, may regard cameras with suspicion.
It is considered very impolite for men to sit next to women on buses.
The punishment for possession of drugs is life imprisonment. For drug trafficking, the death penalty applies.
Travellers cheques are generally accepted in the main cities although it is advisable to take US dollars as well. Accommodation in all hotels must be paid in hard currency, except one-star hotels. Food, beverages, telephone calls etc can be paid in local currency. It is illegal to change money on the streets. Only change money in recognised exchange shops, banks and hotels.

Security
Visitors should keep in touch with developments in the Middle East as any increase in regional tension might affect travel advice. Visitors are advised to carry identity documents at all times. Avoid driving outside the main cities at night.

Getting there
Air
National airline: Syrianair
International airport/s: Damascus International (DAM), 29km south-east of city, with banking, refreshments and duty-free shop. A bus service operates every 30 mins from 0600-2300, into the city centre.
Aleppo (ALP) 10km from city, with banking, refreshments and duty-free shop.
Taxis are available from both airports, and fares should be negotiated beforehand. Journey time into Damascus city centre is 30 minutes, and 20 minutes into Aleppo.
Airport tax: International departures: Syr£200, excluding transit passengers.
Surface
Road: From Istanbul via Ankara the E5 road runs to Damascus via Aleppo. From the east a road runs from Iran via Iraq, and used to be considered excellent, however border crossings are sometimes suspended. From the south the road from Aqaba, (the terminus of the E5) runs via Amman (Jordan), and includes stretches of motorway. Other roads include those from the Lebanon.
Service taxis are faster than buses and run between Damascus-Amman or Irbid (Jordan).
Rail: Routes link Syria with Istanbul and Ankara (Turkey) and Amman (Jordan). Sleeper-cars are available and all trains are air-conditioned.
There are rail lines running from northern Iraq to the Syrian coast, however services are sometimes suspended.
Water: Car ferries sail from Bodrum (Turkey), Rhodes, Heraklion, Santorini and Piraeus (Greece). Cruise ferries are run by Italian, Greek, Cypriot and Turkish companies, with sailings that vary from year to year. Passage may take up to three days. Ferries from Alexandria (Egypt) dock at the Lebanese port of Beirut – the distance to Damascus is shorter than via any Syrian port; visitors should check the viability of this route before travelling.
Main port/s: Latakia, Tartus and Banias.

Getting about
National transport
Air: There are internal flights by Syrianair between Damascus, Aleppo, Latakia, Qamishli and Deir ez-Zor.
Road: The 30,208km road network has some 22,500km of relatively good surfaced roads linking main centres.
Buses: Luxury couch services operate between major towns. Bus tickets, with assigned seats, should be bought prior to boarding. Qadmous, al Ahliah and al Ryan are private bus companies.
Minibuses serve smaller locations; they have no schedule and leave when full.
Microbuses are modern vans used on short routes between cities and on routes to small towns and villages. They are more comfortable than the minibuses and there is no standing room. Departures are more frequent but they are more expensive than the minibuses. Fares are usually paid on board.
Taxis: May be used to travel between cities as they are affordable; either negotiate a fare with the driver or check that the meter runs correctly. Long-haul service (shared) taxis are also available on the more popular routes, they cost more than microbuses but less than a personal taxi hire.
Rail: Two classes of rail service are available, with restaurant cars, sleeping carriages and air-conditioning. The railway links all the major cities and has a regular timetable, but it can be slow so it may not suit the business traveller.
City transport
Taxis: Yellow cabs in Damascus are expensive; always check the meter has been set. Fares are mostly by negotiation. Drivers do not expect a tip.
In other cities, fares are set by government departments.
Buses, trams & metro: From airport to city centre.
Car hire
Private cars are rarely available, but taxis are reasonably priced.

BUSINESS DIRECTORY

Telephone area codes
The international direct dialling (IDD) code for Syria is +963, followed by the area code and subscriber's number:

Aleppo	21	Latakia	41
Damascus	11	Raqqah	22
Hassakah	52	Tartous	43
Homs	31	Zabadani	13

Chambers of Commerce
Federation of Syrian Chambers of Commerce, Mousa bin Nosair Street, PO Box 5909, Damascus (tel: 333-7344; fax: 333-1127; fax: syr-trade@mail.syr; internet: www.fedcommsyr.org).

Aleppo Chamber of Commerce, Amir Palace Hotel Building, Bab Jnein Street, PO Box 1261, Aleppo (tel: 223-8236; fax: 221-3493; e-mail: alepchmb@mail.sy).

Aleppo Chamber of Industry, PO Box 1859, Aleppo (tel: 362-0600; fax: 362-0040; e-mail: alpindus@net.sy).

Damascus Chamber of Commerce, 126 Mouawiah Street, Hariqa, PO Box 1040, Damascus (tel: 221-1339; fax: 222-5874; e-mail: dcc@net.net).

Damascus Chamber of Industry, Mouawiah Street, PO Box 1305,

Damascus (tel: 221-5042; fax: 224-5981; e-mail: dci@mail.sy).

Damascus Countryside Chamber of Commerce, Bagdad Street, PO Box 5859, Damascus (tel: 231-5653; fax: 231-3798).

Banking

Agricultural Co-operative Bank; PO Box 4325, al Naanaa Garden, Damascus (tel: 221-3462, 222-139).

Commercial Bank of Syria (Banque Commerciale de Syrie) PO Box 933, Yousef Azmeh Square, Damascus (tel: 221-8890, 221-8891).

Industrial Bank; PO Box 7578, Almuhandiseen Building, Maisaloun Street, Damascus (tel: 222-8200).

Popular Credit Bank, PO Box 2841, Maisaloun Street, Damascus (tel: 222-7604, 221-8555).

Real Estate Bank, PO Box 2337, Y al Azme Square, Damascus (tel: 221-8602/3).

Central bank

Central Bank of Syria, PO Box 2254, 29 Ayar Street, Damascus (tel: 221-6581; fax: 245-5576).

Stock exchange

Damascus Securities Exchange: www.dse.gov.sy

Travel information

Syrianair, Syrian Arab Airlines, Youssef al Azmeh Square; PO Box 417, Damascus (tel: 223-1838, 223-2154; fax: 221-4923; internet: www.syriaair.com).

Ministry of tourism

Ministry of Tourism, Kwatli Street, Barada Bank, Damascus (tel: 221-0122/223-7940; fax: 224-2636; web: www.syriatourism.org).

Ministries

Ministry of Agriculture and Agrarian Reform, Sa'dallah Al Jaberi Street, Damascus (tel: 221-3613/222-2513; fax: 224-4078/224-4023; web: www.syrianagriculture.org).

Ministry of Al Awkaf, Rukeneddin, Damascus (tel: 441-9079/441-9080; fax: 419-969).

Ministry of Construction and Building, Sa'dallah al-Jaberi Street in Front of the Mail Center, Damascus (tel: 222-3595/ 222-7966/222-3196/222-3597).

Ministry of Communications, Al Salheyeh, Damascus (tel: 222-7033/34; fax: 224-6403).

Ministry of Culture, Al Rawda, George Haddad Street, Damascus (tel: 333-1556/333-8633/338-600; fax: 332-0804).

Ministry of Defense, Omayad Square, Damascus (tel: 777-0700/880-980/ 371-0980/372-0936).

Ministry of Economy and Foreign Trade, Maysaloun Street, Damascus (tel: 221-3514/221-3515; fax: 222-5695; web: www.syrecon.org).

Ministry of Education, Al Mazraa, Al Shahbandar Square, Damascus (tel: 444-4703/4/2/444-4800; fax: 442-0435).

Ministry of Electricity, Kwatli Street, Damascus (tel: 222-3086/222-9654; fax: 222-3686).

Ministry of Environment, Al Salheyeh, Damascus (tel: 222-2600/1/2/3/4; fax: 333-5645).

Ministry of Finance, Al Sabee Bahrat Square, Baghdad Street., Damascus (tel: 221-9600/1/2/3; fax: 222-4701).

Ministry of Foreign Affairs, Muhajereen, Shora Avenue, Damascus (tel: 333-1200/4/333-7200; fax: 332-0686).

Ministry of Health, Parliement Street, Damascus (tel: 333-9600/1/2; fax: 222-3085).

Ministry of Higher Education, Al Rawda, Kasem Amin Avenue, Damascus (tel: 333-0700/1/2/3; fax: 333-7719; web: www.syrianeducation.org).

Ministry of Housing and Utilities, Al-Salheyeh, Yousef Azmeh Square, Damascus (tel: 372-2552/221-7571/ 221-7572/372-2552; fax: 221-7570).

Ministry of Information, Mezzeh Autostrad, Dar al Ba'th Building, Damascus (tel: 666-4600/666-4601; fax: 662-0052; internet: www.moi-syria.com).

Ministry of the Interior, Al Bahsah Street, Damascus (tel: 223-8682/223-8683; fax: 224-6921).

Ministry of Justice, El-Nasre Street, Damascus (tel: 221-4105/220-302; fax: 224-6250).

Ministry of Industry, Maysaloun Street, Damascus (tel: 223-1834; fax: 223-1096; web: www.syrianindustry.org).

Ministry of the Interior, Al Shuhadaa Square, Damascus (tel: 221-1001/ 221-9401; fax: 222-3428).

Ministry of Irrigation, Fardoss Street, Damascus (tel: 221-2741/222-1400; fax: 332-0691).

Ministry of Petroleum and Mineral Resources, Adawi, Insha'at; PO Box 31483, Damascus (tel: 444-5610/445-1624; fax: 445-7786).

Ministry of Social Affairs and Labour, Al Salheyeh, Yousef Azmeh Square, Damascus (tel: 221-0355/222-5948; fax: 224-7499).

Ministry of Supply and Internal Trade, Al Salheyeh, Damascus (tel: 221-9044/221-9241; fax: 221-9803).

Ministry of Transport, Al Jalaa Street, Damascus (tel: 333-6801/2/3; fax: 332-3317; web: www.min-trans.net).

Syrian Cabinet of Ministers, Shahbandar Street, Damascus (tel: 222-600 /222-1000/211-0212).

Other useful addresses

British Embassy, Kotob Building, 11 Mohd Kurd Ali Street, Malki PO Box 37, Damascus (tel: 371-2561/3).

Cotton Marketing Organisation, BP 729, Rue Bab al araj, Aleppo (tel: 238-486).

General Organisation for Cement, PO Box 5265, Damascus (tel: 666-7000/3).

General Organisation for Chemicals and Foodstuffs, PO Box 893, Damascus (tel: 222-8521, 222-5421).

General Organisation for Engineering Industries, PO Box 3120, Damascus (tel: 212-1824/5).

General Organisation for Machinery and Equipment, PO Box 3130, Damascus (tel: 221-8223, 221-8156; fax: 221-1118).

General Organisation for Metals and Building Materials, PO Box 3136, Damascus (tel: 442-0941, 442-0944, 442-0948; fax: 442-0947).

General Organisation for Sugar, PO Box 429, Homs.

General Organisation for the Textile Industries, BP 620, Rue Fardoss, Damascus (tel: 221-6200, 222-7158; fax: 221-6201).

General Organisation for Trading and Distribution, PO Box 15, Damascus (tel: 221-0396).

General Organisation of Free Zones, PO Box 2790, Damascus (tel: 219-137).

International Centre for Agricultural Research in the Dry Areas, Box 5466, Aleppo.

Public Establishment for Distribution and Exploitation of Electric Energy, PO Box 35199, Damascus (tel: 224-5926, 222-3086, 222-9654).

Public Establishment for Electricity Generation and Transmission, PO Box 3386, Damascus (tel: 212-9795, 211-9935; fax: 222-9062).

Syrian Embassy (USA), 2215 Wyoming Avenue, NW, Washington DC 20008 (tel: (+1-202) 232-6313; fax: (+1-202) 234-9548; email: info@syrianembassy.org).

National news agency: SANA

Internet sites

Al Thawra newspaper: www.thawra.com

ArabNet: www.arab.net

Taiwan

KEY FACTS

Official name: Chung-hua Min-kuo (Republic of China)

Head of State: President Ma Ying-jeou (Kuomintang) (took office 20 May 2008)

Head of government: Prime Minister Wu Den-yih (Kuomintang) (from 10 Sep 2009)

Ruling party: Kuomintang (KMT) (Chinese Nationalist Party) (from 12 Jan 2008)

Area: 35,961 square km

Population: 23.20 million (2010)*

Capital: Taipei

Official language: Mandarin Chinese

Currency: Taiwanese dollar (T$) = 100 cents

Exchange rate: T$30.48 per US$ (Oct 2011)

GDP per capita: US$18,558 (2010)*

GDP real growth: 10.90% (2010)

GDP: US$429.80 billion (2010)*

Labour force: 10.92 million (2009)*

Unemployment: 5.85% (2009)

Inflation: 1.00% (2010)*

Balance of trade: US$29.30 billion (2009)

Foreign debt: US$79.80 billion (2009)*

* estimated figure

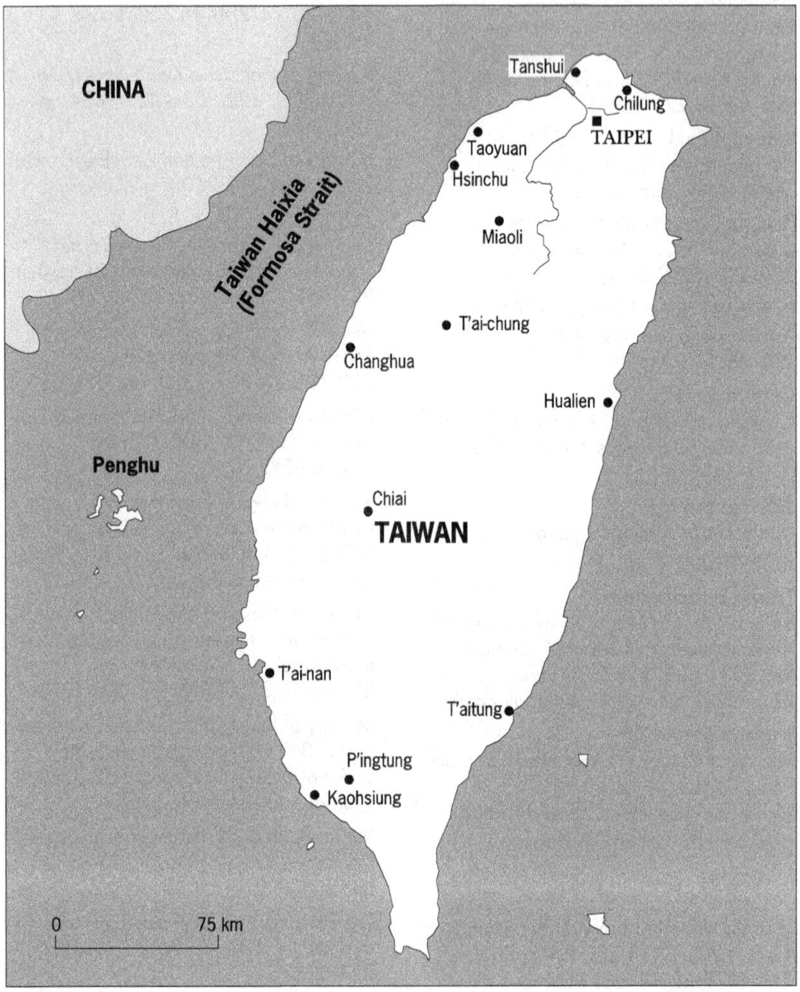

For decades, the island of Formosa, as it was formerly known, was an isolated, authoritarian one-party state ruled by the Kuomintang (KMT) (Nationalist Party), which under Chiang Kai-shek had controlled much of China before the Communists' rise to power in 1949. By 2011 Taiwan had some cause for satisfaction. The economic crisis that engulfed much of Asia in the late 1990's scarcely caused a ripple in the boardrooms of Taipei. The Taiwanese enjoy one of Asia's highest living standards. The Republic of China (ROC) (Taiwan) is a net exporter of capital to the region and Taiwanese companies are themselves seen with increasing frequency on the regional and global business stage. Furthermore, Taiwan's foreign exchange reserves are the third highest of any country in the world. It is one of Asia's powerhouses and a centre for hi-tech exports.

Taiwan has made great strides over the past ten years to open its domestic economy to international competition. For both commercial and strategic reasons, it has sought a role for itself as a regional hub and an alternative centre to Hong Kong and Shanghai from which to develop the People's Republic of China (PRC) (China) market. Lack of direct transportation links with the mainland continue to hamper its efforts in this regard, but there has been rapid progress in other areas that are not dependent on direct links with the mainland.

Taiwan has not, however, succeeded in its bid to establish itself as a regional financial centre, but has none the less become an important market in its own right. Taiwan's industry is becoming increasingly dependent on the export of higher value-added products and is a major purchaser of industrial plant and equipment. Major infrastructure projects underway in the telecommunications, energy and transportation sectors provide opportunities for foreign engineering and technology-based companies. An affluent and fashion conscious population of just over 23 million with a high propensity to spend, provides a growing consumer market. Increasingly, the younger generation takes its cue from Japan rather than the US.

Long-standing tension with the mainland has eased since the China-friendly President Ma Ying-jeou took office in May 2008. In July 2009 the leaders of China and Taiwan had exchanged direct messages for the first time in more than 60 years, albeit in their respective party functions and not as national leaders. And in June 2010, the two countries signed an historic trade pact that was described by some analysts as the most significant agreement in 60 years of separation. Mr Ma's predecessor, Chen Shui-bian, had angered China with moves towards formal independence and relations had been severely strained.

Despite the recent thaw, Taiwanese officials complain that Beijing has kept increasing the number of short-range missiles aimed at Taiwan. In the past the military threat from the mainland has been partly offset by the pivotal relationship between Taipei and Washington, which is the main weapons supplier to the island – one of the world's biggest buyers of arms. Beijing regularly expresses anger at US arms sales to Taiwan.

China insists that nations cannot have official relations with both China and Taiwan, with the result that Taiwan has formal diplomatic ties with only some two dozen countries – Pacific, Latin American and African states in the main. Taiwan has no seat at the United Nations, having lost it to China in 1971. Repeated attempts to regain representation at the UN have been blocked.

Despite its diplomatic isolation, Taiwan has become one of Asia's big traders. It is considered to have achieved an economic miracle, becoming one of the world's top producers of computer technology. And past tensions notwithstanding, Taiwan and China enjoy healthy trade links. China is Taipei's number one export market.

The economy

Taiwan's economy is driven by foreign trade and particularly by exports to the US, Japan and Europe. In the past decade, however, China has become the largest export market. During this period, the drivers of growth have been the semiconductor and related electronics industries; now there is a new emphasis on the emerging 'sunrise opportunities' in the biosciences and nanotechnology. Much of the required technology comes from overseas – like the Japanese before them, the Taiwanese are good at adapting foreign products, but less efficient when it comes to innovation and research.

According to the Asian Development Bank (ADB) Taiwan's trade-dependent economy had already rebounded vigorously from recession in 2009. Surging demand for its manufactured exports in 2010 drove a burst of investment and supported increased private consumption. The 10.8 per cent rise in gross domestic product (GDP) – the fastest in almost a quarter century – was partly a result of the low-base effect from the contraction in the previous year.

Private investment soared by nearly 33 per cent in 2010, after contracting in 2009, with substantial increases in manufacturing, information and communications and construction. Public investment also rose, albeit modestly, as the authorities continued with infrastructure spending, including reconstruction in areas hit by the severe Typhoon Morakot of August 2009. Overall, higher gross fixed capital formation contributed most of the boost to GDP in 2010 (6.1 percentage points of the total).

Rebounding exports and manufacturing spurred employment and income growth, in turn buttressing private consumption. Unemployment declined to 4.7 per cent by end-year, from 5.7 per cent the previous year. Real average monthly earnings in manufacturing rose by 7.5 per cent in 2010, after declines in the two previous years. The stronger labour market buoyed consumer confidence. Private consumption grew by 3.7 per cent in 2010 and added 2.1 percentage points to GDP growth.

Sectorally, growth was dominated by manufacturing (constituting about 84 per cent of industry), which surged by 26.8 per cent and contributed 7.2 percentage points to GDP growth. Construction increased by 10.9 per cent, though its contribution to GDP was slight, as it is a much smaller industry. Services grew by 4.8 per cent, with wholesale and retail trading the major contributors to growth in this sector.

International trade

Strong global demand for manufactured goods drove growth of nearly 40 per cent in exports of electronic products and chemicals and increases of over 30 per cent in metal products and plastics. Total exports shot up by nearly 35 per cent in US dollar terms. The major markets were Hong Kong, China and the US, which collectively took 53 per cent of total.

Merchandise imports bounced back even more, by 43.2 per cent, fuelled by imported materials for manufacturing industries and capital goods required by the investment boom. The merchandise trade surplus therefore fell by 12 per cent to US$26.9 billion. After accounting for small surpluses in

KEY INDICATORS — **Taiwan**

	Unit	2006	2007	2008	2009	2010
Population	m	22.88	22.96	23.04	23.12	*23.20
Gross domestic product (GDP)	US$bn	365.51	383.31	402.70	377.50	*429.80
GDP per capita	US$	15,978	16,606	17,480	16,326	*18,558
GDP real growth	%	4.9	5.7	0.7	-1.9	10.9
Inflation	%	0.6	1.8	3.5	-0.9	*1.0
Unemployment	%	3.9	3.9	4.1	*5.9	–
Exports (fob) (goods)	US$m	223,789.0	219,252.0	255,629.0	203,675.0	–
Imports (fob) (goods)	US$m	200,375.0	219,252.0	240,448.0	174,371.0	–
Balance of trade	US$m	23,414.0	27,425.0	15,181.0	29,304.0	–
Current account	US$m	24,661.0	31,701.0	25,122.0	42,911.0	40,617.0
Foreign debt	US$bn	91.6	93.1	97.8	*79.8	–
Exchange rate	per US$	32.52	32.38	32.95	31.90	31.79

* estimated figure

services and income, the current account surplus declined, to a still significant 9.4 per cent of GDP. The overall balance of payments was in surplus and international reserves rose to US$382 billion by end-2010.

On the back of tighter economic links with China through the Economic Co-operation Framework Agreement (ECFA) signed in 2010 and abundant global liquidity, short-term portfolio inflows picked up and reached US$10 billion in the fourth quarter of 2010. A rapid increase in purchases of government bonds by foreign institutional investors, speculating on an appreciation of the Taiwan dollar, prompted the monetary authorities in November 2010 to put limits on short-term debt that foreigners can hold. The local currency appreciated against the US dollar from T$35.2 in March 2009 to T$29.1 by end-2010.

Consumer prices also rose in 2010, although average inflation was just 1.0 per cent. Of greater concern was a surge in residential property prices caused mainly by speculative buying. The authorities moved to curb bank lending for second homes and directed banks to reduce loan-to-valuation ratios for such properties, which helped to dampen speculation.

Government expenditure fell by 0.8 per cent in 2010 from 2009, as the authorities gradually withdrew 2009's fiscal stimulus measures. Revenue also declined, by 0.4 per cent and the budget deficit narrowed only slightly in terms of the ratio to GDP, to 3.2 per cent from 3.5 per cent in 2009. Outstanding government debt rose to 33.6 per cent of GDP, though still below a 40 per cent limit set by law.

Further growth in world trade in 2011 (though moderating from 2010's sharp rebound) and the continuing expansion of the Chinese economy will underpin growth in 2011. The pace will be around trend, however, as the base effect from the 2009 recession that propelled the 2010 outturn dissipates. Growth is expected to be broad-based, with contributions from both domestic and external demand.

The ECFA with China will also support growth –China and Hong Kong together account for about 40 per cent of Taiwan's exports. The first set of tariff reductions under the agreement came into effect in January 2011. Nearly 2,000 certificates of origin valued at over US$400 million, about 5 per cent of merchandise exports to China, were issued in January–February 2011 for Taiwanese products that receive preferential duties from China.

The number of visitors from across the strait surged by 68 per cent in 2010 and further growth in inbound travel is expected as more tourist groups from China are allowed to visit in 2011 and 2012.

Growth in export orders for manufactured goods (such as mobile telephones and tablet computers) moderated to about 5 per cent in the first 2 months of 2011 compared with the prior-year period. Merchandise exports increased by about 21 per cent in January–February 2011, year on year.

Private consumption is expected to grow by 1.2 per cent in 2011, against the background of a firm labour market. Businesses in sectors with strong external demand – semiconductors and telecommunications equipment for example – are likely to increase investment, but private investment overall is projected to contract by 2.3 per cent from the high base set in 2010.

GDP is forecast by the ADB to grow by 4.8 per cent in 2011 and about 5.0 per cent in 2012. In the view of the ADB, the downside risks to this outlook come from higher than expected global oil and commodity prices, any significant slowdown in China and a prolonged supply disruption to manufactured components from plants in Japan affected by the March 2011 earthquake and *tsunami*.

Risk assessment

Economy	Good
Politics	Fair
Regional stability	Fair

COUNTRY PROFILE

Historical profile

Before the arrival of the Europeans, the island was occupied by indigenous people and immigrants from mainland China.

1590 Portuguese navigators discovered Taiwan and called it *Ilha Formosa*, meaning 'beautiful island' in Portuguese. This is the origin of Taiwan's other name, Formosa.

1624 The Dutch arrived in Taiwan.

1629 The Spaniards, alarmed by growing Dutch control of Taiwan, arrived and occupied the northern part of the island.

1630 The Dutch formally settled on the island.

1630–62 The Dutch and Spanish fought for control of the island. The Spanish were defeated and driven out. The Dutch strengthened their control after the establishment of the Dutch East India Company and Taiwan became an important trading centre. Chinese resistance eventually grew so strong that the Dutch were driven off the island.

1700–1800 Chinese mass migration to the island took place.

1885 Taiwan was officially made a province of China.

1895 China ceded control of Taiwan to Japan following the Sino-Japanese war. The Japanese modernised the country, upgrading infrastructure, restoring the communications network and developing agriculture.

1945 After Japan's defeat in the Second World War, Taiwan became a province of the Republic of China, controlled by the Kuomintang (KMT) (Chinese Nationalist Party).

1949 The KMT was driven out of the mainland by the communist People's Liberation Army (PLA) led by Mao Zedong. President Chiang Kai-shek withdrew his forces to Taiwan. The KMT asserted that it, rather than the new People's Republic of China, constituted the rightful government of mainland China and that it would eventually resume control of all of China.

1954 The US signed a security agreement with the KMT pledging to protect Taiwan.

1971 The People's Republic of China replaced Taiwan as Chinese representatives at the UN.

1975 Chiang Kai-Shek died. His son, Chiang Ching-kuo, became president.

1987 Martial law and one-party rule were dismantled.

1988 After the death of President Chiang Ching-kuo, Taiwan-born Lee Teng-hui became president.

1994 Nationwide local elections were held. The KMT retained its dominance of the political system, although the candidate of the opposition Min-chu Chin-pu Tang (MCT) (Democratic Progressive Party), Chen Shui-bian, was elected mayor of Taipei.

1995 The KMT lost ground to the MCT in the legislative elections.

1996 President Lee Teng-hui comfortably won Taiwan's first direct presidential elections.

1998 The KMT was re-elected, with an increased majority.

1999 Taiwan suffered its worst earthquake for nearly 100 years.

2000 Chen Shui-bian (MCT) became president.

2001 The pro-independence MCT won the parliamentary elections; the KMT lost its majority for the first time in 50 years.

2002 Taiwan joined the World Trade Organisation. Laws were enacted to put the military under the control of the civilian cabinet. President Chen Shui-bian took over the leadership of the MCT.

2004 President Chen Shui-bian (MCT), was re-elected, having survived an assassination attempt on the eve of the elections. Although President Chen's pro-independence Min-chu Chin-pu Tang MCT won the single largest number of seats in the general elections, it narrowly failed to take control of parliament.

2005 Mainland China's National People's Congress passed an anti-secession law, enshrining Beijing's claim of sovereignty and its threat of military force in the event of Taiwan's formal independence; more than one million people took to the streets in Taiwan to express opposition to the law.
2006 Following the defeat of the MCT in local elections, Prime Minister Hsieh resigned and was replaced by Su Tseng-chang. A referendum on the president's suitability for office, following corruption scandals involving the president's family and entourage, led to President Chen devolving some powers to the prime minister's office. The president's wife appeared in court on corruption charges.
2007 Su Tseng-chang resigned and Chang Chun-hsiung was appointed as prime minister. Costa Rica broke diplomatic ties with Taiwan in favour of China and its potential investment in Costa Rica. The UN rejected Taiwan's application for membership.
2008 Electoral reforms were enacted that reduced the number of Legislative Yuan seats. In parliamentary elections the opposition Kuomintang (of the Pan-Blue Coalition) won 81 seats (out of 113), with 72 per cent of the vote. The ruling MCT (Pan-Green Coalition) only managed 27 seats and resulted in President Chen stepping down as leader of the MCT. In presidential elections, Ma Ying-Jeou (Kuomintang) won 58.46 per cent of the vote; Frank Hsieh (MCT) won 41.55 per cent. Ma Ying- Jeou took office as president and appointed Liu Chao-shiuan as prime minister. In formal talks with China (they had been suspended since 1999) an agreement to allow 36 direct flights (18 each) a week between the two countries was signed; a further agreement allowed 3,000 tourists per day to visit each country.
2009 Former president, Chen Shui-bian was sent to trial on embezzlement, bribe-taking and money laundering charges. China and Taiwan agreed to a wide-ranging trade agreement. Typhoon Morakot struck over three days, setting off huge mudslides and leaving around 700 people dead or missing. Premier Liu Chao-shiuan resigned following widespread criticism of his government's response to Typhoon Morakot; Wu Den-yih replaced him.
2010 The Taiwan Strait Tourism Association opened an office in Beijing in May. Although classified as 'non-governmental' it was the first Taiwanese office to open in mainland China since 1949. A landmark trade deal with China was signed on 29 June, which sparked a protest that grew into a brawl in parliament and landed two members in hospital with injuries. In local elections held in December, the president's party won three of five mayoral seats, although the opposition won more of the popular vote. The elections were seen as a test for the president's economic policy towards China.
2011 On 30 June, former president Lee Teng-hui was charged with embezzling US$7.79 million of state funds over 1988–2000.

Political structure

Constitution

The Legislative Yuan, presided over by the prime minister, is the highest government body. It is responsible for passing laws and drafting the budget. It is elected every three years and has the power to dismiss the prime minister.
The 29-member Control Yuan exercises powers of investigation, impeachment and censure over senior officials, including the grand justices of the Judicial Yuan and members of the Examination Yuan, and power of audit over central and local government finances. Its members are appointed by the president with the approval of the legislature.
The Examination Yuan supervises examinations for entry into public office and deals with personnel questions of the civil service.
The Kuo-min Ta-hui (National Assembly) passed a series of constitutional amendments in April 2000 which reduced itself to an *ad hoc* institution deprived of most of its powers. The powers of initiating constitutional amendments, changing the national boundaries, impeaching the president or vice president and approving the appointment of senior officials, were transferred to the Legislative Yuan. The Kuo-min Ta-hui retains the functions of ratifying constitutional amendments and impeachment proceedings against the president.
The National Assembly is to convene for a month from no later than 31 May 2005 to vote on whether public referenda could be used to change the constitution, which means the abolition of the Assembly itself. Other constitutional amendments slated to go before the Assembly are plans to streamline the Legislative Yuan by halving the number of seats from 225 to 113, beginning from 2007, and the extension of legislators' terms from three to four years and whether it should hand over to grand justices the rights to impeach the president.

Form of state

Representative democracy

The executive

The president is directly elected for a four-year term. The president nominates a prime minister to head the Executive Yuan (cabinet), which is the highest administrative organ of the nation, and is responsible to the Legislative Yuan. The Executive Yuan consists of the ministries and commissions and 19 subordinate administrative organs of state.

National legislature

The unicameral Lì fa Yuàn (Legislative Yuan) has 113 members, of which 73 are directly elected by majority votes in single-seat constituencies, 34 are elected by proportional representation from party lists (50 per cent of seats must be allocated to women) and six are reserved for indigenous (aboriginal) people. All members serve for four-year terms.

Legal system

The Judicial Yuan is the highest judicial organ of state. Justices are appointed by the president with the approval of the Control Yuan. Subordinate organs of the Judicial Yuan include the Supreme Court, the high courts, the district courts, the Administrative Court and the Commission on the Disciplinary Sanctions of Public Functionaries.

Last elections

12 January 2008 (parliamentary); 22 March 2008 (presidential).
Results: Parliamentary: KMT won 72 per cent of the vote (81 seats out of 113), the MCT 23.9 per cent (27); 34 seats were allocated on a party list system and six seats were reserved for ethnic minorities. Presidential: Ma Ying-Jeou (Kuomintang) won 58.46 per cent of the vote, Frank Hsieh (MCT) 41.55 per cent; turnout was 76.33 per cent.

Next elections

2012 (parliamentary and presidential)

Political parties

Ruling party

Kuomintang (KMT) (Chinese Nationalist Party) (from 12 Jan 2008)

Main opposition party

Min-chu Chin-pu Tang (MCT) (Democratic Progressive Party)

Population

23.20 million (2010)*

Population density: 640 inhabitants per square km (2010)

Annual growth rate: 0.9 per cent (2010)

Ethnic make-up

Taiwan's population is mostly ethnic Han Chinese. A majority of these are local Taiwanese, who have language links to Fujian province across the Taiwan Strait. There is a powerful minority of immigrants that came from the mainland during the 1940s, as well as a Hakka minority. Taiwan's non-Han aborigines (yuanchumin) are related to the Polynesian and Malay ethnic groups. They comprise dozens of distinct groups, including the Rukai tribe (about 8,000 strong) and the Clouded Leopard People. They have limited rights and may not sell or develop lands. Indigenous rights groups have campaigned to regain political and economic autonomy in the aboriginal territories that were demarcated during the Japanese occupation.

Religions

The majority of people are Buddhist or Taoist with Confucian influence. Most Chinese make no sharp distinction between Buddhism and Taoism in Taiwan, and most practise a hybrid of these two religions. About 2.5 per cent of the population are Christian.

Education

There are 2,600 primary schools with a total enrolment around two million students. Primary school lasts for six years before entry to junior high school, at aged 12, for three years. Dependent on exam results at aged 15, students may move on to either a senior vocational high school or a senior high school (for more academic courses which lead to entrance exams for higher education). There are 986 secondary schools and 188 vocational institutions.

All education is delivered in Chinese however English is a compulsory subject during the secondary cycles. Higher education is offered at colleges and universities from aged 18. The total number of universities and colleges is 150 and the gross enrolment of graduates aged between 18 and 21 years is nearly 70 per cent per cent.

Compulsory years: Six to 15.

Pupils per teacher: 19 in primary school.

Health

Taiwan's public health sector offers a universal health insurance system, the first in Asia to ensure equal access to care for the entire population. Total expenditure on health per capita is approaching developed country standards.

Taiwan has 700 hospitals and 17,000 clinics and an active pharmaceutical industry.

Life expectancy: 77 years (government statistics, 2004).

Fertility rate/Maternal mortality rate: 1.4 births per woman; maternal mortality 7.86 per 100,000 live births (Government statistics).

Birth rate/Death rate: 3.25 per 1,000 (Government statistics).

Child (under 5 years) mortality rate (per 1,000): 6.7 per 1,000 live births (2003)

Welfare

The welfare policy is not universal but is budgeted according to the county or city governments. There is provision for special subsidies and assistance to low-income earners and families, based on variations in regional income distribution for each fiscal year. Some low-income families with children qualify for an additional monthly subsidy.

The elderly comprise a growing proportion of the population. Pensioners (aged from 65 years) of Taipei City and County, Ilan, Hsinchu, Tainan, Chiayi City, Kaohsiung and Penghu counties benefit from organised pension systems. There is serious shortage of housing for elderly people, despite Taiwan's 350 retirement and nursing homes.

Main cities

Taipei (capital, estimated population 2.6 million in 2005), Kaohsiung (1.6 million), Taichung (1.0 million), Tainan (755,800), Panchiao (589,700).

Languages spoken

The second language spoken is Fukienese, a dialect of Mandarin, but very different to it, that is spoken in the Fujian province in China. Fukienese is also called Taiwanese. Other Chinese dialects spoken are Shanghaiese, Hakka and Cantonese. English is spoken only by the elite.

Official language/s

Mandarin Chinese

Media

Press

Dailies: In Chinese, *United Daily News* (http://udn.com), *China Times* (http://news.chinatimes.com), *Liberty Times* (www.libertytimes.com.tw), *Central Daily News* and the *Taiwan Daily*. In English, *The China Post* (www.chinapost.com.tw), *Taiwan News* (www.etaiwannews.com) and *Taipei Times* (www.taipeitimes.com). Local newspapers, in Chinese include *Apple Daily* (http://1-apple.com.tw), and *Taiwan Shin Sheng Daily News* (www.tssdnews.com.tw) from Taipei and *Keng Sheng Daily News* (www.ksnews.com.tw), from Hualien.

Business: In Chinese and English, *Taiwan Economic News* (http://cens.com) and *CommonWealth* (www.cw.com.tw) (monthly) specifically deal with business and financial news. Major newspapers have business sections and the government publishes *Taiwan Journal* (http://taiwanjournal.nat.gov.tw) with information on trade and statistics and *Invest in Taiwan* (http://investintaiwan.nat.gov.tw) with information on local industries.

Periodicals: In English and published by the government, *Taiwan Panorama* (www.taiwan-panorama.com) and *Taiwan Review* (http://taiwanreview.nat.gov.tw) are news and general interest monthlies.

Broadcasting

The Central Broadcasting System (CBS) is the national broadcaster for Taiwan.

Radio: The RTI (Radio Taiwan International) broadcasts nationally and to mainland China. External services are relayed worldwide in up to10 languages.

There are over 170 radio stations, which cater for specific musical genres. UFO Network is one of the most popular private radio station, others include Hit FM (www.hitfm.com.tw) and Kiss Radio Taiwan (www.kiss.com.tw). The only English language station is ICRT FM (www.uforadio.com.tw).

Television: There are three state-owned TV networks (www.pts.org.tw) but most households subscribe to cable TV.

Advertising

A full range of advertising opportunities are available.

News agencies

National news agency: Central News Agency (www.cna.com.tw).

Economy

The structure of the economy reflects the nature of Taiwan's economy, with over 70 per cent of GDP in services, which is underpinned by its entrepreneurial businessmen who invest widely in the Asian region, and its manufacturing exports at over 25 per cent of GDP. With a limited amount of agricultural land available agriculture accounts for less than 2 per cent of GDP.

Taiwan is one the world's leading manufacturers of computers and computer components as well as other electronic consumer goods. However to maintain its manufacturing base Taiwan has to import not only the necessary raw materials for manufacturing but also primary goods in foodstuffs and fuel for its population.

GDP growth was 6.0 per cent in 2007, falling to 0.7 per cent by 2008 as the global economic crisis hit and bank lending was cut, limiting credit and funds for investment. Taiwan did not officially enter recession until 2009 when GDP growth fell to -1.9 per cent; Taiwanese workers were quickly laid-off and capital spending halted as worldwide trade slowed down and the government had to introduce measures to boost the economy, aiming at an annual average growth of 5 per cent over 2009–12. GDP growth soared to 10.9 per cent in 2010, as a result of surging sales of computer components to China. Private investment and consumer confidence were also cited as two of the key drivers of growth.

Political tensions between Taiwan and China have eased since the election of the Koumintang political party in 2008, which undertook to improve their relationship. Taiwan signed a free trade agreement (FTA) with China on 29 June 2010, which cut tariffs on 539 products exported to China (valued at US$13.84 billion), with tariffs on 267 Chinese products exported to Taiwan also cut (valued at US$2.86 billion). The FTA not only has an economic benefit for Taiwan, but politically it eases tension between the two countries.

External trade

Taiwan belongs to the 21-member Asia-Pacific Economic Co-operation (Apec) forum, which is a bloc of countries that border the Pacific with the aim of facilitating trade, economic growth and investment in the region. Taiwan is also a member of the World Trade Organisation (WTO) and an observer member of the Organisation of Economic Co-operation and Development (OECD). Taiwan signed a free trade agreement (FTA) with China on 29 June 2010, which cut tariffs on 539 products exported to China, while tariffs on 267 Chinese products exported to Taiwan were also cut.

The manufacturing sector accounts for over 25 per cent of GDP. Taiwan is a leading global producer of hi-tech goods and the largest supplier of semi-conductors, telecommunication equipment, computers and monitors and optical disks (DVDs). Industrial production includes polycarbonates, refined petroleum and vehicle assembly. With few natural resources it has to import most of its energy needs and raw materials. Nevertheless, the balance of trade is kept level by the high volume of Taiwanese exports.

Imports

Imports are dominated by raw materials, machinery and electrical equipment (around 45 per cent of total), coal, crude oil and natural gas.

Main sources: Japan (typically 21 per cent of total), China (14 per cent), US (10 per cent).

Exports

Main export commodities are electronics, computers and monitors, textiles, refined oil and derivatives, polycarbonates and vehicles.

Main destinations: China (typically 26 per cent of total), Hong Kong (14 per cent), US (12 per cent).

Agriculture

Farming

The agriculture sector contributes 2 per cent to GDP. Taiwan has refocussed its agricultural objectives by reducing its workforce to 633,000 workers and placing an emphasis on quality of food rather than quantity. Taiwan's farm plots are generally small, hindering cost-efficient management. Estimates show that 76 per cent of all farming households have less than one hectare (ha) of arable landand 80 per cent have members working part- or full-time in other occupations.

Rice is still the principal and most valuable crop (in quantiy and cultivated land), followed by betel nuts, pineapples, mangoes, sugar cane, watermelons, tea, bamboo shoots, pears, and peanuts. Industrial crops include cotton, hemp and jute.

Fishing

The fishing industry has gradually developed from small-scale coastal fishing to deep-sea commercial fishing. The deep-water fishing industry is large and expanding, supplemented by aquaculture. Eel is an important aquacultural product as are milkfish, tilapia, groupers, tiger prawn and oyster. Intense aqcuaculture has done some damage to the environment by drawing off huge amounts of water. This has caused land to cave in. The government is tackling the problem by encouraging the recycling of freshwater. The government has been actively engaged in international fishery management and has signed official or private fishery agreements with 29 countries.

The annual fish catch in Taiwan is typically 1.4 million tonnes.

Following the annual meeting of the Commission for the Conservation of Southern Bluefin Tuna (CCSBT), held on Cheju Island, South Korea, all members agreed to a 20 per cut in the roughly 17,000 tonnes in 2009 bluefin tuna catches from 2010. Scientists had warned that without a cut fish stocks could crash as numbers had become dangerously low.

Forestry

The timber industry is limited by inaccessibility, the poor quality of much of the forestry resources and by an official policy of conserving supplies. Taiwan's forested area covers around 2.1 million hectares, which is about half the land area. Forestry products include sawn timber, plywood, paper and fuel for local use.

Industry and manufacturing

The industrial sector contributes around 35 per cent to GDP, with manufacturing accounting for 95 per cent of industrial exports. Heavy industries include motor manufacturing, steel production and shipbuilding. Taiwan's main strength is its high-tech industry. In recent years, Taiwan has moved away from manufacturing electronic toys, deemed to be unhealthy for children, and focussed on electronic components. Most production is exported, accounting for an estimated 55 per cent of total exports and 20 per cent of GDP. The government is hoping to develop Taiwan into a green silicon island. The Taiwan Industrial Technology Association (TITA) was set up to upgrade industries. TITA invests in developing industries such as optoelectronics, aerospace, chemicals, semiconductors, telecommunications and information technology (IT).

Many Taiwanese products have an important share in the global market and the communications industry has been boosted by the liberalisation of the global telecommunications industry.

The main concern for Taiwan's industry is that low-end and mid-range manufacturers are moving to China. To remain competitive, Taiwan needs to focus on developing integrated software design.

Tourism

The government recognises the economic importance of the sector and is actively promoting it and improving facilities.

On 13 June 2008 an agreement was signed with China on to allow 3,000 tourists per day into each country from 18 July. Since then the number of Chinese tourists has increased from 8.5 per cent of foreign visitors in 2008 to 22 per cent in 2009, and by the first quarter of 2010 was the largest group of visitors, exceeding the Japanese. It is estimated that they spent over US$1 billion.

The Taiwan Strait Tourism Association opened an office in Beijing in May. Although classified as 'non-governmental' it was the first Taiwan office to open in mainland China since 1949.

Mining

Mining accounts for less than 1 per cent of GDP. Taiwan has few exploitable mineral resources. Due to the depletion of local sources, nearly all of the rare earth and metallic mining products are imported. Over 20 types of minerals are mined in Taiwan, mainly marble, limestone, serpentine and gravel. Marble is Taiwan's most important mineral resource with reserves conservatively estimated at over 300 million tonnes. Marble, salt, sand and gravel constitute the most valuable mineral products. Taiwan also produces iron and steel from imported iron ore and iron scrap and processed products such as aluminium, copper, lead, nickel, tin and zinc from imported raw materials.

Taiwan has four gold-bearing mines with metal content estimated at 100 tonnes. Taiwan utilises its large trade surpluses to import gold.

Hydrocarbons

Proven oil reserves were 2.38 million barrels in 2008, with production averaging 10,600 barrels per day (bpd). With consumption at 959,000bpd Taiwan must rely on imports to meets its energy needs. Taiwan has four refineries with a total capacity of 1.3 million bpd; the surplus, after domestic supply is met, is exported. The state-owned CPC Corporation is responsible for all aspects of surveying, extracting, refining, transporting and selling petroleum, natural gas and petroleum products. However downstream government has deregulated the CPC's monopoly and other, private companies compete for business.

Taiwan, along with Vietnam, China, Brunei, Malaysia and The Philippines, claims the potentially oil-rich Spratly Islands.

Total natural gas reserves were 6.2 billion cubic metres (cum) in 2008, with production at 396.5 million cum. Consumption, primarily in the form of electricity generation, was over 10 billion cum and imports to meet the shortfall were delivered as liquefied natural gas (LNG) from Asia, Africa and the Middle East.

Proven coal reserves are 1.0 million tonnes, but production has ceased. Taiwan consumes 55 million tonnes of coal per annum, imported mostly from China, Indonesia and Australia. Coal is used for electricity generation, steel production, cement and petrochemical industries.

Energy

Total installed generating capacity was 41.8GW in 2006. The state-owned Taiwan Power Company (Taipower) operates 72 power stations with output at 68 per cent thermally produced, 17 per cent nuclear and most of the rest by hydro-power. Independent power producers are allowed to provide up to 20 per cent of Taiwan's electricity with foreign investors allowed to participate in the electricity sector.

A new, US$35.8 million, solar power plant is planned by Taipower with a capacity of 4,000 kilowatt hours (kWh), scheduled to be completed by the end of 2010.

Financial markets

A computerised over-the-counter (OTC) market, the Taisdaq, was introduced in 1994. Taiwan's financial markets are regulated by the Securities and Futures Commission.

Stock exchange

Taiwan Stock Exchange

Banking and insurance

Foreign banks have been allowed to compete in the Taiwanese market since 1989. In June 2001, the government passed a package of legislation to reform the financial sector. The most important part of this legislation is the financial holding company law, which allows banks, security houses, insurance companies, investment funds, and futures brokerages to be grouped under one entity.

Central bank

Central Bank of China

Main financial centre

Taipei

Offshore facilities

Offshore banking has also been available since 1984. Foreign banks are permitted to set up offshore banking units (OBUs) without first having established a branch in Taiwan.

Time

GMT plus eight hours

Geography

Taiwan is an island 395km long and 144km across. It has high mountains, rising out of the sea along its eastern shore. The western side is flat and fertile. Taipei is located at the northen end of the island and is the largest city.

Hemisphere

Northern

Climate

Subtropical with temperatures ranging from 33 degrees Celsius (C) in Jul–Aug to 12 degrees C in Jan–Feb. Average rainfall is 2,500mm per year, with typhoons from May–Oct and occasional snow in the mountains in Jan–Feb.

Entry requirements

Passports

Required by all and must be valid for six months from date of visit.

Visa

Required by all, except citizens of EU, North America, Australasia and some Asian countries. Visit www.boca.gov.tw for a full list of nationals from *visa-exempt entry* countries and application forms for those who must apply of a visa. Visa free (tourist) visits are limited to 30 days without extension. All business visits of less than six months may be undertaken on visitors visas. Applications require a business letter of intent and itinerary. All visitors must have return/onward passage.

Currency advice/regulations

All currencies imported must be declared in writing on arrival; re-convertion is allowed on production of exchange receipts. The import and export of foreign currency is unlimited; amounts over US$10,000 (or foreign equivalent) must be declared. Import and export of local currency is limited to T$8,000; permission must be obtain from the Ministry of Finance for export of amounts in excess of this.

Travellers cheques are accepted in banks and tourist venues.

Customs

All baggage must be itemised in writing. Personal effects are duty-free.

Prohibited imports

Illegal drugs, gambling aids (including mahjong sets), firearms and explosives, non-canned meat and fresh fruit. Communist propaganda and items originating from China, Cuba, North Korea and members of the CIS.

Health (for visitors)

Mandatory precautions

Vaccination certificate for either yellow fever or cholera if travelling from an infected area.

Advisable precautions

Inoculations and boosters should be current for diphtheria, tetanus, hepatitis A, polio and typhoid. Other vaccinations that may be recommended are cholera, tuberculosis, and Japanese B encephalitis and hepatitis B. Use malaria prophylaxis (which will also provide protection against dengue fever and hepatitis B) including mosquito repellents, sleeping nets and clothing that cover the body after dark. There is a risk of rabies in rural areas. Use only bottled or boiled water for drinks, washing teeth and making ice. Eat only well cooked meals, preferably served hot; vegetables should be cooked and fruit peeled. Dairy products are unpasteurised and should be avoided. Avoid pork and salad and food from street vendors. A full first-aid kit would be useful.

Locally manufactured Western proprietary medicines are easily obtainable, but visitors on regular medication should bring their own supplies – amounts for the length of the visit only.

Visitors should have medical insurance, including emergency evacuation.

Hotels

It is advisable to book hotel rooms in advance. Room facilities usually include TVs and refrigerators. Larger hotels will arrange transport to/from the airport. A 10 per cent service charge is added to the bill. Reasonably priced accommodation is available at Japanese-style hot springs resorts in the mountains.

Credit cards

Major credit and charge cards are accepted in most establishments.

Public holidays (national)

Fixed dates

1 Jan (Founding of the Republic of China), 28 Feb Memorial Day.

Holidays that fall on the weekend are taken on the next working days *in lieu*.

Variable dates

Chinese New Year (Jan/Feb, four days), Tomb Sweeping Day (Mar/Apr), Tuen Ng (Dragon Boat) Festival (May/Jun), Mid-Autumn Moon Festival (Sep/Oct).

Religious and cultural festivals are determined by the Buddhist lunar calendar.

Working hours

Banking

Mon–Fri: 0900–1530; Sat: 0900–1200.

Business

Mon–Fri: 0830–1230, 1330–1730; Sat: 0830–1230.

Government
Mon–Fri: 0830–1230, 1330–1730; Sat: 0830–1230.
Shops
Sun–Sat: 0900–2200 (department stores 1100–2130).

Telecommunications
Mobile/cell phones
There are 900 and 1800 GSM service throughout most of the island.

Electricity supply
110V AC, 60 cycles

Weights and measures
Metric system (some Chinese units in use).

Social customs/useful tips
Shaking hands is the normal form of greeting. When addressing Chinese persons, the family or surname comes first. Business cards are usually exchanged and should be in both Chinese and English. They constitute an important part of the business culture, and Taiwanese expect visitors to carry cards. Cards using mainland (simplified) script are not advisable as this could cause offence.
Visitors should remember that Taiwanese of all backgrounds need to maintain 'face', this means that it is important not to embarrass your Taiwanese counterpart either privately or when in company. Rejection of gifts as small as cigarettes may cause offence, as a sign that the offerer is not considered wealthy. In general, however, the social environment in Taiwan is very liberal and visitors need not fear inadvertently causing offence.
When visiting people's homes, removing shoes is mandatory. The subject of death should be avoided in conversation as it is considered a bad omen.

Getting there
Air
An agreement was signed with China on 13 June 2008 to allow 36 direct flights (18 each) a week to start on 4 July. A further agreement will allow 3,000 tourists per day into each country from 18 July.
National airline: China Airlines (CAL). Taiwan's second carrier, Eva Air, is a major international carrier.
International airport/s: Taiwan Taoyuan International Airport (TTY) (formerly called Chiang Kai-Shek International), 40km south-west of Taipei, with duty-free shop, bar, restaurant, bank, post office, hotel reservations and shops; Kaohsiung International (KHH).
There are bus and taxi services to the closest cities.
Airport tax: None
Surface
Water: Regular ferry services run between Keelung and Kaohsiung ports (Taiwan) and Okinawa (Japan). There are also some sea links between Kaohsiung and Macao.
Main port/s: Keelung (including Suao), Hualien, Taichung.

Getting about
National transport
Air: Domestic air services are operated by China Airlines. Far Eastern Air Transport and seven other carriers connect most of the main cities.
Road: The road network covers 20,000km, most of it surfaced. A good highway links the main centres between Keelung and Kaohsiung. Bad terrain and one-way systems can make road travel difficult outside urban centres.
Buses: Extensive bus services cover coastal, cross-island and inland areas. Express coach services link Taipei, Kaohsiung and other main centres. Advance booking is recommended. Destinations are clearly marked in English at urban bus stations.
Rail: The railway extends the whole length of Taiwan, mainly along the west coast, including high-speed intercity trains. These services are good with air-conditioned express trains linking main centres. Urban train stations have destinations marked in English.
A US$17.8 billion high speed 345km rail system linking Taipei with the southern city of Kaohsiung (journey time 80 minutes) is expected to be operational by the end of 2006.
Water: There are ferry services from Kaohsiung and Chiayi to the Pescadores Islands, from Taitung to the Lanyu and Green Islands.
City transport
Rush-hour traffic in Taipei can be chaotic and stressful. Allow plenty of time for getting to and from the airport.
Taxis: Taxis are plentiful. Metered taxis are available in Taipei, and fares are metered by kilometres and delay time. Have the destination (and the return address) written in Chinese for the taxi driver's reference.
Tipping is not an established practice, though it is becoming more usual.
From Taiwan Taoyuan International Airport to city centre the journey time is 45–60 minutes.
Buses, trams & metro: An underground rail system and a Rapid Mass Transit System are under construction in Taipei and Kaohsiung. Construction of the Taipei system is expected to be fully completed by 2009; Kaohsiung in 2007.
Car hire
Self-drive car hire is available, although chauffeur-driven cars are recommended due to traffic conditions. An international driving licence is required. Driving is on the right-hand side of the road.

BUSINESS DIRECTORY

Telephone area codes
The international direct dialling (IDD) code for Taiwan is +886 followed by the area code and subscriber's number:

Hualien	38	Taichung	4
Kaohsiung	7	Tainan	6
Keelung	32	Taipei	2
Pingtung	8		

Useful telephone numbers
Fire and ambulance: 119.
Police: 110.
English-speaking police: 311-9940, 311-9816 ext 264.
Ambulance: 721-6315.
Women's help-line 581-5469.
International calls: 100.
Directory enquiries:
Chinese language 104
(long-distance: 105).
English language 311-6796.

Chambers of Commerce
American Chamber of Commerce in Taipei, Chia Hsin Building, 96 Chungshan North Road, Section 2, Taipei 104 (tel: 2581-7089; fax: 2542-3376; e-mail: amcham@amcham.com.tw).

British Chamber of Commerce in Taiwan, Fu Key Building, 99 Ren Ai Road, Section 2, Taipei 106 (tel: 2356-0210; fax: 2356-0211; e-mail: info@bcctaipei.com).

Chinese National Association of Industry and Commerce, 390 Fu Hsing South Road, Taipei 106 (tel: 2707-0111; fax : 2701-7601; e-mail: webmaster@nfict.org).

European Chamber of Commerce Taipei, 285 Zhongxiao East Road, Section 4, Taipei (tel: 2740-0236; fax: 2772-0530; e-mail: ecct@ecct.com.tw).

Taiwan Chamber of Commerce, 158 Sung Chiang Road, Taipei 104 (tel: 2536-5455; fax: 2521-1980; e-mail: tcoc@tcoc.org.tw).

Banking
Bank of Taiwan, 120 Chungking S Road, Sec 2, Taipei (tel: 2314-7377; fax: 2331-5840).

Chang Hwa Commercial Bank, 23-1 Chang An E Rd, Sec 1, Taipei City (tel: 2523-0739; fax: 2523-0172).

Chiao Tung Bank, 91 Heng Yang Road, Taipei (tel: 2361-3000; fax: 2311-3263).

Citibank, PO Box 3343, Citicorp Center, 52 Minsheng E Road, Sec 4, Taipei City 105 (tel: 2715-5931; fax: 2712-7388).

First Commercial Bank, 30 Chungking S Road, Sec 1, Taipei 10036 (tel: 2311-111; fax: 2361-0036).

Hua Nan Commercial Bank, 38 Chungking S Road, Sec 1, Taipei (tel: 2371-3111; fax: 2371-5734).

International Commercial Bank of China, 100 Chi Lin Road, Taipei (tel: 2563-3156; fax: 2561-1216).

Shanghai Commercial & Savings Bank Ltd, 2 Min Chuan East Road, Section 1, Taipei City (tel: 2581-7111; fax: 2567-1921).

Standard Chartered Bank, 168 Tun Hwa North Rd, Taipei City 105 (tel: 2716-2621, 2717-2866; fax: 2716-4068).

Taipeibank, 50 Chungshan North Road, Section 2, Taipei City (tel: 2542-5656; fax: 2542-8870).

Taiwan Co-operative Bank, 77 Kuanchien Road, Taipei (tel: 2311-8811; fax: 2331-6567).

Central bank
Central Bank of China, 2 Roosevelt Road, Section 1, Taipei 100 (tel: 2393-6161; fax: 2357-1974; internet: www.cbc.gov.tw).

Stock exchange
Taiwan Stock Exchange: www.twse.com.tw:

Travel information
China Airlines (CAL), 131 Nanking East Road, Section 3, Taipei 104 (tel: 2715-2626; fax: 2717-5120).

Taiwan Taoyuan International Airport, No 9, Hangjan S Rd, Dayuan Shiang, Taoyuan, Taiwan 33758 (tel: 2398-2143, 2398-3274; internet: www.cksairport.gov.tw)

Flight information (24 hours) (tel: 2398-2050).

Sungshan Domestic Airport Travel Information Service Centre (tel: 2349-1580).

Taiwan Visitors' Association, 5th Floor, 9 Ming Chuan East Road, Sec 2, Taipei (tel: 2594-3261; fax: 2594-3265).

Tourist Information Hot Line (tel: 2717-3737).

National tourist organisation offices
Tourism Bureau, 9F Floor, 280 Chung Hsiao East Road, Section 4; PO Box 1490, Taipei (tel: 2721-8541; fax: 2773-5487: internet www.taiwantourism.org).

Ministries
Ministry of Economic Affairs, 15 Foochow Street, Taipei (tel: 2321-2200; fax: 2391-9398).

Ministry of Education (MoE), 5 Chungshan S. Road, Taipei (tel: 2356-6051; fax: 2397-6920).

Ministry of Finance, 2 Aikuo West Road, Taipei (tel: 2322-8000; fax: 2321-1205).

Ministry of Foreign Affairs, 2 Chieh Shou Road, Taipei (tel: 2311-9292; fax: 2314-4972).

Ministry of the Interior (MoI), 5 Hsuchow Road, Taipei (tel: 2356-5000; fax: 2356-6201).

Ministry of Justice (MoJ), 130 Chungking S. Road, Sec. 1, Taipei (tel: 2314-6871; fax: 2389-6239).

Ministry of National Defence, Chiehshou Hall, Chungking S. Road, Taipei (tel: 2311-6117; fax: 2314-4221).

Ministry of Transportation and Communications, 2 Changasha Street, Section 1, Taipei (tel: 2349-2900; fax: 2389-6009).

Monetary Affairs Dept, Ministry of Finance, 2 Aikuo W Road, Taipei (tel: 2321-3836).

President's Office, 122 Chungking South Road, Section 1, Taipei (the First Bureau tel: 2311-3731; fax: 2314-0746; Protocol Section: 2311-5877; Spokesman's Office: 2331-1604).

Other useful addresses
Board of Foreign Trade, 1 Hukou St, Taipei (tel: 2351-0271; fax: 2351-3603).

British Trade and Cultural Office, 9th floor, Fu Key Building, 99 Jen Ali Road, Section 2, Taipei 10625 (tel: 2322-4242; fax: 2394-8673).

China External Trade Development Council (CETRA), 4-8th floor, International Trade Building, 333 Keelung Road, Sec 1, Taipei 10548 (tel: 2725-5200; fax: 2757-6653).

Chinese National Association of Industry & Commerce, 13th floor, 390 Fu Hsing South Rd, Sec 1, Taipei (tel: 2707-0111; fax: 2701-7601).

Chinese National Export Enterprises Association (CNEEA), 6th floor, 285 Nanking E. Road, Sec. 3, Taipei (tel: 2713-8153; fax: 2713-0115).

Chinese National Federation of Industries, 12th floor, 390 Fuhsing South Road, Section 1, Taipei (tel: 2703-3500; fax: 2703-3982).

Chinese Petroleum Corporation, 83 Chung-Hwa Road, Section 1, Taipei 10331 (tel: 2361-0221; fax: 2371-5944).

Council for Economic Planning and Development, 9/F, 87 Nanking East Road, Section 2, Taipei (tel: 2551-3522; fax: 2581-8549).

Directorate-General of Budgets, Accounting & Statistics, Executive Yuan, 1 Chung Hsiao East Road, Section 1, Taipei (internet: www.stat.gov.tw/).

Euro-Asia Trade Organisation, 3rd floor, 9 Roosevelt Road, Sec. 2, Taipei (tel: 2393-2115; fax: 2392-8393).

Government Information Office, Taipei (tel: 2322-8888).

Industrial Development Bureau, MOEA, 41-3 Hsinyi Road, Sec. 3, Taipei (tel: 2754-1255; fax: 2703-0160).

Industrial Development and Investment Centre, MOEA, 4 Chunghsiao W. Road, Sec 1, Taipei (tel: 2389-2111; fax: 2382-0497).

Industry of Free China, 9th Floor, 87 Nanking East Road, Section 2, Taipei (tel: 2543-5988).

International Co-operation Department, MOEA, 15 Foochow St., Taipei (tel: 2321-2200; fax: 2321-3275).

International Economic Co-operation Development Fund, 7th floor, 51 Chung-Ching S. Road, Sec. 2, Taipei (tel: 2396-6316; fax: 2396-9147).

International Telecommunications Administration (ITA), 28 Hangchou S. Rd, Sec. 1, Taipei (tel: 2344-3781).

International Trade Association of the R.O.C., 8th floor, 148 Chunghsiao E. Road, Sec. 4, Taipei (tel: 2772-6252; fax: 2752-2411).

Investment Commission, Ministry of Economic Affairs, 8th Floor, 7 Roosevelt Road, Sec 1, Taipei (tel: 2351-3151; fax: 2396-3970).

Securities and Exchange Commission, 12th Floor, Yangteh Building, 3 Nanhai Road, Taipei (tel: 2341-3191; fax: 2394-8249).

Taipei Economic and Cultural Representative Office (USA), 4201 Wisconsin Avenue, NW, Washington DC 20016 (tel: (+1-202) 895-1800; fax: (+1-202) 363-0999; email: contact@tecro-info.org).

Taipei World Trade Centre Exhibition Hall, 5 Hsinyi Road, Section 5, Taipei (tel: 2886-2725; fax: 2886-1314).

Taiwan Stock Exchange Corp, 85 Yen Ping S Road, Taipei (tel: 2311-4020; fax: 2311-4004).

Taiwan Textile Federation, 22 Ai-Kuo E. Road, Taipei (tel: 2341-7251; fax: 2392-3855).

World Trade Center Taichung, 60 Tienpao St, Taichung (tel: 2254-2271; fax: 2254-2341).

National news agency: Central News Agency (www.cna.com.tw).

Internet sites
Taiwan business directory: www.tbdo.anjes.com.tw

Taiwan business express: www.business.com.tw

Taiwan News, the Voice of Taiwan: www.eTaiwanNews.com

Taiwan Trade Point: www.tradepoint.anjes.com.tw

Tajikistan

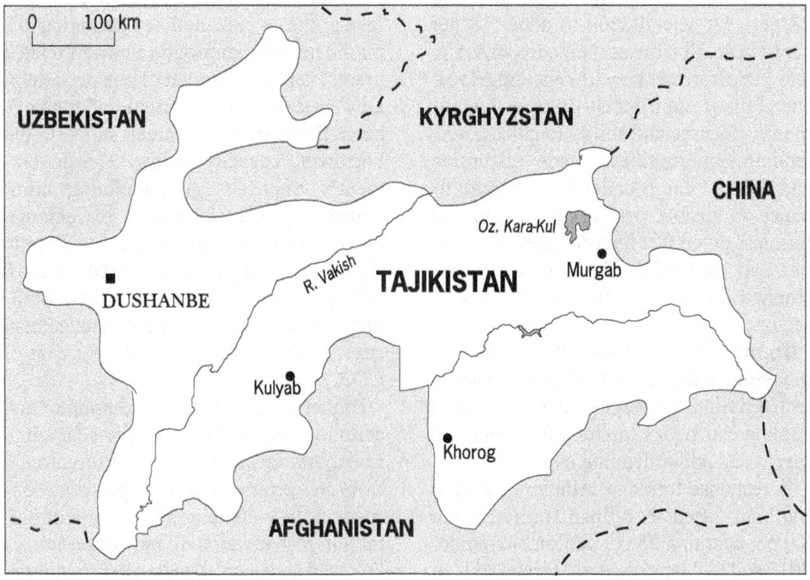

KEY FACTS

Official name: Respublika i Tojikiston (Republic of Tajikistan)

Head of State: President Emomali Rakhmon (leader since 1992; re-elected 2006)

Head of government: Prime Minister Akil Akilov (since 1999)

Ruling party: Hizbi Demokrati Khalkii (HDK) (People's Democratic Party) (elected 2000; re-elected 2010)

Area: 143,100 square km

Population: 7.60 million (2010)*

Capital: Dushanbe

Official language: Tajik (Farsi)

Currency: Somoni (Sm) = 100 dirams

Exchange rate: Sm4.75 per US$ (Oct 2011)

GDP per capita: US$767 (2009)*

GDP real growth: 6.50% (2010)

GDP: US$5.64 billion (2010)

Labour force: 2.10 million (2009)*

Unemployment: 2.20% (2009)*

Inflation: 12.50% (2010)*

Balance of trade: -US$1.63 billion (2010)

* estimated figure

Following the break up of the Soviet Union, an emergent Takistan collapsed into a five-year civil war between its Russia-backed government and an Islamist-led opposition. It is estimated that up to 50,000 people were killed and over one-tenth of the population fled the country. The civil war ended in 1997 with a United Nations-brokered peace agreement.

Poverty is widespread...

The country's economy has never really recovered from the civil war and poverty is widespread. Almost half of Tajikistan's gross domestic product (GDP) is earned by migrants working abroad, especially in Russia, but the recession in 2009 threatened that income. The country is also dependent on oil and gas imports. Economic hardship is seen as contributing to the renewed interest in Islam – including more radical forms – among young Tajiks. Tajikistan has been accused by its neighbours of tolerating the presence of training camps for Islamist rebels on its territory, an accusation which it has strongly denied.

... but the economy improves

Tajikistan's GDP climbed to 6.5 per cent in 2010 from 3.4 per cent in 2009 according to the Asian Development Bank (ADB). Industry grew by about 10 per cent, as favorable weather allowed higher hydropower production (which accounts for most of the electricity generated), in turn allowing small and medium-sized enterprises to maintain continuous operations in winter. Thus industrial growth mainly came from these enterprises, particularly in light manufacturing and food processing, unlike previous years.

Aluminum production suffered due to limited imports of alumina, caused by intermittent disruptions to rail transit through Uzbekistan. These were largely resolved in the second half of the year. Indeed, the two countries have faced several bilateral issues over the years. At present, the main one relates to differences over managing riparian resources. There was an increase in public spending on key infrastructure projects in 2010, such as roads, tunnels and transmission lines, under-pinning growth in construction. Growth in agriculture slowed to a still strong 6.8 per cent after an unusually high 10.5 per cent gain in 2009 (due to a reallocation of land to non-cotton agriculture). Activity in retail trade also fell off, as disruption in rail transit restricted imports, slowing services growth to about 5 per cent. Economic recovery in the Russian Federation lifted remittances by 29 per cent to US$2.4 billion in 2010 the equivalent of 40 per cent of GDP. They remain a key factor in economic and social stability in Tajikistan, supporting domestic demand and private consumption.

The government launched a massive public campaign to collect funds for building the Roghun hydropower plant in January 2010. It believes that, if carried out, this project could end perennial winter power deficits and allow Tajikistan to become a substantial regional electricity exporter. The campaign set out to raise US$1.4 billion to construct the initial phase of Roghun by selling shares to the public. But, after the campaign had raised little more than US$186 million by May 2010, the government suspended it after seeing the adverse impact on household consumption and economic activity. It remains, however, committed to the project.

End-of-period inflation nearly doubled to 9.8 per cent in 2010 from 5.0 per cent in 2009 mainly because of rising food prices – particularly of wheat, following the drought in, and subsequent suspension of exports by, the Russian Federation. Higher global fuel prices and the imposition by Russia (the main supplier of petroleum) of an export duty on hydrocarbons added a further supply-side push. Demand-side pressures from increased remittance spending also stoked inflation, which averaged 6.4 per cent in 2010.

The ADB notes that Tajikistan's banks continued to face tight liquidity conditions and high incidences of non-performing loans. They are constrained by a low deposit base and a limited ability to attract capital inflows, while they have significant exposure to risky credits in agriculture and a shortage of sound investment opportunities.

In a bold move, the Tajik government wrote off about US$500 million of doubtful cotton sector loans. This move cut banks' ratio of non-performing loans from 28 per cent at end-2009 to about 18 per cent a year later, but as their compensation was in the form of very low yielding Treasury bills it contributed little to their liquidity, income and ability to take up new lending opportunities. Trade disruption and delayed cargo deliveries hit trade finance, a sizable part of banks' normal business given that imports represent over one-half of GDP. All these factors restrained credit expansion to the private sector.

To mitigate the banks' difficulties, the government deposited US$50 million collected during the Roghun campaign with commercial banks to strengthen their reserves and add to lending capacity.

In response to rising inflation, the central bank lifted its refinancing rate from 8.0 per cent to 8.25 per cent in November 2010 and to 9.0 per cent in March 2011. In 2010, bank lending rates varied around 25 per cent while deposit rates varied around 6.5 per cent, the large spread reflecting both high levels of doubtful loans and structural difficulties.

Tajikistan continued to pursue a fiscal policy aimed at macro-economic stabilisation while sustaining pro-poor programmes. The government's post-crisis plan, adopted in early 2010, aimed to lift social expenditure to 11.5 per cent of GDP in 2010, but could not meet the target. This was mainly because revenue collection was under stress in the first half of 2009 owing to reduced collection of value-added tax on imports and of customs duties; revenue picked up after the easing of the transit bottleneck.

Although government revenue and expenditure did not fully reach budgeted levels, the overall deficit (excluding the public investment programme and related grants) kept to the target of one per cent of GDP in 2010. Recent fiscal deficits have been financed by external support, but borrowing capacity is low. The government's emphasis on completing infrastructure projects financed by external borrowing raised the debt to-GDP ratio slightly to 34.4 per cent of GDP in 2010 .The government is committed to controlling the debt level – its debt management strategy limits the ratio to 40 per cent of GDP.

Higher global prices for aluminum and cotton underpinned a 40.9 per cent surge in exports in 2010, a marked turnaround from the prior-year's 10.7 per cent contraction. In volume terms, exports of aluminum rose moderately but cotton fell, as less land had been allocated to production. Imports grew by only 8.2 per cent, mainly because of the rail disruptions. The increase in export earnings outpaced the unusually small rise in imports and kept the trade deficit largely unchanged from the previous year. With the strong recovery in remittances, the current account is estimated to have moved to a surplus of 2.2 per cent of GDP from a deficit of 5.9 per cent of GDP in 2009.

Following a large currency depreciation in 2009 that mirrored those of Tajikistan's major trade partners, the somoni was stable against the US dollar in 2010, depreciating by only 0.7 per cent. This reflected market conditions – good export performance and rising remittances in the face of restrained conditions on importing.

Foreign reserves picked up from US$278 million in 2009 to US$640 million. This increase was due to the improvement in the current account, while capital flows and credit disbursements, including those from the IMF, came in broadly as planned. But the level of foreign reserves remained low at year-end, equal to only 2.3 months of projected 2011 imports.

The ADB also notes that Tajikistan's GDP growth was projected to edge up to 6.8 per cent in 2011 and 7.0 per cent in 2012, fuelled by continued remittance inflows and by increases in aluminum and

KEY INDICATORS Tajikistan

	Unit	2006	2007	2008	2009	2010
Population	m	6.38	6.42	*6.46	*6.50	*7.60
Gross domestic product (GDP)	US$bn	2.81	3.71	5.13	4.98	5.64
GDP per capita	US$	*441	578	*795	*767	–
GDP real growth	%	7.0	7.8	0.0	3.9	6.5
Inflation	%	9.9	13.1	20.4	6.5	6.5
lExports (fob) (goods)	US$m	1,511.8	1,556.9	1,574.9	1,038.5	1,302.7
Imports (fob) (goods)	US$m	1,954.6	3,115.0	3,699.0	2,770.4	2,936.4
Balance of trade	US$m	-442.8	-1,558.1	-2,124.2	-1,731.9	-1,633.7
Current account	US$m	-21.4	-495.1	47.6	-179.9	-382.8
Total reserves minus gold	US$m	175.1	–	–	–	–
Foreign exchange	US$m	171.6	–	–	–	–
Exchange rate	per US$	3.43	3.43	3.43	4.14	4.38

* estimated figure

cotton prices in 2011, both of which fell off but are predicted to stay high in 2012. Remittances were forecast to grow by about 7 per cent each year, reaching their pre-crisis high in 2012. They should underpin rising private consumption expenditure, boosting imports and so supporting budget revenues.

Production of aluminum and cotton was also projected to rise moderately in 2011 and 2012, responding to higher global prices (as well as reallocation of land back to cotton), but limited aluminum production capacity and inefficient cotton financing will hold back a stronger response. Agricultural processing, light industry, construction and services will likely continue their strong growth.

Inflation in 2011 and 2012 is projected to increase to 10.5 per cent and 9.5 per cent, reflecting rising global food and fuel prices. The authorities are committed to maintaining a cautious fiscal and monetary stance under their economic programme with the IMF and have undertaken to tighten policies if non-food price pressures emerge.

Rising remittance-fueled consumption spending and expanding public investment are projected to generate much stronger import growth in 2011 and 2012 of about 28 per cent and 10 per cent, assuming normal regional trade and cargo transit arrangements. Exports are set to rise, by around 25 per cent and 1 per cent, largely reflecting global price movements. The trade deficit is expected to deteriorate and even with expected higher remittances the current account balance will move to a deficit of 4.3 per cent and 6.4 per cent of GDP.

Risk assessment

Economy	Fair
Politics	Poor
Regional stability	Fair

COUNTRY PROFILE

Historical profile

1916–17 The Central Asian republics joined in a violent uprising against Russian rule, which was suppressed. After the October Revolution in Russia, the Russian ruler, Lenin, gave the peoples of Central Asia the right of self-determination.
1920s Southern Tajikistan remained under the control of the Khan of Bukhara while northern Tajikistan was incorporated into Soviet-controlled Turkestan, which also included Uzbekistan, Kyrgyzstan, part of northern Turkmenistan and southern Kazakhstan. Soviet nationalities policy, under the direction of Stalin, saw Soviet rule enforced by Red Army troops who put down fierce Muslim resistance in Central Asia after the Russian civil war.
1924 Tajikistan was granted autonomous status in the Socialist Soviet Republic (SSR) of Uzbekistan.
1929 Tajikistan was detached from Uzbekistan and became a separate SSR.
1930s–80s The country underwent a period of agricultural collectivisation and industrialisation, which was unpopular with the population.
1989 Tajik became the official state language.
1990 Social and ethnic tensions erupted in violence in Dushanbe and along the Tajikistan-Kyrgyzstan border. A state of emergency was declared and Soviet troops were sent to Dushanbe to suppress pro-democracy protests. President Kahar Mahkamov resigned after being accused of supporting an attempted coup against the Soviet leader Mikhail Gorbachev.
1991 The collapse of the Soviet Union resulted in Tajikistan declaring independence. Rahmon Nabiyev was appointed president after winning Tajikistan's first direct presidential elections. Tajikistan joined the Commonwealth of Independent States (CIS), following the collapse of the Soviet Union.
1992 Anti-government demonstrations in Dushanbe turned into civil war between pro-government forces and Islamist and pro-democracy groups. Nabiyev was forced to resign and the Hizbi Komunistii Tojikiston (HKT) (Communist Party of Tajikistan) government collapsed. Pro-Communists massacred thousands of government supporters in Dushanbe. The HKT regained power and Imamali Rakhmonov became head of state.
1993 The Supreme Court returned the country to one-party rule after banning all political parties other than the ruling HKT. A CIS peace-keeping force was deployed along the Tajikistan-Afghan border to prevent armed incursions by Islamic guerrilla groups.
1994 A cease-fire between the government and the rebels was agreed. A presidential constitution was approved by national referendum. Rakhmonov won the presidential elections, which were deemed by international observers to be neither free nor fair.
1995 Rakhmonov supporters won the legislative elections, which took place without the participation of any of the opposition groups. Fighting erupted on the Afghan border.
1996 A UN-sponsored cease-fire between the government and Islamist rebels came into effect.
1997 Opposition parties were legalised and as part of a peace treaty between the Tajikistan government and the Islamic United Tajik Opposition (UTO), the government agreed to give 30 per cent of its seats to opposition representatives, retaining 50 per cent for itself, and to give the remaining 20 per cent to independents.
1998 The government removed the ban on religious political parties. Rakhmonov pardoned all opposition leaders in exile. Tajikistan joined the CIS Customs Union.
1999 President Rakhmonov was re-elected for a third term. The UTO armed forces were integrated into the state army.
2000 A new bicameral parliament was set up. The elections were won by the Hizbi Demokrati Khalkii (HDK) (People's Democratic Party). The somoni replaced the Tajik rouble as the currency. Belarus, Kazakhstan, Kyrgyzstan, Russia and Tajikistan (formerly the Customs Five) established the Eurasian Economic Community (EEC).
2001 Tajikistan, China, Russia, Kazakhstan, Kyrgyzstan and Uzbekistan formed the Shanghai Co-operation Organisation (SCO). Rahmon Sanginov, a renegade warlord, declared one of the country's most wanted criminals, was killed in a gun battle with security forces.
2002 Tajikistan became the last Central Asian republic to join NATO's Partnership for Peace (PfP) programme. The number of border guards was doubled to prevent al Qaeda members from crossing the border with Afghanistan to escape US forces.
2003 Russian President Vladimir Putin announced an agreement to increase Russian military presence. A referendum extended President Rakhmonov's term in office by two more consecutive seven-year terms.
2004 A moratorium on the death penalty was introduced. Russia regained control of a former Soviet space-monitoring centre at Nurek and opened a military base in Dushanbe.
2005 The ruling HDK was re-elected. However, international observers said the elections had not reached acceptable international standards. Opposition leader, Mahmadruzi Iskandarov (HDK), had been arrested and released in Moscow after an extradition request was dismissed, was kidnapped and transported to Tajikistan to be re-arrested; he was sentenced on terrorism and corruption charges and received a 23-year sentence.
2006 Incumbent Emomali Rakhmonov won 79 per cent of the vote for president; giving him his fourth term in office. The election was neither free nor fair according to international observers.
2007 A bridge across the Pyanj River, built by the US army, was opened, linking the Tajik town of Nizhny Pyanj with Shir Khan Bandar and extending the trans-Afghanistan road (Regional Road Corridor

Improvement Project) through Central Asia. The president removed the 'ov' from his name and discouraged Russian-style names from use.
2009 Tajikistan reached an agreement with the US to allow non-military shipments destined for Afghanistan to fly over and through its territory.
2010 In parliamentary elections, held on 28 February, the incumbent HDK won an overwhelming majority of 55 seats (out of 63). The Organisation for Security and Co-operation in Europe (OSCE) judged the elections had 'failed on many basic democratic standards' and widespread fraud. The opposition mounted a legal challenge to the results. On 18 August, Russia hosted a regional summit meeting of presidents from Afghanistan, Pakistan, Tajikistan and Russia. Economic and development co-operation was promised between them.
2011 At the beginning of the year Russia began several negotiations towards achieving a security treaty and to return Russian border guards to the joint Tajikistan-Russian border, due to the sharp increase in drugs-trafficking across the border and the risk of regional Islamic violence spilling over into Russia's southern Central Asian states. An agreement was reached between Tajikistan and China which settled a century-old border dispute, following the Tajik parliament's vote on 12 January to cede 1,000 square kilometres of land in the Pamir mountain range to China. Although this only represented 5.5 per cent of the land claimed, China accepted the land as a resolution to the dispute. On 20 August, as part of the anniversary celebrations, President Rakhmon gave an amnesty to 15,000 prisoners who had fought against his forces during the 1990s civil war.

Political structure

Constitution

A presidential constitution was approved by national referendum in 1994. The constitution granted basic economic and political rights and guaranteed religious freedoms. It gave the president powers to appoint the chairs of regions, districts, cities, including Dushanbe, as well as of the Gorno-Badakshan Autonomous Region and the governor of the National Bank of Tajikistan (central bank), subject to the approval of deputies in parliament. The president also has powers of dismissal over these offices. In addition, the president gained the power to declare a state of martial law and issue decrees, as well as immunity from prosecution. Parliament has the power to impeach the president, subject to the findings of the Constitutional Court. If more than two-thirds of deputies vote in favour of impeachment, parliament may dismiss the president from office.

Independence date

9 September 1991

Form of state

Presidential socialist republic

The executive

The president, elected by universal suffrage every seven years, holds executive power. The government consists of the prime minister and cabinet and may present its resignation to the president if it declares it cannot function normally.
In 2003, voters in a referendum favoured allowing President Rakhmonov to run two further consecutive seven-year terms in office after 2006.

National legislature

The bicameral Majlisi Oli (Supreme Assembly) consists of the Majlisi Mamoyandogan (Assembly of Representatives) (lower house), with 63 members, of which 22 are elected by proportional representation and 41 in single-seat constituencies; the Majlisi Milliy (National Assembly) (upper house) has 33 members, of which 25 are elected by subordinate regional assemblies and eight are appointed by the president. All Assembly members serve for five-year terms.

Legal system

The judiciary is constitutionally independent from the legislature and executive. Courts include the Supreme Court, Constitutional Court, Military Court and High Economic Court. In addition there are district and city courts, as well as the Dushanbe City Court. Gorno-Badakshan Autonomous Region has its own court.
The president has powers to appoint and dismiss judges of all courts on petition of the minister of justice, except for judges appointed to the Supreme Court, High Economic Court and Constitutional Court. The latter is composed of seven judges elected from the legal profession, one of whom is a representative of Gorno-Badakshan Autonomous Region.

Last elections

28 February 2010 (parliamentary); 6 November 2006 (presidential)
Results: Parliamentary: Hizbi Demokrati Khalkii (HDK) (People's Democratic Party) won 71.04 per cent of the vote (55 seats out of 63), Islamic Renaissance Party (IRP) 8.2 per cent (two), Hizbi Kommunistii (Communist Party) (CP) 7.01 per cent (two); Agrarian Party (AP) 5.11 per cent (two), Party of Economic Reforms (PER) 5.06 per cent. Turnout was 90.84 per cent.
Presidential: Emomali Rakhmonov won with 79.3 per cent of the vote; four other candidates won less than seven per cent each.

Next elections

2015 (parliamentary); 2011 (presidential)

Political parties

Ruling party

Hizbi Demokrati Khalkii (HDK) (People's Democratic Party) (elected 2000; re-elected 2010)

Main opposition party

Islamic Renaissance Party (IRP)

Population

7.60 million (2010)*
Last census: January 2000: 6,127,000 (provisional)
Population density: 54 inhabitants per square km (2010)
Annual growth rate: 1.6 per cent 2005–2010 (Undata 2010)

Ethnic make-up

Tajik (69.1 per cent), Uzbek (25 per cent), Russian (2.7 per cent), with remaining minorities including Tatar and Kyrgyz groups. Tajikistan is the exception among the Central Asian republics in that its population is predominantly Persian rather than Turkic. The Tajiks are made up of a number of closely related ethnic groups which differ both anthropologically (inhabitants of the Pamir mountains in the north are tall, dark complexioned with light-coloured eyes; those from Kuliab are stocky and dark-skinned; northern Tajiks are fair-complexioned, brown- and black-eyed). Customs and rituals also differ.

Religions

The majority (80 per cent) of ethnic Tajiks and Uzbeks are Sunni Muslims; 5 per cent are Shi'a Muslims. Ethnic Badakhshanis belong to the Ismaili Muslim sect and have the Aga Khan as their spiritual leader. There are also Baptists and Bukhara Jews. There is no official religion.

Education

Public expenditure on education typically amounts to 3 per cent of GDP.
Primary education lasts four years, followed by eight years of secondary schooling which is divided into two cycles of five and three years in either general, technical or vocational education. Successful students may progress to either a university or institute of which there are 29 established.
In 2003, the Asian Development Bank (ADB) approved a US$7.5 million loan for education reforms to give about 90,000 children better access to quality education. About 300 schools, in pilot districts, which were damaged during the civil war and lacked maintenance, received funding for refurbishment and to provide textbooks and learning materials, plus pay for enhancing female teacher training.
The total cost of the project was US$9.38 million, 80 per cent of which was covered by the ADB's loan, while the government provided the balance of US$1.88 million.

Nationwide, the education system is suffering from an exodus of large numbers of qualified teachers to find better paid work. School attendance levels are also falling, as children are pressed into helping their families cope with the widespread poverty and social vulnerability. Gender imbalance is particularly marked at the upper secondary level, with the proportion of girls declining.

Literacy rate: 100 per cent adult rate; 100 per cent youth rate (15–24) (Unesco 2005).

Compulsory years: Seven to 16.

Enrolment rate: 85 per cent gross primary enrolment (ADB); 76 per cent gross secondary enrolment (Unicef).

Pupils per teacher: 24 in primary schools.

Health

The structure of Tajikistan's health system has evolved from the Soviet model of healthcare with few structural changes. The state funds most of the healthcare services in the country. The health ministry runs national-level healthcare services, while local authorities administer most regional services.

State hospitals have limited supplies of free medicines. People have been increasingly forced to pay for their own healthcare, often buying their own medicines off the street.

Tajikistan has substantial environmental problems that pose risks to human health. There is high risk of communicable disease with the breakdown of public health measures such as mosquito control and immunisation. Less than 50 per cent of the rural population have access to clean water. Tajikistan is one of the primary transfer points for the flow of drugs due to transparent border controls and poor custom regulations.

HIV/Aids

HIV prevalence: 0.1 per cent aged 15–49 in 2003 (World Bank)

Life expectancy: 63 years, 2004 (WHO 2006)

Fertility rate/Maternal mortality rate: 3.7 births per woman, 2004 (WHO 2006); maternal mortality 66.5 per 100,000 live births (World Bank).

Birth rate/Death rate: 32.8 births and 8.5 deaths per 1,000 people (2003).

Child (under 5 years) mortality rate (per 1,000): 76 per 1,000 live births (World Bank)

Head of population per physician: 2.03 physicians per 1,000 people, 2003 (WHO 2006)

Welfare

As the poorest of the CIS countries, a significant proportion of Tajikistan's population now faces severe social hardship, especially with most of the country's social welfare budget being spent on pensions. The country relies heavily on overseas assistance, highlighting the failure of the state to create a self-financing welfare system.

Main cities

Dushanbe (capital, estimated population 582,496 in 2005), Khujand (formerly Leninabad) (144,782).

Languages spoken

The Tajik language is very close to Persian, spoken in Iran, and to Dari, spoken in Afghanistan. Although Tajik is spoken locally, in practice, Russian is widely used in government and business. Uzbek is also spoken. The Badakhshanis speak the Pamir languages, but also speak Tajik or Russian. There are three main groups – the Pamir languages, the southern Kulyab and the northern Khodzent dialects.

A State Language law provides for a transition to the Tajik language with Arabic script.

Official language/s

Tajik (Farsi)

Media

Despite a constitutionally guaranteed free press, the government has a heavy influence on all media outlets and has led to widespread self-censorship. Laws prohibit the dissemination of information containing state secrets, inciting racial discrimination and any form of ethnic or religious hatred.

Press

Tajikistan does not possess any pulp mills or paper making industries and has to import all newsprint paper and printing equipment, which has resulted in significantly higher printing costs and an inability to produce daily newspapers. The UN considers this situation denies citizens access to current news.

Weeklies: The four official weeklies are not popular as they are concerned with published resolutions, government decision and official chronicles and lack any innovation. They have deplorable circulation figures of 700–2,000, of which 75 per cent are secured by subscription and only 25 per cent are sold retail.

Government-owned and published three times per week, *Jumhuriyat* and *Sadio Mardumin* Tajik, *Khalq Ovozi* in Uzbek and *Narodnaya Gazeta* in Russian. Private publications include *Neru-i Sukhan* and *Tojikiston* in Takik. Political parties publish *Minbar-i Khalq* (People's Democratic Party), *Nido-i Ranjbar* in Takik (Communist Party), *Golos Tajikistana* in Russian (Communist Party), *Najot* (Islamic Rebirth Party).

Broadcasting

The broadcasting law prohibits dissemination of information containing state secrets, inciting of racial discrimination and any form of ethnic or religious hatred.

Radio: The Government runs Tajik radio with two national networks and in the capital, Radio Sado i Dushanbe. There are two private stations, Asia Plus (www.asiaplus.tj) and Radio Vatan (www.vatan.tj) in the capital and Radio Tiroz (www.tiroz.tj) in Khujand.

External radios stations can be received including BBC, VOA and Voice of Free Tajikistan (run by national exiles).

Television: The state runs three regional networks, Tajik TV, Soghd TV and Khatlon TV. Safina TV (www.safina.tj) the only private operation.

Advertising

All media outlets accept advertising. Alcohol is banned from being advertised

News agencies

National news agency: Khovar (in Russian) (www.khovar.tj).

Avesta news agency (www.avesta.tj/en).

Economy

The economic problems faced by Tajikistan, which has one of the lowest gross domestic products (GDP) of all the Commonwealth of Independent States (CIS), are not insurmountable. In 2009, the service sector constituted 53.9 per cent of GDP, with industry comprising 23.7 per cent, of which manufacturing was 10.8 per cent and agriculture 22.4 per cent. Industry is largely limited to the Tadaz aluminium smelter, the Nurek hydropower station and small obsolete light industry and food processing factories. The country is dependent on cotton and aluminium sales, hydroelectricity and remittances for its foreign exchange, all of which is subject to external shocks, and is in serious need of investment. Natural resources include reserves of gold, silver, uranium, antimony and tungsten.

Although it has great potential for expanding its hydroelectric output, estimated at 300 billion kilowatt hours (kWh), rather than the current 16.5 billion kWh, it does not have the resources to develop the necessary infrastructure. Foreign investors from China and Russia are already assisting in development, but this overrules the potential for private domestic investment that would grow the economy as a whole. Tajikistan also has a serious international dispute with neighbouring Uzbekistan over water rights for the huge Roghun hydroelectricity dam under construction and located on the Vakhsh River.

GDP growth was 7.9 per cent in 2008, falling to 3.9 per cent in 2009 at the depths of the global contraction in trade and when energy and food prices were at record highs. However, growth rebounded to 6.5 per cent in 2010. Although the global economic crisis did not have a

direct influence on the economy, inflation fell from 20.4 per cent in 2008 to 6.5 per cent in 2009 as domestic demand helped lower fuel and food prices; inflation remained at 6.5 per cent in 2010.
Remittances in 2009 fell from a record high of US$2.54 billion in 2008 to US$1.75 billion (35.1 per cent of GDP), but were estimated to have risen again to US$2.06 billion in 2010. Over 75 per cent of the male workforce, including most of the qualified and skilled workers, is employed overseas, mainly in Russia and Kazakhstan, while estimates of unemployment are 11.5 per cent and underemployment even higher at 40 per cent. Subsistence farming occupies around 60 per cent of the workforce but with very low or no wages. GDP per capita was US$732 in 2009 and in 2011, the UN Human Development Index (HDI) ranked Tajikistan 127 (out of 187) for national development in health, education and income. In 2010, 40 per cent of the population experienced at least one indicator of poverty.
Tajikistan, located at the crossroads of Russia, Iran, Pakistan and China, is reported to have become a narcotics hub and a major transit route for opium produced not only in Afghanistan but also increasingly in Tajikistan itself.

External trade

Tajikistan belongs to the Eurasian Economic Community (EAEC), established to promote a customs union between its six member states (Belarus, Kazakhstan, Kyrgyzstan, Russia, Tajikistan, and Uzbekistan), and among other objectives to introduce a standardised currency exchange and rules for trade in goods and services. The EAEC evolved out of the Commonwealth of Independent States (CIS) Customs Union and has begun the process of merging with the Central Asian Co-operation Organisation (CACO). However, by 2010 only three members (Russia, Belarus and Kazakhstan) had instituted a customs union. On 19 October 2011, a free trade agreement (FTA) was signed by Russia with seven of its former Soviet republics: Armenia, Belarus, Kazakhstan, Kyrgyzstan, Moldova and Tajikistan. The FTA must be ratified by all relevant parliaments before its instigation in 2012.
Tajikistan has the potential to mine gold, silver, uranium, antimony and tungsten, which has yet to be exploited commercially. About 75 per cent of all exports are produced by one aluminium smelter, Talco. Cotton is another important commodity and accounts for almost 10 per cent of exports. Both of these products are subject to world prices and Talco is an old Soviet era factory, which along with the general infrastructure is in need of re-investment. Remittances are vital to the country's foreign earnings.

Imports

Main imports are electricity, hydrocarbons, aluminium oxide, machinery, equipment and foodstuffs.
Main sources: Russia (typically 24 per cent of total), China (24 per cent), Kazakhstan (10 per cent).

Exports

The main exports are aluminium, electricity, cotton, gold, fruits and vegetable oil and textiles.
Main destinations: Russia (typically 20 per cent of total), China (18 per cent), Turkey (13 per cent).

Agriculture

Farming

During the Soviet era agriculture was the mainstay of the Tajikistan economy, particularly cotton and wheat. Agriculture typically accounts for around 23 per cent of GDP and employs over 50 per cent of the workforce.
Because of Tajikistan's mountainous nature, only 7 per cent of the land is suitable for farming. Tajikistan is a large net importer of different types of grain. The main agricultural areas are in the lower-lying regions of the south-west and the north-west – part of the Fergana basin. In semi-arid farmland, yield depends on extensive irrigation; aging rural irrigation systems have fallen into serious disrepair after more than a decade of neglect, causing widespread water shortages, silting of irrigation channels, waterlogging, and soil salinity.
Crops constitute about two-thirds, and animal husbandry one-third, of rural production. Cattle, sheep and goats are reared. Important produce is cotton, grain, fruits, grapes, vegetables and tobacco leaves. Lack of processing and packing facilities and inefficient distribution mean that large amounts of the vegetable and fruit crops are wasted and that the country often fails even to meet its domestic needs. Farm machinery has suffered depreciation over the years without replacement, and the quality of seed varieties has fallen.
In a report published in 2005 – *The Curse of Cotton: Central Asia's destructive monoculture* – the International Crisis Group (ICG) said that while the former Soviet cotton producing countries of Uzbekistan, Tajikistan and Turkmenistan continued to exploit their cotton growers there was little hope of improving economic development and tackling poverty. The cotton industry is vital to the economy of Tajikistan, yet while the industry continues to rely on cheap labour (including children), land ownership is uncertain, state intervention discourages competition and the rule of law is limited, there is little incentive for the powerful vested interests to reform the system.
In addition to the economic and social costs to the rural populations, the environmental costs of the monoculture have been devastating. The degradation of the Aral Sea in particular has lead to international concern.

Fishing

Fishing remains important for domestic consumption, but pollution and a lack of investment have reduced fish stocks drastically. Tibet stone loach is a common fish in Tajikistan where it is present up to 4,500 metres altitude, but is of no commercial importance. The typical annual fish catch is over 200 tonnes.

Forestry

The state-owned forestry and wooded land accounts for only 5 per cent of land area with forest cover estimated at over 400,000 hectares (ha). Most of the forests located between 1,000 and 3,000 metre altitude are protected. The main stock of the forests include coniferous and juniper species, which are not available for wood supply.
There are no large-scale primary forest industries and the relatively low per capita consumption of forest products is met mainly by imports from the Russian Federation.

Industry and manufacturing

Industry contributes around 24 per cent to GDP.
Industrial production experienced a significant decline throughout the 1990s. The industrial sector is dominated by some 300 large state-owned enterprises in areas such as heavy industry, transport and wholesale trading and is mainly built around inefficient, labour-intensive production.
Aluminium is Tajikistan's key industrial sector. The country has one of the world's largest aluminium smelters, the state-owned Tadaz aluminium smelter, which has a capacity of 517,000 tonnes a year. Located at Tursunzade in western Tajikistan, the plant is a main source of revenue for the government.
Light industry accounts for around 45 per cent of the value of total industrial production. The main sectors are food processing (mainly dairy products, meat, fruit and cooking oil), tobacco, cotton cleaning, silk, textiles, knitted goods, footwear, tanning, carpet weaving and simple electronics.

Tourism

Tourism is undeveloped. The civil war in the nineties wrecked the tourist sector.Infrastructure was backward even before the civil war and has to be developed afresh. The importance of tourism to the economy is recognised and development is being encouraged, with attention to mountaineering, trekking and eco-tourism.

Environment

The Aral Sea is drying up due to the over-use of water from the two main rivers which feed into it and has lost 40 per cent of its water, dropping by up to 19 metres. This has resulted in desertification of the surrounding land. A UN study published in 2004 reported that there was no possibility of restoring the water and the need must be on preserving what is left.
Hundreds of thousands of people endured the worst winter since the 1960s without heat, electricity or running water before an appeal was made to the UN for aid in 2008. As the first winter snows fell and temperatures dropped to -20 Celsius people began to overload the power system in an attempt to keep warm, while rivers in the mountains that fed the hydroelectric power stations froze and cut off supplies; domestic pipes froze and left millions without drinking water. The UN issued an appeal for US$25 million.
A meeting was held in 2009 to determine water sharing between Tajikistan, Kyrgyzstan, Uzbekistan, Turkmenistan and Kazakhstan failed, as negotiators were unable to find a trade in water for energy and hydrocarbons. Tajikistan and Kyrgyzstan hold around 80 per cent of the water in the Aral Sea but suffer from lack of electricity during freezing winters, while the remaining three states downstream are semi-arid and need water for their cotton industries and agriculture.

Mining

Tajikistan has an established history of mineral production. In the Soviet era, the country used to mine and process uranium amounting to around 500,000 tonnes per year of ore, but with demand falling in the post-Soviet era, uranium production ceased in the 1990s.
Tajikistan holds around 500,000 tonnes of antimony reserves, 6.2 million tonnes of mercury, 60,000 tonnes of silver and 150 tonnes of gold. Lack of modern equipment and techniques means that some resources are not exploited to full capacity. Antimony, bismuth and mercury have been mined, but most deposits are depleted and the mines closing down. Despite large silver reserves, only around one tonne of silver is produced every year.
There are significant deposits of world-class marble; also uranium, radium, arsenic, bismuth, mica and small amounts of potassium salts, molybdenum, sulphur, boron, common salt, carbonates, fluorite, quartz sand, asbestos, lead and zinc. Deposits of semi-precious stones include lapis lazuli, rubies, amethyst and ornamental quartz.

Hydrocarbons

There are negligible proven oil reserves (of 12 million barrels) with production of just 280 barrels per day (bpd). In total, the CIS accounts for over 97 per cent of Tajikistan's oil needs. The state-owned national oil company, Tajikneftegaz, is responsible for all oil exploration, drilling and production.
Proven natural gas reserves were 5.6 billion cubic metres (cum), with production at 28 million cum, however consumption in 2007 was 849 million cum with domestic needs met by imports mainly from Uzbekistan. TajikGas is responsible for distribution of natural and liquefied gas; imports and distribution of petroleum products are carried out by the state-owned Tajiknefteproduct. Gas is supplied via a pipeline running from Uzbekistan to Dushanbe, in exchange for use of a rail corridor by Uzbekistan and gas pipeline across northern Tajikistan.
Tajikistan could have up to six billion tonnes of coal reserves, among of the largest coal deposits in Central Asia, but these are not yet proven. There are six large coal fields, with that at Fan Yagnob estimated to contain two billion tonnes of reserves. Mostly brown coal is mined in Yagnob and Myonadu, with coking coal at Nazarailok in the Karateginsk Valley in the east.

Energy

Total installed generating capacity was 4.42 gigawatts (GW) in 2006, of which 90 per cent was produced by hydropower; 40 per cent is consumed by the aluminium industry.
Tajikistan is a mountainous country with the potential to produce vast quantities of hydro-electricity. The potential is 300 billion kilowatt hours (kWh), whereas current production is 16.5 billion kWh. However, as one of the poorest countries in central Asia it requires foreign investment to develop its resources. Russia and Iran assisted in the construction of a 670MW Sangtuda-1 hydroelectric power station on the Vakhsh River. There are plans for two more, larger, power stations.
Barqi Tojik is the state-owned joint stock company with responsibility for production, transport and distribution of electricity. Energy generation is extremely variable from year to year, depending on the level of rainfall, especially in the winter period. There are two separate electrical networks, the northern grid in the Leninabad region and the southern grid, both linked to Uzbekistan. Both grids are destined to be linked following further investment.

Financial markets

Stock exchange

The Tajik commodity exchange was inaugurated in March 1996.

Banking and insurance

The banking sector remains extremely weak, with the five largest banks (which account for 85 per cent of total commercial bank credit and 90 per cent of deposits) handicapped by substantial non-performing loans. A law on Banks and Banking Activity in May 1998 introduced regulations which are close to international standards.
The restructuring of Agroinvestbank, the largest commercial bank, was completed in March 2004.

Central bank

National Bank of Tajikistan

Time

GMT plus five hours

Geography

Tajikistan is situated in the south-east of Central Asia. To the south of Tajikistan lies Afghanistan, Uzbekistan to the north and west, the People's Republic of China to the east and Kyrgyzstan to the north-east.
The terrain is almost entirely mountainous with more than one-half of the country above 3,000 metres. The main mountain ranges are the western Tian Shan in the north, the southern Tian Shan in the central region and the Pamirs in the south-east. The northern Pamirs are the highest mountains of Tajikistan, and of the former Soviet Union – Lenin Peak 7,134 metres and Ismail Samani Peak (formerly Communism Peak) 7,495 metres. There is a dense river network.

Hemisphere

Northern

Climate

Extreme continental; temperatures range between minus 20 degrees Celsius (C) and 0 degrees C in January, and from 0 degrees C to 30 degrees C in June, depending on altitude. From minus 5 degrees C to 35 degrees C in foothills, valleys and Dushanbe; sub-zero temperatures in the Pamir mountains. Rainfall between 150 and 250mm per annum.

Dress codes

Not overly formal but modest, particularly outside Dushanbe.

Entry requirements

Passports

Required by all, valid for at least six months after date of departure.

Visa

Required by all, except nationals of Russia, Belarus, Kazakstan and Kyrghyzstan. Visas may be obtained at Dushanbe airport by air travellers, but land travellers

must obtain their visas in advance from the nearest Tajik embassies. All applications must be supported by a letter of invitation endorsed by the Ministry of Foreign Affairs. (For details, see www.traveltajikistan.com/visas).
A business visa requires, in addition to a letter of invitation from a local company or organisation, a business letter undertaking full financial responsibility for expenses incurred by the representative and a full itinerary.
Visitors must obtain special permission to visit Gorno-Badakhshan autonomous region.

Currency advice/regulations

There are no restrictions on the import of local and foreign currencies, but it must be declared on arrival. Export of local currency is prohibited. Foreign currency can be exported up to the amount declared on arrival.
Travellers cheques are not generally accepted. Tajikistan is a cash-only economy, although carrying large amounts of cash can be dangerous. US dollars are widely accepted.

Customs

Most personal effects may be imported duty-free, subject to declaration on arrival.

Health (for visitors)

A reciprocal health agreement for urgent medical treatment exists with the United Kingdom. Proof of UK residence will be required. Standards of healthcare are significantly below Western levels. Although emergency treatment can be very expensive, doctors and hospitals often expect immediate cash payment. Uninsured visitors requiring urgent medical evacuation may face extreme difficulties. Comprehensive travel and medical insurance, including evacuation by air ambulance, is essential.

Mandatory precautions

Vaccination certificates are required for yellow fever if travelling from an infected area. Visitors staying for longer than 90 days may be submitted to an Aids test, which carries the possibility of infection with HIV or other pathogens, given the lack of medical supplies in Tajikistan.

Advisable precautions

Water precautions are recommended: water purification tablets may be useful, or drink bottled water. The risk of water-borne diseases, including cholera, is high.
It is advisable to be in date for the following immunisations: polio and tetanus (both within 10 years), typhoid, hepatitis A, and tuberculosis. Anti-malarial precautions are also advisable. There has been a significant increase in the number of cases of diphtheria and professional advice should be sort to determine a suitable precaution.
Any medicines required should be taken by the visitor, and it would be wise to have precautionary antibiotics if going outside major urban centres. A travel kit including a disposable syringe is a reasonable precaution.

Hotels

Visitors are advised to use well-known travel operators with established contacts in Tajikistan. There is a lack of adequate hotel accommodation and there are very few hotels outside the two main towns, Dushanbe and Khodzhent.

Credit cards

Credit cards are not generally accepted.

Public holidays (national)

The Islamic year contains 354 or 355 days, with the result that Muslim feasts advance by 10–12 days against the Gregorian calendar. Dates of feasts vary according to the sighting of the new moon, so cannot be forecast exactly.
Tajikistan uses the Persian calendar, which differs from the Gregorian calendar: there are 31 days in each of the first six months of the Persian calendar, 30 days in each of the next five months and 29 days in the last month, except in leap year when it has 30 days.

Fixed dates

1 Jan (New Year's Day), 8 Mar (Women's Day), 20–22 Mar (Navruz/Persian New Year), 1 May (Labour Day), 9 May (Victory Day), 9 Sep (Independence Day), 6 Nov (Constitution Day), 9 Nov (National Reconciliation Day).

Variable dates

Eid al Adha, Eid al Fitr.

Working hours

Banking

Mon–Fri: 0800–1700.

Business

Mon–Fri: approximately 0900–1800 (appointments are best made in the morning).

Shops

No formal hours, but generally within 0800–2100.

Telecommunications

Mobile/cell phones

Limited 900/1800 GSM services exist particularly around Dushanbe.

Electricity supply

220V AC

Social customs/useful tips

The increasing influence of Islam is widely evident, particularly in rural areas. The Islamic faith can be traced back to the seventh century in Tajikistan and although religious activity was banned during the Soviet era it has begun to play a more important role in everyday life since the late 1980s. Closer links with Iran (Iranian television is beamed into Tajikistan) have been established since independence, although alcohol (generally vodka) is still freely available and consumed. Gratuities are becoming more customary, particularly in international hotels.
'Dushanbe' – Tajik for Monday – is named after the day when, for centuries, merchants have gathered at Dushanbe's famous oriental bazaar.

Security

The prevalence of light weapons and local warlords throughout the country mean that care should be taken at all times. Visitors should avoid demonstrations, crowds, or congregations of military personnel.
Visitors may have their movements, hotel rooms and correspondence (including telephone and fax) monitored by security personnel. Taking photographs of military or otherwise strategically significant installations is not advised. There are periodic nightly curfews. Travel alone or on foot after dark is highly inadvisable. Car hire with a driver is advised rather than the use of public transport. Visitors are reminded to be vigilant and to dress down.

Getting there

Air

National airline: Tajikistan Airlines
International airport/s: Dushanbe (DYU), 3km south of city; restaurant, post office, chemist and left luggage.
There are bus services (nos 3 and 12), hours 0600–1800, and train services (lines 3 and 4), hours 0600–1900, between the airport and city centre, with a journey time of 20 minutes. Taxis operate between 0800—2000, journey time five minutes; as they are not metered the fare should be agreed in advance.
Airport tax: None.

Surface

There are border crossings with neighbouring countries, but not all of them may be open. It is advisable to check in advance.
Road: There are a few primary roads; secondary roads, particularly in mountain areas, are of poor quality. An all-weather road connects the capital Dushanbe to the Samarkand railhead (in Uzbekistan) to the north-west. Vehicles with Tajik licence plates may be refused entry into Uzbekistan.
IN 2007, a bridge was opened across the Pyanj River, build by the US army, linking the Tajik town of Nizhny Pyanj with Shir Khan Bandar in Afghanistan and extended the trans-Afghanistan road (Regional Road Corridor Improvement Project) through Central Asia.
The Regional Road Corridor Improvement Project, estimated at US$18 billion, to

improve Central Asian roads, airports, railway lines and seaports and provide a vital transit route between Europe and Asia was agreed, on 3 November 2007. Six new transit corridors, between Afghanistan, Azerbaijan, China, Kazakhstan, Kyrgyzstan, Mongolia, Tajikistan and Uzbekistan, of mainly roads and rail links, will be constructed, or existing resources upgraded, by 2013. Half the costs with be provided by the Asian Development Bank and other multilateral organisations and the other half by participating countries.
Rail: Tajikistan is linked to the rail network of the former Soviet republics, with the main line running south from Dushanbe to the Uzbekistan border town of Termez and on to Samarkand, Tashkent and the Black Sea. A line running from Andizhan to Samarkand, both in Uzbekistan, cuts through the northern tip of Tajikistan.

Getting about

National transport

Air: There are flights between Dushanbe and Khorog, Khojand and Kulyab, but take-off is dependent on weather conditions and fuel availability.
Road: The road network is generally in a poor condition. Roads are often closed due to weather conditions. Road travel, especially in the east, can be impeded by checkpoints, from which soldiers or other armed groups may shoot if vehicles do not stop. Travel by road should only be undertaken during daylight hours, with the appropriate vehicle and with the utmost precautions.
Buses: Buses run between the main centres when weather conditions permit.
Rail: The railway system is not well-developed, with only around 500km of rail track. The north and south of the country are not linked by rail, because of the mountainous terrain. Passengers are advised to safeguard their possessions.

City transport

Taxis: Taxis can be found at prominent places in the cities. They can also be hailed in the street. It is advisable to use only officially-licensed taxis. As they are not metered, the fare should be agreed in advance. Before setting off, the passenger should be satisfied that the driver is clear about the destination.
Minibus taxis (*marshrutkas*) travel on fixed routes and stop on request, but they can be over-crowded.

Car hire

There are no international car hire companies operating in Tajikistan.

BUSINESS DIRECTORY

Telephone area codes

The international direct dialling (IDD) code for Tajikistan is +992, followed by area code and subscriber's number:

Dushanbe 372

Useful telephone numbers

Police: 02
Fire: 01
Ambulance: 03

Chambers of Commerce

Tajikistan Chamber of Commerce and Industry, 21 Mazayeva Street, 734012 Dushanbe (tel: 279-519; fax: 211-480).

Banking

Agroinvestbank, Prospekt S Sherozi 21, Dushanbe (tel: 210-385; fax: 211-206).

Orienbank, 95/1 Rudaki Ave, Dushanbe (tel: 210-920; fax: 211-662).

Tajikbankbusiness (commercial bank), 29 Shotemur Street, 734025 Dushanbe (tel/fax: 210-634).

Tajikvnesheconombank (Tajikistan Bank for Foreign Economic Affairs), Dushanbe (tel: 233-571, 225-952).

Central bank

National Bank of Tajikistan, Prospekt Rudaki 107A, 734003 Dushanbe (tel: 600-3227; fax: 600-3235; e-mail: info@natbank.tajnet.com).

Travel information

Tajikistan Airlines, Titova Street 32/1, 734006 Dushanbe (tel: 212-247; fax: 510-041; e-mail: mop_gart@tajnet.com).

Tajikistan Republican Council of Tourism and Excursions, Sherozi Avenue 11, 734018 Dushanbe (tel: 332-770; fax: 334-420).

Travel Tajikistan, Proletarskaya 5/11, 734000 Dushanbe (tel: 247-673; fax: 217-184; e-mail: info@traveltajikistan.com).

National tourist organisation offices

National Tourism Company SAYOH, Pushkin Street 14, 734095 Dushanbe (tel: 234—233; fax: 217-184)

Ministries

Council of Ministers, Prospekt Rudaki 48, 734025 Dushanbe (tel: 232-903; fax: 228-120).

EU Co-ordinating Unit, c/o Ministry of External Economic Relations, Prospekt Rudaki 42, Dushanbe (tel: 222-403, 227-077; fax: 228-120).

Ministry of Agriculture, 46 Rudaki Ave, Dushanbe 734051 (tel: 276-249).

Ministry of Communications, 57 Rudaki Ave, 734025 Dushanbe (tel: 232-284; fax: 212-953; International Relations Department (tel: 216-010; fax: 510-277).

Ministry of Construction, 36 Kirova Street, Dushanbe 734025 (tel: 226-143).

Ministry of Economy and External Economic Affairs, 42 Rudaki Ave, 734025 Dushanbe (tel: 232-944).

Ministry of Finance, Prospekt Kuibysheva 3, 734025 Dushanbe (tel: 273-941; fax: 213-329).

Ministry of Foreign Affairs, 40 Rudaki Ave, 734051 Dushanbe (tel: 221-560, 232-971; fax: 227-051).

Ministry of Foreign Economic Relations, 42 Rudaki Ave, Dushanbe (tel: 232-971; fax: 232-964).

Ministry of Grain Products, 42 Rudaki Ave, Dushanbe 734051 (tel: 276-131).

Ministry of Industrial Afairs, 80 Rudaki Avenue, Dushanbe 734023 (tel: 232-249, 231-845; fax: 232-381).

Ministry of Information, Ulitsa Negmata Karabaeva 17, 734018 Dushanbe (tel: 335-851).

Ministry of Justice, 25 Rudaki Ave, 734025 Dushanbe (tel: 214-405; fax: 218-066).

Ministry of Trade and Material Resources, 37 Bokhtar Street, Dushanbe 734002 (tel: 273-434).

Prime Minister's Office, 80 Rudaki Ave, 734023 Dushanbe (tel: 211-871; fax; 215-110).

Other useful addresses

British Embassy, Gulyamov Street 67, Tashkent 700000, Uzbekistan (accredited to Tajikistan) (tel: (+998 71) 120-7852; fax: (+998 71) 120-6549).

State Statistical Committee (SSC), 17 Bokhtar Street, Dushanbe 734025 (tel: 276-882; fax: 275-408).

Tajikistan Embassy (USA), 1005 New Hampshire Avenue, Washington DC 20037 (tel: (+1-202) 223-6090; fax: (+1-202) 223-6091; e-mail: tajikistan@verizon.net).

Tajikistan (TDA) Office, c/o Tajik Bank Business, 23/2 Rudaki Avenue, 734620 Dushanbe (tel: 233-512; fax: 224-844).

Tajikvneshtorg (foreign trade organisation), Prospekt Lenina 41, 734051 Dushanbe (tel: 232-903; fax: 228-120).

National news agency: Khovar (in Russian) (www.khovar.tj).

Internet sites

Tajikistan Privatisation Agency: http://privatization.tajikistan.com

Tajikistan Resource Page: http://www.eurasianet.org/resource/tajikistan/index.shtml

National Tourism Company: http://www.tajiktour.tajnet.com

Tanzania

KEY FACTS

Official name: Jamhuri ya Muungano wa Tanzania (United Republic of Tanzania)

Head of State: President Jakaya Mrisho Kikwete (CCM) (from 2005; re-elected 2010)

Head of government: Prime Minister Mizengo Kayanza Peter Pinda (appointed 8 Feb 2008)

Ruling party: Chama Cha Mapinduzi (CCM) (Party of the Revolution) (since 1977; re-elected 30 Oct 2010)

Area: 945,087 square km

Population: 45.00 million (2010)*

Capital: Dodoma (official, legislative centre); Dar es Salaam (the former capital is the largest city and *de facto* commercial capital)

Official language: KiSwahili and English

Currency: Tanzania shilling (Tsh) = 100 senti (convertible with currencies of Kenya and Uganda)

Exchange rate: Tsh1,659.00 per US$ (Oct 2011)

GDP per capita: US$545 (2010)*

GDP real growth: 6.40% (2010)*

GDP: US$22.50 billion (2010)*

Labour force: 21.23 million (2009)*

Inflation: 10.50% (2010)*

Balance of trade: -US$2.83 billion (2010)

Annual FDI: US$433.44 million (2010)

* estimated figure

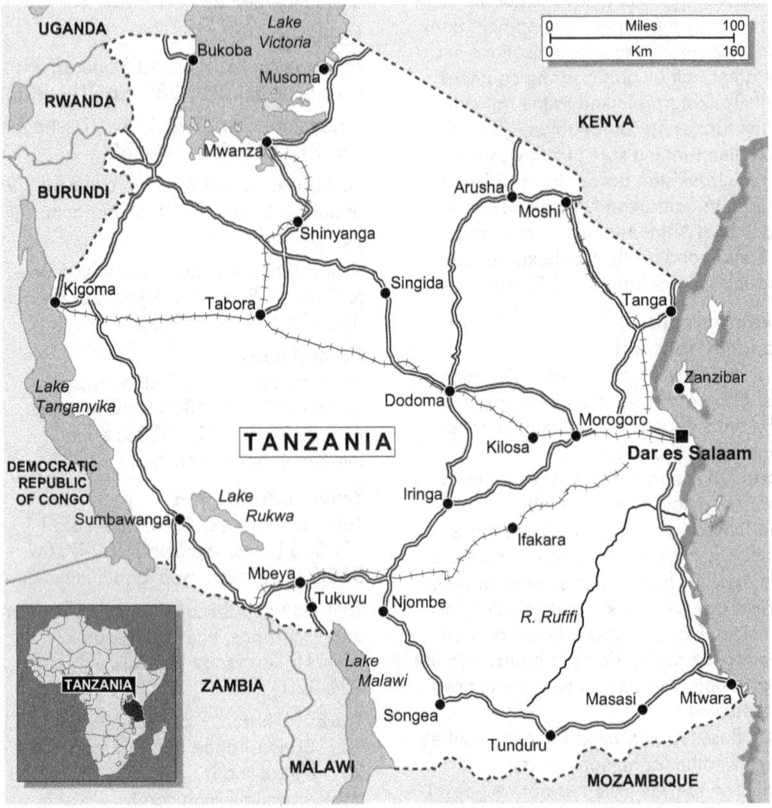

Seven candidates took part in presidential elections held on 31 October 2010 which were won comfortably by incumbent President Jakaya Kikwete (of the Chama Cha Mapinduzi (CCM) (Party of the Revolution)) with 61.17 per cent of the vote, ahead of his closest rival Willibrod Slaa (Chama cha Demokrasia na Maendeleo (Chadema) (Party for Democracy and Progress)) with 26.34 per cent. However 'comfortable' the win, it was, nevertheless well down on the 80 per cent President Kikwete attracted in the last elections in 2005. Turnout in 2010 was a low 43 per cent, possibly a reflection of the general apathy of the population to the CCM.

Parliamentary elections held on the same were also convincingly won by the CCM with 258 seats (out of 343). President Kikwete was sworn into office on 6 November; Mizengo Pinda remained as prime minister.

The National Electoral Commission turned down a demand for a recount by Willibrod Slaa; the chairman agreed that 'there could be irregularities in terms of arithmetic, but not enough to challenge the result'. Nevertheless, and despite the relative calm of the election, some observers did raise concerns about a number of aspects of the election, particularly the poor organisation at the polls by the National Election Commission (NEC) as well as more significant concerns about the slowness of counting the vote. Even so, there were no real concerns about outright fraud or vote rigging.

The opposition Chadema, did however complain of more fundamental problems, so that on 18 November 2010 all its walked out during President Kikwete's inaugural speech to the newly elected parliament. Before the walkout, the party's leadership had also refused to attend the swearing-in of the president on 6

November. Chadema activists, a number of whom were arrested, later made various attempts at launching a nationwide programme to explain their case to their supporters. On 5 January 2011, two people were killed and several dozen hurt following an attempt by a Chadema mob to storm the central police station in Arusha to free party officials and supporters who were being held there.

Zanzibar

The elections in Zanzibar saw no political unrest unlike the 2000 and 2005 elections. This was largely due to the Government of National Unity (GNU), which prompted a political compromise acceptable to all parties. The GNU had been agreed by the Zanzibari electorate in a referendum held in July 2010 – with a 'Yes' vote of 66.4 per cent. In the presidential elections in Zanzibar, Ali Mohamed Shein (CCM) won 50.1 per cent of the vote and Seif Sharif Hamad (Chama Cha Wananchi (CUF) (Civic United Front)) 49.1 per cent. President Shein took office on 3 November.

The Zanzibari president is expected to work closely with President Kikwete to try to make the GNU work in the spirit of compromise in which it was agreed. Specifically, it was agreed that the GNU will include the elected president, two vice presidents (both of whom are appointed by the president), and cabinet ministers who are also presidential appointees commensurate with the number of seats that each political party garnered in the House of Representatives. In line with the agreement, Zanzibari President Shein, appointed the first vice president from the main opposition party in the island, namely the Civic United Front (CUF) and the second from the CCM.

The economy

Tanzania registered eight consecutive years of gross domestic product (GDP) growth in excess of 6 per cent, according to the *African Economic Outlook 2011* (AEO), published jointly by the African Development Bank and the Organisation for Economic Co-operation and Development, until the global economic downturn began to affect growth in 2009. This was one of the most impressive rates of growth for a non-oil-producing sub-Saharan African country in the 2000s. Available data suggest that Tanzania's real GDP growth is firmly on the recovery path with growth at an estimated 6.4 per cent in 2010. Economic prospects for the medium term continue to look bright: inflationary pressures are low, gold prices (a major Tanzanian export) are at historic highs and investor sentiment towards East Africa's second largest economy remains upbeat.

In addition to gold, the country's natural gas sector has potential to add to Tanzania's exports, even though production is not expected to begin until after 2011. The British gas producer BG Group's second discovery off the coast of Tanzania underscores the Ruvuma basin's potential in east Africa, and could likely provide reserves for the region's first liquid natural gas (LNG)-export terminal. Indeed, continuing investment in the country's nascent gas sector will further boost Tanzania's gross fixed capital formation.

Key drivers of growth in the short and medium term include private consumption, exports and gross fixed capital, tourism revenues, foreign investment and aid. The government also intends to direct interventions to ensure that GDP growth is propelled mainly by key sectors, namely agriculture, manufacturing, tourism, mining and infrastructure. Given these factors, which should see the economy continuing its robust expansion in real terms, and in the absence of major adverse effects from the global economy, the forecast is a real GDP growth rate of 6.9 per cent in 2011 and 7.3 per cent in 2012.

The greatest risk to economic growth in the short and medium term is the growing fiscal deficit and the implied potential need to raise bridging funds. In turn, this could translate into an even greater reliance on foreign grants and investment or the government's need to raise such funds from non-concessional borrowing. Any significant disruption to either of these sources of funding would have negative ramifications for macroeconomic stability, and in turn, for economic development.

In October 2010, the Tanzanian National Bureau of Statistics (NBS) altered the weighting and methodology used to calculate the country's consumer price index (CPI). The changes were aimed at making the basket of consumer goods and services used to calculate the CPI more reflective of current rural and urban spending patterns. The most significant adjustment is to the contribution of food, which now makes up 47.8 per cent of the total as opposed to the 55.9 per cent used previously. In general, the new weightings, which were based on the 2007 household budget survey, reflect the course of Tanzania's recent economic development. GDP per capita in 2007 had grown significantly since 2000 when the previous survey was conducted. With more discretionary income for the average Tanzanian, the weightings of several items required adjustment.

The last quarter of 2010 saw the easing of the inflation pressures the country experienced in the first half of the year. Central bank figures indicated rates of 7.2 per cent, 6.3 per cent and 4.5 per cent in June, July and September, respectively. The downward trend was largely attributable to favourable weather conditions in the 2009/10 crop season that, in turn, improved food supplies. Food supply is

KEY INDICATORS **Tanzania**

	Unit	2006	2007	2008	2009	2010
Population	m	*38.20	*38.96	*39.74	*40.54	*45.00
Gross domestic product (GDP)	US$bn	14.20	16.70	20.70	21.00	*22.50
GDP per capita	US$	376	428	520	517	*545
GDP real growth	%	6.7	7.1	7.4	6.7	*6.4
Inflation	%	7.2	7.0	8.4	10.8	*10.5
Industrial output	% change	–	–	7.0	7.0	–
Agricultural output	% change	–	–	4.6	3.2	–
Exports (fob) (goods)	US$m	1,917.6	2,226.6	3,036.7	3,294.6	4,296.8
Imports (fob) (goods)	US$m	3,864.1	4,860.6	6,439.9	5,834.1	7,125.1
Balance of trade	US$m	-1,946.5	-2,634.1	3,403.2	-2,539.5	-2,828.3
Current account	US$m	-1,143.0	-1,496.8	-2,307.2	-1,933.6	-1,978.2
Total reserves minus gold	US$m	2,259.3	2,886.4	2,809.7	3,470.4	3,904.7
Foreign exchange	US$m	2,244.2	2,870.4	2,794.3	3,205.9	3,645.4
Exchange rate	per US$	1,251.90	1,245.00	1,193.31	1,320.30	1,409.30

* estimated figure

expected to remain good at least through the first part of 2011, pointing to possible additional declines in food inflation, and hence, headline inflation. This also assumes stable oil prices as well as continued prudence in monetary and fiscal policies.

International trade and relations

Tanzania, along with the other five East African Community (EAC) partner states (Kenya, Tanzania, Uganda, Rwanda and Burundi), is working on a full monetary union scheduled for 2012, following on the Common Market Protocol for the EAC that became effective in January 2010. Signing of the Framework for Economic Partnership Agreement (FEPA) with the European Union, which was to have been completed by 2010, was once again postponed – in May 2011 the UK Ambassador to Tanzania was quoted as saying he hoped they would be finalised at the end of the year. The negotiations are slated to resume with key issues, which the two parties had failed to agree on during earlier negotiations for FEPA in June 2010. These issues included the most-favoured-national clause, development components and export taxes. The EAC negotiators failed to sign the framework agreement because their European Union partners declined to incorporate important development and trade issues in the document.

Tanzania's long-established economic partners are mostly in Europe. This is true in terms of trade, investment, aid and migration. For example, over 55 per cent of the country's exports as well as 23 per cent of its imports are with the European Union. Japan and India also account for significant proportions of the country's merchandise trade. However, as is the case for much of the continent, recent years have seen the emergence of new economic partners. Strictly speaking, some of the most significant ones are not exactly 'emerging'; they are simply non-Western.

One of the most significant non-Western economic partners for Tanzania is India. Tanzania and India have traditionally enjoyed close, friendly and co-operative relations. Between the 1960s and the 1980s, the political relationship was driven largely by shared ideological commitments to anti-colonialism, anti-racism, socialism in various forms as well as genuine desire for South-South co-operation. Former President Julius Nyerere was held in high esteem in India and was conferred not only the Jawaharlal Nehru Award for International Understanding in 1974, but also the International Gandhi Peace Prize in 1995. During the post-Cold War re-adjustment of policies, both countries initiated economic reform programmes around the same time with external relations aimed at broader international political and economic engagement, cultivation of international business relationships and the promotion of foreign investment. In the 2000s, Indo-Tanzanian ties have evolved into a modern and pragmatic relationship with greater and diversified economic engagement.

According to trade figures, India has exported almost a billion dollars' worth of goods to Tanzania per annum in the 2000s; these consist mostly of mineral fuels, oils, iron and steel, pharmaceuticals, motor vehicles (including auto parts), electrical machinery, plastic products including synthetic polymers, rubber items including tires, cotton fabrics, apparel and clothing and cereals. For its part, Tanzania's major exports to India include vegetables, pulses, cashew nuts, raw cotton, gemstones, cloves and other spices, wood and articles thereof and tanning/dyeing extract.

China is another very significant emerging economic partner for Tanzania. Much like India, Tanzania and China have long enjoyed very strong diplomatic relations, going back to the socialist period of 1961–85 in Tanzania. As one of the major recipients of China's aid to Africa, Tanzania has received more than 100 co-operation projects and programmes totalling several billion dollars since the early 1960s. The majority of earlier aid projects were undertaken in the form of turnkey projects, of which the most well known is the Tanzania-Zambia (Tazara) railway linking Tanzania's Dar es Salaam with Zambia's Kapiri Mposhi. At its construction, Tazara was one of the largest foreign aid projects China had ever undertaken, financed through an interest free loan of US$500 million and built at the height of Cold War hostilities by the Chinese Railway Engineering Corporation (CREC) between 1970 and 1976.

At the same time, Chinese investors and contractors have been particularly successful in the country's construction, water and agriculture sectors, with an estimate of over 100 Chinese-funded enterprises active in the country, and growing. In addition to these, there are many individual Chinese entrepreneurs active in various service sectors such as health, merchandise trade and the hospitality business. There are conflicting statistics on the number of Chinese in the country. In 2000, Tanzania's immigration department indicated that 239 residence permits had been issued to Chinese nationals, making them one of the smaller groups of foreigners in the country. However, China's official Xinhua News Agency reported in 2008 that some 10,000 Chinese people lived in Tanzania.

Doing business

Tanzania fell in both its competitive ranking and its doing business ranking in 2011. According to the World Economic Forum's 2011–12 *Global Competitiveness Report*, Tanzania ranked 120th (out of 142 countries) having slid by 7 positions from 2010–11. This continues the steady trend from 97th (out of 122) in 2006. Tanzania has also slipped in business environment according to the World Bank's *Doing Business* 2011 report. Of 183 countries, Tanzania ranks as 128th in ease of doing business, compared to 125th in the previous edition. The only aspect where Tanzania improved (2 places up from 111 to 109) is cross-border trade – largely because of the coming into full operation of the EAC Customs Union (since January 2010) and the EAC Common Market (since July 2010).

The country's relatively small private sector presents potential opportunities for broader-based growth and reductions in income poverty. Improving Tanzania's overall business environment and its competitiveness have been accorded a high priority by both the government and by the country's development partners. The government is making efforts to improve the country's business environment by continuing several reform programmes, including the Business Environment Strengthening for Tanzania (BEST) Programme, the Tax Modernisation Plan (TMP) and the on-going Second Generation Financial Sector Reform.

Although the country's poverty rate has declined in the 2000s, the absolute number of poor Tanzanians increased by an estimated 1.3 million over the same period. Rapid population growth not only translates into a swelling youth population with few employment opportunities, but also it means a greater strain on the already meagre social services. This structural demographic challenge will persist as long as the country's fertility rate remains high, child mortality continues to decline and life expectancy increases.

Risk assessment

Politics	Fair
Economy	Fair
Regional stability	Fair

COUNTRY PROFILE

Historical profile

1832 The increasing importance of Zanzibar as a spice and slave-trading centre led the Sultan of Oman to transfer his capital there from Muscat. Around this time, Britain signed a number of agreements with Oman to limit the potential threat to Britain's colonies from France. Meanwhile, Germany signed a number of 'friendship' treaties with local chiefs – treaties which formed the basis of the German East Africa Company, which was established to exploit and colonise what became Tanganyika.
1886 The UK and Germany signed an agreement which gave Germany control of mainland Tanzania and the UK control of Zanzibar.
1918 After Germany's defeat in the First World War, the League of Nations mandated the territory to Britain.
1961 Tanganyika gained independence under Julius Nyerere and the Tanganyika Africa National Union (Tanu).
1964 The United Republic of Tanzania was formed following the union of Tanganyika and Zanzibar.
1977 The new constitution established a real one-party state for the whole of Tanzania after the Tanganyika African National Union and Zanzibar's Afro-Shirazi Party merged to create Chama Cha Mapinduzi (CCM) (Party of the Revolution).
1979 Tanzania invaded Uganda, forcing its dictator, Idi Amin, to flee to Saudi Arabia.
1985 Nyerere stepped down as president and was replaced by the president of Zanzibar, Ali Hassan Mwinyi.
1992 The constitution was amended to allow multi-party politics.
1995 The first multi-party elections took place. Benjamin William Mkapa (CCM) was elected president and the CCM was re-elected to government. The Zanzibar opposition Civic United Front (CUF) refused to accept the election results in Zanzibar.
1999 A conciliation agreement was signed between the CCM and the CUF, bringing an end to four years of hostility. Julius Nyerere, the former president and founder figure of modern Tanzania, died.
2000 President Benjamin Mkapa was re-elected for a second term. The CCM was re-elected in the parliamentary elections. Because of unfair elections in Zanzibar, a re-run was held in 16 of its 50 constituencies; it was won by the ruling party, the CCM.
2001 There were clashes in Zanzibar between supporters of CUF and the police. The CCM and the opposition CUF signed a further agreement aimed at ending hostilities on Zanzibar.
2002 The African Development Bank (ADB) signed an agreement with the Deputy Minister for Finance, Alhaj Adbisalaam Issa Khatibu, for a loan of approximately US$47 million to partially finance the Dar es Salaam water supply and sanitation project.
2004 The presidents of Tanzania, Uganda and Kenya signed a protocol in Arusha over a proposed customs union.
2005 Jakaya Kikwete was elected president. The CCM retained an outright majority of seats in parliamentary elections.
2006 A challenge to the legality of the 1964 Act of Union was dismissed by the Zanzibar high court. The African Development Bank cancelled over US$640 million in debt by Tanzania.
2008 President Jakaya Kikwete was elected 2008 chairman of the African Union in January. Governor of the central bank, Daudi Ballali, was sacked after an international audit found evidence of improper payments to local companies of over US$120 million. A corruption scandal forced the president to dissolve his cabinet and the prime minister to resign. Mizengo Pinda was appointed as prime minister.
2009 China granted US$22 million in aid to Tanzania, during the visit of Chinese President Hu Jintao, who also opened a US$56 million, 60,000 seat sports stadium, funded mainly by the Chinese government. Japan agreed to provide around US$22 million under its poverty support credit scheme.
2010 In April around 162,000 Burundi refugees, domiciled since 1972 after some 150,000 Hutus had been killed in Burundi, were granted citizenship. On 14 May, Tanzania along with Uganda and Ethiopia signed an agreement to share the waters of the River Nile. In the new deal the three nations (out of five) that form the source of the river, reserved more of the water for themselves. Egypt and Sudan, which had until then taken the greater share, objected but finally agreed after 13 years of negotiations had failed to resolve the issue earlier. A new micro-finance bank, Access Bank Tanzania, was launched in July, specifically aimed at women who can open an account with minimal capital and an identity card. Seven candidates took part in presidential elections held on 31 October. Incumbent President Jakaya Kikwete (CCM) won 61.17 per cent of the vote, his closest rival Willibrod Slaa (CDM) won 26.34 per cent. The ruling CCM won 258 seats (out of 343) in parliamentary elections, held on the same day. President Kikwete was sworn into office on 6 November; Mizengo Pinda remained in post as prime minister. In presidential elections in Zanzibar, Ali Mohamed Shein (CCM) won 50.1 per cent of the vote and Seif Sharif Hamad (CUF) 49.1 per cent. President Shein took office on 3 November. The National Electoral Commission had turned down a demand for a recount by Willibrod Slaa; the chairman agreed that 'there could be irregularities in terms of arithmetic, but not enough to challenge the result'.
2011 According to government statistics in August the economy was growing by an average 6.7 per cent, despite the chronic shortage of energy, which was having an adverse affect on horticultural cultivation as production of perishable flowers with time-sensitive deliveries were cut. On 22 August, the minister of agriculture warned cashew nut exporters that the government would impose a punitive fine plus 15 per cent of the would-be sales price before shipping if domestic crops of unprocessed cashew nuts were sold abroad directly. Government policy is to enhance the value of Tanzania's cashew nut crop through processing so that 10 per cent of profits are returned to the country and invested in farming equipment. An investigation by the UK's Serious Fraud Office, begun in 2005, which had been investigating alleged bribery by BAE Systems (the defence company) was finally concluded when the company agreed to make an *ex gratia* payment of £29.5 million (US$50 million) to the Tanzanian government. The government agreed to use the money for educational projects. A ferry travelling between the Zanzibar islands of Unguja and Pemba sank on 10 September. Of the some 800 passengers on-board, rescuers managed to save around 620.

Political structure

Constitution
The constitution was introduced in 1965 following the union of Zanzibar and Tanganyika in 1964. Zanzibar is partially autonomous, with 50 political constituencies.
The 1977 constitution established a one-party state for the whole of Tanzania after the two parties merged to create Chama Cha Mapinduzi (CCM) (Party of the Revolution).

Independence date
1961

Form of state
Republic

The executive
Executive power rests with the president, who is elected by direct popular vote for a five-year term. The president can serve a maximum of two terms.
One vice president is appointed by the president, as is the cabinet (in consultation with the prime minister), and the

second vice president is the directly elected president of Zanzibar.

National legislature

The unicameral National Assembly (Bunge) has 274 members of which 232 are elected in single-seat constituencies for a five-year term. The president allocates 37 special seats to women and five seats are allocated to members of the Zanzibar House of Representatives

Legal system

The legal system is based on English common law, the 1977 Union and 1985 Zanzibari constitutions, as amended. The judiciary is relatively independent. A permanent Commission of Enquiry has wide powers to investigate abuses of power. In Zanzibar, *Kadhis* (Islamic courts) have jurisdiction over certain areas of law.

Last elections

31 October 2010 (presidential and parliamentary)

Results: Presidential: Jakaya Kikwete (CCM) won 61.17 per cent of the vote, Willibrod Slaa (CDM) 26.34 per cent, Ibrahim Haruna Lipumba (CUF) 8.06 per cent.

Parliamentary: Chama Cha Mapinduzi (CCM) (Revolutionary Party) won 258 seats (out of 343), Chama Cha Demokrasia Na Maendeleo (CCDM) (Democracy and Progress Party) 44, Chama Cha Wananchi (CCW) (Civic United Front) 34, Tanzania Labour Party (TLP) one, National Convention for Construction and Reform–Mageuzi (NCCR–Mageuzi) four, United Democratic Party one; others ten seats.

Next elections

2015 (presidential and parliamentary)

Political parties

Ruling party

Chama Cha Mapinduzi (CCM) (Party of the Revolution) (since 1977; re-elected 30 Oct 2010)

Main opposition party

Chama Cha Wananchi (CUF) (Civic United Front).

Population

45.00 million (2010)*

Last census: August 2002: 34,443,603 (provisional)

Annual growth rate: 2.3 per cent 1994–2004 (WHO 2006)

Ethnic make-up

About 98 per cent of the population is of indigenous African or Arab (Zanzibar) origin, with the remainder mainly from the Indian sub-continent. Those of Indian, Pakistani and Goan descent tend to work in the towns, mainly dominating the trading environment, but also moving into the industrial sector. The small population of Arab descent is mainly engaged in trade. There are about 10,000 Europeans.

Over 120 tribal groups exist in Tanzania, the most important of which are Sukuma (12 per cent of total population), Makonde (4 per cent), Chagga (4 per cent), Haya (3 per cent), Nyamwezi (3 per cent), Ha (3 per cent), Gogo (3 per cent) and Hehe (3 per cent).

Religions

Islam and Christianity are the main organised religions. However, many people adhere to ancient tribal and animist religions. The religious make-up is believed to be Christianity: 33 per cent, Islam: 33 per cent, traditional beliefs: 33 per cent and Hinduism: 1 per cent.

Education

In 2003, three million seven to 13-year-olds were not in school, most enrolled late and intake and transition rates remained very low. This was the a result of the introduction of 'user fees' during the 1990s, when more than two million Tanzanian children were prevented from entering school and the rate of illiteracy began rising at 2 per cent a year. The education system is beset with problems of poor quality and a lack of participation among enrolled students. This reversed the country's early success of the 1960s when the literacy rate was around 91 per cent (the highest in Africa). The root cause of the problem is the government's debt obligations which have forced it to cut back on education. By 2000, the government was spending twice as much per capita on debt repayments than on education.

In 2001, the government announced in 2001 that it would abolish primary school fees, and the World Bank announced US$150 million interest free credit to expand school access and increase school retention at the primary level. During 2001, Tanzania enrolled 1,100,000 pupils in school, a 41 per cent increase over 779,000 in 2000.

The fees for secondary education, however, widened the gap between those participating in primary and secondary education. Parents must pay fees they cannot afford and teachers are under pressure to act as debt collectors to finance their schools. The situation is particularly dire in rural areas where schools are only able to recover around a third of fees. As a result, the education system is beset with problems of poor quality and a lack of participation among enrolled students. Oxfam, the main non-governmental organisation investing in Tanzanian education, estimates that in poorer schools there is only one desk for every 38 pupils and one textbook for every four children. Meanwhile, teachers are trying to cope with crumbling classrooms, falling salaries, worsening conditions and increasing class sizes.

Moreover, gross inequalities have developed between genders and classes, particularly in the fee-paying secondary schools. This has led to a progressive exclusion and marginalisation of adolescents and the most vulnerable children from basic family and community support.

Literacy rate: 77 per cent adult rate; 92 per cent youth rate (15–24) (Unesco 2005).

Compulsory years: Seven to 14.

Enrolment rate: 67 per cent gross primary enrolment; 6 per cent gross secondary enrolment; of relevant age groups (including repeaters) (World Bank).

Pupils per teacher: 37 in primary schools.

Health

The public health sector has been increasingly deprived of funds in recent years due to the government's move towards privatisation of the health service sector. User fees, introduced in the 1990s to ease the government's fiscal problems, have denied pregnant women and the rural poor access to primary healthcare facilities and essential medicines. While the government claims that mothers and children under five years receive free healthcare, in reality it is very different, particularly for those suffering from HIV/Aids, mental health problems and other diseases. Moreover, medicines which are supposed to be free are often in short supply at state-run hospitals and the number of hospital beds per capita has declined since 1990.

HIV/Aids

On top of inadequate health service provision, HIV/Aids is a continuing problem with infection rates estimated at over 25 per cent in urban areas. Like many African countries, Tanzania cannot afford the expensive Western drugs needed to treat the effects of Aids and initiatives aimed at the promotion of safe sex are often poorly designed and ineffective.

In 2007, officials in Zanzibar released figures that showed the HIV/Aids rate had increase from 0.6 per cent in 2002, to 0.9 per cent of the population in 2006.

HIV prevalence: 8.8 per cent aged 15–49 in 2003 (World Bank)

Life expectancy: 48 years, 2004 (WHO 2006)

Fertility rate/Maternal mortality rate: 4.9 births per woman, 2004 (WHO 2006); maternal mortality 1,100 per 100,000 live births (World Bank)

Birth rate/Death rate: 39.5 births and 17.4 deaths per 1,000 people (2003)

Child (under 5 years) mortality rate (per 1,000): 104 per 1,000 live births (2003); 29.4 per cent of children aged

under five were malnourished (World Bank).
Head of population per physician: 0.02 physicians per 1,000 people, 2002 (WHO 2006)

Welfare
Between 15 million and 18 million of the total population live below the World Bank poverty line. The state does not have the capacity to function as a welfare provider while its ability to increase poor adult literacy rates, especially among women, remains negligible. Rather than building up the capacity and efficiency of state institutions, multilateral and bilateral donors are contracting out welfare services to non-governmental organisations (NGOs), which have little accountability and whose impact is usually localised and short-term.

Main cities
Dodoma (capital, estimated population 168,706 in 2005), Dar es Salaam (former capital and *de facto* commercial capital, estimated population 2.6 million), Arusha (317,169), Mbeya (258,102), Morogoro (235,402), Mwanza (225,244), Zanzibar (219,954), Tanga (190,029).

Languages spoken
KiSwahili is the predominant language with English spoken by most people, especially in the main towns. English is the language most used in business.
Official language/s
KiSwahili and English

Media
The government allows private newspapers and private radio and television operators, although these organisations exercise a strong degree of self-censorship.
Media policies on Zanzibar are different from the mainland; there are no private broadcasters or newspapers although reception of both is received on the islands.
Press
Dailies: A number of newspapers have English and KiSwahili editions including the government-owned *Daily News* and *Harari Leo* (www.dailynews-tsn.com), *Nipashe* and *The Guardian* (www.ippmedia.com); in KiSwahili, *Majira* (www.majira.co.tz), *Tanzania Daima* (www.freemedia.co.tz); in English *This Day* (www.thisday.co.tz).
Weeklies: Including Sunday papers, are *Sunday News*, *Mzalendo* (KiSwahili), *Daily News on Saturday*, *East African*, *Express*, *Heko*, *Mfanyakazi*, *Shangwe*, *Sunday Mail*, *Sunday News*, *Sunday Observer*, *Sunday Times* and *Taifa Letu*. The *Government Gazette* is a weekly, which lists official announcements.
Business: Publications include the weekly *Business Times* (www.businesstimes.co.tz) and *The Express* (www.theexpress.com).
Periodicals: A wide range is published. They include *The African Review*, published by the Department of Political Science of the University of Dar es Salaam; *Foreign Trade News Bulletin* published twice a year by the Ministry of Industry.
Weeklies
Some daily newspapers have Sunday editions. Other publications include *The Arusha Times* (www.arushatimes.co.tz), the *Government Gazette*, which lists official announcements and *Taifa Letu*.
Broadcasting
Radio: The public service Radio Tanzania Dar es Salaam (RTD) and Parapanda Radio Tanzania (PRT), an FM station geared to younger listeners, are adapting to the increasingly commercial media environment. RTD covers 85 per cent of the country with internal services in KiSwahili and external services in English. The Voice of Tanzania and Zanzibar broadcasts on three wavelengths in KiSwahili. The Voice of Tanzania-Zanzibar operates from Zanzibar.
There are many locally based FM radio stations, including Radio Free Africa (www.radiofreeafrica.co.tz), Radio One (www.ippmedia.com), Kiss FM (www.kissfmtz.net), Clouds FM (www.cloudsfm.co.tz) has a network of nine city stations include Zanzibar.
Television: Public service Televisheni ya Taifa (TVT) does not have complete national coverage. Independent Television (ITV) (www.itv.co.tz) is a popular network, Coastal Television Network and Dar es Salaam Television and Star TV (www.startvtz.com) are private, while TV Zanzibar is state run.
News agencies
The Guardian Limited (www.ippmedia.com).

Economy
The economy is dominated by agriculture, which accounted for 28.8 per cent of GDP in 2009, and provided employment for up to 80 per cent of the work force. Major cash crops include coffee, cotton, cashew nuts, tea, sisal and cut flowers. As part of the International Monetary Fund (IMF) set criteria for poverty reduction, food production for domestic consumption has improved and the government's goal is self-sufficiency in basic foods. Industry is dominated by gold mining, which has grown in production and value since 2008, so that by 2010 it represented 30–40 per cent of foreign earnings. Gold represented 39.8 per cent of Tanzania's total goods and services exports, and 26.1 per cent of manufacturing. The service sector in 2009 constituted 46.9 per cent of GDP, of which tourism has grown to become the third pillar in the economy, earning US$1.28 billion in 2008.
Annual GDP growth during the 2000s was an average 6.8 per cent according to the IMF, and was not unduly affected by the global economic crisis; it was 7.4 per cent in 2008, falling to 6.7 per cent in 2009 and rising to an estimated 6.5 per cent in 2010. Growth has been underpinned by a rise in global gold prices and fiscal measures introduced by the government to enhance macro-economic policies in public financial management under the terms of an IMF loan of around US$330 million. However, inflation remained high during this period, at 8.4 per cent in 2008, rising to 11.8 in 2009 before falling somewhat to an estimated 10.6 per cent in 2010. Inflation was projected to fall to 7 per cent in 2011.
Tanzania is East Africa's third-largest economy (after Kenya and Ethiopia), but it remains an unequal society. In 2011, the UN Human Development Index (HDI) ranked Tanzania 152 (out of 187) for national development in health, education and income. Since 2000, Tanzania's progress has grown to match other sub-Saharan African countries. In 2010, 56.3 per cent of the population experienced at least one indicator of poverty, while 67.9 per cent lived on the equivalent of US$1.25 per day. Migrant worker remittances provided only US$16 million (0.1 per cent of GDP) in 2009, as Tanzania is a destination for migrant workers rather than a source of migrant workers.

External trade
Tanzania is a member of the East African Community (EAC) (with Burundi, Kenya, Rwanda and Uganda). The East African Community Common Market Protocol (EACMP) was launched on 1 July 2010, which will lead to the free movement of labour, capital, goods and services between member states as well as employment opportunities and easier flow of investment capital. The signed protocol now requires that legislation in all states must be harmonised to conform to its jurisdiction. Tanzania is also a member of the Southern African Development Community (SADC), the objectives of which include reducing trade barriers, achieving regional development and economic growth and evolving common systems and institutions.
Foreign earnings provided by tourism ranks second to industrial and manufacturing exports, in particular gold, followed by agricultural exports including coffee, which is the principal cash crop, along with cotton, sisal and tobacco. Cloves are Zanzibar's principal export commodity.

In 2009 international donors pledged US$1 billion to upgrade transport links across eastern and southern Africa, in an initiative to carry goods to market cheaper and faster. Not only are roads and rail links being improved, but also time-consuming official procedures were streamlined for efficiency.

Imports

Principal imports are consumer goods, machinery and transport equipment, industrial raw materials and crude oil.

Main sources: India (typically 12 per cent of total), China (11 per cent), South Africa (11 per cent).

Exports

Main exports include gold, coffee, cashew nuts, cotton, sisal, manufactured goods and tobacco.

Main destinations: Switzerland (typically 20 per cent of total), China (13 per cent), Kenya (7 per cent).

Agriculture

Farming

The agricultural sector is the mainstay of the economy. It contributes around 45 per cent of GDP and over 50 per cent of export earnings. Approximately 70 per cent of the population are peasant farmers.

Land laws affecting ownership are complicated and hinder potential investors in agricultural activity. The government has expressed an interest in taking up land reform to attract the private sector.

Tanzania has more than 40 million hectares of arable land, but only six million are cultivated. Only 15 per cent of the country has access to water, and the crops are almost totally dependent on the weather. Coffee, cotton, sisal, tobacco, cashew nuts and tea are the most important crops.

There has been a serious decline in production of most crops. Coffee, cotton and sisal are among the crops which have declined and stagnated, although some export crops are showing signs of growth, including tobacco, tea, cashew nuts and horticulture.

The cashew nut sector has benefited from a return to a system where smallholders deal directly with the buyers. Tanzania supplies more than one-quarter of the global market.

Heavy cotton subsidies in the US have affected cotton production in Tanzania, following the liberalisation of the markets. The effects of subsidies are also felt in traditional industries such as beef, wheat and dairy products and also in non-traditional markets like spices.

Fishing

Tanzania has extensive inland as well as marine fisheries, with the freshwater lakes and rivers accounting for over 80 per cent of production. Foreign vessels trawl Tanzania's exclusive economic zones and take their catches elsewhere for processing; the government wishes to attract some of this business to Tanzania. Nile perch and sardines make up over three-quarters of Tanzania's total fish exports. Tanzania exports around US$150 million of Nile perch and related products annually, 80 per cent of which are sold to the EU market. The industry is well-organised and gives employment to over 300,000 people. The government is encouraging domestic fish consumption by developing local fish markets.

In a meeting of African ministers in Namibia, held in 2009, members discussed illegal and unregulated fishing, which is estimated to cost Africa US$1 billion per annum in lost revenue and the threat to stocks and local artisan fishing.

Forestry

Tanzania has around 33 million hectares of forests and woodlands. The forests have been under intense pressure from population growth and activities such as harvesting of fuelwood, agricultural demands, fires and illegal logging. The government is seeking to create the conditions for private investment in plantation and sustainable management by local communities.

Industry and manufacturing

The industrial and manufacturing sector accounts for 16.7 per cent of GDP and employs 5 per cent of the workforce. Typically, less than a fifth of industrial production is exported.

Most production is geared towards import substitution and the government has traditionally directed public investment towards the sugar and textile industries, tanneries, pulp and paper mills, the fertiliser industry, cement factories, and sisal and cashew nut processing industries. These are engaged in the processing of local minerals and agricultural raw materials for local consumption. Production also includes paper and pulp, cement, textiles and some light engineering.

Growth has been restricted by a lack of foreign exchange needed for the import of raw materials, spare parts and fuel. Foreign aid is aimed at rehabilitating existing industries, but the government is slowly gearing production towards export markets. The high cost of credit inhibits the development of the private sector which is characterised by small enterprises.

Tourism

Tourism is Tanzania's fastest-growing industry. The government's target is over one million visitors by 2011. Tanzania is a comparatively expensive destination, which results in around 50 per cent of visitors entering on short trips from neighbouring countries rather than directly into Tanzania for longer and more lucrative stays. Several tourism and travel organisations inaugurated a joint programme to investigate ways of attracting more visitors directly into the country.

The government has made tourist visas available at the point of entry into Tanzania. The fact that Tanzania has only a small number of embassies abroad makes it difficult for tourists to obtain the necessary entry visas in advance.

Environment

There is concern about gold mining activities taking place in the Eastern Arc Mountains of Tanzania, which are said to be destroying the Amani nature reserve, a UNESCO-designated biosphere reserve and Balangai forest reserve.

It was revealed in 2008 that a new genus of monkey, the *Rungwecebus kipunji*, (known locally as the kipunji) the first to be described since 1925, had been located in two remote forests – Rungwe-Livingstone Forest in the Southern Highlands and the Ndundulu Forest in the Udzungwa Mountains. The *kipunji* are threatened on two fronts – their habitat is at risk from loggers and they are often trapped and killed by farmers as they raid cultivated crops. It is estimated that there are around 1,000 Kipunji in existence.

The *Rungwecebus kipunji* is being considered for inclution on the International Union for Conservation of Nature and Natural Resources (IUCN) Red List of Threatened Species.

Mining

Tanzania is well-endowed with mineral sources, especially gold, base metals, diamonds and other gemstones. Mining accounts for around 2.3 per cent of GDP and is targeted to increase to 10 per cent by 2025.

Gold mining and production have expanded considerably in recent years. 50 tonnes were produced in 2004. Tanzania is the third largest gold producer in Africa. Gold has become a major export, mainly to the EU.

There is significant interest in the Kagera nickel-copper-cobalt belt, which runs north and east bordering with Burundi.

There are considerable reserves of iron, tin, gypsum and kaolin. There is a large phosphate mine at Minjingu, supplying a fertiliser plant at Tanga.

Tanzania is also a significant producer of gems, including a diamond mine in Shinyanga and rubies from Longido. Other gemstones include sapphires and tanzanite, which is unique to Tanzania.

Hydrocarbons

There are no known oil reserves and Tanzania must import all of its domestic needs, which was 32,000 barrels per day

of oil in 2008. International oil and gas exploration companies have been operating offshore in territorial waters since 2007.
Tanzania's only refinery can process 15,000bpd of crude oil. More than 50 per cent of imported oil is consumed by vehicles, with industry consuming 25 per cent and the rest used commercially and in homes. In 2008 petroleum imports accounted for 26 per cent of all imports.
In May 2010, the government in partnership with US-based Noor Oil and Industrial Technologies began construction of a 200,000 barrels per day oil refinery and pipeline. The cost is estimated at US$3.5 billion, with the pipeline connecting Dar es Salaam to Mwanza and Kigoma, with plans to expand the pipeline into a network linking neighbouring countries.
Proved natural gas reserves were 6.5 billion cubic metres in 2007. Offshore reserves have been discovered at Songo Songo Island in the Indian Ocean, Kimbiji and Mnazi Bay near Mtwara. Natural gas is pumped from the offshore Songo Songo field to the Ubungo power station in Dar es Salaam.
A proposal for a natural gas pipeline from the coast at Dar es Salam to the Great Lakes landlocked countries was approved in 2009. The deal will see the sale of Songo Songo natural gas, in return for investment in the construction of the pipeline by initially Kenya and Uganda.
There are proven coal reserves of 200 million tonnes, with typical production at 30,000 tonnes per annum. The coal is bituminous with low sulphur content, typically used in power stations.

Energy
Total installed electricity generating capacity was 919MW in 2006, of which over 60 per cent is hydroelectric and the remainder conventional thermal (diesel and coal). Natual gas from the Songo Songo gas field, supplied through a 200km pipeline to Dar es Salaam, powers the upgraded Ubungo electricity plant and produces 115MW. All power generated is sold to the Tanzania Electric Supply Company (Tanesco) through a 20-year purchase agreement.
Although Tanzania has been implementing a rural electrification programme, progress has been slow due to the very low population density and the high cost of distribution; that wood fuel is still the principal energy source for most people in the country. Photovoltaic panels (solar power) are used to supply electricity in rural schools, health and other community centres, providing a total 1.2WM (maximum at peak times), with a growth rate of 20 per cent per annum.
There is a potential to obtain biogas from the 1.4 million tonnes available from sugar cane and other waste material, but technology and infrastructure is not currently available in Tanzania. With the presences of hot springs in Tanzania comes the potential of geothermal power, which has yet to be exploited. Private individuals have utilised wind-turbines to produce electricity with mixed success.
A proposed new 60MW hydroelectric dam between Tanzania and Burundi at Rusumo Falls, funded by the World Bank, to supply electricity to the mining region, has been questioned since 2008. A series of feasibility studies were undertaken but critics have said that the area as prone to drought.
Of the collection of islands that make up Zanzibar, Unguja the largest and closest island to the mainland has electricity; Pemba an equally large island will receive power through a new US$45 million, marine electricity cable when it is connected to the island in 2009. Although the cable has only 70km to travel the depth of the channel is 800m; it is not expected to be an obstacle to fishing or commercial activities.

Financial markets
Stock exchange
Dar es Salaam Stock Exchange

Banking and insurance
Central bank
Bank of Tanzania
Main financial centre
Dar es Salaam

Time
GMT plus three hours

Geography
Tanzania consists of Tanganyika, on the African mainland, and the nearby islands of Zanzibar and Pemba. Tanganyika lies on the east coast of Africa, bordered by Uganda and Kenya to the north, by the Democratic Republic of Congo (DRC) to the west, and by Zambia, Malawi and Mozambique to the south. Zanzibar and Pemba are in the Indian Ocean about 40km (25 miles) off the coast of Tanganyika, north of Dar es Salaam.
Tanzania is by far the largest country in east Africa. It is divided into three major regions: the coastal plains and river valleys, the central plateau and basin country, and the southern highlands.
The northern coastal area is humid and rainy, with some of the lushest vegetation in Tanzania. Further south the rainfall decreases and the vegetation develops into a drier savanna woodland. Tanzania's major rivers cut across the coastal plains, creating fertile alluvial fans where cotton, sisal and tropical fruits are grown. A few miles inland from the ocean the vegetation switches to tropical savannah woodland.
The central plateau region occupies the major part of the country, wedged between the two rift valleys. The plateau is bordered by Lake Victoria in the north, the Rukwa Valley in the south, Lake Tanganyika and the Ruwenzori Mountains in the west, and the coastal plains in the east. The famous Serengeti Plains and the Masai Steppe are located in the north-east of this central region.
The southern highlands consist of a variety of mountain and hill formations and are sparsely populated.
The islands of Zanzibar and Pemba are located about 35km from the Tanzanian coast in the Indian Ocean. They are low-lying and coral ringed.
Hemisphere
Southern

Climate
Tropical, with variations according to altitude. Rainy seasons April–May and November–December. Warmer on coast, cooler in upland areas. Temperatures range from 23–30 degrees Celsius (C).
Climatically, Tanzania can be divided into two major zones, the wet and humid lowlands around Lake Victoria and the Indian Ocean, and the semi-arid plateau region.
The coastal area is almost always hot and humid with a rainy season that extends for more than 10 months. The most uncomfortable period is December–April when the temperature sometimes exceeds 32 degrees C, with humidity over 90 per cent. The coolest time of the year, and the best time to visit, is June–September when the temperature drops to 15–21 degrees C with relatively low humidity.
The central plateau has distinct wet and dry seasons with great seasonal variations in temperature. Heavy rains fall in March–May and light rains in November–December.
In Dar es Salaam the rainy seasons are usually March–May and November–December, but these can vary from year to year.

Dress codes
Men should wear a lightweight/tropical suit and tie, and women a lightweight suit or formal dress, for business meetings. Women's dress should be modest. On safari it is considered best to avoid bright colours as they may irritate the animals. Visitors to the highlands are advised to take warm clothing. A light raincoat and umbrella are useful during the rainy season.

Entry requirements
Passports
Required by all.

Visa
Required by all; with a few exceptions for citizens of some African states. Details can be found on the visa form, see www.tanzania.go.tz and link to *visa*. Business travellers should submit an application form with a letter of invitation from a local contact; or introduction by an employing company, detailing nature of business and itinerary.
All visitors must have proof of return/onward passage.
Currency advice/regulations
The import and export of local currency is illegal. The import and export of foreign currency is unlimited. A receipt for all money transactions should be obtained and kept until departure.
Travellers cheques are accepted in banks and *bureaux de change*.
Customs
Personal items are duty-free, however a custom's bond may be demanded for video and filming equipment, radios, tape recorders and musical instruments until re-exported. Firearms require a special permit.
The export of local handcraft must be accompanied by sales receipts on departure.
Visitors have to go through customs travelling to and from Zanzibar.

Health (for visitors)
Mandatory precautions
A yellow fever vaccination certificate if arriving from areas of known infection. Zanzibar authorities require yellow fever vaccination certificate if arriving from Tanzania.
Advisable precautions
Visitors should take precautions against all tropical diseases. Vaccinations for diphtheria, polio, tetanus, hepatitis A, typhoid and Yellow fever are recommended. Other vaccinations that may be recommended are cholera, tuberculosis, hepatitis B and meningitis. There is a risk of rabies. HIV/Aids is prevalent.
Malaria is a countrywide problem, except at altitudes above 1,800 metres. Malaria prophylaxis should be taken.
A reasonable precaution could include a first aid kit with a sterile needle kit and disposable syringes.
All water should be regarded as potentially contaminated, use only bottled water (readily available in Dar es Salaam) or boiled and filtered water for drinking, brushing teeth, washing vegetables and reconstituting powdered milk. Local dairy products should be avoided as milk is unpasteurised; vegetables, meat and fish should be well cooked and eaten hot. Fruit should be peeled. Use only well maintained, chlorinated, swimming pools as bilharzia can be contracted from streams and rivers.
Medical insurance is essential, including emergency evacuation, and an adequate supply of personal medicines is necessary.

Hotels
Accommodation tends to be expensive and can be difficult to obtain, especially in Dar es Salaam, so reservations should be made well in advance and confirmation obtained. Bills must be settled with foreign exchange.

Credit cards
Tanzania has a cash economy and major credit cards are only accepted in larger hotels.

Public holidays (national)
Fixed dates
1 Jan (New Year's Day), 12 Jan (Zanzibar Revolution Day), 26 Apr (Union Day), 1 May (Labour Day), 7 Jul (Saba Saba/Industry Day), 8 Aug (Nane Nane/Farmers' Day), 14 Oct (Nyerere Day), 9 Dec (Independence and Republic Day), 25–26 Dec (Christmas).
Variable dates
Eid El Haj, Good Friday and Easter Monday (Mar/Apr), Maulid Day (Apr/May), Eid al Fitr.
Islamic year 1433 (26 Nov 2011–14 Nov 2012): The Islamic year contains 354 or 355 days, with the result that Muslim feasts advance by 10–12 days against the Gregorian calendar. Dates of feasts vary according to the sighting of the new moon, so cannot be forecast exactly.

Working hours
Banking
Mon–Fri: 0800–1300; Sat: 0830–1300. In larger town branch opening hours may be extended Mon–Fri: 1400–1800.
Business
Mon–Fri: 0900–1230, 1500–1700.
Government
Mon–Fri: 0800–1230, 1400–1600.
Shops
Mon–Fri: 0800–1800.

Telecommunications
Mobile/cell phones
GSM services 900/1800/400 are available in populated areas only.

Electricity supply
230V AC, 50 cycles; with a variety of round and square three-pin plug sockets.

Weights and measures
The metric system is in use but UK weights and measures are still used in many industries, for example, building.

Social customs/useful tips
Patience is required when doing business in Tanzania. Visitors should use cameras only in private settings and tourist resorts otherwise permission must be sought.
Visitors should be aware that bridges, railway stations and public buildings are regarded as security installations and should not be photographed. There are no restrictions on alcohol. Almost all business executives speak English.
Business visitors should address Tanzanians as Mr, Mrs or Ms. The term *Ndugu* is equivalent to comrade in English. The normal greeting when meeting an individual is *Jambo*. Handshaking is normal practice both on meeting and parting.
Tanzania has a large number of local traditions, although few will affect the business traveller or tourist. There are no particular taboos, but visitors should be aware of religious customs. Muslims should not be offered pork or ham and many do not drink alcohol. During the Islamic holy month of Ramadan, Muslims do not eat or drink during daylight hours.

Security
Street crime is a serious problem in Tanzania, especially in Dar es Salaam. Be alert at all times. Passports, traveller's cheques, wristwatches and cash are regularly stolen. Use hotel safe deposit boxes and do not carry too much cash.

Getting there
Air
National airline: Air Tanzania.
International airport/s: Dar es Salaam (DAR), 13km from city, duty-free shops, restaurant, bar, bank, shops, post office; Kilimanjaro International (JRO), 50km from Arusha (between Arusha and Moshi), bar, restaurant, post office, shops. Shuttle bus services run to town centres. Zanzibar (ZNZ), 8km from Kisauni. Taxis are available.
Airport tax: Zanzibar only, departure tax: US$25
Surface
Road: The Great North Road runs from Zambia through Tanzania to Kenya; the road is in good condition. Road links from Rwanda, Uganda, Mozambique and Malawi are less reliable.
Rail: The Tanzania-Zambia Railway Authority (Tazara), jointly owned and administered by the Tanzanian and Zambian governments, operates a 1,860km railway link between Dar es Salaam and Kapiri Mposhi (Zambia). Passenger services run twice a week; there are three classes, with sleeper carriages for first- and second-class passengers; bookings are recommended.
Water: Ferry services connect with ports in Burundi, the Democratic Republic of Congo and Zambia (on Lake Tanganyika), Kenya and Uganda (on Lake Victoria) and Malawi (on Lake Malawi).
Main port/s: Dar es Salaam, Mtwara, Tanga and Zanzibar

Getting about

National transport

Air: Air Tanzania operates services between Dar es Salaam, and Zanzibar and other major towns. Precision Air also operates scheduled domestic and regional flights. ZanAir operates flights from Zanzibar. There are charter companies that operate to isolated airfields, national parks and numerous towns.

Road: All-weather roads connect major centres, but minor roads are liable to be impassable in the rainy season except to four-wheel drive vehicles. There are roads from Songea to Makambako and from Mwanza to Musoma.

Buses: Express services link most centres. Routes include: Dar es Salaam-Songea; Dodoma-Moshi; Lindi-Tunduma; Lindi-Mtwara.

Some services may be unreliable.

Rail: There are seven lines run by the Tanzanian Railway Corporation, mostly radiating out from the Dar es Salaam to all regions in the north and west.

Water: Ferry services run from Dar es Salaam to Zanzibar and Pemba Islands every day. A number of steamer services run during the week on Lakes Tanganyika and Victoria. Two ferries operate on Lake Malawi on the Tanzanian side between Itungi port and Mbamba bay, passing through various small ports.

City transport

Taxis: It is advisable to use only authorised taxis, available in main towns. Taxis from hotels have fixed rates for journeys within Dar es Salaam. Fares in any other taxis are by negotiation and should be agreed before the journey. Taxi drivers do not expect tips.

Buses, trams & metro: Bus services operate within Dar es Salaam; a flat fare system operates but they are generally unreliable and overcrowded and unsuitable for business visitors.

Car hire

Car hire, with or without a driver, can be arranged through hotels or at the airport. It is advisable to get a four-wheel-drive if intending to go off main roads.

An international driving licence is necessary and driving is on the left.

BUSINESS DIRECTORY

The addresses listed below are a selection only. While World of Information makes every endeavour to check these addresses, we cannot guarantee that changes have not been made, especially to telephone numbers and area codes. We would welcome any corrections.

Telephone area codes

The international direct dialling (IDD) code for Tanzania is +255, followed by area code and subscriber's number:

Arusha	27	Mwanza	28
Dar es Salaam	22	Tanga	53
Kilimanjaro	27	Zanzibar	54
Moshi	55		

Chambers of Commerce

Arusha Chamber of Commerce, Industry and Agriculture, PO Box 141, Arusha (tel: 250-8556; fax: 250-4191; e-mail: tccia.arusha@cats-net.com).

Tanzania Chamber of Commerce, Industry and Agriculture, Twiga House, Samora Avenue, PO Box 9713, Dar es Salaam (tel: 212-1421; fax: 211-9437; e-mail: tccia.info@cats-net.com).

Zanzibar National Chamber of Commerce, Industry and Agriculture, Darajani, PO Box 1407, Zanzibar (tel: 223-3083; fax: 223-3349; e-mail: znzchamber@zitec.org).

Banking

Access Bank Tanzania Ltd, PO Box 3167, Bagamoyo Road, Dar es Salaam (tel: 255 22 276-1347, 255 22 277-4355; internet: www.accessbank.co.tz)

Akiba Commercial Bank Limited, PO Box 669, TDFL Bldg (Phase II), Upanga Rd, Dar es Salaam (tel: 211-8340–4; fax: 211-4173).

Azania Bancorp Ltd, PO Box 9271, Samora Ave, Dar es Salaam (tel: 211-8026, 211-7998; fax: 223-6741).

Bank of Tanzania, PO Box 2939, 10 Mirambo Street, Dar es Salaam (tel: 211-0945–7, 211-0950–2; fax: 212-8151; 211-2671, 211-2573, 211-3325, 211-2537; email: info@bot-tz.org).

Citibank (T) Limited, PO Box 71625, Ali Hassan Mwinyi Road, Dar es Salaam (tel: 211-7575, 211-7601; fax: 211-3910, 211-7576).

CRDB Limited, PO Box 268, Maktaba St, Dar es Salaam (tel: 211-7442–7).

Diamond Trust Bank (T) Limited, PO Box 115, Jamhuri/Ali Hassan Mwinyi Rd, Dar es Salaam (tel: 211-4888–4892; fax: 211-4210).

Eurafrican Bank (T) Limited, PO Box 3054, NDC Development House, Kivukoni/Ohio Street, Dar es Salaam (tel: 211-0928, 211-1229, 211-0104; fax: 211-3740).

Exim Bank (T) Limited, PO Box 6649, 9 Samora Avenue, Dar es Salaam (tel: 211-9738; fax: 211-9737).

Habib African Bank Limited, PO Box 70086, India St, Dar es Salaam (tel: 211-1107/9).

International Bank of Malaysia (T) Limited, PO Box 9362, Haidery Plaza, Upanga/Kisutu St, Dar es Salaam (tel: 211-0518, 211-0520, 211-0571; fax: 211-0196).

Kenya Commercial Bank Ltd, PO Box 804, Audit House, 36 Upanga Road, Dar es Salaam (tel: 211-5386–8; fax: 211-5391).

Kenya Commercial Bank (T) Limited, PO Box 804, Peugot Hse, Dar es Salaam (tel: 211-5386–8; fax: 211-5391).

NBC Limited, PO Box 1863, NBC House, Sokoine Drive, Dar es Salaam (tel: 211-3914; fax: 211-2887).

National Microfinance Bank, PO Box 9213, Samora Ave, Dar es Salaam (tel: 225 22 211-8785; 255 22 211-0900; fax: 255 22 211-4058)

Stanbic Bank Tanzania Ltd, PO Box 72647, Sukari House, Ohio Street/Sokoine Drive, Dar es Salaam (tel: 211-2195–2200; fax: 211-3742)

Standard Chartered Bank Tanzania Ltd, PO Box 9011, Ohio/Sokoine Drive, Dar es Salaam (tel: 211-7350–52, 211-3787, 211-7377; fax: 211-3770, 211-3775).

Tanzania Investment Bank, PO Box 9373, Samora Avenue, Dar es Salaam (tel: 2111708–13; fax: 211-3438) .

Tanzania Postal Bank, PO Box 9300, Mkwepu Street, Dar es Salaam (tel: 211-2358–60, 211-2385/9, 211-6409, 211-7748; fax: 223-8212).

Central bank

Bank of Tanzania, 10 Mirambo Street, PO Box 2939, Dar es Salaam (tel: 211-0945/6/7, 211-0951/2; fax: 211-3325; e-mail: info@hq.bot-tz.org).

Stock exchange

Dar es Salaam Stock Exchange: www.darstockexchange.com

Travel information

Air Tanzania, PO Box 543, ATC House; 2nd Floor, 773/40 Ohio Street, Dar es salaam, (tel: 211-8411; fax: 211-3114; email: bookings@airtanzania.com; internet: www.airtanzania.com).

Dar es Salaam International Airport, PO Box 19043, Dar es Salaam (tel: 284-4610/19; fax: 284-4343, 284-3022, 284-4209).

Kilimanjaro International Airport, PO Box 995, Arusha (tel: 222-2941; fax: 222-8553).

Precision Air, Along Nyerere-Pugu Road; PO Box 70770 (tel: 286-0701; fax: 286-0725; internet: www.precisionairtz.com).

Scandinavia Express, Nyerere Road, Vingunguti; PO Box 2414, Dar es Salaam (tel: 286-1947–9; fax: 286-1950; internet: www.scandinaviagroup.com).

Tanzanair, Azikiwe & Samora Ave/Airport International Terminal, PO Box 364, Dar es Salaam (tel: 230-232/4, 246-583; fax: 246-296).

Tanzania National Parks, PO Box 3134, Arusha (tel: 250-1930/1931; fax: 254-8216; email: tanapa@yako.habari.co.tz; internet: www.tanapa.com).

Tanzania Railways Corporation, PO Box 468, Dar es Salaam (tel: 211-0599, 211-0600; fax: 211-6525; internet: www.trctz.com).

Tanzania Zambia Railway Authority, Head Office, Nyerere Road; PO Box 2834, Dar es Salaam (tel: 286-5187; fax: 286-5334; internet: www.tazara.co.tz).

Zanair Ltd, PO Box 2113, Zanzibar (tel: 223-3670; internet: www.zanair.com).

Zanzibar Tourist Corporation, PO Box 216, Zanzibar (tel: 223-2344; fax: 223-3430).

National tourist organisation offices

Tanzania Tourist Board, IPS Building, 3rd Floor, PO Box 2485, Dar es Salaam (tel: 211-1244/5; fax: 211-6420; e-mail: safari@ud.co.tz).

Ministries

Ministry of Agriculture and Food Security, PO Box 9192, Dar es Salaam (tel: 286-2480/1; fax: 286-2077; email: psk@kilimo.go.tz).

Ministry of Energy and Minerals, PO Box 9152, Mkwepu Street, Dar es Salaam (tel: 211-7153–59; fax: 211-6719; email: madini@africaonline.co.tz).

Ministry of Finance, Tancot, PO Box 9111, Dar es Salaam (tel: 211-1174–79; fax: 213-8573).

Ministry of Industries and Trade, PO Box 9503, Lumumba Street, Dar es Salaam (tel: 218-1397, 218-0049/50; fax: 218-2481).

Office of the President, State House, Magogoni Road; PO Box 9120, Dar es Salaam (tel: 211-6679; fax: 211-3425).

Office of the President of Zanzibar (vice president), PO Box 776, Zanzibar (tel: 30-814; fax: 33-722).

Prime Minister's Office, Magogoni Road; PO Box 3021, Dar es Salaam (tel: 213-5076, 211-7249/50/51/52).

Other useful addresses

Board of External Trade, PO Box 5402, Dar es Salaam (tel: 233-524).

Board of Internal Trade, PO Box 883, Dar es Salaam (tel: 228-301).

British High Commission, Umoja House, Mirambo Street; PO Box 9200, Dar es Salaam (tel: 211-0101; fax: 211-0102).

Cashew Nut Authority of Tanzania, PO Box 533, Mtwara.

Coffee Authority of Tanzania, PO Box 732, Moshi (tel: 275-4190).

National Development Corporation, Development House, Kivukoni Front/Ohio Street, PO Box 2669, Dar es Salaam (tel: 211-2893, 211-1460/3; fax: 211-3618; e-mail: ndc@cats-net.com; internet: www.ndctz.com).

National Insurance Corporation of Tanzania Ltd, PO Box 9264, Dar es Salaam.

Presidential Parastatal Sector Reform Commission, 2nd Floor, Sukari House, Sokoine Drive/Ohio Street, PO Box 9252, Dar es Salaam (tel: 211-5482, 211-7988/9; fax: 211-3065/6, 212-2870; email: info@psrctz.com; internet: www.psrctz.com).

Radio Tanzania, PO Box 9191, Dar es Salaam.

Southern Paper Mills Co Ltd, (Marketing Dept) Tanzania Elimu Supplies Building, Bandari Road, Dar es Salaam (tel: 211-1602; fax: 211-3233).

State Mining Corporation, PO Box 4958, Dar es Salaam.

Tanzania Electric Supply Company Ltd (TANESCO), PO Box 9024, Dar es Salaam (tel: 211-2891; fax: 211-3836; email: mdtan@intafrica.com).

Tanzania Exporters' Association (TANEXA), c/o Sima International, PO Box 1175, Dar es Salaam.

Tanzania Harbours Authority, PO Box 9184, Dar es Salaam (internet: www.tanzaniaports.com).

Tanzania National Parks, PO Box 3134, Arusha (tel: 250-1930/1931; fax: 254-8216; email: tanapa@yako.habari.co.tz; internet: www.tanapa.com).

Tanzania Petroleum Development Corporation (TPDC), Managing Director, PO Box 2774, Dar es Salaam; Director of Exploration and Production, PO Box 5233, Dar es Salaam; email: tpdcexploration@raha.com); Director of Research & Corporate Services, PO Box 2774, Dar es Salaam.

Tanzania Railways Corporation, PO Box 468, Dar es Salaam.

Tanzania Revenue Authority, PO Bnox 11491, Dar es Salaam (tel: 211-9591/4; fax: 212-8593; email: trais@afsat.com).

Tanzanian Embassy (USA), 2139 R Street, NW, Washington DC 20008 (tel: (+202-1) 939-6129; fax: (+202-1) 797-7408; email: tanz-us@clark.net).

Television Zanzibar, PO Box 314, Zanzibar.

US Embassy, Laibon Road, PO Box 9123, Dar es Salaam.

Internet sites

Africa Business Network: www.ifc.org/abn

AllAfrica.com: http://allafrica.com

African Development Bank: www.afdb.org

Africa Online: www.africaonline.com

Mbendi AfroPaedia (information on companies, countries, industries and stock exchanges in Africa): http://mbendi.co.za

Official government website: www.tanzania.go.tz

Official Zanzibar Government website: www.zanzibargovernment.org

Tanzania Yellow pages: www.yellowpages.co.tz/

Terres Australes

COUNTRY PROFILE

Historical profile

1552–59 Saint Paul and Amsterdam Islands were sighted by survivors of a Portuguese expedition led by Ferdinand Magellan.
1772 Captain Marion Dufresne and ship's mate Crozet saw the group of islands, which became known as the Crozet Archipelago. Yves de Kerguelen sighted another archipelago, later named after him.
1840 Terre Adélie, in Antarctica, was sighted and claimed by the French.
1924 A French government decree placed the administration of the islands with the government of Madagascar (then a French colony).
1947 France established observation stations.
1955 Terres Australes et Antarctiques Francaises were accorded the status of an overseas French territory.
1959 The international community signed the Antarctic Treaty, establishing the legal framework for the management of Antarctica, banning any military activity within the Antarctic continent and guaranteeing the protection of its environment and wildlife.
1961 The Antarctic Treaty came into force.
1993 An agreement between the national institutes in charge of polar research in France and Italy agreed to construct a permanent scientific base, Concordia, approximately 1,000km from the French scientific base of Dumont d'Urville.
2000–01 Concordia was built and completed.
2002 Ten countries began working on a glacial project, the European Programme of Glaciology (EPICA), drilling to study the climate in the Antarctic during the last 500,000 years. Drilling reached 2,871 metres and collected ice samples from 520,000 years ago.
2003 The drilling reached the rock base of the Antarctic continent at a depth of 3,300 metres.
2004 The role of the *Administrator-Superior* was undertaken by a *préfet*, based in Saint Pierre on Réunion.
2005 Michel Champon took office as *préfet*. TAAF celebrated its fiftieth anniversary.
2007 Eric Pilloton was appointed *préfet*.
2008 Rollon Mouchel-Blaisot took office as *Administrator-Superior* for the French Southern and Artic Lands, in Paris.
2007 Eric Pilloton was appointed *préfet*. Nicolas Sarkozy became head of state and president of the French Republic.
2008 Rollon Mouchel-Blaisot took office as *Administrator-Superior* for the French Southern and Arctic Lands, in Paris.
2009 A new advisory committee was established to provide recommendations on how best to administer the largely under-populated region where representative government is unfeasible.
2010 In February, a new plan of action to protect French wetlands within national parks, including Terres Australes, was instigated, with a budget of €20 million (US$27.6 million) for 2010–13. Christian Gaudin took office as *Administrator-Superior* for the French Southern and Arctic Lands, in Paris, on 4 November.
2011 TAAF signed a partnership agreement with Centre National de Documentation Pédogogique (CNDP) (National Centre for Educational Documentation), providing a teaching resource for French schools. On 19 August, Arnaud Quiniou was appointed district chief of Terre Adélie, for one year.

Political structure

Terres Australes et Antarctiques Françaises (TAAF) (French Southern and Antarctic Territories) is a French Térritoire d'Outre Mer (TOM) (Overseas Territory), but is administered under two different international laws. France exercises full sovereignty over the southern islands, unanimously recognised by all nations. Adélie Land (on mainland Antarctica) is administered according to the 1959 Antarctic Treaty, despite the US not recognising France's claim to the Land. The Antarctic Treaty is an international agreement which provides for broad scientific co-operation and demilitarisation of the Antarctic continent and restrained existing territorial claims without prejudicing the solution to the sovereignty problem.
The fully sovereign area is governed by one law and two main decrees. The law of 6 August 1955 confers administrative and financial autonomy on the TOM. The implementation decree of 13 January 1956 defines the TOM's financial system and the decree of 8 September 1956

KEY FACTS

Official name: Le Territoire des Terres Australes et Antarctiques Françaises (TAAF) (French Southern and Antarctic Territories)

Head of State: President of France Nicolas Sarkozy, represented by *Préfet* Rollon Mouchel-Blaisot (appointed 16 Oct 2008) (based in Saint Pierre, on Réunion)

Area: 439,797 square km consisting of: Kerguelen Archipelago 7,215 square km, Crozet Archipelago 115 square km, Amsterdam Island 54 square km, Saint Paul Islands 7 square km, Terre Adélie (in Antarctica) 432,000 square km

Population: 310 (summer total) (150 winter total)

Capital: Port-aux-Françaises (on Kerguelen)

Official language: French

Currency: Euro (€) = 100 cents

Exchange rate: €0.76 per US$ (Oct 2011)

provides for the TOM's administrative organisation.
The TOM is under the authority of a chief administrator, whose official residence is in Paris. The administrator is assisted by an advisory council, which meets twice a year and consists of seven members appointed for five-year terms. The council must be consulted on the TOM's draft budget and it is kept informed and consulted on any proposed new scientific missions or applications for concessions and commercial activities.
The TOM is divided into four districts, each under the authority of a district head appointed by the chief administrator:
Saint Paul and Amsterdam Islands – permanent settlement is Martin de Viviés.
Crozet Islands – settlement is Alfred Faure (Possession Island).
Kerguelen Islands – settlement is Port aux Français.
Adélie Land – settlement is Dumont D'Urville.

Population

310 (summer total) (150 winter total)

Languages spoken

Official language/s
French

Media

There are two publications issued by Terres Australes et Antarctiques Francaises (TAAF). A monthly official journal and a quarterly pamphlet of general interest see publications at www.taaf.fr.

Economy

The Terres Australes have no permanent population, but are temporarily inhabited by scientific research groups. Scientific activities are supported and developed by the Institut Français pour la Récherché et la Technologie Polaires (IFRTP) (French Institute for Polar Research and Technology) and the administration of the TOM is in charge of the logistics. Most of the TOM's economic activities centre on supporting the IFRTP. Fishing is the other main economic activity with fish landed by foreign ships exported to France and Réunion; others activities are philately and tourist cruises.

External trade

Crayfish and other fish are exported to France and Réunion.

Agriculture

Research has indicated the viability of large-scale farming of giant brown macrocystis, a type of seaweed.
Fishing
French vessels fish for crayfish off Amsterdam and Saint Paul. There is an agreement between France and Ukraine to fish for icefish and toothfish.
A research programme which has been carried out since 1970, has shown that trout adapt well to a sub-antarctic environment and the result of sea-ranching salmon was also a biological success. There are estimated to be 60 to 120 million tons of krill in the TOM's coastal waters. Around Saint Paul and Amsterdam Islands, there are plentiful supplies of bull head fish, false cod, crayfish and cape lobster.

Tourism

The French research vessel, *Marion Dufresne*, conducts tourist cruises.

Hydrocarbons

No commercial quantities of hydrocarbons have been located.

Energy

There are three diesel generators in operation, in Amsterdam, powered by imported fuel.

Banking and insurance

Central bank
The Paris-based Institut d'Emission d'Outre-Mer (IEOM) provides all central banking services except foreign exchange reserves.

Time

GMT plus five hours

Geography

Terres Australes consists of several groups of islands in the southern Indian Ocean and a sector of Antarctica.
Adélie Land, a narrow segment of mainland Antarctica, is thick continental ice over barren rock. Les Îles Crozet consists of five large and 15 tiny islands, their combined area is over 330 square km. They are volcanic with black basalt geology and treeless terrain. Pic Marion-Dufresne (1,090 metres) is the highest point on Île de l'Est. The main island of Îles Kerguelen, in the southern Indian Ocean, is volcanic, its highest point is the glaciated Mount Ross. It has around 300 smaller islands forming an archipelago, which combined is 7,000 square km in area. Iles Saint-Paul et Amsterdam are small uninhabited volcanic islands.
Hemisphere
Southern

Climate

The climate of Iles Saint-Paul et Amsterdam is oceanic, damp and mild. The temperature averages 15 degrees Celsius (C). The climate is particularly extreme in the Crozet Archipelago – the islands lie at the centre of an area where tropical and antarctic air masses meet, causing deep depressions and cyclone-forming processes. The Îles Kerguelen have a cool, humid climate due to the proximity of the Antarctic continent. The summers last from December to March and are similar to those beyond the Arctic Circle. The winters from May to October are comparatively mild. The climate is unstable with constant winds, sometimes at a speed of 160kph. The temperature of the surrounding sea averages 4 degrees C.
Adélie Land's climate is harsh. The temperature of the coastal area never rises above 4 degrees C in summer and can fall to minus 37 degrees C in winter.

Entry requirements

Visa
Required by all, except citizens of EU, North America, Australasia and Japan, for stays up to one month; this includes business trips by representatives of overseas companies or organisations. For further exceptions, full details and a copy of the application form visit www.diplomatie.fr/venir/visas/ index.html. Proof of adequate funds for stay and return/onward ticket are necessary.

Health (for visitors)

Advisable precautions
Protective clothing is essential. Sunscreen should be applied and protective eyewear worn in summer in the Antarctic.

Weights and measures

The metric system is in use.

Getting there

Air
There are no air links to or between the bases.
Surface
Water: Relief ships bring new personnel and supplies. A charter vessel calls five times a year to the Antarctic islands and another calls twice a year to Adélie Land.

BUSINESS DIRECTORY

Useful addresses

Institut Français pour la Recherche et la Technologie Polaires (IFRTP), Technopole Brest Iroise, BP 75, 29280 Plouzane, France (tel: (+33-2) 9805-6500; fax: (+33-2) 9805-6555).

Terres Australes et Antarctiques Françaises (TAAF), 34 Rue des Renaudes, 75017 Paris (tel: (+33-1) 4053-4652; fax: (+33-1) 4766-9123).

Internet sites

French tourism:
www.discoverfrance.net/Colonies/Antarctic.shtml

Information about antarctica:
www.gdargaud.net/Antarctica/InfoAntarctica.html

Secretariat of the Antarctic Treaty:
www.ats.aq

Thailand

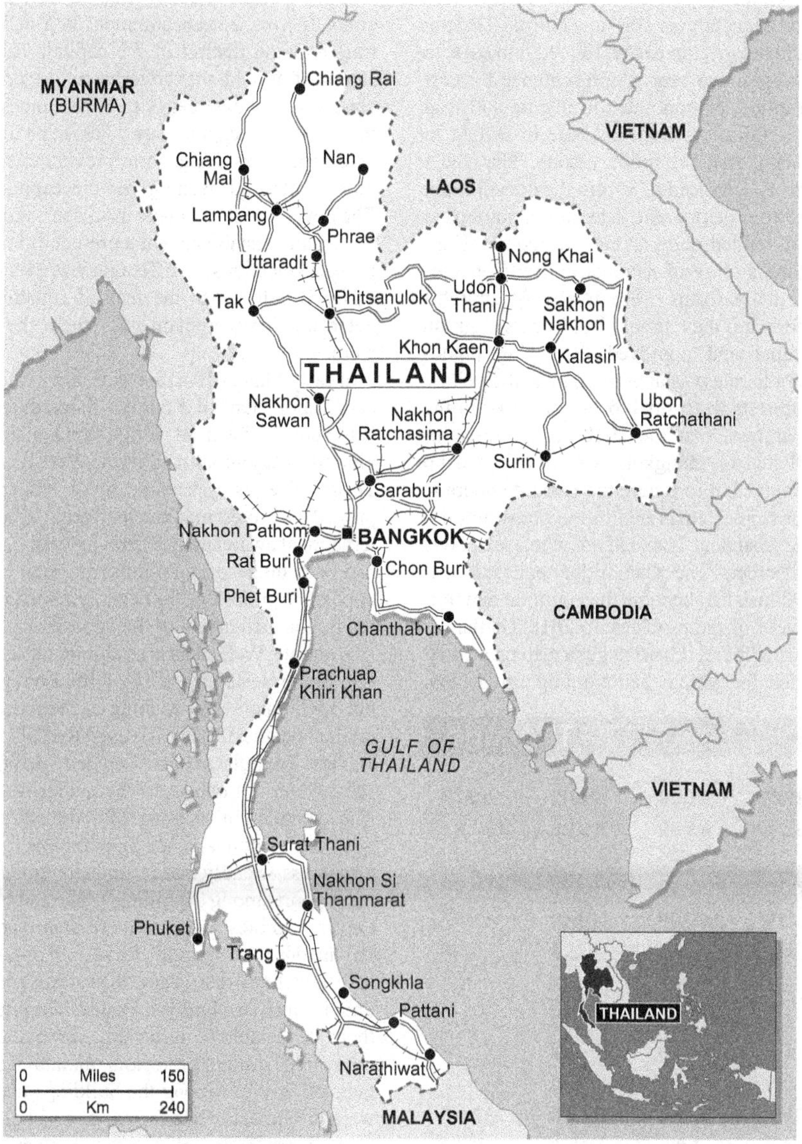

In 2010 Thailand's years of intense and prolonged turmoil were beginning to take their toll. The political temperature remained high, business confidence was falling fast. Outside observers could be forgiven for losing track of events; the ejection of Thaksin Shinawatra's administration in 2006 in a military coup had been followed by the return of Mr Thaksin's allies to power in the elections of December 2007. There followed the collapse of not one, but two, governments in 2008, pushing business confidence to a ten-year low. Abhisit Vejjajiva assumed the premiership in January 2009 at the head of a Phak Prachathipat (PP) (Democrat Party)-led coalition government. However, the discontent of supporters of the ousted governments erupted into violent street

KEY FACTS

Official name: Prathet Thai; Ratcha Anachak Thai (Kingdom of Thailand)

Head of State: King Bhumibol Adulyadej (Rama IX) (since 1946)

Head of government: Prime Minister Yingluck Shinawatra (from 5 Aug 2011)

Ruling party: Coalition led by Phak Puea Thai (PPT) (For Thais Party), with Phak Bhum Jai Thai (BJT) (Thai Pride Party), Phak Chat Thai Pattana (CP) (Thai Nation Development Party) and two other minor parties (from 5 Aug 2011)

Area: 514,000 square km

Population: 67.31 million (2010)*

Capital: Bangkok

Official language: Thai

Currency: Baht (B) = 100 satang

Exchange rate: B31.09 per US$ (Oct 2011)

GDP per capita: US$4,992 (2010)

GDP real growth: 7.80% (2010)

GDP: US$318.90 billion (2010)

Labour force: 38.64 million (2010)

Unemployment: 1.00% (2010)

Inflation: 3.30% (2010)

Oil production: 334,000 bpd (2010)

Balance of trade: US$32.34 million (2010)

Annual FDI: US$6.31 billion (2010)

* estimated figure

protests in early April 2010. As one former minister observed, 'when Moody's get Moody and Standard and Poor's drop your rating, you know you're in trouble.' Declining international confidence led to downgrades by the ratings agencies of Thailand's sovereign and local currency debt in April 2010.

Confusion

At the beginning of 2010 the political crisis had virtually established itself as the *status quo* . This was no ordinary crisis. The prospect of outright civil war lay just over the horizon, a nightmarish scenario not only for a beleaguered and bemused government, but also for Thailand's neighbours. The roots of the crisis dated back to the military's intervention in 2006. Since then, the billionaire Thaksin Shinawatra had become a deeply divisive presence on (and off) Thailand's political stage. His political party was the oddly named Thai Rak Thai (Thais Love Thais). Its policies included the provision of inexpensive healthcare and rural development through locally granted loans. Like it or not, however, Thaksin was the first elected prime minister in Thailand to complete his term of office and the first to be re-elected. Whatever the middle-classes' opinion of him, Thaksin appeared to be doing something right. Hugely popular among Thailand's rural poor, he was just as unpopular with the urban elite who, over the years, had become accustomed to running Thailand's government as they wished. In 2006 the colour of protest had been yellow, the colour adopted by Thaksin's supporters. In suppressing the yellow protestors, the Thai army risked emulating the Sorceror's apprentice, triggering a process they were subsequently unable to control. Thaksin did not give up easily. Forced into exile to avoid a two year prison sentence for corruption, he continued to inspire and lead his followers from his base in Dubai. In 2006, after the military coup, Thailand's army promised to reform the constitution, restore democratic rule and, a somewhat ill-defined undertaking, 'to rebuild Thailand's sense of national unity'. Constitutional reforms were relatively straightforward; they simply had to be set out on paper and approved. Restoring democratic rule was another matter: the yellow protests were small beer compared to the paralysis that the 2010 red protests inflicted on Bangkok. Mr Abhisit had no choice but to ignore the basic democratic principles enshrined in the constitution – or abandon Thailand to wholesale civic disorder. The Cambridge educated Mr Abhisit had become the common denominator of the problem. In 2010 Thailand's army found it hard to get a grip on a situation for which their training fitted them inadequately. In April 2010 the army killed 25 demonstrators in a ham-fisted attempt to suppress a single demonstration.

KEY INDICATORS — Thailand

	Unit	2006	2007	2008	2009	2010
Population	m	65.28	65.74	66.32	*66.98	*67.31
Gross domestic product (GDP)	US$bn	206.70	247.10	272.40	236.90	318.90
GDP per capita	US$	3,166	3,759	4,108	3,940	4,992
GDP real growth	%	5.1	4.9	2.5	-2.3	7.8
Inflation	%	4.6	2.2	5.5	-0.8	3.3
Unemployment	%	1.6	1.4	1.4	1.5	1.0
Industrial output	% change	5.8	5.9	3.3	-4.2	–
Agricultural output	% change	4.8	0.9	3.5	-0.5	–
Oil output	'000 bpd	286.0	309.0	325.0	330.0	334.0
Natural gas output	bn cum	24.3	25.9	28.9	30.9	36.3
Coal output	mtoe	5.4	8.9	5.1	5.3	5.0
Exports (fob) (goods)	US$m	127,929.0	151,130.0	175,279.0	150,713.0	193,610.0
Imports (fob) (goods)	US$m	114,085.0	125,170.0	157,330.0	118,022.0	161,270.0
Balance of trade	US$m	13,844.0	25,960.0	17,948.0	32,691.0	32,340.0
Current account	US$m	2,316.0	15,682.0	1,633.0	20,258.0	14,754.0
Total reserves minus gold	US$m	65,291.0	85,221.0	108,661.0	135,483.0	167,530.0
Foreign exchange	US$m	65,147.0	85,110.0	108,317.0	133,599.0	165,656.0
Exchange rate	per US$	35.88	33.51	33.31	34.28	31.69

* estimated figure

Stalemate

The first four months of 2010 had seen the political stalemate continue and develop, as squatters paralysed the capital Bangkok with the establishment of what became an almost permanent encampment in a central shopping district of the capital. The stand-off forced the government to declare a state of emergency in 17 provinces, including the capital city. The state of emergency was designed to prevent even more protestors heading for the capital. The government had made the dispersal of the squatter establishment a pre-condition for early elections, an offer that was eventually withdrawn in the face of squatter determination to remain just where they were.

In early May 2010 a renegade army officer, Major General Khattiya Sawasdipol was shot in the head while being interviewed by a journalist from the *New York Times*. The assassination, by a sniper, pushed the protest up a notch in terms of international awareness. General Sawasdipol had been the leader of a militant group of opposition protestors; his death symbolised the fragmented nature of the opposition.

To quote W B Yeats, as things turned out, the protests ended 'not with a bang, but a whimper'. Not wishing to see more civilian deaths, in May 2010 the Red Shirt leaders capitulated and handed themselves over, en masse, to the authorities. The capitulation enabled Mr Abhisit to postpone elections, make preparations for a business-friendly budget and strengthen his support among the military. The end of the street protests was no more than that; left unaddressed were the social and political fault lines that years of protests and unquiet had so vividly revealed. Despite their leadership's reluctant surrender, many red shirted protestors maintained their offensive. Among the buildings that were torched after the formal end of hostilities were the Bangkok Stock Exchange and military establishments.

Trouble down south

On top of the political problems confronting the government, the campaign of seperatist violence being waged in Thailand's three southernmost provinces – Pattani, Yala and Narathiwat, which first broke out in 2004 – had by the end of 2009 claimed an estimated 4,000 lives as it too became an entrenched feature of southern politics. The government's initial response had been a series of high profile visits by senior politicians and members of the royal family. All to no avail. The government's opponents are Muslim ethnic Malays. Traditionally, Thailand's south resembled Muslim Malaysia rather than Buddhist Thailand. The sudden growth of a militant opposition opposed to Bangkok's control appeared to take the government by surprise.

There are a number of surprising features to this confrontation. The first is that it appears to be confined to the Thai side of the border; this works well for the insurgents, who are able to seek refuge from Thai forces by simply legging it across the divide. Malaysia seems to be prepared to sit and watch. Secondly, the insurgents do not appear to be seeking publicity for their campaign. Nor does the uprising seem to have attracted much international publicity or awareness. The Thai authorities, conscious of the damage wrought to the tourist industry by the 'red Mist' in Bangkok, have sought to play down the insurgency. Stranger still, the insurgents themselves do not seem overly concerned about international awareness of their grievances and objectives. By mid 2010 hopes were that some form of limited autonomy for the predominantly Muslim states could be peaceably worked out. Hopes, no more than hopes.

Narrow economic base

Despite the resilient economic performance, unsettled domestic politics and the global recession were having an effect on the economy. After the extended period of domestic political turmoil, investor and consumer confidence were low. 2009 saw the first full-year decline in real GDP since the Asian crisis of the 1990s. With political stability, a restoration of domestic and external confidence and full implementation of the public investment programme, Thailand ought to be able to return to sustainable, high growth rates over the medium term. According to the Asian Development Bank (ADB) domestically Thailand has been in an investment slump since 2006. It has been the resilient export performance with average growth of over 10 per cent during 2006–07, that has helped restore GDP growth.

Nevertheless, the economy contracted by 2.3 per cent in 2009, the deepest decline in south-east Asia that year. The antigovernment street protests that began in 2009, coming after a long period of rising political tensions, eroded consumer sentiment and aggravated a decline in tourism prompted by recession in industrial countries.

Manufacturing production fell by 5.1 per cent in 2009, a result of the fall in export demand. Worst-hit industries were those making capital goods and higher-technology products such as automobiles and electrical appliances. However these industries led the recovery in the fourth quarter, when export demand rebounded. Construction activity started to pick up in the second quarter of 2009 as the government accelerated public works under two fiscal stimulus packages. For the full year, though, construction output was flat. Total industrial output fell by 4.3 per cent. Tourist arrivals fell for most of 2009 but then rebounded in the fourth quarter, still showing a full-year decline of about 3 per cent. The services sub-sectors of hotels and restaurants and transport and communications fell particularly sharply from the fourth quarter of 2008 through the third quarter of 2009. Even agriculture had a bad year in 2009, with production down by 0.6 per cent owing, on the one hand, to price declines, notably for paddy, cassava, maize and natural rubber, and, on the other, to pest infestations.

Private consumption contracted by 1.1 per cent in 2009, constrained by the weaker labour market, declines in farm incomes and political strife. Consumer sentiment improved in the second half of the year, when the government rolled out its fiscal stimulus measures. Employment started to pick up and prices for farm products bottomed. In contrast to private consumption, public consumption spending rose by 5.8 per cent in 2009, as the government increased expenditure, including the stimulus measures.

Net exports were positive in 2009 largely because real imports fell much more sharply than exports. The expansionary fiscal policy played an important role in moderating the recession. The first stimulus package of B116 billion (US$3.4 billion) was implemented in March 2009. It included monthly cash payments of B2,000 a person for about 9 million low-income earners, assistance for the aged and extra spending on skills training and public health programmes. Small and medium-sized businesses received tax breaks and the property and tourism industries were given access to concessional loans. Altogether, this package was valued at the equivalent of 1.3 per cent of GDP.

A second stimulus package estimated at B1.43 trillion (US$42 billion) was implemented over three fiscal years starting from October 2009. This programme covers public investment mainly in infrastructure such as transport, water and energy, as well as extra funding for health, education and tourism. The planned outlays represent about 5 per cent of GDP for each of the three years.

Lower prices for imported oil and commodities and weak domestic demand, brought down inflation in 2009 from high levels in the prior year. Government concessions introduced in 2008 to help those on low incomes (such as free electricity, water supply and public transport) contributed to the downward pressure on prices. The consumer price index fell for much of the year, picking up late in the year when oil prices rose.

Fading inflation and the weak economy prompted the Bank of Thailand (central bank) to cut its policy interest rate by 250 basis points, to 1.25 per cent, between early December 2008 and April 2009. Credit growth was sluggish, though – private credit rose by only 3 per cent in 2009 and most of that was for households. The government directed state-owned financial institutions to step up their lending, particularly to small businesses facing a credit squeeze.

Goods exports fell by 13.9 per cent in US dollar terms in 2009, reflecting the fall in external demand, especially in industrial countries (exports to the People's Republic of China and India were little changed from 2008). Sharp falls were recorded in both manufactured and agricultural exports. The slide hit bottom in the first half and by November exports had rebounded on a year-on-year basis. Imports fell by nearly 25 per cent in 2009, a result of the slump in manufactured exports (which require imported raw materials), weak domestic demand and lower prices for oil and commodities.

The trade balance showed a record surplus of US$19.4 billion. With balances in services, income and transfers close to 2008 levels, the trade surplus pushed up the current account surplus to the equivalent of 7.7 per cent of GDP. Net outflows in the capital account slowed last year from 2008 to US$1.3 billion. By year-end, foreign reserves were up by nearly 25 per cent to US$138.4 billion, or 10.6 months of import cover.

Risk assessment

Economy	Good
Politics	Poor
Regional stability	Fair

COUNTRY PROFILE

Historical profile

1767 The former capital of Siam, Ayutthaya, fell to Burmese invaders.

1782 King Rama I – first of the Chakri dynasty – was crowned and founded the capital city Bangkok.
1851–68 King Mongkut (Rama IV) began a period of reform and modernisation while adroitly avoiding European colonisation. Treaties were signed with the US, Great Britain, France and Japan, among others. Barriers against traders were eliminated, allowing expansion.
1868–1910 Chulalongkorn, (Rama V) continued his father's programmes by modernising the legal and administrative systems, reforming the political structure and abolishing slavery. He also began construction of a railway network. Some Siam territories in Indochina were ceded to Britain and France.
1910 Vajiravudha (Rama VI) became King. He introduced compulsory education, among other reforms.
1925 Prajadhipok, the brother of Vajiravudha, became King (Rama VII).
1932 A group of students, led by Pibul Songgram and Pridi Phanomyang forced King Prajadhipok to replace the absolute monarchy with a constitutional monarchy and introduce parliamentary government. A new National Assembly was established.
1933 The first general elections were held.
1935 The King abdicated. A council of regency chose his 10-year old brother, Ananda, to be Rama VIII. He was studying in Switzerland at the time.
1938 Pibul Songgram became prime minister
1939 Siam was renamed Thailand on June 24.
1941–1946 Under the leadership of Pibul, Thailand allied itself with Japan and allowed Japanese troops to traverse the country. Thailand declared war on the US and Britain but the Thai ambassador in Washington withheld the official declaration and so technically the country remained neutral. Pridi Phanomyang led an American-backed anti-Japanese movement.
1945 Pridi became prime minister and Pibul was jailed briefly for war crimes.
1946 King Ananda returned for the second time from studying in Switzerland but died shortly after in mysterious circumstances. He was succeeded by his brother, Bhumipol Adulyadej, as King Rama IX, although he was not formally crowned until 1950. Inflation and corruption marred the government's reputation.
1947 Pibul led an army *coup d'état* and instituted a military dictatorship. Pibul was staunchly anti-Communist and under his rule the Chinese community, suspected of being Communist sympathisers, was harassed.
1950 Bhumibol Adulyadej became King and was crowned Rama IX. Thailand aligned itself with the US during the Cold War and sent troops to fight in the Korean War.
1957 Pibul was overthrown in a coup led by Field Marshal Sarit Thanarat.
1958 Sarit deposed his own premier, took power himself and imposed martial law and dissolved all political parties.
1973 Student riots destabilised the military government and free elections were held. The King appointed a civilian, Sanya Thammasak, as premier.
1974 A new constitution was introduced, legalising political parties.
1975 With the ending of the Vietnam War Thailand became the temporary home to many refugees from Indochina.
1976 The military seized power and Admiral Sa'ngad Chaloryoo annulled the 1974 constitution and re-introduced martial law. A new constitution was introduced. Thanin Kraivixien became prime minister, he imposed a harsh rule and kept unions under tight control while he carried out anti-Communist purges of the civil service and educational institutions.
1977 Thanin was overthrown by General Kriangsak Chomanand.
1978 A new constitution was promulgated in which a bicameral National Assembly was established.
1991 Another military coup led by General Suchinda Krapayoon replaced Kriangsak.
1992 General Krapayoon resigned and elections were held. A coalition led by the Phak Prachathipat (PP) (Democrat Party) was victorious.
1995 The Phak Chat Thai Patthana (CP) (Thai Nation Development Party) won the general election and formed a coalition government.
1997 The constitution was amended to allow the direct election of a prime minister. The baht fell sharply during the Asian financial crisis and led to bankruptcies and unemployment. Chuan Leekpai (PP) was elected prime minister; he worked closely with the IMF to reform the badly damaged economy.
2000 Thailand's first senate election was held. Subsequent rulings against the results by the Election Commission necessitated two further elections.
2001 In general elections, Thaksin Shinawatra became prime minister and the Thai Rak Thai (TRT) (Thais Love Thais) formed a coalition government with the Phak Chart Patthana (PCP) (National Development Party).
2002 The PCT and the Phak Khwam Wang Mai (PKWM) (New Aspiration Party) joined the ruling coalition. Supachai Panitchpakdi became director general of the World Trade Organisation (WTO).
2004 A wave of terrorist attacks by separatist Islamic and ethnic Malays from southern provinces killed over 100 people. Over 100 Islamic insurgents were killed while attacking several police bases in the south and 85 Islamic detainees were killed while in custody following violence at a rally in the south. Millions of domesticated birds were slaughtered following an outbreak of avian flu. Six west coast provinces, including the tourist resorts of Phuket and Khao Lak, were devastated by a *tsunami* which swept the whole region following an earthquake off the coast of Sumatra (Indonesia). The final estimate for Thailand was 8,212 dead or missing and 6,000 people displaced.
2005 The ruling TRT party won the general elections; Thaksin Shinawatra was the first prime minister to win a second term in office.
2006 Amid controversial allegations concerning corruption charges against him, Thaksin Shinawatra called snap general elections which the opposition parties boycotted; they were won by the ruling TRT with 57 per cent of the vote. Despite the victory, the prime minister was forced to step down in favour of his deputy, Chidchai Vanasatidya. But the Supreme Administrative Court ruled that the general elections were invalid and allowed Shinawatra to resume his duties as prime minister. While abroad attending a UN General Assembly meeting Shinawatra was deposed in a bloodless army coup. A ban was placed on all political party activities. Retired ex-army general, Surayud Chulanont was sworn in as prime minister. Shinawatra resigned his leadership of TRT.
2007 Matial law was lifted in Bangkok and 41 (out of 76) provinces two months after its imposition; it continued in border regions and in the north in general. The constitutional court ordered the dissolution of the TRT and barred TRT leader Thaksin Shinawatra from politics for breaking election laws in 2006; the court also barred a further 110 party members from politics for five years. The ban on political party activities was lifted, but the TRT remained dissolved. Former members of TRT agreed to stand as parliamentary candidates for the Palang Prachachon (PPP) (People's Power Party). An arrest warrant was issued for Shinawatra on fraud charges. A referendum agreed constitution changes. King Bhumibol Adulyadej celebrated his eightieth birthday. Although the king has few legal powers, he has been instrumental in calming relations between the military and civilian government and the people. In snap parliamentary elections the PPP won 233 seats (out of 480) and began coalition talks with minor parties.
2008 A coalition government led by the PPP and five minor political parties was

formed. Samak Sundaravej (PPP) was elected as prime minister. Thaksin Shinawatra returned from self-imposed exile, to a welcome of thousands of flag-waving supporters. He was arrested and taken to court immediately to face charges of abuse of power during his tenure as prime minister; he was released on bail. He and his wife went on trial on corruption charges related to a Bangkok real estate deal. His wife was found guilty and he fled Thailand into exile in the UK. Shinawatra was found guilty *in absentia* of corruption and sentenced to two years in jail. Prime Minister Samak Sundaravej was sacked from office by the Constitutional Court for violating electoral laws in 2007. Somchai Wongsawat became prime minister, but was banned from political office until 2013 along with his party, the PPP. Most parliamentary members of PPP joined the newly established Phak Puea Thai (PPT) (For Thais Party). Both main Bangkok international airports were closed for over a week in December as anti-government demonstrators besieged the termini, stranding thousands of visitors and crippling the tourist industry. Opposition leader, Abhisit Vejjajiva (PP), became prime minister. A new government coalition was formed, led by the PP with CP.
2009 Mass rallies showed renewed support of Thaksin Shinawatra, while condemning government efforts to manage the economic crisis. The Asean summit, due to be held in Pattaya, was cancelled after demonstrators stormed the venue. Sonthi Boonyaratglin (who had led the 2006 coup that overthrew Shinawatra) became leader of the Matuphum (Motherland) party (mostly comprised of Muslim politicians) and campaigned on bringing unity to Thailand. A new political party Karn Muang Mai (New Politics Party) was formed, to represent the views of the 'yellow shirts'.
2010 In February, the Supreme Court sequestrated US$1.4 billion of Shinawatra wealth, deemed illegally acquired while Mr Shinawatra was prime minister. Thousands of supporters of Shinawatra, known as 'red shirts', took to the capital's streets for weeks of civil disorder and disruption, calling for new elections. A state of emergency was declared, giving the security forces wide powers, including detention for 30 days without charge. Protestors were finally dispersed by security forces in May, leaving 80 people dead and around 1,800 injured. In May the US put Thailand on a list of countries not doing enough to combat human trafficking, an illegal industry that generates around US$10 billion a year. On 2 June, Prime Minister Vejjajiva survived a parliamentary vote of no-confidence for his handling of the civil unrest. In July the state of emergency was lifted in five states but extended in 19 states. By July over 400 people had been arrested under the emergency rules, which banned the gathering of more than five people and gave the security forces the right to hold suspects for 30 days without charge. The state of emergency was finally lifted in all states in July.
2011 Parliament was dissolved on 10 May and a general election was set for 3 July. In May, PPT elected Yingluck Shinawatra, the sister of ousted-prime minister Taksin Shinawatra, as its leader. In the elections, the opposition PPT in its first contested national election won a convincing majority of 265 seats out of 500, including 48.41 per cent of the proportional vote (61 seats out of 125); the former ruling PP won 159 seats. A five-party government coalition was agreed on 4 July, led by PPT, with CP, BJT and two other minor parties. Parliament voted Yingluck Shinawatra into office as prime minister on 5 August. Of the 500 members 296 voted for her, three against and 197 abstained. She became Thailand's first female head of government. Floodwaters that had been building following months of heavy monsoon rains reached Bangkok on 25 October. In the provinces 356 people were killed and 110,000 families displaced from their homes. By 7 November, as floodwaters reached the outskirts of Bangkok, authorities instigated evacuations (estimated at around 16,000 residents) as it diverted run-off floodwater in an attempt to protect the densely populated capital. By 14 November, nationwide over 562 people had been killed and the floods had effected 22 (out of 77) provinces, while in Bangkok waters in some lower-lying areas were 50cm deep, but in others in general water had begun to recede.

Political structure

Constitution
A new constitution was agreed by referendum in 2007. Aticles of change included: each province to return at least three members of parliament in multi-seat constituencies; making just over half the senate seats to be elected; limiting the powers and privileges of the prime minister – as no prime minister or cabinet may govern while the House of Representatives is dissolved; restricting the term in office to two; banning a prime minister from owning major holdings in private companies and making it easier to impeach a prime minister. Turnout for the referendum was 60 per cent.

Form of state
Constitutional monarchy

The executive
Executive power lies with the cabinet, headed by a prime minister for a term of four years, who must be an elected member of the House of Representatives.

National legislature
The bicameral, Rathasapha (National Assembly) consists of the Sapha Phuthaen Ratsadon (House of Representatives), with 480 representatives, of which 375 are directly elected in single seat-constituencies and 125 are determined by proportional representation along party lines, and the Wuthisapha (Senate) with 150 non-partisan members, of which 76 are directly elected and 74 are appointed by committee. Representatives serve for up to four years and senators serve for fixed terms of six years.

Legal system
Courts follow the traditional pattern of courts of first instance, a court of appeal and a Supreme Court.

Last elections
3 July 2011 (parliamentary)
Results: Parliamentary: Phak Puea Thai (PPT) (For Thais Party) won 48.41 per cent of the vote (265 seats out of 500), Phak Prachathipat (PP) (Democrat Party) 35.15 per cent (159), Phak Bhum Jai Thai (BJT) (Thai Pride Party) 3.94 per cent (34), Phak Chat Thai Pattana (CP) (Thai Nation Development Party) 2.79 per cent (19); seven other political parties each won less than 2 per cent of the vote and shared the remaining 23 seats.

Next elections
July 2015 (parliamentary)

Political parties

Ruling party
Coalition led by Phak Puea Thai (PPT) (For Thais Party), with Phak Bhum Jai Thai (BJT) (Thai Pride Party), Phak Chat Thai Pattana (CP) (Thai Nation Development Party) and two other minor parties (from 5 Aug 2011)

Main opposition party
Phak Prachathipat (PP) (Democrat Party)

Population

67.31 million (2010)*
Last census: April 2000: 60,617,200
Population density: 131 inhabitants per square km (2010)
Annual growth rate: 1.0 per cent 1994–2004 (WHO 2006)

Ethnic make-up
Approximately 80 per cent of the population are Thais, 10 per cent Chinese and 5 per cent Malays. Other ethnic minorities include Laotian, Vietnamese, Kampuchean and a number of hill tribes.

Religions
Buddhist (85 per cent), Muslim (4 per cent), Christian (0.5 per cent), Hindu and Confucian.

Education

Primary schooling lasts for six years until students are aged 13 when they progress

to the lower secondary school. At aged 16 students may either follow a general academic or vocational path in an upper secondary school.
There are 16 universities in Thailand, of which 12 are in Bangkok. There are also 21 recognised private colleges of higher education. Culturally, higher education is biased towards the social sciences and humanities, with science and technology accounting for only 22 per cent of total tertiary enrolment.
The education system in Thailand is undergoing major reforms. The main objective is the eventual decentralisation of education in the country as in 2001, policy was implemented through a central office, regional office, provincial office, then a district office. From August 2002 it will be administered through a central office, a local area education office and the school.
The government hopes to transform the learning process from a teacher-oriented system to a learner-oriented method. There are plans to introduce more technology in education.
Literacy rate: 93 per cent adult rate; 98 per cent youth rate (15–24) (Unesco 2005).
Compulsory years: Six to 16
Enrolment rate: 89 per cent gross primary enrolment; 59 per cent gross secondary enrolment, of relevant age groups (including repeaters), (World Bank).
Pupils per teacher: 21 in primary schools

Health

It is estimated that only 10 per cent of the population have pre-paid health insurance plans. Improve access to healthcare has been promised by the government by implementing a standard B30 (US$0.70) per hospital visit rule across the country. There are fears, however, that the reduced cost will entail a fall in healthcare standards.
The government has as a central objective, the standardisation of healthcare throughout the country. Plans stress the need to reorganise and decentralise public health administration. Private sector healthcare is expanding faster than the public sector, with private healthcare expenditure currently estimated to be running at double the public sector level. Private hospitals (over 370) account for 25 per cent of all hospital beds.
The ministry of health provides free medical services to the poor in all government hospitals. Thailand has well over 1,000 public hospitals, over 13,000 specialised private clinics, over 8,000 health centres and an estimated 0.23 doctors per 1,000 of the population. The health of the Thai population has improved significantly over the last 20–30 years with life expectancy rising by 17 years, the infant mortality rate dropping by about two-thirds and the proportion of the population with access to safe drinking water more than trebling.
HIV/Aids
In a region where conservative leaders have been reluctant to publicly endorse HIV/Aids prevention programmes, Thailand took the initiative in 1994 and introduced a full scale public education and condom distribution programme, so that by 2004 people newly testing HIV positive fell to 21,260, vastly less than the peak of 142,819 in 1991.
HIV prevalence: 1.5 per cent aged 15–49 in 2003 (World Bank)
Life expectancy: 70 years, 2004 (WHO 2006)
Fertility rate/Maternal mortality rate: 1.9 births per woman, 2004 (WHO 2006); maternal mortality 44 deaths per 100,000 (World Bank).
Birth rate/Death rate: 16.4 births and 6.9 deaths per 1,000 people (2003)
Child (under 5 years) mortality rate (per 1,000): 23 per 1,000 live births (2003); 18 per cent of children aged under five were malnourished (World Bank).

Welfare

The social insurance bill provides for cover during illness or accidents unrelated to work, maternity, disability, funeral expenses, child welfare, pensions and unemployment. The welfare system was radically restructured in 1997 with the introduction of a centralised Government Pension Fund (GPF) worth about B71 billion (US$1.57 billion), replacing the old civil service pension scheme with a privately managed autonomous entity.
The labour department of the Ministry of the Interior manages workers' security and welfare and oversees a compensation fund for workers. In 70 out of 73 provinces, employers with more than 20 workers are required by law to contribute to the compensation fund. This fund provides benefits to employees who suffer injury in the workplace, or who fall ill or die as a result of the performance of their work. On average, 60 per cent of the monthly wages will be paid. This amount should not fall below B2,000 (US$46) and should not exceed B9,000 (US$206). Medical expenses are also paid in the case of an injury and in the case of death, the funeral expenses will be covered by the employer.
The public welfare department (PWD) of the Ministry of the Interior provides welfare services to various groups of people such as children and the young, landless farmers, hill tribe minorities, the destitute, the disabled, the handicapped, the aged and those hit by disaster.
Thaksin Shinawatra has ambitious objectives to deal with social problems in Thailand. These include plans to establish family advisory centres and childcare clinics.
Child prostitution in Thailand has received strong international attention. Eradicating the trade in children and women is likely to be a slow process for Thailand, since anti-trafficking laws have been difficult to implement. Female unemployment in Thailand remains high, so many turn to prostitution to earn their living.

Main cities

Bangkok (Krung Thep – City of Angels) (capital, estimated population 7.0 million (m) in 2005), Samut Prakan (1.5m), Si Racha (1.8m), Khlong Luang (834,202), Chon Buri (573,423), Chiang Mai (168,135).

Languages spoken

Business is conducted in Thai. Chinese (mainly the Zhiu Zhou dialect from southern China) is spoken in major towns. Many senior government officials and businessmen speak some English which, along with French and German, is increasingly being used in tourist areas. Malay and indigenous languages are spoken.
Official language/s
Thai

Media

Much of terrestrial television and radio is controlled and operated by the government and military.
Press
Dailies: In Thai, main newspapers includes the mass-circulation *Daily News* (www.dailynews.co.th) and *Thairath* (www.thairath.co.th); other local and regional publications include *Thai Post* (www.thaipost.net) and *Matichon* (www.matichon.co.th), principal in of a media network. In English, the principal example include *The Bangkok Post* (www.bangkokpost.co.th) and *The Nation* (www.nationmultimedia.com) and Chiang Mai (www.chiangmai-mail.com).
Weeklies: Daily newspapers produce weekend editions including, in Thai, *Matichon*.
The UK-based *The Economist* was banned in January 2009 for what the authorities called 'insulting the King' (*lèse majesté*) in an article that questioned the monarch's role in public life.
Business: In Thai, *Krungthep Turakij* (www.bangkokbiznews.com), *Manager* (www.manager.co.th), *Post Today* (www.posttoday.com), *Prachachat Turakij* (www.matichon.co.th/prachachat), *Siam Turakij* (www.siamturakij.com) and *Than Settikij* (www.thannews.th.com); in English, *Business Day* (http://www.biz-day.com),

Thailand News and Press Releases (www.thailand4.com) is a business media outlet.

Periodicals: Various international publications such as *New York Times*, *Newsweek*, *The Economist* and *Asiaweek* are sold by newsagents.

Broadcasting

Radio: The National Broadcasting Service of Thailand (NBT) (www.prd.go.th) operates a national network and external service which broadcasts in nine languages, including English. There are many commercial including MCOT (http://radio.mcot.net) and Bangkok FM (www.bangkokfm.com) and non-commercial radio stations, such as KU Radio network (http://radio.ku.ac.th) operated by Kasetsart University and Army Radio (www.tv5.co.th).

Television: NBT operates Channel 11 (www.prd.go.th); Thailand Independent Television (TiTV) and Modernine TV (http://modernine.mcot.net) are government operated; TV5 (www.tv5.co.th) and BBTV (www.ch7.com) are operated by the Royal Thai Army. Thai TV3 (www.becnews.com) is commercial.

Advertising

Advertising is available in the press, on commercial radio and television, in cinemas and outdoors. Static and mobile loudspeakers are widely used. Tobacco advertising is banned, and alcohol advertising was banned in 2007. While the media is free to report and criticise government policies reporters exercise self-censorship regarding such issues as the monarchy, the military and the judiciary.

News agencies

National news agency: Thai News Agency (MCOT)

Economy

With an export-led economy, the strength of global trade has a significant impact on the Thai economy. The industrial sector constituted 43.3 per cent of GDP in 2009, of which manufacturing accounted for 34.1 per cent, including manufactured items such as computers and electronics, furniture, food stuffs, jewellery and toys and plastic products. As the global economic crisis caused trade to weaken, industrial annual production fell to -4.2 per cent, while manufacturing production fell to -5.1 per cent, particularly in capital goods and hi-tech products such as integrated circuits and hard disk drives, vehicles and electrical goods.

The service sector is the leading constituent of GDP, but only just, constituting 45.1 per cent of GDP in 2009, of which tourism is the most important and typically accounts for around 6.5 per cent of GDP. Thailand has been subject to a series of external and internal shocks since 2008, including the global pandemic swine flu, the mobbing of the international airport in Bangkok by government protestors, the global economic crisis that cut tourist numbers to 6.6 million by the first half of 2009 (7.88 million in the same period in 2008) and the political turmoil at the beginning of 2010, which was estimated to have cut visitor numbers by 1–2 million and cost the economy over US$4 billion. Experience has shown that Thailand's popularity with tourists typically allows a quick reversal of such ill-fortune.

The economy fell into recession at the beginning of 2009 as GDP for the year fell -2.3 per cent. The government introduced a series of stimulus packages from 2008–10, totalling 4.2 per cent of GDP to help kick-start growth. Measures included tax instruments, capital investment and payments to workers on low incomes. Private and public consumption rose by 5.8 per cent in 2009 and by 2010 as world trade picked up, GDP growth had strongly rebounded to 7.8 per cent.

Agriculture constituted 11.6 per cent of GDP in 2009 – Thailand is the world's leading rice exporter. A new government policy aimed at improving the lives of the rural poor was launched on 7 October 2011, whereby the government buys un-milled paddy rice directly from farmers for 50 per cent above the prevailing market price. This will cut out the independent merchants, who have previously exported some one third of Thailand's rice production. Not only will taxpayers be required to fund this scheme (estimated at US$8 billion per annum), but recent international food shortages have occurred, due in part to hoarding of rice by other Asian countries. This cut in exports by the world's leading rice exporter could exacerbate a shortage of rice on the international market. In September 2011, Indonesia protested about the failure by Thailand to supply an agreed 272,000 tonnes of rice.

In 2011, the UN Human Development Index (HDI) ranked Thailand 103 (out of 187) for national development in health, education and income. In 2010, 38.5 per cent of the population experienced at least one indicator of poverty, while 10.8 per cent lived on the equivalent of US$1.25 per day. Remittances in 2009 were US$1.64 billion, (0.6 per cent of GDP) and estimated to have grown to US$1.79 billion in 2010.

External trade

Thailand belongs to the Association of Southeast Asian Nations (Asean) Free Trade Area (Afta) and maintains a list of goods that have preferential import duties between members and a programme of tariff reductions due to be introduced in the next few years. It also belongs to the 21-member Asia-Pacific Economic Co-operation (Apec) forum, which is a bloc of countries that border the Pacific with the aim of facilitating trade, economic growth and investment in the region.

A diversified manufacturing sector provides a wide range of export commodities from rice (Thailand is a world producer), rubber, steel, tin, vehicles, hi-tech electronic goods, garments, seafood and processed food and electricity.

Imports

Principal imports are capital goods, intermediate goods and raw materials, consumer goods, petroleum and natural gas.

Main sources: Japan (typically 19 per cent of total), China (13 per cent), Malaysia (6 per cent).

Exports

Principal exports are vehicles and parts, computers and electronic goods and electrical appliances, textiles and footwear, agricultural and fishery products, rice, natural rubber, jewellery.

Main destinations: US (typically 11 per cent of total), China (11 per cent), Japan (10 per cent).

Agriculture

Farming

Agriculture accounts for around 10 per cent of GDP and employs just over half of the workforce. The rise of the manufacturing industry has meant that agriculture's share of GDP is declining, although farming still provides income for the majority of the population.

About 39 per cent of the total land area is cultivated. Production has generally been increased by expansion of planted acreage, rather than productivity improvements such as irrigation or use of fertilisers. Yield per paddy is one of the lowest in south-east Asia.

Thailand is known as the rice bowl of Asia and is one of the world's leading net exporters of food. The principal rice-growing area is the Chao Phya river basin. Tapioca is mainly produced in the south-east, kenaf in the north-east and maize in the central plain. Thailand is the world's largest exporter of natural rubber. Over 90 per cent of the rubber is produced in the south and most of it is exported through Penang in Malaysia..

Other major crops include sugar, cassava, cotton, jute, tobacco, fruit (especially pineapples), beans, oilseeds and coffee.

Livestock raised includes pigs, cattle, sheep and poultry. Buffaloes, oxen, horses and elephants are used as draught animals.

Crocodiles are farmed for their skins.

Agricultural co-operatives are organised by farmers to help co-ordinate joint farming activities and to provide low interest credits to members. The co-operatives are regulated by the ministry of agriculture and co-operatives.

A new government policy aimed at improving the lives of the rural poor was launched on 7 October 2011, whereby the government buys directly from farmers unmilled paddy rice for 50 per cent above the prevailing market price. This will cut out the independent merchants, who have previously exported some one third of Thailand's rice production. Not only will taxpayers be required to fund this scheme (estimated at US$8 billion per annum), but recent international food shortages have occurred due in part to hoarding of rice by other Asian countries. This cut in exports by the world's leading rice exporter could exacerbate this shortage of rice on the international market. In September 2011, Indonesia protested about the failure by Thailand to supply an agreed 272,000 tonnes of rice.

Fishing

Thailand is the world's main exporter of fish and seafood. Exports typically earn US$4 billion per year. Shrimp products account for over half of the export revenue. Canned tuna is another important export item, typically accounting for 15 per cent of export revenue. The government has focussed on upgrading the fishing industry by cutting production and improving product quality. Shrimp exporters are moving to create more ready-to-eat fish-based products.

Forestry

Forests are estimated to cover 17 per cent of total land area, with a further 18 per cent subject of a reforestation programme following a rapid decrease in the 1980s. There has been a ban on logging in natural forests since 1989 and the government has implemented a number of measures to protect the remaining forests and encourage plantation forest management.

Industry and manufacturing

The majority of industries are in the private sector and most registered factories are small undertakings, but there is a range of medium- and large-concerns. Main industrial products include processed food, precious stones and jewellery, cement, sugar, refined oil, synthetic fibres, textiles, assembled vehicles and parts, paint, steel, paper, pharmaceuticals, galvanised iron sheet, plastics (including artificial flowers), electronics, electrical appliances, glass, tin ingots, condensed milk, tin plate, detergent, hydrochloric acid and caustic soda. The local processing of wood has been encouraged and exports of plywood, veneer, parquet, furniture, household utensils and paper products show significant growth potential.

Tourism

Tourism is Thailand's single most important foreign exchange earner. Despite adverse factors in 2005, notably the 2004 tsunami, but also avian flu and higher fuel costs, as well as the unrest in the south, visitor numbers have remained strong at around 13 million each year. There was a rise in tourists from Asian countries and the government intends to pay particular attention to the new Chinese market and to Japan.

Mining

Mining accounts for around 2.5 per cent of GDP and employs three per cent of the workforce.

Mining has been officially designated a priority economic sector eligible for preferential tax and promotional privileges from the Board of Investment. The Bank of Thailand sets guidelines for private commercial banks to extend loans to the sector at prime lending rates.

Although many reserves remain largely unexploited, Thailand has a rich variety of mineral resources, including antimony, fluorite, iron ore, lead, lignite, limestone, manganese, precious stones, tungsten and zinc.

Tin, which is produced in northern, central and southern Thailand, is the most important mining commodity in terms of revenue. It is estimated that only 30 out of 145 tin mines are still active in the country.

Thailand is the world's biggest gem exporter. Low cost labour has helped Thailand remain a leading exporter. China is expected to become a major competitor in gem production and export. While Thailand's gem industry is more developed, China's lower priced stones have already entered the market.

Hydrocarbons

Proven oil reserves were 500 million barrels in 2007 and production was 309,000 barrels per day (bpd), an increase of 7.4 per cent on 2006 output. Consumption was 911,000bpd, a fall of 1.8 per cent from 2006. The government, in the face of oil price surges, encouraged refiners to reduce imports and increase domestic production; total refinery capacity was one million bpd in 2007.

The publicly owned Petroleum Authority of Thailand (PTT) implements the national energy policy and is responsible for exploration, production, transmission and sale of oil and gas through subsidiary companies. It also manages international trade in hydrocarbons.

Proven natural gas reserves were 330 billion cubic metres (cum) in 2007, while production was 25.9 billion cum. However, as consumption was 35.3 billion cum Thailand was forced to rely on imported natural gas from Myanmar, via an international pipeline, to make up its shortfall. Most of the output is used for electricity generation. Bongkot, in the Gulf of Thailand, is the largest gas field supplying up to 35 per cent of national demand.

A new, US$700 million, 5 million tonne per year, liquefied natural gas (LNG) terminal is under construction at Rayong, southeast of Bangkok, and will be completed by 2011. Capacity will be doubled at a later date to be ready to accept imported LNG from several sources, to fulfil rising domestic demand. Initial supplies of LNG are contracted to arrive from Qatar.

Proven coal reserves were 1.35 billion tonnes in 2007, of less valuable and polluting lignite (brown coal); around 90 per cent of all coal is produced in the north at Mae Moh. Total production was 5.1 million tonnes oil equivalent (mtoe). Thailand imports coal to meet domestic requirements.

Energy

Total installed generating capacity was 26.82GW in 2007 (with a further 11.7GW generated privately for personal consumption). It is estimated that Thailand will need a further 20GW by 2015 to meet future demand. Around 80 per cent of generation is provided by fossil fuel, with natural gas as the principal source, providing around 70 per cent of the total. Around 90 per cent of the country's coal output is used in the Mae Moh power plant in the north of Thailand, providing around 15 per cent of total electricity generation.

Several large hydroelectric projects have been suspended due to environmental and social issues of deforestation and displaced people. Instead over 25 small dams or up to 25MW are planned.

Electricity is imported from Laos and Malaysia. There is a connection with Cambodia under construction, which should become operational by 2016.

Other renewable energy sources include geothermal, biomass gas and wind power.

Financial markets

Stock exchange

The Stock Exchange of Thailand (SET)

Banking and insurance

Thailand set up the Thai Asset Management Corporation (TAMC) in 2001 to take over bad loans in the banking sector. The high level of non-performing loans has prevented Thailand's banks from functioning properly. Banks have been reluctant to lend and this has made economic recovery difficult.

Internal reform also continued in 2001–02 as part of the ongoing restructuring drive. The implementation of risk management systems has been high on the agenda. Siam Commercial Bank, Thailand's most profitable bank is concentrating on upgrading technology and attracting more customers to its internet banking system. Thai Farmers Bank underwent major restructuring, splitting its branches into different departments and making them more customer-oriented.

Central bank

Bank of Thailand

Main financial centre

Bangkok

Time

GMT plus seven hours

Geography

Thailand is situated in the Indo-Chinese peninsula, sharing borders with Myanmar to the west and north, Laos to the east and north, Cambodia to the east and Malaysia to the south.

Thailand can be divided into four regions – the central alluvial plain, the semi-arid plateau of the north-east, the mountainous north and the southern peninsula. It covers an area of 513,115 square km, about the size of France, and measures 1,650km from north to south and 800km from west to east. It has a coastline of 2,400km.

Its narrowest part is the Kra Isthmus, which is about 64km wide, with the Gulf of Thailand to the east and the Andaman Sea to the west.

Hemisphere

Northern

Climate

The climate varies from tropical savannah in the north and tropical monsoon in the south. There are three main seasons: hot (March–May), rainy (June–October) and cool (November–February). In Bangkok temperatures range from 25 degrees Celsius (C) in December to 34 degrees C in April and May.

Dress codes

Light, loose cotton clothing is advisable, although it should be modest. Sweaters may be needed in the evenings and during the cooler season. Businessmen wear shirts and ties, while jackets are worn for official functions or meetings with government officials; jackets and ties may be required for evening wear at larger hotels. Smart attire is also expected of businesswomen.

Entry requirements

Passports

Required by all and must be valid for six months beyond date of visit.

Visa

Required by all; a list of exceptions for certain nationals visiting as tourists are listed at www.thai-la.net, follow link to *visa*.

A business visitor must complete a non-immigrant visa application and produce a letter of invitation from a Thai company, printed on a company letterhead. The letter must include the host company's registration, stating the 'capital investment' and documentation of the payment of the last two years' taxes. Proof of visit for business purposes must also be furnished along with a letter of approval by the Thai Labour Department. Business visas are only valid for up to 90 days. Extensions, for either tourist or business visas, may be granted by the Immigration Bureau in Thailand.

Prohibited entry

Entry is refused to nationals of Afghanistan unless in transit within three hours. Entry may be refused to persons of untidy appearance.

Currency advice/regulations

The import and export of foreign currency is unlimited. The import of local currency is unlimited; export of amounts greater than B50,000 require prior authorisation. Travellers cheques are accepted in most banks.

Customs

Personal effects are allowed duty-free. Radio equipment requires a permit and cameras, computers and luxury jewellery must be declared at customs.

Export of images or statues of Buddha, antiques and archaeologically valuable items is only allowed with a certificate from the Department of Fine Arts. Articles exceeding B10,000 in value require a Certificate of Exportation.

Prohibited imports

Illegal drugs, pornographic material, firearms and ammunition. Live animals and meat, plants and plant material require a permit.

Health (for visitors)

Mandatory precautions

A vaccination certificate for yellow fever is required if travelling from an infected area.

Advisable precautions

Inoculations and boosters should be current for diphtheria, tetanus, hepatitis A, polio and typhoid. Other vaccinations that may be recommended are cholera, tuberculosis, and Japanese B encephalitis and hepatitis B. Use malaria prophylaxis (which will also provide protection against dengue fever and hepatitis B) including mosquito repellents, sleeping nets and clothing that cover the body after dark. There is a risk of rabies in rural areas.

Use only bottled or boiled water for drinks, washing teeth and making ice. Eat only well cooked meals, preferably served hot; vegetables should be cooked and fruit peeled. Dairy products are unpasteurised and should be avoided. Avoid pork and salad and food from street vendors. A full first-aid kit would be useful.

Locally manufactured Western proprietary medicines are easily obtainable, but visitors on regular medication should bring their own supplies – amounts for the length of the visit only.

Visitors should have medical insurance, including emergency evacuation.

Hotels

Choose a hotel in the district in which you are doing business. Most top hotels have good facilities for meetings and can arrange secretarial services if notified in advance. A 10 per cent service charge and 11 per cent tax are added to hotel bills, and it is customary to give small tips for good service.

Credit cards

Major credit and charge cards are widely accepted.

Public holidays (national)

Fixed dates

1 Jan (New Year), 6 Apr (Chakri Day), 13–16 Apr (Songkran/Thai New Year), 1 May (Labour Day), 5 May (Coronation Day), 9 Aug (Sin National Day), 12 Aug (Queen's Birthday), 23 Oct (Chulalongkorn Day), 5 Dec (King's Birthday), 10 Dec (Constitution Day).

Holidays falling on a weekend are taken on the following Monday/Tuesday.

Variable dates

Chinese New Year (Jan/Feb), Makha Bucha Day (Feb), Visakha Bucha Day (May), Asanha Bucha Day (Jul), Buddhist Lent Day (Jul), Naga Fire Ball (Oct), Loy Kratong (Nov).

Religious festivals are determined by the Buddhist lunar calendar.

Working hours

Banking

Mon–Fri: 0830–1530.

Business

Mon–Fri: 0830–1700. Sat: 0830–1200.

Government

Mon–Fri: 0830–1630.

Shops

Mon–Sun: 0900–1800/1900. Some shops are open 24 hours.

Telecommunications

Mobile/cell phones

There are 900, 1800 and 1900 GSM services throughout most of the country.

Electricity supply
220V AC, 50 cycles for domestic use, with plug fittings having two round or flat pins.

Weights and measures
Metric system (local units also in use).

Social customs/useful tips
Always carry business cards and give them to any new acquaintance when introduced. To show respect, offer and accept business cards with both hands, and always read the cards you receive before putting them down.
To the Thais *face* is very important and losing it can be disastrous, with little chance of social recovery; all dealings should be controlled, polite and respectful.
Thai business relationships, networks and associations can be extensive and visitors should expect to spend much time cultivating contacts.
Both men and women should dress in smart, lightweight casual wear. Shorts, bare shoulders, and sandals would be inappropriate in a business setting. Westerners are expected to shake hands and Thais are willing to accommodate this practice. Thai women, however, may still be reluctant to shake hands, and may prefer simply to exchange smiles on being introduced. Thais address each other and foreign visitors by their forename, prefixed by *khun*.
The head is considered the most esteemed part of the body and the feet the least, so visitors should take care not to touch someone's head (even accidentally) or show the soles of their feet.
Images of Buddha are held sacred and cannot be taken out of Thailand without official permission.
Shoes should be removed when entering a Thai house or Buddhist temple. Women must never touch a Buddhist monk, give things to him, or receive things from him, directly.
It is a criminal offence to make critical or defamatory comments about the King or other members of the Royal family, punishable by a sentence of three to 15 years.

Security
Experienced business visitors should not encounter any problems, particularly in central Bangkok. However, Thailand's position in the world drug trade, puts the gullible traveller at risk. It is advisable to lock all luggage and keep it in sight while travelling. Do not accept anything to be taken through customs on behalf of someone else.

Getting there
Air
National airline: Thai Airways International.
International airport/s: The Suvarnabhumi-Bangkok Airport (BKK) (opened in September 2006), 25km east of the city, is the central hub for Thai Airways and the country's principal commercial airport. Facilities include duty-free shopping, restaurants, entertainment, bank, post office, hotel reservations, car hire and business suites. There are train, bus and metered taxi services; limousines, either luxury or 4WD-SUV, are available. In March 2007 Don Muang, the original Bangkok international airport, was re-opened to ease congestion at Suvarnabhumi, caused mostly by the increase in traffic from low-cost airlines. Suvarnabhumi Airport is the world's second largest (after Hong Kong International Airport) single building and terminal (563,000 square metres), it took six years to build and cost around US$3 billion.
Chiang Mai International (CNX); Phuket International (HKT), 35km from Phuket; Hat Yai International (HDY), 9km from Hat Yai.
Other airport/s: Don Muang International, 30km north of Bangkok was decommissioned after the new Suvarnabhumi-Bangkok airport was opened in September 2006. It may re-open for udget airlines to use its facilities.
Airport tax: Departure tax: B700, excluding transit passengers.
Surface
Road: The Asian Highway runs from the northern region through Bangkok and on to southern Thailand, crossing the border with Malaysia and ending in Singapore. The Friendship Bridge in the north links Thailand and Laos.
Rail: There are daily rail services, including the Eastern and Oriental Express, between Singapore, Penang, Kuala Lumpur and Bangkok (including a ferry ride). Trains are air-conditioned with sleeper-coaches (journey time 48 hours). A service runs from Bangkok to Phnom Peng (Cambodia) and through to Saigon (Vietnam). The journey time is over 24 hours and the trains are more basic in facilities.
Water: Passenger liners occasionally visit. International shipping lines that maintain contacts with Thailand may provide passenger services on cargo ships. Limited ferry services are available from Cambodia, Laos and Malaysia.
Main port/s: Bangkok

Getting about
National transport
Considerable investment is earmarked for improving the country's transport facilities. In remote areas conditions are still uncertain, and banditry occurs in the north-west of the country.
Air: Thai Airways and Bangkok Airways operate domestic services to main centres.
Road: There are over 64,000km of national and provincial roads and highways, most of which are paved. Major highways are four-lanes. Toll roads exist around Bangkok.
Buses: Long-distance (air-conditioned) express coaches operate between main centres; local services are not generally recommended.
Rail: Thailand's railway network is controlled by the State Railway of Thailand (SRT), which is responsible for building, operating and maintaining Thailand's 4,600km of railway track.
Rail services are generally recommended: the system is equipped with modern rolling stock, including air-conditioned coaches, sleeping accommodation and restaurant cars on main express services. All main lines originate in Bangkok. Four main routes radiate from Bangkok's main station (Hualompong), with the track to the south extending to the Malaysian border.
Water: There are 1,110–1,600km of navigable inland waterways, depending on the season. Various types of ferries and passenger/cargo boats operate on rivers and in coastal areas.
City transport
Avoid rush-hour travel; hours-long traffic jams are routine in Bangkok, the fastest method of travel is either the metro or a motorbike taxi.
Taxis: Taxis have yellow number plates and, although they are metered, fares should be agreed in advance; a surcharge is imposed during traffic jams. Tipping is not customary.
Taxi drivers rarely understand English and it is best to have the name and address of one's destination written in Thai to show to the driver. There are air-conditioned limousine services provided by main hotels. *Tuk tuks* are motorised trishaws.
Buses, trams & metro: The metro consists of two networks, the underground and the over-ground. Tokens for single trips or cards for frequent travel are not interchangeable between the two networks, however work is underway to unify the system. The metro system is planned to be 91km long with three lines covering major areas of Bangkok by 2009.
Trains: The Bangkok Mass Transit System opened in 1999. The subway, a new mass transit system, opened in 2004.
Helicopter: Royal Orchid Sheraton jointly operates a helicopter service between the airport and the River City shopping complex next to the hotel, with a flight time of seven minutes. There is a five-minute walk by connecting bridge to the hotel.

Car hire
Chauffeur-driven car hire is available in Bangkok, Pattaya, Hat Yai, Phuket and Chiang Mai. It is not advisable to drive yourself in Bangkok. An international driving licence is required and driving is on the left. A driving licence is required to ride motorcycles.

BUSINESS DIRECTORY
The addresses listed below are a selection only. While World of Information makes every endeavour to check these addresses, we cannot guarantee that changes have not been made, especially to telephone numbers and area codes. We would welcome any corrections.

Telephone area codes
The international direct dialling code for Thailand is +66, followed by area code and subscriber's number:

Bangkok	2	Nakhon Ratchasima	44
Chiang Mai	53	Nakhon Sawan	56
Khon Kaen	43	Phuket	76
Lampang	54	Udon Thani	42

Useful telephone numbers
Metropolitan Mobile Police: 123, 191, 246-1338/42
Tourist Assistance Centre: 195, 281-5051
Capital Security Police: 123
Fire: 199, 246-0199
Ambulance: 252-2171/75
Directory (Bangkok): 13
Directory (provinces): 183
International calls: 100
Rail travel: 223-1431

Chambers of Commerce
American Chamber of Commerce in Thailand, Kian Gwan Building, 140 Wireless Road, Bangkok 10330 (tel: 251-9266; fax: 651-4472; e-mail: service@amchamthailand.com).

British Chamber of Commerce Thailand, 208 Wireless Road, Bangkok (tel: 651-5350; fax: 651-5354; e-mail: info@bccthai.com).

Chiang Mai Chamber of Commerce, Hillside Plaza and Condotel, Huai-Kaew Road, Chiang Mai 50300 (tel: 223-256; fax: 222-482).

Khon Kaen Chamber of Commerce, 359 Mittaphab Road, Khon Kaen 4000 (tel: 224-521; fax: 225-719; e-mail: info@kkchamber.com).

Nakhon Ratchasima Chamber of Commerce, 1818 Suranarai Road, Nakhon Ratchasima 30000 (tel: 296-120; fax: 296-124).

Phuket Chamber of Commerce, 1 Montree Road, Phuket 83000 (tel: 217-567; fax: 232-038; e-mail: cham,ber@phuket.ksc.co.th).

Thai Chamber of Commerce, 150 Rajabophit Road, Bangkok 10200 (tel: 225-0086; fax: 225-4913; e-mail: tcc@tcc.or.th).

Banking
Bangkok Bank PCL, 333 Silom Road, Bangkok (tel: 231-4333; fax: 236-8281/2).

Bangkok Bank of Commerce Ltd, 99 Surasak Road, Silom, Bangrak, Bangkok 10500 (tel: 234-9230, 235-5040/9; fax: 234-2939).

Bangkok Metropolitan Bank Ltd, 2 Chalermkhet 4 Street, Pomrab, Bangkok (tel: 223-0561; fax: 224-3768).

Bank of Agriculture and Agricultural Co-operatives, 469 Nakhon Sawan Road, Dusit, Bangkok 10300 (tel: 280-0180).

Bank of America NT & SA, 2/2 Wireless Road, Bangkok 10500 (tel: 251-6333; fax: 253-1905).

Bank of Asia PCL, 191 South Sathorn Road, Bangkok 10120 (tel: 287-2211/3; fax: 287-2973/4).

Bank of Ayuthaya Ltd, 1222 Rama III Road, Bangkok 10120 (tel: 296-2000, 683-1000; fax: 683-1304).

Bank of Toyko Ltd, 62 Silom Road, Bangkok (tel: 236-0119/9103; fax: 236-9110).

Chase Manhattan Bank, Siam Shopping Centre, 965 Rama I Road, Bangkok 10330 (tel: 252-1141).

Citibank NA, 127 Sathorn Tai Road, Bangkok (tel: 213-2441; fax: 213-2517).

Deutsche Bank, 21 Sathorn Tai Road, Bangkok (tel: 240-9401; fax: 240-9425).

Export-Import Bank of Thailand, Boon Pong Tower, 1193 Thanon Phahonyothin, Bangkok 10400 (tel: 271-3700, 278-0047; fax: 271-3204).

First Bangkok City Bank Ltd, 20 Yukhon Road 2, Pomrab, Bangkok (tel: 223-0501; fax: 225-3036).

Hongkong & Shanghai Banking Corporation, 64 Silom Road, Bangkok (tel: 267-3000; fax: 236-7687).

Import-Export Bank of Japan, 138 Silom Road, Bangkok 10500 (tel: 235-7373).

Industrial Finance Corp of Thailand, 1770 New Petchburi Road, Bangkapi, Bangkok 10320 (tel: 253-7111; fax: 253-9677).

International Commercial Bank of China, 36/12 PS Tower, Asoke, 21 Sukhumvit, Phrakhanong, Bangkok 10110 (tel: 259-2000; fax: 259-1330) .

Krung Thai Bank Ltd, 35 Sukhumvit Road, Bangkok (tel: 255-2222; fax: 255-9391/6).

Nakornthon Bank Ltd, 90 Sathonthanee Building, Sathorn Nua Road, Bangrak, Bangkok (tel: 233-2111; fax: 236-4226).

Siam Commercial Bank, 9 Rachadapisek Road, Bangkok (tel: 344-1111; fax: 937-7454).

Siam City Bank Public Company Limited, 1101 New Petchburi Road, Bangkok 10400 (tel: 208-5000/5043; fax: 253-1240).

Standard Chartered Bank, 990 Rama IV Road, Bangkok (tel: 636-1000; fax: 636-1198/9).

Thai Danu Bank Ltd, 393 Silom Road, Bangkok (tel: 233-9160/9; fax: 236-7939).

Thai Farmers Bank, 1 Thai farmers Lane, Rat Burana Road, Bangkok (tel: 470-1122; fax: 470-1571).

Thai Military Bank Ltd, 3000 Phahonyothin Rd, Bangkok 10900 (tel: 299-1111, 273-7020; fax: 273-7121/7124).

Central bank
Bank of Thailand, 273 Samsen Road, Bangkok 10200 (tel: 283-5353; fax: 280-0449).

Stock exchange
The Stock Exchange of Thailand (SET): www.set.or.th

Stock exchange 2
The Market for Alternative Investment (Mai): www.mai.or.th

Travel information
Police (Tourist) (to reports a theft for insurance purposes), 29/1 Soi Lang Suan, Ploenchit Road, Lumpini, Bangkok (tel: 255-2964/8).

Royal Automobile Association of Thailand, 151, Soi Aphaisongkram, Phaholyothin, 10900, Bangkok (tel: 511-2230/1).

Thai Airways, 89 Vibhavadi Rangsit Road, Bangkok 9 10900 (tel: 356-1111; fax: 356-2222; internet: www.thaiairways.com).

Thai Hotels Association, 203-209/2 Rajdamnoen Klang Avenue, Bangkok 10200 (tel: 281-9496, 281-9579; fax: 281-4188).

National tourist organisation offices
Tourism Authority of Thailand, Le Concorde Building, 202 Rachadapisek Road, Huai Khwang, Bangkok 10320 (tel: 694-1222; fax: 694-1329, 694-1221; internet: www.tourismthailand.org).

Ministries
Ministry of Agriculture and Co-operatives, Thanon Ratchadamnoen Nok, Bangkok 10200 (tel: 281-5955, 281-5939; fax: 280-1691).

Ministry of Commerce, Thanon Samamchai, Bangkok 10200 (tel: 282-6171/9; fax: 280-0775).

Ministry of Defence, Thanon Samamchai, Bangkok 10200 (tel: 225-0098, 222-1121; fax: 226-3115).

Ministry of Education, Wang Chan Kasem, Thanon Ratchadamnoen Nok, Bangkok 10300 (tel: 280-0306).

Ministry of Finance, Thanon Rama VI, Bangkok 10400 (tel: 273-9021; fax: 293-9408).

Ministry of Foreign Affairs, Sri Ayutthaya Road, Bangkok 10400 (tel: 643-5000; fax: 643-5180).

Ministry of Industry, Thanon Rama VI, Bangkok 10400 (tel: 202-3000; fax: 202-3048).

Ministry of the Interior, Thanon Atsadang, Bangkok 10200 (tel: 222-1141/55; fax: 223-8851).

Ministry of Justice, Thanon Rachadaphisek, Chatuchak, Bangkok 10900 (tel: 541-2284/91; fax: 541-2307).

Ministry of Labour and Social Welfare, Thanon Mitmaitri, Dindaeng, Bangkok 10400 (tel: 245-4782; fax: 246-1520).

Ministry of Public Health, Thanon Tiwanond, Amphoe Muang, Nonthaburi 11000 (tel: 591-8491; fax: 591-8492).

Ministry of Science, Technology and Environment, Thanon Rama VI, Ratchathewi, Bangkok 10400 (tel: 246-0064; fax: 246-5146).

Ministry of Transport and Communications, 38 Thanon Ratchadanoen Nok, Bangkok 10100 (tel: 283-3000; fax: 281-3959).

Ministry of University Affairs, 328 Thanon Si Ayutthaya, Khet Ratchathewi, Bangkok 10400 (tel: 246-0025, 246-1106/14; fax: 245-8636, 245-8930, 246-8883).

Other useful addresses

Advertising Association of Thailand, 12/14 Prachaniwet 1 Road, Lardyao, Chatuchak, Bangkok 10900 (tel: 591-6461; fax: 589-9470).

ASEAN Investment Promotion Agency, Board of Investment, 555 Vipavadee Rangsit, Chatuchak, Bangkok 10900 (tel: 537-8111; fax: 537-8177; web: www.boi.go.th).

ASEAN Secretariat, 70 A J1 Sisingamangaraja, Jakarta 12110, Indonesia (tel: 62(21)726-2991, 724-3372; fax: 724-3504, 739-8234; web: www.asean.or.id).

Bangkok Mass Transit Authority, 131 Tiumruammitr Road, Huay Kwang, Bangkok 10310 (tel: 246-0339, 246-0741/4, 246-0750/2).

British Embassy, Wireless Road, Bangkok (tel: 253-0191; fax: 255-8619, 255-9278).

Chiangmai Province Commercial Office, Chiangmai City Hall, Chotana Road, Muang District, Chiangmai 50300 (tel: 221-217; fax: 221-121).

Communications Authority of Thailand, 99 Chaeng Watthana Road, Bangkok 10002 (tel: 573-0099).

Customs Department, Atnarong Road, Klongtoey, Bangkok 10110 (tel: 249-0431, 671-7555/7).

Department of Export Promotion, 22/77 Rachadapisek Road, Bangkok 10900 (tel: 513-1909/15, 511-5066/77; fax: 512-1079, 513-1917).

Department of Foreign Trade, Samamchai Road, Bangkok 10110 (tel: 225-1315/29; fax: 224-7269, 225-4763).

Deparetment of Industrial Promotion,Thanon Rama VI, Ratchathewi, Bangkok 10400 (tel: 202-4415/6; fax: 246-0031)

Department of Local Administration, Thanon Asadang, Bangkok 10200 (tel: 222-3852, 222-8847; fax: 222-5858).

Department of Mineral Resources, Rama VI Road, Bangkok 10400 (tel: 246-0034, 246-1161/9).

Eastern Trader's Association for Exporting Fruit-Vegetable, 30/31-32 Trirat Road, Muang District, Chanthaburi 22000 (tel: 325-962; fax: 325-962).

Economic and Social Commission for Asia and the Pacific (ESCAP), United Nations Building, Bangkok (tel: 288-1234; fax: 288-1000).

Election Division, Department of Local Administration, Ministry of Interior, Thanon Asadang, Bangkok 10200 (tel: 221-5871; fax: 222-6886).

Export Promotion Centre-Chanthaburi, 30/31-32 Trirat Road, Chanthaburi 22000 (tel: 325-962/3; fax: 325-962).

Export Promotion Centre-Chiang Mai, 29/19 Singharaj Road, Chiang Mai 50200 (tel: 216-350/1, 221-376; fax: 215-307).

Export Promotion Centre-Hat Yai, 7-15 Jootee-Uthit 1 Road, Hat Yai, Songkla 90110 (tel: 234-349, 231-744; fax: 234-329).

Export Promotion Centre-Khon Kaen, 68/4 Kiang Muang Road, Khon Kaen 40000 (tel: 221-472; fax: 221-476).

Export Promotion Centre-Surat Thani, 148/59 Surat-Nakornsri Road, Bang Kung, Surat Thani , Bangkok 84000 (tel: 286-916; fax: 288-632).

Export Service Centre, Department of Commercial Relations, Ministry of Commerce, 22–77 Thanon Rachadaphisek–Ladprao, Bangkok 10900 (tel: 513-1905).

Federation of Nakhon Ratchasima Industries, 269 Friendship Highway, Tambon Kokgruad Muang District, Nakhon Ratchasima 30280 (tel: 251-028; fax: 251-033).

Federation of Southern Industries, Songkhla Chapter, 165 Southern Industrial Promotion Center Building, 3rd Floor, Karnchanawanitch, Haadyai District, Songkhla 90110 (tel: 211-905).

Federation of Thai Industries, Queen Sirikit National Convention Center, Zone C 4th Floor, 60 New Rachadapisek Road, Klongtoey, Bangkok 10110 (tel: 229-4255; fax: 229-4941).

Federation of Thai Industries, Chiangmai and Nearby Chapter, Northern Industrial Promotion Centre Building, 1st Floor, 158 Tung Hotel Road, Muang District, Chiangmai 50000 (tel: 304-346; fax: 246-353).

Federation of Thai Industries, Khon Kaen Chapter, 359/2 Mittaphab Road, Muang District, Khon Kaen 40000 (tel: 225-679; fax: 225-678).

Federation of Thai Industries, Surathani Chapter, 160/19 Surat-Punpin Road, Makhamtia, Muang District, Surathani 84000 (tel: 285-722).

Federation of Thai Udon Thani Industries and Nearby Chapter, 83/14 Watana Road, Muang District, Udon Thani 41000 (tel: 242-004; fax: 246-498).

Fishery Association of Thailand, 1575 Charoen Nakom Road, Bangkok 10600 (tel: 437-0158/62; fax: 437-1262).

Foreign Bankers Association, 19th Floor, Sathorn Thani Building 2, 92/55 North Sathorn Road, Silom Bangrak, Bangkok 10500 (tel: 236-4730, 236-7224; fax: 236-4731).

General Post Office, 1160 Thanon Jaroenkrung, Bangkok 10501 (tel: 233-1050).

Industrial Estate Authority of Thailand, 618 Nikhom Makkasan Road, Phayathai, Bangkok (tel: 253-0561).

Industrial Finance Corporation, 1770 New Petchaburi Road, Bangkok 10500 (tel: 253-7111, 253-9666; fax: 253-9677, 254-8098).

Lawyers Association, 26 Ratchadamnern Avenue, Bangkok 10220 (tel: 224-1873).

National Statistical Office, Lan Luang Road, Bangkok 10100 (tel: 281-3022; fax: 281-3815, 281-3848).

Northern Industrial Promotion Center, 158 Tung Hotel Road, Muang District, Chiangmai 50000 (tel: 245-361; fax: 248-315).

Northern Investment Promotion Office, 369/1 Charoenrat Road, Watgate, Muang District, Chiangmai 50000 (tel: 248-778; fax: 240-919).

Office of the Board of Investment, 555 Vibhavadi-Rangsit Road, (opposite Central Plaza Hotel), Chatuchak, Bangkok 10900 (tel: 537-8111, 537-8155; fax: 537-8177; email: head@boi.go.th).

Office of Foreign Trade, Sanambin Road, Suthep, Muang District, Chiangmai 50200 (tel: 274-672; fax: 277-901).

Office of the National Culture Commission, Thanon Ratchadapisek, Khet Huay Khwang, Bangkok 10310 (tel: 248-5839, 247-0013/19 (ext 201); fax: 248-5841, 248-5851, 248-5845).

Office of the National Economic and Social Development Board, 962 Krung Kasem, Bangkok 10100 (tel: 282-8434; fax: 282-0891).

Port Authority of Thailand, Thanon Sunthomkosa, (tel: 249-0362).

Prime Minister's Office, Government House, Thanon Nakhon Pathom, Bangkok 10300 (tel: 282-6543, 282-6877; fax: 282-8587, 282-8631).

Religious Affairs Department, Thanon Ratchamnoen Nok, Bangkok 10300 (tel: 281-6080 (ext 43, 74 or 40); fax: 281-5415).

Royal Thai Embassy (US), Suite 401, 1024 Wisconsin Avenue, NW, Washington DC 20007 (tel: (+1-202) 944-3600; fax: (+1-202) 944-3611; email: thai.wsn@thaiembdc.org).

Securities Exchange of Thailand, 32 Sinthon Building, Bangkok 10500 (tel: 250-0001/8).

Southern Industrial Economic Affairs Center, 3rd Floor, Songkhla Industrial Office Building, Karnchanawanitch Road, Muang district, Songkhla 90000 (tel: 321-166; fax: 321-167).

Southern Industrial Promotion Center, Department of Industrial Promotion, 165 Karnchanawanitch, Muang District, Songkhla 90110 (tel: 211-905).

Stock Exchange of Thailand (SET), Sinthon Building, 2nd Floor, 132 Wireless Road, Bangkok 10330 (tel: 254-0960, 254-0969, 256-7100, 256-7109; fax: 254-7120, 256-3040).

Telephone Organisation of Thailand, 89/2 Moo 3 Chaeng Wattana, Bangkok 10002 (tel: 505-1000; fax: 574-9533).

Thai Bankers' Association, 4th Floor, Lake Rachada Office Complex, Building II, Rachadapisek Road, Bangkok 10110 (tel: 264-0883/7; fax: 264-0888).

Thai Mining Association, 79 Prachatipatai Road, Banpanthom, Pranakom, Bangkok 10200 (tel: 282-8947/9; fax: 280-3786, 282-7372).

Thai Petrochemical Industry and Trade Association, 175-177 Surawong Road, Bangkok 10500 (tel: 238-2956/9; fax: 236-3110).

Thai Rice Mill Association, 81 Soi Rong Nam Kheng, Charoenkrung Road, Samphanthawong, Bangkok 10100 (tel: 235-7863, 234-7295; fax: 234-7286).

Trade Statistics Centre, Department of Business Economics, Ratchadamnoen Klang, Bangkok 10200 (tel: 282-6393, 280-1727; fax: 280-0775, 280-0826).

National news agency: Thai News Agency (MCOT)

Internet sites

Airports of Thailand: www.airportthai.co.th

Board of Investment: www.boi.go.th

Commercial directory: www.sino.net.thai/commerce/thaiprod.htm

Eastern and Oriental Express: www.orient-express.com

Thailand government: www.thaigov.go.th

Thailand trade directory: www.sino.net/index.htm

Timor-Leste

KEY FACTS

Official name: República Democrática de Timor-Leste (Democratic Republic of Timor-Leste)

Head of State: President José Ramos-Horta (from 20 May 2007)

Head of government: Prime Minister Xanana Gusmão (CNRT) (from 8 Aug 2007)

Ruling party: Coalition led by Conselho Nacional de Reconstrução do Timor (CNRT) (National Congress for Timorese Reconstruction) with Associação Social-Democrata Timorense (ASDT) (Timorese Social Democratic Association), Partido Social Democrata (PSD) (Social Democratic Party) and Partido Democrático (PD) (Democratic Party) (from Jul 2007)

Area: 19,000 square km

Population: 1.07 million (2010; census figure)

Capital: Díli

Official language: Portuguese and Tetum (Portuguese is the language of documentation).

Currency: US dollar (US$) = 100 cents (adopted as transitional currency, Jan 2000)

GDP per capita: US$588 (2010)

GDP real growth: 6.10% (2010)

GDP: US$628.00 million (2010)

Inflation: 4.90% (2010)

Balance of trade: -US$431.00 million (2009)

Annual FDI: US$279.65 million (2010)

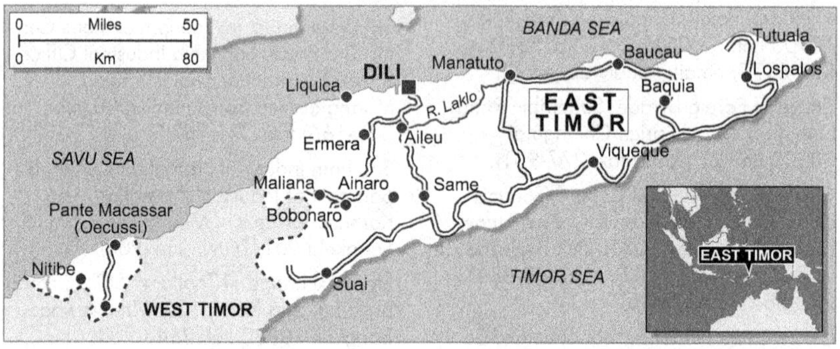

Timor Leste's recent history has been pretty turbulent. Once a Portuguese possession, then a (reluctant) part of Indonesia, its struggle for independence in the face of seemingly implacable opposition from a (then) Indonesian dictatorship was no easy affair. Once the Timor population had voted for independence in 1999, things hardly improved. The territory became independent in 2002 and in 2003 the former Indonesian military commander found himself sentenced to five years in jail for crimes against humanity. The sentence was hardly harsh in view of what had been perpetrated by the retirng Indonesian administration. But the point was made.

Unrest

In February 2008, President Ramos-Horta was shot and severely wounded in an attack led by rebel Alfredo Reinado (who was allegedly involved in the earlier unrest of April/May 2006 and who had escaped from jail on 30 August 2006). Reinado was killed in the attacks. A short time later a convoy including Prime Minister Gusmão was fired on. The Prime Minister was uninjured. President Ramos-Horta returned to East Timor on 17 April 2008, after receiving medical treatment in Australia. An officially-declared 'state of siege' ended in May 2008, following the surrender of rebel leader Gastao Salsinha and most of his followers. Since that time, the security situation has improved and remains stable. Separate presidential and parliamentary elections are due to be held in the first half of 2012.

The economy

According to the Asian Development bank (ADB) economic momentum generated by a rapid build-up in Timor Leste's government spending has resulted in gross domestic product (GDP) (excluding offshore petroleum production and the United Nations (UN) peacekeeping mission) averaging double-digit growth in 2007–10. This measure of GDP rose by 9.5 per cent in 2010, moderating from a very high rate in 2009.

Government expenditure, funded mainly by income from offshore petroleum production, increased steeply from about US$220 million in 2006 to around US$825 million in 2009 and was budgeted at US$967 million for 2010 (although the ADB notes that actual outlays probably fall short of the budget). Much of the additional government spending was on items that fed quickly into the local economy. Private consumption was boosted in 2010 by a continued rise in public sector wages and salaries, as well as cash transfers provided in rural areas through a wide-ranging social safety net. There was a further large expansion in 2010, both in small, rural infrastructure projects and in larger public projects in the capital, Dili. Private investment also climbed as local and overseas-owned businesses geared up to take advantage of the opportunities presented by rising public investment and buoyant consumer spending. A high level of aggregate demand is reflected in a range of indicators, including new vehicle registrations, electricity use and mobile phone subscribers, albeit with some sign of an easing in growth in 2010.

Construction expanded alongside rising investment. Agricultural output, which contributes around 30 per cent of GDP, barely rose in 2010 because of bad weather and continuing transport problems. This followed 2 years of 13 per cent growth in the sector, when it was bolstered by government-led distribution of better seeds and of tractors and by the introduction of extension services. The ministry of agriculture estimated that rice production declined by 6.4 per cent in 2010. Maize production, though, rose by an estimated 10.5 per cent and coffee exports rose from an unusually low 10,000 tons in 2009 to 25,600 tons in 2010.

Merchandise exports, mainly coffee, represent less than 10 per cent of the value of merchandise imports. The wide trade deficit, in the order of 65 per cent of non-petroleum, non-UN GDP, is outweighed by a surplus in the income account attributable to petroleum revenue. In 2010, such revenue rose to an estimated US$2.1 billion and provided for a current account surplus equivalent to 238 per cent of non-petroleum, non-UN GDP.

The ADB noted that bank lending remained constrained by a backlog of non-performing loans and a continuing problem of securing land as collateral. Consequently, commercial bank credit to the private sector was unchanged in 2010 from 2009. Inflation accelerated to average 6.8 per cent in 2010 and was running at 9.2 per cent year-on-year in December 2010. Rising food prices were the main reason, themselves largely due to higher international prices. Inflation was lower for prices set by domestic rather than international conditions, suggesting that inflation was 'cost push' rather than 'demand pull.'

The outlook for the short and medium term rests heavily on developments in government expenditure. The government has budgeted to boost its own-funded spending by about 50 per cent to US$1.27 billion in 2011. Much of the increase is for a multi-year national electrification project and will not be fully spent in 2011, but a sizable increase in actual expenditure is projected for 2011. The government has forecast that its own-funded spending will rise to about US$1.45 billion by 2015. Total infrastructure investment over 2011–15 is projected to exceed US$3 billion. This surge in government outlays will continue to support aggregate demand and construction. Barring disruptive shocks, economic growth is likely to remain high at around 10 per cent over the forecast period.

The United Nations (UN) mission is phasing down toward a scheduled departure at end-2012, which will have a dampening effect on growth, mainly in 2013. Until then, expansion in government expenditure will more than offset that effect.

High world oil prices are boosting public saving, providing the financial resources to sustain the investment surge. Timor Leste's Petroleum Fund held US$6.9 billion in offshore investments at end-2010 and even with large withdrawals planned to finance the budget, the value of the fund is projected to rise above US$14 billion by 2015. Petroleum income exceeding US$2 billion annually is likely to lead to further large budget and current account surpluses in 2011 and 2012. The budget surplus is, however, projected to decline this year as the expansion in government expenditure is expected to outweigh the additional revenue provided by higher world oil prices. From 2012, restraint in recurrent spending and a planned leveling off in public investment are seen easing the downward trend in the budget surplus. Inflation is forecast to average 7.5 per cent in 2011, before decelerating in 2012 as upward pressure on commodity prices eases.

Risk assessment

Economy	Good
Politics	Fair
Regional stability	Fair

COUNTRY PROFILE

Historical profile

Before the arrival of the Portuguese and Dutch, the island of Timor was linked by trade to China and India.

1512 Portuguese navigators landed and established Díli as the colonial capital. Sandalwood, honey, wax and slaves were exported.

1749 The eastern half of Timor became a Portuguese colony (East Timor) and remained so until the mid-1970s, when the Portuguese colonial empire disintegrated. The western half became part of the Dutch East Indies and later Indonesia.

1895 There were several uprisings against Portuguese rule.

1942 The Japanese invaded. Up to 60,000 people were killed during fighting between Australian and Japanese troops.

1945 The end of the Second World War saw the end of Japanese rule.

1974–75 A military coup in Portugal led to a policy of decolonisation. The Portuguese governor and administration withdrew and the capital, Díli, was occupied by the Marxist Frente Revolucionária do Timor-Leste Independente (Fretilin) (Revolutionary Front for Timor-Leste Independence). Indonesian troops occupied the state, setting up a provisional government. An estimated 200,000 people died in the military crackdown and famine that followed.

1976 East Timor was integrated into Indonesia, becoming the 27th Indonesian province, although this act was never officially recognised by the UN.

1985 The rebels suffered a setback when the Australian government recognised Indonesia's incorporation of East Timor. Nevertheless Australia gave shelter to exiled Timorese dissidents.

1991 Portugal took Australia to the International Court of Justice (ICJ), on behalf of East Timor, alleging Australia had failed to observe the rights of the Timorese to national self-determination

KEY INDICATORS — Timor-Leste

	Unit	2006	2007	2008	2009	2010
Population	m	1.01	1.04	*1.06	*1.09	1.07
Gross domestic product (GDP)	US$bn	0.35	0.40	0.50	0.59	0.63
GDP per capita	US$	322	382	469	543	588
GDP real growth	%	-3.4	8.4	12.8	7.4	6.1
Inflation	%	4.1	1.8	2.8	1.7	4.9
Exports (fob) (goods)	US$m	8.0	7.0	14.0	10.0	–
Imports (fob) (goods)	US$m	141.0	176.0	353.0	440.0	–
Balance of trade	US$m	-133.0	-169.0	-339.0	-431.0	–
Current account	US$m	540.0	1,177.0	2,021.0	1,127.0	1,425.0
Total reserves minus gold	US$m	83.8	230.3	210.4	249.9	406.2
Foreign exchange	US$m	83.8	230.3	210.4	237.8	394.3
Exchange rate	per US$	1.00	1.00	1.00	1.00	1.00

* estimated figure

when it had recognised Indonesia's occupation of Timor-Leste in 1975.
1992 Fretilin leader, Xanana Gusmão, was captured by Indonesian troops and convicted of subversion.
1995 The ICJ ruled it did not have jurisdiction in the matter of Australian actions concerning East Timor.
1996 Bishop Carlos Belo and foreign minister-in-exile, José Ramos Horta, jointly won the Nobel Peace Prize.
1998 President Suharto of Indonesia was forced to step down. President B J Habibie considered offering East Timor 'special status' and wider autonomy, but exiled Timorese leaders and Portugal rejected the idea.
1999 The UN Mission organised a referendum, which had a 98.5 per cent turnout, with 78.5 per cent of the population voting for independence. International military intervention halted Indonesian army atrocities and the Indonesian government agreed to grant East Timor extensive autonomy. The first donor conference was held in Tokyo, Japan.
2000 The Lisbon, Portugal, donor conference was held. The UN Transitional Administration for East Timor (UNTAET) established the East Timor Transitional Administration (ETTA). A donor conference was held in Brussels in Belgium.
2001 Gusmão resigned as head of the interim parliament. East Timor voted for an Assembleia Constituinte (Constituent Assembly) in their first democratic election run by the UN. Fretilin won 55 of the 88 seats in the constituent assembly. The ETTA was transformed into the East Timor Public Administration (ETPA) after the elections and Mari Alkatiri was sworn in as chief minister. The gradual reduction of the UNTAET peace-keeping force began.
2002 East Timor became independent as the Democratic Republic of Timor-Leste on 20 May, with independence hero, Xanana Gusmão, as president and Mari Alkatiri as prime minister. The constituent assembly became the newly inaugurated Parlamento Nacional (National Parliament). Timor-Leste became a member of the World Bank Group and joined the UN.
2003 The former Indonesian military chief in Timor-Leste was sentenced by an Indonesian court to five years in jail for crimes against humanity, due to his failure to prevent attacks on civilians following the 1999 independence vote. The Australian parliament ratified the Timor Sea Treaty, which permitted the development of the Bayu-Undan gas field, the royalties from which will fund the country's economic development.
2004 A UN-backed tribunal issued a warrant for the arrest of the Indonesian presidential candidate, General Wiranto, for human rights abuses in Timor-Leste.
2005 Indonesia and Timor-Leste, recognised the location of their shared land border.
2006 Timor-Leste and Australia signed an agreement for the start of oil and gas production in the Greater Sunrise field with an equal share of the proceeds. Prime Minister Alkatiri resigned and was replaced by José Ramos-Horta.
2007 José Ramos-Horta won the presidential elections. General elections did not produce a clear winner but the coalition led by Conselho Nacional de Reconstrução do Timor (CNRT) (National Congress for Timorese Reconstruction), headed by former president Xanana Gusmão, defeated the ruling Fretilin.
2008 The UN troops that had restored peace in 2005 and had since been in control of security began to transfer power to local police forces. President Ramos-Horta was shot and seriously wounded by rebel military forces that attacked his home as parliament extended a state of emergency; he underwent emergency medical treatment in Australia.
2009 The UN voted unanimously to keep its peacekeeping force in Timor-Leste for another year, while the situation remained fragile. The UN formally handed over control of policing for the district of Lautem to local police, thereby beginning the process of devolving domestic security to local forces.
2010 In February a commissioner to investigate officials accused of corruption was sworn into office. Following a seven-month trail of 27 men (mostly ex-soldiers) charged with the assassination attempt on President Ramos-Horta in 2008, 24 were sentenced to imprisonment and three acquitted on 3 March.
2011 The police took over full control from the UN from 27 March, although a group of 1,280 UN police will remain until after the presidential elections in May 2012, when its peacekeeping mission officially ends. On 18 July the government released its Strategic Development Plan (2011–30), with objectives for social, economic and infrastructural goals. On 21 August President Ramos-Horta officially disbanded Forças Armadas para a Liberação Nacional do Timor-Leste (Falintil) (Armed Forces of National Liberation of East Timor), the insurgent army of independence, in a ceremony attended by officials of its former occupiers, Indonesia. On 22 August, former military leader of Falintil, Major General José Maria Vasconcelos (known as Taur Matan Ruak (Two Sharp Eyes)) announced that he would stand as presidential candidate in the upcoming elections.

Political structure

Constitution

The constitution, passed in 2001, became valid on 20 May 2002, when Timor-Leste gained independence.

Independence date

20 May 2002

Form of state

Democratic, sovereign, independent and unitary state.

The executive

The president of the republic is the head of state and supreme commander of the defence force, and is elected by universal suffrage. The term of office is five years and no president can serve more than two terms.
The Council of State is the political advisory body of the president, headed by the president. It comprises the speaker of the national parliament, the prime minister, five citizens elected by the national parliament and five citizens designated by the president for the period corresponding to the president's term of office.

National legislature

The unicameral Parlamento Nacional (National Parliament) has between 52–65 members, serving for five years. Members are elected by a parallel-party list system. The parliament elects the prime minister. Some legislation may be vetoed by the president.

Legal system

The legal system is under reform, putting in place structures under the new constitution.
Since 2000, the International Development Law Organisation (IDLO) has delivered practical training programmes to Timor-Leste's judges and prosecutors as part of a USAID-funded project for upgrading the system of justice.
Amnesty International issued a report in March 2003 which claimed that Timor-Leste's legal framework was incomplete and that there was 'a lack of clarity among judicial and other relevant officials about existing applicable law'. Some of the main problems include a lack of public defenders, delayed processing of court cases and legislation that was inconsistent with international human rights law and standards. It said that these problems encouraged vigilante violence and a loss of confidence in the legal system among police officers.

Last elections

9 April/9 May 2007 (presidential); 1 July 2007 (parliamentary).
Results: Presidential: José Ramos Horta won 69.3 per cent of the vote; Francisco Guterres 30.7 per cent.
Parliamentary: Fretilin won 29 per cent of the vote (21 seats out of 88); Conselho Nacional de Reconstrução do Timor (CNRT) (National Congress for Timorese

Reconstruction) 24.1 per cent (18); Associação Social-Democrata Timorense (ASDT) (Timorese Social Democratic Association) and Partido Social Democrata (PSD) (Social Democratic Party) 15.8 per cent (11); Partido Democrático (PD) (Democratic Party) 11.3 per cent (eight); the remaining five seats were won by two political parties and a coalition of two political parties. Turnout was 80.5 per cent.

Next elections

2012 (parliamentary); 2012 (presidential).

Political parties

Ruling party

Coalition led by Conselho Nacional de Reconstrução do Timor (CNRT) (National Congress for Timorese Reconstruction) with Associação Social-Democrata Timorense (ASDT) (Timorese Social Democratic Association), Partido Social Democrata (PSD) (Social Democratic Party) and Partido Democrático (PD) (Democratic Party) (from Jul 2007)

Main opposition party

Frente Revolucionária do Timor-Leste Independente (Fretilin) (Revolutionary Front for Timor-Leste Independence)

Population

1.07 million (2010; census figure)

Last census: July 2004: 924,642 (provisional)

Population density: 72 inhabitants per square km (2010)

Annual growth rate: 0.5 per cent 1994–2004 (WHO 2006)

Ethnic make-up

Before the arrival of the Europeans, peoples of Asia and Insulindia, mainly Malays, Makasare and Papuans, migrated to Timor-Leste.

Religions

Roman Catholic (91.4 per cent), Protestant (2.6 per cent), Muslim (1.7 per cent). There are also Buddhist and Hindu communities.

Education

Around 70 per cent of school age population attend primary school and 44 per cent are enrolled at secondary school. There is a shortage of teachers due to the fact that 80 per cent of Timor-Leste's teachers were Indonesian and the vast majority left following Indonesia's withdrawal. More than half the population is illiterate. The Roman Catholic Church is attempting to implement a literacy programme for the schools as the country needs to educate its people to manage the new nation's bureaucracy.

Health

Life expectancy: 63 years, 2004 (WHO 2006)

Fertility rate/Maternal mortality rate: 7.8 births per woman, 2004 (WHO 2006)

Child (under 5 years) mortality rate (per 1,000): 87 deaths per 1,000 live births; 42.6 children aged under 5 are malnourished (World Bank).

Head of population per physician: 0.1 physicians per 1,000 people, 2004 (WHO 2006)

Main cities

Díli (capital, estimated population 59,069 in 2005), Los Palos (19,111).

Languages spoken

Tetum and Bahasa Indonesian/Malayu are the local languages. It is estimated that Portuguese is spoken by only 5 per cent of the population, with Tetum spoken by 82 per cent and Indonesian by 43 per cent. Although Tetum is widely spoken, it is an undeveloped language and only recently achieved a standardised grammar and spelling.

Official language/s

Portuguese and Tetum (Portuguese is the language of documentation).

Media

Press

There are two daily publication based in Timor Leste, *Suara Timor Lorosae* (www.suaratimorlorosae.com) and the *Timor Post*; periodicals include *La'o Hamutuk* (www.laohamutuk.org) a joint government and international organisations publication.

Broadcasting

Radio: Around 90 per cent of the public receive transmissions from the national public service provided by Radio Nacional de Timor Leste (RTL). There are two other radio stations, Radio Falintil/Voz da Esperanca is a community radio and Radio Timor Kmanek (RTK) is operated by the Catholic Church.

Television: Fewer residents have access to Televisão de Timor Leste (TTL), but programmes are broadcast for 24 hours a day in Tetum, Indonesian, English and Portuguese. Rural districts show three-hour videotaped summaries of the week's programming on projection screens.

Economy

Crude oil sales and hydrocarbon extraction have become the single greatest source of economic growth since 2004, when it first began production. According to the International Monetary Fund (IMF) in 2010, growth has been achieved through successfully channelling capital from the petroleum fund into the public sector, while sustaining a level of funding to benefit future generations from the profits of the petroleum wealth. The majority of the population is engaged in subsistence farming, with rice as the principal food crop and coffee as the principal export crop; vanilla is being cultivated for future export.

GDP growth was 11 per cent in 2008, in a year when global oil prices were at a record high. Nevertheless, growth was 11.6 per cent in 2009, at a time when oil prices had fallen sharply due to the global economic recession; growth in 2010 fell to 7.2 per cent. The financial assets of the Petroleum Fund were US$6.9 billion in 2010 which has helped to fund much needed development, such as investment in upgrading Dili airport, the electricity grid, the Comoro power station, roads and a new LNG plant.

Timor-Leste is one of the poorest countries in the world, in 2010 the UN Human Development Index (HDI) ranked it as 120 out of 169 countries and that 37.19 per cent of the population lives below the poverty line. Combined unemployment and underemployment are estimated at around 70 per cent, while the country suffers from a serious shortage of skilled workers throughout the economy.

Timor-Leste has been developing its regulatory framework and administrative capacity as well as new investment, insurance and export laws, which should help create a business climate attractive to investors.

External trade

In 2011, Timor Leste does not belong to the World Trade Organisation or any other regional economic block, although plans to join the Association of Southeast Asian Nations (Asean) are underway. The country is the recipient of much foreign aid needed to repair and instigate development of not only the physical infrastructure but social and entrepreneurial structures as well. Production in off-shore oil and natural gas fields have begun and provide the majority of the country's income. Coffee is the principal agricultural product for export and vanilla cultivation for export is being encouraged.

Imports

Principal imports include food, petroleum, building materials, vehicles and machinery.

Main sources: Indonesia (typically over 45 per cent of total), Singapore (15 per cent), Australia (14 per cent).

Exports

Principal exports are oil and natural gas, coffee.

Main destinations: Australia (typically over 50 per cent of total), US (25 per cent), Germany (5 per cent).

Agriculture

Farming

Livestock has been a traditional source of income for the Timorese and the majority of rural families hold livestock. Livestock has a large social and economic function: it is exchanged in marriage, and can be a source of cash income or a savings account. An IMF-sponsored vaccination programme significantly reduced the incidence of disease among farm animals. Investment is required to recommence and improve poultry and livestock farming. Timor-Leste's agriculture has very low productivity due to a lack of technology, modern techniques and money.

The World Bank is encouraging diversification into horticultural products. Vegetables and rice could be grown commercially. The higher elevations in Timor-Leste are ideal for growing pineapples, oranges, mangoes, bananas and papaya.

Coffee is the principal source of foreign exchange. Its production is in the hands of about 45,000 growers with an average of only one-hectare each. There are virtually no large-scale farms. Wet processed *Arabica* beans fetch the highest price but the processing facilities were put out of action during the fighting. *Arabica* beans account for about 80 per cent of the annual harvest. All coffee is produced organically. Renewal and maintenance of the road infrastructure is necessary for the rehabilitation of the coffee industry.

Subsistence farming is giving way to a market economy. The government sees the country's farming future in goods with high margins such as cashew nuts, vanilla and cut flowers. The main priority for now, however, should be food security.

In 2010 an unrelenting rainy season linked to La Niña dragged on for months and left farmers without a June harvest and unsure when to plant for the next one.

Fishing

Although there are extensive rich fishing areas in the seas surrounding Timor-Leste, only traditional coastal fishing was practised as there was no established structure for offshore or deep-sea fishing. The government is contemplating establishing an exclusive economic zone for Timor-Leste and administering fishing and other activities in this area. Domestic fish consumption is very low. There are plans to promote the consumption of dried fish which could be more easily distributed from the coast to inner areas.

A quarter of Timor-Leste's forested areas are in danger of degradation. Deforestation has caused landslides, and a worsening in soil and water quality. In recent years sandalwood, teak, ebony and redwood have been exploited at an unsustainable rate. The forestry sector, if responsibly managed, has potential for good revenue and significant employment opportunities.

Industry and manufacturing

The coffee industry is large and a service sector is developing in urban areas. The manufacturing industry in Timor-Leste is virutally non-existent. Priority areas for investment are industries processing raw materials from forests and marine and agricultural resources, and industries fabricating agricultural machinery, tools and small- and medium-sized fishing boats. The government is promoting the development of native handicrafts for export.

Tourism

Timor-Leste is looking to tourism to give impetus to the economy and its diversification. The sector is being built from scratch, the pre-independence conflict, during which tourism was not an option, having left the infrastructure in ruins. Attention is being focussed in the initial phase on adventure and eco-tourists, who know what to expect and are prepared to rough it. The longer-term aim is to establish a niche market, exploiting local cultural features as well as the natural attractions, which will distinguish Timor-Leste from its regional competitors. Immediate problems are scarce accommodation, high prices, insufficient and expensive air connections and the perception that the country is still unsafe. Measures to attract foreign investment have been adopted.

Environment

Overfelling of sandalwood trees led to devastating erosion in many areas, and forests and farmland were destroyed in the war.

Mining

At the moment there is no significant mining activity. There are indications however that there could be economically interesting deposits of marble, granite, limestone and gold. The government is in the process of setting up a fiscal policy and regulatory framework, which would enable surveys and exploration to begin.

Hydrocarbons

Australia and Timor-Leste signed a treaty in 2006 to equitably share revenue generated by oil and gas fields found between their coastlines.

In 2008 the Italian oil company Eni announced a find of around 80 million barrels of oil in its Kitan 1 and 2 wells drilled in seas between Timor-Leste and Australia. Three other multinational oil companies are exploring in nearby sites. Further licences were auctioned in 2008–09. ConocoPhillips, the third-largest US oil and gas company has offshore natural gas production and Bayu-Undan liquefied natural gas project, plus ongoing exploration projects.

Energy

The national power system had been managed by Indonesians who had left during the violence of 1999. This departure left a lack of people technically capable of maintaining power supplies following independence. Generating capacity is around 38.3MW. The government has been investing in electrical infrastructure but rural areas still have very limited access to electricity and prices are high throughout the country.

A reliance on biomass, predominantly wood fuel, has led to deforestation and more sustainable energy resources are a matter of urgency.

Banking and insurance

The banking system consisted of four commercial banks, but most bank deposits are invested abroad. The banking sector requires a stronger regulatory framework and more investment opportunities if it is to grow.

The Banking and Payments Authority (BPA) provides currency – US dollars – to the country's banks. It also supervises commercial banking, strives to ensure monetary stability and moderate inflation. In the future the BPA will develop into a central bank.

Time

GMT plus eight hours

Geography

The island of Timor is the largest and furthest east of the Lesser Sundar Islands in the Malay Archipelago, between the Indian and Pacific Oceans. Timor-Leste occupies the eastern part of the island, together with the Oecussi-Ambeno enclave in the north-west of the island. The island of Atauro, to the north of Dili, and the small, uninhabited island of Jaco off the eastern tip are also part of the territory. Indonesia, of which the rest of Timor island is a part, lies to the west and north, New Guinea to the east and Australia to the south.

The terrain is mountainous in the interior. The highest point is Mount Ramelau, which rises to 2,963m. A range of mountains runs the length of the country from east to west, dividing the hot northern coastal region from the milder south coastal plain and its rivers and swamps.

Hemisphere

Southern

Climate

The dry season is between July and October when it becomes very hot and dusty with the monsoon winds blowing off the deserts of Australia. Rainy season: Nov–Jun. Temperatures range from 15 degrees Celsius (C) in the mountains to 30 degrees C and above on the north coast. Humidity: 75—85 per cent. There is a risk of tropical cyclones.

Entry requirements

Passports

Required by all, valid for six months beyond date of departure.

Visa

Visas are not required in advance, but are issued to passport-holders on arrival for a fee of US$35 for visits up to 30 days and may be extended.

Currency advice/regulations

The import of currency is permitted, subject to declaration of amounts over US$5,000.

Health (for visitors)

Comprehensive medical and travel insurance is essential as medical services are severely limited. In the event of a medical emergency, evacuation to Australia is probably the only option for treatment, and insurance policies should cover this eventuality. Such treatment carried out locally will require immediate cash payment for doctors' and hospital services.

Advisable precautions

Malaria prophylaxis should be taken. Dengue fever and Japanese encephalitis are common throughout the island and tuberculosis is prevalent, while cholera and rabies may also be present.

Public holidays (national)

Fixed dates

1 Jan (New Year's Day), 1 May (Labour Day), 20 May (Independence Day), 15 Aug (Assumption Day), 30 Aug (Constitution Day), 20 Sep (Liberation Day), 1 Nov (All Saints' Day),12 Nov (Santa Cruz Day), 28 Nov (Independence Manifesto Day), 8 Dec (Immaculate Conception), 25 Dec (Christmas Day).

Variable dates

Good Friday

Working hours

Banking

Mon–Fri: 0930–1530.

Business

Mon–Fri: 0800–1700.

Government

Mon–Fri: 0800–1730.

Social customs/useful tips

Visitors should expect to pay all expenses in hard cash.

Security

The political situation in Timor-Leste is volatile. Visitors should keep away from public demonstrations and public buildings and not venture out after dark.

Getting there

Air

International airport/s: Nicolau Lobato International Airport (DIL), 5km west of Dili. It has limited commercial flights and few gound facilities. There are scheduled services to Western and Northern Australia.

Airport tax: US$10 departure tax.

Surface

The main land route into Timor-Leste from West Timor (Indonesia) is the border crossing at Motaain near the town of Batugede. Entry into the Oecussi-Ambeno enclave is through the border crossing at Oesilo. Travellers entering Timor-Leste from West Timor are issued with Timorese visas on arrival; Indonesian visas for entry into West Timor from Timor-Leste must be obtained in advance.

Water: There are weekly shipping services between Díli and Singapore, and Díli and Darwin, Australia.

Getting about

National transport

Outside the capital, infrastructure is extremely limited.

BUSINESS DIRECTORY

The addresses listed below are a selection only. While World of Information makes every endeavour to check these addresses, we cannot guarantee that changes have not been made, especially to telephone numbers and area codes. We would welcome any corrections.

Telephone area codes

The international direct dialling (IDD) code for Timor-Leste is +670, followed by the subscriber's number.

Banking

Central bank

Banking and Payments Authority of Timor-Leste, Avenida Bispo Medeiros, PO Box 59, Dili (tel: 331-3712; fax: 331-3713; e-mail: info@bancocentral.tl).

Travel information

National tourist organisation offices

Timor-Leste Government Tourism Office, Ministry of Development, Apartado 194, Edificio do Fomento, Rua Dom Aleixo Corte-Real, Dili (tel: 331-0371; fax: 333-9179; e-mail: info@turismotimorleste.com).

Ministries

Ministry of Foreign Affairs and Cooperation, GPA Building 1, Rua Avenida Presidente Nicolau Lobato, PO Box 6, Dili (tel: 333-9600; fax: 333-9025).

Ministry of Health, Edifício dos Serviços Centrais do Ministério da Saúde, Rua de Caicoli, PO Box 374, Dili (tel: 332-2467; fax: 332-5189; e-mail: ministerforhealthtl@yahoo.com).

Ministry of Justice, Avenida Jacinto Candido, Dili (e-mail: moj@mj.gov.tl).

Ministry of Planning and Finance, Building 5, Palaco do Governo, Dili (e-mail: itds@mopf.gov.tl).

Prime Minister's Office, Government Palace, Rua Avenida Presidente Nicolau Lobato, Dili (tel: 723-0140; fax: 332-2026; e-mail: mail@primeministerandcabinet.gov.tp).

Other useful addresses

British Embassy, Deutsche Bank Building, 80 Jalan Imam Bonjol, Jakarta 10310, Indonesia (tel: 331-2652; fax: 331-2652; e-mail: britishembassydili@fco.gov.uk).

Commission for Reception, Truth and Reconciliation in East Timor (CAVR), Comarca Balide, Dalan Balide, PO Box 144, Dili (tel: 331-1263; e-mail: info@cavr-timorleste.org).

Oil, Gas and Energy Directorate, Edificio do Fomento, Rua Dom Aleixo Corte-Real, PO Box 171, Dili (tel: 331-7142; fax: 331-7143; e-mail. emrd@gov.east-timor.org).

US Embassy, Praia de Coquieros, Dili (tel: 332-4684; fax: 331-3206).

Internet sites

East Timor Action Network: http://www.etan.org

Petroleum Transparency: http://www.transparency.gov.tl

Timor Leste government: http://www.timor-leste.gov.tl

Togo

KEY FACTS

Official name: République Togolaise (Togolese Republic)

Head of State: President Faure Gnassingbé (RPT) (from 2005; re-elected 4 Mar 2010)

Head of government: Prime Minister Gilbert Houngbo (RPT) (from 7 Sep 2008)

Ruling party: Rassemblement du Peuple Togolais (RPT) (Rally of the Togolese People) (since 1994; re-elected 2007)

Area: 56,000 square km

Population: 6.03 million (2010)*

Capital: Lomé

Official language: French

Currency: CFA franc (CFAf) = 100 centimes (Communauté Financière Africaine (African Financial Community) franc).

Exchange rate: CFAf488.90 per US$ (Oct 2011); CFAf655.95 per euro (pegged from Jan 1999)

GDP per capita: US$422 (2009)

GDP real growth: 1.80% (2009)*

GDP: US$2.87 million (2009)

Inflation: 1.90% (2009)

Balance of trade: -US$176.70 million (2009)

* estimated figure

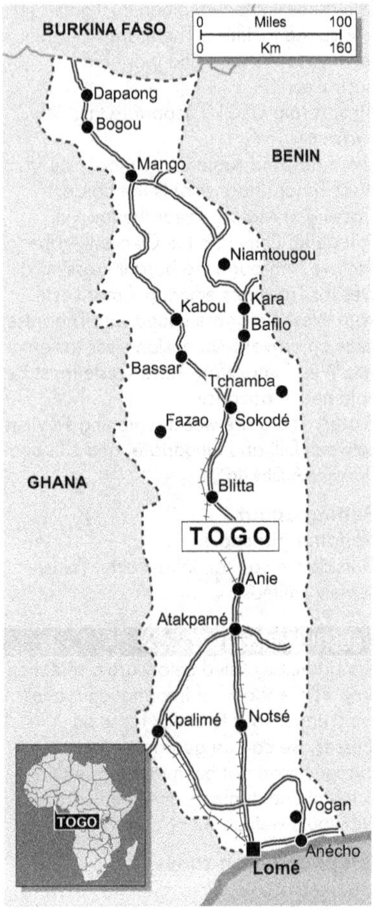

Togo is another of those long, thin countries of Africa that stretch inland from the coast, a result of early explorers and colonisers who just kept on marching in a straight line inland from wherever they landed. In Togo's case it was the Germans who, in 1894, first formed the colony of Togoland. They were forced out by Britain and France in 1914 and in 1922 the country was divided between Britain and France under a League of Nations mandate. This division split the Ewe people, leading to the creation of a nationalist movement which demanded the unification of the two territories. In 1956 British-ruled Togoland was incorporated into Ghana, and on 27 April 1960 French Togoland severed its constitutional ties with France, shed its UN trusteeship status, and became fully independent as the Republic of Togo under a provisional constitution with Sylvanus Olympio as president. All subsequent governments have had to contend with a capital city, Lomé, on the coast with the rest of the country stretching 550km northwards, and a country that in places is a mere 30km wide and 140km at the most.

The best news for the government in 2011 came on 11 May when France cancelled the entire Togolese debt to France, of €101 million (US$104.1 million), as part of France's commitment to the Paris Club (of creditors) agreement of December 2010. An additional US$102 million of Togolese debt will be cancelled by other Paris Club creditors. The debt cancellation was due to economic reforms undertaken since 2006.

The economy

Recovery continued in 2010, according to the *African Economic Outlook 2010* (AEO), published jointly by the African Development Bank and the Organisation for Economic Co-operation and Development, with gross domestic product (GDP) growth of 3.4 per cent compared to 3.2 per cent in 2009. This modest recovery was built on the agriculture sector, which represented 39 per cent of real GDP in 2010. This performance owes a lot to measures taken to support farmers. Fertilisers were made available to cotton producers and the Nouvelle Société Cotonnière du Togo (NSCT) (New Cotton Society of Togo), owned by the state and the Federation of Cotton Producers, started activities to strengthen confidence amongst cotton producers, who are now represented on the NSCT board of directors. Renovation of coffee orchards and maintenance of cocoa plantations continued. Performance would have been better than in 2009 were it not for erratic rainfall during the second quarter of 2010. These climate conditions were particularly adverse to paddy rice and maize, for which production fell by 8.7 per cent and 0.9 per cent, respectively.

The mining sector remains a weak link in the Togolese economy. The state-owned Société Nouvelle des Phosphates du Togo (SNPT) has made substantial investments in the acquisition of new equipment and spare parts aiming to restore production to approximately 1 million metric tons (mt) of phosphate. The year-to-year increase from August 2009 to August 2010 was 8.5 per cent, a disappointing figure considering it was from an already low base. In the 1990s, Togo had been among the 5 largest phosphate producers in Africa, exporting more than 3 million tons. Current production is only 25 per cent of capacity, at approximately 800,000 tons.

The Port of Lomé plays a significant role as an entry port for the Sahel's land-locked countries of Mali, Niger and Burkina Faso. The one-stop window planned for the Port of Lomé will make it possible to strengthen its competitiveness as a trade hub and to increase customs revenues and port revenues in particular.

Trade is now again growing, with a 12.4 per cent added value in 2010 compared to -4.6 per cent in 2009. The transport and communications, and the bank and insurance sub-sectors also performed well thanks to an increase in credits to the economy. The added value of the non-commercial tertiary sector increased by 24.6 per cent in 2010 versus 7.9 per cent in 2009 thanks to an exponential growth in production related to banking services.

On the infrastructure front, in 2011 limitations on electricity supply will be completely removed with the beginning of effective operations of the Contour Global power plant. Togo will have 100MW of additional power. The national road network is to be extended in order to open up the rural areas. No less than 164 kilometres of rural tracks were opened in 2010 while 1,105 kilometres of tracks were renovated. About 17 kilometres of roads were asphalted and at least 30 kilometres of roads were renovated. Official development aid inflows should be maintained in the entire sub-region thanks to the end of the international financial crisis. This is important, as the countries of West Africa are the main importers of Togo's industrial products, cement and concrete-reinforcement steel in particular.

The big unknown variables are climate risks and external shocks. The main risks for 2012 are a possible disappointing production of cotton and phosphates, weak competitiveness of the economy in the West African market and lower volumes of foreign direct investment (FDI).

As far as the labour market is concerned, there was no public-administration hiring in 2010. There was some hiring in the private sector reflecting the policy of reconstruction of economic and road infrastructure, but its importance has not yet been determined.

Togolese emigrant workers' remittances are a valuable addition to Togo's economy. Between August 2009 and August 2010, these increased by 18.2 per cent, up from CFAf64.35 billion (US$131.6 million) to CFAf76.1 billion (US$155.7 million), a considerable contribution to the Togolese economy.

The current-account deficit was estimated for 2010 at CFAf159.7 billion (US$327 million), or CFAf63.2 billion (US$129 million) more than in 2009, an aggravation due to the deterioration in the trade, services and revenues balances. Excluding grants, the deficit in the current balance of payments was estimated at 6.8 per cent of GDP in 2010 versus 6.6 per cent in 2009.

The surplus in the balance of the current account and in financial operations has been estimated for 2010 at CFAf159.7 billion (US$327 million) (10.2 per cent of GDP), or CFAf58.1 billion (US$118 million) more (3.7 per cent of GDP) than the CFAf101.6 billion (US$208 million) surplus of 2009 (6.7 per cent of GDP).

Doing business

Togo's overall ranking in the World Bank's 2011 *Doing Business* report improved to 160th out of 183 countries, from 162nd in 2010. This ranking reflects efforts to promote the private sector. Measures in favour of starting a business included a more incentive regulatory framework and a 40 per cent reduction in registration fees, as well as the time for administrative procedures to be completed now limited to a maximum of three days. Corporate taxes went down by 7 per cent in 2009 and by 3 per cent in 2010. A new investment code is in the works, as well as a new law on the export processing zone aiming to promote investments and the adoption of a charter for small- and medium-sized enterprises and industries (SMEs and SMIs).

There are still many challenges to overcome to achieve a competitive private sector able to play its role driving growth. These include the sluggish bureaucracy handling international trade, protecting investors and contract enforcement, a slow legal system, difficulties in access to credit, and insufficient support to SMEs. Other problems are the absence of a quality-promotion framework and of a culture of intellectual property rights.

International relations

Togo benefits from aid from several emerging countries, in grants or loans, in a variety of fields. These countries are mostly from Asia (China, India and South Korea), but also from Latin America (Brazil and Cuba), the Arab world (Saudi Arabia, Kuwait, Egypt, Morocco, Tunisia, Algeria and, until 2011, Libya), as well as Turkey. Aid is essentially directed to infrastructure (China and Libya), agriculture (South Korea and Brazil), basic education (China), higher education, including scholarships (Morocco, Tunisia, Algeria, Cuba and Turkey), health (India, China, Iran and Cuba) and social housing (India). Given the enormous range of needs, this aid supplements, rather than competes with help from the traditional

KEY INDICATORS — Togo

	Unit	2006	2007	2008	2009	2010
Population	m	6.30	6.46	6.62	*6.79	*6.03
Gross domestic product (GDP)	US$bn	2.22	2.50	2.91	*2.87	–
GDP per capita	US$	352	387	440	*422	–
GDP real growth	%	4.1	2.1	1.1	*1.8	–
Inflation	%	2.2	0.9	8.7	1.9	–
Exports (fob) (goods)	US$m	630.4	676.9	852.6	903.0	–
Imports (fob) (goods)	US$m	949.1	1,072.0	1,307.2	1,315.2	–
Balance of trade	US$m	-318.7	-395.1	-454.6	-412.1	–
Current account	US$m	-176.3	-215.8	-222.0	-176.7	–
Total reserves minus gold	US$m	374.5	438.1	580.0	703.2	714.9
Foreign exchange	US$m	373.9	437.5	579.4	609.8	622.9
Exchange rate	per US$	496.60	454.40	447.81	514.03	495.28

* estimated figure

partners, France, Germany and the European Union.

China, whose grants and loans amounted to US$121.3 million in 2008, is a bigger emerging partner than India, and it is also more important than several of the traditional partners. Beijing was the leading supplier of grants in 2008 with aid estimated at US$118.4 million, followed by the EU (US$29.1 million), the United States (US$25.8 million), France (US$18.2 million) and Germany (US$2.0 million).

The government has attempted to improve its governance through a reform process focused on improving the management of state services and on involving civil society in the development of projects. Reform of the police force, begun in 2010, was taken even further in 2011. The year 2010 was marked by a number of strikes, amongst others in the urban-transport sector following the rise in the prices of fuel.

Risk assessment

Economy	Poor
Politics	Poor
Regional stability	Fair

COUNTRY PROFILE

Historical profile

1894 The country, then known as Togoland, became a German colony.
1914 Britain and France invaded and captured Togoland.
1922 Togoland was divided between Britain and France under a League of Nations mandate.
1930–50s The division of Togoland split the indigenous Ewe people, which led to the creation of a nationalist movement which demanded the unification of the two territories.
1956 British-ruled Togoland was incorporated into Ghana.
1960 The French section of Togoland gained independence as a republic under the presidency of Sylvanus Olympio.
1962 A proposed referendum on unification with Ghana was blocked by President Olympio.
1963 Olympio was executed in a coup by Gnassingbé Eyadéma. Nicolas Grunitzky was appointed president.
1967 Grunitzky was in turn ousted by Major General Gnassingbé Eyadéma.
1979 Eyadéma stood and won as the sole candidate in the presidential election.
1985 France intervened militarily to support the Eyadéma regime, following an attempted coup.
1985–1990 Political pressure for democratic rule increased.
1991 A new government headed by Joseph Koffigoh introduced a national conference to pave the way for multi-party elections. Much of the president's powers were stripped from him. The unrest that followed – orchestrated by the army, which backed Eyadéma – included spontaneous uprisings, a series of attacks on reformers, the prime minister's residence and the bombing of electoral material.
1992 The fragile democratic process of reforms faltered as a series of governments of national unity were imposed, through which much of Eyadéma's powers were re-gained. A new constitution was introduced. Parliamentary elections were postponed and a general strike lasting six months ensued.
1993 Representatives of Germany and France failed to bridge the rift between the government and Eyadéma. The army opened fire on crowds that had gathered at the meeting, killing many and forcing the foreign representatives to depart the country hurriedly. After a series of delays, the country's first multi-party presidential elections were held. Eyadéma, standing for the Rassemblement du Peuple Togolais (RPT) (Rally of the Togolese People), was the only candidate as all other major parties boycotted the election. The EU suspended aid in protest at the abandoned democratic elections.
1994 The RPT won the legislative elections, but needed the support of the Union Togolaise pour la Démocratie (UTD) (Togolese Union for Democracy) to form a majority. The Union des Forces de Changement (UFC) (Union of Forces for Change) boycotted the election.
1996 After winning three delayed by-elections, the RPT no longer required UTD's support.
1998 Opposition parliamentary members were arrested and held in detention. Human rights abuse escalated in the run-up the presidential elections, including extra-judicial executions. Eyadéma won the presidential election; the official results were strongly contested by opposition parties and criticised by the UN.
1999 An independent electoral commission (CENI), was formed, with equal representation of opposition and government. Parliamentary elections were boycotted by all opposition parties after the government unilaterally amended the electoral code and altered the representation on the CENI.
2001 The UN and the Organisation of African Unity (OAU) concluded there were hundreds of summary executions and torture in the run-up to the 1998 presidential election.
2002 The ruling RPT won the parliamentary elections; the main opposition parties boycotted the elections. The constitution was amended allowing unlimited terms in office for a president and required a one-year residency for any candidate – effectively barring the strongest opposition candidate, Gilchrist Olympio (UFC), (exiled son of Sylvanus Olympio, the first president of Togo, executed by Eyadéma).
2003 The opposition parties were unable to agree on a candidate to run against the incumbent Eyadéma, who won the presidential elections; there were allegations of widespread vote rigging.
2004 The French government resumed partial aid to Togo, suspended since 1998.
2005 President Gnassingbé Eyadéma died. Unconstitutionally, the armed forces conferred power on his son, Faure Gnassingbé, but after international pressure he stepped down and later won the presidential elections, against Emmanuel Bob Akitani of the opposition UFC; the opposition disputed the results and there were violent protests in the streets of the capital, Lomé. A clampdown by security forces provoked thousands of opposition supporters to flee to Benin or Ghana. The Constitutional Court confirmed the election of Faure Gnassingbé as president. Edem Kodjo was sworn in as prime minister.
2006 Reconciliation talks – that had been halted on the death of Gnassingbé Eyadéma – were resumed in Burkina Faso between the government and opposition leaders. The EU agreed to re-establish aid and trade if political and economic progress was undertaken. An agreement was reached with opposition parties, excluding Gilchrist Olympio and the UFC, and President Faure Gnassingbé appointed Yawovi Agboyibo, who had helped broker the agreement, to the post of prime minister. Agboyibo's principal undertaking was preparing the country for parliamentary elections in 2007.
2007 Floods that devastated Togo during the summer left 20,000 people homeless at a cost of US$1.1 million. Historic parliamentary elections, which included opposition political parties that had boycotted all elections since 1993, were held. The RTP won 50 seats (out of 81) and the UFC 27. Komlan Mally was appointed prime minister. The EU resumed aid following the successful multi-party elections.
2008 Komlan Mally resigned and Gilbert Houngbo replaced him as prime minister.
2009 The death penalty was abolished. The European Union gave its first grant, of €15 million (US$22.3 million), as budgetary support. There was an attempted coup.
2010 In presidential elections, held in March, incumbent Faure Gnassingbé won 60.9 per cent of the vote, his closest rival Jean-Pierre Fabre won 33.9 per cent. Opposition parties condemned the result

claiming it was fraudulent. A bimonthly Benin newspaper, the *Tribune d'Afrique* was indefinitely banned in Togo by a Togolese court on 1 September, for an article that linked the brother-in-law of President Gnassingbé to drug trafficking. The court also fined the newspaper editor US$113,000 and the chief executive US$3,800. The first census since 1981 was held on 19 November.

2011 On 11 May, France cancelled the entire Togolese debt to France, of €101 million (US$104.1 million), as part of France's commitment to the Paris Club (of creditors) agreement of December 2010. An additional US$102 million of Togolese debt will be cancelled by other Paris Club creditors. The debt cancellation was due to economic reforms undertaken since 2006. Preliminary results of the 2010 census, announced on 11 July, recorded a total population of 5,753,324, composed of 2,799,086 males and 2,954,238 females. President Gnassingbe's half brother, Kpatcha Gnassingbe, the former defence minister, was convicted and sentenced to 20 years in prison for an attempted coup in 2009.

Political structure

Constitution

In 2002 a new, democratic constitution, formally initiating Togo's fourth republic was instituted.

On the death of the president, the chairman of the National Assembly becomes interim president until elections are held. The country is divided into *préfectures*, administered by préfects, and supervised by the interior ministry.

Independence date

27April 1960

Form of state

Republic

The executive

Executive power is vested in the president, who is elected for a period of five years. The prime minister is the head of government and is selected by the president from the parliamentary majority. A Council of Ministers is appointed by the president and the prime minister.

National legislature

The unicameral L'Assemblé Nationale (National Assembly) has 81 members elected by proportional representation from party lists to serve five-year terms.

Legal system

Togo has a French-based court system.

Last elections

4 March 2010 (presidential); 14 October 2007 (parliamentary).

Results: Presidential: Faure Gnassingbé won 60.9 per cent of the vote, Jean-Pierre Fabre 33.9 per cent; turn-out was 64.7 per cent.

Parliamentary: the RTP won 32.71 per cent of the vote (50 seats out of 81), the UFC 30.75 (27), and the Comité d'Action pour la Renouveau (CAR) (Action Committee for Renewal) 6.81 per cent (4). Turnout was 94.8 per cent.

Next elections

2012 (parliamentary); 2015 (presidential).

Political parties

Ruling party

Rassemblement du Peuple Togolais (RPT) (Rally of the Togolese People) (since 1994; re-elected 2007)

Main opposition party

Union des Forces de Changement (UFC) (Union of Forces for Change)

Population

6.03 million (2010)*

Last census: 19 November 2010: 5,753,324 (preliminary figure, July 2011).

The previous census in 1981 recorded a population of 2,719,567.

Population density: 77 inhabitants per square km. Urban population: 34 per cent (1995–2001).

Annual growth rate: 3.2 per cent 1994–2004 (WHO 2006)

Ethnic make-up

African (99 per cent), European (1 per cent).

Religions

Traditional beliefs (50 per cent), Christianity (35 per cent) (mostly Roman Catholic), Islam (15 per cent).

Education

Public expenditure on education is 4–5 per cent of GDP, of which per capita expenditure is 16–17 per cent per student.

Literacy rate: 60 per cent adult rate; 77 per cent youth rate (15–24) (Unesco 2005).

Compulsory years: Six to 15

Enrolment rate: 124 per cent gross primary enrolment, 36 per cent secondary enrolment; of relevant age groups (including repeaters) (World Bank).

Pupils per teacher: 46 in primary schools

Health

HIV/Aids

The impact of HIV/Aids has yet to peak with deaths, orphans and HIV positive pregnant women all showing an increase. By the end of 2003 there were an estimated 10,000 deaths from Aids, although this number could be as high as 16,000; the difference may be due to underreporting or misdiagnosis.

Of the estimated 110,000 people living with HIV/Aids, 9,300, are children (aged 0–14) and 54,000 are women; and 9 per cent of pregnant women tested were positive for HIV in 2003, which bears out the UNAids message that women and children are typically more vulnerable to HIV/Aids in Africa.

Between 2001–03 the number of orphans (aged 0–17) rose from 8,700 to 9,300.

HIV prevalence: 4.1 per cent aged 15–49 in 2003 (World Bank)

Life expectancy: 54 years, 2004 (WHO 2006)

Fertility rate/Maternal mortality rate: 5.2 births per woman, 2004 (WHO 2006)

Birth rate/Death rate: 35.2 births and 11.5 deaths per 1,000 people (2003)

Child (under 5 years) mortality rate (per 1,000): 78 per 1,000 live births; 25 per cent of children aged under five are malnourished (World Bank).

Head of population per physician: 0.04 physicians per 1,000 people, 2004 (WHO 2006)

Main cities

Lomé (capital, estimated population 824,738 in 2005), Sokodé (76,732), Kara (48,570).

Languages spoken

Ewe and Kabyè are widely spoken.

Official language/s

French

Media

Press

There is only one daily newspaper, in French, *Togo Presse* (www.editogo.tg) is national and state-owned. There are several weekly publications including *Nouvelle Combat*, *Carrefour*, *Crocodile*, *Le Regard*, *Le Combat du Peuple*, *Motion d'Information*, *Le Togolais*, *Le Canard*, *Le Changement* and *Le Replublicain*.

Broadcasting

Radio: As the most popular medium, particularly in rural areas, the state-operated Radio Togolaise, broadcasting in French and local languages, runs a national radio network, Radio Lomé (www.radiolome.tg) on FM. Other, external services, are provided by the French service RFI 1 Afrique (www.rfi.fr), VOA and BBC. There are many private commercial radio stations including Zephyr FM (www.zephyr.tg) and Africa No1 (www.africa1.com) from Lomé and Radio Maria Togo (www.radiomaria.tg) operated by the Catholic Church.

Television: All television stations are based in Lomé. The state-owned Télévision Togolaise (TVT) (www.tvt.tg) broadcasts mainly in French, with other local languages. There are several external services broadcasting locally including the French television channel TV5 (www.tv5.org), Euronews (www.euronews.net) and on cable, Media Plus and Canal Plus Horizon.

News agencies
National news agency: Agence Togolaise de Presse (ATOP)
République Togolaise (in French and English) (www.republicoftogo.com)
Le Togolais (in French) (www.letogolais.com)

Economy

Although agriculture is a major component of the economy, comprising over 45 per cent of GDP, it is substantially subsistence farming, typically on farms of one–three hectares. Despite this Togo is self-sufficient in wheat, yams, sorghum, millet and groundnuts. Cotton, coffee and cocoa are the principal cash crops. The reliance on primary production means that Togo is vulnerable to climatic problems and external economic shock in world commodity prices. Trade, particularly of agricultural goods and traditional clothes, which are sold both domestically and to neighbouring countries and provide another important component of GDP. The deep-water harbour and port of Lomé provide significant foreign exchange and underpins the country's role as a trading centre, with goods transiting Togo to landlocked neighbours. The mining industry is centred on Togo's natural resources, which include limestone, marble and phosphates; although Togo is the world's fourth largest supplier of phosphates this sector has declined through a lack of investment. Manufacturing includes small, replacement goods such as shoes, tyres and cloths, plus processed foods and cement.

Estimated GDP growth was 1.8 per cent in 2008, rising to 3.2 per cent in 2009, and is estimated to have risen to 3.4 per cent in 2010. Togo's modest recovery followed the global economic crisis, which cut trade to many markets and weakened investment in general.

Togo is a poor country; the UN Human Development Index (HDI) ranked it 139, out of 169, in 2010, and recorded 38.68 per cent of the population as living below the poverty line, with 54.3 per cent of all households subject to at least three indicators of poverty. Remittances are an important source of earnings for households and foreign exchange for the country. In 2009 remittances amounted to US$307 million (10.3 per cent of GDP), but were estimated to have fallen to US$302 per cent in 2010.

There had been no international aid programmes in Togo from 2003, due to the internal political situation and Togo's record on human rights violations and lack of any democratic institutions. Since 2008 the EU granted €15 million (US$22.3 million), which helped Togo to prepare for its first democratic presidential election, held in 2010. From 16 December 2010, Togo became eligible for debt relief under the IMF's Heavily Indebted Poor Countries (HIPC) initiative, following the country's successful adherence to IMF set criteria, including financial controls, debt management and procurement.

Growth is expected to rise in 2011 as money supply, especially credit to the private sector, expands.

External trade

Togo is a member of the Economic Community of West African States (Ecowas), which was set up to promote economic integration among members. It is also a member of the Union Économique et Monétaire Ouest Africaine (UEMOA) (West African Economic and Monetary Union) (WAEMU). As a member of the Communauté financière d'Afrique (CFA) (Financial Community of Africa), it uses the CFA franc currency along with the seven other CFA members.

Cash crops include coffee, cocoa and cotton although phosphates provide the single largest share of foreign exchange. China has become a major export market for Togolese phosphates. There are reserves of limestone and marble yet to be fully exploited. Togo is a regional hub for trading and transit, with re-exports of consumer goods to neighbouring, landlocked countries.

Its primary exports of gold and cotton are subject to world prices and along with livestock sales provide 80–90 per cent of export earnings. Remittances constitute an important portion of foreign revenue.

Imports
Principal imports are machinery and equipment, foodstuffs and petroleum products.
Main sources: China (typically 37 per cent of total), France (9 per cent), The Netherlands (7 per cent).
Exports
Principal exports are cotton, phosphates, coffee and cocoa.
Main destinations: Germany (typically 18 per cent of total), Ghana (13 per cent), Burkina Faso (11 per cent).
Re-exports
Many goods are re-exported and others transhipped to landlocked, neighbouring countries from the port of Lomé.

Agriculture

The agricultural sector contributes around 40 per cent to GDP and employs around 75 per cent of the workforce.

Traditional methods of cultivation still prevail despite attempts at rapid modernisation.

Self-sufficiency in basic foodstuffs is generally maintained except during drought years. The majority of farmers are smallholders who raise stock and grow maize, millet, yams, cassava, sorghum and rice.

Cotton, coffee and cocoa are the principal export earners.

Forestry
The majority of timber production is used in domestic fuel.

Industry and manufacturing

Activity is centred on the processing of agricultural commodities and the production of phosphoric acid, fertilisers and cement along with beverages, footwear, textiles and plastics.

Tourism

Togo has several distinct environments to offer the tourist, from Atlantic beach resorts to high savannah game parks and tropical forests. Facilities may be basic but should attract eco-tourists wishing to see some unspoiled African landscapes.

Mining

The mining sector contributes around 12 per cent to GDP and employs 5 per cent of the workforce. Mining production is concentrated on phosphates, marble and limestone, although the country has potential for commercial extraction of diamonds, gold and base metals. There are also known reserves of iron ore, bauxite, dolomite and chromite.

Phosphate mining is the second principal export earner after cotton. Reserves are estimated at over 60 million tonnes, mainly located around Lake Togo. There are environmental concerns about the high level of cadmium in Togolese phosphate rock. The possible development of safer but lower-grade carbo-phosphates is being explored. There are 200 identified base metal deposits, including the lead zinc prospect at Pagala which is licensed to Anglo American.

Hydrocarbons

There are no known reserves of hydrocarbons. All domestic energy needs are met by imports, which were 20,000 barrels per day of oil in 2008.

The US$260 million West African Gas Pipeline (WAGP) will supply natural gas from Nigeria's Escravos field to Togo, after its has completed its connection with Ghana (December 2008). The 1,000km pipeline will be managed by Chevron Texaco.

Any use of natural gas or coal is commercially insignificant.

Energy

Total installed generating capacity was 85MW in 2006, producing 20 billion kilowatt hours. According to the UN Environmental Programme, only 54 per cent of the population has access to electricity. Biomass accounts for 80 per cent of primary energy, hydrocarbons 16 per cent

and hydropower and thermal energy 4 per cent. Around 80 per cent of electricity is imported from Ghana. The Adjaralla dam on the Mono River, downstream from the existing Nangbeto Dam, is about to begin construction, and is planned to produce 94MW.
Power stations are traditionally thermal fuelled by oil but will be converted to natural gas when the West African Gas Pipeline (WAGP) brings Nigerian natural gas to Togo.

Financial markets
Stock exchange
Afribourse (Bourse Régionale des Valeurs Moblières) (BRVM)

Banking and insurance
Central bank
Banque Centrale des Etats de l'Afrique de l'Ouest (Central Bank of West African States).
Main financial centre
Lomé.

Time
GMT

Geography
Togo lies in West Africa, forming a narrow strip stretching north from a coastline around 50km wide on the Gulf of Guinea. It is bordered by Ghana to the west, by Benin to the east, and by Burkina Faso, to the north.
Togo is 550km long and varies in width from 40 to 130km. Much of the country is savannah, thicker in the south than the north, with deciduous forests in the central part. The terrain varies from the wide, rolling sandstone Oti Plateau in the north to the low, sandy coastal plain facing the ocean in the south. The narrow coastal strip is fringed by extensive inland lagoons and marshes; Lake Togo is in this area. Further inland are the Ouatchi Plateau and the Mono tableland. The Togo mountains straddle the country from the south-west to north-west; the average elevation is 700m. At the southern extremity of the range is Mount Agou, which at 986m is the highest point in Togo. The main rivers are the Mono, which with its tributaries drains the southern part of the country, and the Oti, which drains the northern plains.
Hemisphere
Northern

Climate
Tropical, mean annual temperature 28 degrees Celsius. Drier in the north. Two rainy seasons between April–June and September–October.

Entry requirements
Passports
Required by all, valid for six months beyond date of departure.
Visa
Required by all, except nationals of Benin, Burkina Faso, Côte d'Ivoire and Niger.
Currency advice/regulations
The import of local currency is restricted to CFAf1 million and export to CFAf25,000. Import of foreign currencies is restricted to CFAf1 million, subject to declaration on arrival, and export to the amount declared.

Health (for visitors)
Mandatory precautions
Yellow fever vaccination certificate required by all.
Advisable precautions
Malaria precautions and prophylaxes are essential. Hepatitis A and B, tetanus, typhoid and polio. There is an HIV/Aids risk and a rabies risk.
All water should be regarded as a potential health risk; only bottled or boiled water should be used for drinking, brushing teeth or making ice. Milk is unpasteurised and should be boiled and dairy products should be avoided. Only hot, cooked food and peeled fruit should be eaten. Medical insurance that includes evacuation is advised.

Hotels
High-standard hotels in Lomé, which should be booked well in advance. Ten per cent tip is usual.

Credit cards
Credit cards accepted.

Public holidays (national)
Fixed dates
1 Jan (New Year's Day), 13 Jan (Liberation Day), 27 Apr (Independence Day), 1 May (Labour Day), 21 Jun (Martyrs' Day), 15 Aug (Assumption Day), 1 Nov (All Saints' Day), 25 Dec (Christmas Day).
Variable dates
Easter Monday, Ascension Day, Whit Monday, Eid al Adha, Birth of the Prophet, Eid al Fitr.
Islamic year 1433 (26 Nov 2011–14 Nov 2012): The Islamic year contains 354 or 355 days, with the result that Muslim feasts advance by 10-12 days against the Gregorian calendar. Dates of feasts vary according to the sighting of the new moon, so cannot be forecast exactly.

Working hours
Banking
Mon–Fri: 0730–1130, 1430–1600.
Business
Mon–Fri: 0700–1200, 1430–1730.
Government
Mon–Fri: 0700–1200, 1430–1730.
Shops
Mon–Fri: 0800–1200, 1430–1730; Sat: 0730–1230.

Telecommunications
Mobile/cell phones
A GSM 900 service is available in populated areas.

Electricity supply
220V AC, 50 cycles.

Social customs/useful tips
Business is conducted in French.

Security
Togo is relatively trouble-free, although visitors should be wary of the occasional car hijacking.

Getting there
Air
International airport/s: Gnassingbé Eyadéma International (LFW), 6km from Lomé; duty-free shop, restaurant, bank, post office, car hire. Taxis operate, from 0600 until the last flight, to the city centre.
Airport tax: None.
Surface
Road: A well-surfaced coastal road, which passes through Lomé, connects Togo with Ghana and Benin and thence to Nigeria. There is a road from Burkina Faso down to Lomé.
Main port/s: Lomé. Kpeme handles phosphate shipments.

Getting about
National transport
Air: Air Togo flies between Lomé, Sokodé, Mango, Lama-Kara, Niamtougou and Dapaong.
Road: Surfaced roads run from Lomé to the borders of neighbouring countries, along the coast west to Ghana and east to Benin, and northwards the length of Togo to Burkina Faso. Other roads may not be passable in the rainy season.
Rail: The main railway lines run from Lomé northwards to Blitta (midway between Atakpamé and Sokodé) and to Kpalimé, and eastwards to Aného.
Water: Ferries serve the ports along the coast.
City transport
Taxis: Readily available in Lomé, while shared taxis ply to other main towns; tipping is not usual.
Car hire
Available, but generally expensive. International driving licence required.

BUSINESS DIRECTORY

The addresses listed below are a selection only. While World of Information makes every endeavour to check these addresses, we cannot guarantee that changes have not been made, especially to telephone numbers and area codes. We would welcome any corrections.

Telephone area codes
The international direct dialling (IDD) code for Togo is +228, followed by subscriber's number.

Chambers of Commerce
Togo Chamber of Commerce, Agriculture and Industry, Angle Avenues de la Présidence et Georges Pompidou, PO Box 360, Lomé (tel: 221-2065; fax: 221-4730; e-mail: ccit@rdd.tg).

Banking
Banque Internationale pour l'Afrique au Togo, BP 346, 13 rue du Commerce, Lomé (tel: 221-3286; fax: 221-1019; e-mail: bia-togo@café.tg).

Banque Togolaise de Développement, BP 65, Place de L'Independance, Angle Avenues des Nîmes et Grunitzky, Lomé (tel 221-3641; fax: 221-4456; e-mail: togo_devbank.btd.tog).

Banque Togolaise pour le Commerce et l'Industrie, BP 363, 169 Boulevard du 13 Janvier, Lomé (tel: 221-4641; fax: 21-3265; e-mail: sda@btci.tg).

Ecobank-Togo, BP 3302, 20 Rue du Commerce, Lomé (tel: 222-6574; fax: 221-4237; e-mail: ecobanktg@ecobank.com).

Société Inter Africaine de Banque, BP 4874, 14 Rue du Commerce, Lomé (tel: 221-1341; fax: 221-5829; e-mail: siab@bibway.com).

Société Nationale d'Investissement et Fonds Annexes BP 2682, 11 Avenue du 24 Janvier, Lomé (tel: 221-6221; fax: 221-6225; e-mail: sni@ids.tg).

Union Togolaise de Banques, BP 359, Boulevard du 13 Janvier, Lomé (tel: 221-6411; fax: 221-2206; utbsdg@café.tg).

Central bank
Banque Centrale des Etats de l'Afrique de l'Ouest, Direction Nationale, BP 120, Rue des Nimes, Lomé (tel: 221-2512; fax: 221-7602).

Stock exchange
Afribourse (Bourse Régionale des Valeurs Moblières) (BRVM): www.brvm.org

Travel information
Ministry of tourism
Ministry of Culture, Tourism and Leisure, BP 3114, Lomé (tel: 221-5400; fax: 221-8927).

National tourist organisation offices
Office national togolais du tourism, BP 1289, Route d'Aného, Lomé, (tel: 221-4313; fax: 221-8927; e-mail: info@togo-tourisme.com).

Other useful addresses
Direction de la Statistique, BP 118, Lomé (tel: 270-662).

Direction des Professions Touristiques, BP 1289, Lomé (tel: 215-662, 214-313).

Kpeme Port Authority, OTP BP 362, Lomé (tel: 213-901; fax: 217-105).

Office des Produits Agricoles du Togo, BP 1334, Lomé (agency dealing with marketing, export, development) (tel: 214-471).

OPTT-Post Office and Telecommunications of Togo, Lomé (tel: 213-737; fax: 210-373).

Togo Embassy (USA), 2208 Massachusetts Avenue, NW, Washington DC 20008 (tel: (+1-202) 234-4212; fax: (+1-202) 232-3190).

National news agency: Agence Togolaise de Presse (ATOP)

Internet sites
Africa Business Network: http://www.ifc.org/abn

AllAfrica.com: http://allafrica.com

African Development Bank: http://www.afdb.org

Africa Online: http://www.africaonline.com

Mbendi AfroPaedia (information on companies, countries, industries and stock exchanges in Africa): http://mbendi.co.za

Republic of Togolais (in French): http://www.republicoftogo.com

Online Togo news: http://www.togodaily.com

Togo Official website: http://www.afrika.com/togo/html

Tokelau

The La Nina weather pattern over the Pacific has lead to a severe drought and water shortage in Tokalau. By 4 October 2011 natural fresh water had run out and the population was relying on boiled water for drinking. The government declared a state of emergency and appealed to New Zealand for help. There are fears that the crisis could escalate across the region and that the lack of water will have an impact on sanitationissues and lead to the need to import extra food and medicines.

COUNTRY PROFILE

Historical profile

Tokelau's three atolls are believed to have been settled by people from Samoa, Cook Islands and Tuvalu. Nineteenth-century whalers and missionaries were among the first European visitors to Tokelau, formerly known as the Union Islands.
1765 Atafu was first sighted by Commodore John Byron and named Duke of York's Island.
1889 The Union Islands became a British protectorate.
1916 At the request of the inhabitants, the United Kingdom annexed the islands and included them within the Gilbert and Ellice Islands Colony (now Kiribati and Tuvalu).
1926 The British government transferred administrative control of the islands to New Zealand (NZ).
1946 The islands were renamed Tokelau Islands.
1948 The Tokelau Islands Act made NZ the formal administering authority.
1976 The islands were renamed Tokelau.
1994 Executive and administrative functions were delegated by NZ to the General Fono (or Council of Faipule when the General Fono is not in session).
1996 Subordinate legislative power was granted to the General Fono by the New Zealand Tokelau Amendment Act.
2001 Tokelau became responsible for its own public service.
2003 A new Principles of Partnership document was signed with NZ.
2004 The UN presented a *Special Case Study* on de-colonisation, urging Tokelau to become independent. The NZ premier Helen Clark visited and signed a three-year agreement on economic support. The General Fono agreed to explore an option of self-government in free association with NZ.
2005 A draft constitution was approved by the General Fono, and agreement was reached on the main elements of the Treaty of Free Association.
2006 A referendum on the Treaty of Free Association with NZ failed with less than the necessary two-thirds majority. Tokelau's status remained unchanged. David Payton was appointed administrator. Census results showed that the population on the three tiny atolls had dropped by 20 per cent over five years.
2007 A second referendum on the Treaty of Free Association also failed to reach a two-thirds majority.
2009 The worst health epidemic since the 1970s struck, with one-in-ten locals falling sick with influenza. Village gatherings were cancelled and schools closed and a New Zealand medical team was dispatched to provide aid.
2010 Kuresa Nasau became head of the on-going government in February. In April, Tokelau declared that its territorial waters had become a whale sanctuary, of over 300,000 square kilometres.
2011 Tokelau's internet domain name (.tk) became the world's third most used country-code, mainly as a source of *phishing* (sending fraudulent e-mails claiming to be from legitimate concerns in order to persuade recipients to reveal personal information, such as credit-card details). A state of emergency was declared on 3 October after fresh water ran out and bottled water dwindled to a week's supply. The shortage was caused by a lack of rainfall blamed on the La Nina weather pattern.The New Zealand Defence Force and Red Cross responded by delivering personnel and water supplies as well as desalination machines, while Samoa organised a shipment of 100,000 litres of water for delivery by 10 October. On 6 October, the government announced that from December Tokelau would switch its relative position from being on the east of the International Dateline to being on the west, so that Tokelau will be one of the first countries to begin the daily cycle and not the last to see the sun set; in effect it moves a day ahead in time and comes into line with its trading partners in Oceania and Australasia and

KEY FACTS

Official name: Tokelau

Head of State: Queen Elizabeth II, represented by Governor General of New Zealand, Anand Satyanand (since 23 Aug 2006) and Administrator David Payton (appointed Oct 2006)

Head of government: *Ulu-o-Tokelau* Kuresa Nasau (from Feb 2010) (on Atafu)

Area: 12 square km (three coral atolls: Nukunonu, Fakaofo, Atafu)

Population: 1,416 (2010)* (1,466 2006, census result); some 6,000 Tokelauans live in New Zealand.

Capital: Each atoll has its own administrative centre

Official language: Tokelauan (English also spoken)

Currency: New Zealand dollar (NZ$) =100 cents; also Tala or Samoan dollar (S$)

Exchange rate: NZ$1.31 per US$ (Oct 2011)

GDP per capita: US$1,035 (2009)*

Balance of trade: -US$2.35 million (2009)

* estimated figure

will coincide with the same move by Samoa. On Thursday 29 December at 11.59.59 Tokelau will lose one day and move forward to Saturday 31 December at 00.00.

Political structure

Constitution

Under the 1948 Tokelau Islands Act (through which New Zealand was the formal administering authority), Tokelau is within the territorial boundaries of New Zealand and Tokelauans are New Zealand citizens.

The 1948 Act was amended and subordinate legislative power was granted to the General Fono by the Tokelau Amendment Act in 1996.

Form of state

Self-administering territory of New Zealand.

The executive

The Head of State is the British Monarch, who is represented by an administrator, appointed from New Zealand. The Ulu o Tokelau (head of government) is a position, which is rotated annually among the three Faipule (leaders) and holds executive power and presides over the Council for Ongoing Goverment (cabinet). The Council consists of the Faipule and Pulenuku (mayors) of each atoll. It has a mandate to manage government business but not to pass laws or introduce taxes.

National legislature

Each island atoll has a Council of Elders (Taupulega) which is the source of authority. The Taupulega delegates authority to the General Fono (parliament) on matters of taxes, law, national policy, budget and management. Parliament sits for three–four days, three–four times a year on the atoll which is home to the current Ulu o Tokelau (head of government). When not in session government business is executed through the Council of Ongoing Government.

The unicameral parliament comprises 20 members, elected by proportional representation between the three islands: Nukunonu six seats, Fakaofo and Atafu seven seats, elected by universal suffrage for a term of three years.

Legal system

The villages have the statutory power to enact their own laws covering village affairs.

Civil and criminal jurisdiction is exercised by commissioners and the New Zealand high court.

There is little crime apart from petty theft and there are no prisons. Punishment generally takes the form of public rebukes, fines or labour.

Last elections

January 2008 (General Fono)

Results: General Fono: all seats were won by independents.

Next elections

2011 (General Fono)

Political parties

There are no organised political parties.

Population

1,416 (2010)* (1,466 2006, census result); some 6,000 Tokelauans live in New Zealand.

Last census: 19 October 2006: 1,151

Annual growth rate: -0.6 per cent (2003)

Ethnic make-up

The residents are mainly Polynesians, with close links to Samoa.

Religions

Christianity

Education

Each atoll has its own school with classes beginning at pre-school and carrying through to Year 10. The Year 11 class is hosted on a different atoll every five years and is made up of students combined from each atoll. After graduation from school, the top eight or 10 students are given a scholarship for further study overseas. Staff members are qualified teachers, usually from Samoa, Fiji and New Zealand.

Health

Tokelau has two doctors, one dentist, eight nurses and three midwives. Tokelau collaborates with the World Health Organisation (WHO) in health promotion projects. There are hospitals on Atafu, Fakaofo and Nukunono.

Life expectancy: 69 years (estimate 2003)

Main cities

Fakaofo (estimated population 540 in 2003), Atafu (140), Nukunonu (90).

Languages spoken

Official language/s

Tokelauan (English also spoken)

Media

Press

There are online news outlets including Event Polynesia, with a sub-heading for Tokelau (www.eventpolynesia.com).

Broadcasting

Radio: There is only one radio station which broadcasts to each of the islands in AM and FM. External service include Pacific Island Radio (www.pacificislandsradio.com), Radio Australia (www.radioaustralia.net.au/pacbeat) and from New Zealand (www.accessradio.org.nz), which provides news for expatriate Tokelauns.

Television: There are no television broadcasts.

News agencies

ABC Pacific Beat:
www.radioaustralia.net.au/pacbeat
Pacific Magazine:
www.pacificmagazine.net

Economy

The economy is based on communal subsistence, agriculture and fishing. The atolls' size, isolation and lack of land-based resources allow little scope for economic development.

Sales of licences to fish for tuna, postage stamps, souvenir coins, handicrafts and remittances from migrant workers are the principal sources of foreign exchange.

Fees from fishing licences, purchased by foreign companies operating within Tokelau's Exclusive Economic Zone, raise up to US$700,000 annually.

Grants from New Zealand account for about 80 per cent of expenditure. Funding from the New Zealand bilateral aid programme, the UN Development Programme (UNDP), the South Pacific Commission, the ILO and other international agencies has been the main source of development assistance. The International Trust Fund, which was set up in 2004 to provide Tokelau with an independent source of revenue, had reached NZ$58 million (US$82.9 million) in 2010.

Since 1982, the General Fono has collected a tax on the salaries of public servants unavailable for communal service (called the Community Services Levy) in order to subsidise copra and handicrafts producers, provide honoraria to members of island councils and supplement village projects.

External trade

Tokelau has a close link to New Zealand which provides a framework for international trade however Tokelau's isolation (25–30 hours by sea from its closest neighbour) hampers trade.

Imports

Imports are foodstuffs, building materials and fuel.

Main sources: New Zealand

Exports

Modest exports of stamps, copra and handicrafts.

Main destinations: New Zealand

Agriculture

The soil is thin and infertile and the land does not rise more than five metres above sea level. Rainfall is erratic and crops are subject to drought and storm damage.

The main subsistence crops are coconut and breadfruit, supplemented by pulaka, ta'amu, pandanus, bananas, pawpaw, with experimental crops of cucumbers, tomatoes, beans, cabbage and watermelon.

Fishing
Fishing for tuna, bonito, trevally and mullet supplies the main source of protein for the inhabitants. The clam industry is an area with some potential. The typical annual marine fish catch is 200t.

Industry and manufacturing
Main industries include copra production, woodwork and the manufacture of woven and plaited goods such as hats, mats, bags and fans. The copra industry suffers from volatile world prices.

Tourism
Tokelau is not a tourist destination, but it does attract a small number of visitors. Access is only by cargo vessel from Samoa once a month. The main accommodation is a small hotel. There is opportunity for swimming and snorkelling.

Hydrocarbons
There are no known hydrocarbon reserves and all domestic energy needs are met by imports from New Zealand.

Banking and insurance
The nearest commercial banking services are in Apia, Samoa, although savings facilities under the control of the administrative officer have been set up on each atoll.

Time
GMT minus 11 hours
GMT plus 13 hours; daylight saving, GMT plus 14 hours (from 31 December 2011).

Geography
Tokelau comprises three atolls (Atafu, Nukunonu and Fakaofo) lying about 480km (300 miles) north of Samoa in the Pacific Ocean.
Hemisphere
Southern

Climate
The average mean temperature is 28 degrees Celsius; warmest in May and coolest in July. Rainfall is heavy but irregular. Severe tropical storms are rare, but possible.

Entry requirements
Tokelau is a dependent territory of New Zealand. Passport and visa requirements are the same as for New Zealand.
Visa
Consent to visit Tokelau should be obtained in advance from the Councils of Elders (*taupulega*). This, together with visas and visitor and cruising permits, can be arranged through the Tokelau Apia Liaison Office in Samoa. Accommodation and a return ticket must be booked before arrival.
Currency advice/regulations
There are no restrictions on the import and export of local or foreign currencies.
Customs
Any firearms must be surrendered until departure.
Prohibited imports
Illegal drugs, plants or plant material, animals or by-products, biological specimens, artifacts made from endangered wildlife and weapons, such as flick knives, are prohibited.

Health (for visitors)
Mandatory precautions
Vaccination certificates required for yellow fever if travelling from infected area.
Advisable precautions
Vaccination for hepatitis A and B, tetanus, typhoid. Rabies is a risk.

Hotels
The Luana Liki Hotel can be found on the atoll of Nukunonu. There are no hotels on Atafu and Fakaofo, although accommodation can be arranged through local families prior to or upon arrival.

Social customs/useful tips
Visitors should be considerate of the island's customs, such as paying due respect to all older persons.
Atafu is officially a dry island. Atafu, Fakaofo and Nukunono have only one co-operative store each. Water is scarce everywhere.

Getting there
Air
There are no air services to Tokelau.
Surface
Water: Tokelau can only be reached by sea. The *MV Tokelau* carries cargo and passengers between Samoa and Tokelau, supplemented by two other vessels (*Samoa Express* and *Lady Naomi*), which ply the route less frequently. Private yachts are the only other means of reaching Tokelau. There are no harbour facilities and only small boats are able to pass through the surrounding reefs; these passes are too shallow for most yachts, which, like the cargo ships, have to anchor outside the reef, although conditions are often unsuitable for such anchorage.

Getting about
National transport
Road: There are no paved roads and few vehicles.
Water: There is a fortnightly catamaran passenger service, which runs between the atolls.

BUSINESS DIRECTORY

The addresses listed below are a selection only. While World of Information makes every endeavour to check these addresses, we cannot guarantee that changes have not been made, especially to telephone numbers and area codes. We would welcome any corrections.

Telephone area codes
The international direct dialling (IDD) code for Tokelau is +690 followed by subscriber's number.

Other useful addresses
Tokelau Apia Liaison Office, PO Box 865, Apia, Samoa (tel: (+685) 20-822; fax: 21-761; e-mail: maka@lesamoa.net).

Tokelau Council of Faipule, PO Box 865, Apia, Samoa (tel: (+685) 20-822; fax: 21-761; e-mail: falani.aukuso@clear.net.nz).

Internet sites
General information on Tokelau: www.dot.tk

Government of Tokelau: www.tokelau.org.nz

Tonga

KEY FACTS

Official name: Kingdom of Tonga

Head of State: King Sia'osi (George) Tupou V (since Sep 2006)

Head of government: Prime Minister Lord Siale'ataonga Tu'ivakano (from 22 Dec 2010)

Ruling party: Coalition

Area: 748 square km (170 islands)

Population: 130,800 (2010)*

Capital: Nuku'alofa (on Tongatapu)

Official language: Tongan

Currency: Tongan dollar or Pa'anga (T$) = 100 seniti

Exchange rate: T$1.72 per US$ (Oct 2011)

GDP per capita: US$3,518 (2010)

GDP real growth: 0.30% (2010)

GDP: US$363.00 million (2010)

Inflation: 4.00% (2010)

Balance of trade: -US$131.21 million (2009)

* estimated figure

Tonga continued its run of gross domestic product (GDP) falls in 2010 with a contraction of 1.2 per cent. A drop in tourism earnings of 13.3 per cent and in remittances of 10.0 per cent contributed to the economy's woes. There was a 4.0 per cent decline in government revenue during the year, leading the government to trim its non-wage operating costs and government funded capital spending. The budget deficit would have been 2.3 per cent without support from donors.

The one bright spot in the economy was increased receipts from sea cucumber exports, which more than made up for declines in fish and agricultural products, so that total exports in 2010 grew by 2.2 per cent. Weak domestic demand led to a fall in imports of 21.0 per cent, giving a current account deficit of US$16.6 million, an improvement over the US$24.8 million in 2009.

The Asian Development Bank expects that donor-funded infrastructure projects will support a return to growth of about 0.5 per cent in 2011.

First elections

The King opened the first democratically elected parliament in Tonga's history on 2 June 2011, after Tonga had held its first elections on 25 November 2010, with an impressive turnout of 89 per cent. The largest party was the Paati Temokalati 'a e 'Otu Motu 'Anga'ofa (PTOMA) (Democratic Party of the Friendly Islands) with 28.49 per cent of the vote (12 seats out of 26). Independents polled 67.3 per cent and won five seats. The People's Democratic Party (PDP), Paati Langafonua Tu'uloa (PLT) (Sustainable Nation Building Party) and Tongan Democratic Labor Party failed to win any seats; nine seats were reserved for representatives of the nobility. As the PTOMA failed to win enough seats to rule independently, coalition talks began immediately. On 21 December, parliament voted by 14 votes for Lord Siale'ataonga Tu'ivakano (elected as a representative by the noblility) as prime minister, by 14 votes against 12 for Samiuela 'Akilisi Pohiva (PTOMA). Prime Minister Lord Tu'ivakano took office on 22 December.

COUNTRY PROFILE

Historical profile

Tonga's dynasty goes back to the tenth century.

1616 Dutch explorers were the first Europeans to visit Tonga.

1773–77 Captain James Cook visited Tonga three times

1875 Taufa'ahau Tupou became George Tupou I and established the Tongan monarchy.

1899 Under the Tripartite Treaty, Britain gained control of Germany's rights in Tonga, Niue, and the Solomon Islands in exchange for withdrawing its claim to Samoa.

1918 Queen Salote Tupou III was crowned.

1953 Queen Salote visited Britain for the coronation of Elizabeth II as Queen.

1965 Queen Salote died and her son was crowned King Taufa'ahau Tupou IV.

1970 Tonga ceased to be a British protectorate and became fully independent within the Commonwealth.

1992 A Pro-Democracy Movement (PDM) emerged.

1994 The PDM formed the first political party, the Tonga Democratic Party, later renamed the People's Party (PP).

1996 In the general election, the PP won a majority of those seats open to popular vote.

1999 The Human Rights and Democracy Movement (HRDM) (formerly the Peoples' Party) won five of the popularly elected nine seats in the Legislative Assembly.

2000 Prince 'Ulukalala Lavaka Ata was appointed prime minister by the King (his father).

2001 Tonga was removed from the Organisation for Economic Co-operation and Development (OECD) blacklist of countries acting as unfair tax havens.

2002 In parliamentary elections, the HRDM won seven of the nine elected seats.

2003 Changes to the constitution were made, giving greater powers to the King and increasing state control of the media.

2004 Royal Tongan Airlines (RTA) was declared bankrupt; with debts of over US$8.5 million and a lack of funds RTA

had been forced to halt its inter-island services.
2005 In parliamentary elections, the HRDM won seven of the nine seats. The People's Democratic Party (PDP) was formed led by Teisina Fuko.
2006 Prince Ulukalala Lavaka Ata resigned and Feleti Sevele (HRDM) became the first commoner to be prime minister. King Taufa'ahau Tupou IV died after a long illness and was succeeded by his eldest son, Sia'osi Taufa'ahau Manumata'ogo Tuku'aho Tupou (known as Crown Prince Tupouto'a). He was sworn in as King Sia'osi (Tongan for George) Tupou V. A pro-democracy demonstration turned into a riot that killed eight people, injured dozens and led to the arrest of over 100 demonstrators and the destruction of the central business district, including an arson attack on a supermarket owned by the prime minister. The King's formal coronation was postponed.
2007 Tonga became the 151st member of the WTO.
2008 The King announced that he would relinquish the monarchy's traditional near-absolute power, changing the country's form of state to a constitutional monarchy by 2010, through a democratic elected parliament.
2009 The Asian Development Bank (ADB) awarded a US$10 million programme grant to help maintain financial stability during the global economic crisis. The reconstruction of the business district of the capital Nuku'alofa was begun, funded by a US$58.8 million loan from China.
2010 Parliament approved the increase in the number of legislative assembly members from nine to 17, to reflect the new, single seat, parliamentary constituencies. A new political party, the Tongan Democratic Labour Party, was formed in June to contest the November elections. In April, the Tonga Broadcasting Commission (TBC) was required to censor parliamentary candidates' political broadcasts and TBC reporters were prohibited from interviewing candidates on the grounds that they 'lacked the necessary training for objective coverage'. On 6 September, Samiuela 'Akilisi Pohiva, along with Uliti Uata (leader of the pressure group Human Rights and Democracy Movement (HRDM)), founded the Paati Temokalati 'a e 'Otu Motu 'Anga'ofa (PTOMA) (Democratic Party of the Friendly Islands). The King officially relinquished most of his powers following Tonga's first egalitarian parliamentary elections, held on 25 November, in which four political parties and over 120 independent candidates took part. The PTOMA won 28.49 per cent of the vote (12 seats out of 26) while independents won a total of 67.3 per cent (five); three other political parties failed to win any seats. Nine seats were reserved for representatives of the nobility. Turnout was 89 per cent. As the PTOMA failed to win enough seats to rule independently, coalition talks began immediately. On 21 December, parliament voted by 14 votes for Lord Siale'ataonga Tu'ivakano (elected as a representative by the noblility) as prime minister, by 14 votes against 12 for Samiuela 'Akilisi Pohiva (PTOMA). Prime Minister Lord Tu'ivakano took office on 22 December.
2011 Opposition leader Samiuela 'Akilisi Pohiva (PTOMA) resigned from the government on 14 January. The trial of the operators of the *MV Princess Ashika* ferry that sank in 2008 with the loss of 74 people was concluded on 4 April. Seven men were sentenced for up to five years in jail (although a few had suspended sentences) and the company fined one million pa'anga (around US$506,000), to be paid in compensation to the women and children's crisis centre in recognition of the loss of the women on-board. The King opened the first democratically elected parliament in Tonga's history on 2 June. On 18 August, Tonga requested development assistance from Australia to help it through its debt crisis. Around one-third of Tonga's GDP is owed in its debt to China.

Political structure

Constitution
The constitution dates from 1875. Changes to the constitution were made in October 2003, giving greater powers to the King and increasing state control of the media.

Form of state
Hereditary monarchy

The executive
Power lies with the King, who appoints the prime minister and the cabinet, which becomes the Privy Council when presided over by the King. The cabinet is comprised of at least two members each from the nobles and popularly elected blocs. The prime minister if appointed for life.

National legislature
The Fale Alea (Legislative Assembly) is a unicameral chamber, with 30 members. Nine members are elected by popular vote for a three-year term, nine members are selected by 33 hereditary nobles, and 12 cabinet ministers sit *ex officio*, including two governors.
The legislative assembly is constituted not to allow political parties to gain power and challenge the monarchy.
In new reforms, to be introduced in 2010, 17 members of parliament will be popularly elected, four will be elected by the nobles and four will be appointed by the King.

Last elections
25 November 2010 (parliamentary)
Results: Parliamentary: Paati Temokalati 'a e 'Otu Motu 'Anga'ofa (PTOMA) (Democratic Party of the Friendly Islands) won 28.49 per cent of the vote (12 seats out of 26), independents 67.3 per cent (five), with less than 3 per cent each the People's Democratic Party (PDP), Paati Langafonua Tu'uloa (PLT) (Sustainable Nation Building Party) and Tongan Democratic Labor Party failed to win any seats; nine seats were reserved for representatives of the nobility. Turnout was 89 per cent.

Next elections
2013 (parliamentary)

Political parties

The constitution does not allow political parties to form a government, but at the discretion of the monarch, some representatives may join the cabinet.

Ruling party
Coalition

KEY INDICATORS — Tonga

	Unit	2006	2007	2008	2009	2010
Population	m	0.10	0.10	0.10	*0.13	*0.13
Gross domestic product (GDP)	US$bn	0.22	0.25	0.26	0.31	0.36
GDP per capita	US$	2,883	3,139	3,267	3,032	3,518
GDP real growth	%	0.6	-3.2	1.2	-0.5	0.3
Inflation	%	7.0	5.1	7.3	3.5	4.0
Exports (fob) (goods)	US$m	9,589.0	12.7	10.9	8.4	*5.2
Imports (fob) (goods)	US$m	86,447.0	134.9	157.8	139.6	*115.7
Balance of trade	US$m	-76,858.0	-122.2	146.9	-131.2	*-110.5
Current account	US$m	-24.0	-28.4	-49.1	-54.2	*-34.0
Total reserves minus gold	US$m	48.0	65.2	69.7	95.7	104.5
Foreign exchange	US$m	44.9	61.9	66.4	81.9	91.0
Exchange rate	per US$	2.03	1.97	1.94	2.03	1.91

* estimated figure

Main opposition party
Paati Temokalati 'a e 'Otu Motu 'Anga'ofa (PTOMA) (Democratic Party of the Friendly Islands). PTOMA had won the largest number of seats in the 2010 elections, but not enough to form a majority government. Once a coalition was formed the party in effect became the main opposition party.
Political situation
The MV *Princess Ashika*, an inter-island ferry, sank in July 2009 six weeks after going into service in Tonga and killed 74 people. It was declared a national tragedy and a Royal Commission was convened to enquired into the details of the sinking. The conclusion of the commission in 2010 was that the Tongan government had not had the *Princess Ashika* surveyed for seaworthiness before purchase and subsequent surveys by the ministry of transport failed to stop the operations of the vessel. Manslaughter charges were later laid against the captains and operator of the ferry.

Population
130,800 (2010)*
Last census: 30 November 2006: 101,991
Population density: 138 inhabitants per square km (2010)
Annual growth rate: 0.6 per cent 1994–2004 (WHO 2006)
Ethnic make-up
The population is mainly of Polynesian descent. Only about 300 inhabitants are of European origin.
Religions
The Wesleyan Methodist church is the major denomination.

Education
In June 2005, New Zealand and the World Bank announced their co-operation in a US$10 million project to improve the quality of education in Tonga.
Literacy rate: 98.5 per cent, adult rate (2003)
Compulsory years: 6 to 14.

Health
Figures from the United Nations Children's Fund (UNCF) (formerly Unicef) revealed in January 2010 that 80 per cent of families in the most vulnerable communities were without funds to buy food; more heads of households were losing their jobs due to the global economic crisis, which had resulted in rising food prices and falling remittances. Malnutrition, particularly among children and women, was becoming of increasing concern as governments in the Pacific region were cutting back on social expenditure in the face of recession.
Life expectancy: 71 years, 2004 (WHO 2006)
Fertility rate/Maternal mortality rate: 3.4 births per woman, 2004 (WHO 2006)
Birth rate/Death rate: 24.5 births and 5.5 deaths per 1,000 people (2003)
Child (under 5 years) mortality rate (per 1,000): 15 per 1,000 live births (World Bank)

Welfare
Statistic by the United Nations Children's Fund (UNCF) (formerly Unicef) revealed in January 2010 that 80 per cent of families in the most vulnerable communities were without funds to buy food, as more heads of households were losing their jobs due to the global economic crisis. Malnutrition, particularly among children and women, was becoming of increasing concern as governments in the Pacific region were cutting back on social expenditure in the face of recession.

Main cities
Nuku'alofa, on Tongatapu (capital, estimated population 22,779 in 2005).

Languages spoken
English is widely spoken. It is used in education and for administrative purposes.
Official language/s
Tongan

Media
Press
A constitutional amendment increased the power of the state to control the media with licensing laws and ownership rules. Publications in Tongan include *Taimi o Vavau* (The Tonga Times) (www.timesoftonga.com).
Weeklies: Weeklies are available in both English and Tongan covering local political and economic news. These include *Ko e Kalonikali Tonga/Tonga Chronicle* and *Tonga Times* (bi-weekly) in Tongan and English editions.
Taimi o Tonga is a bi-lingual weekly publication – the government banned *Taimi o Tonga* in 2003, following a March 2002 sedition charge which was later dropped; its licence was re-approved by the government in October 2004.
Periodicals: In Tongan and English, *Matangi Tonga* (www.matangitonga.to) and *Eva*, are quarterly magazines, *Tonga Star* (www.tongastar.com), is bi-monthly and provides critical analyses of the economic and political affairs. Others include *Lao & Hia* (fortnightly), *Ofa ki Tonga* (Christian publication, *Ko e Tohi Fanongonongo* and *Taumu'a Lelei* (Catholic publication) monthly.
Broadcasting
The public service broadcaster is the Tonga Broadcasting Commission (TBC) (www.Tonga-broadcasting.com), which does not accept advertising.
Radio: The national network, TBC, has three stations include Radio Tonga 1, Kool 90FM and FM103 (a 24 hour Radio Australia relay), broadcasts are in Tongan and English. Private local radio stations include Milennium Radio (www.tongatapu.net.to), UCB Pacific (Christian service), Radio 2000 and Radio Nuku'alofa.
Television: TBC operates Television Tonga. There are several private TV stations including the Friendly Island Broadcasting Network, based in Vava'u, Tonfon TV, a pay-to-view service and OBN TV7 a popular channel that has it service suspended by the government in November 2006. A new channel, TelevisionTonga 2, was launched in 2008, broadcasting a range of programmes including sports, films and foreign programmes.
Advertising
Radio and newspaper advertising is accepted in Tongan and English.
News agencies
ABC Pacific Beat:
www.radioaustralia.net.au/pacbeat
Pacific Magazine:
www.pacificmagazine.net
Pacific Islands New Association (Pina):
www.pina.com.fj

Economy
Tonga is a small, open economy, which has as its heart tourism and agriculture as the generators of wealth. The service sector accounts for around 60 per cent of GDP, of which tourism represents over 28 per cent, and agriculture less than 20 per cent, and industry under 20 per cent. The number of visitors to the islands tops 40,000 per year, the majority of which arrive by air; although a significant minority (over 2,000) arrive by yacht. The greater number are expatriates from New Zealand (over 15,000), and visitors from the US and Australia (around 10,000) constituting the majority of the remainder. Agricultural exports include fish, squash, vanilla, kava, coconuts and its derivatives and root crops. Farms in Tonga are either small, family-run plots, with farmers combining to form co-operatives to grow crops either for local consumption or for export, or large commercial enterprises. Meat is a staple of the diet and Tonga's production is unable to meet domestic demand, so large quantities of either live animals or butchered meat is imported annually. Foreign aid and private remittances typically offset Tonga's regular trade deficit.
GDP growth was 0.8 per cent in 2008, falling to -0.5 per cent in 2009 as a result of the global economic recession when trade in general was cut. Tourist numbers fell which quickly impacted on growth, jobs and foreign exchange. Remittances in

2009 were US$87 million (27.7 per cent of GDP), which were estimated to have grown to US$99 million in 2010.
One of the main problems facing Tonga is job creation. There are around 2,000 school-leavers per year, but only some 500 find jobs and few can emigrate. Unemployment and underemployment are creating social problems. Areas of possible development include offshore oil, fish and vegetable canneries and coconut-based industries. Offshore banking has had to deal with a global crackdown on international money laundering and Tonga has had to undertake anti-corruption measures as a central part of the economic reform programme.

External trade

Tonga is a member of the South Pacific Regional Trade and Economic Co-operation Agreement (Sparteca) along with 12 other regional nations, which allows products duty free access by Pacific Island Forum members to Australian and New Zealand markets (subject to the country of origin restrictions). Tonga is a member of the World Trade Organisation
Tourism and remittances contribute the dominant proportions of foreign earnings. Manufacturing is underdeveloped and agriculture is either large-scale enterprises or small co-operative farming units producing principally squash for export. Fishing, ether by domestic fishermen or licensed foreign trawlers is a growing industry.

Imports

Main imports are foodstuffs, dairy, live animals (cattle, sheep and chickens), building materials, machinery and vehicles, fuels and chemicals.
Main sources: New Zealand (typically 34 per cent of total), Singapore (21 per cent), Australia (12 per cent).

Exports

Main exports are agricultural produce including squash, coconuts, vanilla beans, root crops, tuna, seaweed and sea slugs.
Main destinations: Japan (41.5 per cent total, 2005), US (33.1 per cent), New Zealand (6.3 per cent)

Agriculture

Agriculture and fishing accounts for around 35 per cent of GDP and employs around half the labour force. The soil is generally fertile, but production can suffer from hurricane damage.
All land is held by the Crown and every adult male Tongan is entitled to a smallholding (alienation of land is forbidden). Two-thirds of the kingdom's families raise their own livestock (pigs and poultry) and subsistence crops of manioc, yams, breadfruit, watermelons, tomatoes, cassava, oranges and capsicum. Coconut, vanilla and bananas are produced for export, as is the tranquiliser ingredient, kava.
Cash crops include squash and vanilla crops and aloe vera, which has become a popular crop among farmers as it has a viable export market and there is a new processing plant in Nuku'alofa.

Fishing

Fishing provides additional food and export revenue. Seaweed is in big demand, particularly from Japanese buyers.
The typical annual marine fish catch is over 4,000t, plus over 300t of other seafood.

Forestry

Old coconut tree trunks fulfil up to 25 per cent of timber needs. Typical annual production is 2,000 cubic metres (cum) industrial roundwood, 2,000cum sawnwood and 90,000cum wood fuel.

Industry and manufacturing

The industrial sector accounts for 12.7 per cent of GDP and employs approximately 7.0 per cent of the workforce.
There is a thriving small-industries centre on a mini-industrial area in Nuku'alofa where most of the more advanced products are made. Annual industrial production is almost US$20 million per annum. Manufacturing accounts for 8 per cent of GDP and employs 5 per cent of the labour force. The wide range of products includes shoes, saddles, footballs, knitwear, wooden toys, corrugated iron, plastic piping, bicycle assembly, wire netting, paper, paint, biscuits and processed milk, pulp and passion fruit processing, dumper truck bodies and mini-excavators.

Tourism

Tourism is an important economic activity and foreign exchange earner, but still relatively underdeveloped. There is potential for expansion and efforts are being made to upgrade the infrastructure. Several hundred yachts visit the harbour annually, boosting the local economy by an estimated US$500,000 per annum. The main market is New Zealand, followed by Australia and the US.
Air visitor arrivals, which include holiday visitors, those visiting friends and relatives as well as those visiting for business or to attend a conference, rose by 10 per cent in 2003 to a record high of 40,110.
The sector was dealt a heavy blow in 2004 when Royal Tongan Airlines collapsed. This is particularly serious as the only realistic means of arrival is by air.
The Royal Tonga International Hotel opened in October 2007.

Mining

The US Geological Survey has found huge undersea sediment-filled basins that could hold oil deposits near Tonga, the Solomon Islands and Papua New Guinea. German and Russian researchers have discovered copper and zinc deposits off Tonga.
The government signed an agreement in March 2009 with the Australian company, Blue Water Metals, to prospect undersea for gold, silver, copper and zinc, inside its territorial waters.

Hydrocarbons

There are no known hydrocarbon resources; all domestic energy needs must be met by imported petroleum products, typically 1,000 barrels per day of oil, mainly from New Zealand. Tonga does not import gas or coal.

Banking and insurance

Main financial centre

Nuku'alofa.

Time

GMT plus 13 hours

Geography

Tonga (also known as the Friendly Islands) comprises 172 islands in the south-western Pacific Ocean, about 650km (400 miles) east of Fiji. The Tonga Islands are divided into three main groups – Tongatapu (southern group) Ha'apai (middle group) and Vava'u (northern group). Only 36 of the islands are permanently inhabited.
All are formed from limestone but with two different geological bases, either an uplifted coral foundation or an overlay of a volcanic base. The maximum height of any volcanic range is 1,033 metres, on Kao. Few islands have rivers or lakes and most rely on wells and rainwater for their supply.

Hemisphere

Southern

Climate

From May–November, temperatures are relatively cool and reach between 11–29 degrees Celsius (C). December–April is the wet season, with temperatures reaching 32°C and with high humidity. Average rainfall is 1,700mm per year, but varies from place to place.

Entry requirements

Passports

Required by all, and must be valid six months from date of entry.

Visa

Tourists and business persons listed at www.tongaconsulate.us/visa/visa4tim.htm l may enter for a period not exceeding 31 days providing the visitor holds onward/return passage and proof of adequate funds.
A one month extension is possible if permission is obtained locally from the principal immigration officer; a fee applies.

Currency advice/regulations
No restrictions on import and export of local and foreign currency.
Travellers cheques are accepted in banks and major hotels; Australian dollars and pounds sterling cheques will avoid additional exchange fees.
Customs
Personal items are duty-free. Imports from some countries may require an import licence or be subject to temporary control.
Prohibited imports
Illegal drugs and firearms. Quarantine is required for all imported live animals and plants.

Health (for visitors)
Mandatory precautions
Vaccination certificate for yellow fever if travelling from an infected area.
Advisable precautions
Inoculations and boosters should be current for tetanus, hepatitis A and typhoid. There may be a need for vaccinations for diphtheria, tuberculosis and hepatitis B. Insect repellent should be worn at all times, especially during the early morning and evening. There is a rabies risk.

Hotels
Information regarding various types of tourist accommodation is available in Nuku'alofa and throughout the islands from the Tonga Visitors' Bureau.

Credit cards
Credit and charge cards are accepted.

Public holidays (national)
Fixed dates
1 Jan (New Year's Day), 25 Apr (Anzac Day), 4 May (Crown Prince's Birthday), 4 Jun (Independence Day), 4 Jul (King Taufa'ahau Tupou IV's Birthday), 4 Nov (Constitution Day), 4 Dec (Tupou I Day), 25–26 Dec (Christmas).
Variable dates
Good Friday and Easter Monday (Mar/Apr).

Working hours
Sunday is widely observed as a day of rest, with work, sports and transport services forbidden.
Banking
Mon–Fri: 0930–1530; Sat: 0900–1200.
Business
Mon–Fri: 0800–1700; Sat: 0800–1200.
Government
Mon–Fri: 0830–1630.
Shops
Mon–Fri: 0800–1700; Sat: 0800–1200.

Telecommunications
Mobile/cell phones
There are GSM 900 service available on many inhabited islands.

Electricity supply
240V AC, with Australian style flat three-pin plugs.

Weights and measures
Metric system

Social customs/useful tips
It is customary to shake hands on meeting and taking leave. Business cards are exchanged after introduction. Appointments should be made in advance. Those meeting for the first time are addressed by their title and family name; Tongans address each other by their first name.
Gratuities are not encouraged or customary. Tongans appreciate modesty in dress, casual attire is recommended for most occasions. Beachware is only acceptable at the beach and not in general public. It is an offence to appear in public without a shirt. Drunkenness is frowned upon; alcohol consumption may be restricted.

Getting there
Air
National airline: Air Fiji has provided international access since Royal Tongan Airlines collapsed in 2004.
International airport/s: Fua'amotu International, Tongatapu (TBU), 15km south-east of Nuku'alofa; bank, duty-free shop and car hire. Taxis and buses available to centre.
Airport tax: International departures include a passenger service charge of T$25; not applicable for transit passengers.
Surface
Water: No regular passenger services to the kingdom, but berths may be available on cruise ships visiting Nuku'alofa and Vava'u.
Main port/s: Nuku'alofa (on Tongatapu), Neiafu (on Vava'u), Pangai (on Lifuka), Ha'apai.

Getting about
National transport
No public transport, shipping or air services operate into, out of, or on Tonga on Sundays.
Air: Airlines of Tonga (partly owned by Air Fiji), a new domestic carrier and Peau 'o Vava'u Airways operate inter-island flights.
Road: Total road network of about 400km with 80–90 per cent paved; over 190km are on Tongatapu.
Buses: Buses serve all parts of Tongatapu from Nuku'alofa.
Water: Various shipping lines operate inter-island ferry services. The principal service leaves Nuku'alofa in the afternoon and arrives the following morning in Ha'apia, at Hafeva then Pangia, then goes on to Vava'u; by mid afternoon it retraces its route back to Nuku'alofa. There is no need for advance bookings, schedules may change at short notice due to weather conditions. Charter yachts are available.
City transport
Taxis: Private taxis are for hire. Fares should be agreed before undertaking a journey.
Car hire
Self-drive or chauffeur-driven cars are available. International or national driving licence must be presented to the Police Traffic Department in Nuku'alofa to obtain local driving licence.
Speed limits of 40kph in country areas and slower through towns are enforced. Driving is on the left.

BUSINESS DIRECTORY

The addresses listed below are a selection only. While World of Information makes every endeavour to check these addresses, we cannot guarantee that changes have not been made, especially to telephone numbers and area codes. We would welcome any corrections.

Telephone area codes
The international direct dialling (IDD) code for Tonga is +676 followed by subscriber's number.

Useful telephone numbers
Police: 992
Fire: 999
Ambulance: 933

Chambers of Commerce
Tonga Chamber of Commerce, Tungi Arcade, PO Box 1704, Nuku'alofa (tel: 25-168; email: chamber@kalianet.to).

Banking
Bank of Tonga, PO Box 924, Naku'alofa (tel: 23-933; fax: 23-634).

ANZ Bank, PO Box 910; Cnr Salote and Railway Roads, Nuku'alofa (tel: 24-944; fax: 23-870; email: anztonga@anz.com).

MBf Bank Limited, PO Box 3118; Nuku'alofa, Taufa'ahau Rd, Nuku'alofa (tel: 24-600; fax: 24-662; email: mbfbank@kalianet.to).

Tonga Development Bank; PO Box 126; Nuku'alofa, Fatafehi Rd, Nuku'alofa (tel: 23-333; fax: 23-775; email: tdevbank@tdb.to).

Westpac Bank Tonga, PO Box 924; Taufa'ahau Rd, Nuku'alofa, (tel: 23-933; fax: 23-634; email: westpactonga@westpac.com.au).

Central bank
National Reserve Bank of Tonga, Queen Salote Road, PO Box 25, Nuku'alofa, Tonga (tel: 24-057 fax: 24-201; e-mail: nrbt@reservebank.to).

Travel information
Flight information (0630-1930 hours Mon-Sat) (tel: 32-088).

Fua'amotu International Airport, Ministry of Civil Aviation, PO Box 845, Nuku'alofa (tel: 32-001; fax: 32-003).

Tourist information (tel: 32-060).

Peau Vava'u Limited (domestic airline), Taufa'ahau Road, Nuku'alofa (tel: 878-8896; fax: 28-637; email: administration@peauvavau.to).

National tourist organisation offices

Tonga Visitors' Bureau, PO Box 37, Nuku'alofa (tel: 23-507, 21-733; fax: 22-129; internet: www.vacations.tvb.gov.to).

Ministries

Ministry of Civil Aviation, PO Box 845, Nuku'alofa (tel: 32-001; fax: 32-003).

Ministry of Labour, Commerce and Industries, Salote Road, PO Box 110, Nuku'alofa (tel: 23-688; fax: 23-887).

Office of Prime Minister, Ministry of Agriculture, Fisheries and Forestry, Ministry of Marine, Nuku'alofa (tel: 21-300).

Other useful addresses

Asian Development Bank (ADB), South Pacific Regional Mission, La Casa di Andrea, Lini Highway; PO Box 127, Port Vila, Vanuatu (tel: (+678-2) 23-300; fax: (+678-2) 23-183; adbsprm@adb.org; internet: www.adb.org/SPRM).

Immigration Division, Ministry of Foreign Affairs, Government of Tonga, P O Box 352, Nuku'alofa (tel: 26-970, 26-969; fax: 26-971, 23-360).

Tonga Department of Statistics, PO Box 149, Nuku'alofa (email: dept@stats.gov.to; internet: www.spc.int/prism/country/to/stats).

Internet sites

Government of Tonga: http://pmo.gov.to

Tonga information website: www.tongatapu.net.to

Trinidad and Tobago

KEY FACTS

Official name: Republic of Trinidad and Tobago

Head of State: President George Maxwell Richards (since 2003; re-elected 11 Feb 2008)

Head of government: Prime Minister Kamla Persad-Bissessar (UNC) (from 26 May 2010)

Ruling party: Coalition: People's Partnership led by United National Congress Cwith Congress of the People (CP), Tobago Organisation of the People (TOP), National Joint Action Committee (NJAC) and Movement for Social Justice (MSJ) (from 26 May 2010)

Area: 5,128 square km

Population: 1.34 million (2010)*

Capital: Port-of-Spain

Official language: English

Currency: Trinidad and Tobago dollar (TT$) = 100 cents

Exchange rate: TT$6.40 per US$ (Oct 2011)

GDP per capita: US$15,706 (2010)

GDP: US$20.60 billion (2010)

Labour force: 621,000 (2009)

Unemployment: 5.30% (2009)

Inflation: 10.70% (2010)

Oil production: 146,000 bpd (2010)

Balance of trade: US$2.20 billion (2009)

* estimated figure

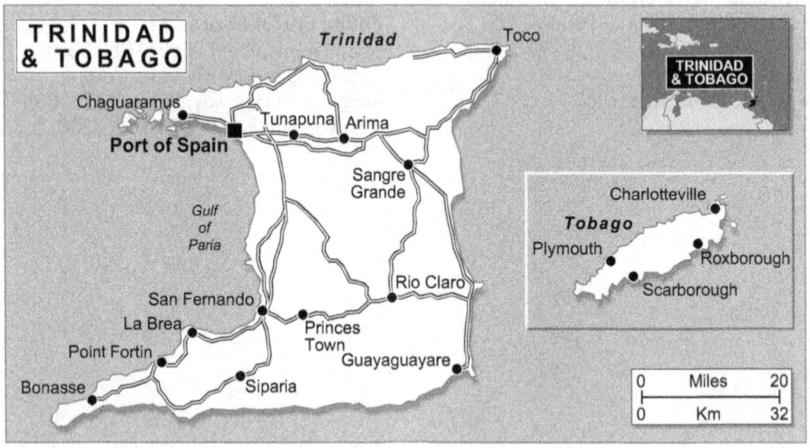

The politics of Trinidad and Tobago are rarely dull. But even by local standards, 2011 turned out to be an exceptionally volatile year. A limited state of emergency in crime hot spots throughout Trinidad and Tobago was declared on 21 August, originally for a period of two weeks, but extended in October for a further three months, until the end of 2011. Prime Minister Kamla Persad-Bissessar also announced the continued curfew in effect for a number of urban areas. In those areas the curfew began at 9 pm and ended at 4 am. The Prime Minister added that the curfew times could be revised on the recommendation of the security forces.

Arrests

Matters came to a head in August 2011 when there were 11 murders in a two day period. It emerged that Trinidad and Tobago's Commissioner of Police, Dwaine Gibbs, was in Brazil on an unauthorised visit about which the Police Service Board had not been notified. Ms Persad-Bissessar gamely stated that the war on crime would continue and called on the country's citizens to 'band together and join hands against the criminals'. This was against a depressing backdrop. In early October the ministry of foreign affairs and communications announced that, since the declaration of the state of emergency, 1,143 people had been arrested. Of these, three hundred and sixty-six were related to gangs, 216 related to drug offences, 228 related to outstanding warrants, 181 related to other serious offences, 82 related to breach of curfew and 30 related to homicide. The ministry's press release also said that the Coast Guard, acting on intelligence, seized a vessel with four persons onboard, including two Trinidadians, and confiscated cocaine with a street value of US$3.2 million. Rumour had it that just before the state of emergency was first declared in Port of Spain customs officers had come across two shipping containers holding weapons and ammunition. Incredibly, despite being placed under police guard, one of the containers was spirited away.

End of the rainbow?

Simmering beneath the surface of Trinidad and Tobago's politics is the nagging question of the racial divide. Although the government saw itself as the 'rainbow' coalition, in 2011 racial tensions were rising over the perceived Indianisation of the civil service. The People's Partnership Coalition (PPC) had gained power in May 2010 after the outgoing prime minister, Patrick Manning, ill-advisedly called elections well before the deadline. The largest party in the PPC is the United National Congress (UNC), very much the fiefdom of the Hon Austin 'Jack' Warner, who hit the world's headlines when details of the corruption surrounding football's ruling body Fifa were made public.

Mr Warner's writ is not confined to the ministry of works and infrastructure, nor indeed to Trinidad and Tobago. His links to other Caribbean countries are just as important.

Sluggish economy

There was still no real evidence of resurgence in economic activity in late 2010. The United Nations Economic Commission for Latin America and the Caribbean (ECLAC) noted that real GDP was expected to have shown growth of 1 per cent for the year, with a potential increase to 2.5 per cent in 2011 if the global economic recovery continued and if consumer and business confidence was restored sufficiently to boost investment and job creation. Economic activity in the non-energy sector was expected to have declined by 1.7 per cent in 2010. The inflation rate was expected to rise to 10 per cent and to average 8 per cent in 2011, while the unemployment rate might reach 7.8 per cent in 2010 and fall back to 7 per cent in 2011. Headline inflation, which measured 1.3 per cent at the end of 2009, spiralled to 16.2 per cent at the end of August 2010, before falling back to 13.2 per cent at the end of September. This was largely due to food prices, which recorded an average increase of 12 per cent over the 12 months to August 2010. However, core inflation remained sticky at 4 per cent. The unemployment rate increased to 6.7 per cent in the first quarter of 2010, up from 5.1 per cent in the previous quarter, although the participation rate declined from 63.6 per cent to 61.9 per cent.

The current account surplus of the balance of payments showed some improvements, increasing from 8.3 per cent of GDP in 2009 to 15.6 per cent of GDP in the first half of 2010. This improvement was linked to the recovery in energy and petroleum prices. The capital and financial account continued to be in deficit as private-sector outflows reached US$1.8 billion and foreign direct investment remained minuscule. At the end of September 2010, gross official reserves amounted to US$9.09 billion or 13.1 months of imports.

The central government ran a lower-than-budgeted fiscal deficit for the 2009/10 fiscal year. The overall deficit (excluding the cost of the government's intervention to bail out the Colonial Life Insurance Company (CLICO), is recorded at TT$3.81 billion (US$595 million) or 3 per cent of GDP. This reflected the recovery in energy sector revenues and lower than planned expenditure. None the less, the government still owed large amounts to contractors and other suppliers, a situation likely to increase the size of the final fiscal deficit. Of particular concern was the non-energy fiscal deficit, estimated at 18 per cent of GDP. Receipts from the non-energy sector were inevitably lower than projected, since the lacklustre economic performance resulted in a shortfall in revenues from customs duties and other taxes.

The central government's budget for 2010/11 was based on a predicted growth rate of 2.5 per cent, an average oil price of US$65 per barrel and a gas price (netback value) of US$2.75 per billion British thermal unit (mmbtu). The objective of this public budget was to encourage growth and job creation through fiscal incentives that would result in the deficit of 5.1 per cent of GDP being financed by local and foreign borrowing. The 2010/11 budget sought to ensure that capital expenditure would stimulate economic recovery. Capital expenditure was projected at TT$7.21 billion (US$1.1 billion), which represented a drop of 4.9 per cent from the previous year due to severe revenue constraints.

However, the fiscal deficit could be larger than budgeted because of the impact of slower growth rates, wage settlements and the 39 per cent increase in the minimum wage to TT$12.50 (around US$2) per hour.

The budget deficit of 2010/11 was projected to push public debt up further to 43 per cent of GDP. Against the background of a weak economy and inflationary pressures the Central Bank of Trinidad and Tobago's policy stance sought to reduce market interest rates and stimulate credit growth. Between April and October 2010, the monetary authorities lowered the policy Repo Rate by 100 basis points from 5 per cent to 4 per cent. In response, commercial banks also reduced their average prime lending rate from 9.5 per cent to 8.9 per cent during the year. Nevertheless, the policy action did not yield the expected results and credit demand remained weak. Consumer credit recorded a year-on-year decline of 2.8 per cent, while business credit declined by 10.1 per cent. In contrast, mortgage loans outstanding grew by 7.1 per cent in August, compared with the corresponding period a year earlier. On a year-on-year basis, the real effective exchange rate appreciated by 14.9 per cent to August 2010. The main contributing factor to this appreciation of the exchange rate was the increase in inflation, which greatly exceeded the 3.3 per cent weighted average inflation rate of Trinidad and Tobago's major trading partners. Additionally, an appreciation of the United States dollar against the euro and pound sterling also caused an indirect appreciation of the Trinidad and Tobago dollar against these currencies.

CLICO

In 2009 the Trinidad and Tobago government had proposed a new bail-out plan for

KEY INDICATORS — Trinidad and Tobago

	Unit	2006	2007	2008	2009	2010
Population	m	1.30	1.30	*1.30	*1.31	*1.34
Gross domestic product (GDP)	US$bn	18.17	20.90	25.90	20.40	20.60
GDP per capita	US$	14,154	19,516	19,870	15,581	15,706
GDP real growth	%	12.0	4.6	2.3	-3.5	0.0
Inflation	%	8.3	7.9	12.1	7.0	10.7
Unemployment	%	6.2	5.6	4.6	5.1	–
Oil output	'000 bpd	174.0	154.0	149.0	151.0	146.0
Natural gas output	bn cum	350.0	390.0	440.0	440.0	42.4
Exports (fob) (goods)	US$m	14,217.0	13,391.0	18,686.0	9,117.5	–
Imports (fob) (goods)	US$m	6,517.0	7,670.0	9,622.0	6,973.0	–
Balance of trade	US$m	7,700.0	5,721.0	9,064.0	2,202.0	–
Current account	US$m	7,271.0	5,364.0	8,775.0	1,614.0	3,627.0
Total reserves minus gold	US$m	6,585.7	6,693.7	9,442.6	9,177.9	9,605.5
Foreign exchange	US$m	6,530.9	6,657.4	9,380.4	8,651.6	9,070.0
Exchange rate	per US$	6.31	6.32	6.28	6.36	6.38

* estimated figure

the failed Colonial Life Insurance Company (CLICO), conscious of the contagion risks that financial difficulties in an institution as vast as the CL Financial Group could have on the entire financial system. The CLICO group controlled over (US$100) billion of assets in at least 28 companies located throughout the Caribbean region and the world. The Group's financial interests covered several industry sectors including banking and financial services, energy, real estate and manufacturing and distribution. The four largest financial institutions in the Group managed assets of over US$38 billion, representing a daunting 25 per cent of Trinidad and Tobago's GDP.

The new government rescue plan proposed that depositors with short-term investments and mutual funds would receive an initial partial payment of a maximum of TT$75,000 (around US$11,200) from the government. Investors and mutual fund depositors whose principal balances exceed TT$75,000 (around US$11,200) would be paid through government bonds amortised over 20 years at zero interest. This plan was rejected by investors but the government insisted that it would be implemented by the end of 2010. In the 2012 budget, presented to parliament in October 2011, the government increased the insurance coverage for depositors to TT$125,000 (around US$20,000).

Energy

Trinidad and Tobago is a country rich in oil and gas, but those riches do not reach the bulk of the population. Impoverishment is high, helped by high levels of corruption. According to the *BP Statistical Review of World Energy, 2011* (BP Statistics), Trinidad and Tobago accounts for the majority of the Caribbean's oil production. In 2010, total proven reserves were 800 billion barrels of oil, with production at 146,000 barrels per day (bpd). Domestic consumption was 43,000bpd allowing it to export a sizeable amount of its production. The largest oil producer in the country is the state-owned Petroleum Company of Trinidad and Tobago (Petrotrin). Other large producers include BP Trinidad and Tobago (BPTT) and BHP Billiton.

Natural gas production in Trinidad and Tobago has climbed dramatically in recent years. In 2006, the country produced 36.4 billion cubic metres (cum) of natural gas, which jumped to 39 billion cum in 2007; this level remained steady up to 2009, before it jumped again to 42.4 billion cum in 2010. Domestic consumption was 19.8 million tonnes of oil equivalent (mtoe) in 2010. Exports of liquefied natural gas (LNG) have facilitated the large increase in production, which amounted to 20.38 billion cum in 2010. Trinidad and Tobago has benefited from a large amount of foreign investment into the sector, with BPTT leading the field. Other important players in the natural gas sector include British Gas (BG) and Chevron. In October 2009, BPTT brought the offshore Savonette onstream gas-field, with a production rate of 16.990 million cubic metre per day.

Trinidad and Tobago was the second largest supplier of LNG to the United States (after Canada) and the fifth largest LNG exporter in the world in 2010. Licences for exploration, extraction and production in the hydrocarbon sector were due to be raised in 2011 as the government sought to maximise its returns on the industry.

Risk assessment

Economy	Fair
Politics	Poor
Regional stability	Good

COUNTRY PROFILE

Historical profile

1498 Trinidad was sighted by a Spanish expedition led by Christopher Columbus.
1532 The island was colonised by the Spanish.
1595 Spanish colonisers were defeated by an English fleet under Sir Walter Raleigh.
1630s The Dutch settled on Tobago and created sugar plantations.
1763 Trinidad was occupied by France, with Spanish consent.
1781 The French seized Tobago.
1797 Trinidad was seized by the British during the Napoleonic wars.
1802 Trinidad was officially transferred to British sovereignty.
1814 Tobago became a British colony of the Windward Island group.
1834 Slavery was abolished and indentured workers were brought in from India to work on the sugar plantations.
1889 Tobago was amalgamated with Trinidad and together the islands became a unified British colony.
1945 Universal suffrage was granted.
1956 Eric Williams founded the People's National Movement (PNM).
1958 Trinidad and Tobago became part of the British-sponsored West Indies Federation.
1959 Britain gave Trinidad and Tobago internal self-government with Williams as prime minister.
1962 When Jamaica opted to leave the West Indies Federation, Trinidad and Tobago followed, becoming independent within the Commonwealth.
1967 Trinidad and Tobago joined the Organisation of American States (OAS).
1968 Anglophone Caribbean states, including Trinidad and Tobago, formed the Caribbean Free Trade Area (Carifta), which became the Caribbean Community and Common Market (Caricom) in 1973.
1970 A state of emergency was declared after the army mutinied against the minority East Indian population.
1972 The state of emergency was lifted.
1976 On 1 August, Trinidad and Tobago became a republic within the Commonwealth. The PNM won the parliamentary elections. Ellis Clarke, previously the governor general, was sworn in as the country's first president and Eric Williams became prime minister.
1981 Eric Williams died and George Chambers became prime minister.
1986 The PNM lost power in the general election - its first defeat since 1957. The Tobago-based National Alliance for Reconstruction (NAR), led by Arthur Robinson, won a decisive victory.
1987 Noor Hassanali became president.
1990 More than 100 Islamic extremists staged a *coup détat*, blowing up the police headquarters, seizing parliament and holding Prime Minister Robinson and several senior officials hostage. The uprising was short-lived.
1991 The harsh economic programme lost the NAR the general elections. The PNM took over and Patrick Manning became prime minister.
1995 The Asian-dominated United National Congress (UNC) won most seats in the general election and formed a coalition government with the support of the NAR. Basdeo Panday became prime minister.
1997 Arthur N R Robinson was elected president. As prime minister in 1989, he had proposed to the UN the founding of the International Criminal Court (ICC) to prosecute individuals for genocide, crimes against humanity and war crimes; the ICC was inaugurated in 2002
1999 Trinidad and Tobago restored the death sentence.
2000 The ruling UNC narrowly won the general election with 19 seats (PNM 16 and NAR one). Three UNC members of parliament defected to the opposition and the government fell in December.
2001 The result of the general election was a tie with the UNC and PNM both winning 18 out of 36 seats. President Robinson appointed Patrick Manning as prime minister, despite the UNC garnering a larger percentage of the vote. With

a hung parliament little legislation was carried out.
2002 Prime Minister Manning finally called the third general election in three years and his PNM won power with 20 seats.
2003 George Maxwell Richards became president. Caroni, the state-owned sugar company closed, with the loss of over 8,000 jobs.
2005 Trinidad became the home of the Caribbean Court of Justice (CCJ), a final court of appeal intended to replace the UK-based Privy Council.
2006 Former prime minister, Basdeo Panday was convicted of financial impropriety and sentenced to two years in prison. Chief Justice, Satnarine Sharma, was accused of misconduct by interfering in the outcome of the case and, following a series of court cases, stepped down as chief justice in 2008. New, commercially viable oil and gas deposits were found off Trinidad. BWIA, the national airline, ceased operations.
2007 Caribbean Airlines began operations; it took over routes previously flown by BWIA. In parliamentary elections, the ruling PNM won 26 seats (out of 41) the UNC won 15; turnout was 66 per cent. Patrick Manning retained the office of prime minister.
2008 As the only candidate standing, President Maxwell Richards was re-elected president by an electoral college.
2009 The Organisation of Eastern Caribbean States (OECS) agreed to support the Trinidad and Tobago intention of joining the OECS Economic Union before 2011, and deepen political ties by 2013. A new, draft constitution was proposed, with changes including an executive president and a diminished role for the prime minister as well as an alternative way of appointing a chief justice.
2010 Two years ahead of schedule, the prime minister called a snap general election in April, following allegations of public corruption and severe criticism of spending on capital works. A coalition was formed in May to contest the elections, led by UNC and including the Congress of the People (CP), Tobago Organisation of the People (TOP), National Joint Action Committee (NJAC) and Movement for Social Justice (MSJ); it was called the People's Partnership. Parliamentary elections were held on 24 May and were won by the People's Partnership coalition. Kamla Persad-Bissessar (UNC) became prime minister on 26 May. On 30 December, the first president of Trinidad and Tobago, Sir Ellis Clarke died, aged 93 years.
2011 On 23 March, Prime Minister Persad-Bissessar said her government was reluctant to use the CCJ instead of the Privy Council, as the judicial process was working without need for change. On 29 September, the government introduced a series of limited state of emergency (SoE) orders and curfews for crime-hotspots to deal with escalating criminal activity and the prevalence of weapons. On 20 October, the Tobago Assembly considered proposed amendments to reform the constitution concerning the relationship between Tobago and Trinidad. The first act would provide an entrenchment of powers for the Tobago Assembly and the second would enhance the status of the Tobago Assembly to enact further legislation – in effect legitimacy would be conferred on to the assembly and any subsequent legislation issued by the assembly. On 4 November the government announced that the SoE and curfews would remain in place as they had had a 'tremendous impact' on violent crime and provided a sense of calm.

Political structure

Constitution
The constitution was adopted in 1976.
Form of state
Republic
The executive
Executive power is divided between the president, who is the head of state, and the prime minister, who is the head of government.
The president is elected every five years by an electoral college made up of members of both houses of parliament.
The prime minister, who has a cabinet composed of members of parliament, is usually the leader of the majority party in the House of Representatives.
National legislature
The parliament is bicameral. The House of Representatives has 36 members elected by universal suffrage for a five-year term. The Senate consists of 31 members appointed by the president: 16 on the prime minister's advice, six on the advice of the leader of the opposition and nine chosen exclusively by the president.
Legal system
An independent judiciary is guaranteed by the constitution. Foreign investors have the same rights as Trinidad and Tobago citizens.
The Supreme Court is the highest legal body. Civil trials are handled by a single judge in the high court without a jury. Decisions made by the high court can be presented for appeal to the three-judge court of appeal. Court of appeal decisions can be appealed to the regional Caribbean Court of Justice (CCJ), which was inaugurated on 16 April 2005.
Last elections
4 February 2008 (presidential *indirect*); 24 May 2010 (parliamentary).
Results: Presidential: Maxwell Richards was elected unopposed by the Electoral College comprised of members of both chambers of parliament.
Parliamentary: the People's Partnership Coalition (led by United National Congress (UNC)) won 42.9 per cent of the vote (29 seats out of 41), the People's National Movement 39.6 per cent (12); turnout was 69.4 per cent.
Next elections
2015 (parliamentary); 2013 (presidential).

Political parties

Ruling party
Coalition: People's Partnership led by United National Congress (UNC) (from 26 May 2010)
Main opposition party
People's National Movement (PNM)

Population

1.34 million (2010)*
Last census: May 2000: 1,262,366
Population density: 251 inhabitants per square km. Urban population: 74 per cent (1995–2001).
Annual growth rate: 0.4 per cent 1994–2004 (WHO 2006)
Ethnic make-up
Black (43 per cent), East Indian (40 per cent), mixed (14 per cent), white (1 per cent), Chinese (1 per cent).
Religions
Roman Catholics (34 per cent), Hindus (30 per cent), Protestants (19 per cent), Muslims (10 per cent).

Education

Primary schooling lasts for seven years followed by secondary, academic and technical or vocational qualifications. World Bank estimates show that the total primary school enrolment of the relevant age group typically stood at 99 per cent for boys and 98 per cent for girls (including repetition rates) between 1994—2000.
The number of pupils per primary school teacher is typically 25. Public expenditure on education typically amounted to 3.6 per cent of annual gross national income between 1994—97.
A new campus of the University of Trinidad and Tobago, costing US$100 million, opened in 2006 including a donation of US$10 million from British Petroleum (BP) towards construction of the university, which was founded as a charitable trust by the government.
Literacy rate: 99 per cent adult rate; 100 per cent youth rate (15–24) (Unesco 2005).
Compulsory years: Five to 11
Pupils per teacher: 25 in primary schools

Health

Improved water sources are available to 86 per cent of the population.

HIV/Aids

The prevalence rate is relatively high, although the number of deaths due to Aids between 2001–03 did not increase significantly, from an estimated 1,500–1,900. There were 29,000 people living with HIV at the end of 2003, of which 700 were children (aged 0–14). Research among young adults (15-24) showed that 95 per cent knew that a healthy–looking person could be HIV positive, and 33 per cent knew of at least two prevention methods and three myths concerning the disease.

HIV prevalence: 0.1 per cent aged 15–49 in 2003 (World Bank)

Life expectancy: 70 years, 2004 (WHO 2006)

Fertility rate/Maternal mortality rate: 1.6 births per woman, 2004 (WHO 2006). Anaemia is common among 53 per cent of pregnant women.

Birth rate/Death rate: 8 deaths and 13 births per 1,000 people (World Bank)

Child (under 5 years) mortality rate (per 1,000): 17 per 1,000 live births (World Bank)

Welfare

Trinidad and Tobago operates social insurance and social assistance systems that were implemented in 1999. The 1999 law ensures state provision for employees, domestic and agricultural workers, but does not cover self-employed workers. Social assistance covers residents aged 65 or older or aged 40 years for those with special needs, based on a means-test. Old age pensions are available to men aged 60–65 and above with 750 weeks of contribution and compulsory retirement. The state also operates a welfare system for benefits covering sickness, maternity, medical provision for workers and family allowance, including a food subsidy. Medical care is available in public hospitals and health offices and centres for recipients of means tested pensions.

Trinidad and Tobago is experiencing a rise in social problems related to young people, despite the economy's improved performance. Restricted access to the secondary education system and unemployment (which reached 30 per cent for the 15–19 age group in 2001), poverty and reduced family care have contributed to youth involvement in crime and drug abuse.

Main cities

Port of Spain (capital, estimated population 50,479 in 2005), San Fernando (centre of the oil industry) (75,246), Arima (33,539).

Scarborough (main town on Tobago, estimated population (16,807).

Languages spoken

Hindi is commonly spoken within the East Indian community.

Official language/s

English

Media

Press

Dailies: There are three national, daily newspapers, including *Daily Express* (www.trinidadexpress.com) and *Trinidad Guardian* (www.guardian.co.tt) and *Newsday* (www.newsday.co.tt); tabloids include *TnT Mirror* an important online news outlet *Trinidad & Tobago News* (www.trinidadandtobagonews.com) and *Tobago News* (www.thetobagonews.com).

Weeklies: Daily newspapers have weekend editions including *Mirror Weekend* and *The Sunday Punch* (politics and satire) plus a magazine *The Bomb* (politics).

Broadcasting

The state-owned Caribbean New Media Group (CNMG) operates radio and television stations.

Radio: Broadcasts may be in English, Hindi and Creole reflecting the islands ethnic diversity with programme contents produced for a variety of listening tastes. The majority of stations are located on Trinidad. CNMG operates four radio stations, Radio 730 AM, Vibe CT 105, Sandeet 106.1 and the most popular 95.1FM City Talk radio. Other private radio stations include i95.5 FM (www.i955fm.com) with news, WeFM (www.96wefm.com) and Power FM (www.power102fm.com).

Television: The commercial channel, TV6, has the largest audiences with a combination of local and foreign (mostly US) programmes. CNMG has two channels. Other channels include Gayelle (www.gayelletv.com) and NCC TV (www.ncctt.org), which are community TVs. Pay-to-view TV includes Jump TV (www.jumptv.com) and Media Zone (www.mediazone.com).

Advertising

Radio is most popular form of advertising, followed by the print media. There are not regulations governing product advertising beyond trademark use.

News agencies

Other news agencies: Cananews: www.cananews.net

Economy

The country is the only significant exporter of oil and gas of the Caribbean islands. With its large hydrocarbons reserves and oil production of 151,000 barrels per day (bpd) and 40.6 billion cubic metres of natural gas in 2009, Trinidad and Tobago had a strong economy that had grown steadily (1993–2008) at 6 per cent per annum. But it was seriously affected by the global economic crisis in 2009 as energy prices fell dramatically and GDP growth dropped to -3.5 per cent and is estimated to have only grown to 0.0 per cent in 2010. Unemployment, which had fallen to 3.9 per cent in 2008 when oil prices had been at a record high, grew to 5.1 per cent in 2009 and peaked at an estimated 7.8 per cent in 2010.

The hydrocarbons sector remains one of the most attractive areas for foreign investment and in turn dominates GDP. Financial services dominates the service sector. The blow to the economy following the collapse of the insurance conglomerate CL Financial in January 2009 caused instability that had to be calmed by a government and central bank bailout of TT$5 billion (US$787 million). But even so, Trinidad and Tobago fell into a recession from a position of strength with low debt and large fiscal surpluses and this provided a buffer during the crisis. The IMF approved the 2010/11 national budget with its expansionist stance and additional expenditure and tax incentives designed to promote private-sector growth.

Another major component of the service sector is the tourist industry, which had shown consistent growth until the global economic crisis struck. By 2005 arrivals were at an all time high of over 463,000, but the industry suffered a fall (2006–09) as annual arrival numbers dropped. The industry contracted by -15 per cent in 2009 alone, recording numbers that roughly matched those in 2000 with arrivals of almost 372,000 (January–November).

In 2010 the government announced that it aimed to increase agriculture's contribution to GDP from an annual 0.6 per cent to 3 per cent by 2013, to enhance the island's food security and diversify the economy. Staple crops include, among others, wheat, maize and rice, cassava, yams and taro. Cash crops for export include sugarcane, citrus and timber. Livestock is typically tropical breeds including goats and sheep and water buffalo, but also includes poultry and pigs.

Trinidad and Tobago has the highest per capita income in the Caribbean and Latin America at US$16,167 in 2010 (a fall from a record high of US$20,827 in 2008). A number of workers go overseas for work to provide remittances for their families; in 2009 remittances were US$99 million (0.4 per cent of GDP) and were estimated to have risen to US$109 million in 2010.

External trade

Trinidad and Tobago is a member of the Caribbean Community and Common Market (Caricom) and operates within the single market (Caribbean Single Market and Economy (CSME)), which became operational in 2006.

Natural gas has replaced oil as the principal export earner, mainly in the form of liquefied natural gas (LNG). The petrochemical sector produces oil derivatives including methanol, ammonia and urea. Natural gas would have allowed for aluminium smelting using domestic gas but in September 2010 the government halted plans for a 125,000 tonnes per year plant on environmental grounds. Manufacturing is dominated by food processing, tobacco and factory assemblies. Agriculture is losing its importance as the sugar industry has contracted.

Imports

Principal imports include machinery, transport equipment, manufactured and consumer goods, foodstuffs and live animals.

Main sources: US (typically 31 per cent of total), Colombia (10 per cent), Russia (8 per cent).

Exports

Principal exports include natural gas, crude oil and petroleum derivatives, petrochemicals, processed food and beverages, tobacco products, sugar, cocoa, coffee, citrus and cut flowers.

Main destinations: US (typically 54 per cent of total), Jamaica (5 per cent), Spain (5 per cent).

Agriculture

Farming

About 23 per cent of the total land area is farmed. Although there is abundant rainfall, it is unevenly distributed, some areas becoming waterlogged, thereby curtailing production. Only 3 per cent of arable land is irrigated. About 60 per cent of the country's agriculture is in private hands and 40 per cent is controlled by the government.

The farming of major cash crops (sugar, coffee, cocoa and citrus fruits) has slumped owing to labour shortages, diseases and falling export demand.

The Agricultural Development Bank (ADB), which is primarily government-owned, provides loans to farmers and finances about 85 per cent of the country's agricultural development.

The Agricultural Development Corporation is charged with developing the agricultural sector. The sector is also the subject of an investment incentive programme, involving tax exemptions for approved projects. Other measures include a US$21 million four-year repair and rehabilitation programme for roads and more funding for water management and flood defence systems.

Fishing

The country does not have a large commercial fishing industry, but relies on small private fishermen whose production does not meet domestic demand. The fishing sector is an important local source of food.

Forestry

Forests cover around one-third of the total land area. Deforestation accounted for an average annual loss of 0.9 per cent, equivalent of 2,000 hectares of forest cover, in 1990–2000. The country has a well-developed commercial forests industry, based primarily on the harvesting of teak and Caribbean pine. Some three-quarters of the wood is used for industrial purposes, and the rest is used for fuel and charcoal. It produces modest quantities of industrial round timber and sawn timber. Much of the domestic demand is met by imports of sawn timber, wood-based panels and paper products.

Industry and manufacturing

Trinidad and Tobago is the most industrialised of the Caribbean islands. The industrial sector typically contributes 44 per cent of GDP, of which manufacturing contributes 8 per cent. Development since the 1970s has centred on heavy export-oriented industries, which are geared towards maximising the country's energy resources.

The principal manufactured products include refined petroleum, petrochemicals, nitrogenous fertilisers, iron, steel, methanol, plastics, sugar, and various import-substitution products. The growth of the petrochemicals sector has helped offset the effects of a decline in the sugar industry.

Tourism

The islands are a mix of mountains and plains with a tropical climate and palm-lined beaches. They have much to offer visitors, but due to the pre-eminence of hydrocarbons to the economy, tourism in Trinidad is not as heavily promoted as by other Caribbean islands. Tourism on Tobago, however, is important and the government invests in capital projects to promote the island. Most tourism is concentrated in resort developments in the south-west, where there are many beaches. In November 2011 a new luxury Magdalena Grand Beach Resort was opened, the first new resort since 1991. Apart from the sea-sports available (Tobago is known for its reef diving) the protected forests of the interior offer eco-friendly holidays.

Infrastructure is improving and air routes to Europe and the US are being expanded. The US is the principal market, followed by the Caribbean and the UK. On 23 September 2011, the minister of transport announced that a private public partnership project had been agreed, to provide a new public ferry service between Trinidad and Tobago and other islands of eastern Caribbean.

Mining

Trinidad and Tobago's mining sector revolves around the petroleum industry. Asphalt and pitch sand are extracted. Other minerals quarried include diorite, limestone, argillite clay and porcelainite. The world's largest supply of natural asphalt is found in La Brea on Trinidad.

Hydrocarbons

Proven oil reserves were 800 million barrels in 2007, with production at 7.3 million barrels, a drop of 12.5 per cent on the 2006 figure of 8.3 million barrels.

The majority of oil fields are located offshore between Trinidad and Tobago and Venezuela, another major oil producer. However in 2007 another oil field off the north-east coast of Trinidad began production of an estimated 310 million barrels of recoverable reserves.

The Pointe-á-Pierre refinery has a capacity of 190,000 barrels per day, production was 168,000 barrels per day in 2008, with over 40,000bpd consisting of natural gas liquids (NGL) (propane, butane, ethane etc).

The state-owned Petrotrin is an integrated oil and gas company which owns many of the offshore fields and the Pointe-á-Pierre refinery. It is responsible for exploration, development and production of hydrocarbons and petroleum products.

The oil and gas sectors account for 40 per cent of GDP and 80 per cent of the country's export earnings.

Proven natural gas reserves were 480 billion cubic metres (cum) in 2007, with production at 39 billion cum, an increase of 7 per cent on the 2006 figure of 36.4 billion cum.

Liquefied natural gas (LNG) has increased in significance, following completion of the major facilities by the Atlantic LNG Company (jointly-owned by the National Gas Company, BP, British Gas, Suez and Repsol-YPF). LNG is exported to the Americas, Europe and Asia for use in electricity, industry and petrochemical production. Trinidad and Tobago ranked seventh largest exporter of LNG in the world in 2007 and supplies the US with 70 per cent of its LNG.

A pipeline from Trinidad and Tobago to Martinique and Guadeloupe, connecting several other Caribbean islands, is being planned.

Coal is neither produced nor imported

Energy

Total installed generating capacity was 1.48 gigawatts (GW) in 2006, of which over 99 per cent of production was generated by fossil fuels, primarily natural gas.

The state-owned Trinidad and Tobago Electricity Commission (T&TEC) is responsible for the overall control of the transmission and distribution network, as well as sales both retail and commercial. It also has a majority shareholding in PowerGen, which is co-owned by US companies Southern Electric International and Amoco, and is responsible for generation, with electricity supplied to the national grid.

Financial markets
Stock exchange
Trinidad and Tobago Stock Exchange (TTSE)

Banking and insurance
The country has a number of international and domestic commercial banks including Citibank, Royal Bank and Scotia Bank.
Central bank
Central Bank of Trinidad and Tobago
Main financial centre
Port of Spain

Time
GMT minus four hours

Geography
Trinidad and Tobago lies in the Caribbean Sea off the eastern coast of Venezuela. Trinidad is the larger of the two islands, Tobago lies 32km north-east of Trinidad. The terrain of Trinidad is principally flat, although three ranges of higher land – peaking at almost 1,000 metres – cross the island from west to east.
Hemisphere
Northern

Climate
The islands have a humid, tropical climate with a rainy season from June to December, and an annual temperature range between 21 and 32 degrees Celsius.

Dress codes
Dress is generally informal and suited to the hot tropical climate. Men generally wear a shirt and tie for business meetings.

Entry requirements
Passports
Required by all, except nationals of Caricom countries, valid for six months beyond date of departure.
Visa
Required by all who are not exempt; a full list can be found at www.visittnt.com/General/things/visa.html. Business travellers should submit an employer's letter stating credentials with the visa application form.
Currency advice/regulations
There are no restrictions on the import of local and foreign currencies, subject to declaration on arrival. Export of local currency is limited to TT$200 and of foreign currency to TT$2,500 per annum.
Prohibited imports
Illegal drugs, weapons and explosives, specific animals (including monkeys and mongoose), animals that have died on transit, products used in relation to certain animals (such as used animal blankets and saddles) as well as dung may not be brought into Trinidad and Tobago.

Health (for visitors)
Mandatory precautions
Yellow fever vaccination certificate if arriving from infected area.
Advisable precautions
Yellow fever, hepatitis A, polio and tetanus vaccinations are advisable. Water precautions should be taken.

Hotels
A range of hotels is available in Trinidad and Tobago. They are generally expensive, although less so in Tobago. A 10 per cent tip is usual. A hotel room tax (in properties of 16 rooms or over) of 10 per cent has replaced value-added tax.
Book well in advance if arriving during Carnival time.

Credit cards
Credit cards are accepted.

Public holidays (national)
Fixed dates
1 Jan (New Year's Day), 30 Mar (Shouter Baptist Liberation Day), 30 May (Indian Arrival Day), 19 Jun (Labour Day), 1 Aug (Emancipation Day), 31 Aug (Independence Day), 24 Sep (Republic Day), 25–26 Dec (Christmas).
Variable dates
Good Friday, Easter Monday, Corpus Christi (May/Jun), Diwali (Hindu, Oct/Nov), Eid al Fitr.

Working hours
Carnival (two-day event immediately preceding Ash Wednesday) is usually taken as an unofficial holiday.
Banking
Mon–Thu: 0800–1400; Fri: 0800–1200, 1500–1700.
Business
Business hours are 0800–1600.
Government
Mon–Fri: 0815–1630.
Shops
Mon–Fri: 0800–1630; Sat: 0800–1200.
Supermarkets stay open later in the evenings and are open all day Saturday. Some open on Sunday. Some close on Thursday afternoon.

Telecommunications
Mobile/cell phones
GSM 850/1900 and 1800 services provide cover for most of the islands.

Electricity supply
Domestic: 115 and 230V AC, 60 cycles.
Industrial: 400V, 60 cycles three-phase.

Weights and measures
Metric system legally in use since 1981, but many traders continue to use the imperial system.

Social customs/useful tips
Both the social and business environment in Trinidad and Tobago are friendly and informal, and it is common to be on a first-name basis with people whom you have met before.

Security
The last major instance of political violence was in 1990, and the islands are generally a safe place to visit. The usual precautions against pickpockets should be taken in crowded areas.

Getting there
Air
National airline: Caribbean Airlines (replacing BWIA in early 2007 as the national airline). CAL receives a fuel subsidy, sometimes refered to as a 'fuel hedge' from the government, giving it an advantage over regional airline LIAT.
International airport/s: Piarco International, 25km east of Port of Spain, Trinidad; duty-free shop, restaurant, bank, post office, car hire.
Crown Point International, 5km west of Scarborough, Tobago.
Airport tax: TT$100, payable in local currency only.
Surface
Water: There are ferry services to neighbouring islands. Cruise ships call at Port of Spain, Trinidad, and Scarborough, Tobago.
Main port/s: Chaguaramas, Point Lisas, Port of Spain, Point-à-Pierre (Trinidad); Scarborough (Tobago).

Getting about
National transport
Air: Tobago Express flies frequent 'airbridge' services throughout the day between Piarco and Crown Point airports. The journey takes about 25 minutes.
Road: There is an extensive road network of around 8,000km. Major highways run north-south and east-west. Traffic jams are common.
Buses: Cheap and generally crowded.
Water: The two islands are connected by ferries between Port of Spain (Trinidad) and Scarborough (Tobago). There are two fast catamaran ferries, with a journey time of around two hours. A daily car ferry takes over six hours and the passage can be uncomfortable.
City transport
Taxis: Shared, route taxis are widely used. Routes with standard fares operated by passenger cars bearing 'H' registration plates and two-coloured Maxi Taxis (yellow stripe in Port of Spain). Negotiate fares for regular taxis in advance. Limousine service available at airport.
Taxis can be hired by distance, by the hour or by the day.

Car hire
National driving licences of most countries accepted for a period of three months from arrival. Insurance required. Cars drive on left. The maximum speed limit is 80kph on highways.

BUSINESS DIRECTORY

The addresses listed below are a selection only. While World of Information makes every endeavour to check these addresses, we cannot guarantee that changes have not been made, especially to telephone numbers and area codes. We would welcome any corrections.

Telephone area codes
This international direct dialling code for Trinidad and Tobago is +1-868 followed by subscriber's number.

Useful telephone numbers
Police: 999, 623-5191
Fire: 990
Ambulance:990, 625-3222/3

Chambers of Commerce
American Chamber of Commerce of Trinidad and Tobago, Trinidad Hilton Hotel and Conference Centre, Lady Young Road, Port of Spain (tel: 627-8570; fax: 627-7405; e-mail: inbox@amchamtt.com).

British-Caribbean Chamber of Commerce, Chamber Building, Columbus Circle, West Moorings, PO Box 499, Port of Spain (tel: 637-6966; fax: 637-7427; e-mail: info@britishcaribbean.com).

Caribbean Association of Industry and Commerce, Trinidad Hilton Hotel and Conference Centre, Lady Young Road, PO Box 442, Port of Spain (tel: 623-4830; fax: 623-6116; e-mail: caic@trinidad.net).

Greater Chaguanas Chamber of Industry and Commerce, Kibon House, 1 Endevour Road, Chaguanas (tel/fax: 671-5754; e-mail: admin@chaguanaschamber.com).

South Trinidad Chamber of Industry and Commerce, Cross Crossing Shopping Centre, Lady Hailes Avenue, PO Box 80, San Fernando (tel: 657-9077; fax: 652-5613; e-mail: execoffice@southchamber.com).

Trinidad and Tobago Chamber of Industry and Commerce, Chamber House, Columbus Circle, West Moorings, PO Box 499, Port of Spain (tel: 637-6966; fax: 637-7425; e-mail: chamber@chamber.org.tt).

Banking
Agricultural Development Bank of Trinidad and Tobago, PO Box 154, Port of Spain (tel: 623-6261/5, 625-6539; fax: 624-3087).

Bank of Commerce, PO Box 69, Port of Spain (tel: 627-9325/8; fax: 627-0904).

Bank of Nova Scotia, The Scotia Building, 56–58 Richmond Street, Port of Spain (tel: 625-3566/5222; fax: 623-0256).

Citibank, PO Box 1249, 12 Queen's Park East, Port of Spain (tel: 625-6445/9, 625-1046/9; fax: 624-8131; 625-6820).

Citicorp Merchant Bank, 12 Queen's Park East, Port of Spain (tel: 623-3344; fax: 624-8131).

CLICO Investment Bank, 1 Rust Street, St. Clair, Port of Spain (tel: 628-3628; fax 628-3639).

First Citizens Bank, Park & Henry Streets, Port of Spain (tel: 623-2423, 623-2576/8; fax: 627-5956).

Republic Bank Ltd, PO Box 1153, Port of Spain, Trinidad (tel: 625-3611, 623-0371; fax: 623-0371); Corner Wilson and Castries St, Scarborough, Tobago (tel: 639-2561).

Royal Merchant Bank & Finance Company, 7th Floor, 55 Independence Square, Port of Spain (tel: 625-3511, 624-5212).

The Royal Bank of Trinidad and Tobago, Head Office, Royal Court, 19-21 Park Street, Port of Spain (tel: 623-4291, 625-3764; fax: 624-4866).

Central bank
Central Bank of Trinidad and Tobago, Eric Williams Plaza, Independence Square, PO Box 1250, Port of Spain (tel: 625-4835; fax: 627-4696; e-mail: info@central-bank.org.tt).

Stock exchange
Trinidad and Tobago Stock Exchange (TTSE): www.stockex.co.tt

Travel information
Caribbean Airlines, Sunjet House, 30 Edward Street, Port of Spain (tel: 669-3000; fax: 669-1680).

Piarco International Airport, Caroni North Bank Road, Piarco (tel: 669-8047; fax: 669-0228).

Tourist Information Office, Crown Point Airport (tel: 639-0509; fax: 639-3566).

Tourist Information Office, Piarco Airport (tel: 669-5196; fax: 669-6045; e-mail: tourism-info@tdc.co.tt).

Trinidad and Tobago Automobile Association (TAA), 41 Woodford Street, Newtown, Port-of-Spain (tel: 622-7194; fax: 622-9079; e-mail: taa@tstt.net.tt).

Ministry of tourism
Ministry of Tourism, 51-55 Frederick Street, Port of Spain (tel: 624-1403; fax: 625-0437; e-mail: mintourism@tourism.gov.tt).

National tourist organisation offices
Tourism Development Company Ltd, Maritime Centre, 29 Tenth Avenue, Barataria (tel: 675-7034; fax: 675-7432; e-mail : info@tdc.co.tt).

Ministries
Ministry of Communications and Information Technology, Kent House, Long Circular Road, Maraval (tel: 628-1323; fax: 622-4783).

Ministry of Community Empowerment, Autorama Building, El Socorro Road, San Juan (tel: 675-6728; fax: 674-4021).

Ministry of Consumer Affairs, Agostini Compound, 3 Duncan Street, Port of Spain (tel: 623-7741; fax: 625-4737).

Ministry of Culture, Algico Building, Jerningham Avenue, Queen's Park East, Port of Spain (tel: 625-3012; fax: 625-3278).

Ministry of Education, Hayes Street, St Clair (tel: 622-2181; fax: 628-7818).

Ministry of Energy and Energy Industries, Level 9, Riverside Plaza, Corner Besson & Piccadilly Streets, Port of Spain (tel: 623-6708; fax: 623-2726).

Ministry of Enterprise Development, Level 15, Riverside Plaza, Corner Besson & Piccadilly Streets, Port of Spain (tel: 623-2931; fax: 627-8488).

Ministry of the Environment, Level 16, Eric Williams Finance Building, Independence Square, Port of Spain (tel: 627-9700; fax: 625-1585).

Ministry of Finance, Level 8, Eric Williams Finance Building, Independence Square, Port of Spain (tel: 627-9700; 627-6108).

Ministry of Food Production and Marine Resources, PO Box 389, St Clair Circle, St Clair (tel: 622-1221; 622-8202).

Ministry of Foreign Affairs, Knowsley Building, 1 Queen's Park West, Port of Spain (tel: 623-4116; fax: 627-0571).

Ministry of Health, Corner Duncan Street & Independence Square, Port of Spain (tel: 627-0012; fax: 623-9528).

Ministry of Housing and Settlements, NHA Building, Corner George Street & South Quay, Port of Spain (tel: 624-5058; fax: 625-2793).

Ministry of Human Development, Sacred Heart Building, 16-18 Sackville Street, Port of Spain (tel: 624-2000; fax: 625-7003).

Ministry of Infrastructure Development, Corner Richmond & London Streets, Port of Spain (tel: 625-1225; fax: 625-8070).

Ministry of Integrated Planning and Development, Level 14, Eric Williams Finance Building, Independence Square, Port of Spain (tel: 623-4308; fax: 623-8123).

Ministry of Labour, Manpower Development and Industrial Relations, Level 11, Riverside Plaza, Corner Besson & Piccadilly Streets, Port of Spain (tel: 623-4241; fax: 624-4091).

Ministry of Legal Affairs, 72-74 South Quay, Port of Spain (tel: 625-4586; fax: 625-9803).

Ministry of Local Government, Kent House, Long Circular Road, Maraval (tel: 628-1325; fax: 622-7410).

Ministry of National Security, Temple Court, 31-33 Abercromby Street, Port of Spain (tel: 623-2441; fax: 625-3925).

Ministry of Sport, ISSA Nicholas Building, Corner Frederick & Duke Streets, Port of Spain (tel: 625-5622; fax: 623-4507).

Ministry of Transport, Corner Richmond & London Streets, Port of Spain (tel: 625-1225; fax: 627-9886).

Office of The Attorney General, Cabildo Chambers, Corner Sackville & St Vincent Streets, Port of Spain (tel: 623-7010; fax: 625-0470).

Office of The Prime Minister, Whitehall, Maraval Road, Port of Spain (tel: 622-1625; fax: 622-0055).

Other useful addresses

Businessmen's Association of Trinidad and Tobago, PO Box 322, Time Plaza, Room 10, 28 Henry Street, Port of Spain (tel: 623-4568).

Caribbean Employers' Confederation, 43 Dundonald Street, Port of Spain (tel: 625-4723).

Caribbean Industrial Research Institute, O'Meara Industrial Estate, Macoya Road, Trincity, Arima (tel: 662-7161/4; fax: 663-4180).

Export Development Corporation, Export House, 10-14 Phillips Street, PO Box 582, Port of Spain (tel: 623-6022/3; fax: 625-0050).

Industrial Development Corporation, 10-12 Independence Square, PO Box 949, Port of Spain (tel: 623-7291/6, 623-7289).

Management Development Centre, Room 212, Salvatoria Building, PO Box 1301, Port of Spain (tel: 623-4951/3).

National Gas Company of Trinidad and Tobago Limited, Goodrich Bay Road, Point Lisas Industrial Estate, Point Lisas (tel: 636-4662; fax: 679-2384).

Petroleum Company of Trinidad and Tobago Limited (PETROTRIN), Administrative Building, Southern Main Road, Pointe-à-Pierre (tel: 658-4200, 658-4230; fax: 658-1315; e-mail: petroweb@petrotrin.com).

Reinsurance Company of Trinidad and Tobago, Trinre House, 52 Jerningham Avenue, Belmont, PO Box 1087, Port of Spain (tel: 623-6194/6602; fax: 624-4021).

Small Business Association of Trinidad and Tobago, Third Floor, MPU Building, 3 Besson Street, Port of Spain (tel: 624-3666).

Shipping Association of Trinidad and Tobago, Room 12a, 64-66 South Quay, Port of Spain (tel: 623-8570).

Telecommunications Services of Trinidad and Tobago Ltd (TSTT), 54 Frederick Street, PO Box 971, Port of Spain (tel: 624-5756/5703; fax: 625-4585; e-mail: tsttceo@tstt.net.tt).

Tobago House of Assembly, (Foreign Investment Proposals in Tobago), Bacolet Street, Scarborough.

Trinidad and Tobago Development Finance Co Ltd, PO Box 187, 8-10 Cipriani Boulevard, Port of Spain (tel: 623-4665/7, 625-4666/8; fax: 624-3563).

Trinidad and Tobago Embassy (USA), 1708 Massachusetts Avenue, NW, Washington DC (tel: (+1-202) 467-6490; fax: (+1-202) 785-3130; e-mail: embttgo@erols.com).

Trinidad and Tobago Export Trading Company Limited, Level 4 Long Circular Mall, Long Circular Road, St. James (tel: 622-7968; fax: 628-2349).

Trinidad and Tobago Manufacturers' Association, 8 Stanmore Avenue, Port of Spain (tel: 623-1029/31, fax: 623-1031).

Internet sites

Government website: http://www.gov.tt

Information on economic trends, investment opportunities, infrastructure, news and events: http://www.tidco.co.tt/

Petroleum Company of Trinidad and Tobago Ltd: http://www.petrotrin.com

Prime Minister's Office: http://www.opm.gov.tt

Statistics Office: http://www.cso.gov.tt

Telecommunications Services of Trinidad and Tobago Ltd: http://www.tstt.net.tt

Trinidad and Tobago company database: http://tradepoint.tidco.co.tt/ttcdbase/

Tristan da Cunha

KEY FACTS

Official name: Tristan da Cunha

Head of State: Head of State: Queen Elizabeth II, represented by Governor Mark Andrew Capes (from 29 Oct 2011) (resides in St Helena)

Head of government: Administrator Sean Burns (from 21 Sep 2010)

Area: 98 square km

Population: 263 (2010)

Capital: Edinburgh of the Seven Seas

Official language: English

Currency: Pound sterling (£) = 100 pence

Exchange rate: £0.64 per US$ (Oct 2011)

COUNTRY PROFILE

Historical profile

1506 The island was sighted by the Portuguese admiral, Tristão da Cunha, on his way to the East Indies.
1810 The first settlers arrived but failed to establish a permanent community.
1816 The island was annexed by Britain and a garrison established to provide additional security for Napoleon who was being held in exile on St Helena.
1817 The garrison was withdrawn but Corporal Glass elected to stay on the island with his wife to guard the remaining stores and incidentally founded the community.
The community gradually developed during the nineteenth century and for a time became relatively prosperous with frequent calls by American whalers in the 1850s. The seven families represented four nations – Britain, Holland, US and Italy. With the decline of sail the island became increasingly isolated and impoverished; sometimes several years passed without a ship calling. The only contact with the outside world was provided by an irregular succession of pastors and a very occasional passing ship.
1938 The island became a dependency of St Helena.
1942 A garrison and radio/meteorological station were built.
1949 The island's extreme isolation ended with the establishment of the crawfish industry when the first fish processing factory was opened.
1950s, The British pound was introduced as the official currency.
1961 The volcano erupted and the community was evacuated, returning some two years later to re-establish the settlement.
1981 The Nationality Act ended the islanders' British citizenship and right of abode.
1999 The Nationality Act came under review in the UK government's 'Partnership for Prosperity and Progress' White Paper.
2000 Development of the crawfish industry ended Tristan's dependence on the UK and gave the islanders economic confidence.
2001 The island was hit by a hurricane which inflicted considerable damage.
2004 A new, long wheel-based type Land Rover fire engine, provided by the UK government, was delivered. Michael Clancy became governor.
2006 An oilrig ran aground on a reef on the southeast side of the island during a hurricane while being towed from South Africa to South America. It took several months and two attempts to re-float the rig. By 2006 very home on the island had a telephone line, and a new satellite service allowed for broadband internet access and live television broadcasts.
2007 David Morley became the resident administrator and Andrew Gurr became governor.
2008 Plans to repair and refurbish the harbour were announced, with work to be undertaken by UK Royal Engineers and materials supplied through the European Development Fund and UK government.
2009 The FCO announced a new constitution for Tristan da Cunha, which included a bill of rights and limits to the power of the governor. It also proposed an executive Legislative Council with either a single constituency for the whole island or two or more constituencies. Tristan da Cunha later voted in favour of the proposed changes. A new, larger and modern fish factory replacing the one that had been burned down in 2008 was opened. Work began, under the auspices of the Tristan Conservation Department, to eradicate the alien plant *Sagina apetala* (Pearlwort) from Gough Island, which was displacing native floral. Funding and management was being provided by the Royal Society for the Protection of Birds (RSPB) from the UK's Overseas Territories Environment Programme.
2010 New island councillors were voted into office in March. In November it was announced that Calshot Harbour is to be repaired by the UK Department for International Development (DfID). It was severely damaged by storms earlier in the year and it was feared that unless emergency repairs were made before the 2011 winter storms the islanders would be cut off. Calshot Harbour is essential to the island's economy, which is primarily based on tourism and fishing. Sean Burns became Administrator on 21 September.
2011 On 19 July Tristan da Cunha's rock lobster fishery was awarded Marine Stewardship Council (MSC) accreditation for sustainable and well-managed fisheries. On 23 September, Governor Gurr's term in office ended and Attorney General Ken

Baddon was sworn in as acting governor on 24 September, until Mark Andrew Capes takes up the post in 29 October.

Political structure

Tristan is the only inhabited island, although there is a meteorological station on Gough Island, maintained by the South African navy.

Although technically under the jurisdiction of St Helena, the island effectively administers itself independently. Responsibility for it, as a British Overseas Territories, is divided between the British Foreign and Commonwealth Office (FCO) and the Department for International Development (DfID). The post of Minister for Overseas Territories within the FCO was created and an Overseas Territories Consultative Council set up.

In 2002, full British citizenship was granted to the inhabitants of Tristan da Cunha.

Constitution

Form of state

As a British Overseas Territory, Tristan da Cunha is a dependency of St Helena.

The executive

Executive authority is exercised by an administrator appointed by the FCO, who acts as chairman of the Island Council (three nominated members, eight elected, two ex-officio members; one member must be a woman), which meets six times a year. A chief islander is also elected, for three years.

National legislature

The Island Council has 15 members: 12 non-partisan members elected by popular vote for a four-year term and three ex officio members.

Last elections

June 2005

Population

263 (2010)

Last census: December 1988: 296

Population density: 3.0 inhabitants per sq km.

Ethnic make-up

English, Scottish, Irish, Dutch and Italian.

Main cities

Edinburgh of the Seven Seas (capital, estimated population 270 in 2003).

Languages spoken

Official language/s

English

Media

Press

News is published by the online newspaper Tristan Times (www.tristantimes.com) and the South Atlantic Remote Territories Media Association (www.sartma.com).

Broadcasting

The Tristan Broadcasting Service provides local and BBC World Service programmes on 93.5FM.

Radio: Atlantic FM was re-launched on 13 January 2008 providing a limited service with local news and information.

Economy

Tristan's commercial economy is based on crawfish (Tristan Rock Lobster), sheep farming, philatelic sales and to a much lesser extent through tourism by the provision of guides and accommodation to visitors and the sale of hand-knitted garments and other woollen handicrafts and souvenirs, which are also sold by mail order.

Since the opening of the first crawfish cannery and freezing plant in 1949, the economy has been transformed from subsistence, sometimes near starvation level, to self-sufficiency. The annual crawfish catch is limited to 340 tonnes, of which 145 tonnes comes from the main island and the balance from the fisheries around Gough, Nightingale and Inaccessible Islands. An agreement was signed with a New Zealand company for catching Patagonian toothfish. Revenue from the industry more than adequately covers the island's running costs and has allowed reserves to be built up. These provided a buffer against the decline in Far Eastern demand. A fire in 2008 burned down the island's only fish processing factory. It was rebuilt to EU standards as a bigger, modern facility able to export lobsters to the EU. The island's oldest inhabitant, Alice Glass (93 years old), opened the new factory in July 2009.

Other economic activities are hampered by poor access with only about 60 days per year suitable for landing. A new harbour has improved conditions and allows for more regular visits, particularly by small yachts. Tristan's fresh water is considered to have special properties and there are plans to develop a mineral water export business, but which by early 2011 had not progressed beyond the feasibility planning stage.

External trade

As a UK Overseas Territory, Tristan da Cunha is a member of the European Union's Association of Overseas Countries and Territories (OCT Association), and some EU regulations apply. Foreign earnings are generated by commercial fishing licences, with postage stamps, coins and handicrafts supplied by mail order.

Agriculture

Farming

The cultivated area is estimated at no more than 15 hectares. Potatoes are the main crop. Cattle, sheep and poultry are kept. Each married couple is allowed to graze seven sheep and two cows on settlement land, or any number on the plateau.

Each family grows potatoes on about an acre of ground. Potatoes were first introduced to the island in 1816 when the first settlers arrived and have been grown on the same land each year without rotation; they are easily grown in volcanic soil.

Fishing

Tristan da Cunha's fisheries zone is rich in unique species – rock lobsters, wreckfish, Tristan red scorpion fish, Tristan wrasse and Atlantic amberjack.

The economy is based on crawfish (rock lobster). Fish provide a major source of protein.

A fire in 2008 burned down the island's only fish processing factory. It was rebuilt to EU standards as a bigger, modern facility able to export lobsters to the EU.

Hydrocarbons

There are no known hydrocarbon reserves and all petroleum needs are met by imports.

Time

GMT

Geography

The Tristan da Cunha archipelago comprises the main island as well as Inaccessible and Nightingale Islands. Gough Island, to the south-east, also comes under Tristan administration, combined their surface area is 201 square kilometres.

The main island of Tristan da Cunha is a single, almost circular, volcanic island that lies 2,400km west of Cape Town in the South Atlantic Ocean. It has only one relatively flat area, where the capital is located. Queen Mary's Peak (2,010 metres) is the highest mountain, at the centre of the island.

Inaccessible Island lies 32km west of Tristan; the three Nightingale Islands 35km south; and Gough Island (Diego Alvarez) 350km south, which has a manned weather station with seven personnel.

Hemisphere

Southern

Climate

Tristan da Cunha has a mild, temperate climate. Temperatures range from 3–25 degrees Celsius. The average annual rainfall is 1,700mm.

Entry requirements

Visa

None required, but visitors must have permission of the Island Council and Administrator to land; this is normally granted. All visitors must have onward/return passage, full medical insurance including emergency evacuation and sufficient funds for a visit. A small landing fee is charged.

Hotels
There is no hotel accommodation on the island.

Working hours
Government
Mon—Fri: 0830—1230, 1300—1630.

Telecommunications
Telephone/fax
The Administrator's office and the factory in Tristan have satellite communications by telephone and fax. Faxes are only available to the government.
A public satellite telephone provides an international service through a radio telephone link via Cape Town Radio.
Postal services
The international postal code for Tristan da Cunha is TDCU 1ZZ.

Getting there
Air
Surface
Shipping is the sole means of regular access to the island.
Water: Calshot Harbour, completed in 1967 and named after the Hampshire village where many islanders lived after the volcanic explosion of 1961, is too small for ocean going boats to berth. Passengers are normally ferried to land in small boats and landing is not guaranteed. Cargo is loaded onto barges and off loaded by crane. Improvements and repairs to the harbour, which is vital to the economy, were agreed in 2006 for completion by 2008. The improvements included deepening the harbour. Finance for the work was to come from the British government and from the EU. However, in 2010 the work still had to be agreed and commissioned.
In 2008 a team of 40 Royal Engineers plus a detachment from the Royal Logistic Corps and a medical support team from the Royal Navy, were transported along with their materials by the RFA *Lyme Bay*, to carry out urgent repairs to the main harbour. Operation Zest was a joint government response involving the foreign and commonwealth office, the department for international development (DfID) (who funded the work) and the ministry of defence. Within months of the successful completion of Operation Zest, the main crane collapsed in April, leaving the islanders with the problem of not only how to bring ashore a new crane, but also the materials to rebuild the fish factory.
The new crane was finally commissioned in January 2009 and further improvements and repairs were finished by April. The Austral storms of 2010 again damaged the harbour walls and it was feared that unless emergency repairs were made before the winter storms of 2011 the islanders would be cut off. In November island administrator, Sean Burns, announced that DfID had agreed to fund the £6 million (US$3.77 million) needed to fund the fifty 10-tonne concrete 'dolosse' blocks specially designed to protect the most vulnerable part of the harbour from future storms.
Calshot Harbour is essential to the island's economy, which is based on tourism and fishing, as well as enabling supplies to be delivered.
The RMS *St Helena* makes an annual visit. The ship is operated under contract by Andrew Weir Shipping Ltd on behalf of the owners, St Helena Line Ltd.
Premier Fishing operates two fishing boats, the *Kelso* and the *Edinburgh*, which make irregular connections between Tristan and Cape Town.
The South African Navy operates the *Agulhas* to approximate sailing dates, mainly for official personnel.
Yachts call frequently and offer an alternative means of reaching the island, as does the occasional cruise ship.

BUSINESS DIRECTORY
The addresses listed below are a selection only. While World of Information makes every endeavour to check these addresses, we cannot guarantee that changes have not been made, especially to telephone numbers and area codes. We would welcome any corrections.

Telephone area codes
The international direct dialling (IDD) code for Tristan de Cunha is +874 (satellite) followed by subscriber's number.

Travel information
Travel information (for air travel and bookings on the RMS St Helena):

Passenger Services Department, Andrew Weir Shipping Ltd, Dexter House, 2 Royal Mint Court, London EC N4XX, UK (tel: (+44-207) 575-6480; fax: (+44-207) 575-6200; email: reservations@aws.co.uk; internet site: www.aws.co.uk).

Premier Fishing, PO Box 181, Cape Town 8000, South Africa. (tel: (+27-21) 419-0124).

St Helena Line, Andrew Weir Shipping (SA) Pty Ltd, 3rd Floor, BP Centre, Thibault Square, Cape Town, South Africa (tel: (+27-21) 425-1165; fax: (+27-21) 421-7485; email: sthelenaline@mweb.co.za).

Miss Kerry Yon, Solomon and Co plc, Jamestown, St Helena, South Atlantic (tel: (+290) 2523; fax: (+290) 2423; email: solco.shipping@helanta.sh).

Ministries
Administrator's Office, Edinburgh of the Seven Seas (e-mail: hmg@cunha.demon.co.uk).

Other useful addresses
The Tristan Resource Centre, Michael Swales, Denstone College, Uttoxeter, Staffs, UK (tel: (+44)-(0)1538) 703-322).

St Helena Desk Officer, Foreign and Commonwealth Office, Room, King Charles Street, London SW1A 2AH, UK (tel: (+44-(0)207) 270-2695).

Miles Apart (books, maps, videos on South Atlantic Islands), 5 Harraton House, Exning, Newmarket, Suffolk CB8 7HF, UK (tel: (+44-(0)1638) 577-627; fax: (+44-(0)1638) 577-874); 5929 Avon Drive, Bethesda, Maryland 20814, US (tel/fax: (+1-301) 571-8942; email: familycarter@msn.com).

Internet sites
Sartma (South Atlantic Remote Territories Media Association): www.sartma.com

Tristan Times: www.tristantimes.com

KEY FACTS

Official name: Jumhuriya at Tunisiya (Republic of Tunisia)

Head of State: President Moncef Marzouki (CPR) (from 19 Nov 2011)

Head of government: Prime Minister Hamadi Jebali (Nahda) (from 19 Nov 2011)

Ruling party: Coalition led by Mouvement de la Renaissance (Nahda) (Renaissance Party), with Congrès pour la République (CPR) (Congress of the Republic) and Forum Démocratique pour le Travail et les Libertés (Ettakatol) (Democratic Forum for Labour and Liberties) (from 19 Nov 2011)

Area: 164,150 square km

Population: 10.55 million (2010)*

Capital: Tunis

Official language: Arabic

Currency: Dinar (D) = 1,000 millimes

Exchange rate: D1.44 per US$ (Oct 2011)

GDP per capita: US$4,200 (2010)

GDP real growth: 3.70% (2010)

GDP: US$44.30 billion (2010)

Labour force: 3.77 million (2010)

Unemployment: 13.00% (2010)

Inflation: 4.40% (2010)

Oil production: 80,000 bpd (2010)

Balance of trade: -US$3.70 billion (2009)

* estimated figure

Tunisia

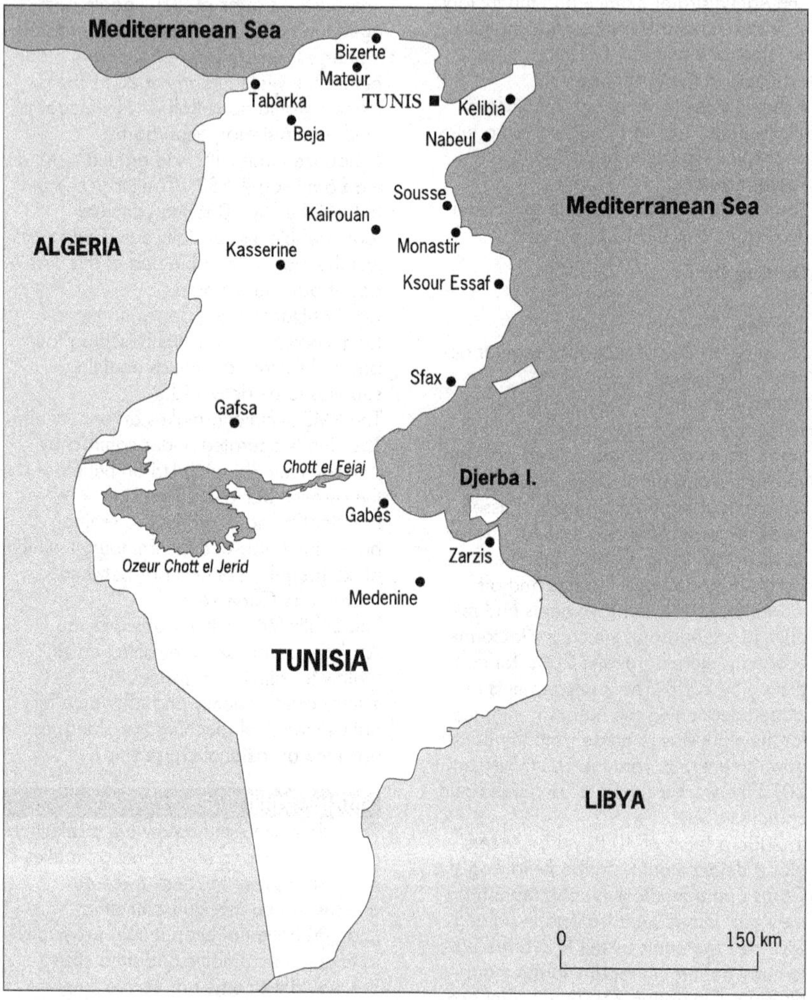

If there was a trigger to the Arab Spring, it was in Tunisia in the self-immolation of street vendor Mohamed Bouazizi on 17 December 2010, followed less than a month later by the flight of President Zine al Abidine Ben Ali to Saudi Arabia. That their country should have been at the forefront of the Arab Spring surprised virtually everyone – both inside and outside Tunisia. Despite the heavy handed rule of Ben Ali, Tunisia had probably been the Arab world's most secular and progressive country. On international poverty comparisons Tunisia fared well, with an official poverty level of only four per cent. Tunisia's education system also ranked highly – seventeenth in the world according to some rankings. Tunisia was the only country where abortion was legal and where Islamic extremism was illegal. Demonstrations against rises in food prices and widespread unemployment escalated in January 2011, a (largely ignored) curfew was imposed and on 13 January Ben Ali said he would not stand again for president in the next elections, scheduled for 2014.

There'll be some changes made

Until 2011, Tunisia had been a republic with an oppressively strong presidential system dominated by a single political party. Ousted president Zine al Abidine Ben Ali had served virtually uncontested as President of the Republic since 1987, when he had deposed President Habib Bourguiba. However, on 14 January 2011, following nearly two months of popular demonstrations and protests calling for his removal from office, Ben Ali abdicated power and voluntarily entered into exile in Saudi Arabia. Shortly after his departure, the Speaker of the Parliament, Fouad Mebazaa, assumed the position of interim President of Tunisia on the basis of Article 57 of the Tunisian constitution. Upon the resignation of Prime Minister Mohamed Ghannouchi on 27 February, Mebazaa appointed former diplomat and cabinet official Béji Caïd Essebsi to the position on 28 February. Prior to Ben Ali's departure, the ruling Democratic Constitutional Rally (RCD), was essentially Tunisia's sole legal political party for 25 years – including when it was known as the Parti Socialiste Destourien (PSD) (Socialist Destourian Party). The RCD was dissolved by judicial ruling on 9 March 2011. Under the former regime, the president was elected to 5-year terms and regional governors and local administrators were appointed by the central government. There was also a bicameral legislative body with a nominally independent judiciary which had generally responded to executive direction, especially in politically sensitive cases.

New brooms

The Tunisian revolution was the signal for widespread calls for political reform, including popular demands for a new constitution, to be drafted by an elected Constituent Assembly. Length and terms of office, authority of the legislature and separation of powers are subject to change under the new constitution. Tunisia's military has traditionally played a professional, apolitical role in defending the country from external threats. Since January 2011 and at the direction of the executive branch, the military has taken on increasing responsibility for domestic security and humanitarian crisis response. Since the revolution, some organisations have reconstituted themselves and hundreds of new ones have emerged. For instance, the Tunisian Human Rights League (LTDH), the first human rights organisation in Africa and the Arab world, operated under restrictions and state intrusion for over half of its existence, but is now completely free to operate. Some independent organisations, such as the Association Tunisienne des Femmes Democrates (ATFD) (Tunisian Association of Democratic Women), the Association of Tunisian Women for Research and Development and the Bar Association also remain active. A lack of political freedom had characterised the Tunisian landscape under the former regime. Tunisia ranked a lowly 154 out of 178 countries in the 2010 Reporters Without Borders's World Press Freedom assessment and the US State Department's annual human rights report consistently cited infringements on freedoms of assembly and expression, as well as reports of torture and abuse of prisoners. With hindsight, it seemed inevitable that an oppressive political environment, coupled with extreme economic inequality, opaque political and economic national decision-making and the government's insensitivity to popular demands for greater economic opportunity, would give rise to a popular revolution.

The months of doubts and instability that characterised the first nine months of 2011 eventually ended with the 23 October elections for the 217-seat Tunisian Constituent Assembly (TCA). The moment of apparent truth saw the inauguration of a notionally representative Constituent Assembly, ushering in a new chapter in recent Tunisian history. The Tunisian people had elected an independent government, whose first responsibility was to draw up a constitution to consolidate and give voice to their collective political wishes. The extent to which this represented a genuinely new start remained to be seen. The lack of transparency and rife corruption that had characterised the Ben Ali period would need a substantial change in political attitudes and professionalism.

Encouragingly, the TCA had a higher percentage of women deputies than many European countries, not to mention the United States. Paradoxically, 42 of the 49 female members represented the Islamist Ennahda party. A woman, Mehrezia Labidi-Maiza of the Ennahda party was also appointed vice president of the Assembly. Tunisia's newly elected coalition government consisted of Islamists, liberals and left wing deputies. One *al Jazeera* report noted that the parties that had 'based their election campaign on provoking fear of others – particularly the Progressive Democratic Party, which stood essentially as the anti-Ennahda party – lost out majorly.' Co-operation not conflict, dialogue not demonisation was the message according to *al Jazeera*. The new Prime Minister, Hammadi Jebali of Ennahda, had, according to *al Jazeera*, spent 16 years in prison, ten of which were in solitary confinement. Tunisia's new president, Moncef Marzouki of the Congrès pour la République (CPR) (Congress of the Republic), had also served time in prison.

Regional importance

Tunisia has long been important in the Mediterranean. Close to vital shipping

KEY INDICATORS — Tunisia

	Unit	2006	2007	2008	2009	2010
Population	m	*10.92	*10.92	*10.33	*10.43	*10.55
Gross domestic product (GDP)	US$bn	30.96	35.60	40.30	43.50	44.30
GDP per capita	US$	3,072	3,483	3,907	4,171	4,200
GDP real growth	%	5.5	6.3	4.5	3.1	3.7
Inflation	%	4.5	3.1	5.0	3.5	4.4
Unemployment	%	14.3	14.1	14.2	13.3	13.0
Industrial output	% change	3.8	7.2	4.0	4.1	–
Agricultural output	% change	3.0	2.1	0.5	3.5	–
Oil output	'000 bpd	69.0	98.0	89.0	86.0	80.0
Exports (fob) (goods)	US$m	11,488.0	15,148.0	19,184.0	14,419.0	–
Imports (fob) (goods)	US$m	14,299.0	18,024.0	23,194.0	18,117.0	–
Balance of trade	US$m	-2,811.0	-2,876.0	-4,010.0	-3,699.0	–
Current account	US$m	-630.0	-904.0	-1,711.0	-1,234.0	-2,125.0
Foreign debt	US$bn	18.5	20.1	20.6	21.4	–
Total reserves minus gold	US$m	6,773.2	7,850.8	8,849.3	11,057.3	9,459.3
Foreign exchange	US$m	6,741.4	7,816.8	8,812.9	10,646.5	9,000.3
Exchange rate	per US$	1.33	1.28	1.23	1.35	1.43

* estimated figure

lanes, it is of strategic significance. French colonial rule ended in 1956 and Tunisia was led for three decades by Habib Bourguiba, who advanced secular ideas. These included emancipation for women – women's rights in Tunisia are among the most advanced in the Arab world – the abolition of polygamy and compulsory free education. Bourguiba insisted on an anti-Islamic fundamentalist line, but increased his own powers to become a virtual dictator. After 31 years, he was retired on grounds of senility and Zine al Abidine Ben Ali came into office.

The economy

According to the International Monetary Fund (IMF) in its (pre-uprising) 2010 assessment, Tunisia's economy had fared relatively well during the global financial crisis, but the country's key challenge was to boost job-generating growth and lower unemployment. The IMF expected gross domestic product (GDP) growth to reach 3.8 per cent in 2010, after slowing to 3 per cent in 2009 as the global downturn took its toll. But unemployment had begun to rise and at 13.3 per cent, remained relatively high, particularly among educated youth.

Over the past two decades, according to the IMF, Tunisia had undertaken wide-ranging structural reforms aimed at enhancing its business environment and improving the competitiveness of its economy. These reforms, accompanied by prudent macro-economic management, had reduced the Tunisian economy's vulnerability to shocks – including the global financial crisis – and provided more options for the authorities to respond to them. But with growth in Tunisia's main trading partners projected at a mere 1.2 per cent in 2010 and 1.5 per cent in 2011, the country's economic recovery remained on a fragile footing. Moreover, the downside risks to prospects for recovery in Europe – by far Tunisia's largest partner in terms of exports, tourism receipts, workers' remittances and foreign direct investment (FDI) – had risen significantly in recent months, posing risks to the country's short-term outlook according to the IMF.

Thanks to prudent macro-economic management, Tunisia still had some leeway to deal with such potential external risks, particularly on the fiscal policy front. But at the end of 2010, in the view of the IMF, the Tunisian authorities needed to remain vigilant in the face of potential inflationary pressures, a recent deterioration of the current account balance and declining external reserves.

To achieve Tunisia's medium-term objectives of boosting employment-generating growth and lowering unemployment, the government was developing an export promotion strategy that sought to diversify target markets and products. To that end, Tunisia had signed a preferential trade agreement with the West African Economic and Monetary Union (WAEMU) and was negotiating free trade agreements with the Central African Economic and Monetary Community (CAEMU). Bilateral negotiations with the European Union (EU) were also under way to extend the Association Agreement to services, agricultural products and processed food; the Agreement currently provides for free trade for industrial products. The authorities have also identified a number of reforms to labour market policies, the educational system and public employment services that will serve to facilitate labour mobility and reduce mismatches between demand and supply in the labour market. The implementation of these reforms was due to be supported by several World Bank Development Policy Loans. Maintaining a stable macro-economic environment that promotes employment and growth also requires determined expenditure control, the IMF assessment said. Key for success in this area was the reform of the social security system. To this end, the government was in discussion with social partners on pension reforms to buttress the pension system's financial sustainability. The government should also explore ways to contain subsidies of food and fuel products, the report noted.

Risk assessment

Economy	Fair
Politics	Improving dramatically
Regional stability	Good

COUNTRY PROFILE

Historical profile

670 The Arabs conquered Carthage.
1207–1574 After the Arab empire collapsed, Tunisia became part of the Moroccan empire of the Almohads before emerging as the independent Hafsid empire.
1600s The Hafsids were defeated by the Ottomans, who developed a system of rule by a local elite descended from the Turks, the Huseinid beys.
1700s Tunisia became a national monarchy.
1881 France invaded Tunisia from Algeria.
1883 Tunisia was declared a French protectorate.
1930s The Néo-Destour nationalist movement developed under Habib Bourguiba, who was jailed by the French.
1942–43 During the Second World War, German and Italian troops, who came to Tunisia to resist allied forces in Algeria, were driven out by the Allies in 1943.
1956 Tunisia gained independence from France under the leadership of Bourguiba.
1957 The monarchy was abolished and the Republic of Tunisia declared.
1961–63 The Tunisian government demanded the withdrawal of French troops from the strategic port of Bizerte; fighting broke out between French and Tunisian forces. French forces left Bizerte following an agreement between the French and Tunisian governments in 1963.
1974 A constitutional amendment named Bourguiba 'President for Life'.
1981 The first multi-party parliamentary elections since independence were won by President Bourguiba's party in a landslide victory.
1982–85 The headquarters of the Palestinian Liberation Organisation (PLO) relocated from Beirut to Tunis, where it stayed until it moved to the Palestinian autonomous areas (Gaza and Jericho) in 1994. In 1985, Israel raided the headquarters in revenge for a PLO attack on a yacht in Larnaca, Cyprus.
1987 In line with the constitution, Prime Minister Zine al Abidine Ben Ali succeeded President Bourguiba, who was declared by his physicians mentally unfit to rule, due to senility.
1989 President Ben Ali won the presidential election; he was re-elected in 1994; both elections were uncontested.
1999 Ben Ali was re-elected for a third term in the first multi-party presidential elections. Mohamed Ghannouchi was appointed prime minister.
2000 Violence erupted in several towns and cities over increasing levels of poverty and price rises in certain basic commodities.
2002 An al Qaeda terrorist bomb killed 19 people in a synagogue in Djerba. A referendum agreed to abolish the three-term limit for incumbent presidents and to raise the age limit of an incumbent president from 70 to 75.
2004 Incumbent Zine al Abidine Ben Ali won 94.5 per cent of the presidential vote, Mohamed Bouchiha won 3.8 per cent. The ruling, Rassemblement Constitutionnel Démocratique (RCD) (Democratic Constitutional Rally), was re-elected with 91.6 per cent of the popular vote.
2005 A second parliamentary legislative body, the Chamber of Advisors, was inaugurated with 112 members, drawn from

professional bodies, local officials and presidential appointees.
2006 A ban on the wearing in public places of the *hijab* (by women) was introduced. The opposition Mouvement des Démocrates Socialistes (MDS) (Movement of Democratic Socialists), elected May Eljeribi as the first female political leader in Tunisia.
2007 The law banning the wearing of the *hijab* was lifted following a ruling by the Administrative Court of Tunis which deemed it unconstitutional.
2009 The international ratings agency Moody's warned that four Tunisian Banks were under review for possible downgrading for local and foreign currency deposit ratings, due to the global financial crisis and the central bank's inability to support its financial institutions. The banks named were Amen Bank, Banque de Tunisie, Banque Internationale Arabe de Tunisie and Societe Tunisienne de Banque. President Zine al Abidine Ben Ali (RCD) was re-elected to a fifth consecutive five-year term in office. Two prominent opposition candidates boycotted the elections. In parliamentary elections, the ruling RCD won 84.6 per cent of the vote (161 seats out of 214).
2010 The annual cereal harvest was halved following a drought during the time of sowing. The agricultural ministry said that the country would need to import over two million tonnes to make up the shortfall. In September the UN announced that Tunisia was among one of the few African states to have achieved their Millennium Development Goals. On 17 December, a street vendor, Mohamed Bouazizi immolated himself in the town of Sidi Bouzid (central Tunisia), in protest at having his fruit and scales confiscated by municipal inspectors. The next day, his family berated the town's governor by throwing coins over at the office gate, crying 'here is your bribe' and were joined by other protesters complaining about corruption, nepotism and officials taking bribes. As crowds grew, police reacted by beating protesters and firing tear gas. Extra police were drafted into Sidi Bouzid on 19 December and by 22 December two more protestors had killed themselves. The first demonstrations of solidarity with Sidi Bouzid were held in Tunis on 27 December. Independent trade union activists called on people to demonstrate and about 1,000 people demanded work and an end to corruption and, for the first time, the resignation of President Ben Ali. The president visited Mohamed Bouazizi in hospital. Security forces stopped the demonstration in Tunis as other demonstrations began in provincial cities of Sousse, Sfax and Meknassy. On 31 December lawyers staged protests and were violently assaulted by security forces, causing various degrees of injury.
2011 Steep rises in food prices and widespread unemployment underlined the angry protests as riots broke out on 8–11 January, which were quelled by security forces, at the cost of 21 deaths. Military personnel were deployed in a number of towns nationwide. On 12 January, the interior minister was sacked. A night-time curfew was launched in Tunis, but was largely ignored as the general population joined protestors, concerned by the weak economy and political frustration with the rule of President Ben Ali. In a speech on 13 January the president announced that he would not stand for election again in 2014. On 14 January, while the country was under a state of emergency, President Ben Ali was forced to resign and went into exile in Saudi Arabia. Prime Minister Mohammed Ghannouchi appointed himself acting president, under Article 56 of the constitution. On 15 January, the Constitutional Court declared that Ben Ali had permanently vacated the presidency and Fouad Mebazaa was appointed interim president, under Article 57 of the constitution. Ghannouchi tried to form a government of unity on 17 January that included members of the opposition. On 26 January, international arrest warrants were issued for Ben Ali and his family, accusing them of illegally acquiring property and other assets and removing state funds aboard. By 1 February, the revised figure of numbers killed during the overthrow of former president Ben Ali was at least 219. The Mebazaa administration decided to suspend and close the offices of the RCD on 6 February, before a final decision was taken on the future of the party. On 7 February the lower house of the senate passed legislation to allow President Mebazaa to rule by decree, thereby side-stepping parliament which was still dominated by Ben Ali supporters. A court dissolved the former ruling RCD and thus prevented the party from putting forward any candidates for future elections. Mohammed Ghannouchi resigned as prime minister on 27 February and Béji Caïd Essebsi was appointed in his place. The moderate Islamist political party Ennahda was legalised on 1 March, allowing it to contest presidential and parliamentary elections. On 3 March, President Mebazaa announced that an interim government would stay in power until the constitution could be rewritten. Elections for members for a council of representatives to rewrite the constitution were scheduled for 24 July. By March round 19,000 Tunisians had fled to the Italian island of Lampedusa, overwhelming local resources and immigration procedures, and prompting Italy to call on the EU for increased funds to deal with the influx. Accusations against ex-president Ben Ali, his family and close associates had, by 14 April, grown to include charges of involuntary manslaughter and drug-trafficking. On 9 June the interim government announced a three month delay to elections originally planned for July. The elections were rescheduled for 23 October. Ben Ali was tried *in abstentia* on 20 June; he denied all charges of embezzlement and misuse of state funds but on 21 June he was found guilty and he and his wife were sentenced to 35 years imprisonment and fined US$66 million between them. On 29 June the ex-president, his daughter and son-in-law were also found guilty *in abstentia* of corrupt property dealing and sentenced to 16 years in goal and jointly fined US$100 million. Ben Ali had earlier in the month been convicted on charges of possessing illegal drugs and weapons and sentenced to 15 years imprisonment. The election for a 217-seat Tunisian Constituent Assembly (TCA) (of which 18 members represent expatriate Tunisians in North America and Europe), was held on 23 October, with a mandate to draft a new constitution. However, as the TCA is also a sovereign entity it may set its own timetable for this drafting, it also has the power to appoint a new government or endorse the current administration until a general election is held. The moderate, centre-right, Hizb Ennahda (Nahda) (Renaissance Party) formed a coalition with Al Mu'tamar min ajl il Jumhuriyyah (also known (in French) as Congrès pour la République (CPR)) (Congress of the Republic); At Takattul ad Dimuqrati min ajl il 'Amal wal Hurriyyat (also known (in French) as Forum Démocratique pour le Travail et les Libertés (Ettakatol)) (Democratic Forum for Labour and Liberties) in 19 November. Hamadi Jebali (Nahda) was appointed as prime minister, Moncef Marzouki (CPR) as president and Mustafa Ben Jaafar (Ettakatol) as speaker of the TCA. Interim-Prime Minister Béji Caid Essebsi resigned on 23 November. The constituent assembly endorsed Marzouki as president on 14 December with 153 votes (out of 217) in favour.

Political structure

Constitution

The constitution was introduced in 1959. Parties must be officially recognised before they can contest elections. Legal opposition parties are guaranteed a minimum of 34 seats in the lower chamber of parliament.
Constitutional amendments in 2002, included unlimited terms of office for the president and a age limit of 75 years and gave the president control over voting

procedures and immunity from prosecution for life.
A new second legislative chamber was also agreed.

Independence date
20 March 1956

Form of state
Republic

The executive
Executive power is held by the president, who is also Head of State, elected by universal suffrage for a five-year term. The president sets state policy; he may appoint and dismiss the prime minister. Cabinet members are proposed by the prime minister and endorsed by the president.
The president can serve unlimited terms of office, up to aged 75.

National legislature
The Tunisian Constituent Assembly (TCA) was elected with 217 (of which 18 members represent expatriate Tunisians in North America and Europe), members in October 2011, with a mandate to draft a new constitution. Although the TCA has 12 months to draft a new constitution it also has sovereignty and may set its own timetable. It has the power to appoint a new government or endorse the current administration until a general election is held.

Legal system
The legal system is based on the French civil law system and Islamic law. There is some judicial review of legislative acts in the Supreme Court.

Last elections
23 October 2011 (Tunisian Constituent Assembly (TCA))
Results: TCA: Hizb Ennahda (Nahda) (Renaissance Party) won 38.9 per cent of the vote (90 seats out of 217), Al Mu'tamar min ajl il Jumhuriyyah (also known (in French) as Congrès pour la République (CPR)) (Congress of the Republic) 8.37 per cent (30), At Takattul ad Dimuqrati min ajl il 'Amal wal Hurriyyat (also known (in French) as Forum Démocratique pour le Travail et les Libertés (Ettakatol)) (Democratic Forum for Labour and Liberties) 6.3 per cent (21), Al 'Aridah ash Sha'biyyah lil Hurriyyah wal 'Adalah wat Tanmiyah (also known (in French) as Pétition Populaire pour la Liberté, la Justice et le Développement (Pétition Populaire) (Popular Petition) 6.27 per cent (20), Hizb ad Dimuqrati at Taqaddumi (also known (in French) as Parti Démocrate Progressiste (PDP) (Progressive Democratic Party) 16; seven other political parties won between 2–5 seats, eight other political parties each won one seat and nine independent candidates were elected.

Next elections
To be announced.

Political parties

Ruling party
Coalition led by Mouvement de la Renaissance (Nahda) (Renaissance Party), with Congrès pour la République (CPR) (Congress of the Republic) and Forum Démocratique pour le Travail et les Libertés (Ettakatol) (Democratic Forum for Labour and Liberties)

Population
10.55 million (2010)*
Last census: September 2004: 9,932,400
Population density: 60 inhabitants per square km. Urban population: 65 per cent (2005 census); 20 per cent of the total population lives in Tunis.
Annual growth rate: 1.21 per cent (census 2004)

Ethnic make-up
Arab-Berber (98 per cent), European (1 per cent), other (1 per cent).

Religions
Islam is the state religion – observance is strong (98 per cent); Christianity (1 per cent); Jewish (1 per cent) – there has been a Jewish population on the southern island of Djerba for 2,000 years and there remains a small Jewish population in Tunis which is descended from those who fled Spain in the late fifteenth century.

Education
Education is free up to university level – the government typically spends as much as 20 per cent of its revenues on an extensive education system. Primary education begins aged six, and lasts for six years. Secondary education begins at 12 and lasts seven years. Registration at primary schools is 95 per cent (100 per cent of boys and 89 per cent of girls) – the highest in north Africa and the Middle East. A compulsory schooling period of nine years has been introduced, although some children still leave school at the age of 12, especially in rural areas. A stronger emphasis has been placed on scientific and technical subjects at secondary level.
Literacy rate: 73 per cent adult rate; 94 per cent youth rate (15–24) (Unesco 2005).
Compulsory years: Six to 16.
Pupils per teacher: 24 in primary schools.

Health
State healthcare is provided free of charge to the families of employees paying social security contributions and at least nominal tax. This covers an estimated 70 per cent of the population. Free state healthcare is also available for those with any kind of disability. The discrepancy between urban and rural access to healthcare diminished during the 1990s, with most rural areas having at least basic health clinics.
There is a well-developed private healthcare sector, with private clinics in towns providing substantially better facilities than state hospitals. Many healthcare professionals have carried out at least part of their training abroad, mostly in France.

HIV/Aids
HIV prevalence: 0.1 per cent aged 15–49 in 2003 (World Bank)
Life expectancy: 72 years, 2004 (WHO 2006)
Fertility rate/Maternal mortality rate: 1.9 births per woman, 2004 (WHO 2006)
Child (under 5 years) mortality rate (per 1,000): 19 per 1,000 live births; 4 per cent of children under aged five are malnourished (World Bank).
Head of population per physician: 1.34 physicians per 1,000 people, 2004 (WHO 2006)

Welfare
The social security system provides pensions for the elderly and disabled, and welfare for orphans and the needy. A total of 945,500 employees, or 47.7 per cent of the workforce, are insured under the social security system. The scheme is financed by compulsory levies from employers and employees. There are no contributions from the state budget. The main social security institution is the Caisse Nationale de la Sécurité Sociale (CNSS) (National Social Security Organisation), which deals with about 45 per cent of outlay.
There is a graded scheme for contributions. The non-agricultural private sector pays most as a proportion of the employee's salary: 11.5 per cent paid by the employer and 6.25 per cent by the employee. In the public sector, where contributions are made to the Caisse Nationale de Retraite et de Prévoyance Sociale (CNRPS) (National Pension Fund), the employer pays 8 per cent and the employee 7 per cent. State pensions are paid to CNSS and CNRPS contributors.

Main cities
Tunis (capital, estimated population 767,564 in 2005), Sfax (229,622), Ariana (243,152), Ettadhamen (165,973), Sousse (192,008), Kairouan (149,122).

Languages spoken
French is the business language. The number of Tunisians speaking English is increasing.

Official language/s
Arabic

Media

The government maintains control of all media reporting by and encourages widespread self-censorship, with fines and imprisonment as ultimate sanctions.

Press

The government uses mandatory pre-screening and controls the advertising revenue to censor 'unacceptable' publications. While the constitution guarantees freedom of expression, the Press Code gives allows wide-ranging powers to ban publications.

There are several independent newspapers and magazines, including two opposition party journals.

Dailies: In Arabic, *Al Horria* (www.tunisieinfo.com/alhorria), published by the RCD political party, *Assabah* (www.assabah.com.tn) and *Essahafa* (www.essahafa.info.tn). Publications from Tunis include *Al Chourouk* (www.alchourouk.com) and *el Wahda* (www.elwahda.org.tn).

In French, *La Presse* (www.lapresse.tn), published by the RCD political party, *Le Renouveau* (www.tunisieinfo.com/LeRenouveau).

Weeklies: In French, *Réalités* (www.realites.com.tn) and *L'Observateur* and *L'Avenir*. In Arabic, *Ar Rai* and *Al Moustaqbal*. Others are *Dialogue*, *Al Tariq al Jadid* and *Al Mauqif*. In English, *Tunisia News* is published in the Maghreb, on Saturdays.

Business: *L'Economiste Maghrebin* (www.leconomiste.com.tn), is published bi-monthly.

Periodicals: There are many magazines published in Arabic, French and one in Italian.

Broadcasting

Radio: Tunisian Radio (www.radiotunis.com), with four stations covering, news, youth, culture and live transmissions. Other private, commercial stations include Radio Mosaique FM (www.mosaiquefm.net), Jawhara FM (www.jawharafm.net) and the religious station Ezzitouna Radio.

Television: La Télévision Tunisienne (http://tunisiatv.com) is the national, state-run TV with two channels, Tunis 7 and Canal 21. The other domestic channel is Hannibal TV (www.hannibaltv.com.tn), with a wide variety of programmes. Pan-Arab channels are readily received.

News agencies

National news agency: Tunisian News Agency (TAP) (in Arabic, French and English)

Economy

The geography of Tunisia has an important influence on its economy. In the southern half of the country desert conditions limit production, while the fertile northern region is heavily populated, with tourism a major source of foreign exchange which influences development decisions. The service sector dominates the economy, constituting around 60 per cent of GDP; industry and manufacturing accounts for over 30 per cent of GDP and agriculture the remainder. From its oil reserves of 600,000 barrels, production in 2009 was 86,000 barrels per day (bpd) (down from a high of 97,000bpd in 2007 when the global price for oil was at a record high). Other industries include mining, (iron ore, phosphates and salt) and manufacturing, of among others items, food processing, clothing and textiles, fabricated and finished products, parts and materials, chemicals, ceramics, glass and crystal, plastics and paper. Tunisia is self-sufficient in seafood, crops, dairy and meat, of which beef and lamb dominates, and it is a leading producer of olive oil, dates and potatoes, as well as other fruits, grains and livestock and seafood, most of which are exported.

GDP growth was 4.5 per cent in 2008, as oil reached an all time high, before falling to 3.1 per cent in 2009 as the global economic crisis cut trade. However, growth began to increase in 2010, to 2.8 per cent, as trade picked up. Remittances in 2009 were US$1.97 billion (5.3 per cent of GDP), but were estimated to have fallen to US$1.96 billion in 2010.

As long-term production in oil and gas has fallen the government has attempted to diversify the economy further, into other industries and an expanded manufacturing base, with a programme to enhance productivity in preparation for global competition. Although agriculture has fallen in its primary significance to the economy it nevertheless employs just under a quarter of the labour force.

The Islamic Development Bank (IDB) and the World Bank announced in October 2010, that they were setting up a regional initiative of up to US$1 billion to help close the infrastructure gap in the Middle East and North Africa (Mena) and help boost economic growth. The World Bank considers that the Mena region requires US$75–100 billion per year to sustain the growth of recent years and boost economic competitiveness. However private sector investment is limited and the new initiative should address the shortfall in investment through Sharia-compliant and conventional investment. The initiative should benefit Egypt, Morocco, Jordan and Tunisia in particular.

Tunisia is a country where 55 per cent of the population is aged less than 25 and where a growing work force has led to an official unemployment rate of around 14 per cent; however with high underemployment this rate may not reflect the true nature of the jobless market. Tunisia has had a closed economy which severely restricted foreign investment and domestic private enterprise. It was the lack of opportunity and corruption that led to the revolution that toppled the Ben Ali regime in January 2011 and Tunisia will not only have to address its underlying economic weaknesses and develop its future direction through reformation but also contend with its foreign debt rating being cut from Baa2 to Baa3 by the international credit ratings agency Moody's on 19 January 2011, following the political strife.

External trade

In 2005 the Greater Arab Free Trade Area (Gafta) was ratified by 17 members, including Tunisia, creating an Arab economic bloc. A customs union was established whereby tariffs within Gafta will be reduced by a percentage each year, until none remain. It is also a signatory of the Euro-Mediterranean Partnership agreement, which provides for the introduction of free trade between the EU and 10 Mediterranean countries by 2012.

Despite natural resources including oil, natural gas, phosphate (of which Tunisia is the world's largest producer) and iron, foreign earnings are dominated by agriculture and tourism.

Imports

Main imports are raw cotton, machinery and electronic equipment, vehicles and hydrocarbons.

Main sources: France (typically 20 per cent of total), Italy (16 per cent), Germany (9 per cent).

Exports

Main export commodities are foodstuffs, textiles, clothing and footwear, steelwork, phosphate, iron ore, manufactured and leather goods, agricultural products, chemicals and hydrocarbons.

Main destinations: France (typically 30 per cent of total), Italy (21 per cent), Germany (9 per cent).

Agriculture

Farming

The government sees agriculture as a principal growth sector, however it is heavily influenced by the climate and rainfall. The principal area of cultivation is in north, along the Mediterranean coast, where ancient oil groves are still located. Major projects to augment irrigation are underway, with a new dam and reservoir supplying the north-east region and waterways being installed. In the desert south, oasis crops of dates are famous and exported throughout the region and Europe. In the central area rainfall directly affects crop production as a wet year will

produce a good harvest; conversely, a dry year risks desertification.
The agricultural investment code offers tax and other financial advantages, while the Agence de Promotion des Investissements Agricoles (APIA) (Agency for the Promotion of Agricultural Investment) channels investment into agriculture. The Banque Nationale Agricole (BNA) provides medium- and long-term credit for agricultural development projects. Since all suitable land is already being farmed, government policy centres on improving yields through new farming techniques and making the most of water resources. Rural depopulation, an inequitable land tenure system, drought, soil erosion, overgrazing and low producer prices remain the major constraints to development.
The country's 55 million olive trees occupy one-third of all arable land and olive oil, at over 70 per cent of production it is the most important agricultural export. Tunisia is the world's fourth, after Italy, Spain, Greece, largest exporter. In 2003 the harvest was 1.2 million tonnes about four times the typical annual yeald. Other main products from the sector are flour, sugar, tomato paste, milk, wine and animal feed.
The recent growth in organic food has encouraged over 240 operations, which have attracted international certification accredited to the EU, producing among others, olive oil and dates.

Fishing

Most seafood production is for domestic consumption and the sector is relatively undeveloped, with extensive small-scale fishing using more traditional methods. The coastal areas around Sfax and the Kerkennah Islands, where the sea is very shallow, are well-known locally for their fishing industry. Total seafood production is typically around 80,000 tonnes, with some 20 per cent of this exported. Catches typically include sardines, pilchards, tuna and whitefish. However, tuna fishing is diminishing as Mediterranean stocks decline.

Forestry

An arid climate, a fast-growing population and animal herds have put Tunisia's already limited woodland areas at serious risk. However efforts to reverse the trend have increased forests by 0.2 per cent or 1,000 hectares.
The oak forests of the country's north provide timber and cork.

Industry and manufacturing

The industrial sector is based primarily on processing domestic raw materials, notably phosphates and agricultural commodities, and textiles, including clothing and leather products. An industrial restructuring programme launched in the mid-1990s has seen high levels of public investment in upgrading businesses' competitiveness in preparation for the liberalisation of markets and European competition. The present strategy is to target specific types of products where relatively cheap labour, proximity to Europe and government incentives can combine to give Tunisia a price and quality advantage over other exporters. The programme has been particularly successful among small- and medium-sized enterprises (SMEs).

Tourism

The tourism sector accounts for around 10 per cent of GDP. One of the country's highest net earners of foreign exchange, it has been an increasingly important source of employment. Over 80 per cent of visitors come from EU countries.
Tunisia is a member of the Euromed Heritage Programme, a computerisation project, sponsored by the EU, which focusses on cultural tourists of archaeology, arts and history, promoting sites through the internet.
The country has a wealth of archaeological sites, traditional habitats and sandy beaches to provide destinations to cater for the wishes of many different holidaymakers.

Mining

The mining sector contributes 3 per cent of GDP and employs 4 per cent of the working population. Tunisia is the world's fifth-largest source of phosphates although the quality of the rock mined is poor. Extraction (largely in Metlaoui and Gafsa) is geared increasingly towards local phosphate processing rather than exporting it in a raw state. Other important minerals mined include iron ore, salt, fluorspar, barytes, lead, zinc, potash and uranium. Foreign investment is being sought by the government for the mining industry.

Hydrocarbons

Total oil reserves stood at 400 million barrels in 2008, with production at 86,930 barrels per day (bpd); consumption was 90,000bpd and Tunisia had to import 3,000bpd to meet its domestic demand. Most of the country's oil deposits are located offshore in the Gulf of Gabés. There is one refinery at Bizerte, with a small capacity of 34,000bpd. The state-owned Societe Tunisienne des Industries de Raffinage (STIR) is overseeing plans for a new 120,000bpd joint Tunisian-Libyan oil refinery, sited in the east at La Skhira.
To replace declining oil reserves, the government is promoting the natural gas sector; local production typically meets 80 per cent of domestic demand.
Proved natural gas reserves were 65 billion cubic metres in 2008. There is a network of pipelines transporting natural gas from fields offshore and in the southwest as well as a number of planned international natural gas pipelines transiting Tunisia from Algeria and Libya, to supply natural gas to Europe via the Transmed pipeline to Italy.
Tunisia does not produce coal but imports around 112,000 tonnes per annum of coke.

Energy

Total installed generating capacity was 3.3GW in 2007. The state-owned electricity and gas company, Société Tunisienne de l'Electricité et du Gaz (STEG) no longer has a monopoly on power generation, although the company retains its monopoly on distribution. Demand for electricity is growing by 7 per cent per annum; around 95 per cent of homes have access to electricity. The government intends to add around 300MW of generating capacity every 2–3 years.

Financial markets

Stock exchange

Bourse de Tunis (Tunis Stock Exchange)

Banking and insurance

Tunisia aims to become the regional financial centre and is keen to build on its status as an economy with investment grade status. However, the banking sector is overcrowded, plagued by bad debts and dominated by the public sector.
The government is determined to rationalise the sector and the government has engaged in a modernisation programme, including privatisation and mergers in a process of consolidation in the sector. The capital base of many banks has improved with the injection of government funds into state-owned banks and the restructuring of non-performing loans.
By June 2010, the Kuwaiti-owned Burgan Bank had completed the purchase of Tunis International Bank from the United Gulf Bank as part of its regional expansion strategy. The US$725 million purchase will allow the Burgan Bank access to other North African markets, to offer specifically investment banking and asset management.

Central bank

Banque Centrale de Tunisie

Main financial centre

Tunis

Time

GMT plus one hour

Geography

Tunisia is in North Africa, between Algeria to its west and Libya to its south-east. The north and eastern borders are a long, 1,148km Mediterranean coastline. It has two islands off its eastern coast, the larger

of which, Ile de Jerba, is connected to the mainland by a 6km causeway, and is the location of Tunisia largest international airport. The other is the island chain of the Iles des Kerkennah.
The mainland has three distinct regions from the fertile north where most of the agricultural crops are grown, and where the Atlas mountains run down to the sea. The middle section is semi-arid desert that is wholly dependent on rainfall for its agricultural produce; the Sahara Desert occupies the southern region, and is largely unproductive. There are no major rivers, irrigation is supplied through rainwater dams and bore-holes.

Hemisphere
Northern

Climate
The northern coastal area has a Mediterranean climate with warm, rainy winters (December–March) and hot summers. The southern and inland area is hot and arid. Temperatures in Tunis range from 6–14 degrees Celsius (C) in January to 21–33 degrees C in August. The wettest month is January and the driest is July.

Dress codes
Formal attire should be worn for business meetings. Women should wear clothes that cover most of the body, including shoulders and legs. In the countryside, western dress and customs are rare and dress should be modest.

Entry requirements
Passports
Required by all, and must be valid for at least six months beyond date of visit.
Visa
Required by all; some exceptions, for visits up to three months, include citizens of US, EU, certain Arab, and many Commonwealth countries. A full list of exceptions can be found at www.tunisia.or.jp/ (see under visas). Business travellers from these countries may visit as a tourist without further reference. Those visitors, both business and tourist, not included on the list should contact the nearest Tunisian consulate for information and visa application form at least three weeks before departure.
Currency advice/regulations
Local currency may not be imported or exported; there are no restrictions on the import of foreign currency. However, the re-export of foreign cash is limited to the amount imported, and the re-conversion of dinars into foreign exchange may not exceed 30 per cent of any foreign currency converted during the visit, or D100, whichever is the greater. Therefore all currency forms should be retained.
Traveller's cheques are widely accepted, and preferably made up of sterling, euros or US dollars.
Customs
Personal items are duty-free and gifts to the value of D100 are allowed.
Antiques require an exit permit.
Prohibited imports
Firearms (except for hunting), explosives, narcotics, immoral or obscene publications, walkie-talkies and material deemed subversive.

Health (for visitors)
Mandatory precautions
Yellow fever vaccination certificate required if arriving from an infected area.
Advisable precautions
Immunisation is recommended against diphtheria, hepatitis, polio, tetanus and typhoid. Rabies is present. Water precautions should be taken outside main towns: boil tap water or drink mineral water and wash fresh foods carefully.

Hotels
Classified into five categories; a government hotel tax is added to the bill. Hotel and restaurant staff expect 10 per cent tip.

Credit cards
Major credit and charge cards are widely accepted. ATMs are common in town centres.

Public holidays (national)
Fixed dates
1 Jan (New Year's Day), 20 Mar (Independence Day), 21 Mar (Youth Day), 9 Apr (Martyrs' Day), 1 May (Labour Day), 25 Jul (Republic Day), 13 Aug (Women's Day), 7 Nov (New Era Day/Accession of President Ben Ali).
Many businesses close during July/August.
Variable dates
Eid al Adha (*Tabaski*, two days), Islamic New Year, Birth of the Prophet, Eid al Fitr (*Korité*, two days).
Islamic year 1433 (26 Nov 2011–14 Nov 2012): The Islamic year contains 354 or 355 days, with the result that Muslim feasts advance by 10–12 days against the Gregorian calendar. Dates of feasts vary according to the sighting of the new moon, so canno be forecast exactly.

Working hours
The weekly day of rest is Sunday, not Friday as is usual in the Muslim world. Tunis is virtually closed down during August.
Banking
Mon–Fri (summer): 0730–1130; Mon–Thu (winter): 0800–1100 and 1400–1615, Fri (winter): 0800–1100 and 1300–1600.
Business
Mon–Sat (summer): 0830–1300; Mon–Fri (winter): 0830–1300, 1500–1745.
Government
Mon–Sat (summer): 0830–1300; Mon–Fri (winter): 0830–1300, 1500–1745.
Government offices' opening hours may vary by half an hour.
Shops
Mon–Sat (summer): 0800–1200 and 1600–1900; Mon–Sat (winter): 0900–1300 and 1500–1900.

Telecommunications
Mobile/cell phones
There are 900 GSM services available, with coverage throughout the inhabited part of the country.

Electricity supply
220V AC, with round two-pin plugs.

Social customs/useful tips
The legacy of French rule is considerable in the towns and a rather formal attitude to courtesy prevails. Senior government or company officials should be addressed as *Monsieur* and government ministers as *Monsieur le Ministre*. It is customary to shake hands on meeting and taking leave. Business cards are exchanged after introduction.
Personal relationships are important in business, and time is usually spent in light conversation, over tea or coffee, before embarking on business matters. Regular visits and personal contact are vital in order to establish a relationship of confidence with agents and customers in Tunisia.
Hospitality is important. It is appropriate to present a small gift in appreciation of hospitality.
Islam affects society at every level. A statute passed in the first year of independence enforced equality of the sexes. Nevertheless, gatherings of men and women are usually separate, the sexes are separated in mosques, and only men may enter a cemetery to attend a funeral.
Alcohol is freely available in towns, although less common in rural areas. Strict Muslims will not drink alcohol, but many Tunisian men do, and it is acceptable for non-Muslim visitors to do so. The minimum drinking age is 21 years.
Mint tea or fresh lemon or orange juice are typical non-alcoholic drinks. It is polite to accept a drink when offered.
During Ramadan visitors are advised not to eat, drink or smoke in public during daylight hours.

Getting there
Air
National airline: Tunisair.
International airport/s: The two largest are Tunis-Carthage (TUN), 8km from the city, with flights by national airlines; travel time to the city is 15–30 minutes and Monastir (MIR) 9km from the city, accepting charter flights. Facilities in both include duty-free shopping, bank, restaurant and car hire.

Smaller airports for regional flights include Djerba-Zarzis (DJE), 9km from Houmek Souk; Sfax-el Maou (SFA), 7km west of city; Tozeur-Nefta (TOE), 10km from city; Tabarka (TBJ), 8km from city. All have duty-free shops and bus and taxi services.

Airport tax: None

Surface

Road: Access is possible by road from Algeria and Libya.

Rail: Access by rail from Algeria.

Water: Passenger traffic comes mostly to Tunis-La Goulette. Regular passenger ferry services operate between Tunis and France, Italy and Malta.

Main port/s: Tunis-La Goulette, Sfax, Bizerte, Gabes, Sousse and Zarzis; of which Tunis-Goulette and Sfax are the largest.

Getting about

National transport

Air: Tuninter operates regular domestic services linking Tunis with Djerba, Monastir, Tozeur and Sfax. The air taxi company, Tunisavia, operates executive flights, from Tunis, throughout the country.

Road: The road network extends for around 19,000km, of which main national roads account for 10,800km. About 57 per cent of the network is paved. There is a 143km motorway between Tunis and Sousse.

Buses: Extensive long-distance services connect all major towns and cities.

Taxis: Long distance taxis (*louages*) operate between all main towns; these are considered the fastest method of road transport.

Rail: A 2,200km network links the main towns. There are two classes, some with air-conditioned, first-class accommodation. It is recommended purchasing a ticket in advance; those purchased onboard may be charged at a much higher price. It is an advantage to book in advance especially for air-conditioned trains.

Water: There are regular ferries from Sfax-Iles Kerkenna and Djerba island.

City transport

Taxis: Taxis are available in all main towns and are fairly easy to obtain. *Louage* taxis have fares shared by several passengers. Taxis are metered, a surcharge is added at night.

Buses, trams & metro: The Société Nationale de Transports operates local buses with extensive services operating in all main towns.

The SMLT light-rail metro that runs four lines through Tunis has a focal point for all at Place de la République and connects to national and suburban lines.

Car hire

Cars are easy to hire at airports and hotels but are expensive and the condition of the cars vary. Roads are being improved but local driving is erratic. International driving permit required if national driving licence doesn't include a photograph. Traffic drives on the right; speed limits are 110kph on major highways and 50kph in towns. Permission must be obtained to drive in Saharan areas.

BUSINESS DIRECTORY

The addresses listed below are a selection only. While World of Information makes every endeavour to check these addresses, we cannot guarantee that changes have not been made, especially to telephone numbers and area codes. We would welcome any corrections.

Telephone area codes

The international direct dialling (IDD) code for Tunisia is +216 followed by subscriber's number.

Chambers of Commerce

American-Tunisian Chamber of Commerce and Industry, 10 Avenue Mosbah Jarbou, Rue 7116, El Manar 3, 2092 Tunis (tel: 7188-9780; fax: 7188-9880; e-mail: tacc@tacc.org.tn).

British-Tunisian Chamber of Commerce and Industry, 23 Rue de Jérusalem, 1002 Tunis (tel: 7180-2284; fax: 7180-1535; e-mail: tbcci@gnet.tn).

Cap Bon Chambre de Commerce et d'Industrie, 3 Rue de Fel, Cité Néapolis, PO Box 113, 8000 Nabeul (tel: 7228-7260; fax: 7228-7417; e-mail: cci.capbon@planet.tn).

Central Chambre de Commerce et d'Industrie, Rue Chédly Khaznadar, 4000 Sousse (7322-5044; fax: 7322-4227; e-mail: ccis.sousse@planet.tn).

French-Tunisian Chambre de Commerce et d'Industrie, 39 Rue 8301, 1002 Tunis (tel: 7184-4310; fax: 7184-5962; e-mail: ctfci@planet.tn).

North-Eastern Chambre de Commerce et d'Industrie, 46 Rue Ibn Khaldoun, 7000 Bizerte (tel: 7243-1044; fax: 7243-2379; e-mail: ccine.biz@gnet.tn).

North-Western Chambre de Commerce et d'Industrie, Hedi Chaker Street, 9000 Beja (tel: 7845-6261; fax: 7845-5789; e-mail: ccino.beja@gnet.tn).

Sfar Chambre de Commerce et d'Industrie, 10 Rue Tahar Sfar, PO Box794, 3018 Sfax (tel: 7429-6120; fax: 7429-6121; e-mail:ccis@planet.tn).

South-Eastern Chambre de Commerce et d'Industrie, 202 Avenue Farhat Hached, 6000 Gabes (tel: 7527-4900; fax: 7527-4688; e-mail: csise@gnet.tn).

South-Western Chambre de Commerce et d'Industrie, Rue des Roses, PO Box 46, 2100 Gafsa (tel: 7622-6650; fax: 7622-4150; e-mail: cciso@planet.tn).

Tunis Chambre de Commerce, 1 Rue des Entrepreneurs, 1000 Tunis (tel: 7135-0300; fax:7135-4744; e-mail: ccitunis@planet.tn).

Banking

Alubaf International Bank – Tunis, PO Box 51, Rue 8007 Montplaisir, 1002 Tunis (tel: 7178-3500 fax: 7179-3905, 7178-4343).

Amen Bank, Avenue Mohamed V, 1002 Tunis (tel: 7134-0511; fax: 7134-9909).

Banque Arabe Tuniso–Libyenne de Développment et de Commerce Extérieur, PO Box 102, 25 Avenue Kheireddine Pacha, 1002 Tunis (tel: 7178-1500; fax: 7178-2818).

Banque du Sud, 95 Avenue de la Liberté, 1002 Tunis (tel: 7184-9400, 7179-2400; fax: 7178-2663).

Banque Internationale Arabe de Tunisie SA, PO Box 520, 70-72 Avenue Habib Bourguiba, 1080 Tunis Cedex (tel: 7134-0722/0733, 7125-2655, ; fax: 7134-0680, 7134-7648).

Banque Nationale Agricole, Rue Hedi Nouira, 1001 Tunis (tel: 7183-1000/1200; fax: 7183-5388, 7183-2807).

Société Tunisienne de Banque SA, Rue Hedi Nouira, 1001 Tunis (tel: 7134-0477, 7125-8000; fax: 7134-0009, 7134-8400, 7134-0446).

Tunis International Bank, PO Box 81, 18 Avenue des Etats Unis D'Amerique, 1002 Tunis (tel: 7178-2411; fax: 7178-9970).

Central bank

Banque Centrale de Tunisie, 25 Rue Hédi Nouira, PO Box 777, 1080 Tunis (tel: 7134-0588; fax: 7134-0615; e-mail: boc@bct.gov.tn).

Stock exchange

Bourse de Tunis (Tunis Stock Exchange): www.bvmt.com.tn

Travel information

Tunisair, Customer Service Unit, Boulevard du 7 Novembre 1987, 2035 L'Ariana, Tunis (tel: 7083-7000 ext: 2572/2510; fax: 7083-6839; reservations tel: 7194-1285; email: resaonline@tunisair.com.tn; internet: www.tunisair.com).

Tunisian Airports Office, Ministère des Technologies de la Communication et du Transport, Direction Générale de l'Aviation Civile, 13 Rue 8006 Montplaisir, 1002 Tunis (tel: 7179-4424; fax: 7179-4227).

Tunisavia, Boulvard de l'Environnement 2035, Aéroport Tunis-Carthage, Tunis (tel: 7128-0555, 7128-0521; email:

siege@tunisavia.com.tn; internet: www.tunisavia.com.tn).

National tourist organisation offices
Tunisian National Tourism Office (ONTT), 1 Ave Mohamed V, 1001Tunis (tel: 7134-1077; fax: 7135-0997; email: info@tourismtunisia.com; internet: www.tourismtunisia.com).

Ministries
Ministry of Agriculture, 30 rue Alain Savery, 1002 Tunis Belvedere (tel: 7128-7133).

Ministry of Communication Technologies, Cabinet de Monsieur le Ministre, 3 bis, rue d'Angleterre, 1000 Tunis.

Ministry of Communications, Belvedere du 9 Avril 1938, 1030 Tunis (tel: 7133-6409; fax: 7135-4628).

Ministry of Economic Development, Direction Générale de la Privatisation, Place Ali Zouaoui, 1000 Tunis (tel: 7135-4467; fax: 7135-0975).

Ministry of Defence, 1008 Montfleury, Tunis (tel: 7156-0244).

Ministry of Education, Boulevard Bab Bnat, Tunis (tel: 71263850; fax: 7156-9307).

Ministry of Equipment and Housing, Av H Cherita –Cite Jardin, 1002 Tunis (tel: 7168-1802).

Ministry of Higher Education, 28 rue de Sousse, 1030 Tunis (tel: 7178-2947).

Ministry of Public Health, Bab Saadoun, Tunis (tel: 7126-0727).

Ministry of Vocational Training and Employment, 21 rue de Lybie – Lafayette, 1002 Tunis (tel: 7178-2432).

Other useful addresses
Agence de Promotion de L'Industrie, 63 rue de Syrie, 1002 Tunis-Belvédère (tel: 7179-2144; fax: 7178-2482).

Agricultural Investment Promotion Agency, 62 rue Alain Savary, 1003 Tunis Khadra, Tunis (tel: 7128-8400, 7128-8091; fax: 7178-2353).

American Embassy, Zone Nord-Est des Berges du Lac, Nord de Tunis, 2045, La Goulette, Tunisia (tel: 7110-7000; fax: 7196-2115).

American Express, c/o Carthage Tours, 59 avenue Habib Bourguiba, 1001 Tunis (tel: 7125-4304; fax: 7135-2740).

Arab League, avenue Khéreddine Pacha, Tunis.

British Embassy, 5 Place de la Victoire, 1000 Tunis (tel: 7124-5100, 7124-5324, 7134-1444; fax: 7135-1487; email: britishemb@planet.tn; internet: www.british-emb.intl.tn).

Central Post Office, rue Charles de Gaulle, Tunis.

CEPEX (agency for promotion of Tunisian exports), 28 rue v Gandhi, 1001 Tunis (tel: 7135-0043, 7135-0801; fax: 7135-3683; email: cepexedpuc@attmail.com).

Entreprise Tunisienne D'Activités Petrolières, 27 avenue Khéreddine Pacha, 1002 Tunis (tel: 7178-2288).

Export Promotion Centre, 28 rue Ghandi, 1001 Tunis (tel: 7135-0344; fax: 7135-3683).

Industrial Land Agency, 2 rue Badii Ezzamen, Cité Mahrajéne, 1002 Tunis-Belvédère, El Menza I (tel: 7179-7360, 7180-0616; fax: 7178-2303).

Institut National de Statistique, 27 rue de Liban, Tunis (tel: 7128-2500).

Maghreb Permanent Consultative Committee, 14 rue Yahia ibn Omar, Mutuelleville, Tunis.

National Sanitation Office, 32 rue Hedi Nouira, Tunis (tel: 7170-4000).

National Water Distribution Company, 67 rue Jawarhel ehru, Montfleury (tel: 7149-3700; fax: 7139-0561).

Office du Commerce de Tunisie, avenue Mohammed V, 1002 Tunis (tel: 7128-8673, 7128-8864, 7168-2903; fax: 7178-8974, 7178-4974).

Prime Ministry, Privatisation General Directorate, 4 Rue ibn Nadim Montplaisir, 1002 Tunis (tel: 7128-2467; fax: 7128-1675).

Tunisian Chemical Group, 5–7 rue Khartoum, 1002 Tunis (tel: 7178-4488).

Tunisian Electricity and Gas Company, 38 rue Kemal Ataturk, Tunis (tel: 7134-1311; fax: 7134-9981).

Tunisian Embassy (USA), 1515 Massachusetts Avenue, NW, Washington DC 20005, USA (tel: (+1-202) 862-1850; fax: (+1-202) 862-1858).

Tunisian External Communication Agency, 2 rue d'Algérie, 1001 Tunis (tel: 7165-1999, 7135-0202; fax: 7134-1902).

Union Tunisienne de l'Industrie, du Commerce et de l'Artisanat, 32 rue Charles de Gaulle, Tunis (tel: 7124-3711).

National news agency: Tunisian News Agency (TAP) (in Arabic, French and English): (tel: 7187-0657; fax: 7188-8999; email: desk.national@email.ati.tn; internet: www.tap.info.tn).

Internet sites
Information on Tunisia: www.tunisiaonline.com

www.investintunisia.tn

www.tunisie.com

Africa Business Network: www.ifc.org/abn

AllAfrica.com: http://allafrica.com

African Development Bank: www.afdb.org

Mbendi AfroPaedia (information on companies, countries, industries and stock exchanges in Africa): http://mbendi.co.za

Radio Tunisia: www.radiotunis.com

Turkey

KEY FACTS

Official name: Türkiye Cumhuriyeti (Republic of Turkey)

Head of State: President Abdullah Gül (from 28 Aug 2007)

Head of government: Prime Minister Recep Tayyip Erdogan (AKP) (from 2003; re-elected 12 Jun 2011)

Ruling party: Adalet ve Kalkinma Partisi (AKP) (Justice and Development Party) (elected 2002; re-elected 12 Jun 2011)

Area: 779,452 square km

Population: 72.70 million (2010)*

Capital: Ankara

Official language: Turkish

Currency: Yeni Turk Lirasi (New Turkish Lira) (YTL) = 100 kurus

Exchange rate: YTL1.86 per US$ (Oct 2011)

GDP per capita: US$10,399 (2010)

GDP real growth: 8.20% (2010)

GDP: US$741.90 billion (2010)

Labour force: 25.66 million (2010)

Unemployment: 11.90% (2010)

Inflation: 8.60% (2010)

Balance of trade: -US$56.45 billion (2010)

* estimated figure

The end of July 2011 saw a sea-change in Turkish politics with the resignation of the country's army commander and the heads of the navy, army and air force. Turkey's military was seen by many Turks as the last bastion of the secular values introduced by Kemal Mustafa Atatürk. Other Turks saw the resignations as the final establishment of civilian rule, the defeat of the army representing a victory for the rule of law. It was certainly a victory for the three components of Prime Minister Erdogan's support, the conservative bourgeois middle class, the formerly disenfranchised and Turkey's fast growing class of 'nouveaux riches'. Mr Erdogan's Anatolian background had helped him to win the support of a Turkish hinterland long neglected by the country's politicians.

Foreign policy

Mr Erdogan's period in office has seen Turkey's foreign policy swing away from a preoccupation with Europe, towards a closer alignment with the Middle East. This was intertwined with a distancing from both Israel and the US. In the case of Syria, Turkey's position is less than straightforward. Turkey, a member of the North Atlantic Treaty Organisation (NATO), is the joker in the pack. By the end of 2011 Ankara seemed to have found itself, perhaps unwillingly and certainly surprisingly, to have assumed the role of Sunni leadership, in the face of Shi'ite heretics, mostly from Iran (but also Iraq, Alawis in Syria and Hezbollah).

European?

Turkey became a European Union (EU) membership candidate country as long ago as 1999 and soon afterwards began to introduce quite far-reaching (by Turkish standards) human rights and economic reforms. The death penalty was abolished, tougher measures were brought in against torture and the penal code was overhauled. Reforms were also introduced in the areas of women's rights and Kurdish (see 'Kurds' below) culture, language, education and broadcasting. Women's rights activists claimed that the reforms do not go far enough and have accused the government of lacking commitment to equality and of simply responding to EU pressure.

After some bargaining, EU membership talks were launched in October 2005. Accession negotiations are expected to take about 10 years. However, progress has been patchy. To start with, Turkey has historically been at odds with its neighbour, Greece, over the divided (since a Turkish invasion in 1974) island of Cyprus and numerous territorial disputes in the Aegean.

The breakthrough in its EU membership talks came shortly after Turkey agreed to recognise Cyprus as an EU member – though it qualified this conciliatory step by declaring that it was not tantamount to full diplomatic recognition. Several European countries continue to have serious misgivings over Turkey's EU membership, notably Germany and France, which seemingly backtracking, have called for Turkey to enter into a so called 'privileged partnership' with the EU instead of enjoying the full membership that had originally been on the table.

In contrast, British prime minister, David Cameron, promised to 'fight' for Turkey's membership of the European Union, saying (in an obvious attack on the Franco-German position) that he was 'angry' at the slow pace of negotiations. In contrast to the vacillation coming from Berlin and Paris, on his first visit to Turkey as prime minister, Cameron said the country could become a 'great European power', helping build links with the Middle East. He also compared hostility to the membership bid in some parts of the EU with the way the UK's entry was once regarded. Mr Cameron suggested the UK would impose provisional restrictions – as with Bulgarians and Romanians after they joined – on the right of Turkish people to live and work in the UK after it joined the EU. But he considered that the rapid rate of Turkey's economic growth would make any restrictions unnecessary in future. Mr Cameron noted how much Turkey had done to defend Europe as a NATO ally and what Turkey was doing in Afghanistan. He expressed frustration that Turkish progress towards EU membership could be frustrated in the way it has been. Mr Cameron added that his view was clear: 'I believe it is just wrong to say that Turkey can guard the camp but not be allowed to sit in the tent.' Under the NATO aegis, Ankara allows the deployment of missile defense systems in its territory, directed not only against Iran but also against Russia.

Turkey, with some justification, had long seen itself as a key member of the North Atlantic Treaty Organisation (NATO) alliance, a role buttressed by its close ties with Israel, but in recent years a distinct chill has crept into Turkish-Israeli relations and since the attacks, in 2010, on a peace flotilla that had sailed from Turkey to Gaza which resulted in 22 Turkish casualties, has been devoting some diplomatic effort to developing better relations with Arab countries.

The Kurds

Turkey is home to a sizeable Kurdish minority, which some estimates put at one fifth of the total population. The Kurds had long complained that the Turkish government was trying to destroy their identity and that they suffered from economic disadvantage and human rights violations. The Kurdistan Workers Party (PKK), the best known and most radical of the Kurdish movements, launched a guerrilla campaign in 1984 claiming an ethnic homeland in the Kurdish heartland in the south-east. Thousands died and hundreds of thousands became refugees in the ensuing conflict with the PKK, which Turkey, the US and the European Union consider to be a terrorist organisation. The Kurdish guerrilla attacks briefly subsided after the high profile 1999 capture of PKK leader Abdullah Ocalan, but soon began to increase again.

Partly in a bid to improve its chances of EU membership, the government began to ease restrictions on the use of the Kurdish language form 2003 onwards. As part of a new 'Kurdish initiative' launched in 2009, Turkey pledged to extend linguistic and cultural rights and to reduce the military presence in the mainly Kurdish south-east. Despite this, fighting continued. A PKK offer in July 2010 to consider a truce if the government were to extend Kurdish civil rights was met with an unfathomable official refusal to respond to what it called 'terrorist' statements.

The economy

The austerity measures drawn up as part of the tough recovery programme agreed with the International Monetary Fund (IMF) in 2002 stood Turkey in good stead when the global financial crisis came round in 2008. Turkey found itself in a better position to weather the storm than many other countries. The level of public debt was already relatively low and although the effects of the recession were still felt, by 2010 the Turkish economy had started to bounce back – to the extent that by the beginning of 2011 concerns were being raised over whether the boom was sustainable.

In the view of the IMF, the Turkish economy continued to grow strongly through the first half of 2011, reaping the benefits of the institutional reforms and the revamped policy frameworks implemented in the previous decade. However, Turkey's growth became increasingly fuelled by domestic demand and imports. This was supported by strong credit growth, reflecting an appreciated currency combined with low interest rates and a surge in short-term capital inflows. The current account deficit widened sharply to near 10 per cent of gross domestic product (GDP). Inflation continued to rise quickly, reflecting pass-through from a large nominal depreciation since late 2010, numerous tax and regulated-price increases and underpinned by tight domestic supply conditions and is forecast to reach 9.5 per cent

KEY INDICATORS — Turkey

	Unit	2006	2007	2008	2009	2010
Population	m	68.13	68.89	69.66	70.54	*72.70
Gross domestic product (GDP)	US$bn	528.69	663.42	730.30	730.30	741.90
GDP per capita	US$	7,760	9,629	8,723	8,723	10,399
GDP real growth	%	6.9	4.9	-4.7	-4.7	8.2
Inflation	%	9.6	8.7	6.3	6.3	8.6
Unemployment	%	9.9	10.2	11.0	14.0	11.9
Industrial output	% change	7.4	5.8	-0.7	-8.4	–
Agricultural output	% change	2.9	-6.5	4.5	3.5	–
Coal output	mtoe	13.4	15.8	17.2	17.4	17.4
Exports (fob) (goods)	US$m	91,937.0	115,306.0	140,739.0	109,635.0	120,902.0
Imports (fob) (goods)	US$m	138,973.0	162,033.0	193,922.0	134,511.0	177,347.0
Balance of trade	US$m	-47,036.0	-46,727.0	-53,183.0	-24,876.0	-56,445.0
Current account	US$m	-32,193.0	-37,575.0	-41,289.0	-13,853.0	-47,739.0
Total reserves minus gold	US$m	60,982.0	73,384.0	70,428.0	70,874.0	80,713.0
Foreign exchange	US$m	60,710.0	73,156.0	70,231.0	69,178.0	79,046.0
Foreign direct investment (FDI)	US$bn	20.2	22.0	19.5	8.4	9.3
Exchange rate	per US$	1.43	1.18	1.30	1.55	1.50

* estimated figure

at end-2011, well above the point target of 5.5 per cent.

The externally-financed demand boom has weakened Turkey's resilience in some areas. Capital inflows are dominated by potentially-volatile financing and short-term external debt has climbed sharply. With banks absorbing much of these inflows, an external funding shortfall will slow down credit. Non-financial companies' net foreign exchange liabilities increased substantially, exposing them to currency depreciation. While the headline fiscal balance continues to improve and the public debt-to-GDP ratio is declining, fiscal performance has been supported by benign economic conditions at home and abroad.

Growth is expected to slow sharply to 2 per cent in 2012 due to weaker capital inflows, reflecting in part concerns about Turkey's large current account deficit. More limited foreign financing would constrain the current account deficit to about 8 per cent of GDP and compress imports. In line with Turkey's previous capital flow-driven corrections, with fewer imports of key raw materials and intermediates, GDP growth is forecast to be sharply scaled down. Inflation is projected to decline to a still-elevated 6.5 per cent, eroding Turkey's external competitiveness.

Risk assessment

Economy	Good
Politics	Fair
Regional stability	Fair

COUNTRY PROFILE

Historical profile

Founded by Constantine the Great in AD330, Turkey (or Asia Minor as it was known) was for more than 1,000 years the heartland of the Eastern Roman (Byzantine) empire. From the eleventh century, invasions from Central Asia led to the Islamic Turkification of the region, headed by the Ottomans, a name derived from their fourteenth century leader Osman Gazi, who had masterminded the comprehensive defeat of the Byzantines at the Battle of Baphaeon in 1301. The modern republic was established in the 1920s by nationalist leader Kemal Atatürk.

1453 The Ottomans gradually expanded their areas of territorial control, creating the Ottoman Empire.

1500s–1800s The Ottoman Empire attempted to widen its territorial control into the Mediterranean and central Europe. This led to conflicts with the major European powers, including the Habsburgs and the Russians. Successive wars eventually undermined the Ottoman Empire.

1914–18 Turkey fought in the First World War on the side of the Germans. The majority of Ottoman possessions came under British or French control after the war.

1920–22 Mustafa Kemal, renamed Atatürk (Father of all the Turks) in 1934, led the country in the War of National Liberation, following the dismemberment of the Ottoman Empire by the *entente* powers at the end of the First World War.

1923 The Republic of Turkey was established; the independence of the Turkish state was recognised by the Treaty of Lausanne. Atatürk was elected as the Republic's first president. Sweeping changes were made in all areas – legal, political, social and economic. The Islamic legal codes were replaced by Western ones. Turkey is the only Muslim country where the principle of secularism is written into the constitution.

1925 Turkey adopted the Gregorian calendar. The fez (a conical, brimless hat), considered to be a sign of Ottoman backwardness, was prohibited.

1928 Islam ceased to be the State religion. The Arabic script was replaced by the Latin alphabet.

1930 Constantinople was officially renamed Istanbul.

1934 Women were given the vote.

1938 Atatürk died and was succeeded by Ismet Inonu.

1945 President Inonu kept Turkey out of the Second World War, except for the last four months, when it fought on the side of the Allies against Germany. Turkey joined the UN.

1950 The first open multi-party elections were won by the Democratic Party.

1952 Turkey joined NATO.

1960 The government was overthrown in a military coup.

1961 A constitution was approved in a referendum; it established a two-chamber parliament. Elections were held and civilian rule was restored.

1963 An agreement was signed with the European Economic Community (EEC).

1965 Süleyman Demirel became prime minister (he went on to occupy this office seven times).

1971 After a wave of strikes and unrest, there was a period of military supervision of government.

1973 Return to civilian rule.

1974 Turkey invaded northern Cyprus and 37 per cent of the island came under Turkish control, enforcing partition between north and south.

1978 The US lifted the trade embargo it had imposed on Turkey after the 1974 invasion.

1980 A military coup followed civil unrest and martial law was declared throughout the country.

1981 All political parties were disbanded.

1982 A new constitution was approved in a referendum. It created a seven-year presidency and reduced parliament to a single chamber.

1983 New political parties were allowed, subject to strict rules. Turgut Ozal became president. Northern Cyprus officially declared its independence as the Kuzey Kýbrýs Türk Cumhuriyeti (KKTC) (Turkish Republic of Northern Cyprus) and introduced its own government and legal system. The independence move was rejected by the international community and only Turkey recognised it as a state.

1984 The Kurdistan Workers' Party (PKK) launched a separatist guerrilla war in the south-east.

1987 Martial law ended, enabling Turkey to become a full and active member of the Organisation of Economic Co-operation and Development (OECD), in addition to becoming an associate member of the EEC.

1990 Turkey allowed the use of its bases for the launch of air strikes against Iraq by the US-led coalition in the war to drive Iraqi forces out of Kuwait.

1992 In an anti-PKK operation, Turkish troops entered Kurdish safe havens in Iraq. Turkey joined the Black Sea alliance.

1993 Following the death of Turgut Ozal, Süleyman Demirel became president. Tansu Ciller was appointed as Turkey's first female prime minister. The PKK declared a unilateral cease-fire in March but by July it had broken down.

1995 Turkey launched a major military offensive against the Kurds in northern Iraq. The Ciller coalition collapsed. Although the pro-Islamist Welfare Party (RP) won the elections, it lacked support to form a government. Two major centre-right parties formed an anti-Islamist coalition. Turkey entered the EU customs union.

1996 The centre-right coalition fell and Necmettin Erbakan was appointed prime minister, heading the first pro-Islamic government since 1923.

1997 The Erbakan coalition government collapsed and Mesut Yilmaz was appointed prime minister.

1998 Corruption allegations forced out the Yilmaz government and Bülent Ecevit was appointed prime minister. The RP was banned.

1999 The PKK leader, Abdullah Ocalan, captured in Kenya, received a death sentence, later commuted to life imprisonment. Two earthquakes in the Izmit region killed over 17,000 people.

2000 After the failure of a move to change the constitution to allow Süleyman Demirel to stay in office, Ahmet Necdet Sezer was elected president.

2001 Parliament voted to change the constitution to bring it closer to the constitutions of EU countries.

2002 To meet EU conditions on opening membership talks, parliament voted for wide reforms. The Islamist Adalet ve Kalkinma Partisi (AKP) (Justice and Development Party) won a landslide victory in parliamentary elections. Abdullah Gül became prime minister. Constitutional changes allowed the AKP leader, Recep Tayyip Erdogan, previously disbarred from public office due to a criminal conviction, to run for parliament.
2003 Recep Tayyip Erdogan was appointed prime minister. Parliament adopted a package of human rights reforms including freedom of speech, giving the Kurdish language some rights and reducing the political role of the military.
2004 EU leaders agreed to open talks towards Turkey's EU accession after Turkey agreed to recognise Cyprus as an EU member. The death penalty was banned.
2005 The new Turkish lira, Yeni Turk Lirasi (YTL), was introduced as six zeroes were dropped from the currency. EU accession negotiations commenced. The Blue Stream gas pipeline under the Black Sea from Russia to the Turkish port of Samsun opened.
2006 The Baku-Tbilisi-Ceyhan oil pipeline opened. Turkey's refusal to open its ports to Cypriot traffic caused deadlock in the EU accession negotiations.
2007 After two rounds in a presidential election, held in parliament, the sole candidate, Abdullah Gül (AKP), failed to win enough votes. Protests against his candidacy due to his Islamist background came from both the public and military, which protested he would challenge the secular constitution. Gül withdrew his candidature. The government was denied the option of reforming the constitution to allow directly elected presidents. To resolve the issue, early general elections were called in which the ruling AKP won 46.76 per cent of the vote (341 seats out of 550). With a majority in parliament the AKP was able to elect Abdullah Gül as the president. The Turkish military launched air strikes against the Kurdish PKK inside Iraq.
2008 Parliament approved a constitutional change to allow women to wear the *hijab* (Islamic headscarf) in universities. The ruling AKP risked a ban on its existence and loss of power when it was accused of undermining the secular constitution by introducing this legislation that was seen by its opponents as creating an Islamic state by stealth. The Constitutional Court overturned the legislation and fined the political party 50 per cent of its treasury funding for one year. An indictment was filed against 86 people for plotting to overthrow the government; they were alleged to belong to the ultra-nationalist and Kemalist group, Ergenekon.
2009 Legislation to allow civilian courts to try military personnel for threats to national security or involvement in organised crime was ratified by the president. An agreement was signed to allow the EU-backed Nabucco gas pipeline to transit Turkey. Turkey agreed 'in principle' to also allow the rival Russian South Stream gas pipeline to transit Turkey. The EU seeks to ensure a supply of energy that is not dependent on Russian oil and gas, and Russia wants to avoid transiting Ukraine, with which it has had several disagreements over payments. Turkey's accession talks (to the EU) were blocked by the Cypriot government when it refused to allow the start of talks in five policy areas unless Turkey changed its position on the Cyprus dispute.
2010 After a four-day marathon parliamentary session in May, parliament approved all but one of 27 amendments to the constitution. However, the government was unable to rally the necessary two-thirds majority required to pass the legislation outright and the changes therefore needed to be decided by referendum. Among the proposed changes were increased power for the government, while reducing the influence of the military, and reform of the judiciary, which critics claim may weaken Turkey's secular society in favour of one more Islamic. A flotilla of six ships, organised by a Turkish human rights organisation, attempted to break the Israeli blockade of the Gaza Strip in May. It was repelled by the Israeli military, with the deaths of Turkish activists. Condemnation of the Israeli military action was voiced by many in the international community. In July the Constitutional Court annulled the changes which would have reduced the powers of the army and the judiciary. On 12 September, a referendum passed with 58 per cent in favour of constitutional reforms covering economic and social rights, individual freedoms and judicial reforms; the proposal to limit the power of the Supreme Court to dissolve political parties failed. The changes brought the constitution into line with EU standards.
2011 Prime Minister Erdogan announced in April that a new waterway would be built to by-pass the Bosphorus, which has become very crowded. He said that Canal Istanbul (the exact route has yet to be announced) would be about 50km long and 150 metres wide. General elections were held on 12 June, in which the ruling AKP won 49.83 per cent of the vote (327 seats out of 550) and the CHP won 25.98 per cent (135). The AKP failed to win the two-thirds majority necessary to allow it to change the constitution in line with its political objectives. Some 30 per cent of the elected members (from the main opposition party (CHP) and minority Kurds) boycotted parliament's swearing in ceremony on 28 June. The CHP later rescinded their boycott but the Baris ve Demokrasi Partisi (BDP) ((Kurdish) Peace and Democracy Party), despite urging by Abdullah Ocalan, leader of the PKK, maintained their boycott. Ironically the constitutional changes proposed by Erdogan, which needed BDP support would benefit the Kurdish community. On 3 July Turkey recognised the rebel Transitional National Council in Benghazi (Libya) as the legitimate representatives of the Libyan people. Angered by the arrest of senior military personnel, Isik Kosaner, chief of the armed forces, resigned on 29 July, along with the army, navy and air force heads. President Gül appointed General Necdet Ozel as head of the army. On 15 August, Turkey warned the Syrian government to stop its military operations, aimed at quelling internal civil disorder, 'immediately and unconditionally'. A UN report, published on 2 September, into the deaths of nine Turkish activists on board a convoy of ships attempting to break the naval blockade of the Gaza Strip in May 2010 concluded that Israel had used 'excessive force', but that the naval blockage was legal. Turkey immediately expelled the Israeli ambassador and cut military ties with Israel. While Turkey demanded an apology from Israel for the killings, it rejected the findings of the report and threatened to set it before the International Court of Justice (ICJ) for a judicial ruling. An earthquake of magnitude 7.2 struck the eastern province of Van on 23 October. Initial estimates put the death toll of over 200 people and over 1,000 people injured, as dozens of buildings were destroyed. On 30 November, Turkey imposed a number of sanctions against Syria that included suspension of financial dealing with and a freeze of assets of the Syrian government and a travel ban on the Syrian leadership; an arms ban is already in place.

Political structure

Constitution

A 1982 referendum approved a new constitution embodying considerable restrictions on personal liberty.
The constitution was amended in 1999 and 2001. The 1999 amendment was undertaken to ease the path of the privatisation programme while an amendment in 2001 was aimed at redefining human rights in view of Turkey's aspirations to join the EU. In 2002, three articles of the constitution were amended, allowing a person with a prison conviction (non-terrorist charge) to stand for parliament. Apart from these additions, the new constitution differs little from the 1926

version, promulgated by Kemal Atatürk, which enshrines Turkey as a secular, democratic and unitary republic.
A referendum will be held in June 2010, following parliamentary proposals, in May, that had failed to gain the necessary two-thirds majority to amend the constitution. Proposals include the prime minister being given increased powers, while reducing the influence of the military on the democratically elected government.
A constitutional referendum was held on 12 September 2010, in which 57.88 per cent of voters agreed to 23 changes to articles within the constitution to bring it into line with European Union standards. Measures included equality of men and women, protection of children and vulnerable adults, personal data protection, increased worker's rights including right of collective bargaining for government employees. The ban on overseas travel was lifted for business people under investigation and with tax debts. The right of citizens to have disputes with government adjudicated by an ombudsman and the right to petition the constitutional court were granted. The abolition of legal safeguards for the 1980 military coup conspirators was enacted as well as further judicial reforms.
The new constitution will allow parliament to select senior judicial candidates and the removal of existing judges. The judiciary would no longer be able to prohibit political parties.

Independence date
29 August 1923

Form of state
Parliamentary democratic republic

The executive
Executive power rests with the president and council of ministers. The president is the head of state. The president, who serves a seven-year term, is elected by the parliament and appoints the prime minister, who in turn chooses the Council of Ministers. A National Security Council guides government policy in areas of security and law and order. It is chaired by the president and is composed of government ministers and armed forces commanders.

National legislature
The unicameral Türkiye Büyük Millet Meclisi (TGNA) (Turkish Grand National Assembly) has 550 representatives, elected by proportional representation from party lists, to serve five-year terms. Only political parties with over 10 per cent of the vote are eligible to sit in the TGNA.
Only political parties gaining more than 10 per cent of the national vote are entitled to parliamentary seats
Voting eligibility: universal direct suffrage over 18 years.

Legal system
The legal system is based on European models and the 1982 constitution.
The court system is divided into three areas: civil, penal and administrative. The highest courts are the Appeal Court for civil and penal cases and the State Council for tax and administrative cases.

Last elections
27 April, 6 May and 28 August 2007 (presidential); 12 June 2011 (parliamentary)
Results: Presidential: (third round) Abdullah Gül (AKP) won 339 votes; Sabahattin Çakmakoglu (MHP) 70; Hüseyin Tayfun Içli (Demokratik Sol Partisi (DSP) (Democratic Left Party)) 13. National assembly member turnout 448.
Parliamentary: Adalet ve Kalkinma Partisi (AKP) (Justice and Development Party) won 49.83 per cent of the vote (327 seats out of 550), Cumhuriyet Halk Partisi (CHP) (Republican People's Party) 25.98 per cent (135), Milliyetçi Hareket Partisi (MHP) (Nationalist Movement Party) 13.01 per cent (53), independent candidates 6.57 per cent (35); 12 other political parties each won less than 2 per cent and failed to win seats. Turnout was 83.16 per cent.

Next elections
2016 (parliamentary); 2014 (presidential).

Political parties

Ruling party
Adalet ve Kalkinma Partisi (AKP) (Justice and Development Party) (elected 2002; re-elected 12 Jun 2011)

Main opposition party
Cumhuriyet Halk Partisi (CHP) (Republican People's Party)

Population

72.70 million (2010)*
Last census: October 2000: 67,803,927
Population density: 84 inhabitants per square km.
Annual growth rate: 1.6 per cent 1994–2004 (WHO 2006)

Internally Displaced Persons (IDP)
Over 1.0 million (UNHCR 2004)

Ethnic make-up
Mainly ethnic Turks, with a large Kurdish minority and small numbers of Armenians, Greeks and Jews.

Religions
Muslim with a small Christian minority. Turkey is a secular state which guarantees complete freedom of worship to non-Muslims.

Education

Although complusory education is free, facilities are extremely limited, forcing a number of students to attend night school or take private tuition to improve their chances of gaining a place at one of Turkey's 29 universities.
Unicef has highlighted the problem of poor education figures for girls, particularly over the age of 11. In traditional families, it is generally not considered necessary to educate girls beyond primary school, so that less than 40 per cent of girls, aged 11–15, in rural areas are enrolled in secondary school. In 2003, a joint Unicef and government programme aimed at addressing the problem has resulted in new schools opened in areas of most need and transport for students who have to travel long distances. Female enrolment figures have slowly begun to rise.
Annual total public expenditure on education is 3–4 per cent of GDP, of which 49 per cent is spent on primary education, 20 per cent on secondary education and 31 per cent on tertiary education (Unicef 2004).
Literacy rate: 87 per cent adult rate; 96 per cent youth rate (15–24) (Unesco 2005).
Compulsory years: Six to 14
Enrolment rate: 105 per cent male, 96 per cent female, gross primary enrolment; 67 per cent male, 48 per cent female, gross secondary enrolment, of relevant age groups (including repeaters), (Unicef 2004).
Pupils per teacher: 23 in primary schools.

Health

Healthcare is provided free of charge. Standards are low, leading many to seek medical services in private hospitals and abroad. Major differences exist in the availability and quality of medical care between major urban centres and eastern parts of the country. Family planning was introduced in the 1960s. Due to opposition from religious groups it did not receive strong support and funding.
Life expectancy: 71 years, 2004 (WHO 2006)
Fertility rate/Maternal mortality rate: 2.4 births per woman, 2004 (WHO 2006)
Birth rate/Death rate: 17.95 births per 1,000 population; 5.95 deaths per 1,000 population (World Bank).
Child (under 5 years) mortality rate (per 1,000): 33 per 1,000 live births; 8 per cent of children under aged five are malnourished (World Bank).
Head of population per physician: 1.35 physicians per 1,000 people, 2003 (WHO 2006)

Welfare

The social security system is based on three major organisations, the Social Insurance Institution (SSK), the Emekli Sandigi (government employees'

retirement fund) and Bag-Kur for the self-employed.
Mass social security began in 1946 with the SSK giving limited benefits and has been gradually expanded. Membership is compulsory for all salaried employees except civil servants, who join Emekli Sandigi. Social insurance law provides for benefits covering work injury and occupational illness, sickness, maternity, old age, disability and death.

Main cities
Ankara (capital, estimated population 3.6 million (m) in 2005), Istanbul (10.1m), Izmir (2.5m), Bursa (1.5m), Adana (1.3m), Gaziantep (1.0m).

Languages spoken
Armenian, Greek and Ladino are used by ethnic minorities. The use of Kurdish was restricted until parliament voted to change the constitution in 2001 and relaxed the restriction. Arabic, Circassian, and Judezmo are also spoken.
Almost all educated Turks have command of a foreign language and English is the dominant language for international business. German and French are also spoken.
Official language/s
Turkish

Media
Press
Dailies: There are several national and regional dailies including in Turkish *Hürriyet* (www.hurriyet.com.tr), *Türkiye* (www.turkiyegazetesi.com.tr) and *Milliyet* (www.milliyet.com.tr), are mass circulation newspapers, *Yeni Asir* (www.yeniasir.com.tr) and *Sabah* (www.sabah.com.tr), *Aksam*(www.aksam.com.tr), *Posta* (www.postagazetesi.net) and *Today's Zaman* (www.todayszaman.com) (with English online articles).
In English, the main publication is *Turkish Daily News* (www.turkishdailynews.com.tr) with *The New Anatolian* (www.thenewanatolian.com).
Weeklies: Some daily newspapers have weekend editions, such as *Sunday's Zaman*. Other magazines, in Turkish, include *Aksiyon* (www.aksiyon.com.tr), *Aydinlik* (www.aydinlik.com.tr), *Yeni Mesaj* (www.yenimesaj.com.tr) and *Yeni Ümit* (www.yeniumit.com.tr). In English *Voices* (www.voicesnewspaper.com) from Altinkum and *Turkish Weekly* (www.turkishweekly.net).
Business: In Turkish, *Dünya Ekonomi Politika* (www.dunyagazetesi.com.tr), (with English online articles), and *Finansal Forum* are important publications; others include *Eko Haber* (www.ekohaber.com.tr) and *Referans* (www.referansgazetesi.com). Ýktisat, Ýþletme ve Finans Dergisi (Journal of Economy, Business and Finance) is a monthly economic publication.
Periodicals: In Turkish, English, and French.*Bizim Anadolu* (www.bizimanadolu.com) is a monthly newspaper. The State Institute of Statistics (www.turkstat.gov.tr) publish yearbooks.
Broadcasting
The national broadcaster is the Türkiye Radyo ve Televizyon Kurumu (TRT) (www.trt.net.tr).
Radio: TRT (www.trt.net.tr) has six stations, providing a national, regional and local network, which includes news, education and cultural programmes, modern and traditional music and programmes for foreign tourists. There are numerous commercial radio stations based in all regions, including Kanal D (www.kanald.com.tr), Radio Sok (www.asyaradyo.com) (Adana), Radyo Marti (www.radyomarti.net) (Antalya), Radyo Net (www.vizeradyonet.com) (Ankara) and Metro FM (www.metrofm.com.tr) (Istanbul).
Television: TRT (www.trt.net.tr) operates four national channels. There are many subscriber cable and satellite television services available with programmes in Turkish, Kurdish and Arabic. Major TV networks include NTV MSNBC (www.ntv.com.tr), Pusula (www.pusula.tv), Samanyolu Haber TV (www.samanyoluhaber.com), Sky Turk (www.skyturk.tv) and Ulusal Kanal (www.ulusalkanal.com.tr).
Advertising
There are opportunities for radio, billboards and print media advertising. There are local codes of practice in operation, as well as statutory requirements.
News agencies
National news agency: Anadolu Agency

Economy
The economy is mixed and dominated by the service sector, which in 2009 contributed 64.7 per cent to GDP, with industry providing 25.9 per cent and agriculture 9.4 per cent. The tourist sector has increased in importance for over a decade, so that by 2008 revenue was US$21.9 billion and over 25 per cent of GDP. In 2009 tourism recorded a total of over 27 million visitors, the majority of which arrived from the OECD (Organisation for Economic Co-Operation and Development) countries of Europe. The volume of tourists did not fall even though the global economic crisis in 2008 cut into the disposable income of foreign holidaymakers. As the euro rose in value during 2008–09 European-Mediterranean holidays became progressively more expensive and Turkey was seen as a more economical destination.
Industrial production is centred on textile and clothing manufacturing, consumer electronics and electrical goods, vehicle assembly and automotive parts and shipbuilding. Turkey is self-sufficient in food production and is a world leader in production of hazelnuts, cherries, figs, apricots, quinces and pomegranates and is second in producing watermelons, cucumbers and chickpeas with its surplus sold for export. Livestock farming and by-products contribute around 30 per cent of overall output; fishing and aquaculture are also important components of the agricultural sector.
GDP growth in 2007 was 4.7 per cent, which fell to 0.7 per cent in 2008 as the economic crisis cut worldwide spending. In the first quarter of 2009 the economy was in recession and average GDP growth was -4.7 per cent; positive growth returned by the end of 2009.
While the banking system was caught up in the economic crisis of toxic debt and credit squeeze worldwide, Islamic banking in Turkey in participating banks grew by 40 per cent in 2009, with the volume of funds up by US$17.8 billion. Services in Islamic banking also include insurance and financial services, real estate and energy investments.
On 1 January 2009, the currency was renamed the Turkish lira, with the issuing of new banknotes and coins.

External trade
Turkey is a member of the regionally based, Islamic, intergovernmental Economic Co-operation Organisation (ECO), comprising 10 regional Central Asian countries that promote economic, technical and cultural development between member countries. Turkey has trade agreements with its neighbours in the Black Sea Economic Co-operation Organisation (BSEC), which promotes trade and investment among the 11 regional member states. Turkey is also a signatory of the Euro-Mediterranean Partnership agreement, which provides for the introduction of free trade between the EU and 10 Mediterranean countries by 2012.
Turkey has been in negotiation for entry to the European Union since 1987, but has yet to resolve the issue of Cyprus and the Turkish Republic of Northern Cyprus (TRNC). In July 2010, negotiations were still underway. Turkey has a customs union with the EU, although this is hampered by Turkish refusal to allow Cypriot vessels to dock at its ports.
Manufacturing consists principally of textiles and clothing and consumer electronics and electrical goods, vehicle assembly and automotive parts and shipbuilding. Turkey exports many agricultural products

and is the world's third largest exporter of tobacco.
A major oil pipeline is in existence and another major natural gas pipeline is proposed through Turkey, connecting the oil and gas fields of Central Asia with Europe.
Imports
Principal imports include hydrocarbons, machinery, chemicals, semi-finished goods, vehicles.
Main sources: Russia (typically 14 per cent of total), Germany (10 per cent), China (9 per cent).
Exports
Principal exports are textiles and clothing, agricultural products, tobacco, iron and steel, electrical and electronic equipment, chemical and industrial products, vehicles and parts.
Main destinations: Germany (typically 10 per cent of total), France (6 per cent), UK Italy (6 per cent).

Agriculture

Farming
Turkey is self-sufficient in fool and agriculture accounts for around 17 per cent of GDP, over 20 per cent of exports and employing about 45 per cent of the labour force. The sector is subsidised, with state support accounting for as much as 7.5 per cent of GDP.
The mainstays of Turkish agriculture are wheat and sheep, although there has been an increase in fruit and vegetable production as well as growth in regional crops such as tea, tobacco, cotton and hazelnuts. Turkey expects to become a leading cotton producer over the next 10 years.
Turkey is the world's largest producer of hazelnuts (70 per cent of the world supply). Production is dominated by Fiskorbirlik, the state-run hazelnut farmers' co-operative.
The GAP south-eastern Anatolian irrigation project, although incomplete, has already raised production and productivity considerably: according to official figures, wheat production nationally has jumped 64 per cent since 1985, barley production by 42 per cent and cotton production by almost 500 per cent. Rice, wheat, soyabeans and potatoes are now produced in more than minimal amounts for the first time. The project will irrigate some 1.8 million hectares (ha), 25 per cent of which will be given over to cotton production.
Agricultural exports including tobacco, cotton, dried fruit (hazelnuts, seedless raisins, figs, apricots), pulses (chickpeas and lentils), live sheep, goats, fresh fruits (applies and citrus fruits) and fresh tomatoes. Cereals, especially wheat and barley, are Turkey's most important crops.
Imports, particularly of dairy products and beef, are growing faster than exports. Significant quantities of rice and processed food products are also imported. Liberal trade policies have opened up markets for imports of both cotton and burley tobacco.
Fishing
Salt water fishing contributes to 77 per cent of the total fishery production, with 62 per cent of the catches obtained from the Black Sea. Anchovies remain the traditional catch with a potential for further processing. Fishery production also thrives on horse mackerel, whiting and bonito.
The main production area for inland fisheries is Lake Van, where gray mullets are mainly caught. The Atatürk Dam and other smaller dams, which were constructed under the Southeast Anatolian Project (GAP), have increased the potential for inland fisheries by over 9,000 tonnes.
Trout constitute more than 60 per cent of the total aquaculture production, 25 per cent of which is obtained from the Aegean Sea. Turkey mainly exports large quantities of canned tuna to the EU and other developed countries.
Forestry
Forest and other wooded land accounts for slightly more than a quarter of the total land area, with forest cover estimated at 10.2 million hectares (ha). Most of the forest is available for wood supply, although it is moderately used for fuel consumption. Only a small area of forest is owned by the state.
Turkey produces a significant quantity of industrial roundwood. Major forest industries rely on local resources for the production of sawnwood, particle board and plywood. The pulp and paper industry is able to meet domestic demand by imports.

Industry and manufacturing

Industry accounts for 25 per cent of GDP and employs approximately 18 per cent of the labour force.
There have been high levels of industrial growth since the mid-1970s, despite low levels of capital investment and plant utilisation. There has also been rapid development of light industry, general diversification and growth in exports of manufactured goods.
Main areas of specialisation include textiles, ready-to-wear clothes, ceramics and glass, iron and steel, chrome, chemicals and light consumer goods.
The industrial sector is still dominated by large state-owned industries. These State Economic Enterprises are mainly engaged in textiles, food processing, chemicals, metals and motor vehicle production. The food processing sector is growing rapidly and agricultural products continue to provide a large proportion of export revenue.
Turkey's non-state industrial sector is dominated by a number of family-run conglomerates. Koc Holding is the largest, with 108 companies operating in 10 core sectors. Koc produces one-third of Turkey's cars, most of its fridges and televisions and owns the biggest supermarket chain. Sabanci Holdings, which has 50 operating companies, is active in chemicals, textiles, cars, banking, and supermarkets. The third-largest conglomerate, Cukorova, is active in commercial vehicles, paper and mobile telephones, although it is concentrating its efforts on the finance sector. There are also dozens of smaller conglomerates with up to 33 companies.
The textile sector, once one of the engines of Turkish economic growth, is losing the interest of the major conglomerates that dominate Turkey's industrial structure.

Tourism

Tourism has grown rapidly in recent years and is a major contributor to the economy. The sector is the second largest earner of foreign currency after exports. 22 million tourists visit Turkey annually Tourist activity is concentrated along the coasts of the Aegean and Mediterranean Seas, where the bulk of accommodation is concentrated. Cultural, mountain and winter tourism are being developed.

Mining

Substantial mineral reserves exist, including copper, zinc, lead, iron ore, coal and lignite. Deposits of borax, wolfram and chromite are internationally significant. Turkey is the world's second-largest producer of boron and a leading exporter of chrome. Etibank controls 60 per cent of all mining activity.

Hydrocarbons

Proven oil reserves were 300 million barrels in January 2009, located mainly in the southeast. Production has fallen by almost a half, from its peak of 85,290 barrels per day (bpd) in 1991 to 46,120bpd in 2008. Consumption was 675,950bpd in 2008 so Turkey relies on imported petroleum products, notably from Russia as well as Middle Eastern countries such as Libya and Algeria. The state-owned Turkish Petroleum Corporation (TPAO) is responsible for exploration, distribution, trading, services and storage of oil and gas. There are five oil refineries processing over 714,000bpd.
Turkey has a strategic position as a hub and transit country for oil and gas pipelines. The Baku-Tbilisi-Ceyhan (BTC) 1,760km oil pipeline was opened in 2005, it carries oil from Azerbaijan's port of Baku, through Georgia, then across

Turkey to its Mediterranean port of Ceyhan. The pipeline has a capacity of one million bpd. The Nabucco natural gas pipeline is planned to follow this and branch off towards Europe at Erzurum in central Turkey. A conference was convened in Prague, in May 2009, for gas exporting countries in Central Asia and the Middle East including Turkey and hosted by the EU. The purpose was to state the EU's seriousness as a buyer of natural gas and its commitment to new gas pipelines and trade between the EU and gas exporters and to end the wrangling that has halted progress on the 3,300km Nabucco pipeline. Other proposed gas pipelines to transit Turkey originate in Egypt, Iraq, Iran and Saudi Arabia.

Turkey has natural gas reserves of 8.5 billion cubic metres (cum) in 2009, with production at 906 million cum per day and consumption at 36.6 billion cum the balance must be imported. Turkey's domestic gas consumption has quadrupled since 1992, reflecting government policy of increasing use of gas. Gas is cleaner, plentiful in neighbouring countries and allows Turkey to diversify energy sources and increase energy security. Turkey can charge transit fees, as well as bring neighbouring post-Soviet republics into its sphere of influence.

Exploration of gas fields centres on the western Black Sea, off Turkey's coast.

Proven coal reserves were 1.8 billion tonnes, of mostly sub-bituminous and lignite (brown) coal which is typically used for power generation and which is generally of poor quality and highly polluting. Since production levels fell in 2003–04 to 10.5 million tonnes of oil equivalent (mtoe), as a result of a lack of investment in the industry, output has grown steadily to 15.8mtoe in 2007 as global oil and gas prices rose.

Energy

Total installed generating capacity was 40.6GW is 2007, almost doubling from the 21.3GW in 1997. Hydropower provides 12.8GW in the energy mix, 3.2GW was under construction with an addition 21GW planned at a later date.

Turkey is a net energy importer (about 60 per cent of its energy requirements) and is Europe's fastest-growing energy market. Demand still outstrips supply and the country experiences blackouts and industrial losses as a result of the energy bottleneck.

The electricity is generated by coal-fired plants and hydropower. There has been rapid expansion of hydroelectricity capacity with over 100 power plants in operation. There are plans to develop nuclear energy (possibly by 2020) as a source of electricity.

The Ministry of Energy and Natural Resources has responsibility for over viewing the private energy companies which generate, distribute and supply electricity wholesale and retail.

On 3 April 2011, the Kurdistan ministry of electricity signed a US$18 million contract with the Turkish energy company Shar to connect electricity power lines between the provinces of Sulaimaniya (Iraq) and Erbil (Turkey).

Financial markets

Stock exchange

Istanbul Menkul Kiymetler Borsasi (IMKB) (Istanbul Stock Exchange)

Commodity exchange

The Istanbul Gold Exchange (IGE) includes silver and platinum spot trading.

Banking and insurance

Central bank

Türkiye Cumhuriyet Merkez Bankasi (TCMB) (Central Bank of the Republic of Turkey)

Time

GMT plus two hours (daylight saving, late March to late October, GMT plus three hours)

Geography

Turkey is mostly situated in Asia Minor on the Anatolian peninsula, which is bordered to the north-east by Georgia and Armenia, to the east by Iran, and to the south by Iraq and Syria. Part of the country reaches into Europe, occupying eastern Thrace (Trakiya), which is separated from the rest of Turkey by the inland Sea of Marmara and is bordered to the west by Greece and Bulgaria. Turkey has an extensive coastline with the Black Sea to the north, the Mediterranean Sea to the south and the Aegean Sea to the west. The Sea of Marmara links the Black Sea and the Aegean Sea.

Turkey is a mountainous country, over three-quarters of which exceeds 500m elevation and averages 1,130m. The highest point is Mount Ararat (Agri Dagi) in the east, reaching 5,165m. There are two major ranges: the North Anatolian mountains in the north and the Taurus mountains in the south. Many short, fast rivers flow down from the mountains, as well as the great Tigris and Euphrates rivers, which rise in the mountains of eastern Turkey, where practically all the water they carry down to the Persian Gulf is generated. There are numerous lakes, the largest of which is Lake Van to the east near the Iranian border.

Hemisphere

Northern

Climate

Coastal regions have a Mediterranean climate, with mild, moist winters and hot, dry summers. The interior plateau has low and irregular rainfall, cold and snowy winters and hot, almost rainless summers.

Ankara: 0–23 degrees Celsius (C) (Jan–Jul); annual rainfall 367mm. Istanbul: 5–23 degrees C (Jan–Jul); annual rainfall 723mm. Ismir: 8–27 degrees C (Jan–Jul); annual rainfall 700mm.

Dress codes

Although the population is predominantly Muslim, Turkey is a secular state and for the visitor daily life in cities and tourist areas is similar to that in Europe. However, in rural areas, standards are much more conservative and women should be cautious in their dress. They should wear clothing which covers most of the body and probably also a headscarf, or at least be able to cover their hair if the need arises. Topless bathing is illegal but tolerated on southern and Aegean tourist beaches.

Dress for formal occasions is conservative and men normally wear a dark business suit or formal dress. Ties are almost always worn for business meetings. Turkish women dress formally for most social occasions.

Entry requirements

Passports

Required by all, valid for at least three months from date of departure, with exception of nationals of Belgium, France, Germany, Greece, Italy, Luxmbourg, Malta, the Netherlands and Spain.

Visa

Required by all, except nationals of some EU and other European, Latin American, Middle East and Asian countries and New Zealand. Details of requirements for individual countries can be found at www.turkishconsulate.org.uk/en/visa.htm.

Currency advice/regulations

There are no restrictions on the import of local or foreign currencies. Visitors bringing in a large amount of foreign currency should have it recorded in their passports by the Turkish authorities. Export of local and foreign currencies is restricted to US$5,000. Currency exchange slips should be retained.

Travellers cheques can be cashed in banks, but cash in euros or US$ is preferred.

Customs

Personal effects and gifts up to the value of eur255.65 may be brought in duty-free. It is advisable to retain invoices and foreign currency exchange slips to cover value of purchases. Export of antiques is prohibited.

Health (for visitors)
Mandatory precautions
Cholera certificate required if travelling from an infected area.
Advisable precautions
Anti-malaria and anti-cholera precautions are advisable. Hepatitis and rabies are prevalent in all areas, and there have been outbreaks of cholera in eastern Turkey. Malaria tablets should be taken for travel to the Adana area and inoculation against cholera and typhoid for travel to the south-eastern region is advised. A tetanus booster if travelling to central and eastern Anatolia is recommended.
Tap water is unpalatable due to heavy chlorination. Bottled water is easily obtainable in food stores. Medicines are easy to purchase without prescription in local pharmacies. The location of a nearby all-night pharmacy is displayed in any pharmacy window. Medical services are adequate in main city hospitals like Istanbul's American and German hospitals.

Hotels
Classified into five categories – deluxe and first- to fourth-class. Prices vary and many hotels reduce their rates between mid-Oct and mid-Apr. A service charge of 15 per cent usually added and tipping is extra; 18 per cent VAT is also added. Advance reservations are advisable. Tap water is safe in major hotels.

Credit cards
Access, Diners Club, Visa, American Express and Eurocard are accepted in most hotels, restaurants and shops, and can be used to withdraw money from automatic cash dispensers at banks.

Public holidays (national)
Fixed dates
1 Jan (New Year's Day), 23 Apr (National Sovereignty/Children's Day), 19 May (Atatürk Commemoration/Youth and Sports Day), 30 Aug (Victory Day), 29 Oct (Republic Day).
Variable dates
Eid al Adha (four days), Eid al Fitr (three days).
Islamic year 1433 (26 Nov 2011–14 Nov 2012): The Islamic year contains 354 or 355 days, with the result that Muslim feasts advance by 10–12 days against the Gregorian calendar. Dates of feasts vary according to the sighting of the new moon, so cannot be forecast exactly.

Working hours
Banking
Mon–Fri: 0830–1230; 1330–1700.
Business
Mon–Fri: 0830–1200; 1300–1730.
Government
Mon–Fri: 0830–1230; 1330–1730.
Shops
Mon–Sat: 0900–1300; 1400–1900.
Many flower shops open late. Pharmacies display the location of one opening late. Many food shops open on Sun.

Telecommunications
Mobile/cell phones
GSM 1800 and 900 services are available throughout most of the country.

Electricity supply
220V AC, 50Hz (110V in parts of Istanbul).

Social customs/useful tips
Hospitality is very important. Turkey is a Muslim country and religion plays an important part in Turkish life. Practically all business entertaining is conducted in restaurants and clubs.
Personal contact is the key to doing business. Bureaucracy tends to be the greatest obstacle for foreigners. Information is most easily and efficiently obtained by going directly to the top of any organisation, government or private.
It is polite when visiting the home of a business associate to bring a gift of chocolates, flowers or cake. When entering you may be asked to take off your shoes and put on slippers. Do not be critical of Ataturk, the founder of the Republic, and avoid discussion of Kurds, Armenians and other minorities.

Security
Levels of petty crime in main cities are comparable to those in most Western European cities.
Ultra-leftist and Kurdish terrorists are active in Istanbul and other western cities but do not constitute more than a minor threat. Visitors to south-eastern Turkey are advised to travel only during daylight hours and on major roads. The police monitor checkpoints on roads throughout the south-eastern region. Drivers and all passengers in the vehicle should be prepared to provide identification if stopped at a checkpoint.

Getting there
Air
National airline: Turkish Airlines
International airport/s: Ankara-Esenboga (ESB), 35km north-east of the city; duty-free shop, bank, restaurants and bars.
Istanbul-Atatüürk (IST), 24km west of the city; duty-free shop, bank, restaurant, bar and car hire.
Istanbul-Sabiha Gökçen (SAW), 32km east of the city. With bank, duty-free shop, restaurants and business centre.
Airport tax: None
Surface
Road: Coach services are available from Austria, France, Germany and Switzerland, as well as a number of countries in the Middle East.
There are connecting routes from the CIS, Greece, Bulgaria and Iran. It is possible to select the northern route via Belgium, Germany, Austria or the southern route through Belgium, Austria and Italy with a car-ferry connection to Turkey.
Rail: Express rail services from Munich, Vienna, Budapest and Bucharest. Connections are available from London (Liverpool Street) via the Hook of Holland and Cologne to Istanbul on the Istanbul Express, which also transports cars from other European cities.
Water: Turkish Maritime Lines (TML), the national shipping organisation, and several other cruise lines operate services to Turkey. There are ferry connections with Italy, Cyprus and Greece. For the one-day ferry from the Greek island of Rhodes to Marmaris, a visa is not required.

Getting about
National transport
Air: Turkish Airlines operate regular services between Istanbul, Izmir, Ankara and other major towns. Bodrum regional airport offers internal flights and connections to other nearby Mediterranean destinations. Travelling by air within Turkey is relatively inexpensive.
Road: The Tarsus-Pozanti-Ayrimi-Gaziantep (Tag) motorway connects the southern Antolian region with the rest of Turkey, providing a vital link for the future growth of the region. There has been an extensive road building and maintenance programme in operation since 1999 involving over 1,400km of motorway.
Buses: Many private companies operate day and night services between all cities. Services are generally quicker than trains and prices are competitively low.
Rail: There is 8,542km of rail track. Most major cities and towns are linked by regular rail services.
Water: There are steamship services between Istanbul and most major coastal towns. Car ferries that offer cabins are highly sought-after and should be booked in advance.
City transport
Taxis: Metered taxis available in major towns and cities. Also available are the much cheaper *Dolmus* taxis, which have fixed routes and carry 8–12 passengers. Tipping not customary. For longer journeys the fare should be agreed beforehand. Drivers rarely speak much English and may be new to the city, so advisable to carry a road map.
Buses, trams & metro: Metros run in three of Turkey's main cities — Ankara, Istanbul and Izmir — and are planned for Bursa and Adana.

Car hire
All international companies are represented. Available at main hotels, airports and travel agents but expensive. International driving licence preferred, but most foreign licences accepted. Driving is on the right.

BUSINESS DIRECTORY

The addresses listed below are a selection only. While World of Information makes every endeavour to check these addresses, we cannot guarantee that changes have not been made, especially to telephone numbers and area codes. We would welcome any corrections.

Telephone area codes

The international direct dialling code (IDD) for Turkey is +90, followed by area code and subscriber's number:

Adana	322	Istanbul	
Ankara	312	(Thrace)	212
Bursa	224	Izmir	232
Dlyarbakir	412	Kayseri	352
Gaziantep	342	Konya	332
Istanbul		Malatya	422
(Anatolia)	216	Samsun	362

Chambers of Commerce

Adana Chamber of Commerce, 52 Abidinpasa Cadessi, Adana (tel: 352-0052; fax: 351-8009; e-mail: basanlik@adan-to.org.tr).

American-Turkish Business Association, Emlak Kredi Bloklari, Levent, 80620 Istanbul (tel: 270-6718; fax: 279-0031; e-mail: taba@taba.org.tr).

Ankara Chamber of Commerce, 2 Sogutozu Mahallesi, 06530 Ankara (tel: 285-7950; fax: 284-2314; info@atonet.org.tr).

British Chamber of Commerce in Turkey, 18 Mesrutiyet Cadessi, Galatasaray, 34435 Istanbul (tel: 249-0658; fax: 252-5551; e-mail: buscenter@bcct.org.tr).

Istanbul Chamber of Commerce, Resadiye Cadessi, Eminonu, 34378 Istanbul (tel: 455-6000; fax: 513-1565; e-mail: ito@ito.org.tr).

Izmir Chamber of Commerce, 126 Ataturk Cadessi , Pasaport, 35210 Izmir (tel: 441-7777; fax: 446-2251; e-mail: info@izto.org.tr).

Kayseri Chamber of Commerce, 6 Tennuri Sokak, 38040 Kayseri (tel: 222-4528; fax: 232-1069; e-mail: kaytic@kayserito.org.tr).

Konya Chamber of Commerce, 1 Vatan Cadessi, 42040 Konya (tel: 353-4850; fax: 353-0546; e-mail: kto@kto.org.tr).

Samsun Chamber of Commerce and Industry, Hancerli Mahallesi, 8 Abbasasa Sokak, 55020 Samsun (tel: 432-3626; fax: 432-9055; e-mail: samsuntso@samsuntso.org.tr).

Turkey Union of Chambers of Commerce, Industry, Maritime Trade and Commodity Exchanges, 149 Ataturk Bulvari, Bakanlyklar, Ankara (tel: 413-8000; fax: 418-3268; e-mail: info@tobb.org.tr).

Banking

Akbank, Sabanci Center, 80745 4.Levent, Istanbul (tel: 270-2666/0044; fax: 269-7383/8081).

Demirbank, Büyükdere Cadessi 122, 80280 Esentepe, Istanbul (tel: 275-1900; fax: 267-4794/2786).

Esbank, Eskisehir Bankasi, Mesrutiyet Cadessi 141, 80050 Tepebasi, Istanbul (tel: 251-7270; fax: 243-2396).

Garanti Bank, 63 Buyukdere Caddesi, Maslak 80670 Istanbul (tel/fax: 335-3535).

Koçbank, Barbaros Bulvari, Morbasan Sokak, Koza Is Merkezi C Blok, 80692 Besiktas, Istanbul (tel: 274-7777; fax: 267-2987).

Pamukbank, Büyükdere Cadessi 82, 80450 Gayrettepe, Istanbul (tel: 275-2424; fax: 275-8606).

Türkiye Is Bankasi, Atatürk Bulvari 191, 06684 Kavaklidere, Ankara (tel: 428-1140; fax: 425-0750/2).

Yapi ve Kredi Bankasi, Büyükdere Cadessi Yapi Kredi Plaza, A Blok, 80620 Levent, Istanbul (tel: 280-1111; fax: 280-1670/1).

Central bank
Türkiye Cumhuriyet Merkez Bankasy, Ystiklal Cadessi 10 Ulus, 06100 Ankara (tel: 310-3646; fax: 310-7434; e-mail: info@tcmb.gov.tr).

Stock exchange
Istanbul Menkul Kiymetler Borsasi (IMKB) (Istanbul Stock Exchange): www.ise.org

Commodity exchange
The Istanbul Gold Exchange (IGE)

Travel information

Turkish Airlines, General Administration Building, Ataturk Airport Yesilkoy, Istanbul (tel: 463-6363; fax: 465-2121; e-mail: turkishairlines@thy.com).

Ministry of tourism
Ministry of Culture and Tourism, Atatürk Bulvari 29, 06050 Opera, Ankara (tel: 309-0850; fax: 312-4359; e-mail: kultur@kultur.gov.tr).

National tourist organisation offices
Tourism Information Office, Gazi Mustafa Kemal Bulvari 121, Ankara (tel: 488-7007; fax: 231-5572).

Ministries

President's Office, Cankaya, Ankara (tel: 468-5030; fax: 427-1330; internet site: www.cankaya.gov.tr).

Prime Minister's Office, Bakanliklar, Ankara (tel: 419-5896; fax: 417-0476: internet site: www.basbakanlik.gov.tr).

Ministry of Agriculture and Rural Affairs, Ataturk Bulvari 153, Ankara (tel: 417-6000; fax: 417-7168).

Ministry of Defence, Ankara (tel: 425-4596; fax: 418-1795).

Ministry of Education, Ataturk Bulvari, Ankara (tel: 419-1410; fax: 417-7027).

Ministry of Energy and Natural Resources, Inonu Bulvari 27, Ankara (tel: 212-6915; fax: 212-3816).

Ministry of the Environment, Eskisehir Yolu, Ankara (tel: 287 9965; fax: 285-2742).

Ministry of Finance, Ankara (tel: 425-0080; fax: 425-0058; internet site: www.maliye.gov.tr).

Ministry of Foreign Affairs, Balgat, Ankara (tel: 287-1665; fax: 287-8811).

Ministry of Forestry, Ataturk Bulvari 153, Ankara (tel: 417-6000; fax: 213-2610).

Ministry of Health, Sihhiye, Ankara (tel: 431-4820; fax: 431-4879).

Ministry of Industry and Trade, Eskisehir Yolu, Ankara (tel: 286-0365; fax: 285-4318).

Ministry of the Interior, Ankara (tel: 418-1368; fax: 418-1795).

Ministry of Justice, Ankara (tel: 419-6050; fax: 417-3954).

Ministry of Labour and Social Security, Inonu Bulvari, Ankara (tel: 212-9700; fax: 215-4962).

Ministry of Public Works and Housing, Vekaletler Cad 1, Ankara (tel: 417-9260; fax: 418-5540).

Ministry of Transport, Ankara (tel: 212-4416; fax: 212-4930).

Other useful addresses

Borsa Komiserligi (stock exchange), Menkul Kiymetler ve Kambiyo Borsasi, Rihtim Caddesi 245, 80030 Karakoy, Istanbul (tel: 298-2100; fax: 298-2500; internet site: http://www.ise.org).

British Consulate General Ankara, Merutiyet Caddesi No 34, Tepebasi, Beyoglu PK33, Ankara (tel: 293-7450; fax: 245-4989).

British Embassy, Sehit Ersan Caddesi 46/A, Cankaya, Ankara (tel: 468-6230/42; fax: 468-3214).

Customs Modernisation Project, Gümrük Müstesarligi, Anafartalar Cad No 6 Kat 14, 06100, Ulus, Ankara (tel: 306-8532, 306-8439; fax: 306-8535).

Director General of Mining, Ankara (tel: 287-9750; fax: 287-9152).

Director General of Press and Publications, Ankara (tel: 468-4967; fax: 468-4966).

Director General of State Water Affairs, Ankara (tel: 418-3415; fax: 418-3409).

Director General of Telecommunications, Ankara (tel: 313-1121; fax: 313-1919).

Embassy of the United States of America, 110 Ataturk Blvd, Ankara (tel: 426-5470, 468-6110; fax: 467-0057/19).

Export Promotion Centre (IGEME), Mithatpasa Cad No 60, Kisilay, Ankara (tel: 418-5351; internet site: http://www.igeme.org.tr).

General Directorate of Foreign Investment, Inönü Bulvari, 06510 Emek, Ankara (tel: 212-8914/5; fax: 212-8916).

Housing Development Administration, Project Implementation Unit, Bilkent Plaza, B1 Blok Kat 1, Bilkent 06530, Ankara (tel: 266-7764, 266-7774; fax: 266-7733).

Modern Tercume Burosu (translation service), Karanfil Sokak 21/4, Yenisehir, Ankara (tel: 417-8122).

Privatisation Administration, Ziya Gokalp Street No 80, Kurtulus 06600 Ankara (tel: 430-0194, 430-4560; fax: 430-6930; e-mail: hascili@oib.gov.tr).

State Institute of Statistics, Necatibey Caddesi 114, Ankara (tel: 417-6440; internet: www.die.gov.tr/ENGLISH/index.html).

State Planning Organisation, Necatibey Caddesi 108, Ankara (tel: 417-6440; internet site: http://www.dpt.gov.tr).

Türk Argus Ajansi (translation service), Lamartin Caddesi 32/4 Taksim, Istanbul (tel: 250-5200).

Türk Haberler Ajansi (news agency), Turkocagi Caddesi 1/4, Cagaloglu, Istanbul (tel: 511-4200).

Turkish Embassy (USA), 2525 Massachusetts Avenue, NW, Washington DC 20008 (tel: (+1-202) 612-6700; fax: (+1- 202) 612-6744; e-mail: info@turkey.org).

Turkish International Co-operation Agency, Kizilirmak Cadessi 31, Kocatepe, Ankara (tel: 417-2790).

Türkiye Radyo Televizyon Kurumu, Nevzat Tandogan Caddesi 2, Kavaklidere, Ankara (tel: 428-2230; fax: 414-2767).

Türk Snayicileri ve Isadamlari Dernegi (association of Turkish industrialists and businessmen), Cumhuriyet Caddesi, 233/9-10 Harbiye, Istanbul (tel: 246-2412, 240-1205).

National news agency: Anadolu Agency, Anadolu Ajansi, Genel Müdürlügü, Gazi Mustafa Kemal Bulvari 128/C, Tandogan, Ankara (tel: 231-7000; internet: www.aa.com.tr).

Other news agencies: Anka News Agency (www.ankaajansi.com.tr)

Turkish News Agency (www.turkishnewsagency.com)

Internet sites

Foreign Trade Secretariat: http://dtm.gov.tr

Republic of Turkey: http://www.turkey.org

State Institute of Statistics: http://www.die.gov.tr

Treasury Secretariat: http://www.treasury.gov.tr

Turkish Foreign Trade and Tourism Centre: http://www.turkex.com

Turkish highways: http://www.kgm.gov.tr/indexe.htm

Turkmenistan

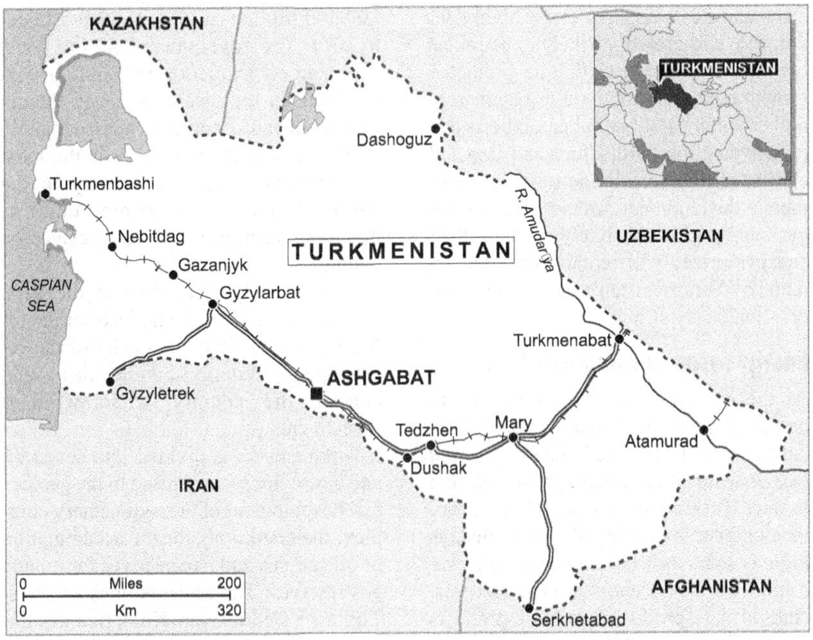

At the end of 2011 President Kurbanguly Berdymukhamedov was still comfortably esconced in power. In March 2007 he had been elected successor to the dictatorial, self styled 'father of the Turkmen' Saparmurad Niyazov who had died in December 2006 of a heart attack. An idea of how democracy works (or doesn't work) in Turkmenistan can be derived from the election statistics. The new president obtained 89.23 per cent of the votes in an election that Western observers and the Turkmen opposition abroad claimed was neither free nor fair. Mr Berdymukhamedov had been education and health minister under Niyazov, so was well schooled in his less than liberal ways. Official figures (never to be trusted in Turkmenistan) were that 98.65 per cent of the electorate had voted. References in Mr Berdymukhamedov's inaugural address to 'mutual benefits and equal rights' were taken with a pinch of salt.

Turkmenistan, the most ethnically homogenous of the Central Asian republics is largely a desert country, with over 80 per cent of its land mass covered by the Kara-Kum desert. The majority of the Turkmen population work in agriculture, principally nomadic cattle raising, intensive agriculture and the hydrocarbons sector.

Even after his death Turkmenistan's domestic scene continued to be heavily influenced by the ideology of the late 'president-for-life' Niyazov. Turkmenistan's international profile was dominated by the country's position as an increasingly central player in the politics of natural gas production and supply. Like most of its Central Asian neighbours, Turkmenistan also strove to minimise any knock-on effect from the Tulip Revolution in Kyrgyzstan. This revolution, in March 2007, had heralded the first and so far only, ousting of an incumbent president in Central Asia since the collapse of the Soviet Union in 1991.

The economy

According to the Asian Development Bank (ADB) the Turkmen economy rebounded in 2010 with government sources estimating gross domestic product (GDP) growth at over 9 per cent, close to the levels seen prior to the global recession. Much of the growth derived from the

KEY FACTS

Official name: Türkmenistan Jumhuriyati (Republic of Turkmenistan)

Head of State: President Gurbanguly Berdymukhamedov (TDP) (from 14 Feb 2007)

Head of government: President Gurbanguly Berdymukhamedov

Ruling party: Türkmenistanyn Demokratik partiýasy (TDP) (Turkmenistan Democratic Party) (from 14 Dec 2008)

Area: 488,100 square km

Population: 5.20 million (2010)*

Capital: Ashgabat

Official language: Turkmen

Currency: New Manat (M) = 100 tennesi (The new manat was introduced on 1 January 2009, with an exchange rate of 5,000 old manat to one new manat).

Exchange rate: M2.84 per US$ (Oct 2011)

GDP per capita: US$3,243 (2009)

GDP real growth: 6.10% (2009)

GDP: US$31.86 billion (2009)

Unemployment: 60.00% (unofficial, 2004)* (no official unemployment data)

Inflation: -2.70% (2009)

Oil production: 216,000 bpd (2010)

Balance of trade: US$2.00 billion (2007)

* estimated figure

resumption of natural gas exports to the Russian Federation, which were suspended for much of 2009, and the opening of new gas pipelines to China and Iran. The strong growth also came from large-scale public investments, a surge in foreign direct investment (FDI) and rapid gains in construction, transport and communications, textiles and agriculture.

Natural gas remains the mainstay of the economy – hydrocarbon exports accounted for over 90 per cent of exports in 2010. Moreover, hydrocarbon production is the main source of government revenue. Gas exports reportedly grew by 34 per cent in 2010 from the previous year. Consumer price inflation for the end of period was estimated to have risen from 0.1 per cent in 2009 to 4.6 per cent in 2010, giving a 2010 average of 3.9 per cent, a switch from deflation of 2.7 per cent in 2009. The inflation partly reflects rising international food and grain prices, which went up by about 12 per cent in 2010. Government controls over certain prices, wages and pensions and a stable exchange rate helped to keep consumer prices in check. The government's expansionary fiscal policy reduced the budget surplus from an estimated 7.8 per cent of GDP in 2009 to 2.8 per cent in 2010.

Much of the spending is guided by the National Programme of Social and Economic Development, which was updated in mid-2010 to cover the period 2011–30. The programme entails large public investment in economic and social infrastructure.

The recovery in gas exports and increased earnings from higher oil export prices helped to narrow the current account deficit from an estimated 16.1 per cent of GDP in 2009 to 4.7 per cent in 2010. The balance of trade in 2010 moved to a small surplus of US$100 million, from a deficit of US$1.8 billion in 2009. Estimated exports were US$10.1 billion for the year, a slight increase from US$9.5 billion in 2009. Imports were estimated to be US$10.0 billion, down from US$11.3 billion the previous year. The outlook for 2011 and 2012 appears to be highly favourable and growth is likely to be robust over the forecast period. The predicted growth rates will continue to result from higher volumes of natural gas exports due to new pipelines with China and Iran and continued implementation of the government's development policies. The global gas supply glut will likely peak in 2011 and gas prices will remain low, but demand by Turkmenistan's established buyers should stay strong.

Energy resources understated?

At the end of 2010 Turkmenistan had proven oil reserves of roughly 600 million barrels according to the US based *Oil and Gas Journal*. It is possible, however, that in fact Turkmenistan's oil reserves are much higher than originally estimated, as high as some two billion barrels plus six billion barrels of undiscovered reserves. Natural gas, crude oil and oil products make up about 80 per cent of the Turkmenistan's exports.

Most of the country's oilfields are situated in the South Caspian Basin in the west of the country. According to the US Energy Information Administration (EIA) Turkmenistan has experienced significant oil production growth since it obtained independence from the USSR, more than doubling from 110,000 barrels per day (bpd) in 1992 to approximately 216,000bpd in 2010. The government has frequently targeted higher oil production, but the oil sector struggles to meet its growth goals due to lagging foreign investment. Foreign investment is limited to joint ventures (JV) and production-sharing agreements (PSAs); Turkmen officials hope to attract US$500 million in oil-sector investment in 2011. The government hopes to boost Turkmen oil extraction to 2 million bpd by 2020. In the meantime, even though Turkmenistan exported approximately 170,000bpd back in 2004, it is the most oil intensive consumer country in the world. It consumes over nine times as much oil per unit of GDP as the average country.

Unfortunately, according to the EIA, slow-paced political and economic reforms have made the majority of the international energy companies that entered the country withdraw their investments.

Turkmenistan is divided into seven oil and gas regions – according to the geological development of the sedimentary complex, the conditions for the accumulation of oil and gas and perspectives for oil and gas reserves. The seven regions are West Turkmen, Central Kara Kum, Beurdeshik-Khiva, Chardzhou, Zaunguz, Murgab and Badkhyz-Karabil. As foreign investment is limited to JVs and PSAs with the state-owned Turkmenneft it has typically been concentrated on offshore oil projects in the Caspian Sea. According to the 2011 *BP Statistical Review of World Energy*, Turkmenistan produced an average of 216,000bpd of crude oil in 2010, 0.3 per cent of the world total and an increase of 2.8 per cent over 2009. Some of the companies currently operating in the country are Dragon Oil, Petronas (Malaysia) and Burren Energy.

Turkmenistan contains several of the world's largest gas fields, located primarily in the Amu'Darya basin in the east, the Murgab Basin and the South Caspian basin in the west. Turkmenistan contains large amounts of natural gas reserves but is constrained by the lack of available natural gas transport infrastructure. According to the *BP Statistical Review of World Energy 2011*, Turkmenistan had proved natural gas reserves of 8 trillion cubic metres at the end of 2010, 4.3 per cent of the world total. This reserve level ranks Turkmenistan among the top four countries in terms of natural gas reserves. Turkmenistan exports most of its natural gas production.

KEY INDICATORS **Turkmenistan**

	Unit	2006	2007	2008	2009	2010
Population	m	5.10	5.19	*5.27	*5.35	*5.20
Gross domestic product (GDP)	US$bn	21.85	25.96	18.27	*31.86	–
GDP per capita	US$	4,280	2,230	3,606	3,243	–
GDP real growth	%	11.1	11.6	10.5	6.1	–
Inflation	%	8.2	6.3	14.5	-2.7	–
Oil output	'000 bpd	163.0	198.0	205.0	209.0	216.0
Natural gas output	bn cum	62.2	67.4	66.1	36.4	42.4
Exports (fob) (goods)	US$m	7,155.0	9,114.0	*11,786.0	*8,946.0	–
Imports (fob) (goods)	US$m	2,558.0	3,780.0	*5,363.0	*8,071.0	–
Balance of trade	US$m	4,557.0	5,334.0	*6,423.0	*875.0	–
Current account	US$m	3,351.0	4,037.0	*3,560.0	*-2,981.0	–
Exchange rate	per US$	5,200.00	5,200.00	5,200.00	14,215.00	2.84

* estimated figure

Risk assessment

Economy	Good
Politics	Poor
Regional stability	Fair

COUNTRY PROFILE

Historical profile

Present-day Turkmenistan was divided three ways between Tsarist Russia and the Khanates of Bukhara and Khiva until 1881, when Russian troops captured Ashgabat and incorporated the country into Russian Turkestan. The fierce Turkmen tribes south of the Amu Darya River were subdued in 1885.

1917 Central Asian peoples were given the right of self-determination by Lenin after the October Revolution in Russia.

1916–21 Turkmens joined other Central Asians states in violently opposing a Russian decree conscripting them for non-combatant duties. They fought against the Bolsheviks during the Russian civil war. In 1921, Turkmenistan formed part of the Turkestan Autonomous Soviet Socialist republic (ASSR).

1924 Turkmenistan was given Union Republic status.

1920s–1930s The Soviet programmes of agricultural collectivisation and secularisation saw an upsurge in armed resistance and popular uprisings in Turkmenistan.

1960s The completion of the Kara-Kum canal led to a rapid expansion in cotton production. The canal is around 800km long and carries water from the Amu Darya River westwards to Mary and Ashgabat.

1971 Muhammad Gapusov was appointed head of the Turkmenistan Communist Party.

1985 Saparmurad Niyazov replaced Gapusov.

1989 Agzybirlik (Unity), a democratic front led by Turkmen intellectuals, was formed, but was banned the following year.

1990 Turkmenistan's Supreme Soviet declared economic and political independence from Moscow and elected Niyazov as its chairman (in effect, state president).

1991 Niyazov supported an attempted military coup against Soviet President Mikhail Gorbachev. Turkmenistan declared independence just before the collapse of the Soviet Union and joined the Commonwealth of Independent States (CIS).

1992 Turkmenistan adopted a new constitution, making the president head of government as well as head of state and giving him the option to appoint a prime minister. Niyazov was re-elected in a direct election in which he was the only candidate allowed to stand.

1993 The manat was introduced as the new national currency. The government began opening up the country to limited foreign investment in the country's oil and gas reserves.

1994 In parliamentary elections, all candidates were returned unopposed. In a referendum, President Niyazov's term of office was extended to 2002 without a new election.

1997 The private ownership of land was legalised.

1998 A natural gas pipeline to Iran was opened.

1999 Parliament made President Niyazov president for life. In parliamentary elections, all the elected officials were privately approved by the President.

2002 Turkmenistan became a full member of the Islamic Development Bank (IDB). The President renamed the months of the year after himself, his mother and his spiritual guide, the Ruhnama.

2003 Russian oil producer, Gazprom, agreed to buy 60 billion cubic metres of gas from Turkmenistan annually. The President cancelled a 1993 dual citizenship agreement with Russia, which sparked a diplomatic row with Moscow.

2004 An agreement on water resources was signed by the presidents of Turkmenistan and Uzbekistan. In parliamentary elections all 50 seats were filled by candidates supporting the president.

2006 President Niyazov died. The State Security Council named Deputy Prime Minister Gurbanguly Berdymukhamedov as acting president.

2007 Gurbanguly Berdymukhamedov was elected president with 89.2 per cent of the vote, beating five other candidates; turnout was 98.7 per cent. Turkmenistan Russia and Kazakhstan agreed to build a new gas pipeline north of the Caspian Sea to ensure gas supplies to Russia.

2008 Natural gas supplies to Iran were cut, during one of the coldest winters in many years. Turkmenistan blamed a technical fault but required Iran to pay more for a resumed supply. A new constitution was adopted that abolished the Khalk Maslakhaty (People's Council) and changed the structure of power including the roles of parliament and the president. The Persian Islamic calendar imposed by the previous president was dropped and the old version re-adopted. The government removed references to the late president Niyazov from the national anthem. Names of months and days, cities, an airport and a meteorite, which were also named after Niyazov and his family, reverted to their original names. In parliamentary elections, 125 seats (out of 125) were won by the Türkmenistanyn Demokratik partiýasy (TDP) (Turkmenistan Democratic Party). They were the first multi-party elections ever held in the country; however due to the lack of time given to register political parties before the elections were called for the newly expanded parliament, opposition parties were unable to field any candidates and the TDP was the only party registered. Opposition groups and Western observers said the elections were a 'sham'; of the 288 candidates running for parliament 90 per cent belonged to the TDP and the rest were state-approved individuals.

2009 The new manat was introduced on 1 January, with an exchange rate of 5,000 old manat to one new manat. President Berdymukhamedov ceremonially began the construction of the latest channel to bring run-off water from the country's cotton fields across thousands of kilometres of desert to create an inland sea. The project, which began in 2000 with two other channels bi-secting the country and hundreds more planned to create feeder funnels, is estimated to cost US$20 billion.

2010 In August, Turkmenistan requested a US$4.1 billion loan from China to develop its untapped South Yolotan natural gas field, which contains proven reserves of 2.8 trillion cubic metres of natural gas, with a further estimated 4–14 trillion cubic metres. The field is one of the world's largest gas fields.

2011 A military arms depot outside Abadan exploded on 7 July, causing many deaths and widespread damage that sparked panic and mass looting. Prolonged power failures in the capital followed. On 4 August it was announced that negotiations between Turkmenistan and the five European partnership countries (Austria, Bulgaria, Hungary, Romania, Turkey) of the Nabucco pipeline were to be held in Poland in September.

Political structure

Constitution

Turkmenistan was the first Central Asian state to adopt a constitution (on 18 May 1992), which upholds political pluralism, separates legislative, executive and judicial powers and guarantees private ownership of property. However, adherence to the principles of the constitution is rare. A new constitution was adopted on 25 September 2008 that abolished the Khalk Maslakhaty (People's Coucil) and changed the structure of power including the roles of parliament and the president. Turkmenistan is divided into five administrative regions: Ashkhabat, Turkmenbashi (formerly Krasnovodsk), Mary, Tashauz and Chardzhou.

Independence date

27 October 2001

Form of state

Republic

The executive
The president is elected by direct popular vote for a five-year term. All candidates must have lived in the country for 15 years before the elections. The president, as head of the executive branch of government, can dissolve the legislature only if the parliament is deadlocked on the election of the Speaker. Parliament would appoint a deputy prime minister as acting president if the president is unable to perform his duties; an acting president cannot run for office as president.
National legislature
The Majlis (Assembly) (established in 2008) has125 members, elected in single seat constituencies by universal adult suffrage (over 18 years of age) for five-year terms. Candidates may be nominated by political parties, public organisations, and interest groups.
Parliament may pass laws, amend the constitution, approve the state budget, set dates for elections of the president, members of the legislature, and local governing bodies and can ratify or reject international treaties. The parliament delivers binding interpretation of laws and determines the legality of executive branch decisions. It may also terminate a president's term of office for reasons of health.
Legal system
The legal system is based on civil law. Members of the Supreme Court, the highest judicial body, are appointed by the president. There is no judicial review of legislative acts or presidential decrees.
Last elections
11 February 2007 (presidential); 14 December 2008 (parliamentary)
Results: Parliamentary: 125 seats (out of 125) were won by the Türkmenistanyn Demokratik partiýasy (TDP) (Turkmenistan Democratic Party).
Presidential: Gurbanguly Berdymukhammedov won 89.2 per cent of the vote; turnout was 98.7 per cent.
Next elections
2013 (parliamentary); 2012 (presidential).

Political parties
Ruling party
Türkmenistanyn Demokratik partiýasy (TDP) (Turkmenistan Democratic Party) (from 14 Dec 2008)
Main opposition party
Due to the lack of time given to register political parties before general elections were called for the newly expanded Mejlis in 2008, opposition parties were unable to field any candidates.

Population
5.20 million (2010)*
Last census: January 1995: 4,483,251
Population density: 11 inhabitants per square km (2010)
Annual growth rate: 1.3 per cent 2005–10 (WHO 2010)
Ethnic make-up
Turkmen (77 per cent), Russian (6.7 per cent), Uzbek (9.2 per cent) and Kazakh (2 per cent).
Religions
The majority of the population are Sunni Muslim (89 per cent). The remainder are predominately Eastern Orthodox Christians (9 per cent).
The government directly controls the hiring, promotion and sacking of Sunni Muslim and Eastern Orthodox clergy.
Turkmenistan has a tradition of Sufism or Islamic mysticism and hosts several important Sufi religious sites.

Education
Secondary specialised education lasts for three to four years. General higher education lasts for four years. The Academy of Sciences in Ashgabat was the Republic's principal college of higher education. However, funding problems meant that by 2000 the Academy was closed. According to the government, 20 per cent of the relevant age group participate in some form of tertiary education. Those doing so are forced to undergo family checks going back three generations, while overseas education is not sanctioned by the government.
Females constitute 53 per cent of students in secondary education, 38 per cent of students in higher education and 29 per cent of students in professional schools. Although there is equal opportunity for females in education, they are often disadvantaged in employment situations.
A series of reforms have taken place since independence, with the aim of reducing the costs of education in general and vocational education in particular. Vocational training schools provide training to general education graduates, or adults who are required to pay fees. Some schools, especially in the bigger cities, are able to make enough income to maintain or even expand their activities. However, as government spending on vocational training in rural areas was reduced in the late 1990s, a number of vocational schools closed.
The quality of education is widely regarded as poor at all levels, and the sector is likely to come under increasing pressures from budgetary cuts and high population growth in the region. In September 2000, President Niyazov announced the axing of 5,000 jobs in the education sector as part of his drive to control the government's budget. Combined with low wages in the sector, this move is likely to undermine morale and reduce Turkmenistan's relatively high education statistics.
Literacy rate: 98 per cent adult rate; 100 per cent youth rate (15–24) (Unesco 2005).
Enrolment rate: 90 per cent gross primary enrolment of relevant age group (including repeaters) (World Bank).

Health
The healthcare system in Turkmenistan has suffered serious under-funding in recent years so that the benefits enjoyed by Turkmenis under the Soviet regime has been lost. Life expectancy has fallen to the lowest of any central Asean state. Free healthcare no longer exists, hospitals outside the capital have been closed, leaving 55 per cent of the population, living in rural areas, forced to travel long distances for treatment.
The availability of prescription drugs is severely limited, although the privatisation of pharmacies has led to an increase in the supply of non-prescription drugs.
There are no private hospitals or clinics in the region although some practitioners offer basic medical services.
Environmental hazards have contributed to widespread respiratory diseases, which prompted the government to ban smoking in public places. Nevertheless government policy on healthcare has ignored the need for Aids awareness, which is thought, by campaigners, to be an heavily underreported.
HIV/Aids
HIV prevalence: 0.1 per cent aged 15–49 in 2003 (World Bank)
Life expectancy: 60 years, 2004 (WHO 2006)
Fertility rate/Maternal mortality rate: 2.5 live births per woman 2005–10 (WHO 2010); maternal mortality 65 per 100,000 live births (World Bank).
Child (under 5 years) mortality rate (per 1,000): 79 deaths per 1,000 live births (World Bank).
Head of population per physician: 4.18 physicians per 1,000 people, 2002 (WHO 2006)

Welfare
The government has attempted to deliver social services during the transitional period, but significant fiscal constraints continue to impede the progress of universal social transfers in the long-run. Taxes collected by the state tax service go to the state budget and the social security fund. The social security system is partly financed by payroll taxes set at 30 per cent of wages and voluntary contributions, while the government bears the full cost of social pensions and other subsidies as needed.
The state provides for different types of welfare payments, including pensions and

several benefits related to disability, child-care, minimum social allowance, workers compensation, unemployment and family allowances. In 2001, the government decided to double public sector salaries.
Pensions are calculated on the number of years employed and the level of income. Pension benefits were doubled in 2003 following a presidential decree.
Maternity leave benefits are paid according to work experience and income. It is usually paid for 112 days. Workers' compensation benefits are paid at the rate of 6 per cent of salary in cases of unhealthy work conditions and 12 per cent of salary for severely harmful work conditions. Those working in desert areas receive compensation at the rate of 10 per cent of their salary.
The government's human rights record remains extremely poor and it continues to commit serious human rights abuses. Interference with citizens' privacy remains a problem. Domestic violence and discrimination against women are prevalent.

Main cities

Ashgabat (capital, estimated population 763,537 in 2005), Turkmenabat (Chärjew) (232,158), Dashhowuz (209,087).

Languages spoken

There is a 28 per cent population of Russian or Uzbek speakers. English is also spoken.
Official language/s
Turkmen

Media

The Turkmen government has an absolute monopoly of the media.
In 2008 the Paris-based Reporters Without Borders condemned Turkmenistan for isolating its population from the world and subjecting it to 'propaganda worthy of a bygone age'.
Press
It has been reported that Turkmenistan is a very repressive climate for journalists, according to international observers, it controls not only printing presses but it monitors media outlets and imposes editorial policies.
In Turkmen, *Turkmenistan* is published six times a week, *Watan* is published three times a week, *Galkynys* is a weekly and represents the Democratic Party of Turkmenistan, *Turkmen Dunyasi* is a monthly and represents the Ashgabat-based World Turkmens Association. *Edebiyat we Sungat* is a literature and the arts magazine. In Russian the *Neytralnyy Turkmenistan* is published six times a week.
Broadcasting
Radio: Turkmen Radio operated two stations, Watan and Char Tarapdan (also in English) (assess may be by www.intervalsignals.net).
Television: There are four channels operated by Turkmenistan state television including TMT 1-2-3 and 4. TMT4 is multinational, transmitting in Turkmen, Russian, English and French. Imported programmes are routinely edited before public broadcasting.
News agencies
National news agency: Turkmen State News Service (TSNS): www.turkmenistan.ru
News Central Asia: www.newscentralasia.net

Economy

Turkmenistan's wealth is almost entirely derived from hydrocarbons and cotton. In 2008 oil exports accounted for 94 per cent of total exports, although in 2009 they fell by 60 per cent with a loss of over US$912 million in revenue. In January 2010, Turkmenistan's proved natural gas reserves were estimated to be the world's fourth largest deposits (7.5 trillion cubic metres (cum)). In 2009 it was ranked 14 for global exports of natural gas. In 2009 natural gas production fell to 36.4 billion cum, falling from a record high of 66.1 billion cum in 2008; both levels reflected demand from Turkmenistan's markets (mainly Europe). In October 2010, Turkmenistan announced that it intended to increase exports of natural gas by 700 per cent by 2030. This followed a summit meeting with Russian's President Medvedev in which negotiations for the sale of natural gas to Europe should be via Russia's state-controlled Gazprom energy company's network of gas pipelines, thereby avoiding the European-backed Nabucco gas pipeline. The Nabucco pipeline in 2011 was not ready to accept Turkmen natural gas; however Turkmenistan has to balance this with its experience of Russia's unilateral closure of its Caspian pipeline, with the loss of revenue in 2009, against possible greater revenue returns if it sold its gas directly to Europe. Turkmenistan and China have a 30-year agreement for the supply of 30 billion cum per year of natural gas. A second natural gas pipeline was opened between Turkmenistan's Dovletabad gas field to Iran in January 2010 and will, when fully operational, double gas exports to Iran to 20 billion cum.
Over 80 per cent of Turkmenistan's land mass is covered by the Kara Kum desert. Even so the majority of the population work in agriculture, principally nomadic cattle raising and intensive agriculture, particularly in cotton cultivation with Turkmenistan one of the world's tenth largest cotton exporters. Production was 304,814 tonnes in 2008/09, falling to 283,041 tonnes in 2009/10, before rising to an estimated 326,586 tonnes in 2010/11. The government has used hydrocarbon revenue to invest in agricultural technology to improve cotton production.
GDP growth was a high of 11.6 per cent in 2007 as world prices for oil were at a peak, however as trade weakened due to the global economic crisis it fell to an estimated 10.5 per cent in 2008 and further still to 6.1 per cent in 2009. Projected GDP growth in 2010 was 9.4 per cent, as global trade began to recover.
Economic data are unreliable and policy-making is opaque. The economy is dominated by the state, which accounts for around 80 per cent of annual output. A central control system is prevalent, with the state fixing prices, output targets and controlling the distribution, marketing and trade of most products. Investors remain largely wary of Turkmenistan, whose economy is characterised by an inadequate legal framework, often contradictory laws, corruption and excessive bureaucracy. Growth is driven by domestic investment – mostly state-led investments in oil and gas extraction, petrochemicals, electricity generation and transmission, textiles, and luxury housing. About 1.5 per cent of GDP is invested by foreign companies developing oil and gas fields under production-sharing agreements.
Life remains austere for many in Turkmenistan and over half the population lives below the poverty line. However the UN was unable to access statistics on poverty to include Turkmenistan in this section of the Human Development Index (2010).

External trade

Turkmenistan is a member of the Economic Co-operation Organisation (ECO), comprising 10 regional Central Asian countries. National statistics are not published; exports are chiefly primary products, cotton and hydrocarbons. Manufacturing and the service sector are underdeveloped and therefore most industrial and community requirements are imported.
Imports
Principal imports are machinery and equipment, vehicles, chemicals, and foodstuffs.
Main sources: China (typically 18 per cent of total), Turkey (16 per cent), Russia (16 per cent).
Exports
The main exports are natural gas (50 per cent of total exports), crude oil, petrochemicals and textiles and cotton fibre.
Main destinations: Ukraine (typically 22 per cent of total), Turkey (10 per cent), Hungary (7 per cent).

Agriculture

Farming

Agriculture typically contributes around 20 per cent to GDP. The cultivated land area is around 32 million hectares (ha), with arable land accounting for 19 million ha. Cotton, a major export earner, is cultivated on over 750,000ha of arable land. Turkmenistan was the second largest producer of cotton in the former Soviet Union and is still a major global producer.

In a report published in 2005 – *The Curse of Cotton: Central Asia's destructive monoculture* – the International Crisis Group (ICG) said that while the former Soviet cotton producing countries of Uzbekistan, Tajikistan and Turkmenistan continued to exploit their cotton growers there was little hope of improving economic development and tackling poverty. The cotton industry is vital to the economy of Turkmenistan, yet while the industry continues to rely on cheap labour (including children), land ownership is uncertain, state intervention discourages competition and the rule of law is limited, there is little incentive for the powerful vested interests to reform the system.

The government has started to diversify production in the agricultural sector away from the cotton monoculture. This has generated a small export surplus in cereal production and a growth of 18 per cent in wheat production. The 23 per cent rise in agricultural output could possibly signal self-sufficiency in grain production.

Turkmenistan is reliant on an inefficient Soviet irrigation system, which diverts water from the Amu Darya River and has contributed to the drying up of the Aral Sea. The irrigation system suffers from poor management and maintenance, with water losses of about 50 per cent, rising salinity and poor drainage.

An absence of storage and packaging facilities means that up to 30 per cent of the grain and cotton harvests are lost annually. Livestock accounts for around one-quarter of agricultural production, including the famous Karakul sheep.

Fishing

Turkmenistan has considerable fishing resources, with estimated total reserves at 50,000 tonnes of Caspian Sea fish and 8,000 tonnes of inland water fish.

Turkmenbashi, on the Caspian Sea, provides an excellent base for accessing marine resources, being located near the main fishing grounds and remaining ice-free throughout the year. The typical annual fish catch is over 12,000 tonnes; the main fish type is kilka, although herring, shad, mullet and crayfish are also harvested.

Forestry

Less than 10 per cent of Turkmenistan has forest cover. All forested land is owned by the state. There is no large-scale forest industry and most wood products are imported from Russia.

Industry and manufacturing

Industry typically contributes around 45 per cent of GDP and employs 25 per cent of the workforce.

The sector is dominated by the processing of hydrocarbons and other raw materials. The sector is labour intensive and the use of energy and raw materials is wasteful. There is some light engineering industry, which mainly concentrates on the production of cables. US-based Coca Cola has a plant in Turkmenistan. Gap, the multinational clothing retailer, in a joint venture with Turkmen, has a fully, vertically integrated jeans production facility, using locally produced cotton,

Tourism

The potential for tourism in Turkmenistan, a large part of which is desert, is limited. Attractions include a number of historical and cultural sites. Mountain and coastal resorts are being developed and hotel accommodation is expanding. Visitor numbers are modest at some 8,000 a year, but increasing slowly. Air connections are improving and Ashgabat Airport has been modernised.

A new tourist zone has been designated, by the Turkmen Caspian Sea, in 2008. The president signed foreign investment agreement worth US$500 million to develop the site in Avaza.

Environment

The Aral Sea is drying up due to the overuse of water from the two main rivers which feed into it and has lost 40 per cent of its water, dropping by up to 19 metres. This has resulted in desertification of the surrounding land. A UN study published in 2004 reported that there was no possibility of restoring the water and the need must be on preserving what was is left.

The government endorsed a 2004 joint strategy to resolve the demands of its water requirements with its neighbours.

An artificial lake (132 cubic metres deep, 3,460 square km in area) in the Kara Kum Desert is planned to be constructed by 2010 at a cost of US$6 billion. It will be situated at the Karashor valley and according to the government will prevent the 4,060 square km large lowlands from being flooded, stop desalinisation of the land and return the area to crop growing. Environmentalists claim it will undermine the agricultural sector and contribute to water loss.

A meeting was held in 2009 to determine water sharing between Tajikistan, Kyrgyzstan, Uzbekistan, Turkmenistan and Kazakhstan failed, as negotiators were unable to find a trade in water for energy and hydrocarbons. Tajikistan and Kyrgyzstan hold around 80 per cent of the water in the Aral Sea but suffer from lack of electricity during freezing winters, while the remaining three states downstream are semi-arid and need water for their cotton industries and agriculture.

Mining

There are large deposits of iodine-bromine, sodium sulphate, magnesium, sulphur, potassium and other salts in Turkmenistan. Prime deposits of ore and rock are located in Tourakyr, Bolshoy Balkhan, Kopet Dag, Badkhyz, Govurdak, Kugitang, Cheleken, Turkmenbashi peninsula, central and south-east Garagum and northern Turkmenistan. Of these, the Zulfagar alunite deposit in Badkhyz in the south contains several million tonnes of ore with a 50 per cent alunite content. Turkmenistan has the third largest deposits of sulphur in the world, located in the Kara Kum desert. Deposits of industrial minerals, notably kaolin and building granite, are also exploited. Non-ferrous and rare metals are mined and used for the production of chemicals. Gold and platinum are also present.

Despite Turkmenistan's vast resources, mineral deposits are under-exploited and not used significantly in domestic industry. Turkmenistan has not traditionally extracted or processed any significant amounts of metal ores, although the government has shown interest in attracting foreign investment to build its own metal-producing facilities.

Hydrocarbons

Proven oil reserves were 1.0 billion barrels in 2010, with production at 1.34 million barrels per day (bpd), an increase of 2.2 per cent on the 2009 figure of 1.0 million bpd. State-owned Turkmenneft accounts for 90.5 per cent of oil extraction and the rest by foreign companies in production-sharing arrangements.

Turkmenistan's oil reserves remain difficult to estimate as potential oil reserves depend on negotiations to define ownership and prospecting rights in the Caspian Sea.

Turkmenistan has two oil refineries – Turkmenbashi and Chardzhou – with a combined capacity of 237,000bpd.

Proven natural gas reserves were 8.0 trillion cubic metres in 2010 making it one of the world's largest deposits; the government claims the actual figure is far higher. Natural gas production was 57.1 billion cubic metres (cum) in 2010, a decrease of -3.8 per cent on the 2009 figure of 19.3 billion cum. The state-owned Turkmengaz accounts for 85 per cent of production with the remainder produced by foreign companies in production-sharing arrangements.

The 1,818km Turkmenistan-China natural gas pipeline, passing through Uzbekistan and Kazakhstan (both of which have undertaken to build their section of the pipeline) to take advantage of natural gas supplies, began construction in 2008 and was scheduled to be completed by 2011. The 188km Turkmenistan section of a 7,000km natural gas pipeline was completed in 2009, at a cost of US$400 million. Natural gas supplies are scheduled to begin flowing from the Caspian Sea, across Central Asia to China by 2009. China has a 30-year agreement for the supply of 30 billion cum per year of natural gas using this pipeline.
Turkmenistan exported 6.5 billion cum of natural gas via its pipeline to Iran in 2010; a second, 25km, gas pipeline was opened in January 2010 which, when fully operational, will double gas exports to Iran to 20 billion cum. Turkmenistan has considered joining the Trans-Caspian Gas Pipeline project but in 2009 Russia offered Turkmenistan greater benefits for the supply of its natural gas to Russia than those offered by Europe for the same gas. The pipeline, opened in 2010, will weaken Moscow's hold over the region, as well as dampen Western hopes. An agreement was signed in December 2010 to build a 1,700km natural gas pipeline supplying gas from Turkmenistan to Afghanistan, Pakistan and India (Tapi). The estimated cost of the Tapi project was between US$3.3 billion (but may go as high as US$10 billion) and was backed by the Asian Development Bank when it was first proposed in the mid-1990s. Any use of coal is commercially insignificant.

Energy

Total installed generating capacity was 12.55 gigawatts (GW) in 2006, which produced 46.66 billion kilowatt hours (kWh), producing a surplus of 4.43kWh to be exported to Iran and Kazakhstan. All power stations are fuelled by domestically produced natural gas. The government aims to increase electricity production to 25.5 billion by 2012, but reaching this target will require significant investment in energy infrastructure.
Turkmenistan is connected to Iranian power lines and exchanges electricity during periods of peak energy consumption, usually summer in Turkmenistan and winter in Iran. The government also plans to sell electricity through Iran to other countries of the Economic Co-operation Organisation (ECO), which includes six former Soviet republics.

Financial markets

Stock exchange

Türkmenistanyn Döwlet Haryt – Çig Mal Biržasy (The State Commodity and Raw Materials Exchange of Turkmenistan)

Commodity exchange

The State Commodity and Raw Materials (SC&RM) exchange trades commodities only.

Banking and insurance

The economic crisis of 1997–98 led to all banks in Turkmenistan becoming 'government commercial banks'. Prior to this move, Turkmenistan had 67 banks, two of which were state-owned banks (Vneshekonombank and Sberbank). Vneshekonombank has become one of the largest banks in Central Asia since its creation in 1991. The bank dominates import/export operations and is a key institution for the operation of foreign investment in Turkmenistan. Sberbank holds 95 per cent of all household deposits. The banking sector is widely viewed as corrupt and inefficient, failing to channel funds effectively, and is constrained by the government's tight control of the credit and foreign exchange markets.

Central bank

Central Bank of Turkmenistan

Main financial centre

Ashgabat

Time

GMT plus five hours

Geography

Turkmenistan is the second largest Central Asian republic and shares lengthy borders with Iran to its south and Uzbekistan to its north and east. The country also borders Kazakhstan to the north-west and Afghanistan to the south-east. The Caspian Sea, where the major port of Turkmenbashi is located, is to the west. The Kara Kum desert comprises over 80 per cent of Turkmenistan's total area. The Kopet Dag mountains extend along Turkmenistan's southern border with Iran and Afghanistan.

Hemisphere

Northern

Climate

Temperatures in Ashgabat range between 0 and 40 degrees Celsius (C). Turkmenistan can be very hot in the summer, with temperatures of 35 degrees C common and a maximum of up to 50 degrees C in some provinces. Winters in the Ashgabat area tend to be mild and temperatures do not usually fall below freezing. However, in mountainous southern areas it is not uncommon for temperatures as low as minus 33 degrees C to be recorded. Ashgabat is the southernmost capital city of the former Soviet republics, on the same latitude as San Francisco and Cordoba.

Dress codes

Smart clothes are required for business visitors.

Entry requirements

Passports

Required by all. Passports must be valid for six months after date of departure.

Visa

Required by all. Business visitors require a full itinerary and an invitation, certified by the Ministry of Foreign Affairs in Ashgabat, from a local, private individual or company to support their application. The Turkmen Chamber of Commerce can provide new business visitors with such a letter. For tourists, these can be obtained from authorised travel agents in Ashgabat. All visitors must provide evidence of sufficient funds for the visit and return/onwards passage.
For further information visit www.turkmenistanembassy.org.
All visa applications made overseas are referred to Ashgabat for a decision. This can take several weeks. There is an accelerated 24 hours service, but a supplementary fee is levied.
On arrival visitors must complete an immigration card and pay a US$10 immigration fee. The authorities retain one copy and the other must be handed back, by the visitor, on departure.
Visitors must register within three days of their arrival, excluding weekends and holidays, with the Turkmenistan State Registration Service. This is carried out by the inviting organisation or individual, and a registration fee is paid. Tourists should register with the State Committee of Turkmenistan for Tourism and Sports. Registration is for the period of the visa; three days before departure, visitors must de-register with the same authorities. Visitors not staying in Ashgabat should register at the local *velayat* office of their place of residence (there is no need to register both in Ashgabat and regionally).
Visitors transiting the country can be registered at entry and exit points if their stay is not longer than five days and they hold a valid transit visa. Transit visitors cannot change their visas in-country, and need to notify the authorities if they intend to vary their route through the country.

Currency advice/regulations

In 2008, local currency began to be exchanged for foreign currency at regulated commercial rates. The import of foreign currency is unlimited but must be declared; export is limited to the amount declared. Visitors should check with the central bank for up-to-date regulations. Ensure you bring enough US dollars to cover all potential needs, Turkmenistan is a cash-only economy. Traveller's cheques and credit cards are not commonly accepted.

Customs

On arrival declare all foreign currency and valuable items such as jewellery, cameras, computers etc.

Prohibited imports
Firearms, illegal drugs and wool carpets.

Health (for visitors)
Mandatory precautions
Vaccination certificate required for yellow fever if travelling from an infected area.
Advisable precautions
Water precautions recommended: water purification tablets may be useful or drink bottled water.
It is advisable to be in date for the following immunisations: polio, diphtheria, tetanus, typhoid, hepatitis A, tuberculosis. Also hepatitis B if you are spending more than 6–8 working weeks in a year in the region.
Anti-malarial precautions are advisable. Inoculation against rabies is advisable if travelling to rural areas. It could be wise to have precautionary antibiotics if going outside major urban centres. A travel kit including a disposable syringe is a reasonable precaution. There is a shortage of routine medications and visitors should take all necessary medicines with them. Medical insurance, including emergency evacuation, is necessary.

Hotels
Rooms are often in short supply and expensive. It is advisable to book in advance through Intourist or other specialist travel agents. A number of major hotel renovations and new building projects have been undertaken in the centre of Ashgabat.

Credit cards
Credit cards are accepted.

Public holidays (national)
Fixed dates
1 Jan (New Year's Day), 12 Jan (Remembrance Day), 19 Feb (National Flag Day), 20 Mar (Novruz Bairam/Persian New Year), 9 May (Victory Day), 18 May (Constitution Day), 6 Oct (Remembrance Day), 27–28 Oct (Independence celebrations), 17 Nov (Students' Day), 12 Dec (Day of Neutrality).
Variable dates
Eid al Adha (Kurban Bairam), Eid al Fitr (Seker Bairam – three days).
Islamic year 1433 (26 Nov 2011–14 Nov 2012): The Islamic year contains 354 or 355 days, with the result that Muslim feasts advance by 10–12 days against the Gregorian calendar. Dates of feasts vary according to the sighting of the new moon, so cannot be forecast exactly.

Working hours
Banking
Mon–Fri: 0930–1730.
Business
Mon–Fri: 0900–1800.
Government
Mon–Fri: 0900–1800.
Shops
Mon–Sat: 0900–1800.

Telecommunications
Mobile/cell phones
The usage of mobile phones is extremely limited; a GSM 900 services exist in Ashgabat, Mary and Turkmenabat.

Electricity supply
220V AC 50Hz. Round two-pin continental plugs are standard.

Social customs/useful tips
Gratuities are becoming more customary, particularly in international hotels. Visitors are advised to carry some form of identity at all times.

Security
It is unwise to venture out on the streets alone at night. Visitors should be vigilant and are advised to dress down. Keep expensive jewellery, watches and cameras out of sight.

Getting there
Air
National airline: Turkmenistan Airlines
International airport/s: Ashgabat Airport (ASB), 4km from city centre. The are limited services from UK, Germany, Russia and the Middle East.
Airport tax: Departure tax: US$25; nationals of CIS countries US$15.
Surface
Road: Primary roads are few; secondary roads, particularly in desert areas, are of poor quality.
There are border crossings with Iran, Afghanistan, Kazakhstan and Uzbekistan. A road links Chardhzhou and Mazar-e-Sharif in Afghanistan.
Rail: A railway service operates from Iran. It runs nearly 300km from the Iranian Silk Road city of Mashhad, crosses the Turkmen border at Sarakhs and joins the Soviet-era Turksib railway at Tedzhen. It gives Turkmenistan access to the Iranian Gulf port of Bandar Abbas.
Water: The only coastline is along the Caspian Sea.
Main port/s: Turkmenbashi, has ferry links to Baku (Azerbaijan).

Getting about
National transport
Air: Akhal Air Company (division of Turkmenistan Airlines) operates domestic services. Daily flights between Ashgabad and Mary.
Road: Roads are poorly maintained and sometimes dangerous. However, new highways are under construction.
Buses: Buses serve Turkmenbashi (formerly Krasnovodsk) and Mary.
Rail: There are lines between Ashgabat, Turkmenbashi, Dashgouz and Mary. Trains to Gushgi are currently prohibited to foreign visitors due to the proximity of the Afghan border.
City transport
Taxis: Volga taxis have a sign on top. Agree a price beforehand. It is safer to use officially marked taxis which should not be shared with strangers.
Car hire
A national licence with authorised translation, or an international driving permit, is required.

BUSINESS DIRECTORY
The addresses listed below are a selection only. While World of Information makes every endeavour to check these addresses, we cannot guarantee that changes have not been made, especially to telephone numbers and area codes. We would welcome any corrections.

Telephone area codes
The international direct dialling (IDD) code for Turkmenistan is +993, followed by area code and subscriber's number:

Ashgabat	12
Mary	522
Turkmenabad (Chardhzhou)	378
Turkmenbashi (Krasnovodsk)	243

Useful telephone numbers
Fire: 01
Police: 02
Ambulance: 03
Gas leak: 04

Chambers of Commerce
Turkmenistan Chamber of Commerce and Industry, 17 Karreyeva Street, Ashgabat 744000 (tel: 355-594; fax: 355-381; e-mail: asccitm@online.tm).

Banking
Daykhanbank, 60 Atabayeva St, Ashgabat (tel: 419-873, 419-875; fax: 419-868).

Garashsyzlyk, 30 A Shevchenko St, Ashgabat (tel: 354-875, 397-393; fax: 397-892).

International Joint-Stock Bank Garaguma, 3 K Kuliyeva St, Ashgabat (tel: 354-062, 475-269; fax: 353-854).

National Bank of Pakistan, Sheraton Turkmen Hotel, 7 Gorogly St, 744000 Ashgabat (tel: 350-465, 512-050; fax: 350-465).

Obabank, 51 Ostrovskogo, Ashgabat (tel: 346-968, 346-558; fax: 246-968).

Prezidentbank, (temporarily at:) 22 Bitarap Turkmenistan Str, Ashgabat (tel: 357-943; fax: 510-812).

The Savings Bank of Turkmenistan, 86 Prospect Mahtumkuly, 744000 Ashgabat (tel: 394-298, 395-4671; fax: 396-553).

Senagat, 42 Turkmenbashy Shayoly Prospect, Ashgabat (tel: 510-305, 350-694; fax: 510-571).

The State Bank for Foreign Economic Affairs of Turkmenistan (Turkmenvnesheconombank), 22 Asudalyk St, 744000 Ashgabat (tel: 235-0252; fax: 239-7982).

Central bank
Central Bank of Turkmenistan, 22 Bitarap Turkmenistan St, 744000, Ashkabad, (tel: 353-442; fax: 356-711; email: cbtmode@cat.glasnet.ru).

Stock exchange
Türkmenistanyn Döwlet Haryt – Çig Mal Biržasy (The State Commodity and Raw Materials Exchange of Turkmenistan): www.exchange.gov.tm

Commodity exchange
The State Commodity and Raw Materials (SC&RM) exchange trades commodities only.

Travel information
Akhal Air Company, Ashgabat Airport, 744088 Ashgabat (tel: 225-6084/1052; fax: 229-0724, 225-4402).

DN Tours, Magtumguly Avenue 48/1, 744000 Ashgabat (tel: 270-438, 270-449; fax: 270-420; email: dntour@online.tm; internet: www.dntours.com).

Intourist, Hotel Ashgabat, Prospekt Makhtumkuli 74, 744023 Ashgabat (tel: 290-026).

Lufthansa Airport Office, Ashgabat Airport (tel: 510-697; fax: 510-728).

Turkmenintour, Ul Makhtumkhuli 74, Ashgabat (tel: 256-932, 255-191; fax: 293-169).

Turkmenistan Airlines, Ashgabat Airport (foreign economic relations) (tel: 290-766; fax: 254-402).

Ministry of tourism
National tourist organisation offices
State Committee of Turkmenistan for Tourism and Sport, 17-1984 Pushkin Street, 744000 Ashgabat, (tel: 354-777, 397-606, 396-740; internet: www.tourism-sport.gov.tm; www.turkmenistan.gov.tm; www.turkmens.com).

Ministries
Ministry of Agriculture, Ulitsa Azadi 63, Ashgabat 744000 (tel: 256-691; fax: 253-557).

Ministry of Automobile Transport, Ulitsa Baba Annanova 2, Ashgabat 744025 (tel: 474-992; fax: 470-391).

Ministry of Communications, Ulitsa Zhitnikova 36, Ashgabat 744000 (tel: 256-665).

Ministry of Construction, Ulitsa Alishera Navoi 56, Ashgabat 744000 (tel: 256-060).

Ministry of Construction Materials Industry, Ulitsa Steklozavodskaya 1, Ashgabat 744000 (tel: 251-560; fax: 251-913).

Ministry of Consumer Goods, Ulitsa Annadurdieva 52, Ashgabat 744000 (tel: 255-442; fax: 254-833).

Ministry of Economy and Finance, Borodinskaya Street no 2, Ashgabat 744000 (tel: 251-653; fax: 256-511).

Ministry of Energy and Industry, Ulitsa N Pomma 6, Ashgabat 744000 (tel: 254-921; fax: 291-670).

Ministry of Foreign Affairs, Prospect Lenina no 11, Ashgabat 744000 (tel: 251-463).

Ministry of Foreign Economic Relations, Ulitsa Kemine 92, Ashgabat 744000 (tel: 297-511; fax: 297-524).

Ministry of Health, Prospect Magtymguly 95, Ashgabat 744000 (tel: 251-063; fax: 255-032).

Ministry of Information, Ulitsa Chekhova 8, Ashgabat (tel: 297-572).

Ministry of Interior Affairs (tel: 251-328).

Ministry of Melioration and Water Resources, Ulitsa Seidi 1, Ashgabat 744000 (tel: 253-032; fax: 298-589).

Ministry of Oil and Gas Industry and Mineral Resources, 28 Gogolia Street, Ashgabat 744000 (tel: 293-827; fax: 510-443).

Ministry of Trade, Pervomayskovo Street no 1, Ashgabat 744000 (tel: 251-047; fax: 295-108).

Office of the President (tel: 254-534).

Other useful addresses
American Business Liaison, Gogol Street no 17, Ashgabat 74000 (tel: 253-386).

British Embassy, 301-308 Office Building, Ak Altin Plaza Hotel, Ashgabat (tel: 251-0861; fax: 632-510).

Central Asia Research Forum, School of Oriental and African Studies, Thornhaugh Street, London WC1H 0XG, UK (tel: (+44-(0)20) 7323-6300; fax: (+44-(0)20) 7436-3844).

Department of Investments, Cabinet of Ministers, Ashgabat (tel: 254-954; fax: 255-112).

EU-TACIS, 92 Kemine Street, Ashgabat (tel: 512-117, 251-020; fax: 511-721).

Kuvyat (state energy corporation), 6 Nurberdi Pomma Street, Ashgabat; Foreign Economic Relations (tel/fax: 254-921).

State Agency for Foreign Investment of Turkmenistan, 53 Azadi Street, Ashgabat 74400 (tel: 350-231; fax: 350-415).

State Committee on Statistics, 72 Magtymgyly Avenue, Ashgabat 744000 (tel: 294-265, 253-596; fax: 254-379).

State Commodity and Raw Materials Exchange, Magtumguly Street 3111, Ashgabat (tel: 254-321; fax: 510-304).

State Customs Office, 7 Stepan Razin, 7440225 Ashgabat (tel: 470-455; fax: 470-221).

State Railway of Turkmenistan, 7 Saparmirat Turkmenbashi Street, 744007 Ashgabat; Engineering Department (tel: 473-936; fax: 473-958); International Services (tel: 473-958; fax: 510-632).

State TV and radio, Prospekt Svobody 89, Ashgabat (tel: 251-515).

Turkmenistan Embassy (USA), 2207 Massachusetts Svenue, NW, Washington DC 20008 (tel: (1-202) 588-1500; fax: (1-202) 588-0697; e-mail: turkmen@earthlink.net).

Turkmenintorg Foreign Trade Organisation, Hivinskaya Str 1, 744000 Ashgabat (tel: 298-774/684/975, 297-521; fax: 298-774/955, 295-987).

National news agency: Turkmen State News Service (TSNS): www.turkmenistan.ru

Internet sites
Turkmenistan Embassy, Washington, US: www.turkmenistanembassy.org

Turkmenistan Information Centre: www.turkmenistan.com

Turks and Caicos Islands

KEY FACTS

Official name: Turks and Caicos Islands

Head of State: Queen Elizabeth II, represented by Governor Damian Roderic Todd (from 12 Sept 2011)

Head of government: Premier Galmo Williams (appointed by governor 25 Mar 2009)

Ruling party: Progressive National Party (PNP) (from 2003; re-elected 2007)

Area: 430 square km

Population: 38,000 (2010)

Capital: Cockburn Town (on Grand Turk)

Official language: English

Currency: US dollar (US$) = 100 cents

Exchange rate: US$1.00 per US$ (fixed)

COUNTRY PROFILE

Historical profile

The first residents of the islands were Amerindians. There are claims that Christopher Columbus actually made his first landing (1492) in the Americas on Grand Turk, and not in the neighbouring Bahamas.

1512 Spanish explorer, Juan Ponce de León, arrived.

1678 British settlers came from Bermuda and set up a salt-panning industry.

1766 Having overridden French and Spanish claims to the islands, Britain appointed a colonial resident.

1799 The islands were annexed to the Bahamas.

1874–1962 The islands were administered from British ruled Jamaica, after which they became a Crown colony and were ruled from the Bahamas.

1972 When the Bahamas gained independence the islands gained their own governor.

1976 A constitution was adopted and the first independent elections were won by the pro-independence People's Democratic Movement (PDM).

1980 The PDM lost the general election to the Progressive National Party (PNP) which was committed to maintaining the status quo.

1982 Plans for independence were reversed.

1985 Chief Minister Norman Saunders, the minister for development and commerce, and a PNP member of the Legislative Council, were arrested and subsequently convicted in the US on drug trafficking charges.

1986 The constitution was suspended following allegations of corruption in local government and a commission of inquiry found the chief minister, Nathaniel Francis, and two of his ministers, unfit to govern. The governor assumed direct control of government and the Executive Council, and ruled through a special Advisory Council.

1988 The constitution was reinstated with revisions.

2002 Jim Poston became governor.

2003 The ruling PDM won the parliamentary election, but in two by-elections, won by the opposition, the PNP gained a majority in parliament. Chief Minister Taylor resigned and Michael Eugene Misick was sworn in on the same day.

2004 The EU's Savings Tax Directive was implemented.

2005 Richard Tauwhare was sworn in as governor.

2006 A new constitution revised the title of the chief minister to premier. A new minimum wage, for all workers, was introduced.

2007 In general elections the ruling PNP won 60 per cent of the vote (13 out of 15 seats); the DPM 40 per cent (two). Michael Misick continued as premier.

2008 Governor Tauwhare resigned and Deputy Governor Mahala Wynns became acting governor. The governor announced he had appointed a Commission of Inquiry (CoI) into allegations of corruption and other serious dishonesty in relation to past and present elected members of the House of Assembly. Gordon Wetherell became governor.

2009 The CoI reported that there were 'clear signs of political amorality and immaturity and of general administrative incompetence' and 'a high probability of systemic corruption or serious dishonesty' in the Turks and Caicos Islands (TCI) government. Prime Minister Misick resigned. The constitution was suspended and power and responsibility for government business reverted to the governor and an advisory council and consultative forum for a minimum period of two years. Galmo Williams and six other members of the House of Assembly were sworn into office as premier and cabinet ministers respectively, although all legislative and executive power remained the responsibility of the governor. The CoI's final report was published and recommended that criminal investigations into the activity of five cabinet ministers, including the former premier, be undertaken by the police.

2010 In April, the Bank of Providenciales was closed down and liquidated by order of the TCI supreme court, at the behest of the official Financial Service Commission (FSC) when it was confirmed that there were insufficient funds to cover withdrawals and the bank was unable to obtain additional financial support. In the first legal actions to be undertaken by the Special Investigative Prosecuting Team, writs of corruption against three businesses that allegedly bribed the former premier Misick

and a former cabinet member were filed in April.
2011 On 9 February, the UK government agreed to provide a financial support package of US$260 million, which included a bridging loan of US$170 million and a five-year loan of US$30 million to shore up the TCI treasury. On 8 March the new, draft TCI constitution was published by the UK Foreign and Commonwealth Office. The final 2008–09 CoI report was published on 31 May, following the last dismissals of legal challenges to the conclusions in the report. It reiterated its initial recommendations that criminal investigations should be undertaken into the activities of former ministers, premier Michael Misick, minister of finance Floyd Hall, minister of natural resources McAllister Hanchell, minister of works Jeffrey Hall and minister of health and education Lillian Boyce. Lack of financial support from the UK government to fund the investigation team had delayed prosecution. On 18 July, the UK minister responsible for Overseas Territories announced that as much as US$5 billion was missing from the TCI treasury due to the fraudulent activities of the Misick administration. The draft constitution was negotiated with civic leaders and the UK government in June and an agreement achieved in July. On 12 September, Damian Roderic Todd took office as governor.

Political structure

Constitution

The constitution was suspended on 25 March 2009 with power and responsibility for government reverting to the governor and an advisory council and consultative forum for a minimum period of two years.
The 1976 constitution was suspended in 1986, restored and revised in 1988 and amended in 1993. It provided for the exercise of a ministerial type of government, through a governor appointed by the British monarch, an Executive Council (ExCo) which had general control of government, and a Legislative Council (LegCo). A new constitution of August 2006 replaced the legislative council with a unicameral house of assembly of 21 members, 15 of whom are directly elected for a four-year term, four nominated from the cabinet, one ex-officio (the attorney-general) and the speaker. The cabinet consists of two ex-officio members (the financial secretary and the attorney-general), the premier and other ministers. The British monarch continues to be head of state, represented by a governor.
Voting: universal suffrage 18 years and over.

Independence date

25 November 1975

Form of state

Caribbean dependency status: overseas territory of the UK.

The executive

The head of state, Queen Elizabeth II, is represented by an appointed governor. The cabinet consists of two ex-officio members (the financial secretary and the attorney-general), the premier and other ministers.

National legislature

The unicameral house of assembly is composed of 21 members, 15 of whom are directly elected for a four-year term, four nominated from the cabinet, one ex-officio (the attorney-general) and the speaker.

Legal system

The legal system is based on laws of England and Wales, with a small number of laws adopted from Jamaica and The Bahamas.

Last elections

9 February 2007 (parliamentary)
Results: Parliamentary: the ruling PNP won 60 per cent of the vote (13 out of 15 seats); the DPM won 40 per cent (two).

Next elections

2011 (parliamentary)

Political parties

Ruling party

Progressive National Party (PNP) (from 2003; re-elected 2007)

Main opposition party

People's Democratic Movement (PDM)

Political situation

Prime Minister Michael Misick resigned in March 2009, perhaps before he could have been sacked, following the critical report by the Commission of Inquiry into allegations of corruption and other serious dishonesty. The commission reported that there were 'clear signs of political amorality and immaturity and of general administrative incompetence' and 'a high probability of systemic corruption or serious dishonesty' in the Turks and Caicos Islands (TCI) government.
While Misick was trenchant in his denouncement of the accusations and declaration of his innocence, the UK government took over control of the government of the TCI, through its governor Gordon Wetherell.
Legal action began against Michael Misick and his brother, and former attorney-at-law, Chalmers (Chal) Misick for corrupt transactions, in 2010

Population

38,000 (2010)
Last census: August 2001: 19,886
Population density: 53 inhabitants per square km.
Annual growth rate: 3.2 per cent (2003)

Ethnic make-up

Afro-Caribbean (95 per cent)

Religions

Baptist (41 per cent), Methodist (19 per cent), Anglican (18 per cent), Seventh-Day Adventist (2 per cent).

Education

The school system is constrained by insufficient infrastructure and is poorly equipped to deal with children of immigrants for whom English is not a first language.
The UK government has a number of projects, which it is working on through the Department for International Development (DFID). By improving teaching methods, the government hopes that around 80 per cent of children will achieve levels in reading and mathematics acceptable to their age.
The primary and secondary curriculum is also under review with plans that it will be standardised.
Compulsory years: Four to 16
Enrolment rate: 94 per cent primary enrollment of relevant age group, 80.2 per cent secondary enrollment.

Health

The UK government has designed an ongoing programme of reforms to improve the health care system. Priorities include human resource development, greater access to financial resources and the prevention and control of HIV/Aids.
The hospital on the island of Grand Turk serves as a referral centre for all of the islands. There are nine community health care clinics throughout the islands.

HIV/Aids

HIV prevalence: Less than 1 per cent in 2004
Life expectancy: 77.7 years (estimate 2003)
Fertility rate/Maternal mortality rate: 4.61 births per woman

Welfare

There is a reciprocal health and welfare agreement with the UK, which entitles nationals of the Turks and Caicos islands to benefits such as income support, housing allowances and child benefits.

Main cities

Cockburn Town (capital, estimated population 5,000 in 2003) situated on Grand Turk island.

Main islands

Grand Turk (business centre), Providenciales (most tourism facilities), South Caicos (fishing and sailing), Salt Cay, Middle Caicos, North Caicos (natural bird sanctuary), Pine Cay and Parrot Cay.
Eight out of 30 islands are inhabited.

Languages spoken

Official language/s

English

Media

Press

There are no dailies but three weekly newspapers all published in . *Turks and Caicos Weekly News* (www.tcweeklynews.com), *Turks and Caicos Free Press* (www.tcifreepress.com) and the *Turks and Caicos Sun* (www.suntci.com). There is an online community newsletter (http://enews.tc). *Times of the Island* (www.timespub.tc) is a quarterly magazine.

Broadcasting

Radio: Radio Turks and Caicos (RTC) (http://tcimall.tc/rtc) broadcasts three channels. Private stations include the religious Radio Vision Christina (www.radiovision.net) and Power 92.5 (WIV) (www.power925fm.com).

Television: The Turks & Caicos Television, is based in Grand Turk, while WIV-TV is based in Providenciales, both are cable television services. Multi-channel satellite television is received from the US and Canada.

Advertising

Advertising is possible through the print media and radio.

Economy

The economy is wholly dependent on its service sector, with tourism and financial services providing the major share of foreign exchange and GDP growth.

The 2008/09 budget announced the Turks and Caicos Islands' (TCI) biggest budget deficit ever. The country was US$36 million in deficit forcing the government to introduce heavy tax hikes to pay for what the government called a 'culture of over-spending' in government departments; the premier's office alone was shown to have spent US$11 million. The UK government became increasingly perturbed at allegations of corruption and mismanagement and launched a Commission of Inquiry. In 2009, the resulting report for the UK Foreign and Commonwealth Office (FCO) into the financial dealing of the Michael Misick administration concluded 'that there was a high probability of systemic corruption in the former Turks and Caicos Islands Government.' In August 2009 the constitution was suspended and power and responsibility for government business reverted to the UK-appointed governor and a locally-drawn advisory council and consultative forum for a minimum period up to 2011.

On 10 April 2010, the Bank of Providenciales was closed down and liquidated by order of the TCI supreme court, at the behest of the official Financial Service Commission (FSC) when it was confirmed that there were insufficient funds to cover withdrawals and the bank was unable to obtain additional financial support.

The first legal actions, to be undertaken by the Special Investigative Prosecuting Team, filed writs of corruption on 30 April 2010 against three businesses that had allegedly bribed former premier Misick and a former cabinet member.

By 2011 the FCO had concluded that the 'fiscal picture in Turks and Caicos Islands represents an unacceptable collapse in the fiscal governance of the Territory', which needed urgently to be addressed. It appointed a chief financial officer tasked with addressing the structural deficit and developing a strategy for putting the economy on a course towards a sustainable fiscal surplus by the financial year 2012/13. On 9 February 2011, the UK government agreed to provide a financial support package of US$260 million, which included a bridging loan of US$170 million and a five-year loan of US$30 million to shore up the TCI treasury.

External trade

As a UK Overseas Territories the Turks and Caicos Islands is a member of the European Union's Association of Overseas Countries and Territories (OCT Association). It is also an associate member of the Caribbean Community (Caricom) and Common Market but does not operate within the single market (Caribbean Single Market and Economy (CSME)), which became operational in 2006.

Foreign earnings derived from the offshore financial sector, tourism and fisheries. All capital goods and foodstuffs are imported.

Imports

Principal imports are food and beverages, tobacco, clothing, consumer goods, manufactures and construction materials.

Main sources: UK and US

Exports

Principal reported exports are lobster, fish, dried and fresh conch, and conch shells.

Main destinations: UK and US

Agriculture

Farming

The agricultural sector is limited to small-scale production for domestic consumption and accounts for around 2 per cent of GDP. The growing tourism sector has encouraged production of fruit and vegetables for hotels and restaurants.

Farming is confined to the rearing of livestock and the growing of maize, beans and some fresh fruit. A hydroponics facility has been developed at Providenciales.

Fishing

The fishing industry grew as the salt industry declined. Over-fishing, low prices and better paid jobs in the growing tourism industry in the 1990s led to a decline in fishing. However, as export prices started to improve, particularly for conch, and the government started to improve conservation techniques and encourage value-added processing, so the industry has rebounded.

Fishing for lobster and conch production accounts for just under 2 per cent of GDP. There is a commercial conch farm on Providenciales.

The typical total annual fish catch is over 1,300mt; shellfish, molluscs and cephalopods account for another 1,000mt per annum.

Industry and manufacturing

The manufacturing sector accounts for less than 1 per cent of GDP. Activity is confined to fish processing (mainly lobsters and conch) and construction work. A rice-milling and packaging plant, supplied with rice from Guyana, is the only significant industrial enterprise.

Construction activity has increased with new tourist and residential developments. The Turks and Caicos Investment Agency is promoting the islands as a location for manufacturing electronic goods.

Tourism

Tourism is the mainstay of the Turks and Caicos economy and continues to expand rapidly, despite the effects of recession in the US and the 2001 terrorist attacks in the US. The main factor influencing growth in the tourism sector has been promotion efforts and improved airline access from North America to Providenciales. 77 per cent of total arrivals come from the US. Wishing to diversify away from dependence on this market, promotions have targeted Europe and Asia. Resort and other facilities continue to be developed, together with a strategic tourism plan for 2004–07. A cruise terminal and pier project in Grand Turk was opened in 2006.

Hydrocarbons

There are no known hydrocarbons reserves, all energy needs are met by imports. The Islands do not import either natural gas or coal.

Banking and insurance

Under an EU tax directive introduced in July 2005 in a number of associate and dependent EU countries, the Turks and Caicos began imposing a withholding tax to be passed to the relevant EU depositor's country but retaining the anonymity of the saver. Withholding taxes began at 15 per cent, and will rise to 35 per cent by 2011. Turks and Caicos has also agreed to supply information on tax fraud, for criminal or civil trials, and notify EU member states about additional malpractices.

Central bank
There is no central bank.
Main financial centre
Cockburn Town, Grand Turk.
Offshore facilities
The Financial Services Commission is an independent statutory body responsible for licensing and supervising all finance-related entities and registering companies.

Time
GMT minus five hours (daylight saving, April to October, GMT minus four hours)

Geography
The Turks and Caicos Islands (TCI) are a group of around 40 islands in the North Atlantic Ocean, split into two groups by a deep channel, which combined covers 500 square km of land. They are situated in the north of the Caribbean, 48km south of the Bahamas and 145km north of Haiti. The islands are limestone plateaux, no higher that 75 metres, most with lush green vegetation. Off their northern shore, TCI has the world's third largest coral reef system.
Hemisphere
Northern

Climate
Tropical, tempered by trade winds. Winter nights sometimes cool, summers are hot. Mean temperature range from 25–29 degrees Celsius.

Entry requirements
Passports
Required by all except visitors from North America who require birth certificate (or, a notarised copy) and photo ID (all US and Canadian nationals require a passport for re-entry to their country from January 2007). Proof of onward/return passage is required.
Visa
Not required except by citizens not found within the list given in www.turksandcaicostourism.com – *Facts and General Information – Visas and Immigration*. Further local information can be found at www.tcimall.tc/government or from the nearest British consulate.
Currency advice/regulations
The import and export of local and foreign currency is unrestricted.
Prohibited imports
Illegal drugs and pornography; firearms require a permit from the commissioner of police prior to arrival.

Health (for visitors)
Mandatory precautions
Yellow fever vaccination certificate required if arriving from an infected area.
Advisable precautions
Typhoid and polio vaccinations. Water precautions.

Hotels
Accommodation is available on Grand Turk, South, Middle and North Caicos, Salt Cay, Pine Cay, and Providenciales, reservations are necessary. There is an 8 per cent room tax and 10–15 per cent service charge added to bills.

Public holidays (national)
Fixed dates
1 Jan (New Year's Day), 12 Jun (Queen's Birthday), 25–26 Dec (Christmas).
Variable dates
Commonwealth Day (second Mon in Mar), Good Friday and Easter Monday (Mar/Apr), National Heroes' Day (last Mon in May), Emancipation Day (first Mon in Aug), National Youth Day (last Fri in Sep), Columbus Day (second Mon in Oct).

Working hours
Banking
Mon–Thu: 0830–1430; Fri: 0830–1230, 1430–1630.
Business
Mon–Fri: 0830–1600.
Government
Mon–Thu (winter): 0800–1230, 1400–1630; Fri: 0800–1230, 1400–1600.
Mon–Thu (summer): 0700–1130, 1300–1530; Fri: 0700–1130, 1300–1500.

Telecommunications
Mobile/cell phones
A GSM 850 service is available.

Electricity supply
120/240 V, 60 cycles

Weights and measures

Getting there
Air
International airport/s: Grand Turk (GDT); South Caicos International (XSC); Providenciales (PDS), duty-free shop, car-hire.
Airport tax: Departure tax: US$35.
Surface
Water: Cruise ships visit regularly.
Main port/s: Cockburn Harbour (South Caicos), Grand Turk, Providenciales.

Getting about
National transport
Air: Air Turks and Caicos serves Providenciales, South, Middle and North Caicos, Salt Cay and Grand Turk. Other scheduled and charter companies operate between the islands.
Road: Main roads on Grand Turk, South Caicos and Providenciales are surfaced.
Taxis: Taxis are unmetered and can be hired for the day, agree a price before travelling.
Water: There are scheduled ferries and island hoppers operating between most of the islands.
Car hire
Available on Grand Turk, Providenciales and South Caicos. National driving licence required, a flat tax of US$10 is levied on all hirings. Driving is on the left.

BUSINESS DIRECTORY

The addresses listed below are a selection only. While World of Information makes every endeavour to check these addresses, we cannot guarantee that changes have not been made, especially to telephone numbers and area codes. We would welcome any corrections.

Telephone area codes
The international direct dialling code (IDD) for Turks and Caicos Islands is +1 649 followed by subscriber's number.

Chambers of Commerce
Grand Turk Chamber of Commerce, PO Box 148, Grand Turk (tel: 946-2324; fax: 946-2504).

Banking
Bordier International Bank and Trust Ltd, PO Box 5, Caribbean Place, Providenciales (tel: 946-4535; fax: 946-4540; email: enquiries@bibt.com).

First Caribbean Bank, PO Box 258, Grand Turk (tel: 946-2831; Fax: 649 946 2695; email: care@firstcaribbeanbank.com).

Scotiabank International, Cherokee Road; PO Box 15, Providenciales (tel: 946-4750; fax: 946-4755; email: bns.turkscaicos@scotiabank.com).

Turks and Caicos Banking Co Ltd (private international banking services), PO Box 123, Harbour House, Front Street, Grand Turk (tel: 946-2368; fax: 946-2365; email: ajbf@turksandcaicosbanking.tc).

Central bank
None

Travel information
Air Turks and Caicos, PO Box 191; 1 InterIsland Plaza, Old Airport Road, Providenciales, (tel: 941-5481; fax: 946-4040; email: fly@airturksandcaicos.com).

SkyKing Airlines, PO Box 398, Providenciales (admin tel: 941-5464 ext 200 / 504; fax: 941-4264; email: cservices@skyking.tc; reservations: 941-3136; fax: 941-5127; email: res@skyking.tc; internet: http://skyking.tc).

Spirit Air (regional flights) 2800 Executive Way, Miramar, Florida 33025, USA (tel: (+1-954) 447-7965; fax: (+1-954) 447-7979; internet: www.spiritair.com).

National tourist organisation offices

Turks and Caicos Tourist Board, Front Street, PO Box 128, Grand Turk (tel: 946-2321/2; fax: 946-2733; email: tci.tourism@tciway.tc; internet: www.turksandcaicostourism.com).

Turks & Caicos Islands Tourist Board, Stubbs Diamond Plaza, Providenciales (tel: 946-4970, 491-5746; fax 941-5494).

Ministries

Governor's Office, Government House, Waterloo, Grand Turk (tel: 946-2309; fax: 946-2903; e-mail: govhouse@tciway.tc).

Main Government Offices, Cockburn Town, Grand Turk (tel: 946-2801).

Ministry of Education, Youth, Sports and Women's Affairs (tel: 946-2801, ext 142; fax: 946-1337; e-mail tci.sports@tciway.tc).

Ministry of Finance, Commerce and Development (tel: 946-2935, 946-2937; fax: 946-2557; e-mail: fsc@tciway.tc).

Ministry of Health and Education (tel: 946-2801; fax: 946-2722).

Other useful addresses

Development Board, PO Box 105, Hibiscus Square, Pond Street, Grand Turk (tel: 946-2058).

Financial Services Commission, Harry Francis Building, Pond Street, Grand Turk (tel: 946-2802; fax: 946-2821).

General Trading Company (Turks & Caicos) Ltd, PMBI, Cockburn Town, Grand Turk (tel: 946-2464).

Government Information Service (GIS), Government Square, Grand Turk (tel: 946-2301 ext 40505/40506; fax: 946-1120).

Immigration And Work Permits, Director Of Immigration, Immigration Department, Southbase, Grand Turk (tel: 946-2939/2700; fax: 946-2924; email: iam@tciway.tc).

TCInvest, Hibiscus Square, Box 105, Grand Turk (tel: 946-2058; fax: 946-1464; email: tcinvest@tciway.tc; internet: www.tcinvest.tc).

Turks & Caicos Hotel Association, Third Turtle Inn, Providenciales (tel: 946-4230).

Turks Islands Importers Ltd (TIMCO), Front Street, PO Box 72, Grand Turk (tel: 946-2480).

Internet sites

Gateway Sites: www.turksandcaicos.tc

Local Information: www.tc/info.htm

Tuvalu

The nine islands (five coral atolls and four reef islands) that constitute the tiny monarchy of Tuvalu continued to feel the impact of the global recession in 2010. Seafarer employment – a significant income source for households – was weak and is likely to remain so. Added to that fishery licences have fallen and the '.tv' domain name, which had been expected to make all Tuvaluans wealthy, has not been the anticipated success after the Australian dollar (Tuvalu's currency) gained parity with the US dollar. The strength of the Australian dollar also had an adverse impact on imports, which became more expensive. Gross domestic product (GDP) growth is expected to be around 0.5 per cent in 2012, after being flat in 2011.

Elections

Parliamentary elections were held on 16 September 2010. Of the 26 non-partisan candidates participating, 10 (out of 15) incumbent MPs retained their seats. On 29 September, Maatia Toafa won nine votes (out of 15) to become prime minister again. However, his first budget was challenged and Willy Telavi joined with the opposition to topple him. Telavi was elected by parliament as prime minister on 24 December. He beat Enele Sopoaga by eight votes to seven.

COUNTRY PROFILE

Historical profile

1819 A. The captain of a ship owned by Edward Ellice, an English member of parliament, visited Funafuta and named the island Ellice Island.

1850–75 European diseases, and the kidnapping of islanders for forced labour on plantations in Fiji and Australia (a practice known as 'blackbirding'), reduced the population from 20,000 to 3,000.

1877 The Western Pacific High Commission was set up by Britain, headquartered in Fiji. The Ellice Islands and other island groups come under its jurisdiction.

1892 A British protectorate was declared over the Ellice Islands and the group was linked administratively with the Gilbert Islands to the north.

1916 The UK annexed the protectorate, which was renamed the Gilbert and Ellice Islands colony.

1975 The Ellice Islands, under the old native name of Tuvalu (eight standing together), became a separate British dependency.

1978 Tuvalu became an independent country within the Commonwealth.

1987 The Tuvalu Trust Fund was established; it provides an average 15 per cent of the country's annual budget.

1989 A UN report on the greenhouse effect listed Tuvalu as one of the island groups which would completely disappear beneath the sea in the twenty-first century unless drastic action was taken.

1996 The 12-member parliament was forced out and Bikenibeu Paeniu became prime minister.

1998 Tomasi Puapua was appointed governor general.

1999 A no-confidence vote forced out Paeniu. Ionatana Ionatana was elected prime minister.

2000 Ionatana Ionatana died suddenly. Tuvalu was formally admitted to the UN.

2001 Parliament elected Faimalaga Luka as prime minister but later lost a no-confidence vote; Koloa Talake was elected as his replacement.

2002 Nine out of 15 MPs were re-elected. Parliament elected Saufatu Sopoanga as prime minister.

2003 The Sopoanga government lost its majority and ruled as a minority government. Faimalaga Luka was sworn in as governor general. The government regained its majority.

2004 During the first six months of the year, there were several very high 'king tides' associated with the new moon. At only four metres above sea level at their highest points, the islands experienced seawater swamping of homes and agricultural land. Prime Minister Sopoanga lost a no-confidence vote; Deputy Prime Minister Maatia Toafa was elected prime minister.

2005 Filoimea Telito was sworn in as governor general. Tuvalu signed the Pacific Islands Air Service Agreement (PIASA), to become the eighth Pacific Islands Forum country to do so. PIASA is designed to ensure open skies policies with more viable routes for airlines in the Pacific.

2006 In general elections, eight out of 15 members of parliament lost their seats, including the entire cabinet. Maatia Toafa

KEY FACTS

Official name: Tuvalu

Head of State: Queen Elizabeth II, represented by Governor General Filoimea Telito (sworn in 15 Apr 2005)

Head of government: Prime Minister Willy Telavi (from 24 Dec 2010)

Area: 26 square km (nine islands – five coral atolls and four reef islands)

Population: 11,909 (2010)*

Capital: Vaiaku in Funafuti administrative division

Official language: Tuvaluan, English

Currency: Australian dollar (A$) = 100 cents)

Exchange rate: A$1.03per US$ (Oct 2011)

GDP real growth: 1.60% (2010)

Inflation: 3.50% (2010)

* estimated figure

retained his seat but lost the premiership when Apisai Ielemia was selected as prime minister.
2008 In a referendum voters agreed to maintain a constitutional monarchy.
2010 The US awarded Tuvalu a grant of US$10,000 to begin a biofuel power generation programme, using copra-bio-diesel, made from the waste of the copra crop (coconut shells and husks). If the initial installation is successful, further biofuel generators will be installed on the nine islands. Tuvalu became the 187th member of the IMF in June. Parliamentary elections were held on 16 September; of the 26 non-partisan candidates participating, 10 (out of 15) incumbent MPs retained their seats. On 29 September, Maatia Toafa won nine votes (out of 15) to become prime minister again. Prime Minister Toafa's first budget was challenged and Willy Telavi joined with the opposition to topple him. Telavi was elected by parliament as prime minister on 24 December. He beat Enele Sopoaga by eight votes to seven.
2011 A two-week state of emergency was declared on 13 January following opposition-led street demonstrations that threatened the residences of the governor general and prime minister. Constituents of the Nukufetau island community demanded that their representative, finance minister Lotoala Metia, should resign. The government introduced a ban on public meetings, lifted on 10 February. By 1 June, the project to supply water to every home in Tuvalu had progressed to installing water tanks and associated plumbing to the seven outer islands. Funding for the work was provided by the UN and EU. A state of emergency was declared on 3 October after fresh water ran out and bottled water dwindled to a week's supply. The US Navy delivered 136,000 litres of bottled water and the New Zealand Red Cross responded by delivering personnel and desalination machines. There were 30 cases of water borne diseases confirmed by 6 October, due to the poor quality of drinking water. The shortage was the result of a lack of rainfall blamed on the La Nina weather pattern. Tuvalu has had no rainfall at all for seven months, and low rainfall for three years. The lack of rain is likely to have an impact on crops giving the island a food shortage problem.

Political structure

Constitution

The constitution dates from 1978. The British sovereign is head of state, represented by a governor general with limited powers. The governor general's powers to veto government measures were abolished under a constitutional amendment in 1986. Each island is ruled by a traditional council of chiefs which runs services and determines development priorities.

Independence date

1 October 1978

Form of state

Constitutional monarchy and parliamentary democracy

The executive

The British monarch is titular Head of State, represented by a governor general, whose functions are largely ceremonial. The governor general is appointed on the advice of the prime minister, in consultation with parliament.
Executive power is exercised by a cabinet of five members and is led by the prime minister. The government is collectively accountable to parliament.

National legislature

The unicameral Fale i Fono (parliament) has 15 members, directly elected for four-year terms. Seven islands send two members each, with one from Nukulaelae (with the smallest population). The parliament has the power to make laws, it can remove the prime minister through a vote of no-confidence and can be dissolved early by the governor general in accordance with the constitution.

Last elections

16 September 2010 (parliamentary)
Results: Parliament: 26 non-partisan candidates stood for election, 15 were chosen including 10 incumbent members.

Next elections

2014 (parliament)

Political parties

There are no organised political parties, although there are opposing political groupings.

Political situation

The politics of Tuvalu are dominated by the very real possibility that this collection of low-lying islands and atolls will disappear as global warming raises sea levels. Progress towards implementation of the Kyoto Protocol on climate change has not been broad or thorough enough and the peoples of all small islands are running out of time. So the action by the representative of Tuvalu, at the UN conference on climate change in Copenhagen (Denmark) in December 2009, when he pleaded with delegates to produce a legally binding agreement before storming out and closing the day's session, could be understood, if not forgiven. Environmental campaigners gave impromptu support for the passionate protest.

Population

11,909 (2010)*
Last census: November 2002: 9,561
Population density: 372 inhabitants per square km (2010)
Annual growth rate: 0.6 per cent 1994–2004 (WHO 2006)

Ethnic make-up

Tuvalu's population is Polynesian in origin.

Religions

Christianity, under which the Church of Tuvalu (Congregationalists) accounts for 97 per cent of the population.

Education

The vast distances between islands make the provision of education harder, as each small community requires a trained teacher. There is only one public, secondary school, located on the island of Vaitupu, where children reside for the academic year.
Compulsory years: Seven to 14.
Pupils per teacher: 19.5 (in primary schools); 12.2 (in secondary schools) (2005)

Health

Tuberculosis has been a long-term problem, which is monitored regularly and remedied under directly observed treatments (Dots), which has notably increased the rate of recoveries.
Figures from the United Nations Children's Fund (UNCF) (formerly Unicef) revealed in January 2010 that 80 per cent of families in the most vulnerable communities were without funds to buy food; more heads of households were losing their jobs due to the global economic crisis, which had resulted in rising food prices and falling remittances. Malnutrition, particularly among children and women, was becoming of increasing concern as governments in the Pacific region were cutting back on social expenditure in the face of recession.
Life expectancy: 61 years, 2004 (WHO 2006)
Fertility rate/Maternal mortality rate: 3.7 births per woman, 2004 (WHO 2006)
Head of population per physician: 0.55 physicians per 1,000 people, 2002 (WHO 2006)

Welfare

Statistic by the United Nations Children's Fund (UNCF) (formerly Unicef) revealed in January 2010 that 80 per cent of families in the most vulnerable communities were without funds to buy food, as more heads of households were losing their jobs due to the global economic crisis. Malnutrition, particularly among children and women, was becoming of increasing concern as governments in the Pacific region were cutting back on social expenditure in the face of recession.

Main cities

Vaiaku in Funafuti administrative division (capital, estimated population 5,300 in 2003).

Languages spoken
Official language/s
Tuvaluan, English

Media
Press
The *Tuvalu Echo* is published fortnightly and the government publishes a newsletter *Sikuleo o Tuvalu*.
Broadcasting
The government operates Radio Tuvalu and the online Tuvalu-News (www.tuvalu-news.tv). Most residents receive foreign television satellite programmes.
Radio: Radio Tuvalu is a government-owned station.
Advertising
Adverts may be placed on radio and in the newspaper, plus through overseas based television services.
News agencies
ABC Pacific Beat:
www.radioaustralia.net.au/pacbeat
Pacific Magazine:
www.pacificmagazine.net
Pacific Islands New Association (Pina):
www.pina.com.fj

Economy
Tuvalu is a mere 26 square kilometres in size and has an economy to match. The small subsistence economy accounts for approximately 30 per cent of GDP. It is supplemented by copra exports and official transfers and investment income from overseas assets. Its smallness means that even a slight change in economic activity will affect GDP. Tuvalu has had to take its revenue where it can and when it was allocated .tv as its country-level domain (CLD) indicator it went into business with a California corporation to take advantage of it. The government sold its share in DotTV Corporation in 2001 for A$20 million (US$10 million) and continues to receive a small royalty.
Other sources of revenue are fishing licences for the exclusive economic zone and remittances from seafarers (some 20 per cent of GDP). The Tuvalu Maritime Training Institute was upgraded over the period 2005–07. This was an important project as it not only increased economic activity but also ensured the Institute retained its accreditation from the International Maritime Organisation.
The Tuvalu Trust Fund (TTF) invests in equities and is normally an important source of income. The government invests its budget surpluses in the TTF as a financial stockpile for years when it runs a deficit. A second fund– the Falekaupule Trust Fund – for the outer islands, has been provided with funds by a loan from the Asian Development Bank (ADB).
The Asian Development Bank estimated GDP growth of 1.5 per cent in 2009 and forecast growth of 1.6 per cent in 2010. A sales tax of 5 per cent exists but the proposals to introduce value added tax (VAT) was being considered in 2009. The introduction of VAT would become important if the Pacific Island Countries Trade Agreement is ratified, since Tuvalu would be expected to loose customs revenue on imports goods from the region.

External trade
Tuvalu is a member of the South Pacific Regional Trade and Economic Co-operation Agreement (Sparteca) along with 12 other regional nations, which allows products duty free access by Pacific Island Forum members to Australian and New Zealand markets (subject to the country of origin restrictions).
Most foreign earnings are provided by sales of stamps and coins by mail order, and remittances.
Imports
Principal imports are food, animals, vehicles, mineral fuels, machinery and manufactured goods.
Main sources: Fiji (typically 46 per cent of total), Japan (19 per cent), China (18 per cent).
Exports
Copra and fish are the principal export commodities; coconut oil is exported to New Zealand.
Main destinations: Germany (typically 62 per cent of total), Italy (21 per cent), Fiji (7 per cent).

Agriculture
Farming
About 80 per cent of the population survive through subsistence agriculture.
Much of the soil is infertile, rainfall is variable and crops are liable to cyclone damage. Copra is the only export crop. Family smallholdings produce subsistence crops of pulaka, taro and other vegetables, bananas and coconuts. Agriculture is under threat from salinisation of the soil caused by rising ocean waters.
Fishing
Fishing and exploitation of the sea are important to the economy, serving mainly local consumption. There is potential to increase income by negotiating fisheries agreements with other countries. The typical annual marine fish catch is 500 tonnes.
In April 2010 the Parties to the Nauru Agreement (PNA) (eight island states including Tuvalu) collectively agreed to close to *purse seine* fishing in 4.55 million square kilometres of high seas in their area, from 1 January 2011, to vessels licensed to fish in their waters. The area involved stretches from Palau and Papua New Guinea in the west to Kiribati in the east, from the Marshall Islands in the north to Tuvalu in the south; it holds an estimated 25 per cent of the world's tuna supply.
On 12 April 2011, a summit of the Parties to the Nauru Agreement (PNA) concluded its strategy for a policy of sustainable fishing in the Pacific. The PNA treaty, which was established in 1989 and expires in 2012, is seen as in need of an overhaul. As a collective region (FSM, Kiribati, Marshall Islands, Nauru, Palau, PNG, Solomon Islands and Tuvalu) control around 25–30 per cent of world stocks of tuna. Only 5 per cent of sales revenue is returned to the PNA and ministers called for specific changes, including an increased share of profits, PNA crews on-board *purse seine* vessels (minimum 10 per cent), conservation and management measures including a limit to fish trapping (fish aggregating devices (FADs)), net mesh rules and the establishment of an observer agency and fisheries information management system.

Industry and manufacturing
A small industry sector (baking, construction, boat building, coconut oil mill, soap making etc) serves local needs, some handicrafts are exported.

Tourism
There is no developed tourist industry owing to Tuvalu's remote location, infrequent flights and lack of amenities, although a Tourism Action Plan has been developed. Air access from Fiji has improved, but the number of visitors, mainly on official or other business and relatives, is small.
Facilities, including the airport, the sole hotel and some guest houses, are concentrated on Funafuti. The other islands are relatively unspoilt, but are not easily accessible.

Environment
The government has publicly acknowledged the problem of the rising sea levels, but feels the situation has been exaggerated by the world media. Claims that the islands will be washed away by 2050 are debateable.

Mining
Tuvalu has no known mineral resources.

Hydrocarbons
There are no known hydrocarbon reserves. All fuel requirements are met by imported petroleum products.
The UN Law of the Sea gave Tuvalu an exclusive economic zone of 12,949 square km for exploration.

Energy
Total installed generating capacity was 1,480kW in 2005. The Energy Department is responsible for policy and planning for the atolls, while the Tuvalu Electricity Corporation supplies energy to

customers. Japan agreed to supply three new 600kW diesel-powered generators and upgrade the distribution grid. The government has placed an emphasis on renewable energy in a bid to reduce reliance on imported fuel; there has been a take-up in the supplementary use of solar-photovoltaic (PV) panels on Vaitupu and Niutao. Niulakita is entirely powered by solar-PV home systems.

Banking and insurance

The state-owned National Bank of Tuvalu (NBT) dominates the country's banking sector. Its monopoly position ensures that it remains in profit.

Tuvalu's currency is the Australian dollar and interest rates are determined by the Reserve Bank of Australia (RBA), so the government has little control over monetary policy. The royalty revenues generated by the '.tv' domain name (after the sale of the DotTV Corporation) have been lower than expected and are paid irregularly.

Central bank

National Bank of Tuvalu

Time

GMT plus 12 hours

Geography

Tuvalu is a scattered group of nine small atolls, extending about 560km (350 miles) from north to south in the western Pacific Ocean. Fiji lies to the south, Kiribati to the north and the Solomon Islands to the west. The Tuvalu archipelago consist of six true atolls and three reef islands. The true atolls are Funafuti, Nanumea, Nui, Nukufetau and Nukulaelae, while Nanumaga, Niulakita and Niutao are single islands. The last three have small salt-water ponds, while Nanumea has a fresh water pond, unusual for an atoll.

At their highest point, these islands are only four metres above sea level, and vulnerable to the rise in sea levels caused through global warming.

Hemisphere

Southern

Climate

Hot and humid, temperatures 26–32 degrees Celsius. Rainfall varies considerably, up to 3,000mm in a year, falling most heavily from November–February. Hurricanes possible.

Entry requirements

Passports

Required by all.

Visa

None required, however visitors must have return/onward tickets and sufficient funds for their stay.

Currency advice/regulations

No restrictions on import and export of local and foreign currency.

Customs

Personal effects allowed duty-free. There are quarantine regulations for plants and animals, and it is inadvisable to carry fruit or plant material. Certain goods may be subject to regulation or import licensing, such as arms, fireworks, drugs, motorcycles, jewellery.

Health (for visitors)

Health facilities are basic.

Mandatory precautions

Vaccination certificate for yellow fever required if travelling from an infected zone.

Advisable precautions

There is rabies risk. Vaccinations for diphtheria, tuberculosis, hepatitis A and B, polio, tetanus and typhoid are recommended.

Hotels

There is only one hotel, the government owned Vaiaku Lagi Hotel. Reservations should be made well in advance. Visitors may be asked to share rooms when there are accommodation shortages. Private guest houses are also available.

Tipping is optional and not expected.

Public holidays (national)

Fixed dates

1 Jan (New Year's Day), 15 May (Gospel Day) 12 Jun (Queen's Official Birthday), 5 Aug (National Children's Day), 1–2 Oct (Tuvalu Days, Anniversary of Independence), 25–26 Dec (Christmas).

Holidays that fall at the weekend are taken either on Friday or Monday.

Variable dates

Commonwealth Day (second Mon in Mar), Good Friday, Easter Monday.

Working hours

Banking

Mon–Thu: 0930–1300; Fri: 0830–1200.

Business

Mon–Fri: 0800–1600.

Government

Mon–Thu: 0730–1615; Fri: 0730–1245.

Shops

Mon–Sat: 0630–1730.

Electricity supply

240V AC (on island of Funafuti only)

Weights and measures

Imperial system (metric units allowed in some instances).

Social customs/useful tips

Tipping is not customary. In business an informal attitude prevails. It is customary to shake hands on meeting and taking leave. Sometimes business cards are exchanged after introduction. Business is conducted in English. Visitors should be perceptive to unfamiliar local customs.

Alcohol is generally available, but there are some limitations on consumption outside licensed premises. The minimum drinking age is 20 years.

Getting there

Air

International airport/s: Funafuti International (FUN), east of Funafuti.

Airport tax: Departure tax: A$10; not applicable to transit passengers

Surface

Water: There are two government-owned ships that sail infrequently between Suva (Fiji) and Funafuti; sailing time is three days.

Getting about

National transport

Road: The only tar roads are on Funafuti. Elsewhere there are tracks. There is a limited number of vehicles, including some minibuses.

Water: An inter-island service is available which can be interupted by bad weather.

City transport

Taxis: There are a few taxis from the airport to the city centre. Hotels offer an airport pick-up service.

BUSINESS DIRECTORY

The addresses listed below are a selection only. While World of Information makes every endeavour to check these addresses, we cannot guarantee that changes have not been made, especially to telephone numbers and area codes. We would welcome any corrections.

Telephone area codes

The international direct dialling (IDD) code for Tuvalu is +688 followed by subscriber's number.

Useful telephone numbers

Police and fire: 20-726

Ambulance: 20-749

Chambers of Commerce

Tuvalu Chamber of Commerce, PO Box 27, Funafuti (tel: 208-46; fax: 208-29).

Banking

Development Bank of Tuvalu, PO Box 9, Vaiaku, Funafuti (tel: 201-99; fax: 208-50).

Central bank

National Bank of Tuvalu; PO Box 13, Vaiaku, Funafuti (tel: 208-03; fax: 208-02; e-mail: gmbt@tuvalu.tu).

Travel information

Air Fiji, 185 Victoria Parade, Suva, Fiji (tel: (+679) 331-5055; email: suvasales@airfiji.com.fi).

Air Marshall Islands, PO Box 1319, Majuro MH 96960, Republic of the Marshall Islands (tel: (+692) 625-3731; fax: (+692) 625-3730; email:

amisales@ntamar.net; internet: www.airmarshallislands.com).

Funafuit International Airport, Vaiaku Funafuti (tel: 20-737, 20-057; email: travel@tuvalu.tv).

Funafuti International Airport, Department of Civil Aviation, Ministry of Works and Communication, Private Mail Bag, Funafuti (tel: 20-737, 20-725, 20-721; fax: 20-722).

South Pacific Tourism Organisation, Level 3, FNPF Place, 343-359 Victoria Parade; PO Box 13119, Suva, Fiji (tel: (+679) 330-4177; internet: www.spto.org).

Tuvalu Marine Department, Vaiaku, Funafuti, (tel: 20-055; fax: 20-722; email: danitaleli@yahoo.co.nz).

National tourist organisation offices

Tuvalu Tourism Office, Private Mail Bag, Vaiaku, Funafuti (tel: 20-184, 20-480; fax: 20-829; lleneuoti@yahoo.com; internet: www.timelesstuvalu.com).

Ministries

Ministry of Commerce and Natural Resources, Vaiaku, Funafuti.

Ministry of Finance, Vaiaku, Funafuti (tel: 20-840).

Statistics Division, c/o Finance Ministry, Vaiaku, Funafuti (tel: 20-839).

Other useful addresses

Asian Development Bank (ADB), South Pacific Regional Mission, La Casa di Andrea, Lini Highway; PO Box 127, Port Vila, Vanuatu (tel: (+678-2) 3300; fax: (+678-2) 3183; email: adbsprm@adb.org; internet: www.adb.org/SPRM).

Broadcasting and Information Office, Vaiaku Funafuti.

Business Development Advisory Board, PO Box 9, Funafuti (tel: 20-850).

Department of Civil Aviation, Ministry of Works and Communications, Private Mail Bag, Funafuti (tel: 20-737, 20-725, 20-721; fax: 20-722).

Department of Commerce, PO Box 33, Funafuti (tel: 20-839).

UN Permanent Mission of Tuvalu, 800 Second Avenue, Suite 400 B, New York, NY 10017 (tel: (+1-212) 490-0534; fax: (+1 212) 808-4975; email: enele@onecommonwealth.org).

Internet sites

South Pacific Tourism Organisation: www.tuvalu.spto.org

Tuvalu home page: www.tuvaluislands.com

KEY FACTS

Official name: Republic of Uganda

Head of State: President Yoweri Kaguta Museveni (NRM) (since 1986; re-elected 18 Feb 2011)

Head of government: Prime Minister Amama Mbabazi (from 24 May 2011)

Ruling party: National Resistance Movement (NRM) (from 1999; re-elected 2011)

Area: 236,036 square km

Population: 30.66 million (2010)*

Capital: Kampala

Official language: English

Currency: Ugandan shilling (Ush) = 100 cents

Exchange rate: Ush2,845.00 per US$ (Oct 2011)

GDP per capita: US$501 (2010)

GDP real growth: 5.20% (2010)

GDP: US$17.00 billion (2010)

Inflation: 9.40% (2010)

Balance of trade: -US$2.10 billion (2010)

Annual FDI: US$817.18 million (2010)

* estimated figure

Uganda

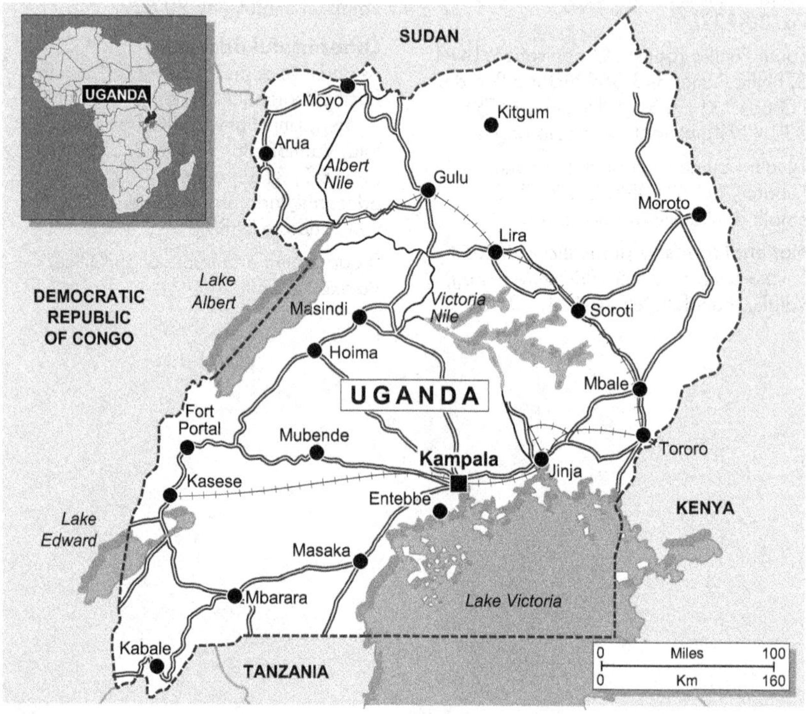

One way and another there was a lot of politiking in Uganda in 2011. The year opened with elections on 18 February. Eight candidates took part in the presidential election, which was won by the incumbent, Yoweri Museveni of the National Resistance Movement (NRM), with 68.4 per cent of the vote. Museveni was sworn in on 12 May for another five-year term, at the end of which he will have lead Uganda for 30 years. His closest rival, Kizza Besigye, leader of the Forum for Democratic Change (FDC) received 26 per cent of the vote. He later alleged that there had been fraud during the election. In parliamentary elections held on the same day the ruling NRM won an overwhelming majority of 263 seats (out of 375). The FDC came in second, a long way behind with 34 seats.

The arrest of Dr Besigye on 17 April as he attempted to join the 'walk-to-work' march protesting against the rising cost of living was followed by a demonstration which police broke up using tear gas and rubber bullets. Dr Besigye was released and left the country for hospital treatment in Kenya. There were a number of further demonstrations that the police broke up, including one in which two persons were killer and another in which demonstrators were sprayed with a pink dye. Police placed Besigye under house arrest on 19 May to prevent the mobilisation of his supporters during the opening of parliament ceremony. On 24 May President Museveni appointed Edward Ssekandi as vice president and Amama Mbabazi as prime minister.

The first trial of a Lords Resistance Army commander began on 11 July in Uganda's International Crimes Division court in Gulu. Thomas Kwoyelo was accused of 53 charges including murder and hostage-taking. Foreign affairs minister, Sam Kutesa, and two other officials resigned on 12 October after being accused of corruption.

The economy

The Ugandan economy recorded weaker growth of 5.1 per cent in 2010 because of receding aggregate demand, mainly in private consumption, and weak external demand for traditional exports, in particular coffee. In spite of the declines, reported the *African Economic Outlook 2011* (AEO), published jointly by the African Development Bank and the Organisation for Economic Co-operation and Development, regional demand for Uganda's exports remained high. Export earnings fell from US$2.9 billion in the financial year 2008/09 to US$2.8 billion in 2009/10. Although lower than 2008/09 levels (US$883 million), remittance receipts of US$820 million in 2009/10 surpassed traditional foreign exchange earners coffee and tourism. Earnings from coffee and tourism in 2009/10 were US$262 million and US$400 million respectively. Sustained public investment in infrastructure and the global recovery are expected to spur growth in the short- to medium-term. The near-term prospects for the oil and gas sector remain uncertain because of disputes between the government and oil exploration firms. The real gross domestic product (GDP) growth rate is projected to increase to 5.6 per cent in 2011 and 6.9 per cent in 2012 because of increasing regional demand and the improved global outlook.

Growth in 2010 was primarily driven by the telecommunications, financial services and construction sectors, while the services and agriculture, forestry, fishing and hunting sectors, which account for 54.4 per cent and 24.8 per cent of GDP respectively, showed weaker growth. Growth in telecommunications was bolstered by expansion in mobile telephony while financial sector growth was boosted by the licensing of an additional commercial bank and expansion in the size and outreach of the existing financial institutions. The rebound in fishing and food production was offset by falling growth for the cash crops of coffee and cotton, leading to stagnation in the agriculture sector. In the recent past the declining GDP share of the agriculture sector has been the result of low productivity, limited value addition and lack of commercialisation. On the demand side, growth was driven by private consumption and investment growth, albeit at rates lower than in 2009. Private consumption and private investment projections are for weaker growth in 2011 but recovery in 2012.

Inflation declined markedly from 13.4 per cent in 2009 to 7.3 per cent in 2010 as a consequence of falling food prices resulting from favourable weather conditions and subsequent improved food production. Indian Ocean pirates, break-downs in the Mombasa oil refineries, and new Kenyan axle loads regulations for trucks contributed to an increase in the price of fuel. Projections are for further reductions in 2011 and 2012. The monetary policy stance over the medium term remains focused on seeking to restrict inflation to the target of 5 per cent. The fiscal policy stance will remain expansionary in view of the government's sustained public investment in infrastructure, including roads and energy. Tax receipts are expected to recover in tandem with the improving economic prospects and tax administration efficiency gains, although these gains will not be sufficient to cover the shortfall in grants. Thus the overall fiscal deficit (including grants) as a percentage of GDP is expected to increase in 2011.

International trade and relations

The external position weakened as a result of a decline in export earnings from the traditional export crops, in particular coffee. International reserves, currently covering slightly under five months of imports, are expected to remain healthy, in part because of the weekly purchase of foreign exchange by the central bank.

The social sector also saw marked improvements with a reduction in the poverty rate from 31 per cent in 2005/06 to 23 per cent in 2009/10 although income inequality worsened. Progress was also recorded in education thanks to the universal primary and secondary education programmes. However, stagnation and reversals were reported for the health-related indicators.

Weak infrastructure, inadequate financial services to the private sector, and weaknesses in public sector management and administration are the major constraints to growth. The National Development Plan (NDP) for 2010/11–2014/15 is expected to prioritise reforms aimed at addressing these constraints.

External relations

The East African Community (EAC) common market protocol came into force on 1 July 2010 establishing a framework for free movement of goods, persons and services within the EAC region (Burundi, Kenya, Tanzania and Uganda). However, relevant legislation and the institutional framework to facilitate the implementation of the common market protocol are not yet in place. Negotiations to eliminate barriers to regional trade are continuing under the auspices of the EAC-Common Market for Eastern and Southern Africa (COMESA)-Southern African Development Community (SADC) tripartite arrangement and are expected to bolster inter-regional trade in East and Southern Africa.

Uganda's major emerging partners in 2009 were China, Hong Kong, India, Singapore and the United Arab Emirates (UAE). The UAE, China and Hong Kong accounted for 29 per cent of total foreign direct investment (FDI) in 2009, with 54 per cent of these investments in equity capital. The bulk of this FDI is

KEY INDICATORS — Uganda

	Unit	2006	2007	2008	2009	2010
Population	m	29.85	30.93	*32.04	*33.20	*30.66
Gross domestic product (GDP)	US$bn	9.49	11.90	14.60	15.80	17.00
GDP per capita	US$	265	385	453	482	501
GDP real growth	%	5.0	8.4	9.5	7.2	5.2
Inflation	%	6.6	6.8	7.3	14.2	9.4
Industrial output	% change	3.4	9.9	6.4	5.2	–
Agricultural output	% change	5.0	-0.3	9.1	3.5	–
Exports (fob) (goods)	US$m	1,187.6	1,686.2	2,687.8	2,987.7	2,164.0
Imports (fob) (goods)	US$m	2,215.6	2,982.5	3,980.2	3,787.3	4,264.4
Balance of trade	US$m	-1,027.9	-1,296.4	-1,292.3	-799.7	-2,100.4
Current account	US$m	-379.0	-744.0	-469.0	-451.1	-1,739.9
Total reserves minus gold	US$m	1,810.9	2,559.8	2,300.6	2,994.5	2,838.3
Foreign exchange	US$m	1,810.8	2,559.5	2,300.4	2,769.3	2,617.5
Exchange rate	per US$	1,831.50	1,723.50	1,720.40	2,030.30	2,117.60

* estimated figure

concentrated in three sectors: finance, insurance and business services; manufacturing; and wholesale, retail, catering, accommodation and tourism. Emerging partners in Asia and the Middle East accounted for 13 per cent of Uganda's export earnings and 57 per cent of imports.

Doing business

Uganda's overall in the World Bank's *Doing Business* index dropped by six places to 112th in 2010 compared to 2009. However, marked improvements were recorded in four of the 10 categories, including employing workers, registering property, paying taxes, and enforcing contracts. For instance, the cost of registering property is only 3.5 per cent of the property value compared to the sub-Saharan African (SSA) average of 10 per cent. In addition, a taxpayer in Uganda needs to work 161 hours annually to pay taxes compared to the SSA and Organisation for Economic Co-operation and Development (OECD)... averages of 306 and 194 hours respectively. There are also no restrictions on employing workers in Uganda and all public sector entities are free to procure from any source. Limited access to credit, inadequate transport and energy infrastructure, human capital deficiencies, and a weak private sector regulatory framework remain the chief obstacles to private sector development in Uganda.

Financial institutions

A total of eight private commercial banks have been licensed since the moratorium against licensing new banks was lifted in 2005. Consequently, the number of commercial banks has increased to 22 with a bank branch network of 390 at the end of June 2010, up from 349 at the end of June 2009, with the deposit base increasing by 35 per cent and loans by 25 per cent. The ratio of non-performing loans to total credit fell from 4 per cent at the end of June 2009 to 3 per cent at the end of June 2010. The overall capital position of the financial sector remained satisfactory with a slight growth in core capital. The Financial and Deposit-taking Institutions Acts are being updated to improve the regulatory framework for financial institutions and to increase the paid-up capital requirements in line with the East African Community Monetary Union convergence criteria.

The Uganda Stock Exchange (USE) recovered strongly in 2009/10 on the back of renewed investor confidence, with the All Share Index (ALSI) increasing by 29.5 per cent at the end of June 2010, compared with a year earlier. Market capitalisation increased by 29.7 per cent during the same period, while turnover declined by 33.6 per cent, largely because of a shift in public preferences. In an effort to expand the securities market, the USE in partnership with the Financial Markets Development Programme of the World Bank and the Private Sector Foundation of Uganda, initiated the small- and medium-sized enterprises (SME) relaunch and listing programme. This project includes identifying eligible issuers, training, and offering technical assistance to the identified SMEs with the potential to list.

Infrastructure and natural resources

Transport costs remain an important barrier to trade and doing business because of the poor transport infrastructure. The International Monetary Fund (IMF) estimates that transport costs amount to effective trade protection of over 20 per cent and an implicit tax on exports of over 25 per cent. Only a fraction of roads are paved while after decades of neglect the railway network is dilapidated and only 26 per cent of it is functional. Consequently, the railway system only carries 3.5 per cent of freight and urgent measures are needed to rehabilitate and standardise the gauge from the current 1.0m to 1.435m, in line with a recent continental agreement. In spite of having a potential of over 5,000 megawatts (MW) of electricity, current capacity is under 600MW with only 11 per cent of the population connected to the power grid. Even after recent investments in the underground fibre optic cable, Internet connections are intermittent and concentrated in the capital Kampala.

The government remains committed to improving the transport and energy infrastructure. In 2010, increased public investment in infrastructure was sustained to promote industrialisation and reduce the cost of doing business. An additional 88MW of power will be generated from various hydropower stations in late 2011. The 250MW Bujagali Hydro Power project is scheduled to start generating 50MW of power in October 2011, increasing Uganda's total installed electricity capacity from 595MW in 2009 to 875MW by 2012. The government has also embarked on plans to upgrade from gravel to tarmac at least 309 kilometres of road and on the reconstruction of some 805 kilometres.

Recent oil discoveries are expected to propel Uganda to the forefront of oil production on the continent. In spite of known reserves of up to 2 billion barrels, the exact implications of oil for Uganda's economy are not yet clear, as much will depend on the timing and scope of production, both of which are in their turn dependent upon continuing exploration work. In the meantime, it is essential that the government build robust institutions and policies as well as a regulatory framework to facilitate the management of oil revenues, which are projected to exceed one third of total government revenues.

Following tax disputes between the government and the two major oil exploration firms (Heritage PLC and Tullow Oil PLC), the government in 2010 suspended the licensing of new oil exploration firms pending the ratification by the Parliament of the oil and gas legislation. This legislation will also pave the way for the massive investment necessary to construct a refinery and a 1,300 kilometre-long oil export pipeline to the East African coast. The government is also planning to set up the Petroleum Regulatory Authority to regulate the sector, as well as the National Oil and Gas Company to spearhead developments in the oil sector.

Emerging or traditional partners?

Data from the Bank of Uganda indicate that official development assistance (ODA) from non-African and non-OECD countries comes exclusively from China, with US$205 million in loans and grants disbursed since 2007, the bulk of this ODA going to infrastructure.

Emerging partners (EPs) differ from their traditional counterparts in several ways, in particular the approach to development co-operation. For instance, while the traditional partners are interested in addressing development challenges in their totality including political governance, human rights and other freedoms, as well as economic governance and management, EPs typically are mostly interested in rates of return on their investments, expanding markets and/or seeking new sources of raw material. Consequently, EPs are complementary to rather than substitutes for the traditional partners.

Another important key difference between the EPs and the traditional partners, in particular the multilateral partners, lies in the conditions attached to development assistance. For instance, while ODA from the multilateral partners usually requires counterpart funds from government, EPs typically finance the entire investment as a turnkey project. In addition, while standard procurement rules and procedures are often followed in the case of investments and ODA from the traditional partners, this is not a requirement for the EPs. In particular, almost all supplies and labour are usually sourced from the EP.

The tenure of engagement between EPs and government usually depends upon either the profitability of the investment or the lifespan of the natural resource of interest. In the case of the former, the EP's commitment is short- to medium-term: in the latter longer term.

The ministry of finance, which is constitutionally mandated to co-ordinate development assistance, conducts all negotiations of loan and grant agreements with both EPs and traditional partners. The Uganda Investment Authority (UIA), a semi-autonomous agency established by the Investment Code Act (1991), operates in partnership with both the private sector and government to spearhead economic growth and development. The UIA's major role is to facilitate and promote private sector investment in Uganda by contributing to and advocating for a competitive doing-business environment.

The NDP is the major framework that governs the engagement between EPs and government. The NDP contains the national development priorities and mechanisms to put into effect these priorities, and the Eps, ODA and FDI is aligned to these national commitments. Traditional partners also use the NDP as a basis for their engagement with government and accordingly ODA and FDI from EPs and traditional partners are complementary. However, EPs have exploited the absence of a robust investment regulatory framework to invest in business ventures such as retail trade and catering activities which would ordinarily be preserved for local citizens. It is felt that his has stifled local entrepreneurship, thereby impeding the development of a local middle class.

Risk assessment

Economy	Fair
Politics	Fair
Regional stability	Fair

COUNTRY PROFILE

Historical profile

By the eighteenth century, the territory, now known as Uganda, was occupied by Nilotic peoples in the north – the Acholi and Langi – and by Bantus and Bagandas, from whom the country gets its name, in the south.

1886–1890 The UK colonised Uganda.

1900 Bugunda in western Uganda became an autonomous region with its own constitutional monarchy.

1958 The UK allowed Uganda self-government.

1962 Uganda became an independent state within the Commonwealth.

1963 Uganda became a republic. Sir Edward Mutesa II, the King of Buganda, became Uganda's first president.

1966 Milton Obote, the defence minister, seized power with the help of Colonel Idi Amin, second-in-command of the army. Obote repressed the Baganda and re-integrated Buganda.

1967 The constitutional role of kings was abolished, along with federal system of government.

1971 Obote was ousted by Idi Amin, who expelled the large Asian (mainly Indian) community and carried out purges in which thousands died. Asians had owned 90 per cent of Uganda's businesses and the economy collapsed.

1979 Tanzania invaded Uganda, causing Amin to flee to Saudi Arabia. Yusufu Lule was briefly appointed president before being replaced by Godfrey Binaisa.

1980 Obote won the presidential election and started to pursue liberal economic policies to obtain aid from western donors, and the economy began to improve.

1985 Ethnic feuding resulted in a coup removing Obote from power.

1986 Yoweri Museveni came to power at the head of the National Resistance Movement (NRM), which had waged a guerrilla war since 1981. He banned multi-party politics, saying they led to ethnic fighting.

1996 President Museveni was elected president for a five-year term.

1998 Uganda intervened in the Democratic Republic of Congo (DRC) on behalf of the rebels who were opposed to the Kabila government.

2001 President Museveni was re-elected. In legislative elections, the supporters of the 'No Party' Movement – formerly the NRM – secured a majority, although they lost over 50 MPs, including 10 ministers. President Museveni's cabinet was headed by incumbent Prime Minister Apolo Nsimbabi. A peace agreement was signed by Rwanda and Uganda in London.

2002 Over 400,000 people were evacuated from villages in the northern war-zone at risk of brutal attacks from the Lord's Resistance Army (LRA).

2003 The LRA announced a cease-fire, but as attacks continued an all-out offensive against the rebels was ordered. As Uganda withdrew the last of its troops from eastern DRC tens of thousands of DRC civilians fleeing fighting in their own country sought asylum in Uganda. Idi Amin died in Saudi Arabia.

2004 LRA rebels killed around 200 people at a camp for displaced persons in the north. President Museveni retired from the army at the rank of general. Faltering peace talks between the government and the LRA began.

2005 The constitution was amended, removing the limit to presidential terms in office, and multi-party politics were restored. The International Criminal Court (ICC) issued arrest warrants for five commanders of the LRA including its leader, Joseph Kony. Opposition presidential candidate, Kizza Besigye, was arrested after he returned from exile and was accused of terrorism and unlawful possession of firearms. Uganda was ordered by the International Court of Justice (ICJ) to pay compensation for rights abuses and plundering the DRC during its occupation in 2003.

2006 Besigye was bailed allowing him to campaign in the presidential election, which was won by Yoweri Museveni. Kizza Besigye was acquitted of the charge against him. A cease-fire was agreed between government forces and the LRA. The UNHCR estimated that there were 1.5 million refugees of the long-running conflict in displacement camps in neighbouring countries; within two months, over 300,000 had returned to their homes.

2007 Racial violence erupted in Kampala, forcing police to protect Asian businesses and a Hindu temple in a conflict over allowing a development within an area of rain forest. Severe flooding caused widespread damage in the north-west.

2008 The LRA signed a permanent cease-fire during talks in Juba, Sudan. However, General Kony refused to sign the peace deal saying he did not understand the workings of the special court to be set up to try rebels. Peace negotiations resumed but broke down within weeks as the government rejected Kony's approach for talks to resume. Interior minister, Ruhaka Rugunda, said that after two years of negotiations there was nothing more to discuss and Kony should have signed the peace agreement earlier. With the peace talks stalled after arrest warrants for Joseph Kony were not withdrawn (by the ICC) as demanded by the LRA, a joint operation against the LRA, based in the Garamba region of the Democratic Republic of Congo (DRC), was launched by the armies of Uganda, Sudan and DRC.

2009 The LRA called for a cease-fire, which was rejected. The government announced that Uganda's army had halted its operations prematurely and had withdrawn from DRC, due to political pressure from DRC, but that the conflict with the LRA continued. Famine in the north-west around Arua district was declared with an

appeal for funds to feed the local population. A law banning female genital mutilation (circumcision) was introduced.
2010 In March, torrential rains on Mount Elgon caused mudslides, near the eastern town of Bududa, which killed at least 100 and made over 5,000 people homeless. A later decision was taken to remove 500,000 people from the area. Traditional tombs of Buganda kings, built mostly of timber and reeds and which were on the list of Unesco World Heritage Sites, caught fire and burned down in March. A decision to rebuild the tombs was taken in April. On 14 May, Uganda, along with Tanzania and Ethiopia signed an agreement to share the waters of the River Nile. In the new deal the three nations (out of five) that form the source of the river, reserved more of the water for themselves. Egypt and Sudan, which had until then taken the greater share, objected but finally agreed after 13 years of negotiations had failed to resolve the issue earlier. Two bombs exploded in Kampala during the Football World Cup final on 11 July, killing some 80 people. The Somali Islamist militant group, al Shabab, claimed responsibility. During the 15th AU Summit meeting held in Kampala later in July President Museveni said that the al Shabab should be 'swept out of Africa'. He called for more AU troops to be sent to Mogadishu. On 30 July three men who had been resident in Kenya were charged with the bombings and several others were later arrested. On 27 August, the government 'repossessed' the Kingfisher oil field, near Lake Albert, in a dispute with its original developers, Heritage Oil, over its refusal to pay US$283 million in tax before selling its assets to Tullow Oil. On 1 December 18 of those accused of the 11 July bombing were released, although three were rearrested and state prosecutors said that 17 others would be tried on charges of terrorism, murder and attempted murder. An outbreak of yellow fever was confirmed in the north in December, the first for some 40 years.
2011 Eight candidates took part in the presidential election held on 18 February. Incumbent, Yoweri Museveni (NRM), won 68.4 per cent of the vote and remains in office for another term. His closest rival Kizza Besigye (FDC) alleged fraud during the election. In parliamentary elections held on 18 February the ruling NRM won an overwhelming majority of 263 seats (out of 375). The arrest of Dr Besigye on 17 April as he attempted to join the 'walk-to-work' march protesting against the rising cost of living was followed by a demonstration which police broke up using tear gas and rubber bullets. Dr Besigye was released and left the country for hospital treatment in Kenya. In a further demonstration, against the manner of Dr Besigye's arrest, on 29 April two demonstrators were reported to have been killed by police. On 10 May police sprayed a pink liquid on opposition leaders and protesters who were heading towards Constitution Square in Kampala to attend a rally. President Museveni was sworn in for his fourth term in office on 12 May; supporters of opposition leader Kizza Besigye stoned the convoy transporting dignitaries to the ceremony. The attacks were in retaliation for alleged police brutality towards Dr Besigye and his supporters. Police placed Besigye under house arrest on 19 May to prevent alleged mobilisation of his supporters during the opening of parliament ceremony. Parliament apparently shelved the controversial anti-gay bill which had been scheduled for debate on 20 May. On 24 May President Yoweri Museveni appointed Edward Ssekandi as vice president and Amama Mbabazi as prime minister. The trial of Thomas Kwoyelo on 53 charges including murder and hostage-taking began on 11 July in Uganda's International Crimes Division court in Gulu. He was the first LRA commander to stand trial. Foreign affairs minister, Sam Kutesa, and two other officials resigned on 12 October after being accused of corruption.

Political structure

Constitution
An elected constituent assembly drafted a constitution which was promulgated on 8 October 1995. It retains the system of non-party government.
In July 2005, the Ugandan parliament voted for a constitutional amendment to allow President Yoweri Museveni to stay longer in office; he should stand down in 2006.

Form of state
Unitary republic

The executive
The president is elected for a five-year term. The president appoints a prime minister and a cabinet composed of representatives of a number of political parties.

National legislature
The unicameral Parliament of Uganda has 319 members, comprising 215 elected constituency representatives, 79 district women representatives, 10 Uganda People's Defence Forces (UPDF) representatives, five youth representatives, five representatives of disabled people and five workers' representatives. In addition there are 13 *ex officio* members.

Legal system
The legal system is based on English common law and the 1995 constitution.

Last elections
18 February 2011 (parliamentary); 18 February 2011 (presidential)
Results: Parliamentary: National Resistance Movement (NRM) won 263 seats (out of 375), Forum for Democratic Change (FDC) 34, Democratic Party (DP) 12, Uganda People's Party (UPP) 10, Conservative Party (CP) one, Justice Forum (JF) one, Independents 43, representatives of the Uganda People's Defence Force 10.
Presidential: Yoweri Museveni (NRM) won 68.4 per cent of the vote, Kizza Besigye (FDC) 26 per cent, Norbert Mao (DP) 1.9 per cent, and Olara Otunnu (Uganda People's Congress (UPC)) 1.6 per cent. Turnout is 59.3 per cent.

Next elections
2016 (parliamentary); February 2016 (presidential).

Political parties

Ruling party
National Resistance Movement (NRM) (from 1999; re-elected 2011)

Main opposition party
Forum for Democratic Change (FDC).

Population

30.66 million (2010)*
Last census: September 2002: 24,442,084
Population density: 114 inhabitants per square km; rural population per sq km of arable land: 349. Urban population: 15 per cent.
There is a high rural density in the south, in a belt from east to west. The north is sparsely populated.
Annual growth rate: 3.2 per cent 1994–2004 (WHO 2006)

Internally Displaced Persons (IDP)
1.6 million (UNHCR 2004)

Ethnic make-up
There are over 20 ethnic groups of which the Baganda, Banyankole and Basoga are the largest. Approximately 99 per cent of the population is of African descent and 1 per cent European or Asian.

Religions
Christianity (71 per cent), traditional beliefs (13 per cent), Islam (5 per cent), others (11 per cent).

Education

Unesco reported that a government's education programme launched in 1997, had successfully increased primary school enrolment from 2.5 million in 1997 to 6.5 million in 2001. The programme provided free primary education to four children including orphaned and disabled children from each household.
Primary school lasts for seven years and, having successfully undertaken exams, students then follow either an acedemic or vocational secondary schooling.

Literacy rate: 69 per cent adult rate; 80 per cent youth rate (15–24) (Unesco 2005).
Compulsory years: None.
Enrolment rate: 74 per cent gross primary; 12 per cent gross secondary; of relevant age groups, (including repeaters) (World Bank).
Pupils per teacher: 35 in primary schools.

Health

The lack of resources and an extreme dependence on foreign aid has resulted in a high infant and maternal mortality rate and low immunisation coverage.
Improved water sources are available to 42 per cent of the population.

HIV/Aids

In 2005 there were an estimated 800,000 people living with HIV/Aids, with 100,000 new infections each year. Even though the prevalence has been falling – down to 6 per cent in 2005 from the high of 30 per cent in the early 1990s – those who are developing Aids is increasing and putting social and economic pressure on the country's resources. The number of people living longer with HIV has been rising due to anti-retroviral (ARV) drugs; there are over 65,000 patients currently receiving ARV medication. Since the beginning of the pandemic in Uganda, an estimated one million people have died of Aids and the government expects another to be treating over 50,000 Aids suffers each year.
Uganda was the first country in sub-Saharan Africa to show a decrease in the number of HIV positive sufferers, due to an extensive, long-term government initiative to combat the spread of the disease (one of the best instituted in Africa).
Rural areas have been badly hit with productivity and output in the agricultural sector significantly fallen as Aids has taken its toll of workers and those that curtail their time in the fields to care for the sick.
A factory in Kampala, to open for production by January 2008, will produce three-in-one tablets of HIV/Aids anti-retorviral and anti-malaria medication. Domestic production reduces the need for and cost of imported drugs. Nevertheless, national distribution remains the largest impediment for healthworkers to manage in a country where only 41 per cent of HIV patients receive anti-retroviral drugs. Uganda has cut its HIV/Aids infection rate from 30 per cent in the 1990s to less than 10 per cent in 2007.
HIV prevalence: 4.1 per cent aged 15–49 in 2003 (World Bank)
Life expectancy: 49 years, 2004 (WHO 2006)
Fertility rate/Maternal mortality rate: 7.1 births per woman, 2004 (WHO 2006); maternal mortality rate 510 per 100,000 live births (World Bank).
Birth rate/Death rate: 46.6 births and 17 deaths per 1,000 people (2003).
Child (under 5 years) mortality rate (per 1,000): 81 per 1,000 live births (2003); 38 per cent of children aged under five are malnourished (World Bank).
Head of population per physician: 0.08 physicians per 1,000 people, 2004 (WHO 2006)

Welfare

The distribution of income in Uganda is less unequal than most countries in Africa, with the richest 20 per cent of the country owning 44.9 per cent of the national wealth while the bottom 20 per cent earning 7.1 per cent of the country's income. Around 10 per cent of the rural population lives under the national poverty line, while around 40 per cent of the urban population is classified as poor. The informal sector employs over 80 per cent of the urban population, implying a high degree of job insecurity and casual labour.

Main cities

Kampala (capital, estimated population 1.3 million in 2005), Gulu (138,946), Jinja (92,483).

Languages spoken

KiSwahili, Luganda and Luo are widely spoken.

Official language/s

English

Media

Press

The Media Council (http://mediavisionsite.com) regulates and censors information.
Dailies: The government publishes two newspapers, *Bukedde* (www.bukedde.co.ug) in Luganda and *The New Vision* (www.newvision.co.ug) in English. *The Monitor* (www.monitor.co.ug) and *Red Pepper* (www.redpepper.ug) (a tabloid) are independent and published in English.
Weeklies: The government publishes three regional newspapers, *Orumuri* (www.orumuri.co.ug) *Rupiny* (www.rupiny.co.ug) and *Etop* (www.etop.co.ug) in local languages. All daily newspapers have Sunday editions. *The Observer Weekly* (www.ugandaobserver.com) and *Entatsi* (in Runyakitara) are independent. .
Business: Apart from daily newspaper with business sections *East African Business Week* (http://www.busiweek.com) is based in Kampala.
Periodicals: In Luganda, *Musizi* is a Catholic monthly publication.

Broadcasting

The Uganda Communications Commission (www.ucc.co.ug) is responsible for the communications industry.
Radio: There has been a large expansion of services with many private local radio stations in operation. The public broadcaster is the Uganda Broadcast Corporation (UBC), with a national FM network with channels on Radio Uganda called Blue, Red, Green and Butebo, which provide programmes in English, KiSwahili and 20 local languages. Private stations include 95N9 Touch FM (www.touch.fm) and Arua One FM (www.aruaonefm.com) and the women's community radio Mama FM (http://interconnection.org/umwa/community_radio.html).
Television: There are over a dozen channels broadcasting by terrestrial, cable and satellite. The state-owned UBC television service is a commercial service, broadcastings mainly in English, KiSwahili and Luganda. Most networks are privately-owned, including WBS Television (www.wbs-tv.com), which is centred on Kampala, as well as Multichoice, Nation TV and Pulse TV; Nkabi Broadcasting Services in based in Jinja. There are several Christian channels including Record Television Network, Top TV and Christian Life Ministries. Foreign channels are provided by Digital Satellite Television DSTV

Economy

In 2010, Uganda became one of the world's latest oil producers as it opened the largest onshore field in Africa, starting at 500–1,000 barrels per day (bpd) rising to 10,000bpd in 2011 and expected to reach 150,000bpd in 2015. However, before the upstream investment deals could be signed, international energy companies were waiting to see how the government dealt with the problem of a protracted tax dispute with Uganda's main oil exploration company. The UK-based Tullow Oil purchased the Ugandan oil interests of Heritage Oil in July 2010 for US$1.4 billion and was asked by the Ugandan authorities to pay the US$404 million capital gains tax on its new acquisition. Tullow believed that Heritage should pay its own tax and then spent 14 months in dispute until March 2011, when an agreement was reach that allowed Tullow to begin production with a consortium of partners, investing up to US$10 billion in an oil development project around the Lake Albertine rift basin, containing over 1 billion barrels of oil. Tullow estimated that by 2018 Uganda could be producing 350,000bpd.
Uganda has other natural resources such as copper, cobalt, salt, phosphate and limestone.

It also has ample fertile land and good rainfall so that agriculture, which constitutes over 20 per cent of GDP, can cultivate for exports of coffee, tea, tobacco, vanilla beans and cut flowers and fish (Nile perch and tilapia) and fish products, it also produces for the domestic market, cassava, potatoes, wheat, vegetables and fruit, while the livestock produces beef and dairy, goat and poultry. Industry and manufacturing, which constitutes over 25 per cent of GDP, includes light manufacturing of textiles and clothes, consumer goods, plus processed agricultural products. Heavy industry includes cement production and other building materials and hydroelectricity.

GDP growth has been consistently high for several years and despite the global economic crisis Uganda's growth rate did not fall below 5 per cent, although growth did fall steadily from a high of 10.8 per cent in 2006 to 8.7 per cent in 2008 to 7.2 per cent in 2009, to 5.8 per cent in 2010. However, inflation was affected by the economic recession as imported food costs reached a record high, pushing inflation to 14.2 per cent in 2009, up from 6.6 per cent in 2006; inflation fell in 2010 to 9.4 per cent.

Remittances are an important resource, not only for the immediate benefit of families but also for the country, and in 2009 US$694 million (5.1 per cent of GDP) was remitted to Uganda, with an estimated US$773 million in 2010. The UN Development Programme reported that Uganda's Human Development Index (HDI) ranking was 143 out of 169 and that its improvement was above the regional average. Nevertheless, 51.53 per cent of the Ugandan population lived below the poverty line in 2010.

The first gold refinery in Uganda was opened in May 2010, in Kampala, with a capacity to produce 10kg of gold per day. The US$1.5 million, Russian-owned refinery will process gold from the Democratic Republic of Congo and other countries in the region.

In May 2010, following 13 years of failed negotiations over distribution of water rights of the Nile River, a split occurred when Tanzania, Uganda, Ethiopia and Rwanda unilaterally demanded a more equitable share. Historical agreements had shared 90 per cent between Egypt and Sudan, leaving just 10 per cent to be shared among the other nine countries of East Africa. Water experts have been engaged to determine how much water each country should be entitled to. Uganda should benefit with more water available for its arid northern region.

External trade

Uganda is a member of the East African Community (EAC) (with Burundi, Kenya, Rwanda and Tanzania). The East African Community Common Market Protocol (EACMP) was launched on 1 July 2010, which will lead to the free movement of labour, capital, goods and services between member states as well as employment opportunities and easier flow of investment capital. The signed protocol now requires that legislation in all states must be harmonised to conform to its jurisdiction. Uganda is also a member of the Common Market for Eastern and Southern Africa (Comesa), and operates a free trade area with 13 of the 19 member states.

With ample, fertile land and good rainfalls agriculture provides the opportunity to cultivate a number of cash crops, including coffee (accounting for around 23 per cent of total agricultural exports), tea, tobacco, vanilla, cotton and cut flowers (flown to European markets within hours of preparation). Industrial production is progressively replacing imports of construction materials, foodstuffs and household goods. Remittances are also an important source of foreign exchange.

Uganda is a landlocked country and any heavy or bulky exports must be transport either by road or train to seaports to Tanzania or Kenya, each adding to a time delay and an increase in the cost of freight.

Imports

Principal imports are capital equipment, vehicles, petroleum, chemicals and pharmaceuticals, medical supplies and cereals.

Main sources: UAE (typically 12 per cent of total), Kenya (11 per cent), India (10 per cent).

Exports

Principal exports are agricultural products, coffee (typically 23 per cent), tea, cotton, live animals, fish and fish products, horticultural products and, from 2010, petroleum.

Main destinations: Sudan (typically 14 per cent of total), Kenya (10 per cent), Switzerland (9 per cent).

Re-exports

Gold, diamonds, coltan and niobium, mostly from neighbouring DRC.

Agriculture

Farming

Around 80 per cent of the population derive their livelihood from agriculture. The area under cultivation has only increased by one-third over the last 30 years.The situation has been worsened by irregular rainfall and climate change. This has eroded the farmers' confidence in applying improved technology to increase productivity, resulting in crop and livestock yields which have been ranked among the lowest in the world. Agricultural development is hampered by shortages of vital inputs, damage caused by civil war, low producer prices and corrupt purchasing bodies.

Uganda's varied climate allows the production of a wide range of produce. Around 75 per cent of Uganda's agricultural output is made up of food crop production, two-thirds of which is used for subsistence. Maize is one of the main food crops and is grown around Lake Victoria as a cash crop. The fertility of Ugandan land could make it a bread basket for East Africa, particularly if the effects of periodic droughts are ameliorated by adequate irrigation techniques.

Coffee is the main cash crop, providing around 70 per cent of agricultural export earnings. Most production is carried out on a small-scale basis. Rehabilitation of coffee holdings has been the main stimulus to economic growth in recent years. The government has encouraged planting of clone coffee which yields in a shorter period of around two years, is more disease resistant and gives higher yields. The private sector controls over 90 per cent of the coffee trade in Uganda. Liberalisation of the coffee market has meant that producers can sell coffee on the open market to the highest bidder, although the dismantling of state marketing boards has meant that they are more vulnerable to price fluctuations and have to deal with often unscrupulous middlemen. The formation of co-operatives has become a basis for reducing the adverse effects of liberalisation. There was concern in 2007 that the economic partnership agreement (EPA) between the EU and Africa, Caribbean and Pacific developing countries would have an adverse affect on coffee growers if the EU did not remove subsidies on its domestic coffee industries. Around 15,000 coffee farmers are certified as organic growers, out of a total number of one million growers. Uganda mostly grows Robusta coffee.

Cotton was once an important cash crop, but due to its labour intensiveness, relatively high cost of production and a poor marketing system, farmers looked towards growing non-traditional cash crops which have a readily available market. Cotton growing is being revived in some eastern areas, and production has been boosted by reforms in agricultural pricing and marketing regimes introduced in the 1990s. Sugar is grown on several vast estates and production is creeping up after collapsing completely in the early 1980s. Tobacco and tea are also important cash crops.

Exports of flowers increased by nearly 20 per cent in 2007 to a record US$32 million.

Fishing
Uganda's fishing industry is important, both for domestic consumption and export. The annual catch is typically around 220,000 tonnes, 40 per cent of which is exported.
The fisheries industry is mostly based on inland capture fisheries from lakes Victoria, Albert, Edward, George and Kyoga. Lake Victoria is Uganda's most important fishery, supplying some 50 per cent of the national catch. Nile perch obtained from Lake Victoria alone amount to 110,000 tonnes and remains the largest fish export item to the markets of Europe, Australia and South-East Asia. Estimates of Lake Kyoga put supplies at 30,000 tonnes, with the nature of the fishery shifting from a prolific Nile perch and tilapia fishery to increased supplies of mukene.
Forestry
Uganda is moderately forested with around 30 per cent forest cover and an additional 48 per cent of other wooded land. The majority of timber production is used in domestic fuel. There is a wide network of protected areas, including 50 parks and nature reserves. A large proportion of household energy needs are met by fuelwood. The sector produces sawnwood from local hardwood species and much of industrial roundwood is used for agricultural purposes. Paper is imported in large quantities.

Industry and manufacturing
Industry accounts for around 21 per cent of GDP. The industrial sector is has seen relatively high levels of growth, particularly in food processing, tobacco, beverages, timber/paper and chemicals/soap. Underutilisation of factory capacity and lack of foreign exchange tend to inhibit progress.
Other industries are textiles, cement, plastics, steel, metal products and brewing. Most of these are operating well below capacity mainly due to shortages of imported materials, spares and fuel, inadequate infrastructure and a lack of skilled manpower.
The building industry is hampered by a lack of finance and skilled manpower and most local building equipment factories still produce at only 50 per cent of their installed capacities. Consequently, many finished products, such as cement, sanitary ware, plumbing pipes and glass are imported.
The textile sector has failed to take advantage of the US's African Growth and Opportunity Act (AGOA), which gives the textile industries from qualifying countries like Uganda access to US markets. Manufacturers have been unable to raise capacity, so they cannot fulfill the demands of US customers. The sector's decline is due to a fall in cotton producton, which has been adversely affected by political instability in the cotton-growing northern regions.

Tourism
The government is investing heavily in tourism to build it up as major currency earner. Insecurity in parts of the country continues to be a handicap, but visitor numbers typically register over 500,000 arrivals per year.
In February 2008 the governments of Democratic Republic of Congo, Rwanda and Uganda agreed to joint measures to protect the mountain gorillas found within their shared border regions. Tourists visiting the area to view the endangered great apes raise a combined US$5 million for the countries concerned.

Environment
In 2008 the governments of Democratic Republic of Congo, Rwanda and Uganda agreed to joint measures to protect the mountain gorillas found within their shared border regions. Tourists visiting the area to view the endangered great apes raise a combined US$5 million for the countries concerned. However, poaching and civil strife have dropped the numbers of gorillas to critically endangered levels, so that a 10-year conservation project which focuses of security and encouraging local people to preserve the animals and habitat is seen as the only hope for the gorilla's survival

Mining
Uganda has deposits of copper, cobalt and iron ore, as well as less viable fields of tungsten, beryl, columbo-tantalite, gold, bismuth, tin, limestone and phosphates. Uganda's mineral potential remains untested due to very little exploration to date.
The first gold refinery in Uganda was opened in Kampala in May 2010, with a capacity to produce 10kg of gold per day. The US$1.5 million, Russian-owned refinery will process gold from the Democratic Republic of Congo and other countries in the region.

Hydrocarbons
Imported petroleum products in 2007 amounted to 13,000bpd. Production of domestic oil should be 6–10,000bpd by the end of 2009.
In January 2009 UK-based oil companies Tullow and Heritage announced, in separate statements, that they had located 'world class' oil discoveries in the Lake Albert Rift Basin in western Uganda, which could total over 400 million barrels of oil. The full potential of the oil field may not be known until 2012–13, following further exploration.
Both companies announced they would invest in a 500,000bpd oil pipeline to Eldoret and then to Nairobi (Kenya). The 320km, Eldoret-Kampala oil pipeline is schedule to begin construction in 2009. Domestic oil will replace 114,000 tonnes of imported petroleum products that are currently transported by road and rail. However in May, President Museveni, who is against a pipeline that would carry only crude oil (and not refined oil) and thereby limit exports to crude oil, announced that he had signed a co-operation agreement with Iran, which would fund a new refinery. This may lead to changes in the pipeline contract. The Italian energy company Eni bought a 50 per cent share in two Ugandan oil fields in November 2009 from the Canadian, Heritage oil exploration company. Eni paid US$1.35 billion in cash with a deferred payment of US$150 million. Oil production, by Tullow Oil, starting at 500–1,000bpd will begin in 2010, rising to 10,000bpd in 2011 and expected to reach 150,000bpd in 2015. Any use of natural gas or coal is commercially insignificant.

Energy
Total installed generating capacity was 313MW in 2006. Uganda relies on imported oil for around 50 per cent of its energy needs, the balance being provided by hydroelectricity. Nalubaale (Owen Falls) power station, operating since the mid-1950s, and its Kiira extension supply almost all of the electricity system's capacity. Less than five per cent of the population has access to electricity, which due to growing demand of 30–40MW per year, has to be rationed. After being dogged by controversy, a 250MW hydro-plant was inaugurated at Bujagali in 2007 for completion in 2011–12. The scheme is a public-private partnership with the government, with World Bank assistance, costing around US$750 million.

Financial markets
Stock exchange
Uganda Securities Exchange

Banking and insurance
Great efforts are being made to improve efficiency in the banking sector, including the placement of local banks under statutory management. However, Uganda's banking sector remains weak. In recent years, the Bank of Uganda's (BoU) (central bank) regulatory powers have been insufficient, with reports that troubled banks have failed to meet their reserve requirements.
In an effort to reverse the situation, the BoU increased the capital requirements of all banks and was granted power to close banks that failed to comply with a number of regulations. As a result, the ratio of

non-performing loans to total assets has fallen and banking system profitability has improved. However, the BoU was forced to seize control of the Uganda Commercial Bank (UCB) after its privatisation due to fraudulent behaviour by the buyer.
The government is planning to increase the availability of credit to poor rural areas through micro-finance and a lighter regulatory framework.
Central bank
Bank of Uganda
Main financial centre
Kampala

Time
GMT plus three hours

Geography
Uganda is a landlocked country in East Africa, bordered by Sudan to the north, the Democratic Republic of Congo (DCR) to the west, Kenya to the east and Rwanda, Tanzania and Lake Victoria to the south.
The terrain is mainly plateau, stretching northwards from Lake Victoria and declining gradually from around 1,500m to 900m towards the Sudan border. Mountain ranges and volcanic hills ring the country. The highest point at 5,110m is Marherita Peak on snow-capped Mount Stanley. Lakes, swampland and rivers occupy around 20 per cent of the country. Lake Victoria occupies much of the south-easten corner of Uganda, stradding the borders with Kenya and Tanzania. In the west the frontier with the DRC passes through lakes Albert and Edward. The White Nile rises in Lake Victoria and travels north through Lakes Kyoga and Albert towards Sudan.
Much of the country is savannah and semi-desert, but there are equatorial forests in the central zone.
Hemisphere
Straddles the equator

Climate
Equatorial, tempered by high altitude. Temperatures are fairly constant throughout the year, hottest months December–February, June–August, with daytime range (in Kampala) of 27–29 degrees Celsius (C) compared with an annual average of 26 degrees C (night-time average 16 degrees C). Heaviest rainfall occurs March–May, October–November; April is wettest month (average fall for month 175 mm).

Dress codes
Lightweight clothing is advisable all year round. Senior officials tend to wear suits, local businessmen and government officials wear suits or safari suits. Light cotton dresses, skirts and blouses or lightweight suits are advised for women. A lightweight raincoat may be needed at any time of the year.

Entry requirements
Passports
Required by all, valid for six months from date of arrival.
Visa
Required by all, except nationals of COMESA and other countries listed on www.ugandaembassy.com/visa.htm (countries with reciprical visa-free entry).
Currency advice/regulations
Import and export of local currency is prohibited. There is no restriction on the import of foreign currency, subject to declaration on arrival, or on the export of foreign currency up to the amount declared on arrival.
Customs
Duty-free allowances are: one litre of spirits or wines, 500ml of perfume or toilet water, 225 grammes of tobacco products.
Prohibited imports
Game trophies require special permit.

Health (for visitors)
Mandatory precautions
A valid international certificate of vaccination against cholera is required for entry into and exit from Uganda. Vaccination must have taken place not less than seven days and no more than six months prior to entering the country. A valid international certificate of vaccination against yellow fever is also required for visitors arriving from infected areas; an outbreak was confirmed in the north in December 2010. The certificate becomes valid 12 days after vaccination and lasts for 10 years.
Advisable precautions
There is a risk of malaria, typhoid is a risk outside main towns. Normal precautions for the tropics with regard to hygiene and drinking water should be taken. Bilharzia risk is present in the lakes and rivers and visitors are advised to swim only in well-maintained swimming pools. A mild form of dysentery is common. Rabies is a risk.
The Aids virus has reached epidemic proportions and precautions should be taken, including a travel kit with disposable syringe and needles. Any medicines required should be brought with the visitor and accompanied by their original packaging.
Medical facilities are limited and visitors should have sufficient insurance to ensure medical evacuation.

Hotels
Private and government-owned, variable standard, but available in all main centres. Should be booked in advance.

Credit cards
Most car hire firms and travel agencies refuse credit cards.

Public holidays (national)
Fixed dates
1 Jan (New Year's Day), 26 Jan (Liberation Day), 8 Mar (Women's Day), 1 May (Labour Day), 3 Jun (Martyrs Day), 9 Jun (National Heroes Day), 9 Oct (Independence Day), 25–26 Dec (Christmas).
Variable dates
Good Friday, Easter Monday, Ascension Day, Eid al Adha, Eid al Fitr.

Working hours
Banking
Mon–Fri: 0900–1400. Some bureaux de change open Sat and Sun.
Business
Mon–Fri: 0830–1245, 1400–1700.
Government
Mon–Fri: 0830–1245, 1400–1700.
Shops
Mon–Fri: 0830–1700; Sat: 0900–1600.

Telecommunications
Mobile/cell phones
GSM 900 services are available throughout most of the country.

Electricity supply
240V AC, 50 cycles.

Social customs/useful tips
Appointments are essential for business meetings. Ugandans have a less urgent sense of time than Europeans, and appointments often run late, particularly if it is raining.
The customary form of greeting is to shake hands. Exchanging business cards is an established ritual.
Visitors should remember that an increasing number of Hindus and Muslims are engaged in commerce and local advice should be obtained if any entertainment is planned. There are many local traditions, but few will affect business visitors and tourists.

Security
There are still areas of the country that are not under secure government control. Rebel activity occasionally targets tourists, and visitors are advised to check with local embassies if they intend to travel away from the main urban centres or main road and rail routes. The government has stepped up its campaign against lawlessness.
Due to rebel raids, including activity spilling over from neighbouring countries, visitors are warned against travelling to certain destinations, particularly the northern and south-western regions, where the Mountains of the Moon and several game parks are located.

Getting there

Air

National airline: The government holds a 20 per cent in Victoria International Airlines, which has a limited number of southern African routes.

International airport/s: Entebbe (EBB), 35km from Kampala; duty-free shop, restaurant, bank, post office, car hire.

Airport tax: None

Surface

Road: There is road access from neighbouring countries, but the Sudanese border crossing is not open to general traffic. There are daily bus services between Nairobi (Kenya) and Kampala.

Rail: There is a joint Kenyan-Ugandan rail link between Nairobi and Kampala, but it has been out of service for some time. Revival of the line is in prospect following transfer of control to a private company in November 2006.

Water: There are ferry services across Lake Victoria from Mwanza (Tanzania) and Kisumu (Kenya).

Getting about

National transport

Road: Uganda has a road network of around 35,000km. Most of the country is served by dirt roads of varying quality, but there are around 3,000km of surface roads connecting the main towns. Many major roads are in good condition.

Buses: Regular services scheduled include Entebbe-Kampala (journey time: 30–45 minutes). There are services between most main centres but they tend to be crowded. An interstate bus service between Kampala and Kigali (Rwanda) is frequently suspended due to military activity. Akamba Bus regularly travels between Kampala and Nairobi (Kenya).

Rail: Two Uganda-Kenya railway agreements were signed in April 2006. In Uganda a concession agreement covers the freight services of Uganda Railways Corporation (URC), while an Interface agreement covers matters common to the Kenya freight and passenger concession and the Uganda freight concession. The Rift Valley Railways Consortium (RVRC) will invest US$15 million over the first five years and a further US$75 million over the remainder of the agreement in Uganda and US$45 and US$300 million respectively in Kenya.

Water: Some freight and passenger transport is available on Lake Victoria.

City transport

Taxis: Available at airport and in Kampala at hotels, the railway station, main park and near major office blocks. The drive from Entebbe airport to Kampala city centre takes 45 minutes.

Matatus (public taxis) are available within Kampala, its suburbs and in all major towns.

Car hire

Car hire is expensive. Services are available, mainly with driver, from a number of rental firms, and through independent taxi drivers. Driving is on the left. A valid international driving licence is required.

BUSINESS DIRECTORY

The addresses listed below are a selection only. While World of Information makes every endeavour to check these addresses, we cannot guarantee that changes have not been made, especially to telephone numbers and area codes. We would welcome any corrections.

Telephone area codes

The international direct dialling (IDD) code for Uganda is +256, followed by area code:

Entebbe	42	Lugazi	44
Fort Portal	483	Masaka	481
Jinja	43	Mbale	45
Kampala	41	Mbarara	485
Kasese	483	Tororo	45

Useful telephone numbers

Ambulance, fire, police: 999

Directory enquiries: 901

International hospital: 340-531, 345-768

Chambers of Commerce

Uganda National Chamber of Commerce and Industry, PO Box 3809, Kampala (tel: 225-8791; fax: 225-8793; e-mail: uncci@uol.co.ug).

Banking

Allied Bank International Uganda Ltd, PO Box 2750, 45 Jinja Road, Kampala (tel: 223-6535; fax: 223-0902; e-mail: allied@alliedbank.co.ug).

Bank of Baroda (Uganda) Ltd, PO Box 7197, 18 Kampala Road, Kampala (tel: 223-3680; fax: 225-8263; e-mail: bobho@spacenet.co.ug).

Barclays Bank of Uganda Ltd, PO Box 7101, 16 Kampala Road, Kampala (tel: 223-0972; fax: 225-9467; e-mail: uganda.barclays@barclays.com).

Cairo International Bank Ltd, PO Box 7052, 30 Kampala Road, Kampala (tel: 223-0136; fax: 223-0130; e-mail: cib@spacenetuganda.com).

Centenary Rural Development Bank Ltd, PO Box 1892, 7 Entebbe Road, Kampala (tel: 225-1276; fax: 225-1273; e-mail: info@centenarybank.co.ug).

Citibank Uganda Ltd, PO Box 7505, Centre Court, 4 Ternan Avenue, Nakasero, Kampala (tel: 234-0625; fax: 234-0624).

Crane Bank Ltd, PO Box 22572, 38 Kampala Road, Kampala (tel: 234-5345; fax: 223-1578; e-mail: cranebank@cranebanklimited.com).

Diamond Trust Bank (U) Ltd, PO Box 7155, 17/19 Kampala Rd, Kampala (tel: 225-9331; fax: 324-2286; e-mail: dtbu@spacenetuganda.com).

East African Development Bank, PO Box 7128, 4 Nile Avenue, Kampala (tel: 223-0021; fax: 225-9763; e-mail: dg@eadb.org).

Nile Bank Ltd, PO Box 2834, Spear House, 22 Jinja Road, Kampala (tel: 234-6904; fax: 225-7779; e-mail: comments@nilebank.co.ug).

Orient Bank Limited, PO Box 3072, 6 Kampala Road, Kampala (tel: 223-6012; fax: 234-8039; e-mail: mail@orient-bank.com).

Stanbic Bank Uganda Ltd, PO Box 7131, 45 Kampala Road, Kampala (tel: 223-1151; fax: 223-1116).

Standard Chartered Bank Uganda Ltd, PO Box 7111, 5 Speke Road, Kampala (tel: 225-8211; fax: 223-1473; e-mail: scb.uganda@standardchartered.com).

Tropical Africa Bank Ltd, PO Box 7292, 27 Kampala Road, Kampala (tel: 223-2857; fax: 221-2296; e-mail: admin@trafbank.com).

Central bank

Bank of Uganda, PO Box 7120, 37–43 Kampala Rd, Kampala (tel: 258-441; fax: 230-878; e-mail: info@boa.or.ug).

Stock exchange

Uganda Securities Exchange:www.use.or.ug

Travel information

Automobile Association of Uganda, 39 William Street, PO Box 10542, Kampala (tel: 225-0814; fax: 234-1245; e-mail: aau@africaonline.co.ug).

Eagle Aviation, Adam House, 11 Portal Avenue, PO Box 7392, Kampala (tel: 234-4292; fax: 234-4501;

e-mail: admin@flyeagleuganda.com).

East African Airlines, Pan Africa House, 3 Kimathi Avenue, PO Box 2389, Kampala (tel: 226-0625; fax: 234-9875; e-mail: info@flyeastafrican.com).

Uganda Wildlife Authority, 7 Kira Road, PO Box 3530, Kampala; (tel: 234-6287; fax: 234-6291; e-mail: uwa@uwa.or.ug).

Ministry of tourism

Ministry of Tourism, Trade and Industry, Farmers House, Parliament Avenue, PO Box 7103, Kampala (tel: 234-3947; fax: 234-7286; e-mail: mintrade@mtti.co.ug).

National tourist organisation offices

Tourism Uganda, 13/15 Kimathi Avenue, Impala House, P.O.Box 7211, Kampala (tel: 234-2196; fax: 234-2188; e-mail: utb@visituganda.com).

Ministries

Ministry of Education and Sports, 17/19 Hannington Rd, PO Box 7063, Kampala (tel: 223-4451; fax: 223-44920; e-mail: pro@education.go.ug).

Ministry of Energy and Mineral Development, Amber House, 29-32 Kampala Road, PO Box 7270, Kampala (tel: 232-3355;fax: 223-0220; e-mail: psmemd@energy.go.ug).

Ministry of Finance, Planning and Economic Development, 2/12 Apollo Kaggwa Road, PO Box 8147, Kampala (tel: 270-7000; fax: 223-0163; e-mail: webmaster@finance.go.ug).

Ministry of Foreign Affairs, Parliament Building, PO Box 7048, Kampala (tel: 225-7525; fax: 225-6722; e-mail: mofa@starcom.co.ug).

Ministry of Gender, Labour and Social Development, Simbamanyo House, 2 Lumumba Avenue, PO Box 7136 , Kampala (tel: 234-7854; fax: 225-6374; e-mail: ps@mglsd.go.ug).

Ministry of Health, 6 Lourdel Road, PO Box 7272, Wandegeya, Kampala (tel: 234-0884; fax: 234-0887; e-mail: info@health.go.ug).

Ministry of Justice and Constitutional Affairs, 1 Parliament Avenue, PO Box 7183, Kampala (tel: 223-0538; fax: 225-4829; e-mail: info@justice.go.ug).

Ministry of Local Government, 1 Pilkington Road, PO Box 7037, Kampala (tel: 234-1224; fax: 225-8127; e-mail: info@molg.go.ug).

Ministry of Public Service, 12 Nakasero Hill Road, PO Box 7003, Kampala (tel: 225-5651; fax: 225-5643; e-mail: ps@publicservice.go.ug).

Ministry of Water, Lands and Environment, Century House, Parliament Avenue, PO Box 7096, Kampala (tel: 234-2931; fax: 223-0891; e-mail: mwle@mwle.go.ug).

Other useful addresses

British High Commission, Commercial Section, 120/12 Parliament Avenue, PO Box 7070, Kampala (tel: 225-7301; fax: 225-7304).

Civil Aviation Authority, PO Box 5536, Kampala (tel: 225-6874; fax: 225-6807).

Export Policy Analysis and Development Unit (EPADU), Impala House, PO Box 10951, Kampala (tel: 223-1390; fax: 223-1329).

Nile International Conference Centre, PO Box 3496, Kampala (tel: 225-8619; fax: 225-9130).

Privatisation Unit, Ministry of Finance and Economic Planning, IPS Building, 6th Floor, 14 Parliament Avenue, PO Box 10944, Kampala (tel: 225-6467; fax: 225-9997; e-mail: pmu@imul.com).

LRA incident tracker
http://www.lracrisistracker.com/

Public Enterprise Reform and Divestiture, IPS Building, PO Box 10944, Kampala (tel: 225-6467; fax: 225-9997).

Uganda Development Corporation, UDC Building, Parliament Avenue, PO Box 7042, Kampala (tel: 223-4383; fax: 224-1588).

Uganda Investment Authority, 28 Kampala Road, PO Box 7418, Kampala (tel: 225-1562; fax: 224-2903; e-mail: info@ugandainvest.com).

Uganda Railway Corporation, PO Box 7150, Kampala (tel: 225-8051; fax: 244-405).

Uganda Tea Corporation Ltd, Kasaku Estate, Jinja-Kampala Rd, PO Box 8955, Lugazi (tel: 48-230/45; fax: 223-0698).

Ugandan Embassy (US), 5911 16th Street, NW, Washington DC 20011 (tel: (+1-202) 726-7100; fax: (+1-202) 726-1727; e-mail: ugembassy@aol.com).

Internet sites

Africa Business Network: www.ifc.org/abn

African Development Bank: www.afdb.org

Africa Online: www.africaonline.com

AllAfrica.com: http://allafrica.com

Mbendi AfroPaedia (information on companies, countries, industries and stock exchanges in Africa): http://mbendi.co.za

Ukraine

By early 2011, any doubts that Ukraine's political pendulum was swinging away from things West European and was hankering after its authoritarian past had been dispelled.

Witch hunt

Ukraine's judicial prosecutors had set their sights on the ministers and officials of the previous government, headed by Yulia Tymoshenko, and the witch hunt that culminated in her arrest had begun in earnest. Mrs Tymoshenko's minister of the interior, Yuri Lutsenko, awaited his trial in jail. Her economy minister, Bohdan Danylyshyn, had sought political asylum in the Czech Republic. Mrs Tymoshenko herself was banned from international travel to enable her to be grilled by the Ukraine's prosecutor general. The October 2010 general elections, the first to be held under President Yanukovich's administration, and won by the Partiya Regioniv (PR) (Party of the Regions), were alleged by most independent observers to be flawed. The pro-Russian Ukrainian president still paid lip service to the idea of European integration without seeming to understand that this lofty ambition presupposed reforming the economy, the judiciary and standards of political behaviour and transparency all round. Ukraine found itself on the fault line between (in the western half of the country) the pro-Europeans and (in the east) the Russian speakers many of whom still harked after the Soviet glory days.

December 2010 had seen the Ukrainian parliament cover itself in glory as deputies traded punches while some even wielded a crowbar after opposition members occupied the rostrum in the chamber, intending to stay overnight to prevent normal parliamentary business getting under way the next day. In the melée, five members of parliament needed to be taken by ambulance to hospital. Their protest was against the opening of the criminal case against Mrs Tymoshenko, charged with illegally using the proceeds from the sale of carbon emission quotas to cover a shortfall in the state pension fund. The eventual outcome of Mrs Tymoshenko's trial was pretty predictable: seven years in jail and a fine of US$190 million. The fine was described as compensation for the damage caused by the terms of a gas deal with Russia struck on Mrs Tymoshenko's watch in 2009. Most Ukrainians were well aware that Mrs Tymoshenko's conviction

KEY FACTS

Official name: Ukraina (Ukraine)

Head of State: President Viktor Fecorovych Yanukovych (Partiya Regioniv (PR) (Party of the Regions)) (from 25 Feb 2010)

Head of government: Prime Minister Mykola Yanovych Azarov (PR) (from 11 Mar 2010)

Ruling party: Partiya Regioniv (PR) (Party of the Regions) (11 Mar 2010)

Area: 603,700 square km

Population: 45.96 million (2010)*

Capital: Kiev (Kyiv)

Official language: Ukrainian

Currency: Hryvna (H) = 100 kopiyka (plural hryvni)

Exchange rate: H8.00 per US$ (Oct 2011)

GDP per capita: US$3,000 (2010)

GDP real growth: 4.20% (2010)

GDP: US$136.40 billion (2010)

Labour force: 22.05 million (2010)

Unemployment: 8.10% (2010)

Inflation: 9.40% (2010)

Balance of trade: -US$8.71 billion (2010)

Annual FDI: US$6.50 billion (2010)

* estimated figure

had more to do with politics and revenge than with justice. The major casualty was, however, Ukrainian justice: Ukrainians no longer knew who to believe or trust. In 2004 Mrs Tymoshenko could galvanise crowds of 150,000. Now, the camera angles were all wrong, the film-star photo-calls had been replaced by less flattering press shots. The European Union's (EU) foreign relations supremo said that Mrs Tymoshenko's case would have 'profound implications for EU-Ukraine bilateral relations, including for the conclusion of the association agreement'. In EU parlance, agreeing an 'association agreement' is the key step towards eventual EU membership.

Russia

The newly adopted Ukrainian tradition of parliamentary violence had first shown itself in April 2010 when opposition members set off smoke bombs and threw eggs at the speaker in a failed attempt to prevent ratification of the treaty that allowed Russia to keep its Black Sea Fleet in Ukraine until 2042. The speaker, sheltering under an umbrella, continued with the vote amid flying eggs. The vote had a hugely symbolic aspect. Not only was it a vital part of Russia's renascent defence policy, its symbolism in the context of Ukrainian politics could not be ignored. The 2010 election results marked a shift in Ukrainian political strategy, reminding those interested that the word 'Ukraine' means 'border'. While paying lip-service to the importance of the EU, President Yanukovych appeared to be gambling on his ability to play the EU against Russia. The plot that is Ukraine's future thickened steadily in early 2011. Mr Yanukovych knows that for the EU, Ukraine, once a key member of the former Soviet Union, holds enormous symbolism. Brussels dare not appear overly critical of Mr Yanukovych and his colleagues for fear of pushing them into a Russian embrace. And that embrace was ready and willing; in mid-2011 Russian Prime Minister (and president elect – again) Vladimir Putin, announced the formation of a Eurasian Union. This, according to Mr Putin, would be a grouping of former Soviet republics into a union to rival the EU. Ukraine is the largest former Soviet republic and any such union risks going off at half cock if Ukraine were not signed up as a member.

Mr Yanukovych, however, was aware that full membership of the EU would bring enormous benefits for Ukraine (investment, exports, visa free travel, grants – and above all –recognition). Russia and its embryonic idea could only offer gas at subsidised prices. And that gas would provide Russia with such leverage over Ukraine, that the risk of reverting to the structures and values of the Soviet Union was very real indeed. Ironically, in October 2011, the biggest single obstacle to any rapprochement with the EU was the fact that Mrs Tymoshenko had been jailed. The Yanukovych balancing act had been flung into reverse so that he had discreetly to amend the criminal code – retrospectively, so that his long time adversary could be freed. A failure to achieve this risked forcing Mr Yanukovych's hand and making the embrace of the Russian bear a little more likely.

Corruption

The Ukraine's wealthiest citizen is one Rinat Akhmetov, who, it is estimated, is worth some US$25 billion. His early career had included a spell working for one Akhat Bragin, who was assassinated while watching a Donetsk Shakhtar football match. Mr Akhmetov subsequently took over the business interests of the murdered Mr Bragin.In 2011 Mr Akhmetov purchased London's most expensive residential property, One Hyde Park, for some US$200 million. The son of a miner Mr Akhmetov has had a dizzy rise to fame and riches; his social elevation has inevitably prompted much speculation, fuelled by countless rumours. In 2007 Mr Akhmetov saw fit to sue for libel, in London, the Kiev English language newspaper, the *Kiev Post*. The legal action ended in 2008 when the *Kiev Post* retracted its comments, specifically one alleging that Mr Akhmetov had acted illegally in business transactions concerning the Dniproenergo thermoelectric generator and the Kryvorizhstal steel mill.

The economy

The International Monetary Fund (IMF) noted that the Ukrainian economy had performed better than expected in 2010, with growth exceeding 4 per cent of GDP, supported by strong exports and recovering investment and private consumption. The government's economic programme was considered to be broadly on track and agreement had been reached on most policies to achieve the government's objectives for 2011. Actions were in hand to support medium-term fiscal consolidation.

To help cushion the impact on households, a more gradual schedule of gas tariff increases were agreed and offsetting budgetary measures identified to support the combined (general government and Naftogaz) deficit of 3.5 per cent of gross domestic product (GDP) for 2011. By the end of 2010 inflation had declined steadily to 8.2 per cent, close to the targets

KEY INDICATORS — Ukraine

	Unit	2006	2007	2008	2009	2010
Population	m	46.47	*46.12	*45.84	*45.71	*45.96
Gross domestic product (GDP)	US$bn	106.47	140.48	180.30	127.10	136.40
GDP per capita	US$	2,291	3,100	3,926	2,542	3,000
GDP real growth	%	7.1	7.3	2.1	-15.1	4.2
Inflation	%	9.0	12.8	25.2	15.9	9.4
Unemployment	%	8.0	6.4	6.4	8.8	7.8
Industrial output	% change	4.3	10.5	3.5	-24.0	–
Agricultural output	% change	0.3	-5.0	15.0	-0.3	–
Natural gas output	bn cum	19.1	19.0	18.7	19.3	18.6
Coal output	mtoe	41.8	39.3	40.2	38.3	38.1
Exports (fob) (goods)	US$m	38,949.0	49,840.0	67,717.0	40,394.0	52,191.0
Imports (fob) (goods)	US$m	44,143.0	60,412.0	84,651.0	45,049.0	60,903.0
Balance of trade	US$m	-5,194.0	-10,572.0	-16,934.0	-4,655.0	-8,712.0
Current account	US$m	-1,617.0	-5,918.0	-12,933.0	-1,801.0	-2,884.0
Foreign debt	US$bn	54.3	80.0	101.7	103.3	–
Total reserves minus gold	US$m	21,844.6	31,786.0	30,800.6	25,556.9	33,327.4
Foreign exchange	US$m	21,843.2	31,783.2	30,791.9	25,493.3	33,319.4
Exchange rate	per US$	5.06	5.06	5.26	7.79	7.94

* estimated figure

of the National Bank of Ukraine (NBU) (central bank). Government objectives included strengthening monetary policy operations, developing the local currency market, improving the foreign currency framework and further strengthening the financial sector.

In its mid-2011 review of the Ukrainian economy, the World Bank was broadly supportive, noting that Ukraine's 'modest recovery' continued as inflation crept up. After the disastrous 14.8 per cent decline in gross domestic product (GDP) in 2009, the economy grew by 4.2 per cent in 2010 and had posted a 5.2 per cent growth rate in the first quarter of 2011. Domestic demand seemed to be the principal driver as retail sales grew by an annual 15.2 per cent in the first 5 months of the year. Industrial production appeared as rather volatile, decelerating from 9.7 per cent in the first quarter of 2011 to 4.9 per cent in April and then returning to an annual growth rate of 8.6 per cent in May 2011. Government interventions of one sort and another managed to keep inflation under 10 per cent in the first quarter of 2011, but the rate rose to 11 per cent in May. Worryingly, producer prices rose by an annual rate of 18 per cent.

Ukraine's current account deficit has widened, but in 2011 remained manageable. The export quotas applied to grain, together with increased domestic demand resulted in a deficit of US$2.9 billion in 2010, roughly ten per cent of GDP. In the period January to April 2011 the deficit widened, increasing by US$1.8 billion, largely due to increased imports and the recovery of domestic demand. But net inflows in the capital account covered the current account deficit and some, enabling the NBU to improve its foreign exchange position in the first 5 months of 2011. However, Ukraine's fiscal position remained fragile and was likely to be further weakened by delays in the introduction of new pension and utility tariff reforms and new spending initiatives. Higher rates of tax collection and a higher inflation tax has enabled the government to keep the budget deficit below target, but in mid-2011 the deficit looked likely to increase. In part this was due to an increase in the deficit incurred by energy monopoly Naftogaz, due to higher import prices and the failure to introduce tariff increases. The budget deficit target of 3.5 per cent of GDP risked being overshot by additional spending increases approved by parliament.

The government has reiterated its goal of achieving robust economic growth over the medium-term. To promote economic activity and improve standards of living the reform momentum needs to be maintained and the regulatory framework further streamlined to improve a still challenging business environment.

Risk assessment

Economy	Good
Politics	Fair
Regional stability	Fair

COUNTRY PROFILE

Historical profile

1917 The Bolsheviks consolidated control over Ukraine, until the incorporation of the republic into the Soviet Union. The Russians retained direct control of eastern Ukraine from 1918 until the country's independence from Russia in 1991. The city of Lviv (formerly Lvov) near the western border was seized from the collapsing Austro-Hungarian Empire.

1920s Russia lost control of parts of western Ukraine to Poland, Czechoslovakia and Romania during the civil war between the Bolsheviks and counter-revolutionary forces supported by Western European armies. Soviet dictator, Josef Stalin, initiated a system of collective agriculture which forced Ukrainian farmers to render fixed quantities of produce to the authorities. These quotas were unrealistic, creating entirely artificial famine conditions during which over five million Ukrainians were estimated to have died.

1932 It is estimated that at least three million, and possibly as many as 10 million, died of starvation in the *Holodomor* or 'famine plague' when the 1932 grain harvest did not meet Kremlin targets and Joseph Stalin sent activists to villages to confiscate all food. The move was part of Stalin's determination to crush the resistance to the collectivisation of farming.

1945 Following the end of the Second World War, the Soviet Union regained control of the lost areas of western Ukraine.

1954 Responsibility for the government of Crimea, an autonomous republic within Ukraine, was transferred from Russia to Ukraine as part of reforms initiated by Nikita Kruschev after Stalin's death.

1986 The Chernobyl nuclear reactor based in Ukraine exploded, causing widespread damage in both Ukraine and neighbouring Belarus.

1991 Under pressure from the opposition parties, in particular Narodniy Rukh Ukrayiny (Rukh) (People's Movement of Ukraine), the government gradually moved towards independence. Political power was transferred from the government of the former Soviet Union to Ukrainian national authorities in Kiev. A majority voted for independence in a referendum, leading to a declaration of independence and the recognition of Ukraine as an independent state by the international community. Leonid Kravchuk won the presidential elections.

1992 Disagreements over economic policy saw the resignation of Ukraine's first prime minister, Vladimir Fokin, who was replaced by Leonid Kuchma.

1993 Arguments over economic policy and labour strikes led to the resignation of Kuchma and Yukhlym Zvyahilsky assumed the post.

1994 Kuchma returned as the main challenger to Kravchuk in the presidential elections, finally defeating Kravchuk in the run-off. Kuchma's attempts to swing the balance of power from parliament in favour of the presidency, in order to reduce the opposition to his economic programme, achieved mixed success.

1996 A new constitution gave the president the power to appoint a government formed by parliamentary deputies.

1997 Valeriy Pustovoitenko became prime minister.

1998 After elections, the Komunistychna Partiya Ukrainy (KPU) (Communist Party of Ukraine) emerged as the largest single party.

1999 Kuchma was re-elected president. He appointed reformist independent deputy Viktor Yushchenko as prime minister.

2000 Over 80 per cent of voters in a referendum supported President Kuchma's proposals for constitutional reform, designed to increase the powers of the presidency.

2001 Yushchenko's pro-reform government was toppled by the KPU-dominated parliament. Anatoly Kinakh became prime minister.

2002 In parliamentary elections, Viktor Yuschenko's Narodnyi Soyuz Nasha Ukraina (NSNU) (People's Union Our Ukraine) bloc gained the highest percentage of votes at 23.6 per cent. Russia, Ukraine, Kazakhstan and Belarus signed an economic union treaty.

2003 Mass demonstrations in Kiev demanded the resignation of President Kuchma. Ukraine and Russia signed an agreement on the joint use of the Kerch Strait and the status of the Azov Sea.

2004 Russian-backed Viktor Yanukovych won the presidential election and opposition supporters gathered in Kiev to protest against election fraud (the Orange Revolution) and the Supreme Court annulled the result. Viktor Yushchenko won the re-run election.

2005 Yushchenko was sworn in as president and Yulia Tymoshenko was approved as prime minister. Yushchenko dismissed Tymoshenko and replaced her with Yuri Yekhanurov. Russia cut off gas supplies after Ukraine refused to agree to a four-fold price increase. The BJT was disbanded and merged with the Vseukrayins'ke Obyednannya Bat'kivshchyna (Fatherland) (All-Ukrainian Union (Fatherland).

2006 Prime Minister Yekhanurov was sacked by parliament. Yushchenko, unwilling to lose his prime minister refused to nominate another candidate and Yekhanurov remained in office. In general elections (judged free and fair by international observers), the ruling NSNU lost ground to both the Partiya Regioniv (PR) (Party of the Regions) led by Viktor Yanukovich and the party created by the president's erstwhile colleague Yulia Tymoshenko of Blok Yulia Tymoshenko (BJT) (Yulia Tymoshenko Bloc). After months when the NSNU and VBJT failed to work out their differences, the PR, KPU and the Sotsialistychna Partiya Ukrainy (SPU) (Socialist Party of Ukraine) formed a coalition government, which sparked disturbances in the parliamentary building. The NSNU announced it would become the main opposition party. President Yushchenko was forced to nominate his archrival, Viktor Yanukovych (PR), as prime minister or call another general election. The Yanukovych cabinet was later approved by parliament.

2007 Months of friction between the pro-Western president and the pro-Russian prime minister lead to a political stalemate, resulting in a presidential decree dissolving parliament. Prime Minister Yanukovych refused to obey the decree, but eventually agreed to early elections. The PR won 34.4 per cent of the vote (175 of 450 seats), BJT won 30.7 per cent (156 seats), Blok Nasha Ukrayina-Narodna Samooborona (NU) (Our Ukraine-People's Self Defense bloc) 14.2 per cent (72), KPU 5.39 per cent (27 seats), Blok Lytvyna (BL) (Lytvyn Bloc) 3.96 per cent (20). Yulia Tymoshenko (BJT) was proposed as prime minister; she lost three rounds of voting but was eventually elected.

2008 Ukraine became a member of the WTO. The Russian state-owned gas producer Gazprom cut supplies of gas by 25 per cent, claiming Ukraine had debts of US$1.5 billion. Gas supplies were resumed when an agreement was reached whereby Gazprom supplied industrial customers directly and cut out a Ukrainian intermediate supply company. The ruling coalition collapsed following the refusal by BJT to back the president's support of Georgia in its dispute with Russia, and the BJT's unwillingness to support the president's veto of several laws aimed at reducing the power of the presidency.

2009 Russia suspended gas supplies to Ukraine again, due to non-payment Ukraine's debt. Gas supplies to the rest of Europe fell, amid accusations by Russia that Ukraine was 'stealing' gas supplies transiting Ukraine and destined for Europe. Within a week a ten-year gas transit deal was signed. The International Court of Justice settled a 40-year disagreement on the maritime boundary dispute between Romania and Ukraine, with a new border extending a line from the land border over an area of the Black Sea and giving each country an area of what is thought to contain rich fields of hydrocarbons.

2010 Former revolutionary leader, Victor Yushchenko, won fewest votes in the first round of presidential elections held in January; he stepped down as president on 23 January. In the run-off held in February, Viktor Yanukovych (PR) won 48.95 per cent and Yulia Tymoshenko (Fatherland) 45.47 per cent. However Tymoshenko refused to accept the result and challenged it with accusations of electoral fraud. She eventually withdrew her objections following a legal ruling that denied her permission to scrutinise certain voting papers. Yanukovych was sworn in as president on 25 February. Prime Minister Tymoshenko and her government lost a vote of no-confidence in parliament on 3 March and were forced to resign, while President Yanukovych began forming a coalition government. Oleksandr Turchynov was named acting prime minister on 4 March; however parliament appointed Mykola Azarov (PR) as prime minister on 11 March. At an international nuclear security summit in Washington held in April, Ukraine agreed to eliminate its stockpile of weapons-grade nuclear material by 2012. The parliamentary session debating the extension of the lease on a Russian naval base on the Black Sea erupted as politicians brawled and the speaker was pelted with eggs and smoke bombs exploded. After order was restored, the lease was extended to 2045, in return for cheaper supplies of Russian natural gas. Local elections held in November were criticised by the US and EU for not meeting 'standards of openness and fairness' and undermining 'further consolidation of democracy'. On 20 December, Yulia Tymoshenko was arrested and charged with misusing state funds as prime minister.

2011 During her trial Yulia Tymoshenko accused President Yanukovych of orchestrating her arrest, aimed at destroying the country's opposition, and on 24 June that the judge was a 'puppet'. On 5 August, Tymoshenko was arrested during her trial for systematically disrupting proceedings; her supporters fought with police as she was driven away from court. On 11 October, Tymoshenko was sentence to seven years in gaol, for abusing her powers in office and paying too much for Russian natural gas imports. She was also ordered to pay damages to the state-owned energy company, the sum of Naftogaz H1.5 billion (US$187.4 million). Criticism of the conviction came from the US and EU, which referred to the trial and result as 'politically motivated' and 'selective justice'.

Political structure

Constitution

The 1996 constitution defines Ukraine as a sovereign, unitary state answerable to individual citizens, with the protection of citizens' rights as its foremost responsibility. The constitution forbids multiple nationality for Ukrainian citizens. The development and protection of the Ukrainian language is a constitutional obligation, but the constitution also guarantees free use of Russian and other minority languages, and requires the state to promote the study of languages of 'international communication'.

The constitution recognises and guarantees the right to local self-government. Local government is based on 24 *oblasts* (regional divisions) and one autonomous republic (Crimea). The *oblasts* are further divided into *rayons* (districts).

The Autonomous Republic of Crimea is bound by the Ukrainian constitution and by acts of the Verkhovna Rada (Supreme Council). However, it has the power to legislate separately on matters such as transport, planning, land use and healthcare.

Constitutional changes agreed in December 2004, which entered into force in January 2006, have given more power to the parliament at the expense of the office of president. Following the parliamentary elections on 26 March 2006, the parliament now nominates the prime minister who must then be approved by the president, replacing the previous system under which the prime minister was nominated by the president and approved by the parliament.

Independence date

24 August 1991

Form of state

Presidential democratic republic

The executive

The highest executive authority rests with the president, who is directly elected for a five-year term and nominates the prime minister and regional governors, whose appointment are subject to the approval of parliament. The president has the power to appoint the cabinet, although parliament must approve it. Members of the cabinet do not necessarily need to be drawn from parliament. The president may rule by decree and did so in 1998, during deadlock in the legislature. Under normal circumstances, the prime minister shares some executive powers with the president and both can propose and approve legislation. This creates the potential for conflict between the two executive branches.

National legislature

The unicameral Verkhovna Rada (Supreme Council) (commonly called the Rada) has 450 deputies, of which 225 are elected by proportional representation (PR) from party lists and 225 in single-seat constituencies. Only parties that obtain over 4 per cent of the vote are allocated PR seats. All deputies are elected for a five-year term.

The Rada elects a speaker and plays an active role in proposing and enacting legislation.

Legal system

The legal system is based on a civil law code and, since the collapse of communism, has been engaged in an ongoing process of reform. The Constitutional Court is the highest interpreter of the constitution and is permitted to carry out judicial review of legislation. There are 18 Supreme Court judges, six each appointed for a nine-year non-renewable term by the president, parliament and a congress of Ukrainian judges.

The Supreme Court is the court of final appeal for civil and criminal cases originally heard in the lower courts. The Supreme Court's judges are appointed by a plenary session of existing judges. The lower courts are organised according to both geography and legal specialisation. The constitution encourages trial by jury and forbids the creation of emergency courts. Judges are granted legal immunity and can only be dismissed by a verdict of the Supreme or Constitutional Courts, or by an order of parliament.

Last elections

17 January / 7 February 2010 (presidential, first round and runoff); 30 September 2007 (parliamentary).

Results: Presidential first round: Viktor Yanukovych (PR) won 35.37 per cent of the vote, Yulia Tymoshenko (Vseukrayins'ke Obyednannya Bat'kivshchyna (Fatherland) (All-Ukrainian Union (Fatherland)) 25.01 per cent, Serhiy Tihpko (independent) 13.05 per cent, Arseniy Yatsenyuk (independent) 6.95 per cent, Victor Yushchenko (independent) 5.45 per cent. Runoff: Yanukovych won 48.95 per cent, Tymoshenko 45.47 per cent

Parliamentary: The Partiya Regioniv (PR) (Party of the Regions) won 34.4 per cent of the vote (175 of 450 seats), BJT won 30.7 per cent (156 seats), Blok Nasha Ukrayina-Narodna Samooborona (NU) (Our Ukraine-People's Self Defense bloc) 14.2 per cent (72), Komunistychna Partiya Ukrainy (KPU) (Communist Party of Ukraine) 5.39 per cent (27 seats), (Narodnyi) Blok Lytvyna (BL) (Lytvyn Bloc) 3.96 per cent (20); turnout was 62.02 per cent.

Next elections

2015 (presidential); 2012 (parliamentary).

Political parties

Ruling party

Partiya Regioniv (PR) (Party of the Regions) (11 Mar 2010)

Main opposition party

Blok Nasha Ukrayina-Narodna Samooborona (NU) (Our Ukraine-People's Self Defense bloc)

Population

45.96 million (2010)*

Last census: December 2001: 48,457,102

Population density: 87 inhabitants per square km. Urban population: 67 per cent (2001 census).

Annual growth rate: -1.0 per cent 1994–2004 (WHO 2006)

Ethnic make-up

Ukrainian (72 per cent), Russian (22 per cent), Belarussian, Moldovan, Polish, Romanian and Tatar (in Crimea). Over 10 million ethnic Russians live in eastern Ukraine; Crimea is about 63 per cent Russian.

Religions

The principal religion is Christianity, of various denominations including Ukrainian Orthodox, Autocephalous Orthodox, and Ukrainian Greek Catholic (Uniate) Church. There is a small Jewish minority, and a Muslim minority mostly located in Crimea.

Education

The reversal of the Russian dominated education system is the primary aim of the government.

Literacy is almost universal in Ukraine, reflecting the high level of educational participation and high quality of teaching. Increased emphasis has also been placed on Ukrainian history, culture and literature.

Elementary schooling must begin by aged seven (parents may choose to enrol their children in school at aged six), and lasts until aged 10. This is followed by secondary basic education, which lasts until aged 15 when examinations determine academic upper secondary education until aged 18, or vocational education which lasts until aged 20.

Ukraine has large scientific and educational centres in Kiev, Odessa, Lviv, Kharkiv and Donetzk, with more than 200 higher educational institutes. There are 10 universities.

Literacy rate: 100 per cent adult rate; 100 per cent youth rate (15–24) (Unesco 2005).

Compulsory years: 6/7 to 16.

Enrolment rate: 78 per cent gross primary enrolment; 105 per cent gross secondary enrolment, of relvant age groups (including repeaters), (Unicef 2004)

Pupils per teacher: 21 in primary schools.

Health

The precipitous economic decline since 1991 has significantly lowered living standards in Ukraine and adversely affected health. Although high soil fertility enables most Ukrainians to enjoy a sufficient diet, nutrition levels remain lower than optimum and high alcohol and tobacco consumption does little to improve matters. Moreover, lacking adequate funds, many health facilities have closed or reduced their level of service since independence. Although the number of doctors is well above the Organisation for Economic Co-operation and Development (OECD) average, they lack the training, facilities and medicines to provide adequate preventative or primary healthcare. One result of this has been outbreaks of tuberculosis, which reached epidemic levels in the late 1990s.

HIV/Aids

HIV prevalence: 0.1 per cent aged 15–49 in 2003 (World Bank)

Life expectancy: 67 years, 2004 (WHO 2006)

Fertility rate/Maternal mortality rate: 1.1 births per woman, 2004 (WHO 2006)

Birth rate/Death rate: 10 births and 16.4 deaths per 1,000 population (2003)

Child (under 5 years) mortality rate (per 1,000): 15 per 1,000 live births (World Bank)

Head of population per physician: 2.95 physicians per 1,000 people, 2003 (WHO 2006)

Welfare

As part of its plan to reduce the fiscal deficit and meet IMF spending restrictions, the government has been forced to alter its social security structure.

More targetting of assistance to vulnerable groups is being planned, with reforms to family benefits, sickness benefits and the employment fund. A social insurance system provides benefits for old age pensions, sickness, maternity, work injury, and employee family allowances.

The pension system is being reformed, with preferential pensions being scaled down. The retirement age is 60 and 55 for men and women, with 25 or 20 years contributions, respectively. Reforms being enacted in 2004 intend to raise this and introduce additional voluntary and

mandatory savings schemes. There are also plans to increase the pension age gradually.
The insurance scheme is funded by employee earnings of 1 per cent on wages up to H150 and 2 per cent on wages of H150 or more (capped at wage of H1,600 per month); employers pay 37 per cent of payroll and central and local governments provide subsidies as needed. There are an estimated 2.2 million Ukrainians who are eligible for extra social security payments as victims of the 1986 Chernobyl disaster.

Main cities

Kiev (Kyiv) (capital, estimated population 2.7 million (m) in 2005), Kharkiv (Kharkov) (1.5m), Odessa (1.0m), Dnepropetrovsk (1.0m), Donetsk (1.0m), Zaporizhzhya (822,931), Lviv (Lvov) (745,632); Sevastapol (349,827); Simferopol (350,616) and Yalta are the major centres of Crimea.

Languages spoken

Ukrainian, Polish and German are widely spoken in western Ukraine, while Russian is widely spoken in the east. Romanian, Bulgarian, Hungarian and Belarusian are also spoken.

Official language/s
Ukrainian

Media

Press

Press freedom in the Ukraine has been described as partial, by the UK-based Freedom House, in 2007. Violence and intimidation of journalists is ongoing, perpetrated by politicos and criminals, while the legal system has not succeeded in finding those responsible for the death of prominent journalist Georgiy Gongadze in 2000.

Dailies: In Ukrainian, *Fakty i Kommentarii* (www.facts.kiev.ua), *Segodnya* (www.segodnya.ua) and *Vecherniye Vesti* are mass-circulations newspapers, others include *Silski Visti* (www.silskivisti.kiev.ua) and *Kievshiye Vedomosti* (www.kv.com.ua), *Ukrayina Moloda* (www.umoloda.kiev.ua) and *Holos Ukrayiny* (http://uamedia.visti.net/golos) the parliamentary newspaper.
In English, *Den* (www.day.kiev.ua), and online Ukryinska Pravda (www2.pravda.com.ua/en).
There are also local newspaper in provincial cities, including *Oga* (www.ogo.ua) from Rivne, *Slovo* (www.slovo.odessa.ua) from Odesa and in Russian, *Zik* (www.zik.com.ua) and *Ekspres* (www.expres.ua) from Lviv, and *Gorod* (www.gorod.donbass.com) from Donetsk in Russian.

Weeklies: Magazines in Ukrainian include *Krytyka* (http://krytyka.kiev.ua), *Zerkalo Nedeli* (www.zn.ua) comments on politics, and *Ji* (www.ji-magazine.lviv.ua), a cultural magazine. In English, *The Ukrainian Observer* (www.ukraine-observer.com) and *Kyiv Post* (www.kyivpost.com).

Business: In Ukrainian, *Kontrakty* (www.kontrakty.com.ua) and *Delovaya Stolitsa* (www.dsnews.com.ua) are newspapers. *Finansovaya Ukraina* covers financial news. In English, the *Eastern Economist* is published weekly.

Broadcasting

The Derzhkominform of Ukraine (state committee, for television and radio broadcasting) is responsible for providing transmission frequencies and dissemination of official information.

Radio: The government operated national service is Ukrayinsko Radio One with three stations (www.nrcu.gov.ua), plus Radio Ukraine International, with external transmissions. There are many private, commercial radio stations which are based regionally or in a city including Trand M Radio (www.trans-m-radio.com), from the Crimea, Shanson Radio (www.shanson.ua), from Kharkov, Melodia FM (www.melodia.ua), Planeta FM (http://planetafm.net), and Dovira FM (www.dovira.com.ua), from Kiev, Mama Radio (http://mama.odessa.fm) from Odessa.

Television: The government-operated network, National TV Company of Ukraine (www.1tv.com.ua), (known as UT1) operates three network channels, which broadcasts over 97 per cent of the territory. There are plans that by 2009 UT1 will acquire public broad broadcaster status and the government will forego its control of the network.
There are a number of commercial channels broadcasting via cable, satellite and terrestrial signals with a range in product content from entertainment, news, music, sports and culture. The most popular TV channel is Inter (http://intertv.com.ua) followed by Studio 1+1 (http://1plus1.tv).

Advertising

The advertising industry is dominated by television. There is a ban on the promotion and advertising of tobacco.

News agencies

National news agency: Ukrinform (Ukranian National News Agency)

Economy

Ukraine's economy has been transformed in many ways since its break with the old Soviet Union in the 1990s. It has always had a potential for strong economic growth with its natural resources of coal, iron ore, mineral deposits, timber and many hectares of fertile agricultural land, coupled with traditional industries such as mining, iron and steel production, light engineering industries such as machinery and transport manufacturing, food-processing, textile and clothing manufacturing as well as modern industries including power generation and communications. However, Ukraine's economic development has been marred by a lack of political consensus on which way to turn to best provide the conditions for a market economy– west towards the European Union or east towards the Russian Federation.
The political instability since 2004 between the factions that proposed partnerships either west or east undermined Ukraine's ability to focus on economic growth. The global economic crisis was particularly hard for the Ukraine in 2008, as its vulnerability was exposed as a steel exporter and a borrower on international markets. As one of the world's least energy-efficient counties Ukraine is highly dependent on natural gas imports from Russia. When global oil prices were at an all-time high in 2008, imported energy cost the country US$22 billion, up from US$15.3 billion in 2007 and falling to US$14.5 billion in 2009. This unwelcome drain on the country's balance of payments intensified the government's financial problems. Confidence in the currency and banking sector was eroded causing a system-wide run on deposits, reducing government revenue.
GDP growth was 2.1 per cent in 2008, down from 7.9 per cent in 2007. However by 2009, growth had plummeted to -15.1 per cent, as both exports and domestic demand dropped. By the first half of 2010 GDP growth was expected to have bounced back to 3.3 per cent.
The International Monetary Fund (IMF) approved a loan of US$16.4 billion in November 2008, which restored macroeconomic and financial stability. However, by late 2009 other structural weaknesses caused growth in the economy to stall and on 14 August 2010 the IMF approved a 29-month, US$15.1 billion loan, with an immediate US$1.89 billion disbursement, under a stand-by arrangement, with other disbursements subject to quarterly reviews by the IMF. The loan was set up to address the structural weaknesses, assist in social programmes for the poor and boost the country's long-term growth prospects.
The IMF considered the Ukraine's recovery to be fragile, as it is dependent on outside conditions. It highlighted the need for the state-owned gas company, Naftogaz, to be restructured and for a programme of increasing prices to customers to bring them up to market levels. The IMF warned that unless the new political regime enhanced policies designed to foster the economic environment through

necessary reforms its loans and help could be wasted.

External trade

Following the break-up of the Soviet Union, trade was formalised with former republics through the Commonwealth of Independent States (CIS), however a free trade zone between members had not, by 2007, been implemented, due to differences in economic objectives, degrees of reforms and economic development. The Ukraine has declared its intentions of applying for membership of the European Union and has begun reforms necessary to align its economy with the EU.

As the world's fifth largest exporter of cereals, and sixth largest exporter of iron, primary industries are important to the economy. Over 30 per cent of all exports are traded to the EU and 25 per cent to Russia. Manufacturing reflects the Ukraine's historic role as an important manufacturing base of the former Soviet Union with production in heavy industry including steel making, shipbuilding, locomotive and aerospace industries, nuclear reactors and boilers, machinery and machine tools. Fees for oil transiting the country from Russia to Europe provide an important source of foreign earnings.

Imports

Principal imports include oil and natural gas (comprising around 30 per cent of all imports), vehicles, machinery, equipment, chemicals and plastics.

Main sources: Russia (30.6 per cent total, 2006), Germany (9.5 per cent), Turkmenistan (7.8 per cent).

Exports

Principal exports are ferrous and non-ferrous metals, fuel and petroleum products, chemicals, tools and machinery, transport equipment and cereals.

Main destinations: Russia (22.5 per cent total, 2006), Italy (6.5 per cent), Turkey (6.2 per cent).

Agriculture

Farming

Historically known as the 'bread basket' of the former Soviet Union, Ukraine used to produce 25 per cent of the total Soviet agricultural output. The agricultural sector, despite Ukraine's rich land resources (with one-third of the world's total acreage of black soil), went into decline for several years as a result of general inefficiency, late payments and a lack of finance for fuel, fertilisers and machinery. Progress of agricultural sector reforms included price and trade reforms, and agriculture-specific institutional reforms will have a significant impact on the future of agricultural production. Economy-wide reforms will allow the sector to absorb technological advances more rapidly.

The main agricultural products are wheat, barley, potatoes, sugar beet and flax. Ukraine is the world's largest producer of sugar beet.

Fishing

The fishery sector is an elaborate organisational complex of oceanic fisheries, pond fish farms, co-operatives, scientific research and education as well as enterprises dealing with processing and the sale of fish products, stock protection and restoration. The sector typically employs more than 60,000 people. The Black Sea fishing industry is concentrated around the ports of Odessa, Mariupol, Sevastopol, Berdyansk and Izmail.

Ukraine has a potential capacity to harvest and rear between 700,000–800,000 tonnes (t) of fish, with an annual output of food fish products from vessels and coastal enterprises amounting to more than 600,000t. The country exports over a third of its fish catch and the industry makes a substantial contribution to the country's trade balance.

Forestry

Ukraine has mainly mixed and steppe forests, which account for one-sixth of the land area, with forest cover estimated at 9.5 million hectares (ha). Nearly two-thirds of the forest is available for wood supply, although consumption of forest products per capita is significantly below the European average. The state owns all the forest area.

The Zavarpattska and Polisia regions are the main centres for the forestry and paper industries. Apart from the smaller wood processing enterprises, most of the forest industry is privatised and caters to domestic demand. The industry is being modernised by improving the sawmills and other manufacturing operations. Small quantities of roundwood and half-finished products are exported to the Middle East and European countries. Wood pulp and paper, mainly from the Russian Federation are imported.

Industry and manufacturing

Most of the sector is concentrated on heavy industry, principally in metallurgy, mining and mechanical engineering. The iron and steel industry is the main earner of hard currency revenues. It is dominated by large companies, such as JSC Zaporozhstal, and the government has been reluctant to introduce privatisation and other reforms. Ukraine has benefited from China's increasing demand for steel. The high-technology industry, having been located in Ukraine in Soviet times, is modern and internationally competitive.

Tourism

The tourism sector is at an early stage of development, having to construct infrastructure practically from scratch after years of Soviet-era neglect. Ukraine's rich cultural and environmental resources offer considerable potential. Tourism is treated as an essential instrument in the modernisation of the economy, but its contribution is as yet modest.

Environment

Extensive pollution is one of the more persistent legacies of the Soviet regime when massive industrialisation was pursued at any cost. The most obvious example is the Chernobyl nuclear power explosion which increased rates of thyroid cancer, leukaemia and birth defects in the surrounding areas. All Ukraine's cities suffer from pollution, both in the air as well as rivers and agricultural land. The Lviv region has the most polluted water in the country. Only about 55 per cent of the Ukranian population has access to safe water.

Mining

The mining sector traditionally accounts for 10 per cent of GDP and employs 3 per cent of the workforce.

Ukraine possesses an estimated 5 per cent of the world's mineral reserves. It has the world's largest supply of titanium, the third-largest deposit of iron ore (more than 200 billion tonnes) and 30 per cent of the world's manganese ore. It also has deposits of mercury, uranium and nickel, and a small amount of gold.

The largest iron ore deposits are in the Krivoy Roj area, with estimated reserves of 18 billion tonnes, Kremenchuk with 4.5 billion tonnes and Kerch and Belozerskie in the Donetsk region. The manganese deposits around Nikopol are thought to be the largest in the world. Gold deposits containing an average of between five and six grammes of gold per tonne of ore exist in the Trans-Carpathian region. The area also contains deposits of zinc and lead.

Other natural resources present in Ukraine include salt, lime, limestone, china clay , sulphur (around Lviv) and granite. Phosphorus deposits of about 20 billion tonnes are also present.

Ukraine typically produces 50 million tonnes per year (tpy) of iron, 1,000 tpy of nickel and 500 tpy of uranium.

Hydrocarbons

Proven oil reserves were 395 million barrels in 2007, the majority of which is located in the Dnieper-Donetsk basin in the eastern part of Ukraine. These reserves are under-exploited while Ukraine typically relies on oil imports from Russia. Ukraine and Russia have been in conflict since the latter began charging market rates for its hydrocarbons. Around 900,000 barrels per day (bpd) of Russian oil and gas transits Ukraine, via pipelines, of which around 250,000bpd is reserved

for domestic use. There are six oil refineries with total capacity of 880,000bpd. Efforts to reduce dependence on Russian oil have included the construction of an international oil terminal at Odessa port.
Proven natural gas reserves were 1.03 trillion cubic metres (cum) in 2007, with annual production of 19 billion cum. However consumption was 84 billion cum in 2007 so Ukraine relies on imported Russian and Turkmenistan natural gas to make up the shortfall.
Two disputes, in 2006 and 2009, over the price of Russian natural gas compared with the levy for transporting the gas across Ukraine territory, resulted in gas supplies being shut off and European customers left without energy during winter. Russia and the EU have both planned and taken measures to avoid future natural gas supplies transiting Ukraine.
Ukraine has 33.9 billion tonnes of coal reserves, but these are under-exploited, with production at 39.6 million tonnes of oil equivalent in 2007. Ukraine is a net importer of coal. Reserves are set to last for the next 400 years.

Energy

Total installed generating capacity was 54 gigawatts (GW) in 2006. There are four major thermal power stations and four nuclear power plants. The last working nuclear reactor at the Chernobyl plant was closed in 2000. Thermal power, much of which is gas-fired, accounts for nearly 50 per cent of the electricity produced in Ukraine, while nuclear energy provides 40 per cent and hydroelectric plants supply the remainder.
A state-owned company, Enerhoatom, oversees the nuclear power plants. Lack of funding has meant that safety standards continue to be lax and strike action and power breakdowns are frequent.
A second reactor at the Khmelnitsky nuclear power plant was switched on in August 2004, the first new nuclear reactor since Chernobyl.
A five-year gas supply deal was reached with Russia in 2006. The price per 1,000 cubic metres (cum) of gas was set at US$230 (up from US$50) but in a complex deal the Russian gas is sold to Gazprom-owned Roskurenergo, which is mixed with cheaper gas from Turkmenistan, Uzbekistan and Kazakhstan and then sold to Ukraine at US$95 per 1,000cum.
Another dispute with Russia was brewing in September 2011 when Ukraine said it would go to court to secure a 'fair' price for gas from Gazprom. Gazprom is also facing a challenge from a number of European customers overt he pricing formula.

Financial markets

Stock exchange
Ukraine Stock Exchange

Banking and insurance

There are seven domestic banks operating in the banking sector, two of which are state-owned and originate from the Soviet era. Foreign investors are permitted to participate in the banking sector, but are only granted a licence after at least a year of running an office in the country.
In February 2004, Ukraine was removed from the OECD Financial Action Task Force (FATF) list of non-co-operative countries on money-laundering after reforms had been implemented.
Central bank
National Bank of Ukraine

Time

GMT plus two hours (daylight saving, late March to late October, GMT plus three hours)

Geography

Ukraine is situated in Eastern Europe. The largest country entirely within Europe, Ukraine covers 603,700 square kilometres, stretching 2,000km from east to west and 1,000km from north to south. The Crimean peninsula in the south juts into the Black Sea, and has the Sea of Azov to the east.
In eastern Ukraine, the country is bordered by Russia to the east and north. In the western part of the country the northern border is with Belarus, and there are western borders with Poland and Slovakia. There are also short borders with Hungary, Romania and Moldova to the south-west, and a small salient of land south of Moldova which borders Bulgaria and has access to the Danube River delta.
The average height above sea level in Ukraine is only 175 metres, and most of the land area is composed of rolling steppes and wooded plains. About two-thirds of the country is covered by a thick layer of humus-rich soil, making it one of the most fertile regions in the world.
The only mountains are in the south on the Crimean peninsula (maximum height 1,545 metres) and the Carpathians in the west (maximum height 2,061 metres).
The main rivers are the Dnepr which drains the central regions of the country and flows into the Black Sea near Kherson and the Dnestr which flows through western Ukraine and Moldova before entering the Black Sea near Odessa.
Hemisphere
Northern

Climate

The moderate continental climate varies little across the country. The Black Sea resorts around Odessa and Yalta are usually warmer and drier than the rest of Ukraine. The average rainfall per year is 1,440mm, with the Crimea receiving only 400mm. Average temperatures in Kiev range from 20 degrees Celsius (C) in July to minus 7 degrees C in January. Average temperatures in Lviv in western Ukraine range from 16 degrees C in July, to minus 5 degrees C in January.

Dress codes

Business clothes are appropriate for meetings, including a suit or jacket with a tie for men and formal clothing for women.

Entry requirements

Passports
Required by all, valid for one month beyond departure date.
Visa
Required by all, except nationals of EU/EEA countries, North America, Japan, Switzerland, Andora, Vatican City, Monaco and San Marino. Letters of invitation are not required for either business or tourist visits by nationals of EU countries, US, Canada, Japan, Switzerland, Slovakia, or Turkey.
Currency advice/regulations
Import and export of local currency is restricted to H1,000; up to H5,000 may be exported subject to customs declaration. Import and export of foreign currencies is restricted to US$1,000 or, subject to customs declaration, up to US$10,000.
Customs
Small amount of personal goods, 200 cigarettes, 1 litre spirits, 2 litres wine and 10 litres beer are allowed duty free.
There are strict regulations governing the export of antiques and items of historical interest. If in doubt seek prior permission from customs authorities.
Prohibited imports
Weapons, illegal drugs and certain pharmaceutical and communcations products are subject to import restrictions; licences are issued by the relevant government ministries.

Health (for visitors)

Mandatory precautions
Vaccination certificates if travelling from a cholera or yellow fever infected area. An HIV/Aids test is required for long-stay visitors only. A UK-issued certificate is usually accepted. All visitors entering Ukraine are required to purchase health insurance at the airport of entry and prior to passing through immigration control. British passport holders are exempt due to a reciprocal agreement between the Ukrainian and British governments.
Advisable precautions
It is advisable to be in date for the following immunisations: polio (within 10 years), tetanus (within 10 years), typhoid fever and hepatitis A (moderate risk only). There

is a rabies risk. Any medicines required by the traveller should be imported and it is advisable to have precautionary antibiotics if travelling outside the major urban centres. However, there are restrictions on the import of some pharmaceuticals and visitors are advised to check with their local Ukrainian embassy prior to travel. A travel kit including a disposable syringe is a reasonable precaution.Water precautions are recommended (water purification tablets may be useful).

Hotels
Kiev has a shortage of hotels. It is worth booking rooms several weeks in advance through the Intourist travel agency.

Credit cards
Credit cards are not widely accepted.

Public holidays (national)
Fixed dates
1 Jan (New Year's Day), 7 Jan (Orthodox Christmas Day), 8 Mar (Women's Day), 1-2 May (Labour/May Days), 9 May (Victory Day), 28 Jun (Constitution Day), 24 Aug (Independence Day).
Variable dates
Orthodox Easter Monday, Orthodox Whit Monday.

Working hours
Banking
Mon–Fri: 0930–1730.
Open 24 hours at Kiev Borispol airport, but only until noon at Odessa.
Business
Mon–Fri: 0900–1800.
Government
Mon–Thu: 0700–1700; Fri: 0900–1200.
Shops
Mon–Sat: 0900–1900.

Social customs/useful tips
Tips are not expected at most cafes, although at more expensive restaurants a tip of between 5 and 10 per cent is appropriate.
Small gifts for your host are appreciated in the event of personal hospitality.
Handshaking is customary on meeting and on leaving. The formal mode of address, *Pan* (Mr) or *Pani* (Mrs) is usual even after several meetings. The use of business cards is widespread. It is important to be on time for meetings and appointments.
Referring to Ukraine as part of the Soviet Union or, even worse, as part of Russia, is a serious insult. The post-independence reaction to decades of 'Russification' led to strong nationalistic feelings, particularly in western Ukraine.

Security
Normal precautions should be taken when visiting Ukraine – avoid displaying large amounts of cash or expensive personal belongings. Avoid travelling alone at night in Kiev, particularly on the metro or in the city's parks.

Getting there
Air
National airline: Ukraine International Airlines
International airport/s: Kiev-Borispol International Airport (KBP), 27km from city centre; bank, post office, duty-free shop, car rental.
Other airport/s: Zhulhany Airport (IEV), 6km from Kiev.
Airport tax: None
Surface
Ukraine is included in the Pan-European Corridor 5 scheme. The project has some 3,270km of railways, linking Kiev in the Ukraine with western Europe via Italy, and 2,850 of new and upgraded roads.
Road: There are roads into Ukraine from all neighbouring countries.
Rail: There are links connecting Kiev and Lviv with all Commonwealth of Independent States member states. Direct rail connections are available to Warsaw in Poland, Budapest in Hungary and Bucharest in Romania.
Water: There are ferry services from Russia to the Crimean ports. Odessa and Yalta on the Black Sea have regular arrivals from Haifa, Istanbul, Limassol, Piraeus and Port Said. Riverboats from Odessa go to a number of Central European cities via the Danube.
Main port/s: The main Crimean ports are Yalta and Sevastopol, with Kerch the main port for the Sea of Azov. Izmail is the main Danube River port, and Odessa is the largest Black Sea port.

Getting about
National transport
Air: The main airports for domestic air traffic are Borispol International and Zhulany, from which there are connections to Chernivitsi, Dniepropetrovsk, Donetsk, Ivano-Frankivsk, Kharkov, Lugansk, Lviv, Mariupol, Odessa, Simferopol, Uzhgorod and Zaporizhzhya. Services during the winter months are often subject to cancellation or delay.
Road: There is an extensive road network comprising approximately 172,00km of road, with around 29,000km of these being main or national roads. Many roads are poorly surfaced and in need of modernisation.
Buses: Ukraine has an extensive bus network, with routes to every city and most smaller towns.
Taxis: Using taxis for long-distance journeys is an option as they are reasonably cheap. Payment is usually requested in hard currency. Agree a price before setting off.
Rail: The Ukrainian rail network links the major cities, most of which are at least *one night's travel apart. There are three types of sleeper carriage: the spalny vahon* is the first class compartment for two people; the *kupe* or *kupeyny* is the second class compartment for four people; and the *platskart* is the third class open carriage with groups of six bunks in each alcove, with more beds along the aisles – avoid the *platskart* unless absolutely necessary.
It is advisable to pre-book tickets before arriving in Ukraine. Foreigners can usually buy rail tickets from separate offices with English-speaking clerks, although the price will be slightly higher.
Although journey times are slower than air, rail travel is more reliable during the winter months.
Water: Passenger transport is available on the Dnepr and Dnestr rivers, which traverse large areas of the country, but price increases, lack of spare parts and cheaper land-based transport have caused a sharp decline in services.
City transport
Taxis: In most cities there are metered official taxis, unofficial 'gypsy cabs' with negotiated fares and fixed route, fixed price shared taxis and minibus services.
Car hire
International agencies are represented in the main cities, in addition to local agencies, offering a range of vehicles. Car hire is relatively cheap.
Speed limits are 60kph (37mph) in built-up areas, 90kph (55mph) in open areas and 110kph (69mph) on motorways. An international driving permit is required. It is illegal to drive having consumed any amount of alcohol.

BUSINESS DIRECTORY
The addresses listed below are a selection only. While World of Information makes every endeavour to check these addresses, we cannot guarantee that changes have not been made, especially to telephone numbers and area codes. We would welcome any corrections.

Telephone area codes
The international direct dialling code (IDD) for Ukraine is + 380, followed by area code and subscriber's number:

Dnepropetrovsk	56	Odessa	48
Donetsk	62	Sevastopol	69
Kharkov	57	Simferopol	65
Kiev	44	Yalta	65
Lviv	32		

Useful telephone numbers
Fire brigade: 01
Militia (Police): 02
Hospital enquiries: 003
Directory enquiries: 09
Address enquiries: 061
Lost property office: 229-7844
Paid enquiries service: 009

Railway timetable: 09
River port: 416-1268
Taxi: 058
Taxi enquiries: 225-0396
Time: 060

Chambers of Commerce

American Chamber of Commerce in Ukraine, 42 Shovkovychna Street, 01601 Kiev (tel: 490-5800; fax: 490-5801; e-mail: acc@amcham.ua).

British-Ukrainian Chamber of Commerce, 34a Grushevskogo Street, 01021 Kiev (tel: 410-5720; fax: 230-2151; e-mail: administrator@bucc.com.ua).

Crimea Chamber of Commerce and Industry, 45 Sevastopolskaya Street, 95013 Simferopol (e-mail: cci@cci.crimea.ua).

Dnipropetrovsk Chamber of Commerce and Industry, 4 Shevchenko Street, 49044 Dnipropetrovsk (tel: 236-2258; fax: 236-2259; e-mail: miv@dcci.dp.ua).

Donetsk Chamber of Commerce and Industry, 12 Dzerzinskogo Avenue, 83000 Donetsk (e-mail: dcci@dtpp.donetsk.ua).

Kharkov Chamber of Commerce and Industry, 3a Kartsarskaya Street, 61012 Kharkov (e-mail: info@kcci.kharkov.ua).

Kiev Chamber of Commerce and Industry, 55 Bogdana Khmelnitskogo Street, 01054 Kiev (tel: 246-8301; fax: 246-9966; e-mail: info@kiev-chamber.org.ua).

Lviv Chamber of Commerce and Industry, 14 Stryisky Park, 79011 Lviv (e-mail: lcci@cscd.lviv.ua).

Odessa Chamber of Commerce and Industry, 47 Bazarna Street, 65011 Odessa (tel: 728-6610; e-mail: orcci@orcci.odessa.ua).

Sevastopol Chamber of Commerce and Industry, 34 Bolshaya Morskaya Street, 99011 Sevastopol (e-mail: stpp@optima.com.ua).

Ukrainian Chamber of Commerce & Industry, 33 Velyka Zhytomyrska, 01601 Kiev (tel: 272-2911; fax: 272-3353; e-mail: ucci@ucci.org.ua).

Banking

Aggio Joint Stock Bank, 9 Leskova Street, 252011 Kiev (tel: 295-0305; fax 295-3164).

Commercial Bank (Ekspobank), 2-4 Volodarskogo Street, 254025 Kiev (tel: 216-1676; fax: 216-6073).

First Ukrainian International Bank (under full management of Bank Mees and Hpe Pierson NV, ABN/AMRO), 8 Prorizna Street, 252034 Kiev (tel: 224-2187; fax: 224-2055).

Gradobank, 1 Dimitrova Street, 252650 Kiev (tel: 261-9191; fax: 268-1530).

Inki Bank, 10/2 Mechnikova Street, 252023 Kiev (tel: 294-9219; fax: 290-6292).

Legbank Commercial Bank for Light Industry, 8/10 Esplanadna (Kuybysheva) Street, 252601 Kiev (tel: 220-6125; fax: 220-8684).

Ukreximbank, 8 Kreshchatyk Street, Kiev (tel: 226-3363; fax: 229-8082).

Ukrainian Bank for Foreign Economic Affairs, 8 Kreshchatyk Street, 252001 Kiev (tel: 293-1698).

Ukrainian Financial Group Joint Stock Commercial Bank, 7 Vokzalnaya Street, 252032 Kiev (tel: 245-4560; fax: 245-4587).

Central bank

National Bank of Ukraine, 9 Institutska Street, Kiev 01601 (tel: 253-0180; fax: 230-2033; e-mail: info@bank.gov.ua).

Stock exchange

Ukraine Stock Exchange: www.ukrse.kiev.ua

Travel information

Ukraine International Airlines, 63A Bogdana Khmelnytskogo Street, 01054 Kiev (tel: 461-5656 ; fax: 216-7994; e-mail: uia@ps.kiev.ua).

Ukrainian Travel Information System, 29A, Electrikov Street, 04176 Kiev (tel/fax: 537-2727; e-mail: info@utis.com.ua)

Ministry of tourism

Ministry of Culture and Tourism, 19 Ivana Franka Street, 01601 Kiev (tel: 235-2378; fax: 235-3257; e-mail: info@mincult.gov.ua).

National tourist organisation offices

State Tourism Administration of Ukraine, 36 Yaroslaviv Val Street, 01034 Kiev (tel: 212-4215; fax: 212-4277; e-mail: info@tourism.gov.ua).

Ministries

Ministry of Agriculture and Foodstuffs, 24 Kreshchatyk Street, 252001 Kiev (tel: 226-2772; fax: 229-8756).

Ministry of the Coal Industry, 4 Bohdana Khmelnitskoho Street, 252001 Kiev (tel: 226-2273, 228-0372; fax: 228-2131).

Ministry of Communications, 22 Kreshchatyk Street, Kiev (tel: 226-2140; fax: 228-6141).

Ministry of Culture, 19 Ivana Franka Street, 252030 Kiev (tel: 224-4911, 226-2645, 226-2902; fax: 225-3257).

Ministry of Defence, 6 Povitroflotsky Avenue, 252168 Kiev (tel: 224-7152; fax: 226-2015).

Ministry of Education, 10 Peremogy Avenue, 252135 Kiev (tel: 216-7210, 216-7763, 216-1575; fax: 274-1049).

Ministry of Engineering, the Defence Industry and Conversion, 6 Pushkinska Street, 252034 Kiev (tel: 229-0390; fax: 228-7653).

Ministry of Environment Protection, 5 Kreshchatyk Street, 252001 Kiev (tel: 226-2428, 228-0644; fax: 229-8383).

Ministry of Finance, 12/2 Hrushevskoho Street, 252008 Kiev (tel: 226-2044; fax: 293-2178).

Ministry of Foreign Affairs, 1 Mihaylivska Square, 252018 Kiev (tel: 226-3379, 293-1581; fax: 226-3169, 293-3302).

Ministry of Foreign Economic Relations, 8 Lvivska Square, 254655 Kiev (tel: 212-3005; fax: 212-5259).

Ministry of Forestry, 5 Kreshchatyk Street, 252001 Kiev (tel: 226-3253, 226-2735, 228-5666; fax: 228-7794).

Ministry of Health, 7 Hrushevskoho Street, 252021 Kiev (tel: 293-6194; fax: 293-6975).

Ministry of Industry, 34 Kreshchatyk Street, 252001 Kiev (tel: 226-2623; fax: 227-4104).

Ministry of Information, 2 Prorizna Street, 252601 Kiev (tel: 226-2871).

Ministry of Internal Affairs, 10 Bogomoltsa Street, 252021 Kiev (tel: 291-3333, 226-3317; fax: 291-3182).

Ministry of Justice, 13 Karl Marx Street, 252001 Kiev (tel: 226-2416; fax: 226-2416).

Ministry of Labour, 28 Pushkinska Street, 252004 Kiev (tel: 226-2445, 226-2639, 226-3215; fax: 224-5905).

Ministry for Nationalities, Migration and Cults Issues, 21/8 Instytutska Street, 252021 Kiev (tel: 293-5335; fax: 293-3531).

Ministry of Power Engineering and Electrification, 30 Kreshchatyk Street, 252001 Kiev (tel: 224-9388; fax: 224-4021).

Ministry for Protection of the Population against the Consequences of Chernobyl, 8 Lvivska Square, 254655 Kiev (tel: 212-5049; fax: 212-5069).

Ministry of Social Welfare, 26-28 Kudriavka Street, 252053 Kiev (tel: 222-5555, 226-2401; fax: 212-2535).

Ministry of Statistics, 3 Shota Rustaveli Street, 252023 Kiev (tel: 226-2021, 227-7057; fax: 227-0783, 227-4266).

Ministry of Transport, 51 Horkoho Street, 252005 Kiev (tel: 226-2266, 227-1029, 227-7087; fax: 227-7351).

Ministry of Youth and Sports Issues, 42 Esplanadna Street, 252023 Kiev (tel: 220-0200, 220-1461; fax: 220-1294).

Ukrainian Ministry for Economics and Issues of European Integration, 12/2

Hrushevskoho Street, 252008 Kiev (tel: 293-4005, 293-9329; fax: 293-6371).

Other useful addresses

British Embassy, 9 Desyatinna, 01025 Kiev (tel: 462-0011/15; fax: 462-0013; internet: wwwbritemb-ukraine.net).

Cabinet of Ministers, 12/2 Hrushevskoho Street, 252001 Kiev (tel: 226-3263; fax: 293-2093).

Committee for Standardisation, Methodology and Certification, 10 Kypska Street, 252021 Kiev (tel: 226-2971).

EBRD Kiev Office, c/o National Hotel, 5 Lipska Street, 252021 Kiev 21 (tel: 291-8847, 291-8977; fax: 291-6246).

EU Co-ordination Unit – TACIS Programme, Agency for International Co-operation and Investment, 1 Mihailivska Ploscha, 252018 Kiev (tel: 212-8312; fax: 230-2513).

European Centre for Macroeconomic Analysis of Ukraine, Kiev (tel & fax: 228-3283; e-mail: ecman@gv.kiev.va).

Foreign Trade Organisation (UKRIMPEX), 22 Vorovsky Street, 252054 Kiev (tel: 216-2174; fax: 216-1926, 216-2996).

International Finance Corporation Field Office, Suite 7, 28-A Lyuteranska Street, 252024 Kiev (tel: 293-4857, 293-8341; fax: 293-0539).

Kiev City Administration, 36 Khreshchatyk Street, Kiev (tel: 220-8065; fax: 228-4718).

Kiev Universal Commodity Exchange (KUCE), 1 Kudryashova Street, 252035 Kiev (tel: 276-7129, 244-0143, fax: 276-7129).

Soros International Economic Advisory Group, Kiev (tel: 296-9877; fax: 269-5263).

State Ukrainian Property Fund, 18/9 Kutuzova Street, 252133 Kiev (tel: 296-6963; fax: 296-6984).

Ukrainian Association of Industrialists and Entrepreneurs, 34 Kreshchatik Street, 252001 Kiev (tel: 224-3122, 228-3069; fax: 226-3152).

Ukrainian Embassy (USA), Suite 711, 3350 M Street, NW, Washington DC 20007 (tel: (+1-202) 333-0606; fax: (+1-202) 333-0606; e-mail: vmar@aol.com).

Ukrainian Exchange (commodities and stock exchange), 15 Proreznaya Street, 252601 Kiev (tel: 228-6481; fax: 229-6376).

Ukrainian League of Enterprises with Foreign Capital, 19A Lyuteranska Street, 252073 Kiev (tel: 229-3544; fax: 229-8739).

Ukrainian National News Agency (UKRINFORM), 8-16b Khemlnitski Street, 252601 Kiev (tel: 226-2469, 229-0143; fax: 229-2439/8007, 228-1659).

Ukrainian Universal Commodity Exchange, 1 Academika Glushkova Avenue, 252085 Kiev (tel: 261-6333, 261-6375; fax: 261-6362).

UKRINTERENERGO (State Foreign Trade Company), 27 Komintern Street, 252032 Kiev (tel: 291-7296; fax: 220-1885).

World Bank Field Office, Suite 2/3, 26 Shovkovychna Street, 252024 Kiev (tel: 293-1110, 293-4045; fax: 293-4236).

National news agency: Ukrinform (Ukranian National News Agency)

8/16 Bohdan Khmelnytsky St, Kiev 01001 (tel: 234-8366; fax: 279-8665; email: office@ukrinform.com; internet: http://news.ukrinform.ua).

Other news agencies: Unian: www.unian.net/eng

Interfax-Ukraine: www.interfax.com.ua/en

Internet sites

Ukraine gateway site: http://www.brama.com

Ukraine Embassy, London: http://www.ukrainet.org

Ukraine Embassy, Washington: http://www.ukremb.com

General information: http://www.bizukraine.com

Tourism and travel: http://www.ukraine.com

Ukraine International Airlines: http://www.ukraine international.com

History and culture: http://www:uazone.net

News on Ukraine: http://www.infoukes.com

Travel and tourism: http://www.travel.kyiv.org

United Arab Emirates

KEY FACTS

Official name: Al Imarat al Arabiyya al Muttahida (United Arab Emirates) (UAE)

Head of State: President Sheikh Khalifa bin Zaid al Nahyan (ruler of Abu Dhabi) (since Nov 2004)

Head of government: Prime Minister Sheikh Mohammed bin Rashed al Maktoum (ruler of Dubai) (from 4 Jan 2006)

Ruling party: There are no official political parties

Area: 83,600 square km

Population: 5.40 million (2010)*

Capital: Abu Dhabi (federal capital); Dubai (commercial capital)

Official language: Arabic

Currency: Dirham (Dh) = 100 fils

Exchange rate: Dh3.67 per US$ (fixed)

GDP per capita: US$59,717 (2010)

GDP real growth: 3.20% (2010)

GDP: US$301.90 billion (2010)

Unemployment: 4.00% (2008)

Inflation: 0.90% (2010)

Oil production: 2.85 million bpd (2010)

Balance of trade: US$63.69 billion (2010)

Annual FDI: US$3.95 billion (2010)

* estimated figure

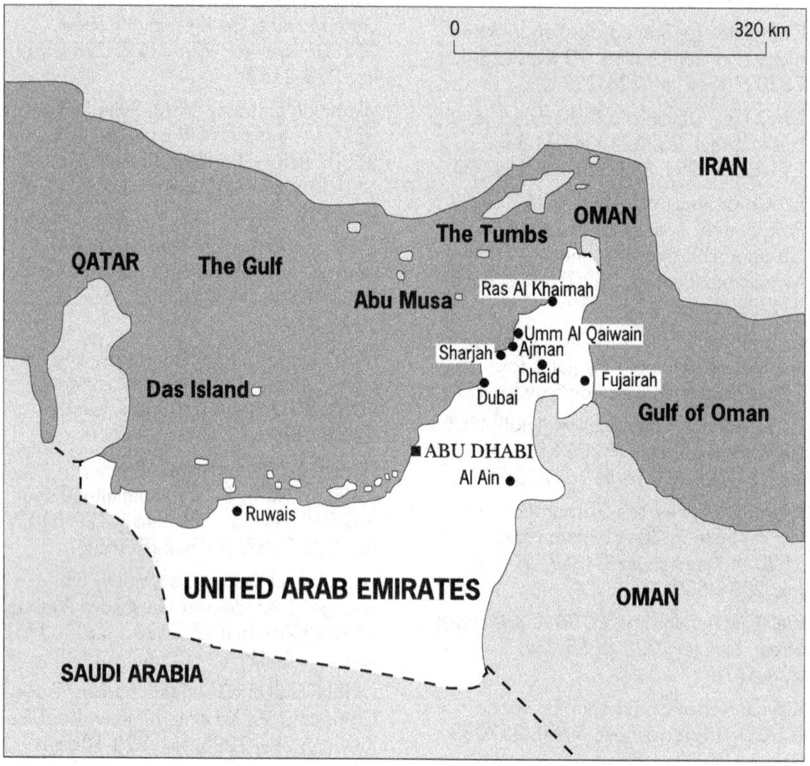

To the relief of international financial markets, not to mention the rulers of Abu Dhabi and the errant Dubai, 2011 was a year in which some sort of economic stability could be seen to be restored to the United Arab Emirates (UAE). Of even greater concern to the authorities, however, was the risk of contagion from the so-called Arab Spring. Perhaps reluctantly, the UAE had contributed troops to the Gulf Co-operation Council (GCC) force sent in to neighbouring Bahrain to 'keep the peace', by which was meant, keep the island state's ruler in place in the face of street protests for greater liberty and freedom of expression.

The turmoil in parts of the Middle East and North Africa also posed downside risks. The re-pricing of risk in the region could result in more difficult financial market conditions. On the positive side, there are indications that the UAE may benefit from increased tourism and investments looking for diversification within the region. Higher oil prices are also benefiting the UAE as a hydrocarbon exporter, though if sustained, they may affect the recovery if demand from Asia falls.

The economy

The UAE government is pursuing economic diversification through investment in infrastructure in transport, trade and tourism. Abu Dhabi has made a concerted effort to increase its industrialisation through projects such as the Khalifa Industrial Zone Abu Dhabi (KIZAD), which will allow 100 per cent foreign ownership of companies. This infrastructure project will be one of the largest integrated industrial zones in the world and will further serve the aims of economic diversification held by the government. It is strategically (diplomatically?) placed mid-way between Abu Dhabi and Dubai.

Although the economic crisis had necessitated the bailing out by Abu Dhabi of the most prominent of Dubai's state-run firms, Dubai World, these financial difficulties did not precipitate a flight of foreign capital. Indeed, the UAE has returned to positive and increasing growth once again, with a gross domestic product (GDP) growth forecast of 3.1 per cent for 2011.

The UAE's non-hydrocarbon GDP growth was projected to increase from 2.1 per cent in 2010 to 3.3 per cent in 2011, led by strong tourism, logistics and trade in Dubai; and large public investment spending in Abu Dhabi. However, the real estate overhang and short term refinancing needs from overleveraged government-related entities (GREs) weighed on the near-term outlook.

Although GREs have contributed significantly to UAE's economic growth, the recent bailouts (in particular of Dubai World), the size of Dubai's GRE debt and the significant short- and medium-term roll-over needs call for containing the risks posed by these entities. This entails better governance within the GREs, as well as assessing, monitoring, reporting and disclosing GRE contingent liabilities in government accounts. Containing GRE borrowing is key for fiscal sustainability at the emirate level.

The UAE's banking sector has remained resilient to shocks, thanks to high capital and strong earnings. Although non-performing loans have doubled since the global economic crisis, banks have increased provisioning. In the light of the ongoing restructuring of Dubai's GREs, the International Monetary Fund (IMF) considers that the Central Bank of the United Arab Emirates should continue to ensure that banks provision adequately, monitor the performance of restructured loans and encourage banks to retain more earnings to handle potential risks in the medium term.

After the alarums of 2010, it should be remembered that the UAE has the fifth-largest oil and gas reserves in the world. Abu Dhabi produces 95 per cent of the country's oil and gas and owns one of the largest sovereign wealth funds in the world, with more than US$300 billion assets under management. In contrast, Dubai, the second largest emirate, has a more diversified economy, driven by re-export trade, services and real estate and is highly leveraged, with a gross debt-to-GDP ratio above 100 per cent.

It should also be remembered that the UAE has had remarkable achievements over the last decade with its open and outward orientation, which has led to a diversified and steadily growing economy. Even so the temporary decline in oil prices, the post-Lehman shut down of international capital markets and the price correction in the property market in Dubai did put significant strains on the economy.

GDP grew by an estimated 3.2 per cent in 2010. But, because of the real estate 'overhang' and continued uncertainties about the solvency of GREs, this growth was below the regional average of 5 per cent. The 12-month consumer price inflation (CPI) rate was subdued at 1.7 per cent in December 2010, up from -0.3 per cent at end-2009.

With exports increasing by 15 per cent in 2010 and imports by 6 per cent, the current account balance is estimated to have reached 7.7 per cent of GDP in 2010. Deposit inflows in the second half of 2010 helped improve the financial account balance. As a result, the central bank's foreign exchange reserves recovered from the losses sustained in 2009 (US$7 billion), reaching US$32 billion by year-end (corresponding to 1.7 months of imports).

The successful restructuring of Dubai World's debt had improved market confidence, allowing top-grade Dubai issuers to regain market access. However, Dubai spreads remain high reflecting the risks posed by further restructuring needs. Many Dubai GREs initiated DW style restructuring talks, while Abu Dhabi stepped up support to some of its GREs.

With continued pressures in Dubai's real estate market in 2010, several GREs and other private companies restructured their bank loans. Dubai banks reduced lending to improve liquidity, while Abu Dhabi banks continued to expand in line with the emirate's fiscal expansion. Nevertheless, overall credit to the private sector remained sluggish and non-performing loans (NPLs) increased to 5.9 per cent from 4.3 per cent in 2009, reflecting mainly the deterioration of loan quality in Dubai banks (8.8 per cent).

Of particular concern to the international financial markets after the DW debacle was the fact that the UAE government made it more than clear that the debt of Dubai World was not guaranteed by the government. What had become clear in the view of the IMF, as a result of the Dubai World affair was the need for the UAE to increase the transparency of its economic and financial data, including the financial accounts and business strategies for GREs and at the same time put in place some form of corporate insolvency regime at the federal level, to provide a transparent framework for debt resolution.

The Dubai World debt announcement certainly undermined the widely held market perception of implicit government support, especially from the government of Abu Dhabi. To the certain relief of the UAE government, the IMF was at pains to point out that developments in Dubai, needed to be seen in the 'wider perspective of the UAE as a whole.' The UAE has a net external creditor position well in excess of 100 per cent of GDP, among the largest in the Fund's membership. If anything the 'crisis' illustrated the contrasting positions between the two major emirates:

KEY INDICATORS — United Arab Emirates

	Unit	2006	2007	2008	2009	2010
Population	m	4.23	*4.49	*4.76	*4.91	*5.40
Gross domestic product (GDP)	US$bn	163.30	207.70	261.40	230.00	301.90
GDP per capita	US$	38,613	46,249	54,849	46,857	59,717
GDP real growth	%	9.4	6.1	5.1	-0.7	3.2
Inflation	%	9.2	11.7	12.3	1.6	0.9
Oil output	'000 bpd	2,969.0	2,915.0	2,980.0	2,599.0	2,849.0
Natural gas output	bn cum	47.4	49.2	50.2	48.8	51.0
Exports (fob) (goods)	US$m	144,600.0	179,100.0	239,800.0	192,200.0	221,900.0
Imports (fob) (goods)	US$m	88,100.0	132,100.0	176,300.0	149,700.0	158,300.0
Balance of trade	US$m	56,500.0	4,700.0	63,500.0	42,500.0	63,600.0
Current account	US$m	35,942.0	19,545.0	22,155.0	9,040.0	23,273.0
Total reserves minus gold	US$m	27,617.4	77,238.8	31,694.5	36,104.2	42,785.3
Foreign exchange	US$m	27,511.9	77,161.9	31,556.6	35,070.4	41,750.9
Exchange rate	per US$	3.67	3.67	3.67	3.67	3.67

* estimated figure

Abu Dhabi, has substantial 'liquid unencumbered external assets'. In contrast Dubai had experienced major economic difficulties based on the weaknesses of the business model it had adopted. However, a number of Dubai's major companies have none the less accumulated substantial assets abroad.

Thanks to the oil...

According to the *Oil & Gas Journal* (OGJ), the UAE had reserves of 97.8 billion barrels of oil on 1 January 2011, making up 7 per cent of global oil reserves. The UAE has been able to maintain its proven reserves over the last decade primarily due to enhanced oil recovery (EOR) technologies increasing extraction rates of mature oil projects combined with higher oil prices making more reserves commercially viable. Few new concessions have been made, as exploration has met with little success and most foreign companies lack market access. However, in late 2008, Occidental Petroleum won the first concession offered in decades, earning the right to develop the Jarn Yahpour and Rahman oil fields.

The oil policy of the UAE government is carried out mainly by the Supreme Petroleum Council (SPC) through the Abu Dhabi National Oil Company (ADNOC), operating 14 subsidiaries which participate at every level of the oil and natural gas sectors. The contract structure is based on a long-term, production-sharing basis with the state mandated to own a majority of the equity stake in a project, often through joint venture companies. The most noteworthy of the oil-producing consortia include the Zakum Development Company (ZADCO), the Abu Dhabi Company for Onshore Operations (ADCO) and the Abu Dhabi Marine Operating Company (ADMA-OPCO). International oil majors operating in the UAE include BP, Shell, Total, ExxonMobil, Petrofac and Partex.

In 2010, the UAE produced approximately 2.81 million barrels per day (bpd) of total oil liquids, of which 2.3 million bpd was crude oil. Crude oil production capacity is currently estimated at 2.6 million bpd. However, increases in capacity have not been reflected in increased production due to limits imposed by OPEC, which constrain UAE's production around its quota of 2.223 million bpd. The government has pushed back plans to increase capacity to 3.5 million bpd to 2018, pending acceptance of fellow Organisation of the Petroleum Exporting Countries (Opec) members.

Much of the oil production in the UAE is from the Zakum oil system, a collection of oil fields which together make up the third largest oil zone in the world. The Upper Zakum field is run by ZADCO, 60 per cent owned by ADNOC with the Japanese Oil Development Company (JODCO) and ExxonMobil holding the remaining stakes. In order to boost production capacity, ZADCO is reviewing the possibility to use extended reach drilling from four artificial islands to expand production from the current 550,000bpd to 750,000bpd by 2015, increasing the oil recovery rate to 70 per cent.

The largest onshore oil fields are operated by ADCO – the Bu Hasa oil field, which produces as much as 600,000bpd, as well as the Murban Bab, Sahil, Asab and Shah oil fields, contributing another 705,000bpd of light, sweet crude. Additionally, two new fields are being developed by ADCO – the Qusahwira and Bab oil fields, adding 250,000bpd by 2014. ADCO will also redevelop Bida al Qemzan field, adding 20,000bpd to its current production of 225,000bpd by the third quarter of 2012. These projects are components of a plan to boost ADCO's aggregate production to 1.8 million bpd from its current 1.4 million bpd by 2017.

ADMA-OPCO operates the main offshore assets in Abu Dhabi, which have been in redevelopment to maximise output. The Umm Shaif and Lower Zakum offshore oil fields have a capacity of 520,000bpd combined, although after an expansion at each they will have a production capacity of 425,000bpd and 300,000bpd, respectively. Two new oil fields have also come into development: Nasr and Umm al Lulu. These will add a further 170,000bpd capacity by 2018.

Dubai and Sharjah produce relatively minor amounts of crude oil. Dubai adds 100,000bpd from four separate fields, the older and more abundant Fateh and Southwest Fateh oil fields, with extra production from the Falah and Rashid fields. Sharjah's only significant oil field is the Mubarak field, which produces 60,000bpd. Sharjah-based Crescent Petroleum operated this field for 35 years before handing control to the government in December 2009. In November 2010, the ruler of Sharjah, Shaikh Sultan bin Muhammad al Qasimi, had issued a decree which created the Sharjah National Oil Corporation (SNOC). The new firm is owned by the emirate of Sharjah and has legal, financial and administrative independence to carry out operations in the upstream and downstream markets, as well as investing in other firms engaging in similar activities. SNOC manages those projects formerly operated by Crescent Petroleum in the emirate.

The Emirates have an extensive network of domestic pipelines linking fields with processing plants and ports. There are also inter-emirate pipelines primarily for natural gas injection to increase oil recovery rates in mature Dubai oil fields. There are two pipelines which deliver natural gas to Dubai for injection and use for electric generation – one originating in Sharjah, while the other begins in Abu Dhabi.

The largest export pipeline project in development currently is the Abu Dhabi Crude Oil Pipeline (ADCOP) Project. The International Petroleum Investment Corporation (IPIC) is spearheading the project, along with the China Petroleum Engineering & Construction Corporation (CPECC), a subsidiary of the China National Petroleum Corporation (CNPC). The 230-mile pipeline is scheduled for completion by August 2011 and will transport 1.5 million bpd from ADCO's Habshan facility to the Fujairah export terminals on the Gulf of Oman coast. Significantly, this will allow more than half of UAE's exports to bypass the strategic chokepoint at the Strait of Hormuz. In late 2011 Iran had threatened to close the strait in response to the application of sanctions by the US and the European Union (EU).

Japan is the main market for UAE petroleum exports, encompassing 40 per cent of its export volumes. South Korea and Thailand are the other major destinations for Emirati crude. The Abu Dhabi National Tanker Company (ADNATCO) is the subsidiary of ADNOC responsible for the transportation of petroleum products.

Fujairah is rapidly expanding its export capability. A second oil terminal, composed of 3 moorings and a new 4-berth facility for tanker bunkering, has been built, as well as storage capacity and a 400,000bpd terminal for refined products and petrochemicals, all of which are expected to be operational before the end of 2012.

According to the OGJ, the UAE possessed 214.4 trillion cubic feet (tcf) of proven natural gas reserves as of 1 January 2011, although some industry estimates place it slightly higher at 227.2tcf. This amounts to the seventh largest natural gas reserves globally, following Russia, Iran, Qatar, Saudi Arabia, Turkmenistan and the United States. The majority of these reserves are located in Abu Dhabi (198.5tcf), with marginal amounts found in Sharjah (10.7tcf), Dubai (4tcf) and Ras al Khaimah (1.2tcf).

In 2010, the UAE produced 51 billion cubic metres of marketed natural gas, which is equal to around 5 billion cubic feet per day (bcf/d). In 2007, domestic consumption outstripped production for the first time. Domestic demand for electricity continues to rise, spurred by subsidies. Most electricity generated in the UAE uses natural gas as a feedstock, causing the government to look for ever increasing volumes to compensate for increased demand from economic expansion and high population growth. The reliance upon natural gas for injection into mature oil fields further compounds the strain on natural gas supplies. Despite the UAE's large natural gas reserves, capital costs and high sulfur content present major impediments to development

While the UAE has a federal structure and some wealth is shared between emirates, each emirate manages its own budget independently. Expatriates constitute 80 per cent of the UAE population and are virtually fully employed. Unemployment among nationals is high (14 per cent in 2009) and concentrated among the youth and in the northern emirates.

Risk assessment

Politics	Fair
Economy	Fair/improving
Regional stability	Good

COUNTRY PROFILE

Historical profile

1498 The Portuguese occupied the region.
1633 The Dutch turned the Portuguese out of their trading posts, to be ousted in their turn, by the British.
1820 Britain and a number of rulers in the Gulf signed a treaty to combat piracy. This began a series of agreements which led to the area becoming known as the Trucial Coast, comprising the Trucial states (Abu Dhabi, Dubai, Sharjah, Ras al Khaimah, Umm al Qaiwain, Fujairah and Ajman).
1892 Exclusive Agreements between the Trucial States and Britain were signed, which effectively gave the British control over foreign affairs, while each emirate retained control over internal affairs.
1952 The seven emirates formed a Trucial council to promote increased co-operation.
1958 Oil was discovered off Abu Dhabi.
1962 Oil was exported for the first time from Abu Dhabi.
1966 Oil was discovered off Dubai.
1968 Britain announced its intention to withdraw from the Gulf by 1971. A British plan to form a single state consisting of Bahrain, Qatar and the Trucial States did not take place.
1971 The independence of Bahrain and Qatar was negotiated. Iran occupied the islands of Greater and Lesser Tumb and Abu Musa. Abu Dhabi, Dubai, Sharjah, Fujairah, Umm al Qaiwain and Ajman formed the United Arab Emirates (UAE), a loose federation. Sheikh Zayed bin Sultan al Nahyan (ruler of Abu Dhabi) was elected president of the federation. Ras al Khaimah's ruler did not join at this point since he optimistically hoped that successful oil exploration would enable him to hold out for a better deal.
1972 Ras al Khaimah joined the federation; the Federal National Council (FNC) was created as a 40-member consultative body, appointed by the seven rulers of the UAE.
1980s The UAE supported Iraq during the Iran-Iraq war.
1981 A political and economic union, Co-operation Council for the Arab States of the Gulf (CCASG) (known as the Gulf Co-operation Council (GCC)) was formed by Bahrain, Kuwait, Oman, Qatar, Saudi Arabia and the UAE. The GCC's inaugural meeting was held in Abu Dhabi.
1991 The UAE joined the US-led alliance against Iraq. The Bank of Credit and Commerce International (BCCI), in which the Abu Dhabi royal family owned a 77.4 per cent stake, collapsed.
1992 Iran insisted that visitors to the islands of Abu Musa and Greater and Lesser Tumb must have Iranian visas.
1993 Abu Dhabi sued BCCI's executives for damages.
1994 A court in Abu Dhabi convicted 11 of the 12 former BCCI executives accused of fraud. They were given prison sentences and ordered to pay compensation.
1996 Iran's dispute with the UAE over the islands of Abu Musa and the Tumbs was further fuelled by Iran when it built an airport on Abu Musa and a power station on Greater Tumb. Two BCCI executives were cleared of fraud charges on appeal.
20101998 Diplomatic relations with Iraq were restored – the UAE had severed them at the outbreak of the Gulf War.
1999 The GCC reiterated its support for the UAE over the three disputed islands of Greater and Lesser Tumb and Abu Musa.
2001 Six thousand prisoners were pardoned by the President on humanitarian grounds. The government ordered financial institutions to freeze the assets of 62 organisations and individuals suspected of funding terrorist movements.
2002 The UAE and Oman signed a final agreement delineating their entire 1,000km border.
2003 Crown Prince Sheikh Khalid bin Saqr al Qasimi, who had been handling day-to-day affairs of state, was dismissed by his father in favour is his brother (a traditionalist), Sheikh Saud bin Saqr al Qasimi.
2004 President Sheikh Zayed died. Sheikh Khalifa bin Zayed al Nahyan succeeded his father as ruler of Abu Dhabi. The Federal National Council (FNC) elected him president of the UAE.
2005 A new terminal for Abu Dhabi International Airport was opened. Sheikh Zayed announced plans to elect half of the 40 members of the FNC, by a limited number of citizens.
2006 Sheikh Maktoum bin Rashed al Maktoum, ruler of Dubai, vice president and prime minister of the UAE, died. He was succeeded by Sheikh Mohammed bin Rashid al Maktoum. The state-owned company, Dubai Ports, purchased the UK shipping line P&O, which in turn controlled the management-company of six of the largest ports in the US, which sparked a US national controversy concerning border security. Dubai Ports was forced to sell its US assets to American International Group within weeks. The working week was changed to bring it into line with Western nations. The first indirect elections of half the membership of the FNC were held; of the more than 300,000 people eligible to vote, only 6,595 were chosen by the authorities and given the right to vote, and of these 1,163 were women.
2008 A common market was created by Bahrain, Kuwait, Oman, Qatar, Saudi Arabia and UAE, the six wealthiest Gulf States. Citizens of these countries are now allowed to travel between and live in any of the six states, where they may find employment, buy properties and businesses and use the educational and health facilities freely. France was given permission to set up a permanent military base in Abu Dhabi. The Emir of Dubai, Sheikh Mohammed bin Rashid al Maktoum, issued a decree appointing his son Sheikh Hamdan bin Mohammed bin Rashid al Maktoum as crown prince of the Emirate. The entire debt owed to the UAE by Iraq was cancelled. The parliamentary term for the FNC was extended from two years to four.
2009 Sheikh Rashid ibn Ahmad al Mu'alla, the ruler of Umm al Qaiwain, died, his son Sheikh Saud ibn Rashid al Mu'alla succeeded him. The UAE federal government bought US$10 billion of Dubai government bonds to ease its liquidity problems. The money was used to pay off debts, which had accumulated in real estate and tourism projects. The Dubai bonds were for five-year terms at 4 per cent annual interest. The UAE

withdrew from the Gulf region monetary union and retained the dirham. The French opened its permanent military base in Abu Dhabi, called the Peace Camp.
2010 The Burj Khalifa, the world's tallest building at 828 metres, with 160 floors, was opened in January. It was originally called the Burj Dubai but was renamed in honour of the ruler of Abu Dhabi and the UAE after Abu Dhabi had loaned Dubai US$10 billion to help pay off its construction debts. In January, the Hamas leader from Palestine, Mahmoud al Mabhouh was killed in a Dubai hotel, with most observers believing the Israeli secret service, Mossad, responsible. The perpetrators used fake UK, Irish, French and German passports to enter and leave the UAE, prompting international condemnation from the countries involved. The population grew by 65 per cent over 2006–10, according to official statistics, and was 8.26 million by June, of which only 948,000 were UAE nationals. Sheikh Saqr bin Muhammad al Qasimi, Emir of Ras al Khaimah, died on 27 October. He was aged 90 and had been the world's oldest and longest serving monarch. An official statement confirmed his fourth son, Sheikh Saud, as the new ruler.
2011 On 9 August the Central Bank announced that the UAE's currency, the dirham, would continue to be pegged to the US dollar 'without change', as bank deposits in June increased by 0.2 per cent from May, and reached Dh1.126 trillion (US$4.134 trillion). UAE became a net lender to the international money markets as its banking system moved from deficit to surplus. A new law was introduced in August that prescribes a jail term of three–five years for anyone spreading rumours using social network media, such as BlackBerry the Internet, Twitter and Facebook. In parliamentary elections held on 24 September, 554 independent candidates took part, including 85 women. Of the 40 members making up the new legislature, 20 were elected and 20 were appointed by the Emirs. Turnout was 27.8 per cent.

Political structure

Constitution

Highest government authority is vested in the Supreme Council of Rulers, which consists of the rulers of the seven emirates — Abu Dhabi, Dubai, Sharjah, Ras al Khaimah, Umm al Qaiwain, Fujairah and Ajman — which comprise the UAE. It is responsible for most internal and external affairs. Abu Dhabi and Dubai hold the power of veto on the Supreme Council.
The Supreme Council meets four times a year, and elects the president and vice president (each for terms of five years). The president appoints the prime minister and the Council of Ministers.
The 40 members of the Federal National Council (FNC), drawn proportionately from each emirate, are appointed by the rulers.
The individual emirates have retained a great degree of autonomy and all local powers which are not specifically reserved for the federal government belong to them. Since 1971, the president has been the ruler of Abu Dhabi and the prime minister and vice president the ruler of Dubai, suggesting that elections are a matter of form and that in fact the two emirates with the largest economic and political muscle tend to dominate the federation.
A constitutional amendment in 1996 removed the word 'interim' from the constitution and designated Abu Dhabi the capital of the UAE.

Independence date

2 December 1971

Form of state

Federal monarchy

The executive

The Head of State is president for a term of seven years, chosen by the seven, hereditary rulers of the Emirates who make up the membership of the Federal Supreme Council (FSC).
The president, vice president and FSC comprise the executive branch. The FSC convenes four-times annually to set policies and sanction federal legislation. Within the FSC, Abu Dhabi and Dubai have effective veto power.

National legislature

The UAE parliament, Majlis al Watani al Ittihadi (Federal National Council) (FNC), has 40 members, Abu Dhabi and Dubai appoint eight members each, Sharjah and Ras al Khaimah appoint six members each and Ajman, Fujairah and Umm al Qaiwain appoint four members each. Of these, half the members are chosen by indirect votes through electoral colleges in each Emirate (the size of each college is 100 times the number of FNC members held by each Emirate) and the other half are appointed by each Emir. All FNC members serve for four-year terms.
Under the constitution the FNC is a consultative body with legislative and supervisory roles, with the authority to review and amend proposed federal legislation, although it cannot veto proposed legislation. It may also assess the performance of any minister or ministry.

Legal system

The federal courts, which consist of the Union Supreme Court and primary tribunals, were established by law in 1979. The former primary tribunals in Abu Dhabi, Sharjah, Ajman and Fujairah became federal primary tribunals and the former primary tribunals of other towns became circuits of the federal primary tribunals. The law applied is *Sharia* (Islamic Law).

Last elections

24 September 2011 (parliamentary)
Results: Parliamentary: 20 independent candidates were elected and 20 candidates were appointed.

Next elections

2011 (presidential); 2010 (FNC)

Political parties

Party political activity is not officially permitted in the UAE.

Ruling party

There are no official political parties

Population

5.40 million (2010)*
Last census: 5 December 2005: 4,106,427
Population density: 30 inhabitants per square km.
Annual growth rate: 6.4 per cent 1994–2004 (WHO 2006)

Ethnic make-up

UAE nationals make up a fifth of the population. Around 80 per cent of the population are expatriates, with those from the Indian subcontinent accounting for about 40 per cent of the population. The second largest group is Iranians, who make up about 17 per cent. Non-UAE Arabs make up about 13 per cent and Westerners about 5 per cent.
Abu Dhabi is dominated by the Bani Yas tribe of which the al Bu Falasah is the most important section (to which the al Maktoums of Dubai belong).

Religions

The majority are Sunni Muslims; about 20 per cent are Shi'a Muslims. Many expatriates from the Indian subcontinent are Christian. The constitution guarantees full religious rights to all. The Apostolic Vicariate of Arabia is in Abu Dhabi.

Education

Primary education is compulsory and is followed by three years' preparatory education which qualifies students for general or technical secondary education. The language of instruction is English.
General secondary education lasts for three years. It consists of a common first year followed by specialisation in science or the humanities. At aged eighteen, students take an examination for progression to higher education.
Technical secondary education lasts for six years following primary school and comprises three main streams: technical, agricultural and commercial in both preparatory and secondary cycles. At aged eighteen, a Technical Secondary Diploma is awarded.
Secondary education is also offered in religious institutions.

Higher education is offered in public and private universities and Higher Colleges of Technology. These include the United Arab Emirates (UAE) University, and the Dubai University College, (a private college).
Emirate and federal politics can at times threaten academic standards. Education is allocated some 20 per cent of the federal budget.
Literacy rate: 77 per cent adult rate; 91 per cent youth rate (15–24) (Unesco 2005).
Compulsory years: 6 to 12.
Enrolment rate: 89 per cent gross primary enrolment; 80 per cent gross secondary enrolment, of relevant age groups (including repeaters) (World Bank).
Pupils per teacher: 16 in primary schools.

Health

Life expectancy: 77 years, 2004 (WHO 2006)
Fertility rate/Maternal mortality rate: 2.5 births per woman, 2004 (WHO 2006); maternal mortality 3 per 100,000 live births (World Bank).
Child (under 5 years) mortality rate (per 1,000): 7.0 per 1,000 live births; 7 per cent of children aged under five are malnourished (World Bank).
Head of population per physician: 2.02 physicians per 1,000 people, 2001 (WHO 2006)

Welfare

There is an extensive and generous welfare system in the UAE, in many ways a model of a successful welfare state. However, this reflects the unique characteristics of the UAE – no social security contributions are levied on employers or employees, and there is no personal taxation. Many services remain free, and there are numerous grants, loans, and subsidies.

Main cities

Abu Dhabi (federal capital estimated population 860,000 in 2007), Dubai (commercial capital, 1.3 million), Sharjah (570,299), Ajman (256,554), Ras al Khaimah (107,662), Umm al Qaiwain (40,629).

Media

Dubai is the hub of the UAE's media industry and the dedicated Dubai Media City, which assures clients freedom of speech, is growing as an important regional centre attracting distinguished international media outlets.
Press
While the press is largely independent, in November 2007, Reporters Without Frontiers reported that press freedom in the UAE was bound by widespread self-censorship which eschewed any criticism of the government to avoid prosecution.
Dailies: Most newspapers are published in either Abu Dhabi or Dubai. Newspapers in Arabic that comment on news and politics include *Al-Bayan* (www.albayan.ae), *Akhbar Al Arab* (www.akhbaralarab.co.ae), also has economic and sports editions, *Emarat al Youm* (www.emaratalyoum.com), *Al Khaleej* (www.alkhaleej.co.ae). In English newspaper include *Emirates Today* (www.emiratestodayonline.com), *Gulf News* (www.gulf-news.com), *Khaleej Times* (www.khaleejtimes.com) and *7 Days* (www.7days.ae).
Weeklies: In Arabic, *Al Azmina Al Arabia* (www.alazmina.info), bi-weekly for politics, culture and economics, *Al-Sada* (www.e-sada.com) is a magazine for women. In English, *The Dubai Life* (www.thedubailife.com) and *Time Out Dubai* (ww.timeoutdubai.com/dubai), covers entertainment and consumer items.
Business: In English monthly publications include the monthly *Capital* (www.capital-me.com), and *UAE Banking & Business Review* (www.sterlingp.ae) and *Gulf Business* (www.gulfbusiness.com) monthly magazine. The CPI Financial services published an online newsletter concerning banking and the financial services (www.cpifinancial.net).
Periodicals: There are over 30 magazines in Arabic and English. *Al Shindagah* (www.alshindagah.com), published six times a year and *Review* (www.sterlingp.ae) covers current affairs, *Al Shumookh* (www.alshumookh.net) monthly magazine lists cultural events.
Broadcasting
The state-owned Emirates Media Incorporated (EMI) operates three satellite TV channels and seven radio stations, four publications and five interactive internet websites.
The switchover to digital signals will be completed by 2013, according to the Director General of the Telecoms Regulatory Authority (TRA), on 26 April 2011.
Radio: Each Emirate has its own radio station, although most are located in either Abu Dhabi or Dubai. There are general interest music and news radio stations, broadcasting throughout the Emirates, while some are dedicated to religious texts or programmes for immigrant populations. Apart from EMI (www.emi.co.ae), another national network is the popular commercial Arabian Radio Network (ARN) (www.arnonline.com), including in English, Dubai 92.
A shortwave world service broadcasts to North America, Asia and Europe.
Television: Of the six TV networks based in UAE, three are pan-Arabic. The state-owned, Dubai Media Incorporated (DMI) produces a number of local TV programmes and operates four domestic channels (http://www.dubaitv.gov.ae), which provides programmes of information, entertainment, religion, culture, news and politics. In 2007 tests were undertaken by DMI to evaluate the viability of mobile digital video broadcasting. MBC (http://www.mbc.net) operates a four channels include the Al Arabiya News Channel (www.alarabiya.net). The private and independent satellite broadcaster Showtime Arabia (www.showtimearabia.com), based in Dubai, which operates over 30 channels showing imported programmes, by subscription. Residents also have a choice of hundreds of regional channels broadcasting via foreign satellite or cable TV companies. Many commercial channels broadcast foreign programmes in English with Arabic subtitles.
Residents have a choice of hundreds of regional channels broadcasting via satellite or cable. Many commercial channels broadcast foreign programmes in English with Arabic subtitles.
There are two local TV stations operating from Ajman (www.ajmantv.com) and Sharjah (www.sharjahtv.ae).
Advertising
The UAE is the region's marketing gateway. Dual English and Arabic usage is common on signs and in many publications.
News agencies
National news agency: Emirates News Agency
Other news agencies: DPM News Agency: www.dpmnewsagency.com

Economy

The UAE is a free-market economy, dominated by hydrocarbons, which accounted for 91.1 per cent of all exports in 2008, when the global price of oil was at an all-time high. However, as the global economic crisis cut demand and oil prices fell, so oil exports fell to an estimated 50.2 per cent in 2009. Oil exports are expected to rise to 63.2 per cent in 2010 as global demand returns. The leading non-oil sectors are manufacturing, in particular Dubai's state-owned aluminium smelter (Dubal). The UAE has made strenuous efforts to attain a reputation as a global commercial logistics hub, investing over US$50 billion in transportation, storage and communications over 2000–10. Abu Dhabi's income from oil in 2010 was Dh278.6 billion (US$75.9 billion), one of the highest in the emirate's history, although much lower than the record

Dh415.8 billion (US$113.3 billion) earned in 2008.

The richest Emirates, Abu Dhabi, Dubai and Sharjah, account for approximately 50 per cent, 30 per cent and 8 per cent respectively of overall GDP. They transfer revenue to other emirates to ensure similar standards in basic public goods and services (health, education and transport) are maintained.

GDP growth was 5.1 per cent in 2008, falling to -0.7 per cent in 2009 as the global economic crisis cut demand for oil. The economy declined so that imports fell and inflation dropped from 11.5 per cent in 2008 to 1.0 per cent in 2009. The crisis resulted in pressures on the banking sector and a contraction in the availability of credit. In March 2009, the credit rating agency Standard and Poor's cut its ratings for six Dubai government-backed entities to A- and Emaar Properties from A- to BBB+. The Dubai building boom was badly hit by the global recession. Dubai World, including a series of artificial islands built in Dubai's shallow waters, was an ambitious multi-million dollar project that had to be bailed out of near collapse in November 2009 by the Dubai government. Although losses were incurred by Dubai, ultimately international financial pressure on the UAE economy was eased when Abu Dhabi agreed to buy fiduciary bonds in February 2010 and allow Dubai to avoid defaulting on an estimated US$87 billion in debt.

The UAE has developed a range of manufacturing industries, financial services and a tourist industry, and is emerging, because of its favourable tax regime, as an important international diamond centre. Overseas companies and foreign direct investment have been attracted to the UAE by the creation of a dozen free trade zones, which offer special advances, while enabling the UAE to expand its non-oil exports. The UAE has made good progress in privatising small agricultural enterprises and has broadened the programme to include larger-scale industrial projects and public utilities. Financial services include a growing sector of Islamic banking, which accounted for 14 per cent in 2009/10.

In July 2011, the IMF estimated that the gross national debt of UAE was US$236.1 billion (6.3 per cent of GDP), of which Abu Dhabi owed US$104 billion and Dubai US$112 billion. Around US$33 billion will mature in 2011, with US$25.8 billion maturing in 2012 and the remainder in 2013.

On 9 August 2011 the Central Bank announced that the UAE's currency, the dirham, would continue to be pegged to the US dollar 'without change', as bank deposits in June increased by 0.2 per cent from May, and reached Dh1.126 trillion (US$4.134 trillion). UAE became a net lender to the international money markets as its banking system moved from deficit to surplus.

External trade

In 2005 the Greater Arab Free Trade Area (Gafta) was ratified by 17 members, including Saudi Arabia, creating an Arab economic bloc. Gafta includes a customs union in which tariffs are reduced by a percentage each year, until none remain. The UAE also belongs to the Gulf Co-operation Council, which negotiates bilateral free trade agreements on behalf of members.

Hydrocarbons accounted for over 90 per cent of exports in 2008 but this dropped to an estimated 50 per cent in 2009. Export of oil and natural gas was US$102.7 billion in 2008, falling to US$56.8 billion in 2009. Dubai produces the UAE's second largest export, aluminium, which accounts for 60 per cent of all non-hydrocarbon exports.

Re-exports are an important sector of external trade and the UAE is the world's leading re-exporter of rice, accounting for 93 per cent of all re-exported rice, valued at US$555 million in 2009. The UAE, likewise is a top importer of rice, reaching 1,238 million tonnes in 2009, of which 49 per cent was re-exported.

The government has encouraged new manufacturing enterprises in metal processing, furniture and jewellery making and food processing. However, the service sector achieves more foreign earnings than any other except oil and natural gas, through tourism, financial services and banking and transport. The Dubai Ports Authority is one of the largest container handling bodies in the world.

Imports

Main imports are machinery and vehicles, pearls and precious stones, chemicals and rice and foodstuffs.

Main sources: China (typically 10 per cent of total), India (10 per cent), US (7 per cent).

Exports

Main exports are crude oil (45 per cent total), natural gas, pearls and precious stones, electronic equipment and vehicles.

Main destinations: Japan (typically 16 per cent of total), India (7 per cent), Iran (3 per cent).

Re-exports

Rice, dried fish and dates and aluminium.

Agriculture

Farming

Agriculture contributes around 4 per cent to GDP and employs 8 per cent of the workforce. A harsh climate and sandy soil make self-sufficiency in food production an unlikely prospect. The northern Emirates of Ras al Khaimah, Fujairah (on the western Gulf of Onan coast) and Ajman supply 25 per cent of local demand. Ajman is the most productive and has been a focal region for agricultural development. Ras al Khaimah and Fujairah produce a more diverse selection of agricultural produce as a result of the higher rainfall they receive. Very few nationals still work on farms, where labour is mostly from Bangladesh and Baluchistan in south-west Pakistan.

Government farm subsidies are generous. Many farms are supported through funding available on easy credit terms, seed allocations and technical advice on fertilisation, irrigation, mechanisation and marketing of crops. Earth-moving and wells are free, and seeds, fertilisers and insecticides are half the market price. Abu Dhabi gives land to its citizens without charge, as well as underwriting other Emirates' grants of land to other UAE citizens via its financing of the federal budget. The main state-funded agricultural research centres and extension services are at al Dhafra, Liwa and Madina Zayed. The Arid Lands Research Centre operates experimental vegetable greenhouses on Saadiyat Island near Abu Dhabi town. The UAE is self-sufficient in various winter vegetables and excess crops of vegetables are sometimes dumped in the desert, due to a lack of processing facilities. The government already buys crops at 'favourable' prices, before selling them at discounted rates in the market.

Water shortages and soil salinity are constant problems. Agriculture is dependent on fast depleting underground aquifers. When these run dry, irrigation will depend almost entirely on desalinated water.

The country's largest dairy farm at Digdagga has a herd of Friesians producing meat and milk for local consumption.

Fishing

Catches cover over 80 per cent of domestic consumption. The UAE ranks fourth in the Arab world in the volume of its annual catch. Around 20 fishing ports and 25 repair workshops have been established along the coastline in Dubai, Sharjah and Ras al Khaimah. Over 15,000 tonnes of fish are imported to supplement domestic sources.

Forestry

The UAE has around 3.8 per cent forest cover, almost all of which is plantation. The government has initiated a long-term programme of afforestation. Abu Dhabi's western region now has about 5,000 hectares of mature tree plantations, including 120 million tamarind, tamarisk, acacia, neem and cork trees, as well as some 30 million date palms.

Industry and manufacturing

The industrial sector typically accounts for under 20 per cent of GDP and employs 45 per cent of the workforce. Non-oil industry,

particularly manufacturing and re-exports, is concentrated in free trade zones.
The government is placing increased emphasis on the expansion of non-oil manufacturing, such as cement, building materials, aluminium, fertilisers, foodstuffs, garments, furniture, plastics, fibreglass and processed metals.
Most non-oil export production is located on Dubai. Dubai has intensified efforts to promote foreign investment and attract regional and global capital. In April 2002, the Dubai Authority for Investment and Development (DAID) was set up to grant concessions, franchises and incentives and to issue licences to large investors. The DAID is authorised to set up, own and develop investment companies on its own or with other organisations.
Dubai's largest manufacturing enterprise, the state-owned Dubai Aluminium Company (Dubal), is expanding production from 536,000 tonnes in 2001 to 710,000 tonnes by 2007. Dubal is based in the thriving free trade area, the Jebel Ali Free Zone. Dubai is also keen to develop information technology (IT); the Dubai Internet City was set up in 2001. IT spending in the UAE was estimated at US$550 million to US$600 million during the first six months of 2004, putting spending for the full year on course to surpass the 2003 total of US$1.1 billion.
Abu Dhabi is planning to develop an industrial base, including petrochemicals, steel and aluminium. A seven-year, US$100 billion investment programme was initiated in 2005. It will be mainly government funded, but it is hoped to attract private private sector and foreign direct investment.

Tourism

Dubai is the largest tourism market in the Emirates, attracting both business travellers and an increasing number of leisure tourists. Tourism is a key element in Dubai's development strategy. With the aim of making Dubai a major tourist destination, investment has been poured into infrastructure, including hotels, a new conference centre, a cruise terminal and, with a view to becoming an aviation hub, airport and airline fleet expansion.
Shortage of prime building land has not deterred planners. The Palm (previously known as the Palm Islands) is a US$3 billion scheme, involving the construction of two man-made islands off the Dubai coast, each in the shape of a palm tree.

Mining

The development of non-hydrocarbon minerals plays a role in the government's policy of diversification away from dependence on the oil sector. Limestone, gypsum and dolerite are exploited.
Celestite is known to exist but has not yet been extracted.
Copper is known to exist in Fujairah and Ras al Khaimah. There is also thought to be talc in Fujairah, chromium in Sharjah, Ajman, Fujairah and Ras al Khaimah, and manganese throughout the northern Emirates. Mineral studies are being undertaken in the Madah region of Fujairah, in Al-Siji in Sharjah and in the Masfouyt and Manama areas of Ajman. Ras al Khaimah already has two quarries, four cement companies and further downstream factories, with annual cement production of 2.3 million tonnes.

Hydrocarbons

The UAE is one of the world's largest producers of crude oil and natural gas, which together account for around 30 per cent of GDP. Under the UAE's constitution, each emirate is responsible for its own production and resource development. Approximately 94 per cent of total reserves is held by Abu Dhabi.
Proven oil reserves were 97.8 billion barrels in 2010, with production at 2.85 million barrels per day (bpd), an increase of 3.5 per cent on the 2.75 million bpd produced in 2009.
Refinery capacity was 673,000bpd in 2010, with production located at Ruwais, Umm al Nar and Jebel Ali. In 2006 Abu Dhabi and ConocoPhilips signed a deal for a new 500,000bpd capacity refinery.
Proven natural gas reserves were 6.00 trillion cubic metres (cum) in 2010, the world's fourth-largest reserves. Production was 51.0 billion cum an increase of 4.5 per cent on the 48.0 billion cum in 2009. Abu Dhabi holds 92.5 per cent of the total reserves, with 5.0 per cent in Sharjah. Domestic consumption has grown, mainly in the production of electricity, particularly during summer. Dubai's consumption has been growing at almost 10 per cent annually, as its industrial sector has grown. In August 2010, the Russian company, Rosneft, signed a joint venture with the Sharjah-based Crescent Petroleum company to invest US$630 million in a 70 billion cubic metre natural gas and 16 million tonne gas condensate, concession. The gas field is planned to be operational by 2013. This is the first upstream project undertaken by an UAE-Russian partnership.
Any use of coal is commercially insignificant.

Energy

Total installed generating capacity was 16.7 gigawatts in 2007, producing 62.8 billion kilowatt hours (kWh). Consumption is among the largest in the region due to expansion of tourism, financial projects and an increased population.
A Gulf Co-operation Council (GCC) project to link the six member states (Saudi Arabia, Qatar, Bahrain, Kuwait, Oman and the United Arab Emirates) to an integrated power-grid began in 2005. The first phase of the GCC power grid was completed in 2009 at a cost of US$1,095 million, linking Saudi Arabia, Bahrain, Kuwait and Qatar through 800km of transmission lines. Kuwait and Saudi Arabia will each receive an extra 1,200MW of power capacity and later, the UAE will receive 900MW, Qatar 750MW, Bahrain 600MW and Oman 400MW. In the first phase, a 400kV overhead line links Kuwait's Al Zour power station with Doha, and a 400kV submarine line to Saudi Arabia with Bahrain. The second phase will link the UAE with Oman. The resulting two mega-grids will be joined in the final phase.
The government is seeking to open up the sector with limited privatisation in order to inject new capital and increase capacity to meet soaring demand. Abu Dhabi is leading the way, with the creation of new independent power and water projects and joint ventures with minority interests held by foreign firms. The Abu Dhabi government has rejected full privatisation of the water and power sector.
The Abu Dhabi Water and Electricity Authority (Adwea) commissioned the building of a 1,500MW power station in October 2011. Other new plants already under construction will supply 2,500MW to the system, (1,600MW by the Shuweihat 3 power plant, to become operational in 2014), for ultimate use among GCC member states.

Financial markets

Stock exchange

Abu Dhabi Securities Exchange (ADX)

Commodity exchange

Dubai Mercantile Exchange (DME)

Banking and insurance

Financial services constitute a key sector throughout the Emirates, with Dubai at the leading edge and hoping to overtake Bahrain as the Gulf's leading financial centre. The UAE's banking sector has attracted more foreign interest than other Gulf states due to its liberal banking regime and low level of taxation.
Development of the sector is focussed on the Dubai International Financial Sector (DIFC), which was launched in 2001 as a link between the financial markets of Africa, Asia, the Middle East and the West. The DIFC has concentrated on the development of asset management, administration, reinsurance and Islamic finance in an attempt to develop a niche market.
By order of the Emir of Dubai, the failing Dubai Bank was taken over by the Emirate's largest lending institute, NBD on 13 October 2011. In May 2011, the government had to save Dubai Bank as loan losses mounted, brought about by the Dubai property bubble; the bank had

remained weak and lacked a diverse business foundation.

Central bank

Central Bank of the United Arab Emirates

Time

GMT plus four hours

Geography

The UAE is bordered by Oman to the east, Saudi Arabia to the west and south, Qatar to the north, and by a coastline of approximately 650km on the southern shore of the Gulf. Much of the land is sand desert or salt flats. Six of the Emirates lie on the Arabian Gulf coast. Fujairah, the seventh, lies on the Gulf of Oman. The region is one of shallow seas and offshore islands and coral reefs. The UAE's two coasts are divided by the Hajjar Mountains stretching through the Musandam Peninsula to the Straits of Hormuz.

Hemisphere

Northern

Climate

Summer temperatures are hot, reaching 49 degrees Celsius (C) in the shade, while January, the coldest winter month, sees temperatures ranging from three to 28 degrees C. Humidity, particularly on the coast, can be extreme. Average annual rainfall is very low, ranging between 100mm and 200mm.

Dress codes

A lightweight suit or lightweight jacket and trousers are advised. A tie is *de rigueur* at business meetings but a jacket need not be worn. Long-sleeved shirts should be worn at business and official meetings. In public places, women should dress discretely and men should wear shirts and long trousers. Bikinis are allowed on certain beaches.

Entry requirements

Passports

Required by all.

Visa

Required by all, except citizens of EU, North America, Australasia, Japan and a few other Asian countries, for visits up to one month. For a full list of exceptions visit www.uae-embassy.org and follow the link from *Travel to UAE* to *consular services* where a visa application form can also be found. All visits for those requiring a visa must be arranged through a sponsor such as tour operator or UAE resident or company. The sponsor organises a visa and will provide a letter of invitation, giving details of the sponsor's residency permit, and a copy of their passport. Visas for business visits are arranged by invitation only. Company credentials must be provided including a trading licence to a sponsor who arranges the visa and will meet the traveller at the airport.

Prohibited entry

Israeli nationals and holders of passports with Israeli visas stamped in them.

Currency advice/regulations

The import and export of local and foreign currency is limited to Dh40,000 (or equivalent). Amounts in excess of this must be declared on entry.

Travellers cheques are widely accepted.

Customs

Personal effects are duty-free. Small quantities of alcohol are allowed entry (non-Muslims only).

Prohibited imports

Firearms and ammunition require a special permit. Illegal drugs (drug trafficking is a capital offence), poppy seeds in all forms, religious propaganda, commercial loose pearls, raw seafood and fruit and vegetables from cholera infected areas are prohibited.

Health (for visitors)

Mandatory precautions

None.

Advisable precautions

Inoculations and boosters should be current for hepatitis A, polio, tetanus and typhoid. There may be a need for vaccinations for tuberculosis, hepatitis B and diphtheria. Anti-malaria precautions are recommended if travelling to the border with Oman, in the east.

NB Some drugs normally taken under a doctor's supervision are classified as narcotics in the UAE. A doctor's prescription should be carried along with any medication that is brought into the country. If suspected of being under the influence of drugs or alcohol, individuals may be required to submit to blood and/or urine tests and may be subject to prosecution.

Hotels

Excellent standards throughout the UAE, and rooms are generally in adequate supply although advance booking is always advisable.

A 20 per cent tax is included in all bills.

Credit cards

Major credit and charge cards are widely accepted.

Public holidays (national)

The working week was altered in 2006, to bring it into line with Western nations (Saturday and Sunday weekend), although a two-day weekend was not made compulsory for the private sector.

Fixed dates

1 Jan (New Year's Day), 6 Aug (Sheikh Zayed's Accession), 2 Dec (National Day).

Variable dates

Eid al Adha (three days), Islamic New Year, Birth of the Prophet, Ascension of the Prophet, Eid al Fitr (two days).

Islamic year 1433 (26 Nov 2011–14 Nov 2012): The Islamic year has 354 or 355 days, with the result that Muslim feasts advance by 10–12 days against the Gregorian calendar each year. Dates of the Muslim feasts vary according to sightings of the new moon, so cannot be forecast exactly.

Working hours

Working hours may vary between Emirates and change from summer to winter. The working week was altered in 2006, to bring it into line with Western nations (Saturday and Sunday weekend), although a two-day weekend was not made compulsory for the private sector. During Ramadan, the Muslim holy month of fasting, working hours are reduced with most people working during daylight hours 0900–1300.

Banking

Mon–Thu: 0800–1300, 1500/1600–1800/1900; Fri: 0800–1300.

Business

Mon–Thu: 0800–1300, 1500/1600–1800/1900; Fri: 0830–1300. Some businesses operate on Saturday.

Government

Mon–Fri: 0700–1430.

Shops

Sat–Thu: 0930–1300, 1630–2130; Fri: 1400/1500–2100. Shopping centres general do not close during the day.

Telecommunications

Mobile/cell phones

There is a 900 GSM service operating throughout the territory – there are plans for 3G and 900/1800 services in the future.

Electricity supply

240/415V AC (Abu Dhabi) and 220/380V AC (Northern Emirates), with three-pin round or flat type plug fittings.

Weights and measures

Metric system (imperial system and local units also used).

Social customs/useful tips

Pork should not be eaten in the presence of Muslims. It is discourteous to eat, drink or smoke in front of Muslims in daylight hours during Ramadan (when it is illegal to do so in public).

Avoid using the term 'Mohammedan'.

Avoid asking personal questions, especially about wives.

Always shake hands on meeting and leaving. You may find the handshake lasts longer than in the West, but this is a sign of friendship. If you have made a good impression, the handshake on departure will be longer than that on arrival.

If coffee is served it is courteous to accept it. Cups will generally be refilled automatically unless the cup is shaken from side to side as it is returned to the server. To take only one cup of coffee is an insult, and to take three or more is considered greedy in some quarters – if in doubt follow the example of your host. Most restaurants and hotels have bars and licensed restaurants, although a licence, which lays down a monthly quota, is required for purchase for consumption at home. Licences are not issued to Muslims. Some Blackberry functions (such as sending emails and accessing the internet) have been banned since October 2010.

Security

Visitors should keep in touch with developments in the Middle East as any increase in regional tension might affect travel advice.

The level of street crime has been traditionally far lower than in the West because of the severity of the penalties imposed. The influx of expatriate workers since the early 1970s has encouraged incidents of theft. Murder and violent crimes such as mugging and rape remain rare. Generally speaking the UAE has a very low incidence of crime.

Getting there

Air

Air Arabia, the Middle East's first low-fare airline, is headquartered in Sharjah and flies within the region and to the Indian subcontinent.

National airline: Etihad Airways and the airline Emirates are owned by the governments of Abu Dhabi and Dubai respectively.

International airport/s: Abu Dhabi International Airport (AUH); 35km from city. It has a new terminal has increased facilities with duty-free shop, bar, bank, hotel reservations, post office, shops, car hire.

Dubai International (DXB), 4km from city, with duty-free shop, bar, bank, hotel reservations, post office, shops, car hire.

Sharjah International (SHJ), 10km from city, with duty-free shop, bar, restaurant, bank (restricted hours), hotel reservations.

Ras al Khaimah International (RKT).

The Al Maktoum International Airport (DWC) (Dubai), was opened in June 2010. When fully operational (expected 2011) the airport will be the largest in the world with five runways, through-flow of five million passengers annually and 250,000 tonnes capacity for cargo.

Other airport/s: Al Ain is Abu Dhabi's second airport 23km from the oasis of Al Ain. Fujairah has an airport.

Airport tax: None

Surface

Road: Road links are through Oman and Saudi Arabia. Buses run between Dubai and Muscat.

Water: Passenger services run between Sharjah and Bandar-é Abbas in Iran.

Getting about

National transport

Air: There are several daily services between Dubai and Abu Dhabi. There are numerous airstrips thoughout the region for charter hire flights.

Road: Good, surfaced roads along the coast links of all the Emirates.

City transport

Taxis: Taxis are plentiful and English is widely understood if not spoken.

Metered taxis are available in Abu Dhabi and the rounding-up of the charge is typical for a tip. It is advisable to negotiate fares in advance in other Emirates as taxis are not usually metered.

City traffic in Dubai has become very congested and it is advisable to allow plenty of time to reach a destination. Taxis on stands outside hotels charge more than those flagged in the street. Fixed fares are available for pre-paid journeys from Dubai airport to the city.

Some hotels offer a courtesy pick-up service; others offer the service but charge. A limousine can be booked through the hotel.

Buses, trams & metro: Dubai's new metro system began operations in 2009 along the 52.9km, 29 station, Red Line, which runs both over and under the city, from the airport terminal to the Jebel Ali seaport terminal. Ticket prices are divided into three zones, with payment via different modes including a pre-paid, smart card. Other lines are under construction. The second metro rail network in Dubai became operational on 9 September 2011. The Green Line runs for around 23km from Etisalat to Dubai Health Care City; however, not all stations were completed and opened.

Car hire

Personal and chauffeur-driven car hire is available. International licences are acceptable only for short-term visitors and requirements should be checked on arrival. Driving is on the right, with speed limits of 60kph in towns and 80–100kph elsewhere.

BUSINESS DIRECTORY

Telephone area codes

The international direct dialling (IDD) code for The United Arab Emirates is +971 followed by the area code:

Abu Dhabi	2	Fujairah	9
Ajman	6	Ras Al-Khaimah	7
Al-Ain	3	Sharjah	6
Dubai	4	Umm Al-Quwain	6

Useful telephone numbers

Directory enquiries: 180
Operator: 100
Call enquiries: 160
Call bookings: 150
Police (Abu Dhabi): 461-461

Chambers of Commerce

Abu Dhabi Chamber of Commerce and Industry, PO Box 662, Abu Dhabi (tel: 621-4000; fax: 621-5867; e-mail: service@adcci-gov.ae).

American Business Council (Dubai and Northern Emirates), PO Box 9281, Dubai (tel: 331-4735; fax: 331-4227; e-mail: amchamdx@emirates.net.ae).

American Business Group (Abu Dhabi), PO Box 43710, Abu Dhabi (tel: 626-2086; fax: 626-2087; e-mail: abgroup@emirates.net.ae).

Ajman Chamber of Commerce and Industry, PO Box 662, Ajman (tel: 742-2177; fax: 742-7591; e-mail: ajmchmbr@emirates.net.ae).

British Business Group (Abu Dhabi), PO Box 43635, Abu Dhabi (tel: 457-234; fax: 450-605; e-mail: bbgauh@emirates.net.ae).

British Business Group (Dubai and Northern Emirates), PO Box 9333, Dubai (tel: 397-0303; fax: 397-0939; e-mail: britbiz@emirates.net.ae).

Dubai Chamber of Commerce and Industry, PO Box 1457, Dubai (tel: 228-1181; fax: 221-1646; e-mail: dcciinfo@dcci.org).

Federation of UAE Chambers of Commerce and Industry, PO Box 3014, Abu Dhabi (tel: 621-4144; fax: 633-9210; e-mail: fcciauh@emirates.net.ae).

Federation of UAE Chambers of Commerce and Industry, PO Box 8886, Dubai (tel: 221-2977; fax: 223-5498; e-mail: fccidxb@emirates.net.ae).

French Business Group (Abu Dhabi), PO Box 73390, Abu Dhabi (tel: 674-1137; fax: 678-6650; e-mail: fbgad@emirates.net.ae).

Fujairah Chamber of Commerce and Industry, PO Box 738, Fujairah (tel: 222-2400; fax: 222-1464; e-mail: fujccia@emirates.net.ae).

Ras Al-Khaimah Chamber of Commerce and Industry, PO Box 87, Ras Al-Khaimah (tel: 233-3511; fax: 233-0233; e-mail: rkchmbr@emirates.net.ae).

Sharjah Chamber of Commerce and Industry, PO Box 580, Sharjah (tel: 568-8888; fax: 568-1119; e-mail:scci@sharjah.gov.ae).

Umm Al-Quwain Chamber of Commerce and Industry, PO Box 436, Umm Al-Quwain (tel: 765-1111; fax: 765-7056; e-mail: uaqcci@emirates.net.ae).

Banking
Abu Dhabi Commercial Bank, Al-Salam Street, PO Box 939, Abu Dhabi.

Arab Bank for Investment & Foreign Trade, PO Box 46733, Abu Dhabi.

Commercial Bank of Dubai Ltd, PO Box 2668, Dubai.

Emirates NDB (result of merger between Emirates Bank International and National Bank of Dubai in 2007), PO Box 2923, Dubai.

Mashreq Bank, P.O. Box 1250, Omar Ibn Al Khatab Rd, Next to Al Ghurair Retail City, Deira, Dubai.

National Bank of Abu Dhabi, PO Box 4, Abu Dhabi.

National Bank of Fujairah, PO Box 786, Abu Dhabi..

National Bank of Sharjah, PO Box 4, Sharjah.

National Bank of Umm Al-Qawain, PO Box 17888, Al-Ain.

RakBank (National Bank of Ras Al-Khaimah), PO Box 5300, Oman Street, Al-Nakheel, Ras Al-Khaimah (tel: 228-1127; fax: 228-3238; email: nbrakho@emirates.net.ae).

Union National Bank, PO Box 865, Abu Dhabi.

Central bank
Central Bank of the United Arab Emirates, Al Bainunah Street; PO Box 854, Abu Dhabi (tel: 665-2220; fax: 666-7494; internet: www.centralbank.ae).

Stock exchange
Abu Dhabi Securities Exchange (ADX): www.adx.ae

Stock exchange 2
Dubai Financial Market: www.dfm.ae

Commodity exchange
Dubai Mercantile Exchange (DME): www.dubaimerc.com

Commodity exchange 2
Dubai Gold and Commodities Exchange (DGCX): www.dgcx.ae

Travel information
Abu Dhabi International Airport, PO Box 28, Abu Dhabi (tel: 575-7500; fax: 575-7285; internet: www.dcaauh.gov.ae).

Abu Dhabi National Hotels Company, PO Box 6806, Abu Dhabi.

Air Arabia, Um Tarafa Area, Al Arouba Street, Rolla, Sharjai (call centre tel: 558-0000; internet: www.airarabia.com)

Dubai Airport (internet: www.dubaiairport.com).

Dubai Tourism P.O.Box 594, Dubai (tel: 223-0000; fax: 223-0022; internet: http://dubaitourism.co.ae).

Emirates Group, Emirates Headquarters, Near Clock Tower, Dubai (tel: 295-1111; internet: www.emirates.com).

Gulf Air, Hamdan St/Airport Road, Abu Dhabi.

Oman Air, PO Box 1058, Central Post Office Seeb International Airport, Muscat, Oman.

Qatar Airways, Almana Tower, Airport Road, PO Box 22550, Doha, Qatar.

Ras Al-Khaimah National Travel Agency, Ras Al-Khaimah.

Ministry of tourism
Department of Tourism and Commerce Marketing, PO Box 594, Dubai (tel: 223-0000; fax: 223-0022; e-mail: info@dubaitourism.co.ae; internet: www.dubaitourism.co.ae).

Ministries
Ministry of Agriculture & Fisheries, PO Box 213, Abu Dhabi.

Ministry of Communication, PO Box 900, Abu Dhabi.

Ministry of Defence, PO Box 2838, Dubai.

Ministry of Economy & Commerce, PO Box 901, Abu Dhabi.

Ministry of Education and Youth, PO Box 295, Abu Dhabi.

Ministry of Electricity & Water, PO Box 629, Abu Dhabi.

Ministry of Finance & Industry, PO Box 433, Abu Dhabi.

Ministry of Foreign Affairs, PO Box 1, Abu Dhabi.

Ministry of Health, PO Box 848, Abu Dhabi.

Ministry of Higher Education & Scientific Research, PO Box 45253, Abu Dhabi.

Ministry of Information & Culture, PO Box 17, Abu Dhabi.

Ministry for the Interior, PO Box 398, Abu Dhabi.

Ministry for Justice and Islamic Affairs & Awqaf, PO Box 2272, Abu Dhabi.

Ministry for Labour & Social Affairs, PO Box 809, Abu Dhabi.

Ministry of Petroleum & Mineral Resources, PO Box 59, Abu Dhabi.

Ministry of Planning, PO Box 904, Abu Dhabi.

Ministry of Public Works & Housing, PO Box 878, Abu Dhabi.

Ministry of State for Cabinet Affairs, PO Box 899, Abu Dhabi..

Minister of State for Supreme Council Affairs, PO Box 545, Abu Dhabi.

Ministry of Youth & Sports, PO Box 539, Abu Dhabi.

Other useful addresses
Abu Dhabi Company for Onshore Oil Operations (ADCO), PO Box 270, Abu Dhabi.

Abu Dhabi Gas Liquifaction Co Ltd, PO Box 3500, Abu Dhabi.

Abu Dhabi National Oil Co (ADNOC), PO Box 898, Abu Dhabi.

Abu Dhabi Water and Electricity Authority, ADWEA Building, Al Falah Street, PO Box 6120, Abu Dhabi.

Ajman Independent Studios, PO Box 442, Ajman.

Arab Monetary Fund (headquarters), PO Box 2818, Abu Dhabi.

British Embassy, Khalid Bin-Walid Street; PO Box 248, Abu Dhabi (tel: 610-1111; fax: 610-1585.

British Embassy, Al-Seef; PO Box 65, Dubai (tel: 309-4445; fax: 309-4302).

Department of Information, Dubai Municipality, PO Box 67, Dubai.

Dubai International Trade Centre, PO Box 9292, Dubai.

Dubai TV, PO Box 1695, Dubai.

Executive Council of Dubai (runs the emirate's political and financial affairs)

Jebel Ali Free Zone Authority, PO Box 3258, Dubai.

Gulf Arab Marketing & Exhibition Co (GAME), PO Box 610, Abu Dhabi.

Ports Authority of Dubai, PO Box 3258, Dubai.

Ports Authority of Sharjah, PO Box 510, Sharjah.

UAE Embassy (USA), 1010 Wisconsin Avenue, NW, Washington DC 20007 (tel: +1-202) 672-1050; fax: (tel: +1-202) 672-1082).

UAE TV Sharjah, PO Box 111, Sharjah.

National news agency: Emirates News Agency: DPM News Agency: www.dpmnewsagency.com

Internet sites
Arab Net: www.arab.net

Arabia OnLine: www.arabia.com

Dubai Metro: http://dubaimetro.eu

Dubai Tourism: http://dubaitourism.co.ae

Etisalat web portal: http://ecompany.ae

UAE Government: www.government.ae

UAE information: www.uae.org.ae

UAE interact: www.uaeinteract.com

Yellow Pages: www.uae-ypages.com

United Kingdom

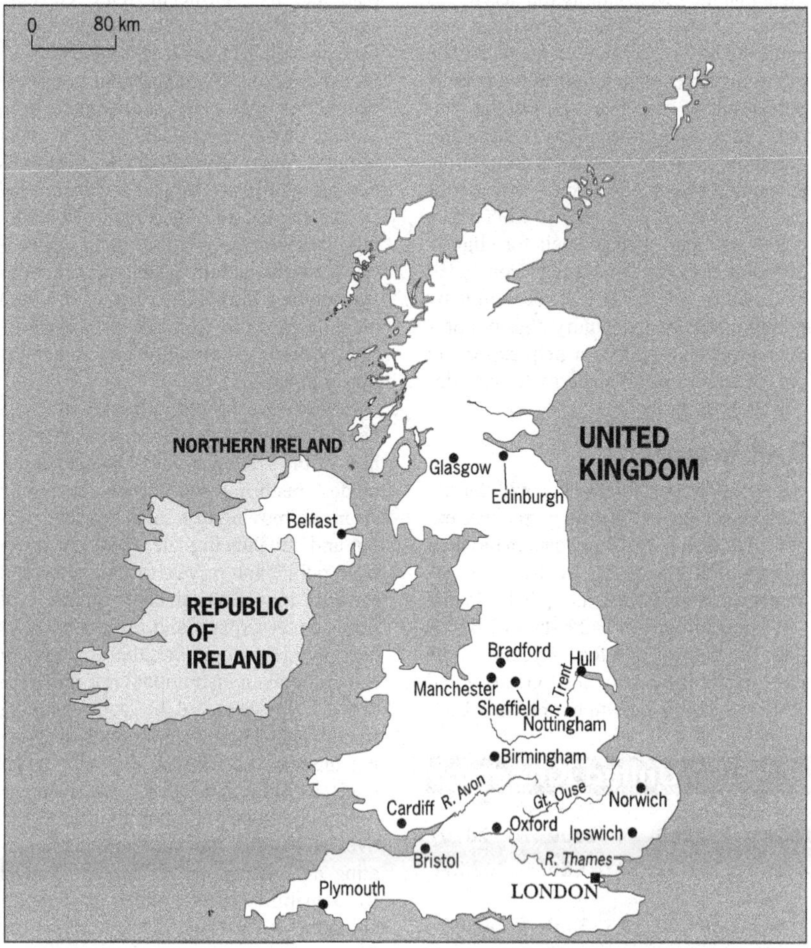

In December 2011 the United Kingdom's (UK) ambivalent relationship with the European Union (EU) became all the more-so following British insistence that French inspired efforts to impose a tax on European financial transactions – the so called 'Tobin's tax' – in all the EU's 27 member states. The UK had claimed that its predominant financial sector should receive preferential treatment as had long been the case for the French agricultural sector. When the motion was voted, the UK found itself in splendid isolation, with all the other 26 states voting in favour. Prime Minister Cameron's veto of the motion was greeted with mixed comments back home. A poll by the London <I>Times<W0> showed that 57 per cent of the public supported his move, and his Euro-sceptic back benchers in parliament were delighted. So were the bankers. However, the public were probably voting against yet more rules from the European Union, whatever they were.

Dicing with debt

Writing in the London *The Observer*, the respected economic commentator William Keegan described the UK's Chancellor of the Exchequer (minister of finance) George Osborne as having 'staked his reputation on a much-publicised plan that has demonstrably failed.' Keegan went on to observe that 'Osborne's strategy was to make a political fetish of deficit reduction relying on a

KEY FACTS

Official name: The United Kingdom of Great Britain and Northern Ireland (UK)

Head of State: Queen Elizabeth II (crowned 2 Jun 1953)

Head of government: Prime Minister David Cameron (from 12 May 2010)

Ruling party: Coalition, led by the Conservative Party, with the Liberal Democrats (from 12 May 2010)

Area: 244,103 square km

Population: 62.22 million (2010)*

Capital: London

Official language: English; English and Welsh in Wales; English and Scottish Gaelic in Scotland.

Currency: Pound sterling (£) = 100 pence

Exchange rate: £0.64 per US$ (Oct 2011)

GDP per capita: US$36,120 (2010)

GDP real growth: 1.30% (2010)

GDP: US$2,247.50 billion (2010)

Labour force: 31.51 million (2010)

Unemployment: 7.90% (2010)

Inflation: 3.30% (2010)

Oil production: 1.34 million bpd (2010)

Balance of trade: -US$152.93 billion (2010)

Visitor numbers: 29.68 million (2009)

Annual FDI: US$46.95 billion (2010)

* estimated figure

widespread public misunderstanding of the difference between household economics and the macro-economic affairs of a nation state.' Criticism indeed.

Depressed, devalued and divided

When David Cameron found himself, thanks to an unlikely coalition with an unelectable Liberal Democrats (LibDems) party, pushed into power in May 2010, he promised to cut the nation's deficits and galvanise the economy with his programme of radical fiscal austerity. In his first budget, Mr Osborne came up with the baffling concept of 'expansionary fiscal contraction', no doubt dreamt up by an ideologically driven civil servant. In his 2011 Autumn Statement Mr Osborne – far from acknowledging the failure of his plan, promised the British electorate more of the same. This, despite the concrete evidence that the British economy was at best flatlining, with unemployment rising and government debt continuing to climb. Neither the Prime Minister nor his Chancellor appeared to have learned that with its export markets languishing in the face of the euro-zone crisis, it made little sense to reduce domestic demand by raising value added tax (VAT) by 2.5 per cent and laying off swathes of public sector workers.

In the second half of 2010 and throughout 2011 Mr Cameron's had government repeated its mantra of austerity and cuts, to such an extent that even those who managed to retain their jobs began to worry about their future. This was not only the case with the electorate, but also with the corporate sector. Many large UK companies were sitting on substantial cash reserves, but such was the perceived economic climate created by the government that they were simply too nervous to spend it. Small- and medium-sized companies (SME's), very much the backbone of the British economy tended not to be in possession of cash reserves. On the contrary, as a group, the SMEs traditionally relied on bank credit. Which brought the economic wheel full circle – the banks that had originally caused the 2008 crash, risked doing so again, albeit for slightly different reasons. Mr Keegan concluded his analysis of the British economy by noting that 'planned penury does not produce growth. Nor does it help exports to preach the virtues of austerity to our principal export markets.'

Bleak forecasts

UK government forecasts could hardly have been bleaker. Overall output was expected to shrink by 0.1 per cent in the final quarter of 2011 and rise by the same percentage in the first quarter of 2012. In late 2011 unemployment had risen to 2.6 million, the highest rate for 17 years. In the view of the International Monetary Fund (IMF) economic growth has recently been sluggish and inflation has been high in the UK, though both indicators are projected to improve gradually over time. Recent increases in indirect taxes and commodity prices will keep headline inflation well above 4 per cent during 2011. However, it should return near the 2 per cent target by end-2012 as these transitory factors dissipate and as significant spare capacity keeps underlying inflation in check. Growth, which has also been adversely affected by spiking commodity prices, is expected to gradually accelerate from around 1.5 per cent in 2011 to 2.5 per cent in the medium term, as low interest rates and global growth support expansion led by net exports and investment. Nonetheless, there are large risks around this central scenario, including from uncertainties surrounding turmoil in parts of the euro area, headwinds from fiscal consolidation, volatile commodity prices and the housing market.

A wide-ranging policy programme has been put in place to aid the post-crisis repair of the UK economy. The agenda includes restoring confidence in public finances, moving to a safer financial sector and rebalancing the economy away from public and private consumption and toward more sustainable sources of growth (net exports and investment). As part of this programme, the government has undertaken institutional reform to address weaknesses in the policy-making framework. These reforms include moving the micro-prudential regulator under the Bank of England (BoE), establishing a Financial Policy Committee (FPC) to oversee macro-prudential policy and creating an independent Office for Budget Responsibility (OBR) aimed at strengthening the credibility of fiscal analysis and forecasts.

The government has made progress on its medium-term fiscal consolidation plan, which is a central component of its overall macro-economic strategy. The cyclically adjusted primary balance (as a per cent of potential gross domestic product (GDP)) is estimated to have improved by about 2 percentage points in 2010/11. In the future the pace of adjustment is projected to ease slightly and become increasingly reliant on spending restraint.

The BoE has maintained an accommodative monetary policy stance, with the Bank Rate at 0.5 per cent and the stock of outstanding asset purchases at £200 billion (US$312.5 billion). This stance reflects the BoE's forecast that inflation will return to target over the forecast horizon, taking into account disinflationary forces

KEY INDICATORS — United Kingdom

	Unit	2006	2007	2008	2009	2010
Population	m	60.24	60.59	61.37	*61.80	*62.22
Gross domestic product (GDP)	US$bn	2,402.00	2,772.57	2,684.20	2,183.60	2,247.50
GDP per capita	US$	39,680	45,922	43,736	35,334	36,120
GDP real growth	%	2.9	3.1	0.5	-4.9	1.3
Inflation	%	2.3	2.3	3.6	2.2	3.3
Unemployment	%	5.4	5.4	5.7	7.6	7.9
Oil output	'000 bpd	1,636.0	1,636.0	1,544.0	1,448.0	1,339.0
Natural gas output	bn cum	80.0	72.4	69.6	64.4	57.1
Coal output	mtoe	11.3	10.4	10.9	10.9	11.0
Exports (fob) (goods)	US$m	447,580.0	442,280.0	468,140.0	356,170.0	410,220.0
Imports (fob) (goods)	US$m	590,470.0	617,800.0	641,600.0	483,940.0	563,150.0
Balance of trade	US$m	-142,890.0	-175,520.0	-173,460.0	-127,760.0	-152,930.0
Current account	US$m	-92,566.0	-115,240.0	-41,160.0	-23,650.0	-71,600.0
Total reserves minus gold	US$m	40,700.0	48,960.0	44,350.0	55.7	68.3
Foreign exchange	US$m	38,890.0	47,500.0	41,550.0	38.0	49.3
Tourist numbers	'000	32,700.0	32,800.0	31,900.0	29,680.0	–
Exchange rate	per US$	0.51	0.49	0.51	0.64	0.64

* estimated figure

from fiscal consolidation. Meanwhile, banks have strengthened their balance sheets and reduced funding vulnerabilities over the last year, with all major banks ahead of schedule in their transition to the Basel III rules. Nonetheless, according to the IMF, the recovery process is not yet complete.

Echoing some of the points made in the IMF forecasts, the Organisation for Economic Co-operation and Development (OECD), in its November 2011 report on the UK, noted that weak international demand, continued retrenchment among households and the much needed fiscal consolidation has halted the recovery. Growth will start to pick up during 2012 as exports and household consumption recover, with further strengthening in 2013. Unemployment is rising and will reach 9 per cent in 2013, while inflation is presently peaking as anticipated and is expected to fall below the 2 per cent target in 2013 as temporary effects from VAT hikes and commodity prices wane. Monetary policy is supportive, with the Bank rate continuing at 0.5 per cent and quantitative easing being resumed. Further expansions of quantitative measures are warranted. The ambitious fiscal consolidation has bolstered credibility and helped maintain low bond yields, leaving room for automatic stabilisers to work fully to cushion the slowdown. The aggressive stance of the coalition government meant that the UK was able to retain its Triple A status with the credit rating agencies. The principle advantages of this were continued low borrowing rates, generally on a par with those of Germany, and easy access to funding when required.

Cameron – fear and frustration

By mid-2011, the heady early days of the coalition government were very much a thing of the past. After his forceful performances in the pre-election debates, the Deputy Prime Minister Nick Clegg had almost become a figure of fun. Meanwhile, the once ebullient prime minister had begun to share some of the electorate's fear and frustration. Mr Cameron's fear came from the realisation that his Plan A was not quite working in a number of ways. His frustration emanated from the irritating presence of non-Conservative ministers and junior ministers who made life difficult on matters related to green politics, social issues and – above all – Europe. As the so-called euro-zone crisis developed, Mr Cameron's backbenchers (i e rank and file Conservative Members of Parliament) began to flex their muscles, taking a 'told you so' stance peppered with *schadenfreude* at the travails across the Channel.

The first obvious split in the coalition took place in May 2011 over the two party's approach to proportional representation system of voting, in contrast to the first-past-the-post system. An unnecessarily complex referendum was held in May 2011 on the Alternative Vote (AV). Agreeing to the referendum had been Mr Cameron's compromise response to Mr Clegg to persuade the LibDems to join his government. In the coalition's honeymoon period, Mr Cameron and his supporters – known as Cameroons – had even considered supporting the Alternative Vote, or at least not opposing it. But by the middle of the year, the gloss had worn off – Mr Cameron had to choose between supporting his party or his coalition. The party won.

This change of heart was seen as a betrayal by the LibDems and called into question their continued support for the coalition government. However, were the coalition to collapse and new elections be called, the biggest losers would certainly be the LibDems. Whereas at the outset of Britain's first peacetime experiment with coalition government both parties had stressed the positives, freely mentioning expressions such as 'catalyst', 'complementary' and 'co-operation', now the arrangement was seen by both sides as a brake rather than a catalyst, dumbing policies down to levels of mutual acceptance. As 2011 wore on, the Conservatives could see that sharing power was actually preventing them from sorting out the what they considered to be the country's problems. This realisation could not, of course, be voiced. But it certainly lead the Conservatives to give thought to what might happen in the next general election.

Hackgate

July 2011 saw Mr Cameron facing a different, far more public, problem. In opposition, he and his right-hand man (later to be appointed Chancellor of the Exchequer) George Osborne, had energetically courted the press magnate Richard Murdoch, owner of the *Times*, *The Sun* and the *News of the World*. The reason for this was, simply, to seek the endorsement of Mr Murdoch's newspapers for the Conservative party in the run-up to the2010 general election. The plan worked: the Murdoch empire switched its endorsement from Labour to the Conservatives. But not well enough to give Mr Cameron the cherished outright majority, just enough to allow him the possibility of forming a coalition government with the LibDems.

Mr Cameron was not alone in his ignorance of the methods customarily used by Mr Murdoch's News International company to obtain information. However, this ignorance, if true, was surprising. Not only had Mr Cameron and his ministers become regular visitors to Mr Murdoch's offices, Mr Cameron had also become an apparently close friend of News International's editor in chief, Rebekah Brooks. He had also employed a former News International editorial director, Andy Coulson, as his press secretary. Earlier in the year, as rumours began to circulate, Mr Coulson had resigned the position. Surprisingly, no-one seemed to have thought fit to warn Mr Cameron about the possible dangers of these appointments and friendships. Or if they had, the advice had been ignored. Either way, the prime minister had been made to look badly lacking in judgement.

The wedding – times change

In 1923 the late Queen Mother, Elizabeth Bowes-Lyon, married the then Duke of York, later to become King George VI. In 2011 an article in the *New Yorker* by Lauren Collins revealed that in 1923 the recently created BBC requested permission to broadcast the ceremony. The request, it seems, was turned down on the grounds that men 'might hear the service, perhaps some of them sitting in public houses, with their hats on.' Almost 90 years later, at the end of April 2011, another royal wedding took place, between the late Queen Mother's great grandson and heir to the throne, Prince William, and Kate Middleton, described rather medievally, as a 'commoner'. Most Britons could well remember the wedding of William's father, Prince Charles, to Diana, in 1981. Rather less, that of the Queen, then Princess, Elizabeth to Prince Philip in 1947. For the majority of Britons, their memories of the royal wedding would be positive. The 1947 wedding shared with that of 2011 the climate of austerity that beset the United Kingdom.

In 2011 the coalition government decided to harness the royal wedding as a catalyst not only for improving the public mood, but also in the hope of converting it into an economic booster. The wedding day was declared a public holiday and street parties became the order of the day, as much of the population decided to take advantage of the spring weather and simply enjoy themselves. Republican voices were almost drowned out by the general festivity. Quoted by Ms Collins, the head of the anti-royalist Republic group (who campaign for a democratic alternative to the monarchy) described the wedding as 'an effort to shore up support for a rather shabby political stitch-up. It's not really appropriate in a modern democracy.' Appropriate or not, the vast majority of the population were happy to go along with it, joined by countless millions of television viewers from virtually every country in the world. The royal couple appeared to have infused the royal family with a new lease of life. Not long after their wedding the couple's first royal engagement was an official visit to Canada, a country not normally known for excessive royal enthusiasm. Such was the success of the visit, that the Canadian government decided to re-insert the adjective 'Royal' into the names of its armed forces.

Energy

The United Kingdom is the largest producer of oil and second-largest producer of natural gas in the European Union (EU). After years of being a net exporter of both fuels, the UK became a net importer of natural gas and crude oil in 2004 and 2005, respectively. According to the US government's Energy Information Administration (EIA) production from UK oil and natural gas fields peaked in the late 1990s and has declined steadily over the past several years, as the discovery of new reserves has not kept pace with the maturation of existing fields. The UK government, aware of the country's increasing reliance on imported fuels, has developed key energy policies to address the domestic production declines. These include enhanced recovery from current and maturing oil and gas fields, ensuring energy security, promoting co-operation with Norway and de-carbonising the UK economy by investing heavily in renewable energy. According to the *Oil and Gas Journal* (OGJ), the UK had 2.9 billion barrels of proven crude oil reserves in 2011, the most of any EU member country. In 2010, the UK produced 1.4 million barrels per day (bpd) and consumed 1.6 million bpd of oil.

The UK Continental Shelf (UKCS), located in the North Sea off the eastern coast of the UK, contains the bulk of the country's oil reserves. There are also sizable reserves in the North Sea north and west of the Shetland Islands. Besides these offshore assets, the UK also has the Wytch Farm field located in the Wessex Basin, the largest onshore oil field in Europe, which has produced more than 400 million barrels of oil over its 35-year life.

Total oil production (including condensates, natural gas liquids and refinery gain) of the 1.4 million bpd in 2010, was a 7 per cent decline compared with the 2009 production levels. The EIA's *Short-Term Energy Outlook* expects UK oil production to continue to decline, falling to 1.2 million bpd by the end of 2012. Nevertheless, exploration interest in the UK remains strong, undoubtedly driven by higher oil prices and the North Sea's proximity to major consuming markets. However, recent increases in the Supplementary Corporate Tax for oil and gas companies by 12 per cent may affect the attractiveness of the UK fields in the longer term.

A total of seven oil fields started production in 2010 and 2011. Two of those, Loirston (ExxonMobil) and Falcon (Taqa) began production in March and July 2011, respectively. Loirston is located in the Viking Graben basin and has 1.79 million barrels of oil equivalent (boe) of reserves. Falcon, located in the East Shetland basin has 3.07 million boe of reserves.

Exports

Most of the UK crude oil grades are light (30° to 40° API) and sweet (relatively small amounts of sulphur), which generally makes them attractive to foreign buyers. Although the UK has become a net importer of oil, it is still one of the largest petroleum producers and exporters in the EU and is home to the Brent benchmark. In 2010, the UK exported 832 thousand bpd, more than half of its total production. Nearly 80 per cent of its crude was shipped to EU countries. Significant volumes of crude oil were destined for the Netherlands (38 per cent of the total), Germany (22 per cent) and the United States (17 per cent). The remaining 23 per cent of crude oil exports were sent to a number of other countries, including France, Sweden, Chile and Denmark.

The United Kingdom is also a significant oil importer, receiving about 1 million bpd in 2010. Considering the slowing decline rate in oil exports accompanied by declining domestic consumption and increasing imports, it appears that the UK is once again becoming an oil transit country. According to Global Trade Atlas, about 72.8 per cent of all crude oil imports originated in Norway (which is not part of EU-27) with another 6.5 per cent arriving from Russia.

Natural gas

According to the OGJ, the UK held an estimated 9 trillion cubic feet (tcf) of proven natural gas reserves in 2011, a 12 per cent decline from the previous year. Most of these reserves occur in three distinct areas: associated fields in the UKCS; non-associated fields in the Southern Gas Basin, located adjacent to the Dutch sector of the North Sea; and non-associated fields in the Irish Sea. The UK government has encouraged the use of natural gas as a substitute for coal and oil in industrial consumption and electricity production. Natural gas consumption in the UK reached 3.3tcf in 2010, increasing about 7 per cent compared with the previous year.

The UK produced 2.0tcf of natural gas in 2010, falling about 5 per cent compared with the previous year, which was a significantly smaller decrease than last year's 15 per cent. However, at 2.0tcf, UK's production reached its lowest level since 1992.

The largest concentration of natural gas production in the UK is the Shearwater-Elgin area of the Southern Gas Basin. The area contains five gas fields, Elgin, Franklin, Halley, Scoter and Shearwater. Most of the leading oil companies in the UK are also the leading natural gas producers, including BP, Shell and ConocoPhillips. The major gas distribution companies in the UK, such as BG Group and E.ON Ruhrgas, also have a presence in the production sector.

Currently, there are 10 nuclear power plants in the UK, with a combined capacity of more than 22 megawatts. Eight of these plants are operated by EDF Energy, which acquired British Energy (BE) in September 2008. These eight plants include seven stations that use advanced, gas-cooled reactors (AGR) and one (Sizewell B) using a pressurised-water reactor (PWR). All of the AGR reactors will reach the end of their designed lifetime by 2023. Reactor 2 of the Oldbury Nuclear Power Plant, a first generation, magnesium-oxide (Magnox) plant, was permanently shut down on 30 June 2011 after operating for 43 years. The plant's Reactor 1 will continue to operate until the end of 2012. Wylfa, also a first-generation nuclear power plant, was slated to be shut down this year. However, in January 2011 the Nuclear Decommissioning Authority announced that the plant will continue to operate until 2012.

In 2008, the UK government announced its support for additional nuclear power plants to meet projected energy needs. The previous (Labour) government issued a series of national policy statements (NPSs) in 2009, identifying potential sites for new plants and outlining its policy that promotes building of new nuclear power plants by 2025. Following the announcement and the NPSs, a number of companies proposed nuclear power plant projects. Among those, EDF proposed four new European pressurised reactors (EPR) totaling 6,400MW, the first one of which would start up in 2017.

The UK had an estimated 228 million tonnes of recoverable coal reserves at the end of 2010 according to the June 2011 issue of the *BP Statistical Review of World Energy*. The country produced 11 million tonnes of oil equivalent (toe) in 2010, remaining one of the top ten coal producers in the EU. Coal production in the UK has declined steadily and dramatically since the early 1990s, but has stabilised over the last couple of years. Decreasing domestic consumption and a surge of low-cost imports have been the principle causes of the production decline. The UK imported 20 million toe in 2010, accounting for more than 60 per cent of its total coal supply.

Risk assessment

Economy	Fair
Politics	Good
Regional stability	Good

COUNTRY PROFILE

Historical profile

1837–1901 The long reign of Queen Victoria saw the British Empire at the height of its power.
1914–1918 Great Britain called on all its colonies and dominions to help it fight alongside its allies, France and Russia, in the First World War against Germany and its allies.
1916 An uprising in Dublin by Irish republicans was supressed after a few days and its leaders were either executed or interned.
1922 The Irish Free State (Eire) was created in southern Ireland; the six north-eastern counties of Ireland remained part of Great Britain.
1939 Britain declared war on Germany having failed to limit its expansionist policies and after Germany had invaded Poland.
1939–45 In the Second World War, Britain was a major member of the allied forces, along with the US and the Soviet Union, against the Axis powers of Germany, Italy and Japan.
1945 Facing near economic collapse as a result of the war, the UK began to relinquish control of its Empire and its role in the world as its power declined.
1945–51 The Labour Party was elected into government. Led by Prime Minister Clement Attlee, the government implemented reforms to education, healthcare, housing and the social security system.
1953 Queen Elizabeth II was crowned on 2 June.
1969 The start of 'The Troubles' in Northern Ireland. Violence between the Catholic civil rights movement and the Unionists, who perceived it as republicanism, intensified.
1973 The UK joined the European Economic Community.
1979 Following a decade marred by economic stagnation and endemic inflation, the Conservative Party (Tories) won a parliamentary majority in the general election. Margaret Thatcher, leader of the party, became the UK's first woman prime minister.
1979–1990 Thatcher's radical domestic policies, including privatisation and local government reforms, did not prevent her securing two further election victories, in addition to a victory in the 1982 Falklands conflict.
1990 Introduction of the community charge and a loss of party confidence stemming from her vociferous opposition to the European Community finally led to Thatcher being replaced by John Major as leader of the Conservative Party and as prime minister.
1992 The treaty on European Union (the Maastricht Treaty) was signed. The Treaty harmonised legislation in key areas of European Union (EU) social policy, immigration and finance, although the UK successfully opted out of the Social Chapter. The UK was forced out of the European Exchange Rate Mechanism (ERM) after the pound dropped below the permitted parity with the deutschmark. The Conservatives won the general election.
1997 The Labour Party, under the leadership of Tony Blair, won an overwhelming victory in the general election.
1998 The UK and Irish governments attempted to bring to an end the problems in Northern Ireland through the signing of the Good Friday Peace Agreement. The political settlement established a precedent for Ireland's direct involvement in Northern Ireland's affairs, with cross-border co-operation and the decommissioning of paramilitary arms.
1999 Scotland's first legislature for 300 years and Wales' first for 600 years were opened in June. Power and conditional authority were also devolved in Northern Ireland in December.
2000 Nationwide cases of foot and mouth broke out; four million cattle were culled and compensation payments totalled £1.1 billion (US$1.5 billion).
2001 The Labour Party won a second landslide parliamentary victory.
2003 British forces joined a US-led invasion of Iraq, prompted in part by an intelligence report that said President Saddam Hussein of Iraq had a stock of weapons of mass destruction (WMD)
2004 The Iraq Survey Group concluded Iraq did not possess WMD. A UK inquiry into the quality of intelligence used to justify UK participation in the Iraq war found no evidence of 'deliberate distortion or culpable negligence' by the government.
2005 The Labour Party won its third term in office but with a significantly reduced majority. On 7 July four bombs exploded (on three underground trains and a bus) during the morning rush hour in London, killing 52 people and injuring over 700. Islamic extremists were later convicted of this terrorism.
2006 Police investigated allegations of peerages being bought through financial donations to the Labour Party. Aleksandr Litvinenko, former Russian security service officer and outspoken critic of Russia's ruling elite was poisoned by radioactive thallium in London. Police traced the source to Russia but authorities there refused to extradite the prime suspect.
2007 Following Northern Ireland elections the Democratic Unionist Party (DUP) and Sinn Féin agreed to share power, ending direct rule from London. The Scottish National Party (SNP) took office after winning Scotland's general election. Prime Minister Blair resigned and was replaced, unopposed, by Gordon Brown.
2008 The first run on a bank by customers since the early 1860s lead the government to nationalise the Northern Rock Bank. The government had to invest £37 billion (US$74 billion) to partly nationalise another three failing banks and guarantee billions more to support the financial sector. In foreign exchange markets the pound sterling dropped against the US dollar as well as other currencies.
2009 The UK fell into recession in the first quarter and the Bank of England's official bank rate was reduced to 1.5 per cent, the lowest level since it began operations in 1694. Halifax-Bank of Scotland announced the largest corporate loss in British history – of around US$41.3 billion (£28 billion). UK troops began leaving Iraq. An inquiry into the Iraq War was announced, to undertake a full investigation of the circumstances, conduct and outcome of the war. The UK climbed out of recession in the last quarter.
2010 Following parliamentary elections held in May, in which the Tories won most votes and seats but not an overall majority, talks began immediately to form a coalition government with the Liberal Democrats (Lib Dems). David Cameron (Tories) became prime minister. An early budget on 22 June, announced public

spending cuts, particularly in welfare. It also included a public sector worker's pay freeze, a VAT rise from 17.5 per cent to 20 per cent and bank levies. In August, the UK public sector borrowing was a record US$24.8 billion (£15.9 billion); January–May borrowing totalled US$89.3 billion (£58.1 billion). In a surprise result, Ed Miliband became leader of the Labour Party. He beat his elder brother, David Miliband, by 50.65 per cent to 49.35 per cent of votes cast. The US, UK, Germany and France placed a ban on all cargo from Yemen in November, following the discovery of improvised bombs sent by agents of al Qaeda.

2011 In a speech delivered to a security conference in Munich, Germany on 6 February, David Cameron said that the UK had 'allowed the weakening of our collective identity' and had tolerated 'segregated communities behaving in ways that run completely counter to our values', which he believed had resulted in 'a process of radicalisation' and extremism. The focus of the argument was Islamic extremism, which he emphasised was a political and not religious ideology that had to be countered by all in Europe and should be led by Islamic communities. On 19 March, the UK joined in a five-country coalition (with Canada, France, Italy and the US) to impose a no-fly zone over Libya. A referendum to change the voting system to proportional representation for the UK parliament was defeated by 67.9 per cent (No) to 32.1 per cent (Yes). In the Scottish Parliamentary elections, held on 5 May, the SNP became the majority party and promised to present a referendum on independence from the UK's Act of Union before the end of its term in office. In Welsh National Assembly elections, held on 5 May, the nationalist Plaid Cymru lost four seats from the previous election, while the Labour Party gained four and won leadership of the assembly, but still required support from other parties to pass legislation. The UK military operations in Iraq ended completely on 20 May, when 81 naval trainers of the Royal Navy left the country, having completed their training of Iraqi sailors, ready to defend Iraqi territorial waters. Rioting and looting broke-out in several major English cities over three nights from 6 August. Order was restored with the deployment of 16,000 police officers in London; magistrate courts stayed open for 24 hours to process those arrested. On 28 October, the 16 Commonwealth Heads of Government in which the British monarch is Head of State unanimously agreed to change the royal line of succession from that of first born son to the first born child (regardless of its gender). The change will be enacted after the succession of Prince William (currently second in line to the throne, after his father Prince Charles). On 29 November, the British embassy in Tehran (Iran) and a British diplomatic compound in northern Tehran were stormed by hundreds of protestors angry at British sanctions against Iran. All UK diplomatic staff and their families were evacuated on 30 November as all Iranian embassy staff in London were told to quit the UK within 48 hours.

Political structure

Constitution

There is no formal written constitution, instead constitutional law is based on legal precedent and legislation both within the UK and from EU supranational institutions. Power within the UK is partially devolved to Scotland, Wales and Northern Ireland. Local councils operate at the level of metropolitan boroughs, counties, districts and parishes, delivering a number of public services such as education and policing, although their powers, particularly regarding taxation and spending, are circumscribed by central government.

Form of state

Parliamentary democratic monarchy

The executive

The monarch is head of state. The monarchy is governed by convention and may not participate in politics or government affairs. It has, however, by unspoken agreement three rights: to be consulted, to encourage and to warn.

The monarch, in regard to democratic principles, accedes to the results of the popular vote and appoints the winner of any general election, and only in extreme circumstances may a monarch dismiss the government.

While government ministers act nominally in the name of the Crown, almost all power rests with the prime minister as head of government and his cabinet of ministers (part of the executive but drawn from the legislature).

The prime minister chooses and chairs the cabinet, who are members of the political party which typically has most seats in the House of Commons. The cabinet consists of around 20 ministers, although its exact composition is not fixed and there are some ministers without portfolio. Secretaries of state are ministers who head specific government departments. Major figures of importance in the cabinet include the chancellor of the exchequer (responsible for economic management), the foreign secretary (foreign policy) and the home secretary (responsible for law and order). Other ministers deal on a functional basis with trade and industry, health, energy, transport and so on. Cabinet ministers head departments of civil servants and have junior ministers (who do not, as a rule, have a seat in the cabinet) to assist them. These ministries are effectively the executive arm of central government, implementing decisions of the cabinet and parliament.

National legislature

The bicameral parliament consists of the House of Commons (lower house) and House of Lords (upper house). Both are commonly referred to as the Commons and Lords respectively. The Commons has 646 members of parliament (MPs), directly elected in single seat constituencies who serve for up to four-year terms. Legislation may be introduced by both houses; the Lords can suggest amendments to and, except for financial legislation, it can refuse to pass legislation, but the Commons has ultimate power.

The Lords has 740 members, including life peers, hereditary peers and Church of England archbishops and bishops who serve for as long as they deem necessary.

Devolution of power to Scotland and Wales took place in 1999 and was Scotland's first legislature for 300 years and Wales' first for 600 years. Elections to the 129-member Scottish Parliament and the 60-member Welsh Assembly are conducted under a system of proportional representation. The Scottish Parliament may raise taxes; however the Welsh Assembly must seek funds from the UK parliament.

Legal system

The judiciary is independent of both the legislature and executive. The legal system in Scotland and Northern Ireland differs from that in England and Wales.

In England and Wales around 300 county courts deal with minor civil cases. Magistrates courts deal with minor criminal cases. Civil and criminal appeals from these courts are heard by crown courts, which sit in about 90 venues. Scotland and Northern Ireland have slightly different judicial systems. The main purpose of a crown court is to try the more important criminal cases. The High Court of Justice is the main civil court, divided into three sections: Chancery Division, Queens Bench Division and the Family Division.

In October the highest court in England, Wales and Northern Ireland, which had been operated by the House of Lords, became the Supreme Court, entirely separate from the legislature.

Since the signing of the Single European Act in 1988, the European Court of Justice (ECJ) has supreme jurisdiction over some aspects of UK law, although this is not often exercised.

Last elections

6 May 2010 (parliamentary); 5 May 2011 (parliamentary Scotland and Wales and UK referendum)

Results: Parliamentary: the Conservative Party won 36.1 per cent of the vote (306 seats out of 650), Labour Party 29 per cent (258), Liberal Democrats 23 per cent (57), Democratic Unionist Party 0.6 per cent (8), Scottish National Party 1.7 per cent (6), Sinn Féin 0.6 per cent (5); three other political parties won less than four seats each. Turnout was 65.1 per cent.
Scottish Parliament: the Scottish National Party won 69 seats (out of 129), Labour Party 37, Liberal Democrats five, others three.
Welsh Assembly: the Labour Party won 30 seats (out of 129), Conservatives 14, Plaid Cymru 11, Liberal Democrats five.
Referendum: 67.9 per cent voted against and 32.1 per cent in favour of changing the voting system for the UK parliament, from 'first-past-the-post' to 'alternative voting' (AV), whereby voters rank their choice of candidates.

Next elections
2014 (parliamentary)

Political parties

Ruling party
Coalition, led by the Conservative Party, with the Liberal Democrats (from 12 May 2010)

Main opposition party
The Labour Party

Population

62.22 million (2010)*
Last census: April 2001: 58,789,187
Population density: 247 inhabitants per square km. Urban population: 90 per cent (1995–2001).
Annual growth rate: 0.3 per cent 1994–2004 (WHO 2006)

Ethnic make-up
The English, Scots, Welsh and Irish peoples combined make up over 90 per cent of the population of the UK; the largest ethnic minorities are those of Caribbean or African descent (875,000 people). The next largest ethnic groups are Indians (840,255 people) and Pakistani and Bangladeshis (639,390 people). Ethnic minority groups represent just under 6 per cent of the population.

Religions
Church of England (25 million (baptised)), Roman Catholic (4.12 million), Muslim (1.5 million), Presbyterian (1.1 million), Methodist (800,000), Sikh (500,000), Hindu (320,000), Jewish (285,000).

Education

The UK has a devolved education system. Alongside the state system are independent schools, often denominational, which are financed by fees, endowments and the state. Pre-school education is not state-funded; it is available for ages two to five, through playgroups and nursery schools. There is a national curriculum and assessment targets for all primary schools and a minimum attainment is set for all children.
The usual age for transfer to secondary schools is 11 in England, Wales and Northern Ireland and 12 in Scotland. About 90 per cent of state secondary school pupils in England, Wales and Scotland attend comprehensive schools, which provide a wide range of secondary education for most children of all abilities. In other areas, the grammar school system has been retained alongside the comprehensive system, with admission through some form of testing at the age of 10 or 11.
All children are tested at the ages of 7, 11 and 14 years, and take General Certificate of Secondary Education (GCSE) or Scottish Certificate of Education (SCE) examinations at 15–16 years. Students can then opt to study at further education institutions for a range of academic and vocational qualifications, such as Advanced level (A-level) or the National Vocational Qualification (NVQ).
Tertiary education typically starts at aged 18, when students go on to university or colleges of higher education. UK higher education has expanded so that first degrees and further post-graduate qualifications are taken at over 162 universities and other colleges of higher education.
Compulsory years: 5 to 16 in England, Wales and Scotland; 4 to 16 in Northern Ireland.
Enrolment rate: 101 per cent gross primary enrolment of relevant age group (including repeaters); 158 per cent gross secondary enrolment; 59 per cent tertiary enrolment (World Bank).
Pupils per teacher: 19 in primary schools

Health

The National Health Service (NHS) benefits from major government spending, with UK citizens provided with free treatment. Most people are required to pay an initial fee for some aspects of treatment such as eye tests, dental care and prescriptions. The NHS accounts for 85 per cent of total healthcare provision in the UK.
The service provided by the NHS is generally of high quality, but delays for many non-urgent operations have encouraged people to take out private health insurance policies. Private health cover is becoming increasingly common as a company benefit.
Latest figures show 83 per cent of children were immunised against measles before aged one year. Many parents have withdrawn their infants from the programme and questioned the efficacy of the triple MMR (measles, mumps and rubella) vaccine, following a hotly contested report that claimed the onset of autism and the MMR vaccination were linked.
The government announced that it would take measures to prohibit visitors or 'health tourists' from accessing NHS services, limiting treatment to accidents and emergency cases only.
Foreign medical providers provide some surgical treatment, outside the administration of local health authorities. This has provided competition for the NHS, to match the provision of treatment at a reduced cost with speedier flow-through.

HIV/Aids
HIV prevalence: 0.2 per cent aged 15–49 in 2003 (World Bank)
Life expectancy: 79 years, 2004 (WHO 2006)
Fertility rate/Maternal mortality rate: 1.7 births per woman, 2004 (WHO 2006)
Birth rate/Death rate: 12 births and 11 deaths per 1,000 people (World Bank)
Child (under 5 years) mortality rate (per 1,000): 5.3 per 1,000 live births (World Bank)

Welfare

The UK has long-established social security and welfare systems. Jobseekers Allowance is provided to most of those registered as unemployed. Additional benefits are paid to families on low incomes or with special needs, for example through the Family Credit Scheme. There is also a wide range of allowances for disabled people. The Housing Benefit Scheme is administered by local authorities and provides assistance with rent and other payments.

Pensions
The UK has an ageing population, with the number of over 65 year-olds projected to outnumber the numbers below 16 years by 2008. The number of those past retirement age is expected to peak at around 15 million in the 2030s. Bills for healthcare and pensions are set to rise significantly, while revenue from income tax falls. Government policy is to actively encourage private pension schemes for all employees, and most people now entering the labour market do not expect to receive a sufficient state pension on retirement. Private pension schemes allow retirement at any time between age 50 and 75.
The State Retirement Pension is paid to men at age 65 and women at age 60, although for women this age is starting to increase with the state retirement age to be equalised at age 65 by April 2020.
A report published in October 2004 found that state pensions were underfunded, and that 9–12 million people (or 40 per cent of the workforce) were not saving enough for their retirement.

In March 2005 the unfunded public workers' pensions liability was estimated at £690 billion (US$1.2 trillion) or 1.5 times the net public sector debt. The government has begun taking action to alleviate the problem but much more will be required and may include some combination of higher taxes, compulsory savings and/or an increase in the retirement age over 65.

In April 2005 the Pension Protection Fund (PPF) began operation. The fund is aimed at workers who lose their pension when their employer declares bankruptcy. The scheme is an insurance plan, to which all final salary pension schemes must belong. Pension schemes pay fees for each member into a fund and when a business collapses the employees should receive at least 90 per cent of the sum they were due when they retire and retired members should receive 100 per cent of the sum. Critics claim this measure will discourage businesses from running final salary pensions, if they are to shoulder yet another financial burden, and that one large enterprise that collapsed could overwhelm the fund.

Main cities

England: London (capital, estimated population 7.5 million in 2004), Birmingham (963,234), Liverpool (457,219), Sheffield (434,468), Leeds (442,921), Bristol (421,795), Manchester (386,849), Leicester (331,731),

Scotland: Edinburgh (capital) (464,290), Glasgow (Scotland) (1.2 million), Aberdeen (198,784), Dundee (153,539).

Wales: Cardiff (capital) (297,997), Swansea (169,412), Newport (116,186), Wrexham (43,079).

Northern Ireland: Belfast (capital) (258,902), Londonderry (Derry) (87,878).

Languages spoken

Other communities such as Indian, Pakistani, Jewish and Chinese maintain their languages.

In 2004 the Bòrd na Gàidhlig (the Bòrd) was established, as a statutory body, working to secure the status of Gaelic as an official language of Scotland.

Official language/s

English; English and Welsh in Wales; English and Scottish Gaelic in Scotland.

Media

Press

The Press Complaints Commission (www.pcc.org.uk) monitors ethical guidelines required by British media.

There are over 2,000 newspapers published in the UK. All major newspapers are in English. The impact of the internet has led all major national news corporations to invest in online editions.

Dailies: Of the 10 daily newspapers published in England, tabloid readership is the greatest, with the most popular, *The Sun* typically selling three million copies. The biggest selling broadsheet is *The Daily Telegraph* with around 900,000 copies sold daily. Broadsheets by popularity include *The Daily Telegraph* (www.telegraph.co.uk), *The Times* (www.timesonline.co.uk), *The Guardian* (www.guardian.co.uk) and *The Independent* (www.independent.co.uk). A free issue newspaper in London *Metro* (www.metro.co.uk) rivals some of the tabloid newspaper circulations.

Influential newspapers in Scotland include the *Daily Record* (www.dailyrecord.co.uk) and *The Herald* (www.theherald.co.uk); in Wales *Western Mail* (http://icwales.icnetwork.co.uk); in Northern Ireland *Belfast Telegraph* (www.belfasttelegraph.co.uk) and *The Irish News* (www.irishnews.com).

There are a number of evening newspapers distributed in major cities including the London *Evening Standard* (www.thisislondon.co.uk), *Manchester Evening News* (www.manchestereveningnews.co.uk), *Bristol Evening Post* (www.epost.co.uk) and *The South Wales Evening Post* (www.thisissouthwales.co.uk). In January 2009, ex-KGB agent Alexander Lebedev bought the ailing *London Evening Standard*, to be run by his son Evgeny Lebedev. An editorial committee will guarantee editorial independence.

Weeklies: Most daily newspapers publish Sunday editions. There are numerous speciality magazines targeting women and men, young and old; the National Magazine Company (www.natmags.co.uk) publishes several of these magazines. Those with serious comment on general interest, with national and international circulation, include *Prospect* (www.prospect-magazine.co.uk), *The Spectator* (www.spectator.co.uk) and *New Statesman* (www.newstatesman.com). Topics can be exclusive, such as *The New Musical Express NME* (www.nme.com), or technology or aimed at ethnic groups, others can be regional and some international. Satirical publications include *Private Eye* (www.private-eye.co.uk) and *Viz* (www.viz.co.uk). There are two tabloid magazines with large circulations *Hello* (www.hellomagazine.com) and *Heat* (www.heatworld.com).

The last edition of the *News of the World* was published on 10 July 2011, following the scandal that a number of staff had systematically hacked into the mobile phones of celebrities, politicians and the bereaved families of military personnel and murder victims.

Business: There are a large number of publications covering all aspects of business, some with international circulation, the most prestigious are *The Financial Times* (www.ft.com) a daily newspaper and *The Economist* (www.economist.com) a weekly magazine. Others include *The Business* (http://info.thebusiness.co.uk), *Independent Business Today* (www.ibpl.co.uk) is a newsletter published by the Institute of Independent Business, *Financial News* (www.efinancialnews.com), and *Investors Chronicle* (www.investorschronicle.co.uk) (weekly). Other regional publications include *Business Brief Channel Islands*, *London Business Matters*, *Business and Finance in Scotland* and *Business Scotsman* (http://business.scotsman.com).

The Bank of England (www.bankofengland.co.uk/publications) regularly publishes news on the British economy. *The Shariah Investor* (www.shariahinvestor.com) has articles concerning Islamic banking.

Periodicals: *Which* (www.which.co.uk) is an influential consumer monthly magazine.

Broadcasting

Public broadcasting is provided by the British Broadcasting Corporation (BBC), a behemoth in the area of worldwide broadcasting. Services are paid for by a licence fee levied against any owner of a television set.

Radio: The BBC operates the largest national network with 11 stations targeting differing audiences, including the World Service, which broadcasts in over 30 languages worldwide. Digital and live online and podcast services are available (www.bbc.co.uk/radio). There is also a BBC local radio network covering the four countries with programmes in English, Welsh and Gaelic.

Private, commercial radio stations thrive throughout the country, although the BBC typically garners the highest listening audiences for both age-related programming and general audience ratings. Popular commercial services include Virgin Radio (www.virgin.com), Classic FM (www.classicfm.co.uk), Talk Sport (www1.talksport.net) and Independent Radio News (IRN) (www.irn.co.uk).

Television: Digital television services are due to be fully implemented by 2012, when all analogue services will be suspended. A number of service providers are transmitting programmes in high definition.

There are five national terrestrial television channels in operation – BBC1 and BBC2 (www.bbc.co.uk), ITV1 (www.itv.com), Channels 4 (www.channel4.com) and 5 (www.channel5.com). All channels

commission their own productions and transmit a range of genre programmes. Free-to-air digital services are provided by all national channels, and some by pay-to-view satellite and cable TV providers. BBC Wales and Channel 4 Wales called S4C provide services in the Welsh language.
Major cable, digital and satellite systems are growing, particularly the Sky network (www.sky.com) and Virgin (www. virgin.com), which includes news and sports channels.

Advertising

There is a highly developed advertising industry covering all forms of media. Numerous terrestrial and digital commercial TV channels accept advertisements subject to principles set by the Advertising Standards Agency (and limited to and average 7–15 minutes per hour). Radio advertising is also effective (limited to 9–12 minutes per hour). The majority of newspapers and magazines carry advertising and relatively high circulation figures make this a particularly useful form of promotion. Newspapers account for around 30 per cent of the media market compared to 40 per cent for television. Cinemas carry short advertisements and posters. Billboards and public transport are also widely used.
There is a ban on tobacco, and advertising limits on food and drinks for children.

News agencies

National news agency: PA Group

Economy

The UK is a major financial centre and one of the world's largest exporters of financial services. The economy is large, open and mixed and characterised by an export-oriented manufacturing sector. The UK is the third richest country in Europe and a member of the G8, a bloc of the wealthiest countries worldwide. This status is in no small measure based on its financial and service industries including insurance, banking and financial transaction services and tourism; the London Stock exchange is Europe's oldest and largest trading forum and globally second only to Wall Street.
GDP growth in 2007 was 2.6 per cent, but as the global economic crisis intensified it fell to 0.5 per cent in 2008. The UK went into recession in the third quarter of 2008, and did not work itself out until third quarter of 2009 ending six consecutive quarters of contraction as output rose by 0.5 per cent. Unemployment had risen in 2009 to a high of 7.8 per cent (youth unemployment was much higher at 19.8 per cent) as inflation fell to a 1.1 per cent, down from 3.6 per cent in 2008 (1.6 per cent above the Bank of England's consumer price index target of 2.0 per cent).
The Bank of England's official bank rate was reduced to 0.5 per cent in March 2009, the lowest level since it began operations in 1694. Sterling fell rapidly and manufacturing contracted by 4.6 per cent, despite the help to exporters of a weak pound.
The global economic crisis hit the UK hard as it is so dependent on its financial services sector for growth. It has high household indebtedness and an unsustainably high housing market. By the third quarter of 2009 insolvencies were at an all time high as cheap credit became scarce. The government was forced, since the run on the Northern Rock Bank in 2007, to commit public funds to prop up the banking sector and later the economy in general. Stimulus packages amounting to 0.2 per cent and 1.4 per cent of GDP were committed in 2008 and 2009 respectively as the UK, in conjunction with other developed countries, tackled its failing economy, through the mechanism of quantitative easing (injecting money directly into the economy). The money was used by the banking sector to provide liquidity for, among other things, inter-bank lending, asset guarantees and by the government in spending to promote growth. The credit ratings agency, Standard and Poor's, review of the UK's economy was revised from stable to negative in May 2009, stating its finances were deteriorating faster than expected. Nevertheless, the agency did not change the UK's triple-A rating, as it saw merit in the government's plans to reduce debt as sound. In June 2010 the Fitch Ratings Agency advised that efforts to cut the budget deficit should be speeded up to prevent the UK from losing its triple-A rating.
A new coalition government was elected in May 2010, which undertook to repay the budget deficit of £163 million (US$239 million) through, among other measures, higher taxes, wage freezes for public workers and social welfare cuts.

External trade

As a member of the European Union, the UK operates within a community-wide free trade area, with tariffs set as a whole. Internationally, the EU has free trade agreements with a number of nations and trading blocs worldwide.
The sector that produces the biggest share of export earnings is banking and financial services, with international banking rated as one of the best and most profitable globally. Despite the decline in heavy industry and manufacturing, output has been maintained by hi-tech industries in aerospace and telecommunications, pharmaceuticals and niche manufacturing that account for 25 per cent of GDP. The UK is still a major exporter of hydrocarbons, but became a net importer of oil and natural gas in 2004. The first liquefied natural gas (LNG) plant opened for imports in 2005.
In 2007, Scotch whisky was awarded greater protection from foreign copiers by British consumer laws. Scotch whisky exports are worth around US$4 billion to the Scottish economy annually and the regulation is seen as a vital measure to protect the integrity of the product.

Imports

Main imports are vehicles, consumer goods, capital machinery, raw materials, fuels and foodstuffs.

Main sources: Germany (typically 13 per cent of total), US (10 per cent), China (9 per cent).

Exports

Main exports are manufactured goods, fuels, chemicals and pharmaceuticals, food, beverages and tobacco.

Main destinations: US (typically 15 per cent total), Germany (11 per cent), France (8 per cent).

Agriculture

Farming

Agriculture contributes one per cent to GDP, employs 2 per cent of the workforce and meets over two-thirds of domestic food consumption needs. The sector is highly efficient and is a significant exporter of agricultural produce, fertilisers and foodstuffs. However, the farming industry remains stuck in long-term recession.
Government policy is to keep the agricultural industry competitive by reducing subsidies and allowing market forces to determine a farm's viability. The National Farmers' Union (NFU), represents around one-third of UK farmers.
Setbacks during the 2000s, included extensive flooding, two outbreaks of foot-and-mouth, the first of which resulted in the culling of over 4 million animals and the second, milder outbreak, a three-kilometre protection zone and a 10km surveillance zone while tests were carried out to find the source of the infection. The outbreak was tracked back to biological research facilities close to the first farm outbreak. Lastly the first case of the insect-borne virus, Bluetongue, affecting livestock was confirmed in 2007. These followed on from the industry's most damaging and widespread outbreak of Bovine *Spongiform Encephalopathy* (BSE) in the mid-1990s, which resulted in the death of nearly 200,000 diseased cattle and the destruction 4.5 million asymptomatic cattle.
UK membership of the EU has created policy disputes between the farmers' organisations, the UK government and the EU. Most of UK agriculture is governed by

the EU's Common Agricultural Policy (CAP), which was reformed fundamentally in 2005. The subsidies paid on farm output, which tended to benefit large farms and encourage overproduction, were replaced by single farm payments not conditional on production. This was expected to reward farms that provided and maintain a healthy environment, food safety and animal welfare standards. The changes were also intended to encourage market conscious production and cut the cost of CAP to the EU taxpayer.

Fishing

Once an important contribution to the economy, the UK's fishing industry is in decline. The total annual marine catch is typically 750,000 tonnes. Cod stocks in the North Sea, Skagerrak, Irish Sea and waters west of Scotland have been in decline for a number of years.

Forestry

Forests cover 24,000 square kilometres, accounting for nearly 10 per cent of total land use. Careful management and replanting programmes mean that forests in the UK are growing by almost 130 square kilometres per annum. Much of the forest plantations have been in the form of non-indigenous coniferous trees, such as the Norwegian Spruce, but in 2005 the government announced a change in policy in favour deciduous woodlands.

The UK typically produces around 7.5 million cubic metres of timber per annum. The UK is far from being self-sufficient in timber or wood products, importing up to 90 per cent of its requirements.

The UK is one of the largest markets for forest products in Europe, with consumption per capita remaining around the European average. Most of the internal demand for pulp and sawnwood is met by imports, although the paper industry depends on the large domestic supply of recovered paper.

Industry and manufacturing

The manufacturing industry is centred in northern England and the Midlands. Heavy industry and mining have steadily declined since the nineteenth century industrial revolution, but more rapidly in recent decades. Regions where heavy industry and manufacturing were once important typically have lower GDP per capita and higher unemployment than in the south-east. Northern England, the Midlands and Wales were dealt several blows between the late 1990s and 2002 as foreign-owned plants, notably in the vehicle manufacturing sector, closed, causing tens of thousands of redundancies. The sector's contribution to GDP has fallen in the last twenty years from over 40 per to around 25 per cent.

The government's involvement in industry has decreased since the 1980s. Policy has focused on small- and medium-sized enterprises (SMEs) and on the development of high-tech industry. The government has reformed its subsidies system to the larger industries, including the phased abolition of subsidies to ship-building operations. The long-awaited turnaround in manufacturing investment has been delayed by rising oil and commodity prices pushing up costs and putting pressure on profit margins.

Tourism

According to the World Tourism Organisation, the UK ranked sixth for international tourist arrivals in 2010, with 28.1 million visitors (France ranked first with 76.8 million); London ranked second for international visitors to cities with 14.6 million (Paris 15.1 million).

The distinct countries within the UK (England, Scotland, Wales and Northern Ireland) all have separate strategies for marketing their tourist destinations.

The direct contribution of travel and tourism to the economy has fallen from a peak in 2007 of US$66.589 billion and an indirect contribution of US$193.149 billion, to a low in 2009 of US$52.811 billion of direct and US$157.129 billion of indirect contribution at a time when the global economic crisis was affecting all aspects of the economy. Direct employment in the tourism industry has remained fairly constant since 2007, at around 3 per cent of all employment.

The prospects for the sector in 2011 were seen as positive with its direct contribution to GDP of US$57.045 billion, returning to roughly the 2005 figure (US$57.373 billion). Likewise, capital investment in the industry was forecast to grow by 1.4 per cent in 2011, having fallen by -17.9 per cent in 2010.

The London Olympics in 2012 will constitute a major boost to the economy, not only for the country but also for local communities that host events and visitors. However, it will require further investment in promotion to encourage tourists to leave London and explore more of the country.

Environment

The Carbon Reduction Commitment (CRC) came into effect on 31 March (2010), requiring around 5,000 big businesses and organisations to cut their carbon emissions, by either buying allowances for their emissions or reducing their emissions by a given amount. Those deemed most efficient will be rewarded and those considered least efficient will be penalised; a league table will be published later.

Mining

The UK is a significant producer of zinc, lead and limestone. There are also deposits of silver, copper, gold, iron ore and potash. Lead and tin production typically reach 2,000 tonnes per annum. Potash production is around 890,000 tonnes, placing UK in the top 10 producers in the world. An estimated 14.6 million tonnes of sandstone, 104.6 million tonnes of sand/gravel and 95.7 million tonnes of limestone are also produced.

Hydrocarbons

Proven oil reserves were 3.6 billion barrels in 2007, with production of 1.6 million barrels per day (bpd). Since production peaked in 1999 at 2.9 million bpd, there has been a steady fall, underscoring the rapid rundown in the UK's domestic oil supplies. All oil production is centred on offshore oil fields in the North Sea. Oil exploration and production are undertaken by independent commercial companies, of which the largest in BP. There is an extensive network of pipelines bringing oil onshore to Scotland and Northern England. Refinery capacity was 1.8 million bpd in 2007.

Proven gas reserves were 410 billion cubic metres (cum) in 2007, with production at 72.4 billion cum. Gas production peaked in 2000, but consumption has continued and the UK became a net importer of gas in 2005. Natural gas imports were 18.8 billion cum in 2007. Natural gas exploration and production, distribution and transmission are undertaken fully by private commercial companies. Two international natural gas pipelines exist between the UK and Belgium and the UK and Norway. Imports of liquefied natural gas (LNG) are delivered to two terminals, one in eastern England and the other a new site in South Wales, opened in May 2009. It is the largest LNG receiving and re-gasification plant in Europe and the world's largest diameter storage tanks, with a capacity of 15.6 million tonnes per year, capable of supplying 20 per cent of the country's natural gas demand.

In February 2011, the major energy company, Centrica, signed a US$3.2 billion contract to buy 2.4 million tonnes of LNG from Qatar over a three-year period. The gas should meet the energy needs of 2.5 million households (around 10 per cent of UK residential gas demand).

The Office of Gas and Electricity Markets (Ofgem), the official regulator of the oil and gas industries, is charged with securing gas and electricity supplies and regulating markets to allow for competition while restricting business monopolies.

Proven coal (anthracite) reserves were 155 million tonnes in 2007; production was 10.4 million tonnes of oil equivalent.

Energy

Total installed generating capacity was 80.4GW in 2008. Around 75 per cent of electricity is generated by conventional thermal power plants (around 50 per cent natural gas, 40 per cent coal, and 10 per cent oil and others), 15 per cent nuclear, 5 per cent hydropower and 2 per cent renewables. Although natural gas power stations are replacing those powered by coal the government announced in April 2009 that four new of coal-fired power stations equipped with carbon capture and storage will be built by 2020.

The energy sector is wholly privatised with private companies competing for market share. Government policy requires companies to produce 10 per cent of generated electricity by renewable sources by 2010. The integrated national grid is also linked to the French grid and the UK imports electricity during times of peak flow. Plans to link the UK grid with those of the Irish Republic and The Netherlands could be completed by 2013.

The largest single producer of power is British Energy (BE), which currently operates eight nuclear power stations, the majority of which are outmoded and due to be decommissioned by 2010. The most modern is the 1,188MW, pressurised-water reactor, Sizewell B, in eastern England. On 2009, the government announced plans to build 10 new nuclear power plants around the UK by 2018. The inclusion of nuclear power in a trinity of renewable energy and clean coal technology is expected to ensure the UK's future energy security while reducing its CO2 emissions. The UK has agreed to reduce its emission of greenhouse gases by 12.5 per cent by 2012, which the government considers can be achieved through the use of new technology and renewable energy.

The UK is reported to have Europe's best wind resources. Onshore wind farms in the UK include the 26-turbines site at Scout Moor in north-western England with a generating capacity of 65MW, which was opened in 2008. Europe's largest onshore wind farm was opened in Whitelee, Scotland, in May 2009, with a 140-turbine site, which may expand by 2010 by a further 36 turbines which would supply a total capacity of 452MW. Several large offshore wind farms are in the planning stage, including a 23-turbine wind farm in the North Sea along the Aberdeenshire Scottish coast and a 341 turbine wind farm off the Essex (south-east) coast which will, during its first phase, produce 630MW. Government policy allows individuals to erect solar panels and wind turbines where appropriate, for private use, with excess electricity sold to the national grid.

Wave power provides electricity to the national grid, from the Pelamis project off the coast of Orkney (Scotland).

On 9 November (2009), the government announced plans to build 10 new nuclear power plants around the UK by 2018. The addition of nuclear power to renewable energy and clean coal technology is expected to ensure the UK's future energy security while reducing its CO2 emissions.

Financial markets

Stock exchange

London Stock Exchange (LSE)

Commodity exchange

Liffe Connect

Banking and insurance

The UK's high street banks have been very profitable since the mid-1990s, despite being the focus of criticism. The UK banking sector is generally regarded as highly concentrated, but the rise of internet and telephone banking has put renewed pressure on high street banks. One consequence has been the decision by several leading banks to reduce the number of small branches in areas of low population density.

It is not yet clear whether a radical switch to internet banking will appeal to customers, or whether the combined (so-called 'clicks and mortar') approach will prove more successful). There is evidence that cost-cutting among British banks has given them a better chance of breaking into European markets. Likewise, to compete in a tighter market, banks are being forced into mergers and take-overs. In 2004 the Banco Santander Central Hispano successful bid for the Abbey National Bank in a £8.5bn (US$15.6 billion) deal that created the world's eighth largest and Europe's fourth largest banking group.

Independent financial centres within the UK, Jersey, Guernsey, and the Isle of Man, are adhering to a new EU tax agreement, which was introduced in 2005. They are imposing a withholding tax, up to 35 per cent, to be passed to the tax department of an EU citizen's country, while retaining the anonymity of the saver, instead of informing the relevant EU country about the amount of money in savings accounts and allowing tax to be levied from the home country.

They also supply information on tax fraud, for criminal or civil trials, and notify EU member states about additional malpractices.

In June 2011 the UK government announced that it will require all commercial banks to separate their retail and investment banking operations, so that bank branches and public savings and loans would not suffer if an investment arm were to become insolvent. Retail banks will also be required to hold more capital to underwrite their operations, greater than the new international 7 per cent minimum.

Central bank

Bank of England. Monetary policy and the Exchange Equalisation Account is managed by the Bank of England. In 1997, the government authorised the Bank of England to set interest rates independently.

Main financial centre

The City of London. Edinburgh is the nation's second largest centre.

Time

GMT (daylight saving, late March to late October, GMT plus one hours)

Geography

The UK consists of a major island (divided into England, Wales and Scotland) together with the northern part of the island of Ireland and a number of other smaller islands, including the Channel Islands, the Isle of Man (both dependencies of the Crown) and other islands which are part of the main countries constituting the UK. There are extensive, though not particularly high, mountain and hill ranges in Wales, Scotland and parts of England. The rest of the country includes flatlands (as in East Anglia) and more gently rolling agricultural land.

Hemisphere

Northern

Climate

The climate is temperate, with a reasonable amount of rainfall. Very hot summers or very cold winters, such as are found on continental Europe, are rare. The temperature rarely goes above 25 degrees Celsius (C), or much below zero, except in mountainous regions such as the Scottish highlands. Rainfall is around 75mm per month on average, although it is higher in Scotland at up to an average of 280mm per month. The wettest month is usually November.

Dress codes

In general, British dress codes follow the conventional North American or European pattern. A suit and tie for men and smart attire for women are advisable at most business occasions.

Entry requirements

Passports

Required by all and must be valid for at least six months after the intended departure date.

Visa

Visas are required by all, except nationals of North America, Australasia, Japan and other EU members. For further exceptions and advice visit www.ukvisas.gov.uk (includes application forms). All visas must be applied for before travelling.

Currency advice/regulations

The import and export of local and foreign currencies is unlimited.

Travellers cheques are widely accepted.

Customs

Personal items are duty-free. There are no duties levied on alcohol and tobacco between EU member states, providing amounts imported are for personal consumption.

Prohibited imports

Illegal drugs, pornography, offensive weapons, counterfiet goods, meat and dairy products.

Firearms require a permit, to be obtained before arrival.

Health (for visitors)

Nationals of the European Economic Area (EEA) countries and Switzerland can access reduced cost and sometimes free medical treatment using a European Health Insurance Card (EHIC) while visiting the EEA. Exceptions include nationals of the 10 countries which joined the EU in 2004 whose EHIC is not valid in Switzerland. Applications for the EHIC should be made before travelling.

Mandatory precautions

There are no mandatory vaccination certificates required, although evidence of good health may be requested if travelling from areas infected with, for instance, yellow fever.

Advisable precautions

There are no major health hazards for foreign visitors. It is recommended that visitors have up-to-date tetanus immunisation.

Hotels

Classified from one- to five-star by AA and RAC (automobile associations), with five being the best. Rating system in Northern Ireland – A star, A, B star, B, C and D. Prices usually includes a 10–15 per cent service charge, but tipping is also expected.

Credit cards

Major credit and charge cards are widely accepted. ATMs are widely available.

Public holidays (national)

Fixed dates

1 Jan (New Year's Day), 2 Jan (Scotland only), 17 Mar (St Patrick's Day) and 12 Jul (Battle of the Boyne, Northern Ireland only), 25–26 Dec (Christmas).

Holidays that fall on the weekend are taken on the following Monday/Tuesday *in lieu*.

Variable dates

Good Friday, Easter Monday, May Day Bank Holiday (first Mon in May), Spring Bank Holiday (last Mon in May) and Summer Bank Holiday (last Mon in Aug).

Scotland has an additional public holiday (first Mon in Aug).

Working hours

Banking

Mon–Fri: 0900–1500/1630. Some banks open Saturday morning and there are variations in hours in Scotland and Northern Ireland.

Business

Mon–Fri: usually 0900–1700.

Government

0900–1700 (Mon–Fri). As flexible working hours are often adopted in government departments, it is advisable to make an appointment before a visit.

Shops

Mon–Sat: generally 0900–1730. An increasing number of shops are also taking advantage of Sunday shopping hours (a maximum of 6 hours) and are open 1000–1600 or 1100–1700.

Telecommunications

Mobile/cell phones

There are 3G, 900 and 1800 GSM services throughout the country and surrounding islands.

Electricity supply

230V AC with flat three-pin plugs.

Social customs/useful tips

A reasonable degree of punctuality is required by those in business. Business cards are usually exchanged at meetings. Gifts are not usually offered to business acquaintances, although when visiting a private home it may be appropriate to take chocolates or wine.

There are few unusual or particularly strict laws. Alcoholic drinks are not allowed into some sporting fixtures, notably soccer matches. Smoking is banned in Scotland and actively discouraged in the rest of the UK in many public places and is banned on all transport services.

Security

Street crime is still much less prevalent in the UK than, for instance, the USA. The police, with a few exceptions, remain unarmed. The number of firearms used in criminal activity is relatively low, although it has increased in recent years.

Getting there

Air

National airline: There are no state-owned airlines, but BA (British Airways) is internationally recognised.

International airport/s: London Heathrow (LHR), 24km west of London is the principal UK airport.

Other satellite airports serve regional cities that provide short-haul international flights. London City (LCY) 10km east of city; London Gatwick (LGW), 46km south of London; London Stansted (STN), 55km north-east of London.

Channel Islands: Guernsey (GCI), 6km south-west of St Peter Port; Jersey (JER), 8km west of St Helier.

Northern Ireland: Belfast International (BFS), 29km north-west of city.

Scotland: Aberdeen (ABZ), 11km north-west of city; Edinburgh (EDI), 11km west of city; Glasgow (Int) (GLA), 14km west of city.

Wales: Cardiff (Int) (CWL), 19km south-west of city.

The Heathrow Express connects Heathrow Airport to west London's Paddington station. Services run, every 15 minutes, between 05.00 and 23.45. The slower London underground connects, initially via the Piccadilly Line, to all mainline stations and city centre.

An extensive airbus service operates from Heathrow airport to the city, including Victoria coach station, Russell Square and Liverpool Street Station.

Rapid train services are available from other London airports to the city centre.

Other airport/s: London Luton (LTN), 51.2km north-west of London; Birmingham International (Int) (BHX), 13km east of city; Bournemouth Int (BOH), Bristol Int (BRS), East Midlands Int (EMA), Humberside Int (HUY), Leeds Bradford Int (LBA), Liverpool John Lennon (LPL), 11km south of Liverpool; Manchester Int (MAN); Newcastle Int (NCL), 8km north-west of Newcastle; Norwich (NWI), Plymouth City (PLH), Southampton Int (SOU), Teeside Int (MME).

Airport tax: All taxes are generally paid within the price of an airline ticket, however a doubling of an environmental tax on all flights leaving the UK may mean passengers are required to pay before boarding.

Surface

Road: There are major road links to all parts of the UK and from the Republic of Ireland to Northern Ireland.

Rail: The newly restored St Pancras International railway station was opened on 6 November 2007; the station is the London terminus for Eurostar, Britain's first high speed train service to Europ. Eurostar connects Paris and Brussels via the channel tunnel, which carries foot and vehicle passengers and freight. The scheduled service operates everyday except Christmas day.

Water: Regular ferry and hovercraft connections with the continent and Ireland.

Main port/s: The main ports are London, Liverpool, Grimsby, Southampton, Milford Haven, Tees and Hartlepool, Dover, Felixstowe, Larne and Holyhead.

Getting about

National transport

Air: Most major cities are linked by regular flights to 21 main commercial airports. A number of small, 'no-frills' airlines have introduced domestic flights that can be very cheap if booked early enough, including connections to Ireland and Scotland and other regional cities.

Road: There is an extensive network of about 370,000km, including 2,800km of motorway, linking all major cities and towns. The M25 circles London as a hub linking other motorways in a network. Traffic can be heavy on these routes, especially as road haulage (wholly in the private sector) use them extensively. Major towns and cities are connected by trunk roads (A roads). Note that roads in rural areas (B roads) can be slow and winding.

Information on planning motorway journeys can be obtained through: www.trafficengland.com

Buses: Express buses between towns and cities are fully in the private sector. Urban and local buses are often still run by local authorities, although private companies operate some routes. For details of services contact www.traveline.org.uk/.

Rail: There is a network of about 18,400km, with relatively expensive first- and second-class services. All principal towns in the UK are connected by regular inter-city services.

Regional companies operate network services. It is advisable to book tickets in advance. These can be obtained on-line (www.thetrainline.com). For more information on UK train services and fare prices, contact: National Rail Enquiries on 0845 748 4950.

Water: There are public and private ferry and car ferry links between Hampshire and the Isle of Wight. Services also provide links with the isles of Scotland, subject to weather conditions, and Northern Ireland. Inshore and inland waterways, are under the control of the British Waterways Board.

City transport

Taxis: Available in all major cities and towns. Taxis can be hailed in the street, at taxi ranks or contacted by telephone. Taxis may charge extra – over and above the metered charge – depending on the number of passengers, the size of luggage items, for journeys at night and at weekends and for journeys exceeding 8km. Tipping is usually in the region of 10 per cent.

Buses, trams & metro: Extensive network linking all parts of the capital. Central London buses are the only ones still formally protected from private competition. Good bus services are also available in all other major towns. London is served by an extensive underground rail (metro) system. The new East London Line train service began in April 2010; it has regular services with connections to the Underground service. Reliable metro services also operate in Glasgow, Liverpool, Manchester (Metrolink Rapid Transit Tram) and Newcastle (Tyne and Wear Metro).

Ferry: There are passenger and car ferry services across the Thames in London and the Mersey in Liverpool.

Car hire

Widely available at airports and in main towns. All major international hire firms are represented. International driving licence or full national licence required. Driving is on the left. Speed limits: motorways/dual carriageways maximum 70mph (113kph), normal roads 40-70mph (64-97kph) (signposted) and built-up areas 30 or 40mph (48 or 64kph) (signposted). Speed cameras are in operation on motorways and other roads and imposed fines are usually forwarded as per car rental agreements.

BUSINESS DIRECTORY

The addresses listed below are a selection only. While World of Information makes every endeavour to check these addresses, we cannot guarantee that changes have not been made, especially to telephone numbers and area codes. We would welcome any corrections.

Telephone area codes

The international direct dialling (IDD) code for United Kingdom is +44, followed by area code and subscriber's number. When dialling from within the UK, add a 0 in front of the area codes below.

Aberdeen	1224	London	20
Belfast	2890 2	Manchester	161
Birmingham	121	Newcastle	191
Cambridge	1223	Nottingham	115
Cardiff	2920	Oxford	1865
Coventry	2476	Perth	1738
Dundee	1382	Plymouth	1752
Edinburgh	131	Portsmouth	2392
Exeter	1392	Sheffield	114
Glasgow	141	Southampton	2380
Liverpool	151	Swansea	1792

Useful telephone numbers

Emergency services	999
Directory enquiries (BT, fee service)	118-500
International directory enquiries (BT, fee service)	118-505

Chambers of Commerce

Birmingham Chamber of Industry and Commerce, 75 Harbourne Road, Birmingham B15 3DH (tel: 454-6171; fax: 455-8670; email: info@birminghamchamber.org.uk).

British Chambers of Commerce, 50 Broadway, St James Park, London SW1H 0RG (tel: 7152-4046; fax: 7565-2049).

Cardiff Chamber of Commerce, Trade and Industry, St David's House East, Wood Street, Cardiff CF10 1ES (tel: 2034-8280; fax: 2037-7653; email: enquiries@cardiffchamber.co.uk).

Edinburgh Chamber of Commerce, 27 Melville Street, Edinburgh EH3 7JF (tel: 477-7000; fax: 477-7002; email: information@ecce.org).

Leeds Chamber of Commerce, 102 Wellington Street, Leeds LS1 4LT (tel: 0113-247-0000; fax: 0113-247-111; email: info@leedschamber.co.uk).

London Chamber of Commerce and Industry, 33 Queen Street, London EC4R 1AP (tel: 7248-4444; fax: 7489-0391; email: lc@londonchamber.co.uk).

Manchester Chamber of Commerce and Industry, Churchgate House, 56 Oxford Street, Manchester M60 7HJ (tel: 237-4102; fax: 237-3277; email: info@mcci.org.uk).

Sheffield Chamber of Commerce and Industry, Albion House, Savile Street, Sheffield S4 7UD (tel: (0)114-201-8888; fax: (0)114-272-0950; email: info@scci.org.uk).

Banking

Abbey National, 2 Triton Square, Regent's Place, London NW1 3AN (tel: 7612-4000; fax: 7612-4230; email: investor@abbeynational.com).

Bank of Scotland, The Mound, Edinburgh EH1 1YZ (tel: 470-7777; fax: 243-5640).

Barclays Bank, 54 Lombard Street, London EC3P 3AH (tel: 7699-5000; fax: 7699-2680).

British Bankers' Association, Pinners Hall, 105-108 Old Broad Street London EC2N 1EX (tel: 7216-8800; fax: 7216-8811).

Chartered Institute of Bankers in Scotland, Drumsheugh House, 38b Drumsheugh Gardens, Edinburgh EH3 7SW (tel: 473-7777; fax:473-7788; email: info@ciobs.org.uk).

Clydesdale Bank, 30 St Vincent Place, Glasgow G1 2HL (tel: 248-7070; fax: 223-2559).

Halifax Plc, Trinity Road, Halifax HX1 2RG (tel: 01422-333-333; fax: 01422-391-777).

HSBC, 10 Lower Thames Street, London EC3R 6AE (tel: 7260-0500; fax: 7260-0501).

Lloyds TSB, 71 Lombard Street, London EC3P 3BS (tel: 7626-1500; fax: 7356-1731).

National Westminster Bank, 135 Bishopsgate, London EC2M 3UR (tel: 7375-5000; fax: 7375-5050).

Royal Bank of Scotland, 36 St Andrew Square, Edinburgh EH2 2YB (tel: 556-8555; fax: 557-6565).

Central bank
Bank of England, Threadneedle Street, London EC2R 8AH (tel: 7601-4444; fax: 7601-5460; internet: www.bankofengland.co.uk).

Stock exchange
London Stock Exchange, Old Broad Street, London EC2N 1HP (tel: 7797-1000; email: enquiries@londonstockexchange.com; www.londonstockexchange.com)

Stock exchange 2
LIFFE (London International Financial Futures and Options Exchange): www.euronext.com

Commodity exchange
Liffe Connect: www.nyse.com/nyseeuronext

Commodity exchange 2
European Climate Exchange (ECX): www.europeanclimateexchange.com

Travel information
Aberdeen Airport, Dyce, Aberdeen AB21 7DU (tel: 1224-722-331; fax: 1224-775-845; email: glal@baa.com).

Belfast International Airport, Aldergrove, Belfast BT 29 4AB (tel: 448-4848; fax: 448-4849; email: info.desk@bial.co.uk).

Birmingham International Airport, Birmingham B26 3QJ (tel: 767-5511; fax: 782-8802; email: custsrvs@bhx.co.uk).

BA, Waterside, PO Box 365, Harmondsworth, Middlesex (tel: 8738-5100; fax: 8738-9838).

Cardiff International Airport, Rhoose CF62 3BD (tel: 1446-711-111; fax: 1446-711-675; email: info@cial.co.uk).

Edinburgh Airport, Edinburgh EH12 9DN (tel: 333-1000; fax: 344 3470; email: glal@baa.com).

Gatwick Airport, West Sussex RH6 0NP (tel: 0870-000-2468; fax: 1293-503-794; email: gatwick_feedback@baa.com).

Glasgow Airport, Paisley, Renfrewshire PA3 2SW (tel: 887-1111; fax: 848-4769; email: glal@baa.com).

Heathrow Airport, 234 Bath Road, Harlington, Middlesex UB3 5AP (tel: 0870-0000-123; fax: 8745-4290; email: lhr1feedback@baa.com).

London City Airport, Royal Docks, London, E16 2PX (customer services tel: 7646-0088; internet: www.londoncityairport.com).

Manchester Airport, Manchester M90 1QX (tel: 489-3000; fax: 489-3813; email: info@manchesterairport.co.uk).

Northern Ireland Tourist Board, 59 North Street, Belfast BT1 1NB (tel: 231-221; fax: 240-960; email: info@nitb.com).

Passport Office, Globe House, 89 Ecclestone Square, London SW1V 1PN (tel: 0870-521-0410; fax: 7271-8403; email: london@ukpa.gov.uk).

Glasgow Prestwick International Airport, Aviation, Prestwick, Ayrshire KA9m 2PL (tel: 1292-511-000; fax: 1292-511-010; email: info@gpia.co.uk).

Stansted Airport, Essex CM24 1QW (tel: 0870-0000-303; fax: 1279-662-066; email: stansted_feedback@baa.com).

VisitScotland, 23 Ravelston Terrace, Edinburgh EH4 3TP (tel: 332-2433; fax: 343-1513; email: info@visitscotland.com).

Wales Tourist Board, Brunel House, 2 Fitzalan Road, Cardiff CF24 0UY (tel: 499-909; fax: 485-031; email: info@visitwales.com).

Ministry of tourism
Department of Culture, Media and Sport, 2-4 Cockspur Street, London SW1Y 5DH (tel: 7211 6200; email: enquiries@culture.gov.uk)

National tourist organisation offices
VisitBritain, Thames Tower, Blacks Road, Hammersmith, London W6 9EL (tel: 8563-3000; fax: 8563-3234; email: comments@englishtourism.org.uk).

Ministries
Cabinet Office, 70 Whitehall, London SW1A 2AS (tel: 7270-1234).

Department of Culture, Media and Sport, 2-4 Cockspur Street, London SW1Y 5DH (tel: 7211-6000; e-mail: enquiries@culture.gov.uk)

Department of Education and Skills, Sanctuary Building, Great Smith Street, London SW1P 3BT (tel: 0870-000-2288; fax: 01928-79-4248; e-mail: info@dfes.gov.uk).

Department of Environment, Food and Rural Affairs, Nobel House, 17 Smith Square, London SW1P 3JR (tel: 7238-6000; fax: 7238-6591).

Department of Health, Richmond House, 79 Whitehall, London SW1A 2NS (tel: 7210-4850; e-mail: dhmail@doh.gsi.gov.uk).

Department of International Development, 94 Victoria Street, London SW1E 5JL (tel: 7917-7000; fax: 7917-0019; e-mail: enquiry@dfid.gov.uk).

Department of Trade and Industry, 1 Victoria Street, London SW1H 0ET (tel: 7215-5000; e-mail: dti.enquiries@dti.gsi.gov.uk).

Department of Transport, Local Government and Regions, Eland House, Bressenden Place, London SW1E 5DU (tel: 7944-3000).

Department of Work and Pensions, Richmond House, 79 Whitehall, London SW1A 2NS (tel: 7238-0800; fax: 238-0763; peo@dwp.gsi.gov.uk).

Foreign and Commonwealth Office, King Charles Street, London SW1A 2AH (tel: 7270-1500).

Home Office, 50 Queen Annes Gate, London SW1H 9AT (tel: 7273-4000; fax: 7273-2065; e-mail: public.enquiries@homeoffice.gti.gov.uk).

Lord Chancellor's Department, Selborne House, 54-60 Victoria Street, London SW1E 6QW (tel: 7210-8500; e-mail: general.enquiries.@lcdhq.gsi.gov.uk).

Ministry of Defence, Main Building, Horse Guards Avenue, London SW1A 2HB (tel: 0870-607-4455).

Northern Ireland Office, 11 Millbank, London SW1P 4PN (tel: 7210-3000; fax: 7210-0249; e-mail: press.nio@nics.gov.uk).

Prime Ministers Office, 10 Downing Street, London SW1A 2AA (tel: 7270-3000).

Scotland Office, Dover House, London SW1A 2AU (tel: 7270-6754; fax: 7270-6812; e-mail: scottish.secretary@scotland.gov.uk).

Treasury, Parliament Street, London SW1P 3AG (tel: 7270-4558; fax: 7270-5244; e-mail: public.enquiries@hm-treasury.gov.uk).

Wales Office, Gwydyr House, London SW1A 2ER (e-mail: wales.office@wales.gsi.gov.uk).

Other useful addresses
Aberdeen Exhibition and Conference Centre, Bridge of Don, Aberdeen (tel: 1224-824-824; fax:1224-825-276; email: aecc@aecc.co.uk).

Advertising Standards Authority, 2 Torrington Place, London WC1E 7HW (tel: 7580-5555; fax: 7631-3051; email: inquiries@asa.org.uk).

BBC Television, Television Centre, Wood Lane, London W12 7RJ (tel: 8743-8000; fax: 8749-7520; email: info@bbc.co.uk).

British Council, 10 Spring Gardens, London SW1A 2BN (tel: 7930-8466; fax: 7389-6347; email: general.enquiries@britishcouncil.org).

British Embassy (USA), 3100 Massachusetts Avenue, NW, Washington DC 20008 (tel: (+1-202) 588-7800; fax: (+1-202) 5588-7870).

British Sky Broadcasting Group (BSkyB), 6 Centaurs Business Park, Grant Way, Isleworth TW7 5QD (tel: 7705-3000; fax: 7705-3060).

British Waterways Board, Willow Grange, Church Road, Watford WD17 4QA (tel: 01923-201-120; email: enquiries.hq@britishwaterways.co.uk).

Chartered Institute of Marketing, Moor Hall, Cookham, Maidenhead, Berkshire SL6 9QH (tel: 1628-427-500; fax: 1628-427-499; email: info@cim.co.uk).

Confederation of British Industry (CBI), Centre Point, 103 New Oxford Street, London WC1A 1DU (tel: 7395-8247; fax: 7240-1578; email: enquiry.desk@cbi.org.uk).

Crown Estate, 16 Carlton House Terrace, London SW1Y 5AH (tel: 7210-4377; fax: 7210-4236; email: pr@crownestate.co.uk).

Customs and Excise, New King's Beam House, 22 Upper Ground, London SE1 9PJ (tel: 7620-1313; fax: 7865-4975; email: enquiries.lon@hmce.gsi.gov.uk).

Design Council, 34 Bow Street, London WC2E 7DL (tel: 7420-5200; fax: 7420-5300; email: info@designcouncil.org.uk).

Guild of Registered Tourist Guides, The Guild House, 52d Borough High Street, London SE1 1XN (tel: 7403-1115; fax: 7378-1705; email: guild@blue-badge.org.uk).

Independent Television News (ITN), 200 Gray's Inn Road, London WC1X 8HF (tel: 7833-3000; fax: 7430-4868; email: info@itn.co.uk).

Institute of Export, Export House, Minerva Business Park, Lynch Wood, Peterborough PE2 6FT (tel: 1733-404-400; fax: 1733-404-444; email: institute@export.org.uk).

Institute of Linguists, Saxon House, 48 Southwark Street, London SE1 1UN (tel: 7940-3100; fax: 7940-3101; email: info@iol.org.uk).

ITV Network Centre, 200 Gray's Inn Road, London WC1X 8HF (tel: 7843-8000; fax: 7843-8158; email: info@itv.co.uk).

Kings Hall Exhibition and Conference Centre, Balmoral, Belfast (tel: 028-9066-5225; fax: 028-9066-1264; email: info@kingshall.co.uk).

National Exhibition Centre, Birmingham B40 1NT (tel: 780-4141; fax: 780-2517; email: centre-exhibitions@necgroup.co.uk).

Office for National Statistics, 1 Drummond Gate, London SW1V 2QQ (tel: 7233-9233; fax: 7533-6262; email: info@statistics.gov.uk).

Press Complaints Commission, 1 Salisbury Square, London EC4Y 8JB (tel: 7353-1248; fax: 7353-8355; email: pcc@pcc.org.uk).

Scottish Exhibition and Conference Centre, Exhibition Way, Fenniston Street, Glasgow G3 8YW (tel: 248-3000; fax: 226-3423; email: info@secc.co.uk).

Trades Union Congress (TUC), Congress House, 23-28 Great Russell Street, London WC1B 3LS (tel: 7636-4030; fax: 7636-0632; email: info@tuc.org.uk).

National news agency: PA Group, 292 Vauxhall Bridge Road, London SE1V 1AE (tel: 120-3200; fax: 120-3201; internet: www.thepagroup.com).

Internet sites

Bank of England: www.bankofengland.co.uk

British Airways: www.british-airways.com

British Chambers of Commerce: www.britishchambers.org.uk/internet_home_page.htm

Confederation of British Industry: www.cbi.org.uk

Department of Trade and Industry: www.dti.gov.uk

Eurostar Train: www.eurostar.com

Kelly's Directory (search engine for UK industry): www.kellys.reedinfo.co.uk

UK export (database of British exporters): www.export.co.uk

UK Online (UK government gateway): www.ukonline.gov.uk

UK trade information: www.ukinfo.com

UK yellow pages: www.yell.co.uk

United States of America

KEY FACTS

Official name: United States of America

Head of State: President Barack Hussein Obama (took office 20 Jan 2009)

Head of government: President Barack Obama

Ruling party: Democratic Party (from Nov 2009)

Area: 9,300,000 square km

Population: 308.75 million (2010; census figure)

Capital: Washington DC

Official language: There is no official language declared in the constitution. English is the *de facto* working language and Spanish is the second, widely spoken, unofficial language.

Currency: US dollar (US$) = 100 cents

Exchange rate: US$1.00 per US$ US$0.78 per euro (Aug 2010)

GDP per capita: US$47,284 (2010)

GDP real growth: 2.90% (2010)

GDP: US$14,657.80 billion (2010)

Labour force: 153.89 million (2010)

Unemployment: 9.60% (2010)

Inflation: 1.60% (2010)

Oil production: 7.51 million bpd (2010)

Balance of trade: -US$642.36 billion (2010)

Foreign debt: US$13,773.00 billion (2009)

In the vast household that is the United States of America (US), 2011 saw the realisation that the parents – the Democratic and Republican parties – could no longer agree on virtually anything. As the country continued to face almost the most intractable problems created by a flatlining economy, the unique public/private partnership that had driven US growth and prosperity in the post Second World War years seemed to have failed. Purpose seemed to have been replaced by pettiness, responsibility by rejection.

Cool to plain cold

By mid-2010 the euphoria that had characterised the opening months of the Obama Presidency had worn a little thin. Not that the US' first black president had failed to introduce the reforms that he had promised the electorate. On the contrary; the most obvious change was the restoration of the US' international dignity, recovering some, but not all, the country's battered moral authority. But the euphoria that had greeted a 'cool' President Obama's election had switched to disappointment as he appeared to be more cold than cool. In 2008, their expectations having been raised, many Democrat voters had thought they were electing another Bill Clinton: instead, as one commentator noted, 'they got an American Gordon Brown (the former British prime minister) – but minus the emotion'. In the midst of crisis, come what may, President Obama appeared to show a calm serenity, described by another observer as 'a stereotyped coolness. Too much Hamlet, not enough Henry IV.' Although Obama had often quoted Martin Luther King's 'fierce urgency of now' speech, in office he had seemed to show neither fierceness nor urgency. Indifference and indecision seemed, too often, to be the case. Certainly, whenever a stand-off with his Republican adversaries loomed large, Obama always seemed to blink first. Obama, said one commentator, 'goes into negotiations already in reverse, not prepared to fight'. The coolness that had once been an asset in financial crises was now simply perceived as indifference. Worse, in the case of the banking crisis, the president had not demanded an investigation. Instead, he had given the banking community a 'get out of jail free' card.

Despair becomes anger

What had started off as a sense of despair among much of the US middle class, had slowly become a sense of anger fuelled by a sense that their president simply didn't connect, that – with the sole exception of health legislation – their president wasn't fighting for them. This was an unfounded criticism. Even die-hard Republicans had to accept that in two years of office, the Obama administration had accomplished a considerable amount. The same Republicans probably chose to overlook the fact that the stimulus package they so derided was in fact introduced by the (Republican) Bush administration.

In October 2008 the Emergency Stabilisation Act, which in turn laid the foundation of the Troubled Assets Relief Programme (TARP) came into law. In the manner of miniature Russian Babushka dolls, TARP allowed President Obama in February 2009 to get his American Recovery and Re-Investment Act on to the statute book. Republican objections to the stimulus package needed to ignore the fact that, by mid-2010, on the economic front, things could have been a great deal worse. Although the economy's performance was less than stellar, as 2010 wore on, it did look as though the feared progression from recession to depression had been avoided.

But the climate of pessimism and gloom made it relatively easy for politicians to harness this negative political energy in the guise of the Tea Party movement, headed up by the Republican Party's former vice presidential candidate, Sarah Palin. The name 'Tea Party' was a reference to the Boston Tea Party, a seminal independence protest in 1773 centred on the platform of 'no representation without representation'. Mrs Palin was described as speaking for a 'vast congregation of the mystified and fearful'. Initially the Republican establishment welcomed this development and the renewed political energy that came with it. But rather in the manner of the Sorcerer's Apprentice, as

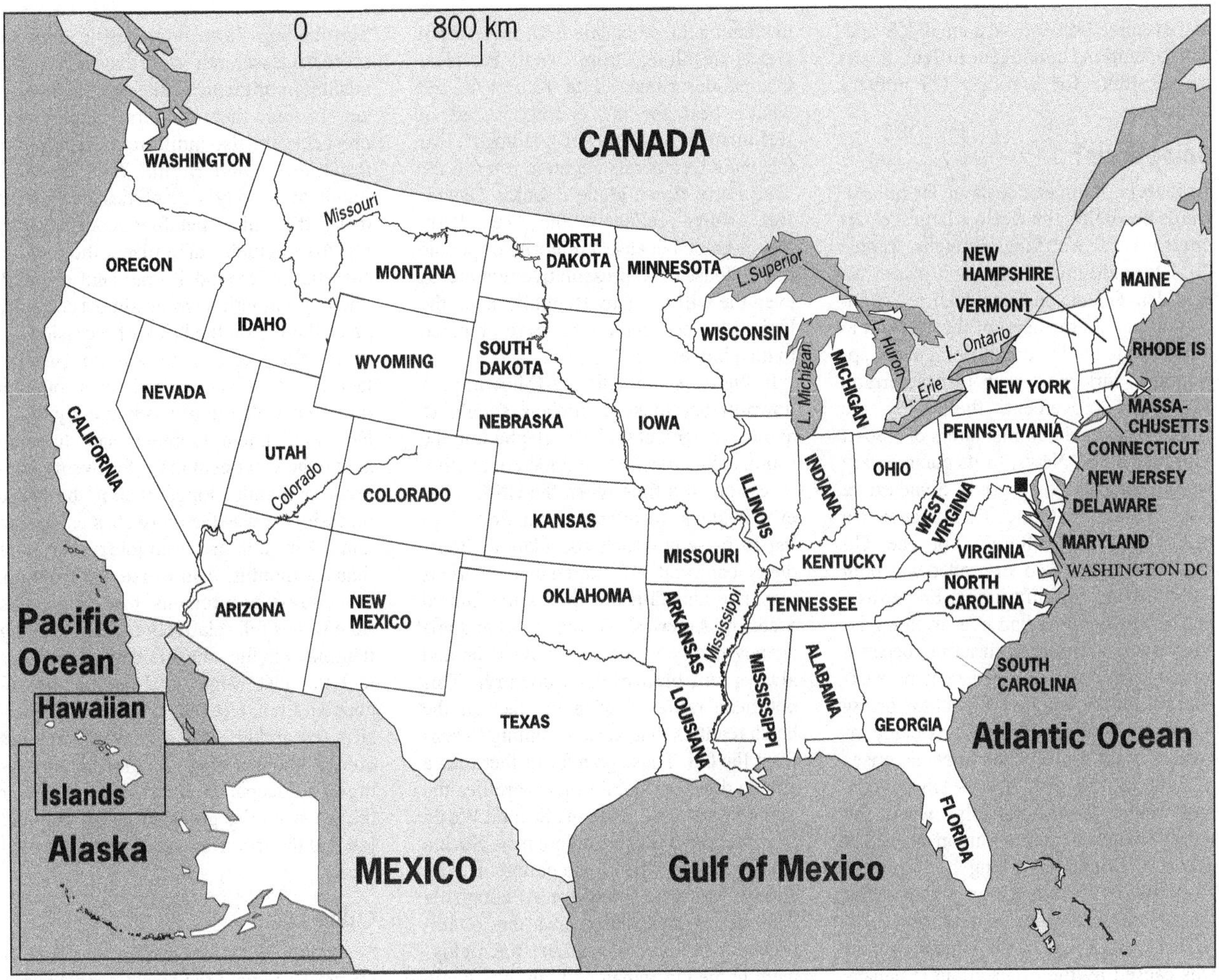

the Tea Party movement grew, it also attracted what one commentator somewhat exaggeratedly described as 'an incoherent typhoon of xenophobic lusts and recriminatory pathologies, already co-opted by political manipulators.' What was clear was that, of some concern for the Republican Party in the run-up to the mid-term elections, the Tea Party movement's opposition to what was described as 'big' government, brought the Grand Old Party (GOP) into disfavour as well. Nowhere was this more apparent than in Delaware where in the Republican election primary the veteran incumbent candidate, nine-term US Representative and former state governor, Mike Castle, lost out to the apparently simplistic and certainly naïve Christine O'Donnell.

Iraq – the end of the road (nearly)

In October 2011 President Obama announced to journalists in the White House briefing room that 'as promised, the rest of our troops in Iraq will come home by the end of the year – after nearly nine years, America's war in Iraq will be over.' The US had tried to extend the military presence of their troops past 31 December. However, according to Max Boot, a senior fellow in national security studies at the United States Council on Foreign Relations writing in the New York based *Wall Street Journal*, the deal breaker was the Iraqis refusal to grant legal immunity for US troops if they are accused of breaking Iraq's laws. Prime Minister Nouri al Maliki was quoted as stating that 'When the Americans asked for immunity, the Iraqi side answered that it was not possible.' So it seemed, the withdrawal was under way.

Criticisms of President Obama's handling of the withdrawal agreement suggested that, not for the first time, the President's aloofness had got the better of him. According to Mr Boot, the same reservations over immunity had loomed in 2008 during the negotiation of what was to be the last Status of Forces Agreement (SFA). At the time there were many more US personnel in Iraq – almost 150,000, compared with less than 50,000 in 2011. It seemed that Mr Bush had spoken on a weekly basis with Mr Maliki by video teleconference. Mr Obama had not spoken with Mr Maliki for months before calling him in late October 2011 to announce the end of negotiations. Surprisingly, Mr Boot also claimed that Mr Obama and his senior aides did not even bother to meet with Iraqi officials at the United Nations General Assembly in September 2011. President Obama's officials had waited until mid-2011 before opening talks on renewing the Status of Forces Agreement, a matter of months before US troops would have to start closing their remaining bases to be able to pull out by the end of the year. The withdrawal from Iraq was thought to be the largest military logistical operation carried out by the US since the Second World War. Mr Boot also pointed out that while the SFA could authorise joint exercises between the two countries and even the presence of a small US Special Operations contingent in Iraq, it was no substitute for a robust US military presence.

Going down?

As if seeing China creep up on the rails towards becoming the world's largest economy wasn't worrying enough, August 2011 brought more doom and gloom for President Obama and a beleaguered Democrat Party. At the heart of the decision to down-grade the US credit rating there appeared to lurk more than just the erratic Tea Party movement, fuelled by the one-dimensional commentators of Rupert Murdoch's Fox News. In its commentary on the August down-grade Standard & Poor's (S&P) made specific reference to a 'toxic political culture'. For the US credit-rating to be down-graded was both embarrassing and infuriating. Embarrassing because no-one had ever even envisaged such a thing; infuriating because although the down-grade made it more expensive for the US government to borrow money, the safe haven sought by many investors in the midst of the financial crises of 2008/09 and 2011 was – US government debt. Unquestionably, when the world's financial markets are in chaos, US Treasury Bonds have long been the answer. In 2011 the question was whether that would continue to be the case.

That a large part of the embarrassment was caused by the often infantile behaviour of US politicians did not seem to trouble very many. Following the down-grade both Republicans and Democrats resorted to blaming the other side for a sequence of events resulting from what President Obama described as 'a refusal to put what's best for the country ahead of self-interest or party or ideology'. Mr Obama's Democrats began to refer to the 'Tea Party down-grade'; senior Senator John Kerry called it the 'Tea Party Down-grade because a minority of people in the House of Representatives countered even the will of many Republicans in the United States Senate who were prepared to do a bigger deal.'

In the days immediately following the down-grade, most politicians sought to avoid eye contact with the elephant in the room, the increasing likelihood of another recession, at a time when the US had not even begun to recover from the first. Hoping to pre-empt such speculation, President Obama gallantly noted that: 'Markets may rise and fall, but this is the United States of America. No matter what some agency may say, we've always been and always will be a triple-A country.' This optimism rather flew in the face of the harsh realities that were beginning to confront the US. These go a lot further than a simple down-grade. At their core lies the myth, perpetrated since the Second World War that the US is a rich country. Such a message does little to encourage a work ethic, or to create enterprise. Although the S&P down-grade came on a day of improved employment figures, unemployment in the US remained high. It is likely to remain that way as long as gross domestic product (GDP) growth remains at its mid-2011 figure of less than one per cent.

KEY INDICATORS — United States of America

	Unit	2006	2007	2008	2009	2010
Population	m	298.93	301.90	304.72	307.37	308.75
Gross domestic product (GDP)	US$bn	13,194.7	13,843.8	14,264.6	14,256.3	14,657.8
GDP per capita	US$	44,118	45,845	46,859	46,381	47,284
GDP real growth	%	2.8	1.9	-0.3	-3.5	3.0
Inflation	%	3.2	2.8	3.8	-0.3	1.6
Unemployment	%	4.6	4.6	5.8	9.3	9.6
Oil output	'000 bpd	6,871.0	6,879.0	6,736.0	7,196.0	7,513.0
Natural gas output	bn cum	524.1	54.6	582.2	69.3	611.0
Coal output	mtoe	595.1	573.7	596.9	539.9	552.2
Exports (fob) (goods)	US$m	1,026,850	1,153,270	1,295,390	1,072,930	1,293,220
Imports (fob) (goods)	US$m	1,861,410	1,964,590	2,112,230	1,576,510	1,935,580
Balance of trade	US$m	-834,550	-811,330	-816,840	-503,580	-470,960
Current account	US$m	-811,483	-738,636	-673,266	-378,430	-470,244
Total reserves minus gold	US$m	54,850	59,520	66,610	119,720	121,390
Foreign exchange	US$m	40,940	45,800	49,580	261,500	261,500

Surrounding these high profile data are scores of lesser indicators that suggest that business confidence, like the stock market, is low, that mid-term employment prospects are also indifferent. Reported in the *International Herald Tribune*, Mark Zandi of Moody's Analytics considered that if the major spending cuts envisaged for 2013 actually take place, they would cost the US around 1.5 per cent of GDP. Such a contraction would almost certainly place the US on the brink of recession.

The US predicament was not just the fact that there were an estimated fourteen million people out of work in early 2011. Nor that unemployment had hovered above the 9 per cent mark for twenty consecutive months, longer than in the 1980s recession. It was the more chastening fact that 6.4 million had been jobless for more than six months. And worse was to come. In contrast to previous recessions, this time wages fell relatively rapidly, making it unlikely in the view of many economists that the lost wage levels would be recouped soon, if ever. Columbia University researcher Till von Wachter was quoted in the *Wall Street Journal* as saying 'The deeper the recession, the lower the wage you're going to get in the next job and the lower the quality of your next job.'

China

So, back to the Chinese question. In 2011 US relations with the world's most populous country had entered a phase of what airline pilots would term 'severe turbulence.' As the largest holder of US Treasury notes – i e US debt – China has sought guarantees that Washington will probably be unable to meet. The risk for the US is the possibility that China seeks to spread its risk, reducing its exposure to dollars by diversifying into the debt of other countries.

Not that this was a theme new to US political thinking. Frank Capra's 1939 melodramatic film *Meet John Doe* was released at a time when the US was barely emerging from the depression of the 1930s. The fictitious John Doe in the film (the creation of a newspaper columnist played by Barbara Stanwyck) resorts to threats of public suicide to protest about the cruelty and lack of fairness of US society. Touching a raw nerve of society, the protests lead to the creation of John Doe clubs all over the US. This phenomenon was uncannily echoed in 2010 by the proliferation of so-called '9/12' clubs and related groups such as 'Liberty Central', the avowedly 'non-partisan' but anti-big government, Tea Party-supporting organisation founded by the wife of no less than a Supreme Court Justice, Clarence Thomas, Virginia 'Ginni' Thomas.

Tea parties

The common denominator of the Tea Party movement seemed to be one of resentment and distrust, animated by a media-fed desire to demonstrate that Middle America was not as prejudiced, bigoted and lacking in political awareness as what they described as 'East Coast Media' would have it. What was unavoidable was what Jonathan Raban described in the UK's *Guardian* as an 'enormous gulf of trust and understanding had opened up between the Obama administration and an unremarkable bunch of ordinary voters.' Mr Raban attributed much of the problem to the administration's failure to communicate. Astonishingly, given his eloquence during his campaign for the presidency, Mr Obama has been lamentably inarticulate in explaining his policies to the electorate. Unheralded was the fact that TARP was due to end at the beginning of October 2010. Despite Republican posturing about this 'socialist' measure, to the neutral observer it appeared to have had considerable success. Most of the money had been repaid and the hard-hit US taxpayer was likely to see a profit on the exercise before long. But US electorates, like any other, have very short memories. Most voters, whether in the Mid-West or wherever, had by mid-2010 probably forgotten that the much derided Emergency Stabilisation Act (which was the enabling legislation for TARP), was signed into law by the Bush Administration early in October 2008, well before the presidential elections.

Perry. Perry who?

Governor 'Rick' Perry of Texas emerged as one of the front runners for the Republican Party's nomination as presidential candidate. This was to cause not only Democats, but also moderate Republicans some concern. Governor Perry claimed that under his leadership Texas had bucked the country's unemployment trend. It later emerged that this was not quite true. The jobs that had been created appeared to be on low salaries and often given to illegal immigrants. Seventeen per cent of Texas children did not have any form of health insurance, placing the state next to last in the national rankings. However successful the state's economy, it ran up a budget deficit of US$27 billion. Governor Perry's riposte was to cut expenditure on both education and health, rather than to use reserve funds or raise some taxes. Governor Perry also placed himself firmly on the side of those refusing to accept that human behaviour might be contributing to global warming. The state's record on penal reform was less than encouraging. Over a period of almost 11 years Texas carried out 234 death penalties. In terms characteristic of Texan bluntness, Governor Perry had also labelled President Obama a 'socialist'.

Ask the man in the street in Peoria what the Fourteenth Amendment to the Constitution was all about and chances are – or at least were – that you'd be met with a blank stare. The first sentence of the amendment in question reads: 'The validity of the public debt of the United States, authorised by law, including debts incurred for payment of pensions and bounties for services in suppressing insurrection or rebellion, shall not be questioned.'

Who is in charge here?

In many respects the US can be thankful not only that its Constitution is written down (countries such as the UK lack this advantage) but also that it is written down so clearly. Much of this is simply common sense, as is the case with the Fourteenth Amendment. The federal budget, its deficit or its surplus, are the consequences of laws approved and enacted by Congress. Thus, if a situation arises whereby the government is no longer able to pay its bills, or pay them on time, the President of the US risks being in breach of his constitutional duty to see that laws are properly enacted. In principle, the Fourteenth Amendment allows the President to raise the debt limit rather than face a damaging default. In mid-2011 the fiscal options open to the President began to look a little limited. So much so, that already in May 2011, the secretary of the treasury, Timothy Geithner drew the attention of analysts and observers to the provisions of the Fourteenth Amendment.

Emerging from behind closed doors sessions with unnamed advisers, Mr Obama appeared to have discounted invoking the Fourteenth Amendment, despite support for the idea from luminaries such as former President Bill Clinton. Thus it was that, to the dismay of most Democrats, the final dénouement of the budget showdown was held by Republicans, as well as by many Democrats, to be a government rout. Mr Obama's intellectual grasp of his government's biggest problem was found to be lacking. The biggest single economic problem facing the US is not so much its deficit, more the lack of domestic (not to mention export) demand. Until unemployment starts to fall and those so employed begin to pay taxes again, the deficit is likely to remain high.

If dismay was the overriding Democrat response, something resembling lunacy characterised Tea Party dominated Republican Party, which flushed with its success in the debt-limit negotiations, sought to introduce legislation in both Congress and the Senate aimed at securing a balanced budget every year. This requirement would hold good regardless of prevailing economic conditions. On top of this, annual government spending was to be limited to 18 per cent of the preceding year's GDP. That the GOP risked taking leave of its senses seemed to be suggested by the fact that the cap could only be increased by a two-thirds 'super majority' of both houses of government. That this was a greater majority than that needed to amend the Constitution itself seemed to be lost on the Tea Party-lovers.

The game changes

If the Republicans needed to take a reality check, many Americans were finding reality hard to ignore. The depressing July 2011 figures continued to show that some fourteen million were out of a job and that almost half of these had been unemployed for over six months. In the wider perspective, things looked just as depressing. Of the Organisation for Economic Co-operation and Development (OECD) members, only Mexico, Spain, Turkey and (surprisingly) New Zealand had higher school dropout rates than the US. Not good reading in the land of opportunity. In fact opportunity was the one thing missing in the mix, alongside prosperity and contentment. But if opportunity had begun to fall by the wayside, so too had equality. Nobel Laureate Joseph Stiglitz was on record as observing that 'The top 1 per cent of Americans now take in roughly one fourth of America's total income every year. In terms of wealth rather than income the top 1 per cent now controls 40 per cent of the total.' Also in 2011, in their excellent book *That Used to be Us* the academics Friedman and Mandelbaum wrote that 'thirty years ago ten per cent of California's general revenue fund went to higher education and 3 per cent to prisons. Today nearly eleven per cent goes to prisons and 8 per cent to higher education.'

It's still the economy...

In 2011 GDP continued to stagnate, unsurprisingly given Washington's increased fixation on deficit reduction. The agreement reached with the Republicans called for a massive reduction of two trillion dollars (your correspondent chooses to spell this out rather than express it numerically for fear of including a zero too many) in government spending over a decade. The cuts came at a time when Federal tax revenues had dropped as low as fifteen per cent of GDP, the lowest level for some sixty years. A background note issued by S&P at the time of the ratings down-grade did not mince its words: 'The fiscal consolidation plan that Congress and the Administration recently agreed to falls short of what, in our view, would be necessary to stabilise the government's medium-term debt dynamics.' The down-grade was more than a shot across the Administration's bows; it represented a cry not so much of despair but of confusion from a financial community uncertain about who was running the country.

... and the economy languishes

In the view of the International Monetary Fund (IMF) the US economy continues to recover from its worst financial crisis since the Great Depression, aided by supportive macro-economic policies. Monetary policy remains highly accommodative, with policy rates near zero and a significantly expanded Federal Reserve balance sheet. Fiscal policy provided a sizable stimulus to demand over 2009–10, but the fiscal impulse for the current fiscal year is likely to be about zero. The financial system continues to strengthen, although lending conditions remain tight for some segments. Household balance-sheet repair has continued amidst still declining house prices and high unemployment rates, weighing on consumption, while construction activity remains depressed. Corporate spending and hiring remain relatively weak, despite record-high profit growth and easy financing conditions for large firms. GDP growth slowed from 2.75 per cent in the second half of 2010 to just under 2 per cent in the first half of 2011, reflecting *inter alia* the impact of higher oil prices and a number of transient factors. The US current account deficit has moved broadly sideways as higher oil prices have offset the effects of strong external demand and the dollar's depreciation. Overall, the slow pace of the recovery is consistent with past international experience in the aftermath of housing and financial crises.

In the view of the IMF the outlook is for continued albeit modest growth. With sluggish private domestic demand, economic slack remains large: in particular, the unemployment rate has declined only modestly from its recent peak. As a result, inflation pressures will likely remain contained, despite the recent firming in core inflation. Risks are elevated and tilted to the downside, especially from the housing market and possible global financial market disruptions from the sovereign crisis in Europe.

On the policy front, the administration and Congressional policymakers have presented medium-term fiscal adjustment proposals and current negotiations suggest that fiscal policy is set to enter a consolidation phase to address its unsustainable trajectory. The Federal Reserve has indicated that economic conditions are likely to warrant an accommodative monetary policy stance for an extended period and any future policy moves would depend on incoming data, including on inflation expectations.

On the financial sector front, the official financial support deployed during the crisis is being wound down and the legislated reform of financial supervision and regulation is being implemented. In particular, the Financial Stability Oversight Committee (FSOC) has ramped up operations and numerous rules are being promulgated. However, many issues remain to be worked out, notably in areas involving systemically important financial institutions and international co-ordination.

The IMF concluded by observing that the US financial system continued to heal, but remained vulnerable to key risks, not least the turmoil in European financial markets and the implications of the US sovereign rating down-grading on higher interest rates on federal debt, both with significant implications for liquidity. Crucial themes are 'dealing with systemically important financial institutions.'

Healthcare legislation – yes or no?

The late-2011 decision by the Supreme Court to hear arguments on a central part of the Obama administration's signature health care legislation looked certain to have significant political implications for President Obama in the 2012 re-election year. The hearing would, the administration hoped, clear up once and for all the legislation's constitutional acceptability. The 2012 hearing would focus on an aspect of the legislation entitled the 'individual mandate' which was due to be implemented by 2014 and required all American citizens to have health insurance or pay a fine. The legislation's largely right-wing, Republican challengers claimed that the mandate, which had already been rejected by a lower court, was unconstitutional. The adjectives used to describe the provision, fuelled by the more vociferous right-wing broadcast media, ran the gamut of political unacceptability from 'socialist' to even 'communist'. The administration and its advisors appeared confident that the legislation would be upheld as constitutional.

For the healthcare legislation, officially known as the Affordable Care Act, to be declared unconstitutional by the Supreme Court in the run-up period to a presidential election would be something of a body-blow for President Obama. As the Republican presidential primaries wound on in early 2012, former Massachusetts governor Mitt Romney appeared to be the front runner, only to be overtaken by Newt Gingrich after the South Carolina primary. The Democrat party's election hopes are pinned on Mr Romney winning the Republican ticket, as the health issue was identified as his weak spot. As Massachusetts governor, he had signed off state health care legislation that served as a template for the Affordable Care Act; in 2004, he had even praised the individual mandate as a conservative idea.

Risk assessment

Economy	Fair
Politics	Fair
Regional stability	Good

COUNTRY PROFILE

Historical profile

1700s As the eighteenth century progressed, an increasing number of European settlers arrived. British attempts to assert authority over its 13 North American colonies led to conflicts with the French and the indigenous population. In order to recoup losses after winning the conflict the British imposed higher taxes (which lead to the slogan 'no taxation without representation'); civil unrest followed and the first stirrings of an independence movement.

1776 Independence from Britain was declared by the colonies.

1781 Rebel states set up a loose confederation, codified in Articles of Confederation, after defeating the British at the Battle of Yorktown.

1783 The British accepted the loss of their colonies under the Treaty of Paris.

1787 The 'founding fathers' drew up the constitution, which created a federal structure for the United States of America.

1788 The constitution came into effect.

1789 George Washington was elected the first US president.

1800s During the nineteenth century, populations expanded across the plains to

the west coast. By 1850, a combination of land purchases, war and diplomacy had created much of the modern-day US.
After 1850, immigrants began arriving from all over the world, mainly attracted by the industrial jobs in the north.
The south remained committed to agriculture and the use of slaves.
1860 When the abolitionist Abraham Lincoln became president, the south seceded from the north and civil war was declared in 1861.
1865 The north won the civil war, but after Lincoln's assassination blacks in the south remained disenfranchised and segregated.
1898 The US's emergence as a world power was demonstrated when Spain lost control of its colonies in Cuba, Guam, the Philippines and Puerto Rico, after being defeated in Cuba by the US.
1914 The US declared its neutrality at the start of the First World War.
1917 The US declared war on Germany after a torpedo attack on the passenger vessel *Lusitania* a year earlier. Over one million US troops had served on the Allied side by the time the war ended in 1918.
1929 The Wall Street crash resulted in a lengthy economic recession referred to as the 'Great Depression'.
1941 After remaining neutral at the outbreak of the Second World War in 1939, the US declared war on the Axis powers following the Japanese air attack on Pearl Harbour.
1944 The US led the Allied liberation of Nazi-occupied Western Europe.
1945 Following the victory in Europe, the US dropped two atomic bombs on the Japanese cities of Hiroshima and Nagasaki, ending the Pacific War.
1947–50s The US's Marshall Plan was instrumental in the rebuilding of post-war Western Europe and Japan, providing financial aid. The Cold War emerged between the capitalist US and Western Europe and the communist Soviet Union and its Eastern European bloc.
1950–53 The US led a UN military force against communist North Korea after it had invaded South Korea. The Chinese intervened on the side of the North Koreans. A cease-fire was agreed in 1953, but no peace treaty was ever signed.
1962 Tensions between the Soviet Union and the US reached a climax during the Cuban missile crisis.
1963 John F Kennedy, the first Catholic and youngest-ever US president, was assassinated in Dallas, Texas in November. Vice President Lyndon B Johnson became president.
1964–73 The US was embroiled in the Vietnam War. The US government provided South Vietnam with military assistance against communist North Vietnam, but was forced to withdraw in 1973 when the war was lost and there was mounting domestic opposition to the high number of casualties.
1974 President Richard Nixon, who was elected in 1969, was forced to resign over the Watergate scandal involving a break-in at Democrat headquarters; tape recordings made in the White House showed he had sanctioned the burglary and subsequent cover-up. Vice President Gerald Ford became president.
1970s and 1980s was a period of great technological advancement and declining industrialisation when US corporations became worldwide leaders and US brands in computers, fast-food and entertainment became global brands. The collapse of the Soviet Union by 1991 left the US as the world's sole superpower.
1979 Iranian students attacked the US embassy in Tehran and held 63 hostages for 444 days. A failed military rescue mission in 1980 damaged the chances of incumbent Jimmy Carter winning the 1980 presidential election.
1980 Ronald Reagan became president. As a conservative popularist his policies were based on reducing federal services and cutting tax, particularly for high-income earners, later dubbed Reagonomics.
1988 George H W Bush won the presidential election.
1989 US troops invaded Panama to oust General Manuel Noriega from power.
1991 In the first Gulf War, a US-led coalition forced Iraq to withdraw from Kuwait.
1992 The Democratic Party (D) candidate Bill Clinton defeated the Republican Party (R) incumbent, George Bush, in presidential elections.
1995 A bomb in Oklahoma killed over 160 people; it was the worst case involving domestic terrorists in US history.
1996 Clinton was re-elected president.
1999 The US led a NATO military campaign against Yugoslavia in response to Serbian violence towards ethnic Albanians in the Kosovo region.
2000 George W Bush was elected president but only after controversial vote counting was declared valid by Florida's Supreme Court.
2001 On 11 September, two passenger jets were flown into the twin towers of the World Trade Centre in New York, demolishing both towers. A third jet was crashed into the Pentagon in Washington. In all, 3,025 people died in the attacks. President Bush declared a 'war on terrorism'. The US launched military action in Afghanistan against the Taliban and Osama bin Laden's extreme Islamist al Qaeda group, blamed for being behind the terrorist attacks. The giant energy provider Enron declared bankruptcy when massive accountancy frauds were uncovered.
2002 President Bush described Iran, Iraq and North Korea as part of an 'axis of evil'. A multi-billion dollar accounting fraud in WorldCom became the biggest failure in US business history to date. The Department of Homeland Security was formed with a remit to protect the US against terrorist attacks.
2003 The space shuttle Columbia broke-up on re-entry killing its crew of seven astronauts. A US-led coalition invaded Iraq. Within two months President Bush declared that 'major combat operations in Iraq have ended'.
2004 The US restored diplomatic relations with Libya after a break of 24 years. Former president, Ronald Reagan died. A Senate report declared the war on Iraq was based on 'flawed' information. Institutional failings in intelligence agencies and the government were held to be responsible for the failure to prevent the 11 September 2001 attack. George W Bush was re-elected president.
2005 New Orleans was devastated by hurricane Katrina; hundreds of people died and thousands made homeless.
2006 The Supreme Court ruled that it would be unconstitutional for Guantanamo Bay prisoners to be tried by military tribunals. Former president Gerald Ford died.
2007 President Bush dispatched a further 20,000 troops to Iraq. The collapse of the sub-prime loans market had a knock-on effect on all major US banks with total losses estimated at US$500 billion. A credit squeeze began and spread abroad.
2008 The government was forced to extend lines of credit for Fanny Mae and Freddy Mac (institutions mandated by the US Congress to provide funding to the housing market), to meet their financial obligations. One of the largest independent US banks, Lehman Brothers, filed for bankruptcy with losses of US$3.9 billion, with a further US$138 billion lost in Federal Reserve-backed advances. The financial crisis deepened in domestic and international markets as the House of Representatives (congress) delayed agreement in funding a US$700 billion rescue plan. In presidential elections, Barack Obama (D) won 52.7 per cent of the vote, John McCain (R) 46 per cent; turnout was 64 per cent. The Democrats also won a majority in the Congress with an increase in its Senate numbers to 57 seats and 255 seats in the congress. The world's leading economies, the Group of 20 (G20), agreed to co-ordinate action to stimulate economic growth; the US treasury injected US$800 billion into financial markets to encourage bank lending.

2009 Barack H Obama was inaugurated as president and quickly moved to approve the American Recovery and Reinvestment Act of 2009 four days after Congress agreed it. The US$787 billion stimulus package (totalling over US$2 trillion since 2008) was designed to stabilise the financial and banking sectors. An additional 17,000 military troops to be deployed to Afghanistan was announced; 38,000 personnel were already deployed and expected to remain until at least 2012. President Obama's US$3.6 trillion budget for 2010 was published and approved by Congress. President Obama committed a further 30,000 US troops to be sent to Afghanistan, bringing US military strength to 100,000. Other foreign troops totalled around 32,000 at the end of 2009.

2010 The US announced in January that people travelling from or through 14 countries (Afghanistan, Algeria, Iraq, Lebanon, Libya, Nigeria, Pakistan, Saudi Arabia, Somalia, Cuba, Iran, Sudan, Syria and Yemen) would be subject to extra screening measures, including pat-downs, scanning and the inspection of hand luggage. The 2010 census took place in April. Censuses have taken place every ten years since 1790; the figures are used to allocate congressional seats and federal funds. The US and Russia signed another nuclear disarmament treaty in Prague (Czech Republic) on 8 April. The treaty limits the number of warheads and launchers each country may possess. The signing took place only after the US scrapped previous plans for a 'missile shield' based in Eastern Europe which Russia considered provocative. In May, BP's Deepwater Horizon oil well off the Louisiana coast ruptured creating the largest oil spill in US history. In July over 90,000 records compiled by the military concerning their operational involvement in Afghanistan, including previously hidden details, were leaked and published on the internet. In November the US, UK, Germany and France placed a ban on all cargo from Yemen, following the discovery of improvised bombs sent by agents of al Qaeda. In mid-term elections held on 3 November, the Republicans won 243 seats (out of 435) in congress, while in the senate, despite losing six seats, the Democrats retained a majority of 51 seats (out of 100) and two incumbent independents voting with the Democrats. On 22 December President Obama signed a landmark law allowing gay people serving in the military to be open about their sexuality.

2011 On 7 March President Obama announced that he was lifting the two-year freeze on new military trials for detainees at the Guantanamo Bay prison. On 19 March, the US joined in a five-country coalition (Canada, France, Italy and the UK) to impose a no-fly zone over Libya. On 4 April President Obama confirmed that he would stand in the 2012 presidential election. The 2010 census showed that Hispanics outnumbered African Americans for the first time in most metropolitan areas. Osama Bin Laden, the leader of al Qaeda, was shot dead by US military special forces in his fortified hideout on the outskirts of Abbottabad in north-west Pakistan on 2 May. His body was flown first to Afghanistan and then buried at sea. On 19 June the Defence Secretary confirmed that 'preliminary' talks between the US and the Taliban in Afghanistan had taken place. In an address from the White House on 23 June President Obama announced the withdrawal of 10,000 US troops from Afghanistan in 2011 and another 23,000 by the end of September 2012. The Nasa Shuttle programme ended on 21 May, when its last shuttle returned from the space-station to earth; it was a victim of government budget cuts. The US Joint Chief of Staff, Admiral Mullens stated to a US Senate inquiry, on 22 September, that the militant Islamist 'Haqqani network (allied to the Taliban), for one, acts as a veritable arm of Pakistan's Inter-Services Intelligence Agency' (ISIA). He referred to two terrorist attacks, one on coalition troops and the other on the US embassy, both in Kabul and in September, of which, he said the Haqqani network had support from the ISIA. Former Republican vice presidential candidate, Sarah Palin, announced on 5 October that she would not run in the 2012 presidential election. Trade agreements with South Korea, Panama and Colombia were agreed by both houses of congress on 12 October. The agreement with South Korea was the biggest deal since the Nafta agreement of 1994. President Obama said the deals would safe-guard American jobs and boost foreign trade. On 21 October, President Obama announced that all US troops (around 39,000) would leave Iraq in an orderly withdrawal by 31 December.

Political structure

Constitution

The constitution of 17 September 1787 came into effect on 4 March 1789. The constitution strictly separates powers between the executive (presidential administration), legislature (Congress – Senate and House of Representatives) and judiciary (Supreme Court).

Independence date

4 July 1776

Form of state

Federal presidential democratic republic

The executive

The president, elected for a maximum of two terms of four years by an electoral college of representatives elected from each state, wields executive power. The president is both the chief of state and head of government.

National legislature

The bicameral Congress consisting of the House of Representatives (typically referred to a The House) and Senate, all legislative power is vested in Congress, which must be equally agreed by both houses. Each house has unique powers, as all revenue-raising bills must originate in the lower house, while all treaties and top appointments by the president are sanctioned by the upper house. All House members are appointed for fixed two-year terms, and re-elected at the same time, whereas Senators are elected for fixed six-year terms and around one-third are elected in rotation every two years.

The House has 435 members which are apportioned among the states by population number. The Senate has 100 members, two from each state regardless of its population. It also has non-voting members for US overseas territories.

Legal system

The legal system is based on English common law. There are judicial reviews of legislative acts. The US accepts compulsory International Court of Jurisdiction (ICJ) authority, although only with reservations. The nine justices of the Supreme Court are appointed for life by the president, with confirmation by the Senate.

Last elections

4 November 2008 (presidential and partial senate); 3 November 2010 (congress and partial senate).

Results: Presidential: Barack Obama (Democratic Party) won 52.7 per cent of the vote, John McCain (Republican Party) 46 per cent; turnout was 64 per cent.

House of Representatives: Republican Party won 243 seats (out of 435), Democratic Party 192 seats.

Senate (2008) (35 seats out of 100): Democratic Party 53.8 per cent of the vote (20 seats); Republican Party 42.4 per cent (15 seats); (Full senate: Democratic Party 60 seats; Republican Party 40 seats).

Senate (2010) (37 seats out of 100): Democratic Party 13 seats (overall total 51, plus two independents members who vote with the Democrats) Republican Party 24 seats (overall total 47).

Next elections

November 2012 (presidential and and partial senate); 2014 (congress and partial senate)

Political parties

Ruling party

Democratic Party (from Nov 2009)

Main opposition party
Republican Party

Population

308.75 million (2010; census figure)
Last census: The census figures are used to allocate federal funds and congressional seats.
April 2000: 281,421,906
Population density: 31 inhabitants per square km. Urban population: 77 per cent.
Annual growth rate: 1.0 per cent 1994–2004 (WHO 2006)
Ethnic make-up
The US has the fourth-largest population in the world and contains a varied social and ethnic mix.
The US is not following the trend of an ageing population as seen in many OECD countries. All categories of ages show an increase, except the 5–13 years old, which declined by 380,000 in 2003–04. This growth in population indicates a high rate of immigration rather than a fertility rate no greater than 2.0 per cent. Approximately 22 per cent of the population is under 14 years of age.
Some 20 per cent of the total population claim British ancestry, 20 per cent German and 18 per cent Irish ancestry.
In January 2003, the Census Bureau announced that Hispanics (Latinos) (13 per cent of the population) had overtaken blacks (12 per cent) as the largest minority group. In July it also reported that the legal Latino population grew by 4.6 million people between 2000–03, accounting for half the nation's total population growth during the period. The Asian population is also growing (around 4 per cent). Native Americans and native Alaskans combined are less than 1 per cent of the population.
Religions
There are some 90 religious organisations in the US with over 50,000 members each. There are approximately 86 million Protestants, 58 million Catholics, six million Jews and over six million members of other faiths. The total number of members of religious groups is estimated to be about 156 million. In the southern United States, the 'bible belt' stretches from California to Florida where the Baptist Church and Evangelism is strong. Numerous protestant sects can be found, each with their own unique outlook.

Education

Under a federal system, each state sets its own educational cycles; each year is a grade, from 1–12. Whichever cycle is adopted it incorporates 12 years. Education is mainly funded at local and state levels with policy set by the local school boards and state education authorities. Some federal funding is available to meet special needs. Schooling is generally compulsory from the age of six (states vary) to 16 years. Pupils at elementary and high schools (up to age 18) generally pay no tuition fees; further education establishments in general charge tuition fees. There is no state assistance for either tuition or living expenses for most university and undergratuate students, although loans are available. Some grant assistance is provided for students from low income and disadvantaged categories and scholarships are available on a competitive and special category basis.
High school graduates who decide to continue their education may enter a technical or vocational institution, a two-year college, or a four-year college or university.
The latest census reports that there are over 32 million elementary school children and over 15 million in high school; combined the projected number is expected to exceed 53 million, a figure not reached since the baby boomers swelled numbers in the early 1960s. The majority of high school students go on to college. Altogether, the system caters for over 72 million individuals in education.
Educational expenditure is typically around 7 per cent of the annual GDP. Elementary and secondary schools spent about 60 per cent of this total, and colleges and universities accounted for the remaining 40 per cent.
Compulsory years: 6 to 16
Enrolment rate: 101 per cent gross primary enrolment; 95.5 per cent gross secondary enrolment, of relevant age groups (including repeaters). (Unicef 2004).
Pupils per teacher: 16 in primary schools.

Health

Healthcare is largely a private-sector concern. Exceptions include the extensive Medicare programme for the elderly and the lesser Medicaid programme for those on welfare. Some emergency hospital treatment is free of charge for the poor.
Health expenditure of 13 per cent of GDP is greater than the Organisation of Economic Co-operation and Development (OECD) average of 8 per cent.
Most people have private health insurance, either as a job benefit or paid for by themselves and is becoming a major financial burden, both for individuals and for the companies who pay for employee health schemes. The premiums for family coverage is over US$9,000 per annum; and for those in worker's health schemes, an employee's share averaged US$2,084, for family cover.
HIV/Aids
HIV prevalence: 0.6 per cent aged 15–49 in 2003 (World Bank)
Life expectancy: 78 years, 2004 (WHO 2006)
Fertility rate/Maternal mortality rate: 2.0 births per woman, 2004 (WHO 2006)
Child (under 5 years) mortality rate (per 1,000): 7.0 per 1,000 live births; 1 per cent of children aged under five are malnourished (World Bank).

Welfare

Income security programmes are in general a mixture of federal and state funding and vary from state to state. The major programmes are unemployment compensation, housing subsidies for low income families and individuals, food stamps, child nutrition, payments to the disabled and family support payments. While states provide some limited form of income security, federal government policy concentrates on encouraging recipients back to work. In addition, the federal government makes social security payments to one in six Americans, either aged or disabled.
Pensions
Medicare trustees, in 2004, reported that the finance for the programme, set up to pay retirees, was deeply underfunded. Retirement payments are made from current revenue and the US$72 billion obligation (inluding the social security pension), to expected numbers of retirees, will outstrip assets and budgets by 2014, leaving the government to either make up the shortfall with tax increases or cut the pension benefits.
A trend by private companies to convert defined benefit and final salary schemes into defined contribution schemes (with uncertain benefits) has increased, with 75 per cent conversion in two decades, and US underfunding of defined benefit schemes estimated at US$278.6 billion. One of the largest providers of a defined benefit pension – United Airlines – has proposed transfering assets to the Pensions Benefit Guaranty Corporation (PBGC), a federal insurer, and divesting itself of a costly legacy. Worry has been expressed that if this and other businesses do likewise it could bankrupt the PBGC and require a government bail out costing tens of billions of dollars.

Main cities

Washington (capital, estimated population 558,891 in 2005), New York (8.2 million (m)), Los Angeles (3.9m), Chicago (2.9m), Houston (2.0m), Philadelphia (1.5m), Phoenix (1.4m), San Diego (1.3m), San Antonio (1.2m), Dallas (1.2m).

Languages spoken

There is no official language declared in the constitution. English is the *de facto* working language and Spanish is the second, widely spoken, unofficial language.

Official language/s

There is no official language declared in the constitution. English is the *de facto* working language and Spanish is the second, widely spoken, unofficial language.

Media

The Constitution guarantees both press and broadcasters freedom of speech, subject to the laws of libel and slander, although even in the latter cases, there are well established public interest defences to these charges.

The law that prevents dual ownership of broadcast and print media outlets was scrapped by the Federal Communications Commission (www.fcc.gov) in December 2007. Media entities will now be able to own both TV channels and newspapers in 20 US cities, but only if there are already eight independently owned media businesses existing in the market concerned, and any TV channel to be purchased is not one of the top four rated stations.

Press

US media organisations since 2000, including the Hearst Corporation, the New York Times Company, the Tribune Company and the Journal Register Company, which all own more than one state- or city-wide publication, have reacted to a downturn in their income (from loss of circulation and a drop in advertising revenue) by either restructuring their newspaper entities or closing them altogether; several major newspapers are under threat of closure.

Dailies: There are over 1,500 daily newspapers, published in either the morning or evening and mostly serving a city, state or region. The majority of newspapers are published in English, while some serve ethnic communities and are published in other languages. The main national dailies include *USA Today* (www.usatoday.com), *New York Times* (www.nytimes.com), *Washington Post* (www.washingtonpost.com), *Los Angeles Times* (www.latimes.com), *Boston Globe* (www.boston.com), distributed nationally in main centres. Other major publications include, the *Philadelphia Enquirer* (www.philly.com), *Baltimore Sun (www.baltimoresun.com), Chicago Sun-Times* (www.suntimes.com), *San Francisco Chronicle* (www.sfgate.com), *Detroit Free Press* (www.freep.com), *Chicago Tribune* (www.chicagotribune.com), *Atlanta Journal* (www.ajc.com) and *Houston Chronicle* (www.chron.com).

Tabloid daily newspapers include the *Daily News* (www.nydailynews.com) and the *New York Post* (www.nypost.com).

Weeklies: There are around 8,000 national magazines, mostly published in English and widely read including *Time* (www.time.com), *Newsweek* (www.newsweek.com) and *US News & World Report* (www.usnews.com). *The Nation* (www.thenation.com), a bi-monthly and *Harvard Political Review* (http://hprsite.squarespace.com) are independent political magazines. Condé Nast (www.condenast.com) publishes over 30 speciality magazines targeting women, men, young and old and special interests. The *Christian Science Monitor* (www.csmonitor.com), became a weekly publication, with a daily website, in 2009.

Business: The *Wall Street Journal* (http://online.wsj.com), the premier financial and business daily, is published in four regional editions. Major business magazines include BarronsWeekly, publicated by the *Wall Street Journal Business Week* (www.businessweek.com), *Forbes* (www.forbes.com) and *Fortune* (http://money.cnn.com with a link to Fortune). Others business news is carried by *Market Watch* (www.marketwatch.com), *Investor's Business Daily* (www.investorsbusinessdaily.com) and *Washington Business Journal* (http://washington.bizjournals.com). Business magazines which target ethnic groups include black entrepreneurs, *Black Enterprise* (www.blackenterprise.com), *Minority Business Entrepreneur* (www.mbemag.com) and Hispanic groups, *Enterprise* (http://hol.hispaniconline.com).

Periodicals: The *Harvard Political Review* (http://hprsite.squarespace.com) is an independent political magazines published four times a year. *The New Yorker* (www.newyorker.com) is an influential literary monthly magazine.

Broadcasting

Radio: Virtually all US households have a radio and there are several national networks with numerous local stations offering a variety of programmes to cater for all tastes. Clear Channel (www.clearchannel.com) is the largest commercial network with over 1,200 stations. CBS Radio (www.cbsradio.com) and ABC Radio Network (http://abcradionetworks.com) provide premium quality radio programmes to its own stations and affiliates (privately-owned stations that broadcast programmes made by others).

Regional networks include Keystone Broadcasting (www.keystonebroadcasting.com), Sheridan Broadcasting Network (SBN), which operates the American Urban Radio Networks (www.aurnol.com), of radio stations and affiliates targeting black American audiences and the non-commercial National Public Radio (www.npr.org), which has member stations broadcasting news, talk and cultural shows. In Spanish, the Hispanic radio network (http://especiales.univision.com), broadcasts in major cities nationwide.

External radio services are provided in over 40 languages to all parts of the world by the Voice of America radio network (www.voanews.com).

Television: Virtually all US households have a television set and 60 per cent have cable TV. In June 2009 all US public television services were switched to digital signals.

With the rapid growth in new technology in digital and satellite broadcasting the dominance of the four major commercial TV broadcasting networks has decreased. New mediums have allowed a wider variety of programmes to be seen at times dictated by the audience and caused steep erosion in viewer numbers for the traditional broadcast stations. Cable TV services include Fox Entertainment Group (www.fox.com), CNN 24-hour news (www.cnn.com) by Turner Broadcasting, MTV (www.mtv.com) broadcasting music and programmes for the young and the pay-TV HBO (www.hbo.com). In the large cities, cable viewers may have 50 or more channels to choose from, allowing advertisers to target their audience. Since viewer ratings determine success all networks compete fiercely with each other for viewers and advertising revenue. The four major networks are Columbia Broadcasting System (CBS) (www.cbs.com), National Broadcasting Corporation (NBC) (www.nbc.com), Capital Cities/ABC (ABC) (http://abc.go.com) and Fox. The a national public broadcasting network PBS (www.npr.org), supported by donations from the government and 'pledges' from viewers.

Business television channels include CNBC (www.cnbc.com), Bloomburg (www.bloomberg.com) and, in 2007, a newly opened Fox Business Network (www.foxbusiness.com), which was launched to challenge CNBC.

Most broadcasting is in English, but there are also TV and radio stations serving local ethnic communities in their own languages. The Hispanic community is relatively well served in Florida, California and New York City.

Worldwide US government services are provided by VOA, International Broadcasting Bureau (http://ibb7-2.ibb.gov).

Advertising

The US is the world leader in mass advertising, utilising all forms of media. Television advertising, the primary medium, is highly competitive with huge budgets and professional presentations. Advertising requirements for high ratings can terminate TV shows regardless of their worth and advertisers may influence policy in other media outlets.

News agencies

Other news agencies: UPI (United Press International):www.upi.com

Associated Press: www.ap.org

Voice of America: www.voanews.com

Economy

The US economy is one of two halves: on the one hand it has the largest economy by GDP worldwide, which significantly drives global growth, but on the other maintains an eye-watering budget deficit – US$1.56 trillion in the September 2011 budget. To do this, the US has both world-class reserves of natural resources including oil, natural gas and minerals, a large mechanised agriculture sector including cotton, wheat and livestock, and a manufacturing sector that produces a wide range of products for its large domestic market and larger foreign markets. It produces a diverse range of goods for export, including hi-tech instruments, electronic, computer and telecommunications equipment, automobiles and aircraft, foods and drinks, iconic and cultural movies, music and literature. If the US does not directly produce manufactured goods it is often the owner of offshore manufacturing processes which export their international brand names worldwide. The US is also a major centre of financial services, including banking, insurance and investment. It is a world leader in scientific research including medicine, computer sciences, astronomy, oceanography and earth sciences. It also has a large, well-funded and innovative military force.

GDP growth was 1.9 per cent in 2007, which as the global economy crisis began to take hold in 2008 fell into recession with an annual rate of -0.3 per cent. The crisis had been sparked by a downturn in the US property market, which had become inflated by cheap loans that encouraged speculative borrowing, particularly through 'subprime' loans. These loans had been re-packaged and sold to banks and other investors worldwide. As the subprime market collapsed investors suffered major losses as stock markets fell significantly and lending almost ceased in a credit squeeze that brought commerce to a standstill. What had begun as defaults in a risky market escalated, as financial institutions and banks worldwide were unable to borrow to cover their debts and had to be rescued by governments, causing national economies to fall into full-blown economic depression. The recession deepened in 2009 as GDP growth fell to -3.5 per cent as consumer spending (which had previously driven growth) fell as wages and salaries shrank, before recovering in 2010, as global trade picked up, with growth of 3 per cent.

In 2008 as the economic crisis took a grip of the global financial system, the US bank rate was cut to an historic low of 0.25 per cent in an attempt to stimulate the US economy. A new US$1.5 trillion bank bailout plan was announced in 2009 and President Obama signed a US$787 billion economic stimulus plan that included measures to create jobs, boost consumer spending and rebuild the infrastructure through the use of tax breaks and federal funding. The unemployment rate in October 2009 rose to 10.2 per cent, the highest rate since 1983; 8.2 million workers had lost their jobs since the beginning of the global economic crisis in 2007. The governor of the US Federal Reserve said the world's financial crisis was the worst since the 1930s. Lehman Brothers, a global investment bank, was declared bankrupt in September 2008, with losses of US$613 billion. The biggest quarterly loss in US corporate history was announced in March 2009 by the insurance giant AIG, at US$61.7 billion. In November 2008, the government had given AIG a financial bailout of US$150 billion to save the company from collapse during the economic crisis. On 18 March the Federal Bank announced that it would buy around US$1.2 trillion worth of long-term government debt to help boost lending.

The reputation of the US as a world leader, not only in financial services and as the stimulus for world trade, but also as a prudent and reputable global partner took a severe blow during the economic crisis. The US government began a review of its banking regulations that is on-going, while federal prosecutors investigate allegations of massive fraud perpetrated on investors, corporate and personal.

In September 2011, the government was unable to pass legislation to allow the US$1.56 trillion budget and suffered an embarrassing loss of its triple A rating as Standard and Poor's downgraded the US credit rating, the first in the history of such ratings.

External trade

The USA is a founder member of the North American Free Trade Agreement (Nafta), under which it has tri-lateral trade agreements with Canada and Mexico. Nafta has FTAs with a number of regional trading blocs. Around 30 per cent of all exports are achieved through Nafta.

The US is the leading global exporter of a number of products including wheat and corn, liquefied natural gas, aluminium, sulphur, phosphates, salt and is the third largest exporter of rice. It is reliant on imported hydrocarbons, but is the world's largest producer of electricity. It has a full range of manufacturing industries, which provide around 20 per cent of GDP, from hi-tech semiconductors and telecommunications to automotive and aerospace assembly fabrication, from pharmaceutical and petrochemical production to metal processing, mineral extraction and foodstuff production including cheese, soya beans and tobacco. The services sector, including financial services, is an important source of foreign earnings.

The US Congress finally ratified free trade agreements (FTA) with Colombia, Panama and South Korea on 13 October 2011. The South Korean FTA had been in negotiations for 16 years and is expected to increase US exports by up to US$10 billion. However, the South Korean parliament has yet to endorse the agreement.

Imports

Principal imports are consumer goods (over 30 per cent of total), oil and natural gas, industrial supplies, agricultural products, capital goods, (over 30 per cent), computers, telecommunications equipment, vehicles and parts, office machines and electric generating and distribution machinery.

Main sources: China (typically 19 per cent of total), Canada (14 per cent), Mexico (11 per cent).

Exports

Main exports are telecommunications and computers equipment (around 50 per cent of total), agricultural products (wheat, corn, rice soya beans, tobacco), industrial materials (aluminium, pig iron, ferroalloys), manufactured goods, vehicles, aircrafts, banking and financial service.

Main destinations: Canada (typically 19 per cent of total), Mexico (12 per cent), China (7 per cent).

Agriculture

Farming

Agriculture accounts for just 2 per cent of total GDP and employs approximately 3 per cent of the country's workforce. However, despite its relatively small contribution to total US GDP, the agricultural sector continues to account for half of the world's corn production and over 20 per cent of world grain output. The US is the world's largest agricultural exporter and exports account for about 25 per cent of farmers' receipts.

Capital-intensive farming techniques produce dairy products, potatoes, fruit, vegetables and poultry for urban markets in the north-eastern states; wheat, barley, maize, oats, soya beans, fodder crops, pigs and cattle in the mid-west and central plains; cotton, tobacco, peanuts, citrus fruits, rice and sugar cane in the south; cattle and sheep in the central and western states; apples, berries and nuts in the Pacific north-west; and vines, apples, citrus fruits, peaches, tomatoes, olives, cotton and rice in California.

In 2007, subsidies for cotton growers were declared illegal by the WTO, following an official complaint by Brazil that such payments constituted unfair trade. Brazil reserved the right to impose sanctions against the US, which could amount to US$4 billion.

Fishing

The fishing industry is well established in the United States and the sector is highly developed on both the Pacific and Atlantic coasts.

Total seafood exports typically amount to over US$3 billion, mainly comprising ground fish (38 per cent), salmon (18 per cent), herring, lobster, shrimps, squid and crab. The top US export markets include Japan (37 per cent), Canada (21 per cent) and the EU (18 per cent). Shrimps account for approximately 36 per cent of total fish and seafood imports.

Forestry

One third of the total land area – 225.9 million hectares (ha) – of the Unites States is covered in forested land. Forests and other wooded areas are mainly concentrated in the east and west of the central plain.

The major part of the forest is classed as semi-natural, with less than a tenth remaining undisturbed, located mainly in Alaska and the west. About nine-tenths of the forest is available for wood supply.

The government owns nearly two fifths of forest and other wooded land, while the remainder is shared among private individuals and institutions, forest industries and some by indigenous peoples.

Forestry is widespread and about half domestic timber needs are met by Oregon and Washington states, with the south-east producing increasing quantities of softwood for pulp. About 30 per cent of global industrial roundwood comes from the US. The US produces and consumes large quantities of sawn timber, wood-based panels and paper. It is also the largest importer and the second-largest exporter, of forest products.

Industry and manufacturing

The industrial sector remains a relatively significant contributor to the US economy. The sector employs over 20 per cent of the total workforce and contributes approximately 22 per cent to total GDP. The manufacturing sector has declined in significance over recent years as the services sectors have expanded.

There has been a shift in the manufacturing sector away from 'smokestack' industries, such as cars, primary metals and heavy machinery, towards high-technology industries, such as aerospace, communications equipment, electronic components and computers. Food, printing and publishing and textiles and clothing are also important.

Tourism

The US has a wide range of sights, cultures, entertainment, sports, interests and experiences to offer any visitor, of which there were just under 55 million in 2009. However, there were just over 61 million US travellers visiting foreign destinations in 2009. The overwhelming number of overseas visitors (over 7.79 million in 2009) either arrived in or visited New York City by at least a ratio of 2:1 over Miami, Los Angeles, Orlando and San Francisco (2.2–2.6 million). At the height of the tourist boom in 2008, before the global economic crisis cut visitor numbers, tourist spending totalled US$767 billion, of which accommodation and food and beverages was just under US$265 billion, and airfares to and within the US over US$112 billion.

The USA is ranked second (behind France) among the world's top destinations for arrivals, but first for tourism spend. In 2010, total visitor numbers were 59.7 million, with 20 million visitors arriving from Canada and 13.4 million from Mexico, 3.9 million from UK and 3.4 million from Japan. The tourism industry accounted for 2.8 per cent of GDP, with visitor spending totalling US$134.4 billion. The sector accounted for 7.72 million jobs of which 5.49 million were directly employed in the tourism industry.

In 2011, travel and tourism is forecast to account for 9.2 per cent of GDP with direct employment 13.7 million jobs (9 per cent of total employment), and US$252.8 billion (11.1 per cent) of total investment.

In May 2011, travel industry representatives complained that too many potential visitors were being either turned away or troubled by visa restrictions on foreign tourists. They called on the government to ease visa rules and have border controls offer a more welcoming demeanour. An estimated 78 million 'unfamiliar tourists' were denied entry or put off applying between 2000–10; only 36 countries worldwide benefit from visa-free, 90-day, entry to the US.

Environment

The US is not a signatory to the Kyoto Protocol.

Mining

The mining sector contributes approximately 4 per cent to total US GDP and employs approximately 4 per cent of the total US workforce.

While there are economically exploitable reserves of virtually every mineral within the US, these are insufficient to meet the needs of the economy in almost all circumstances. The country is 100 per cent dependent on imports for its consumption of bauxite, graphite and manganese among others. Mineral resources include ores of iron, copper (about 13 per cent of worldwide production), lead (17 per cent of worldwide production), gold (15 per cent), silver (12 per cent) and nickel.

The US accounts for approximately 17 per cent of worldwide aluminium production.

Hydrocarbons

Total proven oil reserves were 30.9 billion barrels at the end of 2010. Around 80 per cent of proven reserves are located in just four states: Texas, Louisiana, Alaska and California. Production in 2010 was 7.5 million barrels per day (bpd), which was an increase of 3.2 per cent on the 7.2 million bpd in 2009. As mature oil fields have declined in production there has been a compensating increase as more deepwater oil wells in the Gulf of Mexico and onshore oil fields in Alaska have come on-stream.

The US is the world's largest net importer of oil, receiving over 20 per cent of the world's total, with the largest supplies originating from Canada, the Middle East and Africa. Consumption was 19.5 million bpd in 2010 a figure that has remained largely constant, despite fluctuations since 1997.

Refinery capacity was 17.6 million bpd in 2010. As no new refineries have been built since the 1980s and any new refinery will take years before it become operational the US must continue to import refined oil to meet its domestic demand.

Proven natural gas reserves were 7.7 trillion cubic metres in 2010, with production at 611.0 billion cubic metres (cum), while consumption was 683.4 billion cubic metres.

Net imports have grown to 105.48 billion cum, up from 99 billion cum in 2007, the vast majority of total gas imports (93.25 billion cum) came from Canada.

US coal reserves account for over a quarter of the world's total reserves (around 28 per cent), estimated at 237 trillion tonnes. The US produces 552.2 million tonnes of oil equivalent (end 2010). The states with the largest coal production include Wyoming, West Virginia and Kentucky. More than 90 per cent of US coal output is consumed by the electricity sector. There is a trend towards consumption of coal with lower sulphur content in order to meet environmental targets for sulphur dioxide emissions.

Energy

Total installed generating capacity was 977GW in 2008, producing around 4.2 trillion kilowatt hours (kWh). Electricity demand is growing by 1.5 per cent per annum. This increase will require a significant addition in generating capacity and the government forecasts that 1,300 new power plants will be needed between 2002 and 2020. In 2007 coal-fired

power stations accounted for 48.7 per cent of all generation, with natural gas at 21.5 per cent, nuclear at 19.4 per cent, hydropower at 6 per cent and the remainder by others, including renewables.
The Federal Energy Regulatory Commission (FERC) is responsible for the regulation of the bulk power transmission system and wholesale bulk power markets. Independent utilities companies generate and sell electricity in a competitive market with consumers free to choose their suppliers.
Following California's near miss with energy cuts due to a crisis in cost, the state has encouraged the use of renewable power sources. A contract was let in 2009 for the world's largest photovoltaic energy power station producing in total 2,610MW through a series of solar power plants, to be built by 2016.

Financial markets

Stock exchange
American Stock Exchange (AMX)
Stock exchange 2
Nasdaq OMX
Commodity exchange
Chicago Board Options Exchange (CBOE)
Commodity exchange 2
Chicago Mercantile Exchange (CME)

Banking and insurance

The banking and financial services industry in the US is noted for its complicated regulations, which are overseen by numerous federal and state authorities with overlapping jurisdictions.
Regulatory agencies include the Federal Reserve, the Federal Deposit Insurance Corporation (FDIC), the Securities and Exchange Commission, the Comptroller of the Currency, the Department of Justice and state bank departments. Depositors in banks or savings and loan associations which are members of the FDIC or Federal Savings and Loan Insurance Corporation have their deposits guaranteed to a limit of US$100,000 by the government's system of deposit insurance.
Central bank
Federal Reserve System

Time

There are six time zones
Eastern Standard Time – GMT minus five hours (daylight saving, minus four hours)
Central Standard Time – GMT minus six hours (daylight saving, minus five hours)
Mountain Standard Time – GMT minus seven hours (daylight saving, minus six hours)
Pacific Standard Time – GMT minus eight hours (daylight saving, minus seven hours)
Alaska Time – GMT minus eight hours (no daylight saving)
Hawaii Time – GMT minus 10 hours (no daylight saving)
Daylight saving from March (from 2007, previously daylight saving started in April) to November

Geography

The US is about half the size of Russia and covers a total area of about nine million square km. It stretches from the North Atlantic Ocean to the North Pacific Ocean. The US has borders with Canada (8,893km) (including 2,477km Alaska/Canada), Cuba 29km (US Naval Base at Guantanamo Bay) and Mexico (3,326km).
The western part of the country is dominated by the two major mountain ranges, the Rockies and Sierras. In the eastern US, the lower Appalachian and Allegheny mountains provide the western boundary to the coastal plain. The lowest point is Death Valley, -86 metres; the highest point is Mount McKinley, 6,194 metres.
The central part of the country, the mid-west, is a vast plain, much of it flat and featureless with large wheat fields and known as the breadbasket of the US. Alaska has mountains and broad river valleys. Hawaii is rugged and volcanic. The Everglades in southern Florida comprise the world's largest marsh at 5,659 square kilometres (2,185 square miles), and averages a depth of 150mm.
Hemisphere
Northern

Climate

The size of the land area and the natural mountain barriers give a wide range of climates. It is tropical in Hawaii and Florida, arctic in Alaska, semi-arid in the great plains west of the Mississippi River and arid in the Great Basin of the south-west. California (especially the south) has a Mediterranean-style climate with mild winters and hot summers. The south and Gulf of Mexico areas have a semi-tropical climate. The east coast and the mid-west are invariably very cold in winter and very hot in summer. Snow can be heavy at times, but most cities are equipped for swift snow removal from major streets and the transportation system can cope fairly well in poor weather. Most buildings, cars and public transport are well heated or air-conditioned, according to the season.

Dress codes

There are no overriding dress codes. In the Wall Street financial district of New York and other financial centres, business suits are *de rigueur*, while on the west coast, senior executives might wear anything from suits or sports jackets and trousers to jeans and T-shirts. The more normal business attire would be a business suit, shirt and tie. Despite the reputation US businessmen have for flashy dressing, formal colours are more acceptable, with dark suits, dark socks and sombre ties being the most acceptable form.

Entry requirements

Passports
Required by all.
Extensive information can be gained through http://travel.state.gov.
The US has introduced machine-readable passport (MRP) technology to enhance security measures, screening visitors into and out of the US.
Visitors who do not possess MRP passports are required to apply for a visa for entry.
For Canadian citizens only, under the Nexus programme entry may be achieved using a Nexus photo-identification card.
All arrivals, including US citizens, travelling between Canada, Mexico, Central and South America, the Caribbean and Bermuda through land borders or by sea (including ferries) must have a passport or other biometric, secure documentation as proof of identity since, 23 January 2008.
Visa
Extensive information can be gained through http://travel.state.gov.
Visas are required by all, with some exceptions under the Visa Waiver Program (VWP). This reciprocal programme allows citizens of, among others, most of the EU, Australasia and Japan entry without a visa if they possess a machine readable passport (MRP) and have a return/onward ticket, entry for business and tourist visits up to 90 days.
All citizens of visa-free countries who do not have a MRP must apply for a visa. All other visitors must apply for a visa.
Currency advice/regulations
The import and export of local and foreign currencies is allowed. Amounts over US$10,000 (or foreign equivalent) must be declared.
Gold coins, medals and bullion may be imported unless originating from embargoed countries.
Travellers cheques, in US dollars, are widely accepted.
Customs
Personal items are duty-free. National alcohol allowances may be in excess of state allowances and may result in excess amount being taxed or confiscated.
Certain firearms and ammunition are allowed with a customs permit, obtained in advance.
Prohibited imports
Illegal drugs (personal medication requires a doctor's certificate); soil, plant and animal products (including endangered species); meat, poultry (fresh, dried or canned) and live fish (unless certified disease-free), their eggs (unless canned, pickled or smoked); Cuban cigars (

purchased in any country); wildlife and endangered species (including hunting trophies, shells and crafted items); fireworks and hazardous material; some South American pre-Columbian artefacts; merchandise from embargoed countries and counterfeit items.
These prohibitions apply to transit passengers.

Health (for visitors)
Mandatory precautions
No vaccination certificates are required, however, visitors from countries where cholera or yellow fever is rife, or where an outbreak of infectious disease occurred within six months of arrival, will require vaccination certificates.
Advisable precautions
There are no major health hazards for visitors, and no inoculations or vaccinations are necessary.
All personal medicines must have a physician's certificate declaring their prescribed use. As health costs can be extremely high medical insurance, including emergency evacuation, is necessary.

Hotels
Major hotels have toll-free telephone numbers (with an 800 area code) for reservations. Unless a deposit has been paid, a hotel room will often not be held after 1700/1800, even when the hotel is notified of late arrival. Check-out times vary from 1000–1300 and short extensions can be arranged. Visitors may be charged for overstaying check-out time without making arrangements. Most good hotels have restaurant facilities, bars, free parking and swimming pools. Many hotels provide courtesy transport or an airport bus service.
Road-side motels are numerous and relatively inexpensive.

Credit cards
Major credit and charge cards are widely accepted. A credit card is essential for car hire and usually necessary for hotel bookings.

Public holidays (national)
Fixed dates
1 Jan (New Year's Day), 4 Jul (Independence Day), 11 Nov (Veterans' Day), 25 Dec (Christmas Day).
Any holiday falling on Saturday is taken on Friday before; holidays falling on a Sunday are taken on Monday following.
Variable dates
Martin Luther King's Birthday (third Mon in Jan), Washington's Birthday (third Mon in Feb), Memorial Day (last Mon in May), Labour Day (first Mon in Sep), Columbus Day (second Mon in Oct), Thanksgiving Day (fourth Thu in Nov).
Statutory and public holidays are fixed by state legislation and vary considerably between states.

Working hours
Most offices remain closed on the Friday following Thanksgiving. Working hours vary considerably depending on the industry.
Banking
Mon-Fri: 0900–1500.
Business
Mon-Fri: 0900–1700.
Government
Mon-Fri: 0830–1730.
Shops
Mon-Fri: 0930–1800; Sun: 1200–1700.

Telecommunications
Mobile/cell phones
GSM 850 and 1900 services are available throughout most of the country.

Electricity supply
110–120V AC, 60 cycles single phase, with flat two-point plug fittings.

Weights and measures
Units of measurement used in the US are in general the same as the imperial system. Short ton = hundredweight = 45.4 kilograms, one pound = 0.45 kilogram; one gallon = 3.79 litres, one pint = 0.47 litre. Conversion to metric system is taking place very slowly and on a voluntary basis, with the US Metric Board co-ordinating the process.

Social customs/useful tips
People are likely to use first names in discussions with you. They are also likely to refer to someone else by their surname only. Neither of these usages is considered impolite.
The main cultural role model in the US is that of the pioneer, the isolated man or woman battling against the odds, the story of someone rising from a deprived background to become rich and/or famous. This has led to an admiration for hard work, free enterprise and determination. Gun ownership by civilians is considered, by many, to be a part of American heritage.

Security
The US has a reputation for crime and violence. New York, Baltimore, Chicago, Detroit, Washington and Los Angeles have a high rate of robbery. Washington, Detroit, Baltimore, Dallas, Houston, Philadelphia, Atlanta and Los Angeles have high murder rates.
However, much of the trouble is concentrated in parts of each city and avoiding these neighbourhoods will considerably reduce any risk. Elementary precautions should prevent visitors having too much trouble. Avoid walking in deserted streets, and try to walk on the street-side rather than next to buildings. Always be aware of the kind of neighbourhood it is. At night, except in lively and well-lit areas, call a taxi to collect you rather than walking to look for one.
Although the risk of being mugged is often exaggerated (and crime figures have been falling since the mid-1990s), it is recommended not to resist a robbery attempt. Keep your valuables (especially expensive jewellery) out of sight.

Getting there
Air
International airport/s: The US is accessible by air from all continents and a vast number of countries. Some of the busiest international airports are La Guardia (LGA) (New York), Los Angeles (LAX), Miami International Airport (MIA), O'Hare International Airport (ORD), Hartsfield-Jackson Atlanta Airport (ATL); other important international airports include those in Boston (Logan Airport), Dallas-Fort Worth, Philadelphia, Houston, San Francisco, Washington Dulles International and John F Kennedy Airport (Newark).
Airport tax: Departure taxes are included in the price of a ticket, although local airport departure tax may be charged if the ticket was purchased outside the US.
There is a national programme that allows airports to impose a passenger facility charge of up to US$4.5.
Surface
Road: The US has land borders with Mexico in the south and Canada in the north and there are plenty of efficient overland border crossings between the US and these countries. Border crossings are strictly controlled.
Rail: There are limited passenger services from Mexico, crossing the border at either Yuma, El Paso or Del Rio. Rail links from Canada include Vancouver–Seattle, Toronto–Chicago and Montréal–New York, although these are not all direct and without layovers. Some rail lines run up to the border with Canada, in Michigan
Water: The US has numerous sea and inland water ports and is well served by the international shipping lines.

Getting about
National transport
Inter-state transport can be variable, however the US is generally perceived to have one of the most advanced transport structures in the world, including metro systems in most major cities and sufficient national bus networks. Transport by ferries and helicopters is also widely available. Nevertheless, the easiest and quickest method of crossing great distances in the US is by air.
Air: A highly developed network of airline services connects most towns of importance. Fare systems have been deregulated, leading to sharp competition.
Road: There is a comprehensive network of highways (interstate) that bisect the

counrty from the east to west coast and from the borders with Canada through to Mexico. During the winter even the interstates can be closed or slowed by snow. There is an extensive secondary road system.

Buses: A wide network of air-conditioned long-distance buses link all major cities, but smaller cities and rural areas are generally not well served by public transport. Greyhound is the main bus system in the US and plays an important transport role in most parts of the country.

Rail: Around 245,000km of grade one railroad links approximately 500 stations. Most long-distance trains are air-conditioned and equipped with dining and sleeper carriages. Amtrak is generally comfortable and runs a popular shuttle service between New York and Washington; the New York to Boston route is also well travelled. Much of the national network is in need of new equipment, however, and in terms of time and cost, rail travel compares poorly to air travel on most inter-city routes.

Water: Ferries supply connections for national Highways across the Mississippi at various places.

City transport

Most cities have a good public transport network including a mixture of buses, suburban trains and subways. At night, taxis are the safer option for travel. Fares vary in different cities. Public transport is woefully inadequate in Los Angeles and the cable cars of San Francisco are a special treat. Commuter rail services throughout the US are usually safe and reliable.

Most cities have severe parking problems in downtown areas and it is more convenient to travel by public transport or taxi.

Taxis: It is wise to confirm the approximate cost when entering a cab.

In Los Angeles, taxis do not cruise streets looking for passengers, but there are taxi stands at airports, major hotels, and train and bus terminals.

Taxi fares in Washington DC are based on the unmetered zone system with a basic fare and each zone charged extra; drivers may stop and pick up several passengers following the same general route. Enquire in advance how many zones you will ride.

Buses, trams & metro: There are bus services in all main cities. Many hotels have courtesy bus services to and from airports. In New York City buses are slower than the subway, and especially crowded during rush hours, but the routes are more varied and the stops more frequent, usually every two blocks. The subway is the fastest way to get around. Trains are identified by number or letter which are displayed on the front and sides of the cars. Some are local and some express so be sure the train you board stops where you need to get off. If travelling after 2200, wait for the train in the areas marked for off-peak hours.

A subway connects downtown Chicago and O'Hare International Airport with fast and frequent services from Terminal 2; from the city, the Dearborn Street subway runs to the airport.

Union Station is the transport hub in Washington DC. Connections between Metrorail and Metrobus are available at all Metrorail stations.

Ferry: There are commuter ferries across Boston, San Francisco and New York harbours.

Car hire

Car hire is widely available in major cities. A valid overseas or international driving licence and an international credit card are required. Other methods of payment may not be accepted. Driving is on the right. States are free to set their own speed limits: Montana has no day-time limit but at night the limit is 55mph; 75mph in Kansas, Nevada and Wyoming; 70mph in California, Missouri, Oklahoma, South Dakota and Texas.

For further information on state highways see www.us-highways.com with links to other relevant sites.

BUSINESS DIRECTORY

The addresses listed below are a selection only. While World of Information makes every endeavour to check these addresses, we cannot guarantee that changes have not been made, especially to telephone numbers and area codes. We would welcome any corrections.

Telephone area codes

The international direct dialling code (IDD) for the United States of America is +1, followed by area code and subscriber's number:

Alaska	907	NY, Manhattan	212
Albuquerque	505	Newark	201
Atlanta	404	Montana	406
Austin	512	Oklahoma City	405
Boston	617	Philadelphia	215
Chicago	312	Phoenix	602
Denver	303	Pittsburgh	412
Des Moines	515	Portland	503
Detroit	313	Sacramento	916
Hawaii	808	St Louis	314
Houston	713	St Paul	612
Kansas City	816	Salt Lake City	801
Indianapolis	317	San Francisco	415
Las Vegas	702	Seattle	206
Los Angeles	213	Washington DC	202
Louisville	502	Wichita	316
Memphis	901		
Miami	305		
New Orleans	504		
New York	718		

Useful telephone numbers

Emergency services: 911

Chambers of Commerce

British-American Business Council, 52 Vanderbilt Avenue, 20th Floor, New York NY 10017 (tel: 661-5660; fax: 661-1886; e-mail: info@babc.org).

United States Chamber of Commerce, 1615 H Street, NW, Washington DC 20062 (tel: 659-6000; e-mail: intl@uschambers.com).

Banking

Bank of America, 555 California Street, San Francisco, California, 94104 (tel: 415-622-3456; fax: 510-675-8170).

Bankers Trust, 280 Park Avenue, New York, New York, 10017 (tel: 212-250-2500; fax: 212-250-4029).

Chase Manhattan, 1 Chase Manhattan Plaza, New York, New York, 10081 (tel: 212-552-2222).

Chemical Bank, 270 Park Avenue, New York, New York, 10017 (tel: 212-270-6000; fax: 212-682-3761).

Citibank, 399 Park Avenue, New York, New York, 10043 (tel: 212-559-1000; fax: 212-223-2681).

First National Bank of Chicago, 1 First National Plaza, Chicago, Illinois, 60670 (tel: 312-732-4000; fax: 312-732-5965).

Inter-American Development Bank, 1300 New York Avenue NW, Washington DC 20577 (tel: 202-623-3900; fax: 202-623-2360).

Morgan Guaranty Trust, 60 Wall Street, New York, New York, 10260 (tel: 212-483-2323; fax: 212-233-2623).

Nations Bank, 100 North Tryon Street, Charlotte, North Carolina, 28255 (tel: 704-386-5000; 704-386-0645).

Central bank

Federal Reserve System, 20th Street and Constitution Avenue, NW, Washington DC 20551 (tel: (202) 452-3000; fax: (202) 452-3819).

Stock exchange

American Stock Exchange (AMX): www.amex.com

Stock exchange 2

Nasdaq OMX: www.nasdaqomx.com

Commodity exchange

Chicago Board Options Exchange (CBOE): www.cboe.com

Commodity exchange 2

Chicago Mercantile Exchange (CME): www.cmegroup.com

Travel information

Amtrak (tel: 1-800-872-7245; internet: www.amtrak.com).

California Tourism, PO Box 1499, Sacramento, CA 95812-1499 (1-916-444-4429; internet: www.visitcalifornia.com).

Greyhound Lines Inc, PO Box 660362, MS 470 Dallas, TX 75266- 0362 (tel: 789-7000; internet: www.greyhound.com).

John F Kennedy International Airport, Building 14, Jamaica, New York 11430, (tel: 244-4444; internet: www.kennedyairport.com).

LaGuardia Airport Hangar 7 Center, Third Floor, Flushing, New York 11371 (tel: 533-3400; fax: 533-3421; internet: www.laguardiaairport.com).

Los Angeles International Airport, 1 World Way, Los Angeles, Ca 90045 (tel: 646-5252; internet: www.lawa.org/lax).

Metropolitan Transportation Authority, 347 Madison Avenue, New York, NY 10017-3739 (internet: www.mta.nyc.ny.us).

Miami International Airport, PO Box 592075, Miami, Florida 33159 (tel: 876-7000; fax: 876-7398; internet: www.miami-airport.com).

O'Hare International Airport, PO Box 66142 Chicago, Illinois 60666 (tel: 686-3700, 686-2200; fax: 686-3573; internet: www.ohare.com).

Visit Florida, Welcome Center, The Capitol, West Entrance, Tallahassee FL 32301 (tel: 488-6167; fax: 414-2560; internet: www.visitflorida.com).

Ministries

Department of Agriculture, 1400 Independence Avenue, SW, Washington DC 20250 (tel: 720-3631; internet: www.usda.gov).

Department of Commerce, 1401 Constitution Avenue, NW, Washington DC 20230 (tel: 482-2000; fax: 482-2741; internet: www.commerce.gov).

Department of Defence, The Pentagon, Washington DC 20301-1950 (tel: 692-7100; fax: 428-1982; internet: www.defenselink.mil).

Department of Education, Federal Office Bld 6, 400 Maryland Ave, Washington DC 20202 (tel: 401-3000; fax: 401-0596; internet: www.ed.gov).

Department of Energy, 1000 Independence Avenue, SW, Washington DC 20585 (tel: 586-5000; fax: 586-4403; internet: www.energy.gov).

Department of Health and Human Services, 200 Independence Ave, SW, Room 615F, Washington DC 20201 (tel: 690-7000; fax: 690-7203; internet: www.hhs.gov).

Department of Homeland Security, 3801 Nebraska Avenue, NW, Washington DC 20528 (tel: 282-8000; fax: 282-8401; internet: www.dhs.gov).

Department of Housing and Urban Development, 451 7th Street, SW, Room 10000 Washington DC 20410 (tel: 708-0417; fax: 619-8365; internet: www.hud.gov).

Department of the Interior, 1949 C Street, NW Washington DC 20240 (tel: 208-7351; fax: 208-6956; internet: www.doi.gov).

Department of Justice, 950 Pennsylvania Ave, NW Washington DC 20530-0001 (tel: 514-2001; fax: 307-6777; internet: www.justice.gov).

Department of Labor, 200 Constitution Ave, NW Washington DC 20210 (tel: 693-6000; fax: 693-6111; internet: www.dol.gov).

Department of State, 2201 C Street, NW Washington, DC 20520-0001 (tel: 647-5291; fax: 647-7120; internet: www.state.gov).

Department of Transportation, 400 7th Street, SW Washington DC 20570 (tel: 366-1111; fax: 366-7202; internet: www.dot.gov).

Department of the Treasury, 1500 Pennsylvania Ave, NW Washington DC 20220; (tel: 622-1100; fax: 622-0073; www.untreas.gov).

Office of the President, The White House, 1600 Pennsylvania Ave, Washington DC 20500 (tel: 456-1414; fax: 456-2461; internet: www.whitehouse.gov).

Other useful addresses

British Embassy, 3100 Massachusetts Avenue NW, Washington DC 20008-3600 (tel: 588 6500; fax: 588 7850; internet: www.britainusa.com).

Consumer Product Safety Commission, 4330 East West Highway, Bethseda, MD 20814 (tel: 504-7923; fax: 504-0124; internet: www.cpsc.gov).

Council of Economic Advisers, The White House, 1600 Pennsylvania Avenue NW Washington, DC 20500 (tel: 456-1414).

Environmental Protection Agency, Areil Rios Bld, 1220 Pennsylvania Ave NW, Washington DC 20460 (tel: 814-5000; internet: www.epa.gov).

Federal Trade Commission, 600 Pennsylvania Avenue, NW, Washington DC 20580 (tel: 382-4357; internet: www.ftc.gov).

New York Stock Exchange, 11 Wall Street, New York, NY 10005 (tel: 656-3000; internet: www.nyse.com).

Office of Science and Technology Policy, Executive Office of the President, 725 17th Street, Room 5228 Washington DC 20502 (tel: 456-7116; internet: www.ostp.gov)

Office of the United States Trade Representative, 600 17th Street, NW Washington DC 20508 (tel: 395-7360; internet: www.ustr.gov).

Securities and Exchange Commission, 100 F Street, NE, Washington DC 20549 (tel: 551-6551; internet: www.sec.gov).

United States Information Agency, 301 Fourth Street, SW, Washington DC 20547 (internet: http://usinfo.state.gov).

Internet sites

Alamo Rent A Car: www.alamo.com

American Airlines: www.aa.com

American Chamber of Commerce: www.amcham.com

American Stock Exchange: www.amex.com

Big Book (information on 16m businesses): www.bigbook.com

Big yellow pages (business and residential information):www.bigyellow.com

Continental Airlines: www.flycontinental.com.

Delta Airlines: www.delta.com

Export and Trade Information: www.stat.usa.gov

Federal Agencies: www.fedworld.gov

Lookup USA (locate addresses and telephone numbers of US businesses): www.infousa.com

Northwest Airlines: www.nwa.com

Southwest Airlines: www.southwest.com

Trade US: www.tradeUS.com

United Airlines: www.ual.com

US Bureau of Census: www.census.gov

US Customs and Border Protection www.cbp.gov

US Department of Commerce: www.commerce.gov

US Government gateway site: firstgov.gov/

US Office of Insular affairs: www.doi.gov/oia

US International Trade Administration: www.ita.doc.gov/ita_home

US Virgin Islands

KEY FACTS

Official name: Virgin Islands of the United States

Head of State: President of the United States of America Barack Obama (from 20 Jan 2009)

Head of government: Governor John deJongh (Democrat) (from 2007; re-elected 2 Nov 2010)

Ruling party: Democratic Party of the Virgin Islands (affiliated to the US Democratic Party) (from 2002; re-elected Nov 2008)

Area: 355 square km

Population: 109,775 (2010)*

Capital: Charlotte Amalie (on St Thomas)

Official language: English

Currency: US dollar (US$) = 100 cents

Exchange rate: US$1.00 per US$ (Aug 2010)

* estimated figure

COUNTRY PROFILE

Historical profile

1493 The islands were first sighted by Columbus.
1494–1670 The indigenous Carib and Arawak Indian population endured various waves of European invasions and settlement, including African slaves who were used on sugar cane plantations.
1670 The islands of St John and St Thomas were colonised by Denmark.
1733 Denmark purchased St Croix from France.
1917 Denmark sold the islands to the US for US$25 million.
1927 US citizenship was granted to the islands' population.
1931 The Virgin Islands were placed under the administration of the US State Department.
1936 Universal suffrage and local government were provided for under the Organic Act of the Virgin Islands.
1954 The United States Virgin Islands (USVI) became an unincorporated territory of the United States, under a revised Organic Act, which introduced a form of constitution, with a governor appointed by the president of the US and an elected 15-member unicameral legislature (senate).
1970 A governor was elected for the first time, following the 1968 Elective Governor Act, which also included an elected government for the islands.
1973 The USVI elected a non-voting delegate to the US House of Representatives for the first time.
1995 Damage to the power system occurred when Hurricane Marilyn hit the islands. The US Federal government transferred control of Water Island to the territorial government.
1998 Governor Charles W Turnbull was elected. Three serious hurricanes (Bonnie, George and Mitch) tore through the West Indies and between them killed over 9,700 people. However there was less damage inflicted in US Virgin territories due to reconstruction after previous hurricanes which required buildings to be built to withstand Category 2 storms.
2002 Charles Turnbull was re-elected governor and the Democrats won a majority in the parliamentary election.
2006 John deJongh (D) won the gubernatorial election with 49 per cent of the vote.
2007 An area along the coastline of St John was reserved by the Trust for Public Land to be included in the US Virgin Islands National Park, giving it its largest expansion ever.
2008 A 30-member Constitutional Convention began work on drafting a new constitution. It was the fourth time since 1965 that a new constitution has been envisaged, with previous work stalled over the lack of federal voting rights. John deJongh and the Democrats were re-elected.
2009 USVI received three different funds from the US: US$20.2 million to improve housing for low income residents, around US$71 million for education and US$1.3 million for coral reef restoration. Governor John deJongh rejected the draft constitution submitted by the Constitutional Convention stating it violated federal law, failed to defer federal sovereignty and disregarded basic civil rights. He refused to submit it for consideration in the US.
2010 In January the US Postal Services assigned specific zip codes to islands within the territory: VI followed by 008xx for the five designated destinations. The resident population of the USVI took part in the United States census on 1 April, which, after personal details, included questions on race, housing and internet and mobile phone access. A successful legal challenge to Governor deJongh's refusal to present the draft constitution forced him to comply. President Obama forwarded the draft proposals to the US Congress in May. The US Justice Department restated the concerns of Governor deJongh when the draft was submitted for consideration; as a result Congress rejected the draft requesting that it be reconsidered by the Constitutional Convention on 30 June. In gubernatorial elections held on 2 November, incumbent John deJongh won 56 per cent; Kenneth Mapp (independent) won 44 per cent.
2011 On 24 June the senate passed an austerity act, which will reduce salaries of public workers and allow possible dismissals to reduce costs. The approval was given to avoid the governor's proposal to dismiss up to 600 government employees before April 2012. In August, preliminary results of the 2010 census showed a drop in the population to 106,405, from 108,612 in 2000. It also recorded an

increase in the population of St John and a decline in St Croix.

Political structure

Constitution

USVI is an unincorporated territory of the United States and only certain parts of the US constitution apply. Power is delegated from the US Congress.

Citizens are unable to vote in US federal or presidential elections. However US Virgin Islanders are entitled to vote in presidential primary elections and to send one, non-voting, member to the US House of Representatives for a two-year term.

Form of state

Overseas territory of the United States of America

The executive

Executive authority is exercised by the governor (elected for a four-year term by popular vote) who makes other executive appointments with the concurrence of the legislature.

National legislature

The unicameral legislature, the Senate, has 15 members each serving for two-year terms. The islands are divided into two multimember constituencies with seven senators each. St John is its own constituency and has one senator elected from a list of all-comers.

Legal system

The legal system is based on US laws.

Last elections

2 November 2010 (gubernatorial); 4 November 2008 (Senate)

Results: Gubernatorial: John deJongh won 56 per cent; Kenneth Mapp (independent) won 44 per cent.

Senate: The Democratic Party of the Virgin Islands (Dem) won nine seats (out of 15) independents four and the Independent Citizens Movement (ICM) two.

Next elections

2 November 2014 (gubernatorial); 2012 (parliamentary)

Political parties

Ruling party

Democratic Party of the Virgin Islands (affiliated to the US Democratic Party) (from 2002; re-elected Nov 2008)

Political situation

The economic downturn in the US has had a knock-on effect on the islands. The undercapitalised Virgin Islands Community Bank was sold to FirstBank Virgin Islands in an emergency deal, before a deadline would have resulted in the Federal Deposit Insurance Corporation taking the bank into receivership.

Since then the US House of Representatives has passed a plan to stimulate the economy, including measures to expand mortgage loan opportunities for families at risk of home repossession. It also has islander taxpayers receiving a tax rebate of between US$300–US$600 per person, plus US$300 per child. The money is expected to strengthen the local economy and encourage consumer spending.

In March 2011, the Republican controlled US-Congress voted to rescind the voting rites of representations of the US Virgin Islands, effectively disenfranchising their electorate in policies that directly affect them.

Population

109,775 (2010)*

Last census: April 2000: 108,612

Population density: 352 inhabitants per square km. Urban population: 46 per cent (1994–2000).

Annual growth rate: 3 per cent (2003)

Ethnic make-up

Descendants of former African slaves form the majority (80 per cent) of the population. Whites make up a further 15 per cent. Almost three-quarters (74 per cent) of inhabitants are West Indians (45 per cent Virgin Islands-born, 29 per cent from elsewhere in the Caribbean). Puerto Ricans make up 5 per cent of the population.

Religions

Various Christian denominations predominate, (Baptist, Roman Catholic and Episcopalian).

Education

Compulsory years: Five to 16 years

Health

Life expectancy: 78.3 years (estimate 2003)

Fertility rate/Maternal mortality rate: 2.2 births per woman (World Bank)

Child (under 5 years) mortality rate (per 1,000): 8.3 per 1,000 live births (World Bank).

Main cities

Charlotte Amalie (on St Thomas, capital, estimated population 17,500 in 2005), Christiansted and Frederiksted on St Croix (6,300). The third major island and the least populous is St John (Cruz Bay).

Languages spoken

Spanish and Creole are also spoken.

Official language/s

English

Media

Press

Dailies: The two major dailies are *Virgin Islands Daily News* (www.virginislandsdailynews.com) and *St Croix Avis*. Other publications include an independent community newspaper *St John Times*.

The island is served by on-line news services (www.onepaper.com). The *St Croix Source* provides an alternative news and information source for and about the St Croix community. It is the sister publication of *St Thomas Source* and *St John Source*.

Weeklies: *Tradewinds St John Newspaper* (www.stjohntradewindsnews.com) is published and distributed weekly on St John, as well as to international subscribers. Since 1972, Tradewinds Newspaper has been the island authority. A general tourist publication, *St Thomas This Week Magazine*, is available on-line (www.st-thomas.com/week).

Business: Publications include *Virgin Islands Business Journal*.

Broadcasting

Television services are provided by US commercial broadcasters. WSVI TV 8 (Channel 8) (www.wsvi.tv) is an ABC affiliate and WVGN TV 14 (Channel 11) (www.wvgn.com) is an NBC affiliate; both channels broadcast syndicated US shows. There are several radio stations located on both islands and are identified by their call signs, a few are networked such as VI Radio (www.viradio.com). Most broadcast music while a few are news, talk and religious radio stations.

Economy

The islands have little in the way of natural resources and most industries are dependent on either trade with the US or as an offshore site of the US. Manufacturing includes refined petroleum (shipped to the US), rum (combined, these processes dominate the sector, representing 95 per cent of total output and 85 per cent of all manufacturing employment), textiles, electronic assembly of components, pharmaceuticals and watch assembly.

Crude oil, around half of which is sourced from Venezuela, is processed at the Hovensa oil refinery on Saint Croix, which is one of the world's largest oil refineries, producing 495,000 barrels per day (bpd). Agriculture production is insufficient to provide for the population and most foods have to be imported.

The service sector constitutes the major component of GDP, of which tourism is the single largest sector accounting for around 80 per cent of GDP. Tourism provides the islands' main economic activity, including employment and investment. However, the global economic crisis had an adverse effect on the USVI as tourist numbers fell from 2.55 million in 2008 to 2.22 million in 2009. This led to a drop in economic activity that caused a rise in unemployment that spread across most industries, reaching 8.5 per cent in September 2008 (the highest rate since 2001 when the US was still reeling from the 11 September atrocities and tourists stayed at home). As the USVI came out of recession in 2009/10 employment prospects improved but did not return to the pre-2008 levels. As a consequence, government revenue was projected to remain smaller in 2011 than 2007.

External trade

As an unincorporated territory of the USA the US Virgin Islands are not part of the American Free Trade Agreement (Nafta), despite its heavy reliance on imports and aid from the US. Trade with the US is either directly by air and sea, or indirect via Puerto Rico.

The principal foreign exchange earner is tourism. Hovensa, on St Croix, is one of the world's largest oil refineries; and manufacturing is the next strongest sector producing refined oil and petroleum products and rum. There is a growing financial services sector and USVI has become the home to a number of foreign sales offices.

Imports

Main imports are crude oil, foodstuffs, consumer goods and building materials.

Main sources: US, Puerto Rico

Exports

Main exports refined petroleum products, rum, petrochemicals, clocks and watches.

Main destinations: US and Puerto Rico.

Agriculture

The agricultural sector contributes around 1 per cent to GDP. The US Virgin Islands are mainly hilly with little flat land. The poor quality of the soil and lack of rain precludes large-scale cultivation. Small quantities of sorghum, fruit and vegetables are produced on St Croix and St Thomas. Cattle are the main agricultural product; a special breed of Senepol cattle hardened to the hot temperatures was developed on St Croix for meat export.

There is some commercial fishing, mainly of lobsters, but fishing is mostly for game, not commercial purposes. The typical total fish catch is over 300t, plus over 36t of other seafood, per annum.

Industry and manufacturing

The industrial sector contributes around 17 per cent to GDP. Manufacturing is better developed here than in much of the Caribbean; it is small-scale and export-based (mainly to the US). Manufacturers have the right to stamp 'Made in America' on their products. The main activities are rum distilling (3–4 million gallons per year), watch/clock assembly, ethanol refining, woollen textiles and garments.

The largest single employer is the Hovensa oil refinery on St Croix, which has a capacity of around 500,000 barrels per day (bpd).

Hydrocarbons

There are no known deposits of hydrocarbons; all domestic needs must be met by imports mainly from Trinidad and Tobago. Consumption of petroleum products was 67,000 barrels per day in 2008. The Hovensa refinery is one of the largest in the western hemisphere and one of the world's biggest, with a capacity of around 500,000 barrels per day (bpd), located on St Croix. Less than a quarter of oil imports is consumed locally, the rest being re-exported as refined oil products, mainly to the US.

Any use of imported natural gas is commercially insignificant; around 288,000 tonnes of coal per annum are imported.

Energy

Total installed generating capacity was 323MW in 2006. Residents of the US Virgin Islands have a greater per capita consumption than mainland US or comparable US Pacific islands, due mainly to consumption of output from the Hovensa refinery. A three-part programme to reduce consumption per capita, enhancing energy efficiency of dwellings (weatherisation) and increase the use of renewable energy, was proposed in May 2009.

Banking and insurance

Central bank

Federal Reserve System

Time

GMT minus four hours

Geography

The US Virgin Islands consist of four main inhabited islands (St Croix, St Thomas, St John and Water Island) and about 50 smaller, mostly uninhabited, islands. They are situated at the eastern end of the Greater Antilles, about 64km (40 miles) east of Puerto Rico in the Caribbean Sea. These islands are volcanic in origin and have mountainous interiors.

Hemisphere

Northern

Climate

Sub-tropical with a mean annual temperature of 26 degrees Celsius. Low levels of humidity. Rainy season runs May–November.

Entry requirements

Passports

Required by all.

From 23 January 2007, all travellers arriving by air from Canada, Mexico, Central and South America, the Caribbean and Bermuda must have a biometric passport. For Canadian citzens only, under the Nexus programme entry may be achieved using an Air Nexus Card, which includes a retinal-scan.

From 23 January 2008, all arrivals, including US citizens, travelling between Canada, Mexico, Central and South America, the Caribbean and Bermuda through land borders or by sea (including ferries) must have a passport or other biometric, secure documentation as proof of identity.

Visa

US entry requirements apply; visas required by all with some exceptions under the Visa Waiver Program (VWP). This reciprocal programme allows citizens of, among others, the EU, Australasia and Japan entry without a visa if they possess a MRP and have a return/onward ticket, for business and tourist visits up to 90 days. All citizens of visa-free countries who do not have a MRP must apply for a visa. All other visitors must apply for a visa.

For all information on visas see http://travel.state.gov/visa and follow link to *Visa Types for Temporary Visitors* for specific business visas and extended stays.

Currency advice/regulations

The import of local and foreign currency is unrestricted; amounts over US$10,000 (or equivalent) must be declared.

Customs

Personal items are duty-free. Alcohol and gifts are not duty-free.

Certain firearms and ammunition are allowed with a customs permit, obtained in advance.

Prohibited imports

Illegal drugs (personal medication requires a doctor's certificate); soil, plant and animal products (including endangered species); meat, poultry (fresh, dried or canned) and live fish (unless certified disease-free), their eggs (unless canned, pickled or smoked); Cuban cigars (purchased in any country); wildlife and endangered species (including hunting trophies, shells and crafted items); fireworks and hazardous material; some South American pre-Columbian artefacts; merchandise from embargoed countries and counterfeit items.

These prohibitions apply to transit passengers.

Health (for visitors)

Mandatory precautions

Yellow fever vaccination certificate if arriving from infected area.

Advisable precautions

Health insurance is strongly advised. Adopt precautions when drinking water in rural areas. There is a bilharzia (schistosomiasis) risk when swimming – chlorinated pools are safe. Visitors should consider immunisation against hepatitis A.

Hotels

Advisable to book in advance, especially in winter months. There is an 8 per cent hotel tax. A 15 per cent tip is usual.

Public holidays (national)

Fixed dates

1 Jan (New Year's Day), 6 Jan (Three Kings' Day), 19 Jan (Martin Luther King Day), 3 Jul (Emancipation Day), 4 Jul (US

Independence Day), 25 Jul (Hurricane Supplication Day), 17 Oct (Virgin Islands Thanksgiving Day), 1 Nov (D Hamilton Jackson Day), 11 Nov (Veterans' Day), 25 Dec (Christmas Day).

Variable dates
President's Day (second Mon in Feb), Maundy Thursday, Good Friday, Easter Monday, Memorial Day (fourth Mon in May), Labour Day (first Mon in Sep), Columbus Day (second Mon in Oct), US Thanksgiving Day (fourth Thu in Nov).

Working hours

Banking
Mon–Fri: 0900–1430; Fri: 0900–1400, 1530–1700.
Business
Mon–Fri: 0900–1700
Government
Mon–Fri: 0800–1700.
Shops
Mon–Sat: 0900–1700. Some Sunday opening when cruise ships are in port.

Telecommunications

Mobile/cell phones
There are GSM service available.

Electricity supply

110/120V AC, 60 Hz

Getting there

Air
International airport/s: St Thomas-Cyril E. King (STT), 3km west of Charlotte Amalie, duty-free shop, bar, restaurant, bank, shops, car hire. St Croix-Alexander Hamilton (STX), 14km south-west of Christiansted.
Airport tax: None
Surface
Water: Regular ferry service with the British Virgin Islands.
Main port/s: Charlotte Amalie (St Thomas), Christiansted, Frederiksted, South Shore cargo port (St Croix).

Getting about

National transport
Air: There are frequent services between St Thomas and St Croix (by Sunaire Express).
Road: Throughout the islands there are around 800km of well maintained roads.
Buses: Public service on all main routes and group tours available.
Water: Regular ferry service between St Thomas and St John and the British Virgin Islands.

City transport
Taxis: Widely available; fixed-rate system applies but is not always strictly adhered to.
Higher charges are made for extra passengers, luggage and at night. Taxi vans usually carry multiple passengers; private taxis can be arranged for extra cost.

Car hire
A wide selection of cars is available. National licences are accepted and required. Traffic drives on the left. Speed limit is 35kph in towns and 55kph elsewhere.

BUSINESS DIRECTORY

The addresses listed below are a selection only. While World of Information makes every endeavour to check these addresses, we cannot guarantee that changes have not been made, especially to telephone numbers and area codes. We would welcome any corrections.

Telephone area codes

The international direct dialling code (IDD) for the US Virgin Islands is +1 340 followed by the subscriber's number.

Chambers of Commerce

St Croix Chamber of Commerce, PO Box 4369, Kingshill, St Croix 00851 (tel: 773-1435; fax: 773-8172; e-mail: stcroixchamber@vipowernet.net; internet: www.stxchamber.org).

St Thomas-St John Chamber of Commerce, 6 Main Street, PO Box 324, Charlotte Amalie, St Thomas 00804 (tel: 776-0100; fax: 776-0588; e-mail: chamber@islands.vi).

Banking

Banco Popular de Puerto Rico, Church St, Christiansted, St Croix, VI 00820.

First Virgin Islands Federal Savings Bank, 50 Kronprindesens Gade, Charlotte Amalie, St Thomas, VII 00803 (tel: 776-9494).

Central bank
Federal Reserve System, 20th Street and Constitution Avenue, NW, Washington DC 20551 (tel: (202) 452-3000; fax: (202) 452-3819).

Travel information

National tourist organisation offices
USVI Department of Tourism, PO Box 6400, St Thomas, VI 00804 (tel: 800-372; internet: www.usvitourism.vi).

Other useful addresses

Department of Economic Development and Agriculture (responsible for promotion and development of tourism), PO Box 6400, St Thomas 00804 (tel: 774-8784).

Industrial Development Commission, PO Box 3499, St Croix (tel: 773-6499); PO Box 6400, St Thomas (tel: 774-8784).

Office of the Governor, Government House, 21–22 Kongens Gade, Charlotte Amalie, St Thomas, VI 00801 (tel: 774-0001).

St Croix Hotel and Tourism Association, PO Box 24238, Gallows Bay, St Croix, USVI 00824 (tel: 773-7117; fax: 773-5883, e-mail: hax@noc.usvi.net).

St Thomas and St John Hotel Association, 4-D Contant, St Thomas, USVI 00803 (tel: 774-6835).

Virgin Islands Port Authority, Cyril E King Airport, St Thomas, VI 00801 (tel: 774-1629).

Internet sites

Tourist information: www.here.vi

US Office of Insular Affairs: www.doi.gov/oia

US Virgin Islands Guide: www.usvi.net/

Uruguay

In many respects, to the outside observer, Uruguayans and Argentines would seem to be from the same tribe. Both nations speak a 'plateno' Spanish, share a love of large steaks or 'bifes' and their businessmen criss-cross the River Plate from Montevideo to Buenos Aires as though they were districts of the same city. Long known as the 'Switzerland of South America' Uruguay is where Argentinians, Brazilians and even monied Paraguayans see fit to deposit their 'savings' (*ahorrillos*) and buy holiday apartments in Punta del Este and the more *arriviste* district of José Ignacio. In Montevideo the districts of Pocitos and Carrasco were preferred. Despite the recessions and terrorism and political uncertainty that have beset it, the leafy Montevideo suburbs of Pocitos and the booming resorts of Punta del Este and José Ignacio beach have a very European feel to them.

In the late 1960s Uruguay entered a long period of decline. Governments came and went, terrorist activity and kidnappings became a major problem and a once prosperous country became something of a dusty backwater. Wealthy Argentines continued to vacation in Punta del Este, taking a somewhat proprietorial view of their neighbour across the River Plate. In the twenty-first century the roles began to reverse, as Uruguay's economic wealth and political stability recovered.

Traditionally the Partido Nacional-Blancos (PN) (National-White Party) and Partido Colorado (PC) (Colorado Party) dominated Uruguayan politics. Things

KEY FACTS

Official name: República Oriental del Uruguay (Oriental Republic of Uruguay)

Head of State: President José Mujica (Frente Amplio) (sworn in 1 Mar 2010)

Head of government: President José Mujica

Ruling party: Frente Amplio (FA) (Broad Front) coalition (since 2004)

Area: 176,215 square km

Population: 3.36 million (2010)*

Capital: Montevideo

Official language: Spanish

Currency: Peso Uruguayo (Ur$) = 100 centavos

Exchange rate: Ur$19.85 per US$ (Oct 2011)

GDP per capita: US$11,998 (2010)

GDP real growth: 8.50% (2010)

GDP: US$40.30 billion (2010)

Unemployment: 6.70% (2010)

Inflation: 6.70% (2010)

Balance of trade: -US$256.00 million (2010)

Annual FDI: US$1.63 billion (2010)

* estimated figure

changed with the advent of the Frente Amplio (FA) (Broad Front), a coalition of left-wing parties, which soon became Uruguay's largest political grouping and has ruled Montevideo since 1990. In the October 2004 presidential elections, Tabaré Vázquez ran against the Blanco candidate Jorge Larranaga and the Colorado candidate, former interior minister Stirling. President Vazquez won the elections in the first round, with a decisive 50.5 per cent and his party achieved a parliamentary majority.

Election time

In Uruguay's last presidential election (November 2009), the Conservative ex-president Luis Alberto Lacalle was adopted as the PN's presidential candidate, defeating Senator Jorge Larrañaga, a more middle-of-the-road politician. Some analysts had argued that Sr Lacalle was too conservative for the Uruguayan mood, a prediction which ultimately proved correct. His opponent, the former left-wing rebel José Mujica (FA), had long been seen in the opinion polls as the favourite to become the next president of Uruguay. Sr Mujica, who spent 14 years in jail, had taken 48 per cent of the vote in the first round, just short of the absolute majority he needed and with Luis Lacalle, who took about 28 per cent, in second place. The opinion polls put Sr Mujica ahead by around six to eight percentage points but he was still viewed with suspicion by some of the country's conservatives because he was a founder of the Marxist Tupamaros guerrilla movement which came close to bringing Uruguay to its knees in the late 1960s and early 1970s. Sr Mujica is a close ally of Venezuelan President Hugo Chavez, although he has said he styles himself more along the political lines of Brazil's populist former president, Luiz Inacio 'Lula' da Silva. Sr Mujica's running mate was former finance minister Danilo Astori, is considered a political pragmatist. The two ran on a platform that maintained the economic policies of popular outgoing President Tabaré Vazquez who was constitutionally prohibited from running for office again. In the event, the opposition candidate Luis Lacalle, conceded defeat after Sr Mujica was confirmed as winning some 51 per cent of the vote.

In the municipal elections which were held in May 2010, the governing Frente Amplio coalition managed to keep control over three of the main regional authorities, including the capital Montevideo, where half the Uruguayan population lives. The main opposition National Party ended up with eleven departments and the junior Colorado Party doubled from one to two. The government thus lost control over several departments it had gained in the previous 2005 elections.

In Montevideo, which has been ruled by the Frente Amplio since 1990 with clear majorities above 55per cent, this time the elected mayor of the Uruguayan capital, Communist Ana Olivera only garnered 46 per cent of the vote. This, however, did not mean a gain for the two opposition parties which together remained at virtually the same level as in 2005: below 40 per cent.

Despite their victory, the election's result was interpreted by Frente Amplio officials as a political shot across the bows, as the unprecedentedly high number of blank/void votes clearly expressed a protest likely triggered by the party's (non-participative) system chosen to nominate the (nomenclature) candidate Ms Olivera and the poor performance of the Montevideo governments which, after twenty years, still seemed incapable of solving simple issues such as rubbish collection, transport system, chaotic traffic and the overall municipal taxing scheme which is far from delivering what is expected. What had emerged was that in Uruguay's local elections, local issues appeared to outweigh national interests and allegiances.

The economy

In Uruguay, according to the World Bank, it takes on average 43 days involving 10 different government procedures to register a new business. Amazingly, this makes Uruguay (by a small margin), an above average Latin American republic in terms of bureaucracy. The regional averages are 10.2 procedures and 46.3 days respectively. In Venezuela the figures rises to 16 and an incredible 141 days.

Uruguayan poverty declined, according to the World Bank by nearly 39 per cent between 2003 (from 31.3 per cent of the population) and 2009 (19 per cent). Extreme poverty was further lowered by 57 per cent, from 3 per cent to 1.3 per cent over the same period. This latter development was partially attributed to the expansion of Uruguay's family allowance programme, which was assisted by the World Bank. The unprecedented economic growth was maintained in the period 2004 to 2008, when growth averaged 6.6 per cent. Efforts to decrease the economy's vulnerability successfully resulted in greater resilience in the face of the 2008/09 global recession than seen in most other emerging market economies. The 2.9 per cent expansion rate recorded in 2009 was one of the highest growth rates in the region.

Prudent fiscal policies and enhanced debt management policies brought about a considerable reduction of public debt. Gross public debt declined from 79.3 per cent of gross domestic product (GDP) in 2005 to 60 per cent in 2009. Net public debt declined about 20 percentage points of GDP over the same period.

In its late 2011 summary overview of the Uruguayan economy, the International Monetary Fund (IMF) noted that per capita income in purchasing power terms had doubled from its pre-2002 crisis levels,

KEY INDICATORS **Uruguay**

	Unit	2006	2007	2008	2009	2010
Population	m	*3.31	*3.32	*3.33	*3.35	*3.36
Gross domestic product (GDP)	US$bn	19.32	24.00	31.20	31.50	40.30
GDP per capita	US$	5,977	7,206	9,351	9,426	11,998
GDP real growth	%	7.0	7.5	8.5	2.9	8.5
Inflation	%	6.4	8.1	7.9	7.1	6.7
Unemployment	%	10.8	9.2	7.6	7.3	6.7
Industrial output	% change	–	–	6.1	1.0	–
Agricultural output	% change	–	–	5.7	2.0	–
Exports (fob) (goods)	US$m	3,699.0	5,063.0	7,095.5	6,388.9	8,060.8
Imports (fob) (goods)	US$m	4,701.0	5,554.3	8,806.7	6,660.0	8,316.8
Balance of trade	US$m	-1,002.0	-491.3	-1,771.3	-271.1	-256.0
Current account	US$m	-460.2	-195.0	-1,485.9	211.9	160.2
Total reserves minus gold	US$m	3,085.0	4,114.0	6,533.0	8,029.0	7,644.0
Foreign exchange	US$m	3,084.0	4,114.0	6,349.0	7,644.0	7,168.0
Exchange rate	per US$	24.07	23.47	20.94	22.56	20.06

* estimated figure

unemployment had fallen to record lows and social indicators had also improved. The key factors behind this performance included important policy reforms, prudent macro-economic policies, social policies and a favourable external environment.

The growth momentum continued into 2011 but a slowdown is underway led by weaker exports and slower public investment. GDP growth was forecast at 6 per cent in 2011 and at 4.25 per cent in 2012. Inflation at 7.9 per cent in October 2011 remained above the target range (4-6 per cent). The Banco Central del Uruguay (central bank) tightened monetary policy in the first half of 2011 but left the tightening cycle in pause since late September 2011 to allow the global outlook to become clearer. The fiscal deficit narrowed and Uruguay's gross public debt continued to fall, to 55 per cent of GDP in June 2011.

The IMF considered the outlook for the Uruguayan economy to be positive but with downside risks stemming from the highly uncertain global outlook. Uruguay's economic and financial vulnerabilities are modest and the government has reduced debt vulnerabilities significantly and built important financial buffers; still the spillovers of a deteriorating global outlook could be significant. A long-term policy challenge is to sustain strong and balanced growth with less volatility than in the past.

Other reforms also appear to have been successful. In 2009 the Uruguayan government began undertaking a far-reaching restructuring of the Uruguayan health system. This included results-based financing pilot projects and performance agreements that have expanded access to primary care services and have introduced early disability detection screening, which now covers more than 75 per cent of newborns at risk for disability, ensuring they receive follow up care.

A World Bank supported programme was also instrumental in eradicating foot-and-mouth disease, through the introduction of a tracking system that now covers all Uruguayan cattle, significantly enhancing Uruguay's image as reliable exporter of beef products to standards-sensitive markets. Uruguay is the only country in the world to achieve 100 per cent traceability of cattle. A tracking system monitors the movement of all cattle in the country through a chip placed in the ear. The information is centralised, thus providing for immediate access to the complete history of the animal's movement throughout its life.

Risk assessment

Economy	Good
Politics	Fair
Regional stability	Good

COUNTRY PROFILE

Historical profile

1516 Spanish explorer Juan Díaz de Solis was killed by indigenous people while he was navigating the Rio de la Plata. His death discouraged European exploration for more than a century.
1700s The Portuguese began colonising Uruguay.
1726 The Spanish founded Montevideo and took over Uruguay.
1776 Uruguay became part of the vice royalty of La Plata, which was run from Buenos Aires in Argentina.
1808 The defeat of the Spanish monarchy by Napoleon weakened La Plata, leading to a rebellion in Uruguay which overthrew the vice royalty. The Uruguay resisted Argentine and Brazilian invaders.
1825 Uruguay achieved formal independence from Spain.
1830 A constitution was approved.
1838–65 Uruguay became embroiled in civil war between the conservative Colorados (reds) and the liberal Blancos (whites).
1865–70 Uruguay joined Argentina and Brazil and fought a war against Paraguay, which was eventually defeated.
1904 The Colorados and Blancos fought their last civil war. The Blancos became the Partido Nacional (PN) (National Party) and the Colorados the Partido Colorado (PC).
1903–07 and 1911–16 President José Batlle y Ordonez (PC), introduced the welfare state, extended the right to vote to women, disestablished the Roman Catholic Church and abolished the death penalty.
1933 A military coup led to the abolition of opposition parties.
1951 A new constitution replaced the post of president with a nine-member council.
1962–73 The Tupamaros guerrillas engaged in a campaign of insurgency.
1973–85 A military dictatorship took power, unleashing a campaign of harsh repression.
1984 Violent protests erupted against military rule. The military dictatorship agreed to step down and return the country to constitutional government.
1985 Julio María Sanguinetti (PC) was elected president.
1989 Luis Alberto Lacalle Herrera (PN) (known as Cuqui) was elected president. A referendum agreed to an amnesty for human rights abusers.
1994 Julio María Sanguinetti was elected president.
1999 Jorge Batlle Ibañez (PC) was elected president.
2000 A commission was set up to investigate 'disappearances' under the military regime.
2002 The financial crisis that weakened many economies in Latin America prompted Batlle to introduce fiscal measures including tax increases, while banks were closed to stop the mass withdrawal of savings; a general strike was called.
2003 The government managed to restructure almost half of its US$11 billion foreign debt, pushing the repayment dates back five years. A referendum rejected proposals for the sale of state oil assets to foreign investment.
2004 The World Bank approved a US$6.80 million grant to promote energy efficient goods and service. Left-wing, Tabaré Vázquez (Frente Amplio) won the presidential election and the Frente Amplio (FA) (Broad Front) coalition party won the parliamentary elections.
2006 International Court of Justice (ICJ) rejected the claim by Argentina that the building of two US$1 billion-plus pulp mills, by Finnish company, Botnia, on its border with Uruguay, would pollute the river ecosystem. Uruguay paid back its US$1.1 billion debt to the International Monetary Fund.
2007 Montevideo became the home of the new parliament of Mercosur, South America's leading trading bloc.
2008 The industry minister announced a natural gas field had been found offshore in Uruguayan waters.
2009 In the first general elections with compulsory voting, the incumbent FA won 60 seats out of 99 in the chamber of deputies and 16 seats out of 30 in the Senate. José Mujica (FA) won the run-off presidential election with 54.8 per cent of the vote; his rival, Luis Alberto Lacalle (PN), won 45.2 per cent.
2010 President José Mujica was sworn into office on 1 March. In July a co-operation agreement was signed by the presidents of Uruguay and Brazil, aimed at increasing political and economic integration between the two neighbours. In September Uruguay denied entry to *HMS Gloucester*, the British frigate charged with guarding the Falklands Islands, which had been *en route* to the Falklands when the captain had requested permission to take on fuel and provisions in Montevideo.
2011 On 15 March, Uruguay recognised the Palestinian State, with borders that existed before the (Arab-Israeli) Six-Day War, in 1967. On 2 August, the Inter-American Development Bank (IADB)

approved a US$1.8 billion loan to Uruguay to invest in infrastructure projects.

Political structure

Constitution

The constitution dates from 1967, with a period of suspension during military rule between 1973 and 1985. Voting is by secret ballot and is obligatory for all citizens aged 18 and over. The electorate has to vote in support of a single party list for president, mayors and legislators. A reform to permit cross-party voting for the different positions was defeated at a referendum in 1994.

Form of state

Presidential democratic republic

The executive

Executive power is vested in the president, who is directly elected every five years, usually in October or November. The president is assisted by a vice president and an appointed council of ministers. The president has the power to veto parliamentary resolutions, but the veto can be overturned by a three-fifths majority of Congress.

National legislature

The bicameral Asamblea General (General Assembly) comprises the Cámara de Diputados (Chamber of Deputies) with 99 members and the Cámara de Senadores (Chamber of Senators (Senate)) with 30 members, plus the vice president. Both chambers are elected by proportional representation and members of both serve for five-year terms. Compulsory voting was introduced from October 2009 for the parliamentary and presidential elections.

Legal system

The legal system is based on Spanish civil law. Written law is passed by parliament and promulgated by the president. The ultimate source of the law is the constitution.

Judicial power is exercised by the Supreme Court of Justice which has five members elected by Congress. The Court nominates all other judges and officials.

Last elections

25 October 2009 (parliamentary), 25 October–29 November 2009 (presidential and runoff).

Results: Parliamentary: (Chamber of Deputies) the Frente Amplio (FA) (Broad Front) won 47.49 per cent (50 seats out of 99), the Partido Nacional (PN) (National Party) 28.54 per cent (30), the Partido Colorado (PC) (Colorado Party) 16.67 per cent (17) and the Partido Independiente (PI) (Independent Party) 2.44 per cent (two). Senate: FA 16 seats (out of 30), PN nine, PC five. Turnout was 89.86 per cent.

Presidential (first round): José Mujica (FA) won 47.96 per cent of the vote, Luis Alberto Lacalle (PN) 29.07 per cent, Pedro Bordaberry (PC) 17.02 per cent; two other candidates won less than 3 per cent each. (Runoff): José Mujica won 54.8 per cent of the vote, Luis Alberto Lacalle 45.2 per cent. Turnout was 89.18 per cent.

Next elections

October 2014 (presidential and parliamentary)

Political parties

Ruling party

Frente Amplio (FA) (Broad Front) coalition (since 2004)

Main opposition party

Partido Nacional-Blancos (PN) (National-White Party)

Population

3.36 million (2010)*

Last census: 1 January 2004: 3,241,003

Population density: 19 inhabitants per square km. Urban population: 92 per cent (2002).

Annual growth rate: 0.7 per cent 1994–2004 (WHO 2006)

Ethnic make-up

Around 90 per cent are of European descent, with approximately one-quarter of the population of Italian origin. Minorities are black and *mestizo* (mixed race), but there are no pure Indian groups.

Religions

The majority of Uruguayans are Roman Catholic (66 per cent) with a small minority of Protestants (2 per cent) and Jews (1 per cent). Secular traditions are strong and a third of the population have no professed religious faith.

Education

All education, including university tuition, is provided free of charge. The curriculum is the same in both public and private schools. Secondary education is available from aged 12 and divided into two three-year courses. Technical studies are offered in technical schools and last between two and seven years. There are five universities and enrolment in tertiary education is typically 30 per cent.

Literacy rate: 98 per cent adult rate; 99 per cent youth rate (15–24) (Unesco 2005).

Compulsory years: Six to 14

Enrolment rate: 109.5 per cent gross primary enrolment; 98.5 per cent gross seconday enrolment, of relevant age groups (including repeaters) (Unicef 2004).

Pupils per teacher: 20 in primary schools

Health

HIV/Aids

HIV prevalence: 0.3 per cent aged 15–49 in 2003 (World Bank)

Life expectancy: 75 years, 2004 (WHO 2006)

Fertility rate/Maternal mortality rate: 2.3 births per woman, 2004 (WHO 2006); maternal mortality 26 per 100,000 live births (World Bank).

Child (under 5 years) mortality rate (per 1,000): 12 per 1,000 live births (World Bank)

Head of population per physician: 3.65 physicians per 1,000 people, 2002 (WHO 2006)

Welfare

Uruguay maintains one of the most comprehensive systems of social security in Latin America, including free education, state medical care, pensions and unemployment benefits. Social security spending accounts for around 15 per cent of GDP.

The largest welfare expenditure is the payment of old age pensions. The long tradition of healthcare provision and a relatively low mortality rate have produced an ageing population. The pension age is low (with sometimes less than 30 years' service required). There are some 800,000 old-age pensioners out of a total population of three million and compared to a workforce of only one million, producing one of the highest ratios of pensioners to workers in the world.

There is widespread and vociferous opposition to any modification of the social security system. Many of the welfare benefits, including a workers' charter stipulating maximum hours, minimum wages and paid holidays, date from the beginning of the twentieth century.

Social security is covered by the state budget with about 50 per cent of contributions coming from tax revenues. Despite attempts by the government to raise the percentage derived from taxes, the remaining 50 per cent is still split roughly equally between contributions from workers and employers. Almost 90 per cent of the population is covered for all benefits. Housewives, who are ineligible for retirement benefit, only receive separate pensions after their husbands have died.

Benefits include: a retirement pension at 60 for men, 55 for women or after 30 years of recognised service; an invalidity pension after 10 years of recognised service; an early retirement pension for citizens fulfilling political duties; free maternity care for working women and workers' wives; and sick pay of up to three months for all workers. Unemployment pay of up to six months is provided for all workers who have paid contributions for a year or more. This can reach up to 75 per cent of nominal salary. All medical costs are met by the state during the six-month period.

Main cities

Montevideo (capital, estimated population 1.4 million in 2005), Salto (103,622),

Paysandú (80,352), Las Piedras (72,617), Rivera (69,681).

Languages spoken

Business languages: English and Portuguese. French and Italian are also widely spoken.

Official language/s

Spanish

Media

Press

Dailies: In Spanish, national newspapers, mostly published in Montevideo, include *El País* (www.elpais.com.uy), *Diario Cambio* (www.diariocambio.com.uy), *El Telégrafo* (www.eltelegrafo.com), *La República* (www.larepublica.com.uy), and *Ultimas Noticias* (www.ultimasnoticias.com.uy) an evening newspaper.

Weeklies: In Spanish, there are many magazines, the biggest of which is *Brecha* (www.brecha.com.uy), *Juventud* (www.chasque.apc.org/juventud) is a youth magazine, *Guambia* (www.guambia.com.uy) is a satirical weekly.

In English, the *Uruguay Daily News* (www.uruguaydailynews.com) has an online news digest.

Business: In Spanish, the leading weekly publications are *Crónicas Económicas* (www.cronicas.com.uy) and *Búsqueda (Search)*, while *El Observador* (www.observador.com.uy) is a business-oriented newspaper. *Económico* (www.redtercermundo.org.uy/tm_economico/) is a monthly publication.

Periodicals: There are numerous periodicals and a few trade publications. The government's official journal *Diario Oficial* (www.impo.com.uy) is a monthly publication.

Broadcasting

The government-owned, national broadcaster is Servicio Oficial de Defusión Radiotelevisión y Espectáculos (SODRE) (www.sodre.gub.uy).

Radio: The public radio network has four stations broadcasting cultural, news, educational and entertainment programmes. There are more than 100 private, commercial radio stations, all broadcasting in Spanish, located throughout the country. From Montevideo, Radio Monte Carlo (www.radiomontecarlo.com.uy), Radio El Espectador (/www.espectador.com), Radio Sarandí (www.radiosarandi.com.uy) and 1410 AM Libre (www.1410amlibre.com.uy) transmit news and entertainment programmes.

Television: Over 70 per cent of households own television sets.

The public television channel TV Nacional Uruguay known as TNU (www.tnu.com.uy) broadcasts news, documentaries and cultural programmes nationally. Commercial TV stations include Teledoce (www.teledoce.com), Saeta TV Canal 10 (www.canal10.com.uy) and Monte Carlo TV canal 4 (www.canal4.com.uy) broadcasts foreign Spanish language shows, as well as dubbed US TV shows, and TV Ciudad (www.teveciudad.org.uy) broadcasting cultural shows.

There are pay-for-view television services available through (www.paysandu.com).

Advertising

Television advertising claims nearly half of all media advertising expenditure, while around 25 per cent is spent in the print media. Less than 20 per cent goes to radio advertising. Advertising placement fees, in particular on radio and television, are high by regional standards.

News agencies

Other news agencies: Mercopress (in English): www.mercopress.com

Economy

The wealth of Uruguay is generated by agriculture and manufacturing, including food processing using domestic products. Its natural resources include fertile farmland, plentiful water for hydroelectricity generation and minerals including granite and marble. Its service sector, which constitutes over 62 per cent of GDP, includes a healthy tourist industry as well as ancillary and support industries for agriculture and manufacturing. Agricultural products include wheat, rice, barley and wine. However its single most important component is its cattle production. In 2009 it had 11.9 million head of cattle, falling to 11.8 million in 2010. It exported beef and veal to over 100 countries in 2010 (estimated at 400,000 tonnes in 2011), as well as dairy and leather products plus live animals. Its large flocks of sheep produce lambs' meat and wool for export (around 80 per cent of wool production). In the first six months of 2010, Russia became Uruguay's primary destination for beef exports by volume at 32 per cent, with the EU the primary destination by value at 30 per cent of total market share. A severe drought in 2008–09 caused a fall in beef herd numbers, which affected the amount of beef available for export; numbers were increasing in 2010–11, ready for growth in foreign sales. However, pasture available has been reduced and given over to soybean cultivation and livestock production has become more intense, with an emphasis on maintaining its bovine spongiform encephalopathy-free (BSE) status and improving herd management. Uruguay has been systematically vaccinating its national herd against foot-and-mouth disease (FMD) to avoid foreign import restrictions.

The financial sector is an important component of the economy and following the international financial crisis the Banco Central del Uruguay (central bank) approved US$4 million to strengthen institutional supervision of the sector in December 2009.

GDP growth was 8.5 per cent in 2008; it fell sharply in 2009 to 2.9 per cent as the global economic crisis cut trade in the products Uruguay exports. However as the country had entered the crisis with significant economic momentum it was able to recover quickly, so that GDP growth bounced back to 8.5 per cent in 2010. An adherence to reforms during the period also helped to generate confidence it Uruguay's policy management, while the financial and banking system was under supervision.

Uruguay per capita income is the highest in Latin American. It has grown steadily and almost doubled from US$5,977 to an estimated US$12,824 in 2011, reflecting the general growth in the economy as a whole. Remittances in 2009 were US$101 million (0.3 per cent of GDP), rising to an estimated US$104 million in 2010. Unemployment in Uruguay was at an all time low in 2010 and some sectors were hampered by labour shortages.

External trade

As a member of Mercosur, the world's fourth largest free-trade zone, Uruguay (along with Argentina, Brazil and Paraguay), has access to a market of over 200 million consumers. The EU and Mercosur have been in negotiations to create a mutual free trade zone since 2004 and in 2011 these were still ongoing. Uruguay is also an associate member of the Andean Community (AC), with which Mercosur has negotiated a free trade area.

Foreign trade accounts for around 50 per cent of GDP. Almost 90 per cent of productive land is used for animal husbandry with agriculture the largest exporting sector. Processed meat (fresh, canned and frozen) and animal products account for around 50 per cent of manufacturing activity.

Imports

Main imports are fuels, capital machinery, chemicals and plastics, vehicles, electrical and electronic equipment.

Main sources: Argentina (typically 24 per cent of total), Brazil (21 per cent), China (12 per cent).

Exports

Main exports are meat (particularly beef), rice, wine, raw hides and skins, wool, fish and dairy products.

Main destinations: Brazil (typically 20 per cent of total), Argentina (6 per cent), China (4 per cent).

Agriculture

Farming

Though agricultural production accounts for approximately 6 per cent of total GDP, agricultural-related products make up more than half of the country's exports. The sector also employs around 11 per cent of Uruguay's workforce.

Traditional exports have been hit by protectionism and tough competition from the EU.

The sector is also an important supplier of raw materials (sugar, oilseeds, etc) to industry. It is expanding more rapidly than industry.

Livestock rearing forms the basis of the sector with cattle and sheep being produced for domestic consumption and for export (as meat, wool, hides and skins). Poultry and pigs are largely produced for the home market but exports of dairy products are increasing in importance. Exports of butter and cheese to Mercosur countries are substantial. A severe drought in 2008–09 caused a fall in beef herd numbers, which affected the amount of beef available for export; numbers were increasing in 2010–11, ready for growth in foreign sales. However, pasture available has been reduced and given over to soybean cultivation and livestock production has become more intense, with an emphasis on maintaining its bovine spongiform encephalopathy-free (BSE) status and improving herd management. Uruguay has been systematically vaccinating its national herd against foot-and-mouth disease (FMD) to avoid foreign import restrictions.

There is virtual self-sufficiency in food, although imports of wheat are required at times of low harvests.

Principal crops are wheat (mainly grown on mixed farms), rice (the main export crop, grown almost entirely in the north-east), sugar cane and beet, maize, barley, sorghum, linseed, sunflower seed, vegetables (mainly grown by smallholders) and citrus fruits (mainly oranges and tangerines).

Fishing

The fishing industry typically generates US$80 million in exports per annum. Uruguay suffers from water pollution from its meat and leather industries, which has hit the fishing sector in previous years. If this problem can be permanently erradicated the prospects for the fishing industry will improve markedly.

Forestry

Uruguay has approximately 1.2 million hectares of forested land, which constitutes 5 per cent of the country's total landmass.

Assisted by fiscal incentives, forestry has become a dynamic sector, attracting both foreign and domestic investment. Local forest resources produce modest quantities of sawn timber and pulp with most of paper products imported.

It is estimated that 1.7 million tonnes of timber per year could be exported, but improvements and remodelling of existing facilities and infrastructure would be needed in order to transport the timber.

Industry and manufacturing

Uruguay's industrial sector has been in recession in recent years and has suffered significant reductions in investment. The industry still accounts for a sizeable percentage of the workforce, though this is now falling.

Government industrial policy has promoted export operations, based mainly on agricultural processing and related labour-intensive industries. Although traditional key sectors are still meat processing and packing and while the wool industry and fisheries still have priority, attention has turned to other sectors such as textiles and leather. The penetration of new markets has been a key feature of plans to stimulate manufacturing industry and exports.

Despite a number of new trade agreements with Mercosur, the US and Mexico, industry still suffers deep-seated structural problems. These have included high levels of debt, obsolete machinery and poor investment.

Tourism

Tourism is of considerable importance to Uruguay's economy, accounting for just under 10 per cent of total GDP and employing 10.7 per cent of the country labour force.

The travel and tourism industry suffered a major decline in previous years following the economic crisis in Argentina, which, along with Brazil, is its most important market. However, the sector is now recovering and visitor numbers are rising, which has, in turn, resulted in an increase in capital investment in the sector.

Mining

Mining and quarrying combined make up less than 1 per cent of Uruguay's total GDP. The country has few known mineral reserves and is wholly dependent on imports for raw materials ranging from oil to aluminium.

There are known deposits of iron ore, gold, manganese, copper, zinc and lead. Regulations in 1990 opened up the sector to foreign investment but very few foreign companies are active. Argentina has been the main purchaser of sand from Uruguay while Spain, South Africa and the US have purchased semi-precious stones and granite. Japan and Argentina are also important markets for granite exports.

However, most mine production is consumed domestically.

Hydrocarbons

With no proven oil reserves of its own and a significant demand for oil, Uruguay relies heavily on imports. Consumption in 2008 was 41,000 barrels per day (bpd). There is only one oil refinery, situated near Montevideo, which outputs 50,000bpd which is run by the state-owned Administracion Nacional de Combustible Alcohol y Portland (ANCAP) (National Administration of Fuel, Alcohol and Portland Cement), which has a monopoly on oil importing and refining.

The importance of natural gas in the country's energy sector will increase with the construction of new pipelines and distribution systems. The first pipeline in production carries natural gas from Argentina to western Uruguay, with a capacity of 138,000bpd. There are plans for an extensive pipeline network as the government encourages an increase in gas usage to 30 per cent of primary energy consumption; however the country's economic problems have hindered this target. Currently only negligible quantities are imported.

There are known deposits of low-grade coal although no coal is produced and imports are less two million tonnes per annum.

Energy

Total installed generating capacity was 2.23 gigawatts (GW) in 2007. Production was 5.31 billion kilowatt hours (kWh) in 2006, however consumption was 6.42kWh and the shortfall was covered by imports, predominantly from Argentina and Brazil.

The 1.9GW hydropower plant at Salto Grande (built with Argentina), the 300MW Palmar plant, and two plants on the Rio Negro, provide the majority of energy consumed.

Financial markets

Stock exchange

Bolsa de Valores de Montevideo (BVM) (Montevideo Stock Exchange)

Banking and insurance

Uruguay's banking and financial services sector continues to be dominated by three public banks. The Banco Central del Uruguay (BCU), which does not offer private credit, the Banco de la República Oriental de Uruguay (BROU) and the Banco Hipotecario de Uruguay (BHU) are the kingpins of the financial system.

The BROU is multi-purpose and is the largest credit provider, offering 40 per cent of overall private credit in Uruguay and receiving 33 per cent of deposits. The Banco Hipotecario specialises in mortgage lending.

A new Bank of the South, with a headquarters in Venezuela, will be launched in 2008 to provide an alternative source of development funding for the participating countries. Assets of US$7 billion will underpin its operations.

Central bank

Banco Central del Uruguay

Main financial centre

Montevideo

Time

GMT minus three hours (daylight saving, GMT minus two hours, is determined by presidential decree)

Geography

Uruguay has an area of 176,215 square km and is bordered by Argentina to the west, by Brazil in the north and by the Atlantic and the wide River Plate estuary to the south-east. The largest river, the Uruguay, runs along the border with Argentina.

About 95 per cent of the country is rolling grassland, with few hills above 300 metres. The highest point is the Cerro Catedral at 514 metres. Only about 6 per cent of the land is naturally forested.

The River Negro (Río Negro), the main tributary of the River Uruguay, cuts across the centre of the country, separating the two main ranges of hills, the Cuchilla de Haedo and the Cuchilla Grande. Artificial lakes on the Rio Negro cover 1,199 square km.

Hemisphere

Southern

Climate

The climate is temperate and rainfall is abundant, with an average of about 100 days of rain a year. In January, the hottest summer month, average temperatures range between 21 degrees Celsius (C) on the coast and 26 degrees C inland. In July the average temperatures are between 11 degrees C on the coast and 13 degrees C in the interior, with temperatures occasionally falling to freezing point at night.

Dress codes

Clothing is mostly informal, but jackets and ties or suits for men and skirts for women are usual for business. Uruguayans generally wear more conservative colours than their neighbours in Brazil and Argentina.

Entry requirements

Passports

Required by all except nationals of Argentina, Bolivia, Brazil, Chile, Colombia, Costa Rica, Dominican Republic, Ecuador, Guatemala, Honduras, Paraguay, Peru and the US. Nationals from these countries need a national identity card.

Visa

Required by all except nationals of EU, US, Canada, Japan, Norway, Switzerland, most Latin American countries and certain others for visits up to three months. A Tourist Card will be issued when travellers enter the country (usually given to airline passengers before landing), and must be kept until departure.

Business travellers from the countries mentioned above do not require visas. All other business visitors must have a letter of authorisation from their company or organisation.

The visitor is advised to check with the nearest consulate to determine the validity of their status before travelling.

Currency advice/regulations

The import and export of local and foreign currency is unrestricted.

Travellers cheques, in US dollars (US$50 and US$100 denominations only) are readily accepted. All other currency cheques have very limited acceptance.

Customs

Personal effects are allowed in duty-free, precious jewels and gold (worth more than US$500) must be declared.

Prohibited imports

Precious jewels, gold, firearms, pornography, subversive literature, inflammable articles, acids, illegal drugs, plants, seeds, and foodstuffs as well as some antiquities and business equipment must be declared.

Health (for visitors)

Mandatory precautions

None

Advisable precautions

A typhoid vaccination may be necessary. Water precautions should be taken outside Montevideo.

Excellent health care is available but foreign visitors must pay the full cost.

Hotels

Graded into four classes by the National Tourism Bureau – de luxe, 1, 2A and 2B. There is a 20 per cent value added tax on hotel bills. Service charge is normally included – if not, usually 10 per cent tip.

Credit cards

Major credit and charge cards are readily accepted. ATMs may not accepted foreign cards.

Public holidays (national)

Fixed dates

1 Jan (New Year's Day), 6 Jan (Epiphany), 1 May (Labour Day), 19 Jun (Birth of General Artigas), 18 Jul (Constitution Day), 25 Aug (Independence Day), 12 Oct (Discovery of America Day), 2 Nov (All Souls' Day), 25 Dec (Christmas Day).

Variable dates

Carnival (two days, Feb), Holy Wednesday–Good Friday (Easter–three days, Mar/Apr), Landing of the 33 Patriots (third Mon Apr), Battle of Las Piedras (third Mon May),

Working hours

Banking

Mon–Fri: 1000–1400; summer variations may apply in certain areas.

Business

Mon–Fri: 0830–1200, 1430–1830.

Government

From mid-Mar to mid-Dec: Mon–Fri: 0900–1600. From mid-Dec to mid-Mar: Mon–Fri: 0730–1330.

Shops

Mon–Sat: 0830–1230/1300, 1530/1600–1900/2000; Sun 0830–1200 food shops only.

Telecommunications

Mobile/cell phones

There are 850/1900, 1900 and 1800 GSM services available throughout most of the country.

Electricity supply

220V AC, 50 cycles

Social customs/useful tips

Punctuality is expected and business cards are essential. Uruguay's population is mostly of Italian or Spanish descent, and maintains many European customs, ranging from diet to dress. There is a long tradition of liberal legislation in contrast to many South American countries. Divorce and gambling, for example, are both legal. There is provision in the law for duels in matters of honour, something which much of the population considers an anachronism but which is nevertheless invoked from time to time.

Security

Residents consider the capital relatively safe to walk around at night compared with other South American cities.

Getting there

Air

National airline: Pluna (Primeras Líneas Uruguayas de Navegación Aérea)

International airport/s: Montevideo-Carrasco International (MVD), 19km from city; duty-free shops, bar, restaurant, bank, post office and car hire.

Airport tax: Departure tax: US$26; Buenos Aires only US$14. Not applicable to transit passengers.

Surface

Road: There are a number of border crossings from Brazil, the crossing from Argentina is preferable by car-ferry. A US$176 million programme to improve primary highways is under way.

Water: There are high-speed ferries and a night-ferry service from Buenos Aires–Montevideo (internet: www.buquebus.com). There are also services from Colonia (160km west of

Montevideo) to Buenos Aires by ferry and a hydrofoil service (three times daily). A port departure tax may be levied.
Main port/s: Montevideo River Plate (Rio Plate) harbour includes all the country's main port facilities, served by worldwide cargo lines.

Getting about

National transport

Air: The only internal destinations currently offered are domestic legs of international flights.
Road: Ninety per cent of roads are paved and while urban roads are good, rural roads are only fair. The highway network radiates from Montevideo towards the borders of Brazil and Argentina.
Buses: ONDA, CITA and COT run fast and frequent lines, connecting most towns across the country (routes include: Montevideo-Punta del Este and Montevideo-Paysandú).
Rail: The slow rail system only connects a few villages and is under threat of closure.
Water: Scheduled river services do not exist.

City transport

Taxis: Taxis are widely available in towns and from airports. They can be hailed in the street. Fares are metered, with higher charges for extra passengers and between 0000–0600. They can be hired on a time basis, in which case fares should be negotiated in advance. A 10 per cent tip is usual.
Buses, trams & metro: An extensive bus service links all the capital's suburbs. There is an airport bus to the city centre, travelling time 35 minutes.

Car hire

International driving licence must be accompanied by two photographs; traffic conditions within Montevideo can be difficult and chauffeur-driven cars are recommended. A driving permit for 90 days can be obtained from Montevideo town hall.

BUSINESS DIRECTORY

The addresses listed below are a selection only. While World of Information makes every endeavour to check these addresses, we cannot guarantee that changes have not been made, especially to telephone numbers and area codes. We would welcome any corrections.

Telephone area codes

The international dialling code (IDD) for Uruguay is +598 followed by area code and subscriber's number:

Canelones	33	Minas	44
Florida	352	Montevideo	2
Las Piedras	2	Paysandú	72
Maldonado	42	Punta del Este	42
Mercedes	53	San José de Carrasco	2

Useful telephone numbers

Emergency: 911
Emergency, outside Montevideo: 02911
Roadside assistance: 1707

Chambers of Commerce

American-Uruguayan Chamber of Commerce, Plaza Independencia 831, Edificio Plaza Mayor, 11100 Montevideo (tel: 908-9186; fax: 908-9187; email: info@ccuruguayusa.com).

British-Uruguayan Cámara de Comercio, Avenida Libertador Brigadier General Lavalleja 1641, Piso2, Oficina 201, CP 11.100

Montevideo (tel: 908-0349; fax: 908-0936; email: camurbri@netgate.com.uy).

Uruguay Cámara Nacional de Comercio y Servicios, Rincón 454, 11000 Montevideo (tel: 916-1277; fax: 916-1243; email: info@cncs.com.ny).

Banking

Banco de la República Oriental del Uruguay, Cerrito No. 351 Casa Central, Montevideo.

Banco Exterior, Sarandi No. 402, 11000 Montevideo.

Banco Holandés Unido, Sucursal Montevideo, 25 de Mayo No. 501, 11000 Montevideo.

Banco Pan de Azucar, Rincón No. 518/528, 11000 Montevideo .

Banco Santander, Cerrito No. 449, 11000 Montevideo.

Banco Sudameris, Rincón No. 500, Montevideo.

Banco Surinvest, Rincón No. 530, Montevideo.

Banesto-Banco Uruguay, 25 de Mayo No. 401, 11000 Montevideo.

Citibank, Cerrito No. 455, Montevideo.

Discount Bank (Latin America), Rincón No. 390, Montevideo.

The First National Bank of Boston, Zabala No. 1463, 11000 Montevideo.

ING Bank S.A., Misiones No. 352/60, Montevideo.

Lloyds Bank (BOLSA), Zabala No. 1500, Montevideo.

Nuevo Banco Comercial (NBC), Cerrito No. 400, 11100 Montevideo.

Central bank

Banco Central del Uruguay, Diagonal Fabini 777, 11100 Montevideo. (tel/fax: 1967; e-mail: info@bcu.gub.uy).

Stock exchange

Bolsa de Valores de Montevideo (BVM) (Montevideo Stock Exchange): www.bolsademontevideo.com.uy

Commodity exchange

Bolsa Electronica de Valores de Uruguay (BEVSA): www.bevsa.com.uy

Travel information

Pluna Airlines, Administration Head Offices, Miraflores 1445, Carrasco (tel: 604-2244; fax: 604-2260; email: info@pluna.aero; internet: www.pluna.com.uy).

Ministry of tourism

Ministerio de Turismo del Uruguay (Ministry of Tourism), Rambla 25 de Agosto de 1825 esq, Yacaré, S/N (plano), Montevideo (tel: 188-5100; internet: www.turismo.gub.uy).

Ministries

Ministerio de Defensa Nacional (National Defence), Edificio 'Gral.Artigas', Avda. 8 de Octubre 2628, Montevideo.

Ministerio de Economía y Finanzas (Economy and Finance), Colonia 1089, P3, Montevideo.

Ministerio de Educación y Cultura (Education and Culture), Reconquista 535, Montevideo.

Ministerio de Ganadería, Agricultura y Pesca (Livestock, Agriculture and Fisheries), Constituyente 1476 Montevideo.

Ministerio de Industria, Energía y Minería (Industry, Energy and Mines), Rincón 747, Montevideo.

Ministerio del Interior (Home Office), Mercedes 993, Montevideo.

Ministerio de Relaciónes Exteriores (Foreign Affairs), Av 18 de Julio 1205, Montevideo.

Ministerio de Salud Pública (Public Health), Av 18 De Julio 1892, Montevideo. Ministerio de Trabajo y Seguridad Social (Labour and Social Security), Juncal 1511, Montevideo.

Ministerio de Transporte y Obras Públicas (Transport and Public Works), Rincón 561, Montevideo.

Ministerio de Vivienda, Ordenamiento Territorial y Medio Ambiente (Housing, Territorial Regulation and Environment), Zabala 1427, Montevideo.

Oficina de Planeamiento y Presupuesto (OPP) (Planning and Budget Office), Dr Luis A de Herrera 3350, Montevideo.

Other useful addresses

Aero Consultora Uruguaya, Florida 1280-202, Montevideo.

Asociación de Importadores y Mayoristas de Almacén, Ed de la Bolsa de Comercio, Rincón 454, Montevideo.

British Embassy, Calle Marco Bruto 1073, Montevideo (tel: 622-3630; fax: 622-7815; email: bemonte@internet.com.uy).

Comisión Para el Desarrollo de la Inversión (Committee for Investment Development), Plaza Independencia 776, P1 11100 Montevideo.

Cenci (Centro de Estadísticas Naciónales y Comercio Internacional del Uruguay) Misiones 136, 1 Montevideo.

Comisión Sectorial para el Mercosur, Paysandú esq, Florida, Montevideo.

Compañía Uruguaya de Exportaciónes S.A. (Comurex), Misiones 1372 Oficina 303, Montevideo.

Dirección General de Comercio Exterior (Bureau of Foreign Affairs), Cuareim 1384, P2 11100 Montevideo.

Dirección General de Estadísticas y Censos (DGEC), Cuareim 2052, Montevideo.

Dirección Nacional de Aduanas, Rbla. 25 de Agosto esq. Yacaré, Montevideo.

Export Trade Uruguay S.A., Caramurú 6092, Montevideo.

International Trade Consortium SRL, Rio Negro 1394, P.3, Montevideo.

Laboratorio Tecnológico del Uruguay, Av Italia 6201, Montevideo.

Latin American Integration Association, Cebollati 1461, Casilla de Correo 577, Montevideo.

Unidad Asesora de Promoción Industrial, Rincón 723, P.2, Montevideo.

Unión de Exportadores, Rincón 454, P.2, Montevideo.

Uruguayan Embassy (USA), 1913 'I' Street, NW, Washington DC 20006 (tel: (1-202) 331-1313; fax: (1-202) 331-8142; e-mail: uruwashi@uruwashi.org).

Internet sites

El Observador Económico (Spanish): http://www.observador.com.uy

El Pais digital edition (Spanish): http://www.diarioelpais.com.edicion

Crónicas Económicas: http://www.cronicas.com.uy

Montevideo Free Zone (Zona France de Montevideo): http://www.zfm.com

Uzbekistan

KEY FACTS

Official name: Ozbekiston Respublikasy (Republic of Uzbekistan)

Head of State: President Islam Abduganievich Karimov (since 1991; re-elected 23 Dec 2007)

Head of government: Prime Minister Shavkat Mirziyayev (appointed 11 Dec 2003)

Ruling party: Coalition of O'zbekiston Liberal Demokratik Partiyasi (O'zLiDEp) (Uzbekistan Liberal Democratic Party), O'zbekistan Xalq Demokratik Partiyasi) (OXDP) (People's Democratic Party of Uzbekistan), O'zbekistan Milliy Tiklanish Demokratik Partiyasi (OMTDP) Uzbekistan National Revival Democratic Party) and Adolat Sotsial Demokratik Partiyasi (Adolat) (Justice Social Democratic Party) (from 25 Jan 2010)

Area: 447,400 square km

Population: 28.10 million (2010)*

Capital: Tashkent

Official language: Uzbek

Currency: Sum (Sum) = tiyin

Exchange rate: Sum1,746.60 per US$ (Oct 2011)

GDP per capita: US$1,380 (2010)

GDP real growth: 8.50% (2010)

GDP: US$39.00 billion (2010)

Labour force: 14.44 million (2006)*

Inflation: 9.40% (2010)

Oil production: 87,000 bpd (2010)

Balance of trade: US$1.61 billion (2009)

Foreign debt: US$3.93 billion (2007)

* estimated figure

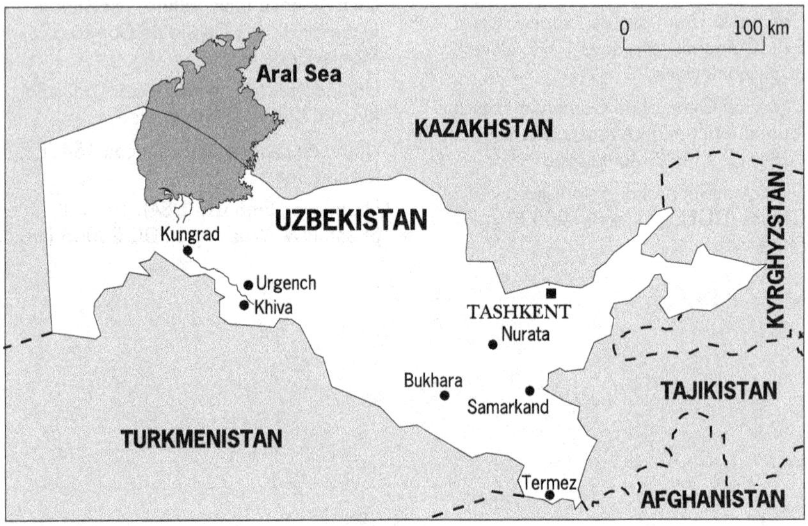

Uzbeks will not remember 2010 as a happy year. Reports of thousands of innocent Uzbeks being killed in genocide perpetrated against them in southern Kyrgyzstan were probably exaggerated, but what was certain was that atrocities were committed against Kyrgyzstan's Uzbek minority. The massacres started in the city of Osh in mid-June 2010 when Kyrgyz groups started attacking Uzbek youth. The massacres soon spread to the city of Djalal-Abad and surrounding villages 45km to the north-west of Osh, a major population centre.

Minorities

According to official data, only 124 people lost their lives. Independent sources put the figure higher, claiming that more than 90 per cent of the dead were Uzbeks. Masked rioters set fire to houses and properties belonging to ethnic Uzbeks and attacked Uzbek neighbourhoods.

Roza Otunbayeva, the newly appointed president of the interim government of Kyrgyzstan, admitted that in the south of the country there were ethnic massacres taking place. She came into power in April when outraged Kyrgyz mobs overthrew Kurmanbek Bakiyev, the previous president. Mrs Otunbayeva asked Russia to send peacekeeping forces after her government was unable to bring the situation under control. However, President Dmitri Medvedev rejected the request. Significantly, mainstream media outlets in Uzbekistan, which is under strict censorship, said nothing about massacres in neighbouring Kyrgyzstan. It was thought that President Islam Karimov's self-made image as protector of the Uzbek nation had taken a dent. The failure to protect the Uzbek minority in southern Kyrgyzstan from being attacked ran counter to President Karimov's desired image as central Asia's strong man.

The pay increases seen in mid-2010 were certainly not the norm in Uzbekistan; they were modest and did not keep pace with rising consumer prices and the depreciation of the national currency. Wage levels remained low, with the minimum legal wage now US$29 a month and pensions starting at US$55. Analysts in Uzbekistan observed that President Karimov announced the pay round partly to offset rising inflation and the widespread economic hardship in the country. But he was just as keen on maintaining calm in the wake of the ethnic violence in Kyrgyzstan, deciding that the carrot was more appropriate than the stick at a sensitive time.

This was not the first time the Uzbek minority has fallen victim to ethnic pogroms in the Kyrgyz Republic. The first massacre of Uzbeks happened in June of 1990 over land disputes. Approximately one thousand Uzbeks were killed in the cities Osh and Ozgen on that occasion. When thousands of Uzbeks from the neighbouring Uzbek cities such as Andijan, Namangan and Ferghana hurried to the Uzbek-Kyrgyz border seeking revenge, the Uzbek government closed the border. Uzbek President Islam Karimov had rejected sending support to Uzbeks in Kyrgyzstan, saying he did not want to create another Nagorno-Karabakh, a reference to the region contested by Azerbaijan and Armenia.

The Kyrgyz never had their own state in Central Asia before the Soviet era. As a territorial entity, Kyrgyzstan was established in December 1936. East Uzbekistan's foothills and mountain territories were 'gifted' to the new Kyrgyz Soviet Republic. Yuldash Akhunbabayev, the first President of Soviet Uzbekistan (1938), couldn't object to a decision made in Moscow. Instead, he stuck to the Moscow line that it didn't matter which side of the border Uzbeks fell on, since both Uzbeks and Kyrgyz were citizens of the Soviet Union. Present-day Kyrgyz cities such as Osh, Djalal-Abad and Ozgen, historically belong to Uzbeks. Even as late as 1970 the Kyrgyz population of these cities was less than 10 per cent. In the fullness of time the Kyrgyz population grew rapidly in the country's southern cities, close to Uzbekistan. At present Kyrgyz make up only half of Osh's 243,000 inhabitants. In some cases 15–20 Kyrgyz may live together in one or two bedroom apartments.

Resource rich...

Uzbekistan is a landlocked country with a gross national income per capita (GNI, Atlas method) of US$1,100 in 2009 according to the World Bank, but resource rich (gold, copper, natural gas, oil, uranium), with great development potential and strategically located in the heart of Central Asia. Uzbekistan is the only country bordering all other Central Asian states so that its development affects energy, water, trade and other issues and ultimately political and social stability within the region. Uzbekistan has well developed capital and social infrastructure, especially compared with neighbouring countries. It accounts for 45 per cent of the region's population and its economic and social prospects are critical not just for the 28 million citizens of Uzbekistan, but also for the whole Central Asian region with a total population of more than 62 million people. An estimated 37 per cent of Uzbekistan's population lives in urban areas, with about three million inhabitants in the capital Tashkent, the largest city.

The economy

Since independence in 1991, Uzbekistan has adopted a refreshingly 'gradual' approach to transition and state-led development, aimed at import substituting industrialisation and energy and food self-sufficiency. This approach resulted in a less painful economic and social transition and performance during the Asian/Russian crisis of 1998 and the global crisis of 2009 than experienced in most countries of the Commonwealth of Independent States (CIS) and, in recent years, a strong macro-economic performance. Despite a significant reduction of the proportion of agriculture in gross domestic product (GDP) from 37 per cent in 1991 to around 18 per cent in 2009, it is still an important sector of the economy, accounting for a third of employment.

In its 2011 assessment of Uzbekistan's economic prospects, the Asian Development Bank (ADB) notes that greater investment and infrastructure development will sustain GDP growth at 8.5 per cent in 2011 and 8.4 per cent in 2012. Industry (particularly construction) and services are expected to be the major contributors. Industrial output will be driven by domestic lending and foreign investment, while services will expand in line with higher domestic demand. Increasing lending coupled with favourable international prices will stimulate output of energy, machinery and metals. Agriculture is expected to be driven by higher vegetable and fruit output, while grain production will improve moderately.

The share of investment in GDP is expected to climb rapidly in the forecast period, partly because the government is seen pursuing the infrastructure development programmes faster. On 15 December 2010, it adopted a presidential decree that envisages spending US$30 billion on 259 industrial projects and US$23.1 billion on new construction in 2011–15. Most financing for both sets of programmes is planned to come from the enterprises' own resources, loans from domestic banks and the Fund for Reconstruction and Development of Uzbekistan (FRD) resources.

The government plans to direct up to 60 per cent of budget spending (US$6.2 billion) toward social programmes – outlays on which are expected to rise by 14 per cent – at the same time as raising allocations for investment (by 37 per cent). It is set to further reduce the tax burden and strengthen revenue collection. The consolidated budget, including the FRD, is forecast to post a surplus of 2.4 per cent in 2011 and 2.0 per cent in 2012. Higher public sector wages and social payments alongside a gradual recovery in remittance inflows will sustain domestic consumption, as will government plans to create many jobs through infrastructure. Higher import costs, a more accommodative fiscal policy and further depreciation of the local currency will stoke price pressures in 2011–12. To counter them, the authorities are likely to adopt a monetary policy that slows money supply growth.

KEY INDICATORS — Uzbekistan

	Unit	2006	2007	2008	2009	2010
Population	m	26.76	27.17	27.55	27.91	*28.10
Gross domestic product (GDP)	US$bn	17.03	22.30	27.90	33.50	39.00
GDP per capita	US$	631	830	1,027	1,199	1,380
GDP real growth	%	7.3	9.5	9.0	8.1	8.5
Inflation	%	14.2	12.3	12.7	14.1	9.4
Industrial output	% change	7.4	6.6	6.8	–	–
Agricultural output	% change	6.2	6.1	4.5	–	–
Oil output	'000 bpd	125.0	114.0	111.0	107.0	87.0
Natural gas output	bn cum	55.4	58.5	62.2	64.4	59.1
Exports (fob) (goods)	US$m	5,615.0	8,026.0	9,817.0	10,890.0	–
Imports (fob) (goods)	US$m	3,994.0	5,730.0	7,612.0	9,277.0	–
Balance of trade	US$m	1,621.0	2,296.0	2,205.0	1,613.0	–
Current account	US$m	1,552.0	1,631.0	3,562.0	*2,198.0	2,602.0
Exchange rate	per US$	1,241.10	1,287.50	1,310.44	1,610.00	1,516.89

* estimated figure

Inflation is forecast at 8.8 per cent in 2011 and 8.5 per cent in 2012. International prices for gold and cotton are seen peaking in 2011, but staying high. Uzbekistan's export prices for natural gas, which have approached international levels, are likely to stay at these high levels. Exports are forecast to grow at 14.0 per cent in 2011 and 3.1 per cent in 2012, supplemented by a gradual improvement in remittance inflows. The steep rise in public investment will likely offset the slower export growth in 2012 in terms of contribution to GDP.

Ubekistan's growth in imports will be driven by an expansion of infrastructure development and by increases in global energy and food prices. Since machinery and equipment are the main import items, the post-2011 investment surge will drive imports even higher. Import growth is therefore put at 11.9 per cent in 2011 and 16.3 per cent in 2012. The current account surplus is projected at 16.3 per cent and 12.6 per cent of GDP.

In the view of the ADB, the downside external risks to these forecasts are related to the pace of economic recovery in Uzbekistan's main trading partners as well as the uncertainty in global financial markets. The immediate challenge is to manage rising pressures from fiscal expansion and global food price increases. To prevent unwanted fiscal-led pressure on monetary policy, the authorities are ready to adapt the structure of budget expenditure and the pace of nominal depreciation of the currency.

Energy rich

Uzbekistan has abundant oil and natural gas reserves. However, several factors such as lack of sufficient foreign investment and inadequate transportation infrastructure have deterred the country from becoming a major energy exporter. Oil production from Uzbekistan has declined since 2003 due to lack of new investment and technological capacity to bring new oilfields online as well as a greater interest in the larger gas potential of the region by energy companies. Uzbekistan contains substantial natural gas reserves but is currently constrained by the lack of available foreign investment and natural gas export pipeline infrastructure. Uzbekistan also serves as a transit country for gas from Turkmenistan to Russia and China.

Risk assessment

Economy	Fair
Politics	Poor
Regional stability	Fair

COUNTRY PROFILE

Historical profile

1865–1876 The Russians took Tashkent and made it the capital of Turkestan, incorporating vast areas of Central Asia. They annexed the emirate of Bukhara and the khanates of Samarkand, Khiva and Kokand

1917 Following the October Revolution in Russia, the Tashkent Soviet was established.

1920 The Tashkent Soviet ousted the emir of Bukhara and the other khans.

1921 Uzbekistan became part of the Turkestan Autonomous Soviet Socialist Republic (ASSR).

1924 The Uzbek Soviet Socialist Republic (SSR) was formed from the Turkestan ASSR, the Bukharan People's Soviet Republic and the Khorezmian People's Soviet Republic; it was given Union Republic status in the Union of Soviet Socialist Republics (USSR).

1930s The Uzbek capital was transferred from Samarkand to Tashkent.

1944 The Soviet leader, Stalin, deported 160,000 Meskhetian Turks from Georgia to Uzbekistan.

1950s–80s Cotton production was boosted as the government undertook major irrigation projects on Uzbekistan's rivers and lakes. The country's water levels fell drastically.

1984 Thousands of Uzbek officials were arrested on corruption charges over the 'cotton affair' when millions of roubles went missing as a result of invented crop yields.

1989 Islam Karimov became the leader of the Communist Party of Uzbekistan. Ethnic violence broke out against the Meskhetian Turks and other minorities in the Ferghana Valley. Birlik (Unity), a nationalist movement, was founded.

1990 The Communist Party of Uzbekistan declared economic and political sovereignty and Islam Karimov became president.

1991 Independence from the USSR was declared. Uzbekistan joined the Commonwealth of Independent States (CIS). The first presidential elections were won by Islam Karimov; only a few opposition groups were allowed to field candidates.

1992 President Karimov banned the political parties Birlik and Erk (Freedom) Democratic Party and members of the opposition were arrested.

1994 Uzbekistan signed an economic integration treaty with Russia and an economic, military and social co-operation treaty with Kazakhstan and Kyrgyzstan.

1995 The ruling Chalk Demokratik Partijasi (CDP) (People's Democratic Party), formerly the Communist Party of Uzbekistan, won the elections. A referendum extended President Karimov's term of office until the year 2000.

1996 Uzbekistan, Kazakhstan and Kyrgyzstan agreed to create a single economic market.

1998 The Islamic Movement of Uzbekistan (IMU), based in Afghanistan and Tajikistan, was formed. It is said to pose a genuine armed threat to Uzbekistan. The activity of the IMU, which aims to overthrow Uzbekistan and establish a separate Islamic polity in the Ferghana valley, has made the Tajikistan-Uzbekistan border a zone of continual near-war. The government severely represses those it suspects of Islamic extremism.

1999 The president blamed bomb blasts in Tashkent on the IMU. A declaration of *jihad* was broadcast by the IMU from a radio station in Iran, demanding the resignation of the Uzbek leadership. The IMU, operating from mountain hideouts, attacked government forces (the first of many future cross-border incursions).

2000 President Karimov was re-elected. Uzbekistan was accused of widespread torture by US-based Human Rights Watch.

2001 The Shanghai Co-operation Organisation (SCO) was formed between Tajikistan, China, Russia, Kazakhstan, Kyrgyzstan and Uzbekistan. The US military were allowed to use bases in Uzbekistan for its troops, and to use Uzbekistan airspace for the US-led military operations in Afghanistan.

2002 Uzbeks voted by referendum to increase the unicameral parliament to two chambers and the presidential term in office from five to seven years. A long-standing border dispute with Kazakhstan was resolved.

2003 The Birlik movement and the opposition Erk party were allowed to hold official meetings; other political parties were denied registration. President Karimov dismissed Prime Minister Otkir Sultanov after the worst cotton harvest ever and appointed Shavkat Mirziyayev to replace him.

2004 The European Bank for Reconstruction and Development (EBRD) cut aid due to the country's poor record on economic reform and human rights. Trading practices were restricted and sparked violent street protests in the eastern city of Kokland. An agreement with Turkmenistan on water resources was signed. Opposition parties were barred from taking part in parliamentary elections.

2005 CDP and independents formed a government. Violence erupted in Andijan after gunmen released inmates from prison and troops opened fire on demonstrators. The death toll was disputed – eyewitnesses said hundreds had been killed and the government only 180.

Fifteen men were convicted of organising the violence and sentenced to 14–20 years in jail.
2006 Two opposition leaders were jailed for eight years for 'economic crimes' by criticising the crackdown in Andijan. Russia agreed to help in the development of Uzbekistan's gas and oil resources.
2007 President Islam Karimov was elected for a third term in office. The result was heavily criticised by international human rights observers as an election that was not considered free or fair.
2008 Igor Vorontsov, the representative of US-based Human Rights Watch, was expelled. Construction of a 525km gas pipeline between Uzbekistan and China began; when completed it is expected to carry 30 billion cubic metres per year.
2009 The president confirmed that non-military supplies bound for Afghanistan could be transported through Uzbekistan, with the use of rail and road links. The EU agreed to lift an embargo on arms sales that had been in place for four years. The EU said there had been 'positive steps' towards improving human rights issues.
2010 Following the second round of parliamentary elections, held on 10 January, O'zbekiston Liberal Demokratik Partiyasi (O'zLiDEp) (Uzbekistan Liberal Democratic Party) won a total of 53 seats (out of 135) and became the single largest party in the national assembly. However, all political parties were supporters of the president and unable to provide an opposition to the administration. In early June, around 400,000 refugees fled ethnic violence in Osh, Kyrgyzstan; while many remained in Uzbekistan for two weeks before returning home a significant number preferred to stay.
2011 On 25 March constitutional amendments were implemented by parliament. The new measures strengthened parliamentary democracy. They are also intended to diminish the role of cliques and the ruling elite. On 2 May, a Kyrgyzstan Inquiry Commission (KIC) published its report into the ethnic violence in Osh in 2010. It concluded that political fanaticism mixed with ethno-nationalism had resulted in violence and that the minority Uzbek community was the overwhelming victim of attack. The report also said that there was evidence of official Kyrgyz complicity. On 11 May, the 153 Kyrgyz families (over 1,000 people) living in Barak, Uzbekistan, used a petition to call on the Kyrgyzstan authorities to relocate them to Kyrgyzstan.

Political structure

Constitution

The constitution was adopted in December 1992. It guarantees respect for all citizens, regardless of language, custom or tradition, and forbids any group or individual to exercise power on behalf of the people of Uzbekistan except for the elected president and legislature. The creation of a state ideology and censorship of the media are also contrary to the constitution; however, media censorship is still practised.
The autonomous region of Karakalpakstan has its own constitution, but is subject to the laws of Uzbekistan. Karakalpakstan has the right to withdraw from Uzbekistan depending on support via a referendum.
On 8 December 1992, Uzbekistan became the second Central Asian state to adopt a post-independence constitution. The already considerable powers of the president were increased, giving him the right to appoint regional governors who report directly to him. The constitution also included guarantees of freedom, of conscience and of travel, and a statement that the country should be a secular democracy. President Karimov has pointed to the Turkish state as his country's model.
On 27 January 2002, a nationwide referendum agreed with the extension of the president's constitutional term in office from five to seven years and authorised the election of a bicameral parliament.

Independence date

1 September 1991

Form of state

Secular, (theoretically) democratic and presidential republic.

The executive

The president is head of state, holds supreme executive power and is directly elected for no more than two consecutive terms. A January 2002 referendum approved a two-year extension of the president's constitutional term of office from five to seven years (it was originally due to expire in 2005 and has been extended to 2007).
The president appoints the prime minister and ministers, subject to confirmation by the legislature, appoints the judges of the lower courts and the governors of the regions.
The Cabinet of Ministers is the government of the country; it is subordinate to the president.

National legislature

The bicameral Oliy Majlis (National Assembly) comprises the Legislative Chamber with 120 members, directly elected in a two-round voting system, for five-year terms, and the Senate with 100 members of which 84 are elected by subordinate assemblies and 16 are appointed by the president.
The minimum voting age is 25 years (the highest in the world).

Legal system

Judicial power is nominally independent of government, but as the judges of the higher courts are selected from among lower court judges, who are themselves appointed by the president, there is in practice significant political control over the system.
The three highest courts are the Constitutional Court, the Supreme Court and the High Commercial Court. The first rules on the validity of legislation and on disputes between the government of Uzbekistan and the Karakalpakstan autonomous region. The second is the highest court of appeal for criminal and civil cases initiated in the lower courts. The third is the highest court of arbitration for civil cases initiated in the lower courts.

Last elections

27 December 2009 / 10 January 2010 (parliamentary); 23 December 2007 (presidential).
Results: Parliamentary: (two rounds combined totals) O'zbekiston Liberal Demokratik Partiyasi (O'zLiDEp) (Uzbekistan Liberal Democratic Party) won 53 seats (out of 135), O'zbekistan Xalq Demokratik Partiyasi) (OXDP) (People's Democratic Party of Uzbekistan) 32, O'zbekistan Milliy Tiklanish Demokratik Partiyasi (OMTDP) Uzbekistan National Revival Democratic Party) 31, Adolat Sotsial Demokratik Partiyasi (Adolat) (Justice Social Democratic Party) 19. Turnout is 79.7 per cent.
Presidential: Islam Karimov won 90.77 per cent of the vote, no other candidate won more than 3.3 per cent. Turnout was 90.6 per cent.

Next elections

December 2014 (presidential); December 2015 (parliamentary)

Political parties

In 1997, legislation came into force prohibiting parties based on ethnic or religious lines, or those advocating war or subversion of the constitutional order.
As a result of amendments to the Law on Elections in August 2003, only registered political parties and voters' initiative groups have the right to field candidates for election.

Ruling party

Coalition of O'zbekiston Liberal Demokratik Partiyasi (O'zLiDEp) (Uzbekistan Liberal Democratic Party), O'zbekistan Xalq Demokratik Partiyasi) (OXDP) (People's Democratic Party of Uzbekistan), O'zbekistan Milliy Tiklanish Demokratik Partiyasi (OMTDP) Uzbekistan National Revival Democratic Party) and Adolat Sotsial Demokratik Partiyasi (Adolat) (Justice Social Democratic Party) (from 25 Jan 2010)

Main opposition party
All parties in the Supreme Assembly are loyal to the president. The banned O'zbekiston Erk Demokratik Partiyasi (OEDP) (Erk Democratic Party) is considered to be the main opposition party to the Karimov regime.

Population
27.91 million (2009)*
Last census: January 1989: 19,810,077
Population density: 64 inhabitants per square km (2010)
Annual growth rate: 1.5 per cent 1994–2004 (WHO 2006)
Ethnic make-up
Uzbek (72 per cent), Russian (8 per cent), Tajik (7 per cent), Kazakh (4 per cent), others (9 per cent). There is a Korean minority estimated at 7 per cent. The Uzbeks are the second most numerous Turkic people in the world after the Turks themselves.
Religions
Muslim (88 per cent, mostly Sunni); Christian Eastern Orthodox (9 per cent).

Education
Although Uzbekistan's overall literacy rate is high, the government is implementing a long-term programme of transition from Cyrillic to Latin script, and in the short-term there is likely to be some changes in the literacy rate.
Primary education begins at aged six and last until aged 10. General secondary education lasts until aged 15, when students may choose between a technical, vocational or academic course for two years. From aged 17, specialised secondary schools offer advanced vocational or academic two-year courses.
There are 16 universities and 42 research institutes in the country, including the state-run Tashkent Islamic University.
The government initiated a National Programme for Personnel Training, giving high priority to introducing new educational technologies and attracting international donors. The reform programme replaced existing schools and it is estimated that seven million pupils will enrol in these new schools, and in sharp contrast with the past, 90 per cent (an unprecedented amount in the New Independent States) of these pupils are expected to enrol in vocational education and training.
In February 2005 a report by the International Crisis Group alleged that thousands of children are forced out of school to work in cotton fields. Uzbekistan is the world's fifth largest cotton producer and during the harvest season children of all ages are used to pick the cotton. Pay for this work may be denied and refusal to work may lead to expulsion from school.
Literacy rate: 99 per cent adult rate; 100 per cent youth rate (15–24) (Unesco 2005).
Compulsory years: Six to 15
Enrolment rate: 100 per cent gross primary school enrolment rate in 2000, 94 per cent at secondary level and 36 per cent at tertiary level.
Pupils per teacher: 21 in primary schools.

Health
Healthcare standards were fairly uniform across the former Soviet Union, but the breakdown in trade and economic crises have brought about a severe shortage of medicines and equipment.
According to a presidential decree in 1999, private healthcare institutions, were exempted from tax in order to facilitate investment in medical equipment; it also included a programme for the development of medical treatment centres in villages over 2001–05. The government also plans to make premises and funds available for private healthcare institutions.
HIV/Aids
HIV prevalence: 0.1 per cent aged 15–49 in 2003 (World Bank)
Life expectancy: 66 years, 2004 (WHO 2006)
Fertility rate/Maternal mortality rate: 2.7 births per woman, 2004 (WHO 2006); maternal mortality 21 per 100,000 live births (World Bank).
Birth rate/Death rate: 23 births and 6 death per 1,000 people (World Bank)
Child (under 5 years) mortality rate (per 1,000): 57 per 1,000 live births; 7.9 per cent of children aged under five are malnourished (World Bank).
Head of population per physician: 2.74 physicians per 1,000 people, 2003 (WHO 2006)

Welfare
Social spending is relatively high compared to most other transitional countries. Social assistance is channelled through traditional local structures using the national Malhalla foundation, which is responsible for meeting the needs of the poor. The Malhalla collects information on the claimants' needs independently of the state. Wages in the agricultural sector have tended to fall behind the national average as a result of high taxes, contributing to increased risks of civil unrest. Expenditure on the social safety net continues to account for 3.5 per cent of GDP and benefits are usually increased in line with wages rather than with official inflation.
There is a comprehensive system of benefits for sickness, disability, maternity and unemployment, as well as a combined state and private pension scheme. However, many of these payments are linked to the declining minimum wage, with the result that those depending on benefits are likely to drop below the poverty line. There are special payments to veterans of the Soviet war in Afghanistan. The government also provides benefits through budget subsidies for housing maintenance and public utilities.

Main cities
Tashkent (capital, estimated population 2.2 million in 2005), Namangan (423,161), Samarkand (374,900), Andizhan (343,232), Bukhara (276,333), Nukus (226,983), Karshi (232,904), Fergana (205,159).

Languages spoken
Uzbek is of Turkic origin and is the most commonly used language, although Russian remains the language of inter-ethnic communication and business. Turkish and Arabic are also spoken. English and other Western languages are increasingly common, particularly in Tashkent and other urban areas.
Official language/s
Uzbek

Media
Although the Uzbek Constitution guarantees press freedom, the state maintains tight control of the media with routine harassment of journalists. The government has control of much of the printing and distribution infrastructure. A law, pass in 2007, holds all media outlets responsible for the objectivity of their output and, as such, self-censorship is widespread.
Press
Dailies: In Uzbek, *Hurriyat* (www.hurriyat.uz), a government-owned publication, *Khalq Sozi* has a Russian editiontion*Narodnoe Slovo* (www.narodnoeslovo.uz), *Uzbekistan Ovozi* and *Tashkent Hakikati*. In Russian, *Pravda Vostoka* (), *Zerkalo XXI* (www.zerkalo21.uz). In English, *Good Morning* and *Ovozi Times*.
Weeklies: In Uzbek, *Mohiyat*.
Business: Russian language publications include *Review* (www.review.uz), *Business Partner Uzbekistana* and *Business-vestnik Vostoka)* (Bvv) (Business News of the East) and *Kommercheskij Vestnik* (Commercial News). In English, publications include *Business Partner* and *Business Review*.
Broadcasting
The National Television and Radio Company (MTRK) (www.mtrk.uz) has a network of four TV channels and five radio stations.
Radio: MTRK national stations include radios' Uzbekistan, Yoshlar (the youth station), Mashal, Tashkent and Oltin Zamin. Private, commercial radio stations include Oriat FM (www.oriat.uz), Uzbegim

Taronasi (www.fm101.uz), Radio Grand (www.grand.uz) and Radio Sezam FM.
Television: MTRK operates four channels, Uzbekistan, Yoshlar, Sport and Tashkent. There are two national and four, privately run TV stations, located in cities around the country including Bagdad TV and Muloqot from the Fergana region, Bekabad from the Tashket region, Aloqa AK from the Syrdarya region and Samarkand TV and Orbita TV.

News agencies

National news agency: Jahon Information Agency

UzA (Uzbekistan National News Agency): www.uza.uz/en

Economy

Reliable statistics for Uzbekistan are not always available; however creditable sources of information were consulted for this report.

Uzbekistan had 600 million barrels of proved oil reserves at the end of 2009, with production of 107,000 barrels per day. It also had 1.68 trillion cubic metres (cum) of proved natural gas reserves, with production of 64.4 billion cum in 2009. Hydrocarbon extraction is the most dominant component of the economy. Of the 15.7 billion cum of natural gas exported in 2009, 11.86 billion cum was sold to Russia and 2.34 billion cum was sold to neighbouring countries. Electricity generation was 50.1 billion kilowatt hours. Mineral resources include uranium, gold and other non-ferrous and rare metals such as copper, molybdenum, zinc, wolfram, lithium and lead. Minerals include kaolin, quartz spar, phosphorus and bentonite clay. The service sector constitutes around 50 per cent of GDP. Manufacturing, particularly the automotive industry has grown, with products assembled for export and aimed at Russia.

Agriculture has fallen in importance in the economy, although cotton production and trade is the third largest source of Uzbekistan's wealth; it is the world's fourth largest producer of cotton. Agriculture constitutes around 18 per cent of GDP, of which cotton comprises over 10 per cent. Oxfam-Australia produced a report in 2010 that stated cotton production in Uzbekistan was 'one of the most exploitative enterprises in the world' as it relies on forced labour, including mandatory employment by school children, students and civil workers, working in poor conditions for very little pay. Other crops include silk, wheat, fruit and vegetables. Farming is typically either large agri-business enterprises or small family-run concerns that provide poor incomes.

GDP growth has remained strong for several years, reaching a high of 9.5 per cent in 2007 as global prices for oil reached a record level. GDP growth did not fall significantly during the global economic crisis of 2008–09 when growth was 9.0 per cent and 8.1 per cent respectively, principally because Uzbekistan is self-sufficient in food and energy, the two commodities that help increase costs for other countries.

While the government has gradually redirected the economy towards an open free-market system, the number of state-owned enterprises, and government influence in their business, remains high. Unemployment and underemployment are long-term problems, for a workforce that is generally well educated. However corruption in the education system has begun to erode the status of Uzbekistan qualifications in the region at a time of high migrant numbers. Estimates of Uzbeks working aboard range from 3–5 million, mostly in Russia, the Middle East and south-east Asia.

Although GDP per capita doubled from US$636 in 2006 to US$1,336 in 2010 the UN Human Development Index ranked Uzbekistan as 102 out of 169 countries for national development in health, education and income in 2010. The intensity of deprivation was 36.2 per cent, however statistics on the level of poverty were unavailable.

Uzbekistan is both an importer and exporter of electricity between its neighbouring countries. It is in disagreement with Tajikistan over that country's building of the Rohgan hydroelectric dam, which it says was planned in the 1970s and based on defunct technology, while the lose of water to be trapped in the dam has the potential of causing long-term damage to Uzbekistan's agricultural production.

As of December 2009, the Asian Development Bank (ADB) had provided US$1.29 billion in financial aid as part of development programmes. The loans were primarily for agriculture and natural resources projects, education, transport and information and communications technology, water supply and other municipal programmes. In April 2010 the ADB agreed to a second line of credit of US$50 million to enhance the established micro-financing service, plus a grant of US$600,000 to increase funding for small and micro-entrepreneurial enterprises in Uzbekistan. The terms of the loans for funds, to be administered by three domestic banks, must include at least a total of 25 per cent set aside for loans to women entrepreneurs.

External trade

Uzbekistan is a member of the Economic Co-operation Organization (ECO), comprising 10 regional Central Asian countries. It belongs to the Eurasian Economic Community (EAEC), which was established to promote a customs union between its six member states (Belarus, Kazakhstan, Kyrgyzstan, Russia, Tajikistan, and Uzbekistan), and among other objectives, to introduce standardised currency exchange and rules for trade in goods and services. The EAEC evolved out of the Commonwealth of Independent States (CIS) Customs Union and has begun the process of merging with the Central Asian Co-operation Organisation (CACO). By March 2011 negotiations for Uzbekistan's membership of the World Trade Organisation were still ongoing.

Natural gas has become the principal export and foreign currency earner, supplanting cotton as the primary export. Other important export products include gold, rare minerals, food, electricity and manufactured goods.

Imports

Principal imports are machinery and equipment (around 50 per cent of total), foodstuffs, chemicals and metals.

Main sources: Russia (typically 27 per cent of total), China (16 per cent), South Korea (12 per cent).

Exports

Principal exports are natural gas, oil, cotton, gold and precious stones, mineral fertilisers, ferrous metals, textiles, food products and vehicles.

Main destinations: Russia (typically 27 per cent of total), Turkey (10 per cent), Kazakhstan (7 per cent).

Agriculture

Farming

Only 9 per cent of the land is suitable for cultivation. Over 1,500 farms operate on a co-operative basis. Family farms dominate 99 per cent of the cotton sector and 93 per cent of the corn sector.

Cotton is the main crop, around a million tonnes a year being produced, three-quarters of it for export. In a report published in 2005 – *The Curse of Cotton: Central Asia's destructive monoculture* – the International Crisis Group (ICG) said that while the former Soviet cotton producing countries of Uzbekistan, Tajikistan and Turkmenistan continued to exploit their cotton growers there was little hope of improving economic development and tackling poverty. The cotton industry is vital to the economy of Uzbekistan, yet while the industry continues to rely on cheap labour (including children), land ownership is uncertain, state intervention discourages competition and the rule of law is limited, there is little incentive for the powerful vested interests to reform the system.

In addition to the economic and social costs to the rural populations, the environmental costs of the monoculture have been devastating. The degradation of the Aral Sea in particular has lead to international concern.

Forestry

Only 8 per cent of Uzbekistan is forested and commercial exploitation is for domestic purposes only as fuel. There is low production of industrial roundwood, because the government has placed restrictions on harvesting due to the poor condition of forests.

Industry and manufacturing

Industry contributed around 25 per cent to GDP in 2004 and employs 18 per cent of the working population.

Main industries include chemical and gas production, heavy engineering, specialising in machinery for the cotton-growing and textile industries, aircraft construction, metal works, textiles and cotton derivatives, canned foods and nitrogenised fertilisers.

Tourism

Uzbekistan, situated on the route of the ancient Silk Road, is a country rich in historical and cultural heritage, giving it considerable tourist potential. Infrastructure is improving and attractions, including skiing, are being developed.

Environment

The Aral Sea had been drying up due to the overuse of water from the two main rivers which feed into it, with the loss of up to 50 per cent of its water. This resulted in desertification of the surrounding land. However, by 2006, a World Bank funded project had begun a reversal, as building works on the river Syr Darya, in Kazakhstan, increased the level of water in the northern section of the Aral Sea. Work continues to allow more water into the southern section and directly benefit Uzbekistan.

Uzbekistan has numerous environmental problems, more than half of irrigated land is heavily salinated and eroded. Surface and underground water sources used for human consumption in parts of the country have also been polluted by industrial and communal discharges.

A meeting was held in April 2009 to determine water sharing between Tajikistan, Kyrgyzstan, Uzbekistan, Turkmenistan and Kazakhstan failed, as negotiators were unable to find a trade in water for energy and hydrocarbons. Tajikistan and Kyrgyzstan hold around 80 per cent of the water in the Aral Sea but suffer from lack of electricity during freezing winters, while the remaining three states downstream are semi-arid and need water for their cotton industries and agriculture.

Mining

Uzbekistan is rich in unexplored mineral deposits – its potential mineral wealth amounts to a value of US$3,000 billion.

There are around 100 deposits of various metals, including gold, silver, uranium, zinc, copper and tungsten, which need developing. Uzbekistan is the fourth-largest uranium producer in the world.

Uzbekistan is the ninth-largest gold producer in the world. Its commercial reserves are associated with open-cast mines of the Muruntau field in the Kyzylkum desert in central Uzbekistan, which have been developed by the main state gold producer Kyzylkumredmetzoloto (Navoi Integrated Mining and Metallurgical Plant) since 1967. Its annual output amounts to 55–60 tonnes, producing 70 per cent of Uzbekistan's total gold production.

The Zarafshan-Newmont joint-venture between Uzbekistan and the US mining company Newmont, set up in 1995, processes about 200 million tonnes of low-grade ore, previously regarded as waste, from the Muruntau open gold pit. The project is due to end in 2012.

Dzhetymtau, located in the Kyzylkum desert is estimated to hold reserves of 400 tonnes of gold and 350,000 tonnes of tungsten ores.

There are silver deposits in the central Kyzylkum region, which also contain gold, platinum group metals, cobalt and nickel, which can be recovered as by-products.

Uzbekistan is the only producer of enriched uranium in the former Soviet Union. All output is exported, since Uzbekistan has no nuclear reactors.

Uzbekistan's proven uranium reserves are around 80,000 tonnes, while estimated reserves are around 178,000 tonnes.

Sugraly is one of Central Asia's biggest uranium fields and holds an estimated 38,000 tonnes of uranium.

Kyzylkumredmetzoloto (Kyzylkum Precious Metals and Gold) is Uzbekistan's only uranium producer and exporter.

Uzbekistan possesses considerable reserves of lead and zinc.

Copper production in Uzbekistan averages 80,000 tonnes per year, principally from the Kalmakir open mine, with the remainder mined at the Sari Checku open pit. The ore is processed at the Almalyk concentrator.

Uzbekistan produces over 100,000 tonnes per year of feldspar, about one-third of the output of the former Soviet Union. The non-ferrous metal industry includes the mining of bismuth, tungsten and molybdenum. Other natural resources include rock salt, potassium salts, anthracite, graphite, ozokerite, sulphur, quartz, limestone, gypsum, bentonites and semi-precious stones.

Hydrocarbons

Proven oil reserves were 600 million barrels at the end of 2009, with production falling from114,000 barrels per day (bpd) in 2007 to 107,000bpd in 2009, due to a lack of new investment and technical difficulties.

There are three refineries – at Fergana, Alty-Arik and Bukhara with total capacity of 222,000bpd.

Proven natural gas reserves were 1.68 trillion cubic metres (cum) in 2009 and Uzbekistan is a major world reserve of natural gas. Of the 15.7 billion cum of natural gas exported in 2009, 11.86 billion cum was sold to Russia and 2.34 billion cum was sold to neighbouring countries

The industry is almost entirely state-controlled, with 14 companies grouped around Uzbekneftegaz (Uzbek Oil and Gas), which is responsible for all aspects of exploration, production, distribution and processing in the hydrocarbons sector. Principal oil and gas fields include Kuanish, Shakhpakthy and Chembar. Other fields have been discovered in the Mamangan and Ferghana regions.

Proven reserves of recoverable coal are 3 billion tonnes, about one-third of which is highly valued anthracite, for which production has increased, while production of less valued bitumin has remained negligible. The industry is in need of modernisation, but production meets all domestic needs of around one million tonnes per annum of which over 80 per cent is used in power stations.

Energy

Total installed generating capacity was 12.55 gigawatts (GW) in 2007, producing over 47 billion kilowatt hours (kWh). Natural gas provides most of the necessary energy for local electricity generation. Uzbekistan is the largest energy producer among the Central Asian republics and a net exporter. The energy sector is almost entirely state-controlled by the joint stock company UzbekEnergo.

Uzbekistan is part of the Central Asian power distribution system, it has 37 electric power plants including the hydroelectric power plants on the Syr Darya, Narin and Chirchik rivers, and thermal power stations at Syr Darya, Tashkent, Novo-Angren, Tachiatasch and Ferghana. Hydroelectric plants produce 15 per cent of electricity and thermal-powered plants 85 per cent.

Financial markets

Stock exchange

Republican Stock Exchange

Banking and insurance

Three state-owned banks dominate the banking sector: Bank Asaka, National Bank of Uzbekistan (NBU) and Narodny Bank.

Central bank
National Bank of Uzbekistan (NBU)
Main financial centre
Tashkent

Time
GMT plus five hours

Geography
Uzbekistan is located in the heart of Central Asia. The fourth-largest republic in the former Soviet Union, Uzbekistan measures approximately 925km from north to south and 1,400km from west to east at its widest points. The republic has a short border with Afghanistan to the south, Kazakhstan lies to the north, Kyrgyzstan and Tajikistan to the east and south-east and Turkmenistan to the south-west.
The western region, including the Karakalpakstan oblast, marks the eastern fringe of the Turkmen desert. The Kyzylkum desert covers most of the area between Tashkent and the Aral Sea. The western reaches of the Tien Shan mountain range protrude from Kyrgyzstan and Tajikistan into south-eastern Uzbekistan. The fertile Ferghana Valley runs from the north-eastern finger of Uzbekistan, east of Tashkent, across the border into Kyrgyzstan. Half of the Aral Sea lies within Uzbekistan, the other half in Kazakhstan. There are two main rivers. The Amu Darya, which enters from Afghanistan at Termez and runs along the border with Turkmenistan before turning north at Khiva and flowing into the southern end of the Aral Sea. The Syr Darya flows from the Tien Shan mountains northwards, east of Tashkent and into Kazakhstan, eventually reaching the northern end of the Aral Sea.
Hemisphere
Northern

Climate
Uzbekistan comprises mostly desert and semi-desert, with extreme continental temperatures: the average stands at minus 8 degrees Celsius (C) in January and 26 degrees C in June. Temperatures in Tashkent vary from minus 1 degree C in January to 29–40 degrees C or more in summer. Rainfall averages between 80 and 90mm per annum on the plains and 890 to 1,000mm per annum in the mountains.

Dress codes
Smart clothes are required for business visitors. Otherwise dress is not overly formal but modest, particularly outside Tashkent.

Entry requirements
Passports
Passports are required by all and must be valid for at least six months after the intended date of departure.
Visa
Required by all. Business travellers must obtain an invitation from a local company or organisation exceptions include nationals of the US, UK, Austria, Belgium, France, Germany, Italy, Japan, Spain and Switzerland who may apply directly. The Uzbek contact should submit a visa support letter to the Ministry of Foreign Affairs in Tashkent before the visitor applies for a visa. When an approval to visit has been agreed a confirmation is sent by the ministry to the embassy and the visitor should contact a consular section to ensure that a visa issuance confirmation of the Ministry of Foreign Affairs is in place before submitting their application.
To download a visa application see www.uzbekembassy.org and *consular section*, see *visa information* for further details.
Travellers on visitor's visas whose stay in Uzbekistan exceeds three days are required to register with the Local Department of the Ministry of Internal Affairs within three working days of arrival. Hotel administration should take care of such registration automatically.
Transit visas issued in other CIS countries are no longer recognised.
Currency advice/regulations
The import and export of local currency is unlimited. The import of foreign currency is unlimited but must be declared on arrival; export is limited to the amount declared. However, proof of legal exchange to local currency must be provided for re-export for imported sums of over US$2,000; retain all currency exchange receipts.
Travellers cheques have limited acceptance.
Customs
Personal items are duty-free, goods to the value of US$10,000 can be imported for personal use; valuable items such as jewellery, cameras, computers must be declared.
The export of antiques and art objects is subject to duty and a special permit from the Ministry of Culture, a certificate stating the age of the item(s) should be obtained when purchased.
Prohibited imports
Firearms, ammunition, illegal drugs, anti-Uzbek propaganda, fruit or vegetables, precious metals, gem stones and furs.

Health (for visitors)
Mandatory precautions
Vaccination certificates are required for yellow fever if travelling from an infected area.
Advisable precautions
Vaccinations for diphtheria, tetanus, hepatitis A and typhoid are recommended.
Other vaccinations that may be advised include tuberculosis and hepatitis B. A non-malignant malaria occasionally occurs in the border area of Afghanistan and Tajikistan, visitors should avoid being bitten by using anti-mosquito sprays and long clothing. There is a risk of rabies. Water precautions are recommended using water purification tablets or drinking bottled water.
Any medicines required by the traveller should be brought into the country and it would be wise to have precautionary antibiotics if going outside major urban centres. A travel kit including a disposable syringe is a reasonable precaution. Medical insurance is essential, including emergency evacuation.

Hotels
Advisable to book in advance through Uzbektourism or other specialist travel agents.

Credit cards
Credit cards are not widely accepted outside Tashkent's top hotels and restaurants.

Public holidays (national)
Fixed dates
1 Jan (New Year's Day), 8 Mar (Women's Day), 20–22 Mar (Nawruz/Persian New Year), 1 May (Labour Day), 9 May (Victory Day), 1 Sep (Independence Day), 18 Nov (Flag Day), 8 Dec (Constitution Day).
Variable dates
Eid al Adha, Persian New Year, Birth of the Prophet, Eid al Fitr.
Islamic year 1433 (26 Nov 2011–14 Nov 2012): The Islamic year contains 354 or 355 days, with the result that Muslim feasts advance by 10–12 days against the Gregorian calendar. Dates of feasts vary according to the sighting of the new moon, so cannot be forecast exactly.

Working hours
Banking
Mon–Fri: 0900–1800; Sat: 0900–1500. Banks at Tashkent airport are open only at arrival of international flights.
Business
Mon–Fri: 0800–1300, 1400–1700. Business hours generally include Saturday mornings.
Government
Mon–Fri: 0800–1300, 1400–1700. Some government offices are open Saturday mornings.
Shops
Mon–Fri: 0800–2000/2100. Shops are closed for lunch for one hour at any time between 1100 and 1500.

Telecommunications
Mobile/cell phones
There are 900 and 900/1800 GSM services located in highly populated areas only.

Electricity supply

220V AC, with round two-pin plugs.

Social customs/useful tips

Business is conducted formally. Appointments are essential when business cards are exchanged.

Personal relationships are the key to doing business in Uzbekistan, with the hierarchy confined to a small group of influential families. Establishing contact within that group can be vital.

Gratuities are illegal.

The giving of small gifts is widely practised, not as bribes but as social niceties. Uzbek hospitality is renowned. It may be regarded as insulting to decline an invitation to a private function. Offering basic food is considered insulting. It is polite to see a visitor off at a train station. If travelling on public transport, make sure to give up your seat to the old, parents with children and the disabled. Superstitions are taken somewhat seriously: for example, do not give an even number of flowers, as this is funereal; do not greet people in a doorway – this is considered unlucky. Local customs of note are ram butting and wrestling, and wedding ceremonies in September which take place in the street. Alcohol is available and smoking is widespread.

Security

Terrorist bombings in Tashkent have prompted many Western governments to advise their citizens not to visit Uzbekistan unless absolutely necessary. Visitors should alert their presence to their own embassies on arrival and take all precautions and advice given regarding safety measures.

It is unwise to venture out on the streets alone at night. Dress inconspicuously, as wealthy-looking foreigners can be a target for muggers. Identification should be carried at all times, and visitors should avoid photographing official buildings. If taking photographs in the vicinity of police or soldiers, it is best to ask their permission first.

Since 1999, there has been an increasing terrorist and kidnapping threat in the north-east of the country, especially in the Ferghana Valley and mountainous regions on the Kyrgyz and Tajik borders. Visitors should register with the Uzbek authorities before entering these areas. Outbreaks of violence can lead to strong reactions from the Uzbekistani army, including widespread road blocks and the closure of some destinations. If stopped by police, visitors should remain calm and polite.

Getting there

Air

National airline: Uzbekistan Airlines

International airport/s: Tashkent International airport (TAS), 11km from city centre. Facilities include duty-free shops, bureau de change, left luggage, restaurants and bar. There are taxis, trains and trolley buses to the city (journey time 10–20 minutes).

Airport tax: Departure tax: US$10

Surface

There are border crossings with Afghanistan, Kazakhstan, Kyrgyzstan, Tajikistan and Turkmenistan, however not all are open and available to international travellers. Check with local authorities before making an abortive trip.

Road: Primary roads along trade routes are being upgraded to increase access for freight. Secondary roads are in poor condition especially in desert areas such as the borders with Turkmenistan and the western borders with Kazakhstan.

The Regional Road Corridor Improvement Project, estimated at US$18 billion, to improve Central Asian roads, airports, railway lines and seaports and provide a vital transit route between Europe and Asia was agreed, on 3 November 2007. Six new transit corridors, between Afghanistan, Azerbaijan, China, Kazakhstan, Kyrgyzstan, Mongolia, Tajikistan and Uzbekistan, of mainly roads and rail links, will be constructed, or existing resources upgraded, by 2013. Half the costs with be provided by the Asian Development Bank and other multilateral organisations and the other half by participating countries.

Rail: Tashkent is the hub of rail services in Central Asia. Lines run west to Ashgabat (Turkmenistan), south to Samarkand and on to Dushanbe (Tajikistan), east to Bishkek (Kyrgyzstan) and Almaty (Kazakhstan) and north to Moscow (Russia). The distances involved do not make this the most convenient means of travel, services are few and slow, and tickets must be purchased with hard currency, preferably US dollars.

Getting about

National transport

Air: Uzbekistan Airways has scheduled flights to many cities and towns around the country providing a realistically quick method of getting around the country. Tashkent, Bukhara, Samarkand and Urgench are all served by internal flights.

Road: The road network is deteriorating and many published statistics on paved and unpaved roads are often a decade out-of-date. Driving can be hazardous for the visitor and it is recommended that arrangements should be made to use a local driver and a four-wheel drive vehicle, particularly if travelling to the Tien Shan mountain ranges. Tashkent roads are relatively well maintained with street lighting. Outside the city however the risks of driving, especially at night, include livestock and farm vehicles (often animal-drawn).

There are security checkpoints at the city limits of Tashkent and other towns throughout the country. A permit is necessary if travelling to Termez and other areas of the Surkhandarya region. The permit can be applied for in Tashkent and usually takes five days to process.

Uzbekistan has a large highway police force, and drivers are frequently stopped for minor infractions or document checks.

Buses: Routes between the main cities are served by modern air-conditioned coach services which are reliable but infrequent. Other regional services are irregular and often used for transporting goods and livestock.

Rail: Tashkent, Samarkand and Bukhara are all connected by an electrified network. Some other routes are in varying states of disrepair, and long-distance travel by train should be avoided.

City transport

Taxis: In each city there are official taxis (with sign on top) and unofficial taxis. Agree rates in advance when using the official taxis. A few dollars are sufficient for a local journey in an unofficial taxi. In Tashkent it is safer to use official taxis or hire cars. Taxis can be hired for an hour, a day or a week.

Buses, trams & metro: An underground railway, trolleybus service and buses provide a comprehensive network in Tashkent.

Car hire

The are very few car hire facilities; a national licence with authorised translation or international driving permit is required.

BUSINESS DIRECTORY

The addresses listed below are a selection only. While World of Information makes every endeavour to check these addresses, we cannot guarantee that changes have not been made, especially to telephone numbers and area codes. We would welcome any corrections.

Telephone area codes

International direct dialling code (IDD) for Uzbekistan is +998, followed by area code and subscriber's number:

Andijan	74	Bukara	65
Ferghana	73	Samarkand	66
Tashkent	71		

Useful telephone numbers

Police: 02

Fire: 01

Ambulance: 03

Chambers of Commerce

American Chamber of Commerce in Uzbekistan, 41 Buyok Turon Street, Tashkent 700000 (tel: 120-6077; fax:

120-7077; e-mail: office@ amcham-uzbekistan.org).

Uzbekistan Chamber of Commodity Producers and Entrepreneurs, 6 Bukhoro Street, Tashkent 700047 (tel: 133-0699; fax: 133-3799; e-mail: root@ptp.co.uz).

Banking

Agrobank, 43 Muqimiy Street, Tashkent 100096. (tel:: 150-5369, 120-8833).

Bank Asaka (specialised state joint stock commercial), 67 Nukus Str, 700015 Tashkent (tel: 120-8111; fax: 120-8173).

Hamkorbank, Avenue Bobur 85, Andijan (tel: 244-73-33; 244-77-18).

Narodny Bank (People's Bank), Tashkent.

National Bank for Foreign Economic Activity of the Republic of Uzbekistan, 101 Amir Temur St, 700084 Tashkent (tel: 137-6077; fax: 133-3200).

Pakhta Bank, 79A Nukus St, Apar 1–2, Tashkent 700015 (tel: 120-5855; fax: 120-7712).

Ravnak Bank, 2 Furkat St, Tashkent 700021 (tel: 144-0753; fax: 144-1091).

Tadbirkorbank, 52 S Azimov St, Tashkent (133-1875; fax: 133-8100).

Uzbekistan-Turkish Bank, No.15/B Drujba Naradov Street, Tashkent (tel: 173-8323, 173-8324; fax: 120-6362).

Uzpromstroybank, 3 Shahrisabzskaya St, Tashkent 700000 (tel: 120-4528; 120-4520).

Central bank

Central Bank of Uzbekistan (CBU), Prospekt Uzbekistana 6, Tashkent 700001 (tel: 133-6829; fax: 136-7704).

Stock exchange

Republican Stock Exchange: www.uzse.uz

Travel information

Sairam Tourism, 13A Movarounnahr St, Tashkent 700060 (tel: 133-7411; fax: 120-6937; internet: www.sairamtour.com).

Tashkent Intourist, 69A Navoi St, Tashkent (tel: 144-1294, 144-0278, fax: 144-0776).

Uzbekistan Airways, 41 Movaraunnakhr Street, Tashkent 700060 (tel: 255-1850; fax: 255-6822; internet: www.uzairways.com).

National tourist organisation offices

Uzbektourism, 47 Khorezm St, 700047 Tashkent (tel: 133-3854; fax: 136-7948; internet: www.uzbektourism.uz).

Ministries

Ministry of Agriculture, 4 Navoi St, 700004 Tashkent (tel: 114-1353, 141-0020; fax: 141-0053).

Ministry of Communication, 1 Alexei Tolstoi St, 700000 Tashkent (tel: 133-8503; fax: 133-1695).

Ministry for Cultural Affairs, 30 Navoi St, 700129 Tashkent (tel: 139-4957).

Ministry of Defence, 100 Academician Abdullaev St, 700000 Tashkent (tel: 133-6667).

Ministry of Energy and Electrification, 6 Horezm St, 700000 Tashkent (tel: 133-6128; fax: 136-2700).

Ministry of Finance, 5 Mustaqillik Sq, 700078 Tashkent (tel: 1391943; fax: 144-5643).

Ministry of Foreign Affairs, 9 Uzbekistan Ave, 700029 Tashkent (tel: 133-6475; fax: 139-4348; internet: http://jahon.mfa.uz).

Ministry of Foreign Economic Relations, Elyor Madjidovich Ganiev, 75 Buyuk Ipak Yuli St, 700077 Tashkent (tel: 1670734, 168-9256, 134-4480; fax: 168-7231, 168-7477).

Ministry of Health, 12 Navoi St, 700012 Tashkent (tel: 141-1680; fax: 141-1641).

Ministry of Higher and Special Secondary Education, 6 Mustaqillik Sq, 700078 Tashkent (tel: 139-4808; fax: 139-4329).

Ministry of Internal Affairs, 1 Herman Lopatin St, 700029 Tashkent (tel: 158-3614; fax: 133-8934).

Ministry of Justice, 5 Hamza St, 700047 Tashkent (tel: 133-5039; fax: 133-5176).

Ministry of Labour, 4 Abai St, 700195 Tashkent (tel: 141-7628; fax: 139-7821).

Ministry of Land Improvement and Water Economy, 5a Abdulla Qodiri St, 700128 Tashkent (tel: 141-1353; fax: 141-4924).

Ministry of Public Education, 5 Mustaqillik Sq, 700078 Tashkent (tel: 139-4214; fax: 139-1173).

Ministry of Social Security, 20a Abdulla Avioni St, 700100 Tashkent (tel: 153-5371).

Other useful addresses

British Embassy, 67 Gulyamov St, Tashkent 700000 (tel: 120-6574; fax: 120-6430; email: brit@emb.uz).

Business-Vestnik Vostoka (BVV) (English newspaper) (32 Matbuotchilar St, Tashkent (tel: 133-9593; email: bvv@bvv.bcc.com.uz).

Cabinet of Ministers, 5 Mustakillik Maidoni, Tashkent (tel: 139-8188; fax: 139-8121).

Central Asia Research Forum, School of Oriental and African Studies, Thornhaugh St, London WC1H 0XG, UK (tel: (+44) 171-323-6300; fax: (+44) 171-436-3844).

EU Co-ordinating Unit, Tarasa Chevchenka St Dom 4, 700029 Tashkent (tel: 138-4018, 156-3479, 156-0417; fax: 132-0652).

Foreign Investment Agency, 4th Floor, 16A Navoi Street, Tashkent (tel: 141-5541, 141-5752; fax: 189-1201).

Government House, 700008 Tashkent (tel: 139-8295; fax: 139-8601).

National Agency for Telecommunications and Postal Services, 1 Tolstoy Street, Tashkent (tel: 133-6503, 133-6645; fax: 139-8732).

National Association of Gold Mining and Diamond Processing Companies, 26 Turaqorghan Thoroughfare, 700019 Tashkent (tel: 148-0720; fax: 144-2603).

National Joint Stock Corporation for Construction in the City of Tashkent, 16a Uzbekistan Ave, 700027 Tashkent (tel: 133-9033; fax: 136-4788).

SME Development Agency, 89 Gargarin St. Samarkand, PO Box 703029 (tel: 124-2966; fax: 131-0107; email: ravshan@samarkand.silk.glas.apc.org).

State Company for Television and Radio Broadcasting, 69 Navoi St, 700011 Tashkent (tel: 133-8106; fax: 144-0021).

State Committee on Agriculture and Construction of the Republic of Uzbekistan, 6 Abai St, 700011 Tashkent (tel: 144-0084/5).

State Committee on Forecasting and Statistics of the Cabinet of Ministers, 45a Uzbekistanskii Ave, 700008 Tashkent (tel: 139-8216, 139-8669; fax: 167-2509, 167-7816).

State Committee on Forests, 49a Uzbekistan Ave, 700017 Tashkent (tel: 145-9180).

State Committee on Geology and Mineral Resources, 11 Taras Shevchenko St, 700060 Tashkent (tel: 133-7206; fax: 156-0283).

State Committee on Precious Metals, 26 Turk-Kurganskiy Proezd, 700019 Tashkent (tel: 148-0720, 148-0663; fax: 144-2603, 148-0481).

State Committee for Privatisation (GKI), Mustaqillik Maydoni 6, Tashkent (tel: 139-8768; fax: 139-8548).

State Committee on the Protection of Nature, 5a Abdulla Qodyri St, 700000 Tashkent (tel: 141-0442; fax: 141-3990).

State Committee on Science and Technology, 29 Hadicha Syleimonova St, 700017 Tashkent (tel: 139-1843; fax: 139-1243).

State Committee for Television and Radio, Ulitsa Khoremzskaya 49, Tashkent (tel: 144-3287).

State Corporation on Industrial and Civil Engineering Construction, 17 Proletar St, 700060 Tashkent (tel: 133-7725; fax: 133-1041).

State Corporation of Local Industries, 5 Mustaqillik Sq, 700078 Tashkent (tel: 139-1058; fax: 139-4853).

State Joint-Stock Association on Trade, 6 Mustaqillik Sq, 700078 Tashkent (tel: 139-4971; fax: 139-1282).

State Property Committee of the Republic of Uzbekistan, Prospekt Uzbekistanskij 55, 700003 Tashkent (fax: 113-94617; 139-2236).

Embassy of Uzbekistan (USA) 1746 Massachusetts Avenue, NW Washington 20036-1903 (tel: (+1-202) 887-5300; fax: (+1-202) 293-6804; internet: www.uzbekistan.org).

Uzbek Information Agency (state news agency), Ulitsa Khamza 2, Tashkent (tel: 139-4982, 133-1622).

Uzbekinvest, 5 Mustaqillik Sq, 700078 Tashkent (tel: 139-1989; fax: 189-1538, 144-5186).

Uzbekiston Ovozi Times (English newspaper), 32 Matbuotchilar St, Tashkent (tel: 133-2036, 133-3855; fax: 133-7914).

Uzbekneftgas (national corporation of the oil and gas industry), 21 Akhunbabaev St, 700047 Tashkent (tel: 133-5757; fax: 132-1062).

Uzbek Post Office, 1 Tolstoy Street, Tashkent (tel: 133-5747; fax: 136-0921).

National news agency: Jahon Information Agency, 9 Uzbekistan Street, Tashkent, 700029 (tel: 133-6591, 153-8682; fax: 120-6443; email: aajohon@mfa.uz; internet: http://jahon.mfa.uz)

Internet sites

The Times of Central Asia: www.times.kg

News and commercial information: www.uzreport.com

General and government information: www.uzland.uz

Regional news and links: www.eurasianet.org

Vanuatu

A fall in tourism revenue in 2010 was the main reason for the slowing in Vanuatu's gross domestic product (GDP) growth to 3.0 per cent after an average of 5.7 per cent for the previous seven years. Agriculture, helped by increases in prices for copra, coconut oil and beef, and construction did well in 2010 after poor performances in 2009. GDP is forecast by the Asian Development Bank to be 4.2 per cent in 2011, and around 4.0 per cent in 2012.

A problem for the future is the inadequate transport infrastructure and services which are holding back rural development. There are also fewer income-generating opportunities on the outer islands, which are in need of improved ports and wharves, as well as more reliable and affordable shipping services.

Prime minister's merry-go-round

While out of the country, Prime Minister Natapei was ousted in a parliamentary vote of no-confidence on 2 December 2010. He was replaced by the deputy prime minister, Sato Kilman, who himself lost a parliamentary vote of no-confidence on 25 April 2011. Serge Vohor was elected prime minister on 26 April; he took office immediately. Kilman and his supporters lost a legal appeal against the procedure of his ousting. On 13 May, the Court of Appeal ruled that the appointment of Vohor as prime minister was unconstitutional and that the decision of the Speaker of the House of Parliament when he ruled to remove Sato Kilman from office as prime minister was 'not in existence'. Kilman was reinstated. On 16 June the Supreme Court invalidated the December 2010 election of Sato Kilman as prime minister, after the parliamentary speaker failed to hold a secret ballot. In the interim Edward Natapei was reinstated. On 20 June Mr Natapei confirmed that he would not stand for re-election. On 26 June parliament re-elected Sato Kilman as prime minister.

COUNTRY PROFILE

Historical profile

Human settlement dates back to around 4,000 BC.

1606 Portuguese explorers, Luis Váez de Torres and Pedro Ferdinand de Queirós, arrived on the island they called Espiritu Santo, at Big Bay.

1792 Captain Cook explored the islands in 1792, calling the group the New Hebrides.

1887 The islands were administered as a joint French-British naval commission.

1906 An Anglo-French Condominium was established. Over half the male population was conscripted as indentured workers into Australia. The native population dropped dramatically, falling to 45,000 by 1935.

1938 A new religion emerged called the John Frum Cargo cult.

1956 The John Frum Cargo religious cult was recognised by the authorities.

1960s An independence movement, NaGriamel, grew; it advocated the return of land to the native Ni-Vanuatu.

1971 With over 36 per cent of the land owned by foreigners, NaGriamel petitioned the United Nations to prevent further sales to non-indigenous people.

1977 The UK, France and local representatives agreed independence plans.

1980 The leader of NaGriamel attempted to gain independence for Espiritu Santo, but the insurrection was put down and the entire state of New Hebrides gained independence on 30 July, under the new name of Vanuatu. The first prime minister was Walter Lini, an Anglican priest.

1981 Vanuatu joined the United Nations.

1995 A coalition government of the Union des Partis Moderés (UPM) (Union of Moderate Parties) (Francophone) and the National United Party (NUP) (Anglophone) took office and Serge Vohor became prime minister.

1998 Donald Kalpokas formed a coalition government, comprising his Vanua'atu Party (VP) (Party of Our Land) and the NUP.

1999 John Bernard Bani was elected president. Parliament elected Barak Sopé prime minister, ousting Donald Kalpokas.

2001 Sopé and his government were ousted following a no-confidence vote. A new government was formed with a coalition of the UPM and the VP; Edward Natapei became prime minister.

2002 An earthquake struck Vanuatu, causing US$700,000 of damage. The UPM won the parliamentary elections.

KEY FACTS

Official name: Ripablik blong Vanuatu (Republic of Vanuatu)

Head of State: President Iolu Abil (from 2 Sep 2009)

Head of government: Prime Minister Sato Kilman (from 26 Jun 2011)

Ruling party: A coalition led by Vanua'aku Pati (VP) with National Unity Party (NUP), Union des Partis Moderés (UPM) (Union of Moderate Parties), Leba Pati (Vanuatu Labour Party) (VLP) and independents (since 2004; re-elected Sep 2008)

Area: 11,880 square km (82 islands)

Population: 241,000 (2010)*

Capital: Port Vila (on Efate)

Official language: Bislama (Ni-Vanuatu Pidgin), English, French

Currency: Vatu (V) = 100 centimes

Exchange rate: V96.25 per US$ (Oct 2011)

GDP per capita: US$2,896 (2010)

GDP real growth: 2.20% (2010)

GDP: US$693.00 million (2010)

Inflation: 2.80% (2010)

Balance of trade: -US$14.00 million (2009)

* estimated figure

2004 Cyclone Ivy caused flooding in many areas and some 1,000 people were evacuated to temporary shelters in Port Vila. In snap elections no clear majority was achieved, the VP, NUP, Vanuatu Republican Party (VRP), National Community Association (NCA) and People's Progressive Party (PPP) formed a coalition government. Alfred Masing Nalo was elected president by an electoral college, but the Supreme Court removed him and after several attempts to resolve the matter, Kalkot Mataskelekele finally became president. Serge Vohor became prime minister and formed a government of national unity. Vohor was ousted in a no-confidence motion and Ham Lini Vanuaroroa was elected prime minister.
2008 Vanuatu completed the domestic requirements of the Pacific Island Countries Trade Agreement (PICTA). In parliamentary elections, the ruling VP and NUP won most seats (11 and eight respectively); Edward Natapei (VP) became prime minister.
2009 Edward Natapei survived a parliamentary vote of no-confidence, despite the disruption caused when four members of parliament were disqualified from attending, due to allegations of bribery during the 2008 general elections. Iolu Abil, supported by Natapei and VT, won the presidential election in parliament. Prime Minister Natapei was expelled from parliament, following his failure to attend three consecutive sessions without prior warning. However, a legal challenge lead to the decision to bar him being ruled as unconstitutional. Mr Natapei apologised to parliament, explaining that he had been absent on official business.
2010 The Gaua volcano became active in April and 3,000 villagers within its vicinity were moved to the west of the island. In August a 7.5 magnitude earthquake struck the island and Port Villa was hit by a magnitude six aftershock on 12 August. Buildings were damaged but there was no reported loss of life. While out of the country, Prime Minister Natapei was ousted in a parliamentary vote of no-confidence on 2 December; he was replaced by the deputy prime minister, Sato Kilman.
2011 Prime Minister Kilman lost a parliamentary vote of no-confidence on 25 April. Serge Vohor was elected prime minister on 26 April; he took office immediately. Kilman and his supporters lost a legal appeal against the procedure of his ousting. On 13 May, the Court of Appeal ruled that the appointment of Serge Vohor as prime minister was unconstitutional and that the decision of the Speaker of the House of Parliament when he ruled to remove Sato Kilman from office as prime minister was 'not in existence'. Kilman was reinstated. On 16 June the Supreme Court invalidated the December 2010 election of Sato Kilman as prime minister, after the parliamentary speaker failed to hold a secret ballot. In the interim Edward Natapei was reinstated. On 20 June Mr Natapei confirmed that he would not stand for re-election. On 26 June parliament re-elected Sato Kilman as prime minister.

Political structure

Constitution

The constitution created a republic, headed by a president with ceremonial powers only. The president is elected by a two-thirds majority in an electoral college from members of parliament and presidents of regional councils including Shefa, Sanma, Penama, Tafea, Malampa and Torba. The president serves a five-year term.
A Malvatumauri (National Council of Chiefs) advises the government on matters of custom, land tenure and the preservation of Vanuatu's traditions. Members of the council are hereditary peers and may not sit in parliament unless given leave to and elected by their peers.

Independence date

30 July 1980

Form of state

Republic

The executive

The executive consists of a Council of Ministers headed by the prime minister who is elected by parliament from among its members. The prime minister and the 12 co-members of the Council of Ministers oversee the administration of the 13 government ministries.
The president, who is head of state, is elected for a five-year term by an electoral college made up of the members of parliament and the presidents of the six provincial governments. A two-thirds majority is required.

National legislature

The 52-member parliament is elected by universal adult suffrage for a four-year term in multi-seat constituencies.

Legal system

Based on English law.

Last elections

1/2 September 2009 (presidential); 2 September 2008 (parliamentary)
Results: Parliamentary: the Vanua'aku Pati (VP) (Party of Our Land) won 11 seats (out of 52), National United Party (NUP) won 8, Union des Partis Moderés (UPM) (Union of Moderate Parties) won 7, Vanuata Republican Party (VRP) 7, Independents 4, People's Progressive Party 4, Green Confederation 2, nine other parties won one seat each.
Edward Natapei (VP) was elected prime minister in parliament, winning 28 votes, against 24 for Maxime Carlot Korman (VRP).
Parliamentary election of presidential: Kalkot Mataskelekele won 49 out of 56 electoral college votes; Willie David Saul won seven.
Presidential: After three rounds of voting by an electoral college in parliament (plus the six heads of provincial governments), Iolu Abil won with 41 votes and Kalkot Mataskelekele 16.

Next elections

18 September 2012 (parliamentary); 2014 (presidential – held in parliament)

Political parties

Ruling party

A coalition led by Vanua'aku Pati (VP) with National Unity Party (NUP), Union des Partis Moderés (UPM) (Union of Moderate Parties), Leba Pati (Vanuatu Labour Party) (VLP) and independents (since 2004; re-elected Sep 2008)

Main opposition party

Political situation

Who owns and who has the right to determine the fate of either tribal or public land has created problems for the government. On the one hand the government wishes to take up partnerships with foreign companies and provide land for commercial endeavours to develop the islands. On the other hand, local people consider traditional lands to be in the ownership of all the community and are not in the government's purvue to sell or lease.
Vanuatu came top of the World Bank's *Ease of Doing Business* in the Pacific in 2010, as well as the *Lonely Planet*'s best destination. At the same time Australia condemned Vanuatu as an offshore tax haven that allowed its citizens to evade tax and criminals to launder money.

Population

241,000 (2010)*
Last census: November 1999: 186,678
Population density: 20 inhabitants per square km (2010)
Annual growth rate: 2.1 per cent 1994–2004 (WHO 2006)

Ethnic make-up

The great majority of the population is Melanesian in origin, with around 5 per cent of European descent.

Religions

About 80 per cent of the population is Christian, although animism is still in evidence, and the cargo cult remains on Tanna Island. There have been localised secessionist movements in Santo, Malekula, Ambrym, Aoba, Pentecost and Maewo.

Education

In 2003, the EU awarded a grant of eur8 million to 14 pacific countries to be used to enhance basic education, and in the case of Vanuatu, to extend compulsory schooling to eight years. The government has backed the 'one laptop per child' programme (OLPC).

Literacy rate: 53 per cent adult rate in 2004

Compulsory years: Six to 12.

Enrolment rate: 117 per cent gross primary enrolment; 28.5 per cent gross secondary enrolment, of relevant age groups (including repeaters) (Unicef 2004).

Health

Life expectancy: 68 years, 2004 (WHO 2006)

Fertility rate/Maternal mortality rate: 4.0 births per woman, 2004 (WHO 2006)

Child (under 5 years) mortality rate (per 1,000): 31 per 1,000 live births (World Bank)

Main cities

Port Vila, on Efate (capital, estimated population 37,735 in 2005), Luganville (Santo) (12,846).

Languages spoken

English is spoken by 60 per cent of the population and French by 40 per cent. There are 115 indigenous languages.

Official language/s

Bislama (Ni-Vanuatu Pidgin), English, French

Media

Press

In English, the only daily is *Vanuatu Daily Post* (www.dailypost.com.vu), other weeklies are *Port Vila Presse* (www.news.vu/en), *The Vanuatu Independent* (www.independent.vu), *Nasara* (), and in Bislama *Ni-Vanuatu*.

Broadcasting

The state-owned Vanuatu Broadcasting and Television Corporation (VBTC) is responsible for public transmissions.

Radio: The VBTC operates Radio Vanuatu AM and Nambawan FM, in Bislama, English and French. External services by RFI Radio France, BBC and Radio Australia are received. Laef FM is a religious radio station.

Television: VBTC operates Television Blong Vanuatu, the only public service. Cable and satellite services are available including Vanuatu TV (http://vanuatu.tv).

News agencies

ABC Pacific Beat: www.radioaustralia.net.au/pacbeat

Pacific Magazine: www.pacificmagazine.net

Pacific Islands New Association (Pina): www.pina.com.fj

Economy

The economy of Vanuatu is dominated by its service sector, which constitutes over 75 per cent of GDP; agriculture, comprising around 15 per cent, is the other major component with industry and manufacturing contributing less than 10 per cent of GDP.

The majority of the population is engaged in subsistence agriculture, with copra as the principal export crop, followed by cocoa, with timber, beef and fish providing smaller earnings. Tourism and the tax-free financial centre helps offset the recurring trade deficit, while providing greater employment. Tourism contributed around 20 per cent of economic output in 2010.

Vanuatu is the oldest offshore financial centre and tax haven in the Pacific, opened in 1971, it has around 2,000 registered financial institutions and trust-fund services, providing an important source of foreign exchange.

GDP growth was 6.3 per cent in 2008 which fell to 3.6 per cent in 2009, and still further to 3.0 per cent in 2010 as tourism was weaker that expected.

The traditional herb kava has been used in the Pacific for generations to alleviate stress and strains. It is typically chewed but can also be brewed. Most Western countries banned its use due to the risk of liver damage by a substance within it. However Vanuatu was at the forefront in international trade talks to get this ban lifted, which was successful in the EU in 2008.

In 2010 a new kava bottling plant (LAV Vanuatu Kava) opened in Rentepau on Efate, with plans to export regionally before expanding into other more distant markets.

The tourism sector is recognised by the government as a key sector in its economic development to provide employment opportunities for its young and rapidly growing population. Although bureaucracy is one of the issues facing new investment, there have been some successful investment proposals approved by the Vanuatu Foreign Investment Board, which have centred on the tourism, international finance and agricultural sectors.

Vanuatu's beef industry has been a success, mainly due to access to export markets, since domestic demand for beef is not sufficient to keep the enterprise going.

External trade

Vanuatu is a member of the South Pacific Regional Trade and Economic Co-operation Agreement (Sparteca) along with 12 other regional nations, which allows products duty free access by Pacific Island Forum members to Australian and New Zealand markets (subject to the country of origin restrictions). It is also a member of the Melanesian Spearhead Group (with Fiji, Papua New Guinea and the Solomon Islands) as a sub-regional trade group, whereby customs tariffs have been harmonised under the Melanesian free trade agreement (MFTA).

Agriculture provides 80 per cent of commodity exports, however tourism is the largest export earner. A new sector in financial services has been introduced by the government.

Imports

Principal imports are machinery and equipment, live animals and foodstuffs, vehicles and fuels.

Main sources: Australia (typically 21 per cent of total), Singapore (12 per cent), New Zealand (11 per cent).

Exports

Main exports are copra, beef, timber, kava and tuna.

Main destinations: Thailand (typically 58 per cent of total), India (19 per cent), Japan (11 per cent).

Agriculture

Farming

The agricultural sector accounts for around 20 per cent of GDP, employs 70 per cent of the workforce and provides up to 80 per cent of the country's exports.

Agricultural production and livestock rearing is mainly carried out by smallholding farmers. More than 90 per cent of all the fruit and vegetables consumed in Vanuatu are imported.

Around 41 per cent of the land area is cultivatable, although only half is utilised. The soil is generally fertile and rainfall adequate, although crops can be subject to cyclone damage. The sector is hampered by a general lack of capital and investment, technical skills as well as the isolation of farmers.

Copra is Vanuatu's main export crop, accounting for approximately one-third of total export earnings and 6 per cent of GDP. A mechanised coconut-desiccating factory opened, in the northern region, capable of processing 24,000 coconuts per day. It is projected that this plant will produce 44 tonnes of coconut oil and 118 tonnes of coconut meat per day expanding export markets.

Kava, used for manufacturing tranquilliser drugs, has become an important export commodity, although production was scaled back due to plant disease and medical concerns over the substance's effects on the liver. Australia and New Zealand lifted a ban on kava after finding that these claims could not be substantiated, although in early 2006 Australia was considering banning the import as it was having an adverse affect on Aborigine communities.

Cattle rearing and forestry are becoming increasingly important foreign exchange earners.

Fishing
An experimental project to seed reefs with trochus raised in hatcheries is under way (the shells are collected and sold as buttons). Investment project permits have been issued for fish farming.
The typical annual fish catch is over 27,000t, with 850t other seafood and 100,000 units pearls and shells.
Forestry
Access only by sea to exploitable forests has limited timber production. The government is working to achieve certification by the International Tropical Timber Organisation (ITTO) to prove that the country's forests are being sustainably managed. This would increase the added value of timber products.

Industry and manufacturing
The industrial sector accounts for approximately 12 per cent of GDP and employs 5 per cent of the workforce. Manufacturing contributes about 5 per cent of GDP. Main industries include copra processing, meat canning, fish processing, soft drinks bottling, furniture making, timber production, metalwork and handicrafts for the growing tourist market.
Japan has played an important part in helping to improve regional commercial centres for transporting and distributing agricultural products and other goods, providing investment for wharves on Tanna and Malekula Islands.

Tourism
Tourism is the main source of foreign exchange. The increased number of cruise ships making stopovers in Vanuatu resulted in a 70 per cent rise in visitors to the islands in February 2011, compared with February 2010. Australia continues to be the main market.
In July 2008 Unesco granted Roi Mata Domain World Heritage status.

Mining
While Vanuatu has mineral resources, including precious metals, these have yet to be exploited. In 2006, the government signed an agreement with a Swiss-American company to exploit the manganese spoil left over at an abandoned mine on Efate. Hundreds of jobs are expected to be created.

Hydrocarbons
There are no known hydrocarbon reserves. All domestic energy needs must be met by imported petroleum products, typically 1,000 barrels per day of oil.

Energy
Total installed generating capacity was around 12MW in 2006, all of which was powered by imported diesel oil. Unelco Vanuatu Limited (Unelco) is responsible for generation and supply of electricity.
The government is encouraging renewable energy companies to invest in Vanuatu, as it became the first country in the Asia-Pacific region to attempt to base its entire economy on renewable energy. It plans to reach that goal by 2020, with electricity generated by geothermal heat, wind and solar power and locally manufactured hydrogen-based fuels, which could also be exported.
In 2009 the Australian company KUTh Energy was awarded two licences to undertake a study into the feasibility of using the hot springs on Efate Island for geothermal energy.
Geothermal energy is planned to provide electricity for Efate by 2014, following the successful connection of the preliminary power plant, near the hot pools by Takara village, to the grid on 7 July 2011.

Banking and insurance
The introduction in 1983 of the International Companies Act helped Vanuatu to develop as an offshore banking centre, attracting some 100 banks. Following the 11 September 2001 terrorist attacks in the US, the US cut off all direct financial dealing with Vanuatu. The aim was to block all financial transactions that could be linked to terrorists, although Vanuatu was not considered to be a haven for terrorist assets. Vanuatu complied with the requirements of the OECD and was removed from the list of nations with 'tax havens' in 2003.
Central bank
Reserve Bank of Vanuatu
Main financial centre
Port Vila

Time
GMT plus 11 hours

Geography
Vanuatu comprises an irregular archipelago of about 80 islands in the south-west Pacific Ocean, spread over a distance of about 900km (560 miles) from north to south. The islands lie about 1,000km (600 miles) west of Fiji and 400km (250 miles) north-east of New Caledonia.
Most islands are mountainous and volcanic in origin. The capital and second largest town are on the islands if Efate and Espiritu Santo, respectively. Mount Tabwemasana, on Espiritu Santo, (height 1,877 metres) is the highest peak in the archipelago.
Hemisphere
Southern

Climate
Temperatures can range from 16–33 degrees Celsius and rainfall varies from 1,000–2,000mm per annum. Cyclones may occur from December to April.

Entry requirements
Passports
Required by all and must be valid for six months from date of arrival.
Visa
Required by all except citizens of the Commonwealth, EU, and the US for stays of up to 30 days. For a full list of exceptions see www.vanuatu.discoverparadise.org and follow link to *resources* to *travel tips* then to *Visa Requirements*. All travellers must hold onward/return tickets and sufficient funds for their stay.
A visa application can be downloaded from the above internet address (and follow links) and must be forwarded to the Principal Immigration Officer, The Immigration Department, Port Vila, Vanuatu, PMB 014 and must be approved before entry.
Prohibited entry
Anyone whose demeanour is not considered acceptable is prohibited entry.
Currency advice/regulations
The import and export of local and foreign currency is unrestricted.
Travellers cheques are widely accepted.
Customs
Personal items are duty-free. All goods of commercial value must be declared.
Prohibited imports
Firearms, ammunitions, illegal drugs, animals, plants and goods carried on behalf of other persons.

Health (for visitors)
Mandatory precautions
Vaccination certificate for yellow fever if travelling from an infected area.
Advisable precautions
Vaccinations for diphtheria, tetanus, hepatitis A and typhoid are recommended. Other vaccinations that may be advised include tuberculosis and hepatitis B. Malaria prophylaxes are required including mosquito nets, insect sprays and long clothing at night. Sunscreen is highly recommended, even in winter.
Any medicines required by the traveller should be brought into the country. Medical insurance is essential, including emergency evacuation.

Hotels
A 10 per cent tax is added to hotel bills.

Credit cards
Major credit cards are widely accepted. ATMs are available in most banks.

Public holidays (national)
Fixed dates
1 Jan (New Year's Day), 21 Feb (Father Lini Day), 5 Mar (Custom Chief's Day), 1 May (Labour Day), 24 Jul (Children's Day), 30 Jul (Independence Day), 15 Aug (Assumption Day), 5 Oct (Constitution

Day), 29 Nov (Unity Day), 25–26 Dec (Christmas).

Variable dates

Good Friday, Easter Monday, Ascension Day.

Working hours

Banking

Mon–Fri: 0830–1500.

Business

Mon–Fri: 0800–1100, 1300–1700.

Government

Mon–Fri: 0730–1700.

Shops

Mon–Fri: 0730–1630/1700 (large supermarkets open until 1930). Sat: 0800–1200. Some shops open Sun morning.

Telecommunications

Mobile/cell phones

There is a 900 GSM service in operation.

Electricity supply

220V AC, 50 Hz with flat, three-pin plugs.

Weights and measures

Metric system

Social customs/useful tips

Tipping and bartering are not considered polite behaviour. It is customary to shake hands on meeting and taking leave.
An informal attitude prevails in business. Sometimes business cards are exchanged after introduction. Business is often conducted in Pidgin, English or French.

Getting there

Air

National airline: Air Vanuatu
International airport/s: Port Vila-Bauerfield (VLI), 6km from Port Vila (on Efate); duty-free shop, currency exchange, hotel reservations, post office, car hire and business lounge.
Airport tax: Departure tax: V2,500, included in ticket price.

Surface

Main port/s: Port Vila and Luganville (Santo)

Getting about

National transport

Air: VanAir operates inter-island services to 16 destinations from Port Vila-Bauerfield airport. A V400 service charge is imposed at every airport for any domestic flight.
Road: There are some 150km of surfaced road on Efate, and 100km on Espiritu Santo, which are passable in dry weather.
Buses: Privately run minivans operate unscheduled and unspecified routes around the islands.
Water: Inter-island sea links are unscheduled but generally good.

City transport

Taxis: Taxi services are plentiful and metered. Journey time from the airport to the city centre is about 10 minutes.
Buses, trams & metro: Buses serve the whole of Port Vila. Journey time from airport to city centre is 10 minutes.

Car hire

Car hire is available in Port Vila and Luganville. International, French and UK licences are acceptable.

BUSINESS DIRECTORY

The addresses listed below are a selection only. While World of Information makes every endeavour to check these addresses, we cannot guarantee that changes have not been made, especially to telephone numbers and area codes. We would welcome any corrections.

Telephone area codes

The international direct dialling code (IDD) for Vanuatu is +678 followed by subscriber's number.

Useful telephone numbers

Police: 22-222
Fire: 22-333
Ambulance: 22-100

Chambers of Commerce

Vanuatu Chamber of Commerce and Industry, PO Box 189, Port Vila (tel: 27-543; fax: 27-542; e-mail: vancci@vanuatu.com.vu).

Banking

ANZ Bank (Vanuatu) Ltd, Private Mail Bag 003, Port Vila (tel: 22-536; fax: 22-814).

Banque d'Hawaii (Vanuatu) Ltd, PO Box 29, Lini Highway, Port Vila (tel: 22-412; fax: 23-579).

European Bank Ltd, PO Box 65, International Bldg, Kumul Highway, Port Vila (tel: 27-700; fax: 22-884).

National Bank of Vanuatu, PO Box 249, Air Vanuatu House, Rue de Paris, Port Vila (tel: 22-201; fax: 22-761).

Central bank

Reserve Bank of Vanuatu, PMB 62, Port Vila, Vanuatu (tel: 23-333; fax: 24-231).

Travel information

Air Vanuatu, Air Vanuatu House, Rue de Paris, Port Vila (tel: 23-838; 23-878; fax: 23-250, 26-591; internet: www.airvanuatu.com).

Bauerfield Port Vila International Airport, Civil Aviation Department, PMB 068, Port Vila (tel: 22-993, 22-819; fax: 23-783).

The Principal Immigration Officer, PMB 014, Port Vila.

Tour Vanuatu, PO Box 409, Port Vila (tel: 22-733; fax: 23-442).

National tourist organisation offices

National Tourism Office of Vanuatu, PO Box 209, Port Vila (tel: 22-515, 22-685; fax: 23-889; internet site: hwww.vanuatutourism.com).

Ministries

Ministry of Finance and Housing, PO Box 31, Port Vila (tel: 22-951).

Ministry of Postal Services, Telecommunications and Meteorology, Private mail Bag 011, Port Vila (tel: 25-059; fax: 23-142).

Ministry of Trade, Co-operatives, Energy and Industry, Port Vila (tel: 23-979).

Prime Minister's Office, Private Mail Bag 053, Port Vila (tel: 22-413).

Other useful addresses

Asian Development Bank (ADB), South Pacific Regional Mission, La Casa di Andrea, Fr Dr W H Lini Highway; PO Box 127, Port Vila (tel: 23-300; fax: 23-183; email: adbsprm@adb.org; internet: www.adb.org/SPRM).

Department for Foreign Affairs, Port Vila (tel: 22-913, 22-347; fax: 23-142).

The Immigration Department, Port Vila, PMB 014, (tel: 22-354; fax: 25-492).

Internet sites

Investment promotion authority: www.investinvanuatu.com

Telephone directory (worldwide): www.teldir.com

Vanuatu government: www.vanuatu.gov.vu

Vanuatu online: www.vol.com.vu

Vanuatu portal: Vatu.com

Vanuatu Broadcasting and Television Corporation: www.vbtc.com.vu

KEY FACTS

Official name: Stato della Cittá del Vaticano (Vatican City State). Santa Sede (The Holy See) – the head organisation of the Roman Catholic Church – operates from the territory of the Vatican City State.

Head of State: Pope Benedict XVI (inaugurated 24 Apr 2005)

Head of government: Archbishop Giovanni Lajolo, President of the Pontifical Commission for the State of Vatican City (appointed 2006); Cardinal Tarcisio Bertone (appointed 2006), Secretary of State of The Holy See, handles diplomatic and political activity.

Area: 0.44 square km

Population: 460 (2010; census figure)

Capital: Vatican City

Official language: Latin; Italian is most commonly spoken.

Currency: Vatican City Lira and Euro (VCL and eur)

Exchange rate: VCL and eur0.75 per US$ (Oct 2011); (the Vatican City State has its own currency which, by agreement with the Italian state, is also legal tender in Italy; its value is pegged to that of the euro).

Vatican City (The Holy See)

COUNTRY PROFILE

Historical profile

1917 The Code of Canon Law was devised. The Law provides codified information and rules on the operations of the Catholic Church.
1922 Achilles Ratti became Pope Pius XI.
1929 The Pope was instrumental in defining the Vatican's position within Italy, which was confirmed by the signing of the Lateran Treaty, when the Vatican City State was formed as a separate state.
1939 When Pius XI died, Eugenio Pacelli became Pope Pius XII, the 261st Pope.
1958 After Pius XII died, Pope John XXIII was elected.
1963 Second Vatican Council assembled (the first council sat in 325 AD), to debate the role of the Church in the modern world, particularly regarding church administration, doctrine and discipline. Foremost in the 16 decrees issued were the reforms in the format of the mass and the liturgy, adoption of local languages instead of Latin for services, and the promotion of ecumenicalism within Christian churches.
1964 Paul VI, appointed Pope in 1963, made the first-ever papal visit to Israel.
1965 Paul VI made the first papal trip to the Western hemisphere, with a visit to the UN headquarters in New York. The Vatican published a document that proclaimed the Jews were not to blame for the death of Jesus Christ.
1967 The Apostolic Constitution was ratified.
1974 The Vatican intervened in Italian politics by urging voters to vote in favour of a referendum to repeal a recently passed law (1971) that made divorce legal. The referendum failed and divorce remained legal.
1978 John Paul I was elected Pope, but died one month later, which made his the shortest reign as Pope. A Polish national, Karol Jozef Wojtyla, succeeded him as John Paul II.
1981 There was an assassination attempt on Pope John Paul II. The Vatican intervened in Italian politics by urging voters to support a referendum to repeal a recently passed law that made abortion legal. The proposal was rejected by almost 68 per cent.
1983 A new and revised Code of Canon Law was introduced.
1993 The Vatican officially recognised Israel as an independent state.
1998 The commandant of the Pope's Swiss Guard, Alois Estermann, and his wife were murdered by a fellow Guardsman. It was the first murder case in the Holy See within living memory.
1999 The Istituto per le Opere di Religione (IOR) (the Institute for Religious Works, otherwise known as the Bank of the Holy See or the Vatican Bank) was sued in the US for helping to conceal in 1945 Nazi-era assets looted from Holocaust survivors and Nazi sympathisers from Croatia.
2000 Pope John Paul II apologised for anti-Semitism by Christians throughout the ages and called for the formation of an independent Palestinian state.
2001 Pope John Paul II appointed 44 new cardinals. The Pope issued a worldwide apology to victims of sexual abuse by Roman Catholic priests and other officers of the Church.
2003 The Vatican hosted a closed-door seminar of top officials and international medical experts on the problem of paedophilia within the Church
2004 The Vatican library, which housed nearly two million books and manuscripts, adopted radio frequency identification (RFID) tags.
2005 Pope John Paul II died aged 84. Joseph Cardinal Ratzinger was elected Pope and chose the name Benedictus XVI. The Pope intervened in Italian politics by successfully urging a boycott of a referendum on Italy's fertility laws. A diplomatic row between the Vatican and Israel broke out when Israel demanded to know why the Pope did not mention Israeli victims during a speech deploring terrorism. The Vatican published a new policy document on homosexuality and the clergy, sparking controversy among liberal and conservative Catholics alike.
2006 The Vatican joined the European Union Schengen area, whereby all travellers may cross borders without a passport or visa. The Vatican excommunicated two bishops consecrated by the breakaway Chinese Catholic Church in an act considered illegal by the authorities. In a speech given at the University of Regensburg in Germany, the Pope quoted a fourteenth century Byzantine emperor who seemed to say that the teachings of

the Prophet Mohammed were 'spread by the sword' and were 'evil and inhuman'. This caused a serious international storm of controversy among Muslims. It took a number of apologies by the Vatican and the Pope to lessen the tension, explaining that this was not necessarily the Pope's belief but was a quotation.
2007 A meeting was held between Pope Benedict and the monarch of Saudi Arabia, King Abdullah. The meeting was the first between the two leaders and concerned Middle East conflict and inter-faith dialogue.
2008 A three-day summit was held between 48 Christian and Muslim officials and scholars to develop an inter-faith, theological dialogue which could diffuse any future religious and political tensions.
2010 In March, in the his Easter address, the Pope condemned media reporting of the child sexual abuse scandal and paedophile priests that had besmirched the reputation of the religious body and said he would not be intimidated by what he described as 'petty gossip'.
2011 A new law of citizenship was enacted on 1 March. The Vatican City now has five categories of inhabitant: the pope; cardinals residing in the city; active members of the Holy See's diplomatic corps; other directors of Vatican offices and services; and official Vatican 'residents' (those that live in the city but are not citizens). In a book published in March, Pope Benedict rejected the idea of Jewish 'collective guilt' for the death of Jesus Christ, arguing there was no basis in scripture for blame of the Jewish people. The Catholic Church had repudiated Jewish 'collective guilt' in 1965. The late Pope John Paul II was beatified (the last stage before sainthood) by Pope Benedict XVI on 1 May. In July the Vatican and Malaysia agreed to establish diplomatic ties. The Vatican's special envoy in Ireland, Papal Nuncio Giuseppe Leanza, was recalled on 25 July after a damning report on the Catholic Church's handling of child abuse by priests.

Political structure

The Vatican City and the Holy See are two different entities: the Vatican is the physical state, while the Holy See is a non-geographical sovereign entity. The Holy See participates in a number of international organisations, such as the UN, as an observer. Italy is in charge of defending the city state, although the Pope's personal guards, the Swiss Guards, belong to the Vatican City.
The Vatican City State employs 1,534 people. It is a sovereign country recognised as a separate subject under international law. The Pope is its absolute monarch and chief of state, but its general administration is overseen by an executive called the Pontifical Commission, appointed by the Pope and headed by a president. The Pope plays little part in the Commission's administration. The Commission runs a police force and post office, has a railway station and issues car licence plates. The term 'Vatican' is commonly used to describe the residence of the Pope – the Apostolic Palace.
The Holy See is exclusively made up of ecclesiastical dignitaries, being the head organisation of the Roman Catholic Church and consisting of the Pope and the Roman Curia. It operates from the territory of the Vatican City State and constitutes a sovereign institution with the status of a subject of international law. The Curia is headed by the Secretariat of State which is presided over by a Cardinal who assumes the title of Secretary of State. The Cardinal Secretary of State is the person primarily responsible for the diplomatic and political activity of The Holy See, in some circumstances representing the person of the Supreme Pontiff himself.
Central offices of The Holy See are: Secretariat of State (two sections), nine congregations, three tribunals, 11 pontifical councils, the Apostolic Chamber, the Administration of the Patrimony of the Apostolic See (APSA) (sometimes referred to as the Vatican Bank), Prefecture of the Economic Affairs of The Holy See, Prefecture of the Papal Household, Office of the Liturgical Celebrations of the Supreme Pontiff, The Holy See Press Office, Vatican Information Service, Central Office of Church Statistics, five pontifical commissions and committees, nine institutions linked to The Holy See, the Synod of Bishops and six pontifical academies. In addition to these central offices, there are 118 pontifical representations to nations and to international organisations. There are 2,674 people working in the Roman Curia: 755 ecclesiastics, 344 religious and 1,575 lay people. There are about 1,000 retired persons.
The Pope is elected for life by a Conclave composed of members of the College of Cardinals. Pope John Paul II changed the rules to make a simple majority sufficient to elect a Pope if no-one has the traditional two-thirds majority after 30 rounds of voting. The College of Cardinals consists of 183 cardinals, of which 117 are electors. Suffrage is limited to cardinals less than 80 years old.
After the Pope's death, the chamberlain becomes acting head of state. An official nine-day mourning period, known as the *novemdiales*, follows the death of the Pope. The Pope's body lies in state in St Peter's Basilica in the Clementine Chapel until the funeral, which takes place between four and six days following the Pope's death. A Conclave, consisting of all the Cardinals under 80 years, meets to elect the next pope no less than 15 days, and no more than 20 days, after the death of the Pope.

Constitution

In 2001, a new basic law, incorporating constitutional amendments adopted since the creation of the Vatican City State under the 1929 Lateran Treaty with Italy, entered into force. It replaced the 1967 document *Regimini Ecclesiae Universae* as the Vatican's constitutional text. It distinguishes between the legislative, executive and judicial branches, continuing to vest absolute authority over all three branches in the Pope as supreme pontiff and sovereign.

Form of state

Theocratic state, non-hereditary, elected monarchy (Bishop of Rome and Pope)

The executive

The Pope is the *ex officio* Head of the State and head of government of Vatican City. He has absolute monarchy powers with total control of legislative, executive and judicial power. He appoints his own advisors. The appointments include president of the Pontifical Commission for the State of Vatican City (head of government).
When a Pope is unable to perform his duties important decisions on the confirmation of bishops, doctrinal issues and the promulgation of laws within the Catholic Church are left in abeyance.
The Roman Curia is the administrative organisation that oversees the Roman Catholic Church, together with the Pope, providing the necessary organisation and objectives of the church.

Population

460 (2010; census figure)
Last census: 26 February 2010: 460
Population density: 1,595 inhabitants per square km.

Ethnic make-up

Predominantly Italian and Swiss.

Religions

Roman Catholic

Main cities

Vatican City (capital)

Languages spoken

Mainly Italian and Latin.

Official language/s

Latin; Italian is most commonly spoken.

Media

Quite apart from the hundreds of publications worldwide, which proclaim the policies and pronouncements of the Catholic Church, there are powerful transmitters that broadcast directly to a global audience.

Press

The only daily newspaper is *L'Osservatore Romano* (www.vatican.va see news services), with weekly editions published in several languages.

The official bulletin of the Holy See is *Acta Apostolicae Sedis*, which is published periodically and on papal pronouncements.

Broadcasting

Radio: Vatican Radio (www.radiovaticana.org) broadcasts in over 40 languages, with modern facilities for podcasts and interactive blogs. It broadcasts from a centre at Santa Maria di Galeria, which has diplomatic privileges similar to a foreign embassy.

Vatican Radio began broadcasting advertising in July 2009, in an effort to offset rising annual costs of US$30 million. Advertisements are vetted to ensure they are in keeping with the Catholic Church's moral standards and ethos.

Television: Centro Televisivo Vaticano (CTV) (www.vatican.va) provides live broadcasts of religious and papal matters, with footage for foreign news broadcasters; it acts as a press centre for broadcast journalists.

News agencies

National news agency: Agenzia Internazionale Fides

Economy

The economy of Vatican City is separate from the Roman Catholic Church (The Holy See), which is a separate entity although headquartered in Vatican City. Vatican City produces very little and typically for local consumption only and without commercial value (market gardening, artwork and manuscripts for church purposes and so forth), income is generated through trade of tourist mementoes (made elsewhere) and services to tourists, plus the sale of postage stamps and publications, and fees for admission to museums as well as donations from its religious followers, all within its territory.

The Holy See is financed from real estate and an internationally diversified portfolio of stocks and bonds, plus donations from Catholic dioceses, institutions and individuals. These fund the ecclesiastical Roman Curia (bureaucracy, diplomatic missions and other international Catholic bodies).

A fundraising collection, used and directed by the Pope for charitable purposes, is the annual *Obolo di San Pietro* (Peter's Pence).

The Istituto per le Opere di Religione (IOR) (Bank of The Holy See) collects money from residents.

The 2009 Peter's Pence collection totalled US$82.5 million. The Holy See posted a budget deficit of US$5.74 million, it was the third consecutive year of deficit, attributed to the global economic crisis that cut dividends on investments and donations from diocese and individuals. The Catholic Church has also had to pay millions of dollars in compensation to victims of abuse during their time in its care.

According to a report published in July 2011 Vatican revenue for 2010 was US$356 million and expenses US$341.6 million, meaning the economy was back in surplus, despite worldwide donations to Peter's Pense falling by US$15 million to US$67.7 million. The Vatican City made eur21 million (US$30.5 million) in entry fees to its museums and other enterprises in 2010, following two years of losses.

Tourism

Tourism and tourist numbers for the Vatican City are difficult to ascertain, as there is no practical border between it and Italy; however, it is estimated that there are some 18 million visitors each year.

Around 100,000 people congregate in St Peter's Square to listen to the Pope's Christmas and Easter messages. The Vatican Museums alone typically attract over four million visitors each year.

Banking and insurance

The Vatican's banking sector has been embroiled in a number of trans-national controversies over the past three decades. The IOR acknowledged 'moral involvement' in the collapse of the Italian private bank, the Banco Ambrosiano, in 1982 and paid US$241million to creditors. Roberto Calvi, who headed the Banco Ambrosiano, fled Italy pending a trial for corruption and was found dead in London in June 1982. Five people, all alleged to have Mafia ties, were charged in Rome with Calvi's murder in April 2005.

In 1999, survivors of Nazi-run concentration camps filed a law suit claiming that the IOR helped conceal assets looted from camp victims by the then pro-Nazi Croatian government.

Central bank

Istituto per le Opere di Religione (IOR) (Bank of The Holy See); European Central Bank (ECB).

Time

GMT plus one hour (daylight saving, late March to late October, GMT plus two hours)

Geography

The State of the Vatican City (The Holy See) is situated entirely within the city of Rome, Italy.

Hemisphere

Northern

Climate

Mediterranean, with hot summers and mild winters. Temperatures range from 4–30 Celsius (C).

Dress codes

Dress should be modest — no shorts or sundresses. Lightweight clothing for summer; medium-weight and light topcoat for winter.

Entry requirements

No formal regulations exist, however visitors must adhere to Italian entry requirements before entry to the city.

Italy: no visa requirements for citizens of Europe, the Americas, Australasia and some Asian countries, visiting for up to 90 days. For a full list, and further information for those citizens not included on the list of visa-free travel, see www.ambwashingtondc.esteri.it and see consular services. A Schengen visa application (offered in several languages) can be downloaded from www.eurovisa.info/ApplicationForm.htm.

Currency advice/regulations

The euro is legal tender alongside the Vatican City Lira.

Health (for visitors)

As for Italy, where no special immunisations are needed.

Public holidays (national)

Fixed dates

1 Jan (New Year's Day), 6 Jan (Epiphany), 25 April (Liberation Day), 1 May (Labour Day), 2 Jun (National Day), 15 Aug (Assumption Day), 1 Nov (All Saints' Day), 8 Dec (Immaculate Conception), 25–26 Dec (Christmas).

Variable dates

Easter Monday

Working hours

Business

Mon–Fri: 0830–1245 and 1630–2000.

Getting there

Air

A heliport is used by Vatican City officials and visiting dignitaries.

A low-cost charter airline was launched 27 August 2007 to carry pilgrims from Rome to Lourdes and other holy sites including the Holy Land, Santiago di Compostela, Fatima and places in Poland and Mexico.

International airport/s: Rome, served by Leonardo da Vinci (Fiumicino) (FCO), 35km from the Vatican City.

Surface

By road or rail through Rome. There is a speed limit of 30kph in the Vatican City.

Getting about

National transport

Rail: The Vatican City has its own small railway which runs into Italy. It covers 862 metres before leaving the City.

BUSINESS DIRECTORY

The addresses listed below are a selection only. While World of Information makes every endeavour to check these addresses, we cannot guarantee that changes have not been made, especially to telephone numbers and area codes. We would welcome any corrections.

Telephone area codes
The international direct dialling (IDD) code for Vatican City is +39 followed by the area code 066982; this is complete in itself, giving access to a central switchboard/operator.

Banking
Central bank
Istituto per le Opere di Religione (IOR), 00120 Città del Vaticano, Rome (tel: 83-354; fax: 85-195); European Central Bank (ECB), Kaiserstrasse 29, D-60311 Frankfurt am Main, Germany (tel: +49(69)13-440; fax: +49(69)1344-6000).

Other useful addresses
American Embassy, Via Delle Terme Deciane 26, 00153 Rome (tel: 646-741; fax: 5730-0682; e-mail: Usinb.holysee@agora.it).

Annuario Pontificio, Palazzo Apostolico, 00120 Città del Vaticano (tel: 698-3064); Press Room, Via della Conciciazione, 54, 00193 Roma (tel: 698-3466).

Apostolic Nunciature (UK), 54 Parkside, Wimbledon, London SW19 5NE, UK (tel: (+44-20) 8946-1410; fax: (+44-20) 8947-2494; email: gb nuntius@eaglenet.co.uk).

Apostolic Nunciature (USA), 3339 Massachusetts Ave, NW, Washington, DC 20008, (+1-202) 333-7121; fax: (+1-202) 337-4036).

British Embassy, Via dei Condotti 91, 00187 Rome (tel: 6992-3561; fax: 6994-0684).

Centro Televisivo Vaticano, Palazzo Belvedere, 00120 Vatican City (tel: 698-5467).

Prefecture of the Economic Affairs of the Holy See, Palazzo delle Congregazioni, Largo del Colonnato 3, 00193 Rome (tel: 84-263; fax: 85-011).

Radio Vaticana, Palazzo Pio, Piazza Pia 3, 00120 Roma (tel: 6988-3551; fax: 6988-3237).

Secretariat of State, Palazzo Apostolico, 00120 Vatican City (tel: 6982).

National news agency: Agenzia Internazionale Fides

Palazzo de Propaganda Fide, 00120 Città del Vaticano (tel: 6988-0115; fax: 6988-0107; email: fides@fides.va; internet: www.fides.org).

Internet sites
Vatican City: www.vatican.va

Vatican Facts: www.vaticanfacts.com

Venezuela

KEY FACTS

Official name: República Bolivariana de Venezuela (Bolivarian Republic of Venezuela)

Head of State: President Hugo Chávez Frías (since 2000, re-elected Dec 2006)

Head of government: President Hugo Chávez (PSUV) (since 2000, re-elected Dec 2006)

Ruling party: Partido Socialista Unido de Venezuela (PSUV) (United Socialist Party of Venezeula) (replaced the defunct Movimiento V República (Quinta) (Fifth Republic Movement) which had won the 2005 election) (from 2007; re-elected 26 Sep 2010)

Area: 916,490 square km

Population: 28.83 million (2010)*

Capital: Caracas

Official language: Spanish

Currency: Bolívar fuerte (Bf) = 100 céntimos (new currency was introduced 1 Jan 2008)

Exchange rate: Bf4.29 per US$ (Oct 2011)

GDP per capita: US$9,960 (2010)

GDP real growth: -1.90% (2010)* (Central Bank)

GDP: US$290.70 billion (2010)

Labour force: 12.00 million (2010)

Unemployment: 8.50% (2010)

Inflation: 28.20% (2010)

Oil production: 2.47 million bpd (2010)

Balance of trade: US$27.17 billion (2010)

* estimated figure

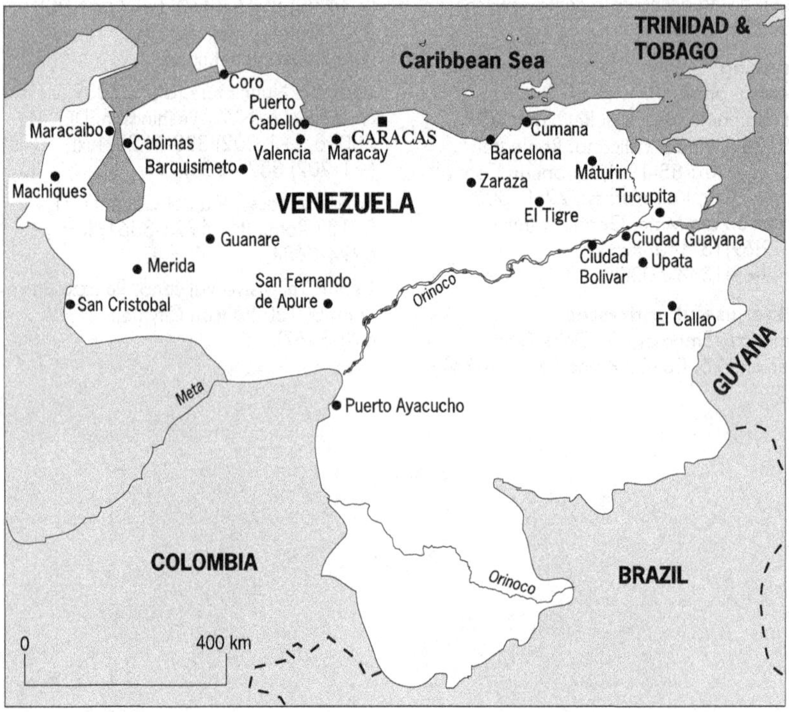

Despite the rhetoric and lip service to the rather vague notion of anti-American socialism embodied in the 'Bolivarian Revolution', domestically, in 2011 Venezuela continued on its rambling path towards a non-functional society under the sometimes absentee presidency of Hugo Chávez. A long period of high oil prices has given the Chávez government a windfall of which it hardly dared dream, but underlying the rhetoric and promises is a fundamental paradox that even Mr Chávez would find it hard to overcome. An unheralded homicide rate (in 2011 there were no less than 56 murders a day) and a record-breaking number of protests, in addition to prolonged food shortages, summed up a year in which President Chávez faced new, unforeseeable personal problems.

The year ended with a paranoiac accusation by the Venezuelan president that not only his cancer, but that of Argentina's Cristina Kirchner, Brasil's ex-President Lula and (when a presidential candidate) Brazil's current President Dilma Rousseff and Paraguay's Fernando Lugo might be part of a sinister US plot. 'Would it be strange?' he asked, 'that they had developed a technology able to induce cancer that we wouldn't be able to detect for another 50 years?' Answering his own question, Chávez concluded his rambling speech 'I don't know, I just leave you with the thought, but it is very strange.'

But as one scandal followed another, in the mist of accusations, dramas, surprises, compromises and tragedy, at the end of 2011, the respected daily newspaper *El Universal* published an overview of the challenges likely to face Venezuela in 2012. The list is not comprehensive; it is more of a digest of some of the more pressing issues.

The Illness

At the end of July 2011, Hugo Chávez confirmed what had long been rumoured. In a radio and television address, broadcast from Havana, Cuba, a troubled Chávez acknowledged that doctors had discovered a tumour with cancerous cells in his body. Chávez had been in Cuba since early June, the final stop on a tour that had included Brazil and Ecuador. Two days later an official statement confirmed that Chávez had undergone surgery to remove a pelvic abscess and was expected to return to Venezuela soon. From Havana, he passed the Indebtedness Law and ordered his team to expedite 'all missions and related things'. Doubts were expressed on the legality of his absence and the fact that he enacted decrees from abroad.

Rumours about his cancer were fuelled by reports in the Miami Spanish-language newspaper *El Nuevo Herald* that Chávez was in 'critical' condition. The reports were probably a combination of speculation, exaggeration and wishful thinking. In Caracas, speculations abounded regarding a possible 'succession' as if it were a monarchical issue. A number of names were thrown into the ring, including those of Nicolás Maduro and Elías Jaua, as well as Diosdado Cabello and Adán Chávez. But to general surprise, at the end of July, Chávez was back. He announced that, after the surgery to remove the abscess, he was told by Fidel Castro about other complications and that a second visit to Cuba was necessary for the 'full extraction of the tumour'. So called analyses of the president's illness filled the news bradcasts for the remainder of 2011, combining political estimates and medical theories.

Protests

2011 saw the most civil protests in Hugo Chávez's long tenure. A report issued by the non-governmental organisation Provea, covering the period from October 2010 to September 2011, indicated that over 4,500 protests were held during this period (well up on the 3,315 of the previous term). The report confirmed that the figure had increased 'for the fifth consecutive time'. 2011 will be remembered, *inter alia*, as the year in which the Venezuelan government finally published murder statistics. In February 2011, the minister of internal affairs, Tareck El Aissami, acknowledged that in 2010 the murder rate in Venezuela was 48 homicides per 100 thousand inhabitants, much higher than the average for Latin America. A survey conducted by the Instituto Nacional Estadística (INE) (National Statistics Institute) and published by daily newspaper *El Nacional* suggested a rate of 75 murders per 100 thousand inhabitants for the period from July 2008 to July 2009. Estimates indicate that by the end of 2011 approximately 19,000 Venezuelans will have been murdered, not including deaths involving police shoot-outs. In Caracas alone, 2,900 homicides by firearm took place.

Shortages

2011 has been one of the worst years in recent history for food shortages, especially milk. The president of the National Livestock Farming Federation, Manuel Cipriano Heredia, listed some of the factors behind the shortage of milk as a prolonged failure to break even, price controls, the fact that only the state is allowed to import milk and, it seems, only 20 per cent of imports actually made it to the private sector. The minister of agriculture and land, Juan Carlos Loyo, attributed the shortage to speculation. Also, Loyo blamed the shortages on the way Venezuelans consumed milk, also accusing the media and increased purchasing power. A survey by Datanálisis in the November–December 2011 period reported milk shortages at 79.8 per cent. At the end of November, the government had seized 260 thousand kilograms of powered milk that was allegedly being hoarded.

Prisoner release

An intriguing and surprising development in mid-2011 was the announcement by the newly appointed minister for correctional services, Iris Varela, of government plans to release 20,000 of the 50,000 prisoners being held in Venezuela's correctional facilities. In an interview with *El Nacional*, Sra Varela declared that the prisoners to be released 'rightly deserved to be released because they have met all legal requirements.' This initiative came after a month-long stand-off between the prison authorities and a large group of protesting inmates who had taken prisoners hostage at the Rodeo II penitentiary outside Caracas. In what had begun as a raid in June to confiscate drugs and weapons inside the complex, the confrontation left no less than ten inmates and three army officers dead. In a twelve year period, over 4,500 inmates have died inside Venezuelan jails and penitentiaries. In 2010 a record 476 prison inmates died and almost 1,000 were injured according to Venezuela's national Observatory of Prisons.

Chinese loans

On 23 November 2011, national oil company Petróleos de Venezuela SA (PdVSA) approved two new credit facilities with China for US$6 billion. Also, the state renewed the US$4 billion Heavy Fund, a credit through which PdVSA undertakes to send 410 thousand barrels per day (bpd) of petroleum to China. Venezuela's loans from China amount to US$32 billion through what is vaguely described as 'financial architecture'. The transactions have been under some scrutiny but, in November, National Assembly member, Miguel Angel Rodríguez,

KEY INDICATORS Venezuela

	Unit	2006	2007	2008	2009	2010
Population	m	*26.96	*27.50	*28.05	*28.61	*28.83
Gross domestic product (GDP)	US$bn	184.25	227.80	319.40	325.70	290.70
GDP per capita	US$	6,834	8,282	11,388	11,383	9,960
GDP real growth	%	10.3	8.4	4.8	-3.3	*-1.9
Inflation	%	13.6	18.7	30.4	27.1	28.2
Unemployment	%	9.3	7.5	7.4	7.9	–
lOil output	'000 bpd	2,824.0	2,613.0	2,566.0	2,437.0	2,471.0
Natural gas output	bn cum	28.7	28.5	31.5	27.9	28.5
Coal output	mtoe	5.9	5.6	4.7	3.6	2.9
Exports (fob) (goods)	US$m	65,210.0	69,165.0	93,542.0	57,595.0	65,786.0
Imports (fob) (goods)	US$m	32,226.0	45,463.0	48,095.0	38,442.0	38,613.0
Balance of trade	US$m	32,984.0	23,702.0	45,447.0	19,153.0	27,173.0
Current account	US$m	27,167.0	20,001.0	39,202.0	37,392.0	14,378.0
Total reserves minus gold	US$m	29,417.0	24,196.0	33,098.0	21,703.0	13,137.0
Foreign exchange	US$m	28,933.0	23,686.0	32,581.0	2,543.3	9,192.0
Exchange rate	per US$	2.15	2.15	2.15	4.29	2.58

* estimated figure

produced internal documents showing that PdVSA was not entitled to undertake such levels of borrowing, without taking into account the government's intention to raise it by another US$116 billion denouncing that the transaction concealed a mechanism allowing President Chávez to use oil resources through a parallel budget not subject to formal oversight.

Falling wages

Given its status as the fifth-largest oil exporter in the world, it is unsurprising that the Venezuelan economy is hugely dependent on its natural resource wealth to generate growth. In 2011, Venezuela's domestic economy had to cope with losing purchasing power as a result of high inflation rates. In 2010, based on reports by the Banco Central de Venezuela (BCV) (Central Bank of Venezuela), wages and salaries inflation ended at 5.4 per cent, a 'more accelerated pace with regard to the prior year', said the BCV's Economic Report. Six out of the 11 measured sectors showed results in the red. The worst performing was the sector related to real estate, business and leasing. It recorded a real drop of 8 per cent in 2010. In the meantime, the wages of community, social and personal service providers plunged 6.1 per cent.

Results in the field of education were also negative, as wages fell down by 4 per cent at the end of 2010. Manufacturing recorded a smaller drop, slipping back by 3.2 per cent. Wages in the trade sector lost 2.8 per cent of their value over the year.

In its 2010 Economic Report, the BCV also referred to the minimum wage which, in real terms, sank 0.7 per cent at the end of 2010, 'A more moderate decline than that noted in 2009 (-4.5 per cent).'

Where's the money gone?

Thanks to rising oil prices, the flow of petrodollars rose sharply in 2011. However, the Venezuelan government borrowed at high interest rates and international reserves remained virtually unchanged because the BCV only received a small portion of foreign exchange. Venezuela received US$89.39 billion from oil revenues in 2011, a 43 per cent increase compared to 2010, according to official data.

However, the Venezuelan authorities oversee the amount of petrodollars transferred to the funds directly managed by the government. As far as these funds are concerned, Venezuela's financial authorities are not obliged to comply with the budget approved by the National Assembly. Nelson Merentes, the BCV president, noted in his end-of-year message that the central bank received US$36.73 billion from state-run oil holding PdVSA, only 41 per cent of total foreign exchange received from oil exports. The limited transfer of petrodollars to the BCV has led to a flatlining of international reserves, in particular of the account to pay imports and of external debt payments. At the end of the year, this amount was US$29.89 billion, showing a minimum increase of 1.3 per cent.

While the Venezuelan government raised the amount of US dollars held in foreign accounts, obtaining a minimum interest rate, it also managed to take on debt at high interest rates. Some analysts think that for the money held in those parallel funds, the Venezuelan government receives, at the most, a 2 per cent interest rate per year. Further, Venezuela needs to pay between 11.75 per cent and 12.75 per cent on bond issues made by PdVSA and the ministry of finance in 2011. Meanwhile, Venezuela's foreign debt at the end of the third quarter of 2011 stood at US$94.6 billion, a 21 per cent increase compared to the same period in 2010.

Saved by oil...?

According to the *Oil and Gas Journal* (OGJ), Venezuela had 211 billion barrels of proven oil reserves in 2011, the second largest in the world. This number constitutes a major upward revision – last year the same publication listed the country's reserves at 99.4 billion barrels. The update results from the inclusion of massive reserves of extra-heavy oil in Venezuela's Orinoco belt.

Venezuela is a significant supplier of crude oil to the world market: in 2009 the country had net oil exports of 1.75 million bpd, eleventh-largest in the world and the largest in the Western Hemisphere. In recent years, crude oil production in the country has fallen, while domestic consumption has risen, causing a decline in net oil exports. The US government's Energy Information Administration (EIA) estimates the Venezuelan net exports fell again in 2010, to 1.59 million bpd.

Venezuela nationalised its oil industry in the 1970s, creating the state-run oil and natural gas company, PdVSA. Along with being Venezuela's largest employer, PdVSA accounts for a significant share of the country's GDP, government revenue and export earnings. In 2002, nearly half of PdVSA's employees walked off the job in protest against the rule of President Chávez, largely bringing the company's operations to a halt. In the wake of the strike, PdVSA fired 18,000 workers – industry analysts speculate that the company has never full recovered from the human capital impacts of this move.

During the 1990s Venezuela took steps to liberalise the petroleum sector. However, since the election of Hugo Chávez in 1999, Venezuela has increased public participation in the oil industry. The Chávez government initially raised tax and royalty rates on new and existing projects and mandated majority PdVSA ownership of all oil projects. In 2009 and 2010 Venezuela nationalised oil field service firms and infrastructure in response to these firms' failure to renegotiate their contracts. Venezuela is also increasing pressure on foreign operators that remain in the country to increase investment to offset recent production declines.

The EIA estimates that Venezuela produced around 2.36 million bpd of oil in 2010. Crude oil represented 2.09 million bpd of this total, with condensates, natural gas liquids (NGLs) accounting for the remaining production. Estimates of Venezuelan production vary from source to source, largely due to measurement methodology. For instance, some analysts directly count the extra-heavy oil produced in Venezuela's Orinoco Belt as part of Venezuela's crude oil production. Others (including the EIA) count the upgraded syncrude, which is about 10 per cent lower than the volume of the original extra-heavy feedstock. The EIA estimates that Venezuela's crude oil production dropped again in 2010, to 2.09 million bpd. Natural decline at older fields, maintenance issues and compliance with Organisation of the Petroleum Exporting Countries (Opec) production cuts are behind this trend. Venezuela's Opec production target is currently 1.99 million bpd.

Venezuela's conventional crude oil is heavy and sour by international standards. As a result, much of Venezuela's oil production must go to specialised domestic and international refineries. The country's most prolific production area is the Maracaibo basin, which contains slightly less than half of Venezuela's oil production. Many of Venezuela's fields are very mature, requiring heavy investment to maintain current capacity. Industry analysts estimate that PdVSA must spend some US$3 billion each year just to maintain production levels at existing fields, given decline rates of at least 25 per cent.

Venezuela contains billions of barrels in extra-heavy crude oil and bitumen deposits, most of which are situated in the

Orinoco Belt in central Venezuela. According to a study released by the US Geological Survey, the mean estimate of recoverable oil resources from the Orinoco Belt is 513 billion barrels of crude oil.

Venezuela's petroleum exports have dropped by almost 50 per cent, since peaking at 3.06 million bpd in 1997. Venezuela sends a large share of its oil exports to the United States because geographic proximity enhances export profitability and because refineries on the US Gulf Coast are specifically designed to handle heavy Venezuelan crude. Currently, Venezuela is the United States' fifth largest supplier of imported petroleum.

However, US imports from Venezuela have declined in recent years. In 2010, the United States imported 987,000bpd of crude oil and petroleum products from Venezuela, just 8.3 per cent of total American imports. Even factoring in 255,000bpd of imports from the US Virgin Islands, which are almost exclusively petroleum products refined from Venezuelan crude, the significance of Venezuela to the American energy sector is in decline

Venezuela has attempted to diversify its export destinations away from the United States. Besides the US, other important destinations of Venezuelan petroleum exports include the Caribbean, Europe and Asia. One of the fastest growing destinations of Venezuelan crude oil exports has been China. In 2010, China imported 125,900bpd of crude oil from Venezuela, up from only 39,000bpd in 2005.

Under the so-called Petrocaribe Initiative, Venezuela provides crude oil and refined products to numerous countries in the Caribbean and Central America, offering favorable financing and long repayment terms that often feature barter arrangements instead of cash transactions. In addition, Venezuela has a separate supply agreement with Cuba. According to industry reports, these preferential supply agreements amount to more than 400,000bpd of Venezuelan exports.

According to the OGJ, Venezuela had 179 trillion cubic feet (tcf) of proven natural gas reserves in 2011, the second largest in the Western Hemisphere behind the United States. In 2009, the country produced 651 billion cubic feet (bcf) of dry natural gas, while consuming 714bcf

The petroleum industry consumes the majority of Venezuela's gross natural gas production, with the largest share of that consumption in the form of gas re-injection to aid crude oil extraction. Due to the declining output of mature oil fields, natural gas use for enhanced oil recovery has increased by more than 50 per cent since 2005.

Sector organisation

PdVSA produces the largest amount of natural gas in Venezuela and it is also the largest natural gas distributor. A number of private companies also currently operate in Venezuela's gas sector. Participants with significant assets include Repsol-YPF (Spain), Chevron (US) and Statoil (Norway).

An estimated 90 per cent of Venezuela's natural gas reserves are associated, meaning that they occur along with oil reserves. Currently, Venezuela is working to increase the production on non-associated gas, largely through the development of its offshore reserves.

Risk assessment

Economy	Poor
Politics	Poor
Regional stability	Fair

COUNTRY PROFILE

Historical profile

1498 Christopher Columbus landed at the mouth of the Orinoco River on 2 August.

1499 Alonso de Ojeda first saw Lake Maracaibo and called the area 'little Venice', or Venezuela, after the houses the local inhabitants built on stilts.

1520s Spanish colonisation began. The most exploitable resource was cocoa.

1567 Caracas was founded.

1620 By this time cocoa had become the principal export. Production attracted many Spanish immigrants.

1749 First rebellion against Spanish rule.

1810–21 Simón Bolívar defeated the Spanish army in a long war and created Greater Colombia out of Venezuela, Colombia, Ecuador, Bolivia and Peru.

1823 The last battles for independence gained Venezuela its freedom from Spanish control.

1830 Bolívar died, José Antonio Paez assumed the presidency.

1859–63 A civil war erupted between conservative centralists and liberal federalists forces, which was won by the latter.

1908–1935 The dictator, Juan Vicente Gómez, ruled the country, instituting a harsh policy of repression while developing Venezuela into an oil-based, technocratic economy. Direct foreign investment in the oil sector also brought interest and influences on domestic policies.

1945–48 Rómulo Ernesto Betancourt Bello (Acción Democrática (AD) (Democratic Action)), set up a new government committed to democracy and social and land reforms. Foreign powers were suspicious of the government's left-wing credentials until Betancourt announced prompt elections would be held, acceptable reforms implemented and no radical action would be taken against foreign oil interests.

1947 A new constitution that provided for a popular vote, by secret ballot, to elect a president was promulgated. Romulo Gallegos Freire (AD) became the first Venezuelan president to be elected by democratic vote.

1948 The government was overthrown in a military *coup d'état* backed by conservative elements opposed to the reforms. A succession of *juntas* formed governments.

1952 Marcos Evangelista Pérez Jiménez seized power and became the next presidential dictator.

1953 The United States of Venezuela was renamed the Bolivian Republic of Venezuela.

1958 Pérez Jiménez was deposed by the military and a governing council allowed free elections, in which Betancourt (AD) was elected president. A pact between the main parties, including the AD and the Partido Demócrata Cristiano de Venezuela (Copei) (Christian Democrat Party of Venezuela), agreed to share power and maintain a pluralistic democracy. Moderate economic reforms, with regard for US interests, were slowly introduced.

1969 Rafael Caldera Rodríguez became Venezuela's first Copei president and managed to achieve a degree of political and economic stability.

1973 Venezuela joined the Andean Community, which also included Ecuador, Colombia, Peru and Bolivia.

1974–79 Carlos Andrés Pérez Rodríguez (AD) held presidential office and used massive oil revenues to nationalise industries and diversify the economy.

1979–84 The election of President Herrera (Copei) coincided with a downturn in global oil prices which led to a series of problems, including rising corruption, capital flight, economic stagnation and high levels of external debt.

1988 Presidential and legislative elections were held in December. Pérez became the first former president to be re-elected.

1989 Public protests against the government's austerity programme, which involved drastic government spending cutbacks in order to stabilise the economy, broke out around the country. The first-ever direct elections of state governors were held.

1992 Lieutenant Colonel Hugo Rafael Chávez Frías led an unsuccessful coup attempt against President Pérez.

1993 Ramon Jose Velasquez became interim president as Pérez was prosecuted on charges of corruption.

1995 Rafael Caldera was elected president.
1996 Ex-president Pérez was convicted of embezzlement and corruption.
1998 Hugo Chávez (Movimiento V República (Quinta) (Fifth Republic Movement)), became president with over 56 per cent of the vote.
1999 President Chávez announced his 'Bolívarian Revolution' that included a unicameral national assembly, a new constitution, reduced civilian control of the military and an increased control by government of the economy. A referendum approved all the amendments. Torrential rains and severe flooding killed around 30,000 people.
2000 Chávez was re-elected president under the new constitutional rules. His coalition won 99 out of 165 assembly seats, not enough to pass laws without support from elsewhere. The assembly granted him the right to legislate by decree.
2001 Chávez passed 49 laws by decree, mostly regarding land redistribution and the oil sector.
2002 Civil unrest interrupted oil exports. A failed *coup d'état* briefly ousted President Chávez, but his supporters forced his reinstatement. Nearly one-half of state-owned oil company PdVSA's employees walked off the job in protest against the rule of Chávez. The strike severely affected PdVSA, practically bringing the company's operations to a halt. PdVSA fired 18,000 workers following the strike, draining the company of technical knowledge and expertise.
2003 The government imported petrol from Brazil as oil facilities were strike-bound.
2004 The electoral authority ruled that opponents of Chávez had collected enough signatures for a referendum on whether President Chávez should serve his remaining term in office. Chávez won 58 per cent of the vote.
2005 Land reforms, including land distribution, were introduced. The Petrocaribe Alliance was created to supply directly 13 Caribbean states, including Cuba, with cheaper Venezuelan oil. Not only was it intended to cut the energy bills of the small island economies, but also to reduce US influence in the region. National assembly elections were boycotted by the opposition and Chávez loyalists made big gains. Quinta won 60 per cent of the vote (116 out of 167 seats).
2006 Parliament approved a new flag, with an eighth star for the province of Guayana Esequiba (a disputed border region with Guyana). Venezuela signed a US$3 billion arms deal with Russia for jet fighters and helicopters. Venezuela became a trading partner of Mercosur, which has a market of around 250 million people and accounts for almost 75 per cent of South America's GDP. Foreign owned oil companies were required to give the state-owned PdVSA, 60 per cent of their Venezuelan operations. Hugo Chávez won a third term in office, with 62 per cent of the vote; his opponent, Manuel Rosales, won 38 per cent.
2007 Nationalisation of electricity and telecommunications companies began. The national assembly granted Chávez the right to legislate by decree until mid-2008. Although Exxon Mobil and ConocoPhilips initially rejected the Venezuelan offer to relinquish majority control of their oil operations, eventually they agreed. A referendum rejected constitutional reforms by 51 to 49 per cent. Hugo Chávez founded a new political party, Partido Socialista Unido de Venezuela (PSUV) (United Socialist Party of Venezeula).
2008 The new Bolívar fuerte (Bf) was introduced at a rate of Bf1 to old B1,000. President Chávez was instrumental in the release of six hostages held by the Colombian Fuerzas Armadas Revolucionarias de Colombia-Ejército del Pueblo (Farc) (Revolutionary Armed Forces of Colombia-Peoples' Army). He also advised Colombian President Uribe that Farc should be considered insurgents instead of terrorists. Colombia took pre-emptive, cross-border strikes against Farc terrorists hiding out in Venezuela and Ecuador, killing over a dozen including the senior Farc leader Raul Reyes. Following the incursion troops were mobilised along the border and Venezuela expelled Colombian diplomats. Relations improved later after Ingrid Betancourt was freed from her Farc captors and President Uribe visited Venezuela for talks. The coalition Mesa de la Unidad Democrática (MUD) (Coalition for Democratic Unity) was formed to provide an opposition to President Hugo Chávez.
2009 A constitutional amendment to remove the limit on times a president and all other elected officials may occupy an office was ratified by 54 per cent. Extensive power cuts were imposed on industry and businesses in an effort to avoid mass power cuts, as electricity output of the country's principal Guri hydroelectric power station began falling due to severely low water levels caused by prolonged drought.
2010 In January the bolívar was devalued; two official exchange rates were established, the first pegged at Bf2.6 per US dollar for all transactions not related to petroleum, the second pegged at Bf4.3 per US dollar for all petroleum related transactions and imports deemed non-essential. President Chávez severed diplomatic ties with Colombia in July as he objected to claims by Colombia that Venezuela was harbouring Farc guerrillas. Diplomatic relations were restored after a meeting with the new president of Colombia, Juan Manuel Santos. In parliamentary elections held on 26 September, the PSUV won 48.2 per cent (96 seats out of 167), MUD 47.2 per cent (64), Patria para Todos (PT) (Fatherland for All) 3.1 per cent (two), others 1.4 per cent (three). In December, the new congress granted the president powers to pass laws by decree, until the middle of 2012.
2011 On 26 April President Chávez ordered a tax increase from 60 to 95 per cent on oil revenues at prices over US$100 per barrel, which alarmed foreign investors. The oil minister said that companies investing in new developments would pay the higher rate only after they had recouped their original expenditure. In 19 of the country's 23 states, electricity services were rationed from May, following failures in transmission lines and the on-going drop in electricity output from the country's principal hydroelectric power station on the Guri Dam. Critics claim the government's failure to invest in the country's energy infrastructure was the reason for the on-going rationing. President Chávez appeared on television from Cuba on 30 June to announce that he had had a cancerous growth removed, but that he was now on the way to 'full recovery'. There had been speculation about his health after he underwent an operation for a pelvic abscess, but had not been seen for some three weeks. He returned to Caracas on 4 July, in time to celebrate Venezuela's 200th anniversary of independence from Spain on the following day. He went back to Cuba for further treatment on 16 July (until 25 July) after delegating a number of presidential powers to vice president Elias Jaua and finance minister Jorge Giordani; the powers included budgetary transfers. In September President Chávez confirmed he would seek re-election in the next presidential election due on 7 October 2012. Also in September opposition politician Leopoldo Lopez began his campaign to challenge President Chávez after the Inter-American Court of Human Rights (IACHR) ruled that he should be allowed to stand in the 2012 presidential election. On 20 October, President Chavez announced that he was free of cancer, following four cycles of chemotherapy in Cuba.

Political structure

Venezuela sends 12 deputies to the Latin American Parliament and five to the Andean Parliament.

Constitution

A new constitution was promulgated in 1999 which set out to strengthen civil and human rights. It extended a presidential

term from five to six years, with one consecutive re-election, revised impeachment mechanism and limited emergency powers. The bicameral parliament was replaced with a single chamber when the senate was abolished, but popular participation by the people was to be encouraged through referenda. A stronger government involvement in the economy included a ban on the privatisation of the country's oil reserves.
A constitutional referendum, held in February 2009, voted by 54.85 per cent in favour of proposed amendments to limit the consecutive number of terms in office served by deputies in the national assembly to two. The presidency was increased to two consecutive five-year terms of office, with the date of the next election re-aligned to the same date as the national assembly.

Independence date
5 July 1811

Form of state
Federal presidential republic

The executive
Executive power rests with the president who is elected by popular, direct, universal suffrage for a six-year term, with one consecutive, renewable term.

National legislature
The unicameral, Asamblea Nacional (National Assembly) has 165 deputies elected through a combination of directly elected and proportional representation through party lists. An additional three deputy seats are reserved for representatives of indigenous peoples. Since 2009 deputies may only serve for two consecutive, five-year terms.

Legal system
The Supreme Court appoints judges in consultation with civil society groups.

Last elections
26 September 2010 (parliamentary); 3 December 2006 (presidential); 15 February 2009 (constitutional referendum)
Results: Presidential: Hugo Rafael Chávez Fríaz (Quinta) won 62.84 per cent of the vote; Manuel Rosales won 36.9 per cent; turnout was 62 per cent; 12 other candidates won less than 1 per cent each. Turnout was 74.69 per cent.
Parliament: Partido Socialista Unido de Venezuela (PSUV) (United Socialist Party of Venezeula) won 48.2 per cent (96 seats out of 165 elected seats), Mesa de la Unidad Democrática (MUD) (Coalition for Democratic Unity) 47.2 per cent (64), Patria para Todos (PT) (Fatherland for All) 3.1 per cent (two), others 1.4 per cent (three).
Constitutional referendum: 54.85 per cent of the electorate voted in favour and 45.15 against the proposed amendments; turnout was 70.33 per cent.

Next elections
7 October 2012 (presidential); 2015 (parliamentary).

Political parties

Ruling party
Partido Socialista Unido de Venezuela (PSUV) (United Socialist Party of Venezeula) (replaced the defunct Movimiento V República (Quinta) (Fifth Republic Movement) which had won the 2005 election) (from 2007; re-elected 26 Sep 2010)

Main opposition party
Mesa de la Unidad Democrática (MUD) (Coalition for Democratic Unity)

Population

28.83 million (2010)*
Last census: October 2001: 23,054,210
Population density: 28 inhabitants per square km. Urban population: 87 per cent (2002).
Annual growth rate: 2.0 per cent 1994–2004 (WHO 2006)

Ethnic make-up
Mestizo (67 per cent), White (21 per cent), Black (10 per cent), Indian (2 per cent).

Religions
Roman Catholic (96 per cent), Protestant (2 per cent).

Education

Pre-primary (one year) and basic education lasts until aged 15. Exams then determine whether students progress onto an academic course for two years or a vocational course for three years. Many institutes of higher education have a selection procedure and often run preparatory courses as part of the admission process. Professional courses last for three years, catering for the industrial, farming, commercial and health sectors.
Universities, institutes, two ecclesiastic university institutes and three military institutes, provide higher education. Institutes and University Colleges generally provide for short courses of study lasting between two and three years. Long courses lasting for five to six years are also available. The universities are both public and private. National public universities are both autonomous and experimental institutions.
Literacy rate: 93 per cent adult rate; 98 per cent youth rate (15–24) (Unesco 2005).
Compulsory years: Five to 17
Enrolment rate: 91 per cent gross primary enrolment; 40 per cent gross seconday enrolment of relevant age groups (including repeaters).
Pupils per teacher: 21 in primary schools

Health

Venezuela has achieved significant long-term advances with regard to health in hospital care but preventive and primary health care remains on a very small scale. Venezuela is vulnerable to natural disasters, the most frequent of which are floods with concurrent landslides, and there is also a risk of earthquakes. The Ministry of Family has assisted non-governmental organisations (NGOs) and community-based groups to participate in social programmes at a household level.

HIV/Aids
HIV prevalence: 0.7 per cent aged 15–49 in 2003 (World Bank)
Life expectancy: 75 years, 2004 (WHO 2006)
Fertility rate/Maternal mortality rate: 2.7 births per woman, 2004 (WHO 2006); maternal mortality 60 per 100,000 live births (World Bank).
Birth rate/Death rate: 4 deaths per 24 births per 1,000 people; infant mortality 19 per 1,000 live births (World Bank).
Child (under 5 years) mortality rate (per 1,000): 18 per 1,000 live birth; 4 per cent of children under aged five are malnourished (World Bank).
Head of population per physician: 1.94 physicians per 1,000 people, 2001 (WHO 2006)

Welfare

Venezuela operates a social insurance system covering employees in private and public employment, unemployed and family members.
The welfare system of benefits covers sickness, maternity, work injury, unemployment and family allowances. Pensioners are also covered for medical benefits. Sickness benefits are covered for up to 52 weeks. Maternity benefit is payable up to six months before and after confinement. Workers' medical benefits include free general and specialist care and hospitalisation. Unemployment benefit covers 60 per cent of the average weekly salary of the last 50 weeks and is paid for up to 13 weeks after waiting for one month following loss of employment. Unemployed persons are entitled to transportation subsidy, training and guidance services.

Pensions
A new system of private pensions was introduced in 1998. In 1999, Venezuela moved away from a pay-as-you-go pension system to one based on 'individual capitalisation funds', along the lines of the Chilean model. Under the mandatory pay-as-you-go system all participants receive pensions in proportion to their contributions, amounting to 12–13 per cent of base salary, and on the basis of the accumulation of the individual fund. The government pays for any deficiency between the accumulated value of the individual capitalised fund and the minimum amount of pension.

Full pensions are paid at aged 60, provided 240 months of contributions have been paid. At the age of 60, the employee has the option of either buying a life annuity from an insurance company, or withdrawing fixed monthly amounts from their individual capitalisation account.
A disability pension is available with 250 weeks of contribution, plus 30 per cent of workers' average earnings, payable after six months of disability.

Main cities

Caracas (capital, estimated population 1.8 million (m) in 2005), Maracaibo (1.8m), Valencia (1.3m), Barquisimeto (869,352), Ciudad Guayana (704,045), Petare (518,800), Maracay (406,812), Ciudad Bolívar (308,469).

Languages spoken

Spanish is spoken by the majority of the population. Indian dialects are spoken by about 200,000 Amerindians in the remote interior.

Official language/s

Spanish

Media

Press

Dailies: In Spanish, *El Nacional* (www.el-nacional.com), *Ultimas Noticias* (www.ultimasnoticias.com.ve), *2001* (www.2001.com.ve) is a tabloid, *El Mundo* (www.elmundo.com.ve) is an evening edition, *El Universal* (www.eluniversal.com), which has an English language edition called *Daily News* (http://english.eluniversal.com).
Weeklies: There are also numerous periodicals including *El Carabobeño* (www.el-carabobeno.com) with supplements and the monthly *Producto* (www.producto.com.ve).
Business: The magazine *Dinero* (www.dinero.com.ve) is a national publication; *Reporte* is a newspaper from Caracas.

Broadcasting

The president broadcasts a weekly programme on the public radio and TV services.
Radio: There are over 280 radio stations and all broadcast in Spanish. The state broadcaster, *Radio Nacional de Venezuela* (www.rnv.gov.ve) operates 15 radio stations in a nationwide network. Private commercial stations include Union Radio Noticias (www.unionradio.com.ve) and Fama FM (www.fama.fm).
The news agency ABN has recordings of National Assembly sessions online, (www.abn.info.ve), in Spanish.
Television: Venezolana de Television (www.vtv.gob.ve) is government run while all others are private and commercial and all broadcast in Spanish. Around 96 per cent of households have a TV set.
Private TV networks include Televen (www.televen.com), Venevision (www.venevision.net) with imported programmes and Telsur (www.telesurtv.net) a pan-Latin station. Radio Caracas Television (RCTV) had its licence withdrawn in 2007.
The owner of Globovision (www.globovision.com), a 24-hour news channel, fled the country in July 2010, to avoid prosecution for supposed business irregularities. President Chávez said that the government may consequently own just under 50 per cent of the company and that he planned to have a government representative on the board. The station had been critical of the president in the past.

Advertising

Television accounts for around 60 per cent of advertising expenditure.

News agencies

National news agency: ABN (Agencia Bolicariana de Noticias)

Economy

Venezuela is an economy dominated by one commodity – albeit a much prized commodity –petroleum. At the end of 2009 oil reserves were 172.3 billion barrels with production at 2.4 million barrels per day (bpd), natural gas reserves were 5.67 trillion cubic metres (cum) with production at 27.9 billion cum and coal reserves were 479 million tonnes, with production at 3.6 million tonnes of oil equivalent (mtoe) per year. Generation of hydroelectricity was 19.5 mtoe, which contributes to exports of electricity. There is a thriving manufacturing sector that contributed around 15 per cent of GDP in 2009, which could grow further if it was unhindered by the lack of private investment. Manufactured goods include clothing, textiles, foodstuffs and beverages, cement, fertilisers, paper, steel, aluminium, and vehicles. Venezuela cannot fully feed itself and must import around 60 per cent of its food needs, which leaves it vulnerable to external shocks.
GDP growth in 2007 was 8.2 per cent, which fell to 4.8 per cent in 2008 as the global economic crisis cut international trade, and oil prices that had been at a record high fell markedly. GDP growth in 2009 was -3.3. Inflation has been a persistent long-term problem. Inflation fell from 99 per cent per annum in 1996 to 13.7 per cent in 2006 but for psychological reasons prices are adjusted automatically during holidays and major festivals regardless of need. Imports outstrip exports (although the trade balance remains in Venezuela's favour due to petroleum exports) due to the scarcity of certain products and a population that is willing to spend readily. Since 2007 inflation has again risen, reaching over 30 per cent in the first quarter of 2010.
The government, under the leadership of President Hugo Chávéz, since gaining control of the national oil company, Petroleos de Venezuela SA (PdVSA) in 2003, has made a marked impression on national economic progress. Under Chávéz the government has introduced legislation that limits foreign ownership of the petroleum sector of upstream activities and in 2009 passed a law reserving all primary hydrocarbon activities to the state. A second law requires private-sector petrochemical producers to become joint ventures with the state-owned Petroquímica de Venezuela (Pequiven) chemical company. Such partial nationalisations have not enamoured Chávéz's administration to foreign interests, particularly in the US.
However, in a 2009 analysis of the Chávéz economic management the US-based Center for Economic and Policy Research (CEPR) reported an impressive list of improved social indicators that were attributed to legislation undertaken since 2003. These included a reduction in the poverty rate by more than 50 per cent (2003–08), with extreme poverty falling by 72 per cent and the number of social security beneficiaries doubling (1999–2009). Economically, the non-oil sector expanded faster than the public sector, unemployment fell from 11.3 per cent to 7.8 per cent and public debt fell from 30.7 per cent of GDP 14.3 per cent, with foreign debt falling from 25.6 per cent to 9.8 per cent (1999–2009).
In January 2010 the bolívar was devalued and two official exchange rates established, the first is pegged at Bf2.6 per US dollar for all transactions not related to petroleum, the second is pegged at Bf4.3 per US dollar for all petroleum related transactions and imports deemed non-essential. This is expected to allow the government to regulate foreign currency exchange, kick-start growth in the private sector and stimulate government and domestic spending. However some have said that it also threatens to weaken GDP growth in 2010.

External trade

As a trading partner of Mercosur, the world's fourth largest free-trade zone, Venezuela has access to a market of over 200 million consumers. Venezuela has been negotiating to join Mercosur since 2004 and has been undertaking required trading alignment, so that full membership is expected to be completed by March 2011. In 2004, twelve South American countries signed an agreement to launch the South American Community of Nations (CSN), modelled on the European Union. In 2007 the name was changed to Union of South American Nations (Unasur). Unasur seeks to integrate with the Andean Community of Nations and Mercosur in a single market by 2014, when tariffs on non-sensitive products are abolished with the remainder eliminated by 2019. However political tensions within the region have hampered the ongoing process.

The export of petroleum plays an overwhelming influence on the economy and provides a trade surplus. Other commodities include heavy industrial products, energy, manufactured goods and agricultural products.

Imports

Principal imports are food, raw materials, machinery and equipment, vehicles, consumer goods and construction materials.

Main sources: US (typically 26 per cent of total), Colombia (15 per cent), China (9 per cent).

Exports

Principal exports are petroleum, aluminium, steel, iron ore, chemicals and plastics, agricultural products, fish, tobacco, textiles and clothing and basic manufactures.

Main destinations: US (typically 40 per cent of total), The Netherlands Antilles (20 per cent), Brazil (3 per cent).

Agriculture

Farming

Land use is divided between arable land (3 per cent), permanent crops cultivation (1 per cent), meadows and pastures (20 per cent), forest and woodland (50 per cent) and other use (26 per cent). The country is subject to periodic droughts. Venezuela's main arable centres are Acarigua, El Tigre, Maracay, Valencia and Barquisimeto.

The agricultural sector is not hugely important to the economy of Venezuela, constituting just 5 per cent of total GDP. There has been little investment in modern farm technology. Inefficient marketing, poor farm management and scant irrigation are all features of the Venezuelan agricultural industry.

The major crops are rice, maize, sorghum, sugar cane, coffee (the main export crop), cocoa and cotton. Tropical fruits, cassava, beans, groundnuts and other vegetables are staple crops for small farmers. Poultry and pig-farming are of growing importance with small quantities of meat exported. Beef production has, however, slumped due to the smuggling of cattle to Colombia (where prices are higher), and cheap imports.

Throughout the 1990s, the government liberalised agricultural imports through lowering tariffs and removing quantitative restrictions in the form of import licences. The overall aim was to boost agricultural efficiency and to refocus production on areas where the country has a comparative advantage.

An agricultural programme is under way, involving the improvement and irrigation of 350,000 hectares of existing agricultural land and the use of about one million new hectares for cultivation. The programme aims to increase output of cereals, sugar and oilseeds (to reduce dependence on imports), and promote crop diversification.

Since the election of Hugo Chávez as president in 1999, the government has introduced land reform measures designed to bring disused agricultural land into production and redistribute land to the rural poor. The measures have been resisted by the land-owning oligarchy in the countryside, particularly cattle ranchers. The national government accelerated its land reform programme and continued to expropriate local agribusinesses throughout 2005.

Fishing

Since coming to power President Chávez has passed legislation that regulates the activities of large trawlers in order to protect small fishing communities.

Generally, the fishing industry has seen good growth, owing to an increase in the tuna catch. The overall typical fish catch is in the region of 435,000mt, including 318,000mt marine fish and 79,000mt shellfish.

Forestry

Approximately half of Venezuela's total landmass is covered with forests and woodland, the majority of which are in the south and east of the country. The forestry sector remains undeveloped and around half the country's wood-derived products are imported.

Industry and manufacturing

Over time heavy industries have arisen with the intention of using local materials as inputs including the refining of aluminium (an increasingly significant export), petrochemicals (ammonia, sulphuric acid, fertilisers, plastics etc) and cement and steel production.

Import-dependent industries include motor vehicle assembly, tyres, rubber, pharmaceuticals, electrical goods and machinery. The traditional home market industries are beverages, textiles, food processing, ceramics and paper/pulp. Major state enterprises include Sidor (steel), Venalum and Alcasa (aluminium) and Pequiven (petrochemicals). Venezuela's aluminium industry is inefficient and heavily indebted.

Manufacturing production remains highly concentrated, with around 10 per cent of all firms accounting for 75 per cent of output. Joint ventures involving state, domestic and foreign private capital were developed in the 1990s to expand the petrochemical and aluminium industries.

Tourism

The travel and tourism industry of Venezuela has been hampered by the political and economic stability in the country. Though capital investment in the sector has risen to represent almost 12 per cent of total capital investment in the economy, employment in the sector is down, as is the industry's percentage contribution to total GDP.

Mining

Venezuela is endowed with a significant range of mineral resources. However, these deposits remain largely undeveloped. The sectors of the industry retaining the most importance include iron ore, bauxite, gold, diamond and nickel laterites. Other sources include zinc, copper, lead, silver, manganese, titanium, nickel, marble, sulphur, phosphates, mercury and uranium.

At present, the mining industry contributes just 1 per cent of the country's total GDP. The government reformed its mining law in 1999, converting mining contracts signed with Corporacion Venezolana de Guayana (CVG) into mining concessions. The government eliminated exploration and surface taxes in the first three years of a concession.

Several foreign investment and joint ventures have propped up the sector. Venezuelan, Canadian and US companies have combined to exploit the extensive kimberlite sills in the region of Guaniamo and aid in the marketing of diamonds. Nickel is mined at Loma de Niquel. The main mineral exploited is iron ore; reserves are estimated at 2,800 million tonnes, 80 per cent high-grade. The largest deposits are located at Cerro Bolívar and San Isidro. Estimated reserves of bauxite at Los Pijiguaos typically amount to some four billion tonnes of high-grade ore.

In September President Chávez suggested that the Las Cristinas gold mining region would be re-nationalised at some point in the future. Crystallex, a Canadian mining company operating in the region and currently planning to build the what would be the largest gold mine in Venezuela, saw a sharp decline in its share price on the back of the news.

Hydrocarbons

Venezuela was a founder member of the Organisation of Petroleum Exporting Countries (Opec) and continues to be one

of the world's most important oil exporters. The country is endowed with the most extensive proven oil reserves in South America. The petroleum industry is the mainstay of the economy.
Total proven oil reserves were 99 billion barrels in 2009. Production in 2007 was 2.6 million barrels per day (bpd); supplies, which if exploited at this current rate, will last into the 2100s. Production is restricted by Venezuela's OPEC quota.
The oil industry has been radicalised since Hugo Chavez became president as he used oil as an extension of his political ideology. He has agreed to oil sales, on preferential terms, in countries in the region to strengthen ties between South America and the Caribbean in an effort to counter US influence. All private oil fields were nationalised in 2007, as Venezuela under President Chavez remained socialist with a strident anti-US message. Nevertheless over 50 per cent of all oil exported is supplied to the US. In May 2009 President Chavez announced that companies that provide services to the oil industry would be nationalised.
The state-run oil and gas company, Petroleos de Venezuela SA (PdVSA), accounts for around 33 per cent of GDP and 50 per cent of government revenue. Although there is an extensive network of domestic pipelines none are yet operational for exports. There are three major oil refineries with 1.28 million bpd capacity in 2009 and all operated by PdVSA.
In December 2010, an announcement by the Venezuelan minister for oil and China's three largest oil companies stated that a series of investment agreements had been signed with PdVSA and these oil companies to invest US$40 billion in Venuzuela's oil and gas sector. The minister also said that Venezuela was exporting 362,000bpd to China and had become one of China's largest oil and gas suppliers. Venezuela plans to export up to 700,000bpd to China by mid-2010s.
Total proven natural gas reserves were 4.8 trillion cubic metres in 2009, the second largest in the Americas, behind the US. Production was 28.5 billion cubic metres in 2007, an increase of 1.9 per cent on the 2006 figure. Exploitation of gas reserves is a priority, since the majority of Venezuela's energy is produced by natural gas. Output has risen from around 14.7 billion cum in 1980 to over 28 billion cum in 2007; there was a high of 32.3 billion cum in 1998.
The government agency Enagas regulates the natural gas sector. Around 70 per cent of gas production is consumed by the oil industry, the majority of which is used as re-injection to aid crude oil extraction. There are natural gas explorations of the country's north coast ongoing, aon areas leased by PdVSA.
The natural gas pipeline network has been enhanced to allow greater domestic access. The international gas pipeline began operation in 2008, supplying 2–4 billion cum per day of Colombian natural gas to western Venezuela. In 2012 a reverse in flow is planned with exports to Colombia of 4 billion cum per day.
Plans for the export of liquefied natural gas (LNG) from 2013 were agreed between PdVSA and three international consortia. Total exports of LNG are expected to be in excess of 10 million tonnes per year.
Venezuela is the second largest producer of coal in Latin America, after Colombia, and has 476 million tonnes of coal reserves (2007). PdVSA operates, through joint ventures between its subsidiary Carbozulia and foreign companies, four mines with production at 5.9 million tonnes of oil equivalent (2007). Domestic consumption is only around 15,000 tonnes per annum and most of Venezuela's bituminous coal is exported to markets in North and South America and Europe.
A joint investment fund with China was increased to US$16 billion in 2009. The fund guarantees energy supplies to China in exchange for cash up front.
In November 2010, the Italian energy company Eni reported that the new Venezuela offshore natural gas and oil field was a 'world-class super-giant gas discovery'. The estimated reserves were increased to 396 billion cubic metres of natural gas and 2.5 billion barrels of oil.

Energy

Total installed generating capacity was 22.2 gigawatts (GW) in 2007.
Hydropower produces over 70 per cent of total electricity generated, with traditional thermal sources constituting the remainder. Construction of more hydroelectric power stations, of 2,250MW, are underway with an additional 2,964MW planned.
Almost half of Venezuela's electricity generating capacity is provided by the 10GW Raul Leoni hydroelectric dam on the Caroní River. Another renewable source of electricity includes a small geothermal energy plant producing 1MW.
Venezuela's grid is connected to that of Colombia, enabling the country to export surplus electricity. However, there have been serious electricity shortages in recent years due to low rainfall and electricity theft, which is estimated to account for a quarter of Venezuelan energy consumption. Extensive power cuts were imposed on industry and businesses in December 2009 in an effort to avoid mass power cuts, as electricity output of the country's principal Guri hydroelectric power station began falling, due to severely low water levels. In May 2011, after blackouts had affected almost half of the country, the government began cutting power for three hours a day in 19 of the country's 23 states.
The electricity sector is dominated by the state-owned Electrificación de Caroni (EDELCA). Cadafe, which includes Cadela, Elecentro, Eleoriente, Eleoccidente, Desurca, and Semda, is the world's second-largest state-owned electricity company.

Financial markets

Stock exchange

Bolsa de Valores de Caracas (BCV) (Caracas Stock Exchange)

Banking and insurance

With the bankruptcy of the second biggest bank in the country, Banco Latino, in 1994, the Venezuelan banking and financial services system went into meltdown. About a third of Venezuela's banks subsequently went into insolvency as depositors panicked, closing accounts and forcing under-capitalised banks to close. Since then, the financial sector in Venezuela has undergone a vigorous restructuring, ensuring that the banks of today are well capitalised with relatively clean balance sheets.
The government has been able to recuperate its losses through the privatisation of several leading banks, and Venezuela's financial system is largely controlled by foreign interests. Foreign participation in Venezuela's banking system rose to around 70 per cent of total banking assets. As elsewhere in Latin America, it was the Spanish banks which had the most influence in the banking system, with Spanish Grupo Santander taking the lead in buying indigenous banks.
Venezuela's banking superintendent privately told several of the country's large banks that President Chávez intended to place official government representatives on their governing boards. In 2008, President Chávez began plans to nationalise the Commercial Bank of Venezuela, owned by the Spanish Grupo Santander. The bank was nationalised in May 2009 and Venezuela paid US$1.05 billion to Grupo Santander. The government closed four banks in December 2009, following suspicions of regulatory violations and the arrest of their owners for misappropriating funds. Of the four, Provivienda and Canarias will be liquidated and Bolivar and Confederado may be rescued; together these banks accounted for around 6 per cent of the banking sector.
A new Bank of the South, (South America) with a headquarters in Venezuela, was to

be launched in 2008, to provide an alternative source of development funding for the participating countries, with assets of US$7 billion to underpin its operations. However as the global economic crisis intensified it undermined the intentions of the new bank so that by 2009 countries in the region were again turning to the IMF and World Bank for assistance.

Central bank

Banco Central de Venezuela

Main financial centre

Caracas

Time

GMT minus four and a half hours (from 9 December 2007)

Geography

Venezuela is on the north coast of South America, bordered by Colombia to the west, Guyana to the east and Brazil to the south.

Venezuela is a mountainous country. A spur of the Andes reaches into the north-west and is home to Pico Bolivar, at 5,007m the highest point in Venezuela. In the south-east, bordering on Brazil, are the densely-forested Guiana Highlands, which make up around half of the country's terrain. The Angel Falls, the highest waterfall in world, is in the Guiana Highlands. The centre of the country, between the mountain ranges and opening to the Caribbean Sea, are plains (*llanos*) and coastal lowlands. The Orinoco, Venezuela's biggest river, rises in the Guiana Highlands, draining most of the country on its way to the north-eastern coast and culminating in an extensive delta, which is marshy and thickly wooded.

Hemisphere

Northern

Climate

Tropical, hot and humid, with more moderate temperatures in highlands.

Dry season from December–April, with mean temperature in Caracas 19 degrees Celsius (C), rising to 28 degrees C during the day; nights are cool. Rainy season from May–November, with mean daytime temperature in Caracas 23 degrees C.

Entry requirements

Passports

Required by all, valid for six months from date of arrival.

Visa

Required by all, except nationals of EU/EEA countries, North America, Australasia, Japan, some South American, Asian and other countries for up to 90 days. For a full list of exemptions and other details, visit www.embavenez-us.org

Currency advice/regulations

There are no restrictions on the import and export of local or foreign currencies

Health (for visitors)

Mandatory precautions

None (yellow fever vaccination certificates may be required by visitor leaving for other countries).

Advisable precautions

Yellow fever, cholera, typhoid, polio vaccinations. Malaria prophylaxis recommended for visits to some rural areas. Rabies is present and dengue fever is becoming more common. There are occasional outbreaks of viral encephalitis.

In north-central regions, to avoid the risk of Bilharzia use only chlorinated swimming pools for bathing.

Bottled water is advisable for new visitors. Unwashed raw foods and undercooked meats are not safe to eat.

Healthcare facilities are good in main cities, but the cost is high and therefore medical insurance is recommended.

Hotels

The selection of first-rate hotels is rather limited. Good standard in Caracas and main centres. Graded into classes by Tourism Department on a one- to five-star basis. Booking in advance is essential. There are some seasonal variations of rates. There is a 10 per cent tourist tax.

Public holidays (national)

Fixed dates

1 Jan (New Year's Day), 19 Apr (Emancipation Day), 1 May (Labour Day), 24 Jun (Battle of Carabobo), 5 Jul (Independence Day), 24 Jul (Simon Bolívar Day), 15 Aug (Assumption Day), 12 Oct (Spanishness Day), 1 Nov (All Saints' Day), 25 Dec (Christmas Day).

Variable dates

Epiphany (first Mon in Jan), Carnival (Feb), Maundy Thursday, Good Friday, Immaculate Conception (Dec).

Working hours

Banking

Mon–Fri: 0830–1130, 1400–1630.

Business

Mon–Fri: 0800–1800 (with long lunch break from noon to 1430).

Government

Mon–Fri: range from 0730–1530 to 0930–1730; long lunch break from noon to 1430.

Shops

Mon–Sat: 0900–1300, 1500–1900.

Telecommunications

Mobile/cell phones

A GSM 900 network is limited to coverage in Caracas and main towns.

Electricity supply

110V AC, 60 cycles

Social customs/useful tips

The normal form of greeting is a handshake or an *abrazo*, a cross between a handshake and a hug. Luncheons are frequently heavy. Wine in restaurants tends to be expensive.

Public services are inefficient and it is advisable to hire professional help to carry out official transactions.

Punctuality is not a strong point and the traffic is often blamed for delays. Business meetings may be cancelled or rescheduled at the last moment.

There is no numbering system for streets in Caracas, and many street names are not marked. Directions are given by building or residence name and the neighbourhood or *urbanización*.

Security

Carry identification at all times as police make spot checks and a person without identification may be detained.

Beware of pickpockets. If unlucky enough to be robbed, do not argue as criminals can quickly become violent. Many Caracas residents carry handguns for personal defence and are prepared to use them.

Getting there

Air

National airline: Aeropostal.

International airport/s: Caracas-Maiquetía International (MQV), 22km north of city, duty-free shopping, bank, restaurants, post office and car hire. Journey time to city by bus 45 minutes running every hour. Taxis are located at a rank.

Other airport/s: Maracaibo-La Chinita (MAR), 17km from city, restaurant, car hire.

Airport tax: US$16.

Surface

Road: It is possible to cross from Colombia by the Caribbean Coastal Highway, or by the Pan-American Highway via San Cristobal. The only road from Brazil (via Santa Elena de Uairen) is very rough and is difficult in the rainy season. There is no direct access from Guyana.

Main port/s: Guanta, La Guaira, Maracaibo, Puerto Cabello.

Getting about

National transport

Air: Several carriers operate services to many destinations in Venezuela. Overbooking is common and it is advisable to arrive at the airport well before minimum check-in time. Cancellations and schedule changes are also likely to occur. Unlimited travel tickets are available.

Road: Roads between main cities are of a high standard, but there are maintenance problems. The road from Caracas to Maiquetía International Airport is closed indefinitely due a collapsed bridge. There are around 36,000km of surfaced roads, including 17,000km motorways and 13,000km highways. The Pan-American Highway runs from Caracas, via Valencia and Barquisimeto, to the Colombian border. Other main highways include: Valencia-Puerto Cabello; Coro-La Ceiba; Caracas-Ciudad Bolívar.

Buses: There are frequent services between major cities. It is advisable to book in advance. Buses are overcrowded, tend to break down and traffic jams are a problem.

Rail: A very limited service available (Barquisimeto-Puerto Cabello; around four trains per day). The first new line since 1937, connecting Caracas and Cua, was inaugurated in October 2006.

City transport

Taxis: Taxis are not metered and it is advisable to agree the fare before travelling. Higher fares are charged for late night journeys. Outside Caracas fares can be expensive for long trips. Licensed taxis are white with yellow number plates and can be hailed in the street. A fleet of black Ford Explorers operates from Caracas airport. Visitors should avoid taxi touts and unlicensed taxis, especially at the airport. Taxis from reliable companies can be booked through the hotels, some of which run their own limousine services. Shared taxis (*por puestos*) are widely used.

Buses, trams & metro: The metro reaches main points all along the Valley of Caracas. It is fast, cheap, clean, comfortable and safe, although pickpockets abound. It links with the metrobus services.

Car hire

Most international rental car companies are available in main towns and at airports. National or international licence accepted. A credit card is required. Insurance cover is recommended.

BUSINESS DIRECTORY

The addresses listed below are a selection only. While World of Information makes every endeavour to check these addresses, we cannot guarantee that changes have not been made, especially to telephone numbers and area codes. We would welcome any corrections.

Telephone area codes

The international direct dialling (IDD) code for Venezuela is +58, followed by area code and subscriber's number:

Barquisimeto	251	Maturin	291
Caracas	212	Merida	274
Ciudad Bolivar	285	Puerto	
Cumana	293	Cabello	242
Maracaibo	261	San Cristobal	276
Maracay	243	Valencia	241

Chambers of Commerce

American-Venezuelan Cámara de Comercio, Torre Credival, 2da Avenida de Campo Alegre, Caracas (tel: 263-0833; fax: 263-1829; e-mail: vanamcham@venamcham.org).

British-Venezuelan Chamber of Commerce, Avenida Francisco de Miranda, Multicentro Empresarial del Este, Caracas (tel: 267-3112; fax: 263-0362; e-mail: britcham@ven.net).

Caracas Cámara de Comercio, Calle Andrés Eloy Blanco 215, Los Caobos, Caracas (tel: 571-3222; fax: 571-0050; e-mail: comercioccs@cantv.net).

Valencia Cámara de Comercio, Avenida Bolivar Norte, Edificio Cámara de Comercio, Valencia (tel: 857-5109; fax: 857-5147; e-mail: camaracomercio@cantv.net).

Venezualan Federación de Cámaras y Asociaciones de Comercio y Producción, Avenida El Empalme, Urbanizacion El Bosque, PO Box 2568, Caracas (tel: 731-1711, 731-0246; e-mail: direje@fedecamaras.org.ve).

Banking

Banco Industrial de Venezuela, Av Universidad Esquina de Traposos, Zona postal 1010, Apartado postal 2054, Caracas (tel: 545-9222/541-8622; fax: 545-8315).

Banco Mercantil, Av Andrés Bello No 1, Edif Mercantil, Aportado postal 789, Caracas 1010-A (tel: 541-4320, 541-6666; fax: 507-1239, 574-3216; e-mail: mercan24@bancomercantil.com; internet site: http://www.bancomercantil.com).

Banco Provincial, Av Este 'O', San Bernardo, Zona postal 1010-A, Apartado postal 1269, Caracas (tel: 574-5611, 574-6611; fax: 574-9408, 574-2065).

Central bank

Banco Central de Venezuela, Avenida Urdaneta esq Las Carmelitas, Apartado 2017, Caracas 1010 (tel: 801-5111; fax: 861-1649; e-mail: biblio@bcv.org.ve).

Stock exchange

Bolsa de Valores de Caracas (BCV) (Caracas Stock Exchange): www.bolsadecaracas.com

Travel information

Caracas-Maiquetía Airport, Ed Vargas, Maiquetia 1161 (tel: 303-1329; fax: 355-1224; e-mail: consejo_admin@iaaim.com.ve).

Ministry of tourism

Ministry of Tourism, Edificio Mintur, Avda Francisco de Miranda con Avda Principal de La Floresta, Caracas (tel: 208-4511; e-mail: webmaster@mintur.gob.ve).

National tourist organisation offices

Inatur (National Institute of Tourism), Edificio Mintur, Avda Francisco de Miranda con Avda Principal de La Floresta, Caracas (tel/fax: 286-3016; fax: 286-3016; e-mail: gpminatur@gmail.com).

Ministries

Ministry of Agriculture and Livestock, Torre Este, Piso 14, Caracas (tel: 509-0445; fax: 574-2432).

Ministry of Defence, Fuerta Tiuna, Conejo Blanco, Caracas 1090 (tel: 622-2745; fax: 662-4078).

Ministry of Education, Esquina de Salas, Edificio Sede Del Ministerio de Educación, Caracas (tel: 564-0672; fax: 564-0379).

Ministry of Energy, Torre Oeste, Parque Central, Piso 16, Caracas (tel: 507-6604; fax: 571-3953).

Ministry of the Environment, Torre Sur, Centro Simon Bolivar, Piso 25, Caracas (tel: 481-6275; fax: 483-1148).

Ministry of Family Affairs, Torre Oeste, Parque Central, Piso 51, Caracas (tel: 575-3690; fax: 573-7481).

Ministry of Finance, Edif Banco la Guaira, Piso 12, Av Mexico, Caracas (tel: 509-8281; fax: 509-7831).

Ministry of Foreign Affairs, Conde a Carmelitas, Torre M.R.E., Piso 2, Caracas 1010 (tel: 862-4484; fax: 861-0894).

Ministry of Foreign Trade, Centro Comercial los Cedros, Mezzanina 3, Avda Libertador, Caracas (tel: 762-2777; fax: 762-3883).

Ministry of Health and Social Security, Edif, Sur, Centro Simón Bolívar, Caracas (tel: 483-1566).

Ministry of Home Affairs, Esquina de Carmelitas, Caracas 1010 (tel: 483-4334; fax: 861-1967).

Ministry of Housing (tel: 509-8676; fax: 509-8437).

Ministry of Industrial Development, Edif Sur, Piso 9, Centro Simón Bolívar, Caracas (tel: 419-296; fax: 483-2607).

Ministry of Justice, Torre Norte, Centro Simón Bolívar, Piso 25 (tel: 483-1170; fax: 483-7515).

Ministry of Labour, Torre Sur, Piso 5, Centro Simón Bolívar, Caracas (tel: 483-1881; fax: 483-5940).

Ministry of Planning, Parque Central, Torre Oeste, Piso 26, Caracas (tel: 507-7902; fax: 573-2834).

Ministry of Public Works and Commercial Affairs, Centro Simón Bolívar, Torre Sur, Piso 6, Caracas (tel: 483-2124-; fax: 412-553).

Ministry of Trade and Industry, Av Libertador Centro Comercial Los Cedros, Piso 2, Caracas (tel: 531-0026; fax: 762-9869).

Ministry of Transport and Communications, Torre Este, Parque Central, Piso 50,

Caracas (tel: 509-10761; fax: 509-1769).

Ministry of Urban Development, Torre Oeste, Parque Central, Piso 51, Caracas (tel: 574-5349; fax: 571-1767).

President's Office, Palacio de Miraflores, Avenida Urdeneta, Caracas 1010 (tel: 861-0811; fax: 861-1101).

Other useful addresses
Asociación Nacional de Comerciantes e Industriales, Plaza Panteón Norte 1, Apdo 33, Caracas.

CVG Bauxita de Venezuela S.A. (Raw Material for Aluminun), Av. La Estancia, Edif, Diamen, Piso 2, Chuao, Caracas (tel: 922-311, 916-187, 916-487; fax: 918-176).

British Embassy, Edificio Torre Las Mercedes, 3 Piso, Avenida La Estancia, Chuao, Caracas 1060 (tel: 911-255, 993-4111, 926-542, 914-253; fax: 993-9989).

Caracas Stock Exchange (fax: 952-2640; internet site: www.caracasstock.com).

Central Information Office (OCI), Parque Central, Torre Oeste, Piso 18, Caracas (tel: 572-7110; fax: 572-2675).

The Commission for State Reform, Torre Oeste, Piso 38, Parque Central, Caracas (tel: 507-8934/8931; fax: 572-3178).

Conapri (National Council for Investment Promotion), Centro Banavén, PB, Local 4, Chuao, Caracas (tel: 923-801; fax: 926-498).

Consejo Venezolana de la Industria, Edif Cámara de Industriales, Esq de Puente Anauco, Caracas.

Corporación Venezolana de Guayana (CVG) (Main Company), Edif. de Administración, Via Caracas, Puerto Ordaz, Ciudad Guayana, C.P. 80915, Edo. Bolivar (tel: 303-333; fax: 226-300, 225-311).

CVG Ferrominera del Orinoco AA (Iron), Av La Estancia, Chuao, Edif, Torre Las Mercedes, Piso 9, Caracas 1070-A (tel: 911-166; fax: 911-639).

Fondo de Inversiones de Venezuela (Privatisation Programme Information), Torre Financiera del Banco Central de Venezuela, Piso 20, Esq de Santa Capilla, Avda Urdaneta, Caracas (tel: 806-5974; fax: 819-169).

PdVSA (Petróleos de Venezuela), Avda Liberator, La Campina, Apdo 169, Caracas 1010-A (tel: 708-1111; fax: 708-4661).

CVG Siderúrgica del Orinoco CA SIDOR. (Aluminium, Iron and Steel), Av La Estancia, Chuao, Edif. General de Seguros, Caracas, 1070-A (tel: 912-333, 911-462).

Superintendencia de Inversiones Extranjeras (SIEX – Superintendency of Foreign Investment), Apdo 213, Edif La Perla, Piso 3, Bolsa a Mercaderes, Caracas (tel: 483-6666; fax: 484-4368, 481-7919).

Unión Patronal Venezolana de Comercio, Edif General Urdaneta, Piso 2, Marrón a Pelota, Apdo 6578, Caracas.

US Embassy, Avda Principal de la Floresta, Esq Francisco de Miranda, La Floresta, Caracas (tel: 285-3111; fax: 285-0336).

Venezuelan Embassy (USA), 1099 30th Street, NW, Washington DC 20007 (tel: (+1-202) 342-2214; fax: (+1-202) 342-6820; e-mail: despacho@embavenez-us.org).

National news agency: ABN (Agencia Bolicariana de Noticias): (internet: www.abn.info.ve).

Internet sites
Venezuela Export Directory: http://www.ddex.com/

Venezuela trade: www.trade-venezuela.com

Vietnam

KEY FACTS

Official name: Cong Hoa Xa Hoi Chu Nghia Viet Nam (The Socialist Republic of Vietnam) (SRV)

Head of State: President Truong Tan Sang (from 25 Jul 2011)

Head of government: Prime Minister Nguyen Tan Dung (from 2006; re-elected 26 Jul 2011)

Ruling party: Dang Cong San Viet Nam (DCSV) (Communist Party of Vietnam)

Area: 329,556 square km

Population: 86.93 million (2010)*

Capital: Hanoi

Official language: Vietnamese

Currency: Dong (D) = 100 xu

Exchange rate: D20,829.50 per US$ (Oct 2011)

GDP per capita: US$1,174 (2010)

GDP real growth: 6.80% (2010)

GDP: US$103.60 billion (2010)

Labour force: 48.26 million (2009)*

Unemployment: 6.50% (2009)*

Inflation: 9.20% (2010)

Oil production: 370,000 bpd (2010)

Balance of trade: -US$5.15 billion (2010)

* estimated figure

The slogan dreamt up for Vietnam's tourist promotion campaign was 'Same, Same – but Different'. In 2011 things certainly were different, as the currency slumped, the black market prospered and inflation continued to rise. Sharing its curious mix of free market economics and the tight political controls of a free market economy with only two other countries, China and Laos, Vietnam could not fall back on text-book solutions to the problems confronting it in early 2011. Often fossilised state-owned companies continue to throttle the economy, accounting for as much as 40 per cent of the capital invested, but only producing 25 per cent of gross domestic product (GDP).

Complex relations

Vietnam's foreign relations remain largely, and predictably, focussed on the two countries which determined the country's international orientation in the second half of the twentieth century. Vietnam's relations with China have never been straightforward. In 1979 Vietnam went on the offensive against its large neighbour to the north following an attempt at incursion by China. Tensions with China have risen, particularly over disputed territory in the China Sea – to the extent of public protests in Hanoi which placed the Vietnamese on the back foot. Vietnam realises that it makes sense to have good relations with China, but at the same time is not prepared to roll over in the face of what the Vietnamese public sees as Chinese indifference.

If Vietnam's relationship with China is complex, that with the other global giant is ten times so. In the first place, Vietnam has to acknowledge that the US relationship with China will always take preference over that with Vietnam. The US-Vietnam relationship also has inevitable emotional overtones which, 40 years after the end of the so-called Vietnamese War, still register. For Vietnam, the US has not only become its major trading partner, but is also seen by Vietnam as an important counterweight to the overwhelming presence of China. Trade links between Vietnam and the US have become more than notional: by 2011 the US had become the largest importer of Vietnamese goods. But in relation to China, Vietnam was a small trading partner. By 2011 US investment in Vietnam totalled around US$10 billion, peanuts alongside that of China. Vietnam's total GDP in 2010 was only US$102 billion, with annual per capita income at some US$1,200. Quoted in the *International Herald Tribune* a study by the Harvard Vietnam programme on the Vietnamese economy compared its prospects with those of Singapore, South Korea and Taiwan. The latter three not only enjoy greater prosperity, each has greater transparency, relatively little corruption, good health and education systems and a workable legal system. The Harvard report did not mince its words, describing Vietnam's educational system as 'abysmal'.

National Congress

2011 saw the holding of the Vietnamese Communist Party's 11th National Congress from 12–19 January. No small matter this – the Congress is only held every five years (the first was held in 1935), giving aspirational politicians a small window of opportunity to shine. The11th National Congress opened with what was described as a 'blunt assessment' of its own shortcomings and a harsh attack on its critics. The outgoing party general secretary, Nong Duc Manh, lauded the country's economic development in his opening address which would later select the country's top leaders and chart its economic path for the next five years.

Mr Manh also warned that Vietnam's current growth rates might be unsustainable and that the republic's companies were lacking in quality, efficiency and competitiveness. He also noted that Vietnam had not been able to reduce corruption and wastefulness, or eliminate what he referred to as 'moral and lifestyle degradation'. Mr Manh also responded to Vietnam's critics after a prominent international human rights group had criticised Vietnam for its harsh crackdown on dissidents ahead of the Congress, saying that 'hostile forces' were using democracy and human rights in an attempt to overthrow the ruling party. In its 2011 survey of perceptions of corruption, Transparency International ranked Vietnam a rather undistinguished 112th out of 193 countries – on a par with Moldova and Kosovo and well behind other south-east Asian states such as Indonesia (100), Thailand (80), Malaysia (60) and Brunei (44). The region's leading performer was Singapore, with a world ranking of 5th.

The 1,400 delegates selected a Central Committee, which in turn appointed a new secretary general to head the *de facto* ruling 17-member Politburo. In affect, according to David Koh of the Institute of Southeast Asian Studies in Singapore, Mr Nguyen Phu Trong had already been chosen as secretary general by the Politburo and recommended to the 10th Central Committee, who accepted it; the 11th Central Committee elected at the 11th National Congress then ratified the choice. Mr Troung Tan Sang, who appeared at the top of the list of Politburo members, replaced Mr Nguyen Minh Triet as President. Prime Minister Nguyen Tan Dung was reappointed by party members to the Politburo, thereby securing his second term in office.

David Koh also commented that there are different views about what the next (rather than new) set of top leaders would achieve. He went on to say that 'The optimists believe that the changes towards better governance to address the myriad problems… may take time but they would surely come, and the slow generational change must be allowed to take its pace. They also think that speed is not crucial; prudence is. The pessimists believe that the problems… stem from the regime that the communist party has established and since there is no will to fundamentally change the system, there is really no point in watching out for any changes; the nation will muddle on. Then there are protagonists who believe that change is possible within this or the next generation, and strong pressures must be put on the leaders to effect these changes as soon as possible. They believe that delaying the changes by one or two generations would be irrevocably late.

'Whatever the views one subscribed to, the 11th Party National Congress did not pass without being noticed but the real work to improve the nation will soon pass on to the bureaucracy and the ability of the PM and the Political Bureau headed by the General Secretary to move strongly ahead without kicking prudence in the teeth. The extent to which these top two men share the same views and approach towards policies, and the extent to which their co-operation is able to persuade fellow decision makers in the Political Bureau to follow their lead, will determine the extent to which Vietnam will soar – or land harshly – in the next five years, until the next Party National Congress in 2016.'

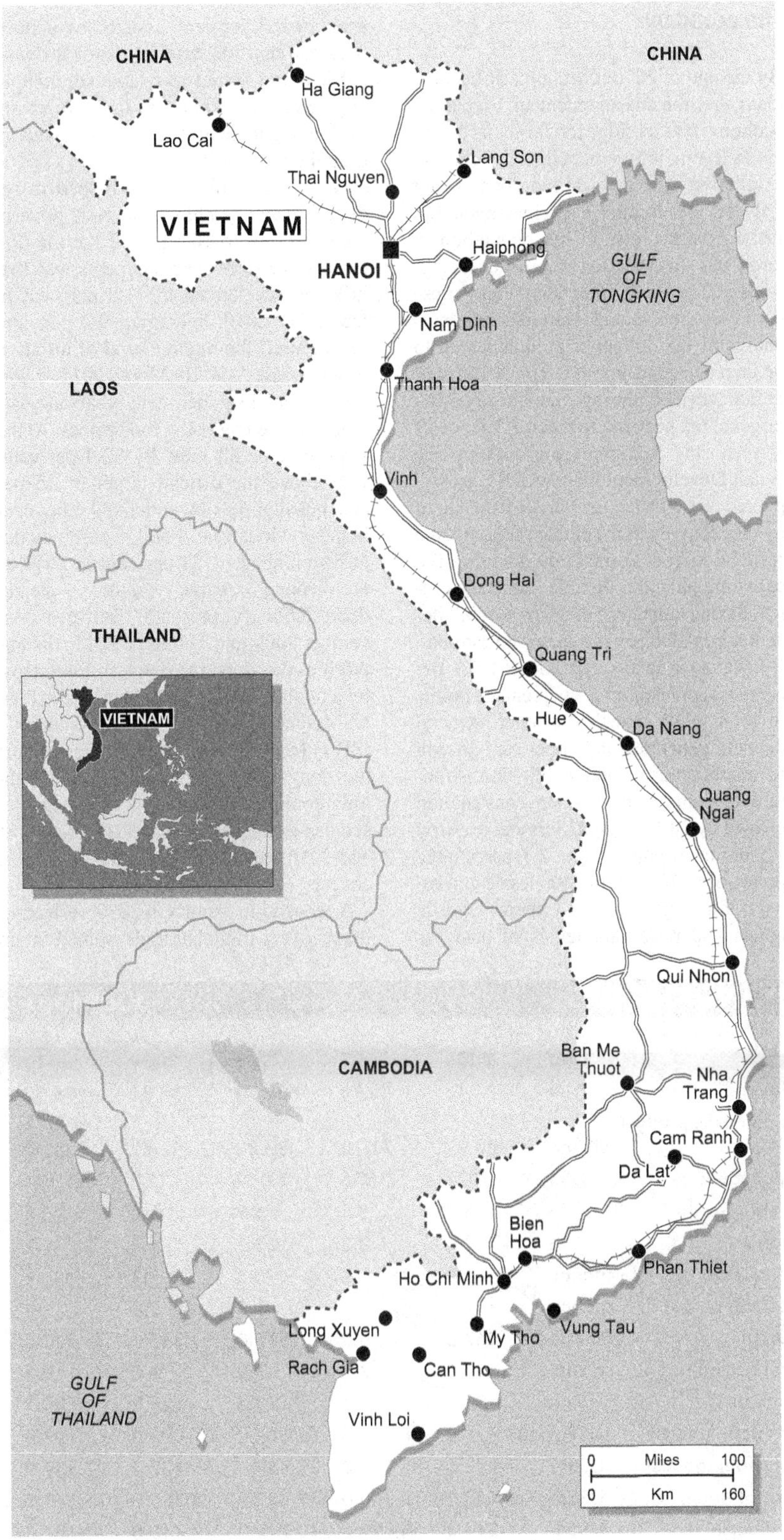

The economy

By the end of 2010 it had already become clear that the management of Vietnam's economy was a bridge too far for its politicians. Rising inflation, budget deficits and a faltering currency caused concern not only to the country's businessmen, but just as worryingly, to the population at large. As the inflation rate edged up towards 12 per cent and canny Vietnamese could see their savings start to shrink, purchases of US dollars or gold appeared to be increasingly attractive. The 2010 fiscal deficit crashed through an already high target of 6.2 per cent, to reach 7.4 per cent.

According to figures prepared by the Asian Development bank (ADB), growth picked up to 6.8 per cent in 2010 bolstered by the recovery in the global economy, the residual effects of the 2009 domestic fiscal stimulus and a flexible monetary policy. Strong consumption growth of 9.7 per cent stimulated private sector investment. By sector, industry expanded by 7.7 per cent and contributed 3.2 percentage points of total GDP growth. Stronger external demand generated an 8.4 per cent growth in manufacturing and public infrastructure investment pushed up construction growth by 10.1 per cent. Services grew by 7.5 per cent, contributing 3.1 percentage points of GDP growth. Wholesale and retail trading climbed by 8.1 per cent, while hotels and restaurant levels of business grew by 8.7 per cent, assisted by a steep 34.8 per cent increase in visitor arrivals. Agricultural output was subdued, though, edging up by 2.8 per cent in 2010, owing to flooding in central regions followed by drought in the north.

Faster economic growth helped to reduce urban unemployment and poverty incidence fell to 10.6 per cent from 12.3 per cent in 2009. The bad news was that inflation accelerated to 11.8 per cent in December 2010, averaging 9.2 per cent for the year, the highest level of inflation in south-east Asia. By March 2011, it was running at 13.9 per cent year-on-year, largely driven by rising food prices. At the same time credit grew by 32.4 per cent, well above the official target of 25 per cent but slightly slower than 39.6 per cent in the previous year. Foreign currency deposits climbed by 21 per cent in 2010 as the dong came under steady depreciationary pressure. Between November 2009 and February 2011, the authorities devalued the dong, in four steps, by a total of about 20 per cent against the US dollar. The State Bank of Vietnam's (SBV) (central bank) capacity to support the dong was constrained by relatively low holdings of foreign exchange reserves, estimated at US$12.4 billion at end-2010 (about 1.9 months of import cover).

A rebound in exports in 2010, reflecting the recovery in global trade, reined in the deficit in merchandise trade to US$7.1 billion on a balance of payments basis, from US$8.3 billion in 2009. Exports rose by 26.4 per cent in US dollars. Customs data showed strong increases in exports of textiles (up by 23 per cent), footwear (25 per cent) and electronics and computers (29 per cent). Crude oil exports fell, however, by 20 per cent, as volumes plunged by 40 per cent owing to depletion of oil fields. Imports rose by 21.2 per cent, reflecting demand for inputs for manufacturing and the country's reliance on imported capital equipment.

Trade with China (PRC) was boosted by a free-trade agreement between the Association of Southeast Asian Nations (ASEAN) and the PRC, from January 2010. Customs data showed that imports from the PRC increased by 23 per cent to about US$18.0 billion and exports there shot up by 49 per cent to US$6.3 billion.

After increases in remittances and tourism receipts, the current account deficit contracted to US$4.3 billion, equivalent to 4.0 per cent of GDP, its narrowest in 4 years. The overall balance of payments showed a deficit of US$1.8 billion in 2010. Net foreign direct investment (FDI) inflows rose by about 3 per cent to US$7.1 billion in 2010. FDI approvals missed the target, however and were well below those of 2009, probably reflecting investor uncertainties over policy direction. FDI approvals for real estate projects fell, but approvals for manufacturing more than doubled. With most fiscal stimulus measures taken during the global recession expiring at end-2009, the overall fiscal deficit in 2010 narrowed to 8.0 per cent of GDP. In real terms, government expenditure was estimated to be little changed from 2009, but revenue and grants rose by about 10 per cent, reflecting stronger non-oil tax receipts.

Preliminary data show that GDP rose by 5.4 per cent year-on-year in January–March 2011, slowing from 7.3 per cent in the fourth quarter of 2010. Agriculture increased by 2.0 per cent, industry by 5.5 per cent and services by 6.3 per cent. Solid expansion in the first quarter was seen elsewhere: industrial production at 14.0 per cent, retail sales at 9 per cent in real terms, international visitor arrivals at 12 per cent and merchandise exports on a customs basis at 44 per cent. GDP is forecast to grow by 6.1 per cent for 2011 as a whole. For the whole year, crude oil production is projected at 15 million metric tons, similar to 2010.

Growth is expected to grow by 6.7 per cent in 2012 as a more stable economic

KEY INDICATORS — Vietnam

	Unit	2006	2007	2008	2009	2010
Population	m	84.16	85.16	*86.18	*87.21	*86.93
Gross domestic product (GDP)	US$bn	60.99	71.10	89.80	92.40	103.60
GDP per capita	US$	724	835	1,042	1,060	1,174
GDP real growth	%	8.2	8.5	6.2	5.3	6.8
Inflation	%	7.5	8.3	23.1	6.7	9.2
Industrial output	% change	–	–	5.5	7.7	–
Agricultural output	% change	–	–	1.8	2.8	–
Oil output	'000 bpd	367.0	340.0	317.0	345.0	370.0
Natural gas output	bn cum	7.0	7.7	7.9	8.0	9.4
Coal output	mtoe	21.8	22.4	23.6	25.2	24.7
Exports (fob) (goods)	US$m	39,826.0	48,561.0	62,685.0	57,096.0	72,192.0
Imports (fob) (goods)	US$m	44,891.0	58,921.0	75,467.0	65,402.0	77,339.0
Balance of trade	US$m	-5,155.0	-10,360.0	-12,782.0	-8,306.0	-5,147.0
Current account	US$m	-244.0	-6,992.0	-10,787.0	-7,440.0	-4,287.0
Total reserves minus gold	US$m	13,384.1	23,602.4	23,890.3	16,447.1	12,466.6
Foreign exchange	US$m	13,382.5	23,594.8	23,882.0	16,027.4	12,054.1
Exchange rate	per US$	16,073.00	16,040.00	16,302.00	19,085.00	18,613.00

* estimated figure

environment stimulates consumption and investment. Inflation is projected to remain high through 2011, peaking at about 16 per cent year-on-year in the third quarter and averaging 13.3 per cent.Vinashin

The high profile scandal surrounding state-owned Vinashin did little to increase public or investor confidence in the government's management of the economy. Vinashin was originally set up as a shipbuilding enterprise, but by 2010 had expanded to over 400 different businesses; the company defaulted in late 2010 on a repayment of US$60 million relating to a US$600 million syndicated loan. Some international credit rating agencies downgraded Vietnam's ratings, citing the government's contingent liabilities and the macro-economic stress. The government indicated it would not bail out Vinashin, signalling to other state-owned firms that they would be held accountable if they overextended their borrowing. Vinashin is to be 'restructured' (i e bailed out) over 3 years to put its finances on a firmer footing. With debts amounting to US$4.5 billion, Vinashin has been exempted from paying taxes and it is thought has been refinanced with interest free loans. The secretive way in which the Vinashin crash was managed by the government did little to improve business transparency.

Some good news

Vietnam's ranking in the World Bank's *Doing Business 2011* report rose to 78 from 88 the previous year. This reflected improvements in the ease of starting a business, obtaining construction permits, access to credit and tax administration. The Socio-Economic Development Strategy for 2011–20, as approved by January 2011, targets rapid average GDP growth of 7–8 per cent. In February 2011, however, the government indicated that it was prepared to give a higher priority to stability than growth in the near term, when it committed to restore stability through a package of policies, notably tighter fiscal and monetary policies in 2011 aimed at curbing inflation and stabilising the external position. The restoration of investor confidence will require sustained and consistent policy actions until inflation is subdued.

The IMF

In its retrospective 2010 assessment of the Vietnamese economy, the International Monetary Fund (IMF) had noted that economic activity held up well during the global crisis, thanks to ambitious stimulus measures. Facing a decline in FDI commitments and expecting sluggish external demand for exports in the wake of the global crisis, the government had shifted policies toward supporting growth. Monetary policy was drastically loosened and a sizable fiscal package (5 per cent of GDP) was executed. As a result, Vietnam's GDP grew by 5.3 per cent in 2009, down from the 6.3 per cent seen in 2008 and the slowest pace since 2000, but nevertheless among the better performers in developing Asia.

Risk assessment

Economy	Fair
Politics	Poor
Regional stability	Fair

COUNTRY PROFILE

Historical profile

1428 After a long period of rule by successive Chinese rulers, Vietnam gained independence from the Ming dynasty's control. The Le dynasty ruled until 1527.
1680 The Portuguese, Dutch, English and French established trading posts in Vietnam.
1771–1802 The Tai Son Rebellion years. The Tai Son brothers wrested control from the ruling Nguyen family. They aimed to seize the wealth of the rich and aid the poor. Most of the members of the Nguyen family were killed, except for Nguyen Anh, the nephew of a Nguyen lord.
1802 Vietnam was unified under the leadership of Nguyen Anh who recaptured much of Vietnam from the Tai Son brothers.
1830–40 The Nguyen dynasty tried to rid Vietnam of French missionaries by forcing the Christian movement underground and executing priests. In response, the missionaries appealed to the French government for military intervention in Vietnam.
1859 The French began their attack on the region, capturing the city of Danang.
1861 The French captured Saigon (now Ho Chi Minh city).
1862 Vietnam agreed to the Treaty of Saigon that gave the French control of three provinces and the island of Poulo Condore, free passage of French ships and freedom for the missionaries.
1883 French rule began over the whole country as part of the Indochina territory that included Cambodia. Under colonial rule, transportation and communications improved but the standard of living among the Vietnamese people remained low. Their suffering contributed to rising nationalist sentiment.
1930 A revolutionary, Ho Chi Minh, formed the Indochinese Communist Party (ICP) to fight against French rule.
1940 The French administration was replaced by Japanese occupation during the war.
1945 The Japanese were expelled by the ICP and French forces. A war of independence against France began.
1954 At a peace conference in Geneva, Vietnam was divided at the seventeenth parallel into communist Democratic Republic of Vietnam (north) and American-backed Republic of Vietnam (south). North Vietnam sponsored a growing guerrilla movement (Viet Cong) in the south, which aimed to re-unite Vietnam.
1964 US armed forces began their official intervention in support of South Vietnam after the US Gulf of Tonkin resolution. The US was committed to South Vietnam.
1967 The US military presence totalled nearly 500,000 troops.
1968 The Communists launched an attack on South Vietnam. This 'Tet Offensive' targeted five major cities. The Communists were forced to retreat within weeks. The US bombing campaign against North Vietnam ended and US troops in South Vietnam were reduced.
1973 The Paris peace accords were signed, temporarily ending hostilities between the US and North Vietnam.
1975 US troops withdrew.
1976 North and South Vietnam were combined to form the Socialist Republic of Vietnam. Saigon was renamed Ho Chi Minh City.
1979 Vietnamese troops invaded Cambodia overthrowing the Pol Pot regime and instituting their own puppet government; Chinese troops invaded Vietnam but were defeated. During this time Vietnam established close relationships with the Soviet Union, which was necessary for its economic development.
1986 Economic reform began with the adoption of the *doi moi* (renovation) reforms.
1992 The state constitution was introduced, which allowed for some liberalisation of the Vietnamese economy.
1993 Full Western aid resumed.
1995 Vietnamese and American rapprochement began. Vietnam joined the Association of Southeast Asian Nations (Asean).
1997 Tran Duc Luong was elected president by the National Assembly, and Phan Van Khai was appointed prime minister.
2000 Vietnam and the US signed an agreement enabling normal trading relations between the two countries.
2001 Nong Duc Manh was appointed secretary general of the Dang Cong San Viet Nam (DCSV) (Communist Party of Vietnam).
2002 Russia closed its naval base in Cam Ranh. Vietnam signed an accord with Russia to construct a US$100 million hydro-electric power station in Vietnam's central highlands. DCSV members won most seats in the National Assembly elections.

2004 The first US commercial flight since 1973 landed in Ho Chi Minh City.
2005 Prime Minister Phan Van Khai visited the US as the first Vietnamese leader since the end of the Vietnam War.
2006 Nguyen Minh Triet and Nguyen Tan Dung replaced Tran Duc Luong and Phan Van Khai as president and prime minister in what was seen as a move towards a younger leadership. A trade agreement with the US was concluded.
2007 Vietnam joined the World Trade Organisation (WTO) after a 12-year accession process. In elections for the National Assembly, the coalition Vietnamese Fatherland Front (led by the Communist Party) won 492 seats (out of 493). The US agreed to fund a study into eliminating the high levels of Agent Orange (a highly toxic defoliant used by the US military during the Vietnam War) from storage sites. Prime Minister Dung was re-appointed and promised to implement economic reforms.
2008 Petrol prices were increased by 31 per cent as the government moved to cut back on subsidies. A two-child limit for families was re-introduced, in an effort to limit population growth. An agreement resolved a 30-year border dispute with China.
2009 Petrovietnam began operating a natural gas pipeline from the offshore Su Tu Vang gas field to electricity power plants in the south-east region with an initial 500,000 cubic metres per day. Tropical storm Mirinae caused the deaths of around 90 people during severe flooding in the central provinces. A deal was signed between the Vietnam and Russian central banks allowing payments for bilateral trade to be made in the dong and the rouble. The currency was devalued by 5 per cent.
2010 In March, the two-child per family limit was relaxed to allow a third, not only to accommodate children of a previous marriage and any that may be handicapped, but also to redress a growing gender imbalance due to abortions following ultrasound scans. The government ordered all online gold trading floors to close by the end of March until new credit institution laws were enacted. The online trading was thought to have been turning over some US$1 billion per day, but was becoming unstable due to lax regulations. On 18 August, the Pepsi Cola Company announced plans to invest US$250 million in a variety of projects around the country. In September, the Coca-Cola Company said it would double its investment to US$400 million in Vietnam.
2011 Nguyen Phu Trong was elected general secretary of the DCSV on 19 January. The dong was devalued by 8.5 per cent in February, leading to an inflation rate of 13.9 per cent year-on-year in March. Fuel prices were increased for the second time in five weeks on 30 March. Public sector wages were increased by 14 per cent in May, in an attempt to shield workers from the high rate of inflation. A decision, by the four-country Mekong River Commission, to implement plans to build the controversial, Mekong Xayaburi dam in Laos was due to be taken on 19 April, but following ecologically and socially adverse reports the decision was postponed. The Mekong River is a food source for millions of people along its length; the dam would reduce food production in favour of electricity production. In parliamentary elections held on 22 May the DCSV won 496 of 500 seats; self-nominated candidates four. Turnout was 99.99 per cent. On 25 July, parliament elected Truong Tan Sang as president, with 487 votes (out of 500). President Troung nominated Prime Minister Nguyen for another term in office. Widespread flooding along the Mekong Delta caused the death of 78 people; over 125,000 homes were inundated, and 4,000 hectares of rice fields submerged. The International Red Cross appealed for US$1 million in assistance for the tens of thousands affected by the rising waters, in the worst flood for over a decade.

Political structure

Constitution

Vietnam has adopted, in broad terms, a Marxist-Leninist political ideology. A number of its political systems are derived from those of China and the former USSR. The political structure is dominated throughout by the Dang Cong San Viet Nam (DCSV) (Communist Party of Vietnam).
Under the 1992 state constitution, the DCSV continues to be ultimately responsible for policy, but the government assumed greater administrative and executive responsibility.
Twenty-four amendments to the 1992 constitution were passed in December 2001. The most important gave equality to the private sector of the economy.
Local government is vested in elected provincial, municipal and district councils.

Independence date

2 September 1945

Form of state

Socialist republic

The executive

Executive power is officially exercised by a Western-style council of ministers under a prime minister. However, in practice, there is a two-way balance with the presidency and party. The president is elected by the National Assembly for a five-year term. Between sessions of the National Assembly, affairs of state are dealt with by the president and the National Assembly's standing committee, the council of state. In any case, membership of the Council of Ministers generally coincides with that of the Politburo and Secretariat of the DCSV, and executive decisions may, *de facto*, be taken by the DCSV even without the co-operation of the government.
The DCSV's 166-member Central Committee meets once or twice a year and is responsible for selecting the Politburo, which has 17 members. The Politburo oversees the DCSV's daily functions and has the power and authority to issue directives to the government. It is the highest policy-making body.

National legislature

The Council of Ministers is responsible to and appointed by the legislative Quoc Hoi (National Assembly), itself elected to a five-year term by universal adult suffrage (voting is mandatory).
The Quoc Hoi is the highest representative and legislative body and the only institution with the authority to enact the constitution, codes and laws and elect the president and vice president, prime minister, president of the supreme people's court and procurator general, among other high officials.
The National Assembly, which is dominated by the ruling DCSV, meets twice a year in plenary session for about two to three weeks at a time. The Assembly's principal purpose is the (generally automatic) approval of Politburo decisions and DCSV-inspired legislation.

Legal system

Vietnam applied French law in the colonial period, but assumed a legal system based on the Soviet mould after the communist takeover. The country has a civil law system, but much of the law is underdeveloped and in the process of being innovated, for example in the case of foreign investment. Civil cases involving such matters as family law are distinguished from 'economic' cases, which include disputes arising from trade, investment and payments involving foreign entities. 'Economic' cases are dealt with by a separate arbitration system, in which the Vietnam International Arbitration Centre (VIAC) is a prominent body.
The People's Supreme Court is Vietnam's highest court. Under it are People's Courts for each province, municipality and district.
The legal system is in the process of being reformed.

Last elections

22 May 2011 (parliamentary); 24 July 2011 (presidential, indirect)
Results: Parliamentary: Dang Cong San Viet Nam (DCSV) (Communist Party of Vietnam) won 496 of 500 seats;

self-nominated candidates four. Turnout was 99.99 per cent.
Presidential: Presidential: Truong Tan Sang won 487 votes (out of 500).

Next elections

No date set (presidential); 2012 (parliamentary)

Political parties

Ruling party

Dang Cong San Viet Nam (DCSV) (Communist Party of Vietnam)

Main opposition party

There are no opposition parties.

Population

86.93 million (2010)*

Last census: April 1999: 76,323,173
Population density: 262 inhabitants per square km (2010)
Annual growth rate: 1.5 per cent 1994–2004 (WHO 2006)

Ethnic make-up

Vietnamese (84 per cent) and Chinese (2 per cent). The remainder are Khmers, Chams and members of some 51 ethnic groups.

Religions

Although the country is officially atheist, many Vietnamese profess to being Buddhists. Christians are a significant minority (five million, mostly Catholics), followed by Caodaists, Hoa Hao Buddhists, Muslims and Hindus. There is a religious revival in Vietnam.

Education

Primary school lasts until age 11. Secondary school education is divided into lower secondary and upper secondary school lasting for four and three years, respectively. There is also provision for technical and vocational secondary education. Universities, specialised colleges, community and junior colleges provide higher education. There are currently over 100 higher education institutions. Distance education is offered in two open universities and other provincial centres.
The Ministry of Labour, Invalids and Social Affairs is expected to build a vocational training school in each province and a job training centre in each district by 2005. Since 1998, the state has invested US$12 million to upgrade infrastructure in job training centres and set up 39 new vocational schools. Trainees at vocational schools have annually increased by 20 per cent. Vietnam will provide vocational training to 1.3 million people annually, including 200,000 technicians, until 2010. As a result, the number of untrained workers will be reduced by 1.6 per cent by that year.
Public expenditure on education typically amounts to 3 per cent of annual gross national income.
Literacy rate: 90 per cent, adult rate (Unesco 2005)
Compulsory years: Six to 14.
Enrolment rate: 105.6 per cent gross primary enrolment; 67.1 per cent gross secondary enrolment, of relevant age groups (including repeaters) (World Bank 2004).
Pupils per teacher: 28, in primary schools.

Health

The government has sought to improve the country's deteriorating healthcare system, which suffers from chronic underfunding and resultant shortages of medicine and equipment, recruitment problems and low staff morale. In 2001, an agreement was signed by the International Finance Corporation to invest US$8 million to establish a foreign-owned, Western-style hospital in Ho Chi Minh City. The new hospital will have modern equipment and advanced medical facilities. It is the first hospital project to be partly funded by private investors and reflects the government's promotion of investment in Vietnam's healthcare system.
The parlous state of Vietnam's healthcare system today dates back to the end of the war in 1975. Although on paper the results are impressive, including the establishment of 9,000 communal clinics and the training of an additional 23,000 doctors to give a ratio of approximately 40 doctors per 10,000 population, the reality is that many clinics are not equipped or stocked and are given inadequate budgets. Many doctors prefer to concentrate their efforts on the more remunerative private treatment of better-off patients.
This difference between private and public expenses partly reflects the system of health fees introduced in the 1990s to supplement the health budget. The new charges (from which civil servants and war veterans are exempt) backfired, resulting in lower bed-occupancy rates – in some cases drops of 40 per cent were registered.

HIV/Aids

The official number of HIV/Aids cases by March 2006 was 104,000, however, some estimates put the real figure at three times this number. Young people, between 15–24 years, account for 40 per cent of the overall infection rate. The government has allocated US$6.7 million and the Asian Development Bank (ADB) allocated US$20 million for a programme, implemented over a five-year period, targetted specifically at the young. In 2004 the US included Vietnam in a list of 15 countries to benefit from a US$15 billion fund, at the beginning of in a five-year aid programme.
HIV prevalence: 0.4 per cent aged 15–49 in 2003 (World Bank)
Life expectancy: 71 years, 2004 (WHO 2006)
Fertility rate/Maternal mortality rate: 2.3 births per woman, 2004 (WHO 2006)
Birth rate/Death rate: 12.7 births and six deaths per 1,000 people (2003).
Child (under 5 years) mortality rate (per 1,000): 19 per 1,000 live births (2003); 37 per cent of children aged under five are malnourished (World Bank).
Head of population per physician: 0.53 physicians per 1,000 people, 2001 (WHO 2006)

Welfare

Vietnam's transition to a market economy has increased problems of unemployment and the availability of social security benefits. The country has about 46.6 million people of working age, accounting for 59 per cent of the total population. Vietnam aims to create 1.4 million jobs annually in the period between 2001–05. The country also plans to reduce unemployment to 5 per cent and increase working time in rural areas.
Although there are social security systems for the victims of war, the collapse of the co-operative system has affected benefits in rural areas. With the introduction of a new Labour Code in 1994, and the Law on Co-operatives in 1996, the Vietnamese government declared its willingness to provide social insurance to workers in all economic sectors. The Vietnam Social Security Organisation, founded in 1995, has a social insurance scheme covering both state and private employees for benefits including retirement, survivorship, sickness, maternity and compensation for work related injuries. The pension scheme is supported by 10 per cent and 5 per cent contributions from the employer and the employee, respectively.
The Ministry of Public Security has undertaken education programmes aimed at halting the increase in the traffic, to China each year, estimated at thousands of women, and young girls aged under 18 – who account for one in six cases.

Main cities

Hanoi (capital, estimated population 1.2 million (m) in 2005), Ho Chi Minh City (formerly Saigon) (3.4m), Hai Phong City (2.6m), Da Nang City (450,909), Bien Hoa (514,450), Hue (275,307), Vung Tau (259,869), Phan Thiet (228,299).

Languages spoken

The Vietnamese alphabet is an adaptation from the Roman, using tonal marks. French is spoken in official circles and some English is spoken in business circles, especially in the south. Business is usually conducted in Vietnamese or English, although many executives speak French and Russian, and a few speak Chinese. English and French are officially taught in secondary schools.

Official language/s
Vietnamese

Media

The Ministry of Culture and Information retains firm control of press and broadcasting and laws circumscribe journalists' ability to report freely.

Press

Dailies: In Vietnamese and most with English versions, *Nhân Dân* (www.nhandan.com.vn), is the Communist Party newspaper, *Tuoi Tre* (www.tuoitre.com.vn) has a wide circulation among the young, *Quân D?i Nhân Dân* (www.qdnd.vn/qdnd), is the army's newpaper.

In English, *Viet Nam News* (vietnamnews.vnanet.vn), *Saigon Giai Phong* (www.saigon-gpdaily.com.vn), is the communist newspaper in Ho Chi Minh City. In French *Le Courrier du Vietnam* (http://lecourrier.vnagency.com.vn).

Weeklies: In English the *Vietnam Courier* is a communist publication and *Doanh Nghiep* is published by the Union of Co-operatives.

Business: In Vietnamese *Tin Nhanh Chúng Khoán* (www.tinnhanhchungkhoan.vn), with stock exchange details, *Nghien Cuu Kinh Te* (www.ie.netnam.vn) a bi-monthly, academic, Economic Studies Review publication.

In English, the *Vietnam Investment Review* (www.vir.com.vn), is a weekly circulated in Vietnam, and distributed throughout Asia, Europe and the US, coupled to the online business news outlet (http://english.vietnamnet.vn). *The Saigon Times Weekly* (www.saigontimesweekly.saigonnet.vn) is another weekly. Monthlies include *Vietnam Economic Times* (www.vneconomy.com.vn/eng) with analysis and business tips, and *Vietnam Business Forum* (http://vibforum.vcci.com.vn), a Chamber of Trade and Commerce publication.

Periodicals: Several commercial periodicals that have recently begun publishing, in Vietnamese, to an international standard include *Nha Dep* a women's magazine, *Dinh Cao* (Sports and Fitness), *M* (Fashion) and *Phu Nu The Gioi* (Woman's World). Other popular publications include *Tuoi Tre* (youth), and *Lao Dong* (Labour).

Broadcasting

Radio: The national radio service, Voice of Vietnam (VOV) (www.vov.org.un) has two networks with six channels broadcasting a wide variety of show including news, current affairs culture and music and an external service with programmes in many languages including English, French and Russian. There are other radio stations, some commercial, operating regionally including Hanoi Radio (www.htv.org.vn), The Voice of Ho Chi Minh (www.voh.com.vn) and Lamp Dong Radio (www.lamdong.gov.vn).

Television: The national broadcaster is Vietnam Television (VTV) (www.vtv.org.vn) with nine channels and is available via satellite. VTV also operates the country's largest cable network VCTV (www.vctv.com.vn) and a direct-to-home (DTH) satellite service which supplies the nine free-to-air channels, nine subscription channels and around 40 international channels. Ho Chi Minh city also has a TV station (HTV) (www.htv.com.vn) with domestic and foreign programmes.

Advertising

As television is the dominant medium it carries the majority of advertising which is regulated by legislation. Advertising content is heavily regulated, while tobacco, liquor and beer are banned and foreign products may require a licence from a relevant ministry to advertise.

News agencies

National news agency: VNA (Vietnam News Agency)

Economy

The economy has moved away from being centrally planned to a greater free-market system, which has expanded and recorded consistently strong growth since the 1990s. The industrial and services sectors contribute GDP of around 39 per cent each. Agriculture remains important and constitutes around 20 per cent of GDP. Industrial production is centred on mineral extraction, including petroleum. In 2009 proven oil reserves were 4.5 billion barrels, with production of 345,000 barrels per day (bpd); natural gas reserves were 680 million cubic metres but commercial production was, in 2010, unexploited. Other minerals include coal, antimony, chromium, gold, zinc, tin and iron. Numerous gem stone deposits include rubies and sapphires. Domestically mined bauxite is used in locally produced aluminium for export. Agriculture is diverse with high productivity, so that Vietnam is a net exporter of food and one of the world largest exporters of rice. In 2010 a bumper harvest ranked Vietnam as the foremost producer of rice in south-east Asia with an estimated 39.9 million tonnes. Other cash crops include coffee, spices, tobacco and rubber. Much of the logged forests are being reforested (five million hectares) to provide timber for future exports. Vietnam also has a large fishing fleet that fishes not only in the seas of south-east Asia but also in the fresh waters of the huge network of tributaries and lakes along the Mekong River. Many varieties of fish and crustaceans are important export products and well as the pearls found in harvested oysters. Manufacturing comprises around 20 per cent of the industrial share of GDP, of which food processing, tobacco and chemicals are major industries. Textiles and clothing manufacturing are also important in the economy, but have been adversely affected by the slowdown in global trade.

GDP growth was 6.3 per cent in 2008, a fall of over 2 percentage points from the high of 8.5 per cent in 2007, and falling to a relative low of 5.3 per cent in 2009. Inflation in 2008 peaked at 23.1 per cent before falling sharply to 6.7 per cent in 2009, which better reflects not only the decrease in global trade that cut exports and the high price of food imports, but also the ambitious stimulus package implemented by the government. Exports in 2010 grew at 25.5 per cent as a whole and in the non-oil sector they grew at 31.5 per cent.

In 2010, the government changed the mechanism from a centrally controlled and subsidised set price to a free market pricing for key commodities such as electricity, natural gas and petroleum.

Remittances in 2009 were US$6.63 billion (7 per cent of GDP), which had fallen from a record high of US$7.20 billion in 2008, but they bounced back to achieve another record of an estimated US$7.21 billion in 2010. Vietnam has benefited from sustained high levels of foreign direct investment (FDI); in 2008 registered FDI was US$71.7 billion and total disbursement was US$11.5 billion; as the global economic crisis hit investment, registered FDI fell by around 70 per cent to US$21.4 billion in 2009, with total disbursement of US$10 billion, 13 per cent lower than in 2008.

Despite the strong growth and healthy economy, the informal economy is still estimated to be 10 per cent of official GDP, but as an entrepreneurial reaction to unemployment rather than tax evasion.

In 2007, the currency was devalued by 9.3 per cent against the US dollar, which was the single largest correction in its exchange rate following the onset of macroeconomic reforms. After several more devaluations it was devalued by 8.5 per cent in February 2011, leading to an inflation rate of 13.9 per cent year-on-year in March.

The initial reform policies, in 1986, collectively known as *Doi Moi* (renovation), restructured the economy from a centrally planned to a multi-sectored economy based on market principles. Although conservative members of the Communist Party wanted to maintain much of the state-controlled economy and limit full privatisation on the Western model, these modernisations have grown the economy and the pressures to continue may already be too great to turn back now.

External trade

Vietnam belongs to the Association of Southeast Asian Nations (Asean) Free Trade Area (Afta) and maintains a list of goods that have preferential import duties between members. There is a programme of tariff reductions being introduced. It is a member of the World Trade Organisation and has an FTA with the US.

In 2010 rice exports totalled 6.5 million tonnes. As regional rice growing had fallen in 2010, export prices were particularly high. The World Bank estimated that the trade balance had fallen to US$7.1 billion in 2010, down from of US$12.8 billion in 2008.

Other exports include coffee, tea and rubber, as well as manufactured goods such as textiles, clothes and footwear. The growing hydrocarbon sector is providing increasing foreign exchange.

Imports

Principal imports include capital machinery and equipment, vehicles, fertiliser, steel products, raw cotton, grain, cement and raw materials.

Main sources: China (typically 24 per cent of total), Japan (11 per cent), South Korea (10 per cent).

Exports

Principal exports include crude oil, rice, seafood, coffee, rubber, tea, garments and shoes.

Main destinations: US (typically 21 per cent of total), Japan (12 per cent), China (9 per cent).

Agriculture

Farming

Agriculture accounts for around 22 per cent of GDP and employs 67 per cent of the workforce. Agricultural goods, including forestry and fishery products, account for more than 50 per cent of total export revenues.

About 15–18 per cent of the total land area is cultivated arable. In the south especially, climate and soils are ideal for rice production. Considerable losses can be sustained from typhoons, flooding and drought.

In the south, 60 per cent of the land is privately farmed; in the north, 95 per cent of farms have been turned into substantial collectives. A contract system on the land spurred a marked improvement in agricultural production.

Ambitious plans include increased use of fertilisers, development of irrigation systems and resettlement of small farmers.

Farmers have boosted rice production by planting high-yield varieties and using more modern farming techniques; government credit of about US$100 million was used mainly in the Mekong Delta.

Half of Vietnam's rice is grown along the Mekong Delta.

Other main food crops include sugar cane, coconut, soya beans, silk, rubber, coffee, tea, tobacco, jute. Livestock raised includes pigs, buffaloes, cattle, sheep, goats, horses and poultry.

The Vietnam National Rubber Corporation development plans for the rubber industry will increase the area under cultivation from 250,000 hectares (ha) to 700,000ha. VNRC estimates 1.7 million ha of total natural land is available for rubber cultivation. The private sector is expected to take a 30–50 per cent share in the development of the industry.

The Vietnam National Coffee Corporation (Vinacaphe) has increased the total area of coffee cultivation to around 200,000ha, principally in the central highlands. Much cultivation in the coffee-growing highlands is under—reported due to a special tax regime. Annual production is thought to be as high as 40,000 tonnes and the government plans to increase production to 100,000 tonnes per year (tpy) by 2010.

Avian flu broke out twice in 2004 and prompted the slaughter of millions of birds.

Fishing

Fishing has traditionally been an important source of export earnings. The sector is facing severe depletion of inshore stocks. Coastal waters were typically overfished by the poorly equipped Vietnamese fleet, whose boats could only stay at sea for short periods of time. Poor infrastructure and processing technology is compounded by a lack of skills required for deep-water fishing on the part of fishermen.

Main fish products are shrimp, freshwater fish, catfish, dried squid and tuna.

Forestry

About 50 per cent of the total land area is forested. Forestry is developing, with 12–15 per cent of the removed volume of timber classified as industrial wood.

Legal exploitation from around one million hectares (ha) of plantations produces a domestic supply of approximately three million cubic metres of wood annually, but insufficient for the processing industry. The industry is estimated to have the potential to approach a turnover of US$1 billion annually, especially following the relaxation of import licences and quotas for domestic processors importing wood. The domestic industry is likely to remain dependent on felled and imported wood of dubious legal status at least over the medium-term. In the longer term, a government replanting programme designed to add five million ha of forest cover by 2010 should change this.

Industry and manufacturing

The heavy industrial base is mostly located in the north, and in the past was adversely affected by conflicts with China. The economy's leading industries were incorporated into the state sector following the Communist takeover and despite limited 'equitisation' (distribution of shares to the public and employees), most remain in state hands. They include oil and gas, food and foodstuff processing, synthetic yarns and fabrics, textiles, engineering, cement, fertilisers, glass, rubber products, tobacco, chemicals, paper and steel. Of some 6,000 state-owned enterprises, only 400 have been equitised, while 2,000 have been organised into 17 'general corporations' (akin to conglomerates) and 77 'special corporations', tending to reinforce monopoly conditions.

Since the *doi moi* reforms of the 1980s, the government has been prioritising lighter, export-oriented and labour-intensive industries. Most of the government's special industrial zones have not yet been fully occupied, and much industry outside the 'legacy' sectors of command-economy industrialisation has been affected by ambivalent sentiment among foreign direct investors.

Tourism

Vietnam is developing as a tourist destination. More facilities are becoming available, although quality and infrastructure, such as roads and power, are inadequate, especially compared to competitors in the region. Visitor numbers have improved year-on-year. The main markets are China, the US, Taiwan, Japan, Hong Kong, Thailand, France, UK and Canada.

Mining

Vietnam is believed to possess a wide range of minerals. The sector is relatively undeveloped, owing to lack of investment and a discouraging legislative environment.

Mining is largely concentrated in the north. Commercially significant quantities of iron ore, apatite, chromite, rubies and gold exist. There are reserves of manganese, titanium ore, bauxite, tin, copper, zinc, lead, nickel, graphite and mica.

Other minerals include phosphates, salt, tin, chromium, wolfram, silver, antimony, pirit, kaolin and limestone.

Vietnam imports a number of metals, including steel.

Hydrocarbons

Proven oil reserves were 4.4 billion barrels in 2010 and production was 370,000 barrels per day (bpd). Vietnam is the third

largest oil producer in south-east Asia (after Indonesia and Malaysia).
The largest oil fields are Back Ho, Rang Dong, Hang Ngoc and Dai Hung. The country's first refinery, a 148,000 barrels per day (bpd) plant, was opened in March 2009 and will provide over 30 per cent of Vietnam's fuel demand. The state-owned PetroVietnam Exploration Production Corporation (PVEP) had to take over the US$3 billion project when foreign companies pulled out claiming its economic efficiency was being compromised by political interests. The refinery is sited in Dung Quat Bay in the central province of Quang Ngai, where unemployment is high but is hundreds of kilometres from either industrial hubs or offshore oil fields. PVEP has began offshore surveys of the country's central costal region. The Russian energy company Lukoil purchased a 50 per cent interest in Vietnam's Hanoi Trough-02 offshore block, which has already identified several prospects. Three exploratory wells are planned for 2011.
Upstream activities in the oil sector are largely controlled by PetroVietnam as the only firm licensed to conduct petroleum activities; foreign investors must conduct their activities in co-operation with it.
Vietnam, along with China, Taiwan, Brunei, Malaysia and The Philippines, claims the potentially oil-rich Spratly Islands.
Proven natural gas reserves were 600 billion cubic metres (cum) in 2010 with production of 9.4 billion cum. In 2009 PVEP announced it had located its largest gas field off the northern coast, in the Hac Long field, with a flow rate of 400,000 cum per day.
Vietnam had coal reserves of 150 million tonnes in 2010, all of which is the valuable anthracite, located in Quang Ninh province. Coal is the principal source of commercial energy, meeting about half of Vietnam's annual primary energy needs. Production totalled 24.7 million tonnes oil equivalent in 2010. Vietnam exports around five million tonnes of coal, mainly to China and Japan.

Energy

Total installed electricity generating capacity was 12.4GW in 2007. The single largest contributor in the energy mix was hydropower with 48 per cent; conventional thermal power stations provided over 50 per cent, of which coal provided most. Natural gas-fired power plants are beginning to be introduced. Although domestic demand is increasing Vietnam still has one of the lowest per capita energy consumption in south-east Asia.
The Asian Development Bank (ADB) has been involved in promoting the Greater Mekong Sub-region (GMS) electricity market to form a regional electricity grid, which incorporates the uneven load demands and different resource bases. By 2008 a regional energy trading and sustainable development scheme was in place and bilateral arrangements included electricity from Laos being exported to Vietnam, which in turn exports electricity to China. Future expansion plans of the GMS network include two other power lines, from Cambodia and Laos. Vietnam has huge potential for hydropower and with growing regional demand for energy should allow expansion of this resource at the same time as natural gas power stations become operational.

Financial markets

The State Capital Investment Corporation (SCIC) and the US-based Morgan Stanley Investment Bank agreed in 2007, to form a securities joint venture; the first in Vietnam's Communist-ruled economy.

Stock exchange

Hochiminh Stock Exchange (HSE)

Banking and insurance

VietcomBank regulates matters relating to exchange control and is responsible for all transactions involving foreign exchange, including bills of exchange, foreign remittances, traveller's cheques and foreign currencies.
In 2005 the government decided that VietcomBank was to be the first state bank to be offered for partial privatisation and ostensibly to operate on purely commercial principles. In preparation for public ownership VietcomBank reduced its portfolio of state enterprised down to 50 per cent and reported a first-half year gross profit of US$82 million in 2005, up by 41 per cent on the previous year. The decision to part-privatise was based on the government's need to sustain economic growth.
There are four large state banks, which account for around 70 per cent of total lending, of which 60 per cent of loans are awarded to state entities and some are of dubious financial viability. Official figures for bad debt levels do not exist but officials in the state bank estimate it could be as high as 20 per cent.

Central bank

State Bank of Vietnam

Main financial centre

Hanoi

Time

GMT plus seven hours

Geography

Vietnam is bordered to the north by the People's Republic of China, to the west and south-west by Laos and Cambodia and to the east by the South China Sea. The country has 3,200km of coastline, 1,150km of land border with China and 1,650km of land border with Laos.
The country is broad in the north and south and narrow in its central region. There are two main cultivated areas, the Red River Delta (15,000 square km) in the north and the Mekong Delta (60,000 square km) in the south. Three-quarters of the country consists of mountains and hills, the highest point being Phan Si Pan mountain in the Hoang Lien Son range in the far north-west of Vietnam.

Hemisphere

Northern

Climate

Located in the tropical monsoon zone, Vietnam's climate is hot and humid with abundant seasonal rainfall.
In the north, climatic changes occur in four seasons: spring (January–April) brings light rain and constant humidity; summer (May to July) is very hot, humid and rainy; autumn (August–October) brings drier weather but sometimes includes storms; winter (October–early January) is cooler. In the centre and the south it is hot year round and there are only two seasons: a rainy season (May–October) and a dry season (October–April).
Average annual temperatures in Hanoi are 29 degrees Celsius (C) in the hot season and 17 degrees C in the cold season; Hue in central Vietnam: 29 degrees C and 21 degrees C; Ho Chi Minh City: 30 degrees C and 24 degrees C.
The average annual rainfall in Hanoi is 1,680mm; Hue: 2,890mm; Ho Chi Minh City: 1979mm.

Dress codes

In Hanoi in the summer (officially from 15 April to 15 October), no jackets are required even for the most formal occasions. In winter, a jacket is more usual but a bush jacket is acceptable even when the weather is warm.
In the south, informal tropical-weight clothing is all that is needed at any time of the year. A jacket and tie is not necessary. In the highlands, where it is cooler, a bush jacket is acceptable any time.

Entry requirements

Passports

Required by all and must be valid for one month beyond the date of departure.

Visa

Required by all. Tourist visas are issued for visits up to one month long and can be extend when in Vietnam.
Business visas are issued only after authorities in Vietnam have approved sponsorship by a local company or organisation. If the business visitor does not have a local sponsor, assistance can be obtained from the embassy.

For a list of embassies worldwide where applications may be obtained see www.mofa.gov.vn/en, see *Countries and Regions*.
All visitors must retain the yellow portion of the immigration arrival-departure card, to be surrendered to authorities when leaving.

Currency advice/regulations
The import and export of local currency is prohibited. The import of foreign currency is unlimited, but amounts over US$3,000 (or equivalent) should be declared on arrival; export is limited to the amount declared.
Major hard currency may be freely traded however outside cities and main towns they are less likely to be accepted.
Travellers cheques (in US dollars) are widely accepted in banks and hotels.

Customs
Personal items are duty-free.
Antiques cannot be exported. Caution is advised when purchasing souvenirs made of ivory, silver, gold and stone, as you may require a permit from customs to take them out of Vietnam.

Prohibited imports
Firearms, anti-government propaganda, pornography and illegal drugs; drug smuggling is a capital offence.

Health (for visitors)

Mandatory precautions
Vaccination certificate required for yellow fever if travelling from an infected area.

Advisable precautions
Vaccinations for diphtheria, tetanus, hepatitis A, cholera and typhoid are recommended. Other vaccinations that may be advised include tuberculosis, hepatitis B, and Japanese encephalitis. Malaria prophylaxes are required including mosquito nets, insect sprays and long clothing at night.
Use only bottled or boiled water for drinks, washing teeth and making ice. Eat only well cooked meals, preferably served hot; vegetables should be cooked and fruit peeled. Avoid pork and salad and food from street vendors. A full first-aid kit, including disposable syringes, would be useful. Any medicines required by the traveller should be brought into the country. Medical insurance is essential, including emergency evacuation.

Hotels

Redevelopment and expansion has increased hotel accommodation in both Ho Chi Minh City and Hanoi where the standard of hotel accommodation is equal to Western hotels. Provincial town also have adequate facilities.
Tipping is discretionary; it is not a Vietnamese tradition although staff in restaurants and hotels may expect to be tipped.

Credit cards

Are accepted in more outlets but only in main towns and cities; where ATMs can be found.

Public holidays (national)

Fixed dates
1 Jan (New Year's Day), 30 Apr (Liberation of Ho Chi Minh City/Saigon), 1 May (May Day), 2 Sep (National Day).

Variable dates
Tet Nguyen Dan (Vietnamese New Year) (Jan/Feb – three days)

Working hours

Banking
Mon–Fri: 0730/0800–1130, 1300–1600.

Business
Mon–Sat: 0730–1130, 1230–1630 in summer (15 Apr to 15 Oct); 0800–1200, 1230–1630 in winter (16 Oct to 14 Apr).

Government
Mon–Sat: 0730–1130, 1230–1630 in summer; 0800–1200, 1230–1630 in winter.

Shops
Many small privately owned shops stay open seven days a week, often until late at night.

Telecommunications

Mobile/cell phones
There are 900 and 900/1800 GSM services available throughout most of the country.

Electricity supply

Electric current is 220V, 50Hz with round two-pin plug. Electricity supplies can be problematic, laptop computers should be protected by a surge suppressor.

Social customs/useful tips

Business is conducted slowly with many familiarisation meetings. Be patient with language difficulties and red tape. The combination of Confucian interaction norms and communist bureaucracy may create large amounts of the latter.
Most Vietnamese names consist of a family name, a middle name and a given name, in that order. The given name is used in address but to do so without a title is considered as expressing either great intimacy between friends or arrogance of the sort a superior would use with his or her inferior. The titles, *Bac* or *Ong* (Mr) (in increasing seniority), *Ba* (Mrs), *Co* or *Chi* (Miss) precedes a Vietnamese given name (sometimes full name). Wives may retain their own names and children take their father's family name. The middle name may be common to all the male members of a family.
It is rude to show the soles of the feet/shoes. Do not touch anyone's head, not even that of a child. When handing over or receiving anything, the right hand should generally be used. On formal occasions it is considered polite to use both hands. Etiquette for male visitors is to shake hands with a man but not with a woman, unless she offers her hand.
Shoes must be removed before entering any religious building. It is also customary to remove shoes before entering a Vietnamese home, but in modern residences the requirement is no longer observed.

Security

Most visits to Vietnam are trouble-free and serious or violent crimes against foreigners are rare. There have been some reports of aggravated theft and assault in areas frequented by tourists in Ho Chi Minh City, prompting the city police chief, Nguyen Chi Dung, to say that tourists who were robbed would receive an apology from the police.
Outside Hanoi and Ho Chi Minh City, the provision of prompt consular assistance is difficult because of poorly developed infrastructure throughout Vietnam, meaning travel and health insurance are well advised. Travel is restricted near military installations and in some border areas.
Unexploded mines, bombs and shells are a hazard in former battlefield areas.

Getting there

Air
National airline: Vietnam Airlines (formerly Hang Khong Vietnam and the General Civil Aviation Administration of Vietnam).
International airport/s: Tan Son Nhat (SGN), 7km from Ho Chi Minh City, facilities include a café, duty-free shopping, VIP services, business lounge, currency exchange, limousine service and car rental with driver.
A new terminal, to handle up to 15 million passengers a year and at cost of US$240 million, was begun in 2004. The first phase of construction is expected to be completed by 2007.
Noi Bai (HAN), 38km from Hanoi, facilities include a café, duty-free shopping and currency exchange.
Danang International Airport, five-minutes drive to Danang City.
Metered taxis are available at all airports.
Airport tax: International departures US$14, excluding transit passengers.

Surface
Road: There is overland access to Vietnam via China (Quang Ninh and Lang Son border crossings in the north), Cambodia (Moc Bai) and Laos (Lao Bao).
Status of overland routes should be checked, as passage has not always been practicable.
Rail: Hanoi and Nanning, in China's Guangxi province, are linked by rail. China and Vietnam have also started a second cross-border rail service. The

761km rail link between Hanoi and Kunming, the capital of Yunnan (south-west China), and which runs through the northern Vietnamese border town of Lao Cai, is being upgraded with work expected to be completed by 2008. There is rail connection linking Hanoi with Pingxiang in China's Guangxi province via the Dong Dang border point in Lang Son province, 200km north of Hanoi. Construction of a new line linking Phnom Penh and Ho Chi Minh City is underway. This project is part of the Asian Development Bank's (ADB) Greater Mekong sub-regional co-operation scheme as part of the Trans-Asia railway.
Services include air-conditioned day and overnight sleeping carriages and restaurant cars.
Water: There are daily and weekly ferry services along the Mekong River from Phnom Penh (Cambodia) to Chau Doc and Can Tho.
Main port/s: Ho Chi Minh City, Haiphong, and Danang.

Getting about

National transport

Air: Vietnam Airlines, provides regular scheduled services between Hanoi, Hue, Danang and Ho Chi Minh City. Flights should be booked well in advance.
Road: There is a 88,000km road network in relatively good condition; roads are better in the south. The coastal Route 1 between Hanoi and Ho Chi Minh City can become impassable in heavy rain. A four-wheel drive vehicle is advisable outside the major centres.
Rail: There is over 2,650km rail network in various degrees of maintenance. The main line between Hanoi-Ho Chi Minh City (travel time 30 hrs minimum) is efficient with first class accommodation with air-conditioning, sleeper carriages and restaurant cars. Long-distance trains are more reliable and comfortable, as well as offering a faster service. Fares for foreigners are comparable to internal air fares.
Water: There are several local ferry services including hydrofoils between Mong Cai and Cat Ba and motorboats between Phu Quoc and Rach Gia.

City transport

Taxis: Taxis serving the hour-long route between downtown Hanoi and the city's airport will typically be ancient and non-air-conditioned vehicles. In Ho Chi Minh City, taxis are modern. Tipping is discretionary; taxi drivers do not expect to be tipped. Taxis and motorbikes are a faster form of hired transport. When travelling by taxi it may be advisable to note down the registration number of the driver (displayed on the rear side of the vehicle), for security reasons.
In Hanoi, cycle-rickshaws (the famous *cyclo*) are available, but slow and best for sightseeing.

Car hire

Personal car hire is not allowed, all hire vehicles come with a driver; hiring can be from half a day to over a week. A four-wheel-drive vehicle is required outside major cities.

BUSINESS DIRECTORY

The addresses listed below are a selection only. While World of Information makes every endeavour to check these addresses, we cannot guarantee that changes have not been made, especially to telephone numbers and area codes. We would welcome any corrections.

Telephone area codes

The international direct dialling code (IDD) for Vietnam is +84, followed by area code and subscriber's number:

Da Nang	51	Ho Chi Minh City	8
Haiphong	31	Lang Son	25
Hanoi	4	Lao Cai	20

Useful telephone numbers

English-language directory enquiries: 108
Police: 113
Fire: 114
Ambulance: 115

Chambers of Commerce

American Chamber of Commerce in Vietnam - Hanoi, Press Club, 59A Ly Thai To Street, Hanoi (tel: 934-2790; fax 934-2787; e-mail: info@amchamhanoi.com).

American Chamber of Commerce in Vietnam - Ho Chi Minh City, New World Hotel, 76 Le Lai Street, Ho Chi Minh City (tel: 824-3562; fax: 824-3572; e-mail: amcham@hcm.vnn.vn).

British Business Group Vietnam - Hanoi, Metropole Hotel, 56 Ly Thai To Street, Hanoi (tel: 936-2420; fax: 936-2419; e-mail: eurochamhanoi@hn.vnn.vn).

British Business Group Vietnam - Ho Chi Minh City, 25 Le Duan Boulevard, Ho Chi Minh City (tel: 829-8430; fax: 822-5172; e-mail: bbgv.hcmc@hcm.fpt.vn).

Vietnam Chamber of Commerce and Industry, 9 Dao Duy Anh Street, Hanoi (tel: 574-3084; fax: 574-2020; e-mail: vcci@hn.vnn.vn).

Banking

ANZ International Merchant Banking Division, 14 Le Thai To Street, Hanoi (tel: 825-8190; fax: 825-8188/9).

Bank of America, 27 Ly Thuong Kiet St, Hanoi (tel: 824-9316; fax: 824-9322).

Crédit Lyonnais, Han Man Officetel, 65 Nguyen du St., Quan 1, Ho Chi Minh City (tel: 299-226; fax: 296-465).

Indovina Bank Ltd (first joint-venture bank), 36 Ton That Dam, D1, Ho Chi Minh City (tel: 822-4995, 823-0130; fax: 823-0131).

Thai Military Bank, Unit 113, 1 Floor, Saigon Trade Center, No. 37 Ton Due Thang Street, Ben Nghe Ward, District 1, Ho Chi Minh City (tel: 910-0606, 910-1388/90; fax: 910-0505).

Industrial and Commercial Bank of Vietnam, 108 Tran Hung Dao, Hanoi (tel: 942-1066, 942-1186; fax: 942-1143).

Central bank

State Bank of Vietnam, 49 Ly Thai To Street, Hoan Kiem District, Hanoi (tel: 825-8388; fax: 825-8385; internet: www.sbv.gov.vn).

Stock exchange

Hochiminh Stock Exchange (HSE): http://hose.vse.vn

Stock exchange 2

Hanoi Securities Trading Centre (HSTC): http://en.hastc.org.vn

Travel information

Ben Thanh Tourist Service, 165 Pham Ngui Lao Street, 1st District, Ho Chi Minh City (tel: 886-0635; fax: 836-1953).

Cathay Pacific Airways, 58 Dong Khoi Road, District 1, Ho Chi Minh City (tel: 822-3203; fax: 822-2679); also at 27 Ly Thuong Kiet Street, Hanoi (tel: 824-9427; fax: 822-2679).

Quang Nam-Da Nang Tourist Company (Da Nang Tourism), 68 Bach Dang Street, Da Nang (tel: 822-112, 821-423, 822-213).

Thua Thien-Hue Tourist Company, No. 9 Ngo Quyen Street, Hue City (tel: 83-288, 82-369).

Sasco Travel (for limousine service), Sasco Building, Tan Son Nhat Airport, Ho Chi Minh City (tel: 848-7142; fax: 848-7141; internet: www.sascotravel.com.vn).

Viet Value Travel Ltd (for car hire), 4th Floor ILU Building, 18 Yen Phu, Ba Dinh, Hanoi (tel: 715-0753; fax: 715-0754; email: vietvaluetravel@yahoo.com; internet: http://vietvaluetravel.com).

Vietnamtourism, 30A Ly Thuong Kiet Street, Hanoi (tel: 825-5552, 826-4148; fax: 855-7583).

Vietnam Airlines (formerly Hang Khong Vietnam and the General Civil Aviation Administration of Vietnam), Gailem Airport, Hanoi (tel: 827-2643; fax: 827-2291).

National tourist organisation offices

Vinatour, 54 Nguyen Du, Hanoi (tel: 942-4490; 942-3997; fax: 942-2707; internet: www.vinatour.com.vn).

Vinatour, 28 Le Thi Hong Gam, District 1, Ho Chi Minh City, (tel: 217- 925,

297-026; fax: 299-868; email: vinatour-saigonoffice@saigonnet.vn).

Ministries

Ministry of Agriculture and Rural Development, 6 Ngoc Ha Street, Hanoi; International Relations Department (tel: 845-9670/71/72; fax: 845-4319).

Ministry of Construction, 37 Le Dai Hanh Street, Hanoi; International Relations Department (tel: 825-5497; fax: 825-2153).

Ministry of Culture and Information, 51-53 Ngo Quyen, Hanoi.

Ministry of Education & Training, 49 Dai Co Viet Street, Hanoi; International Relations Department (tel: 869-4961; fax: 826-3243).

Ministry of Energy, 18 Tran Nguyen Han, Hanoi.

Ministry of Finance, 8 Phgan Huy Chu Street, Hanoi; International Relations Section (tel: 826-2061, 824-0437; fax: 826-2266).

Ministry of Fisheries, 57 Ngoc Khanh, Hanoi.

Ministry of Foreign Affairs, 1 Ton That Dam Street, Hanoi; International Organisation Department (tel: 845-6525, 845-5900; fax: 845-9205).

Ministry of Forestry, 123 Lo Duc, Hanoi.

Ministry of Health, 138 Duong Giang Vo, Hanoi.

Ministry of Industry, 7 Trang Thi Street, Hanoi (fax: 826-9033); International Relations Department (tel: 826-7988, 825-9887).

Ministry of Justice, 25a Cat Linh Street, Hanoi; Internatinol Relations Department (tel: 843-0931; fax: 825-4835).

Ministry of Labour, War Invalids and Social Affairs, 2 Dinh Le Street, Hanoi; International Relations Department (tel: 826-9534; fax: 824-8036).

Ministry of Marine Products, 57 Ngoc Khanh Street, Hanoi; International Relations Department (tel: 832-5607; fax: 832-6702).

Ministry of National Defence, 28A Dien Bien Phy Street, Hanoi (tel: 826-8101; fax: 845-7195); International Relations Department, 33 A Pham Ngu Lao Street, Hanoi (tel: 825-3646).

Ministry of Planning and Investment (background information on aid-financed projects), 2 Hoanag Van Thu, Hanoi; External Economic Relations Department (tel: 845-8241 (ext 3505); fax: 823-0161).

Ministry of Public Health, 138 A Giango Vo, Hanoi; International Relations Department (tel: 844-2463, 846-4050; fax: 846-4051).

Ministry of Sciences, Technology and Environment, 39 Tran Hung Dao Street, Hanoi; International Relations Department (tel: 826-3388; fax: 825-2733).

Ministry of Trade, 31 Trang Tien Street, Hanoi; (tel: 826-2522; fax: 826-4696).

Ministry of Transport, 80 Tran Hung Dao Street, Hanoi; International Relations Department (tel: 825-3301; fax: 825-5851).

Office of the National Assembly, 35 Ngo Quyen, Hanoi (tel: 252-861).

Other useful addresses

ASEAN Investment Promotion Agency, Ministry of Planning and Investment, c/o ASEAN Vietnam, 7 Chu Van An Street, Hanoi (fax: 843-5758).

ASEAN Secretariat, 70 A Jl Sisingamangaraja, Jakarta 12110, Indonesia (tel: (+62-21) 726-2991, 724-3372; fax: (+62-21) 724-3504, 739-8234).

Asian Development Bank, Vietnam Resident Mission, c/o State Bank of Vietnam, Room 401, 16 Tong Dan Street, Hanoi (tel: 824-5908; fax: 824-6171).

British Consulate General, 25 Le Duan, District 1, Ho Chi Minh City (tel: 829-2433; fax: 822-5740).

British Embassy, 31 Hai Ba Trung, Hanoi (tel: 825-2510; fax: 826-5762).

British Embassy Commercial Office, 100 Tue Tinh Street, Hanoi (tel: 822-6875, 822-9455, 822-9457; fax: 822-9457).

Commerical and Tourist Services Centre, 1 Ba Trieu Street, Hanoi (tel: 826-8499; fax: 826-5388).

Department General for Post and Telecomunication, 18 Nguyen Du Street, Hanoi; International Relations Department (tel: 822-6622; fax: 822-6590).

Electricity of Vietnam (EVN), 18 Tran Nguyen Han Street, Hanoi (tel: 826-3725; fax: 824-9462).

Foreign Trade & Investment Development Centre, 92-96 Nguyen Hue Ave, District 1, Ho Chi Minh City (tel: 822-2982; fax: 822-2983).

Investip (will provide business contacts), 1 bis Yet Kieu Street, Hanoi (tel: 826-4707; fax: 826-6185).

The National Oil Service Company of Vietnam, 2 Le Loi Street, Vung Tau Srv, Ho Chi Minh City (tel: 897-562; fax: 897-664).

Petrovietnam, 22 Ngo Quyen Street, Hanoi; International Relations Department (tel: 825-2526; fax: 826-5942).

Saigon Shipping Company (Saigonship), 9 Nguyen Cong Tru Street, District 1, Ho Chi Minh City (tel: 896-316, 896-302; fax: 825-067).

State Committee for Co-operation and Investment Consultancy Service Centre (will provide business contacts), 56 Quoc Tu Giam Street, Hanoi (tel: 825-4970; fax: 825-9271).

Tea Estate Agencies Ltd, 31 Nguyen Gia Thieu Street, Hanoi (tel: 822-8556; fax: 822-7923).

US Embassy, 7 Lang Ha, Dong Da District, Hanoi (tel: 843-1500).

Vietnam Civil Aviation, Gia Lam Airport, Hanoi; International Relations Department (tel: 827-2241).

Vietnam Fund Management Co Ltd (investment into Vietnamese companies and projects), 3 Trieu Viet Vuong Street, Hanoi (tel: 822-8632, 826-6315; fax: 822-8648); 4 Dong Khoi, District 1, Ho Chi Minh City (tel: 829-1074, 829-7206; fax: 823-0685).

Vietnam National Foreign Trade Corporation (TRANSAF), 46 Ngo Quyen, Hanoi.

Vietnamese Embassy (US), Suite 400, 1233 20th Street, NW, Washington DC 20036 (tel: (+1-202) 861-0737; fax: (+1-202) 202-861-0917; email: info@vietnamembassy-usa.org).

National news agency: VNA (Vietnam News Agency), 5 Ly Thuong Kiet Street, Hoan Kiem District, Hanoi (tel: 933-2418; fax: 933-0970; internet: www.vnagency.com.vn).

Internet sites

Asian Development Bank: www.adb.org/vrm

General Statistics Office (GSO): www.gso.gov.vn

Vietnam Access (trade fairs and business opportunities): http://vietnamaccess.com

Vietnam Business Journal: www.viam.com

VietnamNet.vn (news website)

Wallis and Futuna

KEY FACTS

Official name: Wallis and Futuna

Head of State: President of France Nicolas Sarkozy, represented by *Administrateur Supérieur* Philippe Paolantoni (from 8 Sep 2008)

Head of government: President of the Territorial Assembly Pesamino Taputai (DD) (from 11 Apr 2007)

Ruling party: Coalition of various political parties and independent members, of which non are dominant (since 2007)

Area: 144 square km – Wallis (or Uvea): 77.6km; Futuna: 64.4km

Population: 14,000 (2010)*

Capital: Mata Utu (on Wallis)

Official language: Wallisian, Futunian, French

Currency: Comptoirs Français du Pacifique franc (CFPf) = 100 centimes

Exchange rate: CFPf84.51 per US$ (Jan 2009); (pegged CFPf119.25 per euro)

* estimated figure

COUNTRY PROFILE

Historical profile

Around 1400 AD Polynesian navigators from Tonga landed on Uvea and Samoans on Futuna and Alofi.
Historical profile
1616 The islands of Futuna and Alofi were sighted by two Dutch navigators, Willem Cornelius van Schouten and Jacob le Maire, who re-named them the Hoorn Islands.
1767 Samuel Wallis, the English navigator, sighted the island of Uvea, and renamed it Wallis.
1820 The Takumasiva royal dynasty was restored in the kingdom of Uvea (Wallis).
1837 The first European settlers were French, led by missionaries.
1842 Wallis was granted French protection following a local rebellion.
1887 Queen Amelia of Uvea signed a treaty, establishing an official French protectorate.
1888, The Kings of Alo and Sigave (Futuna and Alofi) signed a treaty establishing an official French protectorate.
1924 The protectorates were annexed and became an official French colony
1942 US forces used Wallis as a strategic air base during the Second World War.
1959 Following a referendum, Wallis and Fortuna voted to become a Térritoire d'Outre-Mer (TOM) (Overseas Territory).
1959 Tomasi Kulimoetoke II became the Lavelua (King of Uvea), ending a period of instability within the royal family.
1961 Wallis and Futuna became a TOM and adopted the French constitution.
1999 Sagato Alofi became the the Tuiagaifo (King of Alo); Pasilio Keletaona became the Keletaona (King of Sigave).
2002 The ruling right-wing Rassemblement pour la République (RPR) (Rally for the Republic) and its affiliates retained a majority in the Territorial Assembly elections. Christian Job was appointed *administrateur supérieur*, replacing Alain Waquet. Wallis and Futuna's only newspaper, the weekly *Te Fenua Fo'ou*, closed down after being subjected to threats and raids from the local (traditional) authorities.
2003 Through a constitutional change, Wallis and Fortuna became a collectivités d'outre-mer (COM) (overseas collectivity). A limited census was undertaken.
2004 Xavier de Furst was appointed *administrateur supérieur*.
2006 Richard Didier was appointed *administrateur supérieur, Préfet*.
2007 Following parliamentary elections Pesamino Teputai became president of the territorial assembly. Tomasi Kulimoetoke II, the King of Uvea, died.
2008 Kapiliele (Gabriel) Faupala was chosen by members of the traditional council of ministers to succeed the late King Tomasi, who had designated him to follow him as king. Philippe Paolantoni was appointed *administrateur supérieur*. A census was undertaken recording a population of 13,484.
2009 The results of the 2008 census were published, which showed a decrease in the population (down by 1,460 since 2003), and an ageing population, with 11 per cent over 60 years (up from 7 per cent in 1996).
2010 In June, Micheal Jeanjean was appointed *administrateur supérieur*.
2011 In July, the Minister for Overseas Territories, Marie-Luce Penchard, joined the islands' ceremony in celebration of the fifty years since Wallis and Futuna became a French territory.

Political structure

Constitution

28 September 1958 (French Fifth Republic)
In 1961, Wallis and Futuna became a Térritoire d'Outre-Mer (TOM) (Overseas Territory) of France.
Wallis and Futuna is administered by an administrator (administrateur supérieur) appointed by France and is represented in the French parliament by a deputy and a senator.
The islands are divided into three administrative districts based on the ancient kingdoms: *Uvea* (Wallis), *Alo* (Futuna) and *Sigave* (Futuna).
Wallis and Futuna is the only French territory where a native system of monarchy has been allowed to survive. There are three traditional kings: the Lavelua (King of Uvea), the Tuiagaifo (King of Alo) and the Keletaona (the title of King of Sigave depends on family heritage, and therefore, he has the title of Tui Sigave, Tamolevai or Keletaona).
In *Uvea*, there is a kivalu, the equivalent of a prime minister, who is appointed by the King.

Form of state
Térritoire d'Outre-Mer (TOM) (Overseas Territory) of France

The executive
The President of the French Republic is the head of state, represented by an appointed *administrateur supérieur, Préfet* (supreme administrator) who exercises executive power with the right of veto over some of the territorial assembly decisions.

National legislature
The Assemblée Territoriale (Territorial Assembly) has 20 members, elected by popular vote for five-year terms, (13 from Wallis and seven from Futuna). The assembly deals with local affairs although the administrator has the right of veto over many of the Assembly's decisions.
As Collectivités d'Outre-mer (COM) (overseas collectivity) Wallis and Fortuna is a first-order administrative division of France and citizens vote in French elections for president and return a representative for Wallis and Fortuna to both the French National Assembly and Senate. It is divided into three districts that exactly match the traditional chiefdoms, Uvea, Sigave and Alo.

Legal system
French law is applied while the traditional kings deal with customary law.

Last elections
1 April 2007 (territorial assembly)
Results: Parliamentary: Union pour un Mouvement Populaire (UMP) (Union for a Popular Movement) won four seats (out of 20); Divers Droite (DD) (Various Right groups) won seven seats; Parti Socialiste (PS) (Socialist Party) four seats; Divers Gauche (DG) (Various Left groups) one seat; and unlisted candidates four seats. Turnout was 74.98 per cent.

Next elections
2012 (territorial assembly)

Political parties

Ruling party
Coalition of various political parties and independent members, of which non are dominant (since 2007)

Main opposition party

Population
14,000 (2010)*
Last census: 21 July 2008: 13,484 (provisional)
Population density: 55 inhabitants per square km.
Annual growth rate: 1 per cent (2003)

Ethnic make-up
Polynesian

Religions
Roman Catholic

Education
Compulsory education is provided free-of-charge. Primary education is either provided by public funds or by Roman Catholic missionaries. Secondary education is pubically provided.
Compulsory years: Five to 14

Health
Healthcare is publically funded. There is a 60-bed hospital on Wallis and a 23-bed hospital on Futuna; severe emergency medical cases are evacuation to New Caledonia or Australia.
Life expectancy: 73 (estimate 2003)
Child (under 5 years) mortality rate (per 1,000): 21 per 1,000 live births.

Welfare
While there is no social security benefits offered to the general community, the state assist in the care of old aged pensioners.

Main cities
Mata Utu, on Wallis (capital, estimated population 1,187 in 2005).

Languages spoken

Official language/s
Wallisian, Futunian, French

Media
The islands maintain international and local contacts for news and information through electronic media.

Press

Broadcasting
Radio: The French RFO (http://wallisfutuna.rfo.fr) service provides overseas radio programmes for broadcasting.

Economy
The economy is based on subsistence agriculture and fishing. Licensing of fishing rights, import taxes, remittances from migrant workers and grants from France are the other sources of income.
Tourism is an important source of foreign exchange.

External trade
As a Térritoire d'Outre-Mer (TOM) of France, Wallis and Futuna is integrated as an outermost region of the European Union and EU trade agreements may apply.

Imports
Principal imports are chemicals, machinery, vehicles and consumer goods.
Main sources: France (typically 97 per cent of total), Australia (2 per cent), New Zealand (1 per cent).

Exports
Exports are copra, chemicals and construction materials.
Main destinations: Italy (typically 40 per cent of total), Croatia (15 per cent), US (14 per cent), Denmark (13 per cent)

Agriculture

Farming
Approximately 80 per cent of the labour force depend on agriculture for their livelihood. The soil of the main islands is volcanic and rainfall is adequate.

Fishing
Tuna is fished for local consumption. Licensing of fishing rights to Japan and South Korea provide an important source of revenue.
The typical annual fish catch, for local consumption, is 300t with 4t other seafood.

Forestry
Timber is logged for local consumption and some pine reafforestation has been undertaken.

Industry and manufacturing
Industrial activity is limited to handicrafts.

Hydrocarbons
There are no known hydrocarbon reserves; all needs are met by imports.

Energy
Total installed generating capacity is around 6KW.

Banking and insurance
The only bank is Banque de Wallis et Futuna (a subsidiary of BNP, the French multinational bank).

Central bank
The Paris-based Institut d'Emission d'Outre-Mer (IEOM) provides all central banking services except foreign exchange reserves.

Time
GMT plus twelve hours

Geography
Wallis and Futuna consists of two islands groups – Wallis Island (also known as Uvea) and 22 islets on the surrounding reef, and, to the south-east, Futuna (or Hooru), comprising the two small islands of Futuna and Alofi. Combined, the area of the islands is 274 square kilometres and are 230km apart. They are north-east of Fiji and west of Samoa.
The islands are volcanic with the tallest peak, Mont Singavi (on Futuna) at 765 metres. The main islands had lush rain forests covering them but have been seriously denuded since wood is the major source of fuel. Deforestation has resulted in soil erosion particularly on Futuna. Alofi has no source of fresh water and does not have any permanent settlements.

Hemisphere
Southern

Climate
Hot and humid, although May–October can be dry and cooler. Rainy season from November to April. Average temperature 27 degrees Celsius.

Entry requirements

Passports
Required by all except certain French nationals.

Visa
Required by all, except citizens of EU, North America, Australasia and Japan, for stays up to one month; this includes business trips by representatives of foreign entities with an invitation from a local company or organisation. Proof of adequate funds for stay, an itinerary, a guarantee of repatriation if necessary and return/onward ticket are also required. For further exceptions, full details and a copy of the application form visit www.diplomatie.gouv.fr and follow the link *Getting to France* to *Getting a Visa*.
Currency advice/regulations
As there are only two banks in the country (none at the airport), it is advisable to enter the country with cash, the most practical being the local currency, Comptoirs Français du Pacifique franc (CFPf). Travellers cheques can be exchanged at the banks, but each transaction is accompanied by a large commission; the banks will give advances on Visa or MasterCard.

Health (for visitors)
Mandatory precautions
Vaccination certificates required for yellow fever if travelling from an infected area.
Advisable precautions
Vaccinations for diphtheria, tuberculosis, hepatitis A and B, polio, tetanus and typhoid are recommended. Rabies risk.

Hotels
There are only four hotels with 26 rooms available, all located in Mata Utu on Wallis. Holiday residences are available.

Public holidays (national)
Fixed dates
1 Jan (New Years Day), 28 Apr (Saint Pierre Chanel), 1 May (Labour Day), 8 May (Victory Day 1945), 14 Jul (National Day), 29 Jul (Territory Day), 1 Nov (All Saints Day), 11 Nov (Armistice Day), 25 Dec (Christmas).
Holidays that fall at the weekend are not taken *in lieu*.
Variable dates
Good Friday (Mar/Apr), Ascension (Apr/May) Assumption (Aug).

Working hours
Banking
Mon–Fri: 0730–1545.
Business
Mon–Fri: 0730–1130, 1330–1730. Sat: 0730–1130.
Government
Mon–Fri: 0730–1130, 1215–1600.
Shops
Mon–Fri: 0730–1100, 1400–1800. Half-day Sat and Sun.

Telecommunications
Telephone/fax
Communications are by satellite, although a limited radio link is maintained.

Electricity supply
220V, 50 Hz with round, either two or three pin-plugs.

Weights and measures
Metric system

Getting there
Air
Scheduled but only weekly flights are via either New Caledonia or Fiji, provided by Aircalin. Book well in advance.
National airline: Wallis and Futuna is planning to set up its own airline.
International airport/s: Wallis Hihifo Airport (WLS), 6km from Mata Utu; *bureau de change*, bars, VIP lounge, duty-free, pharmacy, tourist help desk.
Surface
Water: There are no regular passengership services to the islands.
Main port/s: Mata Utu; Leava

Getting about
National transport
There is no public transport or taxis.
Road: There are surfaced roads in Mata Utu and a road network links the main towns on Wallis.
Buses: Minibus services operate on Wallis.
Car hire
Car hire is available on Wallis.

BUSINESS DIRECTORY
The addresses listed below are a selection only. While World of Information makes every endeavour to check these addresses, we cannot guarantee that changes have not been made, especially to telephone numbers and area codes. We would welcome any corrections.

Telephone area codes
The international direct dialling (IDD) code for Wallis and Futuna is +681 followed by the subscriber's number .

Banking
Banque de Wallis et Futuna, PO Box 59, Mata Utu (tel: 722-124; fax: 722-156; internet: www.bnpparibas.com).
Central bank
Institut d'Emission d'Outre-Mer (IEOM), 5 rue Roland Barthes, 75598 Paris Cedex 12, France (tel : (+33 1) 5344-4141; fax : (+33 1) 4347-5134; e-mail: contact@ieom.fr).

Travel information
Aircalin, 8 Rue Frédéric Surleau, BP 3736, Noumea 98846 New Caledonia (tel: (+687) 265-500; fax: (+687) 265-561).

Aircalin, BP 49, Matu Utu, 98600 Wallis (tel: 720-000; fax: 722-711; internet: www.aircalin.com).

Aircalin, BP 50, 98620 Futuna (tel: 723-204; fax: 723-439).

Wallis Hihifo Airport, BP 1, Mata Utu 98600 (tel: 721-200; fax: 721-203; email: aviation.sna@wallis.co.nc).

Other useful addresses
Service des Postes et Télécommunications, BP 00 98600, Mata Utu (tel: 720-700; fax: 722-500; e-mail: spt.get@wallis.co.nc).

Internet sites
Wallis and Futuna (in French): www.wallis.co.nc

Yemen

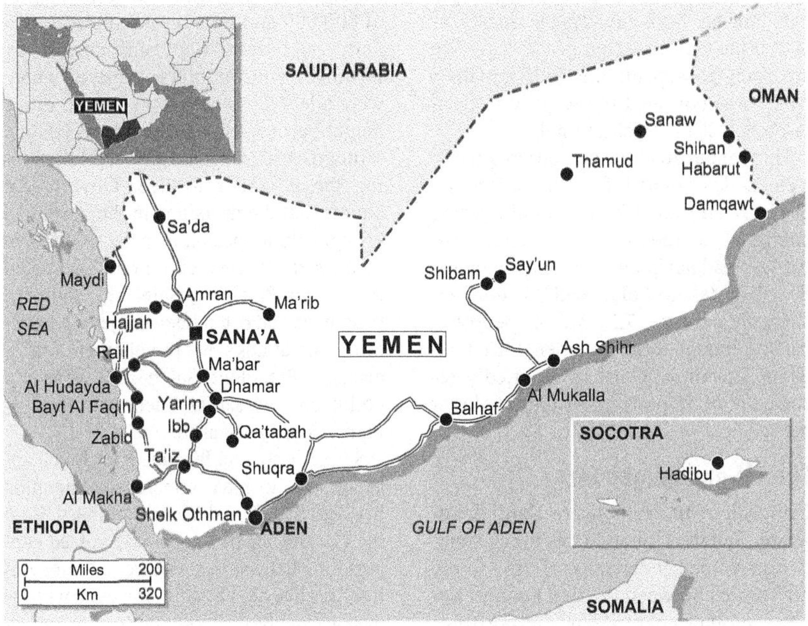

In early December 2011 thousands of citizens from the Yemeni city of Taiz started on a protest march, the 'Life March', from Taiz to the capital Sana'a to demonstrate their opposition to a United Nations (UN) initiative for a so-called 'transition plan'. A UN Security Council resolution in mid-October had condemned human rights abuses allegedly committed by the Yemeni authorities. Had the Peace Plan been acted upon six months earlier, it might possibly have been welcomed by long-suffering Yemenis. But by the end of the year patience was running thin; a tired citizenry had seen the speed with which other Arab leaders, faced with the demands of the Arab Spring had responded – perhaps out of an instinct of self preservation – to the will of their people. They had, legitimately enough, hoped to see similar developments begin with what had become known as the Jasmine Revolution in their own country. By December, what had dawned was not an Arab Spring, more a Yemeni disillusion: not only with their discredited leaders, but with neighbouring countries which, instead of coming to their support, had chosen to turn their backs. Worse, it appeared to some that their President, Ali Abdullah Saleh, in power for a staggering 33 years, had received both tacit support and shelter (since June 2011 after being wounded in an abortive attack on his palace) from a nervous Saudi Arabia. The turning point in the 2011 uprising had been 18 March when a reported 52 protestors were killed by sniper fire.

The Peace Plan

The plan had been drawn up in April 2011 by the Gulf Co-operation Council (GCC) with the support of Saudi Arabia and the United States. Both of these governments had more than a passing interest, not so much with the liberty and wellbeing of Yemen's populations, more with fears that Yemen represented the soft underbelly of an Arabian Peninsula that in 2011 had already felt a few unnerving tremors. As soon as the Peace Plan was put forward, it became more than clear that minimal prior consultation with the figureheads of the Yemeni uprising had taken place. Thus the plan had proposed a reshuffled government comprising the corrupt elites of yesteryear and signally failed to include any

KEY FACTS

Official name: Jamhuriya al Yamaniya (Republic of Yemen)

Head of State: President Ali Abdullah Saleh (GPC) (since 1999; re-elected Sep 2006)

Head of government: Prime Minister Muhammed Salim Basindwa (from 27 Nov 2011)

Ruling party: Al Mutammar al Shabi al Am (GPC) (General People's Congress) (from 1999; re-elected 2003)

Area: 527,968 square km

Population: 23.15 million (2010)*

Capital: Sana'a

Official language: Arabic

Currency: Rial (YR) = 100 fils

Exchange rate: YR218.75 per US$ (Oct 2011)

GDP per capita: US$1,282 (2010)

GDP real growth: 8.00% (2010)

GDP: US$31.30 billion (2010)

Labour force: 6.64 million (2009)

Unemployment: 35.00% (2009)

Inflation: 12.10% (2010)

Oil production: 264,000 bpd (2010)

Balance of trade: -US$2.01 billion (2009)

* estimated figure

Nota

Ali Abdullah Saleh departed for the US on 22 January 2012, the day after members of parliament had approved the law giving him immunity from prosecution. In a farewell speech he asked for forgiveness for 'any shortcomings' during his 33 year rule.

representatives of the pro-democracy movement. It also put forward the idea of a presidential election within 60 days, which in fact the opposition groupings had already agreed to. One of the most insensitive parts of the plan was the complicated suggestion that President Saleh become the Yemen's 'Honorary President' (whatever that meant), in addition to the appointment of a 'Temporary President'. Equally insensitive was the proposal that President Saleh and his aides be granted immunity in respect of the alleged killing and injuring of protestors, not to mention the possible embezzlement from the national coffers.

Election run-up?

After more than half a dozen false starts, presidential elections were eventually set for late February 2012. In November 2011 President Saleh was said to have transferred executive powers to the consensus candidate from Yemen's ruling party, Vice President Abdu Rabo Mansour al Hadi. The opposition coalition Joint Meeting Parties (JMP) supported the nomination. In early December 2011, a 'unity government' consisting of members of the ruling party and the JMP was formed. The new government, which hardly reflected popular demands for increased accountability and transparency, went on to approve a 'national reconciliation plan'. This did not seem to take into account the fundamental demands of the protestors which included the trial of the President, the freezing of his funds abroad, the removal of the entire Sana'a regime and a six month transitional period.

On 23 November dissident army General Ali Mohsen said that he backed the peace accord, lending support to efforts to pull Yemen from the brink of civil war. The General's announcement came a day after both his forces, and troops loyal to outgoing President Ali Abdullah Saleh, began withdrawing from the capital Sana'a as part of the Gulf-brokered peace deal. 'We are ready to support the Gulf initiative, which was bolstered by Security Council resolution 2014,' Mohsen said.

Throughout 2011 the human situation in Yemen deteriorated fast. In September 2011 Oxfam, the UK based aid agency, published a report which stated that 'widespread hunger and chronic malnutrition had taken hold, with a third of Yemenis – some 7.5 million people – lacking enough to eat.' Yemen's Humanitarian Response Plan had reportedly received only 55 per cent of the funding it needed.

Friends and neighbours

Criticism of the response of both Saudi Arabia and the United States to the situation in Yemen inevitably referred to the differences between the two nations' actions in other countries where uprisings had taken hold. One London report observed that over 2011 the US had 'displayed more energy in attacking al Qaeda affiliates in the south of Yemen with drone strikes' than it had in obliging Saleh to step down. The *Washington Post* had reported a significant escalation of drone strikes on Yemen after the US had concluded that the grouping calling itself Al Qaeda in the Arabian Peninsula (AQAP) posed a more significant threat than al Qaeda in Pakistan. Faced with the Jasmine Revolution, the Yemeni government had certainly taken its eye off the ball. Reports were published that the southern city of Aden, with a population of 800,000 and once a vital international port, was virtually surrounded by Islamist militia fighters, some of whom were allegedly linked to al Qaeda. In the neighbouring Abyan Province, Islamic militants had captured the capital, forcing the governor to flee. Government claims that the uprisings in the north had brought about the chaos in the south were dismissed. It was commonly accepted that under President Saleh the southern provinces had often been subject to indiscriminate attacks. More vehement critics accused President Saleh of overseeing collusion between al Qaeda and the Yemeni security apparatus.

Surprisingly, the Jasmine Revolution appeared not to have affected co-operation between the US and Yemeni military. Both the US and Saudi Arabia had voiced support for what was described as a 'co-operative' regime in Yemen. However what is meant exactly by 'co-operative' is generally unclear. More specifically, the looseness of this statement did little to strengthen the resolve of those protesting.

The economy

According to the International Monetary Fund (IMF) in its latest report, published in early 2010, Yemen is one of the poorest countries in the region and progress toward meeting the Millennium Development Goals has been slow. Crude oil output – the mainstay of government revenue and exports – has been in decline since 2000. Barring major new discoveries, exploitable oil reserves could be exhausted in a relatively short period. A new liquefied natural gas (LNG) facility that began production in late 2009 will provide some cushion for the dwindling oil, and recent discoveries of natural gas may prolong the life of the hydrocarbon sector as a whole. Nevertheless, the magnitude of adjustment required by continued declines in oil output is substantial, even over the medium term. Generating strong and sustainable non-hydrocarbon growth, ensuring fiscal and external sustainability and meeting Yemen's pressing social and development needs will be key challenges for a new regime. Recent economic performance in Yemen has raised some

KEY INDICATORS — Yemen

	Unit	2006	2007	2008	2009	2010
Population	m	21.62	22.29	22.98	*23.69	*23.15
Gross domestic product (GDP)	US$bn	19.11	21.70	26.90	25.10	31.30
GDP per capita	US$	884	971	1,171	1,061	1,282
GDP real growth	%	3.2	3.3	3.6	3.9	8.0
Inflation	%	18.3	7.9	19.0	3.7	12.1
Oil output	'000 bpd	390.0	336.0	305.0	298.0	264.0
Natural gas output	bn cum	–	–	–	–	6.2
Exports (fob) (goods)	US$m	7,316.4	7,049.5	8,976.9	5,855.0	–
Imports (fob) (goods)	US$m	5,926.1	7,490.3	9,333.8	7,867.8	–
Balance of trade	US$m	1,390.3	-440.8	-356.9	-2,012.8	–
Current account	US$m	206.0	-1,508.3	-1,251.2	-2,564.9	-1,391.0
Total reserves minus gold	US$m	7,511.5	7,715.4	8,111.4	6,935.6	5,868.4
Foreign exchange	US$m	7,504.4	7,715.4	8,110.9	6,622.0	5,587.8
Exchange rate	per US$	198.48	198.90	199.76	237.65	219.59

* estimated figure

concerns. While direct financial contagion from the global crisis has been limited, Yemen has suffered from a range of indirect effects. The slowdown in world growth appears to have contributed to a slowdown in some areas of economic activity. Non-hydrocarbon economic growth in Yemen appears to have weakened, from 4.8 per cent in 2008 to an estimated 4.1 per cent in 2009 – reflecting slower activity in such areas as agriculture (possibly linked to Yemen's growing water shortages), construction, manufacturing and real estate. Inflation has hit record lows, due largely to the sharp decline in international food prices.

The heaviest impact from the global recession came through lower oil prices. Lower production, combined with the sharp drop in average prices and lower government share of output between 2008 and 2009 resulted in a significant decline in government oil exports. The loss of oil revenue put pressure on the government's fiscal balance. The authorities sought to mitigate the impact through containment of the civil service wage bill and a cabinet decree to slash non-essential current expenditures, but overall the adjustment effort did not keep pace with declining oil receipts. By the time the price of oil had rebounded, production in Yemen had fallen. Non-hydrocarbon revenues, meanwhile, have been stagnant. Full implementation of the General Sales Tax (GST), expected in 2009, had still not materialised in mid-2011.

According to the *Oil and Gas Journal* (OGJ), Yemen had proven crude oil reserves of 3 billion barrels as of 1 January 2011. Yemen's oil reserves and production are sourced from two geological areas: Marib-Jawf basin in the north and Say'un-Masila basin in the south. Marib's Block 18 is estimated to hold the country's main reserves, approximately 84 per cent of the total, according to Yemen's Petroleum Exploration and Production Authority. Yemen's oil reserves are generally light and sweet (low in sulfur content), with API gravities ranging from 28 degrees to 48 degrees, with the highest quality crude coming from the Marib-Jawf Basin. Production has fallen from a high of 457,000 barrels per day (bpd) in 2002 to 264,000bpd in 2010.

The main focus of monetary policy shifted from containing inflation to providing liquidity. With single digit inflation, declining private sector credit and a rapidly expanding fiscal deficit, monetary policy by the Central Bank of Yemen (CBY) has been largely accommodative. In addition to re-injecting sizeable liquidity into the banking system through a repurchase of central bank CDs, the CBY also made the first adjustment to the benchmark deposit rate in nearly ten years – lowering the rate from 13 per cent to 10 per cent during January–May 2009. The impact on broad money growth has been muted given the decrease in net foreign assets. However, the surge in credit to government may have contributed to lower private sector credit growth – which turned negative by mid-2009.

Pressure on the balance of payments was also visible. From September 2008 to September 2009, usable foreign exchange reserves of the CBY declined by US$1.6 billion, or roughly one-fifth of the initial reserve cushion (excluding allocations of Special Drawing Rights (SDRs) in August and September). However, the reserves remained comfortable at US$6.6 billion or about 9 months of imports. The sharp decline in oil exports was the driving force. Strong import demand (especially for food and fuel, which together account for 60 per cent of total imports) and an apparent slowdown in foreign direct investment (FDI) and inward remittances also played a role. Pressure may have eased in the last quarter of the year as oil prices rose, but the current account deficit widened from 4 per cent of GDP in 2008 to about 6 per cent in 2009.

Financial sector soundness indicators continued to improve over the 2009–10 period. While non-performing loans remained high, they were at least declining. Capital ratios were also on the rise, in line with a legal requirement to increase capital by end-2009. However, dollarisation (measured as foreign exchange deposits as a share of total deposits) appears to be rising after several years of steady decline. Given the many challenges ahead, the authorities at the time signaled interest in IMF support – possibly under the Extended Credit Facility (ECF) – to support the design and monitoring of a Yemeni strategy to reduce macro-economic and structural imbalances.

Energy – location, location

Yemen is, according to the US government Energy Information Administration (EIA) important to the global oil trade because of its location on the Bab el-Mandab, one of the world's most strategic shipping lanes, through which an estimated 3.5 million barrels of oil passed daily in 2010. Disruption to shipping in the Bab el-Mandab could prevent tankers from the Persian Gulf and the Gulf of Aden from reaching the Suez Canal/Sumed pipeline complex, requiring a costly diversion around the southern tip of Africa to reach western markets.

In recent years, this region has seen rising piracy off the Somali coast in the Gulf of Aden and southern Red Sea, and reaching further out into the Indian Ocean. Security concerns involving militant groups have also deterred investment in recent years, with numerous attacks on energy infrastructure slowing production and increasing costs. Tribal conflicts have also resulted in attacks on pipelines in the north of the country.

Risk assessment

Economy	Poor
Politics	Poor
Regional stability	Poor

COUNTRY PROFILE

Historical profile

1500s–1600s The Ottomans controlled most of Yemen.

1839 Aden came under British rule, serving as a major refuelling port after the opening of the Suez Canal in 1869.

1918–62 The Ottoman empire broke up and north Yemen gained independence under Imam Yahya. His son, Imam Ahmad succeeded him in 1948 and ruled until his death in 1962. A *coup d'état* overthrew his son and the Yemen Arab Republic (YAR) was established by the military. A civil war between royalists, supported by Saudi Arabia, and republicans, backed by Egypt, ensued.

1967 British withdrew from Aden as local resistance to their presence grew steadily more violent. A communist state in the south was established, comprising Aden and the former protectorate of South Arabia. It was officially known as the People's Democratic Republic of Yemen (PDRY). A nationalisation programme began.

1970s–80s The YAR and the PDRY were in conflict. Ali Abdullah Saleh became president of the YAR in 1978. President Ali Nasser Mohammed of the PDRY fled the country in 1986, after thousands died in political conflict.

1990 The YAR and the PDRY were unified and became the Republic of Yemen, with Ali Abdullah Saleh as president.

1991 A constitution was adopted. Yemen's support for Iraq in the Gulf War led to around a million migrant workers from other gulf states being evicted and returning home.

1993 Democratic elections (the first in the Arabian Peninsula) led to a three-party coalition comprising the former ruling party of the YAR, General People's Congress (GPC), led by Ali Abdullah Saleh,

the former ruling party of the PDRY, Yemeni Socialist Party (YSP), led by al Beedh, and a mainly northern Islamic tribal grouping, the Congregation for Reform (Islah). Disputes within the coalition resulted in an escalating political crisis.
1994 The constitution was amended. In spite of the signing of a conciliation agreement, a series of military confrontations broke out, leading to a full-scale civil war between northern and southern forces. Unity was restored and President Saleh was re-elected by parliament. A coalition government was formed, comprising the GPC and Islah, with the YSP and other smaller parties in opposition.
1995 Yemen and Eritrea clashed over the Hanish islands in the Red Sea.
1997 The ruling GPC won the first election since the 1994 civil war.
1998 Eritrea and Yemen accepted the ruling of the Permanent Court of Arbitration in The Hague that Yemen should have the island of Greater Hanish.
2000 Yemen and Saudi Arabia signed a treaty resolving a 65-year dispute over land and sea boundaries. The US naval vessel, *USS Cole*, was damaged in a suicide attack in Aden; a bomb exploded at the British Embassy.
2001 A referendum approved the extension of the president's term of office by two years to seven years and the parliamentary term by two years to six years. In response to the attack on the Twin Towers in New York, President Saleh told US President Bush that Yemen would join the fight against terrorism.
2002 Jarallah Omar, secretary general of the opposition party, YSP, was assassinated by an Islamic militant. Yemen expelled more than 100 foreign Islamic scholars, suspected of being al Qaeda members. The supertanker *Limburg* was badly damaged in an explosion off the coast of Yemen.
2003 The ruling GPC was re-elected. The 10 chief suspects in the bombing of the *USS Cole* escaped from custody in Aden.
2004 Government troops fought with followers of Hussein al Houthi, the leader of an insurrection in the north. Fifteen men were sentenced on terror charges, some for bombing the supertanker *Limburg*, and two more for bombing the *USS Cole*. Government troops killed Hussein al Houthi
2005 More fighting between government forces and al Houthi supporters caused over 200 deaths. The World Health Organisation confirmed 83 cases of polio; Yemen had been free of the disease. An agreement with the northern insurgents was reached.
2006 Over 625 supporters of the al Houthi uprising were freed from prison under an amnesty. In presidential elections Ali Abdullah Saleh was re-elected.
2007 Dozens of followers of al Houthi were killed in clashes with government troops. Ali Mohamed Mujawar was appointed prime minister. Abdul Malik al Houthi agreed to a ceasefire. Citizens were banned from carrying firearms in the capital and demonstrations without permits were banned.
2008 More violence broke out between supporters loyal to Abdul Malik al Houthi and security forces. Bomb attacks were carried out against local police and official buildings as well as foreign businesses, embassies and tourist targets.
2009 Parliament approved a once-only election postponement to 27 April 2011, allowing further discussions on electoral reforms.
2010 The government stopped issuing visas at international airports in January. A military official was quoted in the defence ministry newspaper *September 26* as saying that 'granting visas to foreigners will take place only through the embassies of Yemen, and after consulting security authorities to verify the identities of travellers'. He went on to say that the move was 'to prevent the infiltration of any suspected terrorist elements' after it was revealed that the Nigerian who had attempted to blow-up an aircraft over Detroit in December 2009 had been trained by al Qaeda elements in Yemen. A siege of the southern Shabwa Province began on 18 September. An estimated 8,000–12,000 civilians fled the town of Huta as a military offensive against al Qaeda got underway on 22 September. The US, UK, Germany and France placed a ban on all cargo from Yemen in November, following the discovery of improvised bombs sent by agents of al Qaeda.
2011 On 2 March a proposal, which included the issue of the transfer of the president's power, negotiated between opposition parties, tribal leaders and religious scholars, was presented to President Saleh. Initial reports were that the report had been positively received. On 10 March President Saleh announced that there would be a referendum later in 2011 on measures to change the constitution, including an election law to move towards a parliamentary system. A 30 day emergency law was passed on 23 March. In an effort to mediate between the president and demonstrators demanding he resign a Gulf Arab initiative lead by Saudi Arabia proposed a transfer of power away from President Saleh. Security forces fired live-rounds into protesting crowds in Sana'a on 17 April, following President Saleh's earlier comment that protestor's behaviour was 'un-Islamic'. From February–April, over 100 people died in civil disturbances as the president said he would step down and hand over power, but only into 'safe hands'. On 26 May the US ordered all non-essential diplomatic staff to leave Yemen. Hundreds of armed members of the Hashid tribe (one of the two main tribal groupings in Yemen), fought with government troops as they marched on Sana'a on 2 June to join forces with other of their tribe already in the capital. Sheikh Sadeq al Ahmar, head of the Hashid tribe, is the son of the founder of the opposition party Islamist Islah. President Saleh was injured by shrapnel in the chest on 3 June, during an attack on his Sana'a palace compound. Saleh left Yemen on 6 June to receive medical treatment in Saudi Arabia. President Saleh appeared on Yemen state television on 7 July, the first time since he was injured. Both hands were bandaged and he did not appear to move his arms. He said that dialogue was needed to resolve Yemen's problems, although any resolution had to be 'within the framework of the constitution and in the framework of the law'. On 7 August President Saleh left hospital, but chose to remain in Saudi Arabia. On 4 June, Abdu Rabu Mansour Hadi became acting prime minister. On 22 August, former prime minister Abdul Aziz Abdul Ghani died of his injuries sustained during the attack on the Sana'a presidential palace on 3 June. On 17 August, President Saleh vowed to return to Yemen and remain in office until 2013. Demonstrations for and against the regime continued in Sana'a. On 15 September, in Yemen's second city Taiz, the elite republican guard, led by President Salah's son Ahmed, opened fire on demonstrators demanding Salah resign; at least 10 people were injured. On 19 September, security forces fired on demonstrators in Sana'a using automatic weapons and killing at least 20 people, while snipers fired from rooftops into a protest camp. President Saleh returned on 23 September. Tawakkul Karman was announced as one of three women to win the 2011 Nobel Peace Prize on 7 October. The three women were honoured for 'their non-violent struggle for the safety of women and for women's rights to full participation in peace-building work'. On 21 October, the UN Security Council called on President Saleh to resign immediately, following weeks of excessive violence meted out by security forces on demonstrators against his regime. On 23 November, President Saleh signed an agreement, brokered by the GCC, to transfer his powers by 23 December, to Vice President Abdrabuh Mansur Hadi. In return Saleh will retain the honorary title of president and have immunity from prosecution. Demonstrators, who had

been protesting since the beginning of the year, condemned the deal; five were killed and 33 injured by security forces. Vice President Hadi designated Muhammed Salim Basindwa, an opposition politician, as prime minister on 27 November.

Political structure

Constitution

The constitution was adopted in 1991 and was amended in 1994 and 2001.
Voting eligibility: 18 years.
A 2001 referendum approved the extension of the president's and parliament's terms of office from five to seven years, and from four to six years, respectively.

Independence date

1918 North Yemen; 1967 South Yemen. 22 May 1990 unification.

Form of state

Republic

The executive

Power is vested in the post of president, who is the Head of State.
The president is elected by popular vote from at least two candidates, endorsed by parliament. He sets a national agenda and is empowered to rule by decree in the case of parliament's absence, call for parliamentary elections, appoint a prime minister to form a government, call for general referenda and form the National Defence Council.
The president can serve a maximum of two, seven-year terms.
The prime minister, in consultation with the president, selects the cabinet to assist in the duties of the executive branch.

National legislature

The bicameral parliament consists of the Majlis al Nuwaab (Assembly of Representatives) with 301 members, elected by popular vote to serve six-year terms and the Shura (Consultative Council) with 111 members, appointed by the president, and serving as advisory body.

Legal system

An independent judiciary was established under the constitution. It is based on *Sharia* (Islamic law), Turkish law, English common law and local tribal customary law. The Supreme Court is based in the capital.

Last elections

20 September 2006 (presidential); 27 April 2003 (parliamentary)
Results: Parliamentary: GPC won 58.01 per cent of the votes (238 seats out of 301); Islah won 22.55 per cent (46 seats); Yemen Socialist Party 3.84 per cent (eight seats). Turnout was 75.98 per cent.
Presidential: Ali Abdullah Saleh won 77.17 per cent of the vote; Faisal Bin Shamlan won 21.81 per cent. Turnout was 65.16 per cent.

Next elections

27 April 2011 (parliamentary); 2013 (presidential)

Political parties

Ruling party

Al Mutammar al Shabi al Am (GPC) (General People's Congress) (from 1999; re-elected 2003)

Main opposition party

At tajammu al yemeni lil Islah (Islah) (Yemeni Congregation for Reform)

Population

23.15 million (2010)*
Last census: 16 December 2004: 19,685,161
Population density: 30 inhabitants per square km. Urban population: 25 per cent (1995–2001).
Annual growth rate: 3.4 per cent 1994–2004 (WHO 2006)

Ethnic make-up

Arabs form 96 per cent of the population. There are ethnic tensions between Arabs and Afro-Arab and South Asian minorities. European communities are concentrated in the major metropolitan areas.

Religions

Muslim (more than 99 per cent), including Shi'ite, Sunni and Zaydi (members of a Shi'ite subsect). Small number of Jews.

Education

Primary education begins at the age of six and lasts for nine years.
Secondary education is provided for academic and vocational courses both lasting three years. The first year comprises a common curriculum, with the option to choose either the scientific or literary subjects for the remaining two years. There are some technical secondary schools, three vocational training centres, a Veterinary Training School and several agricultural secondary schools. There are also religious institutions, which concentrate on Islamic education. Higher education is provided by the University of Sana'a (1970), the University of Aden (1973) and the University of Science and Technology, Sana'a.
Literacy rate: 49 per cent adult rate; 68 per cent youth rate (15–24) (Unesco 2005).
Compulsory years: Six to 15.
Enrolment rate: 70 per cent gross primary enrolment; 34 per cent gross secondary enrolment, of relevant age groups (including repeaters) (World Bank).
Pupils per teacher: 30 in primary schools.

Health

There were cases of polio reported to the World Health Organisation – Global Polio Eradication Initiative in 2006; the country had previously been free of the disease and its re-emergence was due to infected travellers.

HIV/Aids

HIV prevalence: 0.1 per cent aged 15–49 in 2003 (World Bank)
Life expectancy: 59 years, 2004 (WHO 2006)
Fertility rate/Maternal mortality rate: 6.0 births per woman, 2004 (WHO 2006); maternal mortality 350 per 100,000 live births (World Bank).
Child (under 5 years) mortality rate (per 1,000): 82 per 1,000 live births; 46 per cent of children under aged five are malnourished (World Bank).
Head of population per physician: 0.33 physicians per 1,000 people, 2004 (WHO 2006)

Main cities

Sana'a (San'a) (capital, estimated population 2.4 million in 2005), Aden (507,355), Ta'iz (596,672), Hodeida (548,433), Ibb (225,611).

Media

Press

Dailies: In Arabic, the government-owned national newspaper is *Al Thawra* (www.althawranews.net), other regional private publications include *Al Ayyam* (www.al-ayyam.info) and *14 October* (www.14october.com), from Aden, *Akhbar al Youm* (www.alshomoa.net), *Al Thaqafiah* (www.y.net.ye/althaqafiah) and *Al Shoura* from Sanna.
In English, the *Yemen Times* (http://yementimes.com) is a widely read newspaper, *Yemen Observer* (www.yobserver.com) is an independent English online newspaper covering current events.
Weeklies: In Arabic, publications include *26 September* (www.26september.info), *Al Ray News* (www.raynews.net), and *Ektissad ws Aswaq* (www.ekwas.net) on economics, news and analysis.

Broadcasting

High rates of illiteracy has effectively left radio and television as primary sources of news and information for the domestic population.
Radio: The state-run Yemen Radio (www.yemenradio.net) has two networks, from the capital and Aden.
Television: The only terrestrial TV network is Yemen Television with two channels. There is satellite TV with nine international and pan-Arab networks available, including the government-owned Yemen Satellite Channel, offering a wide variety of programmes.

News agencies

National news agency: Saba (Yemen News Agency)

Economy

Petroleum is Yemen's chief revenue source, with 2.7 billion barrels of oil reserves and production of 298,000 barrels per day (bpd) in 2009; there are also 490 million cubic metres of proven natural gas reserves. Production of liquefied natural gas (LNG) began in 2009, with exports to the US, South Korea and Europe. Stocks of oil are being depleted and the non-oil economy is not strong enough to replace its importance to GDP. Agriculture is an important component of GDP, providing the primary occupation of around 50 per cent of the workforce. However the industry suffers from a number of environmental problems including deforestation that has led to soil erosion and desertification and above all a scarcity of water. Through an increased use of irrigation, farmers have switch production from lesser valued, rain-fed cereals to the more valuable, irrigated fruit and vegetables. However, this use of groundwater is depleting the resource as the water-table falls by around two metres per year. The cultivation and use of the mildly narcotic *qat* has increased, so much so that the World Bank estimates that trade and consumption of the plant accounts for over 6 per cent of GDP, while its cultivation alone accounts for 10 per cent of GDP. Farmland given over to its cultivation denies its use for other cash crops necessary for exports. The fishing industry is underinvested and caters for local needs only.

Tourism could provide a greater component of GDP but the threatening security situation and the danger experienced by tourists in the recent past keep visitor numbers to a minimum.

GDP growth has been consistent, from 3.2 per cent in 2006 to 3.9 per cent in 2009. However in 2010 GDP growth jumped to 8 per cent, before falling back to a projected 4 per cent in 2011 – a figure that cannot be sustained given the civil strife experienced at the beginning of the year. Inflation fluctuated widely in this period from 10.8 per cent in 2006 to 7.9 per cent in 2007 then jumping to 19 per cent in 2008 before falling back to 3.7 per cent in 2009.

To improve its revenue income the government fully implemented its general sales tax (GST) in 2010, along with the removal of all exemptions on tax and customs duties and an adjustment of subsidies on domestic fuel prices to make a net fiscal savings of almost 1 per cent of GDP. However the International Monetary Fund (IMF) warned that socially sensitive reforms and weak institutional capacity were at a higher risk of compromise from the ongoing security situation.

Remittances in 2009 were US$1.38 billion (5.2 per cent of GDP) and were estimated to have grown to US$1.47 billion in 2010. The UN Human Development Index (HDI) ranked Yemen as 133 (out of 169 countries) for national development in health, education and income, in 2010. Since 2000, Yemen's HDI has consistently failed to match either world or regional trends, with 53.9 per cent of households experiencing deprivations in the three key indicators and 17.53 per cent of the population living in poverty.

International economic aid is essential to Yemen's short- to medium-term development, not only to provide a more prosperous future for the population but also to nullify the adverse influence of the terrorist group, al Qaeda. In 2008 US$5 billion was pledged in development aid and in March 2011 the Arab League pledged US$329 million for infrastructure development.

External trade

The Greater Arab Free Trade Area (Gafta) has been ratified by 17 members, including Yemen, creating an Arab economic bloc. A customs union has been established whereby tariffs within Gafta are reduced by a percentage each year, until none remain.

Crude oil dominates the export market but reserves are diminishing. A liquefied natural gas (LNG) plant began production in 2009, with exports destined for the US, Europe and South Korea.

The coffee harvest was replaced in prominence by the cultivation of *qat* (an additive, mild hallucinogen), used openly in Yemen but trafficked illegally to the Horn of Africa.

Imports

Main imports are foodstuffs, live animals, vehicles, machinery and equipment.

Main sources: China (typically 11 per cent of total), Japan (7 per cent), Saudi Arabia (6 per cent).

Exports

Crude and refined oil and derivatives, liquefied natural gas (LNG), seafood, fruit and vegetables, tobacco products and animal hides.

Main destinations: China (typically 26 per cent of total), India (23 per cent), Thailand (20 per cent).

Agriculture

With its fertile soil and relatively high levels of rainfall, Yemen possesses the best climatic conditions for agriculture on the Arabian peninsula. Due to its mountainous terrain, terrace agriculture is common practice. In the east and north, herding is the chief activity. In southern Yemen, fertile areas are severely limited and confined to the wadis, comprising only 1 per cent of the total land area.

The main crops are sorghum, wheat, barley, maize, millet, sesame, cotton, coffee, vegetables, dates, fruit, tobacco and qat (a legal narcotic).

The cultivation of *qat*, a widely used mild narcotic shrub dominates production. It is estimated that up to 25 per cent of irrigated land is given over to qat, which generates a value added equivalent of 25 per cent of GDP.

Cereals, fruit and vegetables account for 75 per cent of output, but annual imports of grain are still required. Cereal yields are low and the climate is more suitable for fruit production. Private sector trading companies have invested in agriculture in Tihama and Marib, concentrating on bananas and citrus fruits.

Drought in some places and floods in others, plus general manpower shortages remain serious problems. The Marib Dam provides irrigation and for a region adjacent to the desert (Empty Quarter).

Fishing

Fisheries are one of Yemen's greatest potential sources of wealth after oil. There are some fish exports to Europe and the Middle East.

Industry and manufacturing

The industrial sector contributes over 35 per cent of GDP, of which manufacturing is around 5 per cent. The sector employs around 10 per cent of the working population. Excluding the petroleum sector, industry accounts for only 4 per cent of GDP.

Heavy industry is mostly government-owned while the private sector is encouraged to participate in joint ventures and light industries including food processing, clothing, textiles, leather goods, jewellery, cosmetics, mineral water, fertilisers and cigarettes.

Fish processing is a growth area.

Tourism

The government has been seeking to develop tourism as a potential source of revenue. The country has a moderate climate all-year-round and an ancient civilisation which would prove of great interest to visitors. However, with the rise of terriorist activities and the civil unrest in 2011, tourism has been hampered.

Environment

Yemen has water shortages, especially in the increasingly urbanised areas around Sana'a and other cities.

Mining

Salt is mined at Salif, where deposits total 25 million tonnes. Gypsum and marble are extracted. There are also deposits of zinc, lead, iron, sulphur, gold, silver, copper and nickel.

Hydrocarbons

Proven oil reserves were 2.8 billion barrels in 2007, with production at 336,000 barrels per day (bpd), a fall since a high of 439,970bpd in 2001. Typically, 80 per cent of total oil production is exported. The government is attempting to secure foreign investment to expand production, but political instability and poor security have deterred many major oil companies. Downstream, Yemen has a refining capacity of 143,000bpd with two ageing refineries at Aden (120,000bpd) and Marib (10,000bpd). The government has plans to upgrade these facilities by 150,000bpd and 25,000bpd respectively. A new 50,000bpd refinery at Ras Issa has been planned since 2005 but is yet to be completed.

There is an integrated network of 900km of pipelines which transport crude oil and natural gas from production sites to either domestic users or terminals for export. Proven natural gas reserves were estimated at 490 billion cubic metres in 2007, but commercial production is under-invested. The growth in regional exports of liquefied natural gas (LNG) may stimulate production. The state-owned Yemen LNG has several international contracts to supply LNG in 2009, but all have been delayed. The French energy company GDF Suez has a long-term contract to buy 2.54 million tonnes of LNG per year and the oil companies Total and the Korea Gas Corporation 2.03 million tonnes.

Any use of coal is commercially insignificant.

Energy
Total installed electricity generating capacity was 1.13 gigawatts in 2007, producing over five billion kilowatt hours, all of which was produced in conventional thermal power stations. Only an estimated 35 per cent of the urban and 5 per cent of the rural population has access to the national grid.

The state-owned Public Electricity Corporation (PEC) is responsible for generation and distribution and has organised international development aid to improve electricity supplies. However, to access such investment energy subsidies will have to be terminated – a previous attempt at price increases resulted in riots, leaving the government with a hard choice. The inadequacies of the distribution network are under review with an upgrade in the network expected to follow. A new 340MW natural gas-fired power station in Marib due to be completed in 2007 is still unfinished.

Banking and insurance
Domestic banks are burdened by red tape and private sector credit is crowded out by the state, although the government has announced a reform programme to develop the financial sector.

Central bank
Central Bank of Yemen
Main financial centre
Sana'a

Time
GMT plus three hours

Geography
Yemen is situated in the south of the Arabian peninsula, bordered to the north by Saudi Arabia, to the east by Oman, to the south by the Gulf of Aden, and to the west by the Red Sea. The islands of Perim and Kamaran at the southern end of the Red Sea and the island of Socotra at the entrance to the Gulf of Aden are also part of the Republic.
Hemisphere
Northern

Climate
The semi-desert coastal plain known as the Tihama is hot, humid and dusty. The highlands, which are agreeable in summer but cold in winter, enjoy most of the unreliable rainfall (March–April and July–September).

Entry requirements
Passports
Required by all, valid for six months from date of departure.
Visa
Required by all, except nationals of Iraq, Jordan and Syria.

The government stopped issuing visas at international airports in January 2010. A military official was quoted in the defence ministry newspaper *September 26* as saying that 'granting visas to foreigners will take place only through the embassies of Yemen, and after consulting security authorities to verify the identities of travellers'. He went on to say that the move was 'to prevent the infiltration of any suspected terrorist elements' after it was revealed that the Nigerian who had attempted to blow-up an aircraft over Detroit in December 2009 had been trained by al Qaeda elements in Yemen.

All visitors should start by contacting the nearest Yemeni embassy; the following information was valid in early 2010, but is subject to change. Tourist visas, valid for visits up to two months, require a confirmation letter from a tour company and proof of return/onward passage. Business visas, valid for visits up to two months, require a letter from the applicant's company explaining the purpose of the visit and the nature of business and proof of return/onward passage. Visas valid for six months may be issued to business travellers proposing to make several jouneys, in which case a letter of invitation from a Yemeni company is also required.

Prohibited entry
Israeli nationals or holders of passports with Israeli visas or other indication of a visit to Israel are denied entry or transit facilities.
Currency advice/regulations
The import and export of local currency by non-residents is prohibited. There are no restrictions on the import of foreign currencies, subject to declaration of amounts over US$3,000; export of foreign currencies is restricted to the amount imported and declared.
Customs
600 cigarettes, 60 cigars or 450g of tobacco; two bottles of alcohol; one bottle of perfume, perfumed water or eau de cologne; gifts to a value of YR100,000; and gold ornaments up to 350 grams are allowed duty-free.
Prohibited imports
Firearms, illegal drugs, pornographic literature and all products of Israeli origin are prohibited.

Health (for visitors)
Mandatory precautions
Certificate of vaccination against yellow fever if travelling from infected area.
Advisable precautions
Vaccinations against typhoid and polio are recommended, also anti-malaria precautions (malaria has been endemic in Tihama).

Water precautions are essential; water and milk should be boiled. Local dairy products should be avoided as milk is unpasteurised; vegetables, meat and fish should be well cooked and eaten hot. Use only well maintained, chlorinated swimming pools as bilharzia can be contracted from streams and rivers. Gastric upsets common.

Hotels
Sana'a has several first-class hotels. It is advisable to book in advance. The major hotels have good restaurants.

Credit cards
Major credit cards are acceptable.

Public holidays (national)
Fixed dates
1 May (Labour Day), 22 May (Unity Day), 26 Sep (Revolution Day), 14 Oct (National Day), 30 Nov (Independence Day).
Variable dates
Eid al Adha (four days), Eid al Fitr (four days), Islamic New Year, Birth of the Prophet.

Islamic year 1433 (26 Nov 2011–14 Nov 2012): The Islamic year contains 354 or 355 days, with the result that Muslim feasts advance by 10–12 days against the Gregorian calendar. Dates of feasts vary according to the sighting of the new moon, so cannot be forecast exactly.

Working hours

Banking
Sat–Wed: 0800–1200, Thu: 0800–1130 (closed Fri); in summer: Sat–Wed: 0730–1130, Thu: 0730–1100 (closed Fri).
Business
Sat–Wed: 0800–1230, 1600–1900; Thu: 0800–1200 (closed Fri).
Government
Sat–Thu: 0900–1300.
Shops
Sun-Thu: 0800-1300, 1600-2100.

Telecommunications

Telephone/fax
The telephone directory is in Arabic. For help, ask the telephone operator at your hotel or ring 18 (English spoken).
Mobile/cell phones
There are GSM 900 services available in the south and west of the country.

Electricity supply

Generally 220V AC, with two-pin plug fittings.

Weights and measures

Metric system

Social customs/useful tips

Islamic culture and customs are strictly observed, but visitors are allowed to drink alcohol in hotels or private homes.

Security

Visitors should keep in touch with developments in the Middle East as any increase in regional tension might affect travel advice.

Getting there

Air
National airline: Yemenia (Yemen Airways)
International airport/s: Sana'a International (SAH), 13km north of Sana'a, with duty-free shop, restaurant, bank, car hire; Aden International (ADE), 11km north-east of Aden.
Airport tax: None.
Surface
There are road connections from Saudi Arabia and Oman, but driving to Yemen is advised against.
Main port/s: Aden, Hodeidah and Mukalla

Getting about

National transport
Internal travel may be affected by local night-time curfews and military check points.
Air: Regular scheduled services link Sana'a, Aden, Hodeida, Ta'iz and Marib.
Road: There are metalled roads between main centres.
Buses: There are scheduled services between all main centres.
City transport
Most hosts will send a car to the airport to meet guests.
Taxis: Taxis have yellow licence plates and wait on ranks outside the major hotels and terminals.
Fare is by negotiation and there is a minimum charge system in cities. Always agree the fare before setting off; the hotel will advise what the price should be as the starting point for negotiation. A fixed fare is charged between Sana'a airport and the city centre.
Dahabs (shared taxis) are minibuses which ply set routes in the city. Prices are fixed between destinations and are reasonably cheap.
Buses, trams & metro: Buses wait outside the airport.
Car hire
Available in Sana'a and other main centres.

BUSINESS DIRECTORY

The addresses listed below are a selection only. While World of Information makes every endeavour to check these addresses, we cannot guarantee that changes have not been made, especially to telephone numbers and area codes. We would welcome any corrections.

Telephone area codes

The international direct dialling (IDD) code for Yemen is +967, followed by the area code and subscriber's number:

Aden	2	Sana'a	1
Almahra	5	Taiz	4
Amran	7	Yarim	4
Hodeidah	3	Zabid	3

Chambers of Commerce

Aden Chamber of Commerce, Queen Arwa Road, PO Box 473, Crater, Aden (tel: 221-176; fax: 255-660; e-mail: cciaden@y.net.ye).

Federation of Yemen Chambers of Commerce and Industry, Al-Qiyadah Road, PO Box 16992, Sana'a (tel: 265-038; fax: 261-269; e-mail: fucci@y.net.ye).

Hadhramout Chamber of Commerce and Industry, Mukalla Main Street, PO Box 8302, Mukalla (tel: 353-258; fax: 303-437; e-mail: hdramoutchamber@y.net.ye).

Hodeidah Chamber of Commerce and Industry, Liberty Squaret, PO Box 3370, Hodeidah (tel: 217-401; fax: 211-528; e-mail: hodcii@y.net.ye).

National Chamber of Commerce and Industry, PO Box 5029, Crater, Aden (tel: 51203; fax: 232-412).

Sana'a Chamber of Commerce and Industry, Airport Road, PO Box 195, Sana'a (tel: 232-361; fax: 232-412; e-mail: sanaacomyemen@y.net.ye).

Ta'iz Chamber of Commerce and Industry, Chamber Street, PO Box 5029, Taiz (tel: 210-581; fax: 212-335; e-mail: taizchamber@y.net.ye).

Banking

Arab Bank Plc, PO Box 5130, Madram Street, Maala, Aden (tel: 242-099, 240-043; fax: 242-098).

Credit Agricole Indosuez, PO Box 651, Al Ma'ala Main St, Aden (tel: 247-4024; fax: 247-282).

International Bank of Yemen YSC, PO Box 819, al Maidan - Crater, Off Queen Arwa Rd, Crater, Aden (tel: 255-795; fax: 252-016).

National Bank of Yemen, PO Box 5, Crater, Aden (tel: 252-875, 253-327; fax: 252-875).

Watani Bank for Trade and Investment, PO Box 4424, Queen Arwa St, Agaba, Aden (tel: 2506-1017; fax: 250-618).

Yemen Bank for Reconstruction and Development, PO Box 239, Aden (tel: 252-104, 254-046; fax: 252-141).

Yemen Commercial Bank, PO Box 4230, Aden (tel: 255-813, 253-384; fax: 255-428).

Central bank
Central Bank of Yemen, PO Box 59, Ali Abdulmoghni Street, Sana'a (tel: 274-310 fax: 274-057; e-mail: info@centralbank.gov.ye).

Travel information

Sana'a International Airport, PO Box 1438, Sana'a (tel/fax: 250-819).

Yemenia (Yemen Airways), PO Box 1183, Sana'a (tel: 201-822; fax: 201-821; e-mail: info@yemenia.com).

Ministry of tourism
Ministry of Culture and Tourism, Al-Hasabah, PO Box 129, Sana'a (tel: 235-112; fax: 235-113; e-mail: yementpb@y.net.ye).

National tourist organisation offices
General Tourism Development Authority, Al-Hasabah, PO Box 129, Sana'a (tel: 252-319; fax: 252-316; e-mail: gtda@gtda.gov.ye).

Tourism Promotion Board, Al-Hasabah, PO Box 5607, Sana'a (tel: 251-033; fax: 251-034; e-mail: ytpb@yementourism.com).

Ministries

Ministry of Agriculture and Water Resources, PO Box 2805 (tel: 200-999; fax: 209-509).

Ministry of Civil Service and Administration Reform, PO Box 1992, Sana'a (tel: 200-404; fax: 274-456).

Ministry of Communications, PO Box 17045, Sana's (tel: 271-100; fax: 251-150).

Ministry of Construction, PO Box 1180, Sana'a (tel: 202-288; fax: 274-145).

Ministry of Culture and Tourism (tel: 200-002; fax: 252-316).

Ministry of Defence (tel: 250-330; fax: 251-559).

Ministry of Economy, Supply & Trade, PO Box 1704, Sana'a (tel: 202-471).

Ministry of Education (tel: 274-548; fax: 274-558).

Ministry of Electricity and Water, PO Box 11422, Sana'a (tel: 250-143; fax: 251-554).

Ministry of Finance, PO Box 190, Sana'a (tel: 260-375; fax: 263-040).

Ministry of Fishery Wealth, PO Box 19179, Sana'a (tel: 262-866; fax: 263-165).

Ministry of Foreign Affairs, PO Box 1994, Sana'a (tel: 202-555; fax: 209-540).

Ministry of Higher Education and Scientific Research, PO Box 11327, Sana'a (tel: 200-463; fax: 262-001).

Ministry of Housing and Urban Planning, PO Box 1445, Sana'a (tel: 262-614; fax: 215-613).

Ministry of Immigrants Affairs, PO Box 1299, Sana'a (tel: 215-666; fax: 263-027).

Ministry of Industry, PO Box 607, Sana'a (tel: 252-339; fax: 252-366).

Ministry of Information (tel: 200-050; fax: 282-050).

Ministry of the Interior and Security (tel: 252-701; fax: 251-529).

Ministry of Justice (tel: 252-158; fax: 252-138).

Ministry of Labour and Vocational Training, PO Box 60, Sana'a (tel: 274-922; fax: 274-107).

Ministry of Legal Affairs, PO Box 1292, Sana'a (tel: 262-047; fax: 262-047).

Ministry of Local Government, PO Box 2198, Sana'a (tel: 250-626; fax: 251-513).

Ministry of Oil and Mineral Resources, PO Box 81, Sana'a (tel: 202-312; fax: 202-314).

Ministry of Planning and Development, PO Box 175, Sana'a (tel: 250-118; fax: 251-503).

Ministry of Provision and Trade, PO Box 804, Sana'a (tel: 252-337; fax: 251-366).

Ministry of Public Health, PO Box 274160, Sana'a (tel: 252-222; fax: 244-143).

Ministry of Securities and Social Affairs (tel: 262-809; fax: 209-547).

Ministry of State for Cabinet Affairs (tel: 200-677; fax: 209-518).

Ministry of State for Foreign Affairs, PO Box L994, Sana'a (tel: 202-544; fax: 209-540).

Ministry of State for House of Deputies Affairs (tel: 200-671; fax: 209-518).

Ministry of Transport, PO Box 2781 (tel: 260-904; fax: 263-169).

Ministry of Tourism, PO Box 129, Sana'a (tel: 252-319; fax: 260-186).

Ministry of WAQF and Guidance (tel: 274-438; fax: 274-17).

Ministry of Youth and Sport, PO Box 2701, Sana'a (tel: 215-653; fax: 263-181).

Other useful addresses

British Consulate-General, PO Box 6304, Khormaksar, Aden (tel: 232-712; fax: 231-256).

British Embassy, PO Box 1287, Sana'a (tel: 264-081; fax: 263-059).

Central Planning Organisation, PO Box 175, Sana'a (tel: 250-1018).

Foreign Trade Corporation, PO Box 77, Sana'a (tel: 72-058).

General Post Office, Liberation (Tahreer) Square, (tel: 71-401/2).

Ports and Marine Affairs Corporation, PO Box 3183, Hodeidah.

Republic of Yemen Embassy (USA), Suite 705, 2600 Virginia Avenue, NW, Washington DC 20037 (tel: (+1-202) 965-4760; fax: (+1-202) 337-2017; e-mail: information@yemenembassy.org).

United Nations Development Programme, PO Box 551 Sana'a (tel: 70-593/70-596).

National news agency: Saba (Yemen News Agency)

Internet sites

ArabNet: http://www.arab.net/welcome.html

Arabia.On.Line: http://www.arabia.com

Embassy of the Republic Yemen, Washington DC: http://www.yemenembassy.org

Yemen gateway site: http://www.al-bab.com/yemen/Default.htm

Yemen Times On-line: http://www.yementimes.com

Zambia

KEY FACTS

Official name: Republic of Zambia

Head of State: President Michael Sata (PF) (from 29 Sep 2011)

Head of government: President Michael Sata (Patriotic Front) (from 29 Sep 2011)

Ruling party: To be announced

Area: 752,614 square km

Population: 13.05 million (2010; census figure)

Capital: Lusaka

Official language: English

Currency: Kwacha (K) = 100 ngwee

Exchange rate: K4,822.00 per US$ (Oct 2011)

GDP per capita: US$1,221 (2010)

GDP real growth: 7.60% (2010)

GDP: US$16.20 billion (2010)

Labour force: 5.40 million (2009)*

Inflation: 8.50% (2010)

Balance of trade: -US$2.70 billion (2010)

* estimated figure

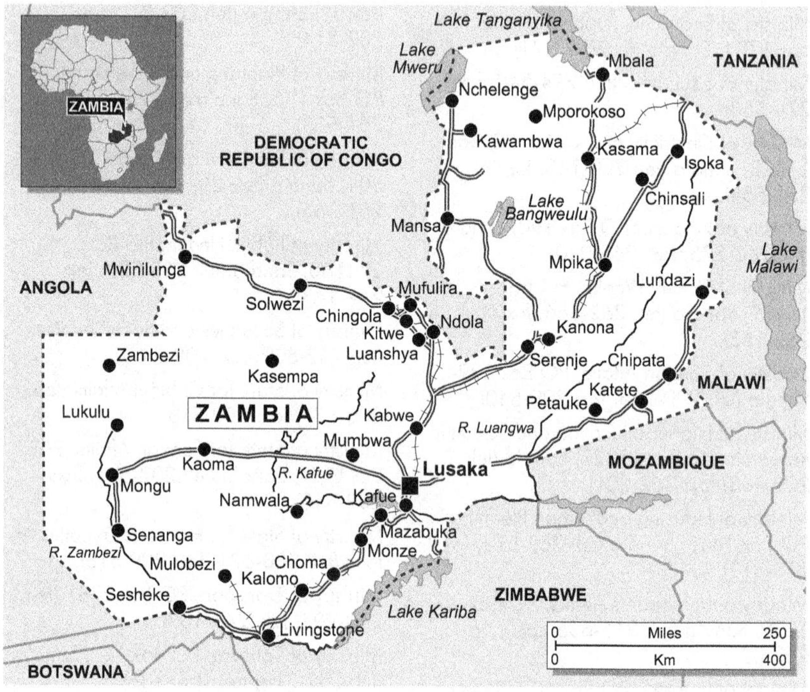

Four of Zambia's seven neighbours had uncomfortably violent transitions to independence, and in the case of the Democratic Republic of the Congo in the north, is still one of Africa's most violent and ungovernable states. Zambia, on the other hand, held its fifth multi-party elections in 2011 and for the second time peacefully switched regimes – the first time, in 1991 when Kenneth Kaunda (KK), who had lead Zambia to independence, and the United National Independence Party (UNIP) were beaten by Frederick Chiluba and the Movement for Multi-party Democracy (MMD). Back then KK set the marker by stepping down gracefully and retiring.

In presidential elections held on 20 September Michael Sata of the Patriotic Front (PF) won 43 per cent of the vote (not significantly more than the 38 per cent he won in the last election in 2006), ahead of incumbent, Rupiah Banda of the MMD with 36.1 per cent. A day later in parliamentary elections the opposition PF won 60 seats (out of 150), ousting the MMD (55 seats) from its 20-years in office. The win was narrow – 38.25 per cent to 33.56 per cent – and not enough for the PF to govern without recourse to one or more of the minor parties when necessary. President Sato's administration took office on 29 September.

In the run up to the elections there had been concerns about Mr Sato's relations with China, Zambia's biggest investment partner. Mr Sato had been very critical in particular about Chinese labour conditions. Although probably an election ploy, the Chinese were sufficiently alarmed to retaliate by threatening to pull out of Zambia if he won.

In the event, to calm fears, of not only the Chinese, President Sata's first official appointment after being sworn in was with the Chinese ambassador. He warned that while he welcomed Chinese companies, they must comply with Zambian law. In his inauguration speech Mr Sato had assured foreign investors that they are all welcome in his country, Africa's biggest copper producer, but said they must improve conditions for their Zambian employees

The economy

Zambia's economy is recovering strongly from the financial and economic crisis with 2010 gross domestic product (GDP) growth estimated at 7.6 per cent, up from 4.5 per cent in 2009. The *African Economic Outlook 2011* (AEO), published jointly by the African Development Bank and the Organisation for Economic Co-operation and Development, estimates that the economy will grow by 6.5 per cent and 6.7 per cent in 2011 and 2012, respectively. However, some caution over the speed of recovery should be taken into account.

Primary industries, mainly agriculture, are performing well. Agriculture was expected to grow 7.6 per cent in 2010. Growth for 2011 and 2012 is projected at 3.2 per cent and 4.6 per cent, respectively. In 2010, Zambia recorded its largest ever maize harvest of about 2.8 million tonnes, compared with 1.9 million tonnes in the previous season. Major staple food crops such as maize, sorghum, rice, groundnuts, Irish potatoes, mixed beans, sweet potatoes and cassava contributed to higher production in 2010. Although average growth for 2011–13 will slow to about 1.2 per cent, the timely provision of inputs, the Fertiliser Input Support Programme (FISP), and expected stable exchange rates and commodity prices, will sustain positive growth in agriculture.

Mining has recovered from the crisis and was expected to show 7.4 per cent growth for 2010. Production is expected to rise 7.5 per cent and 8.5 per cent higher in 2011 and 2012, respectively. Copper production was projected to have increased to 740,000 tonnes in 2010, a level not seen since 1973, and up 8.0 per cent from the 696,900 tonnes in 2009. Much of this growth will have come from the Konkola Copper Mines (KCM) and Lumwana Mines as well as the resumption of production at Luanshya and Bwana Mkubwa mines which were closed during the financial crisis.

With improved copper prices and business environment, the mining sector is expected to grow substantially. Zhonghui Mining Group of China plans to invest more than US$3 billion in Zambia's Copperbelt and North Western Province. There are various other mining projects awaiting an environmental impact assessment. About US$1.0 billion of investment at the Konkola Copper Mines (KCM) aims to increase output of processed copper. KCM plans to spend about US$170 million on a plant with a capacity to process 12 million tonnes of refractory copper ore each year. Vale Mining Company of Brazil and South African-based Rainbow Minerals have jointly agreed to spend more than US$1 billion over five years to develop the Konkola North copper mine on the Copperbelt. The mine is expected to become operational in 2012, with annual output of about 45,000 tonnes which will help reach a nationwide production target of 1 million tonnes by 2013.

New mines will require energy and the government has allocated large amounts of finance for new energy projects such as the 700–800MW Kafue Gorge Lower and the 120MW Itezhi-Tezhi. The Kariba North Bank Extension project, which commenced in 2009, is likely to be completed by 2012. Completion of these projects and other private sector initiatives should increase energy generation capacity by more than 1,000MW a year.

Manufacturing is key to the success of the economy and to creating middle-income jobs. It has particularly benefited from partnerships with emerging economies such as China. Manufacturing was expected to grow by 2.5 per cent in 2010 and the sector is expected to make a big contribution to Zambia's overall growth prospects, reducing dependence on imports with a wider base of locally-produced goods and services. This will depend however on increased agriculture and mining output, and these in turn need stable international commodity prices, exchange rates and climatic conditions.

To revitalise the sector, the government has built infrastructure and made investment easier through the Multi-Facility Economic Zones (MFEZs). At the US$900 million Chambishi economic zone, some 16 manufacturers began operations in 2010. For 2011, it is expected that Chambishi will be producing US$1.5 billion of output per year with an estimated US$600 million of exports and employing up to 6,000 people. Four more economic zones in other parts of the country are planned to open in 2011-13.

Utilities such as electricity, water and gas were expected to grow by 5.9 per cent in 2010. About 5.33 million megawatts (MW) of power were generated in the first half of 2010 compared to 4.98 million MW in the same period of 2009. The increase was mainly due to the completed rehabilitation of generators at Kafue Gorge power station. For 2012 and 2013, growth of about 2.2 per cent is expected.

The government is also constructing new power stations to augment national output and improve supply. Work is ongoing at the Kariba North Bank Extension Project and Kafue Gorge Lower and Itezhi. To increase access to electricity to the vast majority of people in rural areas, authorities have increased funding to the Rural Electrification Authority and approved its programme to build small hydroelectric generators.

Zambia's key construction sector is expected to maintain double-digit growth in the near future, according to the National Council for Construction (NCC). The sector grew by 10 per cent in 2010. Growth is being supported by the new hydro projects, mining developments, housing and

KEY INDICATORS **Zambia**

	Unit	2006	2007	2008	2009	2010
Population	m	*11.87	*11.52	*11.74	*11.97	13.05
Gross domestic product (GDP)	US$bn	10.89	11.40	14.70	12.30	16.20
GDP per capita	US$	917	990	1,248	1,027	1,221
GDP real growth	%	6.2	6.3	5.8	4.5	7.6
Inflation	%	9.0	10.6	12.4	14.0	8.5
Industrial output	% change	6.7	8.3	4.4	34.1	–
Agricultural output	% change	-0.6	0.4	-0.1	21.6	–
Exports (fob) (goods)	US$m	3,375.0	4,593.7	4,961.7	4,319.1	7,413.6
Imports (fob) (goods)	US$m	2,744.0	3,610.6	4,554.3	3,413.4	4,709.9
Balance of trade	US$m	631.0	983.1	407.4	905.7	2,703.7
Current account	US$m	128.0	-755.0	-1,359.7	-703.1	363.1
Total reserves minus gold	US$m	719.7	1,090.0	1,095.6	1,892.1	2,093.8
Foreign exchange	US$m	706.4	1,080.2	1,085.0	1,254.4	1,468.5
Exchange rate	per US$	4,103.80	3,840.00	5,090.00	4,955.00	7,797.10

* estimated figure

commercial property. Sales of domestically produced cement grew by 19.3 per cent in the first half of 2010. The construction boom has seen more cement factories being set up across Zambia. It has also had a spill-over effect in the financial sector with loans and advances at a number of commercial banks rising by 17.3 per cent.

Tourists are also returning as the economic and financial crisis eases. The 2010 FIFA World Cup in South Africa also helped increase bed occupancy rates. The industry saw growth of about 25 per cent in 2010. Preliminary data shows the number of international passengers at Zambia's major airports grew by 17 per cent in the first half of 2010.

The promotion of areas such as the Kafue National Park is expected to boost tourism growth to an annual average of 11.7 per cent in the medium term.

International trade and relations

Zambia's exports are still heavily dependent on copper. The financial crisis slowed demand for Zambian exports and reduced its trade surplus. New partnerships with China and India are expected to restore and increase demand for Zambia's natural resources and guarantee increasing trade surpluses. However, the additional surplus will not cover the deficits in services and income balances. Additional foreign direct investment (FDI) is expected from China which has invested heavily in mining and infrastructure such as hydro-electricity generation projects.

A strategy to make Zambia a middle-income country by 2030 partly involves reducing dependency on aid. However, this will also require substantial economic growth, prudent export diversification and expansion of the domestic revenue base.

Doing business

A good business environment and increased private investment underpinned Zambia's resilience to the financial crisis. The government is committed to accelerating private sector investment to increase and diversify growth. Its Private Sector Development Reform Programme (PSDRP) aims to reduce the cost of doing business and ensure a stable environment for private investment and growth.

To maintain annual economic growth of at least 7.0 per cent still requires a substantial improvement in the business and investment climate. The government's Private Sector Development Programme (PSDP) will focus on improving the business environment and institutions that serve the private sector, including regulations and laws; infrastructure development; business facilitation and economic diversification; trade expansion and economic empowerment.

The private sector reform agencies aim to attack limited credit and its high cost, poor infrastructure, excessive bureaucratic trade procedures, especially at frontiers, lengthy inspection and certification processes, poor technology for border checks and customs techniques, and inadequate skilled personnel. The World Bank's 2011 *Doing Business* report ranked Zambia 76th out of 183 countries.

The government has sought to improve much-criticised public financial management, particularly regarding accountability and transparency. It has published work plans by government agencies and introduced a Treasury Single Account aimed at improving budget execution and management of public finances. The Single Account will help streamline financial management by reducing the hundreds of accounts held at commercial banks. This will reduce unnecessary bank charges. To further improve accountability, the government has increased resources for the ministries responsible for monitoring and evaluating budget execution.

Zambia continues to receive support from donors and international institutions, including the World Bank. The International Finance Corporation (IFC) of the World Bank Group has pledged about US$115 million to support Zambia's long-term growth and diversification away from mining. A large amount will go to the agricultural sector for irrigation. The IFC has also been working closely with Zambia's public and private sector, supporting efforts to increase the ease of doing business, strengthening the private sector and diversifying the economy.

International relations

Zambia, like other African nations, has strengthened co-operation with China, India and Brazil, in line with the shift in global economic power. The change can be seen particularly in infrastructure, mining, manufacturing, and agriculture.

While African nations prefer South-South co-operation for development partnership building, Africa sees the traditional economic giants and the emerging powers as having the same interests: access to the continent's vast energy and raw material resources.

Zambia's exports to the emerging economies are dominated by unprocessed primary products, particularly minerals such as copper. Levels of FDI from emerging economies have significantly increased however compared to those from developed countries.

Zambia has increased co-operation with China since 2005, particularly in mining and commodities. Mining is Zambia's economic backbone and accounts for about 70 per cent of its foreign exchange earnings. However with the global crisis, revenue from copper sales dropped to US$2.9 billion in 2009 from US$3.6 billion in 2008, an 18 per cent decline.

During the crisis, investors from developed countries closed or scaled down mining operations in Zambia, which badly hit the economy and opened the door to players from China, Brazil and India who stepped in to reopen some major mines and manufacturing projects. China's Non-Ferrous Metal Mining Company (NFC) won a contract to reopen the Luanshya Copper Mines – and re-employ about 1,700 miners. In 2009, China invested more than US$400 million in Zambia's mining industry. In addition, Chinese concerns own at least three mining operations, including a new 150,000 tonne-a-year copper smelter for new mines in north-west Zambia. Despite these positive developments, there are mixed views regarding China's interest in Zambia's mining industry.

Zambia and India have also strengthened economic ties. In 2010, India offered lines of credit amounting to US$125 million and the Exim Bank of India and Zambian government signed an agreement on a US$50 million concessional loan for the Itezhi-Tezhi hydro-power project which will generate about 120MW of power. Another US$75 million loan has been extended over two years for health, education and other social sectors.

Combating poverty

The Zambian government has put a high priority on social investment to reduce poverty. About 85 per cent of people in rural areas and 34 per cent in urban districts live below the poverty line. About 64 per cent of the population of more than 13.5 million people live on less than one dollar a day.

Fifty per cent of the 2011 budget was allocated to social spending and infrastructure – both with the aim of combating poverty. The 2010 budget statement said spending will increase on health, education, water and sanitation. With government intervention, access to health services has significantly improved. There are fewer cases of malaria and maternal, infant and child mortality rates have dropped along with HIV/Aids prevalence. It is likely that 2011 expenditure will be lower than 2009–10 due to a fall in aid from developed countries as a result of the financial crisis. The government may struggle to keep up with the good intentions it has expressed.

To help Zambians living below the poverty line, the government in 2010 implemented new tax bands, increasing the minimum monthly salary for which tax must be paid from K700,000 (US$145) to K800,000 (US$166) . It is expected that this measure will give households an extra K85 billion (US$17.6 million) in purchasing power. The threshold will be increased to K1,000,000 (US$207) a month in the 2011 budget.

Risk assessment

Economy	Fair
Politics	Good
Regional stability	Fair

COUNTRY PROFILE

Historical profile

1851 British missionary David Livingstone visited central Africa.
1880s British settlers followed Livingstone and the British South Africa Company, headed by British imperialist and financier, Cecil John Rhodes, opened its first copper mine at Broken Hill (later Kabwe) in 1908.
1924 The colony was put under direct British rule.
1953–63 Northern Rhodesia (later Zambia) was part of the British-sponsored Federation of Rhodesia and Nyasaland.
1960 The United National Independence Party (UNIP) was formed by Kenneth Kaunda to campaign for independence and the dissolution of white minority rule.
1964 Zambia gained independence under the presidency of Kenneth Kaunda. The government supported Marxist rebels in Mozambique, independence movements in Rhodesia (later Zimbabwe) and the African National Congress (ANC) in South Africa. This led to internal security problems and financial difficulties as Zambia's colonial neighbours attempted to destabilise the country.
1964–1970s Key enterprises and land were nationalised.
1972 Zambia became a one-party state with UNIP as the only legal party.
1975 The Tanzania-Zambia Railway Authority (Tazara) open the rail line linking the Zambian Copperbelt to the Tanzanian port of Dar es Salaam, reducing the country's dependence on Rhodesia and South Africa for port access.
1976 Zambia gave support to Rhodesia's bid for independence and its eventual transformation from white minority rule into Zimbabwe.
1989 Zambia began a programme of austerity measures to stabilise the economy, following a long-term fall in the price of Zambia's chief export, copper.
1990 Food riots heightened calls for an end to one-party rule.
1991 Multi-party elections were held in which Kaunda was defeated by Frederick Chiluba and the Movement for Multi-party Democracy (MMD).
1996 The MMD and President Chiluba were re-elected in a landslide victory.
1999 Angolan terrorists attacked sites in Lusaka and the Indeni Oil Refinery in Ndola was sabotaged.
2000 Kaunda resigned as leader of UNIP.
2001 The MMD was re-elected although the opposition said the elections were flawed.
2002 Levy Mwanawasa (MMD) was inaugurated as president. The government excluded genetically modified (GM) maize from its accepted imported foodstuffs.
2003 Former president Frederick Chiluba's immunity from prosecution was removed and he was arrested and charged on 59 counts, including corruption and abuse of office.
2004 The court case against Chiluba was dropped but he was quickly re-arrested and charged with embezzling US$488,000 from state funds.
2005 The World Bank approved a US$3.8 billion debt relief package, which wrote off over 50 per cent of Zambia's debt. The International Monetary Fund (IMF) and Japanese government also cancelled outstanding debt worth around US$577 million and US$692 million respectively. President Mwanawasa appealed for food for millions of Zambian citizens as drought caused widespread hunger.
2006 The government announced that as a result of the US$4 billion of debt relief, healthcare for people living in the rural areas would be provided free of charge. In presidential elections incumbent Levy Mwanawasa (MMD) won with 43.0 per cent of the vote. In parliamentary elections, the MMD won 72 out of 150 directly elected seats. It was announced that the first deposits of oil and gas had been found in the border region with Angola (Africa's second largest oil producer).
2007 A large mining investment zone was inaugurated by Chinese President Hu Jintao. The UK High Court ruled that former president Chiluba had conspired, along with four aides, to defraud Zambia of around US$46 million.
2008 President Mwanawasa died in France, following specialist treatment for a stroke. Vice President Rupiah Banda became interim president until elections could take place. There was no obvious successor; Mwanawasa was reported to have said that the next president should come from a different province from previous presidents Kaunda (Northern), Chiluba (Luapula) and himself (Central), although his wife, Maureen, was said to be 'considering her position'. In the presidential elections, Rupiah Banda (MMD) won with 40.1 per cent of the vote, while Michael Sata (PF), the closest contender won 38.1 per cent. President Banda was sworn into office (on 3 November) until 2011, when former President Mwanawasa's term would have ended.
2009 The government began to liquidate the dept owed to the Co-operative Bank (closed in the 1990s) of US$23 million, of which around US$11.5 million had been paid to the Zambia Co-operative Federation supporting farming investment. Ten Chinese companies committed US$600 million in the Chambishi economic and trade co-operation zone (particularly in mining, construction and steel production). The ministry of finance released US$31.4 million to build sealed roads, mainly from Leopards Hill to Chainda and Ibex Hill. Former president Frederick Chiluba was acquitted of all charges of corruption. The IMF agreed to the immediate disbursement of US$81.2 million as part of the Poverty Reduction and Growth Facility (PRGF) arrangement; the total amount of disbursement approved was US$329.7 million.
2010 In January, around 30,000 small-scale farming households, mostly headed by women, were eligible for a US$20 million loan from the International Fund for Agricultural Development (Ifad). The programme focused on stimulating rural economic development through small-scale production. On 16 June, the Global Fund suspended operations in Zambia due to fraud and the Zambian authorities failure to take appropriate action to safeguard Global Fund grant programmes. A railway line between Zambia and Malawi was inaugurated in August. The Chipata-Mchinji railway line will be extended to Mozambique.
2011 Reuters reported in January that Chinese investment in 2010 exceeded US$1 billion and created over 15,000 jobs. Zambia's first democratically elected president, Frederick Chiluba, died on 18 June at the age of 68. On 9 August the Supreme Court dismissed an opposition claim that President Banda's father had been born in Malawi, which would have made his re-election bid unconstitutional. Presidential elections were held on 20 September in which three candidates took part. Michael Sata (Patriotic Front) (PF) won 43 per cent of the vote; incumbent,

Rupiah Banda (MMD) won 36.1 per cent and Hakainde Hichilema (UPND) 18 per cent. Michael Sata took office as President on 23 September. In a move to reassure foreign investors, President Sata's first official appointment after being sworn in was with the Chinese ambassador. He warned that while he welcomed Chinese companies, they must comply with Zambian law. In parliamentary elections held on 21 September, the opposition PF won 38.25 per cent of the vote, (60 seats out of 150), ousting the MMD from its 20-years in office. President Sato's administration took office on 29 September; Guy Scott, a white parliamentarian, was appointed vice president.

Political structure

Constitution

In November 1991, Zambia's one-party state was replaced by a multi-party democratic system based on a new constitution. In 1995 the ruling Movement for Multi-party Democracy (MMD) revised the constitution. The Zambia Law Association criticised the new constitution on the grounds that it allows parliament to make retrospective laws and that a president could be elected on receiving the highest number of votes cast even if these amounted to less than 50 per cent. It also condemned amendments to the Bill of Rights of the 1991 Constitution without a referendum. A controversial Bill passed by President Chiluba on 28 May 1996 made further amendments to the constitution: future presidential candidates must be second-generation Zambians.

Independence date

24 October 1964 (from UK)

Form of state

Republic

The executive

Executive power is held by the president elected by universal suffrage for a five-year term. The constitution provides for a cabinet appointed from within parliament and gives it extra powers. The president does not have the right to declare martial law. The president must obtain parliamentary approval to impose a state of emergency longer than seven days.

National legislature

The unicameral National Assembly has 158 members in total; 150 are elected by popular vote in single seat constituencies and eight members are appointed by the president, all serve for five-year terms.

Legal system

The president appoints judges and nominates the chief justice. Courts include the Supreme Court of Zambia and the High Court.

Last elections

20 September 2011 (presidential); 23 September 2011 (parliamentary)

Results: Presidential: Michael Sata (Patriotic Front) (PF) won 43 per cent of the vote; Rupiah Banda (MMD) 36.1 per cent and Hakainde Hichilema (UPND) 18 per cent.

Parliamentary: the Patriotic Front (PF) won 38.25 per cent of the vote, (60 seats out of 150), Movement for Multi-party Democracy (MMD) 33.56 per cent (55), United Party for National Development (UPND) 16.99 per cent (28), Alliance for Democracy and Development (ADD) 1.18 per cent (one), Forum for Democracy and Development (FDD) 0.75 per cent (one); three independent candidates each won a seat and 15 other political parties failed to win any seats. Turnout was 53.98 per cent. Two seats remained vacant, pending by-elections.

Eight additional parliamentary members were appointed by the president, to make a total of 158 members of parliament (MP).

Next elections

2016 (presidential and legislative)

Political parties

Ruling party

To be announced

Main opposition party

Movement for Multi-party Democracy (MMD)

Population

13.05 million (2010; census figure)

Last census: October 2000: 9,885,591

Population density: 13 inhabitants per square km. Urban population: 40 per cent.

Annual growth rate: 2.1 per cent 1994–2004 (WHO 2006)

Ethnic make-up

There are 73 ethnic groups in Zambia. The largest single group, comprising 34 per cent of the population, is the Bemba (north-east and Copperbelt areas). Other important groups include the Tonga of the southern province with 16 per cent of the population; the Nyanja of the eastern provinces (14 per cent) who are well represented in the capital, Lusaka; and the Lozi (9 per cent) of the west.

The European population live and work mostly in the urban areas, or on the farmlands along the railway lines. A high proportion of the Asian community is to be found on the Copperbelt and other urban centres.

Religions

Christian, Muslim and indigenous beliefs. Approximately 70 per cent of the population is Christian (mainly Roman Catholic and Protestant).

Education

The HIV/Aids crisis in sub-Saharan Africa has not only undermined public investment in education but has also contributed to the shortage of trained teachers, in 2001 815 primary school teachers, or 45 per cent of teachers trained that year, died of Aids. This has resulted in declining literacy rates and low levels of school enrolment. Enrolment rates for the richest households are more than one-third higher than for the poorest households.

A first cycle primary education begins at age seven, lasting until age 11, then three years in a second cycle primary school prepares children for exams to determine progression to a junior secondary school for two years until aged 16 when successfully completed exams allow progression into senior secondary school for the last two years. There are two universities that provide higher education and several specialist institutions providing professional and vocational training.

The government has developed a strong education sector reform through the Basic Education Sub-sector Investment Programme (Bessip), which has set a target of universal primary school enrolment for just under half a million children by 2005. Annual government expenditure during the first phase of the reform amounted to US$56 million, excluding contributions from international donors for the projects. The scheme aims to construct 2,000 additional classrooms and improve training in rural schools. Zambia spends typically less than 3 per cent of GDP on education.

Literacy rate: 80 per cent adult rate; 89 per cent youth rate (15–24) (Unesco 2005).

Compulsory years: Seven to 13.

Enrolment rate: 89 per cent gross primary enrolment; 27 per cent gross secondary enrolment, of relevant age groups (including repeaters) (World Bank).

Pupils per teacher: 39 in primary schools.

Health

Healthcare is provided free in state-funded hospitals and commercially in private sector clinics. Rural health care is rudimentary and frequently provided only by missionary hospitals and clinics. State funding cut-backs have led to severe shortages of medical equipment and staff. Many medical posts are unfilled for lack of funds. The government is keen to encourage private investment in hospitals and believes foreign investment provides the key to the redevelopment of the health sector.

Improved water sources are available to 64 per cent of the population.

HIV/Aids

Zambia has one of the highest rates of HIV in Africa. It is estimated that 42 per cent of hospital beds are occupied by

HIV/Aids sufferers. The World Bank reported that the Aids epidemic would radically reduce the rate of population growth; it fell from 2.8 per cent annually in 1990–97 to 1.5 per cent in 2003.
The impact on households is severe, with children often kept from attending school in order to help with harvesting of subsistence crops. Studies show that around 55 per cent of households affected by HIV/Aids are unable to pay school fees. Households affected by HIV/Aids have on average 30–35 per cent less income than those who are not affected. Around 60 per cent of families of Aids sufferers endure food shortages and malnutrition as a direct result of the disease.
Nationally HIV/Aids also poses a significant economic threat, with a projected annual loss in GDP growth per capita of 1.15 per cent forecast for the period 2000–10. Government spending on intervention plans was budgeted at US$560 million between 2002–05, of which US$88 million was allocated to antiretroviral treatment and US$126 million to hospital treatment. Zambia, as one of the poorest countries in the world, has been identified as in need of international aid to fight the disease.
A disturbing aspect of the disease that has been identified since 2001 is the gender disparity that has developed. Whereas the highest risk group was previously sexually active males, now women in general and young women in particular lead the male rates — by over 10 per cent in urban areas and over 5 per cent in rural areas. A UN taskforce studying this shift in the demographics has identified socio-economic forces that have left females vulnerable to the disease.
HIV prevalence: 15.6 per cent aged 15–49 in 2003 (World Bank)
Life expectancy: 40 years, 2004 (WHO 2006)
Fertility rate/Maternal mortality rate: 5.5 births per woman, 2004 (WHO 2006); maternal mortality 6.5 per l,000 (World Bank).
Child (under 5 years) mortality rate (per 1,000): 102 per 1,000 live births; 28.1 per cent of children aged under 5 arre malnourished (World Bank).
Head of population per physician: 0.12 physicians per 1,000 people, 2004 (WHO 2006)

Welfare
Zambia is one of the poorest countries in the world, with an estimated 80 per cent of its 11 million people living in desperate poverty. In December 2003 the statistics office stated that 'the food basket... was K528,529 for a family of six. The same family on average was expected to live on K758,961 for all their basic needs'.
The government provides some basic welfare for pensioners, children and people affected by disasters.
The Pension Scheme Regulation Act of 1996 provides a regulatory framework for private pension schemes. The Zambia National Provident Fund (ZNPF) was successfully transformed into the National Pension Scheme Authority (Napsa) in early 2000. The weaknesses of ZNPF, which included poor benefits, delays in payment and ineffective record keeping were critically examined to overcome similar problems for the Napsa. The economic difficulties in Zambia and the low retirement age of 55 made it necessary for Napsa to begin with modest benefits. The scheme offers three principal benefits namely retirement, invalidity and survivors' benefits. Additionally, it provides a funeral grant.
The scheme is based on the principle of social insurance and requires compulsory financial contributions from both employees and their employers at a rate of 5 per cent each. Retirement benefit is paid on the basis of a minimum contributory period of 15 years. The scheme is basic to allow the development of private occupational pension schemes.

Main cities
Lusaka (capital, estimated population 1.3 million in 2004), Ndola (349,300), Kitwe (306,200), Kabwe (219,600), Chingola (151,100), Mufulira (131,500), Luanshya (125,300), Livingstone (111,200).

Languages spoken
English is the usual medium for business. There are 73 identified African languages, all Bantu, of which a number are recognised as official vernaculars – Chitumbuka-Chisenga, Tonga, Silozi, IciBemba, Kaonde, Luvale, Lunda and Chinyanja. Zambian traders usually have a working knowledge of English.
Official language/s
English

Media
Freedom of the press is constrained by legal provisions, which have led to self-censorship.
Press
Since 1996 readership has been falling and prices have risen by 500 per cent so that newspapers have become a luxury item for most Zambians. Most newspapers are distributed in the capital and Copperbelt towns, while the rest of the country receives copies 1–3 days after publication.
Dailies: The government owns two newspapers, *Times of Zambia* (www.times.co.zm) and *Zambia Daily Mail* (www.daily-mail.co.zm); *The Post* (www.postzambia.com) is privately owned.
Weeklies: Dailies publish Sunday papers including *Sunday Mail* and *Sunday Times;* independent publications include *The Monitor* and *National Mirror* (church owned).
Business: Publications include *The Lusaka Times* (www.lusakatimes.com) and the *Zambia Daily Mail* have sections on business and the economy. Periodicals include *The Zambian Marketer* and *Development Zambia* published by (www.langmead.com).
Periodicals: Langmead and Baker (www.langmead.com) publishes several magazines aimed at various special interest groups.
Broadcasting
The state-run Zambia National Broadcasting Corporation (ZNBC) is the dominant organisation in broadcasting.
Radio: ZNBC has four networks with two broadcasting in English, one in local languages and the fourth which carries commercials.
Radio Phoenix (www.radiophoenix.co.zm) is a national commercial radio network; there are a number of local commercial radio stations in operation including Q-FM and Mazabuka Community Radio and Breeze FM (www.breezefm.makeni.net). There are several religious content radio stations.
Television: ZNBC operates the only public terrestrial network with one channel. There is no Zambian based satellite operation, although the MultiChoice Zambia services can be received from South Africa.
News agencies
National news agency: Zambia News Agency

Economy
Zambia's wealth is generated by the primary industries of agriculture and mining. Its main economic zone follows the line of rail southwards from the Copperbelt around Ndola and Kitwe, through Lusaka, the capital, to Livingstone on the border with Zimbabwe. This area has been subject to urbanisation, although the rest of the country is relatively sparsely inhabited. Of the projected US$6.85 billion of total exports in 2010, US$5.46 was earned through copper ore exports. Despite the fall in volume of ore exported, high world prices (41 per cent higher in 2010 than in 2009) ensured record sales which presented Zambia with a trade balance of US$2.12 billion (up from US$906 million in 2009). Other minerals include cobalt, nickel and uranium, coal, gold, silver and emeralds. Industry constitutes around 35 per cent of GDP, of which manufacturing accounts for 10 per cent. Around 60 per cent of the population live rural lives, earning a livelihood from working on the

land. The majority of farms are small-scale with low productivity, leading to food insecurity. Maize is the staple diet and when weather provides the optimum rainfall bumper harvests are attainable. However Zambia is subject to droughts and flooding. Cash crops include coffee, tea, cotton, rice, groundnuts, tobacco, sugarcane and cut flowers. The government is investing in the agricultural sector to improve soil, seeds (including genetically modified) and equipment to increase productivity. Agriculture constitutes around 20 per cent of GDP and the service sector 45 per cent.

GDP growth has remained at around 6.2 per cent per annum since 2006 and only in 2008 did growth fall to 5.7 per cent with this attributed to record high world food prices and the change in government following a presidential election. Since 2008 growth has recovered and was projected to be 6.6 per cent in 2010, rising slightly to 6.8 per cent in 2011.

In the medium-term GDP growth is expected to be led by copper production as the Luanshya Copper Mine is due to re-open in 2011 and infrastructure projects and increased electricity generation provides greater capacity.

The government began economic reforms in 2005, including diversification, to reduce the country's reliance on copper, as the International Monetary Fund (IMF) and World Bank provided large debt relief services to Zambia.

Full donor support and free market reform have had little impact on poverty and per capita income remains low, having only risen from US$947 in 2006 to US$1,286 by 2010 despite the strength of the economy. In the 2010, the UN Human Development Index ranked Zambia as 150 (out of 169 countries) for national development in health, education and income, which was equal to the average for sub-Saharan Africa. The intensity of deprivation was 51.1 per cent; however statistics on the level of poverty were unavailable. Unemployment is a significant problem with half the population either unemployed or underemployed. Remittances in 2009 were US$68 million (0.5 per cent of GDP), which was estimated to have risen to US$71 million in 2010.

External trade

Zambia is a member of the Common Market for Eastern and Southern Africa (Comesa), and operates a free trade area with 13 of the 19 member states. It is also a member of the Southern African Development Community (SADC), the objectives of which include reducing trade barriers, achieving regional development and economic growth and evolving common systems and institutions. In 2009 international donors pledged US$1 billion to upgrade transport links across eastern and southern Africa, in an initiative to carry goods to market cheaper and faster. Not only will roads and rail links be improved, but also time-consuming official procedures will be streamlined for efficiency.

There are valuable reserves in minerals including copper, lead, zinc, cobalt and gemstones. Agricultural products are also important exports along with electricity.

Imports

Principal imports are petroleum and derivatives, capital machinery, electricity, fertiliser, foodstuffs and clothing.

Main sources: South Africa (typically 40 per cent of total), Democratic Republic of Congo (13 per cent), Kuwait (11 per cent).

Exports

Principal exports are copper, cobalt, electricity, maize, tea, cotton, rice, groundnuts, tobacco, sugarcane, vegetables, flowers and cotton.

Main destinations: Switzerland (typically 47 per cent of total), China (11.0 per cent), South Africa (9 per cent).

Agriculture

Farming

About 10 per cent of Zambia's 600 million hectares is arable land but only around 30 million hectares are under cultivation. There are more than 300,000 smallholders, mostly subsistence farmers, earning cash from growing mainly cotton and tobacco. About 500 highly mechanised commercial farms and estates account for 40 per cent of marketed crops and animal produce. The country has abundant perennial and underground water resources. Power generated by hydroelectric installations has been extended to some farming areas. In the wetter northern part of the country, tea and coffee thrive at the higher altitudes, with maize and millet at lower levels. The climate of the central province suits maize, soya beans, cotton and tobacco. The south and west are drier and suit sorghum, tobacco, cotton and groundnuts.

Agriculture accounts for approximately 21 per cent of GDP. Most state-run farms have been privatised. One problem that the industry faces is that much of the land is under tribal authority and difficult to access. In order to tackle this problem, the government has set up areas of virgin land, such as the Tazara Corridor Services (Tazcor), which are open for investment.

Government policy has long been to achieve self-sufficiency in food production, increase exports and improve the supply of inputs to peasant farmers. Measures have included a wide range of production incentives, comprising preferential tax and loan rates, the encouragement of foreign investment and improvements in producer prices. The 2004 budget included a proposal to give away land to local and foreign investors.

Official policy has also encouraged new crops for export which include coffee, flowers and exotic vegetables for European markets. In contrast to these successful new crops, cashew nut production has failed to penetrate European markets. Regional integration means that farmers are finding foreign competition difficult as high production costs, high taxation levels and cheap imports continue to undermine their competitiveness. The country is marginally self-sufficient in food with maize surpluses in times of good weather.

The shutdown of air travel in Europe in April 2010, caused by the Icelandic volcanic ash cloud, resulted in the horticultural sector losing around US$150,000 per day over the six-day period of closure, as flowers and vegetables had to be discarded. V

Fishing

Annual commercial fish production is estimated at 70,000 tonnes. The sector suffers due to infrastructural difficulties, including lack of input supply, such as nets and boats, poor transport and storage facilities. The private sector has stepped up investment in fish marketing and distribution, fish farming and manufacturing of nets and boats.

The Department of Fisheries in Zambia and the Department of National Parks and Wildlife Management in Zimbabwe, with the co-operation of Norway and Denmark, have undertaken a project to facilitate the sustainable utilisation of the shared fisheries resources on Lake Kariba.

Forestry

Forest and other wooded land accounts for 42 per cent and 37 per cent of the total land area respectively. Although nearly half of Zambia's land area is covered by forest, there are only a few commercially exploitable tree species. It is estimated that forests cover some 31.2 million hectares (ha), with most being open savannah woodlands and *miombo* woodland comprising around 80 per cent of the country's vegetation. There are large networks of protected areas constituting 32 per cent of the forests with around 20 national parks and more than 30 game management areas.

Charcoal is a significant cooking and heating fuel in rural areas but, in some regions, woodland has been ravaged and a severe shortage of charcoal is expected unless there is government sponsored replanting. There is some export of sawn timber, while most of the demand for paper products is met by imports.

Industry and manufacturing

Macroeconomic stabilisation and divestiture of state assets has led to a severe

contraction in these sectors of the economy. The government is no longer willing to subsidise the industrial and manufacturing sector. This change contrasts vividly with policy in the 1960s and 1970s whereby vast copper profits were used to establish one of the largest parastatal economies in Africa.
Targetted sectors for development include agriculture-derived processed products and non-traditional exports such as textiles, chemicals and engineering products.

Tourism

Tourism is a growing sector, although Infrastructure remains underdeveloped, including air connections. The cost of air fuel is a serious problem. Nevertheless, visitor numbers continue to grow, rising to over 500,000 per year. The collapse of neighbouring Zimbabwe's tourist industry has benefitted the Zambian tourism, as visitors discover that the Victoria Falls can be viewed from the Zambian side. The government recognises the sector's importance and is aiming to attract a million visitors annually from 2010.

Mining

Zambia has enormous mineral wealth, with major deposits of copper, cobalt, lead, zinc, emeralds, aquamarine, amethyst and tourmaline. It also has small reserves of selenium, manganese, tin, nickel, iron, gold, silver and diamonds.
The mining sector contributes around a fifth of GDP, is Zambia's paramount employer, directly employing 50,000 workers (around 10 per cent of the workforce).
Copper and its by-products, mostly cobalt, account for around 90 per cent of mining production and mining exports.
Zambia is also the second largest producer of cobalt (8,165 tonnes in 2004) after the Democratic Republic of Congo (DRC) (9,979 tons in 2004) and has one of the world's largest reserves. Substantial amounts of cobalt can be recovered from the copper slag heaps, for which Canada's Colossus Resources obtained a 25-year contract with the Zambia Consolidated Copper Mines (ZCCM) signed in 2000. The Nkana and Mufulira cobalt mines and refineries produce 1,800 tonnes per year (tpy) of cobalt. The Nkana and Nchanga mines produce more than half of Zambia's copper and 70 per cent of its cobalt.
In 2002, Anglo American decided to formally quit its mining operations at the Konkola Copper Mines (KCM), which sought a new strategic equity partner. Anglo American's withdrawal followed nine years of negotiations over the privatisation of the mines and two years of operation. The decision was prompted by the drop in KCM's assets and high running costs (including US$350 million expenditure on upgrading facilities), while world metal prices were at the time low. The government pledged to keep the mines open and finally in 2004 a formal agreement with Vedanta Resources Plc was announced whereby Vedanta Resources acquired a 51 per cent controlling stake in KCM for US$48.2 million in cash. Vedanta plans to expand production from the current (2005) 2 million tonnes per year (tpy) to 6 million tpy.
There is very little mining activity outside the Copperbelt although base metal exploration has continued in other regions. Zambia is prospecting for chromium, nickel, tin, tantalite and iron ore. The government allows private sector purchase and export of gemstones. Mining companies can retain 50 per cent of foreign exchange earnings.
Zambia contains approximately a quarter of the world's gem emeralds and accounts for an estimated 20 per cent of output of rough emeralds. Other gemstones mined on a smaller scale include amethysts in the Southern Province near Lake Kariba and Kalomo. Deposits of aquamarine and tourmaline are mined for the jewellery trade. Production of gemstones is estimated to be worth US$200 million annually.
The steep fall in global copper prices from US$9,000 per 8,165 tonnes in 2008 to US$3,000 in March 2009, brought mine shutdowns in the Copperbelt, leaving thousands of miners unemployed.

Hydrocarbons

There are no known oil or gas reserves and Zambia is dependent on imported fuel supplies. Petroleum imports in 2008 were 16,000 barrels per day (bpd). The 1,710km Tazama pipeline from Dar es Salaam, Tanzania, supplies oil to the Indeni refinery at Ndola, which has a capacity of 24,000bpd.
Zambia does not import natural gas.
Proven coal reserves were around 78.2 million tonnes in 2008. Zambia's major coal supplier, Maamba Collieries, used to produce 600,000 tonnes per annum in the 1980s but output has been severely cut due to undercapitalisation. Zambia uses coal in the mining transformation process. All coal produced is consumed and fulfils all domestic demand.

Energy

Total installed generating capacity was 1.64 gigawatts (GW) in 2007, producing around 9.3 billion kilowatt hours.
Hydropower provides virtually all domestic energy, mostly from plants at Kafue Gorge, Kariba North and Livingstone.
The parastatal, Zambian Electricity Supply Company (Zesco), generates, transmits and distributes electricity, with continued responsibility of connecting districts to the national grid. Demand for electricity is expected to grow to 2.5GW by 2013.
The mining industry consumes around 70 per cent of all energy generated; only 10 per cent of the population has access to electricity. New owners of the Maamba Collieries are contracted to build a new 350MW thermal power station.
Zambia also owns the Central African Power Corporation (CAPC) with Zimbabwe. CAPC operates the two Kariba power stations. The country exports energy under the Southern African Development Community (SADC) agreement to Zimbabwe, Botswana, Namibia and Tanzania and is connected to the Democratic Republic of Congo (DRC) (from which Zambia also imported electricity) and South Africa.
The World Bank has agreed to lend Zambia US$75.5 million to boost generation. Contracts for the planned Itezhi-tezhi hydropower plant, on the Kafue River in the southern province, which will have a capacity of 120 megawatts, were let in 2008.

Financial markets

Stock exchange

Lusaka Stock Exchange (LuSE)

Banking and insurance

Zambia's banking sector has undergone a period of crisis and change. The liberalisation of the economy during the 1990s gave rise to the launch of a number of banks. Poor management and over-banking led to the closure of a number of these banks, prompting a wave of concern among investors and depositors who lost money.
In March 2003 the government first directed the Zambia Privatisation Agency (ZPA) to privatise the main state owned commercial bank, Zambia National Commercial Bank. 49 per cent of its shares were to be sold to a qualified investor with management rights, 25.8 per cent were to be offered to the Zambian public through the Zambia Privatisation Trust Fund (ZPTF), 25 per cent were to be retained by the government and the existing minority shareholders, who held 0.2 per cent, were to retain their shares. The ZPA called for tenders to be received by 2005.
The largest commercial banks, Barclays Bank of Zambia and Standard Chartered Bank Zambia, are foreign-owned. However, since January 1972 all foreign-owned banks have been required to incorporate locally.
There are several state-owned development banks and other private financial institutions. The Development Bank of Zambia offers medium- and long-term loans and business consultancy services.The Agricultural Finance Company and Zambia Agricultural Development Bank were merged and

renamed the Lima Bank. The government-owned Zambia State Insurance Corporation (ZSIC) is the major insurance company in Zambia. Other development banks include the state-owned Zambia National Building Society.

Central bank

Bank of Zambia

Main financial centre

Lusaka

Time

GMT plus two hours

Geography

Zambia is landlocked, bordered to the south by Zimbabwe and the Caprivi Strip (an extension of Namibia); to the south-east by Mozambique; to the east by Malawi; to the north-east by Tanzania; to the north and north-west by the Democratic Republic of Congo (DRC); and to the west by Angola.

About nine-tenths of the country is a high rolling plateau (900–1,200 metres above sea level) covered by savannah bush and woodland. The only relief from the monotony of the plateau is the Zambezi and Luangwa rift system. The Luapula River, part of the Congo River system, cuts into the northern part of the plateau.

Zambia takes its name from the Zambezi River. At 2,655km long, this is the third longest river in Africa.

Hemisphere

Southern

Climate

Altitude governs Zambia's climate and it is generally cooler than its neighbours. There are three distinct seasons: cool and dry from May to August; hot and dry from September to October; and rainy from November to April. Rainfall varies widely across the country. The average temperature is 16 degrees Celsius (C) in the winter and 24 degrees C in summer.

The Zambezi and Luangwa river valleys can remain hot and humid all year, typical of tropical lowlands. They are particularly uncomfortable in the rainy season.

Dress codes

The contrast between morning, midday and evening temperatures means that a sweater is often required in the early morning and after sunset between April and September. A light raincoat or umbrella is useful during the wet season from November to April.

Dress is generally informal. Lightweight suits can be worn for most of the year; during the hot season tropical suits are preferable. Tailored safari suits are popular. A hat and sunglasses are useful for protection against the sun.

Most women wear cotton or other lightweight dresses during the day and evening. Warm dresses and lightweight coats are needed during the coldest season, June to August.

Entry requirements

Passports

Required by all; it must be valid for six months beyond the date of stay and with sufficient space for a visa.

Visa

Required by all, exceptions include those listed on the *Visa Application Instructions* (items 4 and 5) and for tourist visits only, see www.zambiaembassy.org. Tourist visas can be obtained at all border crossings, fees will be levied in cash, usually sterling or dollars (exact amounts as change may not be available).

All business visits require a visa, obtained in advance. Applications should include an invitation from a local company or organisation giving brief details of the nature of business, a full itinerary and proof of onward/return passage.

Currency advice/regulations

The import and export of local currency is limited to K100. The import of foreign currency is unlimited but must be declared, and bank notes with denominations over US$5,000 (or equivalent) must be recorded with customs; export is limited to the amount declared. Retain all official currency exchange forms and receipts (they are also necessary for purchase of domestic airline tickets). Use only authorised banks and *bureaux de change* for currency conversions.

Travellers cheques, in major currencies, are widely accepted.

Health (for visitors)

Mandatory precautions

A yellow fever vacination required. A cholera vaccination certificate is required if arriving from an infected area.

Advisable precautions

Vaccinations for diphtheria, tetanus, polio, hepatitis A and typhoid are recommended. Other vaccinations that may be appropriate are tuberculosis, hepatitis B, meningitis, cholera and yellow fever (if travelling to the remote border region with DRC and Angola).

A malignant malaria is present (*falciparum*, which is resistant to chloroquine) from November to May throughout the country and all year in the Zambezi valley. Use malaria prophylaxis including mosquito repellents, sleeping nets and clothing that fully cover the body after dark. Rabies is a risk. Bilharzia is present, use only well-maintained and chlorinated swimming pools. HIV/Aids is prevalent.

All water for drinking, brushing teeth or making ice should be sterilised when outside of the main cities. Bottled water is available. Milk is pasteurised and therefore safe. Vegetables should be cooked and fruit peeled.

Take all prescription medicines; ensure that medical insurance includes evacuation.

Hotels

Several good quality hotels are available. Hotels are graded from one to five stars by the Hotels Board. A service charge of 10 per cent, plus 10 per cent sales tax are added to all bills. Room charges must be settled in foreign currency. Some hotels require a deposit to cover the room rate and an element for food and drink to be converted to Kwacha on arrival. Tipping is not customary in Zambia but is acceptable.

Credit cards

Major credit cards are accepted in most hotels and tourist facilities. ATMs exist in larger branches in city centres only.

Public holidays (national)

Fixed dates

1 Jan (New Year's Day), 12 Mar (Youth Day), 1 May (Labour Day), 25 May (African Day), 24 Oct (Independence Day), 25 Dec (Christmas Day).

Holidays that fall on the weekend are taken on Monday.

Variable dates

Good Friday and Easter Monday (Mar/Apr), Heroes' Day and Unity Day (first Mon and Tue of Jul), Farmers' Day (first Mon of Aug).

Working hours

Banking

Mon–Fri: 0815–1430. Some larger branches open 0816–1030 on first and last Sat of month.

Business

Mon–Fri: 0800–1230, 1400–1630.

Government

Mon–Fri: 0800–1300, 1400–1700.

Shops

Privately owned: Mon–Fri: 0800–1700, Sat: 0800–1300; state-owned: Mon–Sat: 0800–1800, Sun: 0800–1200.

Note: There are wide variations outside city centres.

Telecommunications

Mobile/cell phones

There are 900 GSM services available in large towns and cities.

Electricity supply

230V AC

Social customs/useful tips

Visitors normally entertain business guests in hotels or restaurants, while residents prefer to entertain informally at home or at their clubs. Temporary membership of clubs can normally be obtained on an introduction from friends.

Security
The stealing of cheques has become a problem in Zambia. Visitors are advised to carry travellers' cheques in small denominations and to cash only sufficient for current needs. There has also been a rise in violent crime due to the economic decline and care must be taken when travelling after dark. It is not regarded as advisable to travel by car between Lusaka and the Copperbelt after dark.

Getting there
Air
International airport/s: Lusaka International (LUN), 26km from city; duty-free shop, bar, restaurant, bank, shops, car hire; Livingstone International Airport (LVI).
Airport tax: International departures: US$25, in cash, excluding transit passengers. Domestic departures: K12,000.
Surface
Road: There are tarred roads from Zimbabwe, Botswana, Namibia (Caprivi Strip), Democratic Republic of Congo (DRC), Tanzania and Malawi; motorists should check border post hours, and regulations concerning their vehicles. A customs bond may be required for the import of cars.
During the rainy season many rural roads are impassable. It is not advisable to travel by car between Lusaka and the Copperbelt after dark.
A road bridge across the River Zambezi between Namibia and Zambia opened in May 2004.
Rail: The Tanzania Zambia Railway Authority (Tazara) railway links Zambia to Tanzania – the connection is at Kapiri Mposhi. Zambia Railways Limited (ZRL) connects with Democratic Republic Congo and Zimbabwe where lines run on to Mozambique, South Africa and Botswana.
Water: Services include ferries across the Zambezi river from Botswana (Kazungula) and across Lake Tanganyika from Burundi (Bujumbura) and from Tanzania (Kigoma).

Getting about
National transport
Air: There are regular flights from Lusaka, south to Livingstone and to the Copperbelt in the north. There are several flights a week from Lusaka to other centres including Mfuwe in the Luangwa valley. Charter companies also operate and are in heavy demand. There is a total of around 150 airfields and airstrips.
Road: The total network is almost 40,000km, of which about 6,500km are main roads. Surfaced roads link main centres. During the rainy season many rural roads are impassable.
Buses: Eagle Travel runs regular coach services to numerous locations including tourist sites. Non-tourist services can be irregular and crowded.
Rail: There are three main lines running from Livingstone-Lusaka, Lusaka-Copperbelt and Kapiri Mposhi to the northern border with Tanzania.
There is an overnight train from Livingstone-Lusaka with sleeping carriages, running three time a week. And day-time services that take many more hours, as they stop at more stations along the line. All lengthy trips should be booked at least one week in advance.
The total network is over 2,000km and in need of investment, which through joint ventures, was agreed in 2006 between the governments of Zambia and China. New and refurbished lines, and rolling stock will provide more access to the Indian Ocean through Tanzania and Mozambique.
City transport
Taxis: These are available between airports and hotels and within town centres. They are generally unmetered.
Buses, trams & metro: A number of privately-owned companies run domestic services over a number of routes. Buses are irregular and crowded, especially during the rush hour.
Car hire
Car hire usually comes with a driver; on special request, firms may offer self-drive vehicles. The Zambia Tourist Board has authorised over 16 car-hire firms serving mainly Lusaka, Livingstone and the Copperbelt which are the major urban and tourist centres.

BUSINESS DIRECTORY
The addresses listed below are a selection only. While World of Information makes every endeavour to check these addresses, we cannot guarantee that changes have not been made, especially to telephone numbers and area codes. We would welcome any corrections.

Telephone area codes
The international direct dialling (IDD) code for Zambia is +260, followed by the area code and subscriber's number:

Chingola	2	Livingstone	3
Chipata	6	Luanshya	2
Choma	3	Lusaka	1
Kabwe	2	Mongu	7
Kasama	4	Ndola	2
Kitwe	2	Solwezi	8

Chambers of Commerce
Livingstone Chamber of Commerce and Industry, 29 Airport Road, PO Box 60648, Livingstone (tel/fax: 323-656; email: denmar@zamtel.zm).

Lusaka Chamber of Commerce and Industry, Farmers House, Cairo Rod, PO Box 37997, Lusaka (tel: 221-266; fax: 224-114; email: luschamb@zamnet.zm).

Zambia Association of Chambers of Commerceand Industry, Showgrounds, Great East Road, PO Box 30844, Lusaka (tel: 255-046; fax: 253-007; email: zacci@zamnet.zm).

Banking
Barclays Bank of Zambia, Cairo Rd, PO Box 31936, Lusaka (tel: 228-858/66; fax: 222-519, 226-185).

Cavmont Merchant Bank Ltd, Fourth Floor, Tazara House, Independence Avenue, PO Box 38474, Lusaka (tel: 224 280; fax: 221 643; e-mail: info@cavmont.com.zm).

Citibank, Citibank House, PO Box 30037, Lusaka (tel: 229-025/6/7/8; fax: 226-264).

Indo Zambia Bank, 686 Cairo Rd, PO Box 35411, Lusaka (tel: 225-080, 222-622; fax: 225-090).

Investrust Bank Plc, Investrust House, Plot 4527/8, Freedom Way, PO Box 32344, Lusaka (tel: 238-733; fax: 237 060; e-mail: inquiries@investrustbank.co.zm).

Stanbic Bank, Cairo Rd, Woodgate House, PO Box 31955, Lusaka (tel: 229-071/3, 229-285/6; fax: 221-152, 225-380).

Standard Chartered Bank, PO Box 32238, Lusaka (tel: 229-242; fax: 222-092).

Union Bank, Zimco House, PO Box 34940, Lusaka (tel: 229-397/8; fax: 221-866).

Zambia National Commercial Bank, Cairo Rd, PO Box 33611, Lusaka (tel: 228-979, 221-355; fax: 224-006).

Central bank
Bank of Zambia, Bank Square, Cairo Road, PO Box 30080, Lusaka 10101 (tel: 228-888 fax: 221-722; internet: www.boz.zm).

Stock exchange
Lusaka Stock Exchange (LuSE): www.luse.co.zm

Travel information
Lusaka International Airport, National Airports Corporation Limited, PO Box 30175, Lusaka (tel/fax: 271-359; email: naclaps@zamnet.zm; internet: www.lun.aero).

Tourism Council of Zambia, PO Box 36561, Lusaka (tel: 251-666; fax: 251-501; e-mail: tcz@zamnet.zm; internet: www.zambiatourism.com).

Zambian Airways, Head Office, Lusaka International Airport; PO Box 34777, Lusaka, (tel: 271-230; fax: 271-054; internet: www.zambianairways.com).

Zambian Express, Lusaka (tel: 222-060, 238-162/65; fax: 238-166; e-mail: zamex@zamnet.zm).

Ministry of tourism

Ministry of Tourism, PO Box 30575, Lusaka (tel: 227-645; fax: 225-174).

National tourist organisation offices

Zambia National Tourist Board (ZNTB), Tourist Centre, Mosi-oa-Tunya Road, PO Box 60342, Livingstone (tel: 321-404/5; fax: 321-487; e-mail: zntblive@zamnet.zm); Century House, Cairo Road, Lusaka Square, PO Box 30017, Lusaka (tel: 229-087/90; fax: 225-174; e-mail: zntb@zamnet.zm).

Ministries

Ministry of Agriculture, Food and Fisheries, Mulungushi House, Box RW 50291, Lusaka (tel: 251-537/233; fax: 252-029).

Ministry of Commerce, Trade and Industry, Kwacha House Annex, PO Box 31968/34373, Lusaka (tel: 228-301, 221-184; fax: 226-673).

Ministry of Communication and Transport, PO Box 50065, Lusaka (tel: 251-444/938/740/759; fax: 002-601, 253-260).

Ministry of Community Development and Social Services, Fidelity House, PO Box 31958, Lusaka (tel: 227-840, 228-321; fax: 225-327).

Ministry of Defence, PO Box RW 17X, Lusaka (tel: 251-211, 254-667; fax: 254-670, 221-339, 253-875).

Ministry of Education, PO Box 50093, Lusaka (tel: 227-636; fax: 222-396).

Ministry of Energy and Water Development, Ministerial Headquarters, Lusaka (tel: 263-870; fax: 252-339).

Ministry of Environment and Natural Resources, Mulungushi House, PO Box 30055, Lusaka (tel: 252-711, 250-186; fax: 252-952).

Ministry of Finance, PO Box RW 50062, Lusaka (tel: 250-544, 227-668; fax: 250-501).

Ministry of Foreign Affairs, PO Box 50069, Lusaka (tel: 262-666; fax: 250-634/240, 252-867).

Ministry of Health, PO Box 30205, Lusaka (tel: 227-745, 223-435; fax: 223-435).

Ministry of Home Affairs, PO Box 50997, Lusaka (tel: 254-261/362; fax: 224-656, 254-669).

Ministry of Information and Broadcasting Services, PO Box 50200, Lusaka (tel: 251-766, 253-965; fax: 254-013, 252-391, 250-524).

Ministry of Labour and Social Security, PO Box 32186, Lusaka (tel: 227-640).

Ministry of Lands, Mulungushi House, PO Box 30069, Lusaka (tel: 252-288; fax: 250-130).

Ministry of Legal Affairs, PO Box 50106, Lusaka (tel: 251-588; fax: 253-695).

Ministry of Local Government and Housing, PO Box 34204, Lusaka (tel: 253-077; fax: 252-680).

Ministry of Mines and Minerals Development, PO Box 31969, Lusaka (tel: 252-990; fax: 251-224).

Ministry of Science, Technical Education and Vocational Training, PO Box 50464, Lusaka (tel: 229-673; fax: 252-951).

Ministry of Sports, Youth and Child Development, 4th Floor, Memaco House, Sapele Rd, Lusaka (tel: 227-168; fax: 223-996).

Ministry of Works and Supply, PO Box 50236, Lusaka (tel: 253-266; fax: 222-360).

Other useful addresses

British High Commission, 5210 Independence Avenue; PO Box 50050, 15101 Ridgeway, Lusaka (tel: 251-133; fax: 253-798; email: BHC-lusaka@fco.gov.uk).

Central Statistics Office, PO Box 31908, Lusaka.

Chilanga Cement plc, Kafue Road, PO Box 32639, Lusaka (tel: 225-2853, 701-297; fax: 252-853, 252-655).

Export Board of Zambia, PO Box 30064, Third Floor, State Lottery Building, Cairo Road, North End, Lusaka (tel: 228-106/7; fax: 222-509).

Lusaka Stock Exchange Ltd, Lusaka (tel: 228-594, 228-391; fax: 228-608, 225-969; e-mail: luse@zamnet.zm).

Metal Marketing Corp of Zambia, PO Box 35570, 10101 Lusaka (tel: 228-131/140).

National Air Charters, PO Box 33650, 10101 Lusaka (tel: 229-154, 228-274).

National Commission for Development Planning, PO Box 50268, Lusaka.

National Import & Export Corporation, PO Box 30282, 10101 Lusaka (tel: 228-018).

Nitrogen Chemicals, PO Box 360226, Kafue (tel: 311-531/5; fax: 311-313).

Zambia Consolidated Copper Mines Ltd (ZCCM), 5309 Dedan Kimathi Road, PO Box 30048, Lusaka (tel: 229-115; fax: 221-057).

Zambia Electricity Supply Corporation Ltd (Zesco), PO Box 33304, Stand 6949 Great East Road, Lusaka 10101 (tel: 223-970, 239-343, 225-074; fax: 223-971, 237-601, 239-343, 222-753).

Zambian Embassy (USA), 2419 Massachusetts Avenue, NW, Washington DC 20008 (tel: (+1-202) 265-9717; fax: (+1-202) 332-0826; e-mail: info@zambiainfo.org).

Zambia Industrial & Commercial Copper Industry Service Bureau, PO Box 22100, Kitwe.

Zambia Investment Centre, 5th Floor, Ndeke House, Haile Selassie Avenue, PO Box 34580, Lusaka (tel: 252-130, 252-152; fax: 252-150; e-mail: invest@zamnet.zm).

Zambia National Broadcasting Corporation, PO Box 50015, 10101 Lusaka (tel: 229-648).

Zambia National Oil Company Limited (ZNOC), Lusaka (tel: 222-135; fax: 220-144, 221-265).

Zambia Privatisation Agency (ZPA), Privatisation House, Nasser Road, PO Box 30819, Lusaka (tel: 227-851, 223-859, 227-791; fax: 225-270; e-mail: zpa@zamnet.zm).

Zambia Railways Ltd (ZRL), PO Box 80935, Kabwe (tel: 223-822, 222-201/209; fax: 228-023/025).

Zambia Telecommunications Co Ltd, Lusaka (tel: 611-111, 612-399; fax: 613-055, 615-855).

National news agency: Zambia News Agency, (internet: www.zana.gov.zm).

Internet sites

Africa Business Network: www.ifc.org/abn

African Development Bank: www.afdb.org

Africa Online: www.africaonline.com

AllAfrica.com: http://allafrica.com

Mbendi AfroPaedia (information on companies, countries, industries and stock exchanges in Africa): http://mbendi.co.za

Office of the President: www.statehouse.gov.zm

Zambian Express: www.africa-insites.com

Zambian gateway website: www.zamnet.zm

Zambian Statistical Office: www.zamstats.gov.zm

Zimbabwe

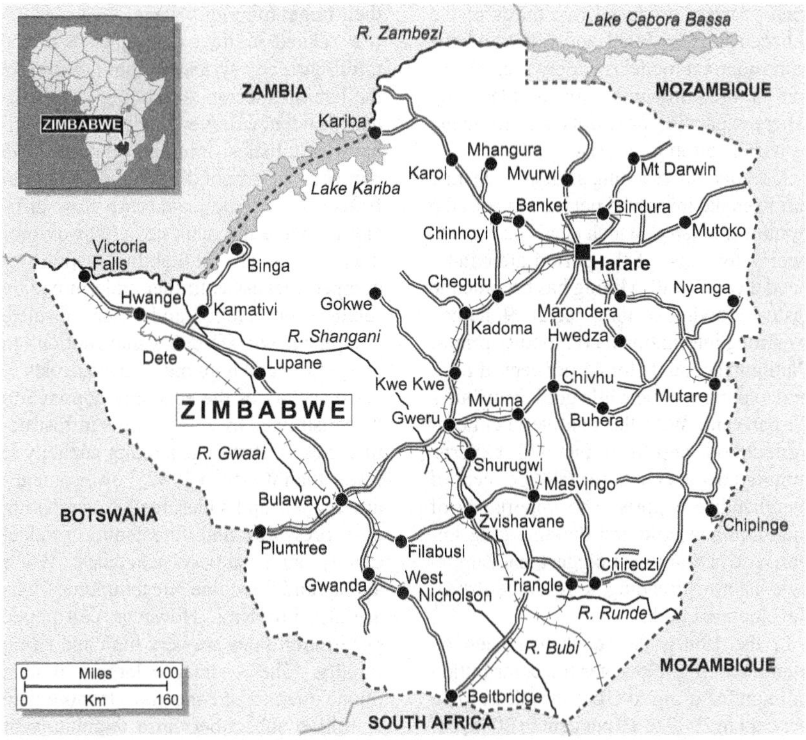

Robert Mugabe won the contested presidential elections in June 2008 by default, Morgan Tsvangirai having withdrawn from the run-off after his supporters had been threatened and attacked by the military and police. But the parliamentary elections were won by Tsvangirai's Movement for Democratic Change (MDC) with 109 seats (out of 210) while the Zimbabwe African National Union-Patriotic Front (Zanu-PF) won 97. The Senate result was a draw with both the MDC and Zanu-PF getting 30 seats. A Government of National Unity (GNU) of the MDC and Zanu-PF was finally established in February 2009, with a remit of drawing up a new constitution by the end of 2010 to be put to a referendum for approval, and to organise new elections within two years.

However, at a meeting held in Zambia in March 2011 the troika of observer states from the Southern African Development Community (SADC) – Tanzania, Angola and Swaziland – noted that there had been insufficient progress and expressed impatience. They resolved that the government in Zimbabwe should make more effort to complete the steps necessary to hold the election and finalise the new constitution.

One of the steps necessary before an election could be held was the drawing up of an electoral role. However, according to a report in June 2011 by the respected South African Institute of Race Relations, the newly created Zimbabwean voters' roll contained 2.6 million bogus entries, including under-aged voters, the registration of 13,396 new voters added to the roll in one constituency (that had not in any way change boundaries) and 14,000 people aged over 100 years. The authors of the report concluded this number of additional votes could determine the result of the next election.

In the meantime, Robert Mugabe continued his absolute rule. There were, however, the beginnings of splits within his party. Ex-military chief Solomon Mujuru,

KEY FACTS

Official name: Republic of Zimbabwe

Head of State: President Robert Gabriel Mugabe (Zanu-PF) (since 1980; re-elected 2008)

Head of government: Prime Minister Morgan Tsvangirai (MDC) (from 11 Feb 2009)

Ruling party: A unity government of the Movement for Democratic Change (MDC) and Zimbabwe African National Union-Patriotic Front (Zanu-PF) (from 15 Sep 2008)

Area: 391,109 square km

Population: 11.73 million (2010)*

Capital: Harare

Official language: English, Shona and Ndebele

Currency: Zimbabwe dollar (Z$) = 100 cents

Exchange rate: Z$378.10 per US$ (Oct 2011), official) (street rate far greater sum)

GDP per capita: US$594 (2010)

GDP real growth: 9.00% (2010)

GDP: US$7.50 billion (2010)

Labour force: 3.84 million (2009)*

Unemployment: 95.00% (2009)*

Inflation: 3.00% (2010)

Foreign debt: US$5.16 billion (2007)

* estimated figure

husband of Vice President Joyce Mujuru, died in a fire at his farm house in August 2011. He was a strategist and rumoured power broker in the divisive Zanu-PF succession politics, and his death will create a void and leave his wife exposed, analysts say.

The economy

After years of hyperinflation (over 11,000,000 per cent at one point, and more) and a Zimbabwe dollar definitely not worth the paper it was written on – a Z$10 million note was introduced in 2008, valued at around US$3.90, then a Z$50 million note... and the maximum that could be withdrawn from a bank in any one day was Z$5 billion. By that time it hardly mattered whether it was a US billion or a UK billion.

The establishment of the GNU and the adoption of macro-economic stabilisation policies including the multi-currency regime resulted in early signs of economic recovery in 2009. Once this happened, the international community started to come to Zimbabwe's aid.

Zimbabwe's economy grew by 5.7 per cent in 2009, by an estimated 8.2 per cent in 2010 and growth of 7.8 per cent is predicted for 2011. These impressive figures are put into perspective however by the steep decline that the country went through in the decade before 2008.

While mining has seen a dramatic improvement since the national unity government took power in early 2009, there has been a considerable loss of industrial output and commercial farming has been decimated with more focus now on smallholder farming. Large-scale farm operations will contribute to agriculture's recovery, especially for sugar, tea and coffee, but smallholder agriculture will play a greater role with important implications for farm financing and marketing. Tobacco production figures for 2010 show that smallholders produced upwards of 75 per cent of the crop compared to less than 10 per cent two years previously. Much of the 2010 expansion of the tobacco crop can be attributed to the extension of contract farming schemes financed indirectly by commercial banks lending to tobacco merchants and processors. Contract growers produced two-thirds of the tobacco crop in 2009 and 2010 and the same contract model is widely used in cotton, a predominantly smallholder crop where expansion prospects are promising as world cotton prices rise.

A second far-reaching structural change has been the improved performance of the mining industry which had performed poorly for most of the period after independence in 1980. Mining has become the fastest growing sector since 2009, helped by strong international commodity prices. Platinum accounts for 45 per cent of mineral export revenue while gold contributes 22 per cent. With the relative decline of agricultural and manufactured exports, mining now accounts for 64.7 per cent of merchandise exports. The importance of platinum and gold and the emerging importance of diamonds suggest that Zimbabwe is now treading a resource-driven development path.

In the 1990s, the focus had been on manufacturing. However the contribution of manufacturing to GDP shrunk from 28 per cent in 2000 to 10 per cent in 2008, before recovering to 17 per cent in 2009. Manufacturing suffers from low capacity utilisation, estimated at 43 per cent in 2009, still an improvement on 2008, when it was below 20 per cent.

The multi-currency system has had an adverse impact on industry competitiveness as manufacturing is heavily import-dependent with 50 per cent of Zimbabwe's imports coming from South Africa. The strengthening of the South African rand against the US dollar has increased input costs significantly. While firms continued to shed jobs in 2010, businesses faced strong wage inflation pressures attributable to high living costs. The poverty line for a family of five is estimated at US$500 a month by Zimbabwe Statistics, which trade unions have set as their target minimum wage.

A related indirect consequence of the multi-currency system is tight liquidity in the banking sector. According to a Business Tendency Survey carried out by Zimbabwe Statistics, mining companies (35 per cent of respondents) and industrial firms (28 per cent) said 'cash flow difficulties' were the main constraint on production and profitability. Industry competitiveness is further undermined by reliance on ageing and often obsolete equipment with frequent interruptions to production and high maintenance costs.

All sectors of the economy continue to be constrained by Zimbabwe's infrastructure deficit. Power generating capacity is lower than it was in 1980. Power outages are frequent and widespread, exacerbating cost pressures and threatening product quality and delivery schedules. Water supply and fixed line telecommunications are also problems. However, cell phone penetration rates are very high and rising rapidly. The country's largest mobile phone operator, Econet, boasts more than 5 million subscribers in a population of about 11.7 million.

Overall, Zimbabwe's economy should grow by more than 5 per cent a year in coming years, but there are risks, including uncertainty over the global recovery in 2011–12.

Doing business

Despite Zimbabwe's much-publicised economic troubles, the country's economy is open with merchandise trade (exports and imports) accounting for 86 per cent of GDP in 2010.

Historically Zimbabwe has always been an import-dependent economy with each 1 per cent increase in real GDP giving rise to a 1.5 per cent increase in imports.

Ten years of chronic inflation, hyperinflation and underinvestment has left Zimbabwe with an uncompetitive economy. The country was ranked fourth from the bottom out of 139 countries in the World Economic Forum's 2010–11 Global Competitiveness Index. For this reason, a weak US dollar has its allure since the dollar price of Zimbabwe's commodity exports would rise while manufactured products

KEY INDICATORS — Zimbabwe

	Unit	2006	2007	2008	2009	2010
Population	m	*11.73	*11.73	*11.73	*11.73	*12.26
Gross domestic product (GDP)	US$bn	3.70	3.60	3.10	5.80	7.50
GDP per capita	US$	319	305	268	464	594
GDP real growth	%	-6.3	-6.9	-14.1	6.0	9.0
Inflation	%	*1,016.7	*10,453.0	156.2	6.5	3.0
Coal output	mtoe	1.8	1.3	1.1	1.1	1.1
Current account	US$m	-470.0	-383.0	-928.0	-1,426.0	-18.3
Foreign debt	US$bn	3.9	–	–	–	–
Exchange rate	per US$	250.00	30,000.00	444.00	378.40	367.00

* estimated figure

would become more attractive regionally and domestically. The downside would be increased prices for key imports, especially fuel and food, which are mainly paid for in South African rand.

With imported goods readily available, Zimbabwean industrialists cannot pass on cost increases to customers as they could in the past. Similarly, exporters cannot rely on a weak exchange rate to ensure competitiveness abroad. As Zimbabwe is not in a position to adjust its exchange rate, restoring and enhancing competitiveness will depend on price restraint, productivity gains, investment in infrastructure and micro-level business reforms designed to reduce business costs.

Reforms are urgent. In the World Bank's 2011 *Doing Business* report, Zimbabwe was ranked 157th out of 183 countries. Among regional competitors, only Angola (163rd) and Democratic Republic of Congo (175th) fared worse.

In 2010, Zimbabwe implemented two important business reforms. First, to ease the opening of businesses, it reduced registration fees and speeded up the name search process, and company and tax registration. Second, the corporate income tax rate was lowered to 25 per cent from 30 per cent. However, there is scope for more change, especially regulations on cross-border trade, construction permits and starting and closing a business. These are all areas where Zimbabwe had a low ranking in the *Doing Business* report.

The Zimbabwe Investment Authority (ZIA) was relaunched in December 2010 as a One Stop Shop with the aim of streamlining and harmonising the handling of investment proposals. Before, the processing of an investment licence could take up to 49 days. The ZIA approved 124 projects in the first nine months of 2010, up from 73 in the same period of 2009. Approvals for the nine months of 2010 were valued at US$387 million, with US$258 million going to the construction industry, followed by US$83 million for mining.

Financing problems lie at the heart of Zimbabwe's infrastructure deficit in transport, power, water and telecommunications. More than 80 per cent of the 88,100km of roads are in need of rehabilitation. The railway network of Zimbabwe has also seen a dramatic decline. The amount of freight carried dropped from more than 14 million tons in 1990 to 9.4 million tons in 2000 and 3.8 million tons in 2008.

International trade and relations

South Africa is by far Zimbabwe's largest trading partner accounting for almost two-thirds of total imports in 2009 and three-quarters of exports. In 2008 regional trade within the SADC and the Common Market for Eastern and Southern Africa (COMESA) accounted for 82 per cent of exports and 86 per cent of imports. South Africa accounted for 82 per cent of Zimbabwe's imports from SADC countries and bought 62 per cent of Zimbabwe's exports to the regional group.

China has become a more important trade partner but its market share is still modest, with 4 per cent of imports and 3.4 per cent of exports. India accounts for 0.85 per cent of imports and 1.4 per cent of exports while the United Arab Emirates provide 0.6 per cent of imports and buy 1.2 per cent of Zimbabwe's exports.

China has provided substantial financial support including US$200 million in credit from China Export-Import Bank to finance agro-inputs and US$60 million for a local company, Farmers World, in 2007. State-owned industries are increasingly reliant on Chinese funding with loans and credits worth more than US$330 million between 2002 and 2007. China's largest direct investment was the takeover of the main ferrochrome exporter Zimasco by Sinosteel, while there are a large number of small- and medium-sized Chinese-owned businesses in mining, retail, and cotton and tobacco trading.

India is a relatively minor player but along with Russia has plans to expand in the diamond sector. Essar African Holdings, Indian owned but registered in Mauritius, bought a controlling stake in the state-owned Zimbabwe Iron and Steel Company (Zisco) at the end of 2010.

The 2010 UN Development Programme (UNDP) Human Development Report ranked Zimbabwe last out of 169 countries, though it did not have accurate data for most social indicators. Poverty levels are high. According to the UNDP report, not only is Zimbabwe one of the world's poorest countries, it is 25 per cent poorer than it was in 1970.

Risk assessment

Economy	Improving
Politics	Poor
Regional stability	Fair

COUNTRY PROFILE

Historical profile

1830s The Ndebele people fled Zulu violence in the south. They moved north and settled in Matabeleland.

1830–1890 European adventurers and missionaries explored much of southern Africa.

1889 Cecil John Rhodes was given a British mandate to colonise what became Southern Rhodesia. He founded the British South Africa Company (BSA) and became wealthy from the diamonds found in the area.

1890 White migration began as settlers arrived and named their first settlement Salisbury, which became the capital of Southern Rhodesia (renamed Harare, after independence).

1893 The BSA crushed an Ndebele uprising.

1922 The white minority voted to become a self-governing British dominion, ending BSA administration.

1930 The Land Apportionment Act restricted black access to land, forcing many into waged labour, and setting the ground for what was to become one of modern Zimbabwe's greatest difficulties, that of white owned farms. Opposition to colonial rule began to grow.

1953 The Central African Federation (CAF) was created, merging Southern Rhodesia (Zimbabwe), Northern Rhodesia (Zambia) and Nyasaland (Malawi).

1960s The Zimbabwe African People's Union (Zapu, mainly Ndebele) and the Zimbabwe African National Union (Zanu mainly Shona) were formed.

1963 The CAF collapsed after Zambia and Malawi elected to become separate independent states.

1964 Ian Smith of the Rhodesian Front (RF) became prime minister. He tried to negotiate independence from Britain with an electoral system that would preserve white minority rule.

1965 The RF made a unilateral declaration of independence (UDI) on 11 November. Despite international sanctions, Smith managed to keep his regime intact until 1980 with the support of apartheid South Africa and Portugal's colonialist regime in Mozambique. Zapu and Zanu began a campaign of guerrilla warfare, operating out of Zambia and Mozambique.

1976 Although Zanu and Zapu formed the Patriotic Front (PF) alliance, co-operation between the two remained limited. The civil war continued and intensified towards the end of the 1970s.

1978 Smith was forced to agree a negotiated settlement. Elections for a transitional legislature were boycotted by the PF. The government of Zimbabwe-Rhodesia, led by Bishop Abel Muzorewa of the United African National Council as prime minister and Canaan Banana as president, failed to gain international recognition. The civil war continued.

1979 A new constitution, favourable to the PF but guaranteeing minority rights, was drawn up at Lancaster House in the UK.

1980 Robert Mugabe's Zanu party won the general election and Zimbabwe gained independence from Britain on 18 April. Mugabe became prime minister. Opposition leader Joshua Nkomo was appointed to the cabinet.
1982 Nkomo was sacked after Mugabe accused him of plotting to overthrow the government. Zapu was largely destroyed by the North Korean-trained Fifth Brigade which Mugabe sent into Matabeleland. According to the Catholic Church a systematic campaign of terror was carried out against the rural population.
1987 Zanu and Zapu put their differences behind them and merged to form the Zimbabwe African National Union-Patriotic Front (Zanu-PF). Mugabe changed the constitution and became executive president.
1997 Concerns over compensation payments to former guerrillas and the consequences of seizing 1,480 of mostly white-owned farms lead to economic crisis. Violent demonstrations ensued.
1998 A general strike due to soaring food prices was supported by 80 per cent of workers. Mugabe decided, without consulting parliament, to intervene in the war in Democratic Republic of Congo (DRC) by sending troops and compounding Zimbabwe's economic crisis.
2000 So-called 'squatters' seized hundreds of white-owned farms in a campaign of intimidation. Mugabe lost a referendum vote for constitutional amendments. Zanu-PF won parliamentary elections by a narrow majority. Protests in Harare, against rises in food prices and demanding Mugabe's resignation, turned into riots.
2001 The finance minister declared that foreign reserves were depleted. The World Bank and IMF cut aid due to the ongoing land seizure programme. A list of 2,030 white-owned farms, required to be handed over under the new land-acquisition law, was published.
2002 Criticism of the president was outlawed and sweeping powers were given to the police to maintain public order. The European Union (EU) imposed sanctions on 20 members of the Zimbabwean government, including the president. Robert Mugabe was re-elected in controversial circumstances. His opponent, Morgan Tsvangirai (Movement for Democratic Change (MDC)), was arrested on charges of treason. Zimbabwe was suspended from the Commonwealth. Media freedom was curtailed.
2003 The currency was devalued by 93 per cent. The US imposed economic sanctions on President Mugabe and 76 other high-ranking government officials, freezing their assets and barring Americans from conducting business with them. The Commonwealth refused to end Zimbabwe's suspension, citing election rigging and persecution of dissidents.
2004 After their plane was impounded in Harare, 70 mercenaries planning a coup in Equatorial Guinea were detained and charged. Canaan Banana, Zimbabwe's first black president, died.
2005 The ruling Zanu-PF was re-elected; the opposition MDC claimed the elections were rigged. Thousands of shanty homes and businesses were demolished by the government, and around 200,000 people made homeless. The government passed a number of constitutional amendments, including the re-introduction of a 66-seat upper house (Senate). Treason charges against Morgan Tsvangirai were dropped. Elections to the upper house resulted, as expected, in the ruling Zanu-PF winning a majority. The Consumer Council reported that the cost of buying groceries increased almost 10-fold during the year; bread rose by some 1,157 per cent.
2006 The Zimbabwe dollar was devalued by 60 per cent; at the same time the central bank dropped three zeros from the currency as new bank notes were issued. The annual inflation rate reached 1,204.6 per cent.
2007 The annual inflation rate jumped by 45.4 per cent in one month to 1,593.6 per cent. By mid-year the inflation rate was estimated to be 15,000 per cent. A new Z$200,000 bank note was introduced in an attempt to tackle Zimbabwe's hyperinflation. Unemployment was estimated at 80 per cent. A Constitutional Amendment Bill, a compromise between the ruling Zanu-PF and the opposition MDC, agreed a redrawing of electoral boundaries and an increased number of parliamentary members. The amendment also agreed that the next presidential election would be held in 2008 to coincide with parliamentary elections, and that parliament would choose Mugabe's successor should he retire mid-term. British Airways, the last foreign long-haul airline flying to Zimbabwe, ended flights to Harare. The RBZ raised the maximum limit on cheques accepted for clearing to Z$500 million. Former prime minister Ian Smith died. The official statistician declared that with the lack of goods in the shops it was impossible to determine an accurate inflation rate.
2008 A new Z$10 million note was introduced valued at around US$3.90 on the black market. The new notes, officially called bearer cheques, were introduced in yet another attempt to stabilise the economy. The official inflation rate was 100,000 per cent; the black-market exchange rate was Z$7.5 million to US$1. It was estimated that around three million people had left the country in search of work abroad while about 80 per cent of the population lived in poverty. The unofficial exchange grew to Z$30–35 million per US$ dollar (compared to the official rate of around Z$31,250 per US$1). In parliamentary elections the opposition MDC won 51.3 per cent (109 seats out of 210), the ruling Zanu-PF won 45.9 per cent (97), independents 2.25 per cent (one). The RBZ introduced a Z$50 million note and increased the maximum withdrawal limit to Z$5 billion per day. A re-count of 23 parliamentary seats confirmed an overall win for the MDC. The result of the presidential election was withheld until a 'verification and collation' process was completed by the electoral commission. While President Mugabe was out of the country attending a UN summit on the on-going global food crisis he banned international aid groups and non-governmental organisations (NGO) from distributing food until they had re-applied for permits. Mugabe forced a rerun of the presidential elections. International observers from Human Rights Watch stated there was a 'campaign of violence' which had 'extinguished any hope of free and fair run-off presidential elections'. Senior officials loyal to Mugabe were linked to violent incidents and with torture camps run by Zanu-PF. African criticism of the violence during the presidential election was voiced by a troika of observer states from the Southern African Development Community (SADC) – Tanzania, Angola and Swaziland – which was monitoring the hustings, and reported that violence was 'escalating throughout Zimbabwe'. The official rebuttal claimed the statement was biased. Morgan Tsvangirai pulled out of the presidential election, citing the violence perpetrated against his supporters. The US announced that it would not recognise the result of the run-off presidential election. Nelson Mandela, condemned the violence and criticised the situation in Zimbabwe as a 'failure of leadership'. Mugabe claimed victory and a sixth term in office. Morgan Tsvangirai refused to attend talks on power-sharing. The central bank issued a Z$500 million banknote to ease cash shortage. The official inflation rate grew to just over 11,250,000 per cent. A new, Z$100 billion note was introduced as the official inflation rate reached 231 million per cent. Mugabe and Tsvangirai signed a Memorandum of Understanding (MoU) that led to an uneasy political settlement. Following the breakdown in the negotiated power-sharing settlement, Prime Minister Tsvangirai was unable to get a passport to travel to Swaziland to take part in regionally sponsored talks with President Mugabe, to resolve the allocation of ministries between Zanu-PF and

the MDC. The talks were postponed and later collapsed altogether.
2009 As the economy continued to fail, the use of US dollars spread, with market traders refusing to take local currency. A new Z$100 trillion note was introduced, valued at US$30 on that day. Other denominations in trillions were also released. Morgan Tsvangirai returned to the country. Further power sharing talks began but immediately stalled. The Zimbabwe dollar was finally officially abandoned in January when it was announced that all commercial transactions may be performed in foreign currencies; at the same time, a licence was granted to the stock exchange for trading to be conducted in foreign currencies. The Zimbabwe dollar had 12 zeros removed from the currency in a revaluation effort to stave off economic collapse; Z$1 trillion was reduced to Z$1. A summit of Southern African leaders urged Mugabe to appoint Morgan Tsvangirai as prime minister; he was sworn in on 11 February. The new coalition government began paying the military, teachers and civil servants in foreign currency, in an attempt to re-start the economy and get people back to work. Prime Minister Tsvangirai estimated that it would take US$5 billion to rebuild the country's economy. The UK offered to pay for re-settlement of an estimated 750 households of aged British residents in Zimbabwe. For the first time since 2000, the World Bank agreed to assist Zimbabwe in rebuilding its economy by offering technical assistance and giving it a token US$22 million as 'a first step' to encourage Zimbabwe to adhere to international fiscal commitments and begin to clear its arrears. Zimbabwe owed the World Bank and the African Development Bank over US$1 billion. Retail prices fell for the first time in years. The Organ of National Healing, Reconciliation and Integration (ONHRI) was inaugurated by the unity government to allow a platform to debate 'national healing' following years of violence and oppression. Vice President Joseph Msika, 85, died. Msika was also deputy president of Zanu-PF and the position is normally seen as a stepping stone to the Zimbabwean presidency. His death is likely to lead to intense lobbying over who succeeds Mugabe. Prime Minister Tsvangirai said the MDC would 'disengage' from working with Zanu-PF after the arrest of Roy Bennett (MDC treasurer-general and deputy agriculture minister designate) in October.
2010 Bishop Abel Muzorewa died, aged 85, in April. He had been one of the most prominent politicians before independence and was briefly prime minister, in 1979, of the interim government of Zimbabwe-Rhodesia. After the Lancaster House Agreement was signed and inclusive elections were held in 1980 he lost out to Robert Mugabe in the general elections. On 10 May, Roy Bennett, was acquitted by the High Court on charges of treason, easing relations between Tsvangirai and Mugabe. The special dispensation that allowed Zimbabweans to cross into South Africa during the political disturbances in 2009 ended in late 2010.
2011 Agreement on a US$700 million loan from China was signed on 21 March. In return, the Chinese government urged Zimbabwe to protect Chinese companies from nationalisation plans. According to a report in June by the respected South African Institute of Race Relations, on the newly created Zimbabwean voters' roll, said the roll contained 2.6 million bogus entries, including underaged voters, the registration of 13,396 new voters added to the roll in one constituency (that did not in any way change boundaries) and 14,000 people aged over 100 years. The authors of the report concluded this number of additional votes could determine the results of next elections. Wikileaks released on line a US diplomatic cable dated June 2008 that reported President Mugabe had prostate cancer. Doctors reportedly said that the illness could cause his death in 'three to five years'.

Political structure

Constitution

The constitution was first instigated in 1979, based on articles agreed in the Lancaster House accord. An amendment in 1987 resulted in the appointment of an executive president as Head of State.
The election laws were amended in January 2002 to ban independent election monitors and deny voting rights to Zimbabweans living abroad.
Further amendments to the constitution, in 2005, included the re-introduction of an upper house – the Senate. The Senate has 66 members – 50 members elected for five-year terms (five from each of the 10 provinces), 10 traditional chiefs and six members appointed by the president.
Constitutional Amendment Bill number 18 became law on 30 October 2007. Under the Bill the next presidential election would be brought forward to 2008 so as to coincide with the parliamentary elections. Seats in the lower house were increased from 150 to 210, and in the Senate from 84 to 93. The most controversial admendment was to allow Mugabe to choose his successor, which would be voted on by the then Zanu-PF-dominated parliament.

Independence date

18 April 1980

Form of state

Republic

The executive

Executive power is vested in the president (elected by universal suffrage every six years), vice presidents and cabinet. Both the vice presidents and cabinet are appointed by the president.

National legislature

Legislative power is vested in the parliament, comprising a 150-member House of Assembly (lower house) and a 66-member Senate (upper house), both elected for five years. The lower house is made up of 120 directly elected members; 20 seats are given to presidential appointees including eight reserved for provincial governors; 10 seats are for representatives of tribal chiefs, chosen by their peers. The Senate comprises 50 members elected by popular vote for five-year terms. Six seats are reserved for presidential appointees and 10 seats are for representatives of tribal chiefs.

Legal system

Based on the constitution and English common law.

Last elections

29 March 2008 (parliamentary and presidential – first round); 27 June 2008 (presidential runoff).
Results: Parliamentary (house of assembly): MDC won 51.3 per cent (109 seats out of 210), Zanu-PF 45.9 per cent (97), Independent 2.25 per cent (one). (Senate) MDC 30 seats, Zanu-PF 30.
Presidential (first round) Morgan Tsvangirai (MDC) won 47.9 per cent, Robert Mugabe (Zanu-PF) 43.2 per cent, Simba Makoni (independent) 8.3 per cent. (Runoff): Mugabe (the only candidate after Tsvangirai withdrew following murderous attacks on his supporters) won 90 per cent of the vote; turnout was 42.4 per cent.

Next elections

March 2014 (presidential, parliamentary)

Political parties

Ruling party

A unity government of the Movement for Democratic Change (MDC) and Zimbabwe African National Union-Patriotic Front (Zanu-PF) (from 15 Sep 2008)

Main opposition party

None as such

Population

11.73 million (2010)*
Last census: August 2002: 11,631,657
Population density: 29 inhabitants per square km. Urban population: 36 per cent (1995–2001).
Annual growth rate: 1.1 per cent 1994–2004 (WHO 2006)
Internally Displaced Persons (IDP)
100,000–200,000 (UNHCR 2004)

Ethnic make-up
Shona (75 per cent) (including the Zezuru clan (18 per cent) and the Karanga clan (22 per cent)); Ndebele (18 per cent); white (1 per cent). There are several minor ethnic groups, and a small number of inhabitants of Asian or mixed racial descent.
Religions
Dual Christian/indigenous beliefs (50 per cent), Christian (25 per cent), indigenous beliefs (24 per cent).

Education
The educational system was one of the best in the region with universal primary school enrolment and secondary education reaching about 50 per cent of those eligible.
The worsening public finances has put the country's education facilities at risk as the government rationalises non-military expenditure. With increases in education levies of between 400 per cent and 2,000 per cent in 2003–04, impoverished families are increasingly unable to find the money to send their children to school. Primary enrolment has declined from 93 per cent in 2000 to 65 per cent in 2003. When schools reassembled for the winter term 2004, they were forced to turn away 800,000 orphans because President Mugabe's government has run out of money to pay their fees.
Literacy rate: 90 per cent adult rate; 98 per cent youth rate (15–24) (Unesco 2005).
Compulsory years: Five to 12.
Enrolment rate: 95.0 per cent gross primary enrolment; 44.5 per cent gross secondary enrolment, of relevant age groups (including repeaters) (World Bank).
Pupils per teacher: 37 in primary schools.

Health
The state of Zimbabwe's healthcare was mixed in the 1990s. Spending on private healthcare (such as private household expenditure and insurance) averaged 3.7 per cent of GDP.
In 2005 the UK gave over US$17.9 million to UN and non-governmental agencies (NGO) to provide food for five million people affected by food shortages. Around US$1 million was allocated to help those who had returned to their rural homes after being evicted under the government's Operation Murambatsvina.
HIV/Aids
The UN stated, in April 2005, that one million children have been made orphans and another 160,000 would lose a parent in 2005. Unicef called on donor countries to look beyond the political administration of Zimbabwe and focus on the victims of the disease. Only US$14 is contributed for each Zimbabwean compared to US$68 for citizens of neighbouring Namibia or US$111 in Mozambique. With one of the highest infection rates in the region, with an estimated 1.8 million people HIV positive in 2003 Zimbabwe's sick can ill-afford international neglect. Poor governance, profligacy and the politicisation of relief by President Mugabe has left donors averse to giving more.
The HIV prevalence rate for females aged 15–24 years is 33 per cent and the incidence of mother-to-child transmission of HIV/Aids is 12 per cent, and these pose another serious impediment to Zimbabwe's embattled population.
HIV prevalence: 24.65 per cent aged 15–49 in 2003 (World Bank)
Life expectancy: 36 years, 2004 (WHO 2006)
Fertility rate/Maternal mortality rate: 3.4 births per woman, 2004 (WHO 2006); maternal mortality 400 per 100,000 live births (World Bank).
Child (under 5 years) mortality rate (per 1,000): 78 per 1,000 live births; 13 per cent of children under aged five are malnourished (World Bank).
Head of population per physician: 0.16 physicians per 1,000 people, 2004 (WHO 2006)

Welfare
Many companies operated some form of social security plan for their employees, which usually included medical aid but the deteriorating economy has curtailed welfare measures. Workers may individually contribute to private insurance and medical aid funds.

Main cities
Harare (capital, estimated population 1.5 million in 2005), Bulawayo (717,670), Chitungwiza (346,582), Mutare (168,112), Gweru (146,339), Epworth (115,787).

Languages spoken
Local languages, Shona and Ndebele spoken by the majority of the population, are written languages and are taught in schools.
Official language/s
English, Shona and Ndebele

Media
The Ministry of Information and Publicity exerts tight control of the media. The *Access to Information* law makes it an offence to report on Zimbabwe unless a state-registered journalist; only Zimbabwean citizens or residents of the country are eligible for registration. Foreign journalists are only allowed into the country to cover specific, usually non-political, events. Through these measures press freedom has been seriously curtailed. Not only are there repressive laws, but violence by either supporters or members of Zanu-PF, have effectively silenced reporters and distorted news and views. In 2007, the Freedom House annual survey showed Zimbabwe had earned the lowest possible score for political rights and civil liberties including, press freedom.
The Zimbabwe Media Commission (ZMC), set up in December 2009, is to spearhead media reforms, including licensing new press, radio and TV outlets. In May 2010 four private newspapers, including the *Daily News* which had been banned in 2003, were granted licences by the ZMC.
Press
Spiralling costs have pushed up the price of production and publications and caused serious falls in circulation numbers.
Dailies: Government-owned newspapers include *The Herald* (www.herald.co.zw) and *The Chronicle* (www.chronicle.co.zw), published in Bulawayo. *The Daily Mirror* (www.zimmirror.co.zw) is independent. *The Daily News* and its weekend edition, critical of the Mugabe government, was suspended in 2003. The ban on *The Daily News* was lifted and began full-time operations on 25 March 2011.
Weeklies: There are more newspapers published at the weekend than daily, including *The Zimbabwe Independent* (www.thezimbabweindependent.com),*The Standard* (www.thezimbabwestandard.com), *The Saturday Mirror* and *The Sunday Mirror* (www.zimmirror.co.zw).
Business: The privately owned *The Financial Gazette* (www.fingaz.co.zw) is a weekly newspaper, published in Harare. Daily newspapers have sections given over to business and economics. *The Farmer* a weekly covers agricultural matters.
Broadcasting
The national, Zimbabwe Broadcasting Corporation (ZBC) is state-run.
Radio: For most Zimbabweans radio is the only source of information and news. ZBC operates four services – Radio 1 (in English), 2 (in Shona and Ndebele) 4 (an educational channel) and Radio 3 is a commercial station aimed at the young. There are no private radio stations although Zimbabwe is targeted by a number of overseas broadcasts. The Voice of the People (VOP) (www.vopradio.co.zw), operated by former staff of ZBC, broadcasts from Madagascar.
Television: ZBC operates one TV channel. Satellite TV is available from South Africa.
News agencies
ZimOnline (from South Africa): www.zimonline.co.za

Zimbabwe Daily News online (from UK): www.zimdaily.com
The Zimbabwe Times (from US): www.thezimbabwetimes.com
Jeune Afrique (in French): www.jeuneafrique.com

Economy

Zimbabwe has huge natural resources, including over 40 different minerals, such as diamonds, gold, silver, platinum, copper, ferrochrome, coal, lithium and nickel, as well as rich soil for crop cultivation such as maize, wheat, coffee, tobacco, cotton, tea and sugarcane. It also has millions of hectares of forest for timber exploitation and pastures for cattle, pigs and sheep and goats. Yet the country has been reduced from the 'breadbasket of Africa' to a bankrupt and economically pariah state by political and ideologically dogmatic leadership.

International financial institutions have either declined to, or been barred from, engaging with their Zimbabwean counterparts as the political regime of President Mugabe instituted greater and more oppressive measures to mould the economy to its ideals of 'Africa for Africans'.

By July 2008 inflation had reached the astronomic height of 231,000,000 per cent and larger and larger bank notes were issued to keep pace, ending with a Z$100 trillion note in January 2009. The Zimbabwe dollar was finally officially abandoned and in a revaluation move in February 2009, 12 zeros were removed – Z$1 trillion became Z$1. The official statistician said that with the lack of goods to purchase it was impossible to determine an accurate inflation rate.

Since late 2008 when the opposition political leader, Morgan Tsvangirai (MDC), became prime minister of a power-sharing government with the Zanu-FP, efforts to restore some semblance of a rational economic policy has lifted the economy from a comatose to a critical but stable condition. In 2009 Tsvangirai began by pleading with world economic institutions to support his efforts for reform. An estimated US$10 billion was needed to rebuild the country and its economy. Individual countries made pledges totalling US$500 million, and for the first time since 2000, in May 2009 the World Bank agreed to offer technical assistance and give a token US$22 million as 'a first step' to encourage Zimbabwe to adhere to international fiscal commitments and begin to clear its arrears (Zimbabwe owed the World Bank and the African Development Bank over US$1 billion).

GDP growth was estimated at 5.7 per cent in 2007, increasing to an estimated 7.5 per cent in 2010. Agricultural production grew by 15 per cent in 2009, and 34 per cent in 2010, with manufacturing and the service sector showing modest growth. The mining sector output grew in value by 8.5 per cent in 2009 and 47 per cent in 2010, with surges in platinum production (64 per cent increase 2008–10) and gold production (125 per cent increase 2008–10). Manufacturing is undercapitalised and capital machinery in need of refurbishment, while being constrained by unreliable power supply, increased labour costs and regulatory burdens. In the 2010 budget corporate tax was cut to 25 per cent (from 30 per cent), income tax was reduced to 35 per cent (from 37.5 per cent) and tax rates for the mining industry rose.

While these improvements have allowed the government to make realistic fiscal plans and submit a budget for approval, the external position of Zimbabwe remains precarious and sustainable economic growth is impeded by a lack of domestic liquidity with very high interest rates, an ailing infrastructure and low domestic demand. The World Bank estimated in 2011 that at Zimbabwe's current pace a recovery to pre-2000 levels would take until around 2020.

In the 2010, UN Human Development Index ranked Zimbabwe last of 169 countries for lack of national development in health, education and income, and well below the average for sub-Saharan Africa. Around three million people have left the country in search of work abroad while an estimated 80 per cent of the remaining population live in poverty. South Africa announced on 7 January 2011 that it would forcibly repatriate 1.3 million Zimbabweans who had not applied to regularise their stay by December 2010; the deadline was later extended to June 2011.

In November 2010, a Kimberly Process meeting extended the ban on the export of diamonds from Zimbabwe, due to its record of systematic human rights abuse of miners within the country and the alleged control of the industry by Zanu-PF for political and financial gain. The poor conditions in the Marange diamond range (the world's largest diamond deposit) were one of the chief reasons for continuing the ban. Even so diamonds worth an estimated US$160 million from these mines were said to have been sold to India, via a South African businessman using certificates he issued as a member of the Kimberly Process, but without authorisation from the body.

International observers are concerned at how the political situation can have such a detrimental effect on the speed of recovery. In March 2011, the South African *Sunday Times* warned of secretive financial support for Robert Mugabe and Zanu-PF by the Chinese financier and mining magnate, Sam Pa. The concern is that such support, in exchange for access to the Marange diamond deposits, could fund an increase in violence against the opposition MDC and its supporters during the 2011 parliamentary elections, seriously distorting the outcome of the vote.

External trade

Zimbabwe is a member of the Common Market for Eastern and Southern Africa (Comesa), but does not operate a free trade area with the other member states as the economy is too weak to maintain the union. It is also a member of the Southern African Development Community (SADC), the objectives of which include reducing trade barriers, achieving regional development and economic growth and evolving common systems and institutions.

Zimbabwe has some of the world's largest reserves in minerals including coal and asbestos, platinum, copper, nickel, gold, iron and chromite. However, the political situation has discouraged virtually all direct foreign investment and mining production has not been maintained or grown. Traditional exports in tobacco have dropped dramatically since 2000, from 237,000 tonnes to 50,000 tonnes in 2006; cotton is the primary agricultural export.

A lack of foreign exchange led to a critical shortage of imported fuel and electricity. A grey economy, with trade in black market goods, has replaced much of the legitimate economy.

Tourism had been a vital foreign exchange earner, but the sector has contracted due to the poor image of Zimbabwe abroad. Remittances, especially in US dollars, have become a necessity for trade within the country. Exports still exist, both primary and manufactured, but intermittent energy supplies hamper production.

In 2009 international donors pledged US$1 billion to upgrade transport links across eastern and southern Africa, in an initiative to carry goods to market cheaper and faster. Not only will roads and rail links be improved, but also time-consuming official procedures are to be streamlined.

Imports

Main imports are food, machinery, fertiliser and general manufactured products.

Main sources: South Africa (typically 60 per cent of total), China (4 per cent), Botswana (4 per cent).

Exports

Main exports were cotton, timber, tobacco, chrome alloy, gold, diamonds, ferroalloys and asbestos.

Main destinations: South Africa (typically 32 per cent of total), Democratic Republic of Congo (10 per cent), Botswana (9 per cent), China (6 per cent).

Agriculture

Farming

Agriculture used to be the dominant sector of the economy. Since 1999 government policy has skewed typical patterns.Whereas Zimbabwe was almost self-sufficient in food with annual exports of around US$70 million, in 2004, imports of food were estimated at US$280 million, in addition to the immense aid provided through the World Food Programme. Since 2000, the government has appropriated white-owned farm property with little or no compensation. Over 200,000 black agricultural workers lost their jobs when corporate and white-owned farms were confiscated and the land given to 124,000 black families. The government has not sought to combine land transfers with the necessary capital and expertise to run the farms and this has resulted in the virtual destruction of the commercial farming sector. The agricultural sector is now firmly small scale, poorly invested, subsistence farming. It is estimated that 85 per cent of Zimbabwe households rely on farm wages for food and other needs.

Concerted measures employed to ensure increased agricultural production are hampered by a lack of farm machinery and foreign exchange to purchase the necessary equipment.

It is estimated that the country has to import 250,000 tonnes of maize to meet expected shortfalls.

Fishing

Despite the existence of five major flood plains, the country has little fishery potential. There are no natural lakes of any significant size and large man-made reservoirs are primarily used for hydroelectric and farming purposes.

Lake Kariba accounts for approximately 80 per cent of the country's total fish production. The industrial fishery thrives on fresh water sardines (kapenta) which were introduced to the lake from Lake Tanganyika. Lake Kariba also supports an artisanal gillnet fishery, which is based on 40 indigenous species near the lake's shores. This type of activity is important for the local economy, as most of the land available along the shore is unsuitable for crop cultivation.

The catch from reservoirs other than Lake Kariba is typically estimated at 2,000 tonnes per year. The bulk of the catch from these small reservoirs is not usually marketed but kept for domestic consumption. The catch from small dams typically constitutes another 2,000 tonnes, while rivers and fish farms are estimated to yield 1,000 tonnes of fish.

Forestry

Timber production is primarily used for fuelwood, which provides three-quarters of domestic energy supplies. The country's main exported forest product is sandalwood.

Industry and manufacturing

Zimbabwe's industrial sector was one of the most advanced and diversified in sub-Saharan Africa. Since 2000, the sector has been undermined by capital flight, a lack of foreign exchange, an overvalued exchange rate, severe fuel shortages and the constant threat of forced nationalisation. The largely liberalised textile sector is also struggling against competition from countries such as South Africa where subsidies and tariffs operate as barriers to free trade.

Other problems include a lack of capacity which can only be improved with increased foreign investment. As supporters of the Zanu-PF begin to attack foreign companies operating in Zimbabwe, prospects for industrial expansion are bleak. Zimbabwe's heavy industries are also facing hard times, despite being targetted by the government as essential to developing import substitutes, which would reduce the loss in foreign exchange. In recent years, Zimbabwe has experienced an expansion in the chemicals and cement sectors.

Tourism

Tourism has stagnated as Zimbabwe is becoming increasingly viewed as a pariah state. Repressive regimes do not attract much tourism and Zimbabwe is losing much foreign exchange from this potentially lucrative industry. The continuing perception in important markets, such as the US, UK and Australia is that Zimbabwe is unsafe, compounded by government travel warnings. Hotels have become dependent on NGOs for business, but this is threatened by proposed government legislation to curb NGO activity.

Government statistics are unreliable. The World Travel and Tourism Council regards the country as one of the lowest ranked for contributions to national GDP. The sector may grow, but not from Western foreign tourists. The expectation is that tourism will decline by around 3.3 per cent between 2006–15. The tourist sector is estimated to have attracted 8.4 per cent of total capital investment but this is a 2.6 per cent fall on previous years.

A symptom of the sector's malaise is the collapse of Victoria Falls as a centre, since tourists find that they can view the falls from Zambia, where tourism has benefited considerably from its neighbour's troubles. Zimbabwe is courting the fledgling Asian market, especially China, which has granted Approved Destination Status to the country.

Mining

The mining sector accounts for around 8 per cent of GDP and employs 5 per cent of the workforce. Many minerals, including chromite, copper and nickel ores, iron ore, tin ore, gold ore, phosphate rock, limestone and iron pyrites are converted to downstream products. The main exceptions are coal, phosphate rock, pyrites and limestone, which, along with a substantial proportion of iron, steel, copper and asbestos production are sold on the domestic market. Import substitution is encouraged. However, high fuel prices have increased costs markedly.

The government's policy on land and assets tenure has left foreign companies concerned that their assets could be seized without cause or warning. The 'economic empowerment provisions' require companies to sell a 20 per cent stake to local black investors and 30 per cent by 2015.

Illegal trade in gold has risen due to the low prices paid to small gold producers. In 2006 Jack Murehwa (Chamber of Mines) said gold mining had shrunk from 24 tonnes a year to 11 because 'the government-set price was below the current market rates'.

A meeting of the international diamond trade organisation that implements the Kimberly Process Certification Scheme (KPCS) whereby exported diamonds are not part of the 'blood diamond' trade, held in June 2010, became deadlocked over whether Zimbabwe should be allowed to resume legitimate trade in diamonds. Exports could amount to over US$1.7 billion per year. Human rights organisations claim miners are subject to forced labour, harassment, torture and killings by security forces. The government stated it would sell its diamonds on the world market, regardless of the KPCS deliberation. In July, the operators of the KPCS allowed partial trade in stockpiles of Zimbabwe diamonds, with full export in September 2010 dependent on a review of conditions. The ban on the exports of diamonds under the Kimberley process from the Marange mines was lifted on 2 November 2011.

Hydrocarbons

There are no known oil deposits. All domestic needs – 13,000 barrels per day in 2008 – are imported. The National Oil Company of Zimbabwe (Noczim) is responsible for supplying the country with petroleum products; supplies are unreliable due to high fuel prices and Noczim's inability to pay its bills.

Any use of natural gas is commercially insignificant.

Proven coal reserves were 502 million tonnes in 2007, production was 1.4 million tonnes. Coal is exclusively used for domestic purposes with around 60 per cent of production used in electricity generation.

Energy

Total installed generating capacity was 2.34 gigawatts (GW) in 2006. Coal provides 60 per cent of local electricity generating capacity with wood, oil and hydroelectric power providing the rest. Zimbabwe faces problems relating to the rising cost of oil and electricity imports. This resulted in severe debts within the electricity sector and extensive power cuts. The Zimbabwe Electricity Supply Authority (Zesa), which oversees generation, transmission and distribution of electricity, has plans for a number of projects aimed at rehabilitating existing power generators, as well as creating new ones. However since the economy collapsed neighbouring countries have halted supplies of electricity to Zimbabwe and there is no revenue to invest in energy infrastructure.

Financial markets

Stock exchange

Zimbabwe Stock Exchange (ZSE)

Banking and insurance

Before the economic crisis that began in 2000, Zimbabwe had a sophisticated banking system. Performance has been adversely affected by the macroeconomic environment, including the government's foreign exchange regime, negative interest rates and the high level of domestic borrowing. The banking sector comprises the Reserve Bank of Zimbabwe (RBZ) (central bank), five commercial banks, four merchant banks, five finance houses (mainly engaged in hire purchase), two discount houses serving the money market, three building societies and the Post Office Savings Bank. In addition, state-owned corporations invest and lend for specific development purposes.

Central bank

Reserve Bank of Zimbabwe

Main financial centre

Harare

Time

GMT plus two hours

Geography

Zimbabwe is a landlocked country in southern central Africa. It is bounded by the Limpopo river and South Africa to the south, by the Zambezi river and Zambia to the north, by Mozambique to the east and by Botswana to the west.

The country falls into three geographical areas: the high veld, the low veld and the Eastern Highlands. The high veld comprises the major part of the country extending across the central area and rising gradually from the south-west to the north-east, with an average altitude of 1,200 metres. The two main cities, Harare (altitude 1,472 metres) and Bulawayo (altitude 1,343 metres) lie in this area. The low veld comprises the Sabi-Limpopo valleys in the south and the Zambezi valley in the north including the spectacular Victoria Falls that form the border with Zambia. Further east the Zambezi is dammed for electricity generation at Kariba, forming a 250km long lake. The Eastern Highlands borders Mozambique and contains two ranges, the Chimanimani Mountains, with peaks reaching 2,436 metres, and the Inyanga Mountains, with peaks up to 2,595 metres.

Hemisphere

Southern

Climate

Most of the country is semi-tropical with day temperatures of 30 degrees Celsius (C), or slightly above on hot days in the rainy season, but falling as low as 0 degrees C at night in the dry winter season. Rainfall is largely confined to the months November to March and is subject to wide annual variations with considerable influence on agricultural production. Heavier rain falls in the Eastern Highlands.

Dress codes

Business dress is generally formal, suits or jacket with a tie and trousers for men. Many hotels and restaurants require smart casual attire, particularly in the evening, with some insisting on jacket and tie, thus excluding denim jeans. Women normally dress conservatively in European style.

Entry requirements

Passports

Required by all.

Visa

Are required by all, except citizens of countries with reciprocal visa-free entry, see www.zimbabweembassy-uk.com and follow link to *Consular*, then *Visa Requirements* then *Category A, B or C* for further information.

Contact the consular section of the nearest embassy for further advice and requirements for a visa, and confirmation the visitor requires a visa. All visitors must have an onward/return ticket and sufficient money for their stay.

Currency advice/regulations

The import and export of local currency is limited to Z$15,000. The import of foreign currency is unlimited but must be declared in writing; export is limited to the amount declared.

The new Zimbabwe dollar went into circulation on 21 August 2006, whereby three zeros were dropped (Z$1,000,000 became Z$1,000). The new notes are now the only legal tender.

Travellers cheques are accepted in banks and major hotels.

Customs

Personal items are duty-free.

Agricultural plant material including seeds and bulbs and fresh meat require an import licence.

Prohibited imports

Illegal drugs, honey, pornographic literature, assault knives and imitation firearms.

Health (for visitors)

Mandatory precautions

Yellow fever vaccination certificate if travelling from an infected area.

Advisable precautions

Vaccinations for diphtheria, tetanus, polio, hepatitis A and typhoid are recommended. Other vaccinations that may be advised include tuberculosis and hepatitis B and cholera. HIV/Aids is prevalent. Anti-malarial prophylaxis is necessary for the Zambezi valley throughout the year and elsewhere from November–June. Bilharzia is endemic, to avoid the risk, only use well maintained, chlorinated swimming pools. Water precautions are necessary, use only boiled or bottled water. Local dairy products should be avoided as milk is unpasteurised; vegetables, meat and fish should be well cooked and eaten hot. Fruit should be peeled. Sun-screen should be used regularly.

Medical services are poor throughout the country and the services of private doctors may be charged in full before treatment begins. Medical insurance is essential, including emergency evacuation, and an adequate supply of personal medicines is necessary.

A reasonable precaution could include a first aid kit with a sterile needle kit and disposable syringes.

Hotels

Several hotels of various standards are available in the main cities, rated from one to five stars by the Tourist Board. Most of the larger ones are air-conditioned. The government imposes a bed tax per person per night, and it is usual to tip 10 per cent.

Credit cards

Major credit and charge cards are widely accepted. Hyperinflation has led to long queues while clients make several withdrawals at ATMs that were designed to issue a maximum of 40 bank notes.

Public holidays (national)

Fixed dates

1 Jan (New Year's Day), 18 Apr (Independence Day), 1 May (Labour Day), 25 May (Africa Day), 22 Dec (Unity Day), 25–26 Dec (Christmas).

Holidays that fall on the weekend are given *in lieu*.

Variable dates
Good Friday, Easter Monday, Heroes' Day and Defence Force's Day (third Mon and Tue Aug)

Working hours
Banking
Mon–Fri: 0830–1500, (Wed) 0830–1300; Sat: 0830–1130.
Business
Mon–Fri: 0745/0830–1600/1700.
Government
Mon–Fri: 0745/0830–1600/1700.
Shops
Mon–Fri: 0800–1300, 1400–1700; Wed half day. Sat: 0800–1200.

Telecommunications
Mobile/cell phones
There are 900 GSM services available in main towns and cities.

Electricity supply
220V 50Hz with either UK style flat, or round, three-pin plugs.

Social customs/useful tips
Zimbabweans generally rise early and go to bed early, particularly on weekdays. Punctuality is generally appreciated in business circles. Hospitality, particularly for meals, is widely offered and may be freely reciprocated. The formal address (Mr, Mrs or Miss with surname) is usual and a given-name terms are only adopted on closer acquaintance. The giving or receiving of gifts, other than between personal friends, is not customary. No particular proscriptions apply to eating, drinking or smoking and there are no particular religious observances or taboos. Tipping (for example, 10 per cent of a restaurant bill) is common.
It is unwise to photograph major government buildings, military personnel or equipment without prior official permission. Photographers should bring their own film as it is not generally available locally.

Security
Physical attacks, car-jacking and credit card fraud are increasing problems. Foreign nationals who are perceived to be wealthy could be targetted by criminals operating in the vicinity of hotels, restaurants and shopping malls in Harare and other major tourist areas. Caution should be exercised at all times.
Visitors should make two photocopies of the biographic page of their passport; one copy should be retained at home and the other carried at all times for identification purposes.

Getting there
Air
British Airways stopped flying to Harare after its flight to London in 2007.
National airline: Air Zimbabwe
International airport/s: Harare International Airport (HRE), 12km from city; post office, restaurant, duty-free shop and bank/bureau de change.
Bulawayo Airport (BUQ), 24km from city.
Other airport/s: Victoria Falls Airport (VFA); Kariba Airport (KAB).
Airport tax: Departure tax varies depending on the destination; all taxes have to be paid in US dollars. To and from UK US$52, to South Africa US$31, to China US$11, to Dubai US$8.
Surface
Road: Direct routes from Zambia via Victoria Falls, Kariba and Chirundu. Entry from South Africa at Beitbridge and from Botswana at Plumtree. There are three main routes from Mozambique in the east. Most of the border posts are closed from 1800 to 0600 hours every day although specific hours vary.
Rail: There are regular services to Zambia via the Victoria Falls and from Botswana via Bulawayo. There is a rail connection from Beira and Maputo (Mozambique). Rail travel from South Africa was suspended in 1999.

Getting about
National transport
Air: Regular inexpensive daily flights to all major destinations.
Road: Network of over 85,000km, of which about one-quarter are classed as main or secondary roads and half are surfaced with gravel. Good roads connect major towns. Nationwide petrol shortages may impede travel.
Buses: Good inter-city network operated by Express Motorways Africa Ltd, Zimbabwe Omnibus Company, plus numerous local operators. Express coach services from Harare to Bulawayo, Mutare, Kariba, Chipinge, Masvingo. Advisable to book in advance.
Rail: National Railways of Zimbabwe operate services between Harare and Gweru, Bulawayo, Victoria Falls, Mutare, Masvingo, Chinhoyi and intermediate towns (there are also certain places served by branch lines). Two classes – some trains carry restaurant cars and couchette sleeping accommodation. (NB Bedding is charged). Advisable to book tickets (and bedding) in advance. The system is badly rundown and lacks investment.
Water: Ferries cross Lake Kariba.
City transport
Taxis: These are not usually hailed in the street, they are available at ranks near main hotels. A 10 per cent tip is usual.
Buses, trams & metro: Urban services in some centres can be sporadic.
Car hire
Self-drive cars are available in main cities and at Harare airport, although their condition may not be well maintained.
However, they are a useful method of transport as most main intercity roads tend to be of good quality, always maintain an adequate supply of fuel as shortages may leave a traveller stranded. Traffic drives on the left and a foreign or international driving licence is acceptable during short visits.

BUSINESS DIRECTORY

Telephone area codes
The international direct dialling code (IDD) for Zimbabwe is + 263, followed by area code and subscriber's number:

Bulawayo	9	Harare	4
Chiredze	31	Mutare	20

Chambers of Commerce
Zimbabwe National Chamber of Commerce, 115 Nelson Mandela Avenue, PO Box 1934, Harare (tel: 799-692; fax: 799-695; e-mail: info@zncc.co.zw).

Banking
Barclays Bank of Zimbabwe Ltd, PO Box 1279, Barclay House, Jason Moyo Avenue/First Street, Harare (tel: 758-280/1/2/3; fax: 752-913).

First Merchant Bank of Zimbabwe, PO Box 2786, FMB House, 67 Samora Machel Avenue, Harare (tel: 703-071, 727-294; fax: 250-682).

Merchant Bank of Central Africa, PO Box 3200, 14th Floor, Old Mutual Centre, Third Street, Jason Moyo Avenue, Harare (tel: 738-081; fax: 708-005).

NMB Bank, PO Box 2564, 1st Floor, Unity Court, Corner 1st Street/Union Avenue, Harare (tel: 759-651/9, 759-601/6; fax: 759-648).

Stanbic Bank Zimbabwe Ltd, PO Box 300, Stanbic Bank Centre, 59 Samora Machel Avenue, Harare (tel: 759-480/3, 759-471/9, 759-479; fax: 749-030).

Standard Chartered Bank Zimbabwe Ltd, PO Box 373, John Boyne House, 38 Speke Ave, Harare (tel: 752-864; fax: 758-076).

Zimbabwe Banking Corporation Ltd, PO Box 3198, Zimbank House, 46 Speke Avenue, Harare (tel: 757-471/94; fax: 757-497, 751-741).

Central bank
Reserve Bank of Zimbabwe, PO Box 1283, 80 Samora Machel Avenue, Harare (tel: 703-000; fax: 707-800; e-mail: rbzmail@rbz.co.zw).

Stock exchange
Zimbabwe Stock Exchange (ZSE): www.zse.co.zw

Travel information
Air Zimbabwe, PO Box AP1, Harare Airport, Harare (tel: 575-111; fax: 575-068).

National tourist organisation offices

Zimbabwe Tourism Authority, 9th Floor, Kopje Plaza, 1 Jason Moyo Avenue, Cnr Jason Moyo/Rotten Row, PO Box CY286, Causeway, Harare (tel: 758-730/34, 752-570, 758-712/14; fax: 758-726/28; e-mail: mktg@ztazim.org; zta@africaonline.co.zw; internet site: http://www.tourismzimbabwe.co.zw).

Ministries

Ministry of Agriculture, Ngungunyana Building 1, Borrowdale Road, P Bag 7701, Causeway, Harare (tel: 706-081, 700-596; fax: 734-646).

Ministry of Defence, Munhumutapa Building, Samora Machel Avenue, P Bag 7713, Causeway, Harare (tel: 700-155, 728-271).

Ministry of Education, Ambassador House, Union Avenue, PO Box CY121, Causeway, Harare (tel: 734-051, 734-067; fax: 734-075).

Ministry of Environment and Tourism, 14th Floor Karigamombe Centre, 53 Samora Machel Avenue, P Bag, 7753, Causeway, Harare (tel: 794-455, 704-701; fax: 794-450).

Ministry of Finance, Munhumutapa Building, Samora Machel Avenue, P Bag, 7705, Causeway, Harare (tel: 794-571, 796-191; fax: 792-750).

Ministry of Foreign Affairs, Munhumutapa Building, Samora Machel Avenue, PO Box 4240, Harare (tel: 727-005, 794-681; fax: 706-293).

Ministry of Health and Child Welfare, Kaguvi Building, 4th Street, PO Box CY198, Causeway, Harare (tel: 730-011, 794-411; fax: 793-634).

Ministry of Higher Education: Old Mutual Centre, 1st Floor, 3rd Street/J Moyo Avenue, PO Box UA 275, Union Avenue, Harare (tel: 702-361, 796-441; fax: 790-923, 728-730).

Ministry of Home Affairs, 11th Floor, Mukwati Building, P Bag 505D, Harare (tel: 723-653, 703-642; fax: 728-768).

Ministry of Industry and International Trade, 13th Floor, Mukwati Building, 4th Street/Livingston Avenue, P Bag 7708, Causeway, Harare (tel: 702-731, 729-801).

Ministry of Information, Posts and Telecommunications, 8th-11th Floor, Linquenda House, Baker Avenue, PO Box CY1276 & CY825, Causeway, Harare (tel: 703-891, 706-891; fax: 735-640).

Ministry of Justice, Legal and Parliamentary Affairs, Corner House, Leopold Takawira Street, P Bag 7704, Causeway, Harare (tel: 790-902, 790-905; fax: 790-901).

Ministry of Lands and Water Development, Ngungunyana Building, 1 Borrowdale Road, P Bag 7701, Causeway, Harare (tel: 706-081, 700-596).

Ministry of Local Government, Rural and Urgan Development, 16th-20th Floors, Mukwati Building, P Bag 7706, Causeway, Harare (tel: 790-601, 728-601).

Ministry of Mines, Zimre Centre, L Takawira Street/Union Avenue, P Bag 7709, Causeway, Harare (tel: 732-881, 732-885; fax: 790-704).

Ministry of National Affairs, Employment Creation and Co-operatives, Zanu PF Building, Rotten Row/Samora Machel Avenue, PO Box 4530, Harare (tel: 734-691, 730-893; fax: 735-338).

Ministry of National Security, Chaminuka Building, 5th Street, Causeway, Harare (tel: 795-965).

Ministry of Public Construction and National Housing, Corner L Takawira Street & H Chitepo Avenue, PO Box CY441, Causeway, Harare (tel: 704-561, 704-021; fax: 702-271).

Ministry of Public Service, Labour and Social Welfare, 12th Floor Compensation House, Central Avenue/4th Street, P Bag 7707, Causeway, Harare (tel: 790-871, 796-451).

Ministry of Sports Recreation and Culture, Pax House, 89 Union Avenue, Harare (tel: 707-411, 794-450; fax: 707-580).

Ministry of Transport and Energy, 4th Floor Atlas House, 62 Robert Mugabe Road, Private Bag 7742, Causeway, Harare (tel: 706-446, 706-161; fax: 708-225, 752-923).

Office of the President and Cabinet, Munhumutapa Building, Samora Machel Avenue/3rd Street, Private Bag 7700, Causeway, Harare (tel: 707-091, 707-098; fax: 734-644, 792-044).

Parliament of Zimbabwe, Baker Avenue Box 8055, Causeway, Harare (tel: 729-722, 795-548).

Other useful addresses

Agricultural Marketing Authority (AMA), Royal Mutual House, 45 Baker Avenue, PO Box 8094, Harare (tel: 730-944).

Attorney-General's Office, Corner House, Leopold Takawira Street, P.Bag 7704, Causeway, Harare (tel: 790-902, 790-905).

British Embassy, 7th Floor, Corner House, Cnr Samora Machel Avenue-Leopold Takawira Street; PO Box 4490, Harare (tel: 772-990, 774-700; fax: 774-605; email: consular.harare@fco.gov.uk).

Chamber of Mines of Zimbabwe, 4 Central Avenue, PO Box 712, Harare (tel: 702-843; fax: 707-983).

Cold Storage Commission (CSC), Josiah Chinamano Road, Bulawayo (tel: 68-961; fax: 67-522).

Commercial Farmers' Union, Agriculture House, PO Box 1241, Leopold Takawira Street, Harare (tel: 791-881).

Confederation of Zimbabwe Industries, Industry House, 109 Rotten Row, PO Box 3794, Harare (tel: 739-833; fax: 702-873).

Cotton Marketing Board (CMB), Kurima House, 89 Baker Avenua, Harare (tel: 739-061; fax: 66-429).

Dairy Marketing Board (DMB), Dolphin House, Leopold Takawira Street, Harare (tel: 705-700).

Grain Marketing Board (GMB), Kurima House, 89 Baker Avenue, Harare (tel: 732-011; fax: 732-019).

Minerals Marketing Corporation of Zimbabwe, Globe House, 51 Jason Moyo Avenue, PO Box 2628, Harare (tel: 703-402, 705-862; fax: 722-441).

Parliament of Zimbabwe, Baker Avenue Box 8055, Causeway, Harare (tel: 729-722, 795-548).

Zimbabwe Broadcasting Corporation (ZBC), Broadcasting Centre, Pockets Hill, PO Box HG444, Highlands, Harare (tel: 486-670, 481-252/9; fax: 498-613).

Zimbabwean Embassy (USA), 1608 New Hampshire Avenue, NW, Washington DC 20009 (tel: (+1-202) 332-7100; fax: (+1-202) 483-9326; e-mail: zimemb@erols.com).

Zimbabwe International Trade Fair, Zift, PO Famona, Bulawayo (tel: 64-911).

Zimbabwe Investment Centre, 109 Rotten Row, PO Box 5950, Harare (tel: 757-931/5; fax: 757-937).

Zimbabwe State Trading Corporation, Globe House, 51 Jason Moyo Avenue, Harare (tel: 729-353).

Zimbabwe Stock Exchange, PO Box UA234, 8th Floor, Southampton House, Union Avenue, Harare (tel: 736-861; fax: 791-045).

Zimbabwe Tourist Development Corporation, PO Box 8052, Causeway, Harare (tel: 793-666).

Internet sites

Africa Business Network: www.ifc.org/abn

AllAfrica.com: www.allafrica.com

African Development Bank: www.afdb.org

The world in 2011

Drawing on the resources of a number of organisations including the United States Department of Economic and Social Affairs, the United Nations Conference on Trade and Development (UNCTAD) and the five United Nations regional commissions, the World Economic Situation and Prospects (WESP) presents a synthesis of informed opinion on the global economic outlook.

The 2011 WESP considered the world economy to be on the brink of another major downturn. Global economic growth started to decelerate on a broad front in mid-2011 after being estimated to have averaged 2.8 per cent over the previous 12 months. This economic slowdown was expected to continue into 2012 and 2013. The United Nations baseline forecast for the growth of world gross product (WGP) was 2.6 per cent for 2012 and 3.2 per cent for 2013, which was below the pre-crisis pace of global growth.

Persistent high unemployment in the United States and low wage growth are holding back aggregate demand and, together with the prospect of prolonged depressed housing prices, this has heightened risks of a new wave of home foreclosures. Growth in the euro zone has slowed considerably since the beginning of 2011 and the ever-simmering sovereign debt crisis weighs heavily on consumer and business confidence across Europe. The failure of policymakers in developed countries to address unemployment and prevent sovereign debt distress and financial sector fragility from escalating posed the most acute risk for the global economy in the outlook for 2012–13, with renewed global recession becoming a distinct possibility.

Meanwhile, developing countries and the economies in transition are expected to continue to stoke the engine of the world economy, growing on average by 5.4 per cent in 2012 and 5.8 per cent in 2013 in the baseline outlook. Among the major developing countries, growth in China and India was expected to remain robust. GDP growth in China slowed from 10.3 per cent in 2010 to 9.3 per cent in 2011 and was projected to further slow to below 9 per cent in 2012–13. India's economy was expected to expand by between 7.7 and 7.9 per cent in 2012–13, down from 8.5 per cent in 2010.

Low-income countries have experienced only a mild slowdown. In per capita terms, income growth slowed from 3.8 per cent in 2010 to 3.5 per cent in 2011 and, despite the global downturn, the poorer countries may see average income growth at or slightly above this rate in 2012 and 2013. The same holds for average growth among the United Nations category of least developed countries (LDCs).

'... developing countries and the economies in transition are expected to continue to stoke the engine of the world economy, growing on average by 5.4 per cent in 2012 '

Against this background, there were several policy directions which could avoid a double-dip recession, including: optimal design of fiscal policies to stimulate more direct job creation and investment in infrastructure, energy efficiency and sustainable energy supply, food security; and stronger financial safety nets; better co-ordination between fiscal and monetary policies; and the provision of sufficient support to developing countries in addressing the fallout from the crisis and the co-ordination of policy measures at the international level.

AFRICA
SEYCHELLES
Victoria
Algiers
Tunis
Rabat
MOROCCO
TUNISIA
Tripoli
Cairo
WESTERN SAHARA
ALGERIA
LIBYA
EGYPT
Nouakchott
MAURITANIA
Dakar
SENEGAL
Banjul
THE GAMBIA
MALI
NIGER
Khartoum
ERITREA
Asmara
Bissau
GUINEA BISSAU
Bamako
BURKINA FASO
Niamey
CHAD
SUDAN
GUINEA
Conakry
Freetown
Ouagadougou
BENIN
NIGERIA
N'Djamena
Djibouti
DJIBOUTI
SIERRA LEONE
Monrovia
COTE D'IVOIRE
TOGO
Abuja
Addis Ababa
ETHIOPIA
LIBERIA
GHANA
Yamoussoukro
Accra
Lome
Cotonou
CENTRAL AFRICAN REPUBLIC
Bangui
CAMEROON
Yaounde
SOMALIA
Mogadishu
Malabo
EQUATORIAL GUINEA
SAO TOME & PRINCIPE
UGANDA
Kampala
KENYA
Libreville
GABON
CONGO
Nairobi
RWANDA
Kigali
Bujumbura
BURUNDI
Brazzaville
Kinshasa
DEMOCRATIC REPUBLIC OF CONGO
TANZANIA
Dar es Salaam
Luanda
CAPE VERDE ISLANDS
Praia
COMOROS
Moroni
ANGOLA
MALAWI
Lilongwe
ZAMBIA
Lusaka
Harare
ZIMBABWE
MOZAMBIQUE
Antananarivo
MADAGASCAR
Windhoek
NAMIBIA
BOTSWANA
Gaborone
Pretoria
Maputo
Mbabane
SWAZILAND
Maseru
SOUTH AFRICA
LESOTHO
MAURITIUS
Port Louis
REUNION
0 Miles 1,000
0 Km 1,600

Traditional or emerging?

The second scramble for Africa has been quietly underway for the last decade. This time it is between the 'emerging' nations of, among others, the original four Bric states (Brazil, Russia, India and China), and the 'traditional' Western, mostly Organisation for Economic Co-operation and Development (OECD), countries lead by the US and the European Union (EU). The prizes are again resource lead – copper, coal, uranium, iron ore, and, most recently, farming land.

For some counties in Africa this seemed a grand opportunity. Especially for those, like Angola, who had run up against transparency issues with the original sources of official development assistance (ODA) who were under ever increasing laws governing, in particular, the environment and fraud. Corrupt leaders found they could no longer demand a new palace in exchange for granting a new mining licence.

> 'China and the other emerging partners offer challenges as well as opportunities.'

The emerging countries are lead by China. Over 2,000 Chinese enterprises have invested in Africa, with accumulated investment of more than US$40 billion. Chinese involvement generally takes one of two forms – joint ventures or wholly Chinese-owned investment, but with government support. These enterprises range from chicken farms in Zambia to vast hydro-electric schemes in Ethiopia, and include textiles, leather products, food, electrical materials and steel.

China and the other emerging partners offer challenges as well as opportunities. By and large the investments come without conditions, can be 'soft' loans and payment by way of barter. But there are disadvantages. Labour is often imported, and not only highly skilled workers, and local workers are poorly paid. Zambia in particular has had problems on the mines where there have been strikes over both wages and safety conditions.

The lesson from Ethiopia's new partnership with emerging economies is the importance of designing optimal investment, trade and industrial policies that can lead to a win-win situation for both Ethiopia and its new partners. Studies recently conducted on the Chinese-Ethiopian economic relationship suggest that Ethiopia lacks a coherent strategy based on a rigorous examination of the facts. There are both positive and negative impacts that may emanate from this emerging partnership. In order for both countries to benefit from it, Ethiopia will have to come up with an appropriate policy response and incentive schemes. The transfer of managerial skills as well as technology, which is of utmost importance to Ethiopian firms, has been extremely limited.

Other drawbacks include smaller projects setting up in competition to local enterprises – the Zambian chicken farm for instance. And others that compete for a share in the same export market – textile garment manufacturers in Uganda exporting within the East African Common Market.

On the positive side, at the November 2011 G20 meeting in Cannes President Hu Jintao of China said that 97 per cent of tariffed exports from least developed countries (LDCs) would be given zero-tariff treatment. Thirty-three counties in Africa are considered as LDCs (with an annual per capita income of under US$745) and this will further facilitate the entry of African commodities into China's market.

At the bilateral level, the IMF documents two examples of China-Equatorial Guinea loans on a concessional and a non-concessional basis. China extended a US$2 billion non-concessional credit line to Equatorial Guinea in 2006. The loans were earmarked for infrastructure (four projects in electrification and improvements to Bata harbour). The Chinese government is also reported to have extended an offer for a US$380 million long-term concessional loan for housing construction.

While governments may welcomes the ease of doing business with the Chinese, some civil servants are becoming increasingly concerned with two issues. First, the limited spin-off and/or multiplier effects of Chinese projects on the national demand for goods and services. Second, the quality of some of the projects executed could be much higher. The latter issue is being addressed with trilateral co-operation approaches in which a company from a traditional partner takes care of the quality control. For example, a Chinese firm is installing a completely new sewerage system in the capital of Equatorial Guinea, while a Spanish engineering company is testing the infrastructure against international safety and quality standards.

China is also building economic and trade co-operation zones in Zambia, Mauritius, Nigeria, Egypt and Ethiopia, involving US$250 million in infrastructure construction.

Traditional partners on the other hand, come with more questions and demands for assurances on transparency and ethical issues.

Currencies (units per US$) – Africa

	Unit	Jan 2007	Jan 2008	Jan 2009	Jan 2010	Jan 2011
Algeria	Algerian dinar	77.71	67.21	72.07	71.76	74.05
Angola	Readjusted kwanza	80.28	75.10	75.10	89.78	92.85
Benin	CFA franc	507.22	454.40	512.85	456.52	505.26
Botswana	Pula	6.18	6.50	8.16	6.68	6.62
Burkina Faso	CFA franc	507.22	454.40	512.85	456.52	505.26
Burundi	Burundi franc	1,000.15	1,139.23	1,234.56	1,230.00	1,233.00
Cameroon	CFA franc	507.22	454.40	512.85	456.52	505.26
Cape Verde	Cape Verde escudo	85.50	75.50	86.20	73.90	82.78
Central African Republic	CFA franc	507.22	454.40	512.85	456.52	505.26
Chad	CFA franc	507.22	454.40	512.85	456.52	505.26
Comoros	Comoros franc	380.41	340.80	384.64	342.39	378.95
Congo	CFA franc	507.55	454.40	512.85	456.52	505.26
Democratic Republic of Congo	Congolese franc	530.00	556.50	692.68	910.35	916.50
Côte d'Ivoire	CFA franc	507.22	454.40	512.85	456.52	505.26
Djibouti	Djibouti franc	174.70	175.47	174.27	160.50	175.75
Egypt	Egyptian pound	5.71	5.54	5.55	5.42	5.80
Equatorial Guinea	CFA franc	507.22	454.40	512.85	456.52	505.26
Eritrea	Nakfa	13.50	13.24	15.20	15.00	15.00
Ethiopia	Ethiopian birr	8.85	9.09	11.05	12.70	16.64
Gabon	CFA franc	507.22	454.40	512.85	456.52	505.26
Gambia	Dalasi	28.25	22.00	26.35	26.70	28.00
Ghana	Ghana Cedi	9,098.50	(a) 0.95	1.31	1.41	1.48
Guinea	Guinean franc	5,556.00	4,242.70	4,930.00	5,010.00	6,940.00
Guinea-Bissau	CFA franc	507.22	454.40	512.85	456.52	505.26
Kenya	Kenya shilling	69.55	62.95	79.75	75.88	81.00
Lesotho	Maloti	7.23	6.84	10.30	7.39	6.77
Liberia	Liberian dollar	58.00	59.15	64.00	70.55	71.00
Libya	Libyan dinar	1.28	1.22	1.27	1.22	1.26
Madagascar	Franc Malgache	2,030.00	1,786.00	1,937.00	2,028.50	2,127.50
Malawi	Kwacha	139.45	139.40	140.60	147.00	150.77
Mali	CFA franc	507.22	454.40	512.84	456.52	505.26
Mauritania	Ouguiya	270.80	252.54	259.77	261.50	282.00
Mauritius	Mauritius rupee	32.57	28.80	32.92	29.70	30.55
Morocco	Moroccan dirham	8.59	7.83	8.66	7.88	8.56
Mozambique	Metical	24.19	23.75	25.80	31.07	32.40
Namibia	Namibian dollar	7.23	6.83	10.30	7.39	6.77
Niger	CFA franc	507.22	454.40	512.85	456.52	505.26
Nigeria	Naira	128.16	118.04	150.80	151.15	152.25
Réunion	Euro	0.77	0.69	0.78	0.69	0.77
Rwanda	Rwanda franc	549.20	545.10	565.44	572.04	595.23
São Tomé and Príncipe	Dobra	6,780.00	14,101.00	14,380.00	15,525.00	1,861.40
Senegal	CFA franc	507.22	454.40	512.85	456.52	505.26
Seychelles	Seychelles rupee	5.49	8.02	16.78	11.20	12.24
Sierra Leone	Leone	2,970.11	2,989.20	3,049.80	3,930.92	4,218.36
Somalia	Somali shilling	1,375.00	1,397.00	1,415.00	1,457.00	1,550.00
South Africa	Rand	7.23	6.83	10.30	7.39	6.77
Sudan	Sudanese dinar	230.29	(b) 2.03	2.23	2.31	2.51
Swaziland	Lilangeni	7.23	6.83	10.30	7.39	6.77
Tanzania	Tanzania shilling	1,282.00	1,158.00	1,395.00	1,343.50	1,475.00
Togo	CFA franc	507.22	454.40	512.85	456.52	505.26
Tunisia	Tunisian dinar	1.32	1.23	1.42	1.31	1.46
Uganda	Ugandan shilling	1,810.00	1,706.70	1,982.50	1,930.00	2,335.00
Zambia	Kwacha	1,245.00	3,840.00	5,110.00	4,444.00	4,750.00
Zimbabwe	Zimbabwe dollar	100,000.00	(c) 3,000,000.00	80,808.10	367.00	378.20

(a)Ghana cedi re-denominated, 2007; (b) Sudanese pound (S£) replaced dinar at rate of S£1 to 100 dinar, 2007; (c) Zimbabwe dollar devalued by 99.9 per cent, 2007

Key indicators 2010

	Population (m)	Area ('000 sq km)	GDP per capita (US$)	Inflation (%)	GDP real growth (%)	Balance of trade (US$m)
Algeria	*35.70	2,381.70	4,366	4.3	3.3	(c) 7,784.0
Angola	19.08	1,246.70	4,329	14.5	3.4	(c) 18,168.0
Benin	*9.85	112.60	*711	(c) 2.2	(c) *2.7	(d) -607.5
Botswana	*1.82	582.00	7,627	8.1	8.6	(c) -753.7
Burkina Faso	*16.43	274.00	(c) 564	(c) 2.6	(c) *3.3	(c) *-513.0
Burundi	*8.50	27.80	180	6.4	3.9	-277.0
Cameroon	*19.41	475.40	1,101	1.3	3.0	-177.0
Cape Verde	0.49	4.03	(c) *3,445	(c) 1.2	(c) *3.6	(c) -676.8
Central African Republic	4.80	623.00	(c) *447	(c) *3.5	(c) 2.4	(c) -153.3
Chad	*11.50	1,284.00	(c) *687	10.1	(c) *-0.9	(c) *171.3
Comoros	*0.73	2.20	1,202	2.7	2.1	(c) *-156.4
Congo	*3.90	342.00	(c) 2,538	(c) *4.3	7.5	(c) 3,600.2
Democratic Republic of Congo	*67.80	2,345.40	186	23.5	7.2	(c) *-3,826.0
Côte d'Ivoire	21.40	322.50	1,036	1.4	2.6	(c) 4,185.2
Djibouti	*0.89	23.20	1,383	4.0	4.5	(c) -373.3
Egypt	*81.12	1,001.50	2,789	11.7	5.1	(c) -16,818.0
Equatorial Guinea	*1.19	28.10	(c) 9,579	12.7	(c) 12.4	(c) 5,936.0
Eritrea	*5.25	125.00	393	12.7	2.2	(c) -501.0
Ethiopia	*85.00	1,251.30	350	2.8	8.0	(c) -5,280.9
Gabon	*1.50	267.70	(c) *7,468	(c) *2.1	(c) *3.5	(c) *1,257.1
Gambia	*1.73	11.30	617	5.0	5.7	-69.0
Ghana	24.22	239.50	1,312	10.7	5.7	-2,540.0
Guinea	*10.54	245.90	448	15.5	1.9	66.0
Guinea-Bissau	*1.51	36.10	(c) *513	(c) -1.6	(c) *2.9	(d) -70.7
Kenya	40.40	582.70	809	4.1	5.6	(c) -4,989.3
Lesotho	*1.89	30.40	837	3.8	3.6	1,147 .0
Liberia	*4.10	111.40	(c) *239	*6.6	*5.6	*-459.0
Libya	*6.36	1,775.50	11,314	2.4	4.2	(d) 40,292.0
Madagascar	*20.10	592.00	392	9.3	0.6	(d) *-699.6
Malawi	15.40	118.50	322	7.4	6.5	(d) 753.6
Mali	*15.37	1,241.20	692	1.2	4.5	(c) -212.6
Mauritania	3.40	1,030.70	2,093	6.1	5.2	(c) -573.0
Mauritius	1.30	1.90	7,593	2.9	4.2	-1,896.0
Morocco	*31.85	711.00	3,249	1.0	3.7	-15,062.0
Mozambique	*21.85	799.40	440	12.7	6.7	-997.0
Namibia	2.14	824.30	5,652	4.2	4.8	(c) -983.5
Niger	*15.20	1,267.00	(c) *340	(c) 4.3	*5.2	(d) -437.4
Nigeria	*158.30	923.80	1,389	13.7	8.4	20,237.0
Réunion	0.79	2.50	–	–	–	–
Rwanda	*10.41	26.30	562	2.3	6.5	(c) -768.0
São Tomé and Príncipe	*0.17	0.90	(c) *1,174	(c) *16.9	(c) *4.3	(c) -74.6
Senegal	*12.51	196.20	981	1.2	4.2	(c) -1,310.8
Seychelles	*0.09	0.50	10,682	-2.4	6.2	-508.0
Sierra Leone	*5.75	72.30	326	17.8	5.0	-373.0
Somalia	8.69	738.00	(b) 283	–	–	–
South Africa	*49.99	1,127.20	7,158	4.3	2.8	3,838.0
South Sudan	(e) *8.26	644.33	448	–	6.5	–
Sudan	(f) *43.20	1,217.15	1,705	13.0	5.1	2,565.0
Swaziland	*1.19	17.40	3,061	4.5	2.0	(c) -131.2
Tanzania	*45.00	945.10	545	10.5	6.4	-2,828.0
Terres Australes	(a)0.00	439.80	–	–	–	–
Togo	6.03	56.00	(c) *422	(c) 1.9	(c) *1.8	(c) -412.1
Tunisia	*10.55	164.20	4,200	4.4	3.7	(c) -3,699.0
Uganda	*30.66	236.00	501	9.4	5.2	-2,100.0
Zambia	13.05	752.60	1,221	8.5	7.6	2,704.0
Zimbabwe	*12.26	391.10	594	3.0	9.0	–

*Estimated figure; (a) 310 people total; 150 winter only; (b) 2006; (c) 2009; (d) 2008; (e) (2008 census, disputed); (f) pre-independence of South Sudan

Commodity conscious Americas

Despite the recent deterioration in the global economic environment, the International Monetary Fund (IMF) projections for the Americas region involve only a modest worsening of the outlook. The IMF's October 2011 *Regional Economic Outlook: Western Hemisphere* cautions, however, that there are severe downside risks. A sharp slowdown in Asia, for example, could affect commodity prices, with negative effects on Latin American commodity exporters. With global monetary policy likely to remain accommodative, capital flows could exacerbate overheating and amplify vulnerabilities in emerging markets. Countries with strong real linkages to the United States could find their room for economic manouvre restricted by the US' priority of reducing public debt. Although much of the Caribbean is recovering from a prolonged recession, the outlook remains constrained by high public debt and weak tourism flows.

> 'Latin America, on average, remained as dependent on commodities today as it was forty years ago'

A number of independent analysts consider that 2012 should be better for Latin America than 2011, if only because the region's two biggest economies, Brazil and Mexico, will probably grow faster than in 2011. Brazil will do better because its policymakers organised a gentle slowdown in the second half of 2011 to avoid the risk of upsets later on in President Dilma Rousseff's four year term. In Mexico, any perceived stronger economic tone of the US economy would itself begin to act as a locomotive.

While much of the Caribbean was finally recovering from a long and protracted recession, the outlook continued to be constrained by high debt levels and weak tourism flows in light of the relatively weak recovery in advanced economies. More needs to be done to bring down high debt levels, as well as addressing financial sector vulnerabilities, without further compromising public finances.

Latin America, on average, remained as dependent on commodities today as it was forty years ago and commodity prices are quite sensitive to global output. Accordingly, faltering global demand could deliver a blow to the region's terms of trade. The lip service Venezuela's president Hugo Chávez pays to anti-Americanism is a reaction – common throughout Latin America – not so much to US economic power, but to the arrogance that often comes with it. Since the early 19th century, when the Monroe Doctrine was promulgated, the US has been perceived in Latin America as treating it with *prepotencia* , which inadequately translates as 'arrogance'. In 2010 that doctrine seemed to have metamorphosed into one of arrogant indifference. Not that the US had failed to assist Latin America with a number of practical measures, notably the fight against drugs. That continued. But the high profile signals being sent out were the sad symbolism of anti-immigration measures on the Mexican border and a feeling that President Obama, like so many presidents, simply had other fish to fry. The Peace Corps initiative of the Kennedy administration may have been sneered at, but it did at least represent a close and constant reminder of US interest and goodwill.

The continued perception and assumption that Latin America is there to be taken for granted represents a failure on the part of the United States body politic to understand the sensibilities and aspirations of Latin Americans. The fundamental irony is that, from Chávez to Correa, Morales to Ortega, whatever Latin American politicians may state publicly, in their heart of hearts most of them know that the sort of country most of their electorate would ideally like to live in would closely resemble the USA. And for most of the region's countries, trade with the USA is of undeniable significance. In *anti-yanqui* Venezuela the two market leaders in the automobile sector are from the US. Venezuela owns one of the largest gasoline retailers in the US, as well as relying on the US to refine much of its crude oil.

Perhaps understandably US responses to Latin American developments have, since 1823 when President James Monroe first articulated the policy, been determined by their likely effect on the US. The US' neighbour to the south, Mexico had always considered itself the region's leader in both development and democracy. In 2011 President Obama's attention and engagement certainly weren't on Latin America. If 'Yes we can' had been the slogan of the 2008 Presidential elections, 'Maybe we can't' was the fear that continued to define the Democrats through the latter part of 2010 and in to 2011. As Massachusetts governor Mitt Romney began to take on the mantle of the Republican presidential candidate, the Republican Party found itself riding a wave of disgruntlement and fear, catalysed by the failure of the economy to create jobs, by the inability of banks to grant credit and by the dramatic falls in real estate values.

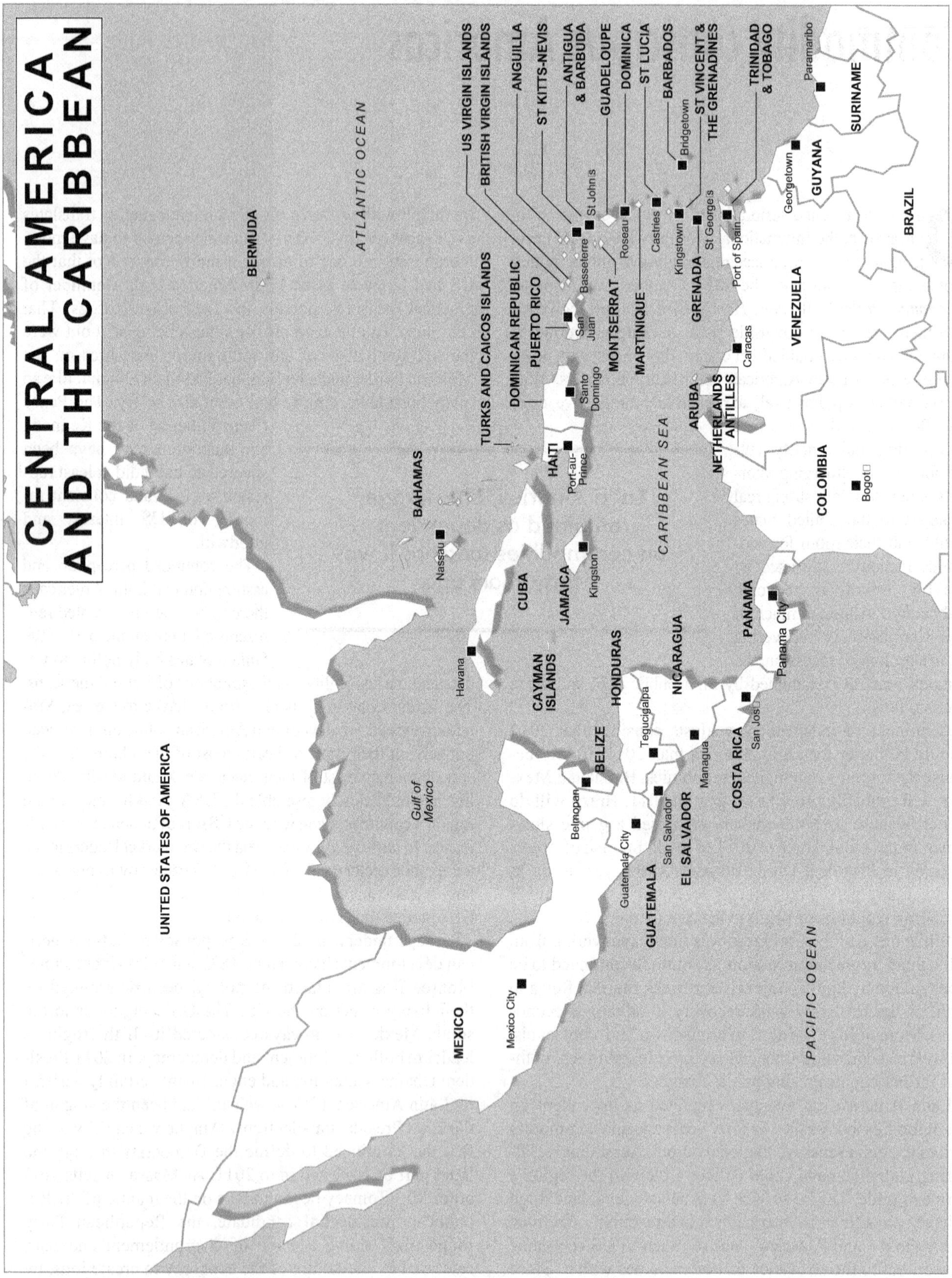
CENTRAL AMERICA AND THE CARIBBEAN
ATLANTIC OCEAN
BERMUDA
BAHAMAS
Nassau
TURKS AND CAICOS ISLANDS
DOMINICAN REPUBLIC
Santo Domingo
HAITI
Port-au-Prince
PUERTO RICO
San Juan
US VIRGIN ISLANDS
BRITISH VIRGIN ISLANDS
ANGUILLA
ST KITTS-NEVIS
Basseterre
ANTIGUA & BARBUDA
St John's
GUADELOUPE
MONTSERRAT
DOMINICA
Roseau
MARTINIQUE
ST LUCIA
Castries
BARBADOS
Bridgetown
ST VINCENT & THE GRENADINES
Kingstown
GRENADA
St George's
TRINIDAD & TOBAGO
Port of Spain
ARUBA
NETHERLANDS ANTILLES
CARIBBEAN SEA
CUBA
Havana
JAMAICA
Kingston
CAYMAN ISLANDS
UNITED STATES OF AMERICA
Gulf of Mexico
MEXICO
Mexico City
BELIZE
Belmopan
GUATEMALA
Guatemala City
HONDURAS
Tegucigalpa
EL SALVADOR
San Salvador
NICARAGUA
Managua
COSTA RICA
San José
PANAMA
Panama City
COLOMBIA
Bogotá
VENEZUELA
Caracas
GUYANA
Georgetown
SURINAME
Paramaribo
BRAZIL
PACIFIC OCEAN

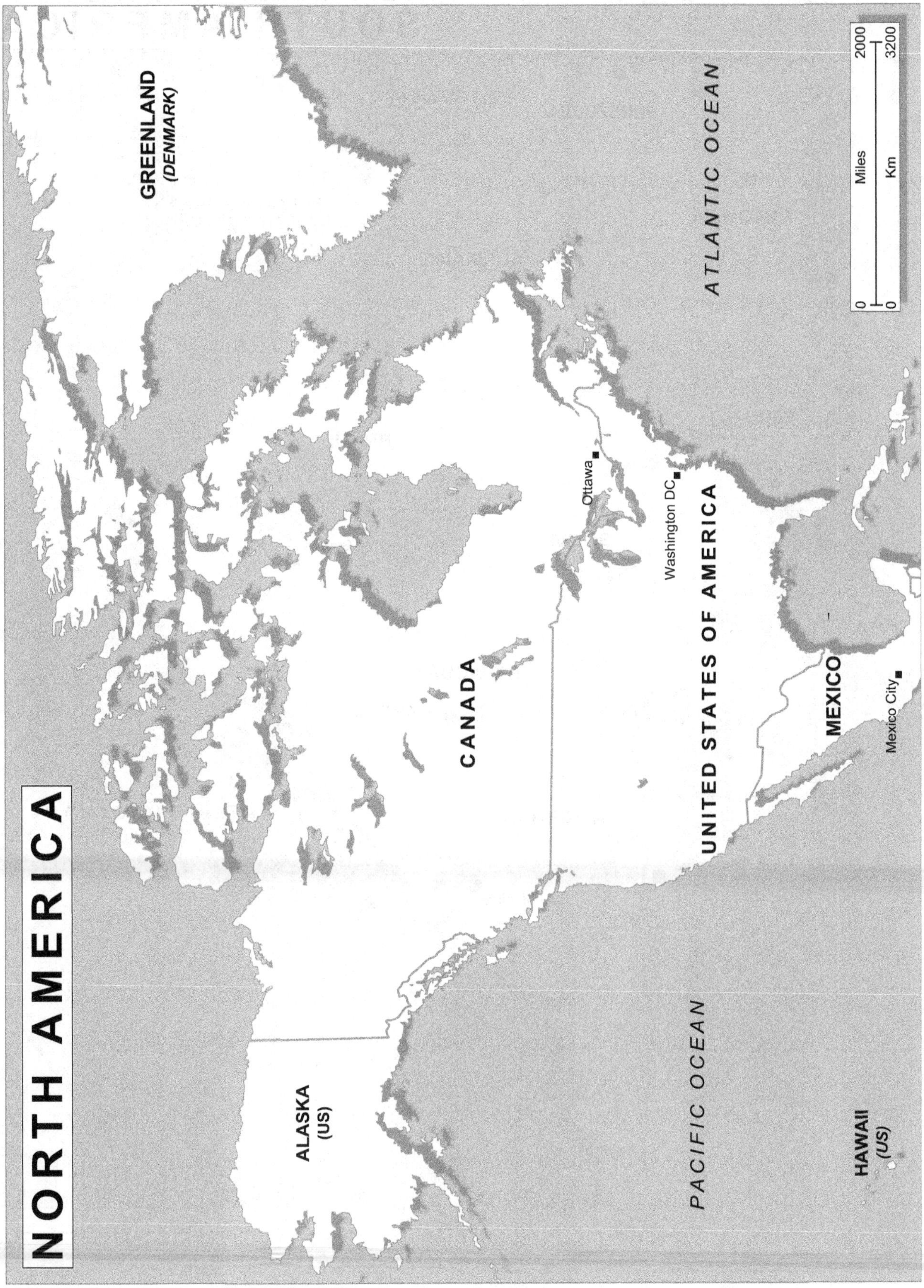
NORTH AMERICA
GREENLAND
(DENMARK)
ATLANTIC OCEAN
Ottawa
Washington DC
CANADA
UNITED STATES OF AMERICA
MEXICO
Mexico City
ALASKA
(US)
PACIFIC OCEAN
HAWAII
(US)
Miles
Km
0
2000
0
3200

SOUTH AMERICA
Caracas
VENEZUELA
GUYANA
Georgetown
Paramaribo
Cayenne
FRENCH GUIANA
SURINAME
Bogot□
COLOMBIA
Quito
ECUADOR
PERU
Lima
BRAZIL
BOLIVIA
La Paz
Bras□lia
PACIFIC OCEAN
PARAGUAY
Asunci□n
CHILE
ARGENTINA
ATLANTIC OCEAN
URUGUAY
Santiago
Buenos Aires
Montevideo
Islas Malvinas (Argentina)
Claimed by UK as Falkland Islands
0 Miles 1000
0 Km 1600

Currencies (units per US$) – Americas

	Unit	Jan 2007	Jan 2008	Jan 2009	Jan 2010	Jan 2011
Argentina	Peso	3.08	3.14	305.38	3.80	3.97
Belize	Belize dollar	1.97	1.97	1.95	1.95	1.95
Bolivia	Peso Boliviano	7.99	7.64	7.02	7.02	6.99
Brazil	Real	2.14	1.78	2.35	1.76	1.68
Chile	Chilean peso	539.90	498.75	621.45	489.90	497.55
Colombia	Colombian peso	2,218.60	1,998.60	2,280.60	1,967.60	1,856.60
Costa Rica	Colón	517.94	498.86	554.47	561.52	511.15
Ecuador	US dollar	1.00	1.00	1.00	1.00	1.00
El Salvador	Colón	1.00	1.00	1.00	1.00	1.00
French Guiana	Euro	0.77	0.69	0.78	0.69	0.77
Guatemala	Quetzal	7.69	7.60	7.80	8.37	8.01
Guyana	Guyana dollar	201.69	204.20	203.25	203.49	203.24
Honduras	Lempira	18.90	18.89	18.90	18.89	18.90
Mexico	Mexican peso	10.97	10.82	14.08	12.69	12.22
Nicaragua	Gold Cordóba	18.03	18.86	19.91	20.88	21.90
Panama	Balboa	1.00	1.00	1.00	1.00	1.00
Paraguay	Guarani	5,680.71	4,685.00	5,135.00	4,715.0	4,555.00
Peru	New sol	3.19	2.97	3.16	2.84	2.80
Suriname	Suriname dollar	2.75	2.75	2.75	2.75	2.75
Uruguay	Peso Uruguayo	24.49	21.68	22.75	19.50	19.95
Venezuela	Bolívar	(c) 2147.50	2,147.30	21,473.00	4.92	4.29
NORTH AMERICA						
Canada	Canadian dollar	1.17	1.02	1.25	1.02	0.99
United States of America	US dollar	1.00	1.00	1.00	1.00	1.00
CARIBBEAN						
Anguilla	EC dollar	2.70	2.70	2.70	2.70	2.70
Antigua	EC dollar	2.70	2.70	2.70	2.70	2.70
Aruba	Aruba guilder	1.79	1.79	1.79	1.79	1.79
Bahamas	Bahamian dollar	1.00	1.00	1.00	1.00	1.00
Barbados	Barbados dollar	2.00	2.00	2.00	2.00	2.00
Bermuda	Bermuda dollar	1.00	1.00	1.00	1.00	1.00
British Virgin Islands	US dollar	1.00	1.00	1.00	1.00	1.00
Cayman Islands	Cayman Islands dollar	0.82	0.82	0.82	0.82	0.82
Curaçao	Netherlands Antilles guilder	1.79	1.79	1.79	1.79	1.79
Cuba	Cuban convertible peso	0.82	0.82	0.82	0.82	0.82
Dominica	EC dollar	2.70	2.70	2.70	2.70	2.70
Dominican Republic	Dominican Republic peso	33.75	33.37	35.30	35.97	175.75
Grenada	EC dollar	2.77	2.70	2.70	2.70	2.70
Guadeloupe	Euro	0.77	0.69	0.78	0.69	0.77
Haiti	Gourde	37.65	36.75	39.75	39.75	39.75
Jamaica	Jamaican dollar	67.13	71.28	83.05	89.17	85.38
Martinique	Euro	0.77	0.69	0.78	0.69	0.77
Montserrat	EC dollar	2.70	2.70	2.70	2.70	2.70
Puerto Rico	US dollar	1.00	1.00	1.00	1.00	1.00
St Kitts Nevis	EC dollar	2.70	2.70	2.70	2.70	2.70
St Lucia	EC dollar	2.70	2.70	2.70	2.70	2.70
St Maartins	Netherlands Antilles guilder	1.79	1.79	1.79	1.79	1.79
St Vincent	EC dollar	2.70	2.70	2.70	2.70	2.70
Trinidad and Tobago	Trinidad and Tobago dollar	6.31	6.30	6.26	6.35	6.41
Turks and Caicos Islands	US dollar	1.00	1.00	1.00	1.00	1.00
US Virgin Islands	US dollar	1.00	1.00	1.00	1.00	1.00

Key indicators 2010

	Population (m)	Area ('000 sq km)	GDP per capita (US$)	Inflation (%)	GDP real growth (%)	Balance of trade (US$m)
Argentina	40.09	2,766.90	9,138	10.5	9.2	14,266.0
Belize	*0.31	23.00	4,159	0.5	2.0	-171.5
Bolivia	*10.52	1,098.60	1,858	2.5	4.2	(f) 774.0
Brazil	190.76	8,512.00	10,816	5.0	7.5	20,221.0
Chile	*17.09	756.60	11,828	1.5	5.3	15,855.0
Colombia	*45.51	1,138.90	6,273	2.3	4.3	2,150.0
Costa Rica	*4.66	51.10	7,843	5.7	4.2	-3,576.0
Ecuador	14.31	270.70	3,984	3.6	3.2	(f) 79.0
El Salvador	*6.18	21.40	3,701	1.2	0.7	-3,612.0
French Guiana	0.20	91.00	–	–	–	–
Guatemala	*14.36	108.90	2,888	3.9	2.6	-4,293.0
Guyana	*0.75	215.00	2,868	3.7	3.6	(f) -394.4
Honduras	*8.05	112.10	2,016	4.7	2.8	(f) -2470.6
Mexico	105.37	1,958.20	8,479	3.9	3.3	-7,590.0
Nicaragua	*5.82	148.00	(f) 1,082	9.2	-1.5	-1,636.0
Panama	3.41	77.10	7,593	3.5	7.5	-4,615.0
Paraguay	*6.45	407.00	2,886	4.7	15.3	-1527.1
Peru	*29.46	1,285.20	5,172	1.5	8.8	6,750.0
Suriname	*0.53	164.00	6,975	6.9	4.4	625.7
Uruguay	*3.35	176.20	11,998	6.7	8.5	-256.0
Venezuela	*28.83	916.50	9,960	28.2	*-1.9	27,173.0
NORTH AMERICA						
Canada	*34.10	9,976.10	46,215	1.8	3.2	-8,682.0
United States of America	308.75	9,300.00	47,284	1.6	3.0	-470,960.0
CARIBBEAN						
Anguilla	(a) - 0.01	0.01	(c) 9,711	1.3	(g) *6.0	–
Antigua	*0.90	0.03	12,849	3.4	-4.1	-404.8
Aruba	*0.11	0.02	(f) 43,986	(g) 1.8	(f) -7.7	-1,077.3
Bahamas	0.35	13.90	21,879	1.7	0.5	-1,888.0
Barbados	*0.27	0.40	14,326	5.1	-0.5	(f) -912.8
Bermuda	0.07	0.01	(c) 80,676	(e) 3.1	(e) 2.5	487.0
British Virgin Islands	0.02	0.15	(d) 16,000	(e) 1.9	(c) 7.2	–
Cayman Islands	0.05	0.30	(c) 46,500	(e) 7.0	(c) 6.5	841.7
Cuba	11.40	110.90	4,051	2.8	6.5	-4,530.0
Curaçao						
Dominica	*0.07	0.80	5,167	2.9	1.0	-159.3
Dominican Republic	9.38	48.40	5,228	6.3	7.8	(f) -6740.8
Grenada	*0.10	0.34	6,534	5.0	-1.4	-218.2
Guadeloupe	0.44	1.80	(e) 7,900	–	–	–
Haiti	*9.99	27.80	673	4.1	-5.1	(f) -1481.1
Jamaica	*2.74	11.00	5,039	12.3	-1.2	(f) -3087.9
Martinique	0.40	1.10	–	–	–	–
Montserrat	(b) - 0.01	0.01	–	–	–	-18.8
Puerto Rico	3.73	8.90	(f) 15,690	2.5	-3.8	(f) *20,156.0
St Kitts Nevis	0.05	0.30	9,636	2.5	-1.5	-142.7
St Lucia	0.17	0.60	5,668	1.8	0.8	-315.2
St Maarten						
St Vincent	*0.11	0.40	5,229	1.5	-2.3	-254.1
Trinidad and Tobago	*1.34	5.10	15,706	10.7	0.0	(f) 2,202.0
Turks and Caicos Islands	(c) 0.02	0.43	–	–	–	–
US Virgin Islands	(c) 0.12	0.40	–	–	–	–

(a) 13,677 people; (b) 9,341 people; (c) 2006; (d) 2004; (e) 2005; (f) 2009; (g) 2008.

Asia keeps on growing

In 2011 the regional implications of the sea change in the relative strengths and weaknesses of China and Japan continued to be pre-eminent. Japan's relative decline was accelerated by the devastating *tsunami* that hit the Tohuku region in March 2011, with a huge casualty toll and widespread property damage. As if things weren't already bad enough, the high profile forced de-commissioning of the Fukushima Dai-ichi nuclear generation plant and the government's equally high-profile ineptitude in handling the affair did little to reassure the world of its super-power status. Chronic political instability and a chronically weak economy only reinforced the impression that Japan, once the region's economic mainspring, had lost its grip.

Politically, the most significant single development in the region was change in Myanmar, where 2011 looked likely to go down in history as the year in which Myanmar's post war history really began to change. This was best symbolised by the December 2011 visit to Yangon (Rangoon) and Naypyidaw by US Secretary of State Hillary Clinton. This was the first visit by such a senior American official for 50 years (the last being John Foster Dulles), and the most high-profile visitor received by Aung San Suu Kyi, winner of the 1991 Nobel Prize for Peace, in Myanmar. The two had a private dinner followed the next day by an official meeting with Ms Suu Kyi and senior officials from her National League for Democracy party (NLD). The NLD has committed itself to re-entering mainstream politics, having boycotted general elections in 2010, and planned to contest by-elections in 2012. After their meeting, Ms Suu Kyi expressed herself 'happy' with the US' engagement.

'Politically, the most significant single development in the region was change in Myanmar.'

Growth in Asia has also moderated since the second quarter of 2011, mainly as a result of weakening external demand. Domestic demand has been generally resilient, and overheating pressures remain elevated in a number of economies, with credit growth still robust and inflation momentum generally high. In line with the weaker global outlook, growth in Asia was expected to be slightly lower in 2011/12 than forecast in April 2011, but the expansion should remain healthy, supported by domestic demand, and inflation is expected to recede modestly after peaking in 2011.

Nevertheless, risks for the Asia and Pacific region are also decidedly tilted to the downside. The sell-off in Asian financial markets in August and September 2011 underscores that an escalation of euro area financial turbulence and a renewed slowdown in the United States could have severe macro-economic and financial spillovers to Asia.

The downside risks to growth amid persistent overheating pressures present Asian policymakers with a delicate balancing act, as they need to guard against risks to growth but also limit the adverse impact of prolonged easy financial conditions on inflation and balance sheet vulnerabilities. In economies where overheating pressures are more elevated and monetary conditions still accommodative, the return to more neutral monetary stances should continue, through both higher interest rates and more flexible exchange rates.

However, in those economies where inflation is within central banks' target ranges and the exposure to severe external shocks is greater, a pause in monetary tightening may be warranted until global uncertainties have lessened. Meanwhile, the normalisation of fiscal policy stances should run its course: in many economies, fiscal positions remain accommodative, with structural deficits higher than their pre-crisis levels. If the downside risks to the global outlook were to materialise, Asian economies have the scope to reverse course and use a range of measures to cushion the impact on economic activity.

At the same time, the weakness in global demand only confirms that Asia would greatly benefit from further progress in rebalancing growth by developing domestic sources of demand. In addition to structural reforms, this would require a reprioritisation of fiscal spending, in order to create fiscal space for critical infrastructure investment and social priority expenditure. These measures would help increase domestic demand over time, as well as make the region more resilient to external shocks, and they would also help to make growth in Asia more 'inclusive'. Despite fast growth and progress in poverty reduction, income inequality in Asia has increased over the last decade. Measures that deepen regional financial integration would also help with rebalancing, by improving access to finance and strengthening domestic demand. Asian low-income and Pacific Island economies face particular challenges in the near and medium term. In low-income countries, the fight against inflation is complicated by strong second-round effects, the need to phase out subsidies, and less well anchored inflation expectations. Pacific Island economies need to undertake further structural reforms to lift potential growth.

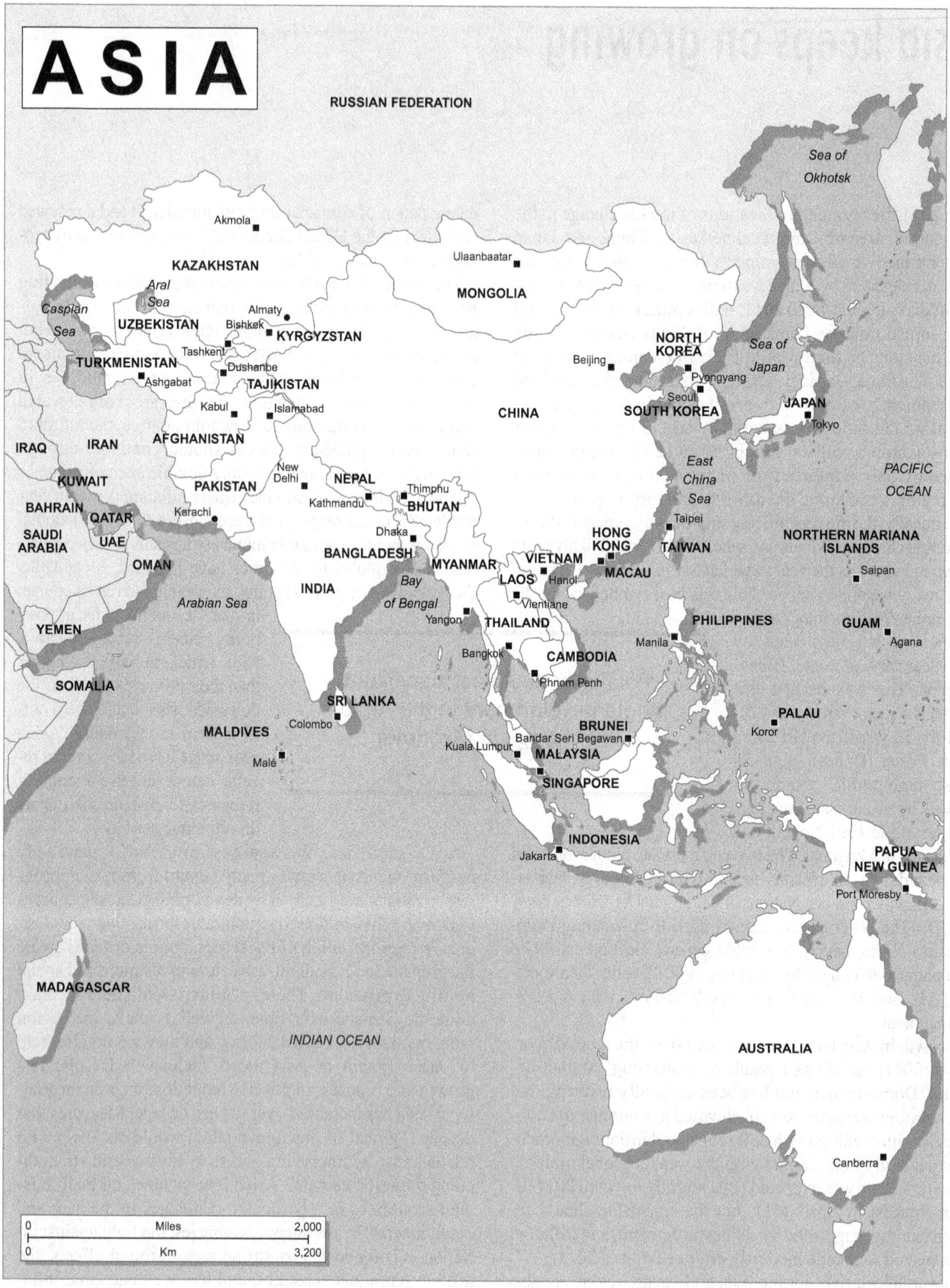
ASIA
RUSSIAN FEDERATION
Sea of Okhotsk
Akmola
KAZAKHSTAN
Ulaanbaatar
MONGOLIA
Aral Sea
Caspian Sea
Almaty
UZBEKISTAN
Bishkek
KYRGYZSTAN
Tashkent
TURKMENISTAN
Ashgabat
Dushanbe
TAJIKISTAN
NORTH KOREA
Beijing
Pyongyang
Sea of Japan
Seoul
SOUTH KOREA
JAPAN
Tokyo
Kabul
Islamabad
CHINA
AFGHANISTAN
IRAQ
IRAN
KUWAIT
New Delhi
NEPAL
PAKISTAN
Thimphu
Kathmandu
BHUTAN
East China Sea
PACIFIC OCEAN
BAHRAIN
QATAR
Karachi
SAUDI ARABIA
UAE
OMAN
Dhaka
BANGLADESH
Taipei
HONG KONG
TAIWAN
NORTHERN MARIANA ISLANDS
MYANMAR
VIETNAM
MACAU
Saipan
INDIA
Bay of Bengal
LAOS
Hanoi
Vientiane
Arabian Sea
Yangon
THAILAND
PHILIPPINES
GUAM
YEMEN
Manila
Agana
Bangkok
CAMBODIA
SOMALIA
Phnom Penh
SRI LANKA
PALAU
Koror
MALDIVES
Colombo
BRUNEI
Bandar Seri Begawan
Kuala Lumpur
MALAYSIA
Male
SINGAPORE
INDONESIA
Jakarta
PAPUA NEW GUINEA
Port Moresby
MADAGASCAR
INDIAN OCEAN
AUSTRALIA
Canberra
0 Miles 2,000
0 Km 3,200

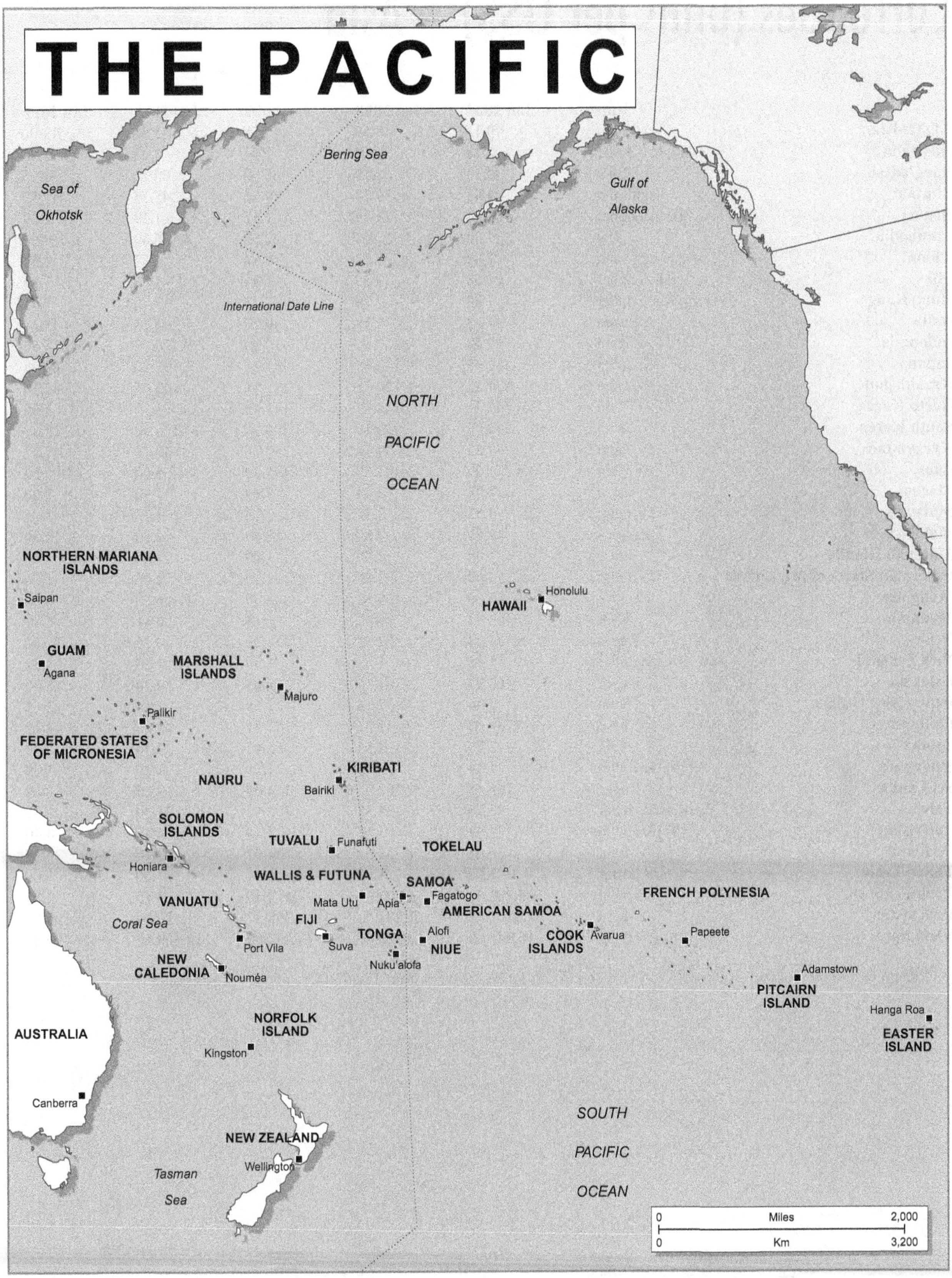
THE PACIFIC
Bering Sea
Sea of Okhotsk
Gulf of Alaska
International Date Line
NORTH PACIFIC OCEAN
NORTHERN MARIANA ISLANDS
Saipan
HAWAII
Honolulu
GUAM
Agana
MARSHALL ISLANDS
Majuro
Palikir
FEDERATED STATES OF MICRONESIA
NAURU
KIRIBATI
Bairiki
SOLOMON ISLANDS
Honiara
TUVALU
Funafuti
TOKELAU
WALLIS & FUTUNA
SAMOA
Mata Utu
Apia
Fagatogo
AMERICAN SAMOA
FRENCH POLYNESIA
VANUATU
Coral Sea
FIJI
Suva
TONGA
Alofi
NIUE
COOK ISLANDS
Avarua
Papeete
Port Vila
NEW CALEDONIA
Nouméa
Nuku'alofa
Adamstown
PITCAIRN ISLAND
Hanga Roa
EASTER ISLAND
AUSTRALIA
NORFOLK ISLAND
Kingston
Canberra
NEW ZEALAND
Wellington
Tasman Sea
SOUTH PACIFIC OCEAN
0 Miles 2,000
0 Km 3,200

Currencies (units per US$) – Asia

	Unit	Jan 2007	Jan 2008	Jan 2009	Jan 2010	Jan 2011
Afghanistan	Afghani	49.18	49.53	47.28	45.36	43.00
Australia	Australian dollar	1.28	1.16	1.54	1.08	1.00
Bangladesh	Taka	70.23	68.59	68.90	69.26	70.95
Bhutan	Ngultrum	44.43	39.34	49.26	45.78	45.39
Brunei	Brunei dollar	1.54	1.45	1.51	1.39	1.29
Cambodia	Riel	4,025.00	3,950.00	4,142.50	4,155.00	4,040.00
China	Renminbi yuan	7.80	7.37	6.84	6.82	6.63
Fiji	Fijian dollar	1.68	1.55	1.84	1.88	1.84
Hong Kong	Hong Kong dollar	7.80	7.79	7.76	7.75	7.77
India	Rupee	44.43	39.35	49.26	45.78	45.38
Indonesia	Rupiah	9,130.00	9,327.50	11,310.00	9,190.00	9,015.50
Japan	Yen	120.35	113.35	89.41	90.86	82.98
Kazakhstan	Tenge	125.33	120.75	121.51	148.05	147.10
North Korea	Won	(a) 142.45	142.45	142.45	(b) 1.30	1.30
South Korea	Won	940.05	930.10	1,390.90	1,123.00	1,122.30
Kyrgyzstan	Som	38.25	34.54	40.28	44.22	47.17
Laos	New kip	8,271.00	9,401.50	8,495.00	8,455.00	8,000.00
Macao	Pataca	8.03	8.03	7.99	7.99	8.00
Malaysia	Ringgit	3.51	3.32	3.63	3.33	3.07
Maldives	Rufiyaa	12.80	12.80	12.80	12.80	12.80
Marshall Islands	US dollar	1.00	1.00	1.00	1.00	1.00
Federated States of Micronesia	US dollar	1.00	1.00	1.00	1.00	1.00
Mongolia	Tugrik	1,165.00	1,169.30	1,408.00	1,456.50	1,276.00
Myanmar	Kyat	6.42	6.42	6.44	6.41	6.41
Nepal	Rupee	71.08	62.95	78.82	73.25	72.62
New Zealand	New Zealand dollar	1.45	1.29	1.90	1.35	1.31
Pakistan	Rupee	60.97	61.14	79.05	84.20	85.80
Papua New Guinea	Kina	2.96	2.75	2.68	2.64	2.65
Philippines	Peso	49.00	41.21	47.41	45.82	44.15
Samoa	Tala	2.70	2.54	3.03	2.44	2.38
Singapore	Singapore dollar	1.54	1.45	1.51	1.39	1.29
Sri Lanka	Rupee	108.45	108.90	114.00	114.25	110.85
Taiwan	Taiwanese dollar	32.76	32.38	33.59	31.79	29.37
Tajikistan	Tajik rouble	3.43	3.43	3.44	4.37	4.40
Thailand	Baht	36.05	33.59	34.91	32.86	30.39
Timor-Leste	US dollar	1.00	1.00	1.00	1.00	1.00
Turkmenistan	New Manat	5,200.00	5,200.00	(c) 2.85	2.85	2.85
Uzbekistan	Sum	1,241.10	1,287.50	1,398.37	1,516.89	1,640.55
Vietnam	New dong	16,047.00	16,040.00	17,477.00	18,469.50	19,499.00

(a) floating exchange rate mid-2003; (b) Won revalued 2009; (c) New Manat from 1 Jan 2009, pegged to US dollar

Key indicators 2010

	Population (m)	Area ('000 sq km)	GDP per capita (US$)	Inflation (%)	GDP real growth (%)	Balance of trade (US$m)
Afghanistan	*29.12	647.50	*515	*7.7	*8.2	(c) *-6.6
Australia	*22.34	7,682.30	55,160	2.7	2.5	18,180.0
Bangladesh	*146.60	144.00	638	8.2	6.0	-5,485.0
Bhutan	*0.73	47.00	1,978	7.1	6.7	(c) -144.7
Brunei	*0.40	5.80	31,239	0.5	4.1	(c) 4,889.5
Cambodia	(14.30	181.00	814	4.0	6.0	(c) -1,573.9
China	*1,334.74	9,597.10	4,382	3.3	10.3	254,180.0
Fiji	*0.88	18.30	3,518	5.4	0.1	(c) -674.9
Hong Kong	*7.07	1.10	31,591	2.4	6.8	-42,965.0
India	*1,190.50	3,287.60	1,265	13.2	10.1	-97,934.0
Indonesia	(b) 237.64	1,919.40	3,015	5.1	6.1	30,623.0
Japan	(b) 128.06	377.70	4	-0.7	4.0	90,970.0
Kazakhstan	*15.90	2,717.30	8,883	7.4	7.3	28,881.0
North Korea	22.80	122.40	–	–	(d) -2.3	(d) -1,380.0
South Korea	*48.90	99.10	20,591	3.0	6.1	41,876.0
Kyrgyzstan	*5.33	198.50	*863	*7.8	*-1.4	-1198.3
Laos	6.31	236.80	984	6.0	7.9	(c) -1,323.0
Macao	*0.544	(a)	(c) 39,264	2.8	25.0	(c) -4,959.0
Malaysia	*28.25	330.40	8,423	1.7	7.2	(c) 40,253.0
Maldives	*0.32	0.30	5,841	5.0	7.1	-798.0
Federated States of Micronesia	*0.11	0.70	(c) 2,497	3.5	-3.2	-119.0
Mongolia	*2.80	1,565.00	2,267	10.2	6.4	-180.0
Myanmar	*53.40	676.60	702	7.3	5.3	(e) 892.0
Nepal	*29.96	147.20	562	9.3	4.6	-4,115.0
New Zealand	*4.37	268.70	32,130	2.3	1.5	2,367.0
Pakistan	*165.15	803.90	1,050	11.7	3.8	-11,416.0
Papua New Guinea	*6.86	462.80	1,488	6.6	7.0	(c) 1,521.2
Philippines	*94.01	300.40	2,007	3.8	7.6	-10,384.0
Samoa	*0.18	2.80	2,780	-0.2	0.0	-245.0
Singapore	*3.77	0.60	43,117	2.8	14.5	46,758.0
Sri Lanka	*20.65	65.60	2,435	5.9	9.1	-3,853.0
Solomon Islands	*0.52	27.50	1,340	1.0	5.6	(c) -75.8
Taiwan	*23.20	36.00	18,458	1.0	10.8	(c) 29,304.0
Tajikistan	*7.60	143.10	(c) *767	6.5	6.5	-1,634.0
Thailand	*67.31	514.00	4,992	3.3	7.8	32.0
Timor-Leste	1.07	19.00	588	4.9	6.1	(c) -431.0
Turkmenistan	*5.20	488.10	(c) 3,243	(c) -2.7	(c) 6.1	(c) *875.0
Uzbekistan	*28.10	447.40	1,380	9.4	8.5	(c) 1,613.0
Vietnam	*86.93	329.60	1,174	9.2	6.8	-5,147.0

*Estimated figure; (a) area 29.2 square km; (b) census figure; (c) 2009; (d) 2007; (e) 2008.

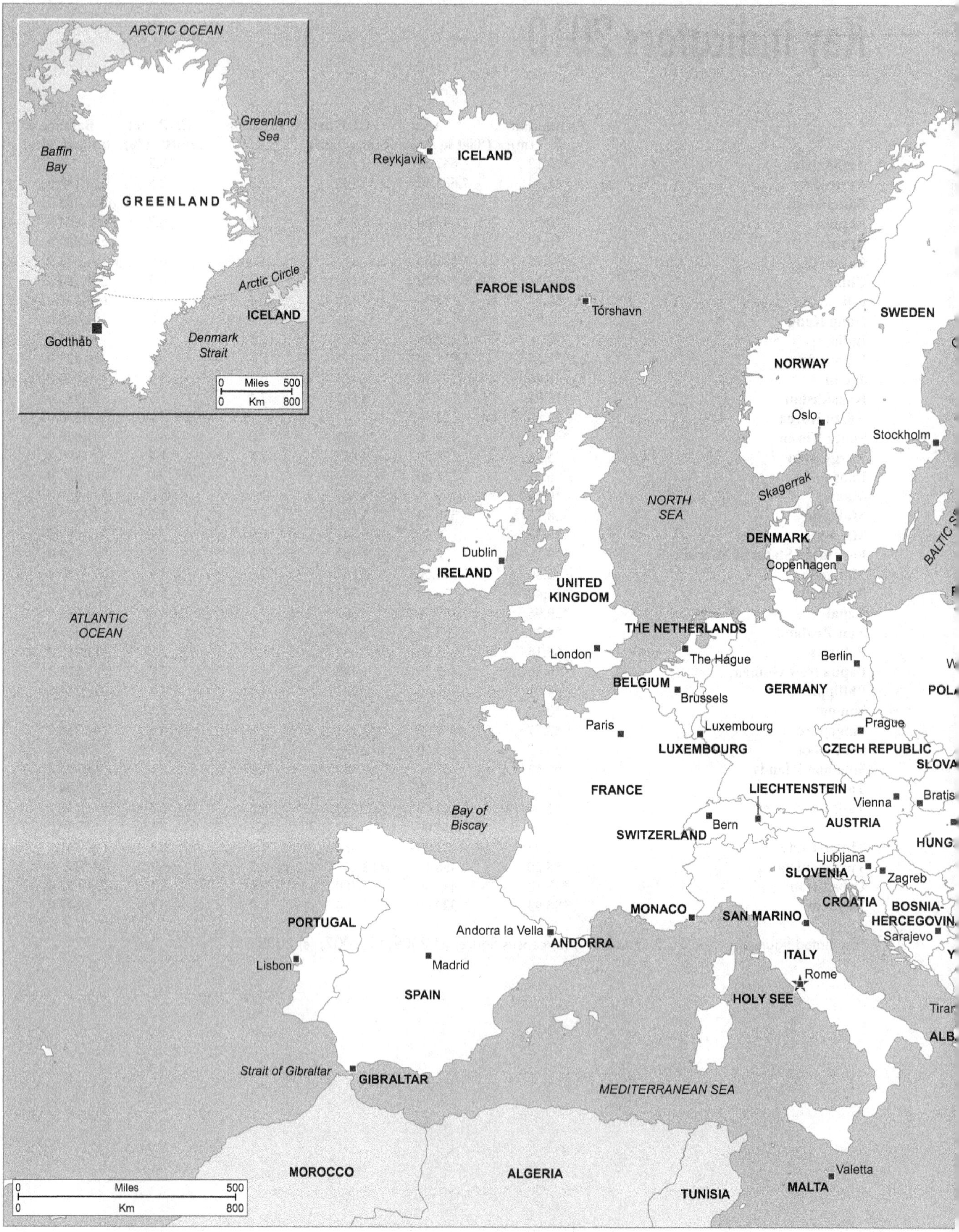
ARCTIC OCEAN
Greenland Sea
Baffin Bay
GREENLAND
Arctic Circle
ICELAND
Godthåb
Denmark Strait
0 Miles 500
0 Km 800
Reykjavik
ICELAND
FAROE ISLANDS
Tórshavn
SWEDEN
NORWAY
Oslo
Stockholm
Skagerrak
NORTH SEA
DENMARK
Copenhagen
BALTIC SEA
Dublin
IRELAND
UNITED KINGDOM
ATLANTIC OCEAN
THE NETHERLANDS
London
The Hague
Berlin
BELGIUM
Brussels
GERMANY
Paris
Luxembourg
Prague
LUXEMBOURG
CZECH REPUBLIC
FRANCE
LIECHTENSTEIN
Vienna
Bratis
Bay of Biscay
Bern
AUSTRIA
SWITZERLAND
HUNG.
Ljubljana
SLOVENIA
Zagreb
CROATIA
BOSNIA-HERCEGOVIN
MONACO
SAN MARINO
PORTUGAL
Andorra la Vella
ANDORRA
Sarajevo
Lisbon
Madrid
ITALY
Rome
SPAIN
HOLY SEE
Tirar
ALB.
Strait of Gibraltar
GIBRALTAR
MEDITERRANEAN SEA
MOROCCO
ALGERIA
Valetta
MALTA
TUNISIA
0 Miles 500
0 Km 800

FINLAND
RUSSIA
ki
Tallinn
ESTONIA
ga
LATVIA
Moscow
HUANIA
Vilnius
Minsk
BELARUS
KAZAKHSTAN
ARAL SEA
UZBEKISTAN
Kiev
UKRAINE
MOLDOVA
Kishinev
TURKMENISTAN
CASPIAN SEA
ROMANIA
Bucharest
de
GEORGIA
Tbilisi
Baku
AZERBAIJAN
BLACK SEA
Yerevan
ARMENIA
A
BULGARIA
Sofia
Skopje
EDONIA
Ankara
TURKEY
CE
IRAN
Athens
SYRIA
Lefkosia
IRAQ
CYPRUS
LEBANON

The euro crumbles

The lingering debate as to how Europe's single currency – the euro – might survive dragged on throughout 2011, with little real prospect of reaching a conclusion. While smiling through gritted teeth for the benefit of European summit photo-calls, the two key players in the drama – France and Germany – had never really sung from the same song sheet. The downgrading of France's Triple A credit rating in early 2012 projected an embarrassingly strong light on just where the differences kicked in. Germany espoused free-market liberalism and economic discipline. France found it hard to break away from a world in which politicians played with monetary policy and governments quietly drew up anti-competition schemes whereby tax rates were harmonised and jobs protected.

Despite its prolonged travails, by the end of the 20th century the European Union (EU) had emerged as the word's largest trading block. In many respects it worked remarkably well: Lithuanians could work in London, Slovaks in Seville. Cars manufactured in Romania could be sold in France, an Irish airline could fly passengers from Barcelona to Bratislava. But the success came at a cost; the bureaucracy exported from Brussels came at an expensive price. A Brussels-centric vision of Europe had also emerged in which trade and commerce existed as support mechanisms for the greater, social, good. The ultimate and intrinsically ironic objective of any greater efficiency was the protection of inefficiency. Retirement ages must be pegged back to 60 or 62 when Europeans were living longer than ever, unemployment benefits should closely match salary levels. Those who pointed out the absurdity of this scenario were branded market 'speculators' bent on bringing down the euro and allowing economic reality to replace a federalist cloud-cuckoo land.

There was, however, something of a role reversal in the region's euro-enthusiasm in 2011. Those states in Europe's north-west that had originally espoused a federalist vision of the EU began to have their doubts. In Germany voters were beginning to express their reluctance to join in seemingly endless bail-outs of the weaker euro-zone economies. The German *hausfrau* was no longer prepared to see her taxes diverted to save the bacon of the spendthrift Greek, Portuguese or possibly even Italian and Spanish governments. Neither France nor Germany were in a poition to criticise economic profligacy in other countries. Instead of respecting and adhering to the provisions and discipline of the Stability and Growth Pact they virtually led the field in flouting them when it suited them to do so. German and French banks were also the leaders of the pack when it came to lending to Greek banks.

If the euro-zone countries were in an economic mess, the same was the case in large parts of the rest of Europe. Growth rates in the gross domestic product (GDP) of the United Kingdom were, by mid-2011, flat-lining in the same way as those of France and Germany. The French and German governments endeavoured to patch together a series of last-ditch measures to save the euro. But the body-language of Messrs Merkel and Sarkozy spoke volumes. The principal message was that Europe's politicians were no longer in charge of what they had mistakenly seen as a political project. The future of the euro had, in 2011, become very much a matter of economic rather than political sense. The financial markets now held serious reservations about the viability of the common currency. Bold, visionary, statements by vote-seeking politicians were no longer enough.

'At the time of the euro's creation and adoption in 2002 it seemed that little, if any, thought had been given to exit mechanisms.'

The political downside of abandoning the euro was politically and financially unpalatable. At the time of the euro's creation and adoption in 2002 it seemed that little, if any, thought had been given to exit mechanisms. For Greece to re-adopt the drachma would involve countless considerations. If speculation was to be avoided, the re-introduction of the drachma would need to take place in complete secrecy. Given the human disposition towards whispering speculation, secrecy in a country like Greece would be virtually impossible. Equally impossible would be the logistics – not to mention the cost – of printing and minting millions of coins and banknotes. These were problems that no government had ever faced; problems which both politicians and central bankers preferred to leave to lesser mortals to sort out – if they can.

Currencies (units per US$) – Europe

	Unit	Jan 2007	Jan 2008	Jan 2009	Jan 2010	Jan 2011
Albania	Lek	96.73	83.21	97.56	96.02	106.41
Andorra	Euro	0.77	0.69	0.78	0.69	0.77
Armenia	Dram	367.25	301.12	305.38	376.00	357.00
Austria	Euro	0.77	0.69	0.78	0.69	0.77
Azerbaijan	New manat	(a) 0.87	0.85	0.81	0.80	0.80
Belarus	Belarus rouble	2,142.00	2,156.50	2,696.00	2,843.00	3,008.00
Belgium	Euro	0.77	0.69	0.78	0.69	0.77
Bosnia-Herzegovina	Bosnian marka	1.51	1.35	1.53	1.36	1.51
Bulgaria	Lev	1.48	1.35	1.53	1.36	1.51
Croatia	Kuna	5.70	5.06	5.78	5.07	5.68
Cyprus	Euro	0.45	(c) 0.69	0.78	0.69	0.77
Czech Republic	Czech koruna	21.50	18.28	21.99	18.04	18.88
Denmark	Danish krone	5.76	5.17	5.83	5.17	5.74
Estonia	Kroon	12.10	10.83	12.23	10.88	(d) 0.77
Faroe Islands	Faroese krone	5.76	5.17	5.83	5.17	5.74
Finland	Euro	0.77	0.69	0.78	0.69	0.77
France	Euro	0.77	0.69	0.78	0.69	0.77
Georgia	Lari	1.71	1.59	1.67	1.70	1.77
Germany	Euro	0.77	0.69	0.78	0.69	0.77
Gibraltar	Gibraltar pound	0.51	0.49	0.73	0.61	0.64
Greece	Euro	0.77	0.69	0.78	0.69	0.77
Greenland	Danish krone	5.76	5.17	5.83	5.17	5.74
Hungary	Forint	195.85	176.03	226.34	186.23	212.86
Iceland	Icelandic krona	70.78	62.93	124.58	125.03	117.58
Ireland	Euro	0.77	0.69	0.78	0.69	0.77
Italy	Euro	0.77	0.69	0.78	0.69	0.77
Kosovo	Euro	–	0.69	0.78	0.69	0.77
Latvia	Lat	0.54	0.48	0.55	0.49	0.54
Liechtenstein	Swiss franc	1.25	1.15	1.17	1.02	0.96
Lithuania	Lit	2.67	2.39	2.70	2.40	2.66
Luxembourg	Euro	0.77	0.69	0.78	0.69	0.77
Macedonia	Macedonian denar	47.12	42.43	47.95	42.70	46.80
Malta	Euro	0.33	(c) 0.69	0.78	0.69	0.77
Moldova	Moldovan leu	13.03	12.14	10.57	12.27	12.34
Monaco	Euro	0.77	0.69	0.78	0.69	0.77
Montenegro	Euro	0.77	0.69	0.78	0.69	0.77
The Netherlands	Euro	0.77	0.69	0.78	0.69	0.77
Norway	Norwegian krone	6.45	5.53	7.04	5.68	5.95
Poland	Zloty	2.99	2.49	3.46	2.81	2.98
Portugal	Euro	0.77	0.69	0.78	0.69	0.77
Romania	New leu	2.67	2.45	3.35	2.86	3.28
Russia	Rouble	26.57	24.68	33.11	29.56	30.77
San Marino	Euro	0.77	0.69	0.78	0.69	0.77
Serbia	Dinar	61.46	54.20	74.53	67.42	81.64
Slovakia	Euro	26.95	(c) 0.69	0.78	0.69	0.77
Slovenia	Euro	(b) 0.77	0.69	0.78	0.69	0.77
Spain	Euro	0.77	0.69	0.78	0.69	0.77
Sweden	Swedish krone	7.02	6.52	8.32	7.06	6.89
Switzerland	Swiss franc	1.25	1.15	1.17	1.02	0.96
Turkey	New Turkish lira	1.43	1.18	1.67	1.45	1.56
Ukraine	Hryvna	5.06	5.06	7.86	8.08	7.97
United Kingdom	UK pound	0.51	0.49	0.73	0.61	0.64
The Holy See	Euro	0.77	0.69	0.78	0.69	0.77

(a) new manat, from 2006; (b) euro adopted, 2007; (c) euro adopted, 2008; (d) euro adopted 1 Jan 2010.

Key indicators 2010

	Population (m)	Area ('000 sq km)	GDP per capita (US$)	Inflation (%)	GDP real growth (%)	Balance of trade (US$m)
Albania	*3.20	28.80	3,716	3.6	3.5	-2,758.0
Andorra	*.09	0.73	(b) *44,900	(b) 2.03	(b) *2.6	–
Armenia	*3.30	29.80	2,846	8.2	2	-2,032.5
Austria	8.39	83.90	44,988	1.7	2.1	-4,303.0
Azerbaijan	*9.19	86.60	(a) *4,807	(a) 1.5	2.7	19,730.0
Belarus	*9.49	208.00	5,800	7.7	7.6	-9,118.0
Belgium	*10.88	30.50	42,630	2.3	2	-2,331.0
Bosnia and Hercegovina	*3.84	51.10	4,319	2.1	0.8	-4,293.0
Bulgaria	*7.53	111.00	6,334	3	0.2	-3,217.0
Croatia	*4.43	56.50	13,720	1	-1.4	-7,877.0
Cyprus	*1.10	9.30	28,237	2.6	1	-6,376.0
Czech Republic	*10.52	78.90	18,288	1.5	2.3	2,814.0
Denmark	*5.55	43.10	56,147	2.3	2.1	8,952.0
Estonia	*1.34	45.10	14,836	2.9	3.1	-331.0
Faroe Islands	0.05	1.40	–	0.5	–	–
Finland	*5.36	338.10	44,489	1.7	3.1	4,404.0
France	*62.97	544.00	41,019	1.7	1.4	-71,210.0
Georgia	*4.41	69.70	2,658	7.1	6.4	-2,572.0
Germany	*81.78	357.00	40,631	1.2	3.5	204,720.0
Gibraltar	0.03	(+)	(c) 38,322	(b) 2.8	(b) 6.0	(d) -194.0
Greece	*11.28	132.00	27,302	4.7	-4.5	-37,537.0
Greenland	0.06	2,166.10	*20,000	(b) 9.4	(a) -2.00	–
Hungary	*10.00	93.00	12,879	4.9	1.2	6,212.0
Iceland	*0.32	103.10	39,026	5.4	-3.5	983.0
Ireland	*4.47	70.30	45,689	-1.6	-0.4	48,273.0
Italy	*60.48	301.30	34,059	1.6	1.3	(a) 3,259.0
Kosovo	(a) *2.13	10.88	(b) 1,303	3.5	*4.0	2,276.0
Latvia	*2.24	64.60	10,695	-1.2	-0.3	-1,546.0
Liechtenstein	*0.03	0.20	*35,000	–	(b) 1.8	–
Lithuania	*3.29	65.20	11,044	1.2	1.2	-1,560.0
Luxembourg	*0.51	2.60	108,832	2.3	3.5	-5,286.0
Macedonia	*2.06	25.70	4,431	1.5	0.7	-1,945.0
Malta	*0.42	0.40	19,746	2	3.1	-1,229.0
Moldova	*4.89	34.00	1,630	7.4	6.9	-2,220.0
Monaco	*0.03	(++)	–	0.7	*1.8	–
Montenegro	*0.63	14.00	6,070	0.5	1.1	-1,745.0
Netherlands	*16.61	41.50	47,172	0.9	1.7	57,290.0
Norway	*4.89	324.00	84,144	2.4	0.3	58,391.0
Poland	*38.18	312.70	12,300	2.6	3.8	-11,414.0
Portugal	*10.64	92.10	21,559	1.4	1.4	-23,751.0
Romania	*21.44	237.50	7,542	6.1	-1.3	-7,805.0
Russia	*142.94	17,075.00	10,437	6.9	4	151,681.0
San Marino	*0.03	0.01	–	2.8	(a) *-13	–
Serbia	*7.43	77.47	5,233	6.2	1.8	-6,344.0
Slovakia	*5.43	49.00	16,104	0.7	4	182.0
Slovenia	*2.05	20.30	23,706	0.8	1.2	-1,602.0
Spain	*46.07	504.80	30,639	2	-0.1	-62,350.0
Sweden	*9.38	449.00	48,875	1.9	5.5	10,879.0
Switzerland	*7.83	41.30	67,246	0.7	2.6	15,870.0
Turkey	*72.70	779.50	10,399	8.6	8.2	-56,445.0
Ukraine	*45.96	603.70	3,000	9.4	4.2	-8,712.0
United Kingdom	*62.22	244.10	36,120	3.3	1.3	-152,930.0

* Estimated figure; (a) 2009; (b) 2008; (c) 2006.
(+) area 5.8 square km; (++) area 1.8 square km

The Arab Spring

In June 2009, in Cairo, President Obama delivered his much awaited keynote speech on the Middle East. Much awaited, but, two years down the line, disappointing. Although his speech set out the stall for US policy in the region, as time went by few of the initiatives detailed have seen the light of day. For whatever reason, the intention to engage more fully with the Iran of President Ahmadinejad has faltered, the strong words used to spell out the administration's intentions in the Isreal-Palestine dispute have not been followed up. A report published by the Washington based Project on Middle East Democracy (POMED) summed up the situation thus: 'President Obama has said the right words, but is unwilling or unable to offer substantive new policies to support the aspirations of people in the Middle East.'

The US administration's failure to make tangible progress led to internal shifts and re-alignments. Writing in the *International Herald Tribune* in late 2010 Roger Cohen attributed the change in policy to the increased importance of Secretary of State Hillary Clinton. She had, according to Mr Cohen, replaced George Mitchell as the administration's special envoy. Once seen as 'the darling' of the Israelis, by 2010 Mrs Clinton appeared to have come to terms with the existence of a Palestinian state was not only 'achievable', but 'inevitable and compatible with Israeli security.' Despite her changed views on Palestine, Mrs Clinton seems not to have lost the trust of the Israeli government. To Mrs Clinton appears to have been trusted the task of persuading the Israeli administration to accept a negotiated solution.

'An interesting aspect of the Arab Spring had been the apparent failure of al Qaeda either to anticipate or infiltrate the uprisings.'

In the first half of 2012 the term 'Arab Spring' became a widespread, if rather vague, generalisation for the mobilisation of popular opinion that began to manifest itself in large parts of the Middle East and North Africa. All generalisations of this sort are inevitably limited; the desire for change may be shared, but local conditions inevitably impose themselves. If there was a trigger, it showed itself in Tunisia in the self-immolation of street vendor Mohamed Bouazizi on 17 December 2010 followed less than a month later by the flight of President Zine al Abidine Bin Ali to Saudi Arabia.

If this was the first rallying point, the pivotal moment was the deposition of Egypt's ruler of 30 years, Hosni Mubarak. Described by one US columnist as a 'nepotisti kleptocracy' the Mubarak regime, undemocratic and tarnished by allegations of corruption, had come to represent so much of what was wrong – not only with Egypt, the region's largest country – but throughout the Middle East. In simple terms, a new generation sought two things: more freedom and more jobs. Underlying both of these demands – and seemingly overlooked by the region's Western allies – was a desire for the dignity of democracy and employment.

The 2011 uprisings lacked the structure and organisation of a true revolution . Strangely, one common denominator of the first wave of uprisings was that the countries in which they took place all had a number of features in common: their Sunni Muslim religion, a predominant Arab culture, recent European colonial rule and – significantly – a long period of Ottoman rule. If, in mid-2011 the political panorama in Egypt was unclear, even confused, in Syria it was ten times so. Syria illustrated just how complex the Middle East could be. Cross currents of religion, sect, tribal loyalties, political and ethnic differences had, in the 30 years rule of the Assad dynasty, been suppressed by coercion and corruption. Feeling themselves safe in the illusory comfort of dictatorship and corruption, the region's rulers had lost touch with two key developments. The first of these was so obvious that the region's rulers failure to take it into account was astonishing; this was the simple demographic fact that more than half their populations was aged less than 30. The second development was that the days of press and broadcast censorship were long gone, replaced by a brave new world of Facebook and Twitter. Access to the uncomfortable truth that their fellow citizens were being killed by those who were supposed to protect them meant that the old world had, effectively, disappeared.

Progress to democracy now looked certain. What was less certain was the speed with which that progress could be accomplished. Differing local conditions meant that while Egypt planned elections for late 2011 and Tunisia as early as July (but not held until October) 2011, the incumbent rulers of Bahrain, Jordan and Morocco paid lip-service to 'reforms', 'debate' and 'discussion' without daring to go so far as to propose any genuine constitutional changes that might sideline them from power. In tiny Bahrain the ruling minority and Sunni al Khalifa family sought the assistance of neighbouring Saudi Arabia and the United Arab

Emirates (UAE) to suppress the largely Shi'a uprising that had established itself in and around Manama's Pearl roundabout. Inhabitants, visitors and seasoned observers were all taken aback by the Bahraini régime's clumsy response. In June 2011 eight leaders of the demonstrations were sentenced by military courts to life imprisonment. Even the doctors who had treated wounded demonstrators were put on trial. The ferocity of the government's crackdown has probably ruled out the prospect of any dialogue. Protestors that had initially sought little more than the release of political prisoners and something resembling a constitutional monarchy now sought the deposition of the ruling family and the departure of the King.

Other Gulf states could only look on nervously. If the writing was on the wall, few of them had much of an idea how to respond to it. Yemen, not a Gulf state, is the poorest of all the Arab countries and at the same time has the youngest population (the average age is 18 and over 73 per cent are aged less than 30. It is also the Arabian Peninsula's only republic. The dramatic flight, after 32 years in power, of Yemen's President Abdullah Ali Saleh (also to Saudi Arabia for 'medical treatment') established an uncomfortably close Arabian Peninsula precedent. In some cases, 'comfort' was seen as the answer. Cash handouts were made to local nationals, suggesting that the only language understood by their rulers was that of the dollar rather than that of democracy or dignity. This response may turn out to have been short-sighted; the Facebook generation could easily see that paying Saudi Arabia's citizens to keep quiet hardly added up to a restoration of dignity or a step towards democracy.

This underlined a potential parting of the ways between a Washington seeking to align itself with the region's demands for democracy and a Riyadh where those very demands represented a serious threat. The Saudi perception was that under the Obama administration the US had become an unreliable ally, one that needed to be replaced. But replaced with what? One option was some sort of extended Gulf Co-operation Council (GCC), possibly developing a closer relationship with China. Russia and China had been conspicuous by their silence rather than for their support of the Arab Spring.

Any Saudi Arabian strategic re-alignment was already reflected elsewhere in the region. Before elections had been held, by mid-2011 post uprising Egypt had, in a matter of months, revised its relationship with Gaza and reassessed its relationship with both Iran and Israel. In Iraq the US presence had long been resented. In each case manifest popular sentiment appeared opposed to any closer relationship with the US. In the longer term, this represented a sea change in US regional influence. Like most of its Western allies, the US had fostered close relationships with the ancient regimes for the sake of stability, but certainly not for the sake of principle.

On assuming power at the beginning of 2009, President Obama had indicated that resolving the Israel-Palestine problem that lay at the heart of so much tension in the Middle East was among his highest priorities. But whatever fine words the President might use, Israeli intransigeance combined with Palestinian divisions resulted in an impasse. Under Benjamin Netanyahu Israel had flagrantly ignored the Obama administration. The rift between Gaza based Hamas and West Bank Fatah meant that cogent dialogue with the Palestinians was impossible. In late 2010, before the Arab Spring got under way, the Palestinian Authority seemed already to have lost confidence in the Obama administration. In practical terms, this meant by-passing the US by seeking United Nations recognition of an independent Palestinian state along the lines drawn up under UN Resolution 181 in 1967 for the West Bank and Gaza. This initiative was opposed in Israel which saw it as the thin end of a dangerous wedge: recognition would enable the Palestinians to increase pressure on Israel to remove settlers and dismantle security fences. If not overtly opposed by the US, the Palestinian move was hardly welcomed. US opposition seemed largely determined by domestic political considerations and the obvious alienation of Israel which, Arab Spring or not, remained the US' most important ally in the region. Some theorists saw in Palestinian moves for UN recognition a game of double bluff designed to force Israel into serious negotiation rather than see the game move beyond their control.

The Arab Spring coincided with the assassination of the al Qaeda leader Osama bin Laden by US Navy Seals in Pakistan in May 2011. An interesting aspect of the Arab Spring had been the apparent failure of al Qaeda either to anticipate or infiltrate the uprisings. The protesters had, it seemed, only one thing in common with the Islamic extremists: the replacement of regional despôts. After that, their motivations and pathways diverged sharply. The Islamic movements sought the installation of suitably conservative Islamic regimes. This was anathema to most of those involved in the demonstrations, many of whom were well aware of al Qaeda's seditious activities in Egypt, where Salafist activists had attacked Christian Copts and in Libya where it was rumoured that al Qaeda forces had joined the Benghazi-based rebel government. In Yemen, al Qaeda 'franchisees' appeared to be well established, its operatives assuming control of the southern city of Zinjibar in the Yemeni uprising's early days.

If the region's embryonic democratic representatives were nervous about any Islamic presence in their countries, it was nothing compared to that of the discredited Syrian government headed by Bashar al Assad. Famously – or infamously – in 1982 the regime of Assad pére had killed as many as 20,000 members of the Muslim Brotherhood in the city of Hama. President Assad had sought to apportion blame for the uprising to both the Muslim Brotherhood and to insurgent forces. Syria was, in the view of most commentators, the country where Islamic extremists might succeed in establishing a government of their own. There were two reasons for this; first, the undeniable strength and organisation of the Muslim Brotherhood in Syria. Second, the strength of the links between Syria and Iran, where an Islamic theocracy has been in power since 1979.

In most Middle East political assessments, Shi'a Iran was the proverbial 'elephant in the room'. Iran's disputed presidential elections in 2009 followed unsuccessful attempts by President Obama to engage the Iranian President Mahmoud Ahmadinejad on the thorny issue of nuclear disarmament. In the disputed election outcome, according to a prescient article in the *New Yorker* by Ryan Lizza, Obama could have opted to side with the leading opposition candidate Mir-Hossein Mousavi. However, he chose not to, thereby revealing divisions within the White House, notably with Hillary Clinton. These were highlighted by the State Department's request that, given its importance to the Iranian opposition, the Twitter social network delay an upgrade that would have temporarily closed the service in Iran. The request was made without White House approval but the glimpse of the obvious, that the US had to side with the region's protest movements, proved to be a pivotal shift in US regional policy.

As reported in the *New Yorker*, the shift was reflected in an August 2010 memorandum prepared by President Obama entitled *Political Reform in the Middle East and North Africa*. The report noted that there was 'evidence of growing citizen discontent with the region's regimes.' It also observed that 'our regional and international credibility will be undermined if we are seen to be backing repressive regimes and ignoring the rights and aspirations of citizens.' Ryan Lizza also noted that the report sought a change in 'the traditional idea that stability in the Middle East always served US interests. In his State of the Union address, Obama heaped praise on the Tunisian uprising, 'where the will of the people proved more powerful than the writ of a dictator.' Sadly, when faced by the Egyptian uprising, the US administration appeared to backtrack, in February 2011 still sending mixed signals of support both for the protestors and for the discredited Mubarak. In the more complex context of Egypt, Obama found himself torn between the views of the US old guard, a hesitant State Department and a worried Israel. None the less, Obama eventually ceased supporting Mubarak and albeit half-heartedly, backed NATO intervention in Libya.

THE MIDDLE EAST AND NORTH AFRICA

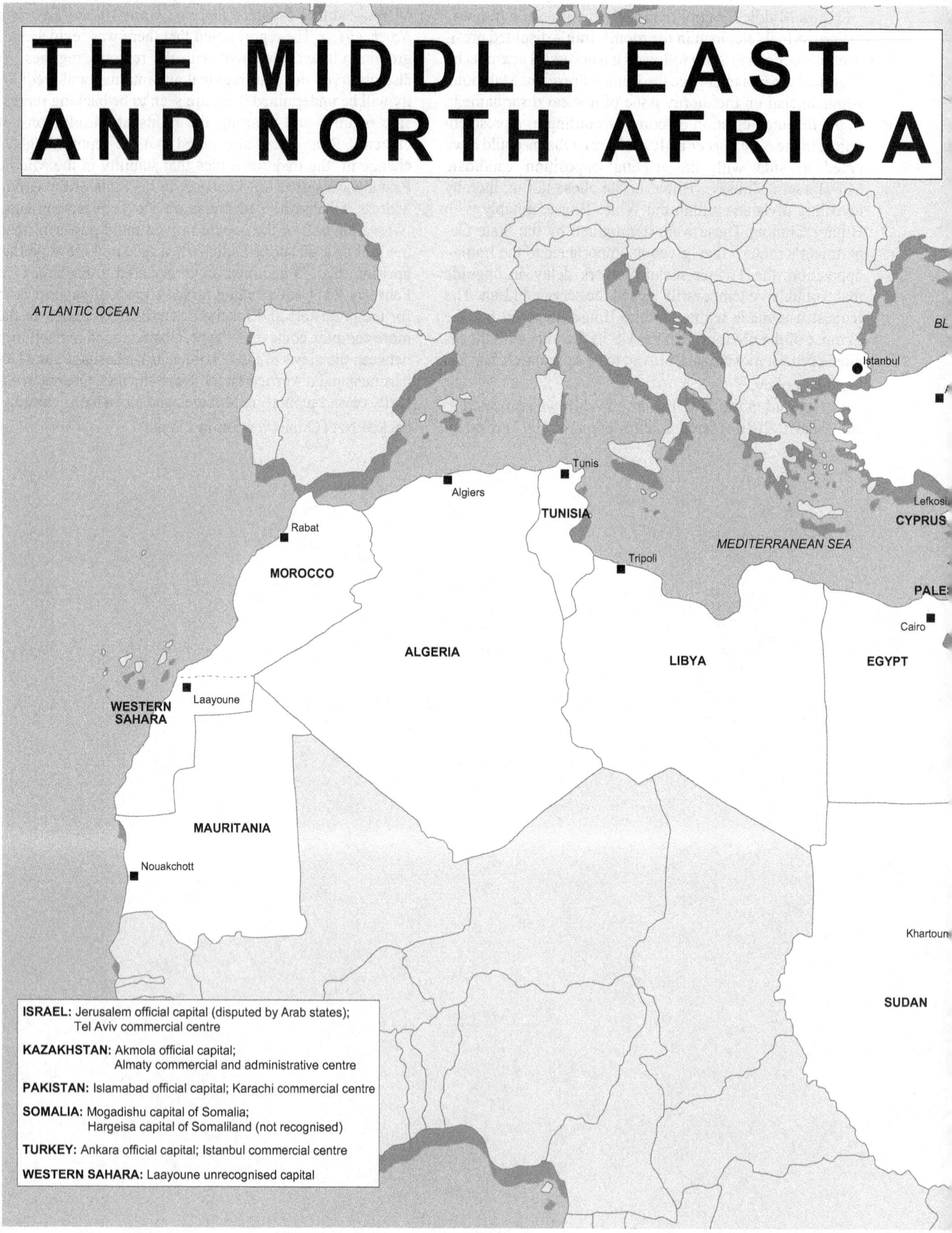
ATLANTIC OCEAN
MEDITERRANEAN SEA
Istanbul
Tunis
Algiers
TUNISIA
Rabat
MOROCCO
Tripoli
ALGERIA
LIBYA
EGYPT
Cairo
Lefkosi
CYPRUS
PALE
Laayoune
WESTERN SAHARA
MAURITANIA
Nouakchott
Khartoun
SUDAN
ISRAEL: Jerusalem official capital (disputed by Arab states); Tel Aviv commercial centre
KAZAKHSTAN: Akmola official capital; Almaty commercial and administrative centre
PAKISTAN: Islamabad official capital; Karachi commercial centre
SOMALIA: Mogadishu capital of Somalia; Hargeisa capital of Somaliland (not recognised)
TURKEY: Ankara official capital; Istanbul commercial centre
WESTERN SAHARA: Laayoune unrecognised capital

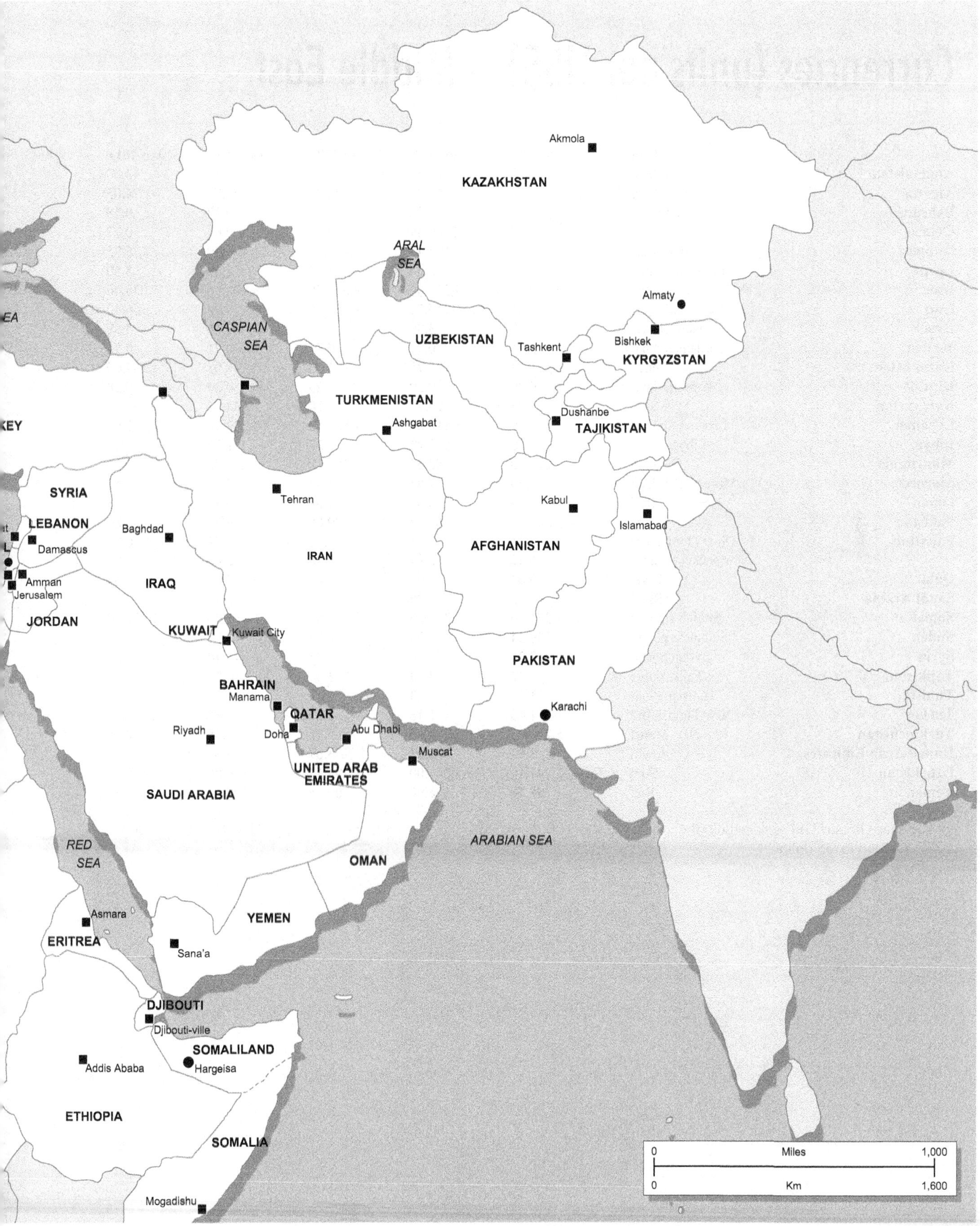
Akmola
KAZAKHSTAN
ARAL SEA
Almaty
CASPIAN SEA
UZBEKISTAN
Tashkent
Bishkek
KYRGYZSTAN
TURKMENISTAN
Ashgabat
Dushanbe
TAJIKISTAN
SYRIA
Tehran
Kabul
LEBANON
Baghdad
Islamabad
Damascus
IRAN
AFGHANISTAN
Amman
IRAQ
Jerusalem
JORDAN
KUWAIT
Kuwait City
PAKISTAN
BAHRAIN
Manama
Karachi
QATAR
Riyadh
Doha
Abu Dhabi
Muscat
UNITED ARAB EMIRATES
SAUDI ARABIA
ARABIAN SEA
RED SEA
OMAN
Asmara
YEMEN
ERITREA
Sana'a
DJIBOUTI
Djibouti-ville
SOMALILAND
Addis Ababa
Hargeisa
ETHIOPIA
SOMALIA
Mogadishu
0 Miles 1,000
0 Km 1,600

Currencies (units per US$) – Middle East

	Unit	Jan 2007	Jan 2008	Jan 2009	Jan 2010	Jan 2011
Afghanistan	Afghani	49.18	49.53	47.28	45.36	43.00
Algeria	Algerian dinar	71.71	67.21	72.07	71.76	74.05
Bahrain	Bahraini dinar	0.38	0.38	0.38	0.37	0.38
Cyprus	Euro	0.45	(b) 0.69	0.78	0.69	0.77
Djibouti	Djibouti franc	174.70	175.47	174.27	160.50	175.75
Egypt	Egyptian pound	5.71	5.54	5.55	5.42	5.80
Iran	Rial	9,230.00	9,332.00	9,865.50	9,900.00	1,035.00
Iraq	New Iraqi dinar	1,314.65	1,216.70	1,153.10	1,150.00	1,166.40
Israel	New Shekel	4.22	3.99	3.98	3.68	3.58
Jordan	Jordanian dinar	0.71	0.71	0.71	0.71	0.71
Kazakhstan	Tenge	125.33	120.75	121.45	148.05	147.10
Kuwait	Kuwaiti dinar	0.29	0.29	0.29	0.29	0.28
Kyrgyzstan	Som	38.25	120.75	40.28	44.22	47.17
Lebanon	Lebanese pound	1,512.00	1,512.00	1,501.50	1,502.50	1,501.00
Libya	Libyan dinar	1.28	1.22	1.27	1.22	1.26
Mauritania	Ouguiya	270.80	252.54	259.77	261.50	282.00
Morocco	Moroccan dirham	8.59	7.83	8.66	7.88	8.56
Oman	Rial	0.39	0.39	0.39	0.38	0.38
Pakistan	Rupee	60.97	61.14	79.05	84.20	85.80
Palestine	Dinar (Jordanian)	0.71	0.71	0.71	0.71	0.71
	New shekel (Israeli)	4.22	3.99	3.98	3.68	3.58
Qatar	Riyal	3.64	3.64	3.64	3.64	3.64
Saudi Arabia	Riyal	3.75	3.75	3.75	3.75	3.75
Somalia	Somali shilling	1,375.00	1,397.00	1,415.00	1,457.00	1,550.00
Sudan	Sudanese pound	(a) 230.24	2.03	2.24	2.31	2.51
Syria	Syrian pound	52.21	51.10	46.05	45.40	46.85
Tajikistan	Tajik rouble	3.43	3.43	3.44	4.37	4.40
Tunisia	Tunisian dinar	1.32	1.23	1.42	1.31	1.46
Turkey	New Turkish lira	1.43	1.18	1.67	1.45	1.57
Turkmenistan	New Manat	5,200.00	5,200.00	(c) 2.85	2.85	2.85
United Arab Emirates	Dirham	3.67	3.67	3.67	3.67	3.67
Uzbekistan	Sum	1,241.10	16,040.00	1,398.37	1,516.89	1,640.55
Yemen	Rial	198.48	198.90	200.15	208.62	213.80

(a) Sudanese pound (S£) replaced dinar at rate of S£1 to 100 dinar, 2007; (b) euro adopted, 2008; (c) New Manat from Jan 2009, pegged to US dollar

Key indicators 2010

	Population (m)	Area ('000 sq km)	GDP per capita (US$)	Inflation (%)	GDP real growth (%)	Balance of trade (US$m)
Afghanistan	*29.12	647.50	*515	*7.7	*8.2	(c) *-6.6
Algeria	*35.70	2,381.70	4,366	4.3	3.3	(c) 7,784.0
Bahrain	1.26	0.70	20,475	2.0	2.9	2,642.0
Cyprus	*1.10	9.30	28,237	2.6	1.0	-6,376.0
Djibouti	*0.89	23.20	1,383	4.0	4.5	(b) -373.3
Egypt	*81.12	1,001.50	2,789	11.7	5.1	(b) -16,818.0
Iran	*74.34	1,648.20	4,741	12.5	3.2	*20,935.0
Iraq	*32.11	434.90	2,564	2.4	0.8	1,654.0
Israel	*7.63	20.80	28,686	2.7	4.6	-2,365.0
Jordan	6.11	91.90	4,500	5.0	2.3	-6,650.0
Kazakhstan	*15.90	2,717.30	8,883	7.4	7.3	28,881.0
Kuwait	*3.58	17.80	36,412	4.1	3.4	47,908.0
Kyrgyzstan	*5.33	198.50	*863	*7.8	*-1.4	-1,198.3
Lebanon	*4.30	10.50	10,044	4.5	7.5	-12,263.0
Libya	*6.36	1,775.50	11,314	2.4	4.2	(c) 40,292.0
Mauritania	3.40	1,030.70	2,093	6.1	5.2	(b) -573.0
Morocco	*31.85	711.00	3,249	1.0	3.7	-15,062.0
Oman	(^)2.69	320.00	18,657	3.3	4.1	18,874.0
Pakistan	*165.15	803.90	1,050	11.7	3.8	-11,416.0
Palestine	*4.17	6.30	–	–	–	–
Qatar	(^)1.69	11.40	74,901	-2.4	16.6	30,728.0
Saudi Arabia	*29.20	2,149.70	16,996	5.4	3.7	153,717.0
Somalia	8.69	738.00	–	–	–	–
Sudan	(a) *43.20	1,217.15	1,705	13.0	5.1	2,564.9
Syria	*20.13	185.20	2,877	4.4	3.2	(b)-3,049.0
Tajikistan	*7.60	143.10	(b) *767	6.5	6.5	-1,634.0
Tunisia	*10.55	164.20	4,200	4.4	3.7	(b) -3,699.0
Turkey	*7.83	41.30	67,246	0.7	2.6	15,870.0
Turkmenistan	*5.20	488.10	(b) 3,243	(b) -2.7	(b) 6.1	(b) *875.0
United Arab Emirates	*5.40	83.60	59,717	0.9	3.2	63,600.0
Uzbekistan	*28.10	447.40	1,380	9.4	8.5	(b) 1,613.0
Yemen	*23.15	528.00	1,282	12.1	8.0	(b)-2,012.8

* Estimated figure; (^) Census figure; (a) pre-independence of South Sudan; (b) 2009; (d=c) 2008.
No current figurework for Palestine and Somalia

FREE ONLINE ACCESS WITH YOUR PURCHASE

Buyers of the 2012 print edition get **Free Access** to Nations of the World Online!

- Immediate Downloads of Individual Country Reports
- Sort by Country, Region and Population
- Access Countries by Trade Group

With online access, searching through this vast amount of text and finding specific country information has never been faster or easier.

http://gold.greyhouse.com

FREE ONLINE ACCESS COUPON

☐ I have enclosed my payment for Nations of the World, 2012. Send my login credentials to the contact below.

Contact Name: ______________________ Invoice#: ______________

Company Name: ______________________________________

Email: ____

Authentication: (fill in as many as applicable to your institution)

IP Address or IP Range:	
Referral URL:	
Library Card Prefix:	
Username & Password:	

Grey House Publishing

Grey House Publishing
PO Box 56 ◆ 4919 Route 22 ◆ Amenia, NY 12501-0056
(800) 562-2139 ◆ (518) 789-8700 ◆ FAX (518) 789-0556
www.greyhouse.com ◆ e-mail: books@greyhouse.com